BUC

USED BOAT PRICE GUIDE

1984-1996 MODELS

Statistically Authenticated
Current Market Prices for ...
OUTBOARDS • INBOARDS • SAILBOATS
OUTDRIVES • POWERBOATS
HOUSEBOATS • CUSTOM BOATS
with Area, Condition and Equipment Scales
and a Complete Cross Referenced Index

96th Edition 2009

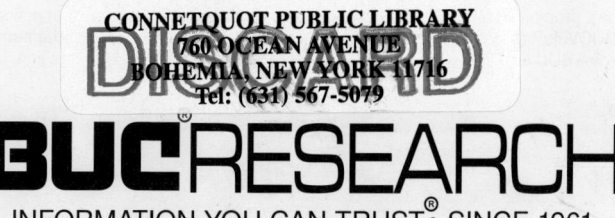

BUC RESEARCH

INFORMATION YOU CAN TRUST® SINCE 1961

PUBLISHED BY

BUC RESEARCH

1314 Northeast 17th Court, Ft Lauderdale, FL 33305
800-327-6929, 954-565-6715, Fax: 954-561-3095

Library of Congress Catalog No. 63-35604

ISBN 978-0-9816019-6-0

Purchase two or more BUC Used Boat Price Guides at discounted prices and receive BUCValuPro.com Memberships FREE*.
See Page iii for login and activation details.

Subscription prices, U.S. and Foreign

BUC Used Boat Price Guide (Vol. I 1997-2008 models) List Price	$95
BUC Used Boat Price Guide (Vol. II 1984-1996 models) List Price	$85
BUC Used Boat Price Guide (Vol. III 1905-1983 models) List Price	$69
Buy Volumes I & II, receive $14 book discount & ONE FREE BUCValuPro.com Membership, a $27.95 per month value.*	**$166**
Buy Volumes I, II & III, receive $34 book discount & TWO FREE BUCValuPro.com Memberships, a $32.95 per month value.*	**$215**

- Plus Postage -
$8 for single Volume I, II or III
$10 for the Two Volume Set (Vol. I & II)
$12 for the Three Volume Set (Vol. I, II & III)
- FLORIDA residents add sales tax -

OVERSEAS AIR SHIPMENT RATES FOR PREPAID ORDERS:
Add $35 for single Volume I, II or III
Add $40 for Two Volume Set (Vol. I & II)
Add $50 for Three Volume Set (Vol. I, II & III)

TO ORDER:
email orders@BUC.com, or call 800-327-6929 or 954-565-6715
If you require 10 or more BUCValuPro.com Login's, please call or email for a customized quotation.

QUANTITY DISCOUNTS for **BUC Used Boat Price Guides** and **BUCValuPro.com** Memberships are also available at
http://wwwBUC.com

Prices, promotions & free trials are subject to change or withdrawal without notice.
*Free BUCValuPro.com Memberships, unless renewed, expire according to the terms on www.BUC.com or upon publication of the next edition whichever comes first.

CONTENTS

Purchase two or more BUC Used Boat Price Guides at discounted prices
and receive BUCValuPro.com Memberships FREE*.

If you have previously registered your BUC Personal Login, go
to: http://www.BUCValuPro.com

To activate a new membership and create your own BUC
Personal Login, go to http://www.BUCValuPro.com/freetrial.
Enter your BUC Customer Number & Free Trial Code: UB94

If you have any questions call:
800-327-6929 or (954) 565-6715

If you have purchased a single copy of the BUC Used Boat Price Guide Volume
I or Volume II, you can receive a FREE BUCValuPro Membership by purchasing
an additional copy or volume. Or, you can supplement your Book purchase with
a BUCValuPro Membership at a special price. (Sign in according to the
instructions above).

Prices, promotions & free trials are subject to change or withdrawal without notice.
*Free BUCValuPro.com Memberships, unless renewed, expire according to the terms on
www.BUC.com or upon publication of the next edition whichever comes first.

PREFACE

This 96th edition of the BUC Used Boat Price Guide contains the current retail price of more than 440,000 used pleasure boats. Over 75,000 additions and other changes have been made since the last edition. The unique formulas used in depreciating or appreciating the various boats utilize the prices of actual used boat sales reported by dealers, brokers and surveyors from all geographical areas of the United States and Canada.

This edition contains a method for adjusting for variation due to area location and condition. Be sure to read the instructions. The cross-referenced trade name index indicates the boat type and length for each trade name. This should facilitate finding listings where two or more manufacturers have used one trade name.

Many other changes have also been made. To gain maximum benefit from this book and a deeper understanding of the subtleties of boat and engine evaluation, we suggest rereading the Introduction and How To Use This Book sections from time to time, especially first time or casual users. Referencing a price without regard to Area, Equipment and Condition Scales is a misusage and likely to be detrimental to your requirements.

Sometimes we are asked why we do not show the original list price of the various boats along with the current retail high for each boat. Since the list price of any boat has little bearing on its ultimate used market value, it only tends to confuse both the user of the price guide and the consumer.

For prices of used boats newer than 1996, see BUC's Used Boat Price Guide Volume I; and for used boats older than 1984, see BUC's Used Boat Price Guide Volume III, the 96th Editions.

Walter J. Sullivan, III
Fort Lauderdale, Florida
January 2009

INTRODUCTION

DEPRECIATION OF BOATS

There are all kinds of depreciation techniques. A straight-line method is often used by accountants and bookkeepers. It's a tidy way to devalue capital equipment over its expected useful life, but the values obtained with this method have no relationship to the market values of recreational boats.

The straight-line depreciation technique generally tends to separate the buyer and seller rather than invite them to negotiate. The only way to accurately determine and project the depreciation curve of a used recreational vessel is to study the market place to see what buyers are actually paying for boats in light of all the current economic factors.

Determining depreciation or appreciation by market demand is not an easy task because it requires analysis of actual used boat sales. BUC analyzes the market through Used Boat Sales Reports received from corresponding dealers, brokers and surveyors, and through analysis of current listing prices. Our expert staff, using the very latest computers and sophisticated software, studies the information statistically for different geographical regions. The various plotted value curves are usually unique to a manufacturer. In some cases, patterns vary across major model lines of the same manufacturer.

Some vessels hold their price after the first year and over a period of years before they show noticeable depreciation. Others drop rapidly in value right from the beginning. Still others may show an initial drop and then a plateau, or drop in a series of steps. Many consumers and some brokers are not aware that boats can actually appreciate in value at times.

The market value of boats depends heavily on current economic conditions, both general and those specifically influencing luxury industries. Rates can fluctuate monthly which is why you should check each evaluation with www.BUCValuPro.com. Alternatively, you may wish to take advantage of BUC's Personalized Boat Evaluation Service by calling our office. There is a small charge for this service but you will have the very latest pricing information customized to your vessel.

Analysis of the recreational boat market is a science as well as a business. Forty-seven years of studying almost 63 billion dollars in used boat transactions has taught us that many common opinions have no basis in fact. For instance, there is no standard relationship between the manufacturer's suggested list price in the year of manufacture and the current retail market value. Another big lesson is that the patterns of depreciation for boats are substantially different from airplanes or automobiles.

Please take note that the prices shown in this guide are current retail prices, also commonly known as actual cash value, fair market value, or just market value. Trade-in value is discussed on page ixx.

DATA RECORDING AND COMPILATION

A network of cooperating dealers, brokers, and surveyors located throughout the United States and Canada complete Used Boat Sales Reports, shown below, and mail them to BUC every six months.

All aspects of each transaction shown on the Used Boat Sales Report are stored in a database where they can be accessed for analysis by our statisticians.

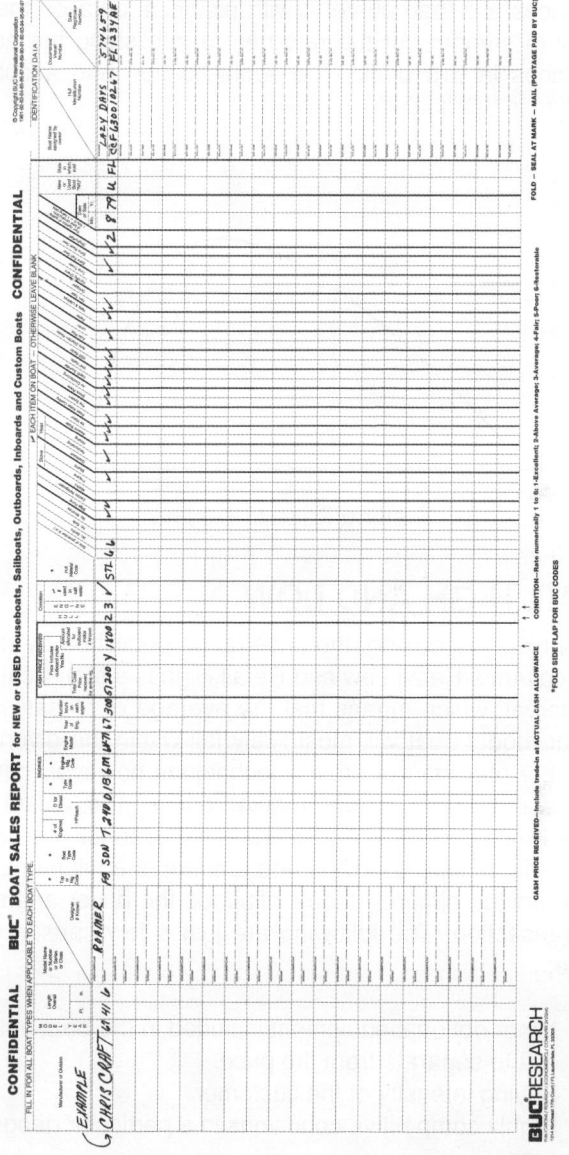

For the purpose of price analysis, sales reports are separated into different geographical areas, typically:

1) North Atlantic Coast
2) South Atlantic and Florida
3) Gulf of Mexico exclusive of Florida Coast
4) Great Lakes and Midwest
5) Northern Pacific Coast (Eureka, CA to Canadian border)
6) Southern Pacific Coast (Eureka, CA to Mexican border)
7) Canada, Great Lakes Area only

Obviously, reported prices of boats reflect myriad variations due to location, condition and the kind and quantity of optional equipment and accessories found on the boat. Special computer programs adjust each reported sale price to reflect a boat in BUC CONDITION with average equipment located in the North Atlantic Area.

The database of reported prices are then passed through various other programs to plot curves by manufacturer, model and year (a typical positively skewed curve is shown below). These prices are then curve fit with historical data on the same company to smooth out the rate before publishing the adjusted Retail Prices in this book. The sophistication and accuracy of this system is unequaled.

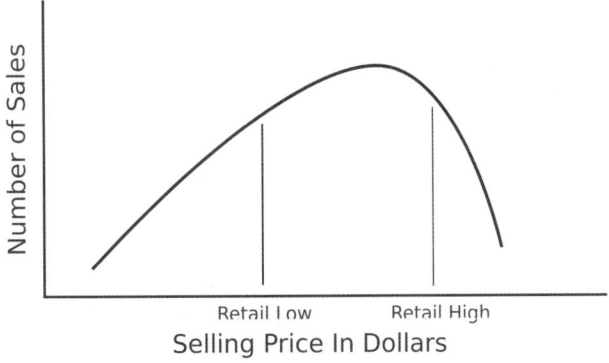

Selling Price In Dollars

RETAIL HIGH AND LOW

Technically speaking, the price range published by BUC under the columns Retail Low and Retail High is a statistical confidence interval, which means that the average of all sales of that particular model boat will most likely fall within the given range. Despite the precision of proven techniques however, compared to BUC's published current market prices, the actual selling prices of boats can show a huge variance even for two boats exactly alike in design, condition and amount of equipment. This is because unique circumstances influence the buyer and seller in every transaction. The following are just a few causes of price variance:

- Minor optional equipment included in the boat but difficult to separate from the price.
- Buying intensity of the customer.
- Highly competitive conditions in a particular geographic area.
- Sales made by firms with different overhead requirements.
- Weather conditions affecting the opportunity of using the boat.
- Terms of payment offered or asked by the buyer and/or his source of credit.
- Distress sales.
- Condition of hull, engine and equipment not properly described.

As you can see the potential causes for price variances are numerous. As a matter of fact, it is not unusual to have a range in reported sales from 30 to 60% of the median price. BUC could, of course, have published the highest and lowest prices reported, but the range in dollars would be so great as to have no practical value to any of our users. The statistically determined Retail Lows and Highs published by BUC are between generally between 8 and 16%. This is a meaningful range on which your business can profitably function.

Knowing the retail price range that has been statistically determined by market data will help you in your decision making. The wider the range, the less firm the price. Conversely, firmer prices exist when the range is small. Very popular well-known boats tend to have prices that are established in a tighter range. In any case, you know that the average of all sales, when adjusted for area and condition, will likely fall between the Retail Low and the Retail High.

Some boats will not have published prices. This is done occasionally when the number or quality of the sales reports is insufficient to be accurate, or if the received reports indicate a sudden price swing. After all, not every used boat is sold and reported every year. Although our statisticians are confident in their comparative techniques, it occasionally happens that we are not able to sufficiently pinpoint the fair market value of some models of boats. When this happens, asterisks (**) will be published in the price columns.

BUC is sometimes asked about the effect of prices reported by those wishing to influence our studies for nefarious purposes, including supporting their own profit or pride. Be assured that false reports are very easy to detect statistically. When a reported price is found to be fictitious, the entire Used Boat Sales Report for that correspondent is deemed useless and their reported prices are removed from the file. This is regrettable. The efforts of the person filing the Sales Reports could have been valid and useful to everyone, but most of all to himself. Ironically, he has excluded the mathematical influence of his local business conditions in the calculation of the very models that he sells.

With all the subtleties to consider, use your new BUC Used Boat Price Guide as a guide, tempered by your own understanding of the market. Most importantly, use the Area and Condition Adjustment Scales found on the inside of the front cover. See page xvi for instructions.

BUC RESEARCH

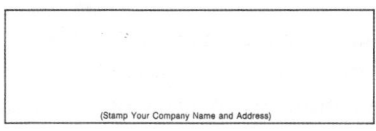

BOAT and YACHT APPRAISAL FORM

BUC's Boat and Yacht Appraisal Form has been designed to assist banks, credit unions, dealers, brokers, surveyors, and others interested in performing a thorough inspection and evaluation of boats, engines, and trailers. It has evolved over many years and includes virtually all the descriptive and equipment items that significantly affect Current Market Value. Because it secures and records a detailed description in a structured way it is a valuable aid to decision making.

The form is designed to be used in conjunction with the latest BUC Used Boat Price Guides. For appraisals of stock, semi-custom, custom and one-of-a-kind boats and yachts on an individual basis, call BUC at 800-327-6929 after completing this form and request BUC's Personalized Boat Evaluation Service℠. The fee for this service can be charged to your credit card or to your account if such has been previously established.

(PLEASE PRINT LEGIBLY)

BOAT DESCRIPTION

• BOAT NAME	RESERVED ☐ YES ☐ NO	EX-NAME		DESIGNER

• MODEL YEAR	MFG. YEAR	• MODEL NAME/NUMBER	• BOAT TYPE •	• TOP/RIG •	• BOAT IS ☐ USED ☐ NEW

• LENGTH OVERALL	LENGTH WATERLINE	BEAM	DRAFT (MAX)	DRAFT (MIN)	WEIGHT (DISPL)	BALLAST (LBS / TYPE)
ft. in.	ft. in.	ft. in.	ft. in.	ft. in.		

• HULL MATERIAL •	HULL CONFIGURATION •	DECK MATERIAL	SLEEPS	STATE ROOMS	SAIL AREA

SPEED(mph)CRUISE@RPM	SPEED(mph)MAX@RPM	GALS/HR CRUISE	GALS/HR MAX	RANGE(miles)	FUEL TANKS(gal)(main)	WATER TANK(gal)(main)
@	@					

COLOR HULL	COLOR DECK	• HULL ID #(HIN)	• DOC VESSEL NUMBER	• STATE NUMBER

ENGINE DESCRIPTION

• TYPE • ☐ OB ☐ IB ☐ JET	• # OF ENGINES	• HORSEPOWER EACH	• FUEL TYPE ☐ GAS ☐ DSL	MANUFACTURER •	MODEL	• MODEL YEAR
HOURS SINCE NEW	HOURS SINCE MAJOR OVERHAUL	OVERHAUL DATE	SERIAL# PORT		SERIAL# STARBOARD	

TRAILER DESCRIPTION

• MANUFACTURER	• MFG YEAR	MODEL	• CAPACITY	• # WHEELS	• TANDEM ☐ YES ☐ NO	TRAILER SERIAL#(VIN)	REGISTRATION #

LOCATION OF BOAT

• MARINA / YARD / STREET ADDRESS / SLIP	• CITY	• STATE	• ZIP	• COUNTRY (if not U.S.)

DOCKMASTER/CONTACT	CAPTAIN ABOARD ☐ YES ☐ NO	CAPTAIN'S NAME	CAPTAIN'S PHONE(A/C & #)	BOAT PHONE(A/C & #)

OWNER DATA

• OWNER NAME	COMPANY	• HOME PHONE(A/C & #)	• BUS PHONE(A/C & #)

• ADDRESS	• CITY	• STATE	• ZIP	• COUNTRY (if not U.S.)

HOMEPORT CITY(if different)	STATE	COUNTRY (if not U.S.)	MARINA

OWNER IS:
☐ FORMER CLIENT
☐ NEW CLIENT, IF NEW SOURCE OF REFERRAL _____

APPRAISER USE ONLY

DATE INSPECTED	INSPECTED BY	STORED: ☐ INSIDE ☐ COVERED ☐ DOCKSIDE ☐ OUTSIDE ☐ UNCOVERED SLIP #_____	REASON FOR APPRAISAL: ☐ INSURANCE ☐ BUY ☐ TRADE-IN ☐ ESTATE ☐ OTHER ☐ SURVEY ☐ SELL ☐ DONATE ☐ BROKER LISTING

CALCULATION SECTION

CURRENT BUC PRICE (Adjusted for Area only) . . . . $ _____ (A)

    Cost to Repair/Replace (column 1 on back page) . . . . $ _____ (B)

    Cost to Repair/Replace (column 2 on back page) . . . . $ _____ (C)

    Total Cost to Recondition Boat for Resale (Add B to C) . . . . $ _____ (D)

CURRENT RESALE VALUE (Subtract D from A) . . . . $ _____ (E)

ALLOWANCE FOR PROFIT ON RESALE (estimated storage, advertising, insurance, profit and other

overhead) . . . . $ _____ (F)

ACTUAL CASH ALLOWANCE/TRADE-IN VALUE (Subtract F from E or multiply E × .75) . . . . $ _____ (G)

> NOTE: The current BUC price is a price for a GOOD BOAT, ready for sale *WITHOUT ANY ADDITIONAL WORK*. See complete definition of BUC Condition in the latest edition of BUC's Used Boat Price Guide.

ITEMS INDICATED WITH A BULLET (•) ARE MANDATORY.   • SEE YOUR BUC USED BOAT PRICE GUIDE, PAGE 1, FOR SUGGESTED ABBREVIATIONS

BUC AF 8406.5

These forms come 50 to a pad and can be ordered
directly from BUC.
Call our toll free number: 800-327-6929 or write:
BUC Research
1314 NE 17th Ct.
Ft Lauderdale, FL 33305

X

Check the box to the left of each item to indicate that the vessel you are appraising has this item. Check a box to the right to indicate whether the item should be repaired or replaced, and insert the cost to repair or replace. Checking the box to the left and not checking either repair or replace will indicate that the item exists on the vessel and is in functional condition. The blank spaces for manufacturer, model, size, number, etc. for some items can be completed at your option. If you elect to use BUC's Personalized Boat Evaluation Service℠, it may be desirable to provide this information since the precision of BUC's Evaluation may depend on such detailed information.

ACCOMMODATIONS & FURNISHINGS

Overall Condition: ☐ Mint ☐ Above Average ☐ Good ☐ Fair ☐ Poor

	Repair ↓	Replace ↓	$
☐ Carpeting ☐ Drapes	☐	☐	
☐ Cushions ☐ Linens	☐	☐	
☐ Dinette	☐	☐	
☐ Furniture: Chairs (#)_____ Table(s) (#)_____ Sofa(s) (#)_____	☐	☐	
☐ Head(s) (#)_____ ☐ Overboard ☐ Recir ☐ Hold; ☐ Elec ☐ Man	☐	☐	
☐ Helmseat	☐	☐	
☐ Insulation: ☐ Thermal ☐ Acoustical	☐	☐	
☐ Owner & Guest Berths: (#)_____ Staterooms: (#)_____	☐	☐	
☐ Master Stateroom is: ☐ Fwd. ☐ Aft ☐ Amidship; has ☐ Head ☐ Shower	☐	☐	
☐ Tub; with: ☐ King ☐ Queen ☐ Double ☐ Twin ☐ Vee Berths			
☐ Guest Berths(#)_____ Guest Heads (#)_____ ☐ Guest Showers(#)_____	☐	☐	
☐ Crew Berths (#)_____ Crew Heads(#)_____ Crew Showers(#)_____	☐	☐	
Separate Captain's Quarters: ☐ Yes ☐ No			
☐ Conv Dinette Sleeps (#)_____ ☐ Conv Settee Sleeps (#)_____	☐	☐	
☐ Stereo ☐ Television(s)(#)_____	☐	☐	
☐ Video Recorder ☐ Wet Bar	☐	☐	

GALLEY & LAUNDRY

Overall Condition: ☐ Mint ☐ Above Average ☐ Good ☐ Fair ☐ Poor

	Repair	Replace	$
☐ Dishwasher	☐	☐	
☐ Clothes Washer ☐ Clothes Dryer	☐	☐	
☐ Galley: ☐ Up ☐ Down	☐	☐	
☐ Garbage Disposal	☐	☐	
☐ Ice Maker: Mfg/Mdl _____	☐	☐	
☐ Refrigeration: ☐ Refrigerator ☐ Ice Box ☐ Deep Freeze	☐	☐	
☐ Stove: ☐ Alcohol ☐ Propane/Butane ☐ Elec w/o Oven			
☐ Electric w/Oven ☐ Microwave Oven	☐	☐	
☐ Water Heater	☐	☐	
☐ Water Maker: Mfg _____ Capacity (gals) _____	☐	☐	
☐ Water System: ☐ Pressure ☐ Manual ☐ Dockside	☐	☐	
☐ Trash Compactor	☐	☐	

•ELECTRONICS & NAVIGATION

Overall Condition: ☐ Mint ☐ Above Average ☐ Good ☐ Fair ☐ Poor

	Repair	Replace	$
☐ Auto Pilot: Mfg/Mdl _____	☐	☐	
☐ Compass(es) (#)_____ Size (1)_____ Size (2)_____	☐	☐	
☐ Depth Sounder: ☐ Flasher/Digital ☐ Recording: Mfg _____	☐	☐	
☐ Direction Finder: Mfg/Mdl _____ ☐ Auto (ADF) ☐ Man (RDF)	☐	☐	
☐ Haller ☐ Intercom	☐	☐	
☐ Loran: Mfg/Mdl _____ ☐ Auto Track ☐ Interface	☐	☐	
☐ Navigation Lights	☐	☐	
☐ Radar: Mfg/Mdl _____ Range (miles) _____	☐	☐	
☐ Radios: ☐ CB; ☐ VHF: Mfg/Mdl _____ Channels _____	☐	☐	
☐ SSB: Mfg/Mdl _____ Channels _____ Watts _____	☐	☐	
☐ Rudder Indicator ☐ Wind Speed Indicator	☐	☐	
☐ Satellite Navigation: Mfg/Mdl _____	☐	☐	
☐ Synchronizers	☐	☐	
☐ Speed & Distance Logs: Mfg/Mdl _____	☐	☐	

•ELECTRICAL EQUIPMENT

Overall Condition: ☐ Mint ☐ Above Average ☐ Good ☐ Fair ☐ Poor

	Repair	Replace	$
☐ Air Cond: Mfg _____ BTUs _____ ☐ Reverse Cycle	☐	☐	
☐ Batteries: (#)_____; Amp hours: _____; ☐ Battery Parallel	☐	☐	
☐ Battery Charger: ☐ Auto ☐ Man; _____ AMPs	☐	☐	
☐ Electrical System: Shippower ☐ 12V ☐ 24V ☐ 32V; Shorepower ☐ 110 ☐ 220	☐	☐	
☐ Dockside Electrical Cable(s) ☐ Constavoit (Converter)	☐	☐	
☐ Generator: Mfg _____ K.W. _____ Hours _____	☐	☐	
☐ Heater only (Separate from A/C)	☐	☐	
☐ Lights	☐	☐	
☐ Switches, fuses, circuit breakers	☐	☐	
☐ Wiring overall	☐	☐	

DECK & SAFETY

Overall Condition: ☐ Mint ☐ Above Average ☐ Good ☐ Fair ☐ Poor

	Repair	Replace	$
☐ Anchor(s) w/Lines: (#)_____; ☐ Anchor Davit(s)	☐	☐	
☐ Bilge Blower(s): (#)_____			
☐ Bilge Pump(s): (#)_____ ☐ Auto ☐ Man	☐	☐	
☐ Bow Rails ☐ Side Stanchions w/Lifelines	☐	☐	
☐ Canvas Covers: ☐ Winter ☐ Mooring ☐ Drop Curtains			
☐ Enclosed Curtains ☐ Bimini Top ☐ Dodger ☐ Cockpit Awning			
☐ Flybridge Curtains ☐ Camper Top	☐	☐	
☐ CG Package: (Anchor, Bell, Compass, Cushions, Fenders,			
Flares, Horn, Jackets, and Lights)	☐	☐	
☐ Deck Wash Down System: ☐ Fresh Water ☐ Salt Water	☐	☐	
☐ Dinghy Davits: ☐ Elec ☐ Man	☐	☐	
☐ Dinghy ☐ Raft: Mfg _____ LOA _____			
☐ Eng _____ HP _____	☐	☐	
☐ Docking Lights: ☐ Transom ☐ Bow	☐	☐	
☐ Fenders and Lines	☐	☐	
☐ Fire System: ☐ CO² ☐ Halon; ☐ Auto ☐ Man	☐	☐	
☐ Life Jackets & Life Rings: (#)_____	☐	☐	
☐ Rails & Lifelines	☐	☐	
☐ Search Lights: ☐ Single ☐ Dual; ☐ Remote Control: ☐ Manual ☐ Electric	☐	☐	
☐ Swim Platform ☐ Swim (Boarding) Ladder	☐	☐	
☐ Windlass ☐ Windshield Wipers	☐	☐	

COST TO REPAIR/REPLACE COLUMN 1 (line B front page) $ _____

•FISHING EQUIPMENT

Overall Condition: ☐ Mint ☐ Above Average ☐ Good ☐ Fair ☐ Poor

	Repair ↓	Replace ↓	$
☐ Bait Freezer ☐ Cockpit Sink	☐	☐	
☐ Downriggers ☐ Fish Gear & Tackle	☐	☐	
☐ Fish Box ☐ Live Well	☐	☐	
☐ Fishing Chairs (#)_____ Mfg _____	☐	☐	
☐ Outriggers: Mfg _____ Length (ft) _____	☐	☐	
☐ Rods (#)_____; ☐ Reels (#)_____; ☐ Rod Holders (#)_____	☐	☐	
☐ Tuna Tower or Half Tower: Mfg _____ Height (ft) _____	☐	☐	
☐ Transom Door	☐	☐	

SAILS & RIGGING

Overall Condition: ☐ Mint ☐ Above Average ☐ Good ☐ Fair ☐ Poor

	Repair	Replace	$
☐ Cruising Equipped ☐ Racing Equipped	☐	☐	
☐ Rigging: Material _____	☐	☐	
☐ Roller Furling, Make/Type: (Main, Jib, etc.) _____	☐	☐	
☐ Sails: ☐ Dacron ☐ Nylon;(#)_____ Types: ☐ Main ☐ Jib ☐ Spinnaker			
☐ (#)1 Genoa ☐ (#)2 Genoa ☐ Mizzen ☐ Staysail;			
# of most: _____	☐	☐	
☐ Winches: (#)_____ Mfg of most: _____	☐	☐	

ENGINE/ENGINE ROOM/CONTROLS/DRIVE

Overall Condition: ☐ Mint ☐ Above Average ☐ Good ☐ Fair ☐ Poor

	Repair	Replace	$
☐ Bow Thrusters: Mfg/Mdl _____	☐	☐	
☐ Clutch: ☐ Mechanical ☐ Hydraulic			
☐ Controls: ☐ Cabin ☐ Cockpit ☐ Bridge ☐ Tower			
☐ Side Console ☐ Center Console			
☐ Ejectors	☐	☐	
☐ Engine Alarm(s) ☐ Emergency Engine Stop	☐	☐	
☐ Engine Block(s)	☐	☐	
☐ Fresh Water Cooling System ☐ Fuel Filters	☐	☐	
☐ Fuel Shut Off Valve: ☐ Stove ☐ Engines	☐	☐	
☐ Fume Detector	☐	☐	
☐ Lube Oil Storage & Transfer System	☐	☐	
☐ Manifolds	☐	☐	
☐ Muffler(s)	☐	☐	
☐ Points & Plugs	☐	☐	
☐ Extra Propeller(s) (#)_____	☐	☐	
☐ Raw Water Sea Strainer(s)	☐	☐	
☐ Reduction Drive: Ratio _____ : _____	☐	☐	
☐ Rudder(s)	☐	☐	
☐ Extra Shaft(s) (#)_____	☐	☐	
☐ Stabilizers: Mfg/Mdl _____	☐	☐	
☐ Steering: ☐ Man ☐ Hydr'l ☐ Wheel ☐ Tiller	☐	☐	
☐ Strut(s)	☐	☐	
☐ Trim Tabs: Mfg _____	☐	☐	
☐ Wiring Harnesses	☐	☐	

PAINT/VARNISH/STAINS

Overall Condition: ☐ Mint ☐ Above Average ☐ Good ☐ Fair ☐ Poor
Boat has: ☐ Awlgrip ☐ Imron

	Repair	Replace	$
☐ Bottom	☐	☐	
☐ Cockpit	☐	☐	
☐ Deck	☐	☐	
☐ Interior	☐	☐	
☐ Super Structure	☐	☐	
☐ Topsides	☐	☐	
☐ Transom	☐	☐	

OTHER MISCELLANEOUS

☐ Cradle
Deck (describe) _____

	Repair	Replace	$
	☐	☐	

Hull (describe) _____

	Repair	Replace	$
	☐	☐	

Super Structure (describe) _____

	Repair	Replace	$
	☐	☐	

Other (describe) _____

COST TO REPAIR/REPLACE COLUMN 2 (line C front page) $ _____

TO ORDER BUC'S PERSONALIZED BOAT EVALUATION SERVICE℠

• YOUR NAME   • COMPANY NAME   • AREA CODE & PHONE NUMBER

• ADDRESS   • CITY   • STATE   • ZIP   • COUNTRY

ARE YOU THE BOAT'S OWNER
☐ YES
☐ NO

ARE YOU CURRENTLY, OR HAVE YOU PREVIOUSLY BEEN, A BUC CUSTOMER?
☐ YES   ☐ NO
IF YES, CUSTOMER NUMBER _____

BUC'S PERSONALIZED BOAT EVALUATION SERVICE HELPS TO ESTABLISH CURRENT MARKET AND OTHER VALUE AS OF A GIVEN DATE. THE FEE IS $45 PER VESSEL. TO DETERMINE VALUES FOR MORE THAN ONE DATE REQUIRES A FEE OF $30 FOR EACH ADDITIONAL DATE. THERE IS A $15.00 SERVICE CHARGE FOR ONE DAY PHONE SERVICE AND $25.00 SERVICE CHARGE FOR PHONE SERVICE WITH TWO HOUR TURNAROUND. FOREIGN CLIENTS MUST ADD COST OF RETURN PHONE CALL.

TO ORDER BY MAIL: COMPLETE THIS FORM AND MAIL TO BUC INFORMATION SERVICES, 1314 NE 17 CT., FT. LAUDERDALE, FL 33305
PLEASE ENCLOSE YOUR CHECK FOR THE FULL AMOUNT DUE (ADD 5% SALES TAX IF FLORIDA RESIDENT) OR USE YOUR CREDIT CARD. PLEASE COMPLETE APPROPRIATE BOXES BELOW.

PAYMENT IS: ☐ BY CHECK   ☐ BY CREDIT CARD: CARD NO.   EXPIRATION DATE
☐ AMERICAN EXPRESS
AMOUNT ENCLOSED $ _____   ☐ MASTER CARD   ☐ VISA

TO ORDER BY PHONE: COMPLETE THIS FORM BEFORE CALLING AND HAVE YOUR CREDIT CARD INFORMATION READILY AVAILABLE (SEE LINE ABOVE) AND CALL 1-800-327-6929 IN U.S. (FLORIDA AND FOREIGN DIAL DIRECT (305) 565-6715.)

These forms come 50 to a pad and can be ordered directly from BUC.
Call our toll free number: 800-327-6929 or write:
BUC Research
1314 NE 17th Ct.
Ft Lauderdale, FL 33305

HOW TO USE THIS BOOK

For proper usage of this publication, it is essential that the user understand the Preface (page v) and the Introduction (page vi). Please read those sections before proceeding with this one.

MINIMUM IDENTIFYING INFORMATION

To arrive at the current retail price of a used boat, the following minimum information is usually required:

1) Manufacturer's name;
2) Model year;
3) The Length Overall;
4) Name and/or Model;
5) Engine Horsepower and Type and whether single, twin, gas or diesel;
6) The Location of the Vessel;
7) A BUC Rating as to its Engine and Hull Condition;
8) Details regarding Extra or Optional Equipment and Accessories.

USING THE INDEX

The index of this book represents thousands of hours of compilation. It is a combination of a manufacturers index and a cross-referenced model name index. This index warrants your attention and understanding because it can save you many hours of fruitless searching.

Unless you are very familiar with a particular listing, it is advisable to look up the manufacturer's name for all boats because it often reveals the unexpected. You will discover that many boat manufacturers have had name changes or have been acquired by other companies. You may also discover more than one manufacturer with the same or similar manufacturing name.

If the name is not listed as a manufacturer, check for a cross-reference, since the common trade names are often mistaken for corporate names. More information on how to use the index can be found on the first page of the index section.

IF YOU DON'T FIND THE BOAT

If you have the necessary information to identify a boat, have properly used the index and are still unable to find the listing, then recheck your source of information. In ninety percent of the cases, the reason for failing to find a listing is improper model year or length data. We gather model data not only directly from the manufacturers themselves, but also from other public sources. Additional models may exist, but BUC has found through various surveys that thirty-four percent of all boats owners cannot or will not properly describe their boat. Even in the trade, twenty-two percent of the inquiries to BUC have incorrect names or specifications.

One of the most common causes of not finding the model is

the confusion between the year of manufacture and the model year. Our listings are categorized by model year, which is not necessarily the same as the calendar year in which the boat was manufactured. Another very common identification problem is confusing the Length Overall (LOA) with the Length On Deck (LOD). Some manufacturers have reported the model to us with the Length On Deck in the LOA field, but list the LOA in their marketing literature. For a boat that has a large swim platform, bowsprit or sloped transom, this can make it difficult to find the model in our book. Sometimes, the numbers in the model name are a clue to solving this riddle.

Yet another area of confusion occurs when people round off inch measurements to the next highest or lowest foot. For example, some boat owner may be so used to bragging about his 31 footer that he has completely forgotten that the actual LOA is 30'1".

It is important to keep these points in mind since most states have titling and registration laws that allow the registrant to offer verbal testimony regarding a boat's specifications. In cases, however, where the boat may not be listed, please bring it to the attention of the research staff.

NOTES ABOUT OUR LISTINGS

Certain listing parameters have been utilized throughout the book with which you should familiarize yourself.

Boats with Engines

When a number appears in the column labeled "HP" under the "ENGINE" description, it can mean several things. If the engine type "TP" is outboard (OB) then the number indicated is the maximum horsepower outboard engine recommended by the manufacturer. The engine is not included in price. If the "TP" is any other inboard installation — HD, IB, IO, JT, SD, TD, VD (see Page 1 for Engine Type abbreviation) — then the number under "HP" is the horsepower of each engine. Single engines have no entry under the column headed "#" but twins will show a "T"; triple, an "R"; quadruple, a "Q". Engines are included in the price of non-outboard power boats. A "D" after the "HP" number indicates a diesel engine.

Older boats offered for sale after the engine has been replaced or rebuilt should receive more favorable treatment when using the BUC CONDITION/EQUIPMENT SCALE. When using the BUC Appraisal Form to determine boat evaluation, the cost of the new engine and installation is not to be added to the BUC price. Allow instead for better condition.

Sailboats

Retail prices for sailboats include standing and running rigging and one set of working sails unless otherwise indicated. The prices do not reflect any racing sails or extra racing equipment although most reported sales for sailboats list extra sails and associated gear. Use the BUC CONDITION/EQUIPMENT SCALE or the BUC APPRAISAL FORM for including the retail value of extra winches, pedestal steerers, etc. Regardless of size, a sailboat is considered an auxiliary when a horsepower appears in the column indicated "HP".

Outboard Boats

Outboard boats are priced without engines or trailer and minimal equipment. Although sales reports often include the value of the engine, these reports have been adjusted accordingly. The price of the motor or the price of a trailer must be added to the boat price.

Custom Built Boats

Custom built boats have no published or suggested list prices. They are usually built to the specifications of the original purchaser and vary considerably in the quality of construction and the manner in which they are equipped, powered and finished. We only assign values to custom built boats using BUC's Personalized Evaluation Service.

Our studies of this unique market have proven that comparison of features and characteristics help to determine each boat's position in the "For Sale" universe. Using powerful statistical computing techniques, our experienced staff will research each boat individually to determine the current market value of the boat, taking into account the vessel's location, condition and its complete inventory of features and equipment. The modest fee for this service can barely compare to the potential cost of a misevaluation. Call BUC (+1-954-565-6715) for complete details about the Personalized Evaluation Service, and to receive the evaluation forms.

Outboard Motors and Trailers

Outboard motors and trailers are only listed in Volume I since older models of these components tend to depreciate based only on condition rather than age. For information on how to use those listings, please see page xx of Volume I of the BUC Used Boat Price Guice.

USING THE LISTINGS

Near the top of every page are column headings. See the example figure on the next page. The numbered columns correspond to these descriptions:

1 LOA	Length Overall expressed in feet and inches.
2 NAME AND/OR MODEL	Descriptive Name or Model Information.
3 TOP/RIG	Indicates kind of Top for outboards and powerboats or the Rig style for sailboats (for example, SLP = Sloop or FB = Flybridge. See Key to BUC Codes on page 1 or inside back cover.)
4 BOAT TYPE	Describes Boat Type (See Key to BUC Codes on page 1 or inside back cover.)
5 HULL MTL	Describes the Hull Material (See Key to BUC Codes on page 1 or inside back cover.)

6 HULL TP	Describes the Hull Configuration (See Key To BUC Codes on page 1 or inside back cover.)
7 ENGINE TP	Describes the type of power plant that is or could be installed (for example IB = Inboard, see Key To BUC Codes on page 1 or inside back cover). If horsepower is shown, the engine is included in price.
8 ENGINE #	The prefix "T" indicates Twin installation; "R", Triple; "Q", Quad. Blank means Single engine.
9 ENGINE HP	The horsepower of each engine included in the price. The suffix "D" indicates Diesel and blank after the number means Gas engine(s). A number followed by a C in the HP column means that the number should be multiplied by 100. For example, T10CD indicates Twin 1000 Horsepower Diesel engines.
10 ENGINE MFG	The manufacturer of the engine(s) listed in the previous column.
11 BEAM FT IN	The boat's Beam in feet and inches.
12 WGT LBS	Approximate Weight in pounds. A number with a "T" suffix (like 35T) indicates the weight in Tons.
13 DRAFT FT IN	The draft of the boat in feet and inches.
14 RETAIL LOW	The current market Retail Low price for the North Atlantic area.
15 RETAIL HIGH	The current market Retail High price for the North Atlantic area.

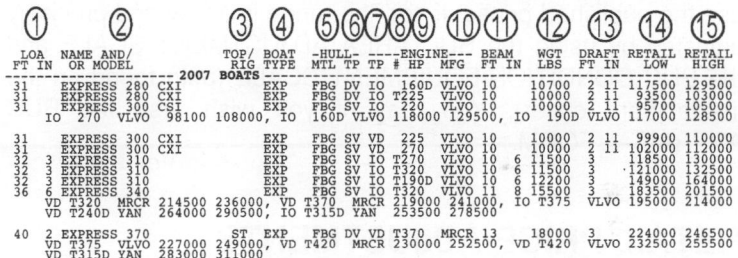

The BUC Used Boat Price Guide is organized first by Manufacturer Name. Within the manufacturer's listing, the boats are separated into groups by Model Year. Within each year, the models are listed in order of increasing Length Overall (LOA) and then by increasing horsepower and number of engines.

When a particular model has more than four different engine options they are stacked in three columns under the basic model description. In other words, the LOA, Name and/or Model, Top/Rig, Boat Type, Hull Material, Hull Type, Beam, Weight and Draft are not repeated but the Engine Type, Number of engines, Horsepower, Fuel, Engine Manufacturer and Retail Price range are listed three to a line under the basic listing. The three columns are separated by commas. Read from left to right on each line and ignore the column headings for these stacked engine options.

If the price difference between two or more engine options is relatively small, then the engine manufacturer is omitted and a range of horsepowers is printed in the horsepower column (shown as a low value and a high value with a dash between them). In this case, apply the retail price range to any engine whose horsepower falls within the horsepower range. See below, for an example of a horsepower range listing.

LOA FT IN	NAME AND/ OR MODEL	TOP/ RIG	BOAT TYPE	-HULL- MTL TP	----ENGINE--- TP # HP MFG	BEAM FT IN	WGT LBS	DRAFT FT IN	RETAIL LOW	RETAIL HIGH
					------ 1998 BOATS ------					
23 7	2300 SC	OP	CUD	FBG SV	IO 220-310	8 4	4700	3 1	16900	20600
23 7	2300 SR	OP	RNBT	FBG SV	IO 220-310	8 4	4100	3 1	14500	17900
25 3	2400 SCR	OP	CR	FBG SV	IO 190-250	8 6	5000	2 11	19400	22300
27 8	2700 SR	OP	CR	FBG SV	IO 250-310	8 3	5850	3 1	23100	27000

Finding A Listing

After properly identifying the boat in question and utilizing the boat manufacturer, trade name and model name Index, refer to the page where the manufacturer's listing starts.

Select the Model Year (for example, ---2003 BOATS---). Read down the list until you find the appropriate Length Overall (LOA). Check the model name of the listing, then the top or rig and the boat type. Next select the correct engine type, the number of engines, the horsepower, fuel type and the engine manufacturer. In some cases, you may have to check the hull material if a particular hull was built with different materials. Models with optional construction variances might follow a group of models with numerous engine options. For example, a 40-foot Express Cruiser with a Flybridge would follow a 40-foot Express Cruiser with a Hard Top.

Under the columns "Retail Low" and "Retail High" is the fair market value price range of the boat in U.S. Dollars for a boat in BUC Condition and located in the North Atlantic area. Obviously, if the boat you are evaluating meets this definition, use the published prices. If not, the range is easily and precisely adjusted by using the BUC AREA ADJUSTMENT SCALE and the BUC CONDITION/EQUIPMENT SCALE (both found on the inside front cover). You may, if you wish, use the BUC APPRAISAL FORM.

RETAIL PRICE ADJUSTMENTS

The prices for used boats listed in BUC's Used Boat Price Guides are for boats that have about average equipment appropriate for the boat's size, are in BUC Condition and are located in the North Atlantic Area. To determine the current retail price of a boat that varies in location, equipment or condition from these assumptions, you must know how to adjust for AREA, CONDITION and EQUIPMENT.

Use of the Area Adjustment Scale

Inside the front cover of each BUC Used Boat Price Guide is an Area Adjustment Scale. This chart shows the percentage that is to be added or subtracted to the Retail Price range in order to obtain the correct price range for a geographical area other than the North Atlantic. To use this scale, find the percentage adjustment where the area and boat type/boat length intersect. The entry in the intersected box will be a plus or minus percent. If the boat does not require a CONDITION/EQUIPMENT adjustment, merely add or subtract the indicated percentage to the published BUC Retail Low and Retail High. If, as is usually the case, the boat requires a CONDITION/EQUIPMENT adjustment, then add the adjustment percentages together (see example below).

Example: A 30' sailboat located on the east coast of Florida	Low	High
Published BUC retail	$70,800	$77,800
South Atlantic Area Adjustment, subtract 5%	-3,540	-3,890
Current Retail market value	$67,260	$73,910

Use of the Condition/Equipment Scale

For a quick determination of the market value of a used boat in other than BUC Condition, use the CONDITION/EQUIPMENT SCALE found inside the front cover. This unique scale has been compiled by studying the selling price of boats reported to us by dealers and brokers to the condition rating they indicate on these reports. Clearly, use of this scale will not be as accurate as a detailed analysis, using, for examle, the BUC APPRAISAL FORM (see below). However, it is quite sufficient for every day use, and especially convenient when interacting with a customer who wants a general idea of the value of his boat.

Banks, finance companies, credit unions, insurance companies, assessors and other government agencies will find themselves using the SCALES almost exclusively. Dealers, brokers and surveyors will use this technique most of the time especially as experience with the BUC Book increases. However, professionals in the industry will also frequently use check lists like the BUC APPRAISAL FORM for an accurate, detailed evaluation, carefully listing and evaluating the price effect of extra equipment and various condition deficiencies.

Example: A 40' sundeck trawler in high Above BUC Condition	Low	High
Published BUC retail	$336,500	$369,500
High end of Above BUC, add 15%	50,475	55,425
Current Retail market value	$386,975	$424,925

Using Both AREA and CONDITION Adjustments

When both the AREA ADJUSTMENT SCALE and the CONDITION/EQUIPMENT SCALE are necessary for the same boat, add the percentages together before adjusting the published Retail Prices.

Example: A 26' sport fisherman in Seattle in Fair Condition	Low	High
Published BUC retail	$70,100	$77,100
Combine Northern Pacific, +15%, and Fair Condition, -10%.		
+5% net adjustment	3,505	3,855
Current Retail market value	$73,605	$80,955

xvii

Use of Appraisal Forms

The BUC APPRAISAL FORM was created to help you record and analyze a boat's condition and equipment inventory. It provides a convenient documentation of the cost to repair, equip or recondition a vessel to bring it up to the level of BUC Condition. These forms can be used everyday in your business to assist with the cost control of trade-in, storage and repair. A reproduction of the form appears on pages x and xi.

To use the BUC APPRAISAL FORM,
1. Find the correct listing in the BUC Used Boat Price Guide.
2. Adjust the Retail High only for Area, not condition.
3. Record the area-adjusted Retail High on line (A) of the Form.
4. Add together the Cost To Repair/Replace from columns 1 and 2 of the back of the page, and put that cost on line (D).
5. Subtract (D) from (A). That is the current High Retail of the boat, on line (E) of the Form.
6. Divide the original Retail Low by the original Retail High to obtain the range percentage. Then multiply this percentage by the adjusted Retail High from step 5, line (E), in order to obtain the adjusted Retail Low.

Example: A 33' Open Express in Texas on the Gulf Coast needing minor repairs. The BUC published Retail range is $173,000-190,000.

BUC published Retail High	$190,000
Adjust for AREA, Gulf Coast, 33', minus 10%	−19,000
Adjusted Retail High	171,000
Dealer estimates the total amount to recondition the boat for resale (to BUC Condition)	−8,500
Current Retail High value for this boat	$162,500
The original Retail Low divided by the original Retail High, 173000÷190000	91%
Current Retail Low value for this boat	$147,875

For the example boat above, the current Retail range, adjusted for area and reconditioning, is $147,875-162,500.

If the completion of the BUC APPRAISAL FORM reveals that the boat has no significant deficiencies, but rather there are extras, or recent major reconditioning, then the situation is somewhat more complicated. One cannot just add the value of the extras to the Retail range. Our studies have shown that money added to a vessel beyond BUC Condition does not necessarily increase the value dollar-for-dollar.

For example, take an older model boat that has had a recent $60,000 re-powering and $40,000 of interior upgrades, and is now in good condition with no deficiencies. It is not correct to just add $100,000 to the BUC Retail Low and High, because some large part of that expense may have just returned the boat to BUC Condition. More likely, professionals in the industry will use their knowledge to evaluate whether this boat is in "Above BUC Condition" or perhaps "Bristol". Then, the appropriate adjustment percentage will be added to the BUC Retail range.

Determination of Trade-In Price
(or actual cash allowance)

We do not calculate or publish a trade-in value because every firm has its own overhead or profit margin. Generally, the trade-in allowance used by most dealers is 70 to 80 percent of the current market retail. The reasons for a variation in the margin are numerous but might typically be: size of the organization, whether salespeople are commissioned or employed, building location, yard costs, showroom expense and financial costs.

There are two common techniques for handling trade-ins. The first is a little round-about. The dealer allows the buyer of a new boat full market value on his trade-in (exactly what he expects to sell it for) but the new boat is not discounted or is discounted very little. This technique has been used successfully by a number of dealers throughout the years. However, the mathematics become tangled and the cost of the used boat to your business and the possible potential profit that could be derived on resale is confused with the new boat sale.

Alternatively, separate the new and used boat sales even if they are involved in the same transaction. For the trade-in, adjust the published BUC price with the Area, Condition and Equipment Scales, and perhaps make-ready repairs such as waxing or bottom painting, along with any factors you might use for local conditions. Then subtract the amount of profit you expect to realize on resale, and subtract your cost of sales overhead, including the cost to store the boat, advertising and salesman's commission. The net result is the trade-in value.

You can divide the net figure resulting after subtracting all those profit and cost items by the adjusted retail price for your area. This coefficient, as a percentage, is your trade-in margin. The trade-in margin can be used to quickly and roughly calculate any other trade-in. Merely multiply your margin by the Retail price after adjusting for area and condition.

BOAT PRICING SECTION
Key to BUC Codes

BOAT TYPE

AIR	Airboat
BASS	Bass
BUOY	Buoy Tender
B/R	Bowrider
CBNCR	Cabin Cruiser
CAMPR	Camper
CANOE	Canoe
CTRCN	Center Console Fisherman
COMM	Commercial
CNV	Convertible
CR	Cruiser
CRCPT	Cruiser with Cockpit
CUD	Cuddy
DECK	Deck Style Boat
DGY	Dinghy
DCCPT	Double Cabin Cockpit
DCFD	Double Cabin Flush Deck
DCMY	Double Cabin Motor Yacht
DNEST	Downeast
EXP	Express
EXPSF	Express Fisherman
FSH	Fisherman
FLATS	Flats Fisherman
FH	Floating Home
FD	Flush Deck
FDCR	Flush Deck Cruiser
FDPH	Flush Deck with Pilothouse
HB	Houseboat
ICE	Ice Boat
JTSKI	Jet Ski
JON	Jon (or John)
KAYAK	Kayak
LNCH	Launch
LRMY	LRC Motor Yacht
LRMYC	LRC Motor Yacht with Cockpit
LRPH	LRC with Raised Pilothouse
LRPHC	LRC with Raised Pilothouse and Cockpit
LRRD	LRC with Raised Aft Deck
LRRDC	LRC with Raised Aft Deck and Cockpit
LRSDN	LRC Sedan
LRTC	LRC with Trunk Cabin
LRTCC	LRC with Trunk Cabin and Cockpit
MS	Motor Sailor
MY	Motor Yacht
MYCPT	Motor Yacht with Cockpit
MYDKH	Motor Yacht with Deckhouse
MYXDH	Motor Yacht with Ext. Deckhouse
MYFD	Motor Yacht with Flush Deck
MYPH	Motor Yacht with Pilothouse
MYSD	Sun Deck Motor Yacht
MYSDC	Sun Deck Motor Yacht with Cockpit
OFF	Offshore
OPFSH	Open Fish
OVNTR	Overnighter
PEDAL	Pedal Boat
PW	Personal Watercraft
PH	Pilothouse
PRAM	Pram
RACE	Racing Runabout
ROW	Row Boat
RNBT	Runabout
SBD	Sailboard
SAIL	Sailboat
SA/CR	Sailboat-Cruising
SA/OD	Sailboat-One Design
SA/RC	Sailboat-Racer/Cruiser
SCDAC	Sail, Cruising-Deckhouse-Aft Cockpit
SCDCA	Sail, Cruising-Deckhouse-Center and Aft Cockpits
SCDCC	Sail, Cruising-Deckhouse-Center Cockpit
SCFAC	Sail, Cruising-Aft Cockpit
SCFCC	Sail, Cruising-Center Cockpit
SCFCA	Sail, Cruising-Center and Aft Cockpits
SCPHO	Sail, Cruising-Pilothouse (Only)
SCPAC	Sail, Cruising-Pilothouse-Aft Cockpit
SCPBR	Sail, Cruising-Pilothouse-Bridge
SCPCC	Sail, Cruising-Pilothouse-Center Cockpit
SCPCA	Sail, Cruising-Pilothouse-Center and Aft Cockpits
SMPHO	Motorsailer-Pilothouse (Only)
SMPAC	Motorsailer-Pilothouse-Aft Cockpit
SMPBR	Motorsailer-Pilothouse—Bridge
SMPCC	Motorsailer-Pilothouse-Center Cockpit
SMPCA	Motorsailer-Pilothouse-Center and Aft Cockpits
SRCAC	Sail, Racer/Cruiser-Aft Cockpit
SRCCC	Sail, Racer/Cruiser-Center Cockpit
SRCCA	Sail, Racer/Cruiser-Center and Aft Cockpits
SROAC	Sail, Racer/Cruiser-One Design
SRRAC	Sail, Racer Only-Aft Cockpit
SRRAD	Sail, Racer Only-Aft Cockpit-Deckpit
SDN	Sedan Cruiser
SDNSF	Sedan Sport Fisherman
SKI	Ski
SPTCR	Sport Cruiser
SF	Sport Fisherman
TRWL	Trawler
TRMY	Trawler Motor Yacht
TRMYC	Trawler Motor Yacht with Cockpit
TRRD	Trawler with Raised Aft Deck
TRRDC	Trawler with Raised Aft Deck and Cockpits
TRSDN	Trawler Sedan
TRTC	Trawler with Trunk Cabin
TRTCC	Trawler with Trunk Cabin and Cockpit
TRPH	Trawler with Raised Pilothouse
TRPHC	Trawler with Raised Pilothouse and Cockpit
TCMY	Triple Cabin Motor Yacht
TUG	Tug Boat
UTL	Utility (or Open)
W/T	Walkthru Windshield
WKNDR	Weekender
YTFS	Yacht Fisherman

HULL CONFIGURATION

BB	Bilge Boards
BK	Bulb Keel
CT	Catamaran
CB	Centerboard
DB	Daggerboard
DV	Deep Vee
DS	Displacement
FL	Flatbottom
KL	Keel
KC	Keel-Centerboard
LB	Leeboards
OR	Outrigger
PN	Pontoon (or Platform)
RB	Round Bottom
SD	Semi Displacement
SV	Semi Vee (or Modified Vee)
SK	Swing Keel (or Drop Keel)

HULL CONFIGURATION (Continued)

TR	Tri Hull (or Cathedral)
TM	Trimaran
TH	Tunnel Hull
TK	Twin Keels (Fin Keels)
WK	Wing Keel

ENGINE TYPE

EL	Electric
HD	Hydraulic Drive
IB	Inboard
IO	Inboard-Outdrive (stern drive)
OB	Outboard
SD	Sail Drive
SE	Seadrive
TD	Tunnel Drive
VD	Vee-Drive
JT	Water Jet Propulsion

HULL MATERIAL

ABS	Acetyl Butyl Styrene
ARX	Airex
AL	Aluminum
A/S	Aluminum over Steel
C/S	Carbon Fiber Sandwich
CDR	Cedar
WCM	Cold Molded Wood
FC	Ferro Cement
FBG	Fiberglass
FBC	Fiberglass Composite
F/S	Fiberglass Sandwich
F/W	Fiberglass over Wood
FOM	Foam
INF	Inflatable
RIB	Inflatable with Rigid Bottom
IRON	Iron
KEV	Kevlar
L/P	Lapstrake Plywood
LEAD	Lead
MHG	Mahogany
M/P	Mahogany over Plywood
MONL	Monel
P/C	Planked Cedar
P/M	Planked Mahogany
P/P	Planked Plywood
PL	Plastic
PLY	Plywood
PVC	Polyvinylchloride
RR	Reinforced Rubber
RIB	Rigid Inflatable
RLX	Royalex
R/N	Rubber over Nylon
STL	Steel
S/S	Stainless Steel
SAN	Styrene Acetyl Nitride
TEK	Teak
V/N	Vinyl over Nylon
VEF	Virtual Engineered Composites
WD	Wood
CVS	Wood/Canvas

TOP or RIG

CAT	Cat Rig
CUT	Cutter Rig
EPH	Enclosed Pilothouse
EPF	Enclosed Pilothouse with Flybridge
EPS	Enclosed Pilothouse with Sun Deck
FB	Flybridge
F+H	Fly Bridge with Half Tower
F+M	Fly Bridge with Marlin Tower
F+T	Fly Bridge with Tuna Tower
GAF	Gaff Rig
HT	Hard Top
H+H	Hard Top with Half Tower
H+M	Hard Top with Marlin Tower
H+T	Hard Top with Tuna Tower
KTH	Ketch Rig
LAT	Lateen (or Gunter Rig)
OP	Open
TH	Open with Half Tower
MT	Open with Marlin Tower
RA	Open with Radar Arch
ST	Open with Soft Top (Bimini Top)
TTP	Open with T-Top
TT	Open with Tuna Tower
SCH	Schooner
SLP	Sloop Rig
SQ	Square Sail Rig
TT	Tuna Tower
YWL	Yawl Rig

MISCELLANEOUS OTHER ABBREVIATIONS

CUS	Custom
DKHS	Deckhouse
DLX	Deluxe
DIN	Dinette
DISPL	Displacement
EXT	Extended
F	Fire Engines
FM	Fixed Mount
FWC	Fresh Water Cooled
HP	Horsepower
LOA	Length Overall
LWL	Length at Waterline
MAX	Maximum
MIN	Minimum
MLD	Molded
MTR	Motor
NA	Not Announced (or not available at time of compilation)
OPT	Power
PRMDK	Promenade Deck
Q	(before HP) Quad Engines
RIV	Riveted
SLPR	Sleeper
SPIN	Spinnaker
STD	Standard
TL	Tilt
TR	Trim
R	(before HP) Triple Engines
T	(after HP) Turbine Engines
TB	Turbocharged
T	(before HP) Twin Engines
WGT	Weight
WELD	Welded

ENGINE MANUFACTURER

ALAS	Alaska Diesel Electric/Lugger
ALBN	Albin
ALLI	Allison Engine Co.
AMER	American Challenger
AMDL	American Diesel Corp.
AMML	American Marine Ltd.
BENZ	Mercedes-Benz
BMW	BMW Marine Products
BPM	BPM Volcano
BMC	British Marine Cmpnts.
SEAG	British Seagull Co.
BUIC	Buick
BUKH	Bukh (USA) Inc.

ENGINE MANUFACTURER (Continued)

CPWR	C-Power (Marine) Ltd.
CADI	Cadillac
CARN	Carniti/Pennsylvania Development
CARY	Cary Marine Engines
CAT	Caterpillar, Inc.
CHAL	Challenger
CHEV	Chevrolet
CC	Chris Craft
CHRY	Chrysler Marine
CBRA	Cobra Power Inc.
COMM	Commander Marine Co.
CNTL	Continental
CORR	Correct Craft
CRUS	Crusader Marine Engines
CUM	Cummins Engine Co. Inc.
CUYA	Cuyuna
DATS	Datsun
DAY	Daytona Marine Engine Corp.
DEER	John Deere
DD	Detroit Diesel
DUTZ	Deutz MWM
DRAK	Drake
EAST	Easthope Industries Ltd.
EICK	Eickert
ESCO	Escort
ESKA	Eska Company
EVIN	Evinrude Motors
FARY	Faryman Diesel Engines
FIAT	Fiat Marine
FIBF	Fiberform
FLAG	Flagship Marine Engine Co. Inc.
FRCE	Force Outboards
FORD	Ford Motor Co.
FUJI	Fuji
GARD	Gardner
GE	General Electric
GM	General Motors
GLAS	Glastron Engines
GRAY	Graymarine Engines
GREN	Greenwich
HAM	CNF Hamelton & Co. Ltd.
HARD	Hardin Marine
HAWK	Hawk Marine Power Inc.
HERC	Hercules Motors Corp.
HINO	Hino Motors Inc.
HOLM	Holman and Moody Inc.
HOME	Homelite
HOND	Honda Marine
HUST	Hustler Hi-Tec Marine
HYDR	Hydro Marine
INDM	Indmar Products Co. Inc.
INT	Interceptor (Crusader) (Eaton)
IF	Isotta Fraschini SPA
ISUZ	Isuzu Diesel of North America
IVCO	Iveco Aifo
JOHN	Johnson Outboard
J&T	Johnson & Towers
KAAM	Kaama
KAWA	Kawasaki
KELV	Kelvin
KERM	Kermath Engine Works
KOHL	Kohler
KRUP	Krupp Mak
KUBT	Kubota
LANC	Lancing Marine
LATH	Lathrop
LEHM	Lehman Power Corp./Ford
LEYL	Leyland Thornycroft
LINC	Lincoln
LIST	Lister Petter Ltd.
LOMB	Lombardini Marine Spa
LYC	Lycoming
MACK	Mack Diesel Power
MAN	MAN Marine Engines
MDS	Marine Drive Systems
MPC	Marine Power Corp.
MRNR	Mariner Outboards
MCCU	McCulloch/Firestone
MRCR	Mercury Marine/Mercruiser
MERC	Mercury Outboards
MERL	Merlin Marine Engines
MAID	Mermaid Marine Engines Ltd.
MITS	Mitsubishi
MITY	Mity Mite
MTU	MTU of North America
MGW	Muncie Gear Works
MWM	M.W.M. Murphy
NANI	Nanni Diesel BV
NAPR	Napier Deltic Paxmans
NISS	Nissan Marine
OMC	OMC Stern Drive
OSCO	Osco Motors Corp.
OWEN	Owens
PACE	Pacemaker
PACK	Packard
PALM	Palmer
PANT	Panther Marine Engines
PARS	Parsons Engineering Ltd.
PATH	Pathfinder Marine
PAX	Paxman Diesels
PEN	Peninsular Engines Inc.
PERK	Perkins North America
PETT	Petter Diesels
PEUG	Peugot Motors of America
PISC	Pisces
PCM	Pleasurecraft Marine Engines Co.
RCA	RCA Marine Division
REN	Renault
RIVA	Riva Marine Engines
RR	Rolls Royce
SAAB	Saab Scania
SABB	Sabb Motor A/S
SABR	Sabre Engines Ltd.
SEAK	Sea King/Montgomery Ward
SEA	Seamaster Marine Division
SEAR	Sears Roebuck & Co.
SETK	Seatek Marine Power
SOLE	Sole Diesel
SOLM	Soloman Technology
STER	Sterling
STRN	Stern Power
S&S	Stewart & Stevenson
SUZU	Suzuki
TAN	Tanaka (USA) Co. Ltd.
THOR	Thornycroft/Leyland
TOHU	Tohatsu
UNIF	Uniflite
UNIV	Universal/Medalist/Atomic
USMA	US Marine Power Corp.
DAF	Van Dorns
DENO	Vetus – Den Ouden, Inc.
VW	Volkswagon Marine Div, N.A. Inc.
VMMD	V-M Marine Diesel
VLVO	Volvo Penta of America
WANK	Wankle
WATE	Watermota Ltd.
WAUK	Waukesha
WEST	Westerbeke Corp.
WICK	Wickstrom
WOLF	Wolfpack Marine
YAMA	Yamaha Motor Corp.
YAN	YanmarDiesel Engine Co. Ltd.

1

A B INFLATABLES
MIAMI FL 33102-5255

See inside cover to adjust price for area

POBA INTERNATIONAL
MIAMI FL 33102-5255

For more recent years, see the BUC Used Boat Price Guide, Volume 1

LOA FT IN	NAME AND/ OR MODEL	TOP/ RIG	BOAT TYPE	-HULL- MTL TP	----ENGINE--- TP # HP MFG	BEAM FT IN	WGT LBS	DRAFT FT IN	RETAIL LOW	RETAIL HIGH
1996 BOATS										
18 8	5.70VS		DGY	FBG DV	OB	8 2	886		6300	7250
24 2	7.40VS		DGY	FBG DV	OB	9 4	1587		12900	14700

A M & T COMPANY
SHIELDS INC
FOUNTAIN VALLEY CA 9270 COAST GUARD MFG ID- AHH

See inside cover to adjust price for area

LOA FT IN	NAME AND/ OR MODEL	TOP/ RIG	BOAT TYPE	-HULL- MTL TP	----ENGINE--- TP # HP MFG	BEAM FT IN	WGT LBS	DRAFT FT IN	RETAIL LOW	RETAIL HIGH
1986 BOATS										
27 3	AERO	ST	SF	FBG DV	IO 425	8 3	4500	1 8	13800	15700
27 3	AERO	ST	SPTCR	FBG DV	IO 330	8 3	4500	1 8	10600	12100
27 3	AERO	ST	SPTCR	FBG DV	IO T185 MRCR	8 3	4900	1 8	11100	12600
35	SUPER-AERO	ST	SF	FBG DV	IO T260 VLVO	8 3	9400	1 10	35400	39300
35	SUPER-AERO	ST	SPTCR	FBG DV	IO T290 VLVO	8 3	9600	1 11	33200	36900
35	SUPER-AERO	ST	SPTCR	FBG DV	IO T330 MRCR	8 3	10200	1 11	34300	38100
35	SUPER-AERO	ST	SPTCR	FBG DV	IO T375	8 3	10200	1 10	35600	39600
40	AERO TIGER	ST	SPTCR	FBG TH	IO T330 MRCR	11 9	10700	1 9	38700	43000
40	AERO TIGER	ST	SPTCR	FBG TH	HD T425	11 9	10650	1 11	65100	71500
40	AERO TIGER	ST	SPTCR	FBG TH	IB T325D CAT	11 9	12800	2 3	86700	95300
50	SABER 500	ST	SPTCR	FBG TH	TD T400 MRCR	16 9	10550	1 11	44300	49200
50	SABER 500	ST	SPTCR	FBG TH	TD T425D S&S	16 9	16980	2 3	85100	93500
60	SABER 600	FB	SPTCR	FBG TH	TD R330 MRCR	16 9	20300	2 6	**	**
1985 BOATS										
27 3	EAGLE	ST	SF	FBG DV	IO 425	8 3	4500	1 8	13200	15000
27 3	EAGLE	ST	SPTCR	FBG DV	IO 330	8 3	4500	1 8	10200	11600
27 3	EAGLE	ST	SPTCR	FBG DV	IO T185 MRCR	8 3	4900	1 8	10700	12100
35	SUPER-EAGLE	ST	SF	FBG DV	IO T260 VLVO	8 3	9400	1 10	34000	37700
35	SUPER-EAGLE	ST	SPTCR	FBG DV	IO T290 VLVO	8 3	9600	1 11	31900	35400
35	SUPER-EAGLE	ST	SPTCR	FBG DV	IO T330 MRCR	8 3	10200	1 11	32900	36600
35	SUPER-EAGLE	ST	SPTCR	FBG DV	IO T375	8 3	10200	1 10	34200	38000
40	AERO	ST	SPTCR	FBG TH	IO T330 MRCR	11 9	10700	1 9	37200	41300
40	AERO	ST	SPTCR	FBG TH	HD T425	11 9	10650	1 11	62300	68500
40	AERO	ST	SPTCR	FBG TH	IB T325D CAT	11 9	12800	2 3	83000	91200
50	SABER 500	ST	SPTCR	FBG TH	TD T400 MRCR	16 9	10550	1 11	42300	47000
50	SABER 500	ST	SPTCR	FBG TH	TD T425D S&S	16 9	16980	2 3	81400	89400
60	SABER 600	FB	SPTCR	FBG TH	TD R330 MRCR	16 9	20300	2 6	**	**
1984 BOATS										
27 3	EAGLE	ST	SF	FBG DV	IO 425	8 3	4500	1 8	12800	14500
27 3	EAGLE	ST	SPTCR	FBG DV	IO 330	8 3	4500	1 8	9850	11200
27 3	EAGLE	ST	SPTCR	FBG DV	IO T185 MRCR	8 3	4900	1 8	10300	11700
35	SUPER-EAGLE	ST	SF	FBG DV	IO T260 VLVO	8 3	9400	1 10	32800	36400
35	SUPER-EAGLE	ST	SPTCR	FBG DV	IO T290 VLVO	8 3	9600	1 11	30800	34200
35	SUPER-EAGLE	ST	SPTCR	FBG DV	IO T330 MRCR	8 3	10200	1 11	31800	35300
35	SUPER-EAGLE	ST	SPTCR	FBG DV	IO T375	8 3	10200	1 10	33000	36600
40	AERO	ST	SPTCR	FBG TH	IO T330 MRCR	11 9	10700	1 9	35900	39800
40	AERO	ST	SPTCR	FBG TH	HD T425	11 9	10650	1 11	59700	65600
40	AERO	ST	SPTCR	FBG TH	IB T325D CAT	11 9	12800	2 3	79500	87400
50	SABER 500	ST	SPTCR	FBG TH	TD T400 MRCR	16 9	10550	1 11	40600	45100
50	SABER 500	ST	SPTCR	FBG TH	TD T425D S&S	16 9	16980	2 3	77900	85600
60	SABER 600	FB	SPTCR	FBG TH	TD R330 MRCR	16 9	20300	2 6	**	**

....For earlier years, see the BUC Used Boat Price Guide, Volume 3

A V S LAMINATES INC
STEIGER CRAFT
BELLPORT NY 11713

See inside cover to adjust price for area

For more recent years, see the BUC Used Boat Price Guide, Volume 1

LOA FT IN	NAME AND/ OR MODEL	TOP/ RIG	BOAT TYPE	-HULL- MTL TP	----ENGINE--- TP # HP MFG	BEAM FT IN	WGT LBS	DRAFT FT IN	RETAIL LOW	RETAIL HIGH
1994 BOATS										
18 9	STEIGER 19	OP	CTRCN	FBG SV	OB	8	2000	9	6050	6950
18 9	STEIGER MOLLY	OP	FSH	FBG SV	OB	8	1900	9	5850	6750
18 9	STEIGER MOLLY	OP	FSH	FBG SV	IO 135 VLVO	8	2400	9	7350	8450
20 6	STEIGER 21	OP	CTRCN	FBG SV	OB	8	2100	9	5750	6600
20 6	STEIGER 21	OP	CTRCN	FBG SV	IO 135 VLVO	8	2600	9	9200	10500
20 6	STEIGER BLOCK ISLAND	OP	FSH	FBG SV	OB	8	2250	9	6000	6900
20 6	STEIGER BLOCK ISLAND	OP	FSH	FBG SV	IO 135 VLVO	8	2750	9	9500	10800
20 6	STEIGER CHESAPEAKE	OP	FSH	FBG SV	OB	8	2500	9	6350	7300
20 6	STEIGER CHESAPEAKE	OP	FSH	FBG SV	IO 135 VLVO	8	3000	9	10000	11300
23	STEIGER 23	OP	CTRCN	FBG SV	OB	8 6	3000	1 1	8500	9800
23	STEIGER 23	OP	CTRCN	FBG SV	IO 245 VLVO	8 6	4000	1 1	14500	16500
23	STEIGER BLOCK ISLAND	OP	FSH	FBG SV	OB	8 6	3700	1 1	9900	11200
23	STEIGER BLOCK ISLAND	OP	FSH	FBG SV	IO 245 VLVO	8 6	4700	1 1	16400	18700
23	STEIGER CHESAPEAKE	OP	CUD	FBG SV	OB	8 6	4000	1 1	10200	11600
23	STEIGER CHESAPEAKE	OP	CUD	FBG SV	IO 245 VLVO	8 6	5000	1 1	16100	18300
24 8	STEIGER BLOCK ISLAND	OP	FSH	FBG SV	OB	9 3	3200	10	9800	11100
24 8	STEIGER BLOCK ISLAND	OP	FSH	FBG SV	IO 245 VLVO	9 3	4200	10	16700	18900
24 8	STEIGER CHESAPEAKE	OP	FSH	FBG SV	OB	9 3	3500	10	10300	11700
24 8	STEIGER CHESAPEAKE	OP	FSH	FBG SV	IO 245 VLVO	9 3	4500	10	17400	19800
1993 BOATS										
18 9	STEIGER 19	OP	CTRCN	FBG SV	OB	8	2000	9	5750	6400
18 9	STEIGER MOLLY	OP	FSH	FBG SV	OB	8	1900	9	5550	6400
18 9	STEIGER MOLLY	OP	FSH	FBG SV	IO 150	8	2400	9	6600	7600
20 6	STEIGER 21	OP	CTRCN	FBG SV	OB	8	2100	9	5450	6250
20 6	STEIGER 21	OP	CTRCN	FBG SV	IO 200	8	2600	9	8350	9600
20 6	STEIGER BLOCK ISLAND	OP	FSH	FBG SV	OB	8	2250	9	5700	6550
20 6	STEIGER BLOCK ISLAND	OP	FSH	FBG SV	IO 200	8	2750	9	8650	9950
20 6	STEIGER CHESAPEAKE	OP	FSH	FBG SV	OB	8	2500	9	6050	6950
20 6	STEIGER CHESAPEAKE	OP	FSH	FBG SV	IO 200	8	3000	9	9200	10400
23	STEIGER 23	OP	CTRCN	FBG SV	OB	8 6	3000	1 1	8100	9300
23	STEIGER 23	OP	CTRCN	FBG SV	IO 300	8 6	4000	1 1	13900	15800
23	STEIGER BLOCK ISLAND	OP	FSH	FBG SV	OB	8 6	3700	1 1	9400	10700
23	STEIGER BLOCK ISLAND	OP	FSH	FBG SV	IO 300	8 6	4700	1 1	15700	17800
23	STEIGER CHESAPEAKE	OP	CUD	FBG SV	OB	8 6	4000	1 1	9800	11100
23	STEIGER CHESAPEAKE	OP	CUD	FBG SV	IO 300	8 6	5000	1 1	15400	17500
24 8	STEIGER BLOCK ISLAND	OP	FSH	FBG SV	OB	9 3	3200	10	9300	10600
24 8	STEIGER BLOCK ISLAND	OP	FSH	FBG SV	IO 300	9 3	4200	10	16100	18300
24 8	STEIGER CHESAPEAKE	OP	FSH	FBG SV	OB	9 3	3500	10	9850	11200
24 8	STEIGER CHESAPEAKE	OP	FSH	FBG SV	IO 300	9 3	4500	10	16800	19100
1989 BOATS										
18 1	BASIC 18		CTRCN	FBG SV	OB	7 6	1000	7	2850	3350
21 6	PECONIC 21		RNBT	FBG SV	OB	7 6	1200	8	4500	5400
21 6	SPORT FISH 21		CTRCN	FBG SV	OB	7 6	1400	8	3450	4000
23	CHESAPEAKE 23		RNBT	FBG SV	OB	8 6	4000	1 1	8050	9250
24 8	BLOCK ISLAND 25	ST	RNBT	FBG SV	OB	9 3	3200	10	**	**
24 8	CHEASAPEAKE 25		UTL	FBG SV	OB	9 3	3500	10	7550	8650
24 8	SPORT FISH 25	OP	CTRCN	FBG SV	OB	9 3	2500	9	6500	7450

ABBATE
VIA FEBO SALA ITALY

See inside cover to adjust price for area

INTERNATIONAL CUSTOM YACHTS
LAUD BY THE SEA FL 33308

LOA FT IN	NAME AND/ OR MODEL	TOP/ RIG	BOAT TYPE	-HULL- MTL TP	----ENGINE--- TP # HP MFG	BEAM FT IN	WGT LBS	DRAFT FT IN	RETAIL LOW	RETAIL HIGH
1985 BOATS										
33	ABBATE OFFSHORE	OP	OFF	FBG DV	IO	9 11	8000	3 2	**	**
35 3	ABBATE OFFSHORE	OP	OFF	FBG DV	IO	8 5	7450	3 2	**	**
41 6	EXECUTIVE ABBATE	OP	OFF	FBG DV	IO	9 11	16300	3 3	**	**
1984 BOATS										
24 7	ABBATE OFFSHORE	OP	OFF	FBG DV	IO 260-330	7 8	5200	3	13200	16200
24 7	ABBATE OFFSHORE	OP	OFF	FBG DV	IO 175D VLVO	7 8	5700	3	16700	19000
24 7	ABBATE OFFSHORE	OP	OFF	FBG DV	IO T140-T145	7 8	5700	3	14900	17500
26 9	ABBATE OFFSHORE	OP	OFF	FBG DV	IO 7 10	7200	3 1	**	**
	IO 330 MRCR 18700		20800, IO T140-T260		19000	22800, IO	19D BMW		21000	23300
33	ABBATE OFFSHORE	OP	OFF	FBG DV	IO T330 MRCR	9 11	8000	3 2	29200	32400
33	ABBATE OFFSHORE	OP	OFF	FBG DV	IO T175D VLVO	9 11	8000	3 2	29300	32400
35 3	ABBATE OFFSHORE	OP	OFF	FBG DV	IO T175 VLVO	8 5	7450	3 2	34900	38700
	IO T270 FIAT 36100		40200, IO T330 MRCR		37900	42100, IO	T175D VLVO	BPM	43300	48200
	IO T175D VLVO 38100		42400							
41 6	EXECUTIVE ABBATE	OP	OFF	FBG DV	IB T270D FIAT	9 11	16300	3 3	106500	117000
41 6	EXECUTIVE ABBATE	OP	OFF	FBG DV	IB T400D IF	9 11	16300	3 3	115500	127000

....For earlier years, see the BUC Used Boat Price Guide, Volume 3

ABBOTT BOATS LTD
SARNIA ONTARIO CANADA   COAST GUARD MFG ID- ZBL See inside cover to adjust price for area

```
LOA   NAME AND/         TOP/ BOAT  -HULL-  ----ENGINE---  BEAM  WGT   DRAFT RETAIL RETAIL
FT IN OR MODEL          RIG  TYPE  MTL TP TP  # HP  MFG   FT IN LBS   FT IN  LOW    HIGH
------------------ 1987 BOATS -----------------------------------------------------------
22    ABBOTT 22         SLP SA/RC FBG KL                   7 6  3100   3 10  6850   7850
27  4 ABBOTT 27         SLP SA/RC FBG KL IB    D           9    6000   5  5 18900  21000
33    ABBOTT 33         SLP SA/RC FBG KL IB    D           8 2  6200   5  5 22900  25400
36  3 ABBOTT 36         SLP SA/RC FBG KL IB    D          10   10000   5  6 38600  42900
------------------ 1986 BOATS -----------------------------------------------------------
22    ABBOTT 22         SLP SA/RC FBG KL OB                7 6  3100   3 10  6450   7400
27    SOLING            SLP SA/OD FBG KL                   6 3  2300   4  6  6350   7250
33  3 ABBOTT 33         SLP SA/RC FBG KL SD  8 VLVO        8 3  6057   5  5 20800  23100
36  3 ABBOTT 36         SLP SA/RC FBG KL SD 10D BUKH      10    9000   5  6 32700  36400
------------------ 1985 BOATS -----------------------------------------------------------
22    ABBOTT 22         SLP SA/RC FBG KL                   7 6  3100   3 10  6050   6950
26  9 SOLING            SLP SA/OD FBG KL                   6 3  2233   4  3  5800   6650
33    ABBOTT 33         SLP SA/RC FBG KL                   8 2  6200   5  5 17100  19400
------------------ 1984 BOATS -----------------------------------------------------------
22    ABBOTT 22         SLP SAIL  FBG KL OB                7 6  3100   3 10  5700   6550
26  9 SOLING            SLP SA/OD FBG KL                   6 3  2300   4  6  5550   6350
33  4 ABBOTT 33         SLP SA/OD FBG KL    8 VLVO         8 3  6300   5  5 19100  21200
33  4 ABBOTT 33         SLP SA/OD FBG KL SD   VLVO         8 3  6057   5  5 18600  20700
```

....For earlier years, see the BUC Used Boat Price Guide, Volume 3

ABLE CUSTOM YACHTS
DIV OF TRENTON MARINE INC
ELLSWORTH ME 04605-9705 COAST GUARD MFG ID- XRA   See inside cover to adjust price for area

For more recent years, see the BUC Used Boat Price Guide, Volume 1

```
LOA   NAME AND/         TOP/ BOAT  -HULL-   ----ENGINE---  BEAM  WGT   DRAFT RETAIL RETAIL
FT IN OR MODEL          RIG  TYPE  MTL TP TP  # HP  MFG    FT IN LBS   FT IN  LOW    HIGH
------------------ 1992 BOATS ------------------------------------------------------------
33  2 ABLE CUSTOM 34    CUT SA/CR F/S KC IB    27D YAN    10  6 11900  3  9  89500  98400
41  9 ABLE CUSTOM 42    SLP SA/CR F/S KL IB    50D YAN    12  8 22000  3  2 188000 206500
42    ABLE 42P          ST  EXP  F/S SV IB  T400D CUM     13  6 23000  3  6 316000 347500
47  8 ABLE WHISTLER 48  CUT SA/CR F/S KL IB    88D YAN    13 11 35900  5 11 320500 352000
50  1 ABLE CUSTOM 50    KTH SA/CR F/S KL IB   100D WEST   13 11 36500  5 11 366000 402000
65    ABLE APOGEE 65    SLP SA/CR F/S KL IB   140D YAN    16  6 50000  6 11 718000 789500
------------------ 1991 BOATS ------------------------------------------------------------
33  2 ABLE CUSTOM 34    CUT SA/CR F/S KC IB    27D YAN    10  6 11900  3  9  84800  93100
41  9 ABLE CUSTOM 42    SLP SA/CR F/S KL IB    50D YAN    12  8 22000  3  2 178000 195500
42    ABLE 42P              EXP  F/S SV IB  T400D CUM     13  6 23000  3  6 301000 330500
47  8 ABLE WHISTLER 48  CUT SA/CR F/S KL IB    88D YAN    13 11 35900  5 11 303500 333500
50  1 ABLE CUSTOM 50    KTH SA/CR F/S KL IB   100D WEST   13 11 36500  5 11 346500 381000
60    ABLE ALTAIR 60    SLP SA/CR F/S KL IB      D        15 10 33960  7     602000 661500
------------------ 1987 BOATS ------------------------------------------------------------
32    WHISTLER 32       CUT SA/CR FDG SK IB      D        10  6 12000  3  8  69000  75800
47  8 WHISTLER 48       CUT SA/CR FDG SK IB      D        13 11 35909  5 10 244000 268000
------------------ 1985 BOATS ------------------------------------------------------------
33  5 INT'L-ONE-DESIGN  SLP SAIL  FBG KL IB      D         6  9  7100  5  4  36400  40400
------------------ 1984 BOATS ------------------------------------------------------------
32  1 WHISTLER 32       CAT SAIL  FBG KC IB    16D YAN    10  6 11986  3  8  58600  64400
33  5 INTERNATL-ONE-DESIGN SLP SAIL FBG KC IB  23D YAN     6  9  7120  5  4  34600  38400
```

....For earlier years, see the BUC Used Boat Price Guide, Volume 3

ACADIA WATERCRAFT
BAR HARBOR ME 04609   See inside cover to adjust price for area

```
LOA   NAME AND/             TOP/ BOAT  -HULL-  ----ENGINE---  BEAM  WGT  DRAFT RETAIL RETAIL
FT IN OR MODEL              RIG  TYPE  MTL TP TP # HP MFG     FT IN LBS  FT IN  LOW    HIGH
------------------ 1992 BOATS -------------------------------------------------------------
24  2 NIMBLE 24 TROPICAL    SLP SAIL  FBG KL IB  12D          8 3  2900  2  6 18900  21000
```

....For earlier years, see the BUC Used Boat Price Guide, Volume 3

ACE SPEEDBOAT CO
ANN NARBOR MI 48108-274 COAST GUARD MFG ID- ACI See inside cover to adjust price for area

```
LOA   NAME AND/      TOP/ BOAT  -HULL-  ----ENGINE---  BEAM  WGT  DRAFT RETAIL RETAIL
FT IN OR MODEL       RIG  TYPE  MTL TP TP # HP  MFG    FT IN LBS  FT IN  LOW    HIGH
------------------ 1985 BOATS -----------------------------------------------------------
21    HACKER 21      OP  RNBT MHG SV IB 220 BMW   5     2100  1  6  9550  10900
26    HACKER 26      OP  RNBT MHG SV IB 350 CRUS  5 6   2600  1  9 20400  22700
------------------ 1984 BOATS -----------------------------------------------------------
21    HACKER 21      OP  RNBT MHG SV IB 190 BMW   5     2000  1  6  8950  10100
26    HACKER 26      OP  RNBT MHG SV IB 350 CRUS  5 6   2500  1  8 19400  21600
```

....For earlier years, see the BUC Used Boat Price Guide, Volume 3

ACHILLES YACHTS LTD
TROSTRE LLANELLI UK   COAST GUARD MFG ID- BMC See inside cover to adjust price for area
FORMERLY BUTLER MOULDINGS

```
LOA   NAME AND/         TOP/ BOAT  -HULL-  ----ENGINE---  BEAM  WGT  DRAFT RETAIL RETAIL
FT IN OR MODEL          RIG  TYPE  MTL TP TP  # HP MFG    FT IN LBS  FT IN  LOW    HIGH
------------------ 1987 BOATS -----------------------------------------------------------
19  6 SEA-LION             FSH  FBG RB OB               7       1250       1250   1500
24  6 ACHILLES 750     SLP SA/RC FBG KL IB    8D        7 3  2800  3  9  8250   9500
25  2 WALRUS               FSH  FBG RB OB               8 6      4100       4100   4750
27  9 ACHILLES 840     SLP SA/RC FBG KL IB   18D        9    5500  5    16600  18800
------------------ 1986 BOATS -----------------------------------------------------------
24  6 ACHILLES 750     SLP SA/CR FBG KL IB              7 3  2800  3  9  6900   7950
24  6 ACHILLES 750     SLP SA/CR FBG KL IB    9D        7 3  2800  3  9  7750   8900
27  9 ACHILLES 840     SLP SA/OD FBG KL SD 9D- 18D      9    5500  5    15400  17700
29 10 ACHILLES 9 METRE CUT SA/OD FBG KL                 9    7000  5  6 18100  20100
------------------ 1985 BOATS -----------------------------------------------------------
19  6 SEA-LION             FSH  FBG RB OB               7       1200       1200   1400
23  9 ACHILLES 24      SLP SA/CR FBG KL OB              7 2  2600  3  9  5900   6800
23  9 ACHILLES 24      CUT SA/OD FBG KL OB              7 2  2600  3  9  5900   6800
24  6 ACHILLES 750     SLP SA/CR FBG KL OB              7 3  2800  3  9  6500   7450
24  6 ACHILLES 750     SLP SA/OD FBG KL OB    9D        7 3  2800  3  9  7250   8350
25  2 WALRUS               FSH  FBG RB OB               8 6      3650       3650   4200
27  9 ACHILLES 840     SLP SA/CR FBG KL SD 9D- 18D      9    5500  5    14400  16500
27  9 ACHILLES 840     CUT SA/OD FBG KL                 9    7000  5    15900  18100
29 10 ACHILLES 9 METRE CUT SA/OD FBG KL                 9    7000  5  6 16600  18800
------------------ 1984 BOATS -----------------------------------------------------------
19  6 SEA-LION         OP  FSH  FBG RB OB               7       1100       1100   1300
23  9 ACHILLES 7 METRE SLP SA/CR FBG KL OB              7 2        4  6  5500   6350
23  9 ACHILLES 24      SLP SA/CR FBG KL OB              7 2  2600  4  6  5650   6500
25  2 WALRUS           OP  FSH  FBG RB OB               8 8      3450       3450   4000
27  9 ACHILLES 840     SLP SA/CR FBG KL IB    D         9    5500  5    13600  15500
29 10 ACHILLES 9 METRE CUT SA/CR FBG KL IB    D         9    7000  5  6 18900  20900
```

....For earlier years, see the BUC Used Boat Price Guide, Volume 3

ACTION CRAFT INC
CAPE CORAL FL 33909-290 COAST GUARD MFG ID- AFQ See inside cover to adjust price for area

For more recent years, see the BUC Used Boat Price Guide, Volume 1

```
LOA   NAME AND/           TOP/ BOAT  -HULL-  ----ENGINE---  BEAM  WGT  DRAFT RETAIL RETAIL
FT IN OR MODEL            RIG  TYPE  MTL TP TP # HP MFG     FT IN LBS  FT IN  LOW    HIGH
------------------ 1996 BOATS -------------------------------------------------------------
16  2 FLYFISHER 1620      OP  CTRCN FBG SV OB           7      750    8   4700   5400
17  5 BAYRUNNER 1760      OP  CTRCN FBG SV OB        6 10      850    8   5450   6300
17  5 BAYRUNNER 1760SE    OP  CTRCN FBG SV OB        6 10     1050    8   6550   7550
18  1 FLATSMASTER 1810    OP  CTRCN FBG DV OB        6 10     1120    8   6150   7100
18  1 FLATSMASTER 1810SE  OP  CTRCN FBG SV OB        6 10     1120    8   8000   9200
18  9 FLATSMASTER 1890    OP  CTRCN FBG SV OB        7  6     1150    9   6500   7500
18  9 FLATSMASTER 1890SE  OP  CTRCN FBG SV OB        7  6     1150    9   8200   9450
20  2 FLATSMASTER 2020    OP  CTRCN FBG SV OB        8        1305    9   8700  10000
20  2 FLATSMASTER 2020SE  OP  CTRCN FBG SV OB        8        1305    9   9400  10700
------------------ 1995 BOATS -------------------------------------------------------------
17  5 BAYRUNNER 1760      OP  CTRCN FBG SV OB        6 10      850    8   5200   6000
17  5 BAYRUNNER 1760SE    OP  CTRCN FBG SV OB        6 10     1050    8   6250   7150
18  1 FLATSMASTER 1810    OP  CTRCN FBG DV OB        6 10     1120    8   6350   7300
18  1 FLATSMASTER 1810SE  OP  CTRCN FBG SV OB        6 10     1120    8   7050   8100
18  9 FLATSMASTER 1890    OP  CTRCN FBG SV OB        7  6     1150    9   6700   7450
18  9 FLATSMASTER 1890SE  OP  CTRCN FBG SV OB        7  6     1150    9   7450   8600
20  2 FLATSMASTER 2020    OP  CTRCN FBG SV OB        8        1305    9   7500   8600
20  2 FLATSMASTER 2020SE  OP  CTRCN FBG SV OB        8        1305    9   8550   9800
21  2 LAGUNA RUNNER 2100  OP  CTRCN FBG SV OB        8        1305   10   7150   8250
21  2 LAGUNA RUNNER 2100TE OP CTRCN FBG SV OB        8        1305   10   9450  10700
------------------ 1994 BOATS -------------------------------------------------------------
17  5 BAYRUNNER 1760SE    OP  CTRCN FBG DV OB        6 10      850    8   4950   5650
17  5 BAYRUNNER 1760SL    OP  CTRCN FBG DV OB        6 10     1050    8   5900   6800
17 10 BLACK TIP 1800          CTRCN FBG DV OB        7  2     1300   11   7100   8200
18  1 FLATSMASTER 1810SL  OP  CTRCN FBG DV OB        6 10     1120    8   6350   7300
18 10 FLATSMASTER 1810SE  OP  CTRCN FBG DV OB        6 10      910    8   5450   6300
19  6 BLACK TIP 2000      OP  CTRCN FBG DV OB        7  9     1700  1 3   9250  10500
```

ACTION CRAFT INC   —CONTINUED

See inside cover to adjust price for area

```
LOA  NAME AND/         TOP/ BOAT  -HULL-  ----ENGINE---  BEAM  WGT  DRAFT RETAIL RETAIL
FT IN OR MODEL         RIG  TYPE  MTL TP TP # HP  MFG  FT IN  LBS  FT IN  LOW   HIGH
------------------- 1994 BOATS -----------------------------------------------------
20  2 FLATSMASTER 2020SE   OP CTRCN FBG SV OB            8     915  9   5650   6500
20  2 FLATSMASTER 2020SL   OP CTRCN FBG DV OB            8    1550  8   8850  10000
------------------- 1993 BOATS -----------------------------------------------------
17  5 BAYRUNNER 1760SE     OP CTRCN FBG SV OB  6 10      850  8   5000   5100
17  5 BAYRUNNER 1760SL     OP CTRCN FBG SV OB  6 10      850  8   4450   5100
18 10 FLATSMASTER 1810SE   OP CTRCN FBG SV OB  6 10      910  8   5450   6250
18 10 FLATSMASTER 1810SL   OP CTRCN FBG SV OB  6 10      910  8   4950   5700
20  2 FLATSMASTER 2020SE   OP CTRCN FBG SV OB            8     915  9   5700   6550
20  2 FLATSMASTER 2020SL   OP CTRCN FBG SV OB            8     915  9   5050   5800
------------------- 1992 BOATS -----------------------------------------------------
17  6 BAYRUNNER 1760       OP CTRCN FBG SV OB                       5000   5750
17  6 BAYRUNNER 1760CB     OP CTRCN FBG SV OB                       5150   5900
17  6 FAST BASSER 1760FB   OP BASS  FBG SV OB               885  8  4700   5450
18  1 FLATSMASTER 1810CBSE OP CTRCN FBG SV OB  6 10         895  8  4800   5500
18  1 FLATSMASTER 1810SE   OP CTRCN FBG SV OB  6 10         895  8  4850   5600
18  8 FLATSMASTER 1880SE   OP CTRCN FBG SV OB  6 10         885  8  4850   5600
18 10 BASS 1810FBSE        OP BASS  FBG SV OB  6 10         905  8  5000   5750
19  6 EAGLE 2000           OP CTRCN FBG SV OB  7  9        1600 1 3 4850   5550
19  6 EAGLE 2000 SE        OP CTRCN FBG SV OB              1600 1 3 4850   5550
------------------- 1991 BOATS -----------------------------------------------------
17  6 BAYRUNNER 1760       OP CTRCN FBG SV OB                       4800   5500
17  6 BAYRUNNER 1760CB     OP CTRCN FBG SV OB                       4900   5650
18  1 FLATSMASTER 1810CBSE OP CTRCN FBG SV OB  6 10         895  8  4600   5250
18  1 FLATSMASTER 1810SE   OP CTRCN FBG SV OB  6 10         895  8  4650   5300
18  8 FLATSMASTER 1880SE   OP CTRCN FBG SV OB  6 10         885  8  4650   5335
18 10 BASS 1810CB          OP CTRCN FBG SV OB  6 10              8  5900   6800
18 10 BASS 1810FBSE        OP BASS  FBG SV OB  6 10         905  8  4800   5550
19  6 EAGLE 2000           OP CTRCN FBG SV OB  7  9        1600 1 3 4600   5300
------------------- 1990 BOATS -----------------------------------------------------
17    COASTLINE 1700CB     OP FSH   FBG SV OB  6 10         880  8  4100   4800
17    COASTLINE 1700FB     OP BASS  FBG SV OB  6 10              8  4100   4750
17    COASTLINE 1710       OP CTRCN FBG SV OB  6 10         880  8  4150   4800
17  5 BAYRUNNER 1736       OP CTRCN FBG SV OB  6 10         850  8  3850   4450
17  5 FLATSMASTER 1736SE   OP CTRCN FBG SV OB  6 10         850  8  4350   5000
18  1 BAYRUNNER 1810       OP CTRCN FBG SV OB  6 10         895  8  4100   4800
18  1 FLATSMASTER 1810SE   OP CTRCN FBG SV OB  6 10         895  8  4650   5350
18  8 BAYRUNNER 1880       OP CTRCN FBG SV OB  6 10         885  8  4150   4850
18  8 FLATSMASTER 1880SE   OP CTRCN FBG SV OB  6 10         885  8  4700   5400
18 10 BASS 1810FB          OP BASS  FBG SV OB  6 10              8  5500   6350
18 10 BASS 1810FBSE        OP BASS  FBG SV OB  6 10              8  5900   6750
18 10 BAYRUNNER 1810CB     OP CTRCN FBG SV OB  6 10              8  5650   6500
19  4 BLUEWATER 1940       OP CTRCN FBG SV OB  6 10              8  5450   6300
19  4 BLUEWATER 1940D      OP CTRCN FBG SV OB  6 10              8  6000   6900
------------------- 1989 BOATS -----------------------------------------------------
17    COASTLINE 1700       OP FSH   FBG SV OB  6 10         880  8  3950   4600
17    COASTLINE 1710 DLX   OP CTRCN FBG SV OB  6 10         880  8  3950   4600
17  5 BAYRUNNER 1736       OP CTRCN FBG SV OB  6 10         850  8  3650   4200
17  5 BAYRUNNER 1750       OP FSH   FBG SV OB  6 10         835  8  3850   4450
17  5 BAYRUNNER 1755       OP CTRCN FBG SV OB  6 10         835  8  3850   4500
17  5 FLATSMASTER 1736SE   OP CTRCN FBG SV OB  6 10         850  8  4200   4850
18  1 BAYRUNNER 1810       OP CTRCN FBG SV OB  6 10         895  8  3900   4550
18  1 FLATSMASTER 1810SE   OP CTRCN FBG SV OB  6 10         895  8  4500   5150
18  8 BAYRUNNER 1880       OP CTRCN FBG SV OB  6 10         885  8  3950   4600
18  8 FLATSMASTER 1880SE   OP CTRCN FBG SV OB  6 10         885  8  4200   5200
------------------- 1988 BOATS -----------------------------------------------------
17  5 BAYRUNNER 1750       OP FSH   FBG SV OB  6 10         835  8  3700   4300
17  5 BAYRUNNER 1755       OP CTRCN FBG SV OB  6 10         835  8  3700   4300
17  5 FLATSMASTER 1736     OP CTRCN FBG SV OB  6 10         850  8  3700   4300
17  5 FLATSMASTER 1736SE   OP CTRCN FBG SV OB  6 10         850  8  3850   4450
18  8 FLATSMASTER 1880     OP CTRCN FBG SV OB  6 10         885  8  3950   4600
18  8 FLATSMASTER 1880SE   OP CTRCN FBG SV OB  6 10         885  8  4150   4800
------------------- 1987 BOATS -----------------------------------------------------
17  5 FASTBASSER           OP BASS  FBG SV OB  6 10              8  3650   4250
17  5 BAYRUNNER 1750       OP FSH   FBG SV OB  6 10         835  8  3550   4150
17  5 BAYRUNNER 1755       OP CTRCN FBG SV OB  6 10         835  8  3550   4150
17  5 FLATSMASTER 1736     OP CTRCN FBG SV OB  6 10         850  8  3350   3900
17  5 FLATSMASTER 1736SE   OP CTRCN FBG SV OB  6 10         850  8  3900   4555
18  8 FLATSMASTER 1880     OP CTRCN FBG SV OB  6 10         885  8  3600   4200
18  8 FLATSMASTER 1880SE   OP CTRCN FBG SV OB  6 10         885  8  4200   4900
------------------- 1985 BOATS -----------------------------------------------------
17  2 STU-APTE FLATSMASTER OP FSH   FBG SV OB  6 10         790  8  3100   3650
17  2 FASTBASSER           OP BASS  FBG SV OB  6 10              8  3400   4000
17  3 STU-APTE FLATSMASTER OP FSH   FBG SV OB  6 10         790  8  3150   3650
17  3 STU-APTE II SE       OP FSH   FBG SV OB  6 10         850  8  3400   4000
17  3 STU-APTE SE          OP FSH   FBG SV OB  6 10         850  8  3300   3800
18  4 CHALLENGER 1820      OP CTRCN FBG SV OB  7           1375 11  5200   5950
18  4 CHALLENGER 1820      OP CTRCN FBG SV SE 115 OMC  7             **     **
------------------- 1984 BOATS -----------------------------------------------------
17  2 STU APTE FLATSMASTER OP CTRCN FBG SV OB  6 10         790  8  3050   3550
17  3 BACK-BAY 1730        OP FSH   FBG SV OB  6 10         900  8  3400   3950
17  3 BASS-CATCHER 1732    OP BASS  FBG SV OB  6 10         925  8  3550   4100
17  3 BONEFISHER 1734      OP CTRCN FBG SV OB  6 10         975  8  3700   4350
17  3 PACEMAKER 1738       OP RNBT  FBG SV OB  6 10         925  8  3550   4150
17  3 STU APTE FLATSMASTER OP CTRCN FBG SV OB  6 10         790  8  3050   3550
17  3 STU APTE FLATSMASTER OP FSH   FBG SV OB  6 10         850  8  3250   3800
18  2 CHALLENGER 1820      OP CTRCN FBG SV OB  7           1375 11  5000   5750
18  2 CHALLENGER 1820      OP CTRCN FBG SV SE 115 OMC  7             **     **
18  2 CHALLENGER XL 1822   OP CTRCN FBG SV OB  7           1400 11  5050   5850
18  2 CHALLENGER XL 1822   OP CTRCN FBG SV SE 115 OMC  7             **     **
```

...For earlier years, see the BUC Used Boat Price Guide, Volume 3

ACTIVE POWERBOATS

EXCESS MARINE   See inside cover to adjust price for area
POMPANO BEACH FL 33064   COAST GUARD MFG ID- ATD
                         FORMERLY THUNDER BOATS

For more recent years, see the BUC Used Boat Price Guide, Volume 1

```
LOA  NAME AND/         TOP/ BOAT  -HULL-  ----ENGINE---  BEAM  WGT  DRAFT RETAIL RETAIL
FT IN OR MODEL         RIG  TYPE  MTL TP TP # HP  MFG  FT IN  LBS  FT IN  LOW   HIGH
------------------- 1994 BOATS -----------------------------------------------------
24  3 THUNDER 24           OFF F/S DV IO 300 MRCR  7 8  4000 1 5  15400  17400
        IO 355-385 16900 20500,  IO 415 MRCR 19700 21900,  IO 465-500 22200 26700
        IO 525 MRCR 25300 28100
31  6 THUNDER 32           OFF F/S DV IO 415-500  8 6  7000 1 6  37900  43700
        IO T300-T415 40300 48900, IO T465-T600 46200 56100, IO T800 MRCR ** **
32  3 ACTIVE THUNDER 32    OFF F/S DV IO T350-T390 9     7800 1 1  48500  56500
32  3 ACTIVE THUNDER 32    OFF F/S DV IO T465-T525 9     7800 1 1  59900  73900
32  3 ACTIVE THUNDER 32    OFF F/S DV IO T575-T800 9     7800 1 1  72300  79500
37    ACTIVE THUNDER 37    OFF F/S CT IO       MRCR 11   9600 1    70200  77100
37    ACTIVE THUNDER 37    OFF F/S CT IO T850  MRCR 11   9600 1    **     **
37    ACTIVE THUNDER 37    OFF F/S CT IO T10C  MRCR 11   9600 1    **     **
------------------- 1993 BOATS -----------------------------------------------------
24  3 THUNDER 24           OFF F/S DV IO 330-365  7 8  4000 1 5  15000  18300
        IO 390 MRCR 17100 19400,  IO 465 20800 23100,  IO 525 MRCR 23600 26300
31  6 THUNDER 31           OFF F/S DV IO T330-T465 8 6 7000 1 6  38500  47500
31  6 THUNDER 31           OFF F/S DV IO T525-T575 8 6 7000 1 6  44800  51600
31  6 THUNDER 31           OFF F/S DV IO T800 MRCR 8 6 7000 1 6  **     **
32  3 ACTIVE THUNDER 32    OFF F/S DV IO T365-T390 9    7800 1 1  46100  52600
32  3 ACTIVE THUNDER 32    OFF F/S DV IO T465-T525 9    7800 1 1  55700  68600
32  3 ACTIVE THUNDER 32    OFF F/S DV IO T575-T800 9    7800 1 1  67200  73800
37    ACTIVE THUNDER 37    OFF F/S CT IO T575 MRCR 11   9600 1    65600  72100
37    ACTIVE THUNDER 37    OFF F/S CT IO T850 MRCR 11   9600 1    **     **
37    ACTIVE THUNDER 37    OFF F/S CT IO T10C MRCR 11   9600 1    **     **
------------------- 1992 BOATS -----------------------------------------------------
16    ACTIVE THUNDER 16    OP RNBT F/S   CT OB          6    550  6     2500   2950
23  8 ACTIVE THUNDER 24    CR      F/S      OB          6   1700  6     9200  10500
24  4 THUNDER 24           OP OFF  F/S      OB          6   4000  2 6  19000  21100
24  4 THUNDER 24           OP OFF  F/S      IO          6   4000  2    14100  17100
24  4 THUNDER 24           OP OFF  F/S      IO 330-365  7 6 4000  2 6  21100  23400
24  4 THUNDER 24           OP OFF  F/S      IO 425-465  8   4000  2    17400  21600
25  8 THUNDER 26           OP OFF  F/S      OB          8              19000  21100
31  6 THUNDER 31           OP OFF  F/S      IO T330-T420 8  7000 3 10  38700  42500
31  6 THUNDER 31           OP OFF  F/S      IO T500-T575 8  7200 3 11  43700  48000
31  6 THUNDER 31           OP OFF  F/S      IO T425 MRCR 8  7200 3 11  44800  42700
32    ACTIVE THUNDER 32/12 OP OFF  F/S   CT OB         11 8 5700 3     52300  57500
32  3 ACTIVE THUNDER 32/12 OP OFF  F/S DV IO T420-T575 11 8 7300 3 6   43300  53200
32  3 ACTIVE THUNDER 32    OP OFF  F/S DV IO T330-T420  8 10 7800 4 1  33100  43400
32  3 ACTIVE THUNDER 32    OP OFF  F/S DV IO T365-T500  8 10 7800 4 1  41300  50300
32  3 ACTIVE THUNDER 32    OP OFF  F/S DV IO T575 MRCR  8 10 7800 4 1  53100  63900
37    ACTIVE THUNDER 37    OP OFF  F/S CT IO T575 MRCR 11 8  9100 4    58200  63900
37    ACTIVE THUNDER 37/12 OP OFF  F/S CT IO T575 MRCR 11 8  9100 4    **     **
37    ACTIVE THUNDER 37/12 OP OFF  F/S CT IO T850D GM  11 8  9100 4    **     **
37    ACTIVE THUNDER 37    OP OFF  F/S CT IO T10CD GM  11 8  9100 4    **     **
42    THUNDER 42           OP OFF  F/S DV IO R365 MRCR  9   10050 3 6  78000  85700
47    ACTIVE THUNDER 47    OP OFF  F/S CT IO Q420 MRCR 14   12000 4 4 132500 145500
```

LOA FT IN	NAME AND/ OR MODEL	TOP/ RIG	BOAT TYPE	-HULL- MTL TP	----ENGINE--- TP # HP MFG	BEAM FT IN	WGT LBS	DRAFT FT IN	RETAIL LOW	RETAIL HIGH
					1991 BOATS					
16	ACTIVE THUNDER 16	OP	RNBT	F/S CT OB		6 6	550	6	2400	2800
23 8	ACTIVE THUNDER 24		CR	F/S OB		6	1700	1 6	8850	10100
24 4	THUNDER 24	OP	OFF	F/S OB		7 6	4000	2 7	18300	20400
24 4	THUNDER 24	OP	OFF	F/S IO	330-365	7 6	4000	3 2	13200	16100
24 4	THUNDER 24	OP	OFF	F/S IO	502 MRCR	7 6	4000	3 2	19800	22000
24 4	THUNDER 24	OP	OFF	F/S DV IO	425 MRCR	7 6	3800	3 2	15900	18100
24 4	THUNDER 24	OP	OFF	F/S DV IO	465 MRCR	7 6	3800	3 2	17600	20000
31 6	THUNDER 31	OP	OFF	F/S OB		8	4600	3 2	36600	40700
31 6	THUNDER 31	OP	OFF	F/S IO	T330-T420	8	7000	3 10	33500	39800
31 6	THUNDER 31	OP	OFF	F/S IO	T500-T575	8	7200	3 11	38200	44900
31 6	THUNDER 31	OP	OFF	F/S DV IO	T425 MRCR	8	7200	3 11	36000	40000
32	ACTIVE THUNDER 32/12	OP	OFF	F/S CT OB		11 8	5700	3	50200	55100
32	ACTIVE THUNDER 32/12	OP	OFF	F/S CT IO	T420-T575	11 8	7300	3 6	40400	49900
32 3	ACTIVE THUNDER 32		OFF	F/S DV OB		8 10	5700	3 2	37400	41600
32 3	ACTIVE THUNDER 32		OFF	F/S DV IO	T365-T500	8 10	7800	4 1	38700	47200
32 3	ACTIVE THUNDER 32		OFF	F/S DV IO	T575 MRCR	8 10	7800	4	44800	49800
37	ACTIVE THUNDER 37/12	OP	OFF	F/S CT IO	T575 MRCR	11 8	9100	4	54600	60000
37	ACTIVE THUNDER 37/12	OP	OFF	F/S CT IO	T850D GM	11 8	9100	4	**	**
37	ACTIVE THUNDER 37/12	OP	OFF	F/S CT IO	T10CD GM	11 8	9500	4 2	**	**
42	THUNDER 42		OFF	F/S DV IO	R365 MRCR	9	10050	3 6	73200	80400
47	ACTIVE THUNDER 47	OP	OFF	F/S CT IO	Q420 MRCR	14	12000	4 4	124000	136000
					1990 BOATS					
17 3	170 BOW RIDER		OP	RNBT FBG OB		7	1200	1 10	5050	5800
17 3	170 BOW RIDER		RNBT	FBG IO	175 MRCR	7	1200	2	3400	3950
23 8	LIGHTNING EXPRESS 24		OFF	F/S CT OB		8	1700	1 6	8400	9650
23 8	LIGHTNING EXPRESS 24		OFF	F/S CT IO	365 MRCR	8	2900	2 3	11000	12500
23 8	LIGHTNING EXPRESS 24		OFF	F/S CT IO	420 MRCR	8	2900	2 3	12900	14700
24 4	THUNDER 24	OP	OFF	F/S OB		7 6	4000	2 7	17200	19600
24 4	THUNDER 24	OP	OFF	F/S IO	330-365	7 6	4000	3 2	12400	15100
24 4	THUNDER 24	OP	OFF	F/S IO	502 MRCR	7 6	4000	3 2	18800	20800
31 6	THUNDER 31	OP	OFF	F/S OB		8	4600	3 2	35100	39000
31 6	THUNDER 31	OP	OFF	F/S IO	T330-T420	8	7000	3 10	31500	37400
31 6	THUNDER 31	OP	OFF	F/S IO	T500-T575	8	7200	3 11	35900	42200
32 3	LIGHTNING EXPRESS 32		OFF	F/S CT IO		8 10	5700	3 2	41400	46000
32 3	LIGHTNING EXPRESS 32		OFF	F/S CT IO	T365-T500	8 10	5200	4 1	36000	43900
32 3	LIGHTNING EXPRESS 32		OFF	F/S CT IO	T575 MRCR	8 10	5200	4 1	40900	45500
37	ACTIVE THUNDER CAT		RACE	F/S CT OB		11 10	3300	3	72000	79100
37	ACTIVE THUNDER CAT		RACE	F/S CT IO	T502 MRCR	11 10	5700	4	61300	67400
37	ACTIVE THUNDER CAT		RACE	F/S CT IO	T575 MRCR	11 10	5700	4	64300	70700
					1989 BOATS					
23 8	LIGHTNING EXPRESS	OP	OFF	FBG TH OB		8	1700	1 6	8100	9300
23 8	LIGHTNING EXPRESS	OP	OFF	FBG TH IO	330 MRCR	8	1700	1 6	8100	9350
23 8	LIGHTNING EXPRESS	OP	OFF	FBG TH IO	365 MRCR	8	1700	1 6	9100	10300
31 6	THUNDER 31	OP	OFF	FBG DV IO	T260-T365	8	7000	2 4	28200	33800
32 3	THUNDER 32	OP	OFF	FBG TH IO	T330-T365	10	6000		33400	38100

ADAMS BLAIR & ASSOCIATES
WASHINGTON DC 20006   See inside cover to adjust price for area

LOA FT IN	NAME AND/ OR MODEL	TOP/ RIG	BOAT TYPE	-HULL- MTL TP	----ENGINE--- TP # HP MFG	BEAM FT IN	WGT LBS	DRAFT FT IN	RETAIL LOW	RETAIL HIGH
					1985 BOATS					
19 10	ETAP 20	SLP	SA/CR	FBG SK OB		7 6	1499	3 9	6100	7050
24 2	ETAP 23	SLP	SA/CR	FBG SK IB		8 2	3320	4 9	12100	13800
25	ETAP 26	SLP	SA/CR	FBG SK IB		9	5000	5 5	19100	21200
27 8	ETAP 28	SLP	SA/CR	FBG SK IB		9	6610	5 5	27200	30200
40	TRINTELLA 40A	SLP	SA/CR	AL KL IB	D	12 9	18000	6 6	108000	118500
42	TRINTELLA 42	SLP	SA/CR	FBG KC IB	D	13 2	18000	7	116500	128000
44 2	TRINTELLA 44A	SLP	SA/CR	AL KL IB	D	13 7	22000	8 9	141500	156000
45	TRINTELLA 45	SLP	SA/CR	FBG KL IB	D	13 5	34000	7 2	179500	197500
49 4 5	TRINTELLA 49A	SLP	SA/CR	AL KL IB	D	14 9	29000	9 6	192000	211000
53	TRINTELLA 53	SLP	SA/CR	FBG KC IB	D	15 5	46000	7 2	259500	285000
53	TRINTELLA 53	SLP	SA/CR	FBG KL IB	D	15 5	46000	7 2	259500	285000
57 1	TRINTELLA 57A	SLP	SA/CR	AL KL IB	D	15 1	38000	7 3	341500	375000

ADMIRALTY LTD
NEWPORT BEACH CA 92663   See inside cover to adjust price for area

LOA FT IN	NAME AND/ OR MODEL	TOP/ RIG	BOAT TYPE	-HULL- MTL TP	----ENGINE--- TP # HP MFG	BEAM FT IN	WGT LBS	DRAFT FT IN	RETAIL LOW	RETAIL HIGH
					1984 BOATS					
41	LORD NELSON	CUT	SA/RC	FBG KL OB		12	30500	5 8	110500	121500

....For earlier years, see the BUC Used Boat Price Guide, Volume 3

ADMIRALTY YACHT SALES INC
ANNAPOLIS MD 21403   See inside cover to adjust price for area

LOA FT IN	NAME AND/ OR MODEL	TOP/ RIG	BOAT TYPE	-HULL- MTL TP	----ENGINE--- TP # HP MFG	BEAM FT IN	WGT LBS	DRAFT FT IN	RETAIL LOW	RETAIL HIGH
					1985 BOATS					
43 4	SEA-FINN 41	KTH	MS	FBG KL		11 10	25350	5	97400	107000

ADVANTAGE BOATS
LAKE HAVASU CITY AZ 86403   See inside cover to adjust price for area

For more recent years, see the BUC Used Boat Price Guide, Volume 1

LOA FT IN	NAME AND/ OR MODEL	TOP/ RIG	BOAT TYPE	-HULL- MTL TP	----ENGINE--- TP # HP MFG	BEAM FT IN	WGT LBS	DRAFT FT IN	RETAIL LOW	RETAIL HIGH
					1996 BOATS					
18	SKI SPORT	SKI	FBG DV OB			6 8	1875		14100	16000
18	SKI SPORT	SKI	FBG DV JT	330		6 8	1875		9450	10700
20	BANSHEE TUNNEL	OFF	FBG SK OB			7 4	2000		16900	19200
20	BANSHEE TUNNEL	OFF	FBG SK JT	330		7 4	2000		12400	14100
21	21 SR	OFF	FBG DV OB			7 9	2900		15800	18000
21	21 SR BR	B/R	FBG DV IO	265		7 9	2900		12300	14000
21	21 SR BR	B/R	FBG DV JT	390		7 9	2900		15800	18000
22	CITATION 22	OFF	FBG DV IO	300		7 11	3750		17200	19600
22	CITATION 22 BR	B/R	FBG DV IO	300		7 11	3520		15500	17600
22	SPORT CAT 22	OFF	FBG CT IO	300		8 3	2800		14800	16800
27	VICTORY 27	OFF	FBG DV IO	365		8 3	4280		28000	31100
27	VICTORY 27	OFF	FBG DV IO	T350		8 3	4280		34300	38100
27	VICTORY 27 BR	B/R	FBG DV IO	365		8 3	4280		26200	29200
30	OFFSHORE 30	OFF	FBG DV IO	365		8 4	5800		33900	37700
30	OFFSHORE 30	OFF	FBG DV IO	T350		8 4	5800		39400	43800
34	OFFSHORE 34	OFF	FBG DV IO	T350		8 6	7340		66100	72700
					1995 BOATS					
18	BOWRIDER	B/R	FBG DV OB			6 8	1875		13400	15200
18	BOWRIDER	B/R	FBG DV JT	330		6 8	1875		9000	10200
18	SKI SPORT	SKI	FBG DV OB			6 8	1875		13400	15200
18	SKI SPORT	SKI	FBG DV JT	330		6 8	1875		9000	10200
20	CLASSIC	OFF	FBG DV OB			7 8	2345		18000	20000
20	CLASSIC	OFF	FBG DV JT	330		7 8	2345		12700	14500
20	CLASSIC BR	B/R	FBG DV OB			7 8	2500		18600	20700
20	CLASSIC BR	B/R	FBG DV JT	330		7 8	2500		13100	14900
21	21 SR	OFF	FBG DV OB			7 9	2900		20200	22500
21	21 SR	OFF	FBG DV JT	365		7 9	2900		15000	17000
21	21 SR BR	B/R	FBG DV OB			7 9	2900		20200	22500
21	21 SR BR	B/R	FBG DV JT	365		7 9	2900		15000	17000
22	CITATION 22	OFF	FBG DV IO	330		7 11	3750		17000	19300
22	CITATION 22 BR	B/R	FBG DV IO	330		7 11	3520		15300	17400
27	VICTORY 27	OFF	FBG DV IO	330		8 3	4280		26100	29000
27	VICTORY 27 BR	B/R	FBG DV IO	365		8 3	4280		24500	27200
30	OFFSHORE 30	OFF	FBG DV IO	T350		8 4	5800		36700	40800
30	OFFSHORE 30 BR	B/R	FBG DV IO	T350		8 4	5800		28500	31700
34	OFFSHORE 34	OFF	FBG DV IO	T350		8 6	7340		61700	67800
34	OFFSHORE 34 BR	B/R	FBG DV IO	T350		8 6	7340		47300	52000
					1994 BOATS					
18	SKI SPORT	SKI	FBG DV JT	330		6 8	1875		8400	9650
20	CLASSIC	OFF	FBG DV OB			7 8	2345		16900	19200
20	CLASSIC	OFF	FBG DV JT	330		7 8	2345		12100	13700
20	CLASSIC BR	B/R	FBG DV OB			7 8	2345		16900	19200
20	CLASSIC BR	B/R	FBG DV JT	330		7 8	2345		9100	10300
21	21 SR	OFF	FBG DV IO	260		7 9	2900		12400	14100
21	21 SR	OFF	FBG DV JT	330		7 9	2900		11700	13300
21	21 SR	OFF	FBG DV JT	365		7 9	2900		14200	16100
21	21 SR BR	B/R	FBG DV IO	260		7 9	2975		11100	12600
21	21 SR BR	B/R	FBG DV JT	330		7 9	2975		19300	21500
21	21 SR BR	B/R	FBG DV JT	365		7 9	2975		14400	16300
22	CITATION 22	OFF	FBG DV IO	330		7 11	3750		15800	18000
22	CITATION 22 BR	B/R	FBG DV IO	330		7 11	3520		14300	16200
24	OFFSHORE 24	OFF	FBG DV IO	330		7 11	4250		19100	21200
24	OFFSHORE BR	B/R	FBG DV IO	330		7 11	4250		18100	20100
27	VICTORY 27	OFF	FBG DV IO	330		8 3	4280		42000	46700
27	VICTORY 27	OFF	FBG DV IO	365		8 3	4280		24400	27100
27	VICTORY 27	OFF	FBG DV IO	T350		8 3	4280		29900	33200

1994 BOATS

LOA FT IN	NAME AND/OR MODEL	TOP/RIG	BOAT TYPE	HULL MTL	TP	TP	HP	BEAM FT IN	WGT LBS	RETAIL LOW	RETAIL HIGH
30	OFFSHORE 30			OFF	FBG	DV	IO	T365	8 4	5800	34900	38700
34	VICTORY 34			OFF	FBG	DV	IO	T350	8 2		61200	67300

LOA FT IN	NAME AND/OR MODEL	RIG	MTL	TP	TP	HP	BEAM FT IN	WGT LBS	RETAIL LOW	RETAIL HIGH
30	OFFSHORE 30	OFF	FBG	DV	IO	T365	8 4	5800	34900	38700
34	VICTORY 34	OFF	FBG	DV	IO	T350	8 2		61200	67300

1993 BOATS

LOA FT IN	NAME AND/OR MODEL	RIG	MTL	TP	TP	HP	BEAM FT IN	WGT LBS	RETAIL LOW	RETAIL HIGH
18	BOWRIDER	B/R	FBG	DV	OB		8 6	1875	12300	14000
18	BOWRIDER	B/R	FBG	DV	JT	333	6 8	1950	8100	9300
18	SKI SPORT	SKI	FBG	DV	JT	333	6 8	1875	7950	9150
18	TUNNEL RUNNER	OFF	FBG	CT	OB		6 5	1950	12600	14300
18	TUNNEL RUNNER	OFF	FBG	CT	JT	333	6 5	1950	7950	9150
19	WARRIOR	OFF	FBG	DV	OB		6 9	2000	13200	15000
19	WARRIOR	OFF	FBG	DV	IO	230	6 9	2000	6500	7450
19	WARRIOR	OFF	FBG	DV	JT	333	6 9	2000	8800	10000
19	WARRIOR BR	B/R	FBG	DV	OB		6 9	2150	13700	15500
19	WARRIOR BR	B/R	FBG	DV	IO	230	6 9	2150	6300	7250
19	WARRIOR BR	B/R	FBG	DV	JT	333	6 9	2150	9050	10300
20	BANSHEE	OFF	FBG	DV	OB		7 2	2000	14800	16800
20	BANSHEE	OFF	FBG	DV	JT	333	7 2	2000	10400	11800
20	CLASSIC	OFF	FBG	DV	OB		7 8	2345	16200	18400
20	CLASSIC	OFF	FBG	DV	IO	230	7 8	2345	8650	9950
20	CLASSIC	OFF	FBG	DV	JT	333	7 8	2345	11400	13000
20	CLASSIC BR	B/R	FBG	DV	OB		7 8	2500	16700	18900
20	CLASSIC BR	B/R	FBG	DV	IO	230	7 8	2500	8350	9600
20	CLASSIC BR	B/R	FBG	DV	JT	333	7 8	2500	11800	13400
21	21 SR	OFF	FBG	DV	OB		7 9	2900	20100	22300
21	21 SR	OFF	FBG	DV	IO	230	7 9	2900	10300	11700
21	21 SR	OFF	FBG	DV	JT	370	7 9	2900	13400	15300
21	21 SR BR	B/R	FBG	DV	OB		7 9	3000	20400	22600
21	21 SR BR	B/R	FBG	DV	IO	280	7 9	3000	10500	11900
21	21 SR BR	B/R	FBG	DV	JT	370	7 9	3000	13700	15600
22	CITATION 22	OFF	FBG	DV	OB		7 11	3750	24900	27700
22	CITATION 22	OFF	FBG	DV	IO	330	7 11	3750	14800	16800
22	CITATION 22 BR	B/R	FBG	DV	OB		7 11	3750	24900	27700
22	CITATION 22 BR	B/R	FBG	DV	IO	330	7 11	3750	13900	15800
24	OFFSHORE 24	OFF	FBG	DV	OB		7 11	4250	31800	35400
24	OFFSHORE 24	OFF	FBG	DV	IO	330	7 11	4250	18000	20000
24	OFFSHORE 24 BR	B/R	FBG	DV	OB		7 11	4250	31800	35400
24	OFFSHORE 24 BR	B/R	FBG	DV	IO	330	7 11	4250	16500	18800
27	VICTORY 27	OFF	FBG	DV	OB		8 2	4820	40600	45100
27	VICTORY 27	OFF	FBG	DV	IO	365	8 2	4820	23800	26500
27	VICTORY 27	OFF	FBG	DV	IO	T350	8 2	4820	28800	32000

1992 BOATS

LOA FT IN	NAME AND/OR MODEL	RIG	MTL	TP	TP	HP	BEAM FT IN	WGT LBS	RETAIL LOW	RETAIL HIGH
18	BOWRIDER	B/R	FBG	DV	OB		8 6	1875	11800	13400
18	BOWRIDER	B/R	FBG	DV	JT	333	6 8	1950	7700	8850
18	SKI SPORT	SKI	FBG	DV	JT	333	6 8	1875	7550	8700
18	TUNNEL RUNNER	OFF	FBG	CT	OB		6 5	1950	12100	13700
18	TUNNEL RUNNER	OFF	FBG	CT	JT	333	6 5	1950	7550	8650
19	WARRIOR	OFF	FBG	DV	OB		6 9	2000	12700	14400
19	WARRIOR	OFF	FBG	DV	IO	230	6 9	2000	6100	7000
19	WARRIOR	OFF	FBG	DV	JT	333	6 9	2000	8250	9500
19	WARRIOR BR	B/R	FBG	DV	OB		6 9	2175	13200	15000
19	WARRIOR BR	B/R	FBG	DV	IO	230	6 9	2150	5900	6750
19	WARRIOR BR	B/R	FBG	DV	JT	333	6 9	2150	8500	9800
20	BANSHEE	OFF	FBG	DV	OB		7 2	2000	14200	16100
20	BANSHEE	OFF	FBG	DV	JT	333	7 2	2000	9850	11200
20	CLASSIC	OFF	FBG	DV	OB		7 8	2345	15500	17700
20	CLASSIC	OFF	FBG	DV	IO	230	7 8	2345	8100	9300
20	CLASSIC	OFF	FBG	DV	JT	333	7 8	2345	10900	12300
20	CLASSIC BR	B/R	FBG	DV	OB		7 8	2500	16000	18200
20	CLASSIC BR	B/R	FBG	DV	IO	230	7 8	2500	7800	9000
20	CLASSIC BR	B/R	FBG	DV	JT	333	7 8	2500	11200	12700
21	21 SR	OFF	FBG	DV	OB		7 9	2900	19300	21400
21	21 SR	OFF	FBG	DV	IO	230	7 9	2900	9700	11000
21	21 SR	OFF	FBG	DV	JT	370	7 9	2900	12700	14500
22	CITATION 22	OFF	FBG	DV	OB		8 6	3200	22200	24700
22	CITATION 22	OFF	FBG	DV	IO	300	7 11	3750	13100	14900
22	CITATION 22 BR	B/R	FBG	DV	OB		7 11	3750	24000	26600
22	CITATION 22 BR	B/R	FBG	DV	IO	300	7 11	3750	12300	14000
24	OFFSHORE 24	OFF	FBG	DV	OB		7 11	4250	30600	34000
24	OFFSHORE 24	OFF	FBG	DV	IO	300	7 11	4250	16800	17900
24	OFFSHORE 24 BR	B/R	FBG	DV	OB		7 11	4250	30600	34000
24	OFFSHORE 24 BR	B/R	FBG	DV	IO	300	7 11	4250	14800	16800
27	VICTORY 27	OFF	FBG	DV	OB		8 2	4820	39000	43400
27	VICTORY 27	OFF	FBG	DV	IO	365	8 2	4820	22300	24800
27	VICTORY 27	OFF	FBG	DV	IO	T350	8 2	4820	27000	30000
30	OFFSHORE 30	OFF	FBG	DV	OB		8 3	4820	53400	58700
30	OFFSHORE 30	OFF	FBG	DV	IO	365	8 3	4820	25000	27800
30	OFFSHORE 30	OFF	FBG	DV	IO	T365	8 3	4820	30000	33300

1991 BOATS

LOA FT IN	NAME AND/OR MODEL	RIG	MTL	TP	TP	HP	BEAM FT IN	WGT LBS	RETAIL LOW	RETAIL HIGH
18	BOWRIDER	B/R	FBG	DV	OB		6 8	1950	11600	13200
18	BOWRIDER	B/R	FBG	DV	JT	330	6 8	1950	7300	8400
18	SKI SPORT	SKI	FBG	DV	JT	330	6 8	1875	7200	8250
18	TUNNEL RUNNER	OFF	FBG	DV	OB		6 5	1950	11600	13200
18	TUNNEL RUNNER	OFF	FBG	CT	JT	330	6 5	1950	7150	8250
19	WARRIOR	OFF	FBG	DV	OB		6 9	2150	12600	14400
19	WARRIOR	OFF	FBG	DV	IO	230	6 9	2000	5700	6550
19	WARRIOR	OFF	FBG	DV	JT	330	6 9	2000	7850	9000
19	WARRIOR BR	B/R	FBG	DV	OB		6 9	2150	12600	14400
19	WARRIOR BR	B/R	FBG	DV	IO	230	6 9	2150	5500	6350
19	WARRIOR BR	B/R	FBG	DV	JT	330	6 9	2150	8100	9300
20	BANSHEE	OFF	FBG	DV	OB		7 2	2000	13700	15500
20	BANSHEE	OFF	FBG	DV	JT	330	7 2	2000	9400	10700
20	CLASSIC	OFF	FBG	DV	OB		8 2	2345	15000	17000
20	CLASSIC	OFF	FBG	DV	IO	230	7 8	2345	7600	8750
20	CLASSIC	OFF	FBG	DV	JT	330	7 8	2345	10300	11700
20	CLASSIC BR	B/R	FBG	DV	OB		7 8	2345	15000	17000
20	CLASSIC BR	B/R	FBG	DV	IO	230	7 8	2500	7350	8450
20	CLASSIC BR	B/R	FBG	DV	JT	330	7 8	2500	10600	12100
21	21 SR	OFF	FBG	DV	OB		7 9	2900	18800	20900
21	21 SR	OFF	FBG	DV	IO	230	7 9	2900	9150	10400
21	21 SR	OFF	FBG	DV	JT	370	7 9	2900	12100	13800
21	21 SR BR	B/R	FBG	DV	OB		7 9	2900	18800	20900
21	21 SR BR	B/R	FBG	DV	IO	230	7 9	2900	8450	9700
21	21 SR BR	B/R	FBG	DV	JT	270	7 9	2900	12100	13800
22	CITATION 22	OFF	FBG	DV	OB		7 11	3750	23100	25600
22	CITATION 22	OFF	FBG	DV	IO	300	7 11	3750	12300	14000
22	CITATION 22 BR	B/R	FBG	DV	OB		7 11	3750	23100	25600
22	CITATION 22 BR	B/R	FBG	DV	IO	300	7 11	3750	11500	13100
24	CELEBRITY 24	OFF	FBG	DV	OB		7 11	4250	29500	32700
24	CELEBRITY 24	OFF	FBG	DV	IO	300	7 11	4250	14800	16800
24	CELEBRITY 24 BR	B/R	FBG	DV	OB		7 11	4250	29500	32700
24	CELEBRITY 24 BR	B/R	FBG	DV	IO	300	7 11	4250	13900	15800
27	VICTORY 27	OFF	FBG	DV	OB		8 2	4820	37600	41800
27	VICTORY 27	OFF	FBG	DV	IO	365	8 2	4820	20900	23200
30	OFFSHORE 30	OFF	FBG	DV	OB		8 3	4820	51400	56500
30	OFFSHORE 30	OFF	FBG	DV	IO	365	8 3	4820	23500	26100

1990 BOATS

LOA FT IN	NAME AND/OR MODEL	RIG	MTL	TP	TP	HP	BEAM FT IN	WGT LBS	RETAIL LOW	RETAIL HIGH
18	BOWRIDER	B/R	FBG	DV	OB		6 8	1950	11300	12800
18	BOWRIDER	B/R	FBG	DV	JT	330	6 8	1950	6950	8000
18	SKI SPORT	SKI	FBG	DV	OB		6 8	1875	6850	7850
18	TUNNEL RUNNER	OFF	FBG	CT	OB		6 5	1950	11300	12800
18	TUNNEL RUNNER	OFF	FBG	CT	JT	330	6 5	1950	6800	7850
19	WARRIOR	OFF	FBG	DV	OB		6 9	2150	12200	13900
19	WARRIOR	OFF	FBG	DV	IO	260	6 9	2000	5600	6450
19	WARRIOR	OFF	FBG	DV	JT	330	6 9	2000	7450	8600
19	WARRIOR BR	B/R	FBG	DV	OB		6 9	2150	12200	13900
19	WARRIOR BR	B/R	FBG	DV	IO	260	6 9	2150	5400	6200
19	WARRIOR BR	B/R	FBG	DV	JT	330	6 9	2150	7700	8850
20	BANSHEE	OFF	FBG	DV	OB		7 2	2000	13200	15000
20	BANSHEE	OFF	FBG	DV	JT	330	7 2	2000	8950	10200
20	CLASSIC	OFF	FBG	DV	OB		7 8	2345	14500	16400
20	CLASSIC	OFF	FBG	DV	IO	260	7 8	2345	7400	8500
20	CLASSIC	OFF	FBG	DV	JT	330	7 8	2345	9800	11100
20	CLASSIC BR	B/R	FBG	DV	OB		7 8	2345	14500	16400
20	CLASSIC BR	B/R	FBG	DV	IO	260	7 8	2500	7150	8200
20	CLASSIC BR	B/R	FBG	DV	JT	330	7 8	2500	10100	11500
22	CITATION 22	OFF	FBG	DV	OB		7 11	3750	22300	24800
22	CITATION 22	OFF	FBG	DV	IO	330	7 11	3750	12200	13900
24	CELEBRITY 24	OFF	FBG	DV	OB		7 11	4250	28500	31600
24	CELEBRITY 24	OFF	FBG	DV	IO	330	7 11	4250	14600	16600
30	OFFSHORE 30	OFF	FBG	DV	OB		8 3	4820	49700	54600
30	OFFSHORE 30	OFF	FBG	DV	IO	365	8 3	4820	22100	24500

1989 BOATS

LOA FT IN	NAME AND/OR MODEL	RIG	MTL	TP	TP	HP	BEAM FT IN	WGT LBS	RETAIL LOW	RETAIL HIGH
18	BOWRIDER	B/R	FBG	DV	OB		6 8	1950	10900	12400
18	BOWRIDER	B/R	FBG	DV	JT	330	6 8	1950	6600	7600
18	SKI SPORT	SKI	FBG	DV	OB		6 8	1875	10700	12100
18	SKI SPORT	SKI	FBG	DV	JT	330	6 8	1875	6500	7500
18	TUNNEL RUNNER	OFF	FBG	CT	OB		6 5	1950	10900	12400

CONTINUED ON NEXT PAGE

LOA FT	LOA IN	NAME AND/ OR MODEL	TOP/ RIG	BOAT TYPE	HULL MTL	HULL TP	ENGINE TP	# HP	MFG	BEAM FT	BEAM IN	WGT LBS	DRAFT FT	DRAFT IN	RETAIL LOW	RETAIL HIGH
		1989 BOATS														
18		TUNNEL RUNNER		OFF	FBG	CT	JT	330		6	5	1950			6500	7450
19		WARRIOR		OFF	FBG	DV	OB			6	9	2000			11400	13000
19		WARRIOR		OFF	FBG	DV	IO	260		6	9	2000			5300	6050
19		WARRIOR BR		B/R	FBG	DV	OB			6	9	2150			11800	13400
19		WARRIOR BR		B/R	FBG	DV	IO	260		6	9	2150			5100	5850
19		WARRIOR BR		B/R	FBG	DV	JT	330		6	9	2150			7300	8400
20		BANSHEE		OFF	FBG	DV	OB			7	2	2000			12800	14500
20		BANSHEE		OFF	FBG	DV	JT	330		7	2	2000			8400	9650
20		CLASSIC		OFF	FBG	DV	OB			7	8	2345			14000	15900
20		CLASSIC		OFF	FBG	DV	IO	260		7	8	2345			6950	8000
20		CLASSIC		OFF	FBG	DV	JT	330		7	8	2345			9400	10700
20		CLASSIC BR		B/R	FBG	DV	OB			7	8	2500			14400	16400
20		CLASSIC BR		B/R	FBG	DV	IO	260		7	8	2500			6750	7750
20		CLASSIC BR		B/R	FBG	DV	JT	330		7	8	2500			9600	10900
22		CITATION 22		OFF	FBG	DV	OB			7	11	3750			21600	24000
22		CITATION 22		OFF	FBG	DV	IO	330		7	11	3750			11500	13100
24		CELEBRITY 24		OFF	FBG	DV	OB			7	11	4250			27600	30600
24		CELEBRITY 24		OFF	FBG	DV	IO	330		7	11	4250			13700	15600
		1988 BOATS														
18		BOWRIDER		B/R	FBG	DV	OB			6	8	1950			10600	12000
18		BOWRIDER		B/R	FBG	DV	JT	325		6	8	1950			6300	7250
18		SKI CLASSIC		SKI	FBG	DV	OB			6	8	1950			10600	12000
18		SKI SPORT		SKI	FBG	DV	OB			6	8	1950			10600	12000
18		SKI SPORT		SKI	FBG	DV	JT	325		6	8	1875			6200	7150
18		TUNNEL RUNNER		OFF	FBG	CT	OB			6	5	1950			10600	12000
18		TUNNEL RUNNER		OFF	FBG	CT	JT	325		6	5	1950			6200	7100
19		WARRIOR		OFF	FBG	DV	OB			6	9	2000			11100	12600
19		WARRIOR		OFF	FBG	DV	JT	330		6	9	2000			6750	7800
19		WARRIOR		OFF	FBG	DV	IO	330		6	9	2000			6000	6900
19		WARRIOR BR		B/R	FBG	DV	OB			6	9	2000			11100	12600
19		WARRIOR BR		B/R	FBG	DV	JT	330		6	9	2150			6950	8000
19		WARRIOR BR		B/R	FBG	DV	IO	330		6	9	2000			5650	6500
20		BANSHEE		OFF	FBG	DV	OB			7	2	2000			12400	14100
20		BANSHEE		OFF	FBG	DV	JT	330		7	2	2000			8000	9200
20		CLASSIC		OFF	FBG	DV	OB			7	8	2345			13600	15400
20		CLASSIC		OFF	FBG	DV	IO	260		7	8	2345			6600	7600
20		CLASSIC		OFF	FBG	DV	JT	330		7	8	2345			8950	10200
20		CLASSIC BR		B/R	FBG	DV	OB			7	8	2345			13600	15400
20		CLASSIC BR		B/R	FBG	DV	JT	330		7	8	2500			9200	10500
20		CLASSIC BR		B/R	FBG	DV	IO	330		7	8	2345			7200	8300
22		CITATION 22		OFF	FBG	DV	OB			7	11	3500			20400	22600
22		CITATION 22		OFF	FBG	DV	IO	330		7	11	3500			10500	11900
24		CITATION 24		OFF	FBG	DV	OB			7	11	3500			23500	26100
24		CITATION 24		OFF	FBG	DV	IO	330		7	11	3500			11500	13000
26		CITATION 26		OFF	FBG	DV	OB			7	11	3500			28000	31100
26		CITATION 26		OFF	FBG	DV	IO	330		7	11	3500			13300	15100
		1987 BOATS														
18		BOWRIDER		B/R	FBG	DV	OB			6	8	1950			10300	11700
18		BOWRIDER		B/R	FBG	DV	JT	260		6	8	1950			6000	6900
18		SKI SPORT		SKI	FBG	DV	JT	260		6	8	1950			6000	6900
18		TUNNEL RUNNER		OFF	FBG	CT	OB			6	5	1950			10300	11700
18		TUNNEL RUNNER		OFF	FBG	CT	JT	330		6	5	1950			5900	6800
20		CLASSIC		OFF	FBG	DV	OB			7	8	2345			13200	15000
20		CLASSIC		OFF	FBG	DV	IO	260		7	8	2345			6300	7200
20		CLASSIC		OFF	FBG	DV	JT	330		7	8	2345			8450	9700
20		CLASSIC BR		B/R	FBG	DV	OB			7	8	2345			13200	15000
20		CLASSIC BR		B/R	FBG	DV	IO	260		7	8	2345			5900	6750
20		CLASSIC BR		B/R	FBG	DV	JT	330		7	8	2500			8700	10000
20		SPORT CRUISER		RNBT	FBG	DV	OB								10800	12300
20		SPORT CRUISER		RNBT	FBG	DV	JT	330							9400	10700
20		SPORT CRUISER		RNBT	FBG	DV	OB								10800	12300
20		SPORT CRUISER		RNBT	FBG	DV	JT	330							9400	10700
24		OFFSHORE 24		OFF	FBG	DV	OB			7	11	4250			26000	28900
24		OFFSHORE 24		OFF	FBG	DV	IO	260		7	11	4250			11300	12900
		1986 BOATS														
18		BOWRIDER		B/R	FBG	DV	OB			6	8	1950			10000	11400
18		BOWRIDER		B/R	FBG	DV	JT	260		6	8	1950			5750	6600
18		BOWRIDER		B/R	FBG	DV	IO	260		6	8	1950			3900	4550
18		SKI SPORT		SKI	FBG	DV	OB			6	8	1950			10000	11400
18		SKI SPORT		SKI	FBG	DV	JT	260		6	8	1950			5750	6600
18		TUNNEL RUNNER		OFF	FBG	CT	OB			6	5	1950			10000	11400
18		TUNNEL RUNNER		OFF	FBG	CT	JT	260		6	5	1950			5650	6450
20		CLASSIC		OFF	FBG	DV	OB			7	8	2345			12900	14600
20		CLASSIC		OFF	FBG	DV	JT	260		7	8	2345			8050	9250
20		CLASSIC		OFF	FBG	DV	IO	260		7	8	2345			6000	6900
20		CLASSIC BR		B/R	FBG	DV	OB			7	8	2345			12900	14600
20		CLASSIC BR		B/R	FBG	DV	JT	260		7	8	2345			8050	9250
20		CLASSIC BR		B/R	FBG	DV	IO	260		7	8	2345			5600	6450
20		SPORT CRUISER		RNBT	FBG	DV	OB								10500	11900
20		SPORT CRUISER		RNBT	FBG	DV	JT	260							9000	10200
20		SPORT CRUISER		RNBT	FBG	DV	IO	260							6250	7150
20		SPORT CRUISER BR		B/R	FBG	DV	OB								12200	13800
20		SPORT CRUISER BR		B/R	FBG	DV	JT	260							9050	10300
20		SPORT CRUISER BR		B/R	FBG	DV	IO	260							6250	7200
24		OFFSHORE 24		OFF	FBG	DV	OB			7	11	4250			25400	28200
24		OFFSHORE 24		OFF	FBG	DV	IO	260		7	11	4250			10800	12300

AEROCRAFT INC

TECUMSEH MI 49286

See inside cover to adjust price for area

LOA FT	LOA IN	NAME AND/ OR MODEL	TOP/ RIG	BOAT TYPE	HULL MTL	HULL TP	ENGINE TP	# HP	MFG	BEAM FT	BEAM IN	WGT LBS	DRAFT FT	DRAFT IN	RETAIL LOW	RETAIL HIGH
		1990 BOATS														
16	6	MALIBU	OP	B/R	FBG	DV	OB			6	11	1388			2700	3100
16	6	MALIBU	OP	B/R	FBG	DV	IO	130-175		6	11	1980			3800	4500
17	6	MONTE CARLO	OP	B/R	FBG	DV	OB			7	4	1478			2850	3350
17	6	MONTE CARLO	OP	B/R	FBG	DV	IO	130-175		7	4	2140			4450	5150
17	6	MONTE CARLO	OP	B/R	FBG	SV	IO	175	OMC	7	4	2140			4450	5100
20	7	MACH II	OP	CUD	FBG	DV	IO	175-260		8		2965			7250	8800
22		MACH III	OP	CUD	FBG	DV	IO	175-260		8		3200			8200	9850
		1989 BOATS														
16	6	MALIBU	OP	B/R	FBG	DV	OB			6	11	1388			2600	3000
16	6	MALIBU	OP	B/R	FBG	DV	IO	128-175		6	11	1980			3550	4250
17	6	MONTE CARLO	OP	B/R	FBG	DV	OB			7	4	1478			2750	3200
17	6	MONTE CARLO	OP	B/R	FBG	DV	IO	128-175		7	4	2140			4100	4850
20	7	MACH II	OP	CUD	FBG	DV	IO	175-260		8		2965			6800	8300
22		MACH III	OP	CUD	FBG	DV	IO	175-260		8		3200			7700	9300
		1988 BOATS														
16	6	MALIBU	OP	RNBT	FBG	DV	OB			6	11	1388			2500	2950
16	6	MALIBU	OP	RNBT	FBG	DV	IO	128-175		6	11	1980			3600	4250
17	6	MONTE CARLO	OP	RNBT	FBG	DV	OB			7	4	1478			2700	3100
17	6	MONTE CARLO	OP	RNBT	FBG	DV	IO	128-175		7	4	2140			4100	4850
20	7	MACH II	OP	CUD	FBG	DV	IO	175-260		8		2965			6450	7850
22		MACH III	OP	CUD	FBG	DV	IO	175-260		8		3200			7300	8800
		1987 BOATS														
16	6	MALIBU	OP	RNBT	FBG	DV	OB			6	11	1388			2450	2850
16	6	MALIBU	OP	RNBT	FBG	DV	IO	120-170		6	11	1980			3450	4050
17	6	MONTE CARLO	OP	RNBT	FBG	DV	OB			7	4	1478			2600	3050
17	6	MONTE CARLO	OP	RNBT	FBG	DV	IO	120-200		7	4	2140			3900	4650
20	7	MACH II	OP	CUD	FBG	DV	IO	170-200		8		2965			6150	7100
22		MACH III	OP	CUD	FBG	DV	IO	170-200		8		3200			6950	8050
		1986 BOATS														
16	6	MALIBU	OP	RNBT	FBG	DV	OB			6	11	1388			2400	2800
16	6	MALIBU	OP	RNBT	FBG	DV	IO	120-170		6	11	1980			3300	3850
17	6	MONTE CARLO	OP	RNBT	FBG	DV	OB			7	4	1478			2550	2950
17	6	MONTE CARLO	OP	RNBT	FBG	DV	IO	120-200		7	4	2140			3750	4450
20	7	MACH II	OP	CUD	FBG	DV	IO	170-200		8		2965			5850	6800
22		MACH III	OP	CUD	FBG	DV	IO	170-200		8		3200			6600	7650
		1985 BOATS														
16	6	MALIBU	OP	RNBT	FBG	DV	OB			6	11	1388			2350	2700
16	6	MALIBU	OP	RNBT	FBG	DV	IO	120-170		6	11	1980			3150	3700
17	6	MONTE CARLO	OP	RNBT	FBG	DV	OB			7	4	1478			2500	2900
17	6	MONTE CARLO	OP	RNBT	FBG	DV	IO	120-200		7	4	2140			3600	4250
20	7	MACH II	OP	CUD	FBG	DV	IO	170-200		8		2965			5600	6500
22		MACH III	OP	CUD	FBG	DV	IO	170-200		8		3200			6350	7350

....For earlier years, see the BUC Used Boat Price Guide, Volume 3

AEROMARINE CORP

BRUNSWICK MD 04011

See inside cover to adjust price for area

LOA FT	LOA IN	NAME AND/ OR MODEL	TOP/ RIG	BOAT TYPE	HULL MTL	HULL TP	ENGINE TP	# HP	MFG	BEAM FT	BEAM IN	WGT LBS	DRAFT FT	DRAFT IN	RETAIL LOW	RETAIL HIGH
		1984 BOATS														
50	4	FD-12 METER	CUT	SA/RC	FBG	KL	IB	D		14	3	35175	6	6	127500	140500

....For earlier years, see the BUC Used Boat Price Guide, Volume 3

ALBEMARLE BOATS INC

BRUNSWICK@DIV OF
EDENTON NC 27932 COAST GUARD MFG ID- XWR

See inside cover to adjust price for area

For more recent years, see the BUC Used Boat Price Guide, Volume 1

LOA FT	IN	NAME AND/ OR MODEL	TOP/ RIG	BOAT TYPE	-HULL- MTL	TP	TP	----ENGINE--- # HP	MFG	BEAM FT	IN	WGT LBS	DRAFT FT	IN	RETAIL LOW	RETAIL HIGH
		1996 BOATS														
23	7	ALBEMARLE 24	OP	CTRCN	FBG	DV	IO	275	VLVO	8		4100			19900	22100
23	7	ALBEMARLE 24	OP	SF	FBG	DV	IO	275-330		8		4100			21500	26100
23	7	ALBEMARLE 24	OP	SF	FBG	DV	IO	200D	VLVO	8		4100			27700	30800
25	10	ALBEMARLE 26	OP	CTRCN	FBG	DV	IO	300	VLVO	8	6	6800			31800	35400
25	10	ALBEMARLE 26	OP	CTRCN	FBG	DV	IO	200D	VLVO	8	6	7500			47900	52600
25	10	ALBEMARLE 26	OP	CUD	FBG	DV	IO	300	VLVO	8	6	7500			32200	35800
25	10	ALBEMARLE 26	OP	EXP	FBG	DV	IO	200D	VLVO	8	6	7500			37900	42100
27	1	ALBEMARLE 27	OP	EXP	FBG	DV	IO	300	VLVO	9	6	9500			38800	43200
27	1	ALBEMARLE 27	OP	EXP	FBG	DV	IO	T330	VLVO	9	6	9500			46100	50700
27	1	ALBEMARLE 27	OP	EXP	FBG	DV	IB	T170D	YAN	9	6	9500			65100	71600
27	1	ALBEMARLE 27	OP	SF	FBG	DV	IO	T275	VLVO	9	6	9500			49000	53900
27	1	ALBEMARLE 27	OP	SF	FBG	DV	IB	T275	VLVO	9	6	9500			48600	53400
27	1	ALBEMARLE 27	OP	SF	FBG	DV	IB	T230D	YAN	9	6	9500			69600	76500
29	6	ALBEMARLE 305	OP	SF	FBG	DV	IB	T300	VLVO	11		14000	2	10	66500	73100
29	6	ALBEMARLE 305	OP	SF	FBG	DV	IB	T300D	CAT	11		14000	2	10	96400	106000
32	2	ALBEMARLE 32 CNV	FB	SF	FBG	DV	IB	T330	VLVO	11		18000	3		84600	93000
32	2	ALBEMARLE 32 CNV	FB	SF	FBG	DV	IB	T300D	CAT	11		18000	3		114500	126000
32	2	ALBEMARLE 32 EXP	OP	SF	FBG	DV	IB	T330	VLVO	11		17000	3		82900	91100
32	2	ALBEMARLE 32 EXP	OP	SF	FBG	DV	IB	T300D	CAT	11		17000	3		110500	121500
		1995 BOATS														
23	7	ALBEMARLE 24	OP	SF	FBG	DV	IO	275-330		8		4100			20000	24300
23	7	ALBEMARLE 24	OP	SF	FBG	DV	IO	200D	VLVO	8		4100			25900	28800
25	10	ALBEMARLE 26	OP	CTRCN	FBG	DV	IO	300	VLVO	8	6	6800			29700	33000
25	10	ALBEMARLE 26	OP	CUD	FBG	DV	IO	300	VLVO	8	6	7500			30100	33400
27	4	ALBEMARLE 27	OP	SF	FBG	DV	IO	T275	VLVO	9	6	9500			46100	50700
27	4	ALBEMARLE 27	OP	SF	FBG	DV	IB	T275	VLVO	9	6	9500			46400	51000
27	4	ALBEMARLE 27	OP	SF	FBG	DV	IB	T230D	PEN	9	6	9500			66900	73600
32	2	ALBEMARLE 32	OP	SF	FBG	DV	IB	T300D	CAT	10	11	17000	3		105000	115500
32	2	ALBEMARLE 32 CNV	FB	SF	FBG	DV	IB	T330	VLVO	10	11	18000	3		79900	87800
32	2	ALBEMARLE 32 CNV	FB	SF	FBG	DV	IB	T300D	CAT	10	11	18000	3		109000	119500
32	2	ALBEMARLE 32 EXP	OP	SF	FBG	DV	IB	T330	VLVO	10	11	17000	3		78300	86100
		1994 BOATS														
23	7	ALBEMARLE 24	OP	SF	FBG	DV	IO	275-330		8		4100			18900	22700
23	7	ALBEMARLE 24	OP	SF	FBG	DV	IO	200D	VLVO	8		4100			24200	26800
25	10	ALBEMARLE 26	OP	CTRCN	FBG	DV	IO	300	VLVO	8	6	6800			27700	30800
25	10	ALBEMARLE 26	OP	CUD	FBG	DV	IO	300	VLVO	8	6	7500			28100	31200
27	4	ALBEMARLE 27	OP	SF	FBG	DV	IO	T275	VLVO	9	6	9500			42600	47400
27	4	ALBEMARLE 27	OP	SF	FBG	DV	IB	T275	VLVO	9	6	9500			43500	48300
27	4	ALBEMARLE 27	OP	SF	FBG	DV	IB	T230D	PEN	9	6	9500			63700	70000
32	2	ALBEMARLE 32	OP	SF	FBG	DV	IB	T300D	CAT	10	11	17000	3		99800	109500
32	2	ALBEMARLE 32 CNV	FB	SF	FBG	DV	IB	T330	VLVO	10	11	18000	3		75600	83100
32	2	ALBEMARLE 32 CNV	FB	SF	FBG	DV	IB	T300D	CAT	10	11	18000	3		103500	114000
32	2	ALBEMARLE 32 EXP	OP	SF	FBG	DV	IB	T330	VLVO	10	11	17000	3		74100	81500
		1993 BOATS														
23	7	ALBEMARLE 24	OP	SF	FBG	DV	IO	275-330		8		4100			17300	21200
23	7	ALBEMARLE 24	OP	SF	FBG	DV	IO	200D	VLVO	8		4100			22600	25100
25	10	ALBEMARLE 26	OP	CTRCN	FBG	DV	IO	T300	VLVO	8	6	6800			30200	33600
25	10	ALBEMARLE 26	OP	CUD	FBG	DV	IO	T300	VLVO	8	6	7500			30300	33600
27	4	ALBEMARLE 27	OP	SF	FBG	DV	IO	T275	VLVO	9	6	8000			36500	40500
27	4	ALBEMARLE 27	OP	SF	FBG	DV	IB	T275	VLVO	9	6	8500			38800	43100
27	4	ALBEMARLE 27	OP	SF	FBG	DV	IB	T230D	PEN	9	6	8500			56400	62000
32	2	ALBEMARLE 32	OP	SF	FBG	DV	IB	T300D	CAT	10	11	17000	3		95100	104500
32	2	ALBEMARLE 32 CNV	FB	SF	FBG	DV	IB	T330	VLVO	10	11	18000	3		71600	78700
32	2	ALBEMARLE 32 CNV	FB	SF	FBG	DV	IB	T300D	CAT	10	11	18000	3		98600	108500
32	2	ALBEMARLE 32 EXP	OP	SF	FBG	DV	IB	T330	VLVO	10	11	17000	3		70300	77200
		1992 BOATS														
23	7	ALBEMARLE 24	OP	SF	FBG	DV	IO	275-330		8		4100			16200	20100
23	7	ALBEMARLE 24	OP	SF	FBG	DV	IO	200D	VLVO	8		4100			21100	23500
27	4	ALBEMARLE 27	OP	SF	FBG	DV	IO	T275	VLVO	9	6	8000			34100	37900
		IB T275 VLVO 36800 40900, IO T200D VLVO 47000 51600, IB T230D PEN													53800	59100
32	2	ALBEMARLE 32	OP	SF	FBG	DV	IB	T330	VLVO	10	11	17000	3		66700	73300
32	2	ALBEMARLE 32	OP	SF	FBG	DV	IB	T300D	CUM	10	11	17000	3		90500	99500
32	2	ALBEMARLE 32	FB	SF	FBG	DV	IB	T330	VLVO	10	11	17000	3		66700	73400
32	2	ALBEMARLE 32	FB	SF	FBG	DV	IB	T300D	CUM	10	11	17000	3		90600	99500
		1991 BOATS														
23	7	ALBEMARLE 24	OP	SF	FBG	DV	IO	275-330		8		4100			15200	18800
23	7	ALBEMARLE 24	OP	SF	FBG	DV	IO	200D	VLVO	8		4100			19800	22000
27	4	ALBEMARLE 27	OP	SF	FBG	DV	IO	T275	VLVO	9	6	8000			32000	35600
		IB T275 VLVO 35000 38900, IO T200D VLVO 43600 48500, IB T230D													50500	55500
32	2	ALBEMARLE 32	OP	SF	FBG	DV	IB	T330	VLVO	10	11	17000	3		63300	69600
32	2	ALBEMARLE 32	OP	SF	FBG	DV	IB	T300D	CUM	10	11	17000	3		86400	95000
32	2	ALBEMARLE 32	FB	SF	FBG	DV	IB	T330	VLVO	10	11	17000	3		63400	69700
32	2	ALBEMARLE 32	FB	SF	FBG	DV	IB	T300D	CUM	10	11	17000	3		86500	95000
		1990 BOATS														
23	7	ALBEMARLE 24	OP	SF	FBG	DV	IO	275-330		8		4100			14300	17700
23	7	ALBEMARLE 24	OP	SF	FBG	DV	IO	200D	VLVO	8		4100			18800	20900
27	4	ALBEMARLE 27	OP	SF	FBG	DV	IO	T275	VLVO	9	6	8000			30100	33500
		IB T275 VLVO 33300 37000, IO T330 VLVO 32300 35900, IB T330 VLVO													34600	38400
		IO T200D VLVO 41000 45600														
32	2	ALBEMARLE 32	FB	SF	FBG	DV	IB	T330	VLVO	10	11	17000	3		60300	66300
32	2	ALBEMARLE 32	FB	SF	FBG	DV	IB	T250D-T300D		10	11	17000	3		79800	90800
		1988 BOATS														
23	7	ALBEMARLE 24	OP	SF	FBG	DV	IO	271	VLVO	8		4500	2	6	13600	15400
23	7	ALBEMARLE 24	OP	SF	FBG	DV	IO	200D	VLVO	8		4500	2	6	17400	19800
23	7	ALBEMARLE 24	HT	SF	FBG	DV	IO	271	VLVO	8		4500	2	6	13600	15400
27	4	ALBEMARLE 27	OP	SF	FBG	DV	IB	T260	VLVO	9	6	8300	3		29500	32800
		IO T271 VLVO 27300 30300, IB T170D GM 40000 44500, IO T200D VLVO													37500	41700
27	4	ALBEMARLE 27	HT	SF	FBG	DV	IO	T271	VLVO	9	6	8500	2	6	27600	30700
27	4	ALBEMARLE 27	TT	SF	FBG	DV	IO	T271	VLVO	9	6	8500	2	6	27600	30700
32	2	ALBEMARLE 32 SPRTFSH	FB	SF	FBG	DV	IB	T350	CRUS	10	11	17000	3		55200	60700
		1987 BOATS														
23	7	ALBEMARLE 24	OP	SF	FBG	DV	IO	271	VLVO	8		4200	2	6	12300	13900
23	7	ALBEMARLE 24	OP	SF	FBG	DV	IO	200D	VLVO	8		4200	2	6	15900	18000
23	7	ALBEMARLE 24	HT	SF	FBG	DV	IO	271	VLVO	8		4200	2	6	12300	13900
27	4	ALBEMARLE 27	OP	SF	FBG	DV	IB	T260	VLVO	9	6	8300	3		28200	31300
27	4	ALBEMARLE 27	OP	SF	FBG	DV	IO	T271	VLVO	9	6	7800	2	6	25100	27900
27	4	ALBEMARLE 27	OP	SF	FBG	DV	IB	T170D	GM	9	6	8300	3		38400	42600
27	4	ALBEMARLE 27	HT	SF	FBG	DV	IO	T271	VLVO	9	6	7800	2	6	25100	27900
27	4	ALBEMARLE 27	TT	SF	FBG	DV	IO	T271	VLVO	9	6	7800	2	6	25100	27900
		1986 BOATS														
23	7	ALBEMARLE 24	OP	SF	FBG	DV	IO	260	VLVO	8		4200	2	6	11600	13100
23	7	ALBEMARLE 24	OP	SF	FBG	DV	IO	165D	VLVO	8		4200	2	6	14700	16700
23	7	ALBEMARLE 24	HT	SF	FBG	DV	IO	260	VLVO	8		4200	2	6	11600	13100
27	4	ALBEMARLE 27	OP	SF	FBG	DV	IO	T260	VLVO	9	6	7800	2	6	23700	26400
		IB T260 VLVO 26900 29900, IO T165D VLVO 31800 35300, IB T170D GM													36800	40900
27	4	ALBEMARLE 27	HT	SF	FBG	DV	IO	T260	VLVO	9	6	7800	2	6	23700	26400
27	4	ALBEMARLE 27	TT	SF	FBG	DV	IO	T260	VLVO	9	6	7800	2	6	23700	26400
		1985 BOATS														
23	7	ALBEMARLE 24	OP	SF	FBG	DV	IO	260	VLVO	8		4400	2	6	11500	13100
23	7	ALBEMARLE 24 DUOPROP	OP	SF	FBG	DV	IO	165D	VLVO	8		4100	2	6	13900	15800
27	4	ALBEMARLE 27	OP	SF	FBG	DV	IO	T260	VLVO	9	6	7800	1	11	22800	25300
27	4	ALBEMARLE 27 DUOPROP	OP	SF	FBG	DV	IO	T165D	VLVO	9	6	7400	2	6	28900	32100
		1984 BOATS														
20	7	ALBEMARLE 21	OP	CUD	FBG	DV	OB			8		2650	2	6	7400	8500
20	7	ALBEMARLE 21	OP	CUD	FBG	DV	IO	170-200		8		3450	2	6	6450	7750
20	7	ALBEMARLE 21	OP	CUD	FBG	DV	IO	130D-165D		8		3600	2	6	8300	9650
23	7	ALBEMARLE 24	OP	SF	FBG	DV	OB			8		3200	2	6	10400	11800
23	7	ALBEMARLE 24	OP	SF	FBG	DV	IO	260		8		4100	2	6	10200	12000
23	7	ALBEMARLE 24	OP	SF	FBG	DV	IO	165D	VLVO	8		4100	2	6	13200	15000
23	7	ALBEMARLE 24	OP	SF	FBG	DV	IO	T138-T188		8		4100	2	6	11400	12900
23	7	ALBEMARLE 24 DUOPROP	OP	SF	FBG	DV	IO	165D	VLVO	8		4100	2	6	13600	15400
27	4	ALBEMARLE 27	OP	SF	FBG	DV	IO	T260	VLVO	9	6	7800	1	11	22000	24400

....For earlier years, see the BUC Used Boat Price Guide, Volume 3

ALBIN BOATS

BLADEN COMPOSITES LLC
BLADENBORO NC 28320 COAST GUARD MFG ID- AUL

See inside cover to adjust price for area

For more recent years, see the BUC Used Boat Price Guide, Volume 1

LOA FT	IN	NAME AND/ OR MODEL	TOP/ RIG	BOAT TYPE	-HULL- MTL	TP	TP	----ENGINE--- # HP	MFG	BEAM FT	IN	WGT LBS	DRAFT FT	IN	RETAIL LOW	RETAIL HIGH
		1996 BOATS														
29	11	TOURNAMENT EXP 28	HT	SF	FBG	SV	IB	300D	PEN	10		7500	3	2	58000	63700
33		TOURNAMENT EXP 31	HT	SF	FBG	SV	IB	T300D	PEN	12	4	14000	3	3	126000	138500
34	4	COMMAND BRIDGE 32	FB	SF	FBG	SV	IB	300D	PEN	12	2	16000	3	10	118000	130000
36	11	CONVERTIBLE SEDAN 35	FB	SF	FBG	SV	IB	370D	CUM	12	4	18000	3	10	116000	127500
36	11	SPORTFISH 35	FB	SF	FBG	SV	IB	T300D	PEN	12	4	18000	3	10	128000	141000
36	11	SPORTFISH LS 35	FB	SF	FBG	SV	IB	T300D	PEN	12	4	18000	3	10	128000	141000
36	11	TOURNAMENT EXP 35	HT	SF	FBG	SV	IB	370D	CUM	12	4	18000	3	10	116000	127500

LOA FT	IN	NAME AND/ OR MODEL	TOP/ RIG	BOAT TYPE	-HULL- MTL	TP	----ENGINE--- TP	# HP	MFG	BEAM FT	IN	WGT LBS	DRAFT FT	IN	RETAIL LOW	RETAIL HIGH
		1995 BOATS														
24	2	ALBIN 24 GET-AWAY	OP	SF	FBG	DV	IB	150D	VLVO	8	6	5500	2	10	35500	39500
24	2	ALBIN 24 GET-AWAY	OP	SF	FBG	SV	IB	250	VLVO	8	6	5250	2	10	28600	31800
28	4	ALBIN 28TE	HT	CR	FBG	SV	IB	340	VLVO	9	9	7000	3	2	41100	45700
28	4	ALBIN 28TE	HT	CR	FBG	SV	IO	216D	VLVO	9	9	7000	3	2	38300	42500
28	4	ALBIN 28TE	HT	CR	FBG	SV	IB	300D-315D		9	9	7500	3	2	54200	59600
32	4	ALBIN 32 SPORTFISH	FB	SF	FBG	DV	IB	300D-350D		12	3	13600	3	10	92300	103500
32	4	ALBIN 32 SPORTFISH	FB	SF	FBG	DV	IB	T300D	PEN	12	3	16400	3	10	115500	127000
32	4	ALBIN 32 SPORTFISH	FB	SF	FBG	SV	IB	300D-315D		12	3	13600	3	10	92300	102000
32	4	ALBIN 32 SPORTFISH	FB	SF	FBG	SV	IB	T300D-T315D		12	3	16400	3	10	115500	128000
34		ALBIN 34 FM CRUISER	FB	CR	FBG	SV	IB	T300D	PEN	11	6	13800	3		115500	127000
35	2	ALBIN 35 SEDAN	FB	SDN	FBG	SV	IB	300D	PEN	12	4	17500	3		129500	142500
		IB 315D CUM 129500 142000, IB 420D CAT 136500 150000, IB T340 VLVO 119500 131000														
		IB T300D CAT 146000 160500, IB T300D PEN 145000 159500, IB T315D CUM 146000 160500														
48	9	ALBIN 49 COCKPIT	FB	TRWL	FBG	DS	IB	T300D	CAT	14	6	35600	4	1	201000	221000
48	9	ALBIN 49 COCKPIT	FB	TRWL	FBG	DS	IB	T315D	CUM	14	6	35600	4	1	200000	220000
48	9	ALBIN 49 COCKPIT	FB	TRWL	FBG	DS	IB	T350D	CAT	14	6	35600	4	1	206500	227000
		1994 BOATS														
24		ALBIN 24 GET-AWAY	OP	SF	FBG	SV	IB	250	MRCR	8	6	5250	2	10	26600	29500
25	8	GET-AWAY	OP	SF	FBG	DV	IB	170D	YAN	8	6	5500	2	10	36500	40500
26	9	ALBIN 27 FAMILY	HT	CBNCR	FBG	DS	IB	180D	MRCR	9	8	6750	2	6	53900	59200
26	9	ALBIN 27 SPORT	HT	EXP	FBG	SV	IB	180D	MRCR	9	8	7050	2	6	46700	51300
27	5	GETAWAY 275	HT	CR	FBG	SV	IO	250	VLVO	8	6	5400	2	10	28000	31100
27	5	GETAWAY 275	HT	CR	FBG	SV	IO	216D	VLVO	8	6	5400	2	10	31100	34600
28	4	ALBIN 28TE	HT	CR	FBG	SV	IB	250	MRCR	9	9	7000	3	2	36900	41000
28	4	ALBIN 28TE	HT	CR	FBG	SV	IB	210D-280D		9	9	7500	3	2	47100	55600
32	4	ALBIN 32 SPORTFISH	FB	SF	FBG	DV	IB	300D-350D		12	3	13500	3	10	87500	98100
32	4	ALBIN 32 SPORTFISH	FB	SF	FBG	DV	IB	T300D	CAT	12	3	16500	3	10	110500	121000
32	4	ALBIN 32 SPORTFISH	FB	SF	FBG	SV	IB	300D	CUM	12	3	13500	3	10	87300	96000
32	4	ALBIN 32 SPORTFISH	FB	SF	FBG	SV	IB	T210D-T300D		12	3	16500	3	10	103500	121000
34		ALBIN 34 CHARTER	FB	CR	FBG	SV	IB	T157D	ISUZ	11	6	13775	3		98200	108000
35	9	ALBIN 36	FB	TRWL	FBG	SV	IB	210D	CUM	13	2	18500	3	6	127000	139500
36	8	PALM-BEACH 37 SUNDK	FB	CR	FBG	DV	IB	T210D	CUM	12	9	17000	3		122000	134000
39	5	ALBIN 40 STANDARD	FB	TRWL	FBG	DS	IB	210D	CUM	13	2	24500	3	6	141000	155000
39	5	ALBIN 40 STANDARD	FB	TRWL	FBG	DS	IB	T210D	CUM	13	2	24500	3	6	150500	165500
39	5	ALBIN 40 SUNDECK	FB	TRWL	FBG	SV	IB	T210D	CUM	13	2	23500	3	6	146000	160500
40		CUSTOM MY 40	FB	MY	FBG	SV	IB	T375D	CAT	14	4	26000	2	6	173500	190500
42	6	ALBIN 43 STANDARD	FB	TRWL	FBG	DS	IB	210D	CUM	14	6	32000	4	1	180000	198000
42	6	ALBIN 43 STANDARD	FB	TRWL	FBG	DS	IB	T210D	CUM	14	6	33000	4	1	194000	213000
42	6	ALBIN 43 SUNDECK	FB	TRWL	FBG	DS	IB	T210D	CUM	14	6	34500	4	1	201500	221500
44		CUSTOM MY 44	FB	MY	FBG	SV	IB	T375D	CAT	14	4	30000	2	6	191000	210000
47	9	NORTH-SEA CUTTER 48	FB	MY	FBG	DV	IB	T307D	VLVO	14		30000	4		187000	205500
47	9	NORTH-SEA CUTTER 48	FB	MY	FBG	DV	IB	T375D	CAT	14		30000	4		203000	223000
48	9	ALBIN 49 COCKPIT	FB	TRWL	FBG	DS	IB	T250D	CUM	14	6	35500	4	1	186000	204500
		1993 BOATS														
24		ALBIN 24 GET-AWAY SF	OP	SF	FBG	SV	IB	250	MRCR	8	6	5250	2	10	25200	28000
25	8	GET-AWAY	OP	SF	FBG	DV	IB	170D	YAN	8	6	5500	2	10	34700	38600
26	9	ALBIN 27 FAMILY CR	HT	CBNCR	FBG	DS	IB	180D	MRCR	9	8	6750	2	6	51300	56400
26	9	ALBIN 27 SPORT	HT	EXP	FBG	SV	IB	180D	MRCR	9	8	7050	2	6	43900	48800
27	5	GETAWAY 275	HT	CR	FBG	SV	IB	250	MRCR	8	6	5400	2	10	30900	34400
27	5	GETAWAY 275	HT	CR	FBG	SV	IB	180D	MRCR	8	6	5400	2	10	35000	38900
28	4	ALBIN 28TE	HT	CR	FBG	SV	IB	250	MRCR	9	9	7000	3	2	34900	38800
28	4	ALBIN 28TE	HT	CR	FBG	SV	IB	230D-270D		9	9	7500	3	2	45900	52400
32		ALBIN 32 SEDAN	FB	SDNSF	FBG	SV	IB	300D-350D		12	3	14000	3	10	84100	94100
32		ALBIN 32 SEDAN	FB	SDNSF	FBG	SV	IB	T250	MRCR	12	3	13500	3		69700	76600
32		ALBIN 32 SEDAN	FB	SDNSF	FBG	SV	IB	T210D	MRCR	12	2	13500	3		86100	94700
32	4	ALBIN 32 SPORTFISH	FB	SF	FBG	DV	IB	300D-350D		12	3	13500	3	10	83300	93400
32	4	ALBIN 32 SPORTFISH	FB	SF	FBG	DV	IB	T300D	CAT	12	3	16500	3	10	105000	115500
32	4	ALBIN 32 SPORTFISH	FB	SF	FBG	SV	IB	300D	CUM	12	3	13500	3	10	83200	91400
32	4	ALBIN 32 SPORTFISH	FB	SF	FBG	SV	IB	T210D-T300D		12	3	16500	3	10	98500	115000
34		ALBIN 34 CHARTER	FB	CR	FBG	SV	IB	T157D	ISUZ	11	6	13775	3		93500	103000
35	9	ALBIN 36	FB	TRWL	FBG	SV	IB	210D	CUM	13	2	18500	3	6	121000	133000
36	8	PALM-BEACH 37 SUNDK	FB	CR	FBG	DV	IB	T210D	CUM	12	9	17000	3		116500	128000
37	2	PALM BEACH 37	FB	TRWL	FBG	DS	IB	T210D	CUM	12	9	16000	3		123000	135500
39	5	ALBIN 40 STANDARD	FB	TRWL	FBG	DS	IB	210D	CUM	13	2	24500	3	6	134500	147500
39	5	ALBIN 40 STANDARD	FB	TRWL	FBG	DS	IB	T210D	CUM	13	2	24500	3	6	143500	157500
39	5	ALBIN 40 SUNDECK	FB	TRWL	FBG	SV	IB	T210D	CUM	13	2	23500	3	6	139000	153000
40		CUSTOM MY 40	FB	MY	FBG	SV	IB	T375D	CAT	14	4	26000	2	6	165000	181500
42	6	ALBIN 43 STANDARD	FB	TRWL	FBG	DS	IB	210D	CUM	14	6	32000	4	1	171500	188500
42	6	ALBIN 43 STANDARD	FB	TRWL	FBG	DS	IB	T210D	CUM	14	6	33000	4	1	184500	203000
42	6	ALBIN 43 SUNDECK	FB	TRWL	FBG	DS	IB	T210D	CUM	14	6	34500	4	1	192000	211000
44		CUSTOM MY 44	FB	MY	FBG	SV	IB	T375D	CAT	14	4	30000	2	6	182000	200000
47	9	NORTH-SEA CUTTER 48	FB	MY	FBG	DV	IB	T307D	VLVO	14		30000	4		178500	196000
47	9	NORTH-SEA CUTTER 48	FB	MY	FBG	DV	IB	T375D	CAT	14		30000	4		193500	212500
48	6	ALBIN 49 TRI-CABIN	FB	TRWL	FBG	SV	IB	T210D	CUM	14	6	38500	4	1	181000	198500
48	6	ALBIN 49 TRI-CABIN	FB	TRWL	FBG	SV	IB	T300D	CUM	14	6	38500	4	1	188000	206500
48	9	ALBIN 49 COCKPIT	FB	TRWL	FBG	DS	IB	T250D	CUM	14	6	35500	4	1	177500	195500
		1992 BOATS														
24		ALBIN 24 GET-AWAY SF	OP	SF	FBG	SV	IB	240	CHRY	8	6	5250	2	10	23700	26400
25	8	GETAWAY	OP	SF	FBG	DV	IB	170D	YAN	8	6	5500	2	10	33100	36800
26	9	ALBIN 27 CRUISER	HT	CR	FBG	DS	IB	78D	PERK	9	8	6500	2	6	35100	38900
26	9	ALBIN 27 CRUISER	HT	CR	FBG	DS	IB	157D	ISUZ	9	8	6750	2	6	39700	44200
26	9	ALBIN 27 EXPRESS	HT	CR	FBG	DS	IB	210D	CUM	9	8	7500	2	8	45800	50300
26	9	ALBIN 27 EXPRESS	HT	EXP	FBG	SV	IB	210D-215D		9	8	7050	2	6	43000	48200
26	9	ALBIN 27 FAMILY CR	HT	CBNCR	FBG	DS	IB	78D	PERK	9	8	6750	2	6	39400	43800
26	9	ALBIN 27 FAMILY CR	HT	CBNCR	FBG	DS	IB	157D	ISUZ	9	8	6750	2	6	47800	52500
26	9	ALBIN 27 SPORT	HT	CR	FBG	DS	IB	78D-157D		9	8	6750	2	6	36500	43500
32	4	ALBIN 32 SPORTFISH	FB	SF	FBG	DV	IB	300D	CAT	12	3	13500	3	10	79500	87300
32	4	ALBIN 32 SPORTFISH	FB	SF	FBG	DV	IB	T300D	CAT	12	3	13500	3	10	90000	98900
32	4	ALBIN 32 SPORTFISH	FB	SF	FBG	SV	IB	300D	CUM	12	3	13500	3	10	79300	87200
32	4	ALBIN 32 SPORTFISH	FB	SF	FBG	SV	IB	T210D-T300D		12	3	16500	3	10	94000	110000
34		ALBIN 34 CHARTER	FB	CR	FBG	SV	IB	T157D	ISUZ	11	6	13775	3		89200	98000
34		ALBIN 34 MOTORYACHT	FB	CR	FBG	SV	IB	T157D	ISUZ	11	6	16500	3		98700	108500
34	3	ALBIN 34 CHARTER	FB	CR	FBG	DV	IB	T157D	ISUZ	11	6	16500	3		96500	106000
35	9	ALBIN 36	FB	TRWL	FBG	SV	IB	135D	SABR	13	2	18500	3	6	112500	123500
35	9	ALBIN 36	FB	TRWL	FBG	SV	IB	210D	CUM	13	2	18500	3	6	115500	126500
36	8	PALM-BEACH 37	FB	DCMY	FBG	DV	IB	T210D	CUM	12	9	16000	3		113000	124000
36	8	PALM-BEACH 37 SUNDCK	FB	CR	FBG	DV	IB	T210D	CUM	12	9	17000	3		111000	122000
39	5	ALBIN 40 STANDARD	FB	TRWL	FBG	DS	IB	135D	LEHM	13	2	24500	3	6	126500	139000
39	5	ALBIN 40 STANDARD	FB	TRWL	FBG	DS	IB	210D	CUM	13	2	24500	3	6	128000	140500
39	5	ALBIN 40 SUNDECK	FB	TRWL	FBG	SV	IB	T135D	LEHM	13	2	23500	3	6	129500	142000
39	5	ALBIN 40 SUNDECK	FB	TRWL	FBG	SV	IB	T210D	CUM	13	2	23500	3	6	132500	145500
42	6	ALBIN 43 STANDARD	FB	TRWL	FBG	DS	IB	210D	CUM	14	6	32000	4	1	163500	180000
42	6	ALBIN 43 STANDARD	FB	TRWL	FBG	DS	IB	T135D	LEHM	14	6	33000	4	1	172000	189000
42	6	ALBIN 43 STANDARD	FB	TRWL	FBG	DS	IB	T210D	CUM	14	6	33000	4	1	176000	193500
42	6	ALBIN 43 SUNDECK	FB	TRWL	FBG	DS	IB	T210D	CUM	14	6	34500	4	1	183000	201000
42	6	ALBIN 43 SUNDECK	FB	TRWL	FBG	SV	IB	T135D	LEHM	14	6	30000	4	1	160000	175500
47	9	NORTH-SEA CUTTER 48	FB	MY	FBG	DV	IB	T307D	VLVO	14		30000	4		170000	187000
47	9	NORTH-SEA CUTTER 48	FB	MY	FBG	DV	IB	T375D	CAT	14		30000	4		184500	202500
48	6	ALBIN 49 TRI-CABIN	FB	TRWL	FBG	SV	IB	T210D	CUM	14	6	38500	4	1	172500	189500
48	6	ALBIN 49 TRI-CABIN	FB	TRWL	FBG	SV	IB	T300D	CUM	14	6	38500	4	1	179000	196500
48	9	ALBIN 49 COCKPIT	FB	TRWL	FBG	DS	IB	T250D	CUM	14	6	35500	4	1	169500	186000
48	9	ALBIN 49 COCKPIT	FB	TRWL	FBG	DS	IB	T300D	CUM	14	6	35500	4	1	173500	190500
		1991 BOATS														
24		ALBIN 24 GET-AWAY SF	OP	SF	FBG	SV	IB	240	CHRY	8	6	5250	2	10	22600	25100
26	9	ALBIN 27 EXPRESS	HT	EXP	FBG	SV	IB	210D-215D		9	8	7050	2	6	41000	46000
26	9	ALBIN 27 FAMILY CR	HT	CBNCR	FBG	DS	IB	78D	PERK	9	8	6750	2	6	38000	42200
26	9	ALBIN 27 FAMILY CR	HT	CBNCR	FBG	DS	IB	157D	ISUZ	9	8	6750	2	6	46000	50600
26	9	ALBIN 27 SPORT CR	HT	CBNCR	FBG	DS	IB	78D	PERK	9	8	6750	2	6	37300	41400
26	9	ALBIN 27 SPORT CR	HT	CBNCR	FBG	DS	IB	157D	ISUZ	9	8	6750	2	6	44800	49800
32	4	ALBIN 32 SPORTFISH	OP	SF	FBG	SV	IB	250D-300D		12	3	13500	3	10	74300	83200
32	4	ALBIN 32 SPORTFISH	FB	SF	FBG	SV	IB	T210D-T300D		12	3	16500	3	10	89700	105000
34	3	ALBIN 34 CHARTER	FB	CR	FBG	SV	IB	T157D	ISUZ	11	6	16500	3		92200	101500
34	3	ALBIN 34 MOTORYACHT	FB	CR	FBG	SV	IB	250D	CUM	11	6	16500	3		90400	99400
34	3	ALBIN 34 MOTORYACHT	FB	CR	FBG	SV	IB	T157D	ISUZ	11	6	16500	3		92200	101500
35	9	ALBIN 36	FB	TRWL	FBG	SV	IB	135D	LEHM	13	2	18500	3	6	108000	119000
35	9	ALBIN 36	FB	TRWL	FBG	SV	IB	210D	CUM	13	2	18500	3	6	110000	121000
35	9	ALBIN 36	FB	TRWL	FBG	SV	IB	T210D	CUM	13	2	18500	3	6	120000	132000
36		ALBIN 36 TRAWLER	FB	TRWL	FBG	DS	IB	135D	SABR	13	2	18500	3	6	84600	93000
36	8	PALM-BEACH 37	FB	DCMY	FBG	DV	IB	T210D	CUM	12	9	16000	3		107500	118500
36	8	PALM-BEACH 37 SUNDCK	FB	CR	FBG	DV	IB	T210D	CUM	12	9	17000	3		106000	116000
39	4	ALBIN CUSTOM 40	FB	MY	FBG	SV	IB	T375D	CAT	14	4	26000	2	6	146500	161000
39	5	ALBIN 40	FB	TRWL	FBG	SV	IB	135D	LEHM	13	2	23500	3	6	117000	128500
		IB 210D CUM 118000 130000, IB T135D LEHM 121000 133000, IB T210D CUM 123500 136000														
39	5	ALBIN 40 SUNDECK	FB	TRWL	FBG	SV	IB	T135D	LEHM	13	2	23500	3	6	126000	138500
39	5	ALBIN 40 SUNDECK	FB	TRWL	FBG	SV	IB	T210D	CUM	13	2	23500	3	6	129000	142000
42	6	ALBIN 43	FB	TRWL	FBG	SV	IB	210D	CUM	14	6	30000	4	1	144000	158000
42	6	ALBIN 43	FB	TRWL	FBG	SV	IB	T135D	LEHM	14	6	30000	4	1	144500	159000
42	6	ALBIN 43	FB	TRWL	FBG	SV	IB	T210D	CUM	14	6	30000	4	1	148000	163000
42	6	ALBIN 43 SUNDECK	FB	TRWL	FBG	SV	IB	T135D	LEHM	14	6	30000	4	1	156500	172000
42	6	ALBIN 43 SUNDECK	FB	TRWL	FBG	SV	IB	T210D	CUM	14	6	30000	4	1	160000	176000
44		ALBIN CUSTOM 44 MY	FB	MY	FBG	SV	IB	T375D	CAT	14	4	30000	2	6	163000	179000
47	9	NORTH-SEA CUTTER 48	FB	MY	FBG	DV	IB	T307D	VLVO	14		30000	4		162000	178000
47	9	NORTH-SEA CUTTER 48	FB	MY	FBG	DV	IB	T375D	CAT	14		30000	4		176000	193000
48	6	ALBIN 49 TRI-CABIN	FB	TRWL	FBG	SV	IB	T210D	CUM	14	6	38500	4	1	164500	180500
48	6	ALBIN 49 TRI-CABIN	FB	TRWL	FBG	SV	IB	T300D	CUM	14	6	38500	4	1	170500	187500

 CONTINUED ON NEXT PAGE

LOA FT	LOA IN	NAME AND/ OR MODEL	TOP/ RIG	BOAT TYPE	HULL MTL	HULL TP	TP	ENGINE # HP	ENGINE MFG	BEAM FT	BEAM IN	WGT LBS	DRAFT FT	DRAFT IN	RETAIL LOW	RETAIL HIGH
		1991 BOATS														
48	9	ALBIN 49 COCKPIT	FB	TRWL	FBG	DS	IB	T250D	CUM	14	6	35500	4	1	161500	177500
48	9	ALBIN 49 COCKPIT	FB	TRWL	FBG	DS	IB	T300D	CUM	14	6	35500	4	1	165500	181500
		1990 BOATS														
26	9	ALBIN 27	HT	CBNCR	FBG	DS	IB	78D	PERK	9	8	6750	2	6	36400	40400
26	9	ALBIN 27	HT	CBNCR	FBG	DS	IB	157D	ISUZ	9	8	6750	2	6	43500	48400
26	9	ALBIN 27 SPORT CR	HT	CBNCR	FBG	DS	IB	78D	PERK	9	8	6750	2	6	35600	39500
26	9	ALBIN 27 SPORT CR	HT	CBNCR	FBG	DS	IB	157D	ISUZ	9	8	6750	2	6	42800	47500
32	4	ALBIN 32 SPORTFISH	OP	SF	FBG	SV	IB	250D-300D		12	3	13500	3	10	71000	79500
34	3	ALBIN 34 FAMILY CR	FB	CR	FBG	SV	IB	250D	CUM	11	6	15000	3	6	81000	89000
34	3	ALBIN 34 FAMILY CR	FB	CR	FBG	SV	IB	T157D	ISUZ	11	6	16500	3		82600	90800
34	3	ALBIN 34 MOTORYACHT	FB	CR	FBG	SV	IB	T157D-T250D		11	6	16500	3		93500	103000
35	9	ALBIN 36	FB	TRWL	FBG	SV	IB	210D	CAT	13	2	18500	3	6	106000	116500
35	9	ALBIN 36	FB	TRWL	FBG	SV	IB	T135D	LEHM	13	2	18500	3	6	109500	120000
35	9	ALBIN 36	FB	TRWL	FBG	SV	IB	T210D	CUM	13	2	18500	3	6	114500	126000
36	8	PALM-BEACH 37	FB	DCMY	FBG	DV	IB	T210D	CAT	12	9	16000	3		104500	115000
36	8	PALM-BEACH 37	FB	DCMY	FBG	DV	IB	T210D	CUM	12	9	16000	3		102500	113000
36	8	PALM-BEACH 37 SUNDCK	FB	CR	FBG	DV	IB	T210D	CAT	12	9	17000	3		103000	113000
36	8	PALM-BEACH 37 SUNDCK	FB	CR	FBG	DV	IB	T210D	CUM	12	9	17000	3		101000	111000
39	4	ALBIN CUSTOM 40	FB	MY	FBG	SV	IB	T320D	CAT	14	4	26000	2	6	134500	147500
39	4	ALBIN CUSTOM 40	FB	MY	FBG	SV	IB	T375D	CAT	14	4	26000	2	6	139500	153500
39	5	ALBIN 40	FB	TRWL	FBG	SV	IB	135D	LEHM	13	2	23500	3	6	111500	122500
		IB 210D CAT 114000 125500, IB 210D CUM 112500 124000, IB T135D LEHM 115000 126500														
		IB T210D CAT 121500 133500, IB T210D CUM 118500 130500														
39	5	ALBIN 40 SUNDECK	FB	TRWL	FBG	SV	IB	T135D	LEHM	13	2	23500	3	6	120500	132500
39	5	ALBIN 40 SUNDECK	FB	TRWL	FBG	SV	IB	T210D	CAT	13	2	23500	3	6	125500	138000
39	5	ALBIN 40 SUNDECK	FB	TRWL	FBG	SV	IB	T210D	CUM	13	2	23500	3	6	122500	135000
42	6	ALBIN 43	FB	TRWL	FBG	SV	IB	135D	LEHM	14	6	30000	4	1	135500	149000
		IB 210D CAT 138500 152000, IB 210D CUM 137500 151000, IB T135D LEHM 138000 151500														
		IB T210D CAT 143000 157500, IB T210D CUM 141000 155000														
42	6	ALBIN 43 SUNDECK	FB	TRWL	FBG	SV	IB	T135D	LEHM	14	6	30000	4	1	149500	164000
42	6	ALBIN 43 SUNDECK	FB	TRWL	FBG	SV	IB	T210D	CAT	14	6	30000	4	1	155000	170000
42	6	ALBIN 43 SUNDECK	FB	TRWL	FBG	SV	IB	T210D	CUM	14	6	30000	4	1	153000	168000
47	9	NORTH-SEA CUTTER 48	FB	MY	FBG	DV	IB	T307D	VLVO	14		30000	4		154500	170000
47	9	NORTH-SEA CUTTER 48	FB	MY	FBG	DV	IB	T375D	CAT	14		30000	4		167500	184500
48	6	ALBIN 49 TRI-CABIN	FB	TRWL	FBG	SV	IB	T225D	CAT	14	6	38500	4	1	159000	175000
48	6	ALBIN 49 TRI-CABIN	FB	TRWL	FBG	SV	IB	T225D	LEHM	14	6	38500	4	1	158000	173500
48	6	ALBIN 49 TRI-CABIN	FB	TRWL	FBG	SV	IB	T375D	CAT	14	6	38500	4	1	171000	187500
48	9	ALBIN 49 COCKPIT	FB	TRWL	FBG	DS	IB	T250D		14	6	35500	4	1	154500	170000
48	9	ALBIN 49 COCKPIT	FB	TRWL	FBG	DS	IB	T250D	CAT	14	6	35500	4	1	156000	171000
48	9	ALBIN 49 COCKPIT	FB	TRWL	FBG	DS	IB	T300D	VLVO	14	6	35500	4	1	156500	172000
		1989 BOATS														
26	9	ALBIN 27	HT	CBNCR	FBG	DS	IB	78D		9	8	6750	2	6	34400	38200
26	9	ALBIN 27	HT	CBNCR	FBG	DS	IB	157D	ISUZ	9	8	6750	2	6	41300	45900
34	3	ALBIN 34 MOTORYACHT	FB	CR	FBG	SV	IB	T157D-T250D		11	6	16500	3	6	84200	97500
35	9	ALBIN 36	FB	TRWL	FBG	SV	IB	135D	LEHM	13	2	18500	3	6	98800	108500
35	9	ALBIN 36	FB	TRWL	FBG	SV	IB	210D	CUM	13	2	18500	3	6	100500	110500
36	8	PALM-BEACH 37	FB	DCMY	FBG	DV	IB	T210D	CUM	12	9	16000	3		98100	108000
36	8	PALM-BEACH 37 SUNDCK	FB	CR	FBG	DV	IB	T210D	CUM	12	9	17000	3		96400	106000
39	5	ALBIN 40	FB	TRWL	FBG	SV	IB	135D	LEHM	13	2	23500	3	6	106500	117000
		IB 210D CUM 107500 118500, IB T135D LEHM 110500 121500, IB T210D CUM 113000 124500														
39	5	ALBIN 40 SUNDECK	FB	TRWL	FBG	SV	IB	T135D	LEHM	13	2	23500	3	6	114500	126000
39	5	ALBIN 40 SUNDECK	FB	TRWL	FBG	SV	IB	T210D	CUM	13	2	23500	3	6	117500	129000
42	6	ALBIN 43	FB	TRWL	FBG	SV	IB	135D	LEHM	14	6	30000	4	1	129500	142500
		IB 210D CUM 131000 144000, IB T135D LEHM 132000 145000, IB T210D CUM 135000 148500														
42	6	ALBIN 43 SUNDECK	FB	TRWL	FBG	SV	IB	T135D	LEHM	14	6	30000	4	1	142500	156500
42	6	ALBIN 43 SUNDECK	FB	TRWL	FBG	SV	IB	T210D	CUM	14	6	30000	4	1	146000	160500
47	9	NORTH-SEA CUTTER 48	FB	MY	FBG	DV	IB	T300D	VLVO	14		30000	4		146500	161000
47	9	NORTH-SEA CUTTER 48	FB	MY	FBG	DV	IB	T375D	CAT	14		30000	4		160000	176000
48	9	ALBIN 49 COCKPIT	FB	TRWL	FBG	DS	IB	T300D	LEHM	14	6	35500	4	1	151000	166000
48	9	ALBIN 49 COCKPIT	FB	TRWL	FBG	DS	IB	T300D	VLVO	14	6	35500	4	1	149500	164000
		1987 BOATS														
26	9	ALBIN 27	HT	CBNCR	FBG	DS	IB	78D	NISS	9	8	6750	2	6	31100	34600
26	9	ALBIN 27	HT	CBNCR	FBG	DS	IB	150D	ISUZ	9	8	6750	2	6	37400	41600
26	9	ALBIN 27	HT	DC	FBG	DS	IB	78D-150D		9	8	6750	2	6	28800	32000
34	3	ALBIN 34 MOTORYACHT	FB	CR	FBG	SV	IB	210D	CUM	11	6	15000	3	6	75800	83300
34	3	ALBIN 34 MOTORYACHT	FB	CR	FBG	SV	IB	T157D-T210D		11	6	16500	3	6	81500	91800
34	3	ALBIN 34 PERF CRUISR	FB	CR	FBG	SV	IB	210D	CUM	11	6	15000	3	6	66800	73500
34	3	ALBIN 34 PERF CRUISR	FB	CR	FBG	SV	IB	T157D-T210D		11	6	16500	3	6	72900	82600
35	9	ALBIN 36	FB	TRWL	FBG	DS	IB	135D	LEHM	13	2	18500	3	6	90600	99600
35	9	ALBIN 36	FB	TRWL	FBG	DS	IO	210D	CUM	13	2	18500	3	6	67500	74200
36	8	PALM-BEACH 37	FB	DCMY	FBG	DV	IB	T210D	CUM	12	9	16000	3		89700	98500
36	8	PALM-BEACH 37 SUNDCK	FB	CR	FBG	DV	IB	T210D	CUM	12	9	17000	3		88100	96800
39	5	ALBIN 40	FB	TRWL	FBG	DS	IB	135D	LEHM	13	2	26000	3	6	103500	113500
		IB 210D CUM 104500 115000, IB T135D LEHM 109000 120000, IB T210D CUM 111500 122500														
39	5	SUN-DECK 40	FB	TRWL	FBG	DS	IB	135D	LEHM	13	2	26000	3	6	108000	118500
		IB 210D CUM 109000 119500, IB T135D LEHM 113500 124500, IB T210D CUM 116000 127000														
42	6	ALBIN 43	FB	TRWL	FBG	DS	IB	T135D	LEHM	14	6	30000	4	1	125000	137500
42	6	ALBIN 43	FB	TRWL	FBG	DS	IB	T210D	CUM	14	6	30000	4	1	128000	140500
42	6	SUN-DECK 43	FB	TRWL	FBG	DS	IB	T135D	LEHM	14	6	32000	4	1	128500	141000
42	6	SUN-DECK 43	FB	TRWL	FBG	DS	IB	T210D	CUM	14	6	32000	4	1	131500	144500
47	9	NORTH-SEA CUTTER 48	FB	MY	FBG	DV	IB	T307D	VLVO	14		30000	4		135000	148500
		IB T320D CAT 138500 152000, IB T357D VLVO 143000 157000, IB T375D CAT 146500 161000														
47	9	PALM-BEACH 48	FB	MY	FBG	DV	IB	T307D	VLVO	14		30000	4		130000	143000
		IB T320D CAT 134500 147500, IB T357D VLVO 134500 148000, IB T375D CAT 139500 153500														
48	9	ALBIN 49 COCKPIT	FB	TRWL	FBG	DS	IB	T225D	LEHM	14	6	35500	4	1	133000	146000
48	9	ALBIN 49 COCKPIT	FB	TRWL	FBG	DS	IB	T275D	LEHM	14	6	35500	4	1	136000	149500
48	11	ALBIN 49 PILOTHOUSE	FB	PH	FBG	DS	IB	T135D	LEHM	15	1	44000	4		142000	156000
		1985 BOATS														
26	9	ALBIN 27	HT	CBNCR	FBG		IB	61D	LEHM	9	8	6750	2	6	27100	30100
26	9	ALBIN 27	HT	CBNCR	FBG	SV	IB	78D-100D		9	8	6750	2	6	28600	33700
26	9	ALBIN 27	HT	DC	FBG		IB	78D	NISS	9	8	6750	2	6	26500	29400
26	9	ALBIN 27	HT	DC	FBG	SV	IB	61D	LEHM	9	8		2	6	18900	21000
32	5	NOVA 33	SLP	SA/CR	F/S	KL	IB	15D	YAN	10	4	8177	5	6	24000	26600
35	9	ALBIN 36	FB	TRWL	FBG	DS	IB	135D		13	2	18500	3	6	83300	91500
35	9	ALBIN 36	FB	TRWL	FBG	DS	IB	135D	LEHM	13	2	18500	3	6	83300	91500
36	6	SUN-DECK 37	FB	TRWL	FBG	DS	IB	T 90D	VLVO	12	6	31500			103500	113500
36	8	PALM-BEACH 37	FB	DCMY	FBG	DV	IB	T 90D	VLVO	12	9	16000	3		78200	85900
36	8	PALM-BEACH 37	FB	DCMY	FBG	DV	IB	T136D	VLVO	12	9	16000	3		78900	86700
36	8	PALM-BEACH 37	FB	DCMY	FBG	DV	IB	T165D	VLVO	12	9	16000	3		79700	87600
40	3	ALBIN 40	FB	TRWL	FBG	DS	IB	135D		13	8	26000			97100	106500
40	3	ALBIN 40	FB	TRWL	FBG	DS	IB	135D	LEHM	13	8	26000	3	6	97100	106500
41	6	NIMBUS 42	SLP	SA/CR	FBG	KL	IB	42D	PATH	12	6	21500	5	10	68000	74700
42	6	ALBIN 43	FB	TRWL	FBG	DS	IB	135D		14	6	30000			109500	120500
42	6	ALBIN 43	FB	TRWL	FBG	DS	IB	T135D	LEHM	14	6	30000	4	1	110500	121500
42	6	SUN-DECK 43	FB	TRWL	FBG	DS	IB	T135D		14	6	30000	4	1	116000	127500
42	6	SUN-DECK 43	FB	TRWL	FBG	DS	IB	T255D	VLVO	14	6	30000	4	1	116000	127500
47	9	PALM-BEACH ALBIN 48	FB	TCMY	FBG	DV	IB	T255D	VLVO	14		31000	4		145000	159000
48	4	ALBIN 49 TRI-CABIN	FB	TRWL	FBG	DS	IB	T135D	LEHM	15		39050	3	8	124500	137000
48	4	ALBIN 49 TRI-CABIN	FB	TRWL	FBG	DS	IB	T158D	VLVO	15		39050	3	8	125500	138000
48	4	ALBIN 49 TRI-CABIN	FB	TRWL	FBG	DS	IB	T210D	CAT	15		40050	3	8	130500	143500
		1984 BOATS														
26	9	ALBIN 27	HT	DC	FBG		IB	61D	LEHM	9	8	6500	2	6	24100	26800
28	7	CUMULUS 28	SLP	SA/RC	FBG	KL	IB	12D	YAN	9	6	7056	5	3	19000	21100
32	5	NOVA 33	SLP	SA/CR	F/S	KL	IB	15D	YAN	10	4	8177	5	6	22500	25000
35	9	ALBIN 36	FB	TRWL	FBG	DS	IB	120D	LEHM	13	2	18500	3	6	80200	88200
40	3	ALBIN 40	FB	TRWL	FBG	DS	IB	120D	LEHM	13	8	26000	3	6	92800	102000
41	6	NIMBUS 42	SLP	SA/CR	FBG	KL	IB	42D	PATH	12	6	21500	5	10	64000	70300
42	6	ALBIN 43	FB	TRWL	FBG	DS	IB	T120D	LEHM	14	6	30000	4	1	109000	120000
47	9	PALM-BEACH ALBIN 48	FB	TCMY	FBG	SV	IB	T148		14		31000	3	6	102500	112500
47	9	PALM-BEACH ALBIN 48	FB	TCMY	FBG	SV	IB	T255D	VLVO	14		25000	3	6	121000	133000
48	4	ALBIN 49 TRI-CABIN	FB	TRWL	FBG	DS	IB	T120D	LEHM	15		39050	3	8	118500	130500
		IB T124D 119000 130500, IB T158D VLVO 120000 132000, IB T210D CAT 125000 137500														

....For earlier years, see the BUC Used Boat Price Guide, Volume 3

ALCAN MARINE PRODUCTS

DIV OF ALCAN CANADA PROD LTD
PRINCEVILLE PQ CANADA COAST GUARD MFG ID- ZCB

See inside cover to adjust price for area

LOA FT	LOA IN	NAME AND/ OR MODEL	TOP/ RIG	BOAT TYPE	HULL MTL	HULL TP	TP	ENGINE # HP	ENGINE MFG	BEAM FT	BEAM IN	WGT LBS	DRAFT FT	DRAFT IN	RETAIL LOW	RETAIL HIGH
		1985 BOATS														
16		STANDARD 16	OP		AL	PN	OB			8		775			1000	1200
16	1	HOLIDAY LX	OP	FSH	AL	SV	OB			6	2	312			385	470
16	1	PRO-BETA 160	OP	BASS	AL		OB			6	1	585			785	945
16	1	PRO-BETA 161	OP	BASS	AL		OB			6	1	585			795	955
16	2	MARLIN SUPREME	ST	RNBT	AL	SV	OB			6	1	800			1150	1350
16	2	SUPER-PRO 165	OP	BASS	AL		OB			6	1	760			1050	1250
18	3	JUMBO LX	OP	UTL	AL	SV	OB			6	9	428			490	590
19	2	SUPER-PRO 19	OP	BASS	AL		OB			7	1	1050			1550	1800
20		STANDARD 19	OP		AL	PN	OB			8		1050			1550	1800
20		VERSAILLE 22	ST		AL	PN	OB			8		1370			1950	2350
20		VOYAGER 19	ST		AL	PN	OB			8		1200			1750	2050

ALCAN MARINE PRODUCTS -CONTINUED See inside cover to adjust price for area

LOA FT	LOA IN	NAME AND/ OR MODEL	TOP/ RIG	BOAT TYPE	HULL MTL	HULL TP	ENGINE TP	ENGINE # HP	ENGINE MFG	BEAM FT	BEAM IN	WGT LBS	DRAFT FT	DRAFT IN	RETAIL LOW	RETAIL HIGH
		1985 BOATS														
20		VOYAGER LX 19	ST		AL	PN	OB			8		1320			1900	2250
24		STANDARD 19	OP		AL	PN	OB			8		1225			1950	2300
24		STANDARD 22	OP		AL	PN	OB			8		1300			2050	2450
24		VERSAILLE 22	ST		AL	PN	OB			8		1625			2600	3050
24		VOYAGER 19	ST		AL	PN	OB			8		1375			2250	2600
24		VOYAGER 22	ST		AL	PN	OB			8		1450			2350	2700
24		VOYAGER LX 19	ST		AL	PN	OB			8		1495			2400	2800
24		VOYAGER LX 22	ST		AL	PN	OB			8		1570			2550	2950
28		STANDARD 22	OP		AL	PN	OB			8		1400			9000	10200
28		VERSAILLE 22	ST		AL	PN	OB			8		1800			9650	10900
28		VOYAGER 22	ST		AL	PN	OB			8		1550			9650	10900
28		VOYAGER LX 22	ST		AL	PN	OB			8		1670			9650	10900
		1984 BOATS														
16	2	MARLIN	ST	RNBT	AL	SV	OB			6	2	800			1100	1300
16	2	MARLIN PRO	ST	CTRCN	AL	SV	OB			6	2	760			995	1200
18	1	JUMBO 1061	OP	UTL	AL	SV	OB			6	9	438			495	595

....For earlier years, see the BUC Used Boat Price Guide, Volume 3

ALCORT SAILBOATS INC

WATERBURY CT 06708 COAST GUARD MFG ID- AMF See inside cover to adjust price for area
FORMERLY ALCORT SAILBOATS INC

LOA FT	LOA IN	NAME AND/ OR MODEL	TOP/ RIG	BOAT TYPE	HULL MTL	HULL TP	ENGINE TP	ENGINE # HP	ENGINE MFG	BEAM FT	BEAM IN	WGT LBS	DRAFT FT	DRAFT IN	RETAIL LOW	RETAIL HIGH
		1988 BOATS														
16	5	TRAC	SLP	SA/OD	FBG	DB				8		359		9	1700	2050
		1987 BOATS														
16	7	TRAC	SLP	SA/OD	FBG					8		330			1550	1850
		1986 BOATS														
16	7	TRAC	SLP	SA/OD	FBG					8		330			1450	1750
18		TRAC	SLP	SA/OD	FBG	CT				8		351		8	1950	2350
		1985 BOATS														
16	7	TRAC	SLP	SA/OD	FBG					8		330			1350	1650
18		TRAC	SLP	SA/OD	FBG	CT				8		351		8	1850	2200
		1984 BOATS														
16	7	TRAC	SLP	SA/OD	FBG					8		330		9	1300	1550
18		TRAC	SLP	SA/OD	FBG	CT				8		351		8	1750	2050

....For earlier years, see the BUC Used Boat Price Guide, Volume 3

ALDEN OCEAN SHELLS INC

ALDEN OCEAN SHELL
ELIOT ME 03903
See inside cover to adjust price for area

FORMERLY MARTIN MARINE CO INC

For more recent years, see the BUC Used Boat Price Guide, Volume 1

LOA FT	LOA IN	NAME AND/ OR MODEL	TOP/ RIG	BOAT TYPE	HULL MTL	HULL TP	ENGINE TP	ENGINE # HP	ENGINE MFG	BEAM FT	BEAM IN	WGT LBS	DRAFT FT	DRAFT IN	RETAIL LOW	RETAIL HIGH
		1988 BOATS														
16		APPLEDORE 16	CAT	SAIL	FBG					2	9	110		5	1050	1250
16		APPLEDORE 16	CAT	SAIL	WD					2	9	70		5	**	**
19		APPLEDORE 19	SCH	SAIL	FBG					3	3	150		5	3300	3800
		1987 BOATS														
16		APPLEDORE 16	CAT	SAIL	FBG					2	9	110		5	970	1150
16		APPLEDORE 16	CAT	SAIL	WD					2	9	70		5	**	**
19		APPLEDORE 19	SCH	SAIL	FBG					3	3	150		5	3100	3600
		1986 BOATS														
16		APPLEDORE 16	CAT	SAIL	FBG					2	9	110		5	915	1100
16		APPLEDORE 16	CAT	SAIL	WD					2	9	70		5	**	**
19		APPLEDORE 19	SCH	SAIL	FBG					3	3	150		5	2900	3400
27		ENERGY 27	CAT	SA/CR	FBG	KL	IB	D		5	5	3000	5	3	11600	13200
48		ENERGY 48		CR	WD	DS	IB	25D		8	3				136000	149500
		1985 BOATS														
16		APPLEDORE 16	CAT	SAIL	FBG					2	9	110		5	860	1050
16		APPLEDORE 16	CAT	SAIL	WD					2	9	70		5	**	**
19		APPLEDORE 19	CAT	SAIL	FBG					3	3	150		5	2750	3200
27		ENERGY 27	CAT	SA/CR	FBG	KL	IB	D		5	5	3000	5	3	10900	12400
48		ENERGY 48		CR	WD	DS	IB	25D		8	3	7500			43800	48600
		1984 BOATS														
16		APPLEDORE 16	CAT	SAIL	FBG					2	9	110		5	800	965
16		APPLEDORE 16	CAT	SAIL	WD					2	9	70		5	**	**
19		APPLEDORE 19	CAT	SAIL	FBG					3	3	150		5	2550	3000

....For earlier years, see the BUC Used Boat Price Guide, Volume 3

ALDEN YACHTS

PORTSMOUTH RI 02871
See inside cover to adjust price for area
FORMERLY JOHN G ALDEN

For more recent years, see the BUC Used Boat Price Guide, Volume 1

LOA FT	LOA IN	NAME AND/ OR MODEL	TOP/ RIG	BOAT TYPE	HULL MTL	HULL TP	ENGINE TP	ENGINE # HP	ENGINE MFG	BEAM FT	BEAM IN	WGT LBS	DRAFT FT	DRAFT IN	RETAIL LOW	RETAIL HIGH
		1996 BOATS														
43	2	ALDEN 43 AC	SLP	SARAC	F/S	KL	IB	63D	WEST	12	6		5	9	235000	258000
44	2	ALDEN 44 AC	CUT	SARAC	F/S	KC	IB	63D	WEST	12	6	24000	4	11	261500	287500
44	10	ALDEN 45 AC	SLP	SARAC	F/S	KL	IB	63D	WEST	12	6		7	5	273500	300500
45	9	ALDEN 46 AC	CUT	SARAC	F/S	KC	IB	63D	WEST	13	6	34700	5	4	352500	387500
48	11	ALDEN 48 AC	CUT	SARAC	F/S	KC	IB	63D	WEST	13	6	34900	5	4	439500	483000
48	11	ALDEN 48 CC	CUT	SARAC	F/S	KC	IB	63D	WEST	13	6	36000	5	4	444000	488000
48	11	ALDEN 50 AC	CUT	SARAC	F/S	KC	IB	63D	WEST	13	6	36500	5	4	446000	490500
48	11	ALDEN 50 CC	CUT	SARAC	F/S	KC	IB	73D	WEST	13	6	37000	5	4	449000	493500
50		ALDEN 50 AC	CUT	SARAC	F/S	KC	IB	73D	WEST	14	4	37500	5	6	480000	527500
50	6	ALDEN 50 MY	FB	MY	F/S	DV	IB	T375D	CAT	15	8	39000	3	10	595500	654500
52	7	ALDEN 52 AC	CUT	SARAC	F/S	KC	IB	73D	WEST	14	4	38000	5	6	570500	627000
52	7	ALDEN 52 CC	CUT	SARAC	F/S	KC	IB	100D	WEST	14	4	40000	5	6	578000	635000
54	1	ALDEN 54 AC	CUT	SARAC	F/S	KC	IB	73D	WEST	14	4	38000	5	6	637000	700000
54	1	ALDEN 54 AC	KTH	SARAC	F/S	KC	IB	73D	WEST	14	4	38000	5	6	637000	700000
54	1	ALDEN 54 CC	CUT	SARAC	F/S	KL	IB	100D	WEST	14	4	40000	5	6	643500	707000
54	1	ALDEN 54 CC	KTH	SARAC	F/S	KC	IB	100D	WEST	14	4	40000	5	6	643500	707000
56		ALDEN 56 EX	OP	EXP	F/S	DV	IB	T425D	CAT	15	8	32000	3	10	484000	532000
72	2	ALDEN 72 AC	CUT	SARAC	F/S	KL	IB	140D	YAN	17	10	78000	10		**	**
		1995 BOATS														
43	2	ALDEN 43 AC	SLP	SARAC	F/S	KL	IB	63D	WEST	12	6		5	9	221000	243000
44	2	ALDEN 44 AC	CUT	SARAC	F/S	KC	IB	63D	WEST	12	6	24000	4	11	246000	270500
44	10	ALDEN 45 AC	SLP	SARAC	F/S	KL	IB	63D	WEST	12	6		7	5	257000	282500
45	9	ALDEN 46 AC	CUT	SARAC	F/S	KC	IB	63D	WEST	13	6	34700	5	4	331500	364500
48	11	ALDEN 48 AC	CUT	SARAC	F/S	KC	IB	63D	WEST	13	6	34900	5	4	413500	454500
48	11	ALDEN 48 CC	CUT	SARAC	F/S	KC	IB	63D	WEST	13	6	36000	5	4	418000	459000
48	11	ALDEN 50 AC	CUT	SARAC	F/S	KC	IB	63D	WEST	13	6	36500	5	4	419500	461000
48	11	ALDEN 50 CC	CUT	SARAC	F/S	KC	IB	73D	WEST	13	6	37000	5	4	422000	464000
50		ALDEN 50 AC	CUT	SARAC	F/S	KC	IB	73D	WEST	14	4	37500	5	6	451500	496000
50	6	ALDEN 50 MY	FB	MY	F/S	DV	IB	T375D	CAT	15	8	39000	3	10	**	**
52	7	ALDEN 52 AC	CUT	SARAC	F/S	KC	IB	73D	WEST	14	4	38000	5	6	536500	589500
52	7	ALDEN 52 CC	CUT	SARAC	F/S	KC	IB	100D	WEST	14	4	40000	5	6	543500	597500
54	1	ALDEN 54 AC	CUT	SARAC	F/S	KC	IB	73D	WEST	14	4	38000	5	6	599000	658000
54	1	ALDEN 54 AC	KTH	SARAC	F/S	KC	IB	73D	WEST	14	4	38000	5	6	599000	658000
54	1	ALDEN 54 CC	CUT	SARAC	F/S	KL	IB	100D	WEST	14	4	40000	5	6	605500	665000
54	1	ALDEN 54 CC	KTH	SARAC	F/S	KC	IB	100D	WEST	14	4	40000	5	6	605500	665000
72	2	ALDEN 72 AC	CUT	SARAC	F/S	KL	IB	140D	YAN	17	10	78000	10		**	**
		1994 BOATS														
43	2	ALDEN 43 AC	SLP	SARAC	F/S	KL	IB	63D	WEST	12	6		5	9	208000	228500
44	2	ALDEN 44 AC	CUT	SARAC	F/S	KC	IB	63D	WEST	12	6	24000	4	11	231500	254500
44	10	ALDEN 45 AC	SLP	SARAC	F/S	KL	IB	63D	WEST	12	6		7	5	242000	266000
45	9	ALDEN 46 AC	CUT	SARAC	F/S	KC	IB	63D	WEST	13	6	34700	5	4	312000	343000
48	11	ALDEN 48 AC	CUT	SARAC	F/S	KC	IB	63D	WEST	13	6	34900	5	4	389000	427500
48	11	ALDEN 48 CC	CUT	SARAC	F/S	KC	IB	63D	WEST	13	6	36000	5	4	393000	432000
48	11	ALDEN 50 AC	CUT	SARAC	F/S	KC	IB	63D	WEST	13	6	36500	5	4	395000	434000
48	11	ALDEN 50 CC	CUT	SARAC	F/S	KC	IB	73D	WEST	13	6	37000	5	4	397000	436500
50		ALDEN 50 AC	CUT	SARAC	F/S	KC	IB	73D	WEST	14	4	37500	5	6	424500	466500
52	7	ALDEN 52 AC	CUT	SARAC	F/S	KC	IB	73D	WEST	14	4	38000	5	6	504500	554500
52	7	ALDEN 52 CC	CUT	SARAC	F/S	KC	IB	100D	WEST	14	4	40000	5	6	511500	562000
54	1	ALDEN 54 AC	CUT	SARAC	F/S	KC	IB	73D	WEST	14	4	38000	5	6	563500	619000
54	1	ALDEN 54 AC	KTH	SARAC	F/S	KC	IB	73D	WEST	14	4	38000	5	6	563500	619000
54	1	ALDEN 54 CC	CUT	SARAC	F/S	KC	IB	100D	WEST	14	4	40000	5	6	569500	625500
54	1	ALDEN 54 CC	KTH	SARAC	F/S	KC	IB	100D	WEST	14	4	40000	5	6	569500	625500
72		ALDEN 72 AC	CUT	SARAC	F/S	KC	IB	140D	YAN	17	10	78000	10		**	**
		1993 BOATS														
43	2	ALDEN 43 AC	SLP	SARAC	F/S	KL	IB	63D	WEST	12	6		5	9	195500	215000
44	2	ALDEN 44 AC	CUT	SARAC	F/S	KC	IB	63D	WEST	12	6	24000	4	11	218000	239500
44	10	ALDEN 45 AC	SLP	SARAC	F/S	KL	IB	63D	WEST	12	6		7	5	227500	250000
45	9	ALDEN 46 AC	CUT	SARAC	F/S	KC	IB	63D	WEST	13	6	34700	5	4	293500	322500
48	11	ALDEN 48 AC	CUT	SARAC	F/S	KC	IB	63D	WEST	13	6	34900	5	4	366000	402000
48	11	ALDEN 48 CC	CUT	SARAC	F/S	KC	IB	63D	WEST	13	6	36000	5	4	369500	406000
48	11	ALDEN 50 AC	CUT	SARAC	F/S	KC	IB	63D	WEST	13	6	36500	5	4	371500	408000
48	11	ALDEN 50 CC	CUT	SARAC	F/S	KC	IB	73D	WEST	13	6	37000	5	4	373500	410500
50		ALDEN 50 AC	CUT	SARAC	F/S	KC	IB	73D	WEST	14	4	37500	5	6	399500	439000
52	7	ALDEN 52 AC	CUT	SARAC	F/S	KC	IB	73D	WEST	14	4	38000	5	6	474500	521500

 CONTINUED ON NEXT PAGE

LOA FT	IN	NAME AND/ OR MODEL	TOP/ RIG	BOAT TYPE	-HULL- MTL	TP	ENGINE TP	# HP	MFG	BEAM FT	IN	WGT LBS	DRAFT FT	IN	RETAIL LOW	RETAIL HIGH
		1993 BOATS														
52	7	ALDEN 52 CC	CUT	SARAC	F/S	KC	IB	100D	WEST	14	4	40000	5	6	481000	528500
54	1	ALDEN 54 AC	CUT	SARAC	F/S	KC	IB	73D	WEST	14	4	38000	5	6	530000	582500
54	1	ALDEN 54 AC	KTH	SARAC	F/S	KC	IB	73D	WEST	14	4	38000	5	6	530000	582500
54	1	ALDEN 54 CC	CUT	SARAC	F/S	KC	IB	100D	WEST	14	4	40000	5	6	535500	588500
54	1	ALDEN 54 CC	KTH	SARAC	F/S	KC	IB	100D	WEST	14	4	40000	5	6	535500	588500
		1992 BOATS														
44	2	ALDEN 44 AC	CUT	SA/CR	F/S	KC	IB	63D	WEST	12	6	24000	4	11	205000	225000
45	9	ALDEN 46 AC	CUT	SA/CR	F/S	KC	IB	63D	WEST	13	6	34700	5	4	276000	303500
48	11	ALDEN 48 AC	CUT	SA/CR	F/S	KC	IB	63D	WEST	13	6	34900	5	4	344000	378000
48	11	ALDEN 48 CC	CUT	SA/CR	F/S	KC	IB	63D	WEST	13	6	36000	5	4	347500	382000
48	11	ALDEN 50 AC	CUT	SA/CR	F/S	KC	IB	63D	WEST	13	6	36500	5	4	349500	384000
48	11	ALDEN 50 CC	CUT	SA/CR	F/S	KC	IB	73D	WEST	13	6	37000	5	4	351500	386000
50		ALDEN 50 AC	CUT	SA/CR	F/S	KC	IB	73D	WEST	14	4	37500	5	6	375500	413000
52	7	ALDEN 52 AC	CUT	SA/CR	F/S	KC	IB	73D	WEST	14	4	38000	5	6	446500	490500
52	7	ALDEN 52 CC	CUT	SA/CR	F/S	KC	IB	100D	WEST	14	4	40000	5	6	452500	497000
54	1	ALDEN 54 AC	CUT	SA/CR	F/S	KC	IB	73D	WEST	14	4	38000	5	6	498500	548000
54	1	ALDEN 54 AC	KTH	SA/CR	F/S	KC	IB	73D	WEST	14	4	38000	5	6	498500	548000
54	1	ALDEN 54 CC	CUT	SA/CR	F/S	KC	IB	100D	WEST	14	4	40000	5	6	503500	553500
54	1	ALDEN 54 CC	KTH	SA/CR	F/S	KC	IB	100D	WEST	14	4	40000	5	6	503500	553500
		1991 BOATS														
44	2	ALDEN 44 AC	CUT	SA/CR	F/S	KC	IB	63D	WEST	12	6	24000	4	11	192500	212000
45	9	ALDEN 46 AC	CUT	SA/CR	F/S	KC	IB	63D	WEST	13	6	34700	5	4	259500	285500
48	11	ALDEN 48 AC	CUT	SA/CR	F/S	KC	IB	63D	WEST	13	6	34900	5	4	323500	355500
48	11	ALDEN 48 CC	CUT	SA/CR	F/S	KC	IB	63D	WEST	13	6	36000	5	4	327000	359500
50		ALDEN 50 AC	CUT	SA/CR	F/S	KC	IB	73D	WEST	14	4	37500	5	6	353500	388500
50	4	ALDEN 50 AC	CUT	SA/CR	F/S	KC	IB	63D	WEST	13	6	36500	5	4	357500	393000
50	4	ALDEN 50 CC	CUT	SA/CR	F/S	KC	IB	73D	WEST	13	6	37000	5	4	359000	394500
52	7	ALDEN 52 AC	CUT	SA/CR	F/S	KC	IB	73D	WEST	14	4	38000	5	6	420000	461500
52	7	ALDEN 52 CC	CUT	SA/CR	F/S	KC	IB	100D	WEST	14	4	40000	5	6	425500	467500
54	1	ALDEN 54 AC	CUT	SA/CR	F/S	KC	IB	73D	WEST	14	4	38000	5	6	469000	515500
54	1	ALDEN 54 CC	CUT	SA/CR	F/S	KC	IB	100D	WEST	14	4	40000	5	6	474000	520500
		1990 BOATS														
44	2	ALDEN 44 AC	CUT	SA/CR	F/S	KC	IB	55D	YAN	12	6	24000	4	11	181000	198500
45	9	ALDEN 46 AC	CUT	SA/CR	F/S	KC	IB	58D	WEST	13	6	34700	5	4	244000	268000
48	11	ALDEN 48 AC	CUT	SA/CR	F/S	KC	IB	58D	WEST	13	6	34900	5	4	304000	334500
48	11	ALDEN 48 CC	CUT	SA/CR	F/S	KC	IB	73D	WEST	13	6	36000	5	4	308000	338500
50		ALDEN 50 AC	CUT	SA/CR	F/S	KC	IB	73D	WEST	14	4	37500	5	6	332500	365000
50	4	ALDEN 50 AC	CUT	SA/CR	F/S	KC	IB	73D	WEST	13	6	36500	5	4	336500	370000
50	4	ALDEN 50 CC	CUT	SA/CR	F/S	KC	IB	58D	WEST	13	6	37000	5	4	337000	370500
52	7	ALDEN 52 AC	CUT	SA/CR	F/S	KC	IB	73D	WEST	14	4	38000	5	6	395000	434000
52	7	ALDEN 52 CC	CUT	SA/CR	F/S	KC	IB	100D	WEST	14	4	40000	5	6	400000	440000
54	1	ALDEN 54 AC	CUT	SA/CR	F/S	KC	IB	73D	WEST	14	4	38000	5	6	441000	484500
54	1	ALDEN 54 CC	CUT	SA/CR	F/S	KC	IB	100D	WEST	14	4	40000	5	6	445500	490000
		1989 BOATS														
44	2	ALDEN 44 AC	CUT	SA/CR	F/S	KC	IB	55D	YAN	12	6	24000	4	11	170000	187000
45	9	ALDEN 46 AC	CUT	SA/CR	F/S	KC	IB	58D	WEST	13	6	34700	5	4	229500	252000
48	11	ALDEN 48 AC	CUT	SA/CR	F/S	KC	IB	58D	WEST	13	6	34900	5	4	286000	314500
48	11	ALDEN 48 CC	CUT	SA/CR	F/S	KC	IB	73D	WEST	13	6	36000	5	4	290000	318500
50		ALDEN 50 AC	CUT	SA/CR	F/S	KC	IB	73D	WEST	14	4	37500	5	6	312500	343500
50	4	ALDEN 50 AC	CUT	SA/CR	F/S	KC	IB	73D	WEST	13	6	36500	5	4	316500	348000
50	4	ALDEN 50 CC	CUT	SA/CR	F/S	KC	IB	73D	WEST	13	6	37000	5	4	318000	349500
52	7	ALDEN 52 AC	CUT	SA/CR	F/S	KC	IB	73D	WEST	14	4	38000	5	6	371500	408500
52	7	ALDEN 52 CC	CUT	SA/CR	F/S	KC	IB	100D	WEST	14	4	40000	5	6	376500	413500
54	1	ALDEN 54 AC	CUT	SA/CR	F/S	KC	IB	73D	WEST	14	4	38000	5	6	415000	456000
54	1	ALDEN 54 CC	CUT	SA/CR	F/S	KC	IB	100D	WEST	14	4	40000	5	6	419000	460500
		1988 BOATS														
44	2	ALDEN 44 AC	CUT	SA/CR	F/S	KC	IB	55D	YAN	12	6	24000	4	11	160000	176000
45	9	ALDEN 46 AC	CUT	SA/CR	F/S	KC	IB	58D	WEST	13	6	34700	5	4	216000	237000
48	11	ALDEN 48 AC	CUT	SA/CR	F/S	KC	IB	58D	WEST	13	6	34900	5	4	269000	296000
48	11	ALDEN 48 CC	CUT	SA/CR	F/S	KC	IB	73D	WEST	13	6	36000	5	4	272500	299500
50		ALDEN 50 AC	CUT	SA/CR	F/S	KC	IB	73D	WEST	14	4	37500	5	6	294000	323000
50	4	ALDEN 50 AC	CUT	SA/CR	F/S	KC	IB	73D	WEST	13	6	36500	5	4	298000	327500
50	4	ALDEN 50 CC	CUT	SA/CR	F/S	KC	IB	73D	WEST	13	6	37000	5	4	299000	328500
52	7	ALDEN 52 AC	CUT	SA/CR	F/S	KC	IB	73D	WEST	14	4	38000	5	6	349500	384000
52	7	ALDEN 52 CC	CUT	SA/CR	F/S	KC	IB	100D	WEST	14	4	39000	5	6	352500	387000
54	1	ALDEN 54 AC	CUT	SA/CR	F/S	KC	IB	73D	WEST	14	4	38000	5	6	390000	429000
54	1	ALDEN 54 CC	CUT	SA/CR	F/S	KC	IB	100D	WEST	14	4	39000	5	6	393000	431500
		1987 BOATS														
44	2	ALDEN 44	CUT	SA/CR	F/S	KC	IB	55D	YAN	12	6	24000	4	11	150500	165500
45	9	ALDEN 46	CUT	SA/CR	F/S	KC	IB	58D	WEST	13	6	34700	5	4	203000	223000
48	11	ALDEN 48	CUT	SA/CR	F/S	KC	IB	58D	WEST	13	6	34900	5	4	253000	278000
50		ALDEN 50	CUT	SA/CR	F/S	KC	IB	73D	WEST	14	4	37500	5	6	276500	304000
52	7	ALDEN 52 CC	CUT	SA/CR	F/S	KC	IB	100D	WEST	14	4	39000	5	6	331500	364000
54	1	ALDEN 54	KTH	SA/CR	F/S	KC	IB	73D	WEST	14	4	38000	5	6	367000	403500
		1986 BOATS														
44	2	ALDEN 44	SLP	SA/CR	F/S	KC	IB	55D	YAN	12	6	24000	4	11	141500	155500
50		ALDEN 50	CUT	SA/CR	F/S	KC	IB	73D	WEST	14	4	37500	5	6	260000	286000
52	7	ALDEN 52	CUT	SA/CR	F/S	KC	IB	73D	WEST	14	4	39000	5	6	311000	341500
54		ALDEN 54	KTH	SA/CR	F/S	KC	IB	73D	WEST	14	4	38000	5	6	343000	377000
		1984 BOATS														
44	2	ALDEN 44	SLP	SA/RC	FBG	KC	IB	50D	PERK	12	6	24500	4	11	125500	138000
75		ALDEN 75	KTH	SA/RC	FBG	KC	IB	100D		18		98400	6	6	**	**

....For earlier years, see the BUC Used Boat Price Guide, Volume 3

ALINDALE MFG CO INC

WILMINGTON NC 28402 COAST GUARD MFG ID- ADL See inside cover to adjust price for area

LOA FT	IN	NAME AND/ OR MODEL	TOP/ RIG	BOAT TYPE	-HULL- MTL	TP	ENGINE TP	# HP	MFG	BEAM FT	IN	WGT LBS	DRAFT FT	IN	RETAIL LOW	RETAIL HIGH
		1984 BOATS														
16	4	SEA-RAIDER	OP	UTL	FBG	SV	OB			6	6	650		10	1050	1250
17		SKIFF	OP	UTL	FBG	FL	OB			5	2	420		5	665	800
17	4	SEA-MARK	OP	UTL	FBG	SV	OB			6	5	710		6	1150	1350
20	9	SEA-MARK	OP	UTL	FBG	SV	OB			8		1250		10	2000	2400

....For earlier years, see the BUC Used Boat Price Guide, Volume 3

ALL FAMILY CRAFT INC

DIV OF PLAYCRAFT BOATS
RICHLAND MO 65556 COAST GUARD MFG ID- CDG See inside cover to adjust price for area

For more recent years, see the BUC Used Boat Price Guide, Volume 1

LOA FT	IN	NAME AND/ OR MODEL	TOP/ RIG	BOAT TYPE	-HULL- MTL	TP	ENGINE TP	# HP	MFG	BEAM FT	IN	WGT LBS	DRAFT FT	IN	RETAIL LOW	RETAIL HIGH
		1996 BOATS														
16		SCREAMER		RNBT	FBG	DV	JT	120		8		900			4950	5700
24	6	PREVIA 250		RNBT	FBG	DV	IO	190		8	6	3800			12100	13800
		1995 BOATS														
21		2150 BR		RNBT	FBG	DV	IO	260	MRCR	8		3350			9150	10400
22	5	2350 BR		RNBT	FBG	DV	IO	260	MRCR	8		3900			10700	12200
		1991 BOATS														
17		1700 BR	OP	RNBT	FBG	DV	OB			7	7	1150			4050	4700
17		1750 BR	OP	RNBT	FBG	DV	IO	115-155		7	7	2200			3800	4700
17	8	1850 BR	OP	RNBT	FBG	DV	IO	115-200		7	3	2400			4050	4950
17	8	1850 BR	OP	RNBT	FBG	DV	IO	205		7	3	2400			4150	5050
19		190 SPORT BR	OP	RNBT	FBG	DV	IO	155-235		8		2700			4950	6150
19	2	2050 BR	OP	RNBT	FBG	DV	IO	155-235		7	7	2650			4800	5950
20	4	2000 CC	OP	CUD	FBG	DV	IO	155-235		7	9	3100			6200	7650
20	8	210 SPORT BR	OP	RNBT	FBG	DV	IO	155-235		8		2950			5950	7350
20	8	210SD	OP	RNBT	FBG	DV	IO	155-235		8		2850			5850	7200
21		2150 BR	OP	RNBT	FBG	DV	IO	155-270		8		3350			6600	8050
21		2150 BR	OP	RNBT	FBG	DV	IO	300		8		3350			7350	8850
21		2150 CC	OP	CUD	FBG	DV	IO	155-270		8		3600			7250	8850
21		2150 CC	OP	CUD	FBG	DV	IO	300		8		3600			8050	9700
22	5	2350 BR	OP	RNBT	FBG	DV	IO	175-270		8		3900			7850	9500
22	5	2350 BR	OP	RNBT	FBG	DV	IO	300		8		3900			8600	10300
22	5	2350 CC	OP	CUD	FBG	DV	IO	175-270		8		4000			8500	10200
22	5	2350 CC	OP	CUD	FBG	DV	IO	300		8		4000			9350	11000
		1990 BOATS														
17		1700 O/B	OP	RNBT	FBG	DV	OB			7	7	1150			3900	4550
17		1750 I/O	OP	RNBT	FBG	DV	IO			7	7	2200			**	**
17	8	1800	OP	RNBT	FBG	DV	OB			7	3	1350			4550	5250
17	8	1850	OP	RNBT	FBG	DV	IO			7	3	2400			**	**
19	2	2050	OP	RNBT	FBG	DV	IO			7	7	2650			**	**
20	4	2000CC	OP	CUD	FBG	DV	IO			7	9	3100			**	**
20	8	210 SPORT BR	OP	RNBT	FBG	DV	IO			8		2950			**	**
20	8	210 SPORT CB	OP	RNBT	FBG	DV	IO			8		2850			**	**
21		2150BR	OP	RNBT	FBG	DV	IO			8		3350			**	**
21		2150CC	OP	CUD	FBG	DV	IO			8		3600			**	**
22	5	2350BR	OP	RNBT	FBG	DV	IO			8		3900			**	**
22	5	2350CC	OP	CUD	FBG	DV	IO			8		4000			**	**
		1989 BOATS														
16	4	1650	OP	RNBT	FBG	DV	IO			6	9	1700			**	**
17		CIERA 17	OP	RNBT	FBG	TR	OB			7	2	2100			5900	6800
17	8	1850	OP	RNBT	FBG	DV	IO			7	3	2400			**	**
19	2	2050	OP	RNBT	FBG	DV	IO			7	7	2650			**	**
19	2	CIERA 19	OP	RNBT	FBG	TR	IO			7	9	2100			**	**
21		2150BR	OP	RNBT	FBG	DV	IO			8		3350			**	**
21		2150CC	OP	CUD	FBG	DV	IO			8		3600			**	**
22	5	2350BR	OP	CUD	FBG	DV	IO			8		4000			**	**

LOA FT	LOA IN	NAME AND/ OR MODEL	TOP/ RIG	BOAT TYPE	-HULL- MTL	-HULL- TP	TP	ENGINE # HP	ENGINE MFG	BEAM FT	BEAM IN	WGT LBS	DRAFT FT	DRAFT IN	RETAIL LOW	RETAIL HIGH
		1989 BOATS														
22	5	2350BR	OP	RNBT	FBG	DV	IO			8		3900			**	**
		1988 BOATS														
17	8	1800		RNBT	FBG	DV	OB			7	3	1350			4250	4900
17	8	1850		RNBT	FBG	DV	IO		MRCR	7	3	2400			**	**
17	8	1850		RNBT	FBG	DV	IO		OMC	7	3	2400			**	**
19	2	2050		RNBT	FBG	DV	IO		MRCR	7	7	2650			**	**
19	2	2050		RNBT	FBG	DV	IO		OMC	7	7	2650			**	**
		1987 BOATS														
16	4	1650		RNBT	FBG	DV	IO			6	8	1700			**	**
21		2150BR		RNBT	FBG	DV	IO			8		3550			**	**
21		2150CC		RNBT	FBG	DV	IO			8		3600			**	**
22	5	2350BR		RNBT	FBG	DV	IO			8		3900			**	**
22	5	2350CC		RNBT	FBG	DV	IO			8		4000			**	**
		1986 BOATS														
16		1600		RNBT	FBG	DV	OB			6	9				2350	2750
16	4	1650		RNBT	FBG	DV	IO			6	9				**	**
17	8	CHARGER 1800VBR		RNBT	FBG	DV	OB			7	3	1350			4000	4650
17	8	CHARGER 1850VBR		RNBT	FBG	DV	IO	140	OMC	7	3	2350			3000	3500
19	2	CHARGER 2050VBR		RNBT	FBG	DV	IO	260	MRCR	7	8	2650			3900	4550
19	2	CHARGER 2150VBR		RNBT	FBG	DV	IO	185	MRCR	7	8				3550	4100
22	5	2300BR		RNBT	FBG		IO	200	OMC	8					5400	6200
22	5	2300CC		RNBT	FBG		IO	230	MRCR	8					5500	6350
		1985 BOATS														
16		1600		RNBT	FBG	DV	OB			6	9				2300	2700
16	4	1650		RNBT	FBG	DV	IO			6	9				**	**
17	8	CHARGER 1800VBR		RNBT	FBG	DV	OB			7	3	1350			3900	4550
17	8	CHARGER 1850VBR		RNBT	FBG	DV	IO	140	OMC	7	3	2350			2900	3350
19	2	CHARGER 2050VBR		RNBT	FBG	DV	IO	260	MRCR	7	8	2650			3750	4350
19	2	CHARGER 2150VBR		RNBT	FBG	DV	IO	185	MRCR	7	8				3400	3950
		1984 BOATS														
16		1600		RNBT	FBG	DV	OB			6	9				2300	2650
16	4	1650		RNBT	FBG	DV	IO			6	9				**	**
16	4	1700	OP	RNBT	FBG		OB			7	2	1100			3100	3600
16	4	1750	OP	RNBT	FBG	DV	IO	120		7	2				2300	2650

....For earlier years, see the BUC Used Boat Price Guide, Volume 3

ALL SEASON INDUSTRIES INC

MARKLE IN 46770 COAST GUARD MFG ID- ALS See inside cover to adjust price for area

LOA FT	LOA IN	NAME AND/ OR MODEL	TOP/ RIG	BOAT TYPE	-HULL- MTL	-HULL- TP	TP	ENGINE # HP	ENGINE MFG	BEAM FT	BEAM IN	WGT LBS	DRAFT FT	DRAFT IN	RETAIL LOW	RETAIL HIGH
		1991 BOATS														
16	10	IMPERIAL 1750	OP	RNBT	FBG	DV	IO	120-175		7	8				2800	3250
18	6	IMPERIAL 1850	OP	RNBT	FBG	DV	IO	120-210		7	8	1900			3100	3750
19	6	IMPERIAL 2000	OP	RNBT	FBG	DV	IO	120-260		8					3650	4450
19	6	IMPERIAL 2000	OP	RNBT	FBG	DV	IO	275	VLVO	8					4100	4750
19	6	IMPERIAL 2020	OP	RNBT	FBG	DV	IO	120-260		8					3400	4200
19	6	IMPERIAL 2020	OP	RNBT	FBG	DV	IO	275	VLVO	8					3850	4450
20	5	IMPERIAL 2150	OP	RNBT	FBG	DV	IO	120-260		8	5				4200	5100
20	5	IMPERIAL 2150	OP	RNBT	FBG	DV	IO	275	VLVO	8	5				4700	5450
21	10	IMPERIAL 2220	OP	RNBT	FBG	DV	IO	167-260		7	7				5000	5950
21	10	IMPERIAL 2220	OP	RNBT	FBG	DV	IO	275	VLVO	7	7				5450	6300
21	10	IMPERIAL 2220	OP	RNBT	FBG	DV	IO	330	VLVO	7	7				6150	7100
21	11	IMPERIAL 2200	OP	RNBT	FBG	DV	IO	167-260		7	7				5050	5950
21	11	IMPERIAL 2200	OP	RNBT	FBG	DV	IO	275	VLVO	7	7				5500	6300
21	11	IMPERIAL 2200	OP	RNBT	FBG	DV	IO	330	VLVO	7	7				6200	7100
22	10	IMPERIAL 2300	OP	RNBT	FBG	DV	IO	167-275		8					6350	7800
22	10	IMPERIAL 2320	OP	FSH	FBG	DV	IO	167-275		8					7250	8900
23	8	IMPERIAL 2400	OP	CR	FBG	DV	IO	167-275		8	6				7450	9150
23	8	IMPERIAL 2400	OP	CR	FBG	DV	IO	330	VLVO	8	6				8700	10000
23	8	IMPERIAL 2400	OP	CR	FBG	DV	IO	200D	VLVO	8	6				10300	11700
26		IMPERIAL 2600	OP	CR	FBG	DV	IO	260-330		10					9750	12200
26		IMPERIAL 2600	OP	CR	FBG	DV	IO	200D	VLVO	10					13900	15700
26		IMPERIAL 2600	OP	SPTCR	FBG	DV	IO	T167-T260		10					11700	14300
		IO T275 VLVO 13100 14900, IO T330 VLVO 14500 16500, IO T200D VLVO													16000	18200
26		RAPPALLO	OP	CR	FBG	DV	IO	175-230		10					10300	12000
		IO 260-330 11800 14700, IO 200D VLVO 16200 18400, IO T167-T260													11700	14300
		IO T275 VLVO 13100 14900, IO T330 VLVO 14500 16500, IO T200D VLVO													18800	20900
27		IMPERIAL 2700	OP	CUD	FBG	DV	IO	260-275		7	6				9600	11300
27		IMPERIAL 2700	OP	CUD	FBG	DV	IO	330	VLVO	7	6				10700	12100
27		IMPERIAL 2700	OP	CUD	FBG	DV	IO	200D	VLVO	7	6				11300	12800
27	10	IMPERIAL 2800	OP	SPTCR	FBG	DV	IO	260-330		10					12200	15000
		IO 200D VLVO 15500 17700, IO T167-T260 13100 16300, IO T275-T330													14900	18300
		IO T200D VLVO 19300 21500														
30		IMPERIAL 3000	OP	CR	FBG	DV	IO	260-330		11					16900	20100
		IO 200D VLVO 19800 22100, IO T260-T330 19300 23000, IO T200D VLVO													23200	25700
34		IMPERIAL 3400	FB	CR	FBG	DV	IO	260-330		11		10000			27000	31000
		IO 200D VLVO 28800 32000, IO T260-T330 29200 34300, IO T200D VLVO													31900	35400
		1990 BOATS														
16	4	IMPERIAL 1700	OP	RNBT	FBG	SV	IO	131		6	11	1870			2300	2700
18	4	IMPERIAL 1900	OP	RNBT	FBG	DV	IO	131		7	8	2140			2900	3400
18	4	IMPERIAL 1950	OP	RNBT	FBG	DV	IO	131		7	8	2140			2900	3400
19	6	IMPERIAL 2000	OP	RNBT	FBG	DV	IO	131		8		2640			3550	4100
19	6	IMPERIAL 2010	OP	FSH	FBG	DV	IO	131		8		2505			3750	4350
19	6	IMPERIAL 2020	OP	RNBT	FBG	DV	IO	131		8		2180			3200	3750
19	6	IMPERIAL 2040	OP	RNBT	FBG	DV	IO	131		8		2575			3500	4050
20	5	IMPERIAL 2150	OP	RNBT	FBG	DV	IO	131		8	5	3135			4650	5350
21	10	IMPERIAL 2200	OP	RNBT	FBG	DV	IO	167		7	7	3275			4900	5650
21	10	IMPERIAL 2220	OP	RNBT	FBG	DV	IO	167		7	7	3475			5100	5900
22	10	IMPERIAL 2300	OP	SPTCR	FBG	DV	IO	167		8		3600			5950	6850
22	10	IMPERIAL 2310	OP	SF	FBG	DV	IO	167		8		3750			7000	8050
22	10	IMPERIAL 2320	OP	SF	FBG	DV	IO	167		8		3950			7250	8350
23	8	IMPERIAL 2400	OP	CR	FBG	DV	IO	167		8	6	4780			7850	9000
26		IMPERIAL 2600	OP	CR	FBG	DV	IO	270		10		5745			10600	12100
26		RAPPALLO	OP	CR	FBG	DV	IO	270		10		6045			11000	12500
27		IMPERIAL 2700	OP	SPTCR	FBG	DV	IO	307		7	6	4000			9550	10800
27	10	IMPERIAL 2800	OP	CR	FBG	DV	IO	270		10		5645			11800	13400
30		ULTRA 3000	OP	CR	FBG	DV	IO	270		11		8000			16000	18200
		1989 BOATS														
16	4	IMPERIAL V164	OP	RNBT	FBG	SV	IO	120		6	11	1870			2200	2550
17		IMPERIAL V173	OP	RNBT	FBG	SV	OB			6	10	960			2250	2600
17		IMPERIAL V174	OP	RNBT	FBG	SV	IO	120		6	10	1860			2250	2600
17	8	IMPERIAL V182	OP	RNBT	FBG	DV	IO	120		7	3	1920			2450	2800
18	4	IMPERIAL V184	OP	RNBT	FBG	DV	IO	120		7	8	1965			2650	3100
19	6	IMPERIAL V200	OP	RNBT	FBG	DV	IO	120		8		2415			3200	3700
19	6	IMPERIAL V202	OP	RNBT	FBG	DV	IO	120		8		2380			3150	3650
19	6	IMPERIAL V204XL	OP	RNBT	FBG	DV	IO	120		8		2380			3150	3700
19	6	IMPERIAL VC200F	OP	FSH	FBG	DV	IO	120		8		2505			3550	4100
20	5	IMPERIAL VC215	OP	RNBT	FBG	DV	IO	120		8	5	2900			4200	4850
21	10	IMPERIAL 220XL	OP	RNBT	FBG	DV	IO	167		7	7	2820			4250	4950
21	10	IMPERIAL V222	OP	RNBT	FBG	DV	IO	167		7	7	2820			4100	4800
22	10	IMPERIAL VC230	OP	SPTCR	FBG	DV	IO	167		8		3600			5650	6450
22	10	IMPERIAL VC230F	OP	SF	FBG	DV	IO	167		8		3750			6600	7600
22	10	IMPERIAL VC230WF	OP	SF	FBG	DV	IO	167		8		3950			6850	7900
23	8	IMPERIAL 240FC	OP	CR	FBG	DV	IO	167		8	6	4200			6700	7700
26		IMPERIAL 260FC	OP	CR	FBG	DV	IO	270		10		5280			8450	9700
26		RAPPOLLO	OP	CR	FBG	DV	IO	270		10		5280			10600	12000
27		IMPERIAL 270XL	OP	SPTCR	FBG	DV	IO	307		7	6	4000			9050	10300
27	10	IMPERIAL 280SF	OP	CR	FBG	DV	IO	270		10		5300			10900	12300
30		ULTRA 3000	OP	CR	FBG	DV	IO	270		11		8000			15100	17100
		1988 BOATS														
16	4	IMPERIAL V164	OP	RNBT	FBG	SV	IO	120		6	11				1900	2300
17		IMPERIAL V173	OP	RNBT	FBG	SV	OB			6	10				2750	3200
17		IMPERIAL V174	OP	RNBT	FBG	SV	IO	120		6	10				2050	2450
17	8	IMPERIAL V182	OP	RNBT	FBG	DV	IO	120		7	3				2100	2500
18	4	IMPERIAL V184	OP	RNBT	FBG	DV	IO	120		7	8				2350	2700
19	6	IMPERIAL V202	OP	RNBT	FBG	DV	IO	120		8					2850	3300
19	6	IMPERIAL V204	OP	RNBT	FBG	DV	IO	120		8					2850	3300
19	6	IMPERIAL V204XL	OP	RNBT	FBG	DV	IO	120		8					2850	3300
19	6	IMPERIAL VC200F	OP	FSH	FBG	DV	IO	120		8					3250	3750
20	5	IMPERIAL VC215	OP	CUD	FBG	DV	IO	120		8	5				3650	4250
21	11	IMPERIAL 220XL	OP	CUD	FBG	DV	IO	167		7	7				4200	4900
21	11	IMPERIAL V222	OP	RNBT	FBG	DV	IO	167		7	7				4050	4750
22	10	IMPERIAL VC230	OP	CUD	FBG	DV	IO	167		8					5350	6100
22	10	IMPERIAL VC230F	OP	FSH	FBG	DV	IO	167		8					5950	6800
22	10	IMPERIAL VC230WF	OP	FSH	FBG	DV	IO	167		8					5950	6800
23	8	IMPERIAL 240FC	OP	CR	FBG	DV	IO	167		8	6				6150	7050
26		IMPERIAL 260FC	OP	CR	FBG	DV	IO	270		10					9200	10500
26		RAPPOLLO	OP	SPTCR	FBG	DV	IO	270		10					9200	10500
27		IMPERIAL 270XL	OP	SPTCR	FBG	DV	IO	307		7	6				8500	9750
27	10	IMPERIAL 280SF	OP	SPTCR	FBG	DV	IO	270		10					10300	11700
		1987 BOATS														
16	3	IMPERIAL V163	OP	RNBT	FBG	SV	OB			6	11	1600			3200	3700
16	4	IMPERIAL V164	OP	RNBT	FBG	SV	IO	120-140		6	11	1870			1900	2300
17		IMPERIAL	OP	RNBT	FBG	SV	OB			6	10	1400			2850	3350
17		IMPERIAL V173	OP	RNBT	FBG	SV	OB			6	10	1400			2850	3350

CONTINUED ON NEXT PAGE

LOA FT IN	NAME AND/ OR MODEL	TOP/ RIG	BOAT TYPE	-HULL- MTL TP	----ENGINE--- TP # HP MFG	BEAM FT IN	WGT LBS	DRAFT FT IN	RETAIL LOW	RETAIL HIGH
					1987 BOATS					
17	IMPERIAL V174	OP	RNBT	FBG SV	IO 120-165	6 10	1810		1950	2350
17	IMPERIAL V175	ST	RNBT	FBG SV	IO 120-165	6 10	1840		1950	2350
17 8	IMPERIAL V184	OP	RNBT	FBG DV	OB	7 8	1370		2850	3300
17 8	IMPERIAL V184	OP	RNBT	FBG DV	IO 120-205	7 8	1370		2000	2450
19 6	IMPERIAL V202	OP	RNBT	FBG DV	IO 120-230	7 11	2040		2650	3200
19 6	IMPERIAL V202	OP	RNBT	FBG DV	IO 260 MRCR	7 11	2040		2850	3300
19 6	IMPERIAL V204	OP	RNBT	FBG DV	IO 120-230	7 11	2036		2650	3200
19 6	IMPERIAL V204	OP	RNBT	FBG DV	IO 260 MRCR	7 11	2036		2850	3300
19 6	IMPERIAL VC200	OP	CUD	FBG DV	IO 120-230	7 11	2130		2800	3350
19 6	IMPERIAL VC200	OP	CUD	FBG DV	IO 260 MRCR	7 11	2130		3000	3500
19 6	IMPERIAL VC200-F	OP	FSH	FBG DV	IO 120-230	7 11	2330		3050	3700
19 6	IMPERIAL VC200-F	OP	FSH	FBG DV	IO 260 MRCR	7 11	2330		3300	3850
20 5	IMPERIAL VC215	OP	CUD	FBG DV	IO		2500		3500	4250
20 5	IMPERIAL VC215	OP	CUD	FBG DV	IO 225-271		2500		3800	4650
20 5	IMPERIAL VC215	OP	CUD	FBG DV	IO 370 MRCR		2500		4950	5650
21 11	IMPERIAL 220XL	OP	CUD	FBG DV	IO MRCR	7 7	2820		**	**
21 11	IMPERIAL 220XL	OP	CUD	FBG DV	IO 165-260	7 7	2820		4000	4900
21 11	IMPERIAL V222	OP	RNBT	FBG DV	IO MRCR	7 7	2820		**	**
21 11	IMPERIAL V222	OP	RNBT	FBG DV	IO 165-260	7 7	2820		3800	4650
22 10	IMPERIAL VC230	OP	CUD	FBG DV	IO 165-260	8	3600		5050	6100
22 10	IMPERIAL VC230-F	OP	FSH	FBG DV	IO 165-260	8	3800		5550	6650
22 10	IMPERIAL VC230WF	OP	FSH	FBG DV	IO 165-260	8	3950		5700	6850
23 8	IMPERIAL 240FC	OP	CR	FBG DV	IO 165-260	8	3950		5650	6750
26	IMPERIAL 260FC	OP	CR	FBG DV	IO 260 MRCR	10	5280		8450	9750
26	IMPERIAL 260FC	OP	CR	FBG DV	IO T140 MRCR	10	5280		8900	10100
26	IMPERIAL 260FC	OP	CR	FBG DV	IO T260 MRCR	10	5280		9900	11300
27	IMPERIAL 270XL	OP	SPTCR	FBG DV	IO MRCR	7 6	4000		**	**
27 10	IMPERIAL 270SF	OP	SF	FBG DV	IO 260 MRCR	10	5300		11100	12600
27 10	IMPERIAL 270SF	OP	SF	FBG DV	IO T140 MRCR	10	5300		11400	12900
27 10	IMPERIAL 270SF	OP	SF	FBG DV	IO T260 MRCR	10	5300		13000	14800
					1986 BOATS					
16 4	IMPERIAL V164	OP	RNBT	FBG SV	OB	6 11	1870		3500	4100
16 4	IMPERIAL V164	OP	RNBT	FBG SV	IO 120-140	6 11	1870		1800	2150
16 4	IMPERIAL V165	OP	RNBT	FBG SV	OB	6 11	1275		2550	3000
17	IMPERIAL V174	OP	RNBT	FBG SV	IO 120-170	6 10	1810		1850	2250
17	IMPERIAL V175	ST	RNBT	FBG SV	IO 120-170	6 10	1840		1850	2250
17	IMPERIAL V185	OP	RNBT	FBG DV	OB	7 8	1370		2750	3200
17 8	IMPERIAL V184	OP	RNBT	FBG DV	OB	7 8	1370		2800	3250
17 8	IMPERIAL V184	OP	RNBT	FBG DV	IO 120-205	7 8	1370		1900	2350
19 6	IMPERIAL V190	OP	RNBT	FBG DV	IO 120-230	7 11	2036		2500	3050
19 6	IMPERIAL V190	OP	RNBT	FBG DV	IO 260 MRCR	7 11	2036		2700	3150
19 6	IMPERIAL V192	OP	RNBT	FBG DV	IO 120-230	7 11	2040		2500	3050
19 6	IMPERIAL V192	OP	RNBT	FBG DV	IO 260 MRCR	7 11	2040		2700	3150
19 6	IMPERIAL VC200	OP	CUD	FBG DV	IO 120-230	7 11	2130		2650	3200
19 6	IMPERIAL VC200	OP	CUD	FBG DV	IO 260 MRCR	7 11	2130		2850	3350
19 6	IMPERIAL VC200-F	OP	FSH	FBG DV	IO 120-230	7 11	2330		2900	3550
19 6	IMPERIAL VC200-F	OP	FSH	FBG DV	IO 260 MRCR	7 11	2330		3150	3650
21 1	IMPERIAL VC210-XS	OP	CUD	FBG DV	IO 170-260	8	2935		3850	4700
22 10	IMPERIAL VC230	OP	CUD	FBG DV	IO 170-260	8	3600		4850	5800
22 10	IMPERIAL VC230-F	OP	FSH	FBG DV	IO 170-260	8	3800		5300	6350
22 10	IMPERIAL VC230WF	OP	FSH	FBG DV	IO 170-260	8	3950		5450	6550
23 8	IMPERIAL 240FC	OP	CR	FBG DV	IO 170-260	8	3950		5400	6450
26	IMPERIAL 260FC	OP	CR	FBG DV	IO 260 MRCR	10	5280		8100	9300
26	IMPERIAL 260FC	OP	CR	FBG DV	IO T140 MRCR	10	5280		8400	9650
26	IMPERIAL 260FC	OP	CR	FBG DV	IO T260 MRCR	10	5280		9450	10800
27 10	IMPERIAL 270SF	OP	SF	FBG DV	IO 260 MRCR	10	5300		10600	12000
27 10	IMPERIAL 270SF	OP	SF	FBG DV	IO T140 MRCR	10	5300		10900	12400
27 10	IMPERIAL 270SF	OP	SF	FBG DV	IO T260 MRCR	10	5300		12400	14100
					1985 BOATS					
17	IMPERIAL V174	OP	RNBT	FBG SV	IO 120-170	6 10	1810		1800	2150
17 8	IMPERIAL V182	OP	RNBT	FBG DV	IO 200 MRCR	7 3	1980		2050	2450
19 6	IMPERIAL V190	OP	RNBT	FBG DV	IO 120-230	7 11	2036		2400	2950
19 6	IMPERIAL V191	OP	RNBT	FBG DV	OB	7 11	1390		2900	3400
19 6	IMPERIAL V192	OP	RNBT	FBG DV	IO 120-230	7 11	2040		2400	2950
19 6	IMPERIAL V192	OP	RNBT	FBG DV	IO 260 MRCR	7 11	2040		2600	3050
19 6	IMPERIAL V193	OP	RNBT	FBG DV	OB	7 11	1390		2900	3400
19 6	IMPERIAL VC200	OP	CUD	FBG DV	IO 120-230	7 11	2130		2550	3100
19 6	IMPERIAL VC200	OP	CUD	FBG DV	IO 260 MRCR	7 11	2130		2750	3200
19 6	IMPERIAL VC200-F	OP	FSH	FBG DV	IO 120-230	7 11	2330		2800	3400
19 6	IMPERIAL VC200-F	OP	FSH	FBG DV	IO 260 MRCR	7 11	2330		3000	3500
21 1	IMPERIAL VC210-XS	OP	CUD	FBG DV	IO 170-260	8	2935		3700	4500
22 10	IMPERIAL VC230	OP	CUD	FBG DV	IO 170-260	8	3600		4650	5600
22 10	IMPERIAL VC230-F	OP	FSH	FBG DV	IO 170-260	8	3800		5100	6100
22 10	IMPERIAL VC230WF	OP	FSH	FBG DV	IO 170-260	8	3950		5250	6300
					1984 BOATS					
17	IMPERIAL V173	OP	RNBT	FBG SV	OB	6 10	900		1800	2150
17	IMPERIAL V174	OP	RNBT	FBG SV	IO 120-170	6 10	1810		1700	2050
17	IMPERIAL V175	ST	RNBT	FBG SV	IO 120-170	6 10	1840		1750	2100
17	IMPERIAL V176	ST	RNBT	FBG DV	OB	6 10	1300		2500	2900
17 8	IMPERIAL V180	OP	RNBT	FBG DV	OB	7 3	1980		1950	2350
17 8	IMPERIAL V181	OP	RNBT	FBG DV	OB	7 3	1270		2500	2900
17 8	IMPERIAL V182	OP	RNBT	FBG DV	IO 120-198	7 3	1980		1950	2350
17 8	IMPERIAL V183	OP	RNBT	FBG DV	OB	7 3	1270		2500	2900
19 6	IMPERIAL V190	OP	RNBT	FBG DV	IO 120-228	7 11	2036		2350	2800
19 6	IMPERIAL V190	OP	RNBT	FBG DV	IO 260 MRCR	7 11	2036		2500	2950
19 6	IMPERIAL V191	OP	RNBT	FBG DV	OB	7 11	1390		2850	3300
19 6	IMPERIAL V192	OP	RNBT	FBG DV	IO 120-228	7 11	2040		2350	2800
19 6	IMPERIAL V192	OP	RNBT	FBG DV	IO 260 MRCR	7 11	2040		2500	2950
19 6	IMPERIAL V193	OP	RNBT	FBG DV	OB	7 11	1390		2850	3300
19 6	IMPERIAL VC200	OP	CUD	FBG DV	IO 120-228	7 11	2130		2450	2950
19 6	IMPERIAL VC200	OP	CUD	FBG DV	IO 260 MRCR	7 11	2130		2650	3100
19 6	IMPERIAL VC200-F	OP	FSH	FBG DV	IO 120-228	7 11	2315		2700	3250
19 6	IMPERIAL VC200-F	OP	FSH	FBG DV	IO 260 MRCR	7 11	2315		2900	3400
19 6	IMPERIAL VC201	OP	RNBT	FBG DV	OB	7 11	1580		3150	3650
21 1	IMPERIAL VC210-XS	OP	CUD	FBG DV	IO 170-260	8	2935		3550	4350
22 10	IMPERIAL VC230	OP	CUD	FBG DV	IO 170-260	8	3600		4500	5400
22 10	IMPERIAL VC230-F	OP	FSH	FBG DV	IO 170-260	8	3800		4900	5900

....For earlier years, see the BUC Used Boat Price Guide, Volume 3

ALLEN BOAT CO
BUFFALO NY 14203   COAST GUARD MFG ID- TGA See inside cover to adjust price for area

For more recent years, see the BUC Used Boat Price Guide, Volume 1

LOA FT IN	NAME AND/ OR MODEL	TOP/ RIG	BOAT TYPE	-HULL- MTL TP	----ENGINE--- TP # HP MFG	BEAM FT IN	WGT LBS	DRAFT FT IN	RETAIL LOW	RETAIL HIGH
					1996 BOATS					
19	INT'L LIGHTNING		SARAC	FBG KL		6 6	700	5	7750	8900
20	HIGHLANDER		SARAC	FBG KL		6 8			8600	9850
					1995 BOATS					
19	INT'L LIGHTNING		SARAC	FBG KL		6 6	700	5	7300	8350
20	HIGHLANDER		SARAC	FBG KL		6 8			8050	9300
					1994 BOATS					
19	INT'L LIGHTNING		SARAC	FBG KL		6 6	700	5	6850	7850
20	HIGHLANDER		SARAC	FBG KL		6 8			7600	8750
					1993 BOATS					
19	INT'L LIGHTNING		SARAC	FBG KL		6 6	700	5	6450	7400
20	HIGHLANDER		SARAC	FBG KL		6 8			7150	8200
					1992 BOATS					
19	LIGHTNING	SLP	SA/OD	FBG CB		6 7	700	7	6050	6950
					1991 BOATS					
19	LIGHTNING	SLP	SA/OD	FBG CB		6 7	700	7	5700	6550
					1990 BOATS					
19	LIGHTNING	SLP	SA/OD	FBG CB		6 7	700	7	5350	6150
					1989 BOATS					
19	LIGHTNING	SLP	SA/OD	FBG CB		6 7	700	7	5050	5800
					1988 BOATS					
19	LIGHTNING	SLP	SA/OD	FBG CB		6 7	700	7	4750	5450
					1987 BOATS					
19	LIGHTNING	SLP	SA/OD	FBG CB		6 7	700	7	4500	5150
					1986 BOATS					
19	LIGHTNING	SLP	SA/OD	FBG CB		6 7	700	7	4150	4850
					1985 BOATS					
19	LIGHTNING	SLP	SA/OD	FBG CB		6 7	700	7	3900	4550
					1984 BOATS					
19	LIGHTNING	SLP	SA/OD	FBG CB		6 7	700	7	3700	4300

....For earlier years, see the BUC Used Boat Price Guide, Volume 3

ALLIAURA MARINE

ALLIAURA SA
LES SABLES D'OLONNE CEDEX

See inside cover to adjust price for area

FORMERLY JEANTOT MARINE

For more recent years, see the BUC Used Boat Price Guide, Volume 1

LOA FT	LOA IN	NAME AND/ OR MODEL	TOP/ RIG	BOAT TYPE	-HULL- MTL	-HULL- TP	ENGINE TP	ENGINE #	ENGINE HP	ENGINE MFG	BEAM FT	BEAM IN	WGT LBS	DRAFT FT	DRAFT IN	RETAIL LOW	RETAIL HIGH
		1996 BOATS															
36	6	PRIVILEGE 36	SLP	SACAC	F/S	CT	IB	T	18D		21	5	14300	3		154000	169000
42		PRIVELEGE 42	CUT	SACAC	F/S	CT	IB	T	27D	YAN	23		20900	3	1	249000	273500
44	1	PRIVILEGE 45	CUT	SACAC	F/S	CT	IB	T	27D	YAN	23		23100	3	1	247500	272000
44	3	EUPHORIE 44	FB	MY	F/S	CT	IB	T	300D	IVCO	21	7	30800	4		352000	387000
51	7	PRIVILEGE 51	CUT	SACAC	F/S	CT	IB	T	27D	YAN	26	5	25300	4	5	420500	462000
65	1	PRIVILEGE 65	CUT	SACAC	F/S	CT	IB	T	80D	YAN	34	4	41900	4	9	1.310M	1.425M
		1995 BOATS															
42		PRIVELEGE 42	CUT	SACAC	F/S	CT	IB	T	27D	YAN	23		20900	3	1	235500	259000
42	8	PRIVILEGE 43	CUT	SACAC	F/S	CT	IB	T	27D	YAN	24		23000	3	11	252500	277000
44	1	PRIVILEGE 45	CUT	SACAC	F/S	CT	IB	T	27D	YAN	23		23100	3	1	234500	257500
44	3	EUPHORIE 44	FB	MY	F/S	CT	IB	T	300D	IVCO	21	7	30800	4		332000	365000
48	9	PRIVILEGE 48	CUT	SACAC	F/S	CT	IB	T	27D	YAN	26	5		6	8	351000	386000
51	7	PRIVILEGE 51	CUT	SACAC	F/S	CT	IB	T	27D	YAN	26	5	25300	4	5	398000	437500
65	1	PRIVILEGE 65	CUT	SACAC	F/S	CT	IB	T	80D	YAN	34	4	41900	4	9	1.240M	1.350M
		1994 BOATS															
40		PRIVILEGE 12	CUT	SACAC		CT	IB	T	27D	YAN	21		14000	3	5	175500	193000
42		EUPHORIE 40	FB	MY		CT	IB	T	150D		22			3	5	225500	248000
43		PRIVILEGE 43	CUT	SACAC		CT	IB	T	27D	YAN	24			4		229500	252500
48		PRIVILEGE 48	CUT	SACAC		CT	IB	T	27D	YAN	26			4	5	319500	351000
		1993 BOATS															
40		PRIVILEGE 12	SLP	SACAC		CT	IB	T	27D	YAN	21		14000	3	5	166500	183000
42		EUPHORIE 40	FB	MY		CT	IB	T	150D		22			3	5	213500	234500
43		PRIVILEGE 43	CUT	SACAC		CT	IB	T	27D	YAN	24			4		217500	239000
48		PRIVILEGE 48	CUT	SACAC		CT	IB	T	27D	YAN	26			4	5	302500	332500
		1991 BOATS															
40		EUPHORIE 40	FB	CR	F/S	CT	IB	T	150D		22		21000	3	3	155500	171000
40		EUPHORIE 40 DXL	FB	CR	F/S	CT	IB	T	300D		22		21000	3	3	169000	185500
40		PRIVILEGE 12	SLP	SA/CR	F/S	CT	IB	T	27D	YAN	21	3	14000	6		149500	164000
48	9	PRIVILEGE 48	SLP	SA/CR	F/S	CT	IB	T	27D	YAN	26	7	22000	6	8	282500	310500
		1990 BOATS															
40		PRIVILEGE 12	SLP	SAIL	F/S	CT	IB	T	27D	YAN	21	3	14000	3	4	141500	155500
48	9	PRIVILEGE 48	CUT	SA/CR	F/S	CT	IB	T	27D	YAN	26	7	22000	6	8	267500	294000
49		PRIVILEGE 14.70	SLP	SAIL	F/S		IB	T	D	VLVO			20000	4		195000	214500
		1989 BOATS															
40		PRIVILEGE 12	SLP	SAIL	F/S	CT	IB	T	27D	PERK	21	3	14000	3	4	134000	147000
49		PRIVILEGE 14,70	CAT	SAIL	F/S		IB	T	D	VLVO			20000	4		185000	203000
		1988 BOATS															
40		PRIVILEGE 12	SLP	SA/CR	F/S	CT	IB	T	27D	YAN	21	3	14000	6		127000	139500

ALLISON BOATS INC

LOUISVILLE TN 37777

COAST GUARD MFG ID- ALT See inside cover to adjust price for area

For more recent years, see the BUC Used Boat Price Guide, Volume 1

LOA FT	LOA IN	NAME AND/ OR MODEL	TOP/ RIG	BOAT TYPE	-HULL- MTL	-HULL- TP	ENGINE TP	ENGINE #	ENGINE HP	ENGINE MFG	BEAM FT	BEAM IN	WGT LBS	DRAFT FT	DRAFT IN	RETAIL LOW	RETAIL HIGH
		1996 BOATS															
20	1	XR-2001 DRAG	OP	RACE	FBG	DV	OB				7		500			5300	6100
20	1	XR-2001 RIVER RACE	OP	RACE	FBG	DV	OB				7		625			6350	7300
20	2	XB-2002 COMP PRO	OP	BASS	FBG	DV	OB				6	5	590			5800	6700
20	2	XB-2002 TOURNAMENT	OP	BASS	FBG	DV	OB				6	11	900			8350	9600
20	3	XB-2003 PRO F+S	OP	BASS	FBG	DV	OB				7	4	975			11200	12700
20	3	XB-2003 PRO SPORT	OP	BASS	FBG	DV	OB				7	4	950			11000	12500
20	3	XB-2003 PRO SPT ELIT	OP	BASS	FBG	DV	OB				7	4	1025			11700	13300
20	3	XB-2003 PRO TOURN	OP	BASS	FBG	DV	OB				7	4	1000			11500	13000
20	3	XS-2003 GRAND SPORT	OP	RNBT	FBG	DV	OB				7	3	900			8450	9750
20	3	XS-2003 GS ELITE	OP	RNBT	FBG	DV	OB				7	3	950			8950	10200
20	3	XS-2003 GS SKI	OP	RNBT	FBG	DV	OB				7	3	900			10500	11900
		1995 BOATS															
20	1	XR-2001 DRAG	OP	RACE	FBG	DV	OB				7		500			5050	5800
20	1	XR-2001 RIVER RACE	OP	RACE	FBG	DV	OB				7		625			6050	6950
20	1	XR-2002 SKI RACER	OP	RNBT	FBG	DV	OB				6	6	625			7200	8250
20	2	XB-2002 BASS RACE	OP	RACE	FBG	DV	OB				6	11	750			7050	8100
20	2	XB-2002 COMP PRO	OP	BASS	FBG	DV	OB				6	5	590			5550	6400
20	2	XB-2002 TOURNAMENT	OP	BASS	FBG	DV	OB				6	11	900			8000	9150
20	3	XB-2003 PRO F+H	OP	BASS	FBG	DV	OB				7	4	960			10500	12000
20	3	XB-2003 PRO SPORT	OP	BASS	FBG	DV	OB				7	4	930			10300	11700
20	3	XB-2003 PRO TOURN	OP	BASS	FBG	DV	OB				7	4	975			10700	12100
20	3	XS-2003 GRAND SPORT	OP	RNBT	FBG	DV	OB				7	3	900			8050	9300
20	3	XS-2003 GS ELITE	OP	RNBT	FBG	DV	OB				7	3	950			8450	9700
20	3	XS-2003 GS SKI	OP	RNBT	FBG	DV	OB				7	3	900			9950	11300
		1994 BOATS															
20	1	XR-2001-DRG DRAG	OP	RACE	FBG	DV	OB				7		500			5750	6600
20	1	XR-2001-RR RIVERRACE	OP	RACE	FBG	DV	OB				7		625			6950	7950
20	1	XR-2002-SR SKI RACER	OP	RNBT	FBG	DV	OB				6	6	625			6850	7900
20	2	XB-2002-BR BASS RACE	OP	RACE	FBG	DV	OB				6	11	750			8100	9350
20	2	XB-2002-CP COMP PRO	OP	BASS	FBG	DV	OB				6	11	825			8850	10100
20	2	XB-2002-T TOURNAMENT	OP	BASS	FBG	DV	OB				6	11	900			9500	10800
20	3	XB-2003 PRO SPORT	OP	BASS	FBG	DV	OB				7	4	930			9800	11100
20	3	XB-2003 PRO SPT F+H	OP	BASS	FBG	DV	OB				7	4	960			10100	11400
20	3	XB-2003PROSPT TRN	OP	BASS	FBG	DV	OB				7	4	975			10200	11600
20	3	XS-2003-GS	OP	RNBT	FBG	DV	OB				7	3	900			9550	10800
20	3	XS-2003-GSE ELITE	OP	RNBT	FBG	DV	OB				7	3	950			9950	11300
20	3	XS-2003-GSS SKI SPT	OP	RNBT	FBG	DV	OB				7	3	900			9550	10800
21		XT-B21-SUPER TRNMENT	OP	BASS	FBG	DV	OB				7	2	995			10200	11600
21		XTB21-T TOURNAMENT	OP	BASS	FBG	DV	OB				7	2	995			10900	12400
		1993 BOATS															
20	1	XR-2001-DRG DRAG	OP	RACE	FBG	DV	OB				7		500			5500	6300
20	1	XR-2001-RR RIVERRACE	OP	RACE	FBG	DV	OB				7		625			6650	7650
20	1	XR-2002-SR SKI RACER	OP	RNBT	FBG	DV	OB				6	6	625			6550	7550
20	2	XB-2002-BR BASS RACE	OP	RACE	FBG	DV	OB				6	11	750			7750	8900
20	2	XB-2002-CP COMP PRO	OP	BASS	FBG	DV	OB				6	11	825			8350	9650
20	2	XB-2002-PT TOURNAMNT	OP	BASS	FBG	DV	OB				6	11	900			9050	10300
20	2	XB-2002-S SPORT	OP	BASS	FBG	DV	OB				6	11	900			9250	10500
20	3	XS-2003-GS	OP	RNBT	FBG	DV	OB				7	3	900			9150	10400
20	3	XS-2003-GSE ELITE	OP	RNBT	FBG	DV	OB				7	3	950			9550	10900
20	3	XS-2003-GSS SKI SPT	OP	RNBT	FBG	DV	OB				7	3	900			9150	10400
21		XT-B21-D PRO DLX	OP	BASS	FBG	DV	OB				7	2	995			10800	12200
21		XTB21-T TOURNAMENT	OP	BASS	FBG	DV	OB				7	2	995			9450	10700
		1992 BOATS															
20	1	XR-2001-DRG DRAG	OP	RACE	FBG	DV	OB				7		500			5250	6050
20	1	XR-2001-RR RIVERRACE	OP	RACE	FBG	DV	OB				7		625			6350	7300
20	1	XR-2002-SR SKI RACER	OP	RNBT	FBG	DV	OB				6	6	625			6300	7250
20	2	XB-2002-BR BASS RACE	OP	RACE	FBG	DV	OB				6	11	750			7450	8550
20	2	XB-2002-CP COMP PRO	OP	BASS	FBG	DV	OB				6	11	825			8050	9250
20	2	XB-2002-PT TOURNAMNT	OP	BASS	FBG	DV	OB				6	11	900			8600	9850
20	2	XB-2002-S SPORT	OP	BASS	FBG	DV	OB				6	11	900			8850	10000
20	3	XS-2003-GS	OP	RNBT	FBG	DV	OB				7	3	900			8700	10000
20	3	XS-2003-GS GRD SPORT	OP	RNBT	FBG	DV	OB				7	3	900			8700	10000
20	3	XS-2003-GSE ELITE	OP	RNBT	FBG	DV	OB				7	3	950			9200	10500
21		XT-B21-D PRO DLX	OP	BASS	FBG	DV	OB				7	2	995			9700	11000
21		XTB21-T TOURNAMENT	OP	BASS	FBG	DV	OB				7	2	950			9300	10600
		1991 BOATS															
20	2	XB-2002-PT TOURNAMNT	OP	BASS	FBG	DV	OB				6	11	900			8250	9450
20	2	XB-2002-S SPORT	OP	BASS	FBG	DV	OB				6	11	900			8400	9650
20	3	XS-2003-GS	OP	RNBT	FBG	DV	OB				7	3	900			7700	8850
20	3	XS-2003-GSE ELITE	OP	RNBT	FBG	DV	OB				7	3	900			9100	10300
21		XTB-21-PT PRO TRNMNT	OP	BASS	FBG	DV	OB				7	2	995			9300	10600
		1990 BOATS															
20	1	XR-2001-D DRAG	OP	RACE	FBG	DV	OB				6	11				5350	6150
20	1	XR-2001-MUP MODUP	OP	RACE	FBG	DV	OB				6	11				6550	7550
20	1	XR-2001-RR RIVERRACR	OP	RACE	FBG	DV	OB				6	11				5950	6850
20	1	XR-2001-SR SPRT RACR	OP	RACE	FBG	DV	OB				6	11				6100	7000
20	2	XB-2002-C BASS RACER	OP	RACE	FBG	DV	OB				6	11				6000	6900
20	2	XB-2002-S SPORT	OP	BASS	FBG	DV	OB				6	11				8350	9600
20	2	XB-2002-T TOURNAMENT	OP	BASS	FBG	DV	OB				6	11				8100	9300
20	2	XR-2002-CS COMSPORT	OP	RNBT	FBG	DV	OB				6	6				8200	9400
20	2	XR-2002-R RACE	OP	RACE	FBG	DV	OB				6	6				5650	6450
20	2	XR-2002-RS RVR SPECL	OP	RACE	FBG	DV	OB				6	6				6350	7300
20	2	XR-2002-S-SKI	OP	RNBT	FBG	DV	OB				6	6				8800	10000
21		XTB-21-T PRO TRNMENT	OP	BASS	FBG	DV	OB				7	2				8400	9650
		1989 BOATS															
20	2	XB-2002 SPORT	OP	RACE	F/S	DV	OB				6	11				5800	6650
20	2	XB-2002 TOURNAMENT	OP	BASS	F/S	DV	OB				6	11				7950	9100
20	2	XB-2002-C	OP	BASS	F/S	DV	OB				6	11	790			6900	7900
20	2	XB-2002-CP	OP	BASS	F/S	DV	OB				6	11	850			7350	8450
20	2	XR-2002 RACE	OP	RACE	F/S	DV	OB				6	5	475			4550	5200
20	2	XR-2002 SKI	OP	SKI	F/S	DV	OB				6	5	675			6000	6900
20	2	XR-2002-COMP	OP	RACE	F/S	DV	OB				6	7	575			5300	6100
20	2	XR-2002-RIVER SPCL	OP	RACE	F/S	DV	OB				6	7	575			5250	6050
21		XTB-21 PRO DELUX	OP	BASS	F/S	DV	OB				7	2	950			8100	9300
21		XTB-21 PRO TOURNAMNT	OP	BASS	F/S	DV	OB				7	2	950			8400	9650
		1988 BOATS															
20	2	XB-2002-C	OP	BASS	F/S	DV	OB				6	11	750			6350	7300
20	2	XB-2002-S	OP	BASS	F/S	DV	OB				6	11	825			6900	7950
20	2	XB-2002-T	OP	BASS	F/S	DV	OB				6	11	810			6800	7800
20	2	XR-2002 RACE	OP	RACE	F/S	DV	OB				6	5	475			4400	5050
20	2	XR-2002 SKI	OP	SKI	F/S	DV	OB				6	5	675			5800	6650

CONTINUED ON NEXT PAGE

ALLISON BOATS INC   -CONTINUED   See inside cover to adjust price for area

LOA FT IN	NAME AND/ OR MODEL	TOP/ RIG	BOAT TYPE	-HULL- MTL TP	----ENGINE--- TP # HP MFG	BEAM FT IN	WGT LBS	DRAFT FT IN	RETAIL LOW	RETAIL HIGH
--------------- 1988 BOATS ---------------										
20 2	XR-2002-COMP	OP	RACE	F/S DV	OB	6 7	575		5150	5900
20 2	XR-2002-RIVER SPCL	OP	RACE	F/S DV	OB	6 7	575		5100	5850
21	XTB-21 PRO DELUX	OP	BASS	F/S DV		7 2	950		**	**
21	XTB-21 PRO TOURNAMNT	OP	BASS	F/S DV	OB	7 2	950		7950	9150
--------------- 1987 BOATS ---------------										
20 2	XB-2002-C	OP	BASS	F/S DV	OB	6 11	750		6150	7050
20 2	XB-2002-S	OP	BASS	F/S DV	OB	6 11	820		6650	7650
20 2	XB-2002-T	OP	BASS	F/S DV	OB	6 11	800		6500	7450
20 5	XR-2002 RACE	OP	RACE	F/S DV	OB	6 5	450		4000	4650
20 5	XR-2002 SKI	OP	SKI	F/S DV	OB	6 5	650		5450	6250
21	XTB-21	OP	BASS	F/S DV	OB	7 2	900		7300	8400
--------------- 1986 BOATS ---------------										
17 2	WS-17	OP	SKI	F/W DV	OB	6 6	790		4800	5550
20 5	XR-2002 RACE	OP	RACE	F/W DV	OB	6 5	450		3900	4550
20 5	XR-2002 SKI	OP	SKI	F/W	OB	6 5	650		5300	6050
21	XTB-21	OP	BASS	F/S DV	OB	7 2	900		7100	8150
--------------- 1985 BOATS ---------------										
17 1	XST 17	OP	BASS	F/W DV	OB	6	625		3750	4350
17 2	WS-17	OP	SKI	F/W DV	OB	6 6	785		4650	5350
18 7	XST 18	OP	BASS	F/W DV	OB	6 5	675		4300	5000
20 5	GT-20	OP	SKI	F/W DV	OB	6 11	800		6150	7050
20 5	XR-2002 RACE	OP	RACE	F/W DV	OB	6 5	475		3950	4600
20 5	XR-2002 SKI	OP	SKI	F/W	OB	6 5	650		5150	5900
21	XTB	OP	BASS	F/S DV	OB	7 2	800		6200	7150
--------------- 1984 BOATS ---------------										
17 1	SST 17	OP	BASS	F/W DV	OB	6	600		3500	4100
17 1	XST 17	OP	BASS	F/W DV	OB	6	625		3650	4250
17 2	WS-17	OP	SKI	F/W DV	OB	6 6	785		4550	5250
18 7	XST 18	OP	BASS	F/W DV	OB	6 5	675		4200	4850
20 5	GT-20	OP	SKI	F/W DV	OB	6 11	800		5950	6850
20 5	RACE 20	OP	RACE	F/W DV	OB	6 5	475		3850	4450
20 5	XR-2002 SKI	OP	SKI	F/W	OB	6 5	650		5000	5750

....For earlier years, see the BUC Used Boat Price Guide, Volume 3

ALLMAND BOATS
JOHN ALLMAND   See inside cover to adjust price for area
MIAMI FL 33157   COAST GUARD MFG ID- JAB

LOA FT IN	NAME AND/ OR MODEL	TOP/ RIG	BOAT TYPE	-HULL- MTL TP	----ENGINE--- TP # HP MFG	BEAM FT IN	WGT LBS	DRAFT FT IN	RETAIL LOW	RETAIL HIGH
--------------- 1985 BOATS ---------------										
30 9	ALLMAND 31	SLP	SA/RC	FBG KL	IB D	11 4	12290	4	25600	28400
34 9	ALLMAND 35	SLP	SA/RC	FBG KL	IB D	11 8	14200	5	29000	32200
34 9	ALLMAND 35 PH	SLP	SA/RC	FBG KL	IB D	11 8	14200	5	29500	32800
--------------- 1984 BOATS ---------------										
30 9	ALLMAND 31	SLP	SA/CR	FBG KL	IB 20D	11 4	12850	4	25200	28000
34 9	ALLMAND 35 PH	SLP	SA/CR	FBG KL	IB 20D	11 8	14200	5	27800	30900
34 9	ALLMAND 35 TRI CBN	SLP	SA/CR	FBG KL	IB 20D	11 8	15100	5 2	29300	32600

....For earlier years, see the BUC Used Boat Price Guide, Volume 3

ALLWEATHER BOATS INC
SEDRO VALLEY WA 98284   COAST GUARD MFG ID- AWT See inside cover to adjust price for area

For more recent years, see the BUC Used Boat Price Guide, Volume 1

LOA FT IN	NAME AND/ OR MODEL	TOP/ RIG	BOAT TYPE	-HULL- MTL TP	----ENGINE--- TP # HP MFG	BEAM FT IN	WGT LBS	DRAFT FT IN	RETAIL LOW	RETAIL HIGH
--------------- 1996 BOATS ---------------										
26 3	ALLWEATHER 8 METER	HT	FDPH	FBG DS	IB 23D PERK	8	4800	3	37100	41200
--------------- 1995 BOATS ---------------										
26 3	ALLWEATHER 8 METER	HT	FDPH	FBG DS	IB 23D PERK	8	4800	3	35200	39100
--------------- 1994 BOATS ---------------										
26 3	ALLWEATHER 8 METER	HT	FDPH	FBG DS	IB 23D PERK	8	4800	3	33400	37100
--------------- 1993 BOATS ---------------										
26 3	ALLWEATHER 8 METER	HT	FDPH	FBG DS	IB 23D PERK	8	4800	3	31700	35200
--------------- 1992 BOATS ---------------										
26 3	ALLWEATHER 8 METER	HT	PH	FBG DS	IB 23D PERK	8	4800	3	30200	33600
--------------- 1991 BOATS ---------------										
26 3	ALLWEATHER 8 METER	HT	PH	FBG DS	IB 23D PERK	8	4800	3	28800	32000
--------------- 1990 BOATS ---------------										
26 3	ALLWEATHER 8 METER	HT	PH	FBG DS	IB 23D	8	4800	3	27200	30500
--------------- 1989 BOATS ---------------										
26 3	ALLWEATHER 8 METER	HT	PH	FBG DS	IB 23D	8	4800	3	27700	30700
--------------- 1988 BOATS ---------------										
26 3	ALLWEATHER 8 METER	HT	PH	FBG DS	IB 23D	8	4800	3	25300	28100
--------------- 1987 BOATS ---------------										
26 3	ALLWEATHER 8 METER	HT	PH	FBG DS	IB 30D YAN	8	4800	3	24400	27100
--------------- 1986 BOATS ---------------										
26 3	ALLWEATHER 8 METER	HT	UTL	FBG DS	IB 30D YAN	8	4800	3	23300	25900
--------------- 1984 BOATS ---------------										
26 3	ALLWEATHER 8 METER	HT	UTL	FBG DS	IB 24D YAN	8	4800	3	21700	24100

....For earlier years, see the BUC Used Boat Price Guide, Volume 3

ALMAR BOATS
TACOMA WA 98421   COAST GUARD MFG ID- AUC See inside cover to adjust price for area

LOA FT IN	NAME AND/ OR MODEL	TOP/ RIG	BOAT TYPE	-HULL- MTL TP	----ENGINE--- TP # HP MFG	BEAM FT IN	WGT LBS	DRAFT FT IN	RETAIL LOW	RETAIL HIGH
--------------- 1996 BOATS ---------------										
17	LITE 17	OP	FSH	AL SV	IB	6 11	700		3000	3500
17	LITE 17	OP	FSH	AL SV	OB	6 11	700		**	**
17	LITE 17 BR	OP	FSH	AL SV	IB	6 11	700		4150	4800
17	LITE 17 BR	OP	FSH	AL SV	OB	6 11	700		**	**
17	LITE 17 RD	OP	FSH	AL SV	IB	6 11	700		3900	4500
17	LITE 17 RD	OP	FSH	AL SV	IB 140 CHEV	6 11	700		6050	6950
18	JETSTREAM 18	OP	FSH	AL SV	OB	7 6	875		4400	5050
18	JETSTREAM 18 BR	OP	FSH	AL SV	IB	7 6	875		4500	5150
18	JETSTREAM 18 BR	OP	FSH	AL SV	OB	7 6	875		**	**
18	JETSTREAM 18 RD	OP	FSH	AL SV	IB	7 6	875		5300	6100
18	JETSTREAM 18 RD	OP	FSH	AL SV	OB	7 6	875		**	**
19	JETSTREAM 19	OP	FSH	AL SV	OB	7 6	940		4500	5200
19	JETSTREAM 19 BR	OP	FSH	AL SV	OB	7 6	940		5700	6500
19	JETSTREAM 19 BR	OP	FSH	AL SV	IB 302 FORD	7 6	940		10100	11400
19	JETSTREAM 19 RD	OP	FSH	AL SV	OB	7 6	940		5400	6200
19	JETSTREAM 19 RD	OP	FSH	AL SV	IB 302 FORD	7 6	940		9600	10900
20	SOUNDER 20	ST	CUD	AL DV	OB	8			9950	11300
20	SOUNDER 20	HT	CUD	AL DV	OB	8			9950	11300
20 6	JETLINE 20	OP	FSH	AL SV	OB	8	2400		8900	10100
20 6	JETLINE 20	OP	FSH	AL SV	IB 351 FORD	8	2400		12400	14000
20 6	JETLINE 20 BR	OP	FSH	AL SV	OB	8	2400		10500	12000
20 6	JETLINE 20 BR	OP	FSH	AL SV	IB 351 FORD	8	2400		13300	15100
20 6	JETLINE 20 RD	OP	FSH	AL SV	OB	8	2400		10000	11300
20 6	JETLINE 20 RD	OP	FSH	AL SV	IB 351 FORD	8	2400		12600	14400
21	SOUNDER 21	ST	CUD	AL DV	OB	8	2800		11200	12700
21	SOUNDER 21	HT	CUD	AL DV	OB	8	2800		11200	12700
22	JETLINE 22	OP	FSH	AL SV	OB	8	2700		10700	12200
22	JETLINE 22 BR	OP	FSH	AL SV	OB	8	2700		12600	14400
22	JETLINE 22 BR	OP	FSH	AL SV	IB 351 FORD	8	2700		14900	16900
22	JETLINE 22 RD	OP	FSH	AL SV	OB	8	2700		12000	13600
22	JETLINE 22 RD	OP	FSH	AL SV	IB 351 FORD	8	2700		14400	16300
22	SOUNDER 22	ST	CUD	AL DV	OB	8	3000		12600	14300
22	SOUNDER 22	ST	CUD	AL DV	IO	8 6	3000		**	**
22	SOUNDER 22	HT	CUD	AL DV	OB	8	3000		12600	14300
22	SOUNDER 22	HT	CUD	AL DV	IO	8 6	3000		**	**
23	SOUNDER 23	ST	CUD	AL DV	OB	8	3350		14500	16500
23	SOUNDER 23	ST	CUD	AL DV	IO	8 6	3350		**	**
23	SOUNDER 23	HT	CUD	AL DV	OB	8	3350		14500	16500
23	SOUNDER 23	HT	CUD	AL DV	IO	8 6	3350		**	**
24	JETLINE 24	OP	FSH	AL SV	OB	8	3000		12900	14700
24	JETLINE 24 BR	OP	FSH	AL SV	OB	8	3000		15100	17100
24	JETLINE 24 BR	OP	FSH	AL SV	IB 130 FORD	8	3000		16400	18600
24	JETLINE 24 RD	OP	FSH	AL SV	OB	8	3000		14200	16200
24	JETLINE 24 RD	OP	FSH	AL SV	IB 460 FORD	8	3000		20200	22500
24	SOUNDER 24	ST	CUD	AL DV	OB	8	4100		18000	20000
24	SOUNDER 24	ST	CUD	AL DV	IO	8 6	4100		**	**
24	SOUNDER 24	HT	CUD	AL DV	OB	8	4700		19200	21400
24	SOUNDER 24	HT	CUD	AL DV	IO	8 6	4400		**	**
25	SOUNDER 25	ST	CUD	AL DV	IO	8 6	4100		18400	20400
25	SOUNDER 25	HT	CUD	AL DV	IO	8 6	4100		**	**
26	SOUNDER 26	ST	CUD	AL DV	OB	8 6	5700		21600	24000
26	SOUNDER 26	HT	CUD	AL DV	OB	9 6	5700		**	**
26	SOUNDER 26	HT	CUD	AL DV	IO	8 6	5700		**	**
27	SOUNDER 27	HT	CUD	AL DV	IO	8 6	5900		**	**
28	SOUNDER 28	HT	CUD	AL DV	IO	9 6	8500		**	**
30	SOUNDER 30	HT	CUD	AL DV	IO T	10 6	9100		**	**
32	SOUNDER 32	HT	CUD	AL DV	IO T	10 6	10500		**	**

LOA FT	LOA IN	NAME AND/ OR MODEL	TOP/ RIG	BOAT TYPE	HULL MTL	HULL TP	ENGINE TP	ENGINE #	ENGINE HP	ENGINE MFG	BEAM FT	BEAM IN	WGT LBS	DRAFT FT	DRAFT IN	RETAIL LOW	RETAIL HIGH
		1995 BOATS															
17		LITE 17 BR	OP	FSH	AL	SV	OB				6	11	700			3950	4600
17		LITE 17 BR	OP	FSH	AL	SV	IB				6	11	700			**	**
17		LITE 17 OB	OP	FSH	AL	SV	OB				6	11	700			2850	3300
17		LITE 17 OB	OP	FSH	AL	SV	IB				6	11	700			**	**
17		LITE 17 RD	OP	FSH	AL	SV	OB				6	11	700			3700	4300
17		LITE 17 RD	OP	FSH	AL	SV	IB		140	CHEV	6	11	700			5700	6550
18		JETSTREAM 18 BR	OP	FSH	AL	SV	OB				7	6	875			4950	5700
18		JETSTREAM 18 BR	OP	FSH	AL	SV	IB				7	6	875			**	**
18		JETSTREAM 18 OB	OP	FSH	AL	SV	OB				7	6	875			5200	6000
18		JETSTREAM 18 RD	OP	FSH	AL	SV	OB				7	6	875			4650	5350
18		JETSTREAM 18 RD	OP	FSH	AL	SV	IB				7	6	875			**	**
19		JETSTREAM 19 BR	OP	FSH	AL	SV	OB				7	6	940			5400	6250
19		JETSTREAM 19 BR	OP	FSH	AL	SV	IB		302	FORD	7	6	940			9500	10800
19		JETSTREAM 19 OB	OP	FSH	AL	SV	OB				7	6	940			4250	4950
19		JETSTREAM 19 RD	OP	FSH	AL	SV	OB				7	6	940			5150	5900
19		JETSTREAM 19 RD	OP	FSH	AL	SV	IB		302	FORD	7	6	940			9050	10300
20		SOUNDER 20	ST	CUD	AL	DV	OB				8					9450	10800
20		SOUNDER 20	HT	CUD	AL	DV	OB				8					9450	10800
20	6	JETLINE 20 BR	OP	FSH	AL	SV	OB				8		2400			10000	11400
20	6	JETLINE 20 BR	OP	FSH	AL	SV	IB		351	FORD	8		2400			12700	14400
20	6	JETLINE 20 OB	OP	FSH	AL	SV	OB				8		2400			8400	9650
20	6	JETLINE 20 OB	OP	FSH	AL	SV	IB		351	FORD	8		2400			11600	13200
20	6	JETLINE 20 RD	OP	FSH	AL	SV	OB				8		2400			9500	10800
20	6	JETLINE 20 RD	OP	FSH	AL	SV	IB		351	FORD	8		2400			12000	13700
21		SOUNDER 21	ST	CUD	AL	DV	OB				8		2800			10600	12100
21		SOUNDER 21	HT	CUD	AL	DV	OB				8		2800			10600	12100
22		JETLINE 22 BR	OP	FSH	AL	SV	OB				8		2700			12000	13700
22		JETLINE 22 BR	OP	FSH	AL	SV	IB		351	FORD	8		2700			14000	15900
22		JETLINE 22 OB	OP	FSH	AL	SV	OB				8		2700			10200	11600
22		JETLINE 22 RD	OP	FSH	AL	SV	OB				8		2700			11400	12900
22		JETLINE 22 RD	OP	FSH	AL	SV	IB		351	FORD	8		2700			13600	15500
22		SOUNDER 22	ST	CUD	AL	DV	OB				8	6	3000			12000	13600
22		SOUNDER 22	ST	CUD	AL	DV	IO				8		3000			**	**
22		SOUNDER 22	HT	CUD	AL	DV	OB				8	6	3000			12000	13600
22		SOUNDER 22	HT	CUD	AL	DV	IO				8		3000			**	**
23		SOUNDER 23	ST	CUD	AL	DV	OB				8	6	3350			13800	15700
23		SOUNDER 23	ST	CUD	AL	DV	IO				8		3350			**	**
23		SOUNDER 23	HT	CUD	AL	DV	OB				8	6	3350			13800	15700
23		SOUNDER 23	HT	CUD	AL	DV	IO				8		3350			**	**
24		JETLINE 24 BR	OP	FSH	AL	SV	OB				8		3000			14300	16300
24		JETLINE 24 BR	OP	FSH	AL	SV	IB		130	FORD	8		3000			15400	17500
24		JETLINE 24 OB	OP	FSH	AL	SV	OB				8		3000			12300	13900
24		JETLINE 24 RD	OP	FSH	AL	SV	OB				8		3000			13500	15400
24		JETLINE 24 RD	OP	FSH	AL	SV	IB		460	FORD	8		3000			19000	21100
24		SOUNDER 24	ST	CUD	AL	DV	OB				8		4100			16800	19000
24		SOUNDER 24	ST	CUD	AL	DV	IO				8	6	4700			**	**
24		SOUNDER 24	HT	CUD	AL	DV	OB				8	6	4700			18500	20600
24		SOUNDER 24	HT	CUD	AL	DV	IO				8		4400			**	**
25		SOUNDER 25	ST	CUD	AL	DV	IO				8	6	4100			**	**
25		SOUNDER 25	HT	CUD	AL	DV	OB				8	6	4100			17100	19500
26		SOUNDER 26	ST	CUD	AL	DV	IO				8	6	5700			**	**
26		SOUNDER 26	HT	CUD	AL	DV	OB				9	6	5700			20600	22900
26		SOUNDER 26	HT	CUD	AL	DV	IO				8	6	5700			**	**
27		SOUNDER 27	HT	CUD	AL	DV	IO				8	6	5900			**	**
28		SOUNDER 28	HT	CUD	AL	DV	IO	T			9	6	8500			**	**
30		SOUNDER 30	HT	CUD	AL	DV	IO	T			10	6	9100			**	**
32		SOUNDER 32	HT	CUD	AL	DV	IO	T			10	6	10500			**	**
		1994 BOATS															
17		LITE 17 BR	OP	FSH	AL	SV	OB				6	11	700			3800	4400
17		LITE 17 BR	OP	FSH	AL	SV	IB				6	11	700			**	**
17		LITE 17 OB	OP	FSH	AL	SV	OB				6	11	700			3350	3900
17		LITE 17 OB	OP	FSH	AL	SV	IB				6	11	700			**	**
17		LITE 17 RD	OP	FSH	AL	SV	OB				6	11	700			3550	4100
17		LITE 17 RD	OP	FSH	AL	SV	IB				6	11	700			**	**
18		JETSTREAM 18 BR	OP	FSH	AL	DV	OB				7	6	875			4700	5450
18		JETSTREAM 18 BR	OP	FSH	AL	DV	IB				7	6	875			**	**
18		JETSTREAM 18 OB	OP	FSH	AL	DV	OB				7	6	875			3650	4250
18		JETSTREAM 18 RD	OP	FSH	AL	DV	OB				7	6	875			4500	5150
18		JETSTREAM 18 RD	OP	FSH	AL	DV	IB				7	6	875			**	**
19		JETSTREAM 19 BR	OP	FSH	AL	DV	OB				7	6	940			5150	5950
19		JETSTREAM 19 BR	OP	FSH	AL	DV	IB				7	6	940			**	**
19		JETSTREAM 19 OB	OP	FSH	AL	DV	OB				7	6	940			4050	4700
19		JETSTREAM 19 RD	OP	FSH	AL	DV	OB				7	6	940			4900	5650
19		JETSTREAM 19 RD	OP	FSH	AL	DV	IB				7	6	940			**	**
20		SOUNDER 20		CUD	AL	SV	OB				8					9100	10300
20		SOUNDER 20	HT	CUD	AL	SV	OB				8					9100	10300
20	6	JETLINE 20 BR	OP	FSH	AL	DV	OB				8		2400			9600	10900
20	6	JETLINE 20 BR	OP	FSH	AL	DV	IB		130	FORD	8		2400			10600	12000
20	6	JETLINE 20 OB	OP	FSH	AL	DV	OB				8		2400			8000	9200
20	6	JETLINE 20 OB	OP	FSH	AL	DV	IB		130	FORD	8		2400			9800	11200
20	6	JETLINE 20 RD	OP	FSH	AL	DV	OB				8		2400			9150	10400
20	6	JETLINE 20 RD	OP	FSH	AL	DV	IB		130	FORD	8		2400			10100	11400
21		SOUNDER 21		CUD	AL	SV	OB				8					10100	11500
21		SOUNDER 21	HT	CUD	AL	SV	OB				8					10100	11500
22		JETLINE 22 BR	OP	FSH	AL	DV	OB				8		2700			11500	13100
22		JETLINE 22 BR	OP	FSH	AL	DV	IB		130	FORD	8		2700			12200	13900
22		JETLINE 22 OB	OP	FSH	AL	DV	OB				8		2700			9750	11100
22		JETLINE 22 OB	OP	FSH	AL	DV	IB		130	FORD	8		2700			11200	12800
22		JETLINE 22 RD	OP	FSH	AL	DV	OB				8		2700			10900	12300
22		JETLINE 22 RD	OP	FSH	AL	DV	IB		130	FORD	8		2700			11800	13400
22		SOUNDER 22		CUD	AL	SV	OB				8	6	3000			11400	13000
22		SOUNDER 22	HT	CUD	AL	SV	OB				8	6	3000			11400	13000
23		SOUNDER 23		CUD	AL	SV	OB				8	6	3350			13200	14900
23		SOUNDER 23	HT	CUD	AL	SV	OB				8	6	3350			13200	14900
24		JETLINE 24 BR	OP	FSH	AL	DV	OB				8		3000			13700	15500
24		JETLINE 24 BR	OP	FSH	AL	DV	IB		130	FORD	8		3000			14500	16400
24		JETLINE 24 OB	OP	FSH	AL	DV	OB				8		3000			11700	13300
24		JETLINE 24 OB	OP	FSH	AL	DV	IB		130	FORD	8		3000			13400	15200
24		JETLINE 24 RD	OP	FSH	AL	DV	OB				8		3000			13000	14800
24		JETLINE 24 RD	OP	FSH	AL	DV	IB		130	FORD	8		3000			14100	16000
24		SOUNDER 24		CUD	AL	SV	OB				8	6	3700			14900	17000
24		SOUNDER 24	HT	CUD	AL	SV	OB				8	6	3700			14900	17000
25		SOUNDER 25		CUD	AL	SV	IB				8	6	4100			**	**
25		SOUNDER 25	HT	CUD	AL	SV	IB				8	6	4100			**	**
26		SOUNDER 26		CUD	AL	SV	IB				8	6	4700			**	**
26		SOUNDER 26	HT	CUD	AL	SV	OB				9	6				19700	21900
26		SOUNDER 26	HT	CUD	AL	SV	IB				8	6	4700			**	**
27		SOUNDER 27	HT	CUD	AL	SV	IB				8	6				**	**
28		SOUNDER 28	HT	CUD	AL	SV	OB				9	6				23200	25800
30		SOUNDER 30	HT	CUD	AL	SV	OB				9	6				29000	32200
32		SOUNDER 32	HT	CUD	AL	SV	OB				10	6				34700	38600

....For earlier years, see the BUC Used Boat Price Guide, Volume 3

ALOHA YACHTS INTERNATIONAL

WHITBY ONTARIO CANADA COAST GUARD MFG ID- ZUY See inside cover to adjust price for area
FORMERLY OUYANG BOAT WORKS LTD

LOA FT	LOA IN	NAME AND/ OR MODEL	TOP/ RIG	BOAT TYPE	HULL MTL	HULL TP	ENGINE TP	ENGINE #	ENGINE HP	ENGINE MFG	BEAM FT	BEAM IN	WGT LBS	DRAFT FT	DRAFT IN	RETAIL LOW	RETAIL HIGH
		1989 BOATS															
26	9	ALOHA 27	SLP	SA/RC	FBG	KL	IB		D		9	6	5200	4	4	18100	20100
28		ALOHA 28	SLP	SA/RC	FBG	KL	IB		D		9	5	6750	4	4	24300	27000
30		ALOHA 30	SLP	SA/RC	FBG	KL	IB		D		10		6800	5	9	25700	28500
32	5	ALOHA 32	SLP	SA/RC	FBG	KL	IB		D		10	10	9800	4	9	38100	42300
34		ALOHA 34	SLP	SA/RC	FBG	KL	IB		D		11	2	13680	5	6	53200	58400
		1986 BOATS															
26	9	ALOHA 27	SLP	SA/CR	FBG	KL	OB				9	6	5200	4	4	14000	15900
26	9	ALOHA 27	SLP	SA/CR	FBG	KL	IB		10D	WEST	9	6	5200	4	4	14700	16700
28		ALOHA 28	SLP	SA/CR	FBG	KL	SD		13D	WEST	9	5	6750	4	4	20200	22400
30		ALOHA 30	SLP	SA/RC	FBG	KL	IB		10D	WEST	10	10	6800	5	9	21200	23600
30		ALOHA 30 SHOAL	SLP	SA/RC	FBG	KL	IB		10D	WEST	10	10	6800	4	6	21400	23800
32	5	ALOHA 32	SLP	SA/CR	FBG	KL	VD		21D	WEST	10	10	9800	4	6	31700	35200
34		ALOHA 34	SLP	SA/CR	FBG	KL	IB		30D	WEST	11	2	13600	5	6	43800	48700
34		ALOHA 34 SHOAL	SLP	SA/CR	FBG	KL	IB		30D	WEST	11	2	13600	4	7	43800	48700
		1985 BOATS															
26	9	ALOHA 27	SLP	SA/CR	FBG	KL	OB				9	6	5200	4	4	13200	15000
28		ALOHA 28	SLP	SA/CR	FBG	KL	IB		13D	WEST	9	5	6750	4	4	19000	21100
30		ALOHA 30	SLP	SA/CR	FBG	KL	IB		10D	WEST	10	8	6800	5	9	20100	22300
32	5	ALOHA 32	SLP	SA/CR	FBG	KL	VD		21D	WEST	10	10	9800	4	6	29800	33100
34		ALOHA 34	SLP	SA/CR	FBG	KL	SE		30D	WEST	11	2	13600	5	6	40800	45300
34		ALOHA 34 SHOAL	SLP	SA/CR	FBG	KL	SE		30D	WEST	11	2	13600	4	7	41200	45800
		1984 BOATS															
26	9	ALOHA 8.2	SLP	SA/CR	FBG	KL	IB		13D	WEST	9	6	5200	4	4	13100	14900
28		ALOHA 8.5	SLP	SA/CR	FBG	KL	SD		13D	WEST	9	5	6750	4	4	18100	20100
32	5	ALOHA 32	SLP	SA/CR	FBG	KL	VD		21D	WEST	10	10	9800	4	6	28000	31200
34		ALOHA 10.4	SLP	SA/CR	FBG	KL	IB		27D	WEST	11	2	13600	5	6	38700	43000

```
ALOHA YACHTS INTERNATIONAL      -CONTINUED      See inside cover to adjust price for area
  LOA  NAME AND/              TOP/ BOAT  -HULL- ----ENGINE--- BEAM   WGT  DRAFT RETAIL RETAIL
  FT IN OR MODEL              RIG  TYPE  MTL TP TP # HP  MFG  FT IN  LBS  FT IN  LOW   HIGH
--------------------- 1984 BOATS --------------------------------------------------------------
  34   ALOHA 10.4 SHOAL       SLP SA/CR FBG KL IB   27D WEST 11  2 13600  4  7 38700 43000

            ....For earlier years, see the BUC Used Boat Price Guide, Volume 3
```

ALSBERG BROTHERS BOATWORKS
CAPITOLA CA 95010   See inside cover to adjust price for area

```
  LOA  NAME AND/              TOP/ BOAT  -HULL- ----ENGINE--- BEAM   WGT  DRAFT RETAIL RETAIL
  FT IN OR MODEL              RIG  TYPE  MTL TP TP # HP  MFG  FT IN  LBS  FT IN  LOW   HIGH
--------------------- 1986 BOATS --------------------------------------------------------------
  27  3 EXPRESS 27            SLP SA/OD F/S KL                8        2450  4  6 12300 14000
  37  1 EXPRESS 37            SLP SA/OD F/S KL               11  6    9500  7  3 56500 62000
--------------------- 1985 BOATS --------------------------------------------------------------
  22  7 EXPRESS 23            SLP SA/OD F/S KL                7  6        3  6 11800 13400
  27  3 EXPRESS 27            SLP SA/OD F/S KL                8        2450  4  6 11600 13200
  37  1 EXPRESS 37            SLP SAIL  F/S KL IB  15D YAN   11  6    9200  7  3 52100 57300
  37  1 EXPRESS 37            SLP SAIL  F/S KL IB  23D YAN   11  6    9500  7  3 52300 57500
--------------------- 1984 BOATS --------------------------------------------------------------
  27  3 EXPRESS 27            SLP SA/OD F/S KL                8        2450  4  6 10900 12400
  37  1 EXPRESS 37            SLP SA/OD F/S KL IB  15D YAN   11  6    9000  7  3 46900 51500
  37  1 EXPRESS 37            SLP SA/OD F/S KL IB  22D YAN   11  6    9000  7    47100 51700
```

ALTECH YACHTS
FT LAUDERDALE FL 33316   See inside cover to adjust price for area

```
  LOA  NAME AND/              TOP/ BOAT  -HULL- ----ENGINE--- BEAM   WGT  DRAFT RETAIL RETAIL
  FT IN OR MODEL              RIG  TYPE  MTL TP TP # HP  MFG  FT IN  LBS  FT IN  LOW   HIGH
--------------------- 1994 BOATS --------------------------------------------------------------
  32 10 TARRAB 33 SPORT       FB  CNV   FBG SV IB  T        13  1        2  6   **    **
  32 10 TARRAB 33 SPORT       FB  CNV   FBG SV IB  T340 MRCR 13  1        2  6 77100 84700
  32 10 TARRAB 33 SPORT       FB  CNV   FBG SV IB  T200D VLVO 13  1        2  6 89500 98400
  44  5 SPORT FISHERMAN       FB  SF    FBG DV IB  T375D CAT  15  6 32000  2  9 189000 207500
      IB T425D CAT 198500 218000, IB T485D J&T 209000 229500, IB T550D J&T 221500 243500
--------------------- 1993 BOATS --------------------------------------------------------------
  32 10 TARRAB 33 SPORT       FB  CNV   FBG SV IB  T        13  1        2  6   **    **
  32 10 TARRAB 33 SPORT       FB  CNV   FBG SV IB  T340 MRCR 13  1        2  6 73000 80200
  32 10 TARRAB 33 SPORT       FB  CNV   FBG SV IB  T200D VLVO 13  1        2  6 85200 93600
  44  5 SPORT FISHERMAN       FB  SF    FBG DV IB  T375D CAT  15  6 32000  2  9 179500 197500
      IB T425D CAT 189000 208000, IB T485D J&T 199000 218500, IB T550D J&T 211000 232000
--------------------- 1991 BOATS --------------------------------------------------------------
  32 10 SPORT CONVERTIBLE     FB  CNV   FBG SV IB  T350 MRCR 13  1 16000  2  6 73200 80400
  44  5 SPORT FISHERMAN       FB  SF    FBG DV IB  T375D CAT  15  6 32000  2  9 163000 179500
      IB T425D CAT 172000 189000, IB T485D J&T 180500 198500, IB T550D J&T 192000 211000
```

ALTRA MARINE PRODUCTS INC
PRINCEVILLE QUE CANADA G0P130   See inside cover to adjust price for area

```
  LOA  NAME AND/              TOP/ BOAT  -HULL- ----ENGINE--- BEAM   WGT  DRAFT RETAIL RETAIL
  FT IN OR MODEL              RIG  TYPE  MTL TP TP # HP  MFG  FT IN  LBS  FT IN  LOW   HIGH
--------------------- 1993 BOATS --------------------------------------------------------------
  16    PRO-162 BT            FSH   AL  SV OB          5  7   470        1950  2300
  16    PRO-162 SC            FSH   AL  SV OB          5  7   523        2200  2550
  16    PRO-163               FSH   AL  SV OB          5  7   391        1600  1900
  16    STARFISH              UTL   AL  SV OB          5  7   266        1050  1300
  16  8 PRO-168               BASS  AL  SV OB          6  4   675        2900  3350
  16  8 PRO-170               BASS  AL  SV OB          6  4   695        2900  3350
  16  8 PRO-171               FSH   AL  SV OB          6  4   670        2800  3250
  16  9 HOLIDAY               UTL   AL  SV OB          6  4   330        1350  1600
  16  9 PRO-169 BT            BASS  AL  SV OB          6  4   600        2600  3000
  16  9 PRO-169 SC            BASS  AL  SV OB          6  4   653        2800  3250
  16 10 PRO-178               FSH   AL  SV OB          6  8   750        3200  3700
  17  4 SUPER PRO-175     OP  CTRCN AL  SV OB          7  1   850        3650  4250

  17  4 SUPER PRO-176     OP  RNBT  AL  SV OB          7  1   960        4000  4650
  17  4 SUPREME 176           RNBT  AL  SV OB          7  1   940        4000  4650
  18  4 JUMBO                 UTL   AL  SV OB          6  8   355        1350  1650
  19  4 SUPER PRO-196     OP  RNBT  AL  SV OB          7  8  1160        5150  5900
  19  4 SUPREME 196           RNBT  AL  SV OB          7  8  1140        5050  5800
  22  6 CORSICA           OP  CUD   AL  DV OB          8      1800        8850 10100
  22  6 CORSICA           OP  CUD   AL  DV IO 130-150  8      2600        9000 10200
--------------------- 1992 BOATS --------------------------------------------------------------
  16    PRO-162 BT            FSH   AL  SV OB          5  7   470        1850  2200
  16    PRO-162 SC            FSH   AL  SV OB          5  7   523        2050  2450
  16    PRO-163               FSH   AL  SV OB          5  7   391        1550  1850
  16    STARFISH              UTL   AL  SV OB          5  7   266        1050  1250
  16  8 PRO-168               BASS  AL  SV OB          6  4   675        2750  3200
  16  8 PRO-170               BASS  AL  SV OB          6  4   695        2750  3200
  16  8 PRO-171               FSH   AL  SV OB          6  4   670        2650  3100
  16  9 HOLIDAY               UTL   AL  SV OB          6  4   330        1300  1550
  16  9 PRO-169 BT            BASS  AL  SV OB          6  4   600        2500  2900
  16  9 PRO-169 SC            BASS  AL  SV OB          6  4   653        2700  3150
  16 10 PRO 178               FSH   AL  SV OB          6  8   750        3050  3550
  17  4 SUPER PRO 175     OP  CTRCN AL  SV OB          7  1   850        3450  4000

  17  4 SUPER PRO 176     OP  RNBT  AL  SV OB          7  1   960        3850  4450
  17  4 SUPREME 176           RNBT  AL  SV OB          7  1   940        3850  4450
  18  4 JUMBO                 UTL   AL  SV OB          6  8   355        1300  1550
  19  4 SUPER PRO 196     OP  RNBT  AL  SV OB          7  8  1160        4950  5650
  19  4 SUPREME 196           RNBT  AL  SV OB          7  8  1140        4850  5600
  22  6 CORSICA           OP  CUD   AL  DV OB          8      1800        8400  9650
  22  6 CORSICA           OP  CUD   AL  DV IO 130-150  8      2600        8300  9600
--------------------- 1991 BOATS --------------------------------------------------------------
  16    PRO-162 BT            FSH   AL  SV OB          5  7   470        1800  2100
  16    PRO-162 SC            FSH   AL  SV OB          5  7   523        2000  2350
  16    PRO-163               FSH   AL  SV OB          5  7   391        1500  1750
  16    STARFISH LX           UTL   AL  SV OB          5  7   273        1000  1200
  16  8 PRO-168               BASS  AL  SV OB          6  4   675        2650  3100
  16  8 PRO-169 BT            BASS  AL  SV OB          6  4   600        2400  2750
  16  8 PRO-169 SC            BASS  AL  SV OB          6  4   653        2600  3000
  16  8 PRO-170               BASS  AL  SV OB          6  4   695        2650  3100
  16  8 PRO-170 TANK          BASS  AL  SV OB          6  4   695        2800  3250
  16  8 PRO-171               FSH   AL  SV OB          6  4   670        2550  3000
  16  8 PRO-171 TANK          FSH   AL  SV OB          6  4   670        2700  3150
  16  9 HOLIDAY LX            UTL   AL  SV OB          6  4   330        1250  1500

  17    SP-175            OP  CTRCN AL  SV OB          6  8   750        2900  3400
  17    SP-175 TANK       OP  CTRCN AL  SV OB          6  8   750        3050  3550
  17    SP-176            OP  RNBT  AL  SV OB          6  8   880        3400  3900
  17    SP-176 TANK       OP  RNBT  AL  SV OB          6  8   880        3550  4100
  17    SP-178            OP  FSH   AL  SV OB          6  8   750        2900  3400
  17    SP-178 TANK       OP  FSH   AL  SV OB          6  8   750        3050  3550
  18  4 JUMBO LX              UTL   AL  SV OB          6  8   355        1250  1500
  19  6 SP-195            OP  CTRCN AL  SV OB          7  1  1050        4450  5100
  19  6 SP-196            OP  RNBT  AL  SV OB          7  1  1120        4700  5350
  22  6 CORSICA           OP  CUD   AL  DV OB          8      1800        8100  9300
  22  6 CORSICA           OP  CUD   AL  DV IO 150-175  8      2600        7800  9100
  22  6 SP-225            OP  CTRCN AL  DV OB          8      1300        6050  6950

  22  6 SP-226            OP  RNBT  AL  DV OB          8      1300        6050  6950
  22  6 SP-226            OP  RNBT  AL  DV IO 150-175  8      2300        7000  8100
--------------------- 1989 BOATS --------------------------------------------------------------
  16    PRO 162           OP  FSH   AL  SV OB          5  7   423        1500  1800
  16    STARFISH LX15     OP  UTL   AL  SV OB          5  7   266         950  1100
  16    STARFISH LX20     OP  UTL   AL  SV OB          5  7   273         955  1150
  16  2 MARLIN SUPREME     ST  RNBT  AL  SV OB          6  1   800        2850  3350
  16  9 HOLIDAY LX        OP  UTL   AL  SV OB          6  4   314        1100  1300
  16  9 PRO 170           OP  BASS  AL  SV OB          6  4   640        2400  2750
  16  9 PRO 171           OP  BASS  AL  SV OB          6  4   570        2150  2500
  17    SUPER PRO 175     OP  CTRCN AL  SV OB          6  8   750        2800  3250
  17    SUPER PRO 176     OP  RNBT  AL  SV OB          6  8   840        3000  3450
  18  6 JUMBO LX          OP  UTL   AL  SV OB          6  8   355        1150  1400
  18  6 PRO 186           OP  BASS  AL  SV OB          6  8   610        2450  2850
  19  6 SUPER PRO 195     OP  CTRCN AL  SV OB          7  1  1050        4100  4750

  19  6 SUPER PRO 196     OP  FSH   AL  SV OB          7  1  1190        4600  5250
  22  6 CORSICA           OP  CUD   AL  DV IO  205     8      2600        7100  8150
  22  6 SUPER PRO 225     OP  FSH   AL  DV OB          8      1300        5650  6500
  22  6 SUPER PRO 226     OP  FSH   AL  DV OB          8      1500        6450  7400
--------------------- 1988 BOATS --------------------------------------------------------------
  16    PRO 162           OP  FSH   AL  SV OB          5  7   423        1450  1750
  16    STARFISH LX15     OP  UTL   AL  SV OB          5  7   266         905  1100
  16    STARFISH LX20     OP  UTL   AL  SV OB          5  7   273         925  1100
  16  2 MARLIN SUPREME     ST  RNBT  AL  SV OB          6  1   800        2800  3250
  16  9 HOLIDAY LX        OP  UTL   AL  SV OB          6  4   314        1050  1250
  16  9 PRO 170           OP  BASS  AL  SV OB          6  4   640        2350  2700
  16  9 PRO 171           OP  BASS  AL  SV OB          6  4   570        2050  2450
  17    SUPER PRO 175     OP  CTRCN AL  SV OB          6  8   750        2700  3150
  17    SUPER PRO 176     OP  RNBT  AL  SV OB          6  8   840        2900  3350
  18  6 JUMBO LX          OP  UTL   AL  SV OB          6  8   355        1150  1350
  18  6 PRO 186           OP  BASS  AL  SV OB          6  8   610        2400  2800
  19  6 SUPER PRO 195     OP  CTRCN AL  SV OB          7  1  1050        3950  4600
```

LOA FT IN	NAME AND/ OR MODEL	TOP/ RIG	BOAT TYPE	HULL MTL	HULL TP	ENGINE TP	HP	MFG	BEAM FT IN	WGT LBS	DRAFT FT IN	RETAIL LOW	RETAIL HIGH
1988 BOATS													
19 6	SUPER PRO 196	OP	FSH	AL	SV	OB			7 1	1190		4450	5100
1987 BOATS													
16	PRO 162	OP	FSH	AL	SV	OB			5 7	423		1400	1700
16	PRO 163	OP	FSH	AL	SV	OB			5 7	408		1350	1600
16	STARFISH LX15	OP	UTL	AL	SV	OB			5 7	266		880	1050
16	STARFISH LX20	OP	UTL	AL	SV	OB			5 7	273		905	1100
16 2	MARLIN SUPREME	ST	RNBT	AL	SV	OB			6 1	800		2700	3150
16 9	HOLIDAY LX	OP	UTL	AL	SV	OB			6 4	314		1050	1250
16 9	PRO 170	OP	BASS	AL	SV	OB			6 4	640		2250	2650
16 9	PRO 171	OP	BASS	AL	SV	OB			6 4	570		2000	2350
17	SUPER PRO 175	OP	CTRCN	AL	SV	OB			6 8	750		2600	3050
17	SUPER PRO 176	OP	UTL	AL	SV	OB			6 8	840		2800	3250
18 6	JUMBO LX	OP	UTL	AL	SV	OB			6 8	355		1100	1300
18 6	PRO 186	OP	BASS	AL	SV	OB			6 8	610		2300	2700
19 6	SUPER PRO 195	OP	CTRCN	AL	SV	OB			7 1	1050		3850	4450
19 6	SUPER PRO 196	OP	FSH	AL	SV	OB			7 1	1190		4250	4950

ALUMACRAFT BOAT COMPANY

ST PETER MN 56082   COAST GUARD MFG ID- ACB   See inside cover to adjust price for area

For more recent years, see the BUC Used Boat Price Guide, Volume 1

LOA FT IN	NAME AND/ OR MODEL	TOP/ RIG	BOAT TYPE	HULL MTL	HULL TP	ENGINE TP	HP	MFG	BEAM FT IN	WGT LBS	DRAFT FT IN	RETAIL LOW	RETAIL HIGH
1996 BOATS													
16	1648	OP	JON	AL	FL	OB			5 10	260		515	620
16	1648 LW	OP	JON	AL	FL	OB			5 10	260		585	700
16	1650 AW TUNNEL	OP	JON	AL	FL	OB			6 2	300		720	870
16	1650AW	OP	JON	AL	FL	OB			6 2	300		615	740
16	MV CRAPPIE PRO	OP	BASS	AL	SV	OB			5 11	700		1600	1900
16	MV TEX	OP	JON	AL	SV	OB			5 10	340		745	895
16	MV TEX CS	OP	JON	AL	SV	OB			5 10	355		775	930
16	MV TEX SPECIAL CS	OP	JON	AL	SV	OB			5 10	425		920	1100
16	MV1648	OP	JON	AL	SV	OB			5 10	260		615	740
16	MV1648 LW	OP	JON	AL	SV	OB			5 10	260		655	790
16	MV1650 AW/DD	OP	FSH	AL	SV	OB			6 2	300		660	795
16	MV1650AW	OP	JON	AL	SV	OB			6 2	300		670	805
16 3	CLASSIC DLX	OP	UTL	AL	SV	OB			6 1	770		1650	2000
16 4	BACKTROLLER 16	OP	FSH	AL	SV	OB			6 1	665		1500	1750
16 4	COMPETITOR 170	OP	FSH	AL	DV	OB			6 7	915		2000	2400
16 4	COMPETITOR 170 CS	OP	FSH	AL	DV	OB			6 7	959		2150	2500
16 5	DOMINATOR	OP	FSH	AL	SV	OB			6 2	825		1850	2200
16 5	DOMINATOR CS	OP	FSH	AL	SV	OB			6 2	839		1850	2200
16 6	LUNKER V16	OP	FSH	AL	SV	OB			5 3	451		1050	1250
16 7	V16 15/20	OP	FSH	AL	SV	OB			5 10	270		670	750
16 8	MV MAVERICK	OP	BASS	AL	SV	OB			5 11	575		1350	1600
16 9	LUNKER V16 LTD	OP	FSH	AL	SV	OB			5 10	605		1400	1650
16 9	LUNKER V16 LTD ANV	OP	FSH	AL	SV	OB			5 10	563		1300	1550
16 10	COMPETITOR 170 SPORT	OP	FSH	AL	DV	OB			6 7	990		2250	2600
16 10	COMPETITOR 170CS ANV	OP	FSH	AL	DV	OB			6 7	917		2050	2450
16 10	TROPHY 170 COMB	OP	RNBT	AL	DV	OB			6 7	1149		2600	3050
16 10	TROPHY 170 PED	OP	RNBT	AL	DV	OB			6 7	1149		2550	2950
16 11	TROPHY 170 ANV	OP	RNBT	AL	DV	OB			6 7	1084		2500	2900
17	PHANTOM V170	OP	BASS	AL	DV	OB			6 9	1102		2500	2900
17	PREDATOR AW	OP	FSH	AL	SV	OB			7 4	900		2000	2400
17	PREDATOR AW ANV	OP	RNBT	AL	SV	OB			7 4	900		2100	2500
17 8	MV SUPER BANDIT	OP	BASS	AL	SV	OB			6 3	900		2150	2500
18	1860 AW TUNNEL	OP	JON	AL	FL	OB			7 4	500		980	1150
18	1860AW	OP	JON	AL	FL	OB			7 4	500		870	1050
18	MV1860AW	OP	JON	AL	SV	OB			7 4	500		935	1100
18	TROPHY 180 COMB	OP	RNBT	AL	DV	OB			6 10	1318		2950	3400
18	TROPHY 180 PED	OP	RNBT	AL	DV	OB			7	1318		2950	3400
18 4	PHANTOM 185 FISH SKI	OP	RNBT	AL	DV	OB			7 8	1440		3150	3650
18 5	PHANTOM V185	OP	RNBT	AL	DV	OB			7 8	1400		3100	3600
18 10	COMPETITOR 190	OP	FSH	AL	DV	OB			7 4	1149		2650	3100
18 10	COMPETITOR 190 CS	OP	FSH	AL	DV	OB			7 4	1270		2850	3300
18 10	TROPHY 190 COMB	OP	RNBT	AL	DV	OB			7 6	1419		3150	3700
18 10	TROPHY 190 PED	OP	RNBT	AL	DV	OB			7 6	1419		3100	3600
18 10	TROPHY 190 PED	OP	RNBT	AL	DV	IO	135-180		7 6	2080		7700	8950
1995 BOATS													
16	1648	OP	JON	AL	FL	OB			5 10	260		515	620
16	1648 LW	OP	JON	AL	FL	OB			5 10	260		550	660
16	1650 AW TUNNEL	OP	JON	AL	FL	OB			6 2	300		685	825
16	1650AW	OP	JON	AL	FL	OB			6 2	300		580	700
16	MV CRAPPIE PRO	OP	BASS	AL	SV	OB			5 11	700		1500	1800
16	MV TEX	OP	JON	AL	SV	OB			5 10	340		705	850
16	MV TEX CS	OP	JON	AL	SV	OB			5 10	355		730	880
16	MV TEX SPECIAL CS	OP	JON	AL	SV	OB			5 10	425		870	1050
16	MV1648	OP	JON	AL	SV	OB			5 10	260		570	685
16	MV1648 LW	OP	JON	AL	SV	OB			5 10	260		605	730
16	MV1650AW	OP	JON	AL	SV	OB			6 2	300		630	760
16 3	CLASSIC DLX	OP	UTL	AL	SV	OB			6 1	770		1600	1900
16 4	BACKTROLLER 16	OP	FSH	AL	SV	OB			6 1	665		1400	1700
16 4	COMPETITOR 170	OP	FSH	AL	DV	OB			6 7	915		1900	2250
16 4	COMPETITOR 170 CS	OP	FSH	AL	DV	OB			6 7	959		2000	2350
16 5	DOMINATOR	OP	FSH	AL	SV	OB			6 2	825		1750	2050
16 5	DOMINATOR CS	OP	FSH	AL	SV	OB			6 2	839		1750	2100
16 6	LUNKER V16	OP	FSH	AL	SV	OB			5 3	451		990	1200
16 7	V16 15/20	OP	FSH	AL	SV	OB			5 10	270		590	710
16 8	MV MAVERICK	OP	BASS	AL	SV	OB			5 11	575		1250	1500
16 9	LUNKER V16 LTD	OP	FSH	AL	SV	OB			5 10	605		1300	1550
16 10	COMPETITOR 170 SPORT	OP	FSH	AL	DV	OB			6 7	990		2050	2450
16 10	TROPHY 170 COMB	OP	RNBT	AL	DV	OB			6 7	1149		2500	2900
16 10	TROPHY 170 PED	OP	RNBT	AL	DV	OB			6 7	1149		2450	2850
17	PHANTOM V170	OP	BASS	AL	DV	OB			6 9	1102		2400	2800
17 8	MV SUPER BANDIT	OP	BASS	AL	SV	OB			6 3	900		2000	2350
18	1860 AW TUNNEL	OP	JON	AL	FL	OB			7 4	500		935	1100
18	1860AW	OP	JON	AL	FL	OB			7 4	500		805	970
18	MV1860AW	OP	JON	AL	SV	OB			7 4	500		880	1050
18	TROPHY 180 COMB	OP	RNBT	AL	DV	OB			6 10	1318		2750	3200
18	TROPHY 180 PED	OP	RNBT	AL	DV	OB			7	1318		2750	3200
18 4	PHANTOM 185 FISH SKI	OP	RNBT	AL	DV	OB			7 8	1440		2950	3450
18 10	COMPETITOR 190	OP	FSH	AL	DV	OB			7 4	1149		2500	2900
18 10	COMPETITOR 190 CS	OP	FSH	AL	DV	OB			7 4	1270		2700	3150
18 10	TROPHY 190 COMB	OP	RNBT	AL	DV	OB			7 6	1419		2950	3450
18 10	TROPHY 190 PED	OP	RNBT	AL	DV	OB			7 6	1419		3000	3500
18 10	TROPHY 190 PED	OP	RNBT	AL	DV	IO	135-180		7 6	2080		7200	8350
1994 BOATS													
16	1648	OP	JON	AL	FL	OB			5 10	260		490	595
16	1648 LW	OP	JON	AL	FL	OB			5 10	260		520	630
16	MV CRAPPIE PRO	OP	BASS	AL	SV	OB			5 11	700		1400	1700
16	MV TEX	OP	JON	AL	SV	OB			5 10	340		665	805
16	MV TEX CS	OP	JON	AL	SV	OB			5 10	355		695	835
16	MV TEX SPECIAL CS	OP	JON	AL	SV	OB			5 10	425		815	980
16	MV1648	OP	JON	AL	SV	OB			5 10	260		540	650
16	MV1648 LW	OP	JON	AL	SV	OB			5 10	260		575	695
16 3	CLASSIC DLX	OP	UTL	AL	SV	OB			6 1	770		1500	1800
16 4	BACKTROLLER 16	OP	FSH	AL	SV	OB			6 1	665		1350	1600
16 4	COMPETITOR 170	OP	FSH	AL	DV	OB			6 7	915		1800	2150
16 4	COMPETITOR 170 CS	OP	FSH	AL	DV	OB			6 7	959		1900	2250
16 5	DOMINATOR	OP	FSH	AL	SV	OB			6 2	825		1650	1950
16 5	DOMINATOR CS	OP	FSH	AL	SV	OB			6 2	839		1650	2000
16 6	LUNKER V16	OP	FSH	AL	SV	OB			5 3	451		935	1100
16 7	V16 15/20	OP	FSH	AL	SV	OB			5 10	270		555	670
16 8	MV MAVERICK	OP	BASS	AL	SV	OB			5 11	575		1200	1450
16 9	LUNKER V16 LTD	OP	FSH	AL	SV	OB			5 10	605		1250	1500
16 10	COMPETITOR 170 SPORT	OP	FSH	AL	DV	OB			6 7	990		1950	2350
16 10	TROPHY 170 COMB	OP	RNBT	AL	DV	OB			6 7	1149		2400	2800
16 10	TROPHY 170 PED	OP	RNBT	AL	DV	OB			6 7	1149		2350	2750
17	PHANTOM V170	OP	BASS	AL	DV	OB			6 9	1102		2250	2600
17 8	MV SUPER BANDIT	OP	BASS	AL	SV	OB			6 3	900		1900	2250
18	TROPHY 180 COMB	OP	RNBT	AL	DV	OB			6 10	1318		2650	3050
18	TROPHY 180 PED	OP	RNBT	AL	DV	OB			7	1318		2650	3050
18 4	COMPETITOR 185	OP	FSH	AL	SV	OB			7 4	1149		2400	2750
18 4	COMPETITOR 185 CS	OP	FSH	AL	SV	OB			7 4	1270		2500	2900
18 4	PHANTOM 185 FISH SKI	OP	RNBT	AL	SV	OB			7 8	1440		2800	3250
18 10	TROPHY 190 COMB	OP	RNBT	AL	DV	OB			7 6	1419		2850	3300
18 10	TROPHY 190 PED	OP	RNBT	AL	DV	OB			7 6	1419		2800	3250
1993 BOATS													
16	1648	OP	JON	AL	FL	OB			5 10	260		505	610
16	1648 LW	OP	JON	AL	FL	OB			5 10	260		515	620
16	MV CRAPPIE PRO	OP	BASS	AL	SV	OB			5 11	660		1250	1500
16	MV TEX	OP	JON	AL	SV	OB			5 10	340		635	765
16	MV TEX CS	OP	JON	AL	SV	OB			5 10	355		660	795
16	MV TEX SPECIAL CS	OP	JON	AL	SV	OB			5 10	425		775	930
16	MV1648	OP	JON	AL	SV	OB			5 10	270		530	640

ALUMACRAFT BOAT COMPANY -CONTINUED See inside cover to adjust price for area

LOA FT	IN	NAME AND/ OR MODEL	TOP/ RIG	BOAT TYPE	-HULL- MTL	TP	----ENGINE--- TP	# HP MFG	BEAM FT	IN	WGT LBS	DRAFT FT IN	RETAIL LOW	RETAIL HIGH
		1993 BOATS												
16		MV1648 LW	OP	JON	AL	SV	OB		5	10	285		545	655
16	3	CLASSIC DLX	OP	UTL	AL	SV	OB		6	1	650		1200	1450
16	4	BACKTROLLER 16	OP	FSH	AL	SV	OB		6	1	583		1100	1350
16	4	COMPETITOR 170	OP	FSH	AL	DV	OB		6	7	873		1650	1950
16	4	COMPETITOR 170 CS	OP	FSH	AL	DV	OB		6	7	917		1700	2050
16	5	DOMINATOR	OP	FSH	AL	SV	OB		6	2	782		1500	1750
16	5	DOMINATOR CS	OP	FSH	AL	SV	OB		6	2	797		1500	1800
16	7	V16 15/20	OP	FSH	AL	SV	OB		5	10	270		530	640
16	8	MV MAVERICK	OP	BASS	AL	SV	OB		5	11	737		1450	1700
16	9	LUNKER V16 LTD	OP	FSH	AL	SV	OB		5	10	563		1100	1300
16	10	TROPHY 170 COMB	OP	RNBT	AL	DV	OB		6	7	897		1750	2100
16	10	TROPHY 170 PED	OP	RNBT	AL	DV	OB		6	7	897		1750	2100
17		PHANTOM V170	OP	BASS	AL	DV	OB		6	9	1049		2000	2400
17	8	MV SUPER BANDIT	OP	BASS	AL	SV	OB		6	3	857		1700	2050
18		TROPHY 180 COMB	OP	FSH	AL	SV	OB		6	10	1084		2100	2500
18		TROPHY 180 PED	OP	RNBT	AL	SV	OB		7		1251		2450	2850
18	4	COMPETITOR 185	OP	FSH	AL	DV	OB		7	4	1178		2300	2700
18	4	COMPETITOR 185 CS	OP	FSH	AL	DV	OB		7	4	1228		2400	2800
18	4	PHANTOM 185 FISH SKI	OP	RNBT	AL	DV	OB		7	8	1386		2600	3050
18	10	TROPHY 190 COMB	OP	RNBT	AL	DV	OB		7	6	1347		2600	3050
18	10	TROPHY 190 PED	OP	RNBT	AL	DV	OB		7	6	1347		2550	3000
		1992 BOATS												
16		1670	OP	JON	AL	SV	OB		5	10	277		510	615
16		1670 LW	OP	JON	AL	SV	OB		5	10	283		515	625
16		MV 1670	OP	JON	AL	SV	OB		5	10	282		515	620
16		MV 1670 LW	OP	JON	AL	SV	OB		5	10	288		525	635
16		MV ANGLER	OP	BASS	AL	SV	OB		5	9	600		1100	1300
16		MV CRAPPIE DLX SS	OP	BASS	AL		OB		5	10	580		1050	1250
16		MV TEX	OP	JON	AL	SV	OB		5	10	290		530	635
16		MV TEX CS	OP	JON	AL	SV	OB		5	10	300		540	650
16		MV TEX SPECIAL	OP	JON	AL	SV	OB		5	10	350		620	745
16		MV TEX SPECIAL CS	OP	JON	AL	SV	OB		5	10	385		675	810
16	3	CLASSIC DLX	OP	UTL	AL	SV	OB		6	1	650		1150	1350
16	4	1674	OP	JON	AL	SV	OB		6	2	348		605	730
16	4	1674 LW	OP	JON	AL	SV	OB		6	2	354		615	740
16	4	BACKTROLLER 16	OP	FSH	AL	SV	OB		6	1	555		1000	1200
16	4	COMPETITOR 170	OP	FSH	AL	DV	OB		6	7	870		1550	1850
16	4	COMPETITOR 170 CS	OP	FSH	AL	DV	OB		6	7	1295		2300	2650
16	4	DOMINATOR	OP	FSH	AL	SV	OB		6	2	795		1450	1700
16	4	DOMINATOR CS	OP	FSH	AL	SV	OB		6	2	825		1500	1750
16	6	LUNKER V16 DLX	OP	FSH	AL	SV	OB		5	9	550		1000	1200
16	8	LUNKER V16 LTD	OP	FSH	AL	SV	OB		5	10	585		1100	1300
16	8	MV MAVERICK	OP	BASS	AL	SV	OB		6		625		1150	1400
16	10	TROPHY 170 COMB	OP	RNBT	AL	DV	OB		6	7	897		1700	2000
16	10	TROPHY 170 PED	OP	RNBT	AL	DV	OB		6	7	897		1650	2000
17		MV CRAPPIE PRO	OP	BASS	AL		OB		6		660		1250	1500
17	2	PHANTOM V170	OP	BASS	AL	DV	OB		6	6	945		1750	2100
17	8	MV SUPER BANDIT	OP	BASS	AL	SV	OB		6	2	740		1450	1700
18		MV 1870-20	OP	JON	AL	SV	OB		5	10	303		400	490
18		TROPHY 180 PED	OP	RNBT	AL	SV	OB		7		1180		2250	2600
18		TROPHY 180 PED	OP	RNBT	AL	SV	IO	155	7		1180		4550	5200
18	4	COMPETITOR 185	OP	FSH	AL	DV	OB		7	4	1149		2150	2500
18	4	COMPETITOR 185 CS	OP	FSH	AL	DV	OB		7	4	1200		2250	2600
18	4	PHANTOM 185 FISH SKI	OP	RNBT	AL	DV	OB		7	2	1375		2500	2950
18	10	TROPHY 190 COMB	OP	RNBT	AL	DV	OB		7	6	1160		2250	2600
18	10	TROPHY 190 COMB	OP	RNBT	AL	DV	IO	130	7	6	2100		5900	6800
18	10	TROPHY 190 PED	OP	RNBT	AL	DV	OB		7	6	1160		2250	2600
18	10	TROPHY 190 PED	OP	RNBT	AL	DV	IO	130	7	6	2100		5900	6750
		1991 BOATS												
16		1670	OP	JON	AL	SV	OB		5	10	277		490	590
16		1670 LW	OP	JON	AL	SV	OB		5	10	283		495	595
16		MV 1670	OP	JON	AL	SV	OB		5	10	282		495	600
16		MV 1670 LW	OP	JON	AL	SV	OB		5	10	288		500	605
16		MV ANGLER	OP	BASS	AL	SV	OB		5	9	600		1050	1250
16		MV CRAPPIE SS	OP	BASS	AL		OB		5	10	580		1000	1200
16		MV TEX	OP	JON	AL	SV	OB		5	10	290		505	605
16		MV TEX CS	OP	JON	AL	SV	OB		5	10	300		520	625
16		MV TEX SPECIAL	OP	JON	AL	SV	OB		5	10	350		590	710
16		MV TEX SPECIAL CS	OP	JON	AL	SV	OB		5	10	385		640	775
16	3	CLASSIC	OP	UTL	AL	SV	OB		6	1	610		1050	1250
16	3	CLASSIC DLX	OP	UTL	AL	SV	OB		6	1	650		1100	1300
16	4	1674	OP	JON	AL	SV	OB		6	2	348		580	695
16	4	1674 LW	OP	JON	AL	SV	OB		6	2	354		585	705
16	4	BACKTROLLER 16	OP	FSH	AL	SV	OB		6	1	555		980	1150
16	4	COMPETITOR	OP	FSH	AL	DV	OB		6	7	870		1500	1750
16	4	COMPETITOR CS	OP	FSH	AL	DV	OB		6	7	1295		2150	2500
16	4	DOMINATOR	OP	FSH	AL	SV	OB		6	2	795		1350	1600
16	4	DOMINATOR CS	OP	FSH	AL	SV	OB		6	2	825		1400	1700
16	6	LUNKER V16 15/20	OP	FSH	AL	SV	OB		5	10	260		465	560
16	6	LUNKER V16 DXL	OP	FSH	AL	SV	OB		5	9	550		980	1150
16	8	LUNKER V16 LTD	OP	FSH	AL	SV	OB		5	10	585		1050	1250
16	8	MV MAVERICK	OP	BASS	AL	SV	OB		6		625		1100	1350
16	10	TROPHY 170 COMB	OP	RNBT	AL	DV	OB		6	7	897		1600	1900
16	10	TROPHY 170 PED	OP	RNBT	AL	DV	OB		6	7	897		1600	1900
16	10	TROPHY 170 SLP	OP	RNBT	AL	DV	OB		6	7	897		1600	1900
17		MV CRAPPIE PRO	OP	BASS	AL		OB		6		660		1200	1400
17	2	PHANTOM V170	OP	BASS	AL	DV	OB		6	6	945		1650	2000
17	8	MV SUPER BANDIT	OP	BASS	AL	SV	OB		6	2	740		1350	1600
18		MV 1870-20	OP	JON	AL	SV	OB		5	10	303		385	465
18	4	COMPETITOR 185	OP	FSH	AL	DV	OB		7	4	1149		2000	2400
18	4	COMPETITOR 185 CS	OP	FSH	AL	DV	OB		7	4	1200		2100	2450
18	10	TROPHY 190 COMB	OP	RNBT	AL	DV	OB		7	6	1160		2100	2500
18	10	TROPHY 190 COMB	OP	RNBT	AL	DV	IO	130	7	6	2100		5550	6350
18	10	TROPHY 190 PED	OP	RNBT	AL	DV	OB		7	6	1160		2050	2450
18	10	TROPHY 190 PED	OP	RNBT	AL	DV	IO	130	7	6	2100		5500	6350
18	10	TROPHY 190 SLP	OP	RNBT	AL	DV	OB		7	6	1160		2100	2500
18	10	TROPHY 190 SLP	OP	RNBT	AL	DV	IO	130-175	7	6	2100		5550	6400
21	8	TROPHY 220	OP	CUD	AL	DV	OB		8	6	2575		4500	5150
21	8	TROPHY 220	OP	CUD	AL	DV	IO	175-260	8	6	3225		9900	11800
		1990 BOATS												
16		1670	OP	JON	AL	SV	OB		5	10	277		470	565
16		1670 LW	OP	JON	AL	SV	OB		5	10	283		475	575
16		MV 1670	OP	JON	AL	SV	OB		5	10	282		475	575
16		MV 1670 LW	OP	JON	AL	SV	OB		5	10	288		485	585
16		MV CRAPPIE SS	OP	BASS	AL		OB		5	10	580		980	1150
16		MV TEX	OP	JON	AL	SV	OB		5	10	290		485	585
16		MV TEX CS	OP	JON	AL	SV	OB		5	10	300		495	600
16		MV TEX SPECIAL	OP	JON	AL	SV	OB		5	10	350		565	680
16		MV TEX SPECIAL CS	OP	JON	AL	SV	OB		5	10	385		615	740
16	3	CLASSIC	OP	UTL	AL	SV	OB		6	1	557		920	1100
16	3	CLASSIC DLX	OP	UTL	AL	SV	OB		6	1	574		945	1150
16	4	BACKTROLLER 16	OP	FSH	AL	SV	OB		6	1	526		890	1050
16	4	COMPETITOR	OP	FSH	AL	DV	OB		6	7	758		1250	1500
16	4	COMPETITOR CS	OP	FSH	AL	DV	OB		6	7	808		1300	1550
16	4	DOMINATOR	OP	FSH	AL	SV	OB		6	2	728		1200	1450
16	4	DOMINATOR CS	OP	FSH	AL	SV	OB		6	2	774		1250	1500
16	6	LUNKER V16 15/20	OP	FSH	AL	SV	OB		5	10	260		445	535
16	6	LUNKER V16 DLX	OP	FSH	AL	SV	OB		5	10	570		970	1150
16	6	LUNKER V16 LTD	OP	FSH	AL	SV	OB		5	10	630		1050	1250
16	10	TROPHY 170 COMB	OP	RNBT	AL	DV	OB		6	7	897		1500	1800
16	10	TROPHY 170 PED	OP	RNBT	AL	DV	OB		6	7	897		1500	1800
16	10	TROPHY 170 SLP	OP	RNBT	AL	DV	OB		6	7	897		1550	1850
17		MV CRAPPIE PRO	OP	BASS	AL		OB		6		660		1150	1350
17	2	PHANTOM V170	OP	BASS	AL	DV	OB		6	6	925		1550	1850
17	8	MV ANGLER	OP	BASS	AL	SV	OB		5	9	577		1050	1250
17	8	MV MAVERICK	OP	BASS	AL	SV	OB		6		625		1100	1350
17	8	MV SUPER BANDIT	OP	BASS	AL	SV	OB		6	2	740		1300	1550
18		MV 1870-20	OP	JON	AL	SV	OB		5	10	303		365	445
18	10	TROPHY 190 COMB	OP	RNBT	AL	DV	OB		7	6	1160		2000	2350
18	10	TROPHY 190 COMB	OP	RNBT	AL	DV	IO	130	7	6	2100		5200	6000
18	10	TROPHY 190 PED	OP	RNBT	AL	DV	OB		7	6	1160		2000	2350
18	10	TROPHY 190 PED	OP	RNBT	AL	DV	IO	130	7	6	2100		5200	5950
18	10	TROPHY 190 SLP	OP	RNBT	AL	DV	OB		7	6	1160		2000	2350
18	10	TROPHY 190 SLP	OP	RNBT	AL	DV	IO	130-175	7	6	2100		5250	6050
21	8	TROPHY 220	OP	CUD	AL	DV	IO	175-260	8	6	3225		9400	11100
		1989 BOATS												
16		1670	OP	JON	AL	FL	OB		5	10	277		450	540
16		1670 LW	OP	JON	AL	FL	OB		5	10	283		455	550
16		MV 1648 W	OP	JON	AL	FL	OB		5	10	321		505	610
16		MV 1670	OP	JON	AL	FL	OB		5	10	282		455	550
16		MV 1670 LW	OP	JON	AL	FL	OB		5	10	288		465	560
16		MV ANGLER	OP	BASS	AL	FL	OB		5	7	485		775	935
16		MV SUPER HAWK SS	OP	BASS	AL		OB		5	10	580		940	1100
16		MV TEX	OP	JON	AL	FL	OB		5	10	290		465	560
16		MV TEX CS	OP	JON	AL	FL	OB		5	10	300		480	580
16	3	CLASSIC 16	OP	UTL	AL	SV	OB		6	1	557		880	1050
16	3	CLASSIC DELUXE	OP	UTL	AL	SV	OB		6	1	574		905	1100
16	4	BACKTROLLER 16	OP	FSH	AL	SV	OB		6	1	526		850	1000

20
CONTINUED ON NEXT PAGE
96th ed. - Vol. II

ALUMACRAFT BOAT COMPANY   -CONTINUED   See inside cover to adjust price for area

LOA FT IN	NAME AND/OR MODEL	TOP/RIG	BOAT TYPE	HULL MTL	HULL TP	ENG TP	ENG # HP	ENG MFG	BEAM FT IN	WGT LBS	DRAFT FT IN	RETAIL LOW	RETAIL HIGH
1989 BOATS													
16 4	COMPETITOR	OP	FSH	AL	DV	OB			6 7	745		1150	1400
16 4	COMPETITOR CS	OP	FSH	AL	DV	OB			6 7	788		1250	1450
16 4	DOMINATOR	OP	FSH	AL		OB			6 2	728		1150	1350
16 4	DOMINATOR CS	OP	FSH	AL		OB			6 2	774		1200	1450
16 4	MV MAVERICK	OP	BASS	AL	SV	OB			6	575		945	1150
16 6	LUNKER V-16 DELUXE	OP	FSH	AL	SV	OB			5 10	500		810	975
16 6	LUNKER V-16 LTD	OP	FSH	AL	SV	OB			5 10	496		800	965
16 6	V-16	OP	FSH	AL	SV	OB			5 10	260		425	515
16 10	TROPHY 170	OP	RNBT	AL	DV	OB			6 7	875		1450	1700
17	BANDIT V-170	OP	BASS	AL	DV	OB			6 8	1135		1800	2100
17	MV SUPER HAWK XL	OP	BASS	AL		OB			6 2	660		1100	1300
17	MV TEX SPECIAL	OP	JON	AL	FL	OB			6 10	350		500	600
17	MV TEX SPECIAL CS	OP	JON	AL	FL	OB			6 10	385		545	660
17 2	PHANTOM V-170	OP	BASS	AL	DV	OB			6 8	925		1500	1800
17 8	MV SUPER-BANDIT	OP	BASS	AL	FL	OB			6 2	740		1250	1500
18	MV 1870	OP	JON	AL	FL	OB			5 10	303		350	430
18 10	TROPHY 190	OP	RNBT	AL	DV	OB			7 6	1150		1900	2250
18 10	TROPHY 190 IO	OP	RNBT	AL		IO	175		7 6	2155		5000	5750
1988 BOATS													
16	1670	OP	JON	AL	FL	OB			5 10	277		430	520
16	1670 LW	OP	JON	AL	FL	OB			5 10	283		440	530
16	MV 1670	OP	JON	AL	FL	OB			5 10	282		435	525
16	MV 1670 LW	OP	JON	AL	FL	OB			5 10	288		445	535
16	MV ANGLER	OP	BASS	AL	FL	OB			5 7	485		745	900
16	MV TEX	OP	JON	AL	FL	OB			5 10	280		435	525
16	MV TEX CS	OP	JON	AL	FL	OB			5 10	300		460	555
16	W1648	OP	JON	AL	FL	OB			5 10	321		490	590
16 3	CLASSIC 16	OP	UTL	AL	SV	OB			6 1	557		845	1000
16 3	CLASSIC DELUXE	OP	UTL	AL	SV	OB			6 1	574		870	1050
16 4	COMPETITOR	OP	BASS	AL	DV	OB			6 7	745		1150	1350
16 4	COMPETITOR CS	OP	BASS	AL	DV	OB			6 7	788		1200	1450
16 4	LUNKER 16SS	OP	FSH	AL	SV	OB			6 1	526		805	970
16 4	MV MAVERICK	OP	BASS	AL	SV	OB			6	575		910	1100
16 6	LUNKER V16 DELUXE	OP	FSH	AL	SV	OB			5 10	500		775	935
16 6	LUNKER V16 LTD	OP	FSH	AL	SV	OB			5 10	496		770	925
16 6	V-16	OP	FSH	AL	SV	OB			5 10	260		405	495
16 10	TROPHY 170	OP	RNBT	AL	DV	OB			6 7	875		1350	1650
17	BANDIT V170	OP	BASS	AL	DV	OB			6 8	1135		1700	2050
17	MV BANDIT	OP	BASS	AL	FL	OB			6	600		975	1150
17	MV TEX SPECIAL	OP	JON	AL	FL	OB			6 10	350		485	585
17	MV TEX SPECIAL CS	OP	JON	AL	FL	OB			6 10	385		530	635
17 2	PHANTOM V170	OP	BASS	AL	DV	OB			6 8	925		1450	1700
17 5	BACKTROLLER 17	OP	FSH	AL	SV	OB			6 2			1100	1350
17 5	PRO 17	OP	UTL	AL	SV	OB			6 2	750	4	1100	1350
17 8	MV SUPER-BANDIT	OP	BASS	AL	FL	OB			6 2	740		1200	1400
18	MV 1870	OP	JON	AL	FL	OB			5 10	303		335	410
18 10	TROPHY 190	OP	RNBT	AL	DV	OB			7 6	1150		1800	2150
1987 BOATS													
16	1670	OP	JON	AL	FL	OB			5 10	277		410	500
16	1670 LW	OP	JON	AL	FL	OB			5 10	283		385	465
16	MV 1670	OP	JON	AL	FL	OB			5 10	282		420	505
16	MV 1670 LW	OP	JON	AL	FL	OB			5 10	288		430	515
16	MV ANGLER	OP	BASS	AL	FL	OB			5 4	485		715	865
16	TEX II MV	OP	JON	AL	FL	OB			5 11	280		420	505
16	TEX III MV	OP	JON	AL	FL	OB			5 11	300		445	535
16	W1648	OP	JON	AL	FL	OB			5 10	283		455	550
16 3	CLASSIC 16	OP	UTL	AL	SV	OB			6 3	557		805	970
16 3	CLASSIC DLX	OP	UTL	AL	SV	OB			6 3	574		830	1000
16 3	T16XL	OP	FSH	AL	SV	OB			5 3	281		415	505
16 4	COMPETITOR	OP	BASS	AL	DV	OB				745		1100	1300
16 4	COMPETITOR CS	OP	BASS	AL	DV	OB				788		1150	1400
16 4	LUNKER 16SS	OP	FSH	AL	SV	OB			5 10	500		740	890
16 4	MAVERICK MV	OP	BASS	AL	SV	OB			6	575		870	1050
16 6	LUNKER V16	OP	FSH	AL	SV	OB			6 3	415		620	750
16 6	V-16	OP	FSH	AL	SV	OB			6	250		375	455
16 10	TROPHY 170	OP	RNBT	AL	DV	OB				875		1300	1550
17	BANDIT MV	OP	BASS	AL	FL	OB			5 11	600		940	1100
17	SUPER-BANDIT	OP	BASS	AL	FL	OB			6 2	740		1100	1350
17 2	PHANTOM V170	OP	BASS	AL	DV	OB				925		1400	1650
17 5	BACKTROLLER	OP	FSH	AL	SV	OB			5 10	675		1050	1250
17 5	PRO 17	OP	UTL	AL	SV	OB			5 10	645	4	945	1150
18	MV 1870	OP	JON	AL	FL	OB			5 10	303		325	395
18 10	TROPHY 190	OP	RNBT	AL	DV	OB				1150		1750	2100
1986 BOATS													
16	1670	OP	JON	AL	FL	OB			5 10	277		395	480
16	1670 LW	OP	JON	AL	FL	OB			5 10	283		370	455
16	MV 1670	OP	JON	AL	FL	OB			5 10	282		400	490
16	MV 1670 LW	OP	JON	AL	FL	OB			5 10	288		410	500
16	MV ANGLER	OP	BASS	AL	FL	OB			5 4	485		690	835
16	TEX II MV	OP	JON	AL	FL	OB			5 11	280		400	485
16	TEX III MV	OP	JON	AL	FL	OB			5 11	300		430	515
16	W1648	OP	JON	AL	FL	OB			5 10	283		440	530
16 3	CLASSIC 16	OP	UTL	AL	SV	OB			6 3	557		775	935
16 3	CLASSIC DLX	OP	UTL	AL	SV	OB			6 3	574		800	960
16 3	T16XL	OP	FSH	AL	SV	OB			5 3	281		400	485
16 4	LUNKER 16SS	OP	FSH	AL	SV	OB			5 10	500		715	860
16 4	MAVERICK MV	OP	BASS	AL	SV	OB			6	575		840	1000
16 6	LUNKER V16	OP	FSH	AL	SV	OB			6 3	415		600	725
16 6	V-16	OP	FSH	AL	SV	OB			6	250		360	440
16 10	SUPREME 1610	OP	RNBT	AL	SV	OB				875		1250	1500
17	BANDIT MV	OP	BASS	AL	FL	OB			5 11	600		905	1100
17	SUPER-BANDIT	OP	BASS	AL	FL	OB			6 2	740		1100	1300
17 5	BACKTROLLER	OP	FSH	AL	SV	OB			5 10	675		1000	1200
17 5	PRO 17	OP	UTL	AL	SV	OB			5 10	645	4	915	1100
18	MV 1870	OP	JON	AL	FL	OB			5 10	303		315	380
18 10	TROPHY 190	OP	RNBT	AL	SV	OB				1150		1700	2000
1985 BOATS													
16	1670	OP	JON	AL	FL	OB			5 10	277		380	465
16	1670 LW	OP	JON	AL	FL	OB			5 10	283		360	435
16	1674	OP	JON	AL	FL	OB			6 2	314		430	520
16	MV 1670	OP	JON	AL	FL	OB			5 10	282		385	470
16	MV 1670 LW	OP	JON	AL	FL	OB			5 10	288		395	480
16	MV ANGLER	OP	BASS	AL	FL	OB			5 4	485		670	805
16	TEX II	OP	JON	AL	FL	OB			5 11	270		375	455
16	TEX III	OP	JON	AL	FL	OB			5 11	280		385	470
16	W1648	OP	JON	AL	FL	OB			5 10	283		425	510
16 3	CLASSIC 16	OP	UTL	AL	SV	OB			6 3	557		750	905
16 3	CLASSIC DLX	OP	UTL	AL	SV	OB			6 3	574		775	930
16 3	T16XL	OP	FSH	AL	SV	OB			5 3	281		385	470
16 4	LUNKER 16	OP	FSH	AL	SV	OB			6 3	415		575	690
16 4	LUNKER 16SS	OP	FSH	AL	SV	OB			5 10	500		690	830
16 4	MAVERICK MV	OP	BASS	AL	SV	OB			6	575		800	965
16 6	V-16	OP	FSH	AL	SV	OB			6	250		350	425
17	BANDIT MV	OP	BASS	AL	FL	OB			5 11	600		875	1050
17	SUPER-BANDIT	OP	BASS	AL	FL	OB			6 2	740		1050	1250
17 5	BACKTROLLER	OP	FSH	AL	SV	OB			5 10	580		855	1000
17 5	PRO 17	OP	UTL	AL	SV	OB			5 10	645	4	880	1050
17 5	SPORTSMAN	OP	FSH	AL	SV	OB			6 2	825		1150	1400
17 5	TROPHY	OP	FSH	AL	SV	OB			7 1	1005		1400	1650
18	1870	OP	JON	AL	FL	OB			5 10	295		295	355
18	1874	OP	JON	AL	FL	OB			6 2	332		340	415
18	MV 1870	OP	JON	AL	FL	OB			5 10	298		295	360
1984 BOATS													
16	1670	OP	JON	AL	FL	OB			5 10	277		370	450
16	1670 LW	OP	JON	AL	FL	OB			5 10	283		360	460
16	1674	OP	JON	AL	FL	OB			6 2	314		415	505
16	MV 1670	OP	JON	AL	FL	OB			5 10	282		375	455
16	MV 1670 LW	OP	JON	AL	FL	OB			5 10	288		385	465
16	MV ANGLER	OP	BASS	AL	FL	OB			5 4	485		645	780
16	MV PRO	OP	BASS	AL	FL	OB			5 4	532		710	855
16	TEX II	OP	JON	AL	FL	OB			5 11	270		360	440
16	TEX III	OP	JON	AL	FL	OB			5 11	280		375	455
16 3	CLASSIC 16	OP	UTL	AL	SV	OB			6 3	557		725	875
16 3	CLASSIC DLX	OP	UTL	AL	SV	OB			6 3	574		750	900
16 3	SUNFISHER 16	OP	UTL	AL	SV	OB			6 3	625		815	980
16 3	T16XL	OP	FSH	AL	SV	OB			5 3	281		375	455
16 4	LUNKER 16	OP	FSH	AL	SV	OB			6 3	415		555	670
16 4	LUNKER 16SS	OP	FSH	AL	SV	OB			5 10	500		670	805
17	BANDIT FISH & SKI	OP	BASS	AL	FL	OB			6 2	780		1050	1250
17	BANDIT MV	OP	BASS	AL	FL	OB			5 11	600		845	1000
17	SUPER-BANDIT	OP	BASS	AL	FL	OB			6 2	740		1000	1200
17 5	BACKTROLLER	OP	FSH	AL	SV	OB			5 10	580		815	985
17 5	PRO 17	OP	UTL	AL	SV	OB			5 10	645	4	855	1000
17 5	SPORTSMAN	OP	FSH	AL	SV	OB			7 1	825		1100	1350
17 5	SUNFISHER 175	OP	FSH	AL	SV	OB			7 1	1005		1350	1600
17 5	TROPHY	OP	FSH	AL	SV	OB			7 1	1005		1300	1550
18	1870	OP	JON	AL	FL	OB			5 10	295		285	345

LOA FT IN	NAME AND/OR MODEL	TOP/RIG	BOAT TYPE	HULL MTL	HULL TP	ENG TP	#	HP	MFG	BEAM FT IN	WGT LBS	DRAFT FT IN	RETAIL LOW	RETAIL HIGH
1984 BOATS														
18	1874	OP	JON	AL	FL	OB				6 2	332		330	400
18	MV 1870	OP	JON	AL	FL	OB				5 10	298		285	350

....For earlier years, see the BUC Used Boat Price Guide, Volume 3

ALUMAWELD BOATS INC

WHITE CITY OR 97503   COAST GUARD MFG ID- AWB See inside cover to adjust price for area

For more recent years, see the BUC Used Boat Price Guide, Volume 1

LOA FT IN	NAME AND/OR MODEL	TOP/RIG	BOAT TYPE	HULL MTL	HULL TP	ENG TP	#	HP	MFG	BEAM FT IN	WGT LBS	DRAFT FT IN	RETAIL LOW	RETAIL HIGH
1994 BOATS														
16	1650H	OP	JON	AL	FL	OB				6 4	386		1400	1650
16	1650HC	OP	JON	AL	FL	OB				6 4	335		1100	1300
16	1650HCLW	OP	JON	AL	FL	OB				6 4	335		1350	1600
16	1650L	OP	JON	AL	FL	OB				6 4	386		1400	1650
16	1650LC	OP	JON	AL	FL	OB				6 3	335		1200	1450
16	1650PF	OP	BASS	AL	SV	OB				6 1	560		2150	2500
16	1650VJ	OP	JON	AL	SV	OB				6 2	300		1100	1300
16	1650VJS	OP	JON	AL	FL	OB				6 2	400		1450	1700
16	H41	OP	BASS	AL	SV	OB				5 6	580		2250	2600
17	1750PFC	OP	BASS	AL	SV	OB				5 11	600		2450	2800
17	1756C	OP	JON	AL	FL	OB				6 5	415		1400	1650
17	1756VJ	OP	JON	AL	FL	OB				6 4	460		1550	1800
17	H51	OP	BASS	AL	SV	OB				6 2	770		2950	3450
17	H52	OP	BASS	AL	SV	OB				6 4	820		3150	3650
17	PRO 52	OP	BASS	AL	FL	OB				6 6	860		3300	3800
17	V50	OP	BASS	AL	SV	OB				5 10	670		2650	3050
17	XP50	OP	BASS	AL	SV	OB				6 2	770		2950	3450
18	1860C	OP	JON	AL	FL	OB				7 5	535		1650	1950
18	1860VJC	OP	JON	AL	FL	OB				7 4	565		1750	2100
18	H56	OP	BASS	AL	SV	OB				7 10	990		3800	4450
18	PRO 56	OP	BASS	AL	FL	OB				6 8	990		3800	4450
20	2060C	OP	JON	AL	FL	OB				7 5	585		1600	1900
20	2060VJC	OP	JON	AL	FL	OB				7 4	615		1700	2000
20 1	H62	OP	BASS	AL	FL	OB				7 7	1130		4250	4900
20 1	H62FS	OP	BASS	AL	FL	OB				7 7	1325		4900	5600
20 1	PRO 62	OP	BASS	AL	FL	OB				7 7	1275		4750	5450
1993 BOATS														
16	1650H	OP	JON	AL	FL	OB				6 4	386		1300	1550
16	1650HC	OP	JON	AL	FL	OB				6 4	335		1100	1300
16	1650HCLW	OP	JON	AL	FL	OB				6 4	335		1250	1500
16	1650L	OP	JON	AL	FL	OB				6 4	386		1300	1550
16	1650PF	OP	BASS	AL	SV	OB				6 1	560		2000	2400
16	1650VJ	OP	JON	AL	SV	OB				6 2	300		1050	1250
16	1650VJS	OP	JON	AL	FL	OB				6 2	400		1350	1600
16	H41	OP	BASS	AL	SV	OB				5 6	580		2100	2450
17	1750PFC	OP	BASS	AL	SV	OB				5 11	600		2300	2700
17	1756C	OP	JON	AL	FL	OB				6 5	415		1300	1550
17	1756CAB	OP	JON	AL	FL	OB				6 5			2600	3000
17	50SM	OP	BASS	AL	SV	OB				5 10			2900	3350
17	50SMB	OP	BASS	AL	SV	OB				5 10			3150	3650
17	H51	OP	BASS	AL	SV	OB				6 2	770		2800	3300
17	H52	OP	BASS	AL	SV	OB				6 4	810		2950	3450
17	V50	OP	BASS	AL	SV	OB				5 10	670		2500	2900
17	XP50	OP	BASS	AL	SV	OB				6 2	770		2800	3300
18	1860C	OP	JON	AL	FL	OB				7 5	535		1550	1850
18	1860CAB	OP	JON	AL	FL	OB				7 5			3400	3950
18	H56	OP	BASS	AL	SV	OB				7 10	990		3650	4200
18	H56FS	OP	BASS	AL	SV	OB				7 10	1010		3700	4300
20	2060C	OP	JON	AL	FL	OB				7 5	585		1500	1800
20	2060CAB	OP	JON	AL	FL	OB				7 5			5050	5800
20	2060HD SPECIAL	OP	JON	AL	FL	OB				7 5			3000	3500
20	2075C SPECIAL	OP	JON	AL	FL	OB				7 5			3550	4100
20 1	H65	OP	BASS	AL	SV	OB				7 9	1130		4000	4700
24	2475C SPECIAL	OP	JON	AL	FL	OB				7 5			6750	7750

ALUMINUM CRUISERS INC

LOUISVILLE KY 40213   COAST GUARD MFG ID- ALC See inside cover to adjust price for area

LOA FT IN	NAME AND/OR MODEL	TOP/RIG	BOAT TYPE	HULL MTL	HULL TP	ENG TP	HP	MFG	BEAM FT IN	WGT LBS	DRAFT FT IN	RETAIL LOW	RETAIL HIGH
1991 BOATS													
32 6	MARINETTE	HT	EXP	AL	DV	IB	T220-T318		12	10000	2	38000	44800
32 6	MARINETTE	HT	SDN	AL	DV	IB	T220-T318		12	10000	2	36600	43800
32 6	MARINETTE FISHERMAN	HT	EXP	AL	DV	IB	T220-T318		12	10000	2	37800	44700
32 6	MARINETTE GRAN	HT	SF	AL	DV	IB	T220-T318		11	7100	2	30000	35800
34	MARINETTE	HT	CNV	AL	DV	IB	T235	CRUS	12 10	13500	2 8	48300	53100
37	MARINETTE	FB	DC	AL	DV	IB	T350	CRUS	13 8	16000	3	65400	71900
41	MARINETTE	FB	CNV	AL	DV	IB	T235	CRUS	14	17000	3	74900	82300
41	MARINETTE	FB	MY	AL	DV	IB	T235	CRUS	14	17000	3	78900	86700
41	MARINETTE 41	FB	CNV	AL	DV	IB	T350	CRUS	14	17000	3	79400	87300
41	MARINETTE 41	FB	MY	AL	DV	IB	T350	CRUS	14	18000	3	82300	90500
1990 BOATS													
32 6	MARINETTE	HT	EXP	AL	DV	IB	T220-T318		12	10000	2	36300	42900
32 6	MARINETTE	HT	SDN	AL	DV	IB	T220-T318		12	10000	2	34800	41600
32 6	MARINETTE FISHERMAN	HT	EXP	AL	DV	IB	T220-T318		12	10000	2	35800	42300
32 6	MARINETTE GRAN	HT	SF	AL	DV	IB	T220-T318		11	7100	2	28500	34000
34	MARINETTE	HT	CNV	AL	DV	IB	T240	CRUS	12 10	13500	2 8	46300	50900
37	MARINETTE	FB	DC	AL	DV	IB	T270	CRUS	13 8	16000	3	60600	66600
37	MARINETTE	FB	DC	AL	DV	IB	T350	CRUS	13 8	16000	3	62400	68600
41	MARINETTE	FB	CNV	AL	DV	IB	T270	CRUS	14	17000	3	76200	80500
41	MARINETTE	FB	CNV	AL	DV	IB	T350	CRUS	14	17000	3	77900	85600
41	MARINETTE	FB	MY	AL	DV	IB	T270	CRUS	14	18000	3	76700	84300
41	MARINETTE	FB	MY	AL	DV	IB	T350	CRUS	14	18000	3	80600	88600
1989 BOATS													
28	MARINETTE	HT	EXP	AL	DV	IB	240	CHRY	11	5800	2	16200	18400
28	MARINETTE	HT	EXP	AL	DV	IB	T220-T318		11	7000	2	19300	22900
28	MARINETTE	HT	EXP	AL	DV	IB	240	CHRY	11	7000	2	19100	23100
28	MARINETTE	HT	SDN	AL	DV	IB	T220-T318		11	7000	2	17100	19400
28	MARINETTE	HT	SDN	AL	DV	IB	240	CHRY	11	6200	2	20900	23300
28	MARINETTE	HT	SF	AL	DV	IB	T220-T318		11	6200	2	19100	22900
28	MARINETTE	FB	EXP	AL	DV	IB	T220-T318		11	7000	2	19100	22900
28	MARINETTE FISHERMAN	HT	EXP	AL	DV	IB	240	CHRY	11	5800	2	16200	18400
28	MARINETTE FISHERMAN	HT	EXP	AL	DV	IB	T220-T318		11	7000	2	20700	24600
28	MARINETTE FISHERMAN	FB	EXP	AL	DV	IB	T220-T318		11	7000	2	20800	24500
29 6	MARINETTE	HT	SDN	AL	DV	IB	240	CHRY	11	6000	2	20200	22400
32 6	MARINETTE	HT	EXP	AL	DV	IB	T220-T318		12	10000	2	33700	39900
32 6	MARINETTE	FB	EXP	AL	DV	IB	T220-T318		12	10000	2	33800	39900
32 6	MARINETTE	FB	SDN	AL	DV	IB	T220-T318		12	10000	2	33100	39600
32 6	MARINETTE	HT	SDN	AL	DV	IB	T220-T318		12	10000	2	33100	39600
32 6	MARINETTE FISHERMAN	FB	EXP	AL	DV	IB	T220-T318		12	10000	2	34900	41200
32 6	MARINETTE FISHERMAN	HT	SF	AL	DV	IB	T220-T318		12	10000	2	34800	41100
32 6	MARINETTE GRAN	FB	SF	AL	DV	IB	T220-T318		12	10000	2	28400	33500
32 6	MARINETTE GRAN	HT	SF	AL	DV	IB	T220-T318		12	10000	2	28400	33500
37	MARINETTE	FB	DC	AL	DV	IB	T270	CRUS	13 8	16000	3	57900	63600
37	MARINETTE	FB	DC	AL	DV	IB	T350	CRUS	13 8	16000	3	59600	65500
41	MARINETTE	FB	CNV	AL	DV	IB	T270	CRUS	14	17000	3	69900	76900
41	MARINETTE	FB	CNV	AL	DV	IB	T350	CRUS	14	17000	3	74400	81700
41	MARINETTE	FB	MY	AL	DV	IB	T350	CRUS	14	18000	3	73300	80500
41	MARINETTE 41	FB	MY	AL	DV	IB	T350	CRUS	14	18000	3	75100	82500
1988 BOATS													
28	MARINETTE	HT	EXP	AL	DV	IB	220-318		11	5800	2	14500	17400
28	MARINETTE	HT	EXP	AL	DV	IB	T220-318		11	7000	2	18400	21600
28	MARINETTE	HT	SDN	AL	DV	IB	220-318		11	5000	2	16100	19800
28	MARINETTE	HT	SDN	AL	DV	IB	T220-318		11	6200	2	20100	22500
28	MARINETTE FISHERMAN	HT	EXP	AL	DV	IB	220-318		11	5800	2	16100	19400
28	MARINETTE FISHERMAN	HT	EXP	AL	DV	IB	T220-T318		11	7000	2	19900	23700
29 6	MARINETTE	HT	SDN	AL	DV	IB	220-318		11	6000	2	19200	22700
29 6	MARINETTE	HT	SF	AL	DV	IB	T220-T318		11	7100	2	22900	25900
32 6	MARINETTE	HT	EXP	AL	DV	IB	T220-T318		11	10000	2	32000	37800
32 6	MARINETTE	HT	SDN	AL	DV	IB	T220-T318		11	10500	2	33500	42400
32 6	MARINETTE FISHERMAN	HT	SDN	AL	DV	IB	T220-T318		11	10000	2	33100	39100
37	MARINETTE	FB	DC	AL	DV	IB	T270	CRUS	13 8	16000	3	55400	60800
37	MARINETTE	FB	DC	AL	DV	IB	T350	CRUS	13 8	16000	3	57000	62600
41	MARINETTE	FB	MY	AL	DV	IB	T270	CRUS	14	17000	3	70000	77000
41	MARINETTE	FB	MY	AL	DV	IB	T350	CRUS	14	18000	3	73300	80900
1987 BOATS													
28	MARINETTE	HT	EXP	AL	DV	IB	220-318		11	5800	2	13800	16800
28	MARINETTE	HT	EXP	AL	DV	IB	T220-318		11	7000	2	17100	20800
28	MARINETTE	HT	SDN	AL	DV	IB	220-318		11	5800	2	13900	16800
28	MARINETTE	HT	SDN	AL	DV	IB	T220-318		11	7000	2	17200	21000
28	MARINETTE	HT	SF	AL	DV	IB	220-318		11	5000	2	13800	16700
28	MARINETTE	FB	SF	AL	DV	IB	T220-T318		11	6200	2	17200	21000
28	MARINETTE	HT	SF	AL	DV	IB	220-318		11	5000	2	13800	16700

ALUMINUM CRUISERS INC -CONTINUED See inside cover to adjust price for area

LOA FT	LOA IN	NAME AND/ OR MODEL	TOP/ RIG	BOAT TYPE	HULL MTL	HULL TP	ENGINE TP	ENGINE # HP	ENGINE MFG	BEAM FT	BEAM IN	WGT LBS	DRAFT FT	DRAFT IN	RETAIL LOW	RETAIL HIGH
		1987 BOATS														
28		MARINETTE	FB	SF	AL	DV	IB	T220-T318		11		6200	2		17200	21000
28		MARINETTE FISHERMAN	HT	EXP	AL	DV	IB	220-318		11		5800	2		15400	18300
28		MARINETTE FISHERMAN	HT	EXP	AL	DV	IB	T220-T318		11		7000	2		19000	22600
28		MARINETTE FISHERMAN	FB	EXP	AL	DV	IB	220-318		11		5800	2		15300	18200
28		MARINETTE FISHERMAN	FB	EXP	AL	DV	IB	T220-T318		11		7000	2		19100	22500
29	6	MARINETTE	HT	SDN	AL	DV	IB	220-318		11		6000	2		18300	21700
29	6	MARINETTE	HT	SDN	AL	DV	IB	T220-T318		11		7100	2		21800	24700
29	6	MARINETTE	FB	SDN	AL	DV	IB	220-318		11		6000	2		18300	21700
29	6	MARINETTE	FB	SDN	AL	DV	IB	T220-T318		11		7100	2		21800	24700
32	6	MARINETTE	HT	EXP	AL	DV	IB	T220-T318		12		10000	2		31200	36800
32	6	MARINETTE	FB	EXP	AL	DV	IB	T220-T318		12		10000	2		31200	36800
32	6	MARINETTE	HT	SDN	AL	DV	IB	T220-T318		12		10500	2		34000	40700
32	6	MARINETTE	FB	SDN	AL	DV	IB	T220-T318		12		10500	2		34000	40700
41		MARINETTE	FB	MY	AL	DV	IB	T270	CRUS	14		18000	3		67000	73600
41		MARINETTE	FB	MY	AL	DV	IB	T350	CHRY	14		18000	3		69500	76400
		1986 BOATS														
28		MARINETTE	HT	EXP	AL	SV	IB	225	CHRY	11		5800	2		13000	14800
28		MARINETTE	HT	EXP	AL	SV	IB	T225	CHRY	11		7000	2		16100	18300
28		MARINETTE	FB	EXP	AL	SV	IB	225	CHRY	11		5800	2		13100	14900
28		MARINETTE	FB	EXP	AL	SV	IB	T225	CHRY	11		7000	2		16200	18400
28		MARINETTE FISHERMAN	HT	EXP	AL	SV	IB	225	CHRY	11		5800	2		14800	16800
28		MARINETTE FISHERMAN	HT	EXP	AL	SV	IB	T225	CHRY	11		7000	2		18400	20400
28		MARINETTE FISHERMAN	FB	EXP	AL	SV	IB	225	CHRY	11		5800	2		14700	16700
28		MARINETTE FISHERMAN	FB	EXP	AL	SV	IB	T225	CHRY	11		7000	2		18300	20300
28		MARINETTE SPORTSMAN	HT	SF	AL	SV	IB	225	CHRY	11		5000	2		13100	14900
28		MARINETTE SPORTSMAN	HT	SF	AL	SV	IB	T225	CHRY	11		6200	2		16300	18500
28		MARINETTE SPORTSMAN	FB	SF	AL	SV	IB	225	CHRY	11		5000	2		13100	14900
28		MARINETTE SPORTSMAN	FB	SF	AL	SV	IB	T225	CHRY	11		6200	2		16300	18500
29	6	MARINETTE	HT	SDN	AL	SV	IB	225	CHRY	11		6000	2		17100	19400
29	6	MARINETTE	HT	SDN	AL	SV	IB	T225	CHRY	11		7100	2		20800	23100
29	6	MARINETTE	FB	SDN	AL	SV	IB	225	CHRY	11		6000	2		17100	19400
29	6	MARINETTE	FB	SDN	AL	SV	IB	T225	CHRY	11		7100	2		20800	23100
32	6	MARINETTE	HT	EXP	AL	SV	IB	T225	CHRY	12		10000	2		29100	32400
32	6	MARINETTE	FB	EXP	AL	SV	IB	T225	CHRY	12		10000	2		29200	32400
32	6	MARINETTE	HT	SDN	AL	SV	IB	T225	CHRY	12		10500	2		32600	36200
32	6	MARINETTE	FB	SDN	AL	SV	IB	T225	CHRY	12		10500	2		32600	36200
32	6	MARINETTE FISHERMAN	HT	EXP	AL	SV	IB	T225	CHRY	12		10000	2		30500	33900
32	6	MARINETTE FISHERMAN	FB	EXP	AL	SV	IB	T225	CHRY	12		10000	2		30500	33800
39		MARINETTE	FB	DC	AL	SV	IB	T350	CRUS	13	6	15000	2	6	54600	60000
39		MARINETTE	FB	SDN	AL	SV	IB	T350	CRUS	13	6	14000	2	6	52000	57200
		1985 BOATS														
28		MARINETTE	HT	EXP	AL	SV	IB	225-260		11		5800	2		13300	15100
28		MARINETTE	HT	EXP	AL	SV	IB	T225-T260		11		5800	2		15300	18200
28		MARINETTE	FB	EXP	AL	SV	IB	235-260		11		5800	2		13300	15400
28		MARINETTE	FD	EXP	AL	SV	IB	T235-T260		11		7000	2		16400	19000
28		MARINETTE	HT	SDN	AL	SV	IB	225		11		6000	2		14800	16800
28		MARINETTE	HT	SDN	AL	SV	IB	T225		11		6000	2		16900	19200
28		MARINETTE	HT	SF	AL	SV	IB	225		11		5000	2		12500	14300
28		MARINETTE	HT	SF	AL	SV	IB	T225		11		5000	2		14700	16700
28		MARINETTE FISHERMAN	FB	EXP	AL	SV	IB	225-260		11		5600	2		13100	15200
28		MARINETTE FISHERMAN	FB	EXP	AL	SV	IB	T225-T260		11		5600	2		15100	18800
28		MARINETTE SPORTSMAN	HT	SF	AL	SV	IB	235-260		11		5000	2		12600	14600
28		MARINETTE SPORTSMAN	HT	SF	AL	SV	IB	T235-T260		11		5000	2		14800	17200
28		MARINETTE SPORTSMAN	FB	SF	AL	SV	IB	235-260		11		5000	2		12600	14600
28		MARINETTE SPORTSMAN	FB	SF	AL	SV	IB	T235-T260		11		5000	2		14800	17200
29	6	MARINETTE	HT	SDN	AL	SV	IB	235-260		11		6200	2		16600	19200
29	6	MARINETTE	HT	SDN	AL	SV	IB	T235-T260		11		6200	2		19100	21200
29	6	MARINETTE	FB	SDN	AL	SV	IB	235-260		11		6200	2		16600	19200
29	6	MARINETTE	FB	SDN	AL	SV	IB	T235-T260		11		6000	2		19100	21200
32	6	MARINETTE	HT	EXP	AL	SV	IB	T225-T260		12		9000	2		28000	31900
32	6	MARINETTE	FB	EXP	AL	SV	IB	T235-T260		12		9000	2		28200	31900
32	6	MARINETTE	HT	SDN	AL	SV	IB	T225-T260		12		9500	2		27400	31300
32	6	MARINETTE	FB	SDN	AL	SV	IB	T235-T260		12		9500	2		27600	31300
32	6	MARINETTE FISHERMAN	FB	EXP	AL	SV	IB	T225-T260		12		8800	2		28000	31800
38	7	MARINETTE	HT	DCMY	AL	SV	IB	T350	CRUS	13	6	13000	2	6	46600	51200
38	7	MARINETTE	FB	DCMY	AL	SV	IB	T350	CRUS	13	6	13000	2	6	46600	51200
38	7	MARINETTE	HT	MY	AL	SV	IB	T350	CRUS	13	6	12000	2	6	43300	48200
38	7	MARINETTE	FB	MY	AL	SV	IB	T350	CRUS	13	6	12000	2	6	43300	48200
39		MARINETTE	FB	DC	AL	SV	IB	T330		13	6	13000	2	6	46300	50900
39		MARINETTE	FB	SDN	AL	SV	IB	T330		13	6	12000	2	6	43000	47800
		1984 BOATS														
28		MARINETTE	HT	EXP	AL	SV	IB	225-250		11		5800	2		12700	14600
28		MARINETTE	HT	EXP	AL	SV	IB	T225-T250		11		7000	2		15600	18000
28		MARINETTE	FB	EXP	AL	SV	IB	225-250		11		5800	2		12700	14600
28		MARINETTE	FB	EXP	AL	SV	IB	T225-T250		11		7000	2		15600	18000
28		MARINETTE	HT	SDN	AL	SV	IB	225-250		11		6000	2		14100	16400
28		MARINETTE	HT	SDN	AL	SV	IB	T225-T250		11		6000	2		16100	18400
28		MARINETTE	FB	SDN	AL	SV	IB	225-250		11		6000	2		14100	16400
28		MARINETTE	FB	SDN	AL	SV	IB	T225-T250		11		6000	2		16100	18400
28		MARINETTE FISHERMAN	FB	EXP	AL	SV	IB	225-250		11		5600	2		12500	14400
28		MARINETTE FISHERMAN	FB	EXP	AL	SV	IB	T225-T250		11		6800	2		15400	17800
28		MARINETTE SPORTSMAN	HT	SF	AL	SV	IB	225-250		11		5000	2		12000	13900
28		MARINETTE SPORTSMAN	HT	SF	AL	SV	IB	T225-T250		11		5000	2		14000	16300
28		MARINETTE SPORTSMAN	FB	SF	AL	SV	IB	225-250		11		5000	2		12000	13900
28		MARINETTE SPORTSMAN	FB	SF	AL	SV	IB	T225-T250		11		5000	2		14000	16300
32	6	MARINETTE	HT	EXP	AL	SV	IB	T225-T250		12		9000	2		26800	30300
32	6	MARINETTE	FB	EXP	AL	SV	IB	T225-T250		12		9000	2		26800	30300
32	6	MARINETTE	HT	SDN	AL	SV	IB	T225-T250		12		9500	2		26200	29700
32	6	MARINETTE	FB	SDN	AL	SV	IB	T225-T250		12		9500	2		26200	29700
32	6	MARINETTE FISHERMAN	FB	EXP	AL	SV	IB	T225-T250		12		8800	2		26700	30200
38	7	MARINETTE	HT	DCMY	AL	SV	IB	T330	CHRY	13	6	13000	2	6	43000	47800
38	7	MARINETTE	FB	DCMY	AL	SV	IB	T330	CHRY	13	6	13000	2	6	43000	47800
38	7	MARINETTE	HT	MY	AL	SV	IB	T330	CHRY	13	6	12000	2	6	40300	44800
38	7	MARINETTE	FB	MY	AL	SV	IB	T330	CHRY	13	6	12000	2	6	40300	44800

....For earlier years, see the BUC Used Boat Price Guide, Volume 3

CHANTIERS AMEL

17812 PERIGNY CEDEX FRANCE

See inside cover to adjust price for area

For more recent years, see the BUC Used Boat Price Guide, Volume 1

LOA FT	LOA IN	NAME AND/ OR MODEL	TOP/ RIG	BOAT TYPE	HULL MTL	HULL TP	ENGINE TP	ENGINE # HP	ENGINE MFG	BEAM FT	BEAM IN	WGT LBS	DRAFT FT	DRAFT IN	RETAIL LOW	RETAIL HIGH
		1996 BOATS														
46		SANTORIN	SLP	SACCC	FBG	WK	IB	50D	VLVO	13	4	20500	6	2	226500	249000
46		SANTORIN	KTH	SACCC	FBG	WK	IB	50D	VLVO	13	4	20500	6	2	226500	249000
53		SUPER MARAMU	KTH	SACCC	FBG	WK	IB	80D	VLVO	15	4	30860	6	7	374500	412000
		1993 BOATS														
45	9	SANTORIN	SLP	SACAC	FBG	KL	IB	D	PERK	13	1	22045	6	2	195500	214500
45	9	SANTORIN	KTH	SACAC	FBG	KL	IB	D	PERK	13	1	22045	6	2	195500	215000
52	5	SUPER MARAMU	KTH	SACAC	FBG	KL	IB	D	PERK	15	1	32000	6	7	309000	340000
		1992 BOATS														
45	9	SANTORIN	SLP	SA/CR	FBG	KL	IB	D	PERK	13	1	22045	6	2	185000	203500
45	9	SANTORIN	KTH	SA/CR	FBG	KL	IB	D	PERK	13	1	22045	6	2	185000	203500
52	5	SUPER MARAMU	KTH	SA/CR	FBG	KL	IB	D	PERK	15	1	32000	6	7	293000	322000
		1991 BOATS														
45	9	SANTORIN	SLP	SA/CR	FBG	KL	IB	D	PERK	13	1	22045	6	2	175500	192500
45	9	SANTORIN	KTH	SA/CR	FBG	KL	IB	D	PERK	13	1	22045	6	2	175500	192500
52	5	SUPER MARAMU	KTH	SA/CR	FBG	KL	IB	D	PERK	15	1	32000	6	7	277500	305000
		1990 BOATS														
32	8	FANGO	SLP	SA/CR	FBG	KL	IB	D	PERK	11	1	11022	5	2	55400	60800
45	9	SANTORIN	SLP	SA/CR	FBG	KL	IB	D	PERK	13	1	22045	6	2	166000	182500
45	9	SANTORIN	KTH	SA/CR	FBG	KL	IB	D	PERK	13	1	22045	6	2	166000	182500
52	5	SUPER MARAMU	KTH	SA/CR	FBG	KL	IB	D	PERK	15	1	32000	6	7	263000	289000
		1989 BOATS														
32	8	FANGO	SLP	SA/CR	FBG	KL	IB	D	PERK	11	1	11022	5	2	52400	57600
45	9	SANTORIN	SLP	SA/CR	FBG	KL	IB	D	PERK	13	1	22045	6	2	157500	173000
45	9	SANTORIN	KTH	SA/CR	FBG	KL	IB	D	PERK	13	1	22045	6	2	157500	173000
52	5	SUPER MARAMU	KTH	SA/CR	FBG	KL	IB	D	PERK	15	1	32000	6	7	249000	273500
		1988 BOATS														
32		FANGO	SLP	SA/CR	FBG	KL	IB	D	PERK	11	1	11022	5	2	49200	54000
39		SHARKI	KTH	SA/CR	FBG	KL	IB	D	PERK	11	8	21390	6	1	110500	121500
48		MARAMU	KTH	SA/CR	FBG	KL	IB	D	PERK	13	1	28440	6	6	182500	200500
53		MANGO	KTH	SA/CR	FBG	KL	IB	D	PERK	14	1	37480	6	7	251000	276000
		1987 BOATS														
32		FANGO	SLP	SA/CR	FBG	KL	IB	D	PERK	11	1	11022	5	2	46900	51500
39		SHARKI	KTH	SA/CR	FBG	KL	IB	D	PERK	11	8	21390	6	1	104500	115000
48		MARAMU	KTH	SA/CR	FBG	KL	IB	D	PERK	13	1	28440	6	6	173000	190000
53		MANGO	KTH	SA/CR	FBG	KL	IB	D	PERK	14	1	37480	6	7	238000	261500
		1986 BOATS														
41		SHARKI	KTH	SA/CR	FBG	KL	IB	D	PERK	11	6	21387	5	7	107500	118500
48		MARAMU	KTH	SA/CR	FBG	KL	IB	D	PERK	13	2	28440	6	3	164000	180000
53		MANGO	KTH	SA/CR	FBG	KL	IB	D	PERK	15	1	36403	6	6	224500	246500
		1985 BOATS														
41		SHARKI	KTH	SA/CR	FBG	KL	IB	D	PERK	11	6	21387	5	7	102000	112000
48		MARAMU	KTH	SA/CR	FBG	KL	IB	D	PERK	13	2	28440	6	3	155500	170500
53		MANGO	KTH	SA/CR	FBG	KL	IB	D	PERK	15	1	36403	6	6	212500	233500

LOA FT	LOA IN	NAME AND/ OR MODEL	TOP/ RIG	BOAT TYPE	HULL MTL	HULL TP	ENGINE TP	# HP	ENGINE MFG	BEAM FT	BEAM IN	WGT LBS	DRAFT FT	DRAFT IN	RETAIL LOW	RETAIL HIGH
		1984 BOATS														
41		SHARKI	KTH	SA/CR	FBG	KL	IB	50D	PERK	11	6	17060	5	7	83800	92100
48		MARAMU	KTH	SA/CR	FBG	KL	IB	60D	PERK	13	2	22297	6	3	134500	148000
52		MANGO	KTH	SA/CR	FBG	KL	IB	80D	PERK	15	1	30032	6	6	183000	201000

....For earlier years, see the BUC Used Boat Price Guide, Volume 3

AMERICA CRUISING YACHT CORP

CLEARWATER FL 33520 See inside cover to adjust price for area

LOA FT	LOA IN	NAME AND/ OR MODEL	TOP/ RIG	BOAT TYPE	HULL MTL	HULL TP	ENGINE TP	# HP	ENGINE MFG	BEAM FT	BEAM IN	WGT LBS	DRAFT FT	DRAFT IN	RETAIL LOW	RETAIL HIGH
		1992 BOATS														
30		AMERI CAT 3014	CAT	SA/CR	FBG	CT	OB			14	4	6300	2	10	36200	40200
40	1	AMERICA 38	SLP	SA/CR	FBG	KL	IB	44D	YAN	12	3	20000	4	6	84500	92900
45	6	AMERICA 43	SLP	SA/CR	FBG	KL	IB	62D	YAN	13	7	26000	4	11	115000	126500
57	2	AMERICA 54	SLP	SA/CR	FBG	KL	IB	110D	YAN	15	4	46000	5	6	235000	258500
61	3	AMERICA 61	SLP	SA/CR	FBG	KL	IB	130D	PERK	16	2	57500	6		371000	408000
73		AMERICA 68	SLP	SA/CR	FBG	KL	IB	165D	PERK	17	4	78500	6	1	**	**
		1991 BOATS														
40	2	IRWIN 38	SLP	SA/CR	FBG	KL	IB	50D	YAN	12	3	20000	4	6	79600	87500
45	6	IRWIN 43	SLP	SA/CR	FBG	KL	IB	62D	YAN	13	7	26000	4	11	108000	119000
50	9	IRWIN 50	SLP	SA/CR	FBG	KL	IB	75D	YAN	14	1	33500	6	6	167000	183500
50	9	IRWIN 50	SLP	SA/CR	FBG	WK	IB	75D	YAN	14	1	33500	5		167000	183500
57	2	IRWIN 54	SLP	SA/CR	FBG	CB	IB	88D	YAN	15	4	46000	12	6	220500	242500
57	2	IRWIN 54	SLP	SA/CR	FBG	KL	IB	88D	YAN	15	4	46000	5	6	220500	242500
58	4	IRWIN 54	KTH	SA/CR	FBG	CB	IB	88D	YAN	15	4	46000	12	6	220500	242500
58	4	IRWIN 54	KTH	SA/CR	FBG	KL	IB	88D	YAN	15	4	46000	5	6	220500	242500
61	3	IRWIN 61 DEEP	SLP	SA/CR	FBG	CB	IB	130D	PERK	16	2	57500	12	9	352000	387000
61	3	IRWIN 61 DEEP	SLP	SA/CR	FBG	KL	IB	130D	PERK	16	2	57500	6		346000	380000
61	3	IRWIN 61 SHOAL	SLP	SA/CR	FBG	CB	IB	130D	PERK	16	2	57500	6		352000	387000
61	3	IRWIN 61 SHOAL	SLP	SA/CR	FBG	KL	IB	130D	PERK	16	2	57500	6		346000	380000
73		IRWIN 68 MKII SHOAL	CUT	SA/CR	FBG	CB	IB	165D	PERK	17	4	78500	6	2	**	**
73		IRWIN 68 MKII SHOAL	CUT	SA/CR	FBG	KL	IB	165D	PERK	17	4	78500	6	1	**	**
73		IRWIN 68 MKII SHOAL	KTH	SA/CR	FBG	CB	IB	165D	PERK	17	4	78500	6	2	**	**
73		IRWIN 68 MKII SHOAL	KTH	SA/CR	FBG	KL	IB	165D	PERK	17	4	78500	6	1	**	**

AMERICAN INTL MARINE CORP

LANCASTER PA 17603 COAST GUARD MFG ID- AIM See inside cover to adjust price for area

LOA FT	LOA IN	NAME AND/ OR MODEL	TOP/ RIG	BOAT TYPE	HULL MTL	HULL TP	ENGINE TP	# HP	ENGINE MFG	BEAM FT	BEAM IN	WGT LBS	DRAFT FT	DRAFT IN	RETAIL LOW	RETAIL HIGH
		1986 BOATS														
20	4	C-20 204		FSH	FBG	SV	OB			7	6	1925			6600	7550
22		C-22 224		FSH	FBG	SV	OB			8		2200			7000	8050
22		CF-22 225		FSH	FBG	SV	OB			8		2200			7950	9150
22		CX 226 FISH		CUD	FBG	SV	IO	190		8					9050	10300
22		CX-22 225		FSH	FBG	SV	OB			8		2200			8900	10100
26		C-26 264		FSH	FBG	SV	OB			8		3475			12900	14600
26		CF-26 265		FSH	FBG	SV	OB			8		3475			14300	16200
26		SX 267		CUD	FBG	SV	IO	260		8					14100	16100
26		SX-26 267		FSH	FBG	SV	OB			8		3475			17100	19500
		1985 BOATS														
20	4	C-20 204	OP	CTRCN	FBG	SV	OB			7	6	1925		10	6450	7400
22		C-22 224	OP	CTRCN	FBG	SV	OB			8		2200		10	7750	8900
22		C-22 224	OP	CTRCN	FBG	SV	SE	205	OMC	8		3160		10	9950	11300
22		C-22 224	OP	CTRCN	FBG	SV	SE	T115	OMC	8		3160		10	9950	11300
22		CF-22 225	OP	CUD	FBG	SV	OB			8		2500		10	8500	9800
22		CF-22 225	OP	CUD	FBG	SV	SE	205	OMC	8		3360		10	10300	11700
22		CF-22 225	OP	CUD	FBG	SV	SE	T115	OMC	8		3360		10	10300	11700
22		CX-22 226	OP	EXP	FBG	SV	OB			8		2500		10	8500	9800
26		C-26 264	OP	CTRCN	FBG	SV	OB			8		3475	2		14400	16400
26		C-26 264	OP	CTRCN	FBG	SV	SE	205	OMC	8		4375	2	8	15300	17400
26		C-26 264	OP	CTRCN	FBG	SV	SE	T115-T205		8		4875	2	8	15800	17900
26		CF-26 265	OP	CUD	FBG	SV	OB			8		3625	2		14600	16600
26		CF-26 265	OP	CUD	FBG	SV	SE	205	OMC			4525	2	8	15500	17600
26		CF-26 265	OP	CUD	FBG	SV	SE	T115-T205				5025	2	8	15900	18100
26		SX-26 267	OP	EXP	FBG	SV	OB			8		4525	2		15500	17600

AMERICAN MULTIHULLS INC

PALATKA FL 32178 COAST GUARD MFG ID- MLP See inside cover to adjust price for area

LOA FT	LOA IN	NAME AND/ OR MODEL	TOP/ RIG	BOAT TYPE	HULL MTL	HULL TP	ENGINE TP	# HP	ENGINE MFG	BEAM FT	BEAM IN	WGT LBS	DRAFT FT	DRAFT IN	RETAIL LOW	RETAIL HIGH
		1995 BOATS														
32		RENAISSANCE 320DL	SLP	SACAC	FBG	CT	IB	T 12D	WEST	16	3	6300	2	10	71800	78900
32		RENAISSANCE 320GL	SLP	SACAC	FBG	CT	IB	T 12D	WEST	16	3	6300	2	10	77800	85500
32		RENAISSANCE 320XL	SLP	SACAC	FBG	CT	IB	T 18D		16	3	6300	2	10	74800	82200
		1994 BOATS														
32		RENAISSANCE 320DL	SLP	SACAC	FBG	CT	IB	T 12D	WEST	16	3	6300	2	10	67100	73800
32		RENAISSANCE 320GL	SLP	SACAC	FBG	CT	IB	T 12D	WEST	16	3	6300	2	10	72700	79900
32		RENAISSANCE 320XL	SLP	SACAC	FBG	CT	IB	T 18D		16	3	6300	2	10	69900	76900

AMERICAN POWERBOATS INC

SEAHAWK BOATS
MIAMI FL 33131 COAST GUARD MFG ID- SBQ See inside cover to adjust price for area

LOA FT	LOA IN	NAME AND/ OR MODEL	TOP/ RIG	BOAT TYPE	HULL MTL	HULL TP	ENGINE TP	# HP	ENGINE MFG	BEAM FT	BEAM IN	WGT LBS	DRAFT FT	DRAFT IN	RETAIL LOW	RETAIL HIGH
		1985 BOATS														
26		SEAHAWK 26	OP	RACE	FBG	DV	IO	260-330		7					6500	8050
26		SEAHAWK 26	OP	RACE	FBG	DV	IO	400	MRCR	7					7750	8950
27	9	SEAHAWK 28	OP	RACE	FBG	DV	IO	T225		8					9550	10800
27	9	SEAHAWK 28	OP	RACE	FBG	DV	IO	T330-T370		8					10700	12900
27	9	SEAHAWK 28	OP	RACE	FBG	DV	IO	T400	MRCR	8					11900	13600
30	9	SEAHAWK 31	OP	RACE	FBG	DV	IO	T330-T400		8					12400	14900
30	9	SEAHAWK 31	OP	RACE	FBG	DV	IO	T440	MRCR	8					13600	15500

AMERICAN RIVER MFG COMPANY

RANCHO CORDOVA CA 95742 COAST GUARD MFG ID- ARU See inside cover to adjust price for area

For more recent years, see the BUC Used Boat Price Guide, Volume 1

LOA FT	LOA IN	NAME AND/ OR MODEL	TOP/ RIG	BOAT TYPE	HULL MTL	HULL TP	ENGINE TP	# HP	ENGINE MFG	BEAM FT	BEAM IN	WGT LBS	DRAFT FT	DRAFT IN	RETAIL LOW	RETAIL HIGH
		1996 BOATS														
36		CUSTOM HOUSEBOAT	HT	HB	STL	PN	IO	130	OMC	12		16236	1	5	32900	36500
36		SL3612	HT	HB	STL	PN	IO	130	OMC	12		18844	1	5	35600	39500
40		RENTAL HOUSEBOAT	HT	HB	STL	PN	IO	130	OMC	12		18291	1	5	33400	37100
40		SL4014	HT	HB	STL	PN	IO	130	OMC	14		23249	1	5	37900	42100
41		PRINCESS	HT	HB	STL	PN	IO	130	OMC	12		18804	1	5	33500	37200
43	9	BON VOYAGE 43	HT	TRWL	STL	PN	IO	T175	OMC	14		26000	1		102000	112000
44		SL4414	HT	HB	STL	PN	IO	130	OMC	14		26066	1	5	38500	42800
46		CUSTOM HOUSEBOAT	HT	HB	STL	PN	IO	130	OMC	14		23318	1	5	37100	41200
47		ESTRALLA	HT	HB	STL	PN	IO	130	OMC	14		23892	1	5	38300	42600
47		SL4714	HT	HB	STL	PN	IO	130	OMC	14		28178	1	5	40800	45400
47		SL4715	HT	HB	STL	PN	IO	130	OMC	15		29368	1	5	41700	46300
47	9	BON VOYAGE 47	HT	TRWL	STL	PN	IO	T175	OMC	14		26214	1		93200	102500
48		CUSTOM HOUSEBOAT	HT	HB	STL	PN	IO	130	OMC	14		24446	1	5	39300	43600
50		DELTA	HT	HB	STL	PN	IO	130	OMC	14		26529	1	5	41900	46500
50		SL5014	HT	HB	STL	PN	IO	130	OMC	14		31589	1	5	44500	49500
50		SL5015	HT	HB	STL	PN	IO	130	OMC	15		31589	1	5	44500	49500
52		CUSTOM HOUSEBOAT	HT	HB	STL	PN	IO	130	OMC	14		37729	1	5	55700	61200
54		CUSTOM HOUSEBOAT	HT	HB	STL	PN	IO	130	OMC	14		28929	1	5	52900	58100
54		SL5414	HT	HB	STL	PN	IO	130	OMC	14		34550	1	5	55600	61100
54		SL5415	HT	HB	STL	PN	IO	130	OMC	15		34550	1	5	55600	61100
55		RIVER QUEEN	HT	HB	STL	PN	IO	130	OMC	14		33695	1	5	55800	61300
57		CUSTOM HOUSEBOAT	HT	HB	STL	PN	IO	130	OMC	14		35099	1	5	57500	63200
58		SL5814	HT	HB	STL	PN	IO	130	OMC	14		37511	1	5	59100	64900
58		SL5815	HT	HB	STL	PN	IO	130	OMC	15		37511	1	5	59100	64900
62		CUSTOM HOUSEBOAT	HT	HB	STL	PN	IO	130	OMC	16		42063	1	5	59000	64900
64		SL6414	HT	HB	STL	PN	IO	130	OMC	14		42427	1	5	60100	66000
64		SL6415	HT	HB	STL	PN	IO	130	OMC	15		42768	1	5	60200	66100
66		CUSTOM HOUSEBOAT	HT	HB	STL	PN	IO	130	OMC	16		45159	1	5	61800	68000
		1995 BOATS														
32		ROVER	HT	HB	AL	PN	IO	130	OMC	8		6100	1	3	22800	25300
32		ROVER	HT	HB	STL	PN	IO	130	OMC	8		6100	1	3	21500	23900
34		WANDERER	HT	HB	AL	PN	IO	130	OMC	8		7018	1	3	25900	28800
34		WANDERER	HT	HB	STL	PN	IO	130	OMC	8		7018	1	3	24000	26600
36		CUSTOM HOUSEBOAT	HT	HB	AL	PN	IO	130	OMC	12		16236	1	5	35100	39000
36		CUSTOM HOUSEBOAT	HT	HB	STL	PN	IO	130	OMC	12		16236	1	5	30700	34100
36		SL3612	HT	HB	AL	PN	IO	130	OMC	12		18844	1	5	38000	42300
36		SL3612	HT	HB	STL	PN	IO	130	OMC	12		18844	1	5	33200	36900
40		RENTAL HOUSEBOAT	HT	HB	AL	PN	IO	130	OMC	12		18291	1	5	35300	39200
40		RENTAL HOUSEBOAT	HT	HB	STL	PN	IO	130	OMC	12		18291	1	5	31100	34600
40		SL4014	HT	HB	AL	PN	IO	130	OMC	14		23249	1	5	39900	44300
40		SL4014	HT	HB	STL	PN	IO	130	OMC	14		23249	1	5	35200	39100

LOA FT	LOA IN	NAME AND/ OR MODEL	TOP/ RIG	BOAT TYPE	-HULL- MTL	-HULL- TP	ENGINE TP	ENGINE # HP	ENGINE MFG	BEAM FT	BEAM IN	WGT LBS	DRAFT FT	DRAFT IN	RETAIL LOW	RETAIL HIGH
		1995 BOATS														
41		PRINCESS	HT	HB	AL	PN	IO	130	OMC	12		18804	1	5	35200	39100
41		PRINCESS	HT	HB	STL	PN	IO	130	OMC	12		18804	1	5	31200	34700
43	9	BON VOYAGE 43	HT	TRWL	AL	PN	IO	175	OMC	14		26000	1		91300	100500
43	9	BON VOYAGE 43	HT	TRWL	STL	PN	IO	T175	OMC	14		26000	1		94900	104500
44		SL4414	HT	HB	AL	PN	IO	130	OMC	14		26066	1	5	39900	44300
44		SL4414	HT	HB	STL	PN	IO	130	OMC	14		26066	1	5	35800	39800
46		CABO SAN LUCUS	HT	COMM	AL	SV	IO	T140		11	6	67000	5	6	**	**
46		CUSTOM HOUSEBOAT	HT	HB	AL	PN	IO	130	OMC	14		23318	1	5	38000	42200
46		CUSTOM HOUSEBOAT	HT	HB	STL	PN	IO	130	OMC	14		23318	1	5	34700	38500
47		ESTRALLAR	HT	HB	AL	PN	IO	130	OMC	14		23892	1	5	39000	43400
47		ESTRALLAR	HT	HB	STL	PN	IO	130	OMC	14		23892	1	5	35600	39600
47		SL4714	HT	HB	AL	PN	IO	130	OMC	14		28178	1	5	41800	46400
47		SL4714	HT	HB	STL	PN	IO	130	OMC	14		28178	1	5	38200	42500
47		SL4715	HT	HB	AL	PN	IO	130	OMC	14		29368	1	5	42500	47200
47		SL4715	HT	HB	STL	PN	IO	130	OMC	15		29368	1	5	38800	43200
47	9	BON VOYAGE 47	HT	TRWL	AL	PN	IO	T175	OMC	14		26214	1	5	87000	95600
47	9	BON VOYAGE 47	HT	TRWL	STL	PN	IO	T175	OMC	14		26214	1		87000	95600
48		CUSTOM HOUSEBOAT	HT	HB	AL	PN	IO	130	OMC	14		24446	1	5	40000	44400
48		CUSTOM HOUSEBOAT	HT	HB	STL	PN	IO	130	OMC	14		24446	1	5	36600	40600
50		DELTA	HT	HB	AL	PN	IO	130	OMC	14		26529	1	5	42600	47400
50		DELTA	HT	HB	STL	PN	IO	130	OMC	14		26529	1	5	39000	43300
50		SL5014	HT	HB	AL	PN	IO	130	OMC	14		31589	1	5	43700	48500
50		SL5014	HT	HB	STL	PN	IO	130	OMC	14		31589	1	5	41400	46000
50		SL5015	HT	HB	AL	PN	IO	130	OMC	14		31589	1	5	47800	52500
50		SL5015	HT	HB	STL	PN	IO	130	OMC	15		31589	1	5	41400	46000
52		CUSTOM HOUSEBOAT	HT	HB	AL	PN	IO	130	OMC	14		37729	1	5	54600	60000
52		CUSTOM HOUSEBOAT	HT	HB	STL	PN	IO	130	OMC	14		37729	1	5	52600	57800
54		CUSTOM HOUSEBOAT	HT	HB	AL	PN	IO	130	OMC	14		28929	1	5	51600	56700
54		CUSTOM HOUSEBOAT	HT	HB	STL	PN	IO	130	OMC	14		28929	1	5	49600	54500
54		SL5414	HT	HB	AL	PN	IO	130	OMC	14		34550	1	5	52400	57600
54		SL5414	HT	HB	STL	PN	IO	130	OMC	14		34550	1	5	52500	57700
54		SL5415	HT	HB	AL	PN	IO	130	OMC	14		34550	1	5	56600	62200
54		SL5415	HT	HB	STL	PN	IO	130	OMC	15		34550	1	5	52500	57700
55		RIVER QUEEN	HT	HB	AL	PN	IO	130	OMC	14		33695	1	5	54700	60100
55		RIVER QUEEN	HT	HB	STL	PN	IO	130	OMC	14		33695	1	5	52700	57900
57		CUSTOM HOUSEBOAT	HT	HB	AL	PN	IO	130	OMC	14		35099	1	5	56500	62100
57		CUSTOM HOUSEBOAT	HT	HB	STL	PN	IO	130	OMC	14		35099	1	5	54100	59500
57	9	BALI	HT	COMM	AL	SV	IO	T120		13	6	50T	5	6	**	**
57	9	COSUMEL	HT	COMM	AL	SV	IO	T120		13	6	50T	5	6	**	**
57	9	HONOLULU	HT	COMM	AL	SV	IO	T205		13	6	50T	5	6	**	**
57	9	KONA	HT	COMM	AL	SV	IO	T120		13	6	50T	5	6	**	**
57	9	LAKEINA	HT	COMM	AL	SV	IO	T120		13	6	50T	5	6	**	**
57	9	MONTEREY	HT	COMM	AL	SV	IO	T206		13	6	50T	5	6	**	**
58		SL5814	HT	HB	AL	PN	IO	130	OMC	14		37511	1	5	55400	60900
58		SL5814	HT	HB	STL	PN	IO	130	OMC	14		37511	1	5	55600	61100
58		SL5815	HT	HB	AL	PN	IO	130	OMC	14		37511	1	5	60700	66700
58		SL5815	HT	HB	STL	PN	IO	130	OMC	15		37511	1	5	55600	61100
62		CATALINA	HT	COMM	AL	SV	IB	T120D		13	6	53T	5	6	**	**
62		CUSTOM HOUSEBOAT	HT	HB	AL	PN	IO	130	OMC	14		42063	1	5	59900	65800
62		CUSTOM HOUSEBOAT	HT	HB	STL	PN	IO	130	OMC	16		42063	1	5	55000	60400
62		GUAM	HT	COMM	AL	SV	IB	T120D		13	6	53T	5	6	**	**
64		SL6414	HT	HB	AL	PN	IO	130	OMC	14		42427	1	5	61000	67100
64		SL6414	HT	HB	STL	PN	IO	130	OMC	14		42427	1	5	56000	61500
64		SL6415	HT	HB	AL	PN	IO	130	OMC	14		47268	1	5	62400	68600
64		SL6415	HT	HB	STL	PN	IO	130	OMC	15		42768	1	5	56100	61600
66		CUSTOM HOUSEBOAT	HT	HB	AL	PN	IO	130	OMC	16		45159	1	5	62800	69000
66		CUSTOM HOUSEBOAT	HT	HB	STL	PN	IO	130	OMC	16		45159	1	5	57600	63300
		1994 BOATS														
32		ROVER	HT	HB	STL	PN	IO	130	OMC	8		6100	1	3	20400	22600
34		WANDERER	HT	HB	STL	PN	IO	130	OMC	8		7018	1	3	22700	25200
36		CUSTOM HOUSEBOAT	HT	HB	STL	PN	IO	130	OMC	12		16236	1	5	28800	32000
36		SL3612	HT	HB	STL	PN	IO	130	OMC	12		18844	1	5	31200	34600
40		RENTAL HOUSEBOAT	HT	HB	STL	PN	IO	130	OMC	12		18291	1	5	29200	32500
40		SL4014	HT	HB	STL	PN	IO	130	OMC	14		23249	1	5	33000	36700
41		PRINCESS	HT	HB	STL	PN	IO	130	OMC	12		18804	1	5	29300	32600
43	9	BON VOYAGE 43	HT	TRWL	STL	PN	IO	T175	OMC	14		26000	1		88600	97300
44		SL4414	HT	HB	STL	PN	IO	130	OMC	14		26066	1	5	33700	37400
46		CUSTOM HOUSEBOAT	HT	HB	STL	PN	IO	130	OMC	14		23318	1	5	32600	36300
47		BON VOYAGE 47	HT	TRWL	STL	PN	IO	T175	OMC	14		26214	1		83300	91500
47		ESTRALLAR	HT	HB	STL	PN	IO	130	OMC	14		23892	1	5	33500	37300
47		SL4714	HT	HB	STL	PN	IO	130	OMC	14		28178	1	5	35800	39800
47		SL4715	HT	HB	STL	PN	IO	130	OMC	15		29368	1	5	36400	40400
48		CUSTOM HOUSEBOAT	HT	HB	STL	PN	IO	130	OMC	14		24446	1	5	34400	38200
50		DELTA	HT	HB	STL	PN	IO	130	OMC	14		26529	1	5	36600	40600
50		SL5014	HT	HB	STL	PN	IO	130	OMC	14		31589	1	5	39000	43300
50		SL5015	HT	HB	STL	PN	IO	130	OMC	15		31589	1	5	39000	43300
52		CUSTOM HOUSEBOAT	HT	HB	STL	PN	IO	130	OMC	14		37729	1	5	49700	54600
54		CUSTOM HOUSEBOAT	HT	HB	STL	PN	IO	130	OMC	14		28929	1	5	47200	51800
54		SL5414	HT	HB	STL	PN	IO	130	OMC	14		34550	1	5	49600	54500
54		SL5415	HT	HB	STL	PN	IO	130	OMC	15		34550	1	5	49600	54500
55		RIVER QUEEN	HT	HB	STL	PN	IO	130	OMC	14		33695	1	5	49800	54700
57		CUSTOM HOUSEBOAT	HT	HB	STL	PN	IO	130	OMC	14		35099	1	5	51400	56500
58		SL5814	HT	HB	STL	PN	IO	130	OMC	14		37511	1	5	52900	58100
58		SL5815	HT	HB	STL	PN	IO	130	OMC	15		37511	1	5	52900	58100
62		CUSTOM HOUSEBOAT	HT	HB	STL	PN	IO	130	OMC	16		42063	1	5	51900	57000
64		SL6414	HT	HB	STL	PN	IO	130	OMC	14		42427	1	5	52800	58100
64		SL6415	HT	HB	STL	PN	IO	130	OMC	15		41952	1	5	52700	57900
66		CUSTOM HOUSEBOAT	HT	HB	STL	PN	IO	130	OMC	16		45159	1	5	53900	59300
		1993 BOATS														
32		ROWER	HT	HB	STL	PN	IO	130	OMC	8		6100	1	3	19600	21800
34		WANDERER	HT	HB	STL	PN	IO	130	OMC	8		7018	1	3	21800	24200
36		CUSTOM HOUSEBOAT	HT	HB	STL	PN	IO	130	OMC	12		17280	1	5	28200	31300
40		RENTAL HOUSEBOAT	HT	HB	STL	PN	IO	130	OMC	12		19200	1	5	28300	31500
41		PRINCESS	HT	HB	STL	PN	IO	130	OMC	12		19680	1	5	28400	31500
46		CUSTOM HOUSEBOAT	HT	HB	STL	PN	IO	130	OMC	14		25760	1	5	32200	35800
47		BON VOYAGE	HT	HB	AL	PN	IO	T175	OMC	14		28000	1		38900	43200
47		ESTRALLER	HT	HB	STL	PN	IO	130	OMC	14		26320	1	5	33000	36700
48		CUSTOM HOUSEBOAT	HT	HB	STL	PN	IO	130	OMC	14		26880	1	5	33800	37600
50		DITTA	HT	HB	STL	PN	IO	130	OMC	14		28000	1	5	35300	39200
52		CUSTOM HOUSEBOAT	HT	HB	STL	PN	IO	130	OMC	14		29120	1	5	43400	48200
54		CUSTOM HOUSEBOAT	HT	HB	STL	PN	IO	130	OMC	14		30240	1	5	45500	50000
55		RIVER QUEEN	HT	HB	STL	PN	IO	130	OMC	14		30800	1	5	46300	50800
57		CUSTOM HOUSEBOAT	HT	HB	STL	PN	IO	130	OMC	14		31920	1	5	47800	52500
62		CUSTOM HOUSEBOAT	HT	HB	STL	PN	IO	130	OMC	16		35504	1	5	47200	51800
66		CUSTOM HOUSEBOAT	HT	HB	STL	PN	IO	130	OMC	16		37872	1	5	49600	54500
		1991 BOATS														
32		ROVER	HT	HB	STL	PN	OB			8		5800	1	3	14100	16000
34		WANDERER	HT	HB	STL	PN	IO	130		8		6000	1	3	30700	34800
36		CUSTOM HOUSEBOAT	HT	HB	STL	PN	IO	130	OMC	12		23028	1	5	21900	24400
36		CUSTOM HOUSEBOAT	HT	HB	STL	PN	IO	130	VLVO	12		23028	1	5	22300	24800
36		PRINCESS	HT	HB	STL	PN	IO	130	OMC	12		14000	1	5	22900	25400
36		PRINCESS	HT	HB	STL	PN	IO	130	VLVO	12		14000	1	5	23100	25700
40		RENTAL HOUSEBOAT	HT	HB	STL	PN	IO	130	OMC	12		24846	1	5	22600	25100
40		RENTAL HOUSEBOAT	HT	HB	STL	PN	IO	130	VLVO	12		24846	1	5	22900	25500
41		CUSTOM DESIGN	HT	HB	STL	PN	IO	130	OMC	14		20700	1	4	26400	29400
41		CUSTOM DESIGN	HT	HB	STL	PN	IO	130	VLVO	14		20700	1	4	26800	29800
45		DELTA	HT	HB	STL	PN	IO	130	OMC	14		21000	1	5	26500	29400
45		DELTA	HT	HB	STL	PN	IO	130	VLVO	14		21000	1	5	26900	29800
46		CUSTOM HOUSEBOAT	HT	HB	STL	PN	IO	130	OMC	14		27270	1	5	30100	33400
46		CUSTOM HOUSEBOAT	HT	HB	STL	PN	IO	130	VLVO	14		27270	1	5	30400	33800
47		CUSTOM DESIGN	HT	HB	STL	PN	IO	130	OMC	14		23700	1	4	28800	32000
47		CUSTOM DESIGN	HT	HB	STL	PN	IO	130	VLVO	14		23700	1	4	29200	32400
49		CUSTOM DESIGN	HT	HB	STL	PN	IO	130	OMC	14		24800	1	4	30300	33600
49		CUSTOM DESIGN	HT	HB	STL	PN	IO	130	VLVO	14		24800	1	4	30600	34100
50		RIVER QUEEN	HT	HB	STL	PN	IO	130	OMC	14		25000	1	5	30800	34200
50		RIVER QUEEN	HT	HB	STL	PN	IO	130	VLVO	14		25000	1	5	31200	34600
52		CUSTOM DESIGN	HT	HB	STL	PN	IO	130	OMC	14		29000	1	4	39700	44100
52		CUSTOM DESIGN	HT	HB	STL	PN	IO	130	VLVO	14		29000	1	4	40200	44600
54		CUSTOM HOUSEBOAT	HT	HB	STL	PN	IO	130	OMC	14		32118	1	5	42100	46700
54		CUSTOM HOUSEBOAT	HT	HB	STL	PN	IO	130	VLVO	14		32118	1	5	42500	47200
62		CUSTOM HOUSEBOAT	HT	HB	STL	PN	IO	130	OMC	16		38178	1	5	42900	47700
62		CUSTOM HOUSEBOAT	HT	HB	STL	PN	IO	130	VLVO	16		38178	1	5	43300	48100
66		CUSTOM HOUSEBOAT	HT	HB	STL	PN	IO	130	OMC	16		40602	1	5	45000	50000
66		CUSTOM HOUSEBOAT	HT	HB	STL	PN	IO	130	VLVO	16		40602	1	5	45900	50400
		1990 BOATS														
32		ROVER	HT	HB	STL	PN	OB			8		5800	1	3	13600	15400
34		WANDERER	HT	HB	STL	PN	IO	120	OMC	8		6000	1	3	29600	32900
36		CUSTOM HOUSEBOAT	HT	HB	STL	PN	IO	130	OMC	12		23028	1	5	21400	23800
36		PRINCESS	HT	HB	STL	PN	IO	135	OMC	12		14000	1	5	22000	24400
40		RENTAL HOUSEBOAT	HT	HB	STL	PN	IO	130	OMC	12		24846	1	5	21700	24100
41		CUSTOM DESIGN	HT	HB	STL	PN	IO	135	OMC	14		20700	1	4	25400	28200
45		DELTA	HT	HB	STL	PN	IO	135	OMC	14		21000	1	5	25500	28300
46		CUSTOM HOUSEBOAT	HT	HB	STL	PN	IO	130	OMC	14		27270	1	5	28900	32100
47		CUSTOM DESIGN	HT	HB	STL	PN	IO	140	OMC	14		23700	1	4	27700	30800
49		CUSTOM DESIGN	HT	HB	STL	PN	IO	140	OMC	14		24800	1	4	29100	32400
50		RIVER QUEEN	HT	HB	STL	PN	IO	135	OMC	14		25000	1	5	29600	32900
52		CUSTOM DESIGN	HT	HB	STL	PN	IO	140	OMC	14		29000	1	4	38300	42500

 CONTINUED ON NEXT PAGE

LOA FT	LOA IN	NAME AND/ OR MODEL	TOP/ RIG	BOAT TYPE	HULL MTL	HULL TP	ENGINE TP	ENGINE # HP	ENGINE MFG	BEAM FT	BEAM IN	WGT LBS	DRAFT FT	DRAFT IN	RETAIL LOW	RETAIL HIGH
		1990 BOATS														
54		CUSTOM HOUSEBOAT	HT	HB	STL	PN	IO	130	OMC	14		32118	1	5	40500	45000
62		CUSTOM HOUSEBOAT	HT	HB	STL	PN	IO	130	OMC	16		38178	1	5	41200	45700
66		CUSTOM HOUSEBOAT	HT	HB	STL	PN	IO	130	OMC	16		40602	1	5	43200	48000
		1989 BOATS														
32		ROVER	HT	HB	STL	PN	OB			8		5800	1	3	13100	14900
34		WANDERER	HT	HB	STL	PN	IO	120	OMC	8		6000	1	3	28600	31800
36		PRINCESS	HT	HB	STL	PN	IO	135	OMC	12		14000	1	5	21500	23900
41		CUSTOM DESIGN	HT	HB	STL	PN	IO	135	OMC	14		20700	1	4	24500	27200
45		DELTA	HT	HB	STL	PN	IO	135	OMC	14		21000	1	5	24600	27300
47		CUSTOM DESIGN	HT	HB	STL	PN	IO	140	OMC	14		23700	1	4	26800	29700
49		CUSTOM DESIGN	HT	HB	STL	PN	IO	140	OMC	14		24800	1	4	28100	31200
50		RIVER QUEEN	HT	HB	STL	PN	IO	135	OMC	14		25000	1	5	28600	31800
52		CUSTOM DESIGN	HT	HB	STL	PN	IO	140	OMC	14		29000	1	4	37000	41100
		1988 BOATS														
32		ROVER	HT	HB	STL	PN	OB			8		5800	1	3	12700	14400
34		WANDERER	HT	HB	STL	PN	IO	120	OMC	8		6000	1	3	27700	30800
36		PRINCESS	HT	HB	STL	PN	IO	135	OMC	12		14000	1	5	20800	23100
45		DELTA	HT	HB	STL	PN	IO	135	OMC	14		21000	1	5	23800	26400
50		RIVER QUEEN	HT	HB	STL	PN	IO	135	OMC	14		25000	1	5	27700	30800
		1987 BOATS														
32		ROVER	HT	HB	STL	PN	OB			7	11	5600	1	3	11800	13400
36		ROVER-MATE	HT	HB	STL	PN	IO	120		12		5800	1	5	10500	11900
50		RIVER QUEEN	HT	HB	STL	PN	IO	140		14		19600	1	5	24200	26900
		1986 BOATS														
32		AMERICAN ROVER	HT	HB	STL	PN	OB			7	11	5600	1	3	11600	13200
32		EXPANDO	HT	HB	STL	PN	IO	120		12		5800	1	5	14400	16300
50		GALAXY	HT	HB	STL	PN	IO	140		14		19600	1	5	23600	26200
		1985 BOATS														
32		AMERICAN ROVER	HT	HB	STL	PN	OB			7	11	5600	1	3	11300	12800
32		EXPANDO	HT	HB	STL	PN	IO	120	OMC	12		5800	1	2	14000	15900
50		GALAXY	HT	HB	STL	PN	IO	140	OMC	14		19600	1	4	23000	25500
		1984 BOATS														
32		AMERICAN ROVER	HT	HB	STL	PN	OB			7	11	5600	1	3	11100	12600
32		EXPANDO	HT	HB	STL	PN	IO	120	OMC	12		5800	1	2	13700	15500
50		GALAXY	HT	HB	STL	PN	IO	140	OMC	14		19600	1	4	22700	25200

....For earlier years, see the BUC Used Boat Price Guide, Volume 3

AMERICAN SKIER

AMERICAN SKIER BOAT CORP
KENTWOOD LA 70444 COAST GUARD MFG ID- SKI

See inside cover to adjust price for area

LOA FT	LOA IN	NAME AND/ OR MODEL	TOP/ RIG	BOAT TYPE	HULL MTL	HULL TP	ENGINE TP	ENGINE # HP	ENGINE MFG	BEAM FT	BEAM IN	WGT LBS	DRAFT FT	DRAFT IN	RETAIL LOW	RETAIL HIGH
		1995 BOATS														
19		ADVANCE SS	OP	SKI	F/S	SV	IB	250	MRCR	7		2250	1	7	7300	8400
19		ADVANCE TOURNAMENT	OP	SKI	F/S	SV	IB	250	MRCR	7		2250	1	7	8050	9250
19		LEGEND TOURNAMENT	OP	SKI	F/S	SV	IB	250	MRCR	7	3	2350	1	7	8000	9200
19	9	TBX TOURNAMENT	OP	SKI	F/S	SV	IB	250	MRCR	7	7	2600	1	7	9200	10400
20	4	VOLANTE LTD	OP	SKI	F/S	SV	IB	250	MRCR	7	6	2700	1	9	9700	11000
20	4	VOLANTE TOURNAMENT	OP	SKI	F/S	SV	IB	250	MRCR	7	6	2700	1	9	9550	10800
		1994 BOATS														
19		ADVANCE SS	OP	SKI	F/S	SV	IB	250	MRCR	7		2250	1	7	6900	7950
19		ADVANCE TOURNAMENT	OP	SKI	F/S	SV	IB	250	MRCR	7		2250	1	7	7600	8750
19		LEGEND TOURNAMENT	OP	SKI	F/S	SV	IB	250	MRCR	7	3	2350	1	7	7550	8700
19	9	TBX TOURNAMENT	OP	SKI	F/S	SV	IB	250	MRCR	7	7	2600	1	7	8600	9900
20	4	VOLANTE LTD	OP	SKI	F/S	SV	IB	250	MRCR	7	6	2700	1	9	9200	10500
20	4	VOLANTE TOURNAMENT	OP	SKI	F/S	SV	IB	250	MRCR	7	6	2700	1	9	9050	10300
24		EAGLE	OP	SKI	F/S	SV	IB	250	MRCR	8		3100	1	9	12500	14200
		1993 BOATS														
19		ADVANCE SS	OP	SKI	F/S	SV	IB	250	FORD	7		2250	1	7	6900	7900
19		ADVANCE TOURNAMENT	OP	SKI	F/S	SV	IB	250	FORD	7		2350	1	7	7050	8100
19		LEGEND TOURNAMENT	OP	SKI	F/S	SV	IB	250	FORD	7	3	2450	1	7	7350	8450
20	4	VOLANTE LTD	OP	SKI	F/S	SV	IB	250	FORD	7	6	2850	1	7	9050	10300
20	4	VOLANTE TOURNAMENT	OP	SKI	F/S	SV	IB	250	FORD	7	6	2850	1	7	8850	10100
24		EAGLE	OP	SKI	F/S	SV	IB	250	FORD	8		3450	1	9	12700	14400
		1992 BOATS														
16	9	170 SE FISH AMERICAN	OP	CTRCN	F/S	DV	OB			7		900			2650	3050
18	6	186 SE	OP	RNBT	F/S	DV	OB			8		1600			4450	5150
19		LEGEND ELEGANCE	OP	SKI	F/S	SV	IB	250	FORD	7	3	2450	1	7	6950	8000
19		SPORT ADVANCE	OP	SKI	F/S	SV	IB	250	FORD	7		2300	1	7	6600	7600
19		SPORT LEGEND	OP	SKI	F/S	SV	IB	250	FORD	7	3	2400	1	7	6900	7900
19	4	200 SE FISH AMER L	OP	CTRCN	F/S	DV	OB			8		1700			5000	5750
19	4	200 SE FISH AMERICAN	OP	CTRCN	F/S	DV	OB			8		1700			4650	5350
20	1	200 SEC	OP	CUD	F/S	DV	IO	155		8		2700			6750	7750
20	4	SPORT VOL LTD 1312	OP	SKI	F/S	SV	IB	250	FORD	7	6	2650	1	7	8100	9350
20	4	SPORT VOLANTE 1312	OP	SKI	F/S	SV	IB	250	FORD	7	6	2650	1	7	7950	9150
20	4	VOL ELEG LTD 1312	OP	SKI	F/S	SV	IB	250	FORD	7	6	2700	1	7	8200	9400
20	4	VOL ELEGANCE 1312	OP	SKI	F/S	SV	IB	250	FORD	7	6	2700	1	7	8050	9250
20	6	215 SEC	OP	RNBT	F/S	DV	OB			8		1750			5500	6300
20	6	215 SEC	OP	RNBT	F/S	DV	IO	155		8		2550			6450	7400
24		EAGLE ELEGANCE	OP	SKI	F/S	SV	IB	250	FORD	8		3375	1	9	11900	13500
24		SPORT EAGLE	OP	SKI	F/S	SV	IB	250	FORD	8		3300	1	9	11700	13300
25		COMANCHE ELEGANCE	OP	CUD	F/S	DV	IO	235	CHEV	8		4700	2	1	13200	15000
25		EAGLE II ELEGANCE	OP	SKI	F/S	DV	IO	235	CHEV	8		3800	2	1	10800	12300
25		SPORT COMANCHE	OP	CUD	F/S	DV	IO	235	CHEV	8		4600	2	1	13000	14800
25		SPORT EAGLE II	OP	SKI	F/S	DV	IO	235	CHEV	8		3700	2	1	10700	12100
		1989 BOATS														
19		ADVANCE		SKI	FBG	SV	IB	255-260		7		2350	1	10	5600	6450
19		CARERRA		SKI	FBG	SV	IB	260	CHEV	7		2350	1	10	5900	6750
19		CARRERA		SKI	FBG	SV	IB	255	FORD	7		2350	1	10	5850	6750
24		EAGLE		SKI	FBG	SV	IB	255-330		8		3400	2	1	10200	12200
		1988 BOATS														
19		ADVANCE		SKI	FBG	SV	IB		CHEV	7		2250	1	10	**	**
19		CARERRA		SKI	FBG	SV	IB		CHEV	7		2250	1	10	**	**
19		CARRERA		SKI	FBG	SV	IB		CHEV	7		2250	1	10	**	**
19		DECO		SKI	FBG	SV	IB			7		2250	1	10	**	**
24		EAGLE		SKI	FBG	SV	IB		CHEV	8		3400	2	1	**	**
		1987 BOATS														
19		ADVANCE		SKI	FBG	SV	IB	255		7		2400			5300	6050
19		BAREFOOT-SKIER		SKI	FBG	SV	IB	T280		7		2400			6650	7650
19		CARRERA		SKI	FBG	SV	IB	275		7		2400			5350	6150
22		CORSICA		SKI	FBG	SV	IB	275		8		3000			7700	8850
		1986 BOATS														
19		ADVANCE		RNBT	FBG	SV	IB	255		7					5150	5900
20	7	BAREFOOT-SKIER		SKI	FBG	SV	IB	255		7	2	2400			5350	6150
20	7	VOLANTE 6.3		SKI	FBG	SV	IB	255		7	2	2400			5900	6800
		1985 BOATS														
18		AMERICAN-SKIER		SKI	FBG	SV	IB	255		7		2200	1	8	4300	5000
20	7	BAREFOOT-SKIER		SKI	FBG	SV	IB	255		7	2	2400	1	8	5050	5800
20	7	VOLANTE 6.3		SKI	FBG	SV	IB	255		7	2	2400			5700	6600
		1984 BOATS														
18		AMERICAN-SKIER		SKI	FBG	SV	IB	225		7			1	8	4200	4900
20	7	BAREFOOT-SKIER		SKI	FBG	SV	IB	255		7	2		1	8	5300	6100
20	7	VOLANTE 6-3		SKI	FBG	SV	IB	225		7	2				5250	6050

....For earlier years, see the BUC Used Boat Price Guide, Volume 3

AMERICAN SLEEK CRAFT INC

SLEEK CRAFT
SANTA FE SPRINGS CA 906 COAST GUARD MFG ID- SLE
FORMERLY SLEEK CRAFT BOATS

See inside cover to adjust price for area

LOA FT	LOA IN	NAME AND/ OR MODEL	TOP/ RIG	BOAT TYPE	HULL MTL	HULL TP	ENGINE TP	ENGINE # HP	ENGINE MFG	BEAM FT	BEAM IN	WGT LBS	DRAFT FT	DRAFT IN	RETAIL LOW	RETAIL HIGH
		1992 BOATS														
20	2	SST	OP	SKI	FBG	TH	OB			7	3	1700			5100	5900
20	2	SST	OP	SKI	FBG	TH	JT	454	CHEV	7	3	1700			7700	8900
20	2	SST MOD-VP	OP	SKI	FBG	TH	OB			7	3	1700			5100	5900
21	3	IMPULSE	OP	SPTCR	FBG	SV	OB			7	3	2600			7350	8450
21	3	IMPULSE	OP	SPTCR	FBG	SV	IO	240	MRCR	7	3	2600			7300	8350
21	3	IMPULSE	OP	SPTCR	FBG	SV	IO	330	MRCR	7	3	2600			8600	9850
21	3	INPULSE	OP	SPTCR	FBG	SV	JT	454	CHEV	7	3	2600			9550	10800
21	3	JR-EXECUTIVE	OP	SPTCR	FBG	SV	OB			7	3	2600			7350	8450
21	3	JR-EXECUTIVE	OP	SPTCR	FBG	SV	IO	240	MRCR	7	3	2600			7300	8350
21	3	JR-EXECUTIVE	OP	SPTCR	FBG	SV	IO	330	MRCR	7	3	2600			8600	9850
21	3	JR-EXECUTIVE	OP	SPTCR	FBG	SV	JT	454	CHEV	7	3	2600			9550	10800
23		EXECUTIVE	OP	CUD	FBG	DV	OB			8		3200			9500	10800
23		EXECUTIVE	OP	CUD	FBG	DV	IO	240	MRCR	8		3200			9250	10500
23		EXECUTIVE	OP	CUD	FBG	DV	IO	330-365		8		3200			10500	13000
23		EXECUTIVE	OP	CUD	FBG	DV	JT	454	CHEV	8		3200			11900	13500
23	6	ENFORCER	OP	OFF	FBG	DV	OB			8		3200			9750	11100
23	6	ENFORCER	OP	OFF	FBG	DV	IO	240	MRCR	8		3200			9500	10800
		IO 330-365 10700 13300, IO 410 MRCR 13200 15000, JT 454 CHEV 12200 13800														
26		ENFORCER	OP	OFF	FBG	DV	OB			8		3500			12700	14500
26		ENFORCER	OP	OFF	FBG	DV	IO	330-365		8		3500			13400	16100
		IO 410 MRCR 15500 17600, JT 454 CHEV 16700 18900, IO T240 MRCR 14500 16400														
		IO T330 MRCR 17200 19500														
26		RAIDER	OP	CUD	FBG	DV	OB			8		3500			12700	14500
26		RAIDER	OP	CUD	FBG	DV	IO	240	MRCR	8		3500			12300	14000

```
LOA  NAME AND/            TOP/ BOAT -HULL- ----ENGINE--- BEAM      WGT  DRAFT RETAIL RETAIL
FT IN  OR MODEL           RIG TYPE MTL TP TP # HP  MFG   FT IN     LBS  FT IN  LOW    HIGH
-------------------- 1992 BOATS -------------------------------------------------------------
26   RAIDER                OP  CUD  FBG DV IO 330-365  8          3500         13800  16700
     JT  454  CHEV  17300  19600, IO T240  MRCR  14900  16900, IO T330  MRCR  16700  19000

28   ENFORCER             OP  OFF  FBG DV OB           8          4300         15900  18100
28   ENFORCER             OP  OFF  FBG DV IO 330-410   8          4300         19800  24200
     IO T240  MRCR  21500 23900, IO T330-T365  24300  28700, IO T410  MRCR  28100  31200

28   RAIDER               OP  CUD  FBG DV OB           8          4300         16300  18500
28   RAIDER               OP  CUD  FBG DV IO 330-410   8          4300         20500  25100
28   RAIDER               OP  CUD  FBG DV IO T240-T330 8          4300         22400  27000
28   RAIDER               OP  CUD  FBG DV IO T365 MRCR 8          4300         25200  28000
30   ENFORCER             OP  OFF  FBG DV OB           8          6500         20500  22800
30   ENFORCER             OP  OFF  FBG DV IO T240-T330 8          6500         29200  35200
30   ENFORCER             OP  OFF  FBG DV IO T365-T410 8          6500         32900  38400
-------------------- 1990 BOATS -------------------------------------------------------------
20 2 SST                  OP  SKI  FBG TH OB           7  3       1700          4750   5500
20 2 SST                  OP  SKI  FBG TH JT 454  CHEV 7  3       1700          7000   8050
20 2 SST MOD-VP           OP  SKI  FBG TH OB           7  3       1700          4750   5500
21 3                      OP  SPTCR FBG SV OB          7  3       2600          6850   7850
21 3                      OP  SPTCR FBG SV IO 330  MRCR 7 3       2600          7550   8650
21 3                      OP  SPTCR FBG SV IO 454  CHEV 7 3       2600          8500   9800
21 3 IMPULSE              OP  SPTCR FBG SV IO 240  MRCR 7 3       2600          6400   7350
21 3 JR-EXECUTIVE         OP  SPTCR FBG SV OB          7  3       2600          6850   7850
21 3 JR-EXECUTIVE         OP  SPTCR FBG SV IO 240  MRCR 7 3       2600          6400   7350
21 3 JR-EXECUTIVE         OP  SPTCR FBG SV IO 330  MRCR 7 3       2600          7550   8650
21 3 JR-EXECUTIVE         OP  SPTCR FBG SV JT 454  CHEV 7 3       2600          8500   9800
23   EXECUTIVE            OP  CUD  FBG DV OB           8          3200          8900  10100

23   EXECUTIVE            OP  CUD  FBG DV IO 240  MRCR 8          3200          8100   9300
23   EXECUTIVE            OP  CUD  FBG DV IO 330-365   8          3200          9250  11400
23   EXECUTIVE            OP  CUD  FBG DV JT 454  CHEV 8          3200         10700  12200
23 6 ENFORCER             OP  OFF  FBG DV OB           8          3200          9150  10400
23 6 ENFORCER             OP  OFF  FBG DV IO 240  MRCR 8          3200          8300   9950
     IO 330-365   9500 11700, IO 410  MRCR 11700 13200, JT 454  CHEV 11000  12500

26   ENFORCER             OP  OFF  FBG DV OB           8          3500         11800  13500
26   ENFORCER             OP  OFF  FBG DV IO 330-365   8          3500         11800  14200
     IO 410  MRCR  13600 15500, JT 454  CHEV 15000  17000, IO T240  MRCR  12700  14500
     IO T330  MRCR 15100 17100

26   RAIDER               OP  CUD  FBG DV OB           8          3500         11800  13500
26   RAIDER               OP  CUD  FBG DV IO 240  MRCR 8          3500         10800  12300
     IO 330-365  12200 14700, JT 454  CHEV 15500  17700, IO T240  MRCR  13100  14900
     IO T330  MRCR 14600 16600

28   ENFORCER             OP  OFF  FBG DV OB           8          4300         14800  16800
28   ENFORCER             OP  OFF  FBG DV IO 330-410   8          4300         17300  21400
28   ENFORCER             OP  OFF  FBG DV IO T240-T330 8          4300         19100  23800
28   ENFORCER             OP  OFF  FBG DV IO T365-T410 8          4300         22800  27500
28   RAIDER               OP  CUD  FBG DV OB           8          4300         15100  17200
28   RAIDER               OP  CUD  FBG DV IO 330-410   8          4300         18300  22200
28   RAIDER               OP  CUD  FBG DV IO T240-T330 8          4300         19800  23800
28   RAIDER               OP  CUD  FBG DV IO T365 MRCR 8          4300         22300  24700
30   ENFORCER             OP  OFF  FBG DV IO 330-410   8          6500         19100  21200
30   ENFORCER             OP  OFF  FBG DV IO T240-T330 8          6500         25700  31000
30   ENFORCER             OP  OFF  FBG DV IO T365-T410 8          6500         29000  33900
-------------------- 1989 BOATS -------------------------------------------------------------
18   REBEL                OP  SKI  FBG SV JT 325       7  2       1700          5200   5950
19   KAUAI                OP  SKI  FBG SV OB           7  2       1825          3900   4550
19   KAUAI                OP  SKI  FBG SV JT 325       7  2       1825          5650   6500
20 2 SST                  OP  SKI  FBG TH OB           7  3       1700          4650   5350
20 2 SST                  OP  SKI  FBG TH JT 325       7  3       1700          6600   7600
20 2 SSV                  OP  SKI  FBG SV JT 325       7  3       1700          6450   7400
21 3 DIPLOMAT             OP  SPTCR FBG SV OB          7  3       2600          6600   7600
21 3 DIPLOMAT             OP  SPTCR FBG SV IO 270  MRCR 7 3       2600          6250   7150
     IO 320-330   6900 8150, IO 365  MRCR 7900  9100, JT 454  CHEV  8100   9350

21 3 DIPLOMAT             OP  SPTCR FBG SV IO 270  MRCR 7 3       2600          6600   7600
21 3 DIPLOMAT             OP  SPTCR FBG TH IO 270  MRCR 7 3       2600          6600   7600
     IO 320-330   7350 8650, IO 365  MRCR 8400  9650, JT 454  CHEV  8550   9850

21 3 JR-EXECUTIVE         OP  SPTCR FBG SV IO 270  MRCR 7 3       2600          6250   7150
     IO 320-330   6900 8150, IO 365  MRCR 7900  9100, JT 454  CHEV  8100   9350

21 3 JR-EXECUTIVE         OP  SPTCR FBG TH IO 270  MRCR 7 3       2600          6600   7600
     IO 320-330   7350 8650, IO 365  MRCR 8400  9650, JT 454  CHEV  8550   9850

23   EXECUTIVE            OP  CUD  FBG DV OB           8          3200          8500   9750
23   EXECUTIVE            OP  CUD  FBG DV IO 270-320   8          3200          7800   9750
     IO 330  MRCR  8650 9950, IO 365  MRCR 9500 10800, JT 454  CHEV 10200  11600

23 6 ENFORCER             OP  OFF  FBG DV OB           8          3200          8850  10000
23 6 ENFORCER             OP  OFF  FBG DV IO 270-320   8          3200          8050   9950
23 6 ENFORCER             OP  OFF  FBG DV IO 330-365   8          3200          8950  11000
23 6 ENFORCER             OP  OFF  FBG DV JT 454  CHEV 8          3200         10500  11900
26   AMBASSADOR           OP  CUD  FBG DV OB           8          3500         11500  13000
26   AMBASSADOR           OP  CUD  FBG DV IO 270-330   8          3500         10600  13000
     IO 365  MRCR 12200 13900, IO 420  MRCR 13600 15400, JT 454  CHEV 14800  16800
     IO T270-T320 12600 15400

26   ENFORCER             OP  OFF  FBG DV OB           8          3500         11500  13000
26   ENFORCER             OP  OFF  FBG DV IO 270-330   8          3500         10200  12600
     IO 365  MRCR 11800 13400, IO 420  MRCR 13100 14900, JT 454  CHEV 14200  16200
     IO T270  MRCR 12600 14300, IO T320-T330 13800 16100, IO T365  MRCR 15400  17500

28   ENFORCER             OP  OFF  FBG DV OB           8          4300         14600  16600
28   ENFORCER             OP  OFF  FBG DV IO 330-365   8          4300         16400  19400
     IO 420  MRCR 18700 20800, IO T270-T330 18900 22700, IO T365  MRCR 21600  24000

28   INTRUDER             OP  CUD  FBG DV OB           8          4300         14600  16600
28   INTRUDER             OP  CUD  FBG DV IO 330-365   8          4300         16800  20000
28   INTRUDER             OP  CUD  FBG DV IO 420  MRCR 8          4300         19100  21200
28   INTRUDER             OP  CUD  FBG DV IO T270-T365 8          4300         19300  23300
30   ENFORCER             OP  OFF  FBG DV OB           8          6500         18700  20800
30   ENFORCER             OP  OFF  FBG DV IO 330-420   8          6500         22700  26900
30   ENFORCER             OP  OFF  FBG DV IO T270-T365 8          6500         24800  30300
30   ENFORCER             OP  OFF  FBG DV IO T420  MRCR 8         6500         29000  32200
36   COMMODORE            OP  OFF  FBG DV IO T270  MRCR 8         10000        37300  41400
     IO T320  MRCR 38400 42700, IO T330  MRCR 38800 43100, IO T365  MRCR 40100  44500
     IO T420  MRCR 42800 47600

36   ENFORCER             OP  OFF  FBG DV IO T270  MRCR 8         8000         33800  37600
     IO 365  MRCR 34400 38200, IO 420  MRCR 35700 39600, IO T270  MRCR 35000  38800
     IO T320  MRCR 36200 40200, IO T330  MRCR 36500 40500, IO T365  MRCR 37700  41900
     IO T420  MRCR 40300 44800
-------------------- 1988 BOATS -------------------------------------------------------------
18   REBEL                OP  SKI  FBG SV JT 325       7  2       1700          4950   5700
19   KAUAI                OP  SKI  FBG SV OB           7  2       1825          3800   4400
19   KAUAI                OP  SKI  FBG SV JT 325       7  2       1825          5400   6200
20 2 SST                  OP  SKI  FBG TH OB           7  3       1700          4500   5150
20 2 SST                  OP  SKI  FBG TH JT 325       7  3       1700          6300   7250
20 2 SST                  OP  SKI  FBG SV JT 325       7  3       1700          6150   7050
21 3 DIPLOMAT             OP  SPTCR FBG SV OB          7  3       2600          6400   7350
21 3 DIPLOMAT             OP  SPTCR FBG SV IO     MRCR 7 3       2600            **     **
     IO 260-270   5800 6750, IO 320  MRCR 6500  7500, JT 454  CHEV  7700   8850

21 3 DIPLOMAT             OP  SPTCR FBG TH OB          7  3       2600          6400   7350
21 3 DIPLOMAT             OP  SPTCR FBG SV IO     MRCR 7 3       2600            **     **
     IO 260-270   6150 7150, IO 320  MRCR 6950  7950, JT 454  CHEV  8150   9350

21 3 JR-EXECUTIVE         OP  SPTCR FBG SV IO     MRCR 7 3       2600            **     **
     IO 260-270   5800 6750, IO 320  MRCR 6500  7500, JT 454  CHEV  7700   8850

21 3 JR-EXECUTIVE         OP  SPTCR FBG TH IO     MRCR 7 3       2600            **     **
     IO 260-270   6150 7150, IO 320  MRCR 6950  7950, JT 454  CHEV  8150   9350

23   EXECUTIVE            OP  CUD  FBG DV OB           8          3200          8250   9500
23   EXECUTIVE            OP  CUD  FBG DV IO 260-270   8          3200            **     **
     IO 260-270   7300 8500, IO 320  MRCR 8000  9200, JT 454  CHEV  9700  11000

23 6 ENFORCER             OP  OFF  FBG DV OB           8          3200          8500   9750
23 6 ENFORCER             OP  OFF  FBG DV IO     MRCR  8          3200            **     **
     IO 260-270   7500 8750, IO 320  MRCR 8200  9450, JT 454  CHEV  9950  11300

26   AMBASSADOR           OP  CUD  FBG DV OB           8          3500         11100  12600
26   AMBASSADOR           OP  CUD  FBG DV IO     MRCR  8          3500            **     **
     IO 260-320   9850 12100, IO 420  MRCR 12800 14600, JT 454  CHEV 14100  16000
     IO T260-T320 11800 14500

26   ENFORCER             OP  OFF  FBG DV OB           8          3500         11100  12600
26   ENFORCER             OP  OFF  FBG DV IO     MRCR  8          3500            **     **
     IO 260-320   9600 11700, IO 420  MRCR 12400 14100, JT 454  CHEV 13600  15400
     IO T        MRCR  **    **, IO T260-T270 11700 13500, IO T320  MRCR 13100  14900

28   ENFORCER             OP  OFF  FBG DV OB           8          4300         14200  16100
28   ENFORCER             OP  OFF  FBG DV IO     MRCR  8          4300            **     **
```

```
 LOA  NAME AND/        TOP/ BOAT  -HULL- ----ENGINE---  BEAM   WGT  DRAFT RETAIL RETAIL
FT IN OR MODEL         RIG  TYPE  MTL TP TP # HP  MFG   FT IN  LBS  FT IN  LOW   HIGH
--------------------- 1988 BOATS -----------------------------------------------------
 28   ENFORCER         OP OFF   FBG DV IO  420 MRCR   8      4300         17400  19700
 28   ENFORCER         OP OFF   FBG DV IO T    MRCR   8      4300           **     **
 28   ENFORCER         OP OFF   FBG DV IO T260-T320   8      4300         17300  21300
 28   INTRUDER         OP CUD   FBG DV OB            8      4300         14200  16100
 28   INTRUDER         OP CUD   FBG DV IO     MRCR   8      4300           **     **
      IO 420 MRCR 18200 20300, IO T    MRCR   **    **, IO T260-T320     18300  21200

 30   ENFORCER         OP OFF   FBG DV OB            8      6500         18100  20200
 30   ENFORCER         OP OFF   FBG DV IO     MRCR   8      6500           **     **
      IO 420 MRCR 22900 25400, IO T    MRCR   **    **, IO T260-T320     23300  27400
      IO T420 MRCR 27500 30500

 36   COMMODORE        OP OFF   FBG DV IO T   MRCR   8     10000           **     **
      IO T260 MRCR 35000 38900, IO T270 MRCR 35200 39100, IO T320 MRCR   36300  40300
      IO T420 MRCR 40300 44800

 36   ENFORCER         OP OFF   FBG DV IO     MRCR   8      8000           **     **
      IO 420 MRCR 33700 37400, IO T    MRCR   **    **, IO T260 MRCR     32900  36500
      IO T270 MRCR 33000 36700, IO T320 MRCR 34100 37900, IO T420 MRCR   38000  42200
--------------------- 1987 BOATS -----------------------------------------------------
 18   REBEL            OP SKI   FBG SV JT  325       6  7    925          4000   4700
 19   KAUAI            OP SKI   FBG SV JT  325       6  7    925          4550   5200
 20 2 ARISTOCRAT T     OP SKI   FBG TH IO  260       7  3                 4000   4700
 20 2 ARISTOCRAT T     OP SKI   FBG TH JT  325       7  3    950          5950   6850
 20 2 ARISTOCRAT V     OP SKI   FBG SV IO  260       7  3                 3900   4500
 20 2 ARISTOCRAT V     OP SKI   FBG SV JT  325       7  3    950          5750   6650
 20 2 SST              OP SKI   FBG TH OB            7  3    800          2350   2700
 20 2 SST              OP SKI   FBG TH JT  325       7  3    950          5950   6850
 20 2 SSV              OP SKI   FBG SV JT  325       7  3    950          5750   6650
 21 3 DIPLOMAT T       OP SPTCR FBG TH OB            7  3                 6250   7150
 21 3 DIPLOMAT T       OP SPTCR FBG TH IO  260       7  3                 5650   6500
 21 3 DIPLOMAT T       OP SPTCR FBG TH JT  325       7  3   1550          6600   7550

 21 3 DIPLOMAT V       OP SPTCR FBG SV OB            7  3                 6250   7150
 21 3 DIPLOMAT V       OP SPTCR FBG SV IO  260       7  3                 5400   6200
 21 3 DIPLOMAT V       OP SPTCR FBG SV JT  325       7  3   1550          6250   7200
 21 3 JR-EXECUTIVE T   OP SPTCR FBG TH JT  325       7  3   1550          6600   7550
 21 3 JR-EXECUTIVE V   OP SPTCR FBG SV JT  325       7  3   1550          6250   7200
 23   EXECUTIVE        OP CUD   FBG DV OB            8                    7500   8650
 23   EXECUTIVE        OP CUD   FBG DV IO  260       8                    6800   7800
 23   EXECUTIVE        OP CUD   FBG DV JT  325       8         1800       7350   8400
 26   AMBASSADOR       OP CUD   FBG DV IO  260       8                    9300  10600
 26   AMBASSADOR       OP CUD   FBG DV JT  325       8         2000      11000  12500
 26   ENFORCER         OP OFF   FBG DV IO  260-330   8                    9100  11300

 28   ENFORCER         OP OFF   FBG DV IO  330       8                   14800  16800
 28   ENFORCER         OP OFF   FBG DV IO T260       8                   16400  18700
 28   INTRUDER         OP CUD   FBG DV IO  330       8                   15100  17200
 28   INTRUDER         OP CUD   FBG DV IO T260       8                   17000  19300
 30   ENFORCER         OP OFF   FBG DV IO T260-T330  8      6500         22200  26300
 36   COMMODORE        OP OFF   FBG DV IO T330       8                   36300  40400
 36   ENFORCER         OP OFF   FBG DV IO T330       8                   30500  33900
--------------------- 1986 BOATS -----------------------------------------------------
 18   REBEL            OP SKI   FBG SV IB  325       6  7    925          3450   4000
 18   SPORTSTER        OP SKI   FBG SV IB  325       6  7    925          3450   4000
 19   KAUAI            OP SKI   FBG SV IB  325       6  7    925          3900   4500
 20 2 ARISTOCRAT T     OP SKI   FBG TH IO  260       7  3   2000          4150   4800
 20 2 ARISTOCRAT T     OP SKI   FBG TH IB  325       7  3    950          5200   6000
 20 2 ARISTOCRAT V     OP SKI   FBG SV IO  260       7  3                 3700   4300
 20 2 ARISTOCRAT V     OP SKI   FBG SV IB  325       7  3                 5100   5850
 20 2 SST              OP SKI   FBG TH OB            7  3    800          2300   2650
 20 2 SST              OP SKI   FBG TH IB  325       7  3    950          5200   6000
 20 2 SSV              OP SKI   FBG SV IB  325       7  3    950          5100   5850
 21 3 DIPLOMAT T       OP SKI   FBG TH IO  260       7  3                 4950   5700
 21 3 DIPLOMAT T       OP SPTCR FBG TH IB  325       7  3   1550          5800   6650

 21 3 DIPLOMAT V       OP SKI   FBG SV IO  260       7  3                 4750   5450
 21 3 DIPLOMAT V       OP SPTCR FBG SV IB  325       7  3   1550          5550   6350
 21 3 JR-EXECUTIVE T   OP SPTCR FBG SV IB  325       7  3   1550          5800   6650
 21 3 JR-EXECUTIVE V   OP SPTCR FBG SV IB  325       7  3   1550          5550   6350
 23   EXECUTIVE        OP CUD   FBG DV OB            8         1800       4900   5650
 23   EXECUTIVE        OP CUD   FBG DV IO  260       8                    6450   7450
 23   EXECUTIVE V      OP CUD   FBG DV IB  325       8         1800       6600   7550
 26   AMBASSADOR V     OP CUD   FBG DV IO  260       8                    8850  10100
 26   AMBASSADOR V     OP CUD   FBG DV IB  405       8         2000      10600  12100
 28   INTRUDER         OP DC    FBG DV IO  260       8                   15300  17400
 30   MONTEREY         OP OFF   FBG DV IO T330       8                   22600  25100
 36   COMMODORE        OP OFF   FBG DV IO T330       8                   34100  37900

 36   CONDOR           OP OFF   FBG DV IO T330       8                   29600  32900
--------------------- 1985 BOATS -----------------------------------------------------
 18   REBEL            OP SKI   FBG SV JT  325       6  7    925          3650   4250
 18   SPORTSTER        OP SKI   FBG SV JT  325       6  7    925          3650   4250
 19   KAUAI            OP SKI   FBG SV JT  325       6  7    925          4100   4750
 20 2 ARISTOCRAT T     OP SKI   FBG TH IO  260       7  3                 3650   4250
 20 2 ARISTOCRAT T     OP SKI   FBG TH JT  325       7  3    950          5400   6250
 20 2 ARISTOCRAT V     OP SKI   FBG SV IO  260       7  3                 3550   4150
 20 2 ARISTOCRAT V     OP SKI   FBG SV JT  325       7  3    950          5250   6050
 20 2 SST              OP SKI   FBG TH OB            7  3    800          2250   2600
 20 2 SST              OP SKI   FBG TH JT  325       7  3    950          5400   6250
 20 2 SSV              OP SKI   FBG SV JT  325       7  3    950          5250   6050
 21 3 DIPLOMAT T       OP SPTCR FBG TH OB            7  3                 5900   6800

 21 3 DIPLOMAT T       OP SPTCR FBG TH IO  260       7  3                 5150   5950
 21 3 DIPLOMAT T       OP SPTCR FBG TH JT  325       7  3   1550          6000   6900
 21 3 DIPLOMAT V       OP SPTCR FBG SV OB            7  3                 5900   6800
 21 3 DIPLOMAT V       OP SPTCR FBG SV IO  260       7  3                 4900   5650
 21 3 DIPLOMAT V       OP SPTCR FBG SV JT  325       7  3   1550          5700   6550
 21 3 JR-EXECUTIVE T   OP SPTCR FBG TH JT  325       7  3   1550          6000   6900
 21 3 JR-EXECUTIVE V   OP SPTCR FBG SV JT  325       7  3   1550          5700   6550
 23   EXECUTIVE        OP CUD   FBG DV OB            8                    7150   8200
 23   EXECUTIVE        OP CUD   FBG DV IO  260       8                    6200   7100
 23   EXECUTIVE        OP CUD   FBG DV JT  325       8         1800       6700   7650
 26   AMBASSADOR       OP CUD   FBG DV IO  260       8                    8450   9700
 26   AMBASSADOR       OP CUD   FBG DV IB  405       8         2000      10200  11500

 30   MONTEREY         OP OFF   FBG DV IO T330       8                   21700  24100
 30   MONTEREY         OP OFF   FBG DV IB T405       8      6500         28800  31900
 36   COMMODORE        OP OFF   FBG DV IO T330       8                   32900  36500
 36   COMMODORE        OP OFF   FBG DV IB T405       8      8000         53700  59000
 36   CONDOR           OP OFF   FBG DV IO T330       8                   28200  31300
 36   CONDOR           OP OFF   FBG DV IB T405       8      8000         47100  51700
--------------------- 1984 BOATS -----------------------------------------------------
 18   REBEL               SKI   FBG SV IB  325       6  7    925          3150   3650
 18   SPORTSTER           SKI   FBG SV IB  325       6  7    925          3150   3650
 19   KAUAI               SKI   FBG SV IB  325       6  7    925          3550   4150
 20 2 ARISTOCRAT          SKI   FBG SV IO  260       7  3    950          3500   4050
 20 2 ARISTOCRAT          SKI   FBG SV IB  325       7  3    950          4650   5350
 20 2 ARISTOCRAT          SKI   FBG TH IO  260       7  3    950          3600   4200
 20 2 ARISTOCRAT          SKI   FBG TH IB  325       7  3    950          4750   5500
 20 2 ARISTOCRAT SST      SKI   FBG TH OB            7  3    800          2200   2550
 20 2 SST                 SKI   FBG TH IB  325       7  3    950          4750   5500
 20 2 SSV                 SKI   FBG SV IB  325       7  3    950          4650   5350
 21 3 DIPLOMAT            SPTCR FBG SV IO  260       7  3   1550          4050   4750
 21 3 DIPLOMAT            SPTCR FBG SV IB  325       7  3   1550          5050   5800

 21 3 DIPLOMAT            SPTCR FBG TH OB            7  3   1550          3900   4550
 21 3 DIPLOMAT            SPTCR FBG TH IO  260       7  3   1550          4250   4950
 21 3 DIPLOMAT            SPTCR FBG TH IB  325       7  3   1550          5300   6050
 21 3 JR-EXECUTIVE        SPTCR FBG SV IO  260       7  3   1550          4050   4750
 21 3 JR-EXECUTIVE        SPTCR FBG SV IB  325       7  3   1550          5050   5800
 21 3 JR-EXECUTIVE        SPTCR FBG TH OB            7  3   1550          3900   4550
 21 3 JR-EXECUTIVE        SPTCR FBG TH IO  260       7  3   1550          4250   4950
 21 3 JR-EXECUTIVE        SPTCR FBG TH IB  325       7  3   1550          5300   6050
 23   EXECUTIVE           CUD   FBG DV OB            8         1800       4700   5400
 23   EXECUTIVE           CUD   FBG DV IO  260       8         1800       4850   5550
 23   EXECUTIVE           CUD   FBG DV IB  326       8         1800       6000   6900

 26   AMBASSADOR          CUD   FBG DV IO  260       8         2000       7300   8350
 26   AMBASSADOR          CUD   FBG DV IB  405       8         2000       9700  11000
 30   MONTEREY            OFF   FBG DV IO T290       8      6500         20100  22400
 30   MONTEREY            OFF   FBG DV IB T405       8      6500         27500  30500
 36   COMMODORE           OFF   FBG DV IO T290       8      8000         30100  33400
 36   COMMODORE           OFF   FBG DV IB T405       8      8000         52200  57400
 36   CONDOR              OFF   FBG DV IO T290       8      8000         25800  28600
 36   CONDOR              OFF   FBG DV IB T405       8      8000         44300  49300

             ....For earlier years, see the BUC Used Boat Price Guide, Volume 3
```

AMPRO INDUSTRIES

DORION VAUDREUIL QUE CA COAST GUARD MFG ID- MYL See inside cover to adjust price for area
FORMERLY MIRAGE YACHTS LTD

LOA FT IN	NAME AND/ OR MODEL	TOP/ RIG	BOAT TYPE	-HULL- MTL TP	----ENGINE--- TP # HP MFG	BEAM FT IN	WGT LBS	DRAFT FT IN	RETAIL LOW	RETAIL HIGH
1994 BOATS										
16	AMPRO 4.8	FSH	FBG	SV OB		6	500		2150	2500
1993 BOATS										
16	AMPRO 4.8	FSH	FBG	SV OB		6	500		2000	2400
1991 BOATS										
16	MISTRAL 16	SLP	SAIL	FBG CB OB		6 1	365	3 10	2000	2400
17 9	GULLWING	OP	SF	FBG SV OB		6 8	1190	7	4550	5250
25 2	MIRAGE 25	SLP	SA/CR	FBG KL OB		9 6	4400	4 4	12200	13900
25 3	TANZER 25	SLP	SA/CR	FBG KL IB	D VLVO	9 7	4200	4 8	12700	14500
27 6	MIRAGE 275	SLP	SA/CR	FBG KL IB	12D VLVO	9 10	6800	4 4	23300	25900
29	MIRAGE 29	SLP	SA/CR	FBG KL IB	18D VLVO	10 6	7000	4 8	25600	28500
29	TANZER 29	SLP	SA/CR	FBG KL IB	18D VLVO	10 3	6900	5 3	25300	28100
32	MIRAGE 32	SLP	SA/CR	FBG KL IB	18D VLVO	10 6	8500	4 10	34100	37900
35 6	MIRAGE 35	SLP	SA/CR	FBG KL IB	27D VLVO	11 8	10000	5	41000	45600
39 2	MIRAGE 39	SLP	SA/CR	FBG KL IB	27D VLVO	12 6	16000	6 2	71100	78100
1990 BOATS										
16	MISTRAL 16	SLP	SAIL	FBG CB OB		6 1	365	3 10	1900	2250
17 9	GULLWING	OP	SF	FBG SV OB		6 8	1190	7	4400	5050
25 2	MIRAGE 25	SLP	SA/CR	FBG KL OB		9 6	4400	4 4	11500	13100
25 3	TANZER 25	SLP	SA/CR	FBG KL IB	D	9 7	4200	4 8	12000	13600
27 6	MIRAGE 275	SLP	SA/CR	FBG KL IB	12D	9 10	6800	4 4	21900	24300
29	MIRAGE 29	SLP	SA/CR	FBG KL IB	18D	10 6	7000	4 8	24100	26800
29	TANZER 29	SLP	SA/CR	FBG KL IB	18D	10 3	6900	5 3	23800	26400
32	MIRAGE 32	SLP	SA/CR	FBG KL IB	18D	10 6	8500	4 10	32100	35600
35 6	MIRAGE 35	SLP	SA/CR	FBG KL IB	27D	11 8	10000	5	38600	42900
39 2	MIRAGE 39	SLP	SA/CR	FBG KL IB	27D	12 6	16000	6 2	66800	73400
1987 BOATS										
25	MIRAGE 25	SLP	SA/RC	FBG KL OB		9 6	4300	4 4	9300	10600
25	MIRAGE 25	SLP	SA/RC	FBG KL SD	8D BUKH	9 6	4300	4 4	10000	11400
27	MIRAGE 27	SLP	SA/RC	FBG KL IB	10D VLVO	9 6	6000	4 4	15500	17600
29	MIRAGE 29	SLP	SA/RC	FBG KL IB	10D VLVO	10 6	7500	4 8	21400	23800
30	MIRAGE 32	SLP	SA/RC	FBG KL IB	20D VLVO	10 6	8500	4 3	25300	28100
33 6	MIRAGE 35	SLP	SA/RC	FBG KL IB	20D- 30D	11 8	10000	5	31300	34800
1986 BOATS										
25	KIRBY 25	SLP	SA/RC	FBG KL OB		8 7	3000	4 4	6250	7200
25	MIRAGE 25	SLP	SA/RC	FBG KL OB		9 6	4500	4 4	9150	10400
28 6	MIRAGE 28	SLP	SA/RC	FBG KL IB	D	10 6	7000	4 6	18700	20800
30	MIRAGE 30	SLP	SA/RC	FBG KL IB	D	10 6	8000	4 9	22400	24800
33	MIRAGE 35	SLP	SA/RC	FBG KL IB		11 8	9500	5	28000	31100
1985 BOATS										
25	KIRBY 25	SLP	SA/RC	FBG KL OB		8 7	3000	4 4	5900	6800
25	MIRAGE 25	SLP	SA/RC	FBG KL OB		9 6	4300	4 4	8150	9350
25	MIRAGE 25	SLP	SA/RC	FBG KL SD	8D BUKH	9 6	4300	4 4	8900	10100
27	MIRAGE 27	SLP	SA/RC	FBG KL IB	9D YAN	9 3	5500	4 4	12600	14300
30	MIRAGE 30	SLP	SA/RC	FBG KL IB	15D YAN	10 6	8000	4 3	21000	23400
33 6	MIRAGE 35	SLP	SA/RC	FBG KL IB	15D- 23D	11 8	9300	5	25700	28600
1984 BOATS										
25	KIRBY 25	SLP	SA/RC	FBG KL OB		8 9	3100	4 2	5700	6550
25	MIRAGE 25	SLP	SA/RC	FBG KL OB		9 6	4300	4 4	7650	8800
25	MIRAGE 25	SLP	SA/RC	FBG KL SD	8D VLVO	9 6	4300	4 4	8250	9450
27	MIRAGE 27	SLP	SA/RC	FBG KL IB	8D VLVO	9 3	5500	4 4	11800	13400
27	MIRAGE 27	SLP	SA/RC	FBG KL IB	8D YAN	9 3	5500	4 4	11800	13400
30	KIRBY 30	SLP	SA/RC	FBG KL IB	8D YAN	10 3	5500	5	13400	15200
30	MIRAGE 30	SLP	SA/RC	FBG KL IB	15D YAN	10 6	7000	4 3	17100	19400
33 6	MIRAGE 33	SLP	SA/RC	FBG KL IB	15D- 20D	11 8	9300	5	24200	26900

....For earlier years, see the BUC Used Boat Price Guide, Volume 3

AMSTERDAM BOATWORKS INC

AMSTERDAM NY 12010 — See inside cover to adjust price for area

LOA FT IN	NAME AND/ OR MODEL	TOP/ RIG	BOAT TYPE	-HULL- MTL TP	----ENGINE--- TP # HP MFG	BEAM FT IN	WGT LBS	DRAFT FT IN	RETAIL LOW	RETAIL HIGH
1985 BOATS										
25 3	CHAMPLAIN	CAT	SAIL	FBG KC OB		7 3	3500	2	7850	9000
25 3	CHAMPLAIN	CAT	SAIL	FBG KC IB	D	7 3	3500	2	8500	9800
25 3	CHAMPLAIN	SLP	SAIL	FBG KC OB		7 3	3500	2	7850	9000
25 3	CHAMPLAIN	SLP	SAIL	FBG KC IB	D	7 3	3500	2	8500	9800

ANACAPRI MARINE INC

MIAMI FL 33142 — COAST GUARD MFG ID- AKR See inside cover to adjust price for area
FOR OLDER MODELS SEE A C MANUFACTURING CO INC

LOA FT IN	NAME AND/ OR MODEL	TOP/ RIG	BOAT TYPE	-HULL- MTL TP	----ENGINE--- TP # HP MFG	BEAM FT IN	WGT LBS	DRAFT FT IN	RETAIL LOW	RETAIL HIGH
1990 BOATS										
16 6	V170	OP	CTRCN	FBG DV OB		6 6	1200	1 2	4650	5300
18 6	V186	OP	CTRCN	FBG DV OB	7 6	1500	1 6	5750	6600	
20 5	V205	OP	CTRCN	FBG DV OB		8	2025		7700	8850
20 5	V205	OP	CTRCN	FBG DV SE		8	2025		**	**
22 3	V230 TORINO	OP	RNBT	FBG DV IO	230-260	8	3400	2 4	12200	13900
22 3	V230 TORINO	OP	CTRCN	FBG DV OB		8	3400	2 4	6850	8050
22 3	V2305 OPEN	OP	RNBT	FBG DV IO	230	8	3040	1 6	11500	13000
22 3	V2305 OPEN	OP	CTRCN	FBG DV IO	260	8	3040	1 6	7100	8150
22 3	V2305 OPEN	OP	CTRCN	FBG DV IB		8	3040	1 6	8200	9450
25	V260 HOLIDAY	OP	RNBT	FBG DV IO		8	4000	2 4	15700	17900
25	V260 HOLIDAY	OP	RNBT	FBG DV IO	230	8	4000	2 4	8850	10000
25	V260 HOLIDAY	OP	RNBT	FBG DV IO	260	8	4000	2 4	11600	13200
25	V260 OPEN	OP	CTRCN	FBG DV IO		8	3900	2 4	15500	17600
25	V260 OPEN	OP	CTRCN	FBG DV IO	230-260	8	3900	2 4	9850	11500
27 9	V280	OP	FSH	FBG DV OB		8			22700	25300
27 9	V280	OP	FSH	FBG DV IB	260-340	8			18200	21100
28 3	V290	OP	SF	FBG DV OB		10	5000		22700	25300
28 3	V290	OP	SF	FBG DV IB	260-340	10	5000	2 4	11600	20000
34	V340	OP	SF	FBG DV IB	260	10			40300	44800
1989 BOATS										
16 6	OPEN FISHERMAN 170	ST	CTRCN	FBG DV OB		6 6	1200	1 2	4500	5150
18 6	OPEN FISHERMAN 186	ST	CTRCN	FBG DV OB		7 6	1500	1 6	5550	6400
20 5	OPEN FISHERMAN V205	ST	FSH	FBG DV OB		8	2025		7450	8600
20 5	OPEN FISHERMAN V205	ST	FSH	FBG DV SE	140	8	2025		7450	8600
20 5	OPEN FISHERMAN V205	ST	FSH	FBG DV IO	165-205	8	2025		4850	5650
20 5	OPEN FISHERMAN V205	ST	FSH	FBG DV SE	225	8	2025		7450	8600
20 5	OPEN FISHERMAN V205	ST	FSH	FBG DV IO	229-230	8	2025		5250	6050
22 3	OPEN FISHERMAN V230	ST	SF	FBG DV IO		8	3040	1 6	11100	12600
22 3	OPEN FISHERMAN V230	ST	SF	FBG DV IO	165-230	8	3040	1 6	7000	8550
	IO 260	7350		8800, IO	130D VLVO	9750	11100, IO T165		8050	9250
22 3	TORINO V230	ST	FSH	FBG DV OB		8	3400	2 4	11800	13500
22 3	TORINO V230	ST	FSH	FBG DV IO	165-235	8	3400	2 4	7050	8550
	IO 260	7400		8800, IO	130D VLVO	10500	11900, IO T165		8050	9250
25	HOLIDAY V260	ST	FSH	FBG DV OB		8	4000	2 4	15200	17300
25	HOLIDAY V260	ST	FSH	FBG DV IO	200-260	8	4000	2 4	9350	11300
25	HOLIDAY V260	ST	FSH	FBG DV IO	200D VLVO	8	4000	2 4	13600	15500
25	HOLIDAY V260	ST	FSH	FBG DV IO	T165-T180	8	4000	2 4	15000	12000
25	OPEN FISHERMAN V260	ST	OPFSH	FBG DV OB		8	3900		15000	17100
25	OPEN FISHERMAN V260	ST	OPFSH	FBG DV IO	200-260	8	3900		9050	11000
25	OPEN FISHERMAN V260	ST	OPFSH	FBG DV IO	200D VLVO	8	3900		13100	14900
25	OPEN FISHERMAN V260	ST	OPFSH	FBG DV IO	T165-T180	8	3900		11200	11700
27 9	PRO FISHERMAN V280	HT	FSH	FBG DV OB		9 9		2 4	22000	24400
27 9	PRO FISHERMAN V280	HT	FSH	FBG DV OB		9 9		2 4	**	**
28 3	OPEN FISHERMAN V290	OP	SF	FBG DV OB		10	5000		22000	24400
28 3	OPEN FISHERMAN V290	OP	SF	FBG DV IO	T260 MRCR	10	5000		17100	19400
	IO T260 OMC	17100		19400, IB T260 MRCR	19100	21200,	IO T330	MRCR	18900	21000
	IB T330 MRCR	20000		22200, IB T200D VLVO	21700	24100,	IB T200D VLVO		23200	25700
1988 BOATS										
16 6	OPEN FISHERMAN 170	ST	CTRCN	FBG DV OB		6 6	1200	1 2	4300	5000
16 6	OPEN FISHERMAN 170	ST	CTRCN	FBG DV SE	OMC	6 6	1200	1 2	**	**
19 6	OPEN FISHERMAN 190	OP	SF	FBG DV OB		7 6	1500	1 6	5500	6350
19 6	OPEN FISHERMAN 190	OP	SF	FBG DV SE	OMC	7 6	1500	1 6	**	**
19 6	OPEN FISHERMAN 190	OP	SF	FBG DV IO	131-175	7 6	1500	1 6	3850	4500
22 3	OPEN FISHERMAN V230	ST	OPFSH	FBG DV IO	D VLVO	8	3040	1 6	**	**
22 3	OPEN FISHERMAN V230	ST	SF	FBG DV IO		8	3040	1 6	10800	12200
22 3	OPEN FISHERMAN V230	ST	SF	FBG DV IO	151-260	8	3040	1 6	**	**
22 3	OPEN FISHERMAN V230	ST	SF	FBG DV IO		8	3040	1 6	6800	8100
22 3	OPEN FISHERMAN V230	ST	SF	FBG DV SE	OMC	8	3040	1 6	**	**
22 3	OPEN FISHERMAN V230	ST	SF	FBG DV SE	T OMC	8	3040	1 6	**	**
22 3	OPEN FISHERMAN V230	ST	SF	FBG DV SE	T151-T190	8	3040	1 6	8000	9200
22 3	TORINO V230	ST	FSH	FBG DV OB		8	3400	2 4	11500	13100
22 3	TORINO V230	ST	FSH	FBG DV OB	OMC	8	3400	2 4	**	**
22 3	TORINO V230	ST	FSH	FBG DV IO	151-260	8	3400	2 4	6850	8100
22 3	TORINO V230	ST	FSH	FBG DV IO	D VLVO	8	3400	2 4	**	**
22 3	TORINO V230	ST	FSH	FBG DV IO	T151-T190	8	3400	2 4	7950	9150
25	HOLIDAY FB V260	FB	CBNCR	FBG DV OB		8	4800	2 4	16200	18400
25	HOLIDAY FB V260	FB	CBNCR	FBG DV OB	OMC	8	4800	2 4	**	**
25	HOLIDAY FB V260	FB	CBNCR	FBG DV IO	230-311	8	4800	2 4	11300	13900
25	HOLIDAY FB V260	FB	CBNCR	FBG DV SE	D OMC	8	4800	2 4	**	**
25	HOLIDAY FB V260	FB	CBNCR	FBG DV SE	T OMC	8	4800	2 4	**	**

LOA FT IN	NAME AND/ OR MODEL	TOP/ RIG	BOAT TYPE	-HULL- MTL	TP	----ENGINE--- TP	# HP	MFG	BEAM FT IN	WGT LBS	DRAFT FT IN	RETAIL LOW	RETAIL HIGH
	1988 BOATS												
25	HOLIDAY FB V260	FB	CBNCR	FBG	DV	IO	T151-T190		8	4800	2 4	12400	14100
25	HOLIDAY FB V260	FB	CBNCR	FBG	DV	IO	T311	VLVO	8	4800	2 4	14300	16200
25	HOLIDAY V260	ST	FSH	FBG	DV	OB			8	4000	2 4	14800	16800
25	HOLIDAY V260	ST	FSH	FBG	DV	SE		OMC	8	4000	2 4	**	**
25	HOLIDAY V260	ST	FSH	FBG	DV	IO	171-271		8	4000	2 4	8850	10800
25	HOLIDAY V260	ST	FSH	FBG	DV	IO	311	VLVO	8	4000	2 4	10100	11500
25	HOLIDAY V260	ST	FSH	FBG	DV	IO	D	VLVO	8	4000	2 4	**	**
25	HOLIDAY V260	ST	FSH	FBG	DV	SE	T	OMC	8	4000	2 4	**	**
25	HOLIDAY V260	ST	FSH	FBG	DV	IO	T151-T190		8	4000	2 4	10100	11500
25	OPEN FISHERMAN V260	ST	OPFSH	FBG	DV	IO	171-271		8	3900		8500	10600
	IO 311 VLVO 9800 11100, IO D VLVO ** **, IO T151 VLVO											9850	11200
25	OPEN FISHERMAN V260	ST	SF	FBG	DV	OB			8	3900		14600	16600
25	OPEN FISHERMAN V260	ST	SF	FBG	DV	SE		OMC	8	3900		**	**
25	OPEN FISHERMAN V260	ST	SF	FBG	DV	IO	230-260		8	3900		9350	10900
25	OPEN FISHERMAN V260	ST	SF	FBG	DV	SE	T	OMC	8	3900		**	**
25	OPEN FISHERMAN V260	ST	SF	FBG	DV	IO	T170-T190		8	3900		10500	12100
28 3	OPEN FISHERMAN V290	OP	SF	FBG	DV	OB			10	5000		21300	23700
28 3	OPEN FISHERMAN V290	OP	SF	FBG	DV	SE	T	OMC	10	5000		**	**
28 3	OPEN FISHERMAN V290	OP	SF	FBG	DV	IO	T260-T271		10	5000		16200	18900
28 3	OPEN FISHERMAN V290	OP	SF	FBG	DV	IO	T D	VLVO	10	5000		**	**
	1987 BOATS												
22 3	PROFESSIONAL V230			FBG	DV	IO	145		8	3000	1 10	5200	6000
	1986 BOATS												
16 6	PROFESSIONAL V170	OP	CTRCN	FBG	DV	OB			6 6	1200	1 2	4100	4750
16 6	PROFESSIONAL V170	OP	CTRCN	FBG	DV	SE	T	OMC	6 6	1200	1 2	**	**
19	PROFESSIONAL V190	OP	CTRCN	FBG	DV	OB			7 6	1500	1 6	5200	6000
19	PROFESSIONAL V190	OP	CTRCN	FBG	DV	IO	131-175		7 6		1 6	3250	3750
19	PROFESSIONAL V190	OP	CTRCN	FBG	DV	SE	T	OMC	7 6		1 6	**	**
22 3	PROFESSIONAL V230	OP	CTRCN	FBG	DV	OB			8			10200	11600
22 3	PROFESSIONAL V230	OP	CTRCN	FBG	DV	SE		OMC	8	3240		**	**
22 3	PROFESSIONAL V230	OP	CTRCN	FBG	DV	IO	151-260		8	3240		6000	7300
22 3	PROFESSIONAL V230	OP	CTRCN	FBG	DV	SE	T	OMC	8	3240		**	**
22 3	PROFESSIONAL V230	OP	CTRCN	FBG	DV	IO	T151-T190		8	3240		7000	8050
22 3	PROFESSIONAL V230	OP	CTRCN	FBG	DV	IO	T D	VLVO	8	3240		**	**
22 3	TORINO V230	OP	CUD	FBG	DV	OB			8	3440	2 4	11000	12500
22 3	TORINO V230	OP	CUD	FBG	DV	SE		OMC	8	3440	2 4	**	**
22 3	TORINO V230	OP	CUD	FBG	DV	IO	151-260		8	3440	2 4	5900	7150
22 3	TORINO V230	OP	CUD	FBG	DV	SE	T	OMC	8	3440	2 4	**	**
22 3	TORINO V230	OP	CUD	FBG	DV	IO	T151-T190		8	3440	2 4	6850	7850
22 3	TORINO V230	OP	CUD	FBG	DV	IO	T D	VLVO	8	3440	2 4	**	**
24 10	HOLIDAY V260	OP	CUD	FBG	DV	OB			8	4000	2 4	13900	15800
24 10	HOLIDAY V260	OP	CUD	FBG	DV	SE		OMC	8	4000	2 4	**	**
24 10	HOLIDAY V260	OP	CUD	FBG	DV	IO	200-260		8	4000	2 4	7500	9050
24 10	HOLIDAY V260	OP	CUD	FBG	DV	IO	290	VLVO	8	4000	2 4	8150	9400
24 10	HOLIDAY V260	OP	CUD	FBG	DV	SE	T	OMC	8	4000	2 4	**	**
24 10	HOLIDAY V260	OP	CUD	FBG	DV	IO	T151-T190		8	4000	2 4	8550	9800
24 10	HOLIDAY V260	OP	CUD	FBG	DV	IO	T D	VLVO	8	4000	2 4	**	**
24 10	HOLIDAY V260	FB	CUD	FBG	DV	OB			8	4000	2 4	13900	15800
24 10	HOLIDAY V260	FB	CUD	FBG	DV	SE		OMC	8	4000	2 4	**	**
24 10	HOLIDAY V260	FB	CUD	FBG	DV	IO	230-260		8	4000	2 4	7500	9050
24 10	HOLIDAY V260	FB	CUD	FBG	DV	IO	290	VLVO	8	4000	2 4	8150	9400
24 10	HOLIDAY V260	FB	CUD	FBG	DV	SE	T	OMC	8	4000	2 4	**	**
24 10	HOLIDAY V260	FB	CUD	FBG	DV	IO	T151-T190		8	4000	2 4	8550	9800
24 10	HOLIDAY V260	FB	CUD	FBG	DV	IO	T D	VLVO	8	4000	2 4	**	**
25	PROFESSIONAL V260	OP	CTRCN	FBG	DV	OB			8	3900		13800	15700
25	PROFESSIONAL V260	OP	CTRCN	FBG	DV	SE		OMC	8	3900		**	**
25	PROFESSIONAL V260	OP	CTRCN	FBG	DV	IO	200-260		8	3900		7900	9550
25	PROFESSIONAL V260	OP	CTRCN	FBG	DV	IO	290	VLVO	8	3900		8650	9950
25	PROFESSIONAL V260	OP	CTRCN	FBG	DV	SE	T	OMC	8	3900		**	**
25	PROFESSIONAL V260	OP	CTRCN	FBG	DV	IO	T151-T190		8	3900		9100	10300
25	PROFESSIONAL V260	OP	CTRCN	FBG	DV	IO	T D	VLVO	8	3900		**	**
28 3	PROFESSIONAL V290	OP	CTRCN	FBG	DV	OB			10	5000		20200	22400
28 3	PROFESSIONAL V290	OP	CTRCN	FBG	DV	SE	T	OMC	10	5000		**	**
28 3	PROFESSIONAL V290	OP	CTRCN	FBG	DV	IO	T260-T290		10	5000		13700	16400
28 3	PROFESSIONAL V290	OP	CTRCN	FBG	DV	IO	T D	VLVO	10	5000		**	**
	1985 BOATS												
20 6	V210			FBG	DV	IO	125		8	2400	1 8	3800	4450
22 3	TORINO V230	OP	CTRCN	FBG	DV	IO	145		8	3400	1 10	5750	6600
22 3	V230	OP	CUD	FBG	DV	IO	145		8	3000	1 10	5000	5750
25	HOLIDAY V260	OP	CUD	FBG	DV	IO	200		8	3800	2	6900	7900
25	PROFESSIONAL V260	OP	CTRCN	FBG	DV	IO	200		8	3800	2	7300	8400
28 2	TOURNAMENT V290	OP	CUD	FBG	DV	IO	T260		10	8000	2 4	14200	16200
	1984 BOATS												
16 6	PROFESSIONAL V170	OP	CTRCN	FBG	DV	OB			6 6	1200	1 2	3900	4550
19	PROFESSIONAL V190	OP	CTRCN	FBG	DV	OB			7 6	1500	1 6	5000	5750
19	PROFESSIONAL V190	OP	CTRCN	FBG	DV	IO	117-138		7 6			3000	3500
22	NEWPORT V220	OP	RNBT	FBG	SV	IO	138-260		8		2 4	5050	6150
	IO 290 VLVO 5600 6450, IO 110D VLVO 5900 6800, IO T117-T138											5850	6750
	IO T165D VLVO 8250 9500												
22	NEWPORT V230	OP	RNBT	FBG	SV	OB			8	3240	2 4	9950	11300
22	NEWPORT V230	OP	RNBT	FBG	SV	IO	117	VLVO	8		2 4	5050	5800
22	TORINO V230	OP	CUD	FBG	SV	OB			8	2720	2 4	9000	10200
22	TORINO V230	OP	CUD	FBG	SV	IO	117-260		8	3440	2 4	5350	6550
	IO 290 VLVO 5950 6850, IO 110D-165D 6400 7800, IO T117-T138											6200	7150
22 3	PROFESSIONAL V230	OP	OPFSH	FBG	SV	OB			8	2400	2 4	8200	9450
22 3	PROFESSIONAL V230	OP	OPFSH	FBG	SV	IO	117-260		8	3040	2 4	5350	6550
	IO 290 VLVO 5950 6850, IO 110D-165D 7650 9300, IO T117-T138											6250	7200
24 10	HOLIDAY V250	OP	CUD	FBG	SV	IB	225-260		8	4000	2 4	8650	10100
	IB 124D VLVO 10500 11900, IO 130D VLVO 7750 8900, IB 158D VLVO											11000	12500
	IO 165D VLVO 8150 9350, IO T117-T138 7750 9000												
24 10	HOLIDAY V250	HT	CUD	FBG	SV	IO	200	VLVO	8	4000	2 4	6950	7950
	IO 225 VLVO 7050 8100, IB 225 VLVO 8650 9950, IO 260 VLVO											7300	8350
	IB 260 VLVO 8900 10100, IO 290 VLVO 7550 8700, IO 130D VLVO											7750	8900
	IB 158D VLVO 11000 12500, IO 165D VLVO 8150 9350, IO T117-T138											7750	9000
	IB T124D VLVO 13800 15600												
24 10	HOLIDAY V250	FB	CUD	FBG	SV	IB	225	VLVO	8	4000	2 4	8650	9950
	IO 260 VLVO 7300 8350, IB 260 VLVO 8900 10100, IO 290 VLVO											7550	8700
	IB 124D VLVO 10500 11900, IO 130D VLVO 7750 8900, IB 158D VLVO											11000	12500
	IO 165D VLVO 8150 9350, IO T117-T138 7750 9000												
24 10	HOLIDAY V260	OP	CUD	FBG	SV	OB			8	3700	2 4	12700	14400
24 10	HOLIDAY V260	OP	CUD	FBG	SV	IO	200-260		8	4000	2 4	6950	8350
24 10	HOLIDAY V260	OP	CUD	FBG	SV	IO	290	VLVO	8	4000	2 4	7550	8700
24 10	HOLIDAY V260	FB	CUD	FBG	SV	OB			8	3700	2 4	12700	14400
24 10	HOLIDAY V260	FB	CUD	FBG	SV	IO	200-225		8	4000	2 4	6950	8100
24 10	PROFESSIONAL V260	OP	OPFSH	FBG	SV	OB			8	3400	2 4	12100	13700
24 10	PROFESSIONAL V260	OP	OPFSH	FBG	SV	IO	200	VLVO	8	3800	2 4	7050	8100
	IO 225 VLVO 7200 8250, IB 225 VLVO 8350 9600, IO 260 VLVO											7400	8550
	IB 260 VLVO 8500 9750, IO 290 VLVO 7700 8850, IB 124D VLVO											10000	11400
	IO 130D VLVO 9350 10600, IB 158D VLVO 10500 12000, IO 165D VLVO											9750	11100
	IO T117-T138 7900 9150												
29	ENTERPRISE V290	OP	EXP	FBG		OB						21100	23400
29	ENTERPRISE V290	OP	EXP	FBG		IO	T260-T330					13000	16000
29	ENTERPRISE V290	OP	EXP	FBG		IO	T370	MRCR				14500	16500
29	ENTERPRISE V290	OP	EXP	FBG		IO	T155D-T158D					13000	14900
29	TOURNAMENT V290	OP	CUD	FBG		OB						21100	23400
29	TOURNAMENT V290	OP	CUD	FBG		IO	T260-T330					14500	17800
29	TOURNAMENT V290	OP	CUD	FBG		IO	T370	MRCR				16400	18700
29	TOURNAMENT V290	OP	CUD	FBG		IO	T155D-T158D					13000	14900

....For earlier years, see the BUC Used Boat Price Guide, Volume 3

ANCHOR INDUSTRIES

MARR'S LEISURE PRODUCTS INC
BRANDON MB CANADA COAST GUARD MFG ID- ZAI

See inside cover to adjust price for area

LOA FT IN	NAME AND/ OR MODEL	TOP/ RIG	BOAT TYPE	-HULL- MTL	TP	----ENGINE--- TP	# HP	MFG	BEAM FT IN	WGT LBS	DRAFT FT IN	RETAIL LOW	RETAIL HIGH
	1984 BOATS												
16 10	EDSON INTRUDER	ST	RNBT	FBG	DV	IO	185		7 4	1220	2 6	1500	1800

....For earlier years, see the BUC Used Boat Price Guide, Volume 3

ANCHOR MARINE INC

IMPORTERS LM GLASFIBER A/S
SISTER BAY WI 54234 COAST GUARD MFG ID- LMJ

See inside cover to adjust price for area

LOA FT IN	NAME AND/ OR MODEL	TOP/ RIG	BOAT TYPE	-HULL- MTL	TP	----ENGINE--- TP	# HP	MFG	BEAM FT IN	WGT LBS	DRAFT FT IN	RETAIL LOW	RETAIL HIGH
	1994 BOATS												
28 8	LM28 IIS	SLP	SACAC	FBG	KL	SD	28D	VLVO	9 6	8810	4 5	72600	79800
33	VITESSE 33 CABRIO	SLP	SACAC	FBG	KL	SD	43D	VLVO	10 2	10580	5 3	95100	104500
34 10	VITESSE 35 CABRIO	SLP	SACAC	FBG	KL	IB	43D	VLVO	10 6	11660	6 3	107500	118000
34 10	VITESSE 36 VISION	SLP	SACAC	FBG	KL	IB	43D	VLVO	10 6	10000	6 3	92800	102000

LOA FT	IN	NAME AND/ OR MODEL	TOP/ RIG	BOAT TYPE	-HULL- MTL	TP	TP	ENGINE # HP	MFG	BEAM FT	IN	WGT LBS	DRAFT FT	IN	RETAIL LOW	RETAIL HIGH
		1993 BOATS														
28	8	LM28 IIS	SLP	SACAC	FBG	KL	SD	28D	VLVO	9	6	8810	4	5	68200	75000
33		VITESSE 33 CABRIO	SLP	SACAC	FBG	KL	SD	43D	VLVO	10	2	10580	5	3	89400	98200
34	10	VITESSE 35 CABRIO	SLP	SACAC	FBG	KL	IB	43D	VLVO	10	6	11660	6	3	101000	111000
34	10	VITESSE 36 VISION	SLP	SACAC	FBG	KL	IB	43D	VLVO	10	6	10000	6	3	87300	95900
		1992 BOATS														
28	8	LM28 IIS	SLP	SA/CR	FBG	KL	SD	28D	VLVO	9	6	8810	4	5	64200	70600
33		VITESSE 33 CABRIO	SLP	SA/CR	FBG	KL	SD	43D	VLVO	10	2	10580	5	3	84100	92400
34	10	VITESSE 35 CABRIO	SLP	SA/CR	FBG	KL	IB	43D	VLVO	10	6	11660	6	3	95000	104500
34	10	VITESSE 36 VISION	SLP	SA/CR	FBG	KL	IB	43D	VLVO	10	6	10000	6	3	82100	90200
		1991 BOATS														
28	8	LM28 IIS	SLP	SA/CR	FBG	KL	SD	28D	VLVO	9	6	8810	4	5	60400	66300
30	8	LM30 IIS	SLP	SA/CR	FBG	KL	SD	28D- 43D		10		11000	4	11	79700	87700
33		VITESSE 33	SLP	SA/CR	FBG	KL	SD	43D	VLVO	10	2	10580	5	3	79100	86900
34	10	VITESSE 35	SLP	SA/CR	FBG	KL	IB	43D	VLVO	10	6	11660	6	3	89400	98200
		1990 BOATS														
26	7	MERMAID 270	SLP	SA/CR	FBG	KL	IB	9D	VLVO	9	6	7480	4	1	43400	48300
26	7	MERMAID 270	SLP	SA/CR	FBG	KL	SD	18D	VLVO	9	6	7480	4	1	43800	48600
28	8	LM28 IIS	SLP	SA/CR	FBG	KL	SD	28D	VLVO	9	6	8810	4	5	56700	62400
28	8	MERMAID 290	SLP	SA/CR	FBG	KL	SD	18D	VLVO	9	6	8300	4	5	53200	58500
30	8	LM30 IIS	SLP	SA/CR	FBG	KL	SD	28D- 43D		10		11000	4	11	74900	82500
30	8	MERMAID 315	SLP	SA/CR	FBG	KL	SD	28D	VLVO	10		10340	4	11	70400	77400
33		VITESSE 33	SLP	SA/CR	FBG	KL	SD	43D	VLVO	10	2	10580	5	3	74400	81700
37		MERMAID 380	SLP	SA/CR	FBG	KL	IB	43D	VLVO	11	9	14330	5	6	108000	118500
		1989 BOATS														
26	7	MERMAID 270	SLP	SA/CR	FBG	KL	IB	9D	VLVO	9	6	7480	4	1	40800	45300
26	7	MERMAID 270	SLP	SA/CR	FBG	KL	SD	18D	VLVO	9	6	7480	4	1	41100	45700
28	8	LM28 IIS	SLP	SA/CR	FBG	KL	SD	28D	VLVO	9	6	8810	4	5	53400	58700
28	8	MERMAID 290	SLP	SA/CR	FBG	KL	SD	18D	VLVO	9	6	8300	4	5	50100	55000
30	8	LM30 IIS	SLP	SA/CR	FBG	KL	SD	28D- 43D		10		11000	4	11	70400	77500
30	8	MERMAID 315	SLP	SA/CR	FBG	KL	SD	28D	VLVO	10		10340	4	11	66200	72700
33		VITESSE 33	SLP	SA/CR	FBG	KL	SD	43D	VLVO	10	2	10580	5	3	69900	76900
37		MERMAID 380	SLP	SA/CR	FBG	KL	IB	43D	VLVO	11	9	14330	5	6	101500	111500
		1988 BOATS														
26	7	MERMAID 270	SLP	SA/CR	FBG	KL	IB	9D	VLVO	9	6	7480	4	1	38300	42600
26	7	MERMAID 270	SLP	SA/CR	FBG	KL	SD	18D	VLVO	9	6	7480	4	1	38600	42900
28	8	LM28 IIS	SLP	SA/CR	FBG	KL	SD	28D	VLVO	9	6	8810	4	5	50200	55200
28	8	MERMAID 290	SLP	SA/CR	FBG	KL	SD	18D	VLVO	9	6	8300	4	5	47300	52000
30	8	LM30 IIS	SLP	SA/CR	FBG	KL	SD	28D- 43D		10		11000	4	11	66200	72800
30	8	MERMAID 315	SLP	SA/CR	FBG	KL	SD	28D	VLVO	10		10340	4	11	62200	68300
32		LM32 IIS	SLP	SA/CR	FBG	KL	SD	43D	VLVO	10	8	13200	4	11	81000	89000
37		MERMAID 380	SLP	SA/CR	FBG	KL	IB	43D	VLVO	11	9	14330	5	6	95400	105000
		1987 BOATS														
26	7	MERMAID 270	SLP	SA/CR	FBG	KL	IB	9D	VLVO	9	6	7480	4	1	36000	40000
26	7	MERMAID 270	SLP	SA/CR	FBG	KL	SD	18D	VLVO	9	6	7480	4	1	36300	40300
27	5	LM27 MARK II	SLP	SA/CR	FBG	KL	IB	28D	VLVO	9		8800	3	1	44900	49900
28	8	LM28 IIS	SLP	SA/CR	FBG	KL	SD	28D	VLVO	9	6	8810	4	5	47400	52100
28	8	MERMAID 290	SLP	SA/CR	FBG	KL	SD	18D	VLVO	9	6	8300	4	5	43900	48800
30	8	LM30 IIS	SLP	SA/CR	FBG	KL	SD	28D- 43D		10		11000	4	11	62200	68400
30	8	MERMAID 315	SLP	SA/CR	FBG	KL	SD	28D	VLVO	10		10340	4	11	58500	64200
32		LM32 IIS	SLP	SA/CR	FBG	KL	SD	43D	VLVO	10	8	13200	4	11	76100	83600
37		MERMAID 380	SLP	SA/CR	FBG	KL	IB	43D	VLVO	11	9	14330	5	6	89700	98500
		1986 BOATS														
26	6	MERMAID 270	SLP	SA/CR	FBG	KL	IB	10D- 24D		9	6	7040	4	1	31700	35700
27	5	LM27 MARK II	SLP	SA/CR	FBG	KL	IB	24D- 36D		9		8800	3	1	42200	47100
28	8	LM28 IIS	SLP	SA/CR	FBG	KL	SD	18D- 36D		9	6	8810	4	5	43900	49200
28	8	MERMAID 290	SLP	SA/CR	FBG	KL	IB	24D- 28D		9	6	8300	4	5	41500	46100
30	8	LM30 IIS	SLP	SA/CR	FBG	KL	SD	24D- 36D		10		11000	4	11	58500	64300
30	8	MERMAID 315	SLP	SA/CR	FBG	KL	SD	24D- 28D		10		10340	4	11	55100	60500
32		LM32 IIS	SLP	SA/CR	FBG	KL	SD	36D		10	8	13200	4	11	71500	78600
		1985 BOATS														
26	6	MERMAID 270	SLP	SA/CR	FBG	KL	IB	8D- 20D		9	6	7040	4	1	29700	33400
27	5	LM27	SLP	SA/CR	FBG	KL	IB	20D- 36D		9		8800	3	1	39500	44300
28	8	LM28	SLP	SA/CR	FBG	KL	SD	18D- 36D		9	6	8810	4	5	41200	46200
30	8	LM30	SLP	SA/CR	FBG	KL	SD	20D- 36D		10		11000	4	11	55000	60600
30	8	MERMAID 315	SLP	SA/CR	FBG	KL	SD	20D- 28D		10		10340	4	11	51800	56900
32		LM32	SLP	SA/CR	FBG	KL	SD	35D- 36D		10	8	13200	4	11	67200	73900
		1984 BOATS														
27	5	LM27	SLP	SA/CR	FBG	KL	IB	35D	VLVO	9		8800	3	1	37300	41400
28	8	LM28	SLP	SA/CR	FBG	KL	SD	23D- 35D		9	6	8810	4	5	38800	43300
30	8	LM30	SLP	SA/CR	FBG	KL	SD	35D	VLVO	10		11000	4	11	51800	56900
30	8	MERMAID 315	SLP	SA/CR	FBG	KL	SD	28D	VLVO	10		10340	4	11	48700	53500
32		LM32	SLP	SA/CR	FBG	KL	SD	35D	VLVO	10	8	13200	4	11	63200	69500

....For earlier years, see the BUC Used Boat Price Guide, Volume 3

ANCHOR PLASTICS INC

DECK BOATS
GATESVILLE TX 76528 COAST GUARD MFG ID- ANP

See inside cover to adjust price for area

LOA FT	IN	NAME AND/ OR MODEL	TOP/ RIG	BOAT TYPE	-HULL- MTL	TP	TP	ENGINE # HP	MFG	BEAM FT	IN	WGT LBS	DRAFT FT	IN	RETAIL LOW	RETAIL HIGH
		1994 BOATS														
17	10	SKI DECK	OP	B/R	FBG	SV	OB			7	7	1200			5350	6150
17	10	SKI DECK XLS	OP	B/R	FBG	SV	IO	180-215		7	7	2105			5950	7400
17	10	SKI DECK XLS	OP	B/R	FBG	SV	IO	230		7	7	2105			6200	7550
17	10	SKI DECK XLS	OP	B/R	FBG	SV	IO	255	VLVO	7	7	2105			6800	7800
		1993 BOATS														
17	10	SKI DECK	OP	B/R	FBG	SV	OB			7	7	1200			5100	5900
17	10	SKI DECK XLS	OP	B/R	FBG	SV	IO	150-210		7	7	1960			5300	6300
19	10	GAN DECKER	OP	B/R	FBG	TH	IO	160-240		7	8	2750			7200	8700

....For earlier years, see the BUC Used Boat Price Guide, Volume 3

THE ANCHORAGE INC

DYER BOATS
WARREN RI 02885 COAST GUARD MFG ID- DYE

See inside cover to adjust price for area

For more recent years, see the BUC Used Boat Price Guide, Volume 1

LOA FT	IN	NAME AND/ OR MODEL	TOP/ RIG	BOAT TYPE	-HULL- MTL	TP	TP	ENGINE # HP	MFG	BEAM FT	IN	WGT LBS	DRAFT FT	IN	RETAIL LOW	RETAIL HIGH
		1987 BOATS														
28	6	DYER 29	ST	CR	FBG	DS	IB	240-350		9	5	6700	2	6	48300	56500
28	6	DYER 29	ST	CR	FBG	DS	IB	200D-300D		9	5	6700	2	6	58800	70600
28	6	DYER 29	HT	CR	FBG	DS	IB	240	CHRY	9	5	6700	2	6	48000	52800
28	6	DYER 29 BASS	ST	CR	FBG	DS	IB	240	CHRY	9	5	6700	2	6	47400	52100
28	6	DYER 29 FLUSHCKPT	ST	CR	FBG	DS	IB	200D	VLVO	9	5	6700	2	6	57100	62800
28	6	DYER 29 LAUNCH	OP	CR	FBG	DS	IB	240	CHRY	9	5	6700	2	6	48000	52800
28	6	DYER 29 SOFTTOP BASS	ST	CR	FBG	DS	IB	240	CHRY	9	5	6700	2	6	48200	53000
39	8	DYER 40	HT	CR	FBG	DS	IB	435D	GM	12	5		2	9	202000	222000
39	8	DYER 40	HT	CR	FBG	DS	IB	T		12	5		2	9	**	**
		1986 BOATS														
28	6	DYER 29	ST	CR	FBG	DS	IB	225-350		9	5	6700	2	6	45600	53900
28	6	DYER 29	ST	CR	FBG	DS	IB	120D-200D		9	5	6700	2	6	50000	61500
28	6	DYER 29	ST	CR	FBG	DS	IB	250D	VLVO	9	5	6700	2	6	57900	63600
28	6	DYER 29	HT	CR	FBG	DS	IB	240	CHRY	9	5	6700	2	6	46000	50500
28	6	DYER 29 BASS	ST	CR	FBG	DS	IB	240	CHRY	9	5	6700	2	6	46000	50500
28	6	DYER 29 FLUSHDECK	ST	CR	FBG	DS	IB	240	CHRY	9	5	6700	2	6	46000	50500
28	6	DYER 29 LAUNCH	OP	CR	FBG	DS	IB	240	CHRY	9	5	6700	2	6	46000	50500
28	6	DYER 29 SOFTTOP BASS	ST	CR	FBG	DS	IB	240	CHRY	9	5	6700	2	6	46000	50500
39	8	DYER 40	HT	CR	FBG	DS	IB			12	5		2	9	**	**
39	8	DYER 40	HT	CR	FBG	DS	IB	T		12	5		2	9	**	**
		1985 BOATS														
28	6	DYERCRAFT 29		BASS	FBG	RB	IB	225		9	5	7000			43500	48300
28	6	DYERCRAFT 29		CR	FBG	RB	IB	225		9	5	7000			43800	48600
28	6	DYERCRAFT 29		LNCH	FBG	RB	IB	58		9	5	7000			33000	36700
39	8	DYERCRAFT 40		CR	FBG	RB	IB	240		12	6				147500	162000
39	8	DYERCRAFT 40		SF	FBG	RB	IB	T250		12	6				168500	185000
39	8	DYERCRAFT 40		UTL	FBG	RB	IB	135		12	6				74900	82300
		1984 BOATS														
28	6	DYERCRAFT 29		CR	FBG	RB	IB	225		9	5	7000			41800	46500
28	6	DYERCRAFT 29	OP	LNCH	FBG	RB	IB	58-170		9	5				36800	40800
28	6	DYERCRAFT 29		OFF	FBG	RB	IB	225		9	5	7000			42200	46900
39	8	DYERCRAFT 40		CR	FBG	RB	IB	110		12	6				140000	153500
39	8	DYERCRAFT 40		DC	FBG	RB	IB	240D		12	6				160500	176500
39	8	DYERCRAFT 40		SF	FBG	RB	IB	T250		12	6				161000	177000

....For earlier years, see the BUC Used Boat Price Guide, Volume 3

ANDERSON & ALEXANDER

SANTA BARBARA CA 93101 COAST GUARD MFG ID- BIL See inside cover to adjust price for area

LOA FT	IN	NAME AND/ OR MODEL	TOP/ RIG	BOAT TYPE	-HULL- MTL	TP	TP	ENGINE # HP	MFG	BEAM FT	IN	WGT LBS	DRAFT FT	IN	RETAIL LOW	RETAIL HIGH
		1986 BOATS														
22		CHAZ 22	HT	FSH	FBG	DV	IO	330		8		4000	1	3	14300	16200
		1985 BOATS														
22		CHAZ 22	HT	FSH	FBG	DV	IO	330		8		4000	1	3	13600	15500

ANDERSSON INTERNATIONAL

KANG KAOHSIUNG TAIWAN ROC — See inside cover to adjust price for area

LOA FT	LOA IN	NAME AND/ OR MODEL	TOP/ RIG	BOAT TYPE	HULL MTL	HULL TP	ENGINE TP	ENGINE # HP	ENGINE MFG	BEAM FT	BEAM IN	WGT LBS	DRAFT FT	DRAFT IN	RETAIL LOW	RETAIL HIGH
		1987 BOATS														
28	11	FIDDLERS-GREEN	CUT	SA/CR	F/S	KL	IB	15D	BMW	9	2	9300	4	3	41600	46300
42	11	INTERNATIONAL 42	SLP	SA/RC	F/S	KL	SD	35D	VLVO	12	8	22000	6	3	102000	112500
49		INTERNATIONAL 49	CUT	SA/RC	F/S	KL	IB	50D	PERK	14		33000	6	9	149500	164500
		1986 BOATS														
28	6	FIDDLERS-GREEN	CUT	SA/CR	F/S	KL	IB	15D	BMW	9	2	9300	4	3	38900	43300
42	11	PACIFIC 42	SLP	SA/RC	F/S	KL	SD	35D	VLVO	12	8	22000	6	3	96100	105500
44	6	FALCON	KTH	SA/CR	FBG	KL	IB	61D	LEHM	13	9	32800	5	10	125000	137500
48	10	PACIFIC 49	CUT	SA/RC	F/S	KL	IB	50D		14		33000	6	9	139500	153500
58	4		SCH	SAIL	F/S	KL	IB	100D		18	4	77000	12		373000	410000
		1985 BOATS														
28	6	FIDDLERS-GREEN	CUT	SA/CR	F/S	KL	IB	20D	YAN	9	2	9300	4	3	36800	40800
42	11	PACIFIC 42	SLP	SA/RC	F/S	KL	SD	35D	VLVO	12	8	22000	6	3	90400	99300
44	6	FALCON	KTH	SA/CR	FBG	KL	IB	D		13	9	32800	5	10	117500	129500
48	10	PACIFIC 48	CUT	SA/RC	F/S	KL	IB	50D		14		33000	6	9	131000	144000
58	4		SCH	SAIL	F/S	KL	IB	100D		18	4	77000	12		350000	384500
		1984 BOATS														
28	6	FIDDLERS-GREEN	CUT	SA/CR	F/S	KL	IB	20	YAN	9	2	9300	4	3	34100	37900
42	11	PACIFIC 42	SLP	SA/RC	F/S	KL	SD	35D	VLVO	12	8	22000	6	3	85000	93400
44	6	FALCON	KTH	SA/CR	FBG	KL	IB	D		13	9	32800	5	10	110500	121500
48	10	PACIFIC 48	CUT	SA/RC	F/S	KL	IB	50D	VLVO	14		33000	6	9	123000	135500
58	4		SCH	SAIL	F/S	KL	IB	100D		18	4	77000	12		329500	362000

N P ANDERSSON LTD

FL SREBRNRUANG
BANGKOK THAILAND — See inside cover to adjust price for area

LOA FT	LOA IN	NAME AND/ OR MODEL	TOP/ RIG	BOAT TYPE	HULL MTL	HULL TP	ENGINE TP	ENGINE # HP	ENGINE MFG	BEAM FT	BEAM IN	WGT LBS	DRAFT FT	DRAFT IN	RETAIL LOW	RETAIL HIGH
		1991 BOATS														
36	8	ANDERSSON 360	HT	LNCH	F/S	DV	IB	250D	CUM	10	9	14000			45900	50400
36	8	ANDERSSON SQUID	HT	FSH	F/S	DV	IB	85D	CUM	10	9	12000			80100	88100
42	5	ANDERSSON 420	FB	MYDKH	F/S	DV	IB	300D	CAT	15	6	23000			237000	260500
47	5	ANDERSSON 470	FB	MYDKH	F/S	DV	IB	T375D	CAT	15	7	30000	3	6	273000	300000
47	6	ANDERSSON 475 FHS	FB	MY	F/S	DV	IB	T300D	CAT	15	6	26000	3		241500	265000
48		ANDERSSON 480	FB	MY	F/S	DV	IB	T375D	CAT	15	7	26000	3		250000	274500
51	7	ANDERSSON 520	FB	MY	F/S	DV	IB	T425D	CAT	15	8	28000	3		276500	303500
52	10	ANDERSSON 530	FB	MYDKH	F/S	DV	IB	375D	CAT	15	8	32000	3	6	214500	235500
52	11	ANDERSSON 525 FHS	FB	MY	F/S	DV	IB	425D	CAT	15	8	30000	3	6	226000	248500

ANGEL MARINE INDUSTRIES CORP

KAOHSIUNG TAIWAN — See inside cover to adjust price for area

LOA FT	LOA IN	NAME AND/ OR MODEL	TOP/ RIG	BOAT TYPE	HULL MTL	HULL TP	ENGINE TP	ENGINE # HP	ENGINE MFG	BEAM FT	BEAM IN	WGT LBS	DRAFT FT	DRAFT IN	RETAIL LOW	RETAIL HIGH
		1987 BOATS														
41	10	ANGEL 42	SLP	SA/CR	FBG	KL	IB	D		12	9	21258	5	10	110500	121500
		1986 BOATS														
41	10	ANGEL 42	SLP	SA/CR		KL	IB	D		12	9	21258	5	10	104000	114500
		1985 BOATS														
41	10	ANGEL 42	SLP	SA/CR	FBG	KL	IB	D		12	9	21258	5	10	89900	98800
41	10	SOUTHERN-OFFSHORE 42	SLP	SA/CR	FBG	KL	IB	D		12	9	21258	5	10	106000	116500

ANGLER BOAT CORP

MIAMI FL 33147 — COAST GUARD MFG ID- ANG See inside cover to adjust price for area

For more recent years, see the BUC Used Boat Price Guide, Volume 1

LOA FT	LOA IN	NAME AND/ OR MODEL	TOP/ RIG	BOAT TYPE	HULL MTL	HULL TP	ENGINE TP	ENGINE # HP	ENGINE MFG	BEAM FT	BEAM IN	WGT LBS	DRAFT FT	DRAFT IN	RETAIL LOW	RETAIL HIGH
		1996 BOATS														
16	8	ANGLER 170 F	OP	CTRCN	FBG	DV	OB			7	2	1170			2350	2750
18		ANGLER 180 F	OP	CTRCN	FBG	DV	OB			7	7	1580			3100	3600
20	4	ANGLER 204 DC	OP	W/T	FBG	DV	OB			8		1900			5150	5900
20	4	ANGLER 204 F	OP	CTRCN	FBG	DV	OB			8		1900			5050	5800
20	4	ANGLER 204 WA	OP	CUD	FBG	DV	OB			8		2200			5800	6650
22		ANGLER 220 F	OP	CTRCN	FBG	DV	OB			8	6	2300			6350	7300
22		ANGLER 220 WA	OP	CUD	FBG	DV	OB			8	6	2500			7100	8150
24		ANGLER 240 F	OP	CTRCN	FBG	DV	OB			8	6	3210			9150	10400
24		ANGLER 240 WA	OP	CUD	FBG	DV	OB			8	6	3310			9800	11100
25	2	ANGLER 252 F	OP	CTRCN	FBG	DV	OB			9	5	4000			10900	12400
25	2	ANGLER 252 WA	OP	CUD	FBG	DV	OB			9	5	4000			11600	13200
		1995 BOATS														
16	8	ANGLER 170 F	OP	CTRCN	FBG	DV	OB			7	2	1170			2250	2600
18		ANGLER 180 F	OP	CTRCN	FBG	DV	OB			7	7	1580			2900	3400
20	4	ANGLER 204 DC	OP	CUD	FBG	DV	OB			8		1900			5000	5700
20	4	ANGLER 204 F	OP	CTRCN	FBG	DV	OB			8		1900			4800	5500
20	4	ANGLER 204 WA	OP	CUD	FBG	DV	OB			8		2200			5450	6300
22		ANGLER 220 F	OP	CTRCN	FBG	DV	OB			8	6	2300			6000	6900
22		ANGLER 220 WA	OP	CUD	FBG	DV	OB			8	6	2500			6650	7650
24		ANGLER 240 F	OP	CTRCN	FBG	DV	OB			8	6	3210			8550	9850
24		ANGLER 240 WA	OP	CUD	FBG	DV	OB			8	6	3310			9250	10500
25	2	ANGLER 252 F	OP	CTRCN	FBG	DV	OB			9	5	4000			10300	11700
25	2	ANGLER 252 WA	OP	CUD	FBG	DV	OB			9	5	4000			11000	12500
		1994 BOATS														
16	8	ANGLER 170 F	OP	CTRCN	FBG	DV	OB			7	2	1170			2050	2450
18		ANGLER 180 F	OP	CTRCN	FBG	DV	OB			7	7	1580			2750	3200
20	4	ANGLER 204 F	OP	CTRCN	FBG	DV	OB			8		1900			4550	5250
20	4	ANGLER 204 WA	OP	CUD	FBG	DV	OB			8		2200			5200	5950
22		ANGLER 220 F	OP	CTRCN	FBG	DV	OB			8	6	2300			5700	6550
22		ANGLER 220 WA	OP	CUD	FBG	DV	OB			8	6	2500			6300	7250
24		ANGLER 240 F	OP	CTRCN	FBG	DV	OB			8	6	3210			8100	9350
24		ANGLER 240 WA	OP	CUD	FBG	DV	OB			8	6	3310			8650	9950
25	2	ANGLER 252 F	OP	CTRCN	FBG	DV	OB			9	5	4000			9800	11200
25	2	ANGLER 252 WA	OP	CUD	FBG	DV	OB			9	5	4000			10400	11800
		1993 BOATS														
16	8	ANGLER 170 F	OP	CTRCN	FBG	DV	OB			7	2	1170			1950	2300
18		ANGLER 180 F	OP	CTRCN	FBG	DV	OB			7	7	1580			2600	3050
20	4	ANGLER 204 F	OP	CTRCN	FBG	DV	OB			8		1900			4300	5000
20	4	ANGLER 204 WA	OP	CUD	FBG	DV	OB			8		2200			4950	5700
22		ANGLER 220 F	OP	CTRCN	FBG	DV	OB			8	6	2300			5450	6250
22		ANGLER 220 WA	OP	CUD	FBG	DV	OB			8	6	2500			6000	6900
25	2	ANGLER 252 F	OP	CTRCN	FBG	DV	OB			9	5	4000			9400	10700
25	2	ANGLER 252 WA	OP	CUD	FBG	DV	OB			9	5	4000			9900	11200
		1992 BOATS														
16	8	FISH 17	OP	CTRCN	FBG	DV	OB			7	2	1110			1750	2100
18		FISH 18	OP	CTRCN	FBG	DV	OB			7	7	1680			2600	3000
18		HORIZON 180	OP	CTRCN	FBG	DV	OB			7	7	1570			2450	2850
18	3	FISH 19	ST	CUD	FBG	SV	OB			7	5	1300			2250	2600
18	3	FISH 19	ST	RNBT	FBG	SV	OB			7	5	1300			2300	2650
18	8	FISH 19	OP	CTRCN	FBG	SV	OB			8		1710			2650	3100
20	4	FISH 20	OP	CTRCN	FBG	DV	OB			8		1950			4150	4850
20	4	HORIZON 204	OP	CTRCN	FBG	DV	OB			8		1820			3950	4600
20	4	HORIZON WA 204	OP	CBNCR	FBG	DV	OB			8		2190			4600	5300
20	4	WALKAROUND 20	OP	FSH	FBG	DV	OB			8		2400			4800	5550
22		FISH 22	OP	CTRCN	FBG	DV	OB			8	6	2400			5350	6150
22		HORIZON 220	OP	CTRCN	FBG	DV	OB			8	6	2150			4950	5650
22		HORIZON WA 220	OP	CBNCR	FBG	DV	OB			8	6	2600			5750	6600
22		WALKAROUND 22	OP	FSH	FBG	DV	OB			8	6	2900			6150	7050
25	2	HORIZON WA 252	OP	CBNCR	FBG	DV	OB			9	5	3850			9000	10200
25	2	WALKAROUND 25	OP	FSH	FBG	DV	OB			9	5	4050			9150	10400
		1991 BOATS														
16	8	FISH 17	OP	CTRCN	FBG	DV	OB			7	2	1110			1700	2000
18		FISH 18	OP	CTRCN	FBG	DV	OB			7	7	1680			2450	2850
18		HORIZON 180	OP	CTRCN	FBG	DV	OB			7	7	1570			2400	2800
18	3	FISH 19	ST	CUD	FBG	SV	OB			7	5	1300			2050	2450
18	3	FISH 19	ST	RNBT	FBG	SV	OB			7	5	1300			2200	2550
18	8	FISH 19	OP	CTRCN	FBG	SV	OB			8		1710			2550	2950
20	4	FISH 20	OP	CTRCN	FBG	DV	OB			8		1950			4000	4650
20	4	HORIZON 204	OP	CTRCN	FBG	DV	OB			8		1820			3800	4400
20	4	HORIZON WA 204	OP	CBNCR	FBG	DV	OB			8		2190			4400	5050
20	4	WALKAROUND 20	OP	FSH	FBG	DV	OB			8		2400			4600	5300
22		FISH 22	OP	CTRCN	FBG	DV	OB			8	6	2400			5150	5900
22		HORIZON 220	OP	CTRCN	FBG	DV	OB			8	6	2150			4750	5450
22		HORIZON WA 220	OP	CBNCR	FBG	DV	OB			8	6	2600			5500	6350
22		WALKAROUND 22	OP	FSH	FBG	DV	OB			8	6	2900			5900	6750
25	2	HORIZON WA 252	OP	CBNCR	FBG	DV	OB			9	5	3850			8500	9750
25	2	WALKAROUND 25	OP	FSH	FBG	DV	OB			9	5	4050			8650	9950
		1990 BOATS														
16	8	17 FISH	OP	CTRCN	FBG	DV	OB			7	2	1110			1600	1900
18		18 FISH	OP	CTRCN	FBG	DV	OB			7	7	1680			2400	2800
18	3	19 FISH	ST	CUD	FBG	SV	OB			7	5	1300			2000	2350
18	3	19 FISH	ST	RNBT	FBG	SV	OB			7	5	1300			2000	2400
18	8	19 FISH	OP	CTRCN	FBG	SV	OB			8		1710			2450	2850
20	4	20 FISH	OP	CTRCN	FBG	DV	OB			8		1950			3850	4450
20	4	20 WALKAROUND	OP	FSH	FBG	DV	OB			8		2400			4450	5100
20	4	20 WALKAROUND	OP	FSH	FBG	DV	IO	165-230		8		3100			5050	5950
22		22 FISH	OP	CTRCN	FBG	DV	OB			8	6	2400			4950	5700
22		22 WALKAROUND	OP	FSH	FBG	DV	OB			8	6	2900			5650	6500
22		22 WALKAROUND	OP	FSH	FBG	DV	IO	230-260		8	6	3500			6400	7550

 CONTINUED ON NEXT PAGE

```
  LOA  NAME AND/    TOP/ BOAT -HULL- ----ENGINE---  BEAM  WGT  DRAFT RETAIL RETAIL
  FT IN  OR MODEL   RIG  TYPE MTL TP TP #  HP  MFG   FT IN LBS  FT IN  LOW    HIGH
-------------------------- 1990 BOATS --------------------------------------------
25  2 25 WALKAROUND  OP FSH  FBG DV OB             9 5  4050          8300   9550
-------------------------- 1989 BOATS --------------------------------------------
16  8 17F            OP CTRCN FBG DV OB            7 2  1110          1550   1800
18  8 18F            OP CTRCN FBG DV OB            7 7  1680          2300   2650
18  3 19BR           ST RNBT  FBG SV OB            7 5  1300          1950   2300
18  3 19CC           ST CUD   FBG SV OB            7 5  1300          1900   2250
18  8 19F            OP CTRCN FBG SV OB            8    1710          2350   2750
20  4 20F            OP CTRCN FBG DV OB            8    1950          3700   4300
20  4 20WA           OP FSH   FBG DV OB            8    2400          4250   4900
20  4 20WA           OP FSH   FBG DV IO 165-230    8    3100          4750   5600
22  2 22F            OP CTRCN FBG DV OB            8 6  2400          4750   5500
22  2 22WA           OP FSH   FBG DV OB            8 6  2900          5450   6250
22  2 22WA           OP FSH   FBG DV IO 230-260    8 6  3500          6050   7150
-------------------------- 1988 BOATS --------------------------------------------
16  8 17F            OP CTRCN FBG DV OB            7 2  1110          1450   1750
18  8 18F            OP CTRCN FBG DV OB            7 7  1680          2200   2550
18  3 19BR           ST RNBT  FBG SV OB            7 5  1300          1850   2200
18  3 19BR           ST RNBT  FBG SV IO 120-130    7 5  1300          2100   2500
18  3 19CC           ST CUD   FBG SV OB            7 5  1300          1800   2150
18  3 19CC           ST CUD   FBG SV IO 120  MRCR  7 5  1300          2200   2550
18  8 19F            OP CTRCN FBG SV OB            8    1710          2250   2600
20  4 20F            OP CTRCN FBG DV OB            8    1950          3600   4200
20  4 20WA           OP FSH   FBG DV OB            8    2400          4100   4750
20  4 20WA           OP FSH   FBG DV IO 165-230    8    3100          4450   5300
22  2 22F            OP CTRCN FBG DV OB            8    2050          4050   4700
22  2 22WA           OP FSH   FBG DV OB            8    2600          4900   5650

22  2 22WA           OP FSH   FBG DV IO 180-260    8    3300          5200   6250
-------------------------- 1987 BOATS --------------------------------------------
16  8 17F            OP CTRCN FBG SV OB            7 2  1110          1400   1700
18  8 18F            OP CTRCN FBG DV OB            7 7  1680          2050   2400
18  3 19BR           ST RNBT  FBG SV OB            7 5  1300          1750   2100
18  3 19BR           ST RNBT  FBG SV IO 120-130    7 5  1300          2000   2350
18  3 19CC           ST CUD   FBG SV OB            7 5  1300          1750   2100
18  3 19CC           ST CUD   FBG SV IO 120  MRCR  7 5  1300          2000   2400
18  8 19F            OP CTRCN FBG SV OB            8    1710          2100   2500
20  4 20F            OP CTRCN FBG DV OB            8    1950          3500   4050
20  4 20WA           OP FSH   FBG DV OB            8    2400          3950   4600
20  4 20WA           OP FSH   FBG DV IO 165-230    8    3100          4200   5000
22  2 22F            OP CTRCN FBG DV OB            8    2050          3950   4550
22  2 22WA           OP FSH   FBG DV OB            8    2600          4750   5450

22  2 22WA           OP FSH   FBG DV IO 180-260    8      3300        4900   5900
27    27CC           ST CUD   FBG DV IO 230-260    8 9                8400   9900
27    27CC           ST CUD   FBG DV IO T180 MRCR  8 9                9600  10900
27    27FB           FB FSH   FBG DV IO 230-260    8 9                9300  10900
27    27FB           FB FSH   FBG DV IO T180 MRCR  8 9               10500  11900
27    27HT           HT FSH   FBG DV IO 230-260    8 9    5540        9750  11400
27    27HT           HT FSH   FBG DV IO T180 MRCR  8 9               10500  11900
-------------------------- 1986 BOATS --------------------------------------------
16  8 V-17F          OP CTRCN FBG SV OB            7 2  1100          1350   1600
18  3 V-19BR         ST RNBT  FBG SV OB            7 5  1300          1700   2050
18  3 V-19BR         ST RNBT  FBG SV IO 120-170    7 5  1300          1900   2250
18  3 V-19CC         ST CUD   FBG SV OB            7 5  1300          1700   2000
18  3 V-19CC         ST CUD   FBG SV IO 120        7 5  1300          1900   2250
18  8 V-19FSH        OP CTRCN FBG SV OB            8    1650          1950   2350
20  1 V-21BR         ST RNBT  FBG SV OB            8    1715          3100   3600
20  1 V-21BR         ST RNBT  FBG SV IO 120-170    8    1715          2650   3100
20  1 V-21BR         ST RNBT  FBG SV IB 175  OMC   8    1715          3800   4400
20  1 V-21BR         ST RNBT  FBG SV IO 198-230    8    1715          2700   3200
20  1 V-21CC         ST CUD   FBG SV OB            8    1715          3100   3600
20  1 V-21CC         ST CUD   FBG SV IO 120-230    8    1715          2750   3350

20  4 V-20WA         OP FSH   FBG DV OB            8    2400          3850   4500
22    V-22F          OP CTRCN FBG SV OB            8    1940          3650   4250
22    V-22F          OP CTRCN FBG SV IO 120-260    8           10     3800   4700
22    V-22F          OP CTRCN FBG SV IO 330  MRCR  8           10     4650   5350
22    V-22WA         OP FSH   FBG DV OB            8    3000          5050   5850
22    V-22WA         OP FSH   FBG DV IO 120-260    8    3000         4350   5300
22    V-22WA         OP FSH   FBG DV IO 330  MRCR  8    3000         5200   6000
23  6 V-24CC         ST CUD   FBG DV OB            8    3000         5600   6450
23  6 V-24CC         ST CUD   FBG DV IO 205-260    8    3400         4700   5600
23  6 V-24CC         ST CUD   FBG DV IO 330  MRCR  8    3400         5400   6200
23  6 V-24XX         ST CUD   FBG DV IO 230  OMC   8    3400         4750   5450
25  9                OP EXP   FBG DV OB            9 9  4900         8400   9650

25  9 FREEDOM 26     OP EXP   FBG DV IB 225  COMM  9 9  4900   2 3   9250  10500
      IO  228 MRCR  7300  8400, IB  255         9400 10700, IO 260 MRCR  7500  8600
      IO T170 MRCR  8250  9500, IB T170 MRCR 10400 11800

25  9 FREEDOM 26     FB EXP   FBG DV OB            9 9  4900   2 3   8400   9700
25  9 FREEDOM 26     FB EXP   FBG DV IB 225  COMM  9 9  4900   2 3   9250  10500
      IO  228 MRCR  7300  8400, IB  255         9400 10700, IO 260 MRCR  7500  8600
      IO T170 MRCR  8250  9500, IB T170 MRCR 10400 12300

25  9 FREEDOM 26     OP SF    FBG DV OB            9 9  4900   2 3   8100   9300
25  9 FREEDOM 26     OP SF    FBG DV IB 225  COMM  9 9  4900   2 3   9050  10300
      IO  228 MRCR  8250  9450, IB  255  MRCR  9200 10500, IO 260 MRCR  8450  9700
      IB 200D PERK 12200 13900, IO T170 MRCR 9300 10600, IB T170-T225 10100 12000

27    V-27CC         ST CUD   FBG SV OB            8 9  3185          9800  11100
27    V-27CC         ST CUD   FBG DV IO 205-260    8 9  3185          6450   8000
      IO  330 MRCR  7750  8900, IO T140-T175 7400  9000, IO T205-T260 8150  9600
      IO T330 MRCR  9150 10400

27    V-27FB         FB SDN   FBG DV OB            8 9  6200          9500  10800
27    V-27FB         FB SDN   FBG DV IO 198-260    8 9               10900  12900
      IO  330 MRCR 12000 13700, IO T140-T205 11800 14500, IO T228-T330 13100 16200
-------------------------- 1985 BOATS --------------------------------------------
16  8 V-17F          OP CTRCN FBG SV OB            7 2  1075   7      1300   1500
18  3 V-19              CUD   FBG SV OB 120        7 5  1230          2250   2600
18  3 V-19BR            RNBT  FBG SV OB            7 5  1230          1550   1850
18  3 V-19BR            RNBT  FBG SV OB 120        7 5  1230          1750   2100
18  3 V-19CC            CUD   FBG SV OB            7 5  1300          1600   1900
18  8 V-19F             FSH   FBG SV OB            8    1570          1850   2200
20  1 V-21              CUD   FBG SV OB 120        8    1775          2650   3050
20  1 V-21BR            RNBT  FBG SV OB            8    1715          3000   3500
20  1 V-21BR            RNBT  FBG SV OB            8    1715          2550   2950
20  1 V-21CC            CUD   FBG SV OB            8    1775          3050   3550
20  4 V-20              FSH   FBG SV OB            8    1800          3150   3650
20  4 V-20WA            FSH   FBG SV IO 120        8                  3700   4300

22    V-22              FSH   FBG SV OB            8    2300          4100   4750
22    V-22F             FSH   FBG SV OB 140        8                  3750   4350
22    V-22F             FSH   FBG SV OB            8    1940          3550   4150
22    V-22WA            FSH   FBG SV IO 170        8    3000          4150   4850
23  6 V-24CC            CUD   FBG DV OB            8    3000          5450   6300
23  6 V-24CC            CUD   FBG DV OB 200        8    3400          4500   5200
25  9 ANGLER 26         EXP   FBG DV OB            9 9  4900          8150   9350
25  9 ANGLER 26         EXP   FBG DV OB            9 9                 **     **
25  9 ANGLER 26      FB SF    FBG SV OB            9 9                7150   8200
25  9 ANGLER 26      FB SF    FBG SV OB            9 9                 **     **
27    V-27CC            CUD   FBG SV OB            8 9  3500          9100  10400
27    V-27CC            CUD   FBG SV OB 230        8 9                7550   8700

27    V-27FB         FB SDN   FBG SV OB            8 9  4000          9050  10300
27    V-27FB         FB SDN   FBG SV IO 230        8 9               10700  12100
-------------------------- 1984 BOATS --------------------------------------------
16  8 V-17F          OP CTRCN FBG SV OB            7 2  1075   7      1250   1500
18  3 V-19BR         ST RNBT  FBG SV OB            7 5  1230          1500   1800
18  3 V-19BR         ST RNBT  FBG SV OB 120-170    7 5  1230          1650   2000
18  3 V-19CC            CUD   FBG SV OB            7 5  1300          1550   1850
18  3 V-19CC            CUD   FBG SV OB 120        7 5                2100   2450
18  8 V-19F          OP FSH   FBG SV OB            8    1570          1750   2100
20  1 V-21BR         ST RNBT  FBG SV OB            8    1715          2950   3400
20  1 V-21BR         ST RNBT  FBG SV OB 120-140    8    1715          2450   2850
      IO 170 MRCR  2450  2850, IB 170 OMC  3400  3950, IO 198-230  2450  2950

20  1 V-21CC         ST CUD   FBG SV OB            8    1775          3000   3500
20  1 V-21CC         ST CUD   FBG SV IO 120-230    8    1775          2550   3050
22    V-22F          OP CTRCN FBG SV OB            8    1940          3500   4050
22    V-22F          OP CTRCN FBG SV IO 120-260    8           10     3450   4250
22    V-22F          OP CTRCN FBG SV IO 330  MRCR  8           10     4200   4900
22    V-22WA         OP FSH   FBG DV OB            8    3000          4850   5550
22    V-22WA         OP FSH   FBG DV IO 120-260    8    3000         3950   4850
22    V-22WA         OP FSH   FBG DV IO 330  MRCR  8    3000         4750   5450
23  6 V-24CC         ST CUD   FBG DV OB            8    3000         5300   6100
23  6 V-24CC         ST CUD   FBG DV IO 200-260    8    3400         4200   5100
23  6 V-24CC         ST CUD   FBG DV IO 330  MRCR  8    3400         4950   5700
25  9                OP EXP   FBG DV OB            9 9  4900         7900   9100

25  9 FREEDOM 26     OP EXP   FBG DV IB 225  COMM  9 9  4900   2 3   8350   9600
      IO  228 MRCR  6600  7600, IB  255         8450  9750, IO 260 MRCR  6850  7900
      IO T170 MRCR  7500  8600, IB T170 MRCR 9450 10700

25  9 FREEDOM 26     FB EXP   FBG DV OB            9 9  4900   2 3   7900   9100
```

```
ANGLER BOAT CORP            -CONTINUED    See inside cover to adjust price for area
LOA   NAME AND/             TOP/ BOAT -HULL- ----ENGINE--- BEAM  WGT  DRAFT RETAIL RETAIL
FT IN   OR MODEL            RIG  TYPE MTL TP TP # HP  MFG   FT IN LBS  FT IN  LOW   HIGH
------------------- 1984 BOATS --------------------------------------------------------
25  9 FREEDOM 26            FB  EXP  FBG DV IB 225  COMM  9  9 4900 2 3  8350  9600
       IO  228 MRCR    6600 7600, IB   255        8450 9750, IO 260 MRCR  6850  7900
       IO T170 MRCR    7500 8600, IB T170-T225        9450 11200

25  9 FREEDOM 26            OP  SF   FBG DV OB          9  9 4900 2 3  7750  8900
25  9 FREEDOM 26            OP  SF   FBG DV IB 225  COMM  9  9 4900 2 3  8150  9400
       IO  228 MRCR    7450 8550, IB  255         8300 9550, IO 260 MRCR  7650  8800
       IB  200D PERK  11200 12700, IO T170  MRCR  8400 9700, IB T170-T225    9250 10900

27   V-27CC               ST  CUD  FBG DV OB          8  9 3500       9250 10500
27   V-27CC               ST  CUD  FBG DV IO 200-260  8  9           7050  8500
       IO  330 MRCR    8050 9250, IO T140-T200   7850 9600, IO T228-T260    8650 10300
       IO T330 MRCR    9950 11300

27   V-27FB               FB  SDN  FBG DV OB          8  9 6200       9050 10300
27   V-27FB               FB  SDN  FBG DV IO 198-260  8  9           9950 11800
       IO  330 MRCR   11000 12500, IO T140-T230 10800 13300, IO T260-T330  12000 14700

27   V-27HS               HT  CUD  FBG DV OB          8  9           9400 10700
27   V-27HS               HT  CUD  FBG DV IO 198-260  8  9           7050  8500
       IO  330 MRCR    8050 9250, IO T140-T200   7850 9600, IO T260  OMC    9050 10300

       ...For earlier years, see the BUC Used Boat Price Guide, Volume 3
```

ANNAPOLIS CUSTOM YACHTS
ARNOLD MD 21012   COAST GUARD MFG ID- AKY See inside cover to adjust price for area

```
LOA   NAME AND/             TOP/ BOAT -HULL- ----ENGINE--- BEAM  WGT  DRAFT RETAIL RETAIL
FT IN   OR MODEL            RIG  TYPE MTL TP TP # HP  MFG   FT IN LBS  FT IN  LOW   HIGH
------------------- 1986 BOATS --------------------------------------------------------
33 10 FARR 33              SLP SAIL KEV KL IB 18D VLVO 11  6 9200 6 9 28100 31300
```

ANSA SAILING NORTH AMER INC
POMPANO BEACH FL   COAST GUARD MFG ID- RWZ See inside cover to adjust price for area

```
LOA   NAME AND/             TOP/ BOAT -HULL- ----ENGINE--- BEAM  WGT   DRAFT RETAIL RETAIL
FT IN   OR MODEL            RIG  TYPE MTL TP TP # HP  MFG   FT IN LBS   FT IN  LOW   HIGH
------------------- 1984 BOATS ---------------------------------------------------------
41 10 ANSA                 SLP SAIL F/S KC IB 28D VLVO 10  2 12127 5     55600  61100
47    ANSA                 SLP SAIL F/S KC IB 90D VLVO 13  2 26000 5 3 105000 115500
```

ANSWER MARINE CORP
MIAMI FL 33147   COAST GUARD MFG ID- AKM See inside cover to adjust price for area

```
LOA   NAME AND/             TOP/ BOAT -HULL- ----ENGINE--- BEAM  WGT  DRAFT RETAIL RETAIL
FT IN   OR MODEL            RIG  TYPE MTL TP TP # HP  MFG   FT IN LBS  FT IN  LOW   HIGH
------------------- 1994 BOATS --------------------------------------------------------
17  1 FISH MACHINE 170F    OP CTRCN FBG DV OB        6 10 1000  8 1500 1800
17  1 FISH MASTER 17BR     OP FSH   FBG DV OB        6 10 1000  8 1500 1800
17  1 PATROL MASTER 17PM   OP CTRCN FBG DV OB        6 10 1000  8 1500 1800
18  6 FISH MACHINE 180F    OP CTRCN FBG DV OB        7  3 1400  9 2100 2450
18  6 PATROL MASTER 18PM   OP CTRCN FBG DV OB        7  3 1400  9 2100 2450
18  6 SEAMAN 19CC          OP CTRCN FBG DV OB        7  3 1377  9 2050 2450
19  2 FISH MASTER          OP FSH   FBG DV OB        7  6 1389  9 2150 2500
19  2 FISHING MACHINE 19   OP CTRCN FBG DV OB        7  6 1416  9 2200 2550
19  6 SPORTS MASTER 20SS   OP SKI   FBG DV OB        7 11 1630 10 2450 2850
20 10 DIVE MASTER 21DM     OP FSH   FBG DV OB        8    1750 10 2750 3200
20 10 FISH MACHINE 210F    OP CTRCN FBG DV OB        8    1670 10 2650 3100
20 10 FISH MASTER 21BR     OP FSH   FBG DV OB        8    1740 10 2750 3200

20 10 PATROL MASTER 21PM   OP CTRCN FBG DV OB        8    1670 10 2650 3100
20 10 SEAMAN 21BR          OP FSH   FBG DV OB        8    1720 10 2750 3200
20 10 SEAMAN 21CC          OP CTRCN FBG DV OB        8    1635 10 2650 3050
22  8 FISH MACHINE 220F    OP CTRCN FBG DV OB        8    2300 1  3700 4300
22  8 FISH MASTER 22WA     OP FSH   FBG DV OB        8    2600 1  4100 4750
23  6 FAMILY SPRTSMAN 24RT OP CUD   FBG DV OB        8    3200 1 3 5050 5800
23  6 FISH MACHINE 240F    OP CTRCN FBG DV OB        8    2800 1 3 4550 5250
23  6 PATROL MASTER 24PM   OP CTRCN FBG DV OB        8    2800 1 3 4550 5250
23  6 SUPER SPORT 24SS     OP CUD   FBG DV OB        8    3300 1 3 5150 5950
------------------- 1993 BOATS --------------------------------------------------------
17  1 FISH MACHINE 170F    OP CTRCN FBG DV OB        6 10 1000  8 1450 1700
17  1 FISH MASTER 17BR     OP FSH   FBG DV OB        6 10 1000  8 1450 1700
17  1 PATROL MASTER 17PM   OP CTRCN FBG DV OB        6 10 1000  8 1450 1700
18  6 FISH MACHINE 180F    OP CTRCN FBG DV OB        7  3 1400  9 2000 2350
18  6 PATROL MASTER 18PM   OP CTRCN FBG DV OB        7  3 1400  9 2000 2350
18  6 SEAMAN 19CC          OP CTRCN FBG DV OB        7  3 1377  9 1950 2350
19  2 FISH MASTER          OP FSH   FBG DV OB        7  6 1389  9 2000 2400
19  2 FISHING MACHINE 19   OP CTRCN FBG DV OB        7  6 1416  9 2050 2400
19  6 SPORTS MASTER 20SS   OP SKI   FBG DV OB        7 11 1630 10 2350 2700
20 10 DIVE MASTER 21DM     OP FSH   FBG DV OB        8    1750 10 2650 3050
20 10 FISH MACHINE 210F    OP CTRCN FBG DV OB        8    1670 10 2550 2950
20 10 FISH MASTER 21BR     OP FSH   FBG DV OB        8    1740 10 2600 3050

20 10 PATROL MASTER 21PM   OP CTRCN FBG DV OB        8    1670 10 2550 2950
20 10 SEAMAN 21BR          OP FSH   FBG DV OB        8    1720 10 2600 3050
20 10 SEAMAN 21CC          OP CTRCN FBG DV OB        8    1635 10 2550 2900
22  8 FISH MACHINE 220F    OP CTRCN FBG DV OB        8    2300 1  3500 4100
22  8 FISH MASTER 22WA     OP FSH   FBG DV OB        8    2600 1  3900 4550
23  6 FAMILY SPRTSMAN 24RT OP CUD   FBG DV OB        8    3200 1  4800 5500
23  6 FISH MACHINE 240F    OP CTRCN FBG DV OB        8    2800 1 3 4250 4950
23  6 PATROL MASTER 24PM   OP CTRCN FBG DV OB        8    2800 1 3 4250 4950
23  6 SUPER SPORT 24SS     OP CUD   FBG DV OB        8    3300 1 3 4900 5650
------------------- 1992 BOATS --------------------------------------------------------
17  1 FISH MACHINE 170F    OP CTRCN FBG DV OB        6 10 1000  8 1350 1600
17  1 FISH MASTER 17BR     OP FSH   FBG DV OB        6 10 1000  8 1350 1600
17  1 PATROL MASTER 17PM   OP CTRCN FBG DV OB        6 10 1000  8 1350 1600
18  6 FISH MACHINE 180F    OP CTRCN FBG DV OB        7  3 1400  9 1900 2250
18  6 FISH MACHINE 18BR    OP FSH   FBG DV OB        7  3 1421  9 1900 2300
18  6 PATROL MASTER 18PM   OP CTRCN FBG DV OB        7  3 1400  9 1900 2250
18  6 SEAMAN 19BR          OP FSH   FBG DV OB        7  3 1400  9 1900 2250
18  6 SEAMAN 19CC          OP CTRCN FBG DV OB        7  3 1377  9 1850 2250
19  2 FISH MASTER          OP FSH   FBG DV OB        7  6 1389  9 1950 2350
19  2 FISHING MACHINE 19   OP CTRCN FBG DV OB        7  6 1416  9 2000 2350
19  6 SPORTS MASTER 20SS   OP SKI   FBG DV OB        7 11 1630 10 2200 2550
20 10 DIVE MASTER 21DM     OP FSH   FBG DV OB        8    1750 10 2500 2900

20 10 FISH MACHINE 210F    OP CTRCN FBG DV OB        8    1670 10 2400 2800
20 10 FISH MASTER 21BR     OP FSH   FBG DV OB        8    1740 10 2450 2900
20 10 PATROL MASTER 21PM   OP CTRCN FBG DV OB        8    1670 10 2400 2800
20 10 SEAMAN 21BR          OP FSH   FBG DV OB        8    1720 10 2450 2900
20 10 SEAMAN 21CC          OP CTRCN FBG DV OB        8    1635 10 2350 2750
22  8 FISH MACHINE 220F    OP CTRCN FBG DV OB        8    2300 1  3350 3900
22  8 FISH MASTER 22WA     OP FSH   FBG DV OB        8    2600 1  3700 4300
23  6 FAMILY SPRTSMAN 24RT OP CUD   FBG DV OB        8    3200 1 3 4550 5250
23  6 FISH MACHINE 240F    OP CTRCN FBG DV OB        8    2800 1 3 4050 4750
23  6 PATROL MASTER 24PM   OP CTRCN FBG DV OB        8    2800 1 3 4050 4750
23  6 SUPER SPORT 24SS     OP CUD   FBG DV OB        8    3300 1 3 4650 5350
------------------- 1991 BOATS --------------------------------------------------------
17  1 FISH MACHINE 170F    OP CTRCN FBG DV OB        6 10 1000  8 1300 1550
17  1 FISH MASTER 17BR     OP FSH   FBG DV OB        6 10 1000  8 1300 1550
17  1 PATROL MASTER 17PM   OP CTRCN FBG DV OB        6 10 1000  8 1300 1550
18  6 FISH MACHINE 180F    OP CTRCN FBG DV OB        7  3 1400  9 1800 2100
18  6 FISH MACHINE 18BR    OP FSH   FBG DV OB        7  3 1421  9 1850 2200
18  6 PATROL MASTER 18PM   OP CTRCN FBG DV OB        7  3 1400  9 1800 2100
18  6 SEAMAN 19BR          OP FSH   FBG DV OB        7  3 1400  9 1800 2150
18  6 SEAMAN 19CC          OP CTRCN FBG DV OB        7  3 1377  9 1750 2100
19  6 SPORTS MASTER 20SS   OP SKI   FBG DV OB        7 11 1630 10 2050 2450
20 10 DIVE MASTER 21DM     OP FSH   FBG DV OB        8    1750 10 2400 2800
20 10 FISH MACHINE 210F    OP CTRCN FBG DV OB        8    1670 10 2300 2700
20 10 FISH MASTER 21BR     OP FSH   FBG DV OB        8    1740 10 2350 2750

20 10 PATROL MASTER 21PM   OP CTRCN FBG DV OB        8    1670 10 2300 2700
20 10 SEAMAN 21BR          OP FSH   FBG DV OB        8    1720 10 2350 2750
20 10 SEAMAN 21CC          OP CTRCN FBG DV OB        8    1635 10 2250 2650
22  8 FISH MACHINE 220F    OP CTRCN FBG DV OB        8    2300 1  3200 3700
22  8 FISH MASTER 22WA     OP FSH   FBG DV OB        8    2600 1  3500 4100
23  6 FAMILY SPRTSMAN 24RT OP CUD   FBG DV OB        8    3200 1 3 4250 5000
23  6 FISH MACHINE 240F    OP CTRCN FBG DV OB        8    2800 1 3 3900 4550
23  6 PATROL MASTER 24PM   OP CTRCN FBG DV OB        8    2800 1 3 3900 4550
23  6 SUPER SPORT 24SS     OP CUD   FBG DV OB        8    3300 1 3 4450 5100
------------------- 1990 BOATS --------------------------------------------------------
17  1 FISH MACHINE 170F    OP CTRCN FBG DV OB        6 10 1000  8 1250 1500
17  1 PATROL MASTER 17PM   OP CTRCN FBG DV OB        6 10 1000  8 1250 1500
18  6 FISH MACHINE 180F    OP CTRCN FBG DV OB        7  3 1400  9 1700 2000
18  6 FISH MASTER 18BR     OP FSH   FBG DV OB        7  3 1421  9 1700 2050
18  6 PATROL MASTER 18PM   OP CTRCN FBG DV OB        7  3 1400  9 1700 2000
18  6 SEAMAN 19BR          OP FSH   FBG DV OB        7  3 1400  9 1700 2000
18  6 SEAMAN 19CC          OP CTRCN FBG DV OB        7  3 1377  9 1700 2000
19  6 SPORTSMAN 20SS       OP SKI   FBG DV OB        7 11 1630 10 2000 2350
20 10 DIVE MASTER 21DM     OP FSH   FBG DV OB        8    1750 10 2300 2650
20 10 FISH MACHINE 210F    OP CTRCN FBG DV OB        8    1670 10 2200 2600
20 10 FISH MASTER 21BR     OP FSH   FBG DV OB        8    1740 10 2300 2650
20 10 PATROL MASTER 21PM   OP CTRCN FBG DV OB        8    1670 10 2200 2550
```

ANSWER MARINE CORP -CONTINUED See inside cover to adjust price for area

LOA FT	LOA IN	NAME AND/ OR MODEL	TOP/ RIG	BOAT TYPE	-HULL- MTL	-HULL- TP	ENGINE TP	ENGINE # HP	ENGINE MFG	BEAM FT	BEAM IN	WGT LBS	DRAFT FT	DRAFT IN	RETAIL LOW	RETAIL HIGH
		1990 BOATS														
20	10	SEAMAN 21BR	OP	FSH	FBG	DV	OB			8		1720		10	2250	2600
20	10	SEAMAN 21CC	OP	CTRCN	FBG	DV	OB			8		1635		10	2150	2500
22	8	FISH MACHINE 22OF	OP	CTRCN	FBG	DV	OB			8		2300	1		3050	3550
22	8	FISH MASTER 22WA	OP	FSH	FBG	DV	OB			8		2600	1		3350	3900
23	6	FAMILY SPRTSMAN 24SS	OP	CUD	FBG	DV	OB			8		3200	1	3	4100	4800
23	6	FISH MACHINE 24OF	OP	CTRCN	FBG	DV	OB			8		2800	1	3	3700	4300
23	6	PATROL MASTER 24PM	OP	CTRCN	FBG	DV	OB			8		2800	1	3	3700	4300
		1989 BOATS														
18	6	FISH MASTER 18	OP	RNBT	FBG	SV	OB			7	3	1200		9	1450	1750
18	6	FISHING MACHINE 18	OP	CTRCN	FBG	SV	OB			7	3	1250		9	1500	1800
20	10	DIVEMASTER 21	OP	W/T	FBG	SV	OB			8		1850		10	2300	2650
20	10	FISH MASTER 21	OP	W/T	FBG	SV	OB			8		1850		10	2300	2650
20	10	FISHING MACHINE 21	OP	CTRCN	FBG	SV	OB			8		1850		10	2300	2650
22	8	FISH MASTER 22	OP	W/T	FBG	SV	OB			8		2600	1		3200	3750
22	8	FISHING MACHINE 22	OP	CTRCN	FBG	SV	OB			8		2300	1		2950	3400
23	6	FAMILY SPORTSMAN 24	OP	FSH	FBG	SV	OB			8		2800	1	3	3550	4100
23	6	FISHING MACHINE 24	OP	CTRCN	FBG	SV	OB			8		2800	1	3	3550	4100
23	6	HARDTOP 24	HT	CUD	FBG	SV	OB			8		3400	1	3	4100	4800
23	6	SUPER SPORT 24	ST	CUD	FBG	SV	OB			8		3300	1	3	4050	4700
		1987 BOATS														
19	6	SPORTMASTER 20	OP	CUD	FBG	DV	OB			8		1630		9	1750	2100
20	10	ANSWER 21	OP	UTL	FBG	SV	IO	170		8		2850		10	6050	6950
20	10	FISHING-MACHINE 21	OP	CTRCN	FBG	SV	OB			8		1710		10	1950	2350
22	6	FISH-MASTER 22	OP	SF	FBG	DV	OB			8		2800	1		3100	3650
22	6	FISH-MASTER 22	OP	SF	FBG	DV	IO	170		8		3600	1		7900	9100
22	6	FISHING-MACHINE 22	OP	CTRCN	FBG	DV	OB			8		2100	1		2500	2900
23	6	FISHING-MACHINE 24	OP	CTRCN	FBG	DV	IO	230		8		3900	1	3	8550	9850
24		FISHING-MACHINE 24	OP	CTRCN	FBG	DV	OB			8		2800	1	3	3350	3900
		1986 BOATS														
18	6	BOWRIDER 18	OP	RNBT	FBG	DV	OB			7	3	1250		9	1350	1600
18	6	BOWRIDER 18	OP	RNBT	FBG	DV	SE	115	OMC	7	3	1250		9	1350	1600
18	6	BOWRIDER 18	OP	RNBT	FBG	DV	IO	120		7	3	1250		9	2900	3550
18	6	BOWRIDER 18	OP	RNBT	FBG	DV	SE	205	OMC	7	3	1250		9	1350	1600
18	6	FISHING-MACHINE 18	OP	OPFSH	FBG	DV	OB			7	3	1250		9	1350	1600
18	6	FISHING-MACHINE 18	OP	OPFSH	FBG	DV	SE	115	OMC	7	3	1250		9	1350	1600
18	6	FISHING-MACHINE 18	OP	OPFSH	FBG	DV	IO	120		7	3			9	4000	4900
18	6	FISHING-MACHINE 18	OP	OPFSH	FBG	DV	SE	205	OMC	7	3	1250		9	1350	1600
18	6	RUNABOUT 18	OP	RNBT	FBG	DV	OB			7	3	1250		9	1350	1600
18	6	RUNABOUT 18	OP	RNBT	FBG	DV	SE	115	OMC	7	3	1250		9	1350	1600
18	6	RUNABOUT 18	OP	RNBT	FBG	DV	IO	120		7	3			9	3650	4450
18	6	RUNABOUT 18	OP	RNBT	FBG	DV	SE	205	OMC	7	3	1250		9	1350	1600
19	6	SPORTSMASTER 20	OP	CUD	FBG	DV	OB			8		1630		9	1700	2050
20	10	DIVEMASTER	ST	UTL	FBG	SV	OB			8		1850		10	1750	2100
20	10	DIVEMASTER	ST	UTL	FBG	SV	SE	115	OMC	8		2850		10	2450	2850
20	10	DIVEMASTER	ST	UTL	FBG	SV	IO	120-200		8		2850		10	5700	6900
20	10	DIVEMASTER	ST	UTL	FBC	SV	SE	205	OMC	8		2850		10	2450	2850
20	10	DIVEMASTER	ST	UTL	FBG	SV	IO	230		8		2850		10	5900	7050
20	10	DIVEMASTER	ST	UTL	FBG	SV	SE	T115	OMC	8		2850		10	2450	2850
20	10	FAMILY-SPORTSMAN 21	ST	CUD	FBG	SV	OB			8		2100		10	2250	2600
20	10	FAMILY-SPORTSMAN 21	ST	CUD	FBG	SV	SE	115	OMC	8		3100		10	2800	3250
20	10	FAMILY-SPORTSMAN 21	ST	CUD	FBG	SV	IO	120-200		8		3100		10	5550	6750
20	10	FAMILY-SPORTSMAN 21	ST	CUD	FBG	SV	SE	205	OMC	8		3100		10	2800	3250
20	10	FAMILY-SPORTSMAN 21	ST	CUD	FBG	SV	IO	230		8		3100		10	5750	6850
20	10	FAMILY-SPORTSMAN 21	ST	CUD	FBG	SV	SE	T115	OMC	8		3100		10	2800	3250
20	10	FISH-MASTER 21	ST	FSH	FBG	DV	OB			8		1850		10	2000	2350
20	10	FISH-MASTER 21	ST	FSH	FBG	DV	SE	115	OMC	8		2550		10	2550	2950
20	10	FISH-MASTER 21	ST	FSH	FBG	DV	IO	120-200		8		2550		10	5300	6450
20	10	FISH-MASTER 21	ST	FSH	FBG	DV	SE	205	OMC	8		2550		10	2550	2950
20	10	FISH-MASTER 21	ST	FSH	FBG	DV	IO	230		8		2550		10	5500	6600
20	10	FISH-MASTER 21	ST	FSH	FBG	DV	SE	T115	OMC	8		2550		10	2550	2950
20	10	FISHING-MACHINE 21	OP	CTRCN	FBG	SV	OB			8		1850		10	2000	2350
20	10	FISHING-MACHINE 21	OP	CTRCN	FBG	SV	SE	115	OMC	8		2850		10	2700	3100
20	10	FISHING-MACHINE 21	OP	CTRCN	FBG	SV	IO	120-200		8		2850		10	5550	6700
20	10	FISHING-MACHINE 21	OP	CTRCN	FBG	SV	SE	205	OMC	8		2850		10	2700	3100
20	10	FISHING-MACHINE 21	OP	CTRCN	FBG	SV	IO	230		8		2850		10	5750	6850
20	10	FISHING-MACHINE 21	OP	CTRCN	FBG	SV	SE	T115	OMC	8		2850		10	2700	3100
22	8	FISH-MASTER 22	ST	SF	FBG	DV	OB			8		2850	1		3100	3600
22	8	FISH-MASTER 22	ST	SF	FBG	DV	IO	170-200		8		3850	1		7950	9500
22	8	FISH-MASTER 22	ST	SF	FBG	DV	SE	205	OMC	8		3850	1		3700	4300
22	8	FISH-MASTER 22	ST	SF	FBG	DV	IO	230-260		8		3850	1		8100	9850
22	8	FISH-MASTER 22	ST	SF	FBG	DV	SE	T115	OMC	8		3850	1		3700	4300
22	8	FISH-MASTER 22	ST	SF	FBG	DV	IO	T140		8		3850	1		8950	10700
22	8	FISHING-MACHINE 22	OP	CTRCN	FBG	DV	OB			8		2850	1		3100	3600
22	8	FISHING-MACHINE 22	OP	CTRCN	FBG	DV	IO	170-200		8		3850	1		7600	9050
22	8	FISHING-MACHINE 22	OP	CTRCN	FBG	DV	SE	205	OMC	8		3850	1		3700	4300
22	8	FISHING-MACHINE 22	OP	CTRCN	FBG	DV	IO	230-260		8		3850	1		7800	9400
22	8	FISHING-MACHINE 22	OP	CTRCN	FBG	DV	SE	T115	OMC	8		3850	1		3700	4300
22	8	FISHING-MACHINE 22	OP	CTRCN	FBG	DV	IO	T140		8		3850	1		8450	10200
23	6	FAMILY-SPORTSMAN 24	ST	CUD	FBG	DV	OB			8		2800		1	3150	3700
23	6	FAMILY-SPORTSMAN 24	ST	CUD	FBG	DV	IO	170-200		8		3900		1	7500	9000
23	6	FAMILY-SPORTSMAN 24	ST	CUD	FBG	DV	SE	205	OMC	8		3900	1	3	4050	4700
23	6	FAMILY-SPORTSMAN 24	ST	CUD	FBG	DV	IO	230-260		8		3900		1	7650	9250
23	6	FAMILY-SPORTSMAN 24	ST	CUD	FBG	DV	SE	T115	OMC	8		3800	1	3	3950	4600
23	6	FAMILY-SPORTSMAN 24	ST	CUD	FBG	DV	IO	T140-T190		8		3900		1	8450	10100
23	6	FISHING-MACHINE 24	OP	CTRCN	FBG	DV	OB			8		2800	1	3	3150	3700
23	6	FISHING-MACHINE 24	OP	CTRCN	FBG	DV	IO	170-200		8		3900		1	8050	9550
23	6	FISHING-MACHINE 24	OP	CTRCN	FBG	DV	SE	205	OMC	8		3900	1	3	4050	4700
23	6	FISHING-MACHINE 24	OP	CTRCN	FBG	DV	IO	230-260		8		3900		1	8200	9850
23	6	FISHING-MACHINE 24	OP	CTRCN	FBG	DV	SE	T115	OMC	8		3900	1	3	4050	4700
23	6	FISHING-MACHINE 24	OP	CTRCN	FBG	DV	IO	T140-T185		8		3900		1	9150	10800
23	6	FLY BRIDGE 24	FB	SF	FBG	DV	OB			8		3500		1	3750	4350
23	6	FLY BRIDGE 24	FB	SF	FBG	DV	IO	200-260		8		4700		1	11500	13800
23	6	FLY BRIDGE 24	FB	SF	FBG	DV	IO	T140-T185		8		4700		1	12800	15100
23	6	HARDTOP 24	HT	SDN	FBG	DV	OB			8				1	3350	3900
23	6	HARDTOP 24	HT	SDN	FBG	DV	IO	170-200		8				1	8000	9500
23	6	HARDTOP 24	HT	SDN	FBG	DV	SE	205	OMC	8			1	3	**	**
23	6	HARDTOP 24	HT	SDN	FBG	DV	IO	230-260		8				1	8150	9800
23	6	HARDTOP 24	HT	SDN	FBG	DV	SE	T115	OMC	8			1	3	**	**
23	6	HARDTOP 24	HT	SDN	FBG	DV	IO	T140-T185		8				1	9050	10700
23	6	SUPERSPORT 24	ST	CUD	FBG	DV	OB			8		3300		1	3600	4150
23	6	SUPERSPORT 24	ST	CUD	FBG	DV	IO	170-185		8		4000		1	7650	9250
23	6	SUPERSPORT 24	ST	CUD	FBG	DV	IO	200		8		4300		1	8150	9600
23	6	SUPERSPORT 24	ST	CUD	FBG	DV	SE	205	OMC	8		4000	1	3	4050	4750
23	6	SUPERSPORT 24	ST	CUD	FBG	DV	IO	230-260		8		4300		1	8250	9900
23	6	SUPERSPORT 24	ST	CUD	FBG	DV	SE	T115	OMC	8		4000	1	3	4050	4750
23	6	SUPERSPORT 24	ST	CUD	FBG	DV	IO	T140-T185		8		4300		1	9150	10800
		1985 BOATS														
18	6	FISHING-MACHINE	OP	OPFSH	FBG	DV	IO	120	OMC	7	3			9	3800	4400
18	6	FISHING-MACHINE 18	OP	OPFSH	FBG	DV	OB			7	3	1250		9	1300	1550
18	6	FISHING-MACHINE 18	OP	OPFSH	FBG	DV	SE	115	OMC	7	3	1250		9	1300	1550
18	6	FISHING-MACHINE 18	OP	OPFSH	FBG	DV	IO	120		7	3			9	3850	4700
18	6	FISHING-MACHINE 18	OP	OPFSH	FBG	DV	SE	205	OMC	7	3	1250		9	1300	1550
18	6	RUNABOUT 18	OP	RNBT	FBG	DV	OB			7	3	1250		9	1300	1550
18	6	RUNABOUT 18	OP	RNBT	FBG	DV	SE	115	OMC	7	3	1250		9	1300	1550
18	6	RUNABOUT 18	OP	RNBT	FBG	DV	IO	120-140		7	3			9	3500	4250
18	6	RUNABOUT 18	OP	RNBT	FBG	DV	SE	205	OMC	7	3	1250		9	1300	1550
19	6	SPORTSMASTER 20	OP	CUD	FBG	DV	OB			8		1630		9	1650	1950
20	10	DIVEMASTER	ST	UTL	FBG	SV	OB			8		1850		10	1700	2000
20	10	DIVEMASTER	ST	UTL	FBG	SV	SE	115	OMC	8		2850		10	2350	2750
20	10	DIVEMASTER	ST	UTL	FBG	SV	IO	120-200		8		2850		10	5450	6600
20	10	DIVEMASTER	ST	UTL	FBG	SV	SE	205	OMC	8		2850		10	2350	2750
20	10	DIVEMASTER	ST	UTL	FBG	SV	IO	230		8		2850		10	5650	6750
20	10	DIVEMASTER	ST	UTL	FBG	SV	SE	T115	OMC	8		2850		10	2350	2750
20	10	FAMILY-SPORTSMAN 21	ST	CUD	FBG	SV	OB			8		2100		10	2150	2500
20	10	FAMILY-SPORTSMAN 21	ST	CUD	FBG	SV	SE	115	OMC	8		3100		10	2700	3100
20	10	FAMILY-SPORTSMAN 21	ST	CUD	FBG	SV	IO	120-200		8		3100		10	5300	6400
20	10	FAMILY-SPORTSMAN 21	ST	CUD	FBG	SV	SE	205	OMC	8		3100		10	2700	3100
20	10	FAMILY-SPORTSMAN 21	ST	CUD	FBG	SV	IO	230		8		3100		10	5500	6550
20	10	FAMILY-SPORTSMAN 21	ST	CUD	FBG	SV	SE	T115	OMC	8		3100		10	2700	3100
20	10	FISH-MASTER 21	ST	FSH	FBG	DV	OB			8		1850		10	1950	2300
20	10	FISH-MASTER 21	ST	FSH	FBG	DV	SE	115	OMC	8		2550		10	2450	2850
20	10	FISH-MASTER 21	ST	FSH	FBG	DV	IO	120-200		8		2550		10	5100	6150
20	10	FISH-MASTER 21	ST	FSH	FBG	DV	SE	205	OMC	8		2550		10	2450	2850
20	10	FISH-MASTER 21	ST	FSH	FBG	DV	IO	230		8		2550		10	5250	6300
20	10	FISH-MASTER 21	ST	FSH	FBG	DV	SE	T115	OMC	8		2550		10	2450	2850
20	10	FISHING-MACHINE 21	OP	CTRCN	FBG	SV	OB			8		1850		10	1950	2300
20	10	FISHING-MACHINE 21	OP	CTRCN	FBG	SV	SE	115	OMC	8		2850		10	2600	3000
20	10	FISHING-MACHINE 21	OP	CTRCN	FBG	SV	IO	120-200		8		2850		10	5300	6400
20	10	FISHING-MACHINE 21	OP	CTRCN	FBG	SV	SE	205	OMC	8		2850		10	2600	3000
20	10	FISHING-MACHINE 21	OP	CTRCN	FBG	SV	IO	230		8		2850		10	5450	6550
20	10	FISHING-MACHINE 21	OP	CTRCN	FBG	SV	SE	T115	OMC	8		2850		10	2600	3000
22	8	FISH-MASTER 22	ST	SF	FBG	DV	OB			8		2850	1		3000	3450
22	8	FISH-MASTER 22	ST	SF	FBG	DV	IO	170-200		8		3850	1		7600	9050
22	8	FISH-MASTER 22	ST	SF	FBG	DV	SE	205	OMC	8		3850	1		3600	4150
22	8	FISH-MASTER 22	ST	SF	FBG	DV	IO	230-260		8		3850	1		7750	9450
22	8	FISH-MASTER 22	ST	SF	FBG	DV	SE	T115	OMC	8		3850	1		3600	4150
22	8	FISH-MASTER 22	ST	SF	FBG	DV	IO	T140		8		3850	1		8500	10200

CONTINUED ON NEXT PAGE

LOA FT	LOA IN	NAME AND/ OR MODEL	TOP/ RIG	BOAT TYPE	-HULL- MTL	-HULL- TP	ENGINE TP	ENGINE # HP	ENGINE MFG	BEAM FT	BEAM IN	WGT LBS	DRAFT FT	DRAFT IN	RETAIL LOW	RETAIL HIGH
		1985 BOATS														
23	6	FAMILY-SPORTSMAN 24	ST	CUD	FBG	DV	OB			8		2800	1	3	3050	3550
23	6	FAMILY-SPORTSMAN 24	ST	CUD	FBG	DV	IO	170-200		8		3900	1	3	7150	8500
23	6	FAMILY-SPORTSMAN 24	ST	CUD	FBG	DV	SE	205	OMC	8		3900	1	3	3900	4550
23	6	FAMILY-SPORTSMAN 24	ST	CUD	FBG	DV	IO	230-260		8		3900	1	3	7300	8850
23	6	FAMILY-SPORTSMAN 24	ST	CUD	FBG	DV	SE	T115	OMC	8		3800	1	3	3850	4450
23	6	FAMILY-SPORTSMAN 24	ST	CUD	FBG	DV	IO	T140-T190		8		3900	1	3	8100	9650
23	6	FISHING-MACHINE 24	OP	CTRCN	FBG	DV	OB			8		2800	1	3	3050	3550
23	6	FISHING-MACHINE 24	OP	CTRCN	FBG	DV	IO	170-200		8		3900	1	3	7650	9100
23	6	FISHING-MACHINE 24	OP	CTRCN	FBG	DV	SE	205	OMC	8		3900	1	3	3900	4550
23	6	FISHING-MACHINE 24	OP	CTRCN	FBG	DV	IO	230-260		8		3900	1	3	7800	9450
23	6	FISHING-MACHINE 24	OP	CTRCN	FBG	DV	SE	T115	OMC	8		3900	1	3	3900	4550
23	6	FISHING-MACHINE 24	OP	CTRCN	FBG	DV	IO	T140-T190		8		3900	1	3	8650	10400
23	6	FLY BRIDGE 24	FB	SF	FBG	DV	OB			8		3500	1	3	3600	4200
23	6	FLY BRIDGE 24	FB	SF	FBG	DV	IO	200-260		8		4700	1	3	10900	13200
23	6	FLY BRIDGE 24	FB	SF	FBG	DV	IO	T140-T190		8		4700	1	3	12200	14400
23	6	FLY BRIDGE 24	FB	SF	FBG	DV	SE	T205	OMC	8		4700	1	3	4250	4950
23	6	FLYBRIDGE 24	FB	SF	FBG	DV	IO	T145		8		5200	1	3	13100	14900
23	6	HARDTOP 24	HT	SDN	FBG	DV	OB			8			1	3	3250	3750
23	6	HARDTOP 24	HT	SDN	FBG	DV	IO	170-200		8			1	3	7650	9050
23	6	HARDTOP 24	HT	SDN	FBG	DV	SE	205	OMC	8			1	3	**	**
23	6	HARDTOP 24	HT	SDN	FBG	DV	IO	230-260		8			1	3	7850	9400
23	6	HARDTOP 24	HT	SDN	FBG	DV	SE	T115	OMC	8			1	3	**	**
23	6	HARDTOP 24	HT	SDN	FBG	DV	IO	T140-T185		8			1	3	8550	10200
23	6	SUPERSPORT 24	ST	CUD	FBG	DV	OB			8		3300	1	3	3450	4050
23	6	SUPERSPORT 24	ST	CUD	FBG	DV	IO	170-185		8		4000	1	3	7300	8850
23	6	SUPERSPORT 24	ST	CUD	FBG	DV	IO	200		8		4300	1	3	7800	9150
23	6	SUPERSPORT 24	ST	CUD	FBG	DV	SE	205	OMC	8		4000	1	3	3950	4600
23	6	SUPERSPORT 24	ST	CUD	FBG	DV	IO	230-260		8		4300	1	3	7850	9500
23	6	SUPERSPORT 24	ST	CUD	FBG	DV	SE	T115	OMC	8		4000	1	3	3950	4600
23	6	SUPERSPORT 24	ST	CUD	FBG	DV	IO	T140-T190		8		4300	1	3	8600	10300
		1984 BOATS														
18	5	RUNABOUT 18	OP	RNBT	FBG	DV	OB			7	3	1250		9	1250	1500
18	5	RUNABOUT 18	OP	RNBT	FBG	DV	IO	140		7	3			9	3100	3600
18	6	FISHING MACHINE 18	OP	OPFSH	FBG	DV	OB			7	3	1250		8	1250	1500
18	6	FISHING MACHINE 18	OP	OPFSH	FBG	DV	IO	140		7	3			9	3700	4300
19	6	SPORTSMASTER 20	OP	CUD	FBG	DV	OB			8		1630		9	1600	1900
20	10	DIVEMASTER	ST	UTL	FBG	SV	OB			8		1850		10	1650	1950
20	10	DIVEMASTER	ST	UTL	FBG	SV	IO	138-200		8		2850		10	5400	6350
20	10	FAMILY-SPORTSMAN 21	ST	CUD	FBG	SV	OB			8		2100		10	2050	2450
20	10	FAMILY-SPORTSMAN 21	ST	CUD	FBG	SV	IO	138-200		8		3100		10	5300	6150
20	10	FISH-MASTER 21	ST	FSH	FBG	DV	OB			8		1850		10	1900	2250
20	10	FISH-MASTER 21	ST	FSH	FBG	DV	IO	138-200		8		2550		10	5050	5900
20	10	FISHING-MACHINE 21	OP	CTRCN	FBG	SV	OB			8		1850		10	1900	2250
20	10	FISHING-MACHINE 21	OP	CTRCN	FBG	SV	IO	138-200		8		2850		10	5250	6150
22	6	FISH-MASTER 22		FSH	FBG	DV	OB			8		2850			2850	3350
22	8	FISH-MASTER	ST	SF	FBG	DV	OB			8		2850	1		2900	3350
22	8	FISH-MASTER	ST	SF	FBG	DV	IO	185-200		8		3850	1		7350	8700
23	6	FAMILY-SPORTSMAN 24	ST	CUD	FBG	DV	OB			8		2800	1	3	2950	3450
23	6	FAMILY-SPORTSMAN 24	ST	CUD	FBG	DV	IO	170-200		8		3800	1	3	6700	8000
23	6	FAMILY-SPORTSMAN 24	ST	CUD	FBG	DV	SE	205	OMC	8		3800	1	3	3700	4300
23	6	FAMILY-SPORTSMAN 24	ST	CUD	FBG	DV	IO	225-290		8		3800	1	3	7050	8650
23	6	FAMILY-SPORTSMAN 24	ST	CUD	FBG	DV	IO	T138-T188		8		3800	1	3	7950	9150
23	6	FAMILY-SPORTSMAN 24	ST	CUD	FBG	DV	SE	T205	OMC	8		3800	1	3	3700	4300
23	6	FISHING-MACHINE 24	OP	CTRCN	FBG	DV	OB			8		2800	1	3	2950	3450
23	6	FISHING-MACHINE 24	OP	CTRCN	FBG	DV	IO	170-200		8		3900	1	3	7350	8750
23	6	FISHING-MACHINE 24	OP	CTRCN	FBG	DV	SE	205	OMC	8		3900	1	3	3750	4350
23	6	FISHING-MACHINE 24	OP	CTRCN	FBG	DV	IO	225-290		8		3900	1	3	7700	9400
23	6	FISHING-MACHINE 24	OP	CTRCN	FBG	DV	IO	T138-T188		8		3900	1	3	8650	9950
23	6	FISHING-MACHINE 24	OP	CTRCN	FBG	DV	SE	T205	OMC	8		3900	1	3	3750	4350
23	6	HARDTOP 24	HT	SDN	FBG	DV	OB			8			1	3	3150	3650
23	6	HARDTOP 24	HT	SDN	FBG	DV	IO	170-200		8			1	3	7350	8700
23	6	HARDTOP 24	HT	SDN	FBG	DV	SE	205	OMC	8			1	3	**	**
23	6	HARDTOP 24	HT	SDN	FBG	DV	IO	225-290		8			1	3	7650	9350
23	6	HARDTOP 24	HT	SDN	FBG	DV	IO	T138-T188		8			1	3	8550	9800
23	6	HARDTOP 24	HT	SDN	FBG	DV	SE	T205	OMC	8			1	3	**	**
23	6	SPORT FISHERMAN	FB	SF	FBG	DV	OB			8		3500	1	3	3500	4050
23	6	SPORT FISHERMAN	FB	SF	FBG	DV	IO	170-200		8		4700	1	3	10400	12200
23	6	SPORT FISHERMAN	FB	SF	FBG	DV	SE	205	OMC	8		4700	1	3	4150	4800
23	6	SPORT FISHERMAN	FB	SF	FBG	DV	IO	225-290		8		4700	1	3	10800	13000
23	6	SPORT FISHERMAN	FB	SF	FBG	DV	IO	T138-T188		8		4700	1	3	12100	13800
23	6	SPORT FISHERMAN	FB	SF	FBG	DV	SE	T205	OMC	8		4700	1	3	4150	4800
23	6	SUPERSPORT 24	ST	CUD	FBG	DV	OB			8		3300	1	3	3350	3900
23	6	SUPERSPORT 24	ST	CUD	FBG	DV	IO	170-198		8		4000	1	3	7000	8550
23	6	SUPERSPORT 24	ST	CUD	FBG	DV	IO	200		8		4300	1	3	7400	8800
23	6	SUPERSPORT 24	ST	CUD	FBG	DV	SE	205	OMC	8		4000	1	3	3850	4450
23	6	SUPERSPORT 24	ST	CUD	FBG	DV	IO	225-230		8		4300	1	3	7700	8900
		IO 260 MRCR 7700 8850, IO 260 OMC 7650 8800, IO 260 VLVO 7900 9100														
		IB 260 OMC 9100 10300, IO 290 VLVO 8200 9400, IO T138-T188 8600 9900														
23	6	SUPERSPORT 24	ST	CUD	FBG	DV	SE	T205	OMC	8		4000	1	3	3850	4450

....For earlier years, see the BUC Used Boat Price Guide, Volume 3

ANTIGUA YACHT CORP

CLEARWATER FL 34622 See inside cover to adjust price for area

LOA FT	LOA IN	NAME AND/ OR MODEL	TOP/ RIG	BOAT TYPE	-HULL- MTL	-HULL- TP	ENGINE TP	ENGINE # HP	ENGINE MFG	BEAM FT	BEAM IN	WGT LBS	DRAFT FT	DRAFT IN	RETAIL LOW	RETAIL HIGH
		1990 BOATS														
44		ANTIGUA 44	SLP	SAIL	FBG	KL	IB	66D	YAN	13	4	32000	4	11	143000	157500
58		ANTIGUA 59 CC	SLP	SA/CR	FBG	KL	IB	135D	PERK	15		55000	5	6	341000	375000
58		ANTIGUA 59 PH	SLP	SA/CR	FBG	KL	IB	135D	PERK	15		55000	5	6	385500	423500
73		ANTIGUA 73 CC	SLP	SA/CR	FBG	KL	IB	270D	CAT	18		92000	7	6	**	**
73		ANTIGUA 73 CC	SLP	SA/CR	FBG	KL	IB	T140D	YAN	18		92000	7	6	**	**
73		ANTIGUA 73 PH	SLP	SA/CR	FBG	KL	IB	T140D	YAN	18		92000	7		**	**
		1989 BOATS														
44		CUTTER SLOOP	SLP	SAIL	FBG	KL	IB	77D	YAN	13	4	32000	4	11	135500	149000
44		CUTTER SLOOP	CUT	SAIL	FBG	KL	IB	77D	YAN	13	4	32000	4	11	135000	148000
53		CUTTER SLOOP	SLP	SA/CR	FBG	KL	IB	135D	YAN	15		50000	5	6	232000	254500
53		CUTTER SLOOP	CUT	SA/CR	FBG	KL	IB	135D	YAN	15		50000	5	6	232000	254500
58		CUTTER SLOOP	SLP	SA/CR	FBG	KL	IB	T 77D	YAN	15		52000	5	6	339000	372500
58		CUTTER SLOOP	CUT	SA/CR	FBG	KL	IB	T 77D	YAN	15		52000	5	6	338500	372000
73		CUTTER SLOOP	SLP	SA/CR	FBG	KL	IB	T240D	CAT	18		90000	7		**	**
73		CUTTER SLOOP	CUT	SA/CR	FBG	KL	IB	T240D	CAT	18		90000	7		**	**

APACHE PERFORMANCE BOATS

N MIAMI BEACH FL 33180 COAST GUARD MFG ID- APH See inside cover to adjust price for area

LOA FT	LOA IN	NAME AND/ OR MODEL	TOP/ RIG	BOAT TYPE	-HULL- MTL	-HULL- TP	ENGINE TP	ENGINE # HP	ENGINE MFG	BEAM FT	BEAM IN	WGT LBS	DRAFT FT	DRAFT IN	RETAIL LOW	RETAIL HIGH
		1995 BOATS														
36		WARRIOR 36	OP	CR	FBG	DV	IO	T385	MRCR	8		10000	3	6	95400	105000
36		WARRIOR 36	OP	CR	FBG	DV	IO	T415	MRCR	8		10000	3	6	98800	108500
36		WARRIOR 36	OP	CR	FBG	DV	IO	T500	MRCR	8		10000	3	6	109000	120000
		1994 BOATS														
21		APACHE SCOUT	OP	RNBT	FBG	DV	OB			7	11	2150			6300	7250
28		APACHE BRAVE	OP	RACE	FBG	DV	OB			8	6	7000			18100	20100
28		APACHE BRAVE	OP	RACE	FBG	DV	IO	T385	MRCR	8	6	7000			40800	45300
28		APACHE OPEN FISH	OP	CTRCN	FBG	DV	OB			8	6	4300			18100	20100
36		WARRIOR 36	OP	CR	FBG	DV	IO	T385	MRCR	8		10000	3	6	89000	97800
36		WARRIOR 36	OP	CR	FBG	DV	IO	T415	MRCR	8		10000	3	6	92100	101500
36		WARRIOR 36	OP	CR	FBG	DV	IO	T500	MRCR	8		10000	3	6	102000	112000
		1993 BOATS														
21		APACHE SCOUT	OP	RNBT	FBG	DV	OB			7	11	2150			6050	6950
28		APACHE BRAVE	OP	OFF	FBG	DV	OB			8	6	7000			17000	19300
28		APACHE BRAVE	OP	OFF	FBG	DV	IO	T300-T350		8	6	7000			41600	49200
28		APACHE OPEN FISH	OP	OPFSH	FBG	DV	OB			8	6	4300			17000	19300
36		WARRIOR 36	OP	CR	FBG	DV	IO	T390	MRCR	8		9500			82200	90300
		IO T425 MRCR 85700 94200, IO T465 MRCR 90100 99000, IO T500 MRCR 93700 103000														
		IO T525 HAWK 95000 104500, IO T575 MRCR 100500 110500, IO T600 MRCR 102000 112500														
		IO T750 HAWK 110500 121500, IO T800 HAWK ** **, IO T800 MRCR ** **														
		IO T900 HAWK ** **, IO T10C HAWK ** **														
		1992 BOATS														
21		APACHE SCOUT	OP	RNBT	FBG	DV	OB			7	11	2150			5800	6650
28		APACHE BRAVE	OP	OFF	FBG	DV	OB			8	6	7000			16300	18600
28		APACHE BRAVE	OP	OFF	FBG	DV	IO	T300-T350		8	6	7000			38900	46000
28		APACHE OPEN FISH	OP	OPFSH	FBG	DV	OB			8	6	4300			16300	18500
36		WARRIOR 36	OP	CR	FBG	DV	IO	T390	MRCR	8		9500			76700	84300
		IO T425 MRCR 80100 88000, IO T465 MRCR 84100 92400, IO T500 MRCR 87500 96100														
		IO T525 HAWK 88700 97500, IO T575 MRCR 93700 103000, IO T600 MRCR 95500 105000														
		IO T750 HAWK 103000 113500, IO T800 HAWK ** **, IO T800 MRCR ** **														
		IO T900 HAWK ** **, IO T10C HAWK ** **														
		1988 BOATS														
22		SCOUT 22	OP	RNBT		DV	OB			7	11	1500	2		3850	4500
22	4	SCOUT	OP	OFF	FBG	DV	OB			7	11	2000			5000	5750
25		ATTACK 25	OP	RNBT			IO	270-330							12600	15300
25		ATTACK 25	OP	RNBT			IO	365	MRCR						14200	16200
28		BRAVE	OP	OFF	FBG	DV	OB			8	6	7000			14200	16200
28		BRAVE	OP	OFF	FBG	DV	IO	365	MRCR	8	6	7000			27800	30900

36 CONTINUED ON NEXT PAGE 96th ed. - Vol. II

APACHE PERFORMANCE BOATS   -CONTINUED   See inside cover to adjust price for area

LOA FT IN	NAME AND/ OR MODEL	TOP/ RIG	BOAT TYPE	-HULL- MTL TP	----ENGINE--- TP # HP MFG	BEAM FT IN	WGT LBS	DRAFT FT IN	RETAIL LOW	RETAIL HIGH
1988 BOATS
28	BRAVE 28	OP	RNBT		IO T270-T365				24100	30200
33	C C O F		OFF	FBG	IO 365 MRCR	9 6	8500		49300	54200
33	C C O F			FBG	OB	9 6	6000		21700	24100
1987 BOATS
22	SCOUT	OP	OFF	FBG DV OB		7 11	2200		5150	5950
22	SCOUT	OP	OFF	FBG DV IB		7 11	2200		**	**
24	ARROW	OP	OFF	FBG DV OB		8 4	2200		5500	6300
24	ARROW	OP	OFF	FBG DV IB		8 4	2200		**	**
33	BRAVE	OP	OFF	FBG DV OB		9 6			21300	23700
33	BRAVE	OP	OFF	FBG DV IB		9 6			**	**
33	RENEGADE	OP	OFF	FBG DV OB		9 6			23900	26600
33	RENEGADE	OP	OFF	FBG DV IB		9 6			**	**

APACHE POWERBOATS
AVENTURA FL 33180   See inside cover to adjust price for area

LOA FT IN	NAME AND/ OR MODEL	TOP/ RIG	BOAT TYPE	-HULL- MTL TP	----ENGINE--- TP # HP MFG	BEAM FT IN	WGT LBS	DRAFT FT IN	RETAIL LOW	RETAIL HIGH
1992 BOATS
41 3	APACHE 41	OP	RACE	KEV DV	IO T575 MRCR	8	12500	3 4	140000	154000
47	APACHE 47	OP	RACE	KEV DV	IO R575 MRCR	8	14750	4	180500	198500
1991 BOATS
41	APACHE KING-CAT	OP	RACE	KEV	IO T575 MRCR	12	10500	3 6	163500	179500
41	APACHE KING-CAT	OP	RACE	KEV	IO T750 MRCR	12	10500	3 6	193000	212000
41 3	APACHE 41	OP	RACE	KEV DV	IO T575 MRCR	8	11500	3 6	131000	144000
47	APACHE 47	OP	RACE	KEV	IO R575 MRCR	8	13500	3 9	176500	194000
64 3	THUNDERCHIEF		OFF	KEV DV	IO T870D GM	14 6	45000	5	**	**
1990 BOATS
41	APACHE KING-CAT	OP	RACE	KEV	IO T575 MRCR	12	10500	3 6	153000	168000
41	APACHE KING-CAT	OP	RACE	KEV	IO T750 MRCR	12	10500	3 6	180500	198500
41 3	APACHE 41	OP	RACE	KEV DV	IO T575 MRCR	8	11500	3 6	122500	134500
47	APACHE 47	OP	RACE	KEV	IO R575 MRCR	8	13500	3 9	165500	181500
64 3	THUNDERCHIEF		OFF	KEV DV	IO T870D GM	14 6	45000	5	**	**
1989 BOATS
41	APACHE KING-CAT	OP	RACE	KEV	IO T575 MRCR	12	10500	3 6	143500	157500
41	APACHE KING-CAT	OP	RACE	KEV	IO T750 MRCR	12	10500	3 6	169000	186000
41 3	APACHE 41	OP	RACE	KEV DV	IO T575 MRCR	8	11500	3 6	115000	126000
47	APACHE 47	OP	RACE	KEV	IO R575 MRCR	8	13500	3 9	155000	170500
64 3	THUNDERCHIEF		OFF	KEV DV	IO T870D GM	14 6	45000	5	**	**
1988 BOATS
41	APACHE KING-CAT	OP	RACE	KEV	IO T575 MRCR	12	10500	3 6	134500	148000
41	APACHE KING-CAT	OP	RACE	KEV	IO T650 MRCR	12	10500	3 6	145500	160000
41 3	APACHE 41	OP	RACE	KEV DV	IO T575 MRCR	8	11600	3 6	108000	118500
64 3	THUNDERCHIEF		OFF	KEV DV	IO T870D GM	14	45000	5	**	**

APHRODITE MARINE AS
KASTRUP DENMARK   See inside cover to adjust price for area

LOA FT IN	NAME AND/ OR MODEL	TOP/ RIG	BOAT TYPE	-HULL- MTL TP	----ENGINE--- TP # HP MFG	BEAM FT IN	WGT LBS	DRAFT FT IN	RETAIL LOW	RETAIL HIGH
1987 BOATS
44 4	CRUISE ROYALE 44	SLP	SAIL		86D VLVO	12 11	25300	6 4	134000	147500

AQUA CRUISER
COLUMBIA TN 38401   COAST GUARD MFG ID- AQU See inside cover to adjust price for area

LOA FT IN	NAME AND/ OR MODEL	TOP/ RIG	BOAT TYPE	-HULL- MTL TP	----ENGINE--- TP # HP MFG	BEAM FT IN	WGT LBS	DRAFT FT IN	RETAIL LOW	RETAIL HIGH
1988 BOATS
29	PLAYMATE RV	HT	HB	FBG CT OB		8	2800	9	1800	2150
30	PLAYMATE HOUSEBOAT	HT	HB	FBG PN OB		8	3300	9	3750	4350
34	AQUACRUISER 34	HT	HB	FBG PN OB		12	5100	10	8900	10100
42	AQUACRUISER 42	HT	HB	FBG PN OB		14	7200	1	8650	9900
50	AQUACRUISER 50	HT	HB	FBG PN OB		14	8800	1	12100	13700
53	LUXURY LINER 52	HT	HB	FBG PN OB		17	10400	1 2	20100	22400
1987 BOATS
25	PLAYMATE RV	HT	HB	FBG CT OB		8	2650	9	**	**
30	PLAYMATE HOUSEBOAT	HT	HB	FBG PN OB		8	3300	9	3650	4250
32	AQUACRUISER 32 SPECL	HT	HB	FBG PN OB		12	3900	9	5550	6350
33	AQUACRUISER 33 SPECL	HT	HB	FBG PN OB		12	4200	9	6300	7250
34	AQUACRUISER 34	HT	HB	FBG PN OB		12	5100	10	8550	9800
38	AQUACRUISER 38	HT	HB	FBG PN OB		12	5700	10	8650	9950
40	AQUACRUISER 40	HT	HB	FBG PN OB		14	7200	1	9650	11000
50	AQUACRUISER 50	HT	HB	FBG PN OB		14	8800	1	11700	13300
53	AQUACRUISER 52	HT	HB	FBG PN OB		16	9900	1 2	19100	21200
1986 BOATS
27	AQUA-CRUISER	HT	HB	FBG PN OB		8	2800	1 2	**	**
29	AQUA-CRUISER	HT	HB	FBG PN OB		8	3200	1 2	3200	3750
33	AQUA-CRUISER	HT	HB	FBG PN OB		12	5300	1 3	8850	10100
37	AQUA-CRUISER	HT	HB	FBG PN OB		12	6800	1 3	10300	11700
38	AQUA-CRUISER	HT	HB	FBG PN OB		14	7200	1 4	10800	12300
48	AQUA-CRUISER	HT	HB	FBG PN OB		14	8000	1 4	**	**
1985 BOATS
26	AQUA-CRUISER	HT	HB	FBG PN OB		8	2800	1 2	**	**
30	AQUA-CRUISER	HT	HB	FBG PN OB		8	3200	1 2	3150	3650
34	AQUA-CRUISER	HT	HB	FBG PN OB		10	5200	1 2	7900	9800
37	AQUA-CRUISER	HT	HB	FBG PN OB		12	6800	1 3	10000	11400
37	AQUA-CRUISER	HT	HB	FBG PN OB		14	7200	1 4	10600	12200
44	AQUA-CRUISER	HT	HB	FBG PN OB		14	8000	1 4	9050	10300
1984 BOATS
28	PLAYMATE	HT	HB	AL PN OB		8	2650	1	**	**
32	AQUA-CRUISER	HT	HB	AL PN OB		10	3475	1	3900	4500
32	PLAYMATE	HT	HB	AL PN OB		10	3400	1	3650	4250
34	AQUA-CRUISER	HT	HB	AL PN OB		10	4005	1	5400	6200
36	LUXURY LINER	HT	HB	FBG PN OB		13	6500	1	9450	10700
38	AQUA-CRUISER	HT	HB	AL PN OB		10	4975	1	6700	7700
44	LUXURY LINER	HT	HB	FBG PN OB		13	8000	1	8650	9950

AQUA SPORT CANADA LTD
LAVAL BOATS   See inside cover to adjust price for area
SPORT CRAFT
FABREVLL PQ CANADA   COAST GUARD MFG ID- ZAS

LOA FT IN	NAME AND/ OR MODEL	TOP/ RIG	BOAT TYPE	-HULL- MTL TP	----ENGINE--- TP # HP MFG	BEAM FT IN	WGT LBS	DRAFT FT IN	RETAIL LOW	RETAIL HIGH
1990 BOATS
18 6	LAWMAN 186	OP	CTRCN AL	SV JT 200-275			2100	6	11400	13900
20 1	LAWMAN SPORT 20	OP	CTRCN FBG	FL JT 200-275		7 9	2200	6	13200	15600
20 6	LAWMAN 206	OP	CTRCN AL	SV JT 320 FORD		7 11	2700	6	15000	17100
1987 BOATS
16	FISHERMAN F-160 BASS	OP	BASS	FBG FL OB		5 11	525		325	395
16	FISHERMAN F-160 DLX	OP	FSH	FBG SV OB		5 11	500		300	365
16	FISHERMAN F-160 LX	OP	FSH	FBG SV OB		5 11	490		295	360
16 9	CONCORDE V-170	OP	RNBT	FBG DV OB		6 7	1000		675	810
17	BIARRITZ 170 B/R	ST	RNBT	FBG DV IO 120-165		6 11	1900		5850	6750
17	CONCORDE V-170	ST	RNBT	FBG DV IO 120-165		6 7	1400		5000	5800
17	RIVIERA B/R-170	OP	RNBT	FBG DV OB		7 10	1100		755	910
20	LAGUNA 200	ST	CUD	FBG DV IO 165-260		8	3000		9650	11600
1986 BOATS
16	LAVAL-CARRERA	OP	RNBT	FBG DV OB		7	1850		1200	1450
16	LAVAL-CONCORDE	OP	RNBT	FBG DV OB		7	630		630	760
16	LAVAL-TARGA	OP	RNBT	FBG DV OB		7	1100		690	835
17	LAVAL-BIARRITZ	OP	RNBT	FBG DV OB		7	1950		1250	1500
1985 BOATS
16	FISHERMAN F-160	OP	FSH	FBG FL OB		5 11	490		280	340
16	FISHERMAN F-160 BASS	OP	BASS	FBG FL OB		5 11	525		300	370
16	FISHERMAN F-160 DLX	OP	FSH	FBG SV OB		6	500		285	345
16 9	CONCORDE V-170	OP	RNBT	FBG DV OB		6 7	1000		620	745
17	CONCORDE V-170	ST	RNBT	FBG DV IO 120-170		6 7	1400		4600	5350
17	RIVIERA B/R-170	OP	RNBT	FBG DV OB		7 10	1100		680	820
1984 BOATS
16	BASE BOAT 16	OP	BASS	FBG FL OB		5 11	525		295	360
16	FISHERMAN 16	OP	FSH	FBG FL OB		5 11	490		275	335
16	FISHERMAN CC DELUXE	OP	FSH	FBG SV OB		6	500		280	340
16 9	CONCORDE V-170	OP	RNBT	FBG DV OB		6 7	1000		585	705
17	CONCORDE V-170	ST	RNBT	FBG DV IO 120-170		6 7	1400		4400	5150

...For earlier years, see the BUC Used Boat Price Guide, Volume 3

AQUA-STAR LTD
ST SAMPSONS GUERNSEY GY2 4LE   See inside cover to adjust price for area

For more recent years, see the BUC Used Boat Price Guide, Volume 1

LOA FT IN	NAME AND/ OR MODEL	TOP/ RIG	BOAT TYPE	-HULL- MTL TP	----ENGINE--- TP # HP MFG	BEAM FT IN	WGT LBS	DRAFT FT IN	RETAIL LOW	RETAIL HIGH
1996 BOATS
27	PACESETTER		RNBT	FBG	IB 300D	9 6	10000	2 10	73500	80700
33	OCEANRANGER		CR	FBG	IB 300D	11 3	14000	3 3	132000	145000
38	OCEANRANGER		CR	FBG	IB 300D	12 7	17000	3 3	161500	177500
43	OCEANRANGER		CR	FBG	IB 300D	13 7	20000	3 3	200500	220000

AQUA-STAR LTD   -CONTINUED   See inside cover to adjust price for area

LOA FT IN	NAME AND/ OR MODEL	TOP/ RIG	BOAT TYPE	-HULL- MTL TP	----ENGINE--- TP # HP MFG	BEAM FT IN	WGT LBS	DRAFT FT IN	RETAIL LOW	RETAIL HIGH
------------------- 1996 BOATS ---
46	NELSON		CR	FBG	IB 300D	14	30000	3 3	254500	280000
54	AQUAIR		CR	FBG	IB 300D	16	44000	3	300500	330500
60	OCEAN		MS	FBG		15		7 7	**	**
62	OCEAN		MS	FBG	IB 300D	16	30000	8	462000	507500
------------------- 1995 BOATS ---
27	PACESETTER		RNBT	FBG	IB 300D	9 6	10000	2 10	69800	76700
33	OCEANRANGER		CR	FBG	IB 300D	11 3	14000	3 3	125500	138000
38	OCEANRANGER		CR	FBG	IB 300D	12 7	17000	3 3	154500	170000
43	OCEANRANGER		CR	FBG	IB 300D	13 7	20000	3 3	191000	210000
46	NELSON		CR	FBG	IB 300D	14	30000	3 3	242500	266500
52	OCEANRANGER		CR	FBG	IB 300D	16	44000	5	300500	330000
62	OCEAN		MS	FBG	IB 300D	16	30000	8	434500	477500
------------------- 1994 BOATS ---
27	PACESETTER		RNBT	FBG	IB 300D	9 6	10000	2 10	66300	72900
33	OCEANRANGER		CR	FBG	IB 300D	11 3	14000	3 3	119000	131000
38	OCEANRANGER		CR	FBG	IB 300D	12 7	17000	3 3	148500	163000
43	OCEANRANGER		CR	FBG	IB 300D	13 7	20000	3 3	182500	200500
46	NELSON		CR	FBG	IB 300D	14	30000	3 3	231500	254500
62	OCEAN		MS	FBG	IB 300D	16	30000	8	408500	449000

....For earlier years, see the BUC Used Boat Price Guide, Volume 3

AQUARIUS MARINE GROUP INC
CLEARWATER FL 33515   See inside cover to adjust price for area

HERITAGE EAST YACHTS INC
CLEARWATER FL

LOA FT IN	NAME AND/ OR MODEL	TOP/ RIG	BOAT TYPE	-HULL- MTL TP	----ENGINE--- TP # HP MFG	BEAM FT IN	WGT LBS	DRAFT FT IN	RETAIL LOW	RETAIL HIGH
------------------- 1987 BOATS ---
40 6	AQUARIUS 41	FB	MY	FBG DV	IB T210D CUM	14 10	26000	3	118000	129500
45	AQUARIUS 45	FB	MY	FBG DV	IB T210D CUM	14 10	31000		121500	133500

AQUARIUS YACHTS INC
SARASOTA FL 33580   COAST GUARD MFG ID- AYW See inside cover to adjust price for area
                       SEE ALSO TOP SAIL YACHTS INC

LOA FT IN	NAME AND/ OR MODEL	TOP/ RIG	BOAT TYPE	-HULL- MTL TP	----ENGINE--- TP # HP MFG	BEAM FT IN	WGT LBS	DRAFT FT IN	RETAIL LOW	RETAIL HIGH
------------------- 1984 BOATS ---
32	PILOT CUTTER	CUT	SA/CR	FBG KL	IB 18D VLVO	9	8900	4	27900	31000

....For earlier years, see the BUC Used Boat Price Guide, Volume 3

AQUASPORT
DIV OF GENMAR INDUSTRIES   See inside cover to adjust price for area
SARASOTA FL 34243   COAST GUARD MFG ID- ASP

For more recent years, see the BUC Used Boat Price Guide, Volume 1

LOA FT IN	NAME AND/ OR MODEL	TOP/ RIG	BOAT TYPE	-HULL- MTL TP	----ENGINE--- TP # HP MFG	BEAM FT IN	WGT LBS	DRAFT FT IN	RETAIL LOW	RETAIL HIGH
------------------- 1996 BOATS ---
16 1	STRIPER 165	OP	CTRCN FBG SV	OB	6	1000	10	3050	3550
17 5	OSPREY 175	OP	CTRCN FBG SV	OB	6 9	1850	1 10	5100	5850
19 6	OSPREY 200	OP	CTRCN FBG SV	OB	7 7	2300	2 2	6150	7050
21 4	EXPLORER 215	OP	CUD FBG DV	OB	8 3	3200	2 9	9650	10900
24	EXPLORER 225	OP	CUD FBG DV	OB	8 6	4100	2 4	12100	13700
24	OSPREY 225	OP	CTRCN FBG DV	OB	8 6	3900	2 4	11800	13500
24 1	EXPLORER 245	OP	CUD FBG DV	OB	8 6	4300	2 10	14300	16200
26 1	EXPLORER 245	OP	CUD FBG DV	OB	8 6	4300	2 5	14300	16200
26 1	OSPREY 245	OP	CTRCN FBG DV	OB	8 6	4100	2 10	13900	15800
------------------- 1995 BOATS ---
17 5	OSPREY 175	OP	CTRCN FBG SV	OB	6 9	1510	2 1	4200	4900
19 6	OSPREY 200	OP	CTRCN FBG SV	OB	7 7	1935	2 4	5350	6150
19 7	OSPREY 195	OP	FSH FBG SV	OB	7 9	2150	2 4	5700	6550
24	EXPLORER 225	OP	CUD FBG DV	OB	8 6	3600	2 4	10900	12400
24	OSPREY 225	OP	CTRCN FBG DV	OB	8 6	3400	2 4	10500	12000
26 1	EXPLORER 245	OP	CUD FBG DV	OB	8 6	3800	2 6	12600	13800
26 1	OSPREY 245	OP	CTRCN FBG DV	OB	8 6	3600	2 6	12200	13800
27 4	EXPLORER 250	OP	CUD FBG DV	OB	9	4200	2 7	13600	15500
------------------- 1994 BOATS ---
17 5	OSPREY 175	OP	CTRCN FBG SV	OB	6 9	1510	2 1	4000	4650
19 6	OSPREY 200	OP	CTRCN FBG SV	OB	7 7	3000	2 4	6000	6900
19 7	OSPREY 195	OP	FSH FBG SV	OB	7 9	2150	2 4	5450	6250
24	EXPLORER 225	OP	CUD FBG DV	OB	8 6	3200	2 4	10600	12200
24	OSPREY 225	OP	CTRCN FBG DV	OB	8 6	3000	2 4	10000	11400
26 1	EXPLORER 245	OP	CUD FBG DV	OB	8 6	3400	2 6	13400	15400
26 1	OSPREY 245	OP	CTRCN FBG DV	OB	8 6	3300	2 6	13400	15200
27 4	EXPLORER 250	OP	CUD FBG DV	OB	9	4070	2 7	17100	19400
------------------- 1993 BOATS ---
17 5	OSPREY 175	OP	CTRCN FBG SV	OB	6 10	1510	2 1	3850	4450
19 6	OSPREY 200	OP	CTRCN FBG SV	OB	7 8	1935	2 3	4900	5600
21	CENTER CONSOLE 210	OP	CTRCN FBG SV	OB	8 6	3000	2 5	7850	9000
21	WALKAROUND 210	OP	FSH FBG SV	OB	8 6	3100	2 5	7950	9150
21	WALKAROUND 210	OP	FSH FBG SV	IO 175-230	8 6	3100	2 5	8800	10500
21	WALKAROUND 210	OP	FSH FBG SV	IO 275 VLVO	8 6	3100	2 5	9800	11200
23	CENTER CONSOLE 230	OP	CTRCN FBG SV	IB	8 6	3200	2 5	9600	10900
23	WALKAROUND 230	OP	SF FBG SV	IB	8 6	3300	2 5	9800	11200
23	WALKAROUND 230	OP	SF FBG SV	IO 180-230	8 6	3300	2 5	10900	12900
23	WALKAROUND 230	OP	SF FBG SV	IO 275 VLVO	8 6	3300	2 5	12000	13600
------------------- 1992 BOATS ---
17 5	OSPREY 175	OP	CTRCN FBG SV	OB	6 10	1510	2 1	3650	4250
19 6	OSPREY 200	OP	CTRCN FBG SV	OB	7 8	1935	2 3	4700	5400
21	CENTER CONSOLE 210	OP	CTRCN FBG SV	OB	8 6	3000	2 5	7500	8650
21	WALKAROUND 210	OP	FSH FBG SV	OB	8 6	3100	2 5	7600	8750
21	WALKAROUND 210	OP	FSH FBG SV	IO 175-230	8 6	3100	2 5	8500	9850
21	WALKAROUND 210	OP	FSH FBG SV	IO 275 VLVO	8 6	3100	2 5	9250	10500
23	CENTER CONSOLE 230	OP	CTRCN FBG SV	IB	8 6	3200	2 5	**	**
23	WALKAROUND 230	OP	SF FBG SV	IB	8 6	3300	2 5	**	**
23	WALKAROUND 230	OP	SF FBG SV	IO 180-230	8 6	3300	2 5	10200	12000
23	WALKAROUND 230	OP	SF FBG SV	IO 275 VLVO	8 6	3300	2 5	11200	12800
31	TOURNAMENT MSTR 310	OP	SF FBG DV	IB T	11	10100	2 6	**	**
------------------- 1991 BOATS ---
17 5	OSPREY 175	OP	CTRCN FBG SV	OB	6 10	1510	2 1	3550	4100
19 6	OSPREY 200	OP	CTRCN FBG SV	OB	7 8	1935	2 3	4500	5200
21	CENTER CONSOLE 210	OP	CTRCN FBG SV	OB	8 6	3000	2 5	7200	8300
21	WALKAROUND 210	OP	FSH FBG SV	OB	8 6	3100	2 5	7350	8500
23	CENTER CONSOLE 230	OP	CTRCN FBG SV	IB	8 6	3200	2 5	**	**
26	WALKAROUND 230	OP	SF FBG SV	IB	8 6	3300	2 5	**	**
31	TOURNAMENT MSTR 310	OP	SF FBG DV	IB T	11	10100	2 6	**	**
------------------- 1990 BOATS ---
17	174	OP	CTRCN FBG SV	OB	6 10	1150		2750	3200
17 5	OSPREY 175	OP	CTRCN FBG SV	OB	6 10	1150		2750	3200
19 6	OSPREY 200	OP	CTRCN FBG SV	OB	7 8	1550	9	3700	4300
21	210 XF BRKT	OP	FSH FBG DV	OB	8 6			7200	8250
21	210 XF CT	OP	FSH FBG DV	OB	8 6			7200	8250
21	210 XF I/O	OP	FSH FBG DV	OB	8 6			7200	8250
22	222 CCP	OP	EXP FBG DV	OB	8	2200	1	6150	7100
22 2	222 XF CT	OP	EXP FBG DV	OB	8	2200	1	6200	7100
23	230 XF BRKT	OP	EXP FBG DV	OB	8 6			8650	9950
23	230 XF CT	OP	EXP FBG DV	OB	8 6			8650	9950
23	230 XF I/O	OP	EXP FBG DV	OB	8 6			8650	9950
24 8	250 CCP BRKT	OP	CTRCN FBG DV	OB	8	2600	1	**	**
26 4	250 XF BRKT	OP	EXP FBG DV	OB	8	2900	1	11800	13400
28 10	281 XF BRKT	OP	EXP FBG DV	OB	8	5400	2	16800	19100
31	290 XF	OP	SF FBG DV	IB T	CRUS 11	10100	2 6	**	**
31	TOURNAMENT MSTR 290	TT	SF FBG DV	IB T	CRUS 11	10100	2 6	**	**
------------------- 1989 BOATS ---
17 10	OSPREY 170	OP	CTRCN FBG SV	OB	6 10	1150		2700	3100
17 10	STRIPER 170	OP	CTRCN FBG SV	OB	6 10	1150		2700	3100
19 6	OSPREY 200	OP	CTRCN FBG SV	OB	7 8	1550	9	3550	4150
19 6	STRIPER 200	OP	CTRCN FBG SV	OB	7 8	1550	9	3550	4150
22 2	EXPRESS FISH 222	OP	FSH FBG DV	OB	8	2200	1	5950	6850
22 2	OSPREY 222	OP	FSH FBG DV	OB	7 11	1800	9	5050	5850
22 2	PROFESSIONAL 222	OP	CTRCN FBG DV	OB	8	2200	1	5950	6850
22 2	SANDPIPER 222	OP	FSH FBG DV	OB	8	2200	1	5950	6850
24 8	PROFESSIONAL 250	OP	CTRCN FBG DV	OB	8	2600	1	7700	8850
26 4	EXPRESS FISH 250	OP	EXP FBG DV	IO	8	2900	1	**	**
28 10	COHO 281	OP	EXP FBG DV	IO	9	5400	2 5	**	**
28 10	FAMILY FISHERMAN 281	OP	EXP FBG DV	IO	9	5400	2 5	**	**
31	EXPRESS FISH 290		SF	FBG DV	IO	11	9500	2 6	**	**
31	TOURNAMENT MASTER		SF	FBG DV	IO	11	9500	2 6	**	**
------------------- 1988 BOATS ---
17	DELL QUAY 170	OP	RNBT FBG TR	OB	7 8	880		2000	2400
17	OSPREY 170	OP	CTRCN FBG SV	OB	6 10	1150	8	2500	2900
17	STRIPER 170	OP	CTRCN FBG SV	OB	6 10	1150	8	2600	3000
17 5	OSPREY 175	OP	CTRCN FBG SV	OB	6 10	1150	8	2550	2950
17 5	STRIPER 175	OP	CTRCN FBG SV	OB	6 10	1150	8	2600	3000
19 6	OSPREY 200	OP	CTRCN FBG SV	OB	7 8	1550	9	3400	3950

38   CONTINUED ON NEXT PAGE   96th ed. - Vol. II

LOA FT	LOA IN	NAME AND/ OR MODEL	TOP/ RIG	BOAT TYPE	-HULL- MTL	-HULL- TP	ENGINE TP	ENGINE # HP	ENGINE MFG	BEAM FT	BEAM IN	WGT LBS	DRAFT FT	DRAFT IN	RETAIL LOW	RETAIL HIGH
		1988 BOATS														
19	6	STRIPER 200	OP	CTRCN	FBG	SV	OB			7	8	1550		9	3450	4000
22	2	222 CCP	OP	CTRCN	FBG	DV	OB			8		2200	1		5750	6600
22	2	EXPRESS FISH 222	OP	FSH	FBG	DV	OB			8		2200	1		6050	7000
22	2	EXPRESS FISH 222	OP	FSH	FBG	DV	IO	231		8		2200	1		5750	6600
22	2	OSPREY 222	OP	CTRCN	FBG	SV	OB			7	11	1800		9	4900	5600
22	2	SANDPIPER 222	OP	FSH	FBG	DV	OB			8		2200	1		5450	6250
24	8	250 CCP	OP	CTRCN	FBG	DV	OB			8		2600	1		7450	8550
26	4	EXPRESS FISH 250	OP	FSH	FBG	DV	OB			8		2900	1		10900	12400
26	4	EXPRESS FISH 250	OP	FSH	FBG	DV	IO	271		8		2900	1		9900	11300
26	4	FISHERMAN 250XF	OP	FSH	FBG	DV	IO	205-260		8		2900	1		9200	11100
26	4	FISHERMAN 250XF	OP	SF	FBG	DV	OB			8		2900	1		10800	12200
28	10	COHO 281	OP	FSH	FBG	DV	IO	260-340		9	8	6400	2	5	19200	22800
28	10	COHO 281 W/BRKT	OP	FSH	FBG	DV	IO			9	8	6400	2	5	**	**
28	10	FAMILY FISH 281	ST	FSH	FBG	DV	IO	260-340		9	8	6400	2	5	19200	22800
28	10	FAMILY FSH 281W/BRKT	ST	FSH	FBG	DV	IO			9	8	6400	2	5	**	**
28	10	FAMILY FSH 281W/BRKT	ST	FSH	FBG	DV	IO		MRCR	9	8	6400	2	5	**	**
28	10	OSPREY 281	OP	CTRCN	FBG	DV	OB			9	8	4700	2		13700	15600
28	10	OSPREY 281	TT	CTRCN	FBG	DV	OB			9	8	4700	2		15700	17900
28	10	OSPREY 281 H/TWR	TT	CTRCN	FBG	DV	OB			9	8	4700	2		17600	20000
28	10	OSPREY 281 W/BRKT	OP	CTRCN	FBG	DV	OB			9	8	4700	2		15600	17700
28	10	OSPREY 281 W/BRKT	TT	CTRCN	FBG	DV	OB			9	8	4700	2		15700	17900
31		EXPRESS FISH 290	ST	FSH	FBG	DV	IO	T260-T340		11		9500	2	6	26500	31300
31		TOURNAMENT MSTER 290	TT	FSH	FBG	DV	IO	T260-T340		11		10100	2	6	32000	37700
		1987 BOATS														
17		OSPREY 170	OP	CTRCN	FBG	SV	OB			6	10	1150		7	2400	2800
17		STRIPER 170	OP	CTRCN	FBG	SV	OB			6	10	1150		7	2500	2900
19	6	OSPREY 200	OP	CTRCN	FBG	SV	OB			7	8	1550		9	3300	3850
19	6	STRIPER 200	OP	CTRCN	FBG	SV	OB			7	8	1550		9	3300	3850
22	2	222 CCP	OP	CTRCN	FBG	DV	OB			8		2200	1		5550	6400
22	2	FISHERMAN 222XF	OP	FSH	FBG	DV	IO	200-260		8		2200	1		5350	6450
22	2	FISHERMAN 222XF	OP	SF	FBG	DV	OB			8		2200	1		5600	6450
22	2	OSPREY 222	OP	CTRCN	FBG	SV	OB			7	11	1800		9	4750	5450
22	2	OSPREY 222	OP	CTRCN	FBG	SV	IB	220-230		7	11	1800	9		6100	7050
22	2	SANDPIPER 222	OP	RNBT	FBG	DV	OB			8		2200	1		5600	6450
24	8	250 CCP	OP	CTRCN	FBG	DV	OB			8		2600	1		7200	8250
24	8	OSPREY 250	OP	CTRCN	FBG	DV	OB			8		2765	1		7500	8600
24	8	OSPREY 250	TT	CTRCN	FBG	DV	OB			8			1		8900	10100
24	8	OSPREY 250 H/TWR	TT	CTRCN	FBG	DV	OB			8			1		8950	10200
24	8	OSPREY 250 H/TWR/BRK		CTRCN	FBG	DV	OB			8			1		9500	10800
24	8	OSPREY 250 W/BRKT	OP	CTRCN	FBG	DV	OB			8		2765	1		7500	8600
24	8	TOURNAMENT MSTER 250	TT	CTRCN	FBG	DV	OB			8			1		9400	10700
26	4	FISHERMAN 250XF	OP	FSH	FBG	DV	IO	200-260		8		2900	1		8600	10600
26	4	FISHERMAN 250XF	OP	SF	FBG	DV	OB			8		2900	1		10400	11800
28	6	FISHERMAN 270XF	TT	FSH	FBG	DV	OB			10		8090	2	5	14400	16300
28	6	FISHERMAN 270XF	TT	FSH	FBG	DV	IO	T220-T270		10		8090	2	5	21600	25100
28	6	FISHERMAN 270XF	TT	SF	FBG	DV	IB			10		8090	2	5	**	**
28	6	FISHERMAN 270XF BRKT	TT	FSH	FBG	DV	OB			10		8090	2	5	15000	17100
28	6	GREAT LAKES FISH		FSH	FBG	DV	OB			10		7855	2	11	14600	16600
28	6	GREAT LAKES FISH		FSH	FBG	DV	IO	350	PCM	10		7855	2	11	20800	23100
28	6	GREAT LAKES FISH		FSH	FBG	DV	IO	T220-T270		10		7855	2	11	21300	24800
28	6	TOURNAMENT MSTER 270	TT	FSH	FBG	DV	OB			10		8690	2	5	14700	16700
28	6	TOURNAMENT MSTER 270	TT	FSH	FBG	DV	IO	T220-T270		10		8690	2	5	22300	25800
28	10	AQUASPORT 281FF	HT	FSH	FBG	DV	IB			9	7	6400	2	5	**	**
28	10	OSPREY 271	OP	CTRCN	FBG	DV	OB			9	7	4700	2		15000	17100
28	10	OSPREY 271	TT	CTRCN	FBG	DV	OB			9	7	4700	2		12500	14200
28	10	OSPREY 271	TT	CTRCN	FBG	SV	OB			9	7	4700	2		15200	17300
28	10	OSPREY 271 W/BRKT	OP	CTRCN	FBG	DV	OB			9	7	4700	2		15000	17100
28	10	OSPREY 271 W/BRKT	TT	CTRCN	FBG	DV	OB			9	7	4700	2		13900	15800
28	10	OSPREY 271 W/BRKT	TT	CTRCN	FBG	SV	OB			9	7	4700	2		18700	20800
31		FISHERMAN 290XF	TT	FSH	FBG	DV	IO	T260-T350		11		9500	2	6	25300	30000
31		FISHERMAN 290XF	TT	FSH	FBG	DV	IO	T D	GM	11		9500	2	6	**	**
31		FISHERMAN 290XF	TT	SF	FBG	DV	IB			11		9500	2	6	**	**
31		TOURNAMENT MSTER 290	TT	FSH	FBG	DV	IO	T260-T350		11		10100	2	6	30400	36100
31		TOURNAMENT MSTER 290	TT	FSH	FBG	DV	IO	T D	GM	11		10100	2	6	**	**
		1986 BOATS														
17		OSPREY 170 CC	OP	CTRCN	FBG	SV	OB			6	10	1150		8	2400	2750
19	6	OSPREY 200 CC	OP	CTRCN	FBG	SV	OB			7	8	1550		9	3200	3700
22	2	AQUASPORT 222 CCP	OP	CTRCN	FBG	DV	OB			8				1	6900	7950
22	2	AQUASPORT 222 XF	OP	FSH	FBG	DV	OB			8		2200	1		5400	6250
22	2	AQUASPORT 222 XF	OP	FSH	FBG	DV	IO	185-200		8		3200	1		6100	7350
22	2	AQUASPORT 222 XF	OP	FSH	FBG	DV	SE	205	OMC	8		2800	1		6450	7400
22	2	AQUASPORT 222 XF	OP	FSH	FBG	DV	IO	225-260		8		3200	1		6500	7700
22	2	OSPREY 222	OP	CTRCN	FBG	SV	OB			7	11	1800		9	4600	5300
22	2	SANDPIPER 222 SP	OP	RNBT	FBG	DV	OB			8		2200	1		5450	6250
22	2	SANDPIPER 222 SP	OP	RNBT	FBG	DV	IO	185-200		8		3200	1		5500	6600
22	2	SANDPIPER 222 SP	OP	RNBT	FBG	DV	SE	205	OMC	8		2800	1		6500	7500
22	2	SANDPIPER 222 SP	OP	RNBT	FBG	DV	IO	225-260		8		3200	1		5800	6900
24	6	AQUASPORT 250 CCP	OP	CTRCN	FBG	DV	OB			8		2600	1		6850	7850
24	6	AQUASPORT 250 XF	OP	FSH	FBG	DV	OB			8		2900	1		7450	8550
24	6	AQUASPORT 250 XF	OP	FSH	FBG	DV	SE	205	OMC	8		3500	1		8500	9750
24	6	AQUASPORT 250 XF	OP	FSH	FBG	DV	IO	225-260		8		3900	1		8350	9850
26	6	AQUASPORT 270 XF	ST	SF	FBG	DV	OB			10		6000	2		11800	13400
26	6	AQUASPORT 270 XF	ST	SF	FBG	DV	SE	T205	OMC	10		7200	2		12000	13700
26	6	AQUASPORT 270 XF	ST	SF	FBG	DV	IB	T220	CRUS	10		8000	2	6	20400	22600
26	6	AQUASPORT 270 XF	ST	SF	FBG	DV	IO	T230-T260		10		8000	2		18500	21100
26	6	AQUASPORT 270 XF	ST	SF	FBG	DV	IB	T270	CRUS	10		8000	2	6	20900	23300
26	6	AQUASPORT 270 XF	TT	SF	FBG	DV	OB			10					12000	13600
26	6	AQUASPORT 270 XF	TT	SF	FBG	DV	SE	T205	OMC	10					11300	12800
26	6	AQUASPORT 270 XF	TT	SF	FBG	DV	IB	T220	CRUS	10					16600	18900
26	6	AQUASPORT 270 XF	TT	SF	FBG	DV	IO	T230-T260		10					14900	17500
26	6	AQUASPORT 270 XF	TT	SF	FBG	DV	IB	T270	CRUS	10					17300	19600
28	6	AQUASPORT 290 XF	OP	SF	FBG	DV	IB	158D	VLVO	11		9500	2	6	32500	36100
28	6	AQUASPORT 290 XF	OP	SF	FBG	DV	IB	T260-T270		11		9500	2	6	27800	31200
28	6	AQUASPORT 290 XF	TT	SF	FBG	DV	IB	158D	VLVO	11		9500	2	6	32500	36100
28	6	AQUASPORT 290 XF	TT	SF	FBG	DV	IB	T260-T270		11		9500	2	6	27800	31200
31		AQUASPORT 290 TM	TT	SF	FBG	DV	IB	158D	VLVO	11		9500	2	6	31100	34600
31		AQUASPORT 290 TM	TT	SF	FBG	DV	IB	T255-T270		11		9500	2	6	29000	32600
		1985 BOATS														
17		OSPREY 170 CC	OP	CTRCN	FBG	SV	OB			6	10	1150		8	2350	2700
19	6	OSPREY 196 CC	OP	CTRCN	FBG	SV	OB			7	8	1550		9	3100	3600
20	2	AQUASPORT 200 CCP	OP	CTRCN	FBG	DV	OB			7	10		1		4800	5550
20	2	AQUASPORT 200 XF	OP	FSH	FBG	DV	OB			7	10		1		4800	5550
22	2	AQUASPORT 222 CCP	OP	CTRCN	FBG	DV	OB			8			1		6700	7700
22	2	AQUASPORT 222 XF	OP	FSH	FBG	DV	OB			8		2200	1		5250	6050
22	2	AQUASPORT 222 XF	OP	FSH	FBG	DV	IO	185-200		8		3200	1		5900	7050
22	2	AQUASPORT 222 XF	OP	FSH	FBG	DV	SE	205	OMC	8		2800	1		6250	7200
22	2	AQUASPORT 222 XF	OP	FSH	FBG	DV	IO	225-260		8		3200	1		6200	7400
22	2	SANDPIPER 222 SP	OP	RNBT	FBG	DV	OB			8		2200	1		5300	6100
22	2	SANDPIPER 222 SP	OP	RNBT	FBG	DV	IO	185-200		8		3200	1		5250	6300
22	2	SANDPIPER 222 SP	OP	RNBT	FBG	DV	SE	205	OMC	8		2800	1		6350	7250
22	2	SANDPIPER 222 SP	OP	RNBT	FBG	DV	IO	225-260		8		3200	1		5600	6650
24	6	AQUASPORT 250 CCP	OP	CTRCN	FBG	DV	OB			8		2600	1		6650	7650
24	6	AQUASPORT 250 XF	OP	FSH	FBG	DV	OB			8		2900	1		7250	8300
24	6	AQUASPORT 250 XF	OP	FSH	FBG	DV	IO	188		8		3900	1		7650	8800
24	6	AQUASPORT 250 XF	OP	FSH	FBG	DV	SE	205	OMC	8		3500	1		8250	9450
24	6	AQUASPORT 250 XF	OP	FSH	FBG	DV	IO	225-260		8		3900	1		8000	9450
26	6	AQUASPORT 270 XF	ST	SF	FBG	DV	OB			10		6000	2		11400	13000
26	6	AQUASPORT 270 XF	ST	SF	FBG	DV	IB	260		10		6800	2	6	15800	17900
26	6	AQUASPORT 270 XF	ST	SF	FBG	DV	SE	T205	OMC	10		7200	2		11700	13300
26	6	AQUASPORT 270 XF	ST	SF	FBG	DV	IB	T220	CRUS	10		8000	2	6	19400	21600
26	6	AQUASPORT 270 XF	ST	SF	FBG	DV	IO	T230-T260		10		8000	2		17300	20200
26	6	AQUASPORT 270 XF	ST	SF	FBG	DV	IB	T270	CRUS	10		8000	2	6	20000	22200
26	6	AQUASPORT 270 XF	TT	SF	FBG	DV	OB			10					11600	13200
26	6	AQUASPORT 270 XF	TT	SF	FBG	DV	SE	T205	OMC	10					11000	12500
26	6	AQUASPORT 270 XF	TT	SF	FBG	DV	IB	T220	CRUS	10					15900	18000
26	6	AQUASPORT 270 XF	TT	SF	FBG	DV	IO	T230-T260		10					14300	16800
26	6	AQUASPORT 270 XF	TT	SF	FBG	DV	IB	T270	CRUS	10					16500	18700
28	6	AQUASPORT 290 XF		SF	FBG	DV	IB	T255		11		9500	2	6	26400	29400
28	6	AQUASPORT 290 XF	OP	SF	FBG	DV	IB	158D	VLVO	11		9500	2	6	31200	34600
28	6	AQUASPORT 290 XF	OP	SF	FBG	DV	IB	T260-T270		11		9500	2	6	26500	29800
28	6	AQUASPORT 290 XF	TT	SF	FBG	DV	IB	158D	VLVO	11		9500	2	6	31200	34600
28	6	AQUASPORT 290 XF	TT	SF	FBG	DV	IB	T260-T270		11		9500	2	6	26500	29800
		1984 BOATS														
17		OSPREY 170 CC	OP	CTRCN	FBG	SV	OB			6	10	1150		8	2250	2650
19	6	OSPREY 196 CC	OP	CTRCN	FBG	SV	OB			7	8	1550		9	3000	3500
19	6	OSPREY 196 CC	OP	CTRCN	FBG	SV	SE			7	8	2050		9	**	**
19	6	OSPREY 196 CC	OP	CTRCN	FBG	SV	IO	115		7	8	1550		9	2700	3150
20	2	AQUASPORT 200 CCP		CTRCN	FBG	DV	OB			7	10	1900	1		4100	4800
20	2	AQUASPORT 200 EF		CUD	FBG	DV	OB			7	10	1800	1		4000	4650
22	2	AQUASPORT 222 CCP	OP	CTRCN	FBG	DV	OB			8		2200	1		5100	5850
22	2	AQUASPORT 222 FF	ST	CUD	FBG	DV	SE			8		2800	1		**	**
22	2	AQUASPORT 222 FF	ST	CUD	FBG	DV	IO			8		3200	1		**	**
22	2	AQUASPORT 222 WT	OP	RNBT	FBG	DV	OB			8		2200	1		5150	5950
22	2	AQUASPORT 222 WT	OP	RNBT	FBG	DV	SE	155	OMC	8		2800	1		6150	7100
22	2	AQUASPORT 222 WT	OP	RNBT	FBG	DV	IO	185-188		8		3200	1		5100	5900
22	2	AQUASPORT 222 WT	OP	RNBT	FBG	DV	SE	205	OMC	8		2800	1		6150	7100
22	2	AQUASPORT 222 WT	OP	RNBT	FBG	DV	IO	228-260		8		3200	1		5200	6150

CONTINUED ON NEXT PAGE

AQUASPORT   -CONTINUED   See inside cover to adjust price for area

LOA FT IN	NAME AND/ OR MODEL	TOP/ RIG	BOAT TYPE	-HULL- MTL TP TP	----ENGINE--- # HP MFG	BEAM FT IN	WGT LBS	DRAFT FT IN	RETAIL LOW	RETAIL HIGH
	--------------- 1984 BOATS ---------------									
22 2	AQUASPORT 222 XF	OP	FSH	FBG DV OB	8	2200	1	5150	5900
22 2	AQUASPORT 222 XF	OP	FSH	FBG DV SE 155 OMC	8	2800	1	6100	7000
22 2	AQUASPORT 222 XF	OP	FSH	FBG DV IO 188 MRCR	8	3200	1	5700	6550
22 2	AQUASPORT 222 XF	OP	FSH	FBG DV SE 205 OMC	8	2800	1	6100	7000
22 2	AQUASPORT 222 XF	OP	FSH	FBG DV IO 228-260	8	3200	1	5800	6850
22 2	OSPREY 222 CC	OP	CTRCN	FBG SV OB	7 11	1800	9	4350	5000
24 6	AQUASPORT 250 CCP	OP	CTRCN	FBG DV OB	8	2600	1	6450	7400
24 6	AQUASPORT 250 XF			SE 155 OMC				3550	4150
24 6	AQUASPORT 250 XF	OP	FSH	FBG DV OB	8	2900	1	7050	8100
24 6	AQUASPORT 250 XF	OP	FSH	FBG DV SE OMC	8	3500	1	**	**
24 6	AQUASPORT 250 XF	OP	FSH	FBG DV SE 155 OMC	8	3500	1	8000	9200
24 6	AQUASPORT 250 XF	OP	FSH	FBG DV IO 228-260	8	3900	1	7550	8900
26 6	AQUASPORT 270 XF	ST	SF	FBG DV OB	10	6000	2	11100	12700
26 6	AQUASPORT 270 XF	ST	SF	FBG DV IB 260	10	6800	2	15100	17100
26 6	AQUASPORT 270 XF	ST	SF	FBG DV SE T155-T205	10	7200	2	11400	12900
26 6	AQUASPORT 270 XF	ST	SF	FBG DV IB T220-T225	10	8000	2 6	18800	20900
	IO T230 MRCR 16700 19000, IB T255 COMM 19000 21100, IO T260 MRCR 17200 19500									
	IB T270 CRUS 19100 21200									
26 6	AQUASPORT 270 XF	TT	SF	FBG DV OB	10			11300	12700
26 6	AQUASPORT 270 XF	TT	SF	FBG DV SE T155-T205	10			10700	12100
26 6	AQUASPORT 270 XF	TT	SF	FBG DV IB T220-T225	10			15200	17200
	IO T230 MRCR 13800 15700, IB T255 COMM 15400 17500, IO T260 MRCR 14300 16300									
	IB T270 CRUS 15800 17900									
28 6	AQUASPORT 290	ST	CR	FBG DV IB T255	11	9500	2 6	25300	28100
28 6	AQUASPORT 290	ST	SF	FBG DV IB T255	11	9500	2 6	25300	28100
28 6	AQUASPORT 290 XF	ST	SF	FBG DV IB T	11	9500	2 6	**	**

....For earlier years, see the BUC Used Boat Price Guide, Volume 3

ARIMA MARINE INTERNATIONAL
AUBURN WA 98002   COAST GUARD MFG ID- AMI See inside cover to adjust price for area

For more recent years, see the BUC Used Boat Price Guide, Volume 1

LOA FT IN	NAME AND/ OR MODEL	TOP/ RIG	BOAT TYPE	-HULL- MTL TP TP	----ENGINE--- # HP MFG	BEAM FT IN	WGT LBS	DRAFT FT IN	RETAIL LOW	RETAIL HIGH
	--------------- 1996 BOATS ---------------									
16 11	SEA CHASER	ST	FSH	FBG SV OB	8	1250		5100	5850
16 11	SEA PACER	ST	FSH	FBG SV OB	8	1300		5250	6050
16 11	SEA RANGER	ST	FSH	FBG SV OB	8	1430		5650	6500
18 11	SEA CHASER	ST	FSH	FBG SV OB	8	1600		6450	7400
18 11	SEA RANGER	ST	FSH	FBG SV OB	8	1650		6600	7550
18 11	SEA RANGER	HT	FSH	FBG SV OB	8	1725		6750	7800
	--------------- 1995 BOATS ---------------									
16 11	SEA CHASER	ST	FSH	FBG SV OB	8	1250		4850	5600
16 11	SEA PACER	ST	FSH	FBG SV OB	8	1300		4950	5700
16 11	SEA RANGER	ST	FSH	FBG SV OB	8	1430		5350	6150
18 11	SEA CHASER	ST	FSH	FBG SV OB	8	1600		6100	7000
18 11	SEA RANGER	ST	FSH	FBG SV OB	8	1650		6200	7150
18 11	SEA RANGER	HT	FSH	FBG SV OB	8	1725		6400	7350
	--------------- 1994 BOATS ---------------									
16 11	SEA CHASER	ST	FSH	FBG SV OB	8	1250		4600	5300
16 11	SEA PACER	ST	FSH	FBG SV OB	8	1300		4750	5450
16 11	SEA RANGER	ST	FSH	FBG SV OB	8	1430		5100	5850
18 11	SEA CHASER	ST	FSH	FBG SV OB	8	1600		5800	6650
18 11	SEA RANGER	ST	FSH	FBG SV OB	8	1650		5900	6800
18 11	SEA RANGER-HARDTOP	HT	FSH	FBG SV OB	8	1725		6050	6950
	--------------- 1991 BOATS ---------------									
16 11	SEA CHASER 17	OP	FSH	FBG SV OB	8	1250		3950	4550
16 11	SEA PACER 17	OP	FSH	FBG SV OB	8	1430		4450	5100
16 11	SEA RANGER 17	OP	CUD	FBG SV OB	8	1430		4450	5150
18 11	SEA RANGER	HT	CUD	FBG SV OB	8	1725		5300	6100
18 11	SEA RANGER 19	OP	CUD	FBG SV OB	8	1650		5150	5950
	--------------- 1984 BOATS ---------------									
16 11	SEA-CHASER	OP	FSH	FBG SV OB	8	1200	11	2900	3400

ARKADY MARINE INC
GREEN BAY WI 54305   See inside cover to adjust price for area

LOA FT IN	NAME AND/ OR MODEL	TOP/ RIG	BOAT TYPE	-HULL- MTL TP TP	----ENGINE--- # HP MFG	BEAM FT IN	WGT LBS	DRAFT FT IN	RETAIL LOW	RETAIL HIGH
	--------------- 1986 BOATS ---------------									
34 8	NIGHTWIND 35	SLP	SA/RC	FBG KC IB	25D	11 6	11900	2 9	48900	53700
	--------------- 1985 BOATS ---------------									
34 8	NIGHTWIND 35	SLP	SA/RC	FBG KC IB	D	11 6	11900	2 9	46300	50800
	--------------- 1984 BOATS ---------------									
34 8	NIGHTWIND 35	SLP	SA/RC	FBG KC IB	25D	11 6	11900	2 9	43000	47800

....For earlier years, see the BUC Used Boat Price Guide, Volume 3

ARONOW MARINE INC
FT LAUDERDALE FL 33301-2985   See inside cover to adjust price for area

LOA FT IN	NAME AND/ OR MODEL	TOP/ RIG	BOAT TYPE	-HULL- MTL TP TP	----ENGINE--- # HP MFG	BEAM FT IN	WGT LBS	DRAFT FT IN	RETAIL LOW	RETAIL HIGH
	--------------- 1995 BOATS ---------------									
31 3	ARONOW 313	OP	RNBT	FBG DV OB	8	5400	1	41500	46100

ARONOW POWERBOATS INC
SANFORD FL 32773   See inside cover to adjust price for area

LOA FT IN	NAME AND/ OR MODEL	TOP/ RIG	BOAT TYPE	-HULL- MTL TP TP	----ENGINE--- # HP MFG	BEAM FT IN	WGT LBS	DRAFT FT IN	RETAIL LOW	RETAIL HIGH
	--------------- 1991 BOATS ---------------									
32	ARONOW 32 LEGACY	OP	OFF	F/S DV IO T365 MRCR	8 4		3	17400	19700
39	ARONOW 39	OP	OFF	F/S CT IO T420 MRCR	11 6	12800	3	43600	48500
40	ARONOW 37 HERITAGE	OP	OFF	F/S DV IO T420 MRCR	8	10200	3	42200	46900
44	ARONOW 42	OP	OFF	F/S DV IO T	9 10	17000	3 6	**	**
47 5	ARONOW 45	OP	OFF	F/S DV IO R420 MRCR	8	14200	3 6	85200	93600
53	ARONOW 47	OP	OFF	F/S DV IO T735D GM	12	35000	3 6	123500	135500
	--------------- 1990 BOATS ---------------									
24	ARONOW 24	OP	OFF	KEV CT OB	8	3600	3	22300	24800
32	ARONOW 32	OP	OFF	F/S DV IO T365 MRCR	8 4		3	16300	18500
39	ARONOW 39	OP	OFF	F/S CT IO T420 MRCR	11 6	12800	3	41500	46100
40	ARONOW 37	OP	OFF	F/S DV IO T420 MRCR	8	10200	3	40800	53400
45	ARONOW 45	OP	OFF	F/S DV IO R420 MRCR	8	14200	3 3	80600	88500
53	ARONOW 47	OP	OFF	F/S DV IO T735D GM	12	35000	3 6	138000	151500
	--------------- 1989 BOATS ---------------									
24	ARONOW 24		OFF	KEV TH OB	8	3400	1 6	20900	24600
27 6	ARONOW 27		OFF	F/S CT OB	10 3	6000	2	33300	37000
27 6	ARONOW 27		OFF	F/S DV IO T270 MRCR	10 3	6800	2	10200	11600
37	ARONOW 37		OFF	F/S DV IO T420 MRCR	8	9000	1 6	36700	40800
37	ARONOW 37		OFF	F/S DV IO T575 MRCR	8	9000	1 6	47500	52200
39 2	ARONOW 39		OFF	F/S CT IO T575 MRCR	11 6	9000	1 6	45500	50000
39 2	ARONOW 39		OFF	F/S DV IO T500D MRCR	11 6	10500	1 10	48700	53500
42	ARONOW 42		RACE	KEV DV OB	8		1 6	62800	69000
42	ARONOW 42		RACE	KEV DV IO R700	8		1 6	73200	80400
45	ARONOW 45		OFF	F/S DV IO R575 MRCR	8	14000	2	97200	107000
45	ARONOW 45		OFF	F/S DV IO R700 MRCR	8	14000	2	105500	116000
47	ARONOW 47		OFF	F/S DV IO T750D GM	12	35000	3	105500	115500

ARRIVA
DIV OF US MARINE   See inside cover to adjust price for area
EVERETT WA

For more recent years, see the BUC Used Boat Price Guide, Volume 1

LOA FT IN	NAME AND/ OR MODEL	TOP/ RIG	BOAT TYPE	-HULL- MTL TP TP	----ENGINE--- # HP MFG	BEAM FT IN	WGT LBS	DRAFT FT IN	RETAIL LOW	RETAIL HIGH
	--------------- 1996 BOATS ---------------									
22 8	ARRIVA 2250BR	OP	RNBT	FBG DV IO 250-300	8 4	3625	3 1	11000	13300
22 8	ARRIVA 2252	OP	CUD	FBG DV IO 250-300	8 4	3625	3 1	11600	13900
24 7	ARRIVA 2550BR	OP	RNBT	FBG DV IO 250-300	8 4	3975	3 3	12800	15300
24 7	ARRIVA 2550BR	OP	RNBT	FBG DV IO 400 MRCR	8 4	3975	3 3	16300	18500
24 7	ARRIVA 2552	OP	CUD	FBG DV IO 250-300	8 4	3975	3 3	13600	16300
24 7	ARRIVA 2552	OP	CUD	FBG DV IO 400 MRCR	8 4	3975	3 3	17300	19600

ARROW GLASS BOAT & MFG CORP
DIV OF GENERAL MARINE IND   See inside cover to adjust price for area
PANAMA CITY FL 32404   COAST GUARD MFG ID- CGM

LOA FT IN	NAME AND/ OR MODEL	TOP/ RIG	BOAT TYPE	-HULL- MTL TP TP	----ENGINE--- # HP MFG	BEAM FT IN	WGT LBS	DRAFT FT IN	RETAIL LOW	RETAIL HIGH
	--------------- 1992 BOATS ---------------									
17 1	CARISMA 5.2	OP	RNBT	FBG DV IO 115 MRCR	6 8	1595		2300	2700
17 1	CARISMA SPORT 5.2	OP	RNBT	FBG DV IO 115 MRCR	6 11	1870		2550	2950

LOA FT IN	NAME AND/ OR MODEL	TOP/ RIG	BOAT TYPE	-HULL- MTL TP TP	--ENGINE-- # HP MFG	BEAM FT IN	WGT LBS	DRAFT FT IN	RETAIL LOW	RETAIL HIGH
1992 BOATS										
17 6	185-S3	OP	RNBT	FBG DV IO	115 MRCR	7 4	2250		2950	3400
17 6	CARISMA 5.4	OP	RNBT	FBG DV IO	115 MRCR	7	1820		2600	3000
18 3	COHO 5.9	OP	CTRCN	FBG DV OB		7 4	1700		3500	4050
18 8	195-SS	OP	RNBT	FBG DV IO	115 MRCR		2370		3400	3950
19 6	CARISMA 5.9	OP	RNBT	FBG DV IO	155 MRCR	7 4	2552		3500	4100
20 1	COHO 6.5	OP	CTRCN	FBG DV OB		8	1775		4000	4700
20 4	CARISMA 6.2	OP	RNBT	FBG DV IO	155 MRCR	8	2702		3700	4300
20 4	FIESTA 6.2	OP	RNBT	FBG DV IO	155 MRCR	8	2802		3750	4350
22	CARISMA 6.9	OP	RNBT	FBG DV IO	155 MRCR	8	2902		4150	4850
22 3	CARRIBEAN	OP	RNBT	FBG DV IO	230 MRCR	8 2	3707		5150	5900
22 4	FIESTA 6.9	OP	RNBT	FBG DV IO	155 MRCR	8	3002		4350	5050
1991 BOATS										
17 1	CARISMA 5.2	OP	RNBT	FBG DV IO	115 MRCR	6 8	1595		2150	2500
17 1	CARISMA SPORT 5.2	OP	RNBT	FBG DV IO	115 MRCR	6 11	1870		2350	2750
17 6	CARISMA 5.4	OP	RNBT	FBG DV IO	115 MRCR	7	1820		2400	2800
18 3	COHO 5.9	OP	CTRCN	FBG DV OB		7 4	1700		3350	3900
19 6	CARISMA 5.9	OP	RNBT	FBG DV IO	155 MRCR	7 4	2552		3300	3850
20 1	COHO 6.5	OP	CTRCN	FBG DV OB		8	1775		3850	4500
20 4	CARISMA 6.2	OP	RNBT	FBG DV IO	155 MRCR	8	2702		3450	4000
20 4	FIESTA 6.2	OP	RNBT	FBG DV IO	155 MRCR	8	2802		3550	4100
22	CARISMA 6.9	OP	RNBT	FBG DV IO	155 MRCR	8	2902		3900	4550
22 3	CARRIBEAN	OP	RNBT	FBG DV IO	230 MRCR	8 2	3707		4850	5550
22 4	FIESTA 6.9	OP	RNBT	FBG DV IO	155 MRCR	8	3002		4050	4700
1988 BOATS										
16 1	CARISMA 5.2	OP	RNBT	FBG DV OB		7	1175		2200	2600
16 1	CARISMA 5.2	OP	RNBT	FBG DV IO		7	1800		**	**
16 1	CARISMA 5.2 FS	OP	RNBT	FBG DV OB		7	1175		2200	2600
16 1	CARISMA 5.2 FS	OP	RNBT	FBG DV IO		7	1800		**	**
17	FREEDOM I	OP	FSH	FBG DV OB		7	950		1850	2200
17	FREEDOM I FISH & SKI	OP	FSH	FBG DV OB		7	950		1850	2200
17 1	CARISMA 5.6	OP	RNBT	FBG DV OB		6 11	1285		2400	2800
17 1	CARISMA 5.6	OP	RNBT	FBG DV IO		7 4	2240		**	**
18 3	CARISMA 5.9	OP	RNBT	FBG DV OB		7 4	2650		**	**
18 3	COHO 5.9	OP	CTRCN	FBG DV OB		7 4	1700		3050	3500
18 8	CARISMA 6	OP	RNBT	FBG DV IO		8	3000		**	**
18 8	FIESTA 6 CC	OP	CUD	FBG DV IO		8	3000		**	**
20 1	CARISMA 6.5	OP	RNBT	FBG DV IO		8	3400		**	**
20 1	COHO 6.5	OP	CTRCN	FBG DV OB		8	1775		3500	4100
20 1	FIESTA 6.5 CC	OP	CUD	FBG DV IO		8	3500		**	**
22 3	CARIBBEAN SPORT 7.3	OP	CUD	FBG DV IO		8	4300		**	**

....For earlier years, see the BUC Used Boat Price Guide, Volume 3

ASTRO BOATS
DIV OF MARINE GROUP
SPRINGFIELD MO 65803

See inside cover to adjust price for area

LOA FT IN	NAME AND/ OR MODEL	TOP/ RIG	BOAT TYPE	-HULL- MTL TP TP	--ENGINE-- # HP MFG	BEAM FT IN	WGT LBS	DRAFT FT IN	RETAIL LOW	RETAIL HIGH
1995 BOATS										
16 11	17CC	OP	FSH	FBG DV OB		7 2	900		3100	3600
16 11	17SCX	OP	FSH	FBG DV OB		7	1385		4550	5250
16 11	STEALTH S17FS	OP	FSH	FBG DV OB		7	1415		4650	5300
17 2	STEALTH S17B	OP	FSH	FBG DV OB		6 10	1290		4250	4950
17 10	STEALTH S18B	OP	FSH	FBG DV OB		7 3	1415		4700	5450
17 10	STEALTH S18FS	OP	FSH	FBG DV OB		7 3	1465		4850	5550
18 4	QUICKFIRE F18	OP	FSH	FBG DV OB		7 5	1265		4400	5050
18 6	18DCX	OP	FSH	FBG DV OB		7 4	1725		5500	6350
18 6	18SCX	OP	FSH	FBG DV OB		7 4	1550		5150	5900
18 8	18FSX	OP	RNBT	FBG DV OB		7 4	1650		5500	6300
19 2	19CC	OP	FSH	FBG DV OB		7 4	1450		5000	5750
19 6	20FSX	OP	RNBT	FBG DV OB		7 11	1900		6250	7200
19 11	21DCX	OP	FSH	FBG DV OB		7 9	1925		6400	7350
19 11	21SCX	OP	FSH	FBG DV OB		7 9	1900		6350	7250
20 1	QUICKFIRE F20	OP	FSH	FBG DV OB		7 7	1450		5400	6200
20 2	STEALTH 20B	OP	FSH	FBG DV OB		7 7	1650		5950	6850
20 2	STEALTH S20DC	OP	FSH	FBG DV OB		7 7	1715		5950	6850
20 2	STEALTH S20FS	OP	FSH	FBG DV OB		7 7	1715		6100	7000
20 6	21CC	OP	FSH	FBG DV OB		8 6	1600		5950	6800
1994 BOATS										
16 6	XF160	OP	FSH	FBG DV OB		6 8	1155		3600	4200
16 11	SCX17	OP	FSH	FBG DV OB		7	1385		4250	4950
16 11	STEALTH S17FS	OP	FSH	FBG DV OB		7	1415		4400	5050
16 11	XF17CC	OP	FSH	FBG DV OB		7 2	900		2950	3400
17 2	STEALTH S17B	OP	FSH	FBG DV OB		6 10	1290		4050	4750
17 4	XF175	OP	FSH	FBG DV OB		7 2	1390		4350	5000
17 4	XF176	OP	FSH	FBG DV OB		7 2	1390		4350	5000
17 10	STEALTH S18B	OP	FSH	FBG DV OB		7 3	1415		4500	5150
17 10	STEALTH S18FS	OP	FSH	FBG DV OB		7 3	1465		4600	5300
18 4	QUICKFIRE F18	OP	FSH	FBG DV OB		7 5	1265		4100	4800
18 6	DCX18	OP	FSH	FBG DV OB		7 4	1725		5200	6000
18 6	SCX18	OP	FSH	FBG DV OB		7 4	1550		4850	5600
18 8	FSX18	OP	RNBT	FBG DV OB		7 4	1650		5200	6000
19 2	XF19CC	OP	FSH	FBG DV OB		7 4	1450		4750	5450
19 6	FSX20	OP	RNBT	FBG DV OB		7 11	1900		5950	6800
19 11	DCX20	OP	FSH	FBG DV OB		7 11	1855		5900	6800
19 11	FDX20	OP	FSH	FBG DV OB		7 11	1830		5850	6700
20 1	QUICKFIRE F20	OP	FSH	FBG DV OB		7 7	1450		5100	5850
20 2	STEALTH S20DC	OP	FSH	FBG DV OB		7 7	1715		5650	6500
20 2	STEALTH S20FS	OP	FSH	FBG DV OB		7 7	1715		5750	6600
20 X	XF21CC	OP	FSH	FBG DV OB		8 6	1600		5600	6450
1993 BOATS										
16 11	FSX17	OP	RNBT	FBG DV OB		7	1415		4250	4950
16 11	SCX17	OP	FSH	FBG DV OB		7	1385		4050	4750
17 2	STEALTH S17B	OP	FSH	FBG DV OB		6 10	1290		3850	4500
17 4	XF175	OP	FSH	FBG DV OB		7 2	1390		4100	4750
17 10	STEALTH S18B	OP	FSH	FBG DV OB		7 3	1415		4200	4900
17 10	STEALTH S18FS	OP	FSH	FBG DV OB		7 3	1465		4350	5000
18 6	DCX18	OP	FSH	FBG DV OB		7 4	1725		4950	5700
18 6	FDX18	OP	FSH	FBG DV OB		7 4	1655		4850	5550
18 6	SCX18	OP	FSH	FBG DV OB		7 4	1550		4600	5300
18 8	FSX18	OP	RNBT	FBG DV OB		7 4	1650		4950	5700
19 6	FSX20	OP	RNBT	FBG DV OB		7 11	1900		5650	6450
19 11	DCX20	OP	FSH	FBG DV OB		7 11	1855		5600	6450
19 11	FDX20	OP	FSH	FBG DV OB		7 11	1830		5550	6400

ATLANTIC CITY CATBOATS
NAVESINK YACHT SALES INC
SEA BRIGHT NJ 07760

See inside cover to adjust price for area

LOA FT IN	NAME AND/ OR MODEL	TOP/ RIG	BOAT TYPE	-HULL- MTL TP TP	--ENGINE-- # HP MFG	BEAM FT IN	WGT LBS	DRAFT FT IN	RETAIL LOW	RETAIL HIGH
1986 BOATS										
21 3	ATLANTIC-CITY-KITTY	CAT	SA/CR	FBG KC		9 6	5300	2	13300	15100
21 3	ATLANTIC-CITY-KITTY	CAT	SA/CR	FBG KC IB	10D- 18D	9 6	5300	2	14400	16800
22 7	ATLANTIC-CITY-SKIFF	ST	CTRCN	FBG SV IB	240 CHRY	8 5	3700	2 4	12000	13700
22 7	ATLANTIC-CITY-SKIFF	ST	CUD	FBG SV IB	240 CHRY	8 5	3700	2 4	12000	13700
24	ATLANTIC-CITY-CAT	CAT	SA/CR	FBG KC IB	18D- 28D	11	8000	2	24500	27600
1985 BOATS										
21 3	ATLANTIC-CITY-KITTY	CAT	SA/CR	FBG KC		9 6	5300	2	12500	14200
21 3	ATLANTIC-CITY-KITTY	CAT	SA/CR	FBG KC IB	10D BMW	9 6	5300	2	13600	15400
22 7	ATLANTIC-CITY-SKIFF	ST	CTRCN	FBG SV IB	240 CHRY	8 5	3700	2 4	11500	13100
22 7	ATLANTIC-CITY-SKIFF	ST	CUD	FBG SV IB	240 CHRY	8 5	3700	2 4	11500	13100
24	ATLANTIC-CITY-CAT	CAT	SA/CR	FBG KC IB	10D BMW	11	8000	2	22700	25300
1984 BOATS										
21 3	ATLANTIC-CITY-KITTY	CAT	SA/CR	FBG KC		9 6	5300	2	11700	13400
21 3	ATLANTIC-CITY-KITTY	CAT	SA/CR	FBG KC IB	12D BMW	9 6	5300	2	12800	14600
24	ATLANTIC-CITY-CAT	CAT	SA/CR	FBG KC IB	12D BMW	11	8000	2	21400	23800

....For earlier years, see the BUC Used Boat Price Guide, Volume 3

ATLANTIC SEACRAFT LTD
DARTMOUTH NS CANADA B2W 3Y4

See inside cover to adjust price for area

LOA FT IN	NAME AND/ OR MODEL	TOP/ RIG	BOAT TYPE	-HULL- MTL TP TP	--ENGINE-- # HP MFG	BEAM FT IN	WGT LBS	DRAFT FT IN	RETAIL LOW	RETAIL HIGH
1985 BOATS										
18 9	LUGGER	YWL	SAIL	FBG CB OB		6 3	850	10	3950	4600
21 9	DRIFTER	YWL	SAIL	FBG CB OB		6 3	2000	2	6850	7850
21 6	DRIFTER	YWL	SAIL	FBG CB IB	7D BMW	6 3	2000	2	8800	10000
21 9	COASTER	YWL	SAIL	FBG CB OB		6 7	1060	1	5150	5900
21 9	LONGBOAT	YWL	SAIL	FBG CB OB		6 7	880	1	4850	5550
22 10	ROB-ROY	LAT	SAIL	FBG CB OB		6 11	2400	1 11	8250	9450
22 10	ROB-ROY	YWL	SAIL	FBG CB IB	7D BMW	6 11	2400	1 11	9850	11200
22 10	ROB-ROY	YWL	SAIL	FBG CB OB		6 11	2400	1 11	8250	9450
22 10	ROB-ROY	YWL	SAIL	FBG CB IB	7D BMW	6 11	2400	1 11	9850	11200
25	GIG	GAF	SAIL	FBG CB OB		7	2500	1 6	9600	10900

LOA FT	LOA IN	NAME AND/ OR MODEL	TOP/ RIG	BOAT TYPE	HULL MTL	HULL TP	ENGINE TP	ENGINE # HP	ENGINE MFG	BEAM FT	BEAM IN	WGT LBS	DRAFT FT	DRAFT IN	RETAIL LOW	RETAIL HIGH
		1984 BOATS														
18	9	LUGGER	YWL	SAIL	FBG	CB	OB			6	3	850		10	3700	4300
21	6	DRIFTER	GAF	SAIL	FBG	CB	OB			7	3	2000	2		6400	7350
21	9	COASTER	YWL	SAIL	FBG	CB	OB			6	7	1060	1		4850	5550
21	9	LONGBOAT	GAF	SAIL	FBG	CB	OB			6	7	880	1		4550	5250
25		GIG	GAF	SAIL	FBG	CB	OB			7		2500	1	6	9100	10300

ATLANTIC YACHT CORPORATION

ST AUGUSTINE BOAT WORKS INC
PALATKA FL 32178
COAST GUARD MFG ID- AYU
FORMERLY ATLANTIC YACHT & SHIPBUILDING CORP

See inside cover to adjust price for area

LOA FT	LOA IN	NAME AND/ OR MODEL	TOP/ RIG	BOAT TYPE	HULL MTL	HULL TP	ENGINE TP	ENGINE # HP	ENGINE MFG	BEAM FT	BEAM IN	WGT LBS	DRAFT FT	DRAFT IN	RETAIL LOW	RETAIL HIGH
		1992 BOATS														
31	5	ATLANTIC 32	OP	CTRCN	FBG	DV	IB	T235	CRUS	12		10500	3		53700	59100
34		ATLANTIC 34 CNV FB	FB	CNV	FBG	SV	IB	T300	CRUS	12		13500	3		77300	84900
34		ATLANTIC 34 CNV FB	FB	CNV	FBG	SV	IB	T250D-T300D		12		13500	3		93500	108000
34		ATLANTIC 34 FB	FB	SF	FBG	SV	IB	T300	CRUS	12		13500	3		72900	80100
34		ATLANTIC 34 FB	FB	SF	FBG	SV	IB	T250D-T300D		12		13500	3		85600	98100
34		ATLANTIC 34 HT	HT	SF	FBG	SV	IB	T300	CRUS	12		13500	3		72900	80100
34		ATLANTIC 34 HT	HT	SF	FBG	SV	IB	T250D-T300D		12		13500	3		85600	98100
34		ATLANTIC 34 SF	OP	CUD	FBG	SV	IB	T300	CRUS	12		13500	3		72900	80100
34		ATLANTIC 34 SF	OP	CUD	FBG	SV	IB	T250D-T300D		12		13500	3		85700	98200
36	7	ATLANTIC 37	FB	DC	FBG	DV	IB	135D	LEHM	13	9	22000	3	3	115500	127000
		IB T235 CRUS 106500 117500, IB T270 CRUS 107500 118000, IB T135D LEHM 118500 130500														
		IB T250D GM 124000 136000, IB T275D LEHM 125500 138000														
38	6	ATLANTIC 38 MEGA CNV	TT	YTFS	FBG	DV	IB	T355	CRUS	16	8	34000	4	6	164500	181000
		IB T425D CAT 221000 242500, IB T425D GM 214500 236000, IB T485D GM 232500 255500														
		IB T540D CAT 221500 243500, IB T550D GM 215500 237000, IB T735D GM 239000 262500														
38	6	ATLANTIC 38 MEGA SF	TT	YTFS	FBG	DV	IB	T300	CRUS	16	8	34000	4	6	162500	178500
38	6	ATLANTIC 38 MEGA SF	TT	YTFS	FBG	DV	IB	T425D	CAT	16	8	34000	4	6	167500	184000
38	6	ATLANTIC 38 MEGA SF	TT	YTFS	FBG	DV	IB	T485D	GM	16	8	34000	4	6	179000	196500
43	8	ATLANTIC 44	FB	MY	FBG	DV	IB	T235	CRUS	14		30000	3	5	166500	183000
		IB T180D GM 179500 197000, IB T320D CAT 204500 224500, IB T375D CAT 214500 236000														
46	9	ATLANTIC 47	FB	MY	FBG	DV	IB	T375D	CAT	16		41000	3	9	217000	238500
46	9	ATLANTIC 47	FB	MY	FBG	DV	IB	T450D	GM	16		41000	3	9	226000	248500
		1991 BOATS														
34		ATLANTIC 34 CONV FB	FB	CNV	FBG	SV	IB	T300	CRUS	12		13500	3		73400	80700
34		ATLANTIC 34 CONV FB	FB	CNV	FBG	SV	IB	T250D-T300D		12		13500	3		89300	103000
34		ATLANTIC 34 FB	FB	SF	FBG	SV	IB	T300	CRUS	12		13500	3		69200	76100
34		ATLANTIC 34 FB	FB	SF	FBG	SV	IB	T250D-T300D		12		13500	3		81700	93600
34		ATLANTIC 34 HT	HT	SF	FBG	SV	IB	T300	CRUS	12		13500	3		69200	76100
34		ATLANTIC 34 HT	HT	SF	FBG	SV	IB	T250D-T300D		12		13500	3		81700	93600
34		ATLANTIC 34 SF	OP	CUD	FBG	SV	IB	T300	CRUS	12		13500	3		69300	76100
34		ATLANTIC 34 SF	OP	CUD	FBG	SV	IB	T250D-T300D		12		13500	3		81800	93700
36	7	ATLANTIC 37	FB	DC	FBG	DV	IB	135D	LEHM	13	9	22000	3	3	110500	121000
		IB T235 CRUS 102000 112000, IB T270 CRUS 102500 112500, IB T135D LEHM 113500 124500														
		IB T250D GM 118000 130000, IB T275D LEHM 120000 131500														
38	6	ATLANTIC 38 MEGA CNV	TT	YTFS	FBG	DV	IB	T355	CRUS	16	8	34000	4	6	157000	172500
		IB T425D CAT 210500 231500, IB T425D GM 205000 225000, IB T485D GM 196500 215500														
		IB T540D CAT 211500 232500, IB T550D GM 205500 226000, IB T735D GM 228000 250500														
38	6	ATLANTIC 38 MEGA SF	TT	YTFS	FBG	DV	IB	T300	CRUS						154000	169500
38	6	ATLANTIC 38 MEGA SF	TT	YTFS	FBG	DV	IB	T425D	CAT	16	8	34000	4	6	159500	175500
38	6	ATLANTIC 38 MEGA SF	TT	YTFS	FBG	DV	IB	T485D	GM						196000	215500
43	8	ATLANTIC 44	FB	MY	FBG	DV	IB	T235	CRUS	14		30000	3	5	158500	174500
		IB T180D GM 171000 188000, IB T320D CAT 195000 214000, IB T375D CAT 204500 225000														
46	9	ATLANTIC 47	FB	MY	FBG	DV	IB	T375D	CAT	16		41000	3	9	207000	227500
46	9	ATLANTIC 47	FB	MY	FBG	DV	IB	T450D	GM	16		41000	3	9	215500	236500
		1990 BOATS														
38	6	ATLANTIC 38	TT	YTFS	FBG	DV	IB	T D	J&T	16	8	34000	4	6	**	**
		1989 BOATS														
34	5	ATLANTIC 34	FB	CNV	FBG	SV	IB	T350	INT	11	8	15600	2	6	73100	80300
34	5	ATLANTIC 34	FB	EXP	FBG	SV	IB	T350	INT	11	8	15300	2	6	69000	75800
34	5	ATLANTIC 34	FB	SDNSF	FBG	SV	IB	T350	INT	11	8	14800	2	6	68300	75000
34	5	ATLANTIC 34	OP	SF	FBG	SV	IB	T350	INT	11	8	14000	2	6	67100	73700
34	5	ATLANTIC 34	OP	SF	FBG	SV	IB	T300D	J&T	11	8	14500	2	6	82900	91100
36	7	ATLANTIC 37	FB	MY	FBG	SV	IB	T250D	GM	13	9	22000	3	3	110000	121000
43	8	ATLANTIC 44	FB	MY	FBG	SV	IB	T320D	CAT	14		30000	3	5	175500	193000
46	9	ATLANTIC 47	FB	MY	FBG	SV	IB	T320D	CAT	16		41000	3	9	181500	199000
46	9	ATLANTIC 47	FB	MY	FBG	SV	IB	T450D	GM	16		41000	3	9	193500	212500
		1988 BOATS														
34		ATLANTIC SPORTSMAN	OP	FSH	FBG	DS	IB	T350	CRUS	12		15000	2	9	63200	69400
34		ATLANTIC SPORTSMAN	OP	FSH	FBG	DS	IB	T250D-T300D		12		15000	2	9	75400	86000
36	7	ATLANTIC LONG RANGE	FB	CR	FBG	DS	IB	135D	LEHM	13	9	22000	3	3	96100	105500
		IB T270 CRUS 89300 98100, IB T135D LEHM 98700 108500, IB T250D GM 103000 113000														
43	8	ATLANTIC LONG RANGE	FB	DCMY	FBG	DS	IB	T350	CRUS	14		30000	3	5	157500	173000
43	8	ATLANTIC LONG RANGE	FB	DCMY	FBG	DS	IB	T300D	GM	14		30000	3	5	172500	189500
43	8	ATLANTIC LONG RANGE	FB	DCMY	FBG	DS	IB	T320D	CAT	14		30000	3	5	177500	195000
46	9	ATLANTIC LONG RANGE	FB	DCMY	FBG	DS	IB	T350	CRUS	16		41000	3	9	164500	180500
46	9	ATLANTIC LONG RANGE	FB	DCMY	FBG	DS	IB	T375D	GM	16		41000	3	9	193500	212500
46	9	ATLANTIC LONG RANGE	FB	DCMY	FBG	DS	IB	T450D	GM	16		41000	3	9	206000	226500
		1987 BOATS														
34		ATLANTIC SPORTSMAN	OP	FSH	FBG	DS	IB	T350	CRUS	12		15000	2	9	60200	66200
34		ATLANTIC SPORTSMAN	OP	FSH	FBG	DS	IB	T250D-T300D		12		15000	2	9	72200	83100
36	7	ATLANTIC LONG RANGE	FB	CR	FBG	DS	IB	135D	LEHM	13	9	22000	3	3	91900	101000
		IB T270 CRUS 85400 93800, IB T135D LEHM 94400 103500, IB T148D VLVO 93400 102500														
		IB T215D GM 96600 106000														
43	8	ATLANTIC LONG RANGE	FB	DCMY	FBG	DS	IB	T350	CRUS	14		30000	3	5	150500	165500
		IB T135D LEHM 151500 166500, IB T210D CAT 152000 167000, IB T300D CAT 166500 183000														
		IB T300D GM 165000 181500														
46	9	ATLANTIC LONG RANGE	FB	DCMY	FBG	DS	IB	T350	CRUS	16		41000	3	9	157000	172500
		IB T210D CAT 157000 172500, IB T300D CAT 172000 189500, IB T300D GM 171500 188500														
		IB T355D CAT 182000 200000, IB T375D GM 185000 203000, IB T435D GM 194500 214000														
		1986 BOATS														
36	7	ATLANTIC LONG RANGE	FB	CR	FBG	DS	IB	135D	LEHM	13	9	22000	3	3	87900	96600
		IB T270 CRUS 81700 89800, IB T135D LEHM 90300 99200, IB T148D VLVO 89400 98200														
		IB T215D GM 92500 101500														
43	8	ATLANTIC LONG RANGE	FB	DCMY	FBG	DS	IB	T350	CRUS	14		30000	3	5	144000	158500
		IB T135D LEHM 145000 159500, IB T210D CAT 145000 159500, IB T300D CAT 159500 175000														
		IB T300D GM 158000 173500														
46	9	ATLANTIC LONG RANGE	FB	DCMY	FBG	DS	IB	T350	CRUS	16		41000	3	9	150500	165000
		IB T210D CAT 150000 165000, IB T300D CAT 165000 181000, IB T300D GM 164500 180500														
		IB T355D CAT 174000 191500, IB T375D GM 177000 194500, IB T435D GM 186000 204500														
		1985 BOATS														
36	7	ATLANTIC LONG RANGE	FB	CR	FBG	DS	IB	135D	LEHM	13	9	22000	3	3	84200	92500
37		ATLANTIC 37		CR	FBG	DS	IB	T215D	GM	13	9	26000	3	3	103000	113500
43	8	ATLANTIC LONG RANGE	FB	DCMY	FBG	DS	IB	T210D	CAT	14		34000	3	5	152500	168000
44		ATLANTIC 44		MY	FBG	DS	IB	T300D		14		32000	3	5	138500	152000
46	9	ATLANTIC LONG RANGE	FB	DCMY	FBG	DS	IB	T275D	GM	16		41000	3	9	153000	168500
		1984 BOATS														
29	7	ATLANTIC LONG RANGE	FB	CR	FBG	DS	IB	165	CRUS	12		13500	3		32500	36100
29	7	ATLANTIC LONG RANGE	FB	CR	FBG	DS	IB	61D-158D		12		13500	3		45800	52900
29	7	ATLANTIC LONG RANGE	FB	CR	FBG	DS	IB	T124D	VLVO	12		13500	3		47600	52400
36	7	ATLANTIC LONG RANGE	FB	CR	FBG	DS	IB	120D	LEHM	13	9	22000	3	3	80800	88800
		IB 124D VLVO 80300 88200, IB T270 CRUS 75000 82400, IB T120D LEHM 82700 90900														
		IB T124D VLVO 81800 89900, IB T158D VLVO 82100 90300, IB T215D GM 84800 93200														
43	8	ATLANTIC LONG RANGE	FB	DCMY	FBG	DS	IB	T350	CRUS	14		30000	3	5	132000	145000
		IB T120D LEHM 132500 145500, IB T210D CAT 133000 146500, IB T235D VLVO 134500 148000														
		IB T300D CAT 146500 160500, IB T300D J&T 145000 159500														
46	9	ATLANTIC LONG RANGE	FB	DCMY	FBG	DS	IB	T350	CRUS	16		41000	3	9	138000	151500
		IB T120D LEHM 154000 169500, IB T235D VLVO 140000 153500, IB T300D CAT 151000 166000														
		IB T300D J&T 151000 166000, IB T355D CAT 160000 175500, IB T375D GM 162500 178500														
		IB T450D GM 173000 190000														
46	9	ATLANTIC LONG RANGE	FB	YTFS	FBG	DS	IB	T350	CRUS	16		41000	3	9	146000	160500
		IB T255D CAT 148500 163000, IB T300D CAT 158000 173500, IB T300D J&T 157500 173500														
		IB T375D S&S 172000 189000, IB T450D GM 185500 203500														

....For earlier years, see the BUC Used Boat Price Guide, Volume 3

AURA YACHTS INC

HURON PARK ONTARIO CANADA
FORMERLY NORTH STAR YACHTS LTD

See inside cover to adjust price for area

LOA FT	LOA IN	NAME AND/ OR MODEL	TOP/ RIG	BOAT TYPE	HULL MTL	HULL TP	ENGINE TP	ENGINE # HP	ENGINE MFG	BEAM FT	BEAM IN	WGT LBS	DRAFT FT	DRAFT IN	RETAIL LOW	RETAIL HIGH
		1986 BOATS														
25	1	COLUMBIA 7.6	SLP	SA/RC	FBG	KL	OB			9	2	4500	3	6	16100	18200
28	7	COLUMBIA 8.7	SLP	SA/RC	FBG	KL	IB	D		10		8500	4	8	34200	38000
35	2	COLUMBIA 10.7	SLP	SA/RC	FBG	KL	IB	D		11	4	14000	5	5	54500	59900

LOA FT IN	NAME AND/ OR MODEL	TOP/ RIG	BOAT TYPE	-HULL- MTL TP	TP	----ENGINE--- # HP MFG	BEAM FT IN	WGT LBS	DRAFT FT IN	RETAIL LOW	RETAIL HIGH
						1986 BOATS					
40	HUGHES 40	KTH	SA/CR	FBG KL	IB	D	13 4	26000	4 9	93300	102500
						1985 BOATS					
25 1	COLUMBIA 7.6	SLP	SA/RC	FBG KL	OB	9 2		4500	3 6	15000	17100
28 7	COLUMBIA 8.7	SLP	SA/RC	FBG KL	IB	D 10		8500	4 8	32000	35600
35 2	COLUMBIA 10.7	SLP	SA/RC	FBG KL	IB	D 11 4		14000	5 5	51300	56400
35 6	AURA A35	SLP	SA/CR	FBG KL		10 4		12000	5 10	40200	44700
40	AURA H40	KTH	SA/CR	FBG KL	IB	D 13 4		26000	4 9	87700	96400
						1984 BOATS					
25 1	COLUMBIA 7.6	SLP	SA/CR	FBG KL	IB	9 2		5000	3 6	16400	18600
28 7	COLUMBIA 8.7	SLP	SA/CR	FBG KL	IB	15D YAN 10		8500	4 8	30100	33500
35 2	COLUMBIA 10.7	SLP	SA/CR	FBG KL	IB	23D YAN 11 4		15000	5 5	51400	56400
35 6	HUGHES 35	SLP	SA/CR	FBG KL	IB	25D UNIV 10 4		12000	5 10	41500	46200
40	HUGHES 40 PREM	SLP	SA/CR	FBG KL	IB	50D PERK 13 4		26000	4 9	83300	91500
40	HUGHES 40 PREM	KTH	SA/CR	FBG KL	IB	50D PERK 13 4		26000	4 9	81900	90000
40	HUGHES 40 STD	SLP	SA/CR	FBG KL	IB	50D PERK 13 4		26000	4 9	80500	88500
40	HUGHES 40 STD	KTH	SA/CR	FBG KL	IB	50D PERK 13 4		26000	4 9	81900	90000

AVALON & TAHOE MFG INC
ALMA MI 48801   COAST GUARD MFG ID- DVN See inside cover to adjust price for area
                         ALSO PLAYBUOY PONTOON MFG INC

For more recent years, see the BUC Used Boat Price Guide, Volume 1

LOA FT IN	NAME AND/ OR MODEL	TOP/ RIG	BOAT TYPE	-HULL- MTL TP	TP	----ENGINE--- # HP MFG	BEAM FT IN	WGT LBS	DRAFT FT IN	RETAIL LOW	RETAIL HIGH
						1986 BOATS					
32	PLAYBUOY	HT	HB	AL	OB	8		3120		2500	2900
40	PLAYBUOY	HT	HB	AL	OB	12 11		8200		9850	11200
						1985 BOATS					
40	PLAYBUOY	HT	HB	AL	OB	12 11		8200		9650	11000
						1984 BOATS					
40	PLAYBUOY	HT	HB	AL	OB	12 11				10100	11400

AVANTI INDUSTRIES INC
CORDOVA TN 38018   See inside cover to adjust price for area

LOA FT IN	NAME AND/ OR MODEL	TOP/ RIG	BOAT TYPE	-HULL- MTL TP	TP	----ENGINE--- # HP MFG	BEAM FT IN	WGT LBS	DRAFT FT IN	RETAIL LOW	RETAIL HIGH
						1988 BOATS					
16	170C	ST	RNBT	FBG SV	OB		6 11	950	11	1200	1450
16 3	170DL	ST	RNBT	FBG SV	OB		6 11	1030	11	1300	1550
16 3	170DLI	ST	RNBT	FBG SV	IO	130	6 11	1770	11	2850	3350
16 3	170FS	ST	RNBT	FBG SV	OB		6 11	1020	11	1300	1550
16 3	170SSI	ST	RNBT	FBG SV	IO	130	6 11	1770	11	3000	3450
16 3	175FS	ST	RNBT	FBG SV	OB		7 7	1200	1 4	1500	1800
17 6	175DL	ST	RNBT	FBG SV	OB		7 7	1200	1 4	1600	1900
17 6	175FSI	ST	RNBT	FBG SV	IO	130	7 7	2100	1 4	3650	4250
17 6	175SSI	ST	RNBT	FBG SV	IO	130	7 7	2100	1 4	3550	4150
17 8	178DLI	ST	RNBT	FBG SV	IO	175	7 7	2250	1 6	3800	4400
17 8	178SSI	ST	RNBT	FBG SV	IO	205	7 7	2475	1 6	3950	4600
17 8	178SSI SPECIAL	ST	RNBT	FBG SV	IO	205	7 7	2475	1 6	4100	4800
19	190CCI	ST	RNBT	FBG SV	IO	175	7 7	3070	1 6	4850	5600
19	190DLI	ST	RNBT	FBG SV	IO	260	7 7	2675	1 6	4700	5400
19	190SSI	ST	RNBT	FBG SV	IO	260	7 7	2675	1 6	4850	5600
						1987 BOATS					
16	170C	ST	RNBT	FBG SV	OB		6 11	950	11	1150	1350
16 3	170DL	ST	RNBT	FBG SV	OB		6 11	1030	11	1200	1450
16 3	170DLI	ST	RNBT	FBG SV	IO	130	6 11	1770	11	2750	3200
16 3	170FS	ST	RNBT	FBG SV	OB		6 11	1020	11	1200	1450
16 3	170SSI	ST	RNBT	FBG SV	IO	130	6 11	1770	11	2850	3300
16 3	175FS	ST	RNBT	FBG SV	OB		7 7	1200	1 4	1450	1700
17 6	175DL	ST	RNBT	FBG SV	OB		7 7	1200	1 4	1450	1750
17 6	175FSI	ST	RNBT	FBG SV	IO	130	7 7	2100	1 4	3450	4050
17 6	175SSI	ST	RNBT	FBG SV	IO	130	7 7	2100	1 4	3400	3950
17 8	178DLI	ST	RNBT	FBG SV	IO	175	7 7	2250	1 6	3600	4200
17 8	178SSI	ST	RNBT	FBG SV	IO	205	7 7	2475	1 6	3750	4350
17 8	178SSI SPECIAL	ST	RNBT	FBG SV	IO	205	7 7	2475	1 6	3900	4550
19	190CCI	ST	RNBT	FBG SV	IO	175	7 7	3070	1 6	4650	5350
19	190DLI	ST	RNBT	FBG SV	IO	260	7 7	2675	1 6	4500	5150
19	190SSI	ST	RNBT	FBG SV	IO	260	7 7	2675	1 6	4650	5350
						1986 BOATS					
16	170C	ST	RNBT	FBG SV	OB		6 11	950	11	1050	1250
16 3	170DL	ST	RNBT	FBG SV	OB		6 11	1030	11	1200	1400
16 3	170DLI	ST	RNBT	FBG SV	IO	140	6 11	1770	11	2600	3050
16 3	170FS	ST	RNBT	FBG SV	OB		6 11	1020	11	1150	1400
16 3	170SSI	ST	RNBT	FBG SV	IO	140	6 11	1770	11	2700	3150
16 3	175FS	ST	RNBT	FBG SV	OB		7 7	1200	1	1400	1650
17 6	175DL	ST	RNBT	FBG SV	OB		7 7	1200	1	1400	1650
17 6	175FSI	ST	RNBT	FBG SV	IO	185-190	7 7	2100	1	3300	3900
17 6	175SSI	ST	RNBT	FBG SV	IO	185-190	7 7	2100	1	3250	3850
17 8	178DLI	ST	RNBT	FBG SV	IO	170-175	7 7	2250	1 6	3450	4000
19	190DLI	ST	RNBT	FBG SV	IO	260	7 7	2475	1	4150	4800
						1985 BOATS					
16	170C	ST	RNBT	FBG SV	OB		6 11	950	11	1000	1200
16 3	170 DLI	ST	RNBT	FBG SV	IO	120	6 11	1650	1 11	2450	2850
16 3	170DL	ST	RNBT	FBG SV	OB		6 11	1030	11	1100	1300
16 3	170DLI	ST	RNBT	FBG SV	IB	120	6 11	1650	11	3000	3500
16 3	170DLI	ST	RNBT	FBG SV	IO	140	6 11	1650	11	2450	2850
16 3	170FS	ST	RNBT	FBG SV	OB		6 11	1020	11	1100	1300
16 3	170FSI	ST	RNBT	FBG SV	IO	120	6 11	1680	11	2450	2850
16 3	170FSI	ST	RNBT	FBG SV	IB	120	6 11	1680	11	3050	3550
16 3	170SSI	ST	RNBT	FBG SV	IO	120	6 11	1685	11	2450	2900
16 3	170SSI	ST	RNBT	FBG SV	IB	120	6 11	1685	11	3050	3550
16 3	170SSI	ST	RNBT	FBG SV	IO	140	6 11	1685	11	2500	2900
16 3	175FS	ST	RNBT	FBG SV	OB		7 7	1200	1 4	1300	1550
17 6	175DL	ST	RNBT	FBG SV	IO	170	7 7	1200	1 4	1350	1600
17 6	175FSI	ST	RNBT	FBG SV	IO	170	7 7	1885	1 4	3000	3500
17 6	175FSI	ST	RNBT	FBG SV	IB	170	7 7	1885	1 4	4000	4650
17 6	175FSI	ST	RNBT	FBG SV	IO	185-190	7 7	1885	1 4	3000	3550
17 6	175SSI	ST	RNBT	FBG SV	IO	170	7 7	1860	1 4	3950	4600
17 6	175SSI	ST	RNBT	FBG SV	IO	185-190	7 7	1860	1 4	3000	3500
19	190DLI	ST	RNBT	FBG SV	IO	170	7 7	1980	1 6	3350	3900
19	190DLI	ST	RNBT	FBG SV	IO	170	7 7	1980	1 6	4500	5200
19	190DLI	ST	RNBT	FBG SV	IO	260	7 7	1980	1 6	3600	4200
						1984 BOATS					
16 3	170 FSI	OP	RNBT	FBG DV	IO	185 OMC	6 11	1680	11	2400	2800

AVON INFLATABLES LTD
AVON RUBBER PLC
STEVENSVILLE MD 21666   COAST GUARD MFG ID- AVB   See inside cover to adjust price for area

IMTRA CORPORATION
CLEARWATER FL 34622

For more recent years, see the BUC Used Boat Price Guide, Volume 1

LOA FT IN	NAME AND/ OR MODEL	TOP/ RIG	BOAT TYPE	-HULL- MTL TP	TP	----ENGINE--- # HP MFG	BEAM FT IN	WGT LBS	DRAFT FT IN	RETAIL LOW	RETAIL HIGH
						1990 BOATS					
17 10	5M RESCUE	OP	CTRCN	FBG DV	OB		6 9	660		4650	5300
						1989 BOATS					
17 10	5M RESCUE	OP	CTRCN	FBG DV	OB		6 9	630		4200	4900
						1988 BOATS					
17 10	5M RESCUE	OP	CTRCN	FBG DV	OB		6 9	630		4050	4700
						1987 BOATS					
17 10	SEARIDER 5M DLX	OP	CTRCN	FBG DV	OB		6 9	630		3900	4500
17 10	SEARIDER 5M RESCUE	OP	CTRCN	FBG DV	OB		6 9	660		4050	4700
						1986 BOATS					
17 10	SEARIDER 5M DLX	OP	CTRCN	FBG DV	OB		6 9	630		3750	4350
17 10	SEARIDER 5M RESCUE	OP	CTRCN	FBG DV	OB		6 9	660		3900	4550
						1985 BOATS					
17 10	SEARIDER 5M DLX	OP	CTRCN	FBG DV	OB		6	630		3650	4200
17 10	SEARIDER 5M RESCUE	OP	CTRCN	FBG DV	OB		6	660		3800	4400
						1984 BOATS					
17 10	SEARIDER 5M DLX	OP	CTRCN	FBG DV	OB		6 8	630		3500	4100
17 10	SEARIDER 5M RESCUE	OP	CTRCN	FBG DV	OB		6 8	660		3650	4250
19 11	6M BASIC COMM	OP		FBG DV	OB		7 9	1056		5900	6800

....For earlier years, see the BUC Used Boat Price Guide, Volume 3

AWESOME BOATS AMERICA INC
FT LAUDERDALE FL 33316   See inside cover to adjust price for area

LOA FT IN	NAME AND/ OR MODEL	TOP/ RIG	BOAT TYPE	-HULL- MTL TP	TP	----ENGINE--- # HP MFG	BEAM FT IN	WGT LBS	DRAFT FT IN	RETAIL LOW	RETAIL HIGH
						1995 BOATS					
76 5	AWESOME 736 SL/EF	FB	MY	KEV DS	IB	T600D MTU				**	**
76 5	AWESOME 736 SL/OF	FB	MY	KEV DS	IB	T600D MTU				**	**

LOA FT IN	NAME AND/ OR MODEL	TOP/ RIG	BOAT TYPE	-HULL- MTL TP	----ENGINE--- TP # HP MFG	BEAM FT IN	WGT LBS	DRAFT FT IN	RETAIL LOW	RETAIL HIGH
				1995 BOATS						
76 6	AWESOME 756 SL/PH	FB	MY	KEV DS	IB T600D MTU				**	**

AZIMUT
VIAREGGIO (LUCCA) ITALY 55049   See inside cover to adjust price for area

For more recent years, see the BUC Used Boat Price Guide, Volume 1

LOA FT IN	NAME AND/ OR MODEL	TOP/ RIG	BOAT TYPE	-HULL- MTL TP	----ENGINE--- TP # HP MFG	BEAM FT IN	WGT LBS	DRAFT FT IN	RETAIL LOW	RETAIL HIGH
				1996 BOATS						
38 3	AZ 36	FB	CR	FBG SV	IB T305D CAT	13	20640	3 3	162500	178500
41 10	AZ 40	FB	MY	FBG SV	IB T350D CAT	13 4	23200	3 7	211500	232000
45 11	AZ 43	FB	CR	FBG SV	IB T440D CAT	14 6	27500	3 4	215000	236500
54 9	AZ 54	EPH	MYCPT	FBG DV	IB T765D MTU	16	33000	4 9	392500	431500
57 10	AZ 58	FB	MY	FBG SV	IB T765D	15 1	40700	4 .1	417500	459000
65	PININFARINA	FB	MY	FBG DV	IB T11CD MTU	16 3	60540	4 11	713000	783500
70	70 SEAJET	FB	MY	FBG DV	IB T11CD MTU	18 3	96000	5 6	943500	1.025M
78	AZ 78 ULTRA	FB	MYFD	FBG SV	IB T11CD MTU	19 5	57T	5 8	**	**
78	AZ 78 ULTRA	HT	SDN	FBG SV	IB T13CD CAT	19 6	57T	5 8	**	**
				1995 BOATS						
38 3	AZ 36	FB	CR	FBG SV	IB T300D	13	20640	3 3	152000	167000
41 10	AZ 40	FB	CR	FBG SV	IB T350D CAT	13 4	23200	3 7	200000	220000
43 4	AZ 42	FB	CR	FBG SV	IB T435D CAT	13 8	29600	3 7	255000	280500
45 11	AZ 43	FB	CR	FBG SV	IB T440D CAT	14 6	27500	3 4	206000	226500
54 9	AZ 54	EPH	MYCPT	FBG DV	IB T765D MTU	16	33000	4 9	376000	413500
65	PININFARINA	FB	MY	FBG DV	IB T11CD MTU	16 3	60540	4 11	684000	751500
78	AZ 78 ULTRA	ST	MY	FBG SV	IB T11CD MTU	19 5	57T	5 8	**	**
78	AZ 78 ULTRA	FB	MY	FBG SV	IB T13CD CAT	19 5	57T	5 8	**	**
78	ULTRA	FB	MY	FBG DV	IB T17CD CAT	19 6	57T	5 8	**	**

AZURE BOAT COMPANY INC
WILMINGTON CA 90744   See inside cover to adjust price for area

LOA FT IN	NAME AND/ OR MODEL	TOP/ RIG	BOAT TYPE	-HULL- MTL TP	----ENGINE--- TP # HP MFG	BEAM FT IN	WGT LBS	DRAFT FT IN	RETAIL LOW	RETAIL HIGH
				1991 BOATS						
34 8	RADOVCICH 34	FB	SF	FBG SV	IB T315 CRUS	13	17500	2 8	82800	90900
34 8	RADOVCICH 34	FB	SF	FBG SV	IB T320D CAT	13	18500	2 8	111000	122000
34 8	RADOVCICH 34	F+T	SF	FBG SV	IB T375D CAT	13	21000	2 8	126000	138500

B & D MFG CO
PLEASANT VIEW TN 37146   See inside cover to adjust price for area

LOA FT IN	NAME AND/ OR MODEL	TOP/ RIG	BOAT TYPE	-HULL- MTL TP	----ENGINE--- TP # HP MFG	BEAM FT IN	WGT LBS	DRAFT FT IN	RETAIL LOW	RETAIL HIGH
				1986 BOATS						
16 6	CHEETAH 166		RNBT	DV IO	120	7 1	1000		2300	2650
17 2	CHEETAH 170		RNBT	DV IO	120	7 5	1260		2650	3100
17 5	CHEETAH 175		FSH	DV OB		6 8	1000		1850	2200
17 6	CHEETAH 176		FSH	DV OB		7 5	1100		2000	2400
17 6	CHEETAH 176		RNBT	DV IO	140	7 5	1260		2750	3200
18 2	CHEETAH 180		RNBT	DV IO	140	7 5	1400		3000	3450
18 11	CHEETAH 200		CUD	DV IO	60	7 8	2400		4000	4650
19 6	CHEETAH 196		FSH	DV OB		7 5	1200		2350	2750
				1985 BOATS						
16 6	CHEETAH 166		FSH	FBG DV OB		7 1	1000		1750	2050
16 6	CHEETAH 166		RNBT	FBG DV IO	120	7 1	1000		2200	2550
17 2	CHEETAH 170		RNBT	FBG DV IO	120	7 5	1260		2550	3000
17 5	CHEETAH 176		FSH	FBG DV OB		7 5	1100		1950	2300
17 6	CHEETAH 176		RNBT	FBG DV IO	140	7 5	1260		2650	3100
18 2	CHEETAH 180		RNBT	FBG DV IO	140	7 5	1400		2850	3350
19 6	CHEETAH 196		FSH	FBG DV OB		7 5	1200		2300	2650

B & R MAST RIGGING
SARASOTA FL 33580   See inside cover to adjust price for area

FORMERLY B&R DESIGNS

LOA FT IN	NAME AND/ OR MODEL	TOP/ RIG	BOAT TYPE	-HULL- MTL TP	----ENGINE--- TP # HP MFG	BEAM FT IN	WGT LBS	DRAFT FT IN	RETAIL LOW	RETAIL HIGH
				1986 BOATS						
30 2	WINDEX 92	SLP	SA/RC	F/S KC	IB 14D YAN	10 6	6300	3 6	23700	26300
31 1	GUYLINE 95	SLP	SA/RC	F/S KC	IB 14D YAN	9 10	6500	4 3	24600	27400
				1985 BOATS						
30 2	WINDEX 92	SLP	SAIL	F/S KC	IB 15D YAN	10 6	6600	3 6	23400	26000
31 1	GUYLINE 95	SLP	SA/RC	F/S KL	IB 8D YAN	9 10	7000	4 3	24900	27700
				1984 BOATS						
30 2	WINDEX 92	SLP	SAIL	F/S KC	IB 15D YAN	10 6	6600	3 6	22000	24400
30 2	WINDEX 92	SLP	SAIL	F/S KL	IB 15D YAN	10 6	6600	3 6	22000	24400

....For earlier years, see the BUC Used Boat Price Guide, Volume 3

B & W CORONET BOATS
DENMARK   See inside cover to adjust price for area

LOA FT IN	NAME AND/ OR MODEL	TOP/ RIG	BOAT TYPE	-HULL- MTL TP	----ENGINE--- TP # HP MFG	BEAM FT IN	WGT LBS	DRAFT FT IN	RETAIL LOW	RETAIL HIGH
				1988 BOATS						
37 6	CORONET-ELVSTROM	SLP	MS	F/S KL	IB 61D VLVO	11 6	14333	5 1	86600	95200
				1987 BOATS						
37 6	CORONET-ELVSTROM	SLP	MS	F/S KL	IB 61D VLVO	11 6	14333	5 1	81500	89600
				1986 BOATS						
37 6	CORONET-ELVSTROM	SLP	MS	F/S KL	IB 61D VLVO	11 6	14333	5 1	76700	84200
				1985 BOATS						
37 6	CORONET-ELVSTROM	SLP	MS	F/S KL	IB 61D VLVO	11 6	14333	5 1	72100	79200
				1984 BOATS						
37 6	CORONET-ELVSTROM	SLP	MS	F/S KL	IB 61D VLVO	11 6	14333	5 1	67800	74500

....For earlier years, see the BUC Used Boat Price Guide, Volume 3

B BOATS INC
TORRANCE CA 90501   See inside cover to adjust price for area

For more recent years, see the BUC Used Boat Price Guide, Volume 1

LOA FT IN	NAME AND/ OR MODEL	TOP/ RIG	BOAT TYPE	-HULL- MTL TP	----ENGINE--- TP # HP MFG	BEAM FT IN	WGT LBS	DRAFT FT IN	RETAIL LOW	RETAIL HIGH
				1996 BOATS						
25	B-25	SLP	SAROD	FBG KL		8 4	2000	5	21200	23500
				1995 BOATS						
25	B-25	SLP	SAROD	FBG KL		8 4	2000	5	20000	22200
32	B-32	SLP	SAROD	FBG KL		10 4	3800	6 6	**	**

BAHA CRUISER BOATS INC
MAYO FL 32066   COAST GUARD MFG ID- VBH See inside cover to adjust price for area

For more recent years, see the BUC Used Boat Price Guide, Volume 1

LOA FT IN	NAME AND/ OR MODEL	TOP/ RIG	BOAT TYPE	-HULL- MTL TP	----ENGINE--- TP # HP MFG	BEAM FT IN	WGT LBS	DRAFT FT IN	RETAIL LOW	RETAIL HIGH
				1996 BOATS						
18 3	BOW RIDER 183	ST	SKI	FBG SV IO	135 VLVO	8	2300		5500	6300
18 3	MACH I 183	ST	SKI	FBG SV IO	135 VLVO	8	2300		5500	6300
20	FISHERMAN 200 WAC	ST	CUD	FBG SV OB		7 3	2800		7650	8750
20	FISHERMAN 200 WAC	ST	CUD	FBG SV OB		7 3	2800		7350	8450
20	MACH I 206	ST	SKI	FBG SV IO	135 VLVO	8	2500		6850	7850
21 4	FISHERMAN 228 WAC	ST	CUD	FBG SV OB		8	3300		9650	11000
21 4	FISHERMAN 228 WAC	ST	CUD	FBG SV OB		8	3300		9400	10700
21 8	CONQUISTARE 218	ST	CUD	FBG SV IO	190 VLVO	8	2800		8650	9950
22 6	WEEKENDER 225	ST	CUD	FBG SV IO	190 VLVO	7 9	2800		8950	10100
23	TARGA 230	OP	SKI	FBG SV IO	190 VLVO	8	3800		11600	13200
24	CENTER CONSOLE 240	OP	CTRCN	FBG SV OB		8 6	3500		12300	13900
24	CENTER CONSOLE 240	OP	CTRCN	FBG SV IO	190 VLVO	8 6	3500		11800	13500
24	FISHERMAN 240 WAC	ST	CUD	FBG SV OB		8 6	3500		12300	14000
24	FISHERMAN 240 WAC	ST	CUD	FBG SV IO	190 VLVO	8 6	3500		11300	12800
24	WEEKENDER 240	ST	WKNDR	FBG SV OB		8 6	3800		13000	14700
24	WEEKENDER 240	ST	WKNDR	FBG SV IO	190 VLVO	8 6	3800		11800	13500
25 1	FISHERMAN 251	HT	CUD	FBG SV OB		8 6	5600		16300	18500
25 1	FISHERMAN 251	HT	CUD	FBG SV IO	235 VLVO	8 6	5600		16800	19100
25 1	FISHERMAN 251	HT	CUD	FBG SV IB	300 VLVO	8 6	5600		19400	21600
26	BOW RIDER 260	ST	B/R	FBG SV IO	300 VLVO	8 6	4600		15000	17100
26	CENTER CONSOLE 260	ST	CTRCN	FBG SV OB		8 6	4200		15300	17400
26	CENTER CONSOLE 260	ST	CTRCN	FBG SV IO	300 VLVO	8 6	4200		16600	18800
26	TARGA 260	OP	SKI	FBG SV IO	300 VLVO	8 6	4200		14700	16700
27 1	CENTER CONSOLE 271	OP	CTRCN	FBG SV IO	300 VLVO	8 6	4500		18300	20400
27 1	CENTER CONSOLE 271	OP	CTRCN	FBG SV IO	300 VLVO	8 6	4500		19400	21600
27 1	CENTER CONSOLE 271	OP	CTRCN	FBG SV IO	300 VLVO	8 6	4500		19200	21300
27 1	CONQUISTARE 271	ST	CR	FBG SV IB	300 VLVO	8 6	6500		21100	23500

BAHA CRUISER BOATS INC -CONTINUED See inside cover to adjust price for area

LOA FT	LOA IN	NAME AND/ OR MODEL	TOP/ RIG	BOAT TYPE	-HULL- MTL	-HULL- TP	ENGINE TP	ENGINE # HP	ENGINE MFG	BEAM FT	BEAM IN	WGT LBS	DRAFT FT	DRAFT IN	RETAIL LOW	RETAIL HIGH
		1996 BOATS														
27	1	CONQUISTARE 271	ST	CR	FBG	SV	IO	T190	VLVO	8	6	6500			22100	24600
27	1	FISHERMAN 271	HT	CUD	FBG	SV	IB	250	VLVO	8	6	5600			21500	23800
27	8	FISHERMAN 278	HT	CUD	FBG	SV	IO	300	VLVO	9	6	6000			21400	23800
27	8	FISHERMAN 278	HT	CUD	FBG	SV	IB	310	VLVO	9	6	6000			24500	27200
27	8	WEEKENDER 278	HT	WKNDR	FBG	SV	IO	300	VLVO	9	6	6800			23900	26500
27	8	WEEKENDER 278	HT	WKNDR	FBG	SV	IB	310	VLVO	9	6	6800			27300	30300
28	2	BOW RIDER 290	ST	B/R	FBG	SV	IO	300	VLVO	8		6000			16900	19200
28	2	BOW RIDER 290	ST	B/R	FBG	SV	IO	T190	VLVO	8		6000			18100	20100
28	2	TARGA 290	ST	SKI	FBG	SV	IO	300	VLVO	8		6000			17300	19600
28	2	TARGA 290	ST	SKI	FBG	SV	IO	T190	VLVO	8		6000			18600	20600
28	5	FISHERMAN 285	HT	CUD	FBG	SV	IB	T205	VLVO	10	6	8000			32500	36100
28	5	FISHERMAN 285	HT	CUD	FBG	SV	IB	T120D	VLVO	10	6	8000			38100	42400
28	5	TOURNAMENT WE 285	ST	WKNDR	FBG	SV	IB	T250	VLVO	10	6	9000			35900	39900
28	5	WEEKENDER 285	HT	WKNDR	FBG	SV	IB	T250	VLVO	10	6	8500			36400	40500
28	5	WEEKENDER 285	HT	WKNDR	FBG	SV	IB	T120D	VLVO	10	6	8500			42200	46900
28	5	WEEKENDER FB 285	FB	WKNDR	FBG	SV	IB	T250	VLVO	10	6	9000			36000	40000
28	5	WEEKENDER FB 285	FB	WKNDR	FBG	SV	IB	T188D	VLVO	10	6	9000			46800	51400
29	5	CONQUISTARE 295	ST	CR	FBG	SV	IO	300	VLVO	9	6	7600			26400	29400
29	5	CONQUISTARE 295	ST	CR	FBG	SV	IO	T190	VLVO	9	6	7600			27500	30600
29	11	FISHERMAN 299	HT	CUD	FBG	SV	IB	310	VLVO	10	6	7000			29600	32800
29	11	FISHERMAN 299	HT	CUD	FBG	SV	IB	T205	VLVO	10	6	7000			31200	34700
31	3	TOURNAMENT WE 313	ST	WKNDR	FBG	SV	IB	T250	VLVO	11	6	13200			48900	53700
31	3	WEEKENDER 313	HT	WKNDR	FBG	SV	IB	T310	VLVO	11	6	11800			49100	54000
31	3	WEEKENDER 313	HT	WKNDR	FBG	SV	IB	T188D	VLVO	11	6	11800			55900	61500
31	3	WEEKENDER FB 313	FB	WKNDR	FBG	SV	IB	T216D	VLVO	11	6	12400			51100	56100
33		CONQUISTARE 330	ST	CR	FBG	SV	IO	T235	VLVO	11		11300			42400	47200
34		BOW RIDER 340	ST	B/R	FBG	SV	IO	T300	VLVO	9	6	9500			34200	38000
34		MACH I 340	ST	SKI	FBG	SV	IO	T300	VLVO	9	6	9500			34400	38200
		1995 BOATS														
20		FISHERMAN 200 WAC	ST	CUD	FBG	SV	OB			7	3	1900			5950	6850
20		FISHERMAN 200 WAC	ST	CUD	FBG	SV	IO	135	VLVO	7	3	1900			5700	6600
21	4	FISHERMAN 228 WAC	ST	CUD	FBG	SV	OB			8		3000			8700	10000
21	4	FISHERMAN 228 WAC	ST	CUD	FBG	SV	IO	190	VLVO	8		3000			8150	9400
21	8	CONQUISTARE 218	ST	CUD	FBG	SV	IO	190	VLVO	8	2	2800			8050	9300
22	6	WEEKENDER 225	ST	CUD	FBG	SV	IO	190	VLVO	7	9	2400			7650	8800
23		TARGA 230	OP	SKI	FBG	SV	IO	300	VLVO	8	2	3800			10900	12300
24		CENTER CONSOLE 240	OP	CTRCN	FBG	SV	OB			8	6	3500			11600	13200
24		CENTER CONSOLE 240	OP	CTRCN	FBG	SV	IO	190	VLVO	8	6	3500			11100	12600
24		FISHERMAN 240 WAC	ST	CUD	FBG	SV	OB			8	6	3500			11600	13200
24		FISHERMAN 240 WAC	ST	CUD	FBG	SV	IO	190	VLVO	8	6	3500			10500	12000
24		WEEKENDER 240	ST	WKNDR	FBG	SV	OB			8	2	3800			12300	14000
24		WEEKENDER 240	ST	WKNDR	FBG	SV	IO	190	VLVO	8	2	3800			11000	12600
25	1	FISHERMAN 271	HT	CUD	FBG	SV	OB			8	6	5600			15300	17400
25	1	FISHERMAN 271	HT	CUD	FBG	SV	IB	250	VLVO	8	6	5600			18600	20600
25	1	FISHERMAN 271	HT	CUD	FBG	SV	IO	255	VLVO	8	6	5600			15900	18000
26		CENTER CONSOLE 260	ST	CTRCN	FBG	SV	OB			8	2	4600			14900	16900
26		CENTER CONSOLE 260	ST	CTRCN	FBG	SV	IO	300	VLVO	8	2	4600			16100	18300
26		TARGA 260	OP	SKI	FBG	SV	OB			8	2	4600			14900	16900
26		TARGA 260	OP	SKI	FBG	SV	IO	300	VLVO	8	2	4600			14300	16300
26		TARGA 260	OP	SKI	FBG	SV	IO	T185	VLVO	8	2	4600			15000	17100
27	1	CENTER CONSOLE 271	OP	CTRCN	FBG	SV	OB			8	6	4800			17100	19400
27	1	CENTER CONSOLE 271	OP	CTRCN	FBG	SV	IB	250	VLVO	8	6	4800			19100	21200
27	1	CENTER CONSOLE 271	OP	CTRCN	FBG	SV	IO	255	VLVO	8	6	4800			17100	19400
27	1	CONQUISTARE 271	ST	CR	FBG	SV	IO	300	VLVO	8	6	6500			19700	21900
27	1	CONQUISTARE 271	ST	CR	FBG	SV	IO	T160	VLVO	8	6	6500			20100	22400
27	8	FISHERMAN 278	HT	CUD	FBG	SV	IO	300	VLVO	9	6	6000			20000	22200
27	8	FISHERMAN 278	HT	CUD	FBG	SV	IB	310	VLVO	9	6	6000			23100	25700
27	8	WEEKENDER 278	HT	WKNDR	FBG	SV	IO	300	VLVO	9	6	6800			22300	24700
27	8	WEEKENDER 278	HT	WKNDR	FBG	SV	IB	310	VLVO	9	6	6800			25800	28700
28	2	BOW RIDER 290	ST	B/R	FBG	SV	IO	300	VLVO	8					15700	17900
28	2	BOW RIDER 290	ST	B/R	FBG	SV	IO	T190	VLVO	8					16500	18700
28	2	TARGA 290	ST	SKI	FBG	SV	IO	300	VLVO	8					16100	18300
28	2	TARGA 290	ST	SKI	FBG	SV	IO	T190	VLVO	8					16900	19200
28	5	FISHERMAN 285	HT	CUD	FBG	SV	IB	T205	VLVO	10	6	8000			30700	34100
28	5	FISHERMAN 285	HT	CUD	FBG	SV	IB	T124D	VLVO	10	6	8000			36500	40500
28	5	WEEKENDER 285	HT	WKNDR	FBG	SV	IB	T250	VLVO	10	6	8500			34400	38200
28	5	WEEKENDER 285	HT	WKNDR	FBG	SV	IB	T124D	VLVO	10	6	8500			40300	44800
28	5	WEEKENDER FB 285	FB	WKNDR	FBG	SV	IB	T250	VLVO	10	6	9000			34000	37800
28	5	WEEKENDER FB 285	FB	WKNDR	FBG	SV	IB	T192D	VLVO	10	6	9000			44200	49100
29	5	CONQUISTARE 295	ST	CR	FBG	SV	IO	300	VLVO	9	6	7600			24600	27400
29	5	CONQUISTARE 295	ST	CR	FBG	SV	IO	T190	VLVO	9	6	7600			25700	28500
29	11	FISHERMAN 299	HT	CUD	FBG	SV	IB	310	VLVO	10	6	7000			27900	31000
29	11	FISHERMAN 299	HT	CUD	FBG	SV	IB	T205	VLVO	10	6	7000			29500	32800
31	3	WEEKENDER 313	HT	WKNDR	FBG	SV	IB	T310	VLVO	11	6	11800			46700	51300
31	3	WEEKENDER 313	HT	WKNDR	FBG	SV	IB	T192D	VLVO	11	6	11800			53400	58600
31	3	WEEKENDER FB 313	FB	WKNDR	FBG	SV	IB	T310	VLVO	11	6	12400			40400	44900
31	3	WEEKENDER FB 313	FB	WKNDR	FBG	SV	IB	T225D	VLVO	11	6	12400			48900	53800
33		CONQUISTARE 330	ST	CR	FBG	SV	IO	T235	VLVO	11		11300			39600	44000
33		CONQUISTARE 330	ST	CR	FBG	SV	IO	T185D	VLVO	11		11300			45500	50000
		1994 BOATS														
20	1	FISHERMAN 200 WAC	OP	FSH	FBG	SV	IO	135-245		7	3				6800	8250
21	4	FISHERMAN 228 WAC	OP	FSH	FBG	SV	IO	135-245		8					7500	9100
21	8	CONQUISTARE 218	ST	CUD	FBG	SV	IO	135-250		8	2	2800	2		7450	9050
22		FISHERMAN 220 WAC	OP	FSH	FBG	SV	IO	135-245		8					7900	9550
22	6	WEEKENDER 225	OP	CUD	FBG	SV	IO	135-245		7	9				7050	8550
23		TARGA 230	OP	SKI	FBG	SV	IO	135-245		8	2				9150	10800
23	3	FISHERMAN 233	OP	SF	FBG	SV	IO	185-250		8	6	4600	2		13200	15400
24		FISHERMAN 240 WAC	OP	CUD	FBG	SV	IO	135-245		8	6				9750	11500
24		WEEKENDER 240	OP	CUD	FBG	SV	IO	135-245		8	2				9650	11400
25	1	FISHERMAN 251	OP	SF	FBG	SV	IO	190-230		8	6	5600	2	8	16200	18900
		IB 237-245 17100 19500, IO 250 VLVO 16800 19100, IO 300 VLVO													18000	20000
		IB 300 VLVO 17500 19900, IO 120D-185D 20400 24200, IB 192D VLVO													21700	24100
		IO 216D VLVO 22400 24900, IB 225D VLVO 22400 24900														
26		TARGA 260	OP	CUD	FBG	SV	IO	135-250		8	2				12200	15200
26		TARGA 260	OP	CUD	FBG	SV	IO	300	VLVO	8	2				14200	16100
26	8	WEEKENDER 271	HT	WKNDR	FBG	SV	IO	190-230		8	8		2	4	16400	19100
		IB 237 VLVO 20200 22400, IO 245-250 17000 19400, IO 300 VLVO													18300	20300
		IB 300 VLVO 20900 23200, IO 120D-185D 19200 23100, IB 192D VLVO													25800	28700
		IO 216D VLVO 21500 23900, IB 225D VLVO 26700 29700														
27	1	CENTER CONSOLE 271	OP	CTRCN	FBG	SV	IO	190-230		8	6	4800	2	4	15000	17700
		IB 237 VLVO 17500 19900, IO 245-250 15800 18000, IO 300 VLVO													16700	19000
		IB 300 VLVO 18700 20800, IO 120D VLVO 17400 19700, IO 185D VLVO													19900	22100
		IB 192D VLVO 19800 22000, IO 216D VLVO 20900 23200, IB 225D VLVO													20900	23200
27	1	CONQUISTARE 271	ST	EXP	FBG	SV	IO	190-300		8	6	6500	2	6	16800	20700
		IO 185D-216D 20100 23100, IO T135-T160 19200 21300, IO T120D VLVO													23300	25900
27	1	FISHERMAN 271	OP	SF	FBG	SV	IO	190-230		8	6	5600	2	8	17500	20600
		IB 237 VLVO 19000 21100, IO 245-250 18700 20900, IO 300 VLVO													19500	21600
		IB 300 VLVO 19800 22000, IO 120D-185D 20100 24700, IB 192D VLVO													22100	24600
		IO 216D VLVO 23100 25700, IB 225D VLVO 23100 25700														
27	8	FISHERMAN 278	OP	SF	FBG	SV	IO	190-250		9	6	6000	2	8	19400	23500
		IO 300 VLVO 22000 24400, IB 300 VLVO 21700 24100, IO T160-T185													22400	25500
		IO T216D VLVO 33400 37100														
27	8	FISHERMAN 278	HT	SF	FBG	SV	IO	245-300		9	6	6000	2	8	20300	23600
27	8	FISHERMAN 278	HT	SF	FBG	SV	IO	185D	VLVO	9	6	6000	2	8	24100	26800
27	8	FISHERMAN 278	HT	SF	FBG	SV	IO	T135-T160		9	6	6500	2	8	21800	24900
27	8	WEEKENDER 278	HT	WKNDR	FBG	SV	IO	190-250		9	8	6800	2	8	19200	22300
		IO 300 VLVO 20800 23100, IB 300 VLVO 24300 27000, IO 185D VLVO													22600	25100
		IB 192D VLVO 27900 31000, IO 216D VLVO 23400 26000, IB 225D VLVO													29000	32200
		IO T135-T185 21200 24700, IB T205 VLVO 26700 29600, IB T124D VLVO													31900	35500
28	5	FISHERMAN 285	OP	SF	FBG	SV	IO	225-250		10	6	8000	2	4	25200	28500
		IO 185D-216D 32400 37000, IB 225D VLVO 33200 36800, IB T225D VLVO													40000	44400
28	5	FISHERMAN 285	HT	SF	FBG	SV	IO	300	VLVO	10	6	7600	2	4	25900	28800
		IB 300 VLVO 26700 29700, IB 296D VLVO 34600 38500, IB T205-T237													29000	33000
		IBT192D-T225D 38200 44400														
28	5	WEEKENDER 285	HT	WKNDR	FBG	SV	IO	225-300		10	6	8100	2	4	23600	27500
		IO 185D-216D 27800 31800, IB 296D VLVO 38300 42600, IB T205-T300													31500	36900
		IBT192D-T225D 42100 48800														
28	5	WEEKENDER FB 285	FB	WKNDR	FBG	SV	IO	225-300		10	6	9000	2	4	24400	28300
		IO 185D-216D 29500 33600, IB 225D-296D 37100 42700, IB T205-T300													31300	36300
		IBT192D-T225D 42100 48600														
29	5	CONQUISTARE 295	ST	EXP	FBG	SV	IO	190-300		9	6	7600	2	4	21400	25100
		IO 185D-216D 23600 27900, IO T135-T190 22800 26600, IO T120D VLVO													26200	29100
29	11	FISHERMAN 299	HT	SF	FBG	SV	IB	300-390		10	6	7000	2	4	26300	30700
29	11	FISHERMAN 299	HT	SF	FBG	SV	IB	225D-296D		10	6	7000	2	4	28800	34300
31	3	FISHERMAN 313	HT	SF	FBG	SV	IB	296D	VLVO	11	6	11800	2	6	48500	53300
31	3	FISHERMAN 313	HT	SF	FBG	SV	IB	T237-T305		11	6	11800	2	6	41800	48400
31	3	FISHERMAN 313	HT	SF	FBG	SV	IB	T192D-T225D		11	6	11800	2	6	50800	57600

 CONTINUED ON NEXT PAGE

```
BAHA CRUISER BOATS INC      -CONTINUED      See inside cover to adjust price for area
LOA   NAME AND/         TOP/ BOAT -HULL- ----ENGINE---  BEAM  WGT DRAFT RETAIL RETAIL
FT IN OR MODEL          RIG  TYPE MTL TP TP # HP  MFG   FT IN  LBS FT IN  LOW   HIGH
---------------------- 1994 BOATS -----------------------------------------------------
31 3 FISHERMAN FB 313    FB   SF  FBG SV IB  296D VLVO 11  6 12400 2  6 50100 55100
31 3 FISHERMAN FB 313    FB   SF  FBG SV IB T237-T300 11  6 12400 2  6 42400 48900
31 3 FISHERMAN FB 313    FB   SF  FBG SV IBT192D-T225D 11 6 11800 2  6 50800 59200
31 3 SEDAN 313           HT   CR  FBG SV IB  296D VLVO 11  6 11950 2  6 48900 53800
31 3 SEDAN 313           HT   CR  FBG SV IB T237-T300 11  6 11950 2  6 42000 48500
31 3 SEDAN 313           HT   CR  FBG SV IBT192D-T225D 11 6 11950 2  6 51200 58000
31 3 SEDAN FB 313        FB   CR  FBG SV IB  296D VLVO 11  6 12800 2  6 51200 56300
31 3 SEDAN FB 313        FB   CR  FBG SV IB T237-T300 11  6 12800 2  6 42800 49300
31 3 SEDAN FB 313        FB   CR  FBG SV IBT192D-T225D 11 6 12800 2  6 53300 58600
33   CONQUISTARE 330     ST   EXP FBG SV IO T160-T250 11     11300 2  6 35400 41400
33   CONQUISTARE 330     ST   EXP FBG SV IOT120D-T216D 11    11300 2  6 39700 48000

34 5 SEDAN 345           HT   CR  FBG SV IB T300  VLVO 11  6 13500 2 10 54400 59700
34 5 SEDAN 345           HT   CR  FBG SV IB T296D VLVO 11  6 13500 2 10 67500 74200
34 5 SEDAN FB 345        FB   CR  FBG SV IB T300  VLVO 11  6 14000 2 10 55000 60500
34 5 SEDAN FB 345        FB   CR  FBG SV IB T292D VLVO 11  6 14000 2 10 68500 75200
---------------------- 1993 BOATS -----------------------------------------------------
21 8 CONQUISTARE 218     ST  CUD FBG SV IO 180-245   8  2 2800  2      7000  8400
23 3 FISHERMAN 223       OP  SF  FBG SV IO 205-245   8  6 4600  2     12400 14300
25 1 FISHERMAN 251       OP  SF  FBG SV IO 205  VLVO 8  6 5600  2  8 15300 17400
     IB 240 VLVO 16200  18400, IO 245 VLVO 15700 17800, IB 192D VLVO 20600 22900

27 1 CENTER CONSOLE 271  OP CTRCN FBG SV IO 205 VLVO 8  6 4800  2  4 14200 16200
     IB 240 VLVO 16600  18900, IO 245 VLVO 14800 16800, IB 192D VLVO 19100 21200

27 1 CENTER CONSOLE 271  ST  EXP FBG SV IO 205-300   8  6 6500  2  6 15800 19300
     IO 120D-185D 17100 21100, IO T135 VLVO 17500 19900, IO T120D VLVO 21800 24200

27 8 FISHERMAN 278       OP  SF  FBG SV IB  240 VLVO 9  6 6000  2  8 19800 22000
     IO 245-300 19100 22100, IB 305 VLVO 20700 23000, IO 185D VLVO 22500 25000
     IB 192D VLVO 22900 25400, IO T135 VLVO 20400 22700, IO T120D VLVO 26500 29400

27 8 WEEKENDER 278       OP WKNDR FBG SV IO 245-300  9  6 6800  2  8 18800 21600
     IB 305 VLVO 23100 25600, IO 185D VLVO 21100 23400, IB 192D VLVO 26600 29500
     IO T135 VLVO 19900 22100, IB T205 VLVO 25300 28100, IB T124D VLVO 30400 33800

28 5 FISHERMAN 285       OP  SF  FBG SV IO 300  VLVO 10 6 7600  2  4 24200 26900
     IB 305 VLVO 25400 28200, IB 296D VLVO 33000 36700, IB T205-T240 27500 31400
     IBT124D-T192D 33000 40500

28 5 WEEKENDER 285       OP WKNDR FBG SV IB 305 VLVO 10 6 8100  2  4 27700 30700
     IB 296D VLVO 36500 40600, IB T205-T240 29900 34100, IBT124D-T192D 36500 44600

28 5 WEEKENDER FB 285    FB WKNDR FBG SV IB 305 VLVO 10 6 8600  2  4 27400 30500
     IB 296D VLVO 36600 40700, IB T205-T240 29700 33700, IBT124D-T192D 36800 44500

29 5 CONQUISTARE 295     ST  EXP FBG SV IO 245-300  9  6 7200  2  4 20300 23500
     IO 185D VLVO 22100 24500, IO T135-T180 21300 24700, IO T120D VLVO 24400 27200

29 11 FISHERMAN 299      OP  SF  FBG SV IO 300 VLVO 10 6 7000  2  4 23600 26300
     IB 305 VLVO 25000 27700, IO 185D VLVO 26100 29000, IB 192D VLVO 26500 29400
     IO T135 VLVO 23700 26400, IO T185D VLVO 32300 35900

31 1 EXPRESS 311         ST  EXP FBG SV IO 300 VLVO 10 6 9300  2  6 28200 31300
     IO 185D VLVO 30600 34000, IO T180-T245 29100 34000, IOT120D-T185D 32400 39000

31 3 FISHERMAN 313       OP  SF  FBG SV IB  296D VLVO 11 6 11800 2  6 46500 51100
31 3 FISHERMAN 313       OP  SF  FBG SV IB T240-T305 11 6 11800 2  6 39700 45900
31 3 FISHERMAN 313       OP  SF  FBG SV IB T192D VLVO 11 6 11800 2  6 48400 53200
31 3 FISHERMAN FB 313    FB  SF  FBG SV IB  296D VLVO 11 6 12400 2  6 47800 52500
31 3 FISHERMAN FB 313    FB  SF  FBG SV IB T240-T305 11 6 12400 2  6 40300 46500
31 3 FISHERMAN FB 313    FB  SF  FBG SV IB T192D VLVO 11 6 11800 2  6 48400 53200
31 3 SEDAN 313           HT  CR  FBG SV IB  296D VLVO 11 6 11950 2  6 46900 51500
31 3 SEDAN 313           HT  CR  FBG SV IB T240-T305 11 6 11950 2  6 39300 46100
31 3 SEDAN 313           HT  CR  FBG SV IB T192D VLVO 11 6 11950 2  6 48700 53600
31 3 SEDAN FB 313        FB  CR  FBG SV IB  296D VLVO 11 6 12800 2  6 48800 53600
31 3 SEDAN FB 313        FB  CR  FBG SV IB T240-T305 11 6 12800 2  6 40600 46900
31 3 SEDAN FB 313        FB  CR  FBG SV IB T192D VLVO 11 6 12800 2  6 50800 55800

33   CONQUISTARE 330     ST  EXP FBG SV IO T180-T245 11    11300 2  6 33400 38600
33   CONQUISTARE 330     ST  EXP FBG SV IOT120D-T185D 11   11300 2  6 37100 43600
34 5 SEDAN 345           HT  CR  FBG SV IB T305  VLVO 11 6 13500 2 10 51600 56700
34 5 SEDAN 345           HT  CR  FBG SV IB T296D VLVO 11 6 13500 2 10 64300 70700
34 5 SEDAN FB 345        FB  CR  FBG SV IB T305  VLVO 11 6 14000 2 10 52300 57400
34 5 SEDAN FB 345        FB  CR  FBG SV IB T296D VLVO 11 6 14000 2 10 65400 71900
---------------------- 1992 BOATS -----------------------------------------------------
21 8 CONQUISTARE 220     ST  CUD FBG SV IO 180-245   8  6 2800  2      6550  7850
23 3 FISHERMAN 230       OP  SF  FBG SV IO 205-245   8  6 4600  2     11600 13400
25 1 FISHERMAN 250       OP  SF  FBG SV IO 205  VLVO 8  6 4800  2  8 12800 14600
     IB 240 VLVO 13800  15700, IO 245 VLVO 13200 15000, IB 192D VLVO 17300 19700
     IO T135 VLVO 16600 16600

25 1 FISHKEELER 250      OP  SF  FBG SV IB  240 VLVO 8  6 5600  2  4 15400 17500
27 1 CENTER CONSOLE 250  OP CTRCN FBG SV IO 205 VLVO 8  6 4800  2  4 13300 15200
     IB 240 VLVO 15800  17900, IO 245 VLVO 13800 15700, IB 192D VLVO 18200 20300

27 1 EXPRESS 250         ST  EXP FBG SV IO 205-300   8  6 5500  2  6 13500 16700
     IO 120D VLVO 13700 15600, IO 185D VLVO 15200 17300, IO T135 VLVO 14600 16600
     IO T120D VLVO 17200 19500

27 6 FISHERMAN 260       OP  SF  FBG SV IB  185 VLVO 9  6 6000  2  4 16600 18800
     IB 240 VLVO 18800 20900, IO 245-300 17300 20700, IB 305 VLVO 19400 21500
     IB 192D VLVO 21700 24200, IO T135 VLVO 18500 20500, IB T205 VLVO 20800 23100
     IO T120D VLVO 23400 26100, IB T124D VLVO 24300 26900

27 6 WEEKENDER 260       OP  SF  FBG SV IB  305 VLVO 9  6 6500  2  4 19400 21500
     IO 245-300 18400 21200, IB 305 VLVO 20100 22300, IO 185D VLVO 22400 24900
     IB 192D VLVO 23200 25700, IO T135 VLVO 20100 22300, IB T205 VLVO 21500 23900
     IO T120D VLVO 24800 27500, IB T124D VLVO 25600 28400

28 2 FISHERMAN 280       OP  SF  FBG SV IO 300 VLVO 10 6 7500  2  4 21300 23700
     IB 305 VLVO 22600 25100, IB 296D VLVO 29200 32400, IB T205-T240 24000 27200
     IBT124D-T192D 28700 35400

28 2 FISHKEELER 280      OP  SF  FBG SV IB T240 VLVO 10 6 7700  2  4 23500 26100
28 2 WEEKENDER 280       OP  SF  FBG SV IB  305 VLVO 10 6 7700  2  4 22900 25500
     IB 296D VLVO 29700 33000, IB T205-T240 24300 29300, IBT124D-T192D 29300 36000

28 2 WEEKENDER FB 280    FB  SF  FBG SV IB  305 VLVO 10 6 8500  2  4 24200 26800
     IB 296D VLVO 31900 35500, IB T205-T240 25600 29100, IBT124D-T192D 31700 38400

29 5 CONQUISTARE 295     ST  EXP FBG SV IO 245-300  9  6 7000  2  4 19100 21800
     IO 185D VLVO 20100 22300, IO T135-T180 19400 22500, IO T120D VLVO 21800 24200

29 11 FISHERMAN 299      OP  SF  FBG SV IO 300 VLVO 10 6 8000  2  4 23000 25600
     IB 305 VLVO 24600 27400, IO 185D VLVO 26700 29600, IB 192D VLVO 27500 30600
     IO T135 VLVO 22700 25300, IO T185D VLVO 31400 34900

31 1 EXPRESS 290         ST  EXP FBG SV IO 300 VLVO 10 6 10000 2  4 26800 29800
     IO 185D VLVO 28400 31500, IO T180-T245 27500 32100, IOT120D-T185D 29500 35400

31 3 FISHERMAN 310       OP  SF  FBG SV IB  296D VLVO 11 6 10500 2  6 40900 45900
31 3 FISHERMAN 310       OP  SF  FBG SV IB T240-T305 11 6 10500 2  6 36600 42500
31 3 FISHERMAN 310       OP  SF  FBG SV IB T305  VLVO 11 6 11500 2  6 43000 47800
31 3 FISHERMAN FB 310    FB  SF  FBG SV IB  296D VLVO 11 6 11500 2  6 43200 47900
31 3 FISHERMAN FB 310    FB  SF  FBG SV IB T240-T305 11 6 11500 2  6 38000 44300
31 3 FISHERMAN FB 310    FB  SF  FBG SV IB T192D VLVO 11 6 11500 2  6 45700 50200
31 3 SEDAN 310           HT  CR  FBG SV IB  296D VLVO 11 6 11750 2  6 37700 42300
31 3 SEDAN 310           HT  CR  FBG SV IB T240-T305 11 6 11750 2  6 37700 44000
31 3 SEDAN 310           HT  CR  FBG SV IB T192D VLVO 11 6 11750 2  6 46300 50900
31 3 SEDAN FB 310        FB  CR  FBG SV IB  296D VLVO 11 6 12750 2  6 38500 44500
31 3 SEDAN FB 310        FB  CR  FBG SV IB T240-T305 11 6 12750 2  6 48300 53100

33   CONQUISTARE 330     ST  EXP FBG SV IB  300 VLVO 11 6 10500 2  6 30100 33500
33   CONQUISTARE 330     ST  EXP FBG SV IO T180-T245 11 6 10500 2  6 30800 35500
33   CONQUISTARE 330     ST  EXP FBG SV IOT120D-T185D 11 6 10500 2  6 33400 39500
34 5 SEDAN 330           HT  CR  FBG SV IB T305  VLVO 11 6 13000 2 10 60400 66300
34 5 SEDAN 330           HT  CR  FBG SV IB T296D VLVO 11 6 13500 2 10 49600 54500
34 5 SEDAN FB 330        FB  CR  FBG SV IB T296D VLVO 11 6 14000 2 10 62400 68500
---------------------- 1991 BOATS -----------------------------------------------------
23 3 FISHERMAN 230       ST  SF  FBG SV IO 205-245  8  6 4600  2     10900 12600
23 3 FISHERMAN 230       OP  SF  FBG SV IO 205-245  8  6 4600  2     10900 12600
23 3 FISHKEELER 250      HT  SF  FBG SV IB  300 VLVO 8 6 5900  2  4 14000 16400
23 3 FISHKEELER 250      HT  SF  FBG SV IB  300 VLVO 8 6 5900  2  4 14400 16400
25 1 FISHERMAN 250       ST  SF  FBG SV IB  300 VLVO 8 6 5600  2  8 12600 14400
25 1 FISHERMAN 250       ST  SF  FBG SV IB  205 VLVO 8 6 5600  2  8 13400 15300
     IB 240 VLVO 14600  16600, IO 245 VLVO 13800 15600, IB 192D VLVO 19800 22000
     IO T135 VLVO 14600 16600

25 1 FISHERMAN 250       HT  SF  FBG DV OB               8 6 5600  2  8 12600 14400
25 1 FISHERMAN 250       HT  SF  FBG SV IO 205 VLVO    8 6 5600  2  8 13400 15300
     IB 240 VLVO 14600  16600, IO 245 VLVO 13800 15600, IB 192D VLVO 19800 22000
     IO T135 VLVO 14600 16600
```

```
      LOA  NAME AND/                 TOP/ BOAT -HULL- ----ENGINE--- BEAM    WGT  DRAFT RETAIL RETAIL
      FT IN OR MODEL                 RIG  TYPE MTL TP TP # HP  MFG  FT IN   LBS  FT IN  LOW   HIGH
      ------------------------- 1991 BOATS ------------------------------------------------------
      27  1 CENTER CONSOLE 250       ST   SF   FBG DV OB        8  6  4800   2 6  14100  16000
      27  1 CENTER CONSOLE 250       SF   FBG  DV IO    205 VLVO 8 6 4800    2 6  13500  15300
             IB  240  VLVO  15000    17000, IO  245  VLVO 14000 15900, IB 192D VLVO  18400  20400

      27  1 EXPRESS XLE 250          ST   EXP  FBG DV IO 205-245   8  6  6000   2 6  13300  16200
          IO  300  VLVO  14900       17000, IO 124D-192D     15100 18700, IO T135  VLVO  14900  16900

      27  1 FISHERMAN 250            ST   SF   FBG DV OB        8  6  5600   2 8  14300  16200
      27  1 FISHERMAN 250            ST   SF   FBG DV IO    205 VLVO 8 6 5600   2 8  14600  16500
             IB  240  VLVO  16100    18300, IO  245  VLVO 15000 17100, IB 192D VLVO  20300  22500
          IO T135  VLVO  15700       17900

      27  1 FISHERMAN 250            HT   SF   FBG DV OB        8  6  5600   2 8  14300  16200
      27  1 FISHERMAN 250            HT   SF   FBG DV IO    205 VLVO 8 6 5600   2 8  14600  16500
             IB  240  VLVO  16100    18300, IO  245  VLVO 15000 17100, IB 192D VLVO  20300  22500
          IO T135  VLVO  15700       17900

      27  6 FISHERMAN 260            ST   SF   FBG DV IB 240  VLVO 9  6  6000   2 8  17500  19900
          IO 245-300    16300        19400, IB  305  VLVO 18600 20700, IO 192D VLVO  20900  23200
             IB 192D VLVO 21800      24200, IO T135-T150    16900 19500, IB T205 VLVO  19800  22000
          IB T124D VLVO  24200       26900

      27  6 FISHERMAN 260            HT   SF   FBG DV IB 240  VLVO 9  6  6000   2 8  17500  19900
          IO 245-300    16300        19400, IB  305  VLVO 18600 20700, IO 192D VLVO  20900  23200
             IB 192D VLVO 21800      24200, IO T135-T150    16900 19500, IB T205 VLVO  19800  22000
          IB T124D VLVO  24200       26900

      27  6 WEEKENDER 260            ST   SF   FBG DV IB 240  VLVO 9  6  6800   2 8  19100  21200
          IO 245-300    17300        20500, IB  305  VLVO 19500 21700, IO 192D VLVO  23000  25600
             IB 192D VLVO 24000      26700, IO T135-T150    18400 20700, IB T205 VLVO  20900  23200
          IB T124D VLVO  26300       29200

      27  6 WEEKENDER 260            HT   SF   FBG DV IB 240  VLVO 9  6  6800   2 8  19100  21200
          IO 245-300    17300        20500, IB  305  VLVO 19500 21700, IO 192D VLVO  23000  25600
             IB 192D VLVO 24000      26700, IO T135-T150    18400 20700, IB T205 VLVO  20900  23200
          IB T124D VLVO  26300       29200

      28  5 FISHERMAN 280            ST   SF   FBG DV IO 300  VLVO 10  6  8000   2 4  20900  23200
             IB  305  VLVO  22500    25000, IB 296D VLVO 30300 33700, IB T205-T240 VLVO  23800  27100
          IBT124D-T192D  29900       36400

      28  5 FISHERMAN 280            HT   SF   FBG DV IO 300  VLVO 10  6  8000   2 4  20900  23200
             IB  305  VLVO  22500    25000, IB 296D VLVO 30300 33700, IB T205-T240 VLVO  23800  27100
          IBT124D-T192D  29900       36400

      28  5 FISHKEELER 280           ST   SF   FBG DV IB T240  VLVO 10  6  8200   2 4  24700  27400
      28  5 FISHKEELER 280           HT   SF   FBG DV IB T240  VLVO 10  6  8200   2 4  24700  27400
      28  5 WEEKENDER 280            ST   SF   FBG DV IB 305  VLVO 10  6  8500   2 4  23100  25700
             IB 296D VLVO  31600     35100, IB T205-T240 24400 27800, IBT124D-T192D  31200  37800

      28  5 WEEKENDER 280            HT   SF   FBG DV IB 305  VLVO 10  6  8500   2 4  23100  25700
             IB 296D VLVO  31600     35100, IB T205-T240 24400 27800, IBT124D-T192D  31200  37800

      28  5 WEEKENDER FB 280         FB   SF   FBG DV IB 305  VLVO 10  6  9000   2 4  23900  26500
             IB 296D VLVO  33000     36600, IB T205-T240 25200 28600, IBT124D-T192D  32700  39300

      29  5 EXPRESS XLE 270          ST   EXP  FBG DV IO 245-300    9  6  7600   2 4  18400  21200
          IO 192D VLVO  20800        23200, IO T135-T180    18900 21700, IO T124D VLVO  22300  24800

      31  1 EXPRESS LXE 290          ST   EXP  FBG DV IO 300  VLVO 10  6  9500   2 6  24900  27700
          IO 192D VLVO  26500        29500, IO T180-T245    25600 29800, IOT124D-T192D  27600  33300

      31  3 FISHERMAN 310            ST   SF   FBG DV IB 296D VLVO 11  6 11800  2 6  41900  46500
      31  3 FISHERMAN 310            ST   SF   FBG DV IB T240-T305 VLVO 11  6 11800  2 6  35800  41400
      31  3 FISHERMAN 310            ST   SF   FBG DV IB T192D VLVO 11  6 12000  2 6  44200  49100
      31  3 FISHERMAN 310            HT   SF   FBG DV IB 296D VLVO 11  6 11800  2 6  41900  46500
      31  3 FISHERMAN 310            HT   SF   FBG DV IB T240-T305 VLVO 11  6 11800  2 6  35800  41400
      31  3 FISHERMAN 310            HT   SF   FBG DV IB T192D VLVO 11  6 12000  2 6  44200  49100
      31  3 FISHERMAN FB 310         FB   SF   FBG DV IB 296D VLVO 11  6 12400  2 6  43200  48000
      31  3 FISHERMAN FB 310         FB   SF   FBG DV IB T240-T305 VLVO 11  6 12400  2 6  36300  41900
      31  3 FISHERMAN FB 310         FB   SF   FBG DV IB T192D VLVO 11  6 12400  2 6  45600  50100
      31  3 SEDAN 310                HT   CR   FBG DV IB 296D VLVO 11  6 11950  2 6  42200  46900
      31  3 SEDAN 310                HT   CR   FBG DV IB T240-T305 VLVO 11  6 11950  2 6  35900  41500
      31  3 SEDAN 310                HT   CR   FBG DV IB T192D VLVO 11  6 11950  2 6  44100  49000

      31  3 SEDAN FB 310             FB   CR   FBG DV IB 296D VLVO 11  6 12800  2 6  44200  49100
      31  3 SEDAN FB 310             FB   CR   FBG DV IB T240-T305 VLVO 11  6 12800  2 6  36600  42300
      31  3 SEDAN FB 310             FB   CR   FBG DV IB T192D VLVO 11  6 12800  2 6  46500  51100
      33    EXPRESS XLE 310          ST   EXP  FBG DV IO    300  VLVO 11  6 11300  2 6  28800  32000
      33    EXPRESS XLE 310          ST   EXP  FBG DV IO T180-T245    11  6 11300  2 6  29400  33900
      33    EXPRESS XLE 310          ST   EXP  FBG DV IOT124D-T192D 11  6 11700  2 6  33200  39100
      34  5 SEDAN 330                HT   CR   FBG DV IB T305  VLVO 12  6 13500  2 10 50300  55000
      34  5 SEDAN 330                HT   CR   FBG DV IB T296D VLVO 12  6 13500  2 10 60300  66200
      34  5 SEDAN FB 330             FB   CR   FBG DV IB T305  VLVO 12  6 14000  2 10 50500  57500
      34  5 SEDAN FB 330             FB   CR   FBG DV IB T296D VLVO 12  6 14000  2 10 61300  67300
      ---------------------- 1990 BOATS ----------------------------------------------------------
      23  3 SPORT FISHERMAN 230      ST   SF   FBG DV IO 205-245    8  6  4800   2    10600  12200
      23  3 SPORT FISHERMAN 230      HT   SF   FBG DV IO 205-245    8  6  4800   2    10600  12200
      27  1 EXPRESS 250              ST   EXP  FBG DV IO 205-300    8  6  6500   2    13100  16000
      27  1 EXPRESS 250              ST   EXP  FBG DV IO 130D-200D  8  6  6500   2    14300  17700
      27  1 EXPRESS 250              ST   EXP  FBG DV IO T110-T135  8  6  6500   2    15900  17900
      27  1 SPORT FISHERMAN 250      ST   SF   FBG DV IO    205 VLVO 8  6 5600   2 8  13700  15600
             IB  240  VLVO  15300    17400, IO  245  VLVO 14100 16100, IB 305-351  VLVO  16000  18600
             IB  454  PCM  18000     20100, IO  200D VLVO 17300 19600, IB 200D VLVO  18700  20800
          IO T110-T135  14400        16800

      27  1 SPORT FISHERMAN 250      HT   SF   FBG DV IO    205 VLVO 8  6 5600   2 8  13700  15600
             IB  240  VLVO  15300    17400, IO  245  VLVO 14100 16100, IB 305-351  VLVO  16000  18600
             IB  454  PCM  18000     20100, IO  200D VLVO 17300 19600, IB 200D VLVO  18700  20800
          IO T110-T135  14400        16800

      27  6 SPORT FISHERMAN 260      ST   SF   FBG DV IO 200  VLVO 9  6  6000   2 8  14800  16800
             IB  240  VLVO  16600    18900, IO 245-302    15300 18200, IB 305-454  VLVO  17000  20700
          IO T110-T150  15500        18400, IO T205  VLVO 17100 19400, IO T130D VLVO  21100  23500
             IB 200D VLVO  25500     28300

      27  6 SPORT FISHERMAN 260      HT   SF   FBG DV IO    VLVO 9  6  6000   2 8    **     **
             IB  240  VLVO  16600    18900, IO 245-300    15300 18200, IB 305-454  VLVO  17300  21400
          IO T110-T150  15500        18400, IB T205-T302    19000 22500, IB T130D VLVO  22400  24900
             IB 200D VLVO  25500     28300

      27  6 WEEKENDER 260            ST   SF   FBG DV IO    VLVO 9  6  6800   2 8  15800  18000
             IB  240  VLVO  18100    20100, IO 245-300    16300 19300, IB 305-454  VLVO  18800  22500
             IB  200D VLVO  22100    24500, IO T110-T150    16500 19500, IB T205-T302 VLVO  19900  23600
             IB T130D VLVO  24300    27100

      27  6 WEEKENDER 260            HT   SF   FBG DV IO    VLVO 9  6  6800   2 8  15800  18000
             IB  240  VLVO  18100    20100, IO 245-300    16300 19300, IB 305-454  VLVO  18800  22500
             IB  200D VLVO  22100    24500, IO T110-T150    16500 19500, IB T205-T302 VLVO  19900  23600
             IB T130D VLVO  24300    27100

      28  5 EXPRESS CR XLE 290       ST   CR   FBG DV IO 300  VLVO 10  6  9800   2 6  19100  21200
          IO    D VLVO    **         **, IO  200D VLVO 23100 25700, IO T180-T245 VLVO  19600  22800
          IOT130D-T200D  24500       29400

      28  5 SPORT FISHERMAN 280      ST   SF   FBG DV IB 305-454    10  6  8000   2 4  21400  25600
             IB 200D-306D  25800     31400, IB T205-T351    22600 27900, IBT130D-T200D VLVO  27800  34100

      28  5 SPORT FISHERMAN 280      HT   SF   FBG DV IB 305-454    10  6  8000   2 4  21400  25600
             IB 200D-306D  25800     31400, IB T205-T351    22600 27900, IBT130D-T200D VLVO  27800  34100

      28  5 WEEKENDER 280            ST   SF   FBG DV IB 305-454    10  6  8500   2 4  22000  26300
             IB 200D-306D  27100     32700, IB T205-T351    23200 28500, IBT130D-T200D VLVO  29100  35400

      28  5 WEEKENDER 280            HT   SF   FBG DV IB 305-454    10  6  8500   2 4  22000  26300
             IB 200D-306D  27100     32700, IB T205-T351    23200 28500, IBT130D-T200D VLVO  29100  35400

      29  5 EXPRESS CR XLE 270       ST   CR   FBG DV IO 245-300    9  6  7600   2 4  16500  19900
          IO  200D VLVO  19000       21200, IO T135-T180    17400 20600, IO T130D VLVO  20500  22800

      31  3 FAMILY FB 310            FB   SF   FBG DV IB 306D VLVO 11  6 12400  2 6  41500  46100
          IB T240-T351  34500        40900, IB T454 PCM  39200 43600, IBT200D-T306D VLVO  43400  52800

      31  3 SEDAN 310                HT   CR   FBG DV IB 306D VLVO 11  6 11950  2 6  38600  42900
          IB T240-T351  28400        34200, IB T454 PCM  33100 36800, IBT200D-T306D VLVO  40400  49500

      31  3 SEDAN FB 310             FB   CR   FBG DV IB 306D VLVO 11  6 12400  2 10 41500  46100
          IB T240-T351  34500        40900, IB T454 PCM  39200 43600, IBT200D-T306D VLVO  43400  52800

      31  3 SPORT FISHERMAN 310      ST   SF   FBG DV IB 306D VLVO 11  6 11800  2 6  40200  44700
          IB T240-T351  34100        40500, IB T454 PCM  38800 43100, IBT200D-T306D VLVO  42200  51800

      31  3 SPORT FISHERMAN 310      HT   SF   FBG DV IB 306D VLVO 11  6 11800  2 6  40200  44700
          IB T240-T351  34100        40500, IB T454 PCM  38800 43100, IBT200D-T306D VLVO  42200  51800

      33    EXPRESS CR XLE 310       ST   CR   FBG DV IO    VLVO 11    11300  2 6    **     **
```

LOA FT	IN	NAME AND/ OR MODEL	TOP/ RIG	BOAT TYPE	-HULL- MTL	TP	ENGINE TP	# HP	MFG	BEAM FT	IN	WGT LBS	DRAFT FT	IN	RETAIL LOW	RETAIL HIGH
		1990 BOATS														
33		EXPRESS CR XLE 310	ST	CR	FBG	DV	IO	T180-T245		11		11300	2	6	27600	31900
33		EXPRESS CR XLE 310	ST	CR	FBG	DV	IO	T130D-T200D		11		11300	2	6	30900	36500
34	5	SEDAN 330	HT	CR	FBG	DV	IB	306D	VLVO	12		13700	2	10	51900	57000
34	5	SEDAN 330	HT	CR	FBG	DV	IB	T305-T454		12		13700	2	10	47800	56600
34	5	SEDAN 330	HT	CR	FBG	DV	IB	T306D	VLVO	12		13700	2	10	58400	64200
34	5	SEDAN FLYBRIDGE 330	HT	CR	FBG	DV	IB	306D	VLVO	12			2	10	48100	52900
34	5	SEDAN FLYBRIDGE 330	HT	CR	FBG	DV	IB	T305-T454		12			2	10	40500	48900
34	5	SEDAN FLYBRIDGE 330	HT	CR	FBG	DV	IB	T306D	VLVO	12			2	10	54500	59900
		1989 BOATS														
22	3	230 SF	HT	SF	FBG	DV	IO	271	VLVO	8	6	4800	2		9900	11300
22	3	230 SF	HT	SF	FBG	DV	IO	271D	VLVO	8	6	4800	2		13600	15400
23	3	230 EXPRESS XLE	ST	CR	FBG	DV	IO	271	VLVO	8	6	5200	2	2	9700	11000
23	3	230 EXPRESS XLE	ST	CR	FBG	DV	IO	T271D	VLVO	8	6	5200	2	2	15700	17800
23	3	230 SF	ST	SF	FBG	DV	IO	271	VLVO	8	6	4800	2		10400	11800
23	3	230 SF	ST	SF	FBG	DV	IO	271D	VLVO	8	6	4800	2		14200	16100
27	6	260 WEEKENDER	ST	SF	FBG	DV	IO	T171	VLVO	9	6	6800	2	6	16500	18700
		IB T171 VLVO 18600 20600, IO T171D VLVO 23200 25700, IB T171D VLVO													24900	27700
27	6	260 WEEKENDER	HT	SF	FBG	DV	IO	T171	VLVO	9	6	6800	2	6	16500	18700
		IB T171 VLVO 18600 20600, IO T171D VLVO 23200 25700, IB T171D VLVO													24900	27700
28	5	280 EXPRESS XLE	ST	CR	FBG	DV	IO	T271	VLVO	10	6	9800	2	6	19800	22000
28	5	280 EXPRESS XLE	ST	CR	FBG	DV	IO	T271D	VLVO	10	6	9800	2	6	27000	30000
28	5	280 SF	ST	SF	FBG	DV	IO	T260	PCM	10	6	8000	2	4	20300	22500
		IO T260 VLVO 20500 22700, IB T260 PCM 22300 24800, IB T260 VLVO													22400	24900
		IO T260D PCM 30100 33400, IO T260D VLVO 29600 32900, IB T260D													32400	35900
28	5	280 SF	HT	SF	FBG	DV	IO	T260	PCM	10	6	8000	2	4	20300	22500
		IO T260 VLVO 20500 22700, IB T260 PCM 22300 24800, IB T260 VLVO													22400	24900
		IO T260D PCM 30100 33400, IO T260D VLVO 29600 32900, IB T260D PCM													32400	35900
28	5	280 WEEKENDER	ST	SF	FBG	DV	IB	T230	PCM	10	6	8500	2	4	22400	24900
		IO T260 PCM 20800 23100, IO T260 VLVO 21000 23300, IB T260 VLVO													23000	25500
		IO T260D PCM 31100 34500, IO T260D VLVO 30600 34000, IB T260D													33400	37100
28	5	280 WEEKENDER	HT	SF	FBG	DV	IO	T260	PCM	10	6	8500	2	4	20800	23100
		IO T260 VLVO 21000 23300, IB T260 PCM 22900 25400, IB T260 VLVO													23000	25500
		IO T260D PCM 31100 34500, IB T260D 33400 37100														
29	5	270 EXPRESS XLE	ST	CR	FBG	DV	IO	T205	VLVO	9	6	7600	2	4	17500	19900
29	5	270 EXPRESS XLE	ST	CR	FBG	DV	IO	T205D	VLVO	9	6	7600	2	4	21700	24200
31	3	FAMILY FB 310	FB	CR	FBG	DV	IB	T340	CUM	11	6	12400	2	6	34800	38700
31	3	FAMILY FB 310	FB	CR	FBG	DV	IB	T340	VLVO	11	6	12400	2	6	34900	38700
31	3	FAMILY FB 310	FB	CR	FBG	DV	IB	T340D		11	6	12400	2	6	47800	52500
31	3	FAMILY FB 310	FB	SF	FBG	DV	IB	T340	CUM	11	6	12400	2	6	34800	38700
31	3	FAMILY FB 310	FB	SF	FBG	DV	IB	T340	VLVO	11	6	12400	2	6	34900	38800
31	3	FAMILY FB 310	FB	SF	FBG	DV	IB	T340D		11	6	12400	2	6	47800	52500
31	3	SPORT FISHERMAN 310	ST	SF	FBG	DV	IB	T340	CUM	11	6	11800	2	6	34400	38300
31	3	SPORT FISHERMAN 310	ST	SF	FBG	DV	IB	T340	VLVO	11	6	11800	2	6	34500	38300
31	3	SPORT FISHERMAN 310	ST	SF	FBG	DV	IB	T340D		11	6	11800	2	6	46700	51300
31	3	SPORT FISHERMAN 310	HT	SF	FBG	DV	IB	T340	CUM	11	6	11800	2	6	34400	38300
31	3	SPORT FISHERMAN 310	HT	SF	FBG	DV	IB	T340	VLVO	11	6	11800	2	6	34500	38300
31	3	SPORT FISHERMAN 310	HT	SF	FBG	DV	IB	T340D		11	6	11800	2	6	46700	51300
33		310 EXPRESS XLE	ST	CR	FBG	DV	IB	T271	VLVO	11		11300	2	6	34600	38500
33		310 EXPRESS XLE	ST	CR	FBG	DV	IB	T271D		11		11300	2	6	44400	49400
34	5	330 EXPRESS FB	HT	CR	FBG	DV	IB	T340	CUM	12		13700	2	8	46400	51000
34	5	330 EXPRESS FB	HT	CR	FBG	DV	IB	T340	VLVO	12		13700	2	8	46500	51100
34	5	330 EXPRESS FB	HT	CR	FBG	DV	IB	T340D		12		13700	2	8	57900	63600
		1988 BOATS														
22	3	SPORT FISHERMAN 230	ST	SF	FBG	SV	IO	230		8	6	4800	2		8900	10400
22	3	SPORT FISHERMAN 230	HT	SF	FBG	SV	IO	230		8	6	4800	2		8900	10400
25	10	EXPRESS CRUISER 260	ST	CR	FBG	SV	IO	260	MRCR	9	6	5200	2	2	10100	11500
25	10	EXPRESS CRUISER 260	ST	CR	FBG	SV	IO	T171	VLVO	9	6	5200	2	2	11000	12500
25	10	SPORT FISHERMAN 260	ST	SF	FBG	SV	IO	271		9	6	6800	2	6	13800	15900
25	10	SPORT FISHERMAN 260	ST	SF	FBG	SV	IB	T171	PCM	9	6	6800	2	6	16100	18200
25	10	SPORT FISHERMAN 260	HT	SF	FBG	SV	IO	271		9	6	6800	2	6	13800	15900
25	10	SPORT FISHERMAN 260	HT	SF	FBG	SV	IB	T171	PCM	9	6	6800	2	6	16100	18200
28	2	EXPRESS CRUISER 280	ST	CR	FBG	SV	IO	340	MRCR	10	6	9800	2	6	17000	19300
28	2	EXPRESS CRUISER 280	ST	CR	FBG	SV	IO	T271	VLVO	10	6	9800	2	6	18800	20900
28	2	EXPRESS FLYBDGE 280	FB	EXP	FBG	SV	IO	340	MRCR	10	6				13700	15500
28	2	EXPRESS FLYBDGE 280	FB	EXP	FBG	SV	IO	T271	VLVO	10	6				15200	17300
28	2	SPORT FISHERMAN 280	ST	SF	FBG	SV	IB	340	MRCR	10	6	8000	2	4	19400	21600
28	2	SPORT FISHERMAN 280	ST	SF	FBG	SV	IB	T230	PCM	10	6	8000	2	4	20500	22800
28	2	SPORT FISHERMAN 280	HT	SF	FBG	SV	IB	340	MRCR	10	6	8000	2	4	19400	21600
28	2	SPORT FISHERMAN 280	HT	SF	FBG	SV	IB	T230	PCM	10	6	8000	2	4	20500	22800
28	2	WEEKENDER 280	ST	WKNDR	FBG	SV	IB	340	MRCR	10	6	8500	2	4	21200	23500
28	2	WEEKENDER 280	ST	WKNDR	FBG	SV	IB	T230	PCM	10	6	8500	2	4	22300	24800
28	2	WEEKENDER 280	HT	WKNDR	FBG	SV	IB	340	MRCR	10	6	8500	2	4	21200	23500
28	2	WEEKENDER 280	HT	WKNDR	FBG	SV	IB	T230	PCM	10	6	8500	2	4	22300	24800
30	10	FAMILY FB 310	FB	CR	FBG	SV	IB	T340		11	2	12400	2	6	32100	35600
30	10	SPORT FISHERMAN 310	ST	SF	FBG	SV	IB	T340		11	2	11800	2	6	31600	35200
30	10	SPORT FISHERMAN 310	HT	SF	FBG	SV	IB	T340		11	2	11800	2	6	31600	35200
33	4	EXPRESS FLYBDGE 330	FB	CR	FBG	SV	IB	T340		12	4	13700	2	8	40200	44700
		1987 BOATS														
22	3	SPORT FISHERMAN 230	ST	SF	FBG	SV	IO	230		8	6	4800	2		8350	9850
22	3	SPORT FISHERMAN 230	HT	SF	FBG	SV	IO	230		8	6	4800	2		8350	9850
25	10	EXPRESS CRUISER 260	ST	CR	FBG	SV	IO	260	MRCR	9	6				9000	10200
25	10	EXPRESS CRUISER 260	ST	CR	FBG	SV	IO	T171	VLVO	9	6				9850	11200
25	10	SPORT FISHERMAN 260	ST	SF	FBG	SV	IO	271		9	6	6800	2	6	13100	15100
25	10	SPORT FISHERMAN 260	ST	SF	FBG	SV	IB	T171	PCM	9	6	6800	2	6	15300	17400
25	10	SPORT FISHERMAN 260	HT	SF	FBG	SV	IO	271		9	6	6800	2	6	13100	15100
25	10	SPORT FISHERMAN 260	HT	SF	FBG	SV	IB	T171	PCM	9	6	6800	2	6	15300	17400
28	2	EXPRESS CRUISER 280	ST	CR	FBG	SV	IO	340	MRCR	10	6	9800	2	6	16200	18400
28	2	EXPRESS CRUISER 280	ST	CR	FBG	SV	IO	T271	VLVO	10	6	9800	2	6	17500	19800
28	2	EXPRESS FLYBDGE 280	FB	EXP	FBG	SV	IO	340	MRCR	10	6				13000	14800
28	2	EXPRESS FLYBDGE 280	FB	EXP	FBG	SV	IO	T271	VLVO	10	6				14500	16500
28	2	SPORT FISHERMAN 280	ST	SF	FBG	SV	IB	340	MRCR	10	6	8000	2	4	18700	20800
28	2	SPORT FISHERMAN 280	ST	SF	FBG	SV	IB	T230	PCM	10	6	8000	2	4	19600	21700
28	2	SPORT FISHERMAN 280	HT	SF	FBG	SV	IB	340	MRCR	10	6	8000	2	4	18700	20800
28	2	SPORT FISHERMAN 280	HT	SF	FBG	SV	IB	T230	PCM	10	6				17400	19800
28	2	WEEKENDER 280	ST	WKNDR	FBG	SV	IB	340	MRCR	10	6	8500	2	4	20200	22400
28	2	WEEKENDER 280	ST	WKNDR	FBG	SV	IB	T230	PCM	10	6	8500	2	4	21300	23700
28	2	WEEKENDER 280	HT	WKNDR	FBG	SV	IB	340	MRCR	10	6	8500	2	4	20200	22400
28	2	WEEKENDER 280	HT	WKNDR	FBG	SV	IB	T230	PCM	10	6	8500	2	4	21300	23700
30	10	FAMILY FLYBRIDGE 310	FB	CR	FBG	SV	IB	T340		11	2	12400	2	6	30600	34000
30	10	SPORT FISHERMAN 310	ST	SF	FBG	SV	IB	T340		11	2	11800	2	6	30200	33500
30	10	SPORT FISHERMAN 310	HT	SF	FBG	SV	IB	T340		11	2	11800	2	6	30200	33500
33	4	EXPRESS FLYBDGE 330	FB	CR	FBG	SV	IB	T340		12	4	13700	2	6	38400	42600
		1986 BOATS														
25	6	EXPRESS CRUISER	OP	EXP	FBG	DV	IO	260		8		4800	2		8250	9500
25	6	SPORTFISHERMAN		SF	FBG	DV	IO	260		8		4600	2		9250	10500
27	7	EXPRESS CRUISER	OP	EXP	FBG	DV	IO	T340		10	6	7000	2	2	15200	17200
27	7	EXPRESS CRUISER	FB	EXP	FBG	DV	IO	T340		10	6	7000	2	2	15200	17200
27	7	SPORT FISHERMAN		SF	FBG	DV	IB	T230		10	6	6500	2	2	16400	18700
27	7	WEEKENDER		WKNDR	FBG	DV	IB	T230		10	6	6800	2	2	18100	20100
29	10	SPORT FISHERMAN		SF	FBG	DV	IB	T340		11	4	9800	2	4	25500	28300
33	4	EXPRESS FLYBRIDGE	FB	EXP	FBG	DV	IB	T340		12		12000	2	4	35500	39400
33	4	SPORT FISHERMAN		SF	FBG	DV	IB	T340		12		10800	2	4	34700	38600
		1985 BOATS														
25	6	EXPRESS CRUISER	OP	EXP	FBG	DV	IO	260		8		4800	2		7900	9100
25	6	SPORTFISHERMAN		SF	FBG	DV	IO	260		8		4600	2		8900	10100
27	7	EXPRESS CRUISER	OP	EXP	FBG	DV	IO	T340		10	6	7000	2	2	14500	16500
27	7	EXPRESS CRUISER	FB	EXP	FBG	DV	IO	T340		10	6	7000	2	2	14500	16500
27	7	SPORT FISHERMAN		SF	FBG	DV	IB	T460		10	6	6500	2	2	19000	21100
27	7	WEEKENDER		WKNDR	FBG	DV	IB	T460		10	6	6800	2	2	20500	22800
29	10	SPORT FISHERMAN		SF	FBG	DV	IB	T340		11	4	9800	2	4	24300	27000
32	4	EXPRESS FLYBRIDGE	FB	EXP	FBG	DV	IB	T680		12		12000	2	4	39200	43600
32	4	SPORT FISHERMAN		SF	FBG	DV	IB	T680		12		10800	2	4	38400	42700
		1984 BOATS														
25	6	DAY CRUISER		SF	FBG	DV	IO	340D		8		4200	1	10	13000	14800
25	6	EXPRESS CRUISER		DC	FBG	DV	IO	340D		8		4600	1	10	13600	15500
27	7	EXPRESS CRUISER		DC	FBG	DV	IO	T340D		10	6	6500	2	4	24300	27000
27	7	EXPRESS FLYBRIDGE	FB	DC	FBG	DV	IO	T340D		10	6	6500	2	4	24300	27000
27	7	SPORT FISHERMAN		SF	FBG	DV	IB	T340D		10	6	6500	2	4	26500	29500
27	7	WEEKENDER		SF	FBG	DV	IB	T230		10	6	6500	2		15000	17100
29	10	SPORT FISHERMAN		SF	FBG	DV	IB	T340		11	4	9800	2		23300	25900
32	4	EXPRESS FLYBRIDGE	FB	SF	FBG	DV	IB	T340D		11	8	13000	2		40800	45300
32	4	SPORT FISHERMAN		SF	FBG	DV	IB	T340D		11		11000	2		38000	42200

....For earlier years, see the BUC Used Boat Price Guide, Volume 3

BAIA YACHTS NA

STUART FL 34994 See inside cover to adjust price for area

CANTIERI DI BAIA
BAIA ITALY 80070

For more recent years, see the BUC Used Boat Price Guide, Volume 1

LOA FT	IN	NAME AND/ OR MODEL	TOP/ RIG	BOAT TYPE	-HULL- MTL	TP	TP	----ENGINE--- # HP	MFG	BEAM FT	IN	WGT LBS	DRAFT FT	IN	RETAIL LOW	RETAIL HIGH
		1986 BOATS														
33	2	BAIA B33	OP	SPTCR	FBG	DV	IO	T330-T440		10	10	9000	2	9	24200	29500
40		BAIA B40	OP	SPTCR	FBG	DV	IO	T370D	CAT	12		22000	2	6	79000	86800
40		BAIA B40	OP	SPTCR	FBG	DV	IB	T435D	GM	12		22000	2	6	121000	133000
49	4	BAIA B50	OP	SPTCR	FBG	DV	IB	T650D	GM	14	2	10400	4		127500	140000
		1985 BOATS														
32	9	BAIA B33	OP	SPTCR	FBG	DV	IO	T370	MRCR	10	7	9000	2	6	23000	25500
49	4	BAIA B50	OP	SPTCR	FBG	DV	IB	T650D	GM	14	2	10400	4		121500	133500

BAJA MARINE CORP

BUCYRUS OH 44820-0151 COAST GUARD MFG ID- AGC See inside cover to adjust price for area
FORMERLY AEROGLASTICS CORP

For more recent years, see the BUC Used Boat Price Guide, Volume 1

LOA FT	IN	NAME AND/ OR MODEL	TOP/ RIG	BOAT TYPE	-HULL- MTL	TP	TP	----ENGINE--- # HP	MFG	BEAM FT	IN	WGT LBS	DRAFT FT	IN	RETAIL LOW	RETAIL HIGH
		1996 BOATS														
18	1	BAJA 180 ISLANDER	OP	RNBT	FBG	SV	IO	135-180		7	10	2400	2	9	4900	5700
19		BAJA 188 ISLANDER	OP	RNBT	FBG	SV	IO	180-250		7	10	2800	2	9	5800	6950
19		BAJA 188 ISLANDER	OP	RNBT	FBG	SV	IO	300	MRCR	7	10	2800	2	9	6600	7600
20	4	BAJA 20 OUTLAW	OP	RNBT	FBG	SV	IO	180-210		7	1	2400	2	9	8100	9450
21		BAJA 208 ISLANDER	OP	RNBT	FBG	SV	IO	180-250		8	4	3350	2	9	8600	10300
		IO 300-330 9550 11500, IO 350 MRCR 10700 12100, IO 385 MRCR													11800	13400
21	6	BAJA 208 ISLANDER	OP	RNBT	FBG	SV	IO	300	MRCR	8	4	3350	2	9	9750	11100
21	7	TWILIGHT CALIBER 22	OP	RNBT	FBG	DV	IO	180-250		8	2	3250	2	10	10700	12600
21	7	TWILIGHT CALIBER 22	OP	RNBT	FBG	DV	IO	300-330		8	2	3250	2	10	11800	14300
21	7	TWILIGHT CALIBER 22	OP	RNBT	FBG	DV	IO	350	MRCR	8	2	3250	2	10	13200	15000
21	7	TWILIGHT CALIBER 22	OP	RNBT	FBG	SV	IO	300	MRCR	8	2	3250	2	10	11800	13500
23	8	BAJA 236	OP	CUD	FBG	SV	IO	250-310		8	6	3925	2	11	14500	17600
23	8	BAJA 236	OP	CUD	FBG	SV	IO	330-350		8	6	3925	2	11	16000	18900
23	8	BAJA 236	OP	CUD	FBG	SV	IO	385	MRCR	8	6	3925	2	11	18400	20500
24		BAJA 240	OP	CUD	FBG	SV	IO	210-300		8	4	3700	2	11	13100	16000
24		BAJA 240	OP	CUD	FBG	SV	IO	330-350		8	4	3700	2	11	14800	17500
24		BAJA 240	OP	CUD	FBG	SV	IO	385-415		8	4	3700	2	11	16800	20600
24		BAJA 240 ISLANDER	OP	RNBT	FBG	SV	IO	210-300		8	4	3800	2	11	11400	14000
24		BAJA 240 ISLANDER	OP	RNBT	FBG	SV	IO	330-350		8	4	3800	2	11	12900	15300
24		BAJA 240 ISLANDER	OP	RNBT	FBG	SV	IO	385-415		8	4	3800	2	11	14600	17900
24		BAJA OUTLAW	OP	CUD	FBG	SV	IO	300-350		8		4000	3	2	16100	20000
24		BAJA OUTLAW	OP	CUD	FBG	SV	IO	385-415		8		4000	3	2	19200	23000
24		BAJA OUTLAW	OP	CUD	FBG	SV	IO	470	MRCR	8		4000	3	2	23800	26500
24	4	BAJA BANDIT II	OP	CUD	FBG	SV	IO	300-350		8		3500	2	9	14000	17400
24	4	BAJA BANDIT II	OP	CUD	FBG	SV	IO	385-415		8		3500	2	9	16600	20400
25	6	BAJA 252	OP	RNBT	FBG	SV	IO	210-300		8	4	4050	3	1	16000	19800
25	6	BAJA 252	OP	RNBT	FBG	SV	IO	330-385		8	4	4050	3	1	18600	22500
25	6	BAJA 252	OP	RNBT	FBG	SV	IO	415-470		8	4	4050	3	1	21500	26700
26		BAJA 260	OP	CUD	FBG	SV	IO	300-385		8	6	4500	2	11	18300	22700
26		BAJA 260	OP	CUD	FBG	SV	IO	415	MRCR	8	6	4500	2	11	21600	24000
27	2	BAJA 272	OP	OFF	FBG	DV	IO	300-385		8	4	4350	3	2	21000	26000
27	2	BAJA 272	OP	OFF	FBG	DV	IO	415-470		8	4	4350	3	2	24400	29500
27	2	BAJA 272 ISLANDER	OP	RNBT	FBG	SV	IO	300-385		8	4	4400	3	2	20100	24900
27	2	BAJA 272 ISLANDER	OP	RNBT	FBG	SV	IO	415-470		8	4	4400	3	2	23400	28200
27	2	BAJA SHOOTER	OP	OFF	FBG	DV	IO	300-385		8	4	4250	3	2	19400	24000
27	2	BAJA SHOOTER	OP	OFF	FBG	DV	IO	415-470		8	4	4250	3	2	22600	27200
28		SPORTFISHERMAN 280	OP	SF	FBG	SV	OB			8	4	4050	2	10	23000	25500
29		BAJA 290	OP	OFF	FBG	DV	IO	T210-T330		9		6410	3	2	25800	32200
29		BAJA 290	OP	OFF	FBG	DV	IO	T350	MRCR	9		6410	3	2	29700	33000
30	6	BAJA 302	OP	OFF	FBG	DV	IO	T250-T350		8	6	6500	3	2	37200	45000
30	6	BAJA 302	OP	OFF	FBG	DV	IO	T385-T500		8	6	6500	3	2	41900	52300
31	10	BAJA 320	OP	OFF	FBG	DV	IO	T330-T500		8	4	7300	3	4	40300	50300
31	10	BAJA 322	OP	OFF	FBG	DV	IO	T300-T415		8	4	7300	3	4	46800	55200
32	1	BAJA 32 OUTLAW	OP	OFF	FBG	DV	IO	T300-T425		8	4	7000	3	4	39300	47500
32	1	BAJA 32 OUTLAW	OP	OFF	FBG	DV	IO	T500	MRCR	8	4	7000	3	4	45000	50000
37	7	BAJA 38 SPECIAL	OP	OFF	FBG	DV	IO	350	MRCR	9	3	9100	3	4	48700	53500
		IO T350 MRCR 52800 58000, IO T385 MRCR 55300 60800, IO T415 MRCR													57800	63600
		IO T470 MRCR 63000 69300, IO T500 MRCR 65900 72400														
42	6	BAJA 420	OP	OFF	FBG	DV	IO	R350	MRCR	9	3	12250	3	10	68400	75200
		IO R385 MRCR 73000 80200, IO R415 MRCR 77400 85100, IO R470 MRCR													86100	94600
		IO R490 MRCR 89200 98000														
		1995 BOATS														
17		BAJA 170 ISLANDER	OP	RNBT	FBG	SV	OB			7	4	1200	2	5	3900	4550
18	1	BAJA 180 ISLANDER	OP	RNBT	FBG	SV	IO	135-180		7	10	2400	2	9	4600	5300
19	1	BAJA 188 ISLANDER	OP	RNBT	FBG	SV	IO	180-265		7	10	2800	2	9	5400	6650
20	4	BAJA 204 HOT SHOT	OP	RNBT	FBG	SV	IO	180-205		7	1	2400	2	9	7300	8450
21	6	BAJA 208 ISLANDER	OP	RNBT	FBG	SV	IO	180-265		8	4	3350	2	9	8200	9950
		IO 300 MRCR 9150 10400, IO 350 MRCR 10100 11500, IO 385 MRCR													11200	12700
21	7	BAJA 22 CALIBER	OP	CUD	FBG	SV	IO	250-300		8	6	3125	2	11	10400	12600
21	7	BAJA 22 CALIBER	OP	CUD	FBG	SV	IO	350	MRCR	8	6	3125	2	11	12400	14100
21	7	TWILIGHT CALIBER 22	OP	RNBT	FBG	DV	IO	180-235		8	2	3250	2	10	10000	11600
		IO 250 MRCR 10400 11800, IO 300 MRCR 11100 12600, IO 350 MRCR													12300	14000
21	7	TWILIGHT CALIBER 22	OP	RNBT	FBG	SV	IO	265	MRCR	8	2	3250	2	10	10500	11900
23	8	BAJA 236	OP	CUD	FBG	SV	IO	235-300		8	6	3925	2	11	13400	16200
23	8	BAJA 236	OP	CUD	FBG	SV	IO	350-385		8	6	3925	2	11	15500	19100
24		BAJA 240	OP	CUD	FBG	SV	IO	235-300		8	4	3700	2	11	12400	15000
24		BAJA 240	OP	CUD	FBG	SV	IO	350-385		8	4	3700	2	11	14400	17800
24		BAJA 240	OP	CUD	FBG	SV	IO	415	MRCR	8	4	3700	2	11	16900	19200
24		BAJA 240 ISLANDER	OP	RNBT	FBG	SV	IO	235-300		8	4	3800	2	11	10800	13000
24		BAJA 240 ISLANDER	OP	RNBT	FBG	SV	IO	350	MRCR	8	4	3800	2	11	12500	14200
24		BAJA 240 ISLANDER	OP	RNBT	FBG	SV	IO	385-415		8	4	3800	2	11	13600	16700
24		BAJA OUTLAW	OP	CUD	FBG	SV	IO	300-350		8		4000	3	2	15000	18600
24		BAJA OUTLAW	OP	CUD	FBG	SV	IO	385-425		8		4000	3	2	18100	22000
24		BAJA OUTLAW	OP	CUD	FBG	SV	IO	470	MRCR	8		4000	3	2	22200	24700
24	4	BAJA BANDIT II	OP	CUD	FBG	SV	IO	300-350		8		3500	2	9	13000	16200
24	4	BAJA BANDIT II	OP	CUD	FBG	SV	IO	385-415		8		3500	2	9	15500	19000
24	4	BAJA BANDIT II	OP	CUD	FBG	SV	IO	425	MRCR	8		3500	2	9	17200	19500
26		BAJA 260	OP	CUD	FBG	SV	IO	300-350		8	6	4500	2	11	16700	20300
26		BAJA 260	OP	CUD	FBG	SV	IO	385-415		8	6	4500	2	11	19100	22400
27	2	BAJA 272	OP	OFF	FBG	DV	IO	300-385		8	4	4350	3	2	19600	24300
27	2	BAJA 272	OP	OFF	FBG	DV	IO	415-470		8	4	4350	3	2	22800	27500
27	2	BAJA 272 ISLANDER	OP	RNBT	FBG	SV	IO	300	MRCR	8	4	4400	3	2	18900	21000
27	2	BAJA 272 ISLANDER	OP	RNBT	FBG	SV	IO	350-425		8	4	4400	3	2	19900	24600
27	2	BAJA 272 ISLANDER	OP	RNBT	FBG	SV	IO	470	MRCR	8	4	4400	3	2	23700	26400
27	2	BAJA SHOOTER	OP	OFF	FBG	DV	IO	300-385		8	4	4250	3	2	18300	22400
27	2	BAJA SHOOTER	OP	OFF	FBG	DV	IO	415-470		8	4	4250	3	2	21100	25400
28		SPORTFISHERMAN 280	OP	SF	FBG	SV	OB			8	4	4050	2	10	21800	24200
29		BAJA 290	OP	OFF	FBG	DV	IO	T235-T300		9		6410	3	2	24600	29000
29		BAJA 290	OP	OFF	FBG	DV	IO	T350	MRCR	9		6410	3	2	27700	30700
29		BAJA 290	OP	OFF	FBG	DV	IO	T385	MRCR	9		6410	3	2	28900	32200
29		BAJA YACHT 290	OP	SPTCR	FBG	SV	IO	T180-T265		10		9000	3	2	27800	33000
31	10	BAJA 320	OP	OFF	FBG	DV	IO	T300-T350		8	4	7300	3	4	36800	42300
31	10	BAJA 320	OP	OFF	FBG	DV	IO	T385	MRCR	8	4	7300	3	4	39000	43300
31	10	BAJA 320	OP	OFF	FBG	DV	IO	T415	MRCR	8	4	7300	3	4	39800	44200
32	1	BAJA 32 CALIBER	OP	OFF	FBG	DV	OB			8	4	7000	3	4	30500	33900
32	1	BAJA 32 CALIBER	OP	OFF	FBG	DV	IO	T300-T470		8	4	7000	3	4	32400	40400
32	1	BAJA 32 CALIBER	OP	OFF	FBG	DV	IO	T490	MRCR	8	4	7000	3	4	36900	41000
34	3	BAJA YACHT 340	OP	SPTCR	FBG	SV	IO	T300-T415		12		12000	3	6	47800	57300
37	7	BAJA 38 SPECIAL	OP	OFF	FBG	DV	IO	T350	MRCR	9	3	9100	3	4	49300	54100
		IO T385 MRCR 51600 56700, IO T415 MRCR 54000 59300, IO T425 MRCR													54800	60200
		IO T470 MRCR 58800 64600, IO T490 MRCR 60600 66600														
42	6	BAJA 420	OP	OFF	FBG	DV	IO	R350	MRCR	9	3	12250	3	10	63800	70100
		IO R385 MRCR 68100 74900, IO R415 MRCR 72200 79400, IO R425 MRCR													72100	79200
		IO R470 MRCR 80300 88200, IO R490 MRCR 83200 91500														
		1994 BOATS														
17		BAJA 170 ISLANDER	OP	RNBT	FBG	SV	OB			7	4	1200	2	5	3750	4350
18	1	BAJA 180 ISLANDER	OP	RNBT	FBG	SV	IO	115-180		7	10	2400	2	9	4250	4950
19	11	BAJA 188 ISLANDER	OP	RNBT	FBG	SV	OB			7	10	2800	2	9	7050	8100
19	11	BAJA 188 ISLANDER	OP	RNBT	FBG	SV	IO	160-250		7	10	2800	2	9	5250	6350
20	4	BAJA 204	OP	RNBT	FBG	SV	IO	180	MRCR	7	1	2400	2	9	5350	6150
21	6	BAJA 208 ISLANDER	OP	RNBT	FBG	SV	IO	180-205		8	4	3350	2	9	7650	8850
21	6	BAJA 208 ISLANDER	OP	RNBT	FBG	SV	IO	250-300		8	4	3350	2	9	7950	9750
21	6	BAJA 208 ISLANDER	OP	RNBT	FBG	SV	IO	350	MRCR	8	4	3350	2	9	9450	10800
21	7	CALIBER 22	OP	CUD	FBG	SV	IO	250-300		8	6	3125	2	11	10700	13000
21	7	CALIBER 22	OP	CUD	FBG	SV	IO	350	MRCR	8	6	3125	2	11	12700	14500
21	7	TWILIGHT CALIBER 22	OP	RNBT	FBG	DV	IO	180-250		8	2	3250	2	10	9350	11000
21	7	TWILIGHT CALIBER 22	OP	RNBT	FBG	DV	IO	300	MRCR	8	2	3250	2	10	10300	11700
21	7	TWILIGHT CALIBER 22	OP	RNBT	FBG	DV	IO	350	MRCR	8	2	3250	2	10	11500	13100
23	8	BAJA 236	OP	CUD	FBG	SV	IO	235	MRCR	8	6	3925	2	11	12500	14200

CONTINUED ON NEXT PAGE

```
BAJA MARINE CORP          -CONTINUED    See inside cover to adjust price for area

LOA  NAME AND/            TOP/ BOAT  -HULL-  ----ENGINE---  BEAM   WGT  DRAFT RETAIL RETAIL
FT IN OR MODEL            RIG TYPE   MTL TP TP # HP  MFG   FT IN  LBS  FT IN  LOW   HIGH
-------------------- 1994 BOATS --------------------------------------------------------
23  8 BAJA 236            OP  CUD   FBG SV IO  250  MRCR 8  6  3925  2 11  12600  14300
23  8 BAJA 236            OP  CUD   FBG SV IO 300-350    8  6  3925  2 11  13300  16500
24    BAJA 240 ISLANDER   OP  RNBT  FBG SV IO  235  MRCR 8  4  3800  2 11  10100  11400
   IO 250   MRCR  10200 11500, IO 300-350    10700 13300, IO  385  MRCR 12700  14400

24    BAJA OUTLAW         OP  CUD   FBG SV IO  300  MRCR 8     4000  3  2  14000  16000
   IO 350-385     15300 18800, IO  415  MRCR 18300 20300, IO  445  MRCR 19000  21700

24  4 BAJA BANDIT II      OP  CUD   FBG SV IO  300  MRCR 8     3500  2  9  12200  13800
   IO 350  MRCR  13300 15100, IO  385  MRCR 14500 16400, IO  415  MRCR 15600  17700
   IO 465  MRCR  18100 20100

26    BAJA 260            OP  CUD   FBG SV IO  250  MRCR 8  6  4500  2 11  14800  16800
26    BAJA 260            OP  CUD   FBG SV IO  300  MRCR 8  6  4500  2 11  15600  17700
26    BAJA 260            OP  CUD   FBG SV IO 385-415    8  6  4500  2 11  18000  21100
27  2 BAJA 272            OP  OFF   FBG DV IO 300-385    8  4  4350  3  2  18500  22600
27  2 BAJA 272            OP  OFF   FBG DV IO 415-445    8  4  4350  3  2  21300  24700
27  2 BAJA 272 ISLANDER   OP  RNBT  FBG DV IO 300-350    8  4  4400  3  2  17300  20900
27  2 BAJA 272 ISLANDER   OP  RNBT  FBG DV IO 385-415    8  4  4400  3  2  19500  22700
27  2 BAJA SHOOTER        OP  OFF   FBG DV IO 300-350    8  4  4250  3  2  16700  20100
27  2 BAJA SHOOTER        OP  OFF   FBG DV IO 385-445    8  4  4250  3  2  19000  22900
28    SPORTSFISHERMAN 280 OP  SF    FBG SV OB            8  4  4050  2 10  20800  23100
29    BAJA 290            OP  OFF   FBG DV IO T300-T385  9     6410  3  2  24400  30000

29    BAJA YACHT 290      OP  SPTCR FBG SV IO T180-T235  10    9000  3  2  25900  30000
29    BAJA YACHT 290      OP  SPTCR FBG SV IO T250  MRCR 10    9000  3  2  27400  30400
31 10 BAJA 320            OP  OFF   FBG DV IO T300  MRCR 8  4  7300  3  4  34400  38200
   IO T385   MRCR  36400 40500, IO T415   MRCR 37200 41300, IO T445  MRCR 37900  42100

32  1 BAJA 32 CALIBER     OP  OFF   FBG DV IO T300-T445  8  4  7000  3  4  30300  37100
34  3 BAJA YACHT 340      OP  SPTCR FBG SV IO T300  MRCR 12   12000  3  6  44100  49000
   IO T350   MRCR  46300 50800, IO T385   MRCR 47600 52300, IO T410  MRCR 50600  53300

37  7 BAJA 38 SPECIAL     OP  OFF   FBG DV IO T350  MRCR 9  3  9100  3  4  46200  50800
   IO T385   MRCR  48200 52900, IO T415   MRCR 50400 55300, IO T445  MRCR 52800  58000
   IO T490   MRCR  56600 62100

42  6 BAJA 420            OP  OFF   FBG DV IO R350  MRCR 9  3 12250  3 10  59600  65500
   IO R385   MRCR  63600 69900, IO R415   MRCR 67400 74100, IO R445  MRCR 71500  78600
   IO R490   MRCR  77700 85400
-------------------- 1993 BOATS --------------------------------------------------------
17    BAJA 170 ISLANDER   OP  RNBT  FBG SV OB            7  4  1200  2  5   3550   4150
18  1 BAJA 180 ISLANDER   OP  RNBT  FBG SV IO 115-180    7 10  2400  2  9   3950   4650
18  7 BAJA 186            OP  RNBT  FBG SV OB            7  5  1400  2  5   4200   4850
19 11 BAJA 188 ISLANDER   OP  RNBT  FBG SV OB            7 10  2800  2  9   6700   7750
19 11 BAJA 188 ISLANDER   OP  RNBT  FBG SV IO 160-235    7 10  2800  2  9   4900   5850
20  3 SPORTSFISHERMAN 203 OP  SF    FBG SV OB            7  4  1500       4900   5650
20  4 BAJA 204            OP  RNBT  FBG SV IO 115-180    7  1  2400  2  9   4950   5750
20  4 BAJA 204 ISLANDER   OP  RNBT  FBG SV IO 115-180    7  1  2500  2  9   6400   7450
21  6 BAJA 208 ISLANDER   OP  RNBT  FBG SV IO 180-205    8  4  3350  2  9   7150   8300
   IO 250   MRCR   7400  8550, IO  300  MRCR  7900  9100, IO  350  MRCR  8900  10100

21  7 BAJA CALIBER        OP  CUD   FBG SV IO 250-300    8  6  3925  2 11   9750  11700
21  7 BAJA CALIBER        OP  CUD   FBG SV IO  350  MRCR 8  6  3925  2 11  11400  12900
23  8 BAJA 236            OP  CUD   FBG SV IO 230-300    8  6  3925  2 11  11600  14100
23  8 BAJA 236            OP  CUD   FBG SV IO 350-390    8  6  3925  2 11  13500  16900
24    BAJA 240            OP  CUD   FBG SV IO 235-300    8  4  3700  2 11  10800  13000
24    BAJA 240            OP  CUD   FBG SV IO 350-390    8  4  3700  2 11  12600  15700
24    BAJA 240            OP  CUD   FBG SV IO  415  MRCR 8  4  3700  2 11  14700  16800
24    BAJA 240 ISLANDER   OP  RNBT  FBG SV IO 235-300    8  4  3800  2 11   9400  11400
24    BAJA 240 ISLANDER   OP  RNBT  FBG SV IO 350-390    8  4  3800  2 11  10900  13600
24    BAJA 240 ISLANDER   OP  RNBT  FBG SV IO  415  MRCR 8  4  3800  2 11  12800  14500
24    BAJA OUTLAW         OP  CUD   FBG SV IO 300-350    8     4000  3  2  13100  16200
   IO 390   MRCR  15700 17800, IO  445  MRCR 18400 20500, IO  465  MRCR 19100  21300

24  4 BAJA BANDIT II      OP  CUD   FBG SV IO  300  MRCR 8     3500  2  9  11400  12900
   IO 350   MRCR  12500 14200, IO  390  MRCR 13700 15500, IO 390-445    11600  17900

26    BAJA 260            OP  CUD   FBG SV IO 230-300    8  6  4500  2 11  13600  16500
26    BAJA 260            OP  CUD   FBG SV IO 350-390    8  6  4500  2 11  15600  18900
26    BAJA 260            OP  CUD   FBG SV IO  415  MRCR 8  6  4500  2 11  17400  19700
27  2 BAJA 272            OP  OFF   FBG DV IO 300-350    8  4  4350  3  2  16900  20400
27  2 BAJA 272            OP  OFF   FBG DV IO 390-445    8  4  4350  3  2  19200  23100
27  2 BAJA SHOOTER        OP  OFF   FBG DV IO 300-350    8  4  4250  3  2  15600  18800
27  2 BAJA SHOOTER        OP  OFF   FBG DV IO 390-445    8  4  4250  3  2  17500  21400
28    SPORTSFISHERMAN 280 OP  SF    FBG SV OB            8  4  4050  2 10  19900  22200
29    BAJA 290            OP  OFF   FBG DV IO T230-T300  9     6410  3  2  21300  25300
29    BAJA 290            OP  OFF   FBG DV IO T350-T390  9     6410  3  2  24100  28200
29    BAJA 290            OP  OFF   FBG DV IO T415  MRCR 9     6410  3  2  26300  29200

29    BAJA YACHT 290      OP  SPTCR FBG SV IO T180-T235  10    9000  3  2  24200  28100
29    BAJA YACHT 290      OP  SPTCR FBG SV IO T250  MRCR 10    9000  3  2  25600  28400
29    BAJA YACHT 290      OP  SPTCR FBG SV IOT140D-T200D 10    9000  3  3  29900  35900
31 10 BAJA 320            OP  OFF   FBG DV IO  465  MRCR 8  4  7300  3  4  30800  34200
31 10 BAJA 320            OP  OFF   FBG DV IO T240-T390  8  4  7300  3  4  30800  37900
31 10 BAJA 320            OP  OFF   FBG DV IO T415  MRCR 8  4  7300  3  4  34700  38600
32  1 BAJA MAGNUM         OP  OFF   FBG DV IO T300-T465  8  4  7000  3  4  29600  36800
34  3 BAJA YACHT 340      OP  SPTCR FBG SV VD T250  MRCR 12   12000  3  6  61400  67400
   IO T300   MRCR  41200 45800, VD T310   MRCR 63100 69300, IO T350  MRCR 42800  47500
   IO T390   MRCR  44200 49100, IO T170D MRCR 42400 47100, VD T200D MRCR 69300  76200

37  7 BAJA 38 SPECIAL     OP  OFF   FBG DV IO T300  MRCR 9  3  9100  3  4  40700  45200
   IO T350   MRCR  42700 47500, IO T390   MRCR 45600 50100, IO T415  MRCR 47300  52000
   IO T445   MRCR  49300 54200, IO T465   MRCR 50900 55900, IO T490  MRCR 52900  58100

42  6 BAJA 420            OP  OFF   FBG DV IO R350  MRCR 9  3 12250  3 10  55700  61200
   IO R390   MRCR  60000 65900, IO R415   MRCR 63000 69200, IO R445  MRCR 66800  73400
   IO R465   MRCR  69400 76300, IO R490   MRCR 72600 79800

45    BAJA YACHT 430      FB  SDN   FBG SV IB T GM   14   19250  3  6    **      **
45    BAJA YACHT 430      FB  SDN   FBG SV IB T375D CAT 14   12000  3  6  97900 107500
45    BAJA YACHT 430      FB  SDN   FBG SV IB T425D CAT 14   19250  3  6 135000 148000
-------------------- 1992 BOATS --------------------------------------------------------
18  1 BAJA 180 ISLANDER   RNBT   FBG SV IO 115-180    7 10  2400       3700   4550
18  6 BAJA 186            RNBT   FBG SV OB            7  1  1200       3550   4100
18  7 SPORTFISHERMAN 186  FSH    FBG SV OB            7  5  1400       3950   4600
18 11 ISLANDER 188        RNBT   FBG SV OB            7 10  2950       5850   6700
18 11 ISLANDER 188        RNBT   FBG SV IO        MRCR 7 10  2950         **     **
   IO    VLVO     **       **, IO 120-230     4900  5750, IO  275  VLVO  5400   6200

20  3 SPORTSFISHERMAN 203 SF     FBG SV OB            7  4  1500       4700   5400
20  4 BAJA 204            RNBT   FBG SV IO 115-235    7  1  2700       4750   5800
20  4 ISLANDER 204        RNBT   FBG SV IO 110-180    7  1  2500       5000   5800
21    ISLANDER 208        RNBT   FBG SV IO 175-245    7  4  3350       6600   8150
21    ISLANDER 208        RNBT   FBG SV IO  300       8  4  3350       7300   8800
21    ISLANDER 208        RNBT   FBG SV IO 250-330    7  9  3350       8150   9350
22  2 SKIER 200           SKI    FBG   IB 230-330    7  9  3300       10700  12600
23  8 BAJA 236            WKNDR  FBG SV IO 230-300    8  6  3800  2 11  10600  12900
23  8 BAJA 236            WKNDR  FBG SV IO 350-390    8  6  3800  2 11  12400  15500
24    BAJA 240            CUD    FBG SV IO 230-245    8  4  3850       10400  12200
24    BAJA 240            CUD    FBG SV IO  390  MRCR 8  4  3850       13200  15000

24    BAJA OUTLAW         RNBT   FBG SV IO 300-350    8     4000  3  2  11500  14300
24    BAJA OUTLAW         RNBT   FBG SV IO  390  MRCR 8     4000  3  2  13700  15600
24    BAJA OUTLAW         RNBT   FBG SV IO  465  MRCR 8     4000  3  2  16600  18900
24    ISLANDER 240        RNBT   FBG SV IO 225-300    8  4  3950       8600  10600
24  4 BANDIT              RNBT   FBG SV IO 225-300    8     3600       10200  12600
24  4 BANDIT              RNBT   FBG SV IO  390  MRCR 8     3600       12400  14000
26    BAJA 260            CUD    FBG SV IO 230-300    8  6  4600       12900  16000
26    BAJA 260            CUD    FBG SV IO 350-390    8  6  4600       14700  17800
26    BAJA 260            CUD    FBG SV IO  465  MRCR 8  6  4600       18300  20300
26 11 BAJA 270            RNBT   FBG SV IO 230-300    8     4350       13200  16400
26 11 BAJA 270            RNBT   FBG SV IO 350-390    8     4350       15100  18200

26 11 BAJA 270            RNBT   FBG SV IO  465  MRCR 8     4350       18400  20500
28    SPORTSFISHERMAN 280 SF     FBG SV OB            8  4  4050       19200  21300
29    BAJA 290            OFF    FBG SV IO T230-T300  9     6410       20000  24000
29    BAJA 290            OFF    FBG SV IO T350-T390  9     6410       22600  26400
29    MOTOR YACHT 290     MY     FBG SV IO T240  MRCR 10        3  2  29500  32700
31 10 BAJA 320            SPTCR  FBG SV IO T240-T390  8  4  7300       25300  34100
32  1 BAJA MAGNUM         SPTCR  FBG SV IO T300-T465  8  4  7500       26500  32900
34  3 MOTOR YACHT 340     MY     FBG SV IO T235 CRUS 12   12000       49700  54600
   IO T300   MRCR  46500 51400, VD T350   MRCR 65300 71700, IO T390  MRCR 49700  54600
   IO T170D  MRCR  53100 58300, IO T200D VLVO 54300 59600, VD T200D MRCR 70300  79200

37  5 BAJA 370            SPTCR  FBG SV IO T300  MRCR 9  3  9100       42600  47400
37  5 BAJA 370            SPTCR  FBG SV IO T350  MRCR 9  3  9100       44800  49800
37  5 BAJA 370            SPTCR  FBG SV IO T390  MRCR 9  3  9100       47700  52400
37  7 BAJA 38 SPECIAL     SPTCR  FBG SV IO T300  MRCR 9  3  9100       38700  42900
   IO T350   MRCR  40600 45100, IO T390   MRCR 42800 47500, IO T465  MRCR 48300  53000

42  6 BAJA 420            SPTCR  FBG SV IO T300  MRCR 9  3 12250  3 10  62600  68800
   IO T390   MRCR  66200 72800, IO T465   MRCR 74000 81300, IO R350  MRCR 61600  71200
   IO R390   MRCR  69300 76200, IO R445   MRCR 76900 84500

50                        CONTINUED ON NEXT PAGE              96th ed. - Vol. II
```

LOA FT	LOA IN	NAME AND/ OR MODEL	TOP/ RIG	BOAT TYPE	HULL MTL	HULL TP	ENGINE TP	ENGINE # HP	ENGINE MFG	BEAM FT	BEAM IN	WGT LBS	DRAFT FT	DRAFT IN	RETAIL LOW	RETAIL HIGH
		1992 BOATS														
45		MOTOR YACHT 430		MY	FBG	SV	IB	T306D	VLVO	14		19250			107000	117500
45		MOTOR YACHT 430		MY	FBG	SV	IB	T375D	CAT	14		12000			110000	121000
45		MOTOR YACHT 430		MY	FBG	SV	IB	T425D	CAT	14		19250			124000	136500
		1991 BOATS														
18	7	SPORTFISHERMAN 186		FSH	FBG	SV	OB			7	5	1400	2	5	3800	4400
19	1	ISLANDER 188		RNBT	FBG	SV	OB			7	10		2	9	4200	4900
19	1	ISLANDER 188		RNBT	FBG	SV	IO		VLVO	7	10		2	9	**	**
		IO YAMA ** **, IO 120-240 4650 5400, IO 275 VLVO 5100 5850														
20	3	SPORTSFISHERMAN 203		SF	FBG	SV	OB			7	4	1500	2	5	4500	5150
20	4	BAJA 204		RNBT	FBG	SV	IO		VLVO	7	1	2500	2	9	**	**
20	4	BAJA 204		RNBT	FBG	SV	IO	115-205		7	1	2500	2	9	4500	5450
20	4	ISLANDER 204		RNBT	FBG	SV	IO	115-205		7	1	2700	2	9	4500	5500
21		ISLANDER 208		RNBT	FBG	SV	IO	175-260		8	4	3350	2	9	6200	7450
21		ISLANDER 208		RNBT	FBG	SV	IO	275-300		8	4	3350	2	9	6900	7900
21		ISLANDER 208		RNBT	FBG	SV	IO	330-360		8	4	3350	2	9	7700	9000
22	2	BAJA 225		RNBT	FBG	SV	IO	155-260		8		3400	2	11	7200	8750
22	2	BAJA 225		RNBT	FBG	SV	IO	275	VLVO	8		3400	2	11	7950	9100
22	2	ISLANDER 225		RNBT	FBG	SV	IO	155-260		8		3400	2	11	6400	7850
22	2	ISLANDER 225		RNBT	FBG	SV	IO	275	VLVO	8		3400	2	11	7150	8250
22	2	SKIER 200		SKI	FBG		IB	250-330		7	9	3300	2	1	10100	12000
24		BAJA 240		CUD	FBG	SV	IO		YAMA	8	4	3850	2	11	**	**
		IO 230-300 9700 11800, IO 330-360 11400 13100, IO 410 MRCR 13000 14800														
24		ISLANDER 240		RNBT	FBG	SV	IO	229-300		8	4	3950	2	11	8050	9650
24		ISLANDER 240		RNBT	FBG	SV	IO	330-360		8	4	3950	2	11	9300	10700
24		ISLANDER 240		RNBT	FBG	SV	IO	410	MRCR	8	4	3950	2	11	10600	12000
24	4	BANDIT 223		RNBT	FBG	SV	IO	230-300		8		3600	2	9	8650	10700
24	4	BANDIT 223		RNBT	FBG	SV	IO	330-360		8		3600	2	9	10300	11900
24	4	BANDIT 223		RNBT	FBG	SV	IO	410	MRCR	8		3600	2	9	11800	13400
26		BAJA 260		CUD	FBG	SV	IO	230-300		8	6	4600	2	11	12100	14700
26		BAJA 260		CUD	FBG	SV	IO	330-360		8	6	4600	2	11	13700	15900
26		BAJA 260		CUD	FBG	SV	IO	410-445		8	6	4600	2	11	15200	18400
26	9	BAJA 270		RNBT	FBG	SV	IO	230-300		8		4350	3	2	12200	14900
26	9	BAJA 270		RNBT	FBG	SV	IO	330-360		8		4350	3	2	13900	16100
26	9	BAJA 270		RNBT	FBG	SV	IO	410-454		8		4350	3	2	15300	18700
28		SPORTSFISHERMAN 280		SF	FBG	SV	OB			8	4	4050	2	10	18500	20500
29		BAJA 290		OFF	FBG	DV	IO	T230-T330		9		6410	3	2	19000	23300
29		BAJA 290		OFF	FBG	DV	IO	T360-T445		9		6410	3	2	21500	26800
29		MOTOR YACHT 290		MY	FBG	SV	IO	T		10			3	2	**	**
30		BAJA 300		RNBT	FBG	SV	IO	T240-T330		8	4	6750	3	2	16200	20200
30		BAJA 300		RNBT	FBG	SV	IO	T360	MRCR	8	4	6750	3	2	18600	20700
31	10	BAJA 320		SPTCR	FBG	SV	IO	T240-T360		8	4	7300	3	4	25600	31300
31	10	BAJA 320		SPTCR	FBG	SV	IO	T410	MRCR	8	4	7300	3	4	29200	32500
34	3	MOTOR YACHT 340		MY	FBG	SV	IO	T300-T360		12		12000	3	4	43100	50300
36	8	MOTOR YACHT 340		MY	FBG	SV	VD	T230	MRCR	12		12000	3	4	55100	60500
		VD T235 CRUS 55600 61000, IO T275 VLVO 36100 40100, VD T300 CRUS 56800 62400														
		VD T300 MRCR 56300 61900, IO T330 VLVO 38100 42300, IO T410 MRCR 41200 45800														
		IO T200D VLVO 39200 43600														
37	4	BAJA 320		SPTCR	FBG	SV	IO	T300	MRCR	9	3	7300	3	4	33000	36600
37	4	BAJA 320		SPTCR	FBG	SV	IO	T360	MRCR	9	3	7300	3	4	35200	39100
37	4	BAJA 320		SPTCR	FBG	SV	IO	T410	MRCR	9	3	9100	3	4	40700	45200
42	6	BAJA 420		SPTCR	FBG	SV	IO	T360	MRCR	9	3	12250	3	10	59800	65700
		IO T410 MRCR 64300 70700, IO T445 MRCR 67700 74400, IO R360 MRCR 62200 68300														
		IO R410 MRCR 67900 74600, IO R445 MRCR 72600 79800														
48		MOTOR YACHT 430		MY	FBG	SV	IB	T D	CAT	14		19250	3	4	**	**
		IB T D CAT ** **, IB T306D VLVO 121500 133500, IB T400D GM 131000 144000														
		1990 BOATS														
16	8	SVF 170	OP	FSH	FBG	SV	OB			7	1	1000			2600	3050
17	4	SVR 174	OP	RNBT	FBG	SV	OB			7	2	1100			2950	3400
17	4	SVR 174	OP	RNBT	FBG	SV	IO	130-205		7	2	1700			2850	3400
18	6	ESS 186	OP	RNBT	FBG	SV	OB			7	1	1200			3100	3600
18	6	FS 186	OP	RNBT	FBG	SV	OB								3950	4600
18	6	SVR 186	OP	RNBT	FBG	SV	OB			7	1	1200			3400	4000
18	6	SVR 186	OP	RNBT	FBG	SV	IO	130-205		7	1	2175			3400	4000
18	7	DSR 190	OP	RNBT	FBG	SV	IO	130-205		7	1	2200			3400	4050
18	7	ES 190	OP	RNBT	FBG	SV	IO	130-205		7	1	2200			3400	4050
19		SK 190	OP	SKI	FBG	SV	IB	250	MRCR	7	1	2500			4900	5600
19	6	ESS 196	OP	RNBT	FBG	SV	OB			7	3	1300			3600	4150
19	6	ESS 196	OP	RNBT	FBG	SV	IO	205-270		7	3	2300			3800	4750
19	6	SVR 196	OP	RNBT	FBG	SV	OB			7	3	1200			3350	3900
19	6	SVR 196	OP	RNBT	FBG	SV	IO	205-270		7	3	2300			3800	4750
20	3	FS 200	OP	FSH	FBG	SV	OB			7	4	1350			3950	4550
20	6	DSR 216	OP	RNBT	FBG	SV	IO	205-270		8		2916			6350	7700
20	6	DVX 216	OP	CUD	FBG	SV	IO	205-270		8		2916			6650	8050
20	10	ES 210	OP	RNBT	FBG	SV	OB			7	3	1400			4150	4850
20	10	ES 210	OP	RNBT	FBG	SV	IO	205-270		7	3	2400			5550	6800
20	10	SVR 210	OP	RNBT	FBG	SV	OB			7	3	1400			4100	4800
20	10	SVR 210	OP	RNBT	FBG	SV	IO	205-270		7	3	2400			5450	6700
22	6	DSR 226	OP	RNBT	FBG	SV	IO	260-270		8	2	3500			7800	9050
22	6	ES 226	OP	RNBT	FBG	SV	IO	260-330		8	2	3500			8550	10400
22	6	ES 226	OP	RNBT	FBG	SV	IO	365	MRCR	8	2	3500			9900	11200
23	6	DVX 235	OP	CUD	FBG	SV	IO	260-330		8		3650			9400	11700
23	6	DVX 235	OP	CUD	FBG	SV	IO	365	MRCR	8		3650			11100	12600
24		ES 240	OP	CUD	FBG	SV	IO	260-330		8		4000			10200	12700
24		ES 240	OP	CUD	FBG	SV	IO	365	MRCR	8		4000			12000	13600
25		ES 250	OP	RNBT	FBG	SV	IO	260-330		8		4000			10100	12600
25		ES 250	OP	RNBT	FBG	SV	IO	365	MRCR	8		4000			11800	13400
26	6	DVX 265	OP	CUD	FBG	SV	IO	260-330		8		4650			13300	16300
26	6	DVX 265	OP	CUD	FBG	SV	IO	365	MRCR	8		4650			15100	17100
28		ES 280	OP	RNBT	FBG	SV	IO	T260-T330		8	4	6750			15500	19200
28		ES 280	OP	RNBT	FBG	SV	IO	T365	MRCR	8	4	6750			18100	20200
28		SF 280	OP	SF	FBG	SV	OB			8	4	2750			17400	19700
30		ES 300	OP	SPTCR	FBG	SV	IO	T330-T365		8	4	7000			24000	27700
32	1	DVX 320	OP	SPTCR	FBG	SV	IO	T330-T420		8	4	7500			29800	35300
35		ES 370	OP	SPTCR	FBG	SV	IO	T365	MRCR	9		10000			46300	50800
35		ES 370	OP	SPTCR	FBG	SV	IO	T420	MRCR	9		10000			48600	53400
35		ES 370	OP	SPTCR	FBG	SV	IO	T575	MRCR	9		10000			56700	62300
40		ES 420	OP	SPTCR	FBG	SV	IO	T365	MRCR	9	2	12000			53600	58900
40		ES 420	OP	SPTCR	FBG	SV	IO	T420	MRCR	9	2	12000			57400	63100
40		ES 420	OP	SPTCR	FBG	SV	IO	R365	MRCR	9	2	12000			57300	62900
		1989 BOATS														
16	8	ANGLER 170	OP	FSH	FBG	SV	OB			7	1	1000			2500	2950
17	4	SUNSPORT 174	OP	RNBT	FBG	SV	OB			7	2	1100			2800	3300
17	4	SUNSPORT 174	OP	RNBT	FBG	SV	IO	130-205		7	2	1700			2700	3200
18	6	FISH-N-SKI 186	OP	RNBT	FBG	SV	OB								3800	4400
18	6	SPORT 186	OP	RNBT	FBG	SV	OB			7	1	1200			2950	3450
18	6	SUNSPORT 186	OP	RNBT	FBG	SV	OB			7	1	1200			3300	3850
18	6	SUNSPORT 186	OP	RNBT	FBG	SV	IO	130-205		7	1	2175			3200	3800
18	7	ISLANDER 190	OP	RNBT	FBG	SV	IO	130-205		7	1	2200			3200	3850
18	7	SPORT 190	OP	RNBT	FBG	SV	IO	130-205		7	1	2200			3200	3850
19		SKI SPORT 190	OP	SKI	FBG	SV	IB	250	MRCR	7	1	2500			4650	5350
19	6	SPORT 196	OP	RNBT	FBG	SV	OB			7	3	1300			3450	4000
19	6	SPORT 196	OP	RNBT	FBG	SV	IO	205-260		7	3	2300			3600	4400
19	6	SPORT 196	OP	RNBT	FBG	SV	IO	270	MRCR	7	3	2300			3850	4500
19	6	SUNSPORT 196	OP	RNBT	FBG	SV	OB			7	3	1200			3250	3750
19	6	SUNSPORT 196	OP	RNBT	FBG	SV	IO	205-260		7	3	2300			3550	4400
19	6	SUNSPORT 196	OP	RNBT	FBG	SV	IO	270	MRCR	7	3	2300			3850	4450
20	3	FISH-N-SKI 200	OP	FSH	FBG	SV	OB			7	4	1350			3750	4400
20	6	FORCE 216	OP	CUD	FBG	SV	IO	205-270		8		2916			6250	7600
20	6	ISLANDER 216	OP	RNBT	FBG	SV	IO	205-270		8		2916			6000	7250
20	10	SPORT 210	OP	RNBT	FBG	SV	OB			7	3	1400			4000	4650
20	10	SPORT 210	OP	RNBT	FBG	SV	IO	205-270		7	3	2400			5250	6450
20	10	SUNSPORT 210	OP	RNBT	FBG	SV	OB			7	3	1400			3950	4600
20	10	SUNSPORT 210	OP	RNBT	FBG	SV	IO	205-270		7	3	2400			5150	6350
22	6	ISLANDER 226	OP	RNBT	FBG	SV	IO	260-270		8	2	3500			7350	8550
22	6	SPORT 226	OP	RNBT	FBG	SV	IO	260-330		8	2	3500			8050	9850
22	6	SPORT 226	OP	RNBT	FBG	SV	IO	365	MRCR	8	2	3500			9400	10700
23	6	FORCE 235	OP	CUD	FBG	SV	IO	260-330		8		3650			8850	11000
23	6	FORCE 235	OP	CUD	FBG	SV	IO	365	MRCR	8		3650			10500	11900
24		SPORT 240	OP	CUD	FBG	SV	IO	260-330		8		4000			9650	12000
24		SPORT 240	OP	CUD	FBG	SV	IO	365	MRCR	8		4000			11300	12900
25		SPORT 250	OP	RNBT	FBG	SV	IO	260-330		8		4000			9550	11900
25		SPORT 250	OP	RNBT	FBG	SV	IO	365	MRCR	8		4000			11100	12600
26	6	FORCE 265	OP	CUD	FBG	SV	IO	260-330		8		4650			12500	15400
26	6	FORCE 265	OP	CUD	FBG	SV	IO	365	MRCR	8		4650			14200	16100
28		SPORT 280	OP	RNBT	FBG	SV	IO	T260-T330		8	4	6750			14700	18100
28		SPORT 280	OP	RNBT	FBG	SV	IO	T365	MRCR	8	4	6750			16700	19000
28		SPORT FISHER 280	OP	SF	FBG	DV	OB			8	4	2750			16700	19000
32	1	FORCE 320	OP	SPTCR	FBG	SV	IO	T330-T365		8	4	7500			28700	33200
32	1	FORCE 320	OP	SPTCR	FBG	SV	IO	T420	MRCR	8	4	7500			33200	36900
35		FORCE 370	OP	SPTCR	FBG	SV	IO	T365	MRCR	9		10000			43200	48000
35		FORCE 370	OP	SPTCR	FBG	SV	IO	T420	MRCR	9		10000			46100	50700
35		FORCE 370	OP	SPTCR	FBG	SV	IO	T575	MRCR	9		10000			53900	59200

CONTINUED ON NEXT PAGE

LOA FT	LOA IN	NAME AND/ OR MODEL	TOP/ RIG	BOAT TYPE	-HULL- MTL	-HULL- TP	ENGINE TP	ENGINE # HP	ENGINE MFG	BEAM FT	BEAM IN	WGT LBS	DRAFT FT	DRAFT IN	RETAIL LOW	RETAIL HIGH
		1988 BOATS														
16	2	SPORT 164	OP	SKI	FBG	SV	OB			6	10	830			2000	2350
16	2	SUNSPORT 164	OP	RNBT	FBG	SV	OB			6	10	850			2050	2450
16	8	ANGLER 170	OP	FSH	FBG	SV	OB			7	1	1000			2450	2800
16	8	SPORT 170	OP	SKI	FBG	SV	OB			7	1	1000			2450	2850
17	4	SUNSPORT 174	OP	RNBT	FBG	SV	OB			7	2	1100			2700	3150
17	4	SUNSPORT 174	OP	RNBT	FBG	SV	IO	130-205		7	2	1700			2550	3050
17	6	ISLANDER 180	OP	RNBT	FBG	SV	IO	130-205		7	6	2000			2850	3400
18	6	FISH-N-SKI 186	OP	RNBT	FBG	SV	OB								3650	4250
18	6	SUNSPORT 186	OP	RNBT	FBG	SV	OB			7	1	1200			3000	3500
18	6	SUNSPORT 186	OP	RNBT	FBG	SV	IO	130-205		7	1	2175			3000	3600
19		SKI SPORT 190	OP	SKI	FBG	SV	IB	250		7	1	2500			4450	5100
19	6	SPORT 196	OP	RNBT	FBG	SV	OB			7	3	1300			3300	3850
19	6	SPORT 196	OP	RNBT	FBG	SV	IO	205	MRCR	7	3	2300			3400	3950
19	6	SPORT 196	OP	RNBT	FBG	SV	IO	260-270		7	3	2300			3700	4350
19	6	SUNSPORT 196	OP	RNBT	FBG	SV	OB			7	3	1200			3100	3600
19	6	SUNSPORT 196	OP	RNBT	FBG	SV	IO	205-270		7	3	2300			3350	4100
20	3	FISH-N-SKI 200	OP	FSH	FBG	SV	OB			7	4	1350			3650	4200
20	6	FORCE 216	OP	RNBT	FBG	SV	IO	205-270		6	8	2916			5200	6350
20	6	ISLANDER 216	OP	RNBT	FBG	SV	IO	205-270		8		2916			5650	6900
20	10	SPORT 210	OP	RNBT	FBG	SV	OB			7	3	1400			3850	4450
20	10	SPORT 210	OP	RNBT	FBG	SV	IO	205-270		7	3	2400			4950	6100
20	10	SUNSPORT 210	OP	RNBT	FBG	SV	OB			7	3	1400			3850	4450
20	10	SUNSPORT 210	OP	RNBT	FBG	SV	IO	205-270		7	3	2400			4900	6000
22	6	ISLANDER 226	OP	RNBT	FBG	SV	IO	260-270		8	2	3500			6800	7900
22	6	SPORT 226	OP	RNBT	FBG	SV	IO	260-330		8	2	3500			7800	9300
22	6	SPORT 226	OP	RNBT	FBG	SV	IO	365	MRCR	8	2	3500			8900	10100
23	6	FORCE 235	OP	CUD	FBG	SV	OB			8		3150			8100	9350
23	6	FORCE 235	OP	CUD	FBG	SV	IO	260-270		8		3650			8300	9600
23	6	FORCE 235	OP	CUD	FBG	SV	IO	330-365		8		3650			9250	11300
24		SPORT 240	OP	CUD	FBG	SV	IO	260-330		8		4000			9200	11400
24		SPORT 240	OP	CUD	FBG	SV	IO	365	MRCR	8		4000			10700	12200
26	6	FORCE 265	OP	CUD	FBG	SV	OB			8		4150			12000	13600
26	6	FORCE 265	OP	CUD	FBG	SV	IO	260-330		8		4650			11800	14600
26	6	FORCE 265	OP	CUD	FBG	SV	IO	365	MRCR	8		4650			13500	15300
26	6	FORCE 265	OP	CUD	FBG	SV	IO	T205-T270		8		4650			13200	16300
28		FORCE 280	OP	SPTCR	FBG	SV	OB			8	4	6500			16500	18800
28		FORCE 280	OP	SPTCR	FBG	SV	IO	T260-T330		8	4	7000			18200	21600
28		FORCE 280	OP	SPTCR	FBG	SV	IO	T365	MRCR	8	4	7000			20500	22700
28		SPORT FISHER 280	OP	SF	FBG	DV	OB			8	4	2750			16100	18300
32	1	FORCE 320	OP	SPTCR	FBG	DV	OB			8	4	8000			22800	25400
32	1	FORCE 320	OP	SPTCR	FBG	SV	IO	T330-T365		8	4	8500			28100	32700
32	1	FORCE 320	OP	SPTCR	FBG	SV	IO	T420	MRCR	8	4	8500			32700	36300
37		FORCE 370	OP	SPTCR	FBG	SV	IO	T365	MRCR	9	3	10000			35800	39800
37		FORCE 370	OP	SPTCR	FBG	SV	IO	T420	MRCR	9	3	10000			38600	42800
		1987 BOATS														
16	2	SPORT 164	OP	SKI	FBG	SV	OB			6	10	830			1900	2300
16	2	SUNSPORT 164	OP	RNBT	FBG	SV	OB			6	10	850			2000	2400
16	8	ANGLER 170	OP	FSH	FBG	SV	OB			7	1	1000			2350	2750
16	8	SPORT 170	OP	SKI	FBG	SV	OB			7	1	1000			2350	2750
17	4	SUNSPORT 174	OP	RNBT	FBG	SV	IO	130-205		7	2	1700			2400	2900
17	6	ISLANDER 180	OP	RNBT	FBG	SV	IO	130-205		7	6	2000			2700	3200
18	4	FISH-N-SKI 184	OP	RNBT	FBG	SV	OB			7	1	1200			2900	3350
19		SKI SPORT 190	OP	SKI	FBG	SV	IB	250-260		7	1	2500			4200	4900
19	6	FORCE 200		CUD	FBG	DV	IO	205-270		8		2700			3850	4750
19	6	ISLANDER 200	OP	RNBT	FBG	SV	IO	205-270		8		2700			3650	4600
19	6	SPORT 196	OP	RNBT	FBG	SV	OB			7	3	2300			4700	5400
19	6	SPORT 196	OP	RNBT	FBG	SV	IO	205-270		7	3	2300			3200	4000
19	6	SPORT 196	OP	RNBT	FBG	SV	IO	330	MRCR	7	3	2300			4000	4650
19	6	SUNSPORT 196	OP	RNBT	FBG	SV	OB			7	3				4050	4700
19	6	SUNSPORT 196	OP	RNBT	FBG	SV	IO	205-270		7	3	2300			3200	4000
19	6	SUNSPORT 196	OP	RNBT	FBG	SV	IO	330	MRCR	7	3	2300			4000	4650
20	3	FISH-N-SKI 200	OP	FSH	FBG	SV	OB			7	4	1350			3500	4050
20	10	SPORT 210	OP	RNBT	FBG	SV	OB			7	3				5050	5800
20	10	SPORT 210	OP	RNBT	FBG	SV	IO	205-270		7	3	2400			4700	5750
20	10	SPORT 210	OP	RNBT	FBG	SV	IO	330	MRCR	7	3	2400			5700	6550
20	10	SUNSPORT 210	OP	RNBT	FBG	SV	OB			7	3				5050	5800
20	10	SUNSPORT 210	OP	RNBT	FBG	SV	IO	205-270		7	3	2400			4700	5750
20	10	SUNSPORT 210	OP	RNBT	FBG	SV	IO	330	MRCR	7	3	2400			5700	6550
21	7	FORCE 220	OP	CUD	FBG	SV	IO	260-270		8		3400			6850	7950
21	7	FORCE 220	OP	CUD	FBG	SV	IO	330	MRCR	8		3400			7650	8800
21	7	ISLANDER 220		RNBT	FBG	DV	IO	260-270		8		3400			6500	7550
22	6	SPORT 220		RNBT	FBG		OB			8		1875			5000	5750
22	6	SPORT 220		RNBT	FBG		IO	260-270		8		2600			5800	6750
22	6	SPORT 220		RNBT	FBG		IO	330	MRCR	8		2600			6550	7550
23	6	FORCE 235	OP	CUD	FBG	DV	IO	260-270		8		3650			7900	9150
23	6	FORCE 235	OP	CUD	FBG	DV	IO	330	MRCR	8		3650			8800	10000
24		SPORT 240	OP	CUD	FBG	DV	OB			8					9700	11000
24		SPORT 240	OP	CUD	FBG	DV	IO	260-270		8		3200			7400	8600
24		SPORT 240	OP	CUD	FBG	DV	IO	330	MRCR	8		3200			8250	9450
24		SPORT 240	OP	CUD	FBG	DV	IO	T205-T270		8		3200			8200	10200
25		AFT 250	OP	SPTCR	FBG	DV	IO	260		8		4800			10400	11900
25		AFT 250	OP	SPTCR	FBG	DV	IO	T130-T170		8		4800			10900	12700
25		FORCE 250	ST	SPTCR	FBG	DV	IO	260-330		8		4500			10000	12300
25		FORCE 250	ST	SPTCR	FBG	DV	IO	T205	MRCR	8		4500			11000	12500
26	6	FORCE 265	OP	CUD	FBG	DV	IO	260-330		8		4650			11300	13800
26	6	FORCE 265	OP	CUD	FBG	DV	IO	T205-T270		8		4650			12600	15500
28		FORCE 280	OP	SPTCR	FBG	DV	IO	T260-T330		8	4	7000			16900	20800
28		FORCE 280	OP	SPTCR	FBG	DV	IO	T370	MRCR	8	4	7000			19600	21800
28		SPORT FISHER 280	OP	SF	FBG	DV	OB			8	4	2750			15500	17700
32	1	FORCE 320	OP	SPTCR	FBG	DV	IO	T370	MRCR	8	4	7500			26700	29700
32	1	FORCE 320	OP	SPTCR	FBG	SV	IO	T330	MRCR	8	4	7500			25500	28300
32	1	FORCE 320	OP	SPTCR	FBG	SV	IO	T420	MRCR	8	4	7500			29100	32300
		1986 BOATS														
16	2	ANGLER 164	OP	BASS	FBG	SV	OB			6	10	900			2000	2400
16	2	FISH'N-SKI 164	OP	RNBT	FBG	SV	OB			6	10	925			2100	2500
16	2	SPORT 164	OP	SKI	FBG	SV	OB			6	10	830			1850	2200
16	2	SUNSPORT 164	OP	RNBT	FBG	SV	OB			6	10	850			1950	2300
16	8	ANGLER 170	OP	FSH	FBG	SV	OB			7	1	1000			2300	2650
16	8	SPORT 170	OP	SKI	FBG	SV	OB			7	1	1000			2300	2650
17	4	SUNSPORT 174	OP	RNBT	FBG	SV	OB			7	2	1700			3550	4100
17	6	ISLANDER 180	OP	RNBT	FBG	SV	IO	140-190		7	6	2000			2550	3050
18	4	ANGLER 184	OP	BASS	FBG	SV	OB			7	1	1100			2600	3050
18	4	FISH'N-SKI 184	OP	RNBT	FBG	SV	OB			7	1	1200			2800	3250
18	4	SPORT 184	OP	SKI	FBG	SV	OB			7	1	1050			2500	2900
18	4	SPORT 184	OP	SKI	FBG	SV	IO	140-190		7	1	1885			2450	2850
18	4	SPORT 184	OP	SKI	FBG	SV	JT	260-360		7	1	1885			3850	4500
18	4	SUNSPORT 184	OP	RNBT	FBG	SV	OB			7	1	1050			2500	2950
18	4	SUNSPORT 184	OP	RNBT	FBG	SV	IO	140-190		7	1	1885			2550	3000
18	4	SUNSPORT 184	OP	RNBT	FBG	SV	JT	260-360		7	1	1885			4050	4700
19	3	SUNSPORT 190	OP	RNBT	FBG	SV	OB			7	3	1200			2900	3350
19	3	SUNSPORT 190	OP	RNBT	FBG	SV	IO	140-230		7	3	2175			2900	3500
		JT 260 CHEV 4550 5250, IO 260 3150 3650, JT 300-360													4550	5250
19	6	FORCE 200		CUD	FBG	DV	IO	170-260		8		2700			3600	4500
19	6	FORCE 200		CUD	FBG	DV	IO	300		8		2700			4150	4800
19	6	ISLANDER 200	OP	RNBT	FBG	SV	IO	140-260		8		2700			3450	4300
20	3	FISH-N-SKI 200	OP	FSH	FBG	SV	OB			7	4	1350			3400	3950
20	3	SPORT 200	OP	SKI	FBG	SV	OB			7	4	1200			3050	3550
20	3	SPORT 200	OP	SKI	FBG	SV	IO	200-230		7	4	2245			4100	4850
		JT 260 CHEV 6250 7200, IO 260 4400 5050, JT 300-360													6250	7200
20	3	SUNSPORT 200	OP	RNBT	FBG	SV	IO	200-230		7	4	2275			4200	5000
		JT 260 CHEV 6450 7400, IO 260 4500 5200, JT 300-360													6450	7400
21	7	FORCE 220	OP	CUD	FBG	SV	IO	200-260		8		3400			6250	7500
21	7	FORCE 220	OP	CUD	FBG	SV	IO	330	MRCR	8		3400			7300	8400
21	7	FORCE 220	OP	CUD	FBG	SV	IO	T170		8		3400			7150	8200
21	7	ISLANDER 220		RNBT	FBG	DV	IO	200-260		8		3400			5950	7100
21	7	ISLANDER 220		RNBT	FBG	DV	IO	300		8		3400			6550	7500
22	6	SPORT 220		RNBT	FBG	SV	OB			8		1875			4850	5600
22	6	SPORT 220		RNBT	FBG	SV	IO	260-300		8		2600			5550	6750
25		AFT 250	OP	SPTCR	FBG	DV	IO	200-260		8		4800			9600	11300
25		AFT 250	OP	SPTCR	FBG	DV	IO	330	MRCR	8		4800			10800	12300
25		AFT 250	OP	SPTCR	FBG	DV	IO	T170		8		4800			10700	12100
25		FORCE 250	ST	SPTCR	FBG	DV	IO	200-260		8		4500			9200	10800
25		FORCE 250	ST	SPTCR	FBG	DV	IO	330	MRCR	8		4500			10400	11800
25		FORCE 250	ST	SPTCR	FBG	DV	IO	T170		8		4500			10300	11700
28		FORCE 280	OP	SPTCR	FBG	DV	IO	T260-T330		8	4	7000			16100	19900
28		FORCE 280	OP	SPTCR	FBG	DV	IO	T370	MRCR	8	4	7000			18900	21000
32	1	FORCE 320	OP	SPTCR	FBG	DV	IO	T370	MRCR	8	4	7500			25300	28100
32	1	FORCE 320	OP	SPTCR	FBG	SV	IO	T330	MRCR	8	4	7500			24300	27000
		1985 BOATS														
16	1	SUNSPORT 160	OP	RNBT	FBG	SV	OB			6	8	845			1850	2200
16	2	ANGLER 164	OP	BASS	FBG	SV	OB			6	10	900			1950	2350
16	2	FISH'N-SKI 164	OP	RNBT	FBG	SV	OB			6	10	925			2050	2400
16	2	SPORT 160	OP	SKI	FBG	SV	OB			6	8	650			1400	1700
16	2	SPORT 164	OP	SKI	FBG	SV	OB			6	10	830			1800	2150
16	2	SUNSPORT 164	OP	RNBT	FBG	SV	OB			6	10	850			1850	2250

CONTINUED ON NEXT PAGE

LOA FT IN	NAME AND/ OR MODEL	TOP/ RIG	BOAT TYPE	-HULL- MTL TP	----ENGINE--- TP # HP MFG	BEAM FT IN	WGT LBS	DRAFT FT IN	RETAIL LOW	RETAIL HIGH
				1985 BOATS						
16 8	SPORT 170	OP	SKI	FBG SV	OB	7 1	1000		2200	2550
16 8	SUNSPORT 170	OP	RNBT	FBG SV	OB	7 1	1000		2250	2650
16 8	SUNSPORT 170	OP	RNBT	FBG SV	IO 140-190	7 1	1500		1950	2400
17 6	ISLANDER 180	OP	RNBT	FBG SV	IO 140-190	7 6	2000		2450	2900
17 6	ANGLER 184	OP	BASS	FBG SV	OB	7 1	1100		2500	2950
18 4	FISH'N-SKI 184	OP	RNBT	FBG SV	OB	7 1	1200		2700	3150
18 4	SPORT 184	OP	SKI	FBG SV	OB	7 1	1050		2450	2850
18 4	SPORT 184	OP	SKI	FBG SV	IO 140-190	7 1	1885		2350	2750
18 4	SPORT 184	OP	SKI	FBG SV	JT 260-360	7 1	1885		3700	4300
18 4	SUNSPORT 184	OP	RNBT	FBG SV	OB	7 1	1050		2450	2850
18 4	SUNSPORT 184	OP	RNBT	FBG SV	IO 140-190	7 1	1885		2450	2900
18 4	SUNSPORT 184	OP	RNBT	FBG SV	JT 260-360	7 1	1885		3850	4450
19 3	SUNSPORT 190	OP	RNBT	FBG SV	OB	7 3	1200		2800	3250
19 3	SUNSPORT 190	OP	RNBT	FBG SV	IO 140-230	7 3	2175		2750	3350
	JT 260 CHEV 4300	5000, IO	260		3000	3500, JT	300-360		4300	5000
19 6	FORCE 200		CUD	FBG DV	OB	8	2700		4650	5350
19 6	FORCE 200		CUD	FBG DV	IO 170-260	8	2700		3450	4300
19 6	FORCE 200		CUD	FBG DV	IO 300	8	2700		3950	4600
19 6	ISLANDER 200	OP	RNBT	FBG SV	IO 140-260	8	2700		3350	4150
20 3	SPORT 200	OP	SKI	FBG SV	OB	7 4	1200		2950	3450
20 3	SPORT 200	OP	SKI	FBG SV	IO 200-230	7 4	2245		3900	4650
	JT 260 CHEV 5950	6850, IO	260		4150	4850, JT	300-360		5950	6850
20 3	SUNSPORT 200	OP	RNBT	FBG SV	IO 200-230	7 4	1200		3000	3450
20 3	SUNSPORT 200	OP	RNBT	FBG SV	IO 200-230	7 4	2275		4050	4800
	JT 260 CHEV 6150	7050, IO	260		4300	5000, JT	300-360		6150	7050
21 7	FORCE 220	OP	CUD	FBG SV	IO 200-260	8	3400		6000	7200
21 7	FORCE 220	OP	CUD	FBG SV	IO 330 MRCR	8	3400		7000	8050
21 7	FORCE 220	OP	CUD	FBG SV	IO T170	8	3400		6850	7850
21 7	ISLANDER 220		RNBT	FBG DV	OB	8	3400		6650	7650
21 7	ISLANDER 220		RNBT	FBG DV	IO 200-260	8	3400		5700	6600
21 7	ISLANDER 220		RNBT	FBG DV	IO 300	8	3400		6250	7200
22 6	SPORT 220		RNBT	FBG	OB	8	1875		4700	5400
22 6	SPORT 220		RNBT	FBG	IO 260-300	8	1875		4750	5850
25	FORCE 250	ST	SPTCR	FBG DV	IO 200-260	8	4500		8850	10500
25	FORCE 250	ST	SPTCR	FBG DV	IO 330 MRCR	8	4500		9950	11300
25	FORCE 250	ST	SPTCR	FBG DV	IO T170	8	4500		9850	11200
28	FORCE 280	OP	SPTCR	FBG DV	IO T260-T330	8 4	7000		15500	19100
28	FORCE 280	OP	SPTCR	FBG DV	IO T370 MRCR	8 4	7000		18200	20200
32 1	FORCE 320	OP	SPTCR	FBG DV	IO T370 MRCR	8 4	7500		24100	26800
32 1	FORCE 320	OP	SPTCR	FBG SV	IO T330 MRCR	8 4	7500		23200	25800
				1984 BOATS						
16 1	SUNSPORT 160	OP	RNBT	FBG SV	OB	6 8	845		1800	2150
16 2	ANGLER 164	OP	BASS	FBG SV	OB	6 10	900		1900	2250
16 2	FISH'N SKI 164	OP	RNBT	FBG SV	OB	6 10	925		1950	2350
16 2	SPORT 160	OP	SKI	FBG SV	OB	6 8	650		1400	1650
16 2	SPORT 164	OP	SKI	FBG SV	OB	6 10	830		1750	2100
16 2	SUNSPORT 164	OP	RNBT	FBG SV	OB	6 10	850		1800	2150
16 8	SPORT 170	OP	SKI	FBG SV	OB	7 1	1000		2150	2500
16 8	SUNSPORT 170	OP	RNBT	FBG SV	OB	7 1	1000		2200	2550
16 8	SUNSPORT 170	OP	RNBT	FBG SV	IO 140-188	7 1	1500		1900	2300
17 6	ISLANDER 180	OP	RNBT	FBG SV	IO 140-188	7 6	2000		2400	2800
18 4	ANGLER 184	OP	BASS	FBG SV	OB	7 1	1100		2450	2850
18 4	FISH'N SKI 184	OP	RNBT	FBG SV	OB	7 1	1200		2650	3050
18 4	SPORT 184	OP	SKI	FBG SV	OB	7 1	1050		2350	2750
18 4	SPORT 184	OP	SKI	FBG SV	IO 140-188	7 1	1885		2300	2700
18 4	SPORT 184	OP	SKI	FBG SV	JT 260-360	7 1	1885		3550	4100
18 4	SUNSPORT 184	OP	RNBT	FBG SV	OB	7 1	1050		2400	2800
18 4	SUNSPORT 184	OP	RNBT	FBG SV	IO 140-188	7 1	1885		2350	2800
18 4	SUNSPORT 184	OP	RNBT	FBG SV	JT 260-360	7 1	1885		3650	4250
19 3	SUNSPORT 190	OP	RNBT	FBG SV	OB	7 3	1200		2700	3150
19 3	SUNSPORT 190	OP	RNBT	FBG SV	IO 140-230	7 3	2175		2700	3250
	JT 260 CHEV 4100	4800, IO	260		2900	3350, JT	300-360		4100	4800
19 3	TWILIGHTER 190	OP	CUD	FBG DV	OB	7 3	1335		2950	3400
19 3	TWILIGHTER 190	OP	CUD	FBG DV	IO 140-230	7 3	2350		2850	3450
	JT 260 CHEV 4100	4800, IO	260		3100	3600, JT	300-360		4100	4800
19 6	ISLANDER 200	OP	RNBT	FBG SV	IO 140-260	8	2700		3200	4000
20 3	SPORT 200		SKI	FBG SV	OB	7 4			3150	3650
20 3	SPORT 200	OP	SKI	FBG SV	IO 198-230	7 4	2245		3800	4500
	JT 260 CHEV 5700	6550, IO	260		4000	4650, JT	300-360		5700	6550
20 3	SUNSPORT 200	OP	RNBT	FBG SV	IO 198-230	7 4	2275		3900	4650
	JT 260 CHEV 5850	6750, IO	260		4150	4800, JT	300-360		5850	6750
21 7	FORCE 220	OP	CUD	FBG SV	IO 198-260	8	3400		5800	6950
21 7	FORCE 220	OP	CUD	FBG SV	IO 330 MRCR	8	3400		6750	7800
21 7	FORCE 220	OP	CUD	FBG SV	IO T170	8	3400		6600	7600
21 7	WEEKENDER 210		EXP	FBG DV	OB	8			4850	5550
22 6	TWILIGHTER 220		CUD	FBG DV	OB	8			7050	8100
22 6	TWILIGHTER 220	OP	CUD	FBG DV	IO 198-260	8	1950		4650	5600
22 6	TWILIGHTER 220	OP	CUD	FBG DV	IO 330 MRCR	8	1950		5600	6450
25	FORCE 250	ST	SPTCR	FBG DV	IO 198-260	8	4500		8450	10100
25	FORCE 250	ST	SPTCR	FBG DV	IO 330 MRCR	8	4500		9600	10900
25	FORCE 250	ST	SPTCR	FBG DV	IO T170	8	4500		9500	10800
25 3	FORCE 250		SPTCR	FBG DV	OB	8			9150	10400
28	FORCE 280	OP	SPTCR	FBG DV	IO T260-T330	8 4	7000		14400	18400
28	FORCE 280	OP	SPTCR	FBG DV	IO T370 MRCR	8 4	7000		17200	19500
28 1	FORCE 280		SPTCR	FBG DV	OB	8 4			14800	16800
32 1	FORCE 320		SPTCR	FBG DV	OB	8 4			22300	24400
32 1	FORCE 320	OP	SPTCR	FBG DV	IO T370 MRCR	8 4	7500		23200	25800
32 1	FORCE 320	OP	SPTCR	FBG SV	IO T330 MRCR	8 4	7500		22400	24900

....For earlier years, see the BUC Used Boat Price Guide, Volume 3

BALTIC YACHTS LTD
SF68555 BOSUND FINLAND   See inside cover to adjust price for area

BALTIC YACHTS USA INC
MARBLEHEAD MA 01945

For more recent years, see the BUC Used Boat Price Guide, Volume 1

LOA FT IN	NAME AND/ OR MODEL	TOP/ RIG	BOAT TYPE	-HULL- MTL TP	----ENGINE--- TP # HP MFG	BEAM FT IN	WGT LBS	DRAFT FT IN	RETAIL LOW	RETAIL HIGH
				1996 BOATS						
34 11	BALTIC 35	SLP	SARAC	F/S KL	IB 18D YAN	11 6	9877	6 1	122000	134000
39 4	BALTIC 40 I	SLP	SARAC	F/S KL	IB 43D VLVO	12 9	14990	7 2	209000	229500
39 4	BALTIC 40 II	SLP	SARAC	F/S KL	IB 43D VLVO	12 9	14990	7 2	217500	239000
39 4	BALTIC 40 III	SLP	SARAC	F/S KL	IB 43D VLVO	12 9	14990	7 2	217500	239000
43 4	BALTIC 43	SLP	SARAC	F/S KL	IB 43D VLVO	13 9	19754	8 1	308000	338500
46 11	BALTIC 47	SLP	SARAC	F/S KL	IB 62D YAN	14 5	24500	8 8	411000	452000
52 6	BALTIC 52	SLP	SARAC	F/S KL	IB 88D YAN	15 5	31967	9 2	629000	691000
58 6	BALTIC 58	SLP	SARAC	F/S KL	IB 100D YAN	16 7	41900	10 6	980500	1.065M
64	BALTIC 64	SLP	SARAC	F/S KL	IB 120D YAN	17 8	56218	10 7	1.175M	1.280M
66 7	BALTIC 67	SLP	SARAC	F/S KL	IB D	17 8	40786	11 4	784500	862000
				1995 BOATS						
39 3	BALTIC 40 II	SLP	SARAC	F/S KL	IB 43D VLVO	12 7	14992	8 3	201000	220500
39 3	BALTIC 40 II	SLP	SARAC	F/S KL	IB 43D VLVO	12 7	14992	8 3	201000	220500
39 3	BALTIC 40 III	SLP	SARAC	F/S KL	IB 43D VLVO	12 7	14992	8 3	201000	220500
43 3	BALTIC 43	SLP	SARAC	F/S KL	IB 43D VLVO	13 8	19754	8 5	288500	317000
52 5	BALTIC 52	SLP	SARAC	F/S KL	IB 88D YAN	15 4	31949	9 8	588000	646500
58 5	BALTIC 58	SLP	SARAC	F/S KL	IB 100D YAN	16 4	41888	10 5	925500	1.005M
64	BALTIC 64	SLP	SARAC	F/S KL	IB 120D YAN	17 3	56218	11	1.105M	1.200M
				1994 BOATS						
34 9	BALTIC 35	SLP	SARAC	F/S KL	IB 18D YAN	11 5	9877	6 7	107500	118000
39 3	BALTIC 40 I	SLP	SARAC	F/S KL	IB 43D VLVO	12 7	14992	8 3	184000	202000
39 3	BALTIC 40 II	SLP	SARAC	F/S KL	IB 43D VLVO	12 7	14992	8 3	191500	210500
39 3	BALTIC 40 III	SLP	SARAC	F/S KL	IB 43D VLVO	12 7	14992	8 3	191500	210500
43 3	BALTIC 43	SLP	SARAC	F/S KL	IB 43D VLVO	13 8	19754	8 5	271500	298500
47 7	BALTIC 48	SLP	SARAC	F/S KL	IB 62D YAN	14 4	24692	8 7	377000	414500
52 5	BALTIC 52	SLP	SARAC	F/S KL	IB 88D YAN	15 4	31967	9 8	553500	608000
58 5	BALTIC 58	SLP	SARAC	F/S KL	IB 100D YAN	16 4	41888	10 5	861000	946000
64	BALTIC 64	SLP	SARAC	F/S KL	IB 120D YAN	17 3	56218	11	1.040M	1.130M
				1993 BOATS						
34 9	BALTIC 35	SLP	SARAC	F/S KL	IB 18D YAN	11 5	9877	6 7	101000	111000
39 3	BALTIC 40	SLP	SARAC	F/S KL	IB 43D VLVO	12 7	14992	8 3	177500	195500
43 3	BALTIC 43	SLP	SARAC	F/S KL	IB 43D VLVO	13 8	19754	8 5	255500	280500
47 7	BALTIC 48	SLP	SARAC	F/S KL	IB 88D YAN	14 4	24692	8 7	355500	390500
48 1	BALTIC 48	SLP	SARAC	F/S KL	IB 88D YAN	14 2	26676	9 2	373500	410500
52 5	BALTIC 52	SLP	SARAC	F/S KL	IB 88D YAN	15 4	31967	9 8	520500	572000
58 5	BALTIC 58	SLP	SARAC	F/S KL	IB 100D YAN	16 4	41888	10 5	810000	890000
64	BALTIC 64	SLP	SARAC	F/S KL	IB 120D YAN	17 3	56218	11	978500	1.065M
				1986 BOATS						
34 11	BALTIC 35	SLP	SA/CR	FBG KL	IB D	11 6	9877	6 1	66000	72600
38	BALTIC 38	SLP	SA/CR	FBG KL	IB D	12 4	14330	7 3	150500	165500
43 6	BALTIC 43JV	SLP	SA/CR	FBG KL	IB D	14 2	19492	8 2	167500	184000
48	BALTIC 48DP	SLP	SA/CR	FBG KL	IB D	14 4	26676	8 8	242500	266500
50 11	BALTIC 51	SLP	SA/CR	FBG KL	IB D	15 3	34390	8 10	312000	343000

LOA FT IN	NAME AND/OR MODEL	TOP/RIG	BOAT TYPE	MTL	TP	TP	# HP	MFG	BEAM FT IN	WGT LBS	DRAFT FT IN	RETAIL LOW	RETAIL HIGH
							1986 BOATS						
54 9	BALTIC 55DP	SLP	SA/CR	FBG	KL	IB	D		16 2	38580	9 7	412000	453000
							1985 BOATS						
34 11	BALTIC 35	SLP	SA/CR	FBG	KC	IB	D		11 6	9877	6 1	62300	68400
37	BALTIC 37	SLP	SA/CR	FBG	KL	IB	D		12	13600	5 9	89200	98000
38	BALTIC 38DP	SLP	SA/CR	FBG	KL	IB	D		12 4	14330	7 3	97400	107000
38 1	BALTIC 39	SLP	SA/CR	FBG	KL	IB	D		12 6	18000	6 10	117500	129000
41 11	BALTIC 42DP	SLP	SA/CR	FBG	KL	IB	D		13 4	18400	7 11	141000	155000
50 11	BALTIC 51	SLP	SA/CR	FBG	KL	IB	D		15 3	34390	8 10	293500	322500
54 9	BALTIC 55DP	SLP	SA/CR	FBG	KC	IB	D		16 6	32600	9 10	379500	417000
62 11	BALTIC 63	SLP	SA/RC	FBG	KL	IB	D		17 1	49800	10 6	560500	616000
74 11	BALTIC 75	SLP	SA/CR	FBG	KC	IB	D		19 4	79990	6 11	**	**
79 8	BALTIC 80	SLP	SA/CR	FBG	KC	IB	D		18 4	83600	12 7	**	**
							1984 BOATS						
37	BALTIC 37	SLP	SA/CR	FBG	KL	SD	23D	VLVO	12	13600	5 9	83600	91800
38	BALTIC 38DP	SLP	SA/CR	FBG	KL	SD	30D	YAN	12 4	14300	7 3	91400	100500
38 1	BALTIC 39	SLP	SA/CR	FBG	KL	SD	23D	VLVO	12 7	18000	6 10	109500	120500
41 11	BALTIC 42	SLP	SA/CR	FBG	KL	IB	D		12 7	19715	7 2	138000	151500
41 11	BALTIC 42DP	SLP	SA/CR	FBG	KL	IB	50D	PERK	13 4	18400	7 11	132000	145000
50 11	BALTIC 51	SLP	SA/CR	FBG	KL	SD	61D	VLVO	15 3	34390	8 11	275500	302500
54 9	BALTIC 55	SLP	SA/CR	FBG	KL	IB	D	PERK	16	36500	9 7	361000	396500
79 8	BALTIC 80	SLP	SA/CR	FBG	KL	IB	D		18 5	83600	12 7	**	**

....For earlier years, see the BUC Used Boat Price Guide, Volume 3

BANANA BOAT LTD
CRANSTON RI 02905   See inside cover to adjust price for area

LOA FT IN	NAME AND/OR MODEL	TOP/RIG	BOAT TYPE	MTL	TP	TP	# HP	MFG	BEAM FT IN	WGT LBS	DRAFT FT IN	RETAIL LOW	RETAIL HIGH
							1986 BOATS						
23 11	BANANA BOAT	OP	OFF	FBG	DV	OB			7 10	3800	1 6	9150	10400
23 11	BANANA BOAT	OP	OFF	FBG	DV	IO	198-260		7 10	3800	1 6	6450	8250
23 11	BANANA BOAT	OP	OFF	FBG	DV	IO	330	MRCR	7 10	3800	1 6	7900	9100
23 11	BANANA BOAT	OP	OFF	FBG	DV	IO	455	MRCR	7 10	2850	1 6	9600	10900
							1985 BOATS						
23 11	BANANA BOAT	OP	OFF	FBG	DV	OB			7 10	2850	1 6	7050	8100
23 11	BANANA BOAT	OP	RACE	FBG	DV	IO			7 10	3800	1 6	8850	10100
23 11	BANANA BOAT	OP	RACE	FBG	DV	IO	198-260		7 10	3800	1 6	6250	7450
23 11	BANANA BOAT	OP	RACE	FBG	DV	IO	330	MRCR	7 10	3800	1 6	7100	8200
23 11	OFFSHORE	OP	OFF	FBG	DV	OB			7 10	2850	1 6	7050	8100
23 11	OFFSHORE	OP	OFF	FBG	DV	IO	455	MRCR	7 10	2850	1 6	9250	10500

BANNO USA INC
CASEVILLE MI 48725   COAST GUARD MFG ID- BUQ See inside cover to adjust price for area

LOA FT IN	NAME AND/OR MODEL	TOP/RIG	BOAT TYPE	MTL	TP	TP	# HP	MFG	BEAM FT IN	WGT LBS	DRAFT FT IN	RETAIL LOW	RETAIL HIGH
							1984 BOATS						
17 10	OLD-WORLD 18	GAF	SAIL	FBG	CB				6 11	1200	1 2	4450	5150

BARBERIS YACHTS/SMI
LARCHMONT NY 10538   See inside cover to adjust price for area

LOA FT IN	NAME AND/OR MODEL	TOP/RIG	BOAT TYPE	MTL	TP	TP	# HP	MFG	BEAM FT IN	WGT LBS	DRAFT FT IN	RETAIL LOW	RETAIL HIGH
							1985 BOATS						
23 4	SHOW 24	SLP	SA/RC	FBG	KL				8 2	2100	4 5	6000	6900
27 6	SHOW 27	SLP	SA/CR	FBG	KL	IB	D		9 8	4840	5 6	14900	16900
29 6	SHOW 30	SLP	SA/CR	FBG	KC	IB	D		10 2	6380	5 7	20400	22700
33 8	SHOW 34	SLP	SA/CR	FBG	KL	IB	D		11 2	10780	6	35000	38900
35 8	SHOW 36	SLP	SA/CR	FBG	KL	IB	D		11 10	10830	6 3	36400	40500
37 8	SHOW 38	SLP	SA/CR	FBG	KL	IB	D		12 7	11220	6 3	41000	45500
41 5	SHOW 42	SLP	SA/CR	FBG	KL	IB	D		13	18480	6 10	73200	80400
							1984 BOATS						
23 4	SHOW 24	SLP	SA/RC	FBG	KL	OB			8 2	2100	4 5	5600	6450
27 6	SHOW 27	SLP	SA/CR	FBG	KL	IB	8D	YAN	9 8	4840	5 6	13900	15800
27 6	SHOW 27 SHOAL	SLP	SA/CR	FBG	KL	IB	8D	YAN	9 8	4840	4 6	13900	15800
29 6	SHOW 30	SLP	SA/CR	FBG	KC	IB	15D	YAN	10 2	6380	5 7	19100	21200
33 8	SHOW 34	SLP	SA/CR	FBG	KL	IB	23D	YAN	11 2	10780	6	32800	36400
37 8	SHOW 38	SLP	SA/CR	FBG	KC	IB	23D	YAN	12 7	11220		38300	42500
37 8	SHOW 38	SLP	SA/CR	FBG	KL	IB	23D	YAN	12 7	11220	6 3	38300	42500
41 5	SHOW 42 DE	SLP	SA/CR	FBG	KC	IB	50D	PERK	13	18480	6 10	68100	74900
41 5	SHOW 42 DE	SLP	SA/CR	FBG	KL	IB	50D	PERK	13	18480	6 10	68100	74900

....For earlier years, see the BUC Used Boat Price Guide, Volume 3

BARETTA MANUFACTURING LTD
CONWAY AR 72032   COAST GUARD MFG ID- BML See inside cover to adjust price for area

LOA FT IN	NAME AND/OR MODEL	TOP/RIG	BOAT TYPE	MTL	TP	TP	# HP	MFG	BEAM FT IN	WGT LBS	DRAFT FT IN	RETAIL LOW	RETAIL HIGH
							1991 BOATS						
18 9	1850 SF	OP	SF	FBG	DV	IO	146	VLVO	7 6	2035		4250	4950
20 1	2000 BR	OP	B/R	FBG	DV	IO	146	VLVO	7 6	2182		4200	4900
20 1	2000 CC	OP	CUD	FBG	DV	IO	146	VLVO	7 6	2530		4850	5600
20 1	2000 CD	OP	RNBT	FBG	DV	IO	205	VLVO	7 6	2546		4800	5500
20 5	2050 BR	OP	B/R	FBG	DV	IO	175	OMC	7 6	2350		4250	4900
20 5	2050 CD	OP	RNBT	FBG	DV	IO	175	OMC	7 6	2650		4650	5350
22 5	2300 BR	OP	B/R	FBG	DV	IO	205	VLVO	7 6	2800		5600	6400
22 5	2300 CC	OP	CUD	FBG	DV	IO	275	VLVO	7 6	2960		6600	7600
22 5	2300 CD	OP	RNBT	FBG	DV	IO	275	VLVO	7 6	2850		6100	7000

BARON YACHTS INC
DECATURT IN 46733   See inside cover to adjust price for area

LOA FT IN	NAME AND/OR MODEL	TOP/RIG	BOAT TYPE	MTL	TP	TP	# HP	MFG	BEAM FT IN	WGT LBS	DRAFT FT IN	RETAIL LOW	RETAIL HIGH
							1991 BOATS						
43 4	BARON 43 EXPRESS	OP	EXP	FBG	SV	IB	T550D	J&T	14 8	29500	3 8	143000	157000

BARTEL BOATS
REMSENBURG NY 11960   COAST GUARD MFG ID- RTC See inside cover to adjust price for area

LOA FT IN	NAME AND/OR MODEL	TOP/RIG	BOAT TYPE	MTL	TP	TP	# HP	MFG	BEAM FT IN	WGT LBS	DRAFT FT IN	RETAIL LOW	RETAIL HIGH
							1996 BOATS						
22	BARTEL 22		RACE	FBG	DV	OB			8	2000		11600	13200
22	BARTEL 22		RACE	FBG	DV	IO	235-250		8	2200		11700	13500
22	BARTEL 22		RACE	FBG	DV	IO	350	MRCR	8	2200		14600	16600
22	BARTEL 22 OF	OP	OPFSH	FBG	DV	OB			8	2200		12500	14200
34	BARTEL 34		OFF	FBG	DV	IO			8	9300		48500	53300
34	BARTEL 34		OFF	FBG	DV	IO	T300-T425		8	9300		86800	105000
34	BARTEL 34		OFF	FBG	DV	IO	T465-T500		8	9300		99000	112550
34	BARTEL 34		OFF	FBG	DV	IO	R390-R425		8	10700		105500	121000
							1995 BOATS						
22	BARTEL 22		RACE	FBG	DV	OB			8	2000		11100	12600
22	BARTEL 22		RACE	FBG	DV	IO	235-250		8	2200		10900	12600
22	BARTEL 22		RACE	FBG	DV	IO	350	MRCR	8	2200		13700	15500
34	BARTEL 34		OFF	FBG	DV	IO			8	3500		45900	51100
34	BARTEL 34		OFF	FBG	DV	IO	T300-T425		8	9300		81000	97900
34	BARTEL 34		OFF	FBG	DV	IO	T465-T500		8	9300		92400	105000
34	BARTEL 34		OFF	FBG	DV	IO	R390-R425		8	10700		98200	113000
							1994 BOATS						
22	BARTEL 22		RACE	FBG	DV	OB			8	2000		10600	12000
22	BARTEL 22		RACE	FBG	DV	IO	235-250		8	2200		10200	11800
22	BARTEL 22		RACE	FBG	DV	IO	350	MRCR	8	2200		12300	14500
34	BARTEL 34		OFF	FBG	DV	IO			8	3500		44000	48900
34	BARTEL 34		OFF	FBG	DV	IO	T300-T425		8	9300		75600	91400
34	BARTEL 34		OFF	FBG	DV	IO	T465-T500		8	9300		86300	97800
34	BARTEL 34		OFF	FBG	DV	IO	R390-R425		8	10700		91700	105500
							1993 BOATS						
22	BARTEL 22		RACE	FBG	DV	OB			8			10100	11500
22	BARTEL 22		RACE	FBG	DV	OB			8			9550	11000
22	BARTEL 22		RACE	FBG	DV	IO	235-250		8	2200		11900	13500
22	BARTEL 22		RACE	FBG	DV	IO	350	MRCR	8	2200		11900	13500
34	BARTEL 34		OFF	FBG	DV	IO			8	3500		42200	46800
34	BARTEL 34		OFF	FBG	DV	IO	T300-T425		8	9300		70700	85400
34	BARTEL 34		OFF	FBG	DV	IO	T465-T500		8	9300		80600	91400
34	BARTEL 34		OFF	FBG	DV	IO	R390-R425		8	10700		91700	98600
							1986 BOATS						
21 8	BARTEL 22	OP	RACE	FBG	DV	OB			8	1700	1 6	6800	7850
21 8	BARTEL 22	OP	RACE	FBG	DV	IO	188-260		8	3000	1 6	7100	8350
21 8	BARTEL 22	OP	RACE	FBG	DV	IO	330		8	3000	1 6	8400	9650
33 8	BARTEL 34	OP	RACE	FBG	DV	OB			8	3000	2 6	47400	52100
33 8	BARTEL 34	OP	RACE	FBG	DV	IB	T330-T370		8	5500	2 6	66700	81200
33 8	BARTEL 34	OP	RACE	FBG	DV	IB	T400		8	5500	2 6	78900	86700
							1985 BOATS						
21 8	BARTEL 22	OP	RACE	FBG	DV	OB			8	1700	1 6	6600	7600
21 8	BARTEL 22	OP	RACE	FBG	DV	IO	188-260		8	3000	1 6	6900	8000
21 8	BARTEL 22	OP	RACE	FBG	DV	IO	330		8	3000	1 6	8050	9250
33 8	BARTEL 34	OP	RACE	FBG	DV	OB			8	3000	2 6	46200	50700

LOA FT	IN	NAME AND/ OR MODEL	TOP/ RIG	BOAT TYPE	-HULL- MTL	TP	TP	----ENGINE--- # HP	MFG	BEAM FT	IN	WGT LBS	DRAFT FT	IN	RETAIL LOW	RETAIL HIGH
		1985 BOATS														
33	8	BARTEL 34	OP	RACE	FBG	DV	IB	T330-T370		8		5500	2	6	63700	77600
33	8	BARTEL 34	OP	RACE	FBG	DV	IB	T400		8		5500	2	6	75400	82800
		1984 BOATS														
21	8	BARTEL 22	OP	RACE	FBG	DV	OB			8		1700	1	6	6450	7400
21	8	BARTEL 22	OP	RACE	FBG	DV	IO	188-260		8		3000	1	6	6550	7900
21	8	BARTEL 22	OP	RACE	FBG	DV	IO	330		8		3000	1	6	7750	8900

....For earlier years, see the BUC Used Boat Price Guide, Volume 3

BASS HARBOR MARINE

BASS HARBOR ME 04653-0010 See inside cover to adjust price for area

LOA FT	IN	NAME AND/ OR MODEL	TOP/ RIG	BOAT TYPE	-HULL- MTL	TP	TP	----ENGINE--- # HP	MFG	BEAM FT	IN	WGT LBS	DRAFT FT	IN	RETAIL LOW	RETAIL HIGH
		1989 BOATS														
35	11	TASHIBA 36 STD	CUT	SAIL	FBG	KL	IB	44D	YAN	11	9	20350	5	6	102000	112000
39	11	TASHIBA 40 PH	CUT	SAIL	FBG	KL	IB	D		12	10	29000	6		118500	130500
39	11	TASHIBA 40 STD	CUT	SAIL	FBG	KL	IB	55D	YAN	12	10	29000	6		118500	130500
		1988 BOATS														
35	4	TASHIBA 31 PH	CUT	SAIL	FBG	KL	IB	D		10	8	13790	5		68300	75000
35	4	TASHIBA 31 PH SHOAL	CUT	SAIL	FBG	KL	IB	D		10	8	13790	4	6	68300	75000
35	4	TASHIBA 31 SHOAL	CUT	SAIL	FBG	KL	IB	D		10	8	13790	4	6	68300	75000
35	4	TASHIBA 31 STD	CUT	SAIL	FBG	KL	IB	27D	YAN	10	8	13790	5		68300	75100
35	11	TASHIBA 36 PH	CUT	SAIL	FBG	KL	IB	D		11	9	20350	5	6	95600	105000
35	11	TASHIBA 36 STD	CUT	SAIL	FBG	KL	IB	44D	YAN	11	9	20350	5	6	95700	105000
39	11	TASHIBA 40 PH	CUT	SAIL	FBG	KL	IB	D		12	10	29000	6		111500	122500
39	11	TASHIBA 40 STD	CUT	SAIL	FBG	KL	IB	55D	YAN	12	10	29000	6		111500	122500
		1987 BOATS														
30	10	TASHIBA 31	CUT	SAIL	FBG	KL	IB	27D	YAN	10	8	13790	5		65900	72500
35	11	TASHIBA 36	CUT	SAIL	FBG	KL	IB	44D	YAN	11	10	20350	5	6	89900	98800
39	10	TASHIBA 40	CUT	SAIL	FBG	KL	IB	55D	YAN	12	10	29000	6		105000	115500

BASS PRO SHOPS

SPRINGFIELD MO 65807 See inside cover to adjust price for area

LOA FT	IN	NAME AND/ OR MODEL	TOP/ RIG	BOAT TYPE	-HULL- MTL	TP	TP	----ENGINE--- # HP	MFG	BEAM FT	IN	WGT LBS	DRAFT FT	IN	RETAIL LOW	RETAIL HIGH
		1986 BOATS														
16		BASS-TRACKER II	OP	BASS	AL	SV	OB			5	9	505			2050	2450
17		TOURNAMENT V-17	OP	BASS	AL	DV	OB			6	2	840			3550	4150
17		TOURNAMENT V-17	OP	BASS	AL	SV	OB			6		595			2600	3000
17	10	BASS-TRACKER 1710	OP	FSH	AL	SV	OB			7	2	1020			3450	4050
17	10	BASS-TRACKER LTD ED	OP	FSH	AL	SV	OB			7	2	1020			5250	6000
		1984 BOATS														
16		BASS-TRACKER II	OP	BASS	AL	SV	OB			5	9	457			1800	2100
16		BASS-TRACKER III	OP	BASS	AL	SV	OB			5	9	595			2350	2700
16		BASS-TRACKER J-3	OP	JON	AL	FL	OB			5	10	250			1000	1200
17		TOURNAMENT TX	OP	BASS	AL	SV	OB			6		615			2550	2950

BAVARIA YACHTBAU GMBH

GIEBELSTADT GERMANY 972 COAST GUARD MFG ID- BVY See inside cover to adjust price for area

BAVARIA YACHTS
ANNAPOLIS MD 21403

FORMERLY INTERNATIONAL YACHTING CENTER

For more recent years, see the BUC Used Boat Price Guide, Volume 1

LOA FT	IN	NAME AND/ OR MODEL	TOP/ RIG	BOAT TYPE	-HULL- MTL	TP	TP	----ENGINE--- # HP	MFG	BEAM FT	IN	WGT LBS	DRAFT FT	IN	RETAIL LOW	RETAIL HIGH
		1996 BOATS														
32	3	SUMBEAM 32	SLP	SACAC	FBG	KL	IB	20D	YAN	10		9500	4	1	50600	55600
49	3	HELMSMAN 50	KTH	SACAC	FBG	KL	IB	62D	VLVO	11	8	23100	6	7	166000	182000
49	3	HELMSMAN 50	KTH	SACAC	FBG	KL	IB	62D	YAN	11	8	23100	6	7	166000	182500
		1995 BOATS														
32	3	SUMBEAM 32	SLP	SACAC	FBG	KL	IB	20D	YAN	10		9500	4	1	47900	52700
49	3	HELMSMAN 50	KTH	SACAC	FBG	KL	IB	62D	VLVO	11	8	23100	6	7	157000	172500
49	3	HELMSMAN 50	KTH	SACAC	FBG	KL	IB	62D	YAN	11	8	23100	6	7	157000	173000
		1994 BOATS														
32	3	SUMBEAM 32	SLP	SACAC	FBG	KL	IB	20D	YAN	10		9500	4	1	45600	50100
49	3	HELMSMAN 50	KTH	SACAC	FBG	KL	IB	62D	VLVO	11	8	23100	6	7	148500	163500
49	3	HELMSMAN 50	KTH	SACAC	FBG	KL	IB	62D	YAN	11	8	23100	6	7	149000	163500
		1993 BOATS														
32	3	SUMBEAM 32	SLP	SACAC	FBG	KL	IB	20D	YAN	10		9500	4	1	42700	47500
49	3	HELMSMAN 50	KTH	SACAC	FBG	KL	IB	62D	VLVO	11	8	23100	6	7	141000	155000
49	3	HELMSMAN 50	KTH	SACAC	FBG	KL	IB	62D	YAN	11	8	23100	6	7	141000	155000
		1992 BOATS														
32	3	SUMBEAM 32	SLP	SA/CR	FBG	KL	IB	20D	YAN	10		9500	4	1	40500	45000
49	3	HELMSMAN 50	KTH	SA/RC	FBG	KL	IB	62D	VLVO	11	8	23100	6	7	133500	146500
49	3	HELMSMAN 50	KTH	SA/RC	FBG	KL	IB	62D	YAN	11	8	23100	6	7	133500	147000
		1991 BOATS														
28		BAVARIA 27		SDN	FBG	SV	IB	200D	VLVO	10	6	7500	2	9	43000	47800
28		BAVARIA 27		SDN	FBG	SV	IB	T130D	VLVO	10	6	7500	2	9	47600	52400
31	6	BAVARIA 31		SDN	FBG	SV	IB	T200D	VLVO	10	6	10000	2	9	67600	74200
32	3	SUMBEAM 32	SLP	SA/CR	FBG	KL	IB	20D	YAN	10		9500	4	1	38400	42600
35		HELMSMAN 35	SLP	SA/CR	FBG	KL	IB	28D	VLVO	11		12000	6		47400	52100
35		HELMSMAN 35	SLP	SA/CR	FBG	KL	IB	28D	YAN	11		12000	6		47500	52200
41	4	BAVARIA 40	FB	CNV	FBG	SV	IB	T306D	VLVO	13	6	22000	3	7	133500	146500
46	10	HELMSMAN 47	SLP	SA/RC	FBG	KL	IB	62D	VLVO	11	8	23100	6	7	110000	121000
46	10	HELMSMAN 47	SLP	SA/RC	FBG	KL	IB	62D	YAN	11	8	23100	6	7	110000	121000
49	3	HELMSMAN 50	KTH	SA/RC	FBG	KL	IB	62D	VLVO	11	8	23100	6	7	126500	139000
49	3	HELMSMAN 50	KTH	SA/RC	FBG	KL	IB	62D	YAN	11	8	23100	6	7	126500	139000
		1990 BOATS														
28		BAVARIA 27		SDN	FBG	SV	IB	200D	VLVO	10	6	7500	2	9	40900	45400
28		BAVARIA 27		SDN	FBG	SV	IB	T130D	VLVO	10	6	7500	2	9	45600	50100
31	6	BAVARIA 31		SDN	FBG	SV	IB	T130D-T200D		10	6	10000	2	9	58300	70900
35		HELMSMAN 35	SLP	SA/CR	FBG	KL	IB	28D	VLVO	11		12000	6		44400	49400
35		HELMSMAN 35	SLP	SA/CR	FBG	KL	IB	28D	YAN	11		12000	6		44500	49400
41	4	BAVARIA 40	FB	CNV	FBG	SV	IB	T200D	VLVO	13	6	22000	3	7	120000	131500
41	4	BAVARIA 40	FB	CNV	FBG	SV	IB	T306D	VLVO	13	6	22000	3	7	127000	139500
43	5	HELMSMAN 43	SLP	SA/RC	FBG	KL	IB	50D	VLVO	11	8	17000	6		76900	84500
43	5	HELMSMAN 43	SLP	SA/RC	FBG	KL	IB	50D	YAN	11	8	17000	6		77000	84600
46	10	HELMSMAN 47	SLP	SA/RC	FBG	KL	IB	62D	VLVO	11	8	23100	6	7	104000	114500
46	10	HELMSMAN 47	SLP	SA/RC	FBG	KL	IB	62D	YAN	11	8	23100	6	7	104000	114500
49	3	HELMSMAN 50	KTH	SA/CR	FBG	KL	IB	62D	VLVO	11	8	23100	6	7	119500	131500
49	3	HELMSMAN 50	KTH	SA/CR	FBG	KL	IB	62D	YAN	11	8	23100	6	7	120000	131500
		1989 BOATS														
28		BAVARIA 27		SDN	FBG	SV	IO		VLVO	10	6	7500	2	9	**	**
		IB VLVO ** **, IB 260 VLVO 30400 33800, IB 200D VLVO 38900 43200														
		IB T150-T175 31700 36300, IB T130D VLVO 43000 47700														
31	6	BAVARIA 31		SDN	FBG	SV	IO		VLVO	10	6	10000	2	9	**	**
		IB VLVO ** **, IB T150-T260 43300 52900, IBT130D-T200D 55500 67200														
31	6	BAVARIA 31DS		SPTCR	FBG	SV	IO		VLVO	10	6	10000	2	9	**	**
		IB VLVO ** **, IB T150-T260 40800 48900, IBT130D-T200D 49200 59100														
31	6	BAVARIA 31FL		SPTCR	FBG	SV	IO		VLVO	10	6	10000	2	9	**	**
		IB VLVO ** **, IB T150-T260 39500 47700, IBT130D-T200D 51700 57800														
35		HELMSMAN 35	SLP	SA/RC	FBG	KL	IB	28D	VLVO	11		12000	6		42100	46800
35		HELMSMAN 35	SLP	SA/RC	FBG	KL	IB	28D	YAN	11		12000	6		42100	46800
38		BAVARIA 35	FB	EXP	FBG	SV	IB	T225	VLVO	11	6	15000	3	7	75900	83400
38		BAVARIA 35	FB	EXP	FBG	SV	IB	T290	VLVO	11	6	15000	3	7	76700	84200
38		BAVARIA 35	FB	EXP	FBG	SV	IB	T175D	VLVO	11	6	15000	3	7	86200	94700
38		HELMSMAN 38	SLP	SA/RC	FBG	KL	IB	28D	VLVO	11		14500	5	5	52000	57200
38		HELMSMAN 38	SLP	SA/RC	FBG	KL	IB	28D	YAN	11		14500	5	5	52100	57200
41	4	BAVARIA 40	FB	CNV	FBG	SV	IB	T200D	VLVO	13	6	22000	3	7	114500	125500
41	4	BAVARIA 40	FB	CNV	FBG	SV	IB	T306D	VLVO	13	6	22000	3	7	121000	133000
43	5	HELMSMAN 43	SLP	SA/RC	FBG	KL	IB	50D	VLVO	11	8	17000	6		72900	80100
43	5	HELMSMAN 43	SLP	SA/RC	FBG	KL	IB	50D	YAN	11	8	17000	6		73000	80200
44	2	BAVARIA 4200SL	FB	MY	FBG	SV	IB	T306D	VLVO	14		25000	4		139000	152500
44	2	BAVARIA 4200SL	FB	MY	FBG	SV	IB	T358D	VLVO	14		25000	4		143000	157000
46	10	HELMSMAN 47	SLP	SA/RC	FBG	KL	IB	62D	VLVO	11	8	23100	6	7	98600	108500
46	10	HELMSMAN 47	SLP	SA/RC	FBG	KL	IB	62D	YAN	11	8	23100	6	7	98800	108500
47	2	BAVARIA 45SL	FB	MY	FBG	SV	IB	T358D	VLVO	14		26500	4		169000	186000
49	3	HELMSMAN 50	KTH	SA/CR	FBG	KL	IB	62D	YAN	11	8	23100	6	7	113500	125000
49	3	HELMSMAN 50	KTH	SA/RC	FBG	KL	IB	62D	VLVO	11	8	23100	6	7	113500	124500
51	6	BAVARIA 48SL	FB	MY	FBG	SV	IB	T400D	BENZ	14	6	31000	4	3	195000	214500
		1988 BOATS														
28		BAVARIA 27		SDN	FBG	SV	IO		VLVO	10	6	7500	2	9	**	**
		IB VLVO ** **, IB 260 VLVO 28900 32200, IB 200D VLVO 37200 41400														
		IB T130-T175 29400 34600														
31	6	BAVARIA 31		SDN	FBG	SV	IO		VLVO	10	6	10000	2	9	**	**
31	6	BAVARIA 31		SDN	FBG	SV	IB	T150-T260		10	6	10000	2	9	41000	50400
31	6	BAVARIA 31		SDN	FBG	SV	IB	T130D-T200D		10	6	10000	2	9	53100	64300
31	6	BAVARIA 31DS		SPTCR	FBG	SV	IO		VLVO	10	6	10000	2	9	**	**
31	6	BAVARIA 31DS		SPTCR	FBG	SV	IB	T150-T260		10	6	10000	2	9	38800	46700
31	6	BAVARIA 31DS		SPTCR	FBG	SV	IB	T130D-T200D		10	6	10000	2	9	47400	56600

CONTINUED ON NEXT PAGE

BAVARIA YACHTBAU GMBH   -CONTINUED   See inside cover to adjust price for area

```
      LOA  NAME AND/      TOP/ BOAT -HULL- ----ENGINE---   BEAM   WGT  DRAFT RETAIL RETAIL
      FT IN OR MODEL      RIG  TYPE MTL TP TP #  HP   MFG   FT IN  LBS  FT IN  LOW    HIGH
----------------------- 1988 BOATS -----------------------------------------------------
31  6 BAVARIA 31FL     SPTCR FBG SV IO        VLVO 10  6 10000  2  9    **     **
31  6 BAVARIA 31FL     SPTCR FBG SV IB T150-T260   10  6 10000  2  9   37700  45200
31  6 BAVARIA 31FL     SPTCR FBG SV IBT130D-T200D  10  6 10000  2  9   44800  55300
35    HELMSMAN 35      SLP SA/RC FBG KL IB 28D VLVO 11    12000  6      39900  44300
35    HELMSMAN 35      SLP SA/RC FBG KL IB 28D YAN  11    12000  6      39900  44400
38    BAVARIA 35       FB  EXP  FBG SV IB T225 VLVO 11  6 15000  3  7   72400  79600
38    BAVARIA 35       FB  EXP  FBG SV IB T290 VLVO 11  6 15000  3  7   73200  80400
38    BAVARIA 35       FB  EXP  FBG SV IB T175D VLVO 11 6 15000  3  7   82300  90400
38    HELMSMAN 38      SLP SA/RC FBG KL IB 28  VLVO 11    14500  5  5   48600  53400
38    HELMSMAN 38      SLP SA/RC FBG KL IB 28  YAN  11    14500  5  5   48600  53400
41  4 BAVARIA 40       FB  CNV  FBG SV IB T200D VLVO 13 6 22000  3  7  109000 120000
41  4 BAVARIA 40       FB  CNV  FBG SV IB T306D VLVO 13 6 22000  3  7  115500 127000

43  5 HELMSMAN 43      SLP SA/RC FBG KL IB 50  VLVO 11  8 17000  6      67900  74600
43  5 HELMSMAN 43      SLP SA/RC FBG KL IB 50  YAN  11  8 17000  6      67900  74600
44  2 BAVARIA 4200SL   FB  MY   FBG SV IB T306D VLVO 14   25000  4     132500 145500
44  2 BAVARIA 4200SL   FB  MY   FBG SV IB T358D VLVO 14   25000  4     136500 150000
46 10 HELMSMAN 47      SLP SA/RC FBG KL IB 62D VLVO 11  8 23100  6  7   93500 102500
46 10 HELMSMAN 47      SLP SA/RC FBG KL IB 62D YAN  11  8 23100  6  7   93600 103000
47  2 BAVARIA 45SL     FB  MY   FBG SV IB T358D VLVO 14   26500  4     161500 177500
49  3 HELMSMAN 50      KTH SA/CR FBG KL IB 62D YAN  11  8 23100  6  7  107500 118000
49  3 HELMSMAN 50      KTH SA/CR FBG KL IB 62D VLVO 11  8 23100  6  7  107500 118000
51  6 BAVARIA 48SL     FB  MY   FBG SV IB T400D BENZ 14 6 31000  4  3  186000 204500
----------------------- 1987 BOATS -----------------------------------------------------
28    BAVARIA 27       FB  SDN  FBG SV IO        VLVO 10  6  7500  2  9   **     **
      IB        VLVO    **   **  IB  260 VLVO 27700   30700, IB 200D VLVO 35600  39600
      IB T130-T175  28100  33000'

31  6 BAVARIA 31       FB  SDN  FBG SV IO        VLVO 10  6 10000  2  9    **     **
31  6 BAVARIA 31       FB  SDN  FBG SV IB T150-T260   10  6 10000  2  9   39300  48300
31  6 BAVARIA 31       FB  SDN  FBG SV IBT130D-T200D  10  6 10000  2  9   50900  61600
31  6 BAVARIA 31DS     FB  SPTCR FBG SV IO        VLVO 10 6 10000  2  9    **     **
31  6 BAVARIA 31DS     FB  SPTCR FBG SV IB T150-T260  10 6 10000  2  9   37100  44300
31  6 BAVARIA 31DS     FB  SPTCR FBG SV IBT130D-T200D 10 6 10000  2  9   46500  54400
31  6 BAVARIA 31FL     FB  SPTCR FBG SV IO        VLVO 10 6 10000  2  9    **     **
31  6 BAVARIA 31FL     FB  SPTCR FBG SV IB T150-T260  10 6 10000  2  9   36000  43200
31  6 BAVARIA 31FL     FB  SPTCR FBG SV IBT130D-T200D 10 6 10000  2  9   44900  53300
35    HELMSMAN 35      SLP SA/RC FBG KL IB 28D VLVO 11    12000  6       37800  42000
35    HELMSMAN 35      SLP SA/RC FBG KL IB 28D YAN  11    12000  6       37800  42000

38    BAVARIA 35       FB  EXP  FBG SV IB T290 VLVO 11  6 15000  3  7    69900  76800
38    BAVARIA 35       FB  EXP  FBG SV IB T175D VLVO 11 6 15000  3  7    78600  86400
38    BAVARIA 35       FB  EXP  FBG SV IB T225D VLVO 11 6 15000  3  7    80500  88500
38    HELMSMAN 38      SLP SA/RC FBG KL IB 28D VLVO 11    14500  5  5    47000  51600
38    HELMSMAN 38      SLP SA/RC FBG KL IB 28D YAN  11    14500  5  5    47000  51700
41  4 BAVARIA 40       FB  CNV  FBG SV IB T200D VLVO 13 6 22000  3  7   104000 114500
41  4 BAVARIA 40       FB  CNV  FBG SV IB T306D VLVO 13 6 22000  3  7   110500 121500
43  5 HELMSMAN 43      SLP SA/RC FBG KL IB 50  VLVO 11  8 17000  6       65400  71900
43  5 HELMSMAN 43      SLP SA/RC FBG KL IB 50  YAN  11  8 17000  6       65500  72000
44  2 BAVARIA 4200SL   FB  MY   FBG SV IB T306D VLVO 14   25000  4      126500 139000
44  2 BAVARIA 4200SL   FB  MY   FBG SV IB T358D VLVO 14   25000  4      130500 143500

46 10 HELMSMAN 47      SLP SA/RC FBG KL IB 62D VLVO 11  8 23100  6  7    88600  97300
46 10 HELMSMAN 47      SLP SA/RC FBG KL IB 62D YAN  11  8 23100  6  7    88700  97400
47  2 BAVARIA 45SL     FB  MY   FBG SV IB T358D VLVO 14   26500  4      154000 169500
49  3 HELMSMAN 47      KTH SA/CR FBG KL IB 62D YAN  11  8 23100  6  7   102000 112000
49  3 HELMSMAN 47      KTH SA/CR FBG KL IB 62D VLVO 11  8 23100  6  7   102000 112000
51  6 BAVARIA 48SL     FB  MY   FBG SV IB T400D BENZ 14 6 31000  4  3   178000 195500
----------------------- 1986 BOATS -----------------------------------------------------
23    FRIENDSHIP       SLP SA/RC FBG KL OB        8      2860  4 10   6150   7100
26  7 FRIENDSHIP       SLP SA/RC FBG KL IB     D  8 10   3900  4 10  10700  12200
28  7 FRIENDSHIP       SLP SA/RC FBG KL IB     D  9  4   7800  5  3  22800  25300
32  7 FRIENDSHIP       SLP SA/RC FBG KL IB     D 10 10   9350  5  6  28700  31900
34  6 FRIENDSHIP       SLP SA/RC FBG KL IB     D 11  5  13500  5  6  40100  44600
41    CORDOVAN         SLP SA/CR FBG KC IB     D 12  2        6  57400  63100
46 10 HELMSMAN         SLP SA/RC FBG KL IB     D 11  8  24700  6     86000  94600
----------------------- 1985 BOATS -----------------------------------------------------
21  4 BAVARIA 606      SLP SA/CR F/S KC OB        8      1980  1  7   4200   4850
23  3 BAVARIA 707      SLP SA/CR F/S KC IB        8      3085  2  3   6300   7250
23  3 BAVARIA 707      SLP SA/CR F/S KC OB        8      3085  2  3   7200   8300
25    BAVARIA 760      SLP SA/CR F/S KC OB        8      3500  2  2   7850   9050
25    BAVARIA 760      SLP SA/CR F/S KC IB     D BMW 8   3500  2  2   8600   9900
25  6 BAVARIA 770      SLP SA/CR F/S KL IB        8      3650  2  3   9250  10500
27    BAVARIA 820      SLP SA/CR F/S KC OB  9D VLVO 9  2 4750  2  3  12300  14000
29  4 BAVARIA 890      SLP SA/CR F/S KL IB 18D VLVO 9  7 7900  5  3  22200  24700
31  6 BAVARIA 940      SLP SA/RC FBG KC IB 18D VLVO 10 5 9600  2  3  28000  31100
32    BAVARIA 960      SLP SA/CR F/S KL IB 18D VLVO 10   8500  5  6  25000  27700
35    BAVARIA 1060     SLP SA/CR F/S KL IB 18D YAN  11 1 12000  5  6  33900  37600
37    BAVARIA 1130     SLP SA/CR F/S KL IB 28D VLVO 11 4 14330  6    40400  44900
```

BAY MARINE & YACHT INC
BAY MACHINE INC
ST PETERSBURG FL 33707   See inside cover to adjust price for area

```
      LOA  NAME AND/      TOP/ BOAT -HULL- ----ENGINE---   BEAM   WGT  DRAFT RETAIL RETAIL
      FT IN OR MODEL      RIG  TYPE MTL TP TP #  HP   MFG   FT IN  LBS  FT IN  LOW    HIGH
----------------------- 1985 BOATS -----------------------------------------------------
33    NAVIGATOR        SLP SA/CR FBG KL IB 15D YAN  9 11 10500  3  8  23700  26300
```

BAY STEALTH BY VIP
VIVIAN INDUSTRIES INC
VIVIAN LA 71082   See inside cover to adjust price for area

For more recent years, see the BUC Used Boat Price Guide, Volume 1

```
      LOA  NAME AND/        TOP/ BOAT -HULL- ----ENGINE---   BEAM   WGT  DRAFT RETAIL RETAIL
      FT IN OR MODEL        RIG  TYPE MTL TP TP #  HP   MFG   FT IN  LBS  FT IN  LOW    HIGH
----------------------- 1996 BOATS -----------------------------------------------------
18  8 BAY STEALTH 1880 CC  OP  CTRCN FBG SV OB    8  6  1600         4200   4850
18  8 BAY STEALTH 1880 CC  OP  CTRCN FBG TH OB    8  6  1600         4200   4850
21  8 BAY STEALTH 2108 CC  OP  CTRCN FBG SV OB    8  6  2180         6000   6900
21  8 BAY STEALTH 2108 CC  OP  CTRCN FBG TH OB    8  6  2180         6100   7000
21  8 BAY STEALTH 2180 CC  OP  CTRCN FBG SV OB    8  6  2180         6400   7350
21  8 BAY STEALTH 2180 CC  OP  CTRCN FBG TH OB    8  6  2180         6500   7450
```

BAYCRAFT MARINE
HAVREGRACE MD 21078   See inside cover to adjust price for area

```
      LOA  NAME AND/      TOP/ BOAT -HULL- ----ENGINE---   BEAM   WGT  DRAFT RETAIL RETAIL
      FT IN OR MODEL      RIG  TYPE MTL TP TP #  HP   MFG   FT IN  LBS  FT IN  LOW    HIGH
----------------------- 1985 BOATS -----------------------------------------------------
19    LIGHTNING        SLP SA/OD CB                 6  6   700  5      3350   3900
----------------------- 1984 BOATS -----------------------------------------------------
17    MOBJACK          SLP SA/OD CB                 5  6        9      2250   2650
19    LIGHTNING        SLP SA/OD CB                 5  6   700  5      3150   3700
```

....For earlier years, see the BUC Used Boat Price Guide, Volume 3

BAYFIELD BOAT YARD LTD
CLINTON ONTARIO CANADA COAST GUARD MFG ID- ZBY See inside cover to adjust price for area

```
      LOA  NAME AND/      TOP/ BOAT -HULL- ----ENGINE---   BEAM   WGT  DRAFT RETAIL RETAIL
      FT IN OR MODEL      RIG  TYPE MTL TP TP #  HP   MFG   FT IN  LBS  FT IN  LOW    HIGH
----------------------- 1989 BOATS -----------------------------------------------------
25    BAYFIELD 25      SLP SA/CR FBG KL IB  9D YAN  8  4  4300  2 11  16400  18700
31    BAYFIELD 29      CUT SA/CR FBG KL IB 18D YAN 10  2  8000  3  9  37100  41300
35    BAYFIELD 32-C    CUT SA/CR FBG KL IB 27D YAN 10  6  9600  3  9  44100  49000
41  3 BAYFIELD 36      CUT SA/CR FBG KL IB 44D YAN 12   18500  5     88400  97100
45  6 BAYFIELD 40      KTH SA/CR FBG KL IB 52D WEST 12  22000  5    113500 125000
----------------------- 1988 BOATS -----------------------------------------------------
25    BAYFIELD 25      SLP SA/CR FBG KL IB  9D YAN  8  4  4300  2 11  15400  17500
31    BAYFIELD 29      CUT SA/CR FBG KL IB 18D YAN 10  2  8000  3  9  34900  38800
35    BAYFIELD 32-C    CUT SA/CR FBG KL IB 27D YAN 10  6  9600  3  9  41100  45700
41  3 BAYFIELD 36      CUT SA/CR FBG KL IB 44D YAN 12   18500  5     83100  91400
45  6 BAYFIELD 40      KTH SA/CR FBG KL IB 52D WEST 12  22000  5    107000 117500
----------------------- 1987 BOATS -----------------------------------------------------
25    BAYFIELD 25      SLP SA/CR FBG KL IB  9D YAN  8  4  4300  2 11  14500  16500
31    BAYFIELD 29      CUT SA/CR FBG KL IB 18D YAN 10  2  7100  3  9  29100  32400
35    BAYFIELD 32-C    CUT SA/CR FBG KL IB 27D YAN 10  6  9600  3  9  38700  43400
41  3 BAYFIELD 36      CUT SA/CR FBG KL IB 44D YAN 12   18500  5     78200  85900
45  6 BAYFIELD 40      CUT SA/CR FBG KL IB 52D WEST 12  22000  4 11 100500 110500
----------------------- 1986 BOATS -----------------------------------------------------
25    BAYFIELD         SLP SA/CR FBG KL IB  9D YAN  8     4300  2 11  13700  15500
31    BAYFIELD 29      CUT SA/CR FBG KL IB 18D YAN 10  2  8000  3  9  30900  34300
35    BAYFIELD 32      CUT SA/CR FBG KL IB 27D YAN 10  6  9600  3  9  36400  40400
41  3 BAYFIELD 36      CUT SA/CR FBG KL IB 44D YAN 12   18500  5     73600  80800
45  6 BAYFIELD 40      CUT SA/CR FBG KL IB 52D WEST 12  22000  4 11  94600 104000
----------------------- 1985 BOATS -----------------------------------------------------
25    BAYFIELD 25      SLP SA/CR FBG KL IB  9D YAN  8     4300  2 11  12900  14600
29    BAYFIELD 29      CUT SA/CR FBG KL IB 15D YAN 10  2  7100  2  9  24700  27500
32    BAYFIELD 32      CUT SA/CR FBG KL IB 23D YAN 10  6  9600  3  9  35300  39200
```

LOA FT	LOA IN	NAME AND/ OR MODEL	TOP/ RIG	BOAT TYPE	-HULL- MTL	-HULL- TP	ENGINE TP	ENGINE # HP	ENGINE MFG	BEAM FT	BEAM IN	WGT LBS	DRAFT FT	DRAFT IN	RETAIL LOW	RETAIL HIGH
		1985 BOATS														
35		BAYFIELD 32C	CUT	SA/CR	FBG	KL	IB	23D	YAN	10	6	9600	3	9	34200	38000
41	3	BAYFIELD 36	CUT	SA/CR	FBG	KL	IB	44D	YAN	12		18500	5		69200	76000
45	6	BAYFIELD 40	CUT	SA/CR	FBG	KL	IB	52D		12		21000	4	11	87000	95600
45	6	BAYFIELD 40	KTH	SA/CR	FBG	KL	IB	52D	WEST	12		22000	5		89000	97800

....For earlier years, see the BUC Used Boat Price Guide, Volume 3

BAYLINER MARINE CORP

DIV OF BRUNSWICK
ARLINGTON WA 98223

COAST GUARD MFG ID- BLB
ALSO SEE TROPHY

See inside cover to adjust price for area

For more recent years, see the BUC Used Boat Price Guide, Volume 1

LOA FT	LOA IN	NAME AND/ OR MODEL	TOP/ RIG	BOAT TYPE	-HULL- MTL	-HULL- TP	ENGINE TP	ENGINE # HP	ENGINE MFG	BEAM FT	BEAM IN	WGT LBS	DRAFT FT	DRAFT IN	RETAIL LOW	RETAIL HIGH
		1996 BOATS														
16	1	CAPRI 1600 LS BR	OP	RNBT	FBG	DV	OB			6	11	1300	2	6	3050	3550
16	9	CAPRI 1700 LS BR	OP	RNBT	FBG	DV	OB			6	11	1362	2	6	3250	3800
16	9	CAPRI 1702 LS CUD	OP	CUD	FBG	DV	OB			6	11	1400	2	6	3350	3900
16	9	CAPRI 1704 SF	OP	RNBT	FBG	DV	OB			6	11	1400	2	6	3350	3900
16	9	CAPRI 1750 LS BR	OP	RNBT	FBG	DV	IO	115	MRCR	7		1850	2	6	4250	4950
17	1	TROPHY 1703	OP	CTRCN	FBG	SV	OB			6	11	1580	2	2	3650	4250
18		TROPHY 1802 CUD	OP	CUD	FBG	SV	OB			7	6	1525	2	10	3650	4250
18	4	CAPRI 1800 LS BR	OP	RNBT	FBG	DV	OB			7	2	1815	2	7	4100	4800
18	4	CAPRI 1850 LS BR	OP	RNBT	FBG	DV	IO	135-180		7	2	2325	2	7	5100	6000
18	4	CAPRI 1850 SS BR	OP	RNBT	FBG	DV	IO	135-180		7	2	2325	2	7	5250	6100
18	4	CAPRI 1851 SS BR	OP	RNBT	FBG	DV	IO	135-180		7	2	2325	2	7	5300	6150
18	4	CAPRI 1854 SF	OP	RNBT	FBG	DV	IO	135-180		7	2	2325	2	7	5500	6350
18	8	CAPRI 1950 CL BR	OP	RNBT	FBG	DV	IO	135	MRCR	7	6	1925	2	10	4950	5700
18	8	CAPRI 1952 CL CUD	OP	CUD	FBG	DV	IO	135	MRCR	7	6	2125	2	10	5450	6250
18	8	CAPRI 1954 CL SF	OP	RNBT	FBG	DV	IO	135	MRCR	7	6	1925	2	10	5250	6000
18	11	TROPHY 1903	OP	CTRCN	FBG	DV	OB			7	8	2087	2	9	4600	5300
20	1	TROPHY 2002 WA	OP	CUD	FBG	DV	OB			8		2700	2	7	5950	6850
20	2	CAPRI 2050 LS BR	OP	RNBT	FBG	DV	IO	135-250		7	6	2550	2	10	6900	8400
20	2	CAPRI 2050 SS	OP	RNBT	FBG	DV	IO	135-235		7	6	2445	2	10	6850	8200
20	2	CAPRI 2051 SS BR	OP	RNBT	FBG	DV	IO	135-235		7	6	2540	2	10	7000	8400
20	2	CAPRI 2052 LS CUD	OP	CUD	FBG	DV	IO	135-235		7	6	2460	2	10	7200	8600
21	5	SKI CHALLENGER 2180	OP	SKI	FBG	SV	VD	250	MRCR	8		3550	2	5	11700	13300
22	3	CIERA EXP 2252 CM	OP	CUD	FBG	DV	IO	180-190		8	1	3800	2	10	10200	11600
22	3	CIERA EXP 2252 CM	OP	CUD	FBG	DV	IO	235	MRCR	8	1	3800	2	10	12000	13700
22	3	CIERA EXP 2252 CP	OP	CUD	FBG	DV	IO	180-235		8	1	3800	2	10	10400	12200
22	6	CAPRI 2250 LS BR	OP	RNBT	FBG	DV	IO	235-300		8	5	3875	3		10400	12800
22	6	CAPRI 2250 SS BR	OP	RNBT	FBG	DV	IO	235-300		8	5	3600	3		11400	13000
22	6	CAPRI 2252 LS CUD	OP	CUD	FBG	DV	IO	235-300		8	5	3875	3		11800	14400
22	7	RENDEZVOUS 2309	OP	RNBT	FBG	TH	OB			8		2827	2	1	7550	8700
22	7	RENDEZVOUS 2359	OP	RNBT	FBG	TH	IO	180-250		8		3450	2	1	9950	11700
22	7	TROPHY 2352 WA	OP	CUD	FBG	DV	IO	180-250		8	6	4050	2	10	12100	14100
23	4	CIERA 2355 SB	OP	CR	FBG	SV	IO	180-235		8	6	4615	2	10	13800	16000
23	5	CIERA EXP 2452	HT	CR	FBG	DV	IO	190-250		8	4	4625	2	11	13900	15800
23	5	CIERA EXP 2452 EXP	HT	CR	FBG	DV	IO	250	MRCR	8	4	4625	2	11	14900	16900
24	7	TROPHY 2502 WA FSH	OP	CUD	FBG	DV	OB			9	6	5560	2	9	12400	14100
26	4	RENDEZVOUS 2609	OP	RNBT	FBG	TH	OB			8	5	4300	2	5	12500	14200
26	4	RENDEZVOUS 2659	OP	RNBT	FBG	TH	IO	180-250		8	5	4800	2	6	14900	17800
26	4	RENDEZVOUS 2659	OP	RNBT	FBG	TH	IO	300	MRCR	8	5	4800	2	6	16400	18700
27	3	TROPHY 2503	OP	CTRCN	FBG	DV	OB			8	5	4150	2	5	14200	16100
27	3	TROPHY 2509 WA	OP	CUD	FBG	DV	OB			8	5	3895	2	5	14200	16200
27	8	CIERA EXP 2859 CR	HT	CR	FBG	DV	IO	250-300		9	9	7600	3	3	24400	28100
27	8	CIERA EXP 2859 CR	HT	CR	FBG	DV	IO	200D	MRCR	9	9	7600	3	3	29400	32700
27	9	CIERA 2655 SB	OP	CR	FBG	SV	IO	235-250		8	5	5175	2	10	17400	20100
30	3	CIERA 2855 SB	OP	CR	FBG	SV	IO	235-300		9	7	6750	3	1	22100	25600
30	3	CIERA 2855 SB	OP	CR	FBG	SV	IO	238D	MRCR	9	7	6750	3	1	24500	27300
30	6	CIERA EXP 2858 CB	FB	CR	FBG	DV	IO	300	MRCR	9	10	8197	3	6	29200	32500
30	6	CIERA EXP 2858 CB	FB	CR	FBG	DV	IO	200D	MRCR	9	10	8197	3	6	31300	34800
32	11	AVANTI 3255 SB	OP	SPTCR	FBG	DV	IO	T250-T300		11		11000	2	11	43700	50100
32	11	AVANTI 3255 SB	OP	SPTCR	FBG	DV	IO	T200D	MRCR	11		11000	2	11	50300	55200
32	11	AVANTI 3258 CB	FB	SPTCR	FBG	DV	IO	T250-T300		11		11900	3	3	48800	55300
32	11	AVANTI 3258 CB	FB	SPTCR	FBG	DV	IO	T200D	MRCR	11		11900	3	3	56900	62500
32	11	MOTORYACHT 3388 CB	FB	MY	FBG	DV	IB	T235	MRCR	11	6	13000	2	11	61800	67900
32	11	MOTORYACHT 3388 CB	FB	MY	FBG	DV	IB	T150D	CUM	11	6	13000	2	11	70800	77800
34	6	AVANTI 3485 SB	OP	SPTCR	FBG	DV	VD	T235-T300		11		11150	3	2	58900	66600
34	6	AVANTI 3485 SB	OP	SPTCR	FBG	DV	VD	T250D-T315D		11		11150	3	2	70800	82300
34	6	AVANTI 3488 CB	FB	SPTCR	FBG	DV	VD	T235-T300		11		11275	3	5	59100	66800
34	6	AVANTI 3488 CB	FB	SPTCR	FBG	DV	VD	T250D-T315D		11		11275	3	5	71100	82600
34	8	MOTORYACHT 3587 AC	FB	MY	FBG	DV	IB	T310	MRCR	13	1	18000	3	6	78600	86400
34	8	MOTORYACHT 3587 AC	FB	MY	FBG	DV	IB	T250D	CUM	13	1	18000	3	6	95400	105000
36		MOTORYACHT 3788 CB	FB	MY	FBG	DV	IB	T310	MRCR	13	5	17000	3	6	79800	87700
36		MOTORYACHT 3788 CB	FB	MY	FBG	DV	IB	T210D	CUM	13	5	17000	3	6	89600	98400
36		MOTORYACHT 3788 CB	FB	MY	FBG	DV	IB	T250D	CUM	13	5	17000	3	6	92000	101000
39		MOTORYACHT 3988 CB	FB	MY	FBG	DV	IB	T310	MRCR	13	11	21000	3	2	102500	112500
39		MOTORYACHT 3988 CB	FB	MY	FBG	DV	IB	T250D	CUM	13	11	21000	3	2	115500	127000
39		MOTORYACHT 3988 CB	FB	MY	FBG	DV	IB	T315D	CUM	13	11	21000	3	2	120000	132000
41	5	MOTORYACHT 4087 AC	FB	MY	FBG	DV	IB	T310	MRCR	13	1	19000	3	6	108000	118500
41	5	MOTORYACHT 4087 AC	FB	MY	FBG	DV	IB	T210D	CUM	13	1	19000	3	6	116000	127500
41	5	MOTORYACHT 4087 AC	FB	MY	FBG	DV	IB	T315D	CUM	13	1	19000	3	6	126500	139000
47	4	MOTORYACHT 4788 PH	EPH	MY	FBG	DV	IB	T310	MRCR	14	11	30000	3	4	165500	181500
47	4	MOTORYACHT 4788 PH	EPH	MY	FBG	DV	IB	T315D	CUM	14	11	30000	3	4	190000	209000
		1995 BOATS														
16	9	CAPRI 1700 LS BR	OP	RNBT	FBG	DV	OB			7		1650	2	6	3600	4200
16	9	CAPRI 1750 LS BR	OP	RNBT	FBG	DV	IO	115	MRCR	7		1850	2	6	3950	4600
17		CAPRI 1702 LS CUD	OP	CUD	FBG	DV	OB			7		1710	2	6	3700	4300
17		CAPRI 1704 SF	OP	RNBT	FBG	DV	OB			7		1550	2	6	3450	4000
17	1	TROPHY 1703	OP	CTRCN	FBG	SV	OB			6	11	1610	2	2	3550	4100
18		TROPHY 1802 CUD	OP	CUD	FBG	SV	OB			7	6	1950	2	5	4050	4700
18	4	CAPRI 1800 LS BR	OP	RNBT	FBG	DV	OB			7	2	1800	2	6	3900	4550
18	4	CAPRI 1850 LS BR	OP	RNBT	FBG	DV	IO	135-180		7	2	2325	2	9	4800	5600
18	4	CAPRI 1850 SS BR	OP	RNBT	FBG	DV	IO	135-180		7	2	2325	2	9	4850	5700
18	4	CAPRI 1851 CL BR	OP	RNBT	FBG	DV	IO	135-180		7	2	2250	2	9	4850	5650
18	4	CAPRI 1854 SF	OP	RNBT	FBG	DV	IO	135-180		7	2	2325	2	9	5150	5950
18	8	CAPRI 1950 CL BR	OP	RNBT	FBG	DV	IO	135	MRCR	7	6	1995	2	8	4800	5550
18	8	CAPRI 1952 CL CUD	OP	CUD	FBG	DV	IO	135	MRCR	7	6	2125	2	8	5100	5850
18	8	CAPRI 1954 CL SF	OP	RNBT	FBG	DV	IO	135	MRCR	7	6	2050	2	8	4900	5600
18	11	TROPHY 1903	OP	CTRCN	FBG	DV	OB			7	8	2087	2	9	4350	5000
20		TROPHY 2003	OP	CTRCN	FBG	DV	OB			8	3	2900	2	5	5700	6600
20	1	TROPHY 2002 WA	OP	CUD	FBG	DV	OB			8		2850	2	5	5800	6650
20	2	CAPRI 2050 LS BR	OP	RNBT	FBG	DV	IO	135-205		7	6	2550	2	11	6450	7550
20	2	CAPRI 2050 LS SE	OP	RNBT	FBG	DV	IO	135-205		7	6	2550	2	11	6700	7800
20	2	CAPRI 2050 SS	OP	RNBT	FBG	DV	IO	135-205		7	6	2550	2	11	6550	7650
20	2	CAPRI 2051 CL BR	OP	RNBT	FBG	DV	IO	135-205		7	5	2380	2	9	6300	7400
20	2	CAPRI 2052 CUD	OP	CUD	FBG	DV	IO	135-205		7	6	2460	2	11	6700	7850
22	3	CLASSIC 22 CUD	OP	CUD	FBG	DV	IO	160-180		8	1	3800	2	10	10300	11800
22	5	RENDEZVOUS 2309 DECK	OP	RNBT	FBG	TR	OB			8		3100	2	3	7600	8700
22	5	RENDEZVOUS 2359 DECK	OP	RNBT	FBG	SV	IO	135-180		8	2	3650	2	3	9600	11000
22	7	CAPRI 2250 LS BR	OP	RNBT	FBG	DV	IO	205-235		8	5	3600	3		9100	10600
22	7	CAPRI 2250 LS BR	OP	RNBT	FBG	DV	IO	300	MRCR	8	5	3600	3		10000	11400
22	7	CAPRI 2250 SS BR	OP	RNBT	FBG	DV	IO	205-300		8	5	3600	3		9250	11500
22	7	TROPHY 2302 WA	OP	CUD	FBG	DV	OB			8	6	3250	2	9	7900	9100
22	7	TROPHY 2352 WA	OP	CUD	FBG	DV	IO	180-235		8	6	3975	2	9	11100	12900
22	7	TROPHY 2359 CUD	HT	SF	FBG	DV	IO	180-235		8	6	4325	2	9	13500	15600
23	4	CIERA 2355 SB	OP	CR	FBG	SV	IO	180-205		8	6	4615	2	6	12900	14800
23	5	CLASSIC 24 EXP	HT	CR	FBG	DV	IO	190-250		8	4	4625	2	11	11400	13300
24	7	TROPHY 2502 WA FSH	OP	CUD	FBG	DV	OB			9	6	5560	1	10	11800	13400
26	1	RENDEZVOUS 2609GA DK	OP	RNBT	FBG	SV	OB			8	4	4000	1	8	10700	12200
26	1	RENDEZVOUS 2609GE DK	OP	RNBT	FBG	SV	OB			8	4	4000	1	8	10800	12300
26	6	RENDEZVOUS 2659 DECK	OP	RNBT	FBG	SV	IO	180-300		8	6	5000	2	6	13400	16800
27	8	CLASSIC 2858 CB	FB	CR	FBG	DV	IO	300	MRCR	9	9	7900	3	3	24100	26700
27	8	CLASSIC 2858 CB	FB	CR	FBG	DV	IO	200D	MRCR	9	9	7900	3	3	28300	31500
27	8	SUPER CLASSIC 2859	HT	CR	FBG	DV	IO	235-300		9	9	7600	3	3	22600	26200
27	8	SUPER CLASSIC 2859	HT	CR	FBG	DV	IO	200D	MRCR	9	9	7600	3	3	27400	30500
27	9	CIERA 2655 SB	OP	CR	FBG	SV	IO	205-235		8	5	5175	3	1	15900	18500
30	3	CIERA 2855 SB	OP	CR	FBG	SV	IO	235-300		9	7	6750	3	4	20600	23900
30	3	CIERA 2855 SB	OP	CR	FBG	SV	IO	238D	MRCR	9	7	6750	3	4	22900	25400
32	1	MOTOR YACHT 3288 CB	FB	MY	FBG	DV	IB	T150D		11	6	12500	2	11	63700	70000
32	11	AVANTI 3255 CB	FB	SPTCR	FBG	DV	IO	T250-T300		11		11900	3		41500	47500
32	11	AVANTI 3255 SB	OP	SPTCR	FBG	DV	IO	T250-T300		11		11000	3		40700	46700
32	11	AVANTI 3255 SB	OP	SPTCR	FBG	DV	IO	T200D	MRCR	11		11000	3		47100	51800
34	8	MOTOR YACHT 3587 AC	FB	MY	FBG	DV	IB	T300	MRCR	13	1	18000	3	1	74000	81300
34	8	MOTOR YACHT 3587 AC	FB	MY	FBG	DV	IB	T250D		13	1	18000	3	1	90800	99800
39		MOTOR YACHT 3988 CB	FB	MY	FBG	DV	IB	T300	MRCR	13	11	21000	3	2	98200	108000
39		MOTOR YACHT 3988 CB	FB	MY	FBG	DV	IB	T250D		13	11	21000	3	2	111500	123000
39		MOTOR YACHT 3988 CB	FB	MY	FBG	DV	IB	T310D		13	11	21000	3	2	116000	127500
45	1	MOTOR YACHT 4587 AC	FB	MY	FBG	DV	IB	T250D		14	3	25000	3		136500	150000
45	1	MOTOR YACHT 4587 AC	FB	MY	FBG	DV	IB	T310D		14	3	25000	3		145500	160000
47	4	MOTOR YACHT 4788 PH	EPH	MY	FBG	DV	IB	T300	MRCR	14	11	30000	3	4	157500	173000
47	4	MOTOR YACHT 4788 PH	EPH	MY	FBG	DV	IB	T250D		14	11	30000	3	4	170000	187000
47	4	MOTOR YACHT 4788 PH	EPH	MY	FBG	DV	IB	T310D		14	11	30000	3	4	185000	203500

CONTINUED ON NEXT PAGE

LOA FT	LOA IN	NAME AND/ OR MODEL	TOP/ RIG	BOAT TYPE	-HULL- MTL	-HULL- TP	ENGINE TP	ENGINE # HP	ENGINE MFG	BEAM FT	BEAM IN	WGT LBS	DRAFT FT	DRAFT IN	RETAIL LOW	RETAIL HIGH
		1994 BOATS														
17		CAPRI 1700 LS BR	OP	RNBT	FBG	DV	OB			7		1550	2	6	3300	3800
17		CAPRI 1750 LS BR	OP	RNBT	FBG	DV	IO	115	MRCR	7		1750	2	6	3650	4250
18	4	CAPRI 1800 LS BR	OP	RNBT	FBG	DV	OB			7	2	1800	2	6	3700	4300
18	4	CAPRI 1850 LS BR	OP	RNBT	FBG	DV	IO	135-180		7	2	2325	2	9	4450	5350
18	4	CAPRI 1850 SS	OP	RNBT	FBG	DV	IO	135-180		7	2	2325	2	9	4650	5400
18	4	CAPRI 1851 SS	OP	RNBT	FBG	DV	IO	135-180		7	2	2250	2	9	4450	5500
18	8	CAPRI 1950 CL BR	OP	RNBT	FBG	DV	IO	115	MRCR	7	6	1995	2	8	4500	5200
18	8	CAPRI 1952 CL CUD	OP	CUD	FBG	DV	IO	115	MRCR	7	6	2125	2	8	4750	5450
18	8	CAPRI 1954 CL SF	OP	RNBT	FBG	DV	IO	115	MRCR	7	6	2050			4550	5250
20	1	TROPHY 2002 WA FSH	OP	CUD	FBG	DV	OB			8		2840	2	5	5500	6350
20	2	CAPRI 2050 LS BR	OP	RNBT	FBG	DV	IO	135-205		7	6	2445	2	11	5200	6450
20	2	CAPRI 2050 SS	OP	RNBT	FBG	DV	IO	135-205		7	6	2445	2	11	5350	6600
20	2	CAPRI 2052 CUD	OP	CUD	FBG	DV	IO	135	MRCR	7	6	2475	2	11	5500	6300
20	2	CAPRI 2052 CUD	OP	CUD	FBG	DV	IO	180-205		7	6	2620	2	11	6500	7800
22	2	CLASSIC 2252 WE	OP	CUD	FBG	DV	IO	160-180		8		3800	2	10	9600	10900
22	5	RENDEZVOUS 2309 DECK	OP	RNBT	FBG	TR	OB			7	11	3100	2	3	7250	8350
22	5	RENDEZVOUS 2359 DECK	OP	RNBT	FBG	SV	OB			7	11	3650	2	3	7950	9150
22	7	TROPHY 2302 WA FSH	OP	CUD	FBG	SV	OB			8	6	3120	2	9	7350	8450
22	7	TROPHY 2352 WA FSH	HT	CUD	FBG	SV	IO	180-235		8	6	4150	2	9	10700	12600
22	7	TROPHY 2359 CUD	HT	SF	FBG	DV	IO	235	MRCR	8	6	4240	2	9	12600	14400
22	7	TROPHY 2359 CUD	HT	SF	FBG	SV	IO	180	MRCR	8	6	4150	2	9	12200	13900
23	4	CIERA 2355 SB	OP	CR	FBG	SV	IO	180-205		8	6	3850	2	6	10500	12200
23	7	CLASSIC 2452 EXP	HT	CR	FBG	SV	IO	190-235		8	6	4625	2	11	10800	12500
24	7	TROPHY 2502 WA FSH	HT	CUD	FBG	DV	OB			9	6	4765	1	10	10600	12000
25		CIERA 2556 CB	FB	CR	FBG	DV	IO	250-300		9	6	5685	3	3	15800	18800
25		CIERA 2556 CB	FB	CR	FBG	DV	IO	170D	MRCR	9	6	5685	3	3	19300	21400
25	11	RENDEZVOUS 2609 DECK	OP	RNBT	FBG	SV	OB			8	4	3300	1	8	10000	11400
27	9	CIERA 2655 SB	OP	CR	FBG	SV	IO	205-235		8	5	4970	3	1	14600	17000
27	10	CLASSIC 2858 CB	FB	CR	FBG	DV	IO	300	MRCR	9	9	7610	3	3	22200	24700
27	10	CLASSIC 2858 CB	FB	CR	FBG	DV	IO	200D	MRCR	9	9	7610	3	3	25700	28500
28		SUPER CLASSIC 2859	FB	CR	FBG	SV	IO	250-300		10		6600			19700	22900
28		SUPER CLASSIC 2859	FB	CR	FBG	SV	IO	200D	MRCR	10		6950			23400	25900
30	3	CIERA 2855 SB	OP	CR	FBG	SV	IO	235-300		9	7	6600	3	4	19100	22300
30	7	CIERA 3055 SB	OP	CR	FBG	SV	IO	300	MRCR	10		8000	3		22200	24600
30	7	CIERA 3055 SB	OP	CR	FBG	SV	IO	T205	MRCR	10		8850	3		24000	26600
30	7	CIERA 3055 SB	OP	CR	FBG	SV	IO	T140D	MRCR	10		9000	3		27600	30700
32	1	MOTOR YACHT 3288	FB	CR	FBG	SV	IB	T140D	MRCR	11	6	11500	2	11	51400	56500
34	7	SUNBRIDGE 3555	OP	SPTCR	FBG	SV	IB	T235	MRCR	11	5	10200	3	8	50900	55900
34	7	SUNBRIDGE 3555	OP	SPTCR	FBG	SV	IB	T170D-T200D		11	5	10200	3	8	57400	64200
36	1	MOTOR YACHT 3688	FB	CR	FBG	SV	IB	T200D		12	2	13700	2	11	73600	80900
36	1	MOTOR YACHT 3688	FB	CR	FBG	SV	IB	T250D		12	2	13700	2	11	76100	83700
38	2	MOTOR YACHT 3888	FB	DCMY	FBG	SV	IB	T200D		13	5	17500	3	2	98100	108000
43	1	MID CABIN 4388	FB	DCMY	FBG	SV	IB	T300D		14	3	19000			122000	134000
43	1	MID CABIN 4388 MY	FB	DCMY	FBG	SV	IB	T240D		14	3	19000	3		116000	127500
43	1	MOTOR YACHT 4387	FB	DCMY	FBG	SV	IB	T300		14	3	20000	3		110000	121000
43	1	MOTOR YACHT 4387	FB	DCMY	FBG	SV	IB	T240D		14	3	20000	3		120500	132500
47	4	MOTOR YACHT 4788	FB	TCMY	FBG	SV	IB	T240D		14	11	30000	3	4	159000	175000
47	4	MOTOR YACHT 4788	FB	TCMY	FBG	SV	IB	T300D		14	11	30000	3	4	175000	192500
51	2	MOTOR YACHT 4587	FB	DCMY	FBG	SV	IB	T240D		14	3	24600	3		128000	140500
51	2	MOTOR YACHT 4587	FB	DCMY	FBG	SV	IB	T300D		14	3	24600	3		138000	152000
		1993 BOATS														
16	7	CAPRI 1700 BR	OP	RNBT	FBG	DV	OB			5	10	1040	2	1	2300	2650
16	7	CAPRI 1750 BR	OP	RNBT	FBG	DV	IO	130	MRCR	5	10		2	9	3150	3650
18		COBRA 1809	OP	BASS	FBG	DV	OB								3750	4350
18	4	CAPRI 1800 BR	OP	RNBT	FBG	DV	OB			7	2	1800	2	9	3500	4100
18	4	CAPRI 1850 BR	OP	RNBT	FBG	DV	IO	130-205		7	2	2250	2	9	3850	4650
18	4	CAPRI 1850 DARE	OP	RNBT	FBG	DV	IO	130-205		7	2	2250	2	9	4500	5200
18	4	CAPRI 1851 SPORT	OP	RNBT	FBG	DV	IO	130-205		7	2	2250	2	9	4000	4800
18	8	CLASSIC 1950 BR	OP	RNBT	FBG	DV	IO	130	MRCR	7	6	1995	2	8	4200	4850
18	8	CLASSIC 1952 CUD	OP	CUD	FBG	DV	IO	130	MRCR	7	6	1995	2	8	4300	5000
18	8	CLASSIC 1954 SF	OP	RNBT	FBG	DV	IO	130	MRCR	7	6	2050			4250	4900
20	1	TROPHY 2002 WA FSH	OP	CUD	FBG	DV	OB			8		2840	2	5	5300	6050
20	1	TROPHY 2003 CC	OP	CTRCN	FBG	DV	OB			8		2710	2	5	5150	5950
20	2	CAPRI 2050 BR	OP	RNBT	FBG	DV	IO	130-230		7	6	2350	2	9	4750	5750
20	2	CAPRI 2051 SPORT	OP	RNBT	FBG	DV	IO	130-230		7	6	2475	2	9	5050	5900
20	2	CAPRI 2052 CUD	OP	FSH	FBG	DV	IO	130	MRCR	7	6	2425	2	9	5350	6150
20	2	CAPRI 2052 FSH	OP	CUD	FBG	DV	IO	205-230		7	6	2425	2	9	5200	6100
20	2	TROPHY 2059 FSH	OP	CUD	FBG	SV	IO	130-175		8		3580	2	11	7650	8800
22		CIERA 2255 SB	OP	CR	FBG	SV	IO	200-205		8		3680	3	4	8700	10000
22	2	CLASSIC 2250 BR	OP	RNBT	FBG	DV	IO	230-260		8		3800			8600	10100
22	2	CLASSIC 2252 WE	OP	CUD	FBG	DV	IO	175	MRCR	8		3680	3	4	8800	10000
22	7	TROPHY 2302 WA FSH	OP	CUD	FBG	SV	OB			8	6	3120	2	9	7050	8100
22	7	TROPHY 2352 WA FSH	HT	CUD	FBG	SV	IO	205-260		8	6	4150	2	9	10100	11800
22	7	TROPHY 2359 CUD	HT	SF	FBG	DV	IO	260	MRCR	8	6	4150	2	9	11800	13500
22	7	TROPHY 2359 CUD	HT	SF	FBG	SV	IO	205	MRCR	8	6	4150	2	9	11500	13000
23	7	CLASSIC 2452 EXP	HT	CR	FBG	SV	IO	190-270		8	6	4625			10100	11900
23	9	ARRIVA 2452 CUD	OP	CUD	FBG	SV	IO	200	MRCR	8	6	3665	2	9	9700	11000
24	7	TROPHY 2502 WA FSH	HT	CUD	FBG	DV	OB			9	6	4765	1	10	10100	11500
25		CIERA 2556 CB	FB	CR	FBG	DV	IO	270-330		9	6	5685	3	3	15000	18100
25		CIERA 2556 CB	FB	CR	FBG	DV	IO	180D	MRCR	9	6	5685	3	3	18400	20500
25	7	CIERA 2655 SB	OP	CR	FBG	SV	IO	160-230		8		4300	3	3	10900	13000
25	11	RENDEZVOUS 2609 DECK	OP	RNBT	FBG	DV	OB			8	4	3300	1	8	9600	10900
27		CIERA 2755 SB	OP	CR	FBG	SV	IO	260-330		8	6	5200	3	3	13800	16800
28		SUPER CLASSIC 2859	FB	CR	FBG	SV	IO	270	MRCR	10		8000			20500	22800
28		SUPER CLASSIC 2859	FB	CR	FBG	SV	IO	330	MRCR	10		8000			21400	23800
28		SUPER CLASSIC 2859	FB	CR	FBG	SV	IO	330D		10		8000			27400	30400
28	1	CIERA 2855 SB	OP	CR	FBG	DV	IO	180D	MRCR	9	6	6649	3	3	18500	20600
28	1	CIERA 2855 SB	OP	CR	FBG	SV	IO	260-330		9	6	6510	3	3	16200	19400
30	7	CIERA 3055 SB	OP	CR	FBG	SV	IO	330	MRCR	10		8000	3		21100	23400
30	7	CIERA 3055 SB	OP	CR	FBG	SV	IO	T205	MRCR	10		8000	3		21800	24200
30	7	CIERA 3055 SB	OP	CR	FBG	SV	IO	T150D	MRCR	10		8000	3		24500	27300
30	7	CIERA 3058 CB	FB	CR	FBG	SV	IO	T205-T260		10		9200	3		26000	30100
30	7	CIERA 3058 CB	FB	CR	FBG	SV	IO	T150D	MRCR	10		9200	3		30000	33300
32	1	MOTOR YACHT 3288	FB	CR	FBG	SV	IB	T		11	6	11500	2	11	**	**
32	1	MOTOR YACHT 3288	FB	CR	FBG	SV	IB	T150D	MRCR	11	6	11500	2	11	49400	54300
34	7	AVANTI 3555 SB	OP	SPTCR	FBG	SV	IO	T260	MRCR	11	5	10200	2	4	34300	38100
34	7	AVANTI 3555 SB	OP	SPTCR	FBG	SV	IO	T180D	MRCR	11	5	10000	2	4	36800	40900
34	7	SUNBRIDGE 3555	OP	OFF	FBG	SV	IB	T150D	MRCR	11	5	10200			56100	61700
36	1	MID CABIN 3688	FB	CR	FBG	DV	IB	T250D		12	2	13700			72500	79700
36	1	MOTOR YACHT 3688	FB	CR	FBG	DV	IB	T210D		12	2	13700	2	11	70600	77500
38	2	MOTOR YACHT 3888	FB	DCMY	FBG	SV	IB	T250D		13	5	17500	3	2	96000	105500
43	1	MID CABIN 4388	FB	DCMY	FBG	SV	IB	T310D		14	3	19000			117500	129500
43	1	MID CABIN 4388 MY	FB	DCMY	FBG	SV	IB	T250D		14	3	19000	3		112000	123000
43	1	MOTOR YACHT 4387	FB	DCMY	FBG	SV	IB	T310		14	3	20000	3		106000	116500
43	1	MOTOR YACHT 4387	FB	DCMY	FBG	SV	IB	T250D		14	3	20000	3		116500	128000
45	4	MOTOR YACHT 4588	FB	TCMY	FBG	SV	IB	T250D		14	11	28000	3		148500	163000
		1992 BOATS														
16	7	CAPRI 1700 BR	OP	RNBT	FBG	DV	OB			5	10	1040	2	1	2200	2550
17	4	COBRA 1704	OP	BASS	FBG	DV	OB			7	6	1650	2	2	3150	3650
17	10	CAPRI 1800 BR	OP	RNBT	FBG	DV	OB			7		1500	2	9	2950	3450
17	10	CAPRI 1850 BR	OP	RNBT	FBG	DV	IO	130-175		7		1880	2	9	3500	4100
17	10	CAPRI 1851 CB	OP	RNBT	FBG	DV	IO	175	MRCR	7		1880	2	9	3500	4100
17	10	CAPRI 1851 SPORT	OP	RNBT	FBG	DV	IO	115	MRCR	7		1880	2	9	3450	4050
17	11	COBRA FISH & SKI	OP	BASS	FBG	DV	OB			7	3	1650	2	2	3200	3700
18	7	ARRIVA 1800 BR	OP	RNBT	FBG	DV	OB			7	9	1995	2	2	3600	4200
18	8	CLASSIC 1950 BR	OP	RNBT	FBG	DV	IO	115	MRCR	7	6	1995	2	8	3900	4550
18	8	CLASSIC 1952 CUD	OP	CUD	FBG	DV	IO	115	MRCR	7	6	1995	2	8	4000	4650
18	8	COBRA 1903 CC	OP	BASS	FBG	DV	OB			8		2000	2	2	3650	4200
19	3	COBRA 1904 SKI	OP	BASS	FBG	DV	OB			7	3	1830	2	2	3550	4150
19	8	ARRIVA 2000 BR	OP	RNBT	FBG	DV	OB			7	4	2120	2	9	4000	4650
19	8	ARRIVA 2050 BR	OP	RNBT	FBG	DV	IO	260	MRCR	7	4	2240	2	9	4700	5400
19	10	CAPRI 2000 BR	OP	RNBT	FBG	DV	OB			7	4	1700	2	9	3500	4100
19	10	CAPRI 2050 BR	OP	RNBT	FBG	DV	IO	115-155		7	4	2150	2	9	4150	5100
19	10	CAPRI 2050 BR	OP	RNBT	FBG	DV	IO	180	MRCR	7	4	2368	2	9	4550	5200
19	10	CAPRI 2051 SPORT	OP	RNBT	FBG	DV	IO	115-180		7	4	2150	2	9	4400	5100
19	10	CAPRI 2052 CUD	OP	CUD	FBG	DV	IO	115-180		7	4	2150	2	9	4450	5450
19	10	CAPRI 2070 BR	OP	RNBT	FBG	DV	IO	120	FRCE	7	4	1730	2	9	3950	4600
19	10	CAPRI 2072 CUD	OP	CUD	FBG	DV	IO	120	FRCE	7	4	1850	2	9	4150	4850
20	1	TROPHY 2000 DUAL	OP	OPFSH	FBG	DV	OB			8		2700	2	5	4950	5700
20	1	TROPHY 2002 DUAL CUD	OP	CUD	FBG	DV	OB			8		2975	2	5	5150	5900
20	1	TROPHY 2002 WA CUD	OP	CUD	FBG	DV	OB			8		2840	2	5	5050	5850
20	1	TROPHY 2003 CC	OP	CTRCN	FBG	DV	OB			8		2710	2	5	4950	5700
20	1	TROPHY 2302 CC	OP	FSH	FBG	SV	OB			8	6	3384	2	9	5150	5950
20	8	TROPHY 2059 CUD	OP	CUD	FBG	SV	IO	115-155		8		3580	2	11	7350	8550
22		CIERA 2255 SB	OP	CR	FBG	SV	IO	155-180		8		3680	3	4	8050	9450
22	2	CLASSIC 2252 WE	OP	CUD	FBG	DV	IO	155	MRCR	8		3680	3	4	8150	9350
22	7	TROPHY 2302 CUD	OP	FSH	FBG	SV	OB			8	6	3120			6700	7800
22	7	TROPHY 2352 CUD	HT	CUD	FBG	SV	IO	155-230		8	6	4150	2	9	9400	11000
22	7	TROPHY 2359 CUD	HT	FSH	FBG	DV	IO	230	MRCR	8	6	4150	2	9	10100	11400
23	8	TROPHY 2359 CUD	HT	SF	FBG	SV	IO	205	MRCR	8		4150	3		11200	12700
23	9	ARRIVA 2452 CUD	OP	CUD	FBG	SV	IO	330	MRCR	8	6	3665	2	9	10400	11800
24	7	TROPHY 2502	HT	FSH	FBG	DV	OB			9	6	4765	1	10	9600	10900
25		CIERA 2556 CB	FB	CR	FBG	DV	IO	230-300		9	6	5546	3	3	13500	16600
25		CIERA 2556 CB	FB	CR	FBG	DV	IO	180D	MRCR	9	6	5685	3	3	16800	19100
25	7	CIERA 2655 SB	OP	CR	FBG	SV	IO	205-230		8		4300	3	3	10500	12300

 CONTINUED ON NEXT PAGE

BAYLINER MARINE CORP -CONTINUED See inside cover to adjust price for area

LOA FT	LOA IN	NAME AND/ OR MODEL	TOP/ RIG	BOAT TYPE	-HULL- MTL	-HULL- TP	ENGINE TP	ENGINE # HP	ENGINE MFG	BEAM FT	BEAM IN	WGT LBS	DRAFT FT	DRAFT IN	RETAIL LOW	RETAIL HIGH
		1992 BOATS														
25	11	RENDEZVOUS 2609 DECK	OP	RNBT	FBG	DV	OB			8	4	3300	1	8	9250	10500
27		CIERA 2755 SB	OP	CR	FBG	SV	IO	230-300		8	6	5200	3	3	12600	15400
28	1	CIERA 2855 CB	OP	CR	FBG	DV	IO	180D	MRCR	9	6	6649	3	3	19200	21300
28	1	CIERA 2855 SB	OP	CR	FBG	SV	IO	230-300		9	6	6510	3	3	14800	17800
30	7	CIERA 3055 SB	OP	CR	FBG	SV	IO	300	MRCR	10		8000	3		19400	21600
30	7	CIERA 3055 SB	OP	CR	FBG	SV	IO	T205	MRCR	10		8766	3		20900	23200
30	7	CIERA 3055 SB	OP	CR	FBG	SV	IO	T150D	MRCR	10		9024	3		24400	27200
30	7	CIERA 3058 CB	FB	CR	FBG	SV	IO	300	MRCR	10		7434	3		22000	24400
30	7	CIERA 3058 CB	FB	CR	FBG	SV	IO	T205	MRCR	10		8200	3		23700	26300
30	7	CIERA 3058 SB	OP	CR	FBG	SV	IO	T150D	MRCR	10		8464	3		26800	29800
32	1	MOTOR YACHT 3288	FB	MY	FBG	SV	IB	T210	USMA	11	6	10000	2	11	41400	46000
32	1	MOTOR YACHT 3288	FB	MY	FBG	SV	IB	T140D	USMA	11	6	10000	2	11	49500	54400
34	7	AVANTI 3555 SB	OP	SPTCR	FBG	SV	IO	T230	MRCR	11	5	10200	2	4	31600	35100
34	7	AVANTI 3555 SB	OP	SPTCR	FBG	SV	IO	T180D	MRCR	11	5	10000	2	4	34500	38300
36	1	MOTOR YACHT 3688	FB	CNV	FBG	DV	IB	T210D	USMA	12	2	14000	2	11	71000	78000
38	2	MOTOR YACHT 3888	FB	DCMY	FBG	SV	IB	T200D	USMA	13	5	17500	3	2	89100	97900
43	1	MID CABIN 4388 MY	FB	DCMY	FBG	SV	IB	T240D	USMA	14	3	19000	3		105000	115500
43	1	MOTOR YACHT 4387	FB	DCMY	FBG	SV	IB	T310	USMA	14	3	20000	3		103500	114000
43	1	MOTOR YACHT 4387	FB	DCMY	FBG	SV	IB	T240D	USMA	14	3	20000	3		109500	120500
45	4	MOTOR YACHT 4588	FB	TCMY	FBG	SV	IB	T240D	USMA	14	11	28000	3		139000	153000
		1991 BOATS														
17	10	CAPRI 1800 BR	OP	RNBT	FBG	DV	OB			7		1490	2	9	2850	3300
17	10	CAPRI 1802 CUD	OP	CUD	FBG	DV	OB			7		1520	2	9	2850	3350
17	10	CAPRI 1850 BR	OP	RNBT	FBG	DV	IO	130	MRCR	7		1870	2	9	3250	3800
17	10	CAPRI 1870 BR	OP	RNBT	FBG	DV	IO	90	FRCE	7		1625	3		3100	3600
18	7	ARRIVA 1800 BR	OP	RNBT	FBG	DV	OB			7	9	1995	2	2	3450	4050
19	8	ARRIVA 2000 BR	OP	RNBT	FBG	DV	OB			7	4	2120	2	9	3850	4450
19	8	ARRIVA 2050 BR	OP	RNBT	FBG	DV	IO	260	MRCR	7	4	2240	2	9	4400	5050
19	10	CAPRI 2000 BR	OP	RNBT	FBG	DV	OB			7	4	1700	2	9	3350	3900
19	10	CAPRI 2002 CUD	OP	CUD	FBG	DV	OB			7	4	1740	2	9	3400	4000
19	10	CAPRI 2050 BR	OP	RNBT	FBG	DV	IO	115-180		7	4	2100	2	9	3950	4900
19	10	CAPRI 2052 CUD	OP	CUD	FBG	DV	IO	115-180		7	4	2150	2	9	4150	5150
19	10	CAPRI 2070 BR	OP	RNBT	FBG	DV	IO	120	FRCE	7	4	1730	2	9	3700	4300
19	10	CAPRI 2072 CUD	OP	CUD	FBG	DV	IO	120	FRCE	7	4	1850	2	9	3900	4550
20	1	TROPHY 2002 CUD	OP	CUD	FBG	DV	OB			8		2840	2	5	4900	5600
20	1	TROPHY 2003	OP	CTRCN	FBG	DV	OB			8		2700	2	5	4750	5450
20	8	TROPHY 2159 CUD	OP	CUD	FBG	SV	IO	115-205		8		3450	2	11	6700	8250
21	7	CAPRI 2250 BR	OP	RNBT	FBG	DV	IO	155-230		8		2630	3	2	5700	7000
21	7	CAPRI 2252 CUD	OP	CUD	FBG	DV	IO	155-230		8		2730	3	2	6100	7500
22		CIERA 2255 SB	OP	CR	FBG	SV	IO	155-205		8		3680	3	4	7550	8800
22	7	TROPHY 2302 CUD	OP	FSH	FBG	SV	OB			8	6	3384			6750	7800
22	7	TROPHY 2352 CUD	OP	CUD	FBG	SV	IO	155-230		8	6	4150	2	9	8800	10300
23	8	TROPHY 2459 CUD	OP	SF	FBG	SV	IO	205	MRCR	8		4025	3		10200	11600
23	9	ARRIVA 2452 CUD	OP	CUD	FBG	SV	IO	330	MRCR	8	6	3665	2	9	9700	11000
25		CIERA 2556 CNV	FB	SF	FBG	SV	IO	230-300		9	6	5685	3	3	14700	17800
25	7	CIERA 2655 SB	OP	CR	FBG	SV	IO	205-230		8		4300			9850	11600
27		CIERA 2755 SB	OP	CR	FBG	SV	IO	230-300		8	6	5200	3	3	11800	14400
28	1	CIERA 2855 SB	OP	CR	FBG	SV	IO	230-300		9	6	6510	3	3	13900	16600
30	7	AVANTI 3055 SB	OP	CR	FBG	SV	IO	300	MRCR	10		8000	3		18000	20000
30	7	AVANTI 3055 SB	OP	CR	FBG	SV	IO	T205	MRCR	10		8766	3		19200	21300
30	7	COMMAND BRIDGE 3058	FB	CR	FBG	SV	IO	300	MRCR	10		7434	3		20600	22900
30	7	COMMAND BRIDGE 3058	FB	CR	FBG	SV	IO	T205	MRCR	10		8200	3		22200	24700
32	1	MOTOR YACHT 3288	FB	MY	FBG	SV	IB	T210	USMA	11	6	11500	2	11	42400	47100
32	1	MOTOR YACHT 3288	FB	MY	FBG	SV	IB	T140D	USMA	11	6	11500	2	11	50000	54900
34	7	AVANTI 3555 SB	OP	SPTCR	FBG	SV	IO	T230	MRCR	11	5	10200	2	4	29600	32900
38	2	MOTOR YACHT 3888	FB	DCMY	FBG	SV	IB	T200D	USMA	13	5	17500	3	2	85000	93400
43	1	MID CABIN 4388 MY	FB	DCMY	FBG	SV	IB	T240D	USMA	14	3	19000	3		100500	110500
43	1	MOTOR YACHT 4387	FB	DCMY	FBG	SV	IB	T330	MRCR	14	3	20000	3		99000	108500
43	1	MOTOR YACHT 4387	FB	DCMY	FBG	SV	IB	T240D	USMA	14	3	20000	3		104500	115000
45	4	MOTOR YACHT 4588	FB	TCMY	FBG	SV	IB	T240D	USMA	14	11	28000	3		132500	146000
		1990 BOATS														
16	7	CAPRI 1700 BR	OP	RNBT	FBG	SV	OB			5	10	1040			1950	2350
17	10	CAPRI 1800 BR	OP	RNBT	FBG	DV	OB			7		1490			2700	3150
17	10	CAPRI 1802 CUD	OP	CUD	FBG	DV	OB			7		1520			2750	3200
17	10	CAPRI 1850 BR	OP	RNBT	FBG	DV	IO	130	MRCR	7		1870			3050	3550
17	10	CAPRI 1870 BR	OP	RNBT	FBG	DV	IO	85		7		1625			2900	3350
18	7	TROPHY 1903	OP	CTRCN	FBG	SV	OB			7	4	2100			3400	3950
19	7	ARRIVA 2001 SKI	OP	SKI	FBG	DV	OB			8		2000			3550	4100
19	10	CAPRI 2000 BR	OP	RNBT	FBG	DV	OB			7	4	1700			3250	3750
19	10	CAPRI 2002 CUD	OP	CUD	FBG	DV	OB			7	4	1740			3300	3800
19	10	CAPRI 2050 BR	OP	RNBT	FBG	DV	IO	130-200		7	4	2100			3700	4400
19	10	CAPRI 2052 CUD	OP	CUD	FBG	DV	IO	115-180		7	4	2150			3900	4550
19	10	CAPRI 2070 BR	OP	RNBT	FBG	DV	IO	120		7	4	1730			3450	4050
19	10	CAPRI 2072 CUD	OP	CUD	FBG	DV	IO	120		7	4	1850			3650	4250
20	8	TROPHY 2159 CUD	OP	CUD	FBG	SV	IO	130-230		8		3450			6300	7450
21	7	CAPRI 2250 BR	OP	RNBT	FBG	DV	IO	130-260		8		2450			5150	6300
21	7	CAPRI 2252 CUD	OP	CUD	FBG	DV	IO	130-260		8		2550			5550	6750
22		CIERA 2255 SB	OP	CR	FBG	SV	IO	130-230		8		3550			6900	8150
22	7	TROPHY 2302 CUD	OP	FSH	FBG	SV	OB			8	6	3120			6100	7000
23	8	TROPHY 2459 CUD	OP	SF	FBG	SV	IO	230		8		4025			9700	11000
23	9	ARRIVA 2450 BR	OP	RNBT	FBG	DV	IO	260	MRCR	8	6	3450			7450	8550
23	9	ARRIVA 2450 BR	OP	RNBT	FBG	DV	IO	330	MRCR	8	6	3450			8200	9450
23	9	ARRIVA 2452 CUD	OP	CUD	FBG	DV	IO	260	MRCR	8	6	3450			7950	9100
23	9	ARRIVA 2452 CUD	OP	CUD	FBG	DV	IO	330	MRCR	8	6	3450			8850	10100
25		CIERA 2556 CNV	OP	SF	FBG	DV	IO	330	MRCR	9	6	5685			15000	17100
25		CIERA 2556 CNV	OP	SF	FBG	SV	IO	260	MRCR	9	6	5685			14000	15900
25	7	CIERA 2651 SB	OP	CR	FBG	SV	IO	230-260		8		4300			9950	11600
26	1	CIERA 2655 SB	OP	CR	FBG	SV	IO	260-330		9	6	5990			12400	15000
27		CIERA 2755 SB	OP	CR	FBG	SV	IO	260-330		8	6	5200			11400	13900
28	8	AVANTI 2955 SB	OP	CR	FBG	SV	IO	330		10	6	7400			18000	20100
28	8	AVANTI 2955 SB	OP	CR	FBG	SV	IO	T230		10	6	7400			19000	21200
28	8	AVANTI 2958 CB	OP	CR	FBG	SV	IO	T230		10	6	8750			20100	22300
28	8	AVANTI 2958 SB	OP	CR	FBG	SV	IO	T260		10	6	8750			20600	22900
32	1	MOTOR YACHT 3288	FB	DCMY	FBG	SV	IB	T240	USMA	11	6	11500			41300	45900
32	1	MOTOR YACHT 3288	FB	DCMY	FBG	SV	IB	T150D	USMA	11	6	11500			48400	53200
34	7	AVANTI 3555 SB	OP	SPTCR	FBG	SV	IO	T260	MRCR	11	5	10250			28400	31500
36	7	AVANTI 3785 SB	OP	SPTCR	FBG	SV	IB	T330	USMA	12	10	13150			48400	53100
38	2	MOTOR YACHT 3888	FB	DCMY	FBG	SV	IB	T240	USMA	13	5	17500			74300	81700
38	2	MOTOR YACHT 3888	FB	DCMY	FBG	SV	IB	T175D	USMA	13	5	17500			80200	88100
43	1	MOTOR YACHT 4387	FB	DCMY	FBG	SV	IB	T330	USMA	14	3	19500			95900	105500
43	1	MOTOR YACHT 4387	FB	DCMY	FBG	SV	IB	T220D	USMA	14	3	19500			95400	105000
45	4	MOTOR YACHT 4588	FB	TCMY	FBG	SV	IB	T330	USMA	14	11	28000			123500	135500
45	4	MOTOR YACHT 4588	FB	TCMY	FBG	SV	IB	T220D	USMA	14	11	28000			122500	134500
		1989 BOATS														
16	10	CAPRI 1700 BR	OP	RNBT	FBG	DV	OB			7		1475	2	9	2550	3000
16	10	CAPRI 1750 BR	OP	RNBT	FBG	DV	IO	128	OMC	7		1780	3		2650	3050
16	10	CAPRI 1770 BR	OP	RNBT	FBG	SV	OB			7		1600	3	1	2700	3150
16	10	CAPRI CUDDY 1702	OP	CUD	FBG	DV	OB			7		1475	2	9	2550	3000
18	7	TROPHY 1903	OP	CTRCN	FBG	SV	OB			7	4	2100	2	9	3600	4200
18	7	TROPHY 1903 SE	OP	CTRCN	FBG	SV	OB			7	4	2100	2	9	2950	3450
18	11	CAPRI 1900 BR	OP	RNBT	FBG	SV	OB			7	4	1655	2	9	2900	3400
18	11	CAPRI 1950 BR	OP	RNBT	FBG	DV	IO	128-200		7	4	2150	2	9	3350	3950
18	11	CAPRI 1970 BR	OP	RNBT	FBG	SV	OB			7	4	1780	3	1	3050	3550
18	11	CAPRI CUDDY 1902	ST	CUD	FBG	SV	OB			7	4	1755	2	9	3000	3500
18	11	CAPRI CUDDY 1952	ST	CUD	FBG	DV	IO	128-200		7	4	2325	2	9	3550	4200
19	3	CAPRI 1901 SKI	OP	SKI	FBG	DV	OB			7	3	1710	3	6	3000	3500
20	5	CAPRI CUDDY 2152	OP	CUD	FBG	SV	IO	130-235		8		2620	3	2	4900	5900
20	5	CIERA 2155 SB	ST	CR	FBG	DV	IO	130-235		8		3400	3	4	5800	6850
20	7	CAPRI 2150 BR	OP	RNBT	FBG	SV	IO	130-235		8		2525	3	2	4650	5550
20	7	TROPHY 2103	OP	CTRCN	FBG	DV	OB			8		2375	2	9	4800	5550
20	7	TROPHY 2103 SE	OP	CTRCN	FBG	SV	OB			8		2375	2	9	3950	4600
20	8	TROPHY CUDDY 2102	HT	FSH	FBG	SV	OB			8		2930	2	9	4850	5600
20	8	TROPHY CUDDY 2159	HT	FSH	FBG	SV	IO	130-235		8		3450	2	11	6250	7400
22	6	TROPHY CUDDY 2302	HT	FSH	FBG	SV	OB			8	6	3120	2	9	5850	6700
23	8	CIERA 2455 SB	ST	CR	FBG	DV	IO	235-260		8		4250	3	3	8300	9700
23	8	TROPHY CUDDY 2459	HT	FSH	FBG	SV	IO	235	OMC	8		4025	3		8400	9650
25		CIERA 2556 CNV	OP	SF	FBG	SV	IO	260-340		9	6	5685	3	3	13200	16200
26	1	CIERA 2655 SB	OP	CR	FBG	SV	IO	260-340		9	6	5990	3	3	11700	14300
27		CIERA 2755 SB	ST	CR	FBG	SV	IO	235	OMC	8	6	5200	3	3	10500	11900
27		CIERA 2755 SB	ST	CR	FBG	SV	IO	340	OMC	8	6	5200	3	3	11600	13200
27	7	CIERA 2855 SB	ST	CR	FBG	DV	IO	260-340		10		6250	3	3	12500	15200
27	7	CIERA 2858 CB		CR	FBG	SV	IO	340	OMC	10		6980	3	3	15700	17800
28	8	AVANTI 2955 SB	OP	CR	FBG	DV	IO	340	OMC	10	6	7400	3	6	16700	19000
28	8	AVANTI 2955 SB	OP	CR	FBG	DV	IO	T235	OMC	10	6	7400	3	6	18000	20000
28	8	AVANTI 2958 CB	FB	CR	FBG	DV	IO	T235-T260		10	6	8750	3	6	19000	21500
31	7	AVANTI 3255 SB	OP	DC	FBG	DV	IO	T235-T260		11	5	10000	3	8	25400	28800
32	1	MOTORYACHT 3288	FB	DCMY	FBG	SV	IB	T225	USMA	11	6	11500	2	11	38900	43200
32	1	MOTORYACHT 3288	FB	DCMY	FBG	SV	IB	T135D	USMA	11	6	11500	2	11	45600	50200
33	9	AVANTI 3485 SB	OP	DCMY	FBG	DV	IB	T330	USMA	12	10	12900	3		40600	45100
33	9	TROPHY 3486 CNV	FB	DCMY	FBG	DV	IB	T330	USMA	12	10	13900	3		48900	53700
33	9	TROPHY 3486 CNV	FB	DCMY	FBG	DV	IB	T220D	USMA	12	10	13900	3		57500	63200
38	2	MOTORYACHT 3888	FB	DCMY	FBG	SV	IB	T175D	USMA	13	5	17500	3	2	76600	84100
38	2	MOTORYACHT 3888 SE	FB	DCMY	FBG	SV	IB	T240	USMA	13	5	17500	3	2	71000	78000
41	7	AVANTI 4285 SB	FB	DCMY	FBG	DV	IB	T330	USMA	14	4	23500	3	10	94500	104000
41	7	AVANTI 4285 SB	FB	DCMY	FBG	DV	IB	T320D	CAT	14	4	23500	3	10	108500	119500
41	7	AVANTI 4285 SB	FB	DCMY	FBG	DV	IB	T400D	USMA	14	4	23500	3	10	115000	126000

 CONTINUED ON NEXT PAGE

LOA FT	LOA IN	NAME AND/ OR MODEL	TOP/ RIG	BOAT TYPE	-HULL- MTL	-HULL- TP	ENGINE TP	ENGINE # HP	ENGINE MFG	BEAM FT	BEAM IN	WGT LBS	DRAFT FT	DRAFT IN	RETAIL LOW	RETAIL HIGH
		1989 BOATS														
45	4	MOTOR YACHT 4588	FB	TCMY	FBG	SV	IB	T220D	USMA	14	11	28000	3		117000	128500
45	4	MOTOR YACHT 4588 SE	FB	TCMY	FBG	SV	IB	T330	USMA	14	11	28000	3		105500	115500
		1988 BOATS														
16	5	BASS TROPHY 1710	OP	BASS	FBG	SV	OB			6	8	1300	2	2	2250	2600
16	5	FISH-N-SKI 1710	OP	BASS	FBG	DV	OB			6	8	1300	2	2	2250	2650
16	10	CAPRI 1700 BR	OP	RNBT	FBG	DV	OB			7		1475	2	9	2500	2900
16	10	CAPRI 1750 BR	OP	RNBT	FBG	DV	IO	128	OMC	7		1780			2500	2900
16	10	CAPRI CUDDY 1700	OP	CUD	FBG	DV	OB			7		1475	2	9	2450	2850
16	10	TROPHY 1710	OP	CTRCN	FBG	SV	OB			7		1275	2	9	2250	2600
17	10	BASS TROPHY 1810	OP	BASS	FBG	SV	OB			7		1470	2	2	2500	2900
17	10	COBRA 1800	OP	RNBT	FBG	SV	OB			7	3	1470	2	2	2500	2900
17	10	FISH-N-SKI 1810	OP	BASS	FBG	DV	OB			7	3	1470	2	2	2500	2900
18	7	CAPRI 1900 BR	OP	RNBT	FBG	SV	OB			7	4	1655	2	9	2750	3200
18	7	CAPRI 1950 BR	OP	RNBT	FBG	DV	IO	130-230		7	4	2150	2	9	3100	3750
18	7	CAPRI CUDDY 1900	ST	CUD	FBG	SV	OB			7	4	1755	2	9	2850	3350
18	7	CAPRI CUDDY 1950	ST	CUD	FBG	DV	IO	130-230		7	4	2325	2	9	3300	4000
18	7	TROPHY 1910	OP	CTRCN	FBG	SV	OB			7	4	1900	2	9	3000	3500
20	5	CAPRI 2150 BR	OP	RNBT	FBG	DV	IO	230	OMC	8		2525	3	2	4550	5250
20	5	CAPRI 2150 BR	OP	RNBT	FBG	SV	IO	130	OMC	8		2525	3	2	4400	5050
20	5	CAPRI CUDDY 2150	OP	CUD	FBG	SV	IO	130-230		8		2620	3	2	4700	5550
20	5	CIERA 2150 SB	ST	CR	FBG	DV	IO	130-230		8		3125	3	4	5200	6150
20	5	TROPHY 2110	OP	CTRCN	FBG	DV	OB			8		2200	2	9	3900	4550
20	8	TROPHY CUDDY 2160	OP	FSH	FBG	SV	OB			8		2825	2	11	4650	5350
20	8	TROPHY CUDDY 2160	HT	FSH	FBG	SV	IO	130-230		8		3305	2	11	5750	6800
22		COBRA 2251 CB	OP	RNBT	FBG	SV	IO	260	OMC	7	11	2300			4800	5500
23	8	CIERA 2450 SB	ST	CR	FBG	DV	IO	230	OMC	8		3675	3	3	7050	8100
23	8	TROPHY CUDDY 2460	HT	FSH	FBG	SV	IO	230	OMC	8		3800			7600	8750
25		CIERA 2560 CNV	OP	SF	FBG	SV	IO	260	OMC	9	6	5350			12000	13600
26	1	CIERA 2650 SB	OP	CR	FBG	SV	IO	260-340		9	6	5100			10700	13200
27	5	CIERA 2850 SB	ST	CR	FBG	DV	IO	260	OMC	10		5775	3	3	12600	14300
27	7	CIERA 2858 CB		CR	FBG	SV	IO	340	OMC	10		6980	3	3	14800	16800
28	8	AVANTI 2950 SB		CR	FBG	DV	IO	340	OMC	9	8	7000	3	6	15300	17400
28	8	AVANTI 2950 SB		CR	FBG	DV	IO	T230	OMC	9	8	7000	3	6	16100	18300
28	8	COMMAND BRIDGE 2950		CR	FBG	DV	IO	T230-T260		9	8	9245	3	6	18300	20800
31	6	AVANTI 3250 SB	FB	DC	FBG	DV	IO	T230-T260		11	5	10200	3	8	23900	27100
32	1	MOTORYACHT 3270	FB	DCMY	FBG	SV	IB	T225		11	6	11200	2	11	38100	42400
32	1	MOTORYACHT 3270	FB	DCMY	FBG	SV	IB	T135D		11	6	11200	2	11	47800	52500
33	9	AVANTI 3450 SB	ST	DCMY	FBG	DV	IB	T330		12	10	12000	3		37600	41800
33	9	CONVERTIBLE 3460	FB	DCMY	FBG	DV	IB	T330		12	10	13000	3		45000	50000
33	9	CONVERTIBLE 3460	FB	DCMY	FBG	DV	IB	T220D		12	10	13000	3		53600	58900
38	2	MOTORYACHT 3870	FB	DCMY	FBG	SV	IB	T175D		13	5	17500	3	2	73200	80400
45	4	MOTORYACHT 4550	FB	TCMY	FBG	SV	IB	T220D		14	11	28000	3		116000	127500
		1987 BOATS														
16	5	BASS STRIKER 1710	OP	BASS	FBG	SV	OB			6	8	1300	2	2	2200	2550
16	5	COBRA 1700	OP	RNBT	FBG	DV	OB			6	8	1300			2200	2550
16	5	FISH-N-SKI 1710	OP	BASS	FBG	DV	OB			6	8	1300			2200	2550
16	10	CAPRI 1700 BOWRIDER	OP	RNBT	FBG	DV	IO	120	OMC	7		1670			2300	2700
16	10	CAPRI 1700 BR	OP	RNBT	FBG	DV	OB			7		1475			2400	2800
16	10	CAPRI 1700 CUDDY	OP	CUD	FBG	DV	OB			7		1475			2400	2800
17	10	BASS STRIKER 1810	OP	BASS	FBG	SV	OB			7	3	1470	2	2	2450	2850
17	10	COBRA 1800	OP	RNBT	FBG	SV	OB			7	3	1470	2	2	2450	2850
17	10	FISH-N-SKI 1810	OP	BASS	FBG	DV	OB			7	3	1470			2400	2800
18	2	TROPHY 1910	OP	CTRCN	FBG	SV	OB			7	4	1900	2	8	2850	3350
18	7	CAPRI 1900 B/R	OP	RNBT	FBG	SV	OB			7	4	1555	2	4	2600	3000
18	7	CAPRI 1950 B/R	OP	RNBT	FBG	DV	IO	130-230		7	4	2125	2	8	2950	3550
18	7	CAPRI CUD 1950	ST	CUD	FBG	DV	IO	130-230		7	4	2325	2	9	3150	3800
18	7	CAPRI CUDDY 1900		RNBT	FBG	SV	OB			7	4	1755	2	9	2750	3200
20	5	CAPRI BR 2150	OP	RNBT	FBG	SV	IO	130-230		8		2425	3		4050	4900
20	5	CAPRI CUD 2150	OP	CUD	FBG	SV	IO	130-230		8		2620	3	3	4450	5300
20	5	CIERA SB 2150	ST	CR	FBG	DV	IO	130	OMC	8		3125	3	4	4900	5650
20	8	TROPHY CUD 2110	OP	FSH	FBG	DV	OB			8		2825	2	9	4500	5200
20	8	TROPHY CUD 2160	HT	FSH	FBG	DV	IO	130	OMC	8		3305	2	11	5450	6300
20	8	TROPHY CUD 2160	HT	FSH	FBG	SV	IO	230	OMC	8		3305	2	11	5600	6450
23	8	CIERA SB 2450	ST	CR	FBG	DV	IO	230	OMC	8		3675	3		6700	7700
23	8	TROPHY CUD 2460	HT	FSH	FBG	DV	IO	230	OMC	8		3800	3		7250	8300
25		CIERA DESIGN ED 2550		CR	FBG	DV	IO	260	OMC	9	6	5095	3		9650	11000
25		TROPHY 2560 CNV	FB	CBNCR	FBG	DV	IO	230-260		9	6	5350	3	2	11700	13500
27		CIERA SB 2750	ST	CBNCR	FBG	DV	IO	260	OMC	8		5000	3	3	12800	14600
27	5	CONTESSA SB 2850	ST	CR	FBG	DV	IO	260	OMC	10		5775		2	11900	13600
27	5	CONTESSA SB 2850	ST	CR	FBG	DV	IO	T230	OMC	10		5775	3	3	13500	15300
27	5	CONTESSA SDN BR 2850	FB	CBNCR	FBG	DV	IO	260-335		10		5994		2	15200	17700
27	5	CONTESSA SDN BR 2850	FB	CBNCR	FBG	DV	IO	T230	OMC	10		5994		2	15700	17800
27	5	TROPHY CUD 2860	HT	FSH	FBG	DV	IO	260	OMC	10		6000	3	3	12800	14600
27	5	TROPHY CUD 2860	HT	FSH	FBG	DV	IB	335	OMC	10		6000	3	3	16300	18600
27	5	TROPHY CUD 2860	TT	FSH	FBG	DV	IB	T230		10		6000	3	3	17400	19800
31	6	AVANTI SUNBR 3250	FB	DC	FBG	DV	IO	T230-T260		11	5	10200	3	8	22700	25800
32	1	MOTORYACHT 3270	FB	DCMY	FBG	SV	IB	T225		11	6	13800	2	11	36400	40400
33	9	AVANTI 3450	ST	DCMY	FBG	DV	IB	T330		12	10	12175	3		36000	40000
33	9	TRI-CABIN 3450	FB	TCMY	FBG	DV	IB	T255		12	10	13700	2	10	39300	43600
33	9	TROPHY CNV 3460	FB	DCMY	FBG	DV	IB	T255		12	10	13000	3		41000	45600
38	2	MOTOR YACHT CB 3870	FB	DCMY	FBG	SV	IB	T175D		13	5	17500	3	2	70000	76900
45	4	PILOTHOUSE 4550	FB	TCMY	FBG	SV	IB	T220D		14	11	28000	3		112000	123000
		1986 BOATS														
16	3	TROPHY 1710	OP	BASS	FBG	SV	OB			6	10	1445	2	2	2300	2650
17	10	CAPRI 1800 B/R	ST	RNBT	FBG	SV	OB					1470	2	2	2350	2750
17	10	TROPHY 1810	OP	BASS	FBG	SV	OB					1470	2	2	2350	2750
18	7	CAPRI 1900 B/R	ST	RNBT	FBG	SV	OB			7	4	1555	2	4	2500	2900
18	7	CAPRI 1950 B/R	ST	RNBT	FBG	DV	IO	125-225		7	4	2000	2	8	2900	3500
18	7	CAPRI CUD 1950	ST	CUD	FBG	DV	IO	125-225		7	4	2200	2	9	3100	3750
18	7	CAPRI CUDDY 1900		RNBT	FBG	SV	OB			7	4	1755	2	9	2700	3100
18	8	TROPHY 1910	OP	CTRCN	FBG	SV	OB			7	6	1900	2	8	2800	3250
20	7	CAPRI BR 2150		RNBT	FBG	SV	IO	125	VLVO	8		2305	3		4000	4650
20	7	CAPRI BR 2150		RNBT	FBG	SV	IO	225	VLVO	8			3		4700	5400
20	7	CAPRI CUD 2150	ST	CUD	FBG	SV	IO	125-225		8		2495	3	3	4400	5200
20	8	CIERA SB2150	ST	CR	FBG	DV	IO	125-225		8		3125	3		4950	5900
20	8	TROPHY 2110	OP	FSH	F/S	DV	OB			8		2875	2	9	4400	5050
20	8	TROPHY CUD 2160		FSH	FBG	DV	IO	125	VLVO	8		3305	2	11	5400	6250
20	8	TROPHY CUD 2160		FSH	FBG	SV	IO	225	VLVO	8			2	11	5300	6100
23	8	CIERA COMM BR 2450	FB	CBNCR	FBG	DV	IO	225-260		8		4525	3		8800	10300
23	8	CIERA SB 2450	ST	CR	FBG	DV	IO	225-260		8		3675	3		6600	7800
23	8	CIERA SPRT CRSR 2450	OP	CR	FBG	DV	IO	260	VLVO	8		2750	3		5750	6600
23	8	TROPHY 2460	OP	FSH	F/S	DV	IO	225	VLVO	8		3650	3		6950	8000
25		CIERA DESIGN ED 2550		CR	FBG	DV	IO	225	VLVO	9	6	5000	3		9100	10400
25		CIERA DESIGN ED 2550		CR	FBG	SV	IO	260	VLVO	9	6		3		8950	10200
25		TROPHY 2560 CNV	FB	CBNCR	FBG	DV	IO	225-260		9	6	5350	3	2	11300	13100
27		CIERA SG 2750	OP	CR	F/S	DV	IO	260	VLVO	8		5440	3	3	10500	11900
27	5	CONTESSA DE 2850	ST	CR	FBG	DV	IO	260	VLVO	10		6470		2	12200	13800
27	5	CONTESSA DE 2850	ST	CR	FBG	DV	IO	T125-T225		10		6470		2	12400	15500
27	5	CONTESSA SDN BR 2850	FB	CBNCR	FBG	DV	IO	260	VLVO	10		6050	3	3	14700	16700
27	5	CONTESSA SDN BR 2850	FB	CBNCR	FBG	DV	IO	T125-T225		10		6770		2	15500	18400
27	5	TROPHY 2860	TT	SF	F/S	DV	IO	260	VLVO	10		5500	3	3	12900	14600
27	5	TROPHY 2860	TT	SF	F/S	DV	IB	T225		10		5500	3	3	16000	18200
31	7	CONQUEST SUNBR 3250	FB	DC	FBG	DV	IO	T260	VLVO	11	11	10180	3	8	26500	29400
32	1	EXPLORER 3270	FB	DCMY	FBG	SV	IB	T225	VLVO	11	6	13800	2	11	34700	38600
32	1	EXPLORER 3270	FB	DCMY	FBG	SV	IB	T105D	USMA	11	6	13800	2	11	42100	46800
38	2	EXPLORER CB 3870	FB	DCMY	FBG	SV	IB	T130D		13	5	19608	3	2	65700	72200
45	4	PILOTHOUSE 4550	FB	TCMY	FBG	SV	IB	T220D		14	11	26000	3		102000	112000
		1985 BOATS														
16	3	TROPHY 1710	OP	BASS	FBG	SV	OB			6	10	1445	2	2	2250	2600
16	6	COBRA 1600	ST	RNBT	FBG	DV	OB			7	2	1150	1	11	1800	2150
18	8	CAPRI 1900 B/R	ST	RNBT	FBG	SV	OB			7	6	1555	2	4	2450	2850
18	8	CAPRI 1950 B/R	ST	RNBT	FBG	DV	IO	125-230		7	6	1995	2	8	2800	3300
18	8	CAPRI CUD 1950	ST	CUD	FBG	DV	IO	125-230		7	6	2200	2	9	3000	3500
18	8	CAPRI CUDDY 1900		RNBT	FBG	SV	OB			7	6	1755	2	9	2600	3050
18	8	TROPHY 1910	OP	CTRCN	FBG	SV	OB			7	6	1900	2	8	2700	3150
20	7	CAPRI BR 2150		RNBT	FBG	SV	IO	140	OMC	8		2400	3		3750	4350
20	7	CAPRI BR 2150		RNBT	FBG	SV	IO	230	OMC	8			3		4300	5000
20	7	CAPRI CUD 2150	ST	CUD	FBG	SV	IO	140-230		8		2590	3	3	4050	4850
20	8	CIERA SB2150	ST	CR	FBG	DV	IO	125-230		8		3125	3		4750	5700
20	8	TROPHY 2110	OP	FSH	F/S	SV	OB			8		2875	2	9	4200	4900
20	8	TROPHY CUD 2160		FSH	FBG	SV	IO	140-230		8		3400	2	11	5100	5850
23	8	CIERA COMM BR 2450	FB	CBNCR	FBG	DV	IO	225-260		8		4525	3		8350	9850
23	8	CIERA SB 2450	ST	CR	FBG	DV	IO	225-260		8		3675	3		6150	7500
23	8	TROPHY 2460	OP	FSH	F/S	SV	IO	225	VLVO	8		3650	3		6650	7650
25		CIERA DESIGN ED 2550		CR	FBG	SV	IO	225-260		9	6	5000	3		8650	9950
27		CIERA SB 2750	OP	CR	F/S	SV	IO	260	OMC	8		5000	3	3	9550	10900
27		CIERA SB 2750	OP	CR	F/S	SV	IO	260	VLVO	8		5000	3	3	9700	11000
27		CIERA SB 2750	OP	CR	F/S	SV	IO	T260		8		5000	3	3	11400	12900
27	5	CONTESSA DE 2850	ST	CR	FBG	DV	IO	260	VLVO	10		5775	2	9	11100	12600
27	5	CONTESSA DE 2850	ST	CR	FBG	DV	IO	T125	VLVO	10		5775	2	9	11300	12800
27	5	CONTESSA DE 2850	ST	CR	FBG	DV	IO	T225	VLVO	10		5775	3	3	12500	14200
27	5	CONTESSA SDN BR 2850	FB	CBNCR	FBG	DV	IO	260	VLVO	10		6050	3	3	14100	16000
27	5	CONTESSA SDN BR 2850	FB	CBNCR	FBG	DV	IO	T125-T225		10		6770	2	9	14900	17600
27	5	TROPHY 2860	TT	SF	F/S	SV	IO	260	VLVO	10		5500	3	3	12300	14000
27	5	TROPHY 2860	TT	SF	F/S	SV	IB	T225		10		5500	3	3	15300	17300
27	5	TROPHY 2860	TT	SF	F/S	SV	IB	T105D		10		5500	3	3	17400	19800

 CONTINUED ON NEXT PAGE

LOA FT	IN	NAME AND/ OR MODEL	TOP/ RIG	BOAT TYPE	-HULL- MTL	TP	TP	----ENGINE--- # HP	MFG	BEAM FT	IN	WGT LBS	DRAFT FT	IN	RETAIL LOW	RETAIL HIGH
		1985 BOATS														
31	7	CONQUEST SUNBR 3250	FB	DC	FBG	DV	IO	T225-T260		11	11	10180	3	8	24800	28200
32	1	EXPLORER 3270	FB	DCMY	FBG	DV	IB	T165	VLVO	11	6	13800	2	11	31600	35200
32	1	EXPLORER 3270	FB	DCMY	FBG	DV	IB	T105D	USMA	11	6	13800	2	11	40400	44900
38	2	EXPLORER CB 3870	FB	DCMY	FBG	SV	IB	T130D		13	5	19608	3	2	62900	69100
45	4	PILOTHOUSE 4550	FB	TCMY	FBG	DV	IB	T220D		14	11	26000	3		99800	109500
		1984 BOATS														
16	3	TROPHY FISH & SKI	OP	BASS	FBG	SV	OB			6	10	1496	2	2	2250	2600
16	6	COBRA 1600	ST	RNBT	FBG	DV	OB			7	2	1140	1	11	1750	2050
18	8	CAPRI 1900 B/R		RNBT	FBG	DV	OB			7	6	1910			2650	3100
18	8	CAPRI 1900 B/R	ST	RNBT	FBG	SV	IO	117	VLVO	7	6	1995	2	4	2650	3100
18	8	CAPRI 1950 B/R	ST	RNBT	FBG	DV	IO	117-200		7	6	1995	2	8	2750	3200
18	8	CAPRI CUD 1950	ST	CUD	FBG	DV	IO	117-200		7	6	2045	2	9	2800	3300
18	8	TROPHY 1910	OP	CTRCN	FBG	SV	OB			7	6	2180	2	8	2850	3300
20	1	EXPLORER 2070	ST	OVNTR	FBG	SV	IO	117	VLVO	8		2870	2	9	4200	4900
20	1	TROPHY FSH 2060	HT	FSH	FBG	SV	IO	117	VLVO	8		2725	2	9	4350	5000
20	7	CAPRI CUD 2150	ST	CUD	FBG	SV	IO	117	VLVO	8		2650	3	3	4150	4800
20	8	CIERA SB2150	ST	CR	FBG	DV	IO	117-225		8		3150	3		4650	5500
20	8	TROPHY 2110	OP	FSH	F/S	SV	OB			8		2875	2	9	4050	4700
22	3	EXPLORER 2270	HT	CR	FBG	SV	IO	117		8		4200	3	2	5950	6850
22	3	TROPHY FSH 2260	HT	FSH	FBG	SV	IO	117	VLVO	8		3600	3		5750	6650
23	8	CIERA COMM BR 2450	FB	CBNCR	FBG	DV	IO	170-260		8		4350	3		7550	9250
23	8	CIERA COMM BR 2450	FB	CBNCR	FBG	DV	IO	T117-T170		8		4350	3		8650	9900
23	8	CIERA SB 2450	ST	CR	FBG	DV	IO	170-260		8		4150	3		6400	7850
23	8	CIERA SB 2450	ST	CR	FBG	DV	IO	T117-T170		8		4150	3		7350	8500
23	8	TROPHY 2460	OP	FSH	F/S	SV	IO	225	VLVO	8		3650	3		6450	7400
27		CIERA SB 2750	OP	CR	F/S	SV	IO	260	VLVO	8		5440	3	3	9750	11100
27	5	CIERA SB 2750	OP	CR	FBG	SV	IO	T125	VLVO	8		5440	3	3	10200	11600
27	5	CONTESSA SB 2850	ST	CR	FBG	DV	IO	260	VLVO	10		6470	3	3	11300	12800
27	5	CONTESSA SB 2850	ST	CR	FBG	DV	IO	T117-T170		10		6470	3	3	11400	13600
27	5	CONTESSA SB 2850	ST	CR	FBG	DV	IO	T225	VLVO	10		6470	3	3	12600	14300
27	5	CONTESSA SDN BR 2850	FB	CBNCR	FBG	DV	IO	260		10		6770	3	3	14100	16100
27	5	CONTESSA SDN BR 2850	FB	CBNCR	FBG	DV	IO	T117-T225		10		6770	3	3	14200	17000
27	5	TROPHY 2860	TT	SF	F/S	SV	IO	260	VLVO	10		6440	3	3	12800	14600
27	5	TROPHY 2860	TT	SF	F/S	SV	IO	T225	VLVO	10		6440	3	3	14300	16300
31	7	CONQUEST SUNBR 3250	ST	DC	FBG	DV	IO	260	VLVO	11	11	10180	3	2	22200	24600
31	7	CONQUEST SUNBR 3250	FB	DC	FBG	DV	IO	T260		11	11	10180	3		24500	27200
31	7	CONQUEST SUNBR 3250	FB	DC	FBG	DV	VD	T350		11	11	10180	3		28700	31900
31	7	CONQUEST SUNBR 3250	FB	DC	FBG	DV	VD	T158D	VLVO	11	11	10180	3		30600	34000
32	1	EXPLORER 3270	FB	DCMY	FBG	DV	IB	T165	VLVO	11	6	13800	2	11	30200	33600
32	1	EXPLORER 3270	FB	DCMY	FBG	DV	IB	T 90D	BMC	11	6	13800	2	11	38200	42400
38	2	MOTORYACHT 3870	FB	DCMY	FBG	SV	IB	T130D	BMC	13	5	19608	3	2	60300	66200
45	4	MOTORYACHT 4550	FB	TCMY	FBG	DV	IB	T200D		14	11	26000	3		90800	99800

....For earlier years, see the BUC Used Boat Price Guide, Volume 3

BAYMASTER BOATS INC

LOS FRESNOS TX 78566 COAST GUARD MFG ID- BKV See inside cover to adjust price for area
FORMERLY KRUGERBRAND INC

For more recent years, see the BUC Used Boat Price Guide, Volume 1

LOA FT	IN	NAME AND/ OR MODEL	TOP/ RIG	BOAT TYPE	-HULL- MTL	TP	TP	----ENGINE--- # HP	MFG	BEAM FT	IN	WGT LBS	DRAFT FT	IN	RETAIL LOW	RETAIL HIGH
		1996 BOATS														
16	4	BAYMASTER T	OP	FSH	FBG	TH	OB			6	6				2300	2700
16	4	BAYMASTER T DXL	OP	FSH	FBG	TH	OB			6	6				2750	3200
16	6	BAYMASTER BACKWATER	OP	FSH	FBG	TH	OB			7	3				4250	4900
16	6	BAYMASTER EXPRESS	OP	FSH	FBG	TH	OB			7	3				3950	4600
16	6	BAYMASTER SPECIAL	OP	FSH	FBG	TH	OB			7	3				3000	3500
16	6	BAYMASTER TV	OP	FSH	FBG	TH	OB			7	3				3100	3600
18	5	BAYMASTER 1850 BW	OP	FSH	FBG	TH	OB			8					4600	5300
18	5	BAYMASTER 1850 EXP	OP	FSH	FBG	TH	OB			8					4350	5000
18	5	BAYMASTER 1850 F&S	OP	FSH	FBG	TH	OB			8					4200	4850
19	3	BAYMASTER BACKWATER	OP	FSH	FBG	TH	OB			7	3				4800	5500
19	3	BAYMASTER EXPRESS	OP	FSH	FBG	TH	OB			7	3				4500	5200
19	5	BAYMASTER 1950 EXP	OP	FSH	FBG	TH	OB			8		1550		10	4700	5400
19	5	BAYMASTER BACKWATER	OP	FSH	FBG	TH	OB			8		1550		10	4900	5650
19	6	PROGLAS BACKWATER	OP	FSH	FBG	TH	OB			8	2				4850	5550
19	6	PROGLAS EXPRESS	OP	FSH	FBG	TH	OB			8	2				4600	5300
20	2	BAYMASTER 202	OP	FSH	FBG	TH	OB			8					4900	5600
21	5	BAYMASTER 2150 BW	OP	FSH	FBG	TH	OB			8		1650			5800	6650
21	5	BAYMASTER 2150 EXP	OP	FSH	FBG	TH	OB			8		1650			5500	6350
21	5	BAYMASTER 2150 F7S	OP	FSH	FBG	TH	OB			8		1650			5300	6100
21	7	BAYMASTER BACKWATER	OP	FSH	FBG	TH	OB			8					6500	7450
21	7	BAYMASTER EXPRESS	OP	FSH	FBG	TH	OB			8					6200	7100
		1995 BOATS														
16	4	BAYMASTER T	OP	FSH	FBG	TH	OB			6	6				2200	2550
16	4	BAYMASTER T DXL	OP	FSH	FBG	TH	OB			6	6				2600	3050
16	6	BAYMASTER BACKWATER	OP	FSH	FBG	TH	OB			7	3				4050	4700
16	6	BAYMASTER EXPRESS	OP	FSH	FBG	TH	OB			7	3				3800	4400
16	6	BAYMASTER SPECIAL	OP	FSH	FBG	TH	OB			7	3				2850	3350
16	6	BAYMASTER TV	OP	FSH	FBG	TH	OB			7	3				2950	3400
18	5	BAYMASTER 1850 BW	OP	FSH	FBG	TH	OB			8					4400	5050
18	5	BAYMASTER 1850 EXP	OP	FSH	FBG	TH	OB			8					4100	4750
18	5	BAYMASTER 1850 F&S	OP	FSH	FBG	TH	OB			8					4000	4650
19	3	BAYMASTER BACKWATER	OP	FSH	FBG	TH	OB			7	3				4600	5300
19	3	BAYMASTER EXPRESS	OP	FSH	FBG	TH	OB			7	3				4250	4950
19	5	BAYMASTER 1950 EXP	OP	FSH	FBG	TH	OB			8		1550		10	4450	5150
19	5	BAYMASTER BACKWATER	OP	FSH	FBG	TH	OB			8		1550		10	4700	5350
19	6	PROGLAS BACKWATER	OP	FSH	FBG	TH	OB			8	2				4650	5350
19	6	PROGLAS EXPRESS	OP	FSH	FBG	TH	OB			8	2				4400	5050
20	2	BAYMASTER 202	OP	FSH	FBG	TH	OB			8					4650	5350
21	5	BAYMASTER 2150 BW	OP	FSH	FBG	TH	OB			8		1650			5500	6350
21	5	BAYMASTER 2150 EXP	OP	FSH	FBG	TH	OB			8		1650			5250	6050
21	5	BAYMASTER 2150 F7S	OP	FSH	FBG	TH	OB			8		1650			5050	5850
21	7	BAYMASTER BACKWATER	OP	FSH	FBG	TH	OB			8					6200	7100
21	7	BAYMASTER EXPRESS	OP	FSH	FBG	TH	OB			8					5900	6750
		1994 BOATS														
16	4	BAYMASTER T	OP	FSH	FBG	TH	OB			6	6				2000	2350
16	4	BAYMASTER T DXL	OP	FSH	FBG	TH	OB			6	6				2600	3000
16	6	BAYMASTER BACKWATER	OP	FSH	FBG	TH	OB			7	3				3850	4500
16	6	BAYMASTER EXPRESS	OP	FSH	FBG	TH	OB			7	3				3700	4300
16	6	BAYMASTER SPECIAL	OP	FSH	FBG	TH	OB			7	3				2700	3150
16	6	BAYMASTER TV	OP	FSH	FBG	TH	OB			7	3				2750	3200
18	5	BAYMASTER 1850 BW	OP	FSH	FBG	TH	OB			8					4100	4800
18	5	BAYMASTER 1850 EXP	OP	FSH	FBG	TH	OB			8					3950	4600
18	5	BAYMASTER 1850 F&S	OP	FSH	FBG	TH	OB			8					3800	4400
19	3	BAYMASTER BACKWATER	OP	FSH	FBG	TH	OB			7	3				4350	5000
19	3	BAYMASTER EXPRESS	OP	FSH	FBG	TH	OB			7	3				4100	4750
19	5	BAYMASTER 1950 EXP	OP	FSH	FBG	TH	OB			8		1550		10	4250	4950
19	5	BAYMASTER BACKWATER	OP	FSH	FBG	TH	OB			8		1550		10	4450	5100
19	6	PROGLAS BACKWATER	OP	FSH	FBG	TH	OB			8	2				4400	5050
19	6	PROGLAS EXPRESS	OP	FSH	FBG	TH	OB			8	2				4150	4850
20	2	BAYMASTER 202	OP	FSH	FBG	TH	OB			8					4500	5150
21	5	BAYMASTER 2150 BW	OP	FSH	FBG	TH	OB			8		1650			5200	6000
21	5	BAYMASTER 2150 EXP	OP	FSH	FBG	TH	OB			8		1650			5050	5800
21	5	BAYMASTER 2150 F7S	OP	FSH	FBG	TH	OB			8		1650			4850	5600
21	7	BAYMASTER BACKWATER	OP	FSH	FBG	TH	OB			8					5850	6750
21	7	BAYMASTER EXPRESS	OP	FSH	FBG	TH	OB			8					5650	6500
		1993 BOATS														
16	4	BAYMASTER T	OP	FSH	FBG	TH	OB			6	6				1900	2250
16	4	BAYMASTER T DXL	OP	FSH	FBG	TH	OB			6	6				2450	2850
16	6	BAYMASTER BACKWATER	OP	FSH	FBG	TH	OB			7	3				3700	4300
16	6	BAYMASTER EXPRESS	OP	FSH	FBG	TH	OB			7	3				3550	4100
16	6	BAYMASTER SPECIAL	OP	FSH	FBG	TH	OB			7	3				2600	3000
16	6	BAYMASTER TV	OP	FSH	FBG	TH	OB			7	3				2650	3050
18	5	BAYMASTER 1850 BW	OP	FSH	FBG	TH	OB			8					3950	4600
18	5	BAYMASTER 1850 EXP	OP	FSH	FBG	TH	OB			8					3800	4400
18	5	BAYMASTER 1850 F&S	OP	FSH	FBG	TH	OB			8					3650	4250
19	3	BAYMASTER BACKWATER	OP	FSH	FBG	TH	OB			7	3				4150	4800
19	3	BAYMASTER EXPRESS	OP	FSH	FBG	TH	OB			7	3				3900	4550
19	6	PROGLAS BACKWATER	OP	FSH	FBG	TH	OB			8	2				4150	4850
19	6	PROGLAS EXPRESS	OP	FSH	FBG	TH	OB			8	2				4000	4650
20	2	BAYMASTER 202	OP	FSH	FBG	TH	OB			8					4250	4950
21	5	BAYMASTER 2150 BW	OP	FSH	FBG	TH	OB			8		1650			5000	5750
21	5	BAYMASTER 2150 EXP	OP	FSH	FBG	TH	OB			8		1650			4850	5550
21	5	BAYMASTER 2150 F7S	OP	FSH	FBG	TH	OB			8		1650			4650	5350
21	7	BAYMASTER BACKWATER	OP	FSH	FBG	TH	OB			8					5600	6450
21	7	BAYMASTER EXPRESS	OP	FSH	FBG	TH	OB			8					5400	6250
		1989 BOATS														
16		BAYMASTER SCOOTER	OP	FSH	FBG	TH	OB			7	1	850	5	1	1900	2250
16	6	BACKWATER EXPRESS	OP	FSH	FBG	TH	OB			7	3	1200	6	1	2700	3150
16	6	BAYMASTER EXPRESS	OP	FSH	FBG	TH	OB			7	3	1200	6	1	2600	3050
18	7	GULFMASTER-V	OP	FSH	FBG	TH	OB			8		1700			3650	4250
19	3	BACKWATER EXPRESS	OP	FSH	FBG	TH	OB			7	3	1300	6	1	3150	3650
19	3	BAYMASTER EXPRESS	OP	FSH	FBG	TH	OB			7	3	1300	6	1	3050	3550
		1988 BOATS														
16		BAYMASTER SCOOTER	OP	FSH	FBG	TH	OB			7	1	850	5	1	1850	2200
16	6	BACKWATER EXPRESS	OP	FSH	FBG	TH	OB			7	3	1200			2650	3050

 CONTINUED ON NEXT PAGE

BAYMASTER BOATS INC   -CONTINUED   See inside cover to adjust price for area

LOA FT IN	NAME AND/ OR MODEL	TOP/ RIG	BOAT TYPE	-HULL- MTL TP	----ENGINE--- TP # HP MFG	BEAM FT IN	WGT LBS	DRAFT FT IN	RETAIL LOW	RETAIL HIGH
				---- 1988 BOATS ----						
16 6	BAYMASTER EXPRESS	OP	FSH	FBG TH OB		7 3	1200	6 5	2550	2950
19 3	BACKWATER EXPRESS	OP	FSH	FBG TH OB		7 3	1300	6 1	3050	3550
19 3	BAYMASTER EXPRESS	OP	FSH	FBG TH OB		7 3	1300	6 1	2950	3400
				---- 1987 BOATS ----						
16 6	BACKWATER EXPRESS	OP	FSH	FBG FL OB		7 3	950	7	2000	2400
16 6	BAYMASTER EXPRESS	OP	FSH	FBG FL OB		7 3	850	6 5	1800	2150
16 7	BCM 17V	OP	OPFSH	FBG DV OB		6 11	1050	10	2250	2650
16 7	BCM 17VT	OP	OPFSH	FBG SV OB		6 11	1150	9	2400	2800
				---- 1984 BOATS ----						
16			FSH	OB		6 11	650	5 6	1250	1500

BB10 MANUFACTURING INC
ANNAPOLIS MD 21403   COAST GUARD MFG ID- BB9 See inside cover to adjust price for area

LOA FT IN	NAME AND/ OR MODEL	TOP/ RIG	BOAT TYPE	-HULL- MTL TP	----ENGINE--- TP # HP MFG	BEAM FT IN	WGT LBS	DRAFT FT IN	RETAIL LOW	RETAIL HIGH
				---- 1988 BOATS ----						
32 10	BB10M FAMILY RACER	SLP	SA/RC	F/S KL OB		7 6	4956	4 10	19500	21700
32 10	BB10M FAMILY RACER	SLP	SA/RC	F/S KL IB	9D YAN	7 6	4956	4 10	19700	21900
				---- 1987 BOATS ----						
32 10	BB10M FAMILY RACER	SLP	SA/RC	F/S KL OB		7 6	4956	4 10	18600	20600
32 10	BB10M FAMILY RACER	SLP	SA/RC	F/S KL IB	9D YAN	7 6	4956	4 10	18700	20800
				---- 1986 BOATS ----						
32 10	BB10M FAMILY RACER	SLP	SA/RC	F/S KL OB		7 6	4956	4 10	17100	19400
32 10	BB10M FAMILY RACER	SLP	SA/RC	F/S KL IB	9D YAN	7 6	4956	4 10	17200	19600
				---- 1985 BOATS ----						
32 10	BB10M FAMILY RACER	SLP	SA/RC	F/S KL IB	9D YAN	7 6	4956	4 10	16200	18400
				---- 1984 BOATS ----						
32 10	BB10M FAMILY RACER	SLP	SA/RC	KL		7 6	4956	4 10	12200	13900
32 10	BB10M FAMILY RACER	SLP	SA/RC	F/S KL OB		7 6	4956	4 10	15100	17200
32 10	BB10M FAMILY RACER	SLP	SA/RC	F/S KL IB	7D BMW	7 6	4956	4 10	15200	17300

....For earlier years, see the BUC Used Boat Price Guide, Volume 3

BEACHCAT BOATS INC
OLDSMAR FL 34677   COAST GUARD MFG ID- MXB See inside cover to adjust price for area

For more recent years, see the BUC Used Boat Price Guide, Volume 1

LOA FT IN	NAME AND/ OR MODEL	TOP/ RIG	BOAT TYPE	-HULL- MTL TP	----ENGINE--- TP # HP MFG	BEAM FT IN	WGT LBS	DRAFT FT IN	RETAIL LOW	RETAIL HIGH
				---- 1985 BOATS ----						
25 4	BEACHCOMBER 25	CAT	SA/CR	FBG CB OB		8	5300	1 3	17200	19500
25 4	BEACHCOMBER 25	CAT	SA/CR	FBG CB IB	D	8	5300	1 3	18700	20800
				---- 1984 BOATS ----						
25 4	BEACH COMBER 25	CAT	SA/CR	FBG CB IB	8D	8	5300		17100	19400

....For earlier years, see the BUC Used Boat Price Guide, Volume 3

BEACHCOMBER FIBERGLASS TECH
STUART FL 33494   COAST GUARD MFG ID- BXG See inside cover to adjust price for area
                           FORMERLY BEACHCOMBER BOAT BUILDING

LOA FT IN	NAME AND/ OR MODEL	TOP/ RIG	BOAT TYPE	-HULL- MTL TP	----ENGINE--- TP # HP MFG	BEAM FT IN	WGT LBS	DRAFT FT IN	RETAIL LOW	RETAIL HIGH
				---- 1988 BOATS ----						
18 4	BEACHCOMBER DORY	SLP	SAIL	FBG CB OB		6	550	6	3150	3650
18 4	BEACHCOMBER DORY	SLP	SAIL	FBG CB OB		6	650	6	3350	3900
				---- 1987 BOATS ----						
18 4	BEACHCOMBER DORY	SLP	SAIL	FBG CB OB		6	550	6	2950	3450
18 4	BEACHCOMBER DORY	SLP	SAIL	FBG CB OB		6	650	6	3150	3700
				---- 1986 BOATS ----						
18 4	BEACHCOMBER DORY	SLP	SAIL	FBG CB OB		6	550	6	2800	3250
18 4	BEACHCOMBER DORY	SLP	SAIL	FBG CB OB		6	650	6	3000	3450
				---- 1985 BOATS ----						
18 4	BEACHCOMBER DORY	SLP	SAIL	FBG CB OB		6	550	6	2600	3050
18 4	BEACHCOMBER OVERNIGH	SLP	SAIL	FBG CB	10	6	600	6	2700	3150
				---- 1984 BOATS ----						
18 4	BEACHCOMBER DORY	SLP	SAIL	FBG CB OB		6	550	6	2450	2850

....For earlier years, see the BUC Used Boat Price Guide, Volume 3

BEACHCRAFT POWER BOATS INC
MIAMI FL 33166   See inside cover to adjust price for area

For more recent years, see the BUC Used Boat Price Guide, Volume 1

LOA FT IN	NAME AND/ OR MODEL	TOP/ RIG	BOAT TYPE	-HULL- MTL TP	----ENGINE--- TP # HP MFG	BEAM FT IN	WGT LBS	DRAFT FT IN	RETAIL LOW	RETAIL HIGH
				---- 1990 BOATS ----						
20 10	STRIKER 21	OP	OPFSH	FBG DV OB		8 4		1 8	6500	7450
24 10	PHANTOM 25	OP	RACE	FBG DV OB		8 2	3000	2	13100	14900
24 10	PHANTOM 25	OP	RACE	FBG DV IO	330	8 2	3000	2	12400	14100
24 10	VIKING 25	OP	OPFSH	FBG DV OB		8 2	2700	2	12300	14000
28	SHADOW 28	OP	RACE	FBG DV OB		8 2	3500	2	19200	21300
28	SHADOW 28	OP	RACE	FBG DV IO	T260	8 2	4500	2	19700	21900
28	SHADOW 28	OP	RACE	FBG DV IO	T365	8 2	4500	2	22300	24700
28	STINGER 28	OP	SF	FBG DV OB		8 2	3300	2	19200	21300
				---- 1989 BOATS ----						
20 10	STRIKER 21	OP	OPFSH	FBG DV OB		8 4		1 8	6250	7200
24 10	PHANTOM 25	OP	RACE	FBG DV OB		8 2	3000	2	12700	14400
24 10	PHANTOM 25	OP	RACE	FBG DV IO	T260 MRCR	8 2	3000	2	12900	14600
24 10	VIKING 25	OP	OPFSH	FBG DV OB		8 2	2700	2	11900	13500
28	SHADOW 28	OP	RACE	FBG DV OB		8 2	3500	2	18800	20900
28	SHADOW 28	OP	RACE	FBG DV IO	T260-T330	8 2	4500	2	18000	22200
28	SHADOW 28	OP	RACE	FBG DV IO	T365 MRCR	8 2	5000	2	21200	23600
28	STINGER 28	OP	SF	FBG DV OB		8 2	3300	2	18800	20900
				---- 1988 BOATS ----						
20 10	STRIKER 21	OP	FSH	FBG SV OB		8 4	2000	1 3	7350	8450
20 10	STRIKER 21	OP	OPFSH	FBG DV OB		8 4	2000	2	7350	8450
24 10	PHANTOM 25	OP	RACE	FBG DV OB		8	2500	1 10	11000	12500
24 10	PHANTOM 25	OP	OPFSH	FBG DV IO		8			**	**
24 10	VIKING 25	OP	RACE	FBG DV OB		8	2500	1 10	11000	12400
28	SPEEDO 28	OP	RACE	FBG DV IO		8	2700	1 10	18200	20200
28	SPEEDO 28	OP	RACE	FBG DV IO		8			**	**
28	STINGER 28	OP	SF	FBG DV OB		8	2700	1 10	18200	20200
				---- 1987 BOATS ----						
20 10	STRIKER 21	OP	CTRCN	FBG DV OB		8 4	2000		7100	8200
23 6	SPORT FISHERMAN 24	OP	RACE	FBG DV OB		8	2500	1 6	9550	10900
24 10	PHANTOM 25	OP	RACE	FBG DV OB		8	2500	1 10	10600	12100
24 10	VIKING 25	OP	FSH	FBG DV OB		8	2500	1 10	10600	12100
28	SPEEDO 28	OP	RACE	FBG DV IO		8	3000	1 10	17300	19700
28	SPEEDO 28	OP	RNBT	FBG DV OB		8	3000	1 8	17300	19700
28	STINGER 28	OP	CTRCN	FBG DV OB		8	2700	1 10	17300	19600
28	STINGER 28SF	OP	CTRCN	FBG DV OB		8	2700	1 8	17300	19600

BECKMANN LTD
SLOCUM RI 02877-0026   COAST GUARD MFG ID- WKL See inside cover to adjust price for area
                      FORMERLY WALTER C BECKMANN LIMITED

For more recent years, see the BUC Used Boat Price Guide, Volume 1

LOA FT IN	NAME AND/ OR MODEL	TOP/ RIG	BOAT TYPE	-HULL- MTL TP	----ENGINE--- TP # HP MFG	BEAM FT IN	WGT LBS	DRAFT FT IN	RETAIL LOW	RETAIL HIGH
				---- 1996 BOATS ----						
20	ROSE 20	OP	LNCH	FBG DS ST	5	SEMP	4 4	1100	1 10	**	**
21 3	COMPROMISE 21	OP	LNCH	FBG DS ST	10	SEMP	5 6	1600	2 2	**	**
22 1	KATHY 22	EPH	TUG	FBG DS IB	28D	YAN	7 10	2400	2 2	**	**
22 1	MASE 22	OP	LNCH	FBG DS ST	10	SEMP	7 10	2400	2 2	**	**
30 1	BRIDGET 30	OP	LNCH	FBG DS ST	10	SEMP	7 10	3500	2 2	**	**
30 1	BRIDGET 30	EPH	TUG	FBG DS IB	28D	YAN	7 10	3500	2 2	**	**
30 1	FIREFLY 30	OP	LNCH	FBG DS ST	20	SEMP	10	8000	4	**	**
30 1	FIREFLY 30	EPH	TUG	FBG DS IB	50D	YAN	10	8000	4	**	**
33 3	FIREFLY 33	EPH	TUG	FBG DS IB	300D	GM	11	18000	3 6	**	**
				---- 1995 BOATS ----						
20	NANCY 20 STEAM	OP	LNCH	FBG DS IB			4 4	900	1 10	**	**
20	SHEHERAZADE 20	OP	LNCH	FBG DS IB			4 4	750	1 10	**	**
20	TARRAGON 20	OP	LNCH	FBG DS IB	10D	BMW	4 4	650	1 10	**	**
21	COMPROMISE 21	OP	LNCH	FBG DS IB			5 10	1400		**	**
23 3	KATHY 22 STEAM	OP	LNCH	FBG DS IB	10D		8	5000	2	**	**
23 3	KATHY 22 TUGBOAT	OP	LNCH	FBG DS IB	10D		8	5000	2	**	**
30	STEAM TUG 30		STL	STL IB			10			**	**
33 7	FIREFLY 33	OP	TUG	FBG DS IB	250D	CUM	11 6	16000	3 3	**	**
48	CLASSIC 48		CR	STL SV IB	325		16	40000		**	**
55	CLASSIC 55		CR	STL SV IB	325		16	50000		**	**
				---- 1994 BOATS ----						
20	NANCY 20 STEAM	OP	LNCH	FBG DS IB	5		4 4	900	1 10	**	**
20	SHEHERAZADE 20	OP	LNCH	FBG DS IB	5		4 4	750	1 10	**	**
20	TARRAGON 20	OP	LNCH	FBG DS IB	10D	BMW	4 4	650	1 10	**	**
21	COMPROMISE 21	OP	LNCH	FBG DS IB	10D		5 10	1400		**	**
23 3	KATHY 22 STEAM	OP	LNCH	FBG DS IB	10D		8	5000	2	**	**

LOA FT	IN	NAME AND/ OR MODEL	TOP/ RIG	BOAT TYPE	HULL MTL	HULL TP	ENG TP	ENG #	ENG HP	ENG MFG	BEAM FT	IN	WGT LBS	DRAFT FT	IN	RETAIL LOW	RETAIL HIGH
		————— 1994 BOATS —————															
23	3	KATHY 22 TUGBOAT	OP	TUG	FBG	DS	IB		8D		8		5000	2		**	**
30		STEAM TUG 30		TUG	STL		IB		20		10					**	**
30		TORPEDO 30		LNCH	WD		IB		30		5					**	**
33	7	FIREFLY 33	OP	TUG	FBG	DS	IB		250D	CUM	11	6	16000	3	3	**	**
45		NORTH-SEA 45		CR	STL	SV	IB		250		14		35000			**	**
45		TERN 45		CR	STL	SV	IB		300		15		35000			**	**
48		CLASSIC 48		CR	STL	SV	IB		300		16		40000			**	**
48		PHOEBE 48		CR	STL	SV	IB				11					**	**
55		CLASSIC 55		CR	STL	SV	IB		325		16		50000			**	**
65		HOLLY 65		CR	STL	SV	IB		350		19		60000			**	**
70		BLACKBIRD 70		CR	STL	SV	IB		375		20		80000			**	**
70		CLASSIC 70		CR	WD	DS	IB		T120		14		50000			**	**
70		CORMORANT 70		CR	STL	SV	IB		375		21		85000			**	**
70		OSPREY 70		CR	STL	SV	IB		375		19		75000			**	**
		————— 1993 BOATS —————															
20		NANCY 20 STEAM	OP	LNCH	FBG	DS	IB		5		4	4	900	1	10	**	**
20		SHEHERAZADE 20	OP	LNCH	FBG	DS	IB		8		4	4	750	1	10	**	**
20		TARRAGON 20	OP	LNCH	FBG	DS	IB		10D	BMW	4	4	650	1	10	**	**
21		TRUSCOTT/COMPROMISE	OP	LNCH	FBG	DS	IB		4		5	10	1400			**	**
23	3	KATHY 22 STEAM	OP	LNCH	FBG	DS	IB		10D		8		5000	2		**	**
23	3	KATHY 22 TUGBOAT	OP	TUG	FBG	DS	IB		8D		8		5000	2		**	**
30		STEAM TUG 30		TUG	STL		IB		20		10					**	**
30		TORPEDO 30		LNCH	WD		IB		30		5					**	**
33	7	FIREFLY 33	OP	TUG	FBG	DS	IB		250D	CUM	11	6	16000	3	3	**	**
45		NORTH-SEA 45		CR	STL	SV	IB		250		14		35000			**	**
45		TERN 45		CR	STL	SV	IB		300		15		35000			**	**
48		CLASSIC 48		CR	STL	SV	IB		300		16		40000			**	**
48		PHOEBE 48		CR	STL	SV	IB				11					**	**
55		CLASSIC 55		CR	STL	SV	IB		325		16		50000			**	**
65		HOLLY 65		CR	STL	SV	IB		350		19		60000			**	**
70		BLACKBIRD 70		CR	STL	SV	IB		375		20		80000			**	**
70		CLASSIC 70		CR	WD	DS	IB		T120		14		50000			**	**
70		CORMORANT 70		CR	STL	SV	IB		375		21		85000			**	**
70		OSPREY 70		CR	STL	SV	IB		375		19		75000			**	**
		————— 1992 BOATS —————															
20		NANCY 20 STEAM	OP	LNCH	FBG	DS	IB		5		4	4	900	1	10	**	**
20		SHEHERAZADE 20	OP	LNCH	FBG	DS	IB		8		4	4	750	1	10	**	**
20		TARRAGON 20	OP	LNCH	FBG	DS	IB		10D	BMW	4	4	650	1	10	**	**
23	3	KATHY 22 STEAM	OP	LNCH	FBG	DS	IB		10D		8		5000	2		**	**
23	3	KATHY 22 TUGBOAT	OP	TUG	FBG	DS	IB		8D		8		5000	2		**	**
30		STEAM TUG 30		TUG	STL		IB		20		10					**	**
33	7	FIREFLY 33	OP	TUG	FBG	DS	IB		250D	CUM	11	6	16000	3	3	**	**
45		NORTH-SEA 45		CR	STL	SV	IB		250		14		35000			**	**
45		TERN 45		CR	STL	SV	IB		300		15		35000			**	**
48		CLASSIC 48		CR	STL	SV	IB		300		16		40000			**	**
48		PHOEBE 48		CR	STL	SV	IB				11					**	**
55		CLASSIC 55		CR	STL	SV	IB		325		16		50000			**	**
65		HOLLY 65		CR	STL	SV	IB		350		19		60000			**	**
70		BLACKBIRD 70		CR	STL	SV	IB		375		20		80000			**	**
70		CLASSIC 70		CR	WD	DS	IB		T120		14		50000			**	**
70		CORMORANT 70		CR	STL	SV	IB		375		21		85000			**	**
70		OSPREY 70		CR	STL	SV	IB		375		19		75000			**	**
		————— 1991 BOATS —————															
20		NANCY 20 STEAM	OP	LNCH	FBG	DS	IB		5		4	4	900	1	10	**	**
20		SHEHERAZADE 20	OP	LNCH	FBG	DS	IB		8		4	4	750	1	10	**	**
20		TARRAGON 20	OP	LNCH	FBG	DS	IB		10D	BMW	4	4	650	1	10	**	**
23	3	KATHY 22 STEAM	OP	LNCH	FBG	DS	IB		10D		8		5000	2		**	**
23	3	KATHY 22 TUGBOAT	OP	TUG	FBG	DS	IB		8D		8		5000	2		**	**
30		STEAM TUG 30		TUG	STL		IB		20		10					**	**
30		TORPEDO 30		LNCH	WD		IB		30		5					**	**
45		NORTH-SEA 45		CR	STL	SV	IB		250		14		35000			**	**
45		TERN 45		CR	STL	SV	IB		300		15		35000			**	**
48		CLASSIC 48		CR	STL	SV	IB		300		16		40000			**	**
48		PHOEBE 48		CR	STL	SV	IB				11					**	**
55		CLASSIC 55		CR	STL	SV	IB		325		16		50000			**	**
65		HOLLY 65		CR	STL	SV	IB		350		19		60000			**	**
70		BLACKBIRD 70		CR	STL	SV	IB		375		20		80000			**	**
70		CLASSIC 70		CR	WD	DS	IB		T120		14		50000			**	**
70		CORMORANT 70		CR	STL	SV	IB		375		21		85000			**	**
70		OSPREY 70		CR	STL	SV	IB		375		19		75000			**	**
		————— 1990 BOATS —————															
20		NANCY 20 STEAM	OP	LNCH	FBG	DS	IB		5		4	4	900	1	10	**	**
20		SHEHERAZADE 20	OP	LNCH	FBG	DS	IB		8		4	4	750	1	10	**	**
20		TARRAGON 20	OP	LNCH	FBG	DS	IB		10D	BMW	4	4	650	1	10	**	**
23	3	KATHY 22 STEAM	OP	LNCH	FBG	DS	IB		10D		8		5000	2		**	**
23	3	KATHY 22 TUGBOAT	OP	TUG	FBG	DS	IB		8D		8		5000	2		**	**
30		STEAM TUG 30		TUG	STL		IB		20		10					**	**
30		TORPEDO 30		LNCH	WD		IB		30		5					**	**
45		NORTH-SEA 45		CR	STL	SV	IB		250		14		35000			**	**
45		TERN 45		CR	STL	SV	IB		300		15		35000			**	**
48		CLASSIC 48		CR	STL	SV	IB		300		16		40000			**	**
48		PHOEBE 48		CR	STL	SV	IB				11					**	**
55		CLASSIC 55		CR	STL	SV	IB		325		16		50000			**	**
65		HOLLY 65		CR	STL	SV	IB		350		19		60000			**	**
70		BLACKBIRD 70		CR	STL	SV	IB		375		20		80000			**	**
70		CLASSIC 70		CR	WD	DS	IB		T120		14		50000			**	**
70		CORMORANT 70		CR	STL	SV	IB		375		21		85000			**	**
70		OSPREY 70		CR	STL	SV	IB		375		19		75000			**	**
		————— 1989 BOATS —————															
20		NANCY 20 STEAM	OP	LNCH	FBG	DS	IB		5		4	4	900	1	10	**	**
20		SHEHERAZADE 20	OP	LNCH	FBG	DS	IB		8		4	4	750	1	10	**	**
20		TARRAGON 20	OP	LNCH	FBG	DS	IB		10D	BMW	4	4	650	1	10	**	**
23	3	KATHY 22 TUGBOAT	OP	TUG	FBG	DS	IB		8D	MITS	8		5000	2		**	**
23	3	KATY 22 STEAM	OP	LNCH	FBG	DS	IB		10D	MITS	8		5000	2		**	**
30		STEAM TUG 30		TUG	STL		IB		20		10					**	**
30		TORPEDO 30		LNCH	WD		IB		30		5					**	**
45		NORTH-SEA 45		CR	STL	SV	IB		250		14		35000			**	**
45		TERN 45		CR	STL	SV	IB		300		15		35000			**	**
48		CLASSIC 48		CR	STL	SV	IB		300		16		40000			**	**
48		PHOEBE 48		CR	STL	SV	IB				11					**	**
55		CLASSIC 55		CR	STL	SV	IB		325		16		50000			**	**
65		HOLLY 65		CR	STL	SV	IB		350		19		60000			**	**
70		BLACKBIRD 70		CR	STL	SV	IB		375		20		80000			**	**
70		CLASSIC 70		CR	WD	DS	IB		T120		14		50000			**	**
70		CORMORANT 70		CR	STL	SV	IB		375		21		85000			**	**
70		OSPREY 70		CR	STL	SV	IB		375		19		75000			**	**
		————— 1988 BOATS —————															
18		AFRICAN QUEEN(STEAM)		LNCH	FBG		IB		5		6	4	3500				
20		COMMODORE 20	OP		FBG		IB				4	4				**	**
20		NANCY 20 STEAM	OP	LNCH	FBG	DS	IB		5		4	4	900	1	10	**	**
20		SCHEHERAZADE 20			FBG						4	4				**	**
20		SHEHERAZADE 20	OP	LNCH	FBG	DS	IB		8		4	4	750	1	10	**	**
20		TARRAGON 20			FBG						4	4				**	**
23	3	KATHY 22	OP	LNCH	FBG	DS	IB		10D	MITS	8		5000	2		**	**
23	3	KATHY 22 TUGBOAT	OP	TUG	FBG	DS	IB		8D	MITS	8		5000	2		**	**
30		STEAM TUG 30		TUG	STL		IB		20		10					**	**
40		MONOCO 40		RNBT	WD	SV	IB		530		9		16000			**	**
45		NORTH-SEA 45		CR	STL	SV	IB		250		14		35000			**	**
45		TERN 45		CR	STL	SV	IB		300		15		35000			**	**
48		CLASSIC 48		CR	STL	SV	IB		300		16		40000			**	**
48		PHOEBE 48		CR	STL	SV	IB				11					**	**
55		CLASSIC 55		CR	STL	SV	IB		325		16		50000			**	**
65		HOLLY 65		CR	STL	SV	IB		350		19		60000			**	**
70		BLACKBIRD 70		CR	STL	SV	IB		375		20		80000			**	**
70		CLASSIC 70		CR	WD	DS	IB		T120		14		50000			**	**
70		CORMORANT 70		CR	STL	SV	IB		375		21		85000			**	**
70		OSPREY 70		CR	STL	SV	IB		375		19		75000			**	**
		————— 1987 BOATS —————															
20		COMMODORE 20			FBG		IB				4	4				**	**
20		NANCY 20			FBG		IB				4	4				**	**
20		NANCY 20 STEAM	OP	LNCH	FBG	DS	IB		5		4	4	900	1	10	**	**
20		SCHEHERAZADE 20			FBG		IB				4	4				**	**
20		SHEHERAZADE 20	OP	LNCH	FBG	DS	IB		8		4	4	750	1	10	**	**
20		TARRAGON 20			FBG		IB				4	4				**	**
20		TARRAGON 20	OP	LNCH	FBG	DS	IB		10D	BMW	4	4	650	1	10	**	**
22	9	SALOME 23	OP	LNCH	FBG	DS	IB				6		1600			**	**
22	9	NIMBUS 23 STEAM	OP	LNCH	FBG	DS	IB				6	4	1900			**	**
22	9	THYME 23	OP	LNCH	FBG	DS	IB		10D	BMW	6	4	1600			**	**
23	3	KATHY 22	OP	LNCH	FBG	DS	IB		10D	BMW	8		3000			**	**
23	3	KATHY 22 TUGBOAT	OP	TUG	FBG	DS	IB		8D	BMW	8		3000			**	**
26		WASQUE 26	OP	SF	FBG	SV	IO		200D		8	7	7000	2	3	**	**
27		BRIDGET 30 TUGBOAT	HT	TUG	FBG	DS	IB		10D	BMW	10		4500	3		**	**
30		ANNIE 30 TUGBOAT	HT	TUG	FBG	DS	IB		200D	BMW	10		6500	4		**	**
30		LINDA 30 TUGBOAT	HT	TUG	FBG	DS	JT		15		10		6500	4		**	**
30		STEAM TUG 30		TUG	STL		IB		20		10					**	**

LOA FT	LOA IN	NAME AND/ OR MODEL	TOP/ RIG	BOAT TYPE	HULL MTL	HULL TP	ENGINE TP	# HP	MFG	BEAM FT	BEAM IN	WGT LBS	DRAFT FT	DRAFT IN	RETAIL LOW	RETAIL HIGH
		1987 BOATS														
30		TORPEDO 30		LNCH	WD		IB	30		5					**	**
40		MONOCO 40		RNBT	WD	SV	IB	530		9		16000			**	**
45		NORTH-SEA 45		CR	STL	SV	IB	250		14		35000			**	**
45		TERN 45		CR	STL	SV	IB	300		15		35000			**	**
48		CLASSIC 48		CR	STL	SV	IB	300		16		40000			**	**
48		PHOEBE 48		CR	STL	SV	IB			11					**	**
55		CLASSIC 55		CR	STL	SV	IB	325		16		50000			**	**
65		HOLLY 65		CR	STL	SV	IB	350		19		60000			**	**
70		BLACKBIRD 70		CR	STL	SV	IB	375		20		80000			**	**
70		CLASSIC 70		CR	WD	DS	IB	T120		14		50000			**	**
70		CORMORANT 70		CR	STL	SV	IB	375		21		85000			**	**
70		OSPREY 70		CR	STL	SV	IB	375		19		75000			**	**
		1986 BOATS														
20		COMMODORE 20	OP	LNCH	FBG	DS	IB	4		4	4	1000			**	**
20		NANCY 20	OP	LNCH	FBG	DS	IB	6		4	4	1000			**	**
20		SCHEHERAZADE 20	OP	LNCH	FBG	DS	IB	4		4	4	1000			**	**
20		TARRAGON 20	OP	LNCH	FBG	DS	IB	10D		4	4	1000			**	**
27		BRIDGET 27 TUG		TUG			IB	45		10		5600			**	**
29		ANNIE 29		SPTCR		SV	IB	300		9		6000			**	**
30		STEAM TUG		TUG	STL		IB			10					**	**
30		TORPEDO 30			WD		IB			5					**	**
30		TUGBOAT 30		TUG			IB	45		10		6500			**	**
40		MONOCO 40		RNBT	WD	SV	IB	530		9		16000			**	**
41		CLASSIC 41		CR	STL	SV	IB	225		12		32000			**	**
45		NORTH-SEA 45		CR	STL	SV	IB	250		14		35000			**	**
45		TERN 45		CR	STL	SV	IB	300		14		35000			**	**
48		CLASSIC 48		CR	STL	SV	IB	300		16		40000			**	**
48		PHOEBE 48		CR	STL	SV	IB			11					**	**
50		STEAM 50		CR	STL	SV	IB			12					**	**
65		HOLLY 65		CR	STL	SV	IB	350		19		60000			**	**
70		BLACKBIRD 70		CR	STL	SV	IB	375		20		80000			**	**
70		CLASSIC 70		CR	WD	RB	IB	T120		14		50000			**	**
70		CORMORANT 70		CR	STL	SV	IB	375		21		85000			**	**
70		OSPREY 70		CR	STL	SV	IB	375		19		75000			**	**
		1985 BOATS														
20		COMMODORE 20			FBG		IB			4	4				**	**
20		NANCY 20			FBG		IB			4	4				**	**
20		NANCY 20 STEAM	OP	LNCH	FBG	DS	IB	5		4	4	900	1	10	**	**
20		SCHEHERAZADE 20			FBG		IB			4	4				**	**
20		SHEHERAZADE 20	OP	LNCH	FBG	DS	IB	8		4	4	750	1	10	**	**
20		TARRAGON 20			FBG		IB			4	4				**	**
20		TARRAGON 20	OP	LNCH	FBG	DS	IB	10D	BMW	4	4	650	1	10	**	**
20	9	SALOME 23	OP	LNCH	FBG	DS	IB	8		6	4	1600	2		**	**
21		NORTH-SEA 21		CR	FBG	SV	IB	16		8		3500			**	**
22	9	NIMBUS 23 STEAM	OP	LNCH	FBG	DS	IB	7		6	4	1900	2		**	**
22	9	THYME 23	OP	LNCH	FBG	DS	IB	10D	BMW	6	4	1600	2		**	**
23	3	KATHY 22	OP	LNCH	FBG	DS	IB	10D	BMW	8		3000	2		**	**
23	3	KATHY 22 TUGBOAT	OP	TUG	FBG	DS	IB	8D	BMW	8		3000	2		**	**
26		NORTH-SEA 26		CR	FBG	SV	IB	20		10		5500			**	**
26		OFFSHORE EXPRESS 26	OP	SF	FBG	SV	IB	200D		8	7	7000	2	3	**	**
26		WASQUE 26	OP	SF	FBG	SV	IB	200D		8	7	7000	2	3	**	**
27		BRIDGET 27 TUGBOAT	HT	TUG	FBG	DS	IB	10D	BMW	10		4500	3		**	**
29		ANNIE 29		TUG	FBG	SV	IB	300		9		6000			**	**
30		ANNIE 30 TUGBOAT	HT	TUG	FBG	DS	IB	20D	BMW	10		6500	4		**	**
30		LINDA 30 TUGBOAT	HT	TUG	FBG	DS	JT	15		10		6500	4		**	**
30		STEAM-TRIG 30			STL		IB	20		10					**	**
30		TORPEDO 30			WD		IB	30		5					**	**
32		NORTH-SEA 32		CR	STL	SV	IB	80		10		12000			**	**
38		NORTH-SEA 38		CR	STL	SV	IB	100		11		20000			**	**
40		MONOCO 40		RNBT	WD	SV	IB	530		9		16000			**	**
41		CLASSIC 41		CR	STL	SV	IB	225		12		32000			**	**
45		NORTH-SEA 45		CR	STL	SV	IB	250		14		35000			**	**
45		TERN 45		CR	STL	SV	IB	300		15		35000			**	**
48		CLASSIC 48		CR	STL	SV	IB	300		16		40000			**	**
48		PHOEBE 48		CR	STL	SV	IB			11					**	**
50		STEAM 50			STL		IB	60		12					**	**
55		CLASSIC 55		CR	STL	SV	IB	325		16		50000			**	**
65		HOLLY 65		CR	STL	SV	IB	350		19		60000			**	**
70		BLACKBIRD 70		CR	STL	SV	IB	375		20		80000			**	**
70		CLASSIC 70		CR	WD	DS	IB	T120		14		50000			**	**
70		CORMORANT 70		CR	STL	SV	IB	375		21		85000			**	**
70		OSPREY 70		CR	STL	SV	IB	375		19		75000			**	**

BENETEAU USA

CHANTIERS BENETEAU S/A-FRANCE
MARION SC 29571 COAST GUARD MFG ID- BEY

See inside cover to adjust price for area

For more recent years, see the BUC Used Boat Price Guide, Volume 1

LOA FT	LOA IN	NAME AND/ OR MODEL	TOP/ RIG	BOAT TYPE	HULL MTL	HULL TP	ENGINE TP	# HP	MFG	BEAM FT	BEAM IN	WGT LBS	DRAFT FT	DRAFT IN	RETAIL LOW	RETAIL HIGH
		1996 BOATS														
21		FIRST 21 CLASSIC	SLP	SARAC	FBG	KL	OB			8	2	2420	2	11	8500	9800
21		FIRST 21.0	SLP	SARAC	FBG	KC	OB			8	2	2420	2	4	9900	11300
28	6	OCEANIS 281	SLP	SACAC	FBG	KL	IB	18D	YAN	9	5	5732	4		30200	33500
32	7	OCEANIS 321	SLP	SACAC	FBG	KL	IB	28D	YAN	11	3	9700	4	3	52900	58100
35		OCEANIS 351	SLP	SACAC	FBG	KL	IB	28D	YAN	12	6	12000	5		64800	71200
35	11	FIRST 36S7	SLP	SARAC	FBG	KL	IB	27D	YAN	12	5	11684	6	1	63800	70200
39	9	OCEANIS 400	SLP	SACAC	FBG	KL	IB	50D	PERK	12	10	16000	4	9	94700	104000
41		OCEANIS 40CC	SLP	SACAC	FBG	KL	IB	50D	YAN	12	9	18740	5	6	111000	122000
42	6	FIRST 42S7	SLP	SARAC	FBG	KL	IB	50D	PERK	13	6	18220	5	11	115000	126000
44	7	OCEANIS 44CC	SLP	SACAC	FBG	KL	IB	80D	PERK	14		20944	5	9	136500	150500
44	10	OCEANIS 440	SLP	SACAC	FBG	KL	IB	78D	PERK	14		20500	5	9	137000	150500
46	5	FIRST 45S5	SLP	SARAC	FBG	KL	IB	60D	PERK	14		21500	5	11	150500	165500
50	9	BENETEAU 50	SLP	SACAC	FBG	KL	IB	80D	PERK	14	8	28660	5	11	214000	235000
53	2	BENETEAU 53F5	SLP	SACAC	FBG	KL	IB	80D	PERK	14	9	30864	6	1	257000	282500
62		BENETEAU 62	SLP	SACAC	FBG	KL	IB	125D	PERK	17		46296	7		**	**
		1995 BOATS														
21		FIRST 21 CLASSIC	SLP	SACAC	FBG	KL	IB	D		8	2	2200	2	11	10900	12400
21		FIRST 21.0	SLP	SACAC	FBG	SK	IB	8D		8	2	2200	2	4	10800	12300
26	5	FIRST 265	SLP	SACAC	FBG	KL	IB	D		9	5	4800	4	2	23200	25800
28	6	OCEANIS 281	SLP	SACAC	FBG	KL	IB	18D		9	5	5732	4		29100	32400
31		FIRST 310 DEEP	SLP	SACAC	FBG	KL	IB	18D	VLVO	10	7	7054	5	11	37000	41100
31		FIRST 310 SHOAL	SLP	SACAC	FBG	KL	IB	18D	VLVO	10	7	7054	4	3	37000	41100
31		FIRST 310R	SLP	SACAC	FBG	KL	IB	18D	VLVO	10	7	7054	4	3	37000	41100
31	1	OCEANIS 300	SLP	SACAC	FBG	KL	IB	18D	VLVO	10	7	7055	5	1	37100	41200
32	7	OCEANIS 321	SLP	SACAC	FBG	WK	IB	18D		11	3	9700	4	3	51100	56200
35		OCEANIS 351	SLP	SACAC	FBG	KL	IB	24D		12	6	12000	5		62600	68800
35	7	FIRST 35S7 DEEP	SLP	SACAC	FBG	KL	IB	27D	PERK	12	6	14520	6	1	74700	82100
35	7	FIRST 35S7 SHOAL	SLP	SACAC	FBG	KL	IB	27D	PERK	12	6	14520	5	1	74700	82100
39	9	OCEANIS 400	SLP	SACAC	FBG	SK	IB	50D	PERK	12	10	16000	5	6	91700	101000
41		OCEANIS 40 CC	SLP	SACAC	FBG	KL	IB	50D		12	9	18740	5	6	99400	109000
42	6	FIRST 42S7 DEEP	SLP	SACAC	FBG	KL	IB	48D	YAN	13	6	18220	7	7	112000	123000
42	6	FIRST 42S7 SHOAL	SLP	SACAC	FBG	KL	IB	48D	YAN	13	6	18220	5	6	112000	123000
44	7	OCEANIS 44 CC	SLP	SACAC	FBG	KL	IB	85D	PERK	14		20944	5	9	132500	145500
44	10	OCEANIS 440	SLP	SACAC	FBG	KL	IB	78D		14		20500	5	9	124500	136500
44	11	FIRST 45F5 DEEP	SLP	SACAC	FBG	KL	IB	50D	PERK	14	1	21500	7	9	153000	168000
44	11	FIRST 45F5 SHOAL	SLP	SACAC	FBG	KL	IB	50D	PERK	14	1	21500	5	10	153000	168000
50	3	OCEANIS 510	SLP	SACAC	FBG	KL	IB	80D	PERK	15	7	30860	6		204000	224000
53	2	FIRST 53F5 DEEP	SLP	SACAC	FBG	KL	IB	80D	PERK	14	9	30864	8	1	248000	272500
53	2	FIRST 53F5 SHOAL	SLP	SACAC	FBG	KL	IB	80D	PERK	14	9	30864	6	3	248000	272500
		1994 BOATS														
21		FIRST 210	SLP	SACAC	FBG	SK	IB	8D		8	2	2200	2	4	10500	11900
26	5	FIRST 265	SLP	SACAC	FBG	KL	IB	D		9	5	4800	4	2	22500	25000
31		FIRST 310 DEEP	SLP	SACAC	FBG	KL	IB	18D	VLVO	10	7	7054	5	11	35900	39900
31		FIRST 310 SHOAL	SLP	SACAC	FBG	KL	IB	18D	VLVO	10	7	7054	4	3	35900	39900
31	1	OCEANIS 300	SLP	SACAC	FBG	KL	IB	18D	VLVO	10	7	7055	5	1	35900	39900
35		OCEANIS 351	SLP	SACAC	FBG	KL	IB	27D	PERK	12	6	12000	5		60500	66500
35	7	FIRST 35S7 DEEP	SLP	SACAC	FBG	KL	IB	27D	PERK	12	6	14520	6	1	72400	79600
35	7	FIRST 35S7 SHOAL	SLP	SACAC	FBG	KL	IB	27D	PERK	12	6	14520	5	1	72400	79600
35	8	OCEANIS 370	SLP	SACAC	FBG	WK	IB	28D	VLVO	12	5	11243	4	2	57500	63200
38	3	FIRST 38S5 DEEP	SLP	SACAC	FBG	KL	IB	43D	VLVO	12	10	14520	6	6	77400	85100
38	3	FIRST 38S5 SHOAL	SLP	SACAC	FBG	KL	IB	43D	VLVO	12	10	14520	5	2	77400	85100
39	9	OCEANIS 400	SLP	SACAC	FBG	SK	IB	50D	PERK	12	10	16000	5	6	88900	97700
42	6	FIRST 42S7 DEEP	SLP	SACAC	FBG	KL	IB	48D	YAN	13	7	18220	7	7	108500	119000
42	6	FIRST 42S7 SHOAL	SLP	SACAC	FBG	KL	IB	48D	YAN	13	7	18220	5	5	108500	119000
44	8	OCEANIS 44 CC	SLP	SACAC	FBG	KL	IB	85D	PERK	14		20944	5	9	129000	141500
44	10	OCEANIS 440/1 AC	SLP	SACAC	FBG	KL	IB	72D	YAN	13	11	20500	5	9	120500	132500
44	10	OCEANIS 440/2 AC	SLP	SACAC	FBG	KL	IB	72D	YAN	13	11	20500	5	9	120000	131500
44	11	FIRST 45F5 DEEP	SLP	SACAC	FBG	KL	IB	50D	PERK	14	1	21500	7	9	148500	163000
44	11	FIRST 45F5 SHOAL	SLP	SACAC	FBG	KL	IB	50D	PERK	14	1	21500	5	10	148500	163000
50	3	OCEANIS 510	SLP	SACAC	FBG	KL	IB	80D	PERK	15	7	30860	6		197000	216500
53	2	FIRST 53F5 DEEP	SLP	SACAC	FBG	KL	IB	80D	PERK	14	9	30864	8	1	240000	263500
53	2	FIRST 53F5 SHOAL	SLP	SACAC	FBG	KL	IB	80D	PERK	14	9	30864	6	3	240000	263500
		1993 BOATS														
21		FIRST 210	SLP	SACAC	FBG	SK	IB	8D		8	2	2200	2	4	10100	11500
26	5	FIRST 265	SLP	SACAC	FBG	KL	OB			9	5	4800	4	2	20500	22800
26	5	FIRST 265	SLP	SACAC	FBG	KL	IB	D		9	5	4800	4	2	21700	24100

CONTINUED ON NEXT PAGE

LOA FT	LOA IN	NAME AND/ OR MODEL	TOP/ RIG	BOAT TYPE	-HULL- MTL	-HULL- TP	ENGINE TP	ENGINE # HP	ENGINE MFG	BEAM FT	BEAM IN	WGT LBS	DRAFT FT	DRAFT IN	RETAIL LOW	RETAIL HIGH
		1993 BOATS														
31		FIRST 310 DEEP	SLP	SACAC	FBG	KL	IB	18D	VLVO	10	7	7054	5	11	34600	38500
31		FIRST 310 SHOAL	SLP	SACAC	FBG	KL	IB	18D	VLVO	10	7	7054	4	3	34600	38500
33	10	OCEANIS 350	SLP	SACAC	FBG	KL	IB	28D	VLVO	11	3	10582	5	2	51800	56900
35	5	FIRST 35S5 DEEP	SLP	SACAC	FBG	KL	IB	28D	VLVO	11	10	11460	6		56300	61900
35	5	FIRST 35S5 SHOAL	SLP	SACAC	FBG	WK	IB	28D	VLVO	11	10	11460	4	9	56300	61900
35	8	OCEANIS 370	SLP	SACAC	FBG	WK	IB	28D	VLVO	12	5	11243	4	2	55500	61000
38	3	FIRST 38S5 DEEP	SLP	SACAC	FBG	KL	IB	43D	VLVO	12	10	14520	6	6	74700	82100
38	3	FIRST 38S5 SHOAL	SLP	SACAC	FBG	WK	IB	43D	VLVO	12	10	14520	5	2	74700	82100
38	4	OCEANIS 390/1	SLP	SACAC	FBG	KL	IB	43D	VLVO	12	10	14300	5	5	73800	81000
38	4	OCEANIS 390/2	SLP	SACAC	FBG	WK	IB	43D	VLVO	12	10	14300	4	6	74300	81700
39	9	OCEANIS 400	SLP	SACAC	FBG	SK	IB	50D	PERK	12	10	16000	5	6	85700	94200
41	4	FIRST 41S5	SLP	SACAC	FBG	WK	IB	50D	PERK	12	9	16800	5	5	94200	103500
41	4	FIRST 41S5 DEEP	SLP	SACAC	FBG	KL	IB	50D	PERK	12	9	16800	7	2	94200	103500
44	10	OCEANIS 440/1	SLP	SACAC	FBG	KL	IB	60D	PERK	13	11	20500	5	9	115500	127000
44	10	OCEANIS 440/2	SLP	SACAC	FBG	WK	IB	60D	PERK	13	11	20500	5	9	114500	125500
44	11	FIRST 45F5	SLP	SACAC	FBG	WK	IB	50D	PERK	14	1	21500	5	10	143000	157000
44	11	FIRST 45F5 DEEP	SLP	SACAC	FBG	KL	IB	50D	PERK	14	1	21500	7	9	143000	157000
47	6	FIRST 48	SLP	SACAC	FBG	KL	IB	80D	PERK	14	2		6	5	148500	163000
50	3	OCEANIS 510	SLP	SACAC	FBG	KL	IB	80D	PERK	15	7	30860	6		190000	208500
53	2	FIRST 53F5	SLP	SACAC	FBG	WK	IB	80D	PERK	14	9	30864	6	3	230500	253500
53	2	FIRST 53F5 DEEP	SLP	SACAC	FBG	KL	IB	80D	PERK	14	9	30864	8	1	230500	253500
		1992 BOATS														
23	4	FIRST 235	SLP	SAIL	FBG	KL				8	2	2310	3	8	8950	10200
23	4	FIRST 235	SLP	SAIL	FBG	WK				8	2	2310	2	9	8950	10200
26	5	FIRST 265	SLP	SAIL	FBG	KL	OB			9	5	4800	4	2	19600	21800
28	3	FIRST 285	SLP	SAIL	FBG	KL	IB	18D	VLVO	9	9	6160	5	3	27900	31000
28	3	FIRST 285	SLP	SAIL	FBG	WK	IB	18D	VLVO	9	9	6160	3	1	27900	31000
31		FIRST 310 DEEP	SLP	SAIL	FBG	KL	IB	18D	VLVO	10	7	7054	5	11	33200	36800
31		FIRST 310 SHOAL	SLP	SAIL	FBG	KL	IB	18D	VLVO	10	7	7054	4	3	33200	36800
32	6	FIRST 32S5	SLP	SAIL	FBG	WK	IB	18D	VLVO	10	10	9260	4	5	43500	48400
32	6	FIRST 32S5 DEEP	SLP	SAIL	FBG	KL	IB	18D	VLVO	10	10	9260	6		43500	48400
33	10	OCEANIS 350	SLP	SAIL	FBG	KL	IB	28D	VLVO	11	3	10582	5	2	49600	54500
33	10	OCEANIS 350	SLP	SAIL	FBG	WK	IB	28D	VLVO	11	3	10582	4	2	49600	54500
35	5	FIRST 35S5 DEEP	SLP	SAIL	FBG	KL	IB	28D	VLVO	11	10	11460	6		53900	59200
35	5	FIRST 35S5 SHOAL	SLP	SAIL	FBG	WK	IB	28D	VLVO	11	10	11460	4	9	53900	59200
35	8	EVASION 36	SLP	SAIL	FBG	KL	IB	43D	VLVO	12	5	12100	4	9	66200	72800
35	8	OCEANIS 370	SLP	SAIL	FBG	KL	IB	28D	VLVO	12	5	11243	5	1	53100	58400
35	8	OCEANIS 370	SLP	SAIL	FBG	WK	IB	28D	VLVO	12	5	11243	4	2	53100	58400
38	3	FIRST 38S5 DEEP	SLP	SAIL	FBG	KL	IB	43D	VLVO	12	10	14520	6	6	71500	78600
38	3	FIRST 38S5 SHOAL	SLP	SAIL	FBG	WK	IB	43D	VLVO	12	10	14520	5	2	71500	78600
38	4	OCEANIS 390	SLP	SAIL	FBG	KL	IB	43D	VLVO	12	10	14300	5	5	70900	77900
38	4	OCEANIS 390	SLP	SAIL	FBG	WK	IB	43D	VLVO	12	10	14300	4	6	70900	77900
41	4	FIRST 41S5	SLP	SAIL	FBG	WK	IB	50D	PERK	12	9	16800	5	5	90200	99100
41	4	FIRST 41S5 DEEP	SLP	SAIL	FBG	KL	IB	50D	PERK	12	9	16800	7	2	90200	99100
44	10	OCEANIS 440	SLP	SAIL	FBG	KL	IB	60D	PERK	13	11	20500	5	9	110000	121000
44	10	OCEANIS 440	SLP	SAIL	FBG	WK	IB	60D	PERK	13	11	20500	5	9	110000	121000
44	11	FIRST 45F5	SLP	SAIL	FBG	WK	IB	50D	PERK	14	1	21500	5	10	137000	150500
44	11	FIRST 45F5 DEEP	SLP	SAIL	FBG	KL	IB	50D	PERK	14	1	21500	7	9	137000	150500
47	6	FIRST 48	SLP	SAIL	FBG	KL	IB	80D	PERK	14	2		6	5	142000	156000
50	3	OCEANIS 510	SLP	SAIL	FBG	KL	IB	80D	PERK	15	7	30860	6		181000	199000
53	2	FIRST 53F5	SLP	SAIL	FBG	WK	IB	80D	PERK	14	9	30864	6	3	220000	241500
53	2	FIRST 53F5 DEEP	SLP	SAIL	FBG	KL	IB	80D	PERK	14	9	30864	8	1	220000	241500
		1991 BOATS														
23	4	FIRST 235	SLP	SAIL	FBG	KL				8	2	2310	3	8	8400	9700
23	4	FIRST 235	SLP	SAIL	FBG	WK				8	2	2310	2	9	8400	9700
28	3	FIRST 285	SLP	SAIL	FBG	KL	IB	18D	VLVO	9	9	6160	5	3	26500	29500
28	3	FIRST 285	SLP	SAIL	FBG	WK	IB	18D	VLVO	9	9	6160	3	1	26500	29500
31		FIRST 310 DEEP	SLP	SAIL	FBG	KL	IB	18D	VLVO	10	7	7054	5	11	31500	35000
31		FIRST 310 SHOAL	SLP	SAIL	FBG	WK	IB	18D	VLVO	10	7	7054	4	3	31500	35000
32	6	FIRST 32S5	SLP	SAIL	FBG	WK	IB	18D	VLVO	10	10	9260	4	5	41400	46000
32	6	FIRST 32S5 DEEP	SLP	SAIL	FBG	KL	IB	18D	VLVO	10	10	9260	6		41400	46000
33	10	OCEANIS 350	SLP	SAIL	FBG	KL	IB	28D	VLVO	11	3	10582	5	2	47400	52100
33	10	OCEANIS 350	SLP	SAIL	FBG	WK	IB	28D	VLVO	11	3	10582	4	2	47400	52100
35	5	FIRST 35S5	SLP	SAIL	FBG	WK	IB	28D	VLVO	11	10	11460	4	9	51300	56400
35	5	FIRST 35S5 DEEP	SLP	SAIL	FBG	KL	IB	28D	VLVO	11	10	11460	6		51300	56400
35	8	OCEANIS 370	SLP	SAIL	FBG	KL	IB	28D	VLVO	12	5	11243	5	1	50600	55600
35	8	OCEANIS 370	SLP	SAIL	FBG	WK	IB	28D	VLVO	12	5	11243	4	2	50600	55600
38	3	FIRST 38S5	SLP	SAIL	FBG	WK	IB	43D	VLVO	12	10	14520	5	2	68100	74800
38	3	FIRST 38S5 DEEP	SLP	SAIL	FBG	KL	IB	43D	VLVO	12	10	14520	6	6	68100	74800
38	4	OCEANIS 390 AFT 1	SLP	SAIL	FBG	KL	IB	43D	VLVO	12	10	14300	5	5	67500	74100
38	4	OCEANIS 390 AFT 1	SLP	SAIL	FBG	WK	IB	43D	VLVO	12	10	14300	4	6	67500	74100
38	4	OCEANIS 390 AFT 2	SLP	SAIL	FBG	KL	IB	43D	VLVO	12	10	14300	5	5	67500	74100
38	4	OCEANIS 390 AFT 2	SLP	SAIL	FBG	WK	IB	43D	VLVO	12	10	14300	4	6	67500	74100
41	4	FIRST 41S5	SLP	SAIL	FBG	WK	IB	50D	PERK	12	9	15840	5	5	82700	90900
41	4	FIRST 41S5 DEEP	SLP	SAIL	FBG	KL	IB	50D	PERK	12	9	15840	7	2	82700	90900
42	9	OCEANIS 430	SLP	SAIL	FBG	KL	IB	50D	PERK	13	10	19800	6		100500	110500
42	9	OCEANIS 430	SLP	SAIL	FBG	WK	IB	50D	PERK	13	10	19800	5	2	100500	110500
44	11	FIRST 45F5	SLP	SAIL	FBG	WK	IB	60D	PERK	14	1	20570	5	10	128000	140500
44	11	FIRST 45F5 DEEP	SLP	SAIL	FBG	KL	IB	60D	PERK	14	1	20570	7	9	128000	140500
47	6	FIRST 48	SLP	SAIL	FBG	KL	IB	80D	PERK	14	2		6	5	135000	148000
50	3	OCEANIS 500 PRESTIGE	SLP	SAIL	FBG	KL	IB	80D	PERK	15	7	28660	6		168500	185500
51	8	FIRST 53F5 DEEP	SLP	SAIL	FBG	KL	IB	80D	PERK	14	9	30864	8	1	188000	206500
51	8	FIRST 53F5 DEEP	SLP	SAIL	FBG	WK	IB	80D	PERK	14	9	30864	6	3	188000	206500
		1990 BOATS														
23	4	FIRST 235	SLP	SAIL	FBG	KL				8	2	2310	3	8	7950	9150
23	4	FIRST 235	SLP	SAIL	FBG	WK				8	2	2310	2	9	7950	9150
28	2	FIRST 285	SLP	SAIL	FBG	KL	IB	D	VLVO	9	8	6160	5	3	25100	27900
28	2	FIRST 285	SLP	SAIL	FBG	WK	IB	D	VLVO	9	8	6160	3	9	25100	27900
32	6	FIRST 32S5	SLP	SAIL	FBG	WK	IB	D	VLVO	10	10	9260	4	5	39200	43600
32	6	FIRST 32S5 DEEP	SLP	SAIL	FBG	KL	IB	D	VLVO	10	10	9260	6		39200	43600
33	10	OCEANIS 350	SLP	SAIL	FBG	KL	IB	28D	VLVO	11	3	10582	5	2	44400	49400
33	10	OCEANIS 350	SLP	SAIL	FBG	WK	IB	28D	VLVO	11	3	10582	4	2	44400	49400
35	5	FIRST 35S5	SLP	SAIL	FBG	KL	IB	28D	VLVO	11	10	11460	6		48600	53400
35	5	FIRST 35S5 SHOAL	SLP	SAIL	FBG	WK	IB	28D	VLVO	11	10	11460	4	9	48600	53400
38	3	FIRST 38S5	SLP	SAIL	FBG	WK	IB	D		12	10	13800	5	2	61700	67800
38	3	FIRST 38S5 DEEP	SLP	SAIL	FBG	KL	IB	D		12	10	13800	6	6	61700	67800
38	3	OCEANIS 390 DEEP	SLP	SAIL	FBG	KL	IB	28D	VLVO	12	10	14300	5	5	63300	69600
38	4	OCEANIS 390	SLP	SAIL	FBG	WK	IB	28D	VLVO	12	10	14300	4	6	63600	69800
41	4	FIRST 41S5	SLP	SAIL	FBG	WK	IB	50D	PERK	12	9	16800	5	5	81200	89300
41	4	FIRST 41S5 DEEP	SLP	SAIL	FBG	KL	IB	50D	PERK	12	9	16800	7	2	81200	89300
42	9	OCEANIS 430	SLP	SAIL	FBG	KL	IB	50D	PERK	13	10	19800	6		95000	104500
42	9	OCEANIS 430	SLP	SAIL	FBG	WK	IB	50D	PERK	13	10	19800	5	2	95000	104500
50	3	OCEANIS 500 PRESTIGE	SLP	SAIL	FBG	KL	IB	80D	PERK	15	7	28660	6		159000	175000
51	2	FIRST 51	SLP	SA/RC	FBG	KL	IB	85D	PERK	14	1	28659	5	9	169000	186000
		1989 BOATS														
23	4	FIRST 235	SLP	SAIL	FBG	KL				8	2	2310	3	8	7550	8650
23	4	FIRST 235	SLP	SAIL	FBG	WK				8	2	2310	2	9	7550	8650
28	1	FIRST 285	SLP	SAIL	FBG	KL	IB	D	VLVO	9	8	6160	5	3	23700	26300
28	1	FIRST 285	SLP	SAIL	FBG	WK	IB	D	VLVO	9	8	6160	3	9	23700	26300
32	6	FIRST 32S5	SLP	SAIL	FBG	WK	IB	D	VLVO	10	10	9260	4	5	37000	41100
32	6	FIRST 32S5 DEEP	SLP	SAIL	FBG	KL	IB	D	VLVO	10	10	9260	6		37000	41100
33	10	OCEANIS 350	SLP	SAIL	FBG	KL	IB	28D	VLVO	11	3	10582	5	2	41900	46600
33	10	OCEANIS 350	SLP	SAIL	FBG	WK	IB	28D	VLVO	11	3	10582	4	2	41900	46600
35	5	FIRST 35S5	SLP	SAIL	FBG	KL	IB	28D	VLVO	11	10	11460	6		46100	50700
35	5	FIRST 35S5 SHOAL	SLP	SAIL	FBG	WK	IB	28D	VLVO	11	10	11460	4	9	46100	50700
38	3	OCEANIS 390	SLP	SAIL	FBG	WK	IB	28D	VLVO	12	8	14300	4	5	59800	65700
38	3	OCEANIS 390 DEEP	SLP	SAIL	FBG	KL	IB	28D	VLVO	12	8	14300	5	4	59800	65700
40	5	FIRST 405 DEEP	SLP	SAIL	FBG	KL	IB	50D	PERK	12	11	20800	7	1	85400	93800
40	5	FIRST 405 SHOAL	SLP	SAIL	FBG	KL	IB	50D	PERK	12	11	20800	5	7	85400	93800
42	7	OCEANIS 430	SLP	SAIL	FBG	KL	IB	50D	PERK	13	1	19800	5	11	89000	97800
47	6	FIRST 48	SLP	SAIL	FBG	KL	IB	80D	PERK	14	2		6	5	120000	132000
50	3	OCEANIS 500	SLP	SAIL	FBG	KL	IB	80D	PERK	15	7	28660	6		150000	164500
51	2	FIRST 51	SLP	SA/RC	FBG	KL	IB	85D	PERK	14	1	28659	9	5	159000	175000
51	2	FIRST 51	SLP	SA/RC	FBG	WK	IB	85D	PERK	14	1	28659	5	9	159000	175000
51	2	FIRST 51	SLP	SAIL	FBG	KL	IB	85D	PERK	14	1	28659	9	5	159000	175000
51	2	FIRST 51	SLP	SAIL	FBG	WK	IB	85D	PERK	14	1	28659	5	9	159000	175000
		1986 BOATS														
21	6	FIRST-CLASS 7		SA/RC		SK				8		1975	4	9	5100	5850
24	6	FIRST 24	SLP	SA/RC		SK	IB	D		8	2	3602	4		10500	12000
25	5	FIRST-CLASS 8		SA/RC		SK		D		8	1	3100	5	9	8550	9850
26	3	FIRST 26	SLP	SA/RC		SK	IB	D		9	2	4814	4	3	14500	16500
28	8	FIRST 29	SLP	SA/RC		KL	IB	D		9	9	7014	5	5	22800	25300
28	9	IDYLLE 8.8		SA/CR		KL				9	8	7385	4	10	21600	24000
32	6	FIRST 325	SLP	SA/RC		KL	IB	D	VLVO	11		9885	4	8	33000	36700
34	4	IDYLLE 10.5		SA/CR		KL				10	9	11152			34100	37900
34	6	FIRST 345	SLP	SA/RC		KL	IB	D		11	5	12651	6	3	41600	46200
37	1	FIRST 375	SLP	SA/RC		KL	IB	D		12	4	16975	6	5	55800	61300
42	3	IDYLLE 13.5		SA/CR		KL				13	4	22046	5	8	76400	84000
43	6	FIRST 435	SLP	SA/RC		KL	IB	D		13	1	21825	7	5	81700	89800
45	7	FIRST 456	SLP	SA/RC		KL	IB	D	PERK	14	1	26500	6	6	96900	106500
		1985 BOATS														
21	7	FIRST-CLASS 7	SLP	SA/RC	FBG	SK				8		1764	4	9	4550	5250
24	6	FIRST 24	SLP	SA/RC	FBG	SK	IB	D		8	2	3300	5	3	9300	10600
25	4	FIRST 26	SLP	SA/RC	FBG	SK	IB	D		9	2	4400	4	3	12200	13900
27	11	FIRST-CLASS 8	SLP	SA/RC	FBG	SK				8	1	2860	5	9	8400	9650
28	5	FIRST 29	SLP	SA/RC	FBG	KL	IB	D		9	9	6614	5	5	20100	22300
28	9	IDYLLE 8.80	SLP	SA/CR	FBG	KL				9	8	6160	4	10	16500	18800
28	9	IDYLLE 8.80 SHOAL	SLP	SA/CR	FBG	KL				9	8	6160	3	6	16500	18800

CONTINUED ON NEXT PAGE

LOA FT	LOA IN	NAME AND/ OR MODEL	TOP/ RIG	BOAT TYPE	-HULL- MTL	-HULL- TP	ENGINE TP	# HP	ENGINE MFG	BEAM FT	BEAM IN	WGT LBS	DRAFT FT	DRAFT IN	RETAIL LOW	RETAIL HIGH
		1985 BOATS														
30	6	FIRST 31	SLP	SA/RC	FBG	KL	IB	15D	VLVO	10	6	7100	4	5	22200	24700
31	6	FIRST 30	SLP	SA/RC	FBG	KL	IB	D		10	6	7100	4	4	22400	24900
32		BENETEAU 305	SLP	SA/RC	FBG	KL	IB	D		10	6	7056	5	5	22300	24700
34	3	BENETEAU 325	SLP	SA/RC	FBG	KL	IB	D		11	1	8380	5	10	26100	29000
34	4	FIRST-CLASS 10	SLP	SA/RC	FBG	SK				9	9	5500	5	11	14200	16100
34	6	FIRST 345	SLP	SA/RC	FBG	KL	IB	D		11	5	10141	6	2	31600	35100
35	2	FIRST 35	SLP	SA/RC	FBG	KL	IB	D		12	2	10500	6	3	32900	36500
36	5	IDYLLE 11.5	SLP	SA/CR	FBG	KL				12	2	11445	4	5	35300	39200
40	2	FIRST 38	SLP	SA/RC	FBG	KL	IB	D		12	9	15655	4	11	55300	60700
42	3	IDYLLE 13.5	SLP	SA/CR	FBG	KL				13	4	22046	5	8	71900	79000
43	8	FIRST 42	SLP	SA/RC	FBG	KL	IB	D		13	2	18600	7	3	71100	78100
44	3	FIRST 435	SLP	SA/RC	FBG	KL	IB	D		13	1	20000	7	9	75800	83300
45	7	FIRST 456	SLP	SA/RC	FBG	KL	IB	D		14	1	22000	7	11	84100	92400
		1984 BOATS														
21	7	FIRST-CLASS 7		SA/RC	FBG	SK	IB			8		1764	4	9	4800	5500
22		CALIFORNIA 6.60		SAIL		KL				8	2	2646	2	11	5600	6450
22		CALIFORNIA 6.60		SAIL		KL	IB	8D	VLVO	8	2	2646	2	11	6850	7850
22	9	EVASION 22		SAIL		KL	IB	17D	VLVO	8	4	3969	3	4	9750	11100
22	10	FIRST 22		SAIL		KL				8	3	2500			5700	6550
22	10	FIRST 22		SAIL		KL	IB			8	3	2500			6200	7150
24	6	FIRST 24	SLP	SA/RC	FBG	SK	IB	D		8	2	3300	5	3	8650	9950
25	4	FIRST 26	SLP	SA/RC	FBG	SK	IB	D		9	2	4400	4	3	11500	13000
26	3	FIRST 24		SAIL		KL	OB			8	3	3307			8500	9750
26	3	FIRST 24		SAIL		KL	IB	8D	VLVO	8	3	3307			9250	10500
27	9	FIRST-CLASS		SAIL		KL				8	9	2867	5	6	7850	9050
27	11	FIRST-CLASS		SA/RC	FBG	SK	IB			8	1	2860	5	9	8100	9350
28		FIRST 25		SAIL		KL	OB			9		3969	4	3	10700	12200
28		FIRST 25		SAIL		KL	IB	8D	VLVO	9		3969	4	3	11200	12700
28	5	FIRST 29	SLP	SA/RC	FBG	KL	IB	D		9	9	6614	5	5	19100	21200
28	9	IDYLLE 8.8		SA/CR	FBG	KL	IB			9	8	6160	4	10	17200	19600
28	10	IDYLLE 8.80		SAIL		KL	IB	17D-	25D	9	8	6174	4	2	17600	20000
28	11	FIRST 28		SAIL		KL	IB	8D-	15D	9	8	5954	5	6	16900	19300
29	6	FIRST 28	SLP	SA/RC	FBG	SK	IB	D		9		5300	4	3	15200	17300
30	9	EVASION 29		SAIL		KL	IB	25D-	40D	10	1	8820	4	7	26100	29000
31	6	FIRST 30	SLP	SA/RC	FBG	KL	IB	D		10	6	7100	4	4	21000	23400
31	10	FIRST 30E		SAIL		KL	IB	8D-	17D	10	6	7056	5	6	20900	23300
31	10	FIRST 30ES		SAIL		KL	IB	17D	VLVO	10	6	6836			20300	22500
32	9	FIRST 32	SLP	SA/RC	FBG	KL	IB	D		11	1	8000	5	10	23600	26200
32	9	FIRST 32 SHOAL	SLP	SA/RC	FBG	KL				11	1	8390	4	5	21700	24100
33	10	FIRST 32		SAIL		KL	IB	17D	VLVO	10	11	8379	5	10	24600	27300
34	4	FIRST-CLASS 10		SA/RC	FBG	SK	IB			9	9	5500	5	11	15400	17500
34	6	FIRST 345	SLP	SA/RC	FBG	KL	IB	D		11	5	10141	6	2	29700	33000
35		EVASION 34		SAIL		KL	IB	36D	VLVO	11	3	12128	5		35500	39400
35		EVASION 34		SAIL		KL	IB	40D	PERK	11	3	12128	5		35400	39300
35		FIRST-CLASS 10		SAIL		KL	IB	8D	YAN	9	6	5513	5	8	15600	17800
35		FIRST-CLASS 10		SAIL		KL	IB	15D	YAN	9	6	5513	5	8	15700	17900
35	2	FIRST 35	SLP	SA/RC	FBG	KL	IB	D		12	2	10500	6	3	30900	34400
36		FIRST 345		SAIL		KL	IB	18D	VLVO	11	4	10143	6	2	30200	33600
36		FIRST 345		SAIL		KL	IB	28D	VLVO	11	4	10143	6	2	30400	33700
36	5	IDYLLE 11.5		SA/CR	FBG	KL	IB			12	2	11445	4	5	33800	37600
36	9	FIRST 35		SAIL		KL	IB	17D	VLVO	12		10474	6	2	31800	35300
36	9	FIRST 35		SAIL		KL	IB	25D	VLVO	12		10474	6	2	31900	35400
36	9	FIRST 35S		SAIL		KL	IB	25D	VLVO	12		10474	6	2	31900	35400
37	9	IDYLLE 11.50		SAIL		KL	IB	36D	VLVO	12		11466	4	3	36000	40000
37	9	IDYLLE 11.50		SAIL		KL	IB	40D	PERK	12		11466	4	3	35800	39800
40	2	FIRST 38	SLP	SA/RC	FBG	KL	IB	D		12	9	15655	4	11	52000	57200
40	2	FIRST 38		SAIL		KL	IB	23D	VLVO	12	7	15666	6	4	51700	56800
40	2	FIRST 38		SAIL		KL	IB	40D	PERK	12	7	15656	6	4	51700	56800
40	2	FIRST 38 S		SAIL		KL	IB	40D	PERK	12	7		6	4	52500	57700
42	3	IDYLLE 13.5		SA/CR	FBG	KL	IB			13	4	22046	5	8	68300	75000
43	4	FIRST 42		SAIL		KL	IB	40D	PERK	13		18743	6	4	65700	72100
43	8	FIRST 42	SLP	SA/RC	FBG	KL	IB	D		13	2	18600	7	3	66800	73400
44	3	IDYLLE 13.50		SAIL		KL	IB	50D	PERK	13	2	22050	5	10	74400	81700
45	7	FIRST 456	SLP	SA/RC	FBG	KL	IB	D		14	1	22000	7	11	79000	86800
46	7	FIRST 456		SAIL		KL	IB	40D	PERK	13	10	22050	7	6	81800	89800
46	7	FIRST 456		SAIL		KL	IB	50D		13		22050	7	6	82200	90300

....For earlier years, see the BUC Used Boat Price Guide, Volume 3

BENNETT BROTHERS YACHTS INC

MAMARONECK NY 10543

See inside cover to adjust price for area

FORMERLY STEVENS YACHTS OF ANNAPOLIS

LOA FT	LOA IN	NAME AND/ OR MODEL	TOP/ RIG	BOAT TYPE	-HULL- MTL	-HULL- TP	ENGINE TP	# HP	ENGINE MFG	BEAM FT	BEAM IN	WGT LBS	DRAFT FT	DRAFT IN	RETAIL LOW	RETAIL HIGH
		1989 BOATS														
42	2	STEVENS CUSTOM 42	CUT	SA/CR	FBG	KL	IB	46D	WEST	12	7	24000	6		152500	167500
49	8	STEVENS CUSTOM 50	CUT	SA/CR	FBG	KL	IB	77D	YAN	14	4	31220	6		245000	269000
50	2	STEVENS CUSTOM 50 PH	CUT	SA/CR	FBG	KL	IB	77D	YAN	14	4	31220	6		252500	277500
		1988 BOATS														
42	2	STEVENS CUSTOM 42	CUT	SA/CR	FBG	KL	IB	46D	WEST	12	7	24000	6		143000	157500
49	8	STEVENS CUSTOM 50	CUT	SA/CR	FBG	KL	IB	70D	WEST	14	4	31220	6		230000	253000
50	2	STEVENS CUSTOM 50 PH	CUT	SA/CR	FBG	KL	IB	70D	WEST	14	4	31220	6		237500	261000
		1987 BOATS														
42	2	STEVENS CUSTOM 42	CUT	SA/CR	FBG	KL	IB	46D	WEST	12	6	24000	6		134500	148000
48	8	STEVENS CUSTOM 50	CUT	SA/CR	FBG	KL	IB	70D	WEST	14	4	31220	6		204000	224000
50	2	STEVENS CUSTOM 50 PH	CUT	SA/CR	FBG	KL	IB	70D	WEST	14	4	31220	6		223000	245500
		1985 BOATS														
40	6	STEVENS 40	CUT	SA/CR	FBG	KL	IB	44D	UNIV	12	7	24000	6		112500	124000
46	10	STEVENS 47	CUT	SA/CR	FBG	KL	IB	44D	UNIV	14	3	32000	6		166500	182500
		1984 BOATS														
40	7	STEVENS CUSTOM 40	CUT	SA/CR	FBG	KL	IB	44D	UNIV	12	7	24000	6		106500	117000
46	10	STEVENS CUSTOM 47	CUT	SA/CR	FBG	KL	IB	44D	UNIV	14	3	32000	6		156500	172000

....For earlier years, see the BUC Used Boat Price Guide, Volume 3

BERTRAM YACHT INC

MIAMI FL 33142

COAST GUARD MFG ID- BER See inside cover to adjust price for area

For more recent years, see the BUC Used Boat Price Guide, Volume 1

LOA FT	LOA IN	NAME AND/ OR MODEL	TOP/ RIG	BOAT TYPE	-HULL- MTL	-HULL- TP	ENGINE TP	# HP	ENGINE MFG	BEAM FT	BEAM IN	WGT LBS	DRAFT FT	DRAFT IN	RETAIL LOW	RETAIL HIGH
		1996 BOATS														
30	6	MOPPIE 30	OP	EXP	FBG	DV	IB	T320	CRUS	11	4	13200	3	1	78600	86400
30	6	MOPPIE 30	OP	EXP	FBG	DV	IB	T300D-T315D		11	4	13200	3	1	106500	117500
35	11	CONVERTIBLE 36	FB	CNV	FBG	DV	IB	T370D	VLVO	13		22500	3	10	190500	209500
35	11	CONVERTIBLE 36	FB	CNV	FBG	DV	IB	T420D	CAT	13		22500	3	10	205000	225000
35	11	CONVERTIBLE 36	FB	CNV	FBG	DV	IB	T420D	CUM	13		22500	3	10	200000	220000
35	11	MOPPIE 36	OP	EXP	FBG	DV	IB	T370D	VLVO	13		20500	3	8	173500	190500
		IB T420D CAT 187500 206000, IB T420D CUM 182500 200500, IB T430D VLVO 181000 199000														
43	4	CONVERTIBLE 43	FB	CNV	FBG	DV	IB	T565D	DD	14	11	41890	4	4	330000	362500
43	4	CONVERTIBLE 43	FB	CNV	FBG	DV	IB	T625D	DD	14	11	41890	4	4	354000	389000
43	4	CONVERTIBLE 43	FB	CNV	FBG	DV	IB	T680D	MAN	14	11	41890	4	4	352500	387500
43	4	MOPPIE 43	OP	EXP	FBG	DV	IB	T565D	DD	15		38290	4	8	311500	342000
		IB T600D MAN 305000 335500, IB T625D DD 319000 350500, IB T680D MAN 314000 345000														
46		MOPPIE 46	OP	EXP	FBG	DV	IB	T760D	DD	15		42000	4	8	348000	382500
46		MOPPIE 46	OP	EXP	FBG	DV	IB	T820D	MAN	15		42000	4	8	359500	395000
46	3	CONVERTIBLE 46	FB	CNV	FBG	DV	IB	T760D	DD	15	1	46100	4	10	381000	418500
46	3	CONVERTIBLE 46	FB	CNV	FBG	DV	IB	T820D	MAN	15	1	46100	4	10	394500	433500
50		CONVERTIBLE 50	FB	CNV	FBG	DV	IB	T820D	MAN	16	2	59500	5		469000	515500
50		CONVERTIBLE 50	FB	CNV	FBG	DV	IB	T900D	DD	16	2	59500	5		496000	545000
54		CONVERTIBLE 54	FB	CNV	FBG	DV	IB	T11CD	DD	16	11	75400	5	2	696000	765000
		IB T11CD MTU 704000 773500, IB T12CD MAN 713500 784000, IB T12CD CAT 723000 794500														
60		CONVERTIBLE 60	FB	CNV	FBG	DV	IB	T12CD	CAT	16	11	92000	5	6	838000	921000
60		CONVERTIBLE 60	FB	CNV	FBG	DV	IB	T16CD	DD	16	11	93500	5	6	932000	1.015M
		1995 BOATS														
30	6	MOPPIE 30	OP	EXP	FBG	DV	IB	T320	CRUS	11	4	13200	3	1	75700	83200
30	6	MOPPIE 30	OP	EXP	FBG	DV	IB	T300D-T315D		11	4	13200	3	1	103000	114000
37	9	CONVERTIBLE 37	FB	CNV	FBG	DV	IB	T435D	CAT	13	3	32410	4		236500	260000
37	9	CONVERTIBLE 37	FB	CNV	FBG	DV	IB	T485D	DD	13	3	32410	4		243000	267000
43	4	CONVERTIBLE 43	FB	CNV	FBG	DV	IB	T550D	DD	14	11	41890	4	4	319000	350500
43	4	CONVERTIBLE 43	FB	CNV	FBG	DV	IB	T600D	MAN	14	11	41890	4	4	330500	363000
43	4	MOPPIE 43	OP	EXP	FBG	DV	IB	T550D	DD	15		36000	4	8	289000	318000
43	4	MOPPIE 43	OP	EXP	FBG	DV	IB	T600D	MAN	15		36000	4	8	285500	314000
46		MOPPIE 46	OP	EXP	FBG	DV	IB	T735D	DD	15		42000	4	8	337000	370500
46	3	CONVERTIBLE 46	FB	CNV	FBG	DV	IB	T735D	DD	15	1	48000	4	10	374000	411500
46	3	CONVERTIBLE 46	FB	CNV	FBG	DV	IB	T820D	MAN	15	1	48000	4	10	392000	430500
50		CONVERTIBLE 50	FB	CNV	FBG	DV	IB	T735D	DD	16	2	59500	5		441000	484500
50		CONVERTIBLE 50	FB	CNV	FBG	DV	IB	T900D	DD	16	2	59500	5		484500	532000
60		CONVERTIBLE 60	FB	CNV	FBG	DV	IB	T12CD	CAT	16	11	92000	5	6	816000	896500
60		CONVERTIBLE 60	FB	CNV	FBG	DV	IB	T14CD	DD	16	11	93500	5	6	857500	942500
		1994 BOATS														
28	6	CRUISER 28	FB	CR	FBG	DV	IB	T260	MRCR	11		13000	3	1	62200	68400
28	6	CRUISER 28	FB	CR	FBG	DV	IB	T230D	VLVO	11		13000	3	1	91000	100000

LOA FT	LOA IN	NAME AND/ OR MODEL	TOP/ RIG	BOAT TYPE	-HULL- MTL	-HULL- TP	ENGINE TP	ENGINE # HP	ENGINE MFG	BEAM FT	BEAM IN	WGT LBS	DRAFT FT	DRAFT IN	RETAIL LOW	RETAIL HIGH
		1994 BOATS														
28	6	MOPPIE 28	OP	CR	FBG	DV	IB	T260	MRCR	11		11515	2	10	58200	64000
28	6	MOPPIE 28	OP	CR	FBG	DV	IB	T230D	VLVO	11		11515	2	10	83100	91400
30	6	MOPPIE 30	OP	CNV	FBG	DV	IB	T310	MRCR	11	4	13200	3	1	78700	86500
30	6	MOPPIE 30	OP	CNV	FBG	DV	IB	T300D		11	4	13200	3	1	112000	123000
37	9	CONVERTIBLE 37	FB	CNV	FBG	DV	IB	T375D	CAT	13	3	32410	4		221500	243500
		IB T425D CAT 229000 252000, IB T450D DD 231000 254000, IB T550D DD													248500	273000
37	9	SPORTFISHERMAN 37	FB	SF	FBG	DV	IB	T450D	DD	13	3	32410	4		229500	252500
43	4	CONVERTIBLE 43	FB	CNV	FBG	DV	IB	T550D	DD	14	11	41890	4	4	311000	342000
43	4	CONVERTIBLE 43	FB	CNV	FBG	DV	IB	T655D	MTU	14	11	41890	4	4	360000	396000
46		MOPPIE 46	OP	EXP	FBG	DV	IB	T735D	DD	15		42000	4	8	329000	361500
50		CONVERTIBLE 50	FB	CNV	FBG	DV	IB	T735D	DD	16	2	59500	5		430500	473000
50		CONVERTIBLE 50	FB	CNV	FBG	DV	IB	T900D	DD	16	2	59500	5		472500	519500
60		CONVERTIBLE 60	FB	CNV	FBG	DV	IB	T11CD	DD	16	11	93500	5	6	751000	825500
		1993 BOATS														
28	6	CRUISER 28 III	FB	CR	FBG	DV	IB	T260	MRCR	11		12060	3		57600	63300
28	6	CRUISER 28 III	FB	CR	FBG	DV	IB	T230D	VLVO	11		12060	3		83400	91600
28	6	MOPPIE 28	OP	CR	FBG	DV	IB	T260	MRCR	11		11515	2	10	56200	61700
28	6	MOPPIE 28	FB	CR	FBG	DV	IB	T230D	VLVO	11		11515	2	10	80600	88600
37	9	CONVERTIBLE 37	FB	CNV	FBG	DV	IB	T375D	CAT	13	3	30710	3	9	207000	227000
		IB T435D CAT 215500 237000, IB T450D DD 224500 246500, IB T550D DD													241000	265000
37	9	SPORTFISHERMAN 37	FB	SF	FBG	DV	IB	T450D	DD	13	3	32410	4		223000	245000
43	4	CONVERTIBLE 43	FB	CNV	FBG	DV	IB	T550D	DD	14	11	41890	4	4	302000	331500
43	4	CONVERTIBLE 43	FB	CNV	FBG	DV	IB	T655D	MTU	14	11	41890	4	4	349500	384000
46		MOPPIE 46	OP	EXP	FBG	DV	IB	T735D	DD	14	11	42000	3	3	319000	350500
50		CONVERTIBLE 50	FB	CNV	FBG	DV	IB	T735D	DD	16	2	59500	5		417500	459000
60		CONVERTIBLE 60	FB	CNV	FBG	DV	IB	T11CD	DD	16	11	93500	5	6	730500	802500
		1992 BOATS														
28	6	BAHIA-MAR	OP	SDN	FBG	DV	IB	T260	MRCR	11		11980	2	11	59400	65300
28	6	BAHIA-MAR	OP	SDN	FBG	DV	IB	T200D-T230D		11		11980	2	11	85800	97300
28	6	FB CRUISER 28 III	FB	CR	FBG	DV	IB	T260	MRCR	11		12060	3		55600	61100
28	6	FB CRUISER 28 III	FB	CR	FBG	DV	IB	T200D-T230D		11		12060	3		78800	88900
28	6	MOPPIE 28	OP	CR	FBG	DV	IB	T260	MRCR	11		11515	2	10	54300	59600
28	6	MOPPIE 28	OP	CR	FBG	DV	IB	T200D	VLVO	11		11515	2	10	76100	83600
28	6	MOPPIE 28	FB	CR	FBG	DV	IB	T230D	VLVO	11		11515	2	10	78300	86000
33		FB CRUISER 33 II	FB	SDN	FBG	DV	IB	T340	MRCR	12	6	22800	3	3	105000	115500
33		FB CRUISER 33 II	FB	SDN	FBG	DV	IB	T270D	CAT	12	6	24900	3	5	155000	170000
33		SPORT FISHERMAN 33II	FB	SDNSF	FBG	DV	IB	T340	MRCR	12	6	20300	3	1	95400	105000
33		SPORT FISHERMAN 33II	FB	SDNSF	FBG	DV	IB	T270D-T320D		12	6	22400	3	3	136500	154000
37	9	CONVERTIBLE 37	FB	CNV	FBG	DV	IB	T340	MRCR	13	3	27910	3	9	154000	169000
		IB T375D CAT 200500 220500, IB T425D CAT 207500 228000, IB T450D DD													217500	239000
		IB T550D DD 234000 257000														
43	4	CONVERTIBLE GLLY DWN	FB	CNV	FBG	DV	IB	T550D	DD	14	11	41890	4	4	286000	314000
43	4	CONVERTIBLE GLLY DWN	FB	CNV	FDG	DV	IB	T655D	MTU	14	11	41890	4	4	331500	364500
43	4	CONVERTIBLE GLLY UP	FB	CNV	FBG	DV	IB	T550D	DD	14	11	41890	4	4	286500	315000
43	4	CONVERTIBLE GLLY UP	FB	CNV	FBG	DV	IB	T655D	MTU	14	11	41890	4	4	332500	365500
50		CONVERTIBLE GLLY DWN	FB	CNV	FBG	DV	IB	T735D	DD	16		59500	4	9	392000	430500
50		CONVERTIBLE GLLY DWN	FB	CNV	FBG	DV	IB	T986D	MTU	16		59500	4	9	444500	488500
50		CONVERTIBLE GLLY UP	FB	CNV	FBG	DV	IB	T735D	DD	16		59500	4	9	394000	433000
50		CONVERTIBLE GLLY UP	FB	CNV	FBG	DV	IB	T986D	MTU	16		59500	4	9	448000	492000
54		CONVERTIBLE 54	FB	CNV	FBG	DV	IB	T900D	DD	16	11	75400	5	2	579500	637000
54		CONVERTIBLE 54	FB	CNV	FBG	DV	IB	T986D	MTU	16	11	75400	5	2	601500	661000
54		CONVERTIBLE 54	FB	CNV	FBG	DV	IB	T11CD	DD	16	11	75400	5	2	622500	684000
60		CONVERTIBLE 60	FB	CNV	FBG	DV	IB	T11CD	DD	16	11	85000	5	4	676500	743500
60		CONVERTIBLE 60	FB	CNV	FBG	DV	IB	T14CD	DD	16	11	85000	5	4	742500	816000
72	6	CONVERTIBLE 72	FB	CNV	FBG	DV	IB	T19CD	MTU	18	5	60T	6	9	**	**
		1991 BOATS														
28	6	BAHIA-MAR	OP	SDN	FBG	DV	IB	T260	MRCR	11		11980	2	11	56500	62100
28	6	BAHIA-MAR	OP	SDN	FBG	DV	IB	T200D	VLVO	11		11980	2	11	82100	90200
28	6	FB CRUISER 28 III	FB	CR	FBG	DV	IB	T260	MRCR	11		12060	3		52900	58100
28	6	FB CRUISER 28 III	FB	CR	FBG	DV	IB	T200D	VLVO	11		12060	3		75400	82800
28	6	MOPPIE 28	OP	CR	FBG	DV	IB	T260	MRCR	11		11515	2	10	51600	56700
28	6	MOPPIE 28	OP	CR	FBG	DV	IB	T200D	VLVO	11		11515	2	10	72800	80000
33		FB CRUISER 33 II	FB	SDN	FBG	DV	IB	T340	MRCR	12	6	22800	3	3	99900	110000
33		FB CRUISER 33 II	FB	SDN	FBG	DV	IB	T270D	CAT	12	6	24900	3	5	148000	163000
33		SPORT FISHERMAN 33II	FB	SDNSF	FBG	DV	IB	T340	MRCR	12	6	20300	3	1	90800	99700
33		SPORT FISHERMAN 33II	FB	SDNSF	FBG	DV	IB	T320D	CAT	12	6	22400	3	3	134000	147500
37	9	CONVERTIBLE 37	FB	CNV	FBG	DV	IB	T340	MRCR	13	3	27910	3	9	147000	161500
37	9	CONVERTIBLE 37	FB	CNV	FBG	DV	IB	T375D	CAT	13	3	30710	3	9	192000	210500
37	9	CONVERTIBLE 37	FB	CNV	FBG	DV	IB	T450D	DD	13	3	32410	3	9	208000	228500
43	4	CONVERTIBLE GLLY DWN	FB	CNV	FBG	DV	IB	T550D	DD	14	11	41890	4	4	282500	310500
43	4	CONVERTIBLE GLLY UP	FB	CNV	FBG	DV	IB	T550D	DD	14	11	41890	4	4	284500	312500
50		CONVERTIBLE GLLY DWN	FB	CNV	FBG	DV	IB	T735D	DD	16		59500	4	9	382500	420500
50		CONVERTIBLE GLLY DWN	FB	CNV	FBG	DV	IB	T986D	MTU	16		59500	4	9	424500	466500
50		CONVERTIBLE GLLY UP	FB	CNV	FBG	DV	IB	T735D	DD	16		59500	4	9	385500	423500
50		CONVERTIBLE GLLY UP	FB	CNV	FBG	DV	IB	T986D	MTU	16		59500	4	9	428000	470000
54		CONVERTIBLE 54	FB	CNV	FBG	DV	IB	T11CD	DD	16	11	75400	5	2	595000	653500
60		CONVERTIBLE 60	FB	CNV	FBG	DV	IB	T14CD	DD	16	11	85000	5	4	709500	779500
72	6	CONVERTIBLE 72	FB	CNV	FBG	DV	IB	T19CD	MTU	18	5	60T	6	9	**	**
		1990 BOATS														
28	6	BAHIA-MAR	OP	SDN	FBG	DV	IB	T260	MRCR	11		11980	2	11	53800	59100
28	6	FB CRUISER 28 III	FB	CR	FBG	DV	IB	T260	MRCR	11		12060	3		50300	55300
28	6	MOPPIE 28	OP	CR	FBG	DV	IB	T260	MRCR	11		11515	2	10	49100	54000
33		FB CRUISER 33II	FB	SDN	FBG	DV	IB	T340	MRCR	12	6	22800	3	3	95000	104500
33		FB CRUISER 33II	FB	SDN	FBG	DV	IB	T270D	CAT	12	6	22800	3	3	134000	147000
33		SPORT FISHERMAN 33II	FB	SDNSF	FBG	DV	IB	T340	MRCR	12	6	20300	3	1	86300	94800
33		SPORT FISHERMAN 33II	FB	SDNSF	FBG	DV	IB	T270D	CAT	12	6	20300	3	1	116500	128000
37	9	CONVERTIBLE 37	FB	CNV	FBG	DV	IB	T340	MRCR	13	3	27910	3	9	140500	154000
37	9	CONVERTIBLE 37	FB	CNV	FBG	DV	IB	T375D	CAT	13	3	27910	3	9	171000	188000
37	9	CONVERTIBLE 37	FB	CNV	FBG	DV	IB	T450D	GM	13	3	27910	3	9	175500	193000
43	4	CONVERTIBLE GLLY DWN	FB	CNV	FBG	DV	IB	T550D	GM	14	11	41890	4	4	266000	292000
43	4	CONVERTIBLE GLLY UP	FB	CNV	FBG	DV	IB	T550D	GM	14	11	41890	4	4	269000	295500
50		CONVERTIBLE GLLY DWN	FB	CNV	FBG	DV	IB	T735D	GM	16		59500	4	9	365000	401000
50		CONVERTIBLE GLLY DWN	FB	CNV	FBG	DV	IB	T840D	MAN	16		59500	4	9	382500	420000
50		CONVERTIBLE GLLY UP	FB	CNV	FBG	DV	IB	T735D	GM	16		59500	4	9	368500	405000
50		CONVERTIBLE GLLY UP	FB	CNV	FBG	DV	IB	T840D	MAN	16		59500	4	9	386000	424000
54		CONVERTIBLE	FB	CNV	FBG	DV	IB	T11CD	GM	16	11	75400	5	2	547500	601500
60		CONVERTIBLE	FB	CNV	FBG	DV	IB	T14CD	GM	16	11	85000	5	4	713000	783500
72		CONVERTIBLE	FB	CNV	FBG	DV	IB	T16CD	GM	18	5	60T	6	9	**	**
72		CONVERTIBLE	FB	CNV	FBG	DV	IB	T19CD	MTU	18	5	60T	6	9	**	**
		1989 BOATS														
28	6	BAHIA-MAR	OP	SDN	FBG	DV	IB	T260	MRCR	11		11980	2	11	51200	56300
28	6	FB CRUISER 28II	FB	CR	FBG	DV	IB	T260	MRCR	11		12060	3		47900	52600
28	6	MOPPIE 28	OP	CR	FBG	DV	IB	T260	MRCR	11		11515	2	10	47000	51700
33		FB CRUISER 33II	FB	SDN	FBG	DV	IB	T340	MRCR	12	6	22800	3	3	90500	99400
33		FB CRUISER 33II	FB	SDN	FBG	DV	IB	T270D	CAT	12	6	24900	3	5	135500	149000
33		SPORT FISHERMAN 33II	FB	SDNSF	FBG	DV	IB	T340	MRCR	12	6	20300	3	1	82200	90300
33		SPORT FISHERMAN 33II	FB	SDNSF	FBG	DV	IB	T270D	CAT	12	6	22400	3	3	119000	131000
37	9	CONVERTIBLE 37	FB	CNV	FBG	DV	IB	T340	MRCR	13	3	27910	3	9	134000	147500
37	9	CONVERTIBLE 37	FB	CNV	FBG	DV	IB	T375D	CAT	13	3	30710	3	10	175000	192000
37	9	CONVERTIBLE 37	FB	CNV	FBG	DV	IB	T450D	GM	13	3	32410	4		186500	204500
43	4	CONVERTIBLE GLLY DWN	FB	CNV	FBG	DV	IB	T550D	GM	14	11	41890			254000	279000
43	4	CONVERTIBLE GLLY UP	FB	CNV	FBG	DV	IB	T550D	GM	14	11	41890			256500	282000
50		CONVERTIBLE	FB	CNV	FBG	DV	IB	T840D	MAN	16	11		4	9	283500	311500
50		CONVERTIBLE GLLY DWN	FB	CNV	FBG	DV	IB	T735D	GM	16		59500	4	9	348500	383000
50		CONVERTIBLE GLLY UP	FB	CNV	FBG	DV	IB	T735D	GM	16		59500	4	9	352000	386500
54		CONVERTIBLE	FB	CNV	FBG	DV	IB	T11CD	GM	16	11	75400	5	2	522500	574500
		1988 BOATS														
28	6	BAHIA-MAR	OP	SDN	FBG	DV	IB	T260	MRCR	11		11300	2	8	47800	52500
28	6	FB CRUISER 28II	FB	CR	FBG	DV	IB	T260	MRCR	11		11820	2	7	44900	49900
28	6	MOPPIE 28	OP	CR	FBG	DV	IB	T260	MRCR	11		10400	2	7	42100	46800
33		FB CRUISER 33II	FB	SDN	FBG	DV	IB	T340	MRCR	12	8				64100	70400
33		FB CRUISER 33II	FB	SDN	FBG	DV	IB	T270D	CAT	12	6	22730	3		122000	134500
33		SPORT FISHERMAN 33II	FB	SDNSF	FBG	DV	IB	T340	MRCR	12	8				65500	71900
33		SPORT FISHERMAN 33II	FB	SDNSF	FBG	DV	IB	T270D	CAT	12	6	21565	3		111000	122000
37	9	CONVERTIBLE 37	FB	CNV	FBG	DV	IB	T340	MRCR	13	3	25500	3	9	119000	130500
37	9	CONVERTIBLE 37	FB	CNV	FBG	DV	IB	T375D	CAT	13	3	28000	3	9	156500	172000
37	9	CONVERTIBLE 37	FB	CNV	FBG	DV	IB	T450D	GM	13	3	25500	3	9	151000	166000
50		CONVERTIBLE	FB	CNV	FBG	DV	IB	T735D	GM	16			4	6	259500	285500
54		CONVERTIBLE	FB	CNV	FBG	DV	IB	T11CD	GM	16	11	65000	4	10	455000	500000
		1987 BOATS														
28	6	28 II FB CRUISER	FB	CR	FBG	DV	IB	T260	MRCR	11		11820	2	7	42800	47600
28	6	BAHIA-MAR	OP	SDN	FBG	DV	IB	T260	MRCR	11		11300	2	8	45600	50100
33		FLYBRIDGE CRUISER	FB	SDN	FBG	DV	IB	T340	MRCR	12	8				61100	67100
33		FLYBRIDGE CRUISER	FB	SDN	FBG	DV	IB	T270D	CAT	12	6	22730	3		117000	128500
33		SPORT FISHERMAN	FB	SDNSF	FBG	DV	IB	T340	MRCR	12	8				62400	68600
33		SPORT FISHERMAN	FB	SDNSF	FBG	DV	IB	T270D	CAT	12	6	21565	3		106500	117000
37	9	CONVERTIBLE 37	FB	CNV	FBG	DV	IB	T340	MRCR	13	3	25500	3	9	114000	125000
		IB T375D CAT 149500 164500, IB T435D GM 152000 167000, IB T450D GM													144500	158500
38	5	CONVERTIBLE 38 III	FB	CNV	FBG	DV	IB	T375D	CAT	13	3	30400	4	1	163500	180000
38	5	SPECIAL 38	TT	SF	FBG	DV	IB	T375D	CAT	13	3	28650	4	1	156000	171500
38	5	SPECIAL 38	TT	SF	FBG	DV	IB	T435D	GM	13	3	28650	4	1	158500	174000
42	6	CONVERTIBLE	FB	CNV	FBG	DV	IB	T475D	GM	14	10	39400	4		204500	224500
42	6	YACHT	FB	MY	FBG	DV	IB	T340	MRCR	14	10	39000	4		169000	186000
42	6	YACHT	FB	MY	FBG	DV	IB	T375D	GM	14	10	39000	4		194000	213000
46	6	CONVERTIBLE 46 III	FB	CNV	FBG	DV	IB	T600D	GM	16		44900	4	6	217500	239000
46	6	YACHT	FB	MY	FBG	DV	IB	T570D	GM	16		45600	4	6	217000	238500
50		CONVERTIBLE	FB	CNV	FBG	DV	IB	T735D	GM	16			4	6	248000	272500

LOA FT	IN	NAME AND/ OR MODEL	TOP/ RIG	BOAT TYPE	-HULL- MTL	TP	ENGINE TP	# HP	MFG	BEAM FT	IN	WGT LBS	DRAFT FT	IN	RETAIL LOW	RETAIL HIGH
		1987 BOATS														
54		CONVERTIBLE	FB	CNV	FBG	DV	IB	T900D	GM	16	11	65000	4	10	404000	444000
54		CONVERTIBLE	FB	CNV	FBG	DV	IB	T11CD	GM	16	11	65000	4	10	435500	478500
		1986 BOATS														
28	6	28 II FB CRUISER	FB	CR	FBG	DV	IB	T260	MRCR	11		11820	2	7	40900	45400
28	6	BAHIA-MAR	OP	SDN	FBG	DV	IB	T260	MRCR	11		11300	2	8	43000	47800
30		SPIRIT	OP	SDN	FBG	DV	IB	T320	CRUS						39800	44300
30		SPIRIT	OP	SDN	FBG	DV	IB	T215D	GM						65700	72200
30	7	EXPRESS CRUISER	OP	EXP	FBG	DV	IB	T320		11	2	16100	3		54800	60200
30	7	EXPRESS CRUISER	OP	EXP	FBG	DV	IB	T215D	GM	11	4	16100	3		76600	84200
30	7	FLYBRIDGE CRUISER	FB	SDN	FBG	DV	IB	T350	CRUS	11	4	13910	3		57500	63200
30	7	SILVER-ANNIV 31	FB	CR	FBG	DV	IB	T340	MRCR	11	2	10600	2	9	48200	53000
33		FLYBRIDGE CRUISER	FB	SDN	FBG	DV	IB	T340	MRCR	12	8				58300	64100
33		FLYBRIDGE CRUISER	FB	SDN	FBG	DV	IB	T270D	CAT	12	6	22730	3		112000	123500
33		SPORT FISHERMAN	FB	SDNSF	FBG	DV	IB	T340	MRCR	12	8				59600	65500
33		SPORT FISHERMAN	FB	SDNSF	FBG	DV	IB	T270D	CAT	12	6	21565	3		102000	112000
35	4	CONVERTIBLE 35 II	FB	CNV	FBG	DV	IB	T340	MRCR	13	3		3	2	73300	80600
35	4	CONVERTIBLE 35 II	FB	CNV	FBG	DV	IB	T320D	CAT	13	3	23000	3	2	125500	138000
37	9	CONVERTIBLE 37	FB	CNV	FBG	DV	IB	T340	MRCR	13	3	25500	3	9	109000	119500
37	9	CONVERTIBLE 37	FB	CNV	FBG	DV	IB	T375D	CAT	13	3	28000	3	9	143000	157500
37	9	CONVERTIBLE 37	FB	CNV	FBG	DV	IB	T435D	GM	13	3	28000	3	9	145500	160000
38	5	CONVERTIBLE 38 III	FB	CNV	FBG	DV	IB	T375D	CAT	13	3	30400	4	1	156500	172000
38	5	SPECIAL 38	TT	SF	FBG	DV	IB	T375D	CAT	13	3	28650	4	1	149500	164000
38	5	SPECIAL 38	TT	SF	FBG	DV	IB	T435D	GM	13	3	28650	4	1	151500	166500
42	6	CONVERTIBLE	FB	CNV	FBG	DV	IB	T475D	GM	14	10	39400	4		195500	215000
42	6	YACHT	FB	MY	FBG	DV	IB	T340	MRCR	14	10	39000	4		162000	178000
42	6	YACHT	FB	MY	FBG	DV	IB	T375D	GM	14	10	39000	4		185500	204000
46	6	CONVERTIBLE	FB	CNV	FBG	DV	IB	T600D	GM	16		44900	4	6	205500	226000
46	6	CONVERTIBLE 46 III	FB	CNV	FBG	DV	IB	T600D	GM	16		44900	4	6	211000	232000
46	6	YACHT	FB	MY	FBG	DV	IB	T570D	GM	16		45600	4	6	207500	228000
54		CONVERTIBLE	FB	CNV	FBG	DV	IB	T820D	GM	16	11	65000	4	10	373500	410500
54		CONVERTIBLE	FB	CNV	FBG	DV	IB	T915D	GM	16	11	65000	4	10	389000	427500
58	3	YACHT	FB	MY	FBG	DV	IB	T675D	GM	17	11	87500	5	4	458500	503500
		1985 BOATS														
26	2	26 II SPORT CONV	OP	SPTCR	FBG	DV	OB			10		5100	3		15200	17200
26	2	26 II SPORT CONV	OP	SPTCR	FBG	DV	IB	T185	CRUS	10		6700	2	4	26300	29200
28	6	BAHIA-MAR	OP	SDN	FBG	DV	IB	T230-T260		11		11300	2	8	40300	45600
28	6	FLYBRIDGE CRUISER	FB	SDN	FBG	DV	IB	T230	MRCR	11		11820	2	8	41100	45700
30	7	EXPRESS CRUISER	OP	EXP	FBG	DV	IB	T320		11	2		3		44700	49700
30	7	EXPRESS CRUISER	OP	EXP	FBG	DV	IB	T350	CRUS	11	4	16100	3		53400	58600
30	7	EXPRESS CRUISER	OP	EXP	FBG	DV	IB	T215D	GM	11	4	16100	3		73500	80700
30	7	FLYBRIDGE CRUISER	FB	SDN	FBG	DV	IB	T320		11	2		3		45500	50000
30	7	FLYBRIDGE CRUISER	FB	SDN	FBG	DV	IB	T350	CRUS	11	4	13910	3		54900	60400
30	7	FLYBRIDGE CRUISER	FB	SDN	FBG	DV	IB	T215D	GM	11	4	15350	3		77400	85100
33		FLYBRIDGE CRUISER	FB	SDN	FBG	DV	IB	T320		12	8		3		54900	60400
33		FLYBRIDGE CRUISER	FB	SDN	FBG	DV	IB	T350	CRUS	12	6	20730	3		72800	80000
33		FLYBRIDGE CRUISER	FB	SDN	FBG	DV	IB	T270D		12	6	22730	3		107500	118500
33		SPORT FISHERMAN	FB	SDNSF	FBG	DV	IB	T320		12	8		3		56300	61900
33		SPORT FISHERMAN	FB	SDNSF	FBG	DV	IB	T350	CRUS	12	6	20930	3		69400	76300
33		SPORT FISHERMAN	FB	SDNSF	FBG	DV	IB	T270D		12	6	21565	3		97800	107500
35	4	CONVERTIBLE 35 II	FB	CNV	FBG	DV	IB	T320		13	3		3	2	69300	76200
		IB T350 CRUS 86200 94700, IB T215D CUM 111500 122500, IB T300D CAT													119000	130500
38	5	CONVERTIBLE 38 III	FB	CNV	FBG	DV	IB	T300D		13	3	30400	3	4	140500	154500
38	5	CONVERTIBLE 38 III	FB	CNV	FBG	DV	IB	T355D	CAT	13	3	30400	4	1	148000	162500
38	5	CONVERTIBLE 38 III	FB	CNV	FBG	DV	IB	T425D	CUM	13	3	30400	4	2	150000	165000
42	6	CONVERTIBLE	FB	CNV	FBG	DV	IB	T450D	CUM	14	10	39400	4		183500	201500
42	6	CONVERTIBLE	FB	CNV	FBG	DV	IB	T475D	GM	14	10	39400	4		187500	206000
42	6	YACHT	FB	MY	FBG	DV	IB	T340	MRCR	14	10	39000	4		155000	170500
42	6	YACHT	FB	MY	FBG	DV	IB	T375D	GM	14	10	39000	4		177500	195000
46	6	CONVERTIBLE	FB	CNV	FBG	DV	IB	T600D	GM	16		44900	4	6	193000	212000
46	6	CONVERTIBLE 46 II	FB	CNV	FBG	DV	IB	T600D	GM	16		44900	4	6	206000	226000
46	6	YACHT	FB	MY	FBG	DV	IB	T570D	GM	16		45600	4	6	198500	218500
54		CONVERTIBLE	FB	CNV	FBG	DV	IB	T820D	GM	16	11	65000	4	10	358000	393000
54		CONVERTIBLE	FB	CNV	FBG	DV	IB	T870D	GM	16	11	65000	4	10	365500	402000
58	3	YACHT	FB	MY	FBG	DV	IB	T675D	GM	17	11	87500	5	4	438500	482000
		1984 BOATS														
26	2	26 II SPORT CONV	OP	SPTCR	FBG	DV	OB			10		5100			14900	17000
26	2	26 II SPORT CONV	OP	SPTCR	FBG	DV	IB	T185-T230		10		6700	3		25100	27900
26	2	26 SPORT CONV	OP	SPTCR	FBG	DV	IO	T165		10		6900	2	4	19900	22100
28	6	FLYBRIDGE CRUISER	FB	SDN	FBG	DV	IB	D		11		11700	3		**	**
28	6	FLYBRIDGE CRUISER	FB	SDN	FBG	DV	IB	T230	MRCR	11		11820	2	8	39300	43600
30	7	EXPRESS CRUISER	OP	EXP	FBG	DV	IB	T320	CRUS	11	4	16100	3		50200	55200
30	7	EXPRESS CRUISER	OP	EXP	FBG	DV	IB	T215D	GM	11	4	16100	3		70500	77500
30	7	FLYBRIDGE CRUISER	FB	SDN	FBG	DV	IB	T320-T350		11	2	13910	3		51400	59300
30	7	FLYBRIDGE CRUISER	FB	SDN	FBG	DV	IB	T215D	GM	11	2	15350	3		74200	81500
33		FLYBRIDGE CRUISER	FB	SDN	FBG	DV	IB	T320-T350		12	8	20730	3		68500	75500
33		FLYBRIDGE CRUISER	FB	SDN	FBG	DV	IB	T270D		12	8	22730	3		103500	113500
33		SPORT FISHERMAN	FB	SDNSF	FBG	DV	IB	T320	CRUS	12	8	20930	3		65500	72000
33		SPORT FISHERMAN	FB	SDNSF	FBG	DV	IB	T270D		12	8	21565	3		93900	103000
35	2	CONVERTIBLE 35 II	FB	CNV	FBG	DV	IB	T320		13	3	22500	3	2	82700	90900
		IB T350 CRUS 81300 89400, IB T215D CUM 106000 116500, IB T300D CAT													113000	124500
38	5	CONVERTIBLE 38 III	FB	CNV	FBG	DV	IB	T300D	CAT	13	3	30400	4		137500	151000
38	5	CONVERTIBLE 38 III	FB	CNV	FBG	DV	IB	T355D	CAT	13	3	30400	4		142000	156000
38	5	CONVERTIBLE 38 III	FB	CNV	FBG	DV	IB	T380D	CUM	13	3	30400	4		140000	154000
42	6	CONVERTIBLE	FB	CNV	FBG	DV	IB	T435D	GM	14	10	39400	4		174500	192000
42	6	CONVERTIBLE	FB	CNV	FBG	DV	IB	T450D	CUM	14	10	39400	4		175500	193000
42	6	YACHT	FB	MY	FBG	DV	IB	T340	MRCR	14	10	39000	4		148500	163000
42	6	YACHT	FB	MY	FBG	DV	IB	T335D		14	10	38650	4		165000	181000
42	6	YACHT	FB	MY	FBG	DV	IB	T375D	GM	14	10	39000	4		170000	187000
46	6	CONVERTIBLE	FB	CNV	FBG	DV	IB	T570D	GM	16		44900	4	6	182000	200000
46	6	CONVERTIBLE 46 II	FB	CNV	FBG	DV	IB	T570D	GM	16		44900	4	6	194000	213500
46	6	YACHT	FB	MY	FBG	DV	IB	T570D	GM	16		45600	4	8	190500	209000
54		CONVERTIBLE	FB	CNV	FBG	DV	IB	T675D	GM	16	11	65000	4	10	320000	351500
54		CONVERTIBLE	FB	CNV	FBG	DV	IB	T800D		16	11	65000	4	10	340000	373500
58	3	CONVERTIBLE	FB	CNV	FBG	DV	IB	T675D	GM	17	11	90000	5	6	417000	458500
58	3	YACHT	FB	MY	FBG	DV	IB	T675D	GM	17	11	87500	5	4	420000	461500
63		MOTOR YACHT 63		MY	FBG	SV	IB	T675D	GM	17	6	52T			512000	562500

....For earlier years, see the BUC Used Boat Price Guide, Volume 3

BESTWAY INDUSTRIES CORP

ACADEMY YACHTS INC
MELVILLE NY 11747

See inside cover to adjust price for area

LOA FT	IN	NAME AND/ OR MODEL	TOP/ RIG	BOAT TYPE	-HULL- MTL	TP	ENGINE TP	# HP	MFG	BEAM FT	IN	WGT LBS	DRAFT FT	IN	RETAIL LOW	RETAIL HIGH
		1990 BOATS														
38		BESTWAY CONVERTIBLE	FB	CNV	C/S	DV	IB	T260D	CAT	14	6	20500	2	6	98700	108500
38		BESTWAY CONVERTIBLE	FB	CNV	C/S	DV	IB	T320D	CAT	14	6	20500	2	6	103000	113500
38		BESTWAY CONVERTIBLE	FB	CNV	C/S	DV	IB	T375D	CAT	14	6	20500	2	6	108000	119000
39	4	CANYON TOUR SF EXP	ST	EXP	FBG	DV	IB	T358D	VLVO	12	9	22000	2	1	119500	131500
39	4	CANYON TOUR SF EXP	ST	EXP	FBG	DV	IB	T375D	CAT	12	9	22000	2	1	128000	141000
39	4	CANYON TOUR SF SDN	FB	CNV	FBG	DV	IB	T358D	VLVO	12	9	24500	2	4	129500	142500
39	4	CANYON TOUR SF SDN	FB	CNV	FBG	DV	IB	T375D	CAT	12	9	24500	2	4	138000	151500
40		BESTWAY 40	FB	DCMY	FBG	SV	IB	T200D	VLVO						124500	136500
40		BESTWAY DC SEDAN	FB	MY	FBG	SV	IB	T210D	CUM	13	6	25700	3	6	126000	138500
41	9	CANYON TOUR SF EXP	ST	EXP	FBG	DV	IB	T358D	VLVO	12	9	24000	2	3	136000	149500
41	9	CANYON TOUR SF EXP	ST	EXP	FBG	DV	IB	T375D	CAT	12	9	24000	2	3	143500	158000
41	9	CANYON TOUR SF SDN	FB	CNV	FBG	DV	IB	T358D	VLVO	12	9	26500	2	5	146500	161000
41	9	CANYON TOUR SF SDN	FB	CNV	FBG	DV	IB	T375D	CAT	12	9	26500	2	5	154500	170000
42		BESTWAY CONVERTIBLE	FB	CNV	FBG	DV	IB	T260D	CAT	14	6	26500	2	6	132500	145500
42		BESTWAY CONVERTIBLE	FB	CNV	FBG	DV	IB	T320D	CAT	14	6	26500	2	6	140500	154500
42		BESTWAY CONVERTIBLE	FB	CNV	C/S	DV	IB	T375D	CAT	14	6	26500	2	6	148500	163000
42		BESTWAY DC SEDAN		MY	FBG	SV	IB	T210D	CUM	14	6	28000	3	3	133000	146000
44		BESTWAY 44 COCKPIT	FB	YTFS	FBG	SV	IB	T210D	CUM	13	6	28000	3	10	141000	155000
44		BESTWAY DC SEDAN	FB	MY	FBG	SV	IB	T320D	CAT	14	6	29900	3	11	165500	182000
46		BESTWAY 46 COCKPIT	FB	YTFS	FBG	SV	IB	T320D	CAT	14	6	32000	3	6	163500	179500
46		BESTWAY 46 DC SEDAN	FB	MY	FBG	SV	IB	T320D	CAT	14	6	33500	3	6	170500	187500
50		BESTWAY 50 COCKPIT	FB	YTFS	FBG	SV	IB	T320D	CAT	14	6	36000	4	2	163000	179500
50		BESTWAY 50 DC SEDAN	FB	MY	FBG	SV	IB	T320D	CAT	14	6	38000	4	2	175000	192500
50		BESTWAY SPORTS SEDAN	FB	CNV	C/S	DV	IB	T375D	CAT	15		39600	2	8	186000	204500
50	7	BESTWAY 50	FB	SDN	FBG	SV	IB	T375D	CAT	15		39600	2	8	185000	203000
50	7	BESTWAY 50	FB	SDN	FBG	SV	IB	T550D	J&T	15		39600	2	8	209500	230000
53		BESTWAY 53 TWIN DECK	FB	MY	FBG	SV	IB	T306D	CAT	16		44000	4	9	185500	204000
		1989 BOATS														
38		BESTWAY CONVERTIBLE	FB	CNV	C/S	DV	IB	T260D	CAT	14	6	20500	2	6	94200	103500
38		BESTWAY CONVERTIBLE	FB	CNV	C/S	DV	IB	T320D	CAT	14	6	20500	2	6	98600	108500
38		BESTWAY CONVERTIBLE	FB	CNV	C/S	DV	IB	T375D	CAT	14	6	20500	2	6	103500	113500
39	4	CANYON TOUR SF EXP	ST	EXP	FBG	DV	IB	T358D	VLVO	12	9	22000	2	1	114500	125500
39	4	CANYON TOUR SF EXP	ST	EXP	FBG	DV	IB	T375D	CAT	12	9	22000	2	1	122500	134500
39	4	CANYON TOUR SF SDN	FB	CNV	FBG	DV	IB	T358D	VLVO	12	9	24500	2	4	123500	136000
39	4	CANYON TOUR SF SDN	FB	CNV	FBG	DV	IB	T375D	CAT	12	9	24500	2	4	131500	144500
40		BESTWAY 40	FB	DCMY	FBG	SV	IB	T200D	VLVO						118500	130500
40		BESTWAY DC SEDAN	FB	MY	FBG	SV	IB	T210D	CUM	13	6	25700	3	6	120500	132500
41	9	CANYON TOUR SF EXP	ST	EXP	FBG	DV	IB	T358D	VLVO	12	9	24000	2	3	130000	143000
41	9	CANYON TOUR SF EXP	ST	EXP	FBG	DV	IB	T375D	CAT	12	9	24000	2	3	137000	150500

68 CONTINUED ON NEXT PAGE 96th ed. - Vol. II

LOA FT	LOA IN	NAME AND/ OR MODEL	TOP/ RIG	BOAT TYPE	HULL MTL	HULL TP	ENGINE TP	ENGINE # HP	ENGINE MFG	BEAM FT	BEAM IN	WGT LBS	DRAFT FT	DRAFT IN	RETAIL LOW	RETAIL HIGH
		1989 BOATS														
41	9	CANYON TOUR SF SDN	FB	CNV	FBG	DV	IB	T358D	VLVO	12	9	26500	2	5	140000	153500
41	9	CANYON TOUR SF SDN	FB	CNV	FBG	DV	IB	T375D	CAT	12	9	26500	2	5	147500	162000
42		BESTWAY CONVERTIBLE	FB	CNV	FBG	DV	IB	T260D	CAT	14	6	26500	2	6	126500	139000
42		BESTWAY CONVERTIBLE	FB	CNV	FBG	DV	IB	T320D	CAT	14	6	26500	2	6	134500	147500
42		BESTWAY CONVERTIBLE	FB	CNV	C/S	DV	IB	T375D	CAT	14	6	26500	2	6	142000	156000
42		BESTWAY DC SEDAN		MY	FBG	SV	IB	T210D	CUM	14	6	28000	3	3	127000	139500
44		BESTWAY 44 COCKPIT	FB	YTFS	FBG	SV	IB	T210D	CUM	13	6	28000	3	10	134500	148000
44		BESTWAY DC SEDAN	FB	MY	FBG	SV	IB	T320D	CAT	14	6	29900	3	11	158000	174000
46		BESTWAY 46 COCKPIT	FB	YTFS	FBG	SV	IB	T320D	CAT	14	6	32000	3	6	156000	171500
46		BESTWAY 46 DC SEDAN	FB	MY	FBG	SV	IB	T320D	CAT	14	6	33500	3	6	163000	179000
50		BESTWAY 50 COCKPIT	FB	YTFS	FBG	SV	IB	T320D	CAT	14	6	36000	4	2	156000	171500
50		BESTWAY 50 DC SEDAN	FB	MY	FBG	SV	IB	T320D	CAT	14	6	38000	4	2	167500	184000
50		BESTWAY SPORTS SEDAN	FB	CNV	C/S	DV	IB	T375D	CAT	15		39600	2	8	177500	195000
50	7	BESTWAY 50	FB	SDN	FBG	SV	IB	T375D	CAT	15		39600	2	8	176500	194000
50	7	BESTWAY 50	FB	SDN	FBG	SV	IB	T550D	J&T	15		39600	2	8	200000	220000
53		BESTWAY 53 TWIN DECK	FB	MY	FBG	SV	IB	T306D	CAT	16		44000	4	9	177500	195000
		1988 BOATS														
39	4	CANYON TOUR SF EXP	ST	EXP	FBG	DV	IB	T358D	VLVO	12	9	22000	2	1	109500	120000
39	4	CANYON TOUR SF EXP	ST	EXP	FBG	DV	IB	T375D	CAT	12	9	22000	2	1	117000	128500
39	4	CANYON TOUR SF SDN	FB	CNV	FBG	DV	IB	T358D	VLVO	12	9	24500	2	4	118000	130000
39	4	CANYON TOUR SF SDN	FB	CNV	FBG	DV	IB	T375D	CAT	12	9	24500	2	4	126000	138500
40		BESTWAY DC SEDAN		MY	FBG	SV	IB	T200D	VLVO	13	6	25700	3	6	113500	124500
41	9	CANYON TOUR SF EXP	ST	EXP	FBG	DV	IB	T358D	VLVO	12	9	24000	2	3	124500	136500
41	9	CANYON TOUR SF EXP	ST	EXP	FBG	DV	IB	T375D	CAT	12	9	24000	2	3	131000	144000
41	9	CANYON TOUR SF SDN	FB	CNV	FBG	DV	IB	T358D	VLVO	12	9	26500	2	5	133500	147000
41	9	CANYON TOUR SF SDN	FB	CNV	FBG	DV	IB	T375D	CAT	12	9	26500	2	5	141000	155000
42		BESTWAY DC SEDAN		MY	FBG	SV	IB	T200D	VLVO	14	6	28000	3	3	119000	131000
44		BESTWAY 44 COCKPIT		YTFS	FBG	SV	IB	T200D	VLVO	13	6	28000	3	10	125500	138000
44		BESTWAY DC SEDAN		MY	FBG	SV	IB	T306D	VLVO	14	6	29900	3	11	145500	160000
46		BESTWAY 46 COCKPIT		YTFS	FBG	SV	IB	T306D	VLVO	14	6	32000	3	6	144000	158500
46		BESTWAY 46 DC SEDAN		MY	FBG	SV	IB	T306D	VLVO	14	6	33500	3	6	151500	166500
50		BESTWAY 50 COCKPIT		YTFS	FBG	SV	IB	T306D	VLVO	14	6	36000	4	2	144500	158500
50		BESTWAY 50 DC SEDAN		MY	FBG	SV	IB	T306D	VLVO	14	6	38000	4	2	156000	171500
53		BESTWAY 53 TWIN DECK		MY	FBG	SV	IB	T306D	CAT	16		44000	4	9	169000	185500
		1987 BOATS														
40		BESTWAY DC SEDAN		MY	FBG	SV	IB	T200D	VLVO	13	6	25700	3	6	108500	119000
42		BESTWAY DC SEDAN		MY	FBG	SV	IB	T200D	VLVO	14	6	26500	3	3	109000	120000
42		BESTWAY DC SEDAN		MY	FBG	SV	IB	T306D	VLVO	14	6	28000	3	3	123500	136000
44		BESTWAY 44 COCKPIT		YTFS	FBG	SV	IB	T200D	VLVO	13	6	28500	3	10	121500	133500
44		BESTWAY DC SEDAN		MY	FBG	SV	IB	T306D	VLVO	14	6	29000	3	4	136500	150000
46	6	BESTWAY 46 COCKPIT		YTFS	FBG	SV	IB	T306D	VLVO	14	6	32000	3	6	138000	151500
46	6	BESTWAY 46 DC SEDAN		MY	FBG	SV	IB	T306D	VLVO	14	6	33000	3	6	143500	158000
50		BESTWAY 50 COCKPIT		YTFS	FBG	SV	IB	T306D	VLVO	14	6	36000	4	2	138000	151500
50		BESTWAY 50 COCKPIT		YTFS	FBG	SV	IB	T358D	VLVO	14	6	37000	4	2	153500	169000
50		BESTWAY 50 DC SEDAN		MY	FBG	SV	IB	T306D	VLVO	14	6	37000	4	2	146000	160500
50		BESTWAY 50 DC SEDAN		MY	FBG	SV	IB	T358D	VLVO	14	6	38000	4	2	159500	175500
53		BESTWAY 53 TWIN DECK		MY	FBG	SV	IB	T375D	CAT	14	6	44000	4		185500	204000

BIDDISON DESIGNS INC

ST PETE FL 33704

See inside cover to adjust price for area

LOA FT	LOA IN	NAME AND/ OR MODEL	TOP/ RIG	BOAT TYPE	HULL MTL	HULL TP	ENGINE TP	ENGINE # HP	ENGINE MFG	BEAM FT	BEAM IN	WGT LBS	DRAFT FT	DRAFT IN	RETAIL LOW	RETAIL HIGH
		1986 BOATS														
18		BIDDISON 18	OP	CTRCN	FBG	DV	OB			7	10	1400			4000	4650
21		BIDDISON 21	OP	CTRCN	FBG	DV	OB			7	11	2150	1		6550	7550
21		BIDDISON 21 WALKAROU	OP	CUD	FBG	DV	OB			7	11	2500	1	3	7250	8350
		1985 BOATS														
21		BIDDISON 21	OP	CTRCN	FBG	DV	OB			7	11	2150	1		6350	7300
21		BIDDISON 21 WALKAROU	OP	CUD	FBG	DV	OB			7	11	2500	1	3	7050	8100
26		BIDDISON 26		SF	FBG	DV	OB			8	6	3000			12100	13800
		1984 BOATS														
21		BIDDISON 21	OP	CTRCN	FBG	DV	OB			7	11	2100	1		6100	7000

....For earlier years, see the BUC Used Boat Price Guide, Volume 3

BIMINI MARINE

BIMINI MARINE
WANCHESE NC 27981

See inside cover to adjust price for area

COAST GUARD MFG ID- WKI
FORMERLY WALKERS CAY INC

LOA FT	LOA IN	NAME AND/ OR MODEL	TOP/ RIG	BOAT TYPE	HULL MTL	HULL TP	ENGINE TP	ENGINE # HP	ENGINE MFG	BEAM FT	BEAM IN	WGT LBS	DRAFT FT	DRAFT IN	RETAIL LOW	RETAIL HIGH
		1994 BOATS														
24	4	TOURNAMENT 245	OP	SF	FBG	SV	IB	T250	VLVO	8		5700	1	11	30300	33700
24	4	TOURNAMENT 245	OP	SF	FBG	SV	IB	T100D	YAN	8		5000	1	11	36900	41000
29		BIMINI 29	OP	SF	FBG	SV	IB	T	VLVO	10	3	9250	2	6	**	**
29		BIMINI 29	OP	SF	FBG	SV	IB	T330	VLVO	10	3	8100	2	6	52700	57900
29		BIMINI 29	OP	SF	FBG	SV	IB	T200D-T225D		10	3	9250	2	6	67800	76700
29		BIMINI 29	MT	SF	FBG	SV	IB	T	VLVO	10	3	9250	2	6	**	**
29		BIMINI 29	MT	SF	FBG	SV	IB	T330	VLVO	10	3	8100	2	6	52700	57900
29		BIMINI 29	MT	SF	FBG	SV	IB	T200D-T225D		10	3	9250	2	6	67800	76700
29		BIMINI 29	TT	SF	FBG	SV	IB	T	VLVO	10	3	9250	2	6	**	**
29		BIMINI 29	TT	SF	FBG	SV	IB	T330	VLVO	10	3	8100	2	6	52700	57900
29		BIMINI 29	TT	SF	FBG	SV	IB	T200D-T225D		10	3	9250	2	6	67800	76700
		1993 BOATS														
24	4	BIMINI 24	OP	CTRCN	FBG	SV	IB	330	VLVO	8		4800	2	2	23400	26000
24	4	BIMINI 24	OP	CTRCN	FBG	SV	IO	200D	VLVO	8		4800	2	2	28800	32000
24	4	BIMINI 24	OP	CTRCN	FBG	SV	IB	200D	VLVO	8		4800	2	2	29000	32200
24	4	TOURNAMENT 245	OP	SF	FBG	SV	IB	T250	VLVO	8		5700	1	11	28700	31900
24	4	TOURNAMENT 245	OP	SF	FBG	SV	IB	T100D	YAN	8		5000	1	11	35200	39100
29		BIMINI 29	OP	SF	FBG	SV	IB	T330	VLVO	10	3	8100	2	6	50000	54900
29		BIMINI 29	OP	SF	FBG	SV	IB	T200D-T225D		10	3	9250	2	6	64500	73100
29		BIMINI 29	MT	SF	FBG	SV	IB	T330	VLVO	10	3	8100	2	6	50000	54900
29		BIMINI 29	MT	SF	FBG	SV	IB	T200D-T225D		10	3	9250	2	6	64500	73100
29		BIMINI 29	TT	SF	FBG	SV	IB	T330	VLVO	10	3	8100	2	6	50000	54900
29		BIMINI 29	TT	SF	FBG	SV	IB	T200D-T225D		10	3	9250	2	6	64500	73100
		1992 BOATS														
24	4	BIMINI 24	OP	CTRCN	FBG	SV	IB	330	VLVO	8		4800	2	2	22200	24700
24	4	BIMINI 24	OP	CTRCN	FBG	SV	IO	200D	VLVO	8		4800	2	2	26900	29900
24	4	BIMINI 24	OP	CTRCN	FBG	SV	IB	200D	VLVO	8		4800	2	2	27600	30700
24	4	BIMINI 24	HT	CTRCN	FBG	SV	IB	200D	VLVO	8		4800	2	2	27600	30700
24	4	TOURNAMENT 245	OP	SF	FBG	SV	IB	T250	VLVO	8		5700	1	11	27300	30300
29		BIMINI 29	OP	SF	FBG	SV	IB	T330	VLVO	10	3	8100	2	6	47700	52400
29		BIMINI 29	OP	SF	FBG	SV	IB	T200D-T225D		10	3	9250	2	6	61600	69700
		1991 BOATS														
24	4	BIMINI	OP	CTRCN	FBG	SV	IB	261D	VLVO	8		4600	2	2	27300	30300
24	4	BIMINI	OP	SF	FBG	SV	IB	330	VLVO	8		4600	2	2	20500	22700
24	4	BIMINI	OP	SF	FBG	SV	IB	T150	VLVO	8		4600	2	2	21300	23600
24	4	BIMINI	TT	SF	FBG	SV	IB	200D	VLVO	8		4900	2	2	26800	29700
24	4	BIMINI CC	OP	CTRCN	FBG	SV	IB	330	VLVO	8		4800	2	2	21100	23500
24	4	BIMINI CC	OP	CTRCN	FBG	SV	IB	200D	VLVO	8		4800	2	2	26400	29300
24	4	CENTER CONSOLE 24	OP	SF	FBG	SV	IB	330	VLVO	8		5000	2	2	21800	24200
24	4	CENTER CONSOLE 24	OP	SF	FBG	SV	IB	200D	VLVO	8		5000	2	2	27100	30100
24	4	TOURNAMENT 245	OP	SF	FBG	SV	IB	T150	VLVO	8		5000	1	11	22600	25100
29		BIMINI	OP	CUD	FBG	SV	IB	T330	VLVO	10	3	8900	2	6	46800	51400
29		BIMINI	OP	CUD	FBG	SV	IB	T200D	VLVO	10	3	8900	2	6	57500	63100
29		BIMINI	TT	CUD	FBG	SV	IB	T330	VLVO	10	3	9300	2	6	47500	52200
29		BIMINI	TT	CUD	FBG	SV	IB	T200D	VLVO	10	3	9300	2	6	59000	64900
29		CUDDY 29	OP	SF	FBG	SV	IB	T200D	VLVO	10	3	9000	2	6	57800	63500
29		CUDDY 29	TT	SF	FBG	SV	IB	T200D	VLVO	10	3	9700	2	6	60600	66600
29		TOURNAMENT 290	TT	SF	FBG	SV	IB	T200D	VLVO	10	3	9900	2	6	61400	67500
		1990 BOATS														
24	4	BIMINI	OP	CTRCN	FBG	SV	IB	261D	VLVO	8		4600	2	2	26100	29000
24	4	BIMINI	OP	SF	FBG	SV	IB	330	VLVO	8		4600	2	2	19500	21600
24	4	BIMINI	OP	SF	FBG	SV	IB	200D	VLVO	8		4600	2	2	24500	27200
24	4	BIMINI	TT	SF	FBG	SV	IB	200D	VLVO	8		4900	2	2	25600	28400
24	4	BIMINI CC	OP	CTRCN	FBG	SV	IB	330	VLVO	8		4800	2	2	20100	22300
24	4	BIMINI CC	OP	CTRCN	FBG	SV	IB	200D	VLVO	8		4800	2	2	25200	28000
29		BIMINI	OP	CUD	FBG	SV	IB	T330	VLVO	10	3	8900	2	6	44000	48900
29		BIMINI	OP	CUD	FBG	SV	IB	T200D	VLVO	10	3	8900	2	6	54900	60300
29		BIMINI	TT	CUD	FBG	SV	IB	T330	VLVO	10	3	9300	2	6	44700	49600
29		BIMINI	TT	CUD	FBG	SV	IB	T200D	VLVO	10	3	9300	2	6	56400	62000
		1989 BOATS														
24	4	BIMINI	OP	CTRCN	FBG	SV	IB	261D	VLVO	8		4600	2	2	25000	27700
24	4	BIMINI	OP	SF	FBG	SV	IB	330	VLVO	8		4600	2	2	18700	20800
24	4	BIMINI	OP	SF	FBG	SV	IB	200D	VLVO	8		4600	2	2	23400	26000
24	4	BIMINI	TT	SF	FBG	SV	IB	200D	VLVO	8		4900	2	2	24400	27200
24	4	BIMINI CC	OP	CTRCN	FBG	SV	IB	330	VLVO	8		4800	2	2	19100	21300
24	4	BIMINI CC	OP	CTRCN	FBG	SV	IB	200D	VLVO	8		4800	2	2	24100	26800
29		BIMINI	OP	CUD	FBG	SV	IB	T330	VLVO	10	3	8900	2	6	41900	46500
29		BIMINI	OP	CUD	FBG	SV	IB	T200D	VLVO	10	3	8900	2	6	52500	57700
29		BIMINI	TT	CUD	FBG	SV	IB	T330	VLVO	10	3	9300	2	6	42500	47200
29		BIMINI	TT	CUD	FBG	SV	IB	T200D	VLVO	10	3	9300	2	6	54000	59300
		1988 BOATS														
24	4	BIMINI	OP	SF	FBG	SV	IB	260	VLVO	8		4600	2	2	16900	19200
24	4	BIMINI	OP	SF	FBG	SV	IB	200D	VLVO	8		4600	2	2	22400	24900
24	4	BIMINI	TT	SF	FBG	SV	IB	200D	VLVO	8		4900	2	2	23400	26000
24	4	BIMINI CC	OP	CTRCN	FBG	SV	IB	460	CHRY	8		4800	2	2	19700	21900

BIMINI MARINE -CONTINUED
See inside cover to adjust price for area

LOA FT IN	NAME AND/ OR MODEL	TOP/ RIG	BOAT TYPE	-HULL- MTL TP	-ENGINE- TP # HP MFG	BEAM FT IN	WGT LBS	DRAFT FT IN	RETAIL LOW	RETAIL HIGH
--- 1988 BOATS ---										
24 4	BIMINI CC	OP	CTRCN	FBG SV	IB 200D VLVO	8	4800	2 2	23100	25600
--- 1987 BOATS ---										
24 4	BIMINI	OP	SF	FBG SV	IB 260 VLVO	8	4600	2 2	16100	18300
24 4	BIMINI	OP	SF	FBG SV	IB 200D VLVO	8	4600	2 2	21500	23900
24 4	BIMINI	TT	SF	FBG SV	IB 165D VLVO	8	4900	2 2	21700	24100
24 4	BIMINI CC	OP	CTRCN	FBG SV	IB 260 VLVO	8	4800	2 2	16700	18900
24 4	BIMINI CC	OP	CTRCN	FBG SV	IB 200D VLVO	8	4800	2 2	22100	24600
--- 1986 BOATS ---										
24 4	BIMINI	OP	SF	FBG SV	IB 165D VLVO	8	4600	2 2	19900	22100
24 4	BIMINI	TT	SF	FBG SV	IB 165D VLVO	8	4900	2 2	20800	23100
--- 1985 BOATS ---										
24 4	BIMINI	OP	SF	FBG SV	IB 165D VLVO	8	4600	2 2	19100	21200
24 4	BIMINI	TT	SF	FBG SV	IB 165D VLVO	8	4900	2 2	20000	22200

BIRCHWOOD YACHTS USA INC
PASADENA MD 21122   COAST GUARD MFG ID- BIR See inside cover to adjust price for area

LOA FT IN	NAME AND/ OR MODEL	TOP/ RIG	BOAT TYPE	-HULL- MTL TP	-ENGINE- TP # HP MFG	BEAM FT IN	WGT LBS	DRAFT FT IN	RETAIL LOW	RETAIL HIGH
--- 1987 BOATS ---										
33	TS 33	FB	SDN	FBG SV	IB T165D VLVO	12 4		3	59900	65900
37	TS 37	FB	DCFD	FBG SV	IB T250D VLVO	12 4	13200	3 6	71400	78500
44	TS 44	FB	SDN	FBG SV	IB T D	15 4		4	**	**
--- 1986 BOATS ---										
31 9	COMMODORE 31	FB	DCFD	FBG SV	IB T165D VLVO	11		3	50900	55900
33	TS 33	FB	SDN	FBG SV	IB T165D VLVO	12 4		3	57500	63200
37	TS 37	FB	DCFD	FBG SV	IB T250D VLVO	12 4	13200	3 6	68100	74800
42	EMPRESS 42	FB	DCMY	FBG SV	IB T D VLVO	14 3		3 9	**	**
42	EMPRESS 42	FB	DCMY	FBG SV	IB T300D VLVO	14 3		3 9	112000	123000
44	TS 44	FB	SDN	FBG SV	IB T D	15 4		4	**	**
48	REGENT 48	FB	DCMY	FBG SV	IB T300D VLVO	15 4		4	175500	192500
52	TS 52	FB	TCMY	FBG	IB T D				**	**
--- 1985 BOATS ---										
27	COUNTESS 27	ST	EXP	FBG SV	IO 165D VLVO	10		2 9	15800	17900
31 9	COMMODORE 31	FB	DCFD	FBG SV	IB T165D VLVO	11		3	49200	54100
33	TS 33	FB	SDN	FBG SV	IB T165D VLVO	12 4		3	55100	60500
37	TS 37	FB	DCFD	FBG SV	IB T165D VLVO	12 4	13200	3 6	61600	67700
42	EMPRESS 42	FB	DCMY	FBG SV	IB T300D VLVO	14 3		3 9	107000	117500
48	REGENT 48	FB	DCMY	FBG SV	IB T300D VLVO	15 4		4	167500	184000
52	TS 52	FB	TCMY	FBG	IB T D				**	**

BLACK THUNDER POWERBOATS
HANNIBAL MO 63401   See inside cover to adjust price for area

For more recent years, see the BUC Used Boat Price Guide, Volume 1

LOA FT IN	NAME AND/ OR MODEL	TOP/ RIG	BOAT TYPE	-HULL- MTL TP	-ENGINE- TP # HP MFG	BEAM FT IN	WGT LBS	DRAFT FT IN	RETAIL LOW	RETAIL HIGH
--- 1996 BOATS ---										
43	XT-430 PERF	OP	OFF	FBG DV	IO T330 MRCR	9 6	9500	2 6	80100	88000
	IO T415 MRCR 90800		99800,	IO T525	MRCR 106500 117000,	IO T600	MRCR	116000	127500	
43	XT-430 SF	OP	SF	FBG DV	IO T350D YAN	9 6	11500	3 2	134000	147000
43	XT-430 SPORT CR	OP	OFF	FBG DV	IO T330 MRCR	9 6	10500	2 6	84600	93000
	IO T415 MRCR 95800		105500,	IO T525	MRCR 112500 123500,	IO T600	MRCR	122500	134500	
	IO T800 MRCR **		**							
--- 1995 BOATS ---										
32	HURRICANE XJ-320	OP	RNBT	FBG DV	IB T465		7000		51800	57000
43	XT-430 PERF	OP	OFF	FBG DV	IO T300 MRCR	9 6	9000	2 6	95300	105000
	IB T415 MRCR 108000		118500,	IB T490	MRCR 117500 129000,	IB T500	MRCR	118500	130500	
	IB T550 MRCR 122500 137500									
43	XT-430 SF	OP	SF	FBG DV	IB T315D		11000		135500	149000
43	XT-430 SPORT CR	OP	OFF	FBG DV	IB T300 MRCR	9 6	11000	2 6	103500	113500
	IB T415 MRCR 117000		128500,	IB T490	MRCR 127000 139500,	IB T500	MRCR	128500	141000	
	IB T550 MRCR 135500 149000									
--- 1993 BOATS ---										
32	SE 320	OP	OFF	F/S DV	IO 300-410	8	5600	2 7	30500	35600
32	XJ 320 HURRICANE	OP	OFF	F/S DV	IO T300-T415	8	7600	2 11	35300	42100
32	XL 320	OP	OFF	F/S DV	IO T300-T415	8	7600	2 11	34500	41300
43	SC 430	OP	OFF	F/S DV	IO T275 MRCR	9 6	13500		70500	77400
43	SC 430	OP	OFF	F/S DV	IO T500 MRCR	9 6	12500		93100	102500
43	SC 430	OP	OFF	F/S DV	IO R415 MRCR	9 6	14500		94500	104000
43	XT 430	OP	OFF	F/S DV	IO T500 MRCR	9 6	10500		85200	93600
43	XT 430	OP	OFF	F/S DV	IO T600 MRCR	9 6	10500		95700	105000
43	XT 430	OP	OFF	F/S DV	IO R415 MRCR	9 6	12000		85800	94300
--- 1992 BOATS ---										
32	SE 320	OP	OFF	F/S DV	IO 300-410	7 4	6000	2 7	28300	33000
32	XJ 320 HURRICANE	OP	OFF	F/S DV	IO T330-T465	8	7500	2 11	33700	40300
32	XL 320	OP	OFF	F/S DV	IO T330-T465	8	7500	2 11	32900	40300
--- 1991 BOATS ---										
32	XJ 320 HURRICANE	OP	OFF	F/S DV	IO T330-T465	8	7500	2 11	31600	38100
32	XL 320	OP	OFF	F/S DV	IO T330-T465	8	7500	2 11	30800	37400
--- 1990 BOATS ---										
32	XJ320 HURRICANE	OP	OFF	F/S DV	IO T365 MRCR	8	7600	2 11	30000	33300
32	XL320	OP	OFF	F/S DV	IO T330-T420	8	7500	2 11	29300	34500

BLACK TIP
CAPE CORAL FL 33909   See inside cover to adjust price for area

LOA FT IN	NAME AND/ OR MODEL	TOP/ RIG	BOAT TYPE	-HULL- MTL TP	-ENGINE- TP # HP MFG	BEAM FT IN	WGT LBS	DRAFT FT IN	RETAIL LOW	RETAIL HIGH
--- 1994 BOATS ---										
17 10	BLACKTIP 1800		CTRCN	FBG SV	OB	7 2	1300	11	4300	5000
19 6	BLACKTIP 2000		CTRCN	FBG SV	OB	7 9	1700		5600	6400
--- 1993 BOATS ---										
17 10	BLACKTIP 1800		CTRCN	FBG SV	OB	7 2	1300	11	4100	4800
19 6	BLACKTIP 2000		CTRCN	FBG SV	OB	7 9	1700		5350	6150

BLACK WATCH CORP
See inside cover to adjust price for area
For more recent years, see the BUC Used Boat Price Guide, Volume 1

LOA FT IN	NAME AND/ OR MODEL	TOP/ RIG	BOAT TYPE	-HULL- MTL TP	-ENGINE- TP # HP MFG	BEAM FT IN	WGT LBS	DRAFT FT IN	RETAIL LOW	RETAIL HIGH
--- 1995 BOATS ---										
26 1	BLACK WATCH 26	OP	SF	FBG DV	OB	9 8	4800	2 2	36200	40200
26 1	BLACK WATCH 26	OP	SF	FBG DV	IB T250 MRCR	9 8	6800	2 6	47500	52200
26 1	BLACK WATCH 26	OP	SF	FBG DV	IB T180D MRCR	9 8	6800	2 6	65200	71600
30 1	BLACK WATCH 30	OP	SF	FBG DV	IB T250 MRCR	10 11	9000	2 3	59600	65500
30 1	BLACK WATCH 30	OP	SF	FBG DV	IBT250D-T300D	10 11	9000	2 3	78600	91700
30 1	BLACK WATCH 30	FB	SF	FBG DV	IB T350D CAT	11	11500	3	112000	123000
30 8	BLACK WATCH 30	FB	SF	FBG DV	IB T250 MRCR	11	11500	3	84700	93000
30 8	BLACK WATCH 30	FB	SF	FBG DV	IBT250D-T300D	11	11500	3	106000	122000
32 8	BLACK WATCH 33	FB	SF	FBG DV	IB T310 MRCR	12 5	11800	2 7	98700	108500
32 10	BLACK WATCH 33	FB	SF	FBG DV	IBT250D-T350D	12 5	11800	2 7	113500	138000
32 10	BLACK WATCH 33	FB	SF	FBG DV	IB T310 MRCR	12 3	13300	2 7	101500	111500
32 10	BLACK WATCH 33	FB	SF	FBG DV	IBT300D-T435D	12 3	13300	2 7	125500	155500
35 10	BLACK WATCH 36	OP	SF	FBG DV	IB T250D CUM	12 5	13900	2 7	144500	158500
35 11	BLACK WATCH 36	FB	SF	FBG DV	IB T310 MRCR	12 4	14900	2 7	130500	143500
35 11	BLACK WATCH 36	FB	SF	FBG DV	IB T300D CUM	12 4	14900	2 7	156000	171500
35 11	BLACK WATCH 36	FB	SF	FBG DV	IB T350D CAT	12 4	14900	2 7	166500	183000
38	BLACK WATCH 36	FB	SF	FBG DV	IB T435D CAT	12 4	14900	2 7	192000	211000
40	TED HOOD 40	FB	SF	FBG DV	IB T300	12 5		2 11	179000	197000
--- 1994 BOATS ---										
26 1	BLACK WATCH 26	OP	SF	FBG DV	OB	9 8	4800	2 2	34400	38200
26 1	BLACK WATCH 26	OP	SF	FBG DV	IB T250 MRCR	9 8	6800	2 6	44500	49400
26 1	BLACK WATCH 26	OP	SF	FBG DV	IB T150D MRCR	9 8	6800	2 6	59400	65300
26 1	BLACK WATCH 26 CLUB	OP	SF	FBG DV	IB T250 MRCR	10 11		2 3	45600	50200
26 1	BLACK WATCH 26 CLUB	OP	SF	FBG DV	IB T150D MRCR	10 11		2 3	60400	66400
30 1	BLACK WATCH 30	OP	SF	FBG DV	IB T250 MRCR	10 11	9000	2 3	56400	62000
30 1	BLACK WATCH 30	OP	SF	FBG DV	IBT250D-T300D	10 11	9000	2 3	74800	87300
30 1	BLACK WATCH 30	FB	SF	FBG DV	IB T350D CAT	11	11500	3	85500	94000
30 8	BLACK WATCH 30	FB	SF	FBG DV	IB T250 MRCR	11	11500	3	80100	88100
30 8	BLACK WATCH 30	FB	SF	FBG DV	IBT250D-T300D	11	11500	3	101000	116000
32 10	BLACK WATCH 33	FB	SF	FBG DV	IB T310 MRCR	12 5	11800	2 7	93500	102500
32 10	BLACK WATCH 33	FB	SF	FBG DV	IBT250D-T350D	12 5	11800	2 7	108000	131000
32 10	BLACK WATCH 33	FB	SF	FBG DV	IB T310 MRCR	12 3	13300	2 7	96100	105500
32 10	BLACK WATCH 33	FB	SF	FBG DV	IBT250D-T350D	12 3	13300	2 7	114500	157500
35 10	BLACK WATCH 36	OP	SF	FBG DV	IB T310 MRCR	12 5	13900	2 7	119000	130500
	IB T250D CUM 137500		151000,	IB T300D	DV MRCR 142500 156500,	IB T350D	CAT	152500	167500	
35 11	BLACK WATCH 36	FB	SF	FBG DV	IB T310 MRCR	12 4	14900	2 7	123500	136000
	IB T250D CUM 143500		157500,	IB T300D	CUM 148500 163500,	IB T350D	CAT	158500	174000	
39 11	BLACK WATCH 40 CLUB	OP	SF	FBG DV	IB T400 MRCR	12 5	19250		176500	194000
39 11	BLACK WATCH 40 CLUB	OP	SF	FBG DV	IB T300D CUM	12 5	19250		199500	219000
39 11	BLACK WATCH 40 CLUB	OP	SF	FBG DV	IB T350D CAT	12 5	19250		213500	234500

LOA FT	LOA IN	NAME AND/ OR MODEL	TOP/ RIG	BOAT TYPE	HULL MTL	HULL TP	ENGINE TP	ENGINE # HP	ENGINE MFG	BEAM FT	BEAM IN	WGT LBS	DRAFT FT	DRAFT IN	RETAIL LOW	RETAIL HIGH
		1993 BOATS														
26	1	BLACK WATCH 26	OP	SF	FBG	DV	OB			9	8	4800	2	2	32700	36400
26	1	BLACK WATCH 26	OP	SF	FBG	DV	IO	330	VLVO	9	8	6500	2	2	37900	42200
26	1	BLACK WATCH 26	OP	SF	FBG	DV	IB	T240	CRUS	9	8	6800	2	6	42400	47100
26	1	BLACK WATCH 26	OP	SF	FBG	DV	IB	T140D	YAN	9	8	6800	2	6	56000	61600
30	1	BLACK WATCH 30	OP	SF	FBG	DV	IB	T350	CRUS	10	11	9000	2	3	57500	63200
30	1	BLACK WATCH 30	OP	SF	FBG	DV	IB	T250D-T300D		10	11	9000	2	3	71300	83100
32	8	BLACK WATCH 30	FB	SF	FBG	DV	IB	T350	CRUS	11		11500	2	3	80500	88500
32	8	BLACK WATCH 30	FB	SF	FBG	DV	IB	T250D-T300D		11		11500	2	3	96100	110500
33	2	BLACK WATCH 33	OP	SF	FBG	DV	IB	T350	CRUS	11	4	11800	2	7	93300	102500
33	2	BLACK WATCH 33	OP	SF	FBG	DV	IB	T250D-T300D		11	4	11800	2	7	105000	121000
35	10	BLACK WATCH 33	OP	SF	FBG	DV	IB	T350	CRUS	11	4	14900	2	7	98800	108500
35	10	BLACK WATCH 33	OP	SF	FBG	DV	IB	T250D	CUM	11	4	14900	2	7	117500	129000
35	10	BLACK WATCH 33	FB	SF	FBG	DV	IB	T300D	CUM	11	4	14900	2	7	122000	134000
35	10	BLACK WATCH 36	OP	SF	FBG	DV	IB	T350	CRUS	11	4	13900	2	7	113500	125000
35	10	BLACK WATCH 36	OP	SF	FBG	DV	IB	T250D	CUM	11	4	13900	2	7	132500	145500
35	10	BLACK WATCH 36	OP	SF	FBG	DV	IB	T300D	CUM	11	4	13900	2	7	137500	151000
35	10	BLACK WATCH 36	FB	SF	FBG	DV	IB	T350	CRUS	11	4	13900	2	7	113500	125000
35	10	BLACK WATCH 36	FB	SF	FBG	DV	IB	T250D	CUM	11	4	13900	2	7	132500	145500
35	10	BLACK WATCH 36	FB	SF	FBG	DV	IB	T300D	CUM	11	4	13900	2	7	137500	151000
		1992 BOATS														
26	1	BLACK WATCH 26	OP	SF	FBG	DV	OB			9	8	4800	2	2	31200	34700
26	1	BLACK WATCH 26	OP	SF	FBG	DV	IO	330	VLVO	9	8	6500	2	2	35500	39500
26	1	BLACK WATCH 26	OP	SF	FBG	DV	IB	T318	CHRY	9	8	6800	2	6	41700	46300
26	1	BLACK WATCH 26	OP	SF	FBG	DV	IB	T140D-T170D		9	8	6800	2	6	53400	61300
26	1	BLACK WATCH 26W/BRCK	OP	SF	FBG	DV	OB			9	8	4800	2	2	34100	37900
30	1	BLACK WATCH 30	OP	SF	FBG	DV	IB	T350	CRUS	10	11	9000	2	3	54600	60000
30	1	BLACK WATCH 30	OP	SF	FBG	DV	IB	T250D	CUM	10	11	9000	2	3	68000	74700
30	1	BLACK WATCH 30	OP	SF	FBG	DV	IB	T300D		10	11	10500	2	3	87500	96200
30	1	BLACK WATCH 30	FB	SF	FBG	DV	IB	T300D	CAT	11		11500	2	3	91900	101000
32	8	BLACK WATCH 30	FB	SF	FBG	DV	IB	T350	CRUS	11		11500	2	3	76400	83900
32	8	BLACK WATCH 30	FB	SF	FBG	DV	IB	T250D-T300D		11		11500	2	3	91700	105500
33	2	BLACK WATCH 33	OP	SF	FBG	DV	IB	T300D	CUM	11		11800	2	7	100500	110500
33	2	BLACK WATCH 33	ST	SF	FBG	DV	IB	T300D	CUM	11		11800	2	7	100500	110500
33	2	BLACK WATCH 33	HT	SF	FBG	DV	IB	T300D	CUM	11		11800	2	7	100500	110500
33	2	BLACK WATCH 33	FB	SF	FBG	DV	IB	T300D	CUM	11		12800	2	7	104000	114000
36	2	BLACK WATCH 36	OP	SF	FBG	DV	IB	T300D	CUM	11	4	12900	2	7	122000	134500
36	2	BLACK WATCH 36	ST	SF	FBG	DV	IB	T300D	CUM	11	4	12900	2	7	122000	134500
36	2	BLACK WATCH 36	HT	SF	FBG	DV	IB	T300D	CUM	11	4	12900	2	7	122500	134500
36	2	BLACK WATCH 36	FB	SF	FBG	DV	IB	T300D	CUM	11	4	13900	2	7	126500	139000
		1991 BOATS														
26	1	BLACK WATCH 26	OP	SF	FBG	DV	OB			9	8	4800	2	2	29800	33200
26	1	BLACK WATCH 26	OP	SF	FBG	DV	IO	330	VLVO	9	8	6500	2	2	33300	37000
26	1	BLACK WATCH 26	OP	SF	FBG	DV	IB	T318	CHRY	9	8	6800	2	6	39600	44000
26	1	BLACK WATCH 26	OP	SF	FBG	DV	IB	T140D-T170D		9	8	6800	2	6	51000	58500
26	1	BLACK WATCH 26W/BRCK	OP	SF	FBG	DV	OB			9	8	4800	2	2	32600	36200
30	1	BLACK WATCH 30	OP	SF	FBG	DV	IB	T325	CRUS	10	11	9000	3		50900	56000
30	1	BLACK WATCH 30	OP	SF	FBG	DV	IB	T250D-T300D		10	11	9800	3		75500	93100
30	1	BLACK WATCH 30	FB	SF	FBG	DV	IB	T325	CRUS	11		11600	3	2	64300	70700
30	1	BLACK WATCH 30	FB	SF	FBG	DV	IB	T250D-T300D		11		11600	3	2	83100	96900
33	2	BLACK WATCH 33	OP	SF	FBG	DV	IB	T300D	CUM	11		11800	2	7	95900	105500
33	2	BLACK WATCH 33	ST	SF	FBG	DV	IB	T300D	CUM	11		11800	2	7	95900	105500
33	2	BLACK WATCH 33	HT	SF	FBG	DV	IB	T300D	CUM	11		11800	2	7	95900	105500
33	2	BLACK WATCH 33	FB	SF	FBG	DV	IB	T300D	CUM	11		12800	2	7	99200	109000
36	2	BLACK WATCH 36	OP	SF	FBG	DV	IB	T300D	CUM	11	4	12900	2	7	116500	128000
36	2	BLACK WATCH 36	ST	SF	FBG	DV	IB	T300D	CUM	11	4	12900	2	7	116500	128000
36	2	BLACK WATCH 36	HT	SF	FBG	DV	IB	T300D	CUM	11	4	12900	2	7	116500	128000
36	2	BLACK WATCH 36	FB	SF	FBG	DV	IB	T300D	CUM	11	4	13900	2	7	120500	132500
		1990 BOATS														
26	1	BLACK WATCH 26	OP	SF	FBG	DV	IB	T318	CHRY	9	8	6800	2	6	37700	41800
26	1	BLACK WATCH 26	OP	SF	FBG	DV	IB	T140D	YAN	9	8	6800	2	6	48700	53500
26	1	BLACK WATCH 26W/BRCK	OP	SF	FBG	DV	OB			9	8	4800	2	2	29900	33200
30	1	BLACK WATCH 30	HT	SF	FBG	DV	IB	T325	CRUS	10	11	9000	3		48500	53200
30	1	BLACK WATCH 30	HT	SF	FBG	DV	IB	T250D-T300D		10	11	9800	3		72100	79200
30	1	BLACK WATCH 30	FB	SF	FBG	DV	IB	T325	CRUS	11		11600	3	2	61200	67200
30	1	BLACK WATCH 30	FB	SF	FBG	DV	IB	T250D-T300D		11		11600	3	2	79400	91600

BLACKBIRD RACING TEAM

B R T
NEW BEDFORD MA 02745 COAST GUARD MFG ID- BBM
FORMERLY BLACKBIRD MARINE

See inside cover to adjust price for area

LOA FT	LOA IN	NAME AND/ OR MODEL	TOP/ RIG	BOAT TYPE	HULL MTL	HULL TP	ENGINE TP	ENGINE # HP	ENGINE MFG	BEAM FT	BEAM IN	WGT LBS	DRAFT FT	DRAFT IN	RETAIL LOW	RETAIL HIGH
		1984 BOATS														
23	6	BRT 7.1 METRE	OP	RACE	FBG	DV	OB			6	8	1900			5850	6700
23	6	BRT 7.1 METRE	OP	RACE	FBG	DV	IO	260	MRCR	6	8	3500			5600	6400
23	6	BRT 7.1 METRE	OP	RACE	FBG	DV	IO	330		6	8	3800			6550	7550
23	6	COBRA	OP	RACE	FBG	DV	IO	370	MRCR	6	8	3800			7150	8250
23	6	ST-TROPEZ	OP	OPFSH	FBG	DV	OB			6	8	3200			9050	10300

....For earlier years, see the BUC Used Boat Price Guide, Volume 3

BLACKFIN YACHT CORP

FT LAUDERDALE FL 33335 COAST GUARD MFG ID- KMA
FORMERLY KARANDA MARINE INC

See inside cover to adjust price for area

For more recent years, see the BUC Used Boat Price Guide, Volume 1

LOA FT	LOA IN	NAME AND/ OR MODEL	TOP/ RIG	BOAT TYPE	HULL MTL	HULL TP	ENGINE TP	ENGINE # HP	ENGINE MFG	BEAM FT	BEAM IN	WGT LBS	DRAFT FT	DRAFT IN	RETAIL LOW	RETAIL HIGH
		1996 BOATS														
29	4	BLACK-FIN COMBI	OP	EXP	FBG	DV	OB			10	6	11000	2	4	43400	48200
29	4	BLACK-FIN COMBI	OP	EXP	FBG	DV	IB	T320	CRUS	10	6	10025	2	5	58200	64000
29	4	BLACK-FIN COMBI	OP	EXP	FBG	DV	IB	T230D-T318D		10	6	12120	2	8	84100	100500
29	4	BLACK-FIN FLYBRIDGE	FB	SF	FBG	DV	IB	T320	CRUS	10	6	11109	2	6	65500	72000
29	4	BLACK-FIN FLYBRIDGE	FB	SF	FBG	DV	IB	T230D-T315D		10	6	13604	2	9	99000	109000
30	8	BLACK-FIN COMBI	OP	EXP	FBG	DV	IB	T320	CRUS	11	10	15500	2	10	77000	84600
30	8	BLACK-FIN COMBI	OP	EXP	FBG	DV	IB	T300D-T370D		11	10	15500	2	10	107500	124000
32	11	BLACK-FIN COMBI	OP	EXP	FBG	DV	IB	T370D-T420D		12		19132	2	11	133000	152000
32	11	BLACK-FIN FLYBRIDGE	FB	SF	FBG	DV	IB	T320	CRUS	12		17645	2	11	102500	113000
32	11	BLACK-FIN FLYBRIDGE	FB	SF	FBG	DV	IB	T370D-T430D		12		21069	2	11	155000	177000
32	11	BLACKFIN COMBI	OP	EXP	FBG	DV	IB	T320	CRUS	12		16428	2	11	100500	110000
32	11	BLACKFIN COMBI	OP	EXP	FBG	DV	IB	T375D	CAT	12		19132	2	11	148000	162500
38	3	BLACK-FIN CNV	FB	SF	FBG	DV	IB	T485D	DD	14	5	35970	4		263500	289500
		IB T550D DD 275500 303000, IB T600D VLVO 268000 294500, IB T625D DD													287500	316000
38	3	BLACK-FIN COMBI		EXP	FBG	DV	IB	T485D	DD	14	5	34170	3	7	250000	275000
		IB T550D DD 262000 288000, IB T600D VLVO 254500 280000, IB T625D DD													274000	301000
		1995 BOATS														
29	4	BLACK-FIN COMBI	OP	EXP	FBG	DV	OB			10	6	11000	2	4	41100	45700
29	4	BLACK-FIN COMBI	OP	EXP	FBG	DV	IB	T270-T320		10	6	10025	2	5	53300	60500
29	4	BLACK-FIN COMBI	OP	EXP	FBG	DV	IB	T230D	VLVO	10	6	12120	2	8	80000	87900
29	4	BLACK-FIN FLYBRIDGE	FB	SF	FBG	DV	IB	T270-T320		10	6	11109	2	6	60100	68000
29	4	BLACK-FIN FLYBRIDGE	FB	SF	FBG	DV	IB	T230D	VLVO	10	6	13604	2	9	94100	103500
30	8	BLACK-FIN COMBI	OP	EXP	FBG	DV	IB	T320	CRUS	11	10	13300	2	7	68800	75600
30	8	BLACK-FIN COMBI	OP	EXP	FBG	DV	IB	T300D		11	10	15500	2	10	102000	112500
32	11	BLACK-FIN FLYBRIDGE	FB	SF	FBG	DV	IB	T320	CRUS	12		17645	2	8	97000	106500
32	11	BLACK-FIN FLYBRIDGE	FB	SF	FBG	DV	IB	T375D	CAT	12		21069	2	11	149000	163500
32	11	BLACKFIN COMBI	OP	EXP	FBG	DV	IB	T320	CRUS	12		16428	2	8	94800	104000
32	11	BLACKFIN COMBI	OP	EXP	FBG	DV	IB	T375D	CAT	12		19132	2	11	140500	154500
38	3	BLACK-FIN CNV	FB	SF	FBG	DV	IB	T435D	CAT	14	5	35970	4		246500	270500
38	3	BLACK-FIN CNV	FB	SF	FBG	DV	IB	T485D	DD	14	5	35970	4		252500	277500
38	3	BLACK-FIN CNV	FB	SF	FBG	DV	IB	T550D	DD	14	5	35970	4		264000	290500
38	3	BLACK-FIN COMBI		EXP	FBG	DV	IB	T435D	CAT	14	5	34170	3	7	233500	256500
38	3	BLACK-FIN COMBI		EXP	FBG	DV	IB	T485D	DD	14	5	34170	3	7	239500	263000
38	3	BLACK-FIN COMBI		EXP	FBG	DV	IB	T550D	DD	14	5	34170	3	7	251000	276000
		1994 BOATS														
29	4	BLACK-FIN COMBI	OP	EXP	FBG	DV	IB	T315	CRUS	10	6	10025	2	5	51900	57000
29	4	BLACK-FIN COMBI	OP	EXP	FBG	DV	IB	T230D-T300D		10	6	12120	2	8	76100	90900
29	4	BLACK-FIN COMBI	TT	EXP	FBG	DV	IB	T315	CRUS	10	6	10025	2	5	51900	57000
29	4	BLACK-FIN COMBI	TT	EXP	FBG	DV	IB	T230D-T300D		10	6	12120	2	8	76100	90900
29	4	BLACK-FIN FLYBRIDGE	FB	SF	FBG	DV	IB	T315	CRUS	10	6	11109	2	6	58400	64200
29	4	BLACK-FIN FLYBRIDGE	FB	SF	FBG	DV	IB	T230D-T300D		10	6	13604	2	11	89500	106000
30	8	BLACK-FIN COMBI	OP	EXP	FBG	DV	IB	T315	CRUS	11	10	15081	2	6	68000	74700
30	8	BLACK-FIN COMBI	OP	EXP	FBG	DV	IB	T300D-T350D		11	10	17788	2	8	106500	117000
30	8	BLACK-FIN COMBI	TT	EXP	FBG	DV	IB	T315	CRUS	11	10	15081	2	6	68000	74700
30	8	BLACK-FIN COMBI	TT	EXP	FBG	DV	IB	T300D-T350D		11	10	17288	2	8	104500	115000
32	11	BLACK-FIN FLYBRIDGE	FB	SF	FBG	DV	IB	T315	CRUS	12		17645	2	8	91600	100500
32	11	BLACK-FIN FLYBRIDGE	FB	SF	FBG	DV	IB	T320D-T435D		12		21069	2	11	136500	158000
32	11	BLACKFIN COMBI	OP	EXP	FBG	DV	IB	T315	CRUS	12		16428	2	8	89500	98300
32	11	BLACKFIN COMBI	OP	EXP	FBG	DV	IB	T320D-T435D		12		19132	2	11	128500	153500
32	11	BLACKFIN FLYBRIDGE	FB	SF	FBG	DV	IB	T375D-T400D		12		20169	2	11	138000	154000
38	3	BLACK-FIN CNV	FB	SF	FBG	DV	IB	T485D	DD	14	5	35970	4		242000	266000
38	3	BLACK-FIN CNV	FB	SF	FBG	DV	IB	T550D	DD	14	5	35970	4		253000	278000
38	3	BLACK-FIN COMBI	OP	EXP	FBG	DV	IB	T485D	DD	14	5	34170	4		229000	252000
38	3	BLACK-FIN COMBI	OP	EXP	FBG	DV	IB	T550D	DD	14	5	34170	4		240000	264000
38	3	BLACK-FIN COMBI	TT	EXP	FBG	DV	IB	T485D	DD	14	5	34170	4		229500	252500
38	3	BLACK-FIN COMBI	TT	EXP	FBG	DV	IB	T550D	DD	14	5	34170	4		240500	264500

LOA FT	LOA IN	NAME AND/ OR MODEL	TOP/ RIG	BOAT TYPE	HULL MTL	HULL TP	ENGINE TP	ENGINE # HP	ENGINE MFG	BEAM FT	BEAM IN	WGT LBS	DRAFT FT	DRAFT IN	RETAIL LOW	RETAIL HIGH
		1993 BOATS														
25	2	BLACK-FIN COMBI	OP	EXP	FBG	DV	OB			8	5	4200	2	5	25100	27900
25	2	BLACK-FIN COMBI	OP	EXP	FBG	DV	IB	315	CRUS	8	5	5200	2	5	24500	27200
25	2	BLACK-FIN COMBI	OP	EXP	FBG	DV	IB	300D		8	5	5200	2	5	35800	39800
25	2	BLACK-FIN FISHERMAN	OP	CUD	FBG	DV	OB			8	5	4200	2	5	25100	27900
25	2	BLACK-FIN FISHERMAN	OP	CUD	FBG	DV	IB	315	CRUS	8	5	5200	2	5	25000	27800
25	2	BLACK-FIN FISHERMAN	OP	CUD	FBG	DV	IB	300D		8	5	5200	2	5	36600	40700
27	9	BLACK-FIN COMBI	OP	EXP	FBG	DV	OB			10		7840	2	10	35100	38900
27	9	BLACK-FIN COMBI	OP	EXP	FBG	DV	IB	T245	CRUS	10		8740	2	9	40100	44500
27	9	BLACK-FIN COMBI	OP	EXP	FBG	DV	IB	T200D	VLVO	10		9200	2	8	56400	62000
27	9	BLACK-FIN COMBI	TT	EXP	FBG	DV	OB			10		6840	2	9	36200	40200
27	9	BLACK-FIN COMBI	TT	EXP	FBG	DV	IB	T245	CRUS	10		8740	2	5	40100	44500
27	9	BLACK-FIN COMBI	TT	EXP	FBG	DV	IB	T200D	VLVO	10		9200	2	8	56400	62000
27	9	BLACK-FIN FISHERMAN	OP	CTRCN	FBG	DV	OB			10		6840	2	9	34500	38300
27	9	BLACK-FIN FISHERMAN	OP	CTRCN	FBG	DV	IB	T245	CRUS	10		8780	2	10	42600	47300
27	9	BLACK-FIN FISHERMAN	OP	CTRCN	FBG	DV	IB	T200D	VLVO	10		9200	2	8	60000	66000
27	9	BLACK-FIN FISHERMAN	TT	CTRCN	FBG	DV	OB			10		7840	2	10	34700	38600
27	9	BLACK-FIN FISHERMAN	TT	CTRCN	FBG	DV	IB	T245	CRUS	10		8740	2	9	42500	47200
27	9	BLACK-FIN FISHERMAN	TT	CTRCN	FBG	DV	IB	T200D	VLVO	10		9200	2	8	60000	66000
29	4	BLACK-FIN COMBI	OP	EXP	FBG	DV	OB			10	6	8000	2	5	37500	41700
29	4	BLACK-FIN COMBI	OP	EXP	FBG	DV	IB	T315	CRUS	10	6	10025	2	5	49200	54100
29	4	BLACK-FIN COMBI	OP	EXP	FBG	DV	IB	T200D-T300D		10	6	12120	2	8	70500	85700
29	4	BLACK-FIN COMBI	TT	EXP	FBG	DV	OB			10	6	8000	2	5	37600	41800
29	4	BLACK-FIN COMBI	TT	EXP	FBG	DV	IB	T315	CRUS	10	6	10025	2	5	49200	54100
29	4	BLACK-FIN COMBI	TT	EXP	FBG	DV	IB	T200D-T300D		10	6	12120	2	8	70500	85700
29	4	BLACK-FIN SPORTFISH	FB	SF	FBG	DV	IB	T315	CRUS	10	6	11109	2	6	55400	60800
29	4	BLACK-FIN SPORTFISH	FB	SF	FBG	DV	IB	T200D-T300D		10	6	13604	2	11	83300	100000
31	9	BLACK-FIN COMBI	OP	EXP	FBG	DV	IB	T315	CRUS	12		15081	2	5	67600	74300
31	9	BLACK-FIN COMBI	OP	EXP	FBG	DV	IB	T300D		12		15000	2	8	90500	110500
31	9	BLACK-FIN COMBI	TT	EXP	FBG	DV	IB	T315	CRUS	12		15081	2	5	67600	74300
31	9	BLACK-FIN COMBI	TT	EXP	FBG	DV	IB	T300D		12		15000	2	8	90500	110500
32	11	BLACK-FIN FLYBRIDGE	FB	SF	FBG	DV	IB	T315	CRUS	12		17645	2	8	86900	95500
32	11	BLACK-FIN FLYBRIDGE	FB	SF	FBG	DV	IB	T320D-T425D		12		21069	2	11	130000	149500
38	3	BLACK-FIN CNV	FB	SF	FBG	DV	IB	T485D	GM	14	5	35970	4		226000	248500
38	3	BLACK-FIN CNV	FB	SF	FBG	DV	IB	T550D	GM	14	5	35970	4		236000	259500
38	3	BLACK-FIN COMBI	OP	EXP	FBG	DV	IB	T425D	CAT	14	5	34170	4		211500	232000
38	3	BLACK-FIN COMBI	OP	EXP	FBG	DV	IB	T485D	GM	14	5	34170	4		214000	235000
38	3	BLACK-FIN COMBI	OP	EXP	FBG	DV	IB	T550D	GM	14	5	34170	4		223500	245500
38	3	BLACK-FIN COMBI	TT	EXP	FBG	DV	IB	T425D	CAT	14	5	34170	4		211500	232500
38	3	BLACK-FIN COMBI	TT	EXP	FBG	DV	IB	T485D	GM	14	5	34170	4		214500	235500
38	3	BLACK-FIN COMBI	TT	EXP	FBG	DV	IB	T550D	GM	14	5	34170	4		224000	246500
		1992 BOATS														
25	2	BLACK-FIN COMBI	OP	EXP	FBG	DV	OB			8	5	4200	2	5	24000	26700
25	2	BLACK-FIN COMBI	OP	EXP	FBG	DV	IB	315	CRUS	8	5	5200	2	5	23200	25800
25	2	BLACK-FIN COMBI	OP	EXP	FBG	DV	IB	300D		8	5	5200	2	5	34100	37900
25	2	BLACK-FIN FISHERMAN	OP	CUD	FBG	DV	OB			8	5	4200	2	5	24000	26700
25	2	BLACK-FIN FISHERMAN	OP	CUD	FBG	DV	IB	315	CRUS	8	5	5200	2	5	23800	26400
25	2	BLACK-FIN FISHERMAN	OP	CUD	FBG	DV	IB	300D		8	5	5200	2	5	34900	38800
27	9	BLACK-FIN COMBI	OP	EXP	FBG	DV	OB			10		7840	2	10	33500	37200
27	9	BLACK-FIN COMBI	OP	EXP	FBG	DV	IB	T245	CRUS	10		8740	2	9	38000	42200
27	9	BLACK-FIN COMBI	OP	EXP	FBG	DV	IB	T200D	VLVO	10		9200	2	8	53800	59100
27	9	BLACK-FIN COMBI	TT	EXP	FBG	DV	OB			10		6840	2	9	34500	38400
27	9	BLACK-FIN COMBI	TT	EXP	FBG	DV	IB	T245	CRUS	10		8740	2	5	38000	42200
27	9	BLACK-FIN COMBI	TT	EXP	FBG	DV	IB	T200D	VLVO	10		9200	2	8	53800	59100
27	9	BLACK-FIN FISHERMAN	OP	CTRCN	FBG	DV	OB			10		6840	2	9	33000	36600
27	9	BLACK-FIN FISHERMAN	OP	CTRCN	FBG	DV	IB	T245	CRUS	10		8780	2	10	40400	44900
27	9	BLACK-FIN FISHERMAN	OP	CTRCN	FBG	DV	IB	T200D	VLVO	10		9200	2	8	57200	62900
27	9	BLACK-FIN FISHERMAN	TT	CTRCN	FBG	DV	OB			10		7840	2	10	33200	36900
27	9	BLACK-FIN FISHERMAN	TT	CTRCN	FBG	DV	IB	T245	CRUS	10		8740	2	9	40300	44800
27	9	BLACK-FIN FISHERMAN	TT	CTRCN	FBG	DV	IB	T200D	VLVO	10		9200	2	8	57300	62900
29	4	BLACK-FIN COMBI	OP	EXP	FBG	DV	OB			10	6	8000	2	5	36000	40000
29	4	BLACK-FIN COMBI	OP	EXP	FBG	DV	IB	T315	CRUS	10	6	10025	2	5	46900	51500
29	4	BLACK-FIN COMBI	OP	EXP	FBG	DV	IB	T200D-T300D		10	6	12120	2	8	67300	81700
29	4	BLACK-FIN COMBI	TT	EXP	FBG	DV	OB			10	6	8000	2	5	36000	40000
29	4	BLACK-FIN COMBI	TT	EXP	FBG	DV	IB	T315	CRUS	10	6	10025	2	5	46900	51500
29	4	BLACK-FIN COMBI	TT	EXP	FBG	DV	IB	T200D-T300D		10	6	12120	2	8	67300	81700
29	4	BLACK-FIN SPORTFISH	FB	SF	FBG	DV	IB	T315	CRUS	10	6	11109	2	6	52500	57700
29	4	BLACK-FIN SPORTFISH	FB	SF	FBG	DV	IB	T200D-T300D		10	6	13604	2	11	79400	95400
31	9	BLACK-FIN COMBI	OP	EXP	FBG	DV	IB	T315	CRUS	12		15081	2	5	64100	70500
31	9	BLACK-FIN COMBI	OP	EXP	FBG	DV	IB	T300D		12		15000	2	8	86300	105000
31	9	BLACK-FIN COMBI	TT	EXP	FBG	DV	IB	T315	CRUS	12		15081	2	5	64100	70500
31	9	BLACK-FIN COMBI	TT	EXP	FBG	DV	IB	T300D		12		15000	2	8	86300	105000
32	11	BLACK-FIN FLYBRIDGE	FB	SF	FBG	DV	IB	T315	CRUS	12		17645	2	8	82400	90600
32	11	BLACK-FIN FLYBRIDGE	FB	SF	FBG	DV	IB	T320D-T425D		12		21069	2	11	124000	142500
38	3	BLACK-FIN CNV	FB	SF	FBG	DV	IB	T485D	GM	14	5	35970	4		215500	237000
38	3	BLACK-FIN CNV	FB	SF	FBG	DV	IB	T550D	GM	14	5	35970	4		225000	247000
38	3	BLACK-FIN COMBI	OP	EXP	FBG	DV	IB	T425D	CAT	14	5	34170	4		201500	221500
38	3	BLACK-FIN COMBI	OP	EXP	FBG	DV	IB	T485D	GM	14	5	34170	4		204000	224000
38	3	BLACK-FIN COMBI	OP	EXP	FBG	DV	IB	T550D	GM	14	5	34170	4		213000	234500
38	3	BLACK-FIN COMBI	TT	EXP	FBG	DV	IB	T425D	CAT	14	5	34170	4		202000	221500
38	3	BLACK-FIN COMBI	TT	EXP	FBG	DV	IB	T485D	GM	14	5	34170	4		204500	224500
38	3	BLACK-FIN COMBI	TT	EXP	FBG	DV	IB	T550D	GM	14	5	34170	4		213500	234500
		1991 BOATS														
25	2	BLACK-FIN COMBI	OP	EXP	FBG	DV	OB			8	5	4200	2	5	23000	25500
25	2	BLACK-FIN COMBI	OP	EXP	FBG	DV	IB	315	CRUS	8	5	5200	2	5	22000	24500
25	2	BLACK-FIN COMBI	OP	EXP	FBG	DV	IB	300D		8	5	5200	2	5	32600	36200
25	2	BLACK-FIN FISHERMAN	OP	CUD	FBG	DV	OB			8	5	4200	2	5	23000	25600
25	2	BLACK-FIN FISHERMAN	OP	CUD	FBG	DV	IB	315	CRUS	8	5	5200	2	5	22600	25100
25	2	BLACK-FIN FISHERMAN	OP	CUD	FBG	DV	IB	300D		8	5	5200	2	5	33400	37100
27	9	BLACK-FIN COMBI	OP	EXP	FBG	DV	OB			10		7840	2	10	32100	35600
27	9	BLACK-FIN COMBI	OP	EXP	FBG	DV	IB	T245	CRUS	10		8740	2	9	36100	40100
27	9	BLACK-FIN COMBI	OP	EXP	FBG	DV	IB	T200D	VLVO	10		9200	2	8	51300	56400
27	9	BLACK-FIN COMBI	TT	EXP	FBG	DV	OB			10		7840	2	10	33000	36600
27	9	BLACK-FIN COMBI	TT	EXP	FBG	DV	IB	T245	CRUS	10		8740	2	5	36100	40100
27	9	BLACK-FIN COMBI	TT	EXP	FBG	DV	IB	T200D	VLVO	10		9200	2	8	51300	56400
27	9	BLACK-FIN FISHERMAN	OP	CTRCN	FBG	DV	OB			10		7840	2	10	31600	35200
27	9	BLACK-FIN FISHERMAN	OP	CTRCN	FBG	DV	IB	T245	CRUS	10		8780	2	10	38400	42700
27	9	BLACK-FIN FISHERMAN	OP	CTRCN	FBG	DV	IB	T200D	VLVO	10		9200	2	8	54600	60100
27	9	BLACK-FIN FISHERMAN	TT	CTRCN	FBG	DV	OB			10		7840	2	10	31800	35400
27	9	BLACK-FIN FISHERMAN	TT	CTRCN	FBG	DV	IB	T245	CRUS	10		8740	2	9	38300	42600
27	9	BLACK-FIN FISHERMAN	TT	CTRCN	FBG	DV	IB	T200D	VLVO	10		9200	2	8	54700	60100
29	4	BLACK-FIN COMBI	OP	EXP	FBG	DV	OB			10	6	9150	2	5	34600	38500
29	4	BLACK-FIN COMBI	OP	EXP	FBG	DV	IB	T245-T315		10	6	10025	2	5	42200	49000
29	4	BLACK-FIN COMBI	OP	EXP	FBG	DV	IB	T200D-T300D		10	6	12120	2	8	64200	78000
29	4	BLACK-FIN COMBI	TT	EXP	FBG	DV	OB			10	6	9150	2	5	34700	38500
29	4	BLACK-FIN COMBI	TT	EXP	FBG	DV	IB	T245-T315		10	6	10025	2	5	42200	49000
29	4	BLACK-FIN COMBI	TT	EXP	FBG	DV	IB	T200D-T300D		10	6	12120	2	8	64200	78000
29	4	BLACK-FIN SPORTFISH	FB	SF	FBG	DV	IB	T245-T315		10	6	11109	2	6	48000	54800
29	4	BLACK-FIN SPORTFISH	FB	SF	FBG	DV	IB	T200D-T300D		10	6	13604	2	9	75800	91100
31	9	BLACK-FIN COMBI	OP	EXP	FBG	DV	IB	T315	CRUS	12		15081	2	5	60900	67000
31	9	BLACK-FIN COMBI	OP	EXP	FBG	DV	IB	T300D		12		17788	2	5	91300	100500
31	9	BLACK-FIN COMBI	TT	EXP	FBG	DV	IB	T315	CRUS	12		15081	2	5	60900	67000
31	9	BLACK-FIN COMBI	TT	EXP	FBG	DV	IB	T300D		12		17788	2	5	91300	100500
31	9	BLACK-FIN FLYBRIDGE	FB	SF	FBG	DV	IB	T315	CRUS	11	11	15460	2	5	68000	74700
31	9	BLACK-FIN FLYBRIDGE	FB	SF	FBG	DV	IB	T300D-T375D		11	11	17815	2	8	101500	117500
32	11	BLACK-FIN FLYBRIDGE	FB	SF	FBG	DV	IB	T375D-T425D		12		20169	2	11	119500	136000
33		BLACK-FIN FLYBRIDGE	FB	SF	FBG	DV	IB	T315	CRUS	12		17645	2	8	78900	86700
33		BLACK-FIN FLYBRIDGE	FB	SF	FBG	DV	IB	T320D	CAT	12		21069	2	11	119000	130500
38	3	BLACK-FIN COMBI	OP	EXP	FBG	DV	IB	T485D	GM	14	5	34170	3	11	194500	214000
38	3	BLACK-FIN COMBI	OP	EXP	FBG	DV	IB	T550D	GM	14	5	34170	3	11	203500	223500
38	3	BLACK-FIN COMBI	TT	EXP	FBG	DV	IB	T485D	GM	14	5	34170	3	11	195000	214000
38	3	BLACK-FIN COMBI	TT	EXP	FBG	DV	IB	T550D	GM	14	5	34170	3	11	203500	224000
38	3	BLACK-FIN CONV	FB	SF	FBG	DV	IB	T485D	GM	14	5	35970	4		203500	224000
38	3	BLACK-FIN CONV	FB	SF	FBG	DV	IB	T550D	GM	14	5	35970	4		212500	233500
		1990 BOATS														
25	2	BLACK-FIN COMBI	OP	EXP	FBG	DV	OB			8	5	4200	2	5	22100	24600
25	2	BLACK-FIN COMBI	OP	EXP	FBG	DV	IB	315	CRUS	8	5	5200	2	5	21000	23300
25	2	BLACK-FIN COMBI	OP	EXP	FBG	DV	IB	300D		8	5	5200	2	5	29700	33300
25	2	BLACK-FIN FISHERMAN	OP	CUD	FBG	DV	OB			8	5	4200	2	5	22100	24600
25	2	BLACK-FIN FISHERMAN	OP	CUD	FBG	DV	IB	315	CRUS	8	5	5200	2	5	21500	23900
25	2	BLACK-FIN FISHERMAN	OP	CUD	FBG	DV	IB	300D		8	5	5200	2	5	30400	34100
27	9	BLACK-FIN COMBI	OP	EXP	FBG	DV	OB			10		7840	2	9	30800	34200
27	9	BLACK-FIN COMBI	OP	EXP	FBG	DV	IB	245	CRUS	10		8780	2	9	31000	34500
27	9	BLACK-FIN COMBI	OP	EXP	FBG	DV	IB	200D	VLVO	10		8780	2	9	40300	44800
27	9	BLACK-FIN COMBI	TT	EXP	FBG	DV	OB			10		7840	2	10	31600	35100
27	9	BLACK-FIN COMBI	TT	EXP	FBG	DV	IB	T245	CRUS	10		8780	2	10	34400	38200
27	9	BLACK-FIN COMBI	TT	EXP	FBG	DV	IB	T200D	VLVO	10		8780	2	10	47700	52400
27	9	BLACK-FIN FISHERMAN	OP	CTRCN	FBG	DV	OB			10		7840	2	10	30500	33800
27	9	BLACK-FIN FISHERMAN	OP	CTRCN	FBG	DV	IB	T245	CRUS	10		8780	2	10	36500	40600
27	9	BLACK-FIN FISHERMAN	OP	CTRCN	FBG	DV	IB	T200D	VLVO	10		8780	2	10	50600	55500
27	9	BLACK-FIN FISHERMAN	TT	CTRCN	FBG	DV	OB			10		7840	2	9	30600	34000
27	9	BLACK-FIN FISHERMAN	TT	CTRCN	FBG	DV	IB	T245	CRUS	10		8780	2	9	36500	40600
27	9	BLACK-FIN FISHERMAN	TT	CTRCN	FBG	DV	IB	T200D	VLVO	10		8780	2	9	50600	55600
29	4	BLACK-FIN COMBI	OP	EXP	FBG	DV	OB			10	6	9150	2	5	33400	37100
29	4	BLACK-FIN COMBI	OP	EXP	FBG	DV	IB	T245-T315		10	6	11120	2	5	41900	48500
29	4	BLACK-FIN COMBI	OP	EXP	FBG	DV	IB	T200D-T300D		10	6	11120	2	5	57700	70700
29	4	BLACK-FIN COMBI	TT	EXP	FBG	DV	OB			10	6	9150	2	5	33400	37100

CONTINUED ON NEXT PAGE

LOA FT	LOA IN	NAME AND/ OR MODEL	TOP/ RIG	BOAT TYPE	-HULL- MTL	-HULL- TP	ENGINE TP	ENGINE # HP	ENGINE MFG	BEAM FT	BEAM IN	WGT LBS	DRAFT FT	DRAFT IN	RETAIL LOW	RETAIL HIGH
		1990 BOATS														
29	4	BLACK-FIN COMBI	TT	EXP	FBG	DV	IB	T245-T315		10	6	11120	2	5	41900	48500
29	4	BLACK-FIN COMBI	TT	EXP	FBG	DV	IB	T200D-T300D		10	6	11120	2	5	57700	70700
29	4	BLACK-FIN SPORTFISH	FB	SF	FBG	DV	IB	T245-T315		10	6	11120	2	6	45700	52400
29	4	BLACK-FIN SPORTFISH	FB	SF	FBG	DV	IB	T200D-T300D		10	6	11120	2	6	62500	76500
31	9	BLACK-FIN COMBI	OP	EXP	FBG	DV	IB	T315	CRUS	12		13960	2	5	56800	62400
31	9	BLACK-FIN COMBI	OP	EXP	FBG	DV	IB	T300D		12		16515	2	5	83300	91500
31	9	BLACK-FIN COMBI	TT	EXP	FBG	DV	IB	T315	CRUS	12		13960	2	5	56800	62400
31	9	BLACK-FIN COMBI	TT	EXP	FBG	DV	IB	T300D		12		16515	2	5	83300	91500
31	9	BLACK-FIN FLYBRIDGE	FB	SF	FBG	DV	IB	T315	CRUS	11	11	15460	2	5	64700	71100
31	9	BLACK-FIN FLYBRIDGE	FB	SF	FBG	DV	IB	T300D-T375D		11	11	17815	2	5	96800	112000
38		BLACK-FIN COMBI	OP	EXP	FBG	DV	IB	T375D	CAT	14		29600	5	1	159000	174500
38		BLACK-FIN COMBI	OP	EXP	FBG	DV	IB	T485D	GM	14		29600	5	1	167000	183500
38		BLACK-FIN COMBI	OP	EXP	FBG	DV	IB	T550D	GM	14		29600	5	1	175000	192500
38		BLACK-FIN COMBI	TT	EXP	FBG	DV	IB	T425D	CAT	14		29600	5	1	165000	181000
38		BLACK-FIN COMBI	TT	EXP	FBG	DV	IB	T485D	GM	14		29600	5	1	167000	184000
38		BLACK-FIN COMBI	TT	EXP	FBG	DV	IB	T550D	GM	14		29600	5	1	175500	193000
38		BLACK-FIN CONV	FB	SF	FBG	DV	IB	T425D	CAT	14		32400	5	1	177500	195000
38		BLACK-FIN CONV	FB	SF	FBG	DV	IB	T485D	GM	14		32400	5	1	180000	197500
38		BLACK-FIN CONV	FB	SF	FBG	DV	IB	T550D	GM	14		32400	5	1	188000	207000
		1989 BOATS														
27	9	BLACK-FIN COMBI	OP	EXP	FBG	DV	OB			10		7840	2	9	29700	33000
27	9	BLACK-FIN COMBI	OP	EXP	FBG	DV	IB	245	CRUS	10		7840	2	9	27600	30700
27	9	BLACK-FIN COMBI	OP	EXP	FBG	DV	IB	200D	VLVO	10		8780	2	9	38600	42900
27	9	BLACK-FIN COMBI	TT	EXP	FBG	DV	OB			10		7840	2	10	30400	33700
27	9	BLACK-FIN COMBI	TT	EXP	FBG	DV	IB	T245	CRUS	10		7840	2	10	31000	34400
27	9	BLACK-FIN COMBI	TT	EXP	FBG	DV	IB	T200D	VLVO	10		8780	2	10	45700	50200
27	9	BLACK-FIN FISHERMAN	OP	CTRCN	FBG	DV	OB			10		7840	2	10	29400	32700
27	9	BLACK-FIN FISHERMAN	OP	CTRCN	FBG	DV	IB	T245	CRUS	10		7840	2	10	32900	36600
27	9	BLACK-FIN FISHERMAN	OP	CTRCN	FBG	DV	IB	T200D	VLVO	10		8780	2	10	48300	53100
27	9	BLACK-FIN FISHERMAN	TT	CTRCN	FBG	DV	OB			10		7840	2	9	29500	32800
27	9	BLACK-FIN FISHERMAN	TT	CTRCN	FBG	DV	IB	T245	CRUS	10		7840	2	9	32900	36600
27	9	BLACK-FIN FISHERMAN	TT	CTRCN	FBG	DV	IB	T200D	VLVO	10		8780	2	9	48300	53100
29	4	BLACK-FIN COMBI	OP	EXP	FBG	DV	OB			10	6	9150	2	5	32300	35900
29	4	BLACK-FIN COMBI	OP	EXP	FBG	DV	IB	T245-T315		10	6	9150	2	5	36800	42900
29	4	BLACK-FIN COMBI	OP	EXP	FBG	DV	IB	T200D	VLVO	10	6	11120	2	5	55200	60700
29	4	BLACK-FIN COMBI	TT	EXP	FBG	DV	OB			10	6	9150	2	5	32300	35900
29	4	BLACK-FIN COMBI	TT	EXP	FBG	DV	IB	T245-T315		10	6	9150	2	5	36800	42900
29	4	BLACK-FIN COMBI	TT	EXP	FBG	DV	IB	T200D	VLVO	10	6	11120	2	5	55200	60700
29	4	BLACK-FIN SPORTFISH	FB	SF	FBG	DV	IB	T245-T315		10	6	10150	2	6	41400	48200
29	4	BLACK-FIN SPORTFISH	FB	SF	FBG	DV	IB	T200D	VLVO	10	6	12120	2	6	63500	69800
31	9	BLACK-FIN COMBI	OP	EXP	FBG	DV	IB	T315	CRUS	11	11	13960	2	5	54000	59300
31	9	BLACK-FIN COMBI	OP	EXP	FBG	DV	IB	T300D	GM	11	11	16515	2	8	79600	87400
31	9	BLACK-FIN COMBI	TT	EXP	FBG	DV	IB	T315	CRUS	11	11	13960	2	5	54000	59300
31	9	BLACK-FIN COMBI	TT	EXP	FBG	DV	IB	T300D	GM	11	11	16515	2	8	79600	87400
31	9	BLACK-FIN FLYBRIDGE	FB	SF	FBG	DV	IB	T315	CRUS	11	11	15460	2	5	61600	67700
31	9	BLACK-FIN FLYBRIDGE	FB	SF	FBG	DV	IB	T300D-T375D		11	11	17815	2	8	92600	107500
38		BLACK-FIN COMBI	OP	EXP	FBG	DV	IB	T375D	CAT	14		28000	5	1	145500	160000
38		BLACK-FIN COMBI	OP	EXP	FBG	DV	IB	T485D	GM	14		28000	5	1	153500	168500
38		BLACK-FIN COMBI	OP	EXP	FBG	DV	IB	T550D	GM	14		25000	3	11	149500	164500
38		BLACK-FIN COMBI	TT	EXP	FBG	DV	IB	T375D	CAT	14		28000	5	1	146000	160000
38		BLACK-FIN COMBI	TT	EXP	FBG	DV	IB	T485D	GM	14		28000	5	1	153500	169000
38		BLACK-FIN COMBI	TT	EXP	FBG	DV	IB	T550D	GM	14		25000	3	11	150000	165000
38		BLACK-FIN CONV	FB	SF	FBG	DV	IB	T375D	CAT	14		29800	5	1	154000	169000
38		BLACK-FIN CONV	FB	SF	FBG	DV	IB	T485D	GM	14		29800	5	1	162000	178000
38		BLACK-FIN CONV	FB	SF	FBG	DV	IB	T550D	GM	14		26800	3	11	158000	174000
		1988 BOATS														
27	9	BLACK-FIN COMBI	OP	CTRCN	FBG	DV	OB			10		7840	2	9	28500	31700
27	9	BLACK-FIN COMBI	OP	CTRCN	FBG	DV	IB	245	CRUS	10		7840	2	9	26400	29300
27	9	BLACK-FIN COMBI	OP	CTRCN	FBG	DV	IB	200D	VLVO	10		8780	2	5	37000	41100
27	9	BLACK-FIN COMBI	TT	CTRCN	FBG	DV	OB			10		7840	2	10	30100	33500
27	9	BLACK-FIN COMBI	TT	CTRCN	FBG	DV	IB	T245	CRUS	10		7840	2	10	29700	33000
27	9	BLACK-FIN COMBI	TT	CTRCN	FBG	DV	IB	T200D	VLVO	10		8780	2	5	43500	48300
27	9	BLACK-FIN FISHERMAN	OP	CTRCN	FBG	DV	OB			10		7840	2	10	28500	31700
27	9	BLACK-FIN FISHERMAN	OP	CTRCN	FBG	DV	IB	T245	CRUS	10		7840	2	10	31400	34900
27	9	BLACK-FIN FISHERMAN	OP	CTRCN	FBG	DV	IB	T200D	VLVO	10		8780	2	5	46500	51100
27	9	BLACK-FIN FISHERMAN	TT	CTRCN	FBG	DV	OB			10		7840	2	9	27000	30000
27	9	BLACK-FIN FISHERMAN	TT	CTRCN	FBG	DV	IB	T245	CRUS	10		7840	2	9	31200	34600
27	9	BLACK-FIN FISHERMAN	TT	CTRCN	FBG	DV	IB	T200D	VLVO	10		8780	2	5	46300	50900
29	4	BLACK-FIN COMBI	OP	FSH	FBG	DV	OB			10	6	9150	2	5	31400	34800
29	4	BLACK-FIN COMBI	OP	FSH	FBG	DV	IB	T245-T315		10	6	9150	2	5	35100	41000
29	4	BLACK-FIN COMBI	OP	FSH	FBG	DV	IB	T200D	VLVO	10	6	11120	2	8	52900	58200
29	4	BLACK-FIN COMBI	TT	FSH	FBG	DV	OB			10	6	9150	2	5	31400	34900
29	4	BLACK-FIN COMBI	TT	FSH	FBG	DV	IB	T245-T315		10	6	9150	2	5	35100	41000
29	4	BLACK-FIN COMBI	TT	FSH	FBG	DV	IB	T200D	VLVO	10	6	11120	2	8	52900	58200
29	4	BLACK-FIN SPORTFISH	FB	SF	FBG	DV	IB	T245-T315		10	6	10150	2	6	39500	45900
29	4	BLACK-FIN SPORTFISH	FB	SF	FBG	DV	IB	T200D	VLVO	10	6	12120	2	9	60800	66800
31	9	BLACK-FIN FLYBRIDGE	FB	SF	FBG	DV	IB	T315	CRUS	11	11	15460	2	5	58700	64500
31	9	BLACK-FIN FLYBRIDGE	FB	SF	FBG	DV	IB	T300D-T375D		11	11	17815	2	8	88600	102500
36	4	BLACK-FIN COMBI	OP	SF	FBG	DV	IB	T315	CRUS	14		27500	3	11	95100	104500
36	4	BLACK-FIN COMBI	OP	SF	FBG	DV	IB	T375D	CAT	14		27500	3	11	119500	131000
36	4	BLACK-FIN COMBI	OP	SF	FBG	DV	IB	T450D	GM	14		27500	3	11	123000	135500
36	4	BLACK-FIN CONV	FB	CNV	FBG	DV	IB	T315	CRUS	14		28400	3	11	102000	112500
36	4	BLACK-FIN CONV	FB	CNV	FBG	DV	IB	T375D	CAT	14		28400	3	11	129500	142500
36	4	BLACK-FIN CONV	FB	CNV	FBG	DV	IB	T485D	GM	14		28400	3	11	137500	151000
		1987 BOATS														
27	9	BLACK-FIN COMBI	OP	CTRCN	FBG	DV	OB			10		7840	2	9	28500	31700
27	9	BLACK-FIN COMBI	OP	CTRCN	FBG	DV	IB	T245	CRUS	10		8780	2	5	29800	33100
27	9	BLACK-FIN COMBI	TT	CTRCN	FBG	DV	OB			10		7840	2	9	27700	30800
27	9	BLACK-FIN COMBI	TT	CTRCN	FBG	DV	IB	T245	CRUS	10		8780	2	5	30000	33300
27	9	BLACK-FIN COMBO	OP	CTRCN	FBG	DV	IB	T200D	VLVO	10		8780	2	9	44300	49200
27	9	BLACK-FIN FISHERMAN	OP	CTRCN	FBG	DV	OB			10		7840	2	9	26800	29800
27	9	BLACK-FIN FISHERMAN	OP	CTRCN	FBG	DV	IB	T245	CRUS	10		8780	2	5	31600	35100
27	9	BLACK-FIN FISHERMAN	OP	CTRCN	FBG	DV	IB	T200D	VLVO	10		8780	2	5	43800	48700
27	9	BLACK-FIN FISHERMAN	TT	CTRCN	FBG	DV	OB			10		7840	2	9	27700	30800
27	9	BLACK-FIN FISHERMAN	TT	CTRCN	FBG	DV	IB	T245	CRUS	10		8780	2	5	31400	34900
29	4	BLACK-FIN 29 SF	FB	SF	FBG	DV	IB	T245-T315		10	6	10150	2	6	37600	43800
29	4	BLACK-FIN 29 SF	FB	SF	FBG	DV	IB	T200D	VLVO	10	6	12120	2	9	58200	64000
29	4	BLACK-FIN 29 SF	TT	SF	FBG	DV	IB	T245-T315		10	6	10150	2	6	37600	43700
29	4	BLACK-FIN 29 SF	TT	SF	FBG	DV	IB	T200D	VLVO	10	6	12120	2	9	58200	63900
29	4	BLACK-FIN COMBI	OP	FSH	FBG	DV	OB			10	6	9150	2	4	30500	33800
29	4	BLACK-FIN COMBI	OP	FSH	FBG	DV	IB	T245-T315		10	6	9150	2	4	33500	39100
29	4	BLACK-FIN COMBI	OP	FSH	FBG	DV	IB	T200D	VLVO	10	6	11120	2	8	50700	55700
29	4	BLACK-FIN COMBI	TT	FSH	FBG	DV	OB			10	6	9150	2	4	30500	33900
29	4	BLACK-FIN COMBI	TT	FSH	FBG	DV	IB	T245-T315		10	6	9150	2	4	33500	39100
29	4	BLACK-FIN COMBI	TT	FSH	FBG	DV	IB	T200D	VLVO	10	6	11120	2	8	50700	55700
31	9	BLACK-FIN	F+T	FSH	FBG	DV	IB	T320D-T375D		11	11	17815	2	8	86200	98500
31	9	BLACK-FIN	FB	SF	FBG	DV	IB	T315	CRUS	11	11	15460	2	5	55900	61500
31	9	BLACK-FIN	FB	SF	FBG	DV	IB	T300D-T375D		11	11	17815	2	8	84800	98400
31	9	BLACK-FIN	F+T	SF	FBG	DV	IB	T315	CRUS	11	11	15460	2	5	55900	61500
36	2	BLACK-FIN COMBI	OP	FSH	FBG	DV	IB	T315	CRUS	14	2	26000	4	1	85000	93400
36	2	BLACK-FIN COMBI	OP	SF	FBG	DV	IB	T375D	CAT	14	2	26000	4	1	107500	118500
36	2	BLACK-FIN COMBI	OP	SF	FBG	DV	IB	T485D	GM	14	2	26000	4	1	114000	125500
36	4	BLACK-FIN	FB	CNV	FBG	DV	IB	T315	CRUS	14		28400	3	11	97800	107500
36	4	BLACK-FIN	FB	CNV	FBG	DV	IB	T375D	CAT	14		28400	3	11	124000	136000
36	4	BLACK-FIN	FB	CNV	FBG	DV	IB	T485D	GM	14		28400	3	11	131500	144500
		1986 BOATS														
27	9	BLACK-FIN COMBI	OP	CTRCN	FBG	DV	OB			10		7840	2	9	27600	30700
27	9	BLACK-FIN COMBI	OP	CTRCN	FBG	DV	SE	T205	OMC	10		8780	2	9	27400	30500
27	9	BLACK-FIN COMBI	OP	CTRCN	FBG	DV	IB	T245	CRUS	10		8780	2	9	28900	32100
27	9	BLACK-FIN COMBI	OP	CTRCN	FBG	DV	IB	T165D-T240D		10		8780		2	38600	47700
27	9	BLACK-FIN COMBI	TT	CTRCN	FBG	DV	OB			10		7840	2	9	27500	30600
27	9	BLACK-FIN COMBI	TT	CTRCN	FBG	DV	IB	165D	VLVO	10		8780	2	9	33100	36800
27	9	BLACK-FIN COMBI	TT	CTRCN	FBG	DV	SE	T205	OMC	10		8780	2	9	27400	30400
27	9	BLACK-FIN COMBI	TT	CTRCN	FBG	DV	IB	T245	CRUS	10		8780	2	9	28800	32000
27	9	BLACK-FIN COMBI	TT	CTRCN	FBG	DV	IB	T240D	GM	10		8780	2	9	42900	47700
27	9	BLACK-FIN FISHERMAN	OP	CTRCN	FBG	DV	OB			10		7840	2	9	26300	29200
27	9	BLACK-FIN FISHERMAN	OP	CTRCN	FBG	DV	SE	T205	OMC	10		8780	2	9	26500	29500
27	9	BLACK-FIN FISHERMAN	OP	CTRCN	FBG	DV	IB	T245	CRUS	10		8780	2	9	29600	32900
27	9	BLACK-FIN FISHERMAN	OP	CTRCN	FBG	DV	IB	T165D-T240D		10		8780		2	39900	49600
27	9	BLACK-FIN FISHERMAN	TT	CTRCN	FBG	DV	OB			10		7840	2	9	26500	29400
27	9	BLACK-FIN FISHERMAN	TT	CTRCN	FBG	DV	SE	T205	OMC	10		8780	2	9	26600	29600
27	9	BLACK-FIN FISHERMAN	TT	CTRCN	FBG	DV	IB	T245	CRUS	10		8780	2	9	29700	33000
27	9	BLACK-FIN FISHERMAN	TT	CTRCN	FBG	DV	IB	T165D-T240D		10		8780	2	9	40500	49600
29	4	BLACK-FIN 29 SF	FB	SF	FBG	DV	IB	T245-T315		10	6	9150	2	5	34500	40300
29	4	BLACK-FIN 29 SF	FB	SF	FBG	DV	IB	T165D-T240D		10	6	11120	2	8	50700	60600
29	4	BLACK-FIN 29 SF	TT	SF	FBG	DV	IB	T245-T315		10	6	9150	2	5	34500	40200
29	4	BLACK-FIN 29 SF	TT	SF	FBG	DV	IB	T165D-T240D		10	6	11120	2	8	50700	60600
29	4	BLACK-FIN COMBI	OP	FSH	FBG	DV	OB			10	6	9150	2	5	29600	32900
29	4	BLACK-FIN COMBI	OP	FSH	FBG	DV	IB	T245-T360		10	6	9150	2	5	32000	38300
29	4	BLACK-FIN COMBI	OP	FSH	FBG	DV	IB	T240D	GM	10	6	11120	2	8	51100	56100
29	4	BLACK-FIN COMBI	TT	FSH	FBG	DV	OB			10	6	9150	2	5	29700	33100
29	4	BLACK-FIN COMBI	TT	FSH	FBG	DV	IB	T245-T360		10	6	9150	2	5	32000	38300
29	4	BLACK-FIN COMBI	TT	FSH	FBG	DV	IB	T240D	GM	10	6	11120	2	8	51100	56100
31	9	BLACK-FIN	FB	SF	FBG	DV	IB	T315-T360		11	11	15460	2	5	53400	60000
31	9	BLACK-FIN	FB	SF	FBG	DV	IB	T240D-T375D		11	11	17815	2	5	78300	94300
31	9	BLACK-FIN	F+T	SF	FBG	DV	IB	T315-T360		11	11	15460	2	8	53400	60000
31	9	BLACK-FIN	F+T	SF	FBG	DV	IB	T240D-T375D		11	11	17815		2	78300	94300

CONTINUED ON NEXT PAGE

LOA FT	IN	NAME AND/ OR MODEL	TOP/ RIG	BOAT TYPE	-HULL- MTL	TP	ENGINE TP	# HP	MFG	BEAM FT	IN	WGT LBS	DRAFT FT	IN	RETAIL LOW	RETAIL HIGH
		1986 BOATS														
36	2	BLACK-FIN	OP	SF	FBG	DV	IB	T315	CRUS	14	2	26000	4	1	84800	93200
36	2	BLACK-FIN	OP	SF	FBG	DV	IB	T375D	CAT	14	2	26000	4	1	107500	118000
36	2	BLACK-FIN	OP	SF	FBG	DV	IB	T450D	GM	14	2	26000	4	1	111000	122000
39		BLACK-FIN 39		SF	FBG	SV	IB	T350D		14	4	32000			141500	155500
		1985 BOATS														
25	2	BLACK-FIN FISHERMAN	OP	SF	FBG	DV	IB	T165		8		6145	2	9	19400	21600
27	8	BLACK-FIN 27	OP	CTRCN	FBG	DV	OB			9	9				26100	29000
27	8	BLACK-FIN 27	OP	CTRCN	FBG	DV	SE	T205	OMC	9	9	6820			26100	29000
27	8	BLACK-FIN 27	OP	CTRCN	FBG	DV	IB	T245	CRUS	9	9	7800			27000	30000
27	8	BLACK-FIN 27	OP	CTRCN	FBG	DV	IB	T165D	VLVO	9	9	7800			35600	39500
27	8	BLACK-FIN 27	TT	CTRCN	FBG	DV	OB			9	9				26100	29000
27	8	BLACK-FIN 27	TT	CTRCN	FBG	DV	SE	T205	OMC	9	9	6820			26100	29000
27	8	BLACK-FIN 27	TT	CTRCN	FBG	DV	IB	T245	CRUS	9	9	7800			27000	30000
27	8	BLACK-FIN 27	TT	CTRCN	FBG	DV	IB	T165D	VLVO	9	9	7800			35600	39500
27	8	BLACK-FIN COMBI	OP	CTRCN	FBG	DV	OB			9	9	7840	2	9	26700	29700
27	8	BLACK-FIN COMBI	OP	CTRCN	FBG	DV	SE	T205	OMC	9	9	8780	2	9	26500	29500
27	8	BLACK-FIN COMBI	OP	CTRCN	FBG	DV	IB	T245-T315		9	9	8780	2	9	27500	31900
27	8	BLACK-FIN COMBI	OP	CTRCN	FBG	DV	IB	T165D	VLVO	9	9	8780	2	9	37000	41100
27	8	BLACK-FIN COMBI	TT	CTRCN	FBG	DV	OB			9	9	7840	2	9	26100	29000
27	8	BLACK-FIN COMBI	TT	CTRCN	FBG	DV	SE	T205	OMC	9	9	8780	2	9	26500	29400
27	8	BLACK-FIN COMBI	TT	CTRCN	FBG	DV	IB	T245-T315		9	9	8780	2	9	27400	31800
27	8	BLACK-FIN COMBI	TT	CTRCN	FBG	DV	IB	T165D	VLVO	9	9	8780	2	9	36900	41000
27	8	BLACK-FIN FISHERMAN	OP	CTRCN	FBG	DV	OB			9	9	7840	2	9	25500	28300
27	8	BLACK-FIN FISHERMAN	OP	CTRCN	FBG	DV	SE	T205	OMC	9	9	8780	2	9	25700	28500
27	8	BLACK-FIN FISHERMAN	OP	CTRCN	FBG	DV	IB	T245-T315		9	9	8780	2	9	28100	32700
27	8	BLACK-FIN FISHERMAN	OP	CTRCN	FBG	DV	IB	T165D	VLVO	9	9	8780	2	9	38100	42400
27	8	BLACK-FIN FISHERMAN	TT	CTRCN	FBG	DV	OB			9	9	7840	2	9	26100	29000
27	8	BLACK-FIN FISHERMAN	TT	CTRCN	FBG	DV	SE	T205	OMC	9	9	8780	2	9	25700	28600
27	8	BLACK-FIN FISHERMAN	TT	CTRCN	FBG	DV	IB	T245-T315		9	9	8780	2	9	28200	32800
27	8	BLACK-FIN FISHERMAN	TT	CTRCN	FBG	DV	IB	T165D	VLVO	9	9	8780	2	9	38200	42500
29	4	BLACK-FIN 29	OP	FSH	FBG	DV	OB			10	6				28900	32100
29	4	BLACK-FIN 29	OP	FSH	FBG	DV	SE	T205	OMC	10	6	9150	2	7	29200	32400
29	4	BLACK-FIN 29	OP	FSH	FBG	DV	IB	T245-T390		10	6	9150	2	5	33000	40500
29	4	BLACK-FIN 29	OP	FSH	FBG	DV	IB	T165D-T250D		10	6	11120	2	8	48700	58800
29	4	BLACK-FIN 29	TT	FSH	FBG	DV	OB			10	6	8400			29000	32300
29	4	BLACK-FIN 29	TT	FSH	FBG	DV	SE	T205	OMC	10	6	9150	2	7	29000	32300
29	4	BLACK-FIN 29	TT	FSH	FBG	DV	IB	T245-T390		10	6	9150	2	5	33000	40500
29	4	BLACK-FIN 29	TT	FSH	FBG	DV	IB	T165D-T250D		10	6	11120	2	8	48700	58200
29	4	BLACK-FIN COMBI	OP	FSH	FBG	DV	OB			10	6				28900	32100
29	4	BLACK-FIN COMBI	OP	FSH	FBG	DV	SE	T205	OMC	10	6	9150	2	7	28600	31700
29	4	BLACK-FIN COMBI	OP	FSH	FBG	DV	IB	T245-T315		10	6	8400	2	7	29600	34600
29	4	BLACK-FIN COMBI	OP	FSH	FBG	DV	IB	T165D	VLVO	10	6	9650	2	10	40500	45000
29	4	BLACK-FIN COMBI	OP	FSH	FBG	DV	IB	T250D	VLVO	10	6	11120	2	8	48500	53300
29	4	BLACK-FIN COMBI	TT	FSH	FBG	DV	OB			10	6				29000	32300
29	4	BLACK-FIN COMBI	TT	FSH	FBG	DV	SE	T205	OMC	10	6	8400	2	7	29000	32300
29	4	BLACK-FIN COMBI	TT	FSH	FBG	DV	IB	T245-T315		10	6	8400	2	10	29600	34600
29	4	BLACK-FIN COMBI	TT	FSH	FBG	DV	IB	T165D-T250D		10	6	9650	2	10	40500	49600
31	9	BLACK-FIN	FB	SF	FBG	DV	IB	T315-T390		11	11	15450	2	5	51000	58300
31	9	BLACK-FIN	FB	SF	FBG	DV	IB	T250D-T300D		11	11	15450	2	5	68800	85900
31	9	BLACK-FIN	FB	SF	FBG	DV	IB	T355D	CAT	11	11	17815	2	8	81200	89200
31	9	BLACK-FIN	F+T	SF	FBG	DV	IB	T315-T410		11	11	15460	2	5	51000	58900
31	9	BLACK-FIN	F+T	SF	FBG	DV	IB	T250D	VLVO	11	11	13680	2	8	64000	70400
31	9	BLACK-FIN	F+T	SF	FBG	DV	IB	T300D-T355D		11	11	17815	2	8	78100	89200
39		BLACK-FIN	FB	SF	FBG	DV	IB	T350		14	4	32000			118500	130000
		IB T355D CAT 141000 155000, IB T355D CAT 139000 152500, IB T410D J&T													143000	157500
		IB T450D J&T 147000 161500, IB T450D J&T 145000 159000														
39		BLACK-FIN	F+T	SF	FBG	DV	IB	T355D	CAT	14	4	32640	3		141000	155000
39		BLACK-FIN	F+T	SF	FBG	DV	IB	T450D	J&T	14	4	32640	3		147000	161500
39		FREEPORT 39	F+T	SF	FBG	DV	IB	T355D	CAT	14	4	28600	3		127500	140000
39		FREEPORT 39	F+T	SF	FBG	DV	IB	T410D	J&T	14	4	28600	3		129500	142500
39		FREEPORT 39	F+T	SF	FBG	DV	IB	T450D	J&T	14	4	28600	3		133500	146500
		1984 BOATS														
25	2	BLACK-FIN COMBI	OP	SF	FBG	DV	OB			8		4500	2	9	19200	21400
25	2	BLACK-FIN COMBI	OP	SF	FBG	DV	IB	350	CRUS	8		5160	2	9	15900	18100
		IB 158D VLVO 19000 21100, IB T260 VLVO 20000 22200, IB T124D VLVO													26800	29800
25	2	BLACK-FIN COMBI	TT	SF	FBG	DV	OB			8		4500	2	9	19200	21400
25	2	BLACK-FIN COMBI	TT	SF	FBG	DV	IB	350	CRUS	8		5160	2	9	15900	18000
		IB 158D VLVO 19000 21100, IB T260 VLVO 20000 22200, IB T124D VLVO													26800	29800
25	2	BLACK-FIN FISHERMAN	OP	SF	FBG	DV	OB			8		4500	2	9	19200	21400
25	2	BLACK-FIN FISHERMAN	OP	SF	FBG	DV	IB	350	CRUS	8		5160	2	9	16000	18100
		IB 158D VLVO 19100 21200, IB T165-T260 18700 22400, IB T124D VLVO													27100	30100
25	2	BLACK-FIN FISHERMAN	TT	SF	FBG	DV	OB			8		4500	2	9	19200	21400
25	2	BLACK-FIN FISHERMAN	TT	SF	FBG	DV	IB	350	CRUS	8		5160	2	9	16000	18200
		IB 158D VLVO 19100 21300, IB T260 VLVO 20200 22400, IB T124D VLVO													27100	30100
29	4	BLACK-FIN	OP	FSH			IB	T270							33800	37500
29	4	BLACK-FIN	OP	FSH	FBG	DV	OB			10	6	6450			28100	31300
29	4	BLACK-FIN	OP	FSH	FBG	DV	SE	T205	OMC	10	6	8400	2	7	28100	31300
29	4	BLACK-FIN	OP	FSH	FBG	DV	IB	T245-T350		10	6	8400	2	7	30600	36800
		IB T410 MRCR 34600 38400, IBT158D-T235D 41700 50600, IB T300D CAT													50600	55600
29	4	BLACK-FIN	TT	FSH	FBG	DV	OB			10	6	6450			28400	31500
29	4	BLACK-FIN	TT	FSH	FBG	DV	SE	T205	OMC	10	6	8400	2	7	28400	31500
29	4	BLACK-FIN	TT	FSH	FBG	DV	IB	T245-T350		10	6	8400	2	10	30600	36800
		IB T410 MRCR 34600 38400, IBT158D-T235D 41700 50600, IB T300D CAT													50600	55600
31	9	BLACK-FIN	FB	SF	FBG	DV	IB	T315-T410		11	11	11640	2	8	45800	53000
31	9	BLACK-FIN	FB	SF	FBG	DV	IB	T235D-T355D		11	11	13680	2	8	60700	73900
31	9	BLACK-FIN	F+T	SF	FBG	DV	IB	T315-T410		11	11	11640	2	8	45800	53000
31	9	BLACK-FIN	F+T	SF	FBG	DV	IB	T235D-T355D		11	11	13680	2	8	60700	73900
32	6	BLACK-FIN COMBI	OP	SF	FBG	DV	OB			9	9	6500	2	8	37400	41600
32	6	BLACK-FIN COMBI	OP	SF	FBG	DV	SE	T205	OMC	9	9	8450	2	8	37600	41800
32	6	BLACK-FIN COMBI	OP	SF	FBG	DV	IB	T350-T410		9	9	8450	2	8	35300	40700
32	6	BLACK-FIN COMBI	OP	SF	FBG	DV	IB	T235D	VLVO	9	9	10470	2	8	47700	52400
32	6	BLACK-FIN COMBI	TT	SF	FBG	DV	OB			9	9	6500	2	8	37600	41700
32	6	BLACK-FIN COMBI	TT	SF	FBG	DV	SE	T205	OMC	9	9	8450	2	8	37700	41800
32	6	BLACK-FIN COMBI	TT	SF	FBG	DV	IB	T350-T410		9	9	8450	2	8	35500	40900
32	6	BLACK-FIN COMBI	TT	SF	FBG	DV	IB	T235D	VLVO	9	9	10470	2	8	48500	53300
39		BLACK-FIN	FB	SF	FBG	DV	IB	T355D	CAT	14	4	32000	3		133000	146000
39		BLACK-FIN	FB	SF	FBG	DV	IB	T450D	GM	14	4	32000	3		138000	151500
39		BLACK-FIN	F+T	SF	FBG	DV	IB	T355D	CAT	14	4	32000	3		133000	146000
39		BLACK-FIN	F+T	SF	FBG	DV	IB	T450D	GM	14	4	32000	3		138000	151500

....For earlier years, see the BUC Used Boat Price Guide, Volume 3

BLAKE BOAT WORKS

GLOUCESTER NC 28528

See inside cover to adjust price for area

LOA FT	IN	NAME AND/ OR MODEL	TOP/ RIG	BOAT TYPE	-HULL- MTL	TP	ENGINE TP	# HP	MFG	BEAM FT	IN	WGT LBS	DRAFT FT	IN	RETAIL LOW	RETAIL HIGH
		1985 BOATS														
25		GAFF SLOOP	SLP	SA/CR	WD	KL	IB	8D	YAN	8		5000	2	6	17200	19500
28		SKIPJACK	SLP	SA/CR	WD	KC	IB	17D	VLVO	10		7000	2	4	27200	30200
		1984 BOATS														
28		SKIPJACK	SLP	SA/CR	WD	KC	SD	17D	VLVO	10		7000	2	4	25600	28400

....For earlier years, see the BUC Used Boat Price Guide, Volume 3

BLUE FIN INDUSTRIES INC

DIV OF BRUNSWICK MARINE GROUP
NAPPANEE IN 46550 COAST GUARD MFG ID- BFF

See inside cover to adjust price for area

LOA FT	IN	NAME AND/ OR MODEL	TOP/ RIG	BOAT TYPE	-HULL- MTL	TP	ENGINE TP	# HP	MFG	BEAM FT	IN	WGT LBS	DRAFT FT	IN	RETAIL LOW	RETAIL HIGH
		1988 BOATS														
16	7	BASS DOMINATOR 1709	OP	BASS	AL	SV	OB			6	2	690			2800	3250
17	1	SPORTSMAN 1700	OP	RNBT	AL	SV	OB			6	4	960			3850	4500
18	10	SPORTSMAN 1900	OP	RNBT	AL	SV	OB			6	10	1090			4600	5300
18	10	SPORTSMAN 1950	OP	RNBT	AL	SV	IO	128		6	10	1582			4050	4750
		1987 BOATS														
17		FISH-N-SKI 7100	OP	FSH	AL	SV	OB			6	5	850			3350	3900
17		SPORTSMAN 7000	OP	RNBT	AL	SV	OB			6	5	830			3300	3800
19		SPORTSMAN 9000	OP	RNBT	AL	SV	OB			7	3	1100			4550	5200
19		SPORTSMAN 9100	OP	RNBT	AL	SV	IO	120	OMC	7	3	1800			4200	4850
		1986 BOATS														
16		BASS AVENGER 7200	OP	FSH	AL	DV	OB			7	5	680			2550	2950
16		PRO-JON	OP	JON	AL	FL	OB			5	9	272			1050	1250
16	1	LAKER	OP	UTL	AL	SV	OB			5	6	275			1000	1200
16	1	PRO-FISH	OP	UTL	AL	SV	OB			5	6	405			1500	1800
16	1	PROSPECTOR	OP	UTL	AL	SV	OB			5	6	365			1350	1600
16	2	SPORTSMAN	OP	RNBT	AL	DV	OB			6	4	758			2850	3300
16	2	SUPER-HAWK	OP	FSH	AL	DV	OB			6	4	758			2850	3300
17		S170 7000	OP	RNBT	AL	DV	OB			7	7	850			3250	3800
17		S170 7025	OP	UTL	AL	DV	OB			7	7	775			2900	3350
18	1	SPORTSMAN	OP	RNBT	AL	DV	OB			6	6	835			3350	3900

CONTINUED ON NEXT PAGE

LOA FT	LOA IN	NAME AND/ OR MODEL	TOP/ RIG	BOAT TYPE	HULL MTL	HULL TP	ENGINE TP	ENGINE # HP	ENGINE MFG	BEAM FT	BEAM IN	WGT LBS	DRAFT FT	DRAFT IN	RETAIL LOW	RETAIL HIGH
		1986 BOATS														
19		ROYALE SEA-KING	OP	RNBT	AL	DV	IO	120	MRCR	7	2	1535			3800	4450
19		ROYALE SPORTSMAN	OP	RNBT	AL	DV	OB			7	2	905			3700	4300
19		ROYALE SPORTSMAN	OP	RNBT	AL	DV	IO	120	MRCR	7	2	1535			3800	4450
19		ROYALE SUPER-HAWK	OP	RNBT	AL	DV	IO	120	MRCR	7	2	1535			3800	4450
19	1	ROYALE SEA-KING	OP	RNBT	AL	DV	OB			6	6	905			3700	4300
21	1	VICTORIAN	OP	CBNCR	AL	DV	OB			7	10	1540			7050	8100
21	1	VICTORIAN	OP	CBNCR	AL	DV	IO			7	10				**	**
21	1	VICTORIAN SEA-KING	OP	RNBT	AL	DV	OB			7	4	2100			9100	10300
21	1	VICTORIAN SEA-KING	OP	RNBT	AL	DV	IO	140	MRCR	7	4	2100			5700	6550
21	1	VICTORIAN SPORTSMAN	OP	RNBT	AL	DV	OB			7	4	1045			5050	5800
21	1	VICTORIAN SPORTSMAN	OP	RNBT	AL	DV	IO	140	MRCR	7	4	1655			5350	6150
		1985 BOATS														
16		PRO-JON	OP	JON	AL	FL	OB			5	9	272			1000	1200
16	1	LAKER	OP	UTL	AL	SV	OB			5	6	275			980	1150
16	1	PRO-FISH	OP	UTL	AL	SV	OB			5	6	405			1450	1750
16	1	PROSPECTOR	OP	UTL	AL	SV	OB			5	6	365			1300	1550
16	1	SEA-HAWK	OP	FSH	AL	SV	OB			5	7	595			2200	2550
16	2	SPORTSMAN	OP	RNBT	AL	DV	OB			6	4	758			2750	3200
16	2	SUPER-HAWK	OP	FSH	AL	DV	OB			6	4	758			2750	3200
18		ROYALE 6300	OP	RNBT	AL	DV	OB			7	2	905			3500	4050
18		ROYALE 6500	OP	RNBT	AL	DV	IO	120	MRCR	7	2	1535			3400	3950
18	1	SEA-KING	OP	RNBT	AL	DV	OB			6	6	905			3500	4050
18	1	SPORTSMAN	OP	RNBT	AL	DV	OB			6	6	835			3250	3800
18	1	SUPER-HAWK	OP	FSH	AL	DV	OB			6	6	835			3250	3800
21	1	ROYALE 6400	OP	RNBT	AL	DV	IO	140	MRCR	7	4	1655			5100	5900
21	1	ROYALE 6600	OP	RNBT	AL	DV	OB			7	4	1045			4900	5650
21	1	SEA-KING	OP	RNBT	AL	DV	OB			7	4	1600			7100	8150
21	1	SPORTSMAN	OP	RNBT	AL	DV	OB			7	4	1600			7100	8150
21	1	SUPER-HAWK	OP	FSH	AL	DV	OB			7	4	1600			7100	8150
21	1	VICTORIAN	OP	CBNCR	AL	DV	OB			7	10	1540			6850	7900
21	1	VICTORIAN	OP	CBNCR	AL	DV	IO			7	10				**	**
		1984 BOATS														
16		PRO-JON	OP	JON	AL	FL	OB			5	9	272			980	1150
16	1	LAKER	OP	UTL	AL	SV	OB			5	6	275			955	1150
16	1	PRO-FISH	OP	UTL	AL	SV	OB			5	6	405			1400	1700
16	1	SEA-HAWK	OP	FSH	AL	SV	OB			5	7	595			2150	2500
16	2	SPORTSMAN	OP	RNBT	AL	DV	OB			6	4	726			2600	3000
16	2	SUPER-HAWK	OP	FSH	AL	DV	OB			6	4	726			2600	3000
18		ROYALE 6300	OP	RNBT	AL	DV	OB			7	2	905			3400	3950
18		ROYALE 6500	OP	RNBT	AL	DV	IO	120	MRCR	7	2	1535			3300	3850
18	1	SEA-KING	OP	RNBT	AL	DV	OB			6	6	905			3400	4000
18	1	SPORTSMAN	OP	RNBT	AL	DV	OB			6	6	835			3200	3700
18	1	SUPER-HAWK	OP	FSH	AL	DV	OB			6	6	835			3150	3700
21	1	ROYALE 6400	OP	RNBT	AL	DV	IO	140	MRCR	7	4	1655			4950	5700
21	1	ROYALE 6600	OP	RNBT	AL	DV	OB			7	4	1045			4800	5550

....For earlier years, see the BUC Used Boat Price Guide, Volume 3

BLUE OCEAN HOLLAND YACHTS BV

AMSTERDAM HOLLAND 3111 See inside cover to adjust price for area

FORMERLY BLUE OCEAN SHIPYARD

LOA FT	LOA IN	NAME AND/ OR MODEL	TOP/ RIG	BOAT TYPE	HULL MTL	HULL TP	ENGINE TP	ENGINE # HP	ENGINE MFG	BEAM FT	BEAM IN	WGT LBS	DRAFT FT	DRAFT IN	RETAIL LOW	RETAIL HIGH
		1987 BOATS														
48		BLUE-OCEAN 48	SLP	SA/RC	AL	KL	IB	D							259500	285000
55		BLUE-OCEAN 55	SLP	SA/RC	AL	KL	IB	D		15	2	55600	7	7	420000	462000
55	7	BLUE-OCEAN 1800 W/O		MY	AL	DV	IB	D		17	7	52000	4	7	**	**
59	7	BLUE-OCEAN 1800 W/CP		MY	AL	DV	IB	D		17	7	52000	4	7	**	**
60		BLUE-OCEAN 60	SLP	SA/RC	AL	SK	IB	D		16	5	63400	12	11	646500	710500
62	3	BLUE-OCEAN 2000 W/O		MY	AL	DV	IB	D		19		64000	4	8	**	**
65		BLUE-OCEAN 65	SLP	SA/RC	AL	SK	IB	D		16	8	70070	12	11	744000	817500
65	6	BLUE-OCEAN 2200 W/O		MY	AL	DV	IB	760D		19		84875	4	10	635500	698500
66	2	BLUE-OCEAN 2000 W/CP		MY	AL	DV	IB	D		19		64000	4	8	**	**
70		BLUE-OCEAN 70	SLP	SA/RC	AL	KL	IB	D		16	8	52050	10	6	426000	468000
70		BLUE-OCEAN 70	SLP	SA/RC	AL	SK	IB	D		16	8	82300	12	11	726500	798500
72	2	BLUE-OCEAN 2200 W/CP		MY	AL	DV	IB	760D		19		84875	4	10	**	**
74		BLUE-OCEAN 2400 W/O		MY	AL	DV	IB	760D		19	8	98985	5		**	**
78	9	BLUE-OCEAN 2400 W/CP		MY	AL	DV	IB	760D		19	8	98985	5		**	**
		1986 BOATS														
55		BLUE-OCEAN 55	SLP	SA/RC	AL	KL	IB	D		15	2	55600	7	7	393000	432000
60		BLUE-OCEAN 60	SLP	SA/RC	AL	SK	IB	D		16	5	63400	12	11	605000	664500
65		BLUE-OCEAN 65	SLP	SA/RC	AL	SK	IB	D		16	8	70070	12	11	697000	766000
		1985 BOATS														
55		BLUE-OCEAN 55	SLP	SA/RC	AL	KL	IB	D		15	2	55600	7	7	367500	404000
60		BLUE-OCEAN 60	SLP	SA/RC	AL	SK	IB	D		16	5	63400	12	11	566000	622000
65		BLUE-OCEAN 65	SLP	SA/RC	AL	SK	IB	D		16	8	70070	12	11	653000	717500
70		BLUE-OCEAN 70	SLP	SA/RC	AL	KL	IB	D		16	8	52050	10	6	377000	414000
70		BLUE-OCEAN 70	SLP	SA/RC	AL	SK	IB	D		16	8	82300	12	11	642500	706500
		1984 BOATS														
55			SLP	SA/RC	AL	KL	IB	D		15	1	55600	7	5	344500	378500
60			SLP	SA/RC	AL	SK	IB	D		16	5	63400	6	7	530500	582500
65			SLP	SA/RC	AL	SK	IB	D		16	8	70100	6	7	612500	673000
70			SLP	SA/RC	AL	KL	IB	D		16	8	52050	10	6	354500	389500
70			SLP	SA/RC	AL	SK	IB	D		16	8	82300	6	7	604500	664500

BLUE SEA INDUSTRIAL CO LT

TAIPEI TAIWAN ROC See inside cover to adjust price for area

LOA FT	LOA IN	NAME AND/ OR MODEL	TOP/ RIG	BOAT TYPE	HULL MTL	HULL TP	ENGINE TP	ENGINE # HP	ENGINE MFG	BEAM FT	BEAM IN	WGT LBS	DRAFT FT	DRAFT IN	RETAIL LOW	RETAIL HIGH
		1986 BOATS														
41		BLUE-SEA 41		EXP	FBG	SV	IB	T165D		14		23000	6		91600	100500
41		BLUE-SEA 41 AC	CUT	SA/CR	FBG	KL	IB	D		14		26000	6		106000	116500
41		BLUE-SEA 41 PH	CUT	MS	FBG	KL	IB	D		14		27500	6	5	109500	120500
		1984 BOATS														
34	2	BLUE-SEA 34	SLP	SA/CR	FBG	KL	IB	30D	YAN	11		22600	5	6	75200	82700
34	2	BLUE-SEA 34	CUT	SA/CR	FBG	KL	IB	30D	YAN	11		22600	5	6	75200	82600
35	6	BLUE-SEA 36	FB	DC	FBG	DS	IB	T 90D	FORD	12	6	19800	3	6	71700	78800
35	6	BLUE-SEA 36	FB	DC	FBG	DS	IB	T120D	FORD	12	6	20600	3	6	73900	81200
35	6	BLUE-SEA 36	FB	SDN	FBG	DS	IB	120D		12	6	19000	3	6	67800	74500
35	6	BLUE-SEA 36	FB	SDN	FBG	DS	IB	T 90D	FORD	12	6	19800	3	6	70200	77100
35	6	BLUE-SEA 36	FB	SDN	FBG	DS	IB	T120D	FORD	12	6	20600	3	6	72400	79500
41		BLUE-SEA 41	CUT	SA/CR	FBG	KL	IB	51D	PERK	14		26000	6		93100	102500
41		BLUE-SEA 41 PH	CUT	SA/CR	FBG	KL	IB	61D	LEHM	14		26000	6		93700	103000
45	5	BLUE-SEA 46	KTH	MS	FBG	KL	IB	80D	FORD	13	9	34720	6		128500	141000

....For earlier years, see the BUC Used Boat Price Guide, Volume 3

BLUE WATER BOATS INC

SALEM OR 97302 COAST GUARD MFG ID- SRV See inside cover to adjust price for area

LOA FT	LOA IN	NAME AND/ OR MODEL	TOP/ RIG	BOAT TYPE	HULL MTL	HULL TP	ENGINE TP	ENGINE # HP	ENGINE MFG	BEAM FT	BEAM IN	WGT LBS	DRAFT FT	DRAFT IN	RETAIL LOW	RETAIL HIGH
		1996 BOATS														
16	2	BLAZER OPEN BOW	ST	RNBT	FBG	SV	IO	115	MRCR	6	9	1850			3500	4100
17	6	BLUE WATER 17	ST	W/T	AL	SV	OB			7	7	1100			4150	4850
17	6	BLUE WATER 17	ST	W/T	AL	SV	IO	115	MRCR	7	7	1700			4200	4900
17	11	FALCON	ST	RNBT	FBG	SV	IO	115-180		7	6	2100			4650	5400
18	3	EAGLE OPEN BOW	ST	RNBT	FBG	SV	IO	115-205		7	6	2175			4800	5650
18	6	EXECUTIVE OVERNIGHT	ST	OVNTR	FBG	SV	IO	115-205		8		2650			5750	6750
18	6	SPORTSMAN 190	OP	OPFSH	FBG	SV	OB			8		1650			5800	6700
19		RIVIERA SPORT	ST	RNBT	FBG	SV	IO	115-205		8	4	2300			5550	6500
19	6	BLUE WATER 19	ST	W/T	AL	SV	OB			8		1200			4800	5500
19	6	BLUE WATER 19	ST	W/T	AL	SV	IO	115-180		8		1800			5300	6250
20	2	MONTE CARLO CUDDY	ST	CUD	FBG	SV	IO	180-250		8		2915			7000	8400
20	2	MONTE CARLO OPEN BOW	ST	RNBT	FBG	SV	IO	180-250		8		2740			6450	7750
20	2	WEEKENDER 202	OP	WKNDR	FBG	SV	OB			8		2500			8550	9850
20	4	MIRAGE	ST	RNBT	FBG	SV	IO	180-250		7	3	2500			5850	7050
20	5	PRO-AM SKIER	ST	SKI	FBG	SV	IB	215	MRCR	7	1	2600			7050	8100
22		MARQUE	ST	CUD	FBG	SV	IO	205-250		8	6	4000			9800	11400
22		MARQUE OPEN BOW	ST	RNBT	FBG	SV	IO	205-250		8	6	3700			8900	10400
		1995 BOATS														
16	2	BLAZER OPEN BOW	ST	RNBT	FBG	SV	IO	145	MRCR	6	9	1850			3250	3800
16	2	HAWK	ST	RNBT	FBG	SV	IO	145	MRCR	6	9	1850			3600	4200
16	11	ASTRO	ST	RNBT	FBG	SV	OB			7	4	1500			5050	5800
16	11	ASTRO OPEN BOW	ST	RNBT	FBG	SV	IO	145-205		7	4	2180			4100	4850
17	5	FALCON	ST	RNBT	FBG	SV	IO	145	MRCR	6	9	2100			3950	4600
17	6	FISH & SKI 172	ST	W/T	AL	SV	OB			7	7	1100			3950	4600
17	6	FISH & SKI 172	ST	W/T	AL	SV	IO	145	MRCR	7	7	1700			3950	4600
18	3	EAGLE OPEN BOW	ST	RNBT	FBG	SV	IO	145-260		7	6	2175			4500	5600
18	6	EXECUTIVE OVERNIGHT	ST	OVNTR	FBG	SV	IO	145-260		8		2650			5400	6650
18	6	EXECUTIVE OVERNIGHT	ST	OVNTR	FBG	SV	IO	280	MRCR	8		2650			6000	6900
18	6	RIVIERA SPORT	ST	RNBT	FBG	SV	IO	145-205		7	1	2300			4550	5300
18	6	SPORTSMAN	ST	W/T	FBG	SV	OB			8		1650			5550	6350
19	6	FISH & SKI 102	ST	W/T	AL	SV	IO	205	MRCR	8		1900			5150	5900
19	6	FISH & SKI 192	ST	W/T	AL	SV	IO	145	MRCR	8		1800			4950	5700
19	6	PRO FISH 192	ST	W/T	AL	SV	OB			8		1200			4600	5250

LOA FT	LOA IN	NAME AND/ OR MODEL	TOP/ RIG	BOAT TYPE	-HULL- MTL	HULL TP	ENGINE TP	ENGINE # HP	ENGINE MFG	BEAM FT	BEAM IN	WGT LBS	DRAFT FT IN	RETAIL LOW	RETAIL HIGH
		1995 BOATS													
20	2	MONTE CARLO CUDDY	ST	CUD	FBG	SV	IO	205-260		8		2915		6500	7900
20	2	MONTE CARLO OPEN BOW	ST	RNBT	FBG	SV	IO	205-280		8		2740		6050	7500
20	2	WEEKENDER	ST	CUD	FBG	SV	OB			8		2450		8050	9300
20	4	MIRAGE	ST	RNBT	FBG	SV	IO	205-270		7	3	2500		5500	6750
20	5	PRO-AM SKIER	ST	SKI	FBG	SV	IB	260	MRCR	7	1	2600		6650	7650
22		MARQUE	ST	CUD	FBG	SV	IO	230-280		8	6	4000		9250	11000
22		MARQUE OPEN BOW	ST	RNBT	FBG	SV	IO	230-280		8	6	3700		8300	9950
22		MARQUE OPEN BOW	ST	RNBT	FBG	SV	IO	330	MRCR	8	6	3700		9500	10800
		1994 BOATS													
16	2	BLAZER OPEN BOW	ST	RNBT	FBG	SV	IO	130-145		6	9	1850		3100	3600
16	2	HAWK	ST	RNBT	FBG	SV	IO	130-145		6	9	1850		3250	3800
16	11	ASTRO	ST	RNBT	FBG	SV	OB			7	4	1500		4850	5550
16	11	ASTRO OPEN BOW	ST	RNBT	FBG	SV	IO	130-205		7	4	2180		3800	4550
17	5	FALCON	ST	RNBT	FBG	SV	IO	145	MRCR	6	9	2100		3700	4300
17	6	BLUEWATER 17	ST	W/T	AL	SV	OB			7	7	1100		3750	4400
17	6	BLUEWATER 17	ST	W/T	AL	SV	IO	145	MRCR	7	7	1700		3700	4300
18		RIVIERA SPORT	ST	RNBT	FBG	SV	IO	145-205		7	1	2300		4050	4850
18	3	EAGLE OPEN BOW	ST	RNBT	FBG	SV	IO	145-230		7	6	2175		4150	5050
18	3	EAGLE OPEN BOW	ST	RNBT	FBG	SV	IO	260	MRCR	7	6	2175		4550	5250
18	6	EXECUTIVE CUDDY II	ST	CUD	FBG	SV	IO	145-260		8		2630		5050	6200
18	6	EXECUTIVE CUDDY II	ST	CUD	FBG	SV	IO	280	MRCR	8		2630		5600	6450
18	6	EXECUTIVE OPEN BOW	ST	RNBT	FBG	SV	IO	145-260		8		2300		4550	5650
18	6	EXECUTIVE OPEN BOW	ST	RNBT	FBG	SV	IO	270	MRCR	8		2300		5000	5750
18	6	EXECUTIVE OVERNIGHT	ST	OVNTR	FBG	SV	IO	145-260		8		2650		5050	6200
18	6	EXECUTIVE OVERNIGHT	ST	OVNTR	FBG	SV	IO	280	MRCR	8		2650		5600	6400
19	6	BLUEWATER 19	ST	W/T	AL	SV	OB			8		1200		4350	5000
19	6	BLUEWATER 19	ST	W/T	AL	SV	IO	145-205		8		1800		4600	5500
20	2	MONTE CARLO CUDDY	ST	CUD	FBG	SV	IO	205-260		8		2915		6100	7300
20	2	MONTE CARLO OPEN BOW	ST	RNBT	FBG	SV	IO	205-280		8		2740		5650	7000
20	4	MIRAGE	ST	RNBT	FBG	SV	IO	205-270		7	3	2500		5150	6300
20	5	PRO-AM SKIER	ST	SKI	FBG	SV	IB	260	MRCR	7	1	2600		6300	7200
22		MARQUE	ST	CUD	FBG	SV	IO	230-280		8	6	4000		8550	10200
22		MARQUE OPEN BOW	ST	RNBT	FBG	SV	IO	230-280		8	6	3700		7800	9350
22		MARQUE OPEN BOW	ST	RNBT	FBG	SV	IO	330	MRCR	8	6	3700		8850	10100
		1993 BOATS													
16	2	BLAZER	ST	RNBT	FBG	SV	OB			6	9	1000		3200	3750
16	2	BLAZER OPEN BOW	ST	RNBT	FBG	SV	IO	130-145		6	9	1850		2900	3400
16	2	HAWK 170	ST	RNBT	FBG	DV	IO	130	MRCR	6	9	1850		3000	3500
16	2	HAWK 170	ST	RNBT	FBG	SV	IO	145	MRCR	6	9	1850		3000	3500
16	11	ASTRO	ST	RNBT	FBG	SV	OB			7	4	1500		4600	5300
16	11	ASTRO OPEN BOW	ST	RNBT	FBG	SV	IO	130-205		7	4	2180		3550	4250
18		RIVIERA SPORT	ST	RNBT	FBG	SV	IO	145-205		7	1	2300		3800	4550
18	3	EAGLE OPEN BOW	ST	RNBT	FBG	SV	IO	145-230		7	6	2175		3900	4700
18	3	EAGLE OPEN BOW	ST	RNBT	FBG	SV	IO	260	MRCR	7	6	2175		4200	4900
18	6	EXECUTIVE CUDDY II	ST	CUD	FBG	SV	IO	145-260		8		2630		4700	5800
18	6	EXECUTIVE CUDDY II	ST	CUD	FBG	SV	IO	270	MRCR	8		2630		5150	5900
18	6	EXECUTIVE OVERNIGHT	ST	OVNTR	FBG	SV	IO	145-260		8		2650		4700	5800
18	6	EXECUTIVE OVERNIGHT	ST	OVNTR	FBG	SV	IO	270	MRCR	8		2650		5150	5900
18	6	SABRE 200	ST	RNBT	FBG	SV	IO	145-230		8		2300		4200	5100
18	6	SABRE 200	ST	RNBT	FBG	SV	IO	260-270		8		2300		4600	5350
20	1	PRO-AM SKIER	ST	SKI	FBG	SV	IB	260	MRCR	7	2	2300		5500	6300
20	2	MONTE CARLO CUDDY	ST	CUD	FBG	SV	IO	175-260		8		2915		5600	6850
20	2	MONTE CARLO OPEN BOW	ST	RNBT	FBG	SV	IO	175-270		8		2740		5200	6450
20	4	MIRAGE	ST	RNBT	FBG	SV	IO	175-270		7	3	2500		4750	5900
22		MARQUE	ST	CUD	FBG	SV	IO	230-270		8	6	4000		8000	9500
		1992 BOATS													
16	2	BLAZER OPEN BOW	ST	RNBT	FBG	SV	IO	130-145		6	9	1850		2750	3250
16	2	BLAZER OUTBOARD	ST	RNBT	FBG	SV	OB			6	9	1000		3050	3550
16	11	ASTRO OPEN BOW	ST	RNBT	FBG	SV	IO	130-205		7	4	2180		3300	3950
16	11	ASTRO OUTBOARD	ST	RNBT	FBG	SV	OB			7	4	1500		4450	5100
18		RIVIERA SPORT	ST	RNBT	FBG	SV	IO	130-205		7	1	2300		3550	4250
18	3	EAGLE OPEN BOW	ST	RNBT	FBG	SV	IO	130-230		7	6	2175		3650	4400
18	3	EAGLE OPEN BOW	ST	RNBT	FBG	SV	IO	260	MRCR	7	6	2175		3950	4600
18	6	EXECUTIVE CUDDY II	ST	CUD	FBG	SV	IO	130-260		8		2630		4400	5450
18	6	EXECUTIVE CUDDY II	ST	CUD	FBG	SV	IO	270	MRCR	8		2630		4800	5500
18	6	EXECUTIVE OPEN BOW	ST	RNBT	FBG	SV	IO	130-260		8		2300		3950	4950
18	6	EXECUTIVE OPEN BOW	ST	RNBT	FBG	SV	IO	270	MRCR	8		2300		4350	5000
18	6	EXECUTIVE OVERNIGHT	ST	OVNTR	FBG	SV	IO	130-260		8		2650		4400	5450
18	6	EXECUTIVE OVERNIGHT	ST	OVNTR	FBG	SV	IO	270	MRCR	8		2650		4800	5500
20	1	PRO-AM SKIER	ST	SKI	FBG	SV	IB	260	MRCR	7	2	2300		5200	6000
20	2	MONTE CARLO CUDDY	ST	CUD	FBG	SV	IO	145-260		8		2915		5200	6400
20	2	MONTE CARLO OPEN BOW	ST	RNBT	FBG	SV	IO	145-270		8		2740		4850	6000
20	4	MIRAGE		RNBT	FBG	SV	IO	145-270		7	3	2500		4400	5500
22		MARQUE	ST	CUD	FBG	SV	IO	175-270		8	6	4000		7350	8950
23	2	OFFSHORE	HT	CUD	FBG	SV	IO	230-270		8	6	4350		8350	9850
23	2	OFFSHORE		OVNTR	FBG	SV	IO	230-270		8	1	4200		8150	9600
		1991 BOATS													
16	2	BLAZER OPEN BOW	ST	RNBT	FBG	SV	IO	130-175		6	9	1850		2600	3050
16	2	BLAZER OUTBOARD	ST	RNBT	FBG	SV	OB			6	9	1000		2950	3450
16	11	ASTRO OPEN BOW	ST	RNBT	FBG	SV	IO	130-205		7	4	2180		3100	3700
16	11	ASTRO OUTBOARD	ST	RNBT	FBG	SV	OB			7	4	1500		4200	4900
18		RIVIERA SPORT	ST	RNBT	FBG	SV	IO	130-205		7	1	2300		3350	3950
18	3	EAGLE OPEN BOW	ST	RNBT	FBG	SV	IO	130-230		7	6	2175		3400	4150
18	3	EAGLE OPEN BOW	ST	RNBT	FBG	SV	IO	260	MRCR	7	6	2175		3700	4300
18	6	EXECUTIVE CUDDY II	ST	CUD	FBG	SV	IO	130-260		8		2630		4100	5100
18	6	EXECUTIVE CUDDY II	ST	CUD	FBG	SV	IO	270	MRCR	8		2630		4500	5150
18	6	EXECUTIVE OPEN BOW	ST	RNBT	FBG	SV	IO	130-230		8		2300		3700	4450
18	6	EXECUTIVE OPEN BOW	ST	RNBT	FBG	SV	IO	260-270		8		2300		4000	4700
18	6	EXECUTIVE OVERNIGHT	ST	OVNTR	FBG	SV	IO	130-260		8		2650		4100	5100
18	6	EXECUTIVE OVERNIGHT	ST	OVNTR	FBG	SV	IO	270	MRCR	8		2650		4500	5150
20	1	PRO-AM SKIER	ST	SKI	FBG	SV	IB	260	MRCR	7	2	2300		4950	5700
20	2	MONTE CARLO OPEN BOW	ST	RNBT	FBG	SV	IO	145-270		8		2740		4550	5650
20	4	MIRAGE		RNBT	FBG	SV	IO	145-260		7	3	2500		4100	5100
20	4	MIRAGE		RNBT	FBG	SV	IO	270	MRCR	7	3	2500		4500	5150
23	2	OFFSHORE		OVNTR	FBG	SV	IO	230-270		8	1	4200		7650	9050
		1990 BOATS													
16	2	BLAZER OPEN BOW	ST	RNBT	FBG	SV	IO	130-175		6	9	1850		2450	2850
16	2	BLAZER OUTBOARD	ST	RNBT	FBG	SV	OB			6	9	1000		2850	3300
16	11	ASTRO OPEN BOW	ST	RNBT	FBG	SV	IO	130-205		7	4	2180		2900	3450
16	11	ASTRO OUTBOARD	ST	RNBT	FBG	SV	OB			7	4	1500		4050	4700
18		RIVIERA SPORT	ST	RNBT	FBG	SV	IO	130-205		7	1	2300		3100	3700
18	3	EAGLE OPEN BOW	ST	RNBT	FBG	SV	IO	130-230		7	6	2175		3150	3850
18	3	EAGLE OPEN BOW	ST	RNBT	FBG	SV	IO	260	MRCR	7	6	2175		3450	4000
18	6	EXECUTIVE CUDDY II	ST	CUD	FBG	SV	IO	130-260		8		2630		3850	4750
18	6	EXECUTIVE CUDDY II	ST	CUD	FBG	SV	IO	270	MRCR	8		2630		4150	4850
18	6	EXECUTIVE OPEN BOW	ST	RNBT	FBG	SV	IO	130-230		8		2300		3450	4200
18	6	EXECUTIVE OPEN BOW	ST	RNBT	FBG	SV	IO	260-270		8		2300		3750	4400
18	6	EXECUTIVE OVERNIGHTR	ST	OVNTR	FBG	SV	IO	130-260		8		2650		3800	4750
18	6	EXECUTIVE OVERNIGHTR	ST	OVNTR	FBG	SV	IO	270	MRCR	8		2650		4150	4850
20	1	PRO-AM		SKI	FBG	SV	IB	260	MRCR	7	2	2300		4700	5400
23	2	OFFSHORE		OVNTR	FBG	SV	IO	230-260		8	1	4200		7200	8400
23	2	OFFSHORE		OVNTR	FBG	SV	IO	350	MRCR	8	1	4200		8300	9550
		1989 BOATS													
16	2	BLAZER OPEN BOW	ST	RNBT	FBG	SV	IO	120-175		6	9	1850		2300	2700
16	2	BLAZER OUTBOARD	ST	RNBT	FBG	SV	OB			6	9	1000		2750	3150
16	11	ASTRO OPEN BOW	ST	RNBT	FBG	SV	IO	120-205		7	4	2180		2700	3250
16	11	ASTRO OUTBOARD	ST	RNBT	FBG	SV	OB			7	4	1500		3900	4550
18	3	EAGLE OPEN BOW	ST	RNBT	FBG	SV	IO	120-230		7	6	2175		2950	3600
18	3	EAGLE OPEN BOW	ST	RNBT	FBG	SV	IO	260	MRCR	7	6	2175		3250	3750
18	6	EXECUTIVE CUDDY I	ST	CUD	FBG	SV	IO	120-230		8		2480		3500	4250
18	6	EXECUTIVE CUDDY I	ST	CUD	FBG	SV	IO	260-270		8		2500		3750	4450
18	6	EXECUTIVE CUDDY II		CUD	FBG	SV	IO	120-230		8		2630		3600	4350
18	6	EXECUTIVE CUDDY II		CUD	FBG	SV	IO	260-270		8		2630		3850	4550
18	6	EXECUTIVE OPEN BOW	ST	RNBT	FBG	SV	IO	120-230		8		2300		3250	3950
18	6	EXECUTIVE OPEN BOW	ST	RNBT	FBG	SV	IO	260-270		8		2300		3500	4150
18	6	EXECUTIVE OVERNIGHTR	ST	OVNTR	FBG	SV	IO	120-230		8		2650		3600	4350
18	6	EXECUTIVE OVERNIGHTR	ST	OVNTR	FBG	SV	IO	260-270		8		2650		3850	4550
20	1	PRO-AM		SKI	FBG	SV	IB	260						4600	5250
		1988 BOATS													
16	2	BLAZER OPEN BOW	ST	RNBT	FBG	SV	IO	120-175		6	9	1850		2150	2550
16	2	BLAZER OUTBOARD	ST	RNBT	FBG	SV	OB			6	9	1000		2650	3050
16	11	ASTRO OPEN BOW	ST	RNBT	FBG	SV	IO	120-205		7	4	2180		2550	3050
18	3	EAGLE OPEN BOW	ST	RNBT	FBG	SV	IO	120-230		7	6	2175		2800	3400
18	3	EAGLE OPEN BOW	ST	RNBT	FBG	SV	IO	260	MRCR	7	6	2175		3050	3550
18	6	EXECUTIVE CUDDY I	ST	CUD	FBG	SV	IO	120-230		8		2480		3250	4000
18	6	EXECUTIVE CUDDY I	ST	CUD	FBG	SV	IO	260	MRCR	8		2500		3550	4150
18	6	EXECUTIVE CUDDY I	ST	CUD	FBG	SV	IO	350	MRCR	8		2500		4500	5150
18	6	EXECUTIVE CUDDY II		CUD	FBG	SV	IO	120-230		8		2630		3400	4100
18	6	EXECUTIVE CUDDY II		CUD	FBG	SV	IO	260	MRCR	8		2630		3650	4250
18	6	EXECUTIVE CUDDY II		CUD	FBG	SV	IO	350	MRCR	8		2630		4550	5250
18	6	EXECUTIVE OPEN BOW	ST	RNBT	FBG	SV	IO	120-230		8		2300		3050	3700
18	6	EXECUTIVE OPEN BOW	ST	RNBT	FBG	SV	IO	260	MRCR	8		2300		3300	3800
18	6	EXECUTIVE OPEN BOW	ST	RNBT	FBG	SV	IO	350	MRCR	8		2300		4150	4800
18	6	EXECUTIVE OVERNIGHTR	ST	OVNTR	FBG	SV	IO	120-230		8		2650		3400	4100
18	6	EXECUTIVE OVERNIGHTR	ST	OVNTR	FBG	SV	IO	260	MRCR	8		2650		3650	4250
18	6	EXECUTIVE OVERNIGHTR	ST	OVNTR	FBG	SV	IO	350	MRCR	8		2650		4550	5250

 CONTINUED ON NEXT PAGE

LOA FT	LOA IN	NAME AND/ OR MODEL	TOP/ RIG	BOAT TYPE	HULL MTL	HULL TP	ENGINE TP	ENGINE # HP	ENGINE MFG	BEAM FT	BEAM IN	WGT LBS	DRAFT FT	DRAFT IN	RETAIL LOW	RETAIL HIGH
		1987 BOATS														
16	4	BLAZER OPEN BOW	ST	RNBT	FBG	SV	IO		MRCR	6	9	1850			**	**
16	4	BLAZER OPEN BOW	ST	RNBT	FBG	SV	IO	120-175		6	9	1850			2000	2450
16	4	BLAZER OUTBOARD	ST	RNBT	FBG	SV	OB			6	9	1000			2550	2950
16	10	SONIC CLOSED BOW	ST	RNBT	FBG	SV	IO		MRCR	7	2	2180			**	**
16	10	SONIC CLOSED BOW	ST	RNBT	FBG	SV	IO	120-205		7	2	2180			2350	2850
16	10	SONIC OPEN BOW	ST	RNBT	FBG	SV	IO		MRCR	7	2	2180			**	**
16	10	SONIC OPEN BOW	ST	RNBT	FBG	SV	IO	120-205		7	2	2180			2450	2900
16	11	ASTRO OPEN BOW	ST	RNBT	FBG	SV	IO		MRCR	7	4	2180			**	**
16	11	ASTRO OPEN BOW	ST	RNBT	FBG	SV	IO	120-205		7	4	2180			2450	2900
18	3	EAGLE	ST	RNBT	FBG	SV	IO		MRCR	7	5	2175			**	**
18	3	EAGLE	ST	RNBT	FBG	SV	IO	120-230		7	5	2175			2650	3200
18	3	EAGLE	ST	RNBT	FBG	SV	IO	260	MRCR	7	5	2175			2850	3350
18	6	EXECUTIVE CUDDY	ST	CUD	FBG	SV	IO		MRCR	8		2480			**	**
		IO 120-230 3100 3750, IO 260 MRCR 3350 3900, IO 350 MRCR													4200	4850
18	6	EXECUTIVE OPEN BOW	ST	RNBT	FBG	SV	IO		MRCR	8		2300			**	**
		IO 120-230 2900 3500, IO 260 MRCR 3100 3600, IO 350 MRCR													3900	4550
18	6	EXECUTIVE OVERNIGHTR	ST	OVNTR	FBG	SV	IO		MRCR	8		2650			**	**
		IO 120-230 3200 3900, IO 260 MRCR 3450 4000, IO 350 MRCR													4250	4950
		1986 BOATS														
16	4	BLAZER OPEN BOW	ST	RNBT	FBG	DV	IO	120-140		6	9	1850			1950	2300
16	10	SONIC B-1810	ST	RNBT	FBG	DV	IO	120-205		7	2	2180			2300	2750
16	10	SONIC V-1810	ST	RNBT	FBG	DV	IO	120-205		7	2	2180			2250	2700
18	2	EAGLE	ST	RNBT	FBG	DV	IO	120-230		7	4	2175			2500	3000
18	2	EAGLE	ST	RNBT	FBG	DV	IO	260		7	4	2175			2700	3150
18	6	EXECUTIVE	ST	OVNTR	FBG	DV	IO	120-230		8		2650			3000	3650
18	6	EXECUTIVE	ST	OVNTR	FBG	DV	IO	260		8		2650			3250	3800
18	6	EXECUTIVE B-2010	ST	RNBT	FBG	DV	IO	120-230		8		2300			2750	3300
18	6	EXECUTIVE B-2010	ST	RNBT	FBG	DV	IO	260		8		2300			2950	3450
18	6	EXECUTIVE C-2010	ST	CUD	FBG	DV	IO	120-230				2500			2950	3550
18	6	EXECUTIVE C-2010	ST	CUD	FBG	DV	IO	260		8		2500			3150	3700
		1985 BOATS														
16	4	BLAZER OPEN BOW	ST	RNBT	FBG	DV	IO	120-140		6	9	1850			1850	2200
16	10	SONIC B-1810	ST	RNBT	FBG	DV	IO	120-190		7	2	2180			2200	2600
16	10	SONIC V-1810	ST	RNBT	FBG	DV	IO	120-190		7	2	2180			2100	2550
18		EAGLE OPEN BOW	OP	B/R	FBG		IO	120-230							2200	2700
18		EAGLE OPEN BOW	OP	B/R	FBG		IO	260							2400	2800
18	3	EAGLE	ST	RNBT	FBG	DV	IO	260	MRCR	7	4	2175			2600	3000
18	6	EXECUTIVE	ST	OVNTR	FBG	DV	IO	170-260		8		2650			2900	3600
18	6	EXECUTIVE B-2010	ST	RNBT	FBG	DV	IO	170-260		8		2300			2650	3300
18	6	EXECUTIVE C-2010	ST	CUD	FBG	DV	IO	170-260		8		2500			2850	3500

BLUE WATER INT`L YACHTS LTD

ROCHELLE NY USA

See inside cover to adjust price for area

LOA FT	LOA IN	NAME AND/ OR MODEL	TOP/ RIG	BOAT TYPE	HULL MTL	HULL TP	ENGINE TP	ENGINE # HP	ENGINE MFG	BEAM FT	BEAM IN	WGT LBS	DRAFT FT	DRAFT IN	RETAIL LOW	RETAIL HIGH
		1987 BOATS														
41	9	ULTIMATE 42	FB	SDN	F/S	SV	IB	T260D	J&T	13		22000	2	10	127000	139500
50	2	ULTIMATE 50	FB	MY	F/S	SV	IB	T450D	J&T	16	10	42000	3	6	196000	215500
50	2	ULTIMATE 50	FB	MY	F/S	SV	IB	T585D	J&T	16	10	42000	3	6	221000	243000
50	2	ULTIMATE 50	FB	MY	F/S	SV	IB	T710D	J&T	16	10	44000	3	6	247500	272000
56	2	ULTIMATE 56	FB	YTFS	F/S	SV	IB	T450D	J&T	16	10	47000	3	6	246000	270500
		1986 BOATS														
41	9	ULTIMATE 42	FB	SDN	F/S	SV	IB	T260D	J&T	13		22000	2	10	121500	133500
50	2	ULTIMATE 50	FB	MY	F/S	SV	IB	T450D	J&T	16	10	42000	3	6	187500	206000
50	2	ULTIMATE 50	FB	MY	F/S	SV	IB	T585D	J&T	16	10	42000	3	6	211500	232500
50	2	ULTIMATE 50	FB	MY	F/S	SV	IB	T710D	J&T	16	10	44000	3	6	237000	260000
56	2	ULTIMATE 56	FB	YTFS	F/S	SV	IB	T450D	J&T	16	10	47000	3	6	235500	258500

BLUEWATER

MORA MN 55051

COAST GUARD MFG ID- BTL See inside cover to adjust price for area
FORMERLY BOATEL YACHTS

For more recent years, see the BUC Used Boat Price Guide, Volume 1

LOA FT	LOA IN	NAME AND/ OR MODEL	TOP/ RIG	BOAT TYPE	HULL MTL	HULL TP	ENGINE TP	ENGINE # HP	ENGINE MFG	BEAM FT	BEAM IN	WGT LBS	DRAFT FT	DRAFT IN	RETAIL LOW	RETAIL HIGH
		1996 BOATS														
49	7	BLUEWATER 482	FB	MY	FBG	SV	IB	T380	CRUS	14		30300	2	4	141500	155500
49	7	BLUEWATER 482	FB	MY	FBG	SV	IB	T315D	CUM	14		30300	2	4	144000	158000
54	7	BLUEWATER 543	FB	MY	FBG	SV	IB	T380	CRUS	14		34800	2		180500	198500
54	7	BLUEWATER 543	FB	MY	FBG	SV	IB	T315D	CUM	14		34800	2	4	178000	195500
54	7	BLUEWATER 543 LE	FB	MY	FBG	SV	IB	T320	CRUS	14		34800	2		173500	190500
54	7	BLUEWATER 543 LE	FB	MY	FBG	SV	IB	T315D	CUM	14		34800	2		179000	196500
54	7	BLUEWATER 543 LEX	FB	MY	FBG	SV	IB	T320	CRUS	14		34800	2		173500	190500
56	10	BLUEWATER 562	FB	MY	FBG	SV	IB	T380	CRUS	14		41000	2	9	219500	241000
56	10	BLUEWATER 562	FB	MY	FBG	SV	IB	T420D	CUM	14		41000	2	9	236000	259000
64		BLUEWATER 622C	FB	MY	FBG	SV	IB	T380	CRUS	14		47700	2	8	287500	316000
64		BLUEWATER 622C	FB	MY	FBG	SV	IB	T420D	CUM	14		47700	2	8	316500	348000
64		BLUEWATER 643	FB	MY	FBG	SV	IB	T380	CRUS	14		48000	2	8	303500	333500
64		BLUEWATER 643	FB	MY	FBG	SV	IB	T420D	CUM	14		48000	2	8	329500	362000
		1995 BOATS														
49	7	BLUEWATER 48	FB	MY	FBG	SV	IB	T502	CRUS	14		30300	2	3	163500	180000
49	7	BLUEWATER 48	FB	MY	FBG	SV	IB	T315D	CUM	14		30300	2	4	144000	158000
54	7	BLUEWATER 54	FB	MY	FBG	SV	IB	T502	CRUS	14		34800	1	11	209000	229500
54	7	BLUEWATER 54	FB	MY	FBG	SV	IB	T315D	CUM	14		34800	2	4	169500	186500
56	10	BLUEWATER 56	FB	MY	FBG	SV	IB	T502	CUM	14		46000	2	2	252000	277000
56	10	BLUEWATER 56	FB	MY	FBG	SV	IB	T420D	CUM	14		37000	2	9	210500	231500
64		BLUEWATER 62 C	FB	MY	FBG	SV	IB	T502	CRUS	14		47700	2		302000	332000
64		BLUEWATER 62 C	FB	MY	FBG	SV	IB	T420D	CUM	14		47700	2	4	286000	314000
64		BLUEWATER 623	FB	MY	FBG	SV	IB	T502	CRUS	14		48000	2	2	309000	339500
64		BLUEWATER 623	FB	MY	FBG	SV	IB	T420D	CUM	14		48000	2	4	306500	337000
		1994 BOATS														
49	7	BLUEWATER 47	FB	MY	FBG	SV	IB	T454	CRUS	14		30300	1	11	156000	171500
49	7	BLUEWATER 47	FB	MY	FBG	SV	IB	T300D	CUM	14		30300	2	4	142500	156500
54	7	BLUEWATER 54	FB	MY	FBG	SV	IB	T454	CRUS	14		34800	1	11	186500	205000
54	7	BLUEWATER 54	FB	MY	FBG	SV	IB	T300D	CUM	14		34800	2	4	159500	175500
64		BLUEWATER 62 C	FB	MY	FBG	SV	IB	T400D	CUM	14		47700	2	4	265500	292000
64		BLUEWATER 623	FB	MY	FBG	SV	IB	T400D	CUM	14		48000	2	4	286500	314500
		1993 BOATS														
49	7	BLUEWATER 46	FB	MY	FBG	SV	IB	T350	CRUS	14		30300			123500	135500
49	7	BLUEWATER 46	FB	MY	FBG	SV	IB	T300D	CUM	14		32000			131000	144000
54	7	BLUEWATER 54	FB	MY	FBG	SV	IB	T350	CRUS	14		34800			152000	167000
54	7	BLUEWATER 54	FB	MY	FBG	SV	IB	T300D	CUM	14		36000			154000	169500
64		BLUEWATER 62	FB	MY	FBG	SV	IB	T400	CRUS	14		48700			280500	308500
64		BLUEWATER 62	FB	MY	FBG	SV	IB	T400D	CUM	14		49900			296500	326000
64		BLUEWATER 62 COCKPIT	FB	MYCPT	FBG	SV	IB	T400	CRUS	14		47700			272500	299500
64		BLUEWATER 62 COCKPIT	FB	MYCPT	FBG	SV	IB	T400D	CUM	14		49000			289500	318000
		1992 BOATS														
49	7	BLUEWATER 45	FB	CR	FBG	SV	IB	T300	CRUS	14		26000	1	11	102500	112500
50	8	BLUEWATER 48	FB	CR	FBG	SV	IB	T300	CRUS	14		28000	1	11	125000	137500
50	8	BLUEWATER 48-2SR	FB	CR	FBG	SV	IB	T300	CRUS	14		28000	1	11	107500	118000
54	7	BLUEWATER 53	FB	CR	FBG	SV	IB	T300	CRUS	14		31000	1	11	129000	142000
59		BLUEWATER 55	FB	MY	FBG	SV	IB	T300D	CUM	14		36000	1	11	149500	164000
64		BLUEWATER 60	FB	MY	FBG	SV	IB	T300D	CUM	14		40000	1	11	181500	199500
		1991 BOATS														
48	8	COCKPIT CRUISER 48/1	FB	CR	FBG	SV	IB	T454	CRUS	14		25000	1	11	98000	107500
48	8	COCKPIT CRUISER 48/1	FB	CR	FBG	SV	IB	T300D	CUM	14		25000	1	11	95500	105000
48	8	COCKPIT CRUISER 48/2	FB	CR	FBG	SV	IB	T454	CRUS	14		25000	1	11	109000	120000
48	8	COCKPIT CRUISER 48/2	FB	CR	FBG	SV	IB	T300D	CUM	14		25000	1	11	104500	114500
54	7	BLUEWATER CRUISER	FB	CR	FBG	SV	IB	T454	CRUS	14		26000	1	11	140500	154500
54	7	BLUEWATER CRUISER	FB	CR	FBG	SV	IB	T300D	CUM	14		26000	1	11	124500	136500
59		BLUEWATER SDN	FB	MY	FBG	SV	IB	T502	CRUS	14		31000	1	11	181500	199500
59		BLUEWATER SDN	FB	MY	FBG	SV	IB	T300D	CUM	14		31000	1	11	142500	156500
64		BLUEWATER CPT	FB	MY	FBG	SV	IB	T502	CRUS	14		36000			172500	189500
64		BLUEWATER CPT	FB	MY	FBG	SV	IB	T300D	CUM	14		36000			173000	190000
		1990 BOATS														
42	6	BLUEWATER CPT CR	FB	CR	FBG	SV	IB	T350	CRUS	14		22000	1	11	85100	93500
42	6	COCKPIT CRUISER 43	FB	CR	FBG	SV	IB	T350	CRUS	14		22000	1	11	91700	101000
46	6	BLUEWATER SDN	FB	MY	FBG	SV	IB	T250D	GM	15		31500	3	6	118500	130500
46	6	BLUEWATER SDN	FB	MY	FBG	SV	IB	T375D	CAT	15		31500	3	6	138500	152000
46	6	BLUEWATER SDN	FB	MY	FBG	SV	IB	T450D	GM	15		31500	3	6	148000	163000
46	6	SEDAN MOTOR YACHT 46	FB	MY	FBG	SV	IB	T350	CRUS	15		31500	2	6	132500	145500
		IB T250D GM 137500 151000, IB T375D CAT 152000 167000, IB T450D GM													156000	171500
47	10	BLUEWATER SDN	FB	MY	FBG	SV	IB	T454	CRUS	14		24000	1	11	131500	144500
47	10	BLUEWATER SDN	FB	MY	FBG	SV	IB	T300D	CUM	14		24000	1	11	123500	136000
47	10	SEDAN MOTOR YACHT 45	FB	MY	FBG	SV	IB	T454	CRUS	14		24000	1	11	128500	141000
47	10	SEDAN MOTOR YACHT 45	FB	MY	FBG	SV	IB	T300D	CUM	14		24000	1	11	120000	132000
48	8	BLUEWATER CPT	FB	CR	FBG	SV	IB			14		25000			**	**
48	8	COCKPIT CRUISER 48	FB	CR	FBG	SV	IB	T454	CRUS	14		25000	1	11	94100	103500
51		BLUEWATER SDN	FB	CR	FBG	SV	IB	T454	CRUS	14		26000	1	11	136500	150000
51		SEDAN CRUISER 52	FB	CR	FBG	SV	IB	T454	CRUS	14		26000	1	11	110000	121000
52	10	BLUEWATER SDN	FB	MY	FBG	SV	IB	T454	CRUS	14		28000			149500	164000
52	10	BLUEWATER SDN	FB	MY	FBG	SV	IB	T300D	CUM	14		28000			127500	140500
52	10	COCKPIT MY 50	FB	MYCPT	FBG	SV	IB	T454	CRUS	14		28000	1	11	151000	166000
52	10	COCKPIT MY 50	FB	MYCPT	FBG	SV	IB	T300D	GM	14		28000	1	11	124500	137000
53	7	BLUEWATER CPT	FB	MY	FBG	SV	IB	T350	CRUS	15		41000	2	10	146500	161000

 CONTINUED ON NEXT PAGE

```
BLUEWATER          -CONTINUED    See inside cover to adjust price for area
LOA  NAME AND/          TOP/ BOAT  -HULL-  ----ENGINE--- BEAM  DRAFT RETAIL RETAIL
FT IN OR MODEL          RIG  TYPE  MTL TP TP # HP MFG  FT IN  LBS  FT IN  LOW   HIGH
-------------------- 1990 BOATS -------------------------------------------------
53  7 BLUEWATER CPT      FB  MY    FBG SV IB T250D GM  15   41000  2 10 136500 150000
53  7 BLUEWATER CPT      FB  MY    FBG SV IB T375D CAT 15   41000  2 10 159500 175000
53  7 BLUEWATER CPT      FB  MY    FBG SV IB T450D GM  15   41000  2 10 174500 192000
53  7 BLUEWATER SDN      FB  MY    FBG SV IB T350  CRUS 15  39000       142500 156500
      IB T250D GM  133500 147000, IB T375D CAT  156000 171500, IB T450D GM  171000 188000

53  7 COCKPIT MY 54      FB  MYCPT FBG SV IB T350  CRUS 15  41000  2  6 152500 167500
      IB T250D GM  136000 149500, IB T375D CAT  165500 182000, IB T450D GM  184000 202000

53  7 SEDAN MOTOR YACHT 54 FB MY   FBG SV IB T350  CRUS 15  39000  2  6 147000 161500
      IB T250D GM  134500 148000, IB T375D CAT  160500 176500, IB T450D GM  177500 195000

59    BLUEWATER SDN      FB  MY    FBG SV IB T502  CRUS 14  29000  1 11 181000 199000
59    BLUEWATER SDN      FB  MY    FBG SV IB T300D CUM  14   29000  1 11 182500 200500
59    SEDAN MOTOR YACHT 55 FB MY   FBG SV IB T502  CRUS 14  29000  1 11 181000 199000
59    SEDAN MOTOR YACHT 55 FB MY   FBG SV IB T300D CUM  14   29000  1 11 182500 200500
64    BLUEWATER CPT      FB  MY    FBG SV IB T502  CRUS 14  35000        **     **
64    BLUEWATER CPT      FB  MY    FBG SV IB T300D CUM  14   35000        **     **
64    COCKPIT MTR YACHT 60 FB MYCPT FBG SV IB T502 CRUS 14  35000  1 11   **     **
64    COCKPIT MTR YACHT 60 FB MYCPT FBG SV IB T300D CUM 14  35000  1 11   **     **
-------------------- 1989 BOATS -------------------------------------------------
42  6 BLUEWATER          FB  SDN   FBG SV IB T270  CRUS 14  22000  1 11  81500  89600
      IB T350  CRUS  84200  92600, IB T135D PERK  86700  95200, IB T165D PERK  88300  97000
      IB T250D GM   91400 100500

42  6 BLUEWATER SPORT CR FB  CR    FBG SV IB T270  CRUS 14  20000  1 11  78700  86500
42  6 BLUEWATER SPORT CR FB  CR    FBG SV IB T350  CRUS 14  20000  1 11  81700  89700
46  6 BLUEWATER          FB  MY    FBG SV IB T350  CRUS 15  31500  3  6  90000  98900
      IB T250D GM   94300 103500, IB T375D CAT  103000 113000, IB T450D J&T  107500 118500

47 10 BLUEWATER CR       FB  CR    FBG SV IB T270  CRUS 14  24000  1 11  82000  90100
      IB T350  CRUS  86400  94900, IB T135D PERK  81700  89800, IB T165D PERK  83500  91800
      IB T250D GM   88700  97500

51    BLUEWATER          FB  CR    FBG SV IB T270  CRUS 14  26000  1 11  88000  96700
      IB T350  CRUS  97500 107000, IB T135D PERK  82000  90100, IB T165D PERK  83300  91600
      IB T250D GM   88100  96900

51    BLUEWATER CPT CR   FB  CR    FBG SV IB T270  CRUS 14  26000  1 11  88300  97100
      IB T350  CRUS  92500 101500, IB T135D PERK  83100  91400, IB T165D PERK  84500  92800
      IB T250D GM   88000  96700

53  7 BLUEWATER          FB  MY    FBG SV IB T350  CRUS 15  39000  2 10 130000 143000
      IB T250D GM  127500 140500, IB T375D CAT  144500 159000, IB T450D J&T  157000 172500

59    BLUEWATER CR       FB  CR    FBG SV IB T270  CRUS 14  29000  1 11 162500 178500
      IB T350  CRUS 163000 179000, IB T135D PERK  150500 165500, IB T165D PERK 152500 168000
      IB T250D GM  158000 173500
-------------------- 1988 BOATS -------------------------------------------------
42  6 BLUEWATER          FB  CR    FBG SV IB T270  CRUS 14  22000  1 11  76700  84300
42  6 BLUEWATER          FB  SDN   FBG SV IB T250  GM  14   22000  1 11  77000  84600
      IB T270  CRUS  77900  85600, IB T350  CRUS  80500  88500, IB T135D PERK  82800  91000
      IB T165D PERK  84300  92700

42  6 BLUEWATER SPORT CR FB  CR    FBG SV IB T240  CHRY 14  20000  1 11  73900  81200
42  6 BLUEWATER SPORT CR FB  CR    FBG SV IB T270  CRUS 14  20000  1 11  75200  82700
42  6 BLUEWATER SPORT CR FB  CR    FBG SV IB T350  CRUS 14  20000  1 11  78000  85700
46  6 BLUEWATER          FB  MY    FBG SV IB T350  CRUS 15  31500  3  6  86000  94500
      IB T210D CAT  89400  98300, IB T250D GM   90100  99000, IB T300D CAT  95900 105500
      IB T305D GM   92700 102000, IB T375D CAT  98400 108000, IB T450D J&T  103000 113000

47 10 BLUEWATER CR       FB  CR    FBG SV IB T135  PERK 14  24000  1 11  72500  79700
      IB T165  PERK  73700  81000, IB T250  GM   77200  84800, IB T270  CRUS  78300  86100
      IB T350  CRUS  82600  90700

51    BLUEWATER          FB  CR    FBG SV IB T270  CRUS 14  26000  1 11  85300  93700
      IB T350  CRUS  94500 104000, IB T135D PERK  79400  87300, IB T165D PERK  80600  88600
      IB T215D GM   82400  90500

51    BLUEWATER CPT CR   FB  CR    FBG SV IB T270  CRUS 14  26000  1 11  83200  91400
      IB T350  CRUS  87100  95700, IB T135D PERK  78300  86100, IB T165D PERK  79700  87500
      IB T215D GM   81000  89000

53  7 BLUEWATER          FB  MY    FBG SV IB T350  CRUS 15  39000  2 10 124500 137000
      IB T210D CAT 121500 133500, IB T250D GM  122500 134500, IB T300D CAT  130000 143000
      IB T305D GM  127500 140000, IB T375D CAT  138500 152000, IB T450D J&T  150500 165500

59    BLUEWATER CR       FB  CR    FBG SV IB T135  PERK 14  29000  1 11 160000 176000
      IB T165  PERK 160500 176500, IB T250  GM  159000 174500, IB T270  CRUS 155500 171000
      IB T350  CRUS 156000 171500
-------------------- 1987 BOATS -------------------------------------------------
42  6 BLUEWATER          FB  CR    FBG SV IB T220  CRUS 14  22000  1 11  72300  79500
42  6 BLUEWATER          FB  CR    FBG SV IB T270  CRUS 14  22000  1 11  73300  80600
42  6 BLUEWATER          FB  SDN   FBG SV IB T270  CRUS 14  22000  1 11  74500  81900
      IB T350  CRUS  77000  84600, IB T135D PERK  79200  87000, IB T165D PERK  80600  88600
      IB T215D GM   81800  89900

46  6 BLUEWATER          FB  MY    FBG SV IB T350  CRUS 15  31500  3  6  82200  90300
      IB T210D CAT  85500  93900, IB T250D GM   86100  94600, IB T300D CAT  91700 100500
      IB T305D GM   88600  97400, IB T355D CAT  92800 102000, IB T450D J&T  98400 108000

51    BLUEWATER          FB  CR    FBG SV IB T270  CRUS 14  26000  1 11  81800  89800
      IB T350  CRUS  90700  99700, IB T135D PERK  76100  83700, IB T165D PERK  77300  85000
      IB T215D GM   79000  86800

51    BLUEWATER CPT CR   FB  CR    FBG SV IB T270  CRUS 14  26000  1 11  79300  87100
      IB T350  CRUS  83000  91300, IB T135D PERK  74600  82000, IB T165D PERK  75900  83400
      IB T215D GM   77200  84900

53  7 BLUEWATER          FB  MY    FBG SV IB T350  CRUS 15  39000  2 10 119500 131500
      IB T210D CAT 116500 128500, IB T250D GM  117500 129000, IB T300D CAT  124500 137000
      IB T305D GM  122500 134500, IB T355D CAT  130500 143500, IB T450D J&T  144500 158500
-------------------- 1986 BOATS -------------------------------------------------
42  6 BLUEWATER          FB  CR    FBG SV IB T220  CRUS 14  22000  1 11  69200  76000
42  6 BLUEWATER          FB  CR    FBG SV IB T270  CRUS 14  22000  1 11  70100  77100
42  6 BLUEWATER          FB  SDN   FBG SV IB T270  CRUS 14  22000  1 11  71300  78300
      IB T350  CRUS  73600  80900, IB T135D PERK  75800  83200, IB T165D PERK  77100  84800
      IB T215D GM   78200  86000

46  6 BLUEWATER          FB  MY    FBG SV IB T350  CRUS 15  31500  3  6  78500  86300
      IB T210D CAT  81700  89800, IB T215D GM   81000  89000, IB T300D CAT  87600  96300
      IB T305D GM   84700  93100, IB T335D CAT  89500  98100, IB T450D J&T  94100 103500

51    BLUEWATER          FB  CR    FBG SV IB T270  CRUS 14  26000  1 11  78200  85900
      IB T350  CRUS  86800  95400, IB T135D PERK  72800  80000, IB T165D PERK  73900  81200
      IB T215D GM   75500  83000

51    BLUEWATER CPT CR   FB  CR    FBG SV IB T270  CRUS 14  26000  1 11  75800  83300
      IB T350  CRUS  79400  87300, IB T135D PERK  71400  78400, IB T165D PERK  72600  79800
      IB T215D GM   73800  81100

53  7 BLUEWATER          FB  MY    FBG SV IB T350  CRUS 15  39000  2 10 114500 126000
      IB T210D CAT 112000 123500, IB T215D GM  110000 120500, IB T300D CAT  119500 131500
      IB T350D GM  122500 134000, IB T355D CAT  125000 137500, IB T450D J&T  138500 152000
-------------------- 1985 BOATS -------------------------------------------------
42  6 BLUE WATER         FB  CR    FBG SV IB T220  CRUS 14  19000  1 11  60100  66100
      IB T270  CRUS  61100  67100, IB T350  CRUS  65300  71800, IB T135D PERK  65300  71800
      IB T165D PERK  66700  73300, IB T215D GM   67700  74400

46  6 BLUEWATER          FB  MY    FBG SV IB T350  CRUS 14  8 31500  3  6  75400  82900
      IB T135D PERK  77400  85100, IB T210D CAT  78200  85900, IB T215D GM   77500  85200
      IB T305D GM   82900  90400, IB T355D CAT  81500  89500, IB T355D GM   83900  93900
      IB T450D J&T   91400 100500

47 10 BLUEWATER          FB  SDN   FBG SV IB T350  CRUS 14  30000  3  8  77100  84800
      IB T135D PERK  73500  80800, IB T210D CAT  77600  85300, IB T215D GM   77700  85400
      IB T300D CAT  82100  90300, IB T305D GM   82300  90400, IB T355D CAT  84700  93100

50    HERCULES           HT  HB    STL CT          14                     42200  46900
51    BLUE WATER         FB  MY    FBG SV IB T220  CRUS 14  23000  1 11  85800  94300
      IB T135D PERK  89100  97900, IB T215D CRUS  84200  92500, IB T300D CAT  92400  95900
      IB T165D PERK  85000  93400, IB T215D GM   89500  98400

51    BLUE WATER CPT CR  FB  CR    FBG SV IB T350  CRUS 14  23000  1 11  77000  80300
      IB T270  CRUS  80100  88000, IB T350  CRUS  84200  92500, IB T135D PERK  73100  80300
      IB T165D PERK  75500  83000, IB T215D GM   78400  86200

10 BLUEWATER             FB  MY    FBG SV IB T350  CRUS 14  33000  3  8 109000 119500
      IB T135D PERK  97800 107500, IB T210D CAT  102500 113000, IB T215D GM  101000 111000
      IB T215D GM  103000 113500, IB T305D GM   108500 119500, IB T355D CAT  116000 127500
      IB T450D J&T  129000 141500

53  7 BLUEWATER          FB  MY    FBG SV IB T350  CRUS 15  35000  3  8 107000 118000

78                    CONTINUED ON NEXT PAGE                96th ed. - Vol. II
```

```
              LOA  NAME AND/      TOP/ BOAT  -HULL-  ----ENGINE---  BEAM   WGT  DRAFT RETAIL RETAIL
              FT IN OR MODEL      RIG  TYPE  MTL TP TP # HP  MFG    FT IN  LBS  FT IN  LOW    HIGH
------------------- 1985 BOATS -----------------------------------------------------------------------
53 7 BLUEWATER         FB  MY  FBG SV IB T135D PERK 15   35000  3  8  98500 108000
     IB T210D CAT 103500 113500, IB T215D GM 101500 111500, IB T300D CAT 111000 122000
     IB T305D GM 109000 119500, IB T355D CAT 116000 127500, IB T450D J&T 129000 141500
------------------- 1984 BOATS -----------------------------------------------------------------------
42 6 BOATEL            FB  CR  FBG SV IB T220  CRUS 14   19000  1 11  57000  62600
     IB T270  CRUS 57900 63600, IB T350  CRUS 59800 65700, IB T 85D PERK 59500 65400

47 10 BLUEWATER        FB  SDN  FBG SV IB T350  CRUS 15   30000  3  8  73900  81200
      IB T 85D PERK 67600 74200, IB T135D PERK 70300 77300, IB T210D CAT 74300 81600
      IB T300D CAT 78700 86500, IB T305D GM 78800 86600

51   BOATEL            FB  CR  FBG SV IB T165      14   21000  1 11  67500  74200
     IB T220  CRUS 80300 88300, IB T350  CRUS 87000 95700, IB T215D GM 82100 90200
     IB T300D CAT 87600 96200

52 10 BLUEWATER        FB  MY  FBG SV IB  215D GM  15   35000  3  8  92800 102000
      IB T350  CRUS 103500 114000, IB T135D PERK 96300 106000, IB T210D CAT 101000 111000
      IB T300D CAT 107500 118000, IB T305D GM 106000 116000

52 10 BLUEWATER        FB  SDN  FBG SV IB T350  CRUS 15   33000  3  8 104500 114500
      IB T135D PERK 94000 103500, IB T210D CAT 98700 108500, IB T300D CAT 106000 116500
      IB T305D GM 104500 114500

54   BLUEWATER         FB  SDN  FBG DV IB T350D     14 8 37000  3  6 119500 131000
     ....For earlier years, see the BUC Used Boat Price Guide, Volume 3
```

BLUEWATER SPORTFISHING BOATS

FT PIERCE FL 34946   COAST GUARD MFG ID- DZV See inside cover to adjust price for area

For more recent years, see the BUC Used Boat Price Guide, Volume 1

```
              LOA  NAME AND/      TOP/ BOAT  ----ENGINE---  BEAM   WGT  DRAFT RETAIL RETAIL
              FT IN OR MODEL      RIG  TYPE  MTL TP TP # HP  MFG   FT IN  LBS  FT IN  LOW    HIGH
------------------- 1996 BOATS -----------------------------------------------------------------------
25 5 BLUEWATER 2550    OP OPFSH FBG DV OB        8  5 2950       19700  21900
```

BLUEWATER YACHT BLD LTD

TAIPEI TAIWAN   COAST GUARD MFG ID- BYY See inside cover to adjust price for area

```
              LOA  NAME AND/      TOP/ BOAT  -HULL-  ----ENGINE---  BEAM   WGT  DRAFT RETAIL RETAIL
              FT IN OR MODEL      RIG  TYPE  MTL TP TP # HP  MFG    FT IN  LBS  FT IN  LOW    HIGH
------------------- 1986 BOATS -----------------------------------------------------------------------
46 7 VAGABOND-VOYAGER  KTH SA/CR FBG KL IB  85D LEHM 13  5 40000  5  6 148500 163000
------------------- 1985 BOATS -----------------------------------------------------------------------
46 7 VAGABOND-VOYAGER  KTH SA/CR FBG KL IB  85D LEHM 13  5 40000  5  6 140500 154500
------------------- 1984 BOATS -----------------------------------------------------------------------
46 7 VAGABOND 47       KTH SA/CR FBG KL IB  85D LEHM 13  5 40000  5  6 133500 146500
     ....For earlier years, see the BUC Used Boat Price Guide, Volume 3
```

BOATEL MARINE INC

PAGE AZ 86040   See inside cover to adjust price for area

```
              LOA  NAME AND/      TOP/ BOAT  -HULL-  ----ENGINE---  BEAM   WGT  DRAFT RETAIL RETAIL
              FT IN OR MODEL      RIG  TYPE  MTL TP TP # HP  MFG    FT IN  LBS  FT IN  LOW    HIGH
------------------- 1995 BOATS -----------------------------------------------------------------------
18  SPORT-A-BOUT       OP RNBT FBG SV OB          8        1100  1  6   1650   2000
20  SPORT-A-BOUT       OP RNBT FBG SV OB          8        1300         1950   2350
36  360                OP HB   STL PN OB         14       12000  2     22700  25200
44  440                OP HB   STL PN OB         14       14000  2     22500  25000
50  500                OP HB   STL PN OB         14       18000  2     28900  32100
52  FH520              FB HB   AL  SV IO T130 OMC 14      24000  2  2  46100  50600
65  PENTHOUSE 650      FB HB   STL PN OB         18       32000  2  6  50400  55400
------------------- 1994 BOATS -----------------------------------------------------------------------
18  SPORT-A-BOUT       OP RNBT FBG SV OB          8        1100  1  6   1600   1900
20  SPORT-A-BOUT       OP RNBT FBG SV OB          8        1300         1850   2200
36  360                OP HB   STL PN OB         14       12000  2     21800  24200
44  440                OP HB   STL PN OB         14       14000  2     21500  23900
50  500                OP HB   STL PN OB         14       18000  2     27200  30300
52  FH520              FB HB   AL  SV IO T130 OMC 14      24000  2  2  43300  48100
54  540                OP HB   STL PN OB         14       26000        41700  46400
55  550                FB HB   STL PN OB         16       28000  2  2  43500  48300
65  PENTHOUSE 650      FB HB   STL PN OB         18       32000  2  6 129000 141500
------------------- 1993 BOATS -----------------------------------------------------------------------
18  SPORT-A-BOUT       OP RNBT FBG SV OB          8        1100  1  6   1500   1800
20  SPORT-A-BOUT       OP RNBT FBG SV OB          8        1300         1750   2100
36  360                OP HB   STL PN OB         14       12000  2     20700  23000
44  440                OP HB   STL PN OB         14       14000  2     20300  22600
50  500                OP HB   STL PN OB         14       18000  2     25800  28700
52  FH520              FB HB   AL  SV IO T130 OMC 14      24000  2  2  41300  45900
54  540                OP HB   STL PN OB         14       26000        39600  44000
55  550                FB HB   STL PN OB         16       28000  2  2  41200  45800
65  PENTHOUSE 650      FB HB   STL PN OB         18       32000  2  6 122500 134500
------------------- 1992 BOATS -----------------------------------------------------------------------
18  SPORT FISHER       OP CTRCN FBG SV OB         8        1100  1  6   1400   1650
18  SPORT-A-BOUT       OP RNBT FBG SV OB          8        1100  1  6   1400   1700
36  HERCULES           OP HB   STL PN OB         14       10000  2     17300  19700
44  HERCULES           OP HB   STL PN OB         14       14000  2     19800  22000
50  HERCULES           OP HB   STL PN OB         14       18000  2     24600  27300
52  FR520              FB HB   AL  SV IO T175 OMC 14      33000  2  2  43800  48600
55  EXECUTIVE          FB HB   STL SV TD T350 CRUS 16     34000  2  2  48100  52900
65  EXECUTIVE PENTHOUSE FB HB  STL PN OB         18       32000  2  6 116500 128000
------------------- 1991 BOATS -----------------------------------------------------------------------
18  SPORT FISHER       OP CTRCN FBG SV OB         8        1100  1  6   1350   1600
18  SPORT-A-BOUT       OP RNBT FBG SV OB          8        1100  1  6   1350   1600
36  HERCULES           OP HB   STL PN OB         14       10000  2     16600  18900
44  HERCULES           OP HB   STL PN OB         14       14000  2     18900  21000
50  HERCULES           OP HB   STL PN OB         14       18000  2     23500  26100
52  FR520              FB HB   AL  SV IO T175 OMC 16      33000  2  2  41500  46100
55  EXECUTIVE          FB HB   STL SV TD         16       24000  2  2  35100  39000
55  EXECUTIVE          FB HB   STL SV TD T350 CRUS 16     34000  2  4  44600  49600
55  EXECUTIVE          FB HB   STL SV TD T454 CRUS 16     34000  2  4  48900  53800
65  EXECUTIVE          FB HB   STL SV TD         16       28000  2  4  34800  38700
65  EXECUTIVE          FB HB   STL SV TD T350 CRUS 16     38000  2  1  42500  47300
65  EXECUTIVE          FB HB   STL SV TD T454 CRUS 16     38000  2  1  46100  50600

65  EXECUTIVE PENTHOUSE FB HB  STL PN OB         18       32000  2  6  36600  40600
------------------- 1990 BOATS -----------------------------------------------------------------------
18  SPORT FISHER       OP CTRCN FBG SV OB         8        1100  1  6   1300   1550
18  SPORT-A-BOUT       OP RNBT FBG SV OB          8        1100  1  6   1300   1550
36  HERCULES           OP HB   STL PN OB         14       10000  2     16000  18200
44  HERCULES           OP HB   STL PN OB         14       14000  2     18200  20200
50  HERCULES           OP HB   STL PN OB         14       18000  2     22600  25400
52  FR520              FB HB   AL  SV IO T175 OMC 14      33000  2  2  39800  44200
55  EXECUTIVE          FB HB   STL SV TD         16       24000  2  2  33700  37400
55  EXECUTIVE          FB HB   STL SV TD T350 CRUS 16     34000  2  4  43400  48200
55  EXECUTIVE          FB HB   STL SV TD T454 CRUS 16     34000  2  4  47100  51700
65  EXECUTIVE          FB HB   STL SV TD         16       28000  2  4  34200  38000
65  EXECUTIVE          FB HB   STL SV TD T350 CRUS 16     38000  2  1  42500  47300
65  EXECUTIVE          FB HB   STL SV TD T454 CRUS 16     38000  2  1  46100  50600

65  EXECUTIVE PENTHOUSE FB HB  STL PN OB         18       32000  2  6  36300  40300
------------------- 1989 BOATS -----------------------------------------------------------------------
18  SPORT-A-BOUT 180   OP RNBT FBG    OB      7  4  1100  1  6   1250   1500
18  SPORTFISH 180      OP RNBT FBG    OB      7  4  1100  1  6   1250   1500
36  HERCULES 36        HT HB   STL PN OB         14       12300  2     16500  18700
36  HERCULES 44        HT HB   STL PN OB         14       12300  2     16500  18700
39  HERCULES 50        HT HB   STL PN OB         14       14400  2     19600  21900
55  VIP 50             HT HB   STL PN OB         14       21000        30300  33600
55  VIP 55             HT HB   STL PN OB         14       21000        30400  33800
60  VIP 65             HT HB   STL PN IO T454 CHEV 16     28000        47500  52200
65  VIP 65             HT HB   STL PN IO        18       30000        35100  39000
------------------- 1988 BOATS -----------------------------------------------------------------------
18  SPORT-A-BOUT 180   OP RNBT        OB      7  4  1100  1  6   1200   1450
18  SPORTFISH 180      OP RNBT        OB      7  4  1100  1  6   1200   1450
------------------- 1986 BOATS -----------------------------------------------------------------------
28  BOATEL 28          HT HB   STL PN OB        8  6            **     **
34  BOATEL 34          HT HB   STL PN OB        8  6     5500   19200  21400
36  BOATEL 36          HT HB   STL PN OB         14       10000        12400  16100
42  BOATEL 42          HT HB   STL PN OB         14       10000        12400  14100
50  BOATEL 50          HT HB   STL PN OB         14       15000        18800  20900
55  BOATEL 55          HT HB   STL PN OB         14       18000        25600  28400
------------------- 1984 BOATS -----------------------------------------------------------------------
36  BOATEL 36          HT HB   STL PN OB         14       10000        13500  15400
44  BOATEL 44          HT HB   STL PN OB         14       15000        15000  17100
50  BOATEL 50          HT HB   STL PN OB         14       15000        17100  19900
51  BOATEL 51          HT HB       SV TD T220    14       21000  1 11  24300  27000
52  BOATEL 53          HT HB   STL PN OB         14                    24300  27000

     ....For earlier years, see the BUC Used Boat Price Guide, Volume 3
```

BOCA GRANDE BOATS

SARASOTA FL 34243   COAST GUARD MFG ID- BQA See inside cover to adjust price for area

LOA FT IN	NAME AND/ OR MODEL	TOP/ RIG	BOAT TYPE	-HULL- MTL TP TP	----ENGINE--- # HP MFG	BEAM FT IN	WGT LBS	DRAFT FT IN	RETAIL LOW	RETAIL HIGH
------- 1996 BOATS -------
26	EXPRESS CRUISER	OP	EXP	FBG SV IB	350 CRUS	9 6	5500	2 2	43000	47800
26	EXPRESS CRUISER	OP	EXP	FBG SV IB	170D-250D	9 6	5500	2 2	48500	58300
26	OPEN FISHERMAN	OP	OPFSH	FBG SV IB	350 CRUS	9 6	4950	2 2	39800	44300
26	OPEN FISHERMAN	OP	OPFSH	FBG SV IB	170D-250D	9 6	4950	2 2	43300	52800
------- 1995 BOATS -------
25 11	BOCA GRANDE	CTRCN	FBG	IB	330 CRUS	9 6	4950	2 2	37600	41800
25 11	BOCA GRANDE	CTRCN	FBG	IB	210D-300D	9 6	4950	2 2	44300	55100
25 11	BOCA GRANDE	CUD	FBG	IB	330 CRUS	9 6	4950	2 2	37600	41800
25 11	BOCA GRANDE	CUD	FBG	IB	210D-300D	9 6	4950	2 2	44300	55100
25 11	BOCA GRANDE	EXP	FBG	IB	330 CRUS	9 6	5125	2 2	38300	42600
25 11	BOCA GRANDE	EXP	FBG	IB	210D-300D	9 6	5125	2 2	45800	56200
------- 1994 BOATS -------
25 11	BOCA GRANDE 26	OP	OPFSH	FBG SV IB	350 CRUS	9 6	4950	2 2	35500	39400
25 11	BOCA GRANDE 26	OP	OPFSH	FBG SV IB	250D CUM	9 6	5300	2 2	45800	50300
25 11	BOCA GRANDE CUDDY	OP	SF	FBG SV IB	350 CRUS	9 6	5500	2 2	38300	42500
25 11	BOCA GRANDE CUDDY	OP	SF	FBG SV IB	250D CUM	9 6	5800	2 2	49700	54600
25 11	DIVE BOAT	OP	UTL	FBG SV IB	170D YAN	9 6	4500	2 6	37500	41700
25 11	PASSENGER LAUNCH	OP	LNCH	FBG SV IB	88D YAN	9 6	4500	2 6	32400	36000
------- 1993 BOATS -------
25 11	BOCA GRANDE 26	OP	OPFSH	FBG SV IB	350 CRUS	9 6	4950	2 2	33600	37300
25 11	BOCA GRANDE 26	OP	OPFSH	FBG SV IB	250D CUM	9 6	5300	2 2	43100	47900
25 11	BOCA GRANDE CUDDY	OP	SF	FBG SV IB	350 CRUS	9 6	5500	2 2	36300	40300
25 11	BOCA GRANDE CUDDY	OP	SF	FBG SV IB	250D CUM	9 6	5800	2 2	47600	52300
25 11	DIVE BOAT	OP	UTL	FBG SV IB	170D YAN	9 6	4500	2 6	35800	39700
25 11	PASSENGER LAUNCH	OP	LNCH	FBG SV IB	88D YAN	9 6	4500	2 6	30900	34300
------- 1992 BOATS -------
25 11	BOCA GRANDE 26	OP	OPFSH	FBG SV IB	350 CRUS	9 6	5000	2 6	32100	35600
25 11	BOCA GRANDE 26	OP	OPFSH	FBG SV IB	250D CUM	9 6	5300	2 6	41100	45700
25 11	BOCA GRANDE CUDDY	OP	SF	FBG SV IB	350 CRUS	9 6	5500	2 6	34400	48300
25 11	BOCA GRANDE CUDDY	OP	SF	FBG SV IB	250D CUM	9 6	5800	2 6	44900	49900
25 11	PASSENGER LAUNCH	OP	LNCH	FBG SV IB	88D YAN	9 6	4500	2 6	29400	32700
------- 1989 BOATS -------
25 11	BOCA CUDDY	OP	CUD	F/S SV IB	350 CRUS	9 6	5300	2 2	29000	32300
25 11	BOCA CUDDY	OP	CUD	F/S SV IB	210D CUM	9 6	5200	2 2	34600	38400
25 11	BOCA FISH	OP	CTRCN	F/S SV IB	350 CRUS	9 6	5000	2 2	28100	31300
25 11	BOCA FISH	OP	CTRCN	F/S SV IB	210D CUM	9 6	5200	2 2	34600	38400
------- 1988 BOATS -------
25 11	BOCA CUDDY	OP	CUD	F/S SV IB	350 CRUS	9 6	5300	2 2	27700	30700
25 11	BOCA FISH	OP	CTRCN	F/S SV IB	350 CRUS	9 6	5000	2 2	26800	29800
------- 1987 BOATS -------
25 11	BOCA CUDDY	OP	CUD	F/S SV IB	350 CRUS	9 6	5300	2 2	26400	29300
25 11	BOCA FISH	OP	CTRCN	F/S SV IB	350 CRUS	9 6	5000	2 2	25600	28400
------- 1986 BOATS -------
25 11	BOCA CUDDY	OP	CUD	F/S SV IB	350 CRUS	9 6	5300	2 2	25200	28000
25 11	BOCA FISH	OP	CTRCN	F/S SV IB	350 CRUS	9 6	5000	2 2	24400	27100

....For earlier years, see the BUC Used Boat Price Guide, Volume 3

BONITO BOATS INC

ORLANDO FL 32805   COAST GUARD MFG ID- BNT See inside cover to adjust price for area

LOA FT IN	NAME AND/ OR MODEL	TOP/ RIG	BOAT TYPE	-HULL- MTL TP TP	----ENGINE--- # HP MFG	BEAM FT IN	WGT LBS	DRAFT FT IN	RETAIL LOW	RETAIL HIGH
------- 1986 BOATS -------
16 4	6VBR	OP	RNBT	FBG	OB		6 5	850		1700	2000
16 4	6VF CENTER CONSOLE	OP	CTRCN	FBG	OB		6 8	800		1600	1900
16 8	170F	OP	CTRCN	FBG	OB		6 10	875		1750	2100
16 8	170VBR	OP	RNBT	FBG	OB		6 10	925		1850	2200
16 8	170VBR	OP	RNBT	FBG	IO 120-140		6 10			2400	2800
16 10	7CC	OP	RNBT	FBG	OB		6 9	1100		2200	2550
16 10	7CC	OP	RNBT	FBG	IO 120-140		6 9	1700		2400	2850
16 10	7CCF	OP	CTRCN	FBG	OB		6 9	900		1800	2150
16 10	7CD SPORT-A-BOUT	OP	RNBT	FBG	OB		6 9	1075		2150	2500
17	5CWF	OP	UTL	FBG	OB		6 2	600		1200	1450
17 6	176B DOUBLE CONSOLE	OP	BASS	FBG	OB		6 9	1000		2100	2450
17 6	176B SINGLE CONSOLE	OP	BASS	FBG	OB		6 9	1000		2000	2350
18	8VBR	OP	RNBT	FBG	OB		6 7	1150		2350	2750
18	8VBR	OP	RNBT	FBG	IO 120-140		6 7	1750		2600	3050
18	8VF	OP	CTRCN	FBG	OB		6 7	1000		2050	2450
18 2	182F	OP	CTRCN	FBG	OB		6 7	1000		2100	2450
18 4	VIBER 185T	OP	BASS	FBG	OB		7 2			2100	2500
19 2	9VBR	OP	RNBT	FBG	OB		7 9	1500		3000	3500
19 2	9VBR	OP	RNBT	FBG	IO 140-200		7 9	2125		3350	3950
19 2	9VF CC/SC	OP	UTL	FBG	OB		7 9	1200		2300	2650
------- 1985 BOATS -------
16 9	170F		FSH	FBG	OB		6 9	800		1600	1900
16 9	170VBR		RNBT	FBG	OB		6 9	850		1650	2000
16 10	7CC	OP	RNBT	FBG	OB		6 9	1100		2150	2500
16 10	7CC	OP	RNBT	FBG	IO 120-140		6 9	1700		2350	2700
16 10	7CCF	OP	CTRCN	FBG	OB		6 9	900		1750	2100
16 10	7CD SPORT-A-BOUT	OP	RNBT	FBG	OB		6 9	1075		2050	2450
17 6	176B DOUBLE CONSOLE	OP	BASS	FBG	OB		6 9	1000		2050	2400
17 6	176B SINGLE CONSOLE	OP	BASS	FBG	OB		6 9	1000		1950	2300
18	8VBR	OP	RNBT	FBG	OB		6 7	1150		2300	2700
18	8VBR	OP	RNBT	FBG	IO 120-140		6 7	1750		2500	2900
18	8VF	OP	CTRCN	FBG	OB		6 7	1000		2000	2400
18 2	182F	OP	CTRCN	FBG	OB		7 2	1000		2050	2400
19 2	9VBR	OP	RNBT	FBG	OB		7 9	1500		2950	3400
19 2	9VBR	OP	RNBT	FBG	IO 140-198		7 9	2125		3200	3800
19 2	9VF CC/SC	OP	UTL	FBG	OB		7 9	1200		2250	2600

....For earlier years, see the BUC Used Boat Price Guide, Volume 3

BONUM MARIN AB

S68101 KRISTI SWEDEN   See inside cover to adjust price for area

FORMERLY LARSSON TRADE AB

LOA FT IN	NAME AND/ OR MODEL	TOP/ RIG	BOAT TYPE	-HULL- MTL TP TP	----ENGINE--- # HP MFG	BEAM FT IN	WGT LBS	DRAFT FT IN	RETAIL LOW	RETAIL HIGH
------- 1986 BOATS -------
25	BONUM 25	DC		FBG DS IB	36D- 55D	8 6	3860	2 4	19600	22700
------- 1985 BOATS -------
25	BONUM 25	DC		FBG DS IB	36D VLVO	8 6	3860	2 4	18800	20800
------- 1984 BOATS -------
25	BONUM 25	DC		FBG DS IB	36D VLVO	8 6	3860	2 4	17300	19700

....For earlier years, see the BUC Used Boat Price Guide, Volume 3

BOOTH ENTERPRISES

VICTORIA BC CANADA V8S COAST GUARD MFG ID- ZQT See inside cover to adjust price for area

For more recent years, see the BUC Used Boat Price Guide, Volume 1

LOA FT IN	NAME AND/ OR MODEL	TOP/ RIG	BOAT TYPE	-HULL- MTL TP TP	----ENGINE--- # HP MFG	BEAM FT IN	WGT LBS	DRAFT FT IN	RETAIL LOW	RETAIL HIGH
------- 1986 BOATS -------
26	THUNDERBIRD	SLP	SA/OD	FBG KL		7 6	4000	4 6	6300	7250
------- 1985 BOATS -------
26	THUNDERBIRD	SLP	SA/OD	FBG KL		7 6	4000	4 6	5950	6850
26	THUNDERBIRD	SLP	SA/RC	FBG KL	OB	7 6	4000	4 6	6250	7200
------- 1984 BOATS -------
17	SALTY	HT	CR	FBG DS IB	7D YAN	6 6	1550	1 6	3350	3900
26	THUNDERBIRD	SLP	SA/OD	FBG KL	OB	7 6	4000	4 6	5850	6750

....For earlier years, see the BUC Used Boat Price Guide, Volume 3

BORRESENS BAADEBYGGERI A/S

7100 VEJLE DENMARK   COAST GUARD MFG ID- BBG See inside cover to adjust price for area

For more recent years, see the BUC Used Boat Price Guide, Volume 1

LOA FT IN	NAME AND/ OR MODEL	TOP/ RIG	BOAT TYPE	-HULL- MTL TP TP	----ENGINE--- # HP MFG	BEAM FT IN	WGT LBS	DRAFT FT IN	RETAIL LOW	RETAIL HIGH
------- 1996 BOATS -------
26 9	SOLING	SLP	SARAC	FBG KL		6 2			35300	39300
29 2	DRAGON	SLP	SARAC	FBG KL		6 4		3 10	33400	37100
30 5	KNARR	SLP	SACAC	FBG KL	OB	6 10		4 3	51400	56500
32 8	BB 10	SLP	SARAC	F/S KL		7 5		4 9	14600	16600
37 7	BB 12 RACING	SLP	SARAC	F/S KL IB	9D YAN	7 7		6 6	133500	146500
------- 1995 BOATS -------
26 9	SOLING	SLP	SARAC	FBG KL		6 2			33200	36900
29 2	DRAGON	SLP	SARAC	FBG KL		6 4		3 10	31300	34800
30 5	KNARR	SLP	SACAC	FBG KL OB		6 10		4 3	48500	53300
32 8	BB 10	SLP	SARAC	F/S KL		7 5		4 9	13800	15700
37 7	BB 11 5 RACING	SLP	SARAC	F/S KL IB	9D YAN	7 7		6 6	125000	137500
------- 1994 BOATS -------
26 9	SOLING	SLP	SARAC	FBG KL		6 2			31200	34700
29 2	DRAGON	SLP	SARAC	FBG KL		6 4		3 10	29500	32700

BORRESENS BAADEBYGGERI A/S -CONTINUED
See inside cover to adjust price for area

LOA FT IN	NAME AND/ OR MODEL	TOP/ RIG	BOAT TYPE	-HULL- MTL TP	TP	----ENGINE--- # HP MFG	BEAM FT IN	WGT LBS	DRAFT FT IN	RETAIL LOW	RETAIL HIGH
						1994 BOATS					
30 5	KNARR	SLP	SACAC	FBG	KL	OB	6 10		4 3	44900	49900
32 8	BB 10	SLP	SARAC	F/S	KL		7 5		4 9	13000	14700
37 7	BB 11 5 RACING	SLP	SARAC	F/S	KL IB	9D YAN	9 7		6 6	117500	129000
39 4	BB 12	SLP	SARAC	F/S	KL IB	18D YAN	9 8		6 6	125500	138000
						1986 BOATS					
26 9	SOLING	SLP	SA/OD	FBG	KL		6 3	2280	4 3	12700	14400
29 2	DRAGON MODERN	CUT	SA/OD	FBG	KL		6 4	3744	3 11	16500	18700
29 2	DRAGON RACING	CUT	SA/OD	FBG	KL		6 4	3744	3 11	20500	22800
30 5	KNARR	CUT	SA/OD	FBG	KL		6 11	4956	4 3	23200	25700
32 9	BB 10M FAMILY RACER	SLP	SA/OD	FBG	KL		7 1	4956	4 10	17100	19400
						1985 BOATS					
26 9	SOLING	SLP	SA/OD	FBG	KL		6 3	2280	4 3	11900	13600
29 2	DRAGON MODERN	CUT	SA/OD	FBG	KL		6 4	3744	3 11	15700	17800
29 2	DRAGON PRESTIGE	CUT	SA/OD	FBG	KL		6 4	3744	3 11	19500	21600
30 5	KNARR	CUT	SA/OD	FBG	KL		6 11	4956	4 3	22300	24800
32 9	BB 10M FAMILY RACER	SLP	SA/OD	FBG	KL		7 1	4956	4 10	16000	18200
32 9	BB 10M FAMILY RACER	CUT	SA/OD	FBG	KL		7 6	4956	4 10	16000	18200
						1984 BOATS					
26 9	SOLING	SLP	SA/OD	FBG	KL		6 3	2280	4 3	11200	12700
29 2	DRAGON MODERN	CUT	SA/OD	FBG	KL		6 4	3744	3 11	14600	16600
29 2	DRAGON PRESTIGE	CUT	SA/OD	FBG	KL		6 4	3744	3 11	18400	20500
30 5	KNARR	CUT	SA/OD	FBG	KL		6 11	4956	4 3	20900	23200

....For earlier years, see the BUC Used Boat Price Guide, Volume 3

VANDEN BOSCH MOTORYACHTS INC
BOCA RATON FL 33431   COAST GUARD MFG ID- MQL See inside cover to adjust price for area

LOA FT IN	NAME AND/ OR MODEL	TOP/ RIG	BOAT TYPE	-HULL- MTL TP	TP	----ENGINE--- # HP MFG	BEAM FT IN	WGT LBS	DRAFT FT IN	RETAIL LOW	RETAIL HIGH
						1986 BOATS					
58	VANDEN-BOSCH 58	FB	MY	STL DV	IB	T165D PERK	16 3	90000	6 6	358500	394000
						1985 BOATS					
58	VANDEN-BOSCH 58		TRWL	STL RB	IB	T165D PERK	16	77000	4 6	313000	344000

BOSSOMS BOATYARD LTD
OXFORD ENGLAND   See inside cover to adjust price for area

LOA FT IN	NAME AND/ OR MODEL	TOP/ RIG	BOAT TYPE	-HULL- MTL TP	TP	----ENGINE--- # HP MFG	BEAM FT IN	WGT LBS	DRAFT FT IN	RETAIL LOW	RETAIL HIGH
						1994 BOATS					
25 8	VERTUE II DEEP	SLP	SACAC	KL	IB	9D YAN	7 10	6100	4 5	21600	24100
						1993 BOATS					
25 8	VENTURE II DEEP	SLP	SACAC	KL	IB	9D YAN	7 10	6100	4 5	20400	22600
						1988 BOATS					
19 5	NELL		LNCH		OB		5 9	1850		**	**
25 8	VERTUE II	SLP	SA/CR	FBG KL	IB	10D YAN	7 10	9200	4 5	23500	26100
31 9	PATRICIA		LNCH		IB		6 6			**	**
						1987 BOATS					
19 5	NELL		LNCH		OB		5 9	1850		**	**
25 8	VERTUE II	SLP	SA/CR	FBG KL	IB	10D YAN	7 10	9200	4 5	22100	24600
31 9	PATRICIA		LNCH		IB		6 6			**	**
						1985 BOATS					
25 8	VERTUE II	SLP	SA/CR	FBG KL	IB	10D YAN	7 10	9200	4 5	19600	21700

....For earlier years, see the BUC Used Boat Price Guide, Volume 3

BOSTON WHALER INC
EDGEWATER FL 32141   COAST GUARD MFG ID- BWC See inside cover to adjust price for area
FORMERLY FISHER PIERCE CO INC

For more recent years, see the BUC Used Boat Price Guide, Volume 1

LOA FT IN	NAME AND/ OR MODEL	TOP/ RIG	BOAT TYPE	-HULL- MTL TP	TP	----ENGINE--- # HP MFG	BEAM FT IN	WGT LBS	DRAFT FT IN	RETAIL LOW	RETAIL HIGH
						1996 BOATS					
16 7	MONTAUK 17	OP	CTRCN	F/S TR	OB		6 2	950	9	5300	6100
17	DAUNTLESS 17	OP	RNBT	F/S DV	OB		7	1500	1	6100	7000
17 6	OUTRAGE 17	OP	CTRCN	F/S DV	OB		7	1700	1	8900	10100
18 5	RAGE 18	OP	CTRCN	F/S DV	JT	285	7	2400	1 2	10400	11800
19 8	DAUNTLESS 20	OP	RNBT	F/S DV	OB		8 4	2350	1	10600	12100
19 8	OUTRAGE 20	OP	CTRCN	F/S DV	OB		8 4	2200	1 3	11100	12700
20 9	OUTRAGE 21	OP	CTRCN	F/S DV	OB		8 6	2500	1 3	12000	13600
23 10	OUTRAGE 24	OP	CTRCN	F/S DV	OB		8 6	3300	1 5	15200	17300
26 7	OFFSHORE 27	OP	CTRCN	F/S SV	OB		10	5800	1 9	40300	44800
						1995 BOATS					
16 7	MONTAUK 17	OP	CTRCN	F/S TR	OB		6 2	900	9	4800	5500
17	DAUNTLESS 17	OP	W/T	F/S DV	OB		7	1550	9	5650	6500
17 3	OUTRAGE 17	OP	CTRCN	F/S DV	OB		6 8	1020	10	5500	6350
18 6	OUTRAGE 19 II	OP	CTRCN	F/S DV	OB		7 2	1450	10	6650	7650
20 9	OUTRAGE 21	OP	CTRCN	F/S DV	OB		8 6	2500	1 2	11400	13000
23 10	OUTRAGE 24	OP	CTRCN	F/S SV	OB		8 6	3100	1 5	13700	15600
26 7	OFFSHORE 27	HT	OFF	F/S DV	OB		10	5800	1 9	43100	47900
						1994 BOATS					
16 7	MONTAUK	OP	CTRCN	F/S DV	OB		6 2	900	9	4550	5250
17 3	OUTRAGE 17	OP	CTRCN	F/S DV	OB		6 8	1020	10	5250	6050
18 6	OUTRAGE 19 II	OP	CTRCN	F/S DV	OB		7 2	1450	10	7300	8400
20 9	OUTRAGE 21	OP	CTRCN	F/S DV	OB		8 6	2500	1 2	10900	12400
23 10	OUTRAGE 24	OP	CTRCN	F/S SV	OB		8 6	3100	1 5	13100	14800
26 7	OFFSHORE 27	OP	OFF	F/S DV	IB	T300	10	5800	1 9	36900	41000
						1993 BOATS					
16 7	MONTAUK	OP	CTRCN	F/S DV	OB		6 2	900	9	4300	5000
17 3	OUTRAGE 17	OP	CTRCN	F/S DV	OB		6 8	1020	10	5000	5750
18 6	OUTRAGE 19	OP	CTRCN	F/S DV	OB		7 2	1450	10	6650	7650
21	WHALER 21 WA	OP	FSH	F/S DV	OB		8 6	2600	1 1	10100	11500
22 3	OUTRAGE 22	OP	OPFSH	F/S DV	OB		7 5	2050	1 2	9200	10500
22 3	OUTRAGE 22 WD	OP	OPFSH	F/S DV	OB		7 5	2300	1 2	9300	10600
22 9	WHALER 23	OP	FSH	F/S DV	OB		8		1 2	12400	14100
22 9	WHALER 23 WA	OP	FSH	F/S DV	IB	T200	8 6	4300	1 5	22600	25800
24 7	OUTRAGE 25	OP	FSH	F/S DV	OB		8	3300	1 4	12300	13900
24 7	OUTRAGE 25 WD	OP	FSH	F/S DV	OB		8	3550	1 4	13700	15600
26 7	OFFSHORE 27	OP	OFF	F/S DV	IO	T300	10	5800	1 9	35000	38900
26 7	WHALER 27 WA	OP	OFF	F/S DV	IO	T300	10	6140	2 6	31400	34900
						1992 BOATS					
16 7	MONTAUK	OP	CTRCN	F/S SV	OB		6 2	900	9	4100	4750
16 7	SPORT GLS 17	OP	UTL	F/S DV	OB		6 8	850	9	3500	4100
17 3	OUTRAGE 17	OP	CTRCN	F/S DV	OB		6 8	1020	10	4800	5500
18 6	OUTRAGE 19	OP	CTRCN	FBG DV	OB		7 2	1450	10	6350	7300
21	WHALER 21 WA	OP	FSH	F/S DV	OB		8 6	2600	1 1	9700	11000
22 3	OUTRAGE 22	OP	OPFSH	F/S DV	OB		7 5	2050	1 2	8850	10000
22 3	OUTRAGE 22 WA	OP	OPFSH	F/S DV	OB		7 5	2300	1 2	9000	10200
22 9	WHALER 23	OP	FSH	F/S DV	OB		8		1 5	11900	13500
22 9	WHALER 23 WA	OP	FSH	F/S DV	IB	T200	8 6	4300	1 5	22000	24500
24 7	OUTRAGE 25	OP	FSH	F/S DV	OB		8	3300	1 4	11800	13400
24 7	OUTRAGE 25 WD	OP	FSH	F/S DV	OB		8	3550	1 4	13100	14800
26 7	OFFSHORE 27	OP	OFF	F/S DV	IB	T300	10	5800	1 9	33200	36900
26 7	WHALER 27 WA	OP	OFF	F/S DV	IO	T300	10	6140	2 6	29400	32600
31 9	WHALER 31	OP	CBNCR	F/S DV	IB	T300D	11 10	12500	3 2	100500	110500
						1991 BOATS					
16 7	MONTAUK	OP	CTRCN	F/S SV	OB		6 2	900	9	3900	4350
16 7	SPORT GLS 17	OP	UTL	F/S DV	OB		6 8	850	9	3400	3950
17 3	OUTRAGE 17	OP	CTRCN	F/S DV	OB		6 8	1020	10	4550	5250
18 6	OUTRAGE 19	OP	CTRCN	FBG DV	OB		7 2	1450	10	6100	7000
21	WHALER 21 WA	OP	FSH	F/S DV	IB	T165D	8 6	2600	1 1	12300	14000
22 3	OUTRAGE 22	OP	OPFSH	F/S DV	OB		7 5	2050	1 2	8400	9650
22 3	OUTRAGE 22 CUDDY	OP	CUD	F/S DV	OB		7 5	2400	1 2	9650	11000
22 3	OUTRAGE 22 CUDDY	OP	CUD	F/S DV	SE	T150	7 5	2950	1 2	10400	11900
22 3	OUTRAGE 22 WD	OP	OPFSH	F/S DV	OB		7 5	2300	1 2	9100	10400
22 9	WHALER 23 WA	OP	FSH	F/S DV	IB	T200	8	4300	1 5	21400	23200
24 7	OUTRAGE 25	OP	FSH	F/S DV	OB		8	3300	1 4	11300	12900
24 7	OUTRAGE 25	OP	FSH	F/S DV	IO	T225	8	3550	1 4	16400	18700
24 7	OUTRAGE 25 WD	OP	FSH	F/S DV	OB		8	3550	1 4	17400	19800
26 7	OFFSHORE 27	OP	OFF	F/S DV	IB	T300	10	5800	1 9	31500	35000
26 7	WHALER 27 WA	OP	OFF	F/S DV	IO	T300	10	5850	2 6	27900	30100
27 11	WHALER 27 WA	OP	OFF	F/S DV	IO	T275	10	4600	1 4	29200	31000
31 9	WHALER 31	OP	CBNCR	F/S DV	IB	T300D	11 10	12500	3 2	95900	105500
						1990 BOATS					
16 7	MONTAUK	OP	CTRCN	F/S DV	OB		6 2	900	9	3750	4350
16	NEWPORT	OP	UTL	F/S DV	OB		6 2	950	9	3450	4000
16 7	SPORT GLS 17	OP	UTL	F/S DV	OB		6 8	850	9	3250	3800
16 7	SUPER-SPORT LTD	OP	UTL	F/S DV	OB		6 8	800	9	3150	3650
18 6	OUTRAGE 22	OP	OPFSH	F/S DV	OB		7 2	1450	10	5850	6700
22 3	OUTRAGE 22	OP	OPFSH	F/S DV	OB		7 5	2050	1 2	8100	9300
22 3	OUTRAGE 22 CUDDY	OP	CUD	F/S DV	OB		7 5	3050	1 2	9350	10600
22 3	OUTRAGE 22 CUDDY	OP	CUD	F/S DV	SE		7 5	3050	1 2	**	**
22 3	OUTRAGE 22 WD	OP	CUD	F/S DV	SE		7 5	3050	1 2	**	**
22 3	REVENGE 22 W/T	OP	CR	F/S DV	OB		7 5	2350	1 2	9350	10700
22 3	REVENGE 22 W/T	OP	CR	F/S DV	SE		7 5	3050	1 2	**	**
24 7	OUTRAGE 25	OP	FSH	F/S DV	OB		8	3300	1 4	10900	12400
24 7	OUTRAGE 25 CUDDY	OP	CUD	F/S DV	OB		8	3500	1 4	12500	14200

96th ed. - Vol. II   CONTINUED ON NEXT PAGE   81

LOA FT	LOA IN	NAME AND/ OR MODEL	TOP/ RIG	BOAT TYPE	-HULL- MTL	-HULL- TP	ENGINE TP	ENGINE # HP	ENGINE MFG	BEAM FT	BEAM IN	WGT LBS	DRAFT FT	DRAFT IN	RETAIL LOW	RETAIL HIGH
		1990 BOATS														
24	7	OUTRAGE 25 CUDDY	OP	CUD	F/S	DV	SE			8		3500	1	4	**	**
24	7	OUTRAGE 25 WD	OP	FSH	F/S	DV	SE			8		3300	1	4	**	**
24	7	REVENGE 25 W/T	OP	CR	F/S	DV	OB			8		4000	1	4	11800	13400
24	7	REVENGE 25 W/T	OP	CR	F/S	DV	SE			8		5170	1	4	**	**
24	7	REVENGE 25 WA	OP	CUD	F/S	DV	SE			8		5170	1	4	**	**
26	7	WHALER 27	OP	OFF	F/S	DV	OB			10		4520	1	9	22800	25400
26	7	WHALER 27	OP	OFF	F/S	DV	IB	T230	MRCR	10		7650	2	6	33400	37200
26	7	WHALER 27 CUDDY	OP	CTRCN	F/S	DV	OB			10		4130	1	9	22600	25100
26	7	WHALER 27 CUDDY	OP	CTRCN	F/S	DV	SE			10		5260	1	9	**	**
26	7	WHALER 27 FULL CABIN	OP	CBNCR	F/S	DV	SE	T		10		7950	1	9	**	**
26	7	WHALER 27 WA	OP	OFF	F/S	DV	SE	T		10		7650	2	6	**	**
26	7	WHALER 27 WD	OP	OFF	F/S	DV	SE	T		10		7650	2	6	**	**
31	9	WHALER 31	OP	CBNCR	F/S	DV	IB	T350	CRUS	11	10	12900			66700	73300
31	9	WHALER 31	OP	CBNCR	F/S	DV	IB	T250D	CUM	11	10	12900			90800	99800
		1989 BOATS														
16	7	MONTAUK	OP	CTRCN	F/S	SV	OB			6	2	900		9	3650	4200
16	7	NEWPORT	OP	CTRCN	F/S	SV	OB			6	2	950		9	3800	4400
16	7	STRIPER	OP	BASS	F/S	SV	OB			6	2	850		9	3450	4000
16	7	SUPER-SPORT	OP	UTL	F/S	SV	OB			6	2	850		9	3500	4100
16	7	SUPER-SPORT LTD	OP	UTL	F/S	SV	OB			6	2	900		9	4550	5200
18	6	OUTRAGE 18	OP	CTRCN	F/S	DV	OB			7	2	1250		10	6000	6900
20	3	OUTRAGE 20	OP	CTRCN	F/S	SV	OB			7	5	1850	1	1	7650	8750
20	3	OUTRAGE 20	OP	CTRCN	F/S	SV	SE			7	5	1850	1	1	**	**
20	3	REVENGE 20 W/T	OP	CR	F/S	DV	OB			7	5	2150	1	1	9450	10700
20	3	REVENGE 20 W/T	OP	CR	F/S	DV	SE			7	5	2150	1	1	**	**
20	3	TEMPTATION 2000	OP	SPTCR	F/S	DV	SE			7	5	2500	1	1	**	**
22	3	OUTRAGE 22	OP	OPFSH	F/S	DV	OB			7	5	2050	1	2	7850	9000
22	3	OUTRAGE 22	OP	OPFSH	F/S	DV	SE			7	5	3050	1	2	**	**
22	3	OUTRAGE 22	OP	OPFSH	F/S	DV	IO	205	MRCR	7	5	3050	1	2	9700	11000
22	3	OUTRAGE 22 CUDDY	OP	CUD	F/S	DV	OB			7	5	2250	1	2	9000	10300
22	3	OUTRAGE 22 CUDDY	OP	CUD	F/S	DV	SE			7	5	3050	1	2	**	**
22	3	REVENGE 22 W/T	OP	CR	F/S	DV	OB			7	5	2350	1	2	9050	10300
22	3	REVENGE 22 W/T	OP	CR	F/S	DV	SE			7	5	3350	1	2	**	**
22	3	TEMPTATION 2200	OP	SPTCR	F/S	DV	SE			7	5	3450	1	2	**	**
22	3	TEMPTATION 2200	OP	SPTCR	F/S	DV	IO			7	5	3450	1	2	**	**
22	3	TEMPTATION 2200	OP	SPTCR	F/S	DV	IO	260	MRCR	7	5	3450	1	2	10400	11800
22	3	TEMPTATION 2200	OP	SPTCR	F/S	DV	IO	330	MRCR	7	5	3450	1	2	11600	13200
24	7	OUTRAGE 25	OP	FSH	F/S	DV	OB			8		3300	1	4	10600	12000
24	7	OUTRAGE 25	OP	FSH	F/S	DV	SE			8		4620	1	4	**	**
24	7	OUTRAGE 25 CUDDY	OP	CUD	F/S	DV	OB			8		3500	1	4	12100	13700
24	7	OUTRAGE 25 CUDDY	OP	CUD	F/S	DV	SE			8		3500	1	4	**	**
24	7	REVENGE 25 W/T	OP	CR	F/S	DV	OB			8		4000	1	4	11400	12900
24	7	REVENGE 25 W/T	OP	CR	F/S	DV	SE			8		5170	1	4	**	**
24	7	REVENGE 25 WAR	OP	CUD	F/S	DV	OB			8		4000	1	4	14000	15900
24	7	REVENGE 25 WAR	OP	CUD	F/S	DV	SE			8		5170	1	4	**	**
24	7	REVENGE 25 WAR	HT	CUD	F/S	DV	OB			8		4000	1	4	14000	15900
24	7	REVENGE 25 WAR	HT	CUD	F/S	DV	SE			8		5170	1	4	**	**
24	7	TEMPTATION 2500	OP	SPTCR	F/S	DV	SE			8		5270	1	4	**	**
24	7	TEMPTATION 2500	OP	SPTCR	F/S	DV	IO			8		5270	1	4	**	**
24	7	TEMPTATION 2500	OP	SPTCR	F/S	DV	IO	330	MRCR	8		5270	1	4	18100	20100
26	7	WHALER 27	OP	OFF	F/S	DV	OB			10		4520	1	9	22000	24400
26	7	WHALER 27	OP	OFF	F/S	DV	SE	T		10		7650	2	6	**	**
26	7	WHALER 27	OP	OFF	F/S	DV	SE	T	OMC	10		7650	2	6	**	**
26	7	WHALER 27	OP	OFF	F/S	DV	IB	T230	MRCR	10		7650	2	6	31800	35400
26	7	WHALER 27 CUDDY	OP	CTRCN	F/S	DV	OB			10		4130	1	9	21900	24300
26	7	WHALER 27 CUDDY	OP	CTRCN	F/S	DV	SE			10		5260	1	9	**	**
26	7	WHALER 27 CUDDY	OP	CTRCN	F/S	DV	SE	T	OMC	10		5260	1	9	**	**
26	7	WHALER 27 FULL CABIN	OP	CBNCR	F/S	DV	SE	T		10		7950	1	9	**	**
26	7	WHALER 27 FULL CABIN	OP	CBNCR	F/S	DV	SE	T	OMC	10		7950	1	9	**	**
26	7	WHALER 27 FULL CABIN	OP	CBNCR	F/S	DV	IB	T230	MRCR	10		7950	2	6	35700	39600
		1988 BOATS														
16	7	MONTAUK	OP	CTRCN	F/S	SV	OB			6	2	900		9	3500	4100
16	7	NEWPORT	OP	CTRCN	F/S	SV	OB			6	2	950		9	3700	4300
16	7	STRIPER	OP	BASS	F/S	SV	OB			6	2	850		9	3300	3850
16	7	SUPER SPORT	OP	UTL	F/S	SV	OB			6	2	850		9	3400	3950
16	7	SUPER SPORT LTD	OP	UTL	F/S	SV	OB			6	2	900		9	4400	5050
18	6	OUTRAGE 18	OP	CTRCN	F/S	DV	OB			7	2	1250		10	5800	6700
20	3	OUTRAGE 20	OP	CTRCN	F/S	SV	OB			7	5	1850		11	7400	8500
20	3	OUTRAGE 20	OP	CTRCN	F/S	SV	SE			7	5	1850	1	1	**	**
20	3	REVENGE 20 W/T	OP	CR	F/S	DV	OB			7	5	2150		11	9200	10500
20	3	REVENGE 20 W/T	OP	CR	F/S	DV	SE			7	5	2150	1	1	**	**
20	3	TEMPTATION 2000	OP	SPTCR	F/S	DV	SE			7	5	2500	1	1	**	**
22	3	OUTRAGE 22	OP	OPFSH	F/S	DV	OB			7	5	2050	1	2	7600	8750
22	3	OUTRAGE 22	OP	OPFSH	F/S	DV	SE			7	5	3050	1	2	**	**
22	3	OUTRAGE 22	OP	OPFSH	F/S	DV	IO			7	5	3050	1	2	**	**
22	3	OUTRAGE 22	OP	OPFSH	F/S	DV	IO	205	MRCR	7	5	3050	1	2	9200	10500
22	3	OUTRAGE 22 CUDDY	OP	CUD	F/S	DV	OB			7	5	2250	1	2	8650	9950
22	3	OUTRAGE 22 CUDDY	OP	CUD	F/S	DV	SE			7	5	3050	1	2	**	**
22	3	OUTRAGE 22 CUDDY	OP	CUD	F/S	DV	IO			7	5	3050	1	2	**	**
22	3	REVENGE 22 W/T	OP	CR	F/S	DV	OB			7	5	2350	1	2	8700	10000
22	3	REVENGE 22 W/T	OP	CR	F/S	DV	SE			7	5	3350	1	2	**	**
22	3	REVENGE 22 W/T	OP	CR	F/S	DV	IO			7	5	3350	1	2	**	**
22	3	REVENGE 22 W/T	OP	CR	F/S	DV	IO	205	MRCR	7	5	3350	1	2	9250	10500
22	3	TEMPTATION 2200	OP	SPTCR	F/S	DV	SE			7	5	3450	1	2	**	**
22	3	TEMPTATION 2200	OP	SPTCR	F/S	DV	IO			7	5	3450	1	2	**	**
22	3	TEMPTATION 2200	OP	SPTCR	F/S	DV	IO	260	MRCR	7	5	3450	1	2	9800	11200
22	3	TEMPTATION 2200	OP	SPTCR	F/S	DV	IO	365	MRCR	7	5	3450	1	2	12000	13600
24	7	OUTRAGE 25	OP	FSH	F/S	DV	OB			8		3300	1	4	10300	11700
24	7	OUTRAGE 25	OP	FSH	F/S	DV	SE			8		4470	1	4	**	**
24	7	OUTRAGE 25	OP	FSH	F/S	DV	IO			8		4470	1	4	**	**
24	7	OUTRAGE 25	OP	FSH	F/S	DV	IO	260	MRCR	8		4470	1	4	14600	16600
24	7	OUTRAGE 25 CUDDY	OP	CUD	F/S	DV	OB			8		3500	1	4	11700	13300
24	7	OUTRAGE 25 CUDDY	OP	CUD	F/S	DV	SE			8		4470	1	4	**	**
24	7	OUTRAGE 25 CUDDY	OP	CUD	F/S	DV	IO			8		4470	1	4	**	**
24	7	OUTRAGE 25 CUDDY	OP	CUD	F/S	DV	IO	260	MRCR	8		4470	1	4	13600	15400
24	7	REVENGE 25 W/T	OP	CR	F/S	DV	OB			8		4000	1	4	11000	12500
24	7	REVENGE 25 W/T	OP	CR	F/S	DV	SE			8		5170	1	4	**	**
24	7	REVENGE 25 W/T	OP	CR	F/S	DV	IO			8		5170	1	4	**	**
24	7	REVENGE 25 W/T	OP	CR	F/S	DV	IO	260	MRCR	8		5170	1	4	15200	17300
24	7	REVENGE 25 WAR	OP	CUD	F/S	DV	OB			8		4000	1	4	13500	15400
24	7	REVENGE 25 WAR	OP	CUD	F/S	DV	SE			8		5170	1	4	**	**
24	7	REVENGE 25 WAR	OP	CUD	F/S	DV	IO			8		5170	1	4	**	**
24	7	REVENGE 25 WAR	OP	CUD	F/S	DV	IO	260	MRCR	8		5170	1	4	15100	17100
24	7	REVENGE 25 WAR	HT	CUD	F/S	DV	OB			8		4000	1	4	13600	15400
24	7	REVENGE 25 WAR	HT	CUD	F/S	DV	IO			8		5170	1	4	**	**
24	7	REVENGE 25 WAR	HT	CUD	F/S	DV	IO	260	MRCR	8		5170	1	4	15100	17100
24	7	TEMPTATION 2500	OP	SPTCR	F/S	DV	SE			8		5270	1	4	**	**
24	7	TEMPTATION 2500	OP	SPTCR	F/S	DV	IO			8		5270	1	4	**	**
24	7	TEMPTATION 2500	OP	SPTCR	F/S	DV	IO	365	MRCR	8		5270	1	4	18100	20100
24	7	TEMPTATION 2500	OP	SPTCR	F/S	DV	SE	T115	OMC	8		5270	1	4	13800	15700
26	7	WHALER 27	OP	OFF	F/S	DV	OB			10		4520	1	9	21200	23500
26	7	WHALER 27	OP	OFF	F/S	DV	SE	T		10		7650	2	6	**	**
26	7	WHALER 27	OP	OFF	F/S	DV	SE	T	OMC	10		7650	2	6	**	**
26	7	WHALER 27	OP	OFF	F/S	DV	IB	T230	MRCR	10		7650	2	6	30300	33700
26	7	WHALER 27 CUDDY	OP	CTRCN	F/S	DV	OB			10		4520	1	9	21500	23900
26	7	WHALER 27 CUDDY	OP	CTRCN	F/S	DV	SE			10		7650	1	9	**	**
26	7	WHALER 27 CUDDY	OP	CTRCN	F/S	DV	SE	T	OMC	10		7650	1	9	**	**
26	7	WHALER 27 FULL CABIN	OP	CBNCR	F/S	DV	SE	T		10		7950	1	9	**	**
26	7	WHALER 27 FULL CABIN	OP	CBNCR	F/S	DV	SE	T	OMC	10		7950	2	6	**	**
26	7	WHALER 27 FULL CABIN	OP	CBNCR	F/S	DV	IB	T230	MRCR	10		7950	2	6	34000	37800
		1987 BOATS														
16	7	MONTAUK	OP	CTRCN	F/S	SV	OB			6	2	900		9	3400	3950
16	7	NEWPORT	OP	CTRCN	F/S	SV	OB			6	2	950		9	3550	4150
16	7	STRIPER	OP	BASS	F/S	SV	OB			6	2	850		9	3200	3700
16	7	SUPER-SPORT	OP	UTL	F/S	SV	OB			6	2	850		9	2950	3400
16	7	SUPER-SPORT LTD	OP	UTL	F/S	SV	OB			6	2	850			4500	5200
18	6	GTX18	OP	RNBT	F/S		OB			7	2	1250		1	5100	5850
18	6	GTX18	OP	RNBT	F/S		IO	190	MRCR	7	2	2950		1	5000	5750
18	6	OUTRAGE 18	OP	CTRCN	F/S	DV	OB			7	2	1250		10	5650	6450
19	10	OUTRAGE 20	OP	CTRCN	F/S	SV	OB			7	5	1650		11	6300	7200
19	10	REVENGE 20	OP	CR	F/S	DV	OB			7	5	1950		11	7350	8450
20	3	TEMPTATION 2000	OP	SPTCR	F/S	DV	SE		OMC	7	5	2250		11	**	**
22	3	OUTRAGE 22	OP	OPFSH	F/S	DV	OB			7	5	2050	1	2	7400	8500
22	3	OUTRAGE 22	OP	OPFSH	F/S	DV	IO	190	MRCR	7	5	3050	1	2	8600	9850
22	3	OUTRAGE 22	OP	OPFSH	F/S	DV	SE	205	OMC	7	5	3050	1	4	10000	11300
22	3	OUTRAGE 22 CUDDY	OP	CUD	F/S	DV	IO	190	MRCR	7	5	3050	1	2	8100	9300
22	3	OUTRAGE 22 CUDDY	OP	CUD	F/S	DV	SE	205	OMC	7	5	3050	1	2	10500	11900
22	3	REVENGE W/T	OP	CR	F/S	DV	OB			7	5	2350	1	4	9550	10900
22	3	REVENGE W/T	OP	CR	F/S	DV	IO	190	MRCR	7	5	3350			8650	9900
22	3	REVENGE W/T	OP	CR	F/S	DV	SE	205	OMC	7	5	3350			12100	13800
22	3	TEMPTATION 2200	OP	SPTCR	F/S	DV	SE	205	OMC	7	5	3350			11300	12800
22	3	TEMPTATION 2200	OP	SPTCR	F/S	DV	IO	260	MRCR	7	5	3350	1	4	9150	10400
22	3	TEMPTATION 2200	OP	SPTCR	F/S	DV	IO	330	MRCR	7	5	3350	1	4	10200	11600
22	3	TEMPTATION 2200	OP	SPTCR	F/S	DV	SE	T115	OMC	7	5	3150	1	4	10900	12400
24	7	OUTRAGE 25	OP	FSH	F/S	DV	SE	205	OMC	8		4670	1	4	12300	14000

CONTINUED ON NEXT PAGE

BOSTON WHALER INC -CONTINUED See inside cover to adjust price for area

LOA FT	LOA IN	NAME AND/ OR MODEL	TOP/ RIG	BOAT TYPE	-HULL- MTL	-HULL- TP	ENGINE TP	ENGINE # HP	ENGINE MFG	BEAM FT	BEAM IN	WGT LBS	DRAFT FT	DRAFT IN	RETAIL LOW	RETAIL HIGH
		1987 BOATS														
24	7	OUTRAGE 25	OP	FSH	F/S	DV	IO	260	MRCR	8		4670	1	4	14200	16200
24	7	OUTRAGE 25	OP	FSH	F/S	DV	SE	T115	OMC	8		4670	1	4	12300	14000
24	7	OUTRAGE 25 CUDDY	OP	CUD	F/S	DV	SE	205	OMC	8		4670	1	4	12600	14300
24	7	OUTRAGE 25 CUDDY	OP	CUD	F/S	DV	IO	260	MRCR	8		4670	1	4	12400	14100
24	7	OUTRAGE 25 CUDDY	OP	CUD	F/S	DV	SE	T115	OMC	8		4670	1	4	12700	14400
24	7	REVENGE 25 WAR	OP	CUD	F/S	DV	SE	205	OMC	8		4670	1	4	15300	17400
24	7	REVENGE 25 WAR	OP	CUD	F/S	DV	IO	260	MRCR	8		4670	1	4	14200	16100
24	7	REVENGE 25 WAR	OP	CUD	F/S	DV	SE	T115	OMC	8		4670	1	4	15200	17300
24	7	REVENGE 25 WAR	HT	CUD	F/S	DV	IO	260	MRCR	8		4670	1	4	13300	15100
24	7	REVENGE 25 WAR	HT	CUD	F/S	DV	SE	T115	OMC	8		4670	1	4	14400	16300
24	7	REVENGE W/T	OP	CR	F/S	DV	SE	205	OMC	8		4700	1	4	13700	15600
24	7	REVENGE W/T	OP	CR	F/S	DV	IO	260	MRCR	8		5170	1	4	14400	16400
24	7	REVENGE W/T	OP	CR	F/S	DV	SE	T115	OMC	8		5170	1	4	14400	16300
24	7	TEMPTATION 2500	OP	SPTCR	F/S	DV	SE	205	OMC	8		5170	1	4	13300	15100
24	7	TEMPTATION 2500	OP	SPTCR	F/S	DV	IO	260-330		8		5170	1	4	14400	17800
24	7	TEMPTATION 2500	OP	SPTCR	F/S	DV	SE	T115	OMC	8		5030	1	4	13100	14900
26	7	WHALER 27	OP	OFF	F/S	DV	SE	T205	OMC	10		7650	2	6	21800	24200
26	7	WHALER 27	OP	OFF	F/S	DV	IB	T230	MRCR	10		7650	2	6	28900	32100
26	7	WHALER 27 CUDDY	OP	CTRCN	F/S	DV	OB			10		4130	1	9	20600	22900
26	7	WHALER 27 CUDDY	OP	CTRCN	F/S	DV	SE	T205	OMC	10		5260	1	9	21300	23700
26	7	WHALER 27 FULL CABIN	OP	CBNCR	F/S	DV	SE	T205	OMC	10		7950	2	6	25700	28600
26	7	WHALER 27 FULL CABIN	OP	CBNCR	F/S	DV	IB	T230	MRCR	10		7950	2	6	32400	36000
		1986 BOATS														
16	7	MONTAUK	OP	CTRCN	F/S	SV	OB			6	2	900		9	3300	3850
16	7	NEWPORT	OP	RNBT	F/S	SV	OB			6	2	950		9	3500	4100
16	7	STRIPER	OP	BASS	F/S	SV	OB			6	2	850		9	3100	3600
16	7	SUPER-SPORT	OP	UTL	F/S	SV	OB			6	2	850		9	3200	3750
18	6	GTX18	OP	RNBT	F/S		OB			7	2	1250		1	6100	7000
18	6	GTX18	OP	RNBT	F/S		IO	188		7	2	1850	1		3750	4350
18	6	GTX18	OP	RNBT	F/S		IO	190-260		7	2	2950		1	4800	5850
18	6	OUTRAGE 18	OP	CTRCN	F/S	DV	OB			7	2	1250		10	5500	6300
18	6	OUTRAGE 18	OP	CTRCN	F/S	DV	SE	115	OMC	7	2				**	**
19	10	OUTRAGE 20	OP	OPFSH	F/S	DV	OB			7	5	1650		11	6150	7050
19	10	REVENGE 20	OP	CR	F/S	DV	OB			7	5	1950		11	7100	8150
22	3	OUTRAGE 22	OP	OPFSH	F/S	DV	OB			7	5	2050	1	2	7200	8300
22	3	OUTRAGE 22	OP	OPFSH	F/S	DV	IO	188-190		7	5	3050			8200	9400
22	3	OUTRAGE 22	OP	OPFSH	F/S	DV	SE	205	OMC	7	5	3050	1	4	9750	11100
22	3	OUTRAGE 22	OP	OPFSH	F/S	DV	SE	T115	OMC	7	5	3050	1	4	9750	11100
22	3	OUTRAGE 22 CUDDY	OP	CUD	F/S	DV	OB			7	5	2250	1	2	8200	9400
22	3	OUTRAGE 22 CUDDY	OP	CUD	F/S	DV	IO	188-190		7	5	3050			7700	8900
22	3	OUTRAGE 22 CUDDY	OP	CUD	F/S	DV	SE	205	OMC	7	5	3050	1	2	10200	11600
22	3	OUTRAGE 22 CUDDY	OP	CUD	F/S	DV	SE	T115	OMC	7	5	3050	1	2	10200	11600
22	3	REVENGE 22	OP	CR	F/S	DV	OB			7	5	2350	1	2	9400	10700
22	3	REVENGE W/T	OP	CR	F/S	DV	OB			7	5	2350	1	4	9350	10600
22	3	REVENGE W/T	OP	CR	F/S	DV	IO	188-190		7	5	3350			8250	9450
22	3	REVENGE W/T	OP	CR	F/S	DV	SE	205	OMC	7	5	3350			11800	13400
22	3	REVENGE W/T	OP	CR	F/S	DV	SE	T115	OMC	7	5	3350			11800	13400
24	7	OUTRAGE 25	OP	FSH	F/S	DV	OB			8		3300	1	4	9750	11100
24	7	OUTRAGE 25	OP	FSH	F/S	DV	IO	188		8		3800	1	4	11200	12700
24	7	OUTRAGE 25	OP	FSH	F/S	DV	SE	205	OMC	8		4670	1	4	12000	13600
24	7	OUTRAGE 25	OP	FSH	F/S	DV	IO	260	MRCR	8		4670	1	4	13600	15400
24	7	OUTRAGE 25	OP	FSH	F/S	DV	SE	T115	OMC	8		4670	1	4	12000	13600
24	7	OUTRAGE 25 CUDDY	OP	CUD	F/S	DV	OB			8		3500	1	4	11100	12600
24	7	OUTRAGE 25 CUDDY	OP	CUD	F/S	DV	IO	188		8		4000	1	4	10900	12400
24	7	OUTRAGE 25 CUDDY	OP	CUD	F/S	DV	SE	205	OMC	8		4670	1	4	12200	13900
24	7	OUTRAGE 25 CUDDY	OP	CUD	F/S	DV	IO	260	MRCR	8		4670	1	4	11800	13400
24	7	OUTRAGE 25 CUDDY	OP	CUD	F/S	DV	SE	T115	OMC	8		4670	1	4	12300	14000
24	7	REVENGE 25 W/T	OP	CR	F/S	DV	IO	188		8		5170	1	4	13200	15000
24	7	REVENGE 25 WAR	OP	CUD	F/S	DV	OB			8		4000	1	4	12800	14600
24	7	REVENGE 25 WAR	OP	CUD	F/S	DV	SE	205	OMC	8		4670	1	4	15000	17000
24	7	REVENGE 25 WAR	OP	CUD	F/S	DV	IO	260	MRCR	8		4670	1	4	13500	15400
24	7	REVENGE 25 WAR	OP	CUD	F/S	DV	SE	T115	OMC	8		4670	1	4	14900	16900
24	7	REVENGE 25 WAR	HT	CUD	F/S	DV	OB			8		4000	1	4	12800	14600
24	7	REVENGE 25 WAR	HT	CUD	F/S	DV	SE	205	OMC	8		4670	1	4	14000	15900
24	7	REVENGE 25 WAR	HT	CUD	F/S	DV	IO	260	MRCR	8		4670	1	4	12700	14400
24	7	REVENGE 25 WAR	HT	CUD	F/S	DV	SE	T115	OMC	8		4670	1	4	14000	15900
24	7	REVENGE W/T	OP	CR	F/S	DV	OB			8		4000	1	4	12200	13900
24	7	REVENGE W/T	OP	CR	F/S	DV	SE	205	OMC	8		4700	1	4	13400	15200
24	7	REVENGE W/T	OP	CR	F/S	DV	IO	260	MRCR	8		5170	1	4	13700	15600
24	7	REVENGE W/T	OP	CR	F/S	DV	SE	T115	OMC	8		5170	1	4	14000	15900
26	7	WHALER 27	OP	OFF	F/S	DV	OB			10		4520			19900	22100
26	7	WHALER 27	OP	OFF	F/S	DV	SE	T205	OMC	10		7650	2	6	21200	23500
26	7	WHALER 27	OP	OFF	F/S	DV	IB	T230	MRCR	10		7650	2	6	27600	30700
26	7	WHALER 27 CUDDY	OP	CTRCN	F/S	DV	OB			10		4130	1	9	20100	22300
26	7	WHALER 27 CUDDY	OP	CTRCN	F/S	DV	SE	205	OMC	10		5260	1	9	20700	23000
26	7	WHALER 27 FULL CABIN	OP	CBNCR	F/S	DV	SE	T205	OMC	10		7950	2	6	25100	27800
26	7	WHALER 27 FULL CABIN	OP	CBNCR	F/S	DV	IB	T230	MRCR	10		7950	2	6	30900	34400
		1985 BOATS														
16	7	MONTAUK	OP	CTRCN	F/S	SV	OB			6	2	900		9	3200	3750
16	7	NEWPORT	OP	RNBT	F/S	SV	OB			6	2	950		9	3400	3950
16	7	STRIPER	OP	BASS	F/S	SV	OB			6	2	850		9	3050	3550
16	7	SUPER-SPORT	OP	UTL	F/S	SV	OB			6	2	850		9	3150	3650
18	6	GTX18	OP	RNBT	F/S		OB			7	2	1250	1		5900	6800
18	6	GTX18	OP	RNBT	F/S		IO	188-260		7	2	2950	1		4600	5600
18	6	OUTRAGE 18	OP	CTRCN	F/S	DV	OB			7	2	1250		10	5350	6150
18	6	OUTRAGE 18	OP	CTRCN	F/S	DV	SE	115-155		7	2				**	**
19	10	OUTRAGE 20	OP	OPFSH	F/S	DV	OB			7	5	1650		11	5950	6850
19	10	REVENGE 20	OP	CR	F/S	DV	OB			7	5	1950		11	6900	7900
22	3	OUTRAGE 22	OP	OPFSH	F/S	DV	OB			7	5	2050	1	2	7050	8100
22	3	OUTRAGE 22	OP	OPFSH	F/S	DV	SE	155	OMC	7	5	3050	1	4	9500	10800
22	3	OUTRAGE 22	OP	OPFSH	F/S	DV	IO	188	MRCR	7	5	3050	1	2	7850	9000
22	3	OUTRAGE 22	OP	OPFSH	F/S	DV	SE	205	OMC	7	5	3050	1	4	9500	10800
22	3	OUTRAGE 22	OP	OPFSH	F/S	DV	SE	T115	OMC	7	5	3050	1	4	9500	10800
22	3	OUTRAGE 22 CUDDY	OP	CUD	F/S	DV	OB			7	5	2250	1	2	8000	9200
22	3	OUTRAGE 22 CUDDY	OP	CUD	F/S	DV	SE	155	OMC	7	5	3050	1	2	10000	11400
22	3	OUTRAGE 22 CUDDY	OP	CUD	F/S	DV	IO	188	MRCR	7	5	3050	1	2	7400	8500
22	3	OUTRAGE 22 CUDDY	OP	CUD	F/S	DV	SE	205	OMC	7	5	3050	1	2	10000	11400
22	3	OUTRAGE 22 CUDDY	OP	CUD	F/S	DV	SE	T115	OMC	7	5	3050	1	2	10000	11400
22	3	REVENGE 22	OP	CR	F/S	DV	OB			7	5	2350	1	2	9250	10500
22	3	REVENGE 22	OP	CR	F/S	DV	SE	155	OMC	7	5	3350	1	2	11700	13200
22	3	REVENGE 22	OP	CR	F/S	DV	IO	170-188		7	5	3350	1	2	7800	9100
22	3	REVENGE 22	OP	CR	F/S	DV	SE	205	OMC	7	5	3350	1	2	11700	13200
22	3	REVENGE 22	OP	CR	F/S	DV	SE	T115	OMC	7	5	3350	1	2	11700	13200
22	3	REVENGE 22 CUDDY	OP	CUD	F/S	DV	OB			7	5	2350	1	2	8450	9750
22	3	REVENGE 22 CUDDY	OP	CUD	F/S	DV	SE	155	OMC	7	5	3350	1	2	10800	12300
22	3	REVENGE 22 CUDDY	OP	CUD	F/S	DV	IO	170-188		7	5	3350	1	2	7800	8950
22	3	REVENGE 22 CUDDY	OP	CUD	F/S	DV	SE	205	OMC	7	5	3350	1	2	10800	12300
22	3	REVENGE 22 CUDDY	OP	CUD	F/S	DV	SE	T115	OMC	7	5	3350	1	2	10800	12300
22	3	REVENGE W/T	OP	CR	F/S	DV	OB			7	5	2350	1	4	9100	10300
22	3	REVENGE W/T	OP	CR	F/S	DV	SE	155	OMC	7	5	3350			11500	13100
22	3	REVENGE W/T	OP	CR	F/S	DV	IO	188	MRCR	7	5	3350			7850	9050
22	3	REVENGE W/T	OP	CR	F/S	DV	SE	205	OMC	7	5	3350			11500	13100
22	3	REVENGE W/T	OP	CR	F/S	DV	SE	T115	OMC	7	5	3350			11500	13100
24	7	FRONTIER 25XC	OP	UTL	F/S	DV	OB			8		3500	1	4	13300	15100
24	7	FRONTIER 25XC	OP	UTL	F/S	DV	IO	188		8		4000	1	4	11000	12500
24	7	FRONTIER 25XC	OP	UTL	F/S	DV	SE	205	OMC	8		4670	1	4	15900	18100
24	7	FRONTIER 25XC	OP	UTL	F/S	DV	IO	260		8		4670	1	4	12800	14600
24	7	FRONTIER 25XC	OP	UTL	F/S	DV	SE	T115-T155		8		4670	1	4	15900	18100
24	7	OUTRAGE 25	OP	FSH	F/S	DV	OB			8		3300	1	4	9500	10800
24	7	OUTRAGE 25	OP	FSH	F/S	DV	IO	188		8		4670	1	4	12400	14100
24	7	OUTRAGE 25	OP	FSH	F/S	DV	SE	205	OMC	8		4670	1	4	11700	13300
24	7	OUTRAGE 25	OP	FSH	F/S	DV	IO	260		8		4670	1	4	13000	14700
24	7	OUTRAGE 25	OP	FSH	F/S	DV	SE	T115-T155		8		4670	1	4	11700	13300
24	7	OUTRAGE 25 CUDDY	OP	CUD	F/S	DV	OB			8		3500	1	4	10800	12300
24	7	OUTRAGE 25 CUDDY	OP	CUD	F/S	DV	IO	188		8		3800	1	4	10100	11500
24	7	OUTRAGE 25 CUDDY	OP	CUD	F/S	DV	SE	205	OMC	8		4670	1	4	12100	13800
24	7	OUTRAGE 25 CUDDY	OP	CUD	F/S	DV	IO	260		8		4670	1	4	11500	13100
24	7	OUTRAGE 25 CUDDY	OP	CUD	F/S	DV	SE	T115-T155		8		4670	1	4	12200	13900
24	7	REVENGE 25	OP	CR	F/S	DV	OB			8		4000	1	4	16000	18200
24	7	REVENGE 25	OP	CR	F/S	DV	SE	205	OMC	8		5000	1	4	17100	19400
24	7	REVENGE 25	OP	CR	F/S	DV	IO	260		8		5000	1	4	12800	14600
24	7	REVENGE 25	OP	CR	F/S	DV	SE	T155	OMC	8		5000	1	4	17100	19400
24	7	REVENGE 25	HT	FSH	F/S	DV	OB			8					15200	17300
24	7	REVENGE 25	HT	FSH	F/S	DV	SE	205	OMC	8					13100	14900
24	7	REVENGE 25	HT	FSH	F/S	DV	IO	260		8					14400	16400
24	7	REVENGE 25	HT	FSH	F/S	DV	SE	T115-T155		8					13100	14900
24	7	REVENGE 25 CUDDY	OP	CUD	F/S	DV	OB			8		4000	1	4	11600	13200
24	7	REVENGE 25 CUDDY	OP	CUD	F/S	DV	SE	205	OMC	8		4670	1	4	12200	13900
24	7	REVENGE 25 CUDDY	OP	CUD	F/S	DV	IO	260		8		4670	1	4	11700	13300
24	7	REVENGE 25 CUDDY	OP	CUD	F/S	DV	SE	T115-T155		8		4670	1	4	12300	14000
24	7	REVENGE 25 WAR	OP	CUD	F/S	DV	OB			8		4000	1	4	12500	14200
24	7	REVENGE 25 WAR	OP	CUD	F/S	DV	SE	205	OMC	8		4670	1	4	14900	17000
24	7	REVENGE 25 WAR	OP	CUD	F/S	DV	IO	260		8		4670	1	4	13200	15100
24	7	REVENGE 25 WAR	OP	CUD	F/S	DV	SE	T115-T155		8		4670	1	4	14800	16800
24	7	REVENGE W/T	OP	CR	F/S	DV	OB			8		4000	1	4	11300	12900
24	7	REVENGE W/T	OP	CR	F/S	DV	SE	205	OMC	8		4700	1	4	13100	14900

CONTINUED ON NEXT PAGE

LOA FT	LOA IN	NAME AND/ OR MODEL	TOP/ RIG	BOAT TYPE	-HULL- MTL	-HULL- TP	ENGINE TP	ENGINE # HP	ENGINE MFG	BEAM FT	BEAM IN	WGT LBS	DRAFT FT	DRAFT IN	RETAIL LOW	RETAIL HIGH
		1985 BOATS														
24	7	REVENGE W/T	OP	CR	F/S	DV	IO	260		8		5170	1	4	13100	14900
24	7	REVENGE W/T	OP	CR	F/S	DV	SE	T115-T155		8		5170	1	4	13700	15500
26	7	WHALER 27	OP	OFF	F/S	DV	OB			10		4520			19400	21600
26	7	WHALER 27	OP	OFF	F/S	DV	SE	T205	OMC	10		7650	2	6	20600	22900
26	7	WHALER 27	OP	OFF	F/S	DV	IB	T230	MRCR	10		7650	2	6	26300	29300
26	7	WHALER 27 FULL CABIN	OP	CBNCR	F/S	DV	SE	T205	OMC	10		7950	2	6	24500	27200
26	7	WHALER 27 FULL CABIN	OP	CBNCR	F/S	DV	IB	T230	MRCR	10		7950	2	6	29500	32800
		1984 BOATS														
16	7	MONTAUK	OP	CTRCN	F/S	SV	OB			6	2	900		9	3150	3650
16	7	NEWPORT	OP	RNBT	F/S	SV	OB			6	2	950		9	3350	3850
16	7	STRIPER	OP	BASS	F/S	SV	OB			6	2	850		9	2950	3450
16	7	SUPER-SPORT	OP	UTL	F/S	SV	OB			6	2	850		9	3050	3550
17		HARPOON 5.2	SLP	SA/OD	F/S	CB	OB			7	6	565		5	3250	3800
17		SUPERCAT 17		SAIL	F/S	CT				8					5900	6800
18	6	GTX18	OP	RNBT	F/S		OB			7	2	1250	1		5750	6650
18	6	GTX18	OP	RNBT	F/S		IO	188-260		7	2	2950	1		4450	5400
18	6	OUTRAGE 18	OP	CTRCN	F/S	DV	OB			7	2	1250		10	5200	6000
19	10	OUTRAGE V-20	OP	OPFSH	F/S	DV	OB			7	5	1650		11	6200	7100
19	10	REVENGE 20	OP	CR	F/S	DV	OB			7	5	1950		11	6700	7700
20	4	HARPOON 6.2	SLP	SA/CR	F/S	CB	OB			8		1700	3	6	6500	7450
22	3	OUTRAGE 22	OP	FSH	F/S	DV	IO	188	MRCR	7	5	3050	1	2	7550	8700
22	3	OUTRAGE 22	OP	OPFSH	F/S	DV	OB			7	5	2050	1	2	6900	7950
22	3	OUTRAGE 22	OP	OPFSH	F/S	DV	IO	170	OMC	7	5	3050	1	2	7500	8600
22	3	OUTRAGE 22 CUDDY	OP	CUD	F/S	DV	OB			7	5	2250	1	2	7850	9000
22	3	OUTRAGE 22 CUDDY	OP	CUD	F/S	DV	IO	170-188		7	5	3050	1	2	7050	8200
22	3	REVENGE 22	OP	CR	F/S	DV	OB			7	5	2350	1	2	9000	10200
22	3	REVENGE 22	OP	CR	F/S	DV	IO	170-188		7	5	3350	1	2	7550	8750
22	3	REVENGE 22 CUDDY	OP	CUD	F/S	DV	OB			7	5	2350	1	2	8300	9550
22	3	REVENGE 22 CUDDY	OP	CUD	F/S	DV	IO	170-188		7	5	3350	1	2	7550	8750
24	7	FRONTIER 25XC	OP	UTL	F/S	DV	OB			8		3500	1	4	12900	14700
24	7	FRONTIER 25XC	OP	UTL	F/S	DV	IO	140-188		8		4670	1	4	11700	13500
24	7	FRONTIER 25XC	OP	UTL	F/S	DV	SE	205	OMC	8		4670	1	4	15500	17600
24	7	FRONTIER 25XC	OP	UTL	F/S	DV	IO	260		8		4670	1	4	12400	14100
24	7	OUTRAGE 25	OP	FSH	F/S	DV	OB			8		3300	1	4	9350	10600
24	7	OUTRAGE 25	OP	FSH	F/S	DV	IO	188	MRCR	8		4670	1	4	12000	13600
24	7	OUTRAGE 25	OP	FSH	F/S	DV	SE	205	OMC	8		4670	1	4	11500	13000
24	7	OUTRAGE 25	OP	FSH	F/S	DV	IO	260		8		4670	1	4	12500	14200
24	7	OUTRAGE 25 CUDDY	OP	CUD	F/S	DV	OB			8		3500	1	4	10600	12000
24	7	OUTRAGE 25 CUDDY	OP	CUD	F/S	DV	IO	188	MRCR	8		4670	1	4	11200	12700
24	7	OUTRAGE 25 CUDDY	OP	CUD	F/S	DV	SE	205	OMC	8		4670	1	4	12400	14100
24	7	OUTRAGE 25 CUDDY	OP	CUD	F/S	DV	IO	260		8		4670	1	4	11600	13200
24	7	REVENGE 25	OP	CR	F/S	DV	OB			8		4000	1	4	14800	16900
24	7	REVENGE 25	OP	CR	F/S	DV	IO	188	MRCR	8		5000	1	4	11900	13500
24	7	REVENGE 25	OP	CR	F/S	DV	SE	205	OMC	8		5000	1	4	16700	19000
24	7	REVENGE 25	OP	CR	F/S	DV	IO	260		8		5000	1	4	12400	14000
24	7	REVENGE 25 CUDDY	OP	CUD	F/S	DV	OB			8		4000	1	4	11400	12900
24	7	REVENGE 25 CUDDY	OP	CUD	F/S	DV	IO	188	MRCR	8		4670	1	4	11400	12900
24	7	REVENGE 25 CUDDY	OP	CUD	F/S	DV	SE	205	OMC	8		4670	1	4	12500	14200
24	7	REVENGE 25 CUDDY	OP	CUD	F/S	DV	IO	260		8		4670	1	4	11800	13500

....For earlier years, see the BUC Used Boat Price Guide, Volume 3

BOTNIA-MARIN OY AB

MAALAHTI FINLAND

See inside cover to adjust price for area

LOA FT	LOA IN	NAME AND/ OR MODEL	TOP/ RIG	BOAT TYPE	-HULL- MTL	-HULL- TP	ENGINE TP	ENGINE # HP	ENGINE MFG	BEAM FT	BEAM IN	WGT LBS	DRAFT FT	DRAFT IN	RETAIL LOW	RETAIL HIGH
		1996 BOATS														
23		TARGA 23		SF	FBG	SV	IO	150D	VLVO	9	3	5100	2	6	37800	42000
25		TARGA 25	FB	SF	FBG	SV	IO	200D	VLVO	9	4	6400	2	6	57600	63300
27		H-BOAT	SLP	SAROD	FBG	KL				7	1	3200	4	3	19900	22200
27		TARGA 27	FB	SF	FBG	SV	IO	230D	VLVO	10		6500	3		60500	66500
29		TARGA 29	FB	SF	FBG	SV	IO	T230D	VLVO	10	6	10200	3		106000	116500
31		TARGA 31	FB	SF	FBG	SV	IO	T230D	VLVO			10400	3		111000	122000
35	5	TARGA 33		SF	FBG	SV	IB	T230D	VLVO	11	6	12000	2	10	123500	135500
		1995 BOATS														
23		TARGA 23		SF	FBG	SV	IO	150D	VLVO	9	3	5100	2	6	35300	39200
25		TARGA 25	FB	SF	FBG	SV	IO	200D	VLVO	9	4	6400	2	6	54100	59500
27		H-BOAT	SLP	SAROD	FBG	KL				7	1	3200	4	3	19000	21100
27		TARGA 27	FB	SF	FBG	SV	IO	230D	VLVO	10		6500	3		57100	62700
29		TARGA 29	FB	SF	FBG	SV	IO	T230D	VLVO	10	6	10200	3		98800	108500
31		TARGA 31	FB	SF	FBG	SV	IO	T230D	VLVO			10400	3		103500	113500
35	5	TARGA 33		SF	FBG	SV	IB	T230D	VLVO	11	6	12000	2	10	117000	128500
		1994 BOATS														
23		TARGA 23		SF	FBG	SV	IO	150D	VLVO	9	3	6000	2	6	36800	40900
25		TARGA 25	FB	SF	FBG	SV	IO	200D	VLVO	9	4	8600	2	6	63100	69300
27		H-BOAT	SLP	SAROD	FBG	KL				7	1	3200	4	3	17400	19800
27		TARGA 27	FB	SF	FBG	SV	IO	230D	VLVO	10		9000	3		67500	74200
29		TARGA 29	FB	SF	FBG	SV	IO	230D	VLVO	10	6	8800	3		70600	77600
29		TARGA 29	FB	SF	FBG	SV	IO	T230D	VLVO	10	6	10200	3		92200	101500
31		TARGA 31	FB	SF	FBG	SV	IO	T230D	VLVO			10400	3		96500	106000
		1993 BOATS														
23		TARGA 23		SF	FBG	SV	IO	130D	VLVO	9	3	6000	2	6	33900	37700
25		TARGA 25		SF	FBG	SV	IO	200D	VLVO	9	4	8600	2	6	52600	57800
27		H-BOAT	SLP	SAROD	FBG	KL				7	1	3200	4	3	16400	18600
27		TARGA 27		SF	FBG	SV	IO	230D	VLVO	10		9000	3		58200	63900
29		TARGA 29		SF	FBG	SV	IO	230D	VLVO	10	6	8800	3		61800	67900
29		TARGA 29		SF	FBG	SV	IO	T230D	VLVO	10	6	10200	3		80400	88400
31		TARGA 31		SF	FBG	SV	IO	T230D	VLVO			10400	3		86000	94600
		1992 BOATS														
23		TARGA 23		SF	FBG	SV	IO	130D	VLVO	9	3	6000	2	6	31700	35200
25		TARGA 25		SF	FBG	SV	IO	200D	VLVO	9	4	8600	2	6	49600	54500
26		TARGA 27		SF	FBG	SV	IO	230D	VLVO	10		9000	3		54300	59600
27		H-BOAT	SLP	SA/OD	FBG	KL				7	1	3200	4	3	15400	17500
29		TARGA 29		SF	FBG	SV	IO	230D	VLVO	10	6	8800	3		58300	64100
29		TARGA 29		SF	FBG	SV	IO	T230D	VLVO	10	6	11000	3		78900	86800
31		TARGA 31		SF	FBG	SV	IO	230D	VLVO	10	6	9500	3		59300	65200
31		TARGA 31		SF	FBG	SV	IO	T230D	VLVO	10	6	11500	3		84100	92400
		1991 BOATS														
25		TARGA 25		SF	FBG	SV	IO	200D	VLVO	9	4	8600	2	6	46400	51000
27		H-BOAT	SLP	SA/OD	FBG	KL				7	1	3200	4	3	14500	16500
29		TARGA 29		SF	FBG	SV	IO	200D		10	6	8800	3		54200	59600
29		TARGA 29		SF	FBG	SV	IO	T200D	VLVO	10	6	10200	3		68100	74800
		1990 BOATS														
25		TARGA 25		SF	FBG	SV	IO	200D	VLVO	9	4	8600	2	6	43000	47800
27		H-BOAT	SLP	SA/OD	FBG	KL				7	1	3200	4	3	13600	15500
29		TARGA 29		SF	FBG	SV	IO	200D		10	6	8800	3		50800	55900
29		TARGA 29		SF	FBG	SV	IO	T200D	VLVO	10	6	10200	3		63800	70100
		1989 BOATS														
25		TARGA 25		SF	FBG	SV	IO	200D		9	4	8600	2	6	41200	45800
27		H-BOAT	SLP	SA/OD	FBG	KL				7	1	3200	4	3	12800	14600
29		TARGA 29		SF	FBG	SV	IO	200D		10	6	8800	3		48200	53000
		1988 BOATS														
25		TARGA 25		SF	FBG	SV	IO	200D		9	4	8600	2	6	38800	43200
27		H-BOAT	SLP	SA/OD	FBG	KL				7	1	3200	4	3	12100	13700
29		TARGA 29		SF	FBG	SV	IO	200D		10	6	11000	3		54200	59600
		1987 BOATS														
25		TARGA 25 BM		SF	FBG	SV	IO	165D		9	4	8600			36000	39900
27		H-BOAT	SLP	SA/OD	FBG	KL				7	1	3200	4	3	11400	12900
		1986 BOATS														
25		TARGA 25 BM		SF	FBG		IO	165D		9	4	8600			34100	37900
27		H-BOAT	SLP	SA/OD	FBG	KL				7	1	3200	4	3	10700	12100
30		BOTNIA 30NF	SLP	SA/RC	FBG	KL				8	7	5700	5		19300	21400
		1985 BOATS														
25		TARGA 25 BM		SF	FBG	SV	IO	165D		9	4	8600			32500	36100
27		H-BOAT	SLP	SA/OD	FBG	KL				7	1	3200	4	3	10000	11400
27	1	H-BOAT	SLP	SA/OD	FBG	KL				7	1	3190	4	3	10100	11400
30		BOTNIA 30NF	SLP	SA/RC	FBG	KL				8	7	5700	5		18300	20300
		1984 BOATS														
27	2	H-BOAT	SLP	SA/OD	FBG	KL				7	2	3190	4	4	9500	10800
30		BOTNIA 30	SLP	SA/CR	FBG	KL	IB	D		8	7		5		29700	33000

....For earlier years, see the BUC Used Boat Price Guide, Volume 3

BOW-WINDS BOATS INC

ZEELAND MI 49464

COAST GUARD MFG ID- BNO See inside cover to adjust price for area

FORMERLY BAND CO

LOA FT	LOA IN	NAME AND/ OR MODEL	TOP/ RIG	BOAT TYPE	-HULL- MTL	-HULL- TP	ENGINE TP	ENGINE # HP	ENGINE MFG	BEAM FT	BEAM IN	WGT LBS	DRAFT FT	DRAFT IN	RETAIL LOW	RETAIL HIGH
		1988 BOATS														
18	3	HERITAGE 18	OP	RNBT	FBG	SV	IB	260-275		7	2	1800	1	10	7850	9050
21	6	CUTLASS	OP	RNBT	FBG	SV	IB	260-340		8		2000	2	3	10600	12600
22	10	ULTRA I	OP	RACE	FBG	DV	IO	260-320		8		1860	2		9600	11900
22	10	ULTRA I	OP	RACE	FBG	DV	IO	330	MRCR	8		1860	2		10900	12400
25	11	ULTRA II	OP	SPTCR	FBG	DV	IO	T260-T330		8		3286	2	3	18800	22600
31	9	ULTRA III	OP	SPTCR	FBG	DV	IO	T320-T365		8	6	3985	2	5	35900	40300
		1987 BOATS														
18	3	HERITAGE 18	OP	RNBT	FBG	SV	IB	260-340		7	2	1800	1	8	7500	9300
21	6	CUTLASS	OP	RNBT	FBG	SV	IB	260-340		8		2000	2	3	10100	12100
22	10	ULTRA I	OP	RACE	FBG	DV	IO	260-270		8		1860	2		9100	10500

LOA FT	IN	NAME AND/ OR MODEL	TOP/ RIG	BOAT TYPE	-HULL- MTL	TP	TP	----ENGINE--- # HP	MFG	BEAM FT	IN	WGT LBS	DRAFT FT	IN	RETAIL LOW	RETAIL HIGH
		1987 BOATS														
22	10	ULTRA I	OP	RACE	FBG	DV	IO	330-340		8		1860	2		10300	11900
25	11	ULTRA II	OP	SPTCR	FBG	DV	IO	330	MRCR	8		3286	2	3	15900	18000
25	11	ULTRA II	OP	SPTCR	FBG	DV	IO	T260-T270		8		3286	2	3	17300	19900
25	11	ULTRA II	OP	SPTCR	FBG	DV	IO	T330-T340		8		3286	2	3	19600	22100
31	9	ULTRA III	OP	SPTCR	FBG	DV	IO	T330-T370		8	6	3985	2	5	34000	38100

....For earlier years, see the BUC Used Boat Price Guide, Volume 3

BRISTOL BOAT COMPANY

BRISTOL RI 02809 COAST GUARD MFG ID- BTY See inside cover to adjust price for area
FOR OLDER MODELS SEE SAILSTAR BOATS INC

LOA FT	IN	NAME AND/ OR MODEL	TOP/ RIG	BOAT TYPE	-HULL- MTL	TP	TP	----ENGINE--- # HP	MFG	BEAM FT	IN	WGT LBS	DRAFT FT	IN	RETAIL LOW	RETAIL HIGH
		1995 BOATS														
35	6	BRISTOL 35.5	SLP	SACAC	FBG	KC	IB	23D	YAN	10	10	15000	5	9	127000	139500
35	6	BRISTOL 35.5	SLP	SACAC	FBG	KL	IB	23D	YAN	10	10	15000	5	9	127000	139500
38	4	BRISTOL 38.8	SLP	SACAC	FBG	CB	IB	47D	YAN	12	1	19150	10	3	176500	194000
41	1	BRISTOL 41.1 AFT	SLP	SACAC	FBG	CB	IB	52D	YAN	12	11	26530	10	6	241500	265500
41	1	BRISTOL 41.1 CC	SLP	SACAC	FBG	CB	IB	52D	YAN	12	11	26530	10	6	255000	280500
41	2	BRISTOL 43.3 AFT	SLP	SACAC	FBG	CB	IB	52D	YAN	12	11	26530	10	6	249000	273500
41	2	BRISTOL 43.3 CC	SLP	SACAC	FBG	CB	IB	52D	YAN	12	11	26530	10	6	249000	273500
45	3	BRISTOL 45.5 AFT	SLP	SACAC	FBG	CB	IB	70D	YAN	13	3	34660	11		319000	351000
45	3	BRISTOL 45.5 CC	SLP	SACAC	FBG	CB	IB	70D	YAN	13	3	34660	11		335500	369000
47	4	BRISTOL 47.7 CC	SLP	SACAC	FBG	CB	IB	70D	YAN	13	3	34660	11		352500	387000
51	1	BRISTOL 51.1 AFT	SLP	SACAC	FBG	CB	IB	70D	YAN	15	2	43700	10	6	434500	477500
51	1	BRISTOL 51.1 CC	SLP	SACAC	FBG	CB	IB	70D	YAN	15	2	43700	10	6	461500	507000
52	5	BRISTOL 53.3 CC	SLP	SACAC	FBG	CB	IB	70D	YAN	15	2	43700	10	6	480500	528500
54	5	BRISTOL 54.4 AFT	SLP	SACAC	FBG	CB	IB	100D	YAN	15	6	54000	11	6	563500	619000
54	5	BRISTOL 54.4 CC	SLP	SACAC	FBG	CB	IB	100D	YAN	15	6	54000	11	6	563500	619000
56	2	BRISTOL 56.6 CC	SLP	SACAC	FBG	CB	IB	100D	YAN	15	2	43700	10	6	660000	725500
65	8	BRISTOL 65.5 CC	SLP	SACAC	FBG	CB	IB	135D	FORD	17	4	71500	13	10	1.025M	1.115M
		1994 BOATS														
35	6	BRISTOL 35.5	SLP	SACAC	FBG	KC	IB	23D	UNIV	10	10	15000	5	9	118500	130000
35	6	BRISTOL 35.5	SLP	SACAC	FBG	KL	IB	23D	UNIV	10	10	15000	5	9	118500	130000
38	4	BRISTOL 38.8	SLP	SACAC	FBG	CB	IB	44D	UNIV	12	1	19150	10	3	165000	181000
40	2	BRISTOL 40	SLP	SACAC	FBG	KL	IB	46D	WEST	10	9	17580	5	5	173500	190500
41	1	BRISTOL 41.1 AFT	SLP	SACAC	FBG	CB	IB	52D	WEST	12	11	26530	10	6	226000	248000
41	1	BRISTOL 41.1 CC	SLP	SACAC	FBG	CB	IB	52D	WEST	12	11	26530	10	6	238500	262000
41	2	BRISTOL 43.3 AFT	SLP	SACAC	FBG	CB	IB	52D	WEST	12	11	26530	10	6	232500	255500
41	2	BRISTOL 43.3 CC	SLP	SACAC	FBG	CB	IB	52D	WEST	12	11	26530	10	6	232500	255500
43	11	BRISTOL 44 AFT	SLP	SACAC	FBG	CB	IB	D		13	6	27500	7	6	259500	285500
43	11	BRISTOL 44 CC	SLP	SACAC	FBG	CB	IB	D		13	6	27500	7	6	259500	285500
45	3	BRISTOL 45.5 AFT	SLP	SACAC	FBG	CB	IB	70D	WEST	13	3	34660	11		298500	327500
45	3	BRISTOL 45.5 CC	SLP	SACAC	FBG	CB	IB	70D	WEST	13	3	34660	11		313500	344500
47	4	BRISTOL 47.7 CC	SLP	SACAC	FBG	CB	IB	70D	WEST	13	3	34660	11		329000	361500
51	1	BRISTOL 51.1 AFT	SLP	SACAC	FBG	CB	IB	70D	WEST	15	2	43700	10	6	406000	446000
51	1	BRISTOL 51.1 CC	SLP	SACAC	FBG	CB	IB	70D	WEST	15	2	43700	10	6	431000	474000
52	5	BRISTOL 53.3 CC	SLP	SACAC	FBG	CB	IB	70D	WEST	15	2	43700	10	6	449000	493500
54	5	BRISTOL 54.4 AFT	SLP	SACAC	FBG	CB	IB	100D	WEST	15	6	54000	11	6	526000	578500
54	5	BRISTOL 54.4 CC	SLP	SACAC	FBG	CB	IB	100D	WEST	15	6	54000	11	6	526000	578500
56	2	BRISTOL 56.6 CC	SLP	SACAC	FBG	CB	IB	100D	WEST	15	2	43700	10	6	616500	677500
65	8	BRISTOL 65.5 CC	SLP	SACAC	FBG	CB	IB	135D	FORD	17	4	71500	13	10	964000	1.050M
		1993 BOATS														
35	6	BRISTOL 35.5	SLP	SACAC	FBG	KC	IB	23D	UNIV	10	10	15000	5	9	110500	121500
35	6	BRISTOL 35.5	SLP	SACAC	FBG	KL	IB	23D	UNIV	10	10	15000	5	9	110500	121500
38	4	BRISTOL 38.8	SLP	SACAC	FBG	CB	IB	44D	UNIV	12	1	19150	10	3	154000	169000
40	2	BRISTOL 40	SLP	SACAC	FBG	KL	IB	46D	WEST	10	9	17580	5	5	162000	178000
41	1	BRISTOL 41.1 AFT	SLP	SACAC	FBG	CB	IB	52D	WEST	12	11	26530	10	6	211000	231500
41	1	BRISTOL 41.1 CC	SLP	SACAC	FBG	CB	IB	52D	WEST	12	11	26530	10	6	222500	244500
41	2	BRISTOL 43.3 AFT	SLP	SACAC	FBG	CB	IB	52D	WEST	12	11	26530	10	6	217000	238500
41	2	BRISTOL 43.3 CC	SLP	SACAC	FBG	CB	IB	52D	WEST	12	11	26530	10	6	217000	238500
43	11	BRISTOL 44 AFT	SLP	SACAC	FBG	CB	IB	D		13	6	27500	7	6	242500	266500
43	11	BRISTOL 44 CC	SLP	SACAC	FBG	CB	IB	D		13	6	27500	7	6	242500	266500
45	3	BRISTOL 45.5 AFT	SLP	SACAC	FBG	CB	IB	70D	WEST	13	3	34660	11		278500	306000
45	3	BRISTOL 45.5 CC	SLP	SACAC	FBG	CB	IB	70D	WEST	13	3	34660	11		293000	322000
47	4	BRISTOL 47.7 CC	SLP	SACAC	FBG	CB	IB	70D	WEST	13	3	34660	11		307500	338000
51	1	BRISTOL 51.1 AFT	SLP	SACAC	FBG	CB	IB	70D	WEST	15	2	43700	10	6	379000	416500
51	1	BRISTOL 51.1 CC	SLP	SACAC	FBG	CB	IB	70D	WEST	15	2	43700	10	6	402500	442500
52	5	BRISTOL 53.3 CC	SLP	SACAC	FBG	CB	IB	70D	WEST	15	2	43700	10	6	419500	461000
54	5	BRISTOL 54.4 AFT	SLP	SACAC	FBG	CB	IB	100D	WEST	15	6	54000	11	6	491500	540000
54	5	BRISTOL 54.4 CC	SLP	SACAC	FBG	CB	IB	100D	WEST	15	6	54000	11	6	491500	540000
56	2	BRISTOL 56.6 CC	SLP	SACAC	FBG	CB	IB	100D	WEST	15	2	43700	10	6	576000	633000
65	8	BRISTOL 65.5 CC	SLP	SACAC	FBG	CB	IB	135D	FORD	17	4	71500	13	10	890500	978500
		1992 BOATS														
35	6	BRISTOL 35.5	SLP	SA/CR	FBG	KC	IB	23D	UNIV	10	10	15000	5	9	103500	113500
35	6	BRISTOL 35.5	SLP	SA/CR	FBG	KL	IB	23D	UNIV	10	10	15000	5	9	103500	113500
38	4	BRISTOL 38.8	SLP	SA/CR	FBG	CB	IB	44D	UNIV	12	1	19150	10	3	143500	158000
40	2	BRISTOL 40	SLP	SA/CR	FBG	KL	IB	46D	WEST	10	9	17580	5	5	151000	166000
41	1	BRISTOL 41.1 AFT	SLP	SA/CR	FBG	CB	IB	52D	WEST	12	11	26530	10	6	197000	216500
41	1	BRISTOL 41.1 CC	SLP	SA/CR	FBG	CB	IB	52D	WEST	12	11	26530	10	6	208000	228500
41	2	BRISTOL 43.3 AFT	SLP	SA/CR	FBG	CB	IB	52D	WEST	12	11	26530	10	6	203000	223000
41	2	BRISTOL 43.3 CC	SLP	SA/CR	FBG	CB	IB	52D	WEST	12	11	26530	10	6	203000	223000
43	11	BRISTOL 44 AFT	SLP	SA/CR	FBG	CB	IB	D		13	6	27500	7	6	226500	249000
43	11	BRISTOL 44 CC	SLP	SA/CR	FBG	CB	IB	D		13	6	27500	7	6	226500	249000
45	3	BRISTOL 45.5 AFT	SLP	SA/CR	FBG	CB	IB	70D	WEST	13	3	34660	11		260000	286000
45	3	BRISTOL 45.5 CC	SLP	SA/CR	FBG	CB	IB	70D	WEST	13	3	34660	11		273500	300500
47	4	BRISTOL 47.7 CC	SLP	SA/CR	FBG	CB	IB	70D	WEST	13	3	34660	11		287000	315500
51	1	BRISTOL 51.1 AFT	SLP	SA/CR	FBG	CB	IB	70D	WEST	15	2	43700	10	6	354000	389500
51	1	BRISTOL 51.1 CC	SLP	SA/CR	FBG	CB	IB	70D	WEST	15	2	43700	10	6	376000	413500
52	5	BRISTOL 53.3 CC	SLP	SA/CR	FBG	CB	IB	70D	WEST	15	2	43700	10	6	392000	430500
54	5	BRISTOL 54.4 AFT	SLP	SA/CR	FBG	CB	IB	100D	WEST	15	6	54000	11	6	459000	504500
54	5	BRISTOL 54.4 CC	SLP	SA/CR	FBG	CB	IB	100D	WEST	15	6	54000	11	6	459000	504500
56	2	BRISTOL 56.6 CC	SLP	SA/CR	FBG	CB	IB	100D	WEST	15	2	43700	10	6	538000	591000
65	8	BRISTOL 65.5 CC	SLP	SA/CR	FBG	CB	IB	135D	FORD	17	4	71500	13	10	832000	914000
		1989 BOATS														
31	2	BRISTOL 31.1	SLP	SA/CR	FBG	KL	IB	18D	UNIV	10	2	11200	5	3	58400	64200
33	4	BRISTOL 33.3	SLP	SA/CR	FBG	KL	IB	21D	UNIV	11	2	14500	5	11	77300	85000
35	6	BRISTOL 35.5	SLP	SA/CR	FBG	KL	IB	24D	UNIV	10	10	15000	5	9	84300	92700
38	4	BRISTOL 38.8	SLP	SA/CR	FBG	CB	IB	44D	UNIV	12	1	19150	10	3	117500	129000
40	2	BRISTOL 40	SLP	SA/CR	FBG	KL	IB	46D	WEST	10	9	17580	5	5	123500	135500
41	1	BRISTOL 41.1 AFT	SLP	SA/CR	FBG	CB	IB	52D	WEST	12	11	26530	10	6	160500	176500
41	1	BRISTOL 41.1 CC	SLP	SA/CR	FBG	CB	IB	52D	WEST	12	11	26530	10	6	169500	186500
42	1	BRISTOL 43.3 CC	SLP	SA/CR	FBG	CB	IB	52D	WEST	12	11	26530	10	6	170000	186500
45	3	BRISTOL 45.5 AFT	SLP	SA/CR	FBG	CB	IB	70D	WEST	13	3	34660	11		212500	233500
45	3	BRISTOL 45.5 CC	SLP	SA/CR	FBG	CB	IB	70D	WEST	13	3	34660	11		223000	245000
47	4	BRISTOL 47.7 CC	SLP	SA/CR	FBG	CB	IB	70D	WEST	13	3	34660	11		234000	257500
51	1	BRISTOL 51.1 AFT	SLP	SA/CR	FBG	CB	IB	70D	WEST	15	2	43700	10	6	289000	317500
51	1	BRISTOL 51.1 CC	SLP	SA/CR	FBG	CB	IB	70D	WEST	15	2	43700	10	6	307000	337000
52	5	BRISTOL 53.3 CC	SLP	SA/CR	FBG	CB	IB	70D	WEST	15	2	43700	10	6	319500	351500
54	5	BRISTOL 54.4 CC	SLP	SA/CR	FBG	CB	IB	100D	WEST	15	2	43700	10	6	361500	397000
56	2	BRISTOL 56.6 CC	SLP	SA/CR	FBG	CB	IB	100D	WEST	15	2	43700	10	6	439000	482500
59	5	BRISTOL 60	SLP	SA/CR	FBG	CB	IB	100D	WEST	16	1		12		511000	561500
65	8	BRISTOL 65.5 CC	SLP	SA/CR	FBG	CB	IB	135D	FORD	17	4	71500	13	10	678500	745500
71	8	BRISTOL 72	KTH	MS	FBG	CB	IB	T200D	PERK	18	1	70T	13		1.110M	1.205M
		1988 BOATS														
31	2	BRISTOL 31.1	SLP	SA/CR	FBG	KL	IB	18D	UNIV	10	2	11200	5	3	57900	63600
31	2	BRISTOL 31S	SLP	SA/CR	FBG	KL	IB	18D	UNIV	10	2	11200	5	3	51200	56300
33	4	BRISTOL 33.3	SLP	SA/CR	FBG	KL	IB	21D	UNIV	11	2	14500	5	11	72300	79400
35	6	BRISTOL 35.5	SLP	SA/CR	FBG	KL	IB	24D	UNIV	10	10	15000	5	9	78800	86600
38	4	BRISTOL 38.8	SLP	SA/CR	FBG	CB	IB	44D	UNIV	12	1	19150	10	3	109500	120500
40	2	BRISTOL 40	SLP	SA/CR	FBG	KL	IB	46D	WEST	10	9	17580	5	5	115500	126500
41	1	BRISTOL 41.1 AFT	SLP	SA/CR	FBG	CB	IB	52D	WEST	12	11	26530	10	6	148500	163500
41	1	BRISTOL 41.1 CC	SLP	SA/CR	FBG	CB	IB	52D	WEST	12	11	26530	10	6	160000	176000
42	1	BRISTOL 43.3 CC	SLP	SA/CR	FBG	CB	IB	52D	WEST	12	11	26530	10	6	159000	174500
45	3	BRISTOL 45.5 AFT	SLP	SA/CR	FBG	CB	IB	70D	WEST	13	3	34660	11		199500	219500
45	3	BRISTOL 45.5 CC	SLP	SA/CR	FBG	CB	IB	70D	WEST	13	3	34660	11		207500	228000
47	4	BRISTOL 47.7 CC	SLP	SA/CR	FBG	CB	IB	70D	WEST	13	3	34660	11		219000	240500
51	1	BRISTOL 51.1 AFT	SLP	SA/CR	FBG	CB	IB	70D	WEST	15	2	43700	10	6	270000	296500
51	1	BRISTOL 51.1 CC	SLP	SA/CR	FBG	CB	IB	70D	WEST	15	2	43700	10	6	287000	315500
52	5	BRISTOL 53.3 CC	SLP	SA/CR	FBG	CB	IB	70D	WEST	15	2	43700	10	6	299000	328500
54	5	BRISTOL 54.4 CC	SLP	SA/CR	FBG	CB	IB	100D	WEST	15	2	43700	10	6	338000	371000
56	2	BRISTOL 56.6 CC	SLP	SA/CR	FBG	CB	IB	100D	WEST	15	2	43700	10	6	410500	451000
59	5	BRISTOL 60	SLP	SA/CR	FBG	CB	IB	100D	WEST	16	1	55864			492000	540500
65	8	BRISTOL 65.5 CC	SLP	SA/CR	FBG	CB	IB	135D	FORD	17	4	71500	13	10	634500	697000
71	8	BRISTOL 72	KTH	MS	FBG	CB	IB	T200D	PERK	18	1	70T	13		1.040M	1.135M
		1987 BOATS														
59	5	BRISTOL 60	SLP	SA/CR	FBG	CB	ID	100D	WEST	16	1	55864			460000	505500
		1986 BOATS														
29	11	BRISTOL 29.9	SLP	SA/RC	FBG	KC	IB	16D	UNIV	10	2	8650	3	6	35500	39400
29	11	BRISTOL 29.9	SLP	SA/RC	FBG	KL	IB	16D	UNIV	10	2	8650	4	4	35300	39300
31	2	BRISTOL 31.1	SLP	SA/RC	FBG	KC	IB	14D-	24D	10	2	11200	3	6	47700	52500
31	2	BRISTOL 31.1	SLP	SA/RC	FBG	KL	IB	14D-	24D	10	2	11200	5	3	47700	52400
35	6	BRISTOL 35.5	SLP	SA/RC	FBG	KC	IB	24D	UNIV	10	10	15000	3	9	68900	75700
35	6	BRISTOL 35.5	SLP	SA/RC	FBG	KC	IB	32D	UNIV	10	10	15000	3	9	69100	75900
35	6	BRISTOL 35.5	SLP	SA/RC	FBG	KL	IB	24D	UNIV	10	10	15000	5	9	68900	75700
35	6	BRISTOL 35.5	SLP	SA/RC	FBG	KL	IB	32D	UNIV	10	10	15000	5	9	69100	75900
38	4	BRISTOL 38.8	SLP	SA/RC	FBG	KL	IB	44D	UNIV	12	1	19150	4	6	95800	105500
40	2	BRISTOL 40	SLP	SA/RC	FBG	KC	IB	40D	WEST	10	9	17580	4		100500	110500

LOA FT	LOA IN	NAME AND/ OR MODEL	TOP/ RIG	BOAT TYPE	HULL MTL	HULL TP	ENGINE TP	# HP	ENGINE MFG	BEAM FT	BEAM IN	WGT LBS	DRAFT FT	DRAFT IN	RETAIL LOW	RETAIL HIGH
		1986 BOATS														
40	2	BRISTOL 40	SLP	SA/RC	FBG	KL	IB	40D	WEST	10	9	17580	5	5	100500	110500
40	2	BRISTOL 40	CUT	SA/RC	FBG	KC	IB	40D	WEST	10	9	17580	4		100500	110500
40	2	BRISTOL 40	CUT	SA/RC	FBG	KL	IB	40D	WEST	10	9	17580	5	5	100500	110500
40	2	BRISTOL 40	YWL	SA/RC	FBG	KC	IB	40D	WEST	10	9	17580	4		100500	110500
40	2	BRISTOL 40	YWL	SA/RC	FBG	KL	IB	40D	WEST	10	9	17580	5	5	100500	110500
41	2	BRISTOL 41.1 AFT	SLP	SA/RC	FBG	KC	IB	50D	WEST	12	11	26530	4	6	126000	138500
41	2	BRISTOL 41.1 CTR	SLP	SA/RC	FBG	KL	IB	50D	WEST	12	11	26530	4	6	144000	158500
45	3	BRISTOL 45.5 AFT	SLP	SA/RC	FBG	KC	IB	58D	WEST	13	3	34660	4	11	171500	188500
45	3	BRISTOL 45.5 AFT	KTH	SA/RC	FBG	KC	IB	58D	WEST	13	3	34660	4	11	177500	195000
45	3	BRISTOL 45.5 CRT	KTH	SA/RC	FBG	KC	IB	58D	WEST	13	3	34660	4	11	177500	195000
45	3	BRISTOL 45.5 CTR	SLP	SA/RC	FBG	KC	IB	58D	WEST	13	3	34660	4	11	184000	202000
54	5	BRISTOL 54.4	KTH	SA/RC	FBG	KC	IB	100D	WEST	15	6	52000	5	4	304000	334000
		1985 BOATS														
29	11	BRISTOL 29.9	SLP	SA/RC	FBG	KC	IB	16D	UNIV	10	2	8650	3	6	33100	36800
29	11	BRISTOL 29.9	SLP	SA/RC	FBG	KL	IB	16D	UNIV	10	2	8650	4	4	33000	36600
31	2	BRISTOL 31.1	SLP	SA/RC	FBG	KC	IB	14D- 24D		10	2	11200	3	6	44400	49300
31	2	BRISTOL 31.1	SLP	SA/RC	FBG	KL	IB	14D- 24D		10	2	11200	5	3	44300	49300
35	6	BRISTOL 35.5	SLP	SA/RC	FBG	KC	IB	24D	UNIV	10	10	15000	3	9	64500	70800
35	6	BRISTOL 35.5	SLP	SA/RC	FBG	KC	IB	32D	UNIV	10	10	15000	3	9	64600	71000
35	6	BRISTOL 35.5	SLP	SA/RC	FBG	KL	IB	24D	UNIV	10	10	15000	5	9	64500	70800
35	6	BRISTOL 35.5	SLP	SA/RC	FBG	KL	IB	32D	UNIV	10	10	15000	5	9	64600	71000
38	4	BRISTOL 38.8	SLP	SA/RC	FBG	KC	IB	44D	UNIV	12	1	19150	4	6	89600	98500
40	2	BRISTOL 40	SLP	SA/RC	FBG	KC	IB	40D	WEST	10	9	17580	4		94100	103500
40	2	BRISTOL 40	SLP	SA/RC	FBG	KL	IB	40D	WEST	10	9	17580	5	5	94100	103500
40	2	BRISTOL 40	CUT	SA/RC	FBG	KC	IB	40D	WEST	10	9	17580	4		94100	103500
40	2	BRISTOL 40	CUT	SA/RC	FBG	KL	IB	40D	WEST	10	9	17580	5	5	94100	103500
40	2	BRISTOL 40	YWL	SA/RC	FBG	KC	IB	40D	WEST	10	9	17580	4		94100	103500
40	2	BRISTOL 40	YWL	SA/RC	FBG	KL	IB	40D	WEST	10	9	17580	5	5	94100	103500
41	2	BRISTOL 41.1 AFT	SLP	SA/RC	FBG	KC	IB	50D	WEST	12	11	26530	4	6	118000	129500
41	2	BRISTOL 41.1 CTR	SLP	SA/RC	FBG	KC	IB	50D	WEST	12	11	26530	4	6	135000	148000
45	3	BRISTOL 45.5 AFT	SLP	SA/RC	FBG	KC	IB	58D	WEST	13	3	34660	4	11	160000	176000
45	3	BRISTOL 45.5 AFT	KTH	SA/RC	FBG	KC	IB	58D	WEST	13	3	34660	4	11	166000	182500
45	3	BRISTOL 45.5 CTR	SLP	SA/RC	FBG	KC	IB	58D	WEST	13	3	34660	4	11	172000	189000
45	3	BRISTOL 45.5 CTR	KTH	SA/RC	FBG	KC	IB	58D	WEST	13	3	34660	4	11	166000	182500
54	5	BRISTOL 54.4	KTH	SA/RC	FBG	KC	IB	100D	WEST	15	6	52000	5	4	284500	312500
		1984 BOATS														
29	11	BRISTOL 29.9	SLP	SA/RC	FBG	KC	IB	16D	UNIV	10	2	8650	3	6	31000	34400
29	11	BRISTOL 29.9	SLP	SA/RC	FBG	KL	IB	16D	UNIV	10	2	8650	4	4	30800	34300
31	2	BRISTOL 31.1	SLP	SA/RC	FBG	KC	IB	14D- 24D		10	2	11200	3	6	41500	46100
31	2	BRISTOL 31.1	SLP	SA/RC	FBG	KL	IB	14D- 24D		10	2	11200	5	3	41500	46100
35	6	BRISTOL 35.5	SLP	SA/RC	FBG	KC	IB	24D	UNIV	10	10	15000	3	9	60300	66300
35	6	BRISTOL 35.5	SLP	SA/RC	FBG	KC	IB	32D	UNIV	10	10	15000	3	9	60400	66400
35	6	BRISTOL 35.5	SLP	SA/RC	FBG	KL	IB	24D	UNIV	10	10	15000	5	9	60300	66300
35	6	BRISTOL 35.5	SLP	SA/RC	FBG	KL	IB	32D	UNIV	10	10	15000	5	9	60400	66400
38	4	BRISTOL 38.8	SLP	SA/RC	FBG	KC	IB	44D	UNIV	12	1	19150	4	6	83800	92100
40	2	BRISTOL 40	SLP	SA/RC	FBG	KC	IB	40D	WEST	10	9	17580	4		88000	96700
40	2	BRISTOL 40	SLP	SA/RC	FBG	KL	IB	40D	WEST	10	9	17580	5	5	88000	96700
40	2	BRISTOL 40	CUT	SA/RC	FBG	KC	IB	40D	WEST	10	9	17580	4		88000	96700
40	2	BRISTOL 40	CUT	SA/RC	FBG	KL	IB	40D	WEST	10	9	17580	5	5	88000	96700
40	2	BRISTOL 40	YWL	SA/RC	FBG	KC	IB	40D	WEST	10	9	17580	4		88000	96700
40	2	BRISTOL 40	YWL	SA/RC	FBG	KL	IB	40D	WEST	10	9	17580	5	5	88000	96700
41	2	BRISTOL 41.1	SLP	SA/RC	FBG	KC	IB	52D		12	11	26530	10		118000	129500
41	2	BRISTOL 41.1 AFT	SLP	SA/RC	FBG	KC	IB	50D	WEST	12	11	26530	4	6	112500	123500
41	2	BRISTOL 41.1 CTR	SLP	SA/RC	FBG	KC	IB	50D	WEST	12	11	26530	4	6	124000	136000
45	3	BRISTOL 45.5 AFT	SLP	SA/RC	FBG	KC	IB	58D	WEST	13	3	34660	4	11	153000	168000
45	3	BRISTOL 45.5 AFT	KTH	SA/RC	FBG	KC	IB	58D	WEST	13	3	34660	4	11	155500	170500
45	3	BRISTOL 45.5 CTR	SLP	SA/RC	FBG	KC	IB	58D	WEST	13	3	34660	4	11	157500	173500
45	3	BRISTOL 45.5 CTR	KTH	SA/RC	FBG	KC	IB	58D	WEST	13	3	34660	4	11	155500	170500
54	5	BRISTOL 54.4	KTH	SA/RC	FBG	KC	IB	100D	WEST	15	6	52000	5	4	266000	292500

....For earlier years, see the BUC Used Boat Price Guide, Volume 3

BRITANNIA BOATS LTD

ANNAPOLIS MD 21403 COAST GUARD MFG ID- BIH See inside cover to adjust price for area

For more recent years, see the BUC Used Boat Price Guide, Volume 1

LOA FT	LOA IN	NAME AND/ OR MODEL	TOP/ RIG	BOAT TYPE	HULL MTL	HULL TP	ENGINE TP	# HP	ENGINE MFG	BEAM FT	BEAM IN	WGT LBS	DRAFT FT	DRAFT IN	RETAIL LOW	RETAIL HIGH
		1986 BOATS														
23		CORNISH-SHRIMPER	SLP	SA/CR	FBG		OB			7	2	2300	4		12500	14200

BRITISH YACHTS LIMITED

REYNOLDSBURG OH 43068 COAST GUARD MFG ID- BYZ See inside cover to adjust price for area
FORMERLY NORTHSHORE YACHT YARDS LTD

LOA FT	LOA IN	NAME AND/ OR MODEL	TOP/ RIG	BOAT TYPE	HULL MTL	HULL TP	ENGINE TP	# HP	ENGINE MFG	BEAM FT	BEAM IN	WGT LBS	DRAFT FT	DRAFT IN	RETAIL LOW	RETAIL HIGH
		1985 BOATS														
19		SKANNER	GAF	SAIL	FBG	KL	IB	7D	BMW	7	2	2500	2	4	9350	10600
25	3	FISHER 25	KTH	SAIL	FBG	KL	IB	23D	VLVO	9	4	9000	3	9	30200	33600
25	3	FISHER POTTER		PH	FBG	DV	IB	25D	VLVO	9	4	9900	3	9	37500	41700
25	3	FISHER POTTER DAYSAI	KTH	SAIL	FBG	KL	IB	25D	VLVO	9	4	9900	3	9	33800	37500
27		VANCOUVER 27	CUT	SA/CR	FBG	KL	IB	22D	WEST	8	8	8960	4	6	32400	36000
29	6	BRITISH YACHTS LTD30	SLP	SAIL	FBG	KL	IB	18D	VLVO	9	6	9866	4	6	38200	42500
30		FISHER 30	KTH	SAIL	FBG	KL	IB	36D	VLVO	9	6	13000	4	3	51700	56800
32		SOUTHERLY 100	SLP	SAIL	FBG	SK	IB	20D	BUKH	9	11	9500	1	10	34700	38600
32		VANCOUVER 32	CUT	SA/CR	FBG	KL	IB	22D	WEST	10	7	14000	4	9	51000	56000
34	4	FISHER 34	KTH	SAIL	FBG	KL	IB	61D	VLVO	11	3	21000	4	9	70600	77600
36	10	SOUTHERLY 115	SLP	SAIL	FBG	SK	IB	36D	BUKH	11	11	14600	2	3	49600	54500
37		FISHER 37	KTH	SAIL	FBG	KL	IB	80D	SABR	12		28000	5	3	85500	93900
37		FISHER 37 AFT CABIN	KTH	SAIL	FBG	KL	IB	80D	SABR	12		28000	5	3	85500	93900
38		VANCOUVER 38	CUT	SA/CR	STL	KL	IB	48D	WEST	11	8	23000	5	6	72100	79200
45	8	FISHER 46	KTH	SAIL	FBG	KL	IB	120D	SABR	15		50000	6	6	140000	153500
48		SOUTHERLY 145	SLP	SAIL	FBG	SK	IB	80D	SABR	13	11	23000	2	6	113500	124500
		1984 BOATS														
25	3	FISHER 25	KTH	SAIL	FBG	KL	IB	23D	VLVO	9	4	9000	3	9	28300	31400
25	3	FISHER POTTER		PH	FBG	DS	IB	25D	VLVO	9	4	9900	3	9	36900	41000
25	3	FISHER POTTER DAYSAI	KTH	SAIL	FBG	KL	IB	25D	VLVO	9	4	9900	3	9	31600	35100
27		VANCOUVER 27	CUT	SA/CR	FBG	KL	IB	20D	WEST	8	8	8960	4	6	30300	33700
29	6	BRITISH YACHTS LTD30	SLP	SAIL	FBG	KL	IB	17D	VLVO	9	6	9866	4	6	35800	39800
30		FISHER 30	KTH	SAIL	FBG	KL	IB	36D	VLVO	9	6	13000	4	3	48400	53200
31	3	FISHER 31	KTH	SAIL	FBG	KL	IB	36D	VLVO	10	4	15120	4	3	54300	59700
32		SOUTHERLY 100	SLP	SAIL	FBG	SK	IB	20D	BUKH	9	11	9500	1	10	32700	36300
32		VANCOUVER 32	CUT	SA/CR	FBG	KL	IB	20D	WEST	10	7	14000	4	9	48000	52700
34	4	FISHER 34	KTH	SAIL	FBG	KL	IB	61D	VLVO	11	3	21000	4	9	66400	73000
36	10	SOUTHERLY 115	SLP	SAIL	FBG	SK	IB	36D	BUKH	11	11	14600	2	3	46900	51500
37		FISHER 37	KTH	SAIL	FBG	KL	IB	80D	SABR	12		28000	5	3	77000	84600
37		FISHER 37 AFT CABIN	KTH	SAIL	FBG	KL	IB	80D	SABR	12		28000	5	3	83800	92000
38		VANCOUVER 38	CUT	SA/CR	STL	KL	IB	48D	WEST	11	8	23000	5	6	67800	74500
45	8	FISHER 46	KTH	SAIL	FBG	KL	IB	120D	SABR	15		50000	6	6	131500	144500
48		SOUTHERLY 145	SLP	SAIL	FBG	SK	IB	80D	SABR	13	11	23000	2	6	107000	117500

....For earlier years, see the BUC Used Boat Price Guide, Volume 3

BUCCANEER BOATS

CORD AR 72524 COAST GUARD MFG ID- BPC See inside cover to adjust price for area

LOA FT	LOA IN	NAME AND/ OR MODEL	TOP/ RIG	BOAT TYPE	HULL MTL	HULL TP	ENGINE TP	# HP	ENGINE MFG	BEAM FT	BEAM IN	WGT LBS	DRAFT FT	DRAFT IN	RETAIL LOW	RETAIL HIGH
		1994 BOATS														
18	9	1800	OP	B/R	FBG	DV	IO	115-175		7	6	2200			4500	5300
18	9	1900	OP	B/R	FBG	DV	IO	155-175		7	6	2200			4550	5450
20	3	2100	OP	B/R	FBG	DV	IO	155-240		7	6	2500			5550	6600
22	6	2300	OP	B/R	FBG	DV	IO	155-250		7	7	2800			6800	8150
		1993 BOATS														
18	9	1800	OP	B/R	FBG	DV	IO	115-175		7	6	2200			4150	4950
18	9	1900	OP	B/R	FBG	DV	IO	155-175		7	6	2200			4200	5100
20	3	2100	OP	B/R	FBG	DV	IO	155-240		7	6	2500			5200	6150
22	6	2300	OP	B/R	FBG	DV	IO	155-250		7	7	2800			6350	7600

BUCHAN YACHTS LTD

LONDON ENGLAND 8S8 5BP See inside cover to adjust price for area

LOA FT	LOA IN	NAME AND/ OR MODEL	TOP/ RIG	BOAT TYPE	HULL MTL	HULL TP	ENGINE TP	# HP	ENGINE MFG	BEAM FT	BEAM IN	WGT LBS	DRAFT FT	DRAFT IN	RETAIL LOW	RETAIL HIGH
		1985 BOATS														
36	2	RED-ADMIRAL	SLP	SA/RC	FBG	KL	SD	23D	VLVO	11	3	12000	6		30100	33500
41	6	SWALLOWTAIL 42	SLP	SA/CR	FBG	KL	IB	51D	PERK	13		19000	6	6	55200	60700
41	6	SWALLOWTAIL 42	SLP	SA/RC	FBG	KC	IB	51D	PERK	13		19000	5		55200	60700
43	6	SWALLOWTAIL 43	KTH	SA/CR	FBG	KC	IB	51D	PERK	13		22500	5		69300	76100
43	6	SWALLOWTAIL 43	KTH	SA/CR	FBG	KL	IB	51D	PERK	13		22500	6	6	69300	76100
		1984 BOATS														
36	2	RED-ADMIRAL	SLP	SA/RC	FBG	KL	SD	23D	VLVO	11	3	12000	6		28400	31500
41	6	SWALLOWTAIL 42	SLP	SA/CR	FBG	KL	IB	50D	PERK	13		19000	6	6	52100	57200
41	6	SWALLOWTAIL 42	SLP	SA/RC	FBG	KC	IB	50D	PERK	13		19000	5		52100	57200
43	6	SWALLOWTAIL 43	KTH	SA/CR	FBG	KC	IB	50D	PERK	12	11	22500	5		65200	71600
43	6	SWALLOWTAIL 43	KTH	SA/CR	FBG	KL	IB	50D	PERK	12	11	22500	6	6	65200	71600

....For earlier years, see the BUC Used Boat Price Guide, Volume 3

BUHLERS YACHTS LTD
DELTA BC CANADA
WEST INDIES

See inside cover to adjust price for area

LOA FT IN	NAME AND/ OR MODEL	TOP/ RIG	BOAT TYPE	-HULL- MTL TP	----ENGINE--- TP # HP MFG	BEAM FT IN	WGT LBS	DRAFT FT IN	RETAIL LOW	RETAIL HIGH
--- 1984 BOATS ---
35	BUHLER 35		FSH	FBG IB	135D PERK 12		6200	3	33300	37000
38	BUHLER 38	CUT	SA/CR	FBG KL OB		18	7300	1 10	19600	21800

....For earlier years, see the BUC Used Boat Price Guide, Volume 3

BULLET BOATS INC
SEASIDE PK NJ 08752   COAST GUARD MFG ID- BUD See inside cover to adjust price for area

LOA FT IN	NAME AND/ OR MODEL	TOP/ RIG	BOAT TYPE	-HULL- MTL TP	----ENGINE--- TP # HP MFG	BEAM FT IN	WGT LBS	DRAFT FT IN	RETAIL LOW	RETAIL HIGH
--- 1984 BOATS ---
22 4	BULLET 22 CALIBER	OP	OFF	FBG DV OB		7 10	1400		5500	6350

....For earlier years, see the BUC Used Boat Price Guide, Volume 3

BURGER BOAT COMPANY
MANITOWOC WI 54220   COAST GUARD MFG ID- BRG See inside cover to adjust price for area

LOA FT IN	NAME AND/ OR MODEL	TOP/ RIG	BOAT TYPE	-HULL- MTL TP	----ENGINE--- TP # HP MFG	BEAM FT IN	WGT LBS	DRAFT FT IN	RETAIL LOW	RETAIL HIGH
--- 1986 BOATS ---
70		HT	MY	AL DV IB		18		5	**	**
70		HT	SF	AL DV IB		18 2		5	**	**
78 10		HT	CR	AL DV IB		18 5		5	**	**
79		HT	MY	AL DV IB		18 5		5	**	**

....For earlier years, see the BUC Used Boat Price Guide, Volume 3

BURNS CRAFT INC
BURNS MANUFACTURING INC
LEXINGTON AL 35648   COAST GUARD MFG ID- BCI
FOR OLDER MODELS SEE NAUTA-CRAFT INC

See inside cover to adjust price for area

LOA FT IN	NAME AND/ OR MODEL	TOP/ RIG	BOAT TYPE	-HULL- MTL TP	----ENGINE--- TP # HP MFG	BEAM FT IN	WGT LBS	DRAFT FT IN	RETAIL LOW	RETAIL HIGH
--- 1988 BOATS ---
37	SUN BRDG DYNSTY 374		SPTCR	FBG SV IB	T350 CRUS 14		20000	3	44300	49200
48	MOTOR YACHT 48	HT	MY	FBG IB	T385D GM	15 3	48000	3 10	117500	129000
--- 1985 BOATS ---
36	FISHERMAN	HT	SF	FBG DV IB	T270 CRUS 14				32300	35900
36	FISHERMAN	HT	SF	FBG DV IB	T350 CRUS 14				33200	36900
36	FISHERMAN	HT	SF	FBG DV IB	T300D CAT 14				37800	42000
36	SPORT CRUISER	ST	OVNTR	FBG DV IB	T270 CRUS 14				33400	37100
36	SPORT CRUISER	ST	OVNTR	FBG DV IB	T300D CAT 14				34300	38100
36	SPORT SEDAN	FB	SDN	FBG DV IB	T270 CRUS 14				**	**
36	SPORT SEDAN	FB	SDN	FBG DV IB	T350 CRUS 14				34000	37800
36	SPORT SEDAN	FB	SDN	FBG DV IB	T300D CRUS 14				35100	39000
36	SPORT SEDAN	FB	SDN	FBG DV IB	T300D CAT 14				43600	48500
40	CONVERTIBLE	FB	SDN	FBG SV IB	T350 CRUS 14				50600	55600
40	CONVERTIBLE	FB	SDN	FBG SV IB	T355D CAT 14				61000	67000
40	MOTOR YACHT	FB	MY	FBG SV IB	T350 CRUS 14				50700	55700
40	MOTOR YACHT	FB	MY	FBG SV IB	T355D CAT 14				61100	67200
40	SPORT FISHERMAN	FB	SF	FBG SV IB	T350 CRUS 14				50500	55500
40	SPORT FISHERMAN	FB	SF	FBG SV IB	T355D CAT 14				60900	66900
48	MOTOR YACHT	FB	MY	FBG SV IB	D J&T 15				**	**
	IB T355D CAT	101000	111000,	IB T375D	101500 111500,	IB T450D J&T			106500	117500
48	SPORT FISHERMAN	FB	SF	FBG SV IB	T D J&T 16 4				**	**
48	SPORT FISHERMAN	FB	SF	FBG SV IB	T375D 15				92500	101500

....For earlier years, see the BUC Used Boat Price Guide, Volume 3

C & B MARINE
CAPITOLA CA 95010   COAST GUARD MFG ID- CNJ See inside cover to adjust price for area

LOA FT IN	NAME AND/ OR MODEL	TOP/ RIG	BOAT TYPE	-HULL- MTL TP	----ENGINE--- TP # HP MFG	BEAM FT IN	WGT LBS	DRAFT FT IN	RETAIL LOW	RETAIL HIGH
--- 1985 BOATS ---
24	ALLEGRA 24	CUT	SA/CR	FBG KL IB	8D 8		6500	3 7	35400	39300
34	TIFFANY-JAYNE	SLP	SAIL	FBG KL IB	15D YAN 8		5790	5 6	37600	41800
34 8	FARR 34	SLP	SAIL	CDR KL IB	18D 11 4		8730	5 9	58600	64400
36 2	ANACAPA 36	KTH	SA/CR	FBG KL IB	D 11		11000	6 3	76200	83700
38 3	FARR 38	SLP	SAIL	CDR KL IB	42D PATH 12		10600	6 4	82100	90200
44	FARR 44	SLP	SAIL	CDR KL IB	42D PATH 13		14516	7 1	149500	164500
44	FARR 44 DECKHOUSE	SLP	SAIL	CDR KL IB	45D BMW 13		15000	7 1	152000	167000
54 10	FARR 55	SLP	SAIL	CDR KL IB	82D PATH 14 7		23180	8 6	403000	443000
--- 1984 BOATS ---
34	TIFFANY-JAYNE	SLP	SAIL	FBG KL IB	13D YAN 8		5790	5 6	35400	39300
34 8	FARR 34	SLP	SAIL	CDR KL IB	18D 11 4		8730	5 9	55100	60600
38 3	FARR 38	SLP	SAIL	FBG KL IB	42D PATH 12		10600	6 4	77200	84800
44	FARR 44	SLP	SAIL	CDR KL IB	42D PATH 13		14516	7 1	140500	154500
44	FARR 44 DECKHOUSE	SLP	SAIL	FBG KL IB	45D BMW 13		15000	7 1	143000	157500
54 10	FARR 55	SLP	SAIL	CDR KL IB	82D PATH 14 7		23180	8 6	378500	416000

....For earlier years, see the BUC Used Boat Price Guide, Volume 3

C & C YACHTS
FAIRPORT HARBOR OH 4400   COAST GUARD MFG ID- ZCC See inside cover to adjust price for area

C & C YACHTS
FAIRPORT HARBOR OH 44077
FORMERLY C & C INTERNATIONAL YACHTS

For more recent years, see the BUC Used Boat Price Guide, Volume 1

LOA FT IN	NAME AND/ OR MODEL	TOP/ RIG	BOAT TYPE	-HULL- MTL TP	----ENGINE--- TP # HP MFG	BEAM FT IN	WGT LBS	DRAFT FT IN	RETAIL LOW	RETAIL HIGH
--- 1996 BOATS ---
21 1	C&C SR 21	SLP	SAROD	F/S DB OB	8		1360	4 6	8900	10100
25 6	C&C SR 25	SLP	SAROD	F/S DB OB	8 6		1860	5 3	12400	14100
30	C&C 30 XL	SLP	SACAC	KEV KL IB	18D YAN 10 8		7500	5 10	49800	54700
30	C&C 30+	SLP	SACAC	KEV KL IB	18D YAN 10 8		8275	5 10	55100	60600
33 1	C&C SR 33	SLP	SACAC	KEV KL IB	18D YAN 11 5		5372	7	36400	40400
35	C&C 36 XL	SLP	SACAC	F/S KL IB	27D YAN 11 7		11200	7 3	77800	85400
35 6	C&C 36+	SLP	SACAC	KEV KL IB	27D YAN 11 7		12000	7 3	83100	91300
51 9	C&C 51 XL	SLP	SACAC	KEV KL IB	85D YAN 15 7		33800	10 4	276500	304000
--- 1995 BOATS ---
21 1	C&C SR 21	SLP	SAROD	F/S DB OB	8		1360	4 6	8250	9500
25 6	C&C SR 25	SLP	SAROD	F/S DB OB	8 6		1860	5 3	11700	13220
27 6	C&C SR 27	SLP	SAROD	F/S DB OB	9 6		3750	5 11	21900	24300
30	C&C 30 XL	SLP	SACAC	KEV KL IB	18D YAN 10 8		7500	5 10	47100	51700
30	C&C 30+	SLP	SACAC	KEV KL IB	18D YAN 10 8		8275	5 10	51800	57000
33 1	C&C SR 33	SLP	SAROD	KEV KL IB	18D YAN 11 5		5372	7	34200	38000
35 6	C&C 34/36 XL	SLP	SACAC	F/S KL IB	27D YAN 11 7		11200	7 3	73100	80400
35 6	C&C 34/36+	SLP	SACAC	KEV KL IB	27D YAN 11 7		12000	7 3	78100	85900
51 9	C&C 51 XL	SLP	SACAC	KEV KL IB	85D YAN 15 7		33800	10 4	260000	285500
51 9	C&C 51+	SLP	SACAC	KEV KC IB	85D YAN 15 7		44000	6	260500	286500
--- 1994 BOATS ---
30	C & C 30 XL	SLP	SACAC	F/S KL IB	18D YAN 10 8		7500	5 10	43800	48700
30	C & C 30+	SLP	SACAC	F/S KL IB	18D YAN 10 8		8275	5 10	48800	53600
35 6	C & C 34/36 R	SLP	SACAC	F/S KL IB	18D YAN 11 7		10500	7 3	64600	71000
35 6	C & C 34/36 XL	SLP	SACAC	F/S KL IB	27D YAN 11 7		11200	7 3	72200	79400
35 6	C & C 34/36+	SLP	SACAC	KEV KL IB	27D YAN 11 7		12000	7 3	76700	76700
39 6	C & C 37/40 R	SLP	SACAC	FBG KL IB	35D YAN 12 7		14900	8 2	108500	119000
39 6	C & C 37/40 XL	SLP	SACAC	F/S KL IB	35D YAN 12 7		15700	8 2	112500	123500
39 6	C & C 37/40+	SLP	SACAC	KEV KL IB	35D YAN 12 7		16700	7 3	117500	129000
44 7	C-STAR 45 CATAMARAN	SLP	SACAC	KEV CT IB	50D YAN 29 8		15950	3 10	204000	224000
45 3	C & C 45 R	SLP	SACAC	KEV KL IB	44D YAN 13 9		19100	7 10	172500	189500
45 3	C & C 45 XL	SLP	SACAC	KEV KL IB	44D YAN 13 9		19100	7 10	172500	189500
45 3	C & C 45+	SLP	SACAC	KEV KC IB	44D YAN 13 9		21000	6	180000	198000
51 9	C & C 51 R	SLP	SACAC	KEV KL IB	85D YAN 15 7		31000	10 4	236500	260000
51 9	C & C 51 XL	SLP	SACAC	KEV KL IB	85D YAN 15 7		31000	6	240500	269000
51 9	C & C 51+	SLP	SACAC	KEV KC IB	85D YAN 15 7		40400	6	245000	269500
--- 1993 BOATS ---
30	C & C 30 XL	SLP	SACAC	F/S KL IB	18D YAN 10 8		7500	5 10	41200	45800
30	C & C 30+	SLP	SACAC	F/S KL IB	18D YAN 10 8		8275	5 10	46100	50700
35 6	C & C 34/36 R	SLP	SACAC	F/S KL IB	18D YAN 11 7		10500	7 3	60800	66800
35 6	C & C 34/36 XL	SLP	SACAC	F/S KL IB	27D YAN 11 7		11200	7 3	67900	74700
35 6	C & C 34/36+	SLP	SACAC	KEV KL IB	27D YAN 11 7		12000	7 3	72200	72200
39 6	C & C 37/40 R	SLP	SACAC	FBG KL IB	35D YAN 12 7		14900	8 2	65700	72200
39 6	C & C 37/40 XL	SLP	SACAC	F/S KL IB	35D YAN 12 7		15700	8 2	102000	112000
39 6	C & C 37/40+	SLP	SACAC	KEV KL IB	35D YAN 12 7		16700	7 3	106000	116500
44 7	C-STAR 45 CATAMARAN	SLP	SACAC	KEV CT IB	50D YAN 29 8		15950	3 10	110500	121500
45 3	C & C 45 R	SLP	SACAC	KEV KL IB	44D YAN 13 9		19100	7 10	135500	150500
45 3	C & C 45 XL	SLP	SACAC	KEV KL IB	44D YAN 13 9		19100	7 10	162500	178500

96th ed. - Vol. II   CONTINUED ON NEXT PAGE   87

LOA FT	LOA IN	NAME AND/ OR MODEL	TOP/ RIG	BOAT TYPE	-HULL- MTL	-HULL- TP	ENGINE TP	# HP	MFG	BEAM FT	BEAM IN	WGT LBS	DRAFT FT	DRAFT IN	RETAIL LOW	RETAIL HIGH
		1993 BOATS														
45	3	C & C 45+	SLP	SACAC	KEV	KC	IB	44D	YAN	13	9	21000	6		169500	186000
51	9	C & C 51 R	SLP	SACAC	KEV	KL	IB	85D	YAN	15	7	31000	10	4	222500	244500
51	9	C & C 51 XL	SLP	SACAC	KEV	KL	IB	85D	YAN	15	7	33900	10	4	230500	253000
51	9	C & C 51+	SLP	SACAC	KEV	KC	IB	85D	YAN	15	7	40400	6		230500	253500
		1991 BOATS														
30		C & C 30	SLP	SAIL	FBG	KL	IB	16D	YAN	10	8	8275	5	10	40300	44800
35	6	C & C 34/36 R	SLP	SAIL	FBG	KL	IB	27D	YAN	11	7	10500	7	3	53800	59100
35	6	C & C 34/36 XL	SLP	SAIL	FBG	KL	IB	27D	YAN	11	7	11200	7	3	60100	66000
35	6	C & C 34/36+	SLP	SAIL	FBG	KL	IB	27D	YAN	11	7	12000	7	3	58100	63800
39	6	C & C 37/40 R	SLP	SAIL	FBG	KL	IB	34D	YAN	12	7	14250	7	10	87300	96000
39	6	C & C 37/40 XL	SLP	SAIL	FBG	KL	IB	34D	YAN	12	7	15000	7	10	90600	99600
39	6	C & C 37/40+	SLP	SAIL	FBG	KL	IB	34D	YAN	12	7	16000	7	3	94900	104500
44		C & C 44 XL	SLP	SAIL	FBG	KL	IB	44D	YAN	13	3	19750	8	6	135500	149000
44		C & C 44+	SLP	SAIL	FBG	KL	IB	44D	YAN	13	3	22500	8	6	145000	159000
51	4	C & C 51 R	SLP	SAIL	FBG	KL	IB	85D	YAN	15	7	31000	10	4	197000	216500
51	4	C & C 51 XL	SLP	SAIL	FBG	KL	IB	85D	YAN	15	7	35900	10	4	208500	229000
57		C & C 57	SLP	SAIL	FBG	KL	IB	85D	YAN	15	6	45000	6		422500	464000
		1987 BOATS														
26	8	C-&-C 27	SLP	SA/RC	FBG	KL	IB	9D	YAN	9	3	4720	4	10	16900	19200
30		C-&-C 30	SLP	SA/RC	FBG	KL	IB	16D	YAN	10	8	8550	5	10	32700	36300
32	7	C-&-C 33	SLP	SA/RC	FBG	KL	IB	16D	YAN	10	6	9450	6	4	37300	41500
34	8	C-&-C 35	SLP	SA/RC	FBG	KL	IB	27D	YAN	11	2	10825	6	5	43500	48400
37	10	C-&-C 38	SLP	SA/RC	FBG	KL	IB	30D	YAN	12	9	14275	7	6	62100	68300
38	9	C-&-C 39	SLP	SA/CR	FBG	KL	IB	44D	YAN	12	3	19500	5	6	82800	91000
40	9	C-&-C 41	SLP	SA/RC	FBG	KL	IB	30D	YAN	12	11	17500	7	10	83800	92100
44	2	C-&-C 44	SLP	SA/RC	FBG	KL	IB	44D	YAN	12	11	22500	8	6	114500	125500
		1986 BOATS														
26	6	C-&-C 27	SLP	SA/CR	FBG	KL	OB			9	3	4420	4	10	14000	15900
26	6	C-&-C 27	SLP	SA/CR	FBG	KL	IB	8D	YAN	9	3	4420	4	10	14900	16900
28	6	C-&-C 29	SLP	SA/CR	FBG	KL	IB	16D	YAN	9	5	6700	5	3	23900	26500
28	6	C-&-C 29 SHOAL	SLP	SA/CR	FBG	KL	IB	16D	YAN	9	5	6700	4		23900	26500
32	7	C-&-C 33	SLP	SA/CR	FBG	KC	IB	16D	YAN	10	6	9450	6	4	35100	39000
34	8	C-&-C 35	SLP	SA/CR	FBG	KL	IB	24D	YAN	11	2	10825	6	5	40900	45500
36	6	CML 37	HT	CR	FBG	DS	IB	T136D	VLVO	12	9	18000	3	2	76100	83600
37	6	C-&-C 38	SLP	SA/RC	FBG	KL	IB	30D	YAN	12	8	14275	7	6	57600	63300
38	6	LANDFALL 39	SLP	SA/CR	FBG	KL	IB	44D	YAN	12	2	19483	5	5	77000	84700
40	9	C-&-C 41	SLP	SA/RC	FBG	KL	IB	30D	YAN	12	11	17500	7	10	78800	86600
42	1	LANDFALL 43	SLP	SA/CR	FBG	KL	IB	58D	WEST	12	8	24600	5	6	103500	113500
44	2	C-&-C 44	SLP	SA/RC	FBG	KL	IB	44D	YAN	13	3	20800	8	3	103500	113500
		1985 BOATS														
24		C-&-C 24	SLP	SA/RC	FBG	KL	OB			8	10	3200	4		8550	9850
26	6	C-&-C 27	SLP	SA/RC	FBG	KL	IB	D		9	3	4420	4	10	14000	15900
28	6	C-&-C 29	SLP	SA/RC	FBG	KL	IB	D		9	5	6700	5	3	22500	25000
31	6	C-&-C 32	SLP	SA/CR	FBG	KC	IB	D		10	3	10485	4		36500	40600
31	6	C-&-C 32	SLP	SA/CR	FBG	KL	IB	D		10	3	9680	5	8	33700	37500
32	6	C-&-C 33	SLP	SA/RC	FBG	KL	IB	D		10		9450	6	4	33000	36700
34	8	C-&-C 35	SLP	SA/RC	FBG	KL	IB	D		11	2	10825	6	5	38500	42700
34	11	LANDFALL 35	SLP	SA/CR	FBG	KL	IB	D		10	8	13000	4	10	46500	51100
37	7	C-&-C 37	SLP	SA/RC	FBG	KL	IB	D		11	8	14300	6	7	54400	59800
37	7	LANDFALL 38	SLP	SA/CR	FBG	KL	IB	D		12		16700	5		61900	68000
38	9	LANDFALL 39	SLP	SA/CR	FBG	KL	IB	D		12	2	17350	5	6	67000	73600
40	9	C-&-C 41	SLP	SA/RC	FBG	KL	IB	D		12	11	17500	7	10	74300	81700
42	1	LANDFALL 43	SLP	SA/CR	FBG	KL	IB	D		12	8	24600	5	6	96900	106500
42	1	LANDFALL 43	KTH	SA/CR	FBG	KL	IB	D		12	8	24600	5	6	96900	106500
		1984 BOATS														
24		C-&-C 24	SLP	SA/CR	FBG	KL	OB			8	10	3200	4		8050	9250
25	2	C-&-C 25	SLP	SAIL	FBG	KL	OB			8	8	4100	4	3	10800	12300
25	2	C-&-C 25	SLP	SAIL	FBG	KL	SD	15	OMC	8	8	4100	4	3	11300	12800
26	6	C-&-C 27	SLP	SA/CR	FBG	KL	OB			9	3	4420	4	10	12400	14100
26	6	C-&-C 27	SLP	SA/CR	FBG	KL	IB	8D	YAN	9	3	4420	4	10	13100	14900
28	6	C-&-C 29	SLP	SA/CR	FBG	KL	IB	15D	YAN	9	5	6700	5	3	21100	23500
28	6	C-&-C 29 SHOAL	SLP	SA/CR	FBG	KL	IB	15D	YAN	9	5	6700	4		21100	23500
31	6	C-&-C 32	SLP	SA/CR	FBG	KC	IB	15D	YAN	10	3	10485	4		34300	38200
31	6	C-&-C 32	SLP	SA/CR	FBG	KL	IB	15D	YAN	10	3	9680	5	8	31700	35200
34	8	C-&-C 35	SLP	SA/CR	FBG	KC	IB	23D	YAN	11	2	11275	4	2	37600	41800
34	8	C-&-C 35	SLP	SA/CR	FBG	KL	IB	23D	YAN	11	2	10825	6	5	36200	40200
34	11	LANDFALL 35	SLP	SA/CR	FBG	KL	VD	27D	WEST	10	8	13000	4	10	43300	48100
37	7	C-&-C 37	SLP	SA/CR	FBG	KC	IB	30D	YAN	11	8	14300	4	7	51200	56300
37	7	C-&-C 37	SLP	SA/CR	FBG	KL	IB	30D	YAN	11	8	14300	6	7	51200	56300
37	7	LANDFALL 38	SLP	SA/CR	FBG	KL	VD	27D	WEST	12		16700	5		58100	63800
38	5	CUSTOM 38	SLP	SA/RC	FBG	KL				12	4	14400	7	6	53400	58600
40	9	C-&-C 41	SLP	SA/RC	FBG	KC	IB	30D	YAN	12	11		5		60500	66500
40	9	C-&-C 41	SLP	SA/RC	FBG	KL	IB	30D	YAN	12	11	17500	7	10	69700	76600
42	1	LANDFALL 43	SLP	SA/CR	FBG	KL	IB	D		12	8	24600	5	6	91100	100000
42	1	LANDFALL 43	KTH	SA/CR	FBG	KL	IB	D		12	8	24600	5	6	91100	100000
47	6	LANDFALL 48	CUT	SA/CR	FBG	KL	IB	85D		14		35600	6		136000	149500
52	1	CUSTOM 52	SLP	SA/RC	FBG	KL				15	6	34000	9	6	171500	188500
52	1	CUSTOM 52 SHOAL	SLP	SA/RC	FBG	KL				15	6	34000	6		171500	188500

....For earlier years, see the BUC Used Boat Price Guide, Volume 3

C & L BOATWORKS

DIV OF WATERHOUSE & MAY LTD
PICKERING ONTARIO CANAD COAST GUARD MFG ID- CLW
See inside cover to adjust price for area
FOR OLDER MODELS SEE CROCE & LOFTHOUSE SAILCRAFT

LOA FT	LOA IN	NAME AND/ OR MODEL	TOP/ RIG	BOAT TYPE	-HULL- MTL	-HULL- TP	ENGINE TP	# HP	MFG	BEAM FT	BEAM IN	WGT LBS	DRAFT FT	DRAFT IN	RETAIL LOW	RETAIL HIGH
		1987 BOATS														
16		CL16	SLP	SA/OD	FBG	CB	OB			6	1	365		8	2200	2550
18	6	SANDPIPER 565	SLP	SAIL	FBG	SK	OB			7	1	1200		10	4100	4750
		1986 BOATS														
16		CL16	SLP	SA/OD	FBG	CB	OB			6	1	365		8	2000	2400
18	6	SANDPIPER 565	SLP	SAIL	FBG	SK	OB			7	1	1200		10	3800	4450
		1985 BOATS														
16		CL16	SLP	SA/OD	FBG	CB	OB			6	1	365		8	1850	2200
18	6	SANDPIPER 565	SLP	SAIL	FBG	SK	OB			7	1	1200		10	3550	4150
		1984 BOATS														
16		CL16	SLP	SA/OD	FBG	CB	OB			6	1	365		8	1750	2100
18	6	SANDPIPER 565	SLP	SAIL	FBG	SK	OB			7	1	1200		10	3350	3900

....For earlier years, see the BUC Used Boat Price Guide, Volume 3

C S Y

TENAFLY NJ 07670
See inside cover to adjust price for area

LOA FT	LOA IN	NAME AND/ OR MODEL	TOP/ RIG	BOAT TYPE	-HULL- MTL	-HULL- TP	ENGINE TP	# HP	MFG	BEAM FT	BEAM IN	WGT LBS	DRAFT FT	DRAFT IN	RETAIL LOW	RETAIL HIGH
		1988 BOATS														
42	4	C-S-Y 42	SLP	SA/CR	FBG	KC	IB	44D	YAN	13	5	22500	5	5	87800	96500
43		C-S-Y 445	SLP	SA/CR	FBG	KC	IB	44D	YAN	13	6	23500	5		92500	101500
44		C-S-Y 44 CLASSIC	SLP	SA/CR	FBG	KC	IB	66D	YAN	13	4	37000	6	6	122500	134500
50	1	C-S-Y 50	SLP	SA/CR	FBG	KC	IB	66D	YAN	14		34500	5	11	152500	167500
50	6	C-S-Y 50.5	SLP	SA/CR	FBG	KC	IB	66D	YAN	15		31500	4	11	153000	168000
		1987 BOATS														
42	4	C-S-Y 42	SLP	SA/CR	FBG	KC	IB	44D	YAN	13	5	22400	5	5	83000	91200
50	1	C-S-Y 50	SLP	SA/CR	FBG	KC	IB	66D	YAN	14		34500	5	11	144500	159000

....For earlier years, see the BUC Used Boat Price Guide, Volume 3

C-DORY MARINE INC

KENT WA 98032
See inside cover to adjust price for area
FORMERLY C-DORY INC

For more recent years, see the BUC Used Boat Price Guide, Volume 1

LOA FT	LOA IN	NAME AND/ OR MODEL	TOP/ RIG	BOAT TYPE	-HULL- MTL	-HULL- TP	ENGINE TP	# HP	MFG	BEAM FT	BEAM IN	WGT LBS	DRAFT FT	DRAFT IN	RETAIL LOW	RETAIL HIGH
		1996 BOATS														
19		C-DORY 19 ANGLER	OP	FSH	FBG	SV	OB			7	10	1500		7	7550	8650
22		C-DORY 22 ANGLER		FSH	FBG	SV	OB			7	8	1700		9	10200	11600
22		C-DORY 22 CRUISER		FSH	FBG	SV	OB			7	8	1950		9	12500	14200
25		C-DORY 25 CRUISE		FSH	FBG	SV	OB			8	6				21600	24000
		1995 BOATS														
16	3	C-DORY 16 SKIFF	OP	FSH	FBG	SV	OB			4	3	170			785	950
17	6	C-DORY 17 CC	OP	FSH	FBG	SV	OB			6	4				6850	7850
19		C-DORY 19 ANGLER	OP	FSH	FBG	SV	OB			7	10	1500		7	7150	8250
22		C-DORY 22 ANGLER		FSH	FBG	SV	OB			7	8	1700		9	9700	11000
22		C-DORY 22 CRUISER		FSH	FBG	SV	OB			7	8	1950		9	11900	13500
25		C-DORY 25 CRUISE		FSH	FBG	SV	OB			8	6				20600	22900
26		PRO ANGLER 26		FSH	FBG	SV	OB					5600			26600	29500
		1994 BOATS														
16	3	C-DORY 16 SKIFF	OP	FSH	FBG	SV	OB			4	3	170			750	905
17	6	C-DORY 17 CC	OP	FSH	FBG	SV	OB			6	4				6550	7500
19		C-DORY 19 ANGLER	OP	FSH	FBG	SV	OB			7	10	1500		7	6850	7850
22		C-DORY 22 ANGLER	OP	FSH	FBG	SV	OB			7	8	1700		9	9300	10600
22		C-DORY 22 CRUISER	OP	FSH	FBG	SV	OB			7	8	1950		9	11400	12900
26		PRO ANGLER 26	OP	FSH	FBG	SV	OB								23400	26000
		1993 BOATS														
16	3	C-DORY 16 SKIFF	OP	FSH	FBG	SV	OB			4	3	170			720	865
17	6	C-DORY 17 CC	OP	FSH	FBG	SV	OB			6	4				6250	7200

LOA FT	LOA IN	NAME AND/ OR MODEL	TOP/ RIG	BOAT TYPE	-HULL- MTL	-HULL- TP	ENGINE TP	ENGINE # HP	ENGINE MFG	BEAM FT	BEAM IN	WGT LBS	DRAFT FT	DRAFT IN	RETAIL LOW	RETAIL HIGH
		1993 BOATS														
19		C-DORY 19 ANGLER	OP	FSH	FBG	SV	OB			7	10	1500		7	6550	7500
22		C-DORY 22 ANGLER	OP	FSH	FBG	SV	OB			7	8	1700		9	8950	10100
22		C-DORY 22 CRUISER	OP	FSH	FBG	SV	OB			7	8	1950		9	10900	12400
		1992 BOATS														
22		C-DORY 22 ANGLER	OP	FSH	FBG	SV	OB			7	8	1700		9	8500	9750
22		C-DORY 22 CRUISER	OP	FSH	FBG	SV	OB			7	8	1950		9	10400	11900
		1991 BOATS														
20	10	C-DORY 21	HT	CR	FBG	DV	OB			7	7	1700		9	8200	9450
22		C-DORY 22 ANGLER	HT	FSH	FBG	DV	OB			7	10	1700		10	8150	9350
22		C-DORY 22 CRUISER	HT	FSH	FBG	DV	OB			7	10	1700		10	9000	10200
25	11	C-DORY 26 PILOTHOUSE	HT	FSH	FBG	DV	OB			8	6	3500	1		20200	22400
25	11	C-DORY 26 PRO-ANGLER	HT	FSH	FBG	DV	OB			8	6	3500	1		19100	21200
		1990 BOATS														
20	10	C-DORY 21	OP	OFF	FBG	DV	OB			7	7	1700		9	7900	9100
22		C-DORY 22 ANGLER	HT	FSH	FBG	DV	OB			7	10	1700		10	7850	9000
22		C-DORY 22 CRUISER	HT	FSH	FBG	DV	OB			7	10	1700		10	8600	9900
25	11	C-DORY 26 PILOTHOUSE	HT	FSH	FBG	DV	OB			8	6	3500	1		19500	21600
25	11	C-DORY 26 PRO-ANGLER	HT	FSH	FBG	DV	OB			8	6	3500	1		18600	20600
		1989 BOATS														
20	10	C-DORY 21	OP	OFF	FBG	DV	OB			7	7	1700		9	7650	8750
22		C-DORY 22 ANGLER		FSH	FBG	DV	OB			7	10	1700		10	7550	8700
22		C-DORY 22 CRUISER		FSH	FBG	DV	OB			7	10	1700		10	8300	9550
25	11	C-DORY 26 PILOTHOUSE		FSH	FBG	DV	OB			8	6	3500	1		18800	20800
25	11	C-DORY 26 PRO-ANGLER		FSH	FBG	DV	OB			8	6	3500	1		18100	20100

C-HAWK BOAT WORKS

BAILEY NC 27807 See inside cover to adjust price for area

FORMERLY TRI-STATE CUSTOM FIBERGLASS

For more recent years, see the BUC Used Boat Price Guide, Volume 1

LOA FT	LOA IN	NAME AND/ OR MODEL	TOP/ RIG	BOAT TYPE	-HULL- MTL	-HULL- TP	ENGINE TP	ENGINE # HP	ENGINE MFG	BEAM FT	BEAM IN	WGT LBS	DRAFT FT	DRAFT IN	RETAIL LOW	RETAIL HIGH
		1995 BOATS														
16		C-HAWK 16	OP	CTRCN	FBG	TR	OB				6	950		8	4000	4600
18		C-HAWK 18	OP	CTRCN	FBG	SV	OB			7	2	1500		10	6050	6950
20	4	C-HAWK 20	OP	CTRCN	FBG	SV	OB			8		1610		10	6900	7900
21	10	C-HAWK 22	OP	CTRCN	FBG	SV	OB			8		1710		10	7650	8800
21	10	C-HAWK 22 SPORT	EPH	SF	FBG	SV	OB			8		2440		10	10300	11700
22	4	C-HAWK 23	OP	CTRCN	FBG	SV	OB			8		1760	1		7950	9150
24	11	C-HAWK 25	OP	CTRCN	FBG	SV	OB			9	6	2680	1		13000	14800
24	11	C-HAWK 25 CABIN	EPH	SF	FBG	SV	OB			9	6	3500	1		15600	17700
24	11	C-HAWK 25 SPORT	EPH	SF	FBG	SV	OB			9	6	3800	1		16500	18700
25	4	C-HAWK 245	OP	CTRCN	FBG	DV	OB			8		2500	1	3	13600	15400
25	4	C-HAWK 245 CABIN	EPH	OFF	FBG	DV	OB			8		3100	1	3	16300	18500
25	9	C-HAWK 26	OP	CTRCN	FBG	DV	OB			8	9	3000	1	6	15900	18100
25	9	C-HAWK 26 W/A	HT	CUD	FBG	DV	OB			8	9	3700	1	6	18600	20600
29		C-HAWK 29 CABIN	EPH	OFF	FBG	DV	OB			10	4	5700	1	6	26500	29500

CABO MARINE INC

CORONA CA 91720 COAST GUARD MFG ID- BOG See inside cover to adjust price for area

LOA FT	LOA IN	NAME AND/ OR MODEL	TOP/ RIG	BOAT TYPE	-HULL- MTL	-HULL- TP	ENGINE TP	ENGINE # HP	ENGINE MFG	BEAM FT	BEAM IN	WGT LBS	DRAFT FT	DRAFT IN	RETAIL LOW	RETAIL HIGH
		1991 BOATS														
20		CABO 204 CENTERCON		CTRCN	FBG	SV	OB			8		2100			4900	5650
20		CABO 206 CUDDYCON		CUD	FBG	SV	OB			8		2200			5050	5800
21		CABO 216 CUDDYCON		CUD	FBG	SV	OB			8		2800			6300	7250
21		CABO 222 CUDDYCON		CUD	FBG	SV	IO	175		8		3500			11500	13000
21		CABO 226 CUDDYCON		CUD	FBG	SV	OB			8		2700			6200	7100
25		CABO 256 CUDDYCON		CUD	FBG	SV	OB			8	6	3700			9650	11000
25		CABO 266 CUDDYCON		CUD	FBG	SV	IO	270		8	6	4200			17300	19700
		1990 BOATS														
20		CABO 204 CUDDYCON		CUD	FBG	SV	OB			8		2100			4750	5450
20		CABO 206 CUDDYCON		CUD	FBG	SV	OB			8		2200			4850	5600
21		CABO 216 CUDDYCON		CUD	FBG	SV	OB			8		2800			6100	7000
22		CABO 222 CUDDYCON		CUD	FBG	SV	IO	260		8		3500			11900	13500
22		CABO 226 CUDDYCON		CUD	FBG	SV	OB			8		2700			6450	7400
25		CABO 256 CUDDYCON		CUD	FBG	SV	OB			8	6	3700			9400	10700
25		CABO 266 CUDDYCON		CUD	FBG	SV	IO	240		8	6	4200			15900	18000
		1989 BOATS														
21		CABO 216 CUDDYCON		CUD	FBG	SV	OB			8		2800			5900	6750
22		CABO 226 CUDDYCON		CUD	FBG	SV	OB			8		2700			6200	7150
25		CABO 256 CUDDYCON		CUD	FBG	SV	OB			8	6	3700			9100	10300
25		CABO 266 CUDDYCON		CUD	FBG	SV	IO	240		8	6	4200			15000	17000
25		CABO 266 CUDDYCON		CUD	FBG	SV	IO	275D		8	6	4200			21000	23300
		1988 BOATS														
21		CABO 216 CUDDYCON		CUD	FBG	SV	OB			8		2800			5700	6550
25		CABO 256 CUDDYCON		CUD	FBG	SV	OB			8	6	4200			9400	10700
		1987 BOATS														
21		CABO 216 CUDDYCON		CUD	FBG	SV	OB			8		2800			5550	6400

CABO RICO YACHTS

FT LAUDERDALE FL 33316 COAST GUARD MFG ID- CQB See inside cover to adjust price for area

For more recent years, see the BUC Used Boat Price Guide, Volume 1

LOA FT	LOA IN	NAME AND/ OR MODEL	TOP/ RIG	BOAT TYPE	-HULL- MTL	-HULL- TP	ENGINE TP	ENGINE # HP	ENGINE MFG	BEAM FT	BEAM IN	WGT LBS	DRAFT FT	DRAFT IN	RETAIL LOW	RETAIL HIGH
		1996 BOATS														
37		CR34	CUT	SACAC	FBG	KL	IB	35D	YAN	11		17000	4	10	166000	182500
37	6	NORTHEAST 37	SLP	SACAC	FBG	KL	IB	100D	YAN	13	8	18900	4	10	196000	215000
41		CHASE 38	F+T	SF	FBG	SV	IB	T550D	J&T	13	9	28000	3	9	204000	224000
41		CR38 PILOTHOUSE	CUT	SACAC	FBG	KL	IB	50D	YAN	11	6	22500	5	2	225500	248000
41		CR38 STD	CUT	SACAC	FBG	KL	IB	50D	YAN	11	6	21000	5		209500	230500
41	5	CAMBRIA 40	CUT	SACAC	FBG	KL	IB	50D	YAN	12	3	22200	5	5	252500	277000
45	11	CAMBRIA 44/46	CUT	SACAC	FBG	KL	IB	62D	YAN	13	6	28600	5	11	350500	385000
48	11	CAMBRIA 48	CUT	SACAC	FBG	KL	IB	62D	YAN	13	5	29400	5	11	408500	449000
48	11	CR45	CUT	SACAC	FBG	KL	IB	75D	YAN	13	2	36000	6		381500	419500
52	6	CAMBRIA 52	CUT	SACAC	FBG	KL	IB	62D	YAN	15	2	28000	6		504000	553500
		1995 BOATS														
37		CR34	CUT	SACAC	FBG	KL	IB	35D	YAN	11		17000	4	10	157000	172500
37	6	NORTHEAST 37	SLP	SACAC	FBG	KL	IB	100D	YAN	13	8	18900	4	10	185500	203500
41		CHASE 38	F+T	SF	FBG	SV	IB	T550D	J&T	13	9	28000	3	9	193000	212500
41		CR38 PILOTHOUSE	CUT	SACAC	FBG	KL	IB	50D	YAN	11	6	22500	5	2	213500	234500
41		CR38 STD	CUT	SACAC	FBG	KL	IB	50D	YAN	11	6	21000	5		198500	218000
41	5	CAMBRIA 40	CUT	SACAC	FBG	KL	IB	50D	YAN	12	3	22200	5	5	239000	262500
45	11	CAMBRIA 44/46	CUT	SACAC	FBG	KL	IB	62D	YAN	13	6	28600	5	11	332000	364500
48	11	CAMBRIA 48	CUT	SACAC	FBG	KL	IB	62D	YAN	13	5	29400	5	11	386500	424500
48	11	CR45	CUT	SACAC	FBG	KL	IB	62D	YAN	13	2	36000	6		360500	396000
52	6	CAMBRIA 52	CUT	SACAC	FBG	KL	IB	62D	YAN	15	2	28000	6		476000	523000
		1994 BOATS														
37		CR34	CUT	SACAC	FBG	KL	IB	35D	YAN	11		17000	4	10	149000	163500
37	6	NORTHEAST 37	CUT	SACAC	FBG	KL	IB	100D	YAN	13	8	18900	4	10	175000	192500
41		CR38 PILOTHOUSE	CUT	SACAC	FBG	KL	IB	50D	YAN	11	6	22500	5	2	202000	222000
41		CR38 STD	CUT	SACAC	FBG	KL	IB	50D	YAN	11	6	21000	5		188000	206500
41	5	CAMBRIA 40	CUT	SACAC	FBG	KL	IB	50D	YAN	12	3	22200	5	5	226000	248500
45	11	CAMBRIA 44/46	CUT	SACAC	FBG	KL	IB	62D	YAN	13	6	28600	5	11	314000	345000
48	11	CAMBRIA 48	CUT	SACAC	FBG	KL	IB	62D	YAN	13	5	29400	5	11	365500	402000
48	11	CR45	CUT	SACAC	FBG	KL	IB	62D	YAN	13	2	36000	6		341000	375000
52	6	CAMBRIA 52	CUT	SACAC	FBG	KL	IB	62D	YAN	15	2	28000	6		450000	494500
		1993 BOATS														
37		CR34	CUT	SACAC	FBG	KL	IB	35D	UNIV	11		17000	4	10	141000	155000
41		CR38 CLASSIC	CUT	SACAC	FBG	KL	IB	46D	UNIV	11	6	21000	5		184500	203000
41		CR38 CO	CUT	SACAC	FBG	KL	IB	46D	UNIV	11	6	21000	5		181000	199000
41		CR38 PILOTHOUSE	CUT	SACAC	FBG	KL	IB	50D	UNIV	11	6	22500	5	2	191500	210000
41		CR38 STD	CUT	SACAC	FBG	KL	IB	46D	UNIV	11	6	21000	5		178000	195500
41		CR38 XL	CUT	SACAC	FBG	KL	IB	50D	UNIV	11	6	21000	5		188500	207000
48	11	CR45	CUT	SACAC	FBG	KL	IB	D		13	2	36000	6		323500	355000
		1992 BOATS														
37		CR34	CUT	SA/CR	FBG	KL	IB	35D	UNIV	11		17000	4	10	133500	146500
41		CR38 CLASSIC	CUT	SA/CR	FBG	KL	IB	46D	UNIV	11	6	21000	5		175500	193000
41		CR38 CO	CUT	SA/CR	FBG	KL	IB	46D	UNIV	11	6	21000	5		171500	188500
41		CR38 PILOTHOUSE	CUT	SA/CR	FBG	KL	IB	50D	UNIV	11	6	22500	5	2	181000	199000
41		CR38 STD	CUT	SA/CR	FBG	KL	IB	46D	UNIV	11	6	21000	5		168000	185000
41		CR38 XL	CUT	SA/CR	FBG	KL	IB	50D	UNIV	11	6	21000	5		178500	196000
48		CR45	CUT	SA/CR	FBG	KL	IB	D		13	2	36000	6		301500	331000
		1991 BOATS														
37		CR 34	CUT	SA/CR	FBG	KL	IB	35D	UNIV	11		17000	4	10	126500	139000
41		CR38 CO	CUT	SA/CR	FBG	KL	IB	46D	UNIV	11	6	21000	5		161000	177000
41		CR38 CO	CUT	SA/CR	FBG	KL	IB	50D	UNIV	11	6	21000	5		161000	177000
41		CR38 PILOTHOUSE	CUT	SA/CR	FBG	KL	IB	50D	UNIV	11	6	22500	5	2	171500	188500
41		CR38 PILOTHOUSE	CUT	SA/CR	FBG	KL	IB	52D	UNIV	11	6	22500	5	2	171500	188500
41		CR38 STD	CUT	SA/CR	FBG	KL	IB	46D	UNIV	11	6	21000	5		158000	173500
41		CR38 STD	CUT	SA/CR	FBG	KL	IB	50D	UNIV	11	6	21000	5		158000	173500
41		CR38 XL	CUT	SA/CR	FBG	KL	IB	46D	UNIV	11	6	21000	5		169000	185500
41		CR38 XL	CUT	SA/CR	FBG	KL	IB	50D	UNIV	11	6	21000	5		169000	186000
		1990 BOATS														
37		CABO RICO 34	CUT	SA/CR	FBG	KL	IB	35D	UNIV	11		15500	4	10	110000	121000
41		CABO RICO 38	CUT	SA/CR	FBG	KL	IB	50D	UNIV	11	6	21000	5		154000	169500
41		CABO RICO 38 PILOT	CUT	SA/CR	FBG	KL	IB	50D	UNIV	11	6	21500	5		157000	172500
41		CHASE 38	F+T	SF	FBG	SV	IB	T550D	J&T	13	9	28000	3	9	150500	165500

CABO RICO YACHTS -CONTINUED See inside cover to adjust price for area

LOA FT	LOA IN	NAME AND/ OR MODEL	TOP/ RIG	BOAT TYPE	HULL MTL	HULL TP	ENGINE TP	ENGINE # HP	ENGINE MFG	BEAM FT	BEAM IN	WGT LBS	DRAFT FT	DRAFT IN	RETAIL LOW	RETAIL HIGH
1989 BOATS																
37		CABO RICO 34	CUT	SA/CR	FBG	KL	IB	35D	UNIV	11		15500	4	10	104000	114500
41		CABO RICO 38	CUT	SA/CR	FBG	KL	IB	50D	UNIV	11	6	21000	5		146000	160500
41		CABO RICO 38 PILOT	CUT	SA/CR	FBG	KL	IB	50D	UNIV	11	6	21500	5		148500	163000
41		CHASE 38	F+T	SF	FBG	SV	IB	T375D	CAT	13	9	28000	3	9	128500	141000
IB T400D J&T 128000 141000, IB T485D J&T 136500 150000, IB T550D J&T 143500 158000																
1988 BOATS																
41		CABO RICO 38	CUT	SA/CR	FBG	KL	IB	46D	WEST	11	6	21000	5		138000	152000
1985 BOATS																
41		CABO-RICO 38	CUT	SA/CR	FBG	KL	IB	46D	WEST	11	6	20000	5		112500	124000
1984 BOATS																
41		CABO-RICO 38	CUT	SA/CR	FBG	KL	IB	50D		11	4	20000	5		106500	117000

....For earlier years, see the BUC Used Boat Price Guide, Volume 3

CADDO BOAT MFG CO

NELSON-DYKES CO INC
DALLAS TX 75224 COAST GUARD MFG ID- LMA See inside cover to adjust price for area

LOA FT	LOA IN	NAME AND/ OR MODEL	TOP/ RIG	BOAT TYPE	HULL MTL	HULL TP	ENGINE TP	ENGINE # HP	ENGINE MFG	BEAM FT	BEAM IN	WGT LBS	DRAFT FT	DRAFT IN	RETAIL LOW	RETAIL HIGH
1985 BOATS																
17	6	CHEETAH I	OP	BASS	FBG	TR	OB			7		1000			2250	2600
17	6	CHEETAH II	OP	BASS	FBG	TR	OB			7		1000			2450	2850
1984 BOATS																
17	6	CHEETAH I	OP	BASS	FBG	TR	OB			7		1000			2200	2550
17	6	CHEETAH II	OP	BASS	FBG	TR	OB			7		1000			2400	2800

....For earlier years, see the BUC Used Boat Price Guide, Volume 3

CAL-PEARSON

BETHESDA MD 20814-3601 COAST GUARD MFG ID- CAB See inside cover to adjust price for area
formerly LEAR SIEGLER MARINE

For more recent years, see the BUC Used Boat Price Guide, Volume 1

LOA FT	LOA IN	NAME AND/ OR MODEL	TOP/ RIG	BOAT TYPE	HULL MTL	HULL TP	ENGINE TP	ENGINE # HP	ENGINE MFG	BEAM FT	BEAM IN	WGT LBS	DRAFT FT	DRAFT IN	RETAIL LOW	RETAIL HIGH
1996 BOATS																
22		CAL 22	SLP	SACAC	FBG	KL				7	6	2100	3	6	8850	10100
26	11	PEARSON 27	SLP	SACAC	FBG	WK	IB	12D	UNIV	9	2	5800	3	4	28600	31700
28	6	PEARSON 28 DEEP	SLP	SACAC	FBG	KL	IB	D		9	10	7000	4	10	36600	40700
28	6	PEARSON 28 SHOAL	SLP	SACAC	FBG	KL	IB	D		9	10	7000	3	6	36600	40700
31	6	PEARSON 31	SLP	SACAC	FBG	KL	IB	18D		10	9	10000	5	9	56300	61800
31	6	PEARSON 31	SLP	SACAC	FBG	WK	IB	18D		10	9	10200	3	11	57400	63100
32	6	PEARSON 33	SLP	SACAC	FBG	WK	IB	18D		11		11080	4	4	62600	68800
33		CAL 33 DEEP	SLP	SACAC	FBG	KL	IB	27D	YAN	11	4	10800	6	2	61200	67200
33		CAL 33 SHOAL	SLP	SACAC	FBG	KL	IB	27D	YAN	11	4	10800	4	8	61200	67200
34	6	PEARSON 34	SLP	SACAC	FBG	WK	IB	30D		11	6	11500	4		65700	72200
37	5	PEARSON 37	SLP	SACAC	FBG	WK	IB	34D	YAN	12	4	16000	4	8	94800	104000
37	6	PEARSON 38	SLP	SACAC	FBG	WK	IB	35D		12	4	15175	4	9	90900	99900
39		CAL 39	SLP	SACAC	FBG	KL	IB	D		12	7	17500	7		108500	119500
39	3	PEARSON 39	SLP	SACAC	FBG	CB	IB	46D		12	5	16800	8	9	107000	117500
39	3	PEARSON 39	SLP	SACAC	FBG	KL	IB	46D		12	5	16800	6	10	107000	117500
1989 BOATS																
22		CAL 22 DEEP	SLP	SA/CR	FBG	KL	OB			7	9	2100	3	6	6000	6900
22		CAL 22 SHOAL	SLP	SA/CR	FBG	KL	OB			7	9	2275	2	10	6300	7250
28	3	CAL 28 DEEP	SLP	SA/CR	FBG	KL	IB	18D	YAN	10	8	7800	5	3	27800	30900
28	3	CAL 28 SHOAL	SLP	SA/CR	FBG	KL	IB	18D	YAN	10	8	7800	3	9	27800	30900
33		CAL 33 DEEP	SLP	SA/CR	FBG	KL	IB	27D	YAN	11	4	10800	6	2	41600	46200
33		CAL 33 SHOAL	SLP	SA/CR	FBG	KL	IB	27D	YAN	11	4	10800	4	8	41600	46200
39		CAL 39 DEEP	SLP	SA/CR	FBG	KL	IB	44D	YAN	12	7	17500	7		74500	81900
39		CAL 39 WING	SLP	SA/CR	FBG	KL	IB	44D	YAN	12	7	17500	5	4	74500	81900
1988 BOATS																
22		CAL 22 DEEP	SLP	SA/CR	FBG	KL	OB			7	9	2100	3	6	5700	6550
22		CAL 22 SHOAL	SLP	SA/CR	FBG	KL	OB			7	9	2275	2	10	5950	6850
28	3	CAL 28 DEEP	SLP	SA/CR	FBG	KL	IB	18D	YAN	10	8	7800	5	3	26400	29300
28	3	CAL 28 SHOAL	SLP	SA/CR	FBG	KL	IB	18D	YAN	10	8	7800	3	9	26400	29300
33		CAL 33 DEEP	SLP	SA/CR	FBG	KL	IB	27D	YAN	11	4	10800	6	2	39400	43800
33		CAL 33 SHOAL	SLP	SA/CR	FBG	KL	IB	27D	YAN	11	4	10800	4	8	39400	43800
39		CAL 39 DEEP	SLP	SA/CR	FBG	KL	IB	44D	YAN	12	7	17500	7		70600	77600
39		CAL 39 WING	SLP	SA/CR	FBG	KL	IB	44D	YAN	12	7	17500	5	4	70600	77600
1987 BOATS																
22		CAL 22 DEEP	SLP	SA/CR	FBG	KL	OB			7	9	2100	3	6	5400	6200
22		CAL 22 SHOAL	SLP	SA/CR	FBG	KL	OB			7	9	2275	2	10	5650	6500
28	3	CAL 28 DEEP	SLP	SA/CR	FBG	KL	IB	18D	YAN	10	8	7800	5	3	25000	27700
28	3	CAL 28 SHOAL	SLP	SA/CR	FBG	KL	IB	18D	YAN	10	8	7800	3	9	25000	27700
33		CAL 33 DEEP	SLP	SA/CR	FBG	KL	IB	22D	YAN	11	4	10800	6	2	37300	41500
33		CAL 33 SHOAL	SLP	SA/CR	FBG	KL	IB	22D	YAN	11	4	10800	4	8	37300	41500
1986 BOATS																
22		CAL 22 DEEP	SLP	SA/CR	FBG	KL	OB			7	9	2100	3	6	5100	5850
22		CAL 22 SHOAL	SLP	SA/CR	FBG	KL	OB			7	9	2275	2	10	5350	6150
28	3	CAL 28	SLP	SA/CR	FBG	KL	IB	14D	WEST	10	8	7200	5	3	21800	24200
28	3	CAL 28 DEEP	SLP	SA/CR	FBG	KL	IB	14D	WEST	10	8	7200	5	3	21800	24200
28	3	CAL 28 SHOAL	SLP	SA/CR	FBG	KL	IB	14D	WEST	10	8	7200	3	9	21800	24200
33		CAL 33	SLP	SA/CR	FBG	KL	IB	22D	YAN	11	4	10800	6	2	35400	39300
33		CAL 33 DEEP	SLP	SA/CR	FBG	KL	IB	22D	YAN	11	4	10800	6	2	35400	39300
33		CAL 33 SHOAL	SLP	SA/CR	FBG	KL	IB	22D	YAN	11	4	10800	4	8	35400	39300
1985 BOATS																
22		CAL 22	SLP	SA/CR	FBG	KL	OB			7	9	2100	3	6	4850	5550
24	4	CAL 24	SLP	SA/CR	FBG	KL	OB			8		3300	4	3	7350	8450
24	4	CAL 24 SHOAL	SLP	SA/CR	FBG	KL	OB			8		3300	3	4	7350	8450
26	8	CAL 27 II	SLP	SA/CR	FBG	KL	OB			9		5200	5		13200	15000
26	8	CAL 27 II	SLP	SA/CR	FBG	KL	IB	8D	YAN	9		5200	5		13800	15700
26	8	CAL 27 II SHOAL	SLP	SA/CR	FBG	KL	OB			9		5200	4		13200	15000
26	8	CAL 27 II SHOAL	SLP	SA/CR	FBG	KL	IB	8D	YAN	9		5200	4		13800	15700
28	3	CAL 28 DEEP	SLP	SA/CR	FBG	KL	IB	13D	WEST	10	7	7200	5	3	20600	22900
28	3	CAL 28 SHOAL	SLP	SA/CR	FBG	KL	IB	13D	WEST	10	7	7200	3	9	20600	22900
33		CAL 33	SLP	SA/CR	FBG	KL	IB	22D	YAN	11	4	10800	6	2	33500	37200
33		CAL 33 SHOAL	SLP	SA/CR	FBG	KL	IB	22D	YAN	11	4	10800	4	8	33500	37200
35		CAL 35	SLP	SA/CR	FBG	KL	IB	32D	UNIV	10	11	13000	5	9	40800	45300
35		CAL 35 SHOAL	SLP	SA/CR	FBG	KL	IB	32D	UNIV	10	11	13000	4	9	40800	45300
39		CAL 39	SLP	SA/CR	FBG	KL	IB	40D	PATH	12		17000	6	8	58500	64300
39		CAL 39 SHOAL	SLP	SA/CR	FBG	KL	IB	40D	PATH	12		17000	5	6	58500	64300
39		CAL 39 TALL RIG	SLP	SA/CR	FBG	KL	IB	40D	PATH	12		17000	6	8	58700	64500
43	6	CAL 44	SLP	SA/CR	FBG	KL	IB	58D	WEST	13	6	25000	6	6	90900	99900
43	6	CAL 44 SHOAL	SLP	SA/CR	FBG	KL	IB	58D	WEST	13	6	25300	5	6	91500	100500
1984 BOATS																
24	4	CAL 24	SLP	SA/CR	FBG	KL	OB			8		3300	4	3	7000	8000
24	4	CAL 24	SLP	SA/CR	FBG	KL	IB	8D	YAN	8		3300	4	3	7800	8950
24	4	CAL 24 SHOAL	SLP	SA/CR	FBG	KL	OB			8		3300	3	4	7000	8000
24	4	CAL 24 SHOAL	SLP	SA/CR	FBG	KL	IB	8D	YAN	8		3300	3	4	7800	8950
26	8	CAL 27 II	SLP	SA/CR	FBG	KL	OB			9		5200	5		12500	14200
26	8	CAL 27 II	SLP	SA/CR	FBG	KL	IB	8D	YAN	9		5200	5		13100	14900
26	8	CAL 27 II SHOAL	SLP	SA/CR	FBG	KL	OB			9		5200	4		12500	14200
26	8	CAL 27 II SHOAL	SLP	SA/CR	FBG	KL	IB	8D	YAN	9		5200	4		13100	14900
30		CAL 9.2	SLP	SA/RC	FBG	KL	IB	D		10	4	7000	5	7	19900	22100
30		CAL 9.2 SHOAL	SLP	SA/RC	FBG	KL	IB	D		10	4	7000	4	7	19900	22100
30		CAL 9.2R	SLP	SA/RC	FBG	KL	IB	D		10	4	7000	5	10	19900	22100
31	6	CAL 31	SLP	SA/CR	FBG	KL	IB	16D	UNIV	10		9170	5		26800	29800
31	6	CAL 31 SHOAL	SLP	SA/CR	FBG	KL	IB	16D	UNIV	10		9170	4	3	26800	29800
35		CAL 35	SLP	SA/CR	FBG	KL	IB	32D	UNIV	10	11	13000	6		38600	42900
35		CAL 35 SHOAL	SLP	SA/CR	FBG	KL	IB	32D	UNIV	10	11	13000	5		38600	42900
39		CAL 39	SLP	SA/CR	FBG	KL	IB	44D	UNIV	12		19000	6	8	60300	66300
39		CAL 39 SHOAL	SLP	SA/CR	FBG	KL	IB	44D	UNIV	12		19000	5	6	60300	66300
39		CAL 39 TALL RIG	SLP	SA/CR	FBG	KL	IB	44D	UNIV	12		19000	6	8	60500	66500
43	6	CAL 44	SLP	SA/CR	FBG	KL	IB	51D	PERK	13	6	25000	6	6	85400	93900
43	6	CAL 44	SLP	SA/CR	FBG	KL	IB	58D	WEST	13	6	25000	6	6	86100	94700
43	6	CAL 44 SHOAL	SLP	SA/CR	FBG	KL	IB	51D	PERK	13	6	25000	5	3	85400	93900
43	6	CAL 44 SHOAL	SLP	SA/CR	FBG	KL	IB	58D	WEST	13	6	25000	5	3	86100	94700

....For earlier years, see the BUC Used Boat Price Guide, Volume 3

CALIBER YACHTS INC

CLEARWATER FL 33762 COAST GUARD MFG ID- CYQ See inside cover to adjust price for area
FORMERLY CALIBER YACHT CORP

For more recent years, see the BUC Used Boat Price Guide, Volume 1

LOA FT	LOA IN	NAME AND/ OR MODEL	TOP/ RIG	BOAT TYPE	HULL MTL	HULL TP	ENGINE TP	ENGINE # HP	ENGINE MFG	BEAM FT	BEAM IN	WGT LBS	DRAFT FT	DRAFT IN	RETAIL LOW	RETAIL HIGH
1996 BOATS																
32	6	CALIBER 30LRC	CUT	SACAC	FBG	KL	IB	18D	YAN	10	10	11000	4		77500	85200
35	9	CALIBER 35LRC	CUT	SACAC	FBG	KL	IB	27D	YAN	11	4	13100	4	6	94800	104000
40	11	CALIBER 40LRC	CUT	SACAC	FBG	KL	IB	50D	YAN	12	8	21600	5		153000	168000
52	11	CALIBER 47LRC	CUT	SACAC	FBG	KL	IB	75D	YAN	13	2	33000	5	2	233000	256500
1995 BOATS																
32	6	CALIBER 30LRC	CUT	SACAC	FBG	KL	IB	18D	YAN	10	10	11000	4		72900	80100
35	9	CALIBER 35LRC	CUT	SACAC	FBG	KL	IB	27D	YAN	11	4	13100	4	6	89200	98000
40	11	CALIBER 40LRC	CUT	SACAC	FBG	KL	IB	50D	YAN	12	8	21600	5		144000	158000
51	11	CALIBER 47LRC	CUT	SACAC	FBG	KL	IB	75D	YAN	13	2	32000	5	3	217000	238500

CALIBER YACHTS INC -CONTINUED
See inside cover to adjust price for area

LOA FT IN	NAME AND/ OR MODEL	TOP/ RIG	BOAT TYPE	-HULL- MTL TP	TP	----ENGINE--- # HP MFG	BEAM FT IN	WGT LBS	DRAFT FT IN	RETAIL LOW	RETAIL HIGH
------------------- 1994 BOATS -------											
32 6	CALIBER 30	CUT	SACAC	FBG KL	IB	18D YAN	10 10	11000	4	68600	75400
35 9	CALIBER 35	CUT	SACAC	FBG KL	IB	27D YAN	11 4	13100	4 6	83900	92200
40 11	CALIBER 40	CUT	SACAC	FBG KL	IB	50D YAN	12 8	21600	5	135500	148500
------------------- 1993 BOATS -------											
36 6	CALIBER 35	SLP	SACAC	FBG KL	IB	28D YAN	11 4	13000	4 6	78400	86100
40 11	CALIBER 40	SLP	SACAC	FBG KL	IB	50D YAN	12 8	21500	5	127000	139500
------------------- 1992 BOATS -------											
36 6	CALIBER 35	SLP	SA/RC	FBG KL	IB	28D YAN	11 4	13000	4 6	73700	81000
40 11	CALIBER 40	SLP	SA/RC	FBG KL	IB	50D YAN	12 8	21500	5	119500	131000
------------------- 1991 BOATS -------											
36 6	CALIBER 35	SLP	SA/RC	FBG KL	IB	28D YAN	11 4	13000	4 6	69300	76200
40 11	CALIBER 40	SLP	SA/RC	FBG KL	IB	50D YAN	12 8	21500	5	112000	123500
------------------- 1990 BOATS -------											
32 6	CALIBER 33	SLP	SA/RC	FBG KL	IB	28D YAN	11 4	11400	4 6	58100	63900
38	CALIBER 38	SLP	SA/RC	FBG KL	IB	50D YAN	12 8	18500	5	91900	101000
------------------- 1989 BOATS -------											
32 6	CALIBER 33	SLP	SA/RC	FBG KL	IB	28D YAN	11 4	11400	4 6	54700	60100
38	CALIBER 38	SLP	SA/RC	FBG KL	IB	44D YAN	12 8	18500	4 6	86300	94800
------------------- 1988 BOATS -------											
27 6	CALIBER 28	SLP	SA/RC	FBG KL	IB	18D YAN	10 10	7200	3 11	27400	30500
27 6	CALIBER 28 TRICABIN	SLP	SA/RC	FBG KL	IB	18D YAN	10 10	7200	3 11	28600	31800
32 6	CALIBER 33	SLP	SA/RC	FBG KL	IB	28D YAN	11 4	11400	4 6	51400	56500
38	CALIBER 38	SLP	SA/RC	FBG KL	IB	44D YAN	12 8	18500	4 6	81200	89200
------------------- 1987 BOATS -------											
27 6	CALIBER 28	SLP	SA/RC	FBG KL	IB	18D YAN	10 10	7200	3 11	25800	28600
27 6	CALIBER 28 TRICABIN	SLP	SA/RC	FBG KL	IB	18D YAN	10 10	7200	3 11	26900	29900
32 6	CALIBER 33	SLP	SA/RC	FBG KL	IB	28D YAN	11 4	11400	4 6	48400	53200
38	CALIBER 38	SLP	SA/RC	FBG KL	IB	44D YAN	12 8	18500	4 6	76400	83900
------------------- 1986 BOATS -------											
27 6	CALIBER 28	SLP	SA/RC	FBG KL	IB	18D YAN	10 10	7200	3 11	24200	26800
27 6	CALIBER 28 TRICABIN	SLP	SA/RC	FBG KL	IB	18D YAN	10 10	7200	3 11	25400	28200
32 6	CALIBER 33	SLP	SA/RC	FBG KL	IB	28D YAN	11 4	11400	4 6	45800	50300
------------------- 1985 BOATS -------											
27 6	CALIBER 28	SLP	SA/RC	FBG KL	IB	18D YAN	10 10	7200	3 11	23300	25900
32 6	CALIBER 33	SLP	SA/RC	FBG KL	IB	28D YAN	11 4	11400	4 6	42600	47300
------------------- 1984 BOATS -------											
27 6	CALIBER 28	SLP	SA/RC	FBG KL	IB	15D YAN	10 10	7300	3 11	22200	24700

....For earlier years, see the BUC Used Boat Price Guide, Volume 3

CAMELOT YACHTS
ONTARIO NY 14519   COAST GUARD MFG ID- KMT See inside cover to adjust price for area

LOA FT IN	NAME AND/ OR MODEL	TOP/ RIG	BOAT TYPE	-HULL- MTL TP	TP	----ENGINE--- # HP MFG	BEAM FT IN	WGT LBS	DRAFT FT IN	RETAIL LOW	RETAIL HIGH
------------------- 1986 BOATS -------											
24 7	CAMELOT 25	SLP	SA/CR	F/S	SD	9D YAN	8 1	4000	3 8	12800	14500
------------------- 1985 BOATS -------											
24 7	CAMELOT 25	SLP	SA/CR	F/S	SD	8D YAN	8	4000	3 8	12000	13600
------------------- 1984 BOATS -------											
24 7	CAMELOT 50	SLP	SA/CR	FBG	SD	8D YAN	8	4000	3 8	11300	12800

....For earlier years, see the BUC Used Boat Price Guide, Volume 3

CAMPER & NICHOLSONS INC
GOSPORT HAMPSHIRE ENGLA COAST GUARD MFG ID- CNL See inside cover to adjust price for area

LOA FT IN	NAME AND/ OR MODEL	TOP/ RIG	BOAT TYPE	-HULL- MTL TP	TP	----ENGINE--- # HP MFG	BEAM FT IN	WGT LBS	DRAFT FT IN	RETAIL LOW	RETAIL HIGH
------------------- 1985 BOATS -------											
30 6	NICHOLSON 31	SLP	SA/CR	FBG KL	IB	D	10 3	14000	5	64400	70800
35 3	NICHOLSON 35	SLP	SA/CR	FBG KL	IB	D	10 5	17000	5 6	76800	84400
39	NICHOLSON 39	KTH	SA/CR	FBG KL	IB	D	11 6	23000	5 6	101500	111500
40	NICHOLSON 40PH	KTH	SA/CR	FBG KL	IB	D	11 6	24400	5 9	108500	119500
43 2	NICHOLSON 44	KTH	SA/CR	FBG KL	IB	D	12 2	28000	5 6	132000	145500
47 8	NICHOLSON 48	KTH	SA/CR	FBG KL	IB	D	12 11	31240	5 6	171500	188500
54 5	NICHOLSON 55	KTH	SA/CR	FBG KL	IB	D	14 4	35000	8 3	273000	300000
57 7	NICHOLSON 58	SLP	SA/CR	FBG KL	IB	D	15 7	52500	8 6	387000	425000
57 7	NICHOLSON 58	KTH	SA/CR	FBG KL	IB	D	15 7	52500	8 6	387000	425500
59 11	NICHOLSON 60	SLP	SA/CR	FBG KL	IB	D	15 7	53000	7 6	411000	451500
59 11	NICHOLSON 60	KTH	SA/CR	FBG KL	IB	D	15 7	53000	7 6	411000	451500
70	NICHOLSON 70	KTH	SA/CR	FBG KL	IB	D	17 1	51T	8 6	781500	859000
------------------- 1984 BOATS -------											
30 6	NICHOLSON 31	SLP	SA/CR	FBG KL	IB	D	10 3	14000	5	60600	66600
35 3	NICHOLSON 35	SLP	SA/CR	FBG KL	IB	D	10 5	17000	5 6	72200	79400
39	NICHOLSON 39	KTH	SA/CR	FBG KL	IB	D	11 6	23000	5 6	95600	105000
40	NICHOLSON 40AFT	KTH	SA/CR	FBG KL	IB	D	11 6	24400	5 9	102000	112000
40	NICHOLSON 40PH	SLP	SA/CR	FBG KL	IB	D	11 6	23300	5 6	98900	108500
43 2	NICHOLSON 44	KTH	SA/CR	FBG KL	IB	D	12 2	28000	5 6	124500	136500
45 2	NICHOLSON 45	KTH	SA/CR	FBG KL	IB	D	7	32000		143500	157500
47 8	NICHOLSON 48	KTH	SA/CR	FBG KL	IB	D	12 11	31240	5 6	161500	177500
54 4	NICHOLSON 55	KTH	SA/CR	FBG KL	IB	D	14 4	35000	8 3	255000	280500
57 7	NICHOLSON 58	SLP	SA/CR	FBG KC	IB	D	15 7	52500	8 6	364000	400000
57 7	NICHOLSON 58	KTH	SA/CR	FBG KC	IB	D	15 7	52500	8 6	364000	400000
59 11	NICHOLSON 60	SLP	SA/CR	FBG KL	IB	D	15 7	53000	6	386000	424500
59 11	NICHOLSON 60	KTH	SA/CR	FBG KL	IB	D	15 7	53000	6	386500	424500
70	NICHOLSON 70	KTH	SA/CR	FBG KL	IB	D	17 1	51T	8 6	734500	807000

....For earlier years, see the BUC Used Boat Price Guide, Volume 3

CAMPER CRAFT MFG
HOLLAND MI 49423   See inside cover to adjust price for area
FORMERLY SEA CAMPER INDUSTRIES

LOA FT IN	NAME AND/ OR MODEL	TOP/ RIG	BOAT TYPE	-HULL- MTL TP	TP	----ENGINE--- # HP MFG	BEAM FT IN	WGT LBS	DRAFT FT IN	RETAIL LOW	RETAIL HIGH
------------------- 1989 BOATS -------											
19	HOBO		CAMPR	FBG DS	OB		8	1500	11	5750	6600
32	AQUA CHALET		HB	AL PN	OB		8	2800	1	1100	1300
32	AQUA CHALET 8161		HB	AL PN	OB		10			1100	1300
36	AQUA CHALET 1201		HB	AL PN	OB		13			10800	12200
36	AQUA CHALET 8201		HB	AL PN	OB		13			10800	12200
40	AQUA CHALET 1261		HB	AL PN	IO	225	13			14000	15900
------------------- 1988 BOATS -------											
19	HOBO		CAMPR	FBG DS	OB		8	1500	11	5550	6400
27	CAMPERCRAFT		HB	FBG DS	IO	130 VLVO	8	3200	11	**	**
30 9	BREAKAWAY		HB	FBG CT	OB		8 6	3600	1 4	2750	3200
34	BREAKAWAY		HB	FBG CT	OB		12	4500	1 4	4250	4950
------------------- 1987 BOATS -------											
19	HOBO		CAMPR	FBG DS	OB		8	1500	11	5400	6200
27	CAMPERCRAFT		HB	FBG DS	IO	130 VLVO	8	3200	11	**	**

CAMPION MARINE INC
KELOWNA BC CANADA V1X 7 COAST GUARD MFG ID- ZBI See inside cover to adjust price for area
For more recent years, see the BUC Used Boat Price Guide, Volume 1

LOA FT IN	NAME AND/ OR MODEL	TOP/ RIG	BOAT TYPE	-HULL- MTL TP	TP	----ENGINE--- # HP MFG	BEAM FT IN	WGT LBS	DRAFT FT IN	RETAIL LOW	RETAIL HIGH
------------------- 1995 BOATS -------											
16	ALLANTE 160 B/R	ST	RNBT	FBG SV	OB		6 7	1020		4100	4750
16 2	EXPLORER	ST	OPFSH	FBG SV	OB		7	1700		6250	7200
16 2	EXPLORER 165	ST	CTRCN	FBG SV	OB		7	1040		4100	4750
17 2	ALLANTE 170 B/R	ST	RNBT	FBG SV	OB		7 2	1300		5200	5950
17 2	ALLANTE 170 B/R	ST	RNBT	FBG SV	IO	115-135	7 2	1940		4750	5450
17 2	ALLANTE 170 C/D	ST	SKI	FBG SV	OB		7 2	1300		5000	5750
17 2	ALLANTE 170 C/D	ST	SKI	FBG SV	IO	115-135	7 2	1940		4500	5200
17 3	ALLANTE 185 CUDDY	ST	CUD	FBG SV	OB		7 3	1300		4500	5950
17 10	ALLANTE 180 B/R	ST	RNBT	FBG SV	IO	115-175	7 7	2090		5100	5900
17 11	EXPLORER 185	ST	FSH	FBG SV	OB		7 7	1700		6250	7200
17 11	EXPLORER 188	ST	FSH	FBG SV	IO	135 MRCR	7 7	2470		6250	7150
18	CHASE 180 B/R	ST	RNBT	FBG SV	IO	175 MRCR	7 7	2150		5200	6000
19	ALLANTE 190 C/D	ST	SKI	FBG SV	OB		7 7	1500		5900	6800
19	ALLANTE 190 C/D	ST	SKI	FBG SV	IO	155-250	7 7	2300		5700	7000
19 1	ALLANTE 190 B/R	ST	RNBT	FBG SV	OB		7 7	1500		6050	6950
19 1	ALLANTE 190 B/R	ST	RNBT	FBG SV	IO	155-250	7 7	2300		5950	7250
19 1	CHASE 190 B/R	ST	RNBT	FBG SV	OB		7 7	1500		6050	6950
19 1	EXPLORER 190	ST	CTRCN	FBG SV	OB		7 8	1700		6500	7450
20 2	ALLANTE 200	ST	CUD	FBG SV	IO	155-250	7 8	2500		6950	8450
20 6	EXPLORER 215	ST	CTRCN	FBG SV	OB		7 10	2500		10300	11700
20 6	EXPLORER 215	ST	CTRCN	FBG SV	IO	135-175	7 10	3400		9200	10500
20 6	VICTORIA 215	HT	SDN	FBG SV	OB		7 10	2600		10300	11700
20 6	VICTORIA 215	HT	SDN	FBG SV	IO	135-175	7 10	3200		8400	9600
22 1	EXPLORER 225	ST	FSH	FBG SV	OB		7 7	3200		13200	15000
23	ALLANTE 233 CUDDY	ST	CUD	F/S SV	IO	230 MRCR	8 1	3400		9300	10600
23	ALLANTE 233 CUDDY	ST	CUD	FBG SV	IO	250-300	8 1	3400		9500	11200
23	CHASE 233	ST	CUD	FBG SV	IO	250 MRCR	8 1	3400		11400	13000
23	CHASE 233	ST	CUD	F/S SV	IO	300 MRCR	8 1	3400		12400	14100
23	CHASE 233	ST	CUD	FBG SV	IO	350 MRCR	8 1	3400		13600	15400

LOA FT	LOA IN	NAME AND/ OR MODEL	TOP/ RIG	BOAT TYPE	-HULL- MTL	-HULL- TP	ENGINE TP	ENGINE # HP	ENGINE MFG	BEAM FT	BEAM IN	WGT LBS	DRAFT FT	DRAFT IN	RETAIL LOW	RETAIL HIGH
		1995 BOATS														
23		CHASE 233	ST	CUD	F/S	SV	IO	390	MRCR	8	1	3400			13800	15700
26		VICTORIA 245	ST	CR	FBG	SV	IO	205-300		8	6	4800			15300	18900
29		VICTORIA 290	ST	CR	FBG	SV	IO	300	MRCR	10		8000			29500	32800
29		VICTORIA 290	ST	CR	FBG	SV	IO	T155-T230		10		8000			29800	35500
29	8	CHASE 300	ST	FSH	FBG	SV	IO	250	MRCR	8	7	4950			36200	40200
		1994 BOATS														
16		ALLANTE 160 B/R	ST	RNBT	FBG	SV	OB			6	7	1020			3850	4500
16	2	EXPLORER	ST	OPFSH	FBG	SV	OB			7	7	1700			5900	6800
16	2	EXPLORER 165	ST	CTRCN	FBG	SV	OB			7	1	1040			3850	4500
17	2	ALLANTE 170 B/R	ST	RNBT	FBG	SV	OB			7	2	1300			4900	5650
17	2	ALLANTE 170 B/R	ST	RNBT	FBG	SV	IO	115-135		7	2	1940			4450	5100
17	2	ALLANTE 170 C/D	ST	SKI	FBG	SV	OB			7	2	1300			4750	5450
17	2	ALLANTE 170 C/D	ST	SKI	FBG	SV	IO	115-135		7	2	1940			4150	4850
17	9	ALLANTE 185 CUDDY	ST	CUD	FBG	SV	OB			7	3	1300			4900	5650
17	10	ALLANTE 180 B/R	ST	RNBT	FBG	SV	IO	115-175		7	2	2090			4750	5500
18		CHASE 180 B/R	ST	SKI	FBG	SV	IO	175	MRCR	7	7	2150			4850	5600
19		ALLANTE 190 C/D	ST	SKI	FBG	SV	OB			7	7	1500			5600	6450
19		ALLANTE 190 C/D	ST	SKI	FBG	SV	IO	155-250		7	7	2300			5350	6500
19	1	ALLANTE 190 B/R	ST	RNBT	FBG	SV	OB			7	7	1500			5750	6600
19	1	ALLANTE 190 B/R	ST	RNBT	FBG	SV	IO	155-250		7	7	2300			5550	6750
19	1	CHASE 190 B/R	ST	RNBT	FBG	SV	OB			7	7	1500			5750	6600
19	1	EXPLORER 190	ST	CTRCN	FBG	SV	OB			7	8	1700			6150	7050
20	2	ALLANTE 200	ST	CUD	FBG	SV	IO	155-250		7	8	2500			6500	7900
20	6	EXPLORER 215	ST	CTRCN	FBG	SV	OB			7	10	2600			9800	11100
20	6	EXPLORER 215	ST	CTRCN	FBG	SV	IO	135-175		7	10	3400			8500	9850
20	6	VICTORIA 215	HT	SDN	FBG	SV	OB			7	10	2600			9800	11100
20	6	VICTORIA 215	HT	SDN	FBG	SV	IO	135-175		7	10	3200			7750	8950
23		ALLANTE 233 CUDDY	ST	CUD	F/S	SV	IO	230	MRCR	8	1	3400			8600	9850
23		ALLANTE 233 CUDDY	ST	CUD	FBG	SV	IO	250-300		8	1	3400			8850	10500
23		CHASE 233	ST	CUD	FBG	SV	IO	250	MRCR	8	1	3400			10800	12200
23		CHASE 233	ST	CUD	F/S	SV	IO	300	MRCR	8	1	3400			11600	13200
23		CHASE 233	ST	CUD	FBG	SV	IO	350	MRCR	8	1	3400			12700	14400
23		CHASE 233	ST	CUD	F/S	SV	IO	390	MRCR	8	1	3400			12800	14600
26		VICTORIA 245	ST	CR	FBG	SV	IO	205-300		8	6	4800			14300	17600
29		VICTORIA 290	ST	CR	FBG	SV	IO	300	MRCR	10		8000			27400	30400
29		VICTORIA 290	ST	CR	FBG	SV	IO	T155-T230		10		8000			27800	33000
		1993 BOATS														
16		ALLANTE 160 B/R	ST	RNBT	FBG	SV	OB			6	7	1020			3650	4250
16	2	EXPLORER	ST	OPFSH	FBG	SV	OB			7	7	1700			5600	6450
16	2	EXPLORER 165	ST	CTRCN	FBG	SV	OB			7	1	1040			3650	4250
17	2	ALLANTE 170 B/R	ST	RNBT	FBG	SV	OB			7	2	1300			4650	5350
17	2	ALLANTE 170 B/R	ST	RNBT	FBG	SV	IO	115-135		7	2	1940			4100	4750
17	2	ALLANTE 170 C/D	ST	SKI	FBG	SV	OB			7	2	1300			4500	5200
17	2	ALLANTE 170 C/D	ST	SKI	FBG	SV	IO	115-135		7	2	1940			3900	4500
17	9	ALLANTE 185 CUDDY	ST	CUD	FBG	SV	OB			7	3	1300			4650	5350
17	10	ALLANTE 180 B/R	ST	RNBT	FBG	SV	IO	115-175		7	2	2090			4450	5200
19		ALLANTE 190 C/D	ST	SKI	FBG	SV	OB			7	7	1500			5300	6100
19		ALLANTE 190 C/D	ST	SKI	FBG	SV	IO	155-250		7	7	2300			5000	6100
19	1	ALLANTE 190 B/R	ST	RNBT	FBG	SV	OB			7	7	1500			5450	6250
19	1	ALLANTE 190 B/R	ST	RNBT	FBG	SV	IO	155-250		7	7	2300			5200	6300
19	1	CHASE 190 B/R	ST	RNBT	FBG	SV	OB			7	7	1500			5450	6250
19	1	CHASE 195	ST	SKI	FBG	SV	IO	155-250		7	8	2300			5050	6150
19	1	EXPLORER 190	ST	CTRCN	FBG	SV	OB			7	8	1700			5850	6700
20	2	ALLANTE 200	ST	CUD	FBG	SV	IO	155-250		7	8	2500			6050	7350
20	6	EXPLORER 215	ST	CTRCN	FBG	SV	OB			7	10	2600			9300	10600
20	6	EXPLORER 215	ST	CTRCN	FBG	SV	IO	135-175		7	10	3400			7950	9200
20	6	VICTORIA 215	HT	SDN	FBG	SV	OB			7	10	2600			9300	10600
20	6	VICTORIA 215	HT	SDN	FBG	SV	IO	135-175		7	10	3200			7250	8350
22	2	VICTORIA 230	ST	CR	FBG	SV	IO	205-300		8	6	4400			10500	12800
23		ALLANTE 233 CUDDY	ST	CUD	F/S	SV	IO	230	MRCR	8	1	3400			8000	9200
23		ALLANTE 233 CUDDY	ST	CUD	FBG	SV	IO	250-300		8	1	3400			8300	9850
23		CHASE 233	ST	CUD	FBG	SV	IO	250	MRCR	8	1	3400			9900	11300
23		CHASE 233	ST	CUD	F/S	SV	IO	300	MRCR	8	1	3400			10800	12300
23		CHASE 233	ST	CUD	FBG	SV	IO	350	MRCR	8	1	3400			11800	13500
23		CHASE 233	ST	CUD	F/S	SV	IO	390	MRCR	8	1	3400			12000	13600
23	10	VICTORIA 250	ST	CR	FBG	SV	IO	205-300		8	9	5500			13700	16500
29		VICTORIA 290	ST	CR	FBG	SV	IO	300	MRCR	10		8000			25600	28400
29		VICTORIA 290	ST	CR	FBG	SV	IO	T155-T230		10		8000			25900	30700
		1992 BOATS														
16		ALLANTE 160 B/R	ST	RNBT	FBG	SV	OB			6	7	950			3250	3750
16	2	EXPLORER 165	ST	CTRCN	FBG	SV	OB			7	1	980			3300	3800
17	2	ALLANTE 170 B/R	ST	RNBT	FBG	SV	OB			7	2	1300			4450	5100
17	2	ALLANTE 170 B/R	ST	RNBT	FBG	SV	IO	120-150		7	2	1300			3300	4100
17	2	ALLANTE 170 C/D	ST	SKI	FBG	SV	OB			7	2	1300			4250	4950
17	2	ALLANTE 170 C/D	ST	SKI	FBG	SV	IO	120		7	2	1300			3100	3850
17	2	ALLANTE 170 C/D	ST	SKI	FBG	SV	IO	150		7	2	1300			3100	3850
17	8	ALLANTE 185 B/R	ST	RNBT	FBG	SV	OB			7	3	1300			4500	5150
17	8	ALLANTE 185 C/D	ST	SKI	FBG	SV	OB			7	3	1300			4350	5000
17	8	ALLANTE 185 C/D	ST	SKI	FBG	SV	IO	120-155		7	3	1300			3300	4050
17	8	ALLANTE 185 C/D	ST	SKI	FBG	SV	IO	205		7	3	1300			3400	4200
17	8	ALLANTE 185 CUDDY	ST	CUD	FBG	SV	OB			7	3	1300			4450	5100
19		ALLANTE 190	ST	SKI	FBG	SV	IO	155	MRCR	7	5	2300			4600	5300
		IO 155 5050 6100, IO 250 MRCR 4900 5600, IO 250													5300	6500
19	1	ALLANTE 195 CUDDY	ST	CUD	FBG	SV	IO	150		7	8	2200			4900	5950
19	1	ALLANTE 195 CUDDY	ST	CUD	FBG	SV	IO	270		7	8	2200			5400	6600
19	1	CHASE 195 SPORT	ST	CUD	FBG	SV	IO	175		7	8	2300			5050	6100
19	1	CHASE 195 SPORT	ST	CUD	FBG	SV	IO	270		7	8	2300			5500	6750
19	1	EXPLORER 190	ST	CTRCN	FBG	SV	OB			7	8	1700			5550	6400
20	6	EXPLORER 215	ST	CTRCN	FBG	SV	OB			7	10	2600			8850	10000
20	6	EXPLORER 215	ST	CTRCN	FBG	SV	IO	155-175		7	10	2600			6300	7600
20	6	VICTORIA 215	HT	SDN	FBG	SV	IO	120-205		7	10	3200			6750	8200
20	6	VICTORIA 215 BRACKET	HT	SDN	FBG	SV	OB			7	10	3200			9550	10800
22	2	VICTORIA 230	ST	CR	FBG	SV	IO	200-270		8	6	4400			9800	12000
23		ALLANTE 233 CUDDY	ST	CUD	F/S	SV	IO	270	MRCR	8	1	3400			7750	8900
23		ALLANTE 233 CUDDY	ST	CUD	FBG	SV	IO	270		8	1	3400			7650	9350
23		ALLANTE 233 CUDDY	ST	CUD	F/S	SV	IO	330	MRCR	8	1	3400			9650	11000
23		ALLANTE 233 CUDDY	ST	CUD	FBG	SV	IO	330		8	1	3400			9500	11500
23		CHASE 233 SPORTS CUD	ST	CUD	F/S	SV	IO	270	MRCR	8	1	3400			9750	11100
23		CHASE 233 SPORTS CUD	ST	CUD	FBG	SV	IO	270		8	1	3400			9550	11400
23		CHASE 233 SPORTS CUD	ST	CUD	F/S	SV	IO	365	MRCR	8	1	3400			10500	11900
23		CHASE 233 SPORTS CUD	ST	CUD	FBG	SV	IO	365		8	1	3400			10300	12600
23	10	VICTORIA 250	ST	CR	FBG	SV	IO	200-270		8	9	5600			13000	15600
29		VICTORIA 290	ST	CR	FBG	SV	IO	300		10		8000			23900	26500
29		VICTORIA 290	ST	CR	FBG	SV	IO	T155		10		8000			24200	26900
		1991 BOATS														
16		ALLANTE 160 B/R	ST	RNBT	FBG	SV	OB			6	7	950			3100	3600
16	2	EXPLORER 165	ST	CTRCN	FBG	SV	OB			7	1	980			3100	3650
17	2	ALLANTE 170 B/R	ST	RNBT	FBG	SV	OB			7	2	1300			4200	4850
17	2	ALLANTE 170 B/R	ST	RNBT	FBG	SV	IO	120-150		7	2	1300			3100	3850
17	2	ALLANTE 170 C/D	ST	SKI	FBG	SV	OB			7	2	1300			4050	4700
17	2	ALLANTE 170 C/D	ST	SKI	FBG	SV	IO	120		7	2	1300			2900	3600
17	2	ALLANTE 170 C/D	ST	SKI	FBG	SV	IO	150		7	2	1300			2900	3650
17	8	ALLANTE 185 B/R	ST	RNBT	FBG	SV	OB			7	3	1300			4250	4900
17	8	ALLANTE 185 B/R	ST	RNBT	FBG	SV	IO	120		7	3	1300			3250	4000
17	8	ALLANTE 185 B/R	ST	RNBT	FBG	SV	IO	205		7	3	1300			3350	4150
17	8	ALLANTE 185 CD	ST	SKI	FBG	SV	OB			7	3	1300			4100	4800
17	8	ALLANTE 185 CD	ST	SKI	FBG	SV	IO	120		7	3	1300			3100	3800
17	8	ALLANTE 185 CD	ST	SKI	FBG	SV	IO	205		7	3	1300			3200	3950
17	8	ALLANTE 185 CUDDY	ST	CUD	FBG	SV	OB			7	3	1300			4200	4850
19	1	ALLANTE 195 B/R	ST	SKI	FBG	SV	IO	150		7	8	2200			4350	5250
19	1	ALLANTE 195 B/R	ST	SKI	FBG	SV	IO	270		7	8	2200			4750	5800
19	1	ALLANTE 195 CUDDY	ST	CUD	FBG	SV	IO	150		7	8	2200			4650	5550
19	1	ALLANTE 195 CUDDY	ST	CUD	FBG	SV	IO	270		7	8	2200			5100	6200
19	1	CHASE 195 SPORT	ST	CUD	FBG	SV	IO	175		7	8	2300			4750	5700
19	1	CHASE 195 SPORT	ST	CUD	FBG	SV	IO	270		7	8	2300			5200	6300
19	1	EXPLORER 190	ST	CTRCN	FBG	SV	OB			7	8	1700			5300	6100
20	6	EXPLORER 215	ST	CTRCN	FBG	SV	OB			7	10	2600			8350	9600
20	6	VICTORIA 215	HT	SDN	FBG	SV	IO	120-205		7	10	3200			6350	7700
20	6	VICTORIA 215 BRACKET	HT	SDN	FBG	SV	OB			7	10	3200			9100	10300
22	2	VICTORIA 230	ST	CR	FBG	SV	IO	200-270		8	6	4400			9250	11200
23		ALLANTE 233 CUDDY	ST	CUD	F/S	SV	IO	270	MRCR	8	1	3400			7400	8500
23		ALLANTE 233 CUDDY	ST	CUD	FBG	SV	IO	270		8	1	3400			7350	8800
23		ALLANTE 233 CUDDY	ST	CUD	F/S	SV	IO	330	MRCR	8	1	3400			9100	10300
23		ALLANTE 233 CUDDY	ST	CUD	FBG	SV	IO	330		8	1	3400			8950	10800
23		CHASE 233 SPORTS CU	ST	CUD	FBG	SV	IO	270		8	1	3400			8950	10600
23		CHASE 233 SPORTS CU	ST	CUD	FBG	SV	IO	365		8	1	3400			9650	11800
23		CHASE 233 SPORTS CUD	ST	CUD	F/S	SV	IO	270-365		8	1	3400			9050	11200
23	10	VICTORIA 250	ST	CR	FBG	SV	IO	200-270		8	9	5600			12200	14600
		1989 BOATS														
16	2	CORTES BOWRIDER	OP	B/R	FBG		IO	140	MRCR						2750	3150
16	2	CORTES BOWRIDER	OP	B/R	FBG	SV	OB			7	1	980			2900	3350
16	2	CORTES CLOSED DECK	OP	RNBT	FBG		OB								2800	3250
16	2	CORTES CLOSED DECK	OP	RNBT	FBG	SV	IO	120	MRCR	7	1	1575			2700	3150
16	2	FISHING MACHINE	OP	CTRCN	FBG	SV	OB			7	1	980			2850	3350
17	8	ALLANTE	OP	CUD	FBG	SV	OB			7	3	1200			3600	4150
17	8	ALLANTE BOWRIDER	OP	B/R	FBG		OB								4850	5550
17	8	ALLANTE BOWRIDER	OP	B/R	FBG		IO	175	MRCR						3650	4200

```
          LOA  NAME AND/       TOP/ BOAT  -HULL-  ----ENGINE---     BEAM   WGT  DRAFT RETAIL RETAIL
          FT IN OR MODEL       RIG  TYPE  MTL TP  TP # HP  MFG      FT IN  LBS  FT IN  LOW   HIGH
          ----------------------- 1989 BOATS ----------------------------------------------------
          17  8 ALLANTE CLOSED DECK  OP  RNBT  FBG SV OB            7  3  1200        3600   4200
          17  8 ALLANTE CLOSED DECK  OP  RNBT  FBG SV IO  130 MRCR 7  3  1820        3250   3750
          19  1 ALLANTE              OP  B/R   FBG SV IO  165 MRCR 7  8  2200        3850   4450
          19  1 ALLANTE              OP  CUD   FBG SV IO  165 MRCR 7  8  2200        4100   4750
          19  1 CHASE CLOSED DECK    OP        FBG    IO  260 MRCR              4450   5100
          20  6 DISCOVERY            SDN       FBG SV OB            7 10  2600        7600   8750
          20  6 DISCOVERY            SDN       FBG SV IO  165 MRCR 7 10  3300        5750   6650
          20  6 FISHING MACHINE      CTRCN     FBG SV OB            7 10  2600        7600   8750
          20  6 FISHING MACHINE      OP CTRCN  FBG SV IO  180 MRCR              5750   6600
          22  2 VICTORIA             CR        FBG SV IO  230 MRCR 8  6  4400        8200   9400
          23 10 HAIDA SUNBRIDGE      CR        FBG SV IO  230 MRCR 8  9  5500       10700  12200
```

...For earlier years, see the BUC Used Boat Price Guide, Volume 3

CANADIAN SAILCRAFT
BRAMPTON ONTARIO CANADA COAST GUARD MFG ID- ZCU See inside cover to adjust price for area

```
          LOA  NAME AND/       TOP/ BOAT  -HULL-  ----ENGINE---     BEAM   WGT  DRAFT RETAIL RETAIL
          FT IN OR MODEL       RIG  TYPE  MTL TP  TP # HP  MFG      FT IN  LBS  FT IN  LOW   HIGH
          ----------------------- 1987 BOATS ----------------------------------------------------
          30    CS 30              SLP SA/RC FBG KL IB  18D VLVO 10  3  8000  5  6  31200  34700
          30    CS 30   SHOAL      SLP SA/RC FBG KL IB  18D VLVO 10  3  8000  4  3  31200  34700
          32  8 CS 33              SLP SA/CR FBG    IB  20D BUKH 10  8 10000  5  9  40500  45000
          32  8 CS 33   SHOAL      SLP SA/RC FBG KL IB  20D BUKH 10  8 10000  4  7  40500  45000
          36  3 MERLIN CS 36       SLP SA/CR FBG    IB  28D VLVO 11  6 13000  6  3  53800  59100
          36  6 CS 36              SLP SA/CR FBG    IB  33D WEST 11  6 15500  6  3  63300  69500
          36  6 CS 36   SHOAL      SLP SA/RC FBG KL IB  33D WEST 11  6 15500  4 11  63300  69500
          39  3 CS 40              SLP SA/CR F/S    IB  43D VLVO 12  8 17000  6  7  74900  82300
          39  3 CS 40   SHOAL      SLP SA/RC FBG KL IB  43D VLVO 12  8 17000  5      74900  82300
          44  1 CS 44              SLP SA/CR FBG    IB  46D WEST 13  6 22000  7  6 114500 126000
          44  1 CS 44   SHOAL      SLP SA/RC FBG KL IB  46D WEST 13  8 22000  5  6 114500 126000
          ----------------------- 1986 BOATS ----------------------------------------------------
          30    CS 30              SLP SA/CR FBG    IB  18D VLVO 10  3  8000  5  6  29600  32900
          30    CS 30              SLP SA/RC FBG KL IB  18D VLVO 10  3  8000  5  6  29500  32800
          30    CS 30   SHOAL      SLP SA/RC FBG KL IB  18D VLVO 10  3  8000  4  3  29700  33000
          32  8 CS 33              SLP SA/CR FBG    IB  20D BUKH 10  8 10000  5  9  38300  42600
          32  8 CS 33   SHOAL      SLP SA/RC FBG KL IB  20D BUKH 10  8 10000  4  7  38300  42600
          36  6 CS 36              SLP SA/CR FBG    IB  33D WEST 11  6 15500  6  3  60000  65900
          36  6 CS 36              SLP SA/CR FBG    IB  30D WEST 11  6 15500  6  3  59900  65800
          36  6 CS 36   SHOAL      SLP SA/RC FBG KL IB  30D WEST 11  6 15500  4 11  59900  65800
          39  3 CS 40              SLP SA/CR F/S    IB  43D VLVO 12  8 17000  6  7  70900  77900
          39  3 CS 40              SLP SA/RC FBG    IB  43D      12  8 17000  6  7  70900  77900
          39  3 CS 40   SHOAL      SLP SA/RC FBG    IB  43D      12  8 17000  5      70900  77900
          44  1 CS 44              SLP SA/CR FBG    IB  46D WEST 13  6 22000  7  6 108500 119000
          44  1 CS 44              SLP SA/RC FBG    IB  46D WEST 13  8 22000  7  6 108500 119000
          44  1 CS 44   SHOAL      SLP SA/RC FBG KL IB  46D WEST 13  8 22000  5  6 108500 119000
          ----------------------- 1985 BOATS ----------------------------------------------------
          27    CS 27              SLP SA/RC FBG KL IB   8D YAN   9  4  6100  5  2  19200  21400
          27    CS 27   SHOAL      SLP SA/RC FBG KL IB   8D YAN   9  4  6500  3 11  20500  22800
          30    CS 30              SLP SA/RC FBG KL IB  18D VLVO 10  3  8000  5  6  28100  31200
          30    CS 30   SHOAL      SLP SA/RC FBG KL IB  18D VLVO 10  3  8500  4  3  29800  33200
          32  8 CS 33              SLP SA/CR FBG KL IB  20D BUKH 10  8 10000  5  9  36300  40400
          32  8 CS 33   SHOAL      SLP SA/RC FBG KL IB  20D BUKH 10  8 10000  4  7  36300  40400
          36  6 CS 36              SLP SA/CR FBG KL IB  30D WEST 11  6 15500  6  3  56800  62400
          36  6 CS 36   SHOAL      SLP SA/RC FBG KL IB  30D WEST 11  6 15500  4 11  56800  62400
          44  1 CS 44              SLP SA/CR FBG    IB  46D WEST 13  6 22000  7  6 103000 113000
          44  1 CS 44   SHOAL      SLP SA/RC FBG KL IB  46D WEST 13  8 22000  5  6 103000 113000
          ----------------------- 1984 BOATS ----------------------------------------------------
          27    CS 27              SLP SA/RC FBG KL IB   8D YAN   9  4  6100  5  2  18400  20500
          27    CS 27   SHOAL      SLP SA/RC FBG KL IB   8D YAN   9  4  6500  3 11  19400  21600
          30    CS 30              SLP SA/RC FBG KL IB  15D      10  3  8000  4  3  26600  29500
          30    CS 30   SHOAL      SLP SA/RC FBG KL IB  15D      10  3  8000  4  3  26600  29500
          32  8 CS 33              SLP SA/CR FBG KL IB  20D BUKH 10  8 10000  5  9  34400  38300
          32  8 CS 33   SHOAL      SLP SA/RC FBG KL IB  20D BUKH 10  8 10000  4  5  34400  38300
          36  6 CS 36              SLP SA/CR FBG KL IB  30D WEST 11  6 15500  6  3  53800  59100
          36  6 CS 36   SHOAL      SLP SA/RC FBG KL IB  30D WEST 11  6 15500  4  5  53800  59100
```

....For earlier years, see the BUC Used Boat Price Guide, Volume 3

CANAVERAL CUSTOM BOATS INC
CAPE CANAVERAL FL 32920 COAST GUARD MFG ID- DBJ See inside cover to adjust price for area
FORMERLY DELTA BOATS INC

For more recent years, see the BUC Used Boat Price Guide, Volume 1

```
          LOA  NAME AND/       TOP/ BOAT  -HULL-  ----ENGINE---     BEAM   WGT  DRAFT RETAIL RETAIL
          FT IN OR MODEL       RIG  TYPE  MTL TP  TP # HP  MFG      FT IN  LBS  FT IN  LOW   HIGH
          ----------------------- 1996 BOATS ----------------------------------------------------
          28  2 CCB 28 CNV          OP  SF    FBG SV IB 240-350      9  6        2  6  36300  42100
                IB 210D-370D  47600 57800, IB 375D-435D  54700 63000, IB T220 PCM 39400  43800
                IB T130D VLVO 49300 54200
          28  2 CCB 28 CNV          HT  SF    FBG SV IB 240-350      9  6        2  6  32500  37700
                IB 250D-264D  42000 51100, IB 300D-420D  46100 55800, IB 435D CAT 53800  59200
                IB T220   PCM 36500 40500, IBT130D-T150D 44600 52700
          28  2 CCB 28 CNV          FB  SF    FBG SV IB 330-350      9  6        2  6  40500  45300
                IB 150D-320D  46600 58100, IB 350D-435D  54200 64200, IB T220 PCM 43200  48000
                IBT130D-T150D 51600 57700
          28  2 CCB 28 CNV CRT      OP  UTL   FBG SV IB 210D-375D    9  6        2  6  47000  58100
          28  2 CCB 28 CNV CRT      OP  UTL   FBG SV IB 400D-435D    9  6        2  6  54000  61300
          28  2 CCB 28 CNV CRT      OP  UTL   FBG SV IBT130D-T150D   9  6        2  6  48900  57600
          28  2 CCB 28 CNV CRT      HT  UTL   FBG SV IB 210D-400D    9  6        2  6  48300  59700
          28  2 CCB 28 CNV CRT      HT  UTL   FBG SV IB 420D-435D    9  6        2  6  56200  61900
          28  2 CCB 28 CNV CRT      HT  UTL   FBG SV IBT130D-T150D   9  6        2  6  50200  57700
          28  2 CCB 28 CNV DUAL     HT  SF    FBG SV IB 240-350      9  6        2  6  40000  46600
                IB 230D-280D  48200 56200, IB 300D-425D  55700 65700, IB T220 PCM 42300  47000
                IBT130D-T150D 53500 58700
          28  2 CCB 28 DIVE CNV     OP  UTL   FBG SV IB 240-350      9  6        2  6  36500  42300
                IB 210D-375D  45900 56700, IB 400D-435D  52100 59800, IB T220 PCM 39600  44000
                IBT130D-T150D 47800 54600
          28  2 CCB 28 DIVE CNV     HT  UTL   FBG SV IB 240-350      9  6        2  6  55200  63200
                IB 210D-375D  47100 58400, IB 400D-425D  54200 61400, IB T220 PCM 59800  65700
                IBT130D-T150D 48700 54400
          28  2 CCB 28 DIVE CRT     OP  UTL   FBG SV IB 150D-210D    9  6        2  6  44500  55000
          28  2 CCB 28 DIVE CRT     OP  UTL   FBG SV IB 250D-435D    9  6        2  6  51800  64600
          28  2 CCB 28 DIVE CRT     OP  UTL   FBG SV IB T130D VLVO   9  6        2  6  51700  56800
          28  2 CCB 28 DIVE CTR     OP  UTL   FBG SV IB 318D VLVO    9  6        2  6  52300  57400
          36  3 CCB 36 SFX          FB  SF    FBG DV IB T370  MRCR 12  2        3    141500 152500
                IB T300D CAT 171000 188000, IB T300D CUM 167000 183500, IB T300D GM 168000 184500
                IB T320D CAT 173500 190500, IB T350D CAT 177000 194500, IB T370D VLVO 169000 185500
                IB T375D CAT 180500 198500, IB T400D CUM 178500 196000, IB T400D GM 183000 201000
                IB T420D CAT 187000 205500, IB T435D CAT 179000 197000, IB T435D CAT 189500 208000
          38    CCB 38 DEER         FB  SF    FBG DV IB 300D CAT 12  5        3    128000 141000
                IB 300D DEER 126500 139000, IB 300D CAT 131000 144000, IB 370D VLVO 127500 140500
                IB 375D CAT 132500 145500, IB 400D GM 131500 144500, IB 370D CAT 133500 149500
                IB 430D VLVO 131000 144000, IB 435D CAT 136500 150000, IB 300D CAT 136000 149500
                IB T250D CUM 135000 148500, IB T250D GM 136000 149500, IB T264D CUM 137000 150500
                IB T300D CAT 144000 158000, IB T320D CAT 139500 153500, IB T300D GM 140500 154000
                IB T318D VLVO 138500 152000, IB T320D CAT 146000 160500, IB T325D VLVO 142500 156500
                IB T350D CAT 149500 164500, IB T370D VLVO 143000 157500, IB T375D CAT 153500 168000
          38    CCB 38 DIVE         OP  UTL   FBG SV IB 264D GM 12  5        3    112500 123500
                IB 280D GM 113000 124000, IB 300D DEER 112500 124000, IB 300D CUM 113000 124500
                IB 300D DEER 113500 125000, IB 318D VLVO 115500 126000, IB 320D CUM 114500 125500
                IB 350D CAT 117500 129500, IB 370D VLVO 116000 127000, IB 430D VLVO 116500 128000
                IB 400D CUM 117500 129500, IB 435D CAT 118000 130000, IB 420D CAT 119000 131000
                IB 435D CAT 123000 128000, IB 485D GM 118000 130500, IB 250D CAT 117000 128500
                IB T220D DEER 121000 133000, IB T250D GM 123500 136000, IB T250D CAT 123500 131000
                IB T264D GM 124000 136500, IB T280D GM 122500 135000, IB T300D CAT 123000 135500
                IB T300D CUM 125000 138500, IB T300D DEER 124500 137500, IB T350D GM 127000 139500
                IB T318D VLVO 129000 142500, IB T320D CAT 132000 145500, IB T350D CUM 129500 142500
          38    CCB 38 DIVE CRT     HT  UTL   FBG DV IB 250D CAT 12  5        3    120500 132500
                IB 264D GM 115500 127000, IB 280D GM 116500 128000, IB 300D CUM 116500 128000
                IB 300D GM 117000 128500, IB 318D VLVO 116000 127500, IB 320D CUM 115500 127000
                IB 370D GM 118000 130000, IB 375D CAT 117500 128500, IB 400D CUM 119500 130500
                IB 430D VLVO 116500 128000, IB 420D CAT 120500 133000, IB 425D CAT 119000 130500
                IB T250D CAT 113000 124500, IB T250D CUM 119000 131000, IB T250D GM 117000 128500
                IB T264D GM 117500 129000, IB T280D GM 118500 130000, IB T300D GM 120000 132000
                IB T300D CUM 120000 131500, IB T318D VLVO 118500 130500, IB T320D CUM 125000 137500
                IB T370D VLVO 133500 146500, IB T375D CAT 130500 143500
```

```
CANAVERAL CUSTOM BOATS INC   -CONTINUED     See inside cover to adjust price for area
LOA  NAME AND/            TOP/ BOAT -HULL- ----ENGINE--- BEAM  WGT  DRAFT RETAIL RETAIL
FT IN  OR MODEL           RIG  TYPE MTL TP TP # HP MFG   FT IN LBS  FT IN  LOW   HIGH
-------------------- 1994 BOATS ---------------------------------------------------------
28   2 DELTA 28 CNV          OP   SF   FBG SV IB 240-350   9  6      2  6  32400  37700
     IB 200D-350D  42300  52400, IB 375D-425D  49400  56500, IB T220  PCM  35200  39100
     IB T130D VLVO 44300  49200
28   2 DELTA 28 CNV          HT   SF   FBG SV IB 240-330   9  6      2  6  30600  35400
     IB 200D-320D  40800  48900, IB 350D-425D  48900  53700, IB T220  PCM  35200  39100
     IB T130D VLVO 42400  47100
28   2 DELTA 28 CNV          FB   SF   FBG SV IB 330-350   9  6      2  6  36100  40400
     IB 200D-350D  43400  52500, IB 375D-425D  49900  57300, IB T220  PCM  38300  42500
     IB T130D VLVO 46600  51200
28   2 DELTA 28 CNV CRT      OP   UTL  FBG SV IB 210D-350D  9  6     2  6  41900  51200
28   2 DELTA 28 CNV CRT      OP   UTL  FBG SV IB 375D-425D  9  6     2  6  47900  54700
28   2 DELTA 28 CNV CRT      OP   UTL  FBG SV IB T130D VLVO 9  6     2  6  43600  48500
28   2 DELTA 28 CNV CRT      HT   UTL  FBG SV IB 210D-350D  9  6     2  6  42700  51800
28   2 DELTA 28 CNV CRT      HT   UTL  FBG SV IB 375D-425D  9  6     2  6  48700  55500
28   2 DELTA 28 CNV CRT      HT   UTL  FBG SV IB T130D VLVO 9  6     2  6  44400  49300
28   2 DELTA 28 CNV DUAL     HT   SF   FBG SV IB 240-350    9  6     2  6  34200  39300
     IB 200D-320D  44900  53100, IB 350D-425D  52900  58100, IBT130D-T220D    46500  54800
28   2 DELTA 28 DIVE CNV     HT   UTL  FBG SV IB 280D GM    9  6     2  6  44400  49300
28   2 DELTA 28 DIVE CRT     OP   UTL  FBG SV IB 200D-400D  9  6     2  6  43500  54200
28   2 DELTA 28 DIVE CRT     OP   UTL  FBG SV IB 425D CAT   9  6     2  6  51300  56300
28   2 DELTA 28 DIVE CRT     OP   UTL  FBG SV IB T130D VLVO 9  6     2  6  45500  50000
36   3 DELTA 36 SFX          FB   SF   FBG DV IB T370  MRCR 12  2         3 165500 181500
     IB T250D GM   158500 174000, IB T264D GM   159500 175500, IB T280D GM   161000 177000
     IB T300D CAT  165500 182000, IB T300D CUM  162000 178000, IB T300D GM   163000 179000
     IB T320D CAT  167500 184500, IB T350D MERL 168000 184500, IB T358D VLVO 166000 182500
     IB T375D CAT  174500 191500, IB T400D CUM  173000 190000, IB T400D GM   177000 194500
     IB T400D MERL 171000 188000, IB T425D CAT  181000 199000, IB T450D MERL 180500 198500
38     DELTA 38             FB   SF   FBG DV IB 300D CAT   12  5        3 117500 129500
     IB 300D GM   116000 127500, IB 320D CAT  118500 130500, IB 350D MERL 118500 130500
     IB 358D VLVO 117000 128500, IB 375D CAT  121500 133500, IB 400D GM   121000 133000
     IB 400D MERL 121000 133000, IB 425D CAT  125000 137000, IB T210D CAT  125000 137000
     IB T240D PERK 127000 139500, IB T250D CUM 124000 136500, IB T250D GM   125000 137000
     IB T264D GM  126000 138500, IB T280D GM   127000 139500, IB T300D CAT  132000 145000
     IB T300D CUM 128000 140500, IB T300D GM   128500 141500, IB T306D VLVO 126000 138500
     IB T320D CAT 134000 147500, IB T350D MERL 133500 146500, IB T375D CAT  140500 154000
     IB T400D CUM 137500 151500, IB T400D GM   138500 152500, IB T400D MERL 139000 152500
38     DELTA 38 DIVE CRT     HT   UTL  FBG DV IB 210D CAT  12  5       3 105500 116000
     IB 240D PERK 110000 120500, IB 250D GM   103500 114000, IB 264D GM   105500 116000
     IB 280D GM   106000 116500, IB 300D CUM  108000 119000, IB 300D CUM  106500 117000
     IB 300D GM   106500 117000, IB 306D VLVO 105500 116000, IB 320D CAT  103500 114000
     IB 350D MERL 113000 124000, IB 358D VLVO 107500 118000, IB 375D CAT  105500 116000
     IB 400D CUM  110500 121500, IB 400D GM   106000 116500, IB 400D MERL 110000 119500
     IB 425D CAT  108500 119000, IB 485D GM   116000 127500, IB T210D CAT  106500 117000
     IB T240D PERK 122500 134500, IB T250D CUM 108500 119000, IB T250D GM   109500 120500
     IB T264D GM  107000 117500, IB T280D GM   108000 118500, IB T300D CAT  122000 134000
     IB T300D CUM 109000 120000, IB T300D GM   119000 131000, IB T306D VLVO 107500 118000
     IB T320D CAT 114000 125000, IB T350D MERL 128000 140500, IB T358D VLVO 120500 132500
     IB T375D CAT 118500 130500, IB T400D CUM  127500 140000, IB T400D GM   119500 131500
     IB T400D MERL 124500 137000, IB T425D CAT  135500 149000
38     DELTA 38 DIVE CRT     HT   UTL  FBG DV IB 250D CUM  12  5       3 105500 109000
46     DELTA 46             FB   TRWL FBG SV IB 280D GM    13  6       4 199500 219000
     IB 358D VLVO 202000 222000, IB 375D CAT  203500 224000, IB 400D CUM  204000 224000
     IB 400D GM   204000 224500, IB 400D MERL 204000 224500, IB 425D CAT  206000 226500
     IB 485D GM   208000 228500, IB 720D GM   219000 240500, IB 10CD CAT  216000 237000
     IB T210D CAT 206000 226500, IB T300D CAT 213500 234500, IB T300D CUM 212000 233000
     IB T300D GM  212000 233000, IB T306D VLVO 211500 232500, IB T320D CAT 212000 233000
46     DELTA 46 SF          FB   SF   FBG DV IB T264D GM   13  6       4 189000 207500
     IB T280D GM  191000 210000, IB T300D CUM 193500 212500, IB T358D VLVO 204000 224000
     IB T375D CAT 211000 232000, IB T400D CUM 215500 236500, IB T400D MERL 215500 236500
     IB T425D CAT 223000 245000, IB T485D CAT 236000 259000
46     DELTA 46 SF          FB   SF   FBG SV IB 375D CAT   13  6       4 180500 198500
     IB 400D CUM  179500 197500, IB 400D MERL 180000 198000, IB 400D MERL 180000 198000
     IB 425D CAT  183500 202000, IB 485D CUM  185500 204000, IB 550D GM   191000 209500
     IB 720D GM   205500 225500, IB 10CD CAT  226500 249000, IB T300D CAT 195500 214500
     IB T300D GM  193000 212000, IB T320D CAT 198000 218000, IB T400D CUM 211000 232000
-------------------- 1993 BOATS ---------------------------------------------------------
28   2 DELTA 28 CNV          OP   SF   FBG SV IB 240-350   9  6      2  6  30700  35700
     IB 200D-350D  40200  49900, IB 375D-425D  47200  53800, IB T220  PCM  33300  37100
     IB T130D VLVO 42200  46900
28   2 DELTA 28 CNV          HT   SF   FBG SV IB 240-330   9  6      2  6  30700  35400
     IB 200D-350D  40100  50000, IB 375D-425D  46100  52700, IB T220  PCM  33300  37000
     IB T130D VLVO 40800  45400
28   2 DELTA 28 CNV          FB   SF   FBG SV IB 330-350   9  6      2  6  34200  38200
     IB 200D-350D  41100  50000, IB 375D-425D  47500  54600, IB T220  PCM  36100  40100
     IB T130D VLVO 43800  48700
28   2 DELTA 28 CNV CRT      OP   SF   FBG SV IB 300D-400D  9  6     2  6  45800  52400
28   2 DELTA 28 CNV CRT      HT   SF   FBG SV IB 300D-400D  9  6     2  6  44700  52000
28   2 DELTA 28 CNV CRT      HT   SF   FBG SV IB T130D VLVO 9  6     2  6  43300  48100
28   2 DELTA 28 CNV CRT      TH   SF   FBG SV IB 210D-350D  9  6     2  6  43700  52900
28   2 DELTA 28 CNV CRT      TH   SF   FBG SV IB 375D-425D  9  6     2  6  49700  54600
28   2 DELTA 28 CNV CRT      TH   SF   FBG SV IB T130D VLVO 9  6     2  6  45700  50200
28   2 DELTA 28 CNV CRT      OP   UTL  FBG SV IB 210D-350D  9  6     2  6  40100  48900
28   2 DELTA 28 CNV CRT      OP   UTL  FBG SV IB 375D-425D  9  6     2  6  41700  46300
28   2 DELTA 28 CNV CRT      HT   UTL  FBG SV IB 210D-320D  9  6     2  6  40600  49000
28   2 DELTA 28 CNV CRT      HT   UTL  FBG SV IB 350D-425D  9  6     2  6  46400  53000
28   2 DELTA 28 CNV CRT      HT   UTL  FBG SV IB T130D VLVO 9  6     2  6  42300  47000
28   2 DELTA 28 DIVE CNV     OP   UTL  FBG SV IB 210D-350D  9  6     2  6  40100  48900
28   2 DELTA 28 DIVE CNV     OP   UTL  FBG SV IB 375D-425D  9  6     2  6  41700  46300
28   2 DELTA 28 DIVE CNV     HT   UTL  FBG SV IB T130D VLVO 9  6     2  6  40600  49000
28   2 DELTA 28 DIVE CNV     HT   UTL  FBG SV IB 210D-350D  9  6     2  6  46300  52900
28   2 DELTA 28 DIVE CNV     HT   UTL  FBG SV IB 375D-425D  9  6     2  6  46900  49300
28   2 DELTA 28 DIVE CNV     TH   UTL  FBG SV IB T130D VLVO 9  6     2  6  46400  53000
28   2 DELTA 28 DIVE CNV     TH   UTL  FBG SV IB 375D-425D  9  6     2  6  41600  47000
28   2 DELTA 28 DIVE CNV     TH   UTL  FBG SV IB 210D-400D  9  6     2  6  43200  50700
28   2 DELTA 28 DIVE CRT     OP   UTL  FBG SV IB 425D CAT   9  6     2  6  41000  54000
28   2 DELTA 28 DIVE CRT     OP   UTL  FBG SV IB T130D VLVO 9  6     2  6  43300  48100
36   3 DELTA 36 SFX          FB   SF   FBG DV IB T370  MRCR 12  2         3 157500 173000
     IB T250D GM   151000 166000, IB T264D GM   152000 167000, IB T280D GM   153500 168500
     IB T300D CAT  157500 173000, IB T300D CUM  154500 170000, IB T300D GM   155000 170500
     IB T320D CAT  159500 175500, IB T350D MERL 160000 176000, IB T358D VLVO 158000 173500
     IB T375D CAT  155500 182500, IB T400D CUM  160500 181000, IB T400D GM   168500 185500
     IB T400D MERL 163000 179000, IB T425D CAT  177500 189500, IB T450D MERL 172000 189000
38     DELTA 38             FB   SF   FBG DV IB 350D MERL  12  5        3 112500 124000
     IB 400D MERL 115000 126500, IB T210D CAT  119000 130500, IB T240D PERK 121000 133000
     IB T250D GM  119000 130500, IB T264D GM   120000 132000, IB T280D GM   121000 133000
     IB T300D CAT 126000 138500, IB T300D CUM  122000 134000, IB T300D GM   122500 135000
     IB T320D CAT 127500 140500, IB T350D MERL 133500 146500, IB T400D GM   132000 145000
38     DELTA 38 COMM        HT   COMM FBG DV IB 300D CAT   12  5        3     **     **
     IB 300D GM    **    **, IB 320D CAT   **    **, IB 358D VLVO  **    **
     IB 375D CAT   **    **, IB 400D GM    **    **, IB 425D CAT   **    **
     IB T210D CAT  **    **, IB T250D GM   **    **, IB T264D GM   **    **
     IB T280D GM   **    **, IB T300D CAT  **    **, IB T300D CUM  **    **
     IB T300D GM   **    **, IB T306D VLVO **    **, IB T300D CAT  **    **
     IB T375D CAT  **    **, IB T400D CUM  **    **, IB T400D GM   **    **
38     DELTA 38 DIVE CRT    HT   UTL  FBG DV IB 210D CAT   12  5        3 100500 110500
     IB 240D PERK 105000 115000, IB 250D GM    99000 108500, IB 264D GM   101000 111000
     IB 280D GM   101500 111500, IB 300D GM   103500 112500, IB 300D CUM  101500 111000
     IB 300D GM   102000 112000, IB 306D VLVO 100500 110500, IB 358D VLVO  98900 108500
     IB 350D MERL 106500 116500, IB 375D CAT  101500 111500, IB 375D CAT  101500 111000
     IB 400D CUM  105500 116000, IB 400D GM   101500 111500, IB 400D MERL 104000 114000
     IB 425D CAT  103500 113500, IB 485D GM   110500 121500, IB T210D CAT 101500 111500
     IB T240D PERK 117000 128500, IB T250D GM  103500 114000, IB T250D GM  104500 115000
     IB T264D GM  102000 112500, IB T280D GM  103500 114000, IB T300D CAT 116500 128000
     IB T300D CUM 104000 114500, IB T300D GM  113500 125000, IB T306D VLVO 102500 112500
     IB T320D CAT 108500 119500, IB T350D MERL 122000 134000, IB T358D VLVO 115000 126500
     IB T375D CAT 113000 124500, IB T400D CUM 121500 133500, IB T400D GM   113500 125500
     IB T400D MERL 119000 130500, IB T425D CAT 129500 142000
38     DELTA 38 DIVE CRT    HT   UTL  FBG DV IB 250D CUM  12  5        3  94600 104000
38   3 DELTA 38             FB   SF   FBG DV IB 358D VLVO 12  5        3 113000 124000
     IB T250D CUM 118000 130000, IB T320D CAT 128000 140500, IB T300D CUM 124500 137000
     IB T306D VLVO 120000 134000, IB T320D CAT 129500 142500, IB T350D MERL 129000 142000
     IB T375D CAT 135500 149000, IB T400D CUM 133000 146500, IB T400D GM   134000 147500
     IB T400D MERL 134500 147500, IB T425D CAT 142000 156000
```

94   CONTINUED ON NEXT PAGE   96th ed. - Vol. II

LOA FT	LOA IN	NAME AND/ OR MODEL	TOP/ RIG	BOAT TYPE	-HULL- MTL	TP	TP	----ENGINE--- # HP MFG	BEAM FT	BEAM IN	WGT LBS	DRAFT FT	DRAFT IN	RETAIL LOW	RETAIL HIGH
		1993 BOATS													
46		DELTA 46	FB	TRWL	FBG	SV	IB	358D VLVO	13	5		4		192500	211500
		IB 375D CAT 194000 213500, IB 400D GM 194500 213500, IB 400D MERL 194500 214000													
		IB 425D CAT 196500 215500, IB 485D GM 198000 218000, IB 720D GM 208500 229000													
		IB 10CD CAT 205500 226000, IB T210D CAT 196500 215500, IB T300D CAT 203000 223000													
		IB T300D CUM 202000 221500, IB T300D GM 202000 222000, IB T306D VLVO 201500 221500													
		IB T320D CAT 204500 225000, IB T358D VLVO 205500 225500, IB T375D CAT 209500 230000													
		IB T400D CUM 209500 230500, IB T400D GM 210000 231000, IB T400D MERL 210000 231000													
		IB T425D CAT 214000 235000, IB T485D GM 217500 239000													
46		DELTA 46 COMM	FB	COMM	FBG	DV	IB	300D CUM						**	**
		IB 350D MERL ** **, IB 358D VLVO ** **, IB 375D CAT ** **													
		IB 400D CUM ** **, IB 400D GM ** **, IB 400D MERL ** **													
		IB 425D CAT ** **, IB 485D GM ** **, IB 550D GM ** **													
		IB 10CD CAT ** **, IB T300D CUM ** **, IB T350D MERL ** **													
		IB T358D VLVO ** **, IB T375D CAT ** **, IB T400D CUM ** **													
		IB T400D GM ** **, IB T400D MERL ** **, IB T425D CAT ** **													
		IB T485D GM ** **, IB T550D GM ** **													
46		DELTA 46 DIVE	OP	UTL	FBG	SV	IB	264D GM						**	**
		IB 280D GM ** **, IB 300D CAT ** **, IB 300D CUM ** **													
		IB 300D GM ** **, IB 320D CAT ** **, IB 350D MERL ** **													
		IB 358D VLVO ** **, IB 375D CAT ** **, IB 400D CUM ** **													
		IB 400D GM ** **, IB 400D MERL ** **, IB 425D CAT ** **													
		IB 485D GM ** **, IB 550D GM ** **, IB 585D CAT ** **													
		IB 650D GM ** **, IB T264D GM ** **, IB T280D GM ** **													
		IB T300D CAT ** **, IB T300D CUM ** **, IB T300D GM ** **													
		IB T320D CAT ** **, IB T350D MERL ** **, IB T358D VLVO ** **													
		IB T375D CAT ** **, IB T400D CUM ** **, IB T400D GM ** **													
		IB T400D MERL ** **, IB T485D GM ** **													
46		DELTA 46 SF	FB	SF	FBG	DV	IB	T264D GM	13	6		4		179500	197500
		IB T280D GM 181500 199500, IB T300D CUM 184000 202500, IB T358D VLVO 194000 213500													
		IB T375D CAT 201000 221000, IB T400D GM 205000 225500, IB T400D MERL 205000 225500													
		IB T425D CAT 212500 233500, IB T485D GM 224500 247000													
46		DELTA 46 SF	FB	SF	FBG	SV	IB	375D CAT	13	6		4		171500	188500
		IB 400D CUM 170500 187500, IB 400D GM 171000 188000, IB 400D MERL 171000 188000													
		IB 425D CAT 174500 192000, IB 485D GM 176500 194000, IB 550D GM 181500 199500													
		IB 720D GM 195500 214500, IB 10CD CAT 216000 237500, IB T300D CAT 185500 204000													
		IB T300D GM 183500 201500, IB T320D CAT 188500 207000, IB T400D CUM 201000 221000													
		1992 BOATS													
28	2	DELTA 28 CNV	OP	SF	FBG	SV	IB	240-350	9	6		2	6	29100	33900
		IB 200D-350D 38300 47700, IB 375D-425D 44500 51500, IB T220 PCM 31600 35200													
		IB T130D VLVO 40200 44600													
28	2	DELTA 28 CNV	HT	SF	FBG	SV	IB	240-330	9	6		2	6	29100	33600
		IB 200D-350D 38200 46700, IB 375D-425D 43600 50300, IB T220 PCM 31600 35200													
		IB T130D VLVO 40100 44500													
28	2	DELTA 28 CNV	FB	SF	FBG	SV	IB	330-350	9	6		2	6	32100	35900
		IB 210D-350D 39500 47700, IB 375D-425D 44800 52000, IB T220 PCM 34200 38000													
		IB T130D VLVO 41700 46400													
28	2	DELTA 28 CNV CRT	TH	SF	FBG	SV	IB	210D-350D	9	6		2	6	41500	50400
28	2	DELTA 28 CNV CRT	TH	SF	FBG	SV	IB	375D-425D	9	6		2	6	47500	52300
28	2	DELTA 28 CNV CRT	TH	SF	FBG	SV	IB	T130D VLVO	9	6		2	6	43200	48000
28	2	DELTA 28 CNV CRT	OP	UTL	FBG	SV	IB	210D-350D	9	6		2	6	38200	46500
28	2	DELTA 28 CNV CRT	OP	UTL	FBG	SV	IB	375D-425D	9	6		2	6	43400	50000
28	2	DELTA 28 CNV CRT	OP	UTL	FBG	SV	IB	T130D VLVO	9	6		2	6	39700	44100
28	2	DELTA 28 CNV CRT	HT	UTL	FBG	SV	IB	130D-300D	9	6		2	6	37200	45200
28	2	DELTA 28 CNV CRT	HT	UTL	FBG	SV	IB	320D-425D	9	6		2	6	41900	50500
28	2	DELTA 28 CNV CRT	HT	UTL	FBG	SV	IB	T210D CAT	9	6		2	6	45900	50400
28	2	DELTA 28 DIVE	OP	UTL	FBG	SV	IB	210D-350D	9	6		2	6	39700	48200
28	2	DELTA 28 DIVE	OP	UTL	FBG	SV	IB	375D-425D	9	6		2	6	44700	51600
28	2	DELTA 28 DIVE	OP	UTL	FBG	SV	IB	T130D VLVO	9	6		2	6	41200	45800
28	2	DELTA 28 DIVE CNV	OP	UTL	FBG	SV	IB	264D-350D	9	6		2	6	39300	46500
28	2	DELTA 28 DIVE CNV	OP	UTL	FBG	SV	IB	400D MERL	9	6		2	6	44500	49400
28	2	DELTA 28 DIVE CNV	HT	UTL	FBG	SV	IB	210D-350D	9	6		2	6	38700	47100
28	2	DELTA 28 DIVE CNV	HT	UTL	FBG	SV	IB	375D-425D	9	6		2	6	43800	50500
28	2	DELTA 28 DIVE CNV	HT	UTL	FBG	SV	IB	T130D VLVO	9	6		2	6	40200	44700
28	2	DELTA 28 DIVE CNV	TH	UTL	FBG	SV	IB	210D-350D	9	6		2	6	38700	47100
28	2	DELTA 28 DIVE CNV	TH	UTL	FBG	SV	IB	375D-425D	9	6		2	6	43800	50500
28	2	DELTA 28 DIVE CNV	TH	UTL	FBG	SV	IB	T130D VLVO	9	6		2	6	40200	44700
28	2	DELTA 28 DIVE CNVCRT	OP	UTL	FBG	SV	IB	210D-320D	9	6		2	6	38200	46000
28	2	DELTA 28 DIVE CNVCRT	OP	UTL	FBG	SV	IB	375D-425D	9	6		2	6	43400	50000
28	2	DELTA 28 DIVE CNVCRT	OP	UTL	FBG	SV	IB	T130D VLVO	9	6		2	6	39700	44100
36	3	DELTA 365	FB	SF	FBG	DV	IB	T370 MRCR	12	2		3		141500	155500
		IB T264D GM 136500 150000, IB T280D GM 137500 151000, IB T300D CUM 138500 152500													
		IB T350D MERL 144000 158000, IB T400D MERL 146500 161000													
36	3	DELTA 36SFX	FB	SF	FBG	DV	IB	T250D GM	12	2		3		135500	149000
		IB T320D CAT 143500 158000, IB T358D VLVO 141500 155500, IB T375D CAT 149500 164500													
		IB T400D GM 151500 166500, IB T425D CAT 155500 171000													
38		DELTA 38	FB	SF	FBG	DV	IB	350D MERL	12	5		3		107500	118000
		IB 400D MERL 110000 120500, IB T210D CAT 113500 124500, IB T240D PERK 115500 127000													
		IB T250D GM 113500 124500, IB T264D GM 114500 125500, IB T280D GM 115500 127000													
		IB T300D CUM 116000 127500, IB T320D CAT 122000 134000, IB T350D MERL 121500 133000													
		IB T375D CAT 127500 140000, IB T400D GM 126000 138500, IB T400D MERL 126000 138500													
38		DELTA 38 COMM	HT	COMM	FBG	DV	IB	320D CAT	12	5		3		**	**
		IB 375D CAT ** **, IB 400D GM ** **, IB 425D CAT ** **													
		IB T210D CAT ** **, IB T250D GM ** **, IB T264D GM ** **													
		IB T280D GM ** **, IB T300D CUM ** **, IB T306D VLVO ** **													
		IB T320D CAT ** **, IB T375D CAT ** **, IB T400D GM ** **													
38		DELTA 38 DIVE CRT	HT	UTL	FBG	DV	IB	210D CAT	12	5		3		95900	105500
		IB 240D PERK 99900 110000, IB 250D GM 94300 103500, IB 264D GM 96000 105500													
		IB 280D GM 96500 106000, IB 300D CUM 96700 106500, IB 306D VLVO 95900 105500													
		IB 320D CAT 94200 103500, IB 350D MERL 102500 112500, IB 375D CAT 96100 105500													
		IB 400D GM 96500 106000, IB 400D MERL 99000 109000, IB 425D CAT 98500 108000													
		IB 485D GM 105500 115500, IB T210D CAT 96800 106500, IB T240D PERK 111000 122000													
		IB T250D CUM 98600 108500, IB T250D GM 99700 109500, IB T264D GM 97400 107000													
		IB T280D GM 98000 107500, IB T300D CUM 99200 109000, IB T306D VLVO 97600 107500													
		IB T320D CAT 103500 114000, IB T350D MERL 116500 128000, IB T375D CAT 108000 118500													
		IB T400D GM 108500 119500, IB T400D MERL 113500 124500, IB T425D CAT 123500 135500													
38		DELTA 38 DIVE CRT	HT	UTL	FBG	SV	IB	250D CUM	12	5		3		90100	99000
46		DELTA 46	FB	TRWL	FBG	SV	IB	375D CAT	13	6		4		185000	203500
		IB 400D GM 185500 203500, IB 400D MERL 185500 203500, IB 425D CAT 187000 205500													
		IB 485D GM 189000 207500, IB T210D CAT 187000 205500, IB T300D CUM 192500 211500													
		IB T306D VLVO 192000 211000, IB T320D CAT 195000 214500, IB T358D VLVO 195500 215000													
		IB T375D CAT 199500 219000, IB T400D GM 200000 220000, IB T400D MERL 200000 220000													
		IB T425D CAT 204000 224000, IB T485D GM 207500 228000													
46		DELTA 46 COMM	FB	COMM	FBG	DV	IB	358D VLVO						**	**
		IB 375D CAT ** **, IB 400D GM ** **, IB 400D MERL ** **													
		IB 425D CAT ** **, IB 485D GM ** **, IB 550D GM ** **													
		IB 10CD CAT ** **, IB T300D CUM ** **, IB T350D MERL ** **													
		IB T358D VLVO ** **, IB T375D CAT ** **, IB T400D GM ** **													
		IB T400D MERL ** **, IB T425D CAT ** **, IB T485D GM ** **													
		IB T550D GM ** **													
46		DELTA 46 DIVE	OP	UTL	FBG	SV	IB	264D GM						**	**
		IB 280D GM ** **, IB 300D CUM ** **, IB 320D CAT ** **													
		IB 350D MERL ** **, IB 358D VLVO ** **, IB 375D CAT ** **													
		IB 400D GM ** **, IB 400D MERL ** **, IB 425D CAT ** **													
		IB 485D GM ** **, IB 550D GM ** **, IB 585D CAT ** **													
		IB 650D GM ** **, IB T264D GM ** **, IB T280D GM ** **													
		IB T300D CUM ** **, IB T320D CAT ** **, IB T350D MERL ** **													
		IB T358D VLVO ** **, IB T375D CAT ** **, IB T400D CUM ** **													
		IB T400D MERL ** **, IB T485D GM ** **													
46		DELTA 46 SF	FB	SF	FBG	DV	IB	T264D GM	13	6		4		171000	188000
		IB T280D GM 173000 190000, IB T300D CUM 175500 192500, IB T358D VLVO 185000 203500													
		IB T375D CAT 191500 210500, IB T400D GM 195500 215000, IB T400D MERL 195500 215000													
		IB T425D CAT 202500 222500, IB T485D GM 214000 235500													
46		DELTA 46 SF	FB	SF	FBG	SV	IB	375D CAT	13	6		4		163000	179000
		IB 400D GM 162500 179000, IB 400D MERL 163000 179000, IB 425D CAT 166000 182500													
		IB 485D GM 168000 184500, IB 550D GM 172500 189500, IB 10CD CAT 206000 226500													
		IB T320D CAT 179500 197000													
		1991 BOATS													
28	2	DELTA 28 CNV	HT	SF	FBG	SV	IB	220-240	9	6		2	6	27400	30700
28	2	DELTA 28 CNV	HT	SF	FBG	SV	IB	130D-306D	9	6		2	6	35200	42600
28	2	DELTA 28 CNV	HT	SF	FBG	SV	IB	320D-425D	9	6		2	6	39700	48100
28	2	DELTA 28 CNV	FB	SF	FBG	SV	IB	240-302	9	6		2	6	29800	33600
28	2	DELTA 28 CNV	FB	SF	FBG	SV	IB	130D-306D	9	6		2	6	35700	43300
28	2	DELTA 28 CNV	FB	SF	FBG	SV	IB	320D-400D	9	6		2	6	40600	47500
28	2	DELTA 28 CNV	OP	UTL	FBG	SV	IB	220-240	9	6		2	6	27600	30900
28	2	DELTA 28 CNV	OP	UTL	FBG	SV	IB	210D-320D	9	6		2	6	37000	45600
28	2	DELTA 28 CNV	OP	UTL	FBG	SV	IB	375D-425D	9	6		2	6	42700	49400

CONTINUED ON NEXT PAGE

```
CANAVERAL CUSTOM BOATS INC  -CONTINUED     See inside cover to adjust price for area
LOA  NAME AND/        TOP/ BOAT  -HULL-  ----ENGINE--- BEAM   WGT  DRAFT RETAIL RETAIL
FT IN OR MODEL        RIG  TYPE  MTL TP TP # HP  MFG   FT IN  LBS  FT IN  LOW   HIGH
-------------------- 1991 BOATS --------------------------------------------------
28  2 DELTA 28 CNV CRT     ST  UTL  FBG SV IB 130D-306D  9  6     2  6  38100  46200
28  2 DELTA 28 CNV CRT     ST  UTL  FBG SV IB 320D-400D  9  6     2  6  43600  50100
28  2 DELTA 28 DIVE        OP  UTL  FBG SV IB 210D-320D  9  6     2  6  36400  43600
28  2 DELTA 28 DIVE        OP  UTL  FBG SV IB 375D-400D  9  6     2  6  41000  45500
28  2 DELTA 28 DIVE CNVCRT OP  UTL  FBG SV IB 210D-400D  9  6     2  6  37900  47300
28  2 DELTA 28 DIVE CNVCRT OP  UTL  FBG SV IB  425D CAT  9  6     2  6  43800  48600
28  2 DELTA 28 DIVE CNVCRT OP  UTL  FBG SV IB T130D VLVO 9  6     2  6  38400  42700
28  2 DELTA 28 DIVE CRT    OP  UTL  FBG SV IB 210D-320D  9  6     2  6  36400  43600
28  2 DELTA 28 DIVE CRT    OP  UTL  FBG SV IB 375D-425D  9  6     2  6  41000  47100
28  2 DELTA 28 DIVE CRT    ST  UTL  FBG SV IB 130D-320D  9  6     2  6  32800  40600
28  2 DELTA 28 DIVE CRT    ST  UTL  FBG SV IB 375D-400D  9  6     2  6  38400  43000

36  3 DELTA 36SFX          FB  SF   FBG DV IB T250D GM   12  2        3  129000 142000
     IB T320D CAT 137000 150500, IB T375D CAT 142500 156500, IB T385D VLVO 137500 151000
     IB T400D GM  142000 156000, IB T425D CAT 148500 163000

38    DELTA 38             FB  SF   FBG DV IB  320D CAT  12  5        3  103000 113000
     IB  375D CAT 105500 116000, IB  400D GM  104500 115000, IB  425D CAT 108000 119000
     IB T250D CUM 107500 118000, IB T306D VLVO 109000 120000, IB T320D CAT 116000 127500
     IB T375D CAT 121500 133500

38    DELTA 38 DIVE        HT  UTL  FBG DV IB  210D CAT  12  5        3  91400  100500
     IB  250D GM   89900  98700, IB  264D GM   91600 100500, IB  320D CAT  92100 101000
     IB  358D VLVO 89100  97900, IB  375D CAT  92800 102000, IB  400D GM   92200 101500
     IB T250D CUM  95400 105000, IB T250D VLVO 96500 106000, IB T264D GM  101000 111000
     IB T320D CAT 103500 114000, IB T358D VLVO 101000 111000, IB T375D CAT 108500 119000
     IB T400D GM  107500 118000, IB T425D CAT 117500 129000

38    DELTA 38 DIVE        HT  UTL  FBG SV IB  250D CUM  12  5        3  85900  94400
38    DELTA 38 DIVE CRT    HT  UTL  FBG SV IB  250D CUM  12  5        3  94100 103500
     IB  250D GM   94600 104000, IB  320D CAT  96800 106500, IB  358D VLVO 97000 106500
     IB  375D CAT 101000 111000, IB  400D GM  100500 110000, IB T250D CUM 103000 113500
     IB T250D GM  104500 114500, IB T320D CAT 111500 122500, IB T358D VLVO 108000 119000
     IB T375D CAT 116000 127500, IB T400D GM  115000 126500

46    DELTA 46             FB  TRWL FBG SV IB  358D VLVO 13  6        4  175000 192000
     IB  375D CAT 176500 194000, IB  400D GM  177000 194500, IB  10CD VLVO 187000 205500
     IB T320D CAT 186000 204500, IB T358D VLVO 186500 205000, IB T375D CAT 190000 209000
     IB T400D GM  191000 209500, IB T425D CAT 194500 213500

46    DELTA DIVE 46        OP  UTL  FBG    IB  375D CAT                      **     **
46    DELTA DIVE 46        OP  UTL  FBG    IB T375D CAT                      **     **
46    DELTA DIVE 46        OP  UTL  FBG    IB T400D CUM                      **     **
-------------------- 1990 BOATS --------------------------------------------------
28  2 DELTA 28 CNV         OP  UTL  FBG SV IB  240  PCM  9  6        2  6  25600  28400
     IB 210D-320D  37500  45600, IB 375D-425D  43200  49000, IB T220  PCM   28700  31800

28  2 DELTA 28 CNV         HT  UTL  FBG SV IB  240  PCM  9  6        2  6  26400  29300
     IB 210D-320D  35300  42500, IB 375D-425D  39900  46100, IB T220  PCM   28600  31800
     IB T130D VLVO 36700  40700

28  2 DELTA 28 CNV         FB  UTL  FBG SV IB  240  PCM  9  6        2  6  26400  29300
     IB 210D-320D  35300  42500, IB 375D-400D  39900  44500, IB T302  PCM   30100  33400
     IB T130D VLVO 36700  40700

28  2 DELTA 28 CNV CRT     ST  UTL  FBG SV IB  250  CUM  9  6        2  6  26500  29300
     IB 210D-320D  38900  47100, IB 375D-400D  44200  49200, IB T130D VLVO 40100  44500

28  2 DELTA 28 DIVE        OP  UTL  FBG SV IB  240  PCM  9  6        2  6  22700  25200
28  2 DELTA 28 DIVE        OP  UTL  FBG SV IB 210D-320D  9  6        2  6  32000  38900
28  2 DELTA 28 DIVE        OP  UTL  FBG SV IB 375D-400D  9  6        2  6  36400  40700
28  2 DELTA 28 DIVE CNVCRT OP  UTL  FBG SV IB  240 PERK  9  6        2  6  29200  32500
28  2 DELTA 28 DIVE CNVCRT OP  UTL  FBG SV IB 210D-425D  9  6        2  6  36500  45500
28  2 DELTA 28 DIVE CNVCRT OP  UTL  FBG SV IB T130D VLVO 9  6        2  6  36700  40700
28  2 DELTA 28 DIVE CRT    OP  UTL  FBG SV IB  240-250   9  6        2  6  28100  31300
28  2 DELTA 28 DIVE CRT    OP  UTL  FBG SV IB 210D-425D  9  6        2  6  35200  43900
28  2 DELTA 28 DIVE CRT    ST  UTL  FBG SV IB 210D-375D  9  6        2  6  31700  39600
28  2 DELTA 28 DIVE CRT    ST  UTL  FBG SV IB  400D GM   9  6        2  6  36100  40100
28  2 DELTA 28 DIVE CRT    ST  UTL  FBG SV IB T130D VLVO 9  6        2  6  33300  37000

36  3 DELTA 365FX          FB  SF   FBG DV IB  250D GM   12  2        3  116000 127000
     IB T320D CAT 118000 130000, IB  400D GM  119500 131500, IB T358D VLVO 129000 141500
     IB T375D CAT 136000 149500, IB T425D CAT 141500 155500

38    DELTA 38             FB  SF   FBG SV IB  320D CAT  12  5        3  98100 108000
     IB  375D CAT 100500 110500, IB  400D GM   99900 110000, IB  425D CAT 103000 113500
     IB T250D CUM 102500 113000, IB T306D VLVO 104500 114500, IB T320D CAT 111000 122000
     IB T375D CAT 116000 127500

38    DELTA 38 DIVE        HT  UTL  FBG SV IB  210D CAT  12  5        3  87200  95800
     IB  250D CUM  83100  91300, IB  250D GM   88300  97100, IB  264D GM   87300  96000
     IB  320D CAT  87800  96500, IB  358D VLVO 86500  95500, IB  375D CAT  90000  98900
     IB  400D GM   89500  98400, IB T210D CAT  95400 105000, IB T250D CUM  92400 101500
     IB T250D GM   93500 102500, IB T264D GM   96200 105500, IB T320D CAT 100000 101500
     IB T358D VLVO 97700 107500, IB T375D CAT 105000 115500, IB T400D GM  104500 114500
     IB T425D CAT 112000 123000

38    DELTA 38 DIVE CRT    HT  UTL  FBG SV IB  250D CUM  12  5        3  87800  96500
     IB  250D GM   88300  97100, IB  320D CAT  92500 101500, IB  358D VLVO 91100 100000
     IB  375D CAT  94800 104000, IB  400D GM   94100 103500, IB T250D CUM  97000 106500
     IB T250D GM   98000 107500, IB T320D CAT 104500 115000, IB T358D VLVO 102000 112000
     IB T375D CAT 109500 120000, IB T400D GM  108000 119000

46    DELTA 46             FB  TRWL FBG SV IB  358D VLVO 13  6        4  167000 183500
     IB  375D CAT 168500 185000, IB  400D GM  169000 185500, IB  10CD VLVO 178500 196000
     IB T320D CAT 177500 195000, IB T358D VLVO 178000 196000, IB T375D CAT 181500 199500
     IB T400D GM  182000 200000, IB T425D CAT 185500 204000

46    DELTA DIVE 46        OP  UTL  FBG    IB  375D CAT                      **     **
46    DELTA DIVE 46        OP  UTL  FBG    IB T375D CAT                      **     **
46    DELTA DIVE 46        OP  UTL  FBG    IB T400D CUM                      **     **
-------------------- 1989 BOATS --------------------------------------------------
28  2 DELTA 28 CNV         OP  UTL  FBG SV IB  240  PCM  9  6        2  6  23400  26000
     IB 210D-320D  35700  43500, IB 375D-400D  41200  45800, IB T220  PCM   27200  30200

28  2 DELTA 28 CNV         HT  UTL  FBG SV IB  240  PCM  9  6        2  6  25100  27800
     IB 210D-320D  35100  40600, IB 375D-400D  38100  42600, IB T220  PCM   27200  30200
     IB T130D VLVO 35100  39000

28  2 DELTA 28 CNV         FB  UTL  FBG SV IB  240  PCM  9  6        2  6  25100  27800
     IB 210D-320D  33800  40600, IB 375D-400D  38100  42600, IB T302  PCM   28600  31800
     IB T130D VLVO 35100  39000

28  2 DELTA 28 CNV CRT     ST  UTL  FBG SV IB  250  CUM  9  6        2  6  25200  28000
     IB 210D-320D  37200  44900, IB 375D-400D  42300  47200, IB T130D VLVO 38500  42700

28  2 DELTA 28 DIVE        OP  UTL  FBG SV IB  240  PCM  9  6        2  6  20700  23100
28  2 DELTA 28 DIVE        OP  UTL  FBG SV IB 210D-320D  9  6        2  6  30500  36800
28  2 DELTA 28 DIVE        OP  UTL  FBG SV IB 375D-400D  9  6        2  6  34600  38600
28  2 DELTA 28 DIVE CNVCRT OP  UTL  FBG SV IB  240 PERK  9  6        2  6  29000  32300
28  2 DELTA 28 DIVE CNVCRT OP  UTL  FBG SV IB 210D-400D  9  6        2  6  34500  44300
28  2 DELTA 28 DIVE CRT    OP  UTL  FBG SV IB T130D VLVO 9  6        2  6  35100  39000
28  2 DELTA 28 DIVE CRT    OP  UTL  FBG SV IB  240-250   9  6        2  6  27000  30000
28  2 DELTA 28 DIVE CRT    OP  UTL  FBG SV IB 210D-375D  9  6        2  6  33200  41400
28  2 DELTA 28 DIVE CRT    ST  UTL  FBG SV IB  400D GM   9  6        2  6  37400  41600
28  2 DELTA 28 DIVE CRT    ST  UTL  FBG SV IB 210D-375D  9  6        2  6  30300  37800
28  2 DELTA 28 DIVE CRT    ST  UTL  FBG SV IB  400D GM   9  6        2  6  34200  38000
28  2 DELTA 28 DIVE CRT    ST  UTL  FBG SV IB T130D VLVO 9  6        2  6  31700  35200

36  3 DELTA 365FX              SF   FBG DV IB  250D GM   12  2        3  110500 121500
     IB  320D CAT 113000 124000, IB  358D VLVO 111500 122500, IB  375D CAT 114500 126000
     IB  400D GM  114000 125500

38    DELTA 38                 SF   FBG SV IB  320D CAT  12  5        3  93700 103000
     IB  375D CAT  96100 105500, IB  400D GM   95400 105000, IB T250D CUM  98100 108000
     IB T306D VLVO 99600 109500, IB T320D CAT 106000 116500, IB T375D CAT 111000 121500

38    DELTA 38 DIVE        HT  UTL  FBG SV IB  210D CAT  12  5        3  83800  92100
     IB  250D CUM  80900  88900, IB  250D GM   81400  89500, IB  264D GM   81600  89700
     IB  320D CAT  84300  92600, IB  358D VLVO 83000  91200, IB  375D CAT  86400  94900
     IB  400D GM   85800  94300, IB T210D CAT  91500 100500, IB T250D CUM  88700  97400
     IB T250D GM   89700  98500, IB T264D GM   90300  99200, IB T320D CAT 100000 110000
     IB T358D VLVO 93600 103000, IB T375D CAT 100500 110500, IB T400D GM   99500 109500

38    DELTA 38 DIVE CRT    HT  UTL  FBG SV IB  250D CUM  12  5        3  85500  94000
     IB  250D GM   86100  94600, IB  264D GM   86200  94700, IB  320D CAT  88800  97600
     IB  358D VLVO 87500  96100, IB  375D CAT  91000  99900, IB  400D GM   90400  99300
     IB T250D CUM  93000 102000, IB T250D GM   94100 103500, IB T264D GM   94400 103500
     IB T400D GM  104000 114000, IB T358D VLVO 97900 107500, IB T375D CAT 105000 115000

46    DELTA 46             FB  TRWL FBG SV IB  320D CAT  13  6        4  159000 174500
     IB  358D VLVO 159500 175000, IB  375D CAT 161000 176500, IB  400D GM  161000 177000
     IB  10CD CAT 170500 187500, IB T358D VLVO 170000 187000, IB T375D CAT 173500 190500
     IB T400D GM  174000 191000

96                        CONTINUED ON NEXT PAGE              96th ed. - Vol. II
```

```
   LOA  NAME AND/               TOP/ BOAT  -HULL-  ----ENGINE--- BEAM   WGT  DRAFT RETAIL RETAIL
   FT IN OR MODEL                RIG TYPE  MTL TP TP # HP  MFG   FT IN  LBS  FT IN  LOW   HIGH
   ------------------- 1988 BOATS --------------------------------------------------------------
   28  2 DELTA 28                OP  SF    FBG DV OB            9  6      2  6  17300 19700
   28  2 DELTA 28                OP  SF    FBG DV IO 240-330    9  6      2  6  21400 25000
      IO 200D-320D  29500  35800, IO 375D-400D  33600  37500, IO T175-T220   22600 25900
      IO T130D VLVO 30900  34300
   28  2 DELTA 28                ST  SF    FBG DV OB            9  6      2  6  17300 19700
   28  2 DELTA 28                HT  SF    FBG DV OB            9  6      2  6  17300 19700
   28  2 DELTA 28                HT  SF    FBG DV IO 240-330    9  6      2  6  21400 25000
      IO 200D-320D  29500  35700, IO 375D-400D  33500  37400, IO T175-T220   22500 25900
      IO T130D VLVO 30900  34300
   28  2 DELTA 28                FB  SF    FBG DV OB            9  6      2  6  17300 19700
   28  2 DELTA 28                FB  SF    FBG DV IO 240-330    9  6      2  6  22500 26100
      IO 200D-320D  29800  36300, IO 375D-400D  34200  38000, IO T175-T220   23600 26900
      IO T130D VLVO 31400  34900
   28  2 DELTA 28 DIVE           OP  UTL   FBG SV IB 240-330    9  6      2  6  23900 27500
   28  2 DELTA 28 DIVE           OP  UTL   FBG SV IB 210D-320D  9  6      2  6  30200 36700
   28  2 DELTA 28 DIVE           OP  UTL   FBG SV IB 375D-400D  9  6      2  6  35300 39300
   28  2 DELTA 28 DIVE           HT  UTL   FBG SV IB 240  PCM   9  6      2  6  23900 26500
      IO 330   MRCR  20900  23200, IB 330   PCM   24800  27500, IB 210D-320D 30200 36700
      IB 375D-400D  36500  40600, IO T175   OMC   20900  23200, IB T220  PCM  25900 28800
      IB T130D VLVO 32500  36100
   28  2 DELTA 28 DIVE           FB  UTL   FBG DV IB T220 PCM   9  6      2  6  25900 28800
   28  2 DELTA 28 DIVE           FB  UTL   FBG SV IB 240  PCM   9  6      2  6  23900 26500
      IO 330   MRCR  20900  23200, IB 330   PCM   24800  27500, IB 210D-320D 32300 38900
      IB 375D-400D  36500  40700, IO T175   OMC   20900  23200, IB T130D VLVO 33600 37300
   28  2 DELTA 28 DIVE CON       OP  UTL   FBG SV IO 175   OMC  9  6      2  6  19300 21500
      IB 220-240    23700  26500, IO 330   MRCR  20900  23200, IB 330   PCM  24800 27500
      IB 210D-320D  30200  36700, IB 375D-400D  35300  39300, IB T130D VLVO 32300 35900
   28  2 DELTA 28 DIVE CRT       OP  UTL   FBG SV IB 210D-375D  9  6      2  6  34800 43100
   28  2 DELTA 28 DIVE CRT       OP  UTL   FBG SV IB 400D GM    9  6      2  6  39300 43700
   28  2 DELTA 28 DIVE CRT       OP  UTL   FBG SV IB T130D VLVO 9  6      2  6  34600 38400
   28  2 DELTA 28 DIVE CRT       HT  UTL   FBG SV IB 210D-320D  9  6      2  6  34400 41100
   28  2 DELTA 28 DIVE CRT       HT  UTL   FBG SV IB 400D GM    9  6      2  6  39000 43400
   28  2 DELTA 28 DIVE CRT       HT  UTL   FBG SV IB T130D VLVO 9  6      2  6  34600 38500
   36  3 DELTA 365FX                 SF    FBG DV IB            MRCR 12   3      **    **
      IB 250D GM  105500 116000, IB 300D GM  106500 117000, IB 320D CAT  108000 118500
      IB 358D VLVO 106500 117000, IB 375D CAT 109500 120000, IB 400D GM  109000 120000
   38    DELTA 38                    SF    FBG SV IB 320D CAT 12  5      3      89600 98400
      IB 375D CAT  91800 101000, IB 400D GM   91200 100000, IB T250D CUM  93800 103000
      IB 375D GM   94200 103500, IB T264D GM  95000 104500, IB T300D GM   97200 107000
      IB T306D VLVO 95200 104500, IB T320D CAT 101000 111000, IB T375D CAT 106000 116500
      IB T400D GM  104500 115000
   38    DELTA 38 COMMERCIAL     HT  COMM  FBG SV IB 320D CAT 12  5      3      **    **
      IB 375D CAT  **     **   , IB T300D GM   **     **   , IB T320D CAT   **    **
   38    DELTA 38 DIVE           HT  UTL   FBG SV IB 210D CAT 12  5      3      70000 76900
      IB 250D CUM  70000  76900, IB 250D GM   69600  76500, IB 264D GM   70600 77600
      IB 320D CAT  70200  77200, IB 358D VLVO 72000  79100, IB 375D CAT  72100 79200
      IB 400D GM   74500  81800, IB T210D CAT 79300  87200, IB T250D CUM  79600 87400
      IB T250D GM  79000  86800, IB T264D GM  80700  88700, IB T320D CAT  80700 88700
      IB T358D VLVO 83500 91800, IB T375D CAT 84300  92700, IB T400D GM   89200 98100
   38    DELTA 38 DIVE CRT       HT  UTL   FBG SV IB 210D CAT 12  5      3      90000 98900
      IB 250D CUM  89800  98700, IB 250D GM   89500  98400, IB 264D GM   89700 98500
      IB 320D CAT  88700  97400, IB 358D VLVO 90900  99800, IB 375D CAT  90400 99400
      IB 400D GM   93800 103000, IB T210D CAT 95400 105000, IB T250D CUM  95500 105000
      IB T250D GM  95000 104500, IB T264D GM  95700 105000, IB T320D CAT  95900 105500
      IB T358D VLVO 99400 109000, IB T375D CAT 99800 109500, IB T400D GM  105000 115500
   46    DELTA 46                FB  SF    FBG SV IB 550D GM  13  6      4     143000 157000
      IB T320D CAT 148500 163000, IB T358D VLVO 151000 166000, IB T375D GM 156500 172000
      IB T375D GM  155500 170500
   46    DELTA 46                FB  TRWL  FBG SV IB 210D CAT 13  6      4     148500 163500
      IB 306D VLVO 151000 165500, IB 310D GM  151000 166000, IB 358D VLVO 187500 206000
      IB T200D VLVO 154000 169000, IB T210D CAT 155500 171000, IB T306D VLVO 159500 175500
   46    DELTA 46 COMMERCIAL     FB  TRWL  FBG SV IB 358D VLVO 13  6      4     117500 129000
      IB 375D CAT 153500 169000, IB 550D GM  149500 170500, IB T358D VLVO 162500 178500
      IB T375D CAT 165500 182500, IB T550D GM  177000 194500
   -------------------- 1986 BOATS --------------------------------------------------------------
   28  2 DELTA CONVERTIBLE       CR        FBG SV OB            9  6   5400         16500 18700
   28  2 DELTA HARDTOP        HT CR        FBG SV OB            9  6   5400         16500 18700
   36  3 CLIMAX 36                SF        FBG DV IB T320D    12  2 17080  3       94900 104500
   38    SPORT FISHERMAN          SF        FBG SV IB T300D    12  5 17500  3       85000 93400
   -------------------- 1985 BOATS --------------------------------------------------------------
   28  2 CHALLENGER              OP  CR    F/S SV IB 250-330    9  6   5400  3      15300 18400
      IB 210D-250D  28500  31600, IB T220   PCM   23100  25700, IB T165D VLVO 24800 27500
   28  2 CHALLENGER              HT  CR    F/S SV IB 250-330    9  6   5750  3      15700 18900
      IB 210D-260D  28500  31600, IB T220   PCM   23100  25700, IB T165D VLVO 23400 26000
   28  2 CHALLENGER              FB  CR    F/S SV IB 250-330    9  6   5950  3      15900 19100
   28  2 CHALLENGER              FB  CR    F/S SV IB 165D-260D  9  6         3      27200 31600
   28  2 CHALLENGER              FB  CR    F/S SV IB T220   PCM 9  6       8  2     23100 25700
   36  3 CLIMAX 36                FB  SF    FBG DV IB T700   PCM 12  2 16500  2     72100 79300
      IB T250D J&T  78200  85900, IB T365D CAT  75000  82500, IB T520D VLVO 81600 89600
      IB T600D CAT  93200 102500
   36  2 CLIMAX 36               F+T SF    FBG DV IB T     D PCM 12  2      3       **    **
      IB T260D VLVO 77200  84800, IB T300D CAT  81500  89500, IB T355D CAT  84600 92900
      IB T520D J&T  84700  93100
   38    COMMERCIAL              HT  OFF   FBG SV IB 195D PCM 12  5 19000  3       75500 82900
      IB 260D J&T  76800  84400, IB 286D VLVO 76200  83700, IB 300D CAT   78600 86400
      IB 310D J&T  78000  85700, IB 360D CAT  80500  88500, IB 425D J&T   81800 89900
      IB T195D PCM 80900  88900, IB T260D CAT 85500  94000, IB T360D CAT  92100 101000
      IB T420D J&T 94600 104000, IB T500D VLVO 96800 106500, IB T572D VLVO 103000 113000
      IB T600D CAT 115000 126000, IB T620D J&T 112500 123500
   38    DIVE                    FB  OFF   FBG SV IB 195D PCM 12  5 19000  3       75500 82900
      IB 210D CAT  76500  84100, IB 220D J&T  76100  83600, IB 250D VLVO  67700 74400
      IB 260D J&T  76800  84400, IB 286D VLVO 76200  83700, IB 300D CAT   70600 77600
      IB 310D J&T  70200  77200, IB 360D CAT  80500  88500, IB 360D CAT   73700 81000
      IB T195D PCM 80900  89000, IB T210D CAT 76600  84200, IB T210D J&T  77400 85000
      IB T250D J&T 76300  83800, IB T286D VLVO 76000  83600, IB T360D CAT 81000 89000
      IB T310D J&T 99700  87600, IB T350D CAT 84600  92900, IB T500D VLVO 96800 106500
   38    PASSENGER 38CGA         FB  OFF   FBG SV IB 250D J&T 12  5 19000  3  6    84500 92900
      IB 300D CAT  86600  95200, IB 310D J&T  85800  94300, IB 350D CAT   80200 88100
      IB 410D J&T  88800  97600, IB T210D J&T 82900 102000, IB T235D VLVO 89800 98700
      IB T250D J&T 90800  99800, IB T260D CAT 85500  94000, IB T286D VLVO 89800 98700
      IB T300D CAT 94700 104000, IB T310D J&T 93800 103000, IB T350D CAT  98100 108000
   38    SPORT FISHERMAN         FB  SF    FBG SV IB 250D J&T 12  5 19000  3  6    76500 84100
      IB 286D VLVO 76100  83600, IB 300D CAT  77500  86300, IB T310D J&T  88500 85700
      IB 350D PERK 77600  85200, IB 410D J&T  81400  89400, IB T210D J&T  81900 90100
      IB T225D LEHM 82200 90300, IB T250D J&T 83700  92000, IB T286D VLVO 91400 91400
      IB T300D CAT 88100  96800, IB T310D J&T 87000  95600, IB T350D PERK 89100 97900
      IB T375D J&T 94100 103500
   38    SPORT FISHERMAN 38      FB  SF    FBG SV IB 350D CAT 12  5 19000  3  6    82800 91000
      IB T195D PCM 81000  89000, IB T260D CAT 85700  94200, IB T350D CAT  94100 103500
   46    COMMERCIAL                  OFF   F/S SV IB 270D VLVO 13  6      4       91700 101000
      IB 310D J&T  94100 103500, IB 355D CAT  96700 106500, IB 410D J&T   98200 108000
      IB 530D CAT 104000 114000
   46    NEPTUNE 46 A/B          FB  TRWL  F/S SV IB 135D LEHM 13  6      4      129500 142500
      IB 165D PERK 133000 143000, IB 300D CAT 133500 146500, IB T135D LEHM 133500 146500
      IB T158D VLVO 133000 146000, IB T165D PERK 135500 148500, IB T210D CAT 137000 150500
      IB T225D LEHM 137000 150500, IB T250D VLVO 136000 149500
   46    NEPTUNE 46A/B           FB  SF    F/S SV IB 675D J&T 13  6      4      131500 144500
      ID T355D CAT 134500 148000, IB T410D J&T 142000 156000, IB T530D CAT  160500 176500
   46    NEPTUNE 46C             FB  SF    F/S SV IB 675D J&T 13  6      4      131500 144500
      IB T355D CAT 133000 146500, IB T410D J&T 140500 154000, IB T530D CAT  160500 176500
   46    NEPTUNE 46C             FB  TRWL  F/S SV IB 135D LEHM 13  6      4      127000 139500
      IB 165D PERK 128000 140500, IB 300D CAT 132000 145000, IB T106D VLVO 130500 143500
      IB T135D LEHM 131000 144000, IB T165D PERK 132500 146000, IB T210D CAT 133500 148500
      IB T225D LEHM 138000 151500, IB T250D VLVO 138000 151500
   -------------------- 1984 BOATS --------------------------------------------------------------
   25    PUMA                    ST  CUD   FBG SV IO 285   PCM  9  6   5800  2      12200 13900
   25    PUMA                    ST  CUD   FBG SV IO 155D VLVO  9  6   5800  2      11400 13000
   25    PUMA                    ST  CUD   FBG SV IB 158D-205D  9  6   5800  2      15600 19200
```

CANAVERAL CUSTOM BOATS INC   -CONTINUED

See inside cover to adjust price for area

LOA FT IN	NAME AND/ OR MODEL	TOP/ RIG	BOAT TYPE	-HULL- MTL TP TP	----ENGINE--- # HP	MFG	BEAM FT IN	WGT LBS	DRAFT FT IN	RETAIL LOW	RETAIL HIGH
------------------- 1984 BOATS -----											
25	PUMA	HT	CUD	FBG SV IB	255	PCM	9 6	5800	2	12200	13900
25	PUMA	HT	CUD	FBG SV IO	155D	VLVO	9 6	5800	2	11400	13000
25	PUMA	HT	CUD	FBG SV IB	158D-205D		9 6	5800	2	15600	19200
25	PUMA	FB	CUD	FBG SV OB			9 6	5800	2	15800	17900
25	PUMA	FB	CUD	FBG SV IB	255	PCM	9 6			10100	11500
25	PUMA	FB	CUD	FBG SV IO	155D	VLVO	9 6	5800	2	11400	13000
25	PUMA	FB	CUD	FBG SV IB	158-205D		9 6	5800	2	15600	19200
36	2 CLIMAX 36	FB	SF	FBG DV IB	T235D VLVO		12 2		3	73100	80300
	IB T240D PERK 75300		82800,	IB T250D J&T	74900 82300,	IB T260D CAT				76200	83700
	IB T286D VLVO 75000		82400,	IB T300D CAT	78000 85700,	IB T310D GM				77200	84800
38	COMMERCIAL	HT	OFF	FBG SV IB	250D J&T		12 5	19000	3	73400	80700
	IB 260D GM 73400		80600,	IB 300D CAT	75300 82800,	IB 310D GM				74500	81900
	IB T286D VLVO 79400		87300,	IB T300D CAT	84200 92500,	IB T310D GM				82600	90700
	IB T410D J&T 89800		98700								
38	PASSENGER 38CGA	FB	OFF	FBG SV IB	300D CAT		12 5	19000	3 6	75300	82800
	IB 310D J&T 74800		82200,	IB 350D CAT	76800 84400,	IB 410D J&T				77900	85600
	IB T250D J&T 80000		88000,	IB T286D VLVO	79400 87300,	IB T300D CAT				84200	92500
38	SPORT FISHERMAN	FB	SF	FBG SV IB	250D J&T		12 5	19000	3	73300	80600
	IB 260D GM 73300		80600,	IB 286D VLVO	72900 80100,	IB 300D CAT				75300	82500
	IB 310D GM 74400		81800,	IB 410D J&T	78000 85700,	IB T250D J&T				80200	88200
	IB T260D GM 83200		91400,	IB T286D VLVO	79700 87500,	IB T300D CAT				84400	92700
	IB T310D GM 82800		91000,	IB T410D J&T	90100 99000						
38	SPORT FISHERMAN 38	FB	SF	FBG SV IB	350D CAT		12 5	19000	3 6	76800	84400
	IB T195D PCM 77600		85200,	IB T260D CAT	79100 86900,	IB T350D GM				87700	96400

....For earlier years, see the BUC Used Boat Price Guide, Volume 3

CANNELL BOATBUILDING CO INC

CAMDEN ME 04843

See inside cover to adjust price for area

LOA FT IN	NAME AND/ OR MODEL	TOP/ RIG	BOAT TYPE	-HULL- MTL TP TP	----ENGINE--- # HP	MFG	BEAM FT IN	WGT LBS	DRAFT FT IN	RETAIL LOW	RETAIL HIGH
------------------- 1986 BOATS -----											
16 11	HERRESHOFF 17	KNCKBT SLP	SA/OD WD				5			4700	5400
------------------- 1985 BOATS -----											
16 11	HERRESHOFF 17	SLP	SA/OD				5			4450	5150

CANOE COVE MFG LTD

SIDNEY BC CANADA   COAST GUARD MFG ID- CVE See inside cover to adjust price for area

LOA FT IN	NAME AND/ OR MODEL	TOP/ RIG	BOAT TYPE	-HULL- MTL TP TP	----ENGINE--- # HP	MFG	BEAM FT IN	WGT LBS	DRAFT FT IN	RETAIL LOW	RETAIL HIGH
------------------- 1994 BOATS -----											
42	CANOE COVE 42	FB	SDN	FBG SV IB	T400		14 2		3 4	155500	170500
	IB T216D GM 161500		177500,	IB T225D CAT	164500 181000,	IB T250D GM				164500	181000
	IB T300D GM 171000		187500,	IB T320D CAT	177000 194500,	IB T320D GM				174000	191000
42	CANOE COVE 42 FD	FB	SDN	FBG SV IB	T400		14 2		3	168500	185500
	IB T216D GM 173500		190500,	IB T225D CAT	177000 194500,	IB T250D GM				177500	195000
	IB T300D GM 183500		202000,	IB T320D CAT	189000 208000,	IB T320D GM				186000	204500
42	CANOE COVE 42 TRICAB	FB	SDN	FBG SV IB	T400		14 2		3	168500	185500
	IB T216D GM 173500		190500,	IB T225D CAT	177000 194500,	IB T250D GM				177500	195000
	IB T300D GM 183500		202000,	IB T320D CAT	189000 208000,	IB T320D GM				186000	204500
45	CANOE COVE 45	FB	SDN	FBG SV IB	T400		14 2		3	148500	163000
	IB T216D GM 151500		166500,	IB T225D CAT	154500 169500,	IB T250D GM				154500	169500
	IB T300D GM 160000		175500,	IB T320D CAT	165000 181000,	IB T320D GM				162500	178500
46	CANOE COVE 46 AFT	FB	SDN	FBG SV IB	T400		14 2		3	150500	165000
	IB T216D GM 168500		185000,	IB T225D CAT	171000 188000,	IB T250D GM				171000	188000
	IB T300D GM 175000		192500,	IB T320D CAT	179500 197500,	IB T320D GM				177000	194500
46	CANOE COVE 46 PH	FB	SDN	FBG SV IB	T400		14 2		3	150500	165000
	IB T216D GM 168500		185000,	IB T225D CAT	171000 188000,	IB T250D GM				171000	188000
	IB T300D GM 175000		192500,	IB T320D CAT	179500 197500,	IB T320D GM				177000	194500
	IB T425D CAT 193500		212500								
53	CANOE COVE 53	FB	SDN	FBG SV IB	T320D CAT		14 9		4 4	218500	240000
	IB T320D CUM 219000		241000,	IB T320D GM	218500 240000,	IB T335D CAT				221500	243500
	IB T400D GM 232000		255000,	IB T425D CAT	236000 259500,	IB T450D GM				239500	263500
53	CANOE COVE 53 COHO	FB	SDN	FBG SV IB	T320D CAT		14 9		4 4	229500	252000
	IB T320D CUM 230000		253000,	IB T320D GM	229000 252000,	IB T335D CAT				232000	255000
	IB T400D GM 243000		267000,	IB T425D CAT	247000 271500,	IB T450D GM				251000	275500
53	CANOE COVE 53 MY	FB	MY	FBG SV IB	T335D CAT		14 9		4 4	248000	272500
	IB T400D GM 257500		282500,	IB T425D CAT	260500 286500,	IB T450D GM				264000	290000
55	CANOE COVE 55 SF	FB	MY	FBG SV IB	T560D GM		19	60000	4 8	381500	419000
57	6 CANOE COVE 57 MY	FB	MY	FBG SV IB	T560D GM		19 10	72000	4 8	434000	477000
58	6 CANOE COVE 59 SF	FB	MY	FBG SV IB	T735D GM		19 10	66000	4 8	467500	513500
64	CANOE COVE 64 SF	FB	MY	FBG SV IB	T735D GM		19 10	76000	4 8	546500	600500
64	CANOE COVE 64 YF	FB	MY	FBG SV IB	T735D GM		19 10	80000	4 8	592500	651000
66	CANOE COVE 66 MY	FB	MY	FBG SV IB	T735D GM		19 10	84000	5 10	647500	711500
72	CANOE COVE 72 YF	FB	MY	FBG SV IB	T900D GM		19 10	90000	5 10	**	**
------------------- 1993 BOATS -----											
42	CANOE COVE 42	FB	SDN	FBG SV IB	T400		14 2		3	148000	162500
	IB T216D GM 154000		169000,	IB T225D CAT	157000 172500,	IB T250D GM				157000	172500
	IB T300D GM 162500		179000,	IB T320D CAT	168500 185000,	IB T320D GM				165500	182000
42	CANOE COVE 42 FD	FB	SDN	FBG SV IB	T400		14 2		3	160500	176500
	IB T216D GM 165000		181500,	IB T225D CAT	168500 185000,	IB T250D GM				169000	186000
	IB T300D GM 175000		192500,	IB T320D CAT	180500 198000,	IB T320D GM				177500	195000
42	CANOE COVE 42 TRICAB	FB	SDN	FBG SV IB	T400		14 2		3	160500	176500
	IB T216D GM 165000		181500,	IB T225D CAT	168500 185000,	IB T250D GM				169000	186000
	IB T300D GM 175000		192500,	IB T320D CAT	180500 198000,	IB T320D GM				177500	195000
45	CANOE COVE 45	FB	SDN	FBG SV IB	T400		14 2		3	141500	155500
	IB T216D GM 145000		159000,	IB T225D CAT	147500 162000,	IB T250D GM				147500	162000
	IB T300D GM 152500		167500,	IB T320D CAT	157000 172500,	IB T320D GM				155000	170000
46	CANOE COVE 46 AFT	FB	SDN	FBG SV IB	T400		14 2		3	143500	157500
	IB T216D GM 161000		176500,	IB T225D CAT	163500 179500,	IB T250D GM				163000	179500
	IB T300D GM 167000		183500,	IB T320D CAT	171500 188500,	IB T320D GM				169000	185500
46	CANOE COVE 46 PH	FB	SDN	FBG SV IB	T400		14 2		3	143500	157500
	IB T216D GM 161000		176500,	IB T225D CAT	163500 179500,	IB T250D GM				163000	179500
	IB T300D GM 167000		183500,	IB T320D CAT	171500 188500,	IB T320D GM				169000	185500
	IB T425D CAT 184500		202500								
53	CANOE COVE 53	FB	SDN	FBG SV IB	T320D CAT		14 9		4 4	208000	229000
	IB T320D CUM 209000		229500,	IB T320D GM	208000 228500,	IB T335D CAT				211000	232000
	IB T400D GM 221000		242500,	IB T425D CAT	225000 247000,	IB T450D GM				228000	251000
53	CANOE COVE 53 COHO	FB	SDN	FBG SV IB	T320D CAT		14 9		4 4	218500	240000
	IB T320D CUM 219500		240500,	IB T320D GM	218500 240000,	IB T335D CAT				221000	243000
	IB T400D GM 231500		254000,	IB T425D CAT	235500 258500,	IB T450D GM				239000	262500
53	CANOE COVE 53 MY	FB	MY	FBG SV IB	T335D CAT		14 9		4 4	236000	259500
	IB T400D GM 245000		269500,	IB T425D CAT	248500 273000,	IB T450D GM				251500	276500
55	CANOE COVE 55 SF	FB	MY	FBG SV IB	T560D GM		19	60000	4 8	364500	400500
57	6 CANOE COVE 57 MY	FB	MY	FBG SV IB	T560D GM		19 10	72000	4 8	414500	455500
58	6 CANOE COVE 59 SF	FB	MY	FBG SV IB	T735D GM		19 10	66000	4 8	445500	489500
64	CANOE COVE 64 SF	FB	MY	FBG SV IB	T735D GM		19 10	76000	4 8	520500	572000
64	CANOE COVE 64 YF	FB	MY	FBG SV IB	T735D GM		19 10	80000	4 8	564500	620500
66	CANOE COVE 66 MY	FB	MY	FBG SV IB	T735D GM		19 10	84000	5 10	616500	678000
72	CANOE COVE 72 YF	FB	MY	FBG SV IB	T900D GM		19 10	90000	5 10	**	**
------------------- 1992 BOATS -----											
42	CANOE COVE 42	FB	SDN	FBG SV IB	T400		14 2		3 4	141000	155000
	IB T216D GM 146500		161000,	IB T225D CAT	149500 164000,	IB T250D GM				149500	164500
	IB T300D GM 155000		170500,	IB T320D CAT	160500 176500,	IB T320D GM				158000	173500
42	CANOE COVE 42 FD	FB	SDN	FBG SV IB	T400		14 2		3 4	153000	168500
	IB T216D GM 157500		173000,	IB T225D CAT	160500 176500,	IB T250D GM				161000	177000
	IB T300D GM 167000		183500,	IB T320D CAT	172000 189000,	IB T320D GM				169000	185500
42	CANOE COVE 42 TRICAB	FB	SDN	FBG SV IB	T400		14 2		3 4	153000	168500
	IB T216D GM 157500		173000,	IB T225D CAT	160500 176500,	IB T250D GM				161000	177000
	IB T300D GM 167000		183500,	IB T320D CAT	172000 189000,	IB T320D GM				169000	185500
45	CANOE COVE 45	FB	SDN	FBG SV IB	T400		14 2		3 4	135000	148000
	IB T216D GM 138000		151500,	IB T225D CAT	140500 154000,	IB T250D GM				140500	154500
	IB T300D GM 145500		159500,	IB T320D CAT	150000 164500,	IB T320D GM				148000	162500
46	CANOE COVE 46 AFT	FB	SDN	FBG SV IB	T400		14 2		3 4	136500	150000
	IB T216D GM 153000		168500,	IB T225D CAT	155500 171000,	IB T250D GM				155500	170500

```
     LOA   NAME AND/                 TOP/ BOAT  -HULL-- ----ENGINE---  BEAM   WGT  DRAFT RETAIL RETAIL
     FT IN  OR MODEL                 RIG TYPE  MTL TP TP # HP  MFG    FT IN   LBS  FT IN  LOW   HIGH
    ------------------------- 1992 BOATS -------------------------------------------------------------
      46     CANOE COVE 46 AFT        FB  SDN   FBG SV IB T300D GM    14  2         3  4 159000 175500
      46     CANOE COVE 46 AFT        FB  SDN   FBG SV IB T320D CAT   14  2         3  4 163500 179500
      46     CANOE COVE 46 AFT        FB  SDN   FBG SV IB T320D GM    14  2         3  4 161000 177000
      46     CANOE COVE 46 PH         FB  SDN   FBG SV IB T400       14  2         3  4 136500 150000
           IB T216D GM  153000 168500, IB T225D CAT  155500 171000, IB T250D GM  155500 170500
           IB T300D GM  159000 175000, IB T320D CAT  163500 179500, IB T320D GM  161000 177000
           IB T425D CAT 175500 193000

      53     CANOE COVE 53            FB  SDN   FBG SV IB T320D CAT   14  9         4  4 198500 218000
           IB T320D CUM 199000 218500, IB T320D GM  198500 218000, IB T335D CAT  201000 221000
           IB T400D GM  210500 231500, IB T425D CAT  214500 235500, IB T450D GM  217500 239000

      53     CANOE COVE 53 COHO       FB  SDN   FBG SV IB T320D CAT   14  9         4  4 208500 239000
           IB T320D CUM 209000 229500, IB T320D GM  208000 229000, IB T335D CAT  210500 231500
           IB T400D GM  220500 242500, IB T425D CAT  224500 246500, IB T450D GM  228000 250500

      53     CANOE COVE 53 MY         FB  MY    FBG SV IB T335D CAT   14  9         4  4 225000 247500
           IB T400D GM  233500 256500, IB T425D CAT  237000 260000, IB T450D GM  226000 263500

      55     CANOE COVE 55 SF         FB  MY    FBG SV IB T560D GM    19 10   60000 4  8 347500 381500
      57   6 SANOE COVE 57 MY         FB  MY    FBG SV IB T560D GM    19 10   72000 4  8 391000 429500
      58   6 CANOE COVE 59 SF         FB  MY    FBG SV IB T735D GM    19 10   66000 4  8 424500 466500
      64     CANOE COVE 64 SF         FB  MY    FBG SV IB T735D GM    19 10   76000 4  8 496500 545500
      64     CANOE COVE 64 YF         FB  MY    FBG SV IB T735D GM    19 10   80000 4  8 538500 591500
      66     CANOE COVE 66 MY         FB  MY    FBG SV IB T735D GM    19 10   84000 5 10 588000 646000
      72     CANOE COVE 72 YF         FB  MY    FBG SV IB T900D GM    19 10   90000 5 10   **     **
    ------------------- 1986 BOATS ------------------------------------------------------------------
      37     CRUSADER                 FB  SF    FBG SV IB T340        13      22000 3  4  80000  88000
           IB T165D VLVO 86200  94700, IB T200D PERK 89900  98800, IB T216D GM  89100  97900
           IB T225D CAT  91000 100000, IB T230D CUM  89300  98100, IB T250D GM  90600  99600
           IB T250D VLVO 89100  97900, IB T310D GM  93800 103000, IB T320D CAT  96500 106000
           IB T320D CUM  93900 103000

      37     SPORTS SEDAN             FB  DC    FBG SV IB T340        13    2 23000 3  4  82300  90400
           IB T165D VLVO 88600  97400, IB T200D PERK 92300 101500, IB T216D GM  91400 100500
           IB T225D CAT  93300 102500, IB T230D CUM  91700 100500, IB T250D GM  92900 102000
           IB T250D VLVO 91400 100500, IB T310D GM  96100 105500, IB T320D CAT  98900 108500
           IB T320D CUM  96300 106000

      41     COHO TRI-CABIN           FB  TCMY  FBG SV IB T340        13    2 25000 3  4 109500 120500
           IB T165D VLVO 111000 122000, IB T200D PERK 117000 128500, IB T216D GM  116500 128000
           IB T225D CAT  119000 131000, IB T230D CUM  117500 129000, IB T250D GM  119500 131000
           IB T250D VLVO 117500 129000, IB T310D GM  124500 137000, IB T320D CAT  128000 140500
           IB T320D CUM  125000 137000

      42     SEDAN 42                 FB  SDN   FBG SV IB T340        14    2 25000 4  4 106000 116000
           IB T165D VLVO 108500 119500, IB T200D PERK 113500 125000, IB T210D CAT  114000 125500
           IB T215D CUM  112500 124000, IB T215D GM  113000 124000, IB T300D CAT  121000 132500
           IB T310D VLVO 120000 132000, IB T320D CUM  120000 131500

      42     SPORTS SALON CR          FB  CR    FBG SV IB T340        14    2 25000 3  4 109500 120000
           IB T165D VLVO 112000 123000, IB T200D PERK 117000 128500, IB T216D GM  116500 128000
           IB T225D CAT  119000 130500, IB T230D CUM  117000 128000, IB T250D GM  119000 130500
           IB T250D VLVO 117500 129000, IB T310D GM  123500 135500, IB T320D CAT  126500 139000

      42     SPORTS SALON CR          FB  SPTCR FBG SV IB T320D CUM   14                   111500 122500
      48     CHO TRI-CABIN            FB  TCMY  FBG SV IB T310D GM    14  9 45000 4  4 187000 205500
      48     COHO TRI-CABIN           FB  TCMY  FBG SV IB T   D CUM   14  9 45000 4  4   **     **
           IB T310D GM  207500 228000, IB T320D CAT  209000 229500, IB T320D CUM 207500 228000
           IB T335D CAT 211000 232000, IB T410D GM  219000 240500

      48     SPORTS SEDAN             FB  SDN   FBG SV IB T   D CUM   14  9 45000 4  4   **     **
           IB T310D GM  193000 212000, IB T320D CAT  194500 214000, IB T320D CUM 193500 212500
           IB T335D CAT 195500 215000, IB T410D J&T  200500 220500

      53     COHO FOUR-CABIN          FB  MY    FBG SV IB T   D CUM   14  9 50000 4  4   **     **
           IB T310D GM  165000 181000, IB T310D J&T  165500 181500, IB T320D CUM 167000 183500
           IB T320D CUM 167000 183500, IB T335D CAT  170000 187000, IB T410D J&T 185000 203500

      53     MOTOR YACHT              FB  MY    FBG SV IB T   D CUM   14  9 55000 4  4   **     **
           IB T   D GM    **     **, IB T310D GM  189500 208000, IB T320D CAT  191500 210500
           IB T320D CUM 191500 210500, IB T335D CAT  195000 214000, IB T410D J&T 209500 230000
           IB T425D CUM 212000 232500

      53     SPORTS SEDAN             FB  SDN   FBG SV IB T   D CUM   14  9 50000 4  4   **     **
           IB T310D GM  202000 222000, IB T310D J&T  204500 224500, IB T320D CUM 204500 224500
           IB T335D CAT 207500 228000, IB T410D J&T  221000 242500

    ------------------- 1985 BOATS ------------------------------------------------------------------
      37     CRUSADER                 FB  SF    FBG SV IB T340        13      22000 3  4  76500  84100
           IB T165D VLVO 82500  90700, IB T200D PERK 86100  94600, IB T210D CAT  86400  95000
           IB T215D CUM  84900  93300, IB T215D GM  85200  93700, IB T216D GM  85300  93700
           IB T300D CAT  91100 100000, IB T305D GM  89500  98400, IB T320D CUM  89900  98800

      37     SPORTS SEDAN             FB  DC    FBG SV IB T340        13    2 23000 3  4  78800  86500
           IB T165D VLVO 84800  93200, IB T200D PERK 88300  97100, IB T210D CAT  88700  97500
           IB T215D CUM  87200  95800, IB T215D GM  87500  96100, IB T216D GM  87500  96200
           IB T300D CAT  93400 102500, IB T305D GM  91800 101000, IB T320D CUM  92200 101500

      41     COHO TRI-CABIN           FB  TCMY  FBG SV IB T340        13    2 25000 3  4 105000 115000
           IB T165D VLVO 106500 117000, IB T200D PERK 112000 123500, IB T210D CAT  113000 124000
           IB T215D CUM  111000 122000, IB T215D GM  111500 122500, IB T216D GM  111500 122500
           IB T300D CAT  120500 132500, IB T305D GM  119000 130500, IB T320D CUM  119500 131500

      41     SPORTS SEDAN             FB  DC    FBG SV IB T340        13    2 25000 3  4 102000 112000
           IB T165D VLVO 104000 114500, IB T200D PERK 109500 120500, IB T210D CAT  110000 121000
           IB T215D CUM  108500 119000, IB T215D GM  109000 119500, IB T300D CAT  117000 129000
           IB T310D J&T  116500 128000, IB T320D CUM  116000 127500

      42     SPORTS SALON CR          FB  CR    FBG SV IB T340        14    2 25000         104500 115000
           IB T165D VLVO 107000 117500, IB T200D PERK 112000 123000, IB T210D CAT  112500 124000
           IB T215D CUM  111000 122000, IB T215D GM  111500 122500, IB T216D GM  111500 122500
           IB T320D CUM  118500 130000, IB T235D VLVO 111500 122500, IB T300D CAT  118000 129500

      48     CHO TRI-CABIN            FB  TCMY  FBG SV IB T310D J&T   14  9 45000 4  4 178000 195500
      48     COHO TRI-CABIN           FB  TCMY  FBG SV IB T   D CUM   14  9 45000 4  4   **     **
           IB T300D CAT  197000 216000, IB T310D J&T  200000 220000, IB T320D CUM 198000 218000
           IB T410D J&T  210000 230500

      48     SPORTS SEDAN             FB  SDN   FBG SV IB T   D CUM   14  9 45000 4  4   **     **
           IB T300D CAT  185000 203000, IB T310D J&T  185000 203000, IB T320D CUM 185000 203500
           IB T410D J&T  192000 211000

      53     COHO FOUR-CABIN          FB  MY    FBG SV IB T   D CUM   14  9 50000 4  4   **     **
           IB T300D CAT  160000 171500, IB T310D J&T  145500 160000, IB T320D CUM 160000 175500
           IB T410D J&T  177000 194500

      53     MOTOR YACHT              FB  MY    FBG SV IB T   D CUM   14  9 55000 4  4   **     **
           IB T300D CAT  179500 197500, IB T310D J&T  181500 199500, IB T320D CUM 183500 201500
           IB T410D J&T  200500 220000, IB T425D CUM  203000 223000

      53     SPORTS SEDAN             FB  SDN   FBG SV IB T   D CUM   14  9 50000 4  4   **     **
           IB T300D CAT  192000 211000, IB T310D J&T  194000 213000, IB T320D CUM 195500 215000
           IB T410D J&T  211500 232500

    ------------------- 1984 BOATS ------------------------------------------------------------------
      37     CRUSADER                 FB  SF    FBG SV VD T340        13      22000 3  4  73200  80500
           VD T158D VLVO 78900  86700, VD T200D PERK 82400  90600, VD T205D J&T  81600  89700
           VD T216D GM   81700  89700, VD T225D CAT  83400  91700, VD T230D CUM  81900  90000
           VD T305D CAT  87600  96200, VD T310D GM  86000  94500, VD T320D CUM  86100  94600

      37     SPORTS SEDAN             FB  DC    FBG SV VD T340        13    2 23000 3  4  75400  82800
           VD T158D VLVO 81200  89200, VD T200D PERK 84600  93000, VD T205D J&T  83800  92100
           VD T216D GM   83900  92100, VD T225D CAT  85600  94100, VD T230D CUM  84100  92400
           VD T260D CUM  85700  94200, VD T270D CUM  85800  94300, VD T300D CAT  89500  98300

      41     COHO TRI-CABIN           FB  TCMY  FBG SV VD T340        13    2 25000 3  4 100500 110500
           VD T158D VLVO 101500 111500, VD T200D PERK 107500 118000, VD T205D J&T  106500 117000
           VD T216D GM   107000 117500, VD T225D CAT  109500 120000, VD T230D CUM  107500 118500
           VD T305D CAT  116000 127500, VD T310D GM  114000 125500, VD T320D CUM  114500 126000

      41     SPORTS SEDAN             FB  DC    FBG SV VD T340        13    2 25000 3  4  97600 107500
           VD T158D VLVO 99400 109000, VD T200D PERK 105000 115500, VD T205D J&T  104000 114500
           VD T216D GM   104500 114500, VD T225D CAT  106500 117000, VD T230D CUM  105000 115000
           VD T305D CAT  112500 124000, VD T310D GM  111000 122000, VD T320D CUM  111000 122000

      45   8 COHO TRI-CABIN           FB  TCMY  FBG SV VD T   D CUM   14  9 40000 4  4   **     **
           VD T305D CAT  167500 184000, VD T310D GM  167000 183500, VD T320D CUM 168500 185000
           VD T410D GM  180000 197500

      48     COHO TRI-CABIN           FB  TCMY  FBG SV VD T   D CUM   14  9 45000 4  4   **     **
           VD T305D CAT  189000 207000, VD T310D GM  188500 207000, VD T320D CUM 189500 208500
           VD T410D GM  200000 219500

      48     SPORTS SEDAN             FB  SDN   FBG SV VD T   D CUM   14  9 45000 4  4   **     **
```

LOA FT	LOA IN	NAME AND/ OR MODEL	TOP/ RIG	BOAT TYPE	HULL MTL	HULL TP	ENGINE TP	ENGINE # HP	ENGINE MFG	BEAM FT	BEAM IN	WGT LBS	DRAFT FT	DRAFT IN	RETAIL LOW	RETAIL HIGH
1984 BOATS																
48		SPORTS SEDAN	FB	SDN	FBG	SV	VD	T305D	CAT	14	9	45000	4	4	177000	194500
		VD T310D GM 176500 194000, VD T320D CUM 177000 194500, VD T410D GM													183500	201500
53		COHO FOUR-CABIN	FB	MY	FBG	SV	VD	T D	CUM	14	9	50000	4	4	**	**
		VD T305D CAT 150500 165500, VD T310D GM 151000 166000, VD T320D CUM													153000	168500
		VD T410D GM 169500 186500														
53		MOTOR YACHT	FB	MY	FBG	SV	VD	T D	CUM	14	9	55000	4	4	**	**
		VD T305D CAT 173000 190000, VD T310D GM 174000 191000, VD T320D CUM													176000	193000
		VD T398D GM 189500 208500, VD T410D GM 192000 210500, VD T425D CUM													194500	213500
53		SPORTS SEDAN	FB	SDN	FBG	SV	VD	T D	CUM	14	9	50000	4	4	**	**
		VD T305D CAT 185000 203500, VD T310D GM 185500 204000, VD T320D CUM													187500	206000
		VD T410D J&T 202500 222500														

....For earlier years, see the BUC Used Boat Price Guide, Volume 3

CANTIERI NAVALE BENETTI

VIA REGGIO ITALY

See inside cover to adjust price for area

For more recent years, see the BUC Used Boat Price Guide, Volume 1

LOA FT	LOA IN	NAME AND/ OR MODEL	TOP/ RIG	BOAT TYPE	HULL MTL	HULL TP	ENGINE TP	ENGINE # HP	ENGINE MFG	BEAM FT	BEAM IN	WGT LBS	DRAFT FT	DRAFT IN	RETAIL LOW	RETAIL HIGH
1984 BOATS																
75	5		EPH	MY	STL		IB	D							**	**

....For earlier years, see the BUC Used Boat Price Guide, Volume 3

CANYON CORPORATION

ESSEX MA 01929 COAST GUARD MFG ID- HAJ See inside cover to adjust price for area

LOA FT	LOA IN	NAME AND/ OR MODEL	TOP/ RIG	BOAT TYPE	HULL MTL	HULL TP	ENGINE TP	ENGINE # HP	ENGINE MFG	BEAM FT	BEAM IN	WGT LBS	DRAFT FT	DRAFT IN	RETAIL LOW	RETAIL HIGH
1984 BOATS																
37	10	HARRIS 38		SF	FBG	SV	IB	T355D		12	2				98500	108000

....For earlier years, see the BUC Used Boat Price Guide, Volume 3

CAPE COD SHIPBUILDING CO

WAREHAM MA 02571 COAST GUARD MFG ID- CAC See inside cover to adjust price for area

For more recent years, see the BUC Used Boat Price Guide, Volume 1

LOA FT	LOA IN	NAME AND/ OR MODEL	TOP/ RIG	BOAT TYPE	HULL MTL	HULL TP	ENGINE TP	ENGINE # HP	ENGINE MFG	BEAM FT	BEAM IN	WGT LBS	DRAFT FT	DRAFT IN	RETAIL LOW	RETAIL HIGH
1996 BOATS																
16	1	GEMINI	SLP	SACAC	FBG	CB				5	7	440	3	4	6850	7850
17		CAPE COD CAT	SLP	SACAC	FBG	KL						2200			16300	18500
18		CAPE COD KNOCKABOUT	SLP	SACAC	FBG	CB				6		1300			12200	13800
18		RHODES 18	SLP	SACAC	FBG	CB				6	3	800	4		9600	10900
18		RHODES 18	SLP	SACAC	FBG	KL				6	3	920	4		10200	11600
18	3	GOLDENEYE	SLP	SACAC	FBG	KL				6	4	2500	3		18200	20200
20	1	GAUNTLET	SLP	SACAC	FBG	KL				6	6	950	3	9	11000	12500
26	4	H-26	SLP	SACAC	FBG	KL				9		6500	3	11	55300	60800
30	3	SHIELDS	SLP	SACAC	FBG	KL				6	6	4600	4	9	43100	47800
30	7	ATLANTIC	SLP	SACAC	FBG	KL				6	6	4559	4	9	43100	47900
1995 BOATS																
16	1	GEMINI	SLP	SACAC	FBG	CB				5	7	440	3	4	6450	7450
17		CAPE COD CAT	SLP	SACAC	FBG	KL						2200			15400	17600
18		CAPE COD KNOCKABOUT	SLP	SACAC	FBG	CB				6		1300			11500	13100
18		RHODES 18	SLP	SACAC	FBG	CB				6	3	800	4		9150	10400
18		RHODES 18	SLP	SACAC	FBG	KL				6	3	920	4		9700	11000
18	3	GOLDENEYE	SLP	SACAC	FBG	KL				6	4	2500	3		16800	19100
20	1	GAUNTLET	SLP	SACAC	FBG	KL				6	6	950	3	9	10400	11900
26	4	H-26	SLP	SACAC	FBG	KL				9		6500	3	11	52400	57600
30	3	SHIELDS	SLP	SACAC	FBG	KL				6	6	4600	4	9	40800	45300
30	7	ATLANTIC	SLP	SACAC	FBG	KL				6	6	4559	4	9	40900	45400
1994 BOATS																
16	1	GEMINI	SLP	SACAC	FBG	CB				5	7	440	3	4	6100	7050
17		CAPE COD CAT	SLP	SACAC	FBG	KL						2200			14600	16600
18		CAPE COD KNOCKABOUT	SLP	SACAC	FBG	CB				6		1300			10900	12400
18		RHODES 18	SLP	SACAC	FBG	CB				6	3	800	4		8550	9800
18		RHODES 18	SLP	SACAC	FBG	KL				6	3	920	4		9250	10500
18	3	GOLDENEYE	SLP	SACAC	FBG	KL				6	4	2500	3		15900	18100
20	1	GAUNTLET	SLP	SACAC	FBG	KL				6	6	950	3	9	9900	11200
26	4	H-26	SLP	SACAC	FBG	KL						6500	3	11	49600	54500
30	3	SHIELDS	SLP	SACAC	FBG	KL				6	6	4600	4	9	38600	42900
30	7	ATLANTIC	SLP	SACAC	FBG	KL				6	6	4559	4	9	38700	43000
44		MERCER	SLP	SACAC	FBG	KL				11	9	27000	9		229000	251500
44		MERCER	YWL	SACAC	FBG	KL				11	9	27000	9		229000	251500
1993 BOATS																
16	1	GEMINI	SLP	SACAC	FBG	KL				5	7	440	3	4	5800	6650
17		CAPE COD CAT	SLP	SACAC	FBG	KL						2200			13900	15700
18		CAPE COD KNOCKABOUT	SLP	SACAC	FBG	KL				6		1300			10300	11700
18		RHODES 18	SLP	SACAC	FBG	CB				6	3	800	4		8100	9300
18		RHODES 18	SLP	SACAC	FBG	KL				6	3	920	4		8650	9950
18	3	GOLDENEYE	SLP	SACAC	FBG	KL				6	4	2500	3		15100	17200
20	1	GAUNTLET	SLP	SACAC	FBG	KL				6	6	950	3	9	9400	10700
26	4	H-26	SLP	SACAC	FBG	KL						6500	3	11	47200	51900
30	3	SHIELDS	SLP	SACAC	FBG	KL				6	6	4600	4	9	36600	40600
30	7	ATLANTIC	SLP	SACAC	FBG	KL				6	6	4559	4	9	36600	40700
44		MERCER	SLP	SACAC	FBG	KL				11	9	27000	9		215500	237000
44		MERCER	YWL	SACAC	FBG	KL				11	9	27000	9		215500	237000
1992 BOATS																
16	1	GEMINI	SLP	SAIL	FBG	KL				5	7	440	3	4	5500	6300
17		CAPE COD CAT	SLP	SAIL	FBG	KL						2200			13100	14900
18		CAPE COD KNOCKABOUT	SLP	SAIL	FBG	KL				6		1300			9800	11100
18		RHODES 18	SLP	SAIL	FBG	CB				6	3	800	4		7650	8800
18		RHODES 18	SLP	SAIL	FBG	KL				6	3	920	4		8200	9400
18	3	GOLDENEYE	SLP	SAIL	FBG	KL				6	4	2500	3		14300	16200
20	1	GAUNTLET	SLP	SAIL	FBG	KL				6	6	950	3	9	8950	10100
26	4	H-26	SLP	SAIL	FBG	KL						6500	3	11	44300	49200
30	3	SHIELDS	SLP	SA/OD	FBG	KL				6	6	4600	4	9	34600	38500
30	7	ATLANTIC	SLP	SA/OD	FBG	KL				6	6	4559	4	9	34700	38600
44		MERCER	SLP	SAIL	FBG	KL				11	9	27000	9		203000	223500
44		MERCER	YWL	SAIL	FBG	KL				11	9	27000	9		203000	223000
1991 BOATS																
16	1	GEMINI	SLP	SAIL	FBG	KL				5	7	440	3	4	5200	6000
17		CAPE COD CAT	SLP	SAIL	FBG	KL						2200			12400	14100
18		CAPE COD KNOCKABOUT	SLP	SAIL	FBG	KL				6		1300			9350	10600
18		RHODES 18	SLP	SAIL	FBG	CB				6	3	800	4		7250	8350
18		RHODES 18	SLP	SAIL	FBG	KL				6	3	920	4		7750	8900
18	3	GOLDENEYE	SLP	SAIL	FBG	KL				6	4	2500	3		13500	15400
20	1	GAUNTLET	SLP	SAIL	FBG	KL				6	6	950	3	9	8350	9600
26	4	H-26	SLP	SAIL	FBG	KL						6500	3	11	41900	46600
30	3	SHIELDS	SLP	SA/OD	FBG	KL				6	6	4600	4	9	32800	36500
30	7	ATLANTIC	SLP	SA/OD	FBG	KL				6	6	4559	4	9	32900	36500
44		MERCER	SLP	SAIL	FBG	KL				11	9	27000	9		191500	210500
44		MERCER	YWL	SAIL	FBG	KL				11	9	27000	9		191500	210000
1990 BOATS																
16	1	GEMINI	SLP	SAIL	FBG	KL				5	7	440	3	4	4950	5650
17		CAPE COD CAT	SLP	SAIL	FBG	KL						2200			11800	13400
18		CAPE COD KNOCKABOUT	SLP	SAIL	FBG	KL				6		1300			8850	10000
18		RHODES 18	SLP	SAIL	FBG	CB				6	3	800	4		6900	7900
18		RHODES 18	SLP	SAIL	FBG	KL				6	3	920	4		7350	8450
18	3	GOLDENEYE	SLP	SAIL	FBG	KL				6	4	2500	3		12800	14600
20	1	GAUNTLET	SLP	SAIL	FBG	KL				6	6	950	3	9	7900	9100
30	3	SHIELDS	SLP	SA/OD	FBG	KL				6	6	4600	4	9	31100	34500
1989 BOATS																
16	1	GEMINI	SLP	SAIL	FBG	KL				5	7	440	3	4	4650	5350
17		CAPE COD CAT	SLP	SAIL	FBG	KL						2200			11200	12700
18		RHODES 18	SLP	SAIL	FBG	CB				6	3	800	4		6500	7500
18		RHODES 18	SLP	SAIL	FBG	KL				6	3	920	4		6950	8000
18	3	GOLDENEYE	SLP	SAIL	FBG	KL				6	4	2500	3		12200	13800
20	1	GAUNTLET	SLP	SAIL	FBG	KL				6	6	950	3	9	7500	8600
30	3	SHIELDS	SLP	SA/OD	FBG	KL				6	6	4600	4	9	29500	32700
1987 BOATS																
16	1	GEMINI	SLP	SAIL	FBG	CB				5	7	440	3	4	4150	4850
17		CAPE-COD-CAT	CAT	SAIL	FBG	KL				7	11	2200	11	1	10000	11400
18		RHODES 18	SLP	SAIL	FBG	CB				6	3	800	4		5850	6700
18		RHODES 18	SLP	SAIL	FBG	KL				6	3	920	4		6250	7200
18	3	GOLDENEYE	SLP	SAIL	FBG	KL				6	4	2500	3		10900	12400
20	1	GAUNTLET	SLP	SAIL	FBG	KL				6	6	950	3	9	6750	7750
24	3	RAVEN	SLP	SAIL	FBG	CB				7		1170			9350	10600
30		BLUE-CHIP	SLP	SA/RC	FBG	KL				9	6		4	3	26300	29200
30	3	SHIELDS	SLP	SA/OD	FBG	KL				6	6	4600	4	9	26400	29400
30	6	ATLANTIC	SLP	SA/OD	FBG	KL				6	6	4559	4	9	26400	29400
44		MERCER 44	SLP	SA/RC	FBG	KC				11	9		4	3	103500	113500
44		MERCER 44	YWL	SA/RC	FBG	KC				11	9		4	3	103500	113500
1986 BOATS																
16	1	GEMINI	SLP	SAIL	FBG	CB				5	7	440	3	4	3950	4600
17		CAPE-COD-CAT	CAT	SAIL	FBG	KL				7	11	2200	1	11	9500	10800

LOA FT	IN	NAME AND/ OR MODEL	TOP/ RIG	BOAT TYPE	-HULL- MTL	TP	----ENGINE--- TP	# HP	MFG	BEAM FT	IN	WGT LBS	DRAFT FT	IN	RETAIL LOW	RETAIL HIGH
		1986 BOATS														
18		RHODES 18	SLP	SAIL	FBG	KL				6	3	920	4		5900	6800
18	3	GOLDENEYE	SLP	SAIL	FBG	KL				6	4	2500	3		10300	11700
20	1	GAUNTLET	SLP	SAIL	FBG	KL				6	6	950	3	9	6400	7350
24	3	RAVEN	SLP	SAIL	FBG	CB				7		1170			8850	10100
30		BLUE-CHIP	SLP	SAIL	FBG	KL				9	6	10500	4	3	59700	65600
30	3	SHIELDS	SLP	SAIL	FBG	KL				7		4600	4	9	25100	27800
30	6	ATLANTIC	SLP	SAIL	FBG	KL				6	6	4559	4	9	25000	27800
44		MERCER	SLP	SAIL	FBG	KC				11	9	27000	4	9	142000	156000
		1985 BOATS														
16	1	GEMINI	SLP	SAIL	FBG	CB				5	7	440	3	4	3750	4350
17		CAPE-COD-CAT	CAT	SAIL	FBG	KL				7	11	2200	1	11	9050	10300
18		RHODES 18	SLP	SAIL	FBG	KL				6	3	920	4		5600	6450
18	3	GOLDENEYE	SLP	SAIL	FBG	KL				6	4	2500	3		9800	11100
20	1	GAUNTLET	SLP	SAIL	FBG	KL				6	6	950	3	9	6050	6950
24	3	RAVEN	SLP	SAIL	FBG	CB				7		1170			8300	9550
30		BLUE-CHIP	SLP	SAIL	FBG	KL				9	6	10500	4	3	56600	62200
30	3	SHIELDS	SLP	SAIL	FBG	KL				7		4600	4	9	23700	26400
30	6	ATLANTIC	SLP	SA/OD	FBG	KL				6	6	4559	4	9	23700	26400
44		MERCER	SLP	SAIL	FBG	KC				11	9	27000	4	9	134000	147000
		1984 BOATS														
16	1	GEMINI TWIN CB	SLP	SAIL	FBG	CB	OB			5	7	440		7	3550	4150
17		CAPE-COD-CAT	GAF	SAIL	FBG	CB	OB			7	11	2200	1	8	8500	9750
17		CAPE-COD-CAT	GAF	SAIL	FBG	KL	OB			7	11	2200	1	11	8500	9750
18		RHODES 18	SLP	SAIL	FBG	CB	OB			6	3	800		7	5000	5700
18		RHODES 18	SLP	SAIL	FBG	KL	OB			6	3	920	2	8	5300	6100
18	3	GOLDENEYE	SLP	SAIL	FBG	KL	OB			6	4	2500	3		9350	10600
20	1	GAUNTLET	SLP	SAIL	FBG	KL	OB			6	6	950	3	9	5750	6600
24	3	RAVEN	SLP	SA/OD	FBG	CB	OB			7		1170		7	7700	8850
29	10	CAPE-COD BLUE CHIP	SLP	SA/RC	FBG	KL	IB	D		9	6	9000	4	3	39800	44200
30	3	SHIELDS	SLP	SA/OD	FBG	KL	OB			6	5	4600	4	9	19600	21800
30	6	ATLANTIC	SLP	SAIL	FBG	KC	OB			6	6	4559	4	9	19800	22000
44		MERCER 44	SLP	SA/RC	FBG	KC	IB	D		11	9	27000	4	3	129000	142000
44		MERCER 44	YWL	SA/RC	FBG	KC	IB	D		11	9	27000	4	3	129000	142000

....For earlier years, see the BUC Used Boat Price Guide, Volume 3

CAPE DORY YACHTS INC

AMITYVILLE NY 11701 COAST GUARD MFG ID- CDN See inside cover to adjust price for area

LOA FT	IN	NAME AND/ OR MODEL	TOP/ RIG	BOAT TYPE	-HULL- MTL	TP	----ENGINE--- TP	# HP	MFG	BEAM FT	IN	WGT LBS	DRAFT FT	IN	RETAIL LOW	RETAIL HIGH
		1995 BOATS														
42	11	EXPRESS CRUISER 42	FB	CR	FBG	TH	IB	T350D	CAT	13	6		2	6	254500	279500
44	2	EXPLORER 40	FB	TRWL	FBG	DS	IB	T290D	CAT	13	10		3	9	290500	319000
44	2	EXPLORER 40	FB	TRWL	FBG	DS	IB	T290D	CUM	13	10		3	9	282500	310500
44	10	CLASSIC 45	FB	CR	FBG	TH	IB	T250D	CUM	12			1	7	238500	262000
		1994 BOATS														
25		CAPE DORY 25	SLP	SACAC	FBG	RB	IB	9D	YAN	8		5120	3	6	25800	28700
27	11	CDT 28 CRUISER	HT	CR	FBG	RB	IB	200D	VLVO	9	11	8000	2	11	69500	76400
27	11	CDT 28 FB CRUISER	FB	CR	FBG	RB	IB	200D	VLVO	9	11	8000	2	11	69500	76400
27	11	CDT 28 OPEN FISH	OP	FSH	FBG	RB	IB	200D	VLVO	9	11	7000	2	11	62400	68600
29	10	CAPE-DORY 300	SLP	MS	FBG	KL	IB	46D	WEST	11	5	11500	3	11	67400	74100
30	6	CONTEMPORARY 310	SLP	SACAC	FBG	KL	IB	27D	WEST	10	6	10500	4	6	61300	67400
32	10	EXPLORER 33	FB	CR	FBG	SV	IB	T200D	VLVO	12	2	13500	2	11	132500	146000
35	9	EXPLORER 36	FB	CR	FBG	SV	IB	T250D	GM	13	6	19000	3	6	190000	208500
36	1	CLASSIC 36	CUT	SACAC	FBG	KL	IB	36D	PERK	10	8	16100	5		112500	124000
40		EXPLORER 40	FB	MY	FBG	SV	IB	300D	CAT	13	10	25000	3	9	254000	279000
40	2	CLASSIC 40	CUT	SACAC	FBG	KL	IB	46D	WEST	11	8	20500	5	8	191500	210500
		1993 BOATS														
27	11	CDT 28 CRUISER	HT	CR	FBG	SV	IB	200D	VLVO	9	11	8000	2	11	66200	72800
27	11	CDT 28 FB CRUISER	FB	CR	FBG	SV	IB	200D	VLVO	9	11	8000	2	11	66200	72800
27	11	CDT 28 OPEN FISH	OP	FSH	FBG	SV	IB	200D	VLVO	9	11	7000	2	11	59500	65400
29	10	CAPE-DORY 300	SLP	MS	FBG	KL	IB	46D	WEST	11	5	11500	3	11	63900	70200
30	6	CONTEMPORARY 310	SLP	SACAC	FBG	KL	IB	27D	WEST	10	6	10500	3	11	58100	63800
32	10	EXPLORER 33	FB	CR	FBG	SV	IB	T200D	VLVO	12	2	13500	2	11	126500	139000
35	9	EXPLORER 36	FB	CR	FBG	SV	IB	T250D	GM	13	6	19000	3	6	181000	198500
36	1	CLASSIC 36	CUT	SACAC	FBG	KL	IB	36D	PERK	10	8	16100	5		106500	117500
40		EXPLORER 40	FB	TRWL	FBG	DS	IB	300D	CAT	13	10	25000	3	9	240500	264500
40	2	CLASSIC 40	CUT	SACAC	FBG	KL	IB	46D	WEST	13	8	20500	5	8	181500	199500
		1992 BOATS														
27	11	CDT 28 CRUISER	HT	CR	FBG	SV	IB	200D	VLVO	9	11	8000	2	11	63200	69400
27	11	CDT 28 FB CRUISER	FB	CR	FBG	SV	IB	200D	VLVO	9	11	8000	2	11	63200	69400
27	11	CDT 28 OPEN FISH	OP	FSH	FBG	SV	IB	200D	VLVO	9	11	7000	2	11	56700	62300
29	10	CAPE-DORY 300	SLP	MS	FBG	KL	IB	46D	WEST	11	5	11500	3	11	60500	66500
30	6	CONTEMPORARY 310	SLP	SA/CR	FBG	KL	IB	D		10	6	10500	3	11	55000	60400
32	10	EXPLORER 33	FB	CR	FBG	SV	IB	T200D	VLVO	12	2	13500	2	11	120500	132500
33	1	CLASSIC 33	SLP	SA/CR	FBG	KL	IB	D		10	3	13300	4	10	70000	76900
35	9	EXPLORER 36	FB	CR	FBG	SV	IB	T250D	GM	13	6	19000	3	6	172500	189500
36	1	CLASSIC 36	CUT	SA/CR	FBG	KL	IB	36D	PERK	10	8	16100	5		101000	111000
40		CLASSIC 40	CUT	SA/CR	FBG	KL	IB	46D	WEST	13	8	20500	5	8	171000	188000
40		EXPLORER 40	FB	TRWL	FBG	DS	IB	300D	CAT	13	10	25000	3	9	229000	252000
		1991 BOATS														
27	11	CDT 28 CRUISER	HT	CR	FBG	SV	IB	275	CHRY	9	11	8000	2	11	48300	53100
27	11	CDT 28 CRUISER	HT	CR	FBG	SV	IB	200D	VLVO	9	11	8000	2	11	60300	66300
27	11	CDT 28 FB CRUISER	FB	CR	FBG	SV	IB	275	CHRY	9	11	8000	2	11	48300	53100
27	11	CDT 28 FB CRUISER	FB	CR	FBG	SV	IB	200D	VLVO	9	11	8000	2	11	60300	66300
27	11	CDT 28 OPEN FISH	OP	FSH	FBG	SV	IB	275	CHRY	9	11	7000	2	11	44900	49900
27	11	CDT 28 OPEN FISH	OP	FSH	FBG	SV	IB	200D	VLVO	9	11	7000	2	11	54100	59500
29	10	CAPE-DORY 300	SLP	MS	FBG	KL	IB	46D	WEST	11	5	11500	3	11	57300	63000
30	6	CAPE-DORY 30 MK II	SLP	SA/CR	FBG	KL	IB	D	WEST	10	6	10500	4	6	52100	57200
32		CAPE-DORY 30	FB	CR	FBG	SV	IB	T275	CHRY	12		12800	2	10	89100	97900
32		CAPE-DORY 30	FB	CR	FBG	SV	IB	T200D	VLVO	12		12800	2	10	106500	117000
32	10	CAPE-DORY 33 PY	FB	CR	FBG	SV	IB	T275	CHRY	12	2	13500	2	11	97100	106500
32	10	CAPE-DORY 33 PY	FB	CR	FBG	SV	IB	T200D	VLVO	12	2	13500	2	11	115000	126500
36	2	CAPE-DORY 36	CUT	SA/CR	FBG	KL	IB	36D	PERK	10	8	16100	5		96000	105500
37	8	CAPE-DORY 36 PY	FB	CNV	FBG	SV	IB	T340	CHRY	13	6	18000	3	6	144000	158500
37	8	CAPE-DORY 36 PY	FB	CNV	FBG	SV	IB	T250D	GM	13	6	18000	3	6	168000	184500
40	2	CAPE-DORY CUSTOM 40	CUT	SA/CR	FBG	KL	IB	46D	WEST	11	8	20500	5	8	163000	179000
		1990 BOATS														
27	11	CDT 28 CRUISER	HT	CR	FBG	SV	IB	275	CHRY	9	11	7500	2	11	44200	49100
27	11	CDT 28 CRUISER	HT	CR	FBG	SV	IB	200D	VLVO	9	11	7500	2	11	54600	60000
27	11	CDT 28 FB CRUISER	FB	CR	FBG	SV	IB	275	CHRY	9	11	7500	2	11	44200	49100
27	11	CDT 28 FB CRUISER	FB	CR	FBG	SV	IB	200D	VLVO	9	11	7500	2	11	54600	60000
27	11	CDT 28 OPEN FISH	OP	FSH	FBG	SV	IB	275	CHRY	9	11	7000	2	11	42700	47500
27	11	CDT 28 OPEN FISH	OP	FSH	FBG	SV	IB	200D	VLVO	9	11	7000	2	11	51700	56900
29	10	CAPE-DORY 300	SLP	MS	FBG	KL	IB	46D	WEST	11	5	11500	3	11	54300	59700
30	6	CAPE-DORY 30 MK II	SLP	SA/CR	FBG	KL	IB		WEST	10	6	10500	4	6	49400	54300
32		CAPE-DORY 30	FB	CR	FBG	SV	IB	T275	CHRY	12		12800	2	10	84700	93100
32		CAPE-DORY 30	FB	CR	FBG	SV	IB	T200D	VLVO	12		12800	2	10	102000	112000
33	1	CAPE-DORY 330	CUT	SA/CR	FBG	KL	IB		WEST	10	3	13300	4	10	62900	69100
34	7	CAPE-DORY 33 PY	FB	CR	FBG	SV	IB	T275	CHRY	12	2	14400	2	11	107500	118000
34	7	CAPE-DORY 33 PY	FB	CR	FBG	SV	IB	T200D	VLVO	12	2	14400	2	11	124500	137000
36	2	CAPE-DORY 36	CUT	SA/CR	FBG	KL	IB	36D	PERK	10	8	16100	5		90900	99900
37	8	CAPE-DORY 36 PY	FB	CNV	FBG	SV	IB	T340	CHRY	13	6	19000	3	6	143000	157000
37	8	CAPE-DORY 36 PY	FB	CNV	FBG	SV	IB	T250D	GM	13	6	19000	3	6	166500	183000
40	2	CAPE-DORY CUSTOM 40	CUT	SA/CR	FBG	KL	IB	46D	WEST	11	8	20500	5	8	154500	169500
		1989 BOATS														
27	11	CAPE-DORY 280 SPORT	HT	SF	FBG	SV	IB	275	CHRY	9	11	6500	2	10	39300	43600
27	11	CDT 28 CRUISER	HT	CR	FBG	SV	IB	275	CHRY	9	11	7500	2	11	42100	46700
27	11	CDT 28 CRUISER	HT	CR	FBG	SV	IB	200D	VLVO	9	11	7500	2	11	52200	57400
27	11	CDT 28 FB CRUISER	FB	CR	FBG	SV	IB	275	CHRY	9	11	7500	2	11	42100	46700
27	11	CDT 28 FB CRUISER	FB	CR	FBG	SV	IB	200D	VLVO	9	11	7500	2	11	52200	57400
27	11	CDT 28 OPEN FISH	OP	FSH	FBG	SV	IB	275	CHRY	9	11	7000	2	11	40700	45200
27	11	CDT 28 OPEN FISH	OP	FSH	FBG	SV	IB	200D	VLVO	9	11	7000	2	11	49500	54400
29	10	CAPE-DORY 300	SLP	MS	FBG	KL	IB	46D	WEST	11	5	11500	3	11	51400	56500
30	6	CAPE-DORY 30 MK II	SLP	SA/CR	FBG	KL	IB	22D	WEST	10	6	10500	4	6	47000	51700
33	1	CAPE-DORY 330	CUT	SA/CR	FBG	KL	IB	24D	UNIV	10	3	13300	4	10	59500	65400
34	7	CAPE-DORY 33 PY	FB	CR	FBG	SV	IB	T275	CHRY	12	2	13500	2	11	99900	110000
34	7	CAPE-DORY 33 PY	FB	CR	FBG	SV	IB	T200D	VLVO	12	2	14400	2	11	119000	131000
36	2	CAPE-DORY 36	CUT	SA/CR	FBG	KL	IB	36D	PERK	10	8	16100	5		86100	94600
37	8	CAPE-DORY 36 PY	FB	CNV	FBG	SV	IB	T340	CHRY	13	6	18000	3	6	131000	144000
37	8	CAPE-DORY 36 PY	FB	CNV	FBG	SV	IB	T250D	GM	13	6	19000	3	6	159000	174500
40	2	CAPE-DORY CUSTOM 40	CUT	SA/CR	FBG	KL	IB	46D	WEST	11	8	20500	5	8	146000	160500
		1988 BOATS														
22	5	TYPHOON SENIOR	SLP	SAIL	FBG	KL	OB			7	5	3300	3	1	10700	12100
25	11	CAPE-DORY 26	SLP	SAIL	FBG	KL	OB			8		5300	3	7	19100	21200
25	11	CAPE-DORY 26-D	SLP	SA/CR	FBG	KL	OD			8		5300	3	7	19100	21200
25	11	CAPE-DORY 26-D	SLP	SA/CR	FBG	KL	IB	D		8		5300	3	7	20000	22200
27	11	CAPE-DORY 280 SPORT	HT	SF	FBG	SV	IB	240	CHRY	9	11	6500	2	10	36600	40700
27	11	CDT 28 CRUISER	HT	CR	FBG	SV	IB	275	CHRY	9	11	7500	2	11	40100	44500
27	11	CDT 28 CRUISER	HT	CR	FBG	SV	IB	200D	VLVO	9	11	7500	2	11	50000	54900
27	11	CDT 28 FB CRUISER	FB	CR	FBG	SV	IB	275	CHRY	9	11	7500	2	11	40100	44500
27	11	CDT 28 FB CRUISER	FB	CR	FBG	SV	IB	200D	VLVO	9	11	7500	2	11	50000	54900
27	11	CDT 28 OPEN FISH	OP	FSH	FBG	SV	IB	275	CHRY	9	11	7000	2	11	38800	43100
28	2	CAPE-DORY 28	SLP	SA/CR	FBG	KL	IB	14D	UNIV	8	11	9000	4		36600	40700
29	10	CAPE-DORY 300	SLP	MS	FBG	KL	IB	46D	WEST	11	5	11500	3	11	48700	53600
30	6	CAPE-DORY 30 MK II	SLP	SA/CR	FBG	KL	IB	22D	WEST	10	6	10500	4	6	44000	48900
32	2	CAPE-DORY 32	SLP	SA/CR	FBG	KL	IB	21D	WEST	9	11	11750	4	11	49600	54500
32	10	CAPE-DORY 33 CNV	FB	CNV	FBG	SV	IB	T200D	VLVO	11	11	13500	2	11	110000	121000

LOA FT	LOA IN	NAME AND/ OR MODEL	TOP/ RIG	BOAT TYPE	-HULL- MTL	-HULL- TP	ENGINE TP	ENGINE # HP	ENGINE MFG	BEAM FT	BEAM IN	WGT LBS	DRAFT FT	DRAFT IN	RETAIL LOW	RETAIL HIGH
		1988 BOATS														
33	1	CAPE-DORY 330	CUT	SA/CR	FBG	KL	IB	24D	UNIV	10	3	13300	4	10	56400	61900
34	7	CAPE-DORY 33 FB CR	FB	CR	FBG	SV	IB			12	2	27000	3	10	**	**
		IB D ** ** , IB T ** ** , IB T D													**	**
36	2	CAPE-DORY 36	CUT	SA/CR	FBG	KL	IB	36D	PERK	10	8	16100	5		81600	89700
37	8	CAPE-DORY 36 CNV	FB	CNV	FBG	SV	IB	T340	CHRY	13	6	18000	3	6	125000	137500
37	8	CAPE-DORY 36 CNV	FB	CNV	FBG	SV	IB	T250D	GM	13	6	18000	3	6	146500	161000
37	8	CAPE-DORY 36 CNV	FB	CNV	FBG	SV	IB	T320D	CAT	13	6	18000	3	6	158000	174000
40	2	CAPE-DORY CUSTOM 40	CUT	SA/CR	FBG	KL	IB	46D	WEST	11	8	20500	5	8	138500	152000
		1987 BOATS														
22	5	TYPHOON SENIOR	SLP	SAIL	FBG	KL	OB			7	5	3300	3	1	10100	11500
25	11	CAPE-DORY 26	SLP	SAIL	FBG	KL	OB			8		5300	3	7	18100	20100
25	11	CAPE-DORY 26-D	SLP	SA/CR	FBG	KL	IB	10D	WEST	8		5300	3	7	19200	21300
27	11	CAPE-DORY 280 SPORT	HT	SF	FBG	SV	IB	240	CHRY	9	11	6500	2	10	34900	38800
27	11	CDT 28 CRUISER	HT	CR	FBG	SV	IB	275	CHRY	9	11	7500	2	11	38200	42500
27	11	CDT 28 CRUISER	HT	CR	FBG	SV	IB	200D	VLVO	9	11	7500	2	11	47900	52600
27	11	CDT 28 FB CRUISER	FB	CR	FBG	SV	IB	275	CHRY	9	11	7500	2	11	38200	42500
27	11	CDT 28 FB CRUISER	FB	CR	FBG	SV	IB	200D	VLVO	9	11	7500	2	11	47900	52600
27	11	CDT 28 OPEN FISH	OP	FSH	FBG	SV	IB	275	CHRY	9	11	7000	2	11	37000	41100
28	2	CAPE-DORY 28	SLP	SA/CR	FBG	KL	IB	14D	UNIV	8	11	9000	4		34700	38500
29	10	CAPE-DORY 300	SLP	MS	FBG	KL	IB	46D	WEST	11	5	11500	3	11	46400	51000
30	6	CAPE-DORY 30 MK II	SLP	SA/CR	FBG	KL	IB	22D	WEST	10	6	10500	4	6	41700	46400
32	2	CAPE-DORY 32	SLP	SA/CR	FBG	KL	IB	21D	WEST	9	11	11750	4	11	47300	51900
33	1	CAPE-DORY 330	CUT	SA/CR	FBG	KL	IB	24D	UNIV	10	3	13300	4	10	53400	58700
36	2	CAPE-DORY 36	CUT	SA/CR	FBG	KL	IB	36D	PERK	10	8	16100	5		77300	85000
40	2	CAPE-DORY CUSTOM 40	CUT	SA/CR	FBG	KL	IB	46D	WEST	11	8	19500	5	8	127000	139500
		1986 BOATS														
22	5	TYPHOON SENIOR	SLP	SAIL	FBG	KL	OB			7	5	3300	3	1	9600	10900
25	11	CAPE-DORY 26	SLP	SAIL	FBG	KL	OB			8		5300	3	7	16700	19000
27	11	CDT 28 CRUISER	HT	CR	FBG	SV	IB	275	CHRY	9	11	7500	2	11	36500	40500
27	11	CDT 28 CRUISER	HT	CR	FBG	SV	IB	165D	VLVO	9	11	7500	2	11	44100	49000
27	11	CDT 28 FB CRUISER	FB	CR	FBG	SV	IB	275	CHRY	9	11	7500	2	11	36500	40500
27	11	CDT 28 FB CRUISER	FB	CR	FBG	SV	IB	165D	VLVO	9	11	7500	2	11	44100	49000
27	11	CDT 28 OPEN FISH	OP	FSH	FBG	SV	IB	260	CHRY	9	11	7000	2	11	35000	38900
28	2	CAPE-DORY 28	SLP	SA/CR	FBG	KL	IB	14D	UNIV	8	11	9000	4		32900	36500
29	10	CAPE-DORY 300	SLP	MS	FBG	KL	IB	46D	WEST	11	5	11500	3	11	43500	48400
30	3	CAPE-DORY 30	CUT	SA/CR	FBG	KL	IB	14D	UNIV	9		10000	4	2	37500	41700
32	2	CAPE-DORY 32	SLP	SA/CR	FBG	KL	IB	21D	WEST	9	11	11750	4	11	44300	49200
33	1	CAPE-DORY 330	CUT	SA/CR	FBG	KL	IB	24D	UNIV	10	3	13300	4	10	50600	55600
36	2	CAPE-DORY 36	CUT	SA/CR	FBG	KL	IB	36D	PERK	10	8	16100	5		73300	80500
40	2	CAPE-DORY 40	CUT	SA/CR	FBG	KL	IB	36D	PERK	11	8	19500	5	8	119000	131000
		1985 BOATS														
18	6	TYPHOON DAYSAILER	SLP	SAIL	FBG	KL	OB			6	4	1900	2	7	6650	7600
18	6	TYPHOON WEEKENDER	SLP	SAIL	FBG	KL	OB			6	4	2000	2	7	6850	7850
22	4	CAPE-DORY 22	SLP	SA/CR	FBG	KL	OB			7	4	3200	3		8900	10100
22	4	CAPE-DORY 22D	SLP	SA/CR	FBG	KL	IB	8D	YAN	7	4	3200	3		10700	12100
22	5	TYPHOON SENIOR	SLP	SAIL	FBG	KL	OB			7	5	3300	3	1	9150	10400
24		CDT 24C	HT	TRWL	FBG	DS	IB	30D	WEST	8		5250	2	7	29700	33000
24		CDT 24S	HT	TRWL	FBG	DS	IB	30D	WEST	8		5250	2	7	22900	25400
25		CAPE-DORY 25D	SLP	SA/CR	FBG	KL	IB	8D	YAN	8		5120	3	6	15700	17800
25	11	CAPE-DORY 26	SLP	SAIL	FBG	KL	OB			8		5300	3	7	15900	18000
27	3	CAPE-DORY 270	SLP	SA/CR	FBG	KC	IB	13D	WEST	9	5	8380	3		28400	31600
27	11	CDT 28 CRUISER	HT	CR	FBG	SV	IB	100D-165D		9	11	7500	2	11	39700	47000
27	11	CDT 28 FB CRUISER	FB	CR	FBG	SV	IB	100D-165D		9	11	7500	2	11	39700	47000
27	11	CDT 28 OPEN FISH	OP	FSH	FBG	SV	IB	260	CHRY	9	11	7000	2	11	33400	37100
28	2	CAPE-DORY 28	SLP	SA/CR	FBG	KL	IB	14D	UNIV	8	11	9000	4		31100	34600
30	3	CAPE-DORY 30	CUT	SA/CR	FBG	KL	IB	14D	UNIV	9		10000	4	2	35600	39500
31	4	CAPE-DORY 31	CUT	SA/CR	FBG	KL	IB	21D	UNIV	9	9	11500	4	9	41100	45700
33	1	CAPE-DORY 33	SLP	SA/CR	FBG	KL	IB	D		10	3	13300	4	10	48000	52700
33	1	CAPE-DORY 33	CUT	SA/CR	FBG	KL	IB	24D	UNIV	10	3	13300	4	10	48000	52700
36	2	CAPE-DORY 36	CUT	SA/CR	FBG	KL	IB	51D	PERK	10	8	16100	5		69600	76500
40	2	CAPE-DORY 40	CUT	SA/CR	FBG	KL	IB	51D	PERK	11	8	19500	5	8	113000	124500
42	3	CDT 42 SPORTFISH	FB	SF	FBG	DV	IB	D		13	8	19000	4		**	**
45	2	CAPE-DORY 45	CUT	SA/CR	FBG	KL	IB	51D	PERK	13		24000	6	3	118000	129500
45	2	CAPE-DORY 45	KTH	SA/CR	FBG	KL	IB	51D	PERK	13		24000	6	3	118000	129500
		1984 BOATS														
18	6	TYPHOON DAYSAILER	SLP	SAIL	FBG	KL				6	4	1900	2	7	6300	7200
18	6	TYPHOON DAYSAILER	SLP	SAIL	FBG	KL	OB			6	4	1900	2	7	6300	7200
18	6	TYPHOON WEEKENDER	SLP	SAIL	FBG	KL				6	4	2000	2	7	6450	7450
18	6	TYPHOON WEEKENDER	SLP	SAIL	FBG	KL	OB			6	4	2000	2	7	6450	7450
22	4	CAPE-DORY 22	SLP	SA/CR	FBG	KL	OB			7	4	3200	3		8350	9600
22	4	CAPE-DORY 22	SLP	SAIL	FBG	KL	OB			7	4	3200	3		8350	9600
22	4	CAPE-DORY 22D	SLP	SA/CR	FBG	KL	IB	8D	YAN	7	4	3200	3		10100	11500
25		CAPE-DORY 25D	SLP	SA/CR	FBG	KL	IB	8D		8		5120	3	6	14900	16900
27	1	CAPE-DORY 27	SLP	SA/CR	FBG	KL	IB	13D		8	6	7500	4		23800	26500
27	3	CAPE-DORY 270	SLP	SA/CR	FBG	KC	IB	13D	WEST	9	5	8380	3		26900	29900
28	1	CAPE-DORY 28	SLP	SA/CR	FBG	KL	IB	D		8	11	9000	4		29500	32800
28	2	CAPE-DORY 28	SLP	SA/CR	FBG	KL	IB	14D	UNIV	8	11	9000	4		29500	32800
30	3	CAPE-DORY 30	CUT	SA/CR	FBG	KL	IB	14D		9		10000	4	2	33700	37500
30	3	CAPE-DORY 30	KTH	SA/CR	FBG	KL	IB	D		9		10000	4	2	33700	37500
31	4	CAPE-DORY 31	SLP	SA/CR	FBG	KL	IB	21D	UNIV	9	9	11500	4	9	38900	43300
31	4	CAPE-DORY 31	CUT	SA/CR	FBG	KL	IB	D		9	9	11500	4	9	38900	43300
33	1	CAPE-DORY 33	SLP	SA/CR	FBG	KL	IB	24D		10	3	13300	4	10	45700	50200
33	1	CAPE-DORY 33	CUT	SA/CR	FBG	KL	IB	D		10	3	13300	4	10	45700	50200
36	2	CAPE-DORY 36	CUT	SA/CR	FBG	KL	IB	D		10	8	16100	5		66000	72500
36	2	CAPE-DORY 36	CUT	SA/CR	FBG	KL	IB	50D	PERK	10	8	16100	5		66000	72500
40	2	CAPE-DORY 40	CUT	SA/CR	FBG	KL	IB	50D	PERK	11	8	19500	5	8	107500	118000
45	2	CAPE-DORY 45	CUT	SA/CR	FBG	KL	IB	55D	PERK	13		24000	6	3	111500	122500
45	2	CAPE-DORY 45	KTH	SA/CR	FBG	KL	IB	55D	PERK	13		24000	6	3	111500	122500
45	3	CAPE-DORY 45	CUT	SA/CR	FBG	KL	IB	D		13		24000	6	3	112500	124000
45	3	CAPE-DORY 45	KTH	SA/CR	FBG	KL	IB	D		13		24000	6	3	112500	124000

....For earlier years, see the BUC Used Boat Price Guide, Volume 3

CAPE-BAY SHIPBUILDERS CORP

KINGSTON MA 02364

See inside cover to adjust price for area

LOA FT	LOA IN	NAME AND/ OR MODEL	TOP/ RIG	BOAT TYPE	-HULL- MTL	-HULL- TP	ENGINE TP	ENGINE # HP	ENGINE MFG	BEAM FT	BEAM IN	WGT LBS	DRAFT FT	DRAFT IN	RETAIL LOW	RETAIL HIGH
		1985 BOATS														
30	11	CAPE-BAY 31/LIBERTY	CUT	SA/CR	FBG	KL	IB	20D		10	5	11400	4	11	36200	40200

CAPITAL YACHTS INC

NEWPORT
HARBOR CITY CA 90710-08 COAST GUARD MFG ID- CPY

See inside cover to adjust price for area

LOA FT	LOA IN	NAME AND/ OR MODEL	TOP/ RIG	BOAT TYPE	-HULL- MTL	-HULL- TP	ENGINE TP	ENGINE # HP	ENGINE MFG	BEAM FT	BEAM IN	WGT LBS	DRAFT FT	DRAFT IN	RETAIL LOW	RETAIL HIGH
		1988 BOATS														
24		NEPTUNE 24	SLP	SAIL	FBG	KL	OB			8		3200	4	8	6850	7900
24		NEPTUNE 24 SHOAL	SLP	SAIL	FBG	CB	OB			8		3200	2		6850	7900
27	2	GULF 27 PILOTHOUSE	SLP	SA/CR	FBG	KL	IB	14D	UNIV	9	4	6900	5	2	18100	20100
27	2	GULF 27 SHOAL PH	SLP	SA/CR	FBG	KL	IB	14D	UNIV	9	4	6900	4		18100	20100
27	2	NEWPORT 27MKIII	SLP	SA/RC	FBG	KL	OB			9	3	6000	5	2	14700	16800
27	2	NEWPORT 27MKIII SHL	SLP	SA/RC	FBG	KL	OB			9	3	6000	3	8	14700	16800
28	4	NEWPORT 28II	SLP	SA/RC	FBG	KL	IB	14D	UNIV	9	9	7000	5	2	18900	21000
28	4	NEWPORT 28II SHOAL	SLP	SA/RC	FBG	KL	IB	14D	UNIV	9	9	7000	4		18900	21000
28	8	GULF 29 PILOTHOUSE	SLP	SA/CR	FBG	KL	IB	14D	UNIV	9	4	7500	5	2	20100	22400
28	8	GULF 29 SHOAL PH	SLP	SA/CR	FBG	KL	IB	14D	UNIV	9	4	7500	4		20100	22400
30	6	NEWPORT 30MKIII	SLP	SA/RC	FBG	KL	IB	14D	UNIV	10	8	8500	5	2	23400	26000
30	6	NEWPORT 30MKIII SHL	SLP	SA/RC	FBG	KL	IB	14D	UNIV	10	8	8500	4		23400	26000
31	2	NEWPORT 31	SLP	SA/RC	FBG	KL	IB	14D	UNIV	10	9	9000	5	2	24900	27700
31	2	NEWPORT 31 SHOAL	SLP	SA/RC	FBG	KL	IB	14D	UNIV	10	9	9000	4		24900	27700
32		GULF 32 PILOTHOUSE	SLP	SA/CR	FBG	KL	IB	32D	UNIV	10		15000	5	2	41200	45700
32		GULF 32 SHOAL PH	SLP	SA/CR	FBG	KL	IB	32D	UNIV	10		15000	4	6	41200	45700
33		NEWPORT 33	SLP	SA/RC	FBG	KL	IB	21D	UNIV	10	10	9700	6		26900	29900
33		NEWPORT 33 SHOAL	SLP	SA/RC	FBG	KL	IB	21D	UNIV	10	10	9700	4		26900	29900
41		NEWPORT 41 MKII SHL	SLP	SA/RC	FBG	KL	IB	32D	UNIV	11	3	18000	5	2	59100	64900
41		NEWPORT 41MKII	SLP	SA/RC	FBG	KL	IB	32D	UNIV	11	3	18000	6	3	59100	64900
		1987 BOATS														
24		NEPTUNE 24	SLP	SAIL	FBG	KL	OB			8		3200	4	8	6500	7500
24		NEPTUNE 24 SHOAL	SLP	SAIL	FBG	CB	OB			8		3200	2		6500	7500
27		NEWPORT 27MKIII	SLP	SA/RC	FBG	KL	IB	D		9	3	6500	5	2	15700	17900
27		NEWPORT 27MKIII SHL	SLP	SA/RC	FBG	KL	IB	D		9	3	6500	3	8	15700	17900
27	2	GULF 27 PILOTHOUSE	SLP	SA/CR	FBG	KL	IB	14D	UNIV	9	4	6900	5	2	16800	19100
27	2	GULF 27 SHOAL PH	SLP	SA/CR	FBG	KL	IB	14D	UNIV	9	4	6900	4		16800	19100
28		NEWPORT 28II	SLP	SA/RC	FBG	KL	IB	14D	UNIV	9	9	7000	5	2	17400	19700
28		NEWPORT 28II SHOAL	SLP	SA/RC	FBG	KL	IB	14D	UNIV	9	9	7000	4		17400	19700
28	8	GULF 29 PILOTHOUSE	SLP	SA/CR	FBG	KL	IB	14D	UNIV	9	4	7500	5	2	19100	21200
28	8	GULF 29 SHOAL PH	SLP	SA/CR	FBG	KL	IB	14D	UNIV	9	4	7500	4		19100	21200
30	6	NEWPORT 30 MKIII	SLP	SA/RC	FBG	KL	IB	14D	UNIV	10	8	8500	5	2	22200	24700
30	6	NEWPORT 30MKIII SHL	SLP	SA/RC	FBG	KL	IB	14D	UNIV	10	8	8500	4		22200	24700
31	2	NEWPORT 31	SLP	SA/RC	FBG	KL	IB	14D	UNIV	10	9	8750	5	2	22900	25500
31	2	NEWPORT 31 SHOAL	SLP	SA/RC	FBG	KL	IB	14D	UNIV	10	9	8750	4		22900	25500
32		GULF 32 PILOTHOUSE	SLP	SA/CR	FBG	KL	IB	32D	UNIV	11		15000	5	2	39000	43300
33		NEWPORT 33	SLP	SA/RC	FBG	KL	IB	21D	UNIV	10	10	9500	6		25000	27700

LOA FT	LOA IN	NAME AND/ OR MODEL	TOP/ RIG	BOAT TYPE	-HULL- MTL	-HULL- TP	ENGINE TP	# HP	MFG	BEAM FT	BEAM IN	WGT LBS	DRAFT FT	DRAFT IN	RETAIL LOW	RETAIL HIGH
		1987 BOATS														
33		NEWPORT 33 SHOAL	SLP	SA/RC	FBG	KL	IB	21D	UNIV	10	10	9500	4		25000	27700
41		NEWPORT 41 MKIII	SLP	SA/RC	FBG	KL	IB	32D	UNIV	11	3	18000	6	3	56000	61500
41		NEWPORT 41 MKIII SHL	SLP	SA/RC	FBG	KL	IB	32D	UNIV	11	3	18000	5	6	56000	61500
		1986 BOATS														
24		NEPTUNE 24	SLP	SAIL	FBG	KL	OB			8		3200	4	8	6150	7100
24		NEPTUNE 24	SLP	SAIL	FBG	SK	OB			8		3200	2		6150	7100
24		NEPTUNE 24 SHOAL	SLP	SAIL	FBG	CB	OB			8		3200	2		6150	7100
27		NEWPORT 27MKIII	SLP	SA/RC	FBG	KL	IB	17D		9	3	6500	5	2	14900	17000
27		NEWPORT 27MKIIISHOAL	SLP	SA/RC	FBG	KL	IB	D		9	3	6500	3	8	14900	16900
27		NEWPORT 27SII	SLP	SA/RC	FBG	KL	IB	14D-	18D	9	3	6500	5	2	14900	17000
27		NEWPORT 27SII SHOAL	SLP	SA/RC	FBG	KL	IB	14D	UNIV	9	3	6500	4	2	14900	16900
27	2	GULF 27	SLP	SA/RC	FBG	KL	IB	14D	UNIV	9	4	6900	5	2	15900	18100
27	2	GULF 27 PILOTHOUSE	SLP	SA/CR	FBG	KL	IB	14D	UNIV	9	4	6900	5	2	15900	18100
27	2	GULF 27 SHOAL	SLP	SA/RC	FBG	KL	IB	14D	UNIV	9	4	6900	4		15900	18100
27	2	GULF 27 SHOAL PH	SLP	SA/CR	FBG	KL	IB	14D	UNIV	9	4	6900	4		15900	18100
28		NEWPORT 28II	SLP	SA/RC	FBG	KL	IB	14D	UNIV	9	9	7000	5	2	16500	18700
28		NEWPORT 28II SHOAL	SLP	SA/RC	FBG	KL	IB	14D	UNIV	9	9	7000	4		16500	18700
28	8	GULF 29	SLP	SA/RC	FBG	KL	IB	14D	UNIV	9	4	7500	5	2	18300	20300
28	8	GULF 29 PILOTHOUSE	SLP	SA/CR	FBG	KL	IB	14D	UNIV	9	4	7500	5	2	18300	20300
28	8	GULF 29 SHOAL	SLP	SA/RC	FBG	KL	IB	14D	UNIV	9	4	7500	4		18300	20300
28	8	GULF 29 SHOAL PH	SLP	SA/CR	FBG	KL	IB	14D	UNIV	9	4	7500	4		18300	20300
30	6	NEWPORT 30 III	SLP	SA/RC	FBG	KL	IB	14D	UNIV	10	8	8500	5	1	21000	23400
30	6	NEWPORT 30 MKIII	SLP	SA/RC	FBG	KL	IB	14D	UNIV	10	8	8500	5	2	21000	23400
30	6	NEWPORT 30III SHOAL	SLP	SA/RC	FBG	KL	IB	14D	UNIV	10	8	8500	4		21000	23400
30	6	NEWPORT 30MKIII SHOA	SLP	SA/RC	FBG	KL	IB	14D	UNIV	10	8	8500	4		21000	23400
32		GULF 32	SLP	SA/CR	FBG	KL	IB	32D	UNIV	10		15000	5	2	36900	41100
32		GULF 32 PILOTHOUSE	SLP	SA/CR	FBG	KL	IB	32D	UNIV	11		15000	5	2	36900	41100
33		NEWPORT 33	SLP	SA/RC	FBG	KL	IB	21D	UNIV	10	10	9500	6		23700	26300
33		NEWPORT 33 SHOAL	SLP	SA/RC	FBG	KL	IB	21D	UNIV	10	10	9500	4		23700	26300
41		NEWPORT 41 MKIII	SLP	SA/RC	FBG	KL	IB	32D	UNIV	11	3	18000	6	3	53000	58300
41		NEWPORT 41SII	SLP	SA/RC	FBG	KL	IB	32D	UNIV	11	3	18000	6	3	53000	58300
		1985 BOATS														
24		NEPTUNE 24	SLP	SAIL	FBG	KL	OB			8		3200	4	8	5850	6700
24		NEPTUNE 24	SLP	SAIL	FBG	SK	OB			8		3200	2		5850	6700
27		NEWPORT 27	SLP	SAIL	FBG	KL	IB	14D	UNIV	9	3	6000	4	3	13000	14800
27		NEWPORT 27 MKIII	SLP	SA/RC	FBG	KL	IB	18D		9	3	6500	4	2	14200	16100
27	2	GULF 27	SLP	SA/RC	FBG	KL	IB	18D	UNIV	9	4	6900	5	2	15100	17200
27	2	GULF 27 PH	SLP	SAIL	FBG	KL	IB	14D	UNIV	9	4	6900	4	2	15100	17100
27	2	GULF 27 SHOAL	SLP	SA/RC	FBG	KL	IB	18D	UNIV	9	4	6900	4		15100	17200
28		NEWPORT 28	SLP	SAIL	FBG	KL	IB	14D	UNIV	9	9	7000	4		15600	17700
28		NEWPORT 28II	SLP	SA/RC	FBG	KL	IB	18D	UNIV	9	9	7000	5	2	15600	17800
28		NEWPORT 28II SHOAL	SLP	SA/RC	FBG	KL	IB	18D	UNIV	9	9	7000	4		15600	17800
28	8	GULF 29	SLP	SA/RC	FBG	KL	IB	18D	UNIV	9	4	7500	5	2	17000	19300
28	8	GULF 29 PH	SLP	SAIL	FBG	KL	IB	14D	UNIV	9	4	7500	4	6	16900	19300
28	8	GULF 29 SHOAL	SLP	SA/RC	FBG	KL	IB	18D	UNIV	9	4	7500	4		17000	19300
30	6	NEWPORT 30	SLP	SAIL	FBG	KL	IB	14D	UNIV	10	8	8500	4		19900	22100
30	6	NEWPORT 30 III	SLP	SA/RC	FBG	KL	IB	18D	UNIV	10	8	8500	5	2	19900	22200
30	6	NEWPORT 30III SHOAL	SLP	SA/RC	FBG	KL	IB	18D	UNIV	10	8	8500	4		19900	22200
32		GULF 32	SLP	SA/CR	FBG	KL	IB	40D	UNIV	11		15000	5	2	35000	38900
32		GULF 32 PH	SLP	SAIL	FBG	KL	IB	32D	UNIV	10		15000	5	2	35000	38900
33		NEWPORT 33	SLP	SA/RC	FBG	KL	IB	18D	UNIV	10	10	9500	6		22400	24900
33		NEWPORT 33	SLP	SAIL	FBG	KL	IB	21D	UNIV	10	10	9500	4		22400	24900
33		NEWPORT 33 SHOAL	SLP	SA/RC	FBG	KL	IB	18D	UNIV	10	10	9500	4		22400	24900
41		NEWPORT 41	SLP	SAIL	FBG	KL	IB	32D	UNIV	11	3	18000	6	3	50300	55200
41		NEWPORT 41 MKII	SLP	SA/RC	FBG	KL	IB	40D	UNIV	11	3	18000	6	3	50400	55400
		1984 BOATS														
24		NEPTUNE 24	SLP	SAIL	FBG	KL	OB			8		3200	5		5550	6350
24		NEPTUNE 24	SLP	SAIL	FBG	SK	OB			8		3200	2		5550	6350
24		RAVEN 24	SLP	SAIL	FBG	CB				7		1170			3200	3700
27		NEWPORT 27SII	SLP	SA/RC	FBG	KL	IB	14D	UNIV	9	2	6500	5	2	13400	15200
27	2	GULF 27	SLP	SA/RC	FBG	KL	IB	14D	UNIV	9	4	6900	5	2	14300	16200
28		NEWPORT 28II	SLP	SA/RC	FBG	KL	IB	14D	UNIV	9	6	7000	5	2	14800	16800
28	8	GULF 29	SLP	SA/RC	FBG	KL	IB	14D	UNIV	9	4	7500	5	2	16100	18200
30		NEWPORT 30 III	SLP	SA/RC	FBG	KL	IB	14D	UNIV	10	8	9000	5	3	19900	22100
32		GULF 32	SLP	SA/CR	FBG	KL	IB	D		10		14000	5	2	31000	34500
33		NEWPORT 33	SLP	SA/RC	FBG	KL	IB	21D	UNIV	10	10	9500	6		21200	23600
41		NEWPORT 41SII	SLP	SA/RC	FBG	KL	IB	32D	UNIV	11	3	18000	6	3	47900	52600

....For earlier years, see the BUC Used Boat Price Guide, Volume 3

CAPRI SAILBOATS

DIV OF CATALINA YACHTS
WOODLAND HILLS CA 91367 COAST GUARD MFG ID- CPS

See inside cover to adjust price for area

For more recent years, see the BUC Used Boat Price Guide, Volume 1

LOA FT	LOA IN	NAME AND/ OR MODEL	TOP/ RIG	BOAT TYPE	-HULL- MTL	-HULL- TP	ENGINE TP	# HP	MFG	BEAM FT	BEAM IN	WGT LBS	DRAFT FT	DRAFT IN	RETAIL LOW	RETAIL HIGH
		1996 BOATS														
16	4	CAPRI 16.5	SLP	SAROD	FBG	KL	OB			7		430	4	5	2950	3450
16	6	CAPRI 16	SLP	SAROD	FBG	WK	OB			6	11	1350	2	5	5400	6200
18		CAPRI 18	SLP	SAROD	FBG	WK	OB			7	7	1500	2	4	5700	6600
22		CAPRI 22 FIN	SLP	SAROD	FBG	KL	OB			8		2200	4		7850	9050
22		CAPRI 22 WING	SLP	SAROD	FBG	WK	OB			8		2250	2	6	8000	9150
26	2	CAPRI 26 FIN	SLP	SARAC	FBG	KL	IB	10D	UNIV	9	10	5250	4	10	21600	24000
26	2	CAPRI 26 WING	SLP	SARAC	FBG	WK	IB	10D	UNIV	9	10	5100	3	5	21000	23300
		1995 BOATS														
16	5	CAPRI 16.5	SLP	SAROD	FBG	KL	OB			7		430	4	5	2800	3250
16	6	CAPRI 16	SLP	SAROD	FBG	WK	OB			6	11	1350	2	5	5050	5800
18		CAPRI 18	SLP	SAROD	FBG	WK	OB			7	7	1500	2	4	5400	6200
22		CAPRI 22	SLP	SAROD	FBG	KL	OB			8		2200	4		7400	8500
22		CAPRI 22	SLP	SAROD	FBG	WK	OB			8		2250	2	8	7500	8600
26	2	CAPRI 26	SLP	SARAC	FBG	KL	IB	10D	UNIV	9	10	5650	4	10	21800	24300
26	2	CAPRI 26	SLP	SARAC	FBG	WK	IB	10D	UNIV	9	10	5500	3	5	21300	23600
37	4	CAPRI 37	SLP	SAROD	FBG	KL	IB	27D	YAN	12		11000	7		52900	58100
		1994 BOATS														
16	6	CAPRI 16	SLP	SAROD	FBG	WK	OB			6	11	1350	2	5	4750	5500
18		CAPRI 18	SLP	SAROD	FBG	WK	OB			7	7	1500	2	4	5050	5800
22		CAPRI 22	SLP	SAROD	FBG	KL	OB			8		2200	4	2	6950	8000
22		CAPRI 22	SLP	SAROD	FBG	WK	OB			8		2250	2	6	7050	8100
26	2	CAPRI 26	SLP	SARAC	FBG	KL	OB			9	10	5250	4	10	18300	20400
26	2	CAPRI 26	SLP	SARAC	FBG	KL	IB	10D	UNIV	9	10	5650	4	10	20500	22800
26	2	CAPRI 26	SLP	SARAC	FBG	WK	OB			9	10	5100	3	5	17400	19800
26	2	CAPRI 26	SLP	SARAC	FBG	WK	IB	10D	UNIV	9	10	5500	3	5	20000	22200
37	4	CAPRI 37	SLP	SAROD	FBG	KL	IB	27D	YAN	12		11000	7		49700	54700
		1993 BOATS														
16	6	CAPRI 16	SLP	SAROD	FBG	WK	OB			6	11	1350	2	5	4500	5200
18		CAPRI 18	SLP	SAROD	FBG	WK	OB			7	7	1500	2	4	4750	5450
22		CAPRI 22	SLP	SAROD	FBG	KL	OB			8		2200	4	2	6550	7500
22		CAPRI 22	SLP	SAROD	FBG	WK	OB			8		2250	2	6	6650	7650
26	2	CAPRI 26	SLP	SARAC	FBG	KL	OB			9	10	5250	4	10	16800	19100
26	2	CAPRI 26	SLP	SARAC	FBG	KL	IB	10D	UNIV	9	10	5650	4	10	19300	21500
26	2	CAPRI 26	SLP	SARAC	FBG	WK	OB			9	10	5100	3	5	16400	18600
26	2	CAPRI 26	SLP	SARAC	FBG	WK	IB	10D	UNIV	9	10	5500	3	5	19000	21100
37	4	CAPRI 37	SLP	SAROD	FBG	KL	IB	27D	YAN	12		11000	7		47100	51700
		1992 BOATS														
16	6	CAPRI 16	SLP	SA/OD	FBG	WK	OB			6	11	1350	2	5	4200	4850
18		CAPRI 18	SLP	SA/OD	FBG	KL	OB			7	7	1500	2		4500	5200
18		CAPRI 18	SLP	SA/OD	FBG	WK	OB			7	7	1500	2	4	4500	5200
22		CAPRI 22	SLP	SA/OD	FBG	KL	OB			8		2150	4	2	6050	7000
22		CAPRI 22	SLP	SA/OD	FBG	WK	OB			8		2150	4	2	6050	7000
26	2	CAPRI 26	SLP	SA/RC	FBG	KL	OB			9	10	5250	4	10	15800	18000
26	2	CAPRI 26	SLP	SA/RC	FBG	KL	IB	10D	UNIV	9	10	5650	4	10	18400	20400
26	2	CAPRI 26	SLP	SA/RC	FBG	WK	OB			9	10	5100	3	5	15400	17500
26	2	CAPRI 26	SLP	SA/RC	FBG	WK	IB	10D	UNIV	9	10	5500	3	5	17500	19900
37	4	CAPRI 37	SLP	SA/OD	FBG	KL	IB	27D	YAN	12		11000	7		43800	48600
		1991 BOATS														
16	6	CAPRI 16	SLP	SA/OD	FBG	WK				6	11	1350	2	5	3950	4600
18		CAPRI 18	SLP	SA/OD	FBG	KL	OB			7	7	1500	2		4200	4850
18		CAPRI 18	SLP	SA/OD	FBG	WK	OB			7	7	1500	2	4	4200	4850
22		CAPRI 22	SLP	SA/OD	FBG	KL	OB			8		2150	4	2	5700	6550
22		CAPRI 22	SLP	SA/OD	FBG	WK	OB			8		2150	4	2	5700	6550
26	2	CAPRI 26	SLP	SA/OD	FBG	KL	OB			9	10	5250	4	10	14900	16900
26	2	CAPRI 26	SLP	SA/OD	FBG	WK	OB			9	10	5100	4	10	14500	16400
		1990 BOATS														
18		CAPRI 18	SLP	SAROD	FBG	KL	OB			7	7	1500	2		3950	4600
22		CAPRI 22	SLP	SAROD	FBG	KL	OB			8		2150	4	2	5350	6150
		1989 BOATS														
18		CAPRI 18	SLP	SAROD	FBG	KL	OB			7	7	1500	2		3700	4300
18		CARPI 18 WING	SLP	SAROD	FBG	WK	OB			7	7	1500	2	4	3700	4300
22		CAPRI 22	SLP	SAROD	FBG	KL	OB			8		2150	4	2	5050	5800
22		CAPRI 22 SHOAL	SLP	SAROD	FBG	WK	OB			8		2240	2		5200	5950
		1988 BOATS														
18		CAPRI 18	SLP	SAROD	FBG	KL	OB			7	7	1500	2		3500	4050
22		CAPRI 22	SLP	SAROD	FBG	KL	OB			8		2150	4	2	4750	5450
22		CAPRI 22 SHOAL	SLP	SAROD	FBG	KL	OB			8		2240	2		4900	5600
24	7	CAPRI 25	SLP	SAROD	FBG	KL	OB			9	2	2785	4	2	6400	7350
		1987 BOATS														
18		CAPRI 18	SLP	SAROD	FBG	KL	OB			7	7	1500	2		3300	3800
22		CAPRI 22	SLP	SAROD	FBG	KL	OB			8		2150	4	2	4500	5150
22		CAPRI 22 SHOAL	SLP	SAROD	FBG	KL	OB			8		2240	2		4600	5300
24	7	CAPRI 25	SLP	SAROD	FBG	KL	OB			9	2	2785	4	2	6050	6950

```
CAPRI SAILBOATS           -CONTINUED    See inside cover to adjust price for area
 LOA   NAME AND/       TOP/ BOAT  -HULL- ----ENGINE---  BEAM   WGT  DRAFT RETAIL RETAIL
FT IN  OR MODEL        RIG  TYPE  MTL TP TP #  HP  MFG  FT IN   LBS  FT IN  LOW    HIGH
------------------------ 1987 BOATS ------------------------------------------------
29  6 CAPRI 30         SLP SAROD FBG KL OB          11  2 4985  5 2 12300  14000
29  6 CAPRI 30         SLP SAROD FBG KL IB  7D BMW  11  2 4985  5 2 12600  14300
------------------------ 1986 BOATS ------------------------------------------------
18    CAPRI 18         SLP SA/OD FBG KL OB           7  7 1500  2    3100   3600
22    CAPRI 22         SLP SA/OD FBG KL OB           8    2150  4 2  4200   4850
22    CAPRI 22 SHOAL   SLP SA/OD FBG KL OB           8    2240  2    4300   5000
24  7 CAPRI 25         SLP SA/OD FBG KL OB           9  2 2785  4 2  5650   6500
29  6 CAPRI 30         SLP SA/OD FBG KL OB          11  2 4985  5 2 11600  13200
29  6 CAPRI 30         SLP SA/OD FBG KL IB  7D BMW  11  2 4985  5 2 11800  13400
------------------------ 1985 BOATS ------------------------------------------------
21    VICTORY 21       SLP SA/OD FBG KL OB           6  3 1350  3    2950   3450
22    CAPRI 22         SLP SA/OD FBG              8         5000   5750
24  7 CAPRI 25         SLP SA/OD FBG KL OB           9  2 2785  4 2  5350   6150
29  6 CAPRI 30         SLP SA/OD FBG KL OB          11  2 4985  5 2 10900  12400
29  6 CAPRI 30         SLP SA/OD FBG KL IB  7D BMW  11  2 4985  5 2 11100  12600
------------------------ 1984 BOATS ------------------------------------------------
21    VICTORY 21       SLP SA/OD FBG KL OB           6  3 1350  3    2750   3250
24  7 CAPRI 25         SLP SA/OD FBG KL OB           9  2 2785  4 2  5000   5750
29  6 CAPRI 30         SLP SA/OD FBG KL OB          11  2 4985  5 2 10300  11700
29  6 CAPRI 30         SLP SA/OD FBG KL IB  7D BMW  11  2 4985  5 2 10500  11900
        ....For earlier years, see the BUC Used Boat Price Guide, Volume 3
```

CAPTIVA YACHTS INC
OLDSMAR FL 33557   COAST GUARD MFG ID- CVI See inside cover to adjust price for area

```
 LOA   NAME AND/       TOP/ BOAT  -HULL- ----ENGINE---  BEAM   WGT  DRAFT RETAIL RETAIL
FT IN  OR MODEL        RIG  TYPE  MTL TP TP #  HP  MFG  FT IN   LBS  FT IN  LOW    HIGH
------------------------ 1986 BOATS ------------------------------------------------
17  9 SANIBEL 17       SLP SAIL  FBG CB            7  4  1300  1    2750   3200
24    CAPTIVA 240      SLP SAIL  FBG CB            8  2  2400  2    4850   5550
34  9 CAPTIVA 35       SLP SA/CR FBG KL           11  8 15100  5 2 35300  39300
------------------------ 1985 BOATS ------------------------------------------------
17  6 SANIBEL 17       SLP SAIL  FBG CB            7  2  1300  1    2600   3000
```

CAR TOP BOATS
P R MARINE
WILMINGTON CA 90744   COAST GUARD MFG ID- PRS See inside cover to adjust price for area

```
 LOA   NAME AND/       TOP/ BOAT  -HULL- ----ENGINE---  BEAM   WGT  DRAFT RETAIL RETAIL
FT IN  OR MODEL        RIG  TYPE  MTL TP TP #  HP  MFG  FT IN   LBS  FT IN  LOW    HIGH
------------------------ 1985 BOATS ------------------------------------------------
16    NORSKA           GAF SAIL  FBG KL OB           6    400 10    1600   1900
```

CARAVELLE POWERBOATS INC
AMERICUS GA 31709   COAST GUARD MFG ID- VCN See inside cover to adjust price for area
FORMERLY CARAVELLE BOATS INC
              For more recent years, see the BUC Used Boat Price Guide, Volume 1

```
 LOA   NAME AND/       TOP/ BOAT  -HULL- ----ENGINE---  BEAM   WGT  DRAFT RETAIL RETAIL
FT IN  OR MODEL        RIG  TYPE  MTL TP TP #  HP  MFG  FT IN   LBS  FT IN  LOW    HIGH
------------------------ 1996 BOATS ------------------------------------------------
17  4 1750 SE BOWRIDER      RNBT FBG DV IO 135       7  1 2000      5150   6250
17  4 1750SE FISH & SKI     RNBT FBG DV IO 135  MRCR 7  1 2000      5150   5950
19    1900SE BOWRIDER       RNBT FBG DV IO 160  MRCR 7  7 2400      6450   7450
19    1900SE CUDDY          CUD  FBG DV IO 160  MRCR 7  7 2400      6650   7650
19    1900SE FISH & SKI     RNBT FBG DV IO 160  MRCR 7  7 2400      6450   7450
20  6 LEGEND 209 BOWRIDER   RNBT FBG DV IO 190  MRCR 8  5 3000      9150  10400
20  6 LEGEND 209 CUDDY      CUD  FBG DV IO 190  MRCR 8  5 3000      9550  10900
20  6 LEGEND 209 FISH&SKI   RNBT FBG DV IO 190  MRCR 8  5 3000      9150  10400
23    INTERCEPTOR 232BR     RNBT FBG DV IO 235  MRCR 8  3 3000     10300  11700
------------------------ 1995 BOATS ------------------------------------------------
17  4 1750 SE BOWRIDER      RNBT FBG DV IO 135       7  1 2000      4700   5700
17  4 1750SE FISH & SKI     RNBT FBG DV IO 135  MRCR 7  1 2000      5050   5800
19    1900SE BOWRIDER       RNBT FBG DV IO 160  MRCR 7  7 2400      5850   6750
19    1900SE CUDDY          CUD  FBG DV IO 160  MRCR 7  7 2400      6250   7150
19    1900SE FISH & SKI     RNBT FBG DV IO 160  MRCR 7  7 2400      6200   7150
20  6 LEGEND 209 BOWRIDER   RNBT FBG DV IO 190  MRCR 8  5 3000      8250   9500
20  6 LEGEND 209 CUDDY      CUD  FBG DV IO 190  MRCR 8  5 3000      8950  10200
20  6 LEGEND 209 FISH&SKI   RNBT FBG DV IO 190  MRCR 8  5 3000      8650   9950
23    INTERCEPTOR 232BR     RNBT FBG DV IO 235  MRCR 8  3 3000      9650  10900
------------------------ 1994 BOATS ------------------------------------------------
17  4 CLASSIC 1750 SE BR ST RNBT FBG SV IO 115  MRCR 7  1 2000      4350   5000
17  4 CLASSIC 1750 SE FS ST RNBT FBG SV IO 115  MRCR 7  1 2000      4650   5350
19    CLASSIC 1900 SE BR ST RNBT FBG SV IO 160  MRCR 7  7 2400      5650   6500
19    CLASSIC 1900 SE CC ST CUD  FBG SV IO 160  MRCR 7  7 2400      5750   6650
19    CLASSIC 1900 SE FS ST RNBT FBG SV IO 160  MRCR 7  7 2400      5650   6500
19  7 LEGEND 2000 BR        RNBT FBG SV IO 180  MRCR 7  8 2550      6000   6900
21    LEGEND 2100 BR        RNBT FBG SV IO 205  MRCR 8  2 3000      8000   9200
21    LEGEND 2100 CC        CUD  FBG SV IO 205  MRCR 8  2 3000      8400   9650
22  8 INTERCEPTOR 2300 BR ST RNBT FBG SV IO 235 MRCR 7  7 2850      8300   9500
22  8 INTERCEPTOR 2300 CC ST CUD FBG SV IO 235  MRCR 7  7 2850      8850  10100
23  2 ROYALE 2350 CC     ST CUD  FBG SV IO 235  MRCR 8    3800     11100  12600
------------------------ 1993 BOATS ------------------------------------------------
17  4 CLASSIC 1750 BR    ST RNBT FBG SV IO 115  MRCR 7  1 2000      4000   4650
17  4 CLASSIC 1750 FS    ST RNBT FBG SV IO 115  MRCR 7  1 2000      4350   5050
18  8 CLASSIC 1900 BR    ST RNBT FBG SV IO 160  MRCR 7  3 2400      5050   5850
18  8 CLASSIC 1900 CC    ST CUD  FBG SV IO 160  MRCR 7  3 2400      5150   5900
18  8 CLASSIC 1900 FS    ST RNBT FBG SV IO 160  MRCR 7  3 2400      5050   5800
19  7 LEGEND 2000 BR        RNBT FBG SV IO 180  MRCR 7  8 2550      5650   6500
21    LEGEND 2100 BR        RNBT FBG SV IO 205  MRCR 8  2 3000      7450   8600
21    LEGEND 2100 CC        CUD  FBG SV IO 205  MRCR 8  2 3000      7850   9000
22  8 INTERCEPTOR 2300 BR ST RNBT FBG SV IO 235 MRCR 7  7 2850      7750   8900
22  8 INTERCEPTOR 2300 CC ST CUD FBG SV IO 235  MRCR 7  7 2850      8250   9400
23  2 ROYALE 2350 CC     ST CUD  FBG SV IO 235  MRCR 8    3800     10400  11800
27    ROYALE 2650 AC     CBNCR   FBG SV IO 300  MRCR 8  6 5400     21300  23700
------------------------ 1992 BOATS ------------------------------------------------
17  4 CLASSIC 1750       ST RNBT FBG SV IO 130       7  3 2010      3900   4550
18    CLASSIC 1900       ST RNBT FBG SV IO 130  MRCR 7  3 2200      4650   5350
18  8 CLASSIC 1900 CC    ST CUD  FBG SV IO 130  OMC  7  3 2200      4550   5250
18  8 ELEGANTE 1900      ST RNBT FBG SV IO 175-185    7 3 2400      4750   5650
20  2 ELEGANTE 2000      ST RNBT FBG SV IO 175        7 7 2650      5950   6850
20  2 ELEGANTE 2000 CC   ST CUD  FBG SV IO 175        7 7 2650      6200   7100
22  8 INTERCEPTOR 2300   ST RNBT FBG SV IO 235-260    7 7 2850      7200   8500
22  8 INTERCEPTOR 2300 CC ST CUD FBG SV IO 235-260    7 7 2850      7600   9050
23  7 ROYALE 2350 CC     ST CUD  FBG SV IO 235-260    8   3960    10200  11800
------------------------ 1991 BOATS ------------------------------------------------
17  4 CLASSIC 1750       ST RNBT FBG SV IO 130        7 3 2010      3650   4250
18  8 CLASSIC 1900       ST RNBT FBG SV IO 130   MRCR 7 3 2200      4400   5050
18  8 CLASSIC 1900       ST RNBT FBG SV IO 175-185    7 3 2200      4500   5200
18  8 CLASSIC 1900 CC    ST CUD  FBG SV IO 130   OMC  7 3 2200      4200   4900
18  8 ELEGANTE 1900      ST RNBT FBG SV IO 175-185    7 3 2400      4600   5400
20  2 ELEGANTE 2000      ST RNBT FBG SV IO 175        7 7 2650      5600   6400
20  2 ELEGANTE 2000 CC   ST CUD  FBG SV IO 175        7 7 2650      5800   6700
22  8 INTERCEPTOR 2300   ST RNBT FBG SV IO 235-260    7 7 2850      6750   8000
22  8 INTERCEPTOR 2300 CC ST CUD FBG SV IO 235-260    7 7 2850      7150   8450
23  7 ROYALE 2350 CC     ST CUD  FBG SV IO 235-260    8   3960     9550  11100
        ....For earlier years, see the BUC Used Boat Price Guide, Volume 3
```

CARIBBEAN BOATS
DIV OF HARDIN MARINE
ANAHEIM CA 92805   COAST GUARD MFG ID- HAO See inside cover to adjust price for area

```
 LOA   NAME AND/       TOP/ BOAT  -HULL- ----ENGINE---  BEAM   WGT  DRAFT RETAIL RETAIL
FT IN  OR MODEL        RIG  TYPE  MTL TP TP #  HP  MFG  FT IN   LBS  FT IN  LOW    HIGH
------------------------ 1986 BOATS ------------------------------------------------
18    MARAUDER          OP SKI  FBG SV JT 333 HARD 6 8 1800     3950   4600
18  4 CARIBBEAN SKI     OP SKI  FBG SV JT 333 HARD 6 8 1800     4050   4700
19    RENEGADE          OP SKI  FBG SV JT 333 HARD 7 1 1850     4450   5100
20    ARIES B/R         OP RNBT FBG SV JT 260 OMC  7 2          3850   4500
20    ARIES B/R         OP RNBT FBG SV JT 333 HARD 7 2          5650   6450
20  2 SPORTCRUZ         OP SPTCR FBG SV JT 260 MRCR 7 2 2300    4250   4950
20  2 SPORTCRUZ         OP SPTCR FBG SV JT 260 HARD 7 2 2243    5700   6500
24  3 EMPEROR           OP OVNTR FBG SV IO 260          3520    6900   7900
26    CARIBBEAN 2600 LTD OP OVNTR FBG SV IO 260 MRCR 8   3960   8500   9800
------------------------ 1985 BOATS ------------------------------------------------
18    MARAUDER          OP SKI  FBG SV JT 333 HARD 6 8 1800     3800   4400
18  4 CARIBBEAN SKI     OP SKI  FBG SV JT 333 HARD 6 8 1800     4050   4400
20    ARIES B/R         OP RNBT FBG SV JT 260 OMC  7 2          3700   4300
20    ARIES B/R         OP RNBT FBG SV JT 260 OMC  7 2          5400   6200
20  2 SPORTCRUZ         OP SPTCR FBG SV JT 260 MRCR 7 2 2300    4050   4750
20  2 SPORTCRUZ         OP SPTCR FBG SV JT 260 HARD 7 2 2243    4900   5600
21  3 BOSS              OP SPTCR FBG SV JT 260 MRCR 7 10        5600   6400
21  3 BOSS              OP SPTCR FBG SV JT 260 MRCR 7 10        6450   7450
22 10 CARIBBEAN 2300    OP OVNTR FBG SV IO 260 MRCR 7 11        6100   7000
26    CARIBBEAN 2600 LTD OP OVNTR FBG SV IO 260 MRCR 8   3960   8200   9400
------------------------ 1984 BOATS ------------------------------------------------
18    MARAUDER          OP SKI  FBG SV JT 333 HARD 6 8 1800     3600   4200
18  4 CARIBBEAN SKI     OP SKI  FBG SV JT 333 HARD 6 8 1800     3700   4300
```

```
CARIBBEAN BOATS            -CONTINUED    See inside cover to adjust price for area
  LOA  NAME AND/         TOP/ BOAT  -HULL- ----ENGINE--- BEAM  WGT  DRAFT RETAIL RETAIL
 FT IN  OR MODEL         RIG  TYPE  MTL TP TP # HP   MFG  FT IN LBS  FT IN  LOW   HIGH
-------------------- 1984 BOATS --------------------------------------------------------
 20    ARIES B/R          OP  RNBT  FBG SV IO  260  OMC  7  2       3600  4150
 20    ARIES B/R          OP  RNBT  FBG SV JT  333  HARD 7  2       5150  5900
 20  2 SPORTCRUZ          OP  SPTCR FBG SV IO  260  MRCR 7  7  2300 3950  4550
 20  2 SPORTCRUZ          OP  SPTCR FBG SV JT  333  HARD 7  7  2243 5200  5950
 21  3 BOSS               OP  SPTCR FBG SV IO  260  MRCR 7 10      4700  5400
 21  3 BOSS               OP  SPTCR FBG SV JT  333  HARD 7 10      6200  7100
 22 10 CARIBBEAN 2300     OP  OVNTR FBG SV IO  260  MRCR 7 11      5900  6750
 26    CARIBBEAN 2600 LTD OP  OVNTR FBG SV IO  260  MRCR 8    3960 7900  9050
```

CARIBE INDUSTRIES INC
LATROBE PA 15650   See inside cover to adjust price for area

```
  LOA  NAME AND/         TOP/ BOAT  -HULL- ----ENGINE--- BEAM  WGT  DRAFT RETAIL RETAIL
 FT IN  OR MODEL         RIG  TYPE  MTL TP TP # HP   MFG  FT IN LBS  FT IN  LOW   HIGH
-------------------- 1993 BOATS --------------------------------------------------------
 16 11 CAPRICE 17 BOW RIDER OP RNBT FBG DV OB           6  5 1800  4250  4950
 16 11 CAPRICE 17 BOW RIDER OP RNBT FBG DV IO 120-205   6  5 1800  4400  5350
 16 11 CAPRICE 17 CLASSIC   OP RNBT FBG DV IO 130-205   6  5 1800  4700  5850
 18 10 CAPRICE 19 BOW RIDER OP RNBT FBG DV OB           7  6 2500  5550  6350
 18 10 CAPRICE 19 BOW RIDER OP RNBT FBG DV IO 130-230   7  6 2500  6500  7850
 18 10 CAPRICE 19 BOW RIDER OP RNBT FBG DV IO 245 VLVO  7  6 2500  7050  8100
 18 10 CAPRICE 19 CLOSD BOW OP RNBT FBG DV OB           7  6 1600  3850  4500
 18 10 CAPRICE 19 CLOSD BOW OP RNBT FBG DV IO 120-245   7  6       6650  7650
 18 10 CARIBE VOYAGER 19   OP CUD  FBG DV SE            7  6 2650  **    **
 18 10 CARIBE VOYAGER 19   OP CUD  FBG DV IO 130-230    7  6 2650  6700  8300
 18 10 CARIBE VOYAGER 19   OP CUD  FBG DV IO 245-260    7  6 2650  7500  8650

 19  2 CARIBE 200         OP RNBT FBG DV IO        OMC  7  8 2900  **    **
 19  2 CARIBE 200         OP RNBT FBG DV IO 130-235     7  8 2900  7050  8650
 19  2 CARIBE 200         OP RNBT FBG DV IO 245-260     7  8 2900  7800  8950
 19  2 COHO               OP SF   FBG DV IO        OMC  7  8 3050  **    **
 19  2 COHO               OP SF   FBG DV IO 130-235     7  8 3050  8650 10700
 19  2 COHO               OP SF   FBG DV IO 245-260     7  8 3050  9550 10900
 19  2 COHO 200           OP SF   FBG DV IO        OMC  7  8 2950  **    **
 19  2 COHO 200           OP SF   FBG DV IO 130-260     7  8 3050  8550 10700
 19  2 SUPER SPORT II     OP RNBT FBG DV IO       VLVO  7  8 3000  **    **
     IO 175-235  7250  9000, IO 245-270  7950  9150, IO  370 OMC 9900 11200

 19  2 VINDICATOR         OP RNBT FBG DV IO       VLVO  7  8 3000  **    **
 19  2 VINDICATOR         OP RNBT FBG DV IO 180-275     7  8 3000  7750  9550
 19  2 VINDICATOR         OP RNBT FBG DV IO 330-370     7  8 3000  9550 11300
 22  3 CARIBE FISHERMAN 23 OP SF  FBG DV OB             8    3500  9450 10700
 22  3 CARIBE FISHERMAN 23 OP SF  FBG DV IO 175-260     8    3500 12100 14800
 22  3 CARIBE VOYAGER 23  OP CUD  FBG DV IO        OMC  8    3500  **    **
 22  3 CARIBE VOYAGER 23  OP CUD  FBG DV IO 205-260     8    3500 10700 13000
-------------------- 1992 BOATS --------------------------------------------------------
 16 11 CAPRICE 17 BOW RIDER OP RNBT FBG DV OB           6  5 1800  4100  4750
 16 11 CAPRICE 17 BOW RIDER OP RNBT FBG DV IO 120-205   6  5 1800  4050  5000
 16 11 CAPRICE 17 CLASSIC   OP RNBT FBG DV IO 130-205   6  5 1800  4400  5450
 18 10 CAPRICE 19 BOW RIDER OP RNBT FBG DV OB           7  6 2500  5300  6100
 18 10 CAPRICE 19 BOW RIDER OP RNBT FBG DV IO 130-230   7  6 2500  6050  7350
 18 10 CAPRICE 19 BOW RIDER OP RNBT FBG DV IO 245 VLVO  7  6 2500  6600  7600
 18 10 CAPRICE 19 CLOSD BOW OP RNBT FBG DV OB           7  6 1600  3700  4350
 18 10 CAPRICE 19 CLOSD BOW OP RNBT FBG DV IO 120-245   7  6       6200  7150
 18 10 CARIBE VOYAGER 19   OP CUD  FBG DV SE            7  6 2650  **    **
 18 10 CARIBE VOYAGER 19   OP CUD  FBG DV IO 130-230    7  6 2650  6250  7750
 18 10 CARIBE VOYAGER 19   OP CUD  FBG DV IO 245-260    7  6 2650  7000  8050

 19  2 CARIBE 200         OP RNBT FBG DV IO        OMC  7  8 2900  **    **
 19  2 CARIBE 200         OP RNBT FBG DV IO 130-235     7  8 2900  6600  8100
 19  2 CARIBE 200         OP RNBT FBG DV IO 245-260     7  8 2900  7300  8400
 19  2 COHO               OP SF   FBG DV IO        OMC  7  8 3050  **    **
 19  2 COHO               OP SF   FBG DV IO 130-235     7  8 3050  8100  9950
 19  2 COHO               OP SF   FBG DV IO 245-260     7  8 3050  9000 10200
 19  2 COHO 200           OP SF   FBG DV IO 130-235     7  8 3050  8000  9750
 19  2 COHO 200           OP SF   FBG DV IO        OMC  7  8 2950  **    **
 19  2 COHO 200           OP SF   FBG DV IO 245-260     7  8 3050  8850 10000
 19  2 SUPER SPORT II     OP RNBT FBG DV IO       VLVO  7  8 3000  **    **
     IO 175-235  6800  8400, IO 245-270  7450  8550, IO  370 OMC 9300 10600

 19  2 VENTURE            OP RNBT FBG DV IO        OMC  7  8 3050  **    **
 19  2 VENTURE            OP RNBT FBG DV IO 130-200     7  8 2950  6650  8300
 19  2 VENTURE            OP RNBT FBG DV IO 205-260     7  8 3050  7250  8500
 19  2 VINDICATOR         OP RNBT FBG DV IO       VLVO  7  8 3000  **    **
 19  2 VINDICATOR         OP RNBT FBG DV IO 180-275     7  8 3000  7200  8950
 19  2 VINDICATOR         OP RNBT FBG DV IO 330-370     7  8 3000  9000 10700
 22  3 CARIBE FISHERMAN 23 OP SF  FBG DV OB             8    3500  9150 10400
 22  3 CARIBE FISHERMAN 23 OP SF  FBG DV IO 175-260     8    3500 11400 13900
 22  3 CARIBE VOYAGER 23  OP CUD  FBG DV IO        OMC  8    3500  **    **
 22  3 CARIBE VOYAGER 23  OP CUD  FBG DV IO 205-260     8    3500 10100 12200
-------------------- 1991 BOATS --------------------------------------------------------
 16 11 CAPRICE 17 BOW RIDER OP RNBT FBG DV OB           6  5 1800  3950  4600
 16 11 CAPRICE 17 BOW RIDER OP RNBT FBG DV IO 120-205   6  5 1800  3800  4700
 16 11 CAPRICE 17 CLASSIC   OP RNBT FBG DV IO 130  OMC  6  5 1800  4100  4750
 16 11 CAPRICE 17 CLASSIC   OP RNBT FBG DV IO 135-205   6  5 1800  4500  5150
 18 10 CAPRICE 19 BOW RIDER OP RNBT FBG DV OB           7  6 2500  5100  5900
 18 10 CAPRICE 19 BOW RIDER OP RNBT FBG DV IO 130-230   7  6 2500  5700  6900
 18 10 CAPRICE 19 BOW RIDER OP RNBT FBG DV IO 245 VLVO  7  6 2500  6200  7150
 18 10 CAPRICE 19 CLOSD BOW OP RNBT FBG DV OB           7  6 2500  4550  5200
 18 10 CAPRICE 19 CLOSD BOW OP RNBT FBG DV IO 120-205   7  6 2500  5500  6300
 18 10 CAPRICE 19 CLOSD BOW OP RNBT FBG DV IO 245 VLVO  7  6 2500  6050  6950
 22  3 CARIBE FISHERMAN 23 OP SF  FBG DV OB             8    3500  8700 10000
 22  3 CARIBE FISHERMAN 23 OP SF  FBG DV IO 175-260     8    3500 10700 13000
-------------------- 1990 BOATS --------------------------------------------------------
 20    CARIBE 200         OP RNBT FBG DV IO 130-262     7  8 2900  6450  7950
 20    CARIBE 200         OP RNBT FBG DV IO 271         7  8 2900  7300  8400
 20    COHO               OP SF   FBG DV IO 130-262     7  8 2900  7650  9500
 20    COHO               OP SF   FBG DV IO 271         7  8 2900  8700 10000
 20    COHO 200           OP SF   FBG DV IO 130-262     7  8 2950  7700  9550
 20    COHO 200           OP SF   FBG DV IO 271         7  8 2950  8850 10100
 20    SUPER RIDER        OP RNBT FBG DV IO 130-262     7  8 3050  6650  8200
 20    SUPER RIDER        OP RNBT FBG DV IO 271         7  8 3050  7500  8600
 20    SUPER SPORT II     OP RNBT FBG DV IO 165-270     7  8 3000  6600  8100
 20    SUPER SPORT II     OP RNBT FBG DV IO 271         7  8 3000  7350  8450
 20    SUPER SPORT II     OP RNBT FBG DV IO 350  OMC    7  8 3000  8300  9550

 20    VINDICATOR         OP RNBT FBG DV IO 200-270     7  8 3000  6750  8150
     IO 271-300  7400  9050, IO 311-350  8100  9600, IO 365 MRCR 8950 10100
     IO 460 OMC 11900 13500
-------------------- 1989 BOATS --------------------------------------------------------
 19  2 CARIBE 200         OP RNBT FBG DV IO 130-235     7  6       5200  6200
 19  2 CARIBE 200         OP RNBT FBG DV IO 260         7  6       5700  6550
 19  2 COHO               OP FSH  FBG DV IO 130-235     7  6       5650  6900
 19  2 COHO               OP FSH  FBG DV IO 260  OMC    7  6       6200  7100
 19  2 COHO 200           OP FSH  FBG DV IO 130-260     7  6       5950  7150
 19  2 SUPER RIDER        OP RNBT FBG DV IO 130-260     7  6       5300  6550
 19  2 SUPER SPORT II     OP RNBT FBG DV IO        OMC  7  6       **    **
 19  2 SUPER SPORT II     OP RNBT FBG DV IO 175-235     7  6       5400  6400
 19  2 SUPER SPORT II     OP RNBT FBG DV IO 260         7  6       5700  6950
 19  2 VINDICATOR         OP CUD  FBG DV IO        OMC  7  6       **    **
 19  2 VINDICATOR         OP CUD  FBG DV IO 200-260     7  6       5400  6650
-------------------- 1988 BOATS --------------------------------------------------------
 19  2 CARIBE 200         OP RNBT FBG DV IO 130-260     7  6       5000  6200
 19  2 COHO               OP FSH  FBG DV IO 130-260     7  6       5500  6750
 19  2 COHO 200           OP FSH  FBG DV IO 130-260     7  6       5500  6200
 19  2 SUPER RIDER        OP RNBT FBG DV IO 130-260     7  6       5000  6200
 19  2 SUPER SPORT II     OP RNBT FBG DV IO        OMC  7  6       **    **
 19  2 SUPER SPORT II     OP RNBT FBG DV IO 175-260     7  6       5000  6200
 19  2 VINDICATOR         OP CUD  FBG DV IO        OMC  7  6       **    **
 19  2 VINDICATOR         OP CUD  FBG DV IO 200-260     7  6       5100  6300
-------------------- 1987 BOATS --------------------------------------------------------
 19  2 CARIBE 200         OP RNBT FBG DV IO 130-260     7  6       4750  5900
 19  2 COHO               OP FSH  FBG DV IO 130-235     7  6       5200  6450
 19  2 COHO 200           OP FSH  FBG DV IO 260         7  6       5200  6450
 19  2 SUPER RIDER        OP RNBT FBG DV IO 130-260     7  6       4750  5900
 19  2 SUPER SPORT II     OP RNBT FBG DV IO        OMC  7  6       **    **
 19  2 SUPER SPORT II     OP RNBT FBG DV IO 175-260     7  6       4750  5900
 19  2 VINDICATOR         OP CUD  FBG DV IO        OMC  7  6       **    **
 19  2 VINDICATOR         OP CUD  FBG DV IO 200-260     7  6       4850  5950
-------------------- 1986 BOATS --------------------------------------------------------
 19  2 CARIBE 200         OP RNBT FBG DV IO 260         7  6       4900  5600
 19  2 COHO 200           OP FSH  FBG DV IO 260         7  6       5050  5800
 19  2 SUPER RIDER        OP RNBT FBG DV IO 260         7  6       4900  5600
 19  2 SUPER SPORT        OP RNBT FBG DV IO 260         7  6       4900  5600
-------------------- 1985 BOATS --------------------------------------------------------
 19  2 CARIBE BOW RIDER   OP RNBT FBG DV IO 260         7  6       4700  5400
 19  2 CARIBE STANDARD    OP RNBT FBG DV IO 260         7  6       4700  5400
 19  2 COHO               OP FSH  FBG DV IO 175         7  6       4700  5600
 19  2 SUPER SPORT        OP RNBT FBG DV IO 260         7  6       4700  5400
-------------------- 1984 BOATS --------------------------------------------------------
 19  2 CARIBE BOW RIDER   OP RNBT FBG DV IO 260         7  6       4550  5250
 19  2 CARIBE STANDARD    OP RNBT FBG DV IO 260         7  6       4550  5250
 19  2 COHO               OP FSH  FBG DV IO 175         7  6       4700  5400
```

CARIBE INDUSTRIES INC   -CONTINUED   See inside cover to adjust price for area

LOA FT IN	NAME AND/ OR MODEL	TOP/ RIG	BOAT TYPE	-HULL- MTL TP TP	----ENGINE--- # HP MFG	BEAM FT IN	WGT LBS	DRAFT FT IN	RETAIL LOW	RETAIL HIGH
				---- 1984 BOATS						
19 2	SUPER SPORT	OP	RNBT	FBG DV IO	260	7 6			4550	5250

....For earlier years, see the BUC Used Boat Price Guide, Volume 3

CARLSON MARINE INC
SCHERERVILLE IN 46375   See inside cover to adjust price for area

LOA FT IN	NAME AND/ OR MODEL	TOP/ RIG	BOAT TYPE	-HULL- MTL TP TP	----ENGINE--- # HP MFG	BEAM FT IN	WGT LBS	DRAFT FT IN	RETAIL LOW	RETAIL HIGH
				---- 1993 BOATS						
36	SABLE 36	SLP	SACAC	F/S CT IB T	18D VLVO	15 6	10000	2 11	73400	80700
				---- 1992 BOATS						
36	SABLE 36	SLP	SAIL	F/S CT IB T	18D VLVO	15 6	10000	2 11	69100	75900
				---- 1991 BOATS						
32	ULTIMATE CONCEPT	SLP	MS	FBG CT OB		13 4	6200	1 6	42000	46700
				---- 1990 BOATS						
32	ULTIMATE CONCEPT	SLP	MS	FBG CT OB		13 4	6200	1 6	39500	43900

CAROLINA CLASSIC BOATS
EDENTON NC 27932   COAST GUARD MFG ID- CAR See inside cover to adjust price for area

For more recent years, see the BUC Used Boat Price Guide, Volume 1

LOA FT IN	NAME AND/ OR MODEL	TOP/ RIG	BOAT TYPE	-HULL- MTL TP TP	----ENGINE--- # HP MFG	BEAM FT IN	WGT LBS	DRAFT FT IN	RETAIL LOW	RETAIL HIGH
				---- 1996 BOATS						
25 2	CAROLINA CLASSIC 25	OP	EXPSF	FBG DV IB	385	8 6	8500	2 6	32900	36600
25 2	CAROLINA CLASSIC 25	HT	SF	FBG DV IO	375 VLVO	8 6	8500	3	35400	39400
25 2	CC 25	FB	SF	FBG DV IO	375 VLVO	8 6	8500	3	36000	40000
25 2	EXPRESS	OP	EXPSF	FBG DV IB	330	8 6	8500	2 6	32100	35700
28 5	CAROLINA CLASSIC 28	MT	EXPSF	FBG DV IB	T230D VLVO	10 6	15000	3	76700	84200
28 5	CAROLINA CLASSIC 28	F+M	EXPSF	FBG DV IO	T330 VLVO	10 6	15000	2 6	50300	55300
28 5	CAROLINA CLASSIC 28	TT	EXPSF	FBG DV IB	T250D CUM	10 6	15000	3	78400	86200
34 9	35 EXPRESS	H+M	EXP	FBG DV IB	T450D CUM	13 6	28000	3	153500	169000
34 9	CAROLINA CLASSIC 35	OP	EXP	FBG DV IB	T450D	13 6	28000	3	171500	188500
34 9	CAROLINA CLASSIC 35	FB	EXP	FBG DV IB	T480D VLVO	13 6	28000	3	173000	190000
34 9	CAROLINA CLASSIC 35	TT	EXPSF	FBG DV IB	T450D CUM	13 6	28000	3	171000	188000
				---- 1995 BOATS						
25 2	CAROLINA CLASSIC 25	OP	EXPSF	FBG DV IB	385	8 6	8500	2 6	31100	34600
25 2	CAROLINA CLASSIC 25	HT	SF	FBG DV IO	375 VLVO	8 6	8500	3	33100	36700
25 2	CC 25	FB	SF	FBG DV IO	375 VLVO	8 6	8500	3	33600	37300
25 2	EXPRESS	OP	EXPSF	FBG DV IB	330	8 6	8500	2 6	30400	33700
28 5	CAROLINA CLASSIC 28	MT	EXPSF	FBG DV IB	T230D VLVO	10 6	15000	3	72800	80000
28 5	CAROLINA CLASSIC 28	F+M	EXPSF	FBG DV IO	T330 VLVO	10 6	15000	2 6	47200	51900
28 5	CAROLINA CLASSIC 28	TT	EXPSF	FBG DV IB	T250D CUM	10 6	15000	3	74500	81900
34 9	35 EXPRESS	H+M	EXP	FBG DV IB	T450D CUM	13 6	28000	3	146000	160500
34 9	CAROLINA CLASSIC 35	OP	EXP	FBG DV IB	T450D	13 6	28000	3	163000	179000
34 9	CAROLINA CLASSIC 35	FB	EXP	FBG DV IB	T480D VLVO	13 6	28000	3	164500	180500
34 9	CAROLINA CLASSIC 35	TT	EXPSF	FBG DV IB	T450D CUM	13 6	28000	3	162500	179000

CAROLINA COAST MARINE
HAMPSTEAD NC 28443   COAST GUARD MFG ID- WHJ See inside cover to adjust price for area

LOA FT IN	NAME AND/ OR MODEL	TOP/ RIG	BOAT TYPE	-HULL- MTL TP TP	----ENGINE--- # HP MFG	BEAM FT IN	WGT LBS	DRAFT FT IN	RETAIL LOW	RETAIL HIGH
				---- 1993 BOATS						
25 6	CAROLINA 26 SF	OP	CTRCN	FBG SV OB		8 2	4800	2 4	23000	25500
25 6	CAROLINA 26 SF	OP	CTRCN	FBG SV IO	330	8 2	4700	2 6	19000	21200
25 6	CAROLINA 26 SF	OP	CTRCN	FBG SV IO	230D VLVO	8 2	4700	2 6	25000	27700
34 8	CUSTOM 35 FBSF	FB	SF	FBG SV IB	T400D VLVO	12 8	16500	2 8	113000	124000
34 8	CUSTOM 35 SF	OP	SF	FBG SV IB	T400D VLVO	12 8	14500	2 8	106500	117000
				---- 1992 BOATS						
25 6	CAROLINA 26 SF	OP	CTRCN	FBG SV OB		8 2	4800	2 4	22100	24500
25 6	CAROLINA 26 SF	OP	CTRCN	FBG SV IO	330	8 2	4700	2 6	17400	19400
25 6	CAROLINA 26 SF	OP	CTRCN	FBG SV IO	230D VLVO	8 2	4700	2 6	23400	26000
34 8	CUSTOM 35 FBSF	FB	SF	FBG SV IB	T400D VLVO	12 8	16500	2 8	107500	118500
34 8	CUSTOM 35 SF	OP	SF	FBG SV IB	T400D VLVO	12 8	14500	2 8	101500	111500

CAROLINA FIBERGLASS PROD CO
SHEARWATER   See inside cover to adjust price for area
WILSON NC 27893

LOA FT IN	NAME AND/ OR MODEL	TOP/ RIG	BOAT TYPE	-HULL- MTL TP TP	----ENGINE--- # HP MFG	BEAM FT IN	WGT LBS	DRAFT FT IN	RETAIL LOW	RETAIL HIGH
				---- 1984 BOATS						
17	17060	OP	JON	FBG FL OB		7 2	475		1200	1450

....For earlier years, see the BUC Used Boat Price Guide, Volume 3

CAROLINA SKIFF LLC
WAYCROSS GA 31501   COAST GUARD MFG ID- EKH See inside cover to adjust price for area

For more recent years, see the BUC Used Boat Price Guide, Volume 1

LOA FT IN	NAME AND/ OR MODEL	TOP/ RIG	BOAT TYPE	-HULL- MTL TP TP	----ENGINE--- # HP MFG	BEAM FT IN	WGT LBS	DRAFT FT IN	RETAIL LOW	RETAIL HIGH
				---- 1994 BOATS						
16 8	1765	OP	UTL	FBG FL OB		6 4	610	3	1900	2300
18 8	1965	OP	UTL	FBG FL OB		6 4	720	3	2250	2600
20 8	2180	OP	UTL	FBG FL OB		7 8	1000	3	2600	3000
23 8	2480	OP	UTL	FBG FL OB		7 8	1200	3	3050	3550
				---- 1993 BOATS						
16 8	1765	OP	UTL	FBG FL OB		6 4	610	3	1800	2150
18 8	1965	OP	UTL	FBG FL OB		6 4	720	3	2100	2500
18 8	1980	OP	UTL	FBG FL OB		6 4	870	3	2550	2950
20 8	2180	OP	UTL	FBG FL OB		7 8	1000	3	2450	2850
23 8	2480	OP	UTL	FBG FL OB		7 8	1200	3	2950	3400
				---- 1992 BOATS						
16 8	1765	OP	UTL	FBG FL OB		6 4	610	3	1750	2050
18 8	1965	OP	UTL	FBG FL OB		6 4	720	3	2000	2350
20 8	2180	OP	UTL	FBG FL OB		7 8	1000	3	2350	2750
23 8	2480	OP	UTL	FBG FL OB		7 8	1200	3	2800	3250
				---- 1991 BOATS						
16 8	1765	OP	UTL	FBG FL OB		6 4		3	1950	2250
18 8	1965	OP	UTL	FBG FL OB		6 4		3	2450	2850
20 8	2180	OP	UTL	FBG FL OB		7 8		3	2800	3250
23 8	2480	OP	UTL	FBG FL OB		7 8		3	3200	3700
				---- 1989 BOATS						
16	CAROLINA 1650		UTL	AL FL OB		6 3	1200		2900	3400
16	CAROLINA 1660		UTL	AL FL OB		7 6	1400		3350	3900
18	CAROLINA 1850		UTL	AL FL OB		7 8	1600		3500	4100
19	CAROLINA 1970		UTL	AL FL OB		7 8	2000		4050	4750
21	CAROLINA 2170		UTL	AL FL OB		8 2	2350		4600	5250
24	CAROLINA 2480		UTL	AL FL OB		8 6	3000		6350	7300

CARRERA POWERBOAT CORP
MIAMI FL 33166   COAST GUARD MFG ID- CBC See inside cover to adjust price for area

LOA FT IN	NAME AND/ OR MODEL	TOP/ RIG	BOAT TYPE	-HULL- MTL TP TP	----ENGINE--- # HP MFG	BEAM FT IN	WGT LBS	DRAFT FT IN	RETAIL LOW	RETAIL HIGH
				---- 1987 BOATS						
26 8	8M SPORTFISH	OP	CTRCN	FBG DV OB		8	3500		12400	14100
26 8	CARRERA SS8M	OP	OFF	FBG DV OB		8	3500		12500	14200
26 8	CARRERA SS8M	OP	OFF	FBG DV IO	260-350	8			12700	15900
26 8	CARRERA SS8M	OP	OFF	FBG DV IO	T260 MRCR	8			14900	16900
26 8	CARRERA SS8M	OP	RACE	FBG DV IO	T350 MRCR	8			17200	19500
26 8	CARRERA SS8M	OP	OFF	FBG DV IO	454 MRCR	8			15400	17400
29 7	CARRERA SS9M	OP	OFF	FBG DV OB		8			17400	19800
29 7	CARRERA SS9M	OP	OFF	FBG DV IO	T330-T420	8	7000		23400	28800
29 7	CARRERA SS9M	OP	OFF	FBG DV IO	T454 MRCR	8	7000		27100	30100
32	32 OPENFISH	OP	OFF	FBG DV OB		8 6	4500		20000	22200
35 8	CORSICA 36	OP	OFF	FBG DV IO	T330 MRCR	8 6	8500		46500	51100
	IO T370 MRCR 48000		52800, IO T420	MRCR 50800	55800, IO T454	MRCR	52900	58100		
				---- 1986 BOATS						
26 8	CARRERA SS8M	OP	RACE	FBG DV OB		8	3500		12000	13600
26 8	CARRERA SS8M	OP	RACE	FBG DV IO	260-350	8			11500	14300
26 8	CARRERA SS8M	OP	RACE	FBG DV IO	T260 MRCR	8			13400	15200
26 8	CARRERA SS8M	OP	RACE	FBG DV IO	T330-T350	8			14900	16700
29 7	CARRERA SS9M	OP	RACE	FBG DV OB		8			16500	18700
29 7	CARRERA SS9M	OP	RACE	FBG DV IO	T300-T370	8	7000		17500	21100
29 7	CARRERA SS9M	OP	RACE	FBG DV IO	T400-T440	8	7000		19700	23300
35 8	CORSICA 36	OP	RACE	FBG DV IO	T330 MRCR	8 6	8500		35000	38900
	IO T370 MRCR 36500		40600, IO T400	MRCR 38000	42200, IO T440	MRCR	40200	44700		

....For earlier years, see the BUC Used Boat Price Guide, Volume 3

CARRI-CRAFT CATAMARANS INC

WAUWATOSA WI 53226-3439 COAST GUARD MFG ID- CRR See inside cover to adjust price for area
FORMERLY CARRI-CRAFT INC

For more recent years, see the BUC Used Boat Price Guide, Volume 1

LOA FT	LOA IN	NAME AND/ OR MODEL	TOP/ RIG	BOAT TYPE	-HULL- MTL	-HULL- TP	ENGINE TP	ENGINE # HP	ENGINE MFG	BEAM FT	BEAM IN	WGT LBS	DRAFT FT	DRAFT IN	RETAIL LOW	RETAIL HIGH
		1995 BOATS														
43		COASTAL CAT 432	FB	MY	F/S	CT	IB	T300D	CAT	14	6	27000	3	2	212500	233500
43		EXPRESS CAT 431	FB	MY	F/S	CT	IO	T300	MRCR	14	6	27000	3	2	164500	181000
48		COASTAL CAT 482	FB	MY	F/S	CT	IB	T300D	CAT	14	6	29000	3	2	162500	178500
48		EXPRESS CAT 481	FB	MY	F/S	CT	IO	T300	MRCR	14	6	29000	3	2	135000	148500
53		COASTAL CAT 532	FB	MY	F/S	CT	IB	T300D	CAT	14	6	31000	3	3	159000	175000
53		EXPRESS CAT 531	FB	MY	F/S	CT	IO	T300	MRCR	14	6	31000	3	3	157500	173000
60		COASTAL CAT 602	FB	MY	F/S	CT	IB	T300D	CAT	14	6	32000	3	4	202000	222000
60		EXPRESS CAT 601	FB	MY	F/S	CT	IB	T300	MRCR	14	6	32000	3	4	202500	222500
		1994 BOATS														
43		SRS-431	FB	SDN	F/S	CT	IB	T200D	MRCR	14	6	26500	2	11	183500	202000
48		BIMINI	FB	SDNSF	F/S	CT	IB	T250	MRCR	14	4	18000	3	2	94900	104500
48		CATALINA	FB	SDN	F/S	CT	IB	T250	MRCR	14	4	21000	3	2	118000	129500
48		SRS-481	FB	SDN	F/S	CT	IB	T300D	CUM	14	6	28000	3		141000	155000
53		SRS-531	FB	MY	F/S	CT	IB	T300D	CUM	14	6	29500	3		148000	162500
60		BIMINI	FB	SDNSF	F/S	CT	IB	T250	MRCR	14	7	20200	3	1	**	**
60		CATALINA	FB	SDN	F/S	CT	IB	T250	MRCR	14	7	22500	3	2	**	**
60		NEW YORKER	FB	TCMY	F/S	CT	IB	T250	MRCR	14	7	23500	3	4	**	**
60		RIVIERA	FB	TCMY	F/S	CT	IB	T250	MRCR	14	7	23500	3	4	**	**
60		SRS-601	FB	MY	F/S	CT	IB	T300D	CUM	14	6	31500	3	2	191500	210500
		1993 BOATS														
48		BIMINI	FB	SDNSF	F/S	CT	IB	T250	MRCR	14	4	18000	3	2	90700	99700
48		CATALINA	FB	SDN	F/S	CT	IB	T250	MRCR	14	4	21000	3	2	112500	124000
60		BIMINI	FB	SDNSF	F/S	CT	IB	T250	MRCR	14	7	20200	3	1	**	**
60		CATALINA	FB	SDN	F/S	CT	IB	T250	MRCR	14	7	22500	3	2	**	**
60		NEW YORKER	FB	TCMY	F/S	CT	IB	T250	MRCR	14	7	23500	3	4	**	**
60		RIVIERA	FB	TCMY	F/S	CT	IB	T250	MRCR	14	7	23500	3	4	**	**
		1992 BOATS														
48		BERLINER		TCMY	F/S	CT	IB	T175		14	6	21000	4		113000	124000
48		BERLINER		TCMY	F/S	CT	IB	T165D		14	6	24000	4		123500	135500
48		BIKINI		UTL	F/S	CT	IB	T125		14	6	17000	3	9	**	**
48		BIMINI		SDNSF	F/S	CT	IB	T125		14	6	16000	3	10	79400	87200
48		CATALINA	FB	SDN	F/S	CT	IB	T145		14	6	20000	3	10	102000	112000
48		CATALINA	FB	SDN	F/S	CT	IB	T150D		14	6	22000	4		111000	122000
48		HANNIBAL		SDN	F/S	CT	IB	T145		14	6	18000	3	10	98700	108500
48		RIVIERA	FB	TCMY	F/S	CT	IB	T205		14	6	23000	4		117500	129000
48		RIVIERA	FB	TCMY	F/S	CT	IB	T180D		14	6	25000	4		126000	138500
60		BERLINER		TCMY	F/S	CT	IB	T205		14	6	24000	4		**	**
60		BERLINER		TCMY	F/S	CT	IB	T210D		14	6	24000	4		**	**
60		BIKINI		UTL	F/S	CT	IB	T145		14	6	17000	3	9	**	**
60		BIMINI		SDNSF	F/S	CT	IB	T145		14	6	19000	3	10	**	**
60		CATALINA	FB	SDN	F/S	CT	IB	T205		14	6	22000	3	10	**	**
60		CATALINA	FB	SDN	F/S	CT	IB	T180D		14	6	22000	3	10	**	**
60		HANNIBAL		SDN	F/S	CT	IB	T175		14	6	21000	3	10	**	**
60		RIVIERA	FB	TCMY	F/S	CT	IB	T230		14	6	25000	4		209000	229500
60		RIVIERA	FB	TCMY	F/S	CT	IB	T210D		14	6	25000	4		195500	215000

....For earlier years, see the BUC Used Boat Price Guide, Volume 3

CARROLL MARINE LTD

BRISTOL RI 02809-0311 COAST GUARD MFG ID- CIR See inside cover to adjust price for area

For more recent years, see the BUC Used Boat Price Guide, Volume 1

LOA FT	LOA IN	NAME AND/ OR MODEL	TOP/ RIG	BOAT TYPE	-HULL- MTL	-HULL- TP	ENGINE TP	ENGINE # HP	ENGINE MFG	BEAM FT	BEAM IN	WGT LBS	DRAFT FT	DRAFT IN	RETAIL LOW	RETAIL HIGH
		1996 BOATS														
30	1	MUMM 30	SLP	SARAC	KEV	KL	IB	10D	YAN	10	1	4500	6	9	45500	50000
30	8	BRENDAN 28	HT	SF	FBG	DV	IB	T260	MPC	11	3	9000	2	4	50300	55300
35	10	MUMM 36	SLP	SARAC	FBG	KL	IB	18D	YAN	11	10	7910	7	4	79700	87600
39	3	CM1200	SLP	SARAC	KEV	KL	IB	30D	YAN	11	10	10000	8		85900	94400
42	11	NELSON/MAREK 43	SLP	SARAC	FBG	KL	IB	43D	YAN	12	6	14750	8	8	150000	165000
43		NELSON/MAREK 43 R/C	SLP	SARAC	FBG	KL	IB	D	YAN	12	6	18100			151000	166000
45		FARR 45 OD	SLP	SARAC	KEV	KL	IB	47D	YAN	13	6	15174	9	5	208500	229000
46	6	NELSON/MAREK 46	SLP	SARAC	KEV	KL	IB	50D	VLVO	13	6	17500	9	1	199000	219000
46	6	NELSON/MAREK 46 CR	SLP	SARAC	FBG	KL	IB	44D	YAN	13	6	18100	9	1	203000	223000
46	6	NELSON/MAREK 46 PC	SLP	SARAC	KEV	KL	IB	44D	YAN	13	6	19750	9	1	204500	224500
		1995 BOATS														
30	8	BRENDAN 28	HT	SF	FBG	DV	IB	T260	MPC	11	3	9000	2	4	47800	52500
33		TRIPP 33	SLP	SARAC	FBG	KL	IB	12D	WEST	10	4	6100	7		41300	45900
35	10	MUMM 36	SLP	SARAC	FBG	KL	IB	18D	YAN	11	10	7910	7	4	75500	83000
39	3	CM1200	SLP	SARAC	KEV	KL	IB	30D	YAN	11	10	10000	8		81300	89400
40	2	CARROLL MARINE 40	SLP	SARAC	FBG	KL	IB	35D	YAN	13		17000	6	6	112500	123500
41	11	FARR ILC40	SLP	SARAC	KEV	KL	IB	30D	YAN	13	11	12500	8	2	130500	143500
42	11	NELSON/MAREK 43	SLP	SARAC	FBG	KL	IB	43D	YAN	12	6	14750	8	8	142000	156000
43		NELSON/MAREK 43 R/C	SLP	SARAC	FBG	KL	IB	D	YAN						135500	149000
46	6	NELSON/MAREK 46	SLP	SARAC	KEV	KL	IB	50D	VLVO	13	6	17500	9	1	188500	207500
		1994 BOATS														
33		TRIPP 33	SLP	SARAC	FBG	KL	IB	12D	WEST	10	4	6100	7		39100	43400
35	10	MUMM 36	SLP	SARAC	FBG	KL	IB	18D	YAN	11	10	7910	7	4	71500	78600
36		TRIPP 36	SLP	SARAC	FBG	KL	IB	27D	YAN	11	4	10000	7		73700	81000
38	6	FRERS 38	SLP	SARAC	FBG	KL	IB	27D	YAN	12	9	14100	7	4	94800	104000
40	2	CARROLL MARINE 40	SLP	SARAC	FBG	KL	IB	35D	YAN	13		17000	6	6	106500	117000
40	3	TRIPP 40 MARK II	SLP	SARAC	FBG	KL	IB	27D	YAN	12	1	12750	7	9	94700	104000
42	11	NELSON/MAREK 43	SLP	SARAC	FBG	KL	IB	43D	VLVO	12	6	14750	8	8	134500	147500
43		NELSON/MAREK 43 R/C	SLP	SARAC	FBG	KL	IB	D	YAN						128500	141000
45		FRERS 45	SLP	SARAC	FBG	WK	IB	44D	YAN	13	11	23500	6	6	161500	177500
47		TRIPP 47	SLP	SACAC	FBG	KL	IB	47D	YAN	13	9	18800	9		185500	204000
47		TRIPP 47	SLP	SARAC	FBG	KL	IB	47D	YAN	13	9	23000	9		200500	220500
		1993 BOATS														
26	8	TRIPP 26	SLP	SARAC	FBG	KL				8	8	2900	6		15200	17200
33		TRIPP 33	SLP	SARAC	FBG	KL	IB	12D	WEST	10	4	6100	7		37000	41100
35	10	FARR 36	SLP	SARAC	FBG	KL	IB	18D	YAN	11	10	7910	7	4	63900	70200
36		TRIPP 36	SLP	SARAC	FBG	KL	IB	27D	YAN	11	4	10000	7		69800	76700
38	6	FRERS 38	SLP	SARAC	FBG	KL	IB	27D	YAN	12	9	14100	7	4	89800	98600
40	2	CARROLL MARINE 40	SLP	SARAC	FBG	KL	IB	35D	YAN	13		17000	6	6	101000	111000
40	3	TRIPP 40 MARK II	SLP	SARAC	FBG	KL	IB	27D	YAN	12	1	12750	7	9	89700	98600
42	11	NELSON/MAREK 43	SLP	SARAC	FBG	KL	IB	43D	VLVO	12	6	14750	8	8	127500	140000
45		FRERS 45	SLP	SARAC	FBG	WK	IB	44D	YAN	13	11	23500	6	6	153000	168000
47		TRIPP 47	SLP	SACAC	FBG	KL	IB	47D	YAN	13	9	18800	9		176000	193500
47		TRIPP 47	SLP	SARAC	FBG	KL	IB	47D	YAN	13	9	23000	9		190000	209000
		1992 BOATS														
33		TRIPP 33	SLP	SAIL	FBG	KL	IB	12D	WEST	10	4	6100	7		35100	39000
33	3	FRERS 33	SLP	SAIL	FBG	KL	IB	18D	YAN	11	3	9400	6	3	49100	54000
33	3	FRERS 33	SLP	SAIL	FBG	WK	IB	18D	YAN	11	3	9400	4	11	49100	54000
36		TRIPP 36	SLP	SAIL	FBG	KL	IB	27D	YAN	11	4	10000	7		66100	72700
38	6	FRERS 38	SLP	SAIL	FBG	KL	IB	27D	YAN	12	9	13500	7		82200	90300
40	3	TRIPP 40	SLP	SAIL	FBG	KL	IB	27D	YAN	12	1	12750	7	6	91000	100000
40	6	FRERS 41	SLP	SAIL	FBG	KL	IB	35D	YAN	13	1	15950	7	3	92700	102000
40	6	FRERS OFFSHORE 41	SLP	SAIL	FBG	KL	IB	35D	YAN	13	1	17500	6	6	101500	111500
45		FRERS 45	SLP	SA/CR	FBG	KL	IB	44D	YAN	13	11	23500	8	3	145000	159000
45		FRERS 45	SLP	SA/CR	FBG	WK	IB	44D	YAN	13	11	23500	6	6	145000	159000
45		FRERS 45 COMP	SLP	SAIL	FBG	KL	IB	44D	YAN	13	11	20000	8	3	139000	153000
47		TRIPP 47	SLP	SAIL	FBG	KL	IB	47D	YAN	13	8	18800	9		166500	183000
		1991 BOATS														
33	3	FRERS 33	SLP	SAIL	FBG	KL	IB	18D	YAN	11	3	9400	6	3	46800	51400
33	3	FRERS 33	SLP	SAIL	FBG	WK	IB	18D	YAN	11	3	9400	4	11	46800	51400
36		TRIPP 36	SLP	SAIL	FBG	KL	IB	27D	YAN	11	4	10000	7		62600	68800
38	6	FRERS 38	SLP	SAIL	FBG	KL	IB	27D	YAN	12	9	13500	7		77800	85500
40	3	TRIPP 40	SLP	SAIL	FBG	KL	IB	27D	YAN	12	1	12750	7	6	86200	94700
40	6	FRERS 41	SLP	SAIL	FBG	KL	IB	35D	YAN	13	1	15950	7	3	87800	96500
40	6	FRERS OFFSHORE 41	SLP	SAIL	FBG	KL	IB	35D	YAN	13	1	17500	6	6	96200	106000
45		FRERS 45	SLP	SA/CR	FBG	KL	IB	44D	YAN	13	11	23500	8	3	137000	150500
45		FRERS 45	SLP	SA/RC	FBG	WK	IB	44D	YAN	13	11	23500	6	6	137000	150500
45		FRERS 45 COMP	SLP	SAIL	FBG	KL	IB	44D	YAN	13	11	20000	8	3	132000	145000
		1990 BOATS														
33	3	FRERS 33	SLP	SAIL	FBG	KL	IB	18D	YAN	11	3	9400	6	3	43800	48700
38		FRERS 38	SLP	SAIL	FBG	KL	IB	35D	YAN	12	9	13500	7		72200	79300
40	6	FRERS 41	SLP	SAIL	FBG	KL	IB	35D	YAN	13	1	15950	7	3	83200	91400
45		FRERS 45	SLP	SAIL	FBG	KL	IB	44D	YAN	13	11	22000	6	3	126000	138500
		1989 BOATS														
29	9	FRERS 30	SLP	SAIL	FBG	KL	IB	18D	YAN	10	11	6800	5	9	31500	35000
33	3	FRERS 33	SLP	SAIL	FBG	KL	IB	18D	YAN	11	3	8600	6	3	38000	42200
38		FRERS 38	SLP	SAIL	FBG	KL	IB	35D	YAN				7		56700	62300
40	6	FRERS 41	SLP	SAIL	FBG	KL	IB	35D	YAN	13	1	15950	7	3	78800	86600
45		FRERS 45	SLP	SAIL	FBG	KL	IB	44D	YAN	13	9	20000	6	3	114000	125500
		1988 BOATS														
29	9	FRERS 30	SLP	SAIL	FBG	KL	IB	18D	YAN	10	11	6800	5	9	29800	33100
33	3	FRERS 33	SLP	SAIL	FBG	KL	IB	18D	YAN	11	3	9400	4	9	39300	43700
40	6	FRERS 41	SLP	SAIL	FBG	KL	IB	35D	YAN	13	1	15950	5	6	74700	82100

CARTER OFFSHORE LTD

ESSEX ENGLAND See inside cover to adjust price for area

LOA FT	LOA IN	NAME AND/ OR MODEL	TOP/ RIG	BOAT TYPE	-HULL- MTL	-HULL- TP	ENGINE TP	ENGINE # HP	ENGINE MFG	BEAM FT	BEAM IN	WGT LBS	DRAFT FT	DRAFT IN	RETAIL LOW	RETAIL HIGH
		1986 BOATS														
34	8	CARTER 35	SLP	SA/CR	FBG	SK	IB	23D	YAN	11		9300	1	9	33500	37200
37	6	CARTER 4+4	SLP	SA/CR	FBG	SK	IB	51D	PERK	12	6	18500	4		68300	75100

```
CARTER OFFSHORE LTD          -CONTINUED     See inside cover to adjust price for area
LOA   NAME AND/        TOP/ BOAT  -HULL- ----ENGINE--- BEAM   WGT  DRAFT RETAIL RETAIL
FT IN  OR MODEL        RIG  TYPE  MTL TP TP # HP  MFG  FT IN  LBS  FT IN  LOW    HIGH
-------------------- 1986 BOATS -----------------------------------------------------
38 9 CARTER OFFSHORE 39 SLP SA/CR AL  SK IB  51D PERK 12  8 15800  2  1  63900  70300
45 2 CARTER 45             SA/CR AL  SK IB  85D PERK 14  4 25000  2  6 124500 136500
-------------------- 1985 BOATS -----------------------------------------------------
34 8 CARTER 35         SLP SA/CR FBG SK IB  23D YAN  11     9300  1  9  31500  35000
37 6 CARTER 4+4        SLP SA/CR FBG SK IB  51D PERK 12  6 18500  4     64200  70600
38 9 CARTER OFFSHORE   SLP SA/CR AL  SK IB  51D PERK 12  8 15800  2  1  60100  66100
39   CARTER 39         SLP SA/CR FBG SK IB      12  8           2  1  81900  90100
45 2 CARTER 45             SA/CR AL  SK IB  85D PERK 14  4 25000  2  6 117000 128500
-------------------- 1984 BOATS -----------------------------------------------------
29 9 CARTER 30         SLP SA/CR FBG KL SD  15D VLVO 10  1  7300  5     22000  24400
34 8 CARTER 35         SLP SA/CR FBG SK IB  23D YAN  11     9300  1  9  29600  32900
37 6 CARTER 4+4        SLP SA/CR FBG SK IB  45D PERK 12  6 18500  2  6  60400  66300
45 2 CARTER 45             SA/CR AL  SK IB  73D PERK 14  4 25000  2  6 110000 120500
50   LUNA 50               SA/CR FBG SK IB 106D      14    26500  2  6 154500 170000
                ....For earlier years, see the BUC Used Boat Price Guide, Volume 3
```

CARVER BOAT CORPORATION
PULASKI WI 54162   COAST GUARD MFG ID- CDR See inside cover to adjust price for area
                For more recent years, see the BUC Used Boat Price Guide, Volume 1

```
LOA  NAME AND/         TOP/ BOAT  -HULL- ----ENGINE--- BEAM   WGT  DRAFT RETAIL RETAIL
FT IN OR MODEL         RIG  TYPE  MTL TP TP # HP  MFG  FT IN  LBS  FT IN  LOW    HIGH
-------------------- 1996 BOATS -----------------------------------------------------
25 7 EXPRESS 250       OP  CR   FBG SV IO 245-300  8  6  6100  3     21300  24800
27 9 SEDAN 280         FB  CBNCR FBG SV IO 300-330  9  6  9778  3  3  34300  39400
     IO 185D-240D  44700 52600, IO T205     36200 40600, IO T130D VLVO 49200  54100

28   EXPRESS 280       OP  CR   FBG SV IO 260-330  9  6  8100  3  3  30700  36200
     IO 216D VLVO 37100 41200, IO T175-T205 32300 37100, IO T130D VLVO 35900  43900

31 3 EXPRESS 310       OP  CR   FBG SV IO T185-T255 10 10 11400  2  9  45700  52600
     IB T265  CRUS 55500 61000, IO T300 MRCR 49000 53800, IO T216D VLVO 55700  61200

31 3 SANTEGO 310       FB  DC   FBG SV IO T164-T215 10 10 12500  2  9  51400  58400
     IO T265  CRUS 54800 60200, IB T265 CRUS 55800 61300, IOT185D-T230D 69800  80100

32 2 AFT CABIN 325     FB  CBNCR FBG SV IB T255-T265 11 10 15100  2 11  62100  68800
32 2 AFT CABIN 325     FB  CBNCR FBG SV IBT185D-T230D 11 10 15100  2 11 79300  91500
32 2 VOYAGER 320       FB  SDN  FBG SV IB T265-T300 11 10 15200  2 11  62400  70100
32 2 VOYAGER 320       FB  SDN  FBG SV IO T220D VLVO 11 10 15200  2 11  67900  74600
32 2 VOYAGER 320       FB  SDN  FBG SV IB T230D YAN 11 10 15200  2 11  81200  89300
34 3 MARINER 330       FB  SDN  FBG SV IB T265  CRUS 12  4 14900  2  9  74100  81400
34 3 MARINER 330       FB  SDN  FBG SV IB T170D YAN 12  4 14900  2  9  84700  93100
37 1 VOYAGER 370       FB  CR   FBG SV IB T300 MRCR 13  3 20350  3  8  98200 108000
     IB T320  CRUS 99500 109500, IB T330 VLVO 99700 109500, IB T230D VLVO 109000 120000
     IB T250D CUM 112000 123000, IB T315D CUM 116500 128000

38 2 AFT CABIN 370     FB  MY   FBG SV IB T300 MRCR 13 10 20660  3  3 113500 124500
     IB T320  CRUS 115000 126000, IB T300D CAT 137500 151000, IB T315D CUM 134500 148000

38 5 SANTEGO 380       FB  CR   FBG SV IB T320  CRUS 13  2 18700  3  4  94500 104000
38 5 SANTEGO 380       FB  CR   FBG SV IB T300D CAT 13  2 18700  3  4 118500 130500
39   AFT CABIN 355     FB  DCMY FBG SV IB T260  CRUS 13  3 19300  3  3  90300  99200
     IB T265  CRUS 90500 99400, IB T300 MRCR 91300 100500, IB T300 VLVO 91600 100500
     IB T320  CRUS 92400 101500, IB T230D VLVO 107500 118000, IB T250D CUM 110000 120500
     IB T315D CUM 115000 126500

40 2 CMY 400           FB  DCCPT FBG SV IB T320 CRUS 13  3 21000  3  3 116500 128000
     IB T330  MRCR 116000 127500, IB T330 VLVO 117000 128500, IB T230D VLVO 126000 138500
     IB T250D CUM 129000 142000, IB T315D CUM 134500 147500

44 3 CMY 430           FB  DCCPT FBG SV IB T380 CRUS 14    28700  3  4 140500 154500
44 4 CMY 430           FB  DCCPT FBG SV IB T315D CUM 14    28700  3  4 150500 165500
44 7 AFT CABIN 440 MY  FB  MY   FBG SV IB T315D CUM 15    30400  4  3 161500 177500
     IB T420  CRUS 176000 193000, IB T315D CUM 184000 202000, IB T350D CAT 192500 212000
     IB T370D CUM 193500 213000, IB T420D CUM 203000 223000, IB T435D CUM 209000 229500

45 9 AFT CABIN 455 MY  FB  MY   FBG DV IB T380  CRUS 15  4 31000  4  7 180500 198500
     IB T315D CUM 195000 214000, IB T350D CAT 204000 224000, IB T370D VLVO 205000 225000
     IB T420D CUM 216500 238000

50   CMY 500           FB  DCCPT FBG DV IB T380  CRUS 15  4 36000  4  7 193500 212500
     IB T315D CUM 200500 220500, IB T350D CAT 208000 229000, IB T370D CUM 206500 227000
     IB T420D CUM 217000 238500
-------------------- 1995 BOATS -----------------------------------------------------
25 7 EXPRESS 250       OP  CR   FBG SV IO 245-300  8  6  6100  3     19800  23100
27 9 SEDAN 280         FB  CBNCR FBG SV IO 275-330  9  6  9778  3  3  33400  36700
     IO 216D-240D 43000 49200, IO T205 33800 37900, IO T130D VLVO 46100 50600

28   EXPRESS 280       OP  CR   FBG SV IO 260-330  9  6  6875  3  3  26400  31300
     IO 216D-240D 30400 35100, IO T175-T205 28000 32300, IO T130D VLVO 32800 36500

31 3 SANTEGO 310       FB  DC   FBG SV IO 230D VLVO 10 10 10000  2  8  52600  57800
     IO T164-T190 44800 50700, IB T260 CRUS 49800 54800, IOT185D-T185D 53900 63100

32 2 AFT CABIN 325     FB  CBNCR FBG SV IB T260-T275 11 10 14221  2 11  58400  64900
32 2 AFT CABIN 325     FB  CBNCR FBG SV IB T180D MRCR 11 10 14221  2 11 73100  80300
32 2 VOYAGER 320       FB  SDN  FBG SV IB T260-T300 11 10 14785  2 11  58400  65900
     IB T200D VLVO 74000 81300, IO T210D CUM 61900 68000, IB T230D VLVO 76100 83600

34 3 MARINER 330       FB  SDN  FBG SV IB T260  CRUS 12  4 14691  2  9  69600  76500
37 1 VOYAGER 370       FB  CR   FBG SV IB T300 MRCR 13  3 20350  3  8  94200 103500
     IB T330  CRUS 95700 105000, IB T330 VLVO 95600 105000, IB T230D VLVO 105400 115000
     IB T250D CUM 107000 118000, IB T315D CUM 111500 122500

38 2 AFT CABIN 370     FB  MY   FBG SV IB T300 MRCR 13 10 20660  3  3 108500 119500
     IB T330  CRUS 110500 121500, IB T330 VLVO 110500 121500, IB T250D CUM 124000 136000
     IB T300D CAT 132000 145000, IB T315D CUM 129000 141500

38 5 SANTEGO 380       FB  CR   FBG SV VD T330  CRUS 13  2 16000  3  4  81300  89300
38 10 AFT CABIN 390    FB  DCMY FBG SV IB T330  CRUS 14    25900  3  4 132000 145000
     IB T420  CRUS 136500 150000, IB T300D CAT 153000 168000
     IB T315D CUM 150000 165000

39   AFT CABIN 355     FB  DCMY FBG SV IB T260  CRUS 13  3 18250  3  3  83200  91400
     IB T260  MRCR 82900 91000, IB T275 VLVO 83600 91900, IB T300 MRCR 84100 92400
     IB T330  CRUS 85500 94000, IB T330 VLVO 85500 94000, IB T230D VLVO 109000 109000
     IB T250D CUM 101000 111000

40 2 CMY 390           FB  DCCPT FBG SV IB T330  CRUS 13  3 17400  3  3 104000 114000
     IB T330  MRCR 103000 113000, IB T330 VLVO 103500 114000, IB T230D VLVO 113000 124000
     IB T240D MRCR 106000 127500, IB T250D CUM 116000 127500, IB T315D CUM 120500 133500

44 3 CMY 430           FB  DCCPT FBG SV IB T330 VLVO 14    28700  3  4 127500 140500
     IB T392  CRUS 136500 150000, IB T420 CRUS 140500 154500, IB T300D CAT 144000 158000
     IB T315D CUM 144500 159000, IB T350D CAT 152500 168000

44 7 AFT CABIN 440 MY  FB  MY   FBG SV IB T330  CRUS 15    28500  4  4 149000 164000
     IB T420  CRUS 162000 178000, IB T300D CAT 169000 186000, IB T315D CUM 169500 186000
     IB T350D CAT 178000 195500, IB T420D CUM 191000 210000, IB T420D CUM 188000 206500
     IB T435D CAT 194000 213000
-------------------- 1994 BOATS -----------------------------------------------------
25 7 EXPRESS 250       OP  CR   FBG SV IO 245-300  8  6          3     18700  21600
27 9 SEDAN 280         FB  CBNCR FBG SV IO 260-330  9  6  8500  2  4  27100  32200
     IO 216D-240D 36600 42100, IO T205 29100 32700, IO T130D VLVO 39200 43600

28   EXPRESS 280       OP  CR   FBG SV IO 260-330  9  6  5900  3  3  23000  27500
     IO 216D-240D 25400 29500, IO T175-T205 24600 28500, IO T130D VLVO 27800 30900

30 2 AFT CABIN 300     FB  CBNCR FBG SV IB T206-T275 11 10 11700  2 11  44300  51000
30 3 SANTEGO 300       FB  DC   FBG SV IB T180D MRCR 11 10 10000  2 11  56600  62200
31 3 SANTEGO 310       FB  DC   FBG SV IB T164-T190 10 10 10000  2  8  43300  47300
31 3 SANTEGO 310       FB  DC   FBG SV IB T185D VLVO 11 10 10000  2  8  53600  58900
32 2 VOYAGER 320       FB  SDN  FBG SV IB T260-T300 11 10 12500  2 11  53600  60600
32 2 VOYAGER 320       FB  SDN  FBG SV IB T210D CUM 11 10 12500  2 11  53700  59000
33 7 SANTEGO 340       FB  DC   FBG SV IB T260     11    11150  3  1  52200  57300
     IO T275  CRUS 50700 55700, IB T300 MRCR 53200 58400, VD T300 VLVO 53200 58500
     IB T320  CRUS 53800 59100, VD T195D VLVO 60200 66100

34 3 MARINER 330       FB  SDN  FBG SV VD T260  CRUS 12  4 12400  2  9  63200  69400
36   AFT CABIN 350     FB  DCMY FBG SV IB T260  CRUS 13  3 16600  2  7  77700  85300
     IB T275  VLVO 78000 85700, IB T300 MRCR 78400 86100, IB T330 CRUS 79800 87700
     IB T250D CUM 88300 97000, IB T240D MRCR 90400 99300, IB T250D CUM 90700 99700

36   VOYAGER 350       FB  CR   FBG SV IB T300 MRCR 13  3 17000  2  7  80100  88100
     IB T330  CRUS 81500 89500, IB T210D CUM 94800 98200, IB T250D VLVO 91600 100500

37 1 VOYAGER 370       FB  CR   FBG SV IB T300 MRCR 13  3 17500  2  7  81000  89000
     IB T330  CRUS 82400 90600, IB T210D CUM 90600 99500, IB T250D CUM 92700 102000

38 2 AFT CABIN 370     FB  MY   FBG SV IB T300 MRCR 13 10 18500  3  1  95200 104500
```

```
CARVER BOAT CORPORATION       -CONTINUED       See inside cover to adjust price for area
     LOA  NAME AND/              TOP/ BOAT  -HULL-  ----ENGINE--- BEAM    WGT   DRAFT  RETAIL RETAIL
     FT IN  OR MODEL             RIG  TYPE  MTL TP TP # HP  MFG   FT IN   LBS   FT IN   LOW   HIGH
     -------------------- 1994 BOATS -------------------------------------------------------------
38  2 AFT CABIN 370        FB  MY   FBG SV IB T330  CRUS 13 10 18500  3  1 96900 106500
    IB T250D CUM  109500 120500, IB T300D CAT  117000 128500, IB T300D CUM  113000 124500

38  5 EXPRESS 380          FB  CR   FBG SV IB T330  CRUS 13  2 16000  3  4 75200  82700
38  5 SANTEGO 380          FB  CR   FBG SV VD T330  CRUS 13  2 16000  3  4 77900  85600
38 10 AFT CABIN 390        FB  DCMY FBG SV IB T300  MRCR 14    22750  3  4 111500 122500
    IB T330  CRUS 113000 124500, IB T420  CRUS 117500 129000, IB T300D CAT  133000 146500
    IB T300D CUM  129000 142000, IB T375D CAT  141000 155000

40  2 CMY 390              FB  DCCPT FBG SV IB T330 CRUS 13  3 17400  2  7 99400 109000
    IB T330  MRCR  98500 108000, IB T210D CUM  108500 119500, IB T240D MRCR 111000 122000
    IB T250D CUM  111000 122000

44    CMY 430              FB  DCCPT FBG SV IB T420 CRUS 14    25620  3  4 127500 140000
    IB T420  MRCR 126500 139000, IB T300D CAT  129500 142500, IB T300D CUM  128000 140500
    IB T350D CAT  138500 152000

44  7 AFT CABIN 440 MY     FB  MY   FBG SV IB T300  MRCR 15    24500  3  6 127000 140000
    IB T330  CRUS 130500 143500, IB T420  CRUS 143500 157500, IB T420  MRCR 142500 157000
    IB T300D CAT  149500 164000, IB T300D CUM  147000 161500, IB T350D CAT  158000 173500
    IB T375D CAT  162500 178500, IB T400D CUM  164500 181000, IB T435D CAT  174000 191000
     -------------------- 1993 BOATS -------------------------------------------------------------
27  9 SEDAN 280            FB  CBNCR FBG SV IO 275-330    9  6  8500  2  4 25800  30100
    IO  200D VLVO  33600  37300, IO T175-T205  27200  30500, IO T130D VLVO  36700  40700

28    EXPRESS 280          OP  CR   FBG SV IO 260-330    9  6  5900  3  3 21500  25700
28    EXPRESS 280          OP  CR   FBG SV IO T175-T205  9  6  5900  3  3 23000  26600
28    EXPRESS 280          OP  CR   FBG SV IO T130D VLVO 9  6  5900  3  3 26000  28900
29  2 MONTEGO 300          OP  CR   FBG SV IO  330       10    6900  2 10 26300  29400
29  2 MONTEGO 300          OP  CR   FBG SV IO T175-T205  10    6900  2 10 26700  30500
29  2 MONTEGO 300          OP  CR   FBG SV IO T130D VLVO 10    6900  2 10 29400  32700
29  2 SANTEGO 300          FB  CBNCR FBG SV IO  330      10    8400  2  8 29100  32600
29  2 SANTEGO 300          FB  CBNCR FBG SV IO T175-T205 10    8400  2  8 29600  33000
29  2 SANTEGO 300          FB  CBNCR FBG SV IO T130D VLVO 10   8400  2  8 38000  42200
30  6 SEDAN 300            FB  SDN  FBG SV IB T220-T300 11 10 12500  2 11 46100  53300
30  6 SEDAN 300            FB  SDN  FBG SV IB T130D VLVO 11 10 12500  2 11 45600  50200

32  9 AFT CABIN 300        FB  CBNCR FBG SV IB T210  CRUS 11 10 11700  2 11 51400  56500
    VD T229  VLVO  52300  57400, IB T260-T275  53000  58300, IBT150D-T180D  58400  67200

33  4 SEDAN 330            FB  CNV  FBG SV IB T260-T275 11  7 12600  2 10 56800  63500
33  4 SEDAN 330            FB  CNV  FBG SV IB T200D VLVO 11  7 12600  2 10 67500  74100
33  7 SANTEGO 340          FB  DC   FBG SV IB T270-T300 11    11150  3  1 47200  52800
34  3 MARINER 330          FB  SDN  FBG SV IB T260-T275 12  4 12600  2  9 59900  66300
36    AFT CABIN 350        FB  DCMY FBG SV IB T260  CRUS 13  3 16600  2  7 74000  81300
    IB T275  VLVO  74300  81700, IB T300  MRCR  74700  82100, IB T330  CRUS  76100  83600
    IB T330  VLVO  76000  83500, IB T200D VLVO  82700  90900, IB T210D CUM   84100  92400
    IB T230D VLVO  84400  92700, IB T300D CUM   89800  98700

36    VOYAGER 350          FB  CR   FBG SV IB T300  MRCR 13  3 17000  2  7 76300  83900
    IB T330  CRUS  77600  85300, IB T330  VLVO  77600  85300, IB T200D VLVO  83800  92100
    IB T210D CUM   85200  93600, IB T230D VLVO  85300  93700, IB T300D CUM   90300  99200

37  1 VOYAGER 370          FB  CR   FBG SV IB T300  MRCR 13  3 17500  2  7 77200  84800
    IB T330  CRUS  78600  86300, IB T330  VLVO  78500  86300, IB T200D VLVO  84700  93300
    IB T210D CUM   86300  94800, IB T230D VLVO  86000  94500, IB T300D CUM   91300 100500

38  2 AFT CABIN 370        FB  MY   FBG SV IB T300  MRCR 13 10 18500  3  1 90700  99600
    IB T330  CRUS  92300 101500, IB T330  VLVO  92300 101500, IB T300D CUM  108000 118500

38  5 EXPRESS 380          FB  CR   FBG SV IB T300  MRCR 13  2 16000  3  4 70300  77200
38  5 EXPRESS 380          FB  CR   FBG SV IB T330  CRUS 13  2 16000  3  4 71700  78800
38  5 EXPRESS 380          FB  CR   FBG SV IB T330  VLVO 13  2 16000  3  4 71600  78700
38  5 SANTEGO 380          FB  CR   FBG SV VD T300  MRCR 13  2 16000  3  4 72800  80000
38  5 SANTEGO 380          FB  CR   FBG SV IB T330  CRUS 13  2 16000  3  4 74200  81600
38  5 SANTEGO 380          FB  CR   FBG SV IB T330  VLVO 13  2 16000  3  4 74200  81500
38 10 AFT CABIN 390        FB  DCMY FBG SV IB T300  MRCR 14    22750  3  4 106000 116500
    IB T330  CRUS 108000 118500, IB T330  VLVO 108000 118500, IB T300D CUM  123000 135500
    IB T375D CAT  134500 147500

40  2 CMY 390              FB  DCCPT FBG SV IB T330 CRUS 13  3 17400  3  1 94700 104000
    IB T330  MRCR  93800 103000, IB T330  VLVO  94600 104000, IB T195D VLVO 101000 111000
    IB T210D CUM  103500 113500, IB T216D VLVO 102000 112500, IB T250D CUM  106000 116500

44  3 CMY 430              FB  DCCPT FBG SV IB T420 MRCR 14    25620  3  4 120500 132500
    IB T300D CUM  122000 134000, IB T375D CAT  136000 149500, IB T425D CUM  141500 155500

44  7 AFT CABIN 440        FB  MY   FBG SV IB T420  CRUS 15    24500  3  6 133500 147000
44  7 AFT CABIN 440        FB  MY   FBG SV IB T420  MRCR 15    24500  3  6 133000 146000
44  7 AFT CABIN 440        FB  MY   FBG SV IB T300D CAT  15    24500  3  6 140000 154000
44  7 AFT CABIN 440 MY     FB  MY   FBG SV IB T300D CUM  15    24500  3  6 140000 154000
44  7 AFT CABIN 440 MY     FB  MY   FBG SV IB T375D CAT  15    24500  3  6 155000 170000
     -------------------- 1992 BOATS -------------------------------------------------------------
26  4 MARINER 2257         OP  DC   FBG SV IO 175-275    8 10            2  9 19100  22800
27  5 COMMAND BRIDGE 26    FB  CBNCR FBG SV IO 275-330   9  6  8500  2  4 24300  28300
27  9 COMMAND BRIDGE 26    FB  CBNCR FBG SV IO T205      9  6  8500  2  4 25600  28700
27  9 COMMAND BRIDGE 26    FB  CBNCR FBG SV IO T130D VLVO 9 6  8500  2  4 34500  38300
28    MONTEGO 528          OP  CR   FBG SV IO 260-330    9  6  5900  3  3 19300  23100
28    MONTEGO 528          OP  CR   FBG SV IO T175-T205  9  6  5900  3  3 20600  23900
28    MONTEGO 528          OP  CR   FBG SV IO T205       10    5900  3  3 23300  25900
29  2 MONTEGO 530          OP  CR   FBG SV IO  330       10    6900  2 10 23900  26700
29  2 MONTEGO 530          OP  CR   FBG SV IO T205       10    6900  2 10 24700  27700
29  2 MONTEGO 530          OP  CR   FBG SV IO T130D VLVO 10    6900  2 10 29700  29500
29  2 SANTEGO 630          FB  CBNCR FBG SV IO  330      10    8400  2  8 26400  29500
29  2 SANTEGO 630          FB  CBNCR FBG SV IO T205      10    8400  2  8 26800  30000

29  2 SANTEGO 630          FB  CBNCR FBG SV IO T130D VLVO 10   8400  2  8 34500  38300
30  2 AFT CABIN 28         FB  CBNCR FBG SV IB T210  CRUS 11 10 11700  2 11 46200  50800
    VD T229  VLVO  47000  51600, IB T260-T275  47700  52500, IB T130D VLVO  58200  63900

30  6 COMMAND BRIDGE 28    FB  SDN  FBG SV IB T220-T300 11 10 12500  2 11 42500  50000
30  6 COMMAND BRIDGE 28    FB  SDN  FBG SV IB T130D VLVO 11 10 12500  2 11 41500  46100
33  4 CONVERTIBLE 32       FB  CNV  FBG SV IB T260  MRCR 11  7 12600  2 10 53100  58300
33  4 CONVERTIBLE 32       FB  CNV  FBG SV IB T260-T275 11  7 12600  2 10 53900  60300
33  4 CONVERTIBLE 32       FB  CNV  FBG SV IB T200D VLVO 11  7 12600  2 10 64300  70700
33  7 SANTEGO 634          FB  DC   FBG SV IB T270-T300 11    11150  3  1 47200  52800
33  7 SANTEGO 634          FB  DC   FBG SV IB T205      11    11150  3  1 55000  60500
34  3 MARINER 3297         FB  SDN  FBG SV IB T260-T275 12  4 12600  2  9 57400  63600
34  4 MONTEGO 534          OP  CR   FBG SV IB T300-T330 12  4 12145  2  9 50500  56500
34  4 MONTEGO 534          OP  CR   FBG SV IB T200D VLVO 12  4 12145  2  9 55600  61100

36    AFT CABIN 33         FB  DCMY FBG SV IB T260  CRUS 13  3 16600  2  7 59900  65800
    IB T275  VLVO  60400  66400, IB T300  VLVO  61200  67200, IB T330  CRUS  62300  68400
    IB T330  VLVO  62300  68400, IB T200D VLVO  76300  83800, IB T300D CUM   83100  91300

38  2 AFT CABIN 36         FB  MY   FBG SV IB T300  MRCR 13 10 18500  3  1 81300  89400
    IB T330  CRUS  82800  90900, IB T330  VLVO  82700  90900, IB T300D CUM   98300 108000

38  5 MONTEGO 538          FB  CR   FBG SV IB T300  MRCR 13  2 16000  3  4 67300  73900
38  5 MONTEGO 538          FB  CR   FBG SV IB T330  CRUS 13  2 16000  3  4 68600  75400
38  5 MONTEGO 538          FB  CR   FBG SV IB T330  VLVO 13  2 16000  3  4 68600  75300
38  5 SANTEGO 638          FB  CR   FBG SV IB T330  MRCR 13  2 16000  3  4 72300  79400
    VD T330  CRUS  73700  81000, VD T330  VLVO  73600  80900, IO T200D VLVO  56100  61600

38 10 AFT CABIN 38         FB  DCMY FBG SV IB T300  MRCR 14    22750  3  4 103500 114000
    IB T330  CRUS 105500 115500, IB T330  VLVO 105500 115500, IB T300D CUM  121000 133000
    IB T306D VLVO 119500 131000

40  3 SANTEGO 640          FB  CR   FBG SV VD T330  CRUS 14    19000  3  7 96800 106500
40  3 SANTEGO 640          FB  CR   FBG SV IB T330  VLVO 14    19000  3  7 97600 106000
40  3 SANTEGO 640          FB  CR   FBG SV IB T300D CUM  14    19000  3  7 111500 122500
40  3 SANTEGO 640          FB  CR   FBG SV IB T300D CUM  14    19000  3  7 95000 104500
42    AFT CABIN 42         FB  MY   FBG SV IB T300  MRCR 15    23600  3  6 137500 151000
    IB T330  CRUS 140500 154500, IB T330  VLVO 140500 154500, IB T300D CUM  149500 163500
    IB T375D CAT  174500 192000

44  3 COCKPIT 43 MY        FB  DCCPT FBG SV IB T330 VLVO 14    25620  3  4 99500 109500
44  3 COCKPIT 43 MY        FB  DCCPT FBG SV IB T420 MRCR 14    25620  3  4 111000 122000
44  3 COCKPIT 43 MY        FB  DCCPT FBG SV IB T300D CUM 14    25620  3  4 123500 136000
45    CALIFORNIAN 4509     FB  MY   FBG SV IB T375D CAT  15  2 40000  4  4 150500 173000
45    CALIFORNIAN 4509     FB  MY   FBG SV IB T425D CUM  15  2 40000  4  4 163000 179000
45    CALIFORNIAN 4509     FB  MY   FBG SV IB T485D GM   15  2 40000  4  4 168000 184500
48  5 CALIFORNIAN 4809     FB  MY   FBG SV IB T425D CAT  15  2 38000  4  5 185500 203500
    IB T425D CAT  174500 192000, IB T485D GM  178000 195500, IB T550D GM  185500 203500

48  5 CALIFORNIAN 5239 MY  FB  MY   FBG SV IB T375D CAT  15  2 44200  4  6 180500 195500
    IB T425D CAT  183000 201000, IB T485D CAT 189000 208000, IB T550D GM  192000 211000

54 11 CALIFORNIAN 5539 CPT FB  MY   FBG SV IB T375D CAT  15  2 46700  4  3 205000 225000
    IB T425D CAT  221000 242000, IB T485D GM  232000 255000, IB T550D GM  248000 272500
     -------------------- 1991 BOATS -------------------------------------------------------------
22 11 MONTEGO 523          OP  CR   FBG SV IO 230-275    8  6  3920  2  7 10800  13100
25  2 MONTEGO 525          OP  CR   FBG SV IO 230-300    9  3  4500  3    12900  15700
25  2 MONTEGO 525          OP  CR   FBG SV IO  330  VLVO 9  3  4500  3    14800  16800
```

```
CARVER BOAT CORPORATION        -CONTINUED      See inside cover to adjust price for area

  LOA  NAME AND/            TOP/ BOAT  -HULL-  ----ENGINE---  BEAM    WGT  DRAFT RETAIL RETAIL
  FT IN  OR MODEL           RIG  TYPE  MTL TP  TP # HP  MFG   FT IN   LBS  FT IN  LOW    HIGH
-------------------- 1991 BOATS -------------------------------------------------------------
27  9 COMMAND BRIDGE 26     FB  CBNCR FBG SV IO  275  VLVO  9  6  8500  2  4  21800  24200
27  9 COMMAND BRIDGE 26     FB  CBNCR FBG SV IO T205       9  6  8500  2  4  22700  25600
27  9 COMMAND BRIDGE 26     FB  CBNCR FBG SV IO T130D VLVO 9  6  8500  2  4  31600  35100
28    MONTEGO 528           OP  CR    FBG SV IO  275-330   9  6  5500  3  3  18200  21300
28    MONTEGO 528           OP  CR    FBG SV IO T175-T205  9  6  5500  3  3  19000  21900
28    MONTEGO 528           OP  CR    FBG SV IO T130D VLVO 9  6  5500  3  3  21000  23300
29  2 MONTEGO 530           OP  CR    FBG SV IO  330       10    6900  2 10  22400  25100
29  2 MONTEGO 530           OP  CR    FBG SV IO T205       10    6900  2 10  23200  26000
29  2 MONTEGO 530           OP  CR    FBG SV IO T130D VLVO 10    6900  2 10  25100  27900
29  2 SANTEGO 630           FB  CBNCR FBG SV IO  330       10    8400  2  8  24800  27700
29  2 SANTEGO 630           FB  CBNCR FBG SV IO T205       10    8400  2  8  25200  28100
29  2 SANTEGO 630           FB  CBNCR FBG SV IO T130D VLVO 10    8400  2  8  32300  35900

30  6 COMMAND BRIDGE 28     FB  SDN   FBG SV IB T220-T275  11 10 12500  2 11  35100  40200
30  6 COMMAND BRIDGE 28     FB  SDN   FBG SV IB T200D VLVO 11 10 12500  2 11  40500  45000
32  9 AFT CABIN 28          FB  SDN   FBG SV IB T220  CRUS 11 10 11700  2 11  37700  41900
      VD T229  VLVO  38000   42200, IB T260-T330   38500  43400, IB T130D VLVO  53000  58200

33  4 CONVERTIBLE 32        FB  CNV   FBG SV VD T229-T260  11  7 12600  2 10  46000  51800
33  4 CONVERTIBLE 32        FB  CNV   FBG SV IB T200D VLVO 11  7 12600  2 10  58400  64200
33  7 SANTEGO 634           FB  DC    FBG SV IB T229-T275  11    11150  3  1  40400  46100
33  7 SANTEGO 634           FB  DC    FBG SV IB T200D VLVO 11    11150  3  1  52500  57700
34    MONTEGO 532           OP  CR    FBG SV IB T275  VLVO 11    13500  3  1  34000  37800
      IO T330  MRCR  35000   38900, IO T330  VLVO  35100  39000, VD T330      43500  48300
      IO T200D VLVO  39100   43500

34  3 MARINER 32            FB  SDN   FBG SV VD T260-T275  12  4 12600  2  9  51500  57200
34  4 MONTEGO 534           OP  CR    FBG SV VD T330       12  4 12145  2  9  48800  53600
34  4 MONTEGO 534           OP  CR    FBG SV IO T200D VLVO 12  4 12145  2  9  53100  58300
35  9 AFT CABIN 33          FB  DCMY  FBG SV IB T229  VLVO 13  3 16600  2  7  55900  61500
      IB T260  CRUS  56900   62500, IB T330  CRUS  59200  65000, IB T330  VLVO  59200  65000

38  2 AFT CABIN 36          FB  MY    FBG SV IB T330  CRUS 13 10 18500  3  1  85500  94000
38  2 AFT CABIN 36          FB  MY    FBG SV IB T330  VLVO 13 10 18500  3  1  85500  93900
38  2 AFT CABIN 36          FB  MY    FBG SV IB T300D CUM  13 10 18500  3  1 107000 117500
38  5 MONTEGO 538           FB  CR    FBG SV IB T330  CRUS 13  2 16000  3  4  65400  71900
38  5 MONTEGO 538           FB  CR    FBG SV IB T330  VLVO 13  2 16000  3  4  65400  71900
38  5 SANTEGO 638           FB  CR    FBG SV IB T330  CRUS 13  2 16000  3  4  70300  77200
38  5 SANTEGO 638           FB  CR    FBG SV IB T330  VLVO 13  2 16000  3  4  70200  77200
38  5 SANTEGO 638           FB  CR    FBG SV IB T200D VLVO 13  2 16000  3  4  52600  57800
38 10 AFT CABIN 38          FB  DCMY  FBG SV IB T330  CRUS 14    22750  3  4 104500 129500
      IB T330  VLVO 104500  115000, IB T300D CUM  119500 131000, IB T306D VLVO 117500 129500
      IB T375D CAT 130000  143000

40  3 SANTEGO 640           FB  CR    FBG SV VD T330  CRUS 14    19000  3  7  92300 101500
      VD T330  VLVO  92200  101500, VD T390  CRUS  94800 104000, VD T300D CUM 106500 117000

40  3 SANTEGO 640 DS        FB  CR    FBG SV VD T300  VLVO 14    19000  3  7  92000 101000
      VD T330  CRUS  93000  102000, VD T390  CRUS  95300 105000, VD T300D CUM 107000 117500

42    AFT CABIN 42          FB  MY    FBG SV IB T330  CRUS 15    23600  3  6 134000 147000
      IB T330  VLVO 134000  147000, IB T390  CRUS 138500 152000, IB T300D CUM 152000 167000
      IB T375D CAT 166500  183000

44  3 COCKPIT 43 MY         FB  DCCPT FBG SV IB T330  CRUS 14    25620  3  4  94800 104000
      IB T330  MRCR  94400  103500, IB T330  VLVO  94800 104000, IB T300D CUM 106000 116500
      IB T306D VLVO 105500  116000, IB T375D CAT 118000 129500

45  3 CALIFORNIAN 4509      FB  MY    FBG SV IB T375D CAT  15  2 40000  4  4 150000 164500
45  3 CALIFORNIAN 4509      FB  MY    FBG SV IB T425D CAT  15  2 40000  4  4 155000 170500
45  3 CALIFORNIAN 4509      FB  MY    FBG SV IB T485D GM   15  2 40000  4  4 159500 175500
48  5 CALIFORNIAN 4809      FB  MY    FBG SV IB T375D CAT  15  2 38000  4  5 161500 177500
      IB T425D CAT 166500  183000, IB T485D GM  169500 186500, IB T550D GM  176500 194000

52  1 CALIFORNIAN 5239 MY   FB  MY    FBG SV IB T375D CAT  15  2 44200  4  4 169500 186500
      IB T425D CAT 174000  191500, IB T485D GM  177000 194500, IB T550D GM  183000 201000

55  1 CALIFORNIAN 5539 CPT  FB  MY    FBG SV IB T375D CAT  15  2 46700  4  3 196500 215500
      IB T425D CAT 208500  229500, IB T485D GM  223000 245000, IB T550D GM  238000 261500

-------------------- 1990 BOATS -------------------------------------------------------------
22 11 MONTEGO 2157          OP  CR    FBG SV IO  175-275   8  6  3920  2  7   9300  11500
23    MONTEGO 2357          OP  CR    FBG SV IO  175-300   9  3  4500  3    10800  13200
25    MONTEGO 2557          OP  CR    FBG SV IO  230-275   9  3  5500  3  3  13200  15800
25    MONTEGO 2557          OP  CR    FBG SV IO  330       9  6  5500  3  3  14500  16900
25    MONTEGO 2557          OP  CR    FBG SV IO T167-T205  9  6  5500  3  3  14700  17100
27  3 MONTEGO 2757          OP  CR    FBG SV IO  300-330   10    6900  2 10  17600  20700
27  3 MONTEGO 2757          OP  CR    FBG SV IO T167-T205  10    6900  2 10  18500  21300
27  3 MONTEGO 2757          OP  CR    FBG SV IO T130D VLVO 10    6900  2 10  20500  23700
27  3 SANTEGO 2767          FB  CBNCR FBG SV IO  300-330   10    8400  2  8  20500  23700
27  3 SANTEGO 2767          FB  CBNCR FBG SV IO T175-T330  10    8400  2  8  21200  25600
27  3 SANTEGO 2767          FB  CBNCR FBG SV IO T130D VLVO 10    8400  2  8  29100  32300

28    ALLEGRA 2587          OP  SPTCR FBG SV IO  275-330   9  6  5100  3  3  14700  17900
28    ALLEGRA 2587          OP  SPTCR FBG SV IO T180-T229  9  6  5100  3  3  15200  18500
28    ALLEGRA 2587          OP  SPTCR FBG SV IO T275-T300  9  6  5100  3  3  16700  19700
28    MARINER 2897          FB  SDN   FBG SV VD T210-T229  11  1 10300  2 10  32100  36200
28    MARINER 2897          FB  SDN   FBG SV IO T130D VLVO 11  1 10300  2 10  46100  50700
28    VOYAGER 2827          FB  SDN   FBG SV IO T210-T229  11  1 10300  2 10  32500  36600
28    VOYAGER 2827          FB  SDN   FBG SV IO T130D VLVO 11  1 10300  2 10  42100  46800
31  6 MONTEGO 3157          OP  CR    FBG SV IO T300  MRCR 11    12100  3  1  28800  32900
      VD T235  CRUS  36400   40400, IO T275  VLVO  29700  33000, IO T300  MRCR  30100  33500
      VD T300  CRUS  37800   42000, IB T330      38500  42800, IO T150D VLVO  32500  36100

32    AFT CABIN 3207        FB  MY    FBG SV IB T229-T235  11  7 12000  2 10  42600  47600
32    AFT CABIN 3207        FB  MY    FBG SV IB T200D VLVO 11  7 12000  2 10  54300  59700
32    CONVERTIBLE 3227      FB  CNV   FBG SV IB T229-T235  11  7 12600  2 10  41900  46800
32    CONVERTIBLE 3227      FB  CNV   FBG SV IB T200D VLVO 11  7 12600  2 10  54100  59400
32  3 MARINER 3297          FB  SDN   FBG SV VD T230-T275  12  4 12600  2  9  44500  51100
32  3 MONTEGO 3257          OP  CR    FBG SV IB T229-T235  11  4 12145  2  9  39600  44000
34    ALLEGRA 3087          OP  SPTCR FBG SV VD T235  CRUS 11    10950  3  1  34300  38100
      IO T260-T275  27700   31300, IO T300  MRCR  28600  31800, VD T300  CRUS  35700  39600
      IO T330  VLVO  29500   32700, VD T200D VLVO  44000  48900

34    SANTEGO 3067          FB  CBNCR FBG SV IO T205-T230  11    11150  3  1  28400  32400
34    SANTEGO 3067          FB  CBNCR FBG SV IO T275  VLVO 11    11150  3  1  35900  39900
34    SANTEGO 3067          FB  CBNCR FBG SV IB T150D VLVO 11    11150  3  1  46200  50800
35    MONTEGO 3557          FB  CR    FBG SV IB T300  CRUS 12              3  1  46600  51400
35    MONTEGO 3557          FB  CR    FBG SV IB T300  MRCR                     46600  51200
35  7 MOTOR YACHT 3608      FB  MY    FBG SV IB T355  CRUS 12  6 18500  3  2  65200  71900
      IB T300  MRCR  64900   71300, IB T355  CRUS  66800  73400, IB T300D CUM  82400  90500

37  6 AFT CABIN 3807        FB  DCMY  FBG SV IB T300  CRUS 14    22750  3  4  86200  94800
      IB T300  MRCR  85600   94100, IB T330  CRUS  86900  95500, IB T300D CUM 100500 110500
      IB T306D VLVO  99200  109000, IB T375D CAT 109500 120500

37  6 SANTEGO 3867          FB  CR    FBG SV IB T300  CRUS 14    19000  3  7  74400  81800
      VD T300  MRCR  74200   81500, IB T355  CRUS  81700  89800, VD T300D CUM 106000 117500

37  6 SANTEGO 3897 DS       FB  CR    FBG SV IB T300  CRUS 14    19000  3  7  75600  83100
      VD T300  MRCR  75400   82900, VD T355  CRUS  82900  91200, VD T300D CUM 108500 119000

41  8 SANTEGO 3467          FB  CR    FBG SV IB T275  VLVO 13  2 16000  3  4  44000  48900
      IO T300  MRCR  44400   49400, VD T300  CRUS  55700  61300, VD T300  MRCR  56600  61100
      IO T300  VLVO  46400   50600, VD T200D VLVO  49800  54700

42    AFT CABIN 4207        FB  MY    FBG SV IB T300  CRUS 15    23600  3  6 112000 123000
      IB T300  MRCR 111000  122000, IB T330  VLVO 113500 124500, IB T355  CRUS 115000 126500
      IB T300D CUM 129000  141500, IB T375D CAT 141000 155000, IB T380D CUM 134500 148000

45  3 CALIFORNIAN 4509      FB  MY    FBG SV IB T375D CAT  15  2 40000  4    142500 156500
45  3 CALIFORNIAN 4509      FB  MY    FBG SV IB T425D CAT  15  2 40000  4    147500 162000
45  3 CALIFORNIAN 4509      FB  MY    FBG SV IB T485D GM   15  2 40000  4    152000 167000
48  5 CALIFORNIAN 4809      FB  MY    FBG SV IB T375D CAT  15  2 38000  4  5 154000 169500
      IB T425D CAT 158500  174500, IB T485D GM  162000 178000, IB T550D GM  168500 185000

48  5 CALIFORNIAN 4839 CPT  FB  MYCPT FBG SV IB T375D CAT  15  2 41000  4  4 140000 154000
      IB T425D CAT 144500  159500, IB T485D GM  148000 162500, IB T550D GM  155000 170000

55  1 CALIFORNIAN 5539 CPT  FB  MY    FBG SV IB T375D CAT  15  2 46700  4  3 187500 206000
      IB T425D CAT 199500  219000, IB T485D GM  213000 234000, IB T550D GM  224000 249500

-------------------- 1989 BOATS -------------------------------------------------------------
22 11 MONTEGO 2157          OP  CR    FBG SV IO  171-260   8 10  3920  2  7   9000  10400
23    MARINER 2257          OP  CBNCR FBG SV IO  205-260   8 10        2  9   7350  8800
23    MARINER 2557          OP  CBNCR FBG SV IO  271  VLVO 8 10        2  9   8150  9350
25    MONTEGO 2557          OP  CR    FBG SV IO  260-330   9  7  5500  3  3  12700  15500
25    MONTEGO 2557          OP  CR    FBG SV IO T171-T180  9  7  5500  3  3  13900  15800
25  2 MONTEGO 2557          OP  CR    FBG SV IO  205-271   9  4  5500  3  3  10200  12400
27  3 MONTEGO 2757          OP  CR    FBG SV IO  271  VLVO 10    6900  2  8  16300  18500
      IO T171-T180  17200   19500, IO T205  MRCR  17500  19900, IB T205  VLVO  18100  20100
      IO T130D VLVO 20900   23200

27  3 SANTEGO 2767          FB  CBNCR FBG SV IO  271  VLVO 10    8400  2  8  19200  21400
27  3 SANTEGO 2767          FB  CBNCR FBG SV IO T171-T205  10    8400  2  8  20100  22600
27  3 SANTEGO 2767          FB  CBNCR FBG SV IO T130D VLVO 10    8400  2  8  27400  30500
```

LOA FT	IN	NAME AND/ OR MODEL	TOP/ RIG	BOAT TYPE	-HULL- MTL	TP	ENGINE TP	# HP	MFG	BEAM FT	IN	WGT LBS	DRAFT FT	IN	RETAIL LOW	RETAIL HIGH
		1989 BOATS														
28		ALLEGRA 2587	OP	SPTCR	FBG	SV	IO	260-330		9	6	5100	3	3	13400	16400
28		ALLEGRA 2587	OP	SPTCR	FBG	SV	IO	T230-T231		9	6	5100	3	3	14900	17500
28		MARINER 2897	FB	SDN	FBG	SV	VD	T220-T231		11	1	10300	2	10	30800	34500
28		MARINER 2897	FB	SDN	FBG	SV	VD	T130D	VLVO	11	1	10300	2	10	41700	46400
28		RIVIERA 2807	ST	CR	FBG	SV	IB	T220-T231		11	1	8900	2	10	29300	32800
28		RIVIERA 2807	ST	CR	FBG	SV	IB	T130D	VLVO	11	1	8900	2	10	37500	41700
28		VOYAGER 2827	FB	SDN	FBG	SV	VD	T220-T231		11	1	10300	2	10	31200	34900
28		VOYAGER 2827	FB	SDN	FBG	SV	VD	T130D	VLVO	11	1	10300	2	10	42200	46800
32		AFT CABIN 3207	FB	MY	FBG	SV	IB	T231-T260		11	7	12000	2	10	40700	46200
32		AFT CABIN 3207	FB	MY	FBG	SV	IB	T200D	VLVO	11	7	12000	2	10	51900	57100
32		CONVERTIBLE 3227	FB	CNV	FBG	SV	VD	T231-T260		11	7	12600	2	10	40000	45400
32	3	MARINER 3297	FB	SDN	FBG	SV	VD	T260-T261		12	4	12600	2	9	43300	48200
32	3	MONTEGO 3257	OP	CR	FBG	SV	VD	T260-T340		12	4	12145	2	9	36800	42800
32	3	MONTEGO 3257	OP	CR	FBG	SV	VD	T200D	VLVO	12	4	12145	2	9	43800	48700
34		ALLEGRA 3087	OP	SPTCR	FBG	SV	VD	T231	VLVO	11		10950	3	1	32500	36100
		IO T260 MRCR 26200 29100, VD T260 33100 36800, IO T271-T330 26500 30700														
		VD T340 MRCR 34800 38600, IO T200D VLVO 31400 34800														
34		SANTEGO 3067	FB	CBNCR	FBG	SV	IO	T230-T271		11		11150	3	1	27400	31100
35	7	AFT CABIN 3607	FB	MY	FBG	SV	IB	T330	CRUS	12	6	18500	3	2	58900	64700
35	7	AFT CABIN 3607	FB	MY	FBG	SV	IB	T340	MRCR	12	6	18500	3	2	58900	64700
35	7	AFT CABIN 3607	FB	MY	FBG	SV	IB	T306D	VLVO	12	6	18500	3	2	73500	80700
37	6	AFT CABIN 3807	FB	DCMY	FBG	SV	IB	T330	CRUS	14		22750	3	4	83100	91300
		IB T340 MRCR 82700 90900, IB T306D VLVO 94700 104000, IB T375D CAT 104500 115000														
37	6	SANTEGO 3867	FB	CR	FBG	SV	VD	T330	CRUS	14		19000	3	7	77700	85400
37	6	SANTEGO 3867	FB	CR	FBG	SV	VD	T340	MRCR	14		19000	3	7	77300	85000
37	6	SANTEGO 3897 DS	FB	CR	FBG	SV	VD	T330	CRUS	14		19000	3	7	77900	85700
37	6	SANTEGO 3897 DS	FB	CR	FBG	SV	VD	T340	MRCR	14		19000	3	7	77500	85200
41	8	SANTEGO 3467	FB	CR	FBG	SV	IO	T271	VLVO	13	2	16000	3	4	41400	46000
		IO T330 MRCR 42600 47400, VD T330 CRUS 54400 59800, VD T340 MRCR 53900 59200														
		IO T200D VLVO 47200 51900														
42		AFT CABIN 4207	FB	MY	FBG	SV	IB	T330	CRUS	15		23600	3	6	110000	121000
		IB T340 MRCR 110000 121000, IB T358D VLVO 130000 143000, IB T375D CAT 137500 151500														
42	5	CALIFORNIAN 4229	FB	CNV	FBG	SV	IB	T375D	CAT	15	2	38000	4	4	130000	142500
42	5	CALIFORNIAN 4229	FB	CNV	FBG	SV	IB	T485D	GM	15	2	38000	4	4	138000	152000
42	5	CALIFORNIAN 4229	FB	CNV	FBG	SV	IB	T575D	GM	15	2	38000	4	4	147000	161500
44		VENETI 4459	FB	MY	FBG	SV	IB	T375D	CAT	15	2	25000	4		99500	109500
45	3	CALIFORNIAN 4509	FB	MY	FBG	SV	IB	T375D	CAT	15	2	40000	4		135500	149000
45	3	CALIFORNIAN 4509	FB	MY	FBG	SV	IB	T400D	GM	15	2	40000	4		137000	150500
45	3	CALIFORNIAN 4509	FB	MY	FBG	SV	IB	T485D	GM	15	2	40000	4		145000	159500
48	5	CALIFORNIAN 4809	FB	MY	FBG	SV	IB	T375D	CAT	15	2	38000	4	8	147000	161500
48	5	CALIFORNIAN 4809	FB	MY	FBG	SV	IB	T485D	GM	15	2	38000	4	8	154500	169500
48	5	CALIFORNIAN 4809	FB	MY	FBG	SV	IB	T575D	GM	15	2	38000	4	8	163000	179500
48	5	CALIFORNIAN 4839	FB	CNV	FBG	SV	IB	T375D	CAT	15	2	40000	4	8	137500	151000
48	5	CALIFORNIAN 4839	FB	CNV	FBG	SV	IB	T485D	GM	15	2	40000	4	8	143500	158000
48	5	CALIFORNIAN 4839	FB	CNV	FBG	SV	IB	T575D	GM	15	2	40000	4	8	151500	166500
48	5	CALIFORNIAN 4839 CPT	FB	MYCPT	FBG	SV	IB	T375D	CAT	15	2	41000	4	8	133500	147000
		IB T400D GM 133500 147000, IB T485D GM 141000 155000, IB T575D GM 150500 165000														
55	1	CALIFORNIAN 5539 CPT	FB	MY	FBG	SV	IB	T375D	CAT	15	2	46700	4	3	179500	197000
55	1	CALIFORNIAN 5539 CPT	FB	MY	FBG	SV	IB	T485D	GM	15	2	46700	4	3	203500	223500
55	1	CALIFORNIAN 5539 CPT	FB	MY	FBG	SV	IB	T575D	GM	15	2	46700	4	3	222000	244000
		1988 BOATS														
21		MONTEGO 2157	OP	CR	FBG	SV	IO		MRCR	8	6	3920	2	7	**	**
21		MONTEGO 2157	OP	CR	FBG	SV	IO	171	VLVO	8	6	3920	2	7	7700	8850
21		MONTEGO 2157	OP	CR	FBG	SV	IO	180-230		8	6	3920	2	7	7500	8800
23		MONTEGO 2357	OP	CR	FBG	SV	IO	205-230		9	3	4500	3		9650	11100
23		MONTEGO 2357	OP	CR	FBG	SV	IO	260-271		9	3	4500	3		9950	11800
25		MONTEGO 2557	OP	CR	FBG	SV	IO	260-271		9	6	5500	3	3	12000	13700
25		MONTEGO 2557	OP	CR	FBG	SV	IO	T171-T180		9	6	5500	3	3	13100	14900
27	3	MONTEGO 2757	OP	CR	FBG	SV	IO	271	VLVO	10		6900	2	10	15400	17600
27	3	MONTEGO 2757	OP	CR	FBG	SV	IO	T180-T205		10		6900	2	8	16200	18800
27	3	SANTEGO 2767	FB	CBNCR	FBG	SV	IO	T171-T205		10		8400	2	8	19200	21300
28		AFT CABIN 2807	ST	CR	FBG	SV	IB	T220-T230		11	1	8900	2	10	29300	32600
28		MARINER 2897	FB	SDN	FBG	SV	VD	T220-T230		11	1	10300	2	10	29300	32600
28		VOYAGER 2827	FB	SDN	FBG	SV	VD	T220-T230		11	1	10300	2	10	29700	33100
30		SANTEGO 3067	FB	CBNCR	FBG	SV	IO	T230-T271		11		11150	3	1	26000	29300
32		AFT CABIN 3207	FB	MY	FBG	SV	IB	T260-T270		11	7	12000	2	10	39600	44400
32		CONVERTIBLE 3227	FB	CNV	FBG	SV	VD	T260-T270		11	7	12600	2	10	38900	43600
32	3	MARINER 3297	FB	SDN	FBG	SV	VD	T260-T270		12	4	12600	2	9	41200	46200
32	3	MONTEGO 3257	OP	CR	FBG	SV	VD	T260-T270		12	4	12145	2	9	35100	39200
32	3	MONTEGO 3257	OP	CR	FBG	SV	VD	T340-T350		12	4	12145	2	9	36700	41100
35	7	AFT CABIN 3607	FB	MY	FBG	SV	IB	T340	MRCR	12	6	18500	3	2	56100	61600
35	7	AFT CABIN 3607	FB	MY	FBG	SV	IB	T350	CRUS	12	6	18500	3	2	56600	62200
35	7	AFT CABIN 3607	FB	MY	FBG	SV	IB	T225D	CRUS	12	6	18500	3	2	67300	74000
35	7	MARINER 3697	FB	SDN	FBG	SV	VD	T340	MRCR	12	6	19500	3	2	59400	65300
35	7	MARINER 3697	FB	SDN	FBG	SV	VD	T350	CRUS	12	6	19500	3	2	60000	65900
37	6	AFT CABIN 3807	FB	DCMY	FBG	SV	IB	T340	MRCR	14		22750	3	4	79000	86900
37	6	AFT CABIN 3807	FB	DCMY	FBG	SV	IB	T350	CRUS	14		22750	3	4	80000	87900
37	6	AFT CABIN 3807	FB	DCMY	FBG	SV	IB	T375D	CAT	14		22750	3	4	99900	110000
37	6	SANTEGO 3867	FB	CR	FBG	SV	VD	T340	MRCR	14		19000	3	7	73900	81200
37	6	SANTEGO 3867	FB	CR	FBG	SV	VD	T350	CRUS	14		19000	3	7	74900	82300
42		AFT CABIN 4207	FB	MY	FBG	SV	IB	T340	MRCR	15		23600	3	6	105500	115500
42		AFT CABIN 4207	FB	MY	FBG	SV	IB	T350	CRUS	15		23600	3	6	107000	117500
42		AFT CABIN 4207	FB	MY	FBG	SV	IB	T375D	CAT	15		23600	3	6	131500	144500
42		COCKPIT 4227 MY	FB	MYCPT	FBG	SV	IB	T340	MRCR	15		23150	3	6	100000	110000
42		COCKPIT 4227 MY	FB	MYCPT	FBG	SV	IB	T350	CRUS	15		23150	3	6	101500	111500
42		COCKPIT 4227 MY	FB	MYCPT	FBG	SV	IB	T375D	CAT	15		23150	3	6	125000	137500
42	5	CALIFORNIAN 42	FB	CNV	FBG	SV	IB	T375D	CAT	15	2	38000	4	4	127000	139500
42	5	CALIFORNIAN 42	FB	CNV	FBG	SV	IB	T450D	GM	15	2	38000	4	4	131500	144500
42	5	CALIFORNIAN 42	FB	CNV	FBG	SV	IB	T550D	GM	15	2	38000	4	4	141000	155000
44		VENETI 44	FB	MY	FBG	SV	IB	T375D	CAT	15	2	25000	4		94700	104000
45		CALIFORNIAN 45	FB	MY	FBG	SV	IB	T320D	CAT	15	2	40000	4		113500	124500
45		CALIFORNIAN 45	FB	MY	FBG	SV	IB	T375D	CAT	15	2	40000	4		118000	129500
45		CALIFORNIAN 45	FB	MY	FBG	SV	IB	T450D	GM	15	2	40000	4		123000	135000
48	5	CALIFORNIAN 48	FB	CNV	FBG	SV	IB	T375D	CAT	15	2	40000	4	8	134000	147500
48	5	CALIFORNIAN 48	FB	CNV	FBG	SV	IB	T450D	GM	15	2	40000	4	8	137500	151000
48	5	CALIFORNIAN 48	FB	CNV	FBG	SV	IB	T550D	GM	15	2	40000	4	8	146000	160500
48	5	CALIFORNIAN 48	FB	MY	FBG	SV	IB	T375D	CAT	15	2	38000	4	8	133000	146500
48	5	CALIFORNIAN 48	FB	MY	FBG	SV	IB	T450D	GM	15	2	38000	4	8	136500	150000
48	5	CALIFORNIAN 48 CPT	FB	MYCPT	FBG	SV	IB	T450D	GM	15	2	41000	4	8	132000	145000
48	5	CALIFORNIAN 48 CPT	FB	MYCPT	FBG	SV	IB	T550D	GM	15	2	41000	4	8	140000	153500
48	5	CALIFORNIAN 48 MCPT	FB	MYCPT	FBG	SV	IB	T375D	CAT	15	2	41000	4	8	125500	138000
55	6	CALIFORNIAN 55 MY	FB	MY	FBG	SV	IB	T450D	GM	15	2	46700	4	3	180500	198000
55	6	CALIFORNIAN 55 MY	FB	MY	FBG	SV	IB	T550D	GM	15	2	46700	4	3	200000	220000
55	6	CALIFORNIAN 55 MY	FB	MY	FBG	SV	IB	T736D	GM	15	2	46700	4	3	233000	256500
		1987 BOATS														
25	8	MONTEGO 2657	OP	CR	FBG	SV	IO	260-271		8		5300	2	10	11600	13500
25	8	SANTA-CRUZ 2667	FB	CBNCR	FBG	SV	IO	260	MRCR	8		5400	2	10	13000	14700
27	3	MONTEGO 2757	OP	CR	FBG	SV	IO	271	VLVO	10		6900	2	10	14700	16700
27	3	MONTEGO 2757	OP	CR	FBG	SV	IO	T180-T205		10		6900	2	8	15400	17800
27	3	SANTEGO 2767	FB	CBNCR	FBG	SV	IO	T180-T205		10		8400	2	8	18200	20300
28		AFT CABIN 2807	ST	CR	FBG	SV	IB	350	CRUS	11	1	8900	2	10	26800	29800
28		AFT CABIN 2807	ST	CR	FBG	SV	IB	T220-T230		11	1	8900	3	5	28000	31100
28		MARINER 2897	FB	SDN	FBG	SV	VD	350	CRUS	11	1	10300	2	10	26900	29800
28		MARINER 2897	FB	SDN	FBG	SV	VD	T220-T230		11	1	10300	3	5	28100	31300
28		VOYAGER 2827	FB	SDN	FBG	SV	VD	350	CRUS	11	1	10300	2	10	27100	30100
28		VOYAGER 2827	FB	SDN	FBG	SV	VD	T220-T230		11	1	10300	3	5	28200	31400
32		AFT CABIN 3207	FB	MY	FBG	SV	IB	T260-T270		11	7	12000	2	10	37800	42300
32		CONVERTIBLE 3227	FB	CNV	FBG	SV	VD	T260-T270		11	7	12600	2	10	37100	41600
32	3	MARINER 3297	FB	SDN	FBG	SV	VD	T260-T270		12	4	12600	2	9	39300	44000
32	3	MONTEGO 3257	OP	CR	FBG	SV	VD	T260-T350		12	4	13000	2	9	33900	39700
35	7	AFT CABIN 3607	FB	MY	FBG	SV	IB	T340	MRCR	12	6	18500	3	2	53500	58800
35	7	AFT CABIN 3607	FB	MY	FBG	SV	IB	T350	CRUS	12	6	18500	3	2	54000	59300
35	7	AFT CABIN 3607	FB	MY	FBG	SV	IB	T225D	CRUS	12	6	18500	3	2	64500	70900
35	7	MARINER 3697	FB	SDN	FBG	SV	VD	T340	MRCR	12	6	19500	3	2	56700	62300
35	7	MARINER 3697	FB	SDN	FBG	SV	VD	T350	CRUS	12	6	19500	3	2	57200	62900
37	6	AFT CABIN 3807	FB	DCMY	FBG	SV	IB	T340	MRCR	14		22750	3	4	75600	83100
37	6	AFT CABIN 3807	FB	DCMY	FBG	SV	IB	T350	CRUS	14		22750	3	4	76500	84000
37	6	AFT CABIN 3807	FB	DCMY	FBG	SV	IB	T375D	CAT	14		22750	3	4	95500	105000
42		AFT CABIN 4207	FB	MY	FBG	SV	IB	T340	MRCR	15		23600	3	6	100500	110500
42		AFT CABIN 4207	FB	MY	FBG	SV	IB	T350	CRUS	15		23600	3	6	102000	112000
42		AFT CABIN 4207	FB	MY	FBG	SV	IB	T375D	CAT	15		23600	3	6	126000	138500
42		COCKPIT 4227 MY	FB	MYCPT	FBG	SV	IB	T340	MRCR	15		23150	3	6	95700	105000
42		COCKPIT 4227 MY	FB	MYCPT	FBG	SV	IB	T350	CRUS	15		23150	3	6	97200	107000
42		COCKPIT 4227 MY	FB	MYCPT	FBG	SV	IB	T375D	CAT	15		23150	3	6	119500	131500
		1986 BOATS														
25	8	MONTEGO 2657	OP	CR	FBG	SV	IO	260	MRCR	8		5300	2	10	11000	12500
25	8	SANTA-CRUZ 2667	FB	CBNCR	FBG	SV	IO	260	MRCR	8		5400	2	10	12400	14000
27	3	MONTEGO 2757	OP	CR	FBG	SV	IO	260	MRCR	10		6900	2	10	13800	15700
27	3	MONTEGO 2757	OP	CR	FBG	SV	IO	T190	MRCR	10		6900	2	10	14800	16800
28		AFT CABIN 2807	ST	CR	FBG	SV	IB	350	CRUS	11	1	8900	2	10	25600	28500
28		AFT CABIN 2807	ST	CR	FBG	SV	IB	T220-T230		11	1	8900	2	10	26700	29700
28		MARINER 2897	FB	SDN	FBG	SV	IB	350	CRUS	11	1	10300	2	10	25600	28400
28		MARINER 2897	FB	SDN	FBG	SV	IB	T220-T230		11	1	10300	2	10	26700	29800

CONTINUED ON NEXT PAGE

LOA FT	LOA IN	NAME AND/ OR MODEL	TOP/ RIG	BOAT TYPE	HULL MTL	HULL TP	ENGINE TP	# HP	MFG	BEAM FT	BEAM IN	WGT LBS	DRAFT FT	DRAFT IN	RETAIL LOW	RETAIL HIGH
		1986 BOATS														
28		VOYAGER 2827	FB	SDN	FBG	SV	IB	350	CRUS	11	1	10300	2	10	25900	28800
28		VOYAGER 2827	FB	SDN	FBG	SV	IB	T220-T230		11	1	10300	2	10	27000	30100
32		AFT CABIN 3207	FB	MY	FBG	SV	IB	T260-T270		11	7	12000	2	10	36100	40400
32		CONVERTIBLE 3227	FB	CNV	FBG	SV	VD	T260-T270		11	7	12600	2	10	35400	39700
32	3	MARINER 3297	FB	SDN	FBG	SV	IB	T260-T270		12	4	12600	2	9	37500	42000
32	9	MONTEREY 2987	OP	EXP	FBG	SV	IB	T260-T270		11	1	9400	2	10	27400	30700
35	7	AFT CABIN 3607	FB	MY	FBG	SV	IB	T340	MRCR	12	6	18500	3	2	51000	56100
35	7	AFT CABIN.3607	FB	MY	FBG	SV	IB	T350	CRUS	12	6	18500	3	2	51500	56600
35	7	AFT CABIN 3607	FB	MY	FBG	SV	IB	T225D	CRUS	12	6	18500	3	2	61800	67900
35	7	MARINER 3697	FB	SDN	FBG	SV	IB	T340	MRCR	12	6	19500	3	2	54100	59400
35	7	MARINER 3697	FB	SDN	FBG	SV	IB	T350	CRUS	12	6	19500	3	2	54600	60000
42		MOTORYACHT 4207	FB	MY	FBG	SV	IB	T340	MRCR	15		23600	3	6	93900	103000
42		MOTORYACHT 4207	FB	MY	FBG	SV	IB	T350	CRUS	15		23600	3	6	95200	104500
42		MOTORYACHT 4207	FB	MY	FBG	SV	IB	T375D	CAT	15		23600	3	6	117000	129000
		1985 BOATS														
25	8	MONTEGO 2657	OP	CR	FBG	SV	IO	260		8		5300	2	10	10600	12200
25	8	SANTA-CRUZ 2667	FB	CBNCR	FBG	SV	IO	260		8		5400	2	10	11900	13700
25	8	SANTA-CRUZ 2667	FB	CBNCR	FBG	SV	IB	270		8		5400	2	10	13700	15500
28		AFT CABIN 2807	ST	CR	FBG	SV	IB	350	CRUS	11	1	8900	2	10	24500	27200
28		AFT CABIN 2807	ST	CR	FBG	SV	IB	T220-T230		11	1	8900	2	10	25500	28300
28		MARINER 2897	FB	SDN	FBG	SV	IB	350	CRUS	11	1	10300	2	10	24100	26800
28		MARINER 2897	FB	SDN	FBG	SV	IB	T220-T230		11	1	10300	2	10	25200	28100
28		VOYAGER 2827	FB	SDN	FBG	SV	IB	350	CRUS	11	1	10300	2	10	25000	27800
28		VOYAGER 2827	FB	SDN	FBG	SV	IB	T220-T230		11	1	10300	2	10	26100	29100
29		MONTEREY 2987	OP	EXP	FBG	SV	IB	T220-T270		11	1	9400	2	10	25900	29900
32		AFT CABIN 3207	FB	MY	FBG	SV	IB	260	MRCR	11	7	12000	2	10	30800	34200
32		AFT CABIN 3207	FB	MY	FBG	SV	IB	T250-T270		11	7	12000	2	10	34200	38600
32		AFT CABIN 3207	FB	MY	FBG	SV	IB	T158D	VLVO	11	7	12000	2	10	41400	46000
32		CONVERTIBLE 3227	FB	CNV	FBG	SV	IB	T250		11	7	12600	2	10	33600	37300
32		CONVERTIBLE 3227	FB	CNV	FBG	SV	VD	T260-T270		11	7	12600	2	10	33800	37900
32		CONVERTIBLE 3227	FB	CNV	FBG	SV	IB	T158D	VLVO	11	7	12600	2	10	41300	45900
32	3	MARINER 3297	FB	SDN	FBG	SV	IB	T270		12	4	12600	2	10	36100	40100
35	7	AFT CABIN 3607	FB	MY	FBG	SV	IB	T340	MRCR	12	6	18500	3	2	48700	53600
		IB T350 CRUS 49200 54100, IB T225D CRUS 59300 65100, IB T225D PCM													59300	65100
35	7	MARINER 3697	FB	SDN	FBG	SV	IB	T340	MRCR	12	6	19500	3	2	51700	56800
35	7	MARINER 3697	FB	SDN	FBG	SV	IB	T350	CRUS	12	6	19500	3	2	52100	57300
42		AFT CABIN 4207	FB	MY	FBG	SV	IB	T350		14	10	23600			93900	103000
		1984 BOATS														
25	8	MONTEREY 2687	OP	EXP	FBG	SV	IO	260		8		5300	2	10	10200	11800
25	8	MONTEREY 2687	OP	EXP	FBG	SV	VD	270	CRUS	8		5300	2	10	12900	14600
25	8	MONTEREY 2687	OP	EXP	FBG	SV	IO	165D	VLVO	8		5300	2	10	11500	13100
25	8	SANTA-CRUZ 2667	FB	CBNCR	FBG	SV	IO	260		8		5400	2	10	11400	13200
25	8	SANTA-CRUZ 2667	FB	CBNCR	FBG	SV	VD	270	CRUS	8		5400	2	10	13200	15000
25	8	SANTA-CRUZ 2667	FB	CBNCR	FBG	SV	IO	165D	VLVO	8		5400	2	10	14600	16600
28		AFT-CABIN 2807	ST	CR	FBG	SV	IB	350	CRUS	11	1	8900	2	10	23500	26100
28		AFT-CABIN 2807	ST	CR	FBG	SV	IB	T220-T250		11	1	8900	2	10	24400	27500
28		AFT-CABIN 2807	ST	CR	FBG	SV	IB	T158D	VLVO	11	1	8900	2	10	33100	36800
28		MARINER 2897	FB	SDN	FBG	SV	IB	350	CRUS	11	1	10300	2	10	23500	26100
28		MARINER 2897	FB	SDN	FBG	SV	IB	T220-T250		11	1	10300	2	10	24100	27700
28		MARINER 2897	FB	SDN	FBG	SV	IB	T158D	VLVO	11	1	10300	2	10	35200	39100
28		VOYAGER 2827	FB	SDN	FBG	SV	IB	T220	CRUS	11	1	10300	2	10	24900	27700
32		AFT-CABIN 3207	FB	MY	FBG	SV	IB	225D	PCM	11	7	12000	2	10	37900	42100
32		AFT-CABIN 3207	FB	MY	FBG	SV	IB	T250-T270		11	7	12000	2	10	32900	37100
32		AFT-CABIN 3207	FB	MY	FBG	SV	IB	T158D	VLVO	11	7	12000	2	10	40100	44500
32		CONVERTIBLE 3227	FB	CNV	FBG	SV	IB	T250-T270		11	7	12600	2	10	32100	36200
32		CONVERTIBLE 3227	FB	CNV	FBG	SV	IB	T158D	VLVO	11	7	12600	2	10	39700	44100
32	9	MARINER 3396	FB	SDN	FBG	SV	VD	T250-T270		12		11620	3	2	30400	34300
32	9	MARINER 3396	FB	SDN	FBG	SV	VD	T158D	VLVO	12		11620	3	2	35900	39800
35	7	AFT CABIN 3607	FB	MY	FBG	SV	IB	225D	CRUS	12	6	18500	3	2	52500	57700
		IB 235D VLVO 52300 57500, IB T350 CRUS 47200 51900, IB T350 PCM													47000	51700
		IB T225D CRUS 56900 62500, IB T225D PCM 56900 62500														
35	7	MARINER 3697	FB	SDN	FBG	SV	IB	T350	CRUS	12	6	19500	3	2	49800	54800
35	7	MARINER 3697	FB	SDN	FBG	SV	IB	T350	PCM	12	6	19500	3	2	49600	54500

....For earlier years, see the BUC Used Boat Price Guide, Volume 3

CARY MARINE

GRAND HAVEN MI 49417 COAST GUARD MFG ID- CRM See inside cover to adjust price for area

LOA FT	LOA IN	NAME AND/ OR MODEL	TOP/ RIG	BOAT TYPE	HULL MTL	HULL TP	ENGINE TP	# HP	MFG	BEAM FT	BEAM IN	WGT LBS	DRAFT FT	DRAFT IN	RETAIL LOW	RETAIL HIGH
		1986 BOATS														
49	10	CARY 50	OP	OFF	FBG	DV	IO	T370	MRCR	14	6		3		108500	119500
		IB T570D GM 216000 237000, IO Q370 MRCR 130500 143500, IO Q500													158000	173500
		IB Q240D REN 223000 245000														
49	10	CARY 50	FB	OFF	FBG	DV	IB	T570D	GM	14	6		3		220000	242000
49	10	CARY 50	FB	OFF	FBG	DV	IO	Q370	MRCR	14	6		3		132000	145500
49	10	CARY 50	FB	OFF	FBG	DV	IB	Q240D	REN	14	6		3		226000	248500
49	10	FLYBRIDGE	FB	SDN	FBG	DV	IB	T570D	GM	14	9		4	1	228000	250500
49	10	SPORT 2+2	OP	OFF	KEV	DV	IO	Q400	MRCR	14	9		3		144500	159000
		1985 BOATS														
49	10	CARY 50	OP	OFF	FBG	DV	IO	Q370	MRCR	14	6	28000	3		144500	158500
49	10	SPORT 2+2	OP	OFF	FBG	DV	IO	Q400	MRCR	14	9	20000	3		147500	162000
		1984 BOATS														
43		CARY 43	OP	OFF	FBG	DV	IO	R370	MRCR	12		16000	2	6	86100	94600
45		CARY 45	OP	OFF	FBG	DV	IO	R330	MRCR	12		18000	2	6	80900	88900
49	10	CARY 50	OP	OFF	FBG	DV	IO	T370	MRCR	14	6	28000	3		119000	131000
		IB T570D GM 228500 251000, IO Q370 MRCR 139500 153000, IO Q500													157000	172500
		IB Q240D REN 244500 268500														
49	10	CARY 50	FB	OFF	FBG	DV	IB	T570D	GM	14	6	28000	3		231500	254500
49	10	CARY 50	FB	OFF	FBG	DV	IO	Q370	MRCR	14	6	28000	3		141000	155000
49	10	CARY 50	FB	OFF	FBG	DV	IB	Q240D	REN	14	6	28000	3		248000	272500
49	10	FLYBRIDGE	FB	SDN	FBG	DV	IB	T570D	GM	14	9	36000	4	1	273500	300500
49	10	SPORT 2+2	OP	OFF	KEV	DV	IO	Q400	MRCR	14	9	20000	3		142000	156000
50		CARY 50	OP	OFF	FBG	DV	IB	Q330		14		27000	3	6	225000	247000

....For earlier years, see the BUC Used Boat Price Guide, Volume 3

CARYSFORT MARINE INC

POMPANO BEACH FL 33062 See inside cover to adjust price for area

LOA FT	LOA IN	NAME AND/ OR MODEL	TOP/ RIG	BOAT TYPE	HULL MTL	HULL TP	ENGINE TP	# HP	MFG	BEAM FT	BEAM IN	WGT LBS	DRAFT FT	DRAFT IN	RETAIL LOW	RETAIL HIGH
		1989 BOATS														
18	6	CARYSFORT 19	OP	OPFSH	FBG	SV	OB			7		1420		8	4100	4750
18	6	CARYSFORT 19TC	OP	UTL	FBG	SV	OB			7		1490		9	3950	4600

CASCADE YACHTS INC

PORTLAND OR 97218 COAST GUARD MFG ID- YCS See inside cover to adjust price for area

For more recent years, see the BUC Used Boat Price Guide, Volume 1

LOA FT	LOA IN	NAME AND/ OR MODEL	TOP/ RIG	BOAT TYPE	HULL MTL	HULL TP	ENGINE TP	# HP	MFG	BEAM FT	BEAM IN	WGT LBS	DRAFT FT	DRAFT IN	RETAIL LOW	RETAIL HIGH
		1996 BOATS														
20		CASCADE CLASSIC 20	CAT	SACAC	FBG	KL	IB	9D	YAN	8		5260	3	6	19800	22000
20		CASCADE CLASSIC 20T	EPH	TUG	FBG	DS	IB	9D	YAN	8		4800	2	3	**	**
22		CASCADE CLASSIC 22	SLP	SACAC	FBG	KL	IB	9D	YAN	7		4000	3		23800	26500
27	5	CASCADE 27	SLP	SACAC	FBG	KL	IB	9D	YAN	8	10	6400	4	6	31300	34800
29		CASCADE 29	SLP	SACAC	FBG	KL	IB	18D	YAN	8	2	8500	4	9	44400	49400
30		CASCADE CLASSIC 30	CUT	SACAC	FBG	KL	IB	27D	YAN	10	6	10975	4	6	59600	65500
30		CASCADE CLASSIC 30T	EPH	TRPH	FBG	DS	IB	27D	YAN	10	6	10000	3		50300	55300
34		CASCADE CLASSIC 34T	EPH	TRWL	FBG	DS	IB	27D	YAN	10	6	9200	2	6	71200	78200
36		CASCADE 36	SLP	SACAC	FBG	KL	IB	27D	YAN	10		13000	5	6	71000	78000
36	1	CASCADE CLASSIC 36T	EPH	TRPHC	FBG	DS	IB	T 38D	YAN	12	6	30000	4	1	106000	116500
39		CASCADE CLASSIC 39	CUT	SACAC	FBG	KL	IB	50D	YAN	12	4	23275	5		120500	132500
39		CASCADE CLASSIC 39PH	CUT	SACIS	FBG	KL	IB	50D	YAN	12	4	23275	5		120500	132500
40		CASCADE CLASSIC 40T	EPH	TRPH	FBG	DS	IB	50D	YAN	12	4	23000	3	6	138000	151500
44		CASCADE 44	CUT	SACAC	FBG	KL	IB	50D	YAN	12		19000	6		122000	134500
		1995 BOATS														
20		CASCADE CLASSIC 20	CAT	SACAC	FBG	KL	IB	9D	YAN	8		2500	2	5	11000	12500
22		CASCADE CLASSIC 22	SLP	SACAC	FBG	KL	IB	9D	YAN	7		4000	3		22600	25100
27	1	CASCADE 27	SLP	SACAC	FBG	KL	IB	9D	YAN	8	10	6000	4	6	27400	30400
29		CASCADE 29	SLP	SACAC	FBG	KL	IB	15D	YAN	8	2	8000	4	9	39500	43900
30		CASCADE CLASSIC 30	CUT	SACAC	FBG	KL	IB	18D	YAN	10	6	12000	4	6	61800	67900
36		CASCADE 36	CUT	SACAC	FBG	KL	IB	T 27D	YAN	10		13000	5	6	68500	75300
36		CASCADE 36		TRWL	FBG	DS	IB	34D	YAN	12	6	30000	4	1	132000	145000
39		CASCADE 39		TRWL	FBG	DS	IB	34D	YAN	12	6	25000	3	6	133500	146500
39		CASCADE CLASSIC 39	CUT	SACAC	FBG	KL	IB	34D	YAN	12	4	23300	5		114000	125000
41	9	CASCADE 42	SLP	SACAC	FBG	KL	IB	55D	YAN	11	8	18450	6		105000	115500
41	9	CASCADE 42	KTH	SACAC	FBG	KL	IB	55D	YAN	11	8	18450	6		105000	115500
42	6	CASCADE 42 HS	SLP	SACAC	FBG	KL	IB	55D	YAN	12		19000	6		109500	120500
42	6	CASCADE 42 HS	KTH	SACAC	FBG	KL	IB	55D	YAN	12		19000	6		109500	120500
44	8	CASCADE 44 HS	CUT	SACAC	FBG	KL	IB	55D	YAN	12		19500	6		120500	132500

LOA FT	LOA IN	NAME AND/ OR MODEL	TOP/ RIG	BOAT TYPE	-HULL- MTL	-HULL- TP	TP	#	ENGINE HP	ENGINE MFG	BEAM FT	BEAM IN	WGT LBS	DRAFT FT	DRAFT IN	RETAIL LOW	RETAIL HIGH
1994 BOATS																	
20		CASCADE CLASSIC 20	CAT	SACAC	FBG	KL	IB		9D	YAN	8		2500	2	5	10400	11900
22		CASCADE CLASSIC 22	SLP	SACAC	FBG	KL	IB		9D	YAN	7		4000	3		21400	23700
27	1	CASCADE 27	SLP	SACAC	FBG	KL	IB		9D	YAN	8	10	6000	4	6	25900	28800
29		CASCADE 29	SLP	SACAC	FBG	KL	IB		15D	YAN	8	2	8000	4	9	37400	41600
30		CASCADE CLASSIC 30	CUT	SACAC	FBG	KL	IB		18D	YAN	10	6	12000	4	6	58500	64300
36		CASCADE 36	CUT	SACAC	FBG	KL	IB	T	27D	YAN	10		13000	5	6	64900	71300
36		CASCADE 36		TRWL	FBG	DS	IB		34D	YAN	12	6	30000	4	1	126500	139000
39		CASCADE 39		TRWL	FBG	DS	IB		34D	YAN	12	6	25000	3	6	128000	140500
39		CASCADE CLASSIC 39	CUT	SACAC	FBG	KL	IB		34D	YAN	12	4	23300	5		107500	118500
41	9	CASCADE 42	SLP	SACAC	FBG	KL	IB		55D	YAN	11	8	18450	6		99400	109000
41	9	CASCADE 42	KTH	SACAC	FBG	KL	IB		55D	YAN	11	8	18450	6		99400	109000
42	6	CASCADE 42 HS	SLP	SACAC	FBG	KL	IB		55D	YAN	12		19000	6		103500	114000
42	6	CASCADE 42 HS	KTH	SACAC	FBG	KL	IB		55D	YAN	12		19000	6		103500	114000
44	8	CASCADE 44 HS	CUT	SACAC	FBG	KL	IB		55D	YAN	12		19500	6		114000	125500
1993 BOATS																	
20		BENFORD	CAT	SACAC	FBG	KL	IB		9D	YAN	8		2500	2	5	9900	11200
22		BENFORD	SLP	SACAC	FBG	KL	IB		9D	YAN	7		4000	3		13300	15200
27	1	CASCADE 27	SLP	SACAC	FBG	KL	IB		9D	YAN	8	10	6000	4	6	24600	27300
29		CASCADE 29	SLP	SACAC	FBG	KL	IB		15D	YAN	8	2	8000	4	9	35400	39300
30		BENFORD	SLP	SACAC	FBG	KL	IB		18D	YAN	10	6	12000	4	6	55400	60800
30		BENFORD	CUT	SACAC	FBG	KL	IB		18D	YAN	10	6	12000	4	6	55400	60800
36		CASCADE 36	SLP	SACAC	FBG	KL	IB	T	27D	YAN	10		13000	5	6	61400	67500
36		LUCANDER		TRWL	FBG	DS	IB		34D	YAN	12	6	30000	4	1	120500	132500
39		BENFORD	CUT	SACAC	FBG	KL	IB		34D	YAN	12	4	23300	5		102000	112000
39		BENFORD		TRWL	FBG	DS	IB		34D	YAN	12	6	25000	3	6	121500	134000
39	8	CASCADE 40	SLP	SACAC	FBG	KL	IB		55D	YAN	11	2		5	10	104000	114500
39	8	CASCADE 40	CUT	SACAC	FBG	KL	IB		55D	YAN	11	2		5	10	104000	114500
41	9	CASCADE 42	SLP	SACAC	FBG	KL	IB		55D	YAN	11	8	18450	6		94100	103500
41	9	CASCADE 42	KTH	SACAC	FBG	KL	IB		55D	YAN	11	8	18450	6		94100	103500
42	6	CASCADE 42 HS	SLP	SACAC	FBG	KL	IB		55D	YAN	12		19000	6		98200	108000
42	6	CASCADE 42 HS	KTH	SACAC	FBG	KL	IB		55D	YAN	12		19000	6		98200	108000
44	8	CASCADE 44 HS	CUT	SACAC	FBG	KL	IB		55D	YAN	12		19500	6		108000	119000
1992 BOATS																	
20		BENFORD	CAT	SA/CR	FBG	KL	IB		9D	YAN	8		2500	2	5	9400	10700
20		BENFORD		TUG	FBG		IB		9D	YAN	8		2500	2	5	**	**
22		BENFORD	SLP	SA/CR	FBG	KL	IB		9D	YAN	7		4000	3		12600	14400
27	1	CASCADE 27	SLP	SAIL	FBG	KL	IB		9D	YAN	8	10	6000	4	6	23300	25900
29		CASCADE 29	SLP	SAIL	FBG	KL	IB		15D	YAN	8	2	8000	4	9	33600	37300
30		BENFORD	SLP	SA/CR	FBG	KL	IB		18D	YAN	10	6	12000	4	6	52500	57700
30		BENFORD	CUT	SA/CR	FBG	KL	IB		18D	YAN	10	6	12000	4	6	52500	57700
36		CASCADE 36	SLP	SA/RC	FBG	KL	IB	T	27D	YAN	10		13000	5	6	58200	63900
36		LUCANDER		TRWL	FBG	DS	IB		34D	YAN	12	6	30000	4	1	115000	126000
39		BENFORD	CUT	SA/CR	FBG	KL	IB		34D	YAN	12	4	23300	5		96700	106000
40		BENFORD		TRWL	FBG	DS	IB		34D	YAN	12	6	25000	3	6	121000	133000
41	9	CASCADE 42	SLP	SA/CR	FBG	KL	IB		55D	YAN	11	8	18450	6		89200	98000
41	9	CASCADE 42	KTH	SA/CR	FBG	KL	IB		55D	YAN	11	8	18450	6		89200	98000
42		CASCADE 44 HS	CUT	SA/CR	FBG	KL	IB		55D	YAN	12		19500	6		92900	102000
42	6	CASCADE 42 HS	SLP	SA/CR	FBG	KL	IB		55D	YAN	12		19000	6		93000	102000
42	6	CASCADE 42 HS	KTH	SA/CR	FBG	KL	IB		55D	YAN	12		19000	6		93000	102000
1991 BOATS																	
20		BENFORD	CAT	SA/CR	FBG	KL	IB		9D	YAN	8		2500	2	5	8900	10100
20		BENFORD		TUG	FBG		IB		9D	YAN	8		2500	2	5	**	**
22		BENFORD	SLP	SA/CR	FBG	KL	IB		9D	YAN	7		4000	3		12000	13600
27	1	CASCADE 27	SLP	SAIL	FBG	KL	IB		9D	YAN	8	10	6000	4	6	22000	24500
29		CASCADE 29	SLP	SAIL	FBG	KL	IB		15D	YAN	8	2	8000	4	9	31800	35300
30		BENFORD	SLP	SA/CR	FBG	KL	IB		18D	YAN	10	6	12000	4	6	49700	54600
30		BENFORD	CUT	SA/CR	FBG	KL	IB		18D	YAN	10	6	12000	4	6	49700	54600
36		CASCADE 36	SLP	SA/RC	FBG	KL	IB	T	27D	YAN	10		13000	5	6	55100	60600
36		LUCANDER		TRWL	FBG	DS	IB		34D	YAN	12	6	30000	4	1	109500	120500
39		BENFORD	CUT	SA/CR	FBG	KL	IB		34D	YAN	12	4	23300	5		91600	100500
40		BENFORD		TRWL	FBG	DS	IB		34D	YAN	12	6	25000	3	6	115500	127000
41	9	CASCADE 42	SLP	SA/CR	FBG	KL	IB		55D	YAN	11	8	18450	6		84500	92800
41	9	CASCADE 42	KTH	SA/CR	FBG	KL	IB		55D	YAN	11	8	18450	6		84500	92800
42		CASCADE 44 HS	CUT	SA/CR	FBG	KL	IB		55D	YAN	12		19500	6		88000	96700
42	6	CASCADE 42 HS	SLP	SA/CR	FBG	KL	IB		55D	YAN	12		19000	6		88100	96800
42	6	CASCADE 42 HS	KTH	SA/CR	FBG	KL	IB		55D	YAN	12		19000	6		88100	96800
1990 BOATS																	
20		BENFORD	CAT	SA/CR	FBG	KL	IB		9D	YAN	8		2500	2	5	8350	9600
20		BENFORD		TUG	FBG		IB		9D	YAN	8		2500	2	5	**	**
22		BENFORD	SLP	SA/CR	FBG	KL	IB		9D	YAN	7		4000	3		11300	12900
27	1	CASCADE 27	SLP	SAIL	FBG	KL	IB		9D	YAN	8	10	6000	4	6	20900	23200
29		CASCADE 29	SLP	SAIL	FBG	KL	IB		15D	YAN	8	2	8000	4	9	30100	33400
30		BENFORD	SLP	SA/CR	FBG	KL	IB		18D	YAN	10	6	12000	4	6	47300	52000
30		BENFORD	CUT	SA/CR	FBG	KL	IB		18D	YAN	10	6	12000	4	6	47300	52000
36		CASCADE 36	SLP	SA/RC	FBG	KL	IB		27D	YAN	10		13000	5	6	51300	56300
36		LUCANDER		TRWL	FBG	DS	IB		34D	YAN	12	6	30000	4	1	104500	115000
39		BENFORD	CUT	SA/CR	FBG	KL	IB		34D	YAN	12	4	23300	5		86700	95300
40		BENFORD		TRWL	FBG	DS	IB		34D	YAN	12	6	25000	3	6	110500	121000
41	9	CASCADE 42	SLP	SA/CR	FBG	KL	IB		55D	YAN	11	8	18450	6		80000	87900
41	9	CASCADE 42	KTH	SA/CR	FBG	KL	IB		55D	YAN	11	8	18450	6		80000	87900
42		CASCADE 44 HS	CUT	SA/CR	FBG	KL	IB		55D	YAN	12		19500	6		83300	91600
42	6	CASCADE 42 HS	SLP	SA/CR	FBG	KL	IB		55D	YAN	12		19000	6		83400	91700
42	6	CASCADE 42 HS	KTH	SA/CR	FBG	KL	IB		55D	YAN	12		19000	6		83500	91700
1989 BOATS																	
27	1	CASCADE 27	SLP	SAIL	FBG	KL	IB		9D	YAN	8	10	6000	4	6	19800	22000
29		CASCADE 29	SLP	SAIL	FBG	KL	IB		15D	YAN	8	2	8000	4	9	28500	31700
36		CASCADE 36	SLP	SA/RC	FBG	KL	IB		27D	YAN	10		13000	5	6	48600	53400
41	9	CASCADE 42	SLP	SA/CR	FBG	KL	IB		51D	PERK	11	8	18450	6		75100	82600
41	9	CASCADE 42	KTH	SA/CR	FBG	KL	IB		51D	PERK	11	8	18450	6		75100	82600
42	6	CASCADE 42 CS	SLP	SA/CR	FBG	KL	IB		51D	PERK	12		19000	6		78400	86200
42	6	CASCADE 42 CS	KTH	SA/CR	FBG	KL	IB		51D	PERK	12		19000	6		78400	86200
1988 BOATS																	
27	1	CASCADE 27	SLP	SAIL	FBG	KL	IB		9D	YAN	8	10	6000	4	6	19000	21100
29		CASCADE 29	SLP	SAIL	FBG	KL	IB		15D	YAN	8	2	8000	4	9	27000	30000
36		CASCADE 36	SLP	SA/RC	FBG	KL	IB		27D	YAN	10		13000	5	6	46300	50800
41	9	CASCADE 42	SLP	SA/CR	FBG	KL	IB		51D	PERK	11	8	18450	6		71200	78200
41	9	CASCADE 42	KTH	SA/CR	FBG	KL	IB		51D	PERK	11	8	18450	6		71200	78200
42	6	CASCADE 42 CS	SLP	SA/CR	FBG	KL	IB		51D	PERK	12		19000	6		74300	81600
42	6	CASCADE 42 CS	KTH	SA/CR	FBG	KL	IB		51D	PERK	12		19000	6		74300	81600
1987 BOATS																	
27	1	CASCADE 27	SLP	SAIL	FBG	KL	IB		9D	YAN	8	10	6000	4	6	17600	20000
29		CASCADE 29	SLP	SAIL	FBG	KL	IB		15D	YAN	8	2	8000	4	9	25600	28400
36		CASCADE 36	SLP	SA/RC	FBG	KL	IB		27D	YAN	10		13000	5	6	43400	48200
41	9	CASCADE 42	SLP	SA/CR	FBG	KL	IB		51D	PERK	11	8	18450	6		67400	74100
41	9	CASCADE 42	KTH	SA/CR	FBG	KL	IB		51D	PERK	11	8	18450	6		67500	74100
42	6	CASCADE 42 CS	SLP	SA/CR	FBG	KL	IB		51D	PERK	12		19000	6		70400	77300
42	6	CASCADE 42 CS	KTH	SA/CR	FBG	KL	IB		51D	PERK	12		19000	6		70400	77300
1986 BOATS																	
22	11	CASCADE 23	SLP	SA/RC	FBG	DB	OB				7	8	2500	1	8	5600	6450
27	1	CASCADE 27	SLP	SA/RC	FBG	KL	IB		8D	FARY	8	10	6500	4	6	18400	20500
27	1	CASCADE 27	SLP	SAIL	FBG	KL	IB		9D	YAN	8	10	6000	4	6	16600	18900
29		CASCADE 29	SLP	SA/RC	FBG	KL	IB		12D	FARY	8	2	8000	4	9	24200	26900
29		CASCADE 29	SLP	SAIL	FBG	KL	IB		15D	YAN	8	2	8000	4	9	24200	26900
36		CASCADE 36	SLP	SA/RC	FBG	KL	IB		24D	FARY	10		13000	5	6	41000	45600
41	9	CASCADE 42	SLP	SA/CR	FBG	KL	IB		32D	FARY	11	8	18450	6		63900	70200
41	9	CASCADE 42	SLP	SA/CR	FBG	KL	IB		51D	PERK	11	8	18450	6		63900	70200
41	9	CASCADE 42	KTH	SA/CR	FBG	KL	IB		32D	FARY	11	8	18450	6		63900	70200
41	9	CASCADE 42	KTH	SA/CR	FBG	KL	IB		51D	PERK	11	8	18450	6		63900	70200
41	9	CASCADE 42 CS	SLP	SA/CR	FBG	KL	IB		32D	FARY	12		19000	6		65100	71500
41	9	CASCADE 42 CS	KTH	SA/CR	FBG	KL	IB		32D	FARY	12		19000	6		65100	71500
42	6	CASCADE 42 CS	SLP	SA/CR	FBG	KL	IB		51D	PERK	12		19000	6		66700	73300
42	6	CASCADE 42 CS	KTH	SA/CR	FBG	KL	IB		51D	PERK	12		19000	6		66700	73300
1985 BOATS																	
22	11	CASCADE 23	SLP	SA/RC	FBG	DB	OB				7	8	2500	1	8	5300	6100
27	1	CASCADE 27	SLP	SAIL	FBG	KL	IB		9D	YAN	8	10	6000	4	6	15800	17900
29		CASCADE 29	SLP	SAIL	FBG	KL	IB		15D	YAN	8	2	8000	4	9	23000	25500
36		CASCADE 36	SLP	SA/RC	FBG	KL	IB		23D		10		13000	6		38800	43200
41	9	CASCADE 42	SLP	SA/CR	FBG	KL	IB		51D	PERK	11	8	18450	6		60600	66600
41	9	CASCADE 42	CUT	SA/CR	FBG	KL	IB		D		11	8	18450	6		60700	66800
42	6	CASCADE 42 CS	SLP	SA/CR	FBG	KL	IB		51D	PERK	12		19000	6		63200	69500
1984 BOATS																	
22	11	CASCADE 23	SLP	SA/RC	FBG	DB	OB				7	8	2500	1	8	5050	5800
27	1	CASCADE 27	SLP	SA/RC	FBG	KL	IB		8D	FARY	8	10	6500	4	6	16200	18400
29		CASCADE 29	SLP	SA/RC	FBG	KL	IB		12D	FARY	8	2	8000	4	9	21700	24100
36		CASCADE 36	SLP	SA/RC	FBG	KL	IB		24D	FARY	10		13000	5	6	36800	40900
41	9	CASCADE 42	SLP	SA/CR	FBG	KL	IB		40D	PERK	11	8	18450	6		57300	62900
41	9	CASCADE 42	CUT	SA/CR	FBG	KL	IB		D		11	8	18450	6		57600	63300
41	9	CASCADE 42	KTH	SA/CR	FBG	KL	IB		40D	PERK	11	8	18450	6		57300	62900
42	6	CASCADE 42 CS	SLP	SA/CR	FBG	KL	IB		40D	PERK	12		19000	6		59800	65700
42	6	CASCADE 42 CS	CUT	SA/CR	FBG	KL	IB		D		12		19000	6		60100	66000
42	6	CASCADE 42 CS	KTH	SA/CR	FBG	KL	IB		40D	PERK	12		19000	6		59800	65700

....For earlier years, see the BUC Used Boat Price Guide, Volume 3

CAT KETCH CORP

MIAMI FL 33146 COAST GUARD MFG ID- CKI See inside cover to adjust price for area

LOA FT	LOA IN	NAME AND/ OR MODEL	TOP/ RIG	BOAT TYPE	HULL MTL	HULL TP	ENGINE TP	#	HP	MFG	BEAM FT	BEAM IN	WGT LBS	DRAFT FT	DRAFT IN	RETAIL LOW	RETAIL HIGH
		1986 BOATS															
27		HERRESHOFF 27	KTH	SA/RC	FBG	KL	IB		10D		9	6	3850	3	10	13800	15700
30	10	HERRESHOFF 31	KTH	SRCAC	FBG	KL	IB		15D		10	4	8640	4		33200	36900
38		HERRESHOFF 38	KTH	SA/RC	FBG	KL	IB		32D	UNIV	11	6	13080	4	5	54900	60400
45		HERRESHOFF 45	KTH	SA/RC	FBG	KL	IB		44D	UNIV	13	6	18500	5		87300	95900
		1985 BOATS															
27		HERRESHOFF 27	KTH	SA/RC	FBG	KL	IB		10D		9	6	3850	3	6	13000	14800
30	10	HERRESHOFF 31	KTH	SRCAC	FBG	KL	IB		11D	UNIV	10	4	8640	4		31300	34700
38		HERRESHOFF 38	KTH	SA/RC	FBG	KL	IB		32D	UNIV	11	6	13080	4	5	51700	56800
45		HERRESHOFF 45	KTH	SA/RC	FBG	KL	IB		44D	UNIV	13	6	18500	5		82100	90200
		1984 BOATS															
30	10	HERRESHOFF 31	KTH	SRCAC	FBG	KL	IB		18D	UNIV	10	4	8640	4		29400	32700
38		HERRESHOFF 38	KTH	SA/RC	FBG	KL	IB		40D	UNIV	11	6	13080	4	5	48700	53600
44		HERRESHOFF 44	KTH	SA/RC	FBG	KL	IB		50D	UNIV	13		18500	5		75200	82700

....For earlier years, see the BUC Used Boat Price Guide, Volume 3

CAT LIMBO MARINE

PALMETTO FL 33561 COAST GUARD MFG ID- XKH See inside cover to adjust price for area

LOA FT	LOA IN	NAME AND/ OR MODEL	TOP/ RIG	BOAT TYPE	HULL MTL	HULL TP	ENGINE TP	#	HP	MFG	BEAM FT	BEAM IN	WGT LBS	DRAFT FT	DRAFT IN	RETAIL LOW	RETAIL HIGH
		1984 BOATS															
31		CAT-LIMBO	HT	FSH	FBG	SV	IB		D		10	2				**	**
31		CAT-LIMBO	HT	FSH	FBG	SV	IB	T	D		10	2				**	**
31		CAT-LIMBO	ST	SF	FBG	SV	IB		D		10	2				**	**
31		CAT-LIMBO	ST	SF	FBG	SV	IB	T	D		10	2				**	**
36		CAT-LIMBO	HT	SDN	FBG	SV	IB		D		13					**	**
36		CAT-LIMBO	HT	SDN	FBG	SV	IB	T	D		13					**	**
36		CAT-LIMBO	FB	SF	FBG	SV	IB		D		13					**	**
36		CAT-LIMBO	FB	SF	FBG	SV	IB	T	D		13					**	**

....For earlier years, see the BUC Used Boat Price Guide, Volume 3

CATALAC CATAMARAN LTD

DORSET ENGLAND See inside cover to adjust price for area

WORLD CATAMARANS
FT LAUDERDALE FL

LOA FT	LOA IN	NAME AND/ OR MODEL	TOP/ RIG	BOAT TYPE	HULL MTL	HULL TP	ENGINE TP	#	HP	MFG	BEAM FT	BEAM IN	WGT LBS	DRAFT FT	DRAFT IN	RETAIL LOW	RETAIL HIGH
		1989 BOATS															
27		CATALAC 8M	SLP	SA/CR	FBG	CT	OB				13	6	6800	2	4	32800	36500
27		CATALAC 8M	SLP	SA/CR	FBG	CT	IB	T	10D	YAN	13	6	6720	2	4	32700	36400
29	3	CATALAC 9M	SLP	SA/CR	FBG	CT	IB	T	10D	YAN	14		8960	2	6	49200	54100
34		CATALAC 10M	SLP	SA/CR	FBG	CT	IB	T	18D	YAN	15	3	13320	2	9	82000	90100
40	10	CATALAC 12M	SLP	SA/CR	FBG	CT	IB	T	35D	YAN	17	6	18500	3	1	146500	161000

CATALINA YACHTS INC

WOODLAND HILLS CA 91367 COAST GUARD MFG ID- CTY See inside cover to adjust price for area

For more recent years, see the BUC Used Boat Price Guide, Volume 1

LOA FT	LOA IN	NAME AND/ OR MODEL	TOP/ RIG	BOAT TYPE	HULL MTL	HULL TP	ENGINE TP	#	HP	MFG	BEAM FT	BEAM IN	WGT LBS	DRAFT FT	DRAFT IN	RETAIL LOW	RETAIL HIGH
		1996 BOATS															
21	6	CATALINA 22 FIN II	SLP	SACAC	FBG	KL	OB				8	4	2290	3	6	9400	10700
21	6	CATALINA 22 II	SLP	SACAC	FBG	CB	OB				8	8	2290	2		9150	10400
21	6	CATALINA 22 WING II	SLP	SACAC	FBG	WK	OB				8	4	2290	2	6	9400	10700
25		CATALINA 250	SLP	SACAC	FBG	CB	OB				8	6	2400	5	9	11300	12800
27		CATALINA 270 FIN	SLP	SACAC	FBG	KL	IB		20D	WEST	9	10	6260	5		31000	34400
27		CATALINA 270 WING	SLP	SACAC	FBG	WK	IB		20D	WEST	9	10	6460	3	6	32000	35500
28	4	CATALINA 28 FIN II	SLP	SACAC	FBG	KL	IB		18D	UNIV	10	4	8300	5	3	42100	46800
28	4	CATALINA 28 WING II	SLP	SACAC	FBG	WK	IB		18D	UNIV	10	4	8600	3	8	43700	48600
29	11	CATALINA 30 III FIN	SLP	SACAC	FBG	KL	IB		23D	UNIV	10	10	10200	5	3	53100	58300
29	11	CATALINA 30 III WING	SLP	SACAC	FBG	WK	IB		23D	UNIV	10	10	10300	3	10	53600	58900
32	6	CATALINA 320 FIN	SLP	SACAC	FBG	KL	IB		27D	WEST	11	9	11300	6		58300	64100
32	6	CATALINA 320 WING	SLP	SACAC	FBG	WK	IB		27D	WEST	11	9	11700	4	3	60300	66300
34	6	CATALINA 34 FIN II	SLP	SACAC	FBG	KL	IB		30D	UNIV	11	9	11950	5	7	61900	68000
34	6	CATALINA 34 WING II	SLP	SACAC	FBG	WK	IB		30D	UNIV	11	9	12550	4	3	64900	71300
36	4	CATALINA 36 FIN II	SLP	SACAC	FBG	KL	IB		30D	UNIV	11	11	13500	5	10	71500	78500
36	4	CATALINA 36 WING II	SLP	SACAC	FBG	WK	IB		30D	UNIV	11	11	14100	4	5	74300	81600
38	5	CATALINA 380 FIN	SLP	SACAC	FBG	KL	IB		42D		12	4	16000	6	6	88700	97400
38	5	CATALINA 380 WING	SLP	SACAC	FBG	WK	IB		42D		12	4	16500	5		90800	99800
40	6	CATALINA 400 3 FIN	SLP	SACAC	FBG	KL	IB		42D	WEST	13	6	18000	6	9	107000	117500
40	6	CATALINA 400 3 WING	SLP	SACAC	FBG	WK	IB		42D	WEST	13	6	18000	5		107000	117500
40	6	CATALINA 400-2 FIN	SLP	SACAC	FBG	KL	IB		42D	WEST	13	6	18000	6	9	107000	117500
40	6	CATALINA 400-2 WING	SLP	SACAC	FBG	WK	IB		42D	WEST	13	6	18000	5		107000	117500
41	10	CATALINA 42-2 FN II	SLP	SACAC	FBG	KL	IB		50D	YAN	13	10	20500	4	10	122000	134000
41	10	CATALINA 42-2 WNG II	SLP	SACAC	FBG	WK	IB		50D	YAN	13	10	20500	4	10	122000	134000
41	10	CATALINA 42-3 FIN II	SLP	SACAC	FBG	KL	IB		50D	YAN	13	10	20500	4	10	124000	136500
41	10	CATALINA 42-3 WNG II	SLP	SACAC	FBG	WK	IB		50D	YAN	13	10	20500	4	10	124000	136500
		1995 BOATS															
21	6	CATALINA 22 FIN II	SLP	SACAC	FBG	KL	OB				7	8	2490	3	6	9350	10600
21	6	CATALINA 22 II	SLP	SACAC	FBG	CB	OB				7	8	2490	2		9050	10300
21	6	CATALINA 22 WING II	SLP	SACAC	FBG	WK	OB				7	8	2490	2	6	9350	10600
25		CATALINA 250	SLP	SACAC	FBG	CB	OB				8	6	2400	5	9	10600	12000
27		CATALINA 270 FIN	SLP	SACAC	FBG	KL	IB		20D	WEST	9	10	6460	5		29900	33200
27		CATALINA 270 WING	SLP	SACAC	FBG	WK	IB		20D	WEST	9	10	6460	3	6	29900	33200
28	6	CATALINA 28 FIN II	SLP	SACAC	FBG	KL	IB		18D	UNIV	10	2	8300	5	3	39400	43800
28	6	CATALINA 28 WING II	SLP	SACAC	FBG	WK	IB		18D	UNIV	10	2	8600	3	10	40900	45500
29	11	CATALINA 30 III FIN	SLP	SACAC	FBG	KL	IB		23D	UNIV	10	10	10200	5	3	49600	54500
29	11	CATALINA 30 III WING	SLP	SACAC	FBG	WK	IB		23D	UNIV	10	10	10300	3	10	50100	55100
32	6	CATALINA 320 FIN	SLP	SACAC	FBG	KL	IB		27D	WEST	11	9	11300	6		54500	59900
32	6	CATALINA 320 WING	SLP	SACAC	FBG	WK	IB		27D	WEST	11	9	11700	4	3	56400	62000
33	9	ISLANDER 34	FB	SDN	FBG	SV	IB	T	210D-T315D		13		21000	3	4	94600	111500
34	6	CATALINA 34 FIN II	SLP	SACAC	FBG	KL	IB		30D	UNIV	11	9	11950	5	7	57900	63600
34	6	CATALINA 34 WING II	SLP	SACAC	FBG	WK	IB		30D	UNIV	11	9	12550	4	3	60600	66600
36	4	CATALINA 36 FIN II	SLP	SACAC	FBG	KL	IB		30D	UNIV	11	11	13500	5	10	66800	73400
36	4	CATALINA 36 WING II	SLP	SACAC	FBG	WK	IB		30D	UNIV	11	11	14100	4	5	69400	76300
40	6	CATALINA 400 3 FIN	SLP	SACAC	FBG	KL	IB		42D	WEST	13	6	18800	6	9	103000	113000
40	6	CATALINA 400 3 WING	SLP	SACAC	FBG	WK	IB		42D	WEST	13	6	18800	5		103000	113000
40	6	CATALINA 400-2 FIN	SLP	SACAC	FBG	KL	IB		42D	WEST	13	6	18000	6	9	99900	110000
40	6	CATALINA 400-2 WING	SLP	SACAC	FBG	WK	IB		42D	WEST	13	6	18800	5		103000	113000
41	10	CATALINA 42-2 FN II	SLP	SACAC	FBG	KL	IB		50D	YAN	13	10	20500	6		114000	125000
41	10	CATALINA 42-2 WNG II	SLP	SACAC	FBG	WK	IB		50D	YAN	13	10	20500	4	10	114000	125000
41	10	CATALINA 42-3 FIN II	SLP	SACAC	FBG	KL	IB		50D	YAN	13	10	20500	6		116000	127500
41	10	CATALINA 42-3 WNG II	SLP	SACAC	FBG	WK	IB		50D	YAN	13	10	20500	4	10	116000	127500
		1994 BOATS															
21	6	CATALINA 22	SLP	SACAC	FBG	CB	OB				7	8	2490	2		8350	9600
21	6	CATALINA 22 FIN	SLP	SACAC	FBG	KL	OB				7	8	2490	3	6	8650	9950
21	6	CATALINA 22 WING	SLP	SACAC	FBG	WK	OB				7	8	2490	2	6	8650	9950
25		CATALINA 250	SLP	SACAC	FBG	CB	OB				8	6	2400	5	9	9850	11200
27		CATALINA 270	SLP	SACAC	FBG	KL	IB		18D	PERK	9	3	6400	5		27300	30300
27		CATALINA 270	SLP	SACAC	FBG	WK	IB		18D	PERK	9	3	6400	3	6	27300	30300
27		CATALINA 270 LE	SLP	SACAC	FBG	KL	IB		18D	PERK	9	3	6400	5		27300	30300
27		CATALINA 270 LE	SLP	SACAC	FBG	WK	IB		18D	PERK	9	3	6400	3	6	27300	30300
28	6	CATALINA 28 FIN	SLP	SACAC	FBG	KL	IB		18D	UNIV	10	2	8300	4	8	36800	40900
28	6	CATALINA 28 WING	SLP	SACAC	FBG	WK	IB		18D	UNIV	10	2	8600	3	10	38200	42500
29	11	CATALINA 30 III	SLP	SACAC	FBG	KL	IB		23D	UNIV	10	10	10200	5	3	46600	51200
29	11	CATALINA 30 III WING	SLP	SACAC	FBG	WK	IB		23D	UNIV	10	10	10300	3	10	47100	51700
32	6	CATALINA 320	SLP	SACAC	FBG	KL	IB		28D	PERK	11	9	11700	6		52600	57800
32	6	CATALINA 320	SLP	SACAC	FBG	WK	IB		28D	PERK	11	9	11700	4	3	52600	57800
33	9	ISLANDER 34	FB	SDN	FBG	SV	IB	T	320	CRUS	13		21000	3	4	71400	78500
33	9	ISLANDER 34	FB	SDN	FBG	SV	IB	T	170D-T300D		13		21000	3	4	88000	105500
34	6	CATALINA 34	SLP	SACAC	FBG	KL	IB		30D	UNIV	11	9	11950	5	7	54100	59400
34	6	CATALINA 34 WING	SLP	SACAC	FBG	WK	IB		30D	UNIV	11	9	12550	4	3	56600	62200
36	4	CATALINA 36 FIN	SLP	SACAC	FBG	KL	IB		30D	UNIV	11	11	13500	5	10	62400	68600
36	4	CATALINA 36 WING	SLP	SACAC	FBG	WK	IB		30D	UNIV	11	11	14100	4	5	64900	71300
40	6	CATALINA 400-2 FIN	SLP	SACAC	FBG	KL	IB		42D	WEST	13	6	18000	6	9	93300	102500
40	6	CATALINA 400-2 WING	SLP	SACAC	FBG	WK	IB		42D	WEST	13	6	18000	5		93300	102500
41	10	CATALINA 42-2 FIN	SLP	SACAC	FBG	KL	IB		48D	YAN	13	10	18000	6		98500	108000
41	10	CATALINA 42-2 WING	SLP	SACAC	FBG	WK	IB		48D	YAN	13	10	18000	4	10	98500	108000
41	10	CATALINA 42-3 FIN	SLP	SACAC	FBG	KL	IB		48D	YAN	13	10	18000	6		100500	110000
41	10	CATALINA 42-3 WING	SLP	SACAC	FBG	WK	IB		48D	YAN	13	10	18000	4	10	100500	110000
		1993 BOATS															
21	6	CATALINA 22	SLP	SACAC	FBG	CB	OB				7	8	2490	2		7800	8950
21	6	CATALINA 22 FIN	SLP	SACAC	FBG	KL	OB				7	8	2490	3	6	8050	9250
21	6	CATALINA 22 WING	SLP	SACAC	FBG	WK	OB				7	8	2490	2	6	8050	9250
27		CATALINA 270	SLP	SACAC	FBG	KL	IB		18D	PERK	9	3	6400	5		23600	26200
27		CATALINA 270	SLP	SACAC	FBG	WK	IB		18D	PERK	9	3	6400	3	6	23600	26200
27		CATALINA 270 LE	SLP	SACAC	FBG	KL	IB		18D	PERK	9	3	6400	5		27300	30400
27		CATALINA 270 LE	SLP	SACAC	FBG	WK	IB		18D	PERK	9	3	6400	3	6	27300	30400
28	6	CATALINA 28 FIN	SLP	SACAC	FBG	KL	IB		18D	UNIV	10	2	8300	4	8	34400	38200
28	6	CATALINA 28 WING	SLP	SACAC	FBG	WK	IB		18D	UNIV	10	2	8600	3	10	35700	39700

CATALINA YACHTS INC -CONTINUED See inside cover to adjust price for area

LOA FT	LOA IN	NAME AND/ OR MODEL	TOP/ RIG	BOAT TYPE	-HULL- MTL	-HULL- TP	ENGINE TP	ENGINE # HP	ENGINE MFG	BEAM FT	BEAM IN	WGT LBS	DRAFT FT	DRAFT IN	RETAIL LOW	RETAIL HIGH
		1993 BOATS														
29	11	CATALINA 30	SLP	SACAC	FBG	KL	IB	23D	UNIV	10	10	10200	5	3	43000	47800
29	11	CATALINA 30 WING	SLP	SACAC	FBG	WK	IB	23D	UNIV	10	10	10300	3	10	43400	48300
32	6	CATALINA 320	SLP	SACAC	FBG	KL	IB	28D	PERK	11	9	11700	6		49100	54000
32	6	CATALINA 320	SLP	SACAC	FBG	WK	IB	28D	PERK	11	9	11700	4	3	49100	54000
33	9	ISLANDER 34	FB	SDN	FBG	SV	IB	T320	CRUS	13		19000	3	4	65200	71700
33	9	ISLANDER 34	FB	SDN	FBG	SV	IB	T170D	YAN	13		19000	3	4	78800	86600
34	6	CATALINA 34	SLP	SACAC	FBG	KL	IB	30D	UNIV	11	9	11950	5	7	50500	55500
34	6	CATALINA 34 WING	SLP	SACAC	FBG	WK	IB	30D	UNIV	11	9	12550	4	3	52900	58100
36	4	CATALINA 36 FIN	SLP	SACAC	FBG	KL	IB	30D	UNIV	11	11	13500	5	10	58300	64000
36	4	CATALINA 36 WING	SLP	SACAC	FBG	WK	IB	30D	UNIV	11	11	14100	4	5	60500	66500
41	10	CATALINA 42-2 FIN	SLP	SACAC	FBG	KL	IB	48D	YAN	13	10	18000	6		92400	101500
41	10	CATALINA 42-2 WING	SLP	SACAC	FBG	WK	IB	48D	YAN	13	10	18000	4	10	92400	101500
41	10	CATALINA 42-3 FIN	SLP	SACAC	FBG	KL	IB	48D	YAN	13	10	18000	6		93100	102500
41	10	CATALINA 42-3 WING	SLP	SACAC	FBG	WK	IB	48D	YAN	13	10	18000	4	10	93100	102500
		1992 BOATS														
21	6	CATALINA 22	SLP	SAIL	FBG	CB	OB			7	8	2490	2		7250	8350
21	6	CATALINA 22 FIN	SLP	SAIL	FBG	KL	OB			7	8	2490	3	6	7500	8650
21	6	CATALINA 22 WING	SLP	SAIL	FBG	WK	OB			7	8	2490	2	6	7500	8650
28	6	CATALINA 28 FIN	SLP	SAIL	FBG	KL	IB	18D	UNIV	10	2	8300	4	8	32100	35600
28	6	CATALINA 28 WING	SLP	SAIL	FBG	WK	IB	18D	UNIV	10	2	8200	3	10	31700	35200
29	11	CATALINA 30	SLP	SAIL	FBG	KL	IB	23D	UNIV	10	10	10200	5	3	40100	44600
29	11	CATALINA 30 WING	SLP	SAIL	FBG	WK	IB	23D	UNIV	10	10	10300	3	10	40500	45000
34	6	CATALINA 34	SLP	SAIL	FBG	KL	IB	30D	UNIV	11	9	11950	5	7	47300	52000
34	6	CATALINA 34 WING	SLP	SAIL	FBG	WK	IB	30D	UNIV	11	9	12550	4	3	49300	54200
36	4	CATALINA 36 FIN	SLP	SAIL	FBG	KL	IB	30D	UNIV	11	11	13500	5	10	54400	59700
36	4	CATALINA 36 WING	SLP	SAIL	FBG	WK	IB	30D	UNIV	11	11	14100	4	5	56500	62100
41	10	CATALINA 42-2 FIN	SLP	SAIL	FBG	KL	IB	50D	YAN	13	10	18000	6		86200	94700
41	10	CATALINA 42-2 WING	SLP	SAIL	FBG	WK	IB	50D	YAN	13	10	18000	4	10	87000	95600
41	10	CATALINA 42-3 FIN	SLP	SAIL	FBG	KL	IB	50D	YAN	13	10	18000	6		86200	94700
41	10	CATALINA 42-3 WING	SLP	SAIL	FBG	WK	IB	50D	YAN	13	10	18000	4	10	87000	95600
		1991 BOATS														
21	6	CATALINA 22	SLP	SAIL	FBG	KL	OB			7	8	2490	2		6850	7850
21	6	CATALINA 22 FIN	SLP	SAIL	FBG	KL	OB			7	8	2490	3	6	7000	8000
21	6	CATALINA 22 WING	SLP	SAIL	FBG	WK	OB			7	8	2490	2	6	7000	8000
25		CATALINA 25 FIN	SLP	SAIL	FBG	KL	IB	D		8		4500	4		14700	16700
25		CATALINA 25 WING	SLP	SAIL	FBG	WK	IB	D		8		4400	2	10	14400	16400
26	10	CATALINA 27 FIN	SLP	SAIL	FBG	KL	IB	D	UNIV	8	10	6850	4		23800	26500
26	10	CATALINA 27 WING	SLP	SAIL	FBG	WK	IB	D	UNIV	8	10	6750	3	5	23500	26100
28	6	CATALINA 28 FIN	SLP	SAIL	FBG	KL	IB	D	UNIV	10	2	8300	4	8	29900	33300
28	6	CATALINA 28 WING	SLP	SAIL	FBG	WK	IB	D	UNIV	10	2	8200	3	10	29600	32900
29	11	CATALINA 30	SLP	SAIL	FBG	KL	IB	D	UNIV	10	10	10200	5	3	37400	41600
29	11	CATALINA 30 WING	SLP	SAIL	FBG	WK	IB	D	UNIV	10	10	10300	3	10	37800	42000
34	6	CATALINA 34	SLP	SAIL	FBG	KL	IB	23D	UNIV	11	9	11950	5	7	43600	48500
34	6	CATALINA 34 WING	SLP	SAIL	FBG	WK	IB	23D	UNIV	11	9	12550	4	3	46200	50800
36	4	CATALINA 36 FIN	SLP	SAIL	FBG	KL	IB	23D	UNIV	11	11	13500	5	10	50600	55600
36	4	CATALINA 36 WING	SLP	SAIL	FBG	WK	IB	23D	UNIV	11	11	14100	4	5	52600	57800
41	10	CATALINA 42-2 FIN	SLP	SAIL	FBG	KL	IB	50D		13	10	18000	6		80600	88600
41	10	CATALINA 42-2 WING	SLP	SAIL	FBG	WK	IB	50D		13	10	18000	4	10	80600	88600
41	10	CATALINA 42-3 FIN	SLP	SAIL	FBG	KL	IB	50D		13	10	18000	6		80600	88600
41	10	CATALINA 42-3 WING	SLP	SAIL	FBG	WK	IB	50D		13	10	18000	4	10	80600	88600
		1990 BOATS														
21	6	CATALINA 22	SLP	SAIL	FBG	KL	OB			7	8	2490	2		6300	7200
21	6	CATALINA 22 FIN	SLP	SAIL	FBG	KL	OB			7	8	2490	3	6	6550	7550
21	6	CATALINA 22 WING	SLP	SAIL	FBG	WK	IB	D		7	8	2490	2	6	8250	9500
25		CATALINA 25 FIN	SLP	SAIL	FBG	KL	IB	D		8		4500	4		13700	15600
25		CATALINA 25 WING	SLP	SAIL	FBG	WK	IB	D		8		4400	2	10	13400	15300
26	10	CATALINA 27 FIN	SLP	SAIL	FBG	KL	IB	D	UNIV	8	10	6850	4		22200	24700
26	10	CATALINA 27 WING	SLP	SAIL	FBG	WK	IB	D	UNIV	8	10	6750	3	5	21900	24300
28	6	CATALINA 28 FIN	SLP	SAIL	FBG	KL	IB	D		10	2	8300	4	8	27900	31000
28	6	CATALINA 28 WING	SLP	SAIL	FBG	WK	IB	D		10	2	8200	3	10	27600	30600
29	11	CATALINA 30	SLP	SAIL	FBG	KL	IB	23D	UNIV	10	10	10200	5	3	34900	38800
29	11	CATALINA 30 WING	SLP	SAIL	FBG	WK	IB	23D	UNIV	10	10	10300	3	10	35300	39200
34	6	CATALINA 34	SLP	SAIL	FBG	KL	IB	30D		11	9	11950	5	7	40700	45200
34	6	CATALINA 34 WING	SLP	SAIL	FBG	WK	IB	30D		11	9	12550	3		42600	47400
36	4	CATALINA 36 FIN	SLP	SAIL	FBG	KL	IB	30D	UNIV	11	11	13500	5	10	47500	52200
36	4	CATALINA 36 WING	SLP	SAIL	FBG	WK	IB	30D	UNIV	11	11	14100	4	2	49100	54000
38	2	CATALINA 38	SLP	SAIL	FBG	KL	IB	D		11	10	15900	6	9	57700	63400
38	2	CATALINA 38 SHOAL	SLP	SAIL	FBG	KL	IB	D		11	10	16700	4	11	60000	65900
41	10	CATALINA 42 FIN	SLP	SAIL	FBG	KL	IB	44D		13	10	18000	6		74500	81900
41	10	CATALINA 42 WING	SLP	SAIL	FBG	WK	IB	44D		13	10	18000	4	10	75600	83000
		1989 BOATS														
21	6	CATALINA 22	SLP	SAIL	FBG	KL	OB			7	8	2490	2		6050	6950
21	6	CATALINA 22 FIN	SLP	SAIL	FBG	KL	OB			7	8	2490	3	6	6050	6950
21	6	CATALINA 22 WING	SLP	SAIL	FBG	WK	OB			7	8	2490	2	6	6050	6950
25		CATALINA 25 FIN	SLP	SAIL	FBG	KL	IB	D		8		4500	4		12800	14500
25		CATALINA 25 WING	SLP	SAIL	FBG	WK	IB	D		8		4400	2	10	12500	14200
26	10	CATALINA 27 FIN	SLP	SAIL	FBG	KL	IB	D	UNIV	8	10	6850	4		20700	23000
26	10	CATALINA 27 WING	SLP	SAIL	FBG	WK	IB	D	UNIV	8	10	6750	3	5	20400	22700
28	6	CATALINA 28 FIN	SLP	SAIL	FBG	KL	IB	D		10	2	8300	4	8	26000	28900
28	6	CATALINA 28 WING	SLP	SAIL	FBG	WK	IB	D		10	2	8200	3	10	25700	28600
29	11	CATALINA 30	SLP	SAIL	FBG	KL	IB	23D	UNIV	10	10	10200	5	3	32600	36200
29	11	CATALINA 30 WING	SLP	SAIL	FBG	WK	IB	23D	UNIV	10	10	10300	3	10	32900	36500
34	6	CATALINA 34	SLP	SAIL	FBG	KL	IB	30D		11	9	11950	5	7	38000	42200
34	6	CATALINA 34 WING	SLP	SAIL	FBG	WK	IB	30D		11	9	12550	3		39800	44200
36	4	CATALINA 36 FIN	SLP	SAIL	FBG	KL	IB	30D	UNIV	11	11	13550	5	10	44000	48900
36	4	CATALINA 36 WING	SLP	SAIL	FBG	WK	IB	30D	UNIV	11	11	14100	4	2	46100	50600
38	2	CATALINA 38	SLP	SAIL	FBG	KL	IB	D		11	10	15900	6	9	53800	59100
38	2	CATALINA 38 SHOAL	SLP	SAIL	FBG	KL	IB	D		11	10	16700	4	11	55900	61500
41	10	CATALINA 42 FIN	SLP	SAIL	FBG	KL	IB	44D		13	10	18000	6		70000	76900
41	10	CATALINA 42 WING	SLP	SAIL	FBG	WK	IB	44D		13	10	18000	4	10	70000	76900
		1988 BOATS														
21	6	CATALINA 22	SLP	SA/CR	FBG	KL	OB			7	8	2250	3	6	5300	6050
21	6	CATALINA 22	SLP	SA/CR	FBG	SK	OB			7	8	2250	2		5250	6000
21	6	CATALINA 22 WING	SLP	SA/CR	FBG	KL	OB			7	8	2250	2	6	5300	6100
25		CATALINA 25	SLP	SA/CR	FBG	KL	OB			8		4550	4		11200	12700
25		CATALINA 25 WING	SLP	SA/CR	FBG	KL	OB			8		4400	2	10	10800	12300
26	10	CATALINA 27	SLP	SA/CR	FBG	KL	OB			8	10	6850	4		18800	20900
26	10	CATALINA 27	SLP	SA/CR	FBG	KL	IB	D	UNIV	8	10	6850	4		19400	21500
26	10	CATALINA 27 WING	SLP	SA/CR	FBG	KL	OB			8	10	6750	3	5	18500	20500
26	10	CATALINA 27 WING	SLP	SA/CR	FBG	KL	IB	D	UNIV	8	10	6750	3	5	19100	21200
29	11	CATALINA 30	SLP	SA/CR	FBG	KL	IB	D	UNIV	10	10	10200	5	3	30400	33800
29	11	CATALINA 30 WING	SLP	SA/CR	FBG	KL	IB	D	UNIV	10	10	10300	3	10	30700	34100
34	6	CATALINA 34	SLP	SA/CR	FBG	KL	IB	25D	UNIV	11	9	11950	5	7	35400	39400
34	6	CATALINA 34 WING	SLP	SA/CR	FBG	KL	IB	25D	UNIV	11	9	12550	3	10	37100	41200
36	4	CATALINA 36	SLP	SA/CR	FBG	KL	IB	D	UNIV	11	11	13500	5	10	41000	45500
36	4	CATALINA 36 WING	SLP	SA/CR	FBG	KL		D	UNIV	11	11	14200	4	2	42100	46800
38	2	CATALINA 38	SLP	SA/CR	FBG	KL	IB	D	UNIV	11	10	15900	6	9	50300	55200
38	2	CATALINA 38 SHOAL	SLP	SA/CR	FBG	KL	IB	D	UNIV	11	10	16700	4	11	52300	57400
		1987 BOATS														
16	8	NACRA 5.0	SLP	SAIL	FBG	CT				8		325	2	3	1850	2200
17		NACRA 5.2	SLP	SAIL	FBG	CT				8		350	2	10	2000	2400
18		CAPRI 18	SLP	SAIL	FBG	KL	OB			7	7	1500	2		3550	4100
18		NACRA 18/2	SLP	SAIL	FBG	CT				11		325	2	10	2000	2400
18	6	NACRA 5.7	SLP	SAIL	FBG	CT				8		229	2	3	1550	1850
19		NACRA 5.8	SLP	SAIL	FBG	CT				8		390	3	2	2450	2850
21	6	CATALINA 22	SLP	SA/CR	FBG	KL	OB			7	8	2490	3	6	5250	6050
21	6	CATALINA 22	SLP	SA/CR	FBG	SK	OB			7	8	2250	2		4900	5650
21	6	CATALINA 22 WING	SLP	SA/CR	FBG	KL	OB			7	8	2350	2	6	5050	5800
22		CAPRI 22	SLP	SAIL	FBG	KL	OB			8		2150	4	2	4900	5600
22		CAPRI 22 WING	SLP	SAIL	FBG	KL	OB			8		2100	2	6	4800	5550
24	7	CAPRI 25	SLP	SAIL	FBG	KL	OB			9	2	2785	4	2	6600	7600
24	7	CAPRI 25 WING	SLP	SAIL	FBG	KL	OB			9	2	2725	3	4	6500	7450
25		CATALINA 25	SLP	SA/CR	FBG	KL	OB			8		4550	4		10400	11800
25		CATALINA 25	SLP	SA/CR	FBG	SK	OB			8		4150	2	8	9550	10800
25		CATALINA 25 WING	SLP	SA/CR	FBG	KL	OB			8		4400	2	10	10100	11500
26	10	CATALINA 27	SLP	SA/CR	FBG	KL	OB			8	10	6850	4		17200	19500
26	10	CATALINA 27	SLP	SA/CR	FBG	KL	IB	D	UNIV	8	10	6850	4		18300	20300
26	10	CATALINA 27 WING	SLP	SA/CR	FBG	KL	OB			8	10	6750	3	5	16900	19200
26	10	CATALINA 27 WING	SLP	SA/CR	FBG	KL	IB	D	UNIV	8	10	6750	3	5	18000	20000
29	6	CAPRI 30	SLP	SAIL	FBG	KL	OB			7	3	4985	5	4	13200	15000
29	6	CAPRI 30 WING	SLP	SAIL	FBG	KL	OB			7	3	5025	4	2	13300	15100
29	11	CATALINA 30	SLP	SA/CR	FBG	KL	IB	D	UNIV	10	10	10200	5	3	28400	31500
29	11	CATALINA 30 WING	SLP	SA/CR	FBG	KL	IB	D	UNIV	10	10	10300	3	10	28700	31900
34	6	CATALINA 34	SLP	SA/CR	FBG	KL	IB	25D	UNIV	11	9	11950	5	7	33100	36800
34	6	CATALINA 34 WING	SLP	SA/CR	FBG	KL	IB	25D	UNIV	11	9	12550	3	10	34700	38500
36	4	CATALINA 36	SLP	SA/CR	FBG	KL	IB	D	UNIV	11	11	13500	5	10	38300	42500
36	4	CATALINA 36 WING	SLP	SA/CR	FBG	KL	IB	D	UNIV	11	11	14200	4	2	40000	44500
38	2	CATALINA 38	SLP	SA/CR	FBG	KL	IB	D	UNIV	11	10	15900	6	9	47200	51900
38	2	CATALINA 38 SHOAL	SLP	SA/CR	FBG	KL	IB	D	UNIV	11	10	16700	4	11	48800	53600
41	3	MORGAN CLASSIC 41	SLP	SAIL	FBG	KL	IB	D	YAN	13	10	23000	4	10	69400	76200
43		MORGAN 43	SLP	SAIL	FBG	KL	IB	44D		13	6	23500	5		75300	82700
		1986 BOATS														
21	6	CATALINA 22	SLP	SA/CR	FBG	KL	OB			7	8	2490	3	6	4900	5650
21	6	CATALINA 22	SLP	SA/CR	FBG	SK	OB			7	8	2250	2		4600	5300
25		CATALINA 25	SLP	SA/CR	FBG	KL	OB			8		4550	4		9750	11100
25		CATALINA 25	SLP	SA/CR	FBG	SK	OB			8		4150	2	8	8950	10200
26	10	CATALINA 27	SLP	SA/CR	FBG	KL	OB			8	10	6850	4		16000	18200
26	10	CATALINA 27	SLP	SA/CR	FBG	KL	IB	D	UNIV	8	10	6850	4		16700	19000

 CONTINUED ON NEXT PAGE

LOA FT IN	NAME AND/ OR MODEL		TOP/ RIG	BOAT TYPE	-HULL- MTL TP	----ENGINE--- TP # HP MFG	BEAM FT IN	WGT LBS	DRAFT FT IN	RETAIL LOW	RETAIL HIGH
						1986 BOATS					
26 10	CATALINA 27	SHOAL	SLP	SA/CR	FBG KL	OB	8 10	7300	3 5	17200	19500
26 10	CATALINA 27	SHOAL	SLP	SA/CR	FBG KL	IB	8 10	7300	3 5	18300	20300
29 11	CATALINA 30		SLP	SA/CR	FBG KL	IB D UNIV	10 10	10200	5 3	26500	29500
29 11	CATALINA 30	SHOAL	SLP	SA/CR	FBG KL	IB D UNIV	10 10	10650	4 4	27700	30800
34 6	CATALINA 34		SLP	SA/CR	FBG KL	IB 25D UNIV	11 9	11950	5 7	30900	34400
34 6	CATALINA 34	SHOAL	SLP	SA/CR	FBG KL	IB 25D UNIV	11 9	11950	4 8	30900	34400
36 4	CATALINA 36		SLP	SA/CR	FBG KL	IB D UNIV	11 11	13500	5 10	35800	39800
36 4	CATALINA 36	SHOAL	SLP	SA/CR	FBG KL	IB D UNIV	11 11	14300	5 1	37700	41800
38 2	CATALINA 38		SLP	SA/CR	FBG KL	IB D UNIV	11 10	15900	6 9	43700	48500
38 2	CATALINA 38	SHOAL	SLP	SA/CR	FBG KL	IB D UNIV	11 10	16700	4 11	45900	50400
						1985 BOATS					
21 6	CATALINA 22	POP TOP	SLP	SA/CR	FBG KL	OB	7 8	2490	3 6	4600	5300
21 6	CATALINA 22	POP TOP	SLP	SA/CR	FBG SK	OB	7 8	2250	2	4250	4950
25	CATALINA 25		SLP	SA/CR	FBG KL	OB	8	4550	4	9150	10400
25	CATALINA 25		SLP	SA/CR	FBG SK	OB	8	4150	2 8	8300	9550
26 10	CATALINA 27		SLP	SA/CR	FBG KL	OB	8 10	6850	4	15000	17100
26 10	CATALINA 27		SLP	SA/CR	FBG KL	IB 14D UNIV	8 10	6850	4	15600	17800
26 10	CATALINA 27	SHOAL	SLP	SA/CR	FBG KL	IB	8 10	7300	3 5	16100	18300
26 10	CATALINA 27	SHOAL	SLP	SA/CR	FBG KL	IB 14D UNIV	8 10	7300	3 5	16700	19000
29 11	CATALINA 30		SLP	SA/CR	FBG KL	IB 14D- 21D	10 10	10200	5 3	24800	27600
29 11	CATALINA 30	SHOAL	SLP	SA/CR	FBG KL	IB 14D- 21D	10 10	10650	4 4	25900	28900
36 4	CATALINA 36		SLP	SA/CR	FBG KL	IB 21D UNIV	11 11	13500	5 10	33400	37100
36 4	CATALINA 36	SHOAL	SLP	SA/CR	FBG KL	IB 21D UNIV	11 11	14300	5 1	35100	39000
38 2	CATALINA 38		SLP	SA/CR	FBG KL	IB 24D UNIV	11 10	15900	6 9	40700	45200
38 2	CATALINA 38	SHOAL	SLP	SA/CR	FBG KL	IB 24D UNIV	11 10	16700	4 11	42300	47000
						1984 BOATS					
21 6	CATALINA 22	POP TOP	SLP	SA/CR	FBG KL	OB	7 8	2490	3 6	4300	5000
21 6	CATALINA 22	POP TOP	SLP	SA/CR	FBG SK	OB	7 8	2250	2	4000	4650
25	CATALINA 25		SLP	SA/CR	FBG KL	OB	8	4550	4	8500	9750
25	CATALINA 25		SLP	SA/CR	FBG SK	OB	8	4150	2 8	7750	8950
26 10	CATALINA 27		SLP	SA/CR	FBG KL	OB	8 10	6850	4	14100	16000
26 10	CATALINA 27		SLP	SA/CR	FBG KL	IB 14D UNIV	8 10	6850	4	14600	16600
26 10	CATALINA 27	SHOAL	SLP	SA/CR	FBG KL	OB	8 10	7300	3 5	15100	17100
26 10	CATALINA 27	SHOAL	SLP	SA/CR	FBG KL	IB 14D UNIV	8 10	7300	3 5	15700	17800
29 11	CATALINA 30		SLP	SA/CR	FBG KL	IB 14D- 21D	10 10	10200	5 3	23200	25900
29 11	CATALINA 30	SHOAL	SLP	SA/CR	FBG KL	IB 14D- 21D	10 10	10650	4 4	24300	27000
35 7	CATALINA 36		SLP	SA/CR	FBG KL	IB 21D UNIV	11 11	15000	5 3	33900	37700
35 7	CATALINA 36	SHOAL	SLP	SA/CR	FBG KL	IB 21D UNIV	11 11	15800	4 7	35500	39500
38 3	CATALINA 38		SLP	SA/CR	FBG KL	IB 24D UNIV	11 10	15900	6 9	38300	42500
38 3	CATALINA 38	SHOAL	SLP	SA/CR	FBG KL	IB 24D UNIV	11 10	16700	4 11	39800	44200

....For earlier years, see the BUC Used Boat Price Guide, Volume 3

CATAMARAN CRUISERS
DIV OF AMERICAN REDI BUILT   See inside cover to adjust price for area
COLUMBIA TN 38401   COAST GUARD MFG ID- ARB

For more recent years, see the BUC Used Boat Price Guide, Volume 1

LOA FT IN	NAME AND/ OR MODEL		TOP/ RIG	BOAT TYPE	-HULL- MTL TP	----ENGINE--- TP # HP MFG	BEAM FT IN	WGT LBS	DRAFT FT IN	RETAIL LOW	RETAIL HIGH
						1996 BOATS					
31	GETAWAY 3108		HB	FBG CT	OB		8 6	5000	1 2	13700	15500
33	GETAWAY 3308		HB	FBG CT	OB		8 6	5000	1 2	13700	15500
35	AQUA CRUISER 1035		HB	FBG CT	OB		10 2	8000	1 2	23000	25500
35	AQUA CRUISER 1235		HB	FBG CT	OB		12	9000	1 2	24800	27600
35	GETAWAY 3510		HB	FBG CT	OB		10 2	8000	1 2	22400	24800
43	AQUA CRUISER 1243		HB	FBG CT	OB		12	11000	1 2	22900	25500
46	AQUA CRUISE-N-HOME		HB	FBG CT	OB		14	14000	1 2	29000	32300
47	AQUA CRUISER 1447		HB	FBG CT	OB		14	13000	1 2	28200	31300
55	AQUA CRUISE-N-HOME		HB	FBG CT	OB		14	17000	1 2	44200	49200
55	AQUA CRUISER 1455		HB	FBG CT	OB		14	16000	1 2	43000	47700
						1995 BOATS					
34	AQUA CRUISER SPC 34		HB	FBG CT	OB		10		1 3	10400	11800
42	AQUA CRUISER SPC 42		HB	FBG CT	OB		12	9900	1 3	20500	22800
46	AQUA CRUISER EXEC		HB	FBG CT	OB		12	14000	1 4	25400	28200
53 6	AQUA CRUISER EXEC		HB	FBG CT	OB		14	14000	1 4	40300	44700
						1994 BOATS					
35	AQUA CRUISER EXEC		HB	FBG CT	OB		10 3	8000	1 2	20400	22700
44	AQUA CRUISER EXEC		HB	FBG CT	OB		12	11600	1 2	21700	24100
45	AQUA CRUISER EXEC		HB	FBG CT	OB		14	13200	1 2	24000	26600
55	AQUA CRUISER EXEC		HB	FBG CT	OB		14	16900	1 2	38100	42300
						1993 BOATS					
34	CATAMARAN 34 DELUXE		HB	FBG CT	OB		8 4	4000	1 3	8100	9300
34	CATAMARAN AQUA DELUX		HB	FBG CT	OB		12 2	9200	1 3	21800	24300
34	WEEKENDER TEN		HB	FBG CT	OB		10 2	4800	1 3	11000	12500
44	CATAMARAN AC DELUXE		HB	FBG CT	OB		12 2	12000	1 3	21100	23400
45	CATAMARAN AC EXEC		HB	FBG CT	OB		14 2	12360	1 3	21900	24300
55	CATAMARAN AC EXEC		HB	FBG CT	OB		14 2	14000	1 3	32500	36100
						1992 BOATS					
34	CATAMARAN AQUA CR		HB	FBG CT	OB		10 2	6800	1 3	15900	18000
35	CATAMARAN AQUA CR		HB	FBG CT	OB		12 2	9200	1 3	20800	23200
35	MINI YACHT 35		HB	FBG CT	OB		8 4	5200	1 3	26000	28900
44	CATAMARAN AC CLASSIC		HB	FBG CT	OB		14 2	12000	1 3	200000	22200
44	CATAMARAN AC EXEC		HB	FBG CT	OB		14 2	12360	1 3	20500	22800
51	CATAMARAN AC CLASSIC		HB	FBG CT	OB		14 2	13000	1 3	24000	26700
51	CATAMARAN AC EXEC		HB	FBG CT	OB		14 2	14000	1 3	25200	28000

CATAMARANS INTERNATIONAL
ANNAPOLIS MD 21403   See inside cover to adjust price for area

LOA FT IN	NAME AND/ OR MODEL	TOP/ RIG	BOAT TYPE	-HULL- MTL TP	----ENGINE--- TP # HP MFG	BEAM FT IN	WGT LBS	DRAFT FT IN	RETAIL LOW	RETAIL HIGH
					1996 BOATS					
39 4	DEAN 400	SLP	SACAC FBG CT	IB T 18D YAN	23 8	13000	3 6	118000	129500
44	ST FRANCIS 44	SLP	SACAC FBG CT	IB T 27D YAN	23 6	13000	2 11	153500	168500

CATAMARINE INC
HULL MA 02045   See inside cover to adjust price for area

LOA FT IN	NAME AND/ OR MODEL		TOP/ RIG	BOAT TYPE	-HULL- MTL TP	----ENGINE--- TP # HP MFG	BEAM FT IN	WGT LBS	DRAFT FT IN	RETAIL LOW	RETAIL HIGH
						1992 BOATS					
32	MALDIVES		SLP	SA/CR F/S CT	OB		17 5	6600	3	66000	72600
37	ANTIGUA		SLP	SA/CR F/S CT	SD T 9D VLVO	19 6	9900	3	93400	102500
39	FIDJI		SLP	SA/CR F/S CT	SD T 18D VLVO	21	13200	3	116000	127500
45	CASAMANCE		SLP	SA/CR F/S CT	SD T 25D VLVO	23	19800	4	194500	214000
53 6	MARQUISES		SLP	SA/CR F/S CT	SD T 50D YAN	27 9	28600		418000	459500
						1991 BOATS					
32	MALDIVES		SLP	SA/CR F/S CT	SD		17 5	6600	3	62100	68200
37	ANTIGUA		SLP	SA/CR F/S CT	SD T 9D YAN	19 6	9900	3	87800	96500
39	FIDJI		SLP	SA/CR F/S CT	SD T 18D YAN	21	13200	3	109500	120000
45	CASAMANCE		SLP	SA/CR F/S CT	SD T 25D VLVO	23	19800	4	183000	201000
53 6	MARQUISES		SLP	SA/CR F/S CT	SD T 50D YAN	27 9	28600		393000	432000

CATANA S A
CANET EN ROUSSILLON FRANCE   See inside cover to adjust price for area

For more recent years, see the BUC Used Boat Price Guide, Volume 1

LOA FT IN	NAME AND/ OR MODEL	TOP/ RIG	BOAT TYPE	-HULL- MTL TP	----ENGINE--- TP # HP MFG	BEAM FT IN	WGT LBS	DRAFT FT IN	RETAIL LOW	RETAIL HIGH
					1996 BOATS					
38 8	CATANA 381	SLP	SACAC FBG CT	IB T 20D YAN	21 7	12362	6 6	199500	219000
41 1	CATANA 411	SLP	SACAC FBG CT	IB T 30D YAN	22 3	14569	6 1	245000	269500
44	CATANA 44	SLP	SACAC FBG CT	IB T 40D YAN	23	16777	7 2	276500	303500
48	CATANA 48	SLP	SACAC FBG CT	IB T 40D YAN	23 7	18764	7 2	436500	480000
52 10	CATANA 531	SLP	SACAC FBG CT	IB T 48D YAN	25	28697	7 6	610000	670000

KENNETH CAVANAUGH
WOLFVILLE NS CANADA   See inside cover to adjust price for area

LOA FT IN	NAME AND/ OR MODEL	TOP/ RIG	BOAT TYPE	-HULL- MTL TP	----ENGINE--- TP # HP MFG	BEAM FT IN	WGT LBS	DRAFT FT IN	RETAIL LOW	RETAIL HIGH
					1984 BOATS					
17	NATIONAL-ONE-DESIGN	SLP	SA/OD FBG DV		5 8	400	3 6	2450	2850

....For earlier years, see the BUC Used Boat Price Guide, Volume 3

CB BOAT WORKS

WEST PERU ME 04290 COAST GUARD MFG ID- ATJ See inside cover to adjust price for area

For more recent years, see the BUC Used Boat Price Guide, Volume 1

LOA FT	IN	NAME AND/ OR MODEL	TOP/ RIG	BOAT TYPE	-HULL- MTL	TP	----ENGINE--- TP	# HP	MFG	BEAM FT	IN	WGT LBS	DRAFT FT	IN	RETAIL LOW	RETAIL HIGH
		1996 BOATS														
16		ALCAR COMMERCIAL	OP	COMM	FBG	SV	OB			6	3	900		6	**	**
16		ALCAR FISHERMAN	OP	CTRCN	FBG	SV	OB			6	3	900		6	2000	2400
16		BUCKSPORT DELUX	OP	UTL	FBG	SV	OB			6	3	600		6	1300	1550
16		C SERIES	OP	CTRCN	FBG	SV	OB			6	3	900		6	1750	2100
16		CB UTILITY DELUXE	OP	UTL	FBG	SV	OB			6	3	600		6	1150	1350
16		KENNEBEC DELUX	OP	UTL	FBG	SV	OB			6	3	600		6	1300	1550
16		SHEEPSCOT DELUX	OP	UTL	FBG	SV	OB			6	3	600		6	1300	1550
17		ALCAR COMMERCIAL	OP	COMM	FBG	SV	OB			7	6	1400	1		**	**
17		ALCAR FISHERMAN	OP	CTRCN	FBG	SV	OB			7	6	1400	1		3100	3600
17		ALCAR SPORTWIN	OP	RNBT	FBG	SV	OB			7	6	1500	1		3050	3550
17		BUCKSPORT DELUXE	OP	UTL	FBG	SV	OB			7	6	900	1		1950	2300
17		C SERIES	OP	CTRCN	FBG	SV	OB			7	6	1400	1		2650	3050
17		CB UTILITY DELUX	OP	UTL	FBG	SV	OB			7	6	900	1		1750	2100
17		KENNEBEC DELUX	OP	UTL	FBG	SV	OB			7	6	900	1		1950	2300
17		SHEEPSCOT DELUX	OP	UTL	FBG	SV	OB			7	6	900	1		1950	2300
18	9	ALCAR LAUNCH	OP	LNCH	FBG	DS	OB			6	6	1500	1	4	**	**
19		ALCAR COMMERCIAL	OP	COMM	FBG	SV	OB			7	6	1600	1		**	**
19		ALCAR FISHERMAN	OP	CTRCN	FBG	SV	OB			7	6	1600	1		3800	4450
19		ALCAR SPORTWIN	OP	RNBT	FBG	SV	OB			7	6	1600	1		3350	3900
19		BUCKSPORT DELUX	OP	UTL	FBG	SV	OB			7	6	1100	1		2300	2650
19		C SERIES	OP	CTRCN	FBG	SV	OB			7	6	1600	1		2850	3300
19		CB UTILITY DELUX	OP	UTL	FBG	SV	OB			7	6	1100	1		2250	2600
19		KENNEBEC DELUX	OP	UTL	FBG	SV	OB			7	6	1100	1		2300	2650
19		SHEEPSCOT DELUX	OP	UTL	FBG	SV	OB			7	6	1100	1		2300	2650
21		ALCAR CLASSIC	ST	RNBT	FBG	SV	OB			8		2200	1	2	5150	5950
21		ALCAR COMMERCIAL	OP	COMM	FBG	SV	OB			8		2200	1	2	**	**
21		ALCAR FISHERMAN	OP	CTRCN	FBG	SV	OB			8		2200	1	2	5550	6400
21		ALCAR SPORTWIN	OP	RNBT	FBG	SV	OB			8		2200	1	2	5150	5950
21		C SERIES	OP	CTRCN	FBG	SV	OB			8		2200	1	2	4750	5450
		1995 BOATS														
16		ALCAR COMMERCIAL	OP	COMM	FBG	SV	OB			6	3	900		6	**	**
16		ALCAR FISHERMAN	OP	CTRCN	FBG	SV	OB			6	3	900		6	1800	2150
16		BUCKSPORT DELUX	OP	UTL	FBG	SV	OB			6	3	600		6	1200	1450
16		C SERIES	OP	CTRCN	FBG	SV	OB			6	3	900		6	1800	2150
16		KENNEBEC DELUX	OP	UTL	FBG	SV	OB			6	3	600		6	1200	1450
16		SHEEPSCOT DELUX	OP	UTL	FBG	SV	OB			6	3	600		6	1200	1450
17		ALCAR COMMERCIAL	OP	COMM	FBG	SV	OB			7	6	1400	1		**	**
17		ALCAR FISHERMAN	OP	CTRCN	FBG	SV	OB			7	6	1400	1		2750	3200
17		ALCAR SPORTWIN	OP	RNBT	FBG	SV	OB			7	6	1500	1		2900	3350
17		C SERIES	OP	CTRCN	FBG	SV	OB			7	6	1400	1		2750	3200
17		CB UTILITY DELUX	OP	UTL	FBG	SV	OB			7	6	900	1		1800	2150
17		KENNEBEC DELUX	OP	UTL	FBG	SV	OB			7	6	900	1		1800	2150
17		SHEEPSCOT DELUX	OP	UTL	FBG	SV	OB			7	6	900	1		1800	2150
18	9	ALCAR LAUNCH	OP	LNCH	FBG	DS	OB			6	6	1500	1	4	**	**
19		ALCAR COMMERCIAL	OP	COMM	FBG	SV	OB			7	6	1600	1		**	**
19		ALCAR FISHERMAN	OP	CTRCN	FBG	SV	OB			7	6	1600	1		3150	3700
19		ALCAR SPORTWIN	OP	RNBT	FBG	SV	OB			7	6	1600	1		3200	3700
19		BUCKSPORT DELUX	OP	UTL	FBG	SV	OB			7	6	1100	1		2150	2500
19		C SERIES	OP	CTRCN	FBG	SV	OB			7	6	1600	1		3150	3700
19		CB UTILITY DELUX	OP	UTL	FBG	SV	OB			7	6	1100	1		2150	2500
19		KENNEBEC DELUX	OP	UTL	FBG	SV	OB			7	6	1100	1		2150	2500
19		SHEEPSCOT DELUX	OP	UTL	FBG	SV	OB			7	6	1100	1		2150	2500
21		ALCAR CLASSIC	ST	RNBT	FBG	SV	OB			8		2200	1	2	4900	5650
21		ALCAR COMMERCIAL	OP	COMM	FBG	SV	OB			8		2200	1	2	**	**
21		ALCAR FISHERMAN	OP	CTRCN	FBG	SV	OB			8		2200	1	2	4900	5650
21		ALCAR SPORTWIN	OP	RNBT	FBG	SV	OB			8		2200	1	2	4900	5650
21		C SERIES	OP	CTRCN	FBG	SV	OB			8		2200	1	2	4900	5650
		1994 BOATS														
16		ALCAR COMMERCIAL	OP	COMM	FBG	SV	OB			6	3	900		6	**	**
16		ALCAR FISHERMAN	OP	CTRCN	FBG	SV	OB			6	3	900		6	2050	2450
16		BUCKSPORT DELUX	OP	UTL	FBG	SV	OB			6	3	600		6	1200	1400
16		C SERIES	OP	CTRCN	FBG	SV	OB			6	3	900		6	1350	1650
16		CB UTILITY DELUX	OP	UTL	FBG	SV	OB			6	3	600		6	1050	1250
16		KENNEBEC DELUX	OP	UTL	FBG	SV	OB			6	3	600		6	1200	1400
16		SHEEPSCOT DELUX	OP	UTL	FBG	SV	OB			6	3	600		6	1200	1400
17		ALCAR COMMERCIAL	OP	COMM	FBG	SV	OB			7	6	1400	1		**	**
17		ALCAR FISHERMAN	OP	CTRCN	FBG	SV	OB			7	6	1400	1		3250	3750
17		ALCAR SPORTWIN	OP	RNBT	FBG	SV	OB			7	6	1500	1		2750	3200
17		BUCKSPORT DELUX	OP	UTL	FBG	SV	OB			7	6	900	1		1750	2100
17		C SERIES	OP	CTRCN	FBG	SV	OB			7	6	1400	1		1950	2300
17		CB UTILITY DELUX	OP	UTL	FBG	SV	OB			7	6	900	1		1600	1900
17		KENNEBEC DELUX	OP	UTL	FBG	SV	OB			7	6	900	1		1750	2100
17		SHEEPSCOT DELUX	OP	UTL	FBG	SV	OB			7	6	900	1		1750	2100
18	9	ALCAR LAUNCH	OP	LNCH	FBG	DS	OB			6	6	1500	1	4	**	**
19		ALCAR COMMERCIAL	OP	COMM	FBG	SV	OB			7	6	1600	1		**	**
19		ALCAR FISHERMAN	OP	CTRCN	FBG	SV	OB			7	6	1600	1		3950	4600
19		ALCAR SPORTWIN	OP	RNBT	FBG	SV	OB			7	6	1600	1		3050	3550
19		BUCKSPORT DELUX	OP	UTL	FBG	SV	OB			7	6	1100	1		2050	2450
19		C SERIES	OP	CTRCN	FBG	SV	OB			7	6	1600	1		2100	2500
19		CB UTILITY DELUX	OP	UTL	FBG	SV	OB			7	6	1100	1		1850	2200
19		KENNEBEC DELUX	OP	UTL	FBG	SV	OB			7	6	1100	1		2050	2450
19		SHEEPSCOT DELUX	OP	UTL	FBG	SV	OB			7	6	1100	1		2050	2450
21		ALCAR CLASSIC	ST	RNBT	FBG	SV	OB			8		2200	1	2	4700	5400
21		ALCAR COMMERCIAL	OP	COMM	FBG	SV	OB			8		2200	1	2	**	**
21		ALCAR FISHERMAN	OP	CTRCN	FBG	SV	OB			8		2200	1	2	5800	6650
21		ALCAR SPORTWIN	OP	RNBT	FBG	SV	OB			8		2200	1	2	4700	5400
21		C SERIES	OP	CTRCN	FBG	SV	OB			8		2200	1	2	3500	4100
		1993 BOATS														
16		ALCAR FISHERMAN	OP	CTRCN	FBG	SV	OB			6	3	900		6	1650	1950
16		BUCKSPORT 16	OP	UTL	FBG	SV	OB			6	3	700		6	1300	1550
16		CB 16 UTILITY	OP	UTL	FBG	SV	OB			6	3	600		6	1100	1300
16		KENNEBEC 16	OP	UTL	FBG	SV	OB			6	3	700		6	1300	1550
16		SHEEPSCOT 16	OP	UTL	FBG	SV	OB			6	3	700		6	1300	1550
17		ALCAR FISHERMAN	OP	CTRCN	FBG	SV	OB			7	6	1400	1		2500	2900
17		ALCAR SPORTWIN	OP	RNBT	FBG	SV	OB			7	6	1500	1		2650	3050
17		BUCKSPORT 17	OP	UTL	FBG	SV	OB			7	6	1000	1		1800	2150
17		CB 17 UTILITY	OP	UTL	FBG	SV	OB			7	6	900	1		1650	1950
17		KENNEBEC 17	OP	UTL	FBG	SV	OB			7	6	1000	1		1800	2150
17		SHEEPSCOT 17	OP	UTL	FBG	SV	OB			7	6	1000	1		1800	2150
18	9	ALCAR LAUNCH	OP	LNCH	FBG	DS	OB			6	6	1500	1	4	**	**
19		ALCAR FISHERMAN	OP	CTRCN	FBG	SV	OB			7	6	1600	1		2900	3350
19		ALCAR SPORTWIN	OP	RNBT	FBG	SV	OB			7	6	1600	1		2900	3400
19		BUCKSPORT 19	OP	UTL	FBG	SV	OB			7	6	1200	1		2100	2450
19		CB 19 UTILITY	OP	UTL	FBG	SV	OB			7	6	1100	1		1900	2300
19		KENNEBEC 19	OP	UTL	FBG	SV	OB			7	6	1200	1		2100	2450
19		SHEEPSCOT 19	OP	UTL	FBG	SV	OB			7	6	1200	1		2100	2450
21		ALCAR CLASSIC	ST	RNBT	FBG	SV	OB			8		2200	1	2	4500	5150
21		ALCAR FISHERMAN	OP	CTRCN	FBG	SV	OB			8		2200	1	2	4500	5150
21		ALCAR SPORTWIN	OP	RNBT	FBG	SV	OB			8		2200	1	2	4500	5150
		1992 BOATS														
16		ALCAR COMMERCIAL	OP	COMM	FBG	SV	OB			6	3	900		6	**	**
16		ALCAR FISHERMAN	OP	CTRCN	FBG	SV	OB			6	3	900		6	1550	1850
17		ALCAR COMMERCIAL	OP	COMM	FBG	SV	OB			7	6	1400	1		**	**
17		ALCAR FISHERMAN	OP	CTRCN	FBG	SV	OB			7	6	1400	1		2400	2750
17		ALCAR SPORTWIN	OP	RNBT	FBG	SV	OB			7	6	1500	1		2550	2950
18	9	ALCAR LAUNCH	OP	LNCH	FBG	DS	OB			6	6	1500	1	4	**	**
19		ALCAR COMMERCIAL	OP	COMM	FBG	SV	OB			8		1600	1		**	**
19		ALCAR FISHERMAN	OP	CTRCN	FBG	SV	OB			8		1600	1		2750	3200
19		ALCAR SPORTWIN	OP	RNBT	FBG	SV	OB			8		1600	1		2800	3250
21		ALCAR CLASSIC	ST	RNBT	FBG	SV	OB			8		2200	1	2	4250	4950
21		ALCAR COMMERCIAL	OP	COMM	FBG	SV	OB			8		2200	1	2	**	**
21		ALCAR FISHERMAN	OP	CTRCN	FBG	SV	OB			8		2200	1	2	4250	4900
21		ALCAR SPORTWIN	OP	RNBT	FBG	SV	OB			8		2200	1	2	4250	4950

CBC LYMAN

FT MYERS FL 33916 COAST GUARD MFG ID- LYM See inside cover to adjust price for area
ALSO LYMAN INDUSTRIES INC

LOA FT	IN	NAME AND/ OR MODEL	TOP/ RIG	BOAT TYPE	-HULL- MTL	TP	----ENGINE--- TP	# HP	MFG	BEAM FT	IN	WGT LBS	DRAFT FT	IN	RETAIL LOW	RETAIL HIGH
		1986 BOATS														
24	4	BISCAYNE 24	OP	RNBT	FBG	RB	IB	225		8	11	4400	2	1	15900	18100
24	4	SPORTSMAN 24	OP	RNBT	FBG	RB	IB	225		8	11	4400	2	1	15300	17400
26		CRUISETTE 26	OP	FSH	FBG	RB	IB	270		10	2	5200	2	4	20900	23200
26		FISHERMAN/SLEEPER 26	OP	FSH	FBG	RB	IB	270		10	2	5200	2	4	20900	23200
		1984 BOATS														
26	2	SLEEPER	OP	UTL	WD	RB	IB	260	VLVO	9	1	4200	2	6	16300	18500

....For earlier years, see the BUC Used Boat Price Guide, Volume 3

CEE BEE MANUFACTURING INC

LYNWOOD CA 90262 — COAST GUARD MFG ID- CBM See inside cover to adjust price for area
FORMERLY CEE BEE MANUFACTURING CO

For more recent years, see the BUC Used Boat Price Guide, Volume 1

LOA FT	LOA IN	NAME AND/ OR MODEL	TOP/ RIG	BOAT TYPE	-HULL- MTL	-HULL- TP	ENGINE TP	ENGINE # HP	ENGINE MFG	BEAM FT	BEAM IN	WGT LBS	DRAFT FT	DRAFT IN	RETAIL LOW	RETAIL HIGH
		1996 BOATS														
17		AVENGER 169	OP	RNBT	FBG	SV	IO	115-180		7	3	1900			6350	7400
17	7	AVENGER 180	OP	SKI	FBG	SV	JT	330	FORD	7	3	2200			9750	11100
17	7	AVENGER 181	OP	SKI	FBG	SV	JT	330	FORD	7	3	2300			9950	11300
17	7	AVENGER 185	OP	SKI	FBG	SV	JT	330	FORD	7	3	2400			10100	11500
18	3	AVENGER 182	OP	BASS	FBG	SV	OB			7	3	1180			5650	6500
18	3	AVENGER 183	OP	SKI	FBG	SV	OB			7	3	900			4200	4850
18	3	AVENGER 183 B/R	OP	SKI	FBG	SV	OB			7	3	900			4800	5500
18	3	AVENGER 184	OP	BASS	FBG	SV	OB			7	3	1100			5350	6150
20	2	AVENGER 200	OP	SKI	FBG	SV	OB			7	5	1100			5650	6500
20	2	AVENGER 200 B/R	OP	SKI	FBG	SV	OB			7	5	1250			6300	7250
20	2	AVENGER 201	OP	SKI	FBG	SV	IO	235		7	5	2300			9350	10600
20	2	AVENGER 202	OP	BASS	FBG	SV	OB			7	5	1200			6100	7000
20	2	AVENGER 203	OP	SKI	FBG	TH	OB			7	5	1250			6300	7250
21	4	AVENGER 220 B/R	OP	B/R	FBG	SV	JT	330	FORD	7	10	3070			15700	17900
21	4	AVENGER 220 B/R	OP	B/R	FBG	SV	IO	350	MRCR	7	10	3070			14500	16500
21	4	AVENGER 221	OP	CR	FBG	SV	IO	235		7	10	3000			12500	14200
21	4	AVENGER 221	OP	CR	FBG	SV	JT	330	FORD	7	10	3000			15500	17600
21	4	AVENGER 222	OP	CR	FBG	SV	OB			7	10	1600			8050	9250
22	6	AVENGER 230	OP	CR	FBG	SV	IO	235		7	10	3200			13900	15800
22	6	AVENGER 230	OP	CR	FBG	SV	JT	330	FORD	7	10	3200			17100	19400
		1995 BOATS														
17		AVENGER 169	OP	RNBT	FBG	SV	IO	115-180		7	3	1900			5900	6900
17	7	AVENGER 180	OP	SKI	FBG	SV	JT	330	FORD	7	3	2200			9250	10500
17	7	AVENGER 181	OP	SKI	FBG	SV	JT	330	FORD	7	3	2300			9400	10700
17	7	AVENGER 185	OP	SKI	FBG	SV	JT	330	FORD	7	3	2400			9600	10900
18	3	AVENGER 182	OP	BASS	FBG	SV	OB			7	3	1180			5400	6200
18	3	AVENGER 183	OP	SKI	FBG	SV	OB			7	3	900			4000	4650
18	3	AVENGER 183 B/R	OP	SKI	FBG	SV	OB			7	3	900			4600	5300
18	3	AVENGER 184	OP	BASS	FBG	SV	OB			7	3	1100			5100	5850
20	2	AVENGER 200	OP	SKI	FBG	SV	OB			7	5	1100			5400	6200
20	2	AVENGER 200 B/R	OP	SKI	FBG	SV	OB			7	5	1250			6000	6900
20	2	AVENGER 201	OP	SKI	FBG	SV	IO	235		7	5	2300			8600	9900
20	2	AVENGER 202	OP	BASS	FBG	SV	OB			7	5	1200			5800	6700
20	2	AVENGER 203	OP	SKI	FBG	TH	OB			7	5	1250			6000	6900
21	4	AVENGER 220 B/R	OP	B/R	FBG	SV	JT	330	FORD	7	10	3070			14900	16900
21	4	AVENGER 220 B/R	OP	B/R	FBG	SV	IO	350	MRCR	7	10	3070			13600	15400
21	4	AVENGER 221	OP	CR	FBG	SV	IO	235		7	10	3000			11700	13300
21	4	AVENGER 221	OP	CR	FBG	SV	JT	330	FORD	7	10	3000			14700	16700
21	4	AVENGER 222	OP	CR	FBG	SV	OB			7	10	1600			7700	8850
22	6	AVENGER 230	OP	CR	FBG	SV	IO	235		7	10	3200			12900	14700
22	6	AVENGER 230	OP	CR	FBG	SV	JT	330	FORD	7	10	3200			16100	18300
		1994 BOATS														
17		AVENGER 169	OP	RNBT	FBG	SV	IO	115-180		7	3	1900			5500	6450
17	7	AVENGER 180	OP	SKI	FBG	SV	JT	330	FORD	7	3	2200			8650	9950
17	7	AVENGER 181	OP	SKI	FBG	SV	JT	330	FORD	7	3	2300			8950	10200
17	7	AVENGER 185	OP	SKI	FBG	SV	JT	330	FORD	7	3	2400			9150	10400
18	3	AVENGER 182	OP	BASS	FBG	SV	OB			7	3	1180			5150	5900
18	3	AVENGER 183 B/R	OP	SKI	FBG	SV	OB			7	3	900			4100	4750
18	3	AVENGER 184	OP	BASS	FBG	SV	OB			7	3	1100			4850	5600
20	2	AVENGER 200 B/R	OP	SKI	FBG	SV	OB			7	5	1100			5150	5950
20	2	AVENGER 201	OP	SKI	FBG	SV	IO	235		7	5	2300			8050	9250
20	2	AVENGER 202	OP	BASS	FBG	SV	OB			7	5	1200			5550	6400
20	2	AVENGER 203	OP	SKI	FBG	TH	OB			7	5	1250			5750	6600
21	4	AVENGER 220 B/R	OP	B/R	FBG	SV	JT	330	FORD	7	10	3070			14100	16000
21	4	AVENGER 220 B/R	OP	B/R	FBG	SV	IO	350	MRCR	7	10	3070			12700	14400
21	4	AVENGER 221	OP	CR	FBG	SV	IO	235		7	10	3000			10900	12400
21	4	AVENGER 221	OP	CR	FBG	SV	JT	330	FORD	7	10	3000			13900	15800
21	4	AVENGER 222	OP	CR	FBG	SV	OB			7	10	1600			7350	8450
22	6	AVENGER 230	OP	CR	FBG	SV	IO	235		7	10	3200			12100	13700
22	6	AVENGER 230	OP	CR	FBG	SV	JT	330	FORD	7	10	3200			15300	17400
		1993 BOATS														
17		AVENGER 169	OP	RNBT	FBG	SV	IO	115-180		7	3	1900			5150	6000
17	7	AVENGER 180	OP	SKI	FBG	SV	JT	330	FORD	7	3	2200			8200	9450
17	7	AVENGER 181	OP	SKI	FBG	SV	JT	330	FORD	7	3	2300			8400	9650
17	7	AVENGER 185	OP	SKI	FBG	SV	JT	330	FORD	7	3	2400			8550	9850
18	3	AVENGER 182	OP	BASS	FBG	SV	OB			7	3	1180			4950	5650
18	3	AVENGER 183	OP	SKI	FBG	SV	OB			7	3	900			3900	4550
18	3	AVENGER 184	OP	BASS	FBG	SV	OB			7	3	1100			4700	5400
20	2	AVENGER 200	OP	SKI	FBG	SV	OB			7	5	1100			4950	5700
20	2	AVENGER 200 B/R	OP	SKI	FBG	SV	OB			7	5	1250			5500	6350
20	2	AVENGER 201	OP	SKI	FBG	SV	IO	235		7	5	2300			7500	8650
20	2	AVENGER 202	OP	BASS	FBG	SV	OB			7	5	1200			5350	6100
20	2	AVENGER 203	OP	SKI	FBG	TH	OB			7	5	1250			5500	6350
21	4	AVENGER 220 B/R	OP	B/R	FBG	SV	JT	330	FORD	7	10	3070			13300	15200
21	4	AVENGER 220 B/R	OP	B/R	FBG	SV	IO	350	MRCR	7	10	3070			11800	13400
21	4	AVENGER 221	OP	CR	FBG	SV	IO	235		7	10	3000			10200	11600
21	4	AVENGER 221	OP	CR	FBG	SV	JT	330	FORD	7	10	3000			13200	15000
21	4	AVENGER 222	OP	CR	FBG	SV	OB			7	10	1600			7050	8100
22	6	AVENGER 230	OP	CR	FBG	SV	IO	235		7	10	3200			11300	12800
22	6	AVENGER 230	OP	CR	FBG	SV	JT	330	FORD	7	10	3200			14500	16500
		1992 BOATS														
17		AVENGER 169	OP	RNBT	FBG	SV	IO	130-175		7	3	1900			4850	5600
17	7	AVENGER 180	OP	SKI	FBG	SV	JT	320	FORD	7	3	2200			7800	8950
17	7	AVENGER 181	OP	SKI	FBG	SV	JT	320	FORD	7	3	2300			7950	9150
17	7	AVENGER 185	OP	SKI	FBG	SV	JT	320	FORD	7	3	2400			8100	9350
18	3	AVENGER 182	OP	BASS	FBG	SV	OB			7	3	1180			4750	5450
18	3	AVENGER 183	OP	SKI	FBG	SV	OB			7	3	900			3750	4350
18	3	AVENGER 184	OP	BASS	FBG	SV	OB			7	3	1100			4500	5200
20	2	AVENGER 200	OP	SKI	FBG	SV	OB			7	5	1100			4750	5450
20	2	AVENGER 200 B/R	OP	SKI	FBG	SV	OB			7	5	1250			5300	6100
20	2	AVENGER 201	OP	SKI	FBG	SV	IO	260		7	5	2300			7250	8350
20	2	AVENGER 202	OP	BASS	FBG	SV	IO	200	OMC	7	5	1200			6600	7600
20	2	AVENGER 203	OP	SKI	FBG	TH	OB			7	5	1250			5300	6100
21	4	AVENGER 221	OP	CR	FBG	SV	IO	260		7	10	3000			9800	11100
21	4	AVENGER 221	OP	CR	FBG	SV	JT	320	FORD	7	10	3000			12500	14200
21	4	AVENGER 222	OP	CR	FBG	SV	OB			7	10	1600			6750	7800
22	6	AVENGER 230	OP	CR	FBG	SV	IO	260		7	10	3200			10800	12300
22	6	AVENGER 230	OP	CR	FBG	SV	JT	320	FORD	7	10	3200			13700	15600
		1991 BOATS														
17		AVENGER 169	OP	RNBT	FBG	SV	IO	130-175		7	3	1900			4550	5300
17	7	AVENGER 180	OP	SKI	FBG	SV	JT	320	FORD	7	3	2200			7400	8500
17	7	AVENGER 181	OP	SKI	FBG	SV	JT	320	FORD	7	3	2300			7550	8700
17	7	AVENGER 185	OP	SKI	FBG	SV	JT	320	FORD	7	3	2400			7700	8850
18	3	AVENGER 182	OP	BASS	FBG	SV	OB			7	3	1180			4600	5300
18	3	AVENGER 183	OP	SKI	FBG	SV	OB			7	3	900			3600	4200
18	3	AVENGER 184	OP	BASS	FBG	SV	OB			7	3	1100			4300	5000
20	2	AVENGER 200	OP	SKI	FBG	SV	OB			7	5	1100			4600	5300
20	2	AVENGER 200 B/R	OP	SKI	FBG	SV	OB			7	5	1250			5100	5850
20	2	AVENGER 201	OP	SKI	FBG	SV	IO	260		7	5	2300			6800	7800
20	2	AVENGER 202	OP	BASS	FBG	SV	IO	200	OMC	7	5	1200			6200	7100
20	2	AVENGER 203	OP	SKI	FBG	TH	OB			7	5	1250			5100	5850
21	4	AVENGER 221	OP	CR	FBG	SV	IO	260		7	10	3000			9250	10500
21	4	AVENGER 221	OP	CR	FBG	SV	JT	320	FORD	7	10	3000			11900	13500
21	4	AVENGER 222	OP	CR	FBG	SV	OB			7	10	1600			6500	7500
22	6	AVENGER 230	OP	CR	FBG	SV	IO	260		7	10	3200			10100	11500
22	6	AVENGER 230	OP	CR	FBG	SV	JT	320	FORD	7	10	3200			13100	14800
		1990 BOATS														
17		AVENGER 169	OP	RNBT	FBG	SV	IO	130-175		7	3	1900			4250	5000
17	7	AVENGER 180	OP	SKI	FBG	SV	JT	320	FORD	7	3	2200			7050	8100
17	7	AVENGER 181	OP	SKI	FBG	SV	JT	320	FORD	7	3	2300			7200	8250
17	7	AVENGER 185	OP	SKI	FBG	SV	JT	320	FORD	7	3	2400			7350	8450
18	3	AVENGER 182	OP	BASS	FBG	SV	OB			7	3	1180			4450	5100
18	3	AVENGER 183	OP	SKI	FBG	SV	OB			7	3	900			3500	4050
18	3	AVENGER 184	OP	BASS	FBG	SV	OB			7	3	1100			4150	4800
20	2	AVENGER 200	OP	SKI	FBG	SV	OB			7	5	1100			4450	5100
20	2	AVENGER 200 B/R	OP	SKI	FBG	SV	OB			7	5	1250			4900	5650
20	2	AVENGER 201	OP	SKI	FBG	SV	IO	260		7	5	2300			6400	7350
20	2	AVENGER 202	OP	BASS	FBG	SV	OB			7	5	1200			4750	5450
20	2	AVENGER 203	OP	SKI	FBG	TH	OB			7	5	1250			4900	5650
21	4	AVENGER 221	OP	CR	FBG	SV	IO	260		7	10	3000			8600	9850
21	4	AVENGER 221	OP	CR	FBG	SV	JT	320	FORD	7	10	3000			11300	12800
21	4	AVENGER 222	OP	CR	FBG	SV	OB			7	10	1600			6300	7250
22	6	AVENGER 230	OP	CR	FBG	SV	IO	260		7	10	3200			9550	10800
22	6	AVENGER 230	OP	CR	FBG	SV	JT	320	FORD	7	10	3200			12400	14100
		1989 BOATS														
16	7	AVENGER 163	OP	SKI	FBG	SV	OB			7	1	750			2700	3150
16	7	AVENGER 165	OP	SKI	FBG	SV	OB			7	1	800			2850	3300
17		AVENGER 169	OP	RNBT	FBG	SV	IO	140-180		7	3	1900			4000	4850
17	7	AVENGER 170	OP	SKI	FBG	SV	JT	320	FORD	7	3	2200			6700	7700
17	7	AVENGER 171	OP	SKI	FBG	SV	JT	320	FORD	7	3	2300			6850	7850
17	7	AVENGER 180	OP	SKI	FBG	SV	JT	320	FORD	7	3	2200			6700	7700
17	7	AVENGER 181	OP	SKI	FBG	SV	JT	320	FORD	7	3	2300			6850	7850
17	7	AVENGER 185	OP	SKI	FBG	SV	JT	320	FORD	7	3	2400			7000	8050
18	3	AVENGER 182	OP	BASS	FBG	SV	OB			7	3	1180			4250	4950

CONTINUED ON NEXT PAGE

LOA FT	LOA IN	NAME AND/ OR MODEL	TOP/ RIG	BOAT TYPE	HULL MTL	HULL TP	ENGINE TP	ENGINE # HP	ENGINE MFG	BEAM FT	BEAM IN	WGT LBS	DRAFT FT	DRAFT IN	RETAIL LOW	RETAIL HIGH
		1989 BOATS														
18	3	AVENGER 183	OP	SKI	FBG	SV	OB			7	3	900			3400	3950
18	3	AVENGER 184	OP	BASS	FBG	SV	OB			7	3	1100			4000	4650
20	2	AVENGER 200	OP	SKI	FBG	SV	OB			7	5	1100			4250	4950
20	2	AVENGER 200 B/R	OP	SKI	FBG	SV	OB			7	5	1250			4750	5500
20	2	AVENGER 201	OP	SKI	FBG	SV	IO	260		7	5	2300			6050	6950
20	2	AVENGER 202	OP	BASS	FBG	SV	OB			7	5	1200			4650	5300
20	2	AVENGER 203	OP	SKI	FBG	TH	OB			7	5	1250			4750	5500
21	4	AVENGER 221	OP	CR	FBG	SV	IO	260		7	10	3000			8100	9300
21	4	AVENGER 221	OP	CR	FBG	SV	JT	320	FORD	7	10	3000			10700	12200
21	4	AVENGER 222	OP	CR	FBG	SV	OB			7	10	1600			6100	7000
22	6	AVENGER 230	OP	CR	FBG	SV	IO	260		7	10	3200			9050	10300
22	6	AVENGER 230	OP	CR	FBG	SV	JT	320	FORD	7	10	3200			11800	13400
		1988 BOATS														
16	7	AVENGER 163	OP	SKI	FBG	SV	OB			7	1	750			2600	3050
16	7	AVENGER 165	OP	SKI	FBG	SV	OB			7	1	800			2750	3200
17		AVENGER 169	OP	RNBT	FBG	SV	IO	140-180		7	3	1900			3800	4600
17	7	AVENGER 170	OP	SKI	FBG	SV	JT	320	FORD	7	3	2200			6400	7350
17	7	AVENGER 171	OP	SKI	FBG	SV	JT	320	FORD	7	3	2300			6500	7500
17	7	AVENGER 180	OP	SKI	FBG	SV	JT	320	FORD	7	3	2200			6400	7350
17	7	AVENGER 181	OP	SKI	FBG	SV	JT	320	FORD	7	3	2300			6500	7500
17	7	AVENGER 185	OP	SKI	FBG	SV	JT	320	FORD	7	3	2400			6650	7650
18	3	AVENGER 182	OP	BASS	FBG	SV	OB			7	3	1180			4100	4800
18	3	AVENGER 183	OP	SKI	FBG	SV	OB			7	3	900			3300	3800
18	3	AVENGER 184	OP	BASS	FBG	SV	OB			7	3	1100			3900	4500
20	2	AVENGER 200	OP	SKI	FBG	SV	OB			7	5	1100			4100	4800
20	2	AVENGER 200 B/R	OP	SKI	FBG	SV	OB			7	5	1250			4650	5350
20	2	AVENGER 201	OP	SKI	FBG	SV	IO	260		7	5	2300			5700	6550
20	2	AVENGER 202	OP	BASS	FBG	SV	OB			7	5	1200			4500	5150
20	2	AVENGER 203	OP	SKI	FBG	TH	OB			7	5	1250			4650	5350
20	10	AVENGER 210	OP	CUD	FBG	SV	IO	260		8		3400			8150	9350
21	4	AVENGER 221	OP	CR	FBG	SV	IO	260		7	10	3000			7650	8800
21	4	AVENGER 221	OP	CR	FBG	SV	JT	320	FORD	7	10	3000			10200	11600
21	4	AVENGER 222	OP	CR	FBG	SV	OB			7	10	1600			5900	6800
22	2	AVENGER 220	OP	SKI	FBG	SV	IO	260		7	11	2800			7250	8350
22	2	AVENGER 220	OP	SKI	FBG	SV	JT	320	FORD	7	11	2800			10300	11700
22	6	AVENGER 230	OP	CR	FBG	SV	IO	260		7	10	3200			8450	9750
22	6	AVENGER 230	OP	CR	FBG	SV	JT	320	FORD	7	10	3200			11300	12800
		1987 BOATS														
16	7	AVENGER 163	OP	SKI	FBG	SV	OB			7	1	750			2550	2950
16	7	AVENGER 165	OP	SKI	FBG	SV	OB			7	1	800			2700	3150
17		AVENGER 169	OP	RNBT	FBG	SV	IO	130-180		7	5	1900			3650	4450
17	7	AVENGER 170	OP	SKI	FBG	SV	JT	320	FORD	7	3	2200			6100	7000
17	7	AVENGER 171	OP	SKI	FBG	SV	JT	320	FORD	7	3	2300			6200	7150
17	7	AVENGER 180	OP	SKI	FBG	SV	JT	320	FORD	7	3	2200			6100	7000
17	7	AVENGER 181	OP	SKI	FBG	SV	JT	320	FORD	7	3	2300			6200	7150
17	7	AVENGER 185	OP	SKI	FBG	SV	JT	320	FORD	7	3	2500			6500	7450
18	3	AVENGER 182	OP	BASS	FBG	SV	OB			7	3	1180			4000	4650
18	3	AVENGER 183	OP	SKI	FBG	SV	OB			7	3	900			3200	3700
18	3	AVENGER 184	OP	BASS	FBG	SV	OB			7	3	1100			3800	4400
20	1	AVENGER 200	OP	SKI	FBG	SV	OB			7	5	1100			4000	4650
20	1	AVENGER 200 B/R	OP	SKI	FBG	SV	OB			7	5	1250			4500	5150
20	1	AVENGER 202	OP	BASS	FBG	SV	OB			7	4	1200			4300	5000
20	2	AVENGER 201	OP	SKI	FBG	SV	IO	260		7	4	2310			5400	6200
20	2	AVENGER 203	OP	SKI	FBG	TH	OB			7	5	1250			4500	5200
20	10	AVENGER 210	OP	CUD	FBG	SV	IO	260		8		3400			7750	8900
21	4	AVENGER 221	OP	CR	FBG	SV	IO	260		7	10	3200			7600	8700
21	4	AVENGER 221	OP	CR	FBG	SV	JT	320	FORD	7	10	3200			10100	11500
21	4	AVENGER 222	OP	CR	FBG	SV	OB			7	10	1900			6600	7550
22	2	AVENGER 220	OP	SKI	FBG	SV	IO	260		7	11	2800			6900	7900
22	2	AVENGER 220	OP	SKI	FBG	SV	JT	320	FORD	7	11	2800			9850	11200
22	6	AVENGER 230	OP	CR	FBG	SV	IO	260		7	10	3200			8050	9250
22	6	AVENGER 230	OP	CR	FBG	SV	JT	320	FORD	7	10	3200			10700	12200
		1985 BOATS														
16	7	AVENGER 163	OP	SKI	FBG	SV	OB			7	1	750			2400	2800
16	7	AVENGER 165	OP	SKI	FBG	SV	OB			7	1	800			2550	2950
17		AVENGER 169	OP	RNBT	FBG	SV	IO	140-190		7	5	1900			3350	4100
17	7	AVENGER 170	OP	SKI	FBG	SV	JT	320	FORD	7	3	2200			5550	6400
17	7	AVENGER 171	OP	SKI	FBG	SV	JT	320	FORD	7	3	2300			5650	6500
17	7	AVENGER 180	OP	SKI	FBG	SV	JT	320	FORD	7	3	2200			5550	6400
17	7	AVENGER 181	OP	SKI	FBG	SV	JT	320	FORD	7	3	2300			5650	6500
17	7	AVENGER 185	OP	SKI	FBG	SV	JT	320	FORD	7	3	2500			5900	6800
18	4	AVENGER 182	OP	BASS	FBG	SV	OB			7	3	1180			3800	4450
18	4	AVENGER 183	OP	SKI	FBG	SV	OB			7	3	900			3050	3500
20	1	AVENGER 200	OP	SKI	FBG	SV	OB			7	5	1100			3800	4400
20	1	AVENGER 200 B/R	OP	SKI	FBG	SV	OB			7	5	1250			4200	4900
20	1	AVENGER 202	OP	BASS	FBG	SV	OB			7	4	1200			4050	4750
20	2	AVENGER 201	OP	SKI	FBG	SV	IO	260		7	4	2310			4950	5700
20	10	AVENGER 210	OP	CUD	FBG	SV	IO	260		8		3400			7100	8150
21	4	AVENGER 221	OP	CR	FBG	SV	IO	260		7	10	3200			6950	8000
21	4	AVENGER 221	OP	CR	FBG	SV	JT	320	FORD	7	10	3200			9300	10600
21	4	AVENGER 222	OP	CR	FBG	SV	OB			7	10	1900			6250	7150
22	2	AVENGER 220	OP	SKI	FBG	SV	IO	260		7	11	2800			6300	7250
22	2	AVENGER 220	OP	SKI	FBG	SV	JT	320	FORD	7	11	2800			9050	10300
22	6	AVENGER 230	OP	CR	FBG	SV	IO	260		7	10	3200			7400	8500
22	6	AVENGER 230	OP	CR	FBG	SV	JT	320	FORD	7	10	3200			9800	11100
		1984 BOATS														
16	7	AVENGER 163	OP	SKI	FBG	SV	OB			7	1	750			2350	2750
16	7	AVENGER 165	OP	SKI	FBG	SV	OB			7	1	800			2500	2900
17		AVENGER 169	OP	RNBT	FBG	SV	IO	140-188		7	5	1900			3250	3950
17	7	AVENGER 170	OP	SKI	FBG	SV	JT	320	FORD	7	3	2200			5300	6100
17	7	AVENGER 171	OP	SKI	FBG	SV	JT	320	FORD	7	3	2300			5400	6250
17	7	AVENGER 180	OP	SKI	FBG	SV	JT	320	FORD	7	3	2200			5300	6100
17	7	AVENGER 181	OP	SKI	FBG	SV	JT	320	FORD	7	3	2300			5400	6250
17	7	AVENGER 185	OP	SKI	FBG	SV	JT	320	FORD	7	3	2500			5650	6500
18	4	AVENGER 182	OP	BASS	FBG	SV	OB			7	3	1180			3700	4300
18	4	AVENGER 183	OP	SKI	FBG	SV	OB			7	3	900			2950	3450
20	1	AVENGER 200	OP	SKI	FBG	SV	OB			7	5	1100			3700	4300
20	1	AVENGER 202	OP	BASS	FBG	SV	OB			7	4	1200			3950	4600
20	2	AVENGER 201	OP	SKI	FBG	SV	IO	260		7	4	2310			4800	5500
20	10	AVENGER 210	OP	CUD	FBG	SV	IO	260		8		3400			6850	7900
21	4	AVENGER 221	OP	CR	FBG	SV	IO	260		7	10	3200			6700	7700
21	4	AVENGER 221	OP	CR	FBG	SV	JT	320	FORD	7	10	3200			8900	10100
21	4	AVENGER 222	OP	CR	FBG	SV	OB			7	10	1900			6100	7000
22	2	AVENGER 220	OP	SKI	FBG	SV	IO	260		7	11	2800			6100	7000
22	2	AVENGER 220	OP	SKI	FBG	SV	JT	320	FORD	7	11	2800			8550	9800
22	6	AVENGER 230	OP	CR	FBG	SV	IO	260		7	10	3200			7100	8200
22	6	AVENGER 230	OP	CR	FBG	SV	JT	320	FORD	7	10	3200			9400	10700

....For earlier years, see the BUC Used Boat Price Guide, Volume 3

CELEBRITY BOATS

DIV SEA DOO / SKI DOO
GRAND-MERE QUEBEC G9T 5 COAST GUARD MFG ID- QDO

See inside cover to adjust price for area

For more recent years, see the BUC Used Boat Price Guide, Volume 1

LOA FT	LOA IN	NAME AND/ OR MODEL	TOP/ RIG	BOAT TYPE	HULL MTL	HULL TP	ENGINE TP	ENGINE # HP	ENGINE MFG	BEAM FT	BEAM IN	WGT LBS	DRAFT FT	DRAFT IN	RETAIL LOW	RETAIL HIGH
		1996 BOATS														
18	2	BOW RIDER 180	OP	RNBT	FBG	DV	IO	135		7	8	2325	2	11	5150	6200
18	2	BOW RIDER 180	OP	RNBT	FBG	DV	IO	160-210		7	8	2500	2	11	5350	6650
18	2	BOW RIDER 180	OP	RNBT	FBG	DV	IO	220	VLVO	7	8	2600	2	11	5900	6800
18	2	FIRESTAR 18	OP	RNBT	FBG	DV	IO	180-210		7	8	2570	2	11	5500	6750
18	2	FIRESTAR 18	OP	RNBT	FBG	DV	IO	220	VLVO	7	8	2670	2	11	6000	6900
18	2	FIRESTAR 18 CNV	OP	B/R	FBG	DV	IO	180-210		7	8	2570	2	11	5300	6500
18	2	FIRESTAR 18 CNV	OP	B/R	FBG	DV	IO	220	VLVO	7	8	2670	2	11	5800	6650
18	3	FISH HAWK 1900 CC	OP	CTRCN	FBG	DV	OB			8		2500	2	7	5650	6500
18	10	BOW RIDER 190	OP	RNBT	FBG	DV	IO	135-180		8		2525	2	11	5700	7100
18	10	BOW RIDER 190	OP	RNBT	FBG	DV	IO	185-250		8		2800	2	11	6350	7700
19	7	BOW RIDER 200	OP	RNBT	FBG	DV	IO	160-210		8	6	2875	2	11	6450	7900
19	7	BOW RIDER 200	OP	RNBT	FBG	DV	IO	220-250		8	6	2975	2	11	7000	8450
19	7	BOW RIDER 200 SS	OP	RNBT	FBG	DV	IO	160-220		8	6	2875	2	11	6850	8450
19	7	BOW RIDER 200 SS	OP	RNBT	FBG	DV	IO	235-250		8	6	2975	2	11	7500	8900
20	8	BOW RIDER 210	OP	RNBT	FBG	DV	IO	160-220		8	6	3050	3	2	7600	9400
20	8	BOW RIDER 210	OP	RNBT	FBG	DV	IO	235-300		8	6	3150	3	2	8300	9950
20	8	CUDDY 210	OP	CUD	FBG	DV	IO	160-250		8	6	3150	3	2	8150	10200
20	8	CUDDY 210	OP	CUD	FBG	DV	IO	265-300		8	6	3150	3	2	9100	10600
20	8	FIRESTAR 21	OP	RNBT	FBG	DV	IO	235-300		8	6	3200	3	2	8350	10000
20	8	FIRESTAR 21 CNV	OP	RNBT	FBG	DV	IO	235-265		8	6	2670	3	2	7600	9500
20	8	FIRESTAR 21 CNV	OP	RNBT	FBG	DV	IO	300	MRCR	8	6	3250	3	2	8900	10100
22	1	BOW RIDER 220	OP	RNBT	FBG	DV	IO	190-265		8	6	3475	3		9200	11000
22	1	BOW RIDER 220	OP	RNBT	FBG	DV	IO	300		8	6	3475	3		9750	12000
22	1	BOW RIDER 220	OP	RNBT	FBG	DV	IO	330-350		8	6	3700	3		10700	12800
22	1	CUDDY 220	OP	CUD	FBG	DV	IO	190-265		8	6	3575	3		9850	11800
22	1	CUDDY 220	OP	CUD	FBG	DV	IO	300-330		8	6	3575	3		10500	13100
22	1	CUDDY 220	OP	CUD	FBG	DV	IO	350	MRCR	8	6	3800	3		12000	13600
22	10	FISH HAWK 2300 CC	OP	CTRCN	FBG	DV	OB			8	6	3250	2	6	8900	10100
22	10	FISH HAWK 2300 CC	OP	CTRCN	FBG	DV	IO	160-250		8	6	4000	2	6	11300	13900
22	10	FISH HAWK 2300 WA	OP	CUD	FBG	DV	OB			8	6	3700	2	8	9600	10900

LOA FT	LOA IN	NAME AND/ OR MODEL	TOP/ RIG	BOAT TYPE	-HULL- MTL	-HULL- TP	ENGINE TP	ENGINE # HP	ENGINE MFG	BEAM FT	BEAM IN	WGT LBS	DRAFT FT	DRAFT IN	RETAIL LOW	RETAIL HIGH
		1996 BOATS														
22	10	FISH HAWK 2300 WA	OP	CUD	FBG	DV	IO	160-250		8	6	4000	2	8	10700	13200
23		BOW RIDER 230	OP	RNBT	FBG	DV	IO	210-265		8	6	3590	3		9550	11600
23		BOW RIDER 230	OP	RNBT	FBG	DV	IO	300		8	6	3590	3		10300	12700
23		BOW RIDER 230	OP	RNBT	FBG	DV	IO	330-350		8	6	3800	3		11300	13400
23		CUDDY 230	OP	CUD	FBG	DV	IO	210-265		8	6	3640	3		10200	12500
23		CUDDY 230	OP	CUD	FBG	DV	IO	300		8	6	3850	3		11500	13600
23		CUDDY 230	OP	CUD	FBG	DV	IO	330-350		8	6	3850	3		12100	14400
24		BOW RIDER 240	OP	RNBT	FBG	DV	IO	210-265		8	6	3750	2	11	10200	12400
24		BOW RIDER 240	OP	RNBT	FBG	DV	IO	300-330		8	6	3750	2	11	11000	13600
24		BOW RIDER 240	OP	RNBT	FBG	DV	IO	350	MRCR	8	6	3950	2	11	12400	14100
24		CUDDY 240	OP	CUD	FBG	DV	IO	210-265		8	6	3850	2	11	11100	13500
24		CUDDY 240	OP	CUD	FBG	DV	IO	300-330		8	6	3850	2	11	12000	14900
24		CUDDY 240	OP	CUD	FBG	DV	IO	350	MRCR	8	6	4050	2	11	13500	15300
24	10	FISH HAWK 2500 WA	OP	CUD	FBG	DV	OB			8	6	3900	2	8	11000	12400
24	10	FISH HAWK 2500 WA	OP	CUD	FBG	DV	IO	190-265		8	6	4400	2	8	12900	15400
24	10	FISH HAWK 2500 WA	OP	CUD	FBG	DV	IO	300		8	6	4400	2	8	13800	16600
26	5	SPORT CRUISER 265	OP	SPTCR	FBG	DV	IO	210-265		8	6	5600	3		16100	19400
		IO 300-330 17400 21200, IO 185D VLVO 20300 22500, IO T135-T180													18400	21700
28	5	SPORT CRUISER 285	OP	SPTCR	FBG	DV	IO	300-330		9	11	7650	3	8	23000	26400
28	5	SPORT CRUISER 285	OP	SPTCR	FBG	DV	IO	T160-T250		9	11	8125	3	4	24300	29400
31		SPORT CRUISER 310	OP	SPTCR	FBG	DV	IO	T190-T250		10	4	8700	2	11	29000	33800
31		SPORT CRUISER 310	OP	SPTCR	FBG	DV	IO	T185D	VLVO	10	4	8900	2	11	34500	38300
		1995 BOATS														
18	2	BOW RIDER 180 CX	OP	B/R	FBG	DV	IO	135	MRCR	7	8	2325	2	11	4500	5200
18	2	BOWRIDER 180 CX	OP	B/R	FBG	DV	IO	135-205		7	8	2325	2	11	4600	5700
18	2	CLOSED DECK 180 CX	OP	RNBT	FBG	DV	IO	135-180		7	8	2325	2	11	4700	5750
18	2	CLOSED DECK 180 CX	OP	RNBT	FBG	DV	IO	185-205		7	8	2500	2	11	5300	6050
18	2	FIRESTAR 18 CD	OP	RNBT	FBG	DV	IO	180-205		7	8	2550	2	11	5100	6250
18	2	FIRESTAR 18 CD	OP	RNBT	FBG	DV	IO	220	VLVO	7	8	2650	2	11	5550	6400
18	2	FIRESTAR 18 CNV	OP	B/R	FBG	DV	IO	180-205		7	8	2570	2	11	4900	6100
18	2	FIRESTAR 18 CNV	OP	B/R	FBG	DV	IO	220	VLVO	7	8	2670	2	11	5400	6200
18	2	STATUS 180 BR	OP	B/R	FBG	DV	IO	135-185		7	8	2325	2	11	5000	6200
18	2	STATUS 180 BR	OP	B/R	FBG	DV	IO	190-205		7	8	2600	2	11	5150	6250
18	2	STATUS 180 CD	OP	RNBT	FBG	DV	IO	135-180		7	8	2325	2	11	5100	6250
18	2	STATUS 180 CD	OP	RNBT	FBG	DV	IO	190-205		7	8	2600	2	11	5400	6450
18	3	FISH HAWK 1900	OP	CTRCN	FBG	DV	OB			8		2050	2	5	4950	5700
18	10	STATUS 190 BR	OP	B/R	FBG	DV	IO	135-180		8		2525	2	11	5150	6450
18	10	STATUS 190 BR	OP	B/R	FBG	DV	IO	185-255		8		2700	2	11	5650	7050
19	7	STATUS 200 BR	OP	B/R	FBG	DV	IO	160-220		8	6	2875	2	11	5850	7350
19	7	STATUS 200 BR	OP	B/R	FBG	DV	IO	235-255		8	6	2975	2	11	6200	7600
19	7	STATUS 200SS BR	OP	B/R	FBG	DV	IO	160-220		8	6	2875	2	11	6250	7750
19	7	STATUS 200SS BR	OP	B/R	FBG	DV	IO	235-255		8	6	2975	2	11	6550	8000
20	8	FIRESTAR 21 CD	OP	RNBT	FBG	DV	IO	235-300		8	6	3200	3	2	7800	9750
20	8	FIRESTAR 21 CNV	OP	B/R	FBG	DV	IO	235-300		8	6	3250	3	2	7750	9650
20	8	STATUS 210 BR	OP	B/R	FBG	DV	IO	160-220		8	6	3050	3	2	6950	8650
20	8	STATUS 210 BR	OP	B/R	FBG	DV	IO	235-255		8	6	3150	3	2	7350	8950
20	8	STATUS 210 CC	OP	CUD	FBG	DV	IO	160-220		8	6	3150	3	2	7600	9400
20	8	STATUS 210 CC	OP	CUD	FBG	DV	IO	235-255		8	6	3250	3	2	7950	9700
22	1	STATUS 220 BR	OP	B/R	FBG	DV	IO	190-255		8	6	3475	3		8200	10100
22	1	STATUS 220 BR	OP	B/R	FBG	DV	IO	275-300		8	6	3475	3		9100	11100
22	1	STATUS 220 BR	OP	B/R	FBG	DV	IO	350	MRCR	8	6	3700	3		10300	11700
22	1	STATUS 220 CC	OP	CUD	FBG	DV	IO	190-275		8	6	3575	3		9000	11200
22	1	STATUS 220 CC	OP	CUD	FBG	DV	IO	300		8	6	3800	3		10200	12100
22	1	STATUS 220 CC	OP	CUD	FBG	DV	IO	350	MRCR	8	6	3800	3		11200	12700
22	10	FISH HAWK 2300	OP	CTRCN	FBG	DV	OB			8	6	2800	2	8	7550	8700
22	10	FISH HAWK 2300	OP	CUD	FBG	DV	OB			8	6	3250	2	8	8400	9650
22	10	FISH HAWK 2300	OP	CUD	FBG	DV	IO	160-255		8	6	4000	2	8	10000	12400
22	10	FISH HAWK 2300 WA	OP	B/R	FBG	DV	IO	190-250		8	6	4100	2	8	9850	11400
23		STATUS 230 BR	OP	B/R	FBG	DV	IO	235-275		8	6	3590	3		9000	10900
23		STATUS 230 BR	OP	B/R	FBG	DV	IO	300-350		8	6	3800	3		9950	12400
23		STATUS 230 CC	OP	CUD	FBG	DV	IO	235-275		8	6	3640	3		9650	11800
23		STATUS 230 CC	OP	CUD	FBG	DV	IO	300-350		8	6	3850	3		10700	13300
24		STATUS 240 BR	OP	B/R	FBG	DV	IO	235-275		8	6	3750	2	11	9650	11700
24		STATUS 240 BR	OP	B/R	FBG	DV	IO	300-350		8	6	3950	2	11	10600	13200
24		STATUS 240 CC	OP	CUD	FBG	DV	IO	235-275		8	6	3850	2	11	10500	12700
24		STATUS 240 CC	OP	CUD	FBG	DV	IO	300-350		8	6	4050	2	11	11600	14300
24	10	FISH HAWK 2500	OP	CUD	FBG	DV	OB			8	6	3450	2	8	9700	11000
24	10	FISH HAWK 2500	OP	CUD	FBG	DV	IO	190-255		8	6	4400	2	8	11700	14400
24	10	FISH HAWK 2500	OP	CUD	FBG	DV	IO	300		8	6	4600	2	8	13200	15400
24	10	FISH HAWK 2500 WA	OP	CUD	FBG	DV	IO	190-275		8	6	4400	2	8	12300	14600
26	5	SPORT CRUISER 265	OP	SPTCR	FBG	DV	IO	230-300		8	6	5500	3		15300	18900
26	5	SPORT CRUISER 265	OP	SPTCR	FBG	DV	IO	185D	VLVO	8	6	5700	3		18300	20400
31		SPORT CRUISER 310	OP	SPTCR	FBG	DV	IO	T190-T275		10	4	8700	2	11	27000	32200
31		SPORT CRUISER 310	OP	SPTCR	FBG	DV	IO	T185D	VLVO	10	4	8800	2	11	32000	35500
		1994 BOATS														
18	2	BOWRIDER 180 CX	OP	B/R	FBG	DV	IO	110-180		7	8	2500	2	11	4250	5150
18	2	BOWRIDER 180 CX	OP	B/R	FBG	DV	IO	185-215		7	8	2500	2	11	4750	5450
18	2	CLOSED DECK 180 CX	OP	RNBT	FBG	DV	IO	110-180		7	8	2500	2	11	4450	5350
18	2	CLOSED DECK 180 CX	OP	RNBT	FBG	DV	IO	185-215		7	8	2500	2	11	4950	5650
18	2	STATUS 180 BR	OP	B/R	FBG	DV	IO	110-215		7	8	2500	2	11	4700	5800
18	2	STATUS 180 CD	OP	RNBT	FBG	DV	IO	110-215		7	8	2500	2	11	4850	6000
18	3	FISH HAWK 1900	OP	CTRCN	FBG	DV	OB			8		2250	2	5	4950	5650
19	7	STATUS 200 BR	OP	B/R	FBG	DV	IO	160-215		8	6	2950	2	11	5750	7100
19	7	STATUS 200 BR	OP	B/R	FBG	DV	IO	225-255		8	6	3050	2	11	6250	7400
19	9	CUDDY CABIN 200	OP	CUD	FBG	DV	IO	160-245		8		3300	2	6	6400	7950
19	9	CUDDY CABIN 200	OP	CUD	FBG	DV	IO	250-255		8		3300	2	6	6700	8050
20	8	STATUS 210 BR	OP	B/R	FBG	DV	IO	160-240		8	6	3050	3	2	6500	8150
20	8	STATUS 210 BR	OP	B/R	FBG	DV	IO	245-255		8	6	3150	3	2	7150	8350
20	8	STATUS 210 CC	OP	CUD	FBG	DV	IO	160-240		8	6	3250	3	2	7200	9000
20	8	STATUS 210 CC	OP	CUD	FBG	DV	IO	245-255		8	6	3350	3	2	7950	9200
22	1	STATUS 220 BR	OP	B/R	FBG	DV	IO	190-255		8	6	3575	3		7800	9600
22	1	STATUS 220 BR	OP	B/R	FBG	DV	IO	300-350		8	6	3800	3		8950	11100
22	1	STATUS 220 CC	OP	CUD	FBG	DV	IO	190-255		8	6	3575	3		8300	10200
22	1	STATUS 220 CC	OP	CUD	FBG	DV	IO	300		8	6	3800	3		9500	11300
22	1	STATUS 220 CC	OP	CUD	FBG	DV	IO	350	MRCR	8	6	3800	3		10500	11900
22	10	FISH HAWK 2300	OP	CTRCN	FBG	DV	OB			8	6	2800	2	6	7200	8250
22	10	FISH HAWK 2300	OP	CUD	FBG	DV	OB			8	6	3250	2	6	8000	9200
22	10	FISH HAWK 2300	OP	CUD	FBG	DV	IO	160-255		8	6	4100	2	8	9500	11700
23		STATUS 230 BR	OP	B/R	FBG	DV	IO	205-255		8	6	3690	3		8350	10200
23		STATUS 230 BR	OP	B/R	FBG	DV	IO	300-350		8	6	3900	3		9450	11700
23		STATUS 230 CC	OP	CUD	FBG	DV	IO	225-255		8	6	3740	3		9400	10900
23		STATUS 230 CC	OP	CUD	FBG	DV	IO	300-350		8	6	3950	3		10200	12600
24		STATUS 240 BR	OP	B/R	FBG	DV	IO	225-255		8	6	3800	2	11	9350	10800
24		STATUS 240 BR	OP	B/R	FBG	DV	IO	300-350		8	6	4000	2	11	10000	12400
24		STATUS 240 CC	OP	CUD	FBG	DV	IO	225-255		8	6	3900	2	11	10100	11700
24		STATUS 240 CC	OP	CUD	FBG	DV	IO	300-350		8	6	4100	2	11	10900	13400
24	10	FISH HAWK 2500	OP	CUD	FBG	DV	OB			8	6	3450	2	8	9250	10500
24	10	FISH HAWK 2500	OP	CUD	FBG	DV	IO	190-275		8	6	4400	2	8	11000	13600
24	10	FISH HAWK 2500	OP	CUD	FBG	DV	IO	300		8	6	4600	2	8	12300	14400
26	5	SPORT CRUISER 265	OP	SPTCR	FBG	DV	IO	225-300		8	6	5550	3		14300	17700
31		SPORT CRUISER 310	OP	SPTCR	FBG	DV	IO	T190-T255		10	4	8800	2	11	25300	29600
31		SPORT CRUISER 310	OP	SPTCR	FBG	DV	IO	T115D-T185D		10	4	8800	2	11	27100	33200
		1993 BOATS														
18	2	BOWRIDER 180 CX	OP	RNBT	FBG	DV	IO	110-180		7	8	2500	2	3	4350	5050
18	2	CLOSED DECK 180 CX	OP	RNBT	FBG	DV	IO	110-180		7	8	2500	2	3	4350	5050
18	2	STATUS 180 BR	OP	RNBT	FBG	DV	IO	110-180		7	8	2500	2	3	4700	5450
18	2	STATUS 180 CD	OP	RNBT	FBG	DV	IO	110-180		7	8	2500	2	3	4700	5450
18	3	FISH HAWK 1900	OP	CTRCN	FBG	DV	OB			8		2250	2	5	4700	5450
18	7	BOWRIDER 190	OP	RNBT	FBG	DV	IO	155-240		7	8	2900	2	5	5150	6050
18	7	BOWRIDER 190 CX	OP	RNBT	FBG	DV	IO	155-180		7	8	2900	2	5	4700	5600
18	7	BOWRIDER 190 CX	OP	RNBT	FBG	DV	IO	190-240		7	8	2900	2	5	5100	6000
19	9	BOWRIDER 200	OP	RNBT	FBG	DV	IO	155-240		8		3050	2	6	5450	6700
19	9	BOWRIDER 200	OP	RNBT	FBG	DV	IO	245-250		8		3050	2	6	5900	6800
19	9	CUDDY CABIN 200	OP	CUD	FBG	DV	IO	155-245		8		3300	2	6	5950	7450
20	8	BOWRIDER 208	OP	RNBT	FBG	DV	IO	175-250		8	6	3150	3		6350	7550
20	8	STATUS 208 BR	OP	RNBT	FBG	DV	IO	155-245		8	6	3350	3		6550	7850
20	8	STATUS 208 CC	OP	CUD	FBG	DV	IO	155-245		8	6	3350	3	1	6900	8500
21	5	BOWRIDER 220	OP	RNBT	FBG	DV	IO	180-250		8		3325	2	7	6600	8100
21	5	BOWRIDER 220	OP	RNBT	FBG	DV	IO	300		8		3325	2	7	7300	8800
21	5	BOWRIDER 220	OP	RNBT	FBG	DV	IO	360	MRCR	8		3325	2	7	8350	9600
21	5	CUDDY CABIN 220	OP	CUD	FBG	DV	IO	180-250		8		3500	2	7	7200	8850
21	5	CUDDY CABIN 220	OP	CUD	FBG	DV	IO	300		8		3500	2	7	7950	9550
21	5	CUDDY CABIN 220	OP	CUD	FBG	DV	IO	360	MRCR	8		3500	2	7	9150	10400
22	1	STATUS 221 BR	OP	RNBT	FBG	DV	IO	155-250		8	6	3850	3	3	7900	9400
22	1	STATUS 221 BR	OP	RNBT	FBG	DV	IO	300		8	6	3850	3	3	8400	10100
22	1	STATUS 221 BR	OP	RNBT	FBG	DV	IO	350	MRCR	8	6	3850	3	3	9350	10600
22	1	STATUS 221 CC	OP	CUD	FBG	DV	IO	155-250		8	6	3950	3	3	8500	10100
22	1	STATUS 221 CC	OP	CUD	FBG	DV	IO	300-350		8	6	3950	3	3	9150	11400
22	10	FISH HAWK 2300	OP	CTRCN	FBG	DV	OB			8	6	2800	2	6	6850	7900
22	10	FISH HAWK 2300	OP	CUD	FBG	DV	OB			8	6	3250	2	6	7650	8750
22	10	FISH HAWK 2300	OP	CUD	FBG	DV	IO	155-240		8	6	3250	2	6	7500	8900
22	10	FISH HAWK 2300 WA	OP	CUD	FBG	DV	IO	155-225		8	6	4100	2	6	9150	10600
22	10	FISH HAWK 2300 WA	OP	CUD	FBG	DV	IO	115D	VLVO	8	6	4100	2	6	10600	12100
23	1	BOWRIDER 230	OP	RNBT	FBG	DV	IO	225-250		8		3500	2	8	7750	9050
23	1	BOWRIDER 230	OP	RNBT	FBG	DV	IO	300		8		3500	2	8	8100	9700

CONTINUED ON NEXT PAGE

CELEBRITY BOATS -CONTINUED See inside cover to adjust price for area

LOA FT	LOA IN	NAME AND/ OR MODEL	TOP/ RIG	BOAT TYPE	-HULL- MTL	-HULL- TP	TP	ENGINE # HP	ENGINE MFG	BEAM FT	BEAM IN	WGT LBS	DRAFT FT	DRAFT IN	RETAIL LOW	RETAIL HIGH
		1993 BOATS														
23	1	BOWRIDER 230	OP	RNBT	FBG	DV	IO	360	MRCR	8		3500	2	8	9250	10500
23	1	CUDDY CABIN 230	OP	CUD	FBG	DV	IO	225-245		8		3700	2	8	8550	9950
23	1	CUDDY CABIN 230	OP	CUD	FBG	DV	IO	300		8		3700	2	8	9000	10700
23	1	CUDDY CABIN 230	OP	CUD	FBG	DV	IO	360	MRCR	8		3700	2	8	10100	11500
24		STATUS 240 BR	OP	RNBT	FBG	DV	IO	225-250		8	6	4000	3	3	8850	10400
24		STATUS 240 BR	OP	RNBT	FBG	DV	IO	300-350		8	6	4000	3	3	9400	11600
24		STATUS 240 CC	OP	CUD	FBG	DV	IO	225-300		8	6	4100	3	3	9800	12000
24		STATUS 240 CC	OP	CUD	FBG	DV	IO	350	MRCR	8	6	4100	3	3	11100	12600
24	2	SPORT CRUISER 245	OP	SPTCR	FBG	DV	IO	225-300		8	6	5750	2	11	12800	15400
24	2	SPORT CRUISER 245	OP	SPTCR	FBG	DV	IO	115D	VLVO	8	6	5750	2	11	14300	16200
24	10	FISH HAWK 2500	OP	CUD	FBG	DV	OB					3900			9500	10800
24	10	FISH HAWK 2500	OP	CUD	FBG	DV	IO	180-300		8	6	4300	2	5	10100	12600
24	10	FISH HAWK 2500	OP	CUD	FBG	DV	IO	115D	VLVO	8	6	4300	2	5	11400	12900
24	10	FISH HAWK 2500 WA	OP	CUD	FBG	DV	IO	205		8	6	4400	2	5	10400	12000
24	10	FISH HAWK 2500 WA	OP	CUD	FBG	DV	IO	300	VLVO	8	6	4400	2	5	11500	13100
28	5	SPORT CRUISER 290	OP	SPTCR	FBG	DV	IO	T180-T250		10	4	8800	3	3	20800	24500
28	5	SPORT CRUISER 290	OP	SPTCR	FBG	DV	IO	T115D	VLVO	10	4	8800	3	3	25000	27700
28	5	SPORT CRUISER 290	OP	SPTCR	FBG	DV	IO	T218D	VLVO	10	4	8800	3	3	28400	31600
28	5	SPORT CURISER 290	OP	SPTCR	FBG	DV	IO	T190	VLVO	10	4	8800	3	3	21300	23700
28	5	SPORT CURISER 290	OP	SPTCR	FBG	DV	IO	T185D	VLVO	10	4	8800	3	3	27300	30400
		1992 BOATS														
18	1	BOWRIDER 181	OP	RNBT	FBG	DV	IO	110-180		7	2	2500	2	3	4050	4700
18	1	BOWRIDER 181 CX	OP	RNBT	FBG	DV	IO	110-180		7	2	2500	2	3	3700	4400
18	2	BOWRIDER 180	OP	RNBT	FBG	DV	IO	110-180		7	8	2500	2	3	4300	5000
18	2	BOWRIDER 180 CX	OP	RNBT	FBG	DV	IO	110-180		7	8	2500	2	3	3800	4550
18	2	CLOSED DECK 180	OP	RNBT	FBG	DV	IO	110-180		7	8	2500	2	3	4300	5000
18	2	CLOSED DECK 180 CX	OP	RNBT	FBG	DV	IO	110-180		7	8	2500	2	3	3800	4550
18	3	FISH HAWK 180	OP	CTRCN	FBG	DV	OB			8		2250	2	5	4550	5200
18	7	BOWRIDER 190	OP	RNBT	FBG	DV	IO	155-240		7	8	2900	2	5	4750	5650
18	7	BOWRIDER 190 CX	OP	RNBT	FBG	DV	IO	155-240		7	8	2900	2	5	4350	5250
19	9	BOWRIDER 200	OP	RNBT	FBG	DV	IO	155-240		8		3050	2	6	5100	6100
19	9	CUDDY CABIN 200	OP	CUD	FBG	DV	IO	155-240		8		3300	2	6	5600	6650
20	6	BOWRIDER 206	OP	RNBT	FBG	DV	IO	155-250		8	6				5850	7050
21	5	BOWRIDER 220	OP	RNBT	FBG	DV	IO	180-240		8		3325	2	7	6150	7300
21	5	BOWRIDER 220	OP	RNBT	FBG	DV	IO	300		8		3325	2	7	6850	7850
21	5	BOWRIDER 220	OP	RNBT	FBG	DV	IO	360	MRCR	8		3325	2	7	7800	9000
21	5	CUDDY CABIN 220	OP	CUD	FBG	DV	IO	180-240		8		3500	2	7	6700	7950
21	5	CUDDY CABIN 220	OP	CUD	FBG	DV	IO	300		8		3500	2	7	7450	8550
21	5	CUDDY CABIN 220	OP	CUD	FBG	DV	IO	360	YAMA	8		3500	2	7	8500	9750
22	4	BOWRIDER 224	OP	RNBT	FBG	DV	IO	230-300		8		3500	2	8	6800	8400
22	4	BOWRIDER 224	OP	RNBT	FBG	DV	IO	360	MRCR	8		3500	2	8	8300	9550
22	4	CUDDY CABIN 224	OP	CUD	FBG	DV	IO	230-300		8		3700	2	8	7500	9250
22	4	CUDDY CABIN 224	OP	CUD	FBG	DV	IO	360	MRCR	8		3700	2	8	9200	10400
22	10	FISH HAWK 210	OP	CTRCN	FBG	DV	OB			8	6	2800	2	6	6600	7550
22	10	FISH HAWK 210	OP	CUD	FBG	DV	OB			8	6	3250	2	6	7300	8400
22	10	FISH HAWK 210	OP	CUD	FBG	DV	IO	155-240		8	6	3250	2	6	7000	8300
23	1	BOWRIDER 230	OP	RNBT	FBG	DV	IO	230-300		8		3500	2	8	7050	8700
23	1	BOWRIDER 230	OP	RNBT	FBG	DV	IO	360	MRCR	8		3500	2	8	8550	9850
23	1	CUDDY 230	OP	CUD	FBG	DV	IO	230-300		8		3700	2	8	7500	9250
23	1	CUDDY 230	OP	CUD	FBG	DV	IO	360	MRCR	8		3700	2	8	9450	10700
23	1	CUDDY 231	OP	CUD	FBG	DV	IO	230-300		8		3700	2	8	8050	9900
24	2	SPORT CRUISER 245	OP	SPTCR	FBG	DV	IO	225-300		8	6	5750	2	11	12000	14400
24	2	SPORT CRUISER 245	OP	SPTCR	FBG	DV	IO	115D	VLVO	8	6	5750	2	11	13400	15200
24	10	FISH HAWK 230	OP	CUD	FBG	DV	OB					3900			9150	10400
24	10	FISH HAWK 230	OP	CUD	FBG	DV	IO	180-300		8	6	4300	2	5	9450	11800
24	10	FISH HAWK 230	OP	CUD	FBG	DV	IO	115D	VLVO	8	6	4300	2	5	10700	12100
28	5	CRUISER 290	OP	SPTCR	FBG	DV	IO	T180-T240		10	4	8800	3	3	19500	22600
		1991 BOATS														
18	1	BOWRIDER 181	OP	RNBT	FBG	DV	IO	155	MRCR	7	2	2500	2	3	3800	4400
18	1	BOWRIDER 181 CX	OP	RNBT	FBG	DV	IO	155	MRCR	7	2	2500	2	3	3500	4100
18	2	BOW RIDER 180	OP	RNBT	FBG	DV	IO	155	MRCR	7	8	2500	2	3	4000	4600
18	2	BOWRIDER 180 CX	OP	RNBT	FBG	DV	IO	155	MRCR	7	8	2500	2	3	3650	4250
18	2	CLOSED DECK 180	OP	RNBT	FBG	DV	IO	155	MRCR	7	8	2500	2	3	4000	4600
18	2	CLOSED DECK 180 CX	OP	RNBT	FBG	DV	IO	155	MRCR	7	8	2500	2	3	3650	4250
18	3	FISH HAWK 180	OP	CTRCN	FBG	DV	OB			8		2250	2	5	4300	5000
18	7	BOW RIDER 190	OP	RNBT	FBG	DV	IO	180	MRCR	7	8	2900	2	5	4500	5200
18	7	BOWRIDER 190 CX	OP	RNBT	FBG	DV	IO	180	MRCR	7	8	2900	2	5	4050	4750
19	9	BOW RIDER 200	OP	RNBT	FBG	DV	IO	230	MRCR	8		3050	2	6	4900	5650
19	9	CUDDY 200	OP	CUD	FBG	DV	IO	230	MRCR	8		3300	2	6	5550	6350
19	9	CUDDY 200 CX	OP	CUD	FBG	DV	IO	230	MRCR	8		3300	2	6	5250	6000
21	5	BOW RIDER 220	OP	RNBT	FBG	DV	IO	230	MRCR	8		3325	2	7	5900	6800
21	5	CUDDY 220	OP	CUD	FBG	DV	IO	230	MRCR	8		3500	2	7	6450	7400
22	4	BOWRIDER 224	OP	RNBT	FBG	DV	IO	230	MRCR	8			2	6	6450	7400
22	4	CUDDY 224	OP	CUD	FBG	DV	IO	230	MRCR	8		3700	2	6	7000	8050
22	10	FISH HAWK 210	OP	CTRCN	FBG	DV	OB			8	6	3100	2	6	6750	7800
22	10	FISH HAWK 210 WA	OP	CUD	FBG	DV	OB			8	6	3475	2	5	7300	8400
23	1	BOW RIDER 230	OP	RNBT	FBG	DV	IO	230	MRCR	8		3500	2	6	6600	7600
23	1	CUDDY 230	OP	CUD	FBG	DV	IO	230	MRCR	8		3700	2	6	7300	8400
25	10	ANDRETTI 260	OP	CUD	FBG	DV	IO		MRCR	8	6	5200	2	7	**	**
25	10	ANDRETTI 260	OP	CUD	FBG	DV	IO	T	MRCR	8	6	6100	3	2	**	**
28	4	SPORT CRUISER 260	OP	SPTCR	FBG	DV	IO		MRCR	8	6	6000	3	5	**	**
28	5	SPORT CRUISER 290	OP	SPTCR	FBG	DV	IO	T230	MRCR	10	4	8800	3	3	19000	21100
29	8	SPORT CRUISER 270	OP	SPTCR	FBG	DV	IO		MRCR	9	9	6900	3	7	**	**
29	8	SPORT CRUISER 270	OP	SPTCR	FBG	DV	IO	T230	MRCR	9	9	7800	3	7	18600	20700
		1990 BOATS														
18	2	OPEN BOW 180	OP	RNBT	FBG	DV	IO	175		7	8	2275	2	3	3450	4000
18	2	SPORT BOW 180	OP	RNBT	FBG	DV	IO	175		7	8	2275	2	3	3450	4000
18	7	CELEBRITY 190	OP	RNBT	FBG	DV	IO	260		7	8	2900	2	5	4250	4950
19	9	BOW RIDER 200	OP	RNBT	FBG	DV	IO	270		8		3050	2	6	4850	5550
19	9	CUDDY 200	OP	CUD	FBG	DV	IO	260		8		3050	2	6	4950	5700
21	5	BOW RIDER 220	OP	RNBT	FBG	DV	IO	330		8		3325	2	7	6400	7350
21	5	CUDDY 220	OP	CUD	FBG	DV	IO	330		8		3325	2	7	6750	7750
23	1	BOW RIDER 230	OP	RNBT	FBG	DV	IO	330		8		3700	2	6	7300	8400
23	1	CUDDY 230	OP	CUD	FBG	DV	IO	330		8		3700	2	6	7750	8900
25	10	ANDRETTI 260	OP	CUD	FBG	DV	IO			8	6	4750	2	7	**	**
25	10	ANDRETTI 260	OP	CUD	FBG	DV	IO	T		8	6	5650	3	2	**	**
28	4	SPORT CRUISER 260	OP	SPTCR	FBG	DV	IO			8	6	6000	3	5	**	**
28	4	SPORT CRUISER 260	OP	SPTCR	FBG	DV	IO	T		8	6	6000	3	5	**	**
29	8	SPORT CRUISER 270	OP	SPTCR	FBG	DV	IO			9	9	6900	3	7	**	**
29	8	SPORT CRUISER 270	OP	SPTCR	FBG	DV	IO	T		9	9	7800	3	7	**	**
31	7	SPORT CRUISER 290	OP	SPTCR	FBG	DV	IO			10	4	7400	3	10	**	**
31	7	SPORT CRUISER 290	OP	SPTCR	FBG	DV	IO	T		10	4	8300	3	10	**	**
		1989 BOATS														
18	1	BOW RIDER 181	ST	RNBT	FBG	DV	IO	120	MRCR	7	2	2275	2	3	3000	3500
18	1	CUDDY CABIN 181	ST	RNBT	FBG	DV	IO	120	MRCR	7	2	2275	2	3	3150	3650
18	2	BOW RIDER 182	ST	RNBT	FBG	DV	IO	120	MRCR	7	8	2900	2	5	3400	3950
18	2	SE BOW RIDER 182	ST	RNBT	FBG	DV	IO	120	MRCR	7	8	2900	2	5	3950	4600
18	7	BOW RIDER 187	ST	RNBT	FBG	DV	IO	120	MRCR	7	8	2900	2	5	3450	4000
18	7	SE BOW RIDER 187	ST	RNBT	FBG	DV	IO	120	MRCR	7	8	2900	2	5	4050	4700
19	2	BOW RIDER 192	ST	RNBT	FBG	DV	IO	120	MRCR	8		3050	2	6	3900	4550
19	2	CUDDY CABIN 192	ST	CUD	FBG	DV	IO	120	MRCR	8		3050	2	6	4050	4700
19	2	SE BOW RIDER 192	ST	RNBT	FBG	DV	IO	120	MRCR	8		3050	2	6	4250	4950
19	2	SE CUDDY CABIN 192	ST	CUD	FBG	DV	IO	120	MRCR	8		3050	2	6	4450	5150
19	9	BOW RIDER 199	ST	RNBT	FBG	DV	IO	120	MRCR	8		3050	2	6	4000	4650
19	9	CUDDY CABIN 199	ST	CUD	FBG	DV	IO	120	MRCR	8		3050	2	6	4200	4850
19	9	SE BOW RIDER 199	ST	RNBT	FBG	DV	IO	120	MRCR	8		3050	2	6	4450	5100
19	9	SE CUDDY CABIN 199	ST	CUD	FBG	DV	IO	120	MRCR	8		3050	2	6	4600	5300
20	8	BOW RIDER 208	ST	RNBT	FBG	DV	IO	165	MRCR	8		3325	2	7	4750	5450
20	8	CUDDY CABIN 208	ST	CUD	FBG	DV	IO	165	MRCR	8		3325	2	7	5000	5750
20	8	SE BOW RIDER 208	ST	RNBT	FBG	DV	IO	165	MRCR	8		3325	2	7	5100	5900
20	8	SE CUDDY CABIN 208	ST	CUD	FBG	DV	IO	165	MRCR	8		3325	2	7	5350	6150
21	5	BOW RIDER 215	ST	RNBT	FBG	DV	IO	165	MRCR	8		3325	2	7	4900	5650
21	5	CUDDY CABIN 215	ST	CUD	FBG	DV	IO	165	MRCR	8		3325	2	7	5400	6200
21	5	SE BOW RIDER 215	ST	RNBT	FBG	DV	IO	165	MRCR	8		3325	2	7	5300	6100
21	5	SE CUDDY CABIN 215	OP	CUD	FBG	DV	IO	165	MRCR	8		3325	2	7	5400	6200
22	4	SE BOW RIDER 224	OP	RNBT	FBG	DV	IO	165	MRCR	8		3700	2	8	5750	6600
22	4	SE CUDDY CABIN 224	OP	CUD	FBG	DV	IO	165	MRCR	8		3700	2	8	6100	7000
23	1	SE BOW RIDER 231	OP	RNBT	FBG	DV	IO	165	MRCR	8		3700	2	8	5950	6850
23	1	SE CUDDY CABIN 231	OP	CUD	FBG	DV	IO	165	MRCR	8		3700	2	8	6350	7300
25	9	ANDRETTI 259	OP	SPTCR	FBG	DV	IO	330	MRCR	8	6	4950	3	5	10300	11700
25	9	SPORT CRUISER 257	OP	SPTCR	FBG	DV	IO	330	MRCR	8	6	5700	3	5	11100	12600
26	8	SPORT CRUISER 268	OP	SPTCR	FBG	DV	IO	260	MRCR	9	9	7500	3	7	13100	14900
28	5	SPORT CRUISER 285	OP	SPTCR	FBG	DV	IO	260	MRCR	10	4	8000	3	10	14200	16200
		1988 BOATS														
18		CHAMPIONLINE 180VBR	ST	RNBT	FBG	DV	IO	120	MRCR	7	2	2000	2	3	2700	3150
18		CHAMPNLN 180VBR S/S	ST	RNBT	FBG	DV	IO	130	MRCR	7	2	2000	2	3	2700	3150
18	10	CHAMPIONLINE 190VBR	ST	RNBT	FBG	DV	IO	130	MRCR	7	8	2150	2	5	3050	3550
18	10	CHAMPNLN 190VBR S/S	ST	RNBT	FBG	DV	IO	165	MRCR	7	8	2200	2	5	2850	3300
18	10	CROWNLINE 190VBR	ST	RNBT	FBG	DV	IO	165	MRCR	7	8	2200	2	5	3400	3950
18	10	CROWNLINE 190VBR S/S	ST	RNBT	FBG	DV	IO	200	MRCR	7	8	2450	2	5	3350	3850
20	3	CHAMPIONLINE 210VBR	ST	CUD	FBG	DV	IO	175	MRCR	8		2650	2	6	4150	4850
20	3	CHAMPIONLINE 210VCC	ST	RNBT	FBG	DV	IO	200	MRCR	8		2850	2	6	4200	4850
20	3	CROWNLINE 210VBR	ST	RNBT	FBG	DV	IO	175	MRCR	8		2900	2	6	4200	4850
20	3	CROWNLINE 210VCC	ST	CUD	FBG	DV	IO	260	MRCR	8		2950	2	6	4700	5400
20	3	CROWNLINE 210VCC S/S	ST	CUD	FBG	DV	IO	200	MRCR	8		2950	2	6	4500	5200
21	6	CHAMPIONLINE 230VBR	ST	RNBT	FBG	DV	IO	200	MRCR	8		3200	2	7	4800	5500
21	6	CHAMPIONLINE 230VCC	ST	CUD	FBG	DV	IO	230	MRCR	8		3250	2	7	5150	5950

CONTINUED ON NEXT PAGE

LOA FT	LOA IN	NAME AND/ OR MODEL	TOP/ RIG	BOAT TYPE	-HULL- MTL	-HULL- TP	ENGINE TP	ENGINE # HP	ENGINE MFG	BEAM FT	BEAM IN	WGT LBS	DRAFT FT	DRAFT IN	RETAIL LOW	RETAIL HIGH
		1988 BOATS														
21	6	CROWNLINE 230VBR	ST	RNBT	FBG	DV	IO	200	MRCR	8		3300	2	7	4900	5600
21	6	CROWNLINE 230VCC	ST	CUD	FBG	DV	IO	230	MRCR	8		3350	2	7	5250	6050
21	6	CROWNLINE 230VCC S/S	OP	CUD	FBG	DV	IO	260	MRCR	8		3350	2	7	5400	6200
22	5	CROWNLINE 250VBR	OP	RNBT	FBG	DV	IO	260	MRCR	8		3900	2	8	5950	6800
22	5	CROWNLINE 250VBR S/S	OP	RNBT	FBG	DV	IO	365	MRCR	8		3900	2	8	7100	8150
22	5	CROWNLINE 250VCC	ST	CUD	FBG	DV	IO	260	MRCR	8		3900	2	8	6300	7200
22	5	CROWNLINE 250VCC	ST	CUD	FBG	DV	IO	330	MRCR	8		3900	2	8	6950	8000
26	2	CROWNLINE 26 CRUISER	OP	CBNCR	FBG	DV	IO	330	MRCR	9	4	6500	2	4	14100	16000
26	2	CROWNLINE 26 CRUISER	OP	CBNCR	FBG	DV	IO	T260	MRCR	9	4	7500	2	4	15700	17900
		1987 BOATS														
16	10	CALAIS 175VBR	ST	RNBT	FBG	DV	IO	120	MRCR	7	8	2250		11	2650	3100
16	10	CELEBRITY 175VBR	ST	RNBT	FBG	DV	IO	130	MRCR	7	8	2350		11	2750	3200
18		CALAIS 183VBR	ST	RNBT	FBG	DV	IO	130	MRCR	7	8	2500	1		3000	3500
18		CELEBRITY 183VBR	ST	RNBT	FBG	DV	IO	165	MRCR	7	8	2600	1		3100	3600
18		CELEBRITY 183VBR S/S	ST	RNBT	FBG	DV	IO	200	MRCR	7	8	2600	1		3150	3650
19		CALAIS 190VBR	ST	RNBT	FBG	DV	IO	165	MRCR	8		2775	1	1	3450	4050
19		CALAIS 190VCC	ST	CUD	FBG	DV	IO	180	MRCR	8		2825	1	1	3650	4250
19		CELEBRITY 190VBR	ST	RNBT	FBG	DV	IO	205	MRCR	8		2825	1	1	3550	4100
19		CELEBRITY 190VBR S/S	ST	RNBT	FBG	DV	IO	230	MRCR	8		2825	1	1	3600	4200
19		CELEBRITY 190VCC	ST	CUD	FBG	DV	IO	200	MRCR	8		2875	1	1	3700	4300
21		CALAIS 210VBR	ST	RNBT	FBG	DV	IO	200	MRCR	8		3250	1	2	4500	5200
21		CALAIS 210VCC	ST	CUD	FBG	DV	IO	230	MRCR	8		3300	1	2	4850	5550
21		CELEBRITY 210VBR	ST	RNBT	FBG	DV	IO	230	MRCR	8		3300	1	2	4650	5300
21		CELEBRITY 210VBR S/S	ST	RNBT	FBG	DV	IO	260	MRCR	8		3300	1	2	4750	5450
21		CELEBRITY 210VCC	ST	CUD	FBG	DV	IO	230	MRCR	8		3350	1	2	4900	5600
22	5	CELEBRITY 225VBR	OP	RNBT	FBG	DV	IO	260	MRCR	8		3900	1	3	5650	6500
22	5	CELEBRITY 225VBR S/S	OP	RNBT	FBG	DV	IO		MRCR	8		3900	1	3	**	**
22	5	CELEBRITY 225VBR S/S	OP	RNBT	FBG	DV	IO	T205	MRCR	8		4500	1	3	6800	7850
22	5	CELEBRITY 225VCC	ST	CUD	FBG	DV	IO	230	MRCR	8		3900	1	3	5850	6700
22	5	CELEBRITY 225VCC S/S	ST	CUD	FBG	DV	IO	260	MRCR	8		3900	1	3	5950	6850
22	5	CELEBRITY 225VCC S/S	ST	CUD	FBG	DV	IO	T180-T205		8		4500	1	3	7150	8300
26	2	CROWNLINE 26 CRUISER	OP	CBNCR	FBG	DV	IO		MRCR	9	4	6500	1	5	**	**
26	2	CROWNLINE 26 CRUISER	OP	CBNCR	FBG	DV	IO	T260	MRCR	9	4	7500	1	5	15000	17000
		1986 BOATS														
16	10	CALAIS 170VBR	ST	RNBT	FBG	DV	IO	120	MRCR	7	6	2050		11	2400	2800
16	10	CELEBRITY 170VBR	ST	RNBT	FBG	DV	IO	140	MRCR	7	6	2200		11	2500	2900
18		CALAIS 180VBR	ST	RNBT	FBG	DV	IO	140	MRCR	7	8	2350		1	2800	3250
18		CELEBRITY 180VBR	ST	RNBT	FBG	DV	IO	170	MRCR	7	8	2450		1	2850	3350
18		CELEBRITY 180VBR S/S	ST	RNBT	FBG	DV	IO	200	MRCR	7	8	2450		1	2900	3350
19		CALAIS 190VBR	ST	RNBT	FBG	DV	IO	170	MRCR	8		2550		1	3150	3700
19		CALAIS 190VCC	ST	CUD	FBG	DV	IO	190	MRCR	8		2600		1	3350	3850
19		CELEBRITY 190VBR	ST	RNBT	FBG	DV	IO	205	MRCR	8		2650		1	3250	3800
19		CELEBRITY 190VBR S/S	ST	RNBT	FBG	DV	IO	230	MRCR	8		2825		1	3450	4000
19		CELEBRITY 190VCC	ST	CUD	FBG	DV	IO	200	MRCR	8		2700		1	3400	3950
21		CALAIS 210VBR	ST	RNBT	FBG	DV	IO	200	MRCR	8		3100		1	4150	4800
21		CALAIS 210VCC	ST	CUD	FBG	DV	IO	230	MRCR	8		3300		1	4650	5350
21		CELEBRITY 210VBR	ST	RNBT	FBG	DV	IO	230	MRCR	8		3300		1	4400	5100
21		CELEBRITY 210VBR S/S	ST	RNBT	FBG	DV	IO	260	MRCR	8		3300		1	4550	5200
21		CELEBRITY 210VCC	ST	CUD	FBG	DV	IO	230	MRCR	8		3350		1	4700	5400
22	5	CELEBRITY 225VCC	ST	CUD	FBG	DV	IO	230	MRCR	8		3900		1	5600	6400
22	5	CELEBRITY 225VCC S/S	ST	CUD	FBG	DV	IO	260	MRCR	8		4075		1	5900	6750
22	5	CELEBRITY 225VCC S/S	ST	CUD	FBG	DV	IO	T190-T205		8		4500	1	3	6850	8200
		1985 BOATS														
16	10	CALAIS 170VBR	ST	RNBT	FBG	DV	IO	120	MRCR	7	6	2200		11	2400	2750
16	10	CELEBRITY 170VBR	ST	RNBT	FBG	DV	IO	140	MRCR	7	6	2200		11	2400	2800
18		CALAIS 180VBR	ST	RNBT	FBG	DV	IO	140	MRCR	7	8	2450	1	2	2750	3150
18		CELEBRITY 180VBR	ST	RNBT	FBG	DV	IO	170	MRCR	7	8	2450	1	2	2750	3200
18		CELEBRITY 180VBR S/S	ST	RNBT	FBG	DV	IO	200	MRCR	7	8	2450	1	2	2800	3250
19		CALAIS 190VBR	ST	RNBT	FBG	DV	IO	170	MRCR	8		2825	1	3	3200	3750
19		CALAIS 190VCC	ST	CUD	FBG	DV	IO	190	MRCR	8		2875	1	3	3400	3950
19		CELEBRITY 190VBR	ST	RNBT	FBG	DV	IO	205	MRCR	8		2825	1	3	3250	3800
19		CELEBRITY 190VBR S/S	ST	RNBT	FBG	DV	IO	230	MRCR	8		2825	1	1	3300	3850
19		CELEBRITY 190VCC	ST	CUD	FBG	DV	IO	200	MRCR	8		2875	1	3	3400	3950
21		CALAIS 210VBR	ST	RNBT	FBG	DV	IO	200	MRCR	8		3300	1	4	4150	4800
21		CALAIS 210VCC	ST	CUD	FBG	DV	IO	230	MRCR	8		3350	1	4	4250	4950
21		CELEBRITY 210VBR	ST	RNBT	FBG	DV	IO	230	MRCR	8		3300	1	4	4200	4900
21		CELEBRITY 210VBR S/S	ST	RNBT	FBG	DV	IO	260	MRCR	8		3300	1	2	4350	5000
21		CELEBRITY 210VCC	ST	CUD	FBG	DV	IO	230	MRCR	8		3350	1	4	4700	5400
22	5	CELEBRITY 225V	ST	CBNCR	FBG	DV	IO	260	MRCR	8		4500	1	5	6800	7800
22	5	CELEBRITY 225VCC	ST	CUD	FBG	DV	IO	230	MRCR	8		3900	1	5	5350	6150
22	5	CELEBRITY 225VCC S/S	ST	CUD	FBG	DV	IO	260	MRCR	8		3900	1	5	5450	6300
		1984 BOATS														
16	10	170V BOW RIDER	ST	RNBT	FBG	SV	IO	140	MRCR	7	6	2200		11	2350	2700
17	6	176V BOW RIDER	ST	RNBT	FBG	SV	IO	140-228		7	8	2400	1		2550	3050
18	8	188V BOW RIDER	ST	RNBT	FBG	SV	IO	198-260		8		2750	1	1	3050	3700
18	8	188V CUDDY	ST	CUD	FBG	SV	IO	228-260		8		2800	1	1	3200	3900
20	5	210V BOW RIDER	ST	RNBT	FBG	SV	IO	228-260		8		3250	1	2	3900	4650
20	5	210V CUDDY	ST	CUD	FBG	SV	IO	228-260		8		3300	1	2	4100	4950
22	5	225V CRUISER	ST	CR	FBG	SV	IO	228-260		8		3950	1	3	5200	6150
22	5	225V CUDDY	ST	CUD	FBG	SV	IO	228-260		8		3600	1	3	4900	5750

....For earlier years, see the BUC Used Boat Price Guide, Volume 3

CELESTIAL YACHT LTD

GEMCRAFT LTD
KOWLOON HONG KONG COAST GUARD MFG ID- CYH

See inside cover to adjust price for area

LOA FT	LOA IN	NAME AND/ OR MODEL	TOP/ RIG	BOAT TYPE	-HULL- MTL	-HULL- TP	ENGINE TP	ENGINE # HP	ENGINE MFG	BEAM FT	BEAM IN	WGT LBS	DRAFT FT	DRAFT IN	RETAIL LOW	RETAIL HIGH
		1985 BOATS														
44		CELESTIAL 44	KTH	SA/CR	F/S	KL	IB	61D		13	2	25000	5	6	89500	98400
48		CELESTIAL 48	KTH	SA/CR	F/S	KL	IB	61D	LEHM	13	6	27000	6		113500	124500

....For earlier years, see the BUC Used Boat Price Guide, Volume 3

CENTURY BOAT COMPANY

C & C MANUFACTURING INC
PANAMA CITY FL 32404 COAST GUARD MFG ID- CGM

See inside cover to adjust price for area

For more recent years, see the BUC Used Boat Price Guide, Volume 1

LOA FT	LOA IN	NAME AND/ OR MODEL	TOP/ RIG	BOAT TYPE	-HULL- MTL	-HULL- TP	ENGINE TP	ENGINE # HP	ENGINE MFG	BEAM FT	BEAM IN	WGT LBS	DRAFT FT	DRAFT IN	RETAIL LOW	RETAIL HIGH
		1996 BOATS														
17		1720 CC	OP	CTRCN	FBG	SV	OB			6	8	1283		8	3500	4050
17	7	RESORTER	OP	RNBT	FBG	SV	IO	250	MRCR			1400	2		4800	5550
18	5	1800 CC	OP	CTRCN	FBG	SV	OB			7		1700		11	4500	5150
18	6	INTRACOASTAL 1860	OP	CTRCN	FBG	SV	OB			8		1600		10	4250	4950
18	9	ARABIAN 190	OP	B/R	FBG	SV	IO	135-180		7	11	1690	1	3	5100	6000
18	9	ARABIAN 190 XL	OP	B/R	FBG	SV	IO	135-180		7	11	1690	1	3	5200	6000
20		1900 CC	OP	CTRCN	FBG	SV	OB			8		2000	1	2	6950	8000
21	3	ARABIAN 210	OP	B/R	FBG	SV	IO	180-250		8		1950	1	8	5900	7100
21	3	ARABIAN 210 XL	OP	B/R	FBG	SV	IO	180-250		8		1950	1	8	6000	7250
21	8	2280 TL	OP	CTRCN	FBG	SV	OB			8		2168		6	8200	9450
21	8	2280 TL	OP	CTRCN	FBG	TH	OB			8		2168		6	8500	9800
21	8	2290 CC	OP	CTRCN	FBG	SV	OB			8		2168		10	7750	8900
21	8	INTRACOASTAL 2180	OP	CTRCN	FBG	SV	OB			8		2146		10	8100	9300
21	11	CORONADO	OP	RNBT	FBG	SV	IB	250-310		7	11	3065	2	4	9700	11300
22		2001 CC	OP	CTRCN	FBG	SV	OB			8	3	2200	1	2	8350	9600
22		2100 CC	OP	CTRCN	FBG	SV	OB			8	3	2200	1	2	7700	8800
22		2100 DC	OP	B/R	FBG	SV	OB			8	3	2300	1	2	7900	9100
22		2100 WA	OP	FSH	FBG	SV	OB			8	3	2200	1	2	7700	8850
23	6	ARABIAN 240	OP	B/R	FBG	SV	IO	235-250		8	9	2790	1	8	8400	10100
23	6	ARABIAN 240	OP	B/R	FBG	SV	IO	265-300		8	9	2790	1	8	9400	10700
23	6	ARABIAN 240 CUDDY	OP	CUD	FBG	SV	IO	235-300		8	9	2790	1	8	9050	11000
23	6	ARABIAN 240 CUDDY	OP	CUD	FBG	SV	IO	385	MRCR	8	9	2790	1	8	11900	13500
23	6	ARABIAN 240 CUDDY XL	OP	CUD	FBG	SV	IO	235-300		8	9	2790	1	8	9150	11200
23	6	ARABIAN 240 CUDDY XL	OP	CUD	FBG	SV	IO	385	MRCR	8	9	2790	1	8	12000	13700
23	6	ARABIAN 240 XL	OP	B/R	FBG	SV	IO	235-300		8	9	2790	1	8	8500	10500
23	6	ARABIAN 240 XL	OP	B/R	FBG	SV	IO	385	MRCR	8	9	2790	1	8	11200	12700
24	7	2200 CC	OP	CTRCN	FBG	SV	OB			8	6	3200	1	2	11500	13100
24	7	2200 WA	OP	FSH	FBG	SV	OB			8	6	3200	1	2	11700	13200
24	7	2300 CC	OP	CTRCN	FBG	SV	OB			8	6	3200	1	2	11900	13600
25	3	2400 CC	OP	CTRCN	FBG	SV	OB			8	6	3400	1	6	12200	13900
25	3	2400 WA	OP	FSH	FBG	SV	OB			8	6	4000	1	6	15000	17000
25	3	2500 CC	OP	CTRCN	FBG	SV	OB			8	6	3400	1	6	14100	16100
27	6	2600 CC	OP	CTRCN	FBG	SV	OB			8	9	3650	1	6	15800	17900
27	6	2600 WA	OP	FSH	FBG	SV	OB			8	9	4250	1	5	13700	15600
30	11	3000 CC	OP	CTRCN	FBG	SV	OB			9	8	5500	1	8	27300	30300
		1995 BOATS														
17		INTRACOASTAL 1720	OP	CTRCN	FBG	SV	OB			6	8	1283		9	3300	3850
17	7	RESORTER	OP	RNBT	FBG	SV	IB	250	MRCR	7		2429	2		6400	7350
18	5	1800CC	OP	CTRCN	FBG	SV	OB			7		1700		11	4200	4900
18	6	INTRACOASTAL 1860	OP	CTRCN	FBG	SV	OB			8		1600		10	4050	4700
18	9	ARABIAN 19	OP	B/R	FBG	SV	IO	135-180		7	10	1690	1	3	4750	5550
20	9	2000CC	OP	CTRCN	FBG	SV	OB			8	3	2200	1	2	7450	8550
21	3	ARABIAN 21	OP	B/R	FBG	SV	IO	205-250		8		1950	1	8	5700	6800
21	8	INTRACOASTAL 2180	OP	CTRCN	FBG	SV	OB			8		2146		10	7700	8850
21	8	INTRACOASTAL 2280	OP	CTRCN	FBG	TH	OB			8		2168		6	7750	8900

CENTURY BOAT COMPANY -CONTINUED See inside cover to adjust price for area

LOA FT	LOA IN	NAME AND/ OR MODEL	TOP/ RIG	BOAT TYPE	HULL MTL	HULL TP	ENGINE TP	ENGINE # HP	ENGINE MFG	BEAM FT	BEAM IN	WGT LBS	DRAFT FT	DRAFT IN	RETAIL LOW	RETAIL HIGH
		1995 BOATS														
21	11	CORONADO	OP	RNBT	FBG	SV	IB	250-310		7	11	3059	2	4	9200	10700
22		2001 CC	OP	CTRCN	FBG	SV	OB			8	3	2350	1	2	8400	9650
22		2100 DC	OP	B/R	FBG	SV	OB			8	3	2400	1	2	8550	9800
23	6	ARABIAN 24	OP	B/R	FBG	SV	IO	235-300		8	9	2840	1	8	7950	9850
23	6	ARABIAN 24	OP	CUD	FBG	SV	IO	300	MRCR	8	9	2840			9250	10500
24	7	2200 CC	OP	CTRCN	FBG	SV	OB			8	6	3200	1	2	12000	13600
24	7	2200 WA	OP	FSH	FBG	SV	OB			8	6	3800	1	1	13400	15200
24	7	2300 CC	OP	CTRCN	FBG	SV	OB			8	6	3200	1	2	12000	13600
25	3	2400 CC	OP	CTRCN	FBG	SV	OB			8	6	3400	1	6	13200	15000
25	3	2400 WA	OP	FSH	FBG	SV	OB			8	6	4000	1	6	14300	16200
25	3	2500 CC	OP	CTRCN	FBG	SV	OB			8	6	3400	1	6	13200	15000
25	3	ANTIGUA 240	OP	CUD	FBG	SV	IO	235-300		8	9	4469	1	9	12500	15200
29	1	ANTIGUA 280	OP	CR	FBG	SV	IO	300	MRCR	9	10	6753	2		20400	22600
29	1	ANTIGUA 280	OP	CR	FBG	SV	IO	T160-T190		9	10	6753	2		20800	23800
30	11	3000 CC	OP	CTRCN	FBG	SV	OB			9	8	5500	1	8	31000	34400
		1994 BOATS														
17		INTRACOASTAL 1720	OP	CTRCN	FBG	SV	OB			6	8	1283			3150	3700
17	2	170 BR	OP	RNBT	FBG	SV	OB			7	2	1355			3350	3850
17	2	180 BR	OP	B/R	FBG	SV	IO	110	YAMA	7	6	2263			4400	5050
17	7	RESORTER 18	OP	RNBT	FBG	SV	IB	235	MRCR	7		2429			6000	6900
18	5	1800	OP	CTRCN	FBG	SV	OB			7		1700			4000	4650
18	6	1860	OP	CTRCN	FBG	SV	OB			8		1600			3850	4500
18	8	190 BR	OP	B/R	FBG	SV	IO	110	YAMA	7	6	2288			4850	5550
18	8	190 CUDDY	OP	CUD	FBG	SV	IO	110	YAMA	7	8	2405			5400	6200
20	6	2000	OP	CTRCN	FBG	SV	OB			8	3	2200			7000	8050
20	6	2100DL	OP	CTRCN	FBG	SV	OB			8	3	2300			7200	8250
20	11	210 BR	OP	B/R	FBG	SV	IO	210	YAMA	8		3203			6650	7650
20	11	210 CUDDY	OP	CUD	FBG	SV	IO	210	YAMA	8		3353			7300	8400
21	8	INTRACOASTAL 2180	OP	CTRCN	FBG	SV	OB			8		2146			7350	8450
21	11	CORONADO	OP	RNBT	FBG	SV	IB	320	MRCR	7	11	3059			9000	10200
22	6	ARROW 230 BR	OP	B/R	FBG	SV	IO	210	YAMA	7	8	2813			6550	7550
22	6	ARROW 230 CUDDY	OP	CUD	FBG	SV	IO	210	YAMA	7	8	2923			7150	8250
23		2200 WA	OP	CUD	FBG	SV	OB			8	6				8900	10100
23	4	232 BR	OP	B/R	FBG	SV	IO	240	YAMA	8	6	3953			9150	10400
23	4	232 CUDDY	OP	CUD	FBG	SV	IO	240	YAMA	8	6	4153			10000	11400
24	7	2200	OP	CTRCN	FBG	SV	OB			8	6	3200			11400	13000
25	3	2400 W/PULPIT	OP	CTRCN	FBG	SV	OB			8	6	3400			12600	14300
25	3	2400 WA W/PULPIT	OP	CUD	FBG	SV	OB			8	6	4000			13600	15500
25	3	ANTIGUA 240	OP	CR	FBG	SV	IO	210	YAMA	8	9	4469			11500	13100
29	1	ANTIGUA 280	OP	CR	FBG	SV	IO	300	YAMA	9	10	6753			19100	21300
		1993 BOATS														
17	6	180 LX	OP	RNBT	FBG	SV	IO	110		7	5	2263			4400	5050
17	7	RESORTER 18	OP	RNBT	FBG	SV	IB	235	MRCR	7		2429			5700	6550
18	4	190 LX BR	OP	RNBT	FDG	SV	IO	110		7	6	2288			4650	5350
18	4	190 LX CD	OP	RNBT	FBG	SV	IO	110		7	5	2338			4650	5350
19	1	ARABIAN CARDELL	OP	RNBT	FBG	SV	IO	240		7	2	2819			5550	6350
19	6	MUSTANG CLX	OP	CUD	FBG	SV	IO	180	YAMA	7	5	2663			5550	6400
19	6	MUSTANG CLX	OP	RNBT	FBG	SV	IO	180	MRCR	7	5	2663			5350	6150
19	6	MUSTANG LX	OP	RNBT	FBG	SV	IO	180		7	5	2563			5250	6050
20	11	210 LX	OP	B/R	FBG	SV	IO	210		8		3203			6200	7150
21		210 CLX	OP	CUD	FBG	SV	IO	210		8		3353			6850	7900
21	11	CORONADO	OP	RNBT	FBG	SV	IB	320	MRCR	7	11	3059			8350	9600
21	11	CORONADO	OP	RNBT	FBG	SV	IB	320	YAMA	7	11	3059			10700	12100
21	11	CORONADO CARDEL	OP	RNBT	FBG	SV	IO	300		7	11	3353			7450	8550
21	11	CORONADO LTD	OP	RNBT	FBG	SV	IB	320	MRCR	7	11	3059			8650	9950
22	6	ARROW 230 BR	OP	RNBT	FBG	SV	IO	180		7	8	2813			6150	7050
22	6	ARROW 230 CC	OP	CUD	FBG	SV	IO	180		7	8	2923			6650	7600
25	3	ANTIGUA 235	OP	CR	FBG	SV	IO		MRCR	8	6	4469			**	**
25	3	ANTIGUA 235	OP	CR	FBG	SV	IO		YAMA	8	6	4469			**	**
29	1	ANTIGUA 275	OP	CR	FBG	SV	IO	260		9	10	6753			17000	19300
		1992 BOATS														
17	6	180 LX	OP	RNBT	FBG	SV	IO	130	MRCR	7	6	1700			3600	4200
17	7	RESORTER 18	OP	RNBT	FBG	SV	IO	260	MRCR	7		1510	2	1	3700	4300
18	4	190 LX		RNBT	FBG	SV	IO	115	MRCR	7	6	2325			4400	5050
19	1	ARABIAN	OP	RNBT	FBG	SV	IO	260	MRCR	7	3	1900	2	3	4450	5150
19	6	MUSTANG II CLX	OP	CUD	FBG	SV	IO	125	MRCR	7	4	2050			4500	5200
19	6	MUSTANG II LX	OP	RNBT	FBG	SV	IO	125	MRCR	7	4	1400	2	2	3900	4500
19	8	RIVIERA 6 METER	OP	RNBT	FBG	SV	IO	260	MRCR	7	4	1375	2	3	4300	5000
19	9	2500 LX	OP	RNBT	FBG	DV	IO	260	MRCR	8		2000	2	1	5000	5750
21		210 LX	OP	RNBT	FBG	SV	IO	260	MRCR	8		2300			5200	6000
21	1	CTS	OP	RNBT	FBG	SV	IO	260	MRCR	7	6	1707	2	2	4650	5350
21	6	SABRE	OP	RNBT	FBG	SV	IO	260	MRCR	8		2000	2	3	5100	5850
21	10	CORONADO	OP	RNBT	FBG	SV	IO	340	MRCR	7	11	2140	2	2	6200	7150
21	10	CORONADO CARDEL	OP	RNBT	FBG	SV	IO	260	MRCR	7	11	2200	2	2	5300	6100
22	6	230 ARROW		RNBT	FBG	SV	IO	155	MRCR	7	7	2792			5650	6500
22	10	ULTRA I	OP	RNBT	FBG	DV	IO	260	MRCR	8		1860	2		5350	6150
23	4	4500 CLX	OP	CUD	FBG	SV	IO	260	MRCR	8	6	3000	2	8	7150	8250
23	4	4500 LX	OP	RNBT	FBG	SV	IO	260	MRCR	8	6	3000	2	8	6750	7750
25		5500 CLX	OP	CUD	FBG	SV	IO	260	MRCR	8	6	3485	2	8	8900	10100
25	5	ARUBA	OP	CR	FBG	SV	IO	260	MRCR	8		3720	2	8	9400	10700
27		MIRADA XL	OP	CR	FBG	SV	IO	260	MRCR	8		4453	2	10	11700	13300
27	2	ULTRA II	OP	OFF	FBG	DV	IO	T260	MRCR	8		3286	2	3	12900	14700
27	3	ANTIGUA 275	OP	CR	FBG	SV	IO	260	MRCR	9	8	5600	1	6	13700	15600
29	7	MERIDIAN XL	OP	CR	FBG	SV	IO	260	MRCR	8		5650	2	10	14500	16500
30	2	MIRAMAR XL	OP	CR	FBG	SV	IO	T175	MRCR	10	1	7440	2	10	18600	20700
31		ULTRA III	OP	OFF	FBG	DV	IO	T260	MRCR	8	4	3788	2	3	21100	23400
32	5	GRANDE 330	OP	CR	FBG	SV	VD	T260	MRCR	10	6	8660	2	10	31000	34400
36		GRANDE 360	OP	CR	FBG	SV	VD	T340	MRCR	13	3	13000	3	4	48300	53100
		1991 BOATS														
17	1	FURY	OP	RNBT	FBG	DV	IO	125		7		1200	2	2	2800	3250
17	7	RESORTER 18	OP	RNBT	FBG	SV	IO	260		7		1510	2	1	3450	4000
17	10	2000 BR	OP	RNBT	FBG	SV	IO	175		7	7	1900	2	1	3650	4250
18	4	180 LX	OP	RNBT	FBG	SV	IO	130		7	6	1700			3600	4150
18	11	3000 BR	OP	RNBT	FBG	SV	IO	205		8		2100	2	1	4300	5000
19	1	ARABIAN	OP	RNBT	FBG	SV	IO	260		7	3	1900	2	3	4150	4800
19	2	MUSTANG CLX	OP	CUD	FBG	SV	IO	125		7	4	1750	2	2	3850	4450
19	2	MUSTANG LX	OP	RNBT	FBG	SV	IO	125		7		1400	2	2	3450	4000
19	6	MUSTANG II CLX	OP	CUD	FBG	SV	IO	125		7	4	2050			4150	4850
19	6	MUSTANG II LX	OP	RNBT	FBG	SV	IO	125		7	4	1400	2	2	3650	4250
19	8	RIVIERA 6 METER	OP	RNBT	FBG	SV	IO	205		7	4	1375	2	3	3800	4400
19	9	2500 LX	OP	RNBT	FBG	DV	IO	175		8		2000	2	1	4400	5050
20	10	3500 CLX	OP	CUD	FBG	DV	IO	200		8		2500	2	2	5000	5750
20	10	3500 LX	OP	RNBT	FBG	DV	IO	200		8		2200	2	2	4550	5250
20	10	4000 CC	OP	CUD	FBG	SV	IO	205		8		2600	2	8	5100	5900
21		210 LX	OP	RNBT	FBG	SV	IO	175		8		2300			4650	5350
21	1	CTS	OP	RNBT	FBG	SV	IO	260		7	6	1707	2	2	4350	5000
21	6	SABRE	OP	RNBT	FBG	SV	IO	260		8		2000	2	3	4750	5500
21	10	CORONADO	OP	RNBT	FBG	SV	IO	340		7	11	2140	2	2	5850	6700
21	10	CORONADO CARDEL	OP	RNBT	FBG	SV	IO	260		7	11	2200	2	2	5000	5700
22	10	ULTRA I	OP	RNBT	FBG	DV	IO	260		8		1860	2		5000	5750
23	4	4500 CLX	OP	CUD	FBG	SV	IO	260		8	6	3000	2	8	6700	7700
23	4	4500 LX	OP	RNBT	FBG	SV	IO	260		8	6	3000	2	8	6300	7250
25		5500 CLX	OP	CUD	FBG	SV	IO	260		8	6	3485	2	8	8250	9500
25	5	ARUBA	OP	CR	FBG	SV	IO	260		8		3720	2	8	8850	10000
27		MIRADA XL	OP	CR	FBG	SV	IO	260		8		4453	2	10	11000	12500
27	2	ULTRA II	OP	OFF	FBG	DV	IO	T260		8		3286	2	3	12100	13800
27	3	ANTIGUA 275	OP	CR	FBG	SV	IO	260		9	8	5600	1	6	12800	14600
29	7	MERIDIAN XL	OP	CR	FBG	SV	IO	260		8		5650	2	10	13600	15500
30	2	MIRAMAR XL	OP	CR	FBG	SV	IO	T260		10	1	7440	2	10	18800	20900
31		ULTRA III	OP	OFF	FBG	DV	IO	T260		8	4	3788	2	3	19700	21900
32	5	GRANDE 330	OP	CR	FBG	SV	VD	T260		10	6	8660	2	10	29400	32700
36		GRANDE 360	OP	CR	FBG	SV	VD	T340		13	3	13000	3	4	46000	50500
		1990 BOATS														
16	1	FURY	OP	RNBT	FBG	DV	IO	125-151		7					2800	3500
17	7	RESORTER	OP	RNBT	FBG	SV	IO	260	MRCR	7					3700	4300
17	10	2000 BR	OP	RNBT	FBG	SV	IO	175-230		7	7				3650	4550
17	10	2000 BR	OP	RNBT	FBG	SV	IO	231-271		7	7				4000	4950
18	11	3000 BR	OP	RNBT	FBG	SV	IO	205-260		8					4400	5350
18	11	3000 BR	OP	RNBT	FBG	SV	IO	271	VLVO	8					4950	5650
19	1	ARABIAN	OP	RNBT	FBG	SV	IO	260-270		7	3				4400	5150
19	1	ARABIAN	OP	RNBT	FBG	SV	IO	330-340		7	3				5150	6000
19	1	MUSTANG LX	OP	RNBT	FBG	SV	IO	125-205		7			2	2	3950	4950
19	2	MUSTANG CLX	OP	CUD	FBG	SV	IO	125-205		7			2	2	4200	5250
19	8	6 METER	OP	RNBT	FBG	SV	IO	205-270		7	4				4500	5550
19	8	6 METER	OP	RNBT	FBG	SV	IO	271	VLVO	7	4				5100	5850
19	8	6 METER	OP	RNBT	FBG	SV	IO	311	VLVO	7	4				5550	6400
19	9	2500 LX	OP	RNBT	FBG	DV	IO	175-260		8					4700	5800
19	9	2500 LX	OP	RNBT	FBG	DV	IO	271	VLVO	8					5300	6100
20	10	3500 CLX	OP	CUD	FBG	DV	IO	200-271		8					5350	6550
20	10	3500 LX	OP	RNBT	FBG	SV	IO	200-270		8					4900	5950
20	10	3500 LX	OP	RNBT	FBG	SV	IO	271	VLVO	8					5450	6250
20	10	4000 CC	OP	CUD	FBG	SV	IO	205-260		8					5500	6750
20	10	4000 CC	OP	CUD	FBG	SV	IO	271-311		8					6000	7350
21	1	SABRE	OP	RNBT	FBG	SV	IB	260-340		7	6				6400	7750
21	6	SABRE	OP	RNBT	FBG	SV	IB	260-340		8					7350	8850
21	10	CORONADO CARDEL	OP	RNBT	FBG	SV	IO	260-270		7	11				5800	6750
21	10	CORONADO CARDEL	OP	RNBT	FBG	SV	IO	330-340		7	11				6500	7550

CONTINUED ON NEXT PAGE

LOA FT	LOA IN	NAME AND/ OR MODEL	TOP/ RIG	BOAT TYPE	-HULL- MTL	-HULL- TP	ENGINE TP	ENGINE # HP	ENGINE MFG	BEAM FT	BEAM IN	WGT LBS	DRAFT FT	DRAFT IN	RETAIL LOW	RETAIL HIGH
		1990 BOATS														
21	10	CORONADO CARDEL	OP	RNBT	FBG	SV	IO	365-370		7	11				7100	8150
22	10	ULTRA I	OP	RNBT	FBG	DV	IO	260-270		8					6400	7450
22	10	ULTRA I	OP	RNBT	FBG	DV	IO	330-370		8					7100	8850
23	4	4500 CLX	OP	CUD	FBG	SV	IO	260-271		8	6				7300	8800
23	4	4500 CLX	OP	CUD	FBG	SV	IO	311-370		8	6				8150	10000
23	4	4500 CLX	OP	CUD	FBG	SV	IO	371	VLVO	8	6				9400	10700
23	4	4500 LX	OP	RNBT	FBG	SV	IO	260-271		8	6				6700	8050
23	4	4500 LX	OP	RNBT	FBG	SV	IO	311-370		8	6				7450	9150
23	4	4500 LX	OP	RNBT	FBG	SV	IO	371	VLVO	8	6				8600	9900
25		5500 CLX	OP	CUD	FBG	SV	IO	260-311		8	6		2	8	9000	11100
25		5500 CLX	OP	CUD	FBG	SV	IO	330-370		8	6		2	8	9750	11800
25		5500 CLX	OP	CUD	FBG	SV	IO	371	VLVO	8	6		2	8	10900	12400
25	5	ARUBA XL 255	OP	CR	FBG	SV	IO	200-271		8					9350	11400
25	5	ARUBA XL 255	OP	CR	FBG	SV	IO	330-370		8					10500	12600
27	1	MIRADA XL 270	OP	CR	FBG	SV	IO	260-340		8					12600	15500
27	1	MIRADA XL 270	OP	CR	FBG	SV	IO	365-370		8					13900	15800
27	2	ULTRA II	OP	RNBT	FBG	DV	IO	260-340		8					9750	12000
27	2	ULTRA II	OP	RNBT	FBG	DV	IO	365-370		8					11000	12500
29	7	MERIDIEN XL 295	OP	CR	FBG	SV	IO	260-370		8					14100	17300
29	7	MERIDIEN XL 295	OP	CR	FBG	SV	IO	T171-T205		8					15000	17500
30	2	MIRAMAR XL 310	OP	CR	FBG	SV	IO	205-271		10	1				14900	17600
30	2	MIRAMAR XL 310	OP	CR	FBG	SV	IO	T175-T260		10	1				16100	19700
31		ULTRA III	OP	RNBT	FBG	DV	IO	260-370		8	4				13000	15600
32	5	GRANDE XL 330	OP	CR	FBG	SV	IO	T260-T330		10	6				23500	28000
36		GRANDE XL 360	OP	CR	FBG	SV	IO	T330	MRCR	13	3				26000	28900
36		GRANDE XL 360	OP	CR	FBG	SV	IO	T415	MRCR	13	3				28800	32000
		1989 BOATS														
16	1	FURY	ST	RNBT	FBG	DV	IO	120	MRCR	7		1050	2	2	2100	2500
17	7	RESORTER 18	OP	RNBT	FBG	SV	IB	260	MRCR	7		1510	2	1	3800	4400
17	10	CENTURY 2000 B/R	ST	RNBT	FBG	SV	IO	200-260		7	7	1900	2	1	3300	4100
18	1	BRONCO LTD	ST	RNBT	FBG	SV	IO	165	MRCR	7		1100	2	2	2700	3150
18	11	CENTURY 3000 B/R	ST	RNBT	FBG	SV	IO	200-260		8		2100	2	1	3800	4650
19	1	ARABIAN 200	OP	SKI	FBG	SV	IO	260	MRCR	7	3	1900	2	3	3550	4150
19	1	ARABIAN 200	OP	SKI	FBG	SV	VD	340	MRCR	7	3	1900	2	3	4800	5550
19	1	CENTURY 2500 SPT LX	ST	RNBT	FBG	SV	IO	200-260		8		2000	2	1	3750	4600
19	7	PALOMINO LTD	ST	RNBT	FBG	SV	IO	165	MRCR	7	4	1400	2	2	3250	3800
19	8	RIVIERA 6-METER	OP	SKI	FBG	SV	IO	200-260		7	4	1375	2	3	3200	4000
20	2	CENTURY 3500 SPT LX	ST	RNBT	FBG	SV	IO	200-260		8		2200	2	2	3850	4750
20	2	CENTURY 3500CC	ST	CUD	FBG	SV	IO	200-260		8		2500	2	2	4250	5200
20	10	CENTURY 4000CC	ST	CUD	FBG	SV	IO	200-260		8		2600	2	8	4550	5500
21	1	CTS	OP	SKI	FBG	SV	IB	260-340		7	6	1707	2	2	4750	5850
21	6	SABRE	ST	RNBT	FBG	SV	IB	260-340		8		2000	2	3	5400	6550
21	10	CORONADO 21	ST	RNBT	FBG	SV	IB	340	MRCR	7	11	2140	2	2	5900	6750
21	10	CORONADO-CARDEL	ST	RNBT	FBG	SV	IO	260	MRCR	7	11	2200	2	2	4450	5100
21	10	CORONADO-CARDEL	ST	RNBT	FBG	SV	IO	330	MRCR	7	11	2200	2	2	5050	5800
21	10	CORONADO-CARDEL	ST	RNBT	FBG	SV	VD	340	MRCR	7	11	2200	2	2	5950	6850
23	3	4500CLX	ST	CUD	FBG	SV	IO	260	MRCR	8	6	4000	2	8	7150	8200
23	3	4500CLX	ST	CUD	FBG	SV	IO	330-350		8	6	4000	2	8	7850	9350
25	2	MIRADA	OP	SPTCR	FBG	SV	IO	260	MRCR	8		4203	2	10	8150	9350
27	7	MERIDIEN	OP	SPTCR	FBG	SV	IO	260-330		8		5400	2	10	11100	13500
27	7	MERIDIEN	OP	SPTCR	FBG	SV	IO	T180	MRCR	8		5400	2	10	12000	13700
27	8	MIRAMAR		SPTCR	FBG	SV	IO	T165-T270		10	1	7140	2	10	14000	17100
29	1	GRANDE 300	ST	DC	FBG	SV	VD	T260	MRCR	10	6	8360	2	10	20500	22800
29	1	GRANDE 300	ST	DC	FBG	SV	VD	T454	MRCR	10	6	8360	2	10	23900	26500
		1988 BOATS														
16	1	FURY	ST	RNBT	FBG	DV	IO	120	MRCR	7		1050	2	2	2000	2350
17	7	RESORTER 18	OP	RNBT	FBG	SV	IB	260	MRCR	7		1510	2	1	3600	4200
17	10	CENTURY 2000 B/R	ST	RNBT	FBG	SV	IO	200-260		7	7	1900	2	1	3100	3900
18	1	BRONCO LTD	ST	RNBT	FBG	SV	IO	165	MRCR	7		1100	2	2	2550	3000
18	11	CENTURY 3000 B/R	ST	RNBT	FBG	SV	IO	200-260		8		2100	2	1	3600	4400
19	1	ARABIAN 200	OP	SKI	FBG	SV	IO	260	MRCR	7	3	1900	2	3	3350	3900
19	1	ARABIAN 200	OP	SKI	FBG	SV	VD	340	MRCR	7	3	1900	2	3	4600	5300
19	1	CENTURY 2500 SPT LX	ST	RNBT	FBG	SV	IO	200-260		8		2000	2	1	3550	4400
19	7	PALOMINO LTD	ST	RNBT	FBG	SV	IO	165	MRCR	7	4	1400	2	2	3100	3600
19	8	RIVIERA 6-METER	OP	SKI	FBG	SV	IO	200-260		7	4	1375	2	3	3050	3800
20	2	CENTURY 3500 SPT LX	ST	RNBT	FBG	SV	IO	200-260		8		2200	2	2	3650	4500
20	2	CENTURY 3500CC	ST	CUD	FBG	SV	IO	200-260		8		2500	2	2	4050	4950
20	10	CENTURY 4000CC	ST	CUD	FBG	SV	IO	200-260		8		2600	2	8	4250	5200
21	1	CTS	OP	SKI	FBG	SV	IB	260-340		7	6	1707	2	2	4550	5550
21	6	SABRE	ST	RNBT	FBG	SV	IB	260-340		8		2000	2	3	5150	6250
21	10	CORONADO 21	ST	RNBT	FBG	SV	IB	340	MRCR	7	11	2140	2	2	5600	6450
21	10	CORONADO-CARDEL	ST	RNBT	FBG	SV	IO	260	MRCR	7	11	2200	2	2	4150	4850
21	10	CORONADO-CARDEL	ST	RNBT	FBG	SV	IO	330	MRCR	7	11	2200	2	2	4800	5500
21	10	CORONADO-CARDEL	ST	RNBT	FBG	SV	VD	340	MRCR	7	11	2200	2	2	5650	6500
23	3	4500CLX	ST	CUD	FBG	SV	IO	260	MRCR	8	6	4000	2	8	6750	7750
23	3	4500CLX	ST	CUD	FBG	SV	IO	350	MRCR	8	6	4000	2	8	7700	8850
23	3	4500CLX	ST	CUD	FBG	SV	IO	454	MRCR	8	6	4000	2	8	10100	11400
25	2	MIRADA	OP	SPTCR	FBG	SV	IO	260	MRCR	8		4203	2	10	7700	8850
27	7	MERIDIEN	OP	SPTCR	FBG	SV	IO	260	MRCR	8		5400	2	10	10500	12000
27	7	MERIDIEN	OP	SPTCR	FBG	SV	IO	T180-T205		8		5400	2	10	11400	13300
27	8	MIRAMAR		SPTCR	FBG	SV	IO	T165-T260		10	1	7140	2	10	13200	16000
29	1	GRANDE 300	ST	DC	FBG	SV	VD	T230-T260		10	6	8360	2	10	19200	21700
		1987 BOATS														
17	7	RESORTER 18	OP	RNBT	FBG	SV	IB	260	MRCR	7		1510	2	1	3450	4000
17	10	CENTURY 2000 B/R	ST	RNBT	FBG	SV	IO	200-260		7	7	1900	2	1	2950	3700
17	10	CENTURY 2500 SPT LX	ST	RNBT	FBG	SV	IO	200-260		8		1950	2	1	3100	3850
18	1	BRONCO II	ST	RNBT	FBG	SV	IO	130	MRCR	7		1100	2	2	2400	2800
18	1	BRONCO II LTD	ST	RNBT	FBG	SV	IO	165	MRCR	7		1100	2	2	2450	2850
18	11	CENTURY 3000 B/R	ST	RNBT	FBG	SV	IO	200-260		8		2100	2	1	3400	4200
19	1	ARABIAN 200	OP	SKI	FBG	SV	IO	260	MRCR	7	3	1900	2	1	3200	3700
19	1	ARABIAN 200	OP	SKI	FBG	SV	VD	340	MRCR	7	3	1900	2	1	4400	5050
19	6	PALOMINO	ST	RNBT	FBG	SV	IO	130	MRCR	7	4	1408	2	2	2900	3400
19	6	PALOMINO LTD	ST	RNBT	FBG	SV	IO	165	MRCR	7	4	1408	2	2	2900	3400
19	8	RIVIERA 6-METER	OP	SKI	FBG	SV	IO	200-260		7	4	1375	2	3	2900	3600
20	2	CENTURY 3500 SPT LX	ST	RNBT	FBG	SV	IO	200-260		8		2200	2	2	3450	4250
20	2	CENTURY 3500CC	ST	CUD	FBG	SV	IO	200-260		8		2500	2	2	3850	4700
20	10	CENTURY 4000CC	ST	CUD	FBG	SV	IO	200-260		8		2600	2	8	4050	4950
21	1	CTS	OP	SKI	FBG	SV	IB	260-340		7	6	1707	2	2	4300	5350
21	6	SABRE	ST	RNBT	FBG	SV	IB	260-340		8		2800	2	3	5700	6850
21	10	CORONADO 21	ST	RNBT	FBG	SV	IB	340	MRCR	7	11	2140	2	2	5350	6150
21	10	CORONADO-CARDEL	ST	RNBT	FBG	SV	IO	260	MRCR	7	11	2200	2	2	3950	4600
21	10	CORONADO-CARDEL	ST	RNBT	FBG	SV	IO	330	MRCR	7	11	2200	2	2	4600	5250
21	10	CORONADO-CARDEL	ST	RNBT	FBG	SV	VD	340	MRCR	7	11	2200	2	2	5400	6200
22	10	ULTRA I	OP	RNBT	FBG	SV	IO	260	MRCR	8		2900	2		4750	5450
22	10	ULTRA I	OP	RNBT	FBG	SV	IO	350	MRCR	8		2900	2		5600	6450
23	3	4500 CLX	ST	CUD	FBG	SV	IO	260	MRCR	8	6	4000	2	8	6400	7400
23	3	4500 CLX	ST	CUD	FBG	SV	IO	350		8	6	4000			7350	8450
25	2	MIRADA	OP	SPTCR	FBG	SV	IO	260	MRCR	8		4203	2	10	7350	8400
25	11	MIRAGE	ST	DC	FBG	SV	IO	T260	MRCR	8		3286	2	3	9450	10800
25	11	ULTRA II	ST	CUD	F/S	DV	IO	T260	MRCR	8		5286	2	3	10400	11800
27	7	MERIDIEN	OP	SPTCR	FBG		IO	260	MRCR	8		5400	2	10	10000	11400
27	7	MERIDIEN	OP	SPTCR	FBG		IO	T180	MRCR	8		5400	2	10	10800	12300
27	7	MERIDIEN	OP	SPTCR	FBG	SV	IO	T205	MRCR	8		5400	2	10	11100	12600
27	8	MIRAMAR		SPTCR	FBG		IO	T165-T260		10	1	7140	2	10	12500	15200
27	8	MIRAMAR		SPTCR	FBG	SV	IO	T205	MRCR	10	1	7140	2	10	13000	14700
29	1	GRANDE 300	ST	DC	FBG	SV	VD	T230-T260		10	6	8360	2	10	18400	20900
		1986 BOATS														
16	5	RIVIERA 5-METER	OP	RNBT	FBG	SV	IO	140-190		7		1000	2	7	1850	2250
17	7	RESORTER 18	OP	RNBT	FBG	SV	IB	230-260		7		1510	2	1	3250	3800
17	10	CENTURY 2000 B/R	ST	RNBT	FBG	SV	IO	200-260		7	7	1900	2	1	2800	3500
17	10	CENTURY 2000 SPT LX	ST	RNBT	FBG	SV	IO	200-260		7	7	1950	2	1	2850	3550
18	1	BRONCO II	ST	RNBT	FBG	SV	IO	205	MRCR	7		1100	2	2	2400	2750
18	1	BRONCO LTD	ST	RNBT	FBG	SV	IO	140	MRCR	7		1100	2	2	2350	2700
18	11	CENTURY 3000 B/R	ST	RNBT	FBG	SV	IO	200-260		8		2100	2	1	3250	4000
19	1	ARABIAN 200	OP	SKI	FBG	SV	IO	260	MRCR	7	3	1900		2	3050	3550
19	1	ARABIAN 200	OP	SKI	FBG	SV	VD	340	MRCR	7	3	1900		2	4150	4800
19	6	PALOMINO	ST	RNBT	FBG	SV	IO	170-205		7	4	1408	2	2	2800	3300
19	8	RIVIERA 6-METER	OP	SKI	FBG	SV	IO	200-260		7	4	1375	2	3	2750	3450
20	2	CENTURY 3500 SPT LX	ST	RNBT	FBG	SV	IO	200-260		8		2200	2	2	3300	4050
20	2	CENTURY 3500CC	ST	CUD	FBG	SV	IO	200-260		8		2500	2	2	3650	4500
20	10	CENTURY 4000CC	ST	CUD	FBG	SV	IO	200-260		8		2600	2	8	3850	4750
21	1	CTS	OP	SKI	FBG	SV	IB	260-340		7	6	1707	2	2	4100	5100
21	10	CORONADO 21	ST	RNBT	FBG	SV	IB	340	MRCR	7	11	2140	2	2	5100	5850
21	10	CORONADO-CARDEL	ST	RNBT	FBG	SV	IO	260	MRCR	7	11	2200	2	2	3750	4400
21	10	CORONADO-CARDEL	ST	RNBT	FBG	SV	IO	330	MRCR	7	11	2200	2	2	4400	5050
21	10	CORONADO-CARDEL	ST	RNBT	FBG	SV	VD	340	MRCR	7	11	2200	2	2	5150	5950
22	3	FIERO	OP	CR	FBG		IO	200-260		8		2330	2	8	3950	4850
22	8	CENTURY 5000CC	ST	CUD	FBG	SV	IO	200-260		8		3000	2	8	4700	5550
25	2	MIRADA	OP	SPTCR	FBG	SV	IO	230-260		8		4203	2	10	6800	8050
25	11	MIRAGE	ST	DC	FBG	SV	IO	T260	MRCR	8		3286	2	3	9100	10300
27	7	MERIDIEN	OP	SPTCR	FBG		IO	260	MRCR	8		5400	2	10	9550	10900
27	7	MERIDIEN	OP	SPTCR	FBG		IO	T190	MRCR	8		5400	2	10	10400	11900
27	7	MERIDIEN	OP	SPTCR	FBG	SV	IO	T170-T185		8		4500	2	10	9600	11800
27	7	MERIDIEN	OP	SPTCR	FBG	SV	IO	T205	MRCR	8		5400	2	10	10600	12100
27	8	MIRAMAR		SPTCR	FBG		IO	T170-T260		10	1	7140	2	10	12000	14500
27	8	MIRAMAR		SPTCR	FBG	SV	IO	T205	MRCR	10	1	7140	2	10	12400	14100

CONTINUED ON NEXT PAGE

LOA FT	LOA IN	NAME AND/ OR MODEL	TOP/ RIG	BOAT TYPE	HULL MTL	HULL TP	ENGINE TP	# HP	MFG	BEAM FT	BEAM IN	WGT LBS	DRAFT FT	DRAFT IN	RETAIL LOW	RETAIL HIGH
		1986 BOATS														
29	1	GRANDE 300	ST	DC	FBG	SV	VD	T230-T260		10	6	8360	2	10	17200	20000
		1985 BOATS														
16	5	RIVIERA 5-METER	OP	RNBT	FBG	SV	IO	170-190		7		1000	2	7	1800	2150
17	7	RESORTER 18	OP	RNBT	FBG	SV	IB	230-260		7		1510	2	1	3100	3650
17	10	CENTURY 2000 B/R	ST	RNBT	FBG	SV	IO	200-260		7	7	1900	2	1	2700	3350
17	10	CENTURY 2000 SPT LX	ST	RNBT	FBG	SV	IO	200-260		7	7	1950	2	1	2750	3400
18	1	BRONCO 180	ST	RNBT	FBG	SV	IO	120-140		7		1100	2	2	2200	2550
18	1	BRONCO 180 LTD	ST	RNBT	FBG	SV	IO	120-140		7		1100	2	2	2250	2650
18	11	CENTURY 3000 B/R	ST	RNBT	FBG	SV	IO	200-260		8		2100	2	1	3100	3850
18	11	CENTURY 3000 SPT LX	ST	RNBT	FBG	SV	IO	200-260		8		2150	2	1	3150	3850
19	1	ARABIAN 200	OP	SKI	FBG	SV	IO	260	MRCR	7	3	1900	2	3	2900	3400
19	1	ARABIAN 200	OP	SKI	FBG	SV	VD	340	MRCR	7	3	1900	2	3	3950	4600
19	6	PALOMINO	ST	RNBT	FBG	SV	IO	120-170		7	4	1408	2	2	2600	3050
19	6	PALOMINO LTD	ST	RNBT	FBG	SV	IO	120-170		7	4	1408	2	2	2700	3150
19	7	MUSTANG 195	OP	RNBT	FBG	SV	IO	120-170		7	5	1300	2	3	2650	3100
19	7	MUSTANG 195 LTD	OP	RNBT	FBG	SV	IO	120-170		7	5	1300	2	3	2700	3150
19	8	RIVIERA 6-METER	OP	SKI	FBG	SV	IO	200-260		7	4	1375	2	3	2650	3300
20	2	CENTURY 3000CC	ST	CUD	FBG	SV	IO	200-260		8		2500	2	3	3500	4300
20	10	CENTURY 4000CC	ST	CUD	FBG	SV	IO	170-260		8		2600	2	8	3700	4550
21	1	CTS	OP	SKI	FBG	SV	IB	260-340		7	7	1707	2	2	3950	4900
21	10	CORONADO 21	ST	RNBT	FBG	SV	IB	340	MRCR	7	11	2140	2	2	4900	5600
21	10	CORONADO-CARDEL	ST	RNBT	FBG	SV	IO	260	MRCR	7	11	2200	2	2	3600	4200
21	10	CORONADO-CARDEL	ST	RNBT	FBG	SV	IO	330	MRCR	7	11	2200	2	2	4150	4850
21	10	CORONADO-CARDEL	ST	RNBT	FBG	SV	VD	340	MRCR	7	11	2200	2	2	4950	5650
22	3	FIERO	OP	CR	FBG		IO	170-260		8		2330	2	8	3800	4650
22	8	CENTURY 5000CC	ST	CUD	FBG	SV	IO	200-260		8		3000	2	8	4500	5400
25	2	MIRADA	OP	SPTCR	FBG	SV	IO	230-260		8		4000	2		6350	7500
26		MIRAGE	OP	SPTCR	FBG	SV	IO	T260	MRCR	8					9550	10800
27	7	MERIDIEN	OP	SPTCR	FBG		IO	260	MRCR	8		4500	2	8	8500	9800
27	7	MERIDIEN	OP	SPTCR	FBG		IO	T190	MRCR	8		4500	2	8	9450	10700
27	7	MERIDIEN	OP	SPTCR	FBG	SV	IO	T170	MRCR	8		4500	2	8	9300	10500
27	8	MIRAMAR		SPTCR	FBG		IO	T170-T260		10	1	6800	2	10	11300	13900
29	1	GRANDE 300	ST	DC	FBG	SV	VD	T230-T260		10	6	8000	2	10	16200	18800
		1984 BOATS														
16	5	CENTURY 1000 B/R	OP	RNBT	FBG	SV	IO	170		7			2	7	2200	2550
16	5	RIVIERA 5-METER	OP	RNBT	FBG	SV	IO	170-188		7		1000	2	7	1750	2100
17	7	RESORTER 18	OP	RNBT	FBG	SV	IB	225-260		7		1510	2	1	2900	3450
17	7	THOROUGHBRED SKIER		RNBT	FBG	SV	IB	250		7		1510	2	1	2950	3450
17	10	CENTURY 2000 B/R	ST	RNBT	FBG	SV	IO	170-228		7	7	1900	2	1	2600	3100
17	10	CENTURY 2000 B/R	ST	RNBT	FBG	SV	IO	260	MRCR	7	7	1900	2	1	2800	3250
17	10	CENTURY 2000 SPT LX	ST	RNBT	FBG	SV	IO	170-228		7	7	1950	2	1	2600	3150
17	10	CENTURY 2000 SPT LX	ST	RNBT	FBG	SV	IO	260	MRCR	7	7	1950	2	1	2800	3300
18	11	CENTURY 3000 B/R	ST	RNBT	FBG	SV	IO	170-260		8		2100	2	1	2950	3700
18	11	CENTURY 3000 SPT LX	ST	RNBT	FBG	SV	IO	170-260		8		2150	2	1	3000	3750
18	11	CENTURY 3000CC	ST	CUD	FBG	SV	IO	170-260		8		2400	2	3	3250	3900
19	1	ARABIAN 200	OP	SKI	FBG	SV	IO	260	MRCR	7	3	1900	2	3	2800	3250
19	1	ARABIAN 200	OP	SKI	FBG	SV	VD	330-340		7	3	1900	2	3	3650	4400
19	7	MUSTANG 195	OP	RNBT	FBG	SV	IO	120-188		7	5	1300	2	3	2600	3050
19	8	RIVIERA 6-METER	OP	SKI	FBG	SV	IO	170-228		7	4	1375	2	3	2500	3050
19	8	RIVIERA 6-METER	OP	SKI	FBG	SV	IO	260	MRCR	7	4	1375	2	3	2750	3200
20	10	CENTURY 4000CC	ST	CUD	FBG	SV	IO	170-260		8		2600	2	8	3550	4400
21	1	CTS	OP	SKI	FBG	SV	IB	225-330		7	7	1707	2	2	3700	4550
21	1	CTS	OP	SKI	FBG	SV	IB	340	MRCR	7	7	1707	2	2	4000	4650
21	10	CORONADO 21	ST	RNBT	FBG	SV	IB	330-340		7	11	2140	2	2	4600	5400
21	10	CORONADO-CARDEL	ST	RNBT	FBG	SV	IO	260	MRCR	7	11	2200	2	2	3500	4050
21	10	CORONADO-CARDEL	ST	RNBT	FBG	SV	VD	330-340		7	11	2200	2	2	4650	5400
22	3	FIERO	OP	CR	FBG		IO	170-260		8		2330	2	8	3650	4500
22	8	CENTURY 5000 SUN EXP	OP	CUD	FBG	SV	IO	170-260		8		3720	2	8	4950	5900
22	8	CENTURY 5000CC	ST	CUD	FBG	SV	IO	170-260		8		3000	2	8	4250	5200
26	4	CENTURY 7000 SUN EXP		CUD	FBG	SV	IO	260		8		4100	2	10	7000	8050
27	7	MERIDIEN	OP	SPTCR	FBG		IO	198-260		8		4500	2	8	7750	9450
27	7	MERIDIEN	OP	SPTCR	FBG		IO	T188	MRCR	8		4500	2	8	9150	10400
27	8	MIRAMAR		SPTCR	FBG		IO	T185-T260		10	1	6800	2	10	11000	13400
27	8	MIRAMAR		SPTCR	FBG		IO	T470	MRCR	10	1	6800	2	10	15800	18000
29	1	GRANDE 300	ST	DC	FBG	SV	IO	330	MRCR	10	6	8000	2	10	13300	15100
29	1	GRANDE 300	ST	DC	FBG	SV	IO	T188	MRCR	10	6	8000	2	10	13500	15400
29	1	GRANDE 300	ST	DC	FBG	SV	VD	T225-T230		10	6	8000	2	10	15400	17500

....For earlier years, see the BUC Used Boat Price Guide, Volume 3

CHAN SIEW TIN COMPANY

SAN FRANCISCO CA 94108 COAST GUARD MFG ID- TXN See inside cover to adjust price for area

ASSOCIATED YACHT BROKERS INC
ALAMEDA CA 94501

LOA FT	LOA IN	NAME AND/ OR MODEL	TOP/ RIG	BOAT TYPE	HULL MTL	HULL TP	ENGINE TP	# HP	MFG	BEAM FT	BEAM IN	WGT LBS	DRAFT FT	DRAFT IN	RETAIL LOW	RETAIL HIGH
		1986 BOATS														
36	2	MT-36	CUT	SA/CR	FBG	KL	IB	33D	YAN	11	2	22000	6		54900	60400
41		MT-41	SLP	SA/CR	FBG	KL	IB	35D	VLVO	12	3	27000	4	10	71300	78300
41		MT-41	KTH	SA/CR	FBG	KL	IB	35D	VLVO	12	3	27000	4	10	71300	78300
41	9	EXCALIBUR	SLP	SA/RC	F/S	KL	SD	35D	VLVO	12	8	21500	6	3	63500	69800
41	9	MT-42 PH	CUT	SA/CR	FBG	KL	IB	51D	PERK	12	11	24750	5	9	69000	75900
41	9	MT-42 PH	KTH	SA/CR	FBG	KL	IB	51D	PERK	12	11	24750	5	9	69100	75900
45	6	EAGLE	CUT	SA/CR	FBG	KL	IB	70D	ISUZ	13		30500	6		89300	98100
45	8	MT-46 PH	CUT	SA/CR	FBG	KL	IB	80D	LEHM	13	6	33500	5	10	94600	104000
49	8	MT-50 PH	CUT	SA/CR	FBG	KL	IB	85D	PERK	14	10	38500	7		118500	130000
50	11	MT-51	KTH	SA/CR	FBG	KL	IB	85D	PERK	14	3	38708	7		127000	140000
50	11	MT-51	CUT	SA/RC	FBG	KL	IB	85D	PERK	14	3	38708	7		127000	140000
		1985 BOATS														
36	2	MT-36	CUT	SA/CR	FBG	KL	IB	33D	YAN	11	2	22000	6		51700	56800
41		MT-41	SLP	SA/CR	FBG	KL	IB	35D	VLVO	12	3	27000	4	10	67000	73700
41		MT-41	KTH	SA/CR	FBG	KL	IB	35D	VLVO	12	3	27000	4	10	67000	73700
41	9	EXCALIBUR	SLP	SA/RC	F/S	KL	SD	35D	VLVO	12	8	21500	6	3	59800	65700
41	9	MT-42 PH	CUT	SA/CR	FBG	KL	IB	51D	PERK	12	11	24750	5	9	64900	71400
41	9	MT-42 PH	KTH	SA/CR	FBG	KL	IB	51D	PERK	12	11	24750	5	9	65000	71400
45	6	EAGLE	CUT	SA/CR	FBG	KL	IB	70D	ISUZ	13		30500	6		84000	92300
45	8	MT-46 PH	CUT	SA/CR	FBG	KL	IB	80D	LEHM	13	6	33500	5	10	89000	97800
49	8	MT-50 PH	CUT	SA/CR	FBG	KL	IB	85D	PERK	14	10	38500	7		111500	122500
50	11	MT-51	KTH	SA/CR	FBG	KL	IB	85D	PERK	14	3	38708	7		119500	131500
50	11	MT-51	CUT	SA/RC	FBG	KL	IB	85D	PERK	14	3	38708	7		119500	131500

....For earlier years, see the BUC Used Boat Price Guide, Volume 3

CHAPARRAL BOATS INC

NASHVILLE GA 31639 COAST GUARD MFG ID- FGB See inside cover to adjust price for area
FORMERLY FIBERGLASS FABRICATORS INC

For more recent years, see the BUC Used Boat Price Guide, Volume 1

LOA FT	LOA IN	NAME AND/ OR MODEL	TOP/ RIG	BOAT TYPE	HULL MTL	HULL TP	ENGINE TP	# HP	MFG	BEAM FT	BEAM IN	WGT LBS	DRAFT FT	DRAFT IN	RETAIL LOW	RETAIL HIGH
		1996 BOATS														
18	3	CHAPARRAL 1830 SS	OP	B/R	FBG	SV	IO	135-190		7	9	2470	1	2	6350	7800
19	3	CHAPARRAL 1930 SS	OP	RNBT	FBG	SV	IO	185-280		8		2745	1	4	7900	9550
19	3	CHAPARRAL 1935 SS	OP	RNBT	FBG	SV	IO	190-235		8		3039	1	4	8050	9950
19	3	CHAPARRAL 1935 SS	OP	RNBT	FBG	SV	IO	250-280		8		3039	1	4	8400	10300
19	3	CHAPARRAL 1950 SS	OP	RNBT	FBG	SV	IO	185-280		8		2890	1	4	8150	10000
20	4	SUNESTA 210	ST	RNBT	FBG	SV	OB			8	4	2452	1	7	6350	7300
20	4	SUNESTA 210	ST	RNBT	FBG	SV	IO	190-235		8	4	2452	1	7	8450	10400
20	4	SUNESTA 210	ST	RNBT	FBG	SV	IO	250-280		8	4	2452	1	7	8900	10800
20	6	CHAPARRAL 2130 SS	OP	B/R	FBG	SV	OB			8	4	2365	1	11	6400	7350
20	6	CHAPARRAL 2130 SS	OP	B/R	FBG	SV	IO	190-250		8	4	3150	1	11	9600	11800
20	6	CHAPARRAL 2130 SS	OP	B/R	FBG	SV	IO	265-300		8	4	3150	1	11	10600	12800
20	6	CHAPARRAL 2135 SS	OP	CUD	FBG	SV	IO	185-280		8	4	3380	1	11	11100	13600
20	6	CHAPARRAL 2135 SS	OP	CUD	FBG	SV	IO	300		8	4	3380	1	11	11900	14200
22	3	CHAPARRAL 2130 BRKT	OP	B/R	FBG	SV	OB			8	4	2365			6400	7350
22	3	CHAPARRAL 2135 BRKT	OP	CUD	FBG	SV	OB			8	4	2590			6650	7600
22	6	SUNESTA 230	ST	RNBT	FBG	SV	OB			8	6	2915	1	7	8300	9550
22	6	SUNESTA 230	ST	RNBT	FBG	SV	IO	190-280		8	6	3640	1	7	11900	14600
23	8	CHAPARRAL 2330 SS	OP	B/R	FBG	SV	OB			8	6	3002	1	10	9250	10500
23	8	CHAPARRAL 2330 SS	OP	B/R	FBG	SV	IO	210-280		8	6	3850	1	10	13100	16000
		IO 300 14100 16600, IO 330-350 14800 17600, IO 385 MRCR 16700 18900														
		IO 415 18400 21800														
23	8	CHAPARRAL 2335 SS	OP	CUD	FBG	SV	OB			8	6	3343	1	10	9850	11200
23	8	CHAPARRAL 2335 SS	OP	CUD	FBG	SV	IO	210-280		8	6	4175	1	10	14800	18100
		IO 300-350 15900 19700, IO 385 MRCR 19100 21200, IO 415 20300 24200														
24		SUNESTA 230	ST	RNBT	FBG	SV	OB			8	6	2915	1	7	8300	9550
24	11	SIGNATURE 24	OP	CR	FBG	SV	IO	190-330		8	6	5360	1	5	18800	23200
24	11	SUNESTA 250	ST	RNBT	FBG	SV	OB			8	6	3865	1	2	11400	12900
24	11	SUNESTA 250	ST	RNBT	FBG	SV	IO	190-280		8	6	3865	1	2	14000	17100
24	11	SUNESTA 250	ST	RNBT	FBG	SV	IO	300-330		8	6	3865	1	2	15100	18600
25	3	CHAPARRAL 2500 SX	OP	B/R	FBG	SV	IO	190-280		8	6	4210	1	8	15000	18300
25	3	CHAPARRAL 2500 SX	OP	B/R	FBG	SV	IO	300-350		8	6	4210	1	8	16200	19800
25	3	CHAPARRAL 2500 SX	OP	B/R	FBG	SV	IO	385-415		8	6	4210	1	8	19000	23400
25	3	CHAPARRAL 2550 SX	OP	CUD	FBG	SV	IO	190-300		8	6	4750	1	10	17500	21700

96th ed. - Vol. II CONTINUED ON NEXT PAGE 125

LOA FT	LOA IN	NAME AND/ OR MODEL	TOP/ RIG	BOAT TYPE	-HULL- MTL	-HULL- TP	ENGINE TP	# HP	MFG	BEAM FT	BEAM IN	WGT LBS	DRAFT FT	DRAFT IN	RETAIL LOW	RETAIL HIGH
		1996 BOATS														
25	3	CHAPARRAL 2550 SX	OP	CUD	FBG	SV	IO	330-385		8	6	4750	1	10	19800	24100
25	3	CHAPARRAL 2550 SX	OP	CUD	FBG	SV	IO	415		8	6	4750	1	10	22900	26800
25	7	SIGNATURE 25	OP	CR	FBG	SV	IO	190-330		8	6	6000	1	5	21100	26300
25	7	SIGNATURE 25	OP	CR	FBG	SV	IO	350-385		8	6	6000	1	5	23700	27700
28	5	SIGNATURE 27	OP	CR	FBG	SV	IO	250-350		9		6120	2	1	22300	27200
		IO 385 MRCR 25600 28500, IO T190 24200 27300, IO T300-T330													27900	32700
31	1	SIGNATURE 29	OP	CR	FBG	SV	IO	330	MRCR	9	9	7200	2	9	31100	34600
31	1	SIGNATURE 29	OP	CR	FBG	SV	IO	T210-T250		9	9	7200	2	9	32300	37200
31	11	SIGNATURE 29	OP	CR	FBG	SV	IO	300-330		9	9	7200	2	9	30500	34600
31	11	SIGNATURE 29	OP	CR	FBG	SV	IO	T190-T250		9	9	7200	2	9	31700	37500
33	2	SIGNATURE 31	OP	CR	FBG	SV	IO	T190-T255		10	9	9750	2	8	43800	51100
		1995 BOATS														
17	6	CHAPARRAL 180 SL	OP	B/R	FBG	SV	IO	135-185		7	7	2140	1	7	5200	6350
17	6	CHAPARRAL 185 SL	OP	RNBT	FBG	SV	IO	135-185		7	7	2210	1	7	5500	6750
18	3	CHAPARRAL 1830 SS	OP	B/R	FBG	SV	IO	135-185		7	9	2470	1	2	5950	7250
19	3	CHAPARRAL 1930 SS	OP	RNBT	FBG	SV	IO	180-235		8		2745	1	4	7100	8750
19	3	CHAPARRAL 1930 SS	OP	RNBT	FBG	SV	IO	250-255		8		2745	1	4	7400	9000
19	3	CHAPARRAL 1950 SS	OP	RNBT	FBG	SV	IO	180-235		8		2890			7300	9000
19	3	CHAPARRAL 1950 SS	OP	RNBT	FBG	SV	IO	250-255		8		2890			7600	9250
20	6	CHAPARRAL 2130 SS	OP	B/R	FBG	SV	IO	180-255		8	4	3150	1	11	9000	11100
20	6	CHAPARRAL 2130 SS	OP	B/R	FBG	SV	IO	275-300		8	4	3150	1	11	10000	12000
20	6	CHAPARRAL 2135 SS	OP	CUD	FBG	SV	IO	180-255		8	4	3380	1	11	10000	12300
20	6	CHAPARRAL 2135 SS	OP	CUD	FBG	SV	IO	275-300		8	4	3380	1	11	11200	13300
22	3	CHAPARRAL 2130 BRKT	OP	B/R	FBG	SV	OB			8	4	2365			6050	6950
22	3	CHAPARRAL 2135 BRKT	OP	CUD	FBG	SV	OB			8	4	2590			6300	7250
22	6	SUNESTA 220	ST	RNBT	FBG	SV	IO	180-275		8	6	3640	1	7	11100	13800
23	8	CHAPARRAL 2330 SS	OP	B/R	FBG	SV	IO	235-275		8	6	3850	1	10	12300	15000
23	8	CHAPARRAL 2330 SS	OP	B/R	FBG	SV	IO	300-350		8	6	3850	1	10	13100	16300
23	8	CHAPARRAL 2330 SS	OP	B/R	FBG	SV	IO	385-415		8	6	3850	1	10	15500	19100
23	8	CHAPARRAL 2335 SS	OP	CUD	FBG	SV	IO	235-275		8	6	4175	1	10	14000	16900
23	8	CHAPARRAL 2335 SS	OP	CUD	FBG	SV	IO	300-350		8	6	4175	1	10	14800	18300
23	8	CHAPARRAL 2335 SS	OP	CUD	FBG	SV	IO	385-415		8	6	4175	1	10	17400	21300
24		SUNESTA 220	ST	RNBT	FBG	SV	OB			8	6	2915	1	7	7900	9100
24	6	SUNESTA 250 CAT	ST	RNBT	FBG	CT	OB			8	6	3020	1	1	9050	10300
24	11	SIGNATURE 24	OP	CR	FBG	SV	IO	190-300		8	6	5360	1	5	17100	21000
24	11	SUNESTA 250	ST	RNBT	FBG	SV	IO	190-275		8	6	3865	1	2	12800	15900
24	11	SUNESTA 250	ST	RNBT	FBG	SV	IO	300		8	6	3865	1	2	14100	16500
25	3	CHAPARRAL 2500 SX	OP	B/R	FBG	SV	IO	235-300		8	6	4210	1	8	14200	17600
25	3	CHAPARRAL 2500 SX	OP	B/R	FBG	SV	IO	350-385		8	6	4210	1	8	16300	19700
25	3	CHAPARRAL 2500 SX	OP	B/R	FBG	SV	IO	415	MRCR	8	6	4210	1	8	18900	21000
25	3	CHAPARRAL 2550 SX	OP	CUD	FBG	SV	IO	235-300		8	6	4750	1	10	16500	20400
25	3	CHAPARRAL 2550 SX	OP	CUD	FBG	SV	IO	350-415		8	6	4750	1	10	19000	23800
28	5	SIGNATURE 27	OP	CR	FBG	SV	IO	235-300		9		6120	2	1	20800	24400
28	5	SIGNATURE 27	OP	CR	FBG	SV	IO	385	MRCR	9		6120	2	1	23900	26600
28	5	SIGNATURE 27	OP	CR	FBG	SV	IO	T180-T185		9		6120	2	1	22400	25400
31	11	SIGNATURE 29	OP	CR	FBG	SV	IO	300-385		9	9	7200	2	9	28400	33700
31	11	SIGNATURE 29	OP	CR	FBG	SV	IO	T180-T255		9	9	7200	2	9	29300	35200
33	2	SIGNATURE 31	OP	CR	FBG	SV	IO	T185-T255		10	9	9750	2	8	40700	47700
		1994 BOATS														
16	8	CHAPARRAL 160 SL LTD	OP	RNBT	FBG	SV	OB			6	6	900	2	7	2250	2600
16	8	CHAPARRAL 165 SL LTD	OP	RNBT	FBG	SV	OB			6	6	1020	2	7	2500	2900
16	8	CHAPARRAL 165 SL LTD	ST	RNBT	FBG	SV	OB			6	6	1020	2	7	2500	2900
17	6	CHAPARRAL 180 SL LTD	OP	RNBT	FBG	SV	IO	110-135		7	7	2150	2	11	5200	6250
17	6	CHAPARRAL 185 SL LTD	OP	RNBT	FBG	SV	IO	110-135		7	7	2225	2	11	5150	6250
18	3	CHAPARRAL 1830 SS	OP	RNBT	FBG	SV	IO	110-185		7	9	2350	2	9	5600	6850
18	9	CHAPARRAL 190 SL LTD	OP	RNBT	FBG	SV	IO	185	VLVO	7	8	2200	2	11	5900	6750
18	9	GEMINI 190	OP	RNBT	FBG	SV	OB			7	8	1800	2	11	4050	4750
19	3	CHAPARRAL 1930 SS	OP	RNBT	FBG	SV	IO	180-240		8		2850	2	10	6750	8300
19	3	CHAPARRAL 1930 SS	OP	RNBT	FBG	SV	IO	250-255		8		2850	2	10	7050	8550
19	3	STRIKER 198	OP	OPFSH	FBG	SV	OB			8		1900	2	2	4100	4750
19	8	CHAPARRAL 190 SL LTD	OP	RNBT	FBG	SV	OB			7	8	2200	2	11	4500	5200
19	8	CHAPARRAL 190 SL LTD	OP	RNBT	FBG	SV	IO	180-185		7	8	2200	2	11	5450	6600
20	3	CHAPARRAL 200 SL LTD	OP	RNBT	FBG	SV	OB			8		2125	2	7	5250	6050
20	3	CHAPARRAL 200 SL LTD	OP	RNBT	FBG	SV	IO	180-215		8		2650	2	7	7400	8900
20	3	CHAPARRAL 200 SL LTD	OP	RNBT	FBG	SV	IO	225-255		8		2850	2	7	8200	9400
20	3	CHAPARRAL 205 SL LTD	OP	CUD	FBG	SV	IO	180-240		8		3000	2	9	8300	10100
20	3	CHAPARRAL 205 SL LTD	OP	CUD	FBG	SV	IO	250-255		8		3000	2	9	8650	10500
20	6	CHAPARRAL 2130 SS	OP	RNBT	FBG	SV	IO	180-255		8	4	3250	2	10	8650	10700
20	6	CHAPARRAL 2130 SS	OP	RNBT	FBG	SV	IO	300		8	4	3250	2	10	9650	11500
22	6	SUNESTA 220	ST	RNBT	FBG	SV	IO	180-255		8	6	3400	2	11	9850	12100
22	7	CHAPARRAL 220 SL LTD	OP	RNBT	FBG	SV	IO	180-255		8	6	3250	2	11	9600	11800
22	7	CHAPARRAL 220 SL LTD	OP	RNBT	FBG	SV	IO	300		8	6	3250	2	11	10600	12600
22	7	CHAPARRAL 225 SL LTD	OP	CUD	FBG	SV	IO	180-255		8	6	3750	2	11	11200	13700
22	7	CHAPARRAL 225 SL LTD	OP	CUD	FBG	SV	IO	300		8	6	3750	2	11	12300	14500
23	3	CHAPARRAL 2300 SX	OP	RNBT	FBG	SV	IO	225-300		8	6	3920	3	3	11700	13900
23	3	CHAPARRAL 2300 SX	ST	RNBT	FBG	SV	IO	235	MRCR	8	6	3920	3	3	11500	13000
23	3	CHAPARRAL 2350 SX	OP	CUD	FBG	SV	IO	225-300		8	6	4120	3	3	12900	15300
23	9	SIGNATURE 24	OP	CR	FBG	SV	IO	185-300		8	6	4800	2	8	14600	18000
24	6	SUNESTA 250	ST	RNBT	FBG	SV	OB			8	6	3020	2	2	8550	9800
25	3	CHAPARRAL 2500 SX	OP	RNBT	FBG	SV	IO	225-300		8	6	4680	3	2	14300	17500
25	3	CHAPARRAL 2500 SX	OP	RNBT	FBG	SV	IO	350-385		8	6	4680	3	2	16100	19400
25	3	CHAPARRAL 2500 SX	OP	RNBT	FBG	SV	IO	415	MRCR	8	6	4680	3	2	18500	20600
25	3	CHAPARRAL 2550 SX	ST	CUD	FBG	SV	IO	225-300		8	6	4850	3	2	15800	19300
25	3	CHAPARRAL 2550 SX	ST	CUD	FBG	SV	IO	350-415		8	6	4850	3	2	18200	22400
26	2	SIGNATURE 27	OP	CR	FBG	DV	IO	250	VLVO	9		6320	2	9	20100	22300
26	2	SIGNATURE 27	OP	CR	FBG	SV	IO	240-300		9		6320	2	9	19700	23300
26	2	SIGNATURE 27	OP	CR	FBG	SV	IO	T180-T185		9		6320	2	9	21300	24200
29	3	SIGNATURE 29	OP	CR	FBG	SV	IO	300		9	9	7200	2	9	26500	29600
29	3	SIGNATURE 29	OP	CR	FBG	SV	IO	T180-T250		9	9	7200	2	9	27400	32700
29	3	SIGNATURE 29	OP	CR	FBG	SV	IO	T190D	VLVO	9	9	7200	2	9	33800	37500
30	6	SIGNATURE 31	OP	CR	FBG	SV	IO	T190-T255		10	9	9750	2	8	38000	44500
30	6	SIGNATURE 31	OP	CR	FBG	SV	IO	T215D	VLVO	10	9	9750	2	9	46700	51400
		1993 BOATS														
16	5	CHAPARRAL 1600 SL	OP	RNBT	FBG	SV	OB			6	2	900	2	7	2050	2450
16	5	CHAPARRAL 1650	ST	RNBT	FBG	SV	OB			6	6	1020	2	7	2350	2750
17	6	CHAPARRAL 180 LTD SL	OP	RNBT	FBG	SV	IO	110-135		7	7	2150	2		4850	5600
17	6	CHAPARRAL 1800 SL	OP	RNBT	FBG	SV	OB			7	7	1525	2	11	3350	3900
17	6	CHAPARRAL 1800 SL	OP	RNBT	FBG	SV	IO	110-187		7	7	2150	2	11	5100	5850
17	6	CHAPARRAL 185 LH	OP	RNBT	FBG	SV	IO	110-135		7	7	2225	2	11	4900	5650
17	6	CHAPARRAL 1850 SL	OP	RNBT	FBG	SV	OB			7	7	1340	2	11	3050	3550
17	6	CHAPARRAL 1850 SL	OP	RNBT	FBG	SV	IO	110-187		7	7	2225	2	11	5200	5950
18	2	STRIKER 190	OP	CTRCN	FBG	SV	OB			8		1900	2	2	3750	4350
18	9	CHAPARRAL 1900 SL	OP	RNBT	FBG	SV	OB			7	8	1625	2	11	3600	4200
18	9	CHAPARRAL 1900 SL	OP	RNBT	FBG	SV	IO	135-187		7	8	2200	2	11	5200	6350
18	9	GEMINI 190	OP	RNBT	FBG	SV	OB			7	8	1800	2	11	3850	4500
19	3	STRIKER 198	OP	OPFSH	FBG	SV	OB			8		1900	2	2	3900	4500
19	3	STRIKER 198	OP	OPFSH	FBG	SV	IO	135-180		8		2500	2	2	6350	7700
20	3	CHAPARRAL 2000 SL	OP	RNBT	FBG	SV	OB			8		2150	2	7	5100	5850
20	3	CHAPARRAL 2000 SL	OP	RNBT	FBG	SV	IO	160-240		8		2850	2	7	7150	8800
20	3	CHAPARRAL 2000 SL	OP	RNBT	FBG	SV	IO	245-250		8		2850	2	7	7800	9000
20	3	CHAPARRAL 205 LTD	OP	CUD	FBG	SV	IO	160-210		8		3000	2	9	7700	9300
20	3	CHAPARRAL 2050 SL	OP	CUD	FBG	SV	IO	160-250		8		3200	2	9	8050	9650
20	3	VILLAIN SLV	OP	RACE	FBG	SV	IO	225-250		8		2800	2	7	7450	8700
22	6	SUNESTA 220	ST	RNBT	FBG	SV	IO	160-250		8	6	3400	2	11	9250	11200
22	7	CHAPARRAL 2200 SL	OP	RNBT	FBG	SV	IO	160-250		8	6	3250	2	11	9000	10900
22	7	CHAPARRAL 2200 SL	OP	RNBT	FBG	SV	IO	300		8	6	3250	2	11	9900	11800
22	7	CHAPARRAL 2250 SL	OP	CUD	FBG	SV	IO	160-250		8	6	3750	2	9	10500	12700
22	7	CHAPARRAL 2250 SL	OP	CUD	FBG	SV	IO	300		8	6	3750	2	9	11500	13600
23	3	CHAPARRAL 2300 SX	OP	RNBT	FBG	SV	IO	225-300		8	6	3920	3	4	11000	13000
23	3	CHAPARRAL 2300 SX	ST	RNBT	FBG	SV	IO	235	MRCR	8	6	3920	3	4	10700	12200
23	3	CHAPARRAL 2350 SX	OP	CUD	FBG	SV	IO	225-300		8	6	4120	3	4	12100	14300
23	9	CHAPARRAL 2450 SL	OP	CUD	FBG	SV	IO	180-250		8	6	4600	2	9	12900	15400
23	9	CHAPARRAL 2450 SL	OP	CUD	FBG	SV	IO	300		8	6	4600	2	9	13900	16300
23	9	SIGNATURE 24	OP	CR	FBG	SV	IO	180-250		8	6	4800	2	8	13400	15900
23	9	SIGNATURE 24	OP	CR	FBG	SV	IO	300		8	6	4800	2	8	14300	16900
24		VILLAIN III	OP	OFF	FBG	SV	IO	300	YAMA	8	4	4200	3	3	13100	14900
24		VILLAIN III	OP	OFF	FBG	SV	IO	390-415		8	4	4200	3	3	15500	18800
24		VILLAIN III	ST	OFF	FBG	SV	IO	300-350		8	4	4200	3	3	13100	15400
24	6	SUNESTA 250	ST	RNBT	FBG	SV	OB			8	6	3020	2	2	8200	9400
25	3	CHAPARRAL 2500 SX	OP	RNBT	FBG	SV	IO	225-300		8	6	4716	3	2	13400	16400
25	3	CHAPARRAL 2500 SX	OP	RNBT	FBG	SV	IO	350-390		8	6	4716	3	2	15100	18300
25	3	CHAPARRAL 2500 SX	OP	RNBT	FBG	SV	IO	415	MRCR	8	6	4680	3	2	16900	19200
25	3	CHAPARRAL 2550 SL	OP	RNBT	FBG	DV	IO	260-275		8	6		3	2	12100	14300
25	3	CHAPARRAL 2550 SL	OP	RNBT	FBG	DV	IO	330-365		8	6		3	2	13200	16000
25	3	CHAPARRAL 2550 SX	ST	CUD	FBG	SV	IO	225-300		8	6	4850	3	2	14800	18100
25	3	CHAPARRAL 2550 SX	ST	CUD	FBG	SV	IO	350-390		8	6	4850	3	2	16600	20200
25	3	CHAPARRAL 2550 SX	ST	CUD	FBG	SV	IO	415	MRCR	8	6	4850	3	2	19100	21200
26	2	SIGNATURE 27	OP	CR	FBG	SV	IO	240-300		9		6320	2	8	18600	21700
26	2	SIGNATURE 27	OP	CR	FBG	SV	IO	T155-T180		9		6320	2	8	19900	22500
27	10	CHAPARRAL 2850 SL	OP	SPTCR	FBG	SV	IO	415	MRCR	9		6460	3	1	24000	26700
27	10	CHAPARRAL 2850 SL	OP	SPTCR	FBG	SV	IO	T235-T250		9		6460	3	1	23400	26300
27	10	CHAPARRAL 2850 SX	OP	SPTCR	FBG	SV	IO	300-390		9		6460	3	1	21400	25900
27	10	CHAPARRAL 2850 SX	OP	SPTCR	FBG	SV	IO	T225-T245		9		6460	3	1	23400	26500
29	3	SIGNATURE 29	OP	CR	FBG	SV	IO	300		9	9	7200	2	8	24800	27700
29	3	SIGNATURE 29	OP	CR	FBG	SV	IO	T155-T180		9	9	7200	2	8	25200	28600

CONTINUED ON NEXT PAGE

LOA FT	LOA IN	NAME AND/ OR MODEL	TOP/ RIG	BOAT TYPE	HULL MTL	HULL TP	ENGINE TP	ENGINE # HP	ENGINE MFG	BEAM FT	BEAM IN	WGT LBS	DRAFT FT	DRAFT IN	RETAIL LOW	RETAIL HIGH
		1993 BOATS														
29	3	SIGNATURE 29	OP	CR	FBG	SV	IO	T120D	VLVO	9	9	7200	2	8	28100	31200
30	6	SIGNATURE 31	OP	CR	FBG	SV	IO	T180-T250		10	9	9750	2	8	35300	41300
30	6	SIGNATURE 31	OP	CR	FBG	SV	IO	T216D	VLVO	10	9	9750	2	8	43300	48100
		1992 BOATS														
16	5	CHAPARRAL 1600 SL	OP	RNBT	FBG	SV	OB			6	2	900	2	7	2000	2350
17	6	CHAPARRAL 1800 LTDSL	OP	RNBT	FBG	SV	IO	110-135		7	7	2100	2	7	4500	5250
17	6	CHAPARRAL 1800 SL	OP	RNBT	FBG	SV	OB			7	7	1525	2	11	3200	3700
17	6	CHAPARRAL 1800 SL	OP	RNBT	FBG	SV	IO	110-180		7	7	2100	2	11	4700	5450
17	6	CHAPARRAL 1850 SL	OP	RNBT	FBG	SV	IO	110-180		7	7	2175	2	11	4700	5450
18	9	CHAPARRAL 1900 SL	OP	RNBT	FBG	SV	OB			7	8	1625	2	11	3450	4000
18	9	CHAPARRAL 1900 SL	OP	RNBT	FBG	SV	IO	135-180		7	8	2200	2	11	4850	5900
19	3	STRIKER 190	OP	CTRCN	FBG	SV	OB			8		1900	2	2	3650	4250
19	3	STRIKER 198	OP	OPFSH	FBG	SV	OB			8		1900	2	4	3650	4250
19	3	STRIKER 198	OP	OPFSH	FBG	SV	IO	135-180		8		2500	2	4	5950	7200
20	3	CHAPARRAL 2000 SL	OP	RNBT	FBG	SV	OB			8		2650	2	7	5450	6250
20	3	CHAPARRAL 2000 SL	OP	RNBT	FBG	SV	IO	155-175		8		2650	2	7	6450	7700
20	3	CHAPARRAL 2000 SL	OP	RNBT	FBG	SV	IO	180	MRCR	8		2650	2	7	6500	7450
20	3	CHAPARRAL 2000 SL	OP	RNBT	FBG	SV	IO	180-250		8		3000	2	9	7200	8300
20	3	CHAPARRAL 2050 SL	OP	CUD	FBG	SV	IO	155-240		8		3000	2	9	7200	8850
20	3	CHAPARRAL 2050 SL	OP	CUD	FBG	SV	IO	245-250		8		3000	2	9	7850	9050
20	3	VILLAIN SLV	OP	RACE	FBG	SV	IO	225-250		8		2800	2	7	6950	8150
21		STRIKER 224	ST	FSH	FBG	SV	OB			8		2900	2	10	6150	7050
22	7	CHAPARRAL 2200 SL	OP	RNBT	FBG	SV	IO	155-250		8	6	3150	2	11	8200	10100
23		STRIKER 234	OP	OPFSH	FBG	SV	OB			8		2975	2	7	7250	8300
23		STRIKER 234	OP	OPFSH	FBG	SV	IO	205-245		8		4000	2	7	10900	13100
23	3	CHAPARRAL 2300 SX	OP	RNBT	FBG	SV	IO	225-300		8	6	3920	3	4	10300	12100
23	3	CHAPARRAL 2300 SX	ST	RNBT	FBG	SV	IO	230	MRCR	8	6	3920	3	4	10000	11400
23	3	CHAPARRAL 2350 SX	OP	CUD	FBG	SV	IO	230-300		8	6	4120	3	4	11000	13400
23	9	CHAPARRAL 2360 SL	OP	CUD	FBG	SV	IO	155-250		8	6	4600	2	9	12100	14400
23	9	CHAPARRAL 2360 SL	OP	CUD	FBG	SV	IO	300		8	6	4600	2	9	13000	15300
23	9	CHAPARRAL 2370 SL	OP	CBNCR	FBG	SV	IO	155-250		8	6	4800	2	9	14200	16900
23	9	CHAPARRAL 2370 SL	OP	CBNCR	FBG	SV	IO	300		8	6	4800	2	9	15200	17900
24		VILLAIN III	OP	OFF	FBG	SV	IO	300	YAMA	8	4	4200	3	3	12300	13900
24		VILLAIN III	OP	OFF	FBG	SV	IO	390	MRCR	8	4	4200	3	3	14500	16500
24		VILLAIN III	ST	OFF	FBG	SV	IO	300-350		8	4	4200	3	3	12300	14500
24	8	STRIKER 234	OP	OPFSH	FBG	SV	IO	205	VLVO	8		4000	2	7	12100	13700
25	3	CHAPARRAL 2500 SX	OP	RNBT	FBG	SV	IO	225-300		8	6	4716	3	2	12600	15400
25	3	CHAPARRAL 2500 SX	OP	RNBT	FBG	SV	IO	350	MRCR	8	6	4716	3	2	14100	16100
25	3	CHAPARRAL 2550 CX	OP	CTRCN	FBG	DV	IO	260-275		8	6		3	2	13600	16000
25	3	CHAPARRAL 2550 CX	OP	CTRCN	FBG	DV	IO	330-365		8	6		3	2	14800	17900
25	3	CHAPARRAL 2550 SX	ST	CUD	FBG	SV	IO	225-300		8	6	5080	3	2	14300	17400
25	3	CHAPARRAL 2550 SX	ST	CUD	FBG	SV	IO	350	MRCR	8	6	5080	3	2	16000	18200
26	2	SIGNATURE 26	OP	CR	FBG	SV	IO	240-300		9		6320	2	9	17200	20800
26	2	SIGNATURE 26	OP	CR	FBG	SV	IO	T155-T180		9		6320	2	9	18600	21200
27	10	CHAPARRAL 2750 SX	OP	SPTCR	FBG	SV	IO	300-350		9		6460	3	1	20000	23300
27	10	CHAPARRAL 2750 SX	OP	SPTCR	FBG	SV	IO	T225-T250		9		6460	3	1	21900	24900
29	3	SIGNATURE 28	OP	CR	FBG	SV	IO	300		9	9	7200	2	9	24700	27600
29	3	SIGNATURE 28	OP	CR	FBG	SV	IO	T155-T180		9	9	7200	2	9	24900	28600
29	3	SIGNATURE 28	OP	CR	FBG	SV	IO	T120D	VLVO	9	9	7200	2	9	28000	31100
30		VILLAIN IV	OP	OFF	FBG	SV	IO	T300	VLVO	8	2	7400	3	6	29400	32700
30		VILLAIN IV	OP	OFF	FBG	SV	IO	T300	YAMA	8	2	7400	3	6	29200	32400
30		VILLAIN IV	OP	OFF	FBG	SV	IO	T390	MRCR	8	2	7400	3	6	31900	35400
30		VILLAIN IV	ST	OFF	FBG	SV	IO	T300-T350		8	2	7400	3	6	29200	34000
30	6	SIGNATURE 30	OP	CR	FBG	SV	IO	T175-T250		10	9	9750	2	9	32900	38700
30	6	SIGNATURE 30	OP	CR	FBG	SV	IO	T185D	VLVO	10	9	9750	2	9	39100	43400
		1991 BOATS														
16	5	CHAPARRAL 1600 SL	OP	RNBT	FBG	SV	OB			6	2	900			1900	2250
17	10	CHAPARRAL 1800 SL	OP	RNBT	FBG	SV	OB			7	7	2100	3	11	3700	4350
17	10	CHAPARRAL 1800 SL	OP	RNBT	FBG	SV	IO	120-175		7	7	2100			4450	5150
17	10	CHAPARRAL 1850 SL	OP	RNBT	FBG	SV	IO	120-175		7	7	2175			4500	5250
18	9	CHAPARRAL 1900 SL	OP	RNBT	FBG	SV	OB			7	8	2200	3	11	3900	4500
18	9	CHAPARRAL 1900 SL	OP	RNBT	FBG	SV	IO	145-205		7	8	2200	3	11	4600	5600
19	3	STRIKER 190	OP	CTRCN	FBG	SV	OB			8		1900			3500	4100
19	3	STRIKER 198	OP	CTRCN	FBG	SV	IO	145-175		8		2500			5600	6450
19	3	STRIKER 198	ST	FSH	FBG	SV	OB			8		1900	2	4	3500	4100
19	3	STRIKER 198	OP	RNBT	FBG	SV	IO	146-205		8		2500			5350	6250
20	3	CHAPARRAL 2000 SL	OP	RNBT	FBG	SV	OB			8		2650	2	7	5250	6050
20	3	CHAPARRAL 2000 SL	OP	RNBT	FBG	SV	IO	175-270		8		2650	2	7	6050	7500
20	3	CHAPARRAL 2000 SL	OP	RNBT	FBG	SV	IO	275	VLVO	8		2650	2	7	6900	7950
20	3	CHAPARRAL 2050 SL	OP	CUD	FBG	SV	IO	175-270		8		3000	2	9	6800	8350
20	3	CHAPARRAL 2050 SL	OP	CUD	FBG	SV	IO	275	VLVO	8		3000	2	9	7700	8850
20	3	VILLAIN SLV	OP	RACE	FBG	SV	IO	260-275		8		2800			6500	8000
21		CHAPARRAL 224	ST	FSH	FBG	SV	OB			8		2900	2	10	5950	6800
21	2	CHAPARRAL 2100 SX	OP	RNBT	FBG	SV	IO	229-275		8	4	2954	3	3	7300	8900
21	2	CHAPARRAL 2150 SX	OP	CUD	FBG	SV	IO	229-275		8	4	3200	3	1	8050	9750
23		STRIKER 234	OP	OPFSH	FBG	SV	IO	229-230		8		4900			12400	14100
23	3	CHAPARRAL 2300 SX	OP	RNBT	FBG	SV	IO	260-330		8	6	3920	3	10	9600	12000
23	3	CHAPARRAL 2300 SX	ST	RNBT	FBG	SV	IO	260	MRCR	8	6	3920	3	10	9600	10900
23	3	CHAPARRAL 2350 SX	OP	CUD	FBG	SV	IO	260-330		8	6	4120	3	4	10600	13100
23	9	CHAPARRAL 2370 SL	OP	CBNCR	FBG	SV	IO	175-275		8	6	4800			13300	16300
23	9	CHAPARRAL 2370 SL	OP	CBNCR	FBG	SV	IO	330		8	6	4800			14900	17600
24		VILLAIN III	OP	OFF	FBG	SV	IO	410	MRCR	8	4	3200			12500	14200
24		VILLAIN III	ST	OFF	FBG	SV	IO	330-365		8	4	3200	3	10	10200	12500
24	8	CHAPARRAL 234	ST	FSH	FBG	SV	IO	175		8		2975	2	7	9250	10500
24	8	CHAPARRAL 234	ST	FSH	FBG	SV	IO	260-275		8		4000	2	7	11600	13800
24	8	STRIKER 238	OP	OPFSH	FBG	SV	OB			8		2975			7600	8700
25	3	CHAPARRAL 2550 CX	OP	CTRCN	FBG	DV	IO	229-330		8	6				12700	15800
25	3	CHAPARRAL 2550 CX	OP	CTRCN	FBG	DV	IO	365	MRCR	8	6				14700	16700
25	3	CHAPARRAL 2550 SX	ST	CUD	FBG	SV	IO	260-275		8	6	4340	3	4	12200	14400
25	3	CHAPARRAL 2550 SX	ST	CUD	FBG	SV	IO	330-365		8	6	4340	3	4	13300	16000
26	1	SIGNATURE 23	OP	SPTCR	FBG	SV	IO	229-260		8		4500	3	1	12900	14800
26	6	SIGNATURE 27	OP	SPTCR	FBG	SV	IO	260-330		8	2	5100	3	6	14300	17800
26	6	SIGNATURE 27	OP	SPTCR	FBG	SV	IO	T175-T205		8	2	5100	3	6	15400	18300
27	10	CHAPARRAL 2750 SX	OP	SPTCR	FBG	SV	IO	330-365		9		6460			19300	22200
27	10	CHAPARRAL 2750 SX	OP	SPTCR	FBG	SV	IO	T260-T275		9		6460			21000	24100
29	3	SIGNATURE 28	OP	CR	FBG	SV	IO	330		9	9	7200			23700	26500
29	3	SIGNATURE 28	OP	CR	FBG	SV	IO	T175-T205		9	9	7200			23800	27400
29	3	SIGNATURE 28	OP	CR	FBG	SV	IO	T130D	VLVO	9	9	7200			26700	29700
30		VILLAIN IV	OP	OFF	FBG	SV	IO	T330-T410		8	2	7400			28400	33900
30		VILLAIN IV	ST	OFF	FBG	SV	IO	T330-T365		8	2	7400	3	6	28100	32400
30	6	SIGNATURE 30	OP	CR	FBG	SV	IO	T150-T275		10	9	9750	2	9	30300	37100
34	4	LASER 32	OP	CR	FBG	SV	IO	T330-T365		10	8	10500	2	10	46000	52000
		1990 BOATS														
16	6	CHAPARRAL 178XL	ST	RNBT	FBG	DV	OB			7	2	1400	2	5	2700	3150
17	10	CHAPARRAL 1800SL	OP	RNBT	FBG	DV	OB			7	7	2100	3	11	3550	4150
17	10	CHAPARRAL 1800SL	OP	RNBT	FBG	DV	IO	125-175		7	7	2100	3	11	3950	4600
17	10	CHAPARRAL 1850SL	OP	RNBT	FBG	DV	IO	125-175		7	7	2175	3	11	4000	4700
18	9	CHAPARRAL 1900SL	OP	RNBT	FBG	DV	OB			7	8	2200	3	11	3650	4250
18	9	CHAPARRAL 1900SL	OP	RNBT	FBG	DV	IO	125-205		7	8	2200	3	11	4250	5300
18	11	CHAPARRAL 187XL	ST	RNBT	FBG	DV	OB			7	2	1500	2	7	2950	3400
19	3	CHAPARRAL 198F	ST	FSH	FBG	DV	OB			8		1900	2	4	3350	3900
19	3	CHAPARRAL 198XL	ST	RNBT	FBG	DV	OB			8		1900	2	7	3500	4050
19	3	CHAPARRAL 198XL	ST	RNBT	FBG	DV	IO	125-175		8		2550	2	7	4850	5650
19	6	CHAPARRAL 1900SX	ST	OFF	FBG	DV	IO	175-230		8		2500	3		5100	6200
20	3	CHAPARRAL 2000SL	OP	RNBT	FBG	DV	OB			8		2650	2	7	5050	5800
20	3	CHAPARRAL 2000SL	OP	RNBT	FBG	DV	IO	145-260		8		2650	2	7	5700	7050
20	3	CHAPARRAL 2000SL	OP	RNBT	FBG	DV	IO	275	VLVO	8		2650	2	7	6500	7450
20	3	CHAPARRAL 2050SL	OP	RNBT	FBG	DV	IO	145-260		8		3000	2	9	6100	7500
20	3	CHAPARRAL 2050SL	OP	RNBT	FBG	DV	IO	275	VLVO	8		3000	2	9	6900	7950
20	6	VILLAIN II ELIM	OP	CR	FBG	DV	IO	260-275		8		2600	2	7	6350	7850
20	10	CHAPARRAL 204	ST	FSH	FBG	DV	OB			8		2200	3	9	4800	5550
21	2	CHAPARRAL 2100SX	OP	OFF	FBG	DV	IO	200-270		8	4	2954	3	3	6850	8350
21	2	CHAPARRAL 2100SX	OP	OFF	FBG	DV	IO	275	VLVO	8	4	2954	3	3	7650	8800
21	2	CHAPARRAL 2150SX	OP	OFF	FBG	DV	IO	200-270		8	4	3200	3	1	7200	8750
21	2	CHAPARRAL 2150SX	OP	OFF	FBG	DV	IO	275	VLVO	8	4	3200	3	1	8000	9200
22	8	CHAPARRAL 224	ST	FSH	FBG	DV	OB			8		2900	2	10	6500	7450
23	3	CHAPARRAL 2300SX	OP	OFF	FBG	DV	IO	229-330		8	6	3920	3	10	9650	12000
23	3	CHAPARRAL 2350SX	OP	OFF	FBG	DV	IO	229-330		8	6	4120	3	4	10000	12400
24		VILLAIN III	ST	CR	FBG	DV	IO	260-275		8	4	3200	3	10	8600	10400
24		VILLAIN III	ST	CR	FBG	DV	IO	330-365		8	4	3200	3	10	9600	11800
24		VILLAIN III ELIM	OP	OFF	FBG	DV	IO	260-275		8	4	3200	3	10	8600	10400
24		VILLAIN III ELIM	OP	OFF	FBG	DV	IO	330-365		8	4	3200	3	10	9600	11800
24	8	CHAPARRAL 234	ST	FSH	FBG	DV	OB			8		2975	2	7	7300	8400
24	8	CHAPARRAL 234	ST	FSH	FBG	DV	IO	229-275		8		4000	2	7	10900	13000
25	3	CHAPARRAL 2550SX	ST	OFF	FBG	DV	IO	260-275		8	6	4340	3	4	11300	13300
25	3	CHAPARRAL 2550SX	ST	OFF	FBG	DV	IO	330-365		8	6	4340	3	4	12300	14800
26	1	SIGNATURE 23	OP	SPTCR	FBG	SV	IO	229-260		8		4500	3	1	12100	14000
26	6	SIGNATURE 27	OP	SPTCR	FBG	SV	IO	260-330		8	2	5100	3	6	13400	16700
26	6	SIGNATURE 27	OP	SPTCR	FBG	SV	IO	200D	VLVO	8	2	5100	3	6	15100	17200
26	6	SIGNATURE 27	OP	SPTCR	FBG	SV	IO	T145-T205		8	2	5100	3	6	14000	17200
30		VILLAIN IV	ST	OFF	FBG	DV	IO	T260-T365		8	2	7400	3	6	24900	30400
33	2	SIGNATURE 30	OP	OFF	FBG	DV	IO	T175-T275		10	9	9750	2	9	36500	42900
33	2	SIGNATURE 30	OP	OFF	FBG	DV	IO	T200D	VLVO	10	9	9750	2	9	40700	45200
34	4	LASER 32	OP	OFF	FBG	DV	IO	T260-T365		10	8	10500	2	10	43400	51600

CONTINUED ON NEXT PAGE

CHAPARRAL BOATS INC -CONTINUED See inside cover to adjust price for area

LOA FT	LOA IN	NAME AND/ OR MODEL	TOP/ RIG	BOAT TYPE	-HULL- MTL	-HULL- TP	ENGINE TP	ENGINE # HP	ENGINE MFG	BEAM FT	BEAM IN	WGT LBS	DRAFT FT	DRAFT IN	RETAIL LOW	RETAIL HIGH
		1989 BOATS														
16	6	CHAPARRAL 178XL	ST	RNBT	FBG	DV	OB			7	2	1400			2600	3000
16	6	CHAPARRAL 178XL	ST	RNBT	FBG	DV	IO	130		7	2	2000			3250	3750
17	8	CHAPARRAL 187XL	ST	RNBT	FBG	DV	OB			7	2	1500			2750	3200
17	8	CHAPARRAL 187XL	ST	RNBT	FBG	DV	IO	130-175		7	2	2100			3550	4150
17	8	CHAPARRAL 187XL	ST	RNBT	FBG	DV	IO	205		7	2	2100			3650	4450
19	3	CHAPARRAL 198CXL	ST	CUD	FBG	DV	IO	165-260		8		2900			5150	6350
19	3	CHAPARRAL 198CXL	ST	CUD	FBG	DV	IO	275	VLVO	8		2900			5900	6750
19	3	CHAPARRAL 198F	ST	FSH	FBG	DV	OB			8		1900			3200	3750
19	3	CHAPARRAL 198F	ST	FSH	FBG	DV	IO	130-175		8		2500			4950	5750
19	3	CHAPARRAL 198XL	ST	RNBT	FBG	DV	OB			8		1900			3350	3900
19	3	CHAPARRAL 198XL	ST	RNBT	FBG	DV	IO	165-260		8		2550			4650	5700
19	3	CHAPARRAL 198XL	ST	RNBT	FBG	DV	IO	275	VLVO	8		2550			5300	6100
19	3	CHAPARRAL 204	ST	FSH	FBG	DV	OB			8		2200			3500	4050
19	3	VILLAIN II	ST	CR	FBG	DV	IO	260-275		8		2600			5150	6050
19	3	VILLAIN II ELIM	OP	CR	FBG	DV	IO	260-275		8		2600			5150	6400
19	6	CHAPARRAL 1900SX	ST	OFF	FBG	DV	IO	175-235		8		2500			4800	5850
21		CHAPARRAL 224	ST	FSH	FBG	DV	OB			8		2900			5550	6350
21		CHAPARRAL 228XL	OP	CUD	FBG	DV	IO	229-275		8		3900			7900	9550
21	2	CHAPARRAL 2100SX	OP	OFF	FBG	DV	IO	200-270		8	4	2800			6300	7650
21	2	CHAPARRAL 2100SX	OP	OFF	FBG	DV	IO	275	VLVO	8	4	2800			7000	8050
21	2	CHAPARRAL 2150SX	OP	OFF	FBG	DV	IO	200-270		8	4	3200			6800	8250
21	2	CHAPARRAL 2150SX	OP	OFF	FBG	DV	IO	275	VLVO	8	4	3200			7550	8650
23		CHAPARRAL 234	ST	FSH	FBG	DV	OB			8		2974			6500	7500
23		CHAPARRAL 234	ST	FSH	FBG	DV	IO	229-275		8		4000			9450	11200
23		CHAPARRAL 248XL	OP	CUD	FBG	DV	IO	229-330		8		4125			9200	11400
23		SIGNATURE 23	OP	SPTCR	FBG	SV	IO	229-275		8	2	4500			9850	11600
23	3	CHAPARRAL 2300SX	OP	OFF	FBG	DV	IO	229-330		8	6	3920			9150	11300
23	3	CHAPARRAL 2350SX	OP	OFF	FBG	DV	IO	229-330		8	6	4100			9400	11600
23	11	VILLAIN III	ST	CR	FBG	DV	IO	260-270		8	5	3200			8100	9750
23	11	VILLAIN III	ST	CR	FBG	DV	IO	330-365		8	5	3200			9100	11100
25	3	CHAPARRAL 2550CX	OP	CTRCN	FBG	DV	IO	229-330		8	6				11200	14000
25	3	CHAPARRAL 2550CX	OP	CTRCN	FBG	DV	IO	340-365		8	6				12400	14900
25	3	CHAPARRAL 2550SX	ST	OFF	FBG	DV	IO	229-330		8	6	4400			10700	13300
25	3	CHAPARRAL 2550SX	ST	OFF	FBG	DV	IO	340-365		8	6	4400			11800	14000
26	6	SIGNATURE 27	OP	SPTCR	FBG	SV	IO	260-330		8	2	5100			12700	15500
26	6	SIGNATURE 27	OP	SPTCR	FBG	SV	IO	T165-T205		8	2	5100			13500	16300
27	10	CHAPARRAL 2850SX	ST	OFF	FBG	DV	IO	330-365		8	4	5900			16000	18800
27	10	CHAPARRAL 2850SX	ST	OFF	FBG	DV	IO	T260-T275		8	4	5900			17400	20400
30		VILLAIN IV	ST	OFF	FBG	DV	IO	T260-T365		8	2	7400			23500	28700
32	2	LASER 32	OP	OFF	FBG	DV	IO	T260-T365		10	8	10500			29400	34700
		1988 BOATS														
16	6	CHAPARRAL 178XL	ST	RNBT	FBG	DV	OB			7	2	1400			2450	2900
16	6	CHAPARRAL 178XL	ST	RNBT	FBG	DV	IO	130		7	2	2000			3050	3550
17	8	CHAPARRAL 187XL	ST	RNBT	FBG	DV	OB			7	2	1500			2650	3050
17	8	CHAPARRAL 187XL	ST	RNBT	FBG	DV	IO	130-175		7	2	2200			3450	4050
18	3	CHAPARRAL 1900SX	ST	OFF	FBG	DV	IO	175-230							3850	4650
18	3	CHAPARRAL 195XLC	ST	RNBT	FBG	DV	IO	130-230		7	8	2400			3850	4700
19	3	CHAPARRAL 198CXL	ST	CUD	FBG	DV	IO	165-230		8		2900			4850	5750
19	3	CHAPARRAL 198F	ST	FSH	FBG	DV	OB			8		1900			3100	3600
19	3	CHAPARRAL 198F	ST	FSH	FBG	DV	IO	130-175		8		2700			4900	5650
19	3	CHAPARRAL 198XL	ST	RNBT	FBG	DV	OB			8		1900			3200	3700
19	3	CHAPARRAL 198XL	ST	RNBT	FBG	DV	IO	165-230		8		2700			4500	5350
19	3	CHAPARRAL 200XLC	ST	RNBT	FBG	DV	IO		MRCR	8		2800			**	**
19	3	CHAPARRAL 200XLC	ST	RNBT	FBG	DV	IO	175-270		8		2800			4650	5650
19	3	CHAPARRAL 204	ST	FSH	FBG	DV	OB			8		2200			3350	3900
19	3	VILLAIN II	ST	CR	FBG	DV	IO	230-270		8		2600			4700	5700
21		CHAPARRAL 215XLC	ST	CR	FBG	DV	IO	200-270		8		3900			7150	8650
21		CHAPARRAL 224	ST	FSH	FBG	DV	OB			8		2900			5350	6150
21	2	CHAPARRAL 2100SX	OP	OFF	FBG	DV	IO	200-270		8	4	2950			6100	7450
21	2	CHAPARRAL 2150SX	OP	OFF	FBG	DV	IO	200-270		8	4	3200			6450	7800
21	9	CHAPARRAL 225XLC	ST	CR	FBG	DV	IO	200-270		8	3	3200	2	4	6600	8000
22		VILLAIN III	ST	CR	FBG	DV	IO	260-270		8		3200			6850	8000
22		VILLAIN III	ST	CR	FBG	DV	IO	330-340		8		3200			7700	8950
22		VILLAIN III	ST	CR	FBG	DV	IO	365	MRCR	8		3200			8400	9700
23		CHAPARRAL 234	ST	FSH	FBG	DV	OB			8		2974			6300	7250
23		CHAPARRAL 234	ST	FSH	FBG	DV	IO	230-260		8		4000			8650	10200
23		CHAPARRAL 235XLC	ST	CR	FBG	DV	IO	230-270		8		4125			8400	9950
23		CHAPARRAL 235XLC	ST	CR	FBG	DV	IO	330-340		8		4125			9450	10900
23		CHAPARRAL 238XLC	ST	CR	FBG	DV	IO	230-260		8	2	4500			9150	10600
23	3	CHAPARRAL 2300SX	OP	OFF	FBG	DV	IO	230-270		8	6	3920			8350	9900
23	3	CHAPARRAL 2350SX	OP	OFF	FBG	DV	IO	230-270		8	6	4100			8600	10200
23	3	CHAPARRAL 238XLC	ST	CR	FBG	DV	IO	230-260							8550	10000
24	4	CHAPARRAL 244	ST	FSH	FBG	DV	IO	230-260		8		3900			9250	10700
24	4	CHAPARRAL 244	ST	FSH	FBG	DV	IO	T130		8		3900			10000	11400
24	6	CHAPARRAL 2550SX	ST	OFF	FBG	DV	IO		MRCR						**	**
		IO OMC ** ** , IO 230-260 9400 10900, IO 350													10900	12300
25	3	CHAPARRAL 2550 CX	OP	CTRCN	FBG	DV	IO	230-270		8	6				10500	12300
25	3	CHAPARRAL 2550 CX	OP	CTRCN	FBG	DV	IO	330-365		8	6				11700	14100
26	6	CHAPARRAL 278XLC	ST	CR	FBG	DV	IO	200-270		8	2	5100			11500	13900
26	6	CHAPARRAL 278XLC	ST	CR	FBG	DV	IO	330-340		8	2	5100			13000	14900
26	6	CHAPARRAL 278XLC	ST	CR	FBG	DV	IO	T165-T175		8	2	5100			12900	14800
27	10	CHAPARRAL 2850SX	ST	OFF	FBG	DV	IO	330-365		8	4	5900	2	5	15100	17800
27	10	CHAPARRAL 2850SX	ST	OFF	FBG	DV	IO	T260-T270		8	4	5900	2	5	16400	18900
30		VILLAIN IV	ST	OFF	FBG	DV	IO	T260-T365		8	2	7400	3		22300	27200
32	2	LASER 32	OP	OFF	FBG	DV	IO	T260-T365		10	8	10500			27900	32900
		1987 BOATS														
16	6	CHAPARRAL 178XL	ST	RNBT	FBG	DV	OB			7	2	1400			2400	2750
16	6	CHAPARRAL 178XL	ST	RNBT	FBG	DV	IO	130		7	2	2000			2900	3400
17		CHAPARRAL 170XL	ST	RNBT	FBG	DV	IO	130							3100	3600
17	8	CHAPARRAL 187XL	ST	RNBT	FBG	DV	OB			7	2	1500			2550	2950
17	8	CHAPARRAL 187XL	ST	RNBT	FBG	DV	IB	130-165		7	2	2200			4200	5100
17	8	CHAPARRAL 187XL	ST	RNBT	FBG	DV	IB	175	OMC	7	2	2200			4700	5400
18	3	CHAPARRAL 195XLC	ST	RNBT	FBG	DV	IO	130-230		7	8	2400			3650	4450
18	3	CHAPARRAL 195XLC	ST	RNBT	FBG	DV	IO	260		7	8	2400			3950	4600
19	3	CHAPARRAL 198CXL	ST	CUD	FBG	DV	IO	130-230		8		2900			4650	5500
19	3	CHAPARRAL 198F	ST	FSH	FBG	DV	OB			8		1900			2950	3450
19	3	CHAPARRAL 198F	ST	FSH	FBG	DV	IO	130-260		8					4900	6000
19	3	CHAPARRAL 198XL	ST	RNBT	FBG	DV	OB			8		1900			3100	3600
19	3	CHAPARRAL 198XL	ST	RNBT	FBG	DV	IO	130-230		8		2700			4250	5100
19	3	CHAPARRAL 200XLC	ST	RNBT	FBG	DV	IO	130-260		8		2800			4350	5350
19	3	CHAPARRAL 204	ST	FSH	FBG	DV	OB			8		2000			3050	3550
19	3	VILLAIN II	ST	CR	FBG	DV	IO	230-260		8		2600			4500	5350
19	3	VILLAIN II	ST	CR	FBG	DV	IO	300	MRCR	8		2600			5000	5750
21		CHAPARRAL 215XLC	ST	CR	FBG	DV	IO	200-260		8		3900			6800	8100
21		CHAPARRAL 215XLC	ST	CR	FBG	DV	IO	350	MRCR	8		3900			8250	9450
21		CHAPARRAL 224	ST	FSH	FBG	DV	OB			8		2900			5200	6000
21	9	CHAPARRAL 225XLC	ST	CR	FBG	DV	IO	165-260		8	3	3200	2	4	6200	7500
21	9	CHAPARRAL 225XLC	ST	CR	FBG	DV	IO	350	MRCR	8	3	3200	2	4	7700	8850
22		VILLAIN III	ST	CR	FBG	DV	IO		MRCR	8		3200			**	**
22		VILLAIN III	ST	CR	FBG	DV	IO	260		8		3200			6500	7500
22		VILLAIN III	ST	CR	FBG	DV	IO	340-350		8		3200			7400	8850
23		CHAPARRAL 234	ST	FSH	FBG	DV	OB			8		2975			6100	7050
23		CHAPARRAL 234	ST	FSH	FBG	DV	IO		MRCR	8		2975			**	**
23		CHAPARRAL 234	ST	FSH	FBG	DV	IO	200-260		8		2975			6650	7950
23		CHAPARRAL 235XLC	ST	CR	FBG	DV	IO		MRCR	8					**	**
23		CHAPARRAL 235XLC	ST	CR	FBG	DV	IO		OMC	8		4125			**	**
23		CHAPARRAL 235XLC	ST	CR	FBG	DV	IO	200-260		8		4125			7900	9350
23		CHAPARRAL 238XLC	ST	CR	FBG	DV	IO		MRCR	8					**	**
23		CHAPARRAL 238XLC	ST	CR	FBG	DV	IO		OMC	8					**	**
23		CHAPARRAL 238XLC	ST	CR	FBG	DV	IO	200-260		8		4500			8450	10000
24	4	CHAPARRAL 244	ST	FSH	FBG	DV	SE		OMC	8		3900			**	**
24	4	CHAPARRAL 244	ST	FSH	FBG	DV	IO		MRCR	8		3900			**	**
24	4	CHAPARRAL 244	ST	FSH	FBG	DV	IO	180-260		8		3900			8500	10200
24	4	CHAPARRAL 244	ST	FSH	FBG	DV	IO	T130-T180		8		3900			9500	10900
25	3	CHAPARRAL 2550 CX	OP	CTRCN	FBG	DV	IO	230-270		8	6				9950	11700
25	3	CHAPARRAL 2550 CX	OP	CTRCN	FBG	DV	IO	330-365		8	6				11100	13400
26	6	CHAPARRAL 278XLC	ST	CR	FBG	DV	IO		MRCR	8					**	**
		IO OMC ** ** , IO 200-260 10900 13000, IO T165-T180													12200	14100
27	10	CHAPARRAL 285XLC	ST	OFF	FBG	DV	IO		MRCR	8	4	5900	2	5	**	**
		IO OMC ** ** , IO T165-T260 14300 17800, IO T350 MRCR													17600	19900
30		VILLAIN IV	ST	OFF	FBG	DV	IO	T260-T350		8	2	7500	3		21200	25500
30		VILLAIN IV	ST	OFF	FBG	DV	IO	T454	MRCR	8	2	7500	3		25700	28500
		1986 BOATS														
16	6	CHAPARRAL 178XL	ST	RNBT	FBG	DV	OB			7	2	1400			2300	2650
16	6	CHAPARRAL 178XL	ST	RNBT	FBG	DV	IO	140		7	2	2000			2800	3250
17		CHAPARRAL 170XL	ST	RNBT	FBG	DV	IO	140							2950	3400
17	8	CHAPARRAL 187XL	ST	RNBT	FBG	DV	OB			7	2	1500			2450	2850
17	8	CHAPARRAL 187XL	ST	RNBT	FBG	DV	IB	140-170		7	2	2200			4050	4950
17	8	CHAPARRAL 187XL	ST	RNBT	FBG	DV	IB	175	OMC	7	2	2200			4500	5150
18	3	CHAPARRAL 195XLC	ST	RNBT	FBG	DV	IO	140-230		7	8	2400			3500	4250
18	3	CHAPARRAL 195XLC	ST	RNBT	FBG	DV	IO	260		7	8	2400			3800	4400
19	3	CHAPARRAL 198CXL	ST	CUD	FBG	DV	IO	170-230		8		2900			4450	5250
19	3	CHAPARRAL 198F	ST	FSH	FBG	DV	OB			8		1900			2850	3350
19	3	CHAPARRAL 198F	ST	FSH	FBG	DV	IO	140-260		8					4650	5750
19	3	CHAPARRAL 198XL	ST	RNBT	FBG	DV	OB			8		1900			2950	3450

128
CONTINUED ON NEXT PAGE
96th ed. - Vol. II

LOA FT	LOA IN	NAME AND/ OR MODEL	TOP/ RIG	BOAT TYPE	HULL MTL	HULL TP	ENGINE TP	ENGINE # HP	ENGINE MFG	BEAM FT	BEAM IN	WGT LBS	DRAFT FT	DRAFT IN	RETAIL LOW	RETAIL HIGH
		1986 BOATS														
19	3	CHAPARRAL 198XL	ST	RNBT	FBG	DV	IO	170-230		8		2700			4050	4850
19	3	CHAPARRAL 200XLC	ST	RNBT	FBG	DV	IO	140-260		8		2800			4150	5100
19	3	CHAPARRAL 204	ST	FSH	FBG	DV	OB			8		2000			2950	3450
19	3	VILLAIN II	ST	CR	FBG	DV	IO	230-260		8		2600			4250	5100
19	3	VILLAIN II	ST	CR	FBG	DV	IO	300	MRCR	8		2600			4750	5450
21		CHAPARRAL 215XLC	ST	CR	FBG	DV	IO			8		3900			**	**
21		CHAPARRAL 215XLC	ST	CR	FBG	DV	IO	190-260		8		3900			6500	7750
21		CHAPARRAL 215XLC	ST	CR	FBG	DV	IO	300	MRCR	8		3900			7100	8150
21		CHAPARRAL 224	ST	FSH	FBG	DV	OB			8		2900			5050	5850
22		VILLAIN III	ST	CR	FBG	DV	IO	260-300		8		3200			6250	7550
23		CHAPARRAL 234	ST	FSH	FBG	DV	OB			8		2975			5950	6850
23		CHAPARRAL 234	ST	FSH	FBG	DV	IO	190-230		8		2975			6350	7400
23		CHAPARRAL 234	ST	FSH	FBG	DV	SE	260	OMC	8		2975			5950	6850
23		CHAPARRAL 234	ST	FSH	FBG	DV	IO	260		8		2975			6600	7600
23		CHAPARRAL 234	ST	FSH	FBG	DV	SE	T260	OMC	8		2975			5950	6850
23		CHAPARRAL 235XLC	ST	CR	FBG	DV	IO	190-300		8		4125			7500	9350
23		CHAPARRAL 238XLC	ST	CR	FBG	DV	SE		OMC	8		4500			**	**
23		CHAPARRAL 238XLC	ST	CR	FBG	DV	IO	190-300		8		4500			8050	9950
23		CHAPARRAL 238XLC	ST	CR	FBG	DV	SE	T	OMC	8		4500			**	**
24	4	CHAPARRAL 244	ST	FSH	FBG	DV	SE		OMC	8		3900			**	**
24	4	CHAPARRAL 244	ST	FSH	FBG	DV	IO	190-260		8		3900			8150	9750
24	4	CHAPARRAL 244	ST	FSH	FBG	DV	SE	T	OMC	8		3900			**	**
24	4	CHAPARRAL 244	ST	FSH	FBG	DV	IO	T140-T175		8		3900			9150	10500
26	6	CHAPARRAL 278XLC	ST	CR	FBG	DV	SE		OMC	8		5100			**	**
26	6	CHAPARRAL 278XLC	ST	CR	FBG	DV	IO	200-300		8		5100			10400	12900
26	6	CHAPARRAL 278XLC	ST	CR	FBG	DV	SE	T	OMC	8		5100			**	**
26	6	CHAPARRAL 278XLC	ST	CR	FBG	DV	IO	T140-T190		8		5100			11400	13600
		1985 BOATS														
17		CHAPARRAL 187VBR		RNBT	FBG	DV	IO	170		7	2	2200			2900	3400
19	3	CHAPARRAL 198CV		CUD	FBG	DV	IO	230		8		2900			4400	5050
19	3	CHAPARRAL 198F		FSH	FBG	DV	IO	290		8					5000	5750
19	3	CHAPARRAL 198VBR		RNBT	FBG	DV	IO	230		8		2700			4000	4650
21		CHAPARRAL 215V		RNBT	FBG	DV	IO	230		8		3900			6000	6900
23		CHAPARRAL 234V		FSH	FBG	DV	IO	228		8					7600	8750
23		CHAPARRAL 235V		CUD	FBG	DV	IO	230		8		4125			7300	8400
23		CHAPARRAL 238V		CR	FBG	DV	IO	260		8		4500			8000	9150
24	4	CHAPARRAL 244V		CUD	FBG	DV	IO	230		8		3900			7550	8700
26	6	CHAPARRAL 278V		CR	FBG	DV	IO	260		8		4500			9850	11200
		1984 BOATS														
16	6	CHAPARRAL 172VBR	ST	RNBT	FBG	DV	IO	120-145		7	2	1900			2500	2950
16	6	CHAPARRAL 177VBR	ST	RNBT	FBG	DV	OB			7	2	1400			2150	2500
16	6	CHAPARRAL 177VBR	ST	RNBT	FBG	DV	IO	120-145		7	2	2000			2600	3000
17	8	CHAPARRAL 187VBR	ST	RNBT	FBG	DV	OB			7	2	1500			2300	2650
17	8	CHAPARRAL 187VBR	ST	RNBT	FBG	DV	IO	120-184		7	2	2200			2900	3400
19	3	CHAPARRAL 198CV	ST	CUD	FBG	DV	IO	140-260		8		2900			4050	5050
19	3	CHAPARRAL 198F	ST	FSH	FBG	DV	OB			8		1900			2700	3150
19	3	CHAPARRAL 198F	ST	FSH	FBG	DV	IO	140-260		8					4350	5350
19	3	CHAPARRAL 198VBR	ST	RNBT	FBG	DV	OB			8		1900			2800	3250
19	3	CHAPARRAL 198VBR	ST	RNBT	FBG	DV	IO	140-260		8		2700			3750	4650
19	3	CHAPARRAL 204V	ST	FSH	FBG	DV	OB			8		2000			2750	3200
21		CHAPARRAL 214V	ST	CUD	FBG	DV	OB			8		2500			4500	5200
21		CHAPARRAL 214V	ST	CUD	FBG	DV	IO	170-260		8		3400			5400	6550
21		CHAPARRAL 215V	ST	RNBT	FBG	DV	IO	185-260		8		3900			5700	6850
23		CHAPARRAL 234V	ST	FSH	FBG	DV	OB			8		2975			5650	6500
23		CHAPARRAL 234V	ST	FSH	FBG	DV	IO	170-260		8					7250	8650
23		CHAPARRAL 235V	ST	CUD	FBG	DV	IO	185		8		4125			6950	8000
23		CHAPARRAL 235V	ST	CUD	FBG	DV	IO	T188		8		4125			7800	8950
23		CHAPARRAL 238V	ST	CR	FBG	DV	IO	198-260		8		4500			7450	8850
23		CHAPARRAL 278V	ST	CR	FBG	DV	IO	198-260		8		4500			7450	8850
24	4	CHAPARRAL 244V	ST	CUD	FBG	DV	IO	185-260		8		3900			7150	8550
24	4	CHAPARRAL 244V	ST	CUD	FBG	DV	IO	T120-T170		8		3900			7900	9250

....For earlier years, see the BUC Used Boat Price Guide, Volume 3

CHARGER BOATS INC

CONCORD LK ONTARIO CANADA
ALSO AMF

See inside cover to adjust price for area

LOA FT	LOA IN	NAME AND/ OR MODEL	TOP/ RIG	BOAT TYPE	HULL MTL	HULL TP	ENGINE TP	ENGINE # HP	ENGINE MFG	BEAM FT	BEAM IN	WGT LBS	DRAFT FT	DRAFT IN	RETAIL LOW	RETAIL HIGH
		1989 BOATS														
16		CHARGER 16 DL	OP	RNBT	FBG	DV	OB			6	1	650		6	2650	3100
17	11	CHARGER 18 STV	OP	RNBT	FBG	TH	OB			6	8	800		8	3550	4100
18		CHARGER 18 DL	OP	RNBT	FBG	DV	OB			6	9	800		8	3550	4100
18		CHARGER 18 SK	OP	SKI	FBG	DV	OB			6	9	800		8	3550	4100
20	4	CHARGER 20 STV	OP	RNBT	FBG	TH	OB			6	8	1000		10	4650	5350
20	4	CHARGER 20 STV	OP	RNBT	FBG	TH	IO	300		6	8	1100		10	6100	7000
20	4	CHARGER 20 SV	OP	RNBT	FBG	DV	OB			6	8	1000		10	4800	5500
20	4	CHARGER 20 SV	OP	RNBT	FBG	DV	IO	300		6	8	1100		10	6250	7150
		1988 BOATS														
16		CHARGER 16 DL	OP	RNBT	FBG	DV	OB			6	1	650		6	2600	3000
17	11	CHARGER 18 STV	OP	RNBT	FBG	TH	OB			6	8	800		8	3400	4000
17	11	CHARGER 18 STV BASS	OP	BASS	FBG	TH	OB			6	8	800		8	3400	4000
18		CHARGER 18 DL	OP	RNBT	FBG	DV	OB			6	9	800		8	3450	4000
18		CHARGER 18 SK	OP	SKI	FBG	DV	OB			6	9	800		8	3450	4000
20	4	CHARGER 20 STV	OP	RNBT	FBG	TH	OB			6	8	1000		10	4550	5200
20	4	CHARGER 20 STV	OP	RNBT	FBG	TH	IO	300		6	8	1100		10	5850	6700
20	4	CHARGER 20 SV	OP	RNBT	FBG	DV	OB			6	8	1000		10	4700	5400
20	4	CHARGER 20 SV	OP	RNBT	FBG	DV	IO	300		6	8	1100		10	5850	6700
		1987 BOATS														
16	1	CHARGER DL	OP	RNBT	FBG	DV	OB			6	6	650		6	2550	2950
17	8	CHARGER STV	OP	RNBT	FBG	TR	OB			6	9	800		8	3300	3850
18		CHARGER DL	OP	RNBT	FBG	DV	OB			6	9	850		8	3500	4100
18		CHARGER SK	OP	SKI	FBG	DV	OB			6	9	800		8	3350	3850
20	1	CHARGER BOWRIDER	OP	RNBT	FBG	DV	OB			8		1400		10	5850	6700
20	3	CHARGER STV	OP	RNBT	FBG	TR	OB			6	9	1000		10	4450	5150
20	6	CHARGER TV	OP	RNBT	FBG	TR	OB			6	2	850		10	3850	4500
		1986 BOATS														
16	1	CHARGER DL	OP	RNBT	FBG	DV	OB			6	6	650		6	2450	2850
18		CHARGER DL	OP	RNBT	FBG	DV	OB			6	9	850		8	3450	4000
18		CHARGER SK	OP	SKI	FBG	DV	OB			6	9	800		8	3250	3750
20	1	CHARGER BOWRIDER	OP	RNBT	FBG	DV	OB			8		1400		10	6100	7000
20	1	CHARGER BOWRIDER	OP	RNBT	FBG	DV	IO	250		8		1400		10	5250	6000
20	1	CHARGER DAYCRUISER	OP	RNBT	FBG	DV	OB			8		1400		10	5950	6800
20	1	CHARGER DAYCRUISER	OP	RNBT	FBG	DV	IO	250		8		1400		10	5250	6000
20	1	CHARGER GT	OP	RNBT	FBG	DV	OB			8		1400		10	5050	5800
20	1	CHARGER GT	OP	RNBT	FBG	DV	IO	250		8		1400		10	5250	6000
20	6	CHARGER TV	OP	RNBT	FBG	TR	OB			6	2	850		10	3750	4350
		1985 BOATS														
16		CHARGER 16	OP	RNBT	F/S	DV	OB			6	6	600		6	2250	2600
18		CHARGER 18DL	OP	RNBT	F/S	DV	OB			6	9	900		8	3500	4100
18		CHARGER 18SK	OP	RNBT	F/S	DV	OB			6	9	800		8	3150	3700
20	2	CHARGER 20	OP	RNBT	F/S	DV	OB			8		1400		10	5550	6400
20	2	CHARGER 20	OP	RNBT	F/S	DV	IO	260		8		1400		10	5150	5900
20	2	CHARGER 20	OP	RNBT	F/S	DV	IO	330		8		1400		10	6050	6950
		1984 BOATS														
18		CHARGER 18DL	OP	RNBT	F/S	DV	OB			6	9	900		8	3450	4000
18		CHARGER 18DL	OP	RNBT	F/S	DV	IO	170-185		6	9	900		8	3000	3550
18		CHARGER 18DL	OP	RNBT	F/S	DV	IO	260		6	9	900		8	3350	3900
18		CHARGER 18SK	OP	RNBT	F/S	DV	OB			6	9	800		8	3100	3600
20	2	CHARGER 20	OP	RNBT	F/S	DV	OB			8		1400		10	5450	6250
20	2	CHARGER 20	OP	RNBT	F/S	DV	IO	260		8		1400		10	4950	5700
20	2	CHARGER 20	OP	RNBT	F/S	DV	IO	330		8		1400		10	5850	6700

....For earlier years, see the BUC Used Boat Price Guide, Volume 3

CHARGER/AFC INC

DIV RICHLAND DIVERSIFIED IND
RICHLAND MO 65556
COAST GUARD MFG ID- RDA
FOR LATER YEARS SEE PLAY-CRAFT PONTOONS

See inside cover to adjust price for area

LOA FT	LOA IN	NAME AND/ OR MODEL	TOP/ RIG	BOAT TYPE	HULL MTL	HULL TP	ENGINE TP	ENGINE # HP	ENGINE MFG	BEAM FT	BEAM IN	WGT LBS	DRAFT FT	DRAFT IN	RETAIL LOW	RETAIL HIGH
		1986 BOATS														
16		1600		RNBT	FBG	DV	OB			6	9				3350	3900
16		162V		BASS	FBG	SV	OB			7	3				2650	3100
16	4	1650		RNBT	FBG	DV	IO			6	9				**	**
16	4	1650	OP	RNBT	FBG	DV	IO	140		6	9	1700			2550	3000
17	1	CHARGER 747XLT	OP	BASS	FBG	SV	OB			6	2	950			3400	3950
17	1	CHARGER 747XLT	OP	BASS	FBG	SV	IO	140		6	2	1700			2700	3150
17	3	FOXFIRE 170T SE	OP	BASS	FBG	DV	OB			7	2				3450	4000
17	3	FOXFIRE 170V SE	OP	BASS	FBG	DV	OB			7	2	1000			3600	4150
17	8	CHARGER 1800VBR	OP	RNBT	FBG	DV	OB			7	3	1350			4650	5350
17	8	CHARGER 1850VBR	OP	RNBT	FBG	DV	IO	140		7	3	2350			3400	3950
17	11	CHARGER 270	OP	BASS	FBG		OB			7		1050			3800	4450
18		180V	OP	BASS	FBG	SV	OB			7	2				4050	4700
18		SPORTSTER	OP	BASS	FBG	SV	OB			6	2				4050	4700
18	11	185T		BASS	FBG	SV	OB			7	3				4300	5000
18	11	185T		BASS	FBG	SV	IO			7	3				**	**
18	11	185V		BASS	FBG	SV	OB			7	3				4050	4750

```
CHARGER/AFC INC              -CONTINUED        See inside cover to adjust price for area

 LOA  NAME AND/       TOP/ BOAT  -HULL- ----ENGINE---  BEAM   WGT  DRAFT RETAIL RETAIL
FT IN  OR MODEL       RIG  TYPE  MTL TP TP #  HP  MFG   FT IN  LBS  FT IN  LOW    HIGH
------------------- 1986 BOATS -------------------------------------------------------
18 11 CHARGER 185T     OP  BASS  FBG SV IO  170        7  3  2200        3850   4450
19  2 CHARGER 2050     OP  RNBT  FBG DV IO  200        7  7  2650        4100   4750
19  2 CHARGER 2050VBR  OP  RNBT  FBG DV IO  260  MRCR  7  8  2650        4400   5050
20  1 2150V            OP  RNBT  FBG DV IO  185        7 11  2950        5050   5800
20  8 200T             OP  BASS  FBG SV OB              7  5              6950   7950
22  5 2300BR           OP  RNBT  FBG DV IO  200        8     3800        6750   7750
22  5 2300CC           OP  RNBT  FBG DV IO  230        8     3800        6850   7850
------------------- 1985 BOATS -------------------------------------------------------
16    1600                  RNBT  FBG DV OB              6  9              3300   3850
16    162V                  BASS  FBG SV OB              7  3              2600   3000
16  4 1650                  RNBT  FBG DV IO              6  9               **     **
16  4 CHARGER 1650     OP  RNBT  FBG DV IO  140        6  9              2400   2800
16  4 CHARGER 1750     OP  RNBT  FBG DV IO  120        7  2              2450   2900
17  1 CHARGER 747XLT   OP  BASS  FBG SV OB              6  2   950        3300   3850
17  1 CHARGER 747XLT   OP  BASS  FBG SV IO  140        6  2  1650        2550   3000
17  1 CHARGER 747XLV   OP  BASS  FBG SV IO  140        6  2              2550   2950
17  3 FOXFIRE 170T SE  OP  BASS  FBG DV OB              7  2              3350   3900
17  3 FOXFIRE 170V SE  OP  BASS  FBG DV OB              7  2  1000        3500   4050
17  8 CHARGER 1800VBR  OP  RNBT  FBG DV OB              7  3  1350        4600   5250
17  8 CHARGER 1850VBR  OP  RNBT  FBG DV IO  140        7  3  2350        3250   3800

17 11 CHARGER 270V     OP        FBG SV OB              7     1050        3700   4350
18 11 185T                  BASS  FBG SV OB              7  3              4200   4850
18 11 185T                  BASS  FBG SV IO              7  3               **     **
18 11 185V                  BASS  FBG SV OB              7  3              3950   4600
18 11 CHARGER 185T     OP  BASS  FBG SV IO  170        7  3              3400   3950
19  2 CHARGER 2050VBR  OP  RNBT  FBG DV IO  200-260    7  7              4000   4850
20  1 2150V            OP  RNBT  FBG DV IO  185        7 11  2950        4850   5550
20  8 200T             OP  BASS  FBG SV OB              7  5              6750   7750
------------------- 1984 BOATS -------------------------------------------------------
16    1600                  RNBT  FBG DV OB              6  9              3200   3750
16    162V                  BASS  FBG SV OB              7  3              2550   2950
16  4 1650                  RNBT  FBG DV IO              6  9               **     **
17  1 CHARGER 747XLT   OP  BASS  FBG SV OB              6  2   950        3250   3800
17  1 CHARGER 747XLT   OP  BASS  FBG SV IO  140        6  2  1650        2500   2900
17  3 FOXFIRE 170T SE  OP  BASS  FBG DV OB              7  2              3250   3800
17  3 FOXFIRE 170V SE  OP  BASS  FBG DV OB              7  2  1000        3400   3950
17  8 CHARGER 1800VBR  OP  RNBT  FBG DV OB              7  3  1350        4500   5150
17  8 CHARGER 180VBR   OP  RNBT  FBG DV IO  140  OMC   7  3  2350        3100   3600
17  8 CHARGER 1850VBR  OP  RNBT  FBG DV IO  140  MRCR  7  3  2350        3150   3650
17 11 CHARGER 270V     OP  RNBT  FBG SV OB              7  3  1800        5450   6300
18 11 185T                  BASS  FBG SV OB              7  3              4200   4900

18 11 185T                  BASS  FBG SV IO              7  3               **     **
18 11 185V                  BASS  FBG SV IO              7  3              3750   4350
19  2 CHARGER 200VBR   OP  RNBT  FBG DV IO  260  OMC   7  8  2650        4000   4650
19  2 CHARGER 2050VBR  OP  RNBT  FBG DV IO  200-260    7  8              3850   4700

       ....For earlier years, see the BUC Used Boat Price Guide, Volume 3
```

CHAUSON FRP CO LTD

```
TAIPEI TAIWAN                          See inside cover to adjust price for area

E TAGLIANETTI YACHT SALES
STATEN ISLAND NY 10309

 LOA  NAME AND/       TOP/ BOAT  -HULL- ----ENGINE---  BEAM   WGT  DRAFT RETAIL RETAIL
FT IN  OR MODEL       RIG  TYPE  MTL TP TP #  HP  MFG   FT IN  LBS  FT IN  LOW    HIGH
------------------- 1991 BOATS -------------------------------------------------------
34  8 CHAUSON 35SD     FB CBNCR FBG SV IBT150D-T275D 12  9      2  2  92400 115000
36  8 CHAUSON 37SD     FB CBNCR FBG SV IB T150D  CUM 12  9      2  2 108000 118500
      IB T210D VLVO 107000 117500, IB T210D CUM 110500 121500, IB T250D CUM 113000 124000
      IB T260D CAT  115500 127000, IB T375D CAT 125000 137500

36  8 CHAUSON 37SF     FB   SF  FBG SV IB T375D CAT  12  9      2  2  94600 104000
41  3 CHAUSON 42SD     FB CBNCR FBG SV IB T150D  CUM 12  9      2  4 124500 137000
      IB T150D VLVO 123500 135500, IB T210D CUM 128000 140500, IB T250D CUM 130500 143500
      IB T260D CAT  134000 147500, IB T375D CAT 145000 159500

41  4 CHAUSON 42SF     FB   SF  FBG SV IB T375D CAT  12  9      2  4 157000 172500
```

CHECKMATE BOATS INC

```
BUCYRUS OH 44820     COAST GUARD MFG ID- CHK See inside cover to adjust price for area

         For more recent years, see the BUC Used Boat Price Guide, Volume 1

 LOA  NAME AND/       TOP/ BOAT  -HULL- ----ENGINE---  BEAM   WGT  DRAFT RETAIL RETAIL
FT IN  OR MODEL       RIG  TYPE  MTL TP TP #  HP  MFG   FT IN  LBS  FT IN  LOW    HIGH
------------------- 1996 BOATS -------------------------------------------------------
17  1 PULSE 170 BR     OP  RNBT  FBG DV OB              7  5  1280        2750   3200
17  1 PULSE 171        OP  RNBT  FBG DV OB              7  5  1235        2650   3050
18  5 PERSUADER 183 BR OP  RNBT  FBG DV IO  180  MRCR  7  4  2625        6850   7900
18  5 PERSUADER 184    OP  RNBT  FBG DV IO  180  MRCR  7  4  2600        6850   7850
18  7 PULSE 185 BR     OP  RNBT  FBG DV OB              7 10  1415        3050   3550
18  7 PULSE 186        OP  RNBT  FBG DV OB              7 10  1460        3100   3600
20  3 PERSUADER 202 BR OP  RNBT  FBG DV IO  180-250    7 10  2790        8400  10100
20  3 PERSUADER 203    OP  RNBT  FBG DV IO  180-250    7 10  2685        8500  10500
20  5 PULSARE 2100     OP  RNBT  FBG DV OB              7 11  1375        3700   4300
20  5 PULSARE 2100 BR  OP  RNBT  FBG DV OB              7 11  1325        3500   4050
21  4 PULSE 210 BR     OP  RNBT  FBG DV OB              7 10  1725        4450   5150
21  4 PULSE 211        OP  RNBT  FBG DV OB              7 10  1680        4300   5000

21  6 CONVINCOR 220    OP  RNBT  FBG DV IO  250-300    7 11  3300       10900  13200
21  6 CONVINCOR 220    OP  RNBT  FBG DV IO  330-350    7 11  3300       12300  14700
21  9 PERSUADER 218 BR OP  RNBT  FBG DV IO  180-250    7 10  2855        9500  11300
21  9 PERSUADER 218 BR OP  RNBT  FBG DV IO  300-330    7 10  2855       10600  12900
21  9 PERSUADER 218 BR OP  RNBT  FBG DV IO  350  MRCR  7 10  2855       12000  13600
21  9 PERSUADER 219    OP  RNBT  FBG DV IO  180-250    7 10  2855        9800  11600
21  9 PERSUADER 219    OP  RNBT  FBG DV IO  300-330    7 10  2855       10900  13200
21  9 PERSUADER 219    OP  RNBT  FBG DV IO  350  MRCR  7 10  2855       12200  13900
23  2 PERSUADER 234 BR OP  RNBT  FBG DV IO  250-300    7 10  3100       11200  13500
23  2 PERSUADER 234 BR OP  RNBT  FBG DV IO  330-350    7 10  3100       12600  15000
23  2 PERSUADER 234 BR OP  RNBT  FBG DV IO  385-415    7 10  3100       14500  18100

23  2 PERSUADER 235    OP  RNBT  FBG DV IO  250-300    7 10  3100       11400  13700
23  2 PERSUADER 235    OP  RNBT  FBG DV IO  330-350    7 10  3100       12800  15200
23  2 PERSUADER 235    OP  RNBT  FBG DV IO  385-415    7 10  3100       14800  18300
24    CONVINCOR 242    OP  OFF   FBG DV IO  250-300    8  3  3900       14700  17600
24    CONVINCOR 242    OP  OFF   FBG DV IO  330-350    8  3  3900       16300  19200
24    CONVINCOR 242    OP  OFF   FBG DV IO  385-415    8  3  3900       18700  22300
25  3 CONVINCOR 253    OP  OFF   FBG DV IO  250-330    8  3  4400       16400  20500
25  3 CONVINCOR 253    OP  OFF   FBG DV IO  350-415    8  3  4400       19100  23800
25  3 CONVINCOR 253 DLX OP OFF   FBG DV IO  250-350    8  3  4400       18000  22300
25  3 CONVINCOR 253 DLX OP OFF   FBG DV IO  385-415    8  3  4400       21300  25100
25  9 PERSUADER 261    OP  OFF   FBG DV IO  250-330    8  2  4400       17300  21300
25  9 PERSUADER 261    OP  OFF   FBG DV IO  350-385    8  2  4400       19700  23300

25  9 PERSUADER 261    OP  OFF   FBG DV IO  415  MRCR  8  2  4400       22400  24900
27 11 CONVINCOR 283    OP  OFF   FBG DV IO  250-350    8  4  5300       23100  28000
      IO 385-415  26200 30500, IO T250-T300 26900 31700, IO T330-T385 30400 36300
      IO T415  MRCR 34700 38500

30  1 CONVINCOR 303    OP  OFF   FBG DV IO  T250-T350  8  4  6500       32200  39500
30  1 CONVINCOR 303    OP  OFF   FBG DV IO  T385-T415  8  4  6500       36900  42800
------------------- 1995 BOATS -------------------------------------------------------
17  1 PULSE 170 BR     OP  RNBT  FBG DV OB              7  5  1280        2600   3000
17  1 PULSE 171        OP  RNBT  FBG DV OB              7  5  1235        2500   2900
18  5 PERSUADER 183 BR OP  RNBT  FBG DV IO  180-205    7  4  2625        6400   7400
18  5 PERSUADER 184    OP  RNBT  FBG DV IO  180-205    7  4  2600        6400   7450
18  7 PULSE 185 BR     OP  RNBT  FBG DV OB              7 10  1415        2900   3400
18  7 PULSE 186        OP  RNBT  FBG DV OB              7 10  1460        2950   3400
20  3 PERSUADER 202 BR OP  RNBT  FBG DV IO  180-250    7 10  2790        7800   9450
20  3 PERSUADER 203    OP  RNBT  FBG DV IO  180-250    7 10  2685        8150   9800
20  5 PULSARE 2100     OP  RNBT  FBG DV OB              7 11  1375        3500   4050
20  5 PULSARE 2100 BR  OP  RNBT  FBG DV OB              7 11  1325        3300   3850
21  4 PULSE 210 BR     OP  RNBT  FBG DV OB              7 10  1725        4200   4850
21  4 PULSE 211        OP  RNBT  FBG DV OB              7 10  1680        4050   4700

21  7 CONVINCOR 216    OP  RNBT  FBG DV IO  250-300    7 11  3300       10200  12300
21  7 CONVINCOR 216    OP  RNBT  FBG DV IO  350  MRCR  7 11  3300       12100  13800
21  9 PERSUADER 218 BR OP  RNBT  FBG DV IO  180-250    7 10  2855        8900  10600
21  9 PERSUADER 218 BR OP  RNBT  FBG DV IO  350  MRCR  7 10  2855        9950  11300
21  9 PERSUADER 218 BR OP  RNBT  FBG DV IO  180-250    7 10  2855       11200  12700
21  9 PERSUADER 218 BR OP  RNBT  FBG DV IO  350  MRCR  7 10  2855       10100  11800
21  9 PERSUADER 219    OP  RNBT  FBG DV IO  180-250    7 10  2855       10200  11600
21  9 PERSUADER 219    OP  RNBT  FBG DV IO  350  MRCR  7 10  2855       11400  13000
22  8 DECKMATE         OP  RNBT  FBG DV IO  180-250    7 10  3100       10800  13400
23  2 PERSUADER 234 BR OP  RNBT  FBG DV IO  250-300    7 10  3100       10400  12600
23  2 PERSUADER 234 BR OP  RNBT  FBG DV IO  350-385    7 10  3100       12300  15000
23  2 PERSUADER 234 BR OP  RNBT  FBG DV IO  415  MRCR  7 10  3100       14800  16900

23  2 PERSUADER 235    OP  RNBT  FBG DV IO  250-300    7 10  3100       10600  12900
23  2 PERSUADER 235    OP  RNBT  FBG DV IO  350-385    7 10  3100       12500  15600
23  2 PERSUADER 235    OP  RNBT  FBG DV IO  415  MRCR  7 10  3100       15000  17100
```

LOA FT	IN	NAME AND/ OR MODEL	TOP/ RIG	BOAT TYPE	-HULL- MTL	TP	TP	----ENGINE--- # HP	MFG	BEAM FT	IN	WGT LBS	DRAFT FT	IN	RETAIL LOW	RETAIL HIGH
		1995 BOATS														
25	3	CONVINCOR 253	OP	OFF	FBG	DV	IO	250-300		8	3	4400			15900	18900
25	3	CONVINCOR 253	OP	OFF	FBG	DV	IO	350-450		8	3	4400			18300	22900
25	3	CONVINCOR 253	OP	OFF	FBG	DV	IO	465-500		8	3	3750			21300	25300
25	9	PERSUADER 261	OP	OFF	FBG	DV	IO	250-300		8	2	3800			14800	17800
		IO 350-385 16900 20500, IO 415-450 19600 23200, IO 490-500													23000	26000
27	11	CONVINCOR 283	OP	OFF	FBG	DV	IO	250-350		8	2	5300			21500	26200
		IO 385-465 24500 30500, IO 490-500 28200 31400, IO T250-T300													25100	29600
		IO T350-T385 28700 33800, IO T415-T450 32300 38100, IO T500 MRCR													37600	41800
30	1	CONVINCOR 303	OP	OFF	FBG	DV	IO	T250-T350		8	4	6500			29900	36600
30	1	CONVINCOR 303	OP	OFF	FBG	DV	IO	T385-T465		8	4	6500			34200	42500
30	1	CONVINCOR 303	OP	OFF	FBG	DV	IO	T490-T500		8	4	6500			39400	43900
		1994 BOATS														
17	1	PULSE 170 BR	OP	RNBT	FBG	DV	OB			7	5	1280			2500	2900
17	1	PULSE 171	OP	RNBT	FBG	DV	OB			7	5	1235			2400	2800
18	5	PERSUADER 183 BR	OP	RNBT	FBG	DV	IO	180-205		7	4	2625			6000	6950
18	5	PERSUADER 184	OP	RNBT	FBG	DV	IO	180-205		7	4	2600			5950	6900
18	7	PULSE 185 BR	OP	RNBT	FBG	DV	OB			7	10	1415			2750	3150
18	7	PULSE 186	OP	RNBT	FBG	DV	OB			7	10	1460			2750	3200
20	3	PERSUADER 202 BR	OP	RNBT	FBG	DV	IO	180-250		7	10	2790			7300	8800
20	3	PERSUADER 203	OP	RNBT	FBG	DV	IO	180-250		7	10	2685			7650	9150
20	5	PULSARE 2100	OP	RNBT	FBG	DV	OB			7	11	1525			3600	4200
20	5	PULSARE 2100 BR	OP	RNBT	FBG	DV	OB			7	11	1525			3500	4100
21	4	PULSE 210 BR	OP	RNBT	FBG	DV	OB			7	10	1725			3950	4600
21	4	PULSE 211	OP	RNBT	FBG	DV	OB			7	10	1680			3850	4450
21	7	CONVINCOR 216	OP	RNBT	FBG	DV	IO	250-300		7	11	3300			9500	11500
21	7	CONVINCOR 216	OP	RNBT	FBG	DV	IO	350	MRCR	7	11	3300			11300	12800
21	7	CONVINCOR 216	OP	RNBT	FBG	DV	IO	385	MRCR	7	11	3300			12500	14200
21	9	PERSUADER 218 BR	OP	RNBT	FBG	DV	IO	180-250		7	10	2855			8300	9900
		IO 300 MRCR 9350 10600, IO 350 MRCR 10500 11900, IO 385 MRCR													11600	13200
21	9	PERSUADER 219	OP	RNBT	FBG	DV	IO	180-250		7	10	2855			8450	10100
		IO 300 MRCR 9450 10700, IO 350 MRCR 10600 12100, IO 385 MRCR													11800	13400
23	2	PERSUADER 234 BR	OP	RNBT	FBG	DV	IO	250-300		7	10	3100			9750	11800
23	2	PERSUADER 234 BR	OP	RNBT	FBG	DV	IO	350-385		7	10	3100			11500	14400
23	2	PERSUADER 234 BR	OP	RNBT	FBG	DV	IO	415	MRCR	7	10	3100			13900	15800
23	2	PERSUADER 235	OP	RNBT	FBG	DV	IO	250-300		7	10	3100			9850	11900
23	2	PERSUADER 235	OP	RNBT	FBG	DV	IO	350-385		7	10	3100			11700	14600
23	2	PERSUADER 235	OP	RNBT	FBG	DV	IO	415	MRCR	7	10	3100			14000	15900
25	3	CONVINCOR 253	OP	OFF	FBG	DV	IO	250-300		8	3	4400			14800	17700
25	3	CONVINCOR 253	OP	OFF	FBG	DV	IO	350-415		8	3	4400			16700	20000
25	3	CONVINCOR 253	OP	OFF	FBG	DV	IO	445-490		8	3	3750			19200	23200
26		ENFORCER 260	OP	OFF	FBG	DV	IO	250-300		8	2	3800			14100	17000
		IO 350-385 16100 19500, IO 415-465 18800 23000, IO 490 MRCR													21700	24100
27	11	CONVINCOR 281	OP	OFF	FBG	DV	OB			8	2	5300			12900	14600
27	11	CONVINCOR 283	OP	OFF	FBG	DV	IO	250-350		8	2	5300			20100	24400
		IO 385-465 22800 28400, IO 490 MRCR 26400 29300, IO T250-T300													23400	27600
		IO T350-T385 26800 31600, IO T415-T465 30200 37000, IO T490 MRCR													34800	38600
28	3	ENFORCER 280	OP	OFF	FBG	DV	IO	250-385		8	2	4600			18400	22900
28	3	ENFORCER 280	OP	OFF	FBG	DV	IO	415-490		8	2	4600			21600	26000
30	1	CONVINCOR 303	OP	OFF	FBG	DV	IO	T250-T350		8	4	6500			27900	34100
30	1	CONVINCOR 303	OP	OFF	FBG	DV	IO	T385-T465		8	4	6500			32000	39500
30	1	CONVINCOR 303	OP	OFF	FBG	DV	IO	T490	MRCR	8	4	6500			36500	40600
		1993 BOATS														
17	1	PULSE 170 BR	OP	RNBT	FBG	DV	OB			7	5	1380			2500	2900
17	1	PULSE 171	OP	RNBT	FBG	DV	OB			7	5	1335			2450	2850
18	5	PERSUADER 183 BR	OP	RNBT	FBG	DV	IO	135-205		7	4	2625			5550	6500
18	5	PERSUADER 184	OP	RNBT	FBG	DV	IO	135-205		7	4	2600			5500	6450
18	7	PULSE 185 BR	OP	RNBT	FBG	DV	OB			7	10	1515			2700	3150
18	7	PULSE 186	OP	RNBT	FBG	DV	OB			7	10	1560			2750	3200
20	3	PERSUADER 202 BR	OP	RNBT	FBG	DV	IO	180-250		7	10	2790			6800	8250
20	3	PERSUADER 203	OP	RNBT	FBG	DV	IO	180-250		7	10	2685			7150	8550
21	2	STARFLITE	OP	RNBT	FBG	DV	OB			7	5	1300			2900	3400
21	2	STARLINER	OP	RNBT	FBG	DV	OB			7	5	1400			3150	3650
21	4	PULSE 210 BR	OP	RNBT	FBG	DV	OB			7	10	1825			3950	4600
21	4	PULSE 211	OP	RNBT	FBG	DV	OB			7	10	1780			3850	4450
21	9	PERSUADER 218 BR	OP	RNBT	FBG	DV	IO	180-250		7	10	2855			7700	9250
21	9	PERSUADER 218 BR	OP	RNBT	FBG	DV	IO	300	MRCR	7	10	2855			8650	9950
21	9	PERSUADER 218 BR	OP	RNBT	FBG	DV	IO	350	MRCR	7	10	2855			9800	11100
21	9	PERSUADER 219	OP	RNBT	FBG	DV	IO	180-250		7	10	2855			7900	9450
21	9	PERSUADER 219	OP	RNBT	FBG	DV	IO	300	MRCR	7	10	2855			8900	10100
21	9	PERSUADER 219	OP	RNBT	FBG	DV	IO	350	MRCR	7	10	2855			9950	11300
22	9	ENFORCER 230	OP	RNBT	FBG	DV	OB			7	10	2550			5450	6250
22	9	ENFORCER 230	OP	RNBT	FBG	DV	IO	250-350		7	10	3200			9050	10900
22	9	ENFORCER 230	OP	RNBT	FBG	DV	IO	390	MRCR	7	10	3200			11900	13600
22	9	ENFORCER 230	OP	RNBT	FBG	DV	IO	445-490		7	10	3200			15800	18600
23	2	PERSUADER 234 BR	OP	RNBT	FBG	DV	IO	250-300		7	10	3100			9150	11000
		IO 350 MRCR 10800 12200, IO 390 MRCR 12000 13600, IO 445 MRCR													14200	16100
23	2	PERSUADER 235	OP	RNBT	FBG	DV	IO	250-300		7	10	3100			9300	11200
		IO 350 MRCR 10900 12400, IO 390 MRCR 12200 13800, IO 445 MRCR													14300	16300
25	1	CONVINCOR 251	OP	OFF	FBG	DV	IO	250-300		7	6	3700			11900	14300
		IO 350-390 13700 17000, IO 445-465 17000 20600, IO 490 MRCR													19300	21500
25	3	CONVINCOR 253	OP	OFF	FBG	DV	IO	250-300		8	3	3750			12500	15100
25	3	CONVINCOR 253	OP	OFF	FBG	DV	IO	350-390		8	3	3750			14400	17700
25	3	CONVINCOR 253	OP	OFF	FBG	DV	IO	445-490		8	3	3750			17600	21700
26		ENFORCER 260	OP	OFF	FBG	DV	IO	250-300		8	2	3800			13200	15900
26		ENFORCER 260	OP	OFF	FBG	DV	IO	350-390		8	2	3800			15100	18400
26		ENFORCER 260	OP	OFF	FBG	DV	IO	445-490		8	2	3800			18400	22500
27	11	CONVINCER 281	OP	OFF	FBG	DV	IO	350	MRCR	8	2	5300			20500	22800
27	11	CONVINCOR 281	OP	OFF	FBG	DV	OB			8	2	5300			12200	13900
27	11	CONVINCOR 281	OP	OFF	FBG	DV	IO	250-300		8	2	5300			18900	21700
		IO 390-465 21500 26600, IO 490 MRCR 24600 27400, IO T250-T300													21900	25800
		IO T350-T390 25000 29700, IO T445-T490 29600 36100														
28	3	ENFORCER 280	OP	OFF	FBG	DV	IO	250-350		8	2	4600			16800	20700
28	3	ENFORCER 280	OP	OFF	FBG	DV	IO	390-465		8	2	4600			19400	24000
28	3	ENFORCER 280	OP	OFF	FBG	DV	IO	490	MRCR	8	2	4600			21800	24300
30	1	CONVINCOR 301	OP	OFF	FBG	DV	IO	T250-T350		8	4	6000			25600	31400
30	1	CONVINCOR 301	OP	OFF	FBG	DV	IO	T390-T465		8	4	6000			29600	36300
30	1	CONVINCOR 301	OP	OFF	FBG	DV	IO	T490	MRCR	8	4	6000			33600	37400
		1992 BOATS														
17	1	PULSE 170 BR	OP	RNBT	FBG	DV	OB			7	5	1380			2400	2800
17	1	PULSE 170 BRSE	OP	RNBT	FBG	DV	OB			7	5	1380			2500	2900
17	1	PULSE 171	OP	RNBT	FBG	DV	OB			7	5	1335			2300	2700
17	1	PULSE 171 SE	OP	RNBT	FBG	DV	OB			7	5	1335			2500	2900
18	7	PULSE 185 BR	OP	RNBT	FBG	DV	OB			7	10	1515			2600	3050
18	7	PULSE 185 BRSE	OP	RNBT	FBG	DV	OB			7	10	1515			2750	3200
18	7	PULSE 186	OP	RNBT	FBG	DV	OB			7	10	1560			2650	3050
18	7	PULSE 186 SE	OP	RNBT	FBG	DV	OB			7	10	1560			2800	3300
20	3	PERSUADER 202 BR	OP	RNBT	FBG	DV	IO	175-250		7	10	2680			6250	7550
20	3	PERSUADER 202 BRSE	OP	RNBT	FBG	DV	IO	175-250		7	10	2680			6400	7700
20	3	PERSUADER 203	OP	RNBT	FBG	DV	IO	175-250		7	10	2680			6650	8000
20	3	PERSUADER 203 SE	OP	RNBT	FBG	DV	IO	175-250		7	10	2680			6850	8200
20	4	PERSUADER 219 SE	OP	RNBT	FBG	DV	IO	230	MRCR	7	10	2760			7100	8150
21	2	STARFLITE	OP	RNBT	FBG	DV	OB			7	5	1300			2800	3250
21	2	STARFLITE SE	OP	RNBT	FBG	DV	OB			7	5	1300			3000	3500
21	2	STARLINER	OP	RNBT	FBG	DV	OB			7	5	1400			3000	3500
21	2	STARLINER SE	OP	RNBT	FBG	DV	OB			7	5	1400			3150	3650
21	4	PULSE 210 BR	OP	RNBT	FBG	DV	OB			7	10	1825			3750	4400
21	4	PULSE 210 BRSE	OP	RNBT	FBG	DV	OB			7	10	1825			3950	4600
21	4	PULSE 211	OP	RNBT	FBG	DV	OB			7	10	1780			3650	4250
21	4	PULSE 211 SE	OP	RNBT	FBG	DV	OB			7	10	1780			3900	4550
21	9	PERSUADER 218 BR	OP	RNBT	FBG	DV	IO	175-250		7	10	2855			6950	8400
21	9	PERSUADER 218 BR	OP	RNBT	FBG	DV	IO	300	MRCR	7	10	2855			7850	9050
21	9	PERSUADER 218 BR	OP	RNBT	FBG	DV	IO	350	MRCR	7	10	2855			9000	10200
21	9	PERSUADER 218 BRSE	OP	RNBT	FBG	DV	IO	175-250		7	10	2855			7150	8600
21	9	PERSUADER 218 BRSE	OP	RNBT	FBG	DV	IO	300	MRCR	7	10	2855			8050	9250
21	9	PERSUADER 218 BRSE	OP	RNBT	FBG	DV	IO	350	MRCR	7	10	2855			9150	10400
21	9	PERSUADER 219	OP	RNBT	FBG	DV	IO	175-250		7	10	2855			7400	8850
21	9	PERSUADER 219	OP	RNBT	FBG	DV	IO	300	MRCR	7	10	2855			8250	9500
21	9	PERSUADER 219	OP	RNBT	FBG	DV	IO	350	MRCR	7	10	2855			9400	10700
21	9	PERSUADER 219 SE	OP	RNBT	FBG	DV	IO	175-250		7	10	2855			7650	9150
21	9	PERSUADER 219 SE	OP	RNBT	FBG	DV	IO	300	MRCR	7	10	2855			8500	9750
21	9	PERSUADER 219 SE	OP	RNBT	FBG	DV	IO	350	MRCR	7	10	2855			9550	10900
22	1	VISION 220 BR	OP	RNBT	FBG	DV	IO	175-250		7	6	3000			7400	8900
22	1	VISION 220 BR	OP	RNBT	FBG	DV	IO	300	MRCR	7	6	3000			8300	9500
22	1	VISION 220 BR	OP	RNBT	FBG	DV	IO	350	MRCR	7	6	3000			9400	10700
22	1	VISION 220 BRSE	OP	RNBT	FBG	DV	IO	175-250		7	6	3000			7600	9050
22	1	VISION 220 BRSE	OP	RNBT	FBG	DV	IO	300	MRCR	7	6	3000			8450	9700
22	1	VISION 220 BRSE	OP	RNBT	FBG	DV	IO	350	MRCR	7	6	3000			9500	10800
22	1	VISION 221	OP	RNBT	FBG	DV	IO	175-250		7	6	2950			7300	8750
22	1	VISION 221	OP	RNBT	FBG	DV	IO	350	MRCR	7	6	2950			9400	10700
22	1	VISION 221 SE	OP	RNBT	FBG	DV	IO	175-250		7	6	2950			7550	9000
22	1	VISION 221 SE	OP	RNBT	FBG	DV	IO	300	MRCR	7	6	2950			8350	9600

CONTINUED ON NEXT PAGE

LOA FT	LOA IN	NAME AND/ OR MODEL	TOP/ RIG	BOAT TYPE	-HULL- MTL	-HULL- TP	ENGINE TP	# HP	MFG	BEAM FT	BEAM IN	WGT LBS	DRAFT FT IN	RETAIL LOW	RETAIL HIGH
		1992 BOATS													
22	1	VISION 221 SE	OP	RNBT	FBG	DV	IO	350	MRCR	7	6	2950		9400	10700
22	9	ENFORCER 230	OP	RNBT	FBG	DV	OB			7	10	2550		5200	5950
22	9	ENFORCER 230	OP	RNBT	FBG	DV	IO	250-350		7	10	3200		8400	10300
22	9	ENFORCER 230	OP	RNBT	FBG	DV	IO	390	MRCR	7	10	3200		11200	12700
22	9	ENFORCER 230 SE	OP	RNBT	FBG	DV	OB			7	10	2550		5450	6250
22	9	ENFORCER 230 SE	OP	RNBT	FBG	DV	IO	250-350		7	10	3200		8650	10600
22	9	ENFORCER 230 SE	OP	RNBT	FBG	DV	IO	390	MRCR	7	10	3200		11500	13000
23	2	PERSUADER 234 BR	OP	RNBT	FBG	DV	IO	175-250		7	10	3100		7900	9500
		IO 300 MRCR 8900 10100, IO 350 MRCR 9900 11200, IO 390 MRCR												11000	12500
23	2	PERSUADER 234 BRSE	OP	RNBT	FBG	DV	IO	175-250		7	10	3100		8100	9700
		IO 300 MRCR 9100 10300, IO 350 MRCR 10100 11400, IO 390 MRCR												11200	12800
23	2	PERSUADER 235	OP	RNBT	FBG	DV	IO	175-250		7	10	3100		8300	9850
		IO 300 MRCR 9250 10500, IO 350 MRCR 10200 11600, IO 390 MRCR												11400	12900
23	2	PERSUADER 235 SE	OP	RNBT	FBG	DV	IO	175-250		7	10	3100		8550	10200
		IO 300 MRCR 9450 10700, IO 350 MRCR 10400 11900, IO 390 MRCR												11600	13200
25	1	CONVINCOR 251	OP	OFF	FBG	DV	IO	250-300		7	6	3700		11100	13400
25	1	CONVINCOR 251	OP	OFF	FBG	DV	IO	350-390		7	6	3700		12800	15900
25	1	CONVINCOR 251	OP	OFF	FBG	DV	IO	445	MRCR	7	6	3700		15900	18000
25	1	CONVINCOR 251 SE	OP	OFF	FBG	DV	IO	250-300		7	6	3700		11400	13700
25	1	CONVINCOR 251 SE	OP	OFF	FBG	DV	IO	350-390		7	6	3700		13100	16200
25	1	CONVINCOR 251 SE	OP	OFF	FBG	DV	IO	445	MRCR	7	6	3700		16100	18300
26		ENFORCER 260	OP	OFF	FBG	DV	IO	250-300		8	2	3800		12400	14900
26		ENFORCER 260	OP	OFF	FBG	DV	IO	350-390		8	2	3800		14100	17200
26		ENFORCER 260	OP	OFF	FBG	DV	IO	445	MRCR	8	2	3800		16900	19200
26		ENFORCER 260 SE	OP	OFF	FBG	DV	IO	250-300		8	2	3800		12700	15200
26		ENFORCER 260 SE	OP	OFF	FBG	DV	IO	350-390		8	2	3800		14400	17600
26		ENFORCER 260 SE	OP	OFF	FBG	DV	IO	445	MRCR	8	2	3800		17200	19500
27	11	CONVINCER 281	OP	OFF	FBG	DV	IO	350	MRCR	8	2	5300		19200	21300
27	11	CONVINCOR 281	OP	OFF	FBG	DV	OB			8	2	5300		11600	13200
27	11	CONVINCOR 281	OP	OFF	FBG	DV	IO	250-300		8	2	5300		17300	20500
		IO 390-445 20100 23900, IO T250-T300 20500 24100, IO T350-T390												23400	27800
		IO T445 MRCR 27700 30800													
27	11	CONVINCOR 281 SE	OP	OFF	FBG	DV	OB			8	2	5300		12000	13600
27	11	CONVINCOR 281 SE	OP	OFF	FBG	DV	IO	250-350		8	2	5300		18100	21800
		IO 390-445 20500 24200, IO T250-T300 20800 24500, IO T350-T390												23700	28200
		IO T445 MRCR 28000 31100													
28	3	ENFORCER 280	OP	OFF	FBG	DV	IO	250-390		8	2	5300		16600	20300
28	3	ENFORCER 280	OP	OFF	FBG	DV	IO	445	MRCR	8	2	4600		19300	21500
28	3	ENFORCER 280 SE	OP	OFF	FBG	DV	IO	250-300		8	2	4600		15600	18800
28	3	ENFORCER 280 SE	OP	OFF	FBG	DV	IO	350-390		8	2	4600		17400	20700
28	3	ENFORCER 280 SE	OP	OFF	FBG	DV	IO	445	MRCR	8	2	4600		19700	21800
30	1	CONVINCOR 301	OP	OFF	FBG	DV	IO	T250-T350		8	4	6000		23900	29300
30	1	CONVINCOR 301	OP	OFF	FBG	DV	IO	T390-T445		8	4	6000		27600	32700
30	1	CONVINCOR 301 SE	OP	OFF	FBG	DV	IO	T250-T350		8	4	6000		24300	29700
30	1	CONVINCOR 301 SE	OP	OFF	FBG	DV	IO	T390-T445		8	4	6000		27900	33000
		1991 BOATS													
16	6	ENTICER	OP	RNBT	FBG	DV	OB			7		750		1300	1550
16	6	PREDICTOR	OP	RNBT	FBG	DV	OB			7		750		1350	1600
16	7	DIPLOMAT	OP	RNBT	FBG	DV	OB			7	5	875		1550	1850
16	7	DIPLOMAT	OP	RNBT	FBG	DV	IO	155-175		7	5	875		2900	3350
16	7	SPORTFIRE	OP	RNBT	FBG	DV	OB			7	5	850		1500	1800
16	7	SPORTFIRE	OP	RNBT	FBG	DV	IO	155-175		7	5	850		2850	3350
17	1	SPECTRA 170	OP	RNBT	FBG	DV	OB			7	5	1100		1850	2200
17	1	SPECTRA 171	OP	RNBT	FBG	DV	OB			7	5	1100		2000	2350
18	3	STARFIRE	OP	RNBT	FBG	DV	IO	155-230		7	5	2450		4650	5550
18	3	STARFIRE SE	OP	RNBT	FBG	DV	IO	155-230		7	5	2450		4750	5650
18	3	STARLET	OP	RNBT	FBG	DV	IO	155-230		7	5	2500		4750	5650
18	7	PULSE 185	OP	RNBT	FBG	DV	OB			7	10	1100		1900	2250
18	7	PULSE 186	OP	RNBT	FBG	DV	OB			7	10	1100		2000	2400
18	7	PULSE 186 SE	OP	RNBT	FBG	DV	OB			7	10	1100		2100	2500
19	7	AMBASSADOR	OP	RNBT	FBG	DV	IO	155-240		7	6	2650		5300	6350
19	7	AMBASSADOR	OP	RNBT	FBG	DV	IO	300	MRCR	7	6	2650		6050	6950
19	7	AMBASSADOR	OP	RNBT	FBG	DV	IO	350	MRCR	7	6	2650		6950	8000
19	7	SENATOR	OP	RNBT	FBG	DV	IO	155-240		7	6	2700		5250	6350
19	7	SENATOR	OP	RNBT	FBG	DV	IO	300	MRCR	7	6	2700		6050	6950
19	7	SENATOR	OP	RNBT	FBG	DV	IO	350	MRCR	7	6	2700		6950	7950
19	7	SENATOR SE	OP	RNBT	FBG	DV	IO	155-240		7	6	2700		5400	6500
19	7	SENATOR SE	OP	RNBT	FBG	DV	IO	300	MRCR	7	6	2700		6200	7100
19	7	SENATOR SE	OP	RNBT	FBG	DV	IO	350	MRCR	7	6	2700		7050	8100
20	2	PACIFICA 198	OP	RNBT	FBG	SV	IO	155-240		7	10	2610		6000	7200
20	2	PACIFICA 199	OP	RNBT	FBG	SV	IO	155-240		7	10	2595		5900	7050
20	2	PACIFICA 199 SE	OP	RNBT	FBG	SV	IO	155-240		7	10	2595		6050	7250
20	3	SPECTRA 200	OP	RNBT	FBG	DV	OB			7	6	1450		2950	3400
20	3	SPECTRA 201	OP	RNBT	FBG	DV	OB			7	6	1500		3000	3500
20	4	STROBE 200	OP	RNBT	FBG	DV	IO	155-240		7	10	2760		5850	7100
20	4	STROBE 201	OP	RNBT	FBG	DV	IO	155-240		7	10	2760		6350	7550
20	4	STROBE 201 SE	OP	RNBT	FBG	DV	IO	155-240		7	10	2760		6500	7700
21	2	STARFLITE	OP	RNBT	FBG	DV	OB			7	5	1300		2700	3150
21	2	STARFLITE SE	OP	RNBT	FBG	DV	OB			7	5	1300		2850	3300
21	2	STARLINER	OP	RNBT	FBG	DV	OB			7	5	1400		2950	3400
21	4	PULSE 210	OP	RNBT	FBG	DV	OB			7	10	1825		3500	4100
21	4	PULSE 211	OP	RNBT	FBG	DV	OB			7	10	1825		3700	4300
21	4	PULSE 211 SE	OP	RNBT	FBG	DV	OB			7	10	1825		3850	4500
22	1	VISION 220	OP	RNBT	FBG	DV	IO	210-240		7	6	1500		5550	6600
22	1	VISION 220	OP	RNBT	FBG	DV	IO	300	MRCR	7	6	1500		6300	7250
22	1	VISION 220	OP	RNBT	FBG	DV	IO	350	MRCR	7	6	1500		7250	8350
22	1	VISION 221	OP	RNBT	FBG	DV	IO	210-240		7	6	2950		7000	8200
22	1	VISION 221	OP	RNBT	FBG	DV	IO	300	MRCR	7	6	2950		7700	8850
22	1	VISION 221	OP	RNBT	FBG	DV	IO	350	MRCR	7	6	2950		8650	9950
22	1	VISION 221 SE	OP	RNBT	FBG	DV	IO	210	OMC	7	6	2950		7000	8050
		IO 230-240 7200 8350, IO 300 MRCR 7850 9000, IO 350 MRCR												8900	10100
22	9	MAXXUM 230	OP	RNBT	FBG	DV	OB			7	10	3200		5850	6750
22	9	MAXXUM 230	OP	RNBT	FBG	DV	IO	210-240		7	10	3200		7650	9000
		IO 300 MRCR 8450 9700, IO 350 MRCR 9450 10700, IO 390 MRCR												10500	12000
22	9	MAXXUM 230 SE	OP	RNBT	FBG	DV	OB			7	10	3200		6050	7000
22	9	MAXXUM 230 SE	OP	RNBT	FBG	DV	IO	210-240		7	10	3200		7850	9200
		IO 300 MRCR 8600 9900, IO 350 MRCR 9600 10900, IO 390 MRCR												10700	12200
23	2	PERSUADER GT	OP	RNBT	FBG	DV	IO	210-240		7	10	3100		7650	9050
		IO 300 MRCR 8450 9700, IO 350 MRCR 9450 10700, IO 390 MRCR												10500	12000
23	2	PERSUADER GT SE	OP	RNBT	FBG	SV	IO	210-240		7	10	3100		7800	9200
		IO 300 MRCR 8600 9900, IO 350 MRCR 9600 10900, IO 390 MRCR												10700	12100
24		ENFORCER GTX	OP	RNBT	FBG	DV	IO	230-300		7	5	3400		8500	10500
		IO 350 MRCR 10100 11500, IO 390 MRCR 11200 12800, IO 465 MRCR												13900	15700
24		ENFORCER SE	OP	RNBT	FBG	SV	IO	230-300		7	5	3400		8700	10700
		IO 350 MRCR 10300 11700, IO 390 MRCR 11400 13000, IO 465 MRCR												14000	15900
25	1	CONVINCER GTX	OP	OFF	FBG	DV	IO	230-300		7	6	3700		10300	12700
25	1	CONVINCER GTX	OP	OFF	FBG	DV	IO	350-390		7	6	3700		12100	14900
25	1	CONVINCOR GTX SE	OP	OFF	FBG	DV	IO	230-300		7	6	3700		10500	12800
25	1	CONVINCOR GTX SE	OP	OFF	FBG	DV	IO	350-390		7	6	3700		12300	15100
27	11	MAXXUM 281	OP	OFF	FBG	DV	OB			8	2	5300		11200	12700
27	11	MAXXUM 281	OP	OFF	FBG	DV	IO	300-350		8	2	5300		17000	20300
		IO 465 MRCR 20700 23000, IO T230-T300 19000 22700, IO T350-T390												22000	26100
		IO T465 MRCR 27000 30000													
27	11	MAXXUM 281 SE	OP	OFF	FBG	DV	OB			8	2	5300		11400	12900
27	11	MAXXUM 281 SE	OP	OFF	FBG	DV	IO	300-390		8	2	5300		17200	21300
		IO 465 MRCR 20900 23200, IO T230-T300 19200 22900, IO T350-T390												22200	26300
		IO T465 MRCR 27100 30200													
28	3	MAXXUM 280	OP	OFF	FBG	DV	IO	300-350		8	2	4600		15200	18200
28	3	MAXXUM 280	OP	OFF	FBG	DV	IO	390-465		8	2	4600		16800	20800
28	3	MAXXUM 280 SE	OP	OFF	FBG	DV	IO	300-350		8	2	4600		15400	18400
28	3	MAXXUM 280 SE	OP	OFF	FBG	DV	IO	390-465		8	2	4600		17000	21000
30	1	MAXXUM 301	OP	OFF	FBG	DV	IO	T300-T390		8	4	6000		23500	28700
30	1	MAXXUM 301	OP	OFF	FBG	DV	IO	T465	MRCR	8	4	6000		28200	31300
30	1	MAXXUM 301 SE	OP	OFF	FBG	DV	IO	T300-T390		8	4	6000		23800	29000
30	1	MAXXUM 301 SE	OP	OFF	FBG	DV	IO	T465	MRCR	8	4	6000		28400	31500
		1990 BOATS													
16	6	ENTICER	OP	RNBT	FBG	DV	OB			7		750		1250	1450
16	6	ENTICER DELUXE	OP	RNBT	FBG	DV	OB			7		750		1350	1600
16	6	PREDICTOR	OP	RNBT	FBG	DV	OB			7		750		1200	1450
16	6	PREDICTOR DELUXE	OP	RNBT	FBG	DV	OB			7		750		1300	1550
17	1	SPECTRA 170	OP	RNBT	FBG	DV	OB			7	5	1100		1750	2100
17	1	SPECTRA 170 DELUXE	OP	RNBT	FBG	DV	OB			7	5	1100		1900	2300
17	1	SPECTRA 171	OP	RNBT	FBG	DV	OB			7	5	1100		1750	2050
17	1	SPECTRA 171 DELUXE	OP	RNBT	FBG	DV	OB			7	5	1100		1950	2300
17	8	DIPLOMAT	OP	RNBT	FBG	DV	OB			7	5	1875		2650	3100
17	8	DIPLOMAT	OP	RNBT	FBG	DV	IO	130-205		7	5	1875		3650	4450
17	8	DIPLOMAT DELUXE	OP	RNBT	FBG	DV	OB			7	5	1875		2850	3350

 CONTINUED ON NEXT PAGE

LOA FT	LOA IN	NAME AND/ OR MODEL	TOP/ RIG	BOAT TYPE	-HULL- MTL	HULL TP	ENGINE TP	# HP	MFG	BEAM FT	BEAM IN	WGT LBS	DRAFT FT	DRAFT IN	RETAIL LOW	RETAIL HIGH
		1990 BOATS														
17	8	DIPLOMAT DELUXE	OP	RNBT	FBG	DV	IO	130		7	5	1875			3800	4400
17	8	SPORTFIRE	OP	RNBT	FBG	DV	OB			7	5	2150			2800	3250
17	8	SPORTFIRE	OP	RNBT	FBG	DV	IO	130-205		7	5	2150			3850	4700
17	8	SPORTFIRE DELUXE	OP	RNBT	FBG	DV	OB			7	5	2150			3100	3600
17	8	SPORTFIRE DELUXE	OP	RNBT	FBG	DV	IO	130		7	5	2150			4050	4700
18	3	STARFIRE	OP	RNBT	FBG	DV	IO	130-205		7	5	2450			4250	5200
18	3	STARFIRE	OP	RNBT	FBG	DV	IO	260		7	5	2450			4750	5450
18	3	STARFIRE DELUXE	OP	RNBT	FBG	DV	IO	130		7	5	2450			4550	5250
18	3	STARLET	OP	RNBT	FBG	SV	IO	130-205		7	5	2500			4350	5250
18	3	STARLET	OP	RNBT	FBG	SV	IO	260		7	5	2500			4800	5500
18	3	STARLET DELUXE	OP	RNBT	FBG	DV	IO	130		7	5	2500			4600	5250
18	7	PULSE 185	OP	RNBT	FBG	DV	OB			7	10	1100			1900	2250
18	7	PULSE 186	OP	RNBT	FBG	DV	OB			7	10	1100			1900	2250
19	7	AMBASSADOR	OP	RNBT	FBG	DV	IO	130-205		7	6	2650			4850	5800
19	7	AMBASSADOR	OP	RNBT	FBG	DV	IO	260-270		7	6	2650			5300	6200
19	7	AMBASSADOR	OP	RNBT	FBG	DV	IO	330-335		7	6	2650			6150	7050
19	7	AMBASSADOR DELUXE	OP	RNBT	FBG	DV	IO	130		7	6	2650			5100	5850
19	7	SENATOR	OP	RNBT	FBG	DV	IO	130-270		7	6	2700			5000	6250
19	7	SENATOR	OP	RNBT	FBG	DV	IO	330-335		7	6	2700			6200	7150
20	2	PACIFICA 198	OP	B/R	FBG	DV	IO	130-205		7	10	2610			5350	6450
20	2	PACIFICA 198	OP	B/R	FBG	DV	IO	260-270		7	10	2610			5850	6850
20	2	PACIFICA 198 DELUXE	OP	B/R	FBG	DV	IO	130		7	10	2610			5600	6450
20	2	PACIFICA 199	OP	RNBT	FBG	DV	IO	130-205		7	10	2595			5450	6550
20	2	PACIFICA 199	OP	RNBT	FBG	DV	IO	260-270		7	10	2595			6000	7000
20	2	PACIFICA 199 DELUXE	OP	RNBT	FBG	DV	IO	130		7	10	2595			5750	6650
20	3	SPECTRA 200	OP	RNBT	FBG	DV	OB			7	6	1500			2800	3250
20	3	SPECTRA 200 DELUXE	OP	RNBT	FBG	DV	OB			7	6	1500			3000	3450
20	3	SPECTRA 201	OP	RNBT	FBG	DV	OB			7	6	1450			2700	3150
20	3	SPECTRA 201 DELUXE	OP	RNBT	FBG	DV	OB			7	6	1450			2900	3400
20	4	STROBE 200	OP	RNBT	FBG	DV	IO	130-205		7	10	2780			5700	6850
20	4	STROBE 200	OP	RNBT	FBG	DV	IO	260-270		7	10	2780			6250	7300
20	4	STROBE 200 DELUXE	OP	RNBT	FBG	DV	IO	130		7	10	2780			6000	6900
20	4	STROBE 201	OP	RNBT	FBG	DV	IO	130-270		7	10	2760			5700	6850
20	4	STROBE 201 DELUXE	OP	RNBT	FBG	DV	IO	130		7	10	2760			6000	6900
20	4	VISION 220	OP	RNBT	FBG	DV	IO	260-270		7	10	2760			6400	7750
20	4	VISION 220	OP	RNBT	FBG	DV	IO	330-335		7	10	2760			7150	8200
20	4	VISION 220	OP	RNBT	FBG	DV	IO	365	MRCR	7	10	2760			7900	9100
20	4	VISION 220 DELUXE	OP	RNBT	FBG	DV	IO	260		7	10	2760			6650	7650
21	2	STARFLITE	OP	RNBT	FBG	DV	OB			7	5	1300			2550	3000
21	2	STARFLITE DELUXE	OP	RNBT	FBG	DV	OB			7	5	1300			2750	3200
21	2	STARLINER	OP	RNBT	FBG	DV	OB			7	5	1400			2700	3150
21	2	STARLINER DELUXE	OP	RNBT	FBG	DV	OB			7	5	1400			2900	3400
22	1	VISION 221	OP	RNBT	FBG	DV	IO	260-270		7	6	2950			6900	8000
22	1	VISION 221	OP	RNBT	FBG	DV	IO	330-335		7	6	2950			7800	8950
22	1	VISION 221	OP	RNBT	FBG	DV	IO	365	MRCR	7	6	2950			8550	9850
22	9	MAXXUM 229	OP	RNBT	FBG	DV	OB			7	10	2550			4900	5650
22	9	MAXXUM 229	OP	RNBT	FBG	DV	IO	260-270		7	10	3200			7600	8800
		IO 330-335 8500 9750, IO 365 MRCR 9350 10600, IO 415 MRCR													10800	12200
25	1	CONVINCOR GTX	OP	RNBT	FBG	DV	IO	260-330		7	6	3700			9450	11800
25	1	CONVINCOR GTX	OP	RNBT	FBG	DV	IO	335-365		7	6	3700			10400	12600
25	1	CONVINCOR GTX	OP	RNBT	FBG	DV	IO	415	MRCR	7	6	3700			12400	14100
27	11	MAXXUM 281	OP	RNBT	FBG	DV	OB			8	2				10700	12100
27	11	MAXXUM 281	OP	RNBT	FBG	DV	IO	330-365		8	2	5300			15300	18100
		IO 415 MRCR 16900 19200, IO T260-T330 16900 21100, IO T365-T415													19900	23800
30	1	MAXXUM 301	OP	OFF	FBG	DV	IO	T330-T415		8	4	6000			22800	27800
		1989 BOATS														
16	6	ENTICER	OP	RNBT	FBG	DV	OB			7		750			1200	1400
16	6	ENTICER DELUXE	OP	RNBT	FBG	DV	OB			7		750			1300	1550
16	6	PREDICTOR II	OP	RNBT	FBG	DV	OB			7		750			1150	1350
16	6	PREDICTOR II DELUXE	OP	RNBT	FBG	DV	OB			7		750			1250	1500
17	1	SPECTRA 170	OP	RNBT	FBG	DV	OB			7	5	1100			1700	2000
17	1	SPECTRA 170 DELUXE	OP	RNBT	FBG	DV	OB			7	5	1100			1850	2200
17	1	SPECTRA 171	OP	RNBT	FBG	DV	OB			7	5	1100			1650	1950
17	1	SPECTRA 171 DELUXE	OP	RNBT	FBG	DV	OB			7	5	1100			1850	2200
17	8	DIPLOMAT	OP	RNBT	FBG	DV	OB			7	5	1875			2550	2950
17	8	DIPLOMAT	OP	RNBT	FBG	DV	IO	130-205		7	5	1875			3500	4200
17	8	DIPLOMAT DELUXE	OP	RNBT	FBG	DV	OB			7	5	1875			2750	3200
17	8	SPORTFIRE	OP	RNBT	FBG	DV	OB			7	5	2150			2700	3150
17	8	SPORTFIRE	OP	RNBT	FBG	DV	IO	130-205		7	5	1775			3450	4100
17	8	SPORTFIRE DELUXE	OP	RNBT	FBG	DV	OB			7	5	2150			3000	3450
18	3	ELUDER	OP	RNBT	FBG	DV	OB			7	5	1025			1650	1950
18	3	ELUDER	OP	RNBT	FBG	DV	IO	130-205		7	5	1025			3200	3800
18	3	ELUDER	OP	RNBT	FBG	DV	IO	260		7	5	1025			3550	4100
18	3	ELUDER DELUXE	OP	RNBT	FBG	DV	OB			7	5	1025			1800	2100
18	3	STARFIRE	OP	RNBT	FBG	DV	IO	130-205		7	5	2450			4100	4900
18	3	STARFIRE	OP	RNBT	FBG	DV	IO	260		7	5	2450			4500	5200
18	3	STARLET	OP	RNBT	FBG	SV	IO	130-205		7	5	2500			4150	4950
18	3	STARLET	OP	RNBT	FBG	SV	IO	260		7	5	2500			4550	5250
18	6	EXCITER	OP	RNBT	FBG	DV	OB			7	5	1000			1600	1900
18	6	EXCITER	OP	RNBT	FBG	DV	IO	130-205		7	5	1000			3300	3900
18	6	EXCITER	OP	RNBT	FBG	DV	IO	260		7	5	1000			3600	4200
18	6	EXCITER DELUXE	OP	RNBT	FBG	DV	OB			7	5	1000			1750	2100
19	7	AMBASSADOR	OP	RNBT	FBG	DV	IO	130-260		7	6	2650			4650	5750
		IO 270 MRCR 5100 5850, IO 320-335 5650 6650, IO 365 MRCR													6450	7450
19	7	SENATOR	OP	RNBT	FBG	DV	IO	130-270		7	6	2700			4700	5900
19	7	SENATOR	OP	RNBT	FBG	DV	IO	320-335		7	6	2700			5700	6700
19	7	SENATOR	OP	RNBT	FBG	DV	IO	365	MRCR	7	6	2700			6500	7500
20	1	SKIMATE	OP	SKI	FBG	DV	OB			7	5	1175			2200	2550
20	1	SKIMATE DELUXE	OP	SKI	FBG	DV	OB			7	5	1175			2450	2850
20	3	SPECTRA 200	OP	RNBT	FBG	DV	OB			7	5	1450			2600	3050
20	3	SPECTRA 200 DELUXE	OP	RNBT	FBG	DV	OB			7	5	1450			2800	3250
20	3	SPECTRA 201	OP	RNBT	FBG	DV	OB			7	5	1500			2700	3100
20	3	SPECTRA 201 DELUXE	OP	RNBT	FBG	DV	OB			7	5	1500			2900	3350
21	2	STARFLITE	OP	RNBT	FBG	DV	OB			7	5	1300			2500	2900
21	2	STARFLITE DELUXE	OP	RNBT	FBG	DV	OB			7	5	1300			2650	3100
21	2	STARLINER	OP	RNBT	FBG	DV	OB			7	5	1400			2650	3050
21	2	STARLINER DELUXE	OP	RNBT	FBG	DV	OB			7	5	1400			2800	3250
22	1	VISION 221	OP	RNBT	FBG	DV	IO	260-270		7	6	2950			6500	7550
22	1	VISION 221	OP	RNBT	FBG	DV	IO	320-335		7	6	2950			7200	8450
22	1	VISION 221	OP	RNBT	FBG	DV	IO	365	MRCR	7	6	2950			8050	9250
22	9	MAXXUM 229	OP	RNBT	FBG	DV	IO	260-270		7	9	3200			7150	8300
22	9	MAXXUM 229	OP	RNBT	FBG	DV	IO	320-340		7	9	3200			7800	9250
22	9	MAXXUM 229	OP	RNBT	FBG	DV	IO	365	MRCR	7	9	3200			8700	10000
24		ENFORCER	OP	RNBT	FBG	DV	IO	260-320		7	5	3400			7800	9750
24		ENFORCER	OP	RNBT	FBG	DV	IO	330-365		7	5	3400			8650	10700
24		ENFORCER	OP	RNBT	FBG	DV	IO	420	MRCR	7	5	3400			10900	12400
24		ENFORCER SX	OP	RNBT	FBG	DV	OB			7	5				5750	6600
25	1	CONVINCOR GTX	OP	RNBT	FBG	DV	OB			7	6	3700			6800	7800
25	1	CONVINCOR GTX	OP	RNBT	FBG	DV	IO	260-335		7	6	3700			9000	11200
25	1	CONVINCOR GTX	OP	RNBT	FBG	DV	IO	365	MRCR	7	6	3700			10500	11900
25	1	CONVINCOR GTX	OP	RNBT	FBG	DV	IO	420	MRCR	7	6	3700			11900	13500
27	11	MAXXUM 281	OP	RNBT	FBG	DV	IO	320-365		8	2	5300			14300	17000
		IO 420 MRCR 16000 18200, IO T260-T320 15900 19600, IO T350 MRCR													18500	20500
30	1	MAXXUM 301	OP	OFF	FBG	DV	IO	T320-T420		8	4	6000			21000	26100
		1988 BOATS														
16	6	ENTICER	OP	RNBT	FBG	DV	OB			7		750			1150	1350
16	6	ENTICER DELUXE	OP	RNBT	FBG	DV	OB			7		750			1250	1450
16	6	PREDICTOR II	OP	RNBT	FBG	DV	OB			7		750			1100	1300
16	6	PREDICTOR II DELUXE	OP	RNBT	FBG	DV	OB			7		750			1200	1450
17	1	SPECTRA 170	OP	RNBT	FBG	DV	OB			7	5	1100			1600	1900
17	1	SPECTRA 170 DELUXE	OP	RNBT	FBG	DV	OB			7	5	1100			1750	2100
17	1	SPECTRA 171	OP	RNBT	FBG	DV	OB			7	5	1100			1600	1900
17	1	SPECTRA 171 DELUXE	OP	RNBT	FBG	DV	OB			7	5	1100			1800	2150
17	8	DIPLOMAT	OP	RNBT	FBG	DV	OB			7	5	1875			2450	2850
17	8	DIPLOMAT	OP	RNBT	FBG	DV	IO	130-205		7	5	1875			3350	3950
17	8	DIPLOMAT DELUXE	OP	RNBT	FBG	DV	OB			7	5	1875			2700	3150
17	8	SPORTFIRE	OP	RNBT	FBG	DV	OB			7	5	1775			2350	2750
17	8	SPORTFIRE	OP	RNBT	FBG	DV	IO	130-205		7	5	1775			3250	3900
17	8	SPORTFIRE DELUXE	OP	RNBT	FBG	DV	OB			7	5	1775			2600	3000
18	3	ELUDER	OP	RNBT	FBG	DV	OB			7	5	1025			1550	1850
18	3	ELUDER	OP	RNBT	FBG	DV	IO	130-205		7	5	1025			3000	3600
18	3	ELUDER	OP	RNBT	FBG	DV	IO	260		7	5	1025			3350	3900
18	3	ELUDER DELUXE	OP	RNBT	FBG	DV	OB			7	5	1025			1700	2050
18	3	STARFIRE	OP	RNBT	FBG	DV	IO	130-205		7	5	2300			3850	4550
18	3	STARFIRE	OP	RNBT	FBG	DV	IO	260		7	5	2300			4150	4800
18	3	STARLET	OP	RNBT	FBG	SV	IO	130-205		7	5	2300			3750	4450
18	3	STARLET	OP	RNBT	FBG	SV	IO	260		7	5	2300			4100	4750
18	3	STARLET FS	OP	RNBT	FBG	DV	IO	130-205		7	5	2300			3750	4450
18	3	STARLET FS	OP	RNBT	FBG	DV	IO	260		7	5	2300			4100	4750
18	6	EXCITER	OP	RNBT	FBG	DV	OB			7	5	1000			1550	1850
18	6	EXCITER	OP	RNBT	FBG	DV	IO	130-205		7	5	1975			3550	4250
18	6	EXCITER	OP	RNBT	FBG	DV	IO	260		7	5	1975			3900	4500
18	6	EXCITER DELUXE	OP	RNBT	FBG	DV	OB			7	5	1000			1700	2050

CONTINUED ON NEXT PAGE

LOA FT	IN	NAME AND/ OR MODEL	TOP/ RIG	BOAT TYPE	-HULL- MTL	TP	ENGINE TP	# HP	MFG	BEAM FT	IN	WGT LBS	DRAFT FT IN	RETAIL LOW	RETAIL HIGH
		1988 BOATS													
19	7	AMBASSADOR	OP	RNBT	FBG	DV	IO		OMC	7	6	2600		**	**
		IO 130-205 4300 5100, IO 260-270 4650 5450, IO 320-330												5350	6150
		IO 365 MRCR 6050 6950													
19	7	SENATOR	OP	RNBT	FBG	DV	IO		OMC	7	6	2600		**	**
		IO 130-270 4450 5550, IO 320-330 5250 6300, IO 365 MRCR												6150	7050
20	1	ENCHANTER	OP	RNBT	FBG	DV	OB			7	6	1275		2400	2750
20	1	ENCHANTER DELUXE	OP	RNBT	FBG	DV	OB			7	6	1275		2400	2750
20	1	SKIMATE	OP	SKI	FBG	DV	OB			7	5	1175		2050	2400
20	1	SKIMATE DELUXE	OP	SKI	FBG	DV	OB			7	5	1175		2350	2750
20	8	ENCHANTER	OP	RNBT	FBG	DV	IO	130-260		7	6	2350		4750	5900
21	2	STARFLITE	OP	RNBT	FBG	DV	OB			7	5	1300		2400	2800
21	2	STARFLITE DELUXE	OP	RNBT	FBG	DV	OB			7	5	1300		2550	3000
21	2	STARLINER	OP	RNBT	FBG	DV	OB			7	5	1400		2500	2950
21	2	STARLINER DELUXE	OP	RNBT	FBG	DV	OB			7	5	1400		2700	3150
22	1	VISION 221	OP	RNBT	FBG	DV	IO		OMC	7	6	3000		**	**
		IO 260-270 6200 7250, IO 320-330 6850 8050, IO 365 MRCR												7700	8850
23		ENFORCER GTX	OP	RNBT	FBG	DV	IO		OMC	7	5	3400		**	**
		IO 260-270 7000 8150, IO 320-330 7650 8950, IO 365 MRCR												8500	9750
24		ENFORCER	OP	RNBT	FBG	DV	IO		OMC	7	5	3400		**	**
		IO 260-320 7400 9200, IO 330-365 8150 10200, IO 420 MRCR												10300	11700
24		ENFORCER SX	OP	RNBT	FBG	DV	OB			7	5			5550	6350
25	1	CONVINCOR	OP	RNBT	FBG	DV	OB			7	6	3700		6500	7500
25	1	CONVINCOR	OP	RNBT	FBG	DV	IO		OMC	7	6	3700		**	**
		IO 260-320 8400 10400, IO 330-365 9350 11300, IO 420 MRCR												11200	12800
28		MAXXUM 281	OP	RNBT	FBG	DV	IO		OMC					**	**
		IO 320-365 10800 12900, IO 420 MRCR 12100 13800, IO T260 MRCR												12100	13700
30	1	MAXXUM 301	OP	OFF	FBG	DV	IO	T	MRCR	8	3	6000		**	**
30	1	MAXXUM 301	OP	OFF	FBG	DV	IO	T320-T420		8	3	6000		19800	24600
		1987 BOATS													
16	6	ENTICER DELUXE	OP	RNBT	FBG	DV	OB			7		750		1200	1450
16	6	ENTICER STANDARD	OP	RNBT	FBG	DV	OB			7		750		1100	1300
16	6	PREDICTOR II DELUXE	OP	RNBT	FBG	DV	OB			7		750		1150	1400
16	6	PREDICTOR II STANDRD	OP	RNBT	FBG	DV	OB			7		750		1050	1250
16	7	DIPLOMAT DELUXE	OP	RNBT	FBG	DV	OB			7	5	875		1350	1600
16	7	DIPLOMAT DELUXE	OP	RNBT	FBG	DV	IO	140		7	5	1875		2950	3450
16	7	DIPLOMAT STANDARD	OP	RNBT	FBG	DV	OB			7	5	875		1250	1500
16	7	DIPLOMAT STANDARD	OP	RNBT	FBG	DV	IO	130-205		7	5	1875		2900	3550
16	7	SPORTFIRE DELUXE	OP	RNBT	FBG	DV	OB			7	5	850		1350	1600
16	7	SPORTFIRE DELUXE	OP	RNBT	FBG	DV	IO	130-175		7	5	1875		3000	3500
16	7	SPORTFIRE STANDARD	OP	RNBT	FBG	DV	OB			7	5	850		1200	1450
16	7	SPORTFIRE STANDARD	OP	RNBT	FBG	DV	IO	130-205		7	6	1875		3000	3550
18	3	ELUDER DELUXE	OP	RNBT	FBG	DV	OB			7	5	1025		1650	1950
18	3	ELUDER DELUXE	OP	RNBT	FBG	DV	IO	140		7	5	2000		3350	3900
18	3	ELUDER STANDARD	OP	RNBT	FBG	DV	OB			7	5	1025		1500	1800
18	3	ELUDER STANDARD	OP	RNBT	FBG	DV	IO	130-205		7	5	2000		3350	4000
18	3	ELUDER STANDARD	OP	RNBT	FBG	DV	IO	260		7	5	2000		3650	4250
18	3	STARFIRE	OP	RNBT	FBG	DV	IO	130-205		7	5	2300		3550	4300
18	3	STARFIRE	OP	RNBT	FBG	DV	IO	260		7	5	2300		3950	4550
18	3	STARFIRE DELUXE	OP	RNBT	FBG	DV	IO	130		7	5	2300		3750	4350
18	3	STARLET	OP	RNBT	FBG	DV	IO	130-205		7	5	2300		3450	4250
18	3	STARLET	OP	RNBT	FBG	DV	IO	260		7	5	2300		3850	4500
18	3	STARLET DELUXE	OP	RNBT	FBG	DV	IO	130		7	5	2300		3650	4250
18	6	EXCITER DELUXE	OP	RNBT	FBG	DV	OB			7	5	1000		1650	1950
18	6	EXCITER DELUXE	OP	RNBT	FBG	DV	IO	130		7	5	1975		3500	4050
18	6	EXCITER STANDARD	OP	RNBT	FBG	DV	OB			7	5	1000		1500	1750
18	6	EXCITER STANDARD	OP	RNBT	FBG	DV	IO	130-205		7	5	1975		3300	4050
18	6	EXCITER STANDARD	OP	RNBT	FBG	DV	IO	260		7	5	1975		3700	4300
19	7	AMBASSADOR		RNBT	FBG	SV	IO	130-205		7	5	2600		4050	4800
19	7	AMBASSADOR		RNBT	FBG	SV	IO	260		7	5	2600		4400	5100
19	7	AMBASSADOR		RNBT	FBG	SV	IO	330		7	5	2600		5100	5850
19	7	AMBASSADOR	OP	RNBT	FBG	DV	IO		MRCR	7	6	2600		**	**
		IO 130-205 4000 4850, IO 260 4450 5100, IO 320 MRCR												5000	5750
19	7	SENATOR		RNBT	FBG	SV	IO	130-260		7	5	2600		4150	5200
19	7	SENATOR		RNBT	FBG	SV	IO	330		7	5	2600		5200	6000
19	7	SENATOR	OP	RNBT	FBG	DV	IO		MRCR	7	6	2600		**	**
		IO 130-205 4100 4950, IO 260 4550 5200, IO 320 MRCR												5100	5850
20	1	ENCHANTER	OP	RNBT	FBG	DV	OB			7	6	1275		2200	2550
20	1	ENCHANTER DELUXE	OP	RNBT	FBG	DV	OB			7	6	1275		2400	2800
20	1	SKIMATE		RNBT	FBG	SV	OB			7	5	1175		2100	2500
20	1	SKIMATE	OP	SKI	FBG	DV	OB			7	5	1175		1950	2350
20	1	SKIMATE DELUXE	OP	SKI	FBG	DV	OB			7	5	1175		2250	2650
20	8	ENCHANTER	OP	RNBT	FBG	DV	IO	130-205		7	6	2350		4450	5350
20	8	ENCHANTER	OP	RNBT	FBG	DV	IO	260		7	6	2350		4850	5600
20	8	ENCHANTER DELUXE	OP	RNBT	FBG	DV	IO	130		7	6	2350		4650	5350
20	8	ENTERTAINER	OP	RNBT	FBG	DV	IO	130-205		7	6	2175		4250	5150
20	8	ENTERTAINER	OP	RNBT	FBG	DV	IO	260		7	6	2175		4700	5400
20	8	ENTERTAINER DELUXE	OP	RNBT	FBG	DV	IO	130		7	6	2175		4500	5150
21	2	STARFLITE		RNBT	FBG	SV	OB			7	5	1300		2400	2800
21	2	STARFLITE	OP	RNBT	FBG	DV	OB			7	6	1300		2400	2800
21	2	STARFLITE DELUXE	OP	RNBT	FBG	DV	OB			7	5	1300		2400	2800
21	2	STARLINER		RNBT	FBG	SV	OB			7	5	1400		2550	2950
21	2	STARLINER	OP	RNBT	FBG	DV	OB			7	5	1400		2500	2900
21	2	STARLINER DELUXE	OP	RNBT	FBG	DV	OB			7	5	1400		2600	3050
22	1	VISION 221		RNBT	FBG	SV	IO	260		7	6	3000		5900	6800
22	1	VISION 221		RNBT	FBG	SV	IO	330		7	6	3000		6650	7650
22	1	VISION 221		RNBT	FBG	SV	IO	365		7	6	3000		7300	8400
23	7	ENFORCER GTX		RNBT	FBG	SV	IO	260		7	5	3200		6600	7600
23	7	ENFORCER GTX		RNBT	FBG	SV	IO	320-330		7	5	3200		7200	8450
23	7	ENFORCER SX		RNBT	FBG	SV	OB			7	5	2500		4450	5100
24		ENFORCER		RNBT	FBG	SV	IO	260		7	5	3400		7000	8050
24		ENFORCER		RNBT	FBG	SV	IO	330-365		7	5	3400		7750	9650
24		ENFORCER	OP	RNBT	FBG	DV	IO		MRCR	7	5	3400		**	**
		IO 260 7000 8050, IO 330 MRCR 7750 8950, IO 370 MRCR												8500	9800
		IO 420 MRCR 9800 11200													
24		ENFORCER SX	OP	RNBT	FBG	DV	OB			7	5			5350	6100
25	1	CONVINCOR		OFF	FBG	DV	IO	260		7	6	3700		8450	9750
25	1	CONVINCOR		OFF	FBG	DV	IO	330-365		7	6	3700		9400	11400
25	1	CONVINCOR	OP	RNBT	FBG	DV	OB			7	6	3700		6250	7200
25	1	CONVINCOR	OP	RNBT	FBG	DV	IO		MRCR	7	5	3400		**	**
		IO 260 8000 9200, IO 330-370 8900 10800, IO 420 MRCR												10300	11700
28		2800 GTS	OP	RNBT	FBG	DV	OB			7	6			9300	10600
30	1	MAXXUM 301		OFF	FBG	DV	IO	T330-T420		8	4	6000		19100	23400
		1986 BOATS													
16	6	ENTICER	OP	RNBT	FBG	DV	OB			7		750		1100	1300
16	6	PREDICTOR II DELUXE	OP	RNBT	FBG	DV	OB			7		750		1150	1350
16	6	PREDICTOR II STANDRD	OP	RNBT	FBG	DV	OB			7		750		1050	1250
16	7	DIPLOMAT	OP	RNBT	FBG	DV	OB			7	5	875		1200	1450
16	7	DIPLOMAT	OP	RNBT	FBG	DV	IO	140-205		7	5	1875		2750	3350
16	7	DIPLOMAT DELUXE	OP	RNBT	FBG	DV	OB			7	5	875		1300	1550
16	7	DIPLOMAT DELUXE	OP	RNBT	FBG	DV	IO	140		7	5	1875		2900	3350
16	7	SPORTFIRE	OP	RNBT	FBG	DV	OB			7	5	850		1150	1400
16	7	SPORTFIRE DELUXE	OP	RNBT	FBG	DV	OB			7	5	850		1300	1550
17	8	SPORTFIRE	OP	RNBT	FBG	DV	IO	140-205		7	6	1875		3050	3650
17	8	SPORTFIRE DELUXE	OP	RNBT	FBG	DV	IO	140		7	5	1875		3000	3500
18	3	ELUDER	OP	RNBT	FBG	DV	OB			7	5	1025		1450	1750
18	3	ELUDER DELUXE	OP	RNBT	FBG	DV	OB			7	5	1025		1600	1900
18	6	EXCITER	OP	RNBT	FBG	DV	OB			7	5	1000		1450	1700
18	6	EXCITER DELUXE	OP	RNBT	FBG	DV	OB			7	5	1000		1600	1900
18	10	ELUDER	OP	RNBT	FBG	DV	IO	140-205		7	5	2000		3250	3950
18	10	ELUDER	OP	RNBT	FBG	DV	IO	260		7	5	2000		3600	4200
18	10	ELUDER DELUXE	OP	RNBT	FBG	DV	IO	140		7	5	2000		3400	3950
18	11	EXCITER	OP	RNBT	FBG	DV	IO	140-205		7	5	1975		3250	3950
18	11	EXCITER	OP	RNBT	FBG	DV	IO	260		7	5	1975		3600	4200
18	11	EXCITER DELUXE	OP	RNBT	FBG	DV	IO	140		7	5	1975		3400	3950
19	7	AMBASSADOR	OP	RNBT	FBG	DV	IO	140-205		7	6	2600		3900	4650
19	7	AMBASSADOR	OP	RNBT	FBG	DV	IO	260		7	6	2600		4200	4900
19	7	SENATOR	OP	RNBT	FBG	DV	IO	140-260		7	6	2600		4000	5000
19	7	SENATOR	OP	RNBT	FBG	DV	IO	300	MRCR	7	6	2600		4600	5300
20	1	ENCHANTER	OP	RNBT	FBG	DV	OB			7	6	1275		2050	2450
20	1	ENCHANTER DELUXE	OP	RNBT	FBG	DV	OB			7	6	1275		2300	2700
20	1	ENTERTAINER	OP	RNBT	FBG	DV	OB			7	6	1150		1900	2250
20	1	ENTERTAINER DELUXE	OP	RNBT	FBG	DV	OB			7	6	1150		2050	2450
20	1	SKIMATE	OP	SKI	FBG	DV	OB			7	5	1175		2000	2400
20	8	ENCHANTER	OP	RNBT	FBG	DV	IO	140-205		7	6	2350		4200	5100
20	8	ENCHANTER	OP	RNBT	FBG	DV	IO	260		7	6	2350		4650	5350
20	8	ENCHANTER DELUXE	OP	RNBT	FBG	DV	IO	140		7	6	2350		4450	5150
20	8	ENTERTAINER	OP	RNBT	FBG	DV	IO	140-205		7	6	2175		4100	4950
20	8	ENTERTAINER	OP	RNBT	FBG	DV	IO	260		7	6	2175		4500	5200

CONTINUED ON NEXT PAGE

LOA FT	IN	NAME AND/ OR MODEL	TOP/ RIG	BOAT TYPE	-HULL- MTL	TP	TP	----ENGINE--- # HP	MFG	BEAM FT	IN	WGT LBS	DRAFT FT	IN	RETAIL LOW	RETAIL HIGH
		1986 BOATS														
20	8	ENTERTAINER DELUXE	OP	RNBT	FBG	DV	IO	140		7	6	2175			4250	4950
21	2	STARFLITE	OP	RNBT	FBG	DV	OB			7	6	1300			2350	2700
21	2	STARFLITE DELUXE	OP	RNBT	FBG	DV	OB			7	5	1300			2350	2700
23		ENFORCER	OP	RNBT	FBG	DV	IO	260-300							6200	7500
		IO 330 MRCR 6900 7950, IO 370 MRCR 7600 8750, IO 400 MRCR 8300 9550														
		IO 440 MRCR 9400 10700														
23		ENFORCER SX	OP	RNBT	FBG	DV	OB								4700	5400
24	7	CONVINCOR	OP	RNBT	FBG	DV	OB			7	8	2400			4450	5100
24	7	CONVINCOR	OP	RNBT	FBG	DV	IO	260		7	8	2400			6000	6850
24	7	CONVINCOR	OP	RNBT	FBG	DV	IO	330	MRCR	7	8	2400			6750	7750
24	7	CONVINCOR	OP	RNBT	FBG	DV	IO	370	MRCR	7	8	2400			7450	8550
28		2800 SX	OP	RNBT	FBG	DV	OB								8950	10200
30		300 SX	OP	RNBT	FBG	DV	IO	T260		8	6				12700	14500
		1985 BOATS														
16	6	ENTICER	OP	RNBT	FBG	DV	OB			7		750			1100	1300
16	6	PREDICTOR II	OP	RNBT	FBG	DV	OB			7		750			1050	1200
16	7	DIPLOMAT	OP	RNBT	FBG	DV	OB			7	5	875			1200	1450
16	7	DIPLOMAT	OP	RNBT	FBG	DV	IO	140-205		7	5	1875			2700	3250
16	7	SPORTFIRE	OP	RNBT	FBG	DV	OB			7	5	850			1200	1400
17	8	SPORTFIRE	OP	RNBT	FBG	DV	IO	140-205		7	6	1875			2900	3500
18	3	ELUDER	OP	RNBT	FBG	DV	OB			7	5	1025			1500	1750
18	6	EXCITER	OP	RNBT	FBG	DV	OB			7	5	1000			1450	1750
18	10	ELUDER	OP	RNBT	FBG	DV	IO	140-205		7	5	2000			3200	3800
18	10	ELUDER	OP	RNBT	FBG	DV	IO	260		7	5	2000			3450	4050
18	11	EXCITER	OP	RNBT	FBG	DV	IO	140-205		7	5	1975			3200	3800
18	11	EXCITER	OP	RNBT	FBG	DV	IO	260		7	5	1975			3450	4050
19	7	AMBASSADOR	OP	RNBT	FBG	DV	IO	140-260		7	6	2600			3800	4750
20	1	ENCHANTER	OP	RNBT	FBG	DV	OB			7	6	1275			2100	2500
20	1	ENTERTAINER	OP	RNBT	FBG	DV	OB			7	6	1150			1900	2300
20	1	SKIMATE	OP	SKI	FBG	DV	OB			7	5	1175			1950	2300
20	8	ENCHANTER	OP	RNBT	FBG	DV	IO	140-260		7	6	2350			4150	5150
20	8	ENTERTAINER	OP	RNBT	FBG	DV	IO	140-260		7	6	2175			4000	5000
21	2	STARFLITE	OP	RNBT	FBG	DV	OB			7	5	1300			2250	2600
23		ENFORCER	OP	RNBT	FBG	DV	IO	260							5950	6800
23		ENFORCER	OP	RNBT	FBG	DV	IO	330	MRCR						6600	7600
23		ENFORCER	OP	RNBT	FBG	DV	IO	370	MRCR						7300	8400
23		ENFORCER SX	OP	RNBT	FBG	DV	OB								4550	5200
24	7	CONVINCOR	OP	RNBT	FBG	DV	OB			7	8	2400			4250	4950
24	7	CONVINCOR	OP	RNBT	FBG	DV	IO	260		7	8	2400			5750	6600
24	7	CONVINCOR	OP	RNBT	FBG	DV	IO	330	MRCR	7	8	2400			6500	7450
24	7	CONVINCOR	OP	RNBT	FBG	DV	IO	370	MRCR	7	8	2400			7150	8200
28		2800 SX	OP	RNBT	FBG	DV	OB								8600	9850
		1984 BOATS														
16	6	ENTICER	OP	RNBT	FBG	DV	OB			7		750			1050	1250
16	6	PREDICTOR II	OP	RNBT	FBG	DV	OB			7		750			995	1200
16	7	DIPLOMAT	OP	RNBT	FBG	DV	OB			7	5	875			1200	1400
16	7	DIPLOMAT	OP	RNBT	FBG	DV	IO	140-185		7	5	1875			2600	3100
16	7	SPORTFIRE	OP	RNBT	FBG	DV	OB			7	5	850			1150	1350
17	8	SPORTFIRE	OP	RNBT	FBG	DV	IO	140-185		7	6	1875			2800	3300
18	3	ELUDER	OP	RNBT	FBG	DV	OB			7	5	1025			1450	1700
18	6	EXCITER	OP	RNBT	FBG	DV	OB			7	5	1000			1400	1700
18	10	ELUDER	OP	RNBT	FBG	DV	IO	140-198		7	5	2000			3100	3650
18	10	ELUDER	OP	RNBT	FBG	DV	IO	260	MRCR	7	5	2000			3350	3900
18	11	EXCITER	OP	RNBT	FBG	DV	IO	140-198		7	5	1975			3100	3650
18	11	EXCITER	OP	RNBT	FBG	DV	IO	260	MRCR	7	5	1975			3350	3900
20	1	ENCHANTER	OP	RNBT	FBG	DV	OB			7	6	1275			2050	2400
20	1	ENTERTAINER	OP	RNBT	FBG	DV	OB			7	6	1150			1850	2200
20	8	ENCHANTER	OP	RNBT	FBG	DV	IO	140-260		7	6	2350			4000	4950
20	8	ENTERTAINER	OP	RNBT	FBG	DV	IO	140-260		7	6	2175			3850	4800
23	1	ENFORCER	OP	RNBT	FBG	DV	OB			7	7	2000			3250	3750
23	3	ENFORCER	OP	RNBT	FBG	DV	IO	260		7	7				5700	6550
24	7	CONVINCOR	OP	RNBT	FBG	DV	OB			7	8	2400			4100	4800
25	3	CONVINCOR	OP	RNBT	FBG	DV	IO	260		7	6				7500	8600

....For earlier years, see the BUC Used Boat Price Guide, Volume 3

CHEETAH BOAT CO

WATSEKA IL 60970

See inside cover to adjust price for area

LOA FT	IN	NAME AND/ OR MODEL	TOP/ RIG	BOAT TYPE	-HULL- MTL	TP	TP	----ENGINE--- # HP	MFG	BEAM FT	IN	WGT LBS	DRAFT FT	IN	RETAIL LOW	RETAIL HIGH
		1995 BOATS														
17	8	1700LS BR	OP	RNBT	FBG	DV	IO	135-250		7	8	1870			4950	6150
17	8	1700LS CB	OP	RNBT	FBG	DV	IO	135-250		7	8	2060			5150	6400
19	6	1900LS BR	OP	RNBT	FBG	DV	IO	135-250		7	8	2350			6100	7400
19	6	1900LS CB	OP	RNBT	FBG	DV	IO	135-250		7	8	2400			6150	7500
19	8	2000LS BR	OP	RNBT	FBG	DV	IO	135-250		7	8	2120			5850	7150
19	8	2000LS CC	OP	CUD	FBG	DV	IO	135-250		7	8	2240			6200	7600
21	1	2100LS BR	OP	RNBT	FBG	DV	IO	135-250		7	9	2600			7200	8750
21	1	2100LS CC	OP	CUD	FBG	DV	IO	135-250		7	9	2750			7800	9400
23	6	2300LS CC	OP	CUD	FBG	DV	IO	205-300		8	6	3700			11300	13900
24	5	2500LS CC	OP	CUD	FBG	DV	IO	205-300		8	6	3900			12300	15100
		1994 BOATS														
17	8	1700LS BR	OP	RNBT	FBG	DV	IO	115-205		7	8	1870			4650	5700
		IO 215-255 5050 6150, IO 300 5550 6850, IO 350 MRCR 6550 7550														
17	8	1700LS CB	OP	RNBT	FBG	DV	IO	115-205		7	8	2060			4850	5950
		IO 215-255 5250 6350, IO 300 5750 7100, IO 350 MRCR 6750 7750														
19	6	1900LS BR	OP	RNBT	FBG	DV	IO	115-225		7	8	2350			5650	7100
		IO 230-235 6200 7100, IO 250 MRCR 6050 6950, IO 250-255 6350 7350														
		IO 300 MRCR 6600 7550, IO 300 VLVO 7000 8050, IO 350 MRCR 7600 8700														
19	6	1900LS CB	OP	RNBT	FBG	DV	IO	115-225		7	8	2400			5750	7150
		IO 230-255 6250 7400, IO 300 6650 8150, IO 350 MRCR 7650 8800														
19	8	2000LS BR	OP	RNBT	FBG	DV	IO	115-215		7	8	2120			5450	6800
		IO 225-255 5950 7100, IO 300 6350 7800, IO 350 MRCR 7400 8500														
19	8	2000LS CC	OP	CUD	FBG	DV	IO	115-215		7	8	2240			5800	7200
		IO 225-255 6300 7550, IO 300 6750 8300, IO 350 MRCR 7850 9000														
21	1	2100LS BR	OP	RNBT	FBG	DV	IO	115-235		7	9	2600			6700	8350
		IO 245-255 7350 8550, IO 300 7650 9300, IO 350 MRCR 8700 10000														
21	1	2100LS CC	OP	CUD	FBG	DV	IO	115-235		7	9	2750			7250	9000
		IO 245-255 7950 9250, IO 300 8250 10000, IO 350 MRCR 9400 10700														
23	6	2300LS CC	OP	CUD	FBG	DV	IO	205-255		8	6	3700			10600	12700
23	6	2300LS CC	OP	CUD	FBG	DV	IO	300-350		8	6	3700			11400	14200
23	6	2300LS CC	OP	CUD	FBG	DV	IO	390	VLVO	8	6	3700			14700	16700
24	5	2500LS CC	OP	CUD	FBG	DV	IO	205-255		8	6	3900			11500	13800
24	5	2500LS CC	OP	CUD	FBG	DV	IO	300-350		8	6	3900			12900	15400
24	5	2500LS CC	OP	CUD	FBG	DV	IO	390	VLVO	8	6	3900			15600	17800
		1993 BOATS														
17	8	1700LS BR	OP	RNBT	FBG	DV	IO	110-275		7	8	1870			4550	5650
17	8	1700LS BR	OP	RNBT	FBG	DV	IO	300-310		7	8	1870			5200	6400
17	8	1700LS BR	OP	RNBT	FBG	DV	IO	350	MRCR	7	8	1870			6100	7050
17	8	1700LS CB	OP	RNBT	FBG	DV	IO	110-275		7	8	2060			4750	5850
17	8	1700LS CB	OP	RNBT	FBG	DV	IO	300-310		7	8	2060			5350	6650
17	8	1700LS CB	OP	RNBT	FBG	DV	IO	350	MRCR	7	8	2060			6300	7250
19	5	1900LS BR	OP	RNBT	FBG	DV	IO	110-245		7	8	2350			5500	6750
		IO 250 MRCR 5600 6450, IO 275 OMC 5750 6600, IO 300 MRCR 6150 7050														
		IO 300-310 6550 7500, IO 350 MRCR 7050 8100														
19	5	1900LS CB	OP	RNBT	FBG	DV	IO	110-275		7	8	2400			5550	6800
19	5	1900LS CB	OP	RNBT	FBG	DV	IO	300-310		7	8	2400			6200	7550
19	5	1900LS CB	OP	RNBT	FBG	DV	IO	350	MRCR	7	8	2400			7100	8200
19	8	2000LS BR	OP	RNBT	FBG	DV	IO	110-275		7	8	2120			5350	6550
19	8	2000LS BR	OP	RNBT	FBG	DV	IO	300-310		7	8	2120			5950	7300
19	8	2000LS BR	OP	RNBT	FBG	DV	IO	350	MRCR	7	8	2120			6900	7900
19	8	2000LS CC	OP	CUD	FBG	DV	IO	110-275		7	8	2240			5650	6950
19	8	2000LS CC	OP	CUD	FBG	DV	IO	300-310		7	8	2240			6300	7750
19	8	2000LS CC	OP	CUD	FBG	DV	IO	350	MRCR	7	8	2240			7300	8400
21	1	2100LS BR	OP	RNBT	FBG	DV	IO	110-275		7	9	2600			6500	7900
21	1	2100LS BR	OP	RNBT	FBG	DV	IO	300-310		7	9	2600			7150	8700
21	1	2100LS BR	OP	RNBT	FBG	DV	IO	350	MRCR	7	9	2600			8100	9350
21	1	2100LS CC	OP	CUD	FBG	DV	IO	110-275		7	9	2750			7050	8550
21	1	2100LS CC	OP	CUD	FBG	DV	IO	300-310		7	9	2750			7700	9400
21	1	2100LS CC	OP	CUD	FBG	DV	IO	350	MRCR	7	9	2750			8850	10100
23	6	2300LSC	OP	CUD	FBG	DV	IO	175-275		8	6	3700			9750	11800
23	6	2300LSC	OP	CUD	FBG	DV	IO	300-350		8	6	3700			10700	13300
24	5	2500LSC	OP	CUD	FBG	DV	IO	175-275		8	6	3900			10500	12800
24	5	2500LSC	OP	CUD	FBG	DV	IO	300-350		8	6	3900			11600	14400
		1992 BOATS														
16	1	1600 FS	OP	RNBT	FBG	SV	OB			6	9				2750	3200
16	1	1600 PRO	OP	RNBT	FBG	SV	OB			6	9				2500	2950
17	8	1700 LS	OP	RNBT	FBG	DV	IO	110-275		7	8	1870			4250	5300
		IO 300 MRCR 4800 5550, IO 300-320 5250 6050, IO 350 MRCR 5750 6600														

CONTINUED ON NEXT PAGE

LOA FT	LOA IN	NAME AND/ OR MODEL	TOP/ RIG	BOAT TYPE	-HULL- MTL	-HULL- TP	TP	ENGINE # HP	ENGINE MFG	BEAM FT	BEAM IN	WGT LBS	DRAFT FT	DRAFT IN	RETAIL LOW	RETAIL HIGH
		1992 BOATS														
17	8	1700 LS CB	OP	RNBT	FBG	DV	IO	110-275		7	8	1870			4250	5300
		IO 300 MRCR 4800 5550, IO 300-320 5250 6050, IO 350 MRCR													5750	6600
18		1800 FS	OP	RNBT	FBG	SV	OB			7	4				4650	5350
18		1800 LS	OP	B/R	FBG	DV	IO	110-240		7	8	1970			4200	5050
		IO 245 OMC 4250 4950, IO 245-275 4600 5300, IO 300-320													4850	6000
		IO 350 MRCR 5700 6550														
18		1800 PRO	OP	RNBT	FBG	SV	OB			7	4				4150	4850
18	9	1900 ES	OP	B/R	FBG	DV	IO	115-230		7	8	2020			4250	5200
19	6	1900 LS	OP	RNBT	FBG	DV	IO	110-275		7	8	2020			4850	5950
19	6	1900 LS	OP	RNBT	FBG	DV	IO	300	MRCR	7	8	2020			5400	6200
19	6	1900 LS	OP	RNBT	FBG	DV	IO	300-350		7	8	2020			5900	7250
19	6	1900 LS CB	OP	RNBT	FBG	DV	IO	110-275		7	8	2020			4850	5950
19	6	1900 LS CB	OP	RNBT	FBG	DV	IO	300	MRCR	7	8	2020			5400	6200
19	6	1900 LS CB	OP	RNBT	FBG	DV	IO	300-350		7	8	2020			5900	7250
19	8	1900 ES	OP	B/R	FBG	DV	IO	110-275		7	8	2120			4850	5950
19	8	1900 ES	OP	B/R	FBG	DV	IO	300	MRCR	7	8	2120			5350	6150
19	8	1900 ES	OP	B/R	FBG	DV	IO	300-350		7	8	2120			5850	7250
19	8	2000 LS	OP	B/R	FBG	DV	IO	110-275		7	8	2120			4850	5900
19	8	2000 LS	OP	B/R	FBG	DV	IO	300	MRCR	7	8	2120			5350	6150
19	8	2000 LS	OP	B/R	FBG	DV	IO	300-350		7	8	2120			5850	7250
19	8	2000 LS CC	OP	RNBT	FBG	DV	IO	110	VLVO	7	8	2240			5100	5850
		IO 115 MRCR 4900 5650, IO 115-240 4850 6000, IO 245-275													5100	6250
		IO 300-320 5700 6950, IO 350 MRCR 6550 7550														
20	10	210 ES	OP	B/R	FBG	DV	IO	110-190		7	8	2220			5200	6400
20	10	210 ES	OP	B/R	FBG	DV	IO	205-275		7	8	2220			5750	6650
20	10	210 ES	OP	B/R	FBG	DV	IO	300-350		7	8	2220			6500	8000
20	10	210 ES BOWRIDER	OP	B/R	FBG	DV	IO	135-230		7	8	2220			5200	6250
20	10	210 ES BOWRIDER	OP	B/R	FBG	DV	IO	300	MRCR	7	8	2220			6000	6900
20	10	210 ES CUDDY	OP	CUD	FBG	DV	IO	110-275		7	8	2340			5950	7250
20	10	210 ES CUDDY	OP	CUD	FBG	DV	IO	300-320		7	8	2340			6600	8050
20	10	210 ES CUDDY	OP	CUD	FBG	DV	IO	350	MRCR	7	8	2340			7550	8700
23	6	HOMBRE 230	OP	SPTCR	FBG	DV	IO	205-275		8	6	3700			9300	11000
23	6	HOMBRE 230	OP	SPTCR	FBG	DV	IO	300-350		8	6	3700			10000	12400
24	5	CALIENTE 250	OP	SPTCR	FBG	DV	IO	205-275		8	6	3900			10000	12000
24	5	CALIENTE 250	OP	SPTCR	FBG	DV	IO	300-350		8	6	3900			10900	13500
		1991 BOATS														
17	8	1700 LS	OP	RNBT	FBG	DV	IO	115-155		7	8	1870			3750	4400
17	8	1700 LS CB	OP	RNBT	FBG	DV	IO	115-155		7	8	1870			3750	4400
18		1800 LS	OP	B/R	FBG	DV	IO	115-155		7	8	1970			3750	4400
18	9	1900 ES	OP	B/R	FBG	DV	IO	115-230		7	8	2020			4000	4850
19	6	1900 LS	OP	RNBT	FBG	DV	IO	115-230		7	8	2020			4400	5250
19	6	1900 LS CB	OP	RNBT	FBG	DV	IO	115-230		7	8	2020			4400	5250
19	8	2000 LS	OP	B/R	FBG	DV	IO	115-230		7	8	2120			4350	5250
19	8	2000 LS CC	OP	RNBT	FBG	DV	IO	115-230		7	8	2240			4600	5500
20	10	210 ES BOWRIDER	OP	B/R	FBG	DV	IO	135-230		7	8	2220			4900	5850
20	10	210 ES BOWRIDER	OP	B/R	FBG	DV	IO	300		7	8	2220			5700	6500
20	10	210 ES CUDDY	OP	CUD	FBG	DV	IO	135-230		7	8	2340			5350	6400
20	10	210 ES CUDDY	OP	CUD	FBG	DV	IO	300		7	8	2340			6200	7100
24	5	CALIENTE 250	OP	SPTCR	FBG	DV	IO	205-300		8	6	3900			9450	11600
27	6	HOMBRE 230	OP	SPTCR	FBG	DV	IO	205-230		8	6	3700			12000	14100
27	6	HOMBRE 230	OP	SPTCR	FBG	DV	IO	300		8	6	3700			13400	15200

C C CHEN BOAT YARD

TAIPEI TAIWAN

See inside cover to adjust price for area

LOA FT	LOA IN	NAME AND/ OR MODEL	TOP/ RIG	BOAT TYPE	-HULL- MTL	-HULL- TP	TP	ENGINE # HP	ENGINE MFG	BEAM FT	BEAM IN	WGT LBS	DRAFT FT	DRAFT IN	RETAIL LOW	RETAIL HIGH
		1987 BOATS														
36	6	VENTURA 37	FB	SDN	FBG	DV	IB	T220D	GM	13		20000	2		83600	91900

CHEOY LEE SHIPYARDS LTD

FT LAUDERDALE FL 33316 COAST GUARD MFG ID- CHL See inside cover to adjust price for area

CHEOY LEE SHIPYARD
LAI CHI KOK KOWLOON HONG KONG

For more recent years, see the BUC Used Boat Price Guide, Volume 1

LOA FT	LOA IN	NAME AND/ OR MODEL	TOP/ RIG	BOAT TYPE	-HULL- MTL	-HULL- TP	TP	ENGINE # HP	ENGINE MFG	BEAM FT	BEAM IN	WGT LBS	DRAFT FT	DRAFT IN	RETAIL LOW	RETAIL HIGH
		1996 BOATS														
50	2	CHEOY-LEE 50	FB	SF	FBG	DS	IB	T235D	DD	16	2	36000	4	10	293500	322500
53	6	CHEOY-LEE 53	CUT	MS	FBG	KL	IB	T 85D	PERK	16	8	63000	7		464500	510000
54	1	LONG RANGE MY 55	FB	MY	FBG	DS	IB	T210D	CAT	17	2	80000	5	4	442000	485500
58	5	CHEOY-LEE 58	FB	SF	FBG	SV	IB	T735D	GM	17	10	58600	4	3	616000	677000
58	10	CHEOY-LEE 58 SPORT	FB	MY	FBG	SV	IB	T800D	CAT	17	11	75000	4	5	754500	829000
60	11	LONG RANGE MY 61	FB	MYCPT	FBG	DS	IB	T210D	CAT	17	2	90000	5	8	490000	538500
63	4	CHEOY LEE-63	KTH	MS	FBG	KL	IB	T210D	CAT	18	6	98500	6	6	964000	1.050M
65	6	LONG RANGE MY 66	FB	MY	FBG	DS	IB	T335D	CAT	18		90000	5	3	601000	660500
70	10	CHEOY-LEE 70 CNV	FB	CNV	FBG	SV	IB	T10CD	DD	20	9	83000	5	2	951500	1.035M
76	3	CHEOY LEE 77 PH	CUT	SACIS	FBG	KL	IB	375D	CAT	22		69T	7	2	**	**
76	6	CHEOY-LEE 77 FAST	FB	MY	FBG	SV	IB	T900D	DD	21	1	61T	5	4	**	**
77	9	CHEOY-LEE 78	KTH	MS	FBG	KL	IB	T210D	CAT	21	6	74T	7	3	**	**
		1995 BOATS														
50		CHEOY-LEE 50	FB	SF	FBG	DS	IB	T625D	GM	15	6	36000	4		356500	391500
53		CHEOY-LEE 53	KTH	MS	FBG	KL	IB	T 82D	PERK	16	8	66000	6		432500	475500
53	6	CHEOY-LEE 53	CUT	MS	FBG	KL	IB	T 82D	PERK	16	8	63000	6		439500	483000
54	10	FULL-WIDTH CABIN	FB	MY	FBG	DS	IB	T210D	CAT	17	2	80000	5	4	428500	471000
54	10	LONG RANGE MY 55	FB	MY	FBG	DS	IB	T210D	CAT	17	2	80000	5	4	424500	466500
58	5	CHEOY-LEE 58	FB	SF	FBG	SV	IB	T735D	GM	17	10	50000	4	3	534500	587500
58	10	CHEOY LEE 58	FB	MYCPT	FBG	SV	IB	T800D	CAT	17	11	68000	4	3	647500	711500
58	10	CHEOY-LEE 58 SPORT	FB	MY	FBG	SV	IB	T800D	CAT	17	11	68000	4	3	683500	751000
60	11	FULL-WIDTH CABIN	FB	MY	FBG	DS	IB	T210D	CAT	17	2	90000	5	4	506500	557000
60	11	LONG RANGE MY 61	FB	MY	FBG	DS	IB	T210D	CAT	16	6	90000	5	4	469000	515500
63	4	CRUISE-EDITION CL63	KTH	MS	FBG	KL	IB	T135D	PERK	18	6	98500	6	6	897000	985500
63	4	LONG RANGE M963	KTH	MS	FBG	KL	IB	T210D	CAT	18	6	98500	6	6	903000	992500
65	5	FULL-WIDTH CABIN	FB	MY	FBG	DS	IB	T355D	CAT	18		80000	5	4	556000	611000
65	5	LONG RANGE MY 66	FB	MY	FBG	DS	IB	T355D	CAT	18		87000	5	3	566000	621500
70	10	CHEOY-LEE 70 CNV	FB	CNV	FBG	SV	IB	T10CD	GM	20	9	83000	3	10	896000	984500
76	3	CHEOY LEE 77 P	CUT	SACIS	FBG	KL	IB	900D	CAT	22		69T	7	2	**	**
76	6	CHEOY-LEE 77 FAST	FB	MY	FBG	SV	IB	T900D	GM	21	1	61T			**	**
77	9	CHEOY-LEE 78	KTH	MS	FBG	KL	IB	T210D	CAT	21	6	74T	7	3	**	**
		1994 BOATS														
36		PEDRICK 36	SLP	SACAC	FBG	KL	IB	32D	UNIV	11	5	16250	5	8	93100	102500
38		PEDRICK 38	SLP	SACAC	FBG	KL	VD	32D	UNIV	11	9	19025	6		112500	124000
40	11	PEDRICK 41	SLP	SACAC	FBG	KL	VD	50D	PERK	12	9	21130	4	4	138000	152000
42	9	CHEOY-LEE 43	CUT	MS	FBG	KL	IB	85D	PERK	13	2	34000	5		199500	219500
43	5	PEDRICK 43 FAST	SLP	SACAC	FBG	KL	IB	44D	UNIV	13		23000	6		167000	183500
46	9	CHEOY-LEE EFFICIENT	FB	MY	FBG	DS	IB	T210D	CAT	15	6	50500	3	10	275500	303000
46	9	PED 47 AFT CPT	SLP	SACAC	FBG	KL	IB	50D	PERK	13	8	34000	6	2	235000	258000
46	9	PED 47 AFT CPT	KTH	SACAC	FBG	KL	IB	50D	PERK	13	8	34000	6	2	234500	257500
46	9	PED 47 CENTER CPT	SLP	SACAC	FBG	KL	IB	50D	PERK	13	8	34000	6	2	246000	270500
46	9	PED 47 CENTER CPT	KTH	SACAC	FBG	KL	IB	50D	PERK	13	8	34000	6	2	246500	271000
50		CHEOY-LEE 50	FB	SF	FBG	DS	IB	T625D	GM	15	6	36000	4		340500	374000
51	11	CHEOY-LEE EFFICIENT	FB	MY	FBG	DS	IB	T210D	CAT	15	6	51500	3	10	279500	307500
53		CHEOY-LEE 53	KTH	MS	FBG	KL	IB	T 85D	PERK	16	8	66000	6		410000	450500
53	6	CHEOY-LEE 53	CUT	MS	FBG	KL	IB	T 85D	PERK	16	8	63000	6		416000	457500
54	10	FULL-WIDTH CABIN	FB	MY	FBG	DS	IB	T210D	CAT	17	2	80000	5	4	409000	449500
54	10	LONG RANGE MY 55	FB	MY	FBG	DS	IB	T210D	CAT	17	2	80000	5	4	406000	446000
55	9	PEDRICK 55 DEEP	SLP	SACAC	FBG	KL	IB	80D	PERK	16		48000	9	5	470500	517000
55	9	PEDRICK 55 SHOAL	SLP	SACAC	FBG	KL	IB	80D	PERK	16		48000	7	6	437500	481000
58	5	CHEOY-LEE 58	FB	YTFS	F/S	SV	IB	T735D	GM	17	10	50000	4	3	543500	597000
58	5	CHEOY-LEE 58 FAST	FB	MY	FBG	SV	IB	T735D	GM	17	10	48000	4	3	540000	593500
60	11	FULL-WIDTH CABIN	FB	DCMY	FBG	DS	IB	T210D	CAT	17	2	90000	5	4	485000	533000
60	11	LONG RANGE MY 61	FB	MY	FBG	DS	IB	T210D	CAT	16	6	90000	5	4	450000	494000
63	4	CRUISE-EDITION CL63	KTH	MS	FBG	KC	IB	T135D	PERK	18	6	98500	6	6	849500	933500
63	4	LONG RANGE M963	KTH	MS	FBG	KC	IB	T210D	CAT	18	6	98500	6	6	855000	940000
65	5	FULL-WIDTH CABIN	FB	MY	FBG	DS	IB	T355D	CAT	18		80000	5	4	532000	585000
65	5	LONG RANGE MY 66	FB	MY	FBG	DS	IB	T355D	CAT	18		87000	5	3	541000	594500
70		CHEOY-LEE 70	FB	MY	FBG	SV	IB	T735D	GM	19	6		4		847000	931000
70	10	CHEOY-LEE 70 CNV	FB	CNV	FBG	SV	IB	T530D	GM	20	9	83000	3	10	770000	846000
76	6	CHEOY-LEE 77 FAST	FB	MY	FBG	SV	IB	T875D	GM	21	1	61T			**	**
78		CHEOY-LEE 78	KTH	MS	FBG	KL	IB	T210D	CAT	21	6	74T	7	3	**	**
		1993 BOATS														
36		PEDRICK 36	SLP	SACAC	FBG	KL	IB	32D	UNIV	11	5	16250	5	8	88200	96900
38		PEDRICK 38	SLP	SACAC	FBG	KL	VD	32D	UNIV	11	9	19025	6		106500	117000
40	11	PEDRICK 41	SLP	SACAC	FBG	KL	VD	50D	PERK	12	9	21130	4	4	131000	144000
42	9	CHEOY-LEE 43	CUT	MS	FBG	KL	IB	85D	PERK	13	2	34000	5		189000	207500
43	5	PEDRICK 43 FAST	SLP	SACAC	FBG	KL	IB	44D	UNIV	13		23000	6		158000	173500
46	9	CHEOY-LEE EFFICIENT	FB	MY	FBG	DS	IB	T210D	CAT	15	6	50500	3	10	262000	288000
46	9	PED 47 AFT CPT	SLP	SACAC	FBG	KL	IB	50D	PERK	13	8	34000	6	2	223000	245000
46	9	PED 47 AFT CPT	KTH	SACAC	FBG	KL	IB	50D	PERK	13	8	34000	6	2	223000	245000
46	9	PED 47 CENTER CPT	SLP	SACAC	FBG	KL	IB	50D	PERK	13	8	34000	6	2	232500	255500
46	9	PED 47 CENTER CPT	KTH	SACAC	FBG	KL	IB	50D	PERK	13	8	34000	6	2	232500	255500
50		CHEOY-LEE 50	FB	SF	FBG	DS	IB	T625D	GM	15	6	36000	4		324000	356000

CONTINUED ON NEXT PAGE

LOA FT	LOA IN	NAME AND/ OR MODEL	TOP/ RIG	BOAT TYPE	-HULL- MTL	-HULL- TP	ENGINE TP	ENGINE # HP	ENGINE MFG	BEAM FT	BEAM IN	WGT LBS	DRAFT FT	DRAFT IN	RETAIL LOW	RETAIL HIGH
		1993 BOATS														
51	11	CHEOY-LEE EFFICIENT	FB	MY	FBG	DS	IB	T210D	CAT	15	6	51500	3	10	266000	292000
53		CHEOY-LEE 53	KTH	MS	FBG	KL	IB	T 85D	PERK	16	8	66000	6		388000	426500
53	6	CHEOY-LEE 53	CUT	MS	FBG	KL	IB	T 85D	PERK	16	8	63000	6		394000	433000
54	10	FULL-WIDTH CABIN	FB	MY	FBG	DS	IB	T210D	CAT	17	2	80000	5	4	391000	429500
54	10	LONG RANGE MY 55	FB	MY	FBG	DS	IB	T210D	CAT	17	2	80000	5	4	386500	425000
55	9	PEDRICK 55 DEEP	SLP	SACAC	FBG	KL	IB	80D	PERK	16		48000	9	5	443500	487500
55	9	PEDRICK 55 SHOAL	SLP	SACAC	FBG	KL	IB	80D	PERK	16		48000	7	6	416000	457500
58	5	CHEOY-LEE 58	FB	YTFS	F/S	SV	IB	T735D	GM	17	10	50000	4	3	518000	569500
58	5	CHEOY-LEE 58 FAST	FB	MY	FBG	SV	IB	T735D	GM	17	10	48000	4	3	514500	565500
60	11	FULL-WIDTH CABIN	FB	DCMY	FBG	DS	IB	T210D	CAT	17	2	90000	5	4	462500	508000
60	11	LONG RANGE MY 61	FB	MY	FBG	DS	IB	T210D	CAT	16	6	90000	5	4	428500	471000
63	4	CRUISE-EDITION CL63	KTH	MS	FBG	KC	IB	T135D	PERK	18	6	98500	6	6	804500	884000
63	4	LONG RANGE M963	KTH	MS	FBG	KC	IB	T210D	CAT	18	6	98500	6	6	810000	890000
65	5	FULL-WIDTH CABIN	FB	MY	FBG	DS	IB	T355D	CAT	18		80000	5	4	508000	558500
65	5	LONG RANGE MY 66	FB	MY	FBG	DS	IB	T355D	CAT	18		87000	5	3	517000	568000
70		CHEOY-LEE 70	FB	MY	FBG	SV	IB	T735D	GM	19	6		4		807000	886500
70	10	CHEOY-LEE 70 CNV	FB	CNV	FBG	SV	IB	T530D	GM	20	9	83000	3	10	733500	806000
76	6	CHEOY-LEE 77 FAST	FB	MY	FBG	SV	IB	T875D	GM	21	1	61T			**	**
78		CHEOY-LEE 78	KTH	MS	FBG	KL	IB	T210D	CAT	21	6	74T	7	3	**	**
		1992 BOATS														
36		PEDRICK 36	SLP	SA/CR	FBG	KL	IB	32D	UNIV	11	5	16250	5	8	83500	91800
38		PEDRICK 38	SLP	SA/CR	FBG	KL	VD	32D	UNIV	11	9	19025	6		101000	111000
40	11	PEDRICK 41	SLP	SA/CR	FBG	KL	VD	50D	PERK	12	9	21130	4	4	124000	136000
42	9	CHEOY-LEE 43	CUT	MS	FBG	KL	IB	85D	PERK	13	2	34000	5		179000	196500
43	5	PEDRICK 43 FAST	SLP	SA/CR	FBG	KL	IB	44D	UNIV	13		23000	6		149500	164500
46	9	CHEOY-LEE EFFICIENT	FB	MY	FBG	DS	IB	T210D	CAT	15	6	50500	3	10	249000	274000
46	9	PED 47 AFT CPT	SLP	SA/CR	FBG	KL	IB	50D	PERK	13	8	34000	6	2	211500	232500
46	9	PED 47 AFT CPT	KTH	SA/CR	FBG	KL	IB	50D	PERK	13	8	34000	6	2	210500	231000
46	9	PED 47 CENTER CPT	SLP	SA/CR	FBG	KL	IB	50D	PERK	13	8	34000	6	2	220000	241500
46	9	PED 47 CENTER CPT	KTH	SA/CR	FBG	KL	IB	50D	PERK	13	8	34000	6	2	221000	243000
50		CHEOY-LEE 50	FB	SF	FBG	DS	IB	T625D	GM	15	6	36000	4		309000	339500
51	11	CHEOY-LEE EFFICIENT	FB	MY	FBG	DS	IB	T210D	CAT	15	6	51500	3	10	253000	278000
53		CHEOY-LEE 53	KTH	MS	FBG	KL	IB	T 85D	PERK	16	8	66000	6		367500	404000
53	6	CHEOY-LEE 53	CUT	MS	FBG	KL	IB	T 85D	PERK	16	8	63000	6		373000	410000
54	10	FULL-WIDTH CABIN	FB	MY	FBG	DS	IB	T210D	CAT	17	2	80000	5	4	373000	410000
54	10	LONG RANGE MY 55	FB	MY	FBG	DS	IB	T210D	CAT	17	2	80000	5	4	369000	405500
55	9	PEDRICK 55 DEEP	SLP	SA/CR	FBG	KL	IB	80D	PERK	16		48000	9	5	422000	463500
55	9	PEDRICK 55 SHOAL	SLP	SA/CR	FBG	KL	IB	80D	PERK	16		48000	7	6	392500	431500
58	5	CHEOY-LEE 58	FB	YTFS	F/S	SV	IB	T735D	GM	17	10	50000	4	3	494500	543000
58	5	CHEOY-LEE FAST 58	FB	MY	FBG	SV	IB	T735D	GM	17	10	48000	4	3	485500	533500
60	11	FULL-WIDTH CABIN	FB	DCMY	FBG	DS	IB	T210D	CAT	17	2	90000	5	4	441000	484500
60	11	LONG RANGE MY 61	FB	MY	FBG	DS	IB	T210D	CAT	16	6	90000	5	4	408500	449000
63	4	CRUISE-EDITION CL63	KTH	MS	FBG	KC	IB	T135D	PERK	18	6	98500	6	6	762000	837500
63	4	LONG RANGE M963	KTH	MS	FBG	KC	IB	T210D	CAT	18	6	98500	6	6	767000	843000
65	5	FULL-WIDTH CABIN	FB	MY	FBG	DS	IB	T355D	CAT	18		80000	5	4	485000	533000
65	5	LONG RANGE MY 66	FB	MY	FBG	DS	IB	T355D	CAT	18		87000	5	3	493500	542500
70		CHEOY-LEE 70	FB	MY	FBG	SV	IB	T735D	GM	19	6		4		769000	845500
70	10	CHEOY-LEE 70 CNV	FB	CNV	FBG	SV	IB	T530D	GM	20	9	83000	3	10	699000	768500
76	6	CHEOY-LEE FAST 77	FB	MY	FBG	SV	IB	T875D	GM	21	1	61T			**	**
78		CHEOY-LEE 78	KTH	MS	FBG	KL	IB	T210D	CAT	21	6	74T	7	3	**	**
		1991 BOATS														
36		PEDRICK 36	SLP	SA/CR	FBG	KL	IB	32D	UNIV	11	5	16250	5	8	79100	86900
38		PEDRICK 38	SLP	SA/CR	FBG	KL	VD	32D	UNIV	11	9	19025	6		95700	105000
40	11	PEDRICK 41	SLP	SA/CR	FBG	KL	VD	50D	PERK	12	9	21130	4	4	117500	129000
42	9	CHEOY-LEE 43	CUT	MS	FBG	KL	IB	85D	PERK	13	2	34000	5		169500	186500
43	5	PEDRICK 43 FAST	SLP	SA/CR	FBG	KL	IB	44D	UNIV	13		23000	6		142000	156000
46	9	CHEOY-LEE EFFICIENT	FB	MY	FBG	DS	IB	T210D	CAT	15	6	50500	3	10	237500	261000
46	9	PED 47 AFT CPT	SLP	SA/CR	FBG	KL	IB	50D	PERK	13	8	34000	6	2	200500	220500
46	9	PED 47 AFT CPT	KTH	SA/CR	FBG	KL	IB	50D	PERK	13	8	34000	6	2	199500	219000
46	9	PED 47 CENTER CPT	SLP	SA/CR	FBG	KL	IB	50D	PERK	13	8	34000	6	2	208000	229000
46	9	PED 47 CENTER CPT	KTH	SA/CR	FBG	KL	IB	50D	PERK	13	8	34000	6	2	209500	230000
50		CHEOY-LEE 50	FB	SF	FBG	DS	IB	T625D	GM	15	6	36000	4		294500	323500
51	11	CHEOY-LEE EFFICIENT	FB	MY	FBG	DS	IB	T210D	CAT	15	6	51500	3	10	241000	264500
53		CHEOY-LEE 53	KTH	MS	FBG	KL	IB	T 85D	PERK	16	8	66000	6		348500	382500
53	6	CHEOY-LEE 53	CUT	MS	FBG	KL	IB	T 85D	PERK	16	8	63000	6		353500	388500
54	10	FULL-WIDTH CABIN	FB	MY	FBG	DS	IB	T210D	CAT	17	2	80000	5	4	357000	392000
54	10	LONG RANGE MY 55	FB	MY	FBG	DS	IB	T210D	CAT	17	2	80000	5	4	352000	387000
55	9	PEDRICK 55 DEEP	SLP	SA/CR	FBG	KL	IB	80D	PERK	16		48000	9	5	386000	424000
55	9	PEDRICK 55 SHOAL	SLP	SA/CR	FBG	KL	IB	80D	PERK	16		48000	7	6	386000	424000
58	5	CHEOY-LEE 58	FB	YTFS	F/S	SV	IB	T735D	GM	17	10	50000	4	3	472000	518500
58	5	CHEOY-LEE FAST 58	FB	MY	FBG	SV	IB	T735D	GM	17	10	48000	4	3	463000	509000
60	11	FULL-WIDTH CABIN	FB	DCMY	FBG	DS	IB	T210D	CAT	17	2	90000	5	4	420500	462500
60	11	LONG RANGE MY 61	FB	MY	FBG	DS	IB	T210D	CAT	16	6	90000	5	4	390000	428500
63	4	CRUISE-EDITION CL63	KTH	MS	FBG	KC	IB	T135D	FORD	18	6	98500	6	6	724000	795500
63	4	CRUISE-EDITION CL63	KTH	MS	FBG	KC	IB	T135D	PERK	18	6	98500	6	6	722000	793500
63	4	CRUISE-EDITION CL63	KTH	MS	FBG	KC	IB	T210D	CAT	18	6	98500	6	6	727000	798500
65	5	FULL-WIDTH CABIN	FB	MY	FBG	DS	IB	T355D	CAT	18		80000	5	4	463500	509500
65	5	LONG RANGE MY 66	FB	MY	FBG	DS	IB	T355D	CAT	18		87000	5	3	472000	518500
66		CHEOY-LEE FAST 66	FB	MY	F/S	SV	IB	T355D	CAT	19		65000	3	9	450500	495000
70		CHEOY-LEE 70	FB	MY	FBG	SV	IB	T735D	GM	19	6		4		734000	806500
70	10	CHEOY-LEE 70 CNV	FB	CNV	FBG	SV	IB	T530D	GM	20	9	83000	3	10	667000	733000
76	6	CHEOY-LEE FAST 77	FB	MY	FBG	SV	IB	T875D	GM	21	1	61T			**	**
78		CHEOY-LEE 78	KTH	MS	FBG	KL	IB	T210D	CAT	21	6	74T	7	3	**	**
		1990 BOATS														
36		PEDRICK 36	SLP	SA/CR	FBG	KL	IB	32D	UNIV	11	5	16250	5	8	74900	82400
38		PEDRICK 38	SLP	SA/CR	FBG	KL	VD	32D	UNIV	11	9	19025	6		90700	99600
40	11	PEDRICK 41	SLP	SA/CR	FBG	KL	VD	50D	PERK	12	9	21130	4	4	111000	122000
42	9	CHEOY-LEE 43	CUT	MS	FBG	KL	IB	85D	PERK	13	2	34000	5		160500	176500
43	5	PEDRICK 43 FAST	SLP	SA/CR	FBG	KL	IB	44D	UNIV	13		23000	6		134500	147500
46	9	CHEOY-LEE EFFICIENT	FB	MY	FBG	DS	IB	T210D	CAT	15	6	50500	3	10	226000	248500
46	9	PED 47 AFT CPT	SLP	SA/CR	FBG	KL	IB	50D	PERK	13	8	34000	6	2	200000	220000
46	9	PED 47 AFT CPT	KTH	SA/CR	FBG	KL	IB	50D	PERK	13	8	34000	6	2	189000	207500
46	9	PED 47 CENTER CPT	SLP	SA/CR	FBG	KL	IB	50D	PERK	13	8	34000	6	2	187000	205500
46	9	PED 47 CENTER CPT	KTH	SA/CR	FBG	KL	IB	50D	PERK	13	8	34000	6	2	198500	218000
50		CHEOY-LEE 50	FB	SF	FBG	DS	IB	T625D	GM	15	6	36000	4		281000	308500
51	11	CHEOY-LEE EFFICIENT	FB	MY	FBG	DS	IB	T210D	CAT	15	6	51500	3	10	229500	252500
53		CHEOY-LEE 53	KTH	MS	FBG	KL	IB	T 85D	PERK	16	8	66000	6		330000	362500
53	6	CHEOY-LEE 53	CUT	MS	FBG	KL	IB	T 85D	PERK	16	8	63000	6		334500	367500
54	10	FULL-WIDTH CABIN	FB	MY	FBG	DS	IB	T210D	CAT	17	2	80000	5	4	341000	375000
54	10	LONG RANGE MY 55	FB	MY	FBG	DS	IB	T210D	CAT	17	2	80000	5	4	337000	370000
55		PEDRICK 55 DEEP	SLP	SA/CR	FBG	KL	IB	80D	PERK	16		48000	9	5	346500	380500
55	9	PEDRICK 55 SHOAL	SLP	SA/CR	FBG	KL	IB	80D	PERK	16		48000	7	6	365500	401500
58	5	CHEOY-LEE 58	FB	YTFS	F/S	SV	IB	T735D	GM	17	10	50000	4	3	451000	495500
58	5	CHEOY-LEE FAST 58	FB	MY	FBG	SV	IB	T735D	GM	17	10	48000	4	3	442000	486000
60	11	FULL-WIDTH CABIN	FB	DCMY	FBG	DS	IB	T210D	CAT	17	2	90000	5	4	401500	441500
60	11	LONG RANGE MY 61	FB	MY	FBG	DS	IB	T210D	CAT	16	6	90000	5	4	372000	409000
63	4	CHEOY-LEE 63	KTH	MS	FBG	KC	IB	T210D	CAT	18	6	98500	6	6	688500	756500
63	4	CRUISE-EDITION CL63	KTH	MS	FBG	KC	IB	T135D	FORD	18	6	98500	6	6	685500	753500
63	4	CRUISE-EDITION CL63	KTH	MS	FBG	KC	IB	T135D	PERK	18	6	98500	6	6	684000	751500
65	5	FULL-WIDTH CABIN	FB	MY	FBG	DS	IB	T355D	CAT	18		80000	5	4	443500	487500
65	5	LONG RANGE MY 66	FB	MY	FBG	DS	IB	T355D	CAT	18		87000	5	3	452000	496500
66		CHEOY-LEE FAST 66	FB	MY	F/S	SV	IB	T355D	CAT	19		65000	3	9	431500	474000
70		CHEOY-LEE 70	FB	MY	FBG	SV	IB	T735D	GM	19	6		4		700500	769500
70	10	CHEOY-LEE 70 CNV	FB	CNV	FBG	SV	IB	T530D	GM	20	9	83000	3	10	636500	699500
76	6	CHEOY-LEE FAST 77	FB	MY	FBG	SV	IB	T875D	GM	21	1	61T			**	**
78		CHEOY-LEE 78	KTH	MS	FBG	KL	IB	T210D	CAT	21	6	74T	7	3	**	**
		1989 BOATS														
36		PEDRICK 36	SLP	SA/CR	FBG	KL	IB	32D	UNIV	11	5	16250	5	8	71000	78000
38		PEDRICK 38	SLP	SA/CR	FBG	KL	VD	32D	UNIV	11	9	19025	6		85900	94400
40	11	PEDRICK 41	SLP	SA/CR	FBG	KL	VD	50D	PERK	12	9	21130	4	4	105500	116000
42	9	CHEOY-LEE 43	CUT	MS	FBG	KL	IB	85D	PERK	13	2	34000	5		152000	167500
43	5	PEDRICK 43 FAST	SLP	SA/CR	FBG	KL	IB	44D	UNIV	13		23000	6		127500	140000
46	9	CHEOY-LEE EFFICIENT	FB	MY	FBG	DS	IB	T215D	GM	15	6	50500	3	10	214000	235500
46	9	PED 47 AFT CPT	SLP	SA/CR	FBG	KL	IB	50D	PERK	13	8	34000	6	2	180000	197500
46	9	PED 47 AFT CPT	KTH	SA/CR	FBG	KL	IB	50D	PERK	13	8	34000	6	2	179000	196500
46	9	PED 47 CENTER CPT	SLP	SA/CR	FBG	KL	IB	50D	PERK	13	8	34000	6	2	187000	205500
46	9	PED 47 CENTER CPT	KTH	SA/CR	FBG	KL	IB	50D	PERK	13	8	34000	6	2	188000	206500
50		CHEOY-LEE 50	FB	SF	FBG	DS	IB	T625D	GM	15	6	36000	4		268000	294500
51	11	CHEOY-LEE EFFICIENT	FB	MY	FBG	DS	IB	T210D	CAT	15	6	51500	3	10	219000	241000
53		CHEOY-LEE 53	KTH	MS	FBG	KL	IB	T 85D	PERK	16	8	66000	6		312500	343500
53	6	CHEOY-LEE 53	CUT	MS	FBG	KL	IB	T 85D	PERK	16	8	63000	6		316500	348000
54	10	FULL-WIDTH CABIN	FB	MY	FBG	DS	IB	T210D	CAT	17	2	80000	5	4	326500	359000
54	10	LONG RANGE MY 55	FB	MY	FBG	DS	IB	T210D	CAT	17	2	80000	5	4	322500	354000
55		PEDRICK 55 DEEP	SLP	SA/CR	FBG	KL	IB	80D	PERK	16		48000	9	5	328000	360500
55	9	PEDRICK 55 SHOAL	SLP	SA/CR	FBG	KL	IB	80D	PERK	16		48000	7	6	346500	380500
58	5	CHEOY-LEE 58	FB	YTFS	F/S	SV	IB	T625D	GM	17	10	50000	4	3	397500	437000
58	5	CHEOY-LEE FAST 58	FB	MY	FBG	SV	IB	T650D	GM	17	10	48000	4	3	394000	433000
60	11	FULL-WIDTH CABIN	FB	DCMY	FBG	DS	IB	T210D	CAT	17	2	90000	5	4	384000	421500
60	11	LONG RANGE MY 61	FB	MY	FBG	DS	IB	T210D	CAT	16	6	90000	5	4	355500	390500
63	4	CHEOY-LEE 63	KTH	MS	FBG	KC	IB	T210D	CAT	18	6	98500	6	6	652500	717000
63	4	CRUISE-EDITION CL63	KTH	MS	FBG	KC	IB	T135D	PERK	18	6	98500	6	6	648000	712000
65	5	FULL-WIDTH CABIN	FB	MY	FBG	DS	IB	T350D	GM	18		80000	5	4	424000	466000
65	6	LONG RANGE MY 66	FB	MY	FBG	DS	IB	T350D	GM	18		87000	5	3	432500	475000
66		CHEOY-LEE FAST 66	FB	MY	F/S	SV	IB	T675D	GM	19		65000	3	9	443000	487000
70		CHEOY LEE 70	FB	MY	FBG		IB	T735D	GM	19	6		4		669000	735000
70		CHEOY LEE 70	FB	MY	FBG		IB	T870D	GM	19	6		4		685000	752500
70	10	CHEOY LEE 70 CNV	FB	CNV	FBG		IB	T10CD	CAT	20	9	83000	3	10	659500	724500

 CONTINUED ON NEXT PAGE

CHEOY LEE SHIPYARDS LTD -CONTINUED See inside cover to adjust price for area

LOA FT	LOA IN	NAME AND/ OR MODEL	TOP/ RIG	BOAT TYPE	-HULL- MTL	-HULL- TP	ENGINE TP	ENGINE # HP	ENGINE MFG	BEAM FT	BEAM IN	WGT LBS	DRAFT FT	DRAFT IN	RETAIL LOW	RETAIL HIGH
1989 BOATS																
70	10	CHEOY LEE 70 CNV	FB	CNV	FBG		IB	T10CD	MTU	20	9	83000	3	10	682000	749500
70	10	CHEOY LEE 70 CNV	FB	CNV	FBG		IB	T11CD	GM	20	9	83000	3	10	667000	733000
76	6	CHEOY-LEE FAST 77	FB	MY	FBG	SV	IB	T875D	GM	21	1	61T			**	**
78		CHEOY-LEE 78	KTH	MS	FBG	KL	IB	T210D	CAT	21	6	74T	7	3	**	**
1988 BOATS																
32	11	CLIPPER 33	CUT	SA/CR	FBG	KL	IB	28D	VLVO	10		12000	4		48600	53400
32	11	CLIPPER 33	KTH	SA/CR	FBG	KL	IB	28D	VLVO	10		12000	4		48600	53400
35	7	CLIPPER 36	KTH	SA/CR	FBG	KL	IB	28D	VLVO	10	9	16250	5	3	66600	73200
36		PEDRICK 36	SLP	SA/CR	FBG	KL	IB	32D	UNIV	11	5	16250	5	8	67300	73900
38		PEDRICK 38	SLP	SA/CR	FBG	KL	VD	32D	UNIV	11	9	19025	6		81400	89400
38	8	CHEOY-LEE	FB	SF	FBG	SV	IB	T215D	CAT	14		21000	3	6	100000	110000
40	11	PEDRICK 41	SLP	SA/CR	FBG	KL	VD	51D	PERK	12	9	21130	4	4	99900	109500
42		CHEOY-LEE 42	FB	SF	FBG	SV	IB	T215D	CAT	14		25374	3	6	128500	141500
42	5	CLIPPER 42 A&B PLAN	SCH	SA/CR	FBG	KL	IB	40D	ISUZ	12	1	23500	5	9	114000	125500
42	5	CLIPPER 42 A&B PLAN	KTH	SA/CR	FBG	KL	IB	40D	ISUZ	12	1	23500	5	9	114500	125500
42	5	CLIPPER 42 C PLAN	SCH	SA/CR	FBG	KL	VD	51D	PERK	12	1	23500	5	9	115000	126000
42	5	CLIPPER 42 C PLAN	KTH	SA/CR	FBG	KL	VD	51D	PERK	12	1	23500	5	9	115000	126500
42	5	CLIPPER 42 PH	KTH	SA/CR	FBG	KL	IB	51D	PERK	12	1	23500	5	9	115000	126500
42	9	CHEOY-LEE 43	CUT	MS	FBG	KL	IB	85D	PERK	13	2	34000	5		144000	158500
46	9	CHEOY-LEE EFFICIENT	FB	MY	FBG	DS	IB	T215D	GM	15	6	50500	3	10	204500	224500
46	9	PED 47 AFT CPT KTH	KTH	SA/CR	FBG	KL	IB	50D	PERK	13	8	34000	6	2	169500	186000
46	9	PED 47 AFT CPT SLP	SLP	SA/CR	FBG	KL	IB	50D	PERK	13	8	34000	6	2	170500	187500
46	9	PED 47 MID CPT KTH	KTH	SA/CR	FBG	KL	IB	50D	PERK	13	8	34000	6	2	178000	196000
46	9	PED 47 MID CPT SLP	SLP	SA/CR	FBG	KL	IB	50D	PERK	13	8	34000	6	2	177000	194500
47	11	CLIPPER 48 LAYOUT A	SCH	SA/CR	FBG	KL	IB	51D	PERK	13		31000	6		178000	195500
47	11	CLIPPER 48 LAYOUT A	KTH	SA/CR	FBG	KL	IB	51D	PERK	13		31000	6		178500	196000
47	11	CLIPPER 48 LAYOUT C	SCH	SA/CR	FBG	KL	IB	51D	PERK	13		31000	6		178000	195500
47	11	CLIPPER 48 LAYOUT C	KTH	SA/CR	FBG	KL	IB	51D	PERK	13		31000	6		178500	196000
48		CHEOY-LEE FAST 48	FB	MY	F/S	SV	IB	T325D	GM	15		37000	4		200000	219500
48		CHEOY-LEE FAST 48	FB	MY	FBG	SV	IB	T350D	GM	15		37000	4		204000	224500
50		CHEOY-LEE 50	FB	SF	FBG	DS	IB	T625D	GM	15	6	36000	4		256000	281500
51	11	CHEOY-LEE EFFICIENT	FB	MY	FBG	DS	IB	T210D	CAT	15	6	51500	3	10	209500	230000
53		CHEOY-LEE 53	KTH	MS	FBG	KL	IB	T 85D	PERK	16	8	66000	6		296000	325500
53		WITTHOLZ DEEP	CUT	SA/CR	FBG	KL	IB	90D	FORD	14	6	44500	7	9	273500	300500
53		WITTHOLZ DEEP	KTH	SA/CR	FBG	KL	IB	90D	FORD	14	6	44500	7	9	264000	290000
53		WITTHOLZ SHOAL	CUT	SA/CR	FBG	KL	IB	90D	FORD	14	6	44500	6	6	263500	289500
53		WITTHOLZ SHOAL	KTH	SA/CR	FBG	KL	IB	90D	FORD	14	6	44500	6	6	274500	302000
53	6	CHEOY-LEE 53	CUT	MS	FBG	KL	IB	T 85D	PERK	16	8	63000	6		299500	329500
54	10	FULL-WIDTH CABIN	FB	MY	FBG	DS	IB	T210D	CAT	17	2	80000	5	4	313000	344000
54	10	LONG RANGE MY 55	FB	MY	FBG	DS	IB	T210D	CAT	17	2	80000	5	4	308500	339000
55		PEDRICK 55 DEEP	SLP	SA/CR	FBG	KL	IB	85D	PERK	16		48000	9	5	311000	342000
55	9	PEDRICK 55 SHOAL	SLP	SA/CR	FBG	KL	IB	85D	PERK	16		48000	7	6	328000	360500
58	5	CHEOY-LEE 58	FB	YTFS	F/S	SV	IB	T625D	GM	17	10	50000	4	3	380500	418000
58	5	CHEOY-LEE FAST 58	FB	MY	FBG	SV	IB	T650D	GM	17	10	48000	4	3	376500	414000
60	11	FULL-WIDTH CABIN	FB	DCMY	FBG	DS	IB	T210D	CAT	17	2	90000	5	4	367000	403000
60	11	LONG RANGE MY 61	FB	MY	FBG	DS	IB	T210D	CAT	16	6	90000	5	4	339500	373500
63	4	CHEOY-LEE 63	KTH	MS	FBG	KC	IB	T D		18	6	98500	6	6	618500	679500
63	4	CRUISE-EDITION CL63	KTH	MS	FBG	KC	IB	T135D	FORD	18	6	96500	6	6	598500	658000
63	4	CRUISE-EDITION CL63	KTH	MS	FBG	KC	IB	T135D	PERK	18	6	98500	6	6	614000	674500
65	5	FULL-WIDTH CABIN	FB	MY	FBG	DS	IB	T350D	GM	18		80000	5	4	406500	446500
65	6	LONG RANGE MY 66	FB	MY	FBG	DS	IB	T350D	GM	18		87000	5	3	414500	455500
66		CHEOY-LEE 66	FB	YTFS	F/S	SV	IB	T675D	GM	19		65000	3	9	423500	465000
66		CHEOY-LEE FAST 66	FB	MY	F/S	SV	IB	T675D	GM	19		65000	3	9	424500	466500
76	6	CHEOY-LEE FAST 77	FB	MY	FBG	SV	IB	T875D	GM	21	1	61T			**	**
78		CHEOY-LEE 78	KTH	MS	FBG	KL	IB	T210D	CAT	21	6	74T	7	3	**	**
1987 BOATS																
32	11	CLIPPER 33	CUT	SA/CR	FBG	KL	IB	28D	VLVO	10		12000	4		46300	50900
32	11	CLIPPER 33	KTH	SA/CR	FBG	KL	IB	28D	VLVO	10		12000	4		46300	50900
35	7	CLIPPER 36	KTH	SA/CR	FBG	KL	IB	25D	VLVO	10	9	16250	5	3	63100	69300
36		PEDRICK 36	SLP	SA/CR	FBG	KL	IB	32D	UNIV	11	5	16250	5	8	63700	70000
38		PEDRICK 38	SLP	SA/CR	FBG	KL	VD	32D	UNIV	11	9	19025	6		77100	84700
38	8	CHEOY LEE	FB	SF	FBG	SV	IB	T215D	CAT	14		21000	3	6	95700	105000
40	9	PED 47 AFT CPT KTH	KTH	SA/CR	FBG	KL	IB	50D	PERK	13	8	34000	6	2	127000	139500
40	11	PEDRICK 41	SLP	SA/CR	FBG	KL	VD	51D	PERK	12	9	21130	4	4	94600	104000
42		CHEOY-LEE 42	FB	SF	FBG	SV	IB	T215D	CAT	14		25374	3	6	123000	135000
42	5	CLIPPER 42 A&B PLAN	SCH	SA/CR	FBG	KL	IB	40D	ISUZ	12	1	23500	5	9	108000	119000
42	5	CLIPPER 42 A&B PLAN	KTH	SA/CR	FBG	KL	IB	40D	ISUZ	12	1	23500	5	9	108500	119000
42	5	CLIPPER 42 C-PLAN	SCH	SA/CR	FBG	KL	VD	51D	PERK	12	1	23500	5	9	109000	119500
42	5	CLIPPER 42 C-PLAN	KTH	SA/CR	FBG	KL	VD	51D	PERK	12	1	23500	5	9	109000	119500
42	5	CLIPPER 42 PH	KTH	SA/CR	FBG	KL	IB	51D	PERK	12	1	23500	5	9	109000	119500
42	9	CHEOY-LEE 43	CUT	MS	FBG	KL	IB	85D	PERK	13	2	34000	5		136500	150000
46	9	CHEOY-LEE EFFICIENT	FB	MY	FBG	DS	IB	T215D	GM	15	6	50500	3	10	195500	214500
46	9	PED 47 AFT CPT SLP	SLP	SA/CR	FBG	KL	IB	50D	PERK	13	8	34000	6	2	161500	177500
46	9	PED 47 MID CPT KTH	KTH	SA/CR	FBG	KL	IB	50D	PERK	13	8	34000	6	2	164500	181000
46	9	PED 47 MID CPT SLP	SLP	SA/CR	FBG	KL	IB	50D	PERK	13	8	34000	6	2	168000	184500
47	11	CLIPPER 48 LAYOUT A	SCH	SA/CR	FBG	KL	IB	51D	PERK	13		31000	6		168500	185500
47	11	CLIPPER 48 LAYOUT A	KTH	SA/CR	FBG	KL	IB	51D	PERK	13		31000	6		169000	185500
47	11	CLIPPER 48 LAYOUT C	SCH	SA/CR	FBG	KL	IB	51D	PERK	13		31000	6		168500	185500
47	11	CLIPPER 48 LAYOUT C	KTH	SA/CR	FBG	KL	IB	51D	PERK	13		31000	6		169000	185500
48		CHEOY LEE FAST	FB	MY	FBG	SV	IB	T350D	GM	15		37000	4		191500	210500
48		CHEOY-LEE 48	FB	MY	F/S	SV	IB	T325D	GM	15		37000	4		190000	208500
50		CHEOY-LEE 50	FB	SF	FBG	DS	IB	T625D	GM	15	6	36000	4		245000	269000
51	11	CHEOY LEE EFFICIENT	FB	MY	FBG	DS	IB	T215D	CAT	15	6	54000	3	10	204000	224000
51	11	CHEOY-LEE EFFICIENT	FB	MY	FBG	DS	IB	T210D	CAT	15	6	51500	3	10	200000	219500
53		CHEOY-LEE 53	KTH	MS	FBG	KL	IB	T 85D	PERK	16	8	66000	6		280500	308500
53		WITTHOLZ DEEP	CUT	SA/CR	FBG	KL	IB	90D	FORD	14	6	44500	7	9	250000	275000
53		WITTHOLZ DEEP	KTH	SA/CR	FBG	KL	IB	90D	FORD	14	6	44500	7	9	250000	274500
53		WITTHOLZ SHOAL	CUT	SA/CR	FBG	KL	IB	90D	FORD	14	6	44500	6	6	258000	283500
53		WITTHOLZ SHOAL	KTH	SA/CR	FBG	KL	IB	90D	FORD	14	6	44500	6	6	260500	286000
53	6	CHEOY LEE 53	CUT	MS	FBG	KL	IB	T 85D	PERK	16	8	63000	6		283500	311500
54	10	FULL WIDTH CABIN	FB	MY	FBG	DS	IB	T210D	CAT	17	2	80000	5	4	299500	329500
54	10	LONG RANGE MY 55	FB	MY	FBG	DS	IB	T210D	CAT	17	2	80000	5	4	295500	325000
55		PEDRICK 55 DEEP	SLP	SA/CR	FBG	KL	IB	85D	PERK	16		48000	9	5	294500	324000
55	9	PEDRICK 55 SHOAL	SLP	SA/CR	FBG	KL	IB	85D	PERK	16		48000	7	6	311000	341500
58	5	CHEOY LEE FAST	FB	MY	FBG	SV	IB	T650D	GM	17	10	48000	4	3	344000	378000
58	5	CHEOY-LEE 58 SPTYHT	FB	YTFS	F/S	SV	IB	T625D	GM	17	10	50000	4	3	351000	385500
60	11	FULL WIDTH CABIN	FB	DCMY	FBG	DS	IB	T210D	CAT	17	2	90000	5	4	349500	384000
60	11	LONG RANGE COCKPIT	FB	LRCPT	FBG	DS	IB	T210D	CAT	16	6	90000	5	4	348500	383000
63	4	CHEOY-LEE 63	KTH	MS	FBG	KC	IB	T210D	CAT	18	6	98500	6	6	585500	643500
63	4	CRUISE EDITION CL63	KTH	MS	FBG	KC	IB	T135D	PERK	18	6	98500	6	6	581500	639000
63	4	CRUISE-EDITION CL63	KTH	MS	FBG	KC	IB	T135D	FORD	18	6	96500	6	6	567000	623500
65	5	CHEOY LEE MY	FB	MY	FBG	DS	IB	T350D	GM	18		80000	5	4	389000	427500
65	6	LONG RANGE MY 66	FB	MY	FBG	DS	IB	T350D	GM	18		87000	5	3	397500	437000
66		CHEOY-LEE 66 SPTYHT	FB	YTFS	F/S	SV	IB	T675D	GM	19		65000	3	9	406000	446000
66		CHEOY-LEE FAST MY	FB	MY	F/S	SV	IB	T675D	GM	19		65000	3	9	407000	447500
66		FULL WIDTH CABIN	FB	MY	FBG	DS	IB	T325D	GM	18		87000	5	3	413500	454500
76	6	CHEOY-LEE FAST MY	FB	MY	FBG	SV	IB	T875D	GM	21	1	61T			**	**
78		LONG RANGE	KTH	MS	FBG	KL	IB	T375D	CAT	21	6	74T	7	3	**	**
1986 BOATS																
27	11	CHEOY-LEE 28	FB	TRWL	FBG	DS	IB	80D	LEHM	10	9	14500	2	10	43500	48300
31	11	CHEOY-LEE 32	SLP	SA/CR	FBG	KL	IB	80D		10	6	11300	4	6	40800	45300
31	11	CHEOY-LEE 32	KTH	SA/CR	FBG	KL	IB	80D		10	6	11300	4	6	40800	45300
31	11	CHEOY-LEE 32	FB	TRWL	FBG	DS	IB	90D	LEHM	12		19000	4	5	62800	69000
31	11	CHEOY-LEE 32 AFT CBN	FB	TRWL	FBG	DS	IB	90D	LEHM	12		19000	4	5	61000	67000
32		CHEOY-LEE 32	FB	TRWL	FBG	DS	IB	120D		12		19000	4	5	66600	73200
32		CHEOY-LEE 32 AFT CBN	FB	TRWL	FBG	DS	IB	120D		12		19000	4	5	66600	73200
32	11	CLIPPER 33	CUT	SA/CR	FBG	KL	IB	25D	VLVO	10		12000	4		43400	48200
32	11	CLIPPER 33	KTH	SA/CR	FBG	KL	IB	25D	VLVO	10		12000	4		43400	48200
34	10	CHEOY-LEE 35	SLP	SA/CR	FBG	KL	IB	25D	VLVO	11	2	14300	5	4	52500	57700
34	10	CHEOY-LEE 35	KTH	SA/CR	FBG	KL	IB	25D	VLVO	11	2	14300	5	4	52500	57700
34	11	CHEOY-LEE 35	FB	TRWL	FBG	DS	IB	135D	LEHM	12		21000	3	7	76600	84200
35	7	CLIPPER 36	CUT	SA/CR	FBG	KL	IB	25D		10	9	16250	5	3	59700	65700
35	7	CLIPPER 36	KTH	SA/CR	FBG	KL	IB	25D	VLVO	10	9	16250	5	3	59800	65700
35	9	MIDSHIPMAN 36	SLP	SA/CR	FBG	KL	IB	D		11	6	15000	4		56000	61500
35	9	MIDSHIPMAN 36	KTH	SA/CR	FBG	KL	IB	D		11	6	15000	4		56000	61500
36		PEDRICK 36	SLP	SA/CR	FBG	KL	IB	32D	UNIV						57900	63600
37	11	CHEOY-LEE 38	SLP	SA/CR	FBG	KL	IB	35D		12		17500	5	8	68200	75000
37	11	CHEOY-LEE 38	KTH	SA/CR	FBG	KL	IB	35D		12		17500	5	8	68200	75000
38		PEDRICK 38	SLP	SA/CR	FBG	KL	VD	32D	UNIV						73900	81200
38	8	CHEOY-LEE	FB	SF	FBG		IB	T210D	GM	14		21000	3	6	89200	98000
40		CHEOY-LEE 40	FB	TRWL	FBG	DS	IB	T135D	LEHM	14	6	38000	4	8	147500	162000
40	9	CHEOY-LEE 41	SLP	SA/CR	FBG	KL	IB	35D		12	6	22000	6		91400	100500
40	9	CHEOY-LEE 41	YWL	SA/CR	FBG	KL	IB	35D		12	6	22000	6		91400	100500
40	9	CHEOY-LEE 41	KTH	SA/CR	FBG	KL	IB	35D		12	6	22000	6		91500	100500
40	11	PEDRICK 41	SLP	SA/CR	FBG	KL	VD	51D	PERK	12	9	21130			89700	98500
42		CHEOY-LEE	FB	SF	FBG		IB	T215D	GM			25374			116000	127000
42	5	CLIPPER 42 A&B PLAN	SCH	SA/CR	FBG	KL	IB	D	ISUZ	12	1	23500	5	9	103000	113000
42	5	CLIPPER 42 A&B PLAN	KTH	SA/CR	FBG	KL	IB	D	ISUZ	12	1	23500	5	9	103000	113000
42	5	CLIPPER 42 C-PLAN	SCH	SA/CR	FBG	KL	VD	51D	PERK	12	1	23500	5	9	103000	113500
42	5	CLIPPER 42 C-PLAN	KTH	SA/CR	FBG	KL	VD	51D	PERK	12	1	23500	5	9	103000	113500
42	5	CLIPPER 42 PH	KTH	SA/CR	FBG	KL	IB	51D	PERK	12	1	23500	5	9	103000	113500
42	9	CHEOY-LEE 43	CUT	MS	FBG	KL	IB	135D	LEHM	13	2	34000	5		131000	144000
42	9	CHEOY-LEE 43	KTH	MS	FBG	KL	IB	135D	LEHM	13	2	34000	5		131000	144000
43	10	CHEOY-LEE 44 AFT	CUT	SA/CR	FBG	KL	IB	37D		13	3	27200	6		120500	132500
43	10	CHEOY-LEE 44 AFT	KTH	SA/CR	FBG	KL	IB	37D		13	3	27200	6		120500	132500

138 CONTINUED ON NEXT PAGE 96th ed. - Vol. II

CHEOY LEE SHIPYARDS LTD -CONTINUED See inside cover to adjust price for area

LOA FT	LOA IN	NAME AND/ OR MODEL	TOP/ RIG	BOAT TYPE	-HULL- MTL	-HULL- TP	ENGINE TP	ENGINE # HP	ENGINE MFG	BEAM FT	BEAM IN	WGT LBS	DRAFT FT	DRAFT IN	RETAIL LOW	RETAIL HIGH
		1986 BOATS														
43	10	CHEOY-LEE 44 MID	CUT	SA/CR	FBG	KL	IB	37D		13	3	27200	6		120500	132500
43	10	CHEOY-LEE 44 MID	KTH	SA/CR	FBG	KL	IB	37D		13	3	27200	6		120500	132500
45	11	CHEOY-LEE 46	FB	TRWL	FBG	DS	IB	T120D	LEHM	14	8	43200	4	8	164500	180500
46	9	CHEOY-LEE EFFICIENT	FB	MY	FBG	DS	IB	T215D	GM	15	6	51500	3	10	188000	206500
47		PEDRICK 47	SLP	SA/CR	FBG	KL	VD	51D	PERK						161000	177000
47	10	CHEOY-LEE 48 AFT CPT	CUT	SA/CR	FBG	KL	IB	37D		13	9	32300	6	6	152500	168000
47	10	CHEOY-LEE 48 AFT CPT	KTH	SA/CR	FBG	KL	IB	37D		13	9	32300	6	6	153500	168500
47	10	CHEOY-LEE 48 MID CPT	CUT	SA/CR	FBG	KL	IB	37D		13	9	32300	6	6	170500	187500
47	10	CHEOY-LEE 48 MID CPT	KTH	SA/CR	FBG	KL	IB	37D		13	9	32300	6	6	171000	187500
47	11	CLIPPER 48 LAYOUT A	SCH	SA/CR	FBG	KL	IB	51D	PERK	13		31000	6		159500	175500
47	11	CLIPPER 48 LAYOUT A	KTH	SA/CR	FBG	KL	IB	51D	PERK	13		31000	6		160000	176000
47	11	CLIPPER 48 LAYOUT C	SCH	SA/CR	FBG	KL	IB	51D	PERK	13		31000	6		159500	175500
47	11	CLIPPER 48 LAYOUT C	KTH	SA/CR	FBG	KL	IB	51D	PERK	13		31000	6		160000	176000
48		CHEOY-LEE 48	FB	MY	F/S	SV	IB	T325D	GM	15		37000	4		181000	199000
48		CHEOY-LEE 48	FB	MY	F/S	SV	IB	T570D	GM	15		37000	4		220500	242500
48		CHEOY-LEE 48 SPTYHT	FB	YTFS	F/S	SV	IB	T325D	GM	15		37000	4		165000	181500
48		CHEOY-LEE 48 SPTYHT	FB	YTFS	F/S	SV	IB	T570D	GM	15		37000	4		212000	233000
50		CHEOY-LEE 50	FB	TRWL	FBG	DS	IB	T120D		15	6	36000			161000	177000
51		CHEOY-LEE 50TC	FB	TRWL	FBG	DS	IB	T120D	LEHM	15	7	67000	5	7	234500	257500
51	9	CHEOY-LEE 52	KTH	MS	FBG	KL	IB	T135D	LEHM	16	5	67800	5	7	255500	280500
51	11	CHEOY-LEE EFFICIENT	FB	MY	FBG		IB	T215D	GM	15	6	51500	3	10	187500	206500
53		CHEOY-LEE 53	KTH	MS	FBG	KL	IB	T135D	LEHM						266500	292500
53		WITTHOLZ DEEP	CUT	SA/CR	FBG	KL	IB	90D	FORD						254000	279000
53		WITTHOLZ DEEP	KTH	SA/CR	FBG	KL	IB	90D	FORD						255500	280500
53		WITTHOLZ SHOAL	CUT	SA/CR	FBG	KL	IB	90D	FORD						265000	291500
53		WITTHOLZ SHOAL	KTH	SA/CR	FBG	KL	IB	90D	FORD						266500	292500
55		CHEOY-LEE 55	FB	TRWL	FBG	DS	IB	T210D	CAT	16	6	80000	5	4	279000	306500
55		LONG RANGE MY 55	FB	MY	FBG	DS	IB	T210D	CAT	17	2	80000	5	4	289500	318000
55		PEDRICK 55	SLP	SA/CR	FBG	KL	IB	85D	PERK	16		48000			279500	307000
58		CHEOY-LEE 58 SPTYHT	FB	YTFS	F/S	SV	IB	T570D	GM						312500	343500
58		CHEOY-LEE 58 SPTYHT	FB	YTFS	F/S	SV	IB	T870D	GM						368500	405000
60	11	CHEOY-LEE COCKPIT	FB	MYCPT	FBG	DS	IB	T210D	CAT	16	6	90000	5	8	334000	367000
63	4	CHEOY-LEE 63	KTH	MS	FBG	KC	IB	T260D	CAT	18	6	98500	6	6	556500	611500
65	6	LONG RANGE MY 66	FB	MY	FBG	DS	IB	T350D	GM	18		87000	5	3	381500	419500
66		CHEOY-LEE 66 SPTYHT	FB	YTFS	F/S	DV	IB	T675D	GM	19		65000	3	9	389500	428000
66		CHEOY-LEE FAST MY	FB	MY	F/S	DV	IB	T675D	GM	19		65000	3	9	390500	429500
66		CHEOY-LEE FAST MY	FB	YTFS	F/S	DV	IB	T870D	GM	19		65000	3	9	413500	454500
70		CHEOY-LEE 70	FB	MY	FBG		IB	T650D		17	9	50T			520500	572000
77		CHEOY-LEE FAST MY	FB	MY	FBG	DV	IB	T870D	GM						**	**
		1985 BOATS														
27	11	CHEOY-LEE 28	FB	TRWL	FBG	DS	IB	80D	LEHM	10	9	14500	2	10	41700	46300
31	11	CHEOY-LEE 32	SLP	SA/CR	FBG	KL	IB	80D		10	6	11300	4	6	38600	42900
31	11	CHEOY-LEE 32	KTH	SA/CR	FBG	KL	IB	80D		10	6	11300	4	6	38600	42900
31	11	CHEOY-LEE 32	FB	TRWL	FBG	DS	IB	90D	LEHM	12		19000	4	5	56000	61600
31	11	CHEOY-LEE 32 AFT CBN	FB	TRWL	FBG	DS	IB	90D	LEHM	12		19000	4	5	62700	68900
32		CHEOY-LEE 32	FB	TRWL	FBG	DS	IB	120D		12		19000	4	5	63900	70200
32		CHEOY-LEE 32 AFT CBN	FB	TRWL	FBG	DS	IB	120D		12		19000	4	5	63900	70200
32	11	CLIPPER 33	CUT	SA/CR	FBG	KL	IB	25D	VLVO	10		12000	4		41100	45700
32	11	CLIPPER 33	KTH	SA/CR	FBG	KL	IB	25D	VLVO	10		12000	4		41100	45700
34	10	CHEOY-LEE 35	SLP	SA/CR	FBG	KL	IB	25D	VLVO	11	2	14300	5	4	49800	54700
34	10	CHEOY-LEE 35	KTH	SA/CR	FBG	KL	IB	25D	VLVO	11	2	14300	5	4	49800	54700
34	11	CHEOY-LEE 35	FB	TRWL	FBG	DS	IB	135D	LEHM	12		21000	3	7	73500	80700
35	7	CLIPPER 36	CUT	SA/CR	FBG	KL	IB	25D		10	9	16250	5	3	56600	62200
35	7	CLIPPER 36	KTH	SA/CR	FBG	KL	IB	25D	VLVO	10	9	16250	5	3	56600	62200
35	9	MIDSHIPMAN 36	SLP	SA/CR	FBG	KL	IB	D		11	6	15000	4		53000	58300
35	9	MIDSHIPMAN 36	KTH	SA/CR	FBG	KL	IB	D		11	6	15000	4		53000	58300
36		PEDRICK 36	SLP	SA/CR	FBG	KL	IB	32D	UNIV						54800	60300
37	11	CHEOY-LEE 38	SLP	SA/CR	FBG	KL	IB	35D		12		17500	5	8	64600	71000
37	11	CHEOY-LEE 38	KTH	SA/CR	FBG	KL	IB	35D		12		17500	5	8	64700	71100
38		PEDRICK 38	SLP	SA/CR	FBG	KL	VD	32D	UNIV						70000	76900
38	8	CHEOY-LEE	FB	SF	FBG		IB	215D		14			3	6	81600	89700
38	8	CHEOY-LEE	FB	SF	FBG		IB	T210D	GM	14		21000	3	6	85200	93700
40		CHEOY-LEE 40	FB	TRWL	FBG	DS	IB	T135D	LEHM	14	6	38000	4	8	141000	155000
40	9	CHEOY-LEE 41	SLP	SA/CR	FBG	KL	IB	35D		12	6	22000	6		86600	95200
40	9	CHEOY-LEE 41	YWL	SA/CR	FBG	KL	IB	35D		12	6	22000	6		86600	95200
40	9	CHEOY-LEE 41	KTH	SA/CR	FBG	KL	IB	35D		12	6	22000	6		86700	95200
40	11	PEDRICK 41	SLP	SA/CR	FBG	KL	VD	51D	PERK	12	9	21130			85000	93400
42		CHEOY-LEE	FB	SF	FBG		IB	T215D	GM			25374			110500	121000
42	5	CLIPPER 42 A&B PLAN	SCH	SA/CR	FBG	KL	IB	D	ISUZ	12	1	23500	5	9	97400	107000
42	5	CLIPPER 42 A&B PLAN	KTH	SA/CR	FBG	KL	IB	D	ISUZ	12	1	23500	5	9	97400	107000
42	5	CLIPPER 42 C-PLAN	SCH	SA/CR	FBG	KL	VD	51D	PERK	12	1	23500	5	9	97700	107500
42	5	CLIPPER 42 C-PLAN	KTH	SA/CR	FBG	KL	VD	51D	PERK	12	1	23500	5	9	97800	107500
42	5	CLIPPER 42 PH	KTH	SA/CR	FBG	KL	IB	51D	PERK	12	1	23500	5	9	97800	107500
42	9	CHEOY-LEE 43	CUT	MS	FBG	KL	IB	135D	LEHM	13	2	34000	5		124000	136500
42	9	CHEOY-LEE 43	KTH	MS	FBG	KL	IB	135D	LEHM	13	2	34000	5		124000	136500
43	10	CHEOY-LEE 44 AFT	CUT	SA/CR	FBG	KL	IB	37D		13	3	27200	6		114500	125500
43	10	CHEOY-LEE 44 AFT	KTH	SA/CR	FBG	KL	IB	37D		13	3	27200	6		114500	125500
43	10	CHEOY-LEE 44 MID	CUT	SA/CR	FBG	KL	IB	37D		13	3	27200	6		114500	125500
43	10	CHEOY-LEE 44 MID	KTH	SA/CR	FBG	KL	IB	37D		13	3	27200	6		114500	125500
45	11	CHEOY-LEE 46	FB	TRWL	FBG	DS	IB	T120D	LEHM	14	8	43200	4	8	156500	172000
46	9	CHEOY-LEE EFFICIENT	FB	MY	FBG	DS	IB	T215D	GM	15	6	51500	3	10	179000	196500
46	9	PEDRICK 47	CUT	SA/CR	FBG	KL	IB	D		13	8	34000	6	2	149000	163500
46	9	PEDRICK 47	KTH	SA/CR	FBG	KL	IB	D		13	8	34000	6	2	149000	163500
47		PEDRICK 47	SLP	SA/CR	FBG	KL	VD	51D	PERK						152500	168000
47	10	CHEOY-LEE 48 AFT CPT	CUT	SA/CR	FBG	KL	IB	37D		13	9	32300	6	6	144500	159000
47	10	CHEOY-LEE 48 AFT CPT	KTH	SA/CR	FBG	KL	IB	37D		13	9	32300	6	6	145000	159500
47	10	CHEOY-LEE 48 MID CPT	CUT	SA/CR	FBG	KL	IB	37D		13	9	32300	6	6	161500	177500
47	10	CHEOY-LEE 48 MID CPT	KTH	SA/CR	FBG	KL	IB	37D		13	9	32300	6	6	162000	178000
47	11	CLIPPER 48 LAYOUT A	SCH	SA/CR	FBG	KL	IB	51D	PERK	13		31000	6		151000	166000
47	11	CLIPPER 48 LAYOUT A	KTH	SA/CR	FBG	KL	IB	51D	PERK	13		31000	6		151500	166500
47	11	CLIPPER 48 LAYOUT C	SCH	SA/CR	FBG	KL	IB	51D	PERK	13		31000	6		151000	166000
47	11	CLIPPER 48 LAYOUT C	KTH	SA/CR	FBG	KL	IB	51D	PERK	13		31000	6		151500	166500
48		CHEOY-LEE 48	FB	MY	F/S	SV	IB	T325D	GM	15		37000	4		173000	190000
48		CHEOY-LEE 48	FB	MY	F/S	SV	IB	T550D		15			4		210000	231000
48		CHEOY-LEE 48	FB	MY	F/S	SV	IB	T570D	GM	15		37000	4		211000	232000
48		CHEOY-LEE 48 SPTYHT	FB	YTFS	F/S	SV	IB	T325D	GM	15		37000	4		157500	173000
48		CHEOY-LEE 48 SPTYHT	FB	YTFS	F/S	SV	IB	T550D		15			4		203500	223500
48		CHEOY-LEE 48 SPTYHT	FB	YTFS	F/S	SV	IB	T570D	GM	15		37000	4		203000	223000
50		CHEOY-LEE 50	FB	TRWL	FBG	DS	IB	T120D		15	6	36000			153500	168500
51		CHEOY-LEE 50TC	FB	TRWL	FBG	DS	IB	T120D	LEHM	15	7	67000	5	7	224000	246500
51	9	CHEOY-LEE 52	KTH	MS	FBG	KL	IB	T135D	LEHM	16	5	67800	5	7	242000	266000
51	11	CHEOY-LEE EFFICIENT	FB	MY	FBG		IB	T215D	GM	15	6	51500	3	10	179000	196500
53		CHEOY-LEE 53	KTH	MS	FBG	KL	IB	T135D	LEHM						252500	277500
53		WITTHOLZ DEEP	CUT	SA/CR	FBG	KL	IB	90D	FORD						240000	264000
53		WITTHOLZ DEEP	KTH	SA/CR	FBG	KL	IB	90D	FORD						242000	266000
53		WITTHOLZ SHOAL	CUT	SA/CR	FBG	KL	IB	90D	FORD						251000	275500
53		WITTHOLZ SHOAL	KTH	SA/CR	FBG	KL	IB	90D	FORD						252500	277500
53	6	LONG RANGE MY 53	FB	MY	FBG	DS	IB	T 90D		16	8				228500	251000
55		CHEOY-LEE 55	FB	TRWL	FBG	DS	IB	T210D	CAT	16	6	80000	5	4	268000	294500
55		LONG RANGE MY 55	FB	MY	FBG	DS	IB	T210D	CAT	17	2	80000	5	4	278000	305500
55		PEDRICK 55	SLP	SA/CR	FBG	KL	IB	85D	PERK	16		48000			264500	291000
58		CHEOY-LEE 58 SPTYHT	FB	YTFS	F/S	SV	IB	T570D	GM						300000	329500
58		CHEOY-LEE 58 SPTYHT	FB	YTFS	F/S	SV	IB	T870D	GM						354000	389000
60	11	CHEOY-LEE COCKPIT	FB	MYCPT	FBG	DS	IB	T210D	CAT	16	6	90000	5	8	320000	351500
63	4	CHEOY-LEE 63	KTH	MS	FBG	KC	IB	T260D	CAT	18	6	98500	6	6	527500	579500
65	6	LONG RANGE MY 66	FB	MY	FBG	DS	IB	T350D	GM	18		87000	5	3	367000	403000
65	6	LONG RANGE MY 66	FB	MY	FBG	DS	IB	T550D		18			5	3	416000	457000
66		CHEOY-LEE 66 SPTYHT	FB	YTFS	F/S	DV	IB	T675D	GM	19		65000	3	9	374000	411000
66		CHEOY-LEE FAST MY	FB	MY	F/S	DV	IB	T675D	GM	19		65000	3	9	375500	412500
66		CHEOY-LEE FAST MY	FB	YTFS	F/S	DV	IB	T870D	GM	19		65000	3	9	396500	435500
70		CHEOY-LEE 70	FB	MY	FBG		IB	T650D		17	9	50T			498500	548000
77		CHEOY-LEE FAST MY	FB	MY	FBG	DV	IB	T870D	GM						**	**
		1984 BOATS														
27	11	CHEOY-LEE 28	FB	TRWL	FBG	DS	IB	80D	LEHM	10	9	14500	2	10	39600	44000
31	11	CHEOY-LEE 32	SLP	SA/CR	FBG	KL	IB	80D		10	6	11300	4	6	36600	40700
31	11	CHEOY-LEE 32	KTH	SA/CR	FBG	KL	IB	80D		10	6	11300	4	6	36600	40700
31	11	CHEOY-LEE 32	FB	TRWL	FBG	DS	IB	80D	LEHM	12		19000	4	5	53300	58600
31	11	CHEOY-LEE 32 AFT CBN	FB	TRWL	FBG	DS	IB	80D	LEHM	12		19000	4	5	60500	66500
32		CHEOY-LEE 32	FB	TRWL	FBG	DS	IB	120D		12		19000	4	5	61300	67300
32		CHEOY-LEE 32 AFT CBN	FB	TRWL	FBG	DS	IB	120D		12		19000	4	5	61300	67300
32	11	CLIPPER 33	CUT	SA/CR	FBG	KL	IB	25D		10		12000	4		38900	43300
32	11	CLIPPER 33	KTH	SA/CR	FBG	KL	IB	25D		10		12000	4		38900	43300
34	10	CHEOY-LEE 35	SLP	SA/CR	FBG	KL	IB	25D		11	2	14300	5	4	47400	52100
34	10	CHEOY-LEE 35	KTH	SA/CR	FBG	KL	IB	25D		11	2	14300	5	4	47400	52100
34	11	CHEOY-LEE 35	FB	TRWL	FBG	DS	IB	120D	LEHM	12		21000	3	7	71000	78000
35	7	CLIPPER 36	CUT	SA/CR	FBG	KL	IB	25D		10	9	16250	5	3	53700	59000
35	7	CLIPPER 36	KTH	SA/CR	FBG	KL	IB	25D		10	9	16250	5	3	53700	59000
35	9	MIDSHIPMAN 36	SLP	SA/CR	FBG	KL	IB	D		11	6	15000	4		50300	55200
35	9	MIDSHIPMAN 36	KTH	SA/CR	FBG	KL	IB	D		11	6	15000	4		50300	55200
37	11	CHEOY-LEE 38	SLP	SA/CR	FBG	KL	IB	35D		12		17500	5	8	61300	67300
37	11	CHEOY-LEE 38	KTH	SA/CR	FBG	KL	IB	35D		12		17500	5	8	61300	67300
38	8	CHEOY-LEE	FB	SF	FBG		IB	T210D	J&T	14		21000	3	6	81900	90000
40		CHEOY-LEE 40	FB	TRWL	FBG	DS	IB	T120D	LEHM	14	6	38000	4	8	134000	147500
40	9	CHEOY-LEE 41	SLP	SA/CR	FBG	KL	IB	35D		12	6	22000	6		82100	90200
40	9	CHEOY-LEE 41	YWL	SA/CR	FBG	KL	IB	35D		12	6	22000	6		82100	90200
40	9	CHEOY-LEE 41	KTH	SA/CR	FBG	KL	IB	35D		12	6	22000	6		82100	90300

 CONTINUED ON NEXT PAGE

LOA FT	LOA IN	NAME AND/ OR MODEL	TOP/ RIG	BOAT TYPE	-HULL- MTL	-HULL- TP	ENGINE TP	ENGINE # HP	ENGINE MFG	BEAM FT	BEAM IN	WGT LBS	DRAFT FT	DRAFT IN	RETAIL LOW	RETAIL HIGH
		1984 BOATS														
40	11	PEDRICK 41	SLP	SA/CR	FBG	KL	IB	37D		12	9	21130			80600	88600
40	11	PEDRICK 41	YWL	SA/CR	FBG	KL	IB	37D		12	9	21130			80600	88600
42		CHEOY-LEE	FB	SF	FBG		IB	T210D	J&T			25374			105500	115500
42	5	CLIPPER 42	SCH	SA/CR	FBG	KL	IB	37D		12	1	23500	5	9	92700	102000
42	5	CLIPPER 42	KTH	SA/CR	FBG	KL	IB	37D		12	1	23500	5	9	92800	102000
42	9	CHEOY-LEE 43	CUT	MS	FBG	KL	IB	120D	LEHM	13	2	34000	5		117500	129000
42	9	CHEOY-LEE 43	KTH	MS	FBG	KL	IB	120D	LEHM	13	2	34000	5		117500	129000
43	10	CHEOY-LEE 44 AFT	CUT	SA/CR	FBG	KL	IB	37D		13	3	27200	6		108500	119000
43	10	CHEOY-LEE 44 AFT	KTH	SA/CR	FBG	KL	IB	37D		13	3	27200	6		108500	119000
43	10	CHEOY-LEE 44 MID	CUT	SA/CR	FBG	KL	IB	37D		13	3	27200	6		108500	119000
43	10	CHEOY-LEE 44 MID	KTH	SA/CR	FBG	KL	IB	37D		13	3	27200	6		108500	119000
45	11	CHEOY-LEE 46	FB	TRWL	FBG	DS	IB	T120D	LEHM	14	8	43200	4	8	149500	164000
46	9	CHEOY-LEE EFFICIENT	FB	MY	FBG	DS	IB	T215D	GM	15	6	51500	3	10	171000	187500
47	10	CHEOY-LEE 48 AFT	CUT	SA/CR	FBG	KL	IB	37D		13	9	32300	6	6	145000	159000
47	10	CHEOY-LEE 48 AFT	KTH	SA/CR	FBG	KL	IB	37D		13	9	32300	6	6	145500	160000
47	10	CHEOY-LEE 48 MID	CUT	SA/CR	FBG	KL	IB	37D		13	9	32300	6	6	145000	159000
47	10	CHEOY-LEE 48 MID	KTH	SA/CR	FBG	KL	IB	37D		13	9	32300	6	6	145500	160000
47	11	CLIPPER 48	SCH	SA/CR	FBG	KL	IB	37D		13		31000	6		143000	157500
47	11	CLIPPER 48	KTH	SA/CR	FBG	KL	IB	37D		13		31000	6		144000	158000
48		CHEOY-LEE 48	FB	MY	F/S	SV	IB	T350D	GM	15		37000	4		169000	185500
		IB T365D 168500 185500, IB T570D GM 202000 222000, IB T650D													211000	232000
48		CHEOY-LEE 48 SPTYHT	FB	YTFS	F/S	SV	IB	T350D	GM	15		37000	4		154500	169500
48		CHEOY-LEE 48 SPTYHT	FB	YTFS	F/S	SV	IB	T570D	GM	15		37000	4		194500	213500
48		CHEOY-LEE SPTYHT	FB	YTFS	F/S	SV	IB	T365D		15		32000	4		149000	164000
48		CHEOY-LEE SPTYHT	FB	YTFS	F/S	SV	IB	T650D		15		32000	4		201500	221500
50		CHEOY-LEE 50	FB	TRWL	FBG	DS	IB	T120D		15	6	36000			146500	161000
51		CHEOY-LEE 50TC	FB	TRWL	FBG	DS	IB	T120D	LEHM	15	7	67000	5	7	214500	236000
51	9	CHEOY-LEE 52	KTH	MS	FBG	KL	IB	T120D	LEHM	16	5	67800	5	7	228500	251500
51	11	CHEOY-LEE EFFICIENT	FB	MY	FBG		IB	T210D	GM	15	6	51500	3	10	170000	187000
51	11	CHEOY-LEE EFFICIENT	FB	MY	FBG		IB	T215D		16		51500	3	10	175000	192500
53		WITTHOLZ 53	KTH	SA/CR	FBG	KL	IB			14	6	45550	7	8	216000	237500
55		CHEOY-LEE 55	FB	MY	FBG	DS	IB	T210D	CAT	17	2	80000	5	4	260500	286000
55		CHEOY-LEE 55	FB	TRWL	FBG	DS	IB	T210D	CAT	16	6	80000	5	4	257500	283000
55	9	CHEOY-LEE-PEDRICK	CUT	SA/CR	FBG	KL	IB			16		48000	7	6	263000	289000
58		CHEOY-LEE 58	FB	YTFS	FBG	SV	IB	T550D		16	6	44000			272000	299000
60	11	CHEOY-LEE COCKPIT	FB	MYCPT	FBG	DS	IB	T210D	CAT	16	6	90000	5	8	306500	337000
63	4	CHEOY-LEE 63	KTH	MS	FBG	KC	IB	T260D	CAT	18	6	98500	6	6	500000	549500
65	6	LONG RANGE MY 66	FB	MY	FBG	DS	IB	T350D	GM	18		87000	5	3	352500	387500
66		CHEOY-LEE 66 SPTYHT	FB	YTFS	FBG	DV	IB	T350D	GM	19		65000	3	9	335000	368000
66		CHEOY-LEE FAST MY	FB	YTFS	FBG	DV	IB	T675D	GM	19		65000	3	9	358500	394000
70		CHEOY-LEE 70	FB	MY	FBG		IB	T650D		17	9	50T			477500	525000

....For earlier years, see the BUC Used Boat Price Guide, Volume 3

CHEYENNE BOAT MFG INC

FRESNO CA 93725 COAST GUARD MFG ID- CYF See inside cover to adjust price for area

LOA FT	LOA IN	NAME AND/ OR MODEL	TOP/ RIG	BOAT TYPE	-HULL- MTL	-HULL- TP	ENGINE TP	ENGINE # HP	ENGINE MFG	BEAM FT	BEAM IN	WGT LBS	DRAFT FT	DRAFT IN	RETAIL LOW	RETAIL HIGH
		1984 BOATS														
18	2	BUBBLE-DECK	OP	SKI	FBG	SV	JT	330	CHEV	6	8				3700	4300
18	2	BUBBLE-DECK	OP	SKI	FBG	SV	VD	330	CHEV	6	8				3400	3950
19		MINI-CRUISER	OP	CR	FBG	SV	IO	260	MRCR	7	4				3300	3850
19		MINI-CRUISER	OP	CR	FBG	SV	JT	330	CHEV	7	4				4450	5100
19		MINI-CRUISER	OP	CR	FBG	SV	VD	330	CHEV	7	4				4100	4750
19		PICKLEFORK HYDRO	OP	SKI	FBG		IB	330	CHEV	7	3				3800	4450
20		MINI-CRUISER	OP	CR	FBG	SV	IO	260	MRCR	7	4				3850	4500
20		MINI-CRUISER	OP	CR	FBG	SV	JT	330	CHEV	7	4				5150	5900
20		MINI-CRUISER	OP	CR	FBG	SV	VD	330	CHEV	7	4				4850	5550
20		TUNNEL BASS	OP	BASS	FBG	TH	OB			7	5				4050	4700
20		TUNNEL CRUISER	OP	CR	FBG	TH	OB			7	5				3850	4450
20		TUNNEL CRUISER	OP	CR	FBG	TH	IO	260	MRCR	7	5				3900	4500
20		TUNNEL CRUISER	OP	CR	FBG	TH	JT	330	CHEV	7	5				5200	5950
20		TUNNEL CRUISER	OP	CR	FBG	TH	VD	330	CHEV	7	5				4850	5600
21		DAY CRUISER	OP	CR	FBG	SV	IO	260	MRCR	7	11				4900	5650
21		DAY CRUISER	OP	CR	FBG	SV	JT	330	CHEV	7	11				6450	7400
21		DAY CRUISER	OP	CR	FBG	SV	VD	330	CHEV	7	11				6100	7050
21		WHALER	OP	CTRCN	FBG	SV	IO	260	MRCR	7	11				4900	5650
21		WHALER	OP	CTRCN	FBG	SV	JT	330	CHEV	7	11				6100	7000
21		WHALER	OP	CTRCN	FBG	SV	VD	330	CHEV	7	11				5800	6650
25	10	FAMILY CRUISER	OP	CUD	FBG	SV	IO	260	MRCR	8					8550	9800
25	10	FAMILY CRUISER	OP	CUD	FBG	SV	IO	330	MRCR	8					9350	10600
25	10	FAMILY CRUISER	OP	CUD	FBG	SV	VD	330	CHEV	8					11100	12600

....For earlier years, see the BUC Used Boat Price Guide, Volume 3

CHIEN HWA BOAT MFG & IND LTD

TAIPEI TAIWAN COAST GUARD MFG ID- CBK See inside cover to adjust price for area

DIST MARIN YACHT SALES
SAN RAFAEL CA 94901

LOA FT	LOA IN	NAME AND/ OR MODEL	TOP/ RIG	BOAT TYPE	-HULL- MTL	-HULL- TP	ENGINE TP	ENGINE # HP	ENGINE MFG	BEAM FT	BEAM IN	WGT LBS	DRAFT FT	DRAFT IN	RETAIL LOW	RETAIL HIGH
		1985 BOATS														
33	6	CHIEN-HWA AFT	FB	TRWL	FBG	DS	IB	120D	LEHM	11	9	16000	3	2	55600	61100
33	6	CHIEN-HWA AFT	FB	TRWL	FBG	DS	IB	T80D-T135D		11	9	16000	3	2	56700	65600
33	6	CHIEN-HWA SDN	FB	TRWL	FBG	DS	IB	120D	LEHM	11	9	16000	3	2	54500	59900
33	6	CHIEN-HWA SDN	FB	TRWL	FBG	DS	IB	T80D-T135D		11	9	16000	3	2	56000	64900

....For earlier years, see the BUC Used Boat Price Guide, Volume 3

CHIEN SUNG

TAIPEI TAIWAN See inside cover to adjust price for area

LOA FT	LOA IN	NAME AND/ OR MODEL	TOP/ RIG	BOAT TYPE	-HULL- MTL	-HULL- TP	ENGINE TP	ENGINE # HP	ENGINE MFG	BEAM FT	BEAM IN	WGT LBS	DRAFT FT	DRAFT IN	RETAIL LOW	RETAIL HIGH
		1993 BOATS														
34	6		FB	TRWL	FBG	DS	IB	135D	LEHM	12		22000			67900	74600
36	5		FB	TRWL	FBG	DS	IB	T210D	CAT	12	2	26000			96800	106500
42			FB	TRWL	FBG	DS	IB	T210D	CAT	13	5	33500			138500	152500
42			FB	TRWL	FBG	DS	IB	T375D	CAT	13	5	33500			149000	164000
45			FB	TRWL	FBG	DS	IB	T135D	LEHM	15	1	37000			153500	169000
45			FB	TRWL	FBG	DS	IB	T400D	DD	15	1	37000			170000	187000
48			FB	TRWL	FBG	DS	IB	T400D	DD	15	5	41000			187000	205500
		1992 BOATS														
34	6		FB	TRWL	FBG	DS	IB	135D	LEHM	12		22000			64700	71100
36	5		FB	TRWL	FBG	DS	IB	T210D	CAT	12	2	26000			92300	101500
42			FB	TRWL	FBG	DS	IB	T210D	CAT	13	5	33500			132000	145000
42			FB	TRWL	FBG	DS	IB	T375D	CAT	13	5	33500			142500	156500
45			FB	TRWL	FBG	DS	IB	T135D	LEHM	15	1	37000			146500	161000
45			FB	TRWL	FBG	DS	IB	T400D	GM	15	1	37000			161000	177000
		1991 BOATS														
34	6		FB	TRWL	FBG	DS	IB	135D	LEHM	12		22000			61800	67900
36	5		FB	TRWL	FBG	DS	IB	T210D	CAT	12	2	26000			88000	96700
42			FB	TRWL	FBG	DS	IB	T210D	CAT	13	5	33500			126000	138500
42			FB	TRWL	FBG	DS	IB	T375D	CAT	13	5	33500			135500	149000
45			FB	TRWL	FBG	DS	IB	T135D	LEHM	15	1	37000			139500	153500
45			FB	TRWL	FBG	DS	IB	T400D	GM	15	1	37000			153500	169000
		1989 BOATS														
34	6		FB	TRWL	FBG	DS	IB	135D	LEHM	12		22000			56500	62100
36	5		FB	TRWL	FBG	DS	IB	T210D	CAT	12	2	26000			80200	88200
42			FB	TRWL	FBG	DS	IB	T210D	CAT	13	5	33500			115000	126500
42			FB	TRWL	FBG	DS	IB	T375D	CAT	13	5	33500			123500	136000
45			FB	TRWL	FBG	DS	IB	T135D	LEHM	15	1	37000			127500	140000
45			FB	TRWL	FBG	DS	IB	T400D	GM	15	1	37000			140000	154000
		1988 BOATS														
34	6		FB	TRWL	FBG	DS	IB	135D	LEHM	12		22000			54100	59400
36	5		FB	TRWL	FBG	DS	IB	T210D	CAT	12	2	26000			76700	84300
42			FB	TRWL	FBG	DS	IB	T210D	GM	13	5	33500			108500	119500
42			FB	TRWL	FBG	DS	IB	T375D	GM	13	5	33500			116500	128000
45			FB	TRWL	FBG	DS	IB	T135D	LEHM	15	1	37000			121500	133500
45			FB	TRWL	FBG	DS	IB	T400D	CAT	15	1	37000			135000	148500
		1987 BOATS														
34	6		FB	TRWL	FBG	DS	IB	135D	LEHM	12		22000			51800	56900
36	5		FB	TRWL	FBG	DS	IB	T210D	CAT	12	2	26000			73300	80600
42			FB	TRWL	FBG	DS	IB	T210D	CAT	13	5	33500			105000	115500
42			FB	TRWL	FBG	DS	IB	T375D	CAT	13	5	33500			113000	124500
45			FB	TRWL	FBG	DS	IB	T135D	LEHM	15	1	37000			116500	128000
45			FB	TRWL	FBG	DS	IB	T400D	GM	15	1	37000			128000	140500

CHINOOK WATER PRODUCTS

CHENEY WEEDER INC
CHENEY WA 99004 COAST GUARD MFG ID- CWZ

See inside cover to adjust price for area

LOA FT	LOA IN	NAME AND/ OR MODEL	TOP/ RIG	BOAT TYPE	HULL MTL	HULL TP	ENGINE TP	# HP	MFG	BEAM FT	BEAM IN	WGT LBS	DRAFT FT	DRAFT IN	RETAIL LOW	RETAIL HIGH
		1988 BOATS														
32		ORCA CAMPER		CAMPR	AL	PN	OB					3000			18600	20700
32		ORCA CUSTOM		CAMPR	AL	PN	OB								18600	20700
		1987 BOATS														
24		TYEE CAMPER		CAMPR	AL	PN	OB					2100			6200	7150
28		KAMLOOPS CAMPER		CAMPR	AL	PN	OB					2400			11800	13400
32		ORCA CAMPER		CAMPR	AL	PN	OB					3000			18100	20100
32		ORCA CUSTOM		CAMPR	AL	PN	OB								18100	20100
		1986 BOATS														
24		TYEE CAMPER		CAMPR	AL	PN	OB					2100			6050	6950
28		KAMLOOPS CAMPER		CAMPR	AL	PN	OB					2400			11500	13100
32		ORCA CAMPER		CAMPR	AL	PN	OB					3000			17300	19600

CHRIS CRAFT BOATS

OMC COMPANY
SARASOTA FL 34243 COAST GUARD MFG ID- CCB

See inside cover to adjust price for area

For more recent years, see the BUC Used Boat Price Guide, Volume 1

LOA FT	LOA IN	NAME AND/ OR MODEL	TOP/ RIG	BOAT TYPE	HULL MTL	HULL TP	ENGINE TP	# HP	MFG	BEAM FT	BEAM IN	WGT LBS	DRAFT FT	DRAFT IN	RETAIL LOW	RETAIL HIGH
		1996 BOATS														
17	2	CONCEPT 17	OP	B/R	FBG	SV	OB			7	6	1800	2	5	5500	6350
17	5	CONCEPT 17 F&S	OP	B/R	FBG	SV	IO	135-190		7	6	2350	2	7	6050	7100
18	6	CONCEPT 18	OP	B/R	FBG	SV	IO	190-205		8		2650	2	8	7250	8450
19	7	CONCEPT 19	OP	B/R	FBG	SV	IO	190-220		7	9	2900	2	6	7950	9300
20	11	CONCEPT 21	OP	B/R	FBG	SV	IO	190-265		8		3200	2	8	9800	11800
20	11	CONCEPT 21	OP	B/R	FBG	SV	IO	T215	VLVO	8		3200	2	8	11900	13600
20	11	CONCEPT 21	OP	CUD	FBG	SV	IO	235-265		8		3100	2	8	10600	12400
20	11	CONCEPT 21 SPORT	OP	RNBT	FBG	SV	IO	190-265		8		3100	2	8	9800	11800
20	11	CONCEPT 21 SPORT	OP	RNBT	FBG	SV	IO	T215	VLVO	8		3100	2	8	11900	13500
21	11	CONCEPT 21	OP	CUD	FBG	SV	IO	190-250		8		3100	2	8	10800	12800
21	11	CONCEPT 21	OP	CUD	FBG	SV	IO	T215	VLVO	8		3100	2	8	13100	14900
22	9	CONCEPT 23	ST	B/R	FBG	SV	IO	235-300		8	3	3800	2	9	12500	14600
22	9	CONCEPT 23	ST	B/R	FBG	SV	IO	T215	VLVO	8	3	3800	2	9	14300	16300
22	9	CONCEPT 23	ST	CUD	FBG	SV	IO	235-300		8	3	3900	2	8	13600	15800
22	9	CONCEPT 23	ST	CUD	FBG	SV	IO	T215	VLVO	8	3	3900	2	8	15500	17600
24	11	CONCEPT 25	ST	CUD	FBG	SV	IO	235-300		8	4	4500	2	9	16600	20300
24	11	CONCEPT 25	ST	CUD	FBG	SV	IO	330	VLVO	8	4	4500	2	9	19100	21200
25	7	CROWNE 26	ST	CR	FBG	SV	IO	250-265		8	6	5100	3	1	19100	21500
25	7	CROWNE 26	ST	CR	FBG	SV	IO	300	VLVO	8	6	5100	3	1	20100	22400
25	7	CROWNE 26	ST	CR	FBG	SV	IO	T300	VLVO	8	6	5100	3	1	24300	27000
25	8	CROWNE 25	ST	CR	FBG	SV	IO	215-300		8	6	4800	3		18200	21700
25	8	CROWNE 25	ST	CR	FBG	SV	IO	139D-216D		8	6	4800	3		19600	24200
25	8	CROWNE 25	ST	CR	FBG	SV	IO	T190	VLVO	8	6	4800	3		20500	22800
27		CONCEPT 27	ST	CR	FBG	SV	IO	300-330		9		5000	2	9	21500	25200
27		CONCEPT 27	ST	CR	FBG	SV	IO	T215-T220		9		5000	2	9	23700	26500
31	6	CROWNE 30	ST	CRCPT	FBG	SV	IO	T190-T265		10		8400	3	2	31700	37600
31	6	CROWNE 30	ST	CRCPT	FBG	SV	IO	T188D	VLVO	10		8400	3	2	39400	43700
34	6	CROWNE 34	ST	CRCPT	FBG	SV	IB	T265-T320		11		10000	2	9	50100	57000
34	6	CROWNE 34	ST	CRCPT	FBG	SV	IB	T216D	VLVO	11		10000	2	9	58400	64200
34	10	CROWNE 33	ST	CRCPT	FBG	SV	IO	T190-T300		11		9500	3	2	52300	61400
34	10	CROWNE 33	ST	CRCPT	FBG	SV	IO	T188D-T216D		11		9500	3	2	57600	64800
39	7	CONTINENTAL 38	ST	CRCPT	FBG	SV	IO	T310	VLVO	12	6	14500	3	1	70500	77400
		IB T310 VLVO 96200 105500, IB T340 VLVO 97200 107000, IB T400 VLVO 100000 110000														
		IB T315D CUM 115000 126000														
		1995 BOATS														
18	6	CONCEPT 18		B/R	FBG	SV	IO	160-190		8		2650	2	9	6250	7600
19	7	CONCEPT 19		B/R	FBG	SV	IO	190-215		7	9	2900	2	7	6900	8050
20	11	CONCEPT 21		B/R	FBG	SV	IO	190-255		8		3200	2	9	8550	10500
20	11	CONCEPT 21 SPORT		RNBT	FBG	SV	IO	190-255		8		3000	2	9	8350	10300
21	11	CONCEPT 21		CUD	FBG	SV	IO	190-255		8		3100	2	9	9450	11500
22	9	CONCEPT 23	ST	B/R	FBG	SV	IO	230-255		8	3	3800	2	11	10900	12900
22	9	CONCEPT 23	ST	B/R	FBG	SV	IO	300-330		8	3	3800	2	11	11700	14000
22	9	CONCEPT 23	ST	CUD	FBG	SV	IO	230-255		8	3	3900	2	10	11900	14000
22	9	CONCEPT 23	ST	CUD	FBG	SV	IO	300-330		8	3	3900	2	10	12700	15100
24	11	CONCEPT 25	ST	CUD	FBG	SV	IO	235-330		8	4	4500	2	11	15200	18600
25	7	CROWNE 26	ST	CR	FBG	SV	IO	225-300		8	6	5100	3	2	16600	20600
27		CONCEPT 27	ST	CR	FBG	SV	IO	215-330		9		5000	2	11	18400	22500
31	6	CROWNE 30	ST	CRCPT	FBG	SV	IO	T190-T255		10		7750	3	2	28000	32900
34	10	CROWNE 33	ST	CRCPT	FBG	SV	IO	T215-T330		11		9500	3	2	38800	46600
34	10	CROWNE 34	ST	CRCPT	FBG	SV	IB	T265-T320		11		10000	2	11	47900	54400
34	10	CROWNE 34	ST	CRCPT	FBG	SV	IB	T225D	VLVO	11		10000	2	11	56200	61700
39	7	CONTINENTAL 38	ST	CRCPT	FBG	SV	IO	T310	VLVO	12	6	14500	3	1	64200	70600
		IO T340 VLVO 66500 73000, IO T400 VLVO 73000 80200, IB T D CUM ** **														
43	2	CONTINENTAL 42	ST	CRCPT	FBG	SV	IO	T340	VLVO	13	8	18700	3	2	78900	86700
43	2	CONTINENTAL 42	ST	CRCPT	FBG	SV	IO	T400	VLVO	13	8	18700	3	2	85700	94200
43	2	CONTINENTAL 42	ST	CRCPT	FBG	SV	IB	T350D	CAT	13	8	18700	3	2	123000	135500
		1994 BOATS														
19	1	CONCEPT 197	ST	B/R	FBG	DV	IO	205	OMC	7	4	2300			5300	6050
20	10	CONCEPT 215	ST	RNBT	FBG	DV	IO	205-275		8		3100			7800	9500
20	10	CONCEPT 217	ST	B/R	FBG	DV	IO	205-275		8		3100			7650	9350
20	10	CONCEPT 218	ST	CUD	FBG	DV	IO	205-275		8		3100			8200	10000
20	10	CONCEPT OR 194	ST	B/R	FBG	DV	OB			7	5	2200			7300	8350
22	8	CONCEPT 237	ST	B/R	FBG	DV	IO	245	VLVO	8	2	2380			8000	9200
22	8	CONCEPT 237	ST	B/R	FBG	DV	IO	250-330		8	2	3800			10100	11800
22	8	CONCEPT 238	ST	CUD	FBG	DV	IO	245-330		8	2	3900			11300	13800
24	11	CONCEPT 248	ST	CUD	FBG	DV	IO	275	OMC	8	4	4200			13400	15300
24	11	CONCEPT 248	ST	CUD	FBG	DV	IO	330		8	4	4200			14400	17100
25	10	CROWNE 262	ST	CR	FBG	SV	IO	245-330		8	6	5100			15900	19300
27	1	CONCEPT 268	ST	CR	FBG	DV	IO	330		9		5000			18900	21200
27	1	CONCEPT 268	ST	CR	FBG	DV	IO	T235	OMC	9		5000			20100	22300
29	7	CROWNE 282	ST	CR	FBG	SV	IO	330	VLVO	10		7750			24500	27200
29	7	CROWNE 282	ST	CR	FBG	SV	IO	T205	OMC	10		7750			25100	27900
31	6	CROWNE 302	ST	CR	FBG	SV	IO	T235-T275		10		8000			30800	35300
34	6	CROWNE 322	ST	CR	FBG	SV	IO	T235-T330		11		9500			42800	50700
34	10	CROWNE 340	ST	CR	FBG	SV	VD	T245-T330		11		10000			53800	61600
39	7	CONTINENTAL 380	ST	CR	FBG	SV	VD	T330	VLVO	12	6	14500			85300	93800
39	7	CONTINENTAL 380	ST	CR	FBG	SV	IB	T300D	CUM	12	6	14500			100000	110000
43	3	CONTINENTAL 421	FB	CR	FBG	SV	VD	T330	VLVO	13	6	18700			103000	113000
43	3	CONTINENTAL 421	FB	CR	FBG	SV	IB	T350D	CAT	13	6	18700			123500	135500
		1993 BOATS														
16	8	CONCEPT 166	OP	RNBT	FBG	DV	OB			7		1100			3200	3700
17	10	CONCEPT 185	ST	B/R	FBG	DV	IO	130-175		7	9	2050			4300	5050
17	10	CONCEPT 186	ST	B/R	FBG	DV	OB			7	9	1640			4500	5150
17	10	CONCEPT 187	ST	B/R	FBG	DV	IO	175	OMC	7	9	2090			4450	5100
18	10	CONCEPT 197	ST	B/R	FBG	DV	IO	200	OMC	7	9	2650			5350	6150
20	10	CONCEPT OR 194	ST	B/R	FBG	DV	OB			7	5	2400			7350	8450
21		CONCEPT 217	ST	B/R	FBG	DV	IO	200-265		8		3050			7050	8500
21		CONCEPT 218	ST	CUD	FBG	DV	IO	200-265		8		3200			7750	9350
23	6	CONCEPT 237	ST	B/R	FBG	DV	IO	225-285		8	5	3750			9550	11400
23	6	CONCEPT 237	ST	B/R	FBG	DV	IO	330	OMC	8	5	3750			10700	12200
23	6	CONCEPT 238	ST	CUD	FBG	DV	IO	225-285		8	5	4000			10700	12700
23	6	CONCEPT 238	ST	CUD	FBG	DV	IO	330	OMC	8	5	4000			11900	13500
25	10	CROWNE 262	ST	CR	FBG	SV	IO	245-285		8	6	5100			14700	17000
26	7	CONCEPT 268	ST	CR	FBG	DV	IO	330-370		9		5000			16400	19700
26	7	CONCEPT 268	ST	CR	FBG	DV	IO	T225	OMC	9		5000			17400	19700
29	7	CROWNE 282	ST	CR	FBG	SV	IO	300-330		10		7750			22100	24900
29	7	CROWNE 282	ST	CR	FBG	SV	IO	T200	OMC	10		7750			23000	25600
31	6	CROWNE 302	ST	CR	FBG	SV	IO	T225-T285		10		8000			28200	32800
34	6	CROWNE 322	ST	CR	FBG	SV	IO	T225-T370		11		9500			39300	48400
34	10	CROWNE 340	ST	CR	FBG	SV	VD	T225-T300		11		10000			49900	56700
34	10	CROWNE 340	ST	CR	FBG	SV	VD	T230D	VLVO	11		10000			58700	64600
39	7	CONTINENTAL 380	ST	CR	FBG	SV	VD	T330	VLVO	12	6	13725			77300	84900
39	7	CONTINENTAL 380	ST	CR	FBG	SV	IB	T306D	VLVO	12	6	13725			89400	98200
43	3	CONTINENTAL 421	FB	CR	FBG	SV	VD	T330	VLVO	13	6	18700			97000	106500
43	3	CONTINENTAL 421	FB	CR	FBG	SV	IB	T306D	VLVO	13	6	18700			108500	119000
		1992 BOATS														
16	8	CAPER 156	OP	RNBT	FBG	DV	OB			7		1100			3050	3550
17	10	CONCEPT 176	ST	RNBT	FBG	DV	OB			7	9	1640			4250	4950
17	10	CONCEPT 177	ST	RNBT	FBG	DV	IO	130-175		7	9	2279			4450	5150
18	6	CONCEPT 186	ST	RNBT	FBG	DV	OB			7	9	2050			4950	5700
18	6	CONCEPT 187	ST	RNBT	FBG	DV	IO	185-200		7	9	2945			5350	6200
21		CONCEPT 207	ST	RNBT	FBG	DV	IO	185-260		8		3245			6900	8300
21		CONCEPT 208	ST	CUD	FBG	DV	IO	185-260		8		3490			7600	9100
23	6	CONCEPT 227	ST	RNBT	FBG	DV	IO	240-285		8	5	3750			9000	10600
23	6	CONCEPT 227	ST	RNBT	FBG	DV	IO	330	OMC	8	5	3750			9950	11300
23	6	CONCEPT 227	ST	RNBT	FBG	DV	IO	205D	OMC	8	5	3750			12000	13700
23	6	CONCEPT 228	ST	CUD	FBG	DV	IO	240-285		8	5	4000			9950	11800
23	6	CONCEPT 228	ST	CUD	FBG	DV	IO	330	OMC	8	5	4250			11500	13100
23	6	CONCEPT 228	ST	CUD	FBG	DV	IO	205D	OMC	8	5	4000			13200	15100
25	8	CROWNE 232	ST	CR	FBG	SV	IO	240-285		8	6	5450			13800	16300
25	8	CROWNE 232	ST	CR	FBG	SV	IO	205D	OMC	8	6	5450			17100	19500
26	7	CONCEPT 258	ST	CUD	FBG	DV	IO	285-330		9		5000			14500	17700

CONTINUED ON NEXT PAGE

LOA FT	LOA IN	NAME AND/ OR MODEL	TOP/ RIG	BOAT TYPE	-HULL- MTL	-HULL- TP	ENGINE TP	ENGINE # HP	ENGINE MFG	BEAM FT	BEAM IN	WGT LBS	DRAFT FT	DRAFT IN	RETAIL LOW	RETAIL HIGH
		1992 BOATS														
26	7	CONCEPT 258	ST	CUD	FBG	DV	IO	370	OMC	9		5200			16300	18600
26	7	CONCEPT 258	ST	CUD	FBG	DV	IO	205D	OMC	9		5000			16300	18500
27	6	CROWNE 252	ST	CR	FBG	SV	IO	260-330		8	6	5900			16300	19700
31	6	CROWNE 272	ST	CR	FBG	SV	IO	330	OMC	10		8000			24900	27600
31	6	CROWNE 272	ST	CR	FBG	SV	IO	T200-T260		10		8000			25600	29900
31	6	CROWNE 272	ST	CR	FBG	SV	IO	T205D	OMC	10		8000			29600	32900
34	9	CROWNE 302	ST	CR	FBG	SV	IO	T200-T330		11		10000			37300	44800
34	9	CROWNE 302	ST	CR	FBG	SV	IO	T205D	OMC	11		10000			42400	47100
41	11	EXPRESS 360	ST	CR	FBG	SV	IB	T460	COMM	13	1	14700			83500	91800
41	11	EXPRESS 360	ST	CR	FBG	SV	IB	T300D	CUM	13	1	14700			89400	98300
		1991 BOATS														
17	10	CONCEPT 166	ST	RNBT	FBG	DV	OB			7	9	1640			4100	4750
17	10	CONCEPT 167	ST	RNBT	FBG	DV	IO	130-150		7	9	2070			3950	4600
18	6	CONCEPT 186	ST	RNBT	FBG	DV	OB			7	9	1900			4550	5250
18	6	CONCEPT 187	ST	RNBT	FBG	DV	IO	175-205		7	9	2380			4450	5150
21		CONCEPT 207	ST	RNBT	FBG	DV	IO	175-260		8		3140			6300	7600
21		CONCEPT 208	ST	CUD	FBG	DV	IO	175-260		8		3390			6900	8350
23	6	CONCEPT 227	ST	RNBT	FBG	DV	IO	200-260		8	5	4109			8800	10300
23	6	CONCEPT 227	ST	RNBT	FBG	DV	IO	330	OMC	8	5	4109			9850	11200
23	6	CONCEPT 228	ST	CUD	FBG	DV	IO	200-260		8	5	4150			9400	11000
23	6	CONCEPT 228	ST	CUD	FBG	DV	IO	330	OMC	8	5	4150			10600	12000
24	6	LIMITED 245	ST	CUD	FBG	DV	IO	330	OMC	8	5	4750			12200	13800
24	6	LIMITED 247	ST	RNBT	FBG	DV	IO	330	OMC	8	5	4800			11400	13000
25	6	CROWNE 232	ST	CR	FBG	SV	IO	235-260		8	6	4600			11400	13200
25	6	CROWNE 232	ST	CR	FBG	SV	IO	330	OMC	8	6	4600			12600	14300
27	6	CROWNE 252	ST	CR	FBG	SV	IO	235-330		8	6	5600			14600	18000
31	6	CROWNE 272	ST	CR	FBG	SV	IO	330	OMC	10		8000			23200	25800
31	6	CROWNE 272	ST	CR	FBG	SV	IO	T175-T260		10		8000			23400	27900
31	6	CROWNE 272	ST	CR	FBG	SV	IO	T200D	VLVO	10		8000			27400	30500
34	9	CROWNE 302	ST	CR	FBG	SV	IO	T200-T340		11		10000			34800	42200
34	9	CROWNE 302	ST	CR	FBG	SV	IO	T200D	VLVO	11		10000			39000	43400
36	2	CATALINA 332	ST	SDN	FBG	SV	VD	T460	COMM	11	10	13100			63400	69600
36	2	CATALINA 332	ST	SDN	FBG	SV	VD	T200D	VLVO	11	10	13100			65300	71700
39	6	EXPRESS 360	ST	CR	FBG	SV	IO	T460	COMM	13	1	14700			52600	57800
39	6	EXPRESS 360	ST	CR	FBG	SV	IO	T300D	CUM	13	1	14700			56400	62000
		1990 BOATS														
16	11	BOWRIDER 177	OP	B/R	FBG	SV	IO	115-175		7	8	2300			3450	4050
18	6	SEAHAWK 190	OP	CTRCN	FBG	SV	OB			7	10	1925	1	1	4250	4950
19	7	BOWRIDER 197	OP	B/R	FBG	SV	IO	150-220		7	10	2800			4700	5500
19	7	CUDDY 198	OP	CUD	FBG	SV	IO	150-220		7	10	2700			4900	5750
21		SEAHAWK 213	OP	CTRCN	FBG	SV	OB			8		2225		10	6300	7250
21		SEAHAWK 215	OP	FSH	FBG	SV	OB			8			1		5100	5850
21		SEAHAWK 215	OP	FSH	FBG	SV	IO	150-210		8		3390			6850	8000
21		SEAHAWK 216	OP	CTRCN	FBG	SV	OB			8		2500		10	6800	7800
21	4	BOWRIDER 217	OP	B/R	FBG	SV	IO	175-220		8	6	3500			6550	7600
21	4	BOWRIDER 217	OP	B/R	FBG	SV	IO	295	OMC	8	6	3500			7150	8200
21	4	CUDDY 218	OP	CUD	FBG	SV	IO	175-220		8	6	3700			7250	8450
21	4	CUDDY 218	OP	CUD	FBG	SV	IO	295	OMC	8	6	3700			7900	9050
21	6	LIMITED 225	OP	RNBT	FBG	SV	IO	210-235		8	7	3700			7050	8200
22		LIMITED 245	OP	RNBT	FBG	SV	IO	220-295		8	7	4750			8650	10500
22		LIMITED 247 BR	OP	RNBT	FBG	SV	IO	220-295		8	7	4800			8850	10600
24	6	SEAHAWK 254	OP	FSH	FBG	SV	OB			8		4800			12600	14300
24	6	SEAHAWK 254	OP	FSH	FBG	SV	IO	210-220		8		4800			10900	12400
24	6	SEAHAWK 265	OP	CTRCN	FBG	SV	OB			8		4800			12500	14300
26		SPORT EXPRESS 260	OP	WKNDR	FBG	SV	IO	295	OMC	9	6	6400			15000	17000
26		SPORT EXPRESS 260	OP	WKNDR	FBG	SV	IO	200D	VLVO	9	6	6400			17500	19900
26		SPORT EXPRESS 260	OP	WKNDR	FBG	SV	IO	T150-T175		9	6	6400			15200	17600
27	9	SPORT EXPRESS 284	OP	WKNDR	FBG	SV	IO	T175-T220		10	2	8214			19900	22900
27	9	SPORT EXPRESS 284	OP	WKNDR	FBG	SV	IO	T130D	VLVO	10	2	8214			24800	27500
30	7	COMMANDER 315	FB	SPTCR	FBG	SV	IB	T270	CRUS	11	10	11400	2	8	33900	37700
30	7	COMMANDER 315	FB	SPTCR	FBG	SV	IB	T205D	GM	11	10	11400	2	8	42400	47100
31	9	CATALINA 322	FB	SDN	FBG	SV	IB	T270-T350		11	11	13100	2	9	41800	49000
31	9	EXPRESS CRUISER 320	OP	SDN	FBG	SV	IB	T270-T354		11	11	11800	2	9	41100	48500
31	9	EXPRESS CRUISER 320	OP	SDN	FBG	SV	IB	T200D	VLVO	11	11	11800	2	9	50900	56000
35	8	EXPRESS CRUISER 360	OP	SDN	FBG	SV	IB	T350	CRUS	12	10	14740	3	3	57200	62800
35	8	EXPRESS CRUISER 360	OP	SDN	FBG	SV	IB	T306D	VLVO	12	10	14740	3	3	69500	76400
37	5	CATALINA 372	FB	DC	FBG	SV	IB	T270	CRUS	13	10	17200	2	9	71200	78300
37	5	CATALINA 372	FB	DC	FBG	SV	IB	T350	CRUS	13	10	17200	2	9	73200	80400
37	5	CATALINA 372	FB	DC	FBG	SV	IB	T306D	VLVO	13	10	17200	2	9	83500	91800
38	10	EXPRESS CRUISER 400	OP	SDN	FBG	SV	IB	T350	CRUS	14		18200	3	8	71600	78700
38	10	EXPRESS CRUISER 400	OP	SDN	FBG	SV	IB	T306D	VLVO	14		18200	3	8	81300	89400
39	3	COMMANDER 392	FB	SDN	FBG	SV	IB	T350	CRUS	13	11	19960	3	9	79000	86800
39	3	COMMANDER 392	FB	SDN	FBG	SV	IB	T375D	CAT	13	11	19960	3	9	99200	109000
42		CATALINA 427	FB	DC	FBG	SV	IB	T350	CRUS	14	9	31000	3	6	113000	124500
42		CATALINA 427	FB	DC	FBG	SV	IB	T375D	CAT	14	9	31000	3	6	134000	147500
42		MOTOR YACHT 42	FB	MY	FBG	SV	IB	T375D	CAT	14	9	31000	3	6	139500	153000
42	3	COMMANDER 422	FB	CNV	FBG	SV	IB	T485D	GM	14		34000	3	11	152500	167500
48		MOTOR YACHT 48	FB	MY	FBG	SV	IB	T375D	CAT	14	9	37000	3	6	149500	164500
50	3	MOTOR YACHT 50	FB	MY	FBG	SV	IB	T550D	GM	15	3	49000	4	4	224500	247000
58	3	MOTOR YACHT 58	FB	MY	FBG	SV	IB	T550D	GM	15	3	58800	4	4	268500	295000
		1989 BOATS														
16	11	CAVALIER 17BR	OP	RNBT	FBG	DV	IO	130		7	1	2020	2	3	3100	3800
18	4	SCORPION 19 CUDDY	OP	CUD	FBG	DV	IO	130-205		7	5	2995	2	6	4450	5450
18	7	SEA-HAWK 190	OP	CTRCN	FBG	SV	OB			8	1	1925	2	2	4100	4800
18	9	CAVALIER 19BR	OP	RNBT	FBG	DV	IO	130-205		7	6	2565	2	6	4050	4900
20	7	SCORPION 21 CUDDY	OP	CUD	FBG	SV	IO	175-260		8		3800	2	10	6550	7950
20	7	SCORPION 21CD	OP	RNBT	FBG	SV	IO	229-260		8		3460	2	10	6200	7100
20	10	LIMITED 205BR	OP	RNBT	FBG	SV	IO	175-205		8	6	3320	2	10	5950	6900
21	3	SEA-HAWK 213	OP	CTRCN	FBG	SV	OB			8		2225	2		6200	7100
21	3	SEA-HAWK 215	OP	RNBT	FBG	SV	IO	160-235		8		3390	2		5950	7150
21	3	SEA-HAWK 215 W/BRCKT	OP	RNBT	FBG	SV	OB			8		2500	2		7050	8100
21	3	SEA-HAWK 216	OP	RNBT	FBG	SV	OB			8		2500	2		6350	7300
21	6	LIMITED 225CD	OP	RNBT	FBG	SV	IO	230-260		8	6	4160	2	10	7300	8550
22		LIMITED 245CD	OP	RNBT	FBG	SV	IO	260-275		8	6	4750	2	10	8400	10100
22		LIMITED 245CD	OP	RNBT	FBG	SV	IO	330-340		8	6	4750	2	10	9250	10600
22		LIMITED 247BR	OP	RNBT	FBG	SV	IO	260-275		8	6	4800	2	10	8450	10200
22		LIMITED 247BR	OP	RNBT	FBG	SV	IO	330-340		8	6	4800	2	10	9300	10700
22	5	SCORPION 21BRSJ	OP	RNBT	FBG	SV	IO	260	MRCR	8		3720	2	10	7000	8050
24	6	AMEROSPORT 250	OP	CR	FBG	SV	IO	229-275		8	6	5520	2	7	11300	13300
24	6	SEA-HAWK 254	OP	WKNDR	FBG	SV	IO	260-275		8		4712	2	8	10000	11800
24	6	SEA-HAWK 254 W/BRCKT	OP	WKNDR	FBG	SV	OB			8		4000	2	8	11000	12500
26	1	AMEROSPORT 262	OP	CR	FBG	SV	IO	275-340		9	6	8050	3	7	16000	18900
26	1	AMEROSPORT 262	OP	CR	FBG	SV	IO	200D	VLVO	9	6	8050	3	7	19700	21900
26	5	SCORPION 26CD	OP	RNBT	FBG	DV	IO	275-340		8		5282	2	9	11100	13300
26	5	STINGER 260	OP	SPTCR	FBG	DV	IO	T260		8		6186	2	6	14900	17000
28		AMEROSPORT 284	OP	CR	FBG	SV	IO	T130-T260		10	2	8750	2	9	16800	20900
28	11	CATALINA 292 SUNBRG	FB	SDN	FBG	SV	IB	T220	CRUS	10	9	7800	2	1	25600	28400
30	7	COMMANDER 315		SDN	FBG	SV	IB	T270	CRUS	11	10	11400	2	8	35300	39200
30	7	COMMANDER 315		SDN	FBG	SV	IB	T205D	GM	11	10	11400	2	8	46300	50900
31	6	STINGER 311	OP	SPTCR	FBG	DV	OB			8		4260	2	6	22300	24800
31	6	STINGER 312	OP	SPTCR	FBG	DV	IB	T330-T365		8		7256	2	6	28600	32600
31	6	STINGER 313	OP	SPTCR	FBG	DV	OB			8		4510	2	6	22300	24800
31	11	AMEROSPORT 322	OP	CR	FBG	SV	IB	T270-T350		11	11	11320	2	9	36100	42100
31	11	AMEROSPORT SEDAN 320	FB	SDN	FBG	SV	VD	T270-T350		11	11	12000	4	1	39900	46900
31	11	AMEROSPORT SEDAN 320	FB	SDN	FBG	SV	VD	T200D	VLVO	11	11	12000	4	1	49600	54500
33	8	STINGER 334	OP	RACE	FBG	DV	IO	T330-T365		8	11	7300	3	1	26000	30500
33	8	STINGER 334	OP	RACE	FBG	DV	IO	T420	MRCR	8	11	7300	3	1	30300	33700
37	5	CATALINA 372	FB	DC	FBG	SV	IB	T270	CRUS	13	10	17200	2	9	68100	74900
37	5	CATALINA 372	FB	DC	FBG	SV	IB	T350	CRUS	13	10	17200	2	9	70000	76900
37	8	STINGER 385	OP	RACE	FBG	DV	IO	T330	MRCR	9		8600	4	1	31500	34900
		IO T340 OMC 31700 35200, IO T365 MRCR 32700 36300, IO T420 MRCR													35200	39100
38		CATALINA 381	FB	DC	FBG	SV	IB	T350	CRUS	14		21600	3		75400	82800
38	7	AMEROSPORT 370	OP	CR	FBG	SV	VD	T350	CRUS	12	10	17500	3	3	69900	76800
38	7	AMEROSPORT 370	OP	CR	FBG	SV	VD	T306D	VLVO	12	10	17500	3	3	79300	87100
39	3	COMMANDER 392	FB	SDN	FBG	SV	IB	T350	CRUS	13	11	18550	3	9	71300	78300
39	3	COMMANDER 392	FB	SDN	FBG	SV	IB	T375D	CAT	13	11	18550	3	9	90500	99500
41	5	STINGER 415	OP	RACE	FBG	DV	IB	T420	MRCR	9		10360	4	1	79600	87400
42		CATALINA 427	FB	DC	FBG	SV	IB	T350	CRUS	14	9	31000	3	6	108500	119000
42		CATALINA 427	FB	DC	FBG	SV	IB	T375D	CAT	14	9	31000	3	6	128500	141000
42	3	COMMANDER 422 CNV	FB	SF	FBG	SV	IB	T485D	GM	14		34000	3	11	140500	154500
43	9	AMEROSPORT 412	OP	CBNCR	FBG	SV	VD	T350	CRUS	14		18200	3	8	79700	87600
43	9	AMEROSPORT 412	OP	CBNCR	FBG	SV	VD	T306D	VLVO	14		18200	3	8	87600	96300
48		CATALINA 480	FB	DCMY	FBG	SV	IB	T350	CRUS	14	9	34000	3	6	121000	133000
48		CATALINA 480	FB	DCMY	FBG	SV	IB	T375D	CAT	14	9	37000	3	6	137500	151500
55	8	COMMANDER 502	FB	SF	FBG	SV	IB	T735D	GM	15	9	50000	4	9	260000	286000
56	4	CONSTELLATION 500	FB	MY	FBG	SV	IB	T550D	GM	15	3	54000	4	4	207000	227500
56	6	CONSTELLATION 501	FB	MY	FBG	SV	IB	T550D	GM	15	3	57000	4	4	217500	239000
		1988 BOATS														
16	8	CAVALIER 17 FISH	OP	RNBT	FBG	DV	OB			6	8	1050			2500	2900
16	11	CAVALIER 17BR	OP	RNBT	FBG	DV	OB			6	8	1020			2450	2850
16	11	CAVALIER 17BR	OP	RNBT	FBG	DV	IO	130		6	9	2070			2900	3400
17	3	SPORTDECK 170	OP	RNBT	FBG	TR	IO	175-205		7	4	2200			3250	3800
18	4	SCORPION 19 CUDDY	OP	CUD	FBG	DV	IO	130-175		7	5	2650			3900	4550
18	6	SPORTDECK 190	OP	RNBT	FBG	TR	IO	205-230		7	8	2300			3700	4400
18	9	CAVALIER 19BR	OP	RNBT	FBG	DV	IO	130-175		7	6	2525			3800	4450
20	6	STINGER 202	OP	RNBT	FBG	DV	IO	175-205		7	8	2300			4250	5000

CONTINUED ON NEXT PAGE

LOA FT	LOA IN	NAME AND/ OR MODEL	TOP/ RIG	BOAT TYPE	-HULL- MTL	-HULL- TP	ENGINE TP	ENGINE # HP	ENGINE MFG	BEAM FT	BEAM IN	WGT LBS	DRAFT FT	DRAFT IN	RETAIL LOW	RETAIL HIGH
		1988 BOATS														
20	7	SCORPION 21 CUDDY	OP	CUD	FBG	DV	IO	175-230		8		3150			5500	6450
20	7	SCORPION 21BR	OP	RNBT	FBG	DV	IO	230-260		8		2968			5200	6100
20	7	SCORPION 21CD	OP	RNBT	FBG	DV	IO	230-260		8		2968			5200	6100
20	7	SKI-JACK 21BR	OP	RNBT	FBG	DV	IO	260	MRCR	8		3307			5700	6550
20	10	LIMITED 205BR	OP	RNBT	FBG	DV	IO	175-205		8	6	3000			5300	6150
21	3	SEA-HAWK 213	OP	CTRCN	FBG	DV	OB			8		2225			6000	6850
21	3	SEA-HAWK 215	OP	RNBT	FBG	DV	OB			8		3253			7450	8600
21	3	SEA-HAWK 215	OP	RNBT	FBG	DV	IO	175-230		8		3253			5500	6500
21	3	SEA-HAWK 216	OP	RNBT	FBG	DV	OB			8		2500			6500	7500
21	6	LIMITED 225CD	OP	RNBT	FBG	DV	IO	230-260		8	6	3300			5950	7000
21	6	SPORTDECK 220	OP	RNBT	FBG	TR	IO	260		7	10	2600			5150	5900
23	4	AMEROSPORT 230	OP	CR	FBG	DV	IO	230-260		8	6	5893			10600	12200
24	6	AMEROSPORT 250	OP	CR	FBG	DV	IO	260-340		8	6	6093			11600	14200
24	6	SEA-HAWK 254	OP	WKNDR	FBG	DV	IO	260		8		4712			9500	10800
26	1	AMEROSPORT 262	OP	CR	FBG	DV	IO	260-340		9	8	6400			12800	15500
26	5	STINGER 260	OP	SPTCR	FBG	DV	IO	T260		8		5764			13700	15500
27	11	AMEROSPORT 283	OP	CR	FBG	DV	IB	T180	CRUS	10	2	6400			19500	21700
28		AMEROSPORT 284	OP	CR	FBG	DV	IB	T230-T260		10	2	8214			21300	24400
28	11	CATALINA 292 SUNBRG	FB	SDN	FBG	DV	IB	T220	CRUS	10	9	7800			24500	27200
30	7	COMMANDER 315		SDN	FBG	DV	IB	T270	CRUS	11	9	11400			33800	37500
31	6	STINGER 311	OP	SPTCR	FBG	DV	OB			8		5080			21500	23900
31	6	STINGER 312	OP	SPTCR	FBG	DV	IB	T330-T365		8		7256			27400	31200
31	6	STINGER 313	OP	SPTCR	FBG	DV	OB			8		4260			21500	23900
31	6	STINGER 314	OP	SPTCR	FBG	DV	OB			8		4790			21500	23900
31	11	AMEROSPORT 320	OP	CR	FBG	DV	IB	T220-T350		11	11	11320			33400	40300
31	11	AMEROSPORT SEDAN 320	FB	SDN	FBG	DV	IB	T220-T350		11	11	12000			36700	44900
37	5	CATALINA 372	FB	DC	FBG	DV	IB	T270	CRUS	13	10	17200			65400	71900
37	8	STINGER 375	OP	RACE	FBG	DV	IB	T330	MRCR	9		9500			56700	62300
		IB T340 OMC 57500 63200, IB T365 MRCR 57900 63600, IB T420 MRCR													60300	66300
38		CATALINA 381	FB	DC	FBG	DV	IB	T350	CRUS	14		21600			72400	79500
38		CATALINA 381	FB	DC	FBG	DV	IB	T350	VLVO	14		21600			72300	79500
38	7	AMEROSPORT 370	OP	CR	FBG	DV	IB	T350	CRUS	13		15000			59300	65100
39	3	COMMANDER 392	FB	SDN	FBG	DV	IB	T350	CRUS	13	11	26000			68500	75200
39	3	COMMANDER 392	FB	SDN	FBG	DV	IB	T375D	CAT	13	11	28000			87000	95600
41	5	STINGER 415	OP	RACE	FBG	DV	IB	T420	MRCR	9		12780			81100	89100
42		CATALINA 426	FB	DC	FBG	DV	IB	T350	CRUS	14	9	30000			100000	110000
42		CATALINA 426	FB	DC	FBG	DV	IB	T D	CAT	14	9	33000			**	**
42	4	COMMANDER 422 CNV	FB	SF	FBG	DV	IB	T D	GM	14		34000			**	**
43	9	AMEROSPORT 412	OP	CBNCR	FBG	DV	IB	T350	CRUS	14		15000			60500	66500
43	9	AMEROSPORT 412	OP	CBNCR	FBG	DV	IB	T D	CAT	14		20000			**	**
46	3	CONSTELLATION 460	FB	MY	FBG	DV	IB	T410D	GM	15	3	49000			148000	162500
48		CATALINA 480	FB	DCMY	FBG	DV	IB	T350	CRUS	14	9	34000			115500	127000
48		CATALINA 480	FB	DCMY	FBG	DV	IB	T D	CAT	14	9	37000			**	**
48	10	COMMANDER 482	FB	MY	FBG	DV	IB	T485D	GM	15	9	48000			154000	169500
56	4	CONSTELLATION 500	FB	MY	FBG	DV	IB	T500D	GM	15	3	54000			195000	214000
56	6	CONSTELLATION 501	FB	MY	FBG	SV	IB	T500D	GM	15	5	57000			201500	221500
		1987 BOATS														
16	11	CAVALIER 17BR	OP	RNBT	FBG	DV	IO	120-140		6	9	1430			2350	2750
16	11	LIMITED 178BR	OP	RNBT	FBG	DV	IO	120-175		6	9	1650			2500	2950
18	4	CAVALIER 19 CUDDY	OP	CUD	FBG	DV	IO	130-200		7	5	1900			3150	3750
18	4	CAVALIER 19BR	OP	RNBT	FBG	DV	IO	130-200		7	5	1775			3000	3550
18	4	LIMITED 196BR	OP	RNBT	FBG	DV	IO	175-230		7	5	2000			3150	3800
18	4	LIMITED 196BR	OP	RNBT	FBG	DV	IO	260		7	5	2000			3450	4000
18	4	LIMITED 197	OP	RNBT	FBG	DV	IO	175-230		7	5	1975			3150	3800
18	4	LIMITED 197	OP	RNBT	FBG	DV	IO	260		7	5	1975			3400	3950
20	4	STINGER 202	OP	RNBT	FBG	DV	IO	175		7	8	1500			3550	4150
20	7	CAVALIER 210	OP	CUD	FBG	DV	IO	175-230		8		2700			4800	5650
20	7	LIMITED 210	OP	RNBT	FBG	DV	IO	230-260		8		2390			4450	5300
20	7	LIMITED 210BR	OP	RNBT	FBG	DV	IO	230-260		8		2425			4500	5300
20	7	SCORPION 210 CUDDY	OP	CUD	FBG	DV	IO	230-260		8		2700			4900	5850
20	7	SCORPION 210BR	OP	RNBT	FBG	DV	IO	230-260		8		2570	2	8	4600	5300
20	7	SCORPION 210S	OP	RNBT	FBG	DV	IO	230-260		8		2375	2	8	4450	5250
20	7	SKI-JACK 210BR	OP	RNBT	FBG	DV	IO	260	MRCR	8		2570			5000	5750
20	7	SKI-JACK 210S	OP	RNBT	FBG	DV	IO	260	MRCR	8		2570			5150	5900
21	3	SEA-HAWK 213	OP	CTRCN	FBG	DV	OB			8		2225			5800	6650
21	3	SEA-HAWK 215	OP	RNBT	FBG	DV	OB			8		2585			6450	7400
21	3	SEA-HAWK 215	OP	RNBT	FBG	DV	IO	180-230		8		2585			4650	5450
21	3	SEA-HAWK 216	OP	RNBT	FBG	DV	OB			8		2500			6300	7250
22	2	LIMITED 230	OP	RNBT	FBG	DV	IO		MRCR	8		2890			**	**
22	2	LIMITED 230	OP	RNBT	FBG	DV	IO	260		8		2890			5400	6200
22	2	SCORPION 230	OP	RNBT	FBG	DV	IO		MRCR	8		2800	2	10	**	**
22	2	SCORPION 230	OP	RNBT	FBG	DV	IO	260		8		2800	2	10	5300	6100
22	2	STINGER 222		RACE	FBG	DV	IO	260		7	10	2190	2	10	4700	5400
22	2	STINGER 222		RACE	FBG	DV	IO	330	MRCR	7	10	2190	2	10	5400	6200
22	2	STINGER 222	OP	SPTCR	FBG	DV	IO	260		8	10	2190			5300	6100
24	6	AMEROSPORT 250	OP	CR	FBG	DV	IO		MRCR	8	6	5400			**	**
24	6	AMEROSPORT 250	OP	CR	FBG	DV	IO	230-260		8	6	5400			9900	11500
24	10	SEA-HAWK 254	OP	WKNDR	FBG	DV	OB			8		3805			10200	11600
24	10	SEA-HAWK 254	OP	WKNDR	FBG	DV	IO	260		8		3805			8050	9250
26	5	STINGER 260	OP	SPTCR	FBG	DV	IO		MRCR	8		3880			**	**
26	5	STINGER 260	OP	SPTCR	FBG	DV	IO	T260		8		3880			11100	12600
27	11	AMEROSPORT 283	OP	CR	FBG	DV	IB	T180	CRUS	10	2	6400			18900	21100
28		AMEROSPORT 284	OP	CR	FBG	DV	IB	260		10	2	6400			16300	18600
28		AMEROSPORT 284	OP	CR	FBG	DV	IB	T230-T260		10	2	6400			18600	21200
28	11	CATALINA 292 SUNBRG	FB	SDN	FBG	DV	IB	T220		10	9	7800	2	3	23400	26000
30		CHRIS-CAT 300	OP	RACE	FBG	CT	IB			8	7	4970			**	**
30		CHRIS-CAT 305	OP	RACE	FBG	CT	IB			8	7	4970			**	**
31	6	SCORPION 311	OP	CTRCN	FBG	DV	OB			8		4260	2	4	20600	22800
31	6	SCORPION 313VF	OP	CTRCN	FBG	DV	OB			8		4260	2	11	20600	22800
31	6	STINGER 312	OP	SPTCR	FBG	DV	IO	T	MRCR	8		5080	3		**	**
31	6	STINGER 312	OP	SPTCR	FBG	DV	IO	T330-T420		8		5080	3		20300	23200
31	6	STINGER 314	OP	SPTCR	FBG	DV	OB			8		4790			20800	23200
31	11	AMEROSPORT 320	OP	CR	FBG	DV	IB	T220-T350		11	11	11320	2	8	32100	38700
31	11	AMEROSPORT SEDAN 320	FB	SDN	FBG	DV	IB	T220-T350		11	11	12000	2	7	35300	43100
33		AMEROSPORT 332	OP	CR	FBG	DV	IB	T270	CRUS	10	2	11560	2	9	33200	36900
33		AMEROSPORT 332	OP	CR	FBG	DV	IB	T350	CRUS	12	1	11560	2	9	37900	42200
33		AMEROSPORT 332	OP	CR	FBG	DV	IB	T250D	GM	12	1	13500	2	9	47700	52500
33		AMEROSPORT 333	FB	CR	FBG	DV	IB	T270-T350		12	1	13000	2	9	37300	43300
33		AMEROSPORT 333	FB	CR	FBG	DV	IB	T250D	GM	12	1	14940	2	9	50100	55000
33		AMEROSPORT 336	OP	CBNCR	FBG	DV	IB	T270-T350		12	1	12360	2	9	41900	47200
35	1	CATALINA 350	FB	DC	FBG	DV	IB	T270	CRUS	13	1	17229	2	10	47800	52500
36		CATALINA 362DC	FB	DC	FBG	DV	IB	T270	CRUS	12	4	15500	2	7	52600	57800
38		CATALINA 381	FB	DC	FBG	DV	IB	T350	CRUS	14		21600	3		69700	76600
38		CATALINA 381	FB	DC	FBG	DV	IB	T250D	VLVO	14		23600	3		81500	89500
38		COMMANDER 382	FB	SDN	FBG	DV	IB	T315D	GM	13	11	28000	3	9	99100	109000
38		COMMANDER 383	FB	SDN	FBG	DV	IB	T350	CRUS	13	11	26000	3	9	82000	90100
38		COMMANDER 383	FB	SDN	FBG	DV	IB	T250D	GM	13	11	28000	3	9	95900	105500
38		COMMANDER 383	FB	SDN	FBG	DV	IB	T300D	GM	13	11	28000	3	9	98300	108000
41		CONSTELLATION 410	FB	MY	FBG	DV	IB	T350	CRUS	14		26565	3	3	92400	101500
41		CONSTELLATION 410	FB	MY	FBG	DV	IB	T300D	GM	14		29213	3	3	110000	121000
41	5	STINGER 415	OP	RACE	FBG	DV	IB	T420	MRCR	9		10000			73500	80800
42		CATALINA 426	FB	DC	FBG	DV	IB	T350	CRUS	14	9	30000	3	6	96300	106000
42		CATALINA 426	FB	DC	FBG	DV	IB	T300D	GM	14	9	33000	3	6	114000	125500
42		CATALINA 426	FB	DC	FBG	DV	IB	T375D	GM	14	9	33000	3	6	120000	132000
42	4	COMMANDER 422 CNV	FB	SF	FBG	DV	IB	T450D	J&T	14		34000	3	11	128000	140500
43	9	AMEROSPORT 412	OP	CBNCR	FBG	DV	IB	T350	CRUS	14		15000	3	2	58200	64000
48		CATALINA 480	FB	DCMY	FBG	DV	IB	T350	CRUS	14	9	34000	3	6	110500	121500
48		CATALINA 480	FB	DCMY	FBG	DV	IB	T250D	GM	14	9	34000	3	6	114000	125000
48		CATALINA 480	FB	DCMY	FBG	DV	IB	T375D	GM	14	9	34000	3	6	120500	132500
48	10	COMMANDER 482	FB	MY	FBG	DV	IB	T600D	GM	14	9	48000	4	9	156500	172000
56	4	CONSTELLATION 500	FB	MY	FBG	SV	IB	T500D	GM	15	5	54000	4	4	184000	202000
56	6	CONSTELLATION 501	FB	MY	FBG	SV	IB	T550D	GM	15	5	57000	4	6	200000	219500
		1986 BOATS														
16	11	CAVALIER 17	OP	RNBT	FBG	DV	OB			6	9	1400			2950	3450
16	11	CAVALIER 17BR	OP	RNBT	FBG	DV	IO	120-140		6	9	1450			2300	2700
16	11	CAVALIER 17CD	OP	RNBT	FBG	DV	IO	120-140		6	9	1430			2300	2700
16	11	LIMITED 178BR	OP	RNBT	FBG	DV	IO	140-185		6	9	1575			2350	2800
16	11	LIMITED 179SL	OP	RNBT	FBG	DV	IO	140-185		6	9	1555			2350	2800
18	4	CAVALIER 19 CUDDY	OP	CUD	FBG	DV	IO	140-200		7	5	1900			3050	3600
18	4	CAVALIER 19BR	OP	RNBT	FBG	DV	IO	140-200		7	5	1775			2900	3450
18	4	CAVALIER 19CD	OP	RNBT	FBG	DV	IO	140-200		7	5	1750			2900	3400
18	4	LIMITED 196BR	OP	RNBT	FBG	DV	IO	185-230		7	5	1900			3000	3600
18	4	LIMITED 196BR	OP	RNBT	FBG	DV	IO	260		7	5	1900			3250	3750
18	4	LIMITED 197SL	OP	RNBT	FBG	DV	IO	185-230		7	5	1875			3000	3600
18	4	LIMITED 197SL	OP	RNBT	FBG	DV	IO	260		7	5	1875			3200	3750
20	7	LIMITED 210BR	OP	RNBT	FBG	DV	IO	230-260		8		2425			4300	5150
20	7	LIMITED 210SL	OP	RNBT	FBG	DV	IO	230-260		8		2390			4250	5100
20	7	SCORPION 210 CUDDY	OP	CUD	FBG	DV	IO	230-260		8		2700			4750	5600
20	7	SCORPION 210BR	OP	RNBT	FBG	DV	IO	230-260		8		2570	2	8	4450	5100
20	7	SCORPION 210S	OP	RNBT	FBG	DV	IO	230-260		8		2375	2	8	4250	5100
20	7	SKI-JACK 210BR	OP	RNBT	FBG	DV	IO	260	MRCR	8		2570			4900	5650
20	7	SKI-JACK 210S	OP	RNBT	FBG	DV	IO	260	MRCR	8		2570			4900	5650
21	3	SCORPION 211VF	OP	FSH	FBG	DV	IO	190-230		8		2375	2	6	4750	5600
21	3	SCORPION 212VF	OP	FSH	FBG	DV	OB			8		2310	1	3	5800	6650
21	3	SCORPION 213VF	OP	CTRCN	FBG	DV	OB			8		2225	1	3	5650	6500

CONTINUED ON NEXT PAGE

LOA FT	LOA IN	NAME AND/ OR MODEL	TOP/ RIG	BOAT TYPE	-HULL- MTL	-HULL- TP	ENGINE TP	ENGINE # HP	ENGINE MFG	BEAM FT	BEAM IN	WGT LBS	DRAFT FT	DRAFT IN	RETAIL LOW	RETAIL HIGH
		1986 BOATS														
21	3	SCORPION 215WA	OP	FSH	FBG	SV	OB			8		2585			6250	7200
21	3	SCORPION 215WA	OP	FSH	FBG	SV	IO	190	MRCR	8		2585	2	6	4950	5700
21	3	SCORPION 215WA	OP	FSH	FBG	SV	SE	205	OMC	8		2585			6250	7200
21	3	SCORPION 215WA	OP	FSH	FBG	SV	IO	230		8		2585	2	6	5050	5850
21	3	SCORPION 216WA	OP	FSH	FBG	SV	OB			8		2500	2	6	6100	7050
21	3	SCORPION 217BR	OP	FSH	FBG	DV	OB			8		2390			5950	6850
21	3	SCORPION 218BR	OP	FSH	FBG	DV	IO	230	OMC	8		2440			4900	5600
21	3	SCORPION 218BR	OP	FSH	FBG	TR	IO	190-230		8		2440			4800	5650
22	2	LIMITED 230SL	OP	RNBT	FBG	DV	IO	260		8		2890			5200	6000
22	2	SCORPION 230S	OP	RNBT	FBG	DV	IO	260		8		2800	2	10	5100	5900
22	2	SCORPION 232AC	FB	EXP	FBG	DV	IO	260		8		3335			6000	6900
22	2	STINGER 222	OP	SPTCR	FBG	DV	OB			7	10	2190			5850	6750
22	2	STINGER 222	OP	SPTCR	FBG	DV	IO	260		7	10	2190			4800	5500
24	10	SCORPION 254WA	OP	FSH	FBG	DV	OB			8		3805			9900	11200
24	10	SCORPION 254WA	OP	FSH	FBG	DV	SE	205	OMC	8		3805			9900	11200
24	10	SCORPION 254WA	OP	FSH	FBG	DV	IO	260		8		3805			8050	9250
24	10	SCORPION 254WA	OP	FSH	FBG	DV	SE	T115	OMC	8		3805			9900	11200
24	10	SCORPION 254WA	OP	FSH	FBG	DV	IO	T140	MRCR	8		3805			8550	9850
25	4	CATALINA 253 MID-CBN	OP	CR	FBG	DV	IO	230	MRCR	9	9	4600	2	3	9100	10300
25	4	CATALINA 255 EXPRESS	OP	CR	FBG	DV	IB	220		9	9	4600	2	3	11400	12900
25	4	CATALINA 255 EXPRESS	HT	CR	FBG	DV	IB	220		9	9	4600	2	3	11400	12900
26	5	LIMITED 260SL	OP	SPTCR	FBG	DV	IO	T260		8		3950			10800	12300
26	5	SCORPION 266AC	OP	SPTCR	FBG	DV	IO	260		8	6	5200	2	11	10300	11700
26	5	SCORPION 266AC	OP	SPTCR	FBG	DV	IO	T140	MRCR	8	6	5200	2	11	10800	12200
26	5	STINGER 260SL	OP	SPTCR	FBG	DV	IO	T260		8		3880			10700	12200
28	2	COMMANDER 282SF	OP	SF	FBG	DV	IB	T260	MRCR	10	10	7500	2	4	19700	21900
28	2	COMMANDER 282SF	HT	SF	FBG	DV	IB	T260	MRCR	10	10	7500	2	4	19700	21900
28	11	CATALINA 291 BRIDGE	FB	EXP	FBG	DV	IB	T220		10	9	7800	2	3	20400	22600
28	11	CATALINA 292 SUNBRG	FB	SDN	FBG	DV	IB	T220		10	9	7800	2	3	22600	25100
28	11	CATALINA 293 EXPRESS	OP	EXP	FBG	DV	IB	220		10	9	6300	2	5	16500	18800
28	11	CATALINA 293 EXPRESS	HT	EXP	FBG	DV	IB	220		10	9	6300	2	5	16500	18800
28	11	CATALINA 294 EXPRESS	OP	EXP	FBG	DV	IB	T220		10	9	7000	2	5	19700	21900
28	11	CATALINA 294 EXPRESS	HT	EXP	FBG	DV	IB	T220		10	9	7000	2	5	19700	21900
30		CHRIS-CAT 300	OP	RACE	FBG	CT	IO	T370-T400		8	7	4970			14200	16800
30		CHRIS-CAT 305	OP	RACE	FBG	CT	OB			8	7	4970			18300	20300
30	10	COMMANDER SPORT 315	FB	SDNSF	FBG	DV	IB	T260-T340		11	9	12000	2	4	29300	34200
30	10	COMMANDER SPORT 315	FB	SDNSF	FBG	DV	IB	T205D	GM	11	9	12000	2	4	37700	41900
31	6	COMPETITION 312	OP	SPTCR	FBG	DV	IO	T400-T460		8					22300	25800
31	6	LIMITED 312SL	OP	SPTCR	FBG	DV	IO	T330-T400		8		5080			19900	22400
31	6	SCORPION 311VF	OP	CTRCN	FBG	DV	OB			8		4260	2	4	20000	22300
31	6	SCORPION 313VF	OP	CTRCN	FBG	DV	OB			8		4260	2	11	20000	22300
31	6	SCORPION 313VF	OP	CTRCN	FBG	DV	SE	T205	OMC	8		4260			20000	22300
31	6	STINGER 312SL	OP	SPTCR	FBG	DV	IO	T330-T400		8		5080	3		19300	22000
31	6	STINGER 314S	OP	SPTCR	FBG	DV	OB			8		4790			20200	22500
33		COMMANDER 332 EXP	OP	EXP	FBG	DV	IB	T260-T340		12	1	12360	2	9	35300	40900
33		COMMANDER 333 SPT	FB	SDN	FBG	DV	IB	T260-T340		12	1	13000	2	9	38300	44700
33		COMMANDER 333 SPT	FB	SDN	FBG	DV	IB	T230D	VLVO	12	1	14940	2	9	52100	57200
33		COMMANDER 336MID-CAB	OP	EXP	FBG	DV	VD	T260-T340		12	1	12360	2	9	35300	40900
33		COMMANDER 338 SUNBRG	FB	SDN	FBG	DV	IB	T260-T340		12	1	13612	2	10	38600	45100
33		COMMANDER EXP 332	OP	EXP	FBG	DV	IB	T230D	VLVO	12	1	14300	2	9	46700	51300
35	1	CATALINA 350	FB	DC	FBG	DV	IB	T260	MRCR	13	1	17229	2	10	45900	50500
36		CATALINA 362DC	FB	DC	FBG	DV	IB	T260		12	4	15500	2	7	50400	55400
36		COMMANDER 360 SPORT	FB	SDNSF	FBG	DV	IB	T340	MRCR	13		22600	3	2	62100	68200
36		COMMANDER 360 SPORT	FB	SDNSF	FBG	DV	IB	T300D	CAT	13		25300	3	2	80000	87900
38		CATALINA 381	FB	DC	FBG	DV	IB	T340	MRCR	14		21600	3		66600	73100
38		CATALINA 381	FB	DC	FBG	DV	IB	T230D	VLVO	14		23600	3		78000	85700
38		COMMANDER 382 SPORT	FB	SDN	FBG	DV	IB	T340	MRCR	13	11	26000	3	9	78400	86100
		IB T250D GM 92600 102000, IB T300D J&T 95400 105000, IB T355D CAT													100500	110500
38		CORINTHIAN 380	FB	DC	FBG	DV	IB	T340	MRCR	14		22500	3		68900	75700
38		CORINTHIAN 380	FB	DC	FBG	DV	IB	T230D	VLVO	14		24500	3		80400	88400
39		COMPETITION 390		RACE	FBG	DV	IO	T400	MRCR	9					33200	36900
39		COMPETITION 390		RACE	FBG	DV	IO	T440	MRCR	9					34800	38700
39		COMPETITION 390		RACE	FBG	DV	IO	T460	MRCR	9					35700	39700
39		STINGER 390X	OP	SPTCR	FBG	DV	IO	T370	MRCR	9		6810	3	3	34900	38700
39		STINGER 390X	OP	SPTCR	FBG	DV	IO	T400	MRCR	9		6810	3	3	36500	40600
41		CONSTELLATION 410	FB	MY	FBG	DV	IB	T340		14		26565	3	3	88300	97000
41		CONSTELLATION 410	FB	MY	FBG	DV	IB	T300D	J&T	14		29213	3	3	107000	117500
42		CATALINA 426	FB	DC	FBG	DV	IB	T340	MRCR	14	9	30000	3	6	92100	101000
42		CATALINA 426	FB	DC	FBG	DV	IB	T250D	GM	14	9	33000	3	6	107000	117500
42		CATALINA 426	FB	DC	FBG	DV	IB	T300D	J&T	14	9	33000	3	6	110500	121500
42	4	COMMANDER 422 CNV	FB	SF	FBG	DV	IB	T340	MRCR	14		34000	3	11	100500	110000
42	4	COMMANDER 422 CNV	FB	SF	FBG	DV	IB	T450D	J&T	14		34000	3	11	123500	135500
45		YACHT HOME 450	FB	HB	FBG	DV	IB	T260	MRCR	14		22000	3	4	53500	58800
45		YACHT HOME 450	FB	HB	FBG	DV	IB	T340	MRCR	14		22000	3	4	54700	60100
45		YACHT HOME 450	FB	HB	FBG	DV	IB	T205D	GM	14		22000	3	4	62900	69200
46	3	CONSTELLATION 460	FB	MY	FBG	DV	IB	T410D	J&T	15	3	49000	4	4	136000	149500
48		CORINTHIAN 480	FB	DCCPT	FBG	DV	IB	T340	MRCR	14	9	34000	3	6	103500	113500
48		CORINTHIAN 480	FB	DCCPT	FBG	DV	IB	T250D	GM	14	9	34000	3	6	107500	118000
48		CORINTHIAN 480	FB	DCCPT	FBG	DV	IB	T355D	CAT	14	9	34000	3	6	114500	126000
48	10	COMMANDER 482 CNV	FB	MY	FBG	DV	IB	T600D	GM	14	9	48000	4	9	149500	164000
56	4	CONSTELLATION 500	FB	MY	FBG	DV	IB	T500D	GM	15	3	54000	4	4	180000	197500
		1985 BOATS														
16	11	SCORPION 167BR	OP	RNBT	FBG	DV	OB			6	9	1250	2	8	2650	3050
16	11	SCORPION 168BRS	OP	RNBT	FBG	DV	IO	117-140		6	9	2050	2	8	2700	3150
16	11	SCORPION 168BRSL	OP	RNBT	FBG	DV	IO	117-140		6	9	2075	2	8	2800	3250
16	11	SCORPION 169S	OP	RNBT	FBG	DV	IO	117-140		6	9	2075	2	8	2600	3050
16	11	SCORPION 169SL	OP	RNBT	FBG	DV	IO	117-140		6	9	2125	2	8	2750	3200
17	3	LIMITED 170	OP	RNBT	FBG	TR	IO	170-185		7	4	2225			2850	3500
18	3	LIMITED 187	OP	RNBT	FBG	DV	IO	200-230		7	5				3400	3950
18	3	SCORPION 186BRS	OP	RNBT	FBG	DV	IO	138-200		7	5	2146	2	8	3150	3650
18	3	SCORPION 186BRSL	OP	RNBT	FBG	DV	IO	138-200		7	5		2	8	3400	4000
18	3	SCORPION 187S	OP	RNBT	FBG	DV	IO	138-200		7	5	2146	2	8	3050	3550
18	3	SCORPION 187SL	OP	RNBT	FBG	DV	IO	138-200		7	5	2146	2	8	3150	3650
18	6	LIMITED 190	OP	RNBT	FBG	TR	IO	200		7	8	2300			3250	3950
18	6	LIMITED 190	OP	RNBT	FBG	TR	IO	260		7	8	2300			3450	4250
20	7	LIMITED 210	OP	RNBT	FBG	DV	IO	230-260		8		3270			4850	5700
20	7	SCORPION 210BRS	OP	RNBT	FBG	DV	IO	225-260		8		3164	2	8	4900	5850
20	7	SCORPION 210BRSL	OP	RNBT	FBG	DV	IO	225-260		8		3350	2	8	5050	6050
20	7	SCORPION 210S	OP	RNBT	FBG	DV	IO	225-260		8		3054	2	8	4800	5700
20	7	SCORPION 210SL	OP	RNBT	FBG	DV	IO	225-260		8		3399	2	8	5100	6100
20	7	SKI-JACK 210BR	OP	RNBT	FBG	DV	IO	260	MRCR	8		3492			5200	5950
20	7	SKI-JACK 210S	OP	RNBT	FBG	DV	IO	260	MRCR	8		3492			5200	5950
21	3	FISHJACK 214VF	OP	CTRCN	FBG	DV	IO	200-260		8		2980	1	3	5150	6200
21	3	SCORPION 211VF	OP	RNBT	FBG	DV	IO	190-230		8		3047	2	6	4700	5700
21	3	SCORPION 212VF	OP	UTL	FBG	DV	OB			8		2370	1	3	5150	5950
21	3	SCORPION 213VF	OP	CTRCN	FBG	DV	OB			8		2300	1	3	5600	6450
21	3	SCORPION 215WA	OP	RNBT	FBG	DV	IO	190-230		8		2950	2	6	4600	5600
21	3	SCORPION 216WA	OP	RNBT	FBG	DV	OB			8		2270	2	6	5650	6500
21	3	SCORPION 217BR	OP	UTL	FBG	DV	OB			8		2100			4700	5400
21	3	SCORPION 218BR	OP	RNBT	FBG	DV	IO	225-230		8		2780			4700	5400
21	3	SCORPION 218BR	OP	RNBT	FBG	TR	IO	190-230		8		2780			4450	5250
21	6	LIMITED 220	OP	RNBT	FBG	TR	IO	260		7	10	2700	2	8	4650	5550
22	2	LIMITED 230SL	OP	RNBT	FBG	DV	IO	260-300		8		3600			5700	6950
22	2	SCORPION 230S	OP	RNBT	FBG	DV	IO	260		8		3550	2	10	5650	6700
22	2	SCORPION 230SL	OP	RNBT	FBG	DV	IO	260		8		3600	2	10	5500	6700
22	2	SCORPION 232AC	FB	EXP	FBG	DV	IO	260		8		4250			6750	8000
24	10	SCORPION 254WA	OP	EXP	FBG	DV	IO	260		8					8100	9550
24	10	SCORPION 254WA	OP	EXP	FBG	DV	IO	T140-T190		8					8550	10100
25	4	CATALINA 251	OP	EXP	FBG	DV	IB	230	MRCR	9	9	4600	2	3	10900	12300
25	4	CATALINA 251	HT	EXP	FBG	DV	IB	230	MRCR	9	9	4600	2	3	10900	12300
25	4	CATALINA 253 MID-CBN	OP	EXP	FBG	DV	IO	230	MRCR	9	9	4600			8600	9850
26		COMMANDER SPORT 268	FB	EXP	FBG	DV	IB	T230	MRCR	10	6	6900	2	2	16500	18700
26	5	SCORPION 265WAC	OP	OPFSH	FBG	DV	IO	260		8	6	4500			9450	10800
26	5	SCORPION 265WAC	OP	OPFSH	FBG	DV	IO	T140-T190		8	6	4500			9850	11800
26	5	SCORPION 266AC	OP	EXP	FBG	DV	IO	260		8	6	4951	2	11	9600	11100
26	5	SCORPION 266AC	OP	EXP	FBG	DV	IO	T140-T190		8	6	4951	2	11	10000	11900
26	5	STINGER 260SL	OP	SPTCR	FBG	DV	IO	T260-T300		8		4752			11000	13200
26	5	STINGER 260SL LIMITD	OP	SPTCR	FBG	DV	IO	T260-T300		8		4752			11200	13400
28	2	COMMANDER 282	OP	SF	FBG	DV	IB	T260	MRCR	10	10		2	4	18600	20700
28	2	COMMANDER 282	HT	SF	FBG	DV	IB	T260	MRCR	10	10		2	4	18600	20700
28	11	CATALINA 280	OP	EXP	FBG	DV	IB	230	MRCR	10	9	6300	2	5	15800	18000
28	11	CATALINA 280	HT	EXP	FBG	DV	IB	230	MRCR	10	9	6300	2	5	15800	18000
28	11	CATALINA 281	OP	EXP	FBG	DV	IB	T230		10	9	7000	2	3	19100	21200
28	11	CATALINA 291 BRIDGE	FB	EXP	FBG	DV	IB	T230	MRCR	10	9	7800	2	3	19500	21700
30		CHRIS-CAT 300	OP	RACE	FBG	CT	IO	T370-T400		8	7	6100			13900	16300
30	10	COMMANDER SPORT 315	FB	SDNSF	FBG	DV	IB	T260-T340		11	9	12000	2	4	27900	32500
30	10	COMMANDER SPORT 315	FB	SDNSF	FBG	DV	IB	T215D	GM	11	9	12000	2	4	36300	40400
31	6	COMPETITION 312	OP	SPTCR	FBG	DV	IO	T400-T460		8					21200	24600
31	6	SCORPION 311VF	OP	CTRCN	FBG	DV	OB			8		4100	2	4	19600	21700
31	6	SCORPION 313VF	OP	CTRCN	FBG	DV	OB			8		3700	2	11	19600	21700
31	6	STINGER 312SL	OP	RACE	FBG	DV	IO	T330-T400		8		6854	3		15800	18900
31	6	STINGER 312SL LIMITD	OP	RACE	FBG	DV	IO	T330-T400		8		7005			15800	19000
31	6	STINGER 314SL	OP	RACE	FBG	DV	OB			8					20300	22500
33		COMMANDER EXP 332		EXP	FBG	DV	IB	T260-T340		12	1	12360	2	9	33500	38800
33		COMMANDER EXP 332		EXP	FBG	DV	IB	T235D	VLVO	12	1	14300	2	9	44200	49100

CONTINUED ON NEXT PAGE

LOA FT	LOA IN	NAME AND/ OR MODEL	TOP/ RIG	BOAT TYPE	-HULL- MTL	-HULL- TP	ENGINE TP	ENGINE # HP	ENGINE MFG	BEAM FT	BEAM IN	WGT LBS	DRAFT FT	DRAFT IN	RETAIL LOW	RETAIL HIGH
		1985 BOATS														
33		COMMANDER EXP 332	OP	EXP	FBG	DV	IB	T260-T340		12	1	11560	2	9	33000	38300
33		COMMANDER EXP 332	OP	EXP	FBG	DV	IB	T235D	VLVO	12	1	13500	2	9	42900	47700
33		COMMANDER EXP 332	FB	EXP	FBG	DV	IB	T260-T340		12	1	12700	2	9	33700	39100
33		COMMANDER EXP 332	FB	EXP	FBG	DV	IB	T235D	VLVO	12	1	14640	2	9	44800	49700
33		COMMANDER MID-CAB336	OP	EXP	FBG	DV	VD	T260-T340		12	1	12360	2	9	33500	38800
33		COMMANDER SPORT 333	FB	SDN	FBG	DV	IB	T260		12	1	13000	2	9	36300	40400
35	1	CATALINA 350	FB	DC	FBG	DV	IB	T260	MRCR	13	1	17229	2	10	43200	48000
36		COMMANDER SPORT 360	FB	SDNSF	FBG	DV	IB	T340	MRCR	13		22600	3	2	59100	65000
36		COMMANDER SPORT 360	FB	SDNSF	FBG	DV	IB	T300D	CAT	13		25300	3	2	76200	83700
38		CATALINA 381	FB	DC	FBG	DV	IB	T340	MRCR	14		21600	3		63400	69600
38		CATALINA 381	FB	DC	FBG	DV	IB	T235D	VLVO	14		23600	3		74500	81800
38		COMMANDER SPORT 382	FB	SDN	FBG	DV	IB	T340	MRCR	13	11	26000	3	9	74600	82000
		IB T215D GM 72900 80100, IB T300D J&T 76900 84500, IB T350D CAT													81300	89300
38		CORINTHIAN 380	FB	DC	FBG	DV	IB	T340	MRCR	14		22500	3		65600	72000
38		CORINTHIAN 380	FB	DC	FBG	DV	IB	T235D	VLVO	14		24500	3		76700	84300
39		COMPETITION 390		RACE	FBG	DV	IO	T400	MRCR	9					31700	35200
39		COMPETITION 390		RACE	FBG	DV	IO	T440	MRCR	9					33300	36900
39		COMPETITION 390		RACE	FBG	DV	IO	T460	MRCR	9					34100	37900
39		STINGER 390X	OP	RACE	FBG	DV	IO	T370	MRCR	9		8940	3	3	30600	34000
39		STINGER 390X	OP	RACE	FBG	DV	IO	T400	MRCR	9		8760	3	3	31700	35200
41		COMMANDER 410	FB	MY	FBG	DV	IB	T340	MRCR	14		26565	3	3	84400	92700
41		COMMANDER 410	FB	MY	FBG	DV	IB	T286D	VLVO	14		29213	3	3	99100	109000
42		CATALINA 426	FB	DC	FBG	DV	IB	T340	MRCR	14	9	30000	3	6	87700	96400
42		CATALINA 426	FB	DC	FBG	DV	IB	T215D	GM	14	9	33000	3	6	99600	109500
42		CATALINA 426	FB	DC	FBG	DV	IB	T300D	J&T	14	9	33000	3	6	105500	116000
42	4	COMMANDER SPORT 422	FB	SDN	FBG	DV	IB	T340	MRCR	14		34000	3	11	100500	110500
42	4	COMMANDER SPORT 422	FB	SDN	FBG	DV	IB	T390D	J&T	14		34000	3	11	115500	126500
42	4	COMMANDER SPORT 422	FB	SDN	FBG	DV	IB	T475D	GM	14		34000	3	11	120500	132000
45		YACHT HOME 450	FB	HB	FBG	DV	IB	T260	MRCR	14		22000	3	4	52200	57300
45		YACHT HOME 450	FB	HB	FBG	DV	IB	T340	MRCR	14		22000	3	4	53900	59200
45		YACHT HOME 450	FB	HB	FBG	DV	IB	T215D	GM	14		22000	3	4	61900	68000
46		AQUA-HOME	HT	HB	FBG	SV	VD	T135D	PERK	14		23700	3		58400	64200
46	3	CONSTELLATION 460	FB	MY	FBG	DV	IB	T410D	J&T	15	3	49000	4	4	129500	142500
48		CORINTHIAN 480	FB	DCCPT	FBG	DV	IB	T340	MRCR	14	9		3	6	**	**
48		CORINTHIAN 480	FB	DCCPT	FBG	DV	IB	T215D	GM	14	9		3	6	101000	111000
48		CORINTHIAN 480	FB	DCCPT	FBG	DV	IB	T350D	CAT	14	9		3	6	109000	119500
48	10	COMMANDER CONVERT	FB	MY	FBG	DV	IB	T600D	GM	14	9	48000	4	9	142500	156500
56	4	CONSTELLATION 500	FB	MY	FBG	DV	IB	T500D	GM	15	3	54000	4	4	171500	188500
		1984 BOATS														
16	11	SCORPION 167BR	OP	RNBT	FBG	DV	OB			6	9	1250	2	8	2550	3000
16	11	SCORPION 168BRS	OP	RNBT	FBG	DV	IO	120-140		6	9	1970	2	8	2400	2850
16	11	SCORPION 168BRSL	OP	RNBT	FBG	DV	IO	120-140		6	9	1970			2450	2900
16	11	SCORPION 169S	OP	RNBT	FBG	DV	IO	120-140		6	9	1970	2	8	2350	2750
16	11	SCORPION 169SL	OP	RNBT	FBG	DV	IO	120-140		6	9	1970	2	8	2400	2800
17	3	ELITE 170	OP	RNBT	FBG	TR	IO	170-188		7	4	2160	2	7	2750	3200
17	3	SPRINT 170	OP	CTRCN	FBG	TR	IO	140		7	4	1846	2	5	2700	3150
18	3	SCORPION 186BR	OP	RNBT	FBG	DV	IO	140-198		7	5	2146	2	8	2900	3450
18	3	SCORPION 187S	OP	RNBT	FBG	DV	IO	140-198		7	5	2146	2	8	2850	3350
18	3	SCORPION 187SL	OP	RNBT	FBG	DV	IO	140-198		7	5	2146	2	8	2950	3450
18	6	ELITE 190	OP	RNBT	FBG	TR	IO	198-260		7	8	2480	2	7	3250	4000
18	6	SPRINT 190	OP	CTRCN	FBG	TR	OB			7	8	1450	2	4	2950	3450
18	6	SPRINT 190	OP	CTRCN	FBG	TR	IO	170-200		7	8		2	7	3600	4200
20	7	SCORPION 210BR	OP	RNBT	FBG	DV	IO	225-260		8		3164	2	8	4750	5700
20	7	SCORPION 210S	OP	RNBT	FBG	DV	IO	225-260		8		3054	2	8	4650	5550
20	7	SCORPION 210SL	OP	RNBT	FBG	DV	IO	225-260		8		3399	2	8	5000	5950
20	7	SKI-JACK 210BR	OP	RNBT	FBG	DV	IO	260	MRCR	8		3492			5050	5800
21	3	FISHJACK 214VF	OP	CTRCN	FBG	DV	IO	198-260		8		3200	1	3	5250	6300
21	3	SCORPION 211VF	OP	RNBT	FBG	DV	IO	185-230		8		3047	2	6	4600	5550
21	3	SCORPION 211VF	OP	RNBT	FBG	DV	IO	260		8		3047	2	6	4800	5750
21	3	SCORPION 212VF	OP	UTL	FBG	DV	OB			8		2100	1	3	4600	5250
21	3	SCORPION 213VF	OP	CTRCN	FBG	DV	OB			8		2100	1	3	5150	5900
21	3	SCORPION 215WA	OP	RNBT	FBG	DV	IO	185-230		8		3447	2	6	4950	5950
21	3	SCORPION 216WA	OP	RNBT	FBG	DV	OB			8		2500	2	6	5850	6750
21	3	SCORPION 217BR	OP	UTL	FBG	DV	OB			8		2200			4750	5450
21	6	LIMITED 220	OP	RNBT	FBG	TR	IO	260		7	10	2700	2	8	4500	5200
22	2	LIMITED 230SL	OP	RNBT	FBG	DV	IO	260	MRCR	8		3476			5200	6000
22	2	SCORPION 230S	OP	RNBT	FBG	DV	IO	260		8		3526	2	10	5450	6500
22	2	SCORPION 230SL	OP	RNBT	FBG	DV	IO	260		8		3570	2	10	5500	6550
22	2	SCORPION 232AC	FB	EXP	FBG	DV	IO	260	MRCR	8					5700	6550
22	2	STINGER 220XL	OP	RNBT	FBG	DV	IO	260	MRCR	8		3476			5600	6450
25	4	CATALINA 251	OP	EXP	FBG	DV	IB	230	MRCR	9	9	4600	2	3	10500	11900
25	4	CATALINA 253 MID-CBN	OP	EXP	FBG	DV	IO	228	MRCR	9	9	4600	2	3	8350	9600
26		COMMANDER SPORT 268	OP	EXP	FBG	DV	IB	T230	MRCR	10	6	6900	2	2	15900	18100
26		COMMANDER SPORT 268	OP	EXP	FBG	DV	IB	T124D	VLVO	10	6	6900	2	2	21300	23600
26	5	SCORPION 264AC	OP	EXP	FBG	DV	IO	260		8	6	4951	2	11	9400	10700
26	5	SCORPION 265WAC	OP	OPFSH	FBG	DV	IO	260		8	6	3435			8150	9400
26	5	SCORPION 265WAC	OP	OPFSH	FBG	DV	IO	T140-T188		8	6	3435			8600	10500
26	5	STINGER 260SL	OP	SPTCR	FBG	DV	IO	T260	MRCR	8		4752			10700	12100
26	5	STINGER 260SL LIMITD	OP	SPTCR	FBG	DV	IO	T260	MRCR	8		4752			10900	12400
28	11	CATALINA 280	OP	EXP	FBG	DV	IB	230	MRCR	10	8	6300	2	5	15200	17300
28	11	CATALINA 280	OP	EXP	FBG	DV	IB	124D	VLVO	10	8	6300	2	5	16100	18300
28	11	CATALINA 281	OP	EXP	FBG	DV	IB	T230	MRCR	10	8	7000	2	3	18400	20400
28	11	CATALINA 291 BRIDGE	FB	EXP	FBG	DV	IB	T230	MRCR	10	8	7800	2	3	19000	21100
30		CHRIS-CAT 300	OP	RACE	FBG	CT	IO	T330-T400		8	7				13000	15900
30		CHRIS-CAT 300	OP	RACE	FBG	CT	IO	T420	KAAM	8	7				14400	16400
30	10	COMMANDER SF316	OP	OPFSH	FBG	DV	IB	T260-T340		11	9	11400	2	10	26000	30200
30	10	COMMANDER SF316	OP	OPFSH	FBG	DV	IB	T215D	GM	11	9	11400	2	10	33200	36900
30	10	COMMANDER SPORT 315	FB	SDNSF	FBG	DV	IB	T260-T340		11	9	12000	2	6	26900	31300
30	10	COMMANDER SPORT 315	FB	SDNSF	FBG	DV	IB	T215D	GM	11	9	12000	2	6	35200	39100
31	6	SCORPION 311VF	OP	CTRCN	FBG	DV	OB			8		3700	1	5	19100	21300
31	6	STINGER 312SL	OP	RACE	FBG	DV	IO	T330-T400		8		6854	3		15400	18400
31	6	STINGER 312SL LIMITD	OP	RACE	FBG	DV	IO	T330-T400							18300	21200
33		COMMANDER 337	FB	DC	FBG	DV	IB	T260-T340		12	4	16000	3		34800	40100
33		COMMANDER EXP 332	OP	EXP	FBG	DV	IB	T260-T340		12	4	11560	2	9	31800	36900
33		COMMANDER EXP 332	OP	EXP	FBG	DV	IB	T158D-T221D		12	4	13500	2	9	39100	45600
33		COMMANDER EXP 332	HT	EXP	FBG	DV	IB	T260-T340		12	4	12360	2	9	32300	37400
33		COMMANDER EXP 332	HT	EXP	FBG	DV	IB	T158D-T221D		12	4	14300	2	9	40500	47000
33		COMMANDER EXP 332	FB	EXP	FBG	DV	IB	T260-T340		12	4	12700	2	9	32500	37700
33		COMMANDER EXP 332	FB	EXP	FBG	DV	IO	T165D	VLVO	12	4	14640	2	9	30200	33600
33		COMMANDER EXP 332	FB	EXP	FBG	DV	IB	T221D	VLVO	12	4	14640	2	9	42900	47600
33		COMMANDER MID-CAB336	OP	EXP	FBG	DV	VD	T260-T340		12	4	12360	2	9	32300	37400
33		COMMANDER SPORT 333	FB	SDN	FBG	DV	IB	T260-T340		12	4	13000	2	9	35000	40900
33		COMMANDER SPORT 333	FB	SDN	FBG	DV	IB	T221D	VLVO	12	4	14940	2	9	47700	52400
35	1	CATALINA 350	FB	DC	FBG	DV	IB	T235	MPC	13	1	17229	2	10	41300	45900
36		COMMANDER SF365	OP	SF	FBG	DV	IB	T340	MRCR	13		20500	2	6	54000	59300
36		COMMANDER SF365	OP	SF	FBG	DV	IB	T300D	CAT	13		20500	2	6	64400	70800
36		COMMANDER SF365	OP	SF	FBG	DV	IB	T320D	CUM	13		20500	2	6	64000	70300
36		COMMANDER SPORT 360	FB	SDNSF	FBG	DV	IB	T340	MRCR	13		22600	3	2	57200	62800
36		COMMANDER SPORT 360	FB	SDNSF	FBG	DV	IB	T300D	CAT	13		25300	3	2	73700	80900
36		COMMANDER SPORT 360	FB	SDNSF	FBG	DV	IB	T320D	CUM	13		25300	3	2	73200	80500
38		CATALINA 381	FB	DC	FBG	DV	IB	T340	MRCR	14		21600	3		61300	67300
38		CATALINA 381	FB	DC	FBG	DV	IB	T221D	VLVO	14		23600	3		71600	78600
38		CORINTHIAN 380	FB	DC	FBG	DV	IB	T340	MRCR	14		22500	3		63400	69700
38		CORINTHIAN 380	FB	DC	FBG	DV	IB	T235D	VLVO	14		24500	3		74200	81500
39		STINGER 390X	OP	RACE	FBG	DV	IO	T370	MRCR	9		8940	3	4	29800	33100
39		STINGER 390X	OP	RACE	FBG	DV	IO	T400	MRCR	9		8760	3	4	30900	34300
41		COMMANDER 410	HT	MY	FBG	DV	IB	T340	MRCR	14		26565	3	4	81600	89700
41		COMMANDER 410	HT	MY	FBG	DV	IB	T286D	VLVO	14		29213	3	4	95900	105500
41		COMMANDER 410	FB	MY	FBG	DV	IB	T340	MRCR	14		26565	3	4	81600	89600
41		COMMANDER 410	FB	MY	FBG	DV	IB	T286D	VLVO	14		29213	3	4	95800	105500
42		COMMANDER 421	F+T	SDNSF	FBG	DV	IB	T462D	GM	14		34750	3	11	119000	130500
46		AQUA-HOME	HT	HB	FBG	SV	IO	T260	MRCR	14		23700	3		53800	59100
		VD T260 MRCR 50100 55100, VD T340 MRCR 51600 56700, VD T135D PERK													57100	62800

....For earlier years, see the BUC Used Boat Price Guide, Volume 3

HANS CHRISTIAN YACHTS AMERICA

ANNAPOLIS MD 21403-2524

See inside cover to adjust price for area

For more recent years, see the BUC Used Boat Price Guide, Volume 1

LOA FT	LOA IN	NAME AND/ OR MODEL	TOP/ RIG	BOAT TYPE	-HULL- MTL	-HULL- TP	ENGINE TP	ENGINE # HP	ENGINE MFG	BEAM FT	BEAM IN	WGT LBS	DRAFT FT	DRAFT IN	RETAIL LOW	RETAIL HIGH
		1995 BOATS														
37		TRADITIONAL 38	CUT	SACAC	FBG	KL	IB	65D	YAN	12	4	26500	6	6	164000	180500
41		TRADITIONAL 41	CUT	SACAC	FBG	KL	IB	62D	YAN	13	3	35500	6	5	212000	233000
43		CHRISTINA 43	CUT	SACAC	FBG	KL	IB	62D	YAN	13	3	30640	6	6	206000	226500
43		TRADITIONAL 43	CUT	SACAC	FBG	KL	IB	62D	YAN	13	3	31500	6	5	209000	230000
44	6	INDEPENDENCE 45 PH		TRWL	FBG	DS	IB	160D	ALAS			36000	4	6	296000	325500
48		TRADITIONAL 48	CUT	SACCC	FBG	KL	IB	110D	YAN	14	3	44000	6	6	295000	324000
52		CHRISTINA 52	CUT	SARAC	FBG	KL	IB	88D	YAN	14		31350	5	11	340500	374000
52		CHRISTINA 52	CUT	SARCC	FBG	KL	IB	88D	YAN	14		31350	5	11	340500	374000
58		CHRISTINA 58	CUT	SARAC	FBG	KL	IB	110D	YAN	16		45000	5	11	572500	629000
58		CHRISTINA 58 PH	CUT	SARAC	FBG	KL	IB	110D	YAN	16		45000	5	11	572500	629000

LOA FT	LOA IN	NAME AND/ OR MODEL	TOP/ RIG	BOAT TYPE	-HULL- MTL	-HULL- TP	TP	ENGINE # HP	ENGINE MFG	BEAM FT	BEAM IN	WGT LBS	DRAFT FT	DRAFT IN	RETAIL LOW	RETAIL HIGH
		1994 BOATS														
41		TRADITIONAL 41	CUT	SACAC	FBG	KL	IB	62D	YAN	13	3	35500	6	5	200500	220500
43		CHRISTINA 43	CUT	SACAC	FBG	KL	IB	62D	YAN	13	3	30640	6	6	195000	214500
43		TRADITIONAL 43	CUT	SACAC	FBG	KL	IB	62D	YAN	13	3	31500	6	5	198000	217500
44	6	INDEPENDENCE 45 PH		TRWL	FBG	DS	IB	160D	ALAS			36000	4	6	283500	311500
48		TRADITIONAL 48	CUT	SACCC	FBG	KL	IB	110D	YAN	14	3	44000	6	6	279000	307000
52		CHRISTINA 52	CUT	SARAC	FBG	KL	IB	88D	YAN	14		31350	5	11	322500	354500
52		CHRISTINA 52	CUT	SARCC	FBG	KL	IB	88D	YAN	14		31350	5	11	322500	354500
58		CHRISTINA 58	CUT	SARAC	FBG	KL	IB	110D	YAN	16		45000	5	11	542000	595500
58		CHRISTINA 58 PH	CUT	SARAC	FBG	KL	IB	110D	YAN	16		45000	5	11	542000	595500
		1993 BOATS														
32	9	HANS-CHRISTAIN 33T	CUT	SACAC	FBG	KL	IB	35D	YAN	11	8	18800	5	6	110500	121500
37	9	HANS-CHRISTIAN 38MK	CUT	SACAC	FBG	KL	IB	62D	YAN	12	6	27500	6		152000	167500
40	11	HANS-CHRISTIAN 41T	CUT	SACAC	FBG	KL	IB	62D	YAN	13	3	35500	6	5	190000	208500
43		CHRISTINA 43	CUT	SACAC	FBG	KL	IB	62D	YAN	13	4	31000	6	6	186000	204500
47	10	HANS-CHRISTIAN 48T	CUT	SACAC	FBG	KL	IB	110D	YAN	14	3	44000	6	6	302500	332500
51	6	CHRISTINA 52	CUT	SACAC	FBG	KL	IB	77D	YAN	14		36000	6		303000	333000
		1992 BOATS														
32	9	HANS-CHRISTAIN 33T	CUT	SA/CR	FBG	KL	IB	35D	YAN	11	8	18500	5	6	103000	113500
37	9	HANS-CHRISTIAN 38MK	CUT	SA/CR	FBG	KL	IB	62D	YAN	12	6	27500	6		144000	158500
37	11	HANS-CHRISTIAN 38T	CUT	SA/CR	FBG	KL	IB	62D	YAN	12	4	26500	6		140500	154500
39	10	HANS-CHRISTIAN C40	CUT	SA/CR	FBG	KL	IB	62D	YAN	12	8	22500	6		131000	144000
40	11	HANS-CHRISTIAN 41T	CUT	SA/CR	FBG	KL	IB	62D	YAN	13	3	35500	6	5	180000	197500
42	8	HANS-CHRISTIAN 43T	CUT	SA/CR	FBG	KL	IB	62D	YAN	13	10	31500	6		175500	193000
42	8	HANS-CHRISTIAN 43T	KTH	SA/CR	FBG	KL	IB	62D	YAN	13	10	31500	6		175500	193000
43		HANS-CHRISTIAN C43	CUT	SA/CR	FBG	KL	IB	62D	YAN	13	4	30640	6	6	175000	192500
44	6	HANS-CHRISTIAN 45I	FB	TRWL	FBG	SV	IB	135D	LEHM	14	6	36000	4	6	248500	273000
44	6	HANS-CHRISTIAN 45I	FB	TRWL	FBG	SV	IB	T135D	LEHM	14	6	36000	4	6	256500	282000
47	10	HANS-CHRISTIAN 48T	CUT	SA/CR	FBG	KL	IB	110D	YAN	14	3	44000	6	6	286500	314500
47	10	HANS-CHRISTIAN 48T	KTH	SA/CR	FBG	KL	IB	110D	YAN	14	3	44000	6	6	286500	314500
47	11	CHRISTINA 48	CUT	SA/CR	FBG	KL	IB	77D	YAN	13	6	29883	6		209500	230500
51	6	CHRISTINA 52	CUT	SA/CR	FBG	KL	IB	77D	YAN	14		26906	6	11	269500	296000
		1991 BOATS														
32	9	HANS-CHRISTAIN 33T	CUT	SA/CR	FBG	KL	IB	35D	YAN	11	8	18500	5	6	97600	107500
37	9	HANS-CHRISTIAN 38MK	CUT	SA/CR	FBG	KL	IB	62D	YAN	12	6	27500	6		136500	150000
37	11	HANS-CHRISTIAN 38T	CUT	SA/CR	FBG	KL	IB	62D	YAN	12	4	26500	6		133000	146000
39	10	HANS-CHRISTIAN C40	CUT	SA/CR	FBG	KL	IB	62D	YAN	12	8	22500	6		124000	136500
40	11	HANS-CHRISTIAN 41T	CUT	SA/CR	FBG	KL	IB	62D	YAN	13	3	35500	6	5	170500	187000
42	8	HANS-CHRISTIAN 43T	CUT	SA/CR	FBG	KL	IB	62D	YAN	13	10	31500	6		166500	183000
42	8	HANS-CHRISTIAN 43T	KTH	SA/CR	FBG	KL	IB	62D	YAN	13	10	31500	6		166500	183000
43		HANS-CHRISTIAN C43	CUT	SA/CR	FBG	KL	IB	62D	YAN	13	4	30640	6	6	166000	182000
44	6	HANS-CHRISTIAN 45I	FB	TRWL	FBG	SV	IB	135D	LEHM	14	6	36000	4	6	237000	260000
44	6	HANS-CHRISTIAN 45I	FB	TRWL	FBG	SV	IB	T135D	LEHM	14	6	36000	4	6	244500	269000
47	10	HANS-CHRISTIAN 48T	CUT	SA/CR	FBG	KL	IB	110D	YAN	14	3	44000	6	6	271500	298000
47	10	HANS-CHRISTIAN 48T	KTH	SA/CR	FBG	KL	IB	110D	YAN	14	3	44000	6	6	271500	298000
47	11	CHRISTINA 48	CUT	SA/CR	FBG	KL	IB	77D	YAN	13	6	29883	6		203500	224000
51	6	CHRISTINA 52	CUT	SA/CR	FBG	KL	IB	77D	YAN	14		26906	6	11	255500	280500
		1990 BOATS														
32	9	HANS-CHRISTAIN 33T	CUT	SA/CR	FBG	KL	IB	35D	YAN	11	6	18800	5	6	93900	103000
37	9	HANS-CHRISTIAN MKII	CUT	SA/CR	FBG	KL	IB	66D	YAN	12	7	27500	6		129500	142500
37	11	HANS-CHRISTIAN T38	CUT	SA/CR	FBG	KL	IB	66D	YAN	12	4	26800	6		127000	139500
39	10	HANS-CHRISTIAN C40	CUT	SA/CR	FBG	KL	IB	66D	YAN	12	8	22506	6		117500	129500
40	11	HANS-CHRISTIAN 41T	CUT	SA/CR	FBG	KL	IB	66D	YAN	13	3	35500	6	5	161500	177500
42	8	HANS-CHRISTIAN 43T	CUT	SA/CR	FBG	KL	IB	66D	YAN	13	10	31500	6		158000	173500
43		HANS-CHRISTIAN C43	CUT	SA/CR	FBG	KL	IB	66D	YAN	13	4	30640	6	6	157000	173000
44	6	HANS-CHRISTIAN 45I	FB	TRWL	F/S	SV	IB	135D	LEHM	14	6	36000	4	6	226000	248500
47	10	HANS-CHRISTIAN 48T	CUT	SA/CR	FBG	KL	IB	110D	YAN	14	3	44000	6	6	257000	282500
47	11	CHRISTINA 48	CUT	SA/CR	FBG	KL	IB	77D	YAN	13	6	29883	6		193000	212000
51	6	CHRISTINA 52	CUT	SA/CR	FBG	KL	IB	77D	YAN	14		26906	6	11	242000	265500
		1989 BOATS														
32	9	HANSA 33LM	CUT	SA/CR	FBG	KL	IB	35		11	8	18500	5	6	78900	86700
32	9	HANSA 33T	CUT	SA/CR	FBG	KL	IB	35		11	8	18500	5	6	96000	105500
37	11	HANS-CHRISTIAN 38T	CUT	SA/CR	FBG	KL	IB	66D	YAN	12	4	26500	6		119500	131500
37	11	HANS-CHRISTIAN 38T	KTH	SA/CR	FBG	KL	IB	35D	YAN	12	4	26500	6		119000	130500
39	10	HANS-CHRISTIAN C40	CUT	SA/CR	FBG	KL	IB	66D	YAN	12	8	22506	6		111500	122500
40	10	HANS-CHRISTIAN 41T	CUT	SA/CR	FBG	KL	IB	66D	YAN	13	3	35500	5	5	152500	168000
42	8	HANS-CHRISTIAN 43T	CUT	SA/CR	FBG	KL	IB	66D	YAN	13	10	31500	6		149500	164000
42	8	HANS-CHRISTIAN 43T	KTH	SA/CR	FBG	KL	IB	66D	YAN	13	10	31500	6		149500	164500
43		HANS-CHRISTIAN C43	CUT	SA/CR	FBG	KL	IB	66D	YAN	13	4	30640	6	6	149000	163500
44	6	HANS-CHRISTIAN I45	FB	TRWL	FBG	SV	IB	135D	LEHM	14	6	36000	4	6	204500	224500
46		HANS-CHRISTIAN MKII		SA/CR	FBG	KL	IB			12	7	26800	6		133500	146500
46		HANS-CHRISTIAN MKII	CUT	SA/CR	FBG	KL	IB	66D	YAN	12	7	26800	6		135500	149000
47	10	CHRISTINA 48	CUT	SA/CR	FBG	KL	IB	77D	YAN	13	6	29883	6	6	182000	200000
47	10	HANS-CHRISTIAN 48T	CUT	SA/CR	FBG	KL	IB	110D	YAN	14	3	44000	7		243500	267500
47	10	HANS-CHRISTIAN 48T	KTH	SA/CR	FBG	KL	IB	110D	YAN	14	3	44000	7		243500	267500
51	6	CHRISTINA 52	SLP	SA/CR	FBG	KL	IB	77D	YAN	14		26906	6	11	229000	252000
		1988 BOATS														
32	9	HANSA 33T	CUT	SA/CR	FBG	KL	IB	37D		11	8	18500	5	6	83000	91200
38		HANS-CHRISTIAN 38T	CUT	SA/CR	FBG	KL	IB	D		12	4	26500	6		113000	124000
38		HANS-CHRISTIAN 38T	KTH	SA/CR	FBG	KL	IB	D		12	4	26500	6		113000	124000
38	6	HANS-CHRISTIAN 39PH	CUT	SA/CR	FBG	KL	IB	D		12	6	28000	6		136500	150000
39	10	HANS-CHRISTIAN C40	CUT	SA/CR	FBG	KL	IB	D		12	6	22506	6		105000	115500
40	10	HANS-CHRISTIAN 41T	CUT	SA/CR	FBG	KL	IB	D		13	3	35500	5	5	145000	159000
42	7	HANS-CHRISTIAN 43T	CUT	SA/CR	FBG	KL	IB	D		13	10	31500	6		141000	155000
42	7	HANS-CHRISTIAN 43T	KTH	SA/CR	FBG	KL	IB	D		13	10	31500	6		141000	155000
43		HANS-CHRISTIAN C43	CUT	SA/CR	FBG	KL	IB	D		13	2	30640	6	6	141000	155000
43	9	HANS-CHRISTIAN 44PH	CUT	SA/CR	FBG	KL	IB	D		14	7	44000	5	6	202000	222000
45	7	HANS-CHRISTIAN 46	FB	MY	FBG	DV	IB	T355D		15		29000	4	2	204000	224000
46		HANS-CHRISTIAN MKII	CUT	SA/CR	FBG	KL	IB	D		12	6	27500	6		129500	142000
46		HANS-CHRISTIAN MKII	KTH	SA/CR	FBG	KL	IB	D		12	6	27500	6		129500	142000
47	10	CHRISTINA 48	CUT	SA/CR	FBG	KL	IB	77D	YAN	13	6	29883	6	6	172500	189500
47	10	HANS-CHRISTIAN 48T	CUT	SA/CR	FBG	KL	IB	110D	YAN	14	3	44000	7		230500	253500
47	10	HANS-CHRISTIAN 48T	KTH	SA/CR	FBG	KL	IB	110D	YAN	14	3	44000	7		230500	253500
51	6	CHRISTINA 52	SLP	SA/CR	FBG	KL	IB	77D	YAN	14		31350	6	11	224000	246500
51	6	CHRISTINA 52	CUT	SA/CR	FBG	KL	IB	77D	YAN	14		31350	6	11	224000	246500
		1987 BOATS														
32	9	HANSA 33	CUT	SA/CR	FBG	KL	IB	37D		11	8	18500	5	6	78700	86400
37	9	HANS-CHRISTIAN MKII	CUT	SA/CR	FBG	KL	IB	D		12	6	27500	6		110000	120500
38		HANS-CHRISTIAN 38T	CUT	SA/CR	FBG	KL	IB	D		12	4	26500	6		107000	117500
38	6	HANS-CHRISTIAN 39PH	CUT	SA/CR	FBG	KL	IB	D		12	6	28000	6		129000	142000
39	10	HANS-CHRISTIAN C40	CUT	SA/CR	FBG	KL	IB	D		12	6	22500	6		99500	109500
40	10	HANS-CHRISTIAN 41T	CUT	SA/CR	FBG	KL	IB	D		13	3	35500	5	5	137000	151000
42	7	HANS-CHRISTIAN 43T	CUT	SA/CR	FBG	KL	IB	D		13		31500	6		133500	147000
42	7	HANS-CHRISTIAN 43T	KTH	SA/CR	FBG	KL	IB	D		13		31500	6		133500	147000
43		HANS-CHRISTIAN C43	CUT	SA/CR	FBG	KL	IB	D		13	2	30640	6	6	133500	147000
43	9	HANS-CHRISTIAN 44PH	CUT	SA/CR	FBG	KL	IB	D		14	7	44000	5	6	191500	210500
45	7	HANS-CHRISTIAN 46	FB	MY	FBG	DV	IB	T355D		15		30000	2	3	198500	218500
47	10	HANS-CHRISTIAN 48T	CUT	SA/CR	FBG	KL	IB	110D	YAN	14	3	44000	7		209000	230000
47	10	HANS-CHRISTIAN 48T	KTH	SA/CR	FBG	KL	IB	110D	YAN	14	3	44000	7		209000	230000
51	6	CHRISTINA 52	CUT	SA/CR	FBG	KL	IB	77D	YAN	14		31350	6	11	212500	233500
		1986 BOATS														
32	9	HANSA 33	CUT	SA/CR	FBG	KL	IB	D		11	6	17900	5	6	72300	79400
37	9	HANS-CHRISTIAN MKII	CUT	SA/CR	FBG	KL	IB	D		12	6	27500	6		104000	114500
38		HANS-CHRISTIAN 38T	CUT	SA/CR	FBG	KL	IB	D		12	4	26500	6		101500	111500
38	6	HANS-CHRISTIAN 39PH	CUT	SA/CR	FBG	KL	IB	D		12	6	28000	6		122500	134500
40	10	HANS-CHRISTIAN 41T	CUT	SA/CR	FBG	KL	IB	D		13	3	35000	5	5	129000	141500
42	7	HANS-CHRISTIAN 43T	CUT	SA/CR	FBG	KL	IB	D		13		31500	6		126500	139000
42	7	HANS-CHRISTIAN 43T	KTH	SA/CR	FBG	KL	IB	D		13		31500	6		126500	139000
43		CRISTINA 43	CUT	SA/CR	FBG	KL	IB	D		13	3	30640	6	6	126500	139000
43	9	HANSA 44PH	KTH	SA/CR	FBG	KL	IB	D		14	7	44000	5	8	181500	199500
47	10	HANS-CHRISTIAN 48T	CUT	SA/CR	FBG	KL	IB	110D	YAN	14	3	44000	6	6	189000	208000
47	10	HANS-CHRISTIAN 48T	KTH	SA/CR	FBG	KL	IB	110D	YAN	14	3	44000	6	6	189000	208000
		1985 BOATS														
32	9	HANSA 33	CUT	SA/CR	FBG	KL	IB	37D		11	6	17900	5	6	68500	75200
37	9	HANS-CHRISTIAN MKII	CUT	SA/CR	FBG	KL	IB	D		12	6	27500	6		98700	108500
38		HANS-CHRISTIAN 38T	CUT	SA/CR	FBG	KL	IB	D		12	4	26500	6		96100	105500
38	6	HANS-CHRISTIAN 39PH	CUT	SA/CR	FBG	KL	IB	D		12	6	28000	6		116000	127500
40	10	HANS-CHRISTIAN 41T	CUT	SA/CR	FBG	KL	IB	D		13	3	35000	5	5	122000	134000
42	7	HANS-CHRISTIAN 43T	CUT	SA/CR	FBG	KL	IB	D		13		31500	6		120000	132000
42	7	HANS-CHRISTIAN 43T	KTH	SA/CR	FBG	KL	IB	D		13		31500	6		120000	132000
45	7	HANS-CHRISTIAN 46	FB	MY	FBG	DV	IB	T355D		15			4	2	203500	223500
47	10	HANS-CHRISTIAN 48T	CUT	SA/CR	FBG	KL	IB	110D	YAN	14	3	44000	6	6	170500	187500
47	10	HANS-CHRISTIAN 48T	KTH	SA/CR	FBG	KL	IB	110D	YAN	14	3	44000	6	6	170500	187500
		1984 BOATS														
32	9	HANS-CHRISTIAN 33	CUT	SA/CR	FBG	KL	IB	D		11	6	18000	5	6	65200	71700
32	9	HANSA 33	CUT	SA/CR	FBG	KL	IB	D		11	6	17900	5	6	64900	71300
37	9	HANS-CHRISTIAN MK II	CUT	SA/CR	FBG	KL	IB	D		12	6	27500	6		93500	102500
37	9	HANS-CHRISTIAN MKII	CUT	SA/CR	FBG	KL	IB	D		12	6	27500	6		93500	102500
38		HANS-CHRISTIAN 38T	CUT	SA/CR	FBG	KL	IB	D		12	4	26500	6		91100	100000
38	6	HANS-CHRISTIAN 39PH	CUT	SA/CR	FBG	KL	IB	D		12	6	28000	6		110000	121000
42	7	HANS-CHRISTIAN 43T	CUT	SA/CR	FBG	KL	IB	D		13		31500	6		113500	125000
42	7	HANS-CHRISTIAN 43T	KTH	SA/CR	FBG	KL	IB	D		13		31500	6		114000	125000
43	9	HANSA 44 PH	KTH	SA/CR	FBG	KL	IB	D		14	7	44000	5	8	163000	179000
47	10	HANS-CHRISTIAN 48T	CUT	SA/CR	FBG	KL	IB	110D	YAN	14	3	44000	6	6	162000	178000
47	10	HANS-CHRISTIAN 48T	KTH	SA/CR	FBG	KL	IB	110D	YAN	14	3	44000	6	6	162000	178000

....For earlier years, see the BUC Used Boat Price Guide, Volume 3

CHUNG HWA BOAT BLDG CO

TAIPEITER TAIWAN   COAST GUARD MFG ID- CHB See inside cover to adjust price for area

```
LOA  NAME AND/          TOP/ BOAT  -HULL- ----ENGINE---  BEAM   WGT  DRAFT  RETAIL RETAIL
FT IN  OR MODEL         RIG TYPE   MTL TP TP # HP  MFG    FT IN  LBS  FT IN   LOW   HIGH
-------------------- 1985 BOATS ------------------------------------------------------------
33  6 CHB 34 DC           FB  TRWL  FBG DS IB 120D-135D 11  9 17500  3  6  58600  64600
37  3 CHB 38 DC           FB  TRWL  FBG SV IB 120D LEHM 13  2 21000  3  9  73300  80600
   IB 135D LEHM 73300  80600, IB T120D LEHM 77100 84800, IB T135D LEHM  77600  85300

37  3 CHB 38 S            FB  TRWL  FBG SV IB 120D LEHM 13  2 21000  3  9  73300  80600
   IB 135D LEHM 73300  80600, IB T120D LEHM 77100 84800, IB T135D LEHM  77600  85300
-------------------- 1984 BOATS ------------------------------------------------------------
33  6 CHB 34 DC           FB  TRWL  FBG DS IB 120D-135D 11  9 17500  3  6  56300  62000
37  3 CHB 38 DC           FB  TRWL  FBG SV IB 120D LEHM 13  2 21000  3  9  70300  77200
   IB 135D LEHM 70300  77200, IB T120D LEHM 73900 81200, IB T135D LEHM  74400  81700

37  3 CHB 38 S            FB  TRWL  FBG SV IB 120D LEHM 13  2 21000  3  9  70300  77200
   IB 135D LEHM 70300  77200, IB T120D LEHM 73900 81200, IB T135D LEHM  74400  81700

44  6 CHB 45 SDN          FB  TRWL  FBG SV IB T120D LEHM 14 10 29000  4     102000 112000
   IB T200D PERK 106500 117000, IB T210D CAT 110000 120000, IB T270D CUM  113000 124000

44 10 CHB 45 DC           FB  TRWL  FBG SV IB T135D LEHM 15    27000  4  2  98700 108500
44 10 CHB 45 DC           FB  TRWL  FBG SV IB T210D CAT  15    28500  4  2 105500 116000
44 10 CHB 45 DC           FB  TRWL  FBG SV IB T270D CUM  15    30000  4  2 110000 121000
44 10 CHB 45 PH           FB  TRWL  FBG SV IB T135D LEHM 15 10 26500  4  2  97600 107500
44 10 CHB 45 PH           FB  TRWL  FBG SV IB T200D PERK 15 10 27000  4  2 102000 112000
44 10 CHB 45 PH           FB  TRWL  FBG SV IB T210D CAT  15 10 26500  4  2 101000 111000
```

....For earlier years, see the BUC Used Boat Price Guide, Volume 3

CIGARETTE RACING TEAM LTD

OPA LOCA FL 33054   COAST GUARD MFG ID- CRT See inside cover to adjust price for area

For more recent years, see the BUC Used Boat Price Guide, Volume 1

```
LOA  NAME AND/          TOP/ BOAT  -HULL- ----ENGINE---  BEAM   WGT  DRAFT  RETAIL RETAIL
FT IN  OR MODEL         RIG TYPE   MTL TP TP # HP  MFG    FT IN  LBS  FT IN   LOW   HIGH
-------------------- 1996 BOATS ------------------------------------------------------------
20   CIGARETTE 20         OP  RACE  FBG DV IO T260  MRCR  7  2 4500  2  8  23700  26400
20   CIGARETTE 20         OP  RACE  FBG DV IO T350  MRCR  7  2 4500  2  8  30400  33800
20   CIGARETTE 20         OP  RACE  FBG DV IO T385-T410 7 2 4500  2  8  34900  43100
31   BULLET 31            OP  RACE  FBG DV IO T300-T450 8 6 8700  2  3  60500  74800
31   BULLET 31            OP  RACE  FBG DV IO T500  MRCR  8  6 8700  2  3  71000  78000
31   BULLET 31 SUPER      OP  RACE  FBG DV IO T490-T600 8 6 8700  2  3  70400  84400
35   CAFE RACER 35        OP  RACE  FBG DV IO T300  MRCR  8    9400  2  3  87500  96200
   IO T415  MRCR  90100  99000, IO T450  MRCR 93900 103000, IO T500  MRCR 100000 110000
   IO T750  HAWK 136500 150500

35   CAFE RACER 35 SUPER  OP  RACE  FBG DV IO T490  MRCR  8    9400  2  3  98900 108500
35   CAFE RACER 35 SUPER  OP  RACE  FBG DV IO T600  HAWK  8    9400  2  3 115000 126500
37  6 TOP GUN 38          OP  RACE  FBG DV IO T415  MRCR  8    9900  2  3  87300  95900
   IO T450  MRCR  91000 100000, IO T500  MRCR 97000 106500, IO T750  HAWK 122000 134000
   IO T800  HAWK    **       **

37  6 TOP GUN 38 SUPER    OP  RACE  FBG DV IO T490  MRCR  8    9900  2  3  95700 105000
37  6 TOP GUN 38 SUPER    OP  RACE  FBG DV IO T600  HAWK  8    9900  2  3 110000 121000
37  6 TOP GUN STAGGERED   OP  RACE  FBG DV IO T750  HAWK  8    9900  2  3 135500 149000
37  6 TOP GUN STAGGERED   OP  RACE  FBG DV IO T800  HAWK  8    9900  2  3    **     **
37  6 TOP GUN STAGGERED   OP  RACE  FBG DV IO T10C  HAWK  8    9900  2  3    **     **
41  7 REVOLUTION 188      OP  RACE  FBG DV IO T500  MRCR  8   11200  2  3 125000 137500
   IO T750  HAWK 155500 171000, IO T800  HAWK   **      **, IO T10C  HAWK    **     **
   IO R465  MRCR 141000 155500, IO R470  MRCR 142500 156500, IO R500  MRCR 150000 165000
   IO R750  HAWK 184000 202500, IO R800  HAWK   **      **, IO R10C  HAWK    **     **

41  7 REVOLUTION 188 SUPER OP RACE  FBG DV IO T490  MRCR  8   11200  2  3 111500 122500
   IO T600  HAWK 123500 136000, IO T900  HAWK   **      **, IO R490  MRCR 133000 146000
   IO R600  HAWK 155500 170500, IO R900  HAWK   **      **

45  7 CIGARETTE 46        OP  RACE  FBG DV IO T750  HAWK  8   15100  3  8 157500 173000
   IO T800  HAWK    **       **, IO T900  HAWK   **      **, IO T10C  HAWK    **     **
   IO R490  MRCR 146500 160500, IO R500  MRCR 148000 162500, IO R600  HAWK 166500 183000
   IO R750  HAWK 195000 214000, IO R800  HAWK   **      **, IO R900  HAWK    **     **
   IO R10C  HAWK    **       **
-------------------- 1995 BOATS ------------------------------------------------------------
20   CIGARETTE 20         OP  RACE  FBG DV IO T260  MRCR  7  2 4500  2  8  22200  24600
20   CIGARETTE 20         OP  RACE  FBG DV IO T350  MRCR  7  2 4500  2  8  28400  31500
20   CIGARETTE 20         OP  RACE  FBG DV IO T385-T410 7 2 4500  2  8  32600  40200
31   BULLET 31            OP  RACE  FBG DV IO T300-T450 8 6 8700  2  3  56500  69800
31   BULLET 31            OP  RACE  FBG DV IO T500  MRCR  8  6 8700  2  3  62700  72700
31   BULLET 31 SUPER      OP  RACE  FBG DV IO T490-T600 8 6 8700  2  3  65700  78700
35   CAFE RACER 35        OP  RACE  FBG DV IO T300  MRCR  8    9400  2  3  81700  89700
   IO T415  MRCR  84100  92400, IO T450  MRCR 87600 96300, IO T500  MRCR 93500 102500
   IO T750  HAWK 127500 140000

35   CAFE RACER 35 SUPER  OP  RACE  FBG DV IO T490  MRCR  8    9400  2  3  92200 101500
35   CAFE RACER 35 SUPER  OP  RACE  FBG DV IO T600  HAWK  8    9400  2  3 107500 118000
37  6 TOP GUN 38          OP  RACE  FBG DV IO T415  MRCR  8    9900  2  3  81400  89500
   IO T450  MRCR  84900  93300, IO T500  MRCR 90400 99400, IO T750  HAWK 113500 125000
   IO T800  HAWK    **       **

37  6 TOP GUN 38 SUPER    OP  RACE  FBG DV IO T490  MRCR  8    9900  2  3  89300  98100
37  6 TOP GUN 38 SUPER    OP  RACE  FBG DV IO T600  HAWK  8    9900  2  3 102500 113000
37  6 TOP GUN STAGGERED   OP  RACE  FBG DV IO T750  HAWK  8    9900  2  3 126500 139000
37  6 TOP GUN STAGGERED   OP  RACE  FBG DV IO T800  HAWK  8    9900  2  3    **     **
37  6 TOP GUN STAGGERED   OP  RACE  FBG DV IO T10C  HAWK  8    9900  2  3    **     **
41  7 REVOLUTION 188      OP  RACE  FBG DV IO T500  MRCR  8   11200  2  3 116500 128000
   IO T750  HAWK 145000 159500, IO T800  HAWK   **      **, IO T10C  HAWK    **     **
   IO R465  MRCR 131500 144500, IO R470  MRCR 133000 146000, IO R500  MRCR 140000 154000
   IO R750  HAWK 172000 189000, IO R800  HAWK   **      **, IO R10C  HAWK    **     **

41  7 REVOLUTION 188 SUPER OP RACE  FBG DV IO T490  MRCR  8   11200  2  3 104000 114500
   IO T600  HAWK 115500 127000, IO T900  HAWK   **      **, IO R490  MRCR 124000 136500
   IO R600  HAWK 145000 159000, IO R900  HAWK   **      **

45  7 CIGARETTE 46        OP  RACE  FBG DV IO T750  HAWK  8   15100  3  8 147000 161500
   IO T800  HAWK    **       **, IO T900  HAWK   **      **, IO T10C  HAWK    **     **
   IO R490  MRCR 136500 150000, IO R500  MRCR 138000 151500, IO R600  HAWK 155500 170500
   IO R750  HAWK 182000 200000, IO R800  HAWK   **      **, IO R900  HAWK    **     **
   IO R10C  HAWK    **       **
-------------------- 1994 BOATS ------------------------------------------------------------
31   BULLET 31            OP  RACE  FBG DV IO T360-T500 8 6 8700  2  3  55100  67900
31   BULLET 31            OP  RACE  FBG DV IO T525  MRCR  8  6 8700  2  3  70800  77800
31   BULLET 31 SUPER      OP  RACE  FBG DV IO T475-T490 8 6 8700  2  3  60500  66500
35   CAFE RACER 35        OP  RACE  FBG DV IO T360  MRCR  8    9400  2  3  67100  81500
   IO T385  MRCR  76000  83500, IO T410  MRCR 78000 88800, IO T500  MRCR  87200  95900
   IO T525  HAWK  99600 109500, IO T750  HAWK 119000 131000, IO T230D VLVO 79900  87800

35   CAFE RACER 35 SUPER  OP  RACE  FBG DV IO T490  MRCR  8    9400  2  3  78500  86300
35   CAFE RACER 35 SUPER  OP  RACE  FBG DV IO T525  HAWK  8    9400  2  3  81000  89000
37  6 TOP GUN 38          OP  RACE  FBG DV IO T410  MRCR  8    9900  2  3  75600  83000
   IO T465  MRCR  80800  88800, IO T500  MRCR 84400 92800, IO T525  HAWK  84400  92700
   IO T750  HAWK 105500 115500, IO T800  HAWK   **      **, IO T230D VLVO 82500  90600

37  6 TOP GUN 38 SUPER    OP  RACE  FBG DV IO T490  MRCR  8    9900  2  3  68400  75200
37  6 TOP GUN 38 SUPER    OP  RACE  FBG DV IO T525  HAWK  8    9900  2  3  69200  76100
37  6 TOP GUN STAGGERED   OP  RACE  FBG DV IO T525  HAWK  8    9900  2  3 108000 118500
   IO T750  HAWK 119000 130500, IO T800  HAWK   **      **, IO T10C  HAWK    **     **
41  7 REVOLUTION 188      OP  RACE  FBG DV IO T465  MRCR  8   11200  2  3 105000 115500
   IO T490  MRCR 108000 118500, IO T500  MRCR 109000 119500, IO T525  HAWK 111500 122500
   IO T750  HAWK 135500 148500, IO T800  HAWK   **      **, IO T10C  HAWK    **     **
   IO T600D SETK 131500 144500, IO R410  MRCR 111500 122500, IO R465  MRCR 123000 135000
   IO R490  MRCR 128500 141000, IO R500  MRCR 130500 143500, IO R750  HAWK 136000 149500
   IO R230D VLVO 118000 130000

45  7 CIGARETTE 46        OP  RACE  FBG DV IO T750  HAWK  8   15100  3  8 137500 151000
   IO T800  HAWK    **       **, IO T10C  HAWK   **      **, IO T600D SETK 147000 161500
   IO R465  MRCR 123500 136000, IO R490  MRCR 127500 140000, IO R500  MRCR 129000 141500
   IO R525  HAWK 133000 146000, IO R750  HAWK 170000 186500, IO R800  HAWK 141500 152000
   IO R10C  HAWK    **       **
-------------------- 1993 BOATS ------------------------------------------------------------
31   BULLET 31            OP  RACE  FBG DV IO T360-T500 8 6 8700  2  3  51500  63500
31   BULLET 31            OP  RACE  FBG DV IO T525  HAWK  8  6 8700  2  3  61400  67400
31   BULLET 31 SUPER      OP  RACE  FBG DV IO T475-T525 8 6 8700  2  3  56600  62200
35   CAFE RACER 35        OP  RACE  FBG DV IO T360  MRCR  8    9400  2  3  69300  76100
   IO T385  MRCR  70800  78000, IO T400  MRCR 72100 79300, IO T410  MRCR  72900  80100
   IO T500  MRCR  81500  89600, IO T525  HAWK 87700 96300, IO T750  HAWK 111500 122500
   IO T230D VLVO  74600  82000

35   CAFE RACER 35 SUPER  OP  RACE  FBG DV IO T490  MRCR  8    9400  2  3  77900  85600
35   CAFE RACER 35 SUPER  OP  RACE  FBG DV IO T525  HAWK  8    9400  2  3  81100  89100
35   CAFE RACER 35 SUPER  OP  RACE  FBG DV IO T600  HAWK  8    9400  2  3  93700 103000
```

```
 LOA  NAME AND/          TOP/ BOAT  -HULL- ----ENGINE---  BEAM  WGT  DRAFT RETAIL RETAIL
FT IN  OR MODEL          RIG  TYPE  MTL TP TP # HP  MFG   FT IN LBS  FT IN  LOW    HIGH
-------------------- 1993 BOATS ------------------------------------------------------
37  6 TOP GUN 38             OP  RACE  FBG DV IO  T410  MRCR  8  9900  2 3  70600  77600
      IO T425 MRCR 64000 70400, IO T465 MRCR 75500 83000, IO T500 MRCR 78900 86700
      IO T525 HAWK 78300 86000, IO T750 HAWK 99400 109500, IO T800 HAWK  **  **
      IO T230D VLVO 77100 84700

37  6 TOP GUN 38 SUPER       OP  RACE  FBG DV IO  T490  MRCR  8  9900  2 3  71000  78000
37  6 TOP GUN 38 SUPER       OP  RACE  FBG DV IO  T525  HAWK  8  9900  2 3  72700  79900
37  6 TOP GUN 38 SUPER       OP  RACE  FBG DV IO  T600  HAWK  8  9900  2 3  89500  98400
37  6 TOP GUN STAGGERED      OP  RACE  FBG DV IO  T425  MRCR  8  9900  2 3  79700  87600
      IO T525 HAWK 93500 102500, IO T750 HAWK 110000 121000, IO T800 HAWK  **  **

41  7 REVOLUTION 188         OP  RACE  FBG DV IO  T425  MRCR  8  11200 2 3  94400  103500
      IO T445 MRCR 96300 106000, IO T500 MRCR 102000 112000, IO T525 HAWK 104500 114500
      IO T750 HAWK 126500 139000, IO T800 HAWK  **  **, IO T10C HAWK  **  **
      IO T600D SETK 122500 135000, IO R360 HAWK 96500 106000, IO R410 MRCR 104500 114500
      IO R425 MRCR 107000 117500, IO R465 MRCR 115000 126500, IO R490 MRCR 120000 132000
      IO R500 MRCR 122000 134500, IO R525 HAWK 127500 140000, IO R750 HAWK 150000 164500
      IO R800 HAWK  **  **, IO R10C HAWK  **  **, IO R230D VLVO 110500 121500

45  7 CIGARETTE 46           OP  RACE  FBG DV IO  T750  HAWK  8  15100 3 8  128500 141000
      IO T800 HAWK  **  **, IO T10C HAWK  **  **, IO T600D SETK 137000 150500
      IO R465 MRCR 115500 127000, IO R490 MRCR 119000 131000, IO R500 MRCR 120500 132500
      IO R525 HAWK 124000 136500, IO R750 HAWK 158500 174500, IO R800 HAWK  **  **
      IO R10C HAWK  **  **
-------------------- 1992 BOATS ------------------------------------------------------
31    BULLET CUSTOM          OP  RACE  FBG DV IO  T360-T445 8 6 8700  2 3  48200  56800
31    BULLET CUSTOM          OP  RACE  FBG DV IO  T525  HAWK  8 6 8700  2 3  55200  60600
31    BULLET PLATINUM        OP  RACE  C/S DV IO  T465-T525 8 6 8700  2 3  52500  60600
35    CAFE RACER             OP  RACE  C/S DV IO  T600  HAWK  8  9400  2 3  87700  96400
35    CAFE RACER             OP  RACE  FBG DV IO  T900  HAWK  8  9400  2 3   **     **
35    CAFE RACER CUSTOM      OP  RACE  FBG DV IO  T360  MRCR  8  9400  2 3  64900  71300
      IO T385 MRCR 66500 73000, IO T400 MRCR 67500 74200, IO T410 MRCR 68300 75000
      IO T525 HAWK 79000 86800, IO T750 HAWK 104000 114500, IO T800 HAWK  **  **
      IO T10C HAWK  **  **

35    CAFE RACER PLATINUM    OP  RACE  C/S DV IO  T465  HAWK  8  9400  2 3  72900  80100
35    CAFE RACER PLATINUM    OP  RACE  C/S DV IO  T525  HAWK  8  9400  2 3  79000  86800
37  6 TOP GUN                OP  RACE  C/S DV IO  T600  HAWK  8  9900  2 3  83800  92100
37  6 TOP GUN STAGGERED      OP  RACE  FBG DV IO  T525  HAWK  8  9900  2 3  87300  95900
37  6 TOP GUN STAGGERED      OP  RACE  FBG DV IO  T800  HAWK  8  9900  2 3   **     **
37  6 TOPGUN CUSTOM          OP  RACE  FBG DV IO  T410  MRCR  8  9900  2 3  66100  72700
      IO T425 MRCR 67300 73900, IO T465 MRCR 70700 77700, IO T525 HAWK 72900 80100
      IO T750 HAWK 98100 108000, IO T800 HAWK  **  **, IO T900 HAWK  **  **
      IO T10C HAWK  **  **

37  6 TOPGUN PLATINUM        OP  RACE  FBG DV IO  T525  HAWK  8  9900  2 3  68700  75400
41  7 REVOLUTION 188         OP  RACE  FBG DV IO  T425  MRCR  8  11200 2 3  88400  97100
      IO T445 MRCR 90200 99100, IO T525 HAWK 97600 107500, IO T750 HAWK 118000 130000
      IO T800 HAWK  **  **, IO T900 HAWK  **  **, IO T10C HAWK  **  **
      IO R360 MRCR 90300 99200, IO R410 MRCR 97600 107500, IO R425 MRCR 100000 110000
      IO R465 MRCR 107500 118000, IO R525 HAWK 119000 131000, IO R750 HAWK 140500 154000
      IO R800 HAWK  **  **
-------------------- 1991 BOATS ------------------------------------------------------
31    BULLET CUSTOM          OP  RACE  FBG DV IO  T     HAWK  8 6 8700  2 3  40600  50200
31    BULLET CUSTOM          OP  RACE  FBG DV IO  T360-T385 8 6 8700  2 3  46600  52500
31    BULLET CUSTOM          OP  RACE  FBG DV IO  T410-T445 8 6 8700  2 3  42100  52600
31    BULLET GTI             OP  RACE  FBG DV IO  T360-T410 8 6 8700  2 3  49100  54000
31    BULLET GTI             OP  RACE  FBG DV IO  T445  MRCR  8 6 8700  2 3   **     **
31    BULLET PLATINUM        OP  RACE  FBG DV IO  T     HAWK  8 6 8700  2 3  52500  57700
31    BULLET PLATINUM        OP  RACE  FBG DV IO  T360  HAWK  8 6 8700  2 3   **     **
35    CAFE RACER CUSTOM      OP  RACE  FBG DV IO  T     HAWK  8  9400  2 3   **     **
      IO T360 MRCR 59900 65900, IO T385 MRCR 62400 68500, IO T400 MRCR 63300 69600
      IO T410 MRCR 63100 69400

35    CAFE RACER GTI         OP  RACE  FBG DV IO  T     HAWK  8  9400  2 3   **     **
      IO T360 MRCR 61800 67900, IO T385 MRCR 62400 68500, IO T410 MRCR 64900 71400
      IO T445 MRCR 66700 73300

35    CAFE RACER PLATINUM    OP  RACE  FBG DV IO  T     HAWK  8  9400  2 3   **     **
37  6 TOPGUN CUSTOM          OP  RACE  FBG DV IO  T     HAWK  8  9900  2 3  63900  70200
      IO T400 MRCR 60500 66500, IO T410 MRCR 61200 67200, IO T445 MRCR  **  **

37  6 TOPGUN GTI             OP  RACE  FBG DV IO  T     HAWK  8  9900  2 3  65400  71900
      IO T400 MRCR 62100 68300, IO T410 MRCR 62900 69100, IO T445 MRCR  **  **

37  6 TOPGUN PLATINUM        OP  RACE  FBG DV IO  T     HAWK  8  9900  2 3   **     **
41  7 REVOLUTION 188         OP  RACE  FBG DV IO  T     HAWK  8  11200 2 3   **     **
      IO T400 MRCR 80900 88900, IO T445 MRCR 84600 92900, IO R HAWK  **  **
      IO R360 MRCR 93100, IO R385 MRCR 87900 96600, IO R410 MRCR 91600 100500
      IO R445 MRCR 97400 107000
-------------------- 1990 BOATS ------------------------------------------------------
31    BULLET                 OP  RACE  FBG DV IO  T330-T410 8 6 8000  1 6  40800  48300
31    BULLET                 OP  RACE  FBG DV IO  T525    8 6 8000  1 6  48200  52900
35    CIGARETTE CAFE RACER   OP  RACE  FBG DV IO  T365  MRCR  8  9000  1 6  57700  63400
      IO T410 MRCR 60600 66600, IO T425 MRCR 61700 67800, IO T525 71000 78000
      IO T540 72600 79700, IO T572 76100 83700

37  6 CIGARETTE TOP GUN      OP  RACE  FBG DV IO  T425  MRCR  8  9800  1 6  59400  65300
      IO T500 65300 71800, IO T540 68800 75600, IO T572 71700 78800
-------------------- 1989 BOATS ------------------------------------------------------
24  4 CIGARETTE FIREFOX 24   OP  RACE  FBG DV IO  365-420   7 5 4800  1 5  19900  24800
24  4 CIGARETTE FIREFOX 24   OP  RACE  FBG DV IO  500   HAWK  7 5 4800  1 5  26400  29300
31    BULLET                 OP  RACE  FBG DV IO  T330-T420 8 6 8000  1 6  38400  45900
31    BULLET                 OP  RACE  FBG DV IO  T500    8 6 8000  1 6  44300  49200
35    CIGARETTE CAFE RACER   OP  RACE  FBG DV IO  T330  MRCR  8  9000  1 6  52600  57800
      IO T365 MRCR 54400 59800, IO T420 MRCR 57900 63600, IO T500 64500 70900
      IO T540 68500 75200, IO T572 71800 78900

37  6 CIGARETTE TOP GUN      OP  RACE  FBG DV IO  T420  MRCR  8  9800  1 6  55700  61200
      IO T500 61600 67700, IO T540 64900 71300, IO T572 67600 74300

41  3 CIGARETTE 41           OP  RACE  FBG DV IO  T   D CAT  9 9 15000 3 9   **     **
-------------------- 1988 BOATS ------------------------------------------------------
21    CIGARETTE 21           OP  RACE  FBG DV OB           7   3300  2 3  23800  26400
24  4 CIGARETTE FIREFOX 24   OP  RACE  FBG DV IO      MRCR  7   4800  1 5   **     **
24  4 CIGARETTE FIREFOX 24   OP  RACE  FBG DV IO  420   MRCR  7 5 4800  1 5  21100  23400
24  4 CIGARETTE FIREFOX 24   OP  RACE  FBG DV IO  500-511 7 5 4800  1 5  25000  28300
31    BULLET                 OP  RACE  FBG DV IO  T     MRCR  8   8000  1 6   **     **
31    BULLET                 OP  RACE  FBG DV IO  T320-T420 8   8000  1 6  36100  43500
31    BULLET                 OP  RACE  FBG DV IO  T500    8   8000  1 6  41900  46600
35    DECATHLON              OP  OPFSH FBG DV OB           8   6150  2 1  68200  75000
35    CAFE RACER SE          OP  RACE  FBG DV IO  T511    8   9000  1 6  62100  68200
35    CAFE RACER SE          OP  RACE  FBG DV IO  T540    8   9000  1 6  64800  71200
35    CAFE RACER SE          OP  RACE  FBG DV IO  T572    8   9000  1 6  68000  74700
35    CIGARETTE CAFE RACER   OP  RACE  FBG DV IO  T     MRCR  8   9000  1 6   **     **
35    CIGARETTE CAFE RACER   OP  RACE  FBG DV IO  T420  MRCR  8   9000  1 6  54800  60200
35    CIGARETTE CAFE RACER   OP  RACE  FBG DV IO  T500    8   9000  1 6  61100  67100
37  6 CIGARETTE SE TOP GUN   OP  RACE  FBG DV IO  T511    8   9800  1 6  59200  65000
37  6 CIGARETTE SE TOP GUN   OP  RACE  FBG DV IO  T540    8   9800  1 6  61400  67500
37  6 CIGARETTE SE TOP GUN   OP  RACE  FBG DV IO  T572    8   9800  1 6  64000  70400
37  6 CIGARETTE TOP GUN      OP  RACE  FBG DV IO  T420  MRCR  8   9800  1 6  52700  58000
37  6 CIGARETTE TOP GUN      OP  RACE  FBG DV IO  T500    8   9800  1 6  58300  64100
41  3 CIGARETTE 41           OP  RACE  FBG DV IO  T   D CAT  9 9 15000 3 9   **     **
-------------------- 1987 BOATS ------------------------------------------------------
19  7 CIGARETTE 20           OP  RACE  FBG DV IO      MRCR  7 2 2450  1 5   **     **
21  7 CIGARETTE 20           OP  RACE  FBG DV OB           7 2 2450  1 5  7600   8750
21  7 CIGARETTE 21           OP  RACE  FBG DV IO  260   MRCR  7 3 3300  2 3  23100  25600
24  3 CIGARETTE FIREFOX 24   OP  RACE  FBG DV IO  370-420 7 4 3850  1 5  18200  22300
24  3 CIGARETTE FIREFOX 24   OP  RACE  FBG DV IO  500-511 7 4 3850  1 5  23700  26900
27 10 CIGARETTE 28           OP  RACE  FBG DV IO      MRCR  7   7000  1 6   **     **
27 10 CIGARETTE 28           OP  RACE  FBG DV IO  T260  MRCR  7   7000  1 6  26700  29600
27 10 DECATHLON              OP  OPFSH FBG DV OB           8 6 5150  2 2  66000  72500
35    CIGARETTE 35L          OP  RACE  FBG DV IO  T330    8   8000  1 6  47800  52600
35    CIGARETTE 35S          OP  RACE  FBG DV IO  T420    8   8000  1 6  52700  58000
35    CIGARETTE CAFE RACER   OP  RACE  FBG DV IO  T330    8   8500  1 6  47800  52600
35    CIGARETTE CAFE RACER   OP  RACE  FBG DV IO  T420    8   8500  1 6  52700  58000
35    CIGARETTE CAFE RACER   OP  RACE  FBG DV IO  T500    8   8500  1 6  59500  65400
37  6 CIGARETTE 38           OP  RACE  FBG DV IO  T420    8   9500  1 6  50200  55200
37  6 CIGARETTE 38           OP  RACE  FBG DV IO  T500    8   9500  1 6  55800  61300
37  6 CIGARETTE 38SE         OP  RACE  FBG DV IO  T511    8   9500  1 6  56600  62300
37  6 CIGARETTE 38SE         OP  RACE  FBG DV IO  T540    8   9500  1 6  58900  64800
41  2 CIGARETTE 41           OP  RACE  FBG DV IO  T   D CAT  9 9 15000 3 9   **     **
-------------------- 1986 BOATS ------------------------------------------------------
19  7 CIGARETTE 20           OP  RACE  FBG DV IO  260-300 7 2 2450  1 5  7250   9050
24    CIGARETTE SPORT        OP  RNBT  FBG DV IO  330     7 10 3850 1 5  13600  15400
24  3 CIGARETTE FIREFOX 24   OP  RACE  FBG DV IO  370-400 7 4 3850  1 5  14800  18000
24  3 CIGARETTE FIREFOX 24   OP  RACE  FBG DV IO  460-511 7 4 3850  1 5  18900  23200
27 10 CIGARETTE 28           OP  RACE  FBG DV IO  T260-T330 8  7000  1 6  25500  30600
35    CIGARETTE 35L          OP  RACE  FBG DV IO  T330  MRCR  8   8000  1 6  45900  50400
35    CIGARETTE 35S          OP  RACE  FBG DV IO  T400  MRCR  8   8500  1 6  49100  53900
```

CIGARETTE RACING TEAM LTD — CONTINUED

See inside cover to adjust price for area

LOA FT IN	NAME AND/OR MODEL	TOP/RIG	BOAT TYPE	-HULL- MTL TP TP	----ENGINE--- # HP MFG	BEAM FT IN	WGT LBS	DRAFT FT IN	RETAIL LOW	RETAIL HIGH
				1986 BOATS						
35	CIGARETTE CAFE RACER	OP	RACE	FBG DV IO	T330 MRCR	8	8500	1 6	45600	50100
35	CIGARETTE CAFE RACER	OP	RACE	FBG DV IO	T400 MRCR	8	8500	1 6	49100	53900
35	CIGARETTE CAFE RACER	OP	RACE	FBG DV IO	T500 MRCR	8	8500	1 6	56800	62500
36	CIGARETTE 36S		RNBT	FBG DV IO	T400	9	9500		40800	45400
36 6	CIGARETTE 36TD		RNBT	FBG DV IO	T300D	9	10500		43800	48700
37 6	CIGARETTE 38	OP	RACE	FBG DV IO	T400 MRCR	8	9500	1 6	47100	51700
37 6	CIGARETTE 38	OP	RACE	FBG DV IO	T500 MRCR	8	9500	1 6	53300	58600
37 6	CIGARETTE 38SE	OP	RACE	FBG DV IO	T511 MRCR	8	9500	1 6	54100	59500
37 6	CIGARETTE 38SE	OP	RACE	FBG DV IO	T540 MRCR	8	9500	1 6	56300	61900
38	CIGARETTE 38L		RNBT	FBG DV IO	T400	8	9500		55500	61000
38	CIGARETTE 38S		RNBT	FBG DV IO	T640	8	9500		72700	79900
38	CIGARETTE 38SE		RNBT	KEV DV IO	T530	8	9500		66200	72700
38	CIGARETTE 38SEL		RNBT	KEV DV IO	T580	8	9500		69600	76500
41 2	CIGARETTE 41	OP	RACE	FBG DV IO	T D CAT	9 9	15000	3 9	**	**
				1985 BOATS						
19 7	SPORT 20	OP	RACE	FBG DV IO	195-260	7 2	2450	1 5	7000	8050
19 7	SPORT 20	OP	RACE	FBG DV IO	300 MRCR	7 2	2500	1 5	7600	8750
24	SPORT 24	OP	RACE	FBG DV IO	400 MRCR	7 10	3850	1 5	15300	17400
26	SPORT 36	OP	RACE	FBG DV IO	T400 MRCR	9 3	9500	1 6	33700	37400
28	SPORT 28	OP	RACE	FBG DV IO	T260-T300	7 10	5000	1 6	17000	20500
35	LTD 35	OP	RACE	FBG DV IO	T330 MRCR	8	8000	1 6	43600	48400
35	SPORT 35	OP	RACE	FBG DV IO	T400 MRCR	8	8500	1 6	47300	52000
35	SPORT EXP 35	OP	RACE	KEV DV IO	T500	8	8500	1 6	54500	59900
35	SPORT EXP 35	OP	RACE	FBG DV IO	T500	8	8500	1 6	54500	59900
36	36S	OP	RACE	FBG DV IO	T400	9	9500	1 6	36700	40800
36	TURBO DIESEL 36	OP	RACE	FBG DV IO	T300D SABR	9 3	10500	1 8	39300	43700
37 6	LTD 38	OP	RACE	FBG DV IO	T400 MRCR	8	9500	1 6	44700	49700
37 6	SPORT 38	OP	RACE	FBG DV IO	T460 MRCR	8	9500	1 6	48500	53200
37 6	SPORT 38	OP	RACE	FBG DV IO	T485 MRCR	8	9500	1 6	50100	55100
37 6	SPORT 38	OP	RACE	FBG DV IO	T500 MRCR	8	9500	1 6	51200	56200
37 6	SPORT EXP 38	OP	RACE	KEV DV IO	T530	8	9500	1 6	55300	58600
37 6	SPORT EXP 38	OP	RACE	FBG DV IO	T530 MRCR	8	9500	1 6	53300	58600
37 6	SPORT EXP LTD 38	OP	RACE	KEV DV IO	T580	8	9500	1 6	57000	62700
37 6	SPORT EXP LTD 38	OP	RACE	KEV DV IO	T580 MRCR	8	9500	1 6	57000	62700
41 2	SPORT 41	OP	RACE	FBG DV IB	T350D CAT	9 9	15000	3 9	136000	149500
				1984 BOATS						
35	35L	OP	RACE	FBG DV IO	T330 MRCR	8	8000	1 6	42000	46700
35	35S	OP	RACE	FBG DV IO	T400 MRCR	8	8500	1 6	45700	50200
36	36S	OP	RACE	FBG DV IO	T400 MRCR	9 3	9500	1 6	35200	39100
36 6	36TD	OP	RACE	FBG DV IO	T300 SABR	9 3	10500	1 8	34600	38400
37 6	38L	OP	RACE	FBG DV IO	T400 MRCR	8	9500	1 8	43100	47900
37 6	38S	OP	RACE	FBG DV IO	T460 MRCR	8	9500	1 8	47000	51700
37 6	38SE	OP	RACE	FBG DV IO	T530	8	8500	1 8	53700	59000
38	38S	OP	RACE	FBG DV IO	T485	8	9500	1 8	50600	55600
41 3	41	OP	RACE	FBG DV IB	T355D CAT	9 9	15000	3 9	133500	147000
43	43S	OP	RACE	KEV DV IB	T300D	11	16000	3 9	126500	139000

....For earlier years, see the BUC Used Boat Price Guide, Volume 3

CIMMARON INC

MEMPHIS TN 38127   COAST GUARD MFG ID- CIM   See inside cover to adjust price for area

LOA FT IN	NAME AND/OR MODEL	TOP/RIG	BOAT TYPE	-HULL- MTL TP TP	----ENGINE--- # HP MFG	BEAM FT IN	WGT LBS	DRAFT FT IN	RETAIL LOW	RETAIL HIGH
				1985 BOATS						
16	SJ16	OP	RNBT	FBG SV JT	BERK	6 7			**	**
16	SJ16	OP	RNBT	FBG SV IB	260 INDM	6 7	1700		3250	3800
18	SJ18	OP	RNBT	FBG SV JT	BERK	7 6			**	**
18	SJ18	OP	RNBT	FBG SV IB	INDM	7 6			**	**
18	SJ18	OP	RNBT	FBG SV IB	260 INDM	7 6			4400	5050
18	SS18	OP	RNBT	FBG SV JT	BERK	7 6			**	**
18	SS18	OP	RNBT	FBG SV IB	INDM	7 6			**	**
18	SS18	OP	RNBT	FBG SV IB	260 INDM	7 6			4550	5250

....For earlier years, see the BUC Used Boat Price Guide, Volume 3

CLASSIC BOAT WORKS INC

MYAKKA CITY FL 34251-80 COAST GUARD MFG ID- KLJ   See inside cover to adjust price for area

LOA FT IN	NAME AND/OR MODEL	TOP/RIG	BOAT TYPE	-HULL- MTL TP TP	----ENGINE--- # HP MFG	BEAM FT IN	WGT LBS	DRAFT FT IN	RETAIL LOW	RETAIL HIGH
				1994 BOATS						
17 1	STUMPJUMPER SEMI-VEE	OP	FSH	FBG SV OB		6	650	6	1750	2050
17 2	STUMPJUMPER GULLWING	OP	FSH	FBG TR OB		6 2	600	7	1600	1900
18 2	STUMPJUMPER V-HULL	OP	FSH	FBG SV OB		7	750	10	2050	2450
				1993 BOATS						
17 1	STUMPJUMPER SEMI-VEE	OP	FSH	FBG SV OB		6	650	6	1650	1950
17 2	STUMPJUMPER GULLWING	OP	FSH	FBG TR OB		6 2	600	7	1550	1850
18 2	STUMPJUMPER V-HULL	OP	FSH	FBG DV OB		7	750	10	1950	2350
				1986 BOATS						
17 2	WHITEHALL 17	OP	UTL	FBG RB OB		4 8	275		510	615
17 8	BAY-SKIFF	OP	UTL	FBG FL OB		6 5	675		1300	1550
19	SEA-SKIFF 20	OP	UTL	FBG RB OB		6 8	1150		2100	2500
				1984 BOATS						
17 2	WHITEHALL 17	OP	LNCH	FBG OB		4 5	325		**	**
17 2	WHITEHALL 17	OP	ROW	FBG OB		4 5	325		**	**
17 2	WHITEHALL 17	CAT	SAIL	FBG OB		4 5	325		1700	2000
17 2	WHITEHALL 17	KTH	SAIL	FBG OB		4 5	325		1650	2000
19	SKIFFIE	OP	LNCH	FBG DS OB		6 8	2000	2	**	**
19	SKIFFIE		SAIL	FBG CB OB		6 8	2000	2	4250	4950
19	SKIFFIE		SAIL	FBG CB IB	D	6 8	2000	2	6350	7300
20 4	DORY		SAIL	FBG OB		5 10	300		2200	2600
20 4	LIFEGUARD DORY		ROW	FBG FL OB		5 10	300		**	**

....For earlier years, see the BUC Used Boat Price Guide, Volume 3

CLASSIC ERA WATERCRAFT INC

FOREST CITY FL 32854   COAST GUARD MFG ID- CQA   See inside cover to adjust price for area

LOA FT IN	NAME AND/OR MODEL	TOP/RIG	BOAT TYPE	-HULL- MTL TP TP	----ENGINE--- # HP MFG	BEAM FT IN	WGT LBS	DRAFT FT IN	RETAIL LOW	RETAIL HIGH
				1990 BOATS						
18 2	SPORT-RIVIERA	OP	RNBT	F/S SV IB	MRCR	6 6	2400	1 10	**	**
18 2	SPORT-RIVIERA	OP	RNBT	F/S SV IB	220-260	6 6	2400	1 10	10000	11600
18 6	SPORTSMAN	OP	RNBT	F/S SV IB	MRCR	7 4	2800	1 8	**	**
18 6	SPORTSMAN	OP	RNBT	F/S SV IB	220-260	7 4	2800	1 8	11900	13700
19 8	SKI-ELITE	OP	RNBT	F/S SV IB	MRCR	7 4	2800	1 8	12600	14500
19 8	SKI-ELITE	OP	RNBT	F/S SV IB	220-260	7 4	2800	1 8	**	**
20 1	RIVIERA W/MODIFIED V	OP	RNBT	F/S SV IB	MRCR	6 6	2900	2 2	**	**
20 1	RIVIERA W/MODIFIED V	OP	RNBT	F/S SV IB	220-260	6 6	2900	2 2	13100	15100
				1989 BOATS						
18 2	SPORT-RIVIERA	OP	RNBT	F/S SV IB	220	6 6	2400	1 10	9600	10900
18 10	SKI-ELITE	OP	RNBT	F/S SV IB	350	7 4	2800	1 8	12500	14200
18 10	SPORTSMAN	OP	RNBT	F/S SV IB	260	7 4	2800	1 8	11700	13300
20 1	RIVIERA W/MODIFIED V	OP	RNBT	F/S SV IB	220	6 6	2900	2 2	12600	14300
				1988 BOATS						
18 2	SPORT-RIVIERA	OP	RNBT	F/S SV IB	220	6 6	2250	1 7	8850	10100
18 10	COMMUTER	OP	RNBT	F/S SV IB	260	7 4	2280		9950	11300
18 10	SKI-ELITE	OP	RNBT	F/S SV IB	260-350	7 4	2200	1 8	9800	12000
18 10	SPORTSMAN	OP	RNBT	F/S SV IB	260	7 4	2280		9950	11300
20 1	RIVIERA	OP	RNBT	F/S SV IB	220	6 6	2650	1 10	11300	12800
20 1	RIVIERA W/MODIFIED V	OP	RNBT	F/S SV IB	220	6 6	2750	1 10	11600	13100
				1987 BOATS						
18 2	SPORT-RIVIERA	OP	RNBT	F/S SV IB	280	6 6	2250	1 7	8550	9850
18 10	COMMUTER	OP	RNBT	F/S SV IB	220	7 4	2280		9400	10700
18 10	SKI-ELITE	OP	RNBT	F/S SV IB	280-350	7 4	2200	1 8	9450	11500
20 1	RIVIERA	OP	RNBT	F/S SV IB	220	6 6	2650	1 10	10800	12200
20 1	RIVIERA W/MODIFIED V	OP	RNBT	F/S SV IB	220	6 6	2650	1 10	10800	12200
				1986 BOATS						
18 2	SPORT-RIVIERA	OP	RNBT	F/S SV IB	280	6 6	2250	1	8200	9400
18 10	SKI-ELITE	OP	RNBT	F/S SV IB	280-350	7 4	2200	1 8	9050	11000
20 1	RIVIERA	OP	RNBT	F/S SV IB	220-260	6 6	2650	1 10	10300	11900
				1985 BOATS						
17 10	SPORT-RIVIERA	OP	RNBT	F/S SV IB	185-220	6 6	1900	1 7	6800	7900
17 10	TENDER	OP	RNBT	F/S SV IB	185-220	6 6	1800	1 7	6650	7700
18 9	SKI-ELITE	OP	RNBT	F/S SV IB	250 PCM	7 4	1900	1 8	7900	9050
18 9	SKI-ELITE	OP	RNBT	F/S SV IB	350	7 4	1900	1 8	8600	9900
20 4	RIVIERA	OP	RNBT	F/S SV IB	185-220	6 7	2200	1 8	9100	10400

CLASSIC YACHTS INC

CHANUTE KS 66720   COAST GUARD MFG ID- DPG   See inside cover to adjust price for area

For more recent years, see the BUC Used Boat Price Guide, Volume 1

LOA FT IN	NAME AND/OR MODEL	TOP/RIG	BOAT TYPE	-HULL- MTL TP TP	----ENGINE--- # HP MFG	BEAM FT IN	WGT LBS	DRAFT FT IN	RETAIL LOW	RETAIL HIGH
				1996 BOATS						
19	CLASSIC BR	B/R		FBG DV IO	225 VLVO	7 8	2960		8350	9550
19	CLASSIC SE	CUD		FBG DV IO	225 VLVO	7 8	3000		9050	10300
21 8	GLOUCESTER 22	SLP	SACAC	FBG KL OB		8	2400	1 8	7200	8300

CLASSIC YACHTS INC -CONTINUED See inside cover to adjust price for area

LOA FT	LOA IN	NAME AND/ OR MODEL	TOP/ RIG	BOAT TYPE	-HULL- MTL	-HULL- TP	ENGINE TP	ENGINE # HP	ENGINE MFG	BEAM FT	BEAM IN	WGT LBS	DRAFT FT	DRAFT IN	RETAIL LOW	RETAIL HIGH
		1996 BOATS														
25	9	CLASSIC 26	SLP	SACAC	FBG	KL	OB			8	4	3900	3	1	13200	15000
25	9	CLASSIC 26 D	SLP	SACAC	FBG	KL	SD	10D	YAN	8	4	4100	3	1	14900	17000
32	11	CLASSIC 33	SLP	SACAC	FBG	KL	SD	27D	YAN	10	8	9590	4		40000	44400
		1994 BOATS														
21	8	GLOUCESTER 22	SLP	SACAC	FBG	CB	OB			8		2400	1	8	6400	7350
25	9	CLASSIC 26	SLP	SACAC	FBG	KL	OB			8	6	4200	3	1	12500	14300
25	9	CLASSIC 26	SLP	SACAC	FBG	KL	IB	8D	VLVO	8	6	4500	3	1	14300	16200
32	11	CLASSIC 33	SLP	SACAC	FBG	KL	IB	18D	YAN	10	8	9700	4		35800	39700
		1993 BOATS														
21	8	GLOUCESTER 22	SLP	SACAC	FBG	CB	OB			8		2400	1	8	6000	6900
25	9	CLASSIC 26	SLP	SACAC	FBG	KL	OB			8	6	4200	3	1	11800	13400
25	9	CLASSIC 26	SLP	SACAC	FBG	KL	IB	8D	VLVO	8	6	4500	3	1	13400	15200
32	11	CLASSIC 33	SLP	SACAC	FBG	KL	IB	18D	YAN	10	8	9700	4		33600	37400

CLEARWATER BAY MARINE WAYS

CLEARWATER FL 33515

See inside cover to adjust price for area

LOA FT	LOA IN	NAME AND/ OR MODEL	TOP/ RIG	BOAT TYPE	-HULL- MTL	-HULL- TP	ENGINE TP	ENGINE # HP	ENGINE MFG	BEAM FT	BEAM IN	WGT LBS	DRAFT FT	DRAFT IN	RETAIL LOW	RETAIL HIGH
		1985 BOATS														
16	6	SUN-CAT	CAT	SA/OD	FBG	CB				7	3	1400		9	3200	3700
		1984 BOATS														
16	6	SUN-CAT CABIN	CAT	SAIL	FBG	CB				7	3	1400		9	3450	4050
16	6	SUN-CAT CABIN	CAT	SAIL	FBG	KL				7	3	1400	2		3300	3850
16	6	SUN-CAT OPEN	CAT	SAIL	FBG	CB				7	3	1400		9	2800	3250
16	6	SUN-CAT OPEN	CAT	SAIL	FBG	KL				7	3	1400	2		2500	2950

....For earlier years, see the BUC Used Boat Price Guide, Volume 3

CLOUD MARINE

DIV OF CLOUD CO INC
LEXINGTON KY 40504 COAST GUARD MFG ID- CID

See inside cover to adjust price for area

LOA FT	LOA IN	NAME AND/ OR MODEL	TOP/ RIG	BOAT TYPE	-HULL- MTL	-HULL- TP	ENGINE TP	ENGINE # HP	ENGINE MFG	BEAM FT	BEAM IN	WGT LBS	DRAFT FT	DRAFT IN	RETAIL LOW	RETAIL HIGH
		1987 BOATS														
46		CLOUD-9 LEISURE CRFT		HB	AL		IO	140	MRCR	14		22000	1	4	20000	22300
46		CLOUD-9 LEISURE CRFT		HB	AL		IO	T151	VLVO	14		22000	1	4	21200	23600
57		CLOUD-9 LEISURE CRFT		HB	AL		IO	T151	VLVO	14		23000	1	4	27600	30700
62		CLOUD-9 LEISURE CRFT		HB	AL		IO	T151	VLVO	14		31000	1	5	31400	34900
		1985 BOATS														
40		CLOUD-9 LEISURE CRAF		HB	AL	SV	IO	125	VLVO	14		15000	1	2	14500	16400
40		CLOUD-9 LEISURE CRAF		HB	AL	SV	IO	T125	VLVO	14			1	2	15700	17800
46		CLOUD-9 LEISURE CRFT		HB	AL		IO	125	VLVO	14		23000	1	4	19700	21800
46		CLOUD-9 LEISURE CRFT		HB	AL		IO	140	MRCR	14		23000	1	4	19500	21600
55		CLOUD-9 LEISURE CRFT		HB	AL		IO	125	VLVO	14		27000	1	4	25900	28700
60		CLOUD-9 LEISURE CRFT		HB	AL		IO	T125	VLVO	14		32000	1	5	29500	32800
65		CLOUD-9 LEISURE CRAF		HB	AL	SV	IO	125	VLVO	15					28900	32100
65		CLOUD-9 LEISURE CRAF		HB	AL	SV	IO	T125	VLVO	15					30200	33500

COBALT BOATS

FIBERGLASS ENGINEERING INC
NEODESHA KS 66757 COAST GUARD MFG ID- FGE

See inside cover to adjust price for area

For more recent years, see the BUC Used Boat Price Guide, Volume 1

LOA FT	LOA IN	NAME AND/ OR MODEL	TOP/ RIG	BOAT TYPE	-HULL- MTL	-HULL- TP	ENGINE TP	ENGINE # HP	ENGINE MFG	BEAM FT	BEAM IN	WGT LBS	DRAFT FT	DRAFT IN	RETAIL LOW	RETAIL HIGH
		1996 BOATS														
18	6	COBALT 190	OP	RNBT	FBG	DV	IO	160-220		8	1	2750	1	8	9300	11300
19	6	COBALT 200	OP	RNBT	FBG	DV	IO	160-250		8	2	2800	1	8	9900	12400
21	11	COBALT 220	OP	RNBT	FBG	DV	IO	190-275		8	5	3140	1	5	13300	16200
		IO 300 14200 16900, IO 330 15000 18100, IO 385-415													17400	21400
22		TRADITION	OP	RNBT	FBG	DV	IO	210-265		8	6	4000	1	7	15300	18600
		IO 300 16500 19600, IO 330 17400 20800, IO 385-415													20000	24000
23	2	COBALT 232	OP	RNBT	FBG	DV	IO	190-265		8	6	3300	1	5	14400	17700
23	2	COBALT 232	OP	RNBT	FBG	DV	IO	300-330		8	6	3300	1	5	16000	19700
23	2	COBALT 232	OP	RNBT	FBG	DV	IO	385-415		8	6	3300	1	5	19100	22900
23	2	COBALT 233	OP	RNBT	FBG	DV	IO	190-265		8	6	3300	1	5	13800	17100
23	2	COBALT 233	OP	RNBT	FBG	DV	IO	300-330		8	6	3300	1	5	15500	19100
23	2	COBALT 233	OP	RNBT	FBG	DV	IO	385-415		8	6	3300	1	5	18600	22200
25		COBALT 252	OP	RNBT	FBG	DV	IO	235-330		8	6	4000	1	8	18700	23200
25		COBALT 252	OP	RNBT	FBG	DV	IO	385-415		8	6	4000	1	8	22400	26500
25		COBALT 253	OP	CUD	FBG	DV	IO	235-300		8	6	4000	1	8	19800	23700
25		COBALT 253	OP	CUD	FBG	DV	IO	330-385		8	6	4000	1	8	22400	26700
25		COBALT 253	OP	CUD	FBG	DV	IO	415	MRCR	8	6	4000	1	8	25600	28500
25		COBALT 253	OP	RNBT	FBG	DV	IO	300-330		8	6	4000	1	8	19600	22200
27	3	COBALT 272	OP	RNBT	FBG	DV	IO	300-385		8	6	4930	1	11	24900	30600
27	3	COBALT 272	OP	RNBT	FBG	DV	IO	415	MRCR	8	6	4930	1	11	28700	31900
		1995 BOATS														
19	6	COBALT 200	OP	RNBT	FBG	DV	IO	180-265		8	2	2800	1	8	9300	11500
21	11	COBALT 220	OP	RNBT	FBG	DV	IO	190-265		8	5	3140	1	5	12000	14700
		IO 275-300 13300 15700, IO 330-385 14800 18400, IO 415 MRCR													18100	20200
22		TRADITION	OP	RNBT	FBG	DV	IO	235-275		8	6	4000	1	7	14500	17600
22		TRADITION	OP	RNBT	FBG	DV	IO	300		8	6	4000	1	7	15400	18300
22		TRADITION	OP	RNBT	FBG	DV	IO	330-385		8	6	4000	1	7	17100	20900
22	3	CONDURRE 222	OP	CUD	FBG	DV	IO	330	VLVO	8	5	3400	1	5	16600	18800
22	3	CONDURRE 222	OP	RNBT	FBG	DV	IO	235-275		8	5	3400	1	5	13000	16000
		IO 300 14000 16700, IO 350-385 15500 19300, IO 415 MRCR													19000	21100
23	2	COBALT 233	OP	CUD	FBG	DV	IO	235-275		8	6	3300	1	5	14200	17400
		IO 300 15200 18100, IO 330-385 16900 20900, IO 415 MRCR													20300	22500
25		COBALT 252	OP	RNBT	FBG	DV	IO	235-300		8	6	4000	1	8	16700	20800
25		COBALT 252	OP	RNBT	FBG	DV	IO	330-385		8	6	4000	1	8	19500	23200
25		COBALT 252	OP	RNBT	FBG	DV	IO	415	MRCR	8	6	4000	1	8	22300	24700
25		COBALT 253	OP	CUD	FBG	DV	IO	235-300		8	6	4000	1	8	18300	22100
25		COBALT 253	OP	CUD	FBG	DV	IO	330-385		8	6	4000	1	8	20900	24900
25		COBALT 253	OP	CUD	FBG	DV	IO	415	MRCR	8	6	4000	1	8	23900	26600
27	3	COBALT 272	OP	RNBT	FBG	DV	IO	300-385		8	6	4930	1	11	23200	28600
27	3	COBALT 272	OP	RNBT	FBG	DV	IO	415	MRCR	8	6	4930	1	11	26800	29800
		1994 BOATS														
19	6	COBALT 200	OP	RNBT	FBG	DV	IO	160-235		8	2	2800	1	6	8550	10500
19	6	COBALT 200	OP	RNBT	FBG	DV	IO	250	VLVO	8	2	2800	1	6	9450	10800
22		COBALT 220	OP	RNBT	FBG	DV	IO	190-250		8	5	2900	1	6	10700	13100
		IO 300 11900 14200, IO 350 MRCR 13300 15100, IO 385-415													14700	18300
22		TRADITION	OP	RNBT	FBG	DV	IO	190-250		8	6	3400	3		11900	14400
22		TRADITION	OP	RNBT	FBG	DV	IO	300		8	6	3400	3		13000	15500
22		TRADITION	OP	RNBT	FBG	DV	IO	350-385		8	6	3400	3		14400	18000
22	3	CONDURRE 222	OP	RNBT	FBG	DV	IO	190-250		8	5	3400	1	5	11900	14500
		IO 300 13100 15600, IO 350-385 14500 18000, IO 415 MRCR													17300	19700
22	3	CONDURRE 223	OP	CUD	FBG	DV	IO	190-250		8	5	3400	1	5	12600	15300
22	3	CONDURRE 223	OP	CUD	FBG	DV	IO	300		8	5	3400	1	5	13900	16500
22	3	CONDURRE 223	OP	CUD	FBG	DV	IO	350-385		8	5	3400	1	5	15300	19100
23	10	COBALT 24X	OP	CUD	FBG	DV	IO	390	VLVO	8		4100	1	8	21300	23700
25	2	COBALT 252	OP	RNBT	FBG	DV	IO	220-300		8	6	4000	1	8	15900	19700
25	2	COBALT 252	OP	RNBT	FBG	DV	IO	350-390		8	6	4000	1	8	18600	23200
25	2	COBALT 252	OP	RNBT	FBG	DV	IO	415	MRCR	8	6	4000	1	8	21000	23300
27	3	CONDURRE 272	OP	RNBT	FBG	DV	IO	300-385		8	6	4930	1	11	21700	26700
27	3	CONDURRE 272	OP	RNBT	FBG	DV	IO	390-415		8	6	4930	1	11	24800	27800
		1993 BOATS														
19	6	CONDURRE 196	OP	B/R	FBG	SV	IO	180	YAMA	8	2	2800	1	8	7600	8750
19	6	CONDURRE 198	OP	B/R	FBG	SV	IO	155-245		8	2	2800	1	6	8100	9800
22		CONDURRE 220	OP	B/R	FBG	SV	IO	190-245							11500	13800
22		CONDURRE 220	OP	B/R	FBG	SV	IO	300							12500	14900
22		CONDURRE 22T	OP	B/R	FBG	SV	IO	225-350		8	6	4000	3		12800	15100
22	3	CONDURRE 222	OP	B/R	FBG	SV	IO	225-300		8	5	3400	1	5	11600	14400
22	3	CONDURRE 222	OP	B/R	FBG	SV	IO	350	YAMA	8	5	3400	1	5	13400	15300
22	3	CONDURRE 223	OP	CUD	FBG	SV	IO	225-300		8	5	3400	1	5	12400	15400
22	3	CONDURRE 223	OP	CUD	FBG	SV	IO	350	MRCR	8	5	3400	1	5	14300	16300
27	4	CONDURRE 272	OP	B/R	FBG	SV	IO	300-390		8	6	4930	1	11	20400	25200
27	4	CONDURRE 272	OP	B/R	FBG	SV	IO	415	MRCR	8	6	4930	1	11	23500	26100
		1992 BOATS														
20	7	CONDURRE 205	ST	RNBT	FBG	DV	IO	175-260		8	3	2700	1		8350	10100
20	7	CONDURRE 205	ST	RNBT	FBG	DV	IO	275	VLVO	8	3	2700	1		9450	10700
20	7	CONDURRE 206	ST	RNBT	FBG	DV	IO	175-260		8	3	2700	1		8200	10100
20	7	CONDURRE 206	ST	RNBT	FBG	DV	IO	275	VLVO	8	3	2700	1		9450	10700
22	3	CONDURRE 222	ST	RNBT	FBG	DV	IO	260-275		8	6	3400	1	5	10800	13000
22	3	CONDURRE 222	ST	RNBT	FBG	DV	IO	330-365		8	6	3400	1	5	12000	14800
22	3	CONDURRE 222	ST	RNBT	FBG	DV	IO	400	MRCR	8	6	3400	1	5	14400	16300
22	3	CONDURRE 223	ST	RNBT	FBG	DV	IO	260-275		8	6	3400	2	1	11100	13300
22	3	CONDURRE 223	ST	RNBT	FBG	DV	IO	330-365		8	6	3400	2	1	12400	15200
22	3	CONDURRE 223	ST	RNBT	FBG	DV	IO	400	MRCR	8	6	3400	2	1	14700	16700
23	10	CONDURRE 243	ST	RNBT	FBG	DV	IO	260-275		8		4100	1	8	13000	15500
23	10	CONDURRE 243	ST	RNBT	FBG	DV	IO	330-365		8		4100	1	8	14300	17400

150 CONTINUED ON NEXT PAGE 96th ed. - Vol. II

LOA FT	LOA IN	NAME AND/ OR MODEL	TOP/ RIG	BOAT TYPE	-HULL- MTL	-HULL- TP	TP	ENGINE # HP	ENGINE MFG	BEAM FT	BEAM IN	WGT LBS	DRAFT FT	DRAFT IN	RETAIL LOW	RETAIL HIGH
		1992 BOATS														
23	10	CONDURRE 243	ST	RNBT	FBG	DV	IO	401	MRCR	8		4100	1	8	16700	19000
25	2	CONDURRE 252	ST	RNBT	FBG	DV	IO	260-275		8	6	4300	1	8	14600	17200
25	2	CONDURRE 252	ST	RNBT	FBG	DV	IO	330-365		8	6	4300	1	8	15900	19100
25	2	CONDURRE 252	ST	RNBT	FBG	DV	IO	400	MRCR	8	6	4300	1	8	18400	20500
25	2	CONDURRE 255	ST	RNBT	FBG	DV	IO	260-275		8	6	4900	1	8	16600	19300
25	2	CONDURRE 255	ST	RNBT	FBG	DV	IO	330-400		8	6	4900	1	8	18200	22400
25	2	CONDURRE 255 CC	ST	RNBT	FBG	DV	IO	225-330		8	6	4900	1	8	15800	19300
25	2	CONDURRE 255 CC	ST	RNBT	FBG	DV	IO	365-400		8	6	4900	1	8	17400	21100
		1991 BOATS														
20	7	CONDURRE 206	ST	RNBT	FBG	DV	IO	175-260		8	3	2700	1		7750	9450
21	1	COBALT 21 BOWRIDER	ST	RNBT	FBG	DV	IO	260-271		8		3600	1	5	9850	11800
21	1	COBALT 21 BOWRIDER	ST	RNBT	FBG	DV	IO	350	MRCR	8		3600	1	5	11500	13100
21	1	COBALT 21 CUDDY	ST	CUD	FBG	DV	IO	260-271		8		3700	1	5	10500	12600
21	1	COBALT 21 CUDDY	ST	CUD	FBG	DV	IO	350	MRCR	8		3700	1	5	12400	14000
22	3	CONDURRE 222	ST	RNBT	FBG	DV	IO	260-271		8		3225	1	5	9700	11600
22	3	CONDURRE 222	ST	RNBT	FBG	DV	IO	330-365		8		3225	1	5	10800	13400
22	3	CONDURRE 223	ST	RNBT	FBG	DV	IO	260-270		8	5	3225	2	1	9900	11800
22	3	CONDURRE 223	ST	RNBT	FBG	DV	IO	330-365		8	5	3225	2	1	11000	13700
23	10	CONDURRE 243	ST	RNBT	FBG	DV	IO	260-330		8		4100	1	8	12200	15200
23	10	CONDURRE 243	ST	RNBT	FBG	DV	IO	365	MRCR	8		4100	1	8	14400	16300
25	2	CONDURRE 252	ST	RNBT	FBG	DV	IO	260-270		8	6	4300	1	8	13700	16000
25	2	CONDURRE 252	ST	RNBT	FBG	DV	IO	330-365		8	6	4300	1	8	14900	17900
25	2	CONDURRE 255	ST	CUD	FBG	DV	IO	260-270		8	6	4900	1	8	16100	18800
25	2	CONDURRE 255	ST	CUD	FBG	DV	IO	330-365		8	6	4900	1	8	17400	20800
26	3	CONDURRE 263	ST	RNBT	FBG	DV	IO	260-330		9	5	5100	1	11	16400	20000
26	3	CONDURRE 263	ST	RNBT	FBG	DV	IO	365	MRCR	9	5	5100	1	11	18800	20900
26	3	CONDURRE 263	ST	RNBT	FBG	DV	IO	T205	MRCR	9	5	5100	1	11	18500	20500
		1990 BOATS														
19		COBALT 19BR	ST	RNBT	FBG	DV	IO		YAMA	7	7	2850	1	5	**	**
19		COBALT 19BR	ST	RNBT	FBG	DV	IO	260-271		7	7	2850	1	5	6650	8150
19		CONDURRE 190	ST	RNBT	FBG	DV	IO	130-175		7	7	2850	1	5	6200	7200
20	1	CONDURRE 202	ST	RNBT	FBG	DV	IO		YAMA	8	4	3200	1	5	**	**
20	1	CONDURRE 202	ST	RNBT	FBG	DV	IO	260-271		8	4	3200	1	5	8350	10100
21	1	COBALT 21 CUDDY	ST	CUD	FBG	DV	IO		YAMA	8		3700	1	5	**	**
21	1	COBALT 21 CUDDY	ST	CUD	FBG	DV	IO	260-271		8		3700	1	5	9900	11900
21	1	COBALT 21 CUDDY	ST	CUD	FBG	DV	IO	350	MRCR	8		3700	1	5	11600	13200
21	1	COBALT 21BR	ST	RNBT	FBG	DV	IO		YAMA	8		3600	1	5	**	**
21	1	COBALT 21BR	ST	RNBT	FBG	DV	IO	260-271		8		3600	1	5	9300	11100
21	1	COBALT 21BR	ST	RNBT	FBG	DV	IO	350	MRCR	8		3600	1	5	10800	12300
22	3	CONDURRE 222	ST	RNBT	FBG	DV	IO		YAMA	8		3225	1	5	**	**
22	3	CONDURRE 222	ST	RNBT	FBG	DV	IO	260-271		8		3225	1	5	9150	10900
22	3	CONDURRE 222	ST	RNBT	FBG	DV	IO	330-365		8		3225	1	5	10200	12600
22	3	CONDURRE 223	ST	RNBT	FBG	DV	IO	260-270		8	5	3225	2	1	9350	11100
22	3	CONDURRE 223	ST	RNBT	FBG	DV	IO	330-365		8	5	3225	2	1	10400	12800
23	10	CONDURRE 243	ST	RNBT	FBG	DV	IO		YAMA	8		4100	1	8	**	**
23	10	CONDURRE 243	ST	RNBT	FBG	DV	IO	260-330		8		4100	1	8	11500	14300
23	10	CONDURRE 243	ST	RNBT	FBG	DV	IO	365	MRCR	8		4100	1	8	13500	15300
25	2	CONDURRE 252	ST	RNBT	FBG	DV	IO	260-270		8	6	4300	1	8	12900	15100
25	2	CONDURRE 252	ST	RNBT	FBG	DV	IO	330-365		8	6	4300	1	8	14000	16900
26	3	CONDURRE 263	ST	RNBT	FBG	DV	IO		YAMA	9	5	5100	1	11	**	**
		IO 260-330 15400 18800, IO 365 MRCR 17300 19700, IO T YAMA													**	**
		IO T205 17000 19700														
		1989 BOATS														
17	2	CONDURRE 172	ST	RNBT	FBG	DV	IO		YAMA	7	5	2475	1	5	**	**
17	2	CONDURRE 172	ST	RNBT	FBG	DV	IO	175-205		7	5	2475	1	5	4900	6000
19		COBALT 19BR	ST	RNBT	FBG	DV	IO		YAMA	7	7	2850	1	5	**	**
19		COBALT 19BR	ST	RNBT	FBG	DV	IO	260-271		7	7	2850	1	5	6250	7700
19	2	CONDURRE 192	ST	RNBT	FBG	DV	IO		YAMA	7	7	2850			**	**
19	2	CONDURRE 192	ST	RNBT	FBG	DV	IO	175-205		7	7	2850			5950	7200
20	1	CONDURRE 202	ST	RNBT	FBG	DV	IO		YAMA	8	4	3200	1	5	**	**
20	1	CONDURRE 202	ST	RNBT	FBG	DV	IO	260-271		8	4	3200	1	5	7850	9550
21	1	COBALT 21 CUDDY	ST	CUD	FBG	DV	IO		YAMA	8		3700	1	5	**	**
21	1	COBALT 21 CUDDY	ST	CUD	FBG	DV	IO	260-271		8		3700	1	5	9400	11200
21	1	COBALT 21 CUDDY	ST	CUD	FBG	DV	IO	350	MRCR	8		3700	1	5	11000	12500
21	1	COBALT 21BR	ST	RNBT	FBG	DV	IO		YAMA	8		3600	1	5	**	**
21	1	COBALT 21BR	ST	RNBT	FBG	DV	IO	260-271		8		3600	1	5	8700	10500
21	1	COBALT 21BR	ST	RNBT	FBG	DV	IO	350	MRCR	8		3600	1	5	10200	11600
22	3	CONDURRE 222	ST	RNBT	FBG	DV	IO		YAMA	8		3225	1	5	**	**
22	3	CONDURRE 222	ST	RNBT	FBG	DV	IO	260-271		8		3225	1	5	8550	10300
22	3	CONDURRE 222	ST	RNBT	FBG	DV	IO	330-365		8		3225	1	5	9600	11900
22	3	CONDURRE 223	ST	CUD	FBG	DV	IO		YAMA	8		3225	1	5	**	**
22	3	CONDURRE 223	ST	CUD	FBG	DV	IO	260-271		8		3225	1	5	9150	10900
22	3	CONDURRE 223	ST	CUD	FBG	DV	IO	330-365		8		3225	1	5	10200	12600
23	10	CONDURRE 243	ST	RNBT	FBG	DV	IO		YAMA	8		4100	1	8	**	**
23	10	CONDURRE 243	ST	RNBT	FBG	DV	IO	260-330		8		4100	1	8	10900	13500
23	10	CONDURRE 243	ST	RNBT	FBG	DV	IO	365	MRCR	8		4100	1	8	12700	14500
26	3	CONDURRE 263	ST	RNBT	FBG	DV	IO		YAMA	9	5	5100	1	11	**	**
		IO 260-330 14500 17700, IO 365 MRCR 16300 18600, IO T YAMA													**	**
		IO T205 17000 19700														
		1988 BOATS														
17	2	CONDURRE 172	ST	RNBT	FBG	DV	IO	175-205		7	5	2475	1	5	4650	5400
19		COBALT 19BR	ST	RNBT	FBG	DV	IO	230-270		7	7	2850	1	5	5750	6900
19		COBALT 19BR	ST	RNBT	FBG	DV	IO	271	VLVO	7	7	2850	1	5	6350	7300
19	2	CONDURRE 192	ST	RNBT	FBG	DV	IO	175-205		7	7	2850			5600	6550
20	1	CONDURRE 202	ST	RNBT	FBG	DV	IO	230-260		8	4	3200	1	5	6900	8250
20	1	CONDURRE 202	ST	RNBT	FBG	DV	IO	271	VLVO	8	4	3200	1	5	7550	8650
20	1	CONDURRE 202SE	ST	RNBT	FBG	DV	IO	230-271		8	4	3200	1	5	7550	9450
21	1	COBALT 21 CUDDY	ST	CUD	FBG	DV	IO	260-271		8		3700	1	5	8900	10700
21	1	COBALT 21 CUDDY	ST	CUD	FBG	DV	IO	350	MRCR	8		3700	1	5	10400	11800
21	1	COBALT 21BR	ST	RNBT	FBG	DV	IO		OMC	8		3600	1	5	**	**
21	1	COBALT 21BR	ST	RNBT	FBG	DV	IO	260-271		8		3600	1	5	8200	9950
21	1	COBALT 21BR	ST	RNBT	FBG	DV	IO	350	MRCR	8		3600	1	5	9700	11000
22	3	CONDURRE 222	ST	RNBT	FBG	DV	IO		OMC	8		3225	1	5	**	**
22	3	CONDURRE 222	ST	RNBT	FBG	DV	IO	260-271		8		3225	1	5	7750	9400
22	3	CONDURRE 222	ST	RNBT	FBG	DV	IO	350	MRCR	8		3225	1	5	9200	10500
22	3	CONDURRE 222SE	ST	RNBT	FBG	DV	IO		OMC	8		3225	1	5	**	**
22	3	CONDURRE 222SE	ST	RNBT	FBG	DV	IO	260-271		8		3225	1	5	8400	10200
22	3	CONDURRE 222SE	ST	RNBT	FBG	DV	IO	350	MRCR	8		3225	1	5	9900	11300
22	3	CONDURRE 223	ST	CUD	FBG	DV	IO		OMC	8		3225	1	5	**	**
22	3	CONDURRE 223	ST	CUD	FBG	DV	IO	260-270		8		3225	1	5	8100	9400
22	3	CONDURRE 223	ST	CUD	FBG	DV	IO	271-350		8		3223	1	5	9100	10900
22	3	CONDURRE 223SE	ST	CUD	FBG	DV	IO		OMC	8		3225	1	5	**	**
22	3	CONDURRE 223SE	ST	CUD	FBG	DV	IO	260-271		8		3225	1	5	9100	10500
22	3	CONDURRE 223SE	ST	CUD	FBG	DV	IO	350	MRCR	8		3225	1	5	10600	12100
22	7	COBALT 23BR	ST	CUD	FBG	DV	IO		OMC	8		3800	1	6	**	**
		IO 260-271 9750 11600, IO 350 MRCR 11200 12800, IO T165-T205													11600	13400
22	7	COBALT CS23	ST	CUD	FBG	DV	IO		OMC	8		3900	1	6	**	**
		IO 260-271 9900 11800, IO 350 MRCR 11400 13000, IO T165-T205													11800	13600
22	7	CONDESA	ST	CUD	FBG	DV	IO		OMC	8		4200	1	6	**	**
		IO 260-271 10500 12400, IO 350 MRCR 12000 13600, IO T165-T205													12400	14300
		1987 BOATS														
17		17BR	ST	RNBT	FBG	DV	IO	175-205		7	4	2475	1	4	4300	5050
18	2	COBALT 18DV	ST	RNBT	FBG	DV	IO	175-260		7	5	2700	1	6	4850	5950
19		COBALT 19BR	ST	RNBT	FBG	DV	IO	230-260		7	7	2850	1	5	5450	6500
21	1	COBALT 21 CUDDY	ST	CUD	FBG	DV	IO	230-260		8		3700	1	5	8150	9650
21	1	COBALT 21BR	ST	RNBT	FBG	DV	IO	230-260		8		3600	1	5	7600	9000
22	3	CONDURRE 223	ST	CUD	FBG	DV	IO	260	MRCR	8		3225	1	5	8100	9350
22	3	CONDURRE 223	ST	CUD	FBG	DV	IO	335	OMC	8		3225	1	5	9200	10500
22	3	CONDURRE 454	ST	CUD	FBG	DV	IO	330	MRCR	8		3225	1	5	9200	10500
22	7	COBALT CS23	ST	CUD	FBG	DV	IO	260		8		3900	1	6	9450	10700
22	7	COBALT CS23	ST	CUD	FBG	DV	IO	T175-T205		8		4700	1	6	11500	13800
22	7	CONDESA	ST	CUD	FBG	DV	IO	260		8		4200	1	6	9950	11300
22	7	CONDESA	ST	CUD	FBG	DV	IO	330-335		8		5200	1	6	12700	14500
22	7	CONDESA	ST	CUD	FBG	DV	IO	T175-T205		8		5200	1	6	12500	14200
26	9	CONDURRE 269	ST	OFF	FBG	DV	IO	T260	MRCR	8		6000	2	6	18100	20200
29	5	CONDURRE 269	ST	OFF	FBG	DV	IO	T330-T420		8		8000	2	8	29600	35600
29	5	CONDURRE 300S	ST	OFF	FBG	DV	IO	T330-T370		8		8000	2	8	23600	27800
29	5	CONDURRE 300S	ST	OFF	FBG	DV	IO	T420		8		8000	2	8	26700	29700
		1986 BOATS														
17		17BR	ST	RNBT	FBG	DV	IO	185	MRCR	7	4	2475	1	4	4100	4800
18	2	COBALT 18DV	ST	RNBT	FBG	DV	IO	175-260		7	5	2700	1	6	4600	5700
19		COBALT 19BR	ST	RNBT	FBG	DV	IO	230-260		7	7	2850	1	5	5200	6200
21	1	COBALT 21 CUDDY	ST	CUD	FBG	DV	IO	230-260		8		3700	1	5	7800	9200
21	1	COBALT 21BR	ST	RNBT	FBG	DV	IO	230-260		8		3600	1	5	7300	8600
22	3	CONDURRE 223	ST	CUD	FBG	DV	IO	260	MRCR	8		3225	1	5	7750	8900
22	7	COBALT CS23	ST	CUD	FBG	DV	IO	260		8		3900	1	6	9050	10300
22	7	COBALT CS23	ST	CUD	FBG	DV	IO	T175-T230		8		4700	1	6	11000	13400
22	7	COBALT CS23	ST	CUD	FBG	DV	IO	T260		8		4900	1	6	12200	13800
22	7	CONDESA	ST	CUD	FBG	DV	IO	260		8		4200	1	6	9500	10800
22	7	CONDESA	ST	CUD	FBG	DV	IO	T175-T230		8		5000	1	6	11500	14000
22	7	CONDESA	ST	CUD	FBG	DV	IO	T260		8		5200	1	6	12700	14400
26	9	CONDURRE 269	ST	OFF	FBG	DV	IO	T260	MRCR	8		6000	2	6	16900	19200

CONTINUED ON NEXT PAGE

LOA FT	IN	NAME AND/ OR MODEL	TOP/ RIG	BOAT TYPE	-HULL- MTL	TP	----ENGINE--- TP	# HP	MFG	BEAM FT	IN	WGT LBS	DRAFT FT	IN	RETAIL LOW	RETAIL HIGH
		1986 BOATS														
29	5	CONDURRE	ST	OFF	FBG	DV	IO	T330-T400		8		8000	2	8	25400	30500
29	5	CONDURRE	ST	OFF	FBG	DV	IO	T440-T475		8		8000	2	8	28800	33300
		1985 BOATS														
17	2	CS7	ST	RNBT	FBG	DV	IO	185-200		7	5	2400	1	6	3950	4900
18	2	COBALT 18DV	ST	RNBT	FBG	DV	IO	185-230		7	5	2700	1	6	4500	5500
18	2	COBALT 18DV	ST	RNBT	FBG	DV	IO	260		7	5	2700	1	6	4750	5750
19		COBALT 19BR	ST	RNBT	FBG	DV	IO	225-260		7	7	2850	1	5	5200	6250
19		COBALT 19CD	ST	RNBT	FBG	DV	IO	225-260		7	7	2850	1	5	5200	6200
19		COBALT CM9	ST	RNBT	FBG	DV	IO	260	MRCR	7	7	2800	1	5	5300	6100
19		COBALT CS9	ST	RNBT	FBG	DV	IO	225-260		7	7	2800	1	5	5150	6100
21	1	COBALT 21 CUDDY	ST	CUD	FBG	DV	IO	225-260		8		3700	1	5	7700	9150
21	1	COBALT 21BR	ST	RNBT	FBG	DV	IO	225-260		8		3600	1	5	7200	8550
22	7	COBALT CM23	ST	CUD	FBG	DV	IO	260	MRCR	8		3900	1	6	9000	10200
22	7	COBALT CS23	ST	CUD	FBG	DV	IO	260		8		3900	1	6	8500	10100
		IO T185 MRCR 9400 10700, IO T185-T230 10600 12800, IO T260													11700	13300
22	7	CONDESA	ST	CUD	FBG	DV	IO	260		8		4200	1	6	9200	10700
22	7	CONDESA	ST	CUD	FBG	DV	IO	T185	MRCR	8		4200	1	6	9850	11200
22	7	CONDESA	ST	CUD	FBG	DV	IO	T185-T260		8		5000	1	6	11100	13800
29	5	CONDURRE	ST	OFF	FBG	DV	IO	T330-T425		8		8000	2	8	24400	30100
29	5	CONDURRE	ST	OFF	FBG	DV	IO	T440-T475		8		8000	2	8	27600	32000
29	7	CONQUEST	ST	OFF	FBG	DV	IO	T330		8		8000	2	8	24100	26800
		1984 BOATS														
17	2	CS7	ST	RNBT	FBG	DV	IO	185-198		7	5	2400	1	6	3750	4500
17	2	CS7	ST	RNBT	FBG	DV	IO	200		7	5	2450	1	6	3850	4750
18	2	COBALT 18DV	ST	RNBT	FBG	DV	IO	185-198		7	5	2700	1	6	4250	5000
18	2	COBALT 18DV	ST	RNBT	FBG	DV	IO	200	OMC	7	5	2700	1	6	4250	4950
18	2	COBALT 18DV	ST	RNBT	FBG	DV	IO	200-260		7	5	2800	1	6	4650	5550
19		COBALT 19BR	ST	RNBT	FBG	DV	IO	225-260		7	7	2850	1	5	5000	6050
19		COBALT 19CD	ST	RNBT	FBG	DV	IO	225-260		7	7	2850	1	5	5000	6000
19		COBALT CM9	ST	RNBT	FBG	DV	IO	228-260		7	7	2800	1	5	4900	5850
19		COBALT CS9	ST	RNBT	FBG	DV	IO	225-260		7	7	2800	1	5	4950	5900
22	7	COBALT CM23	ST	CUD	FBG	DV	IO	260	MRCR	8		3900	1	6	8600	9850
22	7	COBALT CS23	ST	CUD	FBG	DV	IO	260		8		3900	1	6	8200	9750
22	7	COBALT CS23	ST	CUD	FBG	DV	IO	T185-T228		8		4700	1	6	10200	12400
22	7	COBALT CS23	ST	CUD	FBG	DV	IO	T260		8		4900	1	6	11300	12800
22	7	CONDESA	ST	CUD	FBG	DV	IO	260		8		4200	1	6	8850	10400
22	7	CONDESA	ST	CUD	FBG	DV	IO	T185-T260		8		5000	1	6	10700	13300
29	5	CONQUEST	ST	OFF	FBG	DV	IO	T330-T400		8		8000	2	8	23500	28200
29	5	CONQUEST	ST	OFF	FBG	DV	IO	T440-T475		8		8000	2	8	26600	30900

....For earlier years, see the BUC Used Boat Price Guide, Volume 3

COBIA BOAT COMPANY

DIV OF MAVERICK BOAT CO
FT PIERCE FL 34946 COAST GUARD MFG ID- CBA

See inside cover to adjust price for area

For more recent years, see the BUC Used Boat Price Guide, Volume 1

LOA FT	IN	NAME AND/ OR MODEL	TOP/ RIG	BOAT TYPE	-HULL- MTL	TP	----ENGINE--- TP	# HP	MFG	BEAM FT	IN	WGT LBS	DRAFT FT	IN	RETAIL LOW	RETAIL HIGH
		1996 BOATS														
16		MONTE CARLO 166E	OP	RNBT	FBG	DV	OB			7		1460			4200	4900
17	2	CARIBBEAN 173	OP	CTRCN	FBG	SV	OB			7		1376			4000	4650
18		MONTE CARLO 186E	OP	RNBT	FBG	DV	OB			7	5	1850			5050	5800
18		MONTE CARLO 188E	OP	RNBT	FBG	DV	IO	135-185		7	5	2200			5300	6450
18	6	CARIBBEAN 194SF	OP	CTRCN	FBG	SV	OB			8		2430			5750	6600
19	2	MONTE CARLO 198E	OP	RNBT	FBG	DV	IO	180-235		7	7	2500			6150	7350
19	2	MONTE CARLO 198E	OP	RNBT	FBG	DV	IO	250		7	7	2500			6450	7800
19	7	SAN MARINO 205EC	OP	CUD	FBG	DV	IO	180-185		7	7	2600			6650	7950
20	8	CARIBBEAN 204SF	OP	CTRCN	FBG	SV	OB			8		2660			7950	9150
20	8	MONTE CARLO 218E	OP	RNBT	FBG	DV	IO	180-250		8	6	3100			8200	10200
20	8	SAN MARINO 215EC	OP	CUD	FBG	DV	IO	180-250		8	6	3300			9050	11000
22	3	MONTE CARLO 228E	OP	RNBT	FBG	DV	IO	235-250		8	6	3500			9800	11600
22	3	MONTE CARLO 228E	OP	RNBT	FBG	DV	IO	300		8	6	3500			10500	12500
22	3	SAN MARINO 225EC	OP	CUD	FBG	DV	IO	235-250		8	6	3800			10900	13000
22	3	SAN MARINO 225EC	OP	CUD	FBG	DV	IO	300		8	6	3800			11700	13900
22	3	SAN MARINO 6.8EC	OP	CUD	FBG	DV	IO	235-250		8	6	4100			11500	13700
22	3	SAN MARINO 6.8EC	OP	CUD	FBG	DV	IO	300		8	6	4100			12300	14500
23	2	CARIBBEAN 220SW	OP	CUD	FBG	DV	OB			8		3500			9850	11200
23	2	CARIBBEAN 220SW	OP	CUD	FBG	SV	OB			8		3500			9850	11200
24	6	ODYSSEY 246E	OP	RNBT	FBG	SV	OB			8	6	3600			12400	14100
24	6	ODYSSEY 248E	OP	RNBT	FBG	SV	IO	235-300		8	6	4200			12200	15200
25	6	CARIBBEAN 230SW	OP	CTRCN	FBG	SV	OB			8	6	4200			14300	16200
25	6	CARIBBEAN 234SF	OP	CTRCN	FBG	SV	OB			8	6	4100			12300	14000
27	2	SAN MARINO 255EMC	OP	CR	FBG	SV	IO	235-300		8	6				15000	18500
		1995 BOATS														
16		MONTE CARLO 166E	OP	RNBT	FBG	DV	OB			7		1460			4000	4650
17	2	CARIBBEAN 173	OP	CTRCN	FBG	SV	OB			7		1376			3800	4400
18		MONTE CARLO 186E	OP	RNBT	FBG	DV	OB			7	5	1850			5000	5750
18		MONTE CARLO 188E	OP	RNBT	FBG	DV	IO	135-185		7	5	2200			4900	6000
18	6	CARIBBEAN 194SF	OP	CTRCN	FBG	SV	OB			8		2430			5450	6250
19	2	MONTE CARLO 198E	OP	RNBT	FBG	DV	IO	180-235		7	7	2500			5700	6850
19	2	MONTE CARLO 198E	OP	RNBT	FBG	DV	IO	250		7	7	2500			6000	7250
19	7	SAN MARINO 205EC	OP	CUD	FBG	DV	IO	180-185		7	7	2600			6200	7450
20	8	CARIBBEAN 204SF	OP	CTRCN	FBG	SV	OB			8		2660			7550	8700
20	8	MONTE CARLO 218E	OP	RNBT	FBG	DV	IO	180-250		8	6	3100			7650	9500
20	8	SAN MARINO 215EC	OP	CUD	FBG	DV	IO	180-250		8	6	3300			8350	10400
22	3	MONTE CARLO 228E	OP	RNBT	FBG	DV	IO	235-250		8	6	3500			9150	10800
22	3	MONTE CARLO 228E	OP	RNBT	FBG	DV	IO	300		8	6	3500			9700	11600
22	3	SAN MARINO 225EC	OP	CUD	FBG	DV	IO	235-250		8	6	3800			10200	12100
22	3	SAN MARINO 225EC	OP	CUD	FBG	DV	IO	300		8	6	3800			10900	12900
22	3	SAN MARINO 6.8EC	OP	CUD	FBG	DV	IO	235-250		8	6	4100			10800	12700
22	3	SAN MARINO 6.8EC	OP	CUD	FBG	DV	IO	300		8	6	4100			11500	13600
23	2	CARIBBEAN 220SW	OP	CUD	FBG	DV	OB			8		3500			9450	10800
23	2	CARIBBEAN 220SW	OP	CUD	FBG	SV	OB			8		3500			9450	10800
24	6	ODYSSEY 246E	OP	RNBT	FBG	SV	OB			8	6	3600			11800	13400
24	6	ODYSSEY 248E	OP	RNBT	FBG	SV	IO	235-300		8	6	4200			11400	14200
25	6	CARIBBEAN 230SW	OP	CTRCN	FBG	SV	OB			8	6	4200			13600	15400
25	6	CARIBBEAN 234SF	OP	CTRCN	FBG	SV	OB			8	6	4100			11800	13400
27	2	SAN MARINO 255EMC	OP	CR	FBG	SV	IO	235-300		8	6				14000	17300
		1994 BOATS														
16		CHALLENGER 169ER	OP	RNBT	FBG	DV	OB			7		1460			3850	4500
16		MONTE CARLO 166E	OP	RNBT	FBG	DV	OB			7		1460			3800	4400
17		MONTE CARLO 176E	OP	RNBT	FBG	DV	OB			7		1610			4100	4750
17		MONTE CARLO 178E	OP	RNBT	FBG	DV	IO	110-135		7		1800			3750	4650
17	2	CARIBBEAN 174SF	OP	CTRCN	FBG	SV	OB			7		1376			3600	4200
18		CHALLENGER 187ERS	OP	RNBT	FBG	DV	IO	110-185		7	5	2000			4450	5500
18		CHALLENGER 189ER	OP	RNBT	FBG	DV	OB			7	5	1850			4600	5300
18		MONTE CARLO 186E	OP	RNBT	FBG	DV	OB			7	5	1850			4550	5250
18		MONTE CARLO 188E	OP	RNBT	FBG	DV	IO	110-185		7	5	2000			4250	5300
18	2	CARIBBEAN SS180	OP	CTRCN	FBG	SV	OB			7	3	1330			3600	4200
18	2	CARIBBEAN SS190	OP	B/R	FBG	SV	OB			8	7	1780			4500	5150
19	2	CHALLENGER 197ERS	OP	RNBT	FBG	DV	IO	180-240		7	7	2200			5100	6250
19	2	CHALLENGER 197ERS	OP	RNBT	FBG	DV	IO	255	VLVO	7	7	2200			5700	6550
19	2	MONTE CARLO 198E	OP	RNBT	FBG	DV	IO	180-240		7	7	2200			4950	6050
19	2	MONTE CARLO 198E	OP	RNBT	FBG	DV	IO	255	VLVO	7	7	2200			5550	6350
19	7	SAN MARINO 205EC	OP	CUD	FBG	DV	IO	110-210		7	7	2400			5450	6650
20		CARIBBEAN SS200C	OP	CTRCN	FBG	SV	OB			8	9	1890			5600	6450
20	8	CARIBBEAN 204SF	OP	CTRCN	FBG	DV	OB			8		2660			7250	8300
21	6	CARIBBEAN 220SF	OP	CUD	FBG	DV	OB			8		3180			8600	9900
21	6	CARIBBEAN 220SF	OP	CUD	FBG	SV	OB			8		3180			8600	9900
22	3	MONTE CARLO 228ES	OP	RNBT	FBG	DV	IO	210-240		8	6	3500			8350	9950
22	3	MONTE CARLO 228ES	OP	RNBT	FBG	DV	IO	300		8	6	3500			9350	10900
22	3	SAN MARINO 225ECS	OP	CUD	FBG	DV	IO	210-240		8	6	3800			9400	11100
22	3	SAN MARINO 225ECS	OP	CUD	FBG	DV	IO	300		8	6	3800			10300	12100
22	3	SAN MARINO 6.8EC	OP	CUD	FBG	DV	IO	210-240		8	6	4100			9950	11700
22	3	SAN MARINO 6.8EC	OP	CUD	FBG	DV	IO	300		8	6	4100			10900	12700
		1993 BOATS														
16	10	MONTE CARLO 176E	OP	RNBT	FBG	DV	OB					1100			2850	3350
16	10	MONTE CARLO 178E	OP	RNBT	FBG	DV	IO	110-115							3900	4500
16	10	MONTE CARLO 178EL	OP	RNBT	FBG	DV	IO	110-115							3550	4150
17	10	MONTE CARLO 186E	OP	RNBT	FBG	DV	OB					1200			3150	3700
17	10	MONTE CARLO 188E	OP	RNBT	FBG	DV	IO	110-180							4400	5100
17	10	MONTE CARLO 188ELS	OP	RNBT	FBG	DV	IO	110-115							3950	4650
18		CHALLENGER 187ERS	OP	RNBT	FBG	DV	IO	110-180							4450	5150
18	2	SUNSKIFF SS190	OP	RNBT	FBG	DV	OB			7	7	1450			3700	4300
18	2	SUNSKIFF SS200	OP	CTRCN	FBG	DV	OB			7	3	1000			2750	3200
18	7	SPIRIT 1900CC	OP	CUD	FBG	DV	OB			7	7	1200			3250	3750
19	2	CHALLENGER 197ERS	OP	RNBT	FBG	DV	IO	180-240							5100	6150
19	2	MONTE CARLO 198E	OP	RNBT	FBG	DV	IO	180-210							4850	5950
19	2	MONTE CARLO 198E	OP	RNBT	FBG	DV	IO	225-240							5300	6100
19	7	SAN MARINO 205EC	OP	CUD	FBG	DV	IO	180							5650	6750
19	7	SAN MARINO 205EL	OP	CUD	FBG	DV	IO	110-115							5600	6400
20		SUNSKIFF SS215	OP	CTRCN	FBG	DV	OB			7	9	1560			4700	5350
20	8	CARIBBEAN 204SF	OP	CTRCN	FBG	DV	OB			8		2300			6400	7350
21	6	CARIBBEAN 220SF	OP	CUD	FBG	DV	OB			8		2800			7700	8850

LOA FT	LOA IN	NAME AND/ OR MODEL	TOP/ RIG	BOAT TYPE	-HULL- MTL	-HULL- TP	ENGINE TP	ENGINE # HP	ENGINE MFG	BEAM FT	BEAM IN	WGT LBS	DRAFT FT	DRAFT IN	RETAIL LOW	RETAIL HIGH
1993 BOATS																
22	3	MONTE CARLO 228ES	OP	RNBT	FBG	DV	IO	200-295							7450	9250
22	3	MONTE CARLO 228ES	OP	RNBT	FBG	DV	IO	300							8200	9850
22	3	SAN MARINO 225ECS	OP	CUD	FBG	DV	IO	200-295							7800	9700
22	3	SAN MARINO 225ECS	OP	CUD	FBG	DV	IO	300							8600	10300
22	3	SAN MARINO 6.8EC	OP	CUD	FBG	DV	IO	200-295							8300	10300
22	3	SAN MARINO 6.8EC	OP	CUD	FBG	DV	IO	300							9200	10900
1992 BOATS																
16	10	MONTE CARLO 176E	OP	RNBT	FBG	DV	OB								2800	3250
16	10	MONTE CARLO 176ES	OP	RNBT	FBG	DV	OB								2950	3450
16	10	MONTE CARLO 178E	OP	RNBT	FBG	DV	IO	125-135							3500	4300
16	10	MONTE CARLO 178ES	OP	RNBT	FBG	DV	IO	125-135							3350	4150
17	10	MONTE CARLO 186E	OP	RNBT	FBG	DV	OB								3800	4450
17	10	MONTE CARLO 186ES	OP	RNBT	FBG	DV	OB								4000	4650
17	10	MONTE CARLO 188E	OP	RNBT	FBG	DV	IO	125-135							3800	4700
17	10	MONTE CARLO 188ES	OP	RNBT	FBG	DV	IO	125-175							3950	4800
18		CHALLENGER 187ERS	OP	RNBT	FBG	DV	IO	125-175							3900	4850
18	2	SPIRIT 1950VBR	OP	RNBT	FBG	DV	IO	125		7	7	2000			3900	4750
18	2	SUNSKIFF SS190	OP	RNBT	FBG	DV	OB			7	7	1450			3550	4150
18	2	SUNSKIFF SS200	OP	CTRCN	FBG	DV	OB			7	3	1000			2650	3050
18	7	SPIRIT 1950CC	OP	CUD	FBG	DV	IO	125		7	9	2300			4500	5400
19	2	CHALLENGER 197ERS	OP	RNBT	FBG	DV	IO	125-240							4700	5850
19	2	MONTE CARLO 198E	OP	RNBT	FBG	DV	IO	125-175							4550	5500
19	2	MONTE CARLO 198ES	OP	RNBT	FBG	DV	IO	125-240							4700	5850
19	7	SAN MARINO 205EC	OP	CUD	FBG	DV	IO	125-175							5250	6300
20		SUNSKIFF SS215	OP	CTRCN	FBG	DV	OB			7	9	1560			4500	5200
20	8	CARIBBEAN 204SF	OP	CTRCN	FBG	DV	OB			8		2300			6150	7050
21	6	CARIBBEAN 220SF	OP	CUD	FBG	DV	OB			8		2800			7400	8500
22	3	CHALLENGER 227ERS	OP	RNBT	FBG	DV	IO	180-240							7050	8600
22	3	CHALLENGER 227ERS	OP	RNBT	FBG	DV	IO	300							7650	9200
22	3	MONTE CARLO 228E	OP	RNBT	FBG	DV	IO	180-240							6750	8250
22	3	MONTE CARLO 228ES	OP	RNBT	FBG	DV	IO	180-240							7050	8600
22	3	MONTE CARLO 228ES	OP	RNBT	FBG	DV	IO	300							7650	9200
22	3	SAN MARINO 225EC	OP	CUD	FBG	DV	IO	180-240							7350	9000
22	3	SAN MARINO 225ECS	OP	CUD	FBG	DV	IO	180-240							7700	9400
22	3	SAN MARINO 225ECS	OP	CUD	FBG	DV	IO	300							8300	9950
1991 BOATS																
16	5	SPIRIT 1700VBR	ST	RNBT	FBG	DV	OB			7		1100			2600	3050
16	5	SPIRIT 1750VBR	ST	RNBT	FBG	DV	IO	125	MRCR	7		1750			2950	3450
16	10	MONTE CARLO 176E	ST	RNBT	FBG	DV	OB			7					2750	3200
16	10	MONTE CARLO 178E	ST	RNBT	FBG	DV	IO	125	MRCR	7		1450			2800	3250
17	10	MONTE CARLO 186E	ST	RNBT	FBG	DV	OB			7	5	1600			3650	4200
17	10	MONTE CARLO 188E	ST	RNBT	FBG	DV	IO	125	MRCR	7	5	2000			3550	4100
17	10	SPIRIT 1800VBR	ST	RNBT	FBG	DV	OB			7	5	1200			2950	3400
17	10	SPIRIT 1850VBR	ST	RNBT	FBG	DV	IO	125	MRCR	7	5	1900			3450	4050
18	2	SPIRIT 1900VBR	ST	RNBT	FBG	DV	OB			7	7	1450			3400	3950
18	2	SPIRIT 1950VBR	ST	RNBT	FBG	DV	IO	125	MRCR	7	7	2000			3650	4250
18	2	SUNSKIFF 190 FISH	ST	RNBT	FBG	DV	OB			7	7	1450			3400	3950
18	2	SUNSKIFF SS200	OP	CTRCN	FBG	DV	OB			7	3	1000			2550	2950
18	7	SPIRIT 1900CC	ST	CUD	FBG	DV	OB			7	9	1300			3200	3700
18	7	SPIRIT 1950CC	ST	CUD	FBG	DV	IO	125	MRCR	7	9	2300			4150	4850
19	2	MONTE CARLO 198E	ST	RNBT	FBG	DV	IO	125	MRCR	7	7	2200			3800	4400
19	2	MONTE CARLO 198ES	ST	RNBT	FBG	DV	IO	125	MRCR	7	7	2200			4350	5000
19	7	SAN MARINO 205EC	ST	CUD	FBG	DV	IO	125	MRCR	7	7	2200			4300	5000
20		SPIRIT 2150CC	ST	CUD	FBG	DV	IO	175	MRCR	7	9	2520			5000	5750
20		SUNSKIFF SS215	OP	CTRCN	FBG	DV	OB			7	9	1560			4350	5000
20	6	SPIRIT 2250CC	ST	CUD	FBG	DV	IO	175	MRCR	8		3200			6000	6900
21	6	CARIBBEAN 220SF	ST	CUD	FBG	DV	OB			8		2800			7100	8200
22	3	CHALLENGER 227ERS	ST	CUD	FBG	DV	IO	200	MRCR	8	6	3800			7500	8600
22	3	MONTE CARLO 228E	ST	RNBT	FBG	DV	IO	175	MRCR	8	6	3500			6800	7800
22	3	MONTE CARLO 228ES	ST	RNBT	FBG	DV	IO	200	MRCR	8	6	3500			6850	7850
22	3	SAN MARINO 225EC	ST	CUD	FBG	DV	IO	175	MRCR	8	6	3800			7600	8750
22	3	SAN MARINO 225ECS	ST	CUD	FBG	DV	IO	200	MRCR	8	6	3800			7800	8950
23		CARIBBEAN 235SF	ST	CUD	FBG	DV	IO	200	MRCR	8	6	4400			8950	10200
25		CARIBBEAN 255SF	ST	CUD	FBG	DV	IO	200	MRCR	8	6	4800			10300	11700
1990 BOATS																
16	5	1700 VBR	OP	B/R	FBG	DV	OB			7		1100			2500	2950
16	5	1700 VBR	OP	B/R	FBG	DV	IO	115	MRCR	7		1750			2600	3000
16	5	1750 VBR	OP	B/R	FBG	DV	IO	135	MRCR	7		1750			2600	3050
17	10	1800 BVR	OP	B/R	FBG	DV	OB			7	5	1200			2800	3300
17	10	1800 CC	OP	CUD	FBG	DV	OB			7	5	1300			3000	3500
17	10	1850 VBR	OP	B/R	FBG	DV	IO	115-155		7	5	2000			3200	3850
18	2	190 FISH	OP	B/R	FBG	DV	OB			7	7	1450			3300	3850
18	2	1900 CC	OP	CUD	FBG	DV	IO	115	MRCR	7	9	2300			3700	4300
18	2	1900 VBR	OP	B/R	FBG	DV	OB			7	7	1450			3300	3850
18	2	1900 VBR	OP	B/R	FBG	DV	IO	115	MRCR	7	7	2200			3300	3850
18	2	1950 CC	OP	CUD	FBG	DV	IO	115	MRCR	7	9	2300			3950	4550
18	2	1950 VBR	OP	B/R	FBG	DV	IO	135-155		7	7	2200			3450	4200
18	2	SS 200	OP	UTL	FBG	DV	OB			7	3	1000			2300	2700
18	8	1900 CC	OP	CUD	FBG	DV	OB			7	9	1825			3900	4550
18	8	1950 CC	OP	CUD	FBG	DV	IO	135-155		7	9	2300			3950	4800
19	2	MONTE CARLO 198E	OP	B/R	FBG	DV	IO	135-155		7	7	2400			3850	4450
19	2	MONTE CARLO 198ES	OP	B/R	FBG	DV	IO	155-190		7	7	2400			3900	4750
20		2150 CC	OP	CUD	FBG	DV	IO	190	VLVO	7	9	2788			5200	5950
20		2150 CC	OP	CUD	FBG	SV	IO	115-180		7	9	2520			4650	5700
20		SS 215	OP	CTRCN	FBG	DV	OB			7	9	1560			4150	4850
20	10	2250 CC	OP	CUD	FBG	DV	IO	155-205		8		3400			5950	7200
21	6	CARIBBEAN 220 SF	OP	RNBT	FBG	DV	OB			8		2800			6850	7900
21	10	2250 MC	OP	DC	FBG	DV	IO	180-205		8		3800			7800	9300
22	3	MONTE CARLO 225E	OP	B/R	FBG	DV	IO	155-245		8	6	3500			6300	7600
22	3	MONTE CARLO 225E	OP	B/R	FBG	DV	IO	360	MRCR	8	6	3708			8100	9350
22	3	SAN MARINO 225EC	OP	CUD	FBG	DV	IO	180-245		8	6	3800			7000	8600
22	3	SAN MARINO 225ECS	OP	CUD	FBG	DV	IO	180-245		8	6	3800			7300	8850
22	3	SAN MARINO 225ECS	OP	CUD	FBG	DV	IO	300-360		8	6	4064			8500	10600
23		CARIBBEAN 235 SF	OP	CUD	FBG	DV	IO	180-230		8	6	4394			8250	9800
23		CARIBBEAN 235SF	OP	CUD	FBG	DV	IO	245	VLVO	8	6	4394			8700	10000
25		CARIBBEAN 255 SF	OP	CUD	FBG	DV	IO	205-230		8	6	4800			9750	11200
25		CARIBBEAN 255 SF	OP	CUD	FBG	DV	IO	T155-T245		8	6	5511			11700	13500
25		CARIBBEAN 255 SF	OP	CUD	FBG	DV	IO	T300	VLVO	8	6	5057			13400	15200
25		CARIBBEAN 255 SF	OP	CUD	FBG	SV	IO	300	MRCR	8	6	4913			10700	12100
25		CARIBBEAN 255 SF	OP	CUD	FBG	SV	IO	T180	VLVO	8	6	5511			12200	13900
26		SAN MARINO 278 EC	OP	DC	FBG	DV	IO	300		8	6	6800			15600	18000
26		SAN MARINO 278 EC	OP	DC	FBG	DV	IO	T155		8	6	7384			16700	19400
1989 BOATS																
16	5	1700 VBR	OP	B/R	FBG	DV	OB			7		1650			3450	4000
16	5	1750 VBR	OP	B/R	FBG	DV	SE	120	MRCR	7		1750			3600	4200
16	5	MONTE-CARLO 172XL	OP	RNBT	FBG	SV	OB			7		1100			2450	2850
16	5	MONTE-CARLO 172XL	OP	RNBT	FBG	SV	IO	120-130		7		1750			2600	3050
17	10	CHALLENGER 189SRV	OP	RNBT	FBG	SV	IO	175-205		7	4	1900			3300	3800
17	10	MONTE-CARLO 189XL	OP	RNBT	FBG	SV	OB			7	4	1200			2750	3200
17	10	MONTE-CARLO 189XL	OP	RNBT	FBG	SV	IO	120-175		7	4	1900			3050	3550
18		1800 CC	OP	CUD	FBG	DV	OB			7	4	1300			2950	3400
18	2	1900 CC	OP	CUD	FBG	DV	OB			7	7	2000			3900	4550
18	2	1900 VBR	OP	B/R	FBG	DV	OB			7	7	2000			3900	4550
18	2	1950 CC	OP	CUD	FBG	DV	SE	130-165		7	7	2000			3900	4550
18	2	1950 VBR	OP	B/R	FBG	DV	SE	130-165				2000			3900	4500
18	2	2000 SF	OP	CTRCN	FBG	DV	OB			7	3	1450			3200	3700
18	2	MONTE-CARLO 194XL	OP	RNBT	FBG	SV	OB			7	7	1450			3200	3700
18	2	MONTE-CARLO 194XL	OP	RNBT	FBG	SV	IO	130-205		7	7	2000			3250	3900
18	2	SUNSKIFF SS200	OP	UTL	FBG	SV	OB			7	3	1000			2250	2600
18	8	CHALLENGER 197SRV	OP	RNBT	FBG	SV	IO	175-260		7	8	2200			3550	4450
18	8	CHALLENGER 197SRV	OP	RNBT	FBG	SV	IO	270	MRCR	7	8	2200			3850	4500
18	8	ODYSSEY 197SCV	OP	CUD	FBG	SV	OB			7	9	1300			3000	3450
18	8	ODYSSEY 197SCV	OP	CUD	FBG	SV	IO	130-175		7	9	2300			3750	4350
19	7	ALLANTE 207ES	OP	RNBT	FBG	DV	IO	175-260		7	7	2529			3950	4900
19	7	ALLANTE 207ES	OP	RNBT	FBG	DV	IO	270	MRCR	7	7	2529			4300	5000
20		ODYSSEY 215CXL	OP	CUD	FBG	SV	IO	130-205		7	7	2520			4350	5100
20	8	MONTE-CARLO 230XL	OP	RNBT	FBG	SV	IO	175-270		8		2875			4800	5900
21	10	ODYSSEY 228MXL	OP	DC	FBG	SV	IO	175-260		8		3800			7350	8800
21	10	ODYSSEY 230CXL	OP	CUD	FBG	SV	IO	175-260		8		3000			5500	6650
23		ODYSSEY 245FC	OP	CUD	FBG	SV	IO	205-270		8	6	4394			7850	9350
25		ODYSSEY 265FC	OP	CUD	FBG	SV	IO	230-270		8	6	4774			9350	10900
25		ODYSSEY 265FC	OP	CUD	FBG	SV	IO	330	MRCR	8	6	4774			10300	11700
25		ODYSSEY 265FC	OP	CUD	FBG	SV	IO	T130-T175		8	6	4774			9950	11600
26		SAN MARINO 278E	OP	DC	FBG	SV	IO	260-330		8	6	5265			12100	14800
26		SAN MARINO 278E	OP	DC	FBG	SV	IO	T165-T175		8	6	5265			12900	14800
1988 BOATS																
16	5	MONTE-CARLO 172XL	OP	RNBT	FBG	SV	OB			7		1100	1	8	2350	2750
16	5	MONTE-CARLO 172XL	OP	RNBT	FBG	SV	IO	120		7		1750			2500	2900
17	10	CHALLENGER 189SRV	OP	RNBT	FBG	SV	IO	175		7	4	1900			2900	3400
17	10	MONTE-CARLO 189XL	OP	RNBT	FBG	SV	OB			7	4	1200	1	8	2650	3100
17	10	MONTE-CARLO 189XL	OP	RNBT	FBG	SV	IO	120		7	4	1900			2900	3350
18	2	MONTE-CARLO 194XL	OP	RNBT	FBG	SV	OB			7	7	1450	1	8	3100	3600
18	2	MONTE-CARLO 194XL	OP	RNBT	FBG	SV	IO	130		7	7	2000			3100	3600
18	2	SUNSKIFF SS200	OP	UTL	FBG	SV	OB			7	3	1000	1	8	2150	2550
18	8	CHALLENGER 197SRV	OP	RNBT	FBG	SV	IO	175		7	8	2200			3350	3900
18	8	ODYSSEY 197SCV	OP	CUD	FBG	SV	OB			7	9	1300	1	8	2900	3350
18	8	ODYSSEY 197SCV	OP	CUD	FBG	SV	IO	130		7	9	2300			3500	4100

 CONTINUED ON NEXT PAGE

COBIA BOAT COMPANY   -CONTINUED   See inside cover to adjust price for area

LOA FT IN	NAME AND/ OR MODEL	TOP/ RIG	BOAT TYPE	-HULL- MTL TP	TP	----ENGINE--- # HP MFG	BEAM FT IN	WGT LBS	DRAFT FT IN	RETAIL LOW	RETAIL HIGH

------------------- 1988 BOATS -------------------

19 6	ALLANTE 207ES	OP	RNBT	FBG DV	IO	175	7 9	2600		3850	4450
20 2	ODYSSEY 215CXL	OP	CUD	FBG SV	IO	130	7 11	2520		4200	4900
20 8	MONTE-CARLO 230XL	OP	RNBT	FBG SV	IO	200	8	2875		4600	5300
21 10	ODYSSEY 228MXL	OP	DC	FBG SV	IO	200	8	3800		7000	8050
21 10	ODYSSEY 230CXL	OP	CUD	FBG SV	IO	200	8	3000		5250	6000
23	ODYSSEY 245FC	OP	CUD	FBG DV	IO	200	8 6	4394		7400	8500
25	ODYSSEY 265FC	OP	CUD	FBG DV	IO	260	8 6	4774		9050	10300
26	SAN MARINO 278E	OP	DC	FBG DV	IO	260	8 6	5265		11500	13000

------------------- 1987 BOATS -------------------

16 5	MONTE-CARLO 172XL	OP	RNBT	FBG SV	OB		7	1100		2350	2700
16 5	MONTE-CARLO 172XL	OP	RNBT	FBG SV	IO	120	7	1750		2350	2750
17 11	CHALLENGER 189SRV	OP	RNBT	FBG SV	IO	175	7 4	1900		2800	3250
17 11	MONTE-CARLO 189XL	OP	RNBT	FBG SV	OB		7 4	1600		3200	3750
17 11	MONTE-CARLO 189XL	OP	RNBT	FBG SV	IO	120	7 4	1900		2750	3200
18 2	MONTE-CARLO 194XL	OP	RNBT	FBG SV	OB		7 7	1450		3000	3500
18 2	MONTE-CARLO 194XL	OP	RNBT	FBG SV	IO	120	7 7	2000		2950	3400
18 2	SUNSKIFF SS200	OP	UTL	FBG SV	OB		7 3	1000		2050	2450
18 8	CHALLENGER 197SRV	OP	RNBT	FBG SV	IO	175	7 9	2300		3300	3800
18 8	ODYSSEY 197SCV	OP	CUD	FBG SV	OB		7 9	2300		4000	4650
18 8	ODYSSEY 197SCV	OP	CUD	FBG SV	IO	120	7 9	2300		3350	3900
20 2	ODYSSEY 215CXL	OP	CUD	FBG SV	IO	130	7 11	2520		4000	4650
20 8	MONTE-CARLO 230XL	OP	RNBT	FBG SV	IO	165	8	2875		4300	5000
20 2	ODYSSEY 228MXL	OP	DC	FBG SV	IO	165	8	3800		6200	7100
20 8	ODYSSEY 230CXL	OP	CUD	FBG SV	IO	165	8	3000		4450	5100
25	ODYSSEY 256FC	OP	CUD	FBG DV	IO	230	8 6	4775		8300	9550

------------------- 1986 BOATS -------------------

16 5	SPORTSTER 172VBR	OP	RNBT	FBG DV	OB		7	1110		2300	2650
16 5	SPORTSTER 172VBR	OP	RNBT	FBG DV	IO	120	7	1750		2250	2600
17 10	CHALLENGER 189SRV	OP	RNBT	FBG DV	IO	175 OMC	7 4	1900		2600	3050
17 10	MONTE-CARLO 189XL	OP	RNBT	FBG DV	OB		7 4	1200		2500	2900
17 10	MONTE-CARLO 189XL	OP	RNBT	FBG DV	IO	120 OMC	7 4	1900		2600	3000
17 10	MONTE-CARLO 189SCV	OP	CUD	FBG DV	IO	120 OMC	7 4	2000		2700	3150
18 2	SPORTSTER 193VBR	OP	RNBT	FBG DV	IO	120 OMC	7 1	1950		2600	3050
18 2	SUNSKIFF 200	OP	CTRCN	FBG DV	OB		6 9	1000		2200	2550
18 8	CHALLENGER 197SRV	OP	RNBT	FBG DV	IO	230	8 1	2200		3250	3800
18 8	MONTE-CARLO 197XL	OP	RNBT	FBG DV	OB		8 1	1900		3000	3450
18 8	MONTE-CARLO 197XL	OP	RNBT	FBG DV	SE	OMC	8 1	2200		**	**
18 8	MONTE-CARLO 197XL	OP	RNBT	FBG DV	IO	140 OMC	8 1	2200		3100	3600
18 8	ODYSSEY 197CXL	OP	CUD	FBG DV	SE	OMC	8 1	1900		**	**
18 8	ODYSSEY 197CXL	OP	CUD	FBG DV	IO	140	8 1	2300		3300	3850
18 8	SPORTSTER 197SCV	OP	CUD	FBG DV	IO	120	8 1	2300		3300	3850
20 2	MONTE-CARLO 215XL	OP	RNBT	FBG DV	SE	OMC	7 11	1950		**	**
20 2	MONTE-CARLO 215XL	OP	RNBT	FBG DV	IO	140 OMC	7 11	2450		3600	4200
20 2	ODYSSEY 215CXL	OP	CUD	FBG DV	SE	OMC	7 11	2200		**	**
20 2	ODYSSEY 215CXL	OP	CUD	FBG DV	IO	140 OMC	7 11	2520		3800	4450
20 8	MONTE-CARLO 230XL	OP	RNBT	FBG DV	SE	OMC	8	2875		4100	4750
20 8	MONTE-CARLO 230XL	OP	RNBT	FBG DV	IO	175 OMC	8	2200		**	**
20 8	ODYSSEY 230CXL	OP	CUD	FBG DV	SE	OMC	8	2400		**	**
20 8	ODYSSEY 230CXL	OP	CUD	FBG DV	IO	175 OMC	8	3000		4450	5100
20 8	ODYSSEY 230MXL	OP	CUD	FBG DV	SE	OMC	8	3000		**	**
20 8	ODYSSEY 230MXL	OP	CUD	FBG DV	IO	205 OMC	8	3400		4800	5550

------------------- 1985 BOATS -------------------

16 5	ODYSSEY 170SR	OP	RNBT	FBG DV	OB		7	1050		2100	2500
16 5	ODYSSEY 170SR	OP	RNBT	FBG DV	OB		7	1700		2150	2500
16 5	ODYSSEY 170VBR	OP	RNBT	FBG DV	OB		7	1100		2200	2600
16 5	ODYSSEY 170VBR	OP	RNBT	FBG DV	IO	120	7	1750		2200	2550
17 8	ODYSSEY 183CC	OP	CUD	FBG DV	OB		7 4	1300		2600	3050
17 8	ODYSSEY 183CC	OP	CUD	FBG DV	IO	120	7 4	2000		2600	3000
17 8	ODYSSEY 183SR	OP	RNBT	FBG DV	IO	120	7 4	1850		2400	2800
17 8	ODYSSEY 183VBR	OP	RNBT	FBG DV	OB		7 4	1200		2450	2850
17 8	ODYSSEY 183VBR	OP	RNBT	FBG DV	IO	120	7 4	1900		2500	2900
18	SPORTSTER C18VBR	ST	RNBT	FBG DV	IO	120 OMC	7	1950		2450	2850
18	SUNSKIFF CU180	OP	CTRCN	FBG DV	OB		6 11	1000		2100	2500
18 6	ODYSSEY 195CC	OP	CUD	FBG DV	OB		7 11	1550		3050	3500
18 6	ODYSSEY 195CC	OP	CUD	FBG DV	IO	120	7 11	2300		3100	3600
18 6	ODYSSEY 195SCL	OP	RNBT	FBG DV	IO	120	7 11	2200		2950	3450
18 6	ODYSSEY 195VBR	OP	RNBT	FBG DV	OB		7 11	1450		2900	3350
18 6	ODYSSEY 195VBR	OP	RNBT	FBG DV	IO	120 OMC	7 11	2200		2900	3350
20 8	ODYSSEY 214	ST	RNBT	FBG DV	IO	170 OMC	8	2000		4300	4650
21 4	R2165		CUD	FBG DV	IO	185	8	1140		3450	4000
21 6	ODYSSEY 228	ST	RNBT	FBG DV	IO	185 OMC	8	3600		4750	5450
21 6	ODYSSEY 228SD	ST	RNBT	FBG DV	SE	155 OMC	8	3300		6500	7450
21 6	TRITON 228SD	ST	FSH	FBG DV	IO	155 OMC	8	2850		6000	6850
21 6	TRITON 228WAC	ST	FSH	FBG DV	OB		8	2400		5350	6150

------------------- 1984 BOATS -------------------

16	SUNSKIFF CU160	OP	CTRCN	FBG TR	OB		7	800		1550	1850
16 5	ODYSSEY 170SR	OP	RNBT	FBG DV	OB		7	1050		2050	2400
16 5	ODYSSEY 170SR	OP	RNBT	FBG DV	OB		7	1700		2050	2400
16 5	ODYSSEY 170VBR	OP	RNBT	FBG DV	OB		7	1100		2150	2550
16 5	ODYSSEY 170VBR	OP	RNBT	FBG DV	IO	120	7	1750		2050	2450
17 8	ODYSSEY 183CC	OP	CUD	FBG DV	OB		7 3	1300		2550	2950
17 8	ODYSSEY 183CC	OP	CUD	FBG DV	IO	120	7 3	2000		2500	2900
17 8	ODYSSEY 183SR	OP	RNBT	FBG DV	IO	120	7 3	1850		2350	2750
17 8	ODYSSEY 183VBR	OP	RNBT	FBG DV	OB		7 3	1200		2400	2800
17 8	ODYSSEY 183VBR	OP	RNBT	FBG DV	IO	120	7 3	1900		2400	2750
18	SPORTSTER C18VBR	ST	RNBT	FBG DV	IO	120 OMC	6 11	1950		2350	2750
18	SUNSKIFF CU180	OP	CTRCN	FBG DV	OB		6 11	1000		2050	2450
18 6	ODYSSEY 195CC	OP	CUD	FBG DV	IO	120	7 11	1550		2950	3450
18 6	ODYSSEY 195CC	OP	CUD	FBG DV	IO	120-198	7 11	2300		2950	3450
18 6	ODYSSEY 195SCL	OP	RNBT	FBG DV	IO		7 11	2200		2900	3350
18 6	ODYSSEY 195VBR	OP	RNBT	FBG DV	OB		7 11	1450		2850	3300
18 6	ODYSSEY 195VBR	OP	RNBT	FBG DV	IO	120-200	7 11	2200		2750	3350
18 6	SUNSKIFF CU195		FSH	FBG DV	OB		7 11	1100		2300	2700
20 7	SUNSKIFF CU210	OP	CTRCN	FBG DV	OB		7 6	1510		3500	4050
21 4	R2165		CR	FBG DV	IO	188	8	1140		3350	3850
21 6	ODYSSEY 228	ST	RNBT	FBG DV	IO	185-260	8	3600		4600	5500
21 6	ODYSSEY 228SD	ST	RNBT	FBG DV	SE	OMC	8	3300		**	**
21 6	TRITON 228SD	ST	FSH	FBG DV	IO	OMC	8	2850		**	**
21 6	TRITON 228WAC	ST	FSH	FBG DV	OB		8	2400		5250	6050
26	R2665		CR	FBG DV	IO	260	8	1450		5800	6700
26 5	RT260		CR	FBG DV	IB	T228	10 2			13500	15400

....For earlier years, see the BUC Used Boat Price Guide, Volume 3

COMAR S P A
FORLI ITALY 47100   COAST GUARD MFG ID- CDF See inside cover to adjust price for area

COMAR USA INC
IRVINGTON NJ 07111

LOA FT IN	NAME AND/ OR MODEL	TOP/ RIG	BOAT TYPE	-HULL- MTL TP	TP	----ENGINE--- # HP MFG	BEAM FT IN	WGT LBS	DRAFT FT IN	RETAIL LOW	RETAIL HIGH

------------------- 1986 BOATS -------------------

28	COMET 860	SLP	SA/CR	FBG KL	IB	D	9 8	6600	5 3	19700	21900
30 6	COMET 910	SLP	SA/CR	FBG KL	IB	D	10	6974	5 7	21800	24200
32 2	COMET 1000	SLP	SA/CR	FBG KL	IB	D	10 10	10120	5 11	31800	35400
34 4	COMET 1050	SLP	SA/CR	FBG KL	IB	D	11 4	11000	6	34600	38400
37 2	IPERION 37	EXP		FBG SV	IB	T260D	11 10	12800		40100	44500
38 6	COMET IT PLUS	SLP	SA/RC	FBG KL	IB	D	11 10	14300	6 7	49300	54200
39 4	COMET 12	SLP	SA/RC	FBG KL	IB	D	12 10	18700	6 7	62900	69100

------------------- 1985 BOATS -------------------

30 6	COMET 910	SLP	SA/CR	FBG KL	IB	D	10	6974	5 7	20500	22700
32 2	COMET 1000	SLP	SA/CR	FBG KL	IB	D	10 10	10120	5 11	29900	33300
34 4	COMET 1050	SLP	SA/CR	FBG KL	IB	D	11 4	11000	6	32500	36200
36 3	COMET 111	SLP	SA/RC	FBG KL	IB	D	11 10	13850	6 7	41500	46100
38 6	COMET IT PLUS	SLP	SA/RC	FBG KL	IB	D	11 10	14300	6 7	46700	51300
43 2	COMET 13	SLP	SA/RC	FBG KL	IB	D	12 6	22000	6 3	77400	85000
49 3	COMET 15	SLP	SA/RC	FBG KL	IB	D	14 1	30000	6 4	111500	122500

------------------- 1984 BOATS -------------------

30 6	COMET 910 PLUS	SLP	SA/RC	FBG KL	IB	9D	10	6974	4 7	19200	21300
30 6	COMET 910 PLUS SHOAL	SLP	SA/RC	FBG KL	IB	9D	10	6974	4 7	19200	21300
34 4	COMET 1050	SLP	SA/CR	FBG KL	IB	18D	11 4	11000	4 9	30500	33900
34 4	COMET 1050 SHOAL	SLP	SA/CR	FBG KL	IB	18D	11 4	11000	4 9	30500	33900
36 3	COMET III	SLP	SA/CR	FBG KL	IB	25D	11 10	13850	6 7	38900	43300
36 3	COMET III SHOAL	SLP	SA/CR	FBG KL	IB	25D	11 10	13850	5 3	38900	43300

....For earlier years, see the BUC Used Boat Price Guide, Volume 3

COMFORT YACHTS USA
FT LAUDERDALE FL 33316   See inside cover to adjust price for area

LOA FT IN	NAME AND/ OR MODEL	TOP/ RIG	BOAT TYPE	-HULL- MTL TP	TP	----ENGINE--- # HP MFG	BEAM FT IN	WGT LBS	DRAFT FT IN	RETAIL LOW	RETAIL HIGH

------------------- 1985 BOATS -------------------

| 31 2 | COMFORTINA 32 | SLP | SA/RC | FBG KL | IB | 18D VLVO | 10 9 | 9900 | 4 6 | 34300 | 38100 |
| 31 2 | COMFORTINA 32 SHOAL | SLP | SA/RC | FBG KL | IB | 18D VLVO | 10 9 | 9900 | 4 6 | 34300 | 38100 |

154 96th ed. - Vol. II

COMMANDER BOATS

PERRIS CA 92570

See inside cover to adjust price for area

For more recent years, see the BUC Used Boat Price Guide, Volume 1

LOA FT	LOA IN	NAME AND/ OR MODEL	TOP/ RIG	BOAT TYPE	-HULL- MTL	-HULL- TP	---ENGINE--- TP	# HP	MFG	BEAM FT	BEAM IN	WGT LBS	DRAFT FT	DRAFT IN	RETAIL LOW	RETAIL HIGH
1996 BOATS																
18		TIGER	ST	SKI	FBG	SV	OB			7		1150			8650	9950
19		CALIFORNIAN	ST	SKI	FBG	SV	JT	325	CHEV	7		1800			15800	18000
19		COBRA	ST	SKI	FBG	SV	OB			7	1	1350			10200	11600
19		MINI CRUISER	ST	SKI	FBG	SV	JT	325	CHEV	7	2	1900			16300	18500
19		NEWPORT	ST	SKI	FBG	SV	OB			7		1250			9600	10900
19		SUPERSPORT	ST	SKI	FBG	SV	IO	250	MRCR	7	4	1800			12200	13800
20	2	SUNSTREAKER	ST	SKI	FBG	SV	OB			7	4	1550			10900	12400
20	2	SUNSTREAKER	ST	SKI	FBG	SV	IO	250	MRCR	7	4	2000			14200	16100
20	2	SUNSTREAKER	ST	SKI	FBG	SV	JT	325	CHEV	7	4	2000			19000	21200
21		2100 LX	ST	SKI	FBG	SV	OB			8		1850			14500	16400
21		2100 LX	ST	SKI	FBG	SV	IO	250	MRCR	8		2300			16900	19200
21		2100 LX	ST	SKI	FBG	SV	JT	325	CHEV	8		2300			22500	25000
21		CONQUEST	ST	SKI	FBG	SV	IO	250	MRCR	8		2300			16200	18400
21		CONQUEST	ST	SKI	FBG	SV	JT	325	CHEV	8		2300			21400	23800
22	6	HAWK LX	ST	SKI	FBG	SV	IO	300	MRCR	8		2700			20900	23200
22	6	HAWK LX	ST	SKI	FBG	SV	JT	325	CHEV	8		2700			25400	28200
23		2300 LX	ST	SKI	FBG	SV	OB			8		2700			21400	23700
23		2300 LX	ST	SKI	FBG	SV	IO	300	MRCR	8		2700			21400	23800
23		2300 LX	ST	SKI	FBG	SV	JT	325	CHEV	8		2700			26000	28900
24		SUPERCRUISER	ST	CR	FBG	SV	IO	300	MRCR	8		3400			27200	30200
25		2500 LX	ST	CR	FBG	SV	IO	300	MRCR	8		3400			29800	33100
25		SIGNATURE 25	ST	OFF	FBG	DV	IO	300	MRCR	6	9	3100			26800	29800
26		2600 LX	ST	CR	FBG	SV	IO	350	MRCR	8	3	3700			36900	41000
26		SIGNATURE 26	ST	OFF	FBG	DV	IO	350	MRCR	8	2	3300			34200	38000
28		SIGNATURE 28	ST	OFF	FBG	DV	IO	415	MRCR	7	8	3500			39600	44000
28	8	OFFSHORE 29	ST	OFF	FBG	DV	IO	350	MRCR	8	6	5600			53500	58800
28	8	OFFSHORE 29	ST	OFF	FBG	DV	IO	T350	MRCR	8	6	6700			66800	73400
31		OFFSHORE CAT	ST	OFF	FBG	TH	IO	T350-T415		8	6	7500			74300	85700
34		OFFSHORE 34	ST	OFF	FBG	DV	IO	T415	MRCR	8		8000			100000	110000
1995 BOATS																
18		TIGER	ST	SKI	FBG	SV	OB			7		1150			8250	9500
19		CALIFORNIAN	ST	SKI	FBG	SV	JT	325	CHEV	7		1800			14900	17000
19		COBRA	ST	SKI	FBG	SV	OB			7	1	1350			9750	11100
19		MINI CRUISER	ST	SKI	FBG	SV	JT	325	CHEV	7	2	1900			15400	17500
19		NEWPORT	ST	SKI	FBG	SV	OB			7		1250			9200	10500
19		SUPERSPORT	ST	SKI	FBG	SV	IO	230	MRCR	7	4	1800			11100	12600
20	2	SUNSTREAKER	ST	SKI	FBG	SV	OB			7	4	1550			10400	11800
20	2	SUNSTREAKER	ST	SKI	FBG	SV	IO	230	MRCR	7	4	2000			12900	14700
20	2	SUNSTREAKER	ST	SKI	FBG	SV	JT	325	CHEV	7	4	2000			18200	20200
21		2100 LX	ST	SKI	FBG	SV	OB			8		1850			13700	15600
21		2100 LX	ST	SKI	FBG	SV	IO	230	MRCR	8		2300			15400	17500
21		2100 LX	ST	SKI	FBC	SV	JT	325	CHEV	8		2300			21200	23500
21		CONQUEST	ST	SKI	FBG	SV	OB			8		1850			13200	15000
21		CONQUEST	ST	SKI	FBG	SV	IO	230	MRCR	8		2300			14800	16900
21		CONQUEST	ST	SKI	FBG	SV	JT	325	CHEV	8		2300			20300	22600
22	6	HAWK LX	ST	SKI	FBG	SV	OB			8		2200			16600	18900
22	6	HAWK LX	ST	SKI	FBG	SV	IO	300	MRCR	8		2700			19500	21700
22	6	HAWK LX	ST	SKI	FBG	SV	JT	325	CHEV	8		2700			24000	26700
24		SUPERCRUISER	ST	CR	FBG	SV	IO	300	MRCR	8		3400			25400	28200
25		2500 LX	ST	CR	FBG	SV	IO	300	MRCR	8		3400			27800	30900
25		SIGNATURE 25	ST	OFF	FBG	DV	IO	300	MRCR	6	9	3100			25000	27800
26		2600 LX	ST	CR	FBG	SV	IO	300	MRCR	8	3	3700			31900	35500
26		SIGNATURE 26	ST	OFF	FBG	DV	IO	300	MRCR	8	2	3300			29500	32800
28		SIGNATURE 28	ST	OFF	FBG	DV	IO	415	MRCR	7	8	3500			36900	41000
28	8	OFFSHORE 29	ST	OFF	FBG	DV	IO	350	MRCR	8	6	5600			49900	54900
28	8	OFFSHORE 29	ST	OFF	FBG	DV	IO	T350	MRCR	8	6	6700			62300	68500
31		OFFSHORE CAT	ST	OFF	FBG	CT	IO	T350-T415		8	6	7500			67100	77300
34		OFFSHORE 34	ST	OFF	FBG	DV	IO	T415	MRCR	8		8000			93300	102500
1994 BOATS																
18		TIGER	ST	SKI	FBG	SV	OB			7		1150			7900	9050
19		CALIFORNIAN	ST	SKI	FBG	SV	JT	325	CHEV	7		1800			14100	16100
19		COBRA	ST	SKI	FBG	SV	OB			7	1	1350			9350	10600
19		MINI CRUISER	ST	SKI	FBG	SV	JT	325	CHEV	7	2	1900			14600	16600
19		NEWPORT	ST	SKI	FBG	SV	OB			7		1250			8700	10000
19		SUPERSPORT	ST	SKI	FBG	SV	IO	230	MRCR	7	4	1800			10300	11700
20	2	SUNSTREAKER	ST	SKI	FBG	SV	OB			7	4	1550			9950	11300
20	2	SUNSTREAKER	ST	SKI	FBG	SV	IO	230	MRCR	7	4	2000			12100	13700
20	2	SUNSTREAKER	ST	SKI	FBG	SV	JT	325	CHEV	7	4	2000			16800	19100
21		CONQUEST	ST	SKI	FBG	SV	OB			8		1850			12800	14500
21		CONQUEST	ST	SKI	FBG	SV	IO	230	MRCR	8		2300			14100	16100
21		CONQUEST	ST	SKI	FBG	SV	JT	325	CHEV	8		2300			19700	21800
22	6	HAWK LX	ST	SKI	FBG	SV	OB			8		2200			15600	17700
22	6	HAWK LX	ST	SKI	FBG	SV	IO	300	MRCR	8		2700			18400	20500
22	6	HAWK LX	ST	SKI	FBG	SV	JT	325	CHEV	8		2700			22700	25200
24		APOLLO 24	ST	OFF	FBG	DV	IO	300	MRCR	6	9	3100			21600	24000
24		SUPERCRUISER	ST	CR	FBG	SV	IO	300	MRCR	8		3400			23700	26300
24	6	APOLLO 24.5 LX	ST	OFF	FBG	DV	IO	300	MRCR	8	2	3300			24200	26800
25		2500 LX	ST	CR	FBG	SV	IO	300	MRCR	8		3400			25900	28800
26		SUPERCRUISER 26	ST	CR	FBG	SV	IO	300	MRCR	8	3	3700			29800	33100
28		APOLLO 28	ST	OFF	FBG	DV	IO	415	MRCR	7	8	3500			36400	40400
28	8	OFFSHORE 29	ST	OFF	FBG	DV	IO	350	MRCR	8	6	5600			46800	51500
28	8	OFFSHORE 29	ST	OFF	FBG	DV	IO	T350	MRCR	8	6	6700			58200	63900
31		OFFSHORE CAT	ST	OFF	FBG	CT	IO	T350-T415		8	6	7500			62700	72100
34		OFFSHORE	ST	OFF	FBG	DV	IO	T415	MRCR	8		8000			101000	111000
1993 BOATS																
18		TIGER	ST	SKI	FBG	SV	OB			7		1150			7550	8700
19		CALIFORNIAN	ST	SKI	FBG	SV	JT	325	CHEV	7		1800			13400	15200
19		COBRA	ST	SKI	FBG	SV	OB			7	1	1350			8900	10100
19		MINI CRUISER	ST	SKI	FBG	SV	JT	325	CHEV	7	2	1900			13800	15700
19		NEWPORT	ST	SKI	FBG	SV	OB			7		1250			8300	9500
19		SUPERSPORT	ST	SKI	FBG	SV	IO	230	MRCR	7	4	1800			9650	11000
20	2	SUNSTREAKER	ST	SKI	FBG	SV	OB			7	4	1550			9550	10900
20	2	SUNSTREAKER	ST	SKI	FBG	SV	IO	230	MRCR	7	4	2000			11300	12800
20	2	SUNSTREAKER	ST	SKI	FBG	SV	JT	325	CHEV	7	4	2000			16000	18100
21		CONQUEST	ST	SKI	FBG	SV	OB			8		1850			12200	13800
21		CONQUEST	ST	SKI	FBG	SV	IO	230	MRCR	8		2300			13200	15000
21		CONQUEST	ST	SKI	FBG	SV	JT	325	CHEV	8		2300			18800	20900
22	6	HAWK LX	ST	SKI	FBG	SV	OB			8		2200			14800	16800
22	6	HAWK LX	ST	SKI	FBG	SV	IO	300	MRCR	8		2700			16800	19100
22	6	HAWK LX	ST	SKI	FBG	SV	JT	325	CHEV	8		2700			21500	23900
24		APOLLO 24	ST	OFF	FBG	DV	IO	300	MRCR	6	9	3100			20200	22400
24		SUPERCRUISER	ST	CR	FBG	SV	IO	300	MRCR	8		3400			22100	24600
28		APOLLO 28	ST	OFF	FBG	DV	IO	390	MRCR	7	8	3500			32700	36400
28	8	OFFSHORE 29	ST	OFF	FBG	DV	IO	350	MRCR	8	6	5600			43300	48100
28	8	OFFSHORE 29	ST	OFF	FBG	DV	IO	T350	MRCR	8	6	6700			54400	59700
31		OFFSHORE CAT	ST	OFF	FBG	CT	IO	T350-T390		8	6	7500			58600	65900
1992 BOATS																
18		TIGER	ST	SKI	FBG	SV	OB			7		1150			7200	8300
19		CALIFORNIAN	ST	SKI	FBG	SV	JT	325	CHEV	7		1800			12700	14500
19		COBRA	ST	SKI	FBG	SV	OB			7	1	1350			8400	9650
19		MINI CRUISER	ST	SKI	FBG	SV	JT	325	CHEV	7	2	1900			13100	14900
19		NEWPORT	ST	SKI	FBG	SV	OB			7		1250			7950	9100
19		SUPERSPORT	ST	SKI	FBG	SV	IO	230	MRCR	7	4	1800			9100	10300
20	2	SUNSTREAKER	ST	SKI	FBG	SV	OB			7	4	1550			9250	10500
20	2	SUNSTREAKER	ST	SKI	FBG	SV	IO	230	MRCR	7	4	2000			10600	12000
20	2	SUNSTREAKER	ST	SKI	FBG	SV	JT	325	CHEV	7	4	2000			15100	17200
21		CONQUEST	ST	SKI	FBG	SV	OB			8		1850			11600	13200
21		CONQUEST	ST	SKI	FBG	SV	IO	230	MRCR	8		2300			12400	14000
21		CONQUEST	ST	SKI	FBG	SV	JT	325	CHEV	8		2300			17500	19900
24		APOLLO 24	ST	OFF	FBG	DV	IO	300	MRCR	6	9	3100			19100	21200
24		SUPRA	ST	CR	FBG	SV	IO	300	MRCR	8		3400			20700	23000
28		APOLLO 28	ST	OFF	FBG	DV	IO	390	MRCR	7	8	3500			30500	33900
28	8	OFFSHORE 29	ST	OFF	FBG	DV	IO	350	MRCR	8	6	5600			40500	45000
28	8	OFFSHORE 29	ST	OFF	FBG	DV	IO	T350	MRCR	8	6	6700			50900	56000
31		OFFSHORE CAT	ST	OFF	FBG	CT	IO	T350-T390		8	6	7500			54800	61700
1991 BOATS																
18		TIGER	ST	SKI	FBG	SV	OB			7		1150			6950	7950
19		CALIFORNIAN	ST	SKI	FBG	SV	JT	375	CHEV	7		1800			12100	13700
19		COBRA	ST	SKI	FBG	SV	OB			7	1	1350			8050	9250
19		MINI CRUISER	ST	SKI	FBG	SV	JT	325	CHEV	7	2	1900			12500	14200
19		NEWPORT	ST	SKI	FBG	SV	OB			7		1250			7550	8700
20	2	SUNSTREAKER	ST	SKI	FBG	SV	OB			7	4	1550			8850	10100
20	2	SUNSTREAKER	ST	SKI	FBG	SV	IO	260	MRCR	7	4	2000			10300	11700
20	2	SUNSTREAKER	ST	SKI	FBG	SV	JT	325	CHEV	7	4	2000			14400	16400
21		CONQUEST	ST	SKI	FBG	SV	OB			8		1850			11100	12600
21		CONQUEST	ST	SKI	FBG	SV	IO	260	MRCR	8		2300			12000	13600
21		CONQUEST	ST	SKI	FBG	SV	JT	325	CHEV	8		2300			16600	18900
24		APOLLO 24	ST	OFF	FBG	DV	IO	330	MRCR	6	9	3100			19000	21100
24		SUPRA	ST	CR	FBG	SV	IO	330	MRCR	8		3400			20500	22800
28	8	OFFSHORE 29	ST	OFF	FBG	DV	IO	365	MRCR	8	6	5600			38500	42800
28	8	OFFSHORE 29	ST	OFF	FBG	DV	IO	T365	MRCR	8	6	6700			48700	53500
31		OFFSHORE CAT		OFF	FBG	CT	OB			8	6	6900			43200	48000
31		OFFSHORE CAT		OFF	FBG	CT	IO	T365	MRCR	8	6	7500			52100	57200

COMMERCIAL WORK BOATS
MIAMI FL 33178   COAST GUARD MFG ID- UUV See inside cover to adjust price for area

LOA FT IN	NAME AND/ OR MODEL	TOP/ RIG	BOAT TYPE	-HULL- MTL TP	----ENGINE--- TP # HP MFG	BEAM FT IN	WGT LBS	DRAFT FT IN	RETAIL LOW	RETAIL HIGH
				1986 BOATS						
26 9	OFFSHORE 27	HT	OFF	FBG DS IB	85D-200D	10 3	7500	2 6	23200	27300
26 9	OFFSHORE 27	HT	OFF	FBG DS IB	210D-240D	10 3	9000	3	29700	35000
26 9	OFFSHORE 27 EXPRESS	ST	EXP	FBG RB IB	240D PERK	10 3	9500	2 6	31300	34800
26 9	OFFSHORE 27 SEDAN	HT	CR	FBG RB IB	225D GM	10 3	9500	2 6	30600	34000
40 3	OFFSHORE 40	HT	TRWL	FBG DS IB	135D PERK 14		20000	3	80200	88200
	IB 300D CAT 90800		99800, IB	355D CAT	99200 109000, IB T300D CAT				114000 125500
40 3	OFFSHORE 40	FB	TRWL	FBG DS IB	T135D PERK 14		26000	3	106000 116500
40 3	OFFSHORE 40 SEDAN	FB	SF	FBG DS IB	T355D CAT 14		22000	3 6	106000 116500
40 3	OFFSHORE 40 TRAWLER	FB	TRWL	FBG DS IB	210D CAT 14		22000	3 6	88900 97700
55	OFFSHORE 55	HT	TRWL	FBG DS IB	350D GM 16		44000	5 3	128000 140500
				1985 BOATS						
26 9	OFFSHORE 27	HT	OFF	FBG DS IB	85D-200D	10 3	7500	2 6	22300	26200
26 9	OFFSHORE 27	HT	OFF	FBG DS IB	210D-240D	10 3	9000	3	28400	33600
40 3	OFFSHORE 40	HT	TRWL	FBG DS IB	355D CAT 14		24000	3	95000 104500
				1984 BOATS						
26 9	OFFSHORE 27	HT	OFF	FBG DS IB	85D-200D	10 3	7500	2 6	21400	25100
26 9	OFFSHORE 27	HT	OFF	FBG DS IB	225D-240D	10 3	9000	3	27400	32300
40 3	OFFSHORE 40	HT	TRWL	FBG DS IB	135D PERK 14		20000	3	73600	80900
	IB 300D CAT 83300		91500, IB	355D CAT	91000 100000, IB T300D CAT				104500 115000
40 3	OFFSHORE 40	FB	TRWL	FBG DS IB	T135D PERK 14		26000	3	97100 106500

....For earlier years, see the BUC Used Boat Price Guide, Volume 3

COMMODORE YACHT CORP
ST JAMES FL 33956   COAST GUARD MFG ID- XYV See inside cover to adjust price for area

LOA FT IN	NAME AND/ OR MODEL	TOP/ RIG	BOAT TYPE	-HULL- MTL TP	----ENGINE--- TP # HP MFG	BEAM FT IN	WGT LBS	DRAFT FT IN	RETAIL LOW	RETAIL HIGH
				1984 BOATS						
17 2	COMMODORE 17	SLP	SA/CR	FBG CB OB		7 2	1200	1	1900	2300
20	SKIPPER 20	SLP	SA/CR	FBG KL OB		6 8	2000	2	2700	3100
25 10	COMMODORE 26	SLP	SA/CR	FBG KL OB		7 11	4400	2 1	6500	7450
25 10	COMMODORE 26	SLP	SA/CR	FBG KL IB	8D BMW	7 11	4400	2 1	6900	7950

....For earlier years, see the BUC Used Boat Price Guide, Volume 3

COMPODYNE CORPORATION
SARASOTA FL 33580   COAST GUARD MFG ID- BNU See inside cover to adjust price for area
FORMERLY FORCE ENGINEER

LOA FT IN	NAME AND/ OR MODEL	TOP/ RIG	BOAT TYPE	-HULL- MTL TP	----ENGINE--- TP # HP MFG	BEAM FT IN	WGT LBS	DRAFT FT IN	RETAIL LOW	RETAIL HIGH
				1986 BOATS						
23	STILETTO 23	SLP	SA/RC	F/S CT OB		13 10	650	6	8300	9550
26 10	STILETTO CLASSIC	SLP	SA/CR	F/S CT OB		13 10	1565	9	16000	18200
26 10	STILETTO GT	SLP	SA/CR	F/S CT OB		16	1725	10	16500	18700
29 4	STILETTO 30	SLP	SA/CR	F/S CT OB		17 10	2650	11	25600	28400
				1985 BOATS						
23	STILETTO 23	SLP	SA/RC	F/S CT OB		13 10	650	6	7800	9000
26 10	STILETTO 27	SLP	SA/CR	F/S CT OB		13 10	1100	9	13700	15600
26 10	STILETTO GT	SLP	SA/CR	F/S CT OB		16	1725	10	15100	17600
26 10	STILETTO SE	SLP	SA/CR	F/S CT OB		13 10	1565	9	15100	17100
29 4	STILETTO 30 CRUISER	SLP	SA/RC	F/S CT OB		17 10	2650	11	24000	26700
29 4	STILETTO 30 RACER	SLP	SA/RC	F/S CT OB		17 10	2400	11	23400	26000
				1984 BOATS						
26 10	STILETTO 27	SLP	SA/RC	F/S CT OB		13 10	1100	9	12900	14700
26 10	STILETTO CHAMP EDIT	SLP	SA/RC	F/S CT OB		13 10	1200	9	13200	15000
26 10	STILETTO GT	SLP	SA/RC	F/S CT OB		16	1400	9	13800	15700
26 10	STILETTO SE	SLP	SA/CR	F/S CT OB		13 10	1565	9	14200	16100
29 10	STILETTO 30 CRUISER	SLP	SA/RC	F/S CT OB		18	2300	11	22800	25300
29 10	STILETTO 30 RACER	SLP	SA/RC	F/S CT OB		18	2100	10	22200	24700

....For earlier years, see the BUC Used Boat Price Guide, Volume 3

COMPROMIS YACHTS
ZAADNOORDJK WATERSPORT BV   See inside cover to adjust price for area
UITGEEST HOLLAND

LOA FT IN	NAME AND/ OR MODEL	TOP/ RIG	BOAT TYPE	-HULL- MTL TP	----ENGINE--- TP # HP MFG	BEAM FT IN	WGT LBS	DRAFT FT IN	RETAIL LOW	RETAIL HIGH
				1995 BOATS						
20 4	CENTAUR FIXED	SLP	SACAC	F/S KL OB		6 6	1210	2 8	8450	9700
20 4	CENTAUR SWING	SLP	SACAC	F/S KL OB		6 6	1210	3 6	8450	9700
25 11	COMPROMIS 777	SLP	SACAC	F/S KL IB	9D YAN	9 2	5069	4 1	32900	36600
28 6	COMPROMIS 888	SLP	SACAC	F/S KL IB	18D YAN	9 8	7496	4 10	54400	59400
33 6	COMPROMIS 999	SLP	SACAC	F/S KL IB	27D YAN	11 2	10362	4 10	78800	86600
39 6	COMPROMIS 39 CLASS	SLP	SACAC	F/S KL IB	38D YAN	13 3	16889	5 5	138000 151500
				1994 BOATS						
20 4	CENTAUR FIXED	SLP	SACAC	F/S KL OB		6 6	1210	2 8	7950	9100
20 4	CENTAUR SWING	SLP	SACAC	F/S KL OB		6 6	1210	3 6	7950	9100
25 11	COMPROMIS 777	SLP	SACAC	F/S KL IB	9D YAN	9 2	5069	4 1	30900	34400
28 6	COMPROMIS 888	SLP	SACAC	F/S KL IB	18D YAN	9 8	7496	4 10	50800	55900
33 6	COMPROMIS 999	SLP	SACAC	F/S KL IB	27D YAN	11 2	10362	4 10	74100	81400
39 6	COMPROMIS 39	SLP	SACAC	F/S KL IB	38D YAN	13 3	16889	5 5	130000 142500
				1993 BOATS						
20 4	CENTAUR FIXED	SLP	SACAC	F/S KL OB		6 6	1210	2 8	7450	8550
20 4	CENTAUR SWING	SLP	SACAC	F/S KL OB		6 6	1210	3 6	7450	8550
25 11	COMPROMIS 777	SLP	SACAC	F/S KL IB	9D YAN	9 2	5069	4 1	29100	32300
28 6	COMPROMIS 888	SLP	SACAC	F/S KL IB	18D YAN	9 8	7496	4 10	47800	52500
32 6	COMPROMIS 999	SLP	SACAC	F/S KL IB	27D YAN	11 2	10362	4 10	69900	76800
38 6	COMPROMIS 39	SLP	SACAC	F/S KL IB	38D YAN	13 3	16889	5 5	117000 128500
				1992 BOATS						
20 4	CENTAUR FIXED	SLP	SAIL	F/S KL OB		6 6	1210	2 8	7000	8050
20 4	CENTAUR SWING	SLP	SAIL	F/S KL OB		6 6	1210	3 6	7000	8050
25 11	COMPROMIS 777	SLP	SAIL	F/S KL IB	9D YAN	9 2	5069	4 1	27300	30400
28 6	COMPROMIS 888	SLP	SAIL	F/S KL IB	18D YAN	9 8	7496	4 10	44000	49700
32 6	COMPROMIS 999	SLP	SAIL	F/S KL IB	27D YAN	11 2	10362	4 10	65800	72300
38 6	COMPROMIS 39	SLP	SAIL	F/S KL IB	38D YAN	13 3	16889	5 5	110000 121000
				1991 BOATS						
25 9	COMPROMIS 777	SLP	SAIL	F/S KL IB	9D YAN	9 2	5069	4 11	25500	28300
28 6	COMPROMIS 888	SLP	SAIL	F/S KL IB	18D YAN	9 8	7496	4 10	42000	46700
32 6	COMPROMIS 999	SLP	SAIL	F/S KL IB	27D YAN	11 2	10362	4 10	61900	68000
				1988 BOATS						
33	COMPROMIS 999	MS		KL SD	27D YAN		9400		46900	51500
				1987 BOATS						
26 2	COMPROMIS 777	MS		KL SD	9D YAN		4600		18800	20900
29	COMPROMIS 888	MS		KL SD	18D YAN		6800		30000	33300

CONCEPT BOATS
OPA LOCKA FL 33054   See inside cover to adjust price for area

For more recent years, see the BUC Used Boat Price Guide, Volume 1

LOA FT IN	NAME AND/ OR MODEL	TOP/ RIG	BOAT TYPE	-HULL- MTL TP	----ENGINE--- TP # HP MFG	BEAM FT IN	WGT LBS	DRAFT FT IN	RETAIL LOW	RETAIL HIGH
				1994 BOATS						
21 6	CONCEPT 22 SF	OP	RNBT	FBG DV OB		7 6	1900	1 4	5450	6300
27 6	CONCEPT 28 SF	OP	RNBT	FBG DV OB		8	3600	2	15200	17300
				1993 BOATS						
21 6	CONCEPT 22 SF	OP	RNBT	FBG DV OB		7 6	1900	1 4	5200	5950
27 6	CONCEPT 28 SF	OP	RNBT	FBG DV OB		8	3600	2	14300	16200
				1989 BOATS						
25 8	CAY SAL 26	OP	SF	FBG SV OB		8 3	2900	1 5	7600	8750
				1988 BOATS						
25 8	CONCEPT 21	OP	CTRCN	FBG DV OB		8			4500	5150
25 8	CONCEPT 26	OP	CTRCN	FBG DV OB		8	2750	1 5	7150	8200
25 8	CONCEPT 26	OP	CTRCN	FBG DV SE		8 3	2750	1 5	**	**
27 8	CONCEPT 28	TT	CTRCN	FBG DV SE T		10	3300	1 8	11100	12600
27 8	CONCEPT 28	TT	CTRCN	FBG DV SE T		10	3300	1 8	**	**
				1987 BOATS						
25 8	CONCEPT 26	OP	CTRCN	FBG DV OB		8 3	2750	1 5	6900	7950
25 8	CONCEPT 26	OP	CTRCN	FBG DV OB		8 3	2750	1 5	**	**
25 8	CONCEPT 26	OP	CTRCN	FBG DV SE T		8 3	2750	1 5	**	**
27 8	CONCEPT 28	TT	CTRCN	FBG DV SE T		10	3300	1 8	10700	12100
27 8	CONCEPT 28	TT	CTRCN	FBG DV SE T		10	3300	1 8	**	**

CONCORD BOATS
SHERWOOD AR 72116   COAST GUARD MFG ID- CKL See inside cover to adjust price for area

LOA FT IN	NAME AND/ OR MODEL	TOP/ RIG	BOAT TYPE	-HULL- MTL TP	----ENGINE--- TP # HP MFG	BEAM FT IN	WGT LBS	DRAFT FT IN	RETAIL LOW	RETAIL HIGH
				1994 BOATS						
18 4	MACH I DE	ST	RNBT	FBG DV OB		7 6	1050		4500	5200
18 4	MACH I DE	ST	RNBT	FBG DV IO	155-175	7 6	1950		5550	6750
18 4	MACH I DE	ST	RNBT	FBG DV IO	230	7 6	1950		5800	7050
18 4	MACH I GT	OP	B/R	FBG DV OB		7 6	1050		4700	5450

LOA FT	LOA IN	NAME AND/ OR MODEL	TOP/ RIG	BOAT TYPE	-HULL- MTL	-HULL- TP	ENGINE TP	ENGINE # HP	ENGINE MFG	BEAM FT	BEAM IN	WGT LBS	DRAFT FT	DRAFT IN	RETAIL LOW	RETAIL HIGH
		1994 BOATS														
18	4	MACH I GT	OP	B/R	FBG	DV	IO	155-175		7	6	1950			5450	6600
18	4	MACH I GT	OP	B/R	FBG	DV	IO	230		7	6	1950			5700	6950
18	4	MACH I SS	OP	B/R	FBG	DV	OB			7	6	1050			4250	4900
18	4	MACH I SS	OP	B/R	FBG	DV	IO	155-175		7	6	1950			5250	6400
18	4	MACH I SS	OP	B/R	FBG	DV	IO	230		7	6	1950			5450	6600
18	4	SST DE	OP	RNBT	FBG	DV	OB			7	6				4500	5200
18	4	SST DE	OP	RNBT	FBG	DV	IO	115-155		7	6				5500	6650
18	4	SST GT	OP	B/R	FBG	DV	OB			7	6	1050			4700	5400
18	4	SST GT	OP	B/R	FBG	DV	IO	115-155		7	6				5400	6550
18	4	SST SS	OP	B/R	FBG	DV	OB			7	6	1050			4250	4950
18	4	SST SS	OP	B/R	FBG	DV	IO	115-155		7	6				5150	6250
20	3	MACH II DE	OP	RNBT	FBG	DV	OB			7	5	1200			4450	5150
20	3	MACH II DE	OP	RNBT	FBG	DV	IO	180-230		7	5	2400			7000	8700
20	3	MACH II DE	OP	RNBT	FBG	DV	IO	250		7	5	2400			7350	8900
20	3	MACH II DE	OP	RNBT	FBG	DV	IO	300		7	5	2400			8000	9800
20	3	MACH II GT	OP	B/R	FBG	DV	OB			7	5	1200			4650	5350
20	3	MACH II GT	OP	B/R	FBG	DV	IO	180-230		7	5	2400			6950	8600
20	3	MACH II GT	OP	B/R	FBG	DV	IO	250		7	5	2400			7300	8800
20	3	MACH II GT	OP	B/R	FBG	DV	IO	300		7	5	2400			7950	9750
20	3	MACH II SS	OP	B/R	FBG	DV	OB			7	5	1200			4250	4950
20	3	MACH II SS	OP	B/R	FBG	DV	IO	180-230		7	5	2400			6700	8350
20	3	MACH II SS	OP	B/R	FBG	DV	IO	250		7	5	2400			7100	8550
20	3	MACH II SS	OP	B/R	FBG	DV	IO	300		7	5	2400			7750	9450
20	3	MACH II W/PLAT DE	OP	B/R	FBG	DV	OB			7	5	1200			4400	5100
20	3	MACH II W/PLAT GT	OP	B/R	FBG	DV	OB			7	5	1200			4100	4750
20	3	MACH II W/PLAT SS	OP	B/R	FBG	DV	OB			7	5	1200			4750	5450
20	3	MAGNUM 22 DE	OP	RNBT	FBG	DV	OB			7	5	1500			5750	6600
20	3	MAGNUM 22 GT	OP	RNBT	FBG	DV	OB			7	5	1500			5300	6100
20	3	MAGNUM 22 SS	OP	RNBT	FBG	DV	OB			7	5	1500			4950	5700
20	3	MAGNUM II DE	OP	RNBT	FBG	DV	IO	230-250		7	5	2500			7800	9600
20	3	MAGNUM II DE	OP	RNBT	FBG	DV	IO	300		7	5	2500			8700	10600
20	3	MAGNUM II GT	OP	RNBT	FBG	DV	IO	230-250		7	5	2500			7300	9000
20	3	MAGNUM II GT	OP	RNBT	FBG	DV	IO	300		7	5	2500			8200	10000
20	3	MAGNUM II SS	OP	RNBT	FBG	DV	IO	230-250		7	5	2500			7000	8600
20	3	MAGNUM II SS	OP	RNBT	FBG	DV	IO	300		7	5	2500			7650	9350
21	5	MACH III DE	OP	RNBT	FBG	DV	IO	230-250		7	5	2600			7950	9750
21	5	MACH III DE	OP	RNBT	FBG	DV	IO	300		7	5	2600			8900	10700
21	5	MACH III GT	OP	B/R	FBG	DV	OB			7	5	2600			8700	10000
21	5	MACH III GT	OP	B/R	FBG	DV	IO	230-250		7	5	2600			7950	9750
21	5	MACH III GT	OP	B/R	FBG	DV	IO	300		7	5	2600			8900	10700
21	5	MACH III SS	OP	B/R	FBG	DV	OB			7	5	2600			8250	9500
21	5	MACH III SS	OP	B/R	FBG	DV	IO	230-250		7	5	2600			7700	9450
21	5	MACH III SS	OP	B/R	FBG	DV	IO	300		7	5	2600			8450	10300
24	4	007 DE	OP	RNBT	FBG	DV	OB			7	9	3700			12700	14400
24	4	007 DE	OP	RNBT	FBG	DV	IO	230-250		7	9	3700			11700	13900
24	4	007 DE	OP	RNBT	FBG	DV	IO	300-350		7	9	3700			12600	15600
24	4	007 GT	OP	B/R	FBG	DV	OB			7	9	3700			13200	14900
24	4	007 GT	OP	B/R	FBG	DV	IO	230-250		7	9	3700			11700	13900
24	4	007 GT	OP	B/R	FBG	DV	IO	300-350		7	9	3700			12600	15600
24	4	007 SS	OP	B/R	FBG	DV	OB			7	9	3700			12300	14000
24	4	CC-7 DE	OP	RNBT	FBG	DV	IO	230-250		7	9	3900			12200	14400
24	4	CC-7 DE	OP	RNBT	FBG	DV	IO	300-350		7	9	3900			13000	16100
24	4	CC-7 GT	OP	B/R	FBG	DV	IO	230-250		7	9	3900			12200	14400
24	4	CC-7 GT	OP	B/R	FBG	DV	IO	300-350		7	9	3900			13000	16100
24	4	DC-7 DE	OP	CUD	FBG	DV	IO	230-250		7	9	3900			13200	15700
24	4	DC-7 DE	OP	CUD	FBG	DV	IO	300-350		7	9	3900			14100	17500
24	4	DC-7 SS	OP	CUD	FBG	DV	IO	230-250		7	9	3900			12900	15300
24	4	DC-7 SS	OP	CUD	FBG	DV	IO	300-350		7	9	3900			13800	17100
24	4	LS-7 DE	OP	RNBT	FBG	DV	OB			7	9	3300			11700	13300
24	4	LS-7 DE	OP	RNBT	FBG	DV	IO	300-350		7	9	3300			11800	14700
24	4	LS-7 DE	OP	RNBT	FBG	DV	IO	410		7	9	3300			15000	17100
24	4	LS-7 GT	OP	B/R	FBG	DV	OB			7	9	3300			12100	13700
24	4	LS-7 GT	OP	B/R	FBG	DV	IB	300-350		7	9	3300			14000	17100
24	4	LS-7 GT	OP	B/R	FBG	DV	IB	410		7	9	3300			15400	18400
24	4	LS-7 SS	OP	B/R	FBG	DV	OB			7	9	3300			11500	13000
24	4	LS-7 SS	OP	B/R	FBG	DV	IO	300-350		7	9	3300			11800	14700
24	4	LS-7 SS	OP	B/R	FBG	DV	IO	410		7	9	3300			15000	17100
27	10	MAGNUM SPORT 280	OP	CUD	FBG	DV	IO	300-390		8		5000			21200	26000
		IO 450 MRCR 25300 28100, IO T270-T365 24500 30400, IO T410-T465													29100	35100
		1993 BOATS														
18	4	MACH I DE	ST	RNBT	FBG	DV	OB			7	6	1050			4250	4950
18	4	MACH I DE	ST	RNBT	FBG	DV	IO	155-175		7	6	1950			5200	6350
18	4	MACH I DE	ST	RNBT	FBG	DV	IO	230		7	6	1950			5450	6600
18	4	MACH I GT	OP	B/R	FBG	DV	OB			7	6	1050			4500	5200
18	4	MACH I GT	OP	B/R	FBG	DV	IO	155-175		7	6	1950			5100	6200
18	4	MACH I GT	OP	B/R	FBG	DV	IO	230		7	6	1950			5300	6500
18	4	MACH I SS	OP	B/R	FBG	DV	OB			7	6	1050			4100	4750
18	4	MACH I SS	OP	B/R	FBG	DV	IO	155-175		7	6	1950			4900	5950
18	4	MACH I SS	OP	B/R	FBG	DV	IO	230		7	6	1950			5100	6200
18	4	SST DE	OP	RNBT	FBG	DV	OB			7	6				4250	4950
18	4	SST DE	OP	RNBT	FBG	DV	IO	115-155		7	6				5100	6200
18	4	SST GT	OP	B/R	FBG	DV	OB			7	6	1050			4500	5200
18	4	SST GT	OP	B/R	FBG	DV	IO	115-155		7	6				5050	6150
18	4	SST SS	OP	B/R	FBG	DV	OB			7	6	1050			4100	4750
18	4	SST SS	OP	B/R	FBG	DV	IO	115-155		7	6				4800	5850
20	3	MACH II DE	OP	RNBT	FBG	DV	OB			7	5	1200			4250	4900
20	3	MACH II DE	OP	RNBT	FBG	DV	IO	180-230		7	5	2400			6550	8100
20	3	MACH II DE	OP	RNBT	FBG	DV	IO	250		7	5	2400			6900	8300
20	3	MACH II DE	OP	RNBT	FBG	DV	IO	300		7	5	2400			7500	9150
20	3	MACH II GT	OP	B/R	FBG	DV	OB			7	5	1200			4350	5000
20	3	MACH II GT	OP	B/R	FBG	DV	IO	180-230		7	5	2400			6500	8050
20	3	MACH II GT	OP	B/R	FBG	DV	IO	250		7	5	2400			6800	8250
20	3	MACH II GT	OP	B/R	FBG	DV	IO	300		7	5	2400			7450	9100
20	3	MACH II SS	OP	B/R	FBG	DV	OB			7	5	1200			3950	4600
20	3	MACH II SS	OP	B/R	FBG	DV	IO	180-230		7	5	2400			6300	7800
20	3	MACH II SS	OP	B/R	FBG	DV	IO	250		7	5	2400			6600	8000
20	3	MACH II SS	OP	B/R	FBG	DV	IO	300		7	5	2400			7250	8850
20	3	MACH II W/PLAT DE	OP	B/R	FBG	DV	OB			7	5	1200			4850	5550
20	3	MACH II W/PLAT GT	OP	B/R	FBG	DV	OB			7	5	1200			4450	5150
20	3	MACH II W/PLAT SS	OP	B/R	FBG	DV	OB			7	5	1200			4450	5100
20	3	MAGNUM 22 DE	OP	RNBT	FBG	DV	OB			7	5	1500			5500	6300
20	3	MAGNUM 22 GT	OP	RNBT	FBG	DV	OB			7	5	1500			5100	5850
20	3	MAGNUM 22 SS	OP	RNBT	FBG	DV	OB			7	5	1500			4750	5450
20	3	MAGNUM II DE	OP	RNBT	FBG	DV	IO	230-250		7	5	2500			7300	8950
20	3	MAGNUM II DE	OP	RNBT	FBG	DV	IO	300		7	5	2500			8050	9850
20	3	MAGNUM II GT	OP	RNBT	FBG	DV	IO	230-250		7	5	2500			6850	8400
20	3	MAGNUM II GT	OP	RNBT	FBG	DV	IO	300		7	5	2500			7550	9250
20	3	MAGNUM II SS	OP	RNBT	FBG	DV	IO	230-250		7	5	2500			6550	8050
20	3	MAGNUM II SS	OP	RNBT	FBG	DV	IO	300		7	5	2500			7250	8900
21	5	MACH III DE	OP	RNBT	FBG	DV	IO	230-250		7	5	2600			7450	9150
21	5	MACH III DE	OP	RNBT	FBG	DV	IO	300		7	5	2600			8200	9950
21	5	MACH III GT	OP	B/R	FBG	DV	OB			7	5	2600			8300	9550
21	5	MACH III GT	OP	B/R	FBG	DV	IO	230-250		7	5	2600			7450	9150
21	5	MACH III GT	OP	B/R	FBG	DV	IO	300		7	5	2600			8200	10000
21	5	MACH III SS	OP	B/R	FBG	DV	OB			7	5	2600			7900	9100
21	5	MACH III SS	OP	B/R	FBG	DV	IO	230-250		7	5	2600			7200	8850
21	5	MACH III SS	OP	B/R	FBG	DV	IO	300		7	5	2600			7950	9700
24	4	007 DE	OP	RNBT	FBG	DV	OB			7	9	3700			12200	13800
24	4	007 DE	OP	RNBT	FBG	DV	IO	230-250		7	9	3700			11000	13000
24	4	007 DE	OP	RNBT	FBG	DV	IO	300-350		7	9	3700			11800	14600
24	4	007 GT	OP	B/R	FBG	DV	OB			7	9	3700			12600	14300
24	4	007 GT	OP	B/R	FBG	DV	IO	230-250		7	9	3700			11000	13000
24	4	007 GT	OP	B/R	FBG	DV	IO	300-350		7	9	3700			11800	14600
24	4	007 SS	OP	B/R	FBG	DV	OB			7	9	3700			11800	13400
24	4	CC-7 DE	OP	RNBT	FBG	DV	IO	230-250		7	9	3900			11400	13500
24	4	CC-7 DE	OP	RNBT	FBG	DV	IO	300-350		7	9	3900			12200	15100
24	4	CC-7 GT	OP	B/R	FBG	DV	IO	230-250		7	9	3900			11400	13500
24	4	CC-7 GT	OP	B/R	FBG	DV	IO	300-350		7	9	3900			12200	15100
24	4	DC-7 DE	OP	CUD	FBG	DV	IO	230-250		7	9	3900			12400	14600
24	4	DC-7 DE	OP	CUD	FBG	DV	IO	300-350		7	9	3900			13200	16300
24	4	DC-7 SS	OP	CUD	FBG	DV	IO	230-250		7	9	3900			12000	14300
24	4	DC-7 SS	OP	CUD	FBG	DV	IO	300-350		7	9	3900			12900	16000
24	4	LS-7 DE	OP	RNBT	FBG	DV	OB			7	9	3300			11200	12800
24	4	LS-7 DE	OP	RNBT	FBG	DV	IO	300-350		7	9	3300			11000	13700
24	4	LS-7 DE	OP	RNBT	FBG	DV	IO	410		7	9	3300			14100	16000
24	4	LS-7 GT	OP	B/R	FBG	DV	OB			7	9	3300			11600	13100
24	4	LS-7 GT	OP	B/R	FBG	DV	IB	300-350		7	9	3300			13300	16200
24	4	LS-7 GT	OP	B/R	FBG	DV	IB	410		7	9	3300			14600	17400
24	4	LS-7 SS	OP	B/R	FBG	DV	OB			7	9	3300			11000	12500
24	4	LS-7 SS	OP	B/R	FBG	DV	IO	300-350		7	9	3300			11000	13700
24	4	LS-7 SS	OP	B/R	FBG	DV	IO	410		7	9	3300			14100	16000
27	10	MAGNUM SPORT 280	OP	CUD	FBG	DV	IO	300-390		8		5000			19800	24300
		IO 450 MRCR 23600 26300, IO T270-T365 22900 28400, IO T410-T465													27200	32800

 CONTINUED ON NEXT PAGE

LOA FT	LOA IN	NAME AND/ OR MODEL	TOP/ RIG	BOAT TYPE	-HULL- MTL	-HULL- TP	ENGINE TP	ENGINE # HP	ENGINE MFG	BEAM FT	BEAM IN	WGT LBS	DRAFT FT	DRAFT IN	RETAIL LOW	RETAIL HIGH
		1992 BOATS														
18	4	MACH I DE	ST	RNBT	FBG	DV	OB			7	6	1050			4100	4750
18	4	MACH I DE	ST	RNBT	FBG	DV	IO	155-175		7	6	1850			4800	5800
18	4	MACH I DE	ST	RNBT	FBG	DV	IO	230		7	6	1850			5000	6050
18	4	MACH I GT	OP	B/R	FBG	DV	OB			7	6	1050			4300	5000
18	4	MACH I GT	OP	B/R	FBG	DV	IO	155-175		7	6	1850			4700	5700
18	4	MACH I GT	OP	B/R	FBG	DV	IO	230		7	6	1850			4900	5950
18	4	MACH I SS	OP	B/R	FBG	DV	OB			7	6	1050			3900	4550
18	4	MACH I SS	OP	B/R	FBG	DV	IO	155-175		7	6	1850			4500	5450
18	4	MACH I SS	OP	B/R	FBG	DV	IO	230		7	6	1850			4700	5700
20	3	MACH II DE	OP	RNBT	FBG	DV	OB			7	5	1200			4050	4700
20	3	MACH II DE	OP	RNBT	FBG	DV	IO	180-230		7	5	2400			6150	7600
20	3	MACH II DE	OP	RNBT	FBG	DV	IO	250		7	5	2400			6450	7800
20	3	MACH II DE	OP	RNBT	FBG	DV	IO	300		7	5	2400			7000	8600
20	3	MACH II GT	OP	B/R	FBG	DV	OB			7	5	1200			3900	4550
20	3	MACH II GT	OP	B/R	FBG	DV	IO	180-230		7	5	2400			6100	7550
20	3	MACH II GT	OP	B/R	FBG	DV	IO	250		7	5	2400			6400	7750
20	3	MACH II GT	OP	B/R	FBG	DV	IO	300		7	5	2400			7000	8550
20	3	MACH II SS	OP	B/R	FBG	DV	OB			7	5	1200			3600	4150
20	3	MACH II SS	OP	B/R	FBG	DV	IO	180-230		7	5	2400			5850	7300
20	3	MACH II SS	OP	B/R	FBG	DV	IO	250		7	5	2400			6150	7450
20	3	MACH II SS	OP	B/R	FBG	DV	IO	300		7	5	2400			6750	8250
20	3	MACH II W/PLAT DE	OP	B/R	FBG	DV	OB			7	5	1200			4650	5350
20	3	MACH II W/PLAT GT	OP	B/R	FBG	DV	OB			7	5	1200			4250	4900
20	3	MACH II W/PLAT SS	OP	B/R	FBG	DV	OB			7	5	1200			3950	4600
20	3	MAGNUM 22 DE	OP	RNBT	FBG	DV	OB			7	5	1500			5450	6250
20	3	MAGNUM 22 GT	OP	RNBT	FBG	DV	OB			7	5	1500			4800	5500
20	3	MAGNUM 22 SS	OP	RNBT	FBG	DV	OB			7	5	1500			4450	5100
20	3	MAGNUM II DE	OP	RNBT	FBG	DV	IO	230-250		7	5	2500			6850	8400
20	3	MAGNUM II DE	OP	RNBT	FBG	DV	IO	300		7	5	2500			7550	9250
20	3	MAGNUM II GT	OP	RNBT	FBG	DV	IO	230-250		7	5	2500			6350	7850
20	3	MAGNUM II GT	OP	RNBT	FBG	DV	IO	300		7	5	2500			7100	8650
20	3	MAGNUM II SS	OP	RNBT	FBG	DV	IO	230-250		7	5	2500			6100	7550
20	3	MAGNUM II SS	OP	RNBT	FBG	DV	IO	300		7	5	2500			6800	8300
		1988 BOATS														
16	9	SSV	OP	RNBT	FBG	SV	OB			7	2				3400	3950
18	4	MACH I	OP	RNBT	FBG	SV	OB			7	5				3550	4150
18	4	MACH I	OP	RNBT	FBG	SV	IO	130-230		7	6				3700	4500
18	4	MACH I	OP	RNBT	FBG	SV	IO	260		7	6				4050	4700
18	4	MACH I DE	ST	RNBT	FBG	SV	OB			7	5	1050			3550	4150
18	4	MACH I DE	ST	RNBT	FBG	SV	IO	130-230		7	6	1850			3650	4500
18	4	MACH I DE	ST	RNBT	FBG	SV	IO	260		7	6	1850			4000	4650
18	4	MACH I REMOTE	OP	RNBT	FBG	SV	OB			7	8	1050			3350	3900
18	4	MACH I REMOTE DE	OP	RNBT	FBG	SV	OB			7	8	1050			3700	4350
18	4	MAGNUM 200	OP	RNBT	FBG	SV	OB			7	6				3550	4150
18	4	MAGNUM 200 DE	ST	RNBT	FBG		OB			7	6				3550	4150
18	4	MAGNUM I	OP	RNBT	FBG		IO	130-230		7	6				3800	4650
18	4	MAGNUM I	OP	RNBT	FBG		IO	260		7	6				4150	4850
18	4	MAGNUM I DE	ST	RNBT	FBG		IO	130-230		7	6				3800	4650
18	4	MAGNUM I DE	ST	RNBT	FBG		IO	260		7	6				4150	4850
20	3	MACH II	OP	RNBT	FBG	DV	IO		MRCR	7	5	2400			**	**
20	3	MACH II	OP	RNBT	FBG	DV	IO	320-335		7	5	2400			5800	6850
20	3	MACH II	OP	RNBT	FBG	SV	OB			7	5	1200			3150	3700
20	3	MACH II	OP	RNBT	FBG	SV	IO	165-260		7	5	2400			4750	5800
20	3	MACH II DE	OP	RNBT	FBG	DV	IO		MRCR	7	5	2400			**	**
20	3	MACH II DE	OP	RNBT	FBG	DV	IO	320-335		7	5	2400			5800	6850
20	3	MACH II DE	ST	RNBT	FBG	SV	OB			7	5	1200			3500	4050
20	3	MACH II DE	ST	RNBT	FBG	SV	IO	165-260		7	5	2400			4800	5900
20	3	MACH II REMOTE	OP	RNBT	FBG	SV	OB			7	5	1200			3550	4150
20	3	MACH II REMOTE DE	OP	RNBT	FBG	SV	OB			7	5	1200			3500	4050
20	3	MAGNUM 22	OP	RNBT	FBG		OB			7	5				4200	4850
20	3	MAGNUM II	OP	RNBT	FBG		IO	165-260		7	5				4950	6100
20	3	MAGNUM II	ST	RNBT	FBG		IO		MRCR	7	5				**	**
20	3	MAGNUM II	ST	RNBT	FBG		IO	320-335		7	5				5850	6900
22		MAGNUM 22 DE	ST	RNBT	FBG		OB			7	5	1500			4500	5150
22		MAGNUM II	ST	RNBT	FBG	DV	IO		MRCR	7	5	2500			**	**
22		MAGNUM II DE	ST	RNBT	FBG		IO	165-260		7	5	2500			5400	6600
22		MAGNUM II DE	ST	RNBT	FBG	DV	IO		MRCR	7	5	2500			**	**
22		MAGNUM II DE	ST	RNBT	FBG	DV	IO	320-335		7	5	2500			6400	7550
23		LS7		RNBT	FBG	DV	OB			8	9				7300	8400
23		LS7		RNBT	FBG	DV	IO		MRCR	8	9				**	**
		IO OMC ** ** , IO 260 7850 9050, IO 320 MRCR													8550	9850
23		LS7 DE		RNBT	FBG	DV	OB			8	9				8500	9800
23		LS7 DE		RNBT	FBG	DV	IO		MRCR	8	9				**	**
23		LS7 DE		RNBT	FBG	DV	IO		OMC	8	9				**	**
23		LS7 DE		RNBT	FBG	DV	IO	260-320		8	9				8850	10700
23		MAGNUM III DE	ST	RNBT	FBG	SV	OB			7	9	2900			7900	9100
23		MAGNUM III DE	ST	RNBT	FBG	SV	IO		MRCR	7	9	3900			**	**
23		MAGNUM III DE	ST	RNBT	FBG	SV	IO	260-320		7	9	3900			8000	9950
23		MAGNUM III DE	ST	RNBT	FBG	SV	IO	335	OMC	7	9	3900			8900	10100
		1987 BOATS														
16	9	SSV	OP	RNBT	FBG	SV	OB			7	2				3250	3800
16	9	SSV-DE	ST	RNBT	FBG	SV	OB			7	2				3250	3800
18	4	MACH I	OP	RNBT	FBG	SV	OB			7	5				3450	4000
18	4	MACH I	OP	RNBT	FBG	SV	IO	130-230		7	6				3500	4300
18	4	MACH I	OP	RNBT	FBG	SV	IO	260		7	6				3850	4500
18	4	MACH I DE	ST	RNBT	FBG	SV	OB			7	5	1050			3450	4000
18	4	MACH I DE	ST	RNBT	FBG	SV	IO	130-230		7	6	1850			3500	4250
18	4	MACH I DE	ST	RNBT	FBG	SV	IO	260		7	6	1850			3800	4450
18	4	MACH I REMOTE	OP	RNBT	FBG	SV	OB					1050			3250	3800
18	4	MACH I REMOTE DE	OP	RNBT	FBG	SV	OB					1050			3600	4200
18	4	MAGNUM 200	OP	RNBT	FBG	SV	OB			7	6				3450	4000
18	4	MAGNUM 200 DE	ST	RNBT	FBG		OB			7	6				3450	4000
18	4	MAGNUM I	OP	RNBT	FBG		IO	130-230		7	6				3650	4400
18	4	MAGNUM I	OP	RNBT	FBG		IO	260		7	6				3950	4600
18	4	MAGNUM I DE	ST	RNBT	FBG		IO	130-230		7	6				3650	4400
18	4	MAGNUM I DE	ST	RNBT	FBG		IO	260		7	6				3950	4600
20	3	MACH II	OP	RNBT	FBG	DV	IO		MRCR	7	5	2400			**	**
20	3	MACH II	OP	RNBT	FBG	DV	IO	320-335		7	5	2400			5500	6550
20	3	MACH II	OP	RNBT	FBG	SV	OB			7	5	1200			3050	3550
20	3	MACH II	OP	RNBT	FBG	SV	IO		MRCR	7	5	2400			**	**
20	3	MACH II	OP	RNBT	FBG	SV	IO	165-260		7	5	2400			4550	5550
20	3	MACH II	OP	RNBT	FBG	SV	IO	320	MRCR	7	5	2400			5500	6350
20	3	MACH II DE	OP	RNBT	FBG	DV	IO		MRCR			2400			**	**
20	3	MACH II DE	OP	RNBT	FBG	DV	IO	320-335				2400			5500	6550
20	3	MACH II DE	ST	RNBT	FBG	SV	OB			7	5	1200			3400	3900
20	3	MACH II DE	ST	RNBT	FBG	SV	IO		MRCR	7	5	2400			**	**
20	3	MACH II DE	ST	RNBT	FBG	SV	IO	165-260		7	5	2400			4600	5600
20	3	MACH II REMOTE	OP	RNBT	FBG	SV	OB			7	5	1200			3450	4000
20	3	MACH II REMOTE DE	OP	RNBT	FBG	SV	OB					1200			3400	3900
20	3	MAGNUM 22	OP	RNBT	FBG		OB			7	5				4050	4700
20	3	MAGNUM II	OP	RNBT	FBG		IO		MRCR	7	5				**	**
20	3	MAGNUM II	OP	RNBT	FBG		IO	165-260		7	5				4700	5750
20	3	MAGNUM II	ST	RNBT	FBG	DV	IO		MRCR	7	5				**	**
20	3	MAGNUM II	ST	RNBT	FBG	DV	IO	320-335		7	5				5550	6600
22		MAGNUM 22 DE	ST	RNBT	FBG		OB					1500			4300	5000
22		MAGNUM II DE	ST	RNBT	FBG		IO		MRCR			2500			**	**
22		MAGNUM II DE	ST	RNBT	FBG		IO	165-260				2500			5150	6250
22		MAGNUM II DE	ST	RNBT	FBG	DV	IO		MRCR			2500			**	**
22		MAGNUM II DE	ST	RNBT	FBG	DV	IO	320-335				2500			6050	7150
23		MAGNUM III DE	ST	RNBT	FBG	SV	OB			7	9	2900			7650	8800
23		MAGNUM III DE	ST	RNBT	FBG	SV	IO		MRCR	7	9	3900			**	**
23		MAGNUM III DE	ST	RNBT	FBG	SV	IO	260		7	9	3900			7600	8750
23		MAGNUM III DE	ST	RNBT	FBG	SV	IO	335	OMC	7	9	3900			8350	9600
		1985 BOATS														
16	9	SSV	OP	RNBT	FBG	SV	OB			7	2				3100	3600
16	9	SSV	OP	RNBT	FBG	SV	IO	120-140		7	2				2900	3350
16	9	SSV-DE	ST	RNBT	FBG	SV	OB			7	2				3100	3600
16	9	SSV-DE	ST	RNBT	FBG	SV	IO	120-140		7	2				2900	3350
18	4	MACH I	OP	RNBT	FBG	SV	OB			7	5				3250	3750
18	4	MACH I	OP	RNBT	FBG	SV	IO	140-230		7	6				3300	4000
18	4	MACH I	OP	RNBT	FBG	SV	IO	260		7	6				3600	4150
18	4	MACH I DE	ST	RNBT	FBG	SV	OB			7	5	1050			3250	3750
18	4	MACH I DE	ST	RNBT	FBG	SV	IO	140-230		7	6	1850			3250	3950
18	4	MACH I DE	ST	RNBT	FBG	SV	IO	260		7	6	1850			3550	4100
20		MAGNUM 200	OP	RNBT	FBG	SV	OB								3500	4050
20		MAGNUM 200 DE	ST	RNBT	FBG		OB								3500	4050
20		MAGNUM I	OP	RNBT	FBG		IO	140-260							4150	5150
20		MAGNUM I DE	ST	RNBT	FBG		IO	140-260							4150	5150
20	3	MACH II	OP	RNBT	FBG	SV	OB			7	5	1200			3200	3700
20	3	MACH II	OP	RNBT	FBG	SV	IO	170-260		7	5	2400			4200	5200
20	3	MACH II	OP	RNBT	FBG	SV	IO	300	MRCR	7	5	2400			4800	5550
20	3	MACH II DE	ST	RNBT	FBG	SV	OB			7	5	1200			3200	3700
20	3	MACH II DE	ST	RNBT	FBG	SV	IO	170-260		7	5	2400			4200	5200
20	3	MACH II DE	ST	RNBT	FBG	SV	IO	300	MRCR	7	5	2400			4800	5550
22		MAGNUM 22	OP	RNBT	FBG		OB								4050	4700
22		MAGNUM 22 DE	ST	RNBT	FBG		OB					1500			4050	4700

 CONTINUED ON NEXT PAGE

CONCORD BOATS -CONTINUED See inside cover to adjust price for area

LOA FT	LOA IN	NAME AND/ OR MODEL	TOP/ RIG	BOAT TYPE	HULL MTL	HULL TP	ENGINE TP	ENGINE # HP	ENGINE MFG	BEAM FT	BEAM IN	WGT LBS	DRAFT FT	DRAFT IN	RETAIL LOW	RETAIL HIGH
		1985 BOATS														
22		MAGNUM II	OP	RNBT	FBG		IO	170-260				2500			4700	5750
22		MAGNUM II	OP	RNBT	FBG		IO	300	MRCR			2500			5300	6100
22		MAGNUM II DE	ST	RNBT	FBG		IO	170-260				2500			4700	5750
22		MAGNUM II DE	ST	RNBT	FBG		IO	300	MRCR			2500			5300	6100

CONCORDIA YACHT INC

S DARTMOUTH MA 02748 COAST GUARD MFG ID- CNC See inside cover to adjust price for area

LOA FT	LOA IN	NAME AND/ OR MODEL	TOP/ RIG	BOAT TYPE	HULL MTL	HULL TP	ENGINE TP	ENGINE # HP	ENGINE MFG	BEAM FT	BEAM IN	WGT LBS	DRAFT FT	DRAFT IN	RETAIL LOW	RETAIL HIGH
		1986 BOATS														
24	5	AVANCE 245	SLP	SA/RC	FBG	KL	OB			8	5	3850	4	6	15700	17800
33	9	AVANCE 33	SLP	SA/RC	FBG	KL	IB	D		8	7	8800	5	6	44900	49900
35	6	AVANCE 36	SLP	SA/RC	FBG	KL	IB	D		9	2	11000	5	8	57300	63000
37	7	MG 38	SLP	SA/RC	FBG	KL	IB	D		11	3	11000	6	6	61000	67000
40		AVANCE 40	SLP	SA/RC	FBG	KL	IB	D		12	6	19600	7		107500	118000

....For earlier years, see the BUC Used Boat Price Guide, Volume 3

CONSTELLATION MARKETING INC

MANASQUAN NJ 08736 See inside cover to adjust price for area

LOA FT	LOA IN	NAME AND/ OR MODEL	TOP/ RIG	BOAT TYPE	HULL MTL	HULL TP	ENGINE TP	ENGINE # HP	ENGINE MFG	BEAM FT	BEAM IN	WGT LBS	DRAFT FT	DRAFT IN	RETAIL LOW	RETAIL HIGH
		1986 BOATS														
47	9	TRI-STAR-FRERS 48	SLP	SA/RC		KL	IB	D		14	3	27500	6	6	104000	114500
		1985 BOATS														
47	9	TRI-STAR FRERS	KTH	SA/RC	FBG	KL	IB	D		14	3	27500	6	6	98000	107500
47	9	TRI-STAR-FRERS	SLP	SA/RC	FBG	KL	IB	D		14	3	27500	6	6	98000	107500

CONSUL MARINE INC

BELLEVUE WA 98008 COAST GUARD MFG ID- COM See inside cover to adjust price for area

LOA FT	LOA IN	NAME AND/ OR MODEL	TOP/ RIG	BOAT TYPE	HULL MTL	HULL TP	ENGINE TP	ENGINE # HP	ENGINE MFG	BEAM FT	BEAM IN	WGT LBS	DRAFT FT	DRAFT IN	RETAIL LOW	RETAIL HIGH
		1984 BOATS														
26		CONSUL 26	SLP	SAIL	F/W	KL	IB	10D		8	4	3300	3	8	15600	17700

....For earlier years, see the BUC Used Boat Price Guide, Volume 3

CONTEMPORARY YACHTS LTD

ANNAPOLIS MD 21403 COAST GUARD MFG ID- CZY See inside cover to adjust pricc for area

For more recent years, see the BUC Used Boat Price Guide, Volume 1

LOA FT	LOA IN	NAME AND/ OR MODEL	TOP/ RIG	BOAT TYPE	HULL MTL	HULL TP	ENGINE TP	ENGINE # HP	ENGINE MFG	BEAM FT	BEAM IN	WGT LBS	DRAFT FT	DRAFT IN	RETAIL LOW	RETAIL HIGH
		1996 BOATS														
40	7	DEFEVER 41T	FB	TRWL	FBG	DS	IB	150D	CUM	14	2	33000	4		174000	191500
41	6	HAMPTON 42 SD	FB	TRWL	FBG	DS	IB	150D	CUM	14	2	33000	4		177000	194500
41	8	VAGABOND 42 CC	KTH	SACAC	FBG	KL	IB	60D	PERK	12	10	28500	5	6	186500	205000
42	6	HAMPTON 43 PH	CUT	SACAC	FBG	KL	IB	90	PERK	12	11	34810	6	4	209500	230500
42	6	HAMPTON 43 PH	KTH	SACAC	FBG	KL	IB	90	PERK	12	11	34810	6	4	213500	234500
45	10	ULTIMATE 46 EXP	FB	SDNSF	FBG	SV	IB	T375D	CAT	16		36000	3		210500	231500
46	7	VAGABOND 47 CC	KTH	SACAC	FBG	KL	IB	85D	PERK	13	5	40000	5	6	258500	284500
52		VAGABOND 52 CC	SCH	SACAC	FBG	KL	IB	135D	LEHM	13	11	50000	6	6	350000	384500
52		VAGABOND 52 CC	KTH	SACAC	FBG	KL	IB	135D	LEHM	13	11	50000	5	10	363000	399000
52	6	ROYAL 53-C	CUT	SARAC	FBG	KL	IB	85	PERK	14	10	44000	7		348500	383000
52	6	ROYAL 53-C	KTH	SARAC	FBG	KL	IB	85	PERK	14	10	44000	7		366500	402500
55	6	HAMPTON 56 PH	CUT	SACAC	FBG	KL	IB	135D	PERK	15	9	47300	7	8	458500	503500
55	6	HAMPTON 56 PH	KTH	SACAC	FBG	KL	IB	135D	PERK	15	9	47300	7	8	478000	525500
58	5	ROYAL 58 PH	KTH	SACAC	FBG	KL	IB	150D	CUM	16	1	56200	6	6	708500	779000
63		AMARETTI 60	FB	MY	FBG	SV	IB	T770D	VLVO	17	3	63000	3	9	445500	489500
68		HAMPTON 68 PH	KTH	SACAC	FBG	KL	IB	T135D	PERK	17		77000	8	6	1.065M	1.160M
69	9	ROYAL 70 PH	KTH	SACAC	FBG	KL	IB	210D	CUM	19	3	94100	7	8	1.385M	1.505M
		1995 BOATS														
40	7	DEFEVER 41T	FB	TRWL	FBG	DS	IB	150D	CUM	14	2	33000	4		167000	183500
40	7	DEFEVER 41T	FB	TRWL	FBG	DS	IB	T150D	CUM	14	2	33000	4		174500	192000
41	8	VAGABOND 42 CC	KTH	SACAC	FBG	KL	IB	60D	PERK	12	10	28500	5	6	175500	192500
41	10	PLATINUM 42	FB	MY	FBG	DS	IB	T210D	CUM	14	1	23000	3	3	144000	158000
41	10	PLATINUM 42	FB	MY	FBG	DS	IB	T300D	CUM	14	1	23000	3	3	158000	173500
46	7	VAGABOND 47 CC	KTH	SACAC	FBG	KL	IB	85D	PERK	13	5	40000	5	6	243000	267000
46	10	PLATINUM 47 YF	HT	MY	FBG	SV	IB	T210D	CUM	14	1	25800	3	3	165500	182000
50	2	PLATINUM 50	FB	MY	FBG	DS	IB	T485D	J&T	16	10	42000	3	6	279000	307000
52		ROYAL 52 PH	KTH	SACAC	FBG	KL	IB	135D	LEHM	13	11	50000	5	10	400500	440000
52		VAGABOND 52 CC	SCH	SACAC	FBG	KL	IB	135D	LEHM	13	11	50000	6	6	329000	361500
52		VAGABOND 52 CC	KTH	SACAC	FBG	KL	IB	135D	LEHM	13	11	50000	5	10	282000	309500
52	6	ROYAL 53-C	CUT	SARAC	FBG	KL	IB	85	PERK	14	10	44000	7		328000	360500
52	6	ROYAL 53-C	KTH	SARAC	FBG	KL	IB	85	PERK	14	10	44000	7		344500	378500
56	2	PLATINUM 56 YF	HT	MY	FBG	SV	IB	T485D	J&T	16	10	43000	3	6	269500	296000
58	5	ROYAL 58 PH	KTH	SACAC	FBG	KL	IB	150D	CUM	16	1	56200	6	6	666500	732500
69	9	ROYAL 70 PH	KTH	SACAC	FBG	KL	IB	210D	CUM	19	3	94100	7	8	1.300M	1.410M
		1994 BOATS														
40	7	DEFEVER 41T	FB	TRWL	FBG	DS	IB	150D	CUM	14	2	33000	4		160000	176000
40	7	DEFEVER 41T	FB	TRWL	FBG	DS	IB	T150D	CUM	14	2	33000	4		167000	183500
41	8	VAGABOND 42 CC	KTH	SACAC	FBG	KL	IB	60D	PERK	12	10	28500	5	6	165000	181000
41	10	PLATINUM 42	FB	MY	FBG	DS	IB	T210D	CUM	14	1	23000	3	3	138000	151500
41	10	PLATINUM 42	FB	MY	FBG	DS	IB	T300D	CUM	14	1	23000	3	3	151500	166500
46	7	VAGABOND 47 CC	KTH	SACAC	FBG	KL	IB	85D	PERK	13	5	40000	5	6	228500	251000
46	10	PLATINUM 47 YF	HT	MY	FBG	SV	IB	T210D	CUM	14	1	25800	3	3	158500	174000
50	2	PLATINUM 50	FB	MY	FBG	DS	IB	T485D	J&T	16	10	42000	3	6	268000	294500
52		ROYAL 52 PH	KTH	SACAC	FBG	KL	IB	135D	LEHM	13	11	50000	5	10	406000	446500
52		VAGABOND 52 CC	SCH	SACAC	FBG	KL	IB	135D	LEHM	13	11	50000	6	6	309000	339500
52		VAGABOND 52 CC	KTH	SACAC	FBG	KL	IB	135D	LEHM	13	11	50000	5	10	321000	352500
56	2	PLATINUM 56 YF	HT	MY	FBG	SV	IB	T485D	J&T	16	10	43000	3	6	258000	283500
58	5	ROYAL 58 PH	KTH	SACAC	FBG	KL	IB	150D	CUM	16	1	56200	6	6	626500	688500
69	9	ROYAL 70 PH	KTH	SACAC	FBG	KL	IB	210D	CUM	19	3	94100	7	8	1.220M	1.325M
		1993 BOATS														
40	7	DEFEVER 41T	FB	TRWL	FBG	DS	IB	150D	CUM	14	2	33000	4		152500	167500
40	7	DEFEVER 41T	FB	TRWL	FBG	DS	IB	T150D	CUM	14	2	33000	4		159000	175000
41	8	VAGABOND 42 CC	KTH	SACAC	FBG	KL	IB	60D	PERK	12	10	28500	5	6	155000	170500
41	10	PLATINUM 42	FB	MY	FBG	DS	IB	T210D	CUM	14	1	23000	3	3	131500	144500
41	10	PLATINUM 42	FB	MY	FBG	DS	IB	T300D	CUM	14	1	23000	3	3	144000	158500
46	7	VAGABOND 47 CC	KTH	SACAC	FBG	KL	IB	85D	PERK	13	5	40000	5	6	215000	236000
46	10	PLATINUM 47 YF	HT	MY	FBG	SV	IB	T210D	CUM	14	1	25800	3	3	151000	166000
50	2	PLATINUM 50	FB	MY	FBG	DS	IB	T485D	J&T	16	10	42000	3	6	255000	280500
52		VAGABOND 52 CC	SCH	SACAC	FBG	KL	IB	135D	LEHM	13	11	50000	6	6	290500	319500
52		VAGABOND 52 CC	KTH	SACAC	FBG	KL	IB	135D	LEHM	13	11	50000	5	10	301500	331500
56	2	PLATINUM 56 YF	HT	MY	FBG	SV	IB	T485D	J&T	16	10	43000	3	6	246000	270500
58	5	ROYAL 58 PH	KTH	SACAC	FBG	KL	IB	150D	CUM	16	1	56200	6	6	589000	647000
		1987 BOATS														
34	3	SUNRISE 35 AFT CPT	CUT	SA/CR	FBG	KL	IB	30D	YAN	11		19000	5	6	71300	78400
36	5	SUNRISE 36 AFT CPT	CUT	SA/CR	FBG	KL	IB	44D		11	4	22200	5	8	79000	86800
37	11	VAGABOND 38 AFT CPT	CUT	SA/CR	FBG	KL	IB	33	YAN	12		19200	4	11	71300	78400
40	7	DEFEVER 41T	FB	TRWL	FBG	DS	IB	135D	LEHM	14	2	33000	4		115500	127000
41	8	VAGABOND 42 CEN CPT	KTH	SA/CR	FBG	KL	IB	61D	LEHM	12	10	28500	5	6	108000	118500
41	10	PLATINUM 42MY	HT	MY	FBG	SV	IB	T135D	LEHM	14	1	25300	3	3	101000	111000
42	6	SUNRISE 43 CEN CPT	CUT	SA/CR	FBG	KL	IB	80D	YAN	12	2	29500	5	9	112500	123500
42	6	SUNRISE 43 PIL HSE	CUT	SA/CR	FBG	KL	IB	80D	YAN	12	2	29500	5	9	112500	123500
45	2	HARDIN 45 CEN CPT	KTH	SA/CR	FBG	KL	IB	61D	LEHM	13	4	32000	5	6	130500	143500
46	7	VAGABOND 47 CEN CPT	KTH	SA/CR	FBG	KL	IB	90D	VLVO	13	5	40000	5	6	149500	164000
46	10	PLATINUM 47YF	HT	YTFS	FBG	SV	IB	T210D	CAT	14	1	25300	3	3	104000	114000
50	2	PLATINUM 50MY	HT	MY	FBG	SV	IB	T485D	J&T	16	10	42000	3	6	166000	182500
52		VAGABOND 52 CEN CPT	KTH	SA/CR	FBG	KL	IB	135D	LEHM	13	11	48000	5	9	207000	227500
53	9	SUNRISE 54 CEN CPT	CUT	SA/CR	FBG	KL	IB	135D	LEHM	14	2	50000	5	10	228500	251000
53	9	SUNRISE 54 PIL HSE	CUT	SA/CR	FBG	KL	IB	135D	LEHM	14	2	50000	5	10	228500	251000
56	2	PLATINUM 56YF	HT	YTFS	FBG	SV	IB	T485D	J&T	16	10	42000	3	6	189500	208000
		1985 BOATS														
45	2	HARDIN 45	KTH	SA/CR	FBG	KL	IB	80D	LEHM	13	4	32000	5	6	115500	127000
46	7	VAGABOND 47	KTH	SA/CR	FBG	KL	IB	9D	VLVO	13	5	40000	5	6	130500	143500
50	10	VENICE 50	KTH	SA/CR	FBG	KL	IB	80D	LEHM	14	1	52000	6	2	173500	190500
52		VAGABOND 52	KTH	SA/CR	FBG	KL	IB	135D	PERK	13	11	48000	5	6	182000	200000
		1984 BOATS														
41	4	MONARCH 41	KTH	SA/CR	FBG	KL	IB	58D	WEST	12	8	28200	5	6	88500	97300
45	2	HARDIN 45	KTH	SA/CR	FBG	KL	IB	80D	LEHM	13	4	32000	5	6	109000	119500
50	10	VENICE 50	KTH	SA/CR	FBG	KL	IB	80D	LEHM	14	1	52000	6	2	163000	179500

CONTENDER BOATS INC

HOMESTEAD FL 33035 See inside cover to adjust price for area

For more recent years, see the BUC Used Boat Price Guide, Volume 1

LOA FT	LOA IN	NAME AND/ OR MODEL	TOP/ RIG	BOAT TYPE	HULL MTL	HULL TP	ENGINE TP	ENGINE # HP	ENGINE MFG	BEAM FT	BEAM IN	WGT LBS	DRAFT FT	DRAFT IN	RETAIL LOW	RETAIL HIGH
		1996 BOATS														
21	3	CENTER CONSOLE	OP	FSH	FBG	DV	OB			8	3	2100	1	6	13100	14900
23	3	23	TTP	CTRCN	FBG	DV	OB			8	3	2400	1	6	15800	18000

CONTINUED ON NEXT PAGE

CONTENDER BOATS INC -CONTINUED See inside cover to adjust price for area

LOA FT	LOA IN	NAME AND/ OR MODEL	TOP/ RIG	BOAT TYPE	HULL MTL	HULL TP	ENGINE TP	ENGINE # HP	ENGINE MFG	BEAM FT	BEAM IN	WGT LBS	DRAFT FT	DRAFT IN	RETAIL LOW	RETAIL HIGH
		1996 BOATS														
28		CUDDY	TTP	SF	FBG	DV	OB			8	10	4700	18		27000	30000
28		CUT TRANSOM/ CUDDY	OP	CTRCN	FBG	DV	OB			8	10	2700	1	6	20000	22200
29	6	27	TTP	CTRCN	FBG	DV	OB			8	6	3300	2		31500	35000
31		27	TTP	CTRCN	FBG	DV	OB			9	4	3300	1	6	31500	35000
33	6	CUDDY	ST	OPFSH	FBG	DV	OB			9	4	3500	1	6	48100	52800
35		CUDDY	ST	CTRCN	FBG	DV	OB			10		6000	2		56600	62200
35		EXPRESS SIDE CONSOLE	TH	OPFSH	FBG	DV	OB			10		6000	2		56800	62400
35		TWIN CONSOLE	HT	FSH	FBG	DV	OB			10		6000	2		56800	62400
		1995 BOATS														
21		OPEN	OP	OPFSH	FBG	DV	OB			8	6	2100	2		12300	14000
21	3	CENTER CONSOLE	OP	CTRCN	FBG	DV	OB			8	3	2100	1	6	12500	14200
28		25 CENTER CONSOLE	TH	CTRCN	FBG	DV	OB			8	10	2700	1	6	19100	21200
28		25 OPEN	ST	CUD	FBG	DV	OB			8	10	2700	1	6	19400	21500
28		OPEN	TTP	OPFSH	FBG	DV	OB			8	10	4700	18		25700	28600
31		31 CENTER CONSOLE	OP	SF	FBG	DV	OB			9	6	3500	1	6	40700	45200
31	3	27	TTP	CTRCN	FBG	DV	OB			9	6	3300	1	6	30000	33400
32	6	31 CUDDY	TH	CUD	FBG	DV	OB			9	4	4000	1	6	44700	49600
35			TTP	FSH	FBG	DV	IB	T315D	YAN	10		6000	2		83800	92100
35		EXPRESS	TH	EXP	FBG	DV	IB	T315D	YAN	10		7500	2		99300	109000
35		SIDE CONSOLE	TT	SF	FBG	DV	OB			10		5500	2		54500	59900
35		TWIN CONSOLE	HT	CTRCN	FBG	DV	OB			10		6000	2		53900	59200
		1991 BOATS														
25	3	CONTENDER 25 CNV	OP	CTRCN	FBG	DV	OB			8	3	2700	1	6	16600	18900
25	3	CONTENDER 25 CNV	OP	CTRCN	FBG	DV	IO	260-270		8	3	2700	1	6	14300	16200
		IO 340 MRCR 15900 18000, IO 250D CUM 20800 23100, IB 300D CUM													24300	27000
25	3	CONTENDER 25 CUDDY	OP	CUD	FBG	DV	OB			8	3	2700	1	6	16700	19000
25	3	CONTENDER 25 CUDDY	OP	CUD	FBG	DV	IO	260-270		8	3	2700	1	6	13000	14800
25	3	CONTENDER 25 CUDDY	OP	CUD	FBG	DV	IO	340	MRCR	8	3	2700	1	6	14500	16400
25	3	CONTENDER 25 CUDDY	OP	CUD	FBG	DV	IB	250D-300D		8	3	2700	1	6	21700	26500
25	3	CONTENDER 25 OPEN	OP	CTRCN	FBG	DV	OB			8	3	2700	1	6	16600	18900
25	3	CONTENDER 25 OPEN	OP	CTRCN	FBG	DV	IO	260-270		8	3	2700	1	6	13200	15000
25	3	CONTENDER 25 OPEN	OP	CTRCN	FBG	DV	IO	340	MRCR	8	3	2700	1	6	14700	16700
25	3	CONTENDER 25 OPEN	OP	CTRCN	FBG	DV	IB	250D-300D		8	3	2700	1	6	21700	26300
		1990 BOATS														
25	3	CONTENDER 25 CNV	OP	CTRCN	FBG	DV	OB			8	3	2700	1	6	16000	18200
25	3	CONTENDER 25 CNV	OP	CTRCN	FBG	DV	IO	260-270		8	3	2700	1	6	13400	15300
		IO 340 MRCR 14900 16900, IO 250D CUM 19500 21700, IB 300D CUM													23200	25800
25	3	CONTENDER 25 CUDDY	OP	CUD	FBG	DV	OB			8	3	2700	1	6	16200	18400
25	3	CONTENDER 25 CUDDY	OP	CUD	FBG	DV	IO	260-270		8	3	2700	1	6	12200	13900
25	3	CONTENDER 25 CUDDY	OP	CUD	FBG	DV	IO	340	MRCR	8	3	2700	1	6	13600	15500
25	3	CONTENDER 25 CUDDY	OP	CUD	FBG	DV	IB	250D-300D		8	3	2700	1	6	20700	25300
25	3	CONTENDER 25 OPEN	OP	CTRCN	FBG	DV	OB			8	3	2700	1	6	16000	18200
25	3	CONTENDER 25 OPEN	OP	CTRCN	FBG	DV	IO	260-270		8	3	2700	1	6	12400	14100
25	3	CONTENDER 25 OPEN	OP	CTRCN	FBG	DV	IO	340	MRCR	8	3	2700	1	6	13800	15700
25	3	CONTENDER 25 OPEN	OP	CTRCN	FBG	DV	IB	250D-300D		8	3	2700	1	6	20700	24800
		1989 BOATS														
25	3	CONTENDER 25 CNV	OP	CTRCN	FBG	DV	OB			8	3	2700	1	6	15400	17500
25	3	CONTENDER 25 CNV	OP	CTRCN	FBG	DV	IO	260-270		8	3	2700	1	6	12200	13900
25	3	CONTENDER 25 CNV	OP	CTRCN	FBG	DV	IO	350	CRUS	8	3	2700	1	6	13800	15700
25	3	CONTENDER 25 CNV	OP	CTRCN	FBG	DV	IB	240D	PERK	8	3	2700	1	6	20600	22900
25	3	CONTENDER 25 CUDDY	OP	CUD	FBG	DV	OB			8	3	2700	1	6	15600	17800
25	3	CONTENDER 25 CUDDY	OP	CUD	FBG	DV	IO	260-270		8	3	2700	1	6	11500	13100
25	3	CONTENDER 25 CUDDY	OP	CUD	FBG	DV	IO	350	CRUS	8	3	2700	1	6	13100	14900
25	3	CONTENDER 25 CUDDY	OP	CUD	FBG	DV	IB	240D	PERK	8	3	2700	1	6	20600	22900
25	3	CONTENDER 25 OPEN		CTRCN	FBG	DV	OB			8	3	2700	1	6	15400	17500
25	3	CONTENDER 25 OPEN		CTRCN	FBG	DV	IO	260-270		8	3	2700	1	6	12200	13900
25	3	CONTENDER 25 OPEN		CTRCN	FBG	DV	IO	350	CRUS	8	3	2700	1	6	13800	15700
25	3	CONTENDER 25 OPEN		CTRCN	FBG	DV	IB	240D	PERK	8	3	2700	1	6	20600	22900
		1988 BOATS														
25	3	CONTENDER 25 CNV	OP	CTRCN	FBG	DV	OB			8	3	2700	1	6	15500	17600
25	3	CONTENDER 25 CNV	OP	CTRCN	FBG	DV	IO	260-270		8	3	2700	1	6	11900	13500
25	3	CONTENDER 25 CNV	OP	CTRCN	FBG	DV	IO	350	CRUS	8	3	2700	1	6	13400	15300
25	3	CONTENDER 25 CNV	OP	CTRCN	FBG	DV	IB	240D	PERK	8	3	2700	1	6	20100	22300
25	3	CONTENDER 25 CUDDY	OP	CUD	FBG	DV	OB			8	3	2700	1	6	15200	17200
25	3	CONTENDER 25 CUDDY	OP	CUD	FBG	DV	IO	260-270		8	3	2700	1	6	10900	12400
25	3	CONTENDER 25 CUDDY	OP	CUD	FBG	DV	IO	350	CRUS	8	3	2700	1	6	12400	14100
25	3	CONTENDER 25 CUDDY	OP	CUD	FBG	DV	IB	240D	PERK	8	3	2700	1	6	19700	21900
25	3	CONTENDER 25 OPEN	OP	CTRCN	FBG	DV	OB			8	3	2700	1	6	14300	16300
25	3	CONTENDER 25 OPEN	OP	CTRCN	FBG	DV	IO	260-270		8	3	2700	1	6	11200	12800
25	3	CONTENDER 25 OPEN	OP	CTRCN	FBG	DV	IO	350	CRUS	8	3	2700	1	6	12800	14500
25	3	CONTENDER 25 OPEN	OP	CTRCN	FBG	DV	IB	240D	PERK	8	3	2700	1	6	19300	21400
		1987 BOATS														
25	3	CONTENDER 25	OP	CTRCN	FBG	DV	OB			8	3	2600	1	6	14200	16100

CONTESSA YACHTS LTD

HAMPSHIRE ENGLAND

See inside cover to adjust price for area

LOA FT	LOA IN	NAME AND/ OR MODEL	TOP/ RIG	BOAT TYPE	HULL MTL	HULL TP	ENGINE TP	ENGINE # HP	ENGINE MFG	BEAM FT	BEAM IN	WGT LBS	DRAFT FT	DRAFT IN	RETAIL LOW	RETAIL HIGH
		1985 BOATS														
36	3	CONTESSA 38	SLP	SA/CR	F/S	KL				11	4	15900	6	1	67300	73900
38	8	CONTESSA 39	SLP	SA/RC	F/S	KL				12	3	14250	7	3	67500	74100
		1984 BOATS														
24		CONTESSA J24	SLP	SA/OD	F/S	KL				8	11	3100	4		6900	7900
29	5	CONTESSA J29	SLP	SA/OD	F/S	KL				11		6000	5	6	14700	16700
32		CONTESSA 32	SLP	SA/RC	FBG	KL	IB	18D	VLVO	9	6	9500	5	6	34700	38500
33	8	CONTESSA 34	SLP	SA/RC	FBG	KL	IB	28D	VLVO	11	1	9000	5	6	33700	37400
33	8	CONTESSA 34 OD	SLP	SA/OD	FBG	KL	IB	28D	VLVO	11	1	8050	6	4	30100	33500
34	10	CONTESSA 35	SLP	SA/CR	FBG	KL	IB	28D	VLVO	11	1	9500	5	6	36600	40700
38	3	CONTESSA 38	SLP	SA/CR	F/S	KL	IB	36D	VLVO	11	4	15900	6	1	67800	74500
38	8	CONTESSA 39	SLP	SA/RC	F/S	KL	IB	36D	VLVO	12	3	14250	7	2	63800	70100
42	9	CONTESSA 43	SLP	SA/RC	F/S	KL	IB	36D	VLVO	12	6	21000	7	3	105000	115000
42	9	CONTESSA 43	CUT	SA/RC	F/S	KL	IB	36D	VLVO	12	6	21000	7	3	104500	115000
53	5	CONTESSA 54	CUT	SA/CR	F/S	KC	IB	D		15		40585	5	9	228500	251000
53	5	CONTESSA 54	CUT	SA/CR	F/S	KL	IB	D		15		40585	9		228500	251000
53	5	CONTESSA 54	KTH	SA/CR	F/S	KC	IB	D		15		40585	9		239500	263500
53	5	CONTESSA 54	KTH	SA/CR	F/S	KL	IB	D		15		40585	5	9	239500	263500
53	5	CONTESSA 54	KTH	SA/CR	F/S	KL	IB	D		15		40585	9		239500	263500
53	5	CONTESSA 54	SLP	SA/RC	F/S	KC	IB	D		15		40585	5	9	234000	257000
53	5	CONTESSA 54	SLP	SA/RC	F/S	KL	IB	D		15		40585	9		234000	257000

....For earlier years, see the BUC Used Boat Price Guide, Volume 3

CONTEST YACHTS

1671 GD MEDEMBLIK HOLLA COAST GUARD MFG ID- HLY See inside cover to adjust price for area

CONTEST YACHTS
STAMFORD CT 06902

FORMERLY CONYPLEX

For more recent years, see the BUC Used Boat Price Guide, Volume 1

LOA FT	LOA IN	NAME AND/ OR MODEL	TOP/ RIG	BOAT TYPE	HULL MTL	HULL TP	ENGINE TP	ENGINE # HP	ENGINE MFG	BEAM FT	BEAM IN	WGT LBS	DRAFT FT	DRAFT IN	RETAIL LOW	RETAIL HIGH
		1996 BOATS														
34	7	CONTEST 35S	SLP	SACAC	F/S	KL	IB	29D	VLVO	11	2	13040	4	5	104500	115000
36	11	CONTEST 37	SLP	SACAC	F/S	KL	IB	40D	VLVO	16	7	19621			158500	174000
36	11	CONTEST 37	SLP	SACAC	F/S	WK	IB	40D	VLVO	16	7	20944			167500	184000
40		CONTEST 40S	SLP	SACAC	F/S	KL	IB	59D	VLVO	12	8	24230	6	5	208500	229000
43		CONTEST 43	SLP	SACAC	F/S	KL	IB	62D	VLVO	13	2	28437	5	9	252500	277000
48	5	CONTEST 48	SLP	SACAC	F/S	KL	IB	100D	VLVO	13	8	33960	5	9	347000	381500
60		CONTEST 60	SLP	SACAC	F/S	KL	IB	150D	VLVO			60445	7	7	852000	936500
62		CONTEST 62	KTH	SACAC	F/S	KL	IB	150D	VLVO			70000			997000	1.085M
		1995 BOATS														
34	7	CONTEST 35S	SLP	SACAC	F/S	KL	IB	29D	VLVO	11	2	13040	4	5	98300	108000
36	11	CONTEST 37	SLP	SACAC	F/S	KL	IB	40D	VLVO	16	7	19621			149000	164000
36	11	CONTEST 37	SLP	SACAC	F/S	WK	IB	40D	VLVO	16	7	20944			157500	173000
40		CONTEST 40S	SLP	SACAC	F/S	KL	IB	59D	VLVO	12	8	24230	6	5	195500	215000
43		CONTEST 43	SLP	SACAC	F/S	KL	IB	62D	VLVO	13	2	28437	5	9	236500	260000
46	5	CONTEST 46	SLP	SACAC	F/S	KL	IB	100D	VLVO	13	8	33960	5	9	297500	327000
58		CONTEST 58	SLP	SACAC	F/S	KL	IB	150D	VLVO			60445	7	7	756500	831500
62		CONTEST 62	KTH	SACAC	F/S	KL	IB	150D	VLVO			70000			934000	1.015M
		1994 BOATS														
34	7	CONTEST 35S	SLP	SACAC	F/S	KL	IB	29D	VLVO	11	2	13040	4	5	92400	101500
35	8	CONTEST 36S	SLP	SACAC	F/S	WK	IB	40D	VLVO	11	8	17305	4	8	122500	134500
35	8	CONTEST 36S/A	SLP	SACAC	F/S	KL	IB	40D	VLVO	11	8	16315	5	5	116000	127500
35	8	CONTEST 36S/B	SLP	SACAC	F/S	KL	IB	40D	VLVO	11	8	15985	6	2	114000	125500
37	3	CONTEST 38S	SLP	SACAC	F/S	KL	SD	40D	VLVO	12		18063	4	8	132000	145500
40		CONTEST 40S	SLP	SACAC	F/S	KL	IB	59D	VLVO	12	8	24230	6	5	183500	202000
43		CONTEST 43	SLP	SACAC	F/S	KL	IB	62D	VLVO	13	2	28437	5	9	221500	243500
46	5	CONTEST 46	SLP	SACAC	F/S	KL	IB	100D	VLVO	13	8	33960	5	9	278500	306000
58		CONTEST 58	SLP	SACAC	F/S	KL	IB	150D	VLVO			60445	7	7	708500	778500
62		CONTEST 62	KTH	SACAC	F/S	KL	IB	150D	VLVO			70000			866000	951500
		1993 BOATS														
34	7	CONTEST 35	SLP	SACAC	F/S	KL	IB	29D	VLVO	11	2	13040	4	5	86900	95500
35	10	CONTEST 36	SLP	SACAC	F/S	KL	IB	40D	VLVO	11	8	15071	4	8	102000	112500
37	3	CONTEST 38S	SLP	SACAC	F/S	KL	SD	40D	VLVO	12		18063	4	8	124000	136500
40		CONTEST 40S	SLP	SACAC	F/S	KL	IB	59D	VLVO			24230			172500	189500
43		CONTEST 43	SLP	SACAC	F/S	KL	IB	62D	VLVO	13	2	28437	5	9	208000	228500
46	5	CONTEST 46	SLP	SACAC	F/S	KL	IB	100D	VLVO	13	8	33960	5	9	261000	287000
58		CONTEST 58	SLP	SACAC	F/S	KL	IB	150D	VLVO			60445	7	7	663000	728500

CONTEST YACHTS -CONTINUED See inside cover to adjust price for area

LOA FT	LOA IN	NAME AND/ OR MODEL	TOP/ RIG	BOAT TYPE	HULL MTL	HULL TP	ENGINE TP	# HP	MFG	BEAM FT	BEAM IN	WGT LBS	DRAFT FT	DRAFT IN	RETAIL LOW	RETAIL HIGH
		1993 BOATS														
62		CONTEST 62	KTH	SACAC	F/S	KL	IB	150D	VLVO			70000			811000	891000
		1992 BOATS														
34	7	CONTEST 35	SLP	SA/CR	F/S	KL	IB	28D	VLVO	11	2	13040	4	5	81800	89900
35	10	CONTEST 36	SLP	SA/CR	F/S	KL	IB	43D	VLVO	11	8	17300	4	8	108500	119500
37	3	CONTEST 38S	SLP	SA/CR	F/S	KL	SD	43D	VLVO	12		18716	4	8	120500	132500
43		CONTEST 43	SLP	SA/CR	F/S	KL	IB	62D	VLVO	13	2	28437	5	9	195000	214000
46	5	CONTEST 46	SLP	SA/CR	F/S	KL	IB	100D	VLVO	13	8	33960	5	9	244000	268500
		1990 BOATS														
34	7	CONTEST 35S	SLP	SAIL	F/S	KL	SD	28D	VLVO	11	2	13040	5	9	72300	79500
35	10	CONTEST 36S	SLP	SAIL	F/S	KL	IB	43D	VLVO	11	8	15071	6	3	85000	93400
37	3	CONTEST 38SB	SLP	SAIL	F/S	KL	SD	43D	VLVO	12		18063	6	5	103000	113500
37	3	CONTEST 38SB	KTH	SAIL	F/S	KL	SD	43D	VLVO	12		18063	6	5	104000	114000
41		CONTEST 41	SLP	SAIL	F/S	KL	IB	75D	VLVO	12	8	27225	6	3	157500	173000
41		CONTEST 41	KTH	SAIL	F/S	KL	IB	75D	VLVO	12	8	27225	6	3	161000	177000
43		CONTEST 43	SLP	SAIL	F/S	KL	IB	75D	VLVO						177000	194500
46	5	CONTEST 46	SLP	SAIL	F/S	KL	IB	100D	VLVO	13	8	32560	5	7	210000	231000
46	5	CONTEST 46	KTH	SAIL	F/S	KL	IB	100D	VLVO	13	8	32560	5	7	217000	238500
48	3	CONTEST 48S	KTH	SAIL	F/S	KL	IB	100D	VLVO	14	2	37881	6	6	249000	273500
		1989 BOATS														
34	7	CONTEST 35S	SLP	SAIL	F/S	KL	SD	28D	VLVO	11	2	13040	5	9	68000	74700
35	10	CONTEST 36S	SLP	SAIL	F/S	KL	IB	43D	VLVO	11	8	15071	6	3	79900	87800
37	3	CONTEST 38SB	SLP	SAIL	F/S	KL	SD	43D	VLVO	12		18603	6	5	99300	109000
37	3	CONTEST 38SB	KTH	SAIL	F/S	KL	SD	43D	VLVO	12		18603	6	5	100000	110000
41		CONTEST 41	SLP	SAIL	F/S	KL	IB	75D	VLVO	12	8	27225	6	3	147500	162000
41		CONTEST 41	KTH	SAIL	F/S	KL	IB	75D	VLVO	12	8	27225	6	3	151500	166000
42	7	CONTEST 43	SLP	SAIL	F/S	KL	IB	62D	VLVO	13	2	28437	6	5	158000	173500
46	5	CONTEST 46	SLP	SAIL	F/S	KL	IB	100D	VLVO	13	8	32560	5	7	197000	216500
46	5	CONTEST 46	KTH	SAIL	F/S	KL	IB	100D	VLVO	13	8	32560	5	7	203500	223500
48	3	CONTEST 48S	SLP	SAIL	F/S	KL	IB	100D	VLVO	14	2	37881	6	6	225500	248000
48	3	CONTEST 48S	KTH	SAIL	F/S	KL	IB	100D	VLVO	14	2	37881	6	6	233000	256000
		1988 BOATS														
33	6	CONTEST 34S	SLP	SAIL	F/S	KL	SD	28D	VLVO	11		13860	5	5	66700	73300
33	6	CONTEST 34S	KTH	SAIL	F/S	KL	SD	28D	VLVO	11		13860	5	5	66700	73300
34	7	CONTEST 35S	SLP	SAIL	F/S	KL	SD	28D	VLVO	11	2	13040	5	9	63900	70200
35	10	CONTEST 36S	SLP	SAIL	F/S	KL	IB	43D	VLVO	11	8	15071	6	3	75100	82500
37	3	CONTEST 38SB	SLP	SAIL	F/S	KL	SD	43D	VLVO	12		18603	6	5	93200	102500
37	3	CONTEST 38SB	KTH	SAIL	F/S	KL	SD	43D	VLVO	12		18603	6	5	94000	103500
41		CONTEST 41	SLP	SAIL	F/S	KL	IB	75D	VLVO	12	8	27225	6	3	138000	152000
41		CONTEST 41	KTH	SAIL	F/S	KL	IB	75D	VLVO	12	8	27225	6	3	142000	156000
46	5	CONTEST 46	SLP	SAIL	F/S	KL	IB	100D	VLVO	13	8	32560	5	7	184000	202500
46	5	CONTEST 46	KTH	SAIL	F/S	KL	IB	100D	VLVO	13	8	32560	5	7	191000	209500
48	3	CONTEST 48S	SLP	SAIL	F/S	KL	IB	100D	VLVO	14	2	37881	6	6	211000	232000
48	3	CONTEST 48S	KTH	SAIL	F/S	KL	IB	100D	VLVO	14	2	37881	6	6	218500	240000
		1987 BOATS														
33	6	CONTEST 34S	SLP	SAIL	F/S	KL	SD	28D	VLVO	11		13860	5	3	62700	68900
33	6	CONTEST 34S	KTH	SAIL	F/S	KL	SD	28D	VLVO	11		13860	5	3	62800	69000
35	10	CONTEST 36S	SLP	SAIL	F/S	KL	IB	43D	VLVO	11	8	15071	6	3	70500	77500
35	10	CONTEST 36S SHOAL	SLP	SAIL	F/S	KL	IB	43D	VLVO	11	8	15071	5	5	70500	77500
37	3	CONTEST 38SB	SLP	SAIL	F/S	KL	SD	43D	VLVO	12		18603	6	5	87400	96100
37	3	CONTEST 38SB	KTH	SAIL	F/S	KL	SD	43D	VLVO	12		18603	6	5	88400	97100
41		CONTEST 41	SLP	SAIL	F/S	KL	IB	75D	VLVO	12	8	27225	6	3	129500	142500
41		CONTEST 41	KTH	SAIL	F/S	KL	IB	75D	VLVO	12	8	27225	6	3	133500	146500
46	5	CONTEST 46	SLP	SAIL	F/S	KL	IB	100D	VLVO	13	4	32560	5	4	172500	189500
46	5	CONTEST 46	KTH	SAIL	F/S	KL	IB	100D	VLVO	13	9	32560	5	9	178500	196500
48	3	CONTEST 48S	SLP	SAIL	F/S	KL	IB	100D	VLVO	14	2	37881	6	5	197500	217000
48	3	CONTEST 48S	KTH	SAIL	F/S	KL	IB	100D	VLVO	14	2	37881	6	5	204500	224500
		1986 BOATS														
31	10	CONTEST 32	KTH	SA/CR	FBG	KL	IB	D		10	11	14300	5	3	60100	66000
33	6	CONTEST 34S	SLP	SA/CR	FBG	KL	IB	28D	VLVO	11		16896	5	5	71100	78100
33	6	CONTEST 34S	KTH	SA/CR	FBG	KL	IB	28D	VLVO	11		16896	5	5	71100	78200
35	8	CONTEST 36S	SLP	SA/RC	FBG	KL	IB	43D	VLVO	11	8	16315	6	2	70800	77800
37	3	CONTEST 38S	SLP	SA/CR	FBG	KL	IB	43D	VLVO	12		19285	6	5	84600	93000
37	3	CONTEST 38S	KTH	SA/CR	FBG	KL	IB	43D	VLVO	12		19285	6	5	85500	94000
41		CONTEST 41	SLP	SA/CR	FBG	KL	IB	62D	VLVO	12	8	27225	6	3	121000	133000
41		CONTEST 41	KTH	SA/CR	FBG	KL	IB	62D	VLVO	12	8	27225	6	3	125000	137000
43	5	CONTEST 44	KTH	SA/CR	FBG	KL	IB	62D	VLVO	13	1	31085	6	4	145000	159500
48	3	CONTEST 48	KTH	SA/CR	FBG	KL	IB	72D	VLVO	14	2	37881	6	5	191000	209500
63	7	CONTEST 64	KTH	SA/CR	FBG	KL	IB	D		16	3	65000	5	11	492500	541000
		1985 BOATS														
24	9	CONTEST 25	SLP	SA/CR	FBG	KL	IB	D		9		3785	4	11	11200	12700
24	9	CONTEST 250C	SLP	SAIL	F/S	KL	SD	8D	VLVO	9		3788	4	11	11100	12600
27	11	CONTEST 28	SLP	SAIL	F/S	KL	SD	15D	VLVO	9	4	6173	5	4	21400	23800
31	2	CONTEST 31HT	SLP	SAIL	F/S	KL	SD	25D	VLVO	10	4	11157	4	9	43500	48300
31	10	CONTEST 32CS	SLP	SAIL	F/S	KL	SD	25D	VLVO	10	11	13860	5	3	54800	60200
31	10	CONTEST 32CS	KTH	SAIL	F/S	KL	SD	25D	VLVO	10	11	13860	5	3	54800	60200
34	11	CONTEST 35	SLP	SAIL	F/S	KL	SD	35D	VLVO	11	8	14879	6	3	60300	66300
35	10	CONTEST 36S	SLP	SAIL	F/S	KL	IB	36D	VLVO	11	8	15071	6	3	61900	68000
35	10	CONTEST 36S SHOAL	SLP	SAIL	F/S	KL	IB	36D	VLVO	11	8	15071	5	5	62300	68400
37	3	CONTEST 38SB	KTH	SAIL	F/S	KL	SD	35D	VLVO	12		18603	6	5	77900	85600
41		CONTEST 41	KTH	SAIL	F/S	KL	IB	75D	VLVO	12	8	27225	6	3	117500	129000
42	7	CONTEST 44	KTH	SAIL	F/S	KL	IB	61D	VLVO	13	1	29750	6	1	129000	142000
48	3	CONTEST 48	KTH	SAIL	F/S	KL	IB	72D	VLVO	14	2	37881	6	5	178500	196500
48	3	CONTEST 48S	KTH	SAIL	F/S	KL	IB	72D	VLVO	14	2	37881	6	5	178500	196500
63	7	CONTEST 64	KTH	SA/CR	FBG	KL	IB	D		16	3	65000	5	11	460500	506000
		1984 BOATS														
24	9	CONTEST 250C	SLP	SAIL	F/S	KL	SD	8D	VLVO	9		3788	4	11	10400	11900
27	11	CONTEST 28	SLP	SAIL	F/S	KL	SD	15D	VLVO	9	4	6173	5	4	20100	22300
31	2	CONTEST 31HT	SLP	SAIL	F/S	KL	SD	25D	VLVO	10	4	11157	4	9	40900	45500
31	10	CONTEST 32CS	SLP	SAIL	F/S	KL	SD	25D	VLVO	10	11	13860	5	3	51500	56600
31	10	CONTEST 32CS	KTH	SAIL	F/S	KL	SD	25D	VLVO	10	11	13860	5	3	51500	56600
34	11	CONTEST 35	SLP	SAIL	F/S	KL	SD	35D	VLVO	11	8	14879	6	3	56800	62400
35	11	CONTEST 36	SLP	SA/CR	F/S	KL	IB	36D	VLVO	11	8	15700	5	5	60600	66600
37	3	CONTEST 38SB	KTH	SAIL	F/S	KL	SD	35D	VLVO	12		18603	6	5	73200	80400
42	7	CONTEST 44	KTH	SAIL	F/S	KL	IB	52D	VLVO	13	1	29750	6	1	121000	133000
48	3	CONTEST 48	KTH	SAIL	F/S	KL	IB	72D	VLVO	14	2	37881	6	5	168500	185000
63	7	CONTEST 64	KTH	SA/CR	FBG	KL	IB	D		16	3	65000	5	11	434000	477000

....For earlier years, see the BUC Used Boat Price Guide, Volume 3

COOPER YACHT SALES LTD

VANCOUVER BC CANADA V6H COAST GUARD MFG ID- CEL See inside cover to adjust price for area
FORMERLY COOPER ENTERPRISES LTD

LOA FT	LOA IN	NAME AND/ OR MODEL	TOP/ RIG	BOAT TYPE	HULL MTL	HULL TP	ENGINE TP	# HP	MFG	BEAM FT	BEAM IN	WGT LBS	DRAFT FT	DRAFT IN	RETAIL LOW	RETAIL HIGH
		1991 BOATS														
45		MAPLE LEAF 45	SLP	SA/CR	FBG	KL	IB	100D	VLVO	14		25000	6	7	156000	171000
		1990 BOATS														
45		MAPLE LEAF 45	SLP	SA/CR	FBG	KL	IB	100D	VLVO	14		25000	6	7	147500	162000
		1989 BOATS														
41	6	COOPER 42PH	SLP	SA/CR	F/S	KL	IB	50D	LEHM	14		24000	6	7	123500	136000
45		MAPLE-LEAF 45	SLP	SA/CR	F/S	KL	IB	46D	WEST	14		25000	6	7	139000	152500
50	8	COOPER 51	SLP	SA/CR	F/S	KL	IB	85D	LEHM	15		37000	8		185000	203500
50	8	COOPER 51	SLP	SA/RC	F/S	KL	IB	80D	LEHM	15		38350	8		199500	219000
50	8	COOPER 51 SHALLOW	SLP	SA/CR	F/S	KL	IB	85D	LEHM	15		37000	6		210500	231000
67	8	MAPLE-LEAF 68	KTH	SA/CR	F/S	KL	IB	T135D	LEHM	17	10	72000	6	6	532000	585000
72		MAPLE-LEAF PH	KTH	SAIL	F/S	KL	IB	T135D	PERK	17	10	95000	6	10	**	**
		1988 BOATS														
36	7	COOPER 37	SLP	SA/CR	F/S	KL	VD	23D	VLVO	12		13500	5	10	64000	70300
36	7	COOPER 37 SHOAL	SLP	SA/CR	F/S	KL	VD	23D	VLVO	12		13500	5	10	65300	71800
36	7	COOPER 37PH	SLP	SA/CR	F/S	KL	VD	36D		12		13250	5	10	63800	70100
36	7	COOPER 37PH SHOAL	SLP	SA/CR	F/S	KL	VD	28D	VLVO	12		13200	4	8	63500	69800
41	6	COOPER 42PH	SLP	SA/CR	F/S	KL	IB	50D	LEHM	14		24000	6	7	117000	128500
45		MAPLE-LEAF 45	SLP	SA/CR	F/S	KL	IB	46D	WEST	14		25000	6	3	131500	144500
50	8	COOPER 51	SLP	SA/CR	F/S	KL	IB	85D	LEHM	15		37000	8		176000	193500
50	8	COOPER 51	SLP	SA/RC	F/S	KL	IB	80D	LEHM	15		38350	8		189000	207500
50	8	COOPER 51 SHALLOW	SLP	SA/CR	F/S	KL	IB	85D	LEHM	15		37000	6		198500	218000
67	8	MAPLE-LEAF 68	KTH	SA/CR	F/S	KL	IB	T135D	LEHM	17	10	72000	6	6	504000	554000
72		MAPLE-LEAF PH	KTH	SAIL	F/S	KL	IB	T135D	PERK	17	10	95000	6	10	**	**
		1987 BOATS														
36	7	COOPER 37	SLP	SA/CR	F/S	KL	VD	23D	VLVO	12		13500	5	10	60600	66600
36	7	COOPER 37 SHOAL	SLP	SA/CR	F/S	KL	VD	23D	VLVO	12		13500			61900	68000
36	7	COOPER 37PH	SLP	SA/CR	F/S	KL	VD	36D		12		13250	5	10	60500	66500
36	7	COOPER 37PH SHOAL	SLP	SA/CR	F/S	KL	VD	28D	VLVO	12		13200	4	8	60200	66100
41	6	COOPER 42PH	SLP	SA/CR	F/S	KL	IB	50D	LEHM	14		24000	6	7	111000	122000
45		MAPLE LEAF 45	SLP	SA/CR	F/S	KL	IB	46D	WEST	14		25000	6	3	124500	137000
47	8	MAPLE LEAF 48	SLP	SA/CR	F/S	KL	IB	80D	LEHM	14	6	34000	6	6	153000	168000
50	4	MAPLE LEAF 50	SLP	SA/CR	F/S	KL	IB	80D	LEHM	14	6	35000	6	6	172000	189000
50	8	COOPER 51	SLP	SA/CR	F/S	KL	IB	85D	LEHM	15		37000	8		167000	183500
50	8	COOPER 51	SLP	SA/RC	F/S	KL	IB	80D	LEHM	15		38350	8		179000	197000
50	8	COOPER 51 SHALLOW	SLP	SA/CR	F/S	KL	IB	85D	LEHM	15		37000	6		188000	206500
54	5	MAPLE LEAF 54	SLP	SA/CR	F/S	KL	IB	135D	LEHM	14	9	42000	7	2	223000	245500
56	4	MAPLE LEAF 56	SLP	SA/CR	F/S	KL	IB	135D	LEHM	14	9	44000	7	2	291000	319500
67	8	MAPLE LEAF 68	KTH	SA/CR	F/S	KL	IB	T135D	LEHM	17	10	72000	6	6	477500	525000
67	8	MAPLE LEAF PH	KTH	SAIL	F/S	KL	IB	T135D	PERK	17	10	72000	6	6	476000	523000
72		MAPLE LEAF	KTH	SAIL	F/S	KL	IB	T135D	PERK	17	10	95000	6	10	**	**
72		MAPLE LEAF PH	KTH	SAIL	F/S	KL	IB	T135D	PERK	17	10	95000	6	10	**	**
		1986 BOATS														
31	6	COOPER 316	SLP	SA/CR	F/S	KL	VD	18D	VLVO	10	11	10500	5	5	43400	48300
31	8	BANNER 32	SLP	SA/CR	F/S	KL	VD	23D	VLVO	10	11	10500	5	5	43500	48300
36	7	BANNER 37	SLP	SA/CR	F/S	KL	VD	23D	VLVO	12		13500	5	10	57500	63100
36	7	BANNER 37 SHOAL	SLP	SA/CR	F/S	KL	VD	23D	VLVO	12		13500			58600	64400
36	7	COOPER 367	SLP	SA/CR	F/S	KL	VD	36D		12		13250	5	10	57300	63000

CONTINUED ON NEXT PAGE

LOA FT	LOA IN	NAME AND/ OR MODEL	TOP/ RIG	BOAT TYPE	HULL MTL	HULL TP	ENGINE TP	# HP	MFG	BEAM FT	BEAM IN	WGT LBS	DRAFT FT	DRAFT IN	RETAIL LOW	RETAIL HIGH
		1986 BOATS														
36	7	COOPER 367 SHOAL	SLP	SA/CR	F/S	KL	VD	28D	VLVO	12		13200	4	8	57000	62600
41	6	COOPER 416	SLP	SA/CR	F/S	KL	IB	50D	LEHM	14		24000	6	7	105000	115500
45		MAPLE LEAF 45	SLP	SA/CR	F/S	KL	IB	46D	WEST	14		25000	6	3	118000	129500
47	8	MAPLE LEAF 48	SLP	SA/CR	F/S	KL	IB	80D	LEHM	14	6	34000	6	6	145000	159500
50	4	MAPLE LEAF 50	SLP	SA/CR	F/S	KL	IB	80D	LEHM	14	6	35000	6	6	163000	179000
50	8	BANNER 51	SLP	SA/CR	F/S	KL	IB	85D	LEHM	15		37000	8		167500	184000
50	8	BANNER 51 SHALLOW	SLP	SA/CR	F/S	KL	IB	85D	LEHM	15		37000	6		169000	185500
50	8	COOPER 508	SLP	SA/RC	F/S	KL	IB	80D	LEHM	15		38350	8		169500	186500
54	5	MAPLE LEAF 54	SLP	SA/CR	F/S	KL	IB	135D	LEHM	14	9	42000	7	2	211500	232500
56	4	MAPLE LEAF 56	SLP	SA/CR	F/S	KL	IB	135D	LEHM	14	9	44000	7	2	275500	303000
67	8	MAPLE LEAF 68	KTH	SA/CR	F/S	KL	IB	T135D	LEHM	17	10	72000	6	6	452500	497500
		1985 BOATS														
31	6	COOPER 316	SLP	SA/CR	F/S	KL	VD	18D	VLVO	10	11	10500	5	5	41200	45700
31	8	BANNER 32	SLP	SA/CR	F/S	KL	VD	18D- 23D		10	11	10500	5	5	41200	45800
35	3	COOPER 353	SLP	SA/CR	F/S	KL	IB	D		12		13250	5	10	52600	57800
36	7	BANNER 37	SLP	SA/CR	F/S	KL	VD	23D	VLVO	12		13500	5	10	54400	59800
36	7	BANNER 37 SHOAL	SLP	SA/CR	F/S	KL	VD	23D	VLVO	12		13500			55500	61000
36	7	BANNER 37 SHOAL	SLP	SA/CR	F/S	KL	VD	35D	VLVO	12		13500			55200	60700
36	7	BANNER 37 SHOAL	SLP	SA/CR	F/S	KL	VD	35D	VLVO	12		13500	5	10	55200	60700
36	7	COOPER 367	SLP	SA/CR	F/S	KL	VD	25D	VLVO	12		13250	5	10	54100	59500
36	7	COOPER 367	SLP	SA/CR	F/S	KL	VD	36D		12		13250	5	10	53500	58800
36	7	COOPER 367 SHOAL	SLP	SA/CR	F/S	KL	VD	28D	VLVO	12		13200	4	8	54000	59400
36	7	COOPER 367 SHOAL	SLP	SA/CR	F/S	KL	VD	36D		12		13250	4	8	55100	60600
36	10	SEA BIRD 37 CC	CUT	SA/CR	F/S	KL	IB	50D	LEHM	11	8	18000	4		70700	77600
36	10	SEA BIRD 37 CC	KTH	SA/CR	F/S	KL	IB	50D	LEHM	11	8	18000	4		71200	78300
36	10	SEA BIRD 37 MS	SLP	SA/CR	F/S	KL	IB	50D	LEHM	11	8	18000	4		71200	78300
36	10	SEA BIRD 37 MS	CUT	SA/CR	F/S	KL	IB	50D	LEHM	11	8	18000	4		71800	78900
41	6	COOPER 416	SLP	SA/CR	F/S	KL	IB	50D	LEHM	14		24000	6	7	98200	108000
41	6	COOPER 416 SHOAL	SLP	SA/CR	F/S	KL	IB	50D	LEHM	14		24000	5	5	101000	111000
47	8	MAPLE LEAF 48	SLP	SA/CR	F/S	KL	IB	80D	LEHM	14	6	34000	6	6	137500	151000
50	4	MAPLE LEAF 50	SLP	SA/CR	F/S	KL	IB	80D	LEHM	14	6	35000	6	6	154500	169500
50	8	COOPER 508	SLP	SA/RC	F/S	KL	IB	80D	LEHM	15		38350	8		161000	176500
51		BANNER 51	SLP	SA/CR	FBG	KL	IB	85D		15		37000	8		162000	178000
54	5	MAPLE LEAF 54	SLP	SA/CR	F/S	KL	IB	135D	LEHM	14	9	42000	7	2	200500	220500
56	4	MAPLE LEAF 56	SLP	SA/CR	F/S	KL	IB	135D	LEHM	14	9	44000	7	2	261500	287000
63		MAPLE LEAF 63	SLP	SA/CR	F/S	KL	IB	135D	LEHM	16	3	60000	6	6	354000	389000
67	8	MAPLE LEAF 68	KTH	SA/CR	F/S	KL	IB	T135D	LEHM	17	10	72000	6	6	429000	471000
		1984 BOATS														
31	6	BANNER 32	SLP	SA/CR	F/S	KL	VD	18D	VLVO	10	11	10500	5	5	38300	42600
31	6	COOPER 316	SLP	SA/CR	F/S	KL	VD	18D	VLVO	10	11	10500	5	5	39700	44100
35	3	COOPER 367	SLP	SA/CR	F/S	KL	VD	28D	VLVO	12		13250	5	10	49800	54800
36	7	BANNER 37	SLP	SA/CR	F/S	KL	VD	28D	VLVO	12		13500	5	10	52200	57400
36	7	BANNER 37	SLP	SA/RC	F/S	KL	SD	23D	VLVO	12		13500	5	10	52100	57300
36	10	SEA BIRD 37 CC	CUT	SA/CR	F/S	KL	IB	50D	LEHM	11	8	18000	4		67500	74200
36	10	SEA BIRD 37 CC	KTH	SA/CR	F/S	KL	IB	50D	LEHM	11	8	18000	4		67500	74200
36	10	SEA BIRD 37 MS	SLP	SA/CR	F/S	KL	IB	50D	LEHM	11	8	18000	4		67500	74200
36	10	SEA BIRD 37 MS	CUT	SA/CR	F/S	KL	IB	50D	LEHM	11	8	18000	4		67500	74200
41	6	COOPER 416	SLP	SA/CR	F/S	KL	IB	50D	LEHM	14		24000	6	7	94500	104000
47	8	MAPLE LEAF 48	SLP	SA/CR	F/S	KL	IB	80D	LEHM	14	6	34000	6	6	130000	143000
50	4	MAPLE LEAF 50	SLP	SA/CR	F/S	KL	IB	80D	LEHM	14	6	35000	6	6	146500	161000
50	8	COOPER 508	SLP	SA/RC	F/S	KL	IB	80D	LEHM	15		38500	8		152500	167500
54	5	MAPLE LEAF 54	SLP	SA/CR	F/S	KL	IB	135D	LEHM	14	9	42000	7	2	190000	208500
56	4	MAPLE LEAF 56	SLP	SA/CR	F/S	KL	IB	135D	LEHM	14	9	44000	7	2	247500	272000
63		MAPLE LEAF 63	SLP	SA/CR	F/S	KL	IB	135D	LEHM	16	3	60000	6	6	335500	369000
67	8	MAPLE LEAF 68	KTH	MS	F/S	KL	IB	T120D	PERK	17	10	72000	6	6	404500	444500
67	8	MAPLE LEAF 68	KTH	SA/CR	F/S	KL	IB	T135D	LEHM	17	10	72000	6	6	406500	446500

....For earlier years, see the BUC Used Boat Price Guide, Volume 3

COPLAND BOATS

VENTNOR IW ENGLAND COAST GUARD MFG ID- CPP See inside cover to adjust price for area

COPLAND BOATS U S
SEVERNA PK MD 21146

LOA FT	LOA IN	NAME AND/ OR MODEL	TOP/ RIG	BOAT TYPE	HULL MTL	HULL TP	ENGINE TP	# HP	MFG	BEAM FT	BEAM IN	WGT LBS	DRAFT FT	DRAFT IN	RETAIL LOW	RETAIL HIGH
		1986 BOATS														
20		FLYING-FIFTEEN	SLP	SA/OD	FBG	KL				6			2	6	5950	6850
22		HS 22		UTL	FBG	RB	IO	140D		8	3	4500			10600	12000
22	1	FOXTERRIER 22	SLP	SA/OD	FBG	KL				8	2	2800	4	1	9900	11300
24		FOXHOUND 24	SLP	SA/CR	FBG	KL				8	3	3500	4	6	12900	14700
26		HS 26		UTL	FBG	RB	IO	165		8	3	6000			10200	11600
32		INTERNATIONAL-101	SLP	SA/OD	FBG	KL				9		6160	5	5	**	**
36		HS 36		UTL	FBG	RB	IO	T200D		12	6	12000			37300	41500
42		ASK 42		UTL	FBG	RB	IB	T260		14		30000			91900	101000
45		ASK 45		UTL	FBG	RB	IB	T260		14		35000			103500	114000
50		ASK 50		UTL	FBG	RB	IB	T300		14		40000			125500	138000
		1985 BOATS														
18		FOXCUB		SA/CR	FBG	KL				6	5	1400	3	3	5400	6200
20		FLYING-FIFTEEN	SLP	SA/OD	FBG	KL	OB			5		700	2	6	4250	4950
20	1	HARRIER 20	SLP	SA/OD	FBG	KC	OB			8		2000	4		6900	7900
22	1	FOX-TERRIER 22	SLP	SA/OD	FBG	KL	OB			8	2	2650	4	1	9000	10200
22	1	FOX-TERRIER 22	SLP	SA/OD	FBG	SK	OB			8	2	2650	1		9000	10200
23	10	FOXHOUND 24	SLP	SA/CR	FBG	KL	OB			8	4	3200	4	6	11200	12700
23	10	FOXHOUND 24	SLP	SA/CR	FBG	TK	OB			8	4	3200	3		11200	12700
23	10	FOXHOUND 24 SHOAL	SLP	SA/CR	FBG	KL	OB			8	4	3200	3		11200	12700
32		INTERNATIONAL-101	SLP	SA/OD	FBG	KL				9			5	5	**	**
42		ASK 42		UTL	FBG	RB	IB	T260		14		30000			88000	96700
45		ASK 45		UTL	FBG	RB	IB	T260		14		35000			99200	109000
50		ASK 50		UTL	FBG	RB	IB	T300		14		40000			120000	132000
		1984 BOATS														
18		FOXCUB 18	SLP	SAIL	FBG	KL	OB			6	5	1400	3	3	5100	5900
18		FOXCUB 18 SHOAL	SLP	SAIL	FBG	KL	OB			6	5	1400	2		5100	5900
20		FLYING-FIFTEEN	SLP	SA/OD	FBG	KL	OB			5		700	2	6	4000	4650
20	1	HARRIER 20	SLP	SA/OD	FBG	KC	OB			8		2000	4		6450	7450
22		HS 22			FBG		IO	140D		8	3	4500			7400	8550
22	1	FOX-TERRIER 22	SLP	SA/OD	FBG	KL	OB			8	2	2650	4	1	8350	9600
22	1	FOX-TERRIER 22	SLP	SA/OD	FBG	SK	OB			8	2	2650	1		8350	9600
23	10	FOXHOUND 24	SLP	SA/CR	FBG	KL	OB			8	4	3200	4	6	10600	12100
23	10	FOXHOUND 24	SLP	SA/CR	FBG	TK	OB			8	4	3200	3		10600	12100
23	10	FOXHOUND 24 SHOAL	SLP	SA/CR	FBG	KL	OB			8	4	3200	3		10600	12100
26		HS 26			FBG		IO	165D		8	3	6000			11600	13200
32		APHRODITE 101	SLP	SA/OD	FBG	KL				8		6174	5	5	**	**
32		INTERNATIONAL-101	SLP	SA/OD	FBG	KL				7	10	6160			**	**
36		HS 36			FBG		IO	T200D		12	6	12000			32200	35800
42		ASK 42			FBG	RB	IB	T260		14		30000			89800	98700
42		HS 42			FBG		IO	T200D		12	6	15000			45700	50200
45		ASK 45			FBG	RB	IB	T260		14		35000			98800	108500
50		ASK 50			FBG	RB	IB	T300		14		40000			131500	144500
54		HS 54			FBG		IO	T400D		15		25000			123500	136000

....For earlier years, see the BUC Used Boat Price Guide, Volume 3

CORBIN LES BATEAUX INC

NAPIERVILLE QUE CANADA COAST GUARD MFG ID- ZCJ See inside cover to adjust price for area

LOA FT	LOA IN	NAME AND/ OR MODEL	TOP/ RIG	BOAT TYPE	HULL MTL	HULL TP	ENGINE TP	# HP	MFG	BEAM FT	BEAM IN	WGT LBS	DRAFT FT	DRAFT IN	RETAIL LOW	RETAIL HIGH
		1991 BOATS														
36	8	CORBIN 37 LORAC		TRWL	F/S	SV	IB	230	MRCR	13		22000	3	6	52700	57900
38	6	CORBIN 39 AFT CPT A	SLP	SA/CR	F/S	KL	IB	60D	PERK	12	1	22800	5	6	119500	131000
38	6	CORBIN 39 CTR CPT A	SLP	SA/CR	F/S	KL	IB	60D	PERK	12	1	22800	5	6	123000	135500
38	6	CORBIN 39 CTR CPT B	SLP	SA/CR	F/S	KL	IB	60D	PERK	12	1	22800	5	6	127000	139500
		1990 BOATS														
36	8	CORBIN 37 LORAC		TRWL	F/S	SV	IB	230	MRCR	13		22000	3	6	50300	55300
38	6	CORBIN 39 AFT CPT A	SLP	SA/CR	F/S	KL	IB	60D	PERK	12	1	22800	5	6	112000	123000
38	6	CORBIN 39 CTR CPT A	SLP	SA/CR	F/S	KL	IB	60D	PERK	12	1	22800	5	6	116000	127500
38	6	CORBIN 39 CTR CPT B	SLP	SA/CR	F/S	KL	IB	60D	PERK	12	1	22800	5	6	119500	131500
		1989 BOATS														
36	8	CORBIN 37 LORAC		TRWL	F/S	SV	IB	230	MRCR	12	9	17000	3	2	40600	45200
38	6	CORBIN 39 AFT CPT A	SLP	SA/CR	F/S	KL	IB	33D	WEST	12	1	22800	5	6	105500	116000
38	6	CORBIN 39 CTR CPT A	SLP	SA/CR	F/S	KL	IB	33D	WEST	12	1	22800	5	6	109000	119500
38	6	CORBIN 39 CTR CPT B	SLP	SA/CR	F/S	KL	IB	33D	WEST	12	1	22800	5	6	112500	123500
		1988 BOATS														
29		CORBIN 29	SLP	SAIL	FBG		IB	15D	WEST	9	6	5050	4	6	22700	25200
35		CORBIN 35	SLP	SAIL	FBG		IB	30D	WEST	10	6	14000	5		64100	70500
38	6	CORBIN AFT CPT	CUT	SA/CR	F/S	KL	IB	33D	WEST	12	1	22800	5	6	102000	112000
38	6	CORBIN CTR CPT A	KTH	SA/CR	F/S	KL	IB	52D	WEST	12	1	22800	5	6	102500	112500
38	6	CORBIN CTR CPT B	KTH	SA/CR	F/S	KL	IB	52D	WEST	12	1	22800	5	6	104000	114500
		1987 BOATS														
38	6	CORBIN AFT CPT	CUT	SA/CR	F/S	KL	IB	33D	WEST	12	1	22800	5	6	95900	105500
38	6	CORBIN CTR CPT A	KTH	SA/CR	F/S	KL	IB	52D	WEST	12	1	22800	5	6	96500	106000
38	6	CORBIN CTR CPT B	KTH	SA/CR	F/S	KL	IB	52D	WEST	12	1	22800	5	6	97800	107500
		1986 BOATS														
38	6	CORBIN AFT CPT	CUT	SA/CR	F/S	KL	IB	33D	WEST	12	1	22800	5	6	90200	99100
38	6	CORBIN CTR CPT A	KTH	SA/CR	F/S	KL	IB	52D	WEST	12	1	22800	5	6	90400	99300
38	6	CORBIN CTR CPT B	KTH	SA/CR	F/S	KL	IB	52D	WEST	12	1	22800	5	6	92400	101500

LOA FT	IN	NAME AND/ OR MODEL	TOP/ RIG	BOAT TYPE	HULL MTL	HULL TP	ENGINE TP	# HP	MFG	BEAM FT	IN	WGT LBS	DRAFT FT	IN	RETAIL LOW	RETAIL HIGH
		1985 BOATS														
38	9	CORBIN AFT CPT	CUT	SA/CR	F/S	KL	IB	33D	WEST			22000	5	6	83100	91300
38	9	CORBIN CTR CPT	KTH	SA/CR	F/S	KL	IB	52D	WEST	12	2	22000	5	6	84300	92700
		1984 BOATS														
38	9	CORBIN AFT CPT	CUT	SA/CR	F/S	KL	IB	33D	WEST	12	2	22000	5	6	78200	85900
41	6	EDITION-SPECIALE	CUT	SA/CR	FBG	KL	IB	33D	WEST	12	1	22800	5	6	87300	96000
41	6	EDITION-SPECIALE	KTH	SA/CR	FBG	KL	IB	33D	WEST	12	1	22800	5	6	88500	97200

....For earlier years, see the BUC Used Boat Price Guide, Volume 3

CORONET BOATS OF N AMERICA

CORONET BOATS INTERNATIONAL
POMPANO BEACH FL 33062

See inside cover to adjust price for area

LOA FT	IN	NAME AND/ OR MODEL	TOP/ RIG	BOAT TYPE	HULL MTL	HULL TP	ENGINE TP	# HP	MFG	BEAM FT	IN	WGT LBS	DRAFT FT	IN	RETAIL LOW	RETAIL HIGH
		1986 BOATS														
27		SILVER-SPUR		SPTCR	FBG	DV	IB	T145	VLVO	9	2				13800	15700
27		SILVER-SPUR		SPTCR	FBG	DV	IB	T110D	VLVO	9	2				17200	19500
33	3	SEDAN/FISH		SDN	FBG	DV	IB	T260-T290		10	9				34800	39400
33	3	SEDAN/FISH		SDN	FBG	DV	IB	T165D	VLVO	10	9				43000	47800
33	3	SILVER-STAR		SPTCR	FBG	DV	IB	T165-T290		10	9				30600	36300
33	3	SILVER-STAR		SPTCR	FBG	DV	IO	T375	MRCR	10	9				27600	30700
33	3	SILVER-STAR		SPTCR	FBG	DV	IB	T165D	VLVO	10	9				38900	43200
41	10	MOTOR YACHT 42		MY	FBG	DV	IB	T D	GM	13	5				**	**
41	10	MOTOR YACHT 42		MY	FBG	DV	IB	T300D	VLVO	13	5				108000	118500
		1985 BOATS														
21		SUN-RUNNER	ST	CUD	FBG	DV	IO	138-170		7	8	2640	1	2	4100	5000
21		SUN-RUNNER	ST	CUD	FBG	DV	IO	T138	VLVO	7	8	3235	1	2	5550	6350
27		SILVER-SPUR	ST	EXP	FBG	DV	IO	165D	VLVO	9	3	5533	1	7	10500	12000
27		SILVER-SPUR	ST	EXP	FBG	DV	IO	T138	VLVO	9	3	5610	1	7	10500	11900
33	4	CORONET 32 SEDAN	FB	SDN	FBG	DV	IO	T200	VLVO	10	11	11660	1	7	25600	28400
33	4	CORONET 32 SEDAN	FB	SDN	FBG	DV	IO	T165D	VLVO	10	11	11990	1	7	30800	34200
33	4	OCEAN-FARER	ST	EXP	FBG	DV	IO	165D	VLVO	10	11	10373	1	7	26700	29600
33	4	OCEAN-FARER	ST	EXP	FBG	DV	IO	T200	VLVO	10	11	10450	1	7	25800	28700
33	4	SILVER-STAR	OP	EXP	FBG	DV	IO	T200	VLVO	10	11		1	7	25800	28700
33	4	SILVER-STAR	OP	EXP	FBG	DV	IO	T165D	VLVO	10	11		1	7	28800	32000
37	7	BALTIC AFT CAB	ST	EXP	FBG	DV	IB	T255D	VLVO	14	7	20900	2	6	64800	71200
37	7	BALTIC AFT CAB	ST	EXP	FBG	DV	IB	T305D	GM	14	7	21990	2	6	71100	78100
37	7	MEDITERRANIAN	ST	EXP	FBG	DV	IB	T255D	VLVO	14	7	19580	2	6	61600	67700
37	7	MEDITERRANIAN	ST	EXP	FBG	DV	IB	T305D	GM	14	7	20670	2	6	67900	74600
41	7	SILVER-SQUIRE	FB	SDN	FBG	DV	IB	T300D	VLVO	13	6		2	6	105500	116000
41	7	SILVER-SQUIRE	FB	SDN	FBG	DV	IB	T305D	GM	13	6		2	6	107500	118000
		1984 BOATS														
21		CORONET 21 SUNRUNNER	ST	CUD	FBG	DV	IO	138-170		7	8	2640	1	2	4000	4850
21		CORONET 21 SUNRUNNER	ST	CUD	FBG	DV	IO	T138	VLVO	7	8	3235	1	2	5350	6150
23		CORONET 22 DAYCRUISR	ST	CUD	FBG	DV	IO	170-200		8	2	3554	1	2	5500	6550
23		CORONET 22 DAYCRUISR	ST	CUD	FBG	DV	IO	130D	VLVO	8	2	3799	1	2	6850	7900
23		CORONET 22 DAYCRUISR	ST	CUD	FBG	DV	IO	T138	VLVO	8	2	3964	1	2	6750	7750
27		CORONET 26 FAMILY	ST	EXP	FBG	DV	IO	155D	VLVO	9	3	5533	1	8	10000	11400
27		CORONET 26 FAMILY	ST	EXP	FBG	DV	IO	T138	VLVO	9	3	5610	1	8	10100	11500
33	4	CORONET 32 OCEANFARE	ST	EXP	FBG	DV	IO	155D	VLVO	10	11	10373	1	7	25700	28600
33	4	CORONET 32 OCEANFARE	ST	EXP	FBG	DV	IO	T200	VLVO	10	11	10450	1	7	24900	27700
33	4	CORONET 32 SEDAN	FB	SDN	FBG	DV	IO	T200	VLVO	10	11	11660	1	7	24600	27400
33	4	CORONET 32 SEDAN	FB	SDN	FBG	DV	IO	T155D	VLVO	10	11	11990	1	7	29000	32300
37	7	CORONET 38 AFT CABIN	ST	EXP	FBG	DV	IB	T235D	VLVO	13	6	20900	2	6	64500	70900
37	7	CORONET 38 AFT CABIN	ST	EXP	FBG	DV	IB	T305D	GM	13	6	21990	2	6	71100	78100
37	7	CORONET 38 MEDITERRA	ST	EXP	FBG	DV	IB	T235D	VLVO	13	6	19580	2	6	61400	67500
37	7	CORONET 38 MEDITERRA	ST	EXP	FBG	DV	IB	T305D	GM	13	6	20670	2	6	68000	74800
41	7	CORONET 42 AFT CABIN	ST	EXP	FBG	DV	IB	T235D	VLVO	13	6		2	6	72600	79800
41	7	CORONET 42 AFT CABIN	ST	EXP	FBG	DV	IB	T305D	GM	13	6		2	6	77300	84900
41	7	CORONET 42 SEDAN	FB	SDN	FBG	DV	IB	T235D	VLVO	13	6		2	6	97900	107500
41	7	CORONET 42 SEDAN	FB	SDN	FBG	DV	IB	T305D	GM	13	6		2	6	102500	112500
43	9	CORONET 44 YACHT	FB	DCMY	FBG	DV	IB	T286D	VLVO	14	9		3	4	120000	132000
43	9	CORONET 44 YACHT	FB	DCMY	FBG	DV	IB	T375D	GM	14	9		3	4	128500	141500
43	9	CORONET 44 YACHT	FB	DCMY	FBG	DV	IB	T475D	GM	14	9		3	4	137500	151000

....For earlier years, see the BUC Used Boat Price Guide, Volume 3

CORRECT CRAFT INC

ORLANDO FL 32809 COAST GUARD MFG ID- CTC See inside cover to adjust price for area

For more recent years, see the BUC Used Boat Price Guide, Volume 1

LOA FT	IN	NAME AND/ OR MODEL	TOP/ RIG	BOAT TYPE	HULL MTL	HULL TP	ENGINE TP	# HP	MFG	BEAM FT	IN	WGT LBS	DRAFT FT	IN	RETAIL LOW	RETAIL HIGH
		1996 BOATS														
17	6	SKI NAUTIQUE 176		SKI	FBG	SV	IB	260-310		7	7	2250	1	11	11500	13500
19	6	SKI NAUTIQUE		SKI	FBG	SV	IB	260-310		7	7	2500	2		13700	16000
19	6	SKI NAUTIQUE BG ED		SKI	FBG	SV	IB	310	PCM	7	7	2600	2		14700	16700
19	6	SKI NAUTIQUE OB		SKI	FBG	SV	IB	260-310		7	7	2600	2		14000	16000
19	6	SKI NAUTIQUE SIG ED		SKI	FBG	SV	IB	310	PCM	7	7	2600	2		14400	16400
21		NAUTIQUE SUPER SPORT		RNBT	FBG	SV	IB	310	PCM	7	7	3000	2		19800	21900
21		SPORT NAUTIQUE		SKI	FBG	SV	IB	260-310		7	7	2700	2		17600	20500
		1995 BOATS														
19	6	SKI NAUTIQUE		SKI	FBG		IB	260	PCM	7	7	2340	2		12500	14200
19	6	SKI NAUTIQUE		SKI	FBG		IB	270-310		7	7	2340	2		12600	14300
19	6	SKI NAUTIQUE BG		SKI	FBG		IB	310	PCM	7	7	2340	2		13400	15200
19	6	SKI NAUTIQUE OP BOW		SKI	FBG		IB	260-310		7	7	2475	2		12900	15100
19	6	SKI NAUTIQUE SE		SKI	FBG		IB	310	PCM	7	7	2340	2		13100	14900
21		NAUTIQUE SUPERSPORT		SKI	FBG		VD	310	PCM	7	7	2900	2	4	18200	20200
21		SPORT NAUTIQUE		SKI	FBG		IB	260-310		7	7	2700	2		16600	19400
		1994 BOATS														
19	6	SKI NAUTIQUE	OP	SKI	FBG	SV	IB	240-300		7	7	2340	2		11800	13600
19	6	SKI NAUTIZUE	OP	SKI	FBG	SV	IB	300	PCM	7	7	2340	2		12300	14000
20		BAREFOOT NAUTIQUE	OP	SKI	FBG	SV	IB	330	PCM	7	8	3000	2	7	16600	18900
20		NAUTIQUE EXCEL CB	OP	RNBT	FBG	SV	IB	300	PCM	7	8	2900	2	7	16300	18500
20		NAUTIQUE EXCEL OPEN	OP	RNBT	FBG	SV	IB	300	PCM	7	8	3000	2	7	16600	18900
21		SPORT NAUTIQUE	OP	SKI	FBG	SV	IB	285-300		7	7	2700	2		15900	18200
		1993 BOATS														
19	6	SKI NAUTIQUE	OP	SKI	FBG	SV	IB	240-300		7	7	2340	2		11100	13300
19	6	SKI NAUTIZUE	OP	SKI	FBG	SV	IB	300		7	7	2340	2		11200	12800
20		BAREFOOT NAUTIQUE	OP	SKI	FBG	SV	IB	330	PCM	7	8	3000	2	7	15800	17900
20		NAUTIQUE EXCEL CB	OP	RNBT	FBG	SV	IB	300	PCM	7	8	2900	2	7	15400	17500
20		NAUTIQUE EXCEL OPEN	OP	RNBT	FBG	SV	IB	300	PCM	7	8	3000	2	7	15700	17900
21		SPORT NAUTIQUE	OP	SKI	FBG	SV	IB	240-300		7	7	2700	2		14800	17300
		1992 BOATS														
19	6	SKI NAUTIQUE	OP	SKI	FBG	SV	IB	285	PCM	7	7	2300	2		10700	12200
19	6	SKI NAUTIQUE OPENBOW	OP	SKI	FBG	SV	IB	285	PCM	7	7	2475	2		11100	12600
20		BAREFOOT NAUTIQUE	OP	SKI	FBG	SV	IB	330	PCM	7	8	3100	2	7	15300	17300
20		NAUTIQUE EXCEL	OP	SKI	FBG	SV	IB	330	PCM	7	8	3100	2	7	15300	17300
20		NAUTIQUE EXCEL OPENB	OP	SKI	FBG	SV	IB	285	PCM	7	8	3000	2	7	14500	16400
20	4	SPORT NAUTIQUE	OP	SKI	FBG	SV	IB	285	PCM	7	5	2525	1	11	13100	14900
		1991 BOATS														
19	6	SKI NAUTIQUE	OP	SKI	FBG	SV	IB	240		7	7	2300	2		9950	11300
20		BAREFOOT NAUTIQUE	OP	SKI	FBG	SV	IB	330	PCM	7	8	3100	2	7	14100	16000
20		NAUTIQUE EXCEL	OP	SKI	FBG	SV	IB	330	PCM	7	8	3100	2	7	14900	16900
20	4	SPORT NAUTIQUE	OP	SKI	FBG	SV	IB	240		7	5	2525	1	11	12200	13900
		1990 BOATS														
19		BAREFOOT NAUTIQUE	OP	SKI	FBG	DV	IB	330		7		2520	2	2	9800	11100
19	6	SKI NAUTIQUE	OP	SKI	FBG	SV	IB	240		7	7	2300	2		9450	10800
20	4	SPORT NAUTIQUE	OP	SKI	FBG	SV	IB	240		7	5	2525	1	11	11600	13200
		1989 BOATS														
18	9	SKI-NAUTIQUE 2001		SKI	FBG	SV	IB	240-330		7		2400	2		8350	10200
19		BAREFOOT-NAUTIQUE		SKI	FBG	DV	IB	330		7		2400	2	2	9100	10400
20	2	MARTINIQUE B/R		RNBT	FBG	DV	IB	240		7	10	3050	2	9	12900	14600
20	2	MARTINIQUE C/B		RNBT	FBG	DV	IB	240		7	10	2950	2	9	12600	14400
20	4	SPORT-NAUTIQUE	OP	B/R	FBG	DV	IB	240		7	6	2750	1	11	11600	13200
23		FISH-NAUTIQUE	ST	OPFSH	FBG	DV	IB	240		8		4000	2	6	18400	20400
		1988 BOATS														
18	9	SKI-NAUTIQUE 2001		SKI	FBG	SV	IB		COMM	7		2300	2		**	**
18	9	SKI-NAUTIQUE 2001		SKI	FBG	SV	IB		PCM	7		2300	2		**	**
19		BAREFOOT-NAUTIQUE		SKI	FBG	DV	IB		COMM	7		2450	2	2	**	**
19		BAREFOOT-NAUTIQUE		SKI	FBG	DV	IB		PCM	7		2650	2	2	**	**
19		DOMINIQUE		SKI	FBG	DV	IB		COMM	7		2550	2	2	**	**
19		DOMINIQUE		SKI	FBG	DV	IB		PCM	7		2550	2	2	**	**
20	2	MARTINIQUE B/R		RNBT	FBG	DV	IB		COMM	7	10	3100	2	9	**	**
20	2	MARTINIQUE B/R		RNBT	FBG	DV	IB		PCM	7	10	3100	2	9	**	**
20	2	MARTINIQUE C/B		RNBT	FBG	DV	IB		COMM	7	10	3150	2	9	**	**
20	2	MARTINIQUE C/B		RNBT	FBG	DV	IB		PCM	7	10	2950	2	9	**	**
20	2	MARTINIQUE C/C		CUD	FBG	DV	IB		COMM	7	10	3150	2	9	**	**
20	2	MARTINIQUE C/C		CUD	FBG	DV	IB		PCM	7	10	3350	2	9	**	**
23		FISH-NAUTIQUE	ST	OPFSH	FBG	DV	IB		COMM	8		3900	2	6	**	**
23		FISH-NAUTIQUE	ST	OPFSH	FBG	DV	IB		PCM	8		4100	2	6	**	**
		1987 BOATS														
18	9	SKI-NAUTIQUE 2001	OP	SKI	FBG	SV	IB		COMM	7		2300	2		**	**
18	9	SKI-NAUTIQUE 2001	OP	SKI	FBG	SV	IB		PCM	7		2300	2		**	**
19		BAREFOOT-NAUTIQUE	OP	SKI	FBG	DV	IB		COMM	7		2700	2	2	**	**
19		BAREFOOT-NAUTIQUE	OP	SKI	FBG	DV	IB		PCM	7		2900	2	2	**	**
19		DOMINIQUE	OP	SKI	FBG	DV	IB		PCM	7		2900	2	2	**	**
20	2	MARTINIQUE	OP	RNBT	FBG	DV	IB		PCM	7	10	3100	2	9	**	**
20	2	RIVIERA	OP	CUD	FBG	DV	IB		PCM	7	10	3100	2	9	**	**

LOA FT	LOA IN	NAME AND/ OR MODEL	TOP/ RIG	BOAT TYPE	HULL MTL	HULL TP	ENGINE TP	ENGINE # HP	ENGINE MFG	BEAM FT	BEAM IN	WGT LBS	DRAFT FT	DRAFT IN	RETAIL LOW	RETAIL HIGH
		1987 BOATS														
23		FISH-NAUTIQUE	ST	OPFSH	FBG	DV	IB		COMM	8		3900	2	6	**	**
23		FISH-NAUTIQUE	ST	OPFSH	FBG	DV	IB		PCM	8		4100	2	6	**	**
		1986 BOATS														
17	7	BASS-NAUTIQUE	OP	BASS	FBG	SV	OB			7		1100		1	2700	3150
17	7	BASS-NAUTIQUE DUALCN	OP	BASS	FBG	SV	OB			7		1500	1	3	3450	4000
18	9	SKI-NAUTIQUE 2001	OP	SKI	FBG	SV	IB	250-330		7		2350	2	2	7200	8750
19		BAREFOOT-NAUTIQUE	OP	SKI	FBG	DV	IB			6	10	2750	2	2	**	**
19		BAREFOOT-NAUTIQUE	OP	SKI	FBG	DV	IB	250-330		6	10	2750	2	2	7900	9600
20	2	MARTINIQUE	OP	RNBT	FBG	DV	IB	240	PCM	7	10	3200			11500	13100
23		CUDDY-NAUTIQUE	OP	FSH	FBG	DV	IB	250-330		8		4200	2	6	16200	19000
23		FISH-NAUTIQUE	ST	OPFSH	FBG	DV	IB	250-330		8		3790	2	6	15000	17600
26	11	SEA-NAUTIQUE	OP	CUD	FBG	DS	IB	T		10		8000	4		**	**
26	11	SEA-NAUTIQUE	OP	CUD	FBG	DS	IB	T250	PCM	10		8000	4		35200	39200
		1985 BOATS														
17	7	BASS-NAUTIQUE	OP	BASS	FBG	SV	OB			7		1100	1	3	2650	3050
17	7	BASS-NAUTIQUE DUALCN	OP	BASS	FBG	SV	OB			7		1500	1	3	3350	3900
18	9	SKI-NAUTIQUE 2001	OP	SKI	FBG	SV	IB	250-330		7		2350	2	2	6850	8400
19		BAREFOOT-NAUTIQUE	OP	SKI	FBG	DV	IB			6	10	2750	2	2	**	**
19		BAREFOOT-NAUTIQUE	OP	SKI	FBG	DV	IB	250-330		6	10	2750	2	2	7550	9150
19	2	MARTINIQUE	OP	RNBT	FBG	DV	IB	250		7		2600	2	2	7700	8850
20		SOUTHWIND BOWRIDER	OP	RNBT	FBG	DV	IB	250		7	6	2800	2	3	9850	11200
23		CUDDY-NAUTIQUE	OP	FSH	FBG	DV	IB	250-330		8		4200	2	6	15500	18100
23		FISH-NAUTIQUE	ST	OPFSH	FBG	DV	IB	250-330		8		3790	2	6	14300	16800
26	11	SEA-NAUTIQUE	OP	CUD	FBG	DS	IB	T		10		8000	4		**	**
26	11	SEA-NAUTIQUE	OP	CUD	FBG	DS	IB	T250	PCM	10		8000	4		33600	37400
		1984 BOATS														
17	7	BASS-NAUTIQUE	OP	BASS	FBG	SV	OB			7		1000	1	3	2350	2750
17	9	SKI-TIQUE 179	OP	SKI	FBG	SV	IB	220-255		6	4	2200	1	9	5600	6500
18	9	SKI-NAUTIQUE 2001	OP	SKI	FBG	SV	IB	250-330		7		2350	2	2	6550	8000
19		BAREFOOT-NAUTIQUE	OP	SKI	FBG	DV	IB	250-330		6	10	2750	2	2	7200	8750
19	3	MARTINIQUE	OP	RNBT	FBG	DV	IB	250-330		7		2600	2	2	7400	8950
19	11	SOUTHWIND BOWRIDER	OP	RNBT	FBG	DV	IB	250-330		7	6	2800	2	3	8300	10000
23		CUDDY-NAUTIQUE	OP	FSH	FBG	DV	IB	250-351		8		4200	2	6	14800	17600
23		FISH-NAUTIQUE	ST	OPFSH	FBG	DV	IB	250-351		8		3790	2	6	13700	16300
26	11	SEA-NAUTIQUE	OP	CUD	FBG	DS	IB	T240	PCM	10		8000	4		31900	35500

....For earlier years, see the BUC Used Boat Price Guide, Volume 3

CORSA MARINE LTD

MIAMI FL 33054 COAST GUARD MFG ID- MPB See inside cover to adjust price for area

For more recent years, see the BUC Used Boat Price Guide, Volume 1

LOA FT	LOA IN	NAME AND/ OR MODEL	TOP/ RIG	BOAT TYPE	HULL MTL	HULL TP	ENGINE TP	ENGINE # HP	ENGINE MFG	BEAM FT	BEAM IN	WGT LBS	DRAFT FT	DRAFT IN	RETAIL LOW	RETAIL HIGH
		1995 BOATS														
25	6	CORSA S/F	OP	OPFSH	FBG	DV	OB			8		5000	1	6	20300	22500
25	6	CORSA SPRINT	OP	OFF	FBG	DV	IO	300	MRCR	7	4	5900	1	6	13600	15500
30		CORSA O/F	OP	OFF	FBG	DV	OB			8		6800	2		34800	38600
31		CORSA SS	OP	OFF	FBG	DV	IO	T375	MRCR	8		6900	2		25000	27800
32		STUART ANGLER	OP	OPFSH	FBG	DV	IB	T315D	CUM	11		9900	2	10	36200	40200
41	5	CORSA 415		SF	FBG	DV	IO	T540	MRCR	9	6	14200	2		86800	95400
41	5	CORSA S/F	OP	SF	FBG	DV	IB	T400D	CUM	9	6	15500	2		102000	112000
46		SUNBIRD	OP	OFF	FBG	DV	IB	T550D	ALAS	10	6	19900	3		142000	156000
46		SUNBIRD S/F	OP	SF	FBG	DV	IB	T550D	ALAS	10	6	19600	3		133500	147000
		1994 BOATS														
26		CORSA ANGLER SPRINT	OP	OPFSH	FBG	DV	OB			8		2975	2		17100	19400
26		CORSA SPRINT	OP	OFF	FBG	DV	IO	T260		8		5890	2		14800	16900
30		CORSA ANGLER SPORT	OP	OPFSH	FBG	DV	OB			8		6050	2	6	27900	31000
30		CORSA SPORT	OP	OFF	FBG	DV	OB			8		6100	2	6	32800	36500
30		CORSA SPORT	OP	OFF	FBG	DV	IO	T260		8		7340	2	9	22300	24800
31		CORSA SPRINT SS	OP	OFF	FBG	DV	IO	T330		8		6900	2	8	25500	28300
31		CORSA SS	OP	OFF	FBG	DV	OB			8		6100	2	6	35900	39900
32		STUART ANGLER	OP	OPFSH	FBG	DV	OB			11		7875	2	6	37900	42100
32		STUART ANGLER	OP	OPFSH	FBG	DV	IB	T300D		11		9900	3		33800	37600
41		CORSA 2 METER	OP	OFF	FBG	DV	OB			9	6	9250	2		**	**
41		CORSA STUART 2 METER	OP	OFF	FBG	DV	IO	T475		9	6	11850	2	6	55700	61200
53		CORSA ESPERANZA	OP	OFF	FBG	DV	IB	T750D		14	6	21550	7		202500	223000
		1993 BOATS														
26		CORSA ANGLER SPRINT	OP	OPFSH	FBG	DV	OB			8		2975	2		16300	18500
26		CORSA SPRINT	OP	OFF	FBG	DV	IO	T260		8		5890	2		13700	15600
30		CORSA ANGLER SPORT	OP	OPFSH	FBG	DV	OB			8		6050	2	6	26500	29500
30		CORSA SPORT	OP	OFF	FBG	DV	OB			8		6100	2	6	31100	34600
30		CORSA SPORT	OP	OFF	FBG	DV	IO	T260		8		7340	2	9	20800	23100
31		CORSA SPRINT SS	OP	OFF	FBG	DV	IO	T330		8		6900	2	8	24200	26900
31		CORSA SS	OP	OFF	FBG	DV	OB			8		6100	2	6	34000	37800
32		STUART ANGLER	OP	OPFSH	FBG	DV	OB			11		7875	2	6	35700	39600
32		STUART ANGLER	OP	OPFSH	FBG	DV	IB	T300D		11		9900	3		32200	35800
41		CORSA 2 METER	OP	OFF	FBG	DV	OB			9	6	9250	2		**	**
41		CORSA STUART 2 METER	OP	OFF	FBG	DV	IO	T475		9	6	11850	2	6	52100	57200
53		CORSA ESPERANZA	OP	OFF	FBG	DV	IB	T750D		14	6	21550	7		191500	210500
		1992 BOATS														
26		CORSA SPORT	OP	OPFSH	FBG	DV	OB			8		3950	3		16600	18900
26		CORSA SS	OP	OFF	FBG	DV	OB			8		4325	3		18300	20300
30		CORSA 9 METER SPORT	OP	OFF	FBG	DV	OB			8		4990	3	8	29500	32800
30		CORSA 9 METER SPORT	OP	OFF	FBG	DV	IO	T250	MRCR	8		7250	3	8	16900	19200
31		CORSA 9 METER SPRINT	OP	OFF	FBG	DV	IO	T340	MRCR	8		7175	3	10	20000	22300
31		CORSA 9 METER SPRINT	OP	SF	FBG	DV	OB			8		4190	3	8	28200	31300
32		STUART ANGLER	OP	SF	FBG	SV	OB			11		4850	3	9	35300	39200
32		STUART ANGLER	OP	SF	FBG	SV	IO	T340	MRCR	11		7950	3	11	22900	25500
32		STUART ANGLER	OP	SF	FBG	SV	IB	T300D	CAT	11		8890	4		28700	31900
41		CORSA 12 METRE	OP	OFF	FBG	DV	OB			9	6	7990	3	9	**	**
41		CORSA 12 METRE	OP	OFF	FBG	DV	IO	T425	MRCR	9	6	11700	3	9	44400	49300
41		CORSA 12 METRE	OP	OFF	FBG	DV	IB	T375D	CAT	9	6	14250	4	6	86100	94600
54		CORSA CORSAIR	OP	OFF	C/S	DV	IB	T425D	CAT	14	6	22700	7	6	137000	150500
		1989 BOATS														
26		ANGLER SPRINT	OP	OPFSH	FBG	DV	OB			8		2650	2	6	13200	15000
26		SPRINT		OFF	FBG	DV	OB			8		2725	2	6	13700	15600
26		SPRINT		OFF	FBG	DV	IO	T235		8		2725	2	6	7650	8800
30		SPORT		OFF	FBG	DV	OB			8		3225	3		25400	28200
30		SPORT		OFF	FBG	DV	IO	T	MRCR	8		3225	3		**	**
30		SPORT		OFF	FBG	DV	IO	T	OMC	8		3225	3		**	**
30		SPORT FISH		OPFSH	FBG	DV	OB			8		3150	3		21900	24400
30		SPORT FISH		OPFSH	FBG	DV	IO	T		8		3150	3		**	**
31		S S		OFF	FBG	DV	OB			8		3225	3		27800	30900
31		S S		OFF	FBG	DV	IO	T	MRCR	8		3225	3		**	**
31		S S		OFF	FBG	DV	IO	T	OMC	8		3225	3		**	**
32		STUART ANGLER		OPFSH	FBG	DV	OB			11		3990	3	6	29400	32600
32		STUART ANGLER		OPFSH	FBG	DV	IO	T	MRCR	11		3990	3	6	**	**
32		STUART ANGLER		OPFSH	FBG	DV	IO	T	OMC	11		3990	3	6	**	**
41		CORSAIR		OFF	FBG	DV	OB			9	6	7990	4	6	**	**
41		CORSAIR		OFF	FBG	DV	IO	T	MRCR	9	6	5750	4	6	**	**
		IO T OMC ** ** , IO R MRCR ** ** , IO R OMC ** **														
53	6	ESPERANZA		OFF	FBG	DV	IB	T D	GM	14	6	21550	10		**	**
53	6	ESPERANZA		OFF	FBG	DV	IB	R D	GM	14	6	21550	10		**	**
		1988 BOATS														
25	6	SPRINT	OP	SPTCR	FBG	DV	OB			7		3600	2	6	13100	14900
25	6	SPRINT 8M	OP	SPTCR	FBG	DV	IO	420	MRCR	7		4000	2	6	8950	10200
30	6	9 METER O/F	OP	OPFSH	FBG	DV	OB			8		4500	3		22100	24500
30	6	9 METER SS	OP	SPTCR	FBG	DV	IO	T330	MRCR	8		5600	3	6	13800	15600
30	6	9 METER SS-O	OP	SPTCR	FBG	DV	OB			8		4500	3		26000	28900
41		12 METER	OP	OFF	FBG	DV	IO	T420		9	6	8500	4	6	31400	34900
		1986 BOATS														
26		CORSA		FSH	FBG	DV	IB	T185		8			2	6	11300	12800
30		CORSA		FSH	FBG	DV	IB	T185		8			2	6	14200	16200
41		CORSA		CR	FBG	DV	IB	T340		9	6		3	9	45800	50300
		1985 BOATS														
26		CORSA		FSH	FBG	DV	IB	T185		8					10900	12300
30		CORSA		FSH	FBG	DV	IB	T185		8					13400	15200
41		CORSA		CR	FBG	DV	IB	T340		9	6				43300	48100
53	3	CORSA		CR	FBG	DV	IB			13					**	**
		1984 BOATS														
25	6	SPRINT	OP	SPTCR	FBG	DV	IO	260	MRCR	7		3850	2	6	5600	6400
25	6	SPRINT OB	OP	SPTCR	FBG	DV	OB			7		2925	2	6	10500	11900
30		SPORT FISH	OP	SF	FBG	DV	OB			8		4470	2	6	18900	21000
30		SS	OP	SPTCR	FBG	DV	IO	T400	MRCR	8		5850	2	6	12300	14000
30		SS O/B	OP	SPTCR	FBG	DV	OB			8		4470	2	6	21000	23400
32		STUART-ANGLER	OP	SF	FBG	DV	OB			11		5910	3	2	24900	27700
32		STUART-ANGLER	OP	SF	FBG	DV	IB	T350D	CAT	11		8955	3	2	22400	24800
41		CORSAIR	OP	OFF	FBG	DV	OB			9	6	7990	2	9	**	**
41		CORSAIR	OP	SF	FBG	DV	OB			9	6	8250	2	9	**	**
41		CORSAIR	OP	SPTCR	FBG	DV	IO	T400	MRCR	9	6	10700	3	6	29900	33300
41		CORSAIR S/F	OP	SF	FBG	DV	IB	T350D	CAT	9	6	14825	3	9	59600	65500
54		ESPERANZA	HT	SPTCR	FBG	DV	IB	T14CD	GM	14	6	19100	5	5	182500	200500

....For earlier years, see the BUC Used Boat Price Guide, Volume 3

CORSAIR MARINE INC

CHULA VISTA CA 91911   COAST GUARD MFG ID- CSR See inside cover to adjust price for area

For more recent years, see the BUC Used Boat Price Guide, Volume 1

LOA FT IN	NAME AND/ OR MODEL	TOP/ RIG	BOAT TYPE	-HULL- MTL TP	----ENGINE--- TP # HP MFG	BEAM FT IN	WGT LBS	DRAFT FT IN	RETAIL LOW	RETAIL HIGH
--- 1996 BOATS ---
24 2	CORSAIR F-24MKII	SLP	SACAC	F/S TM	OB	17 11	1800	1	26900	29900
27 1	CORSAIR F-27	SLP	SACAC	F/S TM	OB	19 1	2600	1	40400	44900
30 10	CORSAIR F-31	SLP	SACAC	F/S TM	OB	22 5	3850	1 4	70700	77700
--- 1995 BOATS ---
24 2	CORSAIR F-24	SLP	SACAC	F/S TM	OB	17 11	2100	1	26400	29300
27 1	CORSAIR F-27	SLP	SACAC	F/S TM	OB	19 1	2600	1 2	38000	42300
31 10	CORSAIR F-31	SLP	SACAC	F/S TM	OB	22 5	4000	1 4	73200	80500
31 10	CORSAIR F-31	SLP	SACAC	F/S TM	IB	11D UNIV 22 5	4000	1 4	73400	80700
--- 1994 BOATS ---
24 2	CORSAIR F-24	SLP	SACAC	F/S TM	OB	17 11	2100	1	24800	27600
27 1	CORSAIR F-27	SLP	SACAC	F/S TM	OB	19 1	2600	1 2	35800	39700
31 10	CORSAIR F-31	SLP	SACAC	F/S TM	OB	22 5	4000	1 4	68900	75700
31 10	CORSAIR F-31	SLP	SACAC	F/S TM	IB	11D UNIV 22 5	4000	1 4	69000	75900
--- 1993 BOATS ---
24	CORSAIR F-24	SLP	SA/RC	F/S TM	OB	17 11	1800	1	22000	24400
27 1	CORSAIR F-27	SLP	SA/RC	F/S TM	OB	19 1	2600	1 2	33600	37400
--- 1992 BOATS ---
24	F-24 WEEKENDER	SLP	SA/RC	F/S TM	OB	17 11	1800	1	20700	23000
27 1	F-27	SLP	SA/RC	F/S TM	OB	19 1	2600	1 2	31600	35200
--- 1991 BOATS ---
24	F-24	SLP	SA/OD	F/S TM	OB	18 6	1600	1	19100	21200
27 1	F-27	SLP	SA/RC	F/S TM	OB	19 1	2600	1 2	29800	33100
--- 1990 BOATS ---
27 1	F-27	SLP	SA/RC	F/S TM	OB	19 1	2600	1 2	28000	31100

CORSON BOAT CO

MADISON ME 04950   COAST GUARD MFG ID- CBT See inside cover to adjust price for area

LOA FT IN	NAME AND/ OR MODEL	TOP/ RIG	BOAT TYPE	-HULL- MTL TP	----ENGINE--- TP # HP MFG	BEAM FT IN	WGT LBS	DRAFT FT IN	RETAIL LOW	RETAIL HIGH
--- 1986 BOATS ---
16 6	SIXTEEN-SIX	ST	RNBT	FBG SV	OB	6 7	1034		2350	2700
20	FISHERMAN	OP	FSH	FBG SV	OB	7 4	1100		2650	3100
20	V-SPORT	ST	RNBT	FBG SV	OB	7 4	1400		3250	3800
20	V-SPORT	ST	RNBT	FBG SV	IO	120 7 4	2100		3950	4550
--- 1985 BOATS ---
16 6	SIXTEEN-SIX	ST	RNBT	FBG SV	OB	6 7	1034		2300	2650
20	FISHERMAN	OP	FSH	FBG SV	OB	7 4	1100		2600	3050
20	V-SPORT	ST	RNBT	FBG SV	OB	7 4	1400		3200	3700
20	V-SPORT	ST	RNBT	FBG SV	IO	120 7 4	2100		3800	4400

....For earlier years, see the BUC Used Boat Price Guide, Volume 3

CORVETTE CRUISERS LTD

NOTTINGHAM ENGLAND NG23H   See inside cover to adjust price for area

LOA FT IN	NAME AND/ OR MODEL	TOP/ RIG	BOAT TYPE	-HULL- MTL TP	----ENGINE--- TP # HP MFG	BEAM FT IN	WGT LBS	DRAFT FT IN	RETAIL LOW	RETAIL HIGH
32	CORVETTE 32 CLASSQUE	FB	TRWL	FBG DS	IBT130D-T200D 13		13000	4	79400	95500
32	CORVETTE 32 CLASSQUE	FB	TRWL	FBG DS	IBT260D-T600D 13		13000	4	93400	115000
--- 1991 BOATS ---
32	CORVETTE 32 CLASSQUE	FB	TRWL	FBG DS	IBT130D-T200D 13		13000	4	75700	91100
32	CORVETTE 32 CLASSQUE	FB	TRWL	FBG DS	IBT260D-T600D 13		13000	4	89100	109500
--- 1990 BOATS ---
24	CORVETTE 22+2CABRERA	OVNTR	FBG SV	IO	275 VLVO 7	3	3200	1 9	11300	12800
32	CORVETTE 32 CLASSQUE	FB	MY	FBG DS	IB T300 VLVO 13		13000	4	62300	68500

GUY COUACH INC

REX YACHT SALES   See inside cover to adjust price for area
FT LAUDERDALE FL 33316   COAST GUARD MFG ID- GCQ

For more recent years, see the BUC Used Boat Price Guide, Volume 1

LOA FT IN	NAME AND/ OR MODEL	TOP/ RIG	BOAT TYPE	-HULL- MTL TP	----ENGINE--- TP # HP MFG	BEAM FT IN	WGT LBS	DRAFT FT IN	RETAIL LOW	RETAIL HIGH
--- 1986 BOATS ---
36	GUY-COUACH 1100 SPRT	SPTCR	FBG SV	IB T165D VLVO 12	2	15432	3	77000	84600
36	GUY-COUACH 1100 SPRT	SPTCR	FBG SV	IB R165D VLVO 12	2	15432	3	80800	88200
36	GUY-COUACH 1100 YCHT	MY	FBG SV	IB T160D VLVO 12	2	17636	3 1	85700	94200
36	GUY-COUACH 1100 YCHT	MY	FBG SV	IB T270D VLVO 12	2	17636	3 1	91500	100500
45 11	GUY-COUACH 1400 YCHT	MY	FBG SV	IB T286D VLVO 12	11	26455	3 3	136500	150000
45 11	GUY-COUACH 1400 YCHT	MY	FBG SV	IB T475D GM 12	11	26455	3 3	165500	182000
52 10	GUY-COUACH 1600 YCHT	MY	FBG SV	IB T325D GM 14	3	39682	3	189500	208500
52 10	GUY-COUACH 1600 YCHT	MY	FBG SV	IB T475D GM 14	3	39682	3	229500	252500
53 9	GUY-COUACH 1700 SPRT	SPTCR	FBG SV	IB T600D GM 14	3	37477	3 4	263000	291000
55 9	GUY-COUACH 1700 YCHT	MY	FBG SV	IB T475D J&T 17	8	50705	3 11	297500	327000
55 9	GUY-COUACH 1700 YCHT	MY	FBG SV	IB T600D GM 17	8	50705	3 11	332000	364500
56 8	GUY COUACH 1800	MY	FBG SV	IB T700D	17	56217		388000	426500
62 10	GUY-COUACH 2000 YCHT	MY	FBG SV	IB T700D GM 17	8	66130	4 3	477000	524000
70 6	GUY-COUACH 2200 YCHT	MY	FBG SV	IB T700D GM 17	8	70546	4 3	558500	613500
70 6	GUY-COUACH 2200 YCHT	MY	FBG SV	IB T870D GM 17	8	70546	4 3	579500	637000
72	GUY COUACH 2202	MY	FBG SV	IB T700D	20	7	79366		**	**
75 3	GUY COUACH 2402	MY	FBG SV	IB T700D	20	7	85980		**	**
78 8	GUY-COUACH 2400 YCHT	MY	FBG SV	IB T700D GM 17	8	74955	4 5	**	**
78 8	GUY-COUACH 2400 YCHT	MY	FBG SV	IB T870D GM 17	8	74955	4 5	**	**
--- 1985 BOATS ---
36	GUY-COUACH 1100 SPRT	SPTCR	FBG SV	IB 420	12	2	15432	3	67600	74300
36	GUY-COUACH 1100 SPRT	SPTCR	FBG SV	IB T165D	12	2	15432	3	76400	82000
36	GUY-COUACH 1100 SPRT	SPTCR	FBG SV	IB T235D VLVO 12	2	15432	3	76600	84200
36	GUY-COUACH 1100 YCHT	MY	FBG SV	IB 420	12	2	17636	3 1	73900	81200
36	GUY-COUACH 1100 YCHT	MY	FBG SV	IB T158D VLVO 12	2	17636	3 1	82000	90100
36	GUY-COUACH 1100 YCHT	MY	FBG SV	IB T235D VLVO 12	2	17636	3 1	85700	94200
45 11	GUY-COUACH 1400 YCHT	MY	FBG SV	IB T286D VLVO 12	11	26455	3 3	131000	144000
45 11	GUY-COUACH 1400 YCHT	MY	FBG SV	IB T375D GM 12	11	26455	3 3	144500	159000
46	GUY-COUACH 1400 YCHT	MY	FBG SV	IB 650	12	11	26455	3 3	121000	133000
52 10	GUY-COUACH 1600 YCHT	MY	FBG SV	IB 650	14	3	39682	3	180000	197500
52 10	GUY-COUACH 1600 YCHT	MY	FBG SV	IB T450D J&T 14	3	39682	3	214500	235500
53 9	GUY-COUACH 1700 SPRT	SPTCR	FBG SV	IB 900	14	3	37477	3 4	204000	224000
53 9	GUY-COUACH 1700 SPRT	SPTCR	FBG SV	IB T600D GM 14	3	37477	3 4	253500	278500
55 9	GUY-COUACH 1700 YCHT	MY	FBG SV	IB 900	17	8	50705	3 11	263000	289000
55 9	GUY-COUACH 1700 YCHT	MY	FBG SV	IB T450D J&T 17	8	50705	3 11	277500	305000
55 9	GUY-COUACH 1700 YCHT	MY	FBG SV	IB T450D GM 17	8	50705	3 11	330500	363500
62 10	GUY-COUACH 2000 YCHT	MY	FBG SV	IB T700D GM 17	8	66130	4 3	457000	502000
70 6	GUY-COUACH 2200 YCHT	MY	FBG SV	IB 14C	17	8	70546	4 3	500500	550000
70 6	GUY-COUACH 2200 YCHT	MY	FBG SV	IB T700D GM 17	8	70546	4 3	534500	587500
70 6	GUY-COUACH 2200 YCHT	MY	FBG SV	IB T870D GM 17	8	70546	4 3	555000	610000
78 8	GUY-COUACH 2400 YCHT	MY	FBG SV	IB 14C	17	8	74955	4 5	**	**
78 8	GUY-COUACH 2400 YCHT	MY	FBG SV	IB T700D GM 17	8	74955	4 5	**	**
78 8	GUY-COUACH 2400 YCHT	MY	FBG SV	IB T870D GM 17	8	74955	4 5	**	**
--- 1984 BOATS ---
36	GUY-COUACH 1100 SPRT	SPTCR	FBG SV	IB T240D	12	2	15432	3	74700	82100
36	GUY-COUACH 1100 SPRT	SPTCR	FBG SV	IB T286D VLVO 12	2	15432	3	75900	83400
36	GUY-COUACH 1100 YCHT	MY	FBG SV	IB T240D	12	2	17636	3 1	83500	91700
45 11	GUY-COUACH 1400 YCHT	MY	FBG SV	IB T235D	12	11	26455	3 3	118500	130000
	IB T280D 125000 137500, IB T325D 131500 144500, IB T460D GM 148500 163500
52 10	GUY-COUACH 1600 YCHT	MY	FBG SV	IB T325D	14	3	39682	3	178000	196000
52 10	GUY-COUACH 1600 YCHT	MY	FBG SV	IB T450D GM 14	3	39682	3	204500	224500
53 9	GUY-COUACH 1700 SPRT	SPTCR	FBG SV	IB T450D GM 14	3	37477	3 4	203000	223000
53 9	GUY-COUACH 1700 SPRT	SPTCR	FBG SV	IB T600D GM 14	3	37477	3 4	243000	267000
55 9	GUY-COUACH 1700 YCHT	MY	FBG SV	IB T450D GM 17	8	50705	3 11	266000	292000
55 9	GUY-COUACH 1700 YCHT	MY	FBG SV	IB T450D GM 17	8	50705	3 11	317000	348500
62 10	GUY-COUACH 2000 YCHT	MY	FBG SV	IB T600D	17	8	66130	4 3	410500	451000
62 10	GUY-COUACH 2000 YCHT	MY	FBG SV	IB T730D GM 17	8	66130	4 3	445000	489000
70 6	GUY-COUACH 2200 YCHT	MY	FBG SV	IB T730D GM 17	8	70546	4 3	515500	566500
78 8	GUY-COUACH 2400 YCHT	MY	FBG SV	IB T730D GM 17	8	74955	4 5	**	**

COUGAR CUSTOM BOATS & EQUIP

SALMONARM BC CANADA   COAST GUARD MFG ID- ZCZ See inside cover to adjust price for area

LOA FT IN	NAME AND/ OR MODEL	TOP/ RIG	BOAT TYPE	-HULL- MTL TP	----ENGINE--- TP # HP MFG	BEAM FT IN	WGT LBS	DRAFT FT IN	RETAIL LOW	RETAIL HIGH
--- 1989 BOATS ---
18	CLASSIC	OP	RNBT	FBG SV	OB	7 2	1500		5850	6750
18	CLASSIC	OP	RNBT	FBG SV	IO	260 MRCR 7 2	2000		4450	5400
18	CLASSIC	OP	RNBT	FBG SV	JT	325 7 2	2000		6350	7300
18	SPRINT	OP	RACE	FBG FL	VD	6	900		**	**
18 2	1800SS	OP	SKI	FBG SV	JT	325 CHEV 7	1800		5650	6500
18 2	OMEGA	OP	RACE	FBG TH	OB	6 7	1300		5200	5950
19	EXECUTIVE	OP	RNBT	FBG DV	OB	7 9	1000		4450	5100
19	EXECUTIVE	OP	RNBT	FBG DV	IO	260 7 9	1000		4400	5050
19	TUNNEL	OP	RACE	FBG VD	VD	7	900		**	**
19	TUNNEL	OP	SKI	FBG TH	OB	7	675		3050	3550
19	TUNNEL	OP	SKI	FBG TH	JT	325 7	1800		6150	7050

COUGAR CUSTOM BOATS & EQUIP   -CONTINUED   See inside cover to adjust price for area

LOA FT IN	NAME AND/ OR MODEL	TOP/ RIG	BOAT TYPE	-HULL- MTL TP	----ENGINE--- TP # HP MFG	BEAM FT IN	WGT LBS	DRAFT FT IN	RETAIL LOW	RETAIL HIGH
					1989 BOATS					
21	ELITE	OP	RACE	FBG SV VD		7 9	1450		**	**
21	ELITE	OP	SKI	FBG SV IO	260 MRCR	7 9	2500		5850	6700
21	ELITE	OP	SKI	FBG SV JT	325 CHEV	7 9	2500		8250	9500
21	ELITE	OP	SKI	FBG SV VD	405 CHEV	7 9	2500		8550	9850
21	TUNNEL	OP	RACE	FBG TH VD		7 3	1000		**	**
21	TUNNEL	OP	SKI	FBG TH OB		7 3	1200		5750	6600
21	TUNNEL	OP	SKI	FBG TH JT	325	7 3	2000		7300	8400
21	TUNNEL	OP	SKI	FBG TH VD	405 CHEV	7 3	2100		7750	8900
25	OFFSHORE TUNNEL	OP	RACE	FBG TH OB		8	2950		14500	16500
25	OFFSHORE TUNNEL	OP	RACE	FBG TH IO	330-365	8	3100		9450	11500
					1988 BOATS					
18	CLASSIC	OP	RNBT	FBG SV OB		7 2	1500		5650	6500
18	CLASSIC	OP	RNBT	FBG SV IO	260 MRCR	7 2	2000		4150	4850
18	CLASSIC	OP	RNBT	FBG SV JT	325	7 2	2000		6050	6950
18	SPRINT	OP	RACE	FBG FL VD		6	900		**	**
18	1800SS	OP	SKI	FBG SV JT	325 CHEV	6 7	1800		5400	6200
18	2 OMEGA	OP	RACE	FBG TH OB		6 7	1300		5000	5750
19	EXECUTIVE	OP	RNBT	FBG DV OB		7 9	1000		4200	4900
19	EXECUTIVE	OP	RNBT	FBG DV IO	260	7 9	1000		4100	4800
19	TUNNEL	OP	RACE	FBG TH VD		7	900		**	**
19	TUNNEL	OP	SKI	FBG TH OB		7	675		2950	3450
19	TUNNEL	OP	SKI	FBG TH JT	325	7	1800		5850	6700
21	ELITE	OP	RACE	FBG SV VD		7 9	1450		**	**
21	ELITE	OP	SKI	FBG SV IO	260 MRCR	7 9	2500		5500	6350
21	ELITE	OP	SKI	FBG SV JT	325 CHEV	7 9	2500		7850	9050
21	ELITE	OP	SKI	FBG SV VD	405 CHEV	7 9	2500		8150	9350
21	TUNNEL	OP	RACE	FBG TH VD		7 3	1000		**	**
21	TUNNEL	OP	SKI	FBG TH OB		7 3	1200		5500	6350
21	TUNNEL	OP	SKI	FBG TH JT	325	7 3	2000		6950	8000
21	TUNNEL	OP	SKI	FBG TH VD	405 CHEV	7 3	2100		7400	8500
25	OFFSHORE TUNNEL	OP	RACE	FBG TH OB		8	2950		13900	15800
25	OFFSHORE TUNNEL	OP	RACE	FBG TH IO	330-365	8	3100		8950	10900
					1987 BOATS					
18	CLASSIC	OP	RNBT	FBG SV OB		7 2	1500		5450	6250
18	CLASSIC	OP	RNBT	FBG SV IO	260 MRCR	7 2	2000		3950	4600
18	CLASSIC	OP	RNBT	FBG SV JT	325	7 2	2000		5750	6600
18	SPRINT	OP	RACE	FBG FL VD		6	900		**	**
18	2 1800SS	OP	SKI	FBG SV JT	325 CHEV	6 7	1800		5150	5900
18	2 OMEGA	OP	RACE	FBG TH OB		6 7	1300		4850	5600
19	EXECUTIVE	OP	RNBT	FBG DV OB		7 9	1000		4050	4700
19	EXECUTIVE	OP	RNBT	FBG DV IO	260	7 9	1000		3900	4550
19	TUNNEL	OP	RACE	FBG TH VD		7	900		**	**
19	TUNNEL	OP	SKI	FBG TH OB		7	675		2850	3300
19	TUNNEL	OP	SKI	FBG TH JT	325	7	1800		5600	6400
21	ELITE	OP	RACE	FBG SV VD		7 9	1450		**	**
21	ELITE	OP	SKI	FBG SV IO	260 MRCR	7 9	2500		5250	6050
21	ELITE	OP	SKI	FBG SV JT	325 CHEV	7 9	2500		7500	8600
21	ELITE	OP	SKI	FBG SV VD	405 CHEV	7 9	2500		7750	8950
21	TUNNEL	OP	RACE	FBG TH VD		7 3	1000		**	**
21	TUNNEL	OP	SKI	FBG TH OB		7 3	1200		5300	6100
21	TUNNEL	OP	SKI	FBG TH JT	325	7 3	2000		6650	7650
21	TUNNEL	OP	SKI	FBG TH VD	405 CHEV	7 3	2200		7150	8200
					1986 BOATS					
18	SPRINT	OP	RACE	FBG FL VD		6	900		**	**
18	2 1800SS	OP	SKI	FBG SV JT	325 CHEV	6 7	1800		4900	5650
19	EXECUTIVE	OP	RNBT	FBG DV OB		7 9	1000		3900	4550
19	EXECUTIVE	OP	RNBT	FBG DV IO	260	7 9	1000		3750	4350
19	EXECUTIVE B/R	OP	RNBT	FBG DV OB		7 9	1100		4250	4950
19	TUNNEL	OP	RACE	FBG TH VD		7	900		**	**
19	TUNNEL	OP	SKI	FBG TH OB		7	675		2750	3200
19	TUNNEL	OP	SKI	FBG TH JT	325	7	1800		5300	6100
21	ELITE	OP	RACE	FBG SV VD		7 9	1450		**	**
21	ELITE	OP	SKI	FBG SV IO	260 MRCR	7 9	2500		5000	5750
21	ELITE	OP	SKI	FBG SV JT	325 CHEV	7 9	2500		7150	8200
21	ELITE	OP	SKI	FBG SV VD	405 CHEV	7 9	2500		7400	8500
21	TUNNEL	OP	RACE	FBG TH VD		7 3	1000		**	**
21	TUNNEL	OP	SKI	FBG TH OB		7 3	1200		5150	5950
21	TUNNEL	OP	SKI	FBG TH JT	325	7 3	2000		6350	7300
					1985 BOATS					
18	SPRINT	OP	RACE	FBG FL VD		6	900		**	**
18	2 1800SS	OP	SKI	FBG SV JT	325 CHEV	6 7	1800		4700	5400
19	EXECUTIVE	OP	RNBT	FBG DV OB		7 9	1000		3800	4400
19	EXECUTIVE	OP	RNBT	FBG DV IO	260	7 9	1000		3600	4200
19	EXECUTIVE B/R	OP	RNBT	FBG DV OB		7 9	1100		4100	4750
19	TUNNEL	OP	RACE	FBG TH VD		7	900		**	**
19	TUNNEL	OP	SKI	FBG TH OB		7	675		2700	3100
19	TUNNEL	OP	SKI	FBG TH JT	325	7	1800		5100	5850
21	ELITE	OP	RACE	FBG SV VD		7 9	1450		**	**
21	ELITE	OP	SKI	FBG SV IO	260 MRCR	7 9	2500		4800	5550
21	ELITE	OP	SKI	FBG SV JT	325 CHEV	7 9	2500		6850	7850
21	ELITE	OP	SKI	FBG SV VD	405 CHEV	7 9	2500		7100	8150
21	TUNNEL	OP	RACE	FBG TH VD		7 3	1000		**	**
21	TUNNEL	OP	SKI	FBG TH OB		7 3	1200		5000	5750
21	TUNNEL	OP	SKI	FBG TH JT	325	7 3	2000		6050	6950
					1984 BOATS					
18	SPRINT	OP	RACE	FBG FL VD		6	900		**	**
18	2 1800SS	OP	SKI	FBG SV JT	325 CHEV	6 7	1800		4500	5150
19	EXECUTIVE	OP	RNBT	FBG DV OB		7 9	1000		3650	4250
19	EXECUTIVE	OP	RNBT	FBG DV IO	260	7 9	1000		3450	4050
19	EXECUTIVE B/R	OP	RNBT	FBG DV OB		7 9	1100		3950	4600
19	TUNNEL	OP	RACE	FBG TH VD		7	900		**	**
19	TUNNEL	OP	SKI	FBG TH OB		7	675		2600	3000
19	TUNNEL	OP	SKI	FBG TH JT	325 HARD	7	1800		4850	5600
21	ELITE	OP	RACE	FBG SV VD		7 9	1450		**	**
21	ELITE	OP	SKI	FBG SV JT	325 CHEV	7 9	2500		6550	7500

....For earlier years, see the BUC Used Boat Price Guide, Volume 3

COUGAR HOLDINGS LIMITED
SOUTHAMPTON ENGLAND   See inside cover to adjust price for area

LOA FT IN	NAME AND/ OR MODEL	TOP/ RIG	BOAT TYPE	-HULL- MTL TP	----ENGINE--- TP # HP MFG	BEAM FT IN	WGT LBS	DRAFT FT IN	RETAIL LOW	RETAIL HIGH
					1989 BOATS					
25	SPORTCAT 25	OFF	KEV CT OB			8 6		2	10600	12000
27	SPORTCAT 27	OFF	KEV CT OB			10		2 5	13500	15400
30	SPORTCAT 30	OFF	KEV CT IO	T MRCR		10 3		2 6	**	**
33	US-1-33	OFF	KEV DV IO	T15C MRCR		8 3	7200	2 6	**	**
38	US-1-38	OFF	KEV DV IO	T16C MRCR		8 9	8600	2 6	**	**
41	US-1-41	OFF	KEV DV IO	T16CD MRCR		9 3	8600	2 6	**	**
46	US-1-46	OFF	KEV DV IO	R20CD MRCR		9	10000	2 6	**	**
					1985 BOATS					
27	SPORT CATAMARAN	OP	RACE	KEV CT OB		9 4			12100	13800
27	SPORT CATAMARAN	OP	RACE	KEV CT OB		9 4			12100	13800
30	COUGAR SM CAT	OP	RACE	FBG CT IO	T330 MRCR	10 4			17300	19700
30	COUGAR SM CAT	OP	RACE	FBG CT IO	T440 MRCR	10 4			19900	22200
30	COUGAR SM CAT	OP	RACE	FBG CT IB	T440	10 4			28900	32100
45	6 U-S-1	OP	RACE	FBG DV IO	T610 MRCR	9 4	9500	3	61400	67400
45	6 U-S-1	OP	RACE	FBG DV IO	T300D	9 4	9500	3	47200	51800
45	6 U-S-1	OP	RACE	FBG DV IO	R610 MRCR	9 4	9500	3	75700	83200
58		MY	AL	AL CT IO	T13CD S&S	22 10		4	265500	291500
58	COUGAR 58	MY	AL	AL CT IB	T12CD	22	50000		318500	350000
					1984 BOATS					
27	SPORT CATAMARAN	OP	RACE	FBG CT OB		9 4			11800	13400
27	SPORT CATAMARAN	OP	RACE	KEV CT OB		9 4			11800	13400
30	COUGAR SM CAT	OP	RACE	FBG CT IO	T330 MRCR	10 4			16800	19100
30	COUGAR SM CAT	OP	RACE	FBG CT IO	T440 MRCR	10 4			19200	21400
30	COUGAR SM CAT	OP	RACE	FBG CT IB	T440	10 4			27600	30700
30	SPORT CATAMARAN	OP	RACE	FBG CT IB	T340 MRCR	10 4	6200	1 10	25500	28300
	IO T370 MRCR 17600	20000, IB T370 MRCR			26100 29000, IO T440 MRCR				18600	20600
	IB T400 MRCR 26700	29700, IO T440 MRCR			19200 21400, IB T440 MRCR				27600	30700
45	6 U-S-1	OP	RACE	FBG DV IO	T610 MRCR	9 4	9500	3	59200	65100
45	6 U-S-1	OP	RACE	FBG DV IO	T300D	9 4	9500	3	45000	50000
45	6 U-S-1	OP	RACE	FBG DV IO	R610 MRCR	9 4	9500	3	73100	80300
58		MY	FBG CT VD	T13CD S&S		22 10		4	251500	276500

....For earlier years, see the BUC Used Boat Price Guide, Volume 3

COVEY ISLAND BOAT WORKS
WESTERNMAN   See inside cover to adjust price for area
PETITE RIVIERE NS CANADA

LOA FT IN	NAME AND/ OR MODEL	TOP/ RIG	BOAT TYPE	-HULL- MTL TP	----ENGINE--- TP # HP MFG	BEAM FT IN	WGT LBS	DRAFT FT IN	RETAIL LOW	RETAIL HIGH
					1996 BOATS					
64	3 WESTERNMAN 64	CUT	SACAC WD	KL IB	85D PERK	13 6	64000	7 6	545500	599500

COX MARINE LTD
BRIGHTLINGSEA ENGLAND

See inside cover to adjust price for area

LOA FT IN	NAME AND/ OR MODEL	TOP/ RIG	BOAT TYPE	-HULL- MTL TP	----ENGINE--- TP # HP MFG	BEAM FT IN	WGT LBS	DRAFT FT IN	RETAIL LOW	RETAIL HIGH
					1993 BOATS					
22 4	FAMILY FISHER 22		FSH	FBG DS	IB 27D- 50D	8 4	4850	1 6	11500	13600
22 4	MASTER MARINER	SLP	SACAC	FBG KL	IB 50D YAN	8 4	6613	3 3	27000	30000
26 10	FAMILY FISHER 27		FSH	FBG DS	IB 34D- 75D	9 10	7937	3 3	21000	23800
26 10	MOTOR SAILER 27	SLP	SACAC	FBG KL	IB 27D- 50D	9 11	7937	3 3	37500	42200

....For earlier years, see the BUC Used Boat Price Guide, Volume 3

COYOTE MARINE CORP
HOLLYWOOD FL 33023   COAST GUARD MFG ID- HCN See inside cover to adjust price for area

LOA FT IN	NAME AND/ OR MODEL	TOP/ RIG	BOAT TYPE	-HULL- MTL TP	----ENGINE--- TP # HP MFG	BEAM FT IN	WGT LBS	DRAFT FT IN	RETAIL LOW	RETAIL HIGH
					1985 BOATS					
34 4	COYOTE GT	OP	OFF	FBG DV	IO T330-T425	8	7000	1 10	27200	33300
34 4	COYOTE RACER	OP	OFF	FBG DV	IO T700 CHEV	8	6500	1 6	31200	34600
34 4	COYOTE RO	OP	OFF	FBG DV	OB	8	5500	1 6	29000	32200
38 4	COYOTE GT	OP	OFF	FBG DV	IO T370 MRCR	8	8000	1 10	34000	37800
38 4	COYOTE GT	OP	OFF	FBG DV	IO T425	8	8000	1 10	36700	40800
38 4	COYOTE GT	OP	OFF	FBG DV	IO T500 MRCR	8	8000	1 10	41000	45500
38 4	COYOTE GTD	OP	OFF	FBG DV	IO T300D SABR	8	8500	1 10	39600	44000
38 4	COYOTE GTO	OP	OFF	FBG DV	OB	8	3500		34700	38500
38 4	COYOTE RACER	OP	OFF	FBG DV	IO T650 MRCR	8	7500	1 10	30000	33400
38 4	COYOTE SE	OP	OFF	FBG DV	IO T500	8		1 10	41300	45900
					1984 BOATS					
34 4	COYOTE GT	OP	OFF	FBG DV	IO T330-T370	8	7000	1 10	26200	30100
34 4	COYOTE GTO	OP	OFF	FBG DV	OB	8	6000	1 10	28400	31500
34 4	COYOTE RACER	OP	OFF	FBG DV	IO T700 CHEV	8	6500	1 6	30100	33400
34 4	COYOTE RO	OP	OFF	FBG DV	OB	8	5500	1 6	28400	31500
37 4	COYOTE 374		RNBT	FBG DV	IO T370				26700	29700
38 4	COYOTE GT	OP	OFF	FBG DV	IO T370 MRCR	8	8000	1 10	32800	36400
38 4	COYOTE GT	OP	OFF	FBG DV	IO T425	8	8000	1 10	35400	39400
38 4	COYOTE GT	OP	OFF	FBG DV	IO T500 MRCR	8	8000	1 10	39500	43900
38 4	COYOTE GTD	OP	OFF	FBG DV	IO T300D SABR	8	8500	1 10	38200	42500
38 4	COYOTE GTO		RNBT	FBG DV	OB	8	3500		49400	54300
38 4	COYOTE RACER	OP	OFF	FBG DV	IO T650 MRCR	8	7500	1 10	29000	32200

....For earlier years, see the BUC Used Boat Price Guide, Volume 3

CRANCHI
POMPANO BEACH FL 33062   See inside cover to adjust price for area

For more recent years, see the BUC Used Boat Price Guide, Volume 1

LOA FT IN	NAME AND/ OR MODEL	TOP/ RIG	BOAT TYPE	-HULL- MTL TP	----ENGINE--- TP # HP MFG	BEAM FT IN	WGT LBS	DRAFT FT IN	RETAIL LOW	RETAIL HIGH
					1996 BOATS					
25	24 TURCHESE	OP	CUD	FBG DV	IO 275	8	5800	3	28800	32000
28	CORALLO 840	ST	CUD	FBG DV	IO T230	9 6	6620	3 7	36000	40000
28	CORALLO 840	ST	CUD	FBG DV	IO T300D	9 6	6620	3 7	53800	59100
30	GIADA	ST	CUD	FBG DV	IO T150D VLVO	10	6620	3 3	40200	44700
32 6	AQUAMARINA	OP	EXP	FBG DV	IO T200D VLVO	10	12897	3 2	87800	96500
36 10	SMERALDO	OP	EXP	FBG DV	IB T230D VLVO	12 6	14348	3 3	95000	104500
38 2	SMERALDO	OP	EXP	FBG DV	IB T230D VLVO	12 6	14348	3 6	100500	110500
40	MEDITERRANEE 40	RA	EXP	FBG DV	IB T380D VLVO	12 6	15452	3	128000	140500
40	MEDITERRANEE 40	ST	EXP	FBG DV	IB T380D VLVO	12 6	15452	3	128000	140500
40 7	ATLANTIQUE 38	FB	CR	FBG DV	IB T370D VLVO	12 7	15452	3 6	130000	143000
					1995 BOATS					
21 1	START	OP	CUD	FBG DV	IO 230	8 2	5800	2	22300	24800
25	24 TURCHESE	OP	CUD	FBG DV	IO 270	8	5800	3	26700	29700
28	CORALLO 840	ST	CUD	FBG DV	IO T230	9 6	6620	3 7	33600	37300
30	GIADA	ST	CUD	FBG DV	IO T225	10	6620	3 3	35300	39300
30 10	GIADA	ST	CUD	FBG DV	IO T150D	10	6620	3 3	38300	42500
32 7	ACQUAMARINA 31	OP	EXP	FBG DV	IB T200D	10 2	12897	3	69800	76700
40	MEDITERRANEE 40	OP	EXP	FBG DV	IB T380D VLVO	12 6	15452	3	122500	134500
40	MEDITERRANEE 40	ST	EXP	FBG DV	IB T380D	12 6	15452	3	126500	139000
43	ATLANTIQUE 40	FB	MYCPT	FBG DV	IB T370D VLVO	12	19315	3	167000	183500

CRAWFORD BOAT BUILDING
HUMAROCK MA 02047   COAST GUARD MFG ID- RDB See inside cover to adjust price for area
FORMERLY ROGER CRAWFORD BOAT BUILDING

For more recent years, see the BUC Used Boat Price Guide, Volume 1

LOA FT IN	NAME AND/ OR MODEL	TOP/ RIG	BOAT TYPE	-HULL- MTL TP	----ENGINE--- TP # HP MFG	BEAM FT IN	WGT LBS	DRAFT FT IN	RETAIL LOW	RETAIL HIGH
					1996 BOATS					
16	SWAMPSCOTT DORY	CAT	SAROD	FBG CB	OB	6	400	3	5650	6500
16	SWAMPSCOTT ROW DORY	OP	UTL	FBG DS	OB	6	325	3	2550	2950
					1995 BOATS					
16	SWAMPSCOTT DORY	CAT	SAROD	FBG CB	OB	6	400	3	5300	6100
16	SWAMPSCOTT ROW DORY	OP	UTL	FBG DS	OB	6	325	3	2400	2800
					1994 BOATS					
16	SWAMPSCOTT DORY	CAT	SAROD	FBG CB	OB	6	400	3	5000	5750
16	SWAMPSCOTT ROW DORY	OP	UTL	FBG DS	OB	6	325	3	2350	2700
					1993 BOATS					
16	SWAMPSCOTT-DORY	GAF	SAROD	FBG CB	OB	6	400	6	4650	5350
16	SWAMPSCOTT-DORY	OP	UTL	FBG DV	OB	6	300	6	2000	2400
					1992 BOATS					
16	SWAMPSCOTT-DORY	GAF	SAIL	FBG CB	OB	6	400	6	4400	5050
16	SWAMPSCOTT-DORY	OP	UTL	FBG DV	OB	6	300	6	1900	2300
					1991 BOATS					
16	SWAMPSCOTT-DORY	GAF	SAIL	FBG KC	OB	6	400	3	4050	4750
16	SWAMPSCOTT-DORY	OP	UTL	FBG DS	OB	6	300	3	1850	2200
					1990 BOATS					
16	SWAMPSCOTT-DORY	GAF	SAIL	FBG KC	OB	6	425	3	3950	4600
16	SWAMPSCOTT-DORY	OP	UTL	FBG DS	OB	6	325	3	1950	2300
					1989 BOATS					
16	SWAMPSCOTT-DORY	GAF	SAIL	FBG KC	OB	6	425	3	3700	4300
16	SWAMPSCOTT-DORY	OP	UTL	FBG DS	OB	6	325	3	1900	2250
					1988 BOATS					
16	SWAMPSCOTT-DORY	GAF	SAIL	FBG KL	OB	6	425	3	3500	4050
16	SWAMPSCOTT-DORY	OP	UTL	FBG DS	OB	6	325	3	1850	2150
					1987 BOATS					
16	SWAMPSCOTT-DORY	GAF	SAIL	FBG KL	OB	6	425	3	3300	3800
16	SWAMPSCOTT-DORY	OP	UTL	FBG DS	OB	6	325	3	1800	2100
					1985 BOATS					
16	SWAMPSCOTT-DORY	GAF	SAIL	FBG KL	OB	6	425	3	2900	3400
16	SWAMPSCOTT-DORY	OP	UTL	FBG DS	OB	6	325	3	1700	2000
					1984 BOATS					
16	SWAMPSCOTT DORY	GAF	SAIL	FBG CB	OB	6	450	6	2800	3300
16	SWAMPSCOTT DORY	OP	UTL	FBG RB	OB	6	350	6	1800	2150

....For earlier years, see the BUC Used Boat Price Guide, Volume 3

CRESTLINER INC
LITTLE FALLS MN 56345   COAST GUARD MFG ID- CRL See inside cover to adjust price for area

For more recent years, see the BUC Used Boat Price Guide, Volume 1

LOA FT IN	NAME AND/ OR MODEL	TOP/ RIG	BOAT TYPE	-HULL- MTL TP	----ENGINE--- TP # HP MFG	BEAM FT IN	WGT LBS	DRAFT FT IN	RETAIL LOW	RETAIL HIGH
					1996 BOATS					
16	FISH HAWK 16	OP	FSH	AL SV	OB	5 11	500		2250	2600
16	FISH HAWK 16 SC	OP	FSH	AL SV	OB	5 11	500		2450	2850
16	JON 1648	OP	JON	AL SV	OB	5 10	290		1300	1550
16	JON 1648 MSD	OP	JON	AL SV	OB	5 10	290		1250	1500
16	JON 1648 MSD SC	OP	JON	AL SV	OB	5 10	290		2150	2500
16	JON 1648 SC	OP	JON	AL SV	OB	4	290		1300	1550
16	KODIAK 16	OP	UTL	AL SV	OB	5 11	310		1400	1650
16	KODIAK 16 SC	OP	FSH	AL SV	OB	5 11	400		1850	2200
16	PRO 1600	OP	BASS	AL SV	OB	6	560		2650	3050
16 5	1650 SF	OP	RNBT	AL SV	OB	6 2	1130		5300	6050
16 5	FISH HAWK 1650	OP	FSH	AL SV	OB	7 1	870		4000	4650
16 5	FISH HAWK 1650 SC	OP	FSH	AL SV	OB	7 1	870		4250	4950
16 5	PRO AM V1650	OP	FSH	AL SV	OB	6 10	990		4650	5300
16 5	SC PRO AM 1650	OP	FSH	AL SV	OB	6 10	990		4700	5450
17	PRO-1700	OP	BASS	AL SV	OB	6	785		3850	4500
17 2	FISH HAWK 1750	OP	FSH	AL SV	OB	7 7	1350		6000	6900
17 2	FISH HAWK 1750 SC	OP	FSH	AL SV	OB	7 7	1350		6400	7350
17 3	PRO 1800	OP	BASS	AL SV	OB	7 4	1130		5400	6200
17 5	KODIAK 18	OP	UTL	AL SV	OB	6 6	625		2800	3300
17 5	KODIAK 18 SC	OP	UTL	AL SV	OB	6 6	625		3050	3550
17 6	1750 SF	OP	RNBT	AL SV	OB	6 11	1280		6000	6900
17 6	1750 SF	OP	RNBT	AL SV	IO 130-135	6 11	2045		6600	7600
17 6	PRO AM 1750	OP	FSH	AL SV	OB	7 3	1090		5250	6000
17 6	SC PRO AM 1750	OP	FSH	AL SV	OB	7 3	1090		5300	6100
18 6	PHANTOM 1860 SST	OP	FSH	AL SV	OB	6 11	1395		6600	7600
18 10	PRO AM 1850	OP	FSH	AL SV	OB	7 8	1490		6950	8000

LOA FT	LOA IN	NAME AND/ OR MODEL	TOP/ RIG	BOAT TYPE	-HULL- MTL	-HULL- TP	ENGINE TP	ENGINE # HP	ENGINE MFG	BEAM FT	BEAM IN	WGT LBS	DRAFT FT	DRAFT IN	RETAIL LOW	RETAIL HIGH
		1996 BOATS														
18	10	SC PRO AM 1850	OP	FSH	AL	SV	OB			7	8	1490			7050	8100
19		1950SF	OP	RNBT	AL	SV	OB			8		1440			6900	7950
19		1950SF	OP	RNBT	AL	SV	IO	160-205		8		2460			8150	10000
19	2	PHANTOM 1960 SST	OP	FSH	AL	SV	OB			7	3	1670			7800	8950
21	4	EAGLE 2160 SST	OP	CUD	AL	SV	OB			8		2100			11700	13300
21	4	PHANTOM 2160 SST	OP	FSH	AL	SV	OB			8		1910			10800	12300
22	4	EAGLE 2250	ST	FSH	AL	SV	IO	180-235		8	6	3250			13800	16600
23	4	EAGLE 2360 SST	OP	CUD	AL	SV	OB			8	6	2300			13600	15500
24	4	EAGLE 2450	ST	FSH	AL	SV	IO	180-235		8	6	3409			15700	18800
		1995 BOATS														
16		FISH HAWK 1600	OP	FSH	AL	SV	OB			5	8	490			2200	2550
16		JON 1648	OP	JON	AL	SV	OB			5	10	290			1200	1450
16		JON 1648 MSD	OP	JON	AL	SV	OB			5	10	290			1250	1450
16		JON 1648 MSD COMM	OP	JON	AL	SV	OB			5	10	450			2000	2400
16		KODIAK 16	OP	UTL	AL	SV	OB			5	11	310			1300	1550
16		KODIAK 16 DXL	OP	FSH	AL	SV	OB			5	11	400			1750	2050
16		PRO 1600T	OP	BASS	AL	SV	OB			6		560			2500	2900
16	5	FISH HAWK 1650 SC	OP	FSH	AL	SV	OB			6	3	630			2850	3300
16	5	PRO AM V1650	OP	FSH	AL	SV	OB			6	10	990			4200	4850
16	5	SC PRO AM 1650	OP	FSH	AL	SV	OB			6	10	990			4600	5300
16	5	V1650 SF	OP	RNBT	AL	SV	OB			7	4	1130			5000	5750
16	8	FISH HAWK 1700 SC	OP	FSH	AL	SV	OB			6	4	710			3250	3750
17		PRO 1700	OP	BASS	AL	SV	OB			6		785			3600	4200
17	3	PRO 1800	OP	FSH	AL	SV	OB			7	4	1130			5100	5850
17	5	KODIAK 18	OP	UTL	AL	SV	OB			6	6	625			2400	2800
17	5	KODIAK 18 CC	OP	UTL	AL	SV	OB			6	6	625			3150	3650
17	6	PRO AM 1750	OP	FSH	AL	SV	OB			7	3	1090			4800	5500
17	6	SC PRO AM 1750	OP	FSH	AL	SV	OB			7	3	1090			5200	5950
17	6	V1750 SF	OP	RNBT	AL	SV	OB			6	11	1280			5700	6550
17	6	V1750 SF	OP	RNBT	AL	SV	IO	130-135		6	11	2045			6150	7100
18	2	PHANTOM V185	OP	RNBT	AL	SV	IO	130-185		7	3	2280			6900	8050
18	6	PHANTOM 1860 SST	OP	FSH	AL	SV	OB			6	11	1395			6250	7200
18	10	PRO AM V1850	OP	FSH	AL	SV	OB			7	8	1490			6400	7350
18	10	SC PRO AM 1850	OP	FSH	AL	SV	OB			7	8	1490			6850	7900
19		V1950 SF	OP	RNBT	AL	SV	OB			8		1440			6550	7500
19		V1950 SF	OP	RNBT	AL	SV	IO	130	VLVO	8		2460			7900	9100
19		V1950SF	OP	RNBT	AL	SV	IO	135-185		8		2460			7600	9200
19	2	PHANTOM 1960 SST	OP	FSH	AL	SV	OB			7	3	1670			7300	8400
20	4	PHANTOM 2050	OP	RNBT	AL	SV	IO	130-235		8		2510			9150	10800
20	4	SABRE 2050	OP	CUD	AL	SV	IO	130-185		9		2970			11100	12800
21	4	EAGLE 2160 STT	OP	CUD	AL	SV	OB			8		2100			11100	12600
21	4	PHANTOM 2160 SST	OP	FSH	AL	SV	OB			8		1910			10300	11700
22	4	EAGLE 2250	ST	FSH	AL	SV	IO	230-235		8	6	3250			13600	15500
22	4	EAGLE V225	ST	FSH	AL	SV	IO	130-185		8	6	3250			13200	15100
22	4	SABRE 2250	OP	CUD	AL	SV	IO	130-235		8	6	3300			12600	14800
23	4	EAGLE 2360 SST	OP	CUD	AL	SV	OB			8	6	2300			12900	14600
24	4	EAGLE 2450	ST	FSH	AL	SV	IO	130-235		8	6	3409			14800	17600
24	4	SABRE 2450	OP	CUD	AL	SV	IO	130-235		8	6	3610			14500	17200
		1994 BOATS														
16		JON 1648	OP	JON	AL	SV	OB			5	10	290			1100	1300
16		JON 1648 MSD	OP	JON	AL	SV	OB			5	10	290			1100	1350
16		JON 1648 SW	OP	JON	AL	SV	OB			5	10	290			1250	1500
16		PRO 1600	OP	BASS	AL	SV	OB			6		700			2950	3400
16		PRO 1600T	OP	BASS	AL	SV	OB			6		560			2350	2750
16	3	SPORTSMAN 16	OP	FSH	AL	SV	OB			5	8	310			1300	1550
16	3	SPORTSMAN 16 DXL	OP	FSH	AL	SV	OB			5	8	400			1650	2000
16	4	NIGHTHAWK 1640	OP	FSH	AL	SV	OB			6	3	630			2700	3150
16	4	NIGHTHAWK 1640 DXL	OP	FSH	AL	SV	OB			6	3	710			3000	3500
16	5	PRO AM V160	OP	FSH	AL	SV	OB			6	10	990			4150	4800
16	5	V160 SF	OP	RNBT	AL	SV	OB			7	4	1130			4750	5450
17		PRO 1700	OP	BASS	AL	SV	OB			6		785			3450	4000
17	1	SPORTSMAN 17XL	OP	FSH	AL	SV	OB			6	5	625			2800	3250
17	6	PRO AM V170	OP	FSH	AL	SV	OB			7	3	1090			4750	5450
17	6	V170 SF	OP	RNBT	AL	SV	OB			6	11	1280			5400	6200
17	6	V175 SF	OP	RNBT	AL	SV	IO	120-135		6	11	2045			5750	6600
18	2	PHANTOM V185	OP	RNBT	AL	SV	IO	120-185		7	3	2280			6400	7500
18	2	V180 SF	OP	FSH	AL	SV	OB			7	3	1440			6000	6900
18	6	PHANTOM V186 SST	OP	FSH	AL	SV	OB			6	11	1395			5900	6800
18	10	V180 PRO AM	OP	FSH	AL	SV	OB			7	8	1490			6300	7250
19		V195 SF	OP	RNBT	AL	SV	IO	120-160		8		2460			7400	8550
19	2	PHANTOM V196 SST	OP	FSH	AL	SV	OB			7	3	1670			6900	7950
20	4	PHANTOM V205	OP	RNBT	AL	SV	IO	120-235		8		2510			8450	10100
20	4	SABRE V205	OP	CUD	AL	SV	IO	120-160		9		2970			10400	11900
21	4	EAGLE V216 SST	OP	CUD	AL	SV	OB			8		2100			10500	11900
21	4	PHANTOM V216 SST	OP	FSH	AL	SV	OB			8		1910			9700	11000
22	4	EAGLE V225	ST	FSH	AL	SV	IO	120-235		8	6	3250			12300	14400
22	4	SABRE V225	OP	CUD	AL	SV	IO	120-235		8	6	3300			11800	13800
23	4	EAGLE V236 SST	OP	CUD	AL	SV	OB			8	6	2300			12200	13900
24	4	EAGLE V245	ST	FSH	AL	SV	IO	120-235		8	6	3409			13800	16300
24	4	SABRE V245	OP	CUD	AL	SV	IO	120-235		8	6	3610			13500	16000
		1993 BOATS														
16		BACKWATER 1600	OP	JON	AL	SV	OB			5	10	560			2000	2400
16		BACKWATER 1600 PRO	OP	JON	AL	SV	OB			5	10	700			2500	2900
16		JON 1670	OP	JON	AL	SV	OB			5	10	290			1100	1300
16	3	SPORTSMAN 16	OP	FSH	AL	SV	OB			5	8	310			1200	1450
16	4	NIGHTHAWK 1640	OP	FSH	AL	SV	OB			6	3	630			2550	3000
16	4	NIGHTHAWK 1640 DXL	OP	FSH	AL	SV	OB			6	3	710			2850	3350
16	5	V160 SF	OP	FSH	AL	SV	OB			6	6	1130			4500	5150
16	5	V160 TOURNAMENT ED	OP	FSH	AL	SV	OB			6	6	850			3400	3950
17		PRO 1700	OP	FSH	AL	SV	OB			6		785			3250	3800
17		SPORTSMAN 17XL	OP	FSH	AL	SV	OB			6	5	625			2650	3050
17	6	PHANTOM V175 F&S	OP	RNBT	AL	SV	IO	115-135		6	11	2050			5100	6200
17	6	V170 SF	OP	FSH	AL	SV	OB			6	11	1280			5100	5900
17	6	V170 TC	OP	FSH	AL	SV	OB			6	11	1130			4650	5300
18		V180 PRO AM	OP	FSH	AL	SV	OB			6	11	1225			5000	5750
18	2	PHANTOM V185 F&S	OP	RNBT	AL	SV	IO	115-180		7	3	2280			5750	7000
18	2	V180 SF	OP	FSH	AL	SV	OB			7	3	1440			5700	6550
18	6	PHANTOM V186 SST II	OP	FSH	AL	SV	OB			6	11	1395			5650	6450
19		PHANTOM V195 F&S	OP	RNBT	AL	SV	IO	115-180		8		2460			6600	8000
19	2	PHANTOM V196 SST II	OP	FSH	AL	SV	OB			7	3	1670			6550	7550
20	4	PHANTOM V205 F&S	OP	RNBT	AL	SV	IO	115-205		8		2510			7600	9250
21	4	EAGLE V216 SST II	OP	FSH	AL	SV	OB			8		2100			9900	11300
21	4	PHANTOM V216 SST II	OP	FSH	AL	SV	OB			8		1910			9250	10500
21	4	SABRE V216 SST II	OP	CUD	AL	SV	OB			8		2080			9900	11200
22	4	EAGLE V225	ST	FSH	AL	SV	IO	115-230		8	6	3250			11200	13500
22	4	SABRE V225	OP	CUD	AL	SV	IO	115-230		8	6	3300			10700	12900
23	4	EAGLE V236 SST II	OP	FSH	AL	SV	OB			8	6	2300			11600	13200
23	4	SABRE V236 SST II	OP	CUD	AL	SV	OB			8		2200			11200	12700
24	4	EAGLE V245	ST	FSH	AL	SV	IO	115-230		8	6	3409			12600	15300
24	4	SABRE V245	OP	CUD	AL	SV	IO	115-230		8	6	3610			12300	15000
29	3	RAMPAGE 295	OP	CBNCR	FBG	DV	IO	260-330		9	2				35400	41600
		1992 BOATS														
16		BACKWATER 1600	OP	JON	AL	SV	OB			5	10	560			1900	2250
16		BACKWATER 1600 PRO	OP	JON	AL	SV	OB			5	10	700			2400	2750
16		JON 16	OP	JON	AL	SV	OB			5	10	290			1050	1250
16	3	SPORTSMAN 16	OP	FSH	AL	SV	OB			5	8	310			1150	1400
16	3	SPORTSMAN 16W	OP	FSH	AL	SV	OB			6	5	330			1250	1500
16	4	NIGHTHAWK 1640	OP	FSH	AL	SV	OB			6	3	630			2450	2850
16	5	PHANTOM V160 SF	OP	FSH	AL	SV	OB			6	6	1130			4200	4900
16	5	VIKING V160 TOURN	OP	FSH	AL	SV	OB			6	6	850			3250	3750
16	8	FISH HAWK V160 DXL	OP	FSH	AL	SV	OB			6	3	710			2800	3250
17	5	PHANTOM V176 SST II	OP	FSH	AL	SV	OB			6	6	1200			4600	5300
17	6	PHANTOM V170 SF	OP	FSH	AL	SV	OB			6	11	1280			4850	5600
17	6	PHANTOM V175 F&S	OP	RNBT	AL	SV	IO	115-180		6	11	2180			4900	6050
17	6	VIKING V170 TC	OP	FSH	AL	SV	OB			6	11	1130			4400	5050
18		SPORTSMAN 18XL	OP	FSH	AL	SV	OB			6	5	625			2600	3050
18		VIKING V180 PRO AM	OP	FSH	AL	SV	OB			6	11	1225			4800	5500
18	2	PHANTOM V180 SF	OP	FSH	AL	SV	OB			7	3	1440			5450	6250
18	2	PHANTOM V185 F&S	OP	RNBT	AL	SV	IO	115-180		7	3	2410			5800	6700
18	6	PHANTOM V186 SST II	OP	FSH	AL	SV	OB			6	11	1395			5350	6150
19		PHANTOM V195 F&S	OP	RNBT	AL	SV	IO	115-180		8		2460			6200	7500
19	2	EAGLE V196 SST II	OP	CUD	AL	SV	OB			7	3	1565			6000	6850
19	2	PHANTOM V196 SST II	OP	FSH	AL	SV	OB			7	3	1670			6250	7200
19	2	VANGUARD V190 F&S	OP	RNBT	AL	SV	OB			7	2	1750			6450	7400
19	2	VANGUARD V195 F&S	OP	RNBT	AL	SV	IO	115-180		7	2	2385			5750	7000
20		PHANTOM V206 SST II	OP	FSH	AL	SV	OB			8		1725			7400	8500
20	4	PHANTOM V205 F&S	OP	RNBT	AL	SV	IO	115-205		8		2510			7100	8650
21	4	EAGLE V216 SST II	OP	FSH	AL	SV	OB			8		2100			9450	10700
21	4	PHANTOM V216 SST II	OP	FSH	AL	SV	OB			8		1910			8700	10000
21	4	SABRE V216 SST II	OP	CUD	AL	SV	OB			8		2080			9400	10700
22	4	EAGLE V225	ST	FSH	AL	SV	IO	115-230		8	6	3250			10500	12600
22	4	SABRE V225	OP	CUD	AL	SV	IO	115-230		8	6	3300			10000	12000
23	4	EAGLE V236 SST II	OP	FSH	AL	SV	OB			8	6	2300			11000	12500
23	4	SABRE V236 SST II	OP	CUD	AL	SV	OB			8		2200			10600	12100
24	4	EAGLE V245	ST	FSH	AL	SV	IO	115-230		8	6	3409			11800	14300
24	4	SABRE V245	OP	CUD	AL	SV	IO	115-205		8	6	3409			11100	13800
24	4	SABRE V245	OP	CUD	AL	SV	IO	225-230		8	6	3610			12300	14000

 CONTINUED ON NEXT PAGE

CRESTLINER INC -CONTINUED See inside cover to adjust price for area

LOA FT	LOA IN	NAME AND/ OR MODEL	TOP/ RIG	BOAT TYPE	-HULL- MTL	-HULL- TP	ENGINE TP	ENGINE # HP	ENGINE MFG	BEAM FT	BEAM IN	WGT LBS	DRAFT FT IN	RETAIL LOW	RETAIL HIGH
1992 BOATS															
29	3	RAMPAGE 295	OP	CBNCR	FBG	DV	IO	260-330		9	2			33100	39000
1991 BOATS															
16		JON 16	OP	JON	AL	SV	OB			5	10	290		1000	1200
16	3	SPORTSMAN 16W	OP	FSH	AL	SV	OB			6	5	330		1200	1400
16	5	PHANTOM V160 SF	OP	FSH	AL	SV	OB			6	6	1130		4050	4700
16	5	VIKING V160	OP	FSH	AL	SV	OB			6	6	850		3100	3600
16	8	FISH HAWK V16	OP	FSH	AL	SV	OB			6	3	650		2450	2850
16	8	FISH HAWK V16 DXL	OP	FSH	AL	SV	OB			6	3	710		2650	3100
17	5	PHANTOM V176 SST II	OP	FSH	AL	SV	OB			6	6	1200		4400	5050
17	6	PHANTOM V170 SF	OP	FSH	AL	SV	OB			6	11	1280		4650	5350
17	6	PHANTOM V175 F&S	OP	RNBT	AL	SV	IO	135-180		6	11	2180		4650	5650
17	6	VIKING V170 TC	OP	FSH	AL	SV	OB			6	11	1130		4150	4850
18		SPORTSMAN 18XL	OP	FSH	AL	SV	OB			6	5	625		2500	2900
18		VIKING V180 PRO AM	OP	FSH	AL	SV	OB			6	11	1225		4550	5250
18	2	PHANTOM V180 SF	OP	FSH	AL	SV	OB			7	3	1440		5200	5950
18	2	PHANTOM V185 F&S	OP	RNBT	AL	SV	IO	135-180		7	3	2410		5200	6300
18	6	PHANTOM V186 SST II	OP	FSH	AL	SV	OB			6	11	1395		5100	5850
19	2	CC V196 SST II	OP	CTRCN	AL	SV	OB			7	3	1455		5400	6200
19	2	PHANTOM V196 SST II	OP	FSH	AL	SV	OB			7	3	1670		5950	6850
19	2	VANGUARD V190 F&S	OP	RNBT	AL	SV	OB			7	2	1750		6150	7050
19	2	VANGUARD V195	OP	RNBT	AL	SV	IO	135-180		7	2	2385		5400	6550
20		PHANTOM V206 SST II	OP	FSH	AL	SV	OB			8		1725		7050	8100
20	2	CC V206 SST II	OP	CTRCN	AL	SV	OB			8		1625		6800	7800
20	4	PHANTOM V205 F&S	OP	RNBT	AL	SV	IO	135-205		8		2510		6650	8150
21	4	EAGLE V216 SST II	OP	FSH	AL	SV	OB			8		2100		9000	10200
21	4	PHANTOM V216 SST II	OP	FSH	AL	SV	OB			8		1910		8300	9550
21	4	SABRE V216 SST II	OP	CUD	AL	SV	OB			8		2080		9000	10200
21	4	STRIPER V216	OP	CTRCN	AL	SV	OB			8				8200	9400
21	5	VANGUARD V215 SF	OP	CUD	AL	SV	IO	155-245		8		2904		8000	10000
22	4	EAGLE V225	ST	FSH	AL	SV	IO	155-245		8	6	3250		9850	12000
22	4	SABRE V225	OP	CUD	AL	SV	IO	155-230		8	6	3300		9400	11300
23	4	EAGLE V236 SST II	OP	FSH	AL	SV	OB			8	6	2300		10500	12000
23	4	SABRE V236 SST II	OP	CUD	AL	SV	OB			8		2200		10100	11500
24	4	EAGLE V245	ST	FSH	AL	SV	IO	155-245		8	6	3409		11200	13600
24	4	SABRE V245	OP	CUD	AL	SV	IO	155-245		8	6	3610		11000	13400
25	4	EAGLE V256 SST II	OP	FSH	AL	SV	OB			8	6	2560		14100	16000
26	8	SABRE V275	HT	SF	AL	SV	IO	230-245		9	6	4800		18700	21200
29	3	RAMPAGE 295	OP	CBNCR	FBG	DV	IO	260-330		9	2			31000	36500
1990 BOATS															
16	3	ENSIGN 16	OP	FSH	AL	SV	OB			5	8	310		1050	1250
16	3	ENSIGN 16W	OP	FSH	AL	SV	OB			6	5	330		1150	1350
16	3	MUSKIE PRO 16	OP	FSH	AL	DV	OB			5	8	490		1700	2000
16	3	MUSKIE PRO 16W	OP	FSH	AL	DV	OB			6	5	600		2050	2450
16	5	MIRAGE V160	OP	RNBT	AL	DV	OB			6	6	1020		3500	4100
16	5	VIKING V160 DLX	OP	FSH	AL	DV	OB			6	6	710		2500	2900
16	8	COMMANDER V16	OP	FSH	AL	DV	OB			6	3	640		2100	2500
16	8	FISH-HAWK V16	OP	FSH	AL	DV	OB			6	3	640		2450	2850
16	8	FISH-HAWK V16 DLX	OP	FSH	AL	DV	OB			6	3	690		2450	2850
17	3	MAVERICK V170	OP	BASS	AL	DV	OB			6	9	1165		4050	4750
17	6	PHANTOM V170	OP	RNBT	AL	DV	OB			6	6	1075		3850	4450
17	6	PHANTOM V175	OP	RNBT	AL	DV	IO		VLVO	6	11	1960		**	**
17	6	PHANTOM V175	OP	RNBT	AL	DV	IO	175	MRCR	6	11	1960		4150	4800
17	6	VIKING V170 DLX	OP	FSH	AL	DV	OB			6	11	810		2950	3450
18		ENSIGN 18W	OP	FSH	AL	SV	OB			6	5	420		1600	1900
18	1	VANGUARD V195	OP	RNBT	AL	DV	IO	165	MRCR	7	2	2400		4850	5550
18	2	PHANTOM V180	OP	RNBT	AL	DV	OB			7	3	1250		4450	5100
18	2	PHANTOM V180 CC	OP	CTRCN	AL	DV	OB			7	3	1150		4100	4800
18	2	PHANTOM V185	OP	RNBT	AL	DV	IO		VLVO	7	3	2080		**	**
19		SABRE V190 CC	OP	CTRCN	AL	DV	OB			8		1350		4850	5600
19		SABRE V190 OB	OP	RNBT	AL	DV	OB			8		1450		5150	5900
19		SABRE V195 OB	OP	RNBT	AL	DV	IO	205	MRCR	8		2600		5750	6600
20	4	SABRE GL V200 SF	OP	SF	AL	DV	OB			8		1820		7200	8300
20	4	SABRE GL V205 SF	OP	SF	AL	DV	IO	205	MRCR	8		2970		8350	9550
20	4	SABRE V200 CC	OP	CTRCN	AL	DV	OB			8		1520		6250	7150
20	4	SABRE V200 OB	OP	RNBT	AL	DV	OB			8		1620		6650	7650
20	4	SABRE V205 OB	OP	RNBT	AL	DV	IO	230	MRCR	8		2770		6850	7850
21	5	VANGUARD V215	OP	RNBT	AL	DV	IO	260	MRCR	8		2800		7450	8550
21	5	VANGUARD V215 CUD	OP	CUD	AL	DV	IO	260	MRCR	8		3070		8250	9450
22	4	SABRE GL V220 SF	OP	SF	AL	DV	OB			8	6	2100		9000	10200
22	4	SABRE GL V225 SF	OP	SF	AL	DV	OB			8	6	3250		12300	14000
22	4	SABRE V220 OB	OP	RNBT	AL	DV	OB			8	6	1850		8050	9300
22	4	SABRE V225 DAY CR	OP	CBNCR	AL	DV	IO	260	MRCR	8	6	3350		10400	11800
22	4	SABRE V225 OB	OP	RNBT	AL	DV	IO	260	MRCR	8	6	3050		8350	9600
24	4	SABRE GL V240	OP	SF	AL	DV	OB			8	6	2350		10800	12200
24	4	SABRE GL V245	OP	SF	AL	DV	IO	260	MRCR	8	6	3500		12200	13800
24	4	SABRE V245 DAY CR	OP	CBNCR	AL	DV	IO	260	MRCR	8	6	3650		12600	14300
24	4	SABRE V245 MB DAY CR	OP	CBNCR	AL	DV	IO	260	MRCR	8	6	3950		13300	15100
26	8	SABRE V275 MB DAY CR	OP	CBNCR	AL	DV	IO	260	MRCR	9	8	4990		19600	21800
26	8	SABRE V275 SF	OP	SF	AL	DV	IO	260	MRCR	9	8	4850		18200	20200
1989 BOATS															
16		CRUSADER 160	OP	RNBT	FBG	DV	OB			7	8	1080		3500	4100
16		CRUSADER 160	OP	RNBT	FBG	DV	IO	130-165		7	8	1080		2900	3400
16		CRUSADER 160 ANGLR	OP	FSH	FBG	DV	OB			6	6	760		2500	2900
16		CRUSADER 165	OP	RNBT	FBG	DV	OB			7	8	1920		5950	6800
16		CRUSADER 165	OP	RNBT	FBG	DV	IO	130-165		7	8	1920		3700	4350
16	3	ENSIGN 16	OP	FSH	AL	SV	OB			5	8	310		1000	1200
16	3	ENSIGN 16W	OP	FSH	AL	SV	OB			6	5	330		1100	1300
16	3	MUSKIE PRO 16	OP	FSH	AL	DV	OB			5	8	490		1600	1900
16	3	MUSKIE PRO 16W	OP	FSH	AL	DV	OB			6	5	600		2000	2350
16	5	MIRAGE V160	OP	RNBT	AL	DV	OB			6	6	1020		3350	3900
16	5	MIRAGE V160	OP	RNBT	AL	DV	IO	130	MRCR	6	6	1020		2650	3100
16	5	MIRAGE V160 SF	OP	SF	AL	DV	OB			6	6	1020		3350	3900
16	5	MIRAGE V165	OP	RNBT	AL	DV	OB			6	6	1860		5650	6500
16	5	MIRAGE V165	OP	RNBT	AL	DV	IO	130	MRCR	6	6	1860		3400	4000
16	5	MIRAGE V165 SF	OP	SF	AL	DV	OB			6	6	1860		5600	6400
16	5	MIRAGE V165 SF	OP	SF	AL	DV	IO	130	MRCR	6	6	1860		3900	4550
16	5	VIKING V160 DLX	OP	FSH	AL	DV	OB			6	6	710		2400	2800
16	8	COMMANDER V16	OP	FSH	AL	DV	OB			6	3	640		2200	2550
16	8	FISH-HAWK V16	OP	FSH	AL	DV	OB			6	3	640		2200	2550
16	8	FISH-HAWK V16 DLX	OP	FSH	AL	DV	OB			6	3	690		2350	2750
17	1	CRUSADER 170 ANGLR	OP	FSH	FBG	DV	OB			7	4	1125		3700	4300
17	2	CRUSADER 170 SF	OP	SF	FBG	DV	OB			7	8	1290		4200	4850
17	3	MAVERICK V170	OP	BASS	AL	DV	OB			6	9	1165		3900	4550
17	5	MAVERICK V180	OP	BASS	AL	DV	OB			7	2	1225		4050	4700
17	6	PHANTOM V170	OP	RNBT	AL	DV	OB			6	6	1075		3650	4250
17	6	PHANTOM V170	OP	RNBT	AL	DV	IO	130-175		6	11	1075		3200	3750
17	6	PHANTOM V170 SF	OP	SF	AL	DV	OB			6	6	1075		3650	4250
17	6	PHANTOM V170 SF	OP	SF	AL	DV	IO	130-175		6	11	1075		3650	4300
17	6	PHANTOM V175	OP	RNBT	AL	DV	OB			6	11	1960		5750	6600
17	6	PHANTOM V175	OP	RNBT	AL	DV	IO	130-175		6	6	1960		3750	4400
17	6	PHANTOM V175 SF	OP	SF	AL	DV	OB			6	11	1960		5700	6550
17	6	PHANTOM V175 SF	OP	SF	AL	DV	IO	130-175		6	6	1960		4350	5050
17	6	VIKING V170 DLX	OP	FSH	AL	DV	OB			6	11	810		2850	3300
18		CRUSADER 185	OP	B/R	FBG	DV	IO	130-205		7	4	2260		4200	5000
18		ENSIGN 18W	OP	FSH	AL	SV	OB			6	5	420		1550	1850
18		MUSKIE PRO 18W	OP	FSH	AL	DV	OB			6	5	700		2550	2950
18	1	VANGUARD V195	OP	RNBT	AL	DV	IO	165-205		7	2	2400		4600	5350
18	2	PHANTOM V180	OP	CTRCN	AL	DV	OB			7	3	1250		4200	4900
18	2	PHANTOM V180	OP	RNBT	AL	DV	IO	165-205		7	3	1250		3650	4350
18	2	PHANTOM V180 CC	OP	CTRCN	AL	DV	OB			7	3	1250		4200	4900
18	2	PHANTOM V180 SF	OP	SF	AL	DV	OB			7	3	1250		4200	4900
18	2	PHANTOM V180 SF	OP	SF	AL	DV	IO	165-205		7	3	1250		4200	5000
18	2	PHANTOM V185	OP	RNBT	AL	DV	OB			7	3	2080		5950	6850
18	2	PHANTOM V185	OP	RNBT	AL	DV	IO	165-205		7	3	2080		4250	5050
18	2	PHANTOM V185 SF	OP	SF	AL	DV	OB			7	3	2080		5950	6850
18	2	PHANTOM V185 SF	OP	SF	AL	DV	IO	165-205		7	3	2080		5000	5850
18	2	VIKING V180 DLX	OP	FSH	AL	DV	OB			7	3	2080		5950	6850
19		SABRE GL V190 SF	OP	SF	AL	DV	OB			8		1650		5400	6200
19		SABRE GL V190 SF	OP	SF	AL	DV	IO	130-205		8		1650		5150	6150
19		SABRE GL V195 SF	OP	SF	AL	DV	OB			8		2800		6750	7750
19		SABRE GL V195 SF	OP	SF	AL	DV	IO	165-205		8		2800		6550	7650
19		SABRE V190 CB	OP	RNBT	AL	DV	OB			8		1450		4850	5600
19		SABRE V190 CB	OP	RNBT	AL	DV	IO	165-205		8		1450		4250	5050
19		SABRE V190 CC	OP	CTRCN	AL	DV	OB			8		1450		4900	5650
19		SABRE V190 OB	OP	RNBT	AL	DV	OB			8		1450		4950	5700
19		SABRE V190 OB	OP	RNBT	AL	DV	IO	175-205		8		1450		4400	5100
19		SABRE V190 OB	OP	RNBT	AL	SV	IO	165	MRCR	8		1450		4350	5000
19		SABRE V190 SF	OP	SF	AL	DV	IO	165-205		8		1650		5150	6000
19		SABRE V195 CB	OP	RNBT	AL	DV	OB			8		2600		6600	7550
19		SABRE V195 CB	OP	RNBT	AL	DV	IO	165-205		8		2600		5300	6150
19		SABRE V195 OB	OP	RNBT	AL	DV	OB			8		2600		6700	7700
19		SABRE V195 OB	OP	RNBT	AL	DV	IO	165-205		8		2600		5350	6200
19		SABRE V195 SF	OP	RNBT	AL	DV	IO	165-205		8		2600		5350	6250
19		SABRE V195 SF	OP	RNBT	AL	SV	OB			8		2600		6800	7800
19	2	CRUSADER 195	OP	RNBT	FBG	DV	IO	165-260		7	9	2600		5250	6450
19	2	VANGUARD V185	OP	RNBT	AL	DV	IO	130-175		6	11	2100		4450	5150

CONTINUED ON NEXT PAGE

LOA FT	LOA IN	NAME AND/ OR MODEL	TOP/ RIG	BOAT TYPE	-HULL- MTL	-HULL- TP	ENGINE TP	ENGINE # HP	ENGINE MFG	BEAM FT	BEAM IN	WGT LBS	DRAFT FT	DRAFT IN	RETAIL LOW	RETAIL HIGH
		1989 BOATS														
20	4	SABRE GL V200 SF	OP	SF	AL	DV	OB			8		1820			6900	7950
20	4	SABRE GL V200 SF	OP	SF	AL	DV	IO	130-205		8		1820			6150	7250
20	4	SABRE GL V205 SF	OP	SF	AL	DV	OB			8		2970			9150	10400
20	4	SABRE GL V205 SF	OP	SF	AL	DV	IO	130-205		8		2970			7700	9050
20	4	SABRE V200 CB	OP	RNBT	AL	DV	OB			8		1620			6300	7250
20	4	SABRE V200 CB	OP	RNBT	AL	DV	IO	165-230		8		1620			5100	6050
20	4	SABRE V200 CC	OP	CTRCN	AL	DV	OB			8		1620			6250	7200
20	4	SABRE V200 OB	OP	RNBT	AL	DV	OB			8		1620			6400	7400
20	4	SABRE V200 OB	OP	RNBT	AL	DV	IO	165-230		8		1620			5150	6100
20	4	SABRE V205 CB	OP	RNBT	AL	DV	OB			8		2770			8900	10100
20	4	SABRE V205 CB	OP	RNBT	AL	DV	IO	165-230		8		2770			6250	7400
20	4	SABRE V205 OB	OP	RNBT	AL	DV	OB			8		2770			9050	10300
20	4	SABRE V205 OB	OP	RNBT	AL	DV	IO	165-230		8		2770			6300	7450
21	2	CRUSADER 215 CUD	OP	CUD	FBG	DV	IO	205-270		8		2895			7100	8650
21	2	CRUSADER 215 OB	OP	RNBT	FBG	DV	IO	175-270		8		2795			6550	7750
21	2	RAMPAGE 215	OP	RNBT	FBG	DV	IO		MRCR	8		2795			**	**
21	2	RAMPAGE 215	OP	RNBT	FBG	DV	IO	260-270		8		2795			7350	8550
21	5	VANGUARD V215	OP	RNBT	AL	DV	IO	175-230		8		2800			6650	7850
21	5	VANGUARD V215 CUD	OP	CUD	AL	DV	IO	175-230		8		3070			7400	8700
22	4	CRUSADER 2105 WAC	OP	CUD	FBG	DV	IO	205-270		8		3380			8300	10000
22	4	SABRE 225 CB	OP	RNBT	FBG	DV	OB			8		3050			11400	12900
22	4	SABRE GL V220 SF	OP	SF	AL	DV	OB			8	6	2100			8550	9800
22	4	SABRE GL V220 SF	OP	SF	AL	DV	IO	165-230		8	6	2100			7550	8950
22	4	SABRE GL V225 SF	OP	SF	AL	DV	OB			8	6	3250			11800	13400
22	4	SABRE GL V225 SF	OP	SF	AL	DV	IO	165-230		8	6	3250			9450	11000
22	4	SABRE V220 CB	OP	RNBT	AL	DV	OB			8	6	3050			11300	12900
22	4	SABRE V220 CB	OP	RNBT	AL	DV	IO	175-230		8	6	3050			7450	8800
22	4	SABRE V220 OB	OP	RNBT	AL	DV	OB			8	6	3050			11500	13000
22	4	SABRE V220 OB	OP	RNBT	AL	DV	IO	175-230		8	6	3050			7550	8850
22	4	SABRE V225 CB	OP	RNBT	AL	DV	IO	175-230		8	6	3050			7450	8800
22	4	SABRE V225 DAY CR	OP	CBNCR	AL	DV	IO	165-230		8	6	3300			9300	10800
22	4	SABRE V225 OB	OP	RNBT	AL	DV	OB			8	6	3050			11400	12900
22	4	SABRE V225 OB	OP	RNBT	AL	DV	IO	175-230		8	6	3050			7550	8850
24	1	RAMPAGE 245	OP	CUD	FBG	DV	IO		MRCR	8	6	4225			**	**
24	1	RAMPAGE 245	OP	CUD	FBG	DV	IO	260-270		8	6	4225			11200	12900
24	1	RAMPAGE 245	OP	CUD	FBG	DV	IO	365	MRCR	8	6	4225			13100	14900
24	4	SABRE GL V240 SF	OP	SF	AL	DV	OB			8	6	2750			11700	13200
24	4	SABRE GL V240 SF	OP	SF	AL	DV	IO	165-260		8	6	2750			9450	11500
24	4	SABRE GL V245 SF	OP	SF	AL	DV	OB			8	6	3500			13500	15300
24	4	SABRE GL V245 SF	OP	SF	AL	DV	IO	165-260		8	6	3550			11000	13100
24	4	SABRE V240 CB	OP	RNBT	AL	DV	OB			8	6	2150			9600	10900
24	4	SABRE V240 CB	OP	RNBT	AL	DV	IO	175-260		8	6	2150			7000	8600
24	4	SABRE V245 CB	OP	RNBT	AL	DV	OB			8	6	3300			13300	15200
24	4	SABRE V245 CB	OP	RNBT	AL	DV	IO	175-260		8	6	3300			8550	10400
24	4	SABRE V245 DAY CR	OP	CBNCR	AL	DV	IO	175-260		8	6	3600			11400	13400
24	4	SABRE V245 MB DAY CR	OP	CBNCR	AL	DV	IO	175-260		8	6	3900			12000	14100
24	5	VANGUARD V245	OP	CUD	AL	DV	IO	175-260		8	6	3400			9450	11300
26	8	SABRE V275 MB DAY CR	OP	CBNCR	AL	DV	IO	200-270		9	8	4990			18200	20900
26	8	SABRE V275 SF	OP	SF	AL	DV	IO	200-270		9	8	4850			15900	19200
27	2	RAMPAGE 275	OP	CUD	FBG	DV	IO		MRCR	8	6	4700			**	**
27	2	RAMPAGE 275	OP	CUD	FBG	DV	IO	270	MRCR	8	6	4700			14900	17000
27	2	RAMPAGE 275	OP	CUD	FBG	DV	IO	365	MRCR	8	6	4700			16700	18900
29	3	RAMPAGE 295	OP	CBNCR	FBG	DV	IO		MRCR	9	2				**	**
29	3	RAMPAGE 295	OP	CBNCR	FBG	DV	IO	270-365		9	2				27800	33000
		1988 BOATS														
16		CRSDR-160-ANGLR DLX	OP	FSH	FBG	DV	OB			6	5	830			2600	3050
16		CRUSADER 160	OP	RNBT	FBG	DV	OB			7	8	1080			3400	3950
16		CRUSADER 165	OP	RNBT	FBG	DV	IO	120-165		7	8	1080			2750	3250
16		CRUSADER-160-ANGLER	OP	FSH	FBG	DV	OB			6	6	760			2400	2800
16	3	COMMANDER V16	OP	FSH	AL	DV	OB			5	8	340	2	10	1050	1300
16	3	ENSIGN 16	OP	FSH	AL	SV	OB			5	8	310	2	10	980	1150
16	3	ENSIGN 16W	OP	FSH	AL	SV	OB			6	5	330	3	2	1050	1250
16	3	FISH-HAWK V16	OP	FSH	AL	DV	OB			5	8	595	2	10	1900	2250
16	3	FISH-HAWK V16 DLX	OP	FSH	AL	DV	OB			6	4	625	3	2	2000	2350
16	5	MIRAGE V160	OP	RNBT	AL	DV	OB			6	6	1020			3250	3750
16	5	MIRAGE V160 SF	OP	SF	AL	DV	OB			6	6	1020			3200	3750
16	5	MIRAGE V165	OP	RNBT	AL	DV	IO	128-130		6	6	1020			2500	2950
16	5	MIRAGE V165 SF	OP	SF	AL	DV	OB			6	6	1860			5400	6200
16	5	MIRAGE V165 SF	OP	SF	AL	DV	IO	120	MRCR	6	6	1020			2800	3300
16	5	MIRAGE V165 SF	OP	SF	AL	DV	IO	128-130		6	6	1860			3650	4300
16	5	MIRAGE V175	OP	RNBT	AL	DV	IO	120	MRCR	6	6	1020			2550	2950
16	5	VIKING V160 DLX	OP	FSH	AL	DV	OB			6	6	710			2300	2700
17	2	CRSDR-170-ANGLR DLX	OP	FSH	FBG	DV	OB			7	8	1290			4050	4700
17	2	CRUSADER 170	OP	RNBT	FBG	DV	OB			7	8	1290			4050	4700
17	2	CRUSADER 170 SF	OP	SF	FBG	DV	OB			7	8	1290			4050	4700
17	2	CRUSADER 175	OP	RNBT	FBG	DV	IO	120-205		7	8	1290			3300	3950
17	5	PHANTOM V180 MAVERCK	OP	BASS	AL	DV	OB			7	2	1225			3900	4550
17	6	PHANTOM V170	OP	RNBT	AL	DV	OB			6	6	1075			3500	4050
17	6	PHANTOM V170 SF	OP	SF	AL	DV	OB			6	6	1075			3500	4050
17	6	PHANTOM V175	OP	RNBT	AL	DV	IO	120-175		6	6	1075			2900	3400
17	6	PHANTOM V175 SF	OP	SF	AL	DV	IO	120-175		6	6	1075			3300	3900
17	6	PHANTOM-EAGLE	OP	RNBT	AL	DV	OB			6	6	1225			3950	4600
17	6	VIKING V170 DLX	OP	FSH	AL	DV	OB			6	6	810			2750	3200
18		CRUSADER 180	OP	B/R	FBG	DV	OB			7	2	1560			4800	5550
18		CRUSADER 180	OP	B/R	FBG	DV	IO	205	MRCR	7	2	1560			3500	4100
18		CRUSADER 185	OP	B/R	FBG	DV	IO	165-230		7	2	1560			3400	4100
18		CRUSADER 185	OP	B/R	FBG	DV	IO	260		7	2	1560			3700	4300
18		ENSIGN 18W	OP	FSH	AL	SV	OB			6	5	420			1500	1750
18	2	PHANTOM V180	OP	CTRCN	AL	DV	OB			7	3	1150			3800	4450
18	2	PHANTOM V180 CC	OP	CTRCN	AL	DV	OB			7	3	1150			3800	4450
18	2	PHANTOM V180 SF	OP	SF	AL	DV	OB			7	3	1250			4050	4700
18	2	PHANTOM V185	OP	RNBT	AL	DV	IO	120-180		7	3	1250			3400	4050
18	2	PHANTOM V185 SF	OP	SF	AL	DV	IO	120-180		7	3	1250			3950	4650
18	2	VIKING V180 DLX	OP	FSH	AL	DV	OB			7	3	1100			3650	4250
19		SABRE GL V190 SF	OP	SF	AL	DV	OB			8		1575			5000	5750
19		SABRE GL V195 SF	OP	SF	AL	DV	IO	120-205		8		1575			4850	5700
19		SABRE V190 CB	OP	RNBT	AL	DV	OB			8		1450			4700	5400
19		SABRE V190 CC	OP	CTRCN	AL	DV	OB			8		1350			4450	5150
19		SABRE V190 OB	OP	RNBT	AL	DV	OB			8		1450			4750	5500
19		SABRE V195 CB	OP	RNBT	AL	DV	IO	120-205		8		1450			4000	4850
19		SABRE V195 OB	OP	RNBT	AL	DV	IO	120-205		8		1450			4050	4900
20	2	CRUSADER 205 CUD	OP	CUD	FBG	DV	IO		MRCR	7	7	2975			**	**
20	2	CRUSADER 205 CUD	OP	CUD	FBG	DV	IO	165-260		7	7	2975			6200	7600
20	2	CRUSADER 205 OB	OP	RNBT	FBG	DV	IO		MRCR	7	7	2950			**	**
20	2	CRUSADER 205 OB	OP	RNBT	FBG	DV	IO	165-260		7	7	2950			5900	7200
20	2	RAMPAGE 205	OP	CUD	FBG	DV	IO		MRCR	7	7	2925			**	**
20	2	RAMPAGE 205	OP	CUD	FBG	DV	IO	175-260		7	7	2925			6150	7500
20	4	SABRE GL V200 SF	OP	SF	AL	DV	OB			8		1750			6450	7400
20	4	SABRE GL V205 SF	OP	SF	AL	DV	IO	120-205		8		1750			5800	6800
20	4	SABRE V200 CB	OP	RNBT	AL	DV	OB			8		1620			6050	6950
20	4	SABRE V200 CC	OP	CTRCN	AL	DV	OB			8		1520			5750	6600
20	4	SABRE V200 OB	OP	RNBT	AL	DV	OB			8		1620			6150	7100
20	4	SABRE V205 CB	OP	RNBT	AL	DV	IO	120-205		8		1620			4800	5700
20	4	SABRE V205 OB	OP	RNBT	AL	DV	IO	120-205		8		1620			4850	5750
22	4	CRUSADER 2105 WAC	OP	CUD	FBG	DV	IO		MRCR	8		3380			**	**
22	4	CRUSADER 2105 WAC	OP	CUD	FBG	DV	IO	165-260		8		3380			7800	9400
22	4	SABRE GL V220 SF	OP	SF	AL	DV	OB			8		2050			8100	9300
22	4	SABRE GL V225 SF	OP	SF	AL	DV	IO	120-205		8		2050			6850	8000
22	4	SABRE V220 CB	OP	RNBT	AL	DV	OB			8		1850			7300	8400
22	4	SABRE V220 OB	OP	RNBT	AL	DV	OB			8		1850			7400	8500
22	4	SABRE V225 CB	OP	RNBT	AL	DV	IO	120-205		8		1850			5500	6550
22	4	SABRE V225 DAY CR	OP	CBNCR	AL	DV	IO	120-205		8		3300			8500	9900
22	4	SABRE V225 MB DAY CR	OP	CBNCR	AL	DV	IO	120-205		8		3600			9100	10500
22	4	SABRE V225 OB	OP	RNBT	AL	DV	IO	120-205		8		1850			5550	6600
24	1	CRUSADER 245 MB DYCR		CBNCR	FBG	DV	IO	200-260		8		4625			12500	14600
		IO 350-360 14400 16500, IO 454 MRCR 18500 20600, IO T120-T205													13600	15700
24	1	CRUSADER 245 SF	OP	CBNCR	FBG	DV	IO	200-260		8		4350			11900	13900
24	1	CRUSADER 245 SF	OP	CBNCR	FBG	DV	IO	350-360		8		4350			13800	15800
24	1	CRUSADER 245 SF	OP	CBNCR	FBG	DV	IO	454	MRCR	8		4350			17500	19900
24	1	RAMPAGE 245	OP	CUD	FBG	DV	IO	260		8		4225			10500	11900
		IO 350-360 11900 13600, IO 454 MRCR 15200 17200, IO T165-T260													11200	13700
24	4	SABRE GL V240	OP	SF	AL	DV	OB			8		2300			9750	11100
24	4	SABRE GL V245	OP	SF	AL	DV	IO	130-230		8		2300			8000	9700
24	4	SABRE V240 CB	OP	RNBT	AL	DV	OB			8		2100			9050	10300
24	4	SABRE V245 CB	OP	RNBT	AL	DV	IO	130-230		8		2100			6350	7700
24	4	SABRE V245 DAY CR	OP	CBNCR	AL	DV	IO	130-230		8		3600			10500	12300
24	4	SABRE V245 MB DAY CR	OP	CBNCR	AL	DV	IO	130-230		8		3900			11100	13000
26	8	SABRE GL V275 SF	OP	SF	AL	DV	IO	200-260		9	8	4850			15100	18000
26	8	SABRE GL V275 SF	OP	SF	AL	DV	IO	350		9	8	4850			17500	19900
26	8	SABRE GL V275 SF	OP	SF	AL	DV	IO	T120-T175		9	8	4850			16100	19400
26	8	SABRE V275 MB DAY CR	OP	CBNCR	AL	DV	IO	200-350		9	8	4990			16800	20700
26	8	SABRE V275 MB DAY CR	OP	CBNCR	AL	DV	IO	T120-T175		9	8	4990			18200	20300
29	3	RAMPAGE 295	OP	CTRCN	FBG	DV	IO	260-270		9	2				19400	21800

CONTINUED ON NEXT PAGE

LOA FT	LOA IN	NAME AND/ OR MODEL	TOP/ RIG	BOAT TYPE	-HULL- MTL	-HULL- TP	TP	ENGINE # HP	ENGINE MFG	BEAM FT	BEAM IN	WGT LBS	DRAFT FT	DRAFT IN	RETAIL LOW	RETAIL HIGH
		1987 BOATS														
16		CRUSADER 160	OP	RNBT	FBG	SV	OB			7	8	1080			3250	3800
16		CRUSADER 160	OP	RNBT	FBG	SV	IO	120-165		7	8	1080			2600	3050
16		CRUSADER 165	OP	RNBT	FBG	SV	OB			7	8	1920			5500	6300
16		CRUSADER 165	OP	RNBT	FBG	SV	IO	120-165		7	8	1920			3350	3900
16		CRUSADER-160-ANGLER	OP	FSH	FBG	SV	OB			6	6	760			2300	2700
16	3	COMMANDER 16	OP	FSH	AL	SV	OB			5	8	340	2	10	1050	1250
16	3	COMMANDER 16W	OP	FSH	AL	SV	OB			6	5	360	3	2	1100	1300
16	3	COMMANDER II	OP	FSH	AL	SV	OB			6	5	470	3	2	1450	1700
16	3	ENSIGN 16	OP	FSH	AL	SV	OB			5	8	310	2	10	940	1100
16	3	ENSIGN 16W	OP	FSH	AL	SV	OB			6	5	330	3	2	1000	1200
16	3	FISH-HAWK 16	OP	FSH	AL	SV	OB			5	8	595	2	10	1850	2200
16	3	FISH-HAWK 16 XL	OP	FSH	AL	SV	OB			6	4	625	3	2	1950	2300
16	4	NORTHSTAR 16 SF	OP	SF	AL	DV	OB			6	5	990			3000	3500
16	4	VIKING V160	OP	FSH	AL	DV	OB			6	4	680			2100	2450
16	5	MIRAGE V160	OP	RNBT	AL	DV	OB			6	6	1020			3100	3600
16	5	MIRAGE V160	OP	RNBT	AL	DV	IO	120-130		6	6	1020			2400	2800
16	5	MIRAGE V160 SF	OP	SF	AL	DV	OB			6	6	1020			3100	3600
16	5	MIRAGE V160 SF	OP	SF	AL	DV	IO	120-130		6	6	1020			2700	3150
16	5	MIRAGE V165	OP	RNBT	AL	DV	OB			6	6	1860			5250	6000
16	5	MIRAGE V165	OP	RNBT	AL	DV	IO	120-130		6	6	1860			3100	3600
16	5	MIRAGE V165 SF	OP	SF	AL	DV	OB			6	6	1860			5150	5950
16	5	MIRAGE V165 SF	OP	SF	AL	DV	IO	120-130		6	6	1860			3500	4100
16	5	VIKING V160 DLX	OP	FSH	AL	DV	OB			6	6	710			2250	2600
17	2	CRUSADER 170	OP	RNBT	FBG	SV	OB			7	8	1290			3900	4550
17	2	CRUSADER 170	OP	RNBT	FBG	SV	IO	120-205		7	8	1290			3100	3750
17	2	CRUSADER 175	OP	RNBT	FBG	SV	OB			7	8	2440			5950	6850
17	2	CRUSADER 175	OP	RNBT	FBG	SV	IO	120-205		7	8	2440			4050	4800
17	2	CRUSADER-170-ANGLER	OP	FSH	FBG	SV	OB			7	8	1290			3900	4500
17	5	VIKING V170	OP	FSH	AL	DV	OB			6	4	760			2500	2900
17	6	PHANTOM V170	OP	RNBT	AL	DV	OB			6	6	1075			3350	3900
17	6	PHANTOM V170	OP	RNBT	AL	DV	IO	120-175		6	6	1075			2750	3250
17	6	PHANTOM V170 SF	OP	SF	AL	DV	OB			6	6	1075			3350	3900
17	6	PHANTOM V170 SF	OP	SF	AL	DV	IO	120-175		6	6	1075			3150	3700
17	6	PHANTOM V175	OP	RNBT	AL	DV	OB			6	6	1960			5300	6100
17	6	PHANTOM V175	OP	RNBT	AL	DV	IO	120-175		6	6	1960			3350	3950
17	6	PHANTOM V175 SF	OP	SF	AL	DV	OB			6	6	1960			5300	6050
17	6	PHANTOM V175 SF	OP	SF	AL	DV	IO	120-175		6	6	1960			3850	4550
17	6	PHANTOM-EAGLE	OP	RNBT	AL	DV	OB			6	6	1225			3800	4400
17	6	VIKING V170 DLX	OP	FSH	AL	DV	OB			6	6	810			2650	3050
18		CRUSADER 180	OP	B/R	FBG	DV	OB			7	2	1560			4650	5350
18		CRUSADER 180	OP	B/R	FBG	DV	IO	165-230		7	2	1560			3200	3900
18		CRUSADER 180	OP	B/R	FBG	DV	IO	260		7	2	1560			3550	4100
18		CRUSADER 180	OP	B/R	FBG	SV	IO	205	MRCR	7	2	1560			3300	3800
18		CRUSADER 185	OP	B/R	FBG	DV	OB			7	2	2665			6050	6950
18		CRUSADER 185	OP	B/R	FBG	DV	IO	165-230		7	2	2665			4150	5000
18		CRUSADER 185	OP	B/R	FBG	DV	IO	260		7	2	2665			4500	5200
18		FISH-HAWK 18	OP	FSH	AL	SV	OB			6	5	675	3	2	2300	2650
18		VOYAGER 18	OP	FSH	AL	SV	OB			6	5	420	3	2	1400	1700
18	2	PHANTOM V180	OP	CTRCN	AL	DV	OB			7	3	1150			3650	4250
18	2	PHANTOM V180	OP	RNBT	AL	DV	OB			7	3	1250			3950	4550
18	2	PHANTOM V180	OP	RNBT	AL	DV	IO	120-180		7	3	1250			3250	3850
18	2	PHANTOM V180 SF	OP	SF	AL	DV	OB			7	3	1250			3900	4550
18	2	PHANTOM V180 SF	OP	SF	AL	DV	IO	120-180		7	3	1250			3750	4400
18	2	PHANTOM V185	OP	RNBT	AL	DV	OB			7	3	2080			5550	6350
18	2	PHANTOM V185	OP	RNBT	AL	DV	IO	120-175		7	3	2080			3800	4500
18	2	PHANTOM V185 SF	OP	SF	AL	DV	OB			7	3	2080			5500	6350
18	2	PHANTOM V185 SF	OP	SF	AL	DV	IO	120-180		7	3	2080			4500	5200
18	2	VIKING V180 DLX	OP	FSH	AL	DV	OB			7	3	1100			3500	4100
19		SABRE GL V190	OP	SF	AL	DV	OB			8		1575			4800	5550
19		SABRE GL V190	OP	SF	AL	DV	IO	120-205		8		1575			4600	5400
19		SABRE GL V195	OP	SF	AL	DV	OB			8		2725			6250	7150
19		SABRE GL V195	OP	SF	AL	DV	IO	120-205		8		2725			5750	6750
19		SABRE V190	OP	CTRCN	AL	DV	OB			8		1350			4250	4950
19		SABRE V190 CB	OP	RNBT	AL	DV	OB			8		1450			4500	5200
19		SABRE V190 CB	OP	RNBT	AL	DV	IO	120-205		8		1450			3800	4550
19		SABRE V190 OB	OP	RNBT	AL	DV	OB			8		1450			4600	5250
19		SABRE V190 OB	OP	RNBT	AL	DV	IO	120-205		8		1450			3850	4600
19		SABRE V195 CB	OP	RNBT	AL	DV	OB			8		2600			6150	7050
19		SABRE V195 CB	OP	RNBT	AL	DV	IO	120-205		8		2600			4700	5550
19		SABRE V195 OB	OP	RNBT	AL	DV	OB			8		2600			6250	7200
19		SABRE V195 OB	OP	RNBT	AL	DV	IO	120-205		8		2600			4750	5600
20	2	CRUSADER 205 CUD	OP	CUD	FBG	DV	IO		MRCR	7	7	2975			**	**
20	2	CRUSADER 205 CUD	OP	CUD	FBG	DV	IO	165-260		7	7	2975			5900	7200
20	2	CRUSADER 205 OB	OP	RNBT	FBG	DV	IO		MRCR	7	7	2950			**	**
20	2	CRUSADER 205 OB	OP	RNBT	FBG	DV	IO	165-260		7	7	2950			5650	6850
20	2	RAMPAGE 205	OP	CUD	FBG	DV	IO		MRCR	7	7	2925			**	**
20	2	RAMPAGE 205	OP	CUD	FBG	DV	IO	175-260		7	7	2925			5850	7150
20	4	SABRE GL V200	OP	SF	AL	DV	OB			8		1750			6200	7100
20	4	SABRE GL V200	OP	SF	AL	DV	IO	120-205		8		1750			5500	6450
20	4	SABRE GL V205	OP	SF	AL	DV	OB			8		2900			8300	9550
20	4	SABRE GL V205	OP	SF	AL	DV	IO	120-205		8		2900			6850	8000
20	4	SABRE V200	OP	CTRCN	AL	DV	OB			8		1520			5500	6350
20	4	SABRE V200 CB	OP	RNBT	AL	DV	OB			8		1620			5850	6700
20	4	SABRE V200 CB	OP	RNBT	AL	DV	IO	120-205		8		1620			4550	5400
20	4	SABRE V200 OB	OP	RNBT	AL	DV	OB			8		1620			5950	6850
20	4	SABRE V200 OB	OP	RNBT	AL	DV	IO	120-205		8		1620			4600	5400
20	4	SABRE V205 CB	OP	RNBT	AL	DV	OB			8		2770			8200	9400
20	4	SABRE V205 CB	OP	RNBT	AL	DV	IO	120-205		8		2770			5550	6550
20	4	SABRE V205 OB	OP	RNBT	AL	DV	OB			8		2770			8300	9550
20	4	SABRE V205 OB	OP	RNBT	AL	DV	IO	120-205		8		2770			5600	6600
22	4	CRUSADER 2105 WAC	OP	CUD	FBG	DV	IO		MRCR	8		3380			**	**
22	4	CRUSADER 2105 WAC	OP	CUD	FBG	DV	IO	165-260		8		3380			7400	8950
22	4	SABRE GL V220	OP	SF	AL	DV	OB			8		2050			7800	8950
22	4	SABRE GL V220	OP	SF	AL	DV	IO	120-205		8		2050			6500	7600
22	4	SABRE GL V225	OP	SF	AL	DV	OB			8		3200			10800	12200
22	4	SABRE GL V225	OP	SF	AL	DV	IO	120-205		8		3200			8100	9450
22	4	SABRE V220 CB	OP	RNBT	AL	DV	OB			8		1850			7050	8100
22	4	SABRE V220 CB	OP	RNBT	AL	DV	IO	120-205		8		1850			5200	6150
22	4	SABRE V220 OB	OP	RNBT	AL	DV	OB			8		1850			7150	8200
22	4	SABRE V220 OB	OP	RNBT	AL	DV	IO	120-205		8		1850			5250	6200
22	4	SABRE V225 CB	OP	RNBT	AL	DV	OB			8		3000			10400	11800
22	4	SABRE V225 CB	OP	RNBT	AL	DV	IO	120-205		8		3000			6400	7500
22	4	SABRE V225 DAYCRUISR	OP	CBNCR	AL	DV	IO	120-205		8		3300			8050	9400
22	4	SABRE V225 MB DAYCRU	OP	CBNCR	AL	DV	IO	120-205		8		3600			8550	10000
22	4	SABRE V225 OB	OP	RNBT	AL	DV	OB			8		3000			10500	11900
22	4	SABRE V225 OB	OP	RNBT	AL	DV	IO		MRCR	8		3000			**	**
22	4	SABRE V225 OB	OP	RNBT	AL	DV	IO	120-205		8		3000			6450	7600
24	4	SABRE GL V240	OP	SF	AL	DV	OB			8		2300			9400	10700
24	4	SABRE GL V240	OP	SF	AL	DV	IO	130-230		8		2300			7600	9200
24	4	SABRE GL V245	OP	SF	AL	DV	OB			8		3450			12600	14400
24	4	SABRE GL V245	OP	SF	AL	DV	IO	130-230		8		3450			9450	11200
24	4	SABRE V240 CB	OP	RNBT	AL	DV	OB			8		2100			8650	9900
24	4	SABRE V240 CB	OP	RNBT	AL	DV	IO	130-230		8		2100			6050	7350
24	4	SABRE V245 CB	OP	RNBT	AL	DV	OB			8		3250			12200	13900
24	4	SABRE V245 CB	OP	RNBT	AL	DV	IO	130-230		8		3250			7400	8850
24	4	SABRE V245 DAYCRUISR	OP	CBNCR	AL	DV	IO	130-230		8		3600			9950	11700
24	4	SABRE V245 MB DAYCRU	OP	CBNCR	AL	DV	IO	130-230		8		3900			10500	12300
29	3	RAMPAGE 295	OP	CTRCN	FBG	DV	IO	260-270		9	2				18700	20900
		1986 BOATS														
16		ANGLER C160		FSH	AL	RB	OB			6	6	760			2250	2600
16		CRUSADER 160		RNBT	AL	RB	OB			7	10	850			2500	2900
16		CRUSADER 165	OP	RNBT	FBG	SV	IO	120		7	2	2415			3450	4050
16		NORDIC 160		RNBT	AL	TR	OB			6	4	680			2000	2350
16	1	MIRAGE 160		RNBT	AL	SV	OB			6	6	1020			3000	3450
16	1	MIRAGE 165	OP	RNBT	AL	SV	IO	140		6	6	1860			2900	3350
16	3	COMMANDER 16		FSH	AL	RB	OB			5	8	285			825	995
16	3	COMMANDER II 16		FSH	AL	RB	OB			6	5	470			1400	1650
16	3	ENSIGN 16		FSH	AL	RB	OB			5	8	310			910	1100
16	3	FISH-HAWK 16		FSH	AL	RB	OB			5	8	500			1450	1750
16	3	MUSKIE PRO 16		FSH	AL	RB	OB			5	8	490			1450	1700
16	3	MUSKIE PRO 16XL		FSH	AL	RB	OB			6	3	1260			3600	4150
16	3	SUPER-HAWK 16		FSH	AL	RB	OB			6	5	625			1850	2200
16	4	APOLLO 660		RNBT	FBG	SV	OB			6	11	1050			3050	3550
17	1	ANGLER 170		FSH			OB			7	3	1295			3750	4350
17	2	VIKING 170			AL	SV	OB			6	4	740			2300	2700
17	3	CRUSADER 775	OP	RNBT	FBG	SV	IO	140		7	2	2500			3800	4400
17	3	PHANTOM 170			AL	SV	OB			6	5	1140			3400	3950
17	3	PHANTOM 175	OP	RNBT	AL	SV	IO	140		6	5	2010			3200	3700
17	3	PHANTOM-EAGLE			AL	SV	OB			6	5	1290			3750	4350
17	4	CRUSADER 170			FBG		OB			7	2	1250			3650	4250
18		CRUSADER 180		RNBT	FBG	SV	OB			7	2	1560			4450	5150
18		CRUSADER 185	OP	RNBT	FBG	SV	IO	170		7	2	2515			4000	4650
18		MUSKIE PRO 18			AL		OB			6	5	675			2200	2550
18		NORDIC 18		RNBT	FBG	SV	OB			6	10	1225			3700	4300
18		NORDIC 18	OP	RNBT	AL	SV	IO	120		6	10	1850			3300	3850

CONTINUED ON NEXT PAGE

```
LOA  NAME AND/        TOP/ BOAT  -HULL-  ----ENGINE---  BEAM   WGT  DRAFT RETAIL RETAIL
FT IN OR MODEL         RIG  TYPE MTL TP  TP # HP  MFG   FT IN  LBS  FT IN  LOW   HIGH
-------------------- 1986 BOATS ---------------------------------------------------------
18    VOYAGER 18            FSH  FBG RB OB              6  5   375        1250   1450
19    NORDIC 19             RNBT FBG SV OB              7  4  1380        4200   4850
20  2 CRUSADER 205     OP   CUD  FBG SV IO  170         7  7  2976        5650   6500
20  2 CRUSADER 205     OP   RNBT FBG SV IO  185         7  7  3000        5450   6250
20  2 RAMPAGE 205      OP   RNBT FBG SV IO  260         7  7  2925        5650   6500
20  2 SABRE 200             RNBT AL  SV OB              8     1620        5700   6500
20  4 SABRE 205             AL  SV IO  205             8     2660        5300   6100
20  4 SABRE-GREAT LAKES OP       AL  SV IO  205         8     2800        5450   6250
20  4 SABRE-GREAT-LAKES          AL  SV OB              8     1750        6000   6900
20  6 CRUSADER 2105     OP   RNBT FBG SV IO  170        8     3250        5950   6850
21  8 NORDIC 22         OP   RNBT AL  SV IO  140        7  8  2540        5350   6150
21  8 NORDIC 22 DAY CR  OP   RNBT AL  SV IO  170        7  8  2670        5800   6650

22  4 CRUSADER 2105          CUD  FBG SV IO  170        8     3350        7050   8100
22  4 SABRE 220              RNBT AL  SV OB             8     1650        6200   7100
22  4 SABRE 225              AL  SV IO  205             8     1850        5150   5900
22  4 SABRE MID BERTH        CR       SV IO  205         8     3700        7600   8750
22  4 SABRE-DAYCRUISER       CR       SV IO  205         8     3300        7050   8100
22  4 SABRE-GREAT LAKES      CR       SV IO  205         8     3100        6750   7800
22  4 SABRE-GREAT-LAKES      RNBT AL  SV OB             8     2050        7450   8550
24  4 SABRE 240              RNBT FBG RB OB             8     2100        8300   9550
24  4 SABRE 245              AL  SV IO  230             8     3200        7550   8700
24  4 SABRE DAYCRUISER       CR       SV IO  230         8     3600        8450   9700
24  4 SABRE MID BERTH        CR       SV IO  230         8     4000        9150  10400
24  4 SABRE-GREAT-LAKES           SV IO  230             8     2000        6250   7200

24  4 SABRE-GREAT-LAKES      RNBT AL  SV OB             8     2300        9050  10300
-------------------- 1985 BOATS ---------------------------------------------------------
16    CRUSADER 160       OP   RNBT AL  RB OB            7 10   850        2450   2800
16    CRUSADER 160 ANGLER OP  FSH  AL  RB OB            6  6   760        2200   2550
16    CRUSADER 165       OP   RNBT FBG SV IO  120       6  2  2415        3350   3850
16    EXPLORER 16        OP   BASS AL  RB OB            6  4   850        2400   2800
16  2 NORTHSTAR 16       OP   RNBT AL  DV OB            6  4   800        2300   2700
16  3 COMMANDER 16       OP   FSH  FBG RB OB            5  8   285         795    960
16  3 COMMANDER II       OP   FSH  AL  RB OB            6  5   470        1350   1600
16  3 FISH-HAWK 16       OP   BASS AL  RB OB            5  8   500        1400   1700
16  3 MUSKIE PRO         OP   FSH  AL     OB            5  8   490        1400   1650
16  3 MUSKIE PRO XL      OP   FSH  AL     OB            6  3  1260        3450   4050
16  3 SUPER-HAWK 16      OP   BASS AL  RB OB            6  5   625        1750   2100
16  4 APOLLO 660         OP   RNBT FBG SV OB            6 11  1050        2950   3450

17  3 CRUSADER 775       OP   RNBT FBG SV IO  140       7  2  2500        3650   4250
17  3 PHANTOM 170        OP        AL  SV IO            6  5  1140        3250   3800
17  3 PHANTOM 175        OP   RNBT AL  SV IO  140       6  5  2010        3050   3550
17  3 PHANTOM-EAGLE      OP        AL     IO            6  5  1290        3600   4200
17  4 CRUSADER 770       OP        FBG    OB            7  2  1250        3500   4100
18    CRUSADER 180       OP   RNBT FBG SV             7  2  1560        4300   4950
18    CRUSADER 180 ANGLER OP  FSH  FBG SV IO           7  5  1410        4000   4650
18    CRUSADER 185       OP   RNBT FBG SV IO  170       7  2  2515        3800   4450
18    MUSKIE PRO 18      OP        AL     OB            6  5   675        2100   2450
18    NORDIC 18          OP   RNBT AL  DV IO  120       6 10  1850        2300   3700
18    NORDIC 18          OP   RNBT FBG SV OB            6 10   675        3550   4150
18    VOYAGER 18         OP   FSH  FBG RB OB            6  5   375        1200   1400

19    NORDIC 19          OP   RNBT AL  DV IO  140       7  4  2015        3650   4250
19    NORDIC 19          OP   RNBT FBG SV OB            7  4  1380        4050   4750
20  2 CRUSADER 205 CUD   OP   CUD  FBG SV IO  170       7  7  2976        5400   6200
20  2 CRUSADER 205 OP BOW OP  CUD  FBG SV IO  185       7  7  3000        5450   6300
20  2 CRUSADER 205 RAMPAGE OP RNBT FBG SV IO  260       7  7  2925        5450   6250
20  6 CRUSADER 2105      OP   RNBT FBG SV IO  170       8     3250        5750   6600
21  8 NORDIC 22          OP        AL     OB            7  8  1670        5900   6800
21  8 NORDIC 22          OP   CR   AL  DV IO  170       7  8  2670        5550   6400
21  8 NORDIC 22          OP   RNBT AL  DV IO  140       7  8  2670        5250   6050
21  8 NORDIC 22          OP   RNBT FBG SV OB            7  8  1540        5550   6400
21  8 NORDIC 22 DAYCRUISER OP CUD  FBG SV OB            7  8  1670        5950   6850
22  4 CRUSADER 2105 WAC  OP   CUD  FBG SV IO  170       8     3350        6750   7750

23  7 NORSEMAN 24        OP   CR   AL     IO  170       8     3100        6850   7900
-------------------- 1984 BOATS ---------------------------------------------------------
16    CRUSADER 160       OP   RNBT AL  RB OB            7 10   850        2350   2750
16    CRUSADER 160 ANGLER OP  RNBT FBG SV OB            6  6   850        2350   2750
16    CRUSADER 165       OP   RNBT AL  RB OB  120-140   6 10        2850   3350
16    CRUSADER 185       OP   RNBT FBG SV IO  170-230   7  2        2950   3600
16  2 EXPLORER 16        OP   BASS AL  DV OB            7  2        2350   2750
16  2 NORTHSTAR 16       OP   FSH  AL  DV OB            6  4   850   2200   2550
16  2 NORTHSTAR 16 SF    OP   FSH  AL  DV OB            6  4   800   2250   2650
16  3 COMMANDER 11S      OP   FSH  AL  DV OB            6  4   800   1300   1550
16  3 COMMANDER 16       OP   FSH  AL  RB OB            5  8   470    775    935
16  3 COMMANDER II       OP   FSH  AL  RB OB            6  5   470   1300   1550
16  3 FISH-HAWK 16       OP   BASS AL  DV OB            5  8   500   1400   1650
16  3 SUPER-HAWK 16      OP   BASS AL  RB OB            6  5   625   1700   2050

16  4 APOLLO 660         OP   RNBT FBG SV OB            6 11  1050   2900   3350
17  3 CRUSADER 775 RAMPAGE OP RNBT FBG SV IO  170-200   7  2  2500   3550   4150
18    CRUSADER 180 ANGLER OP  RNBT FBG SV IO           7  5  1410   3900   4500
18    CRUSADER 180 ANGLER OP  RNBT FBG SV IO  170 MRCR  7  2  1560   3000   3450
18    FISH-HAWK 18       OP   BASS AL  DV OB            6  5   675   3450   4000
18    NORDIC 18 CLOSED BOW OP RNBT AL  DV SE  115  OMC  6 10  1850   4700   5400
18    NORDIC 18 CLOSED BOW OP RNBT AL  DV IO  120-140   6 10  1850   3050   3550
18    NORDIC 18 CLOSED BOW OP RNBT AL  DV OB            6 10  1225   3450   4000
18    NORDIC 18 OPEN BOW OP   RNBT AL  DV SE  115  OMC  6 10  1850   4700   5400
18    NORDIC 18 OPEN BOW OP   RNBT AL  DV IO  120-140   6 10  1850   3050   3550

18    NORDIC 18 SF       OP   FSH  AL  DV SE            6 10  1150   3250   3800
18    NORDIC 18 SF       OP   FSH  AL  DV SE  115  OMC  6 10  1850   4650   5350
18    NORDIC 18 SF       OP   FSH  AL  DV IO  120-140   6 10  1850   3250   3800
18    VOYAGER 18         OP   FSH  AL  RB OB            7  4   375   1150   1400
19    NORDIC 19 CLOSED BOW OP RNBT AL  DV IO           7  4  1350   3900   4500
19    NORDIC 19 CLOSED BOW OP RNBT AL  DV SE  115  OMC  7  4  2015   5050   5850
19    NORDIC 19 CLOSED BOW OP RNBT AL  DV IO  140-200   7  4  2015   3950   4600
19    NORDIC 19 OPEN BOW OP   RNBT AL  DV OB            7  4  1380   3600   4150
19    NORDIC 19 OPEN BOW OP   RNBT AL  DV SE  115  OMC  7  4  2100   5200   5950
19    NORDIC 19 OPEN BOW OP   RNBT AL  DV IO  140-200   7  4  2100   3600   4250
19    NORDIC 19 SF       OP   FSH  AL  DV OB            7  4  1380   3950   4600
19    NORDIC 19 SF       OP   FSH  AL  DV SE  115  OMC  7  4  2045   5100   5850

19    NORDIC 19 SF       OP   FSH  AL  DV IO  140-200   7  4  2045   3850   4550
20  2 CRUSADER 205       OP   CUD  FBG SV SE  115  OMC  7  2  2784   7250   8350
20  2 CRUSADER 205       OP   CUD  FBG SV IO  185-260   7  2  2784   5050   6100
20  2 CRUSADER 205 RAMPAGE OP CUD  FBG SV SE  115  OMC  7  2       **     **
20  2 CRUSADER 205 RAMPAGE OP CUD  FBG SV SE  155  OMC  7  2       5250   6350
20  2 CRUSADER 205 RAMPAGE OP CUD  FBG SV IO  185-260   7  2  2976  8050   9250
20  6 CRUSADER 2105      OP   CUD  FBG SV SE  115-155   8     3350  5950   7150
20  6 CRUSADER 2105      OP   CUD  FBG SV IO  185-260   8     3350  5750   6650
21  8 NORDIC 22 CLOSED BOW OP RNBT AL  DV OB            7  8  1670  8050   9250
21  8 NORDIC 22 CLOSED BOW OP RNBT AL  DV IO  170-200   7  8  2540  4950   5750

21  8 NORDIC 22 DAYCRUISER OP CUD  AL  DV OB            7  8       6900   7950
21  8 NORDIC 22 DAYCRUISER OP CUD  AL  DV SE           7  8       **     **
21  8 NORDIC 22 DAYCRUISER OP CUD  AL  DV IO  170-198   7  8  2540  6200   7200
21  8 NORDIC 22 OPEN BOW OP   CUD  AL  DV OB            7  8       8000   9200
21  8 NORDIC 22 OPEN BOW OP   CUD  AL  DV SE  155  OMC  7  8       7850   9050
21  8 NORDIC 22 OPEN BOW OP   CUD  AL  DV IO  170-200   7  8  2670  5050   5850
21  8 NORDIC 22 SF       OP   FSH  AL  DV OB            7  8  2670  5750   6600
21  8 NORDIC 22 SF       OP   FSH  AL  DV SE           7  8       **     **
21  8 NORDIC 22 SF       OP   FSH  AL  DV SE  155  OMC  7  8       6400   7400
21  8 NORDIC 22 SF       OP   FSH  AL  DV IO  170-200   7  8  1670  5750   6650
21  8 TRIDENT NORDIC 22  OP   CUD  AL  DV OB            7  8       8800  10000
21  8 TRIDENT NORDIC 22  OP   CUD  AL  DV SE  155  OMC  7  8  2670  5650   6550
21  8 TRIDENT NORDIC 22  OP   CUD  AL  DV IO  170-200   7  8

22  4 CRUSADER 2105 WAC  OP   CUD  FBG SV SE  115-155   8     3200  9750  11100
22  4 CRUSADER 2105 WAC  OP   CUD  FBG SV IO  185-260   8     3200  6350   7600
```

....For earlier years, see the BUC Used Boat Price Guide, Volume 3

CRITCHFIELD MARINE INC

```
LOA  NAME AND/         TOP/ BOAT  -HULL-  ----ENGINE---  BEAM   WGT  DRAFT RETAIL RETAIL
FT IN OR MODEL          RIG  TYPE MTL TP  TP # HP  MFG   FT IN  LBS  FT IN  LOW   HIGH
-------------------- 1995 BOATS ---------------------------------------------------------
16  4 CCV 164           OP   CTRCN FBG DV OB           6  3   700        1700   2050
16  4 VBR 164           OP   B/R  FBG SV OB            6  3   825        2000   2400
16 10 CONTENDER CXR 170 OP   RNBT FBG SV OB            7  2   900        2050   2450
16 11 CCMV 1700         OP   CTRCN FBG DV OB           7  2   850        2250   2650
16 11 CCV 1700          OP   CCV  FBG DV OB            7  2   850        2250   2600
16 11 DSCMV 1700        OP   FSH  FBG DV OB            7  2   875        2000   2400
16 11 SCMV 1700         OP   FSH  FBG DV OB            7  2   850        2300   2700
17 11 VBR 180           OP   B/R  FBG SV OB            6  6   895        2450   2850
18    CCV 1800          OP   CTRCN FBG DV OB           7     950        2450   2850
18    DSCV 1800         OP   W/T  FBG DV OB            7     950        2450   2850
```

LOA FT	LOA IN	NAME AND/ OR MODEL	TOP/ RIG	BOAT TYPE	-HULL- MTL	-HULL- TP	ENGINE TP	ENGINE # HP	ENGINE MFG	BEAM FT	BEAM IN	WGT LBS	DRAFT FT	DRAFT IN	RETAIL LOW	RETAIL HIGH
		1994 BOATS														
16	4	VBR 164	OP	B/R	FBG	SV	OB			6	3	825			1900	2300
16	10	CONTENDER CXR 170	OP	RNBT	FBG	SV	OB			7	2	825			1950	2350
16	11	CCMV 1700	OP	CTRCN	FBG	SV	OB			7	2	900			2150	2550
16	11	CCV 1700	OP	CTRCN	FBG	DV	OB			7	2	850			2150	2500
16	11	DSCMV 1700	OP	FSH	FBG	SV	OB			7	2	875			2050	2450
16	11	SCMV 1700	OP	FSH	FBG	SV	OB			7	2	850			1900	2300
17	11	VBR 180	OP	B/R	FBG	SV	OB			6	6	895			2250	2600
18		CCV 1800	OP	CTRCN	FBG	DV	OB			7		950			2350	2700
		1993 BOATS														
16	4	VBR 164	OP	B/R	FBG	SV	OB			6	3	825			1850	2200
16	10	CONTENDER CXR 170	OP	RNBT	FBG	SV	OB			7	2	825			1850	2250
16	11	CCMV 1700	OP	CTRCN	FBG	SV	OB			7	2	900			2050	2400
16	11	CCV 1700	OP	CTRCN	FBG	DV	OB			7	2	850			2000	2400
16	11	DSCMV 1700	OP	FSH	FBG	SV	OB			7	2	875			2000	2350
16	11	SCMV 1700	OP	FSH	FBG	SV	OB			7	2	850			1850	2200
17	11	VBR 180	OP	B/R	FBG	SV	OB			6	6	895			2150	2500
18		CCV 1800	OP	CTRCN	FBG	DV	OB			7		950			2250	2650
		1992 BOATS														
16	4	VBR 164	OP	B/R	FBG	SV	OB			6	3	825			1750	2100
16	10	CXR 170	OP	RNBT	FBG	SV	OB			7	2	825			1800	2150
16	11	CCMV 1700	OP	CTRCN	FBG	SV	OB			7	2	900			1950	2350
16	11	CCV 1700	OP	CTRCN	FBG	DV	OB			7	2	850			1950	2300
16	11	SCMV 1700	OP	CTRCN	FBG	SV	OB			7	2	850			1750	2100
17	11	VBR 180	OP	B/R	FBG	SV	OB			6	6	895			2000	2400
18		CCV 1800	OP	CTRCN	FBG	DV	OB			7		950			2200	2550

....For earlier years, see the BUC Used Boat Price Guide, Volume 3

CRON HOUSEBOAT CO

GALLATIN TN 37066 COAST GUARD MFG ID- CRH See inside cover to adjust price for area

LOA FT	LOA IN	NAME AND/ OR MODEL	TOP/ RIG	BOAT TYPE	-HULL- MTL	-HULL- TP	ENGINE TP	ENGINE # HP	ENGINE MFG	BEAM FT	BEAM IN	WGT LBS	DRAFT FT	DRAFT IN	RETAIL LOW	RETAIL HIGH
		1996 BOATS														
38		LEISURE CRAFT		HB	AL	SV		150D		12		12000	1	8	34200	38000
42		LEISURE TRAWLER		HB	AL	SV				13		20000	2		39400	43800
44		LEISURE CRAFT		HB	AL	SV		250D		13		16000	2		36200	40300
44		LEISURE TUG	FB	HB	AL	SV				13		22000	2		42600	47300
50		CLIPPER		HB	AL	SV		250D		13	6	22000	2		47500	52200
		1995 BOATS														
38		LEISURE CRAFT		HB	AL	SV		150D		12		12000	1	8	31900	35400
42		LEISURE TRAWLER		HB	AL	SV				13		20000	2		36500	40600
44		LEISURE CRAFT		HB	AL	SV		250D		13		16000	2		33800	37500
44		LEISURE TUG	FB	HB	AL	SV				13		22000	2		39400	43800
50		CLIPPER		HB	AL	SV		250D		13	6	22000	2		43400	48200
		1994 BOATS														
38		LEISURE CRAFT		HB	AL	SV		150D		12		12000	1	8	29800	33100
42		LEISURE TRAWLER		HB	AL	SV				13		20000	2		34100	37900
44		LEISURE CRAFT		HB	AL	SV		250D		13		16000	2		31600	35200
44		LEISURE TUG	FB	HB	AL	SV				13		22000	2		36800	40900
50		CLIPPER		HB	AL	SV		250D		13	6	22000	2		40500	45000
		1993 BOATS														
38		LEISURE CRAFT		HB	AL	SV		150D		12		12000	1	8	28000	31100
42		LEISURE TRAWLER		HB	AL	SV				13		20000	2		32100	35600
44		LEISURE CRAFT		HB	AL	SV		250D		13		16000	2		29800	33200
44		LEISURE TUG	FB	HB	AL	SV				13		22000	2		34700	38600
50		CLIPPER		HB	AL	SV		250D		13	6	22000	2		38200	42500
		1992 BOATS														
38		LEISURE CRAFT		HB	AL	SV		150D		12		12000	1	8	26500	29400
42		LEISURE TRAWLER		HB	AL	SV				13		20000	2		30300	33700
44		LEISURE CRAFT		HB	AL	SV		250D		13		16000	2		28300	31500
44		LEISURE TUG	FB	HB	AL	SV				13		22000	2		33000	36600
50		CLIPPER		HB	AL	SV		250D		13	6	22000	2		36100	40200
		1986 BOATS														
38		LEISURE-CRAFT	HT	HB	AL	FL	OB			11		9000		10	16700	19000
38		LEISURE-CRAFT	HT	HB	AL	FL	IO	140		11		12000		10	23000	25600
52		LEISURE-CRAFT	HT	HB	AL	SV	IO	225		14		24000			40900	45500
		1985 BOATS														
38		LEISURE-CRAFT	HT	HB	STL	FL	OB			11		8900			13800	15700
38		LEISURE-CRAFT	HT	HB	STL	FL	IO	140		11		12000			19900	22100
52		LEISURE-CRAFT	HT	HB	STL	SV	IO	225		14		24000			36600	40600
		1984 BOATS														
38		LEISURE-CRAFT	HT	HB	STL	FL	OB			11		8900		10	13500	15300
40		LEISURE-CRAFT	HT	HB	STL	FL	IO			13		16000	1	4	21600	24000
52		LEISURE-CRAFT	HT	HB	STL	SV	IO	225		14		24000			35800	39700

....For earlier years, see the BUC Used Boat Price Guide, Volume 3

CROSBY YACHT YARD INC

OSTERVILLE MA 02655 COAST GUARD MFG ID- CRY See inside cover to adjust price for area

For more recent years, see the BUC Used Boat Price Guide, Volume 1

LOA FT	LOA IN	NAME AND/ OR MODEL	TOP/ RIG	BOAT TYPE	-HULL- MTL	-HULL- TP	ENGINE TP	ENGINE # HP	ENGINE MFG	BEAM FT	BEAM IN	WGT LBS	DRAFT FT	DRAFT IN	RETAIL LOW	RETAIL HIGH
		1996 BOATS														
21	6	YACHT CLUB LAUNCH		LNCH	FBG	DS	IB	50D	YAN	10		10000	2	9	30800	34200
24		CROSBY STRIPER		CBNCR	FBG	SV	IB	142	MPC	8	9	5200	2	2	30000	33300
26	6	CRUISING TUG	EPH	TUG	FBG	DS	IB	50D	YAN	10	4	12500	3		106000	116500
29	11	CANYON 30		SF	FBG	DV	IB	T320	CRUS	11	6	14000	2	9	106000	116500
29	11	HAWK 29		SPTCR	FBG	DV	IB	T320	CRUS	11	6	13000	2	9	103000	113000
38		TUG 38	EPH	TUG	FBG	DS	IB	150D	CUM	14		22000	4	4	211500	232000
		1995 BOATS														
21	6	YACHT CLUB LAUNCH		LNCH	FBG	DS	IB	50D	CUM	10		10000	2	9	**	**
24		CROSBY STRIPER		CBNCR	FBG	SV	IB	240	CHRY	8	9	5200	2	2	28700	31900
26	6	CRUISING TUG	EPH	TUG	FBG	DS	IB	50D	CUM	10	4	12500	3		100500	110500
29	11	CANYON 30		SF	FBG	DV	IB	T320	CRUS	11	6	14000	2	9	100500	110000
29	11	HAWK 29		SPTCR	FBG	DV	IB	T320	CRUS	11	6	13000	2	9	97400	107000
38		TUG 38	EPH	TUG	FBG	DS	IB	150D	CUM	14		22000	4	4	202500	222500
		1994 BOATS														
24		CROSBY STRIPER		CBNCR	FBG	SV	IB	240	CHRY	8	9	5200	2	2	27100	30100
26	6	CRUISING TUG	EPH	TUG	FBG	DS	IB	50D	CUM	10	4	12500	3		95700	105000
29	11	CANYON 30		SF	FBG	DV	IB	T250D	CUM	11	6	14000	2	9	128000	140500
29	11	HAWK 29		SPTCR	FBG	DV	IB	T502	CRUS	11	6	13000	2	9	103500	114000
38		TUG 38	EPH	TUG	FBG	DS	IB	150D	CUM	14		22000	4	4	194000	213000
		1993 BOATS														
21	6	HARBOR TUG	EPH	TUG	FBG	DS	IB	50D	CUM	10		10000	2	9	**	**
24		CROSBY STRIPER		CBNCR	FBG	SV	IB	240	CHRY	8	9	5200	2	2	25700	28600
26	6	CRUISING TUG	EPH	TUG	FBG	DS	IB	50D	CUM	10	4	12500	3		91200	100000
29	11	CANYON 30		SF	FBG	DV	IB	T300D	CUM	11	6	14000	2	9	127000	139500
29	11	HAWK 29		SPTCR	FBG	DV	IB	T502	CRUS	11	6	13000	2	9	98200	108000
38		TUG 38	EPH	TUG	FBG	DS	IB	150D	CUM	14		22000	4	4	184500	203000
		1992 BOATS														
21	6	TUG TENDER	HT	PH	FBG	DS	IB	66D	YAN	10			2	9	44100	49000
21	6	YACHT CLUB LAUNCH	OP	LNCH	FBG	DS	IB	47D	YAN	10			2	9	25200	28000
24		STRIPER	OP	CTRCN	FBG	DS	IB	250	CHRY	8	9	5200	2	2	24500	27200
24		STRIPER	ST	CUD	FBG	DS	IB	250	CHRY	8	9	5200	2	2	24500	27200
24		STRIPER	ST	CUD	FBG	DS	IB	150D-200D		8	9	5200	2	2	30400	35100
24		STRIPER	ST	CUD	FBG	SD	OB			8	9	5200	2	2	14400	16300
24		STRIPER 24	ST	CUD	FBG	DS	IB	200D	VLVO	8	9	5200	2	2	31600	35100
25		WIANNO SENIOR	GAF	SAIL	FBG	KC				8			2	6	25400	28200
26	6	HARBOR TUG	HT	PH	FBG	DS	IB	66D	YAN	10	4		3		64000	70300
26	6	TOUR TUG	HT	PH	FBG	DS	IB	47D	YAN	10	4		3		63500	69800
26	6	TUG TENDER	HT	PH	FBG	DS	IB	66D	YAN	10	4	10000	3		57400	63100
26	6	TUG TRAWLER	HT	TRWL	FBG	DS	IB	66D	YAN	10	4	10000	3		57400	63100
26	6	YACHT CLUB LAUNCH	OP	LNCH	FBG	DS	IB	47D	YAN	10	4	10000	3		40300	44800
29	4	CANYON 30	ST	CUD	FBG	SV	IB	T300D	CAT	11	5	12000	2	3	114500	125500
29	4	CANYON 30	ST	SF	FBG	SV	IB	T360	CRUS	11	5	12000	2	3	76600	84200
29	4	CANYON 30	ST	SF	FBG	SV	IB	T210D-T300D		11	5	12000	2	3	102000	122500
29	4	HAWK 29	ST	CUD	FBG	SV	IB	T360	CRUS	11	5	12000	2	3	76700	84300
29	4	HAWK 29	ST	CUD	FBG	SV	IB	T210D-T300D		11	5	12000	2	3	102000	122500
38	3	CRUISING TUG	HT	TUG	FBG	DS	IB	110D	CUM	14		14000	4	4	**	**
38	3	TOUR TUG	HT	TUG	FBG	DS	IB	110D	CUM	14		14000	4	4	**	**
		1991 BOATS														
21	6	TUG TENDER	HT	PH	FBG	DS	IB	66D	YAN	10			2	9	42100	46800
21	6	YACHT CLUB LAUNCH	OP	LNCH	FBG	DS	IB	47D	YAN	10			2	9	24000	26700
24		STRIPER		CR	FBG	SV	IB	250	CHRY	8	9	5200	2	2	23300	25900
24		STRIPER	OP	CR	FBG	SV	OB			8	9	5200	2	2	13800	15700
24		STRIPER	OP	CR	FBG	SV	IB	150D	VLVO	8	9	5200	2	2	29000	32300
24		STRIPER EXPRESS	OP	CTRCN	FBG	SV	IB	250	CHRY	8	9	5200	2	2	23300	25900
25	9	WIANNO SENIOR	GAF	SAIL	FBG	KC				8			2	6	28300	31500
26	6	HARBOR TUG		PH	FBG	DS	IB	66D	YAN	10	4		3		61100	67100
26	6	TOUR TUG		LNCH	FBG	DS	IB	47D	YAN	10	4		3		41300	45900
26	6	TUG TENDER	HT	PH	FBG	DS	IB	66D	YAN	10	4	11000	3		60500	66500
26	6	TUG TRAWLER	HT	TRWL	FBG	DS	IB	66D	YAN	10	4	11000	3		60500	66500
26	6	YACHT CLUB LAUNCH	OP	LNCH	FBG	DS	IB	47D	YAN	10	4	11000	3		41100	45600
29	6	CANYON 30		SF	FBG	SV	IB	T360	CRUS	11	5	12000	3		76500	84100
29	6	CANYON 30		SF	FBG	SV	IB	T210D-T300D		11	5	12000	3		97200	115000
29	6	HAWK 29		CUD	FBG	SV	IB	T360	CRUS	11	5	12000	3		76600	84200
29	6	HAWK 29		CUD	FBG	SV	IB	T210D-T300D		11	5	12000	3		97400	115500
29	6	TOMAHAWK 1		CTRCN	FBG	SV	OB			11	5	12000	3		20800	23100
38	3	CROSBY 38		PH	FBG	DS	IB	110D	CUM	14		15800	4	4	119000	131000

 CONTINUED ON NEXT PAGE

LOA FT	LOA IN	NAME AND/ OR MODEL	TOP/ RIG	BOAT TYPE	HULL MTL	HULL TP	ENGINE TP	# HP	ENGINE MFG	BEAM FT	BEAM IN	WGT LBS	DRAFT FT	DRAFT IN	RETAIL LOW	RETAIL HIGH
		1990 BOATS														
21	6	TUG TENDER		TRWL	FBG	DS	IO	50D	PERK	10			2	9	30600	34000
21	6	YACHT CLUB LAUNCH		LNCH	FBG	DS	IO	50D	PERK	10			2	9	16700	18900
24		CROSBY STRIPER	ST	CR	FBG	SV	IB	250	CHRY	8	9	5200	2	2	22200	24600
25		WIANNO SENIOR	SLP	SAIL	FBG	KC				8			2	6	22200	24600
26		TUG TENDER		TRWL	FBG	DS	IO	75D	PERK			11000			43700	48600
26	6	TRAWLER-YACHT		TRWL	FBG	DS	IO	50D	PERK	10	4	11000	3		43700	48600
26	6	YACHT CLUB LAUNCH		LNCH	FBG	DS	IO	75D	PERK	10	4	11000	3		28900	32100
29	4	CANYON 30		SF	FBG	SV	IO	T320-T360		11	5	12000	2	3	62000	70500
29	4	CANYON 30		SF	FBG	SV	IO	T210D	PEN	11	5	12000	2	3	87600	96300
29	4	HAWK 29		CUD	FBG	SV	IO	T210D-T300D		11	5	12000	2	9	69700	83400
38		TUG CROSBY 38		TRWL	FBG	DS	IO	110D	CUM	14			4	4	116500	128000
		1986 BOATS														
21	6	TUGBOAT	HT	PH	FBG	DS	IB	50D- 52D		10		8000	2	9	28600	31800
21	6	YACHT CLUB LAUNCH	OP	LNCH	FBG	DS	IB	46D- 52D		10		7740	2	9	19300	22100
24		CROSBY-STRIPER	OP	CTRCN	FBG	SV	IB	215	EVIN	8	9	5200	2	2	**	**
24		CROSBY-STRIPER	OP	CUD	FBG	SV	OB			8	9	5200	2	2	11700	13200
24		CROSBY-STRIPER	OP	CUD	FBG	SV	IB	215	CHRY	8	9	5200	2	2	**	**
25		WIANNO SR	SLP	SAIL	FBG	CB	OB			8			4		18300	20300
26	6	CRUISING TUGBOAT	HT	TRWL	FBG	DS	IB	200D	PERK	10	4	11000	3		56600	62200
26	6	YACHT CLUB LAUNCH	OP	LNCH	FBG	DS	IB	50D	PERK	10	4	11000	3		33400	37200
29	4	CANYON 30	ST	SF	FBG	SV	IB	350D	PERK	11	5	9500	2	9	63600	69900
29	4	CANYON 30	ST	SF	FBG	SV	IB	T200D	PERK	11	5	12000	2	3	77400	85100
29	4	HAWK 29	ST	CUD	FBG	SV	IB	T200D	PERK	11	5	12000	2	3	77700	85300
		1985 BOATS														
21	6	HARBOR TUG	HT	PH	FBG	DS	IB	51D- 52D		10		8000	2	9	27500	30600
21	6	YACHT-CLUB LAUNCH	OP	LNCH	FBG	DS	IB	51D- 52D		10		8000	2	9	19100	21300
24		CROSBY-STRIPER	OP	CUD	FBG	SV	OB			8	9	5200	2	2	11300	12900
24		CROSBY-STRIPER	OP	CUD	FBG	SV	IB	165-235		8	9	5200	2	2	**	**
24		CROSBY-STRIPER	OP	CUD	FBG	SV	IB	100D-125D		8	9	5200	2	2	**	**
24		CROSBY-STRIPER	HT	CUD	FBG	SV	IB	125D	VLVO	8	9	5200	2	2	**	**
26	6	CRUISING TUG BOAT	HT	PH	FBG	DS	IB	50D	WEST	10	4	11000	3		46700	51300
26	6	EASTERN-RIG	HT	TRWL	FBG	DS	IB	51D	PERK	10	4	11000	3		46900	51600
26	6	HARBOR TUG	HT	PH	FBG	DS	IB	51D	PERK	10	4	11000	3		46900	51600
26	6	TOUR TUG LAUNCH	OP	PH	FBG	DS	IB	50D	WEST	10	4		3		47100	51800
26	6	YACHT-CLUB LAUNCH	OP	LNCH	FBG	DS	IB	50D- 51D		10	4	11000	3		31800	35700
29	4	CANYON 30	OP	SF	FBG	SV	OB			11	5	12000	2	9	16600	18800
29	4	CANYON 30	OP	SF	FBG	SV	IB	350D	PERK	11	5	12000	2	9	71500	78600
29	4	CANYON 30	OP	SF	FBG	SV	IB	T340	MRCR	11	5	12000	2	3	53700	59000
29	4	CANYON 30	OP	SF	FBG	SV	IB	T200D	PERK	11	5	12000	2	3	74300	81600
29	4	HAWK 29	ST	CUD	FBG	SV	OB			11	5	12000	2	9	17100	19400
29	4	HAWK 29	ST	CUD	FBG	SV	IB	350D	PERK	11	4		2	9	52600	57800
29	4	HAWK 29	ST	CUD	FBG	SV	IB	T340	MRCR	11	5	12000	2	9	53700	59100
29	4	HAWK 29	ST	CUD	FBG	SV	IB	T200D	PERK	11	5	12000	2	9	74500	81900
29	4	TOMAHAWK	OP	CTRCN	FBG	SV	OB			11	4	12000	2	9	16600	18800
29	4	TOMAHAWK	OP	CTRCN	FBG	SV	IB	350D	PERK	11	4	12000	2	9	72000	79200
		1984 BOATS														
21	6	TUG BOAT	HT	PH	FBG	DS	IB	50D- 52D		10		8000	2	9	26400	29300
21	6	YACHT-CLUB LAUNCH	OP	LNCH	FBG	DS	IB	50D- 52D		10		7740	2	9	18500	20600
24		CROSBY-STRIPER	OP	CUD	FBG	SV	IB	170-235		8	9	5200	2	2	**	**
24		CROSBY-STRIPER	OP	CUD	FBG	SV	IB	100D	WEST	8	9	5200	2	2	**	**
24		CROSBY-STRIPER	HT	CUD	FBG	SV	IB	125D	VLVO	8	9	5200	2	2	**	**
26	6	CRUISING TUG BOAT	HT	TRWL	FBG	DS	IB	50D	WEST	10	4	11000	3		44300	49200
26	6	EASTERN-RIG	HT	TRWL	FBG	DS	IB	50D	PERK	10	4	11000	3		44500	49500
26	6	TOUR TUG LAUNCH	OP	PH	FBG	DS	IB	50D	PERK	10	4		3		44900	49900
26	6	YACHT-CLUB LAUNCH	OP	LNCH	FBG	DS	IB	50D		10	4	11000	3		30800	34200
29	4	CANYON 30	OP	SF	FBG	SV	IB	300D-350D		11	5	12000	2	9	66700	75400
29	4	CANYON 30	OP	SF	FBG	SV	IB	T340	MRCR	11	5	12000	2	3	51300	56400
29	4	CANYON 30	OP	SF	FBG	SV	IB	T200D	PERK	11	5	12000	2	3	71300	78300
29	4	HAWK 29	ST	CUD	FBG	SV	IB	300D-350D		11	5	12000	2	9	67300	76000
29	4	HAWK 29	ST	CUD	FBG	SV	IB	T340	MRCR	11	5	12000	2	9	51400	56400
29	4	HAWK 29	ST	CUD	FBG	SV	IB	T200D	PERK	11	5	12000	2	9	71500	78600
29	4	HAWK 29	OP	RNBT	FBG	SV	IB	350D	PERK	11	4	12000	2	9	67700	74400

....For earlier years, see the BUC Used Boat Price Guide, Volume 3

CROWNLINE BOATS INC

WEST FRANKFORT IL 62896 COAST GUARD MFG ID- JTC See inside cover to adjust price for area

For more recent years, see the BUC Used Boat Price Guide, Volume 1

LOA FT	LOA IN	NAME AND/ OR MODEL	TOP/ RIG	BOAT TYPE	HULL MTL	HULL TP	ENGINE TP	# HP	ENGINE MFG	BEAM FT	BEAM IN	WGT LBS	DRAFT FT	DRAFT IN	RETAIL LOW	RETAIL HIGH
		1996 BOATS														
17	6	CROWNLINE 176 BR	OP	RNBT	FBG	SV	IO	135	MRCR	7	6	1900	2	11	5100	5850
18	2	CROWNLINE 182 BR	OP	RNBT	FBG	SV	IO	135-180		8		2700	2	3	6550	7550
20		CROWNLINE 200 DB	OP	RNBT	FBG	SV	IO	180-210		8	6	3300	2	4	9700	11100
20	2	CROWNLINE 202 BR	OP	RNBT	FBG	SV	IO	210-250		8	6	3100	2	6	9500	11100
21		CROWNLINE 210 CCR	OP	CUD	FBG	SV	IO	210-300		8	6	3900	2	8	12100	14900
22	5	CROWNLINE 225 BR	OP	RNBT	FBG	SV	IO	250-300		8	6	3500	2	8	11600	14000
22	5	CROWNLINE 225 CCR	OP	CUD	FBG	SV	IO	250-300		8	6	3900	2	8	13200	15900
25		CROWNLINE 250 CR	OP	SPTCR	FBG	SV	IO	250-300		8	6	5600	3		19600	22700
26	6	CROWNLINE 266 BR	OP	RNBT	FBG	DV	IO	250-300		8	6	4400	3		16700	20000
26	6	CROWNLINE 266 CCR	OP	CUD	FBG	DV	IO	300	MRCR	8	6	4500	3		19600	21800
26	6	CROWNLINE 266 CCR	OP	CUD	FBG	DV	IO	415	MRCR	8	6	4500	3		23200	25800
		1995 BOATS														
17	6	CROWNLINE 176 BR	OP	RNBT	FBG	SV	IO	135	MRCR	7	6	1900	2	11	4750	5450
18	2	CROWNLINE 182 BR	OP	RNBT	FBG	SV	IO	135-190		8		2700	2	3	6100	7100
20		CROWNLINE 200 DB	OP	RNBT	FBG	SV	IO	190-235		8	6	3300	2	4	9100	10600
20	2	CROWNLINE 202 BR	OP	RNBT	FBG	SV	IO	205-250		8	6	3100	2	6	8900	10400
21		CROWNLINE 210 CCR	OP	CUD	FBG	SV	IO	205-300		8	6	3900	2	8	11200	13900
22	5	CROWNLINE 225 BR	OP	RNBT	FBG	SV	IO	235-300		8	6	3500	2	8	10700	13000
22	5	CROWNLINE 225 CCR	OP	CUD	FBG	SV	IO	235-300		8	6	3900	2	8	12200	14800
25		CROWNLINE 250 CR	OP	SPTCR	FBG	SV	IO	235-300		8	6	5600	3		18300	21200
26	6	CROWNLINE 266 BR	OP	RNBT	FBG	DV	IO	250-300		8	6	4400	3		15600	18600
26	6	CROWNLINE 266 CCR	OP	CUD	FBG	DV	IO	300	MRCR	8	6	4500	3		18500	20600
26	6	CROWNLINE 266 CCR	OP	CUD	FBG	DV	IO	415	MRCR	8	6	4500	3		21600	24000
		1994 BOATS														
17	6	176 BR	OP	RNBT	FBG	SV	IO	115-135		7	6	1900	2	11	4450	5100
18	2	182 BR	OP	RNBT	FBG	SV	IO	135-190		8		2700	2	3	5700	6600
18	2	182 CD	OP	RNBT	FBG	SV	IO	135-190		7	8	2500	2	3	5300	6200
19	6	196 BR	OP	RNBT	FBG	SV	IO	190-235		8	6	2900	2	6	6650	7850
20		200 DB	OP	RNBT	FBG	SV	IO	190-235		8	6	3300	2	4	8400	9900
21		210 CCR	OP	CUD	FBG	SV	IO	205-300		8	6	3900	2	8	10500	13000
22	5	225 BR	OP	RNBT	FBG	SV	IO	235-300		8	6	3500	2	8	10000	12200
22	5	225 CCR	OP	CUD	FBG	SV	IO	235-300		8	6	3900	2	8	11400	13800
25		250 CR	OP	SPTCR	FBG	SV	IO	235-300		8	6	5600	3		16700	20000
26	6	266 BR	OP	RNBT	FBG	DV	IO	235-300		8	6	4400	3		14300	17400
26	6	266 CCR	OP	CUD	FBG	DV	IO	300	MRCR	8	6	4500	3		16900	19200
26	6	266 CCR	OP	CUD	FBG	DV	IO	T250	MRCR	8	6	4500	3		19400	21500
		1993 BOATS														
18	2	182 BR	OP	RNBT	FBG	SV	IO	115-180		7	8	2500	2	3	4950	5750
18	2	182 CD	OP	RNBT	FBG	SV	IO	180-205		7	8	2500	2	3	5000	5850
19	6	196 BR	OP	RNBT	FBG	SV	IO	205-250		8	6	2900	2	6	6250	7450
20		200 DB	OP	RNBT	FBG	SV	IO	180-205		8	6	3000	2	4	7400	8600
21		210 CCR	OP	CUD	FBG	SV	IO	205-300		8	6	3900	2	8	9800	12100
22	5	225 BR	OP	RNBT	FBG	SV	IO	235-300		8	6	3500	2	8	9400	11400
22	5	225 CCR	OP	CUD	FBG	SV	IO	235-300		8	6	3900	2	8	10600	12900
25		250 CR	OP	SPTCR	FBG	SV	IO	235-300		8	6	5100	3		14600	17500

CRUISERS YACHTS

DIV OF KCS INTERNATIONAL INC See inside cover to adjust price for area
OCONTO WI 54153 COAST GUARD MFG ID- CRS

For more recent years, see the BUC Used Boat Price Guide, Volume 1

LOA FT	LOA IN	NAME AND/ OR MODEL	TOP/ RIG	BOAT TYPE	HULL MTL	HULL TP	ENGINE TP	# HP	ENGINE MFG	BEAM FT	BEAM IN	WGT LBS	DRAFT FT	DRAFT IN	RETAIL LOW	RETAIL HIGH
		1996 BOATS														
25	8	ARIA 2420	ST	CUD	FBG	DV	IO	250-300		8	6	5500	2	9	19200	22700
25	8	ROGUE 2470	ST	CR	FBG	DV	IO	250-300		8	6	5700	2	9	19600	23200
27	7	ROGUE 2670	ST	CR	FBG	DV	IO	300-330		9	6	6100	3	5	22400	26000
27	7	ROGUE 2670	ST	CR	FBG	DV	IO	216D	VLVO	9	6	6400	3	5	26700	29700
27	7	ROGUE 2670	ST	CR	FBG	DV	IO	T205		9	6	6100	3	5	23200	26300
30	8	ROGUE 3175	OP	CR	FBG	DV	IO	T250-T330		10	6	9800	3		39800	48200
30	8	ROGUE 3175	OP	CR	FBG	DV	IO	T216D	VLVO	10	6	9800	3		46800	51400
32	8	ARIA 3120	OP	SPTCR	FBG	DV	IO	T250-T300		10	6	8800	3		37200	43200
32	8	ARIA 3120	OP	SPTCR	FBG	DV	IO	T216D	VLVO	10	6	9800	3		49400	54300
32	8	ARIA 3120	ST	SPTCR	FBG	DV	IO	T250-T330		10	6	8800	3		37200	44300
32	10	ROGUE 3375	OP	CR	FBG	DV	IO	T250		11	8	16000	3		59400	65500
		IO T265 VLVO 60100 66000, VD T265 CRUS 69400 76300, IO T300													61000	67300
		VD T320 CRUS 71200 78300, IO T330 62100 68500, IO T216D VLVO													71800	78900
34	10	ESPRIT 3375	OP	CR	FBG	DV	IO	T260-T310		11	8	12500	3		53900	61100
		IB T320 CRUS 64600 71000, IO T340 MRCR 56700 62300, IB T340 VLVO													65300	71800
35		ROGUE 3580	FB	CNV	FBG	DV	VD	T310	MRCR	13		17100	3		88300	97000
		VD T320 CRUS 89000 97800, VD T340 MRCR 89600 98400, VD T340 VLVO													89900	98800
		VD T380 CRUS 91800 101000, VD T300D CAT 111000 122000, VD T370D VLVO													115000	126500
37	3	ESPRIT 3775	OP	SPTCR	FBG	DV	VD	T310	MRCR	13		16000	3	5	91700	101000

LOA FT	IN	NAME AND/ OR MODEL	TOP/ RIG	BOAT TYPE	-HULL- MTL	TP	TP	----ENGINE--- # HP	MFG	BEAM FT	IN	WGT LBS	DRAFT FT	IN	RETAIL LOW	RETAIL HIGH
		1996 BOATS														
37	3	ESPRIT 3775	OP	SPTCR	FBG	DV	IB	T320	CRUS	13		16000	3	5	92800	102000
		VD T340 VLVO 93900 103000, VD T380 CRUS 95400 105000, VD T300D CAT 114000 125000														
37	4	ESPRIT 3570	OP	CR	FBG	DV	VD	T310	MRCR	13		16000	3	5	76400	83900
		VD T320 CRUS 77000 84600, IO T340 MRCR 68300 75100, IO T340 VLVO 69200 76000														
		VD T380 CRUS 79200 87100, VD T300D CAT 96900 106500														
38	3	AFT CABIN 3650	FB	DCMY	FBG	DV	IB	T310	MRCR	13	8	19400	3	2	93600	103000
		IB T320 CRUS 94500 104000, IB T340 MRCR 94600 104000, IB T340 VLVO 95200 104500														
		IB T380 CRUS 97100 106500, IB T300D CAT 119000 131000, IB T350D CAT 124000 136000														
		IB T370D VLVO 121000 133000														
41	6	AFT CABIN 3950	FB	SDN	FBG	DV	IB	T310	MRCR	14		21000	3	4	116000	127500
		IB T320 CRUS 117500 129000, IB T340 VLVO 118000 129500, IB T380 CRUS 120000 132000														
		IB T300D CAT 146000 160500, IB T350D CAT 151500 166500, IB T370D VLVO 145000 159500														
		1995 BOATS														
25	8	ARIA 2420	ST	CUD	FBG	DV	IO	235	MRCR	8	6	5500	2	9	17500	19900
		IO 235-250 18200 20400, IO 300 MRCR 18900 21000, IO 300 VLVO 19100 21200														
25	8	ROGUE 2470	ST	CR	FBG	DV	IO	235-300		8	6	5700	2	9	18300	21600
26		ROGUE 2670	ST	CR	FBG	DV	IO	300		9	6	6100	3	5	20600	23200
26		ROGUE 2670	ST	CR	FBG	DV	IO	216D	VLVO	9	6	6100	3	5	24000	26600
26		ROGUE 2670	ST	CR	FBG	DV	IO	T180-T185		9	6	6100	3	5	21200	24100
28	11	ROGUE 2970	OP	CR	FBG	DV	IO	185	VLVO	9	6	7800	3	2	25900	28800
28	11	ROGUE 2970	OP	CR	FBG	DV	IO	T180-T250		9	6	7800	3	2	28600	34100
28	11	ROGUE 2970	OP	CR	FBG	DV	IO	T135D	VLVO	9	6	7800	3	2	33500	37200
30	8	ROGUE 3175	OP	CR	FBG	DV	IO	T235-T300		10	6	9800	3		36700	43100
30	8	ROGUE 3175	OP	CR	FBG	DV	IO	T216D	VLVO	10	6	9800	3		43200	48000
32	8	ARIA 3120	OP	SPTCR	FBG	DV	IO	T235-T300		10	6	8800	3		34300	40300
32	8	ARIA 3120	OP	SPTCR	FBG	DV	IO	T216D	VLVO	10	6	8800	3		41200	45800
37	3	ESPRIT 3775	OP	SPTCR	FBG	DV	VD	T310	MRCR	13		16000	3	5	87900	96600
		IB T320 CRUS 89000 97800, VD T380 CRUS 93000 102000, VD T400 MRCR 93300 102500														
		VD T300D CAT 109000 120000														
37	4	ESPRIT 3570	OP	CR	FBG	DV	VD	T310	MRCR	13		16000	3	5	72200	79300
		VD T320 CRUS 72800 80000, VD T380 CRUS 74900 82300, VD T400 MRCR 75300 82700														
		VD T300D CAT 92100 101000														
38	3	AFT CABIN 3650	FB	DCMY	FBG	DV	IB	T310	MRCR	13	8	19400	3	2	89700	98600
		IB T320 CRUS 90600 99600, IB T380 CRUS 93100 102500, IB T400 MRCR 93300 102500														
		IB T300D CAT 114000 125500, IB T306D VLVO 111000 122000, IB T350D CAT 118500 130500														
41	6	AFT CABIN 3950	FB	SDN	FBG	DV	IB	T310	MRCR	14		20000	3	4	107000	117500
		IB T320 CRUS 108000 119000, IB T380 CRUS 110500 121500, IB T400 MRCR 110500 121500														
		IB T300D CAT 129000 142000, IB T306D VLVO 123000 135000, IB T310D DD 129000 142000														
		IB T350D CAT 134500 148000														
42		EXPRESS BRIDGE 4285	FB	DCCPT	FBG	DV	IB	T400D	GM	14	6	25200	3	6	166000	182500
42		EXPRESS BRIDGE 4285	FB	DCCPT	FBG	DV	IB	T435D	CAT	14	6	25200	3	6	176000	193500
		1994 BOATS														
25	8	2420	ST	CUD	FBG	DV	IO	225	VLVO	8	6	5500	2	9	16500	18700
		IO 235 MRCR 16300 18600, IO 245-250 16700 19000, IO 300 MRCR 17200 19600														
		IO 300 VLVO 17600 20000, IO 120D VLVO 18200 20300														
25	8	2470	ST	SPTCR	FBG	DV	IO	225-300		8	6	5700	2	9	16900	20400
25	8	2470	ST	SPTCR	FBG	DV	IO	120D	VLVO	8	6	5700	2	9	18800	20900
26		ROGUE 2670	ST	SPTCR	FBG	DV	IO	225-300		9	6	6100	3	5	18600	21700
26		ROGUE 2670	ST	SPTCR	FBG	DV	IO	185D-216D		9	6	6100	3	5	21700	24900
26		ROGUE 2670	ST	SPTCR	FBG	DV	IO	T180-T187		9	6	6100	3	5	19800	22600
27	2	ROGUE 2870	OP	CR	FBG	DV	IO	300		9	6	7800	3	2	22400	25200
		IO 185D-216D 26000 29600, IO T164-T245 23100 27300, IO T120D VLVO 28300 31400														
28	8	ARIA 3020	OP	SPTCR	FBG	DV	IO	T225-T300		10	6	8800	3		29400	34900
28	8	ARIA 3020	OP	SPTCR	FBG	DV	IO	T120D-T185D		10	6	8800	3		33700	40700
28	8	ARIA 3020	OP	SPTCR	FBG	DV	IO	T216D	VLVO	10	6	8800	3		38100	42300
28	8	ROGUE 3070 EX	OP	CR	FBG	DV	IO	T225-T300		10	6	9800	3		31400	37100
28	8	ROGUE 3070 EX	OP	CR	FBG	DV	IO	T120D-T185D		10	6	9800	3		36600	44400
28	8	ROGUE 3070 EX	OP	CR	FBG	DV	IO	T216D	VLVO	10	6	9800	3		41300	45900
28	8	ROGUE 3175	OP	CR	FBG	DV	IO	T225-T300		10	6	9800	3		29200	34600
28	8	ROGUE 3175	OP	CR	FBG	DV	IO	T185D-T216D		10	6	9800	3		37500	43200
30	10	ESPRIT 3270 EX	ST	CR	FBG	DV	IB	T245-T250		10	10	10000	2	10	44900	50500
30	10	ESPRIT 3270 EX	ST	CR	FBG	DV	IB	T170D	YAN	10	10	10400	2	10	52700	57900
32	10	ESPRIT 3370	ST	SPTCR	FBG	DV	IB	T300-T310		11	10	12000	2	9	58600	66300
32	10	ESPRIT 3370	ST	SPTCR	FBG	DV	IB	T200D-T225D		11	10	13400	2	9	68900	75700
32	10	ESPRIT 3380	FB	SDN	FBG	DV	IB	T300-T310		11	10	14000	2	10	65200	72900
32	10	ESPRIT 3380	FB	SDN	FBG	DV	IB	T200D-T225D		11	10	14800	2	10	79500	87300
35	3	ESPRIT 3675 EX	OP	SPTCR	FBG	DV	IB	T300	VLVO	13		16000	3	5	75100	82500
		VD T310 MRCR 75100 82500, VD T400 MRCR 79400 87200, IB T300D CUM 91100 100000														
		VD T300D CAT 93800 103000														
39		AFT CABIN 3850	FB	DCMY	FBG	DV	IB	T300	VLVO	14		20000	3	4	98300	108000
		IB T310 MRCR 97800 107500, IB T400 MRCR 101000 111000, IB T300D CAT 119000 130500														
		IB T300D CUM 115000 126500, IB T306D VLVO 113500 124500, IB T350D CAT 124000 136000														
42		EXPRESS BRIDGE 4280	FB	DCCPT	FBG	DV	IB	T375D	CAT	14	6	25200	3	6	164500	181000
42		EXPRESS BRIDGE 4280	FB	DCCPT	FBG	DV	IB	T400D	GM	14	6	25200	3	6	165000	181500
42		EXPRESS BRIDGE 4280	FB	DCCPT	FBG	DV	IB	T435D	CAT	14	6	25200	3	6	174500	192000
42		EXPRESS BRIDGE 4285	FB	DCCPT	FBG	DV	IB	T375D	CAT	14	6	25200	3	6	160500	176500
42		EXPRESS BRIDGE 4285	FB	DCCPT	FBG	DV	IB	T400D	GM	14	6	25200	3	6	161000	177000
42		EXPRESS BRIDGE 4285	FB	DCCPT	FBG	DV	IB	T435D	CAT	14	6	25200	3	6	170500	187500
		1993 BOATS														
21		ROGUE 2300 SP	OP	CUD	FBG	DV	IO	230-300		8		3700	2	10	9000	11000
21		ROGUE 2350 SP	OP	B/R	FBG	DV	IO	230-300		8		3600	2	10	8200	10200
23	7	ROGUE 2500 SP	OP	CUD	FBG	DV	IO	300	MRCR	8		5200	3	1	14100	16000
23	8	ROGUE 2530 CC	ST	CUD	FBG	DV	IO	225-245		8		4800	3	1	12800	14800
23	8	ROGUE 2530 CC	ST	CUD	FBG	DV	IO	120D	VLVO	8		4800	3	1	14500	16500
26		ROGUE 2670	ST	SPTCR	FBG	DV	IO	225-300		9	6	6100	3	5	17000	20500
26		ROGUE 2670	ST	SPTCR	FBG	DV	IO	185D-216D		9	6	6100	3	5	20300	23300
26		ROGUE 2670	ST	SPTCR	FBG	DV	IO	T155-T205		9	6	6100	3	5	18800	21200
27	2	ROGUE 2870	OP	CR	FBG	DV	IO	300		9	6	7800	3	2	20900	23500
		IO 185D-216D 24300 27700, IO T155-T245 21400 25500, IO T120D VLVO 26400 29400														
28	8	ARIA 3020	OP	SPTCR	FBG	DV	IO	T225-T300		10	6	8800	3		27400	32600
28	8	ARIA 3020	OP	SPTCR	FBG	DV	IO	T120D-T185D		10	6	8800	3		31500	38100
28	8	ARIA 3020	OP	SPTCR	FBG	DV	IO	T216D	VLVO	10	6	8800	3		35600	39600
28	8	ROGUE 3070 EX	OP	CR	FBG	DV	IO	T225-T300		10	6	9800	3		28700	34000
28	8	ROGUE 3070 EX	OP	CR	FBG	DV	IO	T120D-T216D		10	6	9800	3		34200	42300
30	10	ESPRIT 3270 EX	ST	CR	FBG	DV	IB	T245-T250		10	10	10000	2	10	42600	47900
30	10	ESPRIT 3270 EX	ST	CR	FBG	DV	IB	T170D	YAN	10	10	10400	2	10	50200	55100
32	10	ESPRIT 3370	ST	SPTCR	FBG	DV	IB	T300-T310		11	10	12000	2	9	55500	62800
32	10	ESPRIT 3370	ST	SPTCR	FBG	DV	IB	T200D-T225D		11	10	13400	2	9	65600	72100
32	10	ESPRIT 3380	FB	SDN	FBG	DV	IB	T300-T310		11	10	14000	2	10	61800	69100
32	10	ESPRIT 3380	FB	SDN	FBG	DV	IB	T200D-T225D		11	10	14800	2	10	75700	83200
35	3	ESPRIT 3675 EX	OP	SPTCR	FBG	DV	IB	T300	VLVO	13		16000	3	5	71200	78200
		VD T310 MRCR 71200 78200, VD T400 MRCR 75200 82700, IB T300D CUM 86800 95400														
39		AFT CABIN 3850	FB	DCMY	FBG	DV	IB	T300	VLVO	14		20000	3	4	93600	103000
		IB T310 MRCR 93100 102500, IB T400 MRCR 96400 106000, IB T300D CAT 113000 124500														
		IB T300D CUM 109500 120500, IB T306D VLVO 108000 118500, IB T350D CAT 118000 129500														
42		EXPRESS BRIDGE 4280	FB	DCCPT	FBG	DV	IB	T375D	CAT	14	6	25200	3	6	157000	172500
42		EXPRESS BRIDGE 4280	FB	DCCPT	FBG	DV	IB	T400D	GM	14	6	25200	3	6	157500	173000
42		EXPRESS BRIDGE 4280	FB	DCCPT	FBG	DV	IB	T435D	CAT	14	6	25200	3	6	166500	183000
42		EXPRESS BRIDGE 4285	FB	DCCPT	FBG	DV	IB	T375D	CAT	14	6	25200	3	6	153000	168000
42		EXPRESS BRIDGE 4285	FB	DCCPT	FBG	DV	IB	T400D	GM	14	6	25200	3	6	153500	168500
42		EXPRESS BRIDGE 4285	FB	DCCPT	FBG	DV	IB	T435D	CAT	14	6	25200	3	6	162500	178500
		1992 BOATS														
21		ROGUE 2300 SP	OP	CUD	FBG	DV	IO	230-300		8		3700	2	10	8350	10400
21		ROGUE 2350 SP	OP	B/R	FBG	DV	IO	230-300		8		3600	2	10	7700	9550
23	7	ROGUE 2500 SP	OP	CUD	FBG	DV	IO	300		8		5200	3	1	13200	15000
23	7	ROGUE 2570	OP	CR	FBG	DV	IO	230-300		8		5600	3	1	13300	15900
23	8	ROGUE 2530 CC	ST	CUD	FBG	DV	IO	230-245		8		4800	3	1	11800	13800
23	8	ROGUE 2530 CC	ST	CUD	FBG	DV	IO	120D	VLVO	8		4800	3	1	13600	15500
26		ROGUE 2670	ST	SPTCR	FBG	DV	IO	230-300		9	6	6000	3	5	15600	19000
26		ROGUE 2670	ST	SPTCR	FBG	DV	IO	185D-215D		9	6	6000	3	5	18900	21500
26		ROGUE 2670	ST	SPTCR	FBG	DV	IO	T155-T180		9	6	5800	3	5	16700	19700
27	2	ROGUE 2870	OP	CR	FBG	DV	IO	300		9	6	7800	3	2	19600	22000
		IO 185D-215D 22700 25900, IO T155-T245 20100 23900, IO T120D VLVO 24700 27500														
27	4	ROGUE 3060 EX	OP	CR	FBG	DV	IO	T230-T300		10		7800	3		22000	26200
27	4	ROGUE 3060 EX	OP	CR	FBG	DV	IO	T120D	VLVO	10		7800	3		25800	28700
28	8	ROGUE 3070 EX	OP	CR	FBG	DV	IO	T230-T300		10	6	9800	3		26800	31800
28	8	ROGUE 3070 EX	OP	CR	FBG	DV	IO	T120D-T215D		10	6	9800	3		32000	39600
30	6	ARIA 3020	OP	SPTCR	FBG	DV	IO	T230-T300		10	6	8800	3		27500	32500
30	6	ARIA 3020	OP	SPTCR	FBG	DV	IO	T120D-T185D		10	6	8800	3		29400	35700
30	6	ARIA 3020	OP	SPTCR	FBG	DV	IO	T215D	VLVO	10	6	8800	3		33400	37100
30	10	ESPRIT 3270 EX	ST	CR	FBG	DV	IB	T235-T250		10	10	10400	2	10	40500	45400
32	10	ESPRIT 3370	ST	SPTCR	FBG	DV	IB	T300-T310		11	10	13400	2	9	54000	59600
32	10	ESPRIT 3370	ST	SPTCR	FBG	DV	IB	T200D-T225D		11	10	13400	2	9	62600	68700
32	10	ESPRIT 3380	FB	SDN	FBG	DV	IB	T300-T310		11	10	14800	2	10	59400	65500
32	10	ESPRIT 3380	FB	SDN	FBG	DV	IB	T200D-T225D		11	10	14800	2	10	72200	79300

CONTINUED ON NEXT PAGE

```
      LOA  NAME AND/           TOP/ BOAT -HULL- ----ENGINE--- BEAM    WGT  DRAFT RETAIL RETAIL
      FT IN OR MODEL           RIG  TYPE MTL TP TP # HP  MFG  FT IN   LBS  FT IN  LOW   HIGH
      ---------------------- 1992 BOATS ----------------------------------------------------
35  3 ESPRIT 3670 EX          OP  SPTCR FBG DV IB T300  CRUS 13     16400  3  5  68000  74700
      IB T300 VLVO 68100 74800, IB T310 MRCR 68000 74700, IB T355 CRUS      76500  76500
      IB T400 MRCR 70800 77800, IB T250D IVCO 80200 88100, IB T300D CUM     82800  91000

35  3 ESPRIT 3675 EX          OP  SPTCR FBG DV IB T300  CRUS 13     16400  3  5  68500  75300
      IB T300 VLVO 67600 74200, IB T310 MRCR 68500 75300, VD T355  CRUS     70200  77100
      VD T400 MRCR 71400 78400, IB T250D IVCO 81200 89200, IB T300D CUM     82800  91000

39    AFT CABIN 3850          FB  DCMY  FBG DV IB T300  CRUS 14     20000  3  4  89300  98100
      IB T300 VLVO 89200 98100, IB T310 MRCR 88800 97600, IB T355  CRUS     91000 100000
      IB T400 MRCR 91900 101000, IB T300 CAT 108000 118500, IB T300D CUM   104500 115000
      IB T306D VLVO 103000 113000

42    EXPRESS BRIDGE 4280     FB  DCCPT FBG DV IB T300  CRUS 14  6 23700  3 6 113000 124000
      IB T300 VLVO 112000 123000, IB T310 MRCR 113500 124500, IB T355 CRUS 118500 130500
      IB T410 MRCR 121500 133500, IB T375D CAT 149500 164000, IB T400D GM  150000 165000
      IB T425D CAT 157000 172500

42    EXPRESS BRIDGE 4285     FB  DCCPT FBG DV IB T300  CRUS 14  6 23700  3 6 109500 120500
      IB T300 VLVO 106000 116500, IB T310 MRCR 110000 120500, IB T355 CRUS 115000 126000
      IB T400 MRCR 125500 138000, IB T375D CAT 145500 160000, IB T400D GM  146000 160500
      IB T425D CAT 153500 168500
      ---------------------- 1991 BOATS ----------------------------------------------------
21    ROGUE 2300 SP       OP CUD   FBG DV IO 230-240    8      3700 2  6  7850   9050
23  7 ROGUE 2500 SP       OP CUD   FBG DV IO 300  MRCR  8      5200 3  1 12400  14000
23  7 ROGUE 2570          OP CR    FBG DV IO 230-300    8      5600 3  1 12500  14900
23  8 ROGUE 2530          ST CUD   FBG DV IO 230-245    8      4800 3  1 11000  13000
23  8 ROGUE 2530 CC       ST CUD   FBG DV IO 116 VLVO   8      4800 3  1 12700  14500
26  1 ROGUE 2660 EX       ST SPTCR FBG DV IO 300  MRCR 10      7450      18300  20400
26  1 ROGUE 2660 EX       ST SPTCR FBG DV IO T175-T245 10      7450 3    18800  22100
26  1 ROGUE 2660 EX       ST CR    FBG DV IO T116D VLVO 10     7450 3    23300  25900
27  2 ROGUE 2870          OP CR    FBG DV IO 300        9  6   7800 3  2 18600  20900
        IO 182D VLVO 21300 23600, IO T175-T245 19000 22400, IO T116D VLVO 23100 25600

27  4 ROGUE 3060 EX       OP CR    FBG DV IO T230  VLVO 10     7800 3    20600  22900
27  4 ROGUE 3060 EX       OP CR    FBG DV IO T116D VLVO 10     7800 3    24100  26700
27  4 ROGUE 3060 EX       OP CR    FBG DV IO T245-T300  10     7800 3    21200  24500
28  8 ESPRIT 2970         ST CR    FBG DV IO T230  CRUS 10  8  9600 2  9 24900  27700
28  8 ESPRIT 2970         ST CR    FBG DV IO T250  MRCR 10  8  9600 2  9 31200  34700
28  8 ROGUE 3070 EX       OP CR    FBG DV IO T230-T300  10  6  9800 3    25100  29900
28  8 ROGUE 3070 EX       OP CR    FBG DV IOT116D-T182D 10  6  9800 3    29900  35800
30 10 ESPRIT 3270 EX      ST CR    FBG DV IO T235-T250  10 10 10400 2 10 38500  43200
32 10 ESPRIT 3370         ST SPTCR FBG DV IB T330-T454  11 10 13400 2  9 52100  61500
32 10 ESPRIT 3370         ST SPTCR FBG DV IB T200D VLVO 11 10 13400 2  9 59700  65600
32 10 ESPRIT 3380         FB SDN   FBG DV IB T300-T330  11 10 14800 2 10 56400  63000
32 10 ESPRIT 3380         FB SDN   FBG DV IB T200D VLVO 11 10 14800 2 10 68900  75700

35  3 ESPRIT 3670 EX      OP SPTCR FBG DV VD T240  VLVO 13     16400 3  5 63500  69800
      VD T300 CRUS 64600 71000, VD T330 MRCR 65100 71600, VD T355 CRUS      66200  72700
      VD T410 MRCR 67600 74300

35  3 ESPRIT 3675 EX      OP SPTCR FBG DV VD T300  CRUS 13     16400 3  5 65100  71600
      VD T330 MRCR 65600 72100, VD T355 CRUS 66700 73300, VD T410 MRCR      68200  74900
      VD T240D IVCO 77000 84600

39    AFT CABIN 3850      FB DCMY  FBG DV IB T300  CRUS 14     20000 3  4 85200  93600
      IB T330 MRCR 85200 93600, IB T355 CRUS 86800 95400, IB T410 MRCR      88100  96900
      IB T306D VLVO 98200 108000

42    EXPRESS BRIDGE 4280 FB DCCPT FBG DV IB T300  CRUS 14  6 23700 3  6 105000 115500
      IB T330 MRCR 107500 118500, IB T355 CRUS 110500 121500, IB T410 MRCR 116000 127500
      IB T375D CAT 140000 153500, IB T400D GM 140000 154000, IB T425D CAT  147000 161500

42    EXPRESS BRIDGE 4285 FB DCCPT FBG DV IB T300  CRUS 14  6 23700 3  6 107000 117500
      IB T330 MRCR 109500 120000, IB T355 CRUS 112500 123500, IB T410 MRCR 120500 132500
      IB T375D CAT 142000 156000, IB T400D GM 142500 156500, IB T425D CAT  149000 164000
      ---------------------- 1990 BOATS ----------------------------------------------------
21    ROGUE 2300          OP CUD   FBG DV IO 230-240    8      3600 2  6  7250   8350
21    ROGUE 2320          ST CUD   FBG DV IO 230  MRCR  8      3600 2  6  7250   8300
21    ROGUE 2350          ST B/R   FBG DV IO 230  MRCR  8      3600 2  6  6750   7800
23  7 HOLIDAY 2570        OP CR    FBG DV IO 230-295    8      5300 3  1 11200  13300
23  7 ROGUE 2500          OP RNBT  FBG DV IO 230-295    8      4400 3  1  9100  10900
23  7 ROGUE 2520          ST CUD   FBG DV IO 230-295    8      4400 3  1  9650  11600
23  8 BARNEGAT 2530       ST CUD   FBG DV IO 230-245    8      4400 3  1 11200  12700
23  8 BARNEGAT 2530       ST CUD   FBG DV IO 116 VLVO   8      4400 3  1  9650  11400
23  8 SEA-DEVIL 2515      ST CUD   FBG DV IO 230-271    8      4400 3  1  9750  11700
23  8 SEA-DEVIL 2515      ST CUD   FBG DV IO 116 VLVO   8      4400 3  1 11300  12900
26  1 VEE-SPORT 2660      ST SPTCR FBG DV IO 295-300   10      6600 3    15500  18000
26  1 VEE-SPORT 2660      ST SPTCR FBG DV IO T175-T245 10      6600 3    15900  19600

26  1 VEE-SPORT 2660      ST SPTCR FBG DV IO T116D VLVO 10     6600 3    19900  22100
27  2 HOLIDAY 2870        OP CR    FBG DV IO 295-300    9  6   6200 3  2 15500  17900
        IO 182D VLVO 16800 19100, IO T170-T245 16000 19900, IO T116D VLVO 19100 21200

27  4 ROGUE 3060 EX       OP CR    FBG DV IO T300  VLVO 10     7900 3    21300  23600
27  4 ROGUE 3060 EX       OP CR    FBG DV IO T116D VLVO 10     7900 3    22800  25400
27  4 ROGUE 3060 EX       OP CR    FBG DV IO T245-T295  10     7900 3    20000  23100
28  8 ESPRIT 2970         ST CR    FBG DV IO T235  CRUS 10  8  9000 2  9 22900  25400
28  8 ESPRIT 2970         ST CR    FBG DV IO T250  MRCR 10  8  9000 2  9 28900  32100
28  8 ESPRIT 2980         FB SDN   FBG DV IB T235-T250  10  8  9500 2  9 32100  35900
28  8 ESPRIT 2980         FB SDN   FBG DV IB T200D VLVO 10  8  9500 2  9 45800  50300
28  8 ROGUE 3070 EX       OP CR    FBG DV IO T230-T300  10  6  8400 3    22100  26500
28  8 ROGUE 3070 EX       OP CR    FBG DV IOT116D-T182D 10  6  8400 3    24900  30300
30 10 ESPRIT 3260 EX      ST EXP   FBG DV IO T235-T250  10 10 10500 2 10 36700  41200
30 10 ESPRIT 3270 EX      ST CR    FBG DV IO T235-T250  10 10 10500 2 10 36700  41200
30 10 SEA DEVIL 3210      ST CR    FBG DV IO T235-T250  10 10 10500 2 10 36700  41200

32 10 ESPRIT 3370         ST SPTCR FBG DV IB T300-T330  11 10 12000 2 10 47800  53100
32 10 ESPRIT 3370         ST SPTCR FBG DV IBT200D-T205D 11 10 12000 2 10 54000  59900
32 10 ESPRIT 3380         FB SDN   FBG DV IB T300-T330  11 11 13200 2 10 52400  58600
32 10 ESPRIT 3380         FB SDN   FBG DV IBT200D-T205D 11 11 13200 2 10 62500  69500
35  3 ESPRIT 3670 EX      OP SPTCR FBG DV VD T240  VLVO 13     17500 2  5 64900  71400
      VD T300 CRUS 63500 69700, VD T330 MRCR 63900 70300, VD T355 CRUS      64900  71400
      VD T410 MRCR 66300 72900

42    EXPRESS BRIDGE 4280 FB DCCPT FBG DV IB T300  CRUS 14  6 24000 3  6 102000 112000
      IB T305 VLVO 102500 112500, IB T330 MRCR 104000 114500, IB T355 CRUS 107000 117500
      IB T410 MRCR 111000 122000, IB T375D CAT 139000 153000, IB T400D GM  139500 153500
      IB T425D CAT 146000 160500

42    EXPRESS BRIDGE 4285 FB DCCPT FBG DV IB T300  CRUS 14  6 24000 3  6 102500 112500
      IB T305 VLVO 102500 113000, IB T330 MRCR 104500 114500, IB T355 CRUS 107500 118000
      IB T410 MRCR 112000 123500, IB T375D CAT 139000 154000, IB T400D GM  141000 154500
      IB T425D CAT 147500 162000
      ---------------------- 1989 BOATS ----------------------------------------------------
21    ROGUE 2300          OP CUD   FBG DV IO 260-270    8      3600 2 10  7000   8150
21    ROGUE 2320          ST CUD   FBG DV IO 260  MRCR  8      3600 2 10  7000   8050
21    ROGUE 2350          ST B/R   FBG DV IO 260  MRCR  8      3600 2 10  6550   7550
23  7 HOLIDAY 2570        ST CR    FBG DV IO 260-330    8      5300 3  1 10700  13200
23  7 ROGUE 2500          OP RNBT  FBG DV IO 260-330    8      4400 3  1  8650  10800
23  7 ROGUE 2520          ST CUD   FBG DV IO 260-330    8      4400 3  1  9300  11500
23  8 BARNEGAT 2530       ST CUD   FBG DV IO 260-271    8      4400 3  1  9300  10900
23  8 SEA-DEVIL 2510      ST CUD   FBG DV IO 260-271    8      4400 3  1  9400  11100
24  8 SEA-DEVIL 2510      OP FSH   FBG DV OB                   3400      10300  11700
24  8 SEA-DEVIL 2510      OP FSH   FBG DV SE 225  OMC          4500 2  5 12100  13800
24  8 SEA-DEVIL 2510      OP FSH   FBG DV SE 260  MRCR         4800 2  5 11000  12500
24  8 SEA-DEVIL 2510      OP FSH   FBG DV SE T140  OMC         4500 2  5 12100  13800

26  1 VEE-SPORT 2660      ST SPTCR FBG DV IO 330  MRCR 10      6600 3    15100  17200
26  1 VEE-SPORT 2660      ST SPTCR FBG DV IO T180-T260 10      6600 3    15100  18400
26  1 VEE-SPORT 2660      ST SPTCR FBG DV IO T271  VLVO 10     6600 3    16800  19100
26  2 HOLIDAY 2670        OP EXP   FBG DV IO 260-330    8      5600 3  2 12400  15100
26  2 HOLIDAY 2670        OP EXP   FBG DV IO T180  MRCR 8      5600 3  2 13300  15100
27  4 ROGUE 3060          ST SPTCR FBG DV IO T260-T330 10      7900 3    19100  22700
27  4 ROGUE SPORT 3000    OP SPTCR FBG DV IO T260-T260 10      7900 3    19100  22700
28  8 ESPRIT 2970         ST CR    FBG DV VD T240-T260 10  8   9000 2  9 27400  30800
28  8 ESPRIT 2980         FB SDN   FBG DV IB T240-T260 10  8   9500 2  9 30600  34400
28  8 ESPRIT 2980         FB SDN   FBG DV IB T200D VLVO 10  8  9500 2  9 43300  48100
28  8 SEA-DEVIL 3210      ST SF    FBG DV IB T240-T260 10 10 10500 2 10 29500  33000
30 10 ESPRIT 3260         ST EXP   FBG DV IB T240-T260 10 10 10500 2 10 34000  38200

30 10 ESPRIT 3270         ST EXP   FBG DV IB T240-T260 10 10 10500 2 10 36200  40700
32 10 ESPRIT 3370         ST SPTCR FBG DV IB T320-T400 11 10 12000 2 10 46100  52700
32 10 ESPRIT 3370         ST SPTCR FBG DV IBT200D-T205D 11 11 12000 2 10 51600  57300
32 10 ESPRIT 3380         FB SDN   FBG DV IB T320-T400 11 10 13200 2 10 50500  58400
32 10 ESPRIT 3380         FB SDN   FBG DV IB T205D PEN 11 10 13200 2 10 64400  66400
35  3 ESPRIT 3670              SPTCR FBG DV VD T320  CRUS 13  17500 2 10 60900  66900
35  3 ESPRIT 3670              SPTCR FBG DV VD T340  MRCR 13  17500 2 10 61110  67200
35  3 ESPRIT 3670              SPTCR FBG DV VD T400  CRUS 13  17500 2 10 63200  69400
42    EXPRESS BRIDGE 4280 FB  DCCPT FBG DV IB T320  CRUS 14  6 24000 3  6 99200 109000
      IB T340 MRCR 100500 110000, IB T400 CRUS 106500 117000, IB T375D CAT 133500 146500
      IB T400D GM 133500 147000
```

     CONTINUED ON NEXT PAGE

LOA FT	LOA IN	NAME AND/ OR MODEL	TOP/ RIG	BOAT TYPE	HULL MTL	HULL TP	ENGINE TP	ENGINE # HP	ENGINE MFG	BEAM FT	BEAM IN	WGT LBS	DRAFT FT	DRAFT IN	RETAIL LOW	RETAIL HIGH
		1988 BOATS														
21		ROGUE 2100	OP	CUD	FBG	DV	IO	260-271		7	11	3400	2	10	6350	7700
21		ROGUE 2120	ST	CUD	FBG	DV	IO	200-260		7	11	3400	2	10	6100	7300
21		ROGUE 2120	ST	CUD	FBG	DV	IO	271	VLVO	7	11	3400	2	10	6700	7700
21		ROGUE 2150	ST	B/R	FBG	DV	IO	200-260		7	11	3400	2	10	5700	6850
21		ROGUE 2150	ST	B/R	FBG	DV	IO	271	VLVO	7	11	3400	2	10	6300	7200
22		BARNEGAT 2230	ST	CUD	FBG	DV	IO	200-260		8		3600	2	10	6700	8000
22		BARNEGAT 2230	ST	CUD	FBG	DV	IO	271	VLVO	8		3600	2	10	7350	8400
22		BARNEGAT 2260	ST	CAMPR	FBG	DV	IO	200-260		8		3800	2	10	6950	8300
22		BARNEGAT 2260	ST	CAMPR	FBG	DV	IO	271	VLVO	8		3800	2	10	7600	8700
22		SEA-DEVIL 2210	ST	FSH	FBG	DV	IO	200-260		8		3600	2	10	7100	8450
22		SEA-DEVIL 2210	ST	FSH	FBG	DV	IO	271	VLVO	8		3600	2	10	7750	8900
23	7	HOLIDAY 2470	ST	CR	FBG	DV	IO	230-270		8		3800	3	1	7650	9400
23	7	HOLIDAY 2470	ST	CR	FBG	DV	IO	330	MRCR	8		3800	3	1	8600	9900
23	7	ROGUE 2400	OP	RNBT	FBG	DV	IO	260-271		8		3600	3	1	7100	8550
23	7	ROGUE 2400	OP	RNBT	FBG	DV	IO	330-340		8		3600	3	1	7850	9100
23	7	ROGUE 2420	ST	CUD	FBG	DV	IO	230-271		8		3600	3	1	7400	9100
23	7	ROGUE 2420	ST	CUD	FBG	DV	IO	330	MRCR	8		3600	3	1	8350	9600
23	8	BARNEGAT 2430	ST	CUD	FBG	DV	IO	230-271		8		3600	3	1	7300	9000
23	8	BARNEGAT 2460	ST	CUD	FBG	DV	IO	230-271		8		3600	3	1	7450	9200
23	8	SEA-DEVIL 2410	ST	CUD	FBG	DV	IO	230-271		8		3600	3	1	7400	9150
24	8	SEA-DEVIL 2510	OP	FSH	FBG	DV	OB			8		3150			9500	10800
24	8	SEA-DEVIL 2510	OP	FSH	FBG	DV	SE	225	OMC	8		3700	2	5	10500	11900
24	8	SEA-DEVIL 2510	OP	FSH	FBG	DV	IO	230-271		8		4000	2	5	9050	10900
24	8	SEA-DEVIL 2510	OP	FSH	FBG	DV	SE	T280	OMC	8		3700	2	5	10500	11900
26	1	VEE-SPORT 2660	ST	SPTCR	FBG	DV	IO	330-340		9	11	6600	3		14300	16400
26	1	VEE-SPORT 2660	ST	SPTCR	FBG	DV	IO	T180-T260		9	11	6600	3		14300	17400
26	1	VEE-SPORT 2660	ST	SPTCR	FBG	DV	IO	T271	VLVO	9	11	6600	3		15900	18000
26	2	HOLIDAY 2670	ST	EXP	FBG	DV	IO	260-330		8		5500	3	2	11600	14100
26	2	HOLIDAY 2670	ST	EXP	FBG	DV	IO	T165-T180		8		5500	3	2	12300	14200
27	4	ROGUE 2860	ST	SPTCR	FBG	DV	IO	T180-T271		10		7900	3		16600	20700
27	4	ROGUE 2860	ST	SPTCR	FBG	DV	IO	T330	MRCR	10		7900	3		19400	21500
27	4	ROGUE SPORT 2800	OP	SPTCR	FBG	DV	IO	T260-T330		10		7900	3		18100	21500
28	8	ESPRIT 2970	ST	CR	FBG	DV	VD	T220-T270		10	8	9000	2	9	25800	29600
28	8	ESPRIT 2980	FB	SDN	FBG	DV	IB	T220-T270		10	8	9500	2	9	28700	33200
28	8	ESPRIT 2980	FB	SDN	FBG	DV	IB	T200D	VLVO	10	8	9500	2	9	41400	46100
28	8	SEA-DEVIL 3110	ST	SF	FBG	DV	IB	T220-T270		10	8	9000	2	9	25800	29600
28	8	SEA-DEVIL 3110	ST	SF	FBG	DV	IB	T200D	VLVO	10	8	9000	2	9	35400	39400
30	10	ESPRIT 3160	ST	EXP	FBG	DV	IB	T200-T270		10	10	9500	2	10	31800	36100
30	10	ESPRIT 3170	ST	EXP	FBG	DV	IB	T220-T270		10	10	9500	2	10	33200	38100
32	10	ESPRIT 3360	OP	SPTCR	FBG	DV	IB	T260-T350		11	10	11500	2	9	41500	48600
32	10	ESPRIT 3360	OP	SPTCR	FBG	DV	IB	T200D	VLVO	11	10	11500	2	9	48400	53200
32	10	ESPRIT 3370	ST	SPTCR	FBG	DV	IB	T260-T350		11	10	11500	2	10	41500	48600
32	10	ESPRIT 3370	ST	SPTCR	FBG	DV	IB	T200D	VLVO	11	10	11500	2	10	48400	53200
32	10	ESPRIT 3380	FB	SDN	FBG	DV	IB	T340-T350		11	10	13000	2	10	48500	53700
42		EXPRESS BRIDGE 4280	FB	DCCPT	FBG	DV	IB	T340	MRCR	14	6	24000	3	6	95900	105500
42		EXPRESS BRIDGE 4280	FB	DCCPT	FBG	DV	IB	T350	CRUS	14	6	24000	3	6	97300	107000
42		EXPRESS BRIDGE 4280	FB	DCCPT	FBG	DV	IB	T375D	CAT	14	6	27000	3	6	127500	140000
		1987 BOATS														
18	6	VEE SPORT 1950 B/R	ST	RNBT	FBG	DV	IO	165-230		7	6	2650			3850	4600
21		ROGUE 2100	OP	RNBT	FBG	DV	IO	260-270		7	11	3400			5750	6650
21		VEE SPORT 2120	ST	CUD	FBG	DV	IO	200-260		7	11	3400			5800	6950
22		BARNEGAT 220	ST	CUD	FBG	DV	IO	200-260		8		3600			6400	7600
22		BARNEGAT 220-C	ST	CAMPR	FBG	DV	IO	200-260		8		3800			6650	7900
22		BARNEGAT FSH 220-F	ST	FSH	FBG	DV	IO	200-260		8		3600			6750	8050
23	7	HOLIDAY 244	ST	CR	FBG	DV	IO	230-260		8		3800			7300	8550
23	7	ROGUE 2400	OP	RNBT	FBG	DV	IO	260-270		8		3600			6700	7800
23	7	ROGUE 2400	OP	RNBT	FBG	DV	IO	330-340		8		3600			7450	8650
23	7	ROGUE 2400	ST	RNBT	FBG	DV	IO	260	MRCR	8		3600			6750	7750
23	7	VEE SPORT 2420	ST	CUD	FBG	DV	IO	230-260		8		3600			7000	8250
24	8	HOLIDAY 254	ST	CR	FBG	DV	IO	260		8		4500			9050	10500
24	8	HOLIDAY 254	ST	CR	FBG	DV	IO	T140-T190		8		4500			9500	11100
24	8	SEA-DEVIL 251	OP	FSH	FBG	DV	OB			8		3150			9200	10400
24	8	SEA-DEVIL 251	OP	FSH	FBG	DV	SE	205	OMC	8		3700			10100	11500
24	8	SEA-DEVIL 251	OP	FSH	FBG	DV	IO	230-260		8		4000			8500	10000
24	8	SEA-DEVIL 251	OP	FSH	FBG	DV	SE	T140	OMC	8		3700			10100	11500
26	1	SEA-DEVIL 261	ST	SF	FBG	DV	IB	T220-T270		9	11	6600	3		18300	21000
26	1	VEE EXPRESS 267	ST	SPTCR	FBG	DV	IO	T180-T205		9	11	6600	3		14200	16100
		VD T220 CRUS 18400 20400, IO T230 MRCR 14200 16100, IO T230 OMC 14100 16000														
		VD T230 MRCR 18300 20300, IO T260 MRCR 15100 17200, IO T260 OMC 14900 17000														
		VD T260-T270 18600 21000														
26	1	VEE-SPORT 266	ST	SPTCR	FBG	DV	IO	330-335		9	11	6600	3		13600	15500
26	1	VEE-SPORT 266	ST	SPTCR	FBG	DV	IO	T180-T260		9	11	6600			13000	16000
26	2	HOLIDAY 260	ST	EXP	FBG	DV	IO	260		8		5500			11000	12500
26	2	HOLIDAY 260	ST	EXP	FBG	DV	IO	T165-T180		8		5500			11700	13500
27	4	ROGUE 286	ST	SPTCR	FBG	DV	IO	T180-T260		10		7900			15800	19100
27	4	ROGUE SPORT 286S	OP	SPTCR	FBG	DV	IO	T260-T330		10		7900			16800	20700
28	8	AVANTI-VEE 296	ST	EXP	FBG	DV	IB	T220-T270		10	8	9000	2	9	24600	28300
28	8	AVANTI-VEE 296	ST	EXP	FBG	DV	IB	T200D	VLVO	10	8	9000	2	9	33900	37700
28	8	ELEGANTE 297	ST	SPTCR	FBG	DV	VD	T220-T270		10	8	9000	2	9	24600	28300
28	8	SEA-DEVIL 291	ST	SF	FBG	DV	IB	T220-T270		10	8	9000	2	9	24600	28300
28	8	SEA-DEVIL 291	ST	SF	FBG	DV	IB	T200D	VLVO	10	8	9000	2	9	33900	37700
28	8	VILLA-VEE 298	FB	SDN	FBG	DV	IB	T220-T270		10	8	9500	2	9	27400	31700
28	8	VILLA-VEE 298	FB	SDN	FBG	DV	IB	T200D	VLVO	10	8	9500	2	9	39700	44100
32	10	CHATEAU-VEE 338	FB	SDN	FBG	DV	IB	T340-T350		11	10	13000	2	10	46500	51500
32	10	CHATEAU-VEE 338	FB	SDN	FBG	DV	IB	T250D	VLVO	11	10	13000	2	10	57300	62900
32	10	ESPRIT 337	ST	SPTCR	FBG	DV	IB	T260-T350		11	10	11500	2	10	39600	46400
32	10	ESPRIT 337	ST	SPTCR	FBG	DV	IB	T250D	VLVO	11	10	11500	2	10	48500	53400
32	10	ULTRA-VEE 336	OP	SPTCR	FBG	DV	IB	T260-T350		11	10	11500	2	9	39600	46400
32	10	ULTRA-VEE 336	OP	SPTCR	FBG	DV	IB	T250D	VLVO	11	10	11500	2	9	48500	53400
		1986 BOATS														
18	6	LAZER 1900 B/R	ST	RNBT	FBG	DV	IO	205-230		7	6	2650			3700	4400
20	3	BARON 202	ST	RNBT	FBG	DV	IO	170-230		7	9	3300			4900	5750
20	3	BARON 202	ST	RNBT	FBG	DV	IO	260		7	9	3300			5150	6150
20	3	SEA-DEVIL 201	OP	FSH	FBG	DV	OB			7	9	3300			6250	7150
22		BARNEGAT 220	ST	CUD	FBG	DV	IO	190-260		8		3600			6050	7550
22		BARNEGAT 220-C	ST	CAMPR	FBG	DV	IO	190-230		8		3800			6300	7350
22		BARNEGAT FSH 220-F	ST	FSH	FBG	DV	IO	190-260		8		3600			6400	7950
22		BARON 222	ST	RNBT	FBG	DV	IO	190-260		8		3500			5650	6700
22		HOLIDAY 224	ST	CR	FBG	DV	IO	230-260		8		3650			6250	7600
22		LAZER 2200	ST	RNBT	FBG	DV	IO	230		8					5600	6450
22		LAZER 2200	ST	RNBT	FBG	DV	IO	260		8		3500			6300	7250
24	8	HOLIDAY 254	ST	CR	FBG	DV	IO	260		8		4500			8500	10000
24	8	HOLIDAY 254	ST	CR	FBG	DV	IO	T140-T190		8		4500			9100	10600
24	8	SEA-DEVIL 251	OP	FSH	FBG	DV	OB			8		3150			8900	10100
24	8	SEA-DEVIL 251	OP	FSH	FBG	DV	SE	205	OMC	8		3700			9850	11200
24	8	SEA-DEVIL 251	OP	FSH	FBG	DV	IO	205-260		8		4000			8000	9800
24	8	SEA-DEVIL 251	OP	FSH	FBG	DV	SE	T115	OMC	8		3700			9850	11200
26	1	SEA DEVIL 261	HT	SF	FBG	DV	SE	T205	OMC	9	11	6600	3		13000	14800
26	1	SEA-DEVIL 261	ST	SF	FBG	DV	IB	T220-T270		9	11	6600	3		17100	20100
26	1	VEE EXPRESS 267	ST	SPTCR	FBG	DV	IO	T170-T190		9	11	6600	3		13000	15000
26	1	VEE EXPRESS 267	ST	SPTCR	FBG	DV	SE	T205	OMC	9	11	6600	3		13100	14900
26	1	VEE EXPRESS 267	ST	SPTCR	FBG	DV	IO	T205		9	11	6600	3		13300	15100
		VD T220 CRUS 17100 19500, IO T230 MRCR 13600 15400, IO T230 OMC 13600 15400														
		VD T230 MRCR 17000 19400, IO T260 MRCR 14000 15900, IO T260 OMC 14000 15900														
		IO T260 VLVO 14300 16200, VD T260-T270 17400 20100														
26	1	VEE-SPORT 266	ST	SPTCR	FBG	DV	IO	T170-T260		9	11	6600		3	12800	16000
26	2	HOLIDAY 260	ST	EXP	FBG	DV	IO	230-260		8					10000	12100
26	2	HOLIDAY 260	ST	EXP	FBG	DV	IO	T140-T190		8		5500			11000	13000
28	8	AVANTI-VEE 296	ST	EXP	FBG	DV	IB	T220-T270		10	8	9000	2	9	23500	27000
28	8	AVANTI-VEE 296	ST	EXP	FBG	DV	IB	T165D	VLVO	10	8	9000	2	9	31200	34600
28	8	ELEGANTE 297	ST	SPTCR	FBG	DV	VD	T220-T270		10	8	9000		2	23500	27000
28	8	SEA-DEVIL 291	ST	SF	FBG	DV	IB	T220-T270		10	8	9000	2	9	23500	27000
28	8	SEA-DEVIL 291	ST	SF	FBG	DV	IB	T165D	VLVO	10	8	9000	2	9	31100	34600
28	8	VILLA-VEE 298	FB	SDN	FBG	DV	IB	T220-T270		10	8	9500		2	26100	30200
28	8	VILLA-VEE 298	FB	SDN	FBG	DV	IB	T165D	VLVO	10	8	9500	2	9	36300	40300
32	10	CHATEAU-VEE 338	FB	SDN	FBG	DV	IB	T340-T350		11	10	13000	2	10	43900	49200
32	10	CHATEAU-VEE 338	FB	SDN	FBG	DV	IB	T235D	VLVO	11	10	13000	2	10	54100	59400
32	10	ESPRIT 337	ST	SPTCR	FBG	DV	IB	T260-T350		11	10	11500	2	10	37800	44300
32	10	ESPRIT 337	ST	SPTCR	FBG	DV	IB	T235D	VLVO	11	10	11500	2	10	46200	50700
32	10	ULTRA-VEE 336	OP	SPTCR	FBG	DV	IB	T260-T350		11	10	11500	2	9	37800	44300
32	10	ULTRA-VEE 336	OP	SPTCR	FBG	DV	IB	T235D	VLVO	11	10	11500	2	9	46200	50700
		1985 BOATS														
18	6	LAZER 1900 B/R	ST	RNBT	FBG	DV	IO	230		7	6	2650			3650	4200
20	3	BARON 202	ST	RNBT	FBG	DV	IO	170-260		7	9	3300			4700	5700
20	3	LAZER 2000	ST	RNBT	FBG	DV	IO	260		7	9	3300			5200	6000
20	3	SEA-DEVIL 201	OP	FSH	FBG	DV	OB			7	9	2450			5550	6350
20	3	SEA-DEVIL 201	OP	FSH	FBG	DV	SE	115	OMC	7	9	3300			6050	7000
20	3	SEA-DEVIL 201	OP	FSH	FBG	DV	IO	170-230		7	9	3300			5150	6300
20	3	SEA-DEVIL 201	OP	FSH	FBG	DV	IO	260		7	9	3300			5450	6550
22		BARNEGAT 220	ST	CUD	FBG	DV	IO	165-260		8		3600			6050	7250
22		BARNEGAT 220	HT	CUD	FBG	DV	IO	165-260		8		3600			6050	7250
22		BARNEGAT 220-C	ST	CAMPR	FBG	DV	IO	165-260		8		3800			6250	7500
22		BARNEGAT 220-C	HT	CAMPR	FBG	DV	IO	165-260		8		3800			6250	7500
22		BARNEGAT FSH 220-F	ST	FSH	FBG	DV	IO	165-260		8		3600			6350	7650

 CONTINUED ON NEXT PAGE

LOA FT	LOA IN	NAME AND/ OR MODEL	TOP/ RIG	BOAT TYPE	-HULL- MTL	-HULL- TP	ENGINE TP	ENGINE # HP	ENGINE MFG	BEAM FT	BEAM IN	WGT LBS	DRAFT FT	DRAFT IN	RETAIL LOW	RETAIL HIGH
		1985 BOATS														
22		BARNEGAT FSH 220-F	HT	FSH	FBG	DV	IO	165-260		8		3600			6350	7650
22		BARON 222	ST	RNBT	FBG	DV	IO	165-260		8		3500			5600	6700
22		HOLIDAY 224	ST	CR	FBG	DV	IO	165-260		8		3650			6100	7300
22		LAZER 2200	ST	RNBT	FBG	DV	IO	200		8		3500			5900	6750
22		SEA-DEVIL 221	OP	FSH	FBG	DV	OB			8		2650			6650	7650
22		SEA-DEVIL 221	OP	FSH	FBG	DV	SE	155	OMC	8		3200			7450	8600
22		SEA-DEVIL 221	OP	FSH	FBG	DV	IO	170-188		8		3500			6000	7100
22		SEA-DEVIL 221	OP	FSH	FBG	DV	SE	205	OMC	8		3200			7450	8600
24	8	HOLIDAY 254	ST	CR	FBG	DV	IO	165-260		8		4500			7950	9650
24	8	HOLIDAY 254	ST	CR	FBG	DV	IO	110D	VLVO	8		4500			9000	10200
24	8	HOLIDAY 254	ST	CR	FBG	DV	IO	T140-T188		8		4500			8650	10200
24	8	SEA-DEVIL 251	OP	FSH	FBG	DV	OB			8		3150			8600	9900
24	8	SEA-DEVIL 251	OP	FSH	FBG	DV	SE	155	OMC	8		3700			9600	10900
24	8	SEA-DEVIL 251	OP	FSH	FBG	DV	IO	165-200		8		4000			7750	9050
24	8	SEA-DEVIL 251	OP	FSH	FBG	DV	SE	205	OMC	8		3700			9600	10900
24	8	SEA-DEVIL 251	OP	FSH	FBG	DV	IO	225-260		8		4000			7950	9400
24	8	SEA-DEVIL 251	OP	FSH	FBG	DV	IO	110D	VLVO	8		4000			10200	11600
24	8	SEA-DEVIL 251	OP	FSH	FBG	DV	SE	T115	OMC	8		3700			9600	10900
26	1	SEA DEVIL 261	ST	SF	FBG	DV	SE	T205	OMC	9	11	6600	3		12700	14400
26	1	SEA DEVIL 261	HT	SF	FBG	DV	SE	T205	OMC	9	11	6600	3		12700	14400
26	1	SEA-DEVIL 261	ST	SF	FBG	DV	IB	T160-T270		9	11	6600	3		15500	19200
26	1	SEA-DEVIL 261	HT	SF	FBG	DV	IB	T160-T270		9	11	6600	3		15500	19200
26	1	VEE EXPRESS 267	ST	SPTCR	FBG	DV	VD	260	MRCR	9	11	6600	3		14700	16800
		IO T170 T185 13500 14700, IO T190 MRCR 12600 14300, VD T190 PCM													15900	18100
		IO T200 MRCR 12700 14400, IO T200 OMC 12700 14400, IO T200 VLVO													13200	14900
		VD T200 CRUS 16200 18400														
26	1	VEE EXPRESS 267	ST	SPTCR	FBG	DV	SE	T205	OMC	9	11	6600	3		12700	14500
26	1	VEE EXPRESS 267	ST	SPTCR	FBG	DV	VD	T220		9	11	6600	3		16400	18600
		IO T225 VLVO 13300 15100, IO T230 OMC 13100 14900, VD T230-T250													16300	18700
		IO T260 13500 15600, VD T270 CRUS 16900 19200														
26	1	VEE EXPRESS 267	HT	SPTCR	FBG	DV	IO	T170-T185		9	11	6600	3		12400	14300
		IO T190 MRCR 12600 14300, VD T190 PCM 15900 18100, IO T200 MRCR													12700	14400
		IO T200 OMC 12600 14300, IO T200 VLVO 12900 14700, VD T200 CRUS													16200	18400
26	1	VEE EXPRESS 267	HT	SPTCR	FBG	DV	SE	T205	OMC	9	11	6600	3		12700	14400
26	1	VEE EXPRESS 267	HT	SPTCR	FBG	DV	VD	T220		9	11	6600	3		16400	18600
		IO T225 VLVO 13200 15000, IO T230 OMC 12900 14700, VD T230-T250													16300	18700
		IO T260 OMC 13300 15100, IO T260 VLVO 13600 15500, VD T260-T270													16600	19200
26	1	VEE-SPORT 266	ST	SPTCR	FBG	DV	IO	330	MRCR	9	11	6600	3		12500	14200
26	1	VEE-SPORT 266	ST	SPTCR	FBG	DV	IO	T165-T260		9	11	6600	3		12700	15300
26	1	VEE-SPORT 266	ST	SPTCR	FBG	DV	IO	T110D	VLVO	9	11	6600	3		15200	17200
26	2	HOLIDAY 260	ST	EXP	FBG	DV	IO	195-260		8		5500			9800	11700
26	2	HOLIDAY 260	ST	EXP	FBG	DV	IO	T140-T190		8		5500			10500	12500
28	8	AVANTI-VEE 296	ST	EXP	FBG	DV	IB	T220-T270		10	8	9000	2	9	22400	25800
28	8	AVANTI-VEE 296	ST	EXP	FBG	DV	IB	T165D	VLVO	10	8	9000	2	9	29900	33200
28	8	SEA-DEVIL 291	ST	SF	FBG	DV	IB	T220-T270		10	8	9000	2	9	22400	25800
28	8	SEA-DEVIL 291	ST	SF	FBG	DV	IB	T165D	VLVO	10	8	9000	2	9	29900	33200
28	8	VILLA-VEE 298	FB	SDN	FBG	DV	IB	T220-T270		10	8	9500	2	9	25000	28900
28	8	VILLA-VEE 298	FB	SDN	FBG	DV	IB	T165D	VLVO	10	8	9500	2	9	34800	38700
32	10	CHATEAU-VEE 338	FB	SDN	FBG	DV	IB	T330-T350		11	10	13000	2	10	41600	46900
32	10	CHATEAU-VEE 338	FB	SDN	FBG	DV	IB	T165D-T235D		11	10	13000	2	10	48300	57000
32	10	ULTRA-VEE 336	OP	SPTCR	FBG	DV	IB	T250-T350		11	10	11500	2	9	35900	42300
32	10	ULTRA-VEE 336	OP	SPTCR	FBG	DV	IB	T165D-T235D		11	10	11500	2	9	41100	48700
		1984 BOATS														
20	3	BARON 202	ST	RNBT	FBG	DV	IO	170-260		7	9	3300			4400	5500
20	3	BARON 202SX	ST	RNBT	FBG	DV	IO	170-260		7	9	3300			4650	5750
20	3	SEA-DEVIL 20 201	ST	FSH	FBG	DV	OB			7	9	2450			5400	6200
20	3	SEA-DEVIL 20 201	ST	FSH	FBG	DV	SE	115	OMC	7	9	3300			5950	6800
20	3	SEA-DEVIL 20 201	ST	FSH	FBG	DV	IO	170-230		7	9	3300			5000	6100
20	3	SEA-DEVIL 20 201	ST	FSH	FBG	DV	IO	260		7	9	3300			5250	6300
22		BARNEGAT 220	OP	CUD	FBG	DV	IO	170-260		8		3600			5600	7000
22		BARNEGAT 220-C	HT	CAMPR	FBG	DV	IO	170-260		8		3600			5600	7000
22		BARON 222	ST	RNBT	FBG	DV	IO	170-260		8		3500			5250	6300
22		BARON 222SX	ST	RNBT	FBG	DV	IO	170-260		8		3500			5450	6550
22		HOLIDAY 22 224	ST	CR	FBG	DV	IO	198-260		8		3650			5700	7050
22		SEA-DEVIL 22 221	ST	FSH	FBG	DV	OB			8		2650	2	5	6500	7450
22		SEA-DEVIL 22 221	ST	FSH	FBG	DV	SE	155	OMC	8		3200	2	5	7300	8400
22		SEA-DEVIL 22 221	ST	FSH	FBG	DV	IO	170-188		8		3500	2	5	5800	6850
22		SEA-DEVIL 22 221	ST	FSH	FBG	DV	SE	205	OMC	8		3200	2	5	7300	8400
24	8	HOLIDAY 25 254-4	ST	CR	FBG	DV	IO	198-260		8		4500			7500	9100
24	8	HOLIDAY 25 254-4	ST	CR	FBG	DV	IO	110D	VLVO	8		4500			8500	9800
24	8	HOLIDAY 25 254-4	ST	CR	FBG	DV	IO	T170-T188		8		4500			8400	9750
24	8	HOLIDAY 25 254-6	ST	CR	FBG	DV	IO	198-260		8		4500			7700	9300
24	8	HOLIDAY 25 254-6	ST	CR	FBG	DV	IO	110D	VLVO	8		4500			8700	9950
24	8	HOLIDAY 25 254-6	ST	CR	FBG	DV	IO	T170-T188		8		4500			8550	9950
24	8	SEA-DEVIL 25 251	ST	FSH	FBG	DV	OB			8		3150	2	5	8400	9650
24	8	SEA-DEVIL 25 251	ST	FSH	FBG	DV	SE	155	OMC	8		3700	2	5	9400	10700
24	8	SEA-DEVIL 25 251	ST	FSH	FBG	DV	IO	185-200		8		4000	2	5	7350	8650
24	8	SEA-DEVIL 25 251	ST	FSH	FBG	DV	SE	205	OMC	8		3700	2	5	9400	10700
24	8	SEA-DEVIL 25 251	ST	FSH	FBG	DV	IO	225-260		8		4000	2	5	7650	9100
24	8	SEA-DEVIL 25 251	ST	FSH	FBG	DV	IO	110D	VLVO	8		4000	2	5	9850	11200
24	8	SEA-DEVIL 25 251	ST	FSH	FBG	DV	SE	T115	OMC	8		3700	2	5	9400	10700
26	1	BAR-HARBOR 264	ST	CR	FBG	DV	IO	260		9	11	6000	3	3	10600	12100
26	1	VEE-SPORT 266	ST	SPTCR	FBG	DV	IO	T170-T230		9	11	6600	3		12000	14400
26	1	VEE-SPORT 266	ST	SPTCR	FBG	DV	IO	T260-T330		9	11	6600	3		12900	16100
26	1	VEE-SPORT 266	ST	SPTCR	FBG	DV	IO	T110D	VLVO	9	11	6600	3		14600	16600
28	8	AVANTI-VEE 296	OP	EXP	FBG	DV	IB	T220-T350		10	8	9600	2	9	22100	26700
28	8	AVANTI-VEE 296	OP	EXP	FBG	DV	IB	T124D-T158D		10	8	9600	2	9	28600	33100
28	8	SEA-DEVIL 291	OP	SF	FBG	DV	IB	T220-T350		10	8	9600	2	9	22100	26700
28	8	SEA-DEVIL 291	OP	SF	FBG	DV	IB	T124D-T158D		10	8	9600	2	9	28600	33100
28	8	VILLA-VEE 298	FB	SDN	FBG	DV	IB	T170-T230		10	8	9500	2	9	22800	26600
28	8	VILLA-VEE 298	FB	SDN	FBG	DV	IB	T124D	VLVO	10	8	9500	2	9	31500	35000
28	8	VILLA-VEE 298	FB	SDN	FBG	DV	IB	T235D	VLVO	10	8	9500	2	9	36700	40800
32	10	ULTRA-VEE 336	OP	SPTCR	FBG	DV	IB	T260-T350		11	10	13000	2	9	35500	41400
32	10	ULTRA-VEE 336	OP	SPTCR	FBG	DV	IB	T158D-T235D		11	10	13000	2	9	41800	49400

....For earlier years, see the BUC Used Boat Price Guide, Volume 3

CRUISING WORLD INC

ST PETERSBURG FL 33702 See inside cover to adjust price for area

LOA FT	LOA IN	NAME AND/ OR MODEL	TOP/ RIG	BOAT TYPE	-HULL- MTL	-HULL- TP	ENGINE TP	ENGINE # HP	ENGINE MFG	BEAM FT	BEAM IN	WGT LBS	DRAFT FT	DRAFT IN	RETAIL LOW	RETAIL HIGH
		1988 BOATS														
39	7	CRUISING WORLD 40	SLP	SA/CR	FBG	KL	IB	50D	UNIV	13	3	22500	5	2	94200	103500
		1987 BOATS														
39	7	CRUISING WORLD 40	SLP	SA/CR	FBG	KL	IB	50D	UNIV	13	3	22500	5	2	88600	97300
		1986 BOATS														
21		FAIRLINE 21		CR		DV	IB			8		3100			**	**
26		FAIRLINE 26 SUNFURY		CR		DV	IB			10		6000			**	**
28		FAIRLINE 29 MIRAGE		CR		DV	IB			10		6000			**	**
31		FAIRLINE 31 CORNICHE		CR		DV	IB			12		9000			**	**
33		FAIRLINE 33 TARGA		CR		DV	IB			11		10000			**	**
36		FAIRLINE 36		CR		DV	IB			13		17000			**	**
39	7	OFFSHORE 40	SLP	SA/CR	FBG	KL	IB	44D	UNIV	13	3	21500	5	2	80600	88600
39	7	OFFSHORE 40	SLP	SA/CR	FBG	KL	IB	50D	LEHM	13	3	21500	5	2	80600	88600
39	7	OFFSHORE 40	SLP	SA/CR	FBG	KL	IB	50D	UNIV	13	3	22500	5	2	83300	91500
39	7	OFFSHORE 40	CUT	SA/CR	FBG	KL	IB	50D	LEHM	13	3	21500	5	2	80600	88600
41		FAIRLINE 40		CR		DV	IB			13		18000			**	**
		1985 BOATS														
39	7	OFFSHORE 40	SLP	SA/CR	FBG	KL	IB	50	UNIV	13	3	22500	5	2	77000	84700
39	7	OFFSHORE 40	SLP	SA/CR	FBG	KL	IB	50D	LEHM	13	3	22500	5	2	78300	86000
		1984 BOATS														
39	7	OFFSHORE 40	SLP	SA/CR	FBG	KL	IB	50D	LEHM	13	3	21500	5	2	71400	78400
39	7	OFFSHORE 40	CUT	SA/CR	FBG	KL	IB	50D	LEHM	13	3	21500	5	2	71300	78400

CRUISING YACHTS INT'L INC

HOUSTON TX 77077 COAST GUARD MFG ID- CYI See inside cover to adjust price for area
FORMERLY CRUISING YACHTS INTERNATIONAL

LOA FT	LOA IN	NAME AND/ OR MODEL	TOP/ RIG	BOAT TYPE	-HULL- MTL	-HULL- TP	ENGINE TP	ENGINE # HP	ENGINE MFG	BEAM FT	BEAM IN	WGT LBS	DRAFT FT	DRAFT IN	RETAIL LOW	RETAIL HIGH
		1991 BOATS														
36	9	SLOCUM 37	CUT	SA/CR	F/S	KL	IB	30D	YAN	11	8	27000	6		147000	161500
42	6	SLOCUM 43	CUT	SA/CR	F/S	KL	IB	50D	PERK	12	11	29000	6	4	172000	189000
42	6	SLOCUM 43 PILOTHOUSE	CUT	SA/CR	F/S	KL	IB	61D	LEHM	12	11	29000	6	4	173000	190000
		1990 BOATS														
36	9	SLOCUM 37	CUT	SA/CR	FBG	KL	IB	30D	YAN	11	8	27000	6		138000	152000
36	9	STADMAN 37	CUT	SA/CR	F/S	KL	IB	30D	YAN	11	8	27000	6		138000	152000
42	6	SLOCUM 43	CUT	SA/CR	FBG	KL	IB	51D	PERK	12	11	28104	6	4	159000	174500
42	6	SLOCUM 43 PILOTHOUSE	CUT	SA/CR	FBG	KL	IB	61D	LEHM	12	11	28104	6	4	160000	175500
42	6	STADMAN 43	CUT	SA/CR	F/S	KL	IB	50D	PERK	12	11	29000	6	4	161500	177500
42	6	STADMAN 43 PILOTHSE	CUT	SA/CR	F/S	KL	IB	61D	LEHM	12	11	29000	6	4	162500	179000

LOA FT IN	NAME AND/ OR MODEL		TOP/ RIG	BOAT TYPE	-HULL- MTL TP	----ENGINE--- TP # HP MFG	BEAM FT IN	WGT LBS	DRAFT FT IN	RETAIL LOW	RETAIL HIGH
---	---	--- 1989 BOATS	---								
36 9	SLOCUM 37		CUT	SA/CR FBG	KL IB	30D YAN	11 8	27000	6	139000	143000
42 9	SLOCUM 43		CUT	SA/CR FBG	KL IB	51D PERK	12 11	28104	6 4	149500	164000
42 6	SLOCUM 43	PILOTHOUSE	CUT	SA/CR FBG	KL IB	61D LEHM	12 11	28104	6 4	150500	165000
---	---	--- 1988 BOATS	---								
36 9	SLOCUM 37		CUT	SA/CR FBG	KL IB	35D YAN	11 8	27000	5 11	122500	134500
42 9	SLOCUM 43		CUT	SA/CR FBG	KL IB	50D PERK	12 11	28104	6 4	140500	154500
42 6	SLOCUM 43	PILOTHOUSE	CUT	SA/CR FBG	KL IB	D FORD	12 11	28104	6 4	141500	155500
---	---	--- 1987 BOATS	---								
36 9	SLOCUM 37		CUT	SAIL FBG	KL IB	35D YAN	11 8	27000	5 11	115000	126500
42 9	SLOCUM 43		CUT	SA/CR FBG	KL IB	50D PERK	12 11	28104	6 4	132000	145000
42 6	SLOCUM 43	PILOTHOUSE	CUT	SA/CR FBG	KL IB	D FORD	12 11	28104	6 4	133000	146000
52 9	FINYA 53		CUT	SAIL FBG	KL IB	D PERK	13 11		7	228500	251000
52 9	FINYA 53		KTH	SAIL FBG	KL IB	D PERK	13 11		7	228500	251000
---	---	--- 1986 BOATS	---								
36 9	SLOCUM 37		CUT	SAIL FBG	KL IB	35D YAN	11 8	27000	5 11	108500	119000
42 9	SLOCUM 43		CUT	SA/CR FBG	KL IB	50D PERK	12 11	28104	6 4	124500	136500
50 10	SLOCUM 51		KTH	SAIL FBG	KL IB	85D PERK	16 3	38708	7	194000	213000
---	---	--- 1984 BOATS	---								
36 9	SLOCUM 37			SAIL FBG	KL IB	35D YAN	11 8	27000	5 11	95800	105500
42 9	SLOCUM 43		CUT	SA/CR FBG	KL IB	50D PERK	12 11	28104	6 4	108000	118500
42 6	SLOCUM 43	SHOAL	CUT	SA/CR FBG	KL IB	50D PERK	12 11	28104	5 6	112000	123000

...For earlier years, see the BUC Used Boat Price Guide, Volume 3

CRUSADER BOATS
DIV OF GRANTS FEBERGLASS INC   See inside cover to adjust price for area
MOORE HAVEN FL 33471-80 COAST GUARD MFG ID- GFY

For more recent years, see the BUC Used Boat Price Guide, Volume 1

LOA FT IN	NAME AND/ OR MODEL		TOP/ RIG	BOAT TYPE	-HULL- MTL TP	----ENGINE--- TP # HP MFG	BEAM FT IN	WGT LBS	DRAFT FT IN	RETAIL LOW	RETAIL HIGH
---	---	--- 1996 BOATS	---								
34	CRUSADER 34		EPH	FSH FBG	SV IB		12	5000	3 6	**	**
34	CRUSADER 34		FB	FSH FBG	SV IB	420D CUM	12	12000	3 6	98300	108000
34	CRUSADER 34	WA	FB	FSH FBG	SV IB	420D CUM	12	12000	3 6	98300	108000
---	---	--- 1995 BOATS	---								
34	CRUSADER 34		EPH	FSH FBG	SV IB		12	5000	3 6	**	**
34	CRUSADER 34		FB	FSH FBG	SV IB	420D CUM	12	12000	3 6	93400	102500
34	CRUSADER 34	WA	FB	FSH FBG	SV IB	420D CUM	12	12000	3 6	93400	102500
---	---	--- 1994 BOATS	---								
34	CRUSADER 34		FB	COMM FBG	SV IB	300D CAT	12	10000	3 6	**	**
34	CRUSADER 34		EPH	FSH FBG	SV IB			5000	3 6	**	**
34	CRUSADER 34		FB	FSH FBG	SV IB	420D CUM	12	12000	3 6	88900	97700
34	CRUSADER 34	WA	EPH	COMM FBG	SV IB	300D CAT	12	10000	3 6	**	**
34	CRUSADER 34	WA	FB	FSH FBG	SV IB	420D CUM	12	12000	3 6	88900	97700

...For earlier years, see the BUC Used Boat Price Guide, Volume 3

CRYSTALINER CORP
COSTA MESA CA 92627   See inside cover to adjust price for area

LOA FT IN	NAME AND/ OR MODEL		TOP/ RIG	BOAT TYPE	-HULL- MTL TP	----ENGINE--- TP # HP MFG	BEAM FT IN	WGT LBS	DRAFT FT IN	RETAIL LOW	RETAIL HIGH
---	---	--- 1991 BOATS	---								
29 5	R/S		OP	SF FBG	SV IB	T317 CRUS	11	11000	2 6	41000	45600
29 5	R/S		OP	SF FBG	SV IB	T210D CUM	11	11000	2 6	56700	62300
33 2	R/S		OP	SF FBG	SV IB	T317 CRUS	11	11500	2 6	53500	58800
33 2	R/S		OP	SF FBG	SV IB	T210D CUM	11	11500	2 6	70000	76900
33 2	S/F		FB	SF FBG	SV IB	T317 CRUS	11	13500	2 6	60500	66400
33 2	S/F		FB	SF FBG	SV IB	T300D CUM	11	13575	2 6	83800	92100
---	---	--- 1990 BOATS	---								
29 5	R/S		OP	SF FBG	SV IB	T317 CRUS	11	11000	2 6	38800	43200
29 5	R/S		OP	SF FBG	SV IB	T210D CUM	11	11000	2 6	54100	59500
33 2	R/S		OP	SF FBG	SV IB	T317 CRUS	11	11500	2 6	50700	55700
33 2	R/S		OP	SF FBG	SV IB	T210D CUM	11	11500	2 6	66600	73200
33 2	S/F		FB	SF FBG	SV IB	T317 CRUS	11	13500	2 6	58100	63900
33 2	S/F		FB	SF FBG	SV IB	T300D CUM	11	13575	2 6	79800	87700
---	---	--- 1988 BOATS	---								
21	CRYSTALINER 21			CTRCN FBG	SV IO	175 OMC	7 8	3400	1 6	9150	10400
29 5	CRYSTALINER 29	RS		SF FBG	SV IB	T240-T320	11	10500	3	33200	38400
29 5	CRYSTALINER 29	RS		SF FBG	SV IB	T210D CUM	11	10750	3	48700	53500
33 2	CRYSTALINER 33	RS		SF FBG	SV IB	T320 CRUS	11	11000	3	48600	53400
33 2	CRYSTALINER 33	RS		SF FBG	SV IB	T210D CUM	11	11500	3	62100	68200
33 2	CRYSTALINER 33	SF		SF FBG	SV IB	IBT210D-T250D	11	12250	3	64400	74500
33 2	CRYSTALINER 33	SF	FB	SF FBG	SV IB	T320 CRUS	11	12000	3	51700	56800
---	---	--- 1987 BOATS	---								
21	CRYSTALINER 21			CTRCN FBG	SV IO	175 OMC	7 8	3400	1 6	8550	9850
29 5	CRYSTALINER 29	RS		SF FBG	SV IB	T240 CRUS	11	10500	3	31700	35200
33 2	CRYSTALINER 33	RS		SF FBG	SV IB	T320 CRUS	11	11000	3	46500	51100
33 2	CRYSTALINER 33	SF	FB	SF FBG	SV IB	T320 CRUS	11	12000	3	49700	54600
---	---	--- 1986 BOATS	---								
21	CRYSTALINER 21			CTRCN FBG	SV IB	175	7 8	3400	1 6	9750	11100
29 5	CRYSTALINER 29			UTL FBG	SV IB	T270	11	10500	2 6	31000	34500
33 2	CRYSTALINER 33			SF FBG	SV IB	T350	11	12000	2 6	47700	52400
---	---	--- 1985 BOATS	---								
29 5	CRYSTALINER 29			UTL FBG	SV IB	T270	11	10500	2 6	29700	33000
33 2	CRYSTALINER 33			SF FBG	SV IB	T350	11	12000	2 6	44900	49900
43	CRYSTALINER 43			FSH FBG	SV IB	310D	14			141500	155500
---	---	--- 1984 BOATS	---								
29 5	CRYSTALINER 29			UTL FBG	SV IB	T270	11	10500	2 6	28400	31600
33 2	CRYSTALINER 33			SF FBG	SV IB	T270	11	12000	2 6	41900	46500
43	CRYSTALINER 43			FSH FBG	SV IB	310D	14			135000	148500

...For earlier years, see the BUC Used Boat Price Guide, Volume 3

CSI MARINE
SONIC
STUART FL 34996   COAST GUARD MFG ID- CSI   See inside cover to adjust price for area
                         FORMERLY AMERICAN INDUSTRIES INC

For more recent years, see the BUC Used Boat Price Guide, Volume 1

LOA FT IN	NAME AND/ OR MODEL	TOP/ RIG	BOAT TYPE	-HULL- MTL TP	----ENGINE--- TP # HP MFG	BEAM FT IN	WGT LBS	DRAFT FT IN	RETAIL LOW	RETAIL HIGH
---	---	--- 1996 BOATS								
28	SONIC SS 28	OP	OFF FBG	DV IO	300 MRCR	8 6	6000	1 11	25600	28400
28	SONIC SS 28	OP	OFF FBG	DV IO	T250 MRCR	8 6	6000	1 11	28300	31400
30 6	SONIC SS 31	OP	OFF FBG	DV IO	T300-T415	8 6	7000	1 11	39100	48300
35	SONIC SS 35	OP	OFF FBG	DV IO	T350 MRCR	8 6	8400	2 1	62900	69100
35	SONIC SS 35	OP	OFF FBG	DV IO	T415 MRCR	8 6	8400	2 1	67000	73600
35	SONIC SS 35	OP	OFF FBG	DV IO	T470 MRCR	8 6	8400	2 1	71200	78200
41 6	SONIC SS 42	OP	OFF FBG	DV IO	T415 MRCR	8 6	10000	2 6	86400	94900
41 6	SONIC SS 42	OP	OFF FBG	DV IO	T470 MRCR	8 6	10000	2 6	93600	103000
41 6	SONIC SS 42	OP	OFF FBG	DV IO	R415 MRCR	8 6	12000	2 6	100000	110000
44 6	SONIC SS 45	OP	OFF FBG	DV IO	R415 MRCR	8 6	12500	2 6	96500	106000
44 6	SONIC SS 45	OP	OFF FBG	DV IO	R470 MRCR	8 6	12500	2 6	106500	117500
---	---	--- 1995 BOATS								
28	SONIC SS 28	OP	OFF FBG	DV IO	350 MRCR	8 6	6000	1 11	24900	27700
28	SONIC SS 28	OP	OFF FBG	DV IO	T250 MRCR	8 6	6000	1 11	26400	29300
30 6	SONIC SS 31	OP	OFF FBG	DV IO	T300-T415	8 6	7000	1 11	36500	45000
35	SONIC SS 35	OP	OFF FBG	DV IO	T300 MRCR	8 6	8400	2 1	56500	62100
	IO T350 MRCR 58600	64400, IO T415 MRCR 62500 68700, IO T470 MRCR 66400 72900								
41 6	SONIC SS 42	OP	OFF FBG	DV IO	T415 MRCR	8 6	10000	2 6	80600	88600
41 6	SONIC SS 42	OP	OFF FBG	DV IO	T470 MRCR	8 6	10000	2 6	87300	96000
41 6	SONIC SS 42	OP	OFF FBG	DV IO	R415 MRCR	8 6	12000	2 6	93300	102500
44 6	SONIC SS 45	OP	OFF FBG	DV IO	R415 MRCR	8 6	12500	2 6	90000	98900
44 6	SONIC SS 45	OP	OFF FBG	DV IO	R470 MRCR	8 6	12500	2 6	99600	109500
---	---	--- 1994 BOATS								
28	SONIC SS 28	OP	OFF FBG	DV OB		8 6	6000	1 11	23100	25600
28	SONIC SS 28	OP	OFF FBG	DV IO	350 MRCR	8 6	6000	1 11	23300	25900
28	SONIC SS 28	OP	OFF FBG	DV IO	T250 MRCR	8 6	6000	1 11	24500	27400
30 6	SONIC SS 31	OP	OFF FBG	DV IO	T300-T415	8 6	7000	1 11	33400	42000
35	SONIC SE 35	OP	OFF FBG	DV IO	T350 MRCR	8 6	8400	2 1	51700	56800
35	SONIC SS 35	OP	OFF FBG	DV IO	T415 MRCR	8 6	8400	2 1	63600	69900
35	SONIC SS 35	OP	OFF FBG	DV IO	T470 MRCR	8 6	8400	2 1	65600	72100
35	SONIC SS 35	OP	OFF FBG	DV IO	T300 MRCR	8 6	8400	2 1	52700	52900
41 6	SONIC SS 42	OP	OFF FBG	DV IO	T415 MRCR	8 6	10000	2 6	75300	82700
41 6	SONIC SS 42	OP	OFF FBG	DV IO	R415 MRCR	8 6	12000	2 6	78600	86400
44 6	SONIC SS 45	OP	OFF FBG	DV IO	R415 MRCR	8 6	12500	2 6	87300	95900
44 6	SONIC SS 45	OP	OFF FBG	DV IO	R445 MRCR	8 6	12500	2 6	84000	92300
---	---	--- 1993 BOATS								
28	SONIC SS 28	OP	OFF FBG	DV OB		8 6	5000	1 10	21900	24400
28	SONIC SS 28	OP	OFF FBG	DV IO	T270-T330	8 6	5000	1 10	22400	26700
28	SONIC SS 28	OP	OFF FBG	DV IO	T365 MRCR	8 6	5000	1 10	25400	28200
30 6	SONIC SS 31	OP	OFF FBG	DV IO	T270-T365	8 6	7000	1 10	31000	37400
30 6	SONIC SS 31	OP	OFF FBG	DV IO	T410 MRCR	8 6	7000	1 10	35200	39100

LOA FT	IN	NAME AND/ OR MODEL	TOP/ RIG	BOAT TYPE	-HULL- MTL	TP	ENGINE TP	# HP	MFG	BEAM FT	IN	WGT LBS	DRAFT FT	IN	RETAIL LOW	RETAIL HIGH
		1993 BOATS														
35		SONIC SE 35	OP	OFF	FBG	DV	OB			8	6				**	**
35		SONIC SE 35	OP	OFF	FBG	DV	IO	T330	MRCR	8	6				55100	60500
		IO T365 MRCR 56700 62300, IO T410 MRCR 59200 65100, IO T465 MRCR													62900	69100
41		SONIC SS 41	OP	OFF	FBG	DV	IO	T410	MRCR	8	6	10000	2	6	69000	75900
41		SONIC SS 41	OP	OFF	FBG	DV	IO	T465	MRCR	8	6	10000	2	6	74700	82100
41		SONIC SS 41	OP	OFF	FBG	DV	IO	R410	MRCR	8	6	10000	2	6	75800	83300
44	5	SONIC 445	OP	OFF	FBG	DV	IO	R410	MRCR	8	6	12000	2	9	73200	80400
44	5	SONIC 445	OP	OFF	FBG	DV	IO	R425	MRCR	8	6	12000	2	9	75300	82700
44	5	SONIC 445	OP	OFF	FBG	DV	IO	R465	MRCR	8	6	12000	2	9	81000	89000
		1992 BOATS														
24	2	SONIC SS 24	OP	OFF	FBG	DV	OB			8		4000	1	6	13500	15300
24	2	SONIC SS 24	OP	OFF	FBG	DV	IO	330-365		8		4000	1	6	13800	16800
24	2	SONIC SS 24	OP	OFF	FBG	DV	IO	410-445		8		4000	1	6	16500	20400
27	6	SONIC SS 27	OP	OFF	FBG	DV	OB			8	6	5000	1	10	19800	22100
27	6	SONIC SS 27	OP	OFF	FBG	DV	IO	T270-T330		8	6	5000	1	10	21800	26400
27	6	SONIC SS 27	OP	OFF	FBG	DV	IO	T365	MRCR	8	6	5000	1	10	25200	28100
30	6	SONIC SS 30	OP	OFF	FBG	DV	OB			8	6	7000	1	10	27300	30300
30	6	SONIC SS 30	OP	OFF	FBG	DV	IO	T270-T365		8	6	7000	1	10	27600	33300
30	6	SONIC SS 30	OP	OFF	FBG	DV	IO	T410	MRCR	8	6	7000	1	10	31300	34800
34		SONIC SS 34	OP	OFF	FBG	DV	OB			8	6	8000	2	4	28500	31700
34		SONIC SS 34	OP	OFF	FBG	DV	IO	T330-T445		8	6	8000	2	4	45900	55500
35		SONIC SE 35	OP	OFF	FBG	DV	IO	T330	MRCR	8	6				51500	56600
		IO T365 MRCR 53000 58300, IO T410 MRCR 55400 60900, IO T445 MRCR													57600	63300
38		SONIC SS 38	OP	OFF	FBG	DV	IO	T365	MRCR	8	6	8800	2	6	50900	56000
		IO T410 MRCR 54200 59500, IO T425 MRCR 55400 60900, IO T445 MRCR													57100	62800
41		SONIC SS 41	OP	OFF	FBG	DV	IO	T410	MRCR	8	6	10000	2	6	64600	71000
41		SONIC SS 41	OP	OFF	FBG	DV	IO	T445	MRCR	8	6	10000	2	6	68000	74700
44	5	SONIC 445	OP	OFF	FBG	DV	IO	R365	MRCR	8	6	12000	2	9	63000	69200
		IO R410 MRCR 68500 75200, IO R425 MRCR 70400 77400, IO R445 MRCR													73100	80300
		1991 BOATS														
24	2	SONIC SS 24	OP	OFF	FBG	DV	OB			8		4000	1	6	12900	14600
24	2	SONIC SS 24	OP	OFF	FBG	DV	IO	330-365		8		4000	1	6	13000	15800
24	2	SONIC SS 24	OP	OFF	FBG	DV	IO	410-445		8		4000	1	6	15500	19200
27	6	SONIC SS 27	OP	OFF	FBG	DV	OB			8	6	5000	1	10	19000	21100
27	6	SONIC SS 27	OP	OFF	FBG	DV	IO	T270-T330		8	6	5000	1	10	20500	24800
27	6	SONIC SS 27	OP	OFF	FBG	DV	IO	T365	MRCR	8	6	5000	1	10	23700	26300
30	6	SONIC SS 30	OP	OFF	FBG	DV	OB			8	6	7000	1	10	26000	28900
30	6	SONIC SS 30	OP	OFF	FBG	DV	IO	T270-T365		8	6	7000	1	10	25900	31300
30	6	SONIC SS 30	OP	OFF	FBG	DV	IO	T410	MRCR	8	6	7000	1	10	29400	32700
34		SONIC SS 34	OP	OFF	FBG	DV	OB			8	6	8000	2	4	26900	29900
34		SONIC SS 34	OP	OFF	FBG	DV	IO	T330-T445		8	6	8000	2	4	42600	52300
38		SONIC SS 38	OP	OFF	FBG	DV	IO	T365	MRCR	8	6	8800	2	6	47800	52500
		IO T410 MRCR 50800 55800, IO T425 MRCR 52000 57100, IO T445 MRCR													53600	58900
41		SONIC SS 41	OP	OFF	FBG	DV	IO	T410	MRCR	8	6	10000	2	6	60600	66600
41		SONIC SS 41	OP	OFF	FBG	DV	IO	T425	MRCR	8	6	10000	2	6	61900	68100
41		SONIC SS 41	OP	OFF	FBG	DV	IO	T445	MRCR	8	6	10000	2	6	63800	70100
44	5	SONIC 445	OP	OFF	FBG	DV	IO	R365	MRCR	8	6	12000	2	9	59000	64900
		IO R410 MRCR 64200 70600, IO R425 MRCR 66000 72600, IO R445 MRCR													68500	75300
		1990 BOATS														
24	2	SONIC 24SS	OP	OFF	FBG	DV	OB			8		4200			12700	14400
24	2	SONIC 24SS	OP	OFF	FBG	DV	IO	300	MRCR	8		4200			12000	13700
24	2	SONIC 24SS	OP	OFF	FBG	DV	IO	365	MRCR	8		4200			13500	15300
27	6	SONIC 27SS	OP	OFF	FBG	DV	OB			8	6	5000			18100	20100
27	6	SONIC 27SS	OP	OFF	FBG	DV	IO	300-365		8	6	5000			16600	20300
27	6	SONIC 27SS	OP	OFF	FBG	DV	IO	T270	MRCR	8	6	5000			19300	21400
30	5	SONIC 30SS	OP	OFF	FBG	DV	OB			8	6	7000			24700	27400
30	5	SONIC 30SS	OP	OFF	FBG	DV	IO	T270-T365		8	6	6000			23600	28600
33	4	SONIC 33SS	OP	OFF	FBG	DV	OB			8	6	7000			24900	27700
34	10	SONIC 34SS	OP	OFF	FBG	DV	IO	T300-T420		8	6	8000			43000	52700
35		SONIC 35SE	OP	OFF	FBG	DV	IO	365	MRCR	8	6	8500			42400	47100
35		SONIC 35SE	OP	OFF	FBG	DV	IO	420	MRCR	8	6	8500			43700	48500
35		SONIC 35SE	OP	OFF	FBG	DV	IO	T300	MRCR	8	6	8500			44400	49300
38		SONIC 38SS	OP	OFF	FBG	DV	IO	T365	MRCR	8	6	8800			44700	49600
38		SONIC 38SS	OP	OFF	FBG	DV	IO	T420	MRCR	8	6	8800			48500	53300
38		SONIC 38SS	OP	OFF	FBG	DV	IO	T575	MRCR	8	6	8800			59600	65500
41		SONIC 41SS	OP	OFF	FBG	DV	IO	T420	MRCR	8	6	10000			58300	64000
41		SONIC 41SS	OP	OFF	FBG	DV	IO	T575	MRCR	8	6	10000			71100	78100
		1989 BOATS														
24	2	SONIC 24SS	OP	OFF	FBG	DV	OB			8		4200			12200	13800
24	2	SONIC 24SS	OP	OFF	FBG	DV	IO		MRCR	8		4200			**	**
24	2	SONIC 24SS	OP	OFF	FBG	DV	IO	365	MRCR	8		4200			12700	14400
27	6	SONIC 27SS	OP	OFF	FBG	DV	OB			8	6	5000			17000	19300
27	6	SONIC 27SS	OP	OFF	FBG	DV	IO		MRCR	8	6	5000			**	**
		IO 365 MRCR 16800 19100, IO T MRCR ** **, IO T270 MRCR													18400	20400
30	5	SONIC 30SS	OP	OFF	FBG	DV	OB			8	6	7000			23600	26200
30	5	SONIC 30SS	OP	OFF	FBG	DV	IO	T	MRCR	8	6	6000			**	**
30	5	SONIC 30SS	OP	OFF	FBG	DV	IO	T270-T365		8	6	7000			22800	27500
33	4	SONIC 33SS	OP	OFF	FBG	DV	OB			8	6	7000			23800	26500
34	10	SONIC 34SS	OP	OFF	FBG	DV	IO	T	MRCR	8	6	8000			**	**
34	10	SONIC 34SS	OP	OFF	FBG	DV	IO	T365-T420		8	6	8000			42700	50000
35		SONIC 35SE	OP	OFF	FBG	DV	IO	365	MRCR	8	6	8500			40000	44500
35		SONIC 35SE	OP	OFF	FBG	DV	IO	420	MRCR	8	6	8500			41200	45800
35		SONIC 35SE	OP	OFF	FBG	DV	IO	T	MRCR	8	6	8500			**	**
38		SONIC 38SS	OP	OFF	FBG	DV	IO	T365	MRCR	8	6	8800			42200	46800
38		SONIC 38SS	OP	OFF	FBG	DV	IO	T420	MRCR	8	6	8800			46000	50600
38		SONIC 38SS	OP	OFF	FBG	DV	IO	T575	MRCR	8	6	8800			56200	61800
41		SONIC 41SS	OP	OFF	FBG	DV	IO	T420	MRCR	8	6	10000			55000	60400
41		SONIC 41SS	OP	OFF	FBG	DV	IO	T575	MRCR	8	6	10000			67100	73700
		1988 BOATS														
24	2	SONIC 24SS	OP	OFF	FBG	DV	OB			8		4000			11400	12900
24	2	SONIC 24SS	OP	OFF	FBG	DV	IO		MRCR	8		4000			**	**
24	2	SONIC 24SS	OP	OFF	FBG	DV	IO		OMC	8		4000			**	**
30	5	SONIC 30SS	OP	OFF	FBG	DV	OB			8	6	6600			22700	25200
30	5	SONIC 30SS	OP	OFF	FBG	DV	IO	T	MRCR	8	6	6000			**	**
30	5	SONIC 30SS	OP	OFF	FBG	DV	IO	T	OMC	8	6	6000			**	**
33	4	SONIC 33RS	OP	OFF	FBG	DV	IO	T	MRCR	8	6	7500			**	**
33	4	SONIC 33RS	OP	OFF	FBG	DV	IO	T	OMC	8	6	7500			**	**
33	4	SONIC 33SE	OP	OFF	FBG	DV	OB			8	6	6000			23500	26100
33	4	SONIC 33SS	OP	OFF	FBG	DV	OB			8	6	6000			22200	24700
35		SONIC 35SE	OP	OFF	FBG	DV	IO	T	MRCR	8	6	8000			**	**
35		SONIC 35SE	OP	OFF	FBG	DV	IO	T	OMC	8	6	8000			**	**
35		SONIC 35SS	OP	OFF	FBG	DV	IO	T	MRCR	8	6	7800			**	**
35		SONIC 35SS	OP	OFF	FBG	DV	IO	T	OMC	8	6	7800			**	**
35	4	SONIC 35SE	OP	OFF	FBG	DV	IO	T	MRCR	8	6	8000			**	**
35	4	SONIC 35SE	OP	OFF	FBG	DV	IO	T	OMC	8	6	8000			**	**
35	4	SONIC 35SS	OP	OFF	FBG	DV	IO	T	MRCR	8	6	7800			**	**
35	4	SONIC 35SS	OP	OFF	FBG	DV	IO	T	OMC	8	6	7800			**	**
36		SONIC 36SS	OP	OFF	FBG	DV	IO	T420	MRCR	8	6	8000			33000	36700
41		SONIC 41SE	OP	OFF	FBG	DV	IO	T420	MRCR	8	6	10000			52700	58000
		1987 BOATS														
24	2	SONIC SE	OP	OFF	FBG	DV	OB			8					7250	8350
24	2	SONIC SE	OP	OFF	FBG	DV	IO		MRCR	8					**	**
24	2	SONIC SE	OP	OFF	FBG	DV	IO	330	MRCR	8					9400	10700
24	2	SONIC SE	OP	OFF	FBG	DV	IO	T260		8					9800	11100
24	2	SONIC SS	OP	OFF	FBG	DV	OB			8					7250	8350
24	2	SONIC SS	OP	OFF	FBG	DV	IO		MRCR	8					**	**
		IO 330 MRCR 9150 10400, IO T260-T300 9800 12100, IO T350 MRCR													12400	14000
30	5	SONIC 30SS	OP	OFF	FBG	DV	OB			8		6000			21800	24200
30	5	SONIC 30SS	OP	OFF	FBG	DV	IO	T	MRCR	8		6000			**	**
30	5	SONIC 30SS	OP	OFF	FBG	DV	IO	T330-T420		8		6000			20900	25500
33	4	SONIC 33SS	OP	OFF	FBG	DV	OB			8	2				28500	31700
33	4	SONIC 33SS	OP	OFF	FBG	DV	IO	T330-T425		8	2				31400	37600
33	4	SONIC RS	OP	OFF	FBG	DV	OB			8	2				27000	30000
33	4	SONIC RS	OP	OFF	FBG	DV	IO	T330-T420		8	2				29900	36200
33	4	SONIC SE	OP	OFF	FBG	DV	OB			8	2				29700	33000
33	4	SONIC SE	OP	OFF	FBG	DV	IO	T330-T420		8	2				32600	38600
36		SONIC 36SS	OP	OFF	FBG	DV	IO	T330	MRCR	8	6				28800	32000
36		SONIC 36SS	OP	OFF	FBG	DV	IO	T370	MRCR	8	6				30000	33300
36		SONIC 36SS	OP	OFF	FBG	DV	IO	T420	MRCR	8	6				31800	35400
41		SONIC 41SE	OP	OFF	FBG	DV	IO	T370	MRCR	8	6				48200	53000
41		SONIC 41SE	OP	OFF	FBG	DV	IO	T420	MRCR	8	6				51600	56700
		1986 BOATS														
20	6	SONIC 21	OP	OFF	FBG	DV	OB			8					6650	7650
20	6	SONIC 21	OP	OFF	FBG	DV	JT		CHEV	8					**	**
20	6	SONIC 21	OP	OFF	FBG	DV	IO	260	OMC	8					6600	7600
24	2	SONIC OPEN FISHERMAN	OP	OPFSH	FBG	DV	OB			8					9650	11000
24	2	SONIC OPEN FISHERMAN	OP	OPFSH	FBG	DV	IO	330	MRCR	8					10700	12200
24	2	SONIC OPEN FISHERMAN	OP	OPFSH	FBG	DV	IO	T260		8					11300	12800
24	2	SONIC SE	OP	OFF	FBG	DV	OB			8					7000	8050
24	2	SONIC SE	OP	OFF	FBG	DV	IO	330	MRCR	8					8850	10100
24	2	SONIC SE	OP	OFF	FBG	DV	IO	T260		8					9400	10700
24	2	SONIC SS	OP	OFF	FBG	DV	OB			8					7000	8050
24	2	SONIC SS	OP	OFF	FBG	DV	IO	330	MRCR	8					8850	10100
24	2	SONIC SS	OP	OFF	FBG	DV	IO	T260		8					9400	10700

CONTINUED ON NEXT PAGE

LOA FT	LOA IN	NAME AND/ OR MODEL	TOP/ RIG	BOAT TYPE	HULL MTL	HULL TP	ENGINE TP	ENGINE # HP	ENGINE MFG	BEAM FT	BEAM IN	WGT LBS	DRAFT FT	DRAFT IN	RETAIL LOW	RETAIL HIGH
		1986 BOATS														
33	4	SONIC 33SS	OP	OFF	FBG	DV	OB			8	2				25900	28800
33	4	SONIC 33SS	OP	OFF	FBG	DV	IO	T330-T440		8	2				28700	35200
33	4	SONIC RS	OP	OFF	FBG	DV	OB			8	2				25900	28800
33	4	SONIC RS	OP	OFF	FBG	DV	IO	T330-T440		8	2				28700	35200
33	4	SONIC SE	OP	OFF	FBG	DV	OB			8	2				30000	33300
33	4	SONIC SE	OP	OFF	FBG	DV	IO	T330-T440		8	2				32300	38600
36		SONIC 36SS	OP	OFF	FBG	DV	IO	T330	MRCR						28300	31500
		IO T370 MRCR 29500 32700, IO T400 MRCR 30500 33900, IO T440 MRCR													32000	35600
41		SONIC 41SE	OP	OFF	FBG	DV	IO	T370	MRCR						46300	50900
41		SONIC 41SE	OP	OFF	FBG	DV	IO	T400	MRCR						47900	52700
41		SONIC 41SE	OP	OFF	FBG	DV	IO	T440	MRCR						50700	55700
		1985 BOATS														
20	6	SONIC 21	OP	OFF	FBG	DV	OB			8					6450	7400
20	6	SONIC 21	OP	OFF	FBG	DV	IO	260	OMC	8					6350	7300
20	6	SONIC 21	OP	OFF	FBG	DV	JT	320-333		8					8450	9750
24	2	SONIC OPEN FISHERMAN	OP	OPFSH	FBG	DV	OB			8					9350	10600
24	2	SONIC OPEN FISHERMAN	OP	OPFSH	FBG	DV	IO	330	MRCR	8					10300	11700
24	2	SONIC OPEN FISHERMAN	OP	OPFSH	FBG	DV	IO	T260		8					10800	12300
24	2	SONIC SE	OP	OFF	FBG	DV	OB			8					6800	7800
24	2	SONIC SE	OP	OFF	FBG	DV	IO	330	MRCR	8					8400	9650
24	2	SONIC SE	OP	OFF	FBG	DV	IO	T260		8					9000	10300
24	2	SONIC SS	OP	OFF	FBG	DV	OB			8					6800	7800
24	2	SONIC SS	OP	OFF	FBG	DV	IO	330	MRCR	8					8400	9650
24	2	SONIC SS	OP	OFF	FBG	DV	IO	T260		8					9000	10300
33	4	SONIC RS	OP	OFF	FBG	DV	OB			8	2				23900	26600
33	4	SONIC RS	OP	OFF	FBG	DV	IO	T370-T400		8	2				28200	32300
33	4	SONIC SE	OP	OFF	FBG	DV	OB			8	2				28600	31800
33	4	SONIC SE	OP	OFF	FBG	DV	IO	T330-T425		8	2				28700	35100
		1984 BOATS														
20	6	SONIC 21	OP	OFF	FBG	DV	OB			8					6250	7200
20	6	SONIC 21	OP	OFF	FBG	DV	IO	260		8					6200	7100
20	6	SONIC 21	OP	OFF	FBG	DV	JT	320-333		8					8100	9300
20	6	SONIC 21	OP	OFF	FBG	DV	IO	425		8					9300	10600
24	2	SONIC OPEN FISHERMAN	OP	OFF	FBG	DV	IO	330	MRCR	8					8050	9300
24	2	SONIC OPEN FISHERMAN	OP	OFF	FBG	DV	IO	T260		8					8550	9850
24	2	SONIC OPEN FISHERMAN	OP	OPFSH	FBG	DV	OB			8					9050	10300
24	2	SONIC S	OP	OFF	FBG	DV	OB			8					6550	7500
24	2	SONIC S	OP	OFF	FBG	DV	IO	330	MRCR	8					8050	9300
24	2	SONIC S	OP	OFF	FBG	DV	IO	T260		8					8550	9850
24	2	SONIC SE	OP	OFF	FBG	DV	OB			8					6700	7700
24	2	SONIC SE	OP	OFF	FBG	DV	IO	330-370		8					8250	10200
24	2	SONIC SE	OP	OFF	FBG	DV	IO	T185	MRCR	8					8000	9200
24	2	SONIC SE	OP	OFF	FBG	DV	IO	T260		8					8850	10100
24	2	SONIC SS	OP	OFF	FBG	DV	OB			8					6550	7500
24	2	SONIC SS	OP	OFF	FBG	DV	IO	330	MRCR	8					8050	9300
24	2	SONIC SS/OB	OP	OFF	FBG	DV	IO	T260		8					8550	9850
33	4	SONIC RS		OFF	FBG	DV	OB			8	2				23100	25700
33	4	SONIC RS		OFF	FBG	DV	IO	T330-T400		8	2				26000	30900
33	4	SONIC RS	OP	OFF	FBG	DV	IO	T425		8	2				28600	31800
33	4	SONIC SE		OFF	FBG	DV	OB			8	2				27700	30800
33	4	SONIC SE		OFF	FBG	DV	IO	T330-T400		8	2				29300	34100
33	4	SONIC SE		OFF	FBG	DV	IO	R		8	2				**	**
33	4	SONIC SE	OP	OFF	FBG	DV	IO	T425		8	2				31100	34600

....For earlier years, see the BUC Used Boat Price Guide, Volume 3

CUMBERLAND CRUISER HOUSEBOAT

SOMERSET KY 42501

See inside cover to adjust price for area

LOA FT	LOA IN	NAME AND/ OR MODEL	TOP/ RIG	BOAT TYPE	HULL MTL	HULL TP	ENGINE TP	ENGINE # HP	ENGINE MFG	BEAM FT	BEAM IN	WGT LBS	DRAFT FT	DRAFT IN	RETAIL LOW	RETAIL HIGH
		1987 BOATS														
42		CUMBERLAND CRUISER	HT	HB	AL	SV	IO	145	VLVO	14			1	2	16900	19200
42		CUMBERLAND CRUISER	HT	HB	STL	SV	IO	145	VLVO	14			1	2	15000	17100
44		CUMBERLAND CRUISER	HT	HB	AL	SV	IO	145	VLVO	14			1	2	16800	19100
44		CUMBERLAND CRUISER	HT	HB	STL	SV	IO	145	VLVO	14			1	2	15100	17200
46		CUMBERLAND CRUISER	HT	HB	AL	SV	IO	145	VLVO	14			1	2	19400	21600
46		CUMBERLAND CRUISER	HT	HB	STL	SV	IO	145	VLVO	14			1	2	17400	19800
48		CUMBERLAND CRUISER	HT	HB	AL	SV	IO	145	VLVO	14			1	2	20300	22500
48		CUMBERLAND CRUISER	HT	HB	STL	SV	IO	145	VLVO	14			1	2	18900	21000
50		CUMBERLAND CRUISER	HT	HB	AL	SV	IO	145	VLVO	14			1	2	21700	24100
50		CUMBERLAND CRUISER	HT	HB	STL	SV	IO	145	VLVO	14			1	2	20200	22500
55		CUMBERLAND CRUISER	HT	HB	AL	SV	IO	145	VLVO	14			1	2	25000	27800
55		CUMBERLAND CRUISER	HT	HB	STL	SV	IO	145	VLVO	14			1	2	23300	25900
60		CUMBERLAND CRUISER	HT	HB	AL	SV	IO	145	VLVO	14			1	2	23200	25800
60		CUMBERLAND CRUISER	HT	HB	STL	SV	IO	145	VLVO	14			1	2	21800	24200
		1986 BOATS														
42		CUMBERLAND CRUISER	HT	HB	AL	SV	IO	145	VLVO	14			1	2	16500	18700
42		CUMBERLAND CRUISER	HT	HB	STL	SV	IO	145	VLVO	14			1	2	14600	16600
44		CUMBERLAND CRUISER	HT	HB	AL	SV	IO	145	VLVO	14			1	2	16400	18600
44		CUMBERLAND CRUISER	HT	HB	STL	SV	IO	145	VLVO	14			1	2	14700	16800
46		CUMBERLAND CRUISER	HT	HB	AL	SV	IO	145	VLVO	14			1	2	18900	21000
46		CUMBERLAND CRUISER	HT	HB	STL	SV	IO	145	VLVO	14			1	2	16900	19200
48		CUMBERLAND CRUISER	HT	HB	AL	SV	IO	145	VLVO	14			1	2	20100	22300
48		CUMBERLAND CRUISER	HT	HB	STL	SV	IO	145	VLVO	14			1	2	18400	20500
50		CUMBERLAND CRUISER	HT	HB	AL	SV	IO	145	VLVO	14			1	2	21100	23400
50		CUMBERLAND CRUISER	HT	HB	STL	SV	IO	145	VLVO	14			1	2	19700	21900
55		CUMBERLAND CRUISER	HT	HB	AL	SV	IO	145	VLVO	14			1	2	24400	27100
55		CUMBERLAND CRUISER	HT	HB	STL	SV	IO	145	VLVO	14			1	2	22700	25200
60		CUMBERLAND CRUISER	HT	HB	AL	SV	IO	145	VLVO	14			1	2	22800	25400
60		CUMBERLAND CRUISER	HT	HB	STL	SV	IO	145	VLVO	14			1	2	21200	23600

CUSTOM FIBERGLASS MFG

PORT ANGELES WA 98362 COAST GUARD MFG ID- CFM See inside cover to adjust price for area

LOA FT	LOA IN	NAME AND/ OR MODEL	TOP/ RIG	BOAT TYPE	HULL MTL	HULL TP	ENGINE TP	ENGINE # HP	ENGINE MFG	BEAM FT	BEAM IN	WGT LBS	DRAFT FT	DRAFT IN	RETAIL LOW	RETAIL HIGH
		1993 BOATS														
17	8	1882C	OP	CTRCN	FBG	TR	OB			6	10	950			2400	2750
17	8	1882D	OP	FSH	FBG	TR	OB			6	10	950			2400	2800
17	8	1882S	OP	FSH	FBG	TR	OB			6	10	950			2350	2700
17	8	1882W/T	ST	FSH	FBG	TR	OB			6	10	950			2350	2750
18		1884C	OP	CTRCN	FBG	DV	OB			7		1000			2500	2900
18		1884D	OP	FSH	FBG	DV	OB			7		1000			2550	3000
18		1884S	OP	FSH	FBG	DV	OB			7		1000			2450	2850
18		1884W/T	ST	FSH	FBG	DV	OB			7		1000			2500	2900
20	10	2192C	OP	CTRCN	FBG	DV	OB			7	8	1500			4000	4650
20	10	2192W/T	ST	FSH	FBG	DV	OB			7	8	1500			4000	4650
		1992 BOATS														
16	3	165W/T	OP	RNBT	FBG	DV	OB			6	4	1080			2450	2850
17	8	1882C	OP	CTRCN	FBG	TR	OB			6	10	950			2300	2700
17	8	1882D	OP	FSH	FBG	TR	OB			6	10	950			2350	2750
17	8	1882S	OP	FSH	FBG	TR	OB			6	10	950			2250	2650
17	8	1882W/T	ST	FSH	FBG	TR	OB			6	10	950			2300	2700
18		1884C	OP	CTRCN	FBG	DV	OB			7		1100			2600	3050
18		1884D	OP	FSH	FBG	DV	OB			7		1100			2650	3050
18		1884S	OP	FSH	FBG	DV	OB			7		1100			2550	3000
18		1884W/T	ST	FSH	FBG	DV	OB			7		1100			2600	3050
18	6	1900C	OP	CTRCN	FBG	DV	OB			7		1675			3600	4200
18	6	1900W/T	TT	FSH	FBG	DV	OB			7		1675			3600	4200
20	7	2100WAC	ST	CUD	FBG	DV	OB			8		2400			5350	6150
20	10	2192C	OP	CTRCN	FBG	DV	OB			7	8	1600			4050	4700
20	10	2192W/T	ST	FSH	FBG	DV	OB			7	8	1600			4050	4700
		1989 BOATS														
17	8	1882C	OP	CTRCN	FBG	TR	OB			6	10	950			2050	2400
17	8	1882D	OP	FSH	FBG	TR	OB			6	10	950			2050	2450
17	8	1882S	OP	FSH	FBG	TR	OB			6	10	950			2000	2350
17	8	1882W/T	ST	FSH	FBG	TR	OB			6	10	950			2050	2400
18		1884V-C	OP	CTRCN	FBG	DV	OB			7		1100			2350	2750
18		1884V-D	OP	FSH	FBG	DV	OB			7		1100			2400	2800
18		1884V-S	OP	FSH	FBG	DV	OB			7		1100			2300	2700
18		1884V-W/T	ST	FSH	FBG	DV	OB			7		1100			2350	2750
20	10	2192C	OP	CTRCN	FBG	DV	OB			7	8	1600			3650	4250
20	10	2192W/T	ST	FSH	FBG	DV	OB			7	8	1600			3650	4250
		1988 BOATS														
17	8	1882C	OP	CTRCN	FBG	TR	OB			6	10	950			1950	2350
17	8	1882D	OP	FSH	FBG	TR	OB			6	10	950			2000	2400
17	8	1882S	OP	FSH	FBG	TR	OB			6	10	950			1900	2300
17	8	1882W/T	ST	FSH	FBG	TR	OB			6	10	950			1950	2350
18		1884V-C	OP	CTRCN	FBG	DV	OB			7		1100			2300	2700
18		1884V-D	OP	FSH	FBG	DV	OB			7		1100			2300	2700
18		1884V-S	OP	FSH	FBG	DV	OB			7		1100			2250	2600
18		1884V-W/T	ST	FSH	FBG	DV	OB			7		1100			2300	2700
20	10	2192C	OP	CTRCN	FBG	DV	OB			7	8	1600			3550	4100
20	10	2192W/T	ST	FSH	FBG	DV	OB			7	8	1600			3550	4100

CONTINUED ON NEXT PAGE

LOA FT IN	NAME AND/ OR MODEL	TOP/ RIG	BOAT TYPE	-HULL- MTL TP	----ENGINE--- TP # HP MFG	BEAM FT IN	WGT LBS	DRAFT FT IN	RETAIL LOW	RETAIL HIGH

----------------------- 1987 BOATS -----------------------

17	8	1882C	OP	CTRCN	FBG TR	OB		6	10	950		1900	2300
17	8	1882D	OP	FSH	FBG TR	OB		6	10	950		1950	2350
17	8	1882S	OP	FSH	FBG TR	OB		6	10	950		1850	2200
17	8	1882W/T	ST	FSH	FBG TR	OB		6	10	950		1900	2300
18		1884V-C	OP	CTRCN	FBG DV	OB		7		1100		2250	2600
18		1884V-D	OP	FSH	FBG DV	OB		7		1100		2300	2650
18		1884V-S	OP	FSH	FBG DV	OB		7		1100		2200	2550
18		1884V-W/T	ST	FSH	FBG DV	OB		7		1100		2250	2600
20	10	2192C	OP	CTRCN	FBG DV	OB		7	8	1600		3450	4000
20	10	2192W/T	ST	FSH	FBG DV	OB		7	8	1600		3450	4000

----------------------- 1986 BOATS -----------------------

17	8	1882C	OP	CTRCN	FBG TR	OB		6	10	950		1850	2200
17	8	1882D	OP	FSH	FBG TR	OB		6	10	950		1900	2250
17	8	1882S	OP	FSH	FBG TR	OB		6	10	950		1800	2150
17	8	1882W/T	ST	FSH	FBG TR	OB		6	10	950		1850	2200
17	10	1782C	OP	CTRCN	FBG TR	OB		6	10	900		1800	2150
17	10	1782D	OP	FSH	FBG TR	OB		6	10	900		1800	2150
17	10	1782S	OP	FSH	FBG TR	OB		6	10	900		1750	2100
17	10	1782W/T	ST	FSH	FBG TR	OB		6	10	900		1800	2150
18		1884V-C	OP	CTRCN	FBG DV	OB		7		1100		2200	2550
18		1884V-D	OP	FSH	FBG DV	OB		7		1100		2250	2600
18		1884V-S	OP	FSH	FBG DV	OB		7		1100		2100	2500
18		1884V-W/T	ST	FSH	FBG DV	OB		7		1100		2200	2550
20	3	2088C	OP	CTRCN	FBG TR	OB		7	4	1200		2600	3000
20	3	2088D	OP	FSH	FBG TR	OB		7	4	1200		2650	3050
20	3	2088S	OP	FSH	FBG TR	OB		7	4	1200		2550	2950
20	3	2088W/T	ST	FSH	FBG TR	OB		7	4	1200		2600	3000
20	10	2192C	OP	CTRCN	FBG DV	OB		7	8	1600		3350	3900
20	10	2192W/T	ST	FSH	FBG DV	OB		7	8	1600		3350	3900

----------------------- 1985 BOATS -----------------------

17	8	1882C	OP	CTRCN	FBG TR	OB		6	10	950		1800	2150
17	8	1882D	OP	FSH	FBG TR	OB		6	10	950		1850	2200
17	8	1882S	OP	FSH	FBG TR	OB		6	10	950		1800	2100
17	8	1882W/T	ST	FSH	FBG TR	OB		6	10	950		1800	2150
17	10	1782C	OP	CTRCN	FBG TR	OB		6	10	900		1750	2100
17	10	1782D	OP	FSH	FBG TR	OB		6	10	900		1800	2100
17	10	1782S	OP	FSH	FBG TR	OB		6	10	900		1700	2050
17	10	1782W/T	ST	FSH	FBG TR	OB		6	10	900		1750	2100
18		1884V-C	OP	CTRCN	FBG DV	OB		7		1100		2100	2500
18		1884V-D	OP	FSH	FBG DV	OB		7		1100		2200	2550
18		1884V-S	OP	FSH	FBG DV	OB		7		1100		2050	2450
18		1884V-W/T	ST	FSH	FBG DV	OB		7		1100		2100	2500
20	3	2088C	OP	CTRCN	FBG TR	OB		7	4	1200		2550	2950
20	3	2088D	OP	FSH	FBG TR	OB		7	4	1200		2600	3000
20	3	2088S	OP	FSH	FBG TR	OB		7	4	1200		2500	2900
20	3	2088W/T	ST	FSH	FBG TR	OB		7	4	1200		2550	2950
20	10	2192C	OP	CTRCN	FBG DV	OB		7	8	1600		3300	3800
20	10	2192W/T	ST	FSH	FBG DV	OB		7	8	1600		3300	3800

----------------------- 1984 BOATS -----------------------

17	8	1882C	OP	CTRCN	FBG TR	OB		6	10	950		1800	2100
17	8	1882D	OP	FSH	FBG TR	OB		6	10	950		1800	2150
17	8	1882S	OP	FSH	FBG TR	OB		6	10	950		1750	2100
17	8	1882W/T	ST	FSH	FBG TR	OB		6	10	950		1800	2100
17	10	1782C	OP	CTRCN	FBG TR	OB		6	10	900		1700	2050
17	10	1782D	OP	FSH	FBG TR	OB		6	10	900		1750	2050
17	10	1782S	OP	FSH	FBG TR	OB		6	10	900		1700	2000
17	10	1782W/T	ST	FSH	FBG TR	OB		6	10	900		1700	2050
18		1884V-C	OP	CTRCN	FBG DV	OB		7		1100		2050	2450
18		1884V-D	OP	FSH	FBG DV	OB		7		1100		2100	2500
18		1884V-S	OP	FSH	FBG DV	OB		7		1100		2000	2400
18		1884V-W/T	ST	FSH	FBG DV	OB		7		1100		2050	2450
20	3	2088C	OP	CTRCN	FBG TR	OB		7	4	1200		2450	2900
20	3	2088D	OP	FSH	FBG TR	OB		7	4	1200		2500	2950
20	3	2088S	OP	FSH	FBG TR	OB		7	4	1200		2450	2800
20	3	2088W/T	ST	FSH	FBG TR	OB		7	4	1200		2450	2900
20	10	2192C	OP	CTRCN	FBG DV	OB		7	8	1600		3200	3750
20	10	2192W/T	ST	FSH	FBG DV	OB		7	8	1600		3200	3750

....For earlier years, see the BUC Used Boat Price Guide, Volume 3

CUSTOM LINE INC
AUBURNDALE FL 33823   COAST GUARD MFG ID- CWY See inside cover to adjust price for area

LOA FT IN	NAME AND/ OR MODEL	TOP/ RIG	BOAT TYPE	-HULL- MTL TP	----ENGINE--- TP # HP MFG	BEAM FT IN	WGT LBS	DRAFT FT IN	RETAIL LOW	RETAIL HIGH

----------------------- 1984 BOATS -----------------------

16		RALLY-SPORT 6.3S	OP	RNBT	FBG SV	OB		6	2		1700	2000
17	7	RALLY-SPORT 7.0S	OP	RNBT	FBG SV	OB		7	5		2800	3250
18	3	RALLY-SPORT 7.2S	OP	RNBT	FBG SV	OB		6	8		2850	3300
18	3	RALLY-SPORT 7.2SJ	OP	RNBT	FBG SV JT	320 BERK	6	8		4200	4900
18	3	RALLY-SPORT 7.2SS	OP	SKI	FBG SV	OB		6	8		2200	2550
20	2	RALLY-SPORT 8.1T	OP	RNBT	FBG TH	OB		7	11		4000	4650
20	6	RALLY-SPORT 8.2BR	OP	RNBT	FBG SV	OB		7	9		4750	5450
20	6	RALLY-SPORT 8.2DC	OP	SPTCR	FBG TH	OB		7	9		5400	6200
20	6	RALLY-SPORT 8.2DC	OP	SPTCR	FBG SV	IO	198-260	7	9	4750	5700
20	6	RALLY-SPORT 8.2DC	OP	SPTCR	FBG SV JT	320 BERK	7	9		6500	7450
20	8	RALLY-SPORT 8.3DV	OP	RNBT	FBG SV	OB		7	7		4800	5550
20	8	RALLY-SPORT 8.3DV	OP	RNBT	FBG SV	IO	260 MRCR	7	7		4550	5250
26		RALLY-SPORT 260S	OP	RNBT	FBG SV	OB		7	11		9950	11300
26		RALLY-SPORT 260S	OP	RNBT	FBG SV	IO	260 MRCR	7	11		7950	9150

....For earlier years, see the BUC Used Boat Price Guide, Volume 3

CUSTOM MARINE
DIV OF SAVANNAH DIST CO INC
SAVANNAH GA 31401   COAST GUARD MFG ID- CMN   See inside cover to adjust price for area

LOA FT IN	NAME AND/ OR MODEL	TOP/ RIG	BOAT TYPE	-HULL- MTL TP	----ENGINE--- TP # HP MFG	BEAM FT IN	WGT LBS	DRAFT FT IN	RETAIL LOW	RETAIL HIGH

----------------------- 1984 BOATS -----------------------

| 25 | 7 | RELEASE 26 | OP | OPFSH | FBG DV | IB | 165 | 8 | 4500 | 2 3 | 12800 | 14600 |

....For earlier years, see the BUC Used Boat Price Guide, Volume 3

CUSTOM YACHT TENDERS
LAKE WORTH FL 33460   COAST GUARD MFG ID- CYJ See inside cover to adjust price for area

LOA FT IN	NAME AND/ OR MODEL	TOP/ RIG	BOAT TYPE	-HULL- MTL TP	----ENGINE--- TP # HP MFG	BEAM FT IN	WGT LBS	DRAFT FT IN	RETAIL LOW	RETAIL HIGH

----------------------- 1991 BOATS -----------------------

| 16 | | HANSEN | OP | RNBT | FBG SV | OB | | 5 | 10 | 500 | | 1500 | 1800 |
| 21 | | HANSEN | OP | RNBT | FBG SV | OB | | 7 | 6 | 2600 | | 6250 | 7200 |

----------------------- 1990 BOATS -----------------------

| 16 | | HANSEN | OP | RNBT | FBG SV | OB | | 5 | 10 | 500 | | 1450 | 1750 |
| 21 | | HANSEN | OP | CTRCN | FBG SV | OB | | 7 | 6 | 2600 | | 6050 | 6950 |

----------------------- 1989 BOATS -----------------------

| 16 | | HANSEN | OP | RNBT | FBG SV | OB | | 5 | 10 | 500 | | 1400 | 1650 |
| 21 | | HANSEN | OP | CTRCN | FBG SV | OB | | 7 | 5 | 2000 | | 4900 | 5650 |

----------------------- 1988 BOATS -----------------------

| 16 | | HANSEN | OP | RNBT | FBG SV | OB | | 5 | 10 | 500 | | 1350 | 1600 |
| 21 | | HANSEN | OP | CTRCN | FBG SV | OB | | 7 | 5 | 2000 | | 4800 | 5500 |

----------------------- 1987 BOATS -----------------------

| 16 | | HANSEN | OP | RNBT | FBG SV | OB | | 5 | 10 | 500 | | 1350 | 1600 |
| 21 | | HANSEN | OP | CTRCN | FBG SV | OB | | 7 | 5 | | 4950 | 5700 |

----------------------- 1986 BOATS -----------------------

| 16 | | HANSEN 16 | OP | RNBT | | TH | OB | | 5 | 10 | 500 | | 1300 | 1550 |

....For earlier years, see the BUC Used Boat Price Guide, Volume 3

CUSTOMFLEX INC
TOLEDO OH 43607   COAST GUARD MFG ID- CTF See inside cover to adjust price for area

LOA FT IN	NAME AND/ OR MODEL	TOP/ RIG	BOAT TYPE	-HULL- MTL TP	----ENGINE--- TP # HP MFG	BEAM FT IN	WGT LBS	DRAFT FT IN	RETAIL LOW	RETAIL HIGH

----------------------- 1986 BOATS -----------------------

| 18 | | INTERLAKE | SLP | SA/OD | FBG CB | CB | | 6 | 3 | 650 | 8 | 3550 | 4100 |
| 20 | | HIGHLANDER | SLP | SA/OD | FBG CB | CB | | 6 | 8 | 830 | 8 | 4250 | 4900 |

----------------------- 1985 BOATS -----------------------

| 18 | | INTERLAKE | SLP | SA/OD | FBG CB | CB | | 6 | 3 | 650 | 8 | 3300 | 3850 |
| 20 | | HIGHLANDER | SLP | SA/OD | FBG CB | CB | | 6 | 8 | 830 | 8 | 4000 | 4650 |

----------------------- 1984 BOATS -----------------------

| 18 | | INTERLAKE | SLP | SA/OD | FBG CB | CB | | 6 | 3 | 650 | 8 | 3100 | 3650 |
| 20 | | HIGHLANDER | SLP | SA/OD | FBG CB | CB | | 6 | 8 | 830 | 8 | 3750 | 4350 |

....For earlier years, see the BUC Used Boat Price Guide, Volume 3

CYCLONE MARINE CORP

GROSSE ILE MI 48138   COAST GUARD MFG ID- CMI See inside cover to adjust price for area

LOA FT IN	NAME AND/ OR MODEL	TOP/ RIG	BOAT TYPE	-HULL- MTL TP	----ENGINE--- TP # HP MFG	BEAM FT IN	WGT LBS	DRAFT FT IN	RETAIL LOW	RETAIL HIGH
					1987 BOATS					
21	1 RAM-WING	OP	OFF	FBG CT	OB	8		1	8100	9350
21	1 RAM-WING	OP	OFF	FBG CT	IO 200-260	8		1 3	9500	11300
21	1 RAM-WING	OP	OFF	FBG CT	IO 300 MRCR	8		1 3	10500	11900
21	1 RAM-WING X	OP	RACE	FBG CT	OB	8		1	8100	9350
21	1 RAM-WING X	OP	RACE	FBG CT	IO 400 MRCR	8		1 4	12800	14500
26	6 TWISTER	OP	OFF	FBG CT	OB	8 4		1	15400	17600
26	6 TWISTER	OP	OFF	FBG CT	IO T260-T330	8 4		1 4	20900	25800
26	6 TWISTER	OP	OFF	FBG CT	IO T440 MRCR	8 4		1 4	29600	32900
33	BARRACUDA	TT	SF	FBG CT	OB	9 4		1	34100	37900
33	PHANTOM	OP	OFF	FBG CT	OB	9 4		1	34800	38700
33	PHANTOM	OP	OFF	FBG CT	IO T370-T440	9 4		1 6	51100	59500
33	PHANTOM	OP	OFF	FBG CT	IO T575 MRCR	9 4		1 6	60500	66500
					1985 BOATS					
21	1 RAM-WING	OP	OFF	FBG CT	OB	8		1	7600	8750
21	1 RAM-WING	OP	OFF	FBG CT	IO 200-260	8		1 3	8650	10400
21	1 RAM-WING	OP	OFF	FBG CT	IO 300 MRCR	8		1 3	9650	10900
21	1 RAM-WING X	OP	RACE	FBG CT	OB	8		1	7600	8750
21	1 RAM-WING X	OP	RACE	FBG CT	IO 400 MRCR	8		1 4	11700	13300
26	6 TWISTER	OP	OFF	FBG CT	OB	8 4		1	14500	16500
26	6 TWISTER	OP	OFF	FBG CT	IO T260-T330	8 4		1 4	19100	23700
					1984 BOATS					
23	2 TWISTER S	OP	SPTCR	FBG CT	IO 185	8	3250		9400	10700
23	2 TWISTER SF	OP	SPTCR	FBG CT	OB	8	2500		8250	9500
32	2 PHANTOM S	OP	SPTCR	FBG CT	IO 185-425	9 2	7200		30200	34500
32	2 PHANTOM SE	OP	SPTCR	FBG CT	IO 260 MRCR	9 2	7200		36000	40000
32	2 PHANTOM SE	OP	SPTCR	FBG CT	IO 425 PCM	9 2	7200		43100	47900
32	2 PHANTOM SE	OP	SPTCR	FBG CT	IO 165D-235D	9 2	7200		30700	36500
32	2 PHANTOM SF	OP	SPTCR	FBG CT	OB	9 2	7200		32100	35600
36	6 FURY X	OP	SPTCR	FBG CT	IO T400 PCM	9 6	8500	1 6	51900	57000
38	6 FURY FX	OP	RACE	FBG CT	IO T500	10		1 4	58500	64300
38	6 FURY FX	OP	RACE	FBG CT	IO T600	10		1 4	67000	73600
46	6 FORTRESS	HT	SPTCR	FBG CT	IO T285D S&S	10	14450	1 10	97000	106500
46	6 FORTRESS X	OP	RACE	FBG CT	IO Q500	13 11		1 10	115000	126000

....For earlier years, see the BUC Used Boat Price Guide, Volume 3

D S YACHT SALES LTD

ODESSA ONTARIO CANADA   COAST GUARD MFG ID- ZCW See inside cover to adjust price for area

LOA FT IN	NAME AND/ OR MODEL	TOP/ RIG	BOAT TYPE	-HULL- MTL TP	----ENGINE--- TP # HP MFG	BEAM FT IN	WGT LBS	DRAFT FT IN	RETAIL LOW	RETAIL HIGH
					1985 BOATS					
16	DS-16C	SLP	SA/CR	FBG CB		6	500	7	2350	2700
16	DS-16K	SLP	SA/CR	FBG KL		6	650	1 8	2650	3100
21	8 DS-22C	SLP	SA/CR	FBG CB		8	2400	2	5900	6800
21	8 DS-22K	SLP	SA/CR	FBG KL		8	2300	3 11	5750	6600
23	SONAR	SLP	SA/OD	FBG KL		8	2100	3 9	5750	6600
23	1 KIRBY 23	SLP	SA/RC	FBG KL		8	2400		6250	7200
					1984 BOATS					
16	DS-16	SLP	SAIL	FBG KC		6	650	1 6	2500	2900
21	8 DS-22	SLP	SAIL	FBG KL	OB	8	2400	2	5550	6400
27	3 HM-27	SLP	SA/CR	FBG KL	IB 12D YAN	9 3	7400	4 3	21400	23800

....For earlier years, see the BUC Used Boat Price Guide, Volume 3

DANYACHTS

DIV OF BAESS BOATS INC
WILTON CT 06897   COAST GUARD MFG ID- KBA   See inside cover to adjust price for area

SCANDINAVIAN YACHT MARINE SER
VICTORIA BC CANADA

LOA FT IN	NAME AND/ OR MODEL	TOP/ RIG	BOAT TYPE	-HULL- MTL TP	----ENGINE--- TP # HP MFG	BEAM FT IN	WGT LBS	DRAFT FT IN	RETAIL LOW	RETAIL HIGH
					1984 BOATS					
28	GREAT-DANE 28	SLP	SA/OD	FBG KL	IB	8 2		4 9	33700	37400

....For earlier years, see the BUC Used Boat Price Guide, Volume 3

DARGEL BOAT WORKS INC

DONNA TX 78537   COAST GUARD MFG ID- DBW See inside cover to adjust price for area

For more recent years, see the BUC Used Boat Price Guide, Volume 1

LOA FT IN	NAME AND/ OR MODEL	TOP/ RIG	BOAT TYPE	-HULL- MTL TP	----ENGINE--- TP # HP MFG	BEAM FT IN	WGT LBS	DRAFT FT IN	RETAIL LOW	RETAIL HIGH
					1996 BOATS					
16 11	SKOUT 170 RG	OP	FSH	FBG TH	OB	7 6	950	4	3000	3500
16 11	SKOUT 170 RG EC	OP	FSH	FBG TH	OB	7 6	950	4	2900	3400
18 6	FISHERMAN 186 W/O TH	OP	FSH	FBG SV	OB	8	1350	6	4150	4850
18 6	FISHERMAN 186 W/TH	OP	FSH	FBG TH	OB	8	1350	4	4150	4850
18 6	FISHERMAN 186 WT	OP	W/T	FBG TH	OB	8	1450	5	4450	5100
18 6	SKOUT 186 RG	OP	FSH	FBG TH	OB	7 6	1100	4	3550	4100
19 10	SKOOTER 196	OP	FSH	FBG TH	OB	7 8	1300	4	4300	5000
19 10	SKOOTER 196 EC	OP	FSH	FBG TH	OB	7 8	1300	4	4250	4950
20 3	SKOUT 210 RG	OP	FSH	FBG TH	OB	8 4	1350	4	4600	5250
21	FISHERMAN 210	OP	FSH	FBG SV	OB	8	1500	5	5100	5850
21	FISHERMAN 210 T	OP	FSH	FBG TH	OB	8	1500	5	5100	5850
21	FISHERMAN 210 WT	OP	W/T	FBG TH	OB	8	1650	5	5500	6350
					1995 BOATS					
16 11	SKOUT 170 RG	OP	FSH	FBG TH	OB	7 6	950	4	2900	3350
16 11	SKOUT 170 RG EC	OP	FSH	FBG TH	OB	7 6	950	4	2800	3250
18 6	FISHERMAN 186 W/O TH	OP	FSH	FBG SV	OB	8	1350	6	3950	4600
18 6	FISHERMAN 186 W/TH	OP	FSH	FBG TH	OB	8	1350	4	3950	4600
18 6	FISHERMAN 186 WT	OP	W/T	FBG TH	OB	8	1450	5	4200	4850
19 10	SKOOTER 196	OP	FSH	FBG TH	OB	7 8	1300	4	4150	4800
19 10	SKOOTER 196 EC	OP	FSH	FBG TH	OB	7 8	1300	4	4000	4650
20 3	SKOUT 210 RG	OP	FSH	FBG TH	OB	8 4	1350	4	4350	5000
21	FISHERMAN 210	OP	FSH	FBG SV	OB	8	1500	5	4850	5600
21	FISHERMAN 210	OP	FSH	FBG TH	OB	8	1500	5	4850	5600
21	FISHERMAN 210 WT	OP	W/T	FBG TH	OB	8	1650	5	5250	6050
					1994 BOATS					
16 11	SKOUT 170 RG	OP	FSH	FBG TH	OB	7 6	950	4	2750	3200
16 11	SKOUT 170 RG EC	OP	FSH	FBG TH	OB	7 6	950	4	2650	3100
18 6	FISHERMAN 186 W/TH	OP	FSH	FBG SV	OB	8	1350	6	3800	4400
18 6	FISHERMAN 186 W/TH	OP	FSH	FBG TH	OB	8	1350	4	3800	4400
19 10	SKOOTER 196	OP	FSH	FBG TH	OB	7 8	1300	4	3950	4600
19 10	SKOOTER 196 EC	OP	FSH	FBG TH	OB	7 8	1300	4	3800	4450
20 3	SKOUT 210 RG	OP	FSH	FBG TH	OB	8 4	1350	4	4150	4800
21	FISHERMAN 210	OP	FSH	FBG SV	OB	8	1500	5	4700	5400
21	FISHERMAN 210	OP	FSH	FBG TH	OB	8	1500	5	4700	5400
					1993 BOATS					
16 5	SKOUT 170	OP	FSH	FBG SV	OB	6 9	950	7	2550	2950
16 9	SKOUT 170 CLASSIC	OP	FSH	FBG TH	OB	6 9	980	5	2650	3100
16 11	SKOUT 170 RG	OP	FSH	FBG TH	OB	7 6	950	4	2650	3050
16 11	SKOUT 170 RG EC	OP	FSH	FBG TH	OB	7 6	950	4	2550	2950
18 6	FISHERMAN 186 W/O TH	OP	FSH	FBG SV	OB	8	1350	6	3650	4250
18 6	FISHERMAN 186 W/TH	OP	FSH	FBG TH	OB	8	1350	4	3650	4250
19 10	SKOOTER 196	OP	FSH	FBG TH	OB	7 8	1350	4	3650	4250
19 10	SKOOTER 196 EC	OP	FSH	FBG TH	OB	7 8	1300	4	3800	4400
19 10	SKOUT 200 CLASSIC	OP	FSH	FBG TH	OB	7 8	1500	4	3700	4250
19 10	SKOUT 200 ECONOMY	OP	FSH	FBG TH	OB	7 8	1500	4	4100	4800
20 3	SKOUT 210 RG	OP	FSH	FBG TH	OB	8 4	1350	4	4000	4650
20 3	SKOUT 210 RG EC	OP	FSH	FBG TH	OB	8 4	1350	4	3900	4550
21	FISHERMAN 210	OP	FSH	FBG SV	OB	8	1500	5	4500	5150
21	FISHERMAN 210	OP	FSH	FBG TH	OB	8	1500	5	4500	5150
					1992 BOATS					
16 5	SKOUT 170	OP	FSH	FBG SV	OB	6 9	950	7	2450	2850
16 9	SKOUT 170 CLASSIC	OP	FSH	FBG TH	OB	6 9	980	5	2550	2950
16 11	SKOUT 170 RG	OP	FSH	FBG TH	OB	7 6	950	4	2450	2850
16 11	SKOUT 170 RG EC	OP	FSH	FBG TH	OB	7 6	950	4	2450	2850
18 6	FISHERMAN 186 W/O TH	OP	FSH	FBG SV	OB	8	1350	6	3500	4050
18 6	FISHERMAN 186 W/TH	OP	FSH	FBG TH	OB	8	1350	4	3500	4050
19 10	SKOOTER 196	OP	FSH	FBG TH	OB	7 8	1300	4	3500	4050
19 10	SKOOTER 196 EC	OP	FSH	FBG TH	OB	7 8	1300	4	3650	4200
19 10	SKOUT 200 CLASSIC	OP	FSH	FBG TH	OB	7 8	1500	4	3550	4100
19 10	SKOUT 200 ECONOMY	OP	FSH	FBG TH	OB	7 8	1500	4	4050	4750
20 3	SKOUT 210 RG	OP	FSH	FBG TH	OB	8 4	1350	4	3850	4500
20 3	SKOUT 210 RG EC	OP	FSH	FBG TH	OB	8 4	1350	4	3750	4350
21	FISHERMAN 210	OP	FSH	FBG SV	OB	8	1500	5	4250	4950
21	FISHERMAN 210	OP	FSH	FBG TH	OB	8	1500	5	4250	4950
					1991 BOATS					
16 5	FISHERMAN 170	OP	FSH	FBG SV	OB	6 9	950	7	2350	2750
16 9	SKOUT 170 CLASSIC	OP	FSH	FBG TH	OB	6 9	980	5	2450	2850
16 11	SKOUT 170 RG	OP	FSH	FBG TH	OB	7 6	950	4	2450	2900
16 11	SKOUT 170 RG EC	OP	FSH	FBG TH	OB	7 6	950	4	2350	2700
18 6	FISHERMAN 186 W/O TH	OP	FSH	FBG SV	OB	8	1350	6	3350	3900
18 6	FISHERMAN 186 W/TH	OP	FSH	FBG TH	OB	8	1350	4	3350	3900
19 10	SKOOTER 196	OP	FSH	FBG TH	OB	7 8	1300	4	3500	4100

DARGEL BOAT WORKS INC — CONTINUED

See inside cover to adjust price for area

LOA FT IN	NAME AND/OR MODEL	TOP/RIG	BOAT TYPE	HULL MTL TP	ENGINE TP # HP MFG	BEAM FT IN	WGT LBS	DRAFT FT IN	RETAIL LOW	RETAIL HIGH
1991 BOATS										
19 10	SKOOTER 196 EC	OP	FSH	FBG TH	OB	7 8	1300	4	3400	3950
19 10	SKOUT 200 CLASSIC	OP	FSH	FBG TH	OB	7 8	1500	4	3950	4600
19 10	SKOUT 200 ECONOMY	OP	FSH	FBG TH	OB	7 8	1500	4	3800	4400
20 3	SKOUT 210 RG	OP	FSH	FBG TH	OB	8 4	1350	4	3750	4350
20 3	SKOUT 210 RG EC	OP	FSH	FBG TH	OB	8 4	1350	4	3600	4150
1990 BOATS										
16 5	FISHERMAN 170	OP	FSH	FBG SV	OB	6 9	950	7	2300	2700
16 9	SKOUT 170 CLASSIC	OP	FSH	FBG TH	OB	7	980	5	2350	2750
16 11	SKOUT 170 RG	OP	FSH	FBG TH	OB	7 6	950	4	2400	2750
16 11	SKOUT 170 RG EC	OP	FSH	FBG TH	OB	7 6	950	4	2300	2650
19 10	SKOOTER 196	OP	FSH	FBG TH	OB	7 8	1300	4	3400	3950
19 10	SKOOTER 196 EC	OP	FSH	FBG TH	OB	7 8	1300	4	3250	3800
19 10	SKOUT 200 CLASSIC	OP	FSH	FBG TH	OB	7 8	1500	4	3800	4400
19 10	SKOUT 200 ECONOMY	OP	FSH	FBG TH	OB	7 8	1500	4	3650	4250
20 3	SKOUT 210 RG	OP	FSH	FBG TH	OB	8 4	1350	4	3600	4200
20 3	SKOUT 210 RG EC	OP	FSH	FBG TH	OB	8 4	1350	4	3450	4050
1989 BOATS										
16 5	FISHERMAN 170	OP	FSH	FBG TH	OB	6 9	850	5	1900	2250
16 5	FISHERMAN 170 DLX	OP	FSH	FBG TH	OB	6 9	850	5	2050	2450
16 9	SKOUT	OP	FSH	FBG TH	OB	7	950	5	2250	2600
16 9	SKOUT DLX	OP	FSH	FBG TH	OB	7	1050	4	2450	2850
19 10	SKOOTER 196	OP	FSH	FBG TH	OB	7 8	1125	5	2850	3350
19 10	SKOOTER 196 DLX	OP	FSH	FBG TH	OB	7 8	1200	5	3000	3500
19 10	SKOUT 200	OP	FSH	FBG TH	OB	7 8	1500	5	3550	4150
19 10	SKOUT 200 DLX	OP	FSH	FBG TH	OB	7 8	1500	5	3650	4250
1988 BOATS										
16 9	SKOUT	OP	FSH	FBG TH	OB	7	950	4	2200	2550
16 9	SKOUT DLX	OP	FSH	FBG TH	OB	7	1050	4	2350	2750
19 10	SKOOTER 196	OP	FSH	FBG TH	OB	7 8	1125	5	2750	3200
19 10	SKOOTER 196 DLX	OP	FSH	FBG TH	OB	7 8	1200	5	2950	3400
19 10	SKOUT 200	OP	FSH	FBG TH	OB	7 8	1500	5	3400	3950
19 10	SKOUT 200 DLX	OP	FSH	FBG TH	OB	7 8	1500	5	3600	4200
1987 BOATS										
16	SOOPER-SKOOTER	OP	FSH	FBG TH	OB	7	750	5	1600	1950
16	SOOPER-SKOOTER DLX	OP	FSH	FBG TH	OB	7	800	5	1700	2050
19 6	SKOOTER 196	OP	FSH	FBG TH	OB	7 8	1125	5	2650	3100
1986 BOATS										
16	SOOPER-SKOOTER	OP	FSH	FBG TH	OB	7	750	5	1600	1900
16	SOOPER-SKOOTER DLX	OP	FSH	FBG TH	OB	7	800	5	1700	2000
1985 BOATS										
16	SOOPER-SKOOTER	OP	FSH	FBG TH	OB	7	750	5	1550	1850
16	SOOPER-SKOOTER DLX	OP	FSH	FBG TH	OB	7	800	5	1650	1950

...For earlier years, see the BUC Used Boat Price Guide, Volume 3

DARRAGH LTD
CO MONAGHAN IRELAND

See inside cover to adjust price for area

LOA FT IN	NAME AND/OR MODEL	TOP/RIG	BOAT TYPE	HULL MTL TP	ENGINE TP # HP MFG	BEAM FT IN	WGT LBS	DRAFT FT IN	RETAIL LOW	RETAIL HIGH
1987 BOATS										
19 6	LIGHTNING	ST	SKI	FBG DV	IO 130-205	6 6	1870	1	5300	6250
20 2	MILAN	ST	SPTCR	FBG DV	IO 151 VLVO	7 9	2970	2 1	9650	10900
23	FALCON	ST	SPTCR	FBG DV	IO	8	3600	2 6	**	**
23	FALCON	ST	SPTCR	FBG DV	IO 165-260	8	3600	1 10	11900	14400
23	FALCON	ST	SPTCR	FBG DV	IO 136D-165D	8	3600	1 10	15300	17900
1986 BOATS										
19 6	LIGHTNING	ST	SKI	FBG DV	IO 140-205	6 6	1870	1	5050	5950
23	FALCON	ST	SPTCR	FBG DV	IO 140-260	8	3600	1 10	11300	13700
23	FALCON	ST	SPTCR	FBG DV	IO 136D-165D	8	3600	1 10	14500	17000
1985 BOATS										
19 6	LIGHTNING	ST	SKI	FBG DV	IO 140-165	6 6	1870	1 9	4850	5950
23	FALCON	ST	SPTCR	FBG DV	IO 140 MRCR	8	3600	1 10	10900	12400
23	FALCON	ST	SPTCR	FBG DV	IO 165 BMW	8	3600	1 10	11200	12700
23	FALCON	ST	SPTCR	FBG DV	IO 165D BMW	8	3900	1 10	14900	16900

...For earlier years, see the BUC Used Boat Price Guide, Volume 3

DAVIS BOATWORKS INC
WANSHESE NC 27981-0550
FORMERLY DAVIS YACHTS INC

See inside cover to adjust price for area

For more recent years, see the BUC Used Boat Price Guide, Volume 1

LOA FT IN	NAME AND/OR MODEL	TOP/RIG	BOAT TYPE	HULL MTL TP	ENGINE TP # HP MFG	BEAM FT IN	WGT LBS	DRAFT FT IN	RETAIL LOW	RETAIL HIGH
1987 BOATS										
47	BUDDY-DAVIS	F+T	SF	FBG DV	IB T D GM	16	40000	4	**	**
61	DAVIS 61	FB	SF	FBG DV	IB T D GM	17 6	70000	5	**	**
61	DAVIS 61	FB	SF	FBG DV	IB T750D GM	17 6	70000	5	395500	435000

DAWSON YACHTS
BRIELLE NJ 08330

See inside cover to adjust price for area

LOA FT IN	NAME AND/OR MODEL	TOP/RIG	BOAT TYPE	HULL MTL TP	ENGINE TP # HP MFG	BEAM FT IN	WGT LBS	DRAFT FT IN	RETAIL LOW	RETAIL HIGH
1994 BOATS										
33	DAWSON 33	FB	SDN	FBG SV	IB T D	11 6	13400	2 6	**	**
33	DAWSON 33	OP	SF	FBG SV	IB T D	11 6	11000	2 6	**	**
38	DAWSON 38 CNV	FB	CR	FBG SV	IB T375D CAT	13 8	28000	3 6	153500	168500
38	DAWSON 38 CNV	FB	CR	FBG SV	IB T400D GM	13 8	28000	3 6	152000	167000
38	DAWSON 38 CNV	FB	CR	FBG SV	IB T425D CAT	13 8	28000	3 6	159000	175000
38	DAWSON 38 EXP	OP	SF	FBG SV	IB T375D CAT	13 8	28000	3 6	153500	168500
38	DAWSON 38 EXP	OP	SF	FBG SV	IB T400D GM	13 8	28000	3 6	152000	167000
38	DAWSON 38 EXP	OP	SF	FBG SV	IB T425D CAT	13 8	28000	3 6	159000	175000
1993 BOATS										
33	DAWSON 33	FB	SDN	FBG SV	IB T D	11 6	13400	2 6	**	**
33	DAWSON 33	OP	SF	FBG SV	IB T D	11 6	11000	2 6	**	**
38	DAWSON 38 CNV	FB	CR	FBG SV	IB T375D CAT	13 8	28000	3 6	146000	160500
38	DAWSON 38 CNV	FB	CR	FBG SV	IB T400D GM	13 8	28000	3 6	145000	159000
38	DAWSON 38 CNV	FB	CR	FBG SV	IB T425D CAT	13 8	28000	3 6	151500	166500
38	DAWSON 38 EXP	FB	CR	FBG SV	IB T375D CAT	13 8	28000	3 6	146000	160500
38	DAWSON 38 EXP	OP	SF	FBG SV	IB T400D GM	13 8	28000	3 6	145000	159000
38	DAWSON 38 EXP	OP	SF	FBG SV	IB T425D CAT	13 8	28000	3 6	151500	166500

DEACONS BOAT CENTRE
STHAMPTON ENGLAND

See inside cover to adjust price for area

LOA FT IN	NAME AND/OR MODEL	TOP/RIG	BOAT TYPE	HULL MTL TP	ENGINE TP # HP MFG	BEAM FT IN	WGT LBS	DRAFT FT IN	RETAIL LOW	RETAIL HIGH
1985 BOATS										
23 8	TRAPPER 24	SLP	SAIL	FBG KL	OB	7 5	2640	2 9	7000	8050
23 8	TRAPPER 24	SLP	SAIL	FBG TK	OB	7 5	2640	2 9	7000	8050
25 2	TRAPPER T250	SLP	SAIL	FBG KL	IB	9 2	2987	4 7	8350	9600
25 2	TRAPPER T250	SLP	SAIL	FBG KL	IB 8D YAN	9 2	2987	5 3	9400	10700
25 2	TRAPPER TS240	SLP	SAIL	FBG SK	OB	9 2	2987	4 7	8600	9850
26 2	TRAPPER 26	SLP	SAIL	FBG KL	IB	9 2	2912	4 7	9450	10700
26 2	TRAPPER 26	SLP	SAIL	FBG KL	IB 9D VLVO	9 2	2912	3 8	8600	9900
26 2	TRAPPER 26	SLP	SAIL	FBG KL	IB 9D VLVO	9 2	2912	3 8	9450	10800
26 2	TRAPPER 26	SLP	SAIL	FBG TK	IB	9 2	2912	3 8	9450	10800
26 3	TRAPPER 300	SLP	SAIL	FBG KL	IB 9D	9 5	4410	4 10	13200	15000
26 3	TRAPPER 300	SLP	SAIL	FBG TK	IB 9D	9 5	4410	3 6	13200	15000
29 3	TRAPPER 29	SLP	SAIL	FBG TK	IB 18D	9 8	6000	4 11	19700	21800
29 3	TRAPPER 29	SLP	SAIL	FBG TK	IB 18D	9 8	6000	3 6	19800	22000
31 7	TRAPPER 31	SLP	SAIL	FBG TK	IB 18D VLVO	10 5	8600	3 6	27000	30700
31 7	TRAPPER 31	SLP	SAIL	FBG TK	IB 18D VLVO	10 5	8600	4 2	27800	30900
36 4	TRAPPER 36	SLP	SAIL	FBG KL	IB 28D VLVO	12	12000	4 0	40900	45500
36 4	TRAPPER 36	SLP	SAIL	FBG TK	IB 28D VLVO	12	12000	5 8	41100	45600

...For earlier years, see the BUC Used Boat Price Guide, Volume 3

DEERFOOT YACHTS
FT LAUDERDALE FL 33302

See inside cover to adjust price for area

LOA FT IN	NAME AND/OR MODEL	TOP/RIG	BOAT TYPE	HULL MTL TP	ENGINE TP # HP MFG	BEAM FT IN	WGT LBS	DRAFT FT IN	RETAIL LOW	RETAIL HIGH
1990 BOATS										
61 6	DEERFOOT 61	SLP	SAIL	FBG KL	IB 88D YAN	14 5	45000	6 3	577000	634000
63	PILOTHOUSE 63	SLP	SAIL	FBG KL	IB 110D YAN	14 5	47500	6 3	588000	646000
70	PILOTHOUSE 70	SLP	SAIL	FBG KL	IB 150D	16 5	63000	6 10	735500	808500

...For earlier years, see the BUC Used Boat Price Guide, Volume 3

DEHLER NORTH AMERICA

CHICAGO IL 60616   COAST GUARD MFG ID- XDI See inside cover to adjust price for area
DEHLER YACHTS
MESCHEDE FREIENOHL GERMANY

For more recent years, see the BUC Used Boat Price Guide, Volume 1

LOA FT IN	NAME AND/ OR MODEL	TOP/ RIG	BOAT TYPE	-HULL- MTL TP	----ENGINE--- TP # HP MFG	BEAM FT IN	WGT LBS	DRAFT FT IN	RETAIL LOW	RETAIL HIGH
1996 BOATS										
36 8	DEHLER 37	SLP	SACAC	FBG CB	IB 27D YAN	11 5	12300	5 9	98200	108000
40 8	DEHLER 41 DS	SLP	SACAC	FBG CB	IB 50D YAN	12 8	18300	6 4	159500	175000
1987 BOATS										
22	DEHLER 22	SLP	SA/CR	F/S KL	OB	8	1980		6950	7950
24 11	DEHLER 25	SLP	SA/CR	F/S CB	OB	8 3	3245		11600	13100
30 1	DEHLER 31	SLP	SA/CR	F/S KL	IB D YAN	10 2	7055	3 6	30300	33600
33 10	DEHLER 34	SLP	SA/CR	F/S KL	IB 27D YAN	11 2	7495		32800	36400
38 1	DEHLER 38	SLP	SA/CR	F/S		12 4	12125	6 2	57600	63300
1986 BOATS										
22	DEHLER 22	SLP	SA/CR	F/S KL	OB	8	1980		6500	7500
24 11	DEHLER 25	SLP	SA/CR	F/S CB	OB	8 3	3245		10900	12300
24 11	DEHLER 25	SLP	SA/CR	F/S CB	IB 6D BMW	8 3	3245		11800	13500
30 1	DEHLER 31	SLP	SA/CR	F/S KL	IB D YAN	10 2	7055	3 6	28400	31500
33 10	DEHLER 34	SLP	SA/CR	F/S KL	IB 27D YAN	11 2	7495		30700	34100
1985 BOATS										
24 11	DEHLER 25	SLP	SA/CR	F/S CB	IB 6D BMW	8 2	2645		9650	11000
33 10	DEHLER 34	SLP	SA/CR	F/S KL	IB 27D YAN	11 2	7495		28800	32000
37 6	DEHLER 37	SLP	SA/CR	F/S KL	IB 44D YAN	11 4	12786		52500	57700

DEL-REY YACHTS INC

MIAMI FL 33014   See inside cover to adjust price for area

LOA FT IN	NAME AND/ OR MODEL	TOP/ RIG	BOAT TYPE	-HULL- MTL TP	----ENGINE--- TP # HP MFG	BEAM FT IN	WGT LBS	DRAFT FT IN	RETAIL LOW	RETAIL HIGH
1992 BOATS										
38 9	DEL-REY 39 SPT SUNDK	FB	DCMY	FBG SV	IB T210D CUM	13 8	25000	2 11	114500	126000
42 10	DEL-REY 43 SPT SUNDK	FB	DCMY	FBG SV	IB T250D CUM	15 6	29000	3	139500	153000
43 9	DEL-REY 44 YACHTFSHR	FB	YTFS	FBG SV	IB T250D CUM	13 8	26200	2 11	140000	154000
46 6	DEL-REY 47 SPT SUNDK	FB	DCMY	FBG SV	IB T375D CAT	15 6	32300	4	165500	182000
48 10	DEL-RAY 49 YACHTFSHR	FB	YTFS	FBG SV	IB T375D CAT	15 6	30500	3	162500	179000
52 6	DEL-RAY 53 YACHTFSHR	FB	YTFS	FBG SV	IB T425D CAT	15 6	44000	4	196500	215500
57 10	DEL-RAY 58 YACHTFSHR	FB	YTFS	FBG SV	IB T425D CAT	15 6	45100	4	207500	228000
1991 BOATS										
38 9	DEL-REY 39 SPT SNDCK	FB	DCMY	FBG SV	IB T210D CUM	13 8	25000	2 11	109500	120000
42 10	DEL-REY 43 SPT SNDCK	FB	DCMY	FBG SV	IB T250D CUM	15 6	29000	3	134000	147000
43 9	DEL-REY 44 YACHTFSHR	FB	YTFS	FBG SV	IB T250D CUM	13 8	26200	2 11	133500	147000
46 6	DEL-REY 47 SPT SNDCK	FB	DCMY	FBG SV	IB T375D CAT	15 6	32300	4	158500	174500
48 10	DEL-RAY 49 YACHTFSHR	FB	YTFS	FBG SV	IB T375D CAT	15 6	30500	3	155000	170500
52 6	DEL-RAY 53 YACHTFSHR	FB	YTFS	FBG SV	IB T425D CAT	15 6	44000	4	187500	206000
57 10	DEL-RAY 58 YACHTFSHR	FB	YTFS	FBG SV	IB T425D CAT	15 6	45100	4	198000	217500
1990 BOATS										
38 9	DEL-REY 39 SPT SNDCK	FB	DCMY	FBG SV	IB T210D CUM	13 8	25000	2 11	104500	114500
42 10	DEL-REY 43 SPT SNDCK	FB	DCMY	FBG SV	IB T250D CUM	15 6	29000	3	127500	140500
43 9	DEL-REY 44 YACHTFSHR	FB	YTFS	FBG SV	IB T250D CUM	13 8	26200	2 11	127500	140000
46 6	DEL-REY 47 SPT SNDCK	FB	DCMY	FBG SV	IB T375D CAT	15 6	32300	4	151500	166500
48 10	DEL-RAY 49 YACHTFSHR	FB	YTFS	FBG SV	IB T375D CAT	15 6	30500	3	148000	162500
52 6	DEL-RAY 53 YACHTFSHR	FB	YTFS	FBG SV	IB T425D CAT	15 6	44000	4	178500	196500
57 10	DEL-RAY 58 YACHTFSHR	FB	YTFS	FBG SV	IB T425D CAT	15 6	45100	4	189000	207500
1989 BOATS										
52 6	DEL-REY 53	FB	YTFS	FBG SV	IB T375D CAT	15 6	44100	4	164500	180500

DELL QUAY DORIES

BOSUN MARINE MARKETING INC   See inside cover to adjust price for area
FT LAUDERDALE FL 33311   COAST GUARD MFG ID- DQU
DELL QUAY MARINE LTD
HANTS ENGLAND

LOA FT IN	NAME AND/ OR MODEL	TOP/ RIG	BOAT TYPE	-HULL- MTL TP	----ENGINE--- TP # HP MFG	BEAM FT IN	WGT LBS	DRAFT FT IN	RETAIL LOW	RETAIL HIGH
1986 BOATS										
17	DELL-QUAY FC	OP	CUD	F/S TR	OB	7 1	1035		3800	4450
17	DELL-QUAY SP	OP	CTRCN	F/S TR	OB	7 1	945		3550	4100
1985 BOATS										
17	CUDDY 17 FC	HT	CUD	F/S TR	OB	7 1	1000		3600	4200
17	FISHERMAN 17	OP	CTRCN	F/S TR	OB	7 1	1000		3600	4200
1984 BOATS										
17	CUDDY 17 FC	HT	CUD	F/S TR	OB	7 1	1125		3900	4550
17	FISHERMAN 17	OP	UTL	F/S TR	OB	7 1	957		3300	3850
17	SPORTSMAN	OP	CTRCN	F/S TR	OB	7 1	1034		3650	4250

...For earlier years, see the BUC Used Boat Price Guide, Volume 3

DELTA BOAT CO

FRESNO CA 93722-4913   COAST GUARD MFG ID- DKO See inside cover to adjust price for area

LOA FT IN	NAME AND/ OR MODEL	TOP/ RIG	BOAT TYPE	-HULL- MTL TP	----ENGINE--- TP # HP MFG	BEAM FT IN	WGT LBS	DRAFT FT IN	RETAIL LOW	RETAIL HIGH
1994 BOATS										
16 5	BAYMASTER DV16 IIIC	OP	FSH	AL DV	OB	6 4	405		2000	2400
16 5	BAYMASTER DV16 IIIT	OP	FSH	AL DV	OB	6 4	405		2050	2450
16 5	DELTA ALASKAN 16-1	OP	FSH	AL DV	OB	6 4	375		1700	2000
16 5	DELTA ALASKAN 16-2	OP	FSH	AL DV	OB	6 4	375		1750	2100
16 5	DELTA ALASKAN 16-3	OP	FSH	AL DV	OB	6 4	375		1850	2200
16 5	DELTA ALASKAN 16-4	OP	FSH	AL DV	OB	6 4	375		1900	2250
16 5	DELTA ALASKAN 16-5	OP	FSH	AL DV	OB	6 4	375		2000	2400
16 5	DELTA ALASKAN 16-6	OP	FSH	AL DV	OB	6 4	375		2000	2350
16 5	DELTA ALASKAN 16-7	OP	FSH	AL DV	OB	6 4	375		2050	2400
16 6	RIVER BOAT R16C	OP	FSH	AL DV	OB	5 10	525		2700	3150
16 6	RIVER BOAT R16S	OP	FSH	AL DV	OB	5 10	525		2650	3100
17	NEWPORTER DVO17	OP	CTRCN	AL DV	OB	6 6	460		2450	2850
18 5	BAYMASTER DV18 IVC	OP	FSH	AL DV	OB	6 8	580		3250	3750
18 5	BAYMASTER DV18 IVT	OP	FSH	AL DV	OB	6 8	580		3250	3750
18 5	BAYMASTER SPEC DV181	OP	FSH	AL DV	OB	6 8	580		3550	4150
18 5	BAYMASTER SPEC DV182	OP	FSH	AL DV	OB	6 8	580		3550	4150
18 5	BAYMASTER SPEC DV183	OP	FSH	AL DV	OB	6 8	580		3600	4200
18 5	BAYMASTER SPEC DV18T	OP	FSH	AL DV	OB	6 8	580		3550	4150
18 6	RIVER BOAT R18 DASH	OP	FSH	AL DV	OB	7 6	795		4400	5050
18 6	RIVER BOAT R18C	OP	FSH	AL DV	OB	7 6	795		4300	5000
18 6	RIVER BOAT R18S	OP	FSH	AL DV	OB	7 6	795		4250	4950
18 6	RIVER BOAT R18T	OP	FSH	AL DV	OB	7 6	795		4400	5100
18 6	RIVER BOAT RI18	OP	RNBT	AL DV	IB 215	7 6	1733		8400	9650
19	NEWPORTER DVO19	OP	CTRCN	AL DV	OB	6 6	590		3400	3950
20 6	BAYMASTER DV20 IVC	OP	FSH	AL DV	OB	7	655		3600	4200
20 6	BAYMASTER DV20 IVT	OP	FSH	AL DV	OB	7	655		2950	3450
20 6	BAYMASTER SPEC DV201	OP	FSH	AL DV	OB	7	655		3950	4550
20 6	BAYMASTER SPEC DV202	OP	FSH	AL DV	OB	7	655		3950	4550
20 6	BAYMASTER SPEC DV203	OP	FSH	AL DV	OB	7	655		3950	4600
20 6	BAYMASTER SPEC DV20T	OP	FSH	AL DV	OB	7	655		3950	4550
20 6	RIVER BOAT R20 DASH	OP	FSH	AL DV	OB	7 6	860		4600	5250
20 6	RIVER BOAT R20C	OP	FSH	AL DV	OB	7 6	860		4600	5300
20 6	RIVER BOAT R20S	OP	FSH	AL DV	OB	7 6	860		4600	5250
20 6	RIVER BOAT R20T	OP	FSH	AL DV	OB	7 6	860		4650	5350
20 6	RIVER BOAT RI20	OP	RNBT	AL DV	IB 215	7 6	1798		9050	10300
24 6	RIVER BOAT R24 DASH	OP	FSH	AL DV	OB	7 6	1050		7300	8400
24 6	RIVER BOAT R24C	OP	FSH	AL DV	OB	7 6	1050		7350	8450
24 6	RIVER BOAT R24S	OP	FSH	AL DV	OB	7 6	1050		7300	8400
24 6	RIVER BOAT R24T	OP	FSH	AL DV	OB	7 6	1050		7400	8500
24 6	RIVER BOAT RI24	OP	RNBT	AL DV	IB 215	7 6	2233		12600	14300
1993 BOATS										
16 5	BAYMASTER DV16 IIIC	OP	FSH	AL DV	OB	6 4	405		1950	2300
16 5	BAYMASTER DV16 IIIT	OP	FSH	AL DV	OB	6 4	405		2000	2350
16 5	DELTA ALASKAN 16-1	OP	FSH	AL DV	OB	6 4	375		1650	1950
16 5	DELTA ALASKAN 16-2	OP	FSH	AL DV	OB	6 4	375		1700	2000
16 5	DELTA ALASKAN 16-3	OP	FSH	AL DV	OB	6 4	375		1800	2100
16 5	DELTA ALASKAN 16-4	OP	FSH	AL DV	OB	6 4	375		1800	2150
16 5	DELTA ALASKAN 16-5	OP	FSH	AL DV	OB	6 4	375		1850	2200
16 5	DELTA ALASKAN 16-6	OP	FSH	AL DV	OB	6 4	375		1900	2250
16 5	DELTA ALASKAN 16-7	OP	FSH	AL DV	OB	6 4	375		1950	2300
16 6	RIVER BOAT R16C	OP	FSH	AL DV	OB	5 10	525		2600	3000
16 6	RIVER BOAT R16S	OP	FSH	AL DV	OB	5 10	525		2550	2950
17	NEWPORTER DVO17	OP	CTRCN	AL DV	OB	6 6	460		2350	2700
18 5	BAYMASTER DV18 IVC	OP	FSH	AL DV	OB	6 8	580		3100	3600
18 5	BAYMASTER DV18 IVT	OP	FSH	AL DV	OB	6 8	580		3100	3600
18 5	BAYMASTER SPEC DV181	OP	FSH	AL DV	OB	6 8	580		3400	4000
18 5	BAYMASTER SPEC DV182	OP	FSH	AL DV	OB	6 8	580		3400	4000
18 5	BAYMASTER SPEC DV183	OP	FSH	AL DV	OB	6 8	580		3450	4000
18 5	BAYMASTER SPEC DV18T	OP	FSH	AL DV	OB	6 8	580		3400	4000
18 6	RIVER BOAT R18 DASH	OP	FSH	AL DV	OB	7 6	795		4150	4850
18 6	RIVER BOAT R18C	OP	FSH	AL DV	OB	7 6	795		4100	4800
18 6	RIVER BOAT R18S	OP	FSH	AL DV	OB	7 6	795		4100	4750
18 6	RIVER BOAT R18T	OP	FSH	AL DV	OB	7 6	795		4200	4850

LOA FT	IN	NAME AND/ OR MODEL	TOP/ RIG	BOAT TYPE	-HULL- MTL	TP	---ENGINE--- TP	# HP	MFG	BEAM FT	IN	WGT LBS	DRAFT FT	IN	RETAIL LOW	RETAIL HIGH
		1993 BOATS														
18	6	RIVER BOAT RI18	OP	RNBT	AL	DV	IB	215		7	6	1733			7950	9150
19		NEWPORTER DV019	OP	CTRCN	AL	DV	OB			7		590			3250	3750
20	6	BAYMASTER DV20 IVC	OP	FSH	AL	DV	OB			7		655			3450	4000
20	6	BAYMASTER DV20 IVT	OP	FSH	AL	DV	OB			7		655			3450	4000
20	6	BAYMASTER SPEC DV201	OP	FSH	AL	DV	OB			7		655			3750	4400
20	6	BAYMASTER SPEC DV202	OP	FSH	AL	DV	OB			7		655			3750	4400
20	6	BAYMASTER SPEC DV203	OP	FSH	AL	DV	OB			7		655			3800	4400
20	6	BAYMASTER SPEC DV20T	OP	FSH	AL	DV	OB			7		655			3750	4400
20	6	RIVER BOAT R20 DASH	OP	FSH	AL	DV	OB			7	6	860			4400	5050
20	6	RIVER BOAT R20C	OP	FSH	AL	DV	OB			7	6	860			4400	5100
20	6	RIVER BOAT R20S	OP	FSH	AL	DV	OB			7	6	860			4400	5050
20	6	RIVER BOAT R20T	OP	FSH	AL	DV	OB			7	6	860			4500	5150
20	6	RIVER BOAT RI20	OP	RNBT	AL	DV	IB	215		7	6	1798			8500	9750
24	6	RIVER BOAT R24 DASH	OP	FSH	AL	DV	OB			7	6	1050			7800	8950
24	6	RIVER BOAT R24C	OP	FSH	AL	DV	OB			7	6	1050			7850	9000
24	6	RIVER BOAT R24S	OP	FSH	AL	DV	OB			7	6	1050			7800	8950
24	6	RIVER BOAT R24T	OP	FSH	AL	DV	OB			7	6	1050			7950	9100
24	6	RIVER BOAT RI24	OP	RNBT	AL	DV	IB	215		7	6	2233			11900	13500
		1992 BOATS														
16	5	BAYMASTER DV16 IIIC	OP	FSH	AL	DV	OB			6	4	405			1850	2200
16	5	BAYMASTER DV16 IIIT	OP	FSH	AL	DV	OB			6	4	405			1900	2250
16	5	DELTA ALASKAN 16-1	OP	FSH	AL	DV	OB			6	4	375			1550	1850
16	5	DELTA ALASKAN 16-2	OP	FSH	AL	DV	OB			6	4	375			1600	1950
16	5	DELTA ALASKAN 16-3	OP	FSH	AL	DV	OB			6	4	375			1700	2050
16	5	DELTA ALASKAN 16-4	OP	FSH	AL	DV	OB			6	4	375			1750	2100
16	5	DELTA ALASKAN 16-5	OP	FSH	AL	DV	OB			6	4	375			1850	2200
16	5	DELTA ALASKAN 16-6	OP	FSH	AL	DV	OB			6	4	375			1800	2150
16	5	DELTA ALASKAN 16-7	OP	FSH	AL	DV	OB			6	4	375			1850	2200
16	6	RIVER BOAT R16C	OP	FSH	AL	DV	OB			5	10	525			2500	2900
16	6	RIVER BOAT R16S	OP	FSH	AL	DV	OB			5	10	525			2450	2850
17		NEWPORTER DVO17	OP	CTRCN	AL	DV	OB			6	6	460			2250	2650
18	5	BAYMASTER DV18 IVC	OP	FSH	AL	DV	OB			6	8	580			3000	3500
18	5	BAYMASTER DV18 IVT	OP	FSH	AL	DV	OB			6	8	580			3000	3500
18	5	BAYMASTER SPEC DV181	OP	FSH	AL	DV	OB			6	8	580			3300	3850
18	5	BAYMASTER SPEC DV182	OP	FSH	AL	DV	OB			6	8	580			3300	3850
18	5	BAYMASTER SPEC DV183	OP	FSH	AL	DV	OB			6	8	580			3300	3850
18	5	BAYMASTER SPEC DV18T	OP	FSH	AL	DV	OB			6	8	580			3300	3850
18	6	RIVER BOAT R18 DASH	OP	FSH	AL	DV	OB			7	6	795			4000	4650
18	6	RIVER BOAT R18C	OP	FSH	AL	DV	OB			7	6	795			3950	4600
18	6	RIVER BOAT R18S	OP	FSH	AL	DV	OB			7	6	795			3950	4600
18	6	RIVER BOAT R18T	OP	FSH	AL	DV	OB			7	6	795			4050	4700
18	6	RIVER BOAT RI 18	OP	RNBT	AL	DV	IB	215		7	6	1733			7550	8700
19		NEWPORTER DV019	OP	CTRCN	AL	DV	OB			7		590			3100	3600
20	6	BAYMASTER DV20 IVC	OP	FSH	AL	DV	OB			7		655			3300	3850
20	6	BAYMASTER DV20 IVT	OP	FSH	AL	DV	OB			7		655			3300	3850
20	6	BAYMASTER SPEC DV201	OP	FSH	AL	DV	OB			7		655			3600	4200
20	6	BAYMASTER SPEC DV202	OP	FSH	AL	DV	OB			7		655			3600	4200
20	6	BAYMASTER SPEC DV203	OP	FSH	AL	DV	OB			7		655			3650	4250
20	6	BAYMASTER SPEC DV20T	OP	FSH	AL	DV	OB			7		655			3600	4200
20	6	RIVER BOAT R20 DASH	OP	FSH	AL	DV	OB			7	6	860			4150	4850
20	6	RIVER BOAT R20C	OP	FSH	AL	DV	OB			7	6	860			4200	4900
20	6	RIVER BOAT R20S	OP	FSH	AL	DV	OB			7	6	860			4150	4850
20	6	RIVER BOAT R20T	OP	FSH	AL	DV	OB			7	6	860			4250	4950
20	6	RIVER BOAT RI 20	OP	RNBT	AL	DV	IB	215		7	6	1798			8050	9250
24	6	RIVER BOAT R24 DASH	OP	FSH	AL	DV	OB			7	6	1050			7150	8200
24	6	RIVER BOAT R24C	OP	FSH	AL	DV	OB			7	6	1050			7200	8250
24	6	RIVER BOAT R24S	OP	FSH	AL	DV	OB			7	6	1050			7150	8200
24	6	RIVER BOAT R24T	OP	FSH	AL	DV	OB			7	6	1050			7250	8350
24	6	RIVER BOAT RI 24	OP	RNBT	AL	DV	IB	215		7	6	2233			11300	12800
		1991 BOATS														
16	5	BAYMASTER DV 16 III	OP	FSH	AL	DV	OB			6	4	405			1800	2150
16	5	DELTA ALASKAN 16-1	OP	FSH	AL	DV	OB			6	4	375			1500	1800
16	5	DELTA ALASKAN 16-2	OP	FSH	AL	DV	OB			6	4	375			1550	1850
16	5	DELTA ALASKAN 16-3	OP	FSH	AL	DV	OB			6	4	375			1650	1950
16	5	DELTA ALASKAN 16-4	OP	FSH	AL	DV	OB			6	4	375			1700	2000
16	5	DELTA ALASKAN 16-5	OP	FSH	AL	DV	OB			6	4	375			1800	2150
16	5	DELTA ALASKAN 16-6	OP	FSH	AL	DV	OB			6	4	375			1750	2100
16	5	DELTA ALASKAN 16-7	OP	FSH	AL	DV	OB			6	4	375			1800	2150
16	6	RIVER BOAT R16C	OP	FSH	AL	DV	OB			5	10	525			2400	2800
16	6	RIVER BOAT R16S	OP	FSH	AL	DV	OB			5	10	525			2350	2750
18	5	BAYMASTER DV18 IVC	OP	FSH	AL	DV	OB			6	8	580			2900	3350
18	5	BAYMASTER DV18 IVT	OP	FSH	AL	DV	OB			6	8	580			2900	3350
18	5	BAYMASTER SPEC DV181	OP	FSH	AL	DV	OB			6	8	580			3150	3700
18	5	BAYMASTER SPEC DV182	OP	FSH	AL	DV	OB			6	8	580			3150	3700
18	5	BAYMASTER SPEC DV183	OP	FSH	AL	DV	OB			6	8	580			3200	3700
18	5	BAYMASTER SPEC DV18T	OP	FSH	AL	DV	OB			6	8	580			3150	3700
18	6	RIVER BOAT R18 DASH	OP	FSH	AL	DV	OB			7	6	795			3850	4450
18	6	RIVER BOAT R18C	OP	FSH	AL	DV	OB			7	6	795			3800	4450
18	6	RIVER BOAT R18S	OP	FSH	AL	DV	OB			7	6	795			3800	4400
18	6	RIVER BOAT R18T	OP	FSH	AL	DV	OB			7	6	795			3900	4500
18	6	RIVER BOAT RI 18	OP	RNBT	AL	DV	IB	215		7	6	1733			7150	8250
20	6	BAYMASTER DV20 IVC	OP	FSH	AL	DV	OB			7		655			3200	3700
20	6	BAYMASTER DV20 IVT	OP	FSH	AL	DV	OB			7		655			2600	3050
20	6	BAYMASTER SPEC DV201	OP	FSH	AL	DV	OB			7		655			3500	4050
20	6	BAYMASTER SPEC DV202	OP	FSH	AL	DV	OB			7		655			3500	4050
20	6	BAYMASTER SPEC DV203	OP	FSH	AL	DV	OB			7		655			3500	4100
20	6	BAYMASTER SPEC DV20T	OP	FSH	AL	DV	OB			7		655			3500	4050
20	6	RIVER BOAT R20 DASH	OP	FSH	AL	DV	OB			7	6	860			4000	4700
20	6	RIVER BOAT R20C	OP	FSH	AL	DV	OB			7	6	860			4050	4700
20	6	RIVER BOAT R20S	OP	FSH	AL	DV	OB			7	6	860			4000	4700
20	6	RIVER BOAT R20T	OP	FSH	AL	DV	OB			7	6	860			4100	4750
20	6	RIVER BOAT RI 20	OP	RNBT	AL	DV	IB	215		7	6	1798			7650	8800
24	6	RIVER BOAT R24 DASH	OP	FSH	AL	DV	OB			7	6	1050			6700	7700
24	6	RIVER BOAT R24C	OP	FSH	AL	DV	OB			7	6	1050			6750	7750
24	6	RIVER BOAT R24S	OP	FSH	AL	DV	OB			7	6	1050			6700	7700
24	6	RIVER BOAT R24T	OP	FSH	AL	DV	OB			7	6	1050			6850	7900
24	6	RIVER BOAT RI 24	OP	RNBT	AL	DV	IB	215		7	6	2233			10700	12200
		1990 BOATS														
16	5	BAYMASTER DV 16 IIIC	OP	FSH	AL	DV	OB			6	4	450			1900	2300
16	5	BAYMASTER DV116 IIIT	OP	FSH	AL	DV	OB			6	4	450			1950	2350
16	5	DELTA ALASKAN 16-1	OP	FSH	AL	DV	OB			6	4	375			1450	1750
16	5	DELTA ALASKAN 16-2	OP	FSH	AL	DV	OB			6	4	375			1500	1800
16	5	DELTA ALASKAN 16-3	OP	FSH	AL	DV	OB			6	4	375			1600	1900
16	5	DELTA ALASKAN 16-4	OP	FSH	AL	DV	OB			6	4	375			1650	1950
16	5	DELTA ALASKAN 16-5	OP	FSH	AL	DV	OB			6	4	375			1700	2050
16	5	DELTA ALASKAN 16-6	OP	FSH	AL	DV	OB			6	4	375			1700	2000
16	5	DELTA ALASKAN 16-7	OP	FSH	AL	DV	OB			6	4	375			1750	2050
16	6	RIVER BOAT R16JC	OP	FSH	AL	DV	OB			5	10	525			2350	2700
16	6	RIVER BOAT R16JS	OP	FSH	AL	DV	OB			5	10	525			2350	2700
16	6	RIVER BOAT R16PC	OP	FSH	AL	DV	OB			5	10	505			2250	2600
16	6	RIVER BOAT R16PS	OP	FSH	AL	DV	OB			5	10	505			2250	2600
18	5	BAYMASTER DV18 IVC	OP	FSH	AL	DV	OB			6	8	580			2200	2550
18	5	BAYMASTER DV18 IVT	OP	FSH	AL	DV	OB			6	8	580			2250	2600
18	5	BAYMASTER SPEC DV181	OP	FSH	AL	DV	OB			6	8	580			3050	3550
18	5	BAYMASTER SPEC DV182	OP	FSH	AL	DV	OB			6	8	580			3050	3550
18	5	BAYMASTER SPEC DV183	OP	FSH	AL	DV	OB			6	8	580			3100	3600
18	5	BAYMASTER SPEC DV18T	OP	FSH	AL	DV	OB			6	8	580			3050	3550
18	6	RIVER BOAT R18 DASH	OP	FSH	AL	DV	OB			7	6	795			3700	4300
18	6	RIVER BOAT R18C	OP	FSH	AL	DV	OB			7	6	795			3700	4300
18	6	RIVER BOAT R18S	OP	FSH	AL	DV	OB			7	6	795			3650	4250
18	6	RIVER BOAT R18T	OP	FSH	AL	DV	OB			7	6	795			3750	4400
18	6	RIVER BOAT RI 18	OP	RNBT	AL	DV	IB	215		7	6	1733			6800	7850
20	6	BAYMASTER DV20 IVC	OP	FSH	AL	DV	OB			7		655			2450	2850
20	6	BAYMASTER DV20 IVT	OP	FSH	AL	DV	OB			7		655			2500	2900
20	6	BAYMASTER SPEC DV201	OP	FSH	AL	DV	OB			7		655			3350	3900
20	6	BAYMASTER SPEC DV202	OP	FSH	AL	DV	OB			7		655			3350	3900
20	6	BAYMASTER SPEC DV203	OP	FSH	AL	DV	OB			7		655			3400	3950
20	6	BAYMASTER SPEC DV20T	OP	FSH	AL	DV	OB			7		655			3400	3900
20	6	RIVER BOAT R20 DASH	OP	FSH	AL	DV	OB			7	6	860			3900	4500
20	6	RIVER BOAT R20C	OP	FSH	AL	DV	OB			7	6	860			3900	4550
20	6	RIVER BOAT R20S	OP	FSH	AL	DV	OB			7	6	860			3900	4500
20	6	RIVER BOAT R20T	OP	FSH	AL	DV	OB			7	6	860			3950	4600
20	6	RIVER BOAT RI 20	OP	RNBT	AL	DV	IB	215		7	6	1798			7300	8400
24	6	RIVER BOAT R24 DASH	OP	FSH	AL	DV	OB			7	6	1050			6050	6950
24	6	RIVER BOAT R24C	OP	FSH	AL	DV	OB			7	6	1050			6050	7000
24	6	RIVER BOAT R24S	OP	FSH	AL	DV	OB			7	6	1050			6050	6950
24	6	RIVER BOAT R24T	OP	FSH	AL	DV	OB			7	6	1050			6150	7050
24	6	RIVER BOAT RI 24	OP	RNBT	AL	DV	IB	215		7	6	2233			10200	11600

DENCHO MARINE INC
LONG BEACH CA 90813   See inside cover to adjust price for area
FOR OLDER MODELS SEE DENNIS CHOATE

LOA FT IN	NAME AND/ OR MODEL	TOP/ RIG	BOAT TYPE	-HULL- MTL TP	----ENGINE--- TP # HP MFG	BEAM FT IN	WGT LBS	DRAFT FT IN	RETAIL LOW	RETAIL HIGH
---	--- 1986 BOATS ---									
39 7	ANDREWS 39	SLP	SA/RC	FBG KL	IB D	12 5	13000	7 6	56900	62500
42 3	CHOATE 42	SLP	SA/RC	FBG KL	IB D	13	16500	7 10	72800	80000
48 2	CHOATE 48	SLP	SA/RC	FBG KL	IB D	14	23000	8 8	106000	116500
---	--- 1985 BOATS ---									
39 7	ANDREWS 39	SLP	SA/RC	FBG KL	IB D	12 5	13000	7 6	53400	58700
42 3	CHOATE 42	SLP	SA/RC	FBG KL	IB D	13	16500	7 10	68100	74800
48 2	CHOATE 48	SLP	SA/RC	FBG KL	IB D	14	23000	8 8	99200	109000
---	--- 1984 BOATS ---									
39 7	CHOATE 40	SLP	SA/RC	FBG KL	IB D	12 5	14000	7 6	52800	58000
42 3	CHOATE 42	SLP	SA/RC	FBG KL	IB 30D YAN	13	16500	7 10	63600	69900
48 2	CHOATE 48	SLP	SA/RC	FBG KL	IB 50D VW	14	23000	8 8	92600	101500

DENISON MARINE INC
DANIA FL 33004   COAST GUARD MFG ID- DEI See inside cover to adjust price for area

LOA FT IN	NAME AND/ OR MODEL	TOP/ RIG	BOAT TYPE	-HULL- MTL TP	----ENGINE--- TP # HP MFG	BEAM FT IN	WGT LBS	DRAFT FT IN	RETAIL LOW	RETAIL HIGH
---	--- 1985 BOATS ---									
49	DENISON	HT	MY	AL SV	IB T975D S&S	15		4	171000	187500
72	DENISON	FB	MY	AL SV	IB T975D S&S	20 3		5	**	**

SAMUAL S DEVLIN BOATBUILDING
OLYMPIA WA 98502   COAST GUARD MFG ID- XDK See inside cover to adjust price for area

LOA FT IN	NAME AND/ OR MODEL	TOP/ RIG	BOAT TYPE	-HULL- MTL TP	----ENGINE--- TP # HP MFG	BEAM FT IN	WGT LBS	DRAFT FT IN	RETAIL LOW	RETAIL HIGH
---	--- 1993 BOATS ---									
17 2	OARLING		ROW			3 8			**	**
18 8	WINTER WREN	GAF	SACAC	KL		6 10		2 6	9950	11300
18 8	WINTER WREN II	SLP	SACAC	KL		7 1		3 6	10600	12100
19 2	EIDER	SLP	SACAC	KL		6 4		2 2	10700	12200
19 3	SEA SWIFT	SLP	SACAC			5 5		6	10700	12200
21 7	CAPE COD CAT		SACAC	KL	8D YAN	10	5850		32100	35700
22	SURF SCOTER	PH	F/W DS	IB	30D	7 8	2200	1 11	16200	18400
22 3	KINGFISHER	PH	DS	IB	40D	7 8		2 8	16700	18900
22 6	AUK	MS	KL	IB	D	8 2		3	32200	35700
22 8	ARCTIC JAEGER	SCH	SACAC		IB	7 6		3 1	32300	35900
22 8	ARCTIC TERN	SLP	SACAC	KL		7 6		3 1	13300	15100
24 6	BLACK CROWN	PH	F/W DS	IB	66D	8 5		3	50100	55100
24 6	BLACK CROWN EC	PH	F/W DS	IB	66D	8 5		3	54000	59300
25 4	OYSTA 25	SLP	MS	IB	20D	8 6		3 4	51200	56300
26 2	SHEARWATER		MS	KL	IB 22D	8 10		3 10	53800	59100
27 7	ONYX	SLP	SACAC	KL		8 6		4 6	25000	25000
30	CZARINNA	TRWL	F/W DS	IB T 18D YAN	8 5	8900			58600	64400
30	MOSS ROCK	GAF	MS	KL	IB	12		2	53700	59100
30 6	OYSTA 30	SLP	MS	F/W KL	IB 20D	9 10		4 6	89100	97900
39 9	WHIMBREL		MS	F/W KL	IB 12D	9 8		4 10	96200	105500
40 6	CYGNET	SCH	MS	KL	IB D	11 6			196000	215500
---	--- 1992 BOATS ---									
17 2	OARLING		ROW			3 8			**	**
18 8	WINTER WREN	GAF	SAIL	KL		6 10		2 6	9650	11000
18 8	WINTER WREN II	SLP	SAIL	KL		7 1		3 6	10400	11800
19 2	EIDER	SLP	SAIL	KL		6 4		2 2	10400	11800
19 3	SEA SWIFT	SLP	SAIL			5 5		6	10400	11900
20 3	SURF SCOTER	PH		OB		7 8	2200	1 11	18300	20400
22	SURF SCOTER	PH	F/W DS	OB		7 8	2200	1 11	20200	22400
22	SURF SCOTER	PH		OB	30D	7 8	2200	1 11	15400	17500
22 3	KINGFISHER	PH	DS	IB	40D	8		2 8	15900	18000
22 6	AUK	MS	KL	IB	D	8 2		3	30100	33400
22 8	ARCTIC JAEGER	SCH	SAIL	IB		7 6		3 1	30200	33500
22 8	ARCTIC TERN	SLP	SAIL	KL		7 6		3 1	16000	18200
24 6	BLACK CROWN	PH	F/W DS	IB	66D	8 5		3	46800	51400
24 6	BLACK CROWN EC	PH	F/W DS	IB	66D	8 5		3	52200	57400
25 4	OYSTA 25	SLP	MS	IB	20D	8 6		3 4	48400	53200
26 2	SHEARWATER		MS	KL	IB 22D	8 10		3 10	50200	55200
27 7	ONYX	SLP	SAIL	KL		8 6		4 6	33100	36800
30	CZARINNA	TRWL	F/W DS	IB T 18D YAN	8 5	8900			55800	61300
30	MOSS ROCK	GAF	MS	KL	IB	12		2	50200	55200
30 6	OYSTA 30	SLP	MS	F/W KL	IB 20D	9 10		4 6	83300	91600
39 9	WHIMBREL		MS	F/W KL	IB 12D	9 8		4 10	90000	99000
40 6	CYGNET	SCH	MS	KL	IB D	11 6			183500	201500
---	--- 1984 BOATS ---									
16 4	DIPPER	HT	TRWL	F/W DS	OB	7	1350	1 8	10100	11400
16 4	EIDER	SLP	SA/CR	F/W KL	OB	6 4	1410	2 1	5500	6300
16 4	EIDER	CUT	SA/CR	F/W KL	OB	6 4	1410	2 1	5500	6300
17 2	OARLING	OP	ROW	F/W FL		3 8	92	4	**	**
18 9	WINTER-WREN	SLP	SA/CR	F/W KL	OB	6 10	1825	2 6	6350	7300
19 3	SEA-SWIFT	CAT	SAIL	F/W CB	OB	5 6	380	6	3500	4050
19 3	SEA-SWIFT	KTH	SAIL	F/W CB	OB	5 6	380	6	3300	3850
21 4	ARTIC-TERN	SLP	SA/CR	F/W KL	OB	7 6	2800	3	8450	9750
21 11	ARTIC-JAEGER	SCH	SA/CR	F/W KL	OB	7 6	2820	3 1	8650	9950
24 6	KESTREL		SAIL	F/W					12100	13700
25 4	OYSTA 25	CAT	MS	F/W KL	IB 10D SAAB	8 6	7600	3 4	26300	29200
26 2	SHEARWATER	SCH	SA/CR	F/W KL	IB 22D SABB	8 10	7960	3 10	29100	32300
30 6	OYSTA 30	YWL	MS	F/W KL	IB 10D SAAB	9 10	14100	3 4	58100	63800
39 9	WHIMBREL	SCH	MS	F/W KL	IB 12D BMW	9 6	10900	4 9	46100	50700
39 9	WHIMBREL	CUT	MS	F/W KL	IB 12D BMW	9 6	10900	5	46100	50700

....For earlier years, see the BUC Used Boat Price Guide, Volume 3

DICKERSON BOATBUILDERS INC
TRAPPE MD 21673   COAST GUARD MFG ID- DBB See inside cover to adjust price for area

LOA FT IN	NAME AND/ OR MODEL	TOP/ RIG	BOAT TYPE	-HULL- MTL TP	----ENGINE--- TP # HP MFG	BEAM FT IN	WGT LBS	DRAFT FT IN	RETAIL LOW	RETAIL HIGH
---	--- 1989 BOATS ---									
37	DICKERSON 37 AFT	SLP	SA/CR	F/S KL	VD 33D WEST	11 6	15960	4 6	71200	78200
37	DICKERSON 37 AFT	CUT	SA/CR	F/S KL	VD 33D WEST	11 6	15960	4 6	71200	78200
---	--- 1988 BOATS ---									
37	DICKERSON 37 AFT	SLP	SA/CR	F/S KL	VD 33D WEST	11 6	15960	4 6	66600	73100
37	DICKERSON 37 AFT	CUT	SA/CR	F/S KL	VD 33D WEST	11 6	15960	4 6	66600	73100
---	--- 1987 BOATS ---									
37	DICKERSON 37 AFT	SLP	SA/CR	F/S KL	VD 33D WEST	11 6	15960	4 6	62200	68400
37	DICKERSON 37 AFT	CUT	SA/CR	F/S KL	VD 33D WEST	11 6	15960	4 6	62200	68400
---	--- 1986 BOATS ---									
37	DICKERSON 37	SLP	SA/CR	FBG KL	IB 51D PERK	11 6	16000	4 6	58200	63900
37	FARR 37	SLP	SA/RC	FBG KL	IB D	12	12200	7	42600	47300
50	DICKERSON 50	KTH	SA/CR	FBG KL	IB 62D PERK	13 8	33000	6	173000	190000
---	--- 1985 BOATS ---									
37	DICKERSON 37 AFT	SLP	SA/CR	F/S KL	VD 51D PERK	11 6	15960	4 6	54300	59700
37	DICKERSON 37 AFT	CUT	SA/CR	F/S KL	VD 51D PERK	11 6	15960	4 6	54300	59700
37	DICKERSON 37 CTR	KTH	SA/CR	F/S KL	VD 51D PERK	11 6	15960	4 6	54300	59700
37	FARR 37	SLP	SA/RC	FBG KL	IB D	12	12200	7	39800	44300
50	DICKERSON 50 AFT	SLP	SA/CR	F/S KL	KC VD 62D PERK	13 8	33900	5 2	159000	174500
50	DICKERSON 50 AFT	SLP	SA/CR	F/S KL	VD 62D PERK	13 8	33900	6	159000	174500
50	DICKERSON 50 AFT	CUT	SA/CR	F/S KL	KC VD 62D PERK	13 8	33900	5 2	155500	171000
50	DICKERSON 50 AFT	CUT	SA/CR	F/S KL	VD 62D PERK	13 8	33900	6	155500	171000
50	DICKERSON 50 AFT	KTH	SA/CR	F/S KL	KC VD 62D PERK	13 8	33900	5 2	162500	178500
50	DICKERSON 50 AFT	KTH	SA/CR	F/S KL	VD 62D PERK	13 8	33900	6	162500	178500
---	--- 1984 BOATS ---									
37	DICKERSON 37 AFT	SLP	SA/CR	F/S KL	VD 50D PERK	11 6	15960	4 6	50800	55800
37	DICKERSON 37 AFT	CUT	SA/CR	F/S KL	VD 50D PERK	11 6	15960	4 6	50800	55800
37	DICKERSON 37 CTR	KTH	SA/CR	F/S KL	VD 50D PERK	11 6	15960	4 6	50800	55800
37	FARR 37	SLP	SA/RC	FBG KL	IB D	12	12200	7	37300	41400
50	DICKERSON 50 AFT	SLP	SA/CR	F/S KL	VD 62D PERK	13 8	33900	5 2	149000	163500
50	DICKERSON 50 AFT	SLP	SA/CR	F/S KL	VD 62D PERK	13 8	33900	6	149000	163500
50	DICKERSON 50 AFT	CUT	SA/CR	F/S KL	VD 62D PERK	13 8	33900	5 2	146000	160500
50	DICKERSON 50 AFT	CUT	SA/CR	F/S KL	VD 62D PERK	13 8	33900	6	146000	160500
50	DICKERSON 50 AFT	KTH	SA/CR	F/S KL	VD 62D PERK	13 8	33900	5 2	152000	167000
50	DICKERSON 50 AFT	KTH	SA/CR	F/S KL	VD 62D PERK	13 8	33900	6	152000	167000

....For earlier years, see the BUC Used Boat Price Guide, Volume 3

DIXIE MARINE INC
NEWTON NC 28658   COAST GUARD MFG ID- BKW See inside cover to adjust price for area
FORMERLY SPORTSMAN TRAILERS INC

LOA FT IN	NAME AND/ OR MODEL	TOP/ RIG	BOAT TYPE	-HULL- MTL TP	----ENGINE--- TP # HP MFG	BEAM FT IN	WGT LBS	DRAFT FT IN	RETAIL LOW	RETAIL HIGH
---	--- 1994 BOATS ---									
19	DIXIE V19	OP	RNBT	FBG DV	OB	7 3	1850		2850	3300
19	DIXIE V19	OP	RNBT	FBG DV	IO 135-175	7 3	2500		4450	5150
19	SUNCRUISER V19 SX	OP	RNBT	FBG DV	IO 135-175	7 3	2500		4450	5150
21	DIXIE 521	OP	CUD	FBG DV	IO 135-205	8	3000		6600	7700
21	DIXIE 721	OP	CUD	FBG DV	IO 135-205	8	3000		6600	7700
21	DIXIE 821	OP	CUD	FBG DV	IO 135-260	8	3000		6600	8100

DIXIE MARINE INC   -CONTINUED

See inside cover to adjust price for area

LOA FT IN	NAME AND/ OR MODEL	TOP/ RIG	BOAT TYPE	HULL MTL	HULL TP	ENG TP	# HP	MFG	BEAM FT IN	WGT LBS	DRAFT FT IN	RETAIL LOW	RETAIL HIGH
1994 BOATS													
21	DIXIE 821 W/BRKT	OP	CUD	FBG	DV	OB			8	2200		4600	5300
21	DIXIE DUAL 821W/BRKT	OP	CUD	FBG	DV	OB			8	2200		4600	5300
1993 BOATS													
19	DIXIE V19	OP	RNBT	FBG	DV	OB			7 3	1850		2700	3150
19	DIXIE V19	OP	RNBT	FBG	DV	IO	115-175		7 3	2500		4100	4800
19	SUNCRUISER V19 SX	OP	RNBT	FBG	DV	IO	115-175		7 3	2500		4100	4800
21	DIXIE 521	OP	CUD	FBG	DV	IO	135-205		8	3000		6150	7200
21	DIXIE 721	OP	CUD	FBG	DV	IO	135-205		8	3000		6150	7200
21	DIXIE 821	OP	CUD	FBG	DV	IO	135-205		8	3000		6250	7300
21	DIXIE 821 W/BRKT	OP	CUD	FBG	DV	OB			8	2200		4400	5050
21	DIXIE DUAL 821W/BRKT	OP	CUD	FBG	DV	OB			8	2200		4400	5050
1992 BOATS													
19	DIXIE V19	OP	RNBT	FBG	DV	OB			7 3	1850		2600	3000
19	DIXIE V19	OP	RNBT	FBG	DV	IO	115-175		7 3	2500		3850	4500
19	SUNCRUISER V19 SX	OP	RNBT	FBG	DV	IO	115-175		7 3	2500		3850	4500
21	DIXIE 521	OP	CUD	FBG	DV	IO	135-205		8	3000		5700	6650
21	DIXIE 821	OP	CUD	FBG	DV	IO	135-205		8	3000		5800	6750
21	DIXIE 821 W/BRKT	OP	CUD	FBG	DV	OB			8	2200		4100	4800
21	DIXIE DUAL 821W/BRKT	OP	CUD	FBG	DV	OB			8	2200		4100	4800
1991 BOATS													
19	V19	OP	RNBT	FBG	DV	OB			7 3	1850		2500	2950
19	V19	OP	RNBT	FBG	DV	IO	135-175		7 3	2500		3550	4150
21	521	OP	CUD	FBG	DV	IO	135-175		8	3000		5250	6100
21	821	OP	CUD	FBG	DV	IO	135-175		8	3000		5450	6300
21	821 DUAL BRACKET	OP	CUD	FBG	DV	OB			8	2200		4150	4800
21	821 W/BRACKET	OP	CUD	FBG	DV	OB			8	2200		3750	4350
1990 BOATS													
17	170	OP	RNBT	FBG	DV	OB			6 7	1000		1100	1650
17	170	OP	RNBT	FBG	DV	IO	125	MRCR	6 7	1875		2450	2850
17	170 I/O	OP	RNBT	FBG	DV	IO	145		6 7	1875		2450	2850
18 1	188	OP	RNBT	FBG	DV	IO	175		7 5	1875		2800	3300
18 1	188 I/O	OP	RNBT	FBG	DV	IO	145-205		7 5	1875		2800	3350
18 1	190	OP	RNBT	FBG	DV	OB			7 1	1275		1750	2100
18 1	190	OP	RNBT	FBG	DV	IO	175		7 1	1875		2700	3100
18 1	190 I/O	OP	RNBT	FBG	DV	IO	125-205		7 1	1875		2650	3150
18 1	190 SUN CRUISER	OP	RNBT	FBG	DV	IO	125-205		7 1	1875		2800	3300
18 1	190 SUNCRUISER	OP	RNBT	FBG	DV	IO	175		7 1	1875		2800	3250
19	199	OP	RNBT	FBG	DV	IO	260		7 6	2700		3850	4500
19	299	OP	RNBT	FBG	DV	IB	260	MRCR	7 6	2700		4800	5550
21	521	OP	CUD	FBG	DV	IO	125-205		8	3000		4950	5800
21	521 I/O	OP	CUD	FBG	DV	IO	230-260		8	3000		5100	6050
21	721	OP	CUD	FBG	DV	IO	125-205		8	3000		4950	5850
21	721 I/O	OP	CUD	FBG	DV	IO	230-260		8	3000		5100	6050
21	721 SUN CRUISER	OP	CUD	FBG	DV	IO	260		8	3000		5450	6250
21	721 SUNCRUISER	OP	CUD	FBG	DV	IO	125-230		8	3000		5150	6100
21	821	OP	CUD	FBG	DV	IO	125-205		8	3000		5100	6000
21	821 I/O	OP	CUD	FBG	DV	IO	230-260		8	3000		5300	6250
21	821 W/BRACKET	OP	CUD	FBG	DV	OB			8	3000		4550	5250
24	924 I/O	OP	CUD	FBG	DV	IO	205-260		8 4			7600	9000
1989 BOATS													
17	170	OP	RNBT	FBG	DV	OB			6 7	1000		1350	1600
17	170 DELUXE	OP	RNBT	FBG	DV	IO	128-130		6 7	1875		2300	2700
18 1	188	OP	RNBT	FBG	DV	IO	175		7 5	1875		2650	3100
18 1	190	OP	RNBT	FBG	DV	OB			7 1	1275		1700	2000
18 1	190	OP	RNBT	FBG	DV	IO	165-175		7 1	1875		2450	2900
18 1	190 SUNCRUISER	OP	RNBT	FBG	DV	IO	165-175		7 1	1875		2650	3100
19	199	OP	RNBT	FBG	DV	IO	260		7 6	2700		3800	4200
19	299	OP	RNBT	FBG	DV	IB		MRCR	7 6	2700		**	**
19	299	OP	CUD	FBG	DV	IO	130-205		8	3000		4500	5350
21	521	OP	CUD	FBG	DV	IO	130-205		8	3000		4700	5500
21	721	OP	CUD	FBG	DV	IO	130-205		8	3000		5000	5800
21	721 SUNCRUISER	OP	CUD	FBG	DV	IO	130-205		8	3000		4800	5600
21	821	OP	CUD	FBG	DV	IO	130-205		8	3000		4800	5600
21	821 W/BRACKET	OP	CUD	FBG	DV	OB			8	3000		4350	5000
21	921 W/BRACKET	OP	CTRCN	FBG	DV	OB			8	2200		3600	4200
1988 BOATS													
16 4	166	OP	RNBT	FBG	TR	OB			6 4	755		990	1200
17	170	OP	RNBT	FBG	DV	OB			6 7	1000		1300	1550
17	170	OP	RNBT	FBG	DV	IO	120-130		6 7	1875		2150	2550
17	170 DELUXE	OP	RNBT	FBG	DV	IO	130		6 7	1875		2250	2600
17	171	OP	RNBT	FBG	DV	OB			6 7	1175		1500	1750
18 1	188	OP	RNBT	FBG	DV	IO	175-205		7 5	1875		2500	2950
18 1	188	OP	RNBT	FBG	DV	OB			7 1	1275		1650	1950
18 1	190	OP	RNBT	FBG	DV	IO	130-205		7 1	1875		2400	2900
18 1	190	OP	RNBT	FBG	DV	IO	260		7 1	1875		2650	3050
19	199	OP	RNBT	FBG	DV	IO	205-260		7 6	2700		3200	3950
19	299	OP	RNBT	FBG	DV	IB		MRCR	7 6	2700		**	**
19	299	OP	RNBT	FBG	DV	IB		PCM	7 6	2700		**	**
21	521	OP	CUD	FBG	DV	SE		OMC	8	3000		**	**
21	521	OP	CUD	FBG	DV	IO	165-205		8	3000		4450	5200
21	521 W/BRACKET	OP	CUD	FBG	DV	IO	165-260		8	3000		4150	4800
21	721	OP	CUD	FBG	DV	IO	165-260		8	3000		4450	5450
21	721 W/BRACKET	OP	CUD	FBG	DV	SE		OMC	8	3000		4150	4800
21	821	OP	CUD	FBG	DV	SE			8	3000		**	**
21	821	OP	CUD	FBG	DV	IO	130-205		8	3000		4500	5350
21	821	HT	CUD	FBG	DV	SE		OMC	8	3000		**	**
21	821	HT	CUD	FBG	DV	IO	130-205		8	3000		4500	5250
21	821 W/BRACKET	OP	CUD	FBG	DV	OB			8	3000		4150	4800
21	821 W/BRACKET	HT	CUD	FBG	DV	OB			8	3000		4150	4800
21	921 W/BRACKET	OP	CTRCN	FBG	DV	OB			8	2200		3450	4000

....For earlier years, see the BUC Used Boat Price Guide, Volume 3

DOCKRELL YACHTS LTD

PARSIPPANY NJ 07054   COAST GUARD MFG ID- JLD   See inside cover to adjust price for area

LOA FT IN	NAME AND/ OR MODEL	TOP/ RIG	BOAT TYPE	HULL MTL	HULL TP	ENG TP	# HP	MFG	BEAM FT IN	WGT LBS	DRAFT FT IN	RETAIL LOW	RETAIL HIGH
1995 BOATS													
22	DOCKRELL 22	SLP	SACAC	FBG	KL	IB	D		7 8	1200	2	4950	5700
27	DOCKRELL 27	CUT	SACAC	FBG	KL	IB	D		8	7000	3	20700	23000
37	DOCKRELL 37	CUT	SACAC	FBG	KL	IB	D		10 2	11500	8 4	49200	54100
1994 BOATS													
22	DOCKRELL 22	SLP	SACAC	FBG	KL	IB	D		7 8	1200	2	4700	5400
27	DOCKRELL 27	CUT	SACAC	FBG	KL	IB	D		8	7000	3	19400	21600
37	DOCKRELL 37	CUT	SACAC	FBG	KL	IB	D		10 2	11500	8 4	46600	51200
1993 BOATS													
22	DOCKRELL 22	SLP	SACAC	FBG	KL	IB	D		7 8	1200	2	4400	5050
27	DOCKRELL 27	CUT	SACAC	FBG	KL	IB	D		8	7000	3	18500	20500
37	DOCKRELL 37	CUT	SACAC	FBG	KL	IB	D		10 2	11500	8 4	43300	48100
1992 BOATS													
22	DOCKRELL 22	SLP	SACAC	FBG	KL	IB	D		7 8	1200	2	4100	4750
27	DOCKRELL 27	CUT	SACAC	FBG	KL	IB	D		8	7000	3	17000	19300
37	DOCKRELL 37	CUT	SACAC	FBG	KL	IB	D		10 2	11500	8 4	40700	45300
1991 BOATS													
22	DOCKRELL 22	SLP	SACAC	FBG	KL	IB	D		7 8	1200	2	3850	4500
27	DOCKRELL 27	CUT	SACAC	FBG	KL	IB	D		8	7000	3	16000	18200
37	DOCKRELL 37	CUT	SACAC	FBG	KL	IB	D		10 2	11500	8 4	38300	42600
1990 BOATS													
22	DOCKRELL 22	SLP	SACAC	FBG	KL	IB	D		7 8	1200	2	3650	4200
27	DOCKRELL 27	CUT	SACAC	FBG	KL	IB	D		8	7000	3	15000	17100
37	DOCKRELL 37	CUT	SACAC	FBG	KL	IB	D		10 2	11500	8 4	36100	40100
1989 BOATS													
22	DOCKRELL 22	SLP	SACAC	FBG	KL	IB	D		7 8	1200	2	3400	3950
27	DOCKRELL 27	CUT	SACAC	FBG	KL	IB	D		8	7000	3	14100	16100
37	DOCKRELL 37	CUT	SACAC	FBG	KL	IB	D		10 2	11500	8 4	33900	37700
1988 BOATS													
22	DOCKRELL 22	SLP	SACAC	FBG	KL	IB	D		7 8	1200	2	3200	3750
27	DOCKRELL 27	CUT	SACAC	FBG	KL	IB	D		8	7000	3	13300	15100
37	DOCKRELL 37	CUT	SACAC	FBG	KL	IB	D		10 2	11500	8 4	31900	35400
1987 BOATS													
22	DOCKRELL 22	SLP	SA/CR	FBG	KL	IB	D		7 8	1200	2	3000	3500
27	DOCKRELL 27	CUT	SA/CR	FBG	KL	IB	D		8	7000	3	12500	14200
37	DOCKRELL 37	CUT	SA/CR	FBG	KL	IB	D		10 2	11500	8 4	30000	33300
1986 BOATS													
17	DOCKRELL 17	SLP	SA/CR	FBG	SK	OB			7 4	1100	10	1750	2100
22	DOCKRELL 22	SLP	SA/CR	FBG	KC	OB			7 6	2150	1 4	2850	3300
27	DOCKRELL 27	CUT	SA/CR	FBG	KL	IB	D		8 3	7000	3	11800	13400
37	DOCKRELL 37	CUT	SA/CR	FBG	KL	IB	D		10 2	11500	8 4	28200	31400
1985 BOATS													
27	DOCKRELL 27	CUT	SA/CR	FBG	KL	IB	D		8	7000	3	11100	12600
37	DOCKRELL 37	CUT	SA/CR	FBG	KL	IB	D		10 2	11500	8 4	26500	29500
1984 BOATS													
17	DOCKRELL 17	SLP	SA/CR	FBG	SK	OB			7 4	1100	10	1550	1850
22	DOCKRELL 22	SLP	SA/CR	FBG	KC	OB			7 6	2150	1 4	2500	2900
27	DOCKRELL 27	CUT	SA/CR	FBG	KC	IB	15D	YAN	8	7000	3	10400	11900
37	DOCKRELL 37	CUT	SA/CR	FBG	KC	IB	30D	PANT	10 2	11500	3 9	25000	27800

....For earlier years, see the BUC Used Boat Price Guide, Volume 3

DODSON BOATYARD INC
STONINGTON CT 06378   See inside cover to adjust price for area

LOA FT IN	NAME AND/ OR MODEL	TOP/ RIG	BOAT TYPE	-HULL- MTL TP	----ENGINE--- TP # HP MFG	BEAM FT IN	WGT LBS	DRAFT FT IN	RETAIL LOW	RETAIL HIGH
			1985 BOATS							
39 11 JONMERI 40		SLP	SA/RC	FBG KL		12 7	18900	6 10	104500	115000

DOLPHIN BOATS INC
PRINCETON FL 33032   COAST GUARD MFG ID- DFL See inside cover to adjust price for area

For more recent years, see the BUC Used Boat Price Guide, Volume 1

LOA FT IN	NAME AND/ OR MODEL	TOP/ RIG	BOAT TYPE	-HULL- MTL TP	----ENGINE--- TP # HP MFG	BEAM FT IN	WGT LBS	DRAFT FT IN	RETAIL LOW	RETAIL HIGH
			1996 BOATS							
17 10	BACKCOUNTRY 18	OP	FSH	FBG DV	OB	7 7	900	10	6400	7400
20 10	DOLPHIN BRACKET DRV	OP	FSH	FBG DV	OB	7 7	1600	1 1	9700	11000
22 10	BULL DOLPHIN	OP	FSH	FBG DV	OB	8 2	2300	1 1	14000	15900
			1995 BOATS							
17 10	BACKCOUNTRY 18	OP	FSH	FBG DV	OB	7 7	900	10	6100	7000
			1994 BOATS							
17 10	BACKCOUNTRY 18	OP	FSH	FBG DV	OB	7 7	900	10	5800	6700
19 6	COMMERCIAL	OP	FSH	FBG DV	OB	7 7	1500	1 1	9400	10700
19 6	SUPER DOLPHIN	OP	FSH	FBG DV	OB	7 7	1550	1 1	9600	10900
21	SUPER BRACKET DRIVE	OP	FSH	FBG DV	OB	7 7	1550	1 1	8650	9900
21 6	BULL DOLPHIN	OP	FSH	FBG DV	OB	8 2	1900	1 1	10400	11800
			1993 BOATS							
17 10	BACKCOUNTRY 18	OP	FSH	FBG DV	OB	7 7	900	10	5550	6400
19 6	COMMERCIAL	OP	FSH	FBG DV	OB	7 7	1500	1 1	9000	10200
19 6	SUPER DOLPHIN	OP	FSH	FBG DV	OB	7 7	1550	1 1	9200	10500
21	SUPER BRACKET DRIVE	OP	FSH	FBG DV	OB	7 7	1550	1 1	8250	9500
21 6	BULL DOLPHIN	OP	FSH	FBG DV	OB	8 2	1900	1 1	10000	11400
			1992 BOATS							
17 10	BACKCOUNTRY 18	OP	FSH	FBG DV	OB	7 7	900	10	5300	6100
19 6	COMMERCIAL	OP	FSH	FBG DV	OB	7 7	1500	1 1	8550	9800
19 6	SUPER DOLPHIN	OP	FSH	FBG DV	OB	7 7	1550	1 1	8850	10000
21	SUPER BRACKET DRIVE	OP	FSH	FBG DV	OB	7 7	1550	1 1	7950	9150
21 6	BULL DOLPHIN	OP	FSH	FBG DV	OB	8 2	1900	1 1	9600	10900
			1991 BOATS							
17 10	BACKCOUNTRY 18	OP	FSH	FBG DV	OB	7 7	900	10	5100	5900
19 6	COMMERCIAL	OP	FSH	FBG DV	OB	7 7	1500	1 1	8200	9400
19 6	SUPER DOLPHIN	OP	FSH	FBG DV	OB	7 7	1550	1 1	8400	9650
21	SUPER BRACKET DRIVE	OP	FSH	FBG DV	OB	7 7	1550	1 1	7650	8800
21 6	MARLIN	OP	FSH	FBG DV	OB	8 2	1900	1 1	9300	10600
			1990 BOATS							
17 10	BACKCOUNTRY 18	OP	FSH	FBG DV	OB	7 7	900	10	4950	5650
19 6	COMMERCIAL	OP	FSH	FBG DV	OB	7 7	1500	1 1	7900	9100
19 6	SUPER DOLPHIN	OP	FSH	FBG DV	OB	7 7	1550	1 1	8100	9300
21	SUPER BRACKET DRIVE	OP	FSH	FBG DV	OB	7 7	1550	1 1	7400	8500
21 6	MARLIN	OP	FSH	FBG DV	OB	8 2	1900	1 1	8950	10200
			1989 BOATS							
17 10	BACKCOUNTRY 18	OP	FSH	FBG DV	OB	7 7	900	10	4800	5500
19 6	COMMERCIAL	OP	FSH	FBG DV	OB	7 7	1500	1 1	7650	8800
19 6	SUPER DOLPHIN	OP	FSH	FBG DV	OB	7 7	1550	1 1	7850	9000
21	SUPER BRACKET DRIVE	OP	FSH	FBG DV	OB	7 7	1550	1 1	7150	8200
21 6	MARLIN	OP	FSH	FBG DV	OB	8 2	1900	1 1	8550	9850
			1988 BOATS							
17 10	BACKCOUNTRY 18	OP	FSH	FBG DV	OB	7 7	900	10	4650	5350
19 6	COMMERCIAL	OP	FSH	FBG DV	OB	7 7	1500	1 1	7400	8500
19 6	SUPER-DOLPHIN	OP	FSH	FBG DV	OB	7 7	1550	1 1	7600	8750
21	SUPER BRACKET DRIVE	OP	FSH	FBG DV	OB	7 7	1550	1 1	6900	7950
			1987 BOATS							
17 10	BACKCOUNTRY 18	OP	FSH	FBG SV	OB	7 7	900	10	4550	5200
19 6	COMMERCIAL	OP	FSH	FBG DV	OB	7 7	1500	1 1	7200	8300
19 6	SUPER-DOLPHIN	OP	FSH	FBG DV	OB	7 7	1550	1 1	7400	8500
21	SUPER BRACKET DRIVE	OP	FSH	FBG DV	OB	7 7	1550	1 1	6700	7700
			1986 BOATS							
17 10	BACKCOUNTRY	OP	FSH	FBG SV	OB	7 7	900	10	4400	5050
19 6	COMMERCIAL	OP	FSH	FBG DV	OB	7 7	1500	1	7050	8100
19 6	SUPER SPORTER	OP	FSH	FBG DV	OB	7 7	1550	1	7200	8300
21	SUPER FISHER	OP	FSH	FBG DV	OB	7 7	1550	1	6500	7500
			1985 BOATS							
17 10	DOLPHIN BACKCOUNTRY	OP	FSH	FBG SV	OB	7 6	900	10	4250	4950
19 6	DOLPHIN COMMERCIAL	OP	FSH	FBG DV	OB	7 7	1600	1 1	7200	8250
19 6	SUPER-DOLPHIN	OP	FSH	FBG DV	OB	7 7	1550	1 1	7050	8100
19 6	SUPER-DOLPHIN	OP	FSH	FBG DV	SE	115	OMC	7 7	2000	1 1	8350	9550
			1984 BOATS							
17 10	DOLPHIN BACKCOUNTRY	OP	FSH	FBG SV	OB	7 6	1000	11	4600	5300
19 6	DOLPHIN COMMERCIAL	OP	FSH	FBG DV	OB	7 7	1600	1 1	7050	8100
19 6	SUPER-DOLPHIN	OP	FSH	FBG DV	OB	7 7	1550	1 1	6900	7900

....For earlier years, see the BUC Used Boat Price Guide, Volume 3

DONG SUNG VENUS INC
TOWSON MD 21204   See inside cover to adjust price for area

LOA FT IN	NAME AND/ OR MODEL	TOP/ RIG	BOAT TYPE	-HULL- MTL TP	----ENGINE--- TP # HP MFG	BEAM FT IN	WGT LBS	DRAFT FT IN	RETAIL LOW	RETAIL HIGH
			1986 BOATS							
46	VENUS 46	KTH	SA/RC	FBG KL	IB	D	13 6	30000	6	120500	132500
			1985 BOATS							
46	VENUS 46	KTH	SA/CR	FBG KL	IB	62D PERK	13 6	30000	6	111500	123000
			1984 BOATS							
46 6	VENUS 46	KTH	SA/CR	FBG KL	IB	80D LEHM	13 6	29000	6 2	105500	116000

DONZI MARINE CORP
DIV AMERICAN MARINE HLDNGS INC   See inside cover to adjust price for area
SARASOTA FL 34243   COAST GUARD MFG ID- DMR

For more recent years, see the BUC Used Boat Price Guide, Volume 1

LOA FT IN	NAME AND/ OR MODEL	TOP/ RIG	BOAT TYPE	-HULL- MTL TP	----ENGINE--- TP # HP MFG	BEAM FT IN	WGT LBS	DRAFT FT IN	RETAIL LOW	RETAIL HIGH
			1996 BOATS							
16 5	CLASSIC 16	RNBT	F/W DV	IO	205 MRCR	6 11	1850	1 1	7550	8700
16 11	JET BOAT 152	JTSKI	FBG SV	JT	170 MRCR	6 6	1100	11	**	**
18	CLASSIC 18	RNBT	F/W DV	IO	270 MRCR	7	2600	1 3	10700	12200
18 4	MEDALLION 182	ST	RNBT	FBG SV	IO	235 MRCR	7 9	3200	2 6	9750	11100
18 4	MEDALLION 182 XL	ST	RNBT	FBG SV	IO	235 MRCR	7 9	3200	2 6	10000	11400
20 10	MEDALLION 210	ST	CUD	FBG SV	IO	300 MRCR	8 6	4000	2 9	12700	14500
20 10	MEDALLION 210 XL	ST	CUD	FBG SV	IO	300 MRCR	8 6	4000	2 9	13000	14800
20 10	MEDALLION 212	ST	RNBT	FBG DV	IO	300 MRCR	8 6	3600	2 8	11300	12900
20 10	MEDALLION 212 XL	ST	RNBT	FBG DV	IO	300 MRCR	8 6	3600	2 8	11500	13100
22 7	CLASSIC 22	OP	CUD	FBG DV	IO	412 MRCR	7	3400	1 4	18800	20900
26 5	255 LXC	OP	CUD	FBG DV	IO	415 MRCR	8 6	5700	1 0	26300	29200
27 8	27 ZX	OP	OFF	FBG DV	IO	500 MRCR	8 6	6000	2 1	27300	30300
29 3	275 LXC	OP	EXP	FBG SV	IO	415 MRCR	8 6	6500	1 10	26000	28900
32 8	33 ZX	OP	OFF	FBG SV	IO	T525 MRCR	9 3	9500	2 4	64500	70900
32 10	3250 LXC		WKNDR	FBG SV	IO	T330 MRCR	11		2 7	53000	58300
37 9	33 ZX	OP	OFF	FBG DV	IO	T525 MRCR	9 3	11500	2 4	97600	107500
			1995 BOATS							
16 8	CLASSIC 16	OP	RNBT	FBG DV	IO	180-215	6 10	1845	2 2	7000	8600
18	CLASSIC 18	OP	RNBT	FBG DV	IO	215-250	7	2600	2 3	9350	11400
18	CLASSIC 18	OP	RNBT	FBG DV	IO	255-275	7	2600	2 3	10300	12200
18 3	MEDALLION 182	OP	B/R	FBG DV	IO	180-185	7 8	2500	2 6	7200	8550
18 3	MEDALLION 182XL	OP	B/R	FBG DV	IO	180-185	7 8	2500	2 6	7450	8800
21	MEDALLION 210	OP	CUD	FBG DV	IO	235-275	8 6	3500	2 8	10100	12600
21	MEDALLION 210	OP	CUD	FBG DV	IO	300	8 6	3500	2 8	10900	13300
21	MEDALLION 210XL	OP	CUD	FBG DV	IO	235-275	8 6	3500	2 8	10300	12800
21	MEDALLION 210XL	OP	CUD	FBG DV	IO	300	8 6	3500	2 8	11100	13500
21	MEDALLION 212	OP	B/R	FBG DV	IO	190-275	8 6	3200	2 8	9150	11200
21	MEDALLION 212	OP	B/R	FBG DV	IO	300	8 6	3200	2 8	9650	11800
21	MEDALLION 212XL	OP	B/R	FBG DV	IO	190-275	8 6	3200	2 8	9400	11400
21	MEDALLION 212XL	OP	B/R	FBG DV	IO	300	8 6	3200	2 8	9850	12100
21	MEDALLION 255	OP	B/R	FBG DV	IO	235-300	8 6	5200	3 3	12900	16100
21	MEDALLION 255	OP	B/R	FBG DV	IO	350-385	8 6	5200	3 3	14800	18100
22 8	CLASSIC 22	OP	RNBT	FBG DV	IO	205-235	7	3300	2 9	11600	13900
	IO 250 MRCR 12000	13600, IO 255-300			12500	15200, IO 350 MRCR				14200	16200
29 3	MEDALLION 275	OP	CUD	FBG DV	IO	300-415	8 6	6500	3 5	23500	28700
32 8	33ZX	OP	OFF	FBG DV	IO	T350-T500	9 2	7500	3 5	57300	70600
38 2	38ZX	OP	OFF	FBG DV	IO	T385 MRCR	9 2	9750	3 5	72500	79700
38 2	38ZX	OP	OFF	FBG DV	IO	T500 MRCR	9 2	9750	3 5	86200	94700
			1994 BOATS							
16 8	CLASSIC 16	OP	RNBT	FBG DV	IO	180-205	6 10	1845		6550	8050
18	CLASSIC 18	OP	RNBT	FBG DV	IO	205-250	7	2600		8600	10600
18 3	MEDALLION 182	OP	B/R	FBG DV	IO	205-250	7 8	2500		6850	7950
21	MEDALLION 210	OP	CUD	FBG DV	IO	190-250	8 6	3500		9400	11100
21	MEDALLION 210	OP	CUD	FBG DV	IO	300 MRCR	8 6	3500		10400	11800
21	MEDALLION 212	OP	CUD	FBG DV	IO	190-255	8 6	3200	2 8	9250	10900
21	MEDALLION 212	OP	CUD	FBG DV	IO	300	8 6	3200	2 8	9850	11800
22 8	CLASSIC 22	OP	RNBT	FBG DV	IO	230-235	7	3300		11400	13000
	IO 250 MRCR 11200	12700, IO 255-300			11700	14200, IO 350 MRCR				13300	15100

DONZI MARINE CORP -CONTINUED See inside cover to adjust price for area

LOA FT	IN	NAME AND/ OR MODEL	TOP/ RIG	BOAT TYPE	-HULL- MTL	TP	TP	----ENGINE--- # HP	MFG	BEAM FT	IN	WGT LBS	DRAFT FT	IN	RETAIL LOW	RETAIL HIGH
		1994 BOATS														
22	8	CLASSIC 22	OP	RNBT	FBG	DV	IO	415	MRCR	7		3300			16000	18200
		1993 BOATS														
16	8	CLASSIC 16	OP	RNBT	FBG	DV	IO	200	OMC	6	10	1845			6100	7050
18		CLASSIC 18	OP	RNBT	FBG	DV	IO	265-285		7		2600			8500	10100
22	8	CLASSIC 22	OP	RNBT	FBG	DV	IO	285-330		7		3300			10800	13300
22	8	CLASSIC 22	OP	RNBT	FBG	DV	IO	370	OMC	7		3300			12900	14700
23	8	Z-24	OP	OFF	FBG	DV	IO	330-370		8	6	4200			16000	19600
23	8	Z-24	OP	OFF	FBG	DV	IO	420	OMC	8	6	4200			19600	21800
28	9	Z-28	OP	OFF	FBG	DV	IO	T285-T370		8	7	6800			28300	34700
		1992 BOATS														
16	8	SWEET 16	OP	RNBT	FBG	DV	IO	185-200		6	10	1845	1	2	5650	6600
18		CLASSIC 18	OP	RNBT	FBG	DV	IO	260-285		7		2600	1	2	7250	8750
22	8	CLASSIC 22	OP	RNBT	FBG	DV	IO	285-330		7		3300	1	8	9350	11400
23	8	Z-24	OP	OFF	FBG	DV	IO	330-370		8	6	4200	1	6	16100	19800
28	9	Z-28	OP	FSH	FBG	DV	OB			8	8	6800	1	10	22100	24600
29	11	Z-30	OP	OFF	FBG	DV	IO	T330-T370		9		7500	2	3	33500	38700
32	6	F-33	OP	CTRCN	FBG	DV	OB			9		5300	1	6	29100	32300
32	11	Z-33	OP	OFF	FBG	DV	IO	T370-T420		9		8100	1	4	49200	56100
35	5	F-33 CC	OP	FSH	FBG	DV	OB			9		6435	1	6	31600	35100
		1991 BOATS														
16	8	SWEET 16	OP	RNBT	FBG	DV	IO	175-250		6	10	1845	1	2	5300	6550
18		CLASSIC 18	OP	RNBT	FBG	DV	IO	260-270		7		2600	1	2	6800	7950
18	6	F-19	OP	FSH	FBG	DV	IO	120-150		8	6	2700		11	9000	10200
20	8	F-21 CC	OP	CTRCN	FBG	DV	OB			8	6	3328	1	4	8200	9450
20	8	F-21 WA	OP	FSH	FBG	DV	IO	235	OMC	8	6	4000	1	4	11100	12700
20	8	F-21 WA BRKT	OP	FSH	FBG	DV	OB			8	6		1	4	5550	6400
20	8	F-21WIA	OP	FSH	FBG	DV	IO	175-235		8	6	4000			10900	13100
22	6	F-23 CC	OP	CTRCN	FBG	DV	OB			9	4	2500	1	1	8250	9450
22	6	F-23 CC	OP	FSH	FBG	DV	OB			9	4	4450	1	3	11400	13000
22	6	F-23 W/A	OP	FSH	FBG	DV	OB			9	4	4655	1	1	11600	13100
22	6	F-23 WA	OP	FSH	FBG	DV	OB			9	4	4655	1	1	11600	13100
22	6	F-23 WA BRKT	OP	FSH	FBG	DV	OB			9	4	2800	1	1	9100	10300
22	6	F-23 WA BRKT	OP	FSH	FBG	DV	IO	260	OMC	9	4	2800	1	1	10400	11800
22	8	CLASSIC 22	OP	RNBT	FBG	DV	IO	270	OMC	7		3300	1	8	8500	9800
22	8	CLASSIC 22	OP	RNBT	FBG	DV	IO	350	OMC	7		3300	1	8	9900	11300
23	8	CLASSIC 22	OP	RNBT	FBG	DV	IO	370	OMC	7		3300	1	6	10900	12400
23	8	Z-24	OP	OFF	FBG	DV	IO	270-330		8	6	4200	1	6	14000	17200
23	8	Z-24	OP	OFF	FBG	DV	IO	370	OMC	8	6	4200	1	6	16400	18600
24	3	F-23 WA	OP	FSH	FBG	DV	IO	235	OMC	9	4	5075	1	1	16200	18400
25	5	F-25 CC	OP	FSH	FBG	DV	OB			9	5		1	10	13300	15100
25	5	F-25 WA	OP	FSH	FBG	DV	OB			9	5	5872	1	8	15300	17400
25	5	F-25 WA	OP	FSH	FBG	DV	IO	330	OMC	9	5	6200	1	8	21300	23700
29	11	Z-30	OP	OFF	FBG	DV	IO	T330-T370		9		7500	2	3	31400	36300
32	6	F-33	OP	CTRCN	FBG	DV	OB			9		5300	1	6	28000	31200
32	11	Z-33	OP	OFF	FBG	DV	IO	T330-T370		9		8100	1	4	44600	50900
35	5	F-33 CC	OP	FSH	FBG	DV	OB			9		6435	1	6	30400	33700
		1990 BOATS														
16	8	SWEET 16	OP	RNBT	FBG	DV	IO	175-205		6	10	1845	1	2	5000	5800
17	11	DL-180	OP	B/R	FBG	DV	IO	130-175		7	4	2400	1	2	6200	7150
17	11	GT-180	OP	B/R	FBG	DV	IO	130-175		7	4	2400	1	2	5850	7000
18		CLASSIC 18	OP	RNBT	FBG	DV	IO	260-270		7		2600	1	2	6400	7500
18	6	F-18	OP	FSH	FBG	DV	OB			8	6	2000		11	5100	5900
18	7	GT-190	OP	B/R	FBG	DV	IO	150-205		7	4	2800	1	2	6900	8050
21		DL-210	OP	B/R	FBG	DV	IO	175-260		8	2	3100	1	2	7750	9300
21		DL-210	OP	CUD	FBG	DV	IO	175-260		8	2	3100	1	2	8250	9950
21		F-21 CC	OP	CTRCN	FBG	DV	OB			8	6	3328	1	4	8300	9550
21		F-21 WA	OP	FSH	FBG	DV	OB			8	6		1	4	5450	6250
21		F-21 WA W/BRACKET	OP	FSH	FBG	DV	OB			8	6	3328	1	4	8300	9550
21		F-21 WA W/BRACKET	OP	FSH	FBG	DV	SE		OMC	8	6	3550	1	4	**	**
21		F-21 WA W/BRACKET	OP	FSH	FBG	DV	IO	260	OMC	8	6	4000	1	4	10900	12400
21		GT-210	OP	B/R	FBG	DV	IO	175-260		8	2	3100	1	2	7450	9000
21		GT-210	OP	CUD	FBG	DV	IO	175-260		8	2	3100	1	2	7950	9650
22	8	CLASSIC 22	OP	RNBT	FBG	DV	IO	270	OMC	7		3300	1	8	8000	9200
22	8	CLASSIC 22	OP	RNBT	FBG	DV	IO	340	OMC	7		3300	1	8	9150	10400
23		DL-230	OP	CUD	FBG	DV	IO	175-260		8	2	3800	1	2	10500	12500
23		GT-230	OP	CUD	FBG	DV	IO	175-260		8	2	3800	1	2	10200	12100
23	8	BLACK WIDOW 24	OP	OFF	FBG	DV	IO	260-270		8	6	4200	1	6	12100	13900
23	8	BLACK WIDOW 24	OP	OFF	FBG	DV	IO	340-370		8	6	4200	1	6	13400	16200
24	3	F-23 CC	OP	CTRCN	FBG	DV	OB			9	4	2500	1	1	8550	9850
24	3	F-23 WA	OP	FSH	FBG	DV	OB			9	4	2800	1	1	9150	10400
24	3	F-23 WA W/BRACKET	OP	FSH	FBG	DV	OB			9	4	2800	1	1	9700	11000
24	3	F-23 WA W/BRACKET	OP	FSH	FBG	DV	SE		OMC	9	4	2800	1	1	**	**
24	3	F-23 WA W/BRACKET	OP	FSH	FBG	DV	IO	260	OMC	9	4	2800	1	1	10600	12000
25		GT-250	OP	CUD	FBG	DV	IO	235-270		8	6	4800	1	3	14000	16400
27		PESCADOR 250	OP	FSH	FBG	DV	IO	260	OMC	8	6	4550	1	4	16800	19100
27		PESCADOR 250 W/BRKT	OP	CUD	FBG	DV	OB			8	6	3550	1	4	15800	18000
29	11	BLACK WIDOW 30	OP	OFF	FBG	DV	IO	T340-T370		9		7500	2	3	27600	31600
32		LEVANTE 300	OP	CR	FBG	DV	IO	T200-T260		11	2	9800	1	9	28700	33300
32	6	F-33	OP	CTRCN	FBG	DV	OB			9		5300	1	6	27100	30100
32	11	CROSSBOW Z33	OP	OFF	FBG	DV	IO	T340-T370		9		8100	1	4	35900	40800
		1989 BOATS														
17		R 17	OP	B/R	FBG	DV	IO	128-175		7	4	2400	2	5	4950	5800
18		2-PLUS-3	OP	RNBT	FBG	DV	IO	270	MRCR	7		2250	2	3	6800	7800
18		2-PLUS-3	OP	RNBT	FBG	DV	IO	350	OMC	7		2250	2	3	8400	9650
18	7	R 19 BR	OP	B/R	FBG	DV	IO	175-205		7	4	2800	2	5	6050	7050
21		R 21 BR	OP	B/R	FBG	DV	IO	175-260		8	2	3100	2	5	6650	8000
21		R 21 CC	OP	CUD	FBG	DV	IO	175-260		8	2	3100	2	5	7100	8550
22	6	Z 22	OP	RNBT	FBG	DV	IO	260-270		8	5	3200	2	10	9300	10700
22	6	Z 22	OP	RNBT	FBG	DV	IO	330-350		8	5	3200	2	10	10300	12100
22	8	2-PLUS-3	OP	RNBT	FBG	DV	IO	330-340		7		3300	2	9	9950	11400
22	11	F 23	OP	FSH	FBG	DV	OB			8	6	2700			8350	9550
23		R 23 CC	OP	CUD	FBG	DV	IO	175-260		8	4	3800	2	5	9150	10800
24	7	Z 25	OP	RNBT	FBG	DV	IO	330-365		8	6	4200	2	10	13200	16000
24	7	Z 25	OP	RNBT	FBG	DV	IO	420	MRCR	8	6	4200	2	10	15900	18100
25		F 25 WA EL PESCADOR	OP	FSH	FBG	DV	OB			8	6	3550	2	5	11300	12800
25		F 25 WA EL PESCADOR	OP	FSH	FBG	DV	IO	260		8	6	4550	2	5	13800	15700
25		F 25 WA EL PESCADOR	OP	FSH	FBG	DV	IO	330-340		8	6	4750	2	5	15300	17600
25		R 25 CC	OP	CUD	FBG	DV	IO	260-340		9		4450	2	5	12000	14900
32	4	Z 33	OP	RNBT	FBG	DV	IO	T330-T365		9		8100	2	11	29900	35300
32	4	Z 33	OP	RNBT	FBG	DV	IO	T420-T460		9		8100	2	11	35800	43100
33	1	F 33	OP	FSH	FBG	DV	OB			9		5300			26200	29100
		1988 BOATS														
17		R 17	OP	B/R	FBG	DV	IO	128-130		7	4	2400	2	5	4700	5450
18		2-PLUS-3	OP	RNBT	FBG	DV	IO	270	MRCR	7		2250	2	3	6400	7400
18		2-PLUS-3	OP	RNBT	FBG	DV	IO	350	OMC	7		2250	2	3	7950	9100
18	7	R 19 BR	OP	B/R	FBG	DV	IO	128-205		7	4	2800	2	5	5650	6700
21		R 21	OP	B/R	FBG	DV	IO	175-260		8	2	3100	2	5	6300	7600
22	6	Z 21	OP	RNBT	FBG	DV	IO	330-350		8	5	3200	2	10	9800	11900
22	6	Z 21	OP	RNBT	FBG	DV	IO	460	OMC	8	5	3200	2	10	13800	15700
22	6	ZB 21	OP	RNBT	FBG	DV	IO	330-350		8	5	3200	2	10	9700	11700
22	6	ZB 21	OP	RNBT	FBG	DV	IO	460	OMC	8	5	3200	2	10	13600	15500
22	8	2-PLUS-3	OP	RNBT	FBG	DV	IO	330	MRCR	7		3300	2	9	9450	10700
22	8	2-PLUS-3	OP	RNBT	FBG	DV	IO	460	OMC	7		3300	2	9	13400	15200
22	11	F 23	OP	FSH	FBG	DV	OB			8	6	2700			8100	9300
23		R 23	OP	CUD	FBG	DV	IO	175-260		8	4	3800	2	5	8600	10300
24	7	Z 25	OP	RNBT	FBG	DV	IO	330-365		8	6	4200	2	10	12500	15200
24	7	Z 25	OP	RNBT	FBG	DV	IO	420-460		8	6	4200	2	10	15100	18500
25		R 25	OP	CUD	FBG	DV	IO	260-330		9		4450	2	5	11300	14000
25		R 25	OP	CUD	FBG	DV	IO	460	OMC	9		4450	2	5	15600	17700
32	4	Z 33	OP	RNBT	FBG	DV	IO	T	MRCR	9		8100	2	11	**	**
32	4	Z 33	OP	RNBT	FBG	DV	IO	T365-T420		9		8100	2	11	29600	37000
32	4	Z 33	OP	RNBT	FBG	DV	IO	T460	OMC	9		8100	2	11	36100	40100
33	1	F 33	OP	FSH	FBG	DV	OB			9		5300			25400	28300
36		WIDEBODY 36	OP	RNBT	FBG	DV	IO	350		12	8	14500			30200	33500
65		Z 65	ST	SF	FBG	DV	IB	T11CD	GM	18	8	72000			473000	520000
65		Z 65	ST	SF	FBG	DV	IB	T14CD	GM	18	8	72000			525500	577500
		1987 BOATS														
18		2-PLUS-3	OP	RNBT	FBG	DV	IO	270	MRCR	7		2250	2	3	6100	7000
20	1	MINX	OP	RNBT	FBG	DV	IO	270	MRCR	7		2700	2	3	5800	6650
20	1	MINX	OP	RNBT	FBG	DV	IO	320	MRCR	7		2700	2	1	6450	7400
21		HORNET III	OP	RNBT	FBG	DV	IO	300-320		7	10	3150	2	3	7850	9400
21		HORNET III	OP	RNBT	FBG	DV	IO	370	MRCR	7	10	3150	2	3	9400	10700
22	6	Z 21		RNBT	FBG	DV	IO	270-320		8	5	2800	2	9	7800	9750
22	6	Z 21		RNBT	FBG	DV	IO	330	MRCR	8	5	2800	2	9	8700	9950
22	6	ZB 21		RNBT	FBG	DV	IO	270	MRCR	8	5	2800	2	9	7700	8850
22	6	ZB 21		RNBT	FBG	DV	IO	320-330		8	5	2800	2	9	8400	9850
22	8	2-PLUS-3	OP	RNBT	FBG	DV	IO	270	MRCR	7		2900	2	9	7450	8550
22	8	2-PLUS-3	OP	RNBT	FBG	DV	IO	320-330		7		2900	2	9	8100	9550
22	8	2-PLUS-3	OP	RNBT	FBG	DV	IO	370	MRCR	7		2900	2	9	9350	10600
22	11	FC 23		RNBT	FBG		IO	260	MRCR	8	6	3500			8250	9500
22	11	ZF 23		FSH	FBG	DV	OB			8	6	2700	1	6	8500	9750
24	7	Z 25	OP	RNBT	FBG	DV	IO	270-330		8	6	3800	2	10	10300	12700
24	7	Z 25	OP	RNBT	FBG	DV	IO	370	MRCR	8	6	3800	2	10	12100	13800
24	7	Z 25	OP	RNBT	FBG	DV	IO	420	MRCR	8	6	3800	2	10	13600	15500
28	4	Z 29	OP	RNBT	FBG	DV	IO	T270-T330		8	6	5500	2	10	15200	18600
32	4	Z 33	OP	RNBT	FBG	DV	IO	T330-T370		8	10	6800	2	11	25200	29600
32	4	Z 33	OP	RNBT	FBG	DV	IO	T420-T425		8	10	6800	2	11	29400	34200
33	1	ZF 33		FSH	FBG	DV	OB			9		4200	1	6	26700	29700
35		Z 35	OP	SF	FBG	DV	IB	T460	OMC	9	8	7600	3	2	54500	59800

190 CONTINUED ON NEXT PAGE 96th ed. - Vol. II

LOA FT	LOA IN	NAME AND/ OR MODEL	TOP/ RIG	BOAT TYPE	-HULL- MTL	-HULL- TP	ENGINE TP	ENGINE # HP	ENGINE MFG	BEAM FT	BEAM IN	WGT LBS	DRAFT FT	DRAFT IN	RETAIL LOW	RETAIL HIGH
		1987 BOATS														
65		Z 65	ST	SF	FBG	SV	IB	T11CD	GM	18	8	72000	4	2	453500	498500
65		Z 65	ST	SF	FBG	SV	IB	T14CD	GM	18	8	72000	4	2	504000	554000
		1986 BOATS														
18		2-PLUS-3	OP	RNBT	FBG	DV	IO	260	MRCR	7		2250		1	5700	6600
20	1	MINX	OP	RNBT	FBG	DV	IO	260-300		7		2700		1	5450	6700
21		HORNET III	OP	RNBT	FBG	DV	IO	260-300		7	10	3150		1	7100	8650
21		HORNET III	OP	RNBT	FBG	DV	IO	330	MRCR	7	10	3150		1	8000	9200
22	8	2-PLUS-3	OP	RNBT	FBG	DV	IO	260-300		7		2900		1	7000	8550
22	8	2-PLUS-3	OP	RNBT	FBG	DV	IO	330	MRCR	7		2900		1	7950	9100
24	7	Z 25	OP	RNBT	FBG	DV	IO	260-330		8	6	3800		1	9750	12200
24	7	Z 25	OP	RNBT	FBG	DV	IO	370	MRCR	8	6	3800		1	11600	13200
28	4	Z 29	OP	RNBT	FBG	DV	IO	T260-T300		8	6	5500	1	10	14300	17100
32	4	Z 33	OP	RNBT	FBG	DV	IO	T330-T400		8	10	6800		1	23900	29400
32	4	Z 33	OP	RNBT	FBG	DV	IO	T440	MRCR	8	10	6800		1	29000	32300
65		Z 65 TOURNAMENT FSH	ST	SF	FBG	SV	IB	T14CD	GM	18	8	72000	4	2	484000	531500
		1985 BOATS														
18		2-PLUS-3	OP	RNBT	FBG	DV	IO	260		7		2450	2	3	5700	7000
18		2-PLUS-3	OP	RNBT	FBG	DV	IO	290-330		7		2450	2	3	6500	7800
21		HORNET III	OP	RNBT	FBG	DV	IO	260		7	10	3150	2	3	6800	8150
21		HORNET III	OP	RNBT	FBG	DV	IO	290-330		7	10	3150	2	3	7450	8850
22	8	2-PLUS-3	OP	RNBT	FBG	DV	IO	260		7	2	3000	2	3	6900	8050
22	8	2-PLUS-3	OP	RNBT	FBG	DV	IO	290-330		7	2	3500	2	3	8250	9500
22	8	CRITERION II	OP	RNBT	FBG	DV	IO	330	MRCR	7	2	3900	2	9	8450	9700
		1984 BOATS														
18		2-PLUS-3	OP	RNBT	FBG	DV	IO	255-290		7		2450	2	3	5800	7200
18		2-PLUS-3	OP	RNBT	FBG	DV	IO	330	MRCR	7		2900	2	4	7100	8150
20	3	HORNET II	OP	RNBT	FBG	DV	IO	260	MRCR	7	10	3400	2	3	6650	7650
20	3	HORNET II	OP	RNBT	FBG	DV	IO	290	VLVO	7	10	3400	2	3	7250	8350
20	3	HORNET II	OP	RNBT	FBG	DV	IO	330	MRCR	7	10	3800	2	4	8000	9200
21		HORNET III	OP	RNBT	FBG	DV	IO	260		7	10	3150	2	3	6550	7850
21		HORNET III	OP	RNBT	FBG	DV	IO	290-330		7	10	3150	2	3	7200	8500
22	8	2-PLUS-3	OP	RNBT	FBG	DV	IO	260		7	2	3000	2	3	6700	7800
22	8	2-PLUS-3	OP	RNBT	FBG	DV	IO	290-330		7	2	3500	2	3	8000	9150
22	8	CRITERION	OP	RNBT	FBG	DV	IO	330	MRCR	7	2	3600	2	4	7750	8900
22	8	CRITERION II	OP	RNBT	FBG	DV	IO	330	MRCR	7		3900	2	9	8100	9300

....For earlier years, see the BUC Used Boat Price Guide, Volume 3

DORADO MARINE

OZONA FL 34660 COAST GUARD MFG ID- ELO See inside cover to adjust price for area

LOA FT	LOA IN	NAME AND/ OR MODEL	TOP/ RIG	BOAT TYPE	-HULL- MTL	-HULL- TP	ENGINE TP	ENGINE # HP	ENGINE MFG	BEAM FT	BEAM IN	WGT LBS	DRAFT FT	DRAFT IN	RETAIL LOW	RETAIL HIGH
		1996 BOATS														
23		DORADO 23	OP	OPFSH	F/S	SV	OB			8		1900		11	9750	11100
30		DORADO 30	OP	OPFSH	F/S	SV	OB			8	8	4900	1	6	32900	36500
30		DORADO 30	OP	OPFSH	F/S	SV	IO	210	VLVO	8	8	4900	1	6	33300	37000
30		DORADO 30	OP	OPFSH	F/S	SV	IO	200D-230D		8	8	4900	1	6	38400	44500
36		DORADO 36 EXP	FB	SF	F/S	SV	IO	T370D	VLVO	13		13500	3	4	106500	117000
40		DORADO 40 CC	OP	CTRCN	F/S	SV	IB	300D	DD	13		14500	1	6	93600	103000
40		DORADO 40 DIVE	OP	COMM	F/S	SV	IB	300D	DD	13		14500	1	6	**	**
40		DORADO 40 EXP	OP	EXP	F/S	SV	IB	T300D	DD	13		14500	1	6	123500	135500
40		DORADO 40 SC	FB	CR	F/S	SV	IB	T300D	DD	13		14500	1	6	151500	166500
40		DORADO 40 SF	FB	SF	F/S	SV	IB	T300D	DD	13		14500	1	6	150000	165000
		1995 BOATS														
23		DORADO 23	OP	OPFSH	F/S	SV	OB			8		1900		11	9300	10600
30		DORADO 30	OP	OPFSH	F/S	SV	IO	230D	VLVO	8	8	4900	1	6	41700	46300
		1994 BOATS														
23		DORADO 23	OP	OPFSH	F/S	SV	OB			8		1900		11	8850	10100
30		DORADO 30	OP	OPFSH	F/S	SV	IO	230D	VLVO	8	8	4900	1	6	34500	38400
		1991 BOATS														
23		DORADO 23	OP	SF	F/S	SV	IO	130D	VLVO	8			1	6	13900	15800
30		DORADO 30	OP	SF	F/S	SV	IO	200D	VLVO	8	8	4900	1	6	26900	29900
		1990 BOATS														
24		DORADO 24	OP	SF	F/S	SV	OB			8		1800	1	6	7200	8250
24		DORADO 24	OP	SF	F/S	SV	IB	180		8		2800	2		10700	12100
24		DORADO 24	OP	SF	F/S	SV	IO	130D		8		2800	2		14300	16300
30		COMMERCIAL 30	OP	SF	F/S	SV	IB	210D		8	8	4900	2		26900	29900
30		DORADO 30	OP	SF	F/S	SV	OB			8	8	3900	1	6	25000	27800
30		DORADO 30	OP	SF	F/S	SV	IB	330		8	8	4900	2		26900	29900
30		DORADO 30	OP	SF	F/S	SV	IO	200D		8	8	4900	2		25500	28300
30		DORADO 30	OP	SF	F/S	SV	IB	300D		8	8	4900	2		30400	33700
		1989 BOATS														
23	8	DORADO 24	OP	SF	F/S	SV	OB			8		1100	1	6	4400	5050
23	8	DORADO 24	OP	SF	F/S	SV	IB	185		8		2100	2		8850	10100
23	8	DORADO 24	OP	SF	F/S	SV	IO	130D		8		2100	1	6	12100	13800
30		COMMERCIAL 30	OP	SF	F/S	SV	OB			8	8	3900	1	6	22300	24800
30		COMMERCIAL 30	OP	SF	F/S	SV	IB	330		8	8	4900	2		22100	24500
30		COMMERCIAL 30	OP	SF	F/S	SV	IO	200D		8	8	4900	1	6	21300	23700
30		DORADO 30	OP	SF	F/S	SV	OB			8	8	3900	1	6	25700	28500
30		DORADO 30	OP	SF	F/S	SV	IB	330		8	8	4900	2		29200	32400
30		DORADO 30	OP	SF	F/S	SV	IO	200D		8	8	4900	1	6	27800	30900

DORAL INTERNATIONAL

MIDLAND ON CANADA L4R 4P4 See inside cover to adjust price for area
FORMERLY DORAL BOATS INC

For more recent years, see the BUC Used Boat Price Guide, Volume 1

LOA FT	LOA IN	NAME AND/ OR MODEL	TOP/ RIG	BOAT TYPE	-HULL- MTL	-HULL- TP	ENGINE TP	ENGINE # HP	ENGINE MFG	BEAM FT	BEAM IN	WGT LBS	DRAFT FT	DRAFT IN	RETAIL LOW	RETAIL HIGH
		1996 BOATS														
16	8	DORAL 170	OP	B/R	FBG	DV	OB			6	11	1078	1	7	2650	3050
20	1	DORAL 185	OP	B/R	FBG	DV	OB			7	9	2500	1	5	5750	6650
20	1	DORAL 185	OP	B/R	FBG	DV	IO	135-190		7	9	2500	1	5	9050	10300
20	1	DORAL 200	OP	B/R	FBG	DV	IO	190-250		7	9	2500	1	5	9250	10800
20	1	DORAL 216	OP	CUD	FBG	DV	OB			7	9	2825	1	5	6050	6950
20	1	DORAL 216	OP	CUD	FBG	DV	IO	190-250		7	9	2825	1	5	10400	12300
23		DORAL 230CC	OP	CUD	FBG	DV	IO	190-300		8	6	3350	1	4	14100	17500
		IO 330 MRCR 16200 18500, IO 385 MRCR 19000 21100, IO 140D MRCR 18700 20800														
25	4	DORAL 250SC	OP	CR	FBG	DV	IO	210-300		8	8	4500	2	8	19800	23800
25	4	DORAL 250SC	OP	CR	FBG	DV	IO	330-385		8	8	4500	2	8	22300	27100
25	4	DORAL 250SC	OP	CR	FBG	DV	IO	140D	MRCR	8	8	4500	2	8	22700	25300
27		DORAL 270SC	OP	CR	FBG	DV	IO	210-330		8	8	5100	2	8	23600	29300
27		DORAL 270SC	OP	CR	FBG	DV	IO	385	MRCR	8	8	5100	2	8	28300	31500
27		DORAL 270SC	OP	CR	FBG	DV	IO	140D	MRCR	8	8	5100	2	8	24800	27600
30		DORAL 300SC	OP	CR	FBG	DV	IO	T190-T280		10	3	8000	2	9	36700	44500
30		DORAL 300SC	OP	CR	FBG	DV	IO	T140D-T200D		10	3	8000	2	9	42600	51700
30		DORAL 300SE	OP	CR	FBG	DV	IO	T190-T280		10	3	8000	2	9	38200	46100
30		DORAL 300SE	OP	CR	FBG	DV	IO	T140D-T200D		10	3	8000	2	9	43900	52900
36	10	DORAL 350SC	OP	CR	FBG	DV	IO	T300	MRCR	12		11904	3	2	57600	63400
36	10	DORAL 350SC	OP	CR	FBG	DV	IO	T200D	MRCR	12		11904	3	2	70800	77800
		1995 BOATS														
16	8	PRESTIGE 170	OP	B/R	FBG	DV	OB			6	11	1078			2500	2900
18	7	PRESTIGE 180	OP	B/R	FBG	DV	OB			7	4	1365			3200	3750
18	7	PRESTIGE 185	OP	B/R	FBG	DV	IO	135-180		7	4	2415			6450	7450
20	1	PRESTIGE 205	OP	B/R	FBG	DV	IO	180-235		7	9	2825	2	5	9100	10700
22	1	PRESTANCIA 240 MC	OP	CR	FBG	SV	IO	250	MRCR	8	8	4500	2	8	16000	18200
22	1	PRESTANCIA 240 MC	OP	CR	FBG	SV	IO	150D	MRCR	8	8	4500	2	8	19900	22100
23	7	PRESTIGE 230	OP	CUD	FBG	DV	IO	180-235		8	3	3350	2	7	13300	15500
24		PRESTANCIA 255 MC	OP	CR	FBG	SV	IO	250-300		8	8	4800	2	8	18800	21600
24		PRESTANCIA 255 MC	OP	CR	FBG	SV	IO	150D	MRCR	8	8	4800	2	8	22500	25000
25	4	PRESTANCIA 270 MC	OP	CR	FBG	SV	IO	150D	MRCR	9	6	7175	2	9	32100	35700
25	4	PRESTANCIA 270 MC	OP	CR	FBG	SV	IO	T180	MRCR	9	6	7175	2	9	28300	31500
28		PRESTANCIA 300 MC	OP	CR	FBG	SV	IO	180D	MRCR	10		8275	2	11	37100	41200
28		PRESTANCIA 300 MC	OP	CR	FBG	SV	IO	T180-T235		10		8275	2	11	32900	38200
		1994 BOATS														
16	8	PRESTIGE 170	OP	B/R	FBG	DV	OB			6	11	1078			2400	2800
18	7	PRESTIGE 180	OP	B/R	FBG	DV	OB			7	4	1365			3050	3550
18	7	PRESTIGE 185	OP	B/R	FBG	DV	IO	135-180		7	4	2415			6000	7000
20	1	PRESTIGE 205	OP	B/R	FBG	DV	IO	180-235		7	9	2825	2	5	8400	9950
22	1	PRESTANCIA 240 MC	OP	CR	FBG	SV	IO	250	MRCR	8	8	4500	2	8	15000	17000
22	1	PRESTANCIA 240 MC	OP	CR	FBG	SV	IO	150D	MRCR	8	8	4500	2	8	18800	20900
23	7	PRESTIGE 230	OP	CUD	FBG	DV	IO	180-235		8	3	3350	2	7	12400	14400
24		PRESTANCIA 255 MC	OP	CR	FBG	SV	IO	250-300		8	8	4800	2	8	17200	20400
24		PRESTANCIA 255 MC	OP	CR	FBG	SV	IO	150D	MRCR	8	8	4800	2	8	21000	23300
25	4	PRESTANCIA 270 MC	OP	CR	FBG	SV	IO	150D	MRCR	9	6	7175	2	9	30000	33300
25	4	PRESTANCIA 270 MC	OP	CR	FBG	SV	IO	T180	MRCR	9	6	7175	2	9	26500	29400
28		PRESTANCIA 300 MC	OP	CR	FBG	SV	IO	180D	MRCR	10		8275	2	11	34600	38500
28		PRESTANCIA 300 MC	OP	CR	FBG	SV	IO	T180-T235		10		8275	2	11	30700	35600
		1992 BOATS														
17	8	IMAGE 180 BR	OP	B/R	FBG	DV	OB			7	4	1615			3100	3600
17	8	IMAGE 185 BR	OP	B/R	FBG	DV	IO	175	MRCR	7	4	2415			5000	5750
19	1	CACHET 205 EX	OP	CUD	FBG	SV	IO	175	MRCR	7	9	2825			6600	7550
19	1	IMAGE 200 BR	OP	B/R	FBG	DV	IO	175	MRCR	7	9	2675			6000	6850
20	3	CACHET 230 EX	OP	CUD	FBG	SV	IO	175	MRCR	8	6	3350			9350	10600
22	1	PRESTANCIA 240 MC	OP	CR	FBG	SV	IO	175	MRCR	8	2	4300			12000	13600
23	7	CACHET 250 EX	OP	CR	FBG	SV	IO	205	MRCR	8	8	4620			14000	15900
23	7	PRESTANCIA 255 MC	OP	CR	FBG	SV	IO	T205	MRCR	8	8	4800			16000	18200
25	4	PRESTANCIA 270 MC	OP	CR	FBG	SV	IO	T175	MRCR	9	6	7175	2	9	23100	25700

LOA FT IN	NAME AND/ OR MODEL	TOP/ RIG	BOAT TYPE	-HULL- MTL TP	----ENGINE--- TP # HP MFG	BEAM FT IN	WGT LBS	DRAFT FT IN	RETAIL LOW	RETAIL HIGH
	------------- 1992 BOATS -------------									
28	PRESTANCIA 300 MC	OP	CR	FBG SV IO	T175 MRCR	10	8275	2 11	26800	29700
33 7	BOCA GRANDE 350 MC	OP	CR	FBG SV IB	T300 MRCR	12 6	13900	3	67200	73900
	------------- 1991 BOATS -------------									
17 8	IMAGE 185	OP	B/R	FBG DV OB		7 4	1615		3000	3450
17 8	IMAGE 185	OP	B/R	FBG DV IO	175 MRCR	7 4	2415		4700	5400
19 1	CACHET 205	OP	CUD	FBG SV IO	175 MRCR	7 9	2825		6200	7100
19 1	IMAGE 200	OP	B/R	FBG DV IO	175 MRCR	7 9	2675		5600	6450
20 3	CACHET 230	OP	CUD	FBG SV IO	175 MRCR	8 6	3350		8700	10000
20 3	IMAGE 220	OP	B/R	FBG DV IO	175 MRCR	8 6	2975		7550	8700
21	PHAZAR	OP	CUD	FBG SV IO		8	3650		**	**
21 8	CACHET 240	OP	CR	FBG SV IO		8 2	3950		**	**
22 1	PRESTANCIA 240	OP	CR	FBG SV IO	MRCR	8 2	4300		11300	12800
23 7	CACHET 250	OP	CR	FBG SV IO	T205 MRCR	8 2	4620		14600	16600
23 7	PRESTANCIA 255	OP	CR	FBG SV IO	T205 MRCR	8 2	4800		15000	17100
24 6	PRESTANCIA 260	OP	CR	FBG SV IO	T	8 2	4925		**	**
25 4	PRESTANCIA 270	OP	CR	FBG SV IO	T175 MRCR	9 6	7175	2 9	21700	24100
28	PRESTANCIA 300	OP	CR	FBG SV IO	T175 MRCR	10	8275	2 11	25100	27900
33 7	BOCA GRANDE 350	OP	CR	FBG SV IB	T300 MRCR	12 6	13900	3	63900	70200
	------------- 1990 BOATS -------------									
17 4	SPIRIT 175 BR	OP	B/R	FBG SV OB		7 11	1300	3 6	2450	2850
17 4	SPIRIT 175 BR	OP	B/R	FBG SV IO	155-205	7 11	2100	3 6	3900	4600
19 6	CLASSIC 200 BR	OP	B/R	FBG SV IO	155-205	7 10	2625	3 10	5350	6200
20 1	ECLIPSE	OP	CUD	FBG SV IO	155-205	7 9	2825	4 2	6900	7950
20 1	MIRAGE	OP	B/R	FBG DV IO	155-205	7 9	2675	3 5	6250	7250
21 9	VANTAGE	OT	RNDT	FBG EV IO	175-260	7 6	2975	4 2	7750	9300
21 9	VANTAGE	OP	CUD	FBG SV IO	175-260	8	2975	4 2	8650	9900
22 5	PHAZAR	OP	RNBT	FBG DV IO	300 MRCR	8 6	2975	4 9	9900	11800
22 5	PHAZAR	OP	CUD	FBG SV IO	270-300	8	3650	4 9	11800	13400
23	CONCEPT	OP	CUD	FBG SV IO	360 MRCR	8	3650	4 2	10400	12800
24	CAVALIER 240	OP	CUD	FBG SV IO	175-300	8	3850		11700	13700
24	TARA	OP	CR	FBG SV IO	175-260	8 2	3950		11000	12900
26 10	CITATION 260	OP	CR	FBG SV IO	230-260	8 2	4925		15300	17800
27 1	MONTICELLO 270	OP	CR	FBG SV IO	240 MRCR	9 6	7175		19900	22100
27 1	MONTICELLO 270	OP	CR	FBG SV IO	T155-T205	9 6	7175		21000	24200
30 3	PRESTANCIA 300	OP	CR	FBG SV IO	T175-T260	10	8275		26000	30900
	------------- 1989 BOATS -------------									
17 4	SPIRIT BR 175	OP	RNBT	FBG DV IO		7 1	1300		2400	2800
17 4	SPIRIT BR 175	OP	RNBT	FBG DV SE	130-205	7 1	2000		3250	3800
17 4	SPIRIT CD 175	OP	RNBT	FBG DV IO		7 1	1300		2300	2700
17 4	SPIRIT CD 175	OP	RNBT	FBG DV SE	130-205	7 1	2000		3200	3700
19 6	CLASSIC BR 200	OP	RNBT	FBG SV IO	175-205	7 6	2500		5050	5900
19 6	CLASSIC CD 200	OP	RNBT	FBG SV IO	175-205	7 6	2500		4950	5800
22 5	PHAZAR	OP	RNBT	FBG DV IO	MRCR	8	3100		**	**
22 5	PHAZAR	OP	RNBT	FBG DV IO	340 OMC	8	3100		9050	10300
24	CAVALIER 240	OP	CUD	FBG SV IO	205-260	8 2	4000		10500	12300
24	TARA 240	OP	CUD	FBG SV IO	205-260	8 2	3800		10100	11900
26 10	CITATION 260	OP	CUD	FBG SV IO	260	8 2	4600		14400	16300
27 1	MONTICELLO 270	OP	CR	FBG SV IO	MRCR	9 6	6300	2 9	**	**
27 1	MONTICELLO 270	OP	CR	FBG SV IO	260-340	9 6	6300	2 9	17500	21300
27 1	MONTICELLO 270	OP	CR	FBG SV IO	T175-T205	9 6	6300	2 9	19000	21300
30 3	PRESTANCIA 300	OP	CR	FBG SV IO	T175-T260	10	7600	2 11	24000	28700

DOUGLAS MARINE CORP
DOUGLAS MI 49406   COAST GUARD MFG ID- DUX See inside cover to adjust price for area

For more recent years, see the BUC Used Boat Price Guide, Volume 1

LOA FT IN	NAME AND/ OR MODEL	TOP/ RIG	BOAT TYPE	-HULL- MTL TP	----ENGINE--- TP # HP MFG	BEAM FT IN	WGT LBS	DRAFT FT IN	RETAIL LOW	RETAIL HIGH
	------------- 1996 BOATS -------------									
21	SKATER 21	OP	RNBT	FBG TR OB		7 6	1300		9400	10700
24 3	SKATER 24	OP	RNBT	FBG TR OB		7 11	1700		13000	14800
24 3	SKATER 24 RACE	OP	RACE	FBG TR OB		7 11	1700		13000	14800
28	SKATER 28	OP	RNBT	FBG TR OB		8 4	2100		36000	40000
28	SKATER 28 RACE	OP	RACE	FBG TR OB		8 4	2100		36000	40000
28	SKATER 28 RACE	ST	RACE	FBG TR OB		8 4	2100		36400	40400
32	SKATER 32	OP	RNBT	FBG	OB		8 6	2750		58800	64600
32	SKATER 32	OP	RNBT	FBG	IB T		8 6	2900		**	**
32	SKATER 32 RACE	OP	RACE	FBG	OB T		8 6	2550		58200	63900
32	SKATER 32 RACE	OP	RACE	FBG	IB T		8 6	2700		**	**
36	SKATER 36	OP	RNBT	FBG	IB T		10	3200		93800	103000
36	SKATER 36	OP	RNBT	FBG	IB T		10	3400		**	**
36	SKATER 36 RACE	OP	RACE	FBG	OB		10	3300		94600	104000
36	SKATER 36 RACE	OP	RACE	FBG	IB T		10	3400		**	**
40	SKATER 40	OP	RNBT	FBG TR IB T		10 11	4750		**	**
45 7	SKATER 46	OP	RNBT	FBG TR IB T		12	5000		**	**
	------------- 1995 BOATS -------------									
21	SKATER 21	OP	RNBT	FBG TR OB		7 6	1300		8900	10100
24 3	SKATER 24	OP	RNBT	FBG TR OB		7 11	1700		12300	14000
24 3	SKATER 24 RACE	OP	RACE	FBG TR OB		7 11	1700		12300	14000
28	SKATER 28	OP	RNBT	FBG TR OB		8 4	2100		34100	37800
28	SKATER 28 RACE	OP	RACE	FBG TR OB		8 4	2100		34100	37800
28	SKATER 28 RACE	ST	RACE	FBG TR OB		8 4	2100		34400	38200
32	SKATER 32	OP	RNBT	FBG	IB T		8 6	2750		55600	61000
32	SKATER 32	OP	RNBT	FBG	IB T		8 6	2900		**	**
32	SKATER 32 RACE	OP	RACE	FBG	IB T		8 6	2550		55000	60400
32	SKATER 32 RACE	OP	RACE	FBG	IB T		8 6	2700		**	**
36	SKATER 36	OP	RNBT	FBG	IB T		10	3200		88700	97500
36	SKATER 36	OP	RNBT	FBG	IB T		10	3400		**	**
36	SKATER 36 RACE	OP	RACE	FBG	IB T		10	3300		89400	98300
36	SKATER 36 RACE	OP	RACE	FBG	IB T		10	3400		**	**
40	SKATER 40	OP	RNBT	FBG TR IB T		10 11	4750		**	**
45 7	SKATER 46	OP	RNBT	FBG TR IB T		12	5000		**	**
	------------- 1994 BOATS -------------									
21	SKATER 21	OP	RNBT	FBG TR OB		7 6	1300		8350	9550
24 3	SKATER 24	OP	RNBT	FBG TR OB		7 11	1700		11700	13300
24 3	SKATER 24 RACE	OP	RACE	FBG TR OB		7 11	1700		11700	13300
28	SKATER 28	OP	RNBT	FBG TR OB		8 4	2100		32300	35900
28	SKATER 28 RACE	OP	RACE	FBG TR OB		8 4	2100		32300	35900
28	SKATER 28 RACE	ST	RACE	FBG TR OB		8 4	2100		32600	36200
32	SKATER 32	OP	RNBT	FBG	OB		8 6	2750		52600	57800
32	SKATER 32	OP	RNBT	FBG	OB		8 6	2900		**	**
32	SKATER 32 RACE	OP	RNBT	FBG	IB T		8 6	2550		52300	57500
32	SKATER 32 RACE	OP	RNBT	FBG	IB T		8 6	2700		**	**
40	SKATER 40	OP	RNBT	FBG TR IB T		10 11	4750		**	**
45 7	SKATER 46	OP	RNBT	FBG TR IB T		12	5000		**	**
	------------- 1993 BOATS -------------									
21	SKATER 21	OP	RNBT	FBG TR OB		7 6	1300		7900	9100
24 3	SKATER 24	OP	RNBT	FBG TR OB		7 11	1700		11200	12700
24 3	SKATER 24 RACE	OP	RACE	FBG TR OB		7 11	1700		11200	12700
28	SKATER 28	OP	RNBT	FBG TR OB		8 4	2100		30700	34100
28	SKATER 28 RACE	OP	RACE	FBG TR OB		8 4	2100		30700	34100
28	SKATER 28 RACE	ST	RACE	FBG TR OB		8 4	2100		31000	34400
32	SKATER 32	OP	RNBT	FBG	OB		8 6	2750		50200	55100
32	SKATER 32	OP	RNBT	FBG	OB		8 6	2900		**	**
32	SKATER 32 RACE	OP	RNBT	FBG	OB		8 6	2550		50200	55100
32	SKATER 32 RACE	OP	RNBT	FBG	OB		8 6	2700		**	**
40	SKATER 40	OP	RNBT	FBG TR IB T		10 11	4750		**	**
45 7	SKATER 45	OP	RNBT	FBG TR IB T		12	5000		**	**
	------------- 1985 BOATS -------------									
17 7	SKATER 18	OP	RNBT	FBG TH OB		7 11	1100	10	4400	5050
17 7	SKATER 18S	OP	RNBT	FBG TH OB		7 11	950	10	3850	4450
24 3	SKATER 24	OP	RNBT	FBG TH OB		7 11	1700	1 6	8000	9200

....For earlier years, see the BUC Used Boat Price Guide, Volume 3

DRAGONFLY SAILBOATS
OYSTER BAY NY 11771   See inside cover to adjust price for area

For more recent years, see the BUC Used Boat Price Guide, Volume 1

LOA FT IN	NAME AND/ OR MODEL	TOP/ RIG	BOAT TYPE	-HULL- MTL TP	----ENGINE--- TP # HP MFG	BEAM FT IN	WGT LBS	DRAFT FT IN	RETAIL LOW	RETAIL HIGH
	------------- 1996 BOATS -------------									
20	DRAGONFLY 600	SLP	SACAC	F/S TM		16	586		**	**
26 2	DRAGONFLY 800 SW	SLP	SACAC	F/S TM		19 8	2315		47000	51700
30 8	DRAGONFLY 920 SW SLP	SLP	SACAC	F/S TM		22	3693		89200	98100
33	DRAGONFLY 1000 SW	SLP	SACAC	F/S TM	IB	18D VLVO	25	5100		129500	142000
	------------- 1995 BOATS -------------									
20	DRAGONFLY 600	SLP	SACAC	F/S TM		16	586		**	**
26 2	DRAGONFLY 800 SW	SLP	SACAC	F/S TM		19 8	2315		43600	48500
33	DRAGONFLY 1000 SW	SLP	SACAC	F/S TM	IB	18D VLVO	25	5100		121500	133500

DREYER BOAT YARD
MARYSVILLE WA 98270   COAST GUARD MFG ID- FCF See inside cover to adjust price for area

For more recent years, see the BUC Used Boat Price Guide, Volume 1

LOA FT IN	NAME AND/ OR MODEL	TOP/ RIG	BOAT TYPE	-HULL- MTL TP	----ENGINE--- TP # HP MFG	BEAM FT IN	WGT LBS	DRAFT FT IN	RETAIL LOW	RETAIL HIGH
					1985 BOATS					
29	BOWPICKER		FSH	FBG SV	IO 260 VLVO	10	7000	11	8850	10100
29	BOWPICKER		FSH	FBG SV	IO 260 VLVO	10	8500		11800	13500
32	COMBO	FB	FSH	FBG SV	IB 260 VLVO	10 6	8500	1 1	11800	13500
37	COMBO	FB	FSH	FBG SV	IB 11000	12	11000	2 6	21500	23900
39	COMBO	FB	FSH	FBG SV	IB 210D GM	12 7	13000	3	41400	46000
		FB	FSH	FBG SV	IB 230D GM	14	16500	3 7	49400	54200

....For earlier years, see the BUC Used Boat Price Guide, Volume 3

DRIFTER MARINE ENT INC
PHOENIX AZ 85061   COAST GUARD MFG ID- DRZ See inside cover to adjust price for area

LOA FT IN	NAME AND/ OR MODEL	TOP/ RIG	BOAT TYPE	-HULL- MTL TP	----ENGINE--- TP # HP MFG	BEAM FT IN	WGT LBS	DRAFT FT IN	RETAIL LOW	RETAIL HIGH
					1984 BOATS					
18 8	DRIFTER 17	SLP	SAIL	FBG KC	OB	6 7	1100	1 10	2700	3100

....For earlier years, see the BUC Used Boat Price Guide, Volume 3

DUFFY & DUFFY CUSTOM YACHTS
BROOKLIN ME 04616   COAST GUARD MFG ID- DUJ See inside cover to adjust price for area
FORMERLY DUFFY & DUFFY FIBERGLASS BOATS

LOA FT IN	NAME AND/ OR MODEL	TOP/ RIG	BOAT TYPE	-HULL- MTL TP	----ENGINE--- TP # HP MFG	BEAM FT IN	WGT LBS	DRAFT FT IN	RETAIL LOW	RETAIL HIGH
					1995 BOATS					
26	BASS 26 SEDAN	ST	CUD	F/S DS	IB 390 MPC	9 6	6500	2 10	53400	58700
26	BASS 26 SEDAN	ST	CUD	F/S DS	IB 300D CUM	9 6	6500	2 10	69100	75900
31	DUFFY 31	ST	CBNCR	F/S DS	IB 360D CUM	11 4	9000	3	131500	144500
35	DUFFY 35	ST	CBNCR	F/S DS	IB 375D CAT	12 3	14900	3	182000	200000
35	DUFFY 35	ST	SF	F/S DS	IB 300D CUM	12 3	14900	3	157000	172500
38 6	DUFFY 38 CRUISER	ST	LRCPT	F/S DS	IB T375D CAT	14	36000	4 4	337500	370500
38 6	DUFFY 38 SPORT CR	ST	SPTCR	F/S DS	IB T540D CAT	14	36000	4 4	394500	433500
42	DUFFY 42 AFT CABIN	ST	DCMY	F/S DS	IB 600D MERL	14	26000	4 6	292000	321000
42	DUFFY 42 SPORT CR	ST	SPTCR	F/S DS	IB T300D CUM	14	26000	4 6	289500	318000
48	DUFFY 48 AFT CABIN	ST	DCMY	F/S DS	IB T565D DD	17 6	40000	5	549500	604000
48	DUFFY 48 CRUISER	ST	LRCPT	F/S DS	IB 10CD MAN	17 6	40000	5	421500	463500
48	DUFFY 48 YACHT FISH	ST	YTFS	F/S DS	IB T530D GM	17 6	40000	5	502500	552000
					1994 BOATS					
26	BASS 26 SEDAN	ST	CUD	F/S DS	IB 390 MPC	9 6	6500	2 10	50400	55400
26	BASS 26 SEDAN	ST	CUD	F/S DS	IB 300D CUM	9 6	6500	2 10	65600	72100
31	DUFFY 31	ST	CBNCR	F/S DS	IB 360D CUM	11 4	9000	3	125000	137500
35	DUFFY 35	ST	CBNCR	F/S DS	IB 375D CAT	12 3	14900	3	173500	190500
35	DUFFY 35	ST	SF	F/S DS	IB 300D CUM	12 3	14900	3	149500	164500
38 6	DUFFY 38 CRUISER	ST	LRCPT	F/S DS	IB T375D CAT	14	36000	4 4	320000	352000
38 6	DUFFY 38 SPORT CR	ST	SPTCR	F/S DS	IB T540D CAT	14	36000	4 4	374000	411000
42	DUFFY 42 AFT CABIN	ST	DCMY	F/S DS	IB 600D MERL	14	26000	4 6	277000	304500
42	DUFFY 42 SPORT CR	ST	SPTCR	F/S DS	IB T300D CUM	14	26000	4 6	274500	302000
48	DUFFY 48 AFT CABIN	ST	DCMY	F/S DS	IB T540D CAT	17 6	40000	5	518500	569500
48	DUFFY 48 YACHT FISH	ST	YTFS	F/S DS	IB T530D GM	17 6	40000	5	477500	524500
					1993 BOATS					
26	DUFFY 26	CR		FBG DS	IB 210D CUM	9 6	6500	2 10	55400	60800
30 6	DUFFY 30 BASS	OP		FBG DS	IB 210D CUM	10 9	7500	3	66400	72900
31	DUFFY 31	HT	CR	FBG DS	IB 250D CUM	11	7500	3	71500	78600
35	DUFFY 35	FB	SPTCR	FBG DS	IB 375D CAT	12 3	14900	3	148000	163000
42	DUFFY 42	FB	SDN	FBG SV	IB 375D CAT	14 6	24000	4 6	224000	246500
48 3	DUFFY 48	FB	CR	FBG SV	IB 900D GM	17 4	32000	5	298000	327500
					1992 BOATS					
26	DUFFY 26	CR		FBG DS	IB 210D CUM	9 6	6500	2 10	52700	58000
30 6	DUFFY 30 BASS	OP		FBG DS	IB 210D CUM	10 9	7500	3	63300	69600
31	DUFFY 31	HT	CR	FBG DS	IB 250D CUM	11	7500	3	68200	74900
35	DUFFY 35	FB	SPTCR	FBG DS	IB 375D CAT	11 10	12000	3 3	128500	141500
42	DUFFY 42	FB	SDN	FBG SV	IB 375D CAT	14 6	24000	4 6	213000	234000
48 3	DUFFY 48	FB	CR	FBG SV	IB 900D GM	17 4	32000	5	282500	310000
					1991 BOATS					
26	DUFFY 26	FB	CR	FBG DS	IB 210D CUM	9 6	6500	2 10	50300	55300
30 6	DUFFY 30 BASS	OP	CR	FBG DS	IB 210D CUM	10 9	7500	3	60400	66400
31	DUFFY 31	HT	CR	FBG DS	IB 250D CUM	11	7500	3	65100	71500
35	DUFFY 35	FB	SPTCR	FBG DS	IB 375D CAT	11 10	12000	3 3	122500	135000
42	DUFFY 42	FB	SDN	FBG SV	IB 375D CAT	14 6	24000	4 6	203000	223000
48 3	DUFFY 48	FB	CR	FBG DV	IB 900D GM	17 4		5	250000	274500
					1990 BOATS					
30 6	DUFFY 30 BASS	OP	CR	FBG DS	IB 210D CUM	10 9	7500	3	57700	63400
31	DUFFY 31	HT	CR	FBG DS	IB 250D CUM	11	7500	3	62200	68300
35	DUFFY 35	FB	SPTCR	FBG DS	IB 375D CAT	11 10	12000	3 3	117500	129000
42	DUFFY 42	FB	SDN	FBG SV	IB 375D CAT	14 6	24000	4 6	193000	212500
48 3	DUFFY 48	FB	CR	FBG DV	IB 900D GM	17 4		5	238000	261500
					1989 BOATS					
30 6	DUFFY 30	OP	BASS	FBG DS	IB 210D CUM	10 9	7500	3	58200	64000
31	DUFFY 31	HT	CR	FBG DS	IB 250D CUM	11	7500	3	59400	65300
35	DUFFY 35	FB	SPTCR	FBG DS	IB 375D CAT	11 10	12000	3 3	112000	123000
42	DUFFY 42	FB	SDN	FBG SV	IB 375D CAT	14 6	24000	4 6	184000	202500
					1988 BOATS					
26	DUFFY 26	HT	CR	FBG DS	IB 210D CUM	9 6	6000	3	40500	45000
30 6	DUFFY 30 BASS	OP	CR	FBG DS	IB 210D CUM	10 9	7500	3	52800	58000
31	DUFFY 31	HT	CR	FBG DS	IB 210D CUM	11	7500	3	56400	60300
35	DUFFY 35	FB	SPTCR	FBG DS	IB 375D CAT	11 10	12000	3 3	107500	118000
42	DUFFY 42	FB	SDN	FBG SV	IB 375D CAT	14 6	24000	4 6	176000	193000
50 2	DUFFY 50	HT	TRWL	FBG SV	IB 600D GM	16 3	52000	9	342000	376000
					1987 BOATS					
26	DUFFY 26	HT	CR	FBG DS	IB 210D CUM	9 6	6000	3	39000	43300
30 6	DUFFY 30 BASS	OP	CR	FBG DS	IB 210D CUM	10 9	7500	3	50600	55600
31	DUFFY 31	HT	CR	FBG DS	IB 210D CUM	11	7500	3	52500	57700
35	DUFFY 35	FB	SPTCR	FBG DS	IB 375D CAT	11 10	12000	3 3	103000	113000
42	DUFFY 42	FB	SDN	FBG SV	IB 375D CAT	14 6	24000	4 6	168000	184500
50 2	DUFFY 50	HT	TRWL	FBG SV	IB 600D GM	16 3	52000	9	326500	359000
					1985 BOATS					
30 6	DUFFY 30	HT	CR	FBG DV	IB D		10 9	7500	3	** **
35	DUFFY 35	HT	CR	FBG DS	IB		11 10	8000	3 3	** **
41	DUFFY 41	HT	CR	FBG DS	IB D		13 10	26000	4	** **
50 2	DUFFY 50	HT	TRWL	FBG DS	IB D		16 3	52000	9	** **
56 5	DUFFY 56	HT	TRWL	FBG DS	IB D		17 2	60000	7 4	** **
					1984 BOATS					
30 6	DUFFY 30	HT	CR	FBG DS	IB		10 9	7500	3	** **
35	DUFFY 35	HT	CR	FBG DS	IB		11 10	8000	3 3	** **
41	DUFFY 41	HT	CR	FBG DV	IB D		13 10	26000	4 2	** **
50 2	DUFFY 50	HT	TRWL	FBG DS	IB D		16 3	52000	9	** **
56 5		HT	TRWL	FBG DS	IB D		17 2	60000	7 4	** **

....For earlier years, see the BUC Used Boat Price Guide, Volume 3

DUFOUR YACHTS
PERIGNY FRANCE 17185   COAST GUARD MFG ID- DUF See inside cover to adjust price for area

DUFOUR YACHTS USA INC
ANNAPOLIS MD 21403

For more recent years, see the BUC Used Boat Price Guide, Volume 1

LOA FT IN	NAME AND/ OR MODEL	TOP/ RIG	BOAT TYPE	-HULL- MTL TP	----ENGINE--- TP # HP MFG	BEAM FT IN	WGT LBS	DRAFT FT IN	RETAIL LOW	RETAIL HIGH
					1996 BOATS					
35	CLASSIC 35	SLP	SCFAC	FBG KL	IB 30D VLVO	11 5	10000	5 11	57300	63000
40 5	CLASSIC	SLP	SACAC	FBG KL	IB 50D	12 10	13000	7	91500	100500
41	CLASSIC	SLP	SRCAC	FBG KL	IB 50D VLVO	13 1	16538	6 5	98400	108000
43 4	NAUTITECH	CAT	SCFAC	FBG CT	IB 30D VLVO	21	16500	3	162000	178000
43	NAUTITECH 435	SLP	SACAC	FBG CT	IB T 56D	14 8	16500	6 4	163000	179000
45 9	CLASSIC 45	SLP	SACAC	FBG KL	IB 50D	14 1	24251	6 4	163000	179000
47	NAUTITECH 475	SLP	SRCAC	FBG CT	IB T 50D	25	15500	4	215000	236000
47	NAUTITECH 475	CUT	SMPCC	F/S CT	IB T 50D	25	15500	4	215000	236000
49 6	48	SLP	SRCAC	FBG KL	IB 60D VLVO	15 2	29800	6 11	205000	225500
					1995 BOATS					
35	35	SLP	SA/CR	FBG KL	IB 28D VLVO	11 5	10000	5 11	54300	59600
47	NAUTITECH 475	SLP	SRCAC	FBG CT	IB T 50D VLVO	25	15500	4	205500	226000
49 6	PRESTIGE 48	SLP	SRCAC	FBG KL	IB 60D VLVO	15 2	29800	6 11	194500	213500
56 6	PRESTIGE 56 CC	SLP	SCFAC	FBG CT	IB 110D	15 9	38500	7	353000	388000
64 8	NAUTITECH 65	SLP	SCFAC	FBG KL	IB 110D	15 9	38500	7	316500	348000
78	PRESTIGE 80	SLP	SCFAC	F/S KL	IB T120D	18	21230		**	**
					1984 BOATS					
25 1	DUFOUR 25	SLP	SA/CR	FBG CB	OB	8 11	3940	2 6	9950	11300
25 1	DUFOUR 25	SLP	SA/CR	FBG KL	OB	8 11	3940	4 4	10700	12200
25 1	DUFOUR 25	SLP	SA/CR	FBG KL	OB 8D VLVO	8 11	3940	4 4	10700	12200
25 1	DUFOUR 25	SLP	SA/CR	FBG CB	OB	8 11	3940	4 4	9550	10900
25 1	DUFOUR 25 SHOAL	SLP	SA/CR	FBG KL	SD	8 11	3940	3 3	10400	11800
25 1	DUFOUR 25 SHOAL	SLP	SA/CR	FBG KL	SD 8D VLVO	8 11	3940	3 3	10400	11800
27 2	DUFOUR 28	SLP	SA/CR	FBG KL	SD 17D VLVO	9 7	6160	4 11	18100	20100
27 2	DUFOUR 28	SLP	SA/CR	FBG KL	SD 17D VLVO	9 7	6160	4 11	17100	19400
27 2	DUFOUR 28 SHOAL	SLP	SA/CR	FBG KL	SD 17D VLVO	9 7	6160	3 11	17600	19900

LOA FT	LOA IN	NAME AND/ OR MODEL	TOP/ RIG	BOAT TYPE	HULL MTL	HULL TP	ENGINE TP	#	HP	MFG	BEAM FT	BEAM IN	WGT LBS	DRAFT FT	DRAFT IN	RETAIL LOW	RETAIL HIGH
		1984 BOATS															
27	2	DUFOUR 28 TALL RIG	SLP	SA/CR	FBG	KL	SD		17D	VLVO	9	7	6160	4	11	17600	19900
30	6	DUFOUR/FRERS 31	SLP	SA/CR	FBG	CB	SD		17D	VLVO	10	8	8360			25700	28500
30	6	DUFOUR/FRERS 31	SLP	SA/CR	FBG	KL	SD		17D	VLVO	10	8	8360	5	7	25300	28100
30	6	DUFOUR/FRERS 31 SHOA	SLP	SA/CR	FBG	KL	SD		17D	VLVO	10	8	8360	4	5	25000	27700
30	6	DUFOUR/FRERS 31CS	SLP	SA/RC	FBG	KL	SD		17D	VLVO	10	8	8360	5	7	25300	28100
34	11	VALENTIJN AFT	SLP	SA/CR	FBG	KL	SD		25D	VLVO	11	2	10560	6		31200	34700
34	11	VALENTIJN AFT CS	SLP	SA/CR	FBG	KL	SD		25D	VLVO	11	2	10560	6		31700	35200
34	11	VALENTIJN AFT SHOAL	SLP	SA/CR	FBG	KL	SD		25D	VLVO	11	2	10560	4	11	31200	34700
34	11	VALENTIJN OFF	SLP	SA/CR	FBG	KL	SD		25D	VLVO	11	2	10579	6		31300	34700
34	11	VALENTIJN OFF CS	SLP	SA/CR	FBG	KL	SD		25D	VLVO	11	2	10579	6		31700	35300
34	11	VALENTIJN OFF SHOAL	SLP	SA/CR	FBG	KL	SD		25D	VLVO	11	2	10579	4	11	31300	34700
38	5	FRERS 39	SLP	SA/CR	FBG	KC	IB		40D	PERK	12	6	14960			46000	50600
38	5	FRERS 39	SLP	SA/CR	FBG	KL	IB		40D	PERK	12	6	14960	6	7	46000	50600
38	5	FRERS 39CS	SLP	SA/CR	FBG	KL	IB		50D	PERK	12	6	14960	6	7	46100	50700
40	1	VALENTIJN 40	SLP	SA/CR	AL	KL	IB		85D	PERK	12	11	19845	6	9	60300	66300
45	3	DUFOUR 46 KETCH	KTH	SA/CR	FBG	KL	IB		85D	PERK	13	1	26400	6	11	84100	92400

....For earlier years, see the BUC Used Boat Price Guide, Volume 3

DURA NAUTIC INC

GREENTOWN PA 18426 COAST GUARD MFG ID- DNU See inside cover to adjust price for area

LOA FT	LOA IN	NAME AND/ OR MODEL	TOP/ RIG	BOAT TYPE	HULL MTL	HULL TP	ENGINE TP	#	HP	MFG	BEAM FT	BEAM IN	WGT LBS	DRAFT FT	DRAFT IN	RETAIL LOW	RETAIL HIGH
		1988 BOATS															
16		OFFSHORE 16	OP	UTL	AL	SV	OB				5	10	380			1200	1400
		1987 BOATS															
16		OFFSHORE 16	OP	UTL	AL	SV	OB				5	10	380			1150	1350
		1985 BOATS															
16		OFFSHORE 16	OP	UTL	AL	SV	OB				5	10	380			1100	1300
16		OFFSHORE 1660	OP	RNBT	AL	SV	OB				5	10	405			1150	1400
16		RANGER	OP	RNBT	AL	SV	OB				5	10	625			1800	2150
		1984 BOATS															
16		OFFSHORE 16	OP	UTL	AL	SV	OB				5	10	380			1050	1300
16		OFFSHORE 1660	OP	RNBT	AL	SV	OB				5	10	405			1150	1350
16		RANGER 16	OP	RNBT	AL	SV	OB				5	10	625			1750	2100

....For earlier years, see the BUC Used Boat Price Guide, Volume 3

DURACRAFT MARINE CORP

COLUMBIA SC 29203 COAST GUARD MFG ID- DCA See inside cover to adjust price for area

For more recent years, see the BUC Used Boat Price Guide, Volume 1

LOA FT	LOA IN	NAME AND/ OR MODEL	TOP/ RIG	BOAT TYPE	HULL MTL	HULL TP	ENGINE TP	#	HP	MFG	BEAM FT	BEAM IN	WGT LBS	DRAFT FT	DRAFT IN	RETAIL LOW	RETAIL HIGH
		1988 BOATS															
16		1642 COMPETITOR	OP	BASS	AL	SV	OB						525			1250	1500
16		1642 PACER	OP	BASS	AL	SV	OB						560			1350	1600
16	4	1620SSCP	OP	BASS	AL	SV	OB						725			1750	2050
16	4	1620SV	OP	UTL	AL	SV	OB						320			750	905
16	4	1660CBF	OP	UTL	AL	SV	OB				7		530			1250	1500
17	11	1720 PLUS	OP	BASS	AL	SV	OB				5	5	760			1950	2300
18		1854XL	OP	BASS	AL	SV	OB				5	11	910			2350	2700
18	4	1860CBF	OP	UTL	AL	SV	OB				7		585			1350	1600
18	4	1860ST	OP	BASS	AL	SV	OB				7		1090			2700	3150
20	4	2060CBF	OP	UTL	AL	SV	OB				7		645			1350	1600
20	4	2060CBF W/CABIN	OP	UTL	AL	SV	OB				7		945			2050	2450
		1987 BOATS															
16		1642SSCP	OP	BASS	AL	SV	OB				5	1	560			1300	1550
16	4	1660CBF	OP	UTL	AL	SV	OB				7		530			1250	1450
17		1720 SV	OP	UTL	AL	SV	OB				5	7	340			775	930
17	4	1720SSCP	OP	BASS	AL	SV	OB				5	7	760			1850	2200
17	4	SUPER-STAR FISH&SKI	OP	RNBT	AL	SV	OB				5	7	760			1850	2200
17	11	1720 PLUS	OP	BASS	AL	SV	OB				5	5	760			1900	2250
18	4	1860CBF	OP	UTL	AL	SV	OB				7		585			1300	1600
18	4	1860FR	OP	BASS	AL	SV	OB				7		1090			2650	3050
18	4	1860ST	OP	BASS	AL	SV	OB				7		1090			2650	3050
20	4	2060CBF	OP	UTL	AL	SV	OB				7		645			1300	1550
20	4	2060CBF W/CABIN	OP	UTL	AL	SV	OB				7		945			2000	2400
		1986 BOATS															
16		1642SS	OP	BASS	AL	SV	OB				5	1	465			1050	1250
16		1642SSCP	OP	BASS	AL	SV	OB				5	1	560			1250	1500
16	4	1660CBF	OP	UTL	AL	SV	OB				7		530			1200	1400
17		1720 SV	OP	UTL	AL	SV	OB				5	7	340			755	910
17	4	1720SSCP	OP	BASS	AL	SV	OB				5	7	730			1750	2050
17	4	SUPER-STAR FISH&SKI	OP	RNBT	AL	SV	OB				5	7	730			1750	2050
18	4	1860CBF	OP	UTL	AL	SV	OB				7		585			1300	1550
18	4	1860FR	OP	BASS	AL	SV	OB				7		1090			2550	3000
18	4	1860ST	OP	BASS	AL	SV	OB				7		1090			2550	3000
20	4	2060CBF	OP	UTL	AL	SV	OB				7		645			1250	1500
20	4	2060CBF W/CABIN	OP	UTL	AL	SV	OB				7		945			1950	2300
		1985 BOATS															
16		1642SS	OP	BASS	AL	SV	OB				5	1	465			1000	1200
16		1642SSCP	OP	BASS	AL	SV	OB				5	1	560			1250	1450
16	4	1660CBF	OP	UTL	AL	SV	OB				7		530			1150	1400
17		1720 SV	OP	UTL	AL	SV	OB				5	7	340			735	890
17	4	1720SSCP	OP	BASS	AL	SV	OB				5	7	730			1700	2000
17	4	SUPER-STAR FISH&SKI	OP	RNBT	AL	SV	OB				5	7	730			1700	2000
18	4	1860CBF	OP	UTL	AL	SV	OB				7		585			1250	1500
20	4	2060CBF	OP	UTL	AL	SV	OB				7		645			1250	1500
		1984 BOATS															
16		1642SS	OP	BASS	AL	SV	OB				5	1	465			1000	1200
16		1642SSCP	OP	BASS	AL	SV	OB				5	1	560			1200	1450
16	4	1660CBF	OP	UTL	AL	SV	OB				7		530			1150	1350
16	8	1720	OP	FSH	AL	FL	OB				5	4	315			705	850
16	8	1720DS	OP	FSH	AL	FL	OB				5	4	325			725	875
17		1720 SV	OP	UTL	AL	SV	OB				5	7	340			720	870
17	4	1720SSCP	OP	BASS	AL	SV	OB				5	7	730			1650	1950
17	4	SUPER-STAR FISH&SKI	OP	RNBT	AL	SV	OB				5	7	730			1650	1950
18	4	1860CBF	OP	UTL	AL	SV	OB				7		585			1250	1450
20	4	2060CBF	OP	UTL	AL	SV	OB				7		645			1200	1450

....For earlier years, see the BUC Used Boat Price Guide, Volume 3

DURBECK'S INC

HOLMES BEACH FL 33510 COAST GUARD MFG ID- DBK See inside cover to adjust price for area

LOA FT	LOA IN	NAME AND/ OR MODEL	TOP/ RIG	BOAT TYPE	HULL MTL	HULL TP	ENGINE TP	#	HP	MFG	BEAM FT	BEAM IN	WGT LBS	DRAFT FT	DRAFT IN	RETAIL LOW	RETAIL HIGH
		1990 BOATS															
46	9	D46 FLUSH DECK	CUT	SA/CR	FBG	KL	IB		85D	PERK	13	8	38000	5	3	162500	178500
46	9	D46 FLUSH DECK	KTH	SA/CR	FBG	KL	IB		85D	PERK	13	8	38000	5	3	162500	178500
		1989 BOATS															
46	9	D46 FLUSH DECK	CUT	SA/CR	FBG	KL	IB		85D	PERK	13	8	38000	5	3	152500	168000
46	9	D46 FLUSH DECK	KTH	SA/CR	FBG	KL	IB		85D	PERK	13	8	38000	5	3	153000	168000
46	9	D46 GREAT CABIN	CUT	SA/CR	FBG	KL	IB		85D	PERK	13	8	37375	5	2	151500	166500
46	9	D46 GREAT CABIN	KTH	SA/CR	FBG	KL	IB		85D	PERK	13	8	37375	5	2	152000	167000
		1988 BOATS															
46	9	D46 FLUSH DECK	CUT	SA/CR	FBG	KL	IB		85D	PERK	13	8	38000	5	3	143500	158000
46	9	D46 FLUSH DECK	KTH	SA/CR	FBG	KL	IB		85D	PERK	13	8	38000	5	3	144000	158000
46	9	D46 GREAT CABIN	CUT	SA/CR	FBG	KL	IB		85D	PERK	13	8	37375	5	2	142500	156500
46	9	D46 GREAT CABIN	KTH	SA/CR	FBG	KL	IB		85D	PERK	13	8	37375	5	2	143000	157000
		1987 BOATS															
46	9	D46 FLUSH DECK	CUT	SA/CR	FBG	KL	IB		62D	PERK	13	8	35825	5	1	131500	144500
46	9	D46 FLUSH DECK	KTH	SA/CR	FBG	KL	IB		62D	PERK	13	8	35825	5	1	131500	144500
46	9	D46 GREAT CABIN	CUT	SA/CR	FBG	KL	IB		62D	PERK	13	8	37375	5	2	134000	147000
46	9	D46 GREAT CABIN	KTH	SA/CR	FBG	KL	IB		62D	PERK	13	8	37375	5	2	134000	147500
46	9	D46 WORLD CRUISING	CUT	SA/CR	FBG	KL	IB		85D	PERK	13	8	38925	5	3	136500	150000
46	9	D46 WORLD CRUISING	KTH	SA/CR	FBG	KL	IB		85D	PERK	13	8	38925	5	3	136500	150000
		1986 BOATS															
45	10	D46 TRAWLER	HT	TRWL	FBG	DS	IB		135D	PERK	15		62500	5	3	270000	297000
46	9	D46 FLUSH DECK	CUT	SA/CR	FBG	KL	IB		62D	PERK	13	8	35825	5	1	123500	136000
46	9	D46 FLUSH DECK	KTH	SA/CR	FBG	KL	IB		62D	PERK	13	8	35825	5	1	124000	136000
46	9	D46 GREAT CABIN	CUT	SA/CR	FBG	KL	IB		62D	PERK	13	8	37375	5	2	126000	138500
46	9	D46 GREAT CABIN	KTH	SA/CR	FBG	KL	IB		62D	PERK	13	8	37375	5	2	126000	138500
46	9	D46 WORLD CRUISING	CUT	SA/CR	FBG	KL	IB		85D	PERK	13	8	38925	5	3	128500	141000
46	9	D46 WORLD CRUISING	KTH	SA/CR	FBG	KL	IB		85D	PERK	13	8	38925	5	3	128500	141500
		1985 BOATS															
45	10	D46 TRAWLER	HT	TRWL	FBG	DS	IB		135D	PERK	15		62500	5	3	257500	283000
46	9	D46 FLUSH DECK	CUT	SA/CR	FBG	KL	IB		62D	PERK	13	8	35825	5	1	116500	128000
46	9	D46 FLUSH DECK	KTH	SA/CR	FBG	KL	IB		62D	PERK	13	8	35825	5	1	116500	128000
46	9	D46 GREAT CABIN	CUT	SA/CR	FBG	KL	IB		62D	PERK	13	8	37375	5	2	118500	130000
46	9	D46 GREAT CABIN	KTH	SA/CR	FBG	KL	IB		62D	PERK	13	8	37375	5	2	118500	130500
46	9	D46 WORLD CRUISING	CUT	SA/CR	FBG	KL	IB		85D	PERK	13	8	38925	5	3	120500	132500
46	9	D46 WORLD CRUISING	KTH	SA/CR	FBG	KL	IB		85D	PERK	13	8	38925	5	3	121000	133000
48		D48 TRAWLER		TRWL	FBG	DS	IB		190		15		63500			184000	202000
50		D50 TRAWLER		TRWL	FBG	DS	IB		190		15		64500			197500	217000
50	9	D50 FISHERMAN	KTH	SA/CR	FBG	KL	IB		85D	PERK	13	10	45000	5	3	150000	165000
50	9	D50 FLUSH DECK	CUT	SA/CR	FBG	KL	IB		85D	PERK	13	10	44600	5	1	149500	164500
50	9	D50 FLUSH DECK	KTH	SA/CR	FBG	KL	IB		85D	PERK	13	10	44600	5	1	149500	164500

LOA FT	LOA IN	NAME AND/ OR MODEL	TOP/ RIG	BOAT TYPE	-HULL- MTL	-HULL- TP	TP	ENGINE # HP	ENGINE MFG	BEAM FT	BEAM IN	WGT LBS	DRAFT FT	DRAFT IN	RETAIL LOW	RETAIL HIGH
		1985 BOATS														
50	9	D50 GREAT CABIN	CUT	SA/CR	FBG	KL	IB	85D	PERK	13	10	46450	5	2	151500	166500
50	9	D50 GREAT CABIN	KTH	SA/CR	FBG	KL	IB	85D	PERK	13	10	46450	5	2	151500	166500
50	9	D50 WORLD CRUISING	CUT	SA/CR	FBG	KL	IB	85D	PERK	13	10	48300	5	3	153000	168000
50	9	D50 WORLD CRUISING	KTH	SA/CR	FBG	KL	IB	85D	PERK	13	10	48300	5	3	153000	168500
52		D52 TRAWLER		TRWL	FBG	DS	IB	190		15		65500			204000	224500
62		D620 WORLD CRUISING	KTH	SA/CR	FBG	KL	IB	120D	WEST	13	11	54700	5	3	275500	302500
64	11	DURBECK 65 MOTORSHIP		MY	F/S	DS	IB	175D		18		63T	6		628500	691000
64	11	DURBECK 65 MOTORSHIP		MY	F/S	DS	IB	T200		18		63T			638500	701500
		1984 BOATS														
45	10	D46 TRAWLER	HT	TRWL	FBG	DS	IB	135D	PERK	15		62500	5	3	245500	269500
46	9	D46 FLUSH DECK	CUT	SA/CR	FBG	KL	IB	62D	PERK	13	8	35825	5	1	109500	120000
46	9	D46 FLUSH DECK	KTH	SA/CR	FBG	KL	IB	62D	PERK	13	8	35825	5	1	109500	120500
46	9	D46 GREAT CABIN	CUT	SA/CR	FBG	KL	IB	62D	PERK	13	8	37375	5	2	111500	122500
46	9	D46 GREAT CABIN	KTH	SA/CR	FBG	KL	IB	62D	PERK	13	8	37375	5	2	111500	122500
46	9	D46 WORLD CRUISING	CUT	SA/CR	FBG	KL	IB	85D	PERK	13	8	38925	5	3	113500	125000
46	9	D46 WORLD CRUISING	KTH	SA/CR	FBG	KL	IB	85D	PERK	13	8	38925	5	3	113500	125000
48		SNAPPER D 48	HT	TRWL	FBG	DS	IB	131D	GM	15		65000	5	6	171500	188500
50		D50 TRAWLER		TRWL	FBG	DS	IB	190		15		64500			189000	207500
50	9	D50 FISHERMAN	KTH	SA/CR	FBG	KL	IB	85D	PERK	13	10	45000	5	3	141000	155000
50	9	D50 FLUSH DECK	CUT	SA/CR	FBG	KL	IB	85D	PERK	13	10	44600	5	1	140500	154500
50	9	D50 FLUSH DECK	KTH	SA/CR	FBG	KL	IB	85D	PERK	13	10	44600	5	1	141000	154500
50	9	D50 GREAT CABIN	CUT	SA/CR	FBG	KL	IB	85D	PERK	13	10	46450	5	2	142500	156500
50	9	D50 GREAT CABIN	KTH	SA/CR	FBG	KL	IB	85D	PERK	13	10	46450	5	2	142500	156500
50	9	D50 WORLD CRUISING	CUT	SA/CR	FBG	KL	IB	85D	PERK	13	10	48300	5	3	144000	158000
50	9	D50 WORLD CRUISING	KTH	SA/CR	FBG	KL	IB	85D	PERK	13	10	48300	5	3	144000	158500
52		D52 TRAWLER		TRWL	FBG	DS	IB	190		15		65500			196500	215500
62		D620 WORLD CRUISING	KTH	SA/CR	FBG	KL	IB	120D	WEST	13	11	54700	5	3	259000	284500
64	11	DURBECK 65 MOTORSHIP		MY	F/S	DS	IB	175D		18		63T	6		604500	664000
65		DURBECK 65 MOTORSHIP		MY	F/S	DS	IB	T200		18		63T			615000	675500

....For earlier years, see the BUC Used Boat Price Guide, Volume 3

DUSKY MARINE INC

DANIA FL 33004 COAST GUARD MFG ID- DUS See inside cover to adjust price for area

For more recent years, see the BUC Used Boat Price Guide, Volume 1

LOA FT	LOA IN	NAME AND/ OR MODEL	TOP/ RIG	BOAT TYPE	-HULL- MTL	-HULL- TP	TP	ENGINE # HP	ENGINE MFG	BEAM FT	BEAM IN	WGT LBS	DRAFT FT	DRAFT IN	RETAIL LOW	RETAIL HIGH
		1996 BOATS														
16	8	DUSKY 17	OP	OPFSH	FBG	SV	OB			7	4	1300		6	3300	3850
17	9	DUSKY 18	OP	CTRCN	FBG	SV	OB			7		1200		10	3200	3750
19	1	DUSKY 19	OP	OPFSH	FBG	SV	OB			7	10	1900	1		4700	5400
20	3	DUSKY 203	OP	OPFSH	FBG	SV	OB			7	4	2000	1		7150	8200
20	3	DUSKY 203	OP	OPFSH	FBG	SV	IB	180	VLVO	7	4	2000	2	8	11300	12900
		IO 205 VLVO 10900 12400, IB 220 CRUS 11500 13000, IO 245 VLVO 11400 12900														
		IB 270 CRUS 11700 13300														
20	3	DUSKY 203FAC	OP	FSH	FBG	SV	OB			8		2300	1		7750	8900
20	3	DUSKY 203FAC	OP	FSH	FBG	SV	SE	180-245		8		2300	1		7750	8900
23	3	DUSKY 233	OP	OPFSH	FBG	SV	OB			8		3200	1	1	9200	10500
23	3	DUSKY 233	OP	OPFSH	FBG	SV	IO	180-205		8		3200	1	1	12800	14700
		IB 220 CRUS 13800 15700, IO 245-250 13300 15100, IB 270 CRUS 14000 15900														
		IO 300 13700 16300, IB 350 CRUS 14700 16700, IB 225D VLVO 19500 21700														
		IBT200D-T210D 25700 30800, IB T250D CUM 29800 33100														
23	3	DUSKY 233CSS	OP	CUD	FBG	SV	OB			8		3600	1	1	9950	11300
23	3	DUSKY 233CSS	OP	CUD	FBG	SV	IO	180-205		8		3600	1	1	13100	15000
		IB 220 CRUS 14900 17000, IO 245-250 13500 15400, IB 270 CRUS 15100 17200														
		IO 300 13900 16500, IB 350 CRUS 15800 18000, IB 200D-250D 20100 24600														
23	3	DUSKY 233FAC	OP	FSH	FBG	SV	OB			8		3600	1	1	9900	11300
23	3	DUSKY 233FAC	OP	FSH	FBG	SV	IO	180-245		8		3600	1	1	13900	16300
23	3	DUSKY 233FAC	OP	FSH	FBG	SV	IO	300	VLVO	8		3600	1	1	15400	17500
23	3	DUSKY 233FC	OP	CUD	FBG	SV	OB			8		3500	1	1	9500	10800
23	3	DUSKY 233FC	OP	CUD	FBG	SV	IO	180-205		8		3500	1	1	12600	14500
		IB 220 CRUS 14700 16600, IO 245-250 13100 14800, IB 270 CRUS 14600 16600														
		IO 300 13700 16200, IB 350 CRUS 15300 17400, IB 225D VLVO 20300 22600														
		IBT200D-T210D 26000 31800, IB T250D CUM 30300 33700														
25	6	DUSKY 256	OP	OPFSH	FBG	SV	OB			8		3800	1	1	11600	13200
25	6	DUSKY 256	OP	OPFSH	FBG	SV	IO	205	VLVO	8		3800	1	1	16300	18600
		IB 220 CRUS 18200 20300, IO 245-250 17000 19300, IB 270 CRUS 18800 20900														
		IO 300 18100 20600, IB 350 CRUS 19800 22000, IB 225D VLVO 22400 24900														
		IBT200D-T210D 29900 35200, IB T250D CUM 34400 38200														
25	6	DUSKY 256CSS	OP	CUD	FBG	SV	OB			8		4100	1	1	12100	13800
25	6	DUSKY 256CSS	OP	CUD	FBG	SV	IO	205	VLVO	8		4100	1	1	16200	18400
		IB 220 CRUS 19100 21200, IO 245-250 17000 19400, IB 270 CRUS 19700 21900														
		IO 300 17500 20600, IB 350 CRUS 21000 23300, IB 225D VLVO 24000 26600														
		IBT200D-T210D 31700 37700, IB T250D CUM 36300 40300														
25	6	DUSKY 256FAC	OP	FSH	FBG	SV	OB			8		4100	1	1	12000	13600
25	6	DUSKY 256FAC	OP	FSH	FBG	SV	IO	180	VLVO	8		4100	1	1	17000	19300
		IB 220 CRUS 19200 21300, IO 245-250 18200 20300, IB 270 CRUS 19600 21800														
		IO 300 18900 21500, IB 350 CRUS 20800 23100, IB 225D VLVO 24000 26700														
		IBT200D-T210D 31600 37100, IB T250D CUM 36000 40000														
25	6	DUSKY 256FC	OP	CUD	FBG	SV	OB			8		4000	1	1	11800	13400
25	6	DUSKY 256FC	OP	CUD	FBG	SV	IO	205	VLVO	8		4000	1	1	16000	18200
		IB 220 CRUS 18600 20700, IO 245-250 16400 18600, IB 270 CRUS 19200 21300														
		IO 300 17300 19900, IB 350 CRUS 20200 22500, IB 225D VLVO 23600 26200														
		IBT200D-T210D 30900 36700, IB T250D CUM 35300 39200														
		1995 BOATS														
16	8	DUSKY 17	OP	OPFSH	FBG	SV	OB			7	4	1300		6	3150	3650
19	1	DUSKY 19	OP	OPFSH	FBG	SV	OB			7	10	1800	1		4250	4950
20	3	DUSKY 203	OP	OPFSH	FBG	SV	OB			8		2000	1		6750	7800
20	3	DUSKY 203	OP	OPFSH	FBG	SV	IB	180	VLVO	8		2000	2	8	11300	12900
		IO 205 VLVO 10700 12200, IB 220 CRUS 11500 13000, IO 245 VLVO 11200 12700														
		IB 270 CRUS 11700 13200														
20	3	DUSKY 203FAC	OP	FSH	FBG	SV	OB			8		2300	1		7400	8500
20	3	DUSKY 203FAC	OP	FSH	FBG	SV	SE	180-245		8		2300	1		7400	8500
23	3	DUSKY 233	OP	OPFSH	FBG	SV	OB			8		2700	1	1	7600	8750
23	3	DUSKY 233	OP	OPFSH	FBG	SV	IO	180-205		8		4500	1	1	15200	17700
		IB 220 CRUS 16900 19200, IO 245 VLVO 16200 18400, IB 270 CRUS 17200 19500														
		IO 300 VLVO 18200 20200, IB 350 CRUS 18800 20900, IB T200D VLVO 28200 31400														
		IBT210D-T250D 31900 38400														
23	3	DUSKY 233FAC	OP	FSH	FBG	SV	OB			8		3400	1	1	9100	10300
23	3	DUSKY 233FAC	OP	FSH	FBG	SV	IO	180-245		8		5200	1	1	17200	20900
23	3	DUSKY 233FAC	OP	FSH	FBG	SV	IO	300	VLVO	8		5600	1	1	20000	22200
23	3	DUSKY 233FC	OP	CUD	FBG	SV	OB			8		3000	1	1	8000	9200
23	3	DUSKY 233FC	OP	CUD	FBG	SV	IO	180-245		8		5300	1	1	16100	19100
		IB 270-350 19400 23000, IBT200D-T210D 30900 37900, IB T250D CUM 36300 40300														
25	6	DUSKY 256	OP	OPFSH	FBG	SV	OB			8		3700	1	1	10900	12400
25	6	DUSKY 256	OP	OPFSH	FBG	SV	IO	205	VLVO	8		5400	1	1	19400	21500
		IB 220 CRUS 21300 23700, IO 245 VLVO 20100 22300, IB 270 CRUS 22400 24800														
		IO 300 VLVO 21900 24400, IB 350 CRUS 23900 26600, IBT200D-T210D 35000 42400														
		IB T250D CUM 40900 45400														
25	6	DUSKY 256CSS	OP	CUD	FBG	SV	OB			8		3800	1	1	11200	12700
25	6	DUSKY 256CSS	OP	CUD	FBG	SV	IO	205-245		8		5400	1	1	18500	21400
		IB 270 CRUS 22100 24600, IO 300 VLVO 20600 22800, IB 350 CRUS 23700 26400														
		IBT200D-T210D 36000 43600, IB T250D CUM 41600 46200														
25	6	DUSKY 256FAC	OP	FSH	FBG	SV	OB			8		3800	1	1	11000	12500
25	6	DUSKY 256FAC	OP	FSH	FBG	SV	IB	220	CRUS	8		5700	2	9	22200	24700
		IO 245 VLVO 20500 22800, IB 270 CRUS 22400 24900, IO 300 VLVO 22100 24500														
		IB 350 CRUS 24100 26700, IB T200D VLVO 33000 36600, IBT210D-T250D 38200 45100														
25	6	DUSKY 256FC	OP	CUD	FBG	SV	OB			8		3800	1	1	10900	12400
25	6	DUSKY 256FC	OP	CUD	FBG	SV	IO	205	VLVO	8		5200	1	1	18000	20000
		IB 220 CRUS 21400 23700, IO 245 VLVO 18300 20300, IB 270 CRUS 22100 24600														
		IO 300 VLVO 20500 22800, IB 350 CRUS 23400 26000, IBT200D-T210D 35400 42400														
		IB T250D CUM 40100 44600														
		1994 BOATS														
16	8	DUSKY 17	OP	OPFSH	FBG	SV	OB			7	4	1300		6	2950	3450
19	1	DUSKY 19	OP	OPFSH	FBG	SV	OB			7	10	1800	1		4050	4700
20	3	DUSKY 203	OP	OPFSH	FBG	SV	OB			8		2000	1		6450	7400
20	3	DUSKY 203	OP	OPFSH	FBG	SV	IB	180	VLVO	8		2000	2	8	10700	12200
		IO 205 VLVO 10000 11400, IB 220 CRUS 10800 12300, IO 245 VLVO 10400 11800														
		IB 270 CRUS 11000 12500														
20	3	DUSKY 203FAC	OP	FSH	FBG	SV	OB			8		2300	1		7050	8100
20	3	DUSKY 203FAC	OP	FSH	FBG	SV	SE	180-245		8		2300	1		7050	8100
23	3	DUSKY 233	OP	OPFSH	FBG	SV	OB			8		2700	1	1	7250	8350
23	3	DUSKY 233	OP	OPFSH	FBG	SV	IO	180-205		8		4500	1	1	14200	16500
		IB 220 CRUS 15900 18100, IO 245 VLVO 15100 17200, IB 270 CRUS 16200 18400														
		IO 300 VLVO 16600 18900, IB 350 CRUS 17500 19900, IB T200D VLVO 26900 29800														
		IBT210D-T250D 30400 36500														
23	3	DUSKY 233CSS	OP	CUD	FBG	SV	OB			8		2700	1	1	7500	8600

CONTINUED ON NEXT PAGE

LOA FT	IN	NAME AND/ OR MODEL	TOP/ RIG	BOAT TYPE	-HULL- MTL	TP	ENGINE TP	# HP	MFG	BEAM FT	IN	WGT LBS	DRAFT FT	IN	RETAIL LOW	RETAIL HIGH
		1994 BOATS														
23	3	DUSKY 233CSS	OP	CUD	FBG	SV	IO	180-205		8		5400	1	1	15800	18300
		IB 220 CUM 17000 19300, IO 245 VLVO 16400 18700, IB 270 CRUS													18300	20300
		IO 300 VLVO 17600 20000, IB 350 CRUS 19100 21200, IBT200D-T210D													28900	35200
		IB T250D CUM 33500 37200														
23	3	DUSKY 233FAC	OP	FSH	FBG	SV	OB			8		3400	1	1	8600	9900
23	3	DUSKY 233FAC	OP	FSH	FBG	SV	IO	180-245		8		5200	1	1	16000	19600
23	3	DUSKY 233FAC	OP	FSH	FBG	SV	IO	300	VLVO	8		5600	1	1	18800	20900
23	3	DUSKY 233FC	OP	CUD	FBG	SV	OB			8		3000	1	1	7600	8750
23	3	DUSKY 233FC	OP	CUD	FBG	SV	IO	180-245		8		5300	1	1	15000	17800
		IB 270-350 18600 21800, IBT200D-T210D 29400 36000, IB T250D CUM													34500	38400
25	6	DUSKY 256	OP	OPFSH	FBG	SV	OB			8		3700	1	1	10400	11800
25	6	DUSKY 256	OP	OPFSH	FBG	SV	IO	205	VLVO	8		5400	1	1	18200	20300
		IB 220 CRUS 20200 22400, IO 245 VLVO 18900 21000, IB 270 CRUS													21200	23500
		IO 300 VLVO 20500 22700, IB 350 CRUS 22700 25200, IBT200D-T210D													33300	40400
		IB T250D CUM 38900 43200														
25	6	DUSKY 256CSS	OP	CUD	FBG	SV	OB			8		3800	1	1	10700	12200
25	6	DUSKY 256CSS	OP	CUD	FBG	SV	IO	205-245		8		5400	1	1	16900	20000
		IB 270 CRUS 20900 23300, IO 300 VLVO 19200 21300, IB 350 CRUS													22500	25000
		IBT200D-T210D 34300 41500, IB T250D CUM 39500 43900														
25	6	DUSKY 256FAC	OP	FSH	FBG	SV	OB			8		3800	1	1	10500	11900
25	6	DUSKY 256FAC	OP	FSH	FBG	SV	IB	220	CRUS	8		5700	2	9	21000	23400
		IO 245 VLVO 19300 21400, IB 270 CRUS 21200 23600, IO 300 VLVO													20600	22900
		IB 350 CRUS 22800 25300, IB T200D VLVO 31300 34800, IBT210D-T250D													36300	42900
25	6	DUSKY 256FC	OP	CUD	FBG	SV	OB			8		3800	1	1	10300	11700
25	6	DUSKY 256FC	OP	CUD	FBG	SV	IO	205	VLVO	8		5200	1	1	16400	18700
		IB 220 CRUS 20200 22500, IO 245 VLVO 16700 19000, IB 270 CRUS													20900	23300
		IO 300 VLVO 19200 21300, IB 350 CRUS 22200 24700, IBT200D-T210D													33700	40300
		IB T250D CUM 38100 42400														
25	11	DUSKY 26	OP	SF	FBG	SV	OB			11	3	6000	2	5	17000	19300
25	11	DUSKY 26	OP	SF	FBG	SV	IB	T220-T270		11	3	7500	2	5	31400	35900
		IB T350 CRUS 35500 39500, IBT200D-T210D 44100 54900, IB T250D CUM													52300	57500
		1993 BOATS														
16	8	DUSKY 17	OP	OPFSH	FBG	SV	OB			7	4	1300		6	2850	3300
19	1	DUSKY 19	OP	OPFSH	FBG	SV	OB			7	10	1800	1		3850	4500
20	3	DUSKY 203	OP	OPFSH	FBG	SV	OB			8		2000	1		6150	7100
20	3	DUSKY 203	OP	OPFSH	FBG	SV	IB	180	VLVO	8		3800	2	8	14500	16500
		IO 205 VLVO 13400 15200, IB 220 CRUS 14800 16800, IO 245 VLVO													14000	15900
		IB 270 CRUS 15400 17400														
20	3	DUSKY 203FAC	OP	FSH	FBG	SV	OB			8		2300	1		6700	7700
20	3	DUSKY 203FAC	OP	FSH	FBG	SV	SE	180-245		8		2300	1		6700	7700
23	3	DUSKY 233	OP	OPFSH	FBG	SV	OB			8		2700	1	1	6950	7950
23	3	DUSKY 233	OP	OPFSH	FBG	SV	IO	180-205		8		4500	1	1	13300	15400
		IB 220 CRUS 15100 17200, IO 245 VLVO 14100 16000, IB 270 CRUS													15400	17500
		IO 300 VLVO 15400 17500, IB 350 CRUS 16500 18800, IB T200D VLVO													25600	28400
		IBT210D-T250D 28900 34800														
23	3	DUSKY 233CSS	OP	CUD	FBG	SV	OB			8		2700	1	1	7150	8200
23	3	DUSKY 233CSS	OP	CUD	FBG	SV	IO	180-205		8		5400	1	1	14800	17100
		IB 220 CUM 16100 18200, IO 245 VLVO 15300 17400, IB 270 CRUS													17000	19300
		IO 300 VLVO 16400 18600, IB 350 CRUS 18300 20300, IBT200D-T210D													27500	33500
		IB T250D CUM 31900 35500														
23	3	DUSKY 233FAC	OP	FSH	FBG	SV	OB			8		3400	1	1	8200	9450
23	3	DUSKY 233FAC	OP	FSH	FBG	SV	IO	180-245		8		5200	1	1	14900	18200
23	3	DUSKY 233FAC	OP	FSH	FBG	SV	IO	300	VLVO	8		5600	1	1	17200	19500
23	3	DUSKY 233FC	OP	CUD	FBG	SV	OB			8		3000	1	1	7300	8350
23	3	DUSKY 233FC	OP	CUD	FBG	SV	IO	180-245		8		5300	1	1	14000	16400
		IB 270-350 17200 20900, IBT200D-T210D 28000 34300, IB T250D CUM													32900	36500
25	6	DUSKY 256	OP	OPFSH	FBG	SV	OB			8		3700	1	1	9900	11300
25	6	DUSKY 256	OP	OPFSH	FBG	SV	IO	205	VLVO	8		5400	1	1	16700	18900
		IB 220 CRUS 19100 21300, IO 245 VLVO 17300 19700, IB 270 CRUS													20100	22300
		IO 300 VLVO 19300 21400, IB 350 CRUS 21500 23900, IBT200D-T210D													31700	38400
		IB T250D CUM 37000 41100														
25	6	DUSKY 256CSS	OP	CUD	FBG	SV	OB			8		3800	1	1	10300	11700
25	6	DUSKY 256CSS	OP	CUD	FBG	SV	IO	205	VLVO	8		5400	1	1	15800	17900
		IB 210 CUM 19100 21300, IO 245 VLVO 16400 18600, IB 270 CRUS													19800	22000
		IO 300 VLVO 18100 20100, IB 350 CRUS 21300 23700, IBT200D-T210D													32700	39500
		IB T250D CUM 37700 41800														
25	6	DUSKY 256FAC	OP	FSH	FBG	SV	OB			8		3800	1	1	10000	11400
25	6	DUSKY 256FAC	OP	FSH	FBG	SV	IB	220	CRUS	8		5700	2	9	20000	22200
		IO 245 VLVO 18000 20000, IB 270 CRUS 20100 22400, IO 300 VLVO													19300	21400
		IB 350 CRUS 21600 24000, IB T200D VLVO 29800 33200, IBT210D-T250D													34600	40800
25	6	DUSKY 256FC	OP	CUD	FBG	SV	OB			8		3800	1	1	9800	11200
25	6	DUSKY 256FC	OP	CUD	FBG	SV	IO	205	VLVO	8		5200	1	1	15300	17400
		IB 220 CRUS 19200 21300, IO 245 VLVO 15600 17700, IB 270 CRUS													19800	22100
		IO 300 VLVO 18100 20100, IB 350 CRUS 21000 23400, IBT200D-T210D													32100	38400
		IB T250D CUM 36300 40400														
25	11	DUSKY 26	OP	SF	FBG	SV	OB			11	3	6000	2	5	16100	18300
25	11	DUSKY 26	OP	SF	FBG	SV	IB	T220-T270		11	3	7500	2	5	29800	34000
		IB T350 CRUS 33700 37400, IB T200D VLVO 42000 46700, IBT210D-T250D													47800	54700
		1992 BOATS														
16	8	DUSKY 17	OP	OPFSH	FBG	SV	OB			7	4	1300		6	2700	3150
19	1	DUSKY 19	OP	OPFSH	FBG	SV	OB			7	10	1800	1		3650	4250
20	3	DUSKY 203	OP	OPFSH	FBG	SV	OB			8		2000	1		5900	6800
20	3	DUSKY 203	OP	OPFSH	FBG	SV	IB	180	VLVO	8		2000	2	8	9650	11000
20	3	DUSKY 203	OP	OPFSH	FBG	SV	SE	205	VLVO	8		2000	1		5900	6800
20	3	DUSKY 203	OP	OPFSH	FBG	SV	IB	220	CRUS	8		2000	2	8	9750	11100
20	3	DUSKY 203	OP	OPFSH	FBG	SV	SE	245	VLVO	8		2000	1		5900	6800
20	3	DUSKY 203	OP	OPFSH	FBG	SV	IB	270	CRUS	8		2000	2	8	9900	11300
20	3	DUSKY 203FAC	OP	FSH	FBG	SV	OB			8		2300	1		6450	7400
20	3	DUSKY 203FAC	OP	FSH	FBG	SV	SE	180-245		8		2300	1		6450	7400
23	3	DUSKY 233	OP	OPFSH	FBG	SV	OB			8		2700	1	1	6650	7650
23	3	DUSKY 233	OP	OPFSH	FBG	SV	SE	180-205		8		2700	1	1	6650	7650
23	3	DUSKY 233	OP	OPFSH	FBG	SV	IB	220	CRUS	8		2700	2	9	10100	11400
23	3	DUSKY 233	OP	OPFSH	FBG	SV	SE	245	VLVO	8		2700	1	1	6650	7650
23	3	DUSKY 233	OP	OPFSH	FBG	SV	IB	270	CRUS	8		2700	2	9	10200	11600
23	3	DUSKY 233	OP	OPFSH	FBG	SV	SE	300	VLVO	8		2700	1	1	6650	7650
23	3	DUSKY 233	OP	OPFSH	FBG	SV	IB	350	CRUS	8		2700	2	9	10800	12300
23	3	DUSKY 233	OP	OPFSH	FBG	SV	IB	T200D-T306D		8		2700	2	9	23500	28300
23	3	DUSKY 233CSS	OP	CUD	FBG	SV	OB			8		2700	1	1	6850	7850
23	3	DUSKY 233CSS	OP	CUD	FBG	SV	SE	180-205		8		3000	1	1	7350	8450
23	3	DUSKY 233CSS	OP	CUD	FBG	SV	IB	220	CRUS	8		2700	2	9	10200	11600
23	3	DUSKY 233CSS	OP	CUD	FBG	SV	SE	245	VLVO	8		2700	1	1	6750	7750
23	3	DUSKY 233CSS	OP	CUD	FBG	SV	IB	270	CRUS	8		2700	2	9	10400	11800
23	3	DUSKY 233CSS	OP	CUD	FBG	SV	SE	300	VLVO	8		2700	1	1	6750	7750
23	3	DUSKY 233CSS	OP	CUD	FBG	SV	IB	350	CRUS	8		2700	2	9	11000	12500
23	3	DUSKY 233CSS	OP	CUD	FBG	SV	IB	T200D-T306D		8		2700	2	9	24100	28600
23	3	DUSKY 233FAC	OP	FSH	FBG	SV	OB			8		3000	1	1	7200	8250
23	3	DUSKY 233FAC	OP	FSH	FBG	SV	SE	180-300		8		3000	1	1	7200	8250
23	3	DUSKY 233FC	OP	CUD	FBG	SV	OB			8		3000	1	1	7000	8000
23	3	DUSKY 233FC	OP	CUD	FBG	SV	SE	180-205		8		3000	1	1	7050	8150
23	3	DUSKY 233FC	OP	CUD	FBG	SV	IB	220	CRUS	8		3000	2	9	10500	11900
23	3	DUSKY 233FC	OP	CUD	FBG	SV	SE	245	OMC	8		3000	1	1	7100	8150
23	3	DUSKY 233FC	OP	CUD	FBG	SV	IB	270	CRUS	8		3000	2	9	10600	12100
23	3	DUSKY 233FC	OP	CUD	FBG	SV	SE	300	OMC	8		3000	1	1	7100	8150
23	3	DUSKY 233FC	OP	CUD	FBG	SV	IB	350	CRUS	8		3000	2	9	11200	12800
23	3	DUSKY 233FC	OP	CUD	FBG	SV	IB	T200D-T306D		8		3000	2	9	24200	28700
25	6	DUSKY 256	OP	OPFSH	FBG	SV	OB			8		3000	1	1	8650	9950
25	6	DUSKY 256	OP	OPFSH	FBG	SV	SE	205	VLVO	8		3000	1	1	8650	9950
25	6	DUSKY 256	OP	OPFSH	FBG	SV	IB	220	CRUS	8		3000	2	9	12800	14500
25	6	DUSKY 256	OP	OPFSH	FBG	SV	SE	245	VLVO	8		3000	1	1	8650	9950
25	6	DUSKY 256	OP	OPFSH	FBG	SV	IB	270	CRUS	8		3000	2	9	13300	15100
25	6	DUSKY 256	OP	OPFSH	FBG	SV	SE	300	VLVO	8		3000	1	1	8650	9950
25	6	DUSKY 256	OP	OPFSH	FBG	SV	IB	350	CRUS	8		3000	2	9	14300	16200
25	6	DUSKY 256	OP	OPFSH	FBG	SV	IB	T200D-T306D		8		3000	2	9	25300	30500
25	6	DUSKY 256CSS	OP	CUD	FBG	SV	OB			8		3000	1	1	8950	10200
25	6	DUSKY 256CSS	OP	CUD	FBG	SV	SE	205	VLVO	8		3000	1	1	8700	10000
25	6	DUSKY 256CSS	OP	CUD	FBG	SV	IB	220	CRUS	8		3000	2	9	13100	14900
25	6	DUSKY 256CSS	OP	CUD	FBG	SV	SE	245	VLVO	8		3000	1	1	8900	10100
25	6	DUSKY 256CSS	OP	CUD	FBG	SV	IB	270	CRUS	8		3000	2	9	13600	15500
25	6	DUSKY 256CSS	OP	CUD	FBG	SV	SE	300	VLVO	8		3000	1	1	8850	10100
25	6	DUSKY 256CSS	OP	CUD	FBG	SV	IB	350	CRUS	8		3000	2	9	14700	16600
25	6	DUSKY 256CSS	OP	CUD	FBG	SV	IB	T200D-T306D		8		3000	2	9	26300	30500
25	6	DUSKY 256FAC	OP	FSH	FBG	SV	OB			8		3000	1	1	8650	9950
25	6	DUSKY 256FAC	OP	FSH	FBG	SV	SE	180	VLVO	8		3000	1	1	8650	9950
25	6	DUSKY 256FAC	OP	FSH	FBG	SV	IB	220	CRUS	8		3000	2	9	12900	14700
25	6	DUSKY 256FAC	OP	FSH	FBG	SV	SE	245	VLVO	8		3000	1	1	8650	9950
25	6	DUSKY 256FAC	OP	FSH	FBG	SV	IB	270	CRUS	8		3000	2	9	13400	15300
25	6	DUSKY 256FAC	OP	FSH	FBG	SV	SE	300	VLVO	8		3000	1	1	8650	9950
25	6	DUSKY 256FAC	OP	FSH	FBG	SV	IB	350	CRUS	8		3000	2	9	14500	16500

CONTINUED ON NEXT PAGE

LOA FT	LOA IN	NAME AND/ OR MODEL	TOP/ RIG	BOAT TYPE	HULL MTL	HULL TP	ENGINE TP	ENGINE # HP	ENGINE MFG	BEAM FT	BEAM IN	WGT LBS	DRAFT FT	DRAFT IN	RETAIL LOW	RETAIL HIGH
		1992 BOATS														
25	6	DUSKY 256FAC	OP	FSH	FBG	SV	IBT200D-T306D			8		3000	2	9	25800	30300
25	6	DUSKY 256FC	OP	CUD	FBG	SV	OB			8		3300	1	1	8900	10100
25	6	DUSKY 256FC	OP	CUD	FBG	SV	SE	205	VLVO	8		3300	1	1	9100	10400
25	6	DUSKY 256FC	OP	CUD	FBG	SV	IB	220	CRUS	8		3300	2	9	13300	15100
25	6	DUSKY 256FC	OP	CUD	FBG	SV	SE	245	VLVO	8		3300	1	1	9000	10200
25	6	DUSKY 256FC	OP	CUD	FBG	SV	IB	270	CRUS	8		3300	2	9	13800	15700
25	6	DUSKY 256FC	OP	CUD	FBG	SV	SE	300	VLVO	8		3300	1	1	9000	10200
25	6	DUSKY 256FC	OP	CUD	FBG	SV	IB	350	CRUS	8		3300	2	9	14800	16800
25	6	DUSKY 256FC	OP	CUD	FBG	SV	IBT200D-T306D			8		3300	2	9	26600	31100
25	11	DUSKY 26	OP	SF	FBG	SV	OB			11	3	6000	2	5	15500	17600
25	11	DUSKY 26	OP	SF	FBG	SV	IB	T220-T350		11	3	7500	2	5	28200	34200
25	11	DUSKY 26	OP	SF	FBG	SV	IBT200D-T240D			11	3	7500	2	5	42400	49800
		1991 BOATS														
16	8	DUSKY 17	OP	OPFSH	FBG	SV	OB			7	4	1300		6	2600	3000
16	8	DUSKY 17	OP	OPFSH	FBG	SV	SE	115	OMC	7	4	1300		6	2600	3000
19	1	DUSKY 19	OP	OPFSH	FBG	SV	OB			7	10	1800	1		3450	4050
19	1	DUSKY 19	OP	OPFSH	FBG	SV	SE	115-140		7	10	1800	1		3450	4050
20	3	DUSKY 203	OP	OPFSH	FBG	SV	OB			8		2000	1		5700	6550
20	3	DUSKY 203	OP	OPFSH	FBG	SV	SE	140	OMC	8		2000	1		5700	6550
20	3	DUSKY 203	OP	OPFSH	FBG	SV	IB	185-220		8		2000	2	8	9250	10600
20	3	DUSKY 203	OP	OPFSH	FBG	SV	SE	225	OMC	8		2000	1		5700	6550
20	3	DUSKY 203	OP	OPFSH	FBG	SV	IB	270	CRUS	8		2000	2	8	9450	10700
20	3	DUSKY 203FAC	OP	FSH	FBG	SV	OB			8		2000	1		5700	6550
20	3	DUSKY 203FAC	OP	FSH	FBG	SV	SE	140-225		8		2000	1		5700	6550
23	3	DUSKY 233	OP	OPFSH	FBG	SV	OB			8		2700	1	1	6400	7350
23	3	DUSKY 233	OP	OPFSH	FBG	SV	SE	140	OMC	8		2700	1	1	6400	7350
23	3	DUSKY 233	OP	OPFSH	FBG	SV	IB	220	CRUS	8		2700	2	9	9550	10900
23	3	DUSKY 233	OP	OPFSH	FBG	SV	SE	225	OMC	8		2700	1	1	6400	7350
23	3	DUSKY 233	OP	OPFSH	FBG	SV	IB	270	CRUS	8		2700	2	9	9700	11000
23	3	DUSKY 233	OP	OPFSH	FBG	SV	SE	300	OMC	8		2700	1	1	6400	7350
23	3	DUSKY 233	OP	OPFSH	FBG	SV	IB	350	CRUS	8		2700	2	9	10300	11700
23	3	DUSKY 233	OP	OPFSH	FBG	SV	SE	T140	OMC	8		2700	1	1	6400	7350
23	3	DUSKY 233	OP	OPFSH	FBG	SV	IBT200D-T306D			8		2700	2	9	22500	27000
23	3	DUSKY 233CSS	OP	CUD	FBG	SV	OB			8		2700	1	1	6600	7550
23	3	DUSKY 233CSS	OP	CUD	FBG	SV	SE	140	OMC	8		2700	1	1	6400	7350
23	3	DUSKY 233CSS	OP	CUD	FBG	SV	IB	220	CRUS	8		2700	2	9	9700	11000
23	3	DUSKY 233CSS	OP	CUD	FBG	SV	SE	225	OMC	8		2700	1	1	6500	7450
23	3	DUSKY 233CSS	OP	CUD	FBG	SV	IB	270	CRUS	8		2700	2	9	9850	11200
23	3	DUSKY 233CSS	OP	CUD	FBG	SV	SE	300	OMC	8		2700	1	1	6500	7450
23	3	DUSKY 233CSS	OP	CUD	FBG	SV	IB	350	CRUS	8		2700	2	9	10400	11800
23	3	DUSKY 233CSS	OP	CUD	FBG	SV	SE	T140	OMC	8		2700	1	1	6450	7450
23	3	DUSKY 233CSS	OP	CUD	FBG	SV	IBT200D-T306D			8		2700	2	9	23000	27300
23	3	DUSKY 233FAC	OP	FSH	FBG	SV	OB			8		2700	1	1	6400	7350
23	3	DUSKY 233FAC	OP	FSH	FBG	SV	SE	140-300		8		2700	1	1	6400	7350
23	3	DUSKY 233FAC	OP	FSH	FBG	SV	SE	T140	OMC	8		2700	1	1	6400	7350
23	3	DUSKY 233FC	OP	CUD	FBG	SV	OB			8		2700	1	1	6200	7100
23	3	DUSKY 233FC	OP	CUD	FBG	SV	SE	140	OMC	8		2700	1	1	6400	7350
23	3	DUSKY 233FC	OP	CUD	FBG	SV	IB	220	CRUS	8		2700	2	9	9400	10700
23	3	DUSKY 233FC	OP	CUD	FBG	SV	SE	225	OMC	8		2700	1	1	6300	7200
23	3	DUSKY 233FC	OP	CUD	FBG	SV	IB	270	CRUS	8		2700	2	9	9550	10800
23	3	DUSKY 233FC	OP	CUD	FBG	SV	SE	300	OMC	8		2700	1	1	6300	7250
23	3	DUSKY 233FC	OP	CUD	FBG	SV	IB	350	CRUS	8		2700	2	9	10100	11500
23	3	DUSKY 233FC	OP	CUD	FBG	SV	SE	T140	OMC	8		2700	1	1	6300	7250
23	3	DUSKY 233FC	OP	CUD	FBG	SV	IBT200D-T306D			8		2700	2	9	22500	26700
25	6	DUSKY 256	OP	OPFSH	FBG	SV	OB			8		3000	1	1	8350	9600
25	6	DUSKY 256	OP	OPFSH	FBG	SV	SE	140	OMC	8		3000	1	1	8350	9600
25	6	DUSKY 256	OP	OPFSH	FBG	SV	IB	220	CRUS	8		3000	2	9	12100	13800
25	6	DUSKY 256	OP	OPFSH	FBG	SV	SE	225	OMC	8		3000	1	1	8350	9600
25	6	DUSKY 256	OP	OPFSH	FBG	SV	IB	270	CRUS	8		3000	2	9	12600	14300
25	6	DUSKY 256	OP	OPFSH	FBG	SV	SE	300	OMC	8		3000	1	1	8350	9600
25	6	DUSKY 256	OP	OPFSH	FBG	SV	IB	350	CRUS	8		3000	2	9	13600	15400
25	6	DUSKY 256	OP	OPFSH	FBG	SV	SE	T140	OMC	8		3000	1	1	8350	9600
25	6	DUSKY 256	OP	OPFSH	FBG	SV	IBT200D-T306D			8		3000	2	9	24200	29100
25	6	DUSKY 256CSS	OP	CUD	FBG	SV	OB			8		3000	1	1	8550	9800
25	6	DUSKY 256CSS	OP	CUD	FBG	SV	SE	140	OMC	8		3000	1	1	8350	9600
25	6	DUSKY 256CSS	OP	CUD	FBG	SV	IB	220	CRUS	8		3000	2	9	12400	14100
25	6	DUSKY 256CSS	OP	CUD	FBG	SV	SE	225	OMC	8		3000	1	1	8450	9700
25	6	DUSKY 256CSS	OP	CUD	FBG	SV	IB	270	CRUS	8		3000	2	9	12900	14700
25	6	DUSKY 256CSS	OP	CUD	FBG	SV	SE	300	OMC	8		3000	1	1	8450	9700
25	6	DUSKY 256CSS	OP	CUD	FBG	SV	IB	350	CRUS	8		3000	2	9	13900	15800
25	6	DUSKY 256CSS	OP	CUD	FBG	SV	SE	T140	OMC	8		3000	1	1	8250	9500
25	6	DUSKY 256CSS	OP	CUD	FBG	SV	IBT200D-T306D			8		3000	2	9	25100	29100
25	6	DUSKY 256FAC	OP	FSH	FBG	SV	OB			8		3000	1	1	8350	9600
25	6	DUSKY 256FAC	OP	FSH	FBG	SV	SE	140	OMC	8		3000	1	1	8350	9600
25	6	DUSKY 256FAC	OP	FSH	FBG	SV	IB	220	CRUS	8		3000	2	9	12300	14000
25	6	DUSKY 256FAC	OP	FSH	FBG	SV	SE	225	OMC	8		3000	1	1	8350	9600
25	6	DUSKY 256FAC	OP	FSH	FBG	SV	IB	270	CRUS	8		3000	2	9	12800	14500
25	6	DUSKY 256FAC	OP	FSH	FBG	SV	SE	300	OMC	8		3000	1	1	8350	9600
25	6	DUSKY 256FAC	OP	FSH	FBG	SV	IB	350	CRUS	8		3000	2	9	13800	15600
25	6	DUSKY 256FAC	OP	FSH	FBG	SV	SE	T140	OMC	8		3000	1	1	8350	9600
25	6	DUSKY 256FAC	OP	FSH	FBG	SV	IBT200D-T306D			8		3000	2	9	24600	28900
25	6	DUSKY 256FC	OP	CUD	FBG	SV	OB			8		3000	1	1	8150	9350
25	6	DUSKY 256FC	OP	CUD	FBG	SV	SE	140	OMC	8		3000	1	1	8350	9600
25	6	DUSKY 256FC	OP	CUD	FBG	SV	IB	220	CRUS	8		3000	2	9	12100	13800
25	6	DUSKY 256FC	OP	CUD	FBG	SV	SE	225	OMC	8		3000	1	1	8250	9450
25	6	DUSKY 256FC	OP	CUD	FBG	SV	IB	270	CRUS	8		3000	2	9	12600	14300
25	6	DUSKY 256FC	OP	CUD	FBG	SV	SE	300	OMC	8		3000	1	1	8250	9450
25	6	DUSKY 256FC	OP	CUD	FBG	SV	IB	350	CRUS	8		3000	2	9	13600	15400
25	6	DUSKY 256FC	OP	CUD	FBG	SV	SE	T140	OMC	8		3000	2	9	8400	9700
25	6	DUSKY 256FC	OP	CUD	FBG	SV	IBT200D-T306D			8		3000	2	9	24600	28600
25	11	DUSKY 26	OP	SF	FBG	SV	OB			11	3	6000	2	5	14900	16900
25	11	DUSKY 26	OP	SF	FBG	SV	IB	T220-T350		11	3	7500	2	5	26800	32500
25	11	DUSKY 26	OP	SF	FBG	SV	IBT200D-T240D			11	3	7500	2	5	40500	47500
		1990 BOATS														
16	8	DUSKY 17	OP	OPFSH	FBG	SV	OB			7	4	1300		6	2450	2850
16	8	DUSKY 17	OP	OPFSH	FBG	SV	SE	115	OMC	7	4	1300		6	2450	2850
19	1	DUSKY 19	OP	OPFSH	FBG	SV	OB			7	10	1800	1		3350	3850
19	1	DUSKY 19	OP	OPFSH	FBG	SV	SE	115-140		7	10	1800	1		3350	3850
20	3	DUSKY 203	OP	OPFSH	FBG	SV	OB			8		2000	1		5450	6300
20	3	DUSKY 203	OP	OPFSH	FBG	SV	SE	140	OMC	8		2000	1		5450	6300
20	3	DUSKY 203	OP	OPFSH	FBG	SV	IB	185-220		8		2000	2	8	8700	10100
20	3	DUSKY 203	OP	OPFSH	FBG	SV	SE	225	OMC	8		2000	1		5450	6300
20	3	DUSKY 203	OP	OPFSH	FBG	SV	IB	270	CRUS	8		2000	2	8	9000	10200
20	3	DUSKY 203FAC	OP	FSH	FBG	SV	OB			8		2400	1		6100	7000
20	3	DUSKY 203FAC	OP	FSH	FBG	SV	SE	140-225		8		2400	1		6100	7000
23	3	DUSKY 233	OP	OPFSH	FBG	SV	OB			8		2700	1	1	6150	7050
23	3	DUSKY 233	OP	OPFSH	FBG	SV	SE	140	OMC	8		2700	1	1	6150	7050
23	3	DUSKY 233	OP	OPFSH	FBG	SV	IB	220	CRUS	8		2700	2	9	9150	10400
23	3	DUSKY 233	OP	OPFSH	FBG	SV	SE	225	OMC	8		2700	1	1	6150	7050
23	3	DUSKY 233	OP	OPFSH	FBG	SV	IB	270	CRUS	8		2700	2	9	9250	10500
23	3	DUSKY 233	OP	OPFSH	FBG	SV	SE	300	OMC	8		2700	1	1	6150	7050
23	3	DUSKY 233	OP	OPFSH	FBG	SV	IB	350	CRUS	8		2700	2	9	9750	11100
23	3	DUSKY 233	OP	OPFSH	FBG	SV	SE	T140	OMC	8		2700	1	1	6150	7050
23	3	DUSKY 233	OP	OPFSH	FBG	SV	IBT200D-T306D			8		2700	2	9	21500	25800
23	3	DUSKY 233CSS	OP	CUD	FBG	SV	OB			8		3000	1	1	6650	7650
23	3	DUSKY 233CSS	OP	CUD	FBG	SV	SE	140	OMC	8		3000	1	1	6800	7800
23	3	DUSKY 233CSS	OP	CUD	FBG	SV	IB	220	CRUS	8		3000	2	9	9800	11100
23	3	DUSKY 233CSS	OP	CUD	FBG	SV	SE	225	OMC	8		3000	1	1	6800	7800
23	3	DUSKY 233CSS	OP	CUD	FBG	SV	IB	270	CRUS	8		3000	2	9	9900	11300
23	3	DUSKY 233CSS	OP	CUD	FBG	SV	SE	300	OMC	8		3000	1	1	6750	7800
23	3	DUSKY 233CSS	OP	CUD	FBG	SV	IB	350	CRUS	8		3000	2	9	10500	11900
23	3	DUSKY 233CSS	OP	CUD	FBG	SV	SE	T140	OMC	8		3000	1	1	6750	7750
23	3	DUSKY 233CSS	OP	CUD	FBG	SV	IBT200D-T306D			8		3000	2	9	22600	26800
23	3	DUSKY 233FAC	OP	FSH	FBG	SV	OB			8		3000	1	1	6650	7650
23	3	DUSKY 233FAC	OP	FSH	FBG	SV	SE	140-300		8		3000	1	1	6650	7650
23	3	DUSKY 233FAC	OP	FSH	FBG	SV	SE	T140	OMC	8		3000	1	1	6650	7650
23	3	DUSKY 233FC	OP	CUD	FBG	SV	OB			8		3000	1	1	6650	7650
23	3	DUSKY 233FC	OP	CUD	FBG	SV	SE	140	OMC	8		3000	1	1	6550	7550
23	3	DUSKY 233FC	OP	CUD	FBG	SV	IB	220	CRUS	8		3000	2	9	9500	10800
23	3	DUSKY 233FC	OP	CUD	FBG	SV	SE	225	OMC	8		3000	1	1	6550	7550
23	3	DUSKY 233FC	OP	CUD	FBG	SV	IB	270	CRUS	8		3000	2	9	9600	10900
23	3	DUSKY 233FC	OP	CUD	FBG	SV	SE	300	OMC	8		3000	1	1	6550	7550
23	3	DUSKY 233FC	OP	CUD	FBG	SV	IB	350	CRUS	8		3000	2	9	10200	11500
23	3	DUSKY 233FC	OP	CUD	FBG	SV	SE	T140	OMC	8		3000	1	1	6600	7550
23	3	DUSKY 233FC	OP	CUD	FBG	SV	IBT200D-T306D			8		3000	2	9	22100	26100
25	6	DUSKY 256	OP	OPFSH	FBG	SV	OB			8		3000	1	1	8050	9250
25	6	DUSKY 256	OP	OPFSH	FBG	SV	SE	140	OMC	8		3000	1	1	8050	9250
25	6	DUSKY 256	OP	OPFSH	FBG	SV	IB	220	CRUS	8		3000	2	9	11500	13100
25	6	DUSKY 256	OP	OPFSH	FBG	SV	SE	225	OMC	8		3000	1	1	8050	9250
25	6	DUSKY 256	OP	OPFSH	FBG	SV	IB	270	CRUS	8		3000	2	9	12000	13600
25	6	DUSKY 256	OP	OPFSH	FBG	SV	SE	300	OMC	8		3000	1	1	8050	9250
25	6	DUSKY 256	OP	OPFSH	FBG	SV	IB	350	CRUS	8		3000	2	9	12900	14700
25	6	DUSKY 256	OP	OPFSH	FBG	SV	SE	T140	OMC	8		3000	1	1	8050	9250
25	6	DUSKY 256	OP	OPFSH	FBG	SV	IBT200D-T306D			8		3000	2	9	23100	27800
25	6	DUSKY 256CSS	OP	CUD	FBG	SV	OB			8		3300	1	1	8550	9800

CONTINUED ON NEXT PAGE

LOA FT	LOA IN	NAME AND/ OR MODEL	TOP/ RIG	BOAT TYPE	-HULL- MTL	-HULL- TP	ENGINE TP	ENGINE # HP	ENGINE MFG	BEAM FT	BEAM IN	WGT LBS	DRAFT FT	DRAFT IN	RETAIL LOW	RETAIL HIGH
		1990 BOATS														
25	6	DUSKY 256CSS	OP	CUD	FBG	SV	SE	140	OMC	8		3300	1	1	8450	9750
25	6	DUSKY 256CSS	OP	CUD	FBG	SV	IB	220	CRUS	8		3300	2	9	12300	14000
25	6	DUSKY 256CSS	OP	CUD	FBG	SV	SE	225	OMC	8		3300	1	1	8450	9750
25	6	DUSKY 256CSS	OP	CUD	FBG	SV	IB	270	CRUS	8		3300	2	9	12800	14500
25	6	DUSKY 256CSS	OP	CUD	FBG	SV	SE	300	OMC	8		3300	1	1	8450	9700
25	6	DUSKY 256CSS	OP	CUD	FBG	SV	IB	350	CRUS	8		3300	2	9	13700	15500
25	6	DUSKY 256CSS	OP	CUD	FBG	SV	SE	T140	OMC	8		3300	1	1	8450	9700
25	6	DUSKY 256CSS	OP	CUD	FBG	SV	IB	T200D-T306D		8		3300	2	9	24700	28900
25	6	DUSKY 256FAC	OP	FSH	FBG	SV	OB			8		3300	1	1	8350	9600
25	6	DUSKY 256FAC	OP	FSH	FBG	SV	SE	140	OMC	8		3300	1	1	8350	9600
25	6	DUSKY 256FAC	OP	FSH	FBG	SV	IB	220	CRUS	8		3300	2	9	12200	13800
25	6	DUSKY 256FAC	OP	FSH	FBG	SV	SE	225	OMC	8		3300	1	1	8350	9600
25	6	DUSKY 256FAC	OP	FSH	FBG	SV	IB	270	CRUS	8		3300	2	9	12600	14300
25	6	DUSKY 256FAC	OP	FSH	FBG	SV	SE	300	OMC	8		3300	1	1	8350	9600
25	6	DUSKY 256FAC	OP	FSH	FBG	SV	IB	350	CRUS	8		3300	2	9	13500	15400
25	6	DUSKY 256FAC	OP	FSH	FBG	SV	SE	T140	OMC	8		3300	1	1	8350	9600
25	6	DUSKY 256FAC	OP	FSH	FBG	SV	IB	T200D-T306D		8		3300	2	9	24200	28600
25	6	DUSKY 256FC	OP	CUD	FBG	SV	OB			8		3300	1	1	8150	9400
25	6	DUSKY 256FC	OP	CUD	FBG	SV	SE	140	OMC	8		3300	1	1	8250	9450
25	6	DUSKY 256FC	OP	CUD	FBG	SV	IB	220	CRUS	8		3300	2	9	12000	13600
25	6	DUSKY 256FC	OP	CUD	FBG	SV	SE	225	OMC	8		3300	1	1	8250	9500
25	6	DUSKY 256FC	OP	CUD	FBG	SV	IB	270	CRUS	8		3300	2	9	12400	14100
25	6	DUSKY 256FC	OP	CUD	FBG	SV	SE	300	OMC	8		3300	1	1	8250	9500
25	6	DUSKY 256FC	OP	CUD	FBG	SV	IB	350	CRUS	8		3300	2	9	13400	15200
25	6	DUSKY 256FC	OP	CUD	FBG	SV	SE	T140	OMC	8		3300	2	9	8250	9500
25	6	DUSKY 256FC	OP	CUD	FBG	SV	IB	T200D-T306D		8		3300	2	9	24300	28300
25	11	DUSKY 26	OP	SF	FBG	SV	OB			11	3	6000	1		14300	16300
25	11	DUSKY 26	OP	SF	FBG	SV	IB	T220-T350		11	3	7500	2	5	25500	30900
25	11	DUSKY 26	OP	SF	FBG	SV	IB	T200D-T240D		11	3	7500	2	5	38700	45400
		1989 BOATS														
16	8	DUSKY 17	OP	OPFSH	FBG	SV	OB			7	4	1300			2350	2750
16	8	DUSKY 17	OP	OPFSH	FBG	SV	SE	115	OMC	7	4	1300			2350	2750
19	1	DUSKY 19	OP	OPFSH	FBG	SV	OB			7	10	1800			3200	3700
19	1	DUSKY 19	OP	OPFSH	FBG	SV	SE	115-140		7	10	1800			3200	3700
20	3	DUSKY 203	OP	OPFSH	FBG	SV	OB			8		2000			5300	6100
20	3	DUSKY 203	OP	OPFSH	FBG	SV	SE	140	OMC	8		2000			5300	6100
20	3	DUSKY 203	OP	OPFSH	FBG	SV	IB	185-220		8		2000			8250	9600
20	3	DUSKY 203	OP	OPFSH	FBG	SV	SE	225	OMC	8		2000			5300	6100
20	3	DUSKY 203	OP	OPFSH	FBG	SV	IB	270	CRUS	8		2000			8500	9750
20	3	DUSKY 203	OP	OPFSH	FBG	SV	SE	T140	OMC	8		2000			5300	6100
20	3	DUSKY 203FAC	OP	FSH	FBG	SV	OB			8		2400			5900	6800
20	3	DUSKY 203FAC	OP	FSH	FBG	SV	SE	140-225		8		2400			5900	6800
20	3	DUSKY 203FAC	OP	FSH	FBG	SV	SE	T140	OMC	8		2400			5900	6800
23	3	DUSKY 233	OP	OPFSH	FBG	SV	OB			8		2700			5950	6850
23	3	DUSKY 233	OP	OPFSH	FBG	SV	SE	140	OMC	8		2700			5950	6850
23	3	DUSKY 233	OP	OPFSH	FBG	SV	IB	220	CRUS	8		2700			8600	9900
23	3	DUSKY 233	OP	OPFSH	FBG	SV	SE	225	OMC	8		2700			5950	6850
23	3	DUSKY 233	OP	OPFSH	FBG	SV	IB	270	CRUS	8		2700			8800	10000
23	3	DUSKY 233	OP	OPFSH	FBG	SV	SE	275	OMC	8		2700			5950	6850
23	3	DUSKY 233	OP	OPFSH	FBG	SV	IB	350	CRUS	8		2700			9350	10600
23	3	DUSKY 233	OP	OPFSH	FBG	SV	SE	T140	OMC	8		2700			5950	6850
23	3	DUSKY 233	OP	OPFSH	FBG	SV	IB	T200D-T306D		8		2700			20500	24700
23	3	DUSKY 233CSS	OP	CUD	FBG	SV	OB			8		2800			6100	7050
23	3	DUSKY 233CSS	OP	CUD	FBG	SV	SE	140	OMC	8		2800			6100	7050
23	3	DUSKY 233CSS	OP	CUD	FBG	SV	IB	220	CRUS	8		2800			8900	10100
23	3	DUSKY 233CSS	OP	CUD	FBG	SV	SE	225	OMC	8		2800			6100	7050
23	3	DUSKY 233CSS	OP	CUD	FBG	SV	IB	270	CRUS	8		2800			9000	10200
23	3	DUSKY 233CSS	OP	CUD	FBG	SV	SE	275	OMC	8		2800			6100	7050
23	3	DUSKY 233CSS	OP	CUD	FBG	SV	IB	350	CRUS	8		2800			9450	10700
23	3	DUSKY 233CSS	OP	CUD	FBG	SV	SE	T140	OMC	8		2800			6100	7050
23	3	DUSKY 233CSS	OP	CUD	FBG	SV	IB	T200D-T306D		8		2800			20700	24900
23	3	DUSKY 233FAC	OP	FSH	FBG	SV	OB			8		2700			5950	6850
23	3	DUSKY 233FAC	OP	FSH	FBG	SV	SE	140-275		8		2700			5950	6850
23	3	DUSKY 233FAC	OP	FSH	FBG	SV	SE	T140	OMC	8		2700			5950	6850
23	3	DUSKY 233FC	OP	CUD	FBG	SV	OB			8					7200	8250
23	3	DUSKY 233FC	OP	CUD	FBG	SV	SE	140	OMC	8		2700			5950	6850
23	3	DUSKY 233FC	OP	CUD	FBG	SV	IB	220	CRUS	8		2700			8600	9900
23	3	DUSKY 233FC	OP	CUD	FBG	SV	SE	225	OMC	8		2700			5950	6850
23	3	DUSKY 233FC	OP	CUD	FBG	SV	IB	270	CRUS	8		2700			8800	10000
23	3	DUSKY 233FC	OP	CUD	FBG	SV	SE	275	OMC	8		2700			5950	6850
23	3	DUSKY 233FC	OP	CUD	FBG	SV	IB	350	CRUS	8		2700			9350	10600
23	3	DUSKY 233FC	OP	CUD	FBG	SV	SE	T140	OMC	8		2700			5950	6850
23	3	DUSKY 233FC	OP	CUD	FBG	SV	IB	T200D	VLVO	8		2700			17300	19600
23	3	DUSKY 233FC	OP	CUD	FBG	SV	IB	T220D-T306D		8		2700			21300	24700
25	6	DUSKY 256	OP	OPFSH	FBG	SV	OB			8		3000			7750	8900
25	6	DUSKY 256	OP	OPFSH	FBG	SV	SE	140	OMC	8		3000			7750	8900
25	6	DUSKY 256	OP	OPFSH	FBG	SV	IB	220	CRUS	8		3000			11000	12500
25	6	DUSKY 256	OP	OPFSH	FBG	SV	SE	225	OMC	8		3000			7750	8900
25	6	DUSKY 256	OP	OPFSH	FBG	SV	IB	270	CRUS	8		3000			11400	13000
25	6	DUSKY 256	OP	OPFSH	FBG	SV	SE	275	OMC	8		3000			7750	8900
25	6	DUSKY 256	OP	OPFSH	FBG	SV	IB	350	CRUS	8		3000			12300	14000
25	6	DUSKY 256	OP	OPFSH	FBG	SV	SE	T140	OMC	8		3000			7750	8900
25	6	DUSKY 256	OP	OPFSH	FBG	SV	IB	T200D-T306D		8		3000			22100	26600
25	6	DUSKY 256CSS	OP	CUD	FBG	SV	OB			8		3300			8050	9300
25	6	DUSKY 256CSS	OP	CUD	FBG	SV	SE	140	OMC	8		3300			8050	9300
25	6	DUSKY 256CSS	OP	CUD	FBG	SV	IB	220	CRUS	8		3300			11600	13100
25	6	DUSKY 256CSS	OP	CUD	FBG	SV	SE	225	OMC	8		3300			8050	9300
25	6	DUSKY 256CSS	OP	CUD	FBG	SV	IB	270	CRUS	8		3300			12000	13600
25	6	DUSKY 256CSS	OP	CUD	FBG	SV	SE	275	OMC	8		3300			8050	9300
25	6	DUSKY 256CSS	OP	CUD	FBG	SV	IB	350	CRUS	8		3300			12900	14600
25	6	DUSKY 256CSS	OP	CUD	FBG	SV	SE	T140	OMC	8		3300			8050	9300
25	6	DUSKY 256CSS	OP	CUD	FBG	SV	IB	T200D-T306D		8		3300			23200	27400
25	6	DUSKY 256FAC	OP	FSH	FBG	SV	OB			8		3200			7950	9150
25	6	DUSKY 256FAC	OP	FSH	FBG	SV	SE	140	OMC	8		3200			7950	9150
25	6	DUSKY 256FAC	OP	FSH	FBG	SV	IB	220	CRUS	8		3200			11400	13000
25	6	DUSKY 256FAC	OP	FSH	FBG	SV	SE	225	OMC	8		3200			7950	9150
25	6	DUSKY 256FAC	OP	FSH	FBG	SV	IB	270	CRUS	8		3200			11800	13500
25	6	DUSKY 256FAC	OP	FSH	FBG	SV	SE	275	OMC	8		3200			7950	9150
25	6	DUSKY 256FAC	OP	FSH	FBG	SV	IB	350	CRUS	8		3200			12700	14500
25	6	DUSKY 256FAC	OP	FSH	FBG	SV	SE	T140	OMC	8		3200			7950	9150
25	6	DUSKY 256FAC	OP	FSH	FBG	SV	IB	T200D-T306D		8		3200			23000	27100
25	6	DUSKY 256FC	OP	CUD	FBG	SV	OB			8		3200			7950	9150
25	6	DUSKY 256FC	OP	CUD	FBG	SV	SE	140	OMC	8		3200			7950	9150
25	6	DUSKY 256FC	OP	CUD	FBG	SV	IB	220	CRUS	8		3200			11400	13000
25	6	DUSKY 256FC	OP	CUD	FBG	SV	SE	225	OMC	8		3200			7950	9150
25	6	DUSKY 256FC	OP	CUD	FBG	SV	IB	270	CRUS	8		3200			11800	13500
25	6	DUSKY 256FC	OP	CUD	FBG	SV	SE	275	OMC	8		3200			7950	9150
25	6	DUSKY 256FC	OP	CUD	FBG	SV	IB	350	CRUS	8		3200			12700	14500
25	6	DUSKY 256FC	OP	CUD	FBG	SV	SE	T140	OMC	8		3200			7950	9150
25	6	DUSKY 256FC	OP	CUD	FBG	SV	IB	T200D-T306D		8		3200			23000	27000
25	11	DUSKY 26	OP	SF	FBG	SV	OB			11	3	6000			13900	15700
25	11	DUSKY 26	OP	SF	FBG	SV	IB	T220-T350		11	3	7500			24300	29400
25	11	DUSKY 26	OP	SF	FBG	SV	IB	T200D-T240D		11	3	7500			37000	43400
		1988 BOATS														
16	6	DUSKY 17	OP	OPFSH	FBG	SV	OB			7	3	1200			2100	2450
16	6	DUSKY 17	OP	OPFSH	FBG	SV	SE	115	OMC	7	3	1200			2100	2450
19	1	DUSKY 19	OP	OPFSH	FBG	SV	OB			7	10	1800			3050	3550
19	1	DUSKY 19	OP	OPFSH	FBG	SV	SE	115-140		7	10	1800			3050	3550
20	3	DUSKY 203	OP	OPFSH	FBG	SV	OB			8		2000			5150	5900
20	3	DUSKY 203	OP	OPFSH	FBG	SV	SE	140	OMC	8		2000			5150	5900
20	3	DUSKY 203	OP	OPFSH	FBG	SV	IB	185-220		8		2000			7850	9150
20	3	DUSKY 203	OP	OPFSH	FBG	SV	SE	225	OMC	8		2000			5150	5900
20	3	DUSKY 203	OP	OPFSH	FBG	SV	IB	270	CRUS	8		2000			8100	9300
20	3	DUSKY 203	OP	OPFSH	FBG	SV	SE	T140	OMC	8		2000			5150	5900
20	3	DUSKY 203FAC	OP	FSH	FBG	SV	OB			8		2400			5700	6600
20	3	DUSKY 203FAC	OP	FSH	FBG	SV	SE	140-225		8		2400			5700	6600
20	3	DUSKY 203FAC	OP	FSH	FBG	SV	SE	T140	OMC	8		2400			5700	6600
23	3	DUSKY 233	OP	OPFSH	FBG	SV	OB			8		2700			5750	6650
23	3	DUSKY 233	OP	OPFSH	FBG	SV	SE	140	OMC	8		2700			5750	6650
23	3	DUSKY 233	OP	OPFSH	FBG	SV	IB	220	CRUS	8		2700			8200	9450
23	3	DUSKY 233	OP	OPFSH	FBG	SV	SE	225	OMC	8		2700			5750	6650
23	3	DUSKY 233	OP	OPFSH	FBG	SV	IB	270	CRUS	8		2700			8300	9550
23	3	DUSKY 233	OP	OPFSH	FBG	SV	SE	275	OMC	8		2700			5750	6650
23	3	DUSKY 233	OP	OPFSH	FBG	SV	IB	350	CRUS	8		2700			8900	10100
23	3	DUSKY 233	OP	OPFSH	FBG	SV	SE	T140	OMC	8		2700			5750	6650
23	3	DUSKY 233	OP	OPFSH	FBG	SV	IB	T200D-T306D		8		2700			19700	23600
23	3	DUSKY 233CSS	OP	CUD	FBG	SV	OB			8		2800			5950	6800
23	3	DUSKY 233CSS	OP	CUD	FBG	SV	SE	140	OMC	8		2800			5950	6800
23	3	DUSKY 233CSS	OP	CUD	FBG	SV	IB	220	CRUS	8		2800			8350	9600
23	3	DUSKY 233CSS	OP	CUD	FBG	SV	SE	225	OMC	8		2800			5950	6800
23	3	DUSKY 233CSS	OP	CUD	FBG	SV	IB	270	CRUS	8		2800			8450	9750
23	3	DUSKY 233CSS	OP	CUD	FBG	SV	SE	275	OMC	8		2800			5950	6800
23	3	DUSKY 233CSS	OP	CUD	FBG	SV	IB	350	CRUS	8		2800			9050	10300
23	3	DUSKY 233CSS	OP	CUD	FBG	SV	SE	T140	OMC	8		2800			5950	6800
23	3	DUSKY 233CSS	OP	CUD	FBG	SV	IB	T200D-T306D		8		2800			19800	23800

 CONTINUED ON NEXT PAGE

```
     LOA  NAME AND/       TOP/ BOAT -HULL- ----ENGINE--- BEAM  WGT  DRAFT RETAIL RETAIL
     FT IN OR MODEL        RIG TYPE MTL TP TP # HP  MFG   FT IN LBS  FT IN  LOW   HIGH
--------------------------- 1988 BOATS ----------------------------------------------
23  3 DUSKY 233FAC   OP FSH   FBG SV OB            8       2700          5750  6650
23  3 DUSKY 233FAC   OP FSH   FBG SV SE 140-275    8       2700          5750  6650
23  3 DUSKY 233FAC   OP FSH   FBG SV SE T140 OMC   8       2700          5750  6650
23  3 DUSKY 233FC    OP CUD   FBG SV OB            8            12 1     6950  8000
23  3 DUSKY 233FC    OP CUD   FBG SV SE 140  OMC   8       2700          5750  6650
23  3 DUSKY 233FC    OP CUD   FBG SV IB 220  CRUS  8       2700          8200  9450
23  3 DUSKY 233FC    OP CUD   FBG SV SE 225  OMC   8       2700          5750  6650
23  3 DUSKY 233FC    OP CUD   FBG SV IB 270  CRUS  8       2700          8300  9550
23  3 DUSKY 233FC    OP CUD   FBG SV SE 275  OMC   8       2700          5750  6650
23  3 DUSKY 233FC    OP CUD   FBG SV IB 350  CRUS  8       2700          8900 10100
23  3 DUSKY 233FC    OP CUD   FBG SV SE T140 OMC   8       2700          5750  6650

23  3 DUSKY 233FC    OP CUD   FBG SV IB T200D VLVO 8       2700         16500 18800
23  3 DUSKY 233FC    OP CUD   FBG SV IBT220D-T306D 8       2700         20400 23600
25  6 DUSKY 256      OP OPFSH FBG SV OB            8       3000          7550  8650
25  6 DUSKY 256      OP OPFSH FBG SV SE 140  OMC   8       3000          7550  8650
25  6 DUSKY 256      OP OPFSH FBG SV IB 220  CRUS  8       3000         10500 11900
25  6 DUSKY 256      OP OPFSH FBG SV SE 225  OMC   8       3000          7550  8650
25  6 DUSKY 256      OP OPFSH FBG SV IB 270  CRUS  8       3000         10900 12400
25  6 DUSKY 256      OP OPFSH FBG SV SE 275  OMC   8       3000          7550  8650
25  6 DUSKY 256      OP OPFSH FBG SV IB 350  CRUS  8       3000         11700 13300
25  6 DUSKY 256      OP OPFSH FBG SV SE T140 OMC   8       3000          7550  8650
25  6 DUSKY 256      OP OPFSH FBG SV IBT200D-T306D 8       3000         21100 25500

25  6 DUSKY 256CSS   OP CUD   FBG SV OB            8       3300          7850  9000
25  6 DUSKY 256CSS   OP CUD   FBG SV SE 140  OMC   8       3300          7850  9000
25  6 DUSKY 256CSS   OP CUD   FBG SV IB 220  CRUS  8       3300         11000 12500
25  6 DUSKY 256CSS   OP CUD   FBG SV SE 225  OMC   8       3300          7850  9000
25  6 DUSKY 256CSS   OP CUD   FBG SV IB 270  CRUS  8       3300         11400 13000
25  6 DUSKY 256CSS   OP CUD   FBG SV SE 275  OMC   8       3300          7850  9000
25  6 DUSKY 256CSS   OP CUD   FBG SV IB 350  CRUS  8       3300         12300 13900
25  6 DUSKY 256CSS   OP CUD   FBG SV SE T140 OMC   8       3300          7850  9000
25  6 DUSKY 256CSS   OP CUD   FBG SV IBT200D-T306D 8       3300         22200 26200
25  6 DUSKY 256FAC   OP FSH   FBG SV OB            8       3200          7750  8900
25  6 DUSKY 256FAC   OP FSH   FBG SV SE 140  OMC   8       3200          7750  8900
25  6 DUSKY 256FAC   OP FSH   FBG SV IB 220  CRUS  8       3200         10900 12400

25  6 DUSKY 256FAC   OP FSH   FBG SV SE 225  OMC   8       3200          7750  8900
25  6 DUSKY 256FAC   OP FSH   FBG SV IB 270  CRUS  8       3200         11300 12800
25  6 DUSKY 256FAC   OP FSH   FBG SV SE 275  OMC   8       3200          7750  8900
25  6 DUSKY 256FAC   OP FSH   FBG SV IB 350  CRUS  8       3200         12100 13800
25  6 DUSKY 256FAC   OP FSH   FBG SV SE T140 OMC   8       3200          7750  8900
25  6 DUSKY 256FAC   OP FSH   FBG SV IBT200D-T306D 8       3200         22000 25900
25  6 DUSKY 256FC    OP CUD   FBG SV OB            8       3200          7750  8900
25  6 DUSKY 256FC    OP CUD   FBG SV SE 140  OMC   8       3200          7750  8900
25  6 DUSKY 256FC    OP CUD   FBG SV IB 220  CRUS  8       3200         10900 12400
25  6 DUSKY 256FC    OP CUD   FBG SV SE 225  OMC   8       3200          7750  8900
25  6 DUSKY 256FC    OP CUD   FBG SV IB 270  CRUS  8       3200         11300 12800
25  6 DUSKY 256FC    OP CUD   FBG SV SE 275  OMC   8       3200          7750  8900

25  6 DUSKY 256FC    OP CUD   FBG SV IB 350  CRUS  8       3200         12100 13800
25  6 DUSKY 256FC    OP CUD   FBG SV SE T140 OMC   8       3200          7750  8900
25  6 DUSKY 256FC    OP CUD   FBG SV IBT200D-T306D 8       3200         22000 25900
25 11 DUSKY 26       OP SF    FBG SV OB           11 3     6000         13400 15300
25 11 DUSKY 26       OP SF    FBG SV IB T220-T350 11 3     7500         23100 28000
25 11 DUSKY 26       OP SF    FBG SV IBT200D-T240D 11 3    7500         35400 41500
--------------------------- 1986 BOATS ----------------------------------------------
16  6 DUSKY 17       OP OPFSH FBG SV OB            7 3     1200     6   1950  2350
20  3 DUSKY 203      OP OPFSH FBG DV OB            8       2000 1   6   4850  5600
20  3 DUSKY 203      OP OPFSH FBG DV IO 175        8       2700 1   1   6700  7700
20  3 DUSKY 203      OP OPFSH FBG DV IB 220        8       2900 1   1   8400  9650
23  3 DUSKY 233      OP CUD   FBG DV IO 205        8       3500 2   8   6800  7800
23  3 DUSKY 233      OP OPFSH FBG DV OB            8       2700 1   2   5450  6300
23  3 DUSKY 233      OP OPFSH FBG DV IO 175        8       3400 2   8   7000  8000
23  3 DUSKY 233      OP OPFSH FBG DV IB 220        8       3600 2   8   8850 10100
23  3 DUSKY 233 CSS  OP CUD   FBG DV OB            8       2800 1   2   5600  6450
23  3 DUSKY 233 FAC  OP CUD   FBG DV OB            8       2700 1   2   5450  6300
23  3 DUSKY 233FC    OP CTRCN FBG DV OB            8       2700 1   2   5450  6300
25  6 DUSKY 256      OP OPFSH FBG DV OB            8       3000 1   2   7150  8200

25  6 DUSKY 256      OP OPFSH FBG DV IO 230        8       3700 2   9   8800 10000
25  6 DUSKY 256      OP OPFSH FBG DV IB 270        8       4000 2   9  11200 12700
25  6 DUSKY 256 CC   OP CUD   FBG DV OB            8       3300          7200  8300
25  6 DUSKY 256 CSS  OP CUD   FBG DV OB            8       3300          7650  8750
25  6 DUSKY 256 CSS  OP CUD   FBG DV IO 230        8       4000 2   9   8900 10100
25  6 DUSKY 256 FAC  OP CR    FBG DV OB            8       3200          7300  8400
25  6 DUSKY 256CC    OP CUD   FBG DV IO 230        8       4000 2   9   8550  9800
25  6 DUSKY 256FC    OP CUD   FBG SV OB            8            1   2   7950  9150
25 11 DUSKY 26       OP SF    FBG SV OB           11 3     6000 2   9  12700 14500
25 11 DUSKY 26       OP SF    FBG IB T           11 3     7500 2   9    **    **
--------------------------- 1985 BOATS ----------------------------------------------
16  6 DUSKY 17       OP OPFSH FBG SV OB            7 3     1200     6   1900  2250
19  3 DUSKY 19       OP OPFSH FBG SV OB            7 10    1800          2750  3200
20  3 DUSKY 203      OP OPFSH FBG DV OB            8                     5000  5750
20  3 DUSKY 203      OP OPFSH FBG DV OB            8                     6700  7700
23  3 DUSKY 233      OP OPFSH FBG DV IO 220        8       2700 1   2   5350  6150
23  3 DUSKY 233      OP OPFSH FBG DV IO 170        8       3500 2   8   6850  7850
23  3 DUSKY 233      OP OPFSH FBG DV IB 220        8       3500 2   8   8200  9450
23  3 DUSKY 233CSS   OP CUD   FBG DV OB            8       2800 1   2   5500  6300
23  3 DUSKY 233CSS   OP CUD   FBG DV IO 200        8       3500 2   8   6500  7500
23  3 DUSKY 233CSS   OP CUD   FBG DV IB 220        8       3500 2   8   8200  9450
23  3 DUSKY 233FAC   OP CR    FBG DV OB            8       2700 1   2   5350  6150
23  3 DUSKY 233FC    OP CTRCN FBG DV OB            8       2700 1   2   5350  6150

23  3 DUSKY 233FC    OP CTRCN FBG DV IB 220        8       3500 2   8   8200  9450
25  6 DUSKY 256      OP CTRCN FBG DV IO 230        8       3000 1   2   6950  8200
25  6 DUSKY 256      OP OPFSH FBG DV OB            8       4700          9700 11000
25  6 DUSKY 256      OP OPFSH FBG DV IB 270        8       4700 2   9  11800 13400
25  6 DUSKY 256CC    OP CUD   FBG DV OB            8       3300 1   2   8600  9900
25  6 DUSKY 256CC    OP CUD   FBG DV IO 230        8                     8600  9900
25  6 DUSKY 256CC    OP CUD   FBG DV IB 270        8                    11000 12500
25  6 DUSKY 256CSS   OP CUD   FBG DV IB 270        8       3300 1   2   7450  8600
25  6 DUSKY 256FAC   OP CR    FBG DV IB 270        8       3200 1   2   7150  8200
25  6 DUSKY 256FAC   OP CR    FBG DV OB            8                    10900 12400

25  6 DUSKY 256FC    OP OPFSH FBG DV IB 270        8       3100 1   2   9400 10700
25 11 DUSKY 26       OP SF    FBG SV IB T220      11 3     7500 2   9  19900 22100
--------------------------- 1984 BOATS ----------------------------------------------
16  6 DUSKY 17       OP OPFSH FBG SV OB            7 3     1200     6   1850  2150
20  3 DUSKY 20       OP OPFSH FBG SV OB            8       2000 1   6   4700  5400
20  3 DUSKY 20       OP OPFSH FBG DV SE 115 OMC    8       3000 1   1   5650  6500
20  3 DUSKY 20       OP OPFSH FBG DV IO 170-200    8       3000 1   1   6550  7600
          IB 220-225  8000  9200, IO 230 OMC  6700  7750, IB 255-270  7900  9350
          IB 158D VLVO 11400 12900, IO 165D VLVO 10500 11900, IB 165D PERK 12800 14600

20  3 DUSKY 20       OP OPFSH FBG DV SE T115 OMC   8       3000 1   1   5650  6500
23  3 DUSKY 233      OP OPFSH FBG DV SE 170-200    8       2800 1   2   5400  6200
23  3 DUSKY 233      OP OPFSH FBG DV IB 205 OMC    8       3500 2   8   6550  7600
23  3 DUSKY 233      OP OPFSH FBG DV IB 220-225    8       3500 2   8   6300  7250
23  3 DUSKY 233      OP OPFSH FBG DV IB            8       3500 2   8   6850  9150
          IO 230 OMC   6700  7700, IB 255 COMM  7900 9050, IO 260 OMC  6850  7850
          IB 270-350   8050  9750, IB 158D VLVO 10900 12400, IO 165D VLVO 10000 11400

23  3 DUSKY 233      OP OPFSH FBG DV SE T115 OMC   8       3500 2   8   6300  7250
23  3 DUSKY 233CSS   OP CUD   FBG DV OB            8       2800 1   2   5000  5750
23  3 DUSKY 233CSS   OP CUD   FBG DV IO 170-200    8       3500 2   8   6000  6950
23  3 DUSKY 233CSS   OP CUD   FBG DV IB 205 OMC    8       3500 2   8   6100  6900
23  3 DUSKY 233CSS   OP CUD   FBG DV IB 220-225    8       3500 2   8   8000  9150
          IO 230 OMC   6100  7000, IB 255 COMM  7900 9050, IO 260 OMC  6250  7200
          IB 270-350   8050  9750, IB 158D VLVO 10900 12400, IO 165D VLVO 7750  8900

23  3 DUSKY 233CSS   OP CUD   FBG DV SE T115 OMC   8       3500 2   8   6150  7050
23  3 DUSKY 233FAC   OP CUD   FBG DV OB            8       2800 1   2   5750  6600
23  3 DUSKY 233FAC   OP CUD   FBG DV IO 170-200    8       3500 2   8   6450  7450
23  3 DUSKY 233FAC   OP CUD   FBG DV IB 205 OMC    8       3500 2   8   6500  7500
23  3 DUSKY 233FAC   OP CUD   FBG DV IB 230-260    8       3500 2   8   6550  7700
23  3 DUSKY 233FAC   OP CUD   FBG DV IO 165D VLVO  8       3500 2   8   8200  9450
23  3 DUSKY 233FAC   OP CUD   FBG DV SE T115 OMC   8       3500 2   8   6500  7450
23  3 DUSKY 233FC    OP CTRCN FBG DV IO 170-200    8       3500 1   2   6200  7200
23  3 DUSKY 233FC    OP CTRCN FBG DV IB 205 OMC    8       3500 2   8   6550  7600
23  3 DUSKY 233FC    OP CTRCN FBG DV OB            8       3500 1   2   6300  7250

23  3 DUSKY 233FC    OP CTRCN FBG DV IB 220-225    8       3500 2   8   8000  9150
          IO 230 OMC   6700  7700, IB 255 COMM  7900 9050, IO 260 OMC  6850  7850
          IB 270-350   8050  9750, IB 158D VLVO 10900 12400, IB 165D-235D 12000 14300

23  3 DUSKY 233FC    OP CTRCN FBG DV SE T115 OMC   8       3500 2   8   6300  7250
25  6 DUSKY 256      OP OPFSH FBG DV IO 170-200    8       3000 1   2   6800  7850
25  6 DUSKY 256      OP OPFSH FBG DV IB 205 OMC    8       4700 2   9   9000 10400
25  6 DUSKY 256      OP OPFSH FBG DV IB 220-225    8       4700 2   9   8150  9400
25  6 DUSKY 256      OP OPFSH FBG DV IB            8       4700 2   9  11100 12600
          IO 230 OMC   9350 10600, IB 255 COMM 10100 11500, IO 260 OMC  8600  9900
```

```
 LOA  NAME AND/           TOP/ BOAT -HULL- ----ENGINE--- BEAM  WGT DRAFT RETAIL RETAIL
FT IN OR MODEL            RIG  TYPE MTL TP TP # HP  MFG   FT IN LBS FT IN  LOW    HIGH
------------------- 1984 BOATS
25  6 DUSKY 256           OP  OPFSH FBG DV IB 270   CRUS  8      4000 2 9 10300 11700
      IB  350   CRUS 12000 13600, IO 165D VLVO 12500 14200, IB 165D-235D 14500 17300
      IB  355D  CAT  19200 21400
25  6 DUSKY 256           OP  OPFSH FBG DV SE T115  OMC   8      4700 2 9  8150  9400
25  6 DUSKY 256CC         OP  CUD   FBG DV OB            8                 7600  8700
25  6 DUSKY 256CC         OP  CUD   FBG DV IO 170-200    8                 7800  8150
25  6 DUSKY 256CC         OP  CUD   FBG DV SE 205  OMC   8                 7400  8500
25  6 DUSKY 256CC         OP  CUD   FBG DV IB 220-225    8                10300 11700
      IO  230   OMC  8150  9400, IB 255  COMM 10400 11800, IO 260   OMC   8400  9650
      IB  270-350 10600 12800, IO 165D VLVO  9550 10800, IB 165D-235D 13900 16700
      IB  355D  CAT  19000 21100
25  6 DUSKY 256CC         OP  CUD   FBG DV SE T115  OMC   8           2 6  7400  8500
25  6 DUSKY 256CSS        OP  CUD   FBG DV OB            8            2 6  8050  9250
25  6 DUSKY 256CSS        OP  CUD   FBG DV IO 170-200    8            2 6  8050  9450
25  6 DUSKY 256CSS        OP  CUD   FBG DV SE 205  OMC   8            2 6  7650  8800
25  6 DUSKY 256CSS        OP  CUD   FBG DV IB 220-225    8            2 6 10600 12100
      IO  230   OMC  8450  9700, IB 255  COMM 10700 12200, IO 260   OMC   8650  9950
      IB  270-350 10900 13200, IO 165D VLVO  9800 11100, IB 165D-235D 14100 17000
      IB  355D  CAT  19000 21200
25  6 DUSKY 256CSS        OP  CUD   FBG DV SE T115  OMC   8           2 6  7600  8750
25  6 DUSKY 256CSS        OP  CUD   FBG DV IB T165  CRUS  8           2 6 11700 13300
25  6 DUSKY 256FAC        OP  CR    FBG DV OB            0                 7750  8900
25  6 DUSKY 256FAC        OP  CR    FBG DV IO 170-200    8                 7800  9150
25  6 DUSKY 256FAC        OP  CR    FBG DV SE 205  OMC   8                       8650
25  6 DUSKY 256FAC        OP  CR    FBG DV IB 220-225    8                10300 11700
      IO  230   OMC  8150  9350, IB 255  COMM 10400 11800, IO 260   OMC   8350  9600
      IB  270-350 10600 12800, IO 165D VLVO  9400 10700, IB 165D-235D 13600 16400
      IB  355D  CAT  18700 20800
25  6 DUSKY 256FAC        OP  CR    FBG DV SE T115  OMC   8      3100 1 2  7500  8650
25  6 DUSKY 256FC         OP  OPFSH FBG DV OB            8      3100 1 2  6900  7950
25  6 DUSKY 256FC         OP  OPFSH FBG DV IO 170-200    8      3100 1 2  6900  8150
25  6 DUSKY 256FC         OP  OPFSH FBG DV SE 205  OMC   8      3100 1 2  6900  7950
25  6 DUSKY 256FC         OP  OPFSH FBG DV IB 220-225    8      3100 1 2  8650  9950
      IO  230   OMC  7300  8400, IB 255  COMM  8900 10100, IO 260   OMC   7550  8650
      IB  270-350  9100 11000, IO 165D VLVO  9350 10600, IB 165D-235D 11000 13500
      IB  355D  CAT  15800 18000
25  6 DUSKY 256FC         OP  OPFSH FBG DV SE T115  OMC   8      3100 1 2  6900  7950
25 11 DUSKY 26            OP  SF    FBG SV OB        11  3 6000 2 9 12200 13800
25 11 DUSKY 26            OP  SF    FBG SV IB T165  CRUS 11 3 7500 2 9 18800 20900
25 11 DUSKY 26            OP  SF    FBG SV SE T205  OMC  11 3 7500 2 9 12700 14400
25 11 DUSKY 26            OP  SF    FBG SV IB T220  CRUS 11 3 7500 2 9 19200 21400
      IB T225   COMM 19100 21200, IB T225 CRUS 19300 21400, IB T255-T350 19400 23300
      IBT165D-T235D 28600 33300
```

....For earlier years, see the BUC Used Boat Price Guide, Volume 3

DYNA CRAFT LTD
KUAN-TIEN IND ZONE TAINAN MSN   See inside cover to adjust price for area

```
 LOA  NAME AND/           TOP/ BOAT -HULL- ----ENGINE--- BEAM   WGT DRAFT RETAIL RETAIL
FT IN OR MODEL            RIG  TYPE MTL TP TP # HP  MFG   FT IN  LBS FT IN  LOW    HIGH
------------------- 1996 BOATS
45  4 DYNA 45             FB  MY    FBG SV IB T375D CAT  14  7 31876 4 2 225500 248000
49  6 DYNA 50 PILOTHOUSE  EPH MY    FBG SV IB T435D CAT  15  6 41380 4 1 285500 314000
52  6 DYNA 53 PILOTHOUSE  EPH MY    FBG SV IB T550D DD   15  6 40380 3 6 310500 341500
52  6 DYNA 53 YACHTFISHER FB  SF    FBG SV IB T550D DD   15  6 38000 3 6 314500 345500
66    DYNA 66 LAGUNA      FB  MY    FBG SV IB T12CD CAT  18  1 77000 5 1 748500 822500
------------------- 1994 BOATS
45  4 DYNA 45             FB  SDN   FBG SV IB T485D GM   15  6 38000 3 6 242500 266500
45  6 DYNA 46 SD          HT  DC    FBG SV IB T485D GM   15  6 35000 3 6 240500 264500
49  6 DYNA 50             FB  PH    FBG SV IB T550D GM   15  6 38000 3 6 259000 284500
52  6 DYNA 53 YF          HT  DCCPT FBG SV IB T550D GM   15  6 38000 3 6 267000 293500
53    DYNA 53             FB  SDN   FBG SV IB T550D GM   15  6 38000 3 6 271000 297500
66    DYNA 66             FB  MY    FBG SV IB T10CD MTU  18  1 60000 5 1 589000 647000
------------------- 1993 BOATS
45  4 DYNA 45             FB  PH    FBG SV IB T485D GM   15  6 38000 3 6 232500 255500
45  6 DYNA 46             HT  DC    FBG SV IB T485D GM   15  6 35000 3 6 203000 223000
49  6 DYNA 50             FB  PH    FBG SV IB T550D GM   15  6 38000 3 6 246500 271000
52  6 DYNA 53             HT  DCCPT FBG SV IB T550D GM   15  6 38000 3 6 251000 276000
------------------- 1992 BOATS
45  4 DYNA 45             FB  PH    FBG SV IB T485D GM   15  6 38000 3 6 222000 243500
45  6 DYNA 46             HT  DC    FBG SV IB T485D GM   15  6 35000 3 6 193500 212500
49  6 DYNA 50             FB  PH    FBG SV IB T550D GM   15  6 38000 3 6 235500 258000
52  6 DYNA 53             HT  DCCPT FBG SV IB T550D GM   15  6 38000 3 6 239500 263000
52  6 DYNA 53             HT  TCMY  FBG SV IB T550D GM   15  6 40000 3 6 254000 279000
------------------- 1991 BOATS
45  6 DYNA 46             HT  DC    FBG SV IB T375D CAT  15  6 35000 3 6 176500 194000
      IB T400D GM  175500 193000, IB T425D CAT  181500 199500, IB T450D GM  180500 198500
      IB T450D J&T 181500 199000, IB T485D GM  185500 203500
49  6 DYNA 50             FB  PH    FBG SV IB T375D CAT  15  6 38000 3 6 205000 225000
      IB T400D GM  204000 224500, IB T425D CAT  211000 232000, IB T450D GM  205000 225000
      IB T450D J&T 213500 234500, IB T485D GM  215000 236000, IB T550D GM  218000 239500
      IB T550D GM  223500 246000, IB T550D GM  227000 249500
52  6 DYNA 53             HT  DCCPT FBG SV IB T375D CAT  15  6 38000 3 6 203500 224500
      IB T400D GM  203500 224000, IB T425D CAT  212500 233500, IB T450D GM  204000 224500
      IB T450D J&T 219500 241000, IB T485D GM  217500 239000, IB T550D GM  225500 248000
      IB T550D GM  228500 251500
52  6 DYNA 53             HT  TCMY  FBG SV IB T375D CAT  15  6 40000 3 6 216000 237500
      IB T400D GM  215500 237000, IB T425D CAT  225000 247000, IB T450D GM  221000 242500
      IB T450D J&T 228500 251500, IB T485D GM  230500 253500, IB T550D GM  238500 262500
      IB T550D GM  242500 266500
------------------- 1990 BOATS
45  6 DYNA 46             HT  DC    FBG SV IB T375D CAT  15  6 35000 3 6 168000 185000
      IB T400D GM  167500 184000, IB T450D GM  172000 189000, IB T550D GM  182500 200500
      IB T485D GM  175500 193000, IB T485D J&T 176500 194000, IB T550D GM  184000 202000
49  6 DYNA 50             FB  PH    FBG SV IB T375D CAT  15  6 38000 3 6 195500 214500
      IB T400D GM  194500 214000, IB T450D GM  200500 220500, IB T550D GM  213500 234500
      IB T485D GM  205000 225000, IB T485D J&T 208000 228500, IB T550D GM  216500 238000
52  6 DYNA 53             HT  DCCPT FBG SV IB T375D CAT  15  6 38000 3 6 195000 214500
      IB T400D GM  194500 214000, IB T450D J&T 201500 221500, IB T550D GM  202000 222000
      IB T485D GM  208000 228000, IB T485D J&T 215500 237000, IB T550D GM  218500 240000
52  6 DYNA 53             HT  TCMY  FBG SV IB T375D CAT  15  6 40000 3 6 206500 227000
      IB T400D GM  206000 226500, IB T450D GM  214000 235500, IB T550D GM  222000 244000
      IB T485D GM  220000 242000, IB T485D J&T 228000 250500, IB T550D GM  231500 254500
      IB T550D GM  240000 263500
```

DYNA-GLASS COMPANY
OPA LOCKA FL 33054   See inside cover to adjust price for area

```
 LOA  NAME AND/           TOP/ BOAT -HULL- ----ENGINE--- BEAM  WGT DRAFT RETAIL RETAIL
FT IN OR MODEL            RIG  TYPE MTL TP TP # HP  MFG   FT IN LBS FT IN  LOW    HIGH
------------------- 1988 BOATS
29  4 ESPIRIT COASTAL CR  SLP  SA/RC F/S CT         18       2200 1    14600 16600
29  4 ESPIRIT DL          SLP  SA/RC F/S CT         16       2200 1    14600 16600
29  4 ESPIRIT STANDARD    SLP  SA/RC F/S CT         18       1850   11 14000 15900
```

DYNACAT
PALO ALTO CA 94303   COAST GUARD MFG ID- DYR See inside cover to adjust price for area

```
 LOA  NAME AND/           TOP/ BOAT -HULL- ----ENGINE--- BEAM  WGT DRAFT RETAIL RETAIL
FT IN OR MODEL            RIG  TYPE MTL TP TP # HP  MFG   FT IN LBS FT IN  LOW    HIGH
------------------- 1985 BOATS
19    SEA-SPRAY 19        SLP  SA/OD FBG CT         8  3  355   5  3600  4150
```

....For earlier years, see the BUC Used Boat Price Guide, Volume 3

DYNASTY BOAT CORPORATION
SARASOTA FL 34243   COAST GUARD MFG ID- OFF See inside cover to adjust price for area
                          FORMERLY OFFSHORE MARINE INDUSTRIES

```
 LOA  NAME AND/           TOP/ BOAT -HULL- ----ENGINE--- BEAM  WGT DRAFT RETAIL RETAIL
FT IN OR MODEL            RIG  TYPE MTL TP TP # HP  MFG   FT IN LBS FT IN  LOW    HIGH
------------------- 1995 BOATS
16  8 17TBB               OP  FSH   FBG TR OB       6  2  910   10 2850  3300
16  8 17TRICC             OP  CTRCN FBG TR OB       6  2  850   10 2700  3100
16  8 17TRIDSC            OP  SF    FBG TR OB       6  2  850   10 2750  3200
```

DYNASTY BOAT CORPORATION -CONTINUED See inside cover to adjust price for area

LOA FT	IN	NAME AND/ OR MODEL	TOP/ RIG	BOAT TYPE	-HULL- MTL	TP	----ENGINE--- TP	# HP	MFG	BEAM FT	IN	WGT LBS	DRAFT FT	IN	RETAIL LOW	RETAIL HIGH
		------------- 1995 BOATS														
16	8	17TRISC	OP	SF	FBG	TR	OB			6	2	850		10	2600	3050
17		17VBFB	OP	BASS	FBG	SV	OB			6	4	920		10	2900	3400
17		17VCC	OP	CTRCN	FBG	TR	OB			6	9	930		10	2950	3400
17		17VDSC	OP	SF	FBG	TR	OB			6	9	930		10	2950	3400
17		18RVCC ROLLED EDGE	OP	SF	FBG	TR	OB			7	6	1140	1		3350	3900
18		18VBFB	OP	CTRCN	FBG	TR	OB			7	2	1240			4500	5150
18		18VCC	OP	CTRCN	FBG	TR	OB			7	2	1240	1		3300	3850
18	5	ULTIMA 18VCCL	OP	BASS	FBG	SV	OB			7	5	1280	1		4000	4650
18	5	ULTIMA 19VBFB	OP	BASS	FBG	SV	OB			7	5	1380	1		4250	4950
18	8	19VCC	OP	CTRCN	FBG	DV	OB			7	2	1280			4050	4700
18	8	19VCCL W/CAP LINER	OP	CTRCN	FBG	DV	OB			7	3	1440			4450	5150
18	8	DYNASTY 19VBR	OP	B/R	FBG	DV	OB			7	2	1495			4600	5300
19	8	22VCCL	OP	CTRCN	FBG	DV	OB			7	8	2250			6200	7150
19	8	22VDSCL	OP	SF	FBG	DV	OB			7	10	2330	1	4	6350	7250
20	7	21VCC	OP	CTRCN	FBG	DV	OB			7	11	1470	1		4800	5500
21		21VCCL	OP	CTRCN	FBG	DV	OB			7	11	1760	1		5600	6450
21	9	22VCC	OP	CTRCN	FBG	DV	OB			7	8	1850	1	3	6000	6900
21	9	22VDSC	OP	SF	FBG	DV	OB			7	10	2040	1	3	6500	7500
21	9	22VDSCS	OP	SF	FBG	DV	OB			7	10	2140			6750	7750
21	9	22VDSCSL	OP	SF	FBG	DV	OB			7	10	2390			7350	8450
25		22VCAB	OP	CUD	FBG	DV	OB			7	10	2845			10200	11600
25		25VCAB	OP	CUD	FBG	DV	OB			9	2	3970			12200	13900
25		25VCC	OP	CTRCN	FBG	DV	OB			9	1	3440			11300	12900
25		THUNDERBOLT 25	OP	SF	FBG	DV	OB			9	1	3670			11700	13300
27		27VCAB	OP	CUD	FBG	DV	OB			9	2	4000			15700	17900
27		27VCC	OP	CTRCN	FBG	DV	OB			9	2	3700			15600	17800
27		27VDSC	OP	SF	FBG	DV	OB			9	2	3760			15700	17800
		------------- 1994 BOATS														
16	8	17TBB	OP	FSH	FBG	TR	OB			6	2	910		10	2700	3150
16	8	17TRICC	OP	CTRCN	FBG	TR	OB			6	2	850		10	2550	3000
16	8	17TRIDSC	OP	SF	FBG	TR	OB			6	2	850		10	2600	3050
16	8	17TRISC	OP	SF	FBG	TR	OB			6	2	850		10	2500	2900
17		17VBFB	OP	BASS	FBG	SV	OB			6	4	920		10	2800	3250
17		17VCC	OP	CTRCN	FBG	TR	OB			6	9	930		10	2800	3250
17		17VDSC	OP	SF	FBG	TR	OB			6	9	930		10	2800	3250
17		18RVCC ROLLED EDGE	OP	SF	FBG	TR	OB			7	6	1140	1		3200	3750
18		18VBFB	OP	CTRCN	FBG	TR	OB			7	2	1240			4350	5000
18		18VCC	OP	CTRCN	FBG	TR	OB			7	2	1240	1		3100	3600
18	5	ULTIMA 18VCCL	OP	BASS	FBG	SV	OB			7	5	1280	1		3850	4450
18	5	ULTIMA 19VBFB	OP	BASS	FBG	SV	OB			7	5	1380	1		4050	4700
18	8	19VCC	OP	CTRCN	FBG	DV	OB			7	2	1280			3850	4500
18	8	19VCCL W/CAP LINER	OP	CTRCN	FBG	DV	OB			7	3	1440			4200	4900
18	8	DYNASTY 19VBR	OP	B/R	FBG	DV	OB			7	2	1495			4400	5050
19	8	22VCCL	OP	CTRCN	FBG	DV	OB			7	8	2250			5950	6850
19	8	22VDSCL	OP	SF	FBG	DV	OB			7	10	2330	1	4	6050	6950
20	7	21VCC	OP	CTRCN	FBG	DV	OB			7	11	1470	1		4600	5300
21		21VCCL	OP	CTRCN	FBG	DV	OB			7	11	1760	1		5350	6200
21	9	22VCC	OP	CTRCN	FBG	DV	OB			7	8	1850	1	3	5750	6600
21	9	22VDSC	OP	SF	FBG	DV	OB			7	10	2040	1	3	6200	7150
21	9	22VDSCS	OP	SF	FBG	DV	OB			7	10	2140			6450	7400
21	9	22VDSCSL	OP	SF	FBG	DV	OB			7	10	2390			7000	8050
25		22VCAB	OP	CUD	FBG	DV	OB			7	10	2845			9700	11000
25		25VCAB	OP	CUD	FBG	DV	OB			9	2	3970			11700	13300
25		25VCC	OP	CTRCN	FBG	DV	OB			9	1	3440			10800	12300
25		THUNDERBOLT 25	OP	SF	FBG	DV	OB			9	1	3670			11200	12700
27		27VCAB	OP	CUD	FBG	DV	OB			9	2	4000			15000	17100
27		27VCC	OP	CTRCN	FBG	DV	OB			9	2	3700			14900	17000
27		27VDSC	OP	SF	FBG	DV	OB			9	2	3760			15000	17000
		------------- 1993 BOATS														
16	8	17TBB	OP	FSH	FBG	TR	OB			6	2	910		10	2600	3050
16	8	17TRICC	OP	CTRCN	FBG	TR	OB			6	2	850		10	2450	2850
16	8	17TRIDSC	OP	SF	FBG	TR	OB			6	2	850		10	2550	2950
16	8	17TRSC	OP	SF	FBG	TR	OB			6	2	850		10	2350	2750
17		17VBFB	OP	BASS	FBG	SV	OB			6	4	920		10	2650	3100
17		17VCC	OP	CTRCN	FBG	TR	OB			6	9	930		10	2700	3150
17		17VSC	OP	SF	FBG	TR	OB			6	9	930		10	2700	3150
17		18RVCC ROLLED EDGE	OP	SF	FBG	TR	OB			7	6	1140	1		3100	3600
17		18RVDSC ROLLED EDGE	OP	SF	FBG	TR	OB			7	6	1140	1		3350	3900
18		18VBFB	OP	CTRCN	FBG	TR	OB			7	2	1240			4150	4800
18		18VCC	OP	CTRCN	FBG	TR	OB			7	2	1240	1		2950	3450
18		18VDSC	OP	SF	FBG	TR	OB			7	2	1240	1		3550	4100
18	5	ULTIMA 18VCCL	OP	BASS	FBG	SV	OB			7	5	1280	1		3700	4300
18	5	ULTIMA 19VBFB	OP	BASS	FBG	SV	OB			7	5	1380	1		3900	4550
18	8	19VBR	OP	B/R	FBG	DV	OB			7	2	1495			4150	4850
18	8	19VCC	OP	CTRCN	FBG	DV	OB			7	2	1280			3700	4300
18	8	19VCCL W/CAP LINER	OP	CTRCN	FBG	DV	OB			7	3	1440			4050	4700
20	7	21VCC	OP	CTRCN	FBG	DV	OB			7	11	1470	1		4400	5050
21		21VCCL	OP	CTRCN	FBG	DV	OB			7	11	1760	1		5150	5900
21		22VDSCL	OP	SF	FBG	DV	OB			7	10	2330	1	4	6300	7250
21	9	22VCC	OP	CTRCN	FBG	DV	OB			7	8	1850	1	3	5500	6350
21	9	22VCCL	OP	CTRCN	FBG	DV	OB			7	8	2250			6450	7400
21	9	22VCCL	OP	SF	FBG	DV	OB			7	10	2040	1	3	5950	6850
22		22VCAB	OP	CUD	FBG	DV	OB			7	10	2845			7700	8850
22		22VDSCS	OP	SF	FBG	DV	OB			7	10	2140			6250	7200
22		22VDSCSL	OP	SF	FBG	DV	OB			7	10	2390			6800	7850
24		24VCC	OP	CTRCN	FBG	DV	OB			9	1				9900	11300
25		25VCAB	OP	CUD	FBG	DV	OB			9	2	3970			11200	12700
25		25VCC	OP	CTRCN	FBG	DV	OB			9	1	3440			10400	11800
25		25VDSC	OP	SF	FBG	DV	OB			9	1	3670			10700	12200
26		26VCC	OP	CTRCN	FBG	DV	OB			9	2	3490			11900	13600
26		26VDSC	OP	CUD	FBG	DV	OB			9	2	3590			12000	13700
26	8	27VCAB	OP	CUD	FBG	DV	OB			9	2	4000			13700	15500
26	8	27VCC	OP	CTRCN	FBG	DV	OB			9	2	3700			13500	15400
26	8	27VDSC	OP	SF	FBG	DV	OB			9	2	3760			13600	15400
		------------- 1992 BOATS														
16	8	17TBB	OP	FSH	FBG	TR	OB			6	2	910		10	2500	2900
16	8	17TRICC	OP	CTRCN	FBG	TR	OB			6	2	850		10	2350	2750
16	8	17TRIDSC	OP	SF	FBG	TR	OB			6	2	850		10	2450	2850
16	8	17TRSC	OP	SF	FBG	TR	OB			6	2	850		10	2300	2700
17		17VCC	OP	CTRCN	FBG	TR	OB			6	9	930		10	2600	3000
17		17VSC	OP	SF	FBG	TR	OB			6	9	930		10	2600	3000
17		18RVCC ROLLED EDGE	OP	SF	FBG	TR	OB			7	6	1140	1		2950	3450
17		18RVDSC ROLLED EDGE	OP	SF	FBG	TR	OB			7	6	1140	1		3200	3750
18		18VBFB	OP	CTRCN	FBG	TR	OB			7	2	1240			3950	4600
18		18VCC	OP	CTRCN	FBG	TR	OB			7	2	1240	1		2850	3300
18		18VDSC	OP	SF	FBG	TR	OB			7	2	1240	1		3400	3950
18	8	19VBR	OP	B/R	FBG	DV	OB			7	2	1495			4000	4650
18	8	19VCC	OP	CTRCN	FBG	DV	OB			7	2	1280			3550	4150
18	8	19VCCL W/CAP LINER	OP	CTRCN	FBG	DV	OB			7	3	1440			3900	4550
20	7	21VCC	OP	CTRCN	FBG	DV	OB			7	11	1470	1		4200	4850
21		21VCCL	OP	CTRCN	FBG	DV	OB			7	11	1760	1		4950	5700
21		22VDSCL	OP	SF	FBG	DV	OB			7	10	2330	1	4	6050	7000
21	9	22VCC	OP	CTRCN	FBG	DV	OB			7	8	1850	1	3	5300	6100
21	9	22VCCL	OP	CTRCN	FBG	DV	OB			7	8	2250			6200	7100
21	9	22VCCL	OP	SF	FBG	DV	OB			7	10	2040	1	3	5750	6600
22		22VCAB	OP	CUD	FBG	DV	OB			7	10	2845			7400	8500
22		22VDSCS	OP	SF	FBG	DV	OB			7	10	2140			6000	6900
22		22VDSCSL	OP	SF	FBG	DV	OB			7	10	2390			6550	7500
24		24VCC	OP	CTRCN	FBG	DV	OB			9	1				9500	10800
25		25VCAB	OP	CUD	FBG	DV	OB			9	2	3970			10800	12200
25		25VCC	OP	CTRCN	FBG	DV	OB			9	1	3440			9950	11300
25		25VDSC	OP	SF	FBG	DV	OB			9	1	3670			10300	11700
26		26VCC	OP	CTRCN	FBG	DV	OB			9	2	3490			11500	13000
26		26VDSC	OP	CUD	FBG	DV	OB			9	2	3590			11600	13100
26	8	27VCAB	OP	CUD	FBG	DV	OB			9	2	4000			13100	14900
26	8	27VCC	OP	CTRCN	FBG	DV	OB			9	2	3700			13000	14800
26	8	27VDSC	OP	SF	FBG	DV	OB			9	2	3760			13000	14800
		------------- 1991 BOATS														
16	8	17TBB	OP	FSH	FBG	TR	OB			6	2	910		10	2400	2800
16	8	17TRICC	OP	CTRCN	FBG	TR	OB			6	2	850		10	2300	2650
16	8	17TRIDSC	OP	SF	FBG	TR	OB			6	2	850		10	2350	2750
16	8	17TRSC	OP	SF	FBG	TR	OB			6	2	850		10	2200	2600
17		17VCC	OP	CTRCN	FBG	TR	OB			6	9	930		10	2500	2900
17		17VSC	OP	SF	FBG	TR	OB			6	9	930		10	2500	2900
17		18RVCC ROLLED EDGE	OP	SF	FBG	TR	OB			7	6	1140	1		2850	3300
17		18RVDSC ROLLED EDGE	OP	SF	FBG	TR	OB			7	6	1140	1		3100	3600
18		18VBFB	OP	CTRCN	FBG	TR	OB			7	2	1240			3800	4450
18		18VCC	OP	CTRCN	FBG	TR	OB			7	2	1240	1		2750	3200
18		18VDSC	OP	SF	FBG	TR	OB			7	2	1240	1		3300	3800
18	8	19VBR	OP	B/R	FBG	DV	OB			7	2	1495			3850	4500
18	8	19VCC	OP	CTRCN	FBG	DV	OB			7	2	1280			3450	4000
18	8	19VCCL W/CAP LINER	OP	CTRCN	FBG	DV	OB			7	3	1440			3750	4350
20	7	21VCC	OP	CTRCN	FBG	DV	OB			7	11	1470	1		4050	4700
21		21VCCL	OP	CTRCN	FBG	DV	OB			7	11	1760	1		4750	5500
21		22VDSCL	OP	SF	FBG	DV	OB			7	10	2330	1	4	5850	6700
21	9	22VCC	OP	CTRCN	FBG	DV	OB			7	8	1850	1	3	5100	5850
21	9	22VCCL	OP	CTRCN	FBG	DV	OB			7	8	2250			5950	6850

 CONTINUED ON NEXT PAGE

LOA FT	IN	NAME AND/ OR MODEL	TOP/ RIG	BOAT TYPE	-HULL- MTL	TP	----ENGINE--- TP	# HP	MFG	BEAM FT	IN	WGT LBS	DRAFT FT	IN	RETAIL LOW	RETAIL HIGH
1991 BOATS																
21	9	22VCCL	OP	SF	FBG	DV	OB			7	10	2040	1	3	5500	6350
22		22VCAB	OP	CUD	FBG	DV	OB			7	10	2845			7100	8200
22		22VDSCS	OP	SF	FBG	DV	OB			7	10	2140			5800	6650
22		22VDSCSL	OP	SF	FBG	DV	OB			7	10	2390			6300	7250
24		24VCC	OP	CTRCN	FBG	DV	OB			9	1				9250	10500
25		25VCAB	OP	CUD	FBG	DV	OB			9	2	3970			10400	11800
25		25VCC	OP	CTRCN	FBG	DV	OB			9	1	3440			9600	10900
25		25VDSC	OP	SF	FBG	DV	OB			9	1	3670			9950	11300
26		26VCC	OP	CTRCN	FBG	DV	OB			9	2	3490			11000	12600
26		26VDSC	OP	CUD	FBG	DV	OB			9	2	3590			11100	12600
26	8	27VCAB	OP	CUD	FBG	DV	OB			9	2	4000			12600	14400
26	8	27VCC	OP	CTRCN	FBG	DV	OB			9	2	3700			12500	14200
26	8	27VDSC	OP	SF	FBG	DV	OB			9	2	3760			12600	14300
1990 BOATS																
16	8	17TBB	OP	FSH	FBG	TR	OB			6	2	910		10	2350	2700
16	8	17TRICC	OP	CTRCN	FBG	TR	OB			6	2	850		10	2200	2600
16	8	17TRIDSC	OP	SF	FBG	TR	OB			6	2	850		10	2300	2700
16	8	17TRSC	OP	SF	FBG	TR	OB			6	2	850		10	2100	2450
17		17VCC	OP	CTRCN	FBG	TR	OB			6	9	930		10	2400	2800
17		17VDSC	OP	SF	FBG	TR	OB			6	9	930		10	2400	2800
17		18RVCC ROLLED EDGE	OP	SF	FBG	TR	OB			7	6	1140	1		2800	3250
17		18RVDSC ROLLED EDGE	OP	SF	FBG	TR	OB			7	6	1140	1		2950	3450
18		18VBFB	OP	CTRCN	FBG	TR	OB			7	2	1240			3650	4250
18		18VCC	OP	CTRCN	FBG	TR	OB			7	2	1240	1		2700	3100
18		18VDSC	OP	SF	FBG	TR	OB			7	2	1240	1		3150	3700
18	8	19VBR	OP	B/R	FBG	DV	OB			7	2	1495			3700	4350
18	8	19VCC	OP	CTRCN	FBG	DV	OB			7	2	1280			3300	3850
18	8	19VCCL W/CAP LINER	OP	CTRCN	FBG	DV	OB			7	3	1440			3600	4200
20	7	21VCC	OP	CTRCN	FBG	DV	OB			7	11	1470	1		3900	4550
21		21VCCL	OP	CTRCN	FBG	DV	OB			7	11	1760	1		4650	5350
21		22VDSCL	OP	SF	FBG	DV	OB			7	10	2330	1	4	5650	6500
21	9	22VCC	OP	CTRCN	FBG	DV	OB			7	8	1850	1	3	4950	5650
21	9	22VCCL	OP	CTRCN	FBG	DV	OB			7	8	2250			5750	6600
21	9	22VDSC	OP	SF	FBG	DV	OB			7	10	2040	1	3	5350	6150
22		22VCAB	OP	CUD	FBG	DV	OB			7	10	2845			6900	7900
22		22VDSCS	OP	SF	FBG	DV	OB			7	10	2140			5600	6450
22		22VDSCSL	OP	SF	FBG	DV	OB			7	10	2390			6100	7000
24		24VCC	OP	CTRCN	FBG	DV	OB			9	1				8900	10100
25		25VCAB	OP	CUD	FBG	DV	OB			9	2	3970			10000	11400
25		25VCC	OP	CTRCN	FBG	DV	OB			9	1	3440			9350	10600
25		25VDSC	OP	SF	FBG	DV	OB			9	1	3670			9600	10900
26		26VCC	OP	CTRCN	FBG	DV	OB			9	2	3490			10700	12100
26		26VDSC	OP	CUD	FBG	DV	OB			9	2	3590			10800	12200
26	8	27VCAB	OP	CUD	FBG	DV	OB			9	2	4000			12200	13900
26	8	27VCC	OP	CTRCN	FBG	DV	OB			9	2	3700			12100	13800
26	8	27VDSC	OP	SF	FBG	DV	OB			9	2	3760			12100	13800
1989 BOATS																
16	8	17TBB	OP	FSH	FBG	TR	OB			6	2	910		10	2300	2650
16	8	17TRICC	OP	CTRCN	FBG	TR	OB			6	2	850		10	2100	2500
16	8	17TRIDSC	OP	SF	FBG	TR	OB			6	2	850		10	2250	2600
16	8	17TRISC	OP	SF	FBG	TR	OB			6	2	850		10	2000	2400
17		17VCC	OP	CTRCN	FBG	DV	OB			6	9	930		10	2350	2700
17		17VDSC	OP	SF	FBG	DV	OB			6	9	930		10	2350	2700
17		18RVCC ROLLED EDGE	OP	SF	FBG	DV	OB			7	6	1140	1		2700	3150
17		18RVDSC ROLLED EDGE	OP	SF	FBG	DV	OB			7	6	1140	1		2850	3300
18		18VBFB	OP	CTRCN	FBG	DV	OB			7	2	1240			3550	4100
18		18VCC	OP	CTRCN	FBG	DV	OB			7	2	1240	1		2600	3000
18		18VDSC	OP	SF	FBG	DV	OB			7	2	1240	1		3050	3550
18	8	19VBR	OP	B/R	FBG	DV	OB			7	2	1495			3600	4200
18	8	19VCC	OP	CTRCN	FBG	DV	OB			7	2	1280			3200	3750
18	8	19VCCL W/CAP LINER	OP	CTRCN	FBG	DV	OB			7	3	1440			3500	4100
20	7	21VCC	OP	CTRCN	FBG	DV	OB			7	11	1470	1		3750	4400
21		21VCCL	OP	CTRCN	FBG	DV	OB			7	11	1760			4500	5150
21		22VDSCL	OP	SF	FBG	DV	OB			7	10	2330	1	4	5450	6300
21	9	22VCC	OP	CTRCN	FBG	DV	OB			7	8	1850	1	3	4800	5500
21	9	22VCCL	OP	CTRCN	FBG	DV	OB			7	8	2250			5550	6400
21	9	22VDSC	OP	SF	FBG	DV	OB			7	10	2040	1	3	5150	5950
22		22VCAB	OP	CUD	FBG	DV	OB			7	10	2845			6650	7650
22		22VDSCS	OP	SF	FBG	DV	OB			7	10	2140			5400	6250
22		22VDSCSL	OP	SF	FBG	DV	OB			7	10	2390			5900	6800
24		24VCC	OP	CTRCN	FBG	DV	OB			9	1				8550	9800
25		25 THUNDERBOLT VDSC	OP	SF	FBG	DV	OB			9	1	3670			9350	10600
25		25VCAB	OP	CUD	FBG	DV	OB			9	2	3970			9700	11000
25		25VCC	OP	CTRCN	FBG	DV	OB			9	1	3440			9050	10300
26		26VCC	OP	CTRCN	FBG	DV	OB			9	2	3490			10300	11700
26		26VDSC	OP	CUD	FBG	DV	OB			9	2	3590			10400	11800
26	8	27VCAB	OP	CUD	FBG	DV	OB			9	2	4000			11800	13400
26	8	27VCC	OP	CTRCN	FBG	DV	OB			9	2	3700			11700	13300
26	8	27VDSC	OP	SF	FBG	DV	OB			9	2	3760			11700	13300
1988 BOATS																
16	8	17TBB	OP	FSH	FBG	TR	OB			6	2	910		10	2200	2600
16	8	17TRICC	OP	CTRCN	FBG	TR	OB			6	2	850		10	2050	2400
16	8	17TRIDSC	OP	SF	FBG	TR	OB			6	2	850		10	2150	2500
16	8	17TRISC	OP	SF	FBG	TR	OB			6	2	850		10	1950	2350
17		17VCC	OP	CTRCN	FBG	DV	OB			6	9	930		10	2300	2650
17		17VDSC	OP	SF	FBG	DV	OB			6	9	930		10	2300	2650
17		18RVCC ROLLED EDGE	OP	SF	FBG	DV	OB			7	6	1140	1		2650	3050
17		18RVDSC ROLLED EDGE	OP	SF	FBG	DV	OB			7	6	1140	1		2750	3200
18		18VBFB	OP	CTRCN	FBG	DV	OB			7	2	1240			3300	3800
18		18VCC	OP	CTRCN	FBG	DV	OB			7	2	1240	1		2650	3100
18		18VDSC	OP	SF	FBG	DV	OB			7	2	1240	1		3000	3450
18	8	19VBR	OP	B/R	FBG	DV	OB			7	2	1495			3500	4050
18	8	19VCC	OP	CTRCN	FBG	DV	OB			7	2	1280			3100	3600
18	8	19VCCL W/CAP LINER	OP	CTRCN	FBG	DV	OB			7	3	1440			3400	3950
20	7	21VCC	OP	CTRCN	FBG	DV	OB			7	11	1470	1		3650	4250
21		21VCCL	OP	CTRCN	FBG	DV	OB			7	11	1760			4350	5000
21		22VDSCL	OP	SF	FBG	DV	OB			7	10	2330	1	4	5300	6100
21	9	22VCC	OP	CTRCN	FBG	DV	OB			7	8	1850	1	3	4650	5350
21	9	22VCC W/CAP LINER	OP	CTRCN	FBG	DV	OB			7	8	2250			5400	6200
21	9	22VDSC	OP	SF	FBG	DV	OB			7	10	2040	1	3	5000	5750
22		22VCAB	OP	CUD	FBG	DV	OB			7	10	2845			6450	7400
22		22VDSCS	OP	SF	FBG	DV	OB			7	10	2140			5250	6050
22		22VDSCSL	OP	SF	FBG	DV	OB			7	10	2390			5700	6600
24		24VCC	OP	CTRCN	FBG	DV	OB			9	1				8250	9500
25		25 THUNDERBOLT VDSC	OP	SF	FBG	DV	OB			9	1	3670			9100	10300
25		25VCAB	OP	CUD	FBG	DV	OB			9	2	3970			9400	10700
25		25VCC	OP	CTRCN	FBG	DV	OB			9	1	3440			8650	9950
26		26VCC	OP	CTRCN	FBG	DV	OB			9	2	3490			10000	11400
26		26VDSC	OP	CUD	FBG	DV	OB			9	2	3590			10100	11500
26	8	27VCAB	OP	CUD	FBG	DV	OB			9	2	4000			11500	13000
26	8	27VCC	OP	CTRCN	FBG	DV	OB			9	2	3700			11400	12900
26	8	27VDSC	OP	SF	FBG	DV	OB			9	2	3760			11400	12900
1987 BOATS																
16	8	17TRICC	OP	CTRCN	FBG	TR	OB			6	2	850		10	2000	2350
16	8	17TRIDSC	OP	SF	FBG	TR	OB			6	2	850		10	2000	2350
16	8	17TRISC	OP	SF	FBG	TR	OB			6	2	850		10	1950	2350
17		17VBR	OP	B/R	FBG	DV	OB			6	9	930		10	2250	2600
17		17VCC	OP	CTRCN	FBG	DV	OB			6	9	930		10	2250	2600
17		17VDSC	OP	SF	FBG	DV	OB			6	9	930		10	2200	2600
17		18RVCC ROLLED EDGE	OP	SF	FBG	DV	OB			7	6	1140	1		2600	3000
17		18RVDSC ROLLED EDGE	OP	SF	FBG	DV	OB			7	6	1140	1		2650	3100
18		18VBR	OP	B/R	FBG	DV	OB			7	2	1140	1		2700	3150
18		18VCC	OP	CTRCN	FBG	DV	OB			7	2	1240	1		2900	3350
18		18VDSC	OP	SF	FBG	DV	OB			7	2	1240	1		2900	3350
18	8	19VBR	OP	B/R	FBG	DV	OB			7	2	1495			3400	3950
18	8	19VCC	OP	CTRCN	FBG	DV	OB			7	2	1495			3400	3950
18	8	19VCC W/CAP LINER	OP	CTRCN	FBG	DV	OB			7	3	1440			3300	3850
20	7	21VCC	OP	CTRCN	FBG	DV	OB			7	11	1470	1		3550	4150
21	9	22VCC	OP	CTRCN	FBG	DV	OB			7	8	1850	1	3	4550	5200
21	9	22VCC W/CAP LINER	OP	CTRCN	FBG	DV	OB			7	8	1850			4550	5200
21	9	22VDSC	OP	SF	FBG	DV	OB			7	10	2040	1	3	4850	5600
24		24VCC	OP	CTRCN	FBG	DV	OB			9	1				8050	9250
25		25 THUNDERBOLT	OP	SF	FBG	DV	OB			9	1	3670			8800	10000
25		25VCC	OP	CTRCN	FBG	DV	OB			9	1				8400	9650
1986 BOATS																
17		17HD	OP	RNBT	FBG	DV	OB			6	3	825		10	1750	2100
17		17TRICC	OP	RNBT	FBG	TR	OB			6	3	825		10	1950	2350
17		17TRIDSC	OP	RNBT	FBG	TR	OB			6	3	825		10	2000	2400
17		17TRISC	OP	RNBT	FBG	TR	OB			6	3	825		10	1900	2250
17		17VBR	OP	RNBT	FBG	DV	OB			6	9	825		10	2150	2500
17		17VBR	OP	RNBT	FBG	DV	IO	170		6	9	2050	1	1	3200	3700
17		17VCC	OP	CTRCN	FBG	DV	OB			6	9	825		10	1900	2250
17		17VDSC	OP	RNBT	FBG	DV	OB			6	9	825		10	1700	2000
17		17VDSC	OP	RNBT	FBG	DV	IO	170		6	9	2050	1	1	2950	3400
18		18RVCC ROLLED EDGE	OP	RNBT	FBG	DV	OB			7	2	1240		1	2600	3050
18		18RVDSC	OP	RNBT	FBG	DV	IO	170		7	2	2050	1	2	3250	3800
18		18RVDSC ROLLED EDGE	OP	RNBT	FBG	DV	OB			7	2	1240		1	2700	3150

 CONTINUED ON NEXT PAGE

LOA FT	LOA IN	NAME AND/ OR MODEL	TOP/ RIG	BOAT TYPE	HULL MTL	HULL TP	ENGINE TP	ENGINE # HP	ENGINE MFG	BEAM FT	BEAM IN	WGT LBS	DRAFT FT	DRAFT IN	RETAIL LOW	RETAIL HIGH
1986 BOATS																
18		18VBR	OP	RNBT	FBG	DV	OB			7	2	1240		1	3100	3600
18		18VBR	OP	RNBT	FBG	DV	IO	170		7	2	2050	1	2	3450	4000
18		18VCC	OP	CTRCN	FBG	DV	OB			7	2	1240		1	2800	3250
18		18VDSC	OP	RNBT	FBG	DV	OB			7	2	1240		1	2900	3350
18		18VDSC	OP	RNBT	FBG	DV	IO	170		7	2	2050	1	2	3350	3900
20	6	21VCC	OP	CTRCN	FBG	DV	OB			8		1470		1	3450	4000
20	6	21VDSC	OP	RNBT	FBG	DV	OB			8		1470	1	1	3450	4000
20	6	21VDSC	OP	RNBT	FBG	DV	IO	170-205		8		2280	1	3	4100	4950
21	9	22VCC	OP	CTRCN	FBG	DV	OB			7	10	1880	1	3	4450	5150
21	9	22VCC	OP	CTRCN	FBG	DV	IO	170-205		7	10	3250	1	6	5850	6800
21	9	22VDSC	OP	RNBT	FBG	DV	OB			7	10	1880	1	3	4450	5150
21	9	22VDSC	OP	RNBT	FBG	DV	IO	170-205		7	10	3250	1	6	5300	6150

....For earlier years, see the BUC Used Boat Price Guide, Volume 3

DYNASTY BOATS INC

DIV OF GODFREY MARINE
VINEMONT AL 35179 COAST GUARD MFG ID- MJI

See inside cover to adjust price for area

For more recent years, see the BUC Used Boat Price Guide, Volume 1

LOA FT	LOA IN	NAME AND/ OR MODEL	TOP/ RIG	BOAT TYPE	HULL MTL	HULL TP	ENGINE TP	ENGINE # HP	ENGINE MFG	BEAM FT	BEAM IN	WGT LBS	DRAFT FT	DRAFT IN	RETAIL LOW	RETAIL HIGH
1994 BOATS																
16	9	ELANTI 171	OP	RNBT	FBG	DV	IO	110-115		7	1	1700			7650	8800
16	9	ELANTI 176 B/R	OP	RNBT	FBG	DV	OB			7	1	1150			1900	2250
17	10	ELANTI 181	OP	RNBT	FBG	DV	IO	110-180		7	3	1775			8450	9850
18	6	CLASSIC 190 CUDDY	OP	CUD	FBG	DV	IO	110-240		7	9	2370			10800	12800
18	6	ELAN 191	OP	CUD	FBG	DV	IO	115-190		7	9	2370			11000	12600
18	6	REGENCY 190 B/R	OP	RNBT	FBG	DV	IO	110-240		7	9	2100			9900	11900
18	7	RELEASE 192	OP	FSH	FBG	DV	OB			8		2000			2850	3350
18	8	ELAN 195	OP	RNBT	FBG	DV	IO	110-210		7	10	2160			10200	11900
20	6	RELEASE 212	OP	FSH	FBG	DV	OB			8		2400			3950	4600
20	8	ELAN 211 B/R	OP	RNBT	FBG	DV	IO	160-240		8		2725			13000	15300
20	8	ELAN 215	OP	CUD	FBG	DV	IO	160-240		8		2925			14000	16500
23		ELAN 230 CUDDY	ST	CUD	FBG	DV	IO	235	MRCR	8		3500			18500	20500
26	11	FRIENDSHIP 260 AC	OP	CR	FBG	DV	IO	T240-T300		8	6	6500			38000	45200
1993 BOATS																
16	9	ELANTI 171	OP	RNBT	FBG	DV	IO	110-115		7	1	1700			7150	8200
16	9	ELANTI 176 B/R	OP	RNBT	FBG	DV	OB			7	1	1150			1800	2150
17	10	ELANTI 181	OP	RNBT	FBG	DV	IO	110-180		7	3	1775			7900	9200
18	6	CLASSIC 190 CUDDY	OP	CUD	FBG	DV	IO	110-240		7	9	2370			10100	12100
18	6	REGENCY 190 B/R	OP	RNBT	FBG	DV	IO	110-240		7	9	2100			9350	11200
18	7	RELEASE 192	OP	FSH	FBG	DV	OB			8		2000			2700	3150
18	8	ELAN 195	OP	RNBT	FBG	DV	IO	110-210		7	10	2160			9600	11200
20	6	RELEASE 212	OP	FSH	FBG	DV	OB			8		2400			3750	4350
20	8	ASSAULT 210	OP	CUD	FBG	DV	IO	190-240		8		3000			13400	15600
20	8	ASSAULT 210	OP	CUD	FBG	DV	IO	300		8		3000			15000	17000
20	8	ELAN 211 B/R	OP	RNBT	FBG	DV	IO	160-240		8		2725			12300	14400
20	8	ELAN 215	OP	CUD	FBG	DV	IO	160-240		8		2925			13100	15400
26	11	FRIENDSHIP 260 AC	OP	CR	FBG	DV	IO	T240-T300		8	6	6500			35500	42200
1992 BOATS																
16	9	ELANTI 171	OP	RNBT	FBG	DV	IO	115-135		7	1	1700			6700	7750
16	9	ELANTI 171 B/R	OP	RNBT	FBG	DV	OB			7	1	1405			2050	2400
16	10	REGENCY 170 B/R	OP	RNBT	FBG	DV	IO	115-155		7	2	1945			7200	8300
17	10	ELANTI 181	OP	RNBT	FBG	DV	IO	115-180		7	3	1775			7400	8600
17	10	ELANTI 186	OP	RNBT	FBG	DV	OB			7	1	1650			2400	2800
18	6	CLASSIC 190 CUDDY	OP	CUD	FBG	DV	IO	115-230		7	9	2370			9500	11300
18	6	REGENCY 190 B/R	OP	RNBT	FBG	DV	IO	115-230		7	9	2100			8600	10300
18	7	RELEASE 192	OP	FSH	FBG	DV	OB			8		2000			2600	3050
18	8	ELANTI 191	OP	RNBT	FBG	DV	IO	115-180		7	10	2160			8950	10300
20	6	RELEASE 212	OP	FSH	FBG	DV	OB			8		2400			3550	4150
20	8	ASSAULT 210	OP	CUD	FBG	DV	IO	115-230		8		3000			12500	14600
20	8	ELAN 208 B/R	OP	RNBT	FBG	DV	IO	115-230		8		2725			11400	13400
20	8	ELANTI 211 CUDDY	OP	CUD	FBG	DV	IO	230	YAMA	8		2725			12300	13900
22		REGENCY 220	OP	CUD	FBG	DV	IO	115-230		8		3500			14000	16200
22		REGENCY 220 FISH	OP	CUD	FBG	DV	IO	115-230		8		3500			15200	17800
22		RELEASE 222	OP	FSH	FBG	DV	OB			8		2400			3950	4600
23		ASSAULT 230	OP	CUD	FBG	DV	IO	115-230		8		3600			15600	18200
23		ELAN 228 B/R	OP	RNBT	FBG	DV	IO	115-230		8		3400			14400	16800
26	8	RELEASE 252	OP	FSH	FBG	DV	OB			8		3900			7800	8950
26	11	FREINDSHIP 260 AC	OP	CR	FBG	DV	IO	T360	YAMA	8	6	6500			39000	43400
1991 BOATS																
16	9	ELAN 171	OP	RNBT	FBG	DV	IO	115-135		7	1	1700			6350	7300
16	9	ELAN 171 B/R	OP	RNBT	FBG	DV	OB			7	1	1405			1950	2300
16	10	CLASSIC 170 B/R	OP	RNBT	FBG	DV	IO	115-155		7	2	1945			6600	7650
16	10	CLASSIC 190 B/R	OP	RNBT	FBG	DV	IO	115-155		7	2	1945			7050	8100
16	10	REGENCY 170 B/R	OP	RNBT	FBG	DV	IO	115-155		7	2	1945			6600	7650
17	10	ELAN 181	OP	RNBT	FBG	DV	IO	115-180		7	3	1775			6900	8050
18	6	CLASSIC 190 CUDDY	OP	CUD	FBG	DV	IO	115-230		7	9	2370			8900	10500
18	6	REGENCY 190 B/R	OP	RNBT	FBG	DV	IO	115-230		7	9	2100			8050	9700
18	8	ELAN 191	OP	RNBT	FBG	DV	IO	115-180		7	10	2160			8300	9650
20	8	ASSAULT 210	OP	CUD	FBG	DV	IO	115-230		8		3000			11700	13800
20	8	ELAN 208 B/R	OP	RNBT	FBG	DV	IO	115-230		8		2725			10800	12700
22		REGENCY 220	OP	CUD	FBG	DV	IO	115-230		8		3500			13100	15300
22		REGENCY 220 FISH	OP	CUD	FBG	DV	IO	115-230		8		3500			14300	16600
23		ASSAULT 230	OP	CUD	FBG	DV	IO	115-230		8		3600			14600	17000
23		ELAN 228 B/R	OP	RNBT	FBG	DV	IO	115-230		8		3400			13400	15700
1990 BOATS																
16	10	APOLLO CLASSIC 170	OP	RNBT	FBG	DV	IO	130-175		7	2	1945			6500	7500
16	10	APOLLO CLASSIC 170LS	OP	RNBT	FBG	DV	IO	130-175		7	2	1945			6700	7750
16	10	CHALLENGER 170	OP	RNBT	FBG	DV	IO	130-175		7	2	1945			6150	7150
16	10	CHALLENGER 170LS	OP	RNBT	FBG	DV	IO	130-175		7	2	1945			6300	7300
16	10	REGENCY 170	OP	RNBT	FBG	DV	IO	130	MRCR	7	2	1945			6200	7150
16	10	REGENCY 170LS	OP	RNBT	FBG	DV	OB			7	2	1965			2450	2850
18	6	APOLLO CLASSIC 190	OP	RNBT	FBG	DV	IO	130-260		7	9	2110			7600	9500
18	6	APOLLO CLASSIC 190FS	OP	RNBT	FBG	DV	IO	130-260		7	9	2110			8850	10500
18	6	APOLLO CLASSIC 190LS	OP	RNBT	FBG	DV	IO	130-260		7	9	2110			7850	9700
18	6	CHALLENGER 190	OP	RNBT	FBG	DV	IO	130-175		7	9	2110			7150	8350
18	6	CHALLENGER 190	OP	RNBT	FBG	DV	IO	260	MRCR	7	9	2110			7850	9050
18	6	CHALLENGER 190LS	OP	RNBT	FBG	DV	IO	130-175		7	9	2110			7400	8600
18	6	CHALLENGER 190LS	OP	RNBT	FBG	DV	IO	260	MRCR	7	9	2110			8050	9250
18	6	CUDDY 190	OP	CUD	FBG	DV	IO	130-260		7	9	2370			8150	10200
18	6	CUDDY 190LS	OP	CUD	FBG	DV	IO	130-260		7	9	2370			8300	10300
18	6	REGENCY 190	OP	RNBT	FBG	DV	IO	130-175		7	9	2110			7100	8250
18	6	REGENCY 190	OP	RNBT	FBG	DV	IO	260	MRCR	7	9	2110			7800	8950
18	6	REGENCY 190LS	OP	RNBT	FBG	DV	IO	130-175		7	9	2110			7300	8500
18	6	REGENCY 190LS	OP	RNBT	FBG	DV	IO	260	MRCR	7	9	2110			8000	9200
18	8	ELAN 188	OP	RNBT	FBG	DV	IO	130-175		7	10	2160			7800	9050
20	8	ELAN 208	OP	RNBT	FBG	DV	IO	130-175		8		2475			9350	10700
20	8	ELAN 208CB	OP	RNBT	FBG	DV	IO	130-260		8		2475			9850	11700
20	8	ELAN 208CB LS	OP	RNBT	FBG	DV	IO	130-260		8		2475			10000	11900
20	8	ELAN 208LS	OP	RNBT	FBG	DV	IO	130-260		8		2475			9550	11400
22		CUDDY 220 LS	OP	CUD	FBG	DV	IO	130-280		8		3400			12600	15400
1986 BOATS																
17		TRITON	ST	RNBT	FBG	SV	IO	120-185		7	2	1800			5000	5850
18	6	APOLLO BR	ST	RNBT	FBG	SV	IO	120-230		7	9	2000			5750	7000
18	6	APOLLO BR	ST	RNBT	FBG	SV	IO	260		7	9	2000			6350	7300
18	6	APOLLO CLOSED BOW	ST	RNBT	FBG	SV	IO	120-230		7	9	2000			5850	7100
18	6	APOLLO CLOSED BOW	ST	RNBT	FBG	SV	IO	260		7	9	2000			6400	7350
18	6	APOLLO CUDDY	ST	RNBT	FBG	SV	IO	120-260		7	9	2000			6350	7750
18	6	MAGNUM	ST	RNBT	FBG	SV	IO	200-260		7	8	2100			6200	7500
1985 BOATS																
17		TRITON	ST	RNBT	FBG	SV	IO	120-140		7	2	1700			4700	5450
18	6	APOLLO	ST	RNBT	FBG	SV	IO	140-200		7	9	2000			5750	6700
18	6	APOLLO	ST	SKI	FBG	SV	IO	140-200		7	9	2000			5600	6500

EAGLE TRAWLER YACHTS

MILLER YACHT SALES INC
S TOMS RIVER NJ 08753 COAST GUARD MFG ID- ETY

See inside cover to adjust price for area

LOA FT	LOA IN	NAME AND/ OR MODEL	TOP/ RIG	BOAT TYPE	HULL MTL	HULL TP	ENGINE TP	ENGINE # HP	ENGINE MFG	BEAM FT	BEAM IN	WGT LBS	DRAFT FT	DRAFT IN	RETAIL LOW	RETAIL HIGH
1986 BOATS																
39	11	EAGLE DBL CBN	FB	TRWL	FBG	DS	IB	120D	LEHM	14			4		128500	141500
39	11	EAGLE DBL CBN	FB	TRWL	FBG	DS	IB	T120D	LEHM	14			4		135000	148500
39	11	EAGLE SEDAN	FB	TRWL	FBG	DS	IB	120D	LEHM	14			4		128500	141500
39	11	EAGLE SEDAN	FB	TRWL	FBG	DS	IB	T120D	LEHM	14			4		135000	148500
1985 BOATS																
39	11	EAGLE DBL CBN	FB	TRWL	FBG	DS	IB	120D	LEHM	14			4		123000	135000
39	11	EAGLE DBL CBN	FB	TRWL	FBG	DS	IB	T120D	LEHM	14			4		129000	142000
39	11	EAGLE SEDAN	FB	TRWL	FBG	DS	IB	120D	LEHM	14			4		123000	135000
39	11	EAGLE SEDAN	FB	TRWL	FBG	DS	IB	T120D	LEHM	14			4		129000	142000
1984 BOATS																
39	11	EAGLE DBL CBN	FB	TRWL	FBG	DS	IB	128		14			4		93900	103000
IB 120D LEHM 117500 129500, IB 128D 118000 129500, IB T120D LEHM 123500 136000																

CONTINUED ON NEXT PAGE

EAGLE TRAWLER YACHTS -CONTINUED See inside cover to adjust price for area

LOA FT	LOA IN	NAME AND/ OR MODEL	TOP/ RIG	BOAT TYPE	HULL MTL	HULL TP	ENGINE TP	ENGINE # HP	ENGINE MFG	BEAM FT	BEAM IN	WGT LBS	DRAFT FT	DRAFT IN	RETAIL LOW	RETAIL HIGH
		1984 BOATS														
39	11	EAGLE SEDAN	FB	TRWL	FBG	DS	IB	128		14			4		93900	103000
		IB 120D LEHM 117500 129500, IB 128D 118000 129500, IB T120D LEHM 123500 136000														

....For earlier years, see the BUC Used Boat Price Guide, Volume 3

EAST/WEST CUSTOM BOATS INC

KITTERY PT ME 03905 COAST GUARD MFG ID- EWV See inside cover to adjust price for area

LOA FT	LOA IN	NAME AND/ OR MODEL	TOP/ RIG	BOAT TYPE	HULL MTL	HULL TP	ENGINE TP	ENGINE # HP	ENGINE MFG	BEAM FT	BEAM IN	WGT LBS	DRAFT FT	DRAFT IN	RETAIL LOW	RETAIL HIGH
		1984 BOATS														
18	3	DRASCOMBE-LUGGER	YWL	SAIL	P/P	CB	OB			6	3	600		8	4150	4850
21	9	DRASCOMBE-LONGBOAT	YWL	SAIL	P/P	CB	OB			6	7	700	1		5300	6100

....For earlier years, see the BUC Used Boat Price Guide, Volume 3

EASTERN BOATS INC

EASTERN BOATS
MILTON NH 03851 COAST GUARD MFG ID- SCG
FORMERLY SEACOAST BOAT BUILDERS
See inside cover to adjust price for area

For more recent years, see the BUC Used Boat Price Guide, Volume 1

LOA FT	LOA IN	NAME AND/ OR MODEL	TOP/ RIG	BOAT TYPE	HULL MTL	HULL TP	ENGINE TP	ENGINE # HP	ENGINE MFG	BEAM FT	BEAM IN	WGT LBS	DRAFT FT	DRAFT IN	RETAIL LOW	RETAIL HIGH
		1996 BOATS														
18	3	CLASSIC 18	OP	CTRCN	FBG	SD	OB			6	8	1000	1		5650	6500
18	3	CUDDY 18	OP	CUD	FBG	SD	OB			6	8	1150	1		6350	7300
18	9	SEAWAY 19 CC	OP	CTRCN	FBG	SD	OB			7	6	1200		10	6700	7700
22	3	CENTER CONSOLE 22	OP	CTRCN	FBG	SD	OB			7	8	1400	1	2	7550	8650
22	3	LOBSTER 22	EPH	OFF	FBG	SD	OB			7	8	2000	1	2	10300	11700
22	3	SPORT FISH 22	EPH	FSH	FBG	SD	OB			7	8	1800	1	2	9450	10700
26	4	CENTER CONSOLE 27	HT	CTRCN	FBG	DS	IO	200	MRCR	8	4	3600	1	2	19300	21500
26	4	LOBSTER 27	EPH	OFF	FBG	DS	IO	200	MRCR	8	4	4800	2	2	20700	23000
26	11	EASTERN JC 27	FB	CBNCR	FBG	SV	VD	250	MRCR	10			2	10	31600	35100
29	9	EASTERN 30 SISU	FB	CBNCR	FBG	SV	IB	310	MRCR	10	6	11400	2	11	60000	66000
31	4	EASTERN JC 31	FB	CBNCR	FBG	SV	IB	310	MRCR	11	2	11600	3	3	68600	75300
35		EASTERN JC 35	FB	CBNCR	FBG	SV	IB	350D	CUM	12		16000	3	6	119500	131500
		1995 BOATS														
18	3	CLASSIC 18	OP	CTRCN	FBG	SD	OB			6	8	1000	1		5400	6200
18	3	CUDDY 18	OP	CUD	FBG	SD	OB			6	8	1150	1		6050	7000
18	9	SEAWAY 19 CC	OP	CTRCN	FBG	SD	OB			7	6	1200		10	6400	7350
22	3	CENTER CONSOLE 22	OP	CTRCN	FBG	SD	OB			7	8	1400	1	2	7200	8250
22	3	LOBSTER 22	EPH	OFF	FBG	SD	OB			7	8	2000	1	2	9850	11200
22	3	SPORT FISH 22	EPH	FSH	FBG	SD	OB			7	8	1800	1	2	9050	10300
26	4	CENTER CONSOLE 27	HT	CTRCN	FBG	DS	IO	200	MRCR	8	4	3600	1	2	18200	20200
26	4	LOBSTER 27	EPH	OFF	FBG	DS	IO	200	MRCR	8	4	4800	2	2	19300	21500
29	9	EASTSERN 30 SISU	FB	CBNCR	FBG	SV	IB	310	MRCR	10	6	11400	2	11	56800	62400
31	4	EASTERN JC 31	FB	CBNCR	FBG	SV	IB	310	MRCR	11	2	11600	3	3	64800	71200
35		EASTERN JC 35	FB	CBNCR	FBG	SV	IB	350D	CUM	12		16000	3	6	113500	125000
		1994 BOATS														
18	3	CLASSIC 18	OP	CTRCN	FBG	SD	OB			6	8	1000	1		5150	5950
18	3	CUDDY 18	OP	CUD	FBG	SD	OB			6	8	1150	1		5800	6650
18	9	SEAWAY 19 CC	OP	CTRCN	FBG	SD	OB			7	6	1200		10	6100	7000
22	3	CENTER CONSOLE 22	OP	CTRCN	FBG	SD	OB			7	8	1400	1	2	6900	7900
22	3	LOBSTER 22	EPH	OFF	FBG	SD	OB			7	8	2000	1	2	9400	10700
22	3	SPORT FISH 22	EPH	FSH	FBG	SD	OB			7	8	1800	1	2	8550	9850
26	4	CENTER CONSOLE 27	HT	CTRCN	FBG	DS	IO	200	MRCR	8	4	3600	1	2	16600	18900
26	4	LOBSTER 27	EPH	OFF	FBG	DS	IO	200	MRCR	8	4	4800	2	2	18200	20300
		1993 BOATS														
18	3	CLASSIC 18	OP	CTRCN	FBG	SD	OB			6	8	1000	1		4950	5700
18	3	CUDDY 18	OP	CUD	FBG	SD	OB			6	8	1500	1		6800	7850
18	9	SEAWAY 19 CC	OP	CTRCN	FBG	SD	OB			7	6	1200		10	5850	6700
22	3	CENTER CONSOLE 22	OP	CTRCN	FBG	SD	OB			7	8	1400	1	2	6600	7600
22	3	LOBSTER 22	EPH	OFF	FBG	SD	OB			7	8	2000	1	2	9100	10300
22	3	SPORT FISH 22	EPH	FSH	FBG	SD	OB			7	8	1800	1	2	8200	9450
26	4	CENTER CONSOLE 27	HT	CTRCN	FBG	DS	IO	200	MRCR	8	4	3600	1	2	15500	17600
26	4	LOBSTER 27	EPH	OFF	FBG	DS	IO	200	MRCR	8	4	4800	2	2	16700	18900
		1992 BOATS														
18	3	CLASSIC 18	OP	CTRCN	FBG	SD	OB			6	8	1000	1		4750	5450
18	3	CUDDY 18	OP	CUD	FBG	SD	OB			6	8	1500	1		6550	7500
18	9	SEAWAY 19 CC	OP	CTRCN	FBG	SD	OB			7	6	1200		10	5600	6450
22	3	CENTER CONSOLE 22	OP	CTRCN	FBG	SD	OB			7	8	1400	1	2	6350	7300
22	3	LOBSTER 22	EPH	OFF	FBG	SD	OB			7	8	2000	1	2	8600	9900
22	3	SPORT FISH 22	EPH	FSH	FBG	SD	OB			7	8	1800	1	2	7900	9100
26	4	CENTER CONSOLE 27	HT	CTRCN	FBG	DS	IO	200	MRCR	8	4	3600	1	2	14500	16500
26	4	LOBSTER 27	EPH	OFF	FBG	DS	IO	200	MRCR	8	4	4800	2	2	15600	17700
		1991 BOATS														
18	3	CLASSIC 18	OP	CTRCN	FBG	SD	OB			6	8	1000	1		4600	5300
18	3	CUDDY 18	OP	CUD	FBG	SD	OB			6	8	1500	1		6300	7250
18	9	SEAWAY 19 CC	OP	CTRCN	FBG	SD	OB			7	6	1200		10	5400	6200
22	3	CENTER CONSOLE 22	OP	CTRCN	FBG	SD	OB			7	8	1400	1	2	6100	7000
22	3	LOBSTER 22	EPH	OFF	FBG	SD	OB			7	8	2000	1	2	8300	9550
22	3	SPORT FISH 22	EPH	FSH	FBG	SD	OB			7	8	1800	1	2	7600	8750
26	4	CENTER CONSOLE 27	HT	CTRCN	FBG	DS	IO	200	MRCR	8	4	3600	1	2	13600	15500
26	4	LOBSTER 27	EPH	OFF	FBG	DS	IO	200	MRCR	8	4	4800	2	2	14600	16600
		1990 BOATS														
18	3	CLASSIC 18	OP	CTRCN	FBG	SD	OB			6	8	1000	1		4450	5100
18	3	CUDDY 18	OP	CUD	FBG	SD	OB			6	8	1500	1		6100	7000
18	9	SEAWAY 19 CC	OP	CTRCN	FBG	SD	OB			7	6	1200		10	5200	6000
22	3	CENTER CONSOLE 22	OP	CTRCN	FBG	SD	OB			7	8	1400	1	2	5900	6750
22	3	LOBSTER 22	EPH	OFF	FBG	SD	OB			7	8	2000	1	2	8000	9200
22	3	SPORT FISH 22	EPH	FSH	FBG	SD	OB			7	8	1800	1	2	7350	8450
26	4	CENTER CONSOLE 27	HT	CTRCN	FBG	DS	IO	200	MRCR	8	4	3600	1	2	12800	14600
26	4	LOBSTER 27	EPH	OFF	FBG	DS	IO	200	MRCR	8	4	4800	2	2	13800	15600
		1989 BOATS														
18	3	CLASSIC 18	OP	CTRCN	FBG	SD	OB			6	8	1000	1		4250	4950
18	3	CUDDY 18	OP	CUD	FBG	SD	OB			6	8	1500	1		5900	6750
18	9	SEAWAY 19 CC	OP	CTRCN	FBG	SD	OB			7	6	1200		10	5050	5800
22	3	CENTER CONSOLE 22	OP	CTRCN	FBG	SD	OB			7	8	1400	1	2	5700	6550
22	3	LOBSTER 22	EPH	OFF	FBG	SD	OB			7	8	2000	1	2	7700	8850
22	3	SPORT FISH 22	EPH	FSH	FBG	SD	OB			7	8	1800	1	2	7100	8150
26	4	CENTER CONSOLE 27	HT	CTRCN	FBG	DS	IO	200	MRCR	8	4	3600	1	2	12100	13700
26	4	LOBSTER 27	EPH	OFF	FBG	DS	IO	200	MRCR	8	4	4800	2	2	13000	14800

EBBTIDE CORP

WHITE BLUFF TN 37187 COAST GUARD MFG ID- ETC See inside cover to adjust price for area

For more recent years, see the BUC Used Boat Price Guide, Volume 1

LOA FT	LOA IN	NAME AND/ OR MODEL	TOP/ RIG	BOAT TYPE	HULL MTL	HULL TP	ENGINE TP	ENGINE # HP	ENGINE MFG	BEAM FT	BEAM IN	WGT LBS	DRAFT FT	DRAFT IN	RETAIL LOW	RETAIL HIGH
		1995 BOATS														
16	3	DYNA-TRAK 160SS	OP	RNBT	FBG	SV	OB			6	8	1050			2850	3300
16	8	DYNA-TRAK 170	OP	BASS	FBG	SV	OB			6	9	1000			2750	3200
18		CAMPIONE 185	OP	B/R	FBG	DV	IO	135-185		7		2200			5050	6250
18		CAMPIONE 185 F & S	OP	B/R	FBG	DV	IO	135-185		7		2200			5450	6750
18		DYNA-TRAK 179	OP	BASS	FBG	SV	OB			7	3	1050			3000	3500
18		DYNA-TRAK 180	OP	BASS	FBG	SV	OB			7	3	1150			2800	3250
18		DYNA-TRAK 180SS	OP	RNBT	FBG	SV	OB			7	3	1200			3350	3900
18		DYNA-TRAK 181DC	OP	BASS	FBG	SV	OB			7	3	1150			3500	4050
18		DYNA-TRAK 181SC	OP	BASS	FBG	SV	OB			7	3	1150			3400	4000
18		DYNA-TRAK 181SS	OP	BASS	FBG	SV	OB			7	3	1380			3700	4350
18		EBBTIDE 182SE	OP	B/R	FBG	DV	IO	135		7		2200			4850	5850
18		EBBTIDE 182XL	OP	RNBT	FBG	DV	IO	135		7		2200			5100	6150
18	5	DYNA-TRAK 186SC	OP	BASS	FBG	SV	OB			7	7	1380			3750	4400
18	9	EBBTIDE 190 SPORT	OP	BASS	FBG	SV	OB			7	8	1550			4150	4800
18	10	MYSTIQUE 1900	OP	B/R	FBG	DV	IO	160-205		7	8	2550			6250	7550
18	10	MYSTIQUE 1900	OP	B/R	FBG	DV	IO	230-235		7	8	2550			6800	7800
19	1	CAMPIONE 195	OP	B/R	FBG	DV	IO	135-235		7	6	2600			6550	7950
19	1	CAMPIONE 195 CUD	OP	CUD	FBG	DV	IO	135-185		7	6	2750			6950	8400
19	1	EBBTIDE 192SE	OP	B/R	FBG	DV	IO	135-185		7	6	2600			6250	7600
19	1	EBBTIDE 192XL	OP	B/R	FBG	DV	IO	135-185		7	6	2600			6050	7400
19	4	DYNA-TRAK 194CC	OP	BASS	FBG	SV	OB			7	8	1450			4100	4750
19	4	DYNA-TRAK 194DC	OP	BASS	FBG	SV	OB			7	8	1450			4100	4750
19	4	DYNA-TRAK 194SC	OP	BASS	FBG	SV	OB			7	8	1450			4000	4650
19	10	DYNA-TRAK 201SS	OP	BASS	FBG	SV	OB			8		1750			4800	5500
20	4	CAPIONE 205	OP	B/R	FBG	DV	IO	160-250		8		2950			8100	10000
20	4	CAPIONE 205	OP	B/R	FBG	DV	IO	255	VLVO	8		2950			9050	10300
20	6	MYSTIQUE 2100	OP	B/R	FBG	DV	IO	160-255		8	6	3250			9100	11200
20	6	MYSTIQUE 2100	OP	B/R	FBG	DV	IO	300	MRCR	8	6	3250			10100	11500
22	1	CAPIONE 225	OP	B/R	FBG	DV	IO	205-300		8	3	3500			10200	12700
22	4	EBBTIDE 224 CLASSIC	OP	CUD	FBG	DV	IO	205-255		8	3	3950			12100	14600
22	11	MYSTIQUE 2300 DB	OP	RNBT	FBG	SV	OB			8	6	4000			10400	11900
22	11	MYSTIQUE 2300 DB	OP	RNBT	FBG	SV	IO	180-255		8	6	4000			11800	14400
23	2	MYSTIQUE 2300	OP	CUD	FBG	DV	IO	230-300		8	6	3900			13100	15400
23	2	MYSTIQUE 2300	OP	CUD	FBG	DV	IO	350-385		8	6	3900			14900	18300
		1994 BOATS														
16	3	DYNA-TRAK 160CC	OP	RNBT	FBG	SV	OB			6	8	1050			2700	3150
16	8	DYNA-TRAK 170	OP	BASS	FBG	SV	OB			6	9	1000			2600	3050
18		DYNA-TRAK 178SS	OP	RNBT	FBG	SV	OB			7	3	1200			3200	3700

LOA FT	LOA IN	NAME AND/ OR MODEL	TOP/ RIG	BOAT TYPE	HULL MTL	HULL TP	ENGINE TP	# HP	MFG	BEAM FT	BEAM IN	WGT LBS	DRAFT FT IN	RETAIL LOW	RETAIL HIGH
1994 BOATS															
18		DYNA-TRAK 179	OP	BASS	FBG	SV	OB			7	3	1050		2850	3300
18		DYNA-TRAK 180	OP	BASS	FBG	SV	OB			7	3	1150		2600	3000
18		DYNA-TRAK 181DC	OP	BASS	FBG	SV	OB			7	3	1150		3350	3900
18		DYNA-TRAK 181SC	OP	BASS	FBG	SV	OB			7	3	1150		3300	3850
18		DYNA-TRAK 181SS	OP	BASS	FBG	SV	OB			7	3	1380		3550	4150
18		EBBTIDE 178SS	OP	BASS	FBG	SV	OB			7	3	1200		3200	3700
18		EBBTIDE 182	OP	RNBT	FBG	SV	IO	110-135		7		2200		4750	5700
18		EBBTIDE 182SE	OP	RNBT	FBG	SV	IO	110-185		7		2200		4950	5950
18		EBBTIDE 182SE F/S	OP	RNBT	FBG	SV	IO	110-185		7		2200		5400	6550
18	5	DYNA-TRAK 186SC	OP	BASS	FBG	SV	OB			7	6	1380		3600	4200
18	9	EBBTIDE 190SF	OP	BASS	FBG	SV	OB			7	8	1550		3950	4600
18	10	CAMPIONE 1900	OP	RNBT	FBG	SV	IO	160-215		7	8	2550		6050	7400
19	1	EBBTIDE 190SE	OP	RNBT	FBG	SV	IO	160-215		7	6	2600		5850	7250
19	1	EBBTIDE 190SE CUDDY	OP	CUD	FBG	SV	IO	160-185		7	6	2750		6500	7850
19	1	EBBTIDE 190SE F/S	OP	RNBT	FBG	SV	IO	160-215		7	6	2600		6300	7750
19	4	DYNA-TRAK 194CC	OP	BASS	FBG	SV	OB			7	8	1450		3900	4550
19	4	DYNA-TRAK 194DC	OP	BASS	FBG	SV	OB			7	8	1450		3900	4550
19	4	DYNA-TRAK 194SC	OP	BASS	FBG	SV	OB			7	8	1450		3800	4400
19	10	DYNA-TRAK 201SS	OP	BASS	FBG	SV	OB			8		1750		4600	5300
20	4	CAMPIONE 2040	OP	RNBT	FBG	SV	IO	180-255		8		2950		8150	10200
20	4	EBBTIDE 204SE	OP	RNBT	FBG	SV	IO	180-250		8		2950		7450	9100
20	4	EBBTIDE 204SE	OP	RNBT	FBG	SV	IO	255	VLVO	8		2950		8150	9350
22	1	CAMPIONE 2200	OP	RNBT	FBG	SV	IO	205-300		8	3	3500		9650	12000
22	4	CATALINA 224	OP	CUD	FBG	SV	IO	205-255		8	3	3950		11300	13600
23	2	CAMPIONE 2300GS	OP	CUD	FBG	SV	IO	230-300		8	6	3900		12200	14400
23	2	CAMPIONE 2300GS	OP	CUD	FBG	SV	IO	350	MRCR	8	6	3900		13900	15800
1987 BOATS															
16	6	MONTEGO 170	OP	RNBT	FBG	SV	OB			6	8	1050		2050	2450
16	6	MONTEGO 170	OP	RNBT	FBG	SV	IO	120-130		6	8	1925		2700	3150
16	6	MONTEGO 170XL	OP	RNBT	FBG	SV	IO	130-175		6	8	1925		2900	3400
16	8	CAMPIONE 166	OP	RNBT	FBG	SV	OB			7	5	855		1750	2050
16	8	DYNA-TRAK 166	OP	BASS	FBG	SV	OB			6	7	1000		1800	2150
16	8	DYNA-TRAK 166SS	OP	SKI	FBG	SV	OB			6	7	1050		2050	2450
16	8	DYNA-TRAK 166STE	OP	BASS	FBG	SV	OB			6	7	1000		2200	2550
17	9	RIVIERA 180	OP	RNBT	FBG	SV	IO	130-175		7	1	2300		3150	3700
17	9	RIVIERA 180XL	OP	RNBT	FBG	SV	IO	130-205		7	1	2300		3550	4100
18		CAMPIONE 180	OP	RNBT	FBG	SV	OB			7	2	1075		2250	2650
18		DYNA-TRAK 180SS	OP	SKI	FBG	SV	OB			7	2	1200		2250	2650
18		DYNA-TRAK 180SSLE	OP	SKI	FBG	SV	OB			7	2	1200		2600	3000
18		DYNA-TRAK 180STE	OP	BASS	FBG	SV	OB			7	2	1150		2350	2750
18		DYNA-TRAK 180TCSTE	OP	BASS	FBG	SV	OB			7	2	1150		2400	2750
18	9	CATALINA 190	ST	CUD	FBG	SV	OB			7	6	1650		3150	3650
18	9	CATALINA 190	ST	RNBT	FBG	SV	OB			7	6	1550		3000	3500
18	9	CATALINA 190	ST	RNBT	FBG	SV	IO	175-205		7	6	2550		3800	4450
18	9	CATALINA 190	ST	SF	FBG	SV	OB			7	6	1550		3000	3500
18	9	CATALINA 190XL	ST	RNBT	FBG	SV	IO	175-270		7	6	2550		3950	4900
18	9	CATALINA 190XL CUDDY	ST	CUD	FBG	SV	IO	175-260		7	6	2650		4100	5050
18	9	CATALINA 190XL CUDDY	ST	CUD	FBG	SV	IO	270	MRCR	7	6	2650		4500	5150
19	11	CAMPIONE 200	OP	RNBT	FBG	SV	IO	230-270		8		2550		4450	5350
19	11	DYNA-TRAK 196SS	OP	SKI	FBG	SV	OB			8		1675		3350	3900
19	11	DYNA-TRAK 196STE	OP	BASS	FBG	SV	OB			8		1600		3250	3800
22	4	CATALINA 224XL CUDDY	ST	CUD	FBG	SV	IO	230-270		8	2	3950		7400	8750
22	4	CATALINA 224XL CUDDY	ST	CUD	FBG	SV	IO	330	MRCR	8	2	3950		8350	9600
1986 BOATS															
16	5	MONTEGO		RNBT	FBG	DV	OB			6	10	1050		2000	2400
16	5	MONTEGO		RNBT	FBG	DV	IO	140		6	10	1050		2050	2450
16	6	DYNA-TRAK 166			FBG	SV	OB			6	10	1000		1900	2250
17	8	RIVIERA		RNBT	FBG	TR	IO	140		7	1	2300		3150	3700
17	11	DYNA-TRAK 180			FBG	SV	OB			7	2	1200		2350	2750
17	11	DYNA-TRAK 180 STE			FBG	SV	OB			7	2	1150		2300	2650
18	9	CATALINA		CUD	FBG	DV	IO	170		7	8	2650		3950	4600
18	9	CATALINA		RNBT	FBG	DV	IO			6	10	2550		**	**
18	9	CATALINA		RNBT	FBG	DV	IO	175		7	8	1550		3050	3550
18	9	CATALINA CUDDY		CUD	FBG	DV	OB			7	8	1650		3050	3550
19	5	DYNA-TRAK 195 STE			FBG		OB			7	11	1600		3050	3550
22	2	CATALINA XL		CUD	FBG	DV	IO	230		6	10	3950		6600	7600
1985 BOATS															
16	5	MONTEGO		RNBT	FBG	DV	IO	140		6	10			2450	2850
17	8	RIVIERA		RNBT	FBG	TR	IO	140		7	1			3000	3500
17	8	RIVIERA SS		RNBT	FBG	TR	IO	140		7	1			3000	3500
18	9	CATALINA		RNBT	FBG	DV	IO	170		7	8			3600	4200
18	9	CATALINA SS		RNBT	FBG	DV	IO	170		7	8			3600	4200

....For earlier years, see the BUC Used Boat Price Guide, Volume 3

EBKO INDUSTRIES INC

HASTINGS NE 68902 COAST GUARD MFG ID- EBK See inside cover to adjust price for area

LOA FT	LOA IN	NAME AND/ OR MODEL	TOP/ RIG	BOAT TYPE	HULL MTL	HULL TP	ENGINE TP	# HP	MFG	BEAM FT	BEAM IN	WGT LBS	DRAFT FT IN	RETAIL LOW	RETAIL HIGH
1992 BOATS															
16	3	MONTE-CARLO 165	OP	RNBT	FBG	DV	OB			7		950		2400	2750
16	3	MONTE-CARLO 165	OP	RNBT	FBG	DV	IO	115-175		7		1800		3550	4150
16	3	MONTE-CARLO 165FS	OP	RNBT	FBG	DV	OB			7		950		2850	3350
16	3	MONTE-CARLO 165FS	OP	RNBT	FBG	DV	IO	115-175		7		1800		3800	4550
16	3	MONTE-CARLO 165SS	OP	RNBT	FBG	DV	IO	115-175		7		1800		3750	4350
17	3	BLUEWATER V175	OP	RNBT	FBG	DV	IO	155-260		7	8			4400	5400
17	3	MONTE-CARLO 173	OP	RNBT	FBG	DV	OB			7	8	1170		3250	3750
17	3	MONTE-CARLO 180FS	OP	RNBT	FBG	DV	OB			7	2	1050		2950	3450
17	3	MONTE-CARLO 180FS	OP	RNBT	FBG	DV	IO	115-205		7	2	1900		4100	5000
17	10	BLUEWATER V185	OP	RNBT	FBG	DV	IO	155-270		7		1850		4600	5600
17	10	MONTE-CARLO 1800	OP	RNBT	FBG	DV	IO	115-205		7		1850		4050	4850
17	10	MONTE-CARLO 1800SS	OP	RNBT	FBG	DV	IO	115-205		7		1850		4250	5050
18	7	MONTE-CARLO 195	OP	RNBT	FBG	DV	OB			7	8	1250		3550	4100
18	7	MONTE-CARLO 195FS	OP	RNBT	FBG	DV	IO	115-205		7	7	2050		4800	5650
18	7	MONTE-CARLO 195FS	OP	RNBT	FBG	SV	OB			7	7	1250		3900	4550
18	7	MONTE-CARLO 195FS	OP	RNBT	FBG	SV	IO	235	OMC	7	7	2000		5000	5750
19		BLUEWATER V190	OP	RNBT	FBG	DV	IO	155-270		7	2	2000		5000	6150
19		BLUEWATER V190	OP	RNBT	FBG	DV	IO	300-330		7	2	2000		5550	6850
19		MONTE-CARLO 1900	OP	RNBT	FBG	DV	IO	115-205		7	2	2000		4650	5500
19		MONTE-CARLO 1900SS	OP	RNBT	FBG	DV	IO	115-205		7	2	2000		4750	5750
20	6	BLUEWATER V210	OP	CUD	FBG	DV	IO	155-270		7	7			5850	7250
20	6	BLUEWATER V210	OP	CUD	FBG	DV	IO	300-330		7	7			6750	8300
20	6	BLUEWATER V210	OP	RNBT	FBG	DV	IO	155-300		7	7	2100		5950	7400
20	6	BLUEWATER V210	OP	RNBT	FBG	DV	IO	330-340		7	7	2100		6850	8250
20	6	MONTE-CARLO 2100	OP	RNBT	FBG	DV	IO	115-270		7	7	2100		5450	6700
20	6	MONTE-CARLO 2100SS	OP	RNBT	FBG	DV	IO	115-270		7	7	2100		5650	6750
25	8	SPECTRE 2650	OP	CBNCR	FBG	DV	IO	230-370		9	6	6200		19900	24400
26		SPECTRE 2600	OP	CUD	FBG	DV	IO	300-370		8		4700		14500	18000
26		SPECTRE 2600	OP	CUD	FBG	DV	IO	390	MRCR	8		4700		16500	18700
1990 BOATS															
16	3	CHEROKEE PK165	OP	RNBT	FBG	DV	OB			7				2350	2750
16	3	CHEROKEE PK165	OP	RNBT	FBG	DV	IO	175						3250	3800
16	3	CIMMARON 1651	ST	RNBT	FBG	DV	OB			6	9	750		1900	2250
16	3	CIMMARON 1651FS	ST	RNBT	FBG	SV	OB			6	9	910		2300	2700
16	3	CIMMARON 1651SS	ST	RNBT	FBG	DV	IO	140		6	9	750		2300	2700
16	3	MONTE-CARLO 165	OP	RNBT	FBG	DV	OB			7		950		2150	2500
16	3	MONTE-CARLO 165	OP	RNBT	FBG	DV	IO	175		7		1800		3150	3650
16	3	MONTE-CARLO 165FS	OP	RNBT	FBG	DV	OB			7		950		2650	3100
16	3	MONTE-CARLO 165FS	OP	RNBT	FBG	DV	IO	175		7		1800		3550	4150
16	3	MONTE-CARLO 165SS	OP	RNBT	FBG	DV	IO	175		7		1800		3250	3800
16	3	SKIMASTER PK165	OP	RNBT	FBG	DV	OB			7		1800		4200	4900
16	3	SKIMASTER PK165	OP	RNBT	FBG	DV	IO	125		7		1800		3250	3800
17	3	CHEROKEE PK1785	OP	RNBT	FBG	DV	OB			7	2			2650	3100
17	3	CHEROKEE PK180	OP	RNBT	FBG	DV	IO	205		7	2			3750	4350
17	3	CIMMARON 1785	ST	RNBT	FBG	DV	IO	205		7	2	1900		3500	4050
17	3	CIMMARON 1785FS	ST	RNBT	FBG	DV	OB			7	2	930		2450	2850
17	3	CIMMARON 1785FS	ST	RNBT	FBG	DV	IO	205		7	2	1900		3800	4450
17	3	MONTE-CARLO 173	OP	RNBT	FBG	DV	OB			7	8	1170		2950	3450
17	3	MONTE-CARLO 180FS	ST	RNBT	FBG	DV	OB			7	2	970		2550	2950
17	3	MONTE-CARLO 180FS	ST	RNBT	FBG	DV	IO	205		7	2	1900		3850	4500
17	3	SKIMASTER PK1785	OP	RNBT	FBG	DV	OB			7	2			2650	3100
17	3	SKIMASTER PK180	OP	RNBT	FBG	DV	IO	205		7	2			3750	4350
17	10	CIMMARON 180/EURO	OP	RNBT	FBG	DV	IO	205		7				3800	4400
17	10	CIMMARON 180/EUROSS	OP	RNBT	FBG	DV	IO	205		7				3900	4500
18	7	CHEROKEE PK195	OP	RNBT	FBG	DV	IO	230		7	8			4500	5150
18	7	CHEROKEE PK195SS	OP	CUD	FBG	DV	IO	230		7	8			4700	5400
18	7	CIMMARON 1821	ST	RNBT	FBG	DV	OB			7	8	1250		2650	3050
18	7	CIMMARON 1821FS	ST	RNBT	FBG	DV	OB			7	8	1250		3500	4050
18	7	CIMMARON 1821FS	ST	RNBT	FBG	DV	IO	230		7	8	2000		4400	5050
18	7	MONTE-CARLO 195	ST	CUD	FBG	SV	IO	230		7	7	2200		4700	5400
18	7	MONTE-CARLO 195	OP	RNBT	FBG	DV	OB			7	8	1250		3250	3750
18	7	MONTE-CARLO 195	ST	RNBT	FBG	SV	IO	230		7	7	2000		4400	5050
18	7	MONTE-CARLO 195FS	ST	RNBT	FBG	SV	OB			7	8	1250		3600	4200
18	7	MONTE-CARLO 195FS	ST	RNBT	FBG	SV	IO	230		7	8	2000		4500	5150
18	7	SKIMASTER PK195	OP	RNBT	FBG	DV	IO	230		7	8			4500	5150
18	7	SKIMASTER PK195SS	OP	CUD	FBG	DV	IO	230		7	8			4700	5400

LOA FT	LOA IN	NAME AND/ OR MODEL	TOP/ RIG	BOAT TYPE	-HULL- MTL	-HULL- TP	ENGINE TP	ENGINE # HP	ENGINE MFG	BEAM FT	BEAM IN	WGT LBS	DRAFT FT	DRAFT IN	RETAIL LOW	RETAIL HIGH
		1990 BOATS														
19		CIMMARON 190/EURO	OP	RNBT	FBG	DV	IO	205		7	2				4200	4850
19		CIMMARON 190/SS EURO	OP	RNBT	FBG	DV	IO	205		7	2				4400	5100
19		MONTE-CARLO 1900ESS	ST	RNBT	FBG	DV	IO	120		7	2	2125			4400	5050
19		MONTE-CARLO 1900EURO	ST	RNBT	FBG	DV	IO	120		7	2	2125			4100	4750
20	3	CIMMARON 211 SPTCDDY	OP	CUD	FBG	DV	IO	260							7150	8250
20	3	MONTE-CARLO 210	ST	CUD	FBG	SV	IO	260		8		3400			7150	8250
20	6	MONTE-CARLO 2100ESS	ST	RNBT	FBG	DV	IO	130		7	8	2740			5750	6600
20	6	MONTE-CARLO 2100EURO	ST	RNBT	FBG	DV	IO	130		7	8	2740			5450	6250
		1989 BOATS														
16	3	CIMMARON 1631	ST	RNBT	FBG	DV	IO	140		6	7				2950	3450
16	3	CIMMARON 1631XFS	ST	RNBT	FBG	SV	OB			6	7	910			2250	2600
16	3	MONTE-CARLO 163X	OP	RNBT	FBG	DV	OB			6	8	910			2250	2600
16	3	MONTE-CARLO 165	OP	RNBT	FBG	DV	OB			7		950			2050	2450
16	3	MONTE-CARLO 165FS	OP	RNBT	FBG	DV	OB			7		950			2550	2950
16	3	MONTE-CARLO 165FS	OP	RNBT	FBG	DV	IO	175		7		1800			3350	3850
16	3	MONTE-CARLO 165SM	OP	RNBT	FBG	DV	IO	175		7		1800			2900	3350
16	3	MONTE-CARLO 165SS	OP	RNBT	FBG	DV	IO	175		7		1800			3150	3650
17	3	BIARRITZ 175BR	ST	RNBT	FBG	DV	IO	205		7	7	2050			3700	4300
17	3	BIARRITZ 175SS	ST	RNBT	FBG	DV	IO	205		7	7	2050			3800	4450
17	3	CIMARRON 1785	ST	RNBT	FBG	DV	IO	205		7	2	1900			3350	3850
17	3	CIMARRON 1785FS	ST	RNBT	FBG	DV	IO	205		7	2	1900			3700	4300
17	3	CIMMARON 1785	ST	RNBT	FBG	DV	OB			7	2	930			2350	2750
17	3	CIMMARON 1785FS	ST	RNBT	FBG	DV	OB			7	2	970			2450	2850
17	3	MONTE-CARLO 173	OP	RNBT	FBG	DV	OB			7	7	1170			2850	3300
17	3	MONTE-CARLO 180	OP	RNBT	FBG	DV	IO	205		7	2	1900			3500	4100
17	3	MONTE-CARLO 180FS	ST	RNBT	FBG	DV	OB			7	2	970			2450	2850
17	3	MONTE-CARLO 180FS	ST	RNBT	FBG	DV	IO	130		7	2	1900			3400	3950
18	3	BIARRITZ 185BR	ST	RNBT	FBG	DV	IO	260		7	7	2300			4450	5100
18	3	BIARRITZ 185SS	ST	RNBT	FBG	DV	IO	260		7	7	2300			4550	5250
18	6	BIARRITZ 190BR	ST	RNBT	FBG	DV	IO	260		8		2750			5050	5800
18	6	BIARRITZ 190SS	ST	RNBT	FBG	DV	IO	260		8		2750			5150	5950
18	7	CIMARRON 1821FS	ST	RNBT	FBG	DV	IO	230		7	7	2000			4500	5150
18	7	CIMMARON 1821	ST	CUD	FBG	DV	IO	230		7	7	2200			4400	5050
18	7	CIMMARON 1821	ST	RNBT	FBG	DV	OB			7	7	1250			2650	3100
18	7	CIMMARON 1821	ST	RNBT	FBG	DV	IO	230		7	7	2000			3900	4500
18	7	CIMMARON 1821FS	ST	RNBT	FBG	DV	OB			7	7	1250			3550	4150
18	7	CIMMARON 1821FS	ST	RNBT	FBG	DV	IO	130		7	7	2000			3900	4550
18	7	MONTE-CARLO 195	ST	CUD	FBG	SV	IO	230		7	7	2200			4500	5150
18	7	MONTE-CARLO 195	OP	RNBT	FBG	DV	OB			7	7	1250			3100	3650
18	7	MONTE-CARLO 195	ST	RNBT	FBG	SV	IO	230		7	7	2000			4000	4600
18	7	MONTE-CARLO 195FS	ST	RNBT	FBG	DV	OB			7	7	1250			3100	3650
18	7	MONTE-CARLO 195FS	ST	RNBT	FBG	DV	IO	130		7	7	2000			3950	4600
18	9	MONTE-CARLO 1900ERSS	ST	RNBT	FBG	DV	IO	130		7	2	2125			3900	4550
18	9	MONTE-CARLO 1900EURO	ST	RNBT	FBG	DV	IO	130		7	2	2125			3900	4550
20	2	MONTE-CARLO 2100ERSS	ST	RNBT	FBG	DV	IO	130		7	7	2740			5150	5950
20	2	MONTE-CARLO 2100EURO	ST	RNBT	FBG	DV	IO	130		7	7	2740			5150	5950
20	3	BIARRITZ 210BR	ST	RNBT	FBG	DV	IO	260		8		3100			6000	6900
20	3	BIARRITZ 210SS	ST	RNBT	FBG	DV	IO	260		8		3100			6200	7100
20	3	MONTE-CARLO 210	ST	CUD	FBG	SV	IO	260		8		3400			6750	7750
		1988 BOATS														
16	3	CIMMARON 1631	ST	RNBT	FBG	DV	IO	140		6	7				2900	3350
16	3	CIMMARON 1631X	ST	RNBT	FBG	DV	OB			6	7	910			2000	2350
16	3	CIMMARON 1631X	ST	RNBT	FBG	DV	IO	140		6	7				2750	3200
16	3	CIMMARON 1631XFS	ST	RNBT	FBG	SV	OB			6	7	910			2300	2650
16	3	MONTE-CARLO 163X	OP	RNBT	FBG	DV	OB			6	8	910			2150	2500
16	3	MONTE-CARLO 165	OP	RNBT	FBG	DV	OB			7		950			2050	2450
16	3	MONTE-CARLO 165FS	OP	RNBT	FBG	DV	OB			7		950			2400	2800
16	3	MONTE-CARLO 165FS	OP	RNBT	FBG	DV	IO	175		7		1800			3100	3600
16	3	MONTE-CARLO 165SM	OP	RNBT	FBG	DV	IO	175		7		1800			2800	3250
16	3	MONTE-CARLO 165SS	OP	RNBT	FBG	DV	IO	175		7		1800			2950	3450
17	3	BIARRITZ 175BR	ST	RNBT	FBG	DV	IO	205		7	7	2050			3500	4050
17	3	BIARRITZ 175SS	ST	RNBT	FBG	DV	IO	205		7	7	2050			3600	4200
17	3	CIMARRON 1785FS	ST	RNBT	FBG	DV	IO	205		7	2	1900			3400	3950
17	3	CIMARRON 1785GS	ST	RNBT	FBG	DV	IO	205		7	2	1900			3250	3800
17	3	CIMMARON 1785	ST	RNBT	FBG	DV	OB			7	2	930			2300	2650
17	3	MONTE-CARLO 173	OP	RNBT	FBG	DV	OB			7	7	1170			2750	3200
17	3	MONTE-CARLO 180	OP	RNBT	FBG	DV	IO	205		7	2	1900			3300	3850
18	3	BIARRITZ 185BR	ST	RNBT	FBG	DV	IO	260		7	7	2300			4150	4800
18	3	BIARRITZ 185SS	ST	RNBT	FBG	DV	IO	260		7	7	2300			4300	4950
18	6	BIARRITZ 190BR	ST	RNBT	FBG	DV	IO	260		8		2750			4750	5450
18	6	BIARRITZ 190SS	ST	RNBT	FBG	DV	IO	260		8		2750			4900	5650
18	7	CIMMARON 1821	ST	CUD	FBG	DV	IO	230		7	7	2200			3900	4500
18	7	CIMMARON 1821	ST	RNBT	FBG	DV	IO	230		7	7	2000			3650	4250
18	7	CIMMARON 1821SS	ST	RNBT	FBG	DV	IO	230		7	7	2000			3800	4400
18	7	MONTE-CARLO 195	ST	CUD	FBG	SV	IO	230		7	7	2200			4500	5150
18	7	MONTE-CARLO 195	OP	RNBT	FBG	DV	OB			7	7	1250			3000	3500
18	7	MONTE-CARLO 195	ST	RNBT	FBG	SV	IO	230		7	7	2000			4200	4900
20	3	BIARRITZ 210BR	ST	RNBT	FBG	DV	IO	260		8		3100			5700	6550
20	3	BIARRITZ 210SS	ST	RNBT	FBG	DV	IO	260		8		3100			5850	6750
20	3	MONTE-CARLO 210	ST	CUD	FBG	SV	IO	260		8		3400			6400	7350
		1987 BOATS														
16	2	EBKO V165	ST	RNBT	FBG	SV	OB			7		910			2050	2450
16	2	FISH-&-SKI V165	ST	RNBT	FBG	SV	OB			7		950			2150	2550
16	2	SKIMASTER 165 I/O	OP	RNBT	FBG	DV	IO	120	MRCR	7		1800			2750	3200
16	3	1631XLT	OP	RNBT	FBG	DV	OB			6	7	910			1900	2250
16	3	CIMMARON 1631	ST	RNBT	FBG	DV	OB			6	7	910			2100	2500
16	3	CIMMARON 1631X	ST	RNBT	FBG	SV	OB			6	7	910			2000	2350
16	3	EBKO V163X	ST	RNBT	FBG	DV	OB			6	7	910			2050	2450
16	3	FISH & SKI 1631X	OP	RNBT	FBG	DV	OB			6	7	910			2200	2600
17	3	BIARRITZ 175	ST	RNBT	FBG	DV	IO	165	MRCR	7	6	2010			3200	3750
17	3	BIARRITZ SS 175	ST	RNBT	FBG	DV	IO	165	MRCR	7	6	2010			3300	3850
17	3	CIMMARON 1785	ST	RNBT	FBG	DV	IO	120	MRCR	7	2	1900			3050	3550
17	3	CIMMARON 1785	ST	RNBT	FBG	SV	OB			7	2	930			2200	2550
17	3	EBKO V173	ST	RNBT	FBG	SV	OB			7	5	1170			2650	3100
17	3	FISH-&-SKI 1785	ST	RNBT	FBG	SV	OB			7	2	970			2300	2650
17	3	MONTE-CARLO 180	OP	RNBT	FBG	DV	IO	120	MRCR	7	1	1900			3050	3550
18	3	BIARRITZ 185	ST	RNBT	FBG	DV	IO	165	MRCR	7	7	2210			3600	4150
18	3	BIARRITZ SS 185	ST	RNBT	FBG	DV	IO	165	MRCR	7	7	2210			3700	4300
18	6	BIARRITZ 190	ST	RNBT	FBG	DV	IO	165		8		2750			4200	4900
18	6	BIARRITZ SS 190	ST	RNBT	FBG	DV	IO	165	MRCR	8		2750			4400	5050
18	7	CIMMARON 1821	ST	CUD	FBG	DV	IO	120	MRCR	7	7	2200			3600	4150
18	7	CIMMARON 1821	ST	RNBT	FBG	DV	IO	120	MRCR	7	7	2000			3350	3900
18	7	CIMMARON SS 1821	ST	RNBT	FBG	DV	IO	120		7	7	2000			3500	4050
18	7	EBKO V195	ST	RNBT	FBG	SV	OB			7	7	1250			2900	3400
18	7	MONTE-CARLO V195	ST	CUD	FBG	SV	IO	120	MRCR	7	7	2200			3950	4600
18	7	MONTE-CARLO V195	ST	RNBT	FBG	SV	IO	120	MRCR	7	7	2000			3700	4350
20	3	BIARRITZ B/R 210	ST	RNBT	FBG	DV	IO	165	MRCR	8		3200			5250	6000
20	3	BIARRITZ SS 210	ST	RNBT	FBG	DV	IO	165		8		3200			5400	6200
20	3	MONTE-CARLO 210	ST	CUD	FBG	SV	IO	165		8					5750	6650
		1986 BOATS														
16	2	165 I/OX	OP	RNBT	FBG	DV	IO	120	MRCR	7		1800			2650	3050
16	2	EBKO V165	ST	RNBT	FBG	SV	OB			7		910			2000	2350
16	2	FISH-&-SKI V165	ST	RNBT	FBG	SV	OB			7		950			2050	2450
16	2	MONTE-CARLO V165	ST	RNBT	FBG	SV	IO	120	MRCR	7		1800			2650	3050
16	3	1631X FISH & SKI	OP	RNBT	FBG	DV	OB			6	9	910			2200	2550
16	3	1631XLT	OP	RNBT	FBG	DV	OB			6	9	910			1850	2200
16	3	CIMMARON 1631	ST	RNBT	FBG	DV	OB			6	9	910			2050	2450
16	3	CIMMARON 1631	ST	RNBT	FBG	DV	IO	120	MRCR	6	9	1850			2650	3050
16	3	CIMMARON 1631X	ST	RNBT	FBG	SV	OB			6	9	910			1900	2250
16	3	EBKO V163X	ST	RNBT	FBG	DV	OB			6	8	910			2000	2350
17	3	180	OP	RNBT	FBG	DV	IO	120	MRCR	7	1				2950	3400
17	3	BIARRITZ 175	ST	RNBT	FBG	DV	IO	170	MRCR	7	7	2010			3100	3600
17	3	BIARRITZ SS 175	ST	RNBT	FBG	DV	IO	170	MRCR	7	7	2010			3200	3750
17	3	CIMMARON 1785	ST	RNBT	FBG	DV	IO	120	MRCR	7	2	1900			2950	3400
17	3	CIMMARON 1785	ST	RNBT	FBG	SV	OB			7	2	930			2100	2500
17	3	EBKO V173	ST	RNBT	FBG	SV	OB			6	8	1170			2600	3000
17	3	FISH-&-SKI 1785	ST	RNBT	FBG	SV	OB			7	2	970			2200	2600
18	3	BIARRITZ 185	ST	RNBT	FBG	DV	IO	170	MRCR	7	7	2210			3400	4000
18	3	BIARRITZ SS 185	ST	RNBT	FBG	DV	IO	170	MRCR	7	7	2210			3550	4100
18	6	BIARRITZ SS 190	ST	RNBT	FBG	DV	IO	170	MRCR	8		2750			4100	4750
18	7	CIMMARON 1821	ST	CUD	FBG	DV	IO	120	MRCR	7	7	2200			3400	4000
18	7	CIMMARON 1821	ST	RNBT	FBG	DV	IO	120	MRCR	7	7	2000			3150	3650
18	7	CIMMARON 1821 FISH	ST	FSH	FBG	DV	IO	120	MRCR	7	7	2200			3600	4200
18	7	MONTE-CARLO FISH	ST	FSH	FBG	SV	IO	120	MRCR	7	7	2200			4000	4650
18	7	MONTE-CARLO V195	ST	CUD	FBG	SV	IO	120	MRCR	7	7	2200			3800	4400
18	7	MONTE-CARLO V195	ST	RNBT	FBG	SV	IO	120	MRCR	7	7	2000			3600	4200
20	3	BIARRITZ B/R 210	ST	RNBT	FBG	DV	IO	170	MRCR	8		3200			5050	5800
20	3	SUN-CRUISER 210	ST	RNBT	FBG	DV	IO	170	MRCR	8		3550			5400	6250
		1985 BOATS														
16	2	CIMMARON 1621	ST	RNBT	FBG	SV	OB			6	4	910			1900	2300
16	2	EBKO V165	ST	RNBT	FBG	SV	OB			7		910			1900	2300
16	2	FISH-&-SKI V165	ST	RNBT	FBG	SV	OB			7		950			2000	2400
16	2	MONTE-CARLO V165	ST	RNBT	FBG	SV	IO	120-190		7		1800			2550	3150
16	2	MONTE-CARLO V165	ST	RNBT	FBG	SV	IO	200-205		7		1800			2600	3250
16	2	MONTE-CARLO V165	ST	RNBT	FBG	SV	IO	225-230		7		1800			2850	3300
16	3	CIMMARON 1631	ST	RNBT	FBG	DV	OB			6	9	910			2050	2400
16	3	CIMMARON 1631	ST	RNBT	FBG	DV	IO	117-170		6	9	1850			2700	3150

CONTINUED ON NEXT PAGE

LOA FT IN	NAME AND/ OR MODEL	TOP/ RIG	BOAT TYPE	-HULL- MTL TP	----ENGINE--- TP # HP MFG	BEAM FT IN	WGT LBS	DRAFT FT IN	RETAIL LOW	RETAIL HIGH
			--- 1985 BOATS ---							
16 3	CIMMARON 1631X	ST	RNBT	FBG SV	OB	6 9	910		1850	2150
16 3	EBKO V163X	ST	RNBT	FBG DV	OB	6 8	910		1950	2300
17 3	BIARRITZ 175	ST	RNBT	FBG DV	IO 170-205	7 7	2010		2950	3700
17 3	BIARRITZ 175	ST	RNBT	FBG DV	IO 225-260	7 7	2010		3250	4000
17 3	BIARRITZ SS 175	ST	RNBT	FBG DV	IO 170-205	7 7	2010		3100	3800
17 3	BIARRITZ SS 175	ST	RNBT	FBG DV	IO 225-260	7 7	2010		3350	4150
17 3	CIMMARON 1785	ST	RNBT	FBG DV	IO 120-190	7 2	1900		2800	3450
17 3	CIMMARON 1785	ST	RNBT	FBG DV	IO 200-205	7 2	1900		2900	3550
17 3	CIMMARON 1785	ST	RNBT	FBG DV	IO 225-230	7 2	1900		3150	3650
17 3	EBKO V173	ST	RNBT	FBG SV	OB	7 2	930		2050	2450
17 3	FISH-&-SKI 1785	ST	RNBT	FBG SV	OB	7 2	970		2150	2500
18 3	BIARRITZ	ST	RNBT	FBG DV	IO 170-185	7 7	2210		3250	3850
18 3	BIARRITZ	ST	RNBT	FBG DV	IO 225-260	7 7	2210		3600	4350
18 3	BIARRITZ 185	ST	RNBT	FBG DV	IO 170 MRCR	7 7	2210		3300	3800
18 3	BIARRITZ SS	ST	RNBT	FBG DV	IO 170-185	7 7	2210		3350	3950
18 3	BIARRITZ SS	ST	RNBT	FBG DV	IO 225-260	7 7	2210		3700	4500
18 3	BIARRITZ SS 185	ST	RNBT	FBG DV	IO 170 MRCR	7 7	2210		3400	3950
18 6	BIARRITZ 190	ST	RNBT	FBG DV	IO 170-205	8	2750		3850	4750
18 6	BIARRITZ 190	ST	RNBT	FBG DV	IO 225-260	8	2750		4150	5050
18 6	BIARRITZ SS 190	ST	RNBT	FBG DV	IO 170-230	8	2750		4000	4950
18 6	BIARRITZ SS 190	ST	RNBT	FBG DV	IO 260	8	2750		4250	5200
18 7	CIMMARON 1821	ST	CUD	FBG DV	IO 117-230	7 7	2200		3600	4300
18 7	CIMMARON 1821	ST	RNBT	FBG DV	IO 117-230	7 7	2000		3400	4050
18 7	CIMMARON 1821	ST	RNBT	FBG DV	IO T120 OMC	7 7	2000		3800	4400
18 7	CIMMARON 1821 FISH	ST	FSH	FBG DV	IO 120-190	7 7	2200		3550	4350
18 7	CIMMARON 1821 FISH	ST	FSH	FBG DV	IO 200-230	7 7	2200		3650	4550
18 7	MONTE-CARLO FISH	ST	FSH	FBG SV	IO 120-205	7 7	2200		3750	4650
18 7	MONTE-CARLO V195	ST	CUD	FBG SV	IO 225-230	7 7	2200		4100	4750
18 7	MONTE-CARLO V195	ST	CUD	FBG SV	IO 170-205	7 7	2200		4300	4550
18 7	MONTE-CARLO V195	ST	CUD	FBG SV	IO 225-230	7 7	2200		3900	4500
18 7	MONTE-CARLO V195	ST	RNBT	FBG SV	IO 120-205	7 7	2000		3300	4050
18 7	MONTE-CARLO V195	ST	RNBT	FBG SV	IO 225-230	7 7	2000		3600	4200
			--- 1984 BOATS ---							
16 2	CIMMARON 1621	ST	RNBT	FBG SV	OB	6 4	910		1900	2250
16 2	CIMMARON 1621	ST	RNBT	FBG DV	IO 117-185	6 4	1800		2500	2900
16 3	CIMMARON 1631	ST	RNBT	FBG DV	OB	6 9	910		1900	2250
16 3	CIMMARON 1631	ST	RNBT	FBG DV	IO 117-170	6 9	1850		2600	3000
16 3	CIMMARON 1631X	ST	RNBT	FBG DV	OB	6 9	910		1900	2250
16 3	EBKO V163	ST	RNBT	FBG SV	OB	6 8	915		1900	2250
16 3	EBKO V163X	ST	RNBT	FBG SV	OB	6 8	910		1900	2250
16 3	SCORPION	ST	RNBT	FBG DV	IO 117-170	6 8	1850		2600	3000
17	CIMMARON 1721	ST	RNBT	FBG DV	OB	6 8	1020		2200	2550
17	CIMMARON 1721	ST	RNBT	FBG DV	IO 117-188	6 8	1900		2700	3200
17 3	EBKO V173	ST	RNBT	FBG SV	OB	6 8	1170		2450	2850
17 3	SEVILLE	ST	RNBT	FBG SV	IO 170-230	7 7	2010		3050	3300
17 3	SEVILLE	ST	RNBT	FBG SV	IO 170	7 7	2010		2900	3400
18 3	BIARRITZ	ST	RNBT	FBG DV	IO 170-230	7 7	2210		3350	4000
18 3	BIARRITZ	ST	RNBT	FBG DV	IO 260	7 7	2210		3600	4450
18 3	BIARRITZ SS	ST	RNBT	FBG DV	IO 170-230	7 7	2210		3350	4150
18 3	BIARRITZ SS	ST	RNBT	FBG DV	IO 260	7 7	2210		3700	4550
18 3	BIARRITZ SS	ST	RNBT	FBG DV	IO 170-260	7 7	2210		2350	2700
18 6	COBRA	ST	RNBT	FBG DV	IO 225-260	8	2750		4050	4950
18 7	CIMMARON 1821	ST	CUD	FBG DV	IO 117-230	7 7	2200		3500	4050
18 7	CIMMARON 1821	ST	RNBT	FBG DV	IO 117-230	7 7	2000		3100	3750
18 7	CIMMARON 1821	ST	RNBT	FBG DV	IO T120 OMC	7 7	2000		3650	4250
18 7	MONTE-CARLO	ST	CUD	FBG DV	IO 117-140	7 7	2000		3350	4050
18 7	MONTE-CARLO	ST	CUD	FBG DV	IO 170-188	7 7	2200		3500	4250
18 7	MONTE-CARLO	ST	CUD	FBG DV	IO 225-230	7 7	2200		3800	4450
18 7	MONTE-CARLO	ST	RNBT	FBG DV	IO 117-230	7 7	2000		3450	4200
20 3	LE-BARON	ST	RNBT	FBG DV	IO 225-260	8	3200		5000	5950

....For earlier years, see the BUC Used Boat Price Guide, Volume 3

EDDYLINE NORTHWEST LTD
EVERETT WA 98204   COAST GUARD MFG ID- EDY See inside cover to adjust price for area

LOA FT IN	NAME AND/ OR MODEL	TOP/ RIG	BOAT TYPE	-HULL- MTL TP	----ENGINE--- TP # HP MFG	BEAM FT IN	WGT LBS	DRAFT FT IN	RETAIL LOW	RETAIL HIGH
			--- 1995 BOATS ---							
21 5	DOUEKIE	CAT	SACAC	F/S KL	OB	6 8	850		5450	6300
23 2	SAKOHNET 23	SLP	SAROD	F/S KC	OB	6 1	2000	5 2	8650	9950
23 4	STONE HORSE	CAT	SACAC	F/S KL	IB 12D WEST	7 1	4490	3 6	19000	21100
26 11	CONCH 27	OP	CTRCN	F/S DV	IO	9 4	4400	1 4	17500	19900
26 11	CONCH 27	OP	CTRCN	F/S DV	IO 235D	9	4400	1 4	19300	21500
28 3	SHEARWATER	YWL	SACAC	F/S KL	OB	6 6	2400	6	11500	13100

....For earlier years, see the BUC Used Boat Price Guide, Volume 3

EDEY & DUFF LTD
MATTAPOISETT MA 02739   COAST GUARD MFG ID- EAD See inside cover to adjust price for area

For more recent years, see the BUC Used Boat Price Guide, Volume 1

LOA FT IN	NAME AND/ OR MODEL	TOP/ RIG	BOAT TYPE	-HULL- MTL TP	----ENGINE--- TP # HP MFG	BEAM FT IN	WGT LBS	DRAFT FT IN	RETAIL LOW	RETAIL HIGH
			--- 1996 BOATS ---							
21 5	DOVEKIE	CAT	SACAC	F/S LB	OB	6 8	850	4	8850	10100
23	SAKONNET 23	SLP	SACAC	FBG KL	OB	6 1	2010	5 2	13900	15800
23 4	STONE HORSE	CAT	SACAC	F/S KL	IB 12D WEST	7 1	4490	3 6	30100	33500
26 11	CONCH 27	OP	CTRCN	F/S DV	IO	9 4	4400	1 4	47100	51700
26 11	CONCH 27	OP	CTRCN	F/S DV	IO 235D VLVO	9	4400	1 4	15600	17700
28 3	SHEARWATER	YWL	SACAC	F/S LB	OB	6 6	2400	6	18900	21000
			--- 1995 BOATS ---							
21 5	DOVEKIE	CAT	SACAC	F/S LB	OB	6 8	850	4	8250	9500
23 4	STONE HORSE	CAT	SACAC	F/S KL	IB 12D WEST	7 1	4490	3 6	28300	31500
26 11	CONCH 27	OP	CTRCN	F/S DV	IO	9 4	4400	1 4	44300	49200
26 11	CONCH 27	OP	CTRCN	F/S DV	IO 235D VLVO	9	4400	1 4	14500	16500
28 3	SHEARWATER	YWL	SACAC	F/S LB	OB	6 6	2400	6	17400	19800
			--- 1994 BOATS ---							
21 5	DOVEKIE	CAT	SACAC	F/S KL	OB	6 8	850	4	7750	8900
23 4	STONE HORSE	CAT	SACAC	F/S KL	IB 12D WEST	7 1	4490	3 6	26600	29600
26 11	CONCH 27	OP	CTRCN	F/S DV	IO	9 4	4400	1 4	42300	47000
26 11	CONCH 27	OP	CTRCN	F/S DV	IO 235D VLVO	9	4400	1 4	13600	15500
28 3	SHEARWATER	YWL	SACAC	F/S LB	OB	6 6	2400	6	16400	18600
			--- 1993 BOATS ---							
21 5	DOVEKIE	CAT	SACAC	F/S LB	OB	6 8	850	4	7300	8400
23 4	STONE HORSE	CAT	SACAC	F/S KL	IB 12D WEST	7 1	4490	3 6	25100	27800
26 11	CONCH 27	OP	CTRCN	F/S DV	IB 300D CUM	9	4400	1 4	14400	16400
28 3	SHEARWATER	CAT	SACAC	F/S LB	OB	6 6	2400	6	15400	17500
			--- 1987 BOATS ---							
21 5	DOVEKIE	CAT	SA/CR	FBG LB	OB	6 8	600	2 6	4600	5300
23 4	STONE-HORSE	SLP	SA/CR	FBG KL	IB	7 1	4500	3 6	17000	19300
28 3	SHEARWATER	CAT	SA/RC	FBG LB	OB	6 6	1200	3 4	6050	6950
			--- 1986 BOATS ---							
21 5	DOVEKIE	CAT	SA/CR	FBG LB	OB	6 8	600	2 6	4300	5000
23 4	STONE-HORSE	SLP	SA/CR	FBG KL	IB D	7 1	4500	3 6	16000	18200
28 3	SHEARWATER	YWL	SA/RC	FBG LB	OB	6 6	1200	3 4	5700	6550
			--- 1985 BOATS ---							
21 6	DOVEKIE	CAT	SA/CR	FBG LB	OB	6 8	600	2 6	4050	4700
23 4	STONE-HORSE	SLP	SA/CR	FBG KL	IB D	7 1	4500	3 6	15000	17100

....For earlier years, see the BUC Used Boat Price Guide, Volume 3

EDGEWATER POWERBOATS
EDGEWATER FL 32132   See inside cover to adjust price for area

For more recent years, see the BUC Used Boat Price Guide, Volume 1

LOA FT IN	NAME AND/ OR MODEL	TOP/ RIG	BOAT TYPE	-HULL- MTL TP	----ENGINE--- TP # HP MFG	BEAM FT IN	WGT LBS	DRAFT FT IN	RETAIL LOW	RETAIL HIGH
			--- 1996 BOATS ---							
16 6	EDGEWATER 170CC	OP	CTRCN	FBG SV	OB	6 8	1200	1	5900	6800
16 6	EDGEWATER 170DC	OP	RNBT	FBG SV	OB	6 8	1200	1	6150	7050
17 7	EDGEWATER 180CC	OP	CTRCN	FBG SV	OB	7 3	1400	1 1	6800	7800
17 7	EDGEWATER 180DC	OP	RNBT	FBG SV	OB	7 3	1400	1 1	7100	8150
21 3	EDGEWATER 210CC	OP	CTRCN	FBG SV	OB	8 6	2600	1 5	14300	16200
24 7	EDGEWATER 240CC	OP	CTRCN	FBG SV	OB	8 6	3200	1 6	19900	22100
24 7	EDGEWATER 240DC	OP	RNBT	FBG SV	OB	8 6	3200	1 6	20900	23200
26 7	EDGEWATER 260CC	OP	CTRCN	FBG SV	OB	8 6	3600	1 6	26800	29800

EDSON BOAT COMPANY

ANCHOR DIVISION
DIV MARR'S LEISURE PRODUCT INC
BRANDON MAN CANADA R7A COAST GUARD MFG ID- ZAI

See inside cover to adjust price for area

LOA FT	LOA IN	NAME AND/ OR MODEL	TOP/ RIG	BOAT TYPE	HULL MTL	HULL TP	ENGINE TP	ENGINE # HP	ENGINE MFG	BEAM FT	BEAM IN	WGT LBS	DRAFT FT	DRAFT IN	RETAIL LOW	RETAIL HIGH
		1989 BOATS														
16	1	FIRENZA	ST	RNBT	FBG	DV	OB			6	11				2250	2600
16	1	FIRENZA IO	ST	RNBT	FBG	DV	IO	130		6	11				1800	2150
16	9	AVANTI	OP	RNBT	FBG	SV	OB			7	2	1247			3150	3650
16	9	XR-17	ST	RNBT	FBG	SV	OB			7	2	1310			3300	3800
17	1	SUNBIRD	ST	RNBT	FBG	SV	OB			7	2	1452			3550	4150
17	1	SUNBIRD IO	ST	RNBT	FBG	SV	IO	180		7	2	2382			3050	3550
17	1	SUNSPORT	ST	RNBT	FBG	DV	IO	180		7	2	2305			3000	3500
18	8	CHALLENGER EDSON	ST	RNBT	FBG	DV	IO	235		7	6	2700			3800	4400
18	8	CORSAIR EDSON	ST	RNBT	FBG	DV	IO	235		7	6	2714			3800	4400
20	9	MONACO	ST	CUD	FBG	DV	IO	260		8					5500	6350
		1988 BOATS														
16	9	AVANTI GT	ST	RNBT	FBG	SV	OB			7	2	1180			2850	3350
16	9	AVANTI SS	OP	RNBT	FBG	SV	OB			7	2	1180			2900	3400
16	9	SPORTFIRE GT	ST	RNBT	FBG	SV	OB			7	2	1180			2900	3400
16	9	SPORTFIRE GT	ST	RNBT	FBG	SV	IO	180		7	2	1180			2100	2500
16	9	XR-17	ST	RNBT	FBG	SV	OB			7	2	1180			2950	3450
17	1	SUNBIRD GT	ST	RNBT	FBG	SV	OB			7	2	1295			3150	3700
17	1	SUNBIRD GT	ST	RNBT	FBG	SV	IO	180		7	2	1295			2250	2650
17	1	SUNSPORT	ST	RNBT	FBG	DV	IO	180		7	2	1295			2250	2650
18	8	CHALLENGER GT EDSON	ST	RNBT	FBG	DV	OB			7	6	1300			3300	3850
18	8	CHALLENGER GT EDSON	ST	RNBT	FBG	DV	IO	230		7	6	1300			2750	3200
18	8	CORSAIR GT EDSON	ST	RNBT	FBG	DV	IO	230		7	6	1300			2750	3200
		1987 BOATS														
16	9	AVANTI GT	ST	RNBT	FBG	SV	OB			7	2	1180			2850	3300
16	9	AVANTI SS	OP	RNBT	FBG	SV	OB			7	2	1180			2850	3300
16	9	SPORTFIRE GT	ST	RNBT	FBG	SV	OB			7	2	1180			2850	3300
16	9	SPORTFIRE GT	ST	RNBT	FBG	SV	IO	185		7	2	1180			2000	2350
18	8	CHALLENGER GT EDSON	ST	RNBT	FBG	DV	OB			7	6	1300			3250	3750
18	8	CHALLENGER GT EDSON	ST	RNBT	FBG	DV	IO	260		7	6	1300			2750	3200
18	8	CORSAIR GT EDSON	ST	RNBT	FBG	DV	IO	260		7	6	1300			2700	3150
		1986 BOATS														
16	2	GLASTRON SSV-167	ST	RNBT	FBG	SV	OB			6	6	860			2000	2400
16	4	GLASTRON SSV-168	ST	RNBT	FBG	SV	IO	140		6	7	880			1550	1850
16	7	GLASTRON CVX-16	OP	RNBT	FBG	SV	OB			6	7	700			1700	2000
16	10	INTRUDER GT EDSON	ST	RNBT	FBG	DV	IO	185		7	4	1220			1950	2350
18	8	CHALLENGER GT EDSON	ST	RNBT	FBG	DV	OB			7	6	1300			3150	3650
18	8	CHALLENGER GT EDSON	ST	RNBT	FBG	DV	IO	260		7	6	1300			2600	3050
18	8	CORSAIR GT EDSON	ST	RNBT	FBG	DV	OB			7	6	1300			3150	3650
18	8	CORSAIR GT EDSON	ST	RNBT	FBG	DV	IO	260		7	6	1300			2600	3050
		1985 BOATS														
16		GLASTRON CVX-16SSDLX	OP	RNBT	FBG	SV	OB			6	7	700			1600	1900
16	2	GLASTRON SSV-167	ST	RNBT	FBG	SV	OB			6	6	860			1950	2350
16	4	GLASTRON SSV-168	ST	RNBT	FBG	SV	IO	140		6	7	880			1500	1750
16	7	GLASTRON CVX-16	OP	RNBT	FBG	SV	OB			6	7	700			1650	1950
16	10	INTRUDER GT EDSON	ST	RNBT	FBG	DV	IO	185		7	4	1220			1900	2250
18	8	CHALLENGER GT EDSON	ST	RNBT	FBG	DV	IO	260		7	6	1300			2500	2900
		1984 BOATS														
16	2	GLASTRON SSV-167	ST	RNBT	FBG	SV	OB			6	6	860			1900	2300
16	4	GLASTRON SSV-168	ST	RNBT	FBG	SV	IO	140		6	7	880			1450	1700
16	7	GLASTRON CVX-16	OP	RNBT	FBG	SV	OB			6	7	700			1600	1900
16	10	INTRUDER GT EDSON	ST	RNBT	FBG	DV	IO	185		7	4	1220			1800	2150
18	8	CHALLENGER GT EDSON	ST	RNBT	FBG	DV	IO	260		7	6	1300			2400	2800

....For earlier years, see the BUC Used Boat Price Guide, Volume 3

EGG HARBOR YACHTS

EGG HARBOR CITY NJ 0821 COAST GUARD MFG ID- EGH See inside cover to adjust price for area

For more recent years, see the BUC Used Boat Price Guide, Volume 1

LOA FT	LOA IN	NAME AND/ OR MODEL	TOP/ RIG	BOAT TYPE	HULL MTL	HULL TP	ENGINE TP	ENGINE # HP	ENGINE MFG	BEAM FT	BEAM IN	WGT LBS	DRAFT FT	DRAFT IN	RETAIL LOW	RETAIL HIGH
		1996 BOATS														
34	6	GOLDEN EGG 35	FB	SF	FBG	SV	IB	T380	CRUS	13	2	20925	3	2	106000	116500
34	6	GOLDEN EGG 35	FB	SF	FBG	SV	IB	T350D-T420D		13	2	22800	3	2	143000	164500
38	6	GOLDEN EGG 38	FB	SF	FBG	SV	IB	T380	CRUS	15		26300	3	10	147500	162000
		IB T420D CAT 208000 228500, IB T430D VLVO 198000 217500, IB T485D DD													216000	237500
42	2	GOLDEN EGG 42	FB	SF	FBG	SV	IB	T420D	CAT	15		36300	3	10	248000	273000
		IB T430D VLVO 241500 265000, IB T485D DD 259000 285000, IB T550D DD													272000	299000
		IB T625D DD 285000 313500														
58	6	GOLDEN EGG 58	FB	SF	FBG	SV	IB	T900D	DD	17	6	82000	5	3	638000	701000
		IB T10CD DD 677500 744500, IB T11CD DD 683000 751000, IB T11CD MTU													689500	758000
		IB T12CD CAT 709500 779500														
		1995 BOATS														
34	6	GOLDEN EGG 34	FB	SF	FBG	SV	IB	T320-T380		13	2	20925	3	2	110000	124000
34	6	GOLDEN EGG 34	FB	SF	FBG	SV	IB	T350D-T420D		13	2	22800	3	2	153000	176500
38	6	GOLDEN EGG 38	FB	SF	FBG	SV	IB	T380	CRUS	15		26300	3	10	141500	155500
		IB T420D CAT 199500 219000, IB T430D VLVO 190000 209000, IB T485D DD													207500	228000
42	2	GOLDEN EGG 42	FB	SF	FBG	SV	IB	T420D	CAT	15		36000	3	10	236500	260000
		IB T430D VLVO 231500 254500, IB T485D DD 248500 273000, IB T550D DD													261000	287000
54	6	GOLDEN EGG 54	FB	SF	FBG	SV	IB	T735D	DD	17	6	72600	5	3	494000	543000
54	6	GOLDEN EGG 54	FB	SF	FBG	SV	IB	T760D	DD	17	6	72600	5	3	500000	549500
54	6	GOLDEN EGG 54	FB	SF	FBG	SV	IB	T900D	DD	17	6	72600	5	3	530000	582500
58	6	GOLDEN EGG 58	FB	SF	FBG	SV	IB	T900D	DD	17	6	82000	5	3	611000	671500
		IB T10CD DD 650000 714500, IB T11CD DD 655500 720000, IB T12CD CAT													680500	748000
		1994 BOATS														
34	6	GOLDEN EGG 34	FB	SF	FBG	SV	IB	T355-T380		13	2	17500	3	2	98000	109000
34	6	GOLDEN EGG 34	FB	SF	FBG	SV	IB	T325D-T350D		13	2	17500	3	2	122500	138000
38	6	DOUBLE CABIN 38	FB	DC	FBG	SV	IB	T355	CRUS	15		27000	3	10	137500	151000
		IB T380 CRUS 139000 152500, IB T350D DD 162500 178500, IB T435D CAT													175000	192000
38	6	GOLDEN EGG 38	FB	SF	FBG	SV	IB	T380	CRUS	15		22500	3	10	118500	130000
		IB T350D DD 141500 155500, IB T435D CAT 154000 169500, IB T485D CAT													161500	177500
42	2	DOUBLE CABIN 42	FB	DC	FBG	SV	IB	T380	CRUS	15		32000	3	10	175000	192500
		IB T350D CAT 199500 219500, IB T435D CAT 213500 234500, IB T485D DD													220500	242500
42	2	GOLDEN EGG 42	FB	DC	FBG	SV	IB	T435D	CAT	15		31000	3	10	206500	227000
42	2	GOLDEN EGG 42	FB	SF	FBG	SV	IB	T485D	DD	15		31000	3	10	216500	237500
42	2	GOLDEN EGG 42	FB	SF	FBG	SV	IB	T550D	DD	15		31000	3	10	228500	251000
54	6	GOLDEN EGG 54	FB	SF	FBG	SV	IB	T735D	DD	17	6	64000	5	3	432000	474500
54	6	GOLDEN EGG 54	FB	SF	FBG	SV	IB	T900D	DD	17	6	64000	5	3	465500	511500
59	6	GOLDEN EGG 58	FB	SF	FBG	SV	IB	T900D	DD	17	6	72000	5	3	525000	577000
59	6	GOLDEN EGG 58	FB	SF	FBG	SV	IB	T10CD	GM	17	6	72000	5	3	565000	621000
		1993 BOATS														
34	6	GOLDEN EGG 34	FB	SF	FBG	SV	IB	T300-T360		13	2	17500	3	2	90700	102500
34	6	GOLDEN EGG 34	FB	SF	FBG	SV	IB	T350D	CAT	13	2	17500	3	2	119500	131500
38	6	DOUBLE CABIN 38	FB	DC	FBG	SV	IB	T300	CRUS	15		27000	3	10	129000	142000
38	6	DOUBLE CABIN 38	FB	DC	FBG	SV	IB	T360	CRUS	15		27000	3	10	131000	144000
38	6	DOUBLE CABIN 38	FB	DC	FBG	SV	IB	T375D	CAT	15		27000	3	10	159000	174500
38	6	GOLDEN EGG 38	FB	SF	FBG	SV	IB	T360	CRUS	15		22500	3	10	111500	122500
38	6	GOLDEN EGG 38	FB	SF	FBG	SV	IB	T375D	CAT	15		22500	3	10	139000	153000
38	6	GOLDEN EGG 38	FB	SF	FBG	SV	IB	T425D	CAT	15		22500	3	10	145500	160000
42	2	DOUBLE CABIN 42	FB	DC	FBG	SV	IB	T360	CRUS	15		32000	3	10	165000	181000
42	2	DOUBLE CABIN 42	FB	DC	FBG	SV	IB	T375D	CAT	15		32000	3	10	194000	213000
42	2	DOUBLE CABIN 42	FB	DC	FBG	SV	IB	T425D	CAT	15		32000	3	10	201500	221500
42	2	GOLDEN EGG 42	FB	DC	FBG	SV	IB	T425D	CAT	15		31000	3	10	195500	214500
42	2	GOLDEN EGG 42	FB	SF	FBG	SV	IB	T485D	DD	15		31000	3	10	206000	226500
54	6	GOLDEN EGG 54	FB	SF	FBG	SV	IB	T735D	DD	17	6	64000	5	3	411500	452000
54	6	GOLDEN EGG 54	FB	SF	FBG	SV	IB	T900D	DD	17	6	64000	5	3	443500	487500
59	6	GOLDEN EGG 58	FB	SF	FBG	SV	IB	T900D	DD	17	6	72000	5	3	500500	549500
59	6	GOLDEN EGG 58	FB	SF	FBG	SV	IB	T10CD	GM	17	6	72000	5	3	538500	591500
		1992 BOATS														
33		FAMILY CRUISER 33	FB	CR	FBG	SV	IB	T210	CRUS	13	2	14500	2	10	69400	76300
33		FAMILY CRUISER 33	FB	CR	FBG	SV	IB	T300	CRUS	13	2	14500	2	10	72500	79700
33		FAMILY CRUISER 33	FB	CR	FBG	SV	IB	T300D	CUM	13	2	14500	2	10	92600	101500
34	6	GOLDEN EGG 34	FB	SF	FBG	SV	IB	T454-T502		13	2	17500	3	2	92900	105000
34	6	GOLDEN EGG 34	FB	SF	FBG	SV	IB	T375D	CAT	13	2	17500	3	2	116000	127500
37	4	FAMILY CRUISER 37	FB	CR	FBG	SV	IB	T300	CRUS	14	5	21000	3	10	95400	105000
37	4	FAMILY CRUISER 37	FB	CR	FBG	SV	IB	T355	CRUS	14	5	21000	3	10	97200	107000
37	4	FAMILY CRUISER 37	FB	CR	FBG	SV	IB	T320D	CAT	14	5	21000	3	10	116500	128000
38	6	DOUBLE CABIN 38	FB	DC	FBG	SV	IB	T454	CRUS	15		27000	3	10	130500	143500
38	6	DOUBLE CABIN 38	FB	DC	FBG	SV	IB	T502	CRUS	15		27000	3	10	134000	147000
38	6	DOUBLE CABIN 38	FB	DC	FBG	SV	IB	T375D	CAT	15		27000	3	10	151500	166500
38	6	GOLDEN EGG 38	FB	SF	FBG	SV	IB	T502	CRUS	15		22500	3	10	115500	126500
38	6	GOLDEN EGG 38	FB	SF	FBG	SV	IB	T375D	CAT	15		22500	3	10	132500	145500
38	6	GOLDEN EGG 38	FB	SF	FBG	SV	IB	T425D	CAT	15		22500	3	10	138500	152500
42	2	DOUBLE CABIN 42	FB	DC	FBG	SV	IB	T502	CRUS	15		32000	3	10	171500	188500
42	2	DOUBLE CABIN 42	FB	DC	FBG	SV	IB	T375D	CAT	15		32000	3	10	185000	203000
42	2	DOUBLE CABIN 42	FB	DC	FBG	SV	IB	T425D	CAT	15		32000	3	10	192500	211500
42	2	GOLDEN EGG 42	FB	DC	FBG	SV	IB	T502	CRUS	15		27000	3	10	150500	165500
42	2	GOLDEN EGG 42	FB	DC	FBG	SV	IB	T425D	CAT	15		31000	3	10	186000	204500
42	2	GOLDEN EGG 42	FB	SF	FBG	SV	IB	T485D	DD	15		31000	3	10	196500	216000

LOA FT	LOA IN	NAME AND/ OR MODEL	TOP/ RIG	BOAT TYPE	-HULL- MTL	-HULL- TP	ENGINE TP	ENGINE # HP	ENGINE MFG	BEAM FT	BEAM IN	WGT LBS	DRAFT FT	DRAFT IN	RETAIL LOW	RETAIL HIGH
1992 BOATS																
54	6	GOLDEN EGG 54	FB	SF	FBG	SV	IB	T735D	DD	17	6	64000	5	3	392000	431000
54	6	GOLDEN EGG 54	FB	SF	FBG	SV	IB	T900D	DD	17	6	64000	5	3	423000	464500
59	6	GOLDEN EGG 58	FB	SF	FBG	SV	IB	T900D	DD	17	6	72000	5	3	477000	524000
59	6	GOLDEN EGG 58	FB	SF	FBG	SV	IB	T10CD	GM	17	6	72000	5	3	513000	564000
62	8	GOLDEN EGG 58	FB	SF	FBG	SV	IB	T10CD	CAT	17	6	72000	5	3	496000	545000
1991 BOATS																
25		FAMILY CRUISER 25	OP	CR	FBG	SV	IO			8	4	5900	2	4	**	**
33		FAMILY CRUISER 33	FB	CR	FBG	SV	IB	T210	CRUS	13	2	14500	2	10	66000	72500
33		FAMILY CRUISER 33	FB	CR	FBG	SV	IB	T300	CRUS	13	2	14500	2	10	68900	75700
33		FAMILY CRUISER 33	FB	CR	FBG	SV	IB	T300D	CUM	13	2	14500	2	10	88400	97100
34	6	GOLDEN EGG 34	FB	SF	FBG	SV	IB	T454-T502		13	2	17500	3	2	88200	99800
34	6	GOLDEN EGG 34	FB	SF	FBG	SV	IB	T375D	CAT	13	2	17500	3	2	111000	122000
37	4	FAMILY CRUISER 37	FB	CR	FBG	SV	IB	T300	CRUS	14	5	21000	3	10	91000	100000
37	4	FAMILY CRUISER 37	FB	CR	FBG	SV	IB	T355	CRUS	14	5	21000	3	10	92700	102000
37	4	FAMILY CRUISER 37	FB	CR	FBG	SV	IB	T320D	CAT	14	5	21000	3	10	111500	122500
38	6	DOUBLE CABIN 38	FB	DC	FBG	SV	IB	T454	CRUS	15		27000	3	10	124500	137000
38	6	DOUBLE CABIN 38	FB	DC	FBG	SV	IB	T502	CRUS	15		27000	3	10	128000	140500
38	6	DOUBLE CABIN 38	FB	DC	FBG	SV	IB	T375D	CAT	15		27000	3	10	144500	159000
38	6	GOLDEN EGG 38	FB	SF	FBG	SV	IB	T502	CRUS	15		22500	3	10	110000	121000
38	6	GOLDEN EGG 38	FB	SF	FBG	SV	IB	T375D	CAT	15		22500	3	10	126500	139000
38	6	GOLDEN EGG 38	FB	SF	FBG	SV	IB	T425D	CAT	15		22500	3	10	132000	145500
42	2	DOUBLE CABIN 42	FB	DC	FBG	SV	IB	T502	CRUS	15		32000	3	10	163500	180000
42	2	DOUBLE CABIN 42	FB	DC	FBG	SV	IB	T375D	CAT	15		32000	3	10	176500	193500
42	2	DOUBLE CABIN 42	FB	DC	FBG	SV	IB	T425D	CAT	15		32000	3	10	183500	201500
42	2	GOLDEN EGG 42	FB	DC	FBG	SV	IB	T502	CRUS	15		27000	3	10	144000	158000
42	2	GOLDEN EGG 42	FB	DC	FBG	SV	IB	T425D	CAT	15		31000	3	10	177500	195000
42	2	GOLDEN EGG 42	FB	SF	FBG	SV	IB	T485D	DD	15		31000	3	10	187500	206000
54	6	GOLDEN EGG 54	FB	SF	FBG	SV	IB	T735D	DD	17	6	64000	5	3	374000	411000
54	6	GOLDEN EGG 54	FB	SF	FBG	SV	IB	T900D	DD	17	6	64000	5	3	403500	443000
59	6	GOLDEN EGG 58	FB	SF	FBG	SV	IB	T900D	DD	17	6	72000	5	3	455000	500000
59	6	GOLDEN EGG 58	FB	SF	FBG	SV	IB	T10CD	GM	17	6	72000	5	3	489500	538000
62	8	GOLDEN EGG 58	FB	SF	FBG	SV	IB	T10CD	CAT	17	6	72000	5	3	474000	521000
1990 BOATS																
34	6	GOLDEN EGG 34	FB	SF	FBG	SV	IB	T454	CRUS	13	2	17500	3	2	83900	92200
34	6	GOLDEN EGG 34	FB	SF	FBG	SV	IB	T375D-T400D		13	2	17500	3	2	106000	117500
38	6	DOUBLE CABIN 38	FB	DC	FBG	SV	IB	T454	CRUS	15		27000	3	10	119000	130500
38	6	DOUBLE CABIN 38	FB	DC	FBG	SV	IB	T375D	CAT	15		27000	3	10	138000	151500
38	6	GOLDEN EGG 38	FB	SF	FBG	SV	IB	T454	CRUS	15		22500	3	10	102000	112000
		IB T502 CRUS 105000 115500, IB T375D CAT 120500 132500, IB T400D GM 119500 131000														
42	2	DOUBLE CABIN 42	FB	DC	FBG	SV	IB	T502	CRUS	15		32000	3	10	156500	171500
42	2	DOUBLE CABIN 42	FB	DC	FBG	SV	IB	T375D	CAT	15		32000	3	10	168500	185000
42	2	GOLDEN EGG 42	FB	DC	FBG	SV	IB	T502	CRUS	15		27000	3	10	137000	151000
42	2	GOLDEN EGG 42	FB	SF	FBG	SV	IB	T375D	CAT	15		31000	3	10	163500	180000
42	2	GOLDEN EGG 42	FB	SF	FBG	SV	IB	T400D	GM	15		31000	3	10	164000	180500
42	2	GOLDEN EGG 42	FB	SF	FBG	SV	IB	T485D	GM	15		31000	3	10	176000	193500
54	6	GOLDEN EGG 54	FB	SF	FBG	SV	IB	T735D	GM	17	6	64000	5	3	357000	392500
54	6	GOLDEN EGG 54	FB	SF	FBG	SV	IB	T900D	GM	17	6	64000	5	3	385000	423000
59	6	GOLDEN EGG 58	FB	SF	FBG	SV	IB	T900D	GM	17	6	72000	5	3	438500	482000
59	6	GOLDEN EGG 58	FB	SF	FBG	SV	IB	T10CD	CAT	17	6	72000	5	3	451500	496500
59	6	GOLDEN EGG 58	FB	SF	FBG	SV	IB	T10CD	GM	17	6	72000	5	3	467500	513500
1989 BOATS																
33		CONVERTIBLE SEDAN	FB	SDN	FBG	SV	IB	T340	MRCR	13	2	16500	2	5	70500	77500
33		CONVERTIBLE SEDAN	FB	SDN	FBG	SV	IB	T320D	CAT	13	2	16500	2	5	97000	106500
35		SPORT FISHERMAN	FB	SF	FBG	SV	IB	T340	MRCR	13	2	17000	3	2	76800	84400
35		SPORT FISHERMAN	FB	SF	FBG	SV	IB	T300D	GM	13	2	17000	3	2	95600	105000
35		SPORT FISHERMAN	FB	SF	FBG	SV	IB	T375D	CAT	13	2	17000	3	2	102500	113000
37		CONVERTIBLE SEDAN	FB	SDN	FBG	SV	IB	T340	MRCR	14	5	24000	3	10	91700	100500
37		CONVERTIBLE SEDAN	FB	SDN	FBG	SV	IB	T375D	CAT	14	5	24000	3	10	116000	127500
38		DOUBLE CABIN	FB	DC	FBG	SV	IB	T340	MRCR	14	5	27000	3	10	107000	117500
38		DOUBLE CABIN	FB	DC	FBG	SV	IB	T320D	CAT	14	5	27000	3	10	126500	139000
41		CONVERTIBLE SEDAN	FB	SDN	FBG	SV	IB	T375D	CAT	14	5	29000	3	10	150500	165000
41		CONVERTIBLE SEDAN	FB	SDN	FBG	SV	IB	T485D	GM	14	5	29000	3	10	158000	173500
41		SPORT FISHERMAN	FB	SF	FBG	SV	IB	T375D	CAT	14	5	28000	3	10	147000	161500
41		SPORT FISHERMAN	FB	SF	FBG	SV	IB	T485D	GM	14	5	28000	3	10	156500	172000
43		DOUBLE CABIN	FB	DC	FBG	SV	IB	T375D	CAT	14	5	32000	3	10	162000	178000
43		SPORT FISHERMAN	FB	SF	FBG	SV	IB	T375D	CAT	14	5	31000	3	10	156500	172000
43		SPORT FISHERMAN	FB	SF	FBG	SV	IB	T485D	GM	14	5	31000	3	10	169500	186000
54		CONVERTIBLE SEDAN	FB	SDN	FBG	SV	IB	T735D	GM	17	6	64000	5	3	358500	394000
59	6	SPORT FISHERMAN	FB	SF	FBG	SV	IB	T735D	GM	17	6	72000	5	3	392000	430500
59	6	SPORT FISHERMAN	FB	SF	FBG	SV	IB	T900D	GM	17	6	72000	5	3	419500	461000
59	6	SPORT FISHERMAN	FB	SF	FBG	SV	IB	T11CD	GM	17	6	72000	5	3	450000	494500
1988 BOATS																
33		CONVERTIBLE SEDAN	FB	CNV	FBG	SV	IB	T340	MRCR	13	2	16500	2	5	67200	73800
33		CONVERTIBLE SEDAN	FB	CNV	FBG	SV	IB	T320D	CAT	13	2	16500	2	5	92900	102000
35		SPORT FISHERMAN	FB	SF	FBG	SV	IB	T340	MRCR	13	2	17000	3	2	73200	80500
35		SPORT FISHERMAN	FB	SF	FBG	SV	IB	T320D	CAT	13	2	17000	3	2	94000	103500
35		SPORT FISHERMAN	FB	SF	FBG	SV	IB	T375D	CAT	13	2	17000	3	2	98200	108000
37		CONVERTIBLE SEDAN	FB	CNV	FBG	SV	IB	T340	MRCR	14	5	24000	3	10	87600	96300
37		CONVERTIBLE SEDAN	FB	CNV	FBG	SV	IB	T320D	CAT	14	5	24000	3	10	106500	117000
37		CONVERTIBLE SEDAN	FB	CNV	FBG	SV	IB	T375D	CAT	14	5	24000	3	10	111000	122000
38		DOUBLE CABIN	FB	DC	FBG	SV	IB	T340	MRCR	14	5	27000	3	10	102000	112500
38		DOUBLE CABIN	FB	DC	FBG	SV	IB	T320D	CAT	14	5	27000	3	10	120500	132500
41		CONVERTIBLE SEDAN	FB	CNV	FBG	SV	IB	T340	MRCR	14	5	29000	3	10	119000	131000
41		CONVERTIBLE SEDAN	FB	CNV	FBG	SV	IB	T375D	CAT	14	5	29000	3	10	143500	157500
41		CONVERTIBLE SEDAN	FB	CNV	FBG	SV	IB	T485D	GM	14	5	29000	3	10	152000	167500
41		SPORT FISHERMAN	FB	SF	FBG	SV	IB	T340	MRCR	14	5	28000	3	10	116000	127500
41		SPORT FISHERMAN	FB	SF	FBG	SV	IB	T375D	CAT	14	5	28000	3	10	140500	154500
41		SPORT FISHERMAN	FB	SF	FBG	SV	IB	T485D	GM	14	5	28000	3	10	149500	164500
43		DOUBLE CABIN	FB	DC	FBG	SV	IB	T375D	CAT	14	5	32000	3	10	154500	170000
43		SPORT FISHERMAN	FB	SF	FBG	SV	IB	T375D	CAT	14	5	31000	3	10	149500	164500
43		SPORT FISHERMAN	FB	SF	FBG	SV	IB	T485D	GM	14	5	31000	3	10	162000	178000
59	6	SPORT FISHERMAN	FB	SF	FBG	SV	IB	T710D	GM	17	6	72000	5	3	370000	407000
59	6	SPORT FISHERMAN	FB	SF	FBG	SV	IB	T870D	GM	17	6	72000	5	3	396000	435500
59	6	SPORT FISHERMAN	FB	SF	FBG	SV	IB	T10CD	GM	17	6	72000	5	3	416000	457000
1987 BOATS																
33		CONVERTIBLE SEDAN	FB	CNV	FBG	SV	IB	T350	CRUS	13	2	17000	2	5	65000	71500
33		CONVERTIBLE SEDAN	FB	CNV	FBG	SV	IB	T250D-T320D		13	2	17000	2	5	84400	99100
35		SPORT FISHERMAN	FB	SF	FBG	SV	IB	T350	CRUS	13	2	17000	2	5	70400	77400
35		SPORT FISHERMAN	FB	SF	FBG	SV	IB	T320D	CAT	13	2	17000	2	5	90100	99000
35		SPORT FISHERMAN	FB	SF	FBG	SV	IB	T375D	CAT	13	2	17000	2	5	94100	103500
37		CONVERTIBLE SEDAN	FB	CNV	FBG	SV	IB	T350	CRUS	14	5	24000	3		84700	93100
37		CONVERTIBLE SEDAN	FB	CNV	FBG	SV	IB	T320D	CAT	14	5	24000	3		101500	111500
37		CONVERTIBLE SEDAN	FB	CNV	FBG	SV	IB	T375D	CAT	14	5	24000	3		106000	116500
38		DOUBLE CABIN	FB	DC	FBG	SV	IB	T350	CRUS	14	5	27000	3		98700	108500
38		DOUBLE CABIN	FB	DC	FBG	SV	IB	T320D	CAT	14	5	27000	3		115500	127000
41		CONVERTIBLE SEDAN	FB	CNV	FBG	SV	IB	T350	CRUS	14	5	28000	3		112000	123000
41		CONVERTIBLE SEDAN	FB	CNV	FBG	SV	IB	T375D	CAT	14	5	28000	3		134000	147000
41		CONVERTIBLE SEDAN	FB	CNV	FBG	SV	IB	T485D	GM	14	5	28000	3		142500	156500
41		SPORT FISHERMAN	FB	SF	FBG	SV	IB	T350	CRUS	14	5	28000	3		112000	123500
41		SPORT FISHERMAN	FB	SF	FBG	SV	IB	T375D	CAT	14	5	28000	3		134500	147500
41		SPORT FISHERMAN	FB	SF	FBG	SV	IB	T485D	GM	14	5	28000	3		143000	157000
43		DOUBLE CABIN	FB	DC	FBG	SV	IB	T375D	CAT	14	5	32000	3		148000	162500
43		SPORT FISHERMAN	FB	SF	FBG	SV	IB	T375D	CAT	14	5	32000	3		145500	160000
43		SPORT FISHERMAN	FB	SF	FBG	SV	IB	T485D	GM	14	5	32000	3		157500	173000
59	6	SPORT FISHERMAN	FB	SF	FBG	SV	IB	T100D	GM	17	6		5	3	210500	231000
59	6	SPORT FISHERMAN	FB	SF	FBG	SV	IB	T710D	GM	17	6		5	3	281500	309000
59	6	SPORT FISHERMAN	FB	SF	FBG	SV	IB	T870D	GM	17	6		5	3	300500	330000
1986 BOATS																
33		EXPRESS FISHERMAN		FSH	FBG	SV	IB	T350	CRUS	13	2	17000	2	5	58300	64000
33		EXPRESS FISHERMAN		FSH	FBG	SV	IB	T215D-T270D		13	2	17000	2	5	73100	83300
33		SEDAN CRUISER	FB	SDN	FBG	SV	IB	T350	CRUS	13	2	17000	2	5	62100	68200
33		SEDAN CRUISER	FB	SDN	FBG	SV	IB	T215D-T270D		13	2	17000	2	5	79000	92000
33		TOURNAMENT FISHERMAN	FB	SDNSF	FBG	SV	IB	T350	CRUS	13	2	17000	2	5	58200	64000
33		TOURNAMENT FISHERMAN	FB	SDNSF	FBG	SV	IB	T215D-T270D		13	2	17000	2	5	73100	84700
36		SEDAN CRUISER	FB	SDN	FBG	SV	IB	T350	CRUS	13	3	20000	2	9	70200	77100
36		SEDAN CRUISER	FB	SDN	FBG	SV	IB	T300D	CAT	13	3	20000	2	9	84000	92400
36		TOURNAMENT FISHERMAN	FB	SDNSF	FBG	SV	IB	T350	CRUS	13	3	20000	2	9	68500	75300
36		TOURNAMENT FISHERMAN	FB	SDNSF	FBG	SV	IB	T300D	CAT	13	3	20000	2	9	81100	89100
40		MOTOR YACHT	FB	MY	FBG	SV	IB	T350	CRUS	14	1	30000	2	11	115500	126500
40		MOTOR YACHT	FB	MY	FBG	SV	IB	T300D	CAT	14	1	30500	2	11	131500	144500
40		MOTOR YACHT	FB	MY	FBG	SV	IB	T375D	J&T	14	1	30800	2	11	136000	149500
40		SEDAN CRUISER	FB	SDN	FBG	SV	IB	T350	CRUS	14		28000	2	9	109000	120000
40		SEDAN CRUISER	FB	SDN	FBG	SV	IB	T430D	GM	14		28000	2	9	131000	144000
40		TOURNAMENT FISHERMAN	FB	SDNSF	FBG	SV	IB	T350	CRUS	14		28000	2	9	109000	119500
40		TOURNAMENT FISHERMAN	FB	SDNSF	FBG	SV	IB	T430D	GM	14		28900	2	9	134000	147000
40	10	TOURNAMENT FISHERMAN	FB	SDNSF	FBG	SV	IB	T350	CRUS	14	5	28000	3		106500	117000
40	10	TOURNAMENT FISHERMAN	FB	SDNSF	FBG	SV	IB	T355D	CAT	14	5	28900	3		128500	141000
40	10	TOURNAMENT FISHERMAN	FB	SDNSF	FBG	SV	IB	T480D	GM	14	5	28900	3		137500	151000
48		GOLDEN EGG	FB	SDNSF	FBG	SV	IB	T500D	S&S	15		44000	3	5	152000	167000
48		GOLDEN EGG	FB	SDNSF	FBG	SV	IB	T675D	J&T	15		44000	3	5	166500	183000
60		TOURNAMENT FISHERMAN	FB	SDNSF	FBG	SV	IB	T710D	J&T	17	6	62600	4	6	293500	322500
60		TOURNAMENT FISHERMAN	FB	SDNSF	FBG	SV	IB	T875D	J&T	17	6	63700	4	6	321500	353000
60		TOURNAMENT FISHERMAN	FB	SDNSF	FBG	SV	IB	T10CD	J&T	17	6	63900	4	6	340500	374000
1985 BOATS																
33		EXPRESS FISHERMAN		FSH	FBG	SV	IB	T350	CRUS	13	2	17000	2	5	55700	61200
33		EXPRESS FISHERMAN		FSH	FBG	SV	IB	T215D-T270D		13	2	17000	2	5	70200	79900
33		SEDAN CRUISER	FB	SDN	FBG	SV	IB	T350	CRUS	13	2	17000	2	5	59300	65200

 CONTINUED ON NEXT PAGE

LOA FT IN	NAME AND/ OR MODEL	TOP/ RIG	BOAT TYPE	-HULL- MTL TP	TP	----ENGINE--- # HP	MFG	BEAM FT IN	WGT LBS	DRAFT FT IN	RETAIL LOW	RETAIL HIGH
						1985 BOATS						
33	SEDAN CRUISER	FB	SDN	FBG	SV	IBT215D-T270D		13 2	17000	2 5	75700	88200
33	TOURNAMENT FISHERMAN	FB	SDNSF	FBG	SV	IB T350	CRUS	13 2	17000	2 5	55600	61100
33	TOURNAMENT FISHERMAN	FB	SDNSF	FBG	SV	IBT215D-T270D		13 2	17000	2 5	70100	81200
36	SEDAN CRUISER	FB	SDN	FBG	SV	IB T350	CRUS	13 3	20000	2 9	67200	73900
36	SEDAN CRUISER	FB	SDN	FBG	SV	IB T300D	CAT	13 3	20000	2 9	80500	88400
36	TOURNMENT FISHERMAN	FB	SDNSF	FBG	SV	IB T350	CRUS	13 3	20000	2 9	65600	72100
36	TOURNAMENT FISHERMAN	FB	SDNSF	FBG	SV	IB T300D	CAT	13 3	20000	2 9	77600	85300
37 5	SEDAN CRUISER	FB	SDN	FBG	SV	IB T350	CRUS	14 5	24000	3	79600	87400
37 5	SEDAN CRUISER	FB	SDN	FBG	SV	IB T300D	CAT	14 5	24000	3	93600	103000
37 5	SEDAN CRUISER	FB	SDN	FBG	SV	IB T375D	J&T	14 5	24000	3	97100	106500
37 5	TOURNAMENT FISHERMAN	FB	SDNSF	FBG	SV	IB T350	CRUS	14 5	24000	3	79000	86800
37 5	TOURNAMENT FISHERMAN	FB	SDNSF	FBG	SV	IB T300D	CAT	14 5	24000	3	92600	102100
37 5	TOURNAMENT FISHERMAN	FB	SDNSF	FBG	SV	IB T375D	J&T	14 5	24000	3	95900	105500
40	MOTOR YACHT	FB	MY	FBG	SV	IB T350	CRUS	14 1	30000	2 11	110500	121500
40	MOTOR YACHT	FB	MY	FBG	SV	IB T300D	CAT	14 1	30500	2 11	126000	138500
40	MOTOR YACHT	FB	MY	FBG	SV	IB T375D	J&T	14 1	30800	2 11	130500	143500
40	SEDAN CRUISER	FB	SDN	FBG	SV	IB T350	CRUS	14	28000	2 9	104500	114500
40	SEDAN CRUISER	FB	SDN	FBG	SV	IB T430D	GM	14	28000	2 9	125500	138000
40	TOURNAMENT FISHERMAN	FB	SDNSF	FBG	SV	IB T350	CRUS	14	28000	2 9	104500	114500
40	TOURNAMENT FISHERMAN	FB	SDNSF	FBG	SV	IB T430D	GM	14	28900	2 9	128000	141000
40 10	TOURNAMENT FISHERMAN	FB	SDNSF	FBG	SV	IB T350	CRUS	14 5	28000	3	102000	112000
40 10	TOURNAMENT FISHERMAN	FB	SDNSF	FBG	SV	IB T355D	CAT	14 5	28900	3	123000	135000
40 10	TOURNAMENT FISHERMAN	FB	SDNSF	FBG	SV	IB T480D	GM	14 5	28900	3	131500	144500
48	COLDEN DGG	FB	SDNSF	FBG	SV	IB T500D	S&S	15	44000	3 5	145000	159500
48	GOLDEN-EGG	FB	SDNSF	FBG	SV	IB T675D	J&T	15	44000	3 5	159500	175000
60	TOURNAMENT FISHERMAN	FB	SDNSF	FBG	SV	IB T675D		17 6	62600	4 6	276000	303500
	IB T710D J&T	282000	309500,	IB T875D	J&T	308500	339000,	IB T10CD	J&T	326500	359000	
						1984 BOATS						
33	EXPRESS FISHERMAN	TT	FSH	FBG	SV	IB T350	CRUS	13 2	17000	2 5	53200	58500
33	EXPRESS FISHERMAN	TT	FSH	FBG	SV	IBT250D-T270D		13 2	17500	2 5	70200	78000
33	TOURNAMENT FISHERMAN	FB	SDNSF	FBG	SV	IB T350	CRUS	13 2	17000	2 5	53200	58400
33	TOURNAMENT FISHERMAN	FB	SDNSF	FBG	SV	IBT250D-T270D		13 2	17500	2 5	70100	77900
36	SEDAN CRUISER	FB	SDN	FBG	SV	IB T350		13 3	17000	2 9	58900	64700
36	TOURNAMENT FISHERMAN	FB	SDNSF	FBG	SV	IB T350	CRUS	13 3	20000	2 9	62800	69100
	IB T250D J&T	72300	79500,	IB T270D	CUM	72700	79900,	IB T300D	CAT	75500	83000	
40	MOTOR YACHT	FB	MY	FBG	SV	IB T350	CRUS	14 1	30000	2 11	106000	116000
	IB T250D J&T	117500	129000,	IB T270D	CUM	116500	128000,	IB T300D	CAT	121000	133000	
40	TOURNAMENT FISHERMAN	FB	SDNSF	FBG	SV	IB T350	CRUS	14	28000	3	100000	110000
40	TOURNAMENT FISHERMAN	FB	SDNSF	FBG	SV	IB T250D	J&T	14	28900	3	112000	123000
40	TOURNAMENT FISHERMAN	FB	SDNSF	FBG	SV	IB T450D	J&T	14	28900	3	125500	138000
41	TOURNAMENT FISHERMAN	FB	SDNSF	FBG	SV	IB T350	CRUS	14	28000	3	97400	107000
	IB T300D CAT	112500	123500,	IB T450D	J&T	124000	136000,	IB T570D	J&T	136500	150000	
48	GOLDEN EGG	FB	SDNSF	FBG	SV	IB T570D	J&T	15	44000	3 5	146000	160000
48	GOLDEN-EGG	FB	SDNSF	FBG	SV	IB 550D	J&T	15	44000	4 4	126500	139000
	IB T530	128000	140500,	IB T600D	J&T	147500	162500,	IB T675D	J&T	152500	167500	
60	TOURNAMENT FISHERMAN	FB	SDNSF	FBG	SV	IB T675D	J&T	17 6	63700	4 6	268500	295000
60	TOURNAMENT FISHERMAN	FB	SDNSF	FBG	SV	IB T10CD	J&T	17 6	63900	4 6	313500	345000

....For earlier years, see the BUC Used Boat Price Guide, Volume 3

WILLIAM EICKHOLT & ASSOC INC
SEATTLE WA 98148   See inside cover to adjust price for area

LOA FT IN	NAME AND/ OR MODEL	TOP/ RIG	BOAT TYPE	-HULL- MTL TP	TP	----ENGINE--- # HP	MFG	BEAM FT IN	WGT LBS	DRAFT FT IN	RETAIL LOW	RETAIL HIGH
						1988 BOATS						
50 4	FD-12 METER	CUT	SAIL	F/S KL	IB	60D	LEHM	14 3	35175	6 6	169500	186500
50 4	FD-12 METER CTRCPT	CUT	SAIL	F/S KL	IB	60D	LEHM	14 3	35175	6 6	184500	202500
50 4	FD-12 METER CTRCPT	KTH	SAIL	F/S KL	IB	60D	LEHM	14 3	35175	6 6	186500	205000
						1987 BOATS						
50 4	FD-12 METER	CUT	SAIL	F/S KL	IB	60D	LEHM	14 3	35175	6 6	156500	171500
50 4	FD-12 METER CTRCPT	CUT	SAIL	F/S KL	IB	60D	LEHM	14 3	35175	6 6	172500	190000
50 4	FD-12 METER CTRCPT	KTH	SAIL	F/S KL	IB	60D	LEHM	14 3	35175	6 6	173500	191000
						1986 BOATS						
37 8	SUNBEAM-38	SLP	SAIL	F/S KL	IB	36D	YAN	11 6	16500	5 5	75500	82900
50 4	FD-12 METER	CUT	SAIL	F/S KL	IB	60D	LEHM	14 3	35175	6 6	141500	155500
50 4	FD-12 METER CTRCPT	CUT	SAIL	F/S KL	IB	60D	LEHM	14 3	35175	6 6	164500	181000
50 4	FD-12 METER CTRCPT	KTH	SAIL	F/S KL	IB	60D	LEHM	14 3	35175	6 6	161500	177500
						1985 BOATS						
37 8	SUNBEAM-38	SLP	SAIL	F/S KL	IB	36D	YAN	11 6	16500	5 5	70300	77200
50 4	FD-12 METER	CUT	SAIL	F/S KL	IB	60D	LEHM	14 3	35175	6 6	138000	152000
50 4	FD-12 METER CTRCPT	CUT	SAIL	F/S KL	IB	60D	LEHM	14 3	35175	6 6	146000	160500
50 4	FD-12 METER CTRCPT	KTH	SAIL	F/S KL	IB	60D	LEHM	14 3	35175	6 6	150500	165000
						1984 BOATS						
51	FD 12 METER	CUT	SA/CR	FBG KL	IB	D		14 4	35000	6 6	138000	152000
51	FD 12 METER	KTH	SA/CR	FBG KL	IB	D		14 4	35000	6 6	146000	160000

....For earlier years, see the BUC Used Boat Price Guide, Volume 3

ELANTE EXPRESS CRUISERS
DIV OF TANKERS INTL INC   See inside cover to adjust price for area
SALINA KS 67401   COAST GUARD MFG ID- ELT

For more recent years, see the BUC Used Boat Price Guide, Volume 1

LOA FT IN	NAME AND/ OR MODEL	TOP/ RIG	BOAT TYPE	-HULL- MTL TP	TP	----ENGINE--- # HP	MFG	BEAM FT IN	WGT LBS	DRAFT FT IN	RETAIL LOW	RETAIL HIGH
						1996 BOATS						
34 8	ELANTE 348	OP	EXP	FBG DV	IO	T300	VLVO	11	10000	2 6	77200	84800
34 8	ELANTE 348	OP	EXP	FBG DV	IO	T270D	MRCR	11	10000	2 7	90200	99100
						1995 BOATS						
34 8	ELANTE 348	OP	EXP	FBG DV	IO	T300	VLVO	11	10000	2 6	72000	79100
34 8	ELANTE 348	OP	EXP	FBG DV	IO	T270D	MRCR	11	10000	2 7	84100	92400
						1994 BOATS						
34 8	ELANTE 348	OP	EXP	FBG DV	IO	T300	VLVO	11	10000	2 6	54500	59900
34 8	ELANTE 348	OP	EXP	FBG DV	IO	T185D	VLVO	11	10000	2 6	71800	78900
						1993 BOATS						
34 8	ELANTE 348	OP	EXP	FBG DV	IO	T300	VLVO	11	10000	2 6	51300	56300
34 8	ELANTE 348	OP	EXP	FBG DV	IB	T300	VLVO	11	10000	2 6	59000	64800
						1992 BOATS						
34 8	ELANTE 348	OP	EXP	FBG DV	IO	T330	VLVO	11	10000	2 6	70900	77900
34 8	ELANTE 348	OP	EXP	FBG DV	IB	T330D	VLVO	11	10000	2 6	87200	95800
						1991 BOATS						
34 8	ELANTE 348	OP	EXP	FBG DV	IO	T330D	VLVO	11	10000	2 6	66300	72800
34 8	ELANTE 348	OP	EXP	FBG DV	IB	T330D	VLVO	11	10000	2 6	83100	91300

ELCO ELECTRIC LAUNCH INC
ELCO   See inside cover to adjust price for area
ATHENS NY 12015
FORMERLY ELECTRIC LAUNCH COMPANY INC

For more recent years, see the BUC Used Boat Price Guide, Volume 1

LOA FT IN	NAME AND/ OR MODEL	TOP/ RIG	BOAT TYPE	-HULL- MTL TP	TP	----ENGINE--- # HP	MFG	BEAM FT IN	WGT LBS	DRAFT FT IN	RETAIL LOW	RETAIL HIGH
						1995 BOATS						
24	CLASSIC 24	RNBT	FBG	SV	IO	220	MRCR	8 5	4500	2 4	**	**
24	CLASSIC 24	RNBT	FBG	SV	IO	220	VLVO	8 5	4500	2 4	**	**
24	CLASSIC 24 EXP CR	CRCPT	FBG	SV	IO	220	MRCR	8 5	5000	2 4	**	**
24	CLASSIC 24 EXP CR	CRCPT	FBG	SV	IB	220	VLVO	8 5	5000	2 4	**	**
24	CLASSIC 24 SPORT	SPTCR	FBG	SV	IO	220	MRCR	8 5	4500	2 4	**	**
24	CLASSIC 24 SPORT	SPTCR	FBG	SV	IB	220	VLVO	8 5	4500	2 4	**	**
						1990 BOATS						
24	CLASSIC 24 RUNABOUT	ST	RNBT	FBG	RB	IB	220	CRUS	8 6	4000	2 6	** **

ELEGANT MOTORS INC
SARASOTA FL   See inside cover to adjust price for area

LOA FT IN	NAME AND/ OR MODEL	TOP/ RIG	BOAT TYPE	-HULL- MTL TP	TP	----ENGINE--- # HP	MFG	BEAM FT IN	WGT LBS	DRAFT FT IN	RETAIL LOW	RETAIL HIGH
						1986 BOATS						
32	ELEGANT	RNBT	FBG	DV	IB	T330		8			29600	32900
32 8	ELEGANT	RNBT	FBG	DV	IO	T330		8			22000	24400
						1985 BOATS						
32	ELEGANTE	RNBT	FBG	DV	IB	T330		8			28300	31500
32 8	ELEGANTE	RNBT	FBG	DV	IO	T330		8			21000	23300
						1984 BOATS						
32	ELEGANTE	RNBT	FBG	DV	IB	T330		8			27100	30100
32 8	ELEGANTE	RNBT	FBG	DV	IO	T330		8			20100	22400

....For earlier years, see the BUC Used Boat Price Guide, Volume 3

ELIMINATOR BOATS
MIRA LOMA CA 91752   COAST GUARD MFG ID- ELB See inside cover to adjust price for area

For more recent years, see the BUC Used Boat Price Guide, Volume 1

LOA FT IN	NAME AND/ OR MODEL	TOP/ RIG	BOAT TYPE	-HULL- MTL TP	ENGINE TP # HP MFG	BEAM FT IN	WGT LBS	DRAFT FT IN	RETAIL LOW	RETAIL HIGH
				1996 BOATS						
18 7	DAYTONA 19	OP	SKI	KEV TH OB		7 1	2000		6950	8000
18 7	DAYTONA 19	OP	SKI	KEV TH JT		7 1	2000		**	**
20	SKIER 207	OP	B/R	SV JT	CHEV	7 9	2800		**	**
20 7	SKIER 207	OP	B/R	SV IO 250	MRCR	7 9	2800		13200	15000
21	DAYTONA 21	OP	RNBT	KEV TH OB		7 8	2200		9150	10400
21	DAYTONA 21	OP	RNBT	KEV TH JT	CHEV	7 8	2200		**	**
21	DAYTONA 21	OP	RNBT	KEV TH IO 250	MRCR	7 8	2200		12200	13900
21 5	SKIER 215	OP	B/R	SV JT	CHEV	8 3	3100		**	**
21 5	SKIER 215	OP	B/R	SV IO 250	MRCR	8 3	3100		15100	17100
22 2	DAYTONA 22	OP	RNBT	KEV TH OB		7 6	2800		11500	13000
22 2	DAYTONA 22	OP	RNBT	KEV TH IO 250	MRCR	7 6	2800		14300	16300
22 11	EAGLE XP 220	OP	RNBT	SV IO 250	MRCR	8 3	3000		16000	18200
23	EAGLE 230 BR	OP	RNBT	SV JT	CHEV	8 3	3100		**	**
23	EAGLE 230 BR	OP	RNBT	SV IO 250	MRCR	8 3	3100		16400	18600
23 6	EAGLE XP 236 CLOSED	OP	CUD	SV IO 250	MRCR	8 3	3400		19100	21200
23 6	EAGLE XP 236 OPEN	OP	B/R	SV IO 250	MRCR	8 3	3400		19100	21200
23 6	EAGLE XP 236 OPEN	OP	RNBT	SV IO 250	MRCR	8 3	3400		18100	20100
25	DAYTONA 25	OP	RNBT	KEV TH OB		8	2800		13700	15600
25	DAYTONA 25	OP	RNBT	KEV TH IO 250	MRCR	8	2800		18000	20200
25 4	EAGLE XP 250 CLOSED	OP	CUD	SV IO 250	MRCR	8 3	4100		24200	26900
25 4	EAGLE XP 250 OPEN	OP	B/R	SV IO 250	MRCR	8 3	4100		22300	24800
25 4	EAGLE XP 250 OPEN	OP	CUD	SV IO 250	MRCR	8 3	4100		24200	26900
27	DAYTONA 27	OP	RNBT	KEV TH IO 250	MRCR	9	4500		27000	30000
27	DAYTONA 27	OP	RNBT	KEV TH IO T250	MRCR	9	4500		32100	35700
28 3	EAGLE XP 280 CLOSED	OP	CUD	SV IO 250	MRCR	8 3	4800		29600	32800
28 3	EAGLE XP 280 OPEN	OP	B/R	SV IO 250	MRCR	8 3	4800		23400	24800
28 3	EAGLE XP 280 OPEN	OP	CUD	SV IO 250	MRCR	8 3	4800		29600	32800
33 11	EAGLE XP 340 CLOSED	OP	CUD	SV IO T250	MRCR	8 6	7000		65200	71700
33 11	EAGLE XP 340 OPEN	OP	CUD	SV IO T250	MRCR	8 6	7000		65200	71700
37 11	EAGLE 380 OFFSHORE	OP	CUD	SV IO T250	MRCR	8 6	9200		67700	74400
				1995 BOATS						
18 7	DAYTONA 19	OP	SKI	KEV TH OB		7 1	2000		6650	7650
18 7	DAYTONA 19	OP	SKI	KEV TH JT		7 1	2000		**	**
20 7	SKIER 207	OP	B/R	SV JT	CHEV	7 9	2800		**	**
20 7	SKIER 207	OP	B/R	SV IO 250	MRCR	7 9	2800		12300	14000
21	DAYTONA 21	OP	RNBT	KEV TH OB		7 8	2200		8600	9900
21	DAYTONA 21	OP	RNBT	KEV TH JT	CHEV	7 8	2200		**	**
21	DAYTONA 21	OP	RNBT	KEV TH IO 250	MRCR	7 8	2200		11400	12900
21 5	SKIER 215	OP	B/R	SV JT	CHEV	8 3	3100		**	**
21 5	SKIER 215	OP	B/R	SV IO 250	MRCR	8 3	3100		14100	16000
22 2	DAYTONA 22	OP	RNBT	KEV TH OB		7 6	2800		10900	12400
22 2	DAYTONA 22	OP	RNBT	KEV TH IO 250	MRCR	7 6	2800		13400	15200
22 11	EAGLE XP 220	OP	RNBT	SV IO 250	MRCR	8 3	3000		14900	17000
23	EAGLE 230 BR	OP	RNBT	SV JT	CHEV	8 3	3100		**	**
23	EAGLE 230 BR	OP	RNBT	SV IO 250	MRCR	8 3	3100		15300	17400
23 6	EAGLE XP 236 OPEN	OP	CUD	SV IO 250	MRCR	8 3	3400		17600	20000
23 6	EAGLE XP 236 OPEN	OP	CUD	SV IO 250	MRCR	8 3	3400		17600	20000
23 6	EAGLE XP 236 OPEN	OP	RNBT	SV IO 250	MRCR	8 3	3400		16500	18800
25	DAYTONA 25	OP	RNBT	KEV TH OB		8	2800		13000	14800
25	DAYTONA 25	OP	RNBT	KEV TH IO 250	MRCR	8	2800		16400	18700
25 4	EAGLE XP 250	OP	CUD	SV IO 250	MRCR	8 3	4100		22600	25100
25 4	EAGLE XP 250	OP	B/R	SV IO 250	MRCR	8 3	4100		20800	23200
25 4	EAGLE XP 250	OP	CUD	SV IO 250	MRCR	8 3	4100		22600	25100
27	DAYTONA 27	OP	RNBT	KEV TH IO 250	MRCR	9	4500		25200	28000
27	DAYTONA 27	OP	RNBT	KEV TH IO T250	MRCR	9	4500		30000	33300
28 3	EAGLE XP 280 CLOSED	OP	CUD	SV IO 250	MRCR	8 3	4800		27600	30600
28 3	EAGLE XP 280 OPEN	OP	B/R	SV IO 250	MRCR	8 3	4800		21800	24200
28 3	EAGLE XP 280 OPEN	OP	CUD	SV IO 250	MRCR	8 3	4800		27600	30600
33 11	EAGLE XP 340 CLOSED	OP	CUD	SV IO T250	MRCR	8 6	7000		60800	66900
33 11	EAGLE XP 340 OFF	OP	CUD	SV IO T250	MRCR	8 6	7000		60800	66900
37 11	EAGLE 380 OFFSHORE	OP	CUD	SV IO T250	MRCR	8 6	9200		63200	69400
				1986 BOATS						
18 7	DAYTONA 19	OP	SKI	KEV TH OB		6 9	700		2150	2500
18 7	DAYTONA 19	OP	SKI	TH JT 330		6 9			7900	9100
19	ELIMINATOR 19	OP	RNBT	SV TH 330		7	8400		9650	
19 3	ELIMINATOR 19	OP	SKI	SV IB 260		7			7350	8450
20	LIBERTY 20	OP	RNBT	SV OB 700		7 4	700		2300	2700
20 7	LIBERTY 20	OP	RNBT	SV IO 330		7 9			9500	10800
20 7	ELIMINATOR 20	OP	RNBT	SV IO 260		7 9			7000	8050
20 7	ELIMINATOR 20	OP	RNBT	SV IO 330		7 9			10000	11400
21	DAYTONA 21	OP	RNBT	KEV TH OB 1125		7 7			3550	4100
21	DAYTONA 21	OP	RNBT	KEV TH IO 330		7 7			10100	11500
21	MONACO 21	OP	RNBT	SV IO 260		8			7250	8350
21	MONACO 21	OP	RNBT	SV JT 330		8			10400	11800
23	DAYTONA 23		RNBT	KEV TH JT 330		8			12500	14200
23	DAYTONA 23		RNBT	KEV TH IO 330		8			9900	11200
23	DAYTONA 23	OP	RNBT	KEV TH OB 2300		8			6800	7850
24 6	MOJAVE 24		CUD	SV IO 260		8			12000	13600
24 6	MOJAVE 24		CUD	SV JT 330		8			16000	18200
24 6	PRO-AM 25		CUD	SV IO 260		8			12000	13600
24 6	PRO-AM 25		CUD	SV JT 330		8			15800	18000
30	OFFSHORE 30		OFF	KEV SV IO T260		8			24400	26700
30	OFFSHORE 30		OFF	KEV SV JT T330		8			32400	36000
				1985 BOATS						
20 7	SPORT 20		SPTCR	IO 260		7 9			7350	8450
21	DAYTONA 21		SKI	IO 260		7 8			7000	8050
21 3	MANACO 21		CR	IO 260		8			7750	8900
21 3	MOJAVE 31		CR	IO 260		8			7750	8900
21 3	WHALER 21		CR	IO 260		8			7750	8900
23	DAYTONA 23		CR	IO 260		8			9050	10300
24 7	MOJAVE 24		CR	IO 260		8			11400	12900
24 7	PRO-AM 25		CR	IO 260		8			11400	12900
30	OFFSHORE 30		OFF	IO T260		8			23000	25600

....For earlier years, see the BUC Used Boat Price Guide, Volume 3

ELITE CRAFT INC
COLOMA MI   See inside cover to adjust price for area

LOA FT IN	NAME AND/ OR MODEL	TOP/ RIG	BOAT TYPE	-HULL- MTL TP	ENGINE TP # HP MFG	BEAM FT IN	WGT LBS	DRAFT FT IN	RETAIL LOW	RETAIL HIGH
				1990 BOATS						
18 2	SPORTS RIVIERA	OP	RNBT	F/S DV IO		6	2400	1 10	**	**
19 8	SKI ELITE	OP	RNBT	F/S DV IO		7 4	2800	1 8	**	**
19 8	SPORTSMAN	OP	RNBT	F/S DV IO		7 4	2800	1 8	**	**
20 1	RIVIERA	OP	RNBT	F/S DV IO		6 6	2900	2 2	**	**

....For earlier years, see the BUC Used Boat Price Guide, Volume 3

ELITE YACHTS DE FRANCE INC
ANNAPOLIS MD 21403   COAST GUARD MFG ID- EYD See inside cover to adjust price for area

LOA FT IN	NAME AND/ OR MODEL	TOP/ RIG	BOAT TYPE	-HULL- MTL TP	ENGINE TP # HP MFG	BEAM FT IN	WGT LBS	DRAFT FT IN	RETAIL LOW	RETAIL HIGH
				1989 BOATS						
28 6	ELITE 286	SLP	SA/CR FBG KL IB	15D VLVO		10 2	5296	5 4	23600	26200
31 6	ELITE 326	SLP	SA/CR FBG KL IB	18D VLVO		11 2	7200	5 7	32200	35800
33 7	ELITE 346	SLP	SA/CR FBG KC IB	18D VLVO		11 9	8474	5 7	37000	41100
36 4	ELITE 364	SLP	SA/CR FBG KL IB	28D VLVO		11 9	11000	5 9	48400	53100
41 9	ELITE 426	SLP	SA/CR FBG KL IB	43D VLVO		13 10	19874	6 6	90000	98900
45 11	ELITE 45	SLP	SA/CR FBG KL IB	50D PERK		14	22050	5 3	108000	118500
				1988 BOATS						
28 6	ELITE 286	SLP	SA/CR FBG KL IB	9D VLVO		10 2	5296	5 4	22000	24500
31 6	ELITE 326	SLP	SA/CR FBG KL IB	18D VLVO		11 2	7200	5 7	30200	33600
33 7	ELITE 346	SLP	SA/CR FBG KC IB	18D VLVO		11 9	8474	5 7	34700	38600
36 4	ELITE 364	SLP	SA/CR FBG KL IB	28D VLVO		11 9	11000	5 9	44900	49900
41 9	ELITE 426	SLP	SA/CR FBG KL IB	43D VLVO		13 10	19874	6 6	84300	92600
45 11	ELITE 45	SLP	SA/CR FBG KL IB	43D VLVO		13 10	19874	6 6	84300	92600
45 11	ELITE 45	SLP	SA/CR FBG KL IB	50D PERK		14	22050	5 3	101500	111500
				1987 BOATS						
24 8	ELITE 25	SLP	SA/CR FBG KC OB			8 10	3960	2 5	13300	15200
24 8	ELITE 25	SLP	SA/CR FBG KL IB	9D VLVO		8 10	3960	4 7	14600	16600
24 8	ELITE 25	SLP	SA/CR FBG KC IB			8 10	3960	2 5	13300	15200
24 8	ELITE 25	SLP	SA/CR FBG KL IB	9D VLVO		8 10	3960	4 7	14600	16600
29 4	ELITE 286	SLP	SA/CR FBG KL IB	9D		10		4 7	21700	24100
31	ELITE 30 RACING	SLP	SA/RC FBG KL IB	9D VLVO		10 6	5732	5 7	22500	25100
31	ELITE 30 SPECIAL	SLP	SA/CR FBG KL IB	9D- 18D		10 6	5732	5 7	22600	25100
32 4	ELITE 324	SLP	SA/CR FBG KL IB	18D		10 6	8600	4 3	33700	37400
35 2	ELITE 346	SLP	SA/RC FBG KC IB	27D YAN		11 9	10590	4 7	40400	44900
35 2	ELITE 346	SLP	SA/CR FBG KL IB	27D YAN		11 9	10590	4 7	40300	44700
36 4	ELITE 364	SLP	SA/CR FBG KL IB	27D YAN		11 9	11000	5 9	42100	46700
36 4	ELITE 364	SLP	SA/CR FBG KL IB	27D YAN		11 9	11000	5 9	42200	46900

LOA FT	LOA IN	NAME AND/ OR MODEL	TOP/ RIG	BOAT TYPE	-HULL- MTL	-HULL- TP	TP	ENGINE # HP	ENGINE MFG	BEAM FT	BEAM IN	WGT LBS	DRAFT FT	DRAFT IN	RETAIL LOW	RETAIL HIGH
		1987 BOATS														
45	11	ELITE 45	SLP	SA/CR	FBG	KL	IB	50D	PERK	14		22050	5	3	95000	104500
45	11	ELITE 45	SLP	SA/RC	FBG	KL	IB	50D	PERK	14		22050	7	7	95000	104500
		1986 BOATS														
25	9	ELITE 25	SLP	SA/CR	FBG	KC	OB			8	10	3750	2	5	12500	14200
25	9	ELITE 25	SLP	SA/CR	FBG	KC	IB	9D	VLVO	8	10	3750	2	5	13500	15300
25	9	ELITE 25	SLP	SA/CR	FBG	KL	OB			8	10	3750	2	5	12500	14200
25	9	ELITE 25	SLP	SA/CR	FBG	KL	IB	9D	VLVO	8	10	3750	2	5	13500	15300
28	8	ELITE 29	SLP	SA/RC	FBG	KC	IB	9D- 18D		10	8	6160	5	7	22400	25000
28	8	ELITE 29	SLP	SA/RC	FBG	KL	IB	9D- 18D		10	8	6160	5	7	21700	24300
28	8	ELITE 29 MKII	SLP	SA/RC	FBG	KC	IB	9D- 18D		10	8	6160	5	7	23500	26300
28	8	ELITE 29 MKII	SLP	SA/RC	FBG	KL	IB	9D- 18D		10	8	6160	5	7	23100	25800
31		ELITE 30 RACE MKII	SLP	SA/RC	FBG	KL	IB	9D- 18D		10	8	5732	5	7	21900	24300
31		ELITE 30 RACING	SLP	SA/RC	FBG	KL	IB	9D- 18D		10	8	5732	5	7	20500	22900
31		ELITE 30 SPEC MKII	SLP	SA/CR	FBG	KL	IB	9D- 18D		10	8	5732	5	7	21900	24400
31		ELITE 30 SPECIAL	SLP	SA/CR	FBG	KL	IB	9D- 18D		10	8	5732	5	7	20500	22800
31	9	ELITE 32 MKI	SLP	SA/RC	FBG	KC	IB	18D	VLVO	10	7	8000	3	1	28100	31300
31	9	ELITE 32 MKI	SLP	SA/RC	FBG	KL	IB	18D	VLVO	10	7	8000	5	7	27400	30400
31	9	ELITE 32 MKII	SLP	SA/RC	FBG	KC	IB	18D	VLVO	10	7	8000	3	1	31800	35400
31	9	ELITE 32 MKII	SLP	SA/RC	FBG	KL	IB	18D	VLVO	10	7	8000	5	7	31400	34800
34	6	ELITE 346 MKI	SLP	SA/RC	FBG	KL	IB	18D- 28D		11	10	11200	5	10	38000	42300
34	6	ELITE 346 MKII	SLP	SA/RC	FBG	KL	IB	18D- 28D		11	10	11200	5	10	41600	46200
37	1	ELITE 37 MKI	SLP	SA/RC	FBG	KC	IB	28D	VLVO	12	2	12400	4	1	43900	48800
37	1	ELITE 37 MKI	SLP	SA/RC	FBG	KL	IB	28D	VLVO	12	2	12400	5	11	42300	47000
37	1	ELITE 37 MKII	SLP	SA/RC	FBG	KC	IB	28D	VLVO	12	2	12400	4	11	47500	52200
37	1	ELITE 37 MKII	SLP	SA/RC	FBG	KL	IB	28D	VLVO	12	2	12400	5	11	46100	50700
45	9	ELITE 45	SLP	SA/RC	FBG	KL	IB	50D	BMW	14	2	22050	7	6	88900	97700
45	9	ELITE 45	SLP	SA/RC	FBG	KL	IB	50D	PERK	14	2	22050	5	9	88500	97300
		1985 BOATS														
24	8	ELITE 25	SLP	SA/CR	FBG	KL	OB			8	10	3960	4	9	11800	13400
25	9	ELITE 25	SLP	SA/CR	FBG	KC	OB			8	10	3750	2	5	11700	13300
25	9	ELITE 25	SLP	SA/CR	FBG	KC	IB	9D	VLVO	8	10	3750	2	5	12700	14400
25	9	ELITE 25	SLP	SA/CR	FBG	KL	OB			8	10	3750	2	5	11700	13300
25	9	ELITE 25	SLP	SA/CR	FBG	KL	IB	9D	VLVO	8	10	3750	2	5	12700	14400
28	8	ELITE 29	SLP	SA/RC	FBG	KL	IB	9D	VLVO	10	8	6160	5	7	21300	23700
31		ELITE 30 RACING	SLP	SA/RC	FBG	KL	IB	9D	VLVO	10	8	5732	5	7	19900	22200
31	9	ELITE 32 MKI	SLP	SA/RC	FBG	KC	IB	18D	VLVO	10	7	8000	3	1	26500	29400
31	9	ELITE 32 MKI	SLP	SA/RC	FBG	KL	IB	18D	VLVO	10	7	8000	5	7	25900	28800
31	9	ELITE 32 MKII	SLP	SA/RC	FBG	KC	IB	18D	VLVO	10	7	8000	3	1	29800	33100
31	9	ELITE 32 MKII	SLP	SA/RC	FBG	KL	IB	18D	VLVO	10	7	8000	5	7	29400	32600
34	6	ELITE 346 MKI	SLP	SA/RC	FBG	KL	IB	28D	VLVO	11	10	11200	5	10	36100	40100
34	6	ELITE 346 MKII	SLP	SA/RC	FBG	KL	IB	28D	VLVO	11	10	11200	5	10	38700	43000
37	1	ELITE 37 MKI	SLP	SA/RC	FBG	KC	IB	18D	VLVO	12	2	12400	4	1	42100	46800
37	1	ELITE 37 MKI	SLP	SA/RC	FBG	KL	IB	18D	VLVO	12	2	12400	5	11	41800	46500
37	1	ELITE 37 MKII	SLP	SA/RC	FBG	KC	IB	28D	VLVO	12	2	12400	4	11	42100	46800
37	1	ELITE 37 MKII	SLP	SA/RC	FBG	KL	IB	28D	VLVO	12	2	12400	5	11	42100	46800
45	9	ELITE 45 MKI	SLP	SA/RC	FBG	KL	IB	51D	PERK	14	2	22050	5	9	80400	88400
45	9	ELITE 45 MKII	SLP	SA/RC	FBG	KL	IB	51D	PERK	14	2	22050	7	6	85700	94200
49	4	ELITE 50	SLP	SA/CR	FBG	SK	IB	D		14	7	26700	5	2	105000	115500
63	8	ELITE 64	SLP	SA/CR	FBG	KL	IB	D		16	5	55000	8		243000	267500
		1984 BOATS														
25	9	ELITE 25	SLP	SA/RC	FBG	KC	OB			8	10	3750	2	5	11000	12500
25	9	ELITE 25	SLP	SA/RC	FBG	KC	IB	10D	VLVO	8	10	3750	2	5	12000	13600
25	9	ELITE 25	SLP	SA/RC	FBG	KL	OB			8	10	3750	4	7	11000	12500
25	9	ELITE 25	SLP	SA/RC	FBG	KL	IB	10D	VLVO	8	10	3750	4	7	12000	13600
28	8	ELITE 29	SLP	SA/CR	FBG	KL	IB	9D- 10D		10	6	6150	5	7	20000	22300
28	8	ELITE 29	SLP	SA/RC	FBG	KL	IB	10D	VLVO	10	6	6160			20100	22300
31	9	ELITE 32	SLP	SA/CR	FBG	KL	IB	9D		10	7	8000	5	7	26200	29100
31	9	ELITE 32 MKI	SLP	SA/RC	FBG	KC	IB	10D	VLVO	10	7	8000	3	1	26200	29200
31	9	ELITE 32 MKI	SLP	SA/RC	FBG	KL	IB	10D	VLVO	10	7	8000	5	7	26200	29100
31	9	ELITE 32 MKII	SLP	SA/RC	FBG	KC	IB	18D	VLVO	10	7	8000	3	1	26300	29200
31	9	ELITE 32 MKII	SLP	SA/RC	FBG	KL	IB	18D	VLVO	10	7	8000	5	7	26200	29100
37	1	ELITE 37 MKI	SLP	SA/RC	FBG	KC	IB	18D	VLVO	12	2	12400	4	1	39400	43800
37	1	ELITE 37 MKI	SLP	SA/RC	FBG	KL	IB	18D	VLVO	12	2	12400	5	11	39300	43600
37	1	ELITE 37 MKII	SLP	SA/RC	FBG	KC	IB	28D	VLVO	12	2	12400	4	1	39500	43900
37	1	ELITE 37 MKII	SLP	SA/RC	FBG	KL	IB	28D	VLVO	12	2	12400	5	11	39400	43800
45	1	ELITE 45	SLP	SA/RC	FBG	KC	IB	82D		14	5	22000	4	6	77000	84600
45	1	ELITE 45	SLP	SA/RC	FBG	KC	IB	85D	PERK	14	5	22200	4	6	76900	84600
45	1	ELITE 45	SLP	SA/RC	FBG	KL	IB	82D		14	5	22000	6	7	77000	84600
45	1	ELITE 45	SLP	SA/RC	FBG	KL	IB	85D	PERK	14	5	22200	6	7	76900	84600
45	1	ELITE 45	KTH	SA/RC	FBG	KC	IB	85D	PERK	14	5	22200	4	6	79400	87200
45	1	ELITE 45	KTH	SA/RC	FBG	KL	IB	85D	PERK	14	5	22200	6	7	79400	87200
46	1	ELITE 45	SLP	SA/RC	FBG	KL	IB	82D		14	5	22200	6	7	80100	88000
49	4	ELITE 50	SLP	SA/RC	FBG	KL	IB	85D	PERK	14	7	26700	6	7	98100	108000
49	4	ELITE 50	KTH	SA/RC	FBG	KL	IB	85D	PERK	14	7	26700	6	7	99600	109500
49	4	ELITE 50 SHOAL	SLP	SA/RC	FBG	KL	IB	85D	PERK	14	7	26700	5		98900	108500
49	4	ELITE 50 SHOAL	KTH	SA/RC	FBG	KL	IB	85D	PERK	14	7	26700	5		100500	110500
50	9	ELITE 50	SLP	SA/RC	FBG	KL	IB	82D		14	7	26700	6	7	108000	119000
50	9	ELITE 51	SLP	SA/RC	FBG	KC	IB	82D	PERK	14	7	26700	4	7	108000	118500
50	9	ELITE 51	SLP	SA/RC	FBG	KL	IB	D		14	7	26700	6	7	108000	119000
50	9	ELITE 51	SLP	SA/RC	FBG	KL	IB	82D	PERK	14	7	26700	6	7	108000	118500
50	9	ELITE 51	KTH	SA/RC	FBG	KC	IB	82D	PERK	14	7	26700	4	7	109000	119500
50	9	ELITE 51	KTH	SA/RC	FBG	KL	IB	82D	PERK	14	7	26700	6	7	109000	119500
63	8	ELITE 64	SLP	SA/RC	FBG	KL	IB	125D		16	5	55000	8		228500	251000
63	8	ELITE 64	SLP	SA/RC	FBG	KL	IB	135D	PERK	16	5	55000	8		227000	249500
63	8	ELITE 64 SHOAL	SLP	SA/RC	FBG	KL	IB	135D	PERK	16	5	55000	6		229500	252000

ELIZABETHAN MARINE LTD

WOOLSTON ENGLAND

See inside cover to adjust price for area

LOA FT	LOA IN	NAME AND/ OR MODEL	TOP/ RIG	BOAT TYPE	-HULL- MTL	-HULL- TP	TP	ENGINE # HP	ENGINE MFG	BEAM FT	BEAM IN	WGT LBS	DRAFT FT	DRAFT IN	RETAIL LOW	RETAIL HIGH
		1985 BOATS														
19	6	MIRROR OFFSHORE MKII	SLP	SAIL	FBG	KL	OB			6	9	1700	1	11	1850	2200
23		ELIZABETHAN 23	SLP	SA/RC	FBG	KC	OB			7	1	3475	2	6	3300	3850
23		ELIZABETHAN 23	SLP	SA/RC	FBG	KC	IB	9D	YAN	7	1	3475	2	6	3650	4250
25		ITCHEN-FERRY MKII	SLP	SAIL	FBG	KL	IB	9D	YAN	8		6272	3		6750	7750
29	6	ELIZABETHAN 30	SLP	SA/RC	FBG	KL	IB	15D	BUKH	9	3	7168	5		9550	10800
30	8	MERIDIAN	SLP	MS	FBG	KL	IB	35D		10	3	15680	4	1	21700	24100
30	8	MERIDIAN	KTH	MS	FBG	KL	IB	35D		10	3	15680	4	1	21700	24100
33		ELIZABETHAN 33	SLP	SAIL	FBG	KL	IB	20D	BUKH	9	4	12768	4	7	18100	20100
33		ELIZABETHAN 33	KTH	SAIL	FBG	KL	IB	20D	BUKH	9	4	12768	4	7	18200	20300

ELLIOTT BAY STEAM LAUNCH CO

ELLIOTT BAY COMPANY
PORTLAND OR 97202 COAST GUARD MFG ID- EBQ

See inside cover to adjust price for area

LOA FT	LOA IN	NAME AND/ OR MODEL	TOP/ RIG	BOAT TYPE	-HULL- MTL	-HULL- TP	TP	ENGINE # HP	ENGINE MFG	BEAM FT	BEAM IN	WGT LBS	DRAFT FT	DRAFT IN	RETAIL LOW	RETAIL HIGH
		1985 BOATS														
23	4	DIESEL RENTAL		CUD	FBG	DS	IB	8		6	4	200	1	6	19600	21700
23	4	DIESEL RENTAL	OP	LNCH	FBG	DS	IB	8		6	4	1200	1	6	11300	12800
23	4	JACK-SALMON		CNV	FBG	DS	IB	8		6	4	1200	1	6	7000	8000
23	4	LIMOSINE	HT	CNV	FBG	DS	IB	8D	YAN	6	4	1400	1	6	9650	11000
23	4	STEAM LAUNCH	ST	LNCH	FBG	DS	IB	4		6	4	2000	1	6	11200	12800
23	4	STEAM LAUNCH	HT	LNCH	FBG	DS	IB	4		6	4	2200	1	6	11200	12800
23	4	STEAM LAUNCH KIT	OP	LNCH	FBG	DS	IB	4		6	4	2000	1	6	11200	12800
23	4	WATER-TAXI	HT	LNCH	FBG	DS	IB	8D	YAN	6	4	1200	1	6	15000	17100
		1984 BOATS														
23	4	DIESEL RENTAL		CUD	FBG	DS	IB	8		6	4	200	1	6	18800	20900
23	4	DIESEL RENTAL	OP	LNCH	FBG	DS	IB	8		6	4	1200	1	6	10800	12300
23	4	JACK-SALMON		CNV	FBG	DS	IB	8		6	4	1200	1	6	6650	7650
23	4	JACK-SALMON		CUD	FBG	DS	IB	8D	YAN	6	4	1200	1	6	9550	10800
23	4	JACK-SALMON	HT	PH	FBG	DS	IB	8		6	4	1300	1	6	6650	7600
23	4	LIMOSINE	HT	CNV	FBG	DS	IB	8D	YAN	6	4	1400	1	6	9300	10600
23	4	STEAM LAUNCH	ST	LNCH	FBG	DS	IB	4		6	4	2000	1	6	10700	12200
23	4	STEAM LAUNCH	HT	LNCH	FBG	DS	IB	4		6	4	2200	1	6	10700	12200
23	4	STEAM LAUNCH KIT	OP	LNCH	FBG	DS	IB	4		6	4	2000	1	6	10700	12200
23	4	WATER-TAXI	HT	LNCH	FBG	DS	IB	8D	YAN	6	4	1200	1	6	14300	16300

....For earlier years, see the BUC Used Boat Price Guide, Volume 3

ELLIS BOAT COMPANY

SOUTHWEST HARBOR ME 046 COAST GUARD MFG ID- RDL See inside cover to adjust price for area

LOA FT	LOA IN	NAME AND/ OR MODEL	TOP/ RIG	BOAT TYPE	-HULL- MTL	-HULL- TP	TP	ENGINE # HP	ENGINE MFG	BEAM FT	BEAM IN	WGT LBS	DRAFT FT	DRAFT IN	RETAIL LOW	RETAIL HIGH
		1986 BOATS														
20	1	ELLIS 20		UTL	FBG	FL	OB			7	4	1200		11	2400	2750
24	4	ELLIS 24			FBG	SV	IB	125		8	6				25500	28300
24	4	ELLIS 24	HT	CUD	FBG	SV	IO	125		8	6				21500	23900
28		ELLIS 28		FSH	FBG	DS	IB	150		9	6	1200			35400	39400
		1985 BOATS														
20	1	ELLIS 20		UTL	FBG	DS	OB			7	4	1200		11	2350	2700
28		ELLIS 28		FSH	FBG	DS	IB			9	6	1200			**	**
		1984 BOATS														
20	1	ELLIS 20	OP	UTL	FBG	DS	OB			7	4	1200		11	2300	2700

....For earlier years, see the BUC Used Boat Price Guide, Volume 3

EMBASSY YACHTS LTD

STATEN ISLAND NY 10308 See inside cover to adjust price for area

LOA FT	IN	NAME AND/ OR MODEL	TOP/ RIG	BOAT TYPE	HULL MTL	HULL TP	ENGINE TP	# HP	MFG	BEAM FT	IN	WGT LBS	DRAFT FT	IN	RETAIL LOW	RETAIL HIGH
		1992 BOATS														
44	4	SUNDECK 44	FB	MY			IB	T375D							131500	144500
		1989 BOATS														
44	4	SUNDECK 44	FB	MY			IB	T375D							114000	125500
		1988 BOATS														
44	4	SUNDECK 44	FB	MY			IB	T375D							109000	120000
		1987 BOATS														
44	4	SUNDECK 44	FB	MY			IB	T375D							104500	114500

EMPIRE TRADING CO LTD

SYRACUSE NY 13206 COAST GUARD MFG ID- EMX See inside cover to adjust price for area

LOA FT	IN	NAME AND/ OR MODEL	TOP/ RIG	BOAT TYPE	HULL MTL	HULL TP	ENGINE TP	# HP	MFG	BEAM FT	IN	WGT LBS	DRAFT FT	IN	RETAIL LOW	RETAIL HIGH
		1986 BOATS														
40		EMPIRE-TRADER JUNK		SAIL	WD	KL	IB	135D	PERK	13	6		5		72400	79500
		1985 BOATS														
40		EMPIRE-TRADER JUNK		SAIL	WD	KL	IB	135D	PERK	13	6		5		68100	74800

ENDEAVOUR CATAMARAN CORP

CLEARWATER FL 33762 COAST GUARD MFG ID- ECR See inside cover to adjust price for area

For more recent years, see the BUC Used Boat Price Guide, Volume 1

LOA FT	IN	NAME AND/ OR MODEL	TOP/ RIG	BOAT TYPE	HULL MTL	HULL TP	ENGINE TP	# HP	MFG	BEAM FT	IN	WGT LBS	DRAFT FT	IN	RETAIL LOW	RETAIL HIGH
		1996 BOATS														
30		ENDEAVOUR CAT MKII	SLP	SACAC	FBG	CT	OB			14	6	7000	2	10	66900	73500
34		ENDEAVOUR CAT 34	SLP	SACAC	FBG	CT	OB			14	6	8800	2	10	99700	109500
		1995 BOATS														
30		ENDEAVOUR CAT 30	SLP	SACAC	FBG	CT	OB			14	6	7000	2	10	62900	69200
36		ENDEAVOUR CAT 36	SLP	SACAC	FBG	CT	OB			17		6500	2	6	90000	98900
		1994 BOATS														
30		ENDEAVOUR CAT 30	SLP	SACAC	FBG	CT	OB			14	6	7000	2	10	59200	65000
36		ENDEAVOUR CAT 36	SLP	SACAC	FBG	CT	OB			17		6500	2	6	84700	93000
		1993 BOATS														
30		ENDEAVOUR CAT 30	SLP	SACAC	FBG	CT	OB			14	6	7000	2	10	55700	61200
		1992 BOATS														
30		ENDEAVOUR CAT 30	SLP	SAIL	FBG	CT	OB			14	6	7000	2	10	52400	57500
		1991 BOATS														
30		ENDEAVOUR CAT 30	SLP	SAIL	FBG	CT	OB			14	6	7000	2	10	49300	54100

ENDEAVOUR YACHT CORP

CLEARWATER FL 34620 COAST GUARD MFG ID- ECR See inside cover to adjust price for area

For more recent years, see the BUC Used Boat Price Guide, Volume 1

LOA FT	IN	NAME AND/ OR MODEL	TOP/ RIG	BOAT TYPE	HULL MTL	HULL TP	ENGINE TP	# HP	MFG	BEAM FT	IN	WGT LBS	DRAFT FT	IN	RETAIL LOW	RETAIL HIGH
		1996 BOATS														
40		MANTA 40	CAT	SACAC	FBG	KL	IB	T 29D	VLVO	21		18000	3	4	129000	142000
44	6	ENDEAVOUR 45	SLP	SACAC	FBG	KL	IB	62D	YAN	13	3	26000	5		190500	209000
52	4	ENDEAVOUR 52	SLP	SACAC	FBG	KL	IB	88D	YAN	15		35000	5	6	326500	359000
54	6	ENDEAVOUR 54	SLP	SACAC	FBG	KL	IB	T 75D	YAN	15	9	55000	5	6	415000	456000
59	3	ENDEAVOUR 59	SLP	SACAC	FBG	KL	IB	140D	YAN	15	11	65000	5	10	632000	694500
		1995 BOATS														
38		MANTA 38	CAT	SACAC	FBG	KL	IB	T 27D	VLVO	21		18000	3	4	217000	238500
44	6	ENDEAVOUR 45	SLP	SACAC	FBG	KL	IB	62D	YAN	13	3	26000	5		177500	195500
52	4	ENDEAVOUR 52	SLP	SACAC	FBG	KL	IB	88D	YAN	15		35000	5	6	305000	335000
54	6	ENDEAVOUR 54	SLP	SACAC	FBG	KL	IB	T 75D	YAN	15	9	55000	5	6	387500	425500
59	3	ENDEAVOUR 59	SLP	SACAC	FBG	KL	IB	140D	YAN	15	11	65000	5	10	590000	648500
		1994 BOATS														
38		MANTA 38	CAT	SACAC	FBG	KL	IB	T 27D	VLVO	21		18000	3	4	101500	111500
44	6	ENDEAVOUR 45	SLP	SACAC	FBG	KL	IB	62D	YAN	13	3	26000	5		166000	182500
52	4	ENDEAVOUR 52	SLP	SACAC	FBG	KL	IB	88D	YAN	15		35000	5	6	284500	313000
54	6	ENDEAVOUR 54	SLP	SACAC	FBG	KL	IB	T 75D	YAN	15	9	55000	5	6	361500	397500
59	3	ENDEAVOUR 59	SLP	SACAC	FBG	KL	IB	140D	YAN	15	11	65000	5	10	551000	605500
		1993 BOATS														
44	6	ENDEAVOUR 45	SLP	SACAC	FBG	KL	IB	62D	YAN	13	3	26000	5		155000	170500
52	4	ENDEAVOUR 52	SLP	SACAC	FBG	KL	IB	88D	YAN	15		35000	5	6	266000	292000
54	6	ENDEAVOUR 54	SLP	SACAC	FBG	KL	IB	T 75D	YAN	15	9	55000	5	6	338000	371000
59	3	ENDEAVOUR 59	SLP	SACAC	FBG	KL	IB	140D	YAN	15	11	65000	5	10	514500	565500
		1992 BOATS														
44	6	ENDEAVOUR 45	SLP	SAIL	FBG	KL	IB	62D	YAN	13	3	26000	5		145000	159000
52	4	ENDEAVOUR 52	SLP	SAIL	FBG	KL	IB	88D	YAN	15		35000	5	6	248500	273000
54	6	ENDEAVOUR 54	SLP	SAIL	FBG	KL	IB	T 75D	YAN	15	9	55000	5	6	315500	346500
59	3	ENDEAVOUR 59	SLP	SAIL	FBG	KL	IB	140D	YAN	15	11	65000	5	10	480500	528000
68	5	ENDEAVOUR 68	SLP	SAIL	FBG	KL	IB	T140D	YAN	18		86500	6	9	720000	791000
		1991 BOATS														
44	6	ENDEAVOUR 45	SLP	SAIL	FBG	KL	IB	62D	YAN	13	3	26000	5		135500	148500
52	4	ENDEAVOUR 52	SLP	SAIL	FBG	KL	IB	88D	YAN	15		35000	5	6	232000	255000
54	6	ENDEAVOUR 54	SLP	SAIL	FBG	KL	IB	T 75D	YAN	15	9	55000	5	6	295000	324000
59	3	ENDEAVOUR 59	SLP	SAIL	FBG	KL	IB	140D	YAN	15	11	65000	5	10	449000	493500
68	5	ENDEAVOUR 68	SLP	SAIL	FBG	KL	IB	T140D	YAN	18		86500	6	9	671000	737500
		1990 BOATS														
42	3	ENDEAVOUR 42	SLP	SAIL	FBG	KL	IB	62D	YAN	13		24000	5		110000	121000
52	4	ENDEAVOUR 52	SLP	SAIL	FBG	KL	IB	88D	YAN	15		35000	5	6	217000	238000
54	4	ENDEAVOUR 54 MS	SLP	SAIL	FBG	KL	IB	T 75D	YAN	15	7	55000	5		272500	299500
56	4	ENDEAVOUR 56	SLP	SAIL	FBG	KL	IB	140D	YAN	15	7	55005	5	6	354000	389000
		1988 BOATS														
33	10	ENDEAVOUR 34	SLP	SA/CR	FBG	KL	IB	23D	YAN	11	6	11350	4	6	39300	43600
38	3	ENDEAVOUR 38C	SLP	SA/CR	FBG	KL	IB	44D	YAN	12	5	17600	5		65900	72400
42	3	ENDEAVOUR 42C	SLP	SA/CR	FBG	KL	IB	66D	YAN	13		25000	5		98400	108000
51		ENDEAVOUR 51C	SLP	SA/CR	FBG	KL	IB	85D	YAN	15		37500	7	6	176500	194000
		1987 BOATS														
32	7	ENDEAVOUR 33	SLP	SA/CR	FBG	KL	IB	23D	YAN	11	6	11350	4	6	36300	40400
35	5	ENDEAVOUR 35	SLP	SA/CR	FBG	KL	IB	30D	YAN	12	2	13250	4	11	43700	48500
38	3	ENDEAVOUR 38C	SLP	SA/CR	FBG	KL	IB	44D	YAN	12	5	17600	5		61600	67700
42	3	ENDEAVOUR 42C	SLP	SA/CR	FBG	KL	IB	66D	YAN	13		25000	5		92000	101000
51		ENDEAVOUR 51C	SLP	SA/CR	FBG	KL	IB	85D	YAN	15		37500	7	6	165000	181000
		1986 BOATS														
32	7	ENDEAVOUR 33	SLP	SA/CR	FBG	KL	IB	23D	YAN	11	6	11350	4	6	34000	37800
35	5	ENDEAVOUR 35	SLP	SA/CR	FBG	KL	IB	30D	YAN	12	2	13250	4	11	40800	45400
38	3	ENDEAVOUR 38C	SLP	SA/CR	FBG	KL	IB	44D	YAN	12	5	17600	5		57600	63300
42	3	ENDEAVOUR 42C	SLP	SA/CR	FBG	KL	IB	62D	PERK	13		25000	5		85300	93800
51		ENDEAVOUR 51	SLP	SA/CR	FBG	KL	IB	85D	PERK	15		37500	7	6	153500	168500
		1985 BOATS														
32	7	ENDEAVOUR 33	SLP	SA/CR	FBG	KL	IB	23D	YAN	11	6	11350	4	6	31800	35300
35	5	ENDEAVOUR 35	SLP	SA/CR	FBG	KL	IB	30D	YAN	12	2	13250	4	11	38200	42400
38	3	ENDEAVOUR 38	SLP	SA/CR	FBG	KL	IB	30D	YAN	12	6	17600	4	11	53700	59000
38	3	ENDEAVOUR 38C	SLP	SA/CR	FBG	KL	IB	44D	YAN	12	5	17600	5		53900	59200
40		ENDEAVOUR 40	SLP	SA/CR	FBG	KL	IB	51D	PERK	13		25000	5		74400	81800
40		ENDEAVOUR 40	KTH	SA/CR	FBG	KL	IB	51D	PERK	13		25000	5		74400	81800
40		ENDEAVOUR 40C	SLP	SA/CR	FBG	KL	IB	D		13		25000	5		74900	82300
42	3	ENDEAVOUR 42C	SLP	SA/CR	FBG	KL	IB	62D	PERK	13		25000	5		79800	87700
51		ENDEA 51C	SLP	SA/CR	FBG	KL	IB	85D	PERK	15		37500	7	6	143500	157500
51		ENDEAVOUR 51	SLP	SA/CR	FBG	KL	IB	D		15		37500	7	6	144000	158500
51		ENDEAVOUR 51 SHOAL	SLP	SA/CR	FBG	KL	IB	D		15		37500	5		144000	158500
		1984 BOATS														
32	7	ENDEAVOUR 33	SLP	SA/CR	FBG	KL	IB	23D	YAN	11	6	11350	4	6	29700	33000
35	5	ENDEAVOUR 35	SLP	SA/CR	FBG	KL	IB	30D	YAN	12	2	13250	4	11	35700	39700
38	3	ENDEAVOUR 38	SLP	SA/CR	FBG	KL	IB	30D	YAN	12	6	17600	4	11	50200	55200
40		ENDEAVOUR 40	SLP	SA/CR	FBG	KL	IB	30D		13		25000	5		69600	76400
40		ENDEAVOUR 40	SLP	SA/CR	FBG	KL	IB	50D	PERK	13		25000	5		69600	76500
40		ENDEAVOUR 40	KTH	SA/CR	FBG	KL	IB	50D	PERK	13		25000	5		69600	76500

....For earlier years, see the BUC Used Boat Price Guide, Volume 3

ENTERPRISE BOAT CO INC

CORWIN SERIES
RANCHO CORDOVA CA 95670 COAST GUARD MFG ID- ENT See inside cover to adjust price for area

LOA FT	IN	NAME AND/ OR MODEL	TOP/ RIG	BOAT TYPE	HULL MTL	HULL TP	ENGINE TP	# HP	MFG	BEAM FT	IN	WGT LBS	DRAFT FT	IN	RETAIL LOW	RETAIL HIGH
		1988 BOATS														
16	10	E17FRIO	ST	RNBT	FBG	TR	IO	130-230		7	3	2150	1	6	3050	3700
16	10	E17FROB	ST	RNBT	FBG	TR	OB			7	3	1400	1	6	2850	3300
17		17VBRIO	ST	RNBT	FBG	SV	IO	130-230		7	3	2100	1	6	3050	3700
17		17VBROB	ST	RNBT	FBG	SV	OB			7	3	1300	1	6	2700	3150
18	1	181VIO	OP	RNBT	FBG	DV	IO	175-205		7	4	1200	1	6	2750	3250
20		202DVIO	ST	RNBT	FBG	DV	IO	130-230		7	4	2500	1	2	3850	4600
20	2	202DVIO	ST	RNBT	FBG	DV	IO	175	OMC	7	4	2500	1	2	3900	4500
20	2	202DVOB	ST	RNBT	FBG	DV	OB			7	4	1650	1	2	3550	4100
		1987 BOATS														
16	10	E17FRIO	ST	RNBT	FBG	TR	IO	130-230		7	3	2150	1	6	2900	3550
16	10	E17FROB	ST	RNBT	FBG	TR	OB			7	3	1400	1	6	2750	3200
17		17VBRIO	ST	RNBT	FBG	SV	IO	130-230		7	3	2100	1	6	2900	3550
17		17VBROB	ST	RNBT	FBG	SV	OB			7	3	1300	1	6	2600	3050
18	1	181VIO	OP	RNBT	FBG	DV	IO	175-205		7	4	1200	1	6	2650	3100
20		202DVIO	ST	RNBT	FBG	DV	IO	130-230		7	4	2500	1	2	3650	4400
20	2	202DVIO	ST	RNBT	FBG	DV	IO	175	OMC	7	4	2500	1	2	3700	4300

 CONTINUED ON NEXT PAGE

LOA FT IN	NAME AND/ OR MODEL	TOP/ RIG	BOAT TYPE	-HULL- MTL TP	----ENGINE--- TP # HP MFG	BEAM FT IN	WGT LBS	DRAFT FT IN	RETAIL LOW	RETAIL HIGH
					1987 BOATS					
20 2	202DVOB	ST	RNBT	FBG DV	OB	7 4	1650	1 2	3450	4000
					1986 BOATS					
16 10	E17FR		RNBT	FBG TR	OB	7 3	1400	1 6	2700	3150
16 10	E17FRIO		RNBT	FBG TR	IO 170	7 3	2150	1 6	2800	3300
17	17BR		RNBT	FBG SV	OB	7 3	1350	1 6	2650	3050
17	17VBRIO		RNBT	FBG SV	IO 170	7 3	2100	1 6	2800	3250
18 1	181VIO		RNBT	FBG DV	IO 170	7 4	1200	1 6	2550	2950
20 2	202DV		RNBT	FBG DV	OB	7 4	1700	1 2	3450	4000
20 2	202DVIO		RNBT	FBG DV	IO 170	7 4	2500	1 6	3550	4150
					1985 BOATS					
16	16EIO	ST	RNBT	FBG TR	IO 120-170	6 8	1850	11	2250	2700
16	16EOB	ST	RNBT	FBG TR	OB	6 8	1150	9	2250	2600
16 10	E17FRIO	ST	RNBT	FBG TR	IO 120-230	7 3	2150	1 6	2650	3250
16 10	E17FROB	ST	RNBT	FBG TR	OB	7 3	1400	1 6	2650	3050
16 10	E17IO	ST	RNBT	FBG TR	IO 120-230	7 3	2200	1 6	2700	3300
16 10	E17OB	ST	RNBT	FBG TR	OB	7 3	1400	1 6	2650	3050
17	17VBRIO	ST	RNBT	FBG SV	IO 120-230	7 3	2100	1 6	2650	3250
17	17VBROB	ST	RNBT	FBG SV	OB	7 3	1300	1 6	2500	2900
18 1	181VIO	OP	RNBT	FBG DV	IO 170	7 4	1200	1 6	2450	2850
20	202DVIO	ST	RNBT	FBG DV	IO 120-230	7 4	2500	1 2	3350	4000
20 2	202DVIO	ST	RNBT	FBG DV	IO 170 OMC	7 4	2500	1 2	3400	3950
20 2	202DVOB	ST	RNBT	FBG DV	OB	7 4	1650	1 2	3250	3800
					1984 BOATS					
16	16EIO	ST	RNBT	FBG TR	IO 120-170	6 8	1850	11	2200	2600
16	16EOB	ST	RNBT	FBG TR	OB	6 8	1150	9	2200	2550
16 10	E17CIO	ST	CR	FBG TR	IO 140-170	7 3	2450	1 9	2800	3300
16 10	E17COB	ST	CR	FBG TR	OB	7 3	1700	1 6	2800	3450
16 10	E17FRIO	ST	RNBT	FBG TR	IO 120-230	7 3	2150	1 6	2550	3150
16 10	E17FROB	ST	RNBT	FBG TR	OB	7 3	1400	1 6	2550	3000
16 10	E17IO	ST	RNBT	FBG TR	IO 120-230	7 3	2200	1 6	2600	3150
16 10	E17OB	ST	RNBT	FBG TR	OB	7 3	1400	1 6	2550	3000
17	17VBRIO	ST	RNBT	FBG SV	IO 120-230	7 3	2100	1 6	2550	3100
17	17VBROB	ST	RNBT	FBG SV	OB	7 3	1300	1 6	2450	2850
18 1	181VIO	OP	RNBT	FBG DV	IO 170-230	7 4	1200	1 6	2350	2800
20	202DVIO	ST	RNBT	FBG DV	IO 120-230	7 4	2500	1 2	3200	3900
20 2	202DVIO	ST	RNBT	FBG DV	IO 170 OMC	7 4	2500	1 2	3250	3800
20 2	202DVOB	ST	RNBT	FBG DV	OB	7 4	1650	1 2	3200	3700

....For earlier years, see the BUC Used Boat Price Guide, Volume 3

ENTERPRISE MARINE CORP

EMC JOINER SHOP   See inside cover to adjust price for area
NEWCASTLE ME 04553   COAST GUARD MFG ID- EMG

LOA FT IN	NAME AND/ OR MODEL	TOP/ RIG	BOAT TYPE	-HULL- MTL TP	----ENGINE--- TP # HP MFG	BEAM FT IN	WGT LBS	DRAFT FT IN	RETAIL LOW	RETAIL HIGH
					1984 BOATS					
23	CATNIPS	CAT	SA/RC FBG	CB	IB 12D BMW	10	6000	2 3	18600	20700
23	JAMES-W-HART	CAT	SA/RC WD	CB	IB 12D BMW	10	6000	2 3	18600	20700

ENVISION BOATS INC

MONMOUTH IL 61462   COAST GUARD MFG ID- EVN See inside cover to adjust price for area

For more recent years, see the BUC Used Boat Price Guide, Volume 1

LOA FT IN	NAME AND/ OR MODEL	TOP/ RIG	BOAT TYPE	-HULL- MTL TP	----ENGINE--- TP # HP MFG	BEAM FT IN	WGT LBS	DRAFT FT IN	RETAIL LOW	RETAIL HIGH
					1996 BOATS					
26	FANTASEA 2600	B/R	FBG DV	IO	300	8 6	4500		13700	15600
26	FANTASEA 2600	B/R	FBG DV	IO	T250	8 6	4500		15400	17500
26	P'ZAZZ 2600	CUD	FBG DV	IO	300	8 6	5700		17000	19300
26	P'ZAZZ 2600	CUD	FBG DV	IO	T250	8 6	4500		16800	19100
29	COMBO 2900	B/R	FBG DV	IO	350	8 6	5400		18200	20200
29	COMBO 2900	B/R	FBG DV	IO	T300	8 6	6500		21100	23500
29	CONCEPT 2900	CUD	FBG DV	IO	385	8 6	6500		24600	27300
29	CONCEPT 2900	CUD	FBG DV	IO	T300	8 6	6500		26800	29800
29	SOLARIS 2900	B/R	FBG DV	IO	300	8 6	5400		17000	19300
32	ILLUSION 3200	CUD	FBG DV	IO	415	8 6	7200		30000	33300
32	ILLUSION 3200	CUD	FBG DV	IO	T415	8 6	7200		35100	39000
32	INTRUDER 3200	B/R	FBG DV	IO	415	8 6	6000		25400	28200
32	INTRUDER 3200	B/R	FBG DV	IO	T470	8 6	7200		30900	34400
					1995 BOATS					
26	FANTASEA 2600	B/R	FBG DV	IO	300	8 6	4500		12800	14500
26	FANTASEA 2600	B/R	FBG DV	IO	T250	8 6	4500		14300	16300
26	P'ZAZZ 2600	CUD	FBG DV	IO	350	8 6	4500		14900	16900
26	P'ZAZZ 2600	CUD	FBG DV	IO	T250	8 6	5700		17500	19900
29	COMBO 2900	B/R	FBG DV	IO	350	8 6	5400		16600	18800
29	COMBO 2900	B/R	FBG DV	IO	T300	8 6	6500		19700	21900
29	CONCEPT 2900	CUD	FBG DV	IO	385	8 6	5400		21900	24400
29	CONCEPT 2900	CUD	FBG DV	IO	T300	8 6	6500		25000	27800
32	ILLUSION 3200	CUD	FBG DV	IO	415	8 6	7200		28000	31100
32	ILLUSION 3200	CUD	FBG DV	IO	T415	8 6	7200		32800	36400
					1994 BOATS					
26	FANTASEA 2600	B/R	FBG DV	IO	300	8 6	4500		11900	13600
26	FANTASEA 2600	B/R	FBG DV	IO	T250	8 6	4500		13400	15200
26	P'ZAZZ 2600	CUD	FBG DV	IO	350	8 6	4500		13900	15800
26	P'ZAZZ 2600	CUD	FBG DV	IO	T250	8 6	5700		16300	18600
29	COMBO 2900	B/R	FBG DV	IO	350	8 6	5400		15500	17600
29	COMBO 2900	B/R	FBG DV	IO	T300	8 6	6500		18600	20700
29	CONCEPT 2900	CUD	FBG DV	IO	385	8 6	5400		20500	22700
29	CONCEPT 2900	CUD	FBG DV	IO	T300	8 6	6500		23300	25900
32	BOWRIDER 3200	B/R	FBG DV	IO	415	8 6	7200		22300	24800
32	BOWRIDER 3200	B/R	FBG DV	IO	T415	8 6	7200		25900	28800
32	ILLUSION 3200	CUD	FBG DV	IO	415	8 6	7200		26100	29000
32	ILLUSION 3200	CUD	FBG DV	IO	T415	8 6	7200		30600	34000
					1993 BOATS					
29	CONCEPT 2900	CUD	FBG DV	IO	385	8 6	6500		20000	22200
29	CONCEPT 2900	CUD	FBG DV	IO	T300	8 6	6500		21800	24200
29	CONCEPT 2900 COMBO	CUD	FBG DV	IO	350	8 6	6500		19400	21600
29	CONCEPT 2900 COMBO	CUD	FBG DV	IO	T300	8 6	6500		21800	24200
32	ILLUSION 3200	CUD	FBG DV	IO	415	8 6	7200		24400	27100
32	ILLUSION 3200	CUD	FBG DV	IO	T415	8 6	7200		28600	31800

ERICKSON POWERBOATS INC

VICTORY MARINE   See inside cover to adjust price for area
W PALM BEACH FL 33407   COAST GUARD MFG ID- ERQ

LOA FT IN	NAME AND/ OR MODEL	TOP/ RIG	BOAT TYPE	-HULL- MTL TP	----ENGINE--- TP # HP MFG	BEAM FT IN	WGT LBS	DRAFT FT IN	RETAIL LOW	RETAIL HIGH
					1986 BOATS					
23 3	VICTORY		RNBT	KEV DV	OB	8 6	1900		4400	5050
32 6	VICTORY CUD		CUD	KEV DV	OB	9 6	3600	2 6	18200	20200
32 6	VICTORY SPORT			KEV DV	OB	9 6	3600	2 6	18200	20200
					1985 BOATS					
32 6	VICTORY 33	OP	CUD	F/S DV	OB	9 6	3550	2 6	17400	19700
32 6	VICTORY 33	OP	OPFSH	F/S DV	OB	9 6	3400	2 6	17300	19700
32 6	VICTORY 33	OP	RACE	F/S DV	OB	9 6	3700	2 6	23000	25500

ERICSON YACHTS INC

FULLERTON CA 92631   COAST GUARD MFG ID- PCS See inside cover to adjust price for area

For more recent years, see the BUC Used Boat Price Guide, Volume 1

LOA FT IN	NAME AND/ OR MODEL	TOP/ RIG	BOAT TYPE	-HULL- MTL TP	----ENGINE--- TP # HP MFG	BEAM FT IN	WGT LBS	DRAFT FT IN	RETAIL LOW	RETAIL HIGH
					1996 BOATS					
34 10	ERICSON 34	SLP	SACAC FBG	KL	IB 30D YAN	11 4	13000	6 3	79700	87600
34 10	ERICSON 34	SLP	SACAC WK	KL	IB 30D YAN	11 4	13000	5 1	79700	87600
37 10	ERICSON 38 CR ED	SLP	SACAC FBG	KL	IB 38D YAN	12	15500	6 3	101500	111500
37 10	ERICSON 38 CR ED	SLP	SACAC WK	KL	IB 38D YAN	12	15500	5 3	101500	111500
					1995 BOATS					
34 10	ERICSON 34	CUT	SACAC FBG	KL	IB 28D VLVO	11 4	13000	6 3	74300	81700
34 10	ERICSON 34	CUT	SACAC WK	KL	IB 28D VLVO	11 4	13000	5 1	74300	81700
37 10	ERICSON 38	SLP	SACAC WK	KL	IB 38D YAN	12	15500	5 3	94700	104000
					1993 BOATS					
34 10	ERICSON 34	SLP	SACAC FBG	KL	IB 43D VLVO	11 4	13000	6 3	65000	71400
34 10	ERICSON 34	SLP	SACAC WK	KL	IB 43D VLVO	11 4	13000	5 1	65000	71400
37 10	ERICSON 38	SLP	SACAC FBG	KL	IB 43D VLVO	12	15500	6 3	82600	90800
37 10	ERICSON 38	SLP	SACAC WK	KL	IB 43D VLVO	12	15500	5 3	82600	90800
37 10	ERICSON 38 REGATTA	SLP	SACAC FBG	KL	IB 43D VLVO	12			82600	90800
					1990 BOATS					
25	OLSON 25 DEEP	SLP	SA/CR FBG	KL	IB	9	2900	4 6	10000	11400
25 9	ERICSON 26	SLP	SA/CR FBG	WK	IB 10D UNIV	9 3	5250	3 11	19300	21400
25 9	ERICSON 26 DEEP	SLP	SA/CR FBG	KL	IB 10D UNIV	9 3	5250	4 1	19300	21400
25 9	ERICSON 26 SHOAL	SLP	SA/CR FBG	KL	IB 10D UNIV	9 3	5250	3 11	19300	21400
28	ERICSON 28	SLP	SA/CR FBG	KL	IB 10D UNIV	10	7500	4 6	29100	32400
28	ERICSON 28 DEEP	SLP	SA/CR FBG	KL	IB 10D UNIV	10	7500	5	29100	32400
28	ERICSON 28 SHOAL	SLP	SA/CR FBG	KL	IB 10D UNIV	10	7500	4	29100	32400

LOA FT	LOA IN	NAME AND/ OR MODEL	TOP/ RIG	BOAT TYPE	-HULL- MTL	-HULL- TP	TP	ENGINE # HP	ENGINE MFG	BEAM FT	BEAM IN	WGT LBS	DRAFT FT	DRAFT IN	RETAIL LOW	RETAIL HIGH
		1990 BOATS														
29	11	OLSON 911S	SLP	SA/CR	FBG	KL	IB	14D	UNIV	10	4	8100	5	5	32300	35900
32	6	ERICSON 32	SLP	SA/CR	FBG	WK	IB	23D	UNIV	10	10	9800	4	5	39200	43600
32	6	ERICSON 32 DEEP	SLP	SA/CR	FBG	KL	IB	23D	UNIV	10	10	9800	6	1	39200	43600
32	6	ERICSON 32 SHOAL	SLP	SA/CR	FBG	KL	IB	23D	UNIV	10	10	9800	4	4	39200	43600
32	6	ERICSON 32-200	SLP	SA/CR	FBG	WK	IB	23D	UNIV	10	10	9800	4	5	39200	43600
32	6	ERICSON 32-200 DEEP	SLP	SA/CR	FBG	KL	IB	23D	UNIV	10	10	9800	6	1	39200	43600
32	6	ERICSON 32-200 SHOAL	SLP	SA/CR	FBG	KL	IB	23D	UNIV	10	10	9800	4	4	39200	43600
34		OLSON 34	SLP	SA/CR	FBG	WK	IB	23D	UNIV	10	10	10600	4	11	42800	47500
34		OLSON 34 FIN	SLP	SA/CR	FBG	KL	IB	23D	UNIV	10	10	10600	6		42800	47500
34	10	ERICSON 34	SLP	SA/CR	FBG	WK	IB	23D	UNIV	11	4	13000	5		52800	58000
34	10	ERICSON 34 DEEP	SLP	SA/CR	FBG	KL	IB	23D	UNIV	11	4	13000	6	2	52800	58000
34	10	ERICSON 34 SHOAL	SLP	SA/CR	FBG	KL	IB	23D	UNIV	11	4	13000	4	11	52800	58000
35	6	ERICSON 35	SLP	SA/CR	FBG	WK	IB	23D	UNIV	11	4	13000	4	11	53500	58700
35	6	ERICSON 35 DEEP	SLP	SA/CR	FBG	KL	IB	23D	UNIV	11	4	13000	6	2	53500	58700
35	6	ERICSON 35 SHOAL	SLP	SA/CR	FBG	KL	IB	23D	UNIV	11	4	13000	4	11	53500	58700
37	8	ERICSON 38	SLP	SA/CR	FBG	WK	IB	32D	UNIV	12		15500	5		66700	73300
37	8	ERICSON 38 DEEP	SLP	SA/CR	FBG	KL	IB	32D	UNIV	12		15500	6	6	66700	73300
37	8	ERICSON 38 SHOAL	SLP	SA/CR	FBG	KL	IB	32D	UNIV	12		15500	4	11	66700	73300
		1989 BOATS														
25		OLSON 25 DEEP	SLP	SA/RC	FBG	KL				9		2900	4	6	9400	10700
25	9	ERICSON 26	SLP	SA/CR	FBG	WK	IB	11D	UNIV	9	3	5250	3	11	18300	20300
25	9	ERICSON 26 DEEP	SLP	SA/CR	FBG	KL	IB	11D	UNIV	9	3	5250	4	11	18300	20300
25	9	ERICSON 26 SHOAL	SLP	SA/CR	FBG	KL	IB	11D	UNIV	9	3	5250	3	11	18300	20300
28		ERICSON 28	SLP	SA/CR	FBG	WK	IB	11D	UNIV	10		7500	4		27300	30300
28		ERICSON 28 DEEP	SLP	SA/CR	FBG	KL	IB	11D	UNIV	10		7500	5	6	27300	30300
28		ERICSON 28 SHOAL	SLP	SA/CR	FBG	KL	IB	11D	UNIV	10		7500	4		27300	30300
29	11	OLSON 911S	SLP	SA/CR	FBG	KL	IB	14D	UNIV	10	4	8100	5	5	30200	33500
32	6	ERICSON 32	SLP	SA/CR	FBG	WK	IB	23D	UNIV	10	10	9800	4	5	36700	40700
32	6	ERICSON 32 DEEP	SLP	SA/CR	FBG	KL	IB	23D	UNIV	10	10	9800	7		36700	40700
32	6	ERICSON 32 SHOAL	SLP	SA/CR	FBG	KL	IB	23D	UNIV	10	10	9800	4	4	36700	40700
32	6	ERICSON 32-200	SLP	SA/CR	FBG	WK	IB	23D	UNIV	10	10	9800	4	5	36700	40700
32	6	ERICSON 32-200 DEEP	SLP	SA/CR	FBG	KL	IB	23D	UNIV	10	10	9800	7		36700	40700
32	6	ERICSON 32-200 SHOAL	SLP	SA/CR	FBG	KL	IB	23D	UNIV	10	10	9800	4	4	36700	40700
34		OLSON 34 DEEP	SLP	SA/CR	FBG	KL	IB	23D	UNIV	10	10	10600	6		40000	44400
34		OLSON 34 DEEP	SLP	SA/CR	FBG	WK	IB	23D	UNIV	10	10	10600	4	11	40000	44400
34	10	ERICSON 34	SLP	SA/CR	FBG	WK	IB	23D	UNIV	11	4	13000	5		49400	54200
34	10	ERICSON 34 DEEP	SLP	SA/CR	FBG	KL	IB	23D	UNIV	11	4	13000	6	2	49400	54200
34	10	ERICSON 34 SHOAL	SLP	SA/CR	FBG	KL	IB	23D	UNIV	11	4	13000	4	11	49400	54200
35	6	ERICSON 35	SLP	SA/CR	FBG	WK	IB	23D	UNIV	11	4	13000	4	11	50000	54900
35	6	ERICSON 35 DEEP	SLP	SA/CR	FBG	KL	IB	3D	UNIV	11	4	13000	6	2	49600	54500
35	6	ERICSON 35 SHOAL	SLP	SA/CR	FBG	KL	IB	23D	UNIV	11	4	13000	4	11	50000	54900
37	8	ERICSON 38	SLP	SA/CR	FBG	WK	IB	32D	UNIV	12		15500	5		62400	68500
37	8	ERICSON 38 DEEP	SLP	SA/CR	FBG	KL	IB	32D	UNIV	12		15500	6	6	62400	68500
37	8	ERICSON 38 SHOAL	SLP	SA/CR	FBG	KL	IB	32D	UNIV	12		15500	4	11	62400	68500
		1987 BOATS														
25	9	ERICSON 26	SLP	SAIL	FBG	KL	IB	10D	UNIV	9	3	5250	4	11	15600	17700
25	9	ERICSON 26 SHOAL	SLP	SAIL	FBG	KL	IB	10D	UNIV	9	3	5250	3	11	15600	17700
28		ERICSON 28	SLP	SAIL	FBG	KL	IB	10D	UNIV	10		7500	4		23800	26400
28		ERICSON 28 COMP	SLP	SAIL	FBG	KL	IB	10D	UNIV	10		7500	5	6	23800	26400
29	11	ERICSON 30	SLP	SAIL	FBG	KL	IB	14D	UNIV	10	6	9000	5	10	29400	32600
29	11	ERICSON 30 SHOAL	SLP	SAIL	FBG	KL	IB	14D	UNIV	10	6	9000	4		29400	32600
32	6	ERICSON 32	SLP	SAIL	FBG	KC	IB	23D	UNIV	10	10	9800	3	11	32000	35600
32	6	ERICSON 32 SHOAL	SLP	SAIL	FBG	KL	IB	23D	UNIV	10	10	9800	4	4	32000	35600
34	11	ERICSON 34 MKII	SLP	SAIL	FBG	KL	IB	23D	UNIV	11	4	13000	6	2	43000	47700
35	6	ERICSON 35 COMP	SLP	SAIL	FBG	KL	IB	23D	UNIV	11	4	13000	6	2	43400	48200
35	6	ERICSON 35 STD	SLP	SAIL	FBG	KL	IB	23D	UNIV	11	4	13000	4	11	43400	48200
37	6	ERICSON 38-200	SLP	SAIL	FBG	KL	IB	30D	YAN	12		14900	6	6	52400	57600
37	6	ERICSON 38-200	SLP	SAIL	FBG	KL	IB	32D	UNIV	12		14900	6	6	52400	57600
37	6	ERICSON 38-200 SHOAL	SLP	SAIL	FBG	KL	IB	30D	YAN	12		14900	4	11	52400	57600
37	6	ERICSON 38-200 SHOAL	SLP	SAIL	FBG	KL	IB	32D	UNIV	12		14900	4	11	52400	57600
37	8	ERICSON 38 COMP	SLP	SA/RC	FBG	KL	IB	32D	UNIV	12		14900	6	6	52800	58000
37	8	ERICSON 38 STD	SLP	SAIL	FBG	KL	IB	32D	UNIV	12		14900	4	11	52800	58000
37	8	ERICSON 381 COMP	SLP	SA/RC	FBG	KL	IB	32D	UNIV	12		14400	6	6	51300	56400
37	8	ERICSON 381 STD	SLP	SAIL	FBG	KL	IB	32D	UNIV	12		14400	4	11	51300	56400
		1986 BOATS														
25	9	ERICSON 26	SLP	SAIL	FBG	KL	IB	8D	YAN	9	3	5250	4	11	14500	16500
25	9	ERICSON 26 SHOAL	SLP	SAIL	FBG	KL	IB	8D	YAN	9	3	5250	3	11	14500	16500
28		ERICSON 28	SLP	SAIL	FBG	KL	IB	10D	UNIV	10		7500	4		22300	24700
28		ERICSON 28 COMP	SLP	SAIL	FBG	KL	IB	10D	UNIV	10		7500	5	6	22300	24700
29	11	ERICSON 30	SLP	SAIL	FBG	KL	IB	14D	UNIV	10	6	9000	5	10	27500	30500
29	11	ERICSON 30 SHOAL	SLP	SAIL	FBG	KL	IB	14D	UNIV	10	6	9000	4		27500	30500
32	6	ERICSON 32	SLP	SAIL	FBG	KC	IB	21D	UNIV	10	10	9800	3	11	30000	33300
32	6	ERICSON 32 SHOAL	SLP	SAIL	FBG	KL	IB	21D	UNIV	10	10	9800	4	4	30000	33300
33	6	ERICSON 33	SLP	SAIL	FBG	KL	IB	21D	UNIV	11	2	9500	5	11	29200	32400
35	6	ERICSON 35 COMP	SLP	SAIL	FBG	KL	IB	21D	UNIV	11	4	13000	6	2	40600	45100
35	6	ERICSON 35 STD	SLP	SAIL	FBG	KL	IB	21D	UNIV	11	4	13000	4	11	40600	45100
35	7	ERICSON 36	SLP	SAIL	FBG	KL	IB	21D	UNIV	11	10	11600	6	3	36600	40700
37	6	ERICSON 38-200	SLP	SAIL	FBG	KL	IB			12		14900	6	6	48300	53100
37	6	ERICSON 38-200 SHOAL	SLP	SAIL	FBG	KL	IB			12		14900	4	11	48300	53100
37	8	ERICSON 38 COMP	SLP	SA/RC	FBG	KL	IB	32D	UNIV	12		14900	6	6	49400	54200
37	8	ERICSON 38 STD	SLP	SAIL	FBG	KL	IB	32D	UNIV	12		14900	4	11	49400	54200
37	8	ERICSON 381 COMP	SLP	SA/RC	FBG	KL	IB	32D	UNIV	12		14400	6	6	48000	52700
37	8	ERICSON 381 STD	SLP	SAIL	FBG	KL	IB	32D	UNIV	12		14400	4	11	48000	52700
		1985 BOATS														
25	9	ERICSON 26	SLP	SAIL	FBG	KL	IB	8D	YAN	9	3	5250	4	11	13600	15400
25	9	ERICSON 26 SHOAL	SLP	SAIL	FBG	KL	IB	8D	YAN	9	3	5250	3	11	13600	15400
28	6	ERICSON 28	SLP	SAIL	FBG	KL	IB	11D	UNIV	10	6	7500	5		21000	23300
28	6	ERICSON 28 SHOAL	SLP	SAIL	FBG	KL	IB	11D	UNIV	10	6	7500	4		21000	23300
29	11	ERICSON 30	SLP	SAIL	FBG	KL	IB	14D	UNIV	10	6	9000	5	10	25700	28500
29	11	ERICSON 30 SHOAL	SLP	SAIL	FBG	KL	IB	14D	UNIV	10	6	9125	4		26000	28900
32	6	ERICSON 32	SLP	SAIL	FBG	KC	IB	21D	UNIV	10	10	9800	3	11	28000	31100
32	6	ERICSON 32	SLP	SAIL	FBG	KL	IB	21D	UNIV	10	10	9800	6	2	28000	31100
32	6	ERICSON 32 SHOAL	SLP	SAIL	FBG	KL	IB	21D	UNIV	10	10	9800	4	4	28000	31100
33	6	ERICSON 33	SLP	SAIL	FBG	KL	IB	21D	UNIV	11	2	9500	5	11	27300	30300
35	6	ERICSON 35	SLP	SAIL	FBG	KL	IB	21D	UNIV	11	4	13000	6	2	38000	42200
35	6	ERICSON 35 SHOAL	SLP	SAIL	FBG	KL	IB	21D	UNIV	11	4	13000	4	11	38000	42200
35	7	ERICSON 36	SLP	SAIL	FBG	KL	IB	21D	UNIV	11	10	11600	6	3	34200	38000
37	8	ERICSON 38 COMP	SLP	SA/RC	FBG	KL	IB	32D	UNIV	12		14900	6	6	46400	51000
37	8	ERICSON 38 STD	SLP	SAIL	FBG	KL	IB	32D	UNIV	12		14900	4	11	46400	51000
37	8	ERICSON 381 COMP	SLP	SA/RC	FBG	KL	IB	32D	UNIV	12		14400	6	6	44600	49600
37	8	ERICSON 381 STD	SLP	SAIL	FBG	KL	IB	32D	UNIV	12		14400	4	1	44600	49600
		1984 BOATS														
19		SUPER-CAT	SLP	SA/OD	F/S	CT				8		375			2300	2650
25	9	ERICSON 26	SLP	SAIL	FBG	KL	IB	8D	YAN	9	3	5200	4	11	12600	14300
25	9	ERICSON 26 SHOAL	SLP	SAIL	FBG	KL	IB	8D	YAN	9	3	5200	3	11	12600	14300
28	6	ERICSON 28	SLP	SAIL	FBG	KL	IB	11D	UNIV	10	6	7500	5		19600	21800
28	6	ERICSON 28 SHOAL	SLP	SAIL	FBG	KL	IB	11D	UNIV	10	6	7500	4		19600	21800
29	11	ERICSON 30	SLP	SAIL	FBG	KL	IB	16D-	18D	10	6	9000	5	10	24000	26700
29	11	ERICSON 30 SHOAL	SLP	SAIL	FBG	KL	IB	18D	UNIV	10	6	9125	4		24400	27100
33	6	ERICSON 33	SLP	SAIL	FBG	KL	IB	21D	UNIV	11	2	9500	5	11	25500	28400
35	6	ERICSON 35	SLP	SAIL	FBG	KL	IB	21D	UNIV	11	4	13000	6	2	35500	39400
35	6	ERICSON 35 SHOAL	SLP	SAIL	FBG	KL	IB	21D	UNIV	11	4	13000	4	11	35500	39400
35	7	ERICSON 36	SLP	SAIL	FBG	KL	IB	21D	UNIV	11	10	11600	6	3	32000	35600
35	7	ERICSON 36	SLP	SAIL	FBG	KL	IB	24D		11	10	11600	6	3	32000	35600
37	8	ERICSON 38	SLP	SAIL	FBG	KL	IB	32D	UNIV	12		14900	6	6	42900	47700
37	8	ERICSON 38 SHOAL	SLP	SAIL	FBG	KL	IB	32D	UNIV	12		14900	4	11	42900	47700
37	8	ERICSON 381	SLP	SAIL	FBG	KL	IB	32D	UNIV	12		14400	6	6	41800	46400
37	8	ERICSON 381 SHOAL	SLP	SAIL	FBG	KL	IB	32D	UNIV	12		14400	4	1	41800	46400

....For earlier years, see the BUC Used Boat Price Guide, Volume 3

ESCAPE SAILBOAT CO

GRAND RAPIDS MI 49512-5 COAST GUARD MFG ID- SLI See inside cover to adjust price for area
FORMERLY SUNFISH LASER

For more recent years, see the BUC Used Boat Price Guide, Volume 1

LOA FT	LOA IN	NAME AND/ OR MODEL	TOP/ RIG	BOAT TYPE	-HULL- MTL	-HULL- TP	TP	ENGINE # HP	ENGINE MFG	BEAM FT	BEAM IN	WGT LBS	DRAFT FT	DRAFT IN	RETAIL LOW	RETAIL HIGH
		1994 BOATS														
16	9	DAYSAILER	SLP	SAROD	FBG	CB				6	3	575			3150	3700
16	9	DAYSAILER RACE	SLP	SARAC	FBG	CB				6	3	575			3150	3700
		1993 BOATS														
16	9	DAYSAILER	SLP	SAROD	FBG	CB				6	3	575			3000	3450
16	9	DAYSAILER RACE	SLP	SARAC	FBG	CB				6	3	575			3000	3450
		1992 BOATS														
16	9	DAYSAILER	SLP	SAIL	FBG	CB				6	3	575			2800	3250

ESPRIT CATAMARANS

OPA LOCKA FL 33054 COAST GUARD MFG ID- ECK See inside cover to adjust price for area

LOA FT	LOA IN	NAME AND/ OR MODEL	TOP/ RIG	BOAT TYPE	-HULL- MTL	-HULL- TP	TP	ENGINE # HP	ENGINE MFG	BEAM FT	BEAM IN	WGT LBS	DRAFT FT	DRAFT IN	RETAIL LOW	RETAIL HIGH
		1986 BOATS														
29	3	ESPRIT CRUISER	SLP	SAIL	FBG	CT	OB			18		2450		1	16000	18200
29	3	ESPRIT STANDARD	SLP	SAIL	FBG	CT	OB			18		2100		11	15400	17500

ESPRIT CATAMARANS   -CONTINUED   See inside cover to adjust price for area

LOA FT IN	NAME AND/ OR MODEL	TOP/ RIG	BOAT TYPE	-HULL- MTL TP	----ENGINE--- TP # HP MFG	BEAM FT IN	WGT LBS	DRAFT FT IN	RETAIL LOW	RETAIL HIGH
---	--- 1985 BOATS	---	---	---	---	---	---	---	---	---
29 3	ESPRIT CRUISER	SLP	SAIL	FBG CT	OB	18	2450	1	15100	17100
29 3	ESPRIT STANDARD	SLP	SAIL	FBG CT	OB	18	2100	11	14500	16400

ESSEX BAY BOAT CO INC
PORTSMOUTH NH 03802-438 COAST GUARD MFG ID- ESI See inside cover to adjust price for area

LOA FT IN	NAME AND/ OR MODEL	TOP/ RIG	BOAT TYPE	-HULL- MTL TP	----ENGINE--- TP # HP MFG	BEAM FT IN	WGT LBS	DRAFT FT IN	RETAIL LOW	RETAIL HIGH
---	--- 1986 BOATS	---	---	---	---	---	---	---	---	---
19 6	ESSEX-BAY 17	SLP	SAIL	CDR KL		7 2	3600	2 4	7850	9050
24 11	ESSEX-BAY 22	CUT	SAIL	CDR KL		9	5600	2 11	14700	16700
30 3	ESSEX-BAY 30-R	SLP	SA/RC	CDR KL		11	6100	6	18500	20500
30 9	ESSEX-BAY 27	CUT	SA/CR	CDR KL IB	15D	11	10500	3 6	39100	43500
38 9	ESSEX-BAY 39-OR	SLP	SA/RC	CDR KL IB	30D	13	16900	6	69200	76000
61 6	ESSEX-BAY 56	SCH	SA/CR	CDR KL IB	80D	17 9	42000	6 2	271000	298000
---	--- 1985 BOATS	---	---	---	---	---	---	---	---	---
19 6	ESSEX-BAY 17	SLP	SAIL	CDR KL		7 2	3600	2 4	7350	8450
24 11	ESSEX-BAY 22	CUT	SAIL	CDR KL		9	5600	2 11	13800	15700
30 3	ESSEX-BAY 30-R	SLP	SA/RC	CDR KL		11	6100	6	16900	19200
30 9	ESSEX-BAY 27	CUT	SA/CR	CDR KL IB	15D	11	10500	3 6	36600	40700
38 9	ESSEX-BAY 39-OR	SLP	SA/RC	CDR KL IB	30D	13	16900	6	64700	71100
61 6	ESSEX-BAY 56	SCH	SA/CR	CDR KL IB	80D	17 9	42000	6 2	253500	278500
---	--- 1984 BOATS	---	---	---	---	---	---	---	---	---
19 6	ESSEX-BAY 17	SLP	SAIL	CDR KL		7 2	3600	2 4	6900	7950
24 11	ESSEX-BAY 22	CUT	SAIL	CDR KL		9	5600	2 11	12900	14700
30 3	ESSEX-BAY 30-R	SLP	SA/RC	CDR KL		11	6100	6	15800	18000
30 9	ESSEX-BAY 27	CUT	SA/CR	CDR KL IB	15D	11	10500	3 6	34200	38000
38 9	ESSEX-BAY 39-OR	SLP	SA/RC	CDR KL IB	30D	13	16900	6	60500	66500
61 6	ESSEX-BAY 56	SCH	SA/CR	CDR KL IB	80D	17 9	42000	6 2	237000	260500

....For earlier years, see the BUC Used Boat Price Guide, Volume 3

P EVANSON YACHT CO INC
RIVERSIDE NJ 08075   COAST GUARD MFG ID- PEB See inside cover to adjust price for area

LOA FT IN	NAME AND/ OR MODEL	TOP/ RIG	BOAT TYPE	-HULL- MTL TP	----ENGINE--- TP # HP MFG	BEAM FT IN	WGT LBS	DRAFT FT IN	RETAIL LOW	RETAIL HIGH
---	--- 1984 BOATS	---	---	---	---	---	---	---	---	---
19 9	CELEBRITY	SLP	SA/OD	FBG CB	OB	6 4	800	10	3450	4050

....For earlier years, see the BUC Used Boat Price Guide, Volume 3

EXCALIBUR MARINE CORP
SARASOTA FL 33580   COAST GUARD MFG ID- NAP See inside cover to adjust price for area

LOA FT IN	NAME AND/ OR MODEL	TOP/ RIG	BOAT TYPE	-HULL- MTL TP	----ENGINE--- TP # HP MFG	BEAM FT IN	WGT LBS	DRAFT FT IN	RETAIL LOW	RETAIL HIGH
---	--- 1984 BOATS	---	---	---	---	---	---	---	---	---
27 6		OP	FSH	FBG DV	OB	7		1 11	9800	11200
27 6		OP	OFF	FBG DV	OB	7		1 11	9850	11200
27 6	SPEEDSTER	OP	OFF	FBG DV	IO T330	7		1 11	8900	10100
30 6	EXCALIBUR-CAT 30	OP	OFF	FBG CT	OB	10 9		1	13900	15800
30 6	EXCALIBUR-CAT 30	OP	OFF	FBG DV	IO T330	9 10		1	13900	15800
31 6		OP	OFF	FBG DV	OB	8		2 4	15200	17300
31 6	SPEEDSTER	OP	OFF	FBG DV	IO T330	8		2 4	15100	17200
32 8	SPEEDSTER	OP	OFF	FBG DV	IO T370	9 6	8200	2 6	19400	21500
37 6	SPEEDSTER	OP	OFF	FBG DV	IO T370	8	7800	1 11	26100	29000
39 3		OP	FSH	FBG DV	OB	8			**	**
39 3	EXCALIBUR-HAWK	OP	OFF	FBG DV	IO T370	9		2 2	27000	30000
41 6	EXCALIBUR-EAGLE	OP	OFF	FBG DV	IO T370	9		2 6	31800	35300

....For earlier years, see the BUC Used Boat Price Guide, Volume 3

EXPLORER YACHTS INC
FRISCO CO 80443   See inside cover to adjust price for area

For more recent years, see the BUC Used Boat Price Guide, Volume 1

LOA FT IN	NAME AND/ OR MODEL	TOP/ RIG	BOAT TYPE	-HULL- MTL TP	----ENGINE--- TP # HP MFG	BEAM FT IN	WGT LBS	DRAFT FT IN	RETAIL LOW	RETAIL HIGH
---	--- 1996 BOATS	---	---	---	---	---	---	---	---	---
47 9	EXPLORER 4750	SLP	SACAC	FBG KL IB	100D YAN	14 5	33750	5 9	197500	217000

....For earlier years, see the BUC Used Boat Price Guide, Volume 3

EXPRESS CATAMARANS
ALGONAC MI 48001   COAST GUARD MFG ID- EMS See inside cover to adjust price for area
FORMERLY EXPRESS MARINE

LOA FT IN	NAME AND/ OR MODEL	TOP/ RIG	BOAT TYPE	-HULL- MTL TP	----ENGINE--- TP # HP MFG	BEAM FT IN	WGT LBS	DRAFT FT IN	RETAIL LOW	RETAIL HIGH
---	--- 1995 BOATS	---	---	---	---	---	---	---	---	---
25 6	NITRO 2500	OP	OFF	FBG CT	OB	8	1950	10	18600	20700
29	NITRO 2800	OP	OFF	FBG CT	OB	8 11	2800	10	37000	41100
31	EXPRESS 3100 PLSR	OP	OFF	FBG CT	IO 410 MRCR	8 11	6500	2	77000	84600
31	EXPRESS 3100 RACE	OP	OFF	FBG CT	OB	8 11	6500	2	45700	50200
31	EXPRESS 3100 RACE	OP	OFF	FBG CT	IO 410 MRCR	8 11	6500	2	77000	84600
33	EXPRESS 3300 PLSR	OP	OFF	FBG CT	IO 420-525	10	7600	2	103000	119000
33	NITRO 3300 RACE	OP	OFF	FBG CT	IO 575-800	10	7600	2	144000	175500
35	NITRO 3500 RACE	OP	OFF	FBG CT	IO	10	7600	2	**	**
39 4	EXPRESS 39	OP	OFF	FBG CT	IO T750 HAWK	12	8500	2 6	159500	175500
48	EXPRESS 48 PLEASURE	OP	OFF	FBG CT	IO T900 HAWK	11	10000	2 6	**	**
48	EXPRESS 48 PLEASURE	OP	OFF	FBG CT	IO R575 MRCR	11	10000	2 6	210000	231000
48	EXPRESS 48 RACE	OP	OFF	FBG CT	IO T	11	10000	2 6	**	**
48	EXPRESS 48 RACE	OP	OFF	FBG CT	IO R	11	10000	2 6	**	**
---	--- 1994 BOATS	---	---	---	---	---	---	---	---	---
25 6	NITRO 2500	OP	OFF	FBG CT	OB	8	1950	10	17400	19800
29	NITRO 2900	OP	OFF	FBG CT	OB	8 11	2800	10	35300	39300
31	EXPRESS 3100 PLSR	OP	OFF	FBG CT	OB	8 11	6500	2	71800	79000
31	EXPRESS 3100 RACE	OP	OFF	FBG CT	OB	8 11	6500	2	43200	47900
31	EXPRESS 3100 RACE	OP	OFF	FBG CT	IO 410 MRCR	8 11	6500	2	71800	79000
33	EXPRESS 3300 PLSR	OP	OFF	FBG CT	IO 420-525	10	7600	2	96300	111000
33	NITRO 3300 RACE	OP	OFF	FBG CT	IO 575-800	10	7600	2	134000	164000
35	NITRO 3500 RACE	OP	OFF	FBG CT	IO	10	7600	2	**	**
39 4	EXPRESS 39	OP	OFF	FBG CT	IO T750 HAWK	12	8500	2 6	148500	163000
48	EXPRESS 48 PLEASURE	OP	OFF	FBG CT	IO T900 HAWK	11	10000	2 6	**	**
48	EXPRESS 48 PLEASURE	OP	OFF	FBG CT	IO R575 MRCR	11	10000	2 6	197000	216500
48	EXPRESS 48 RACE	OP	OFF	FBG CT	IO T	11	10000	2 6	**	**
48	EXPRESS 48 RACE	OP	OFF	FBG CT	IO R	11	10000	2 6	**	**
---	--- 1993 BOATS	---	---	---	---	---	---	---	---	---
25 6	NITRO 2500	OP	OFF	FBG CT	OB	8	1950	10	17200	19500
29	NITRO 2900	OP	OFF	FBG CT	OB	8 11	2800	10	33900	37600
31	EXPRESS 3100 PLSR	OP	OFF	FBG CT	IO 410 MRCR	8 11	6500	2	67000	73700
31	EXPRESS 3100 RACE	OP	OFF	FBG CT	OB	8 11	6500	2	41400	46000
31	EXPRESS 3100 RACE	OP	OFF	FBG CT	IO 410 MRCR	8 11	6500	2	67000	73700
33	EXPRESS 3300 PLSR	OP	OFF	FBG CT	IO 420-525	10	7600	2	89900	103500
33	NITRO 3300 RACE	OP	OFF	FBG CT	IO 575-800	10	7600	2	125000	153000
35	NITRO 3500 RACE	OP	OFF	FBG CT	IO	10	7600	2	**	**
39 4	EXPRESS 39	OP	OFF	FBG CT	IO T750 HAWK	12	8500	2 6	138000	151500
48	EXPRESS 48 PLEASURE	OP	OFF	FBG CT	IO T900 HAWK	11	10000	2 6	**	**
48	EXPRESS 48 PLEASURE	OP	OFF	FBG CT	IO R575 MRCR	11	10000	2 6	184500	202500
48	EXPRESS 48 RACE	OP	OFF	FBG CT	IO T	11	10000	2 6	**	**
48	EXPRESS 48 RACE	OP	OFF	FBG CT	IO R	11	10000	2 6	**	**
---	--- 1992 BOATS	---	---	---	---	---	---	---	---	---
25 6	NITRO 2500	OP	OFF	FBG CT	OB	8	1950	10	16200	18400
29	NITRO 2900	OP	OFF	FBG CT	OB	8 11	2800	10	32600	36200
31	EXPRESS 3100 PLSR	OP	OFF	FBG CT	IO 410 MRCR	8 11	6500	2	62700	68900
31	EXPRESS 3100 RACE	OP	OFF	FBG CT	OB	8 11	6500	2	39800	44200
31	EXPRESS 3100 RACE	OP	OFF	FBG CT	IO 410 MRCR	8 11	6500	2	62700	68900
33	EXPRESS 3300 PLSR	OP	OFF	FBG CT	IO 420-525	10	7600	2	84000	96800
33	NITRO 3300 RACE	OP	OFF	FBG CT	IO 575-800	10	7600	2	117000	143500
35	NITRO 3500 RACE	OP	OFF	FBG CT	IO	10	7600	2	**	**
39 4	EXPRESS 39	OP	OFF	FBG CT	IO T750 HAWK	12	8500	2 6	128500	141000
48	EXPRESS 48 PLEASURE	OP	OFF	FBG CT	IO T900 HAWK	11	10000	2 6	**	**
48	EXPRESS 48 PLEASURE	OP	OFF	FBG CT	IO R575 MRCR	11	10000	2 6	173500	190500
48	EXPRESS 48 RACE	OP	OFF	FBG CT	IO T	11	10000	2 6	**	**
48	EXPRESS 48 RACE	OP	OFF	FBG CT	IO R	11	10000	2 6	**	**
---	--- 1991 BOATS	---	---	---	---	---	---	---	---	---
25 6	NITRO 2500	OP	OFF	FBG CT	OB	8	1950	10	15300	17700
29	NITRO 2900	OP	OFF	FBG CT	OB	8 11	2800	10	31400	34900
31	EXPRESS 3100 PLSR	OP	OFF	FBG CT	IO 365-420	8 11	6500	2	57900	65000
31	EXPRESS 3100 RACE	OP	OFF	FBG CT	OB	8 11	6500	2	38300	42600
31	EXPRESS 3100 RACE	OP	OFF	FBG CT	IO 365-420	8 11	6500	2	57900	65000
33	EXPRESS 3300 PLSR	OP	OFF	FBG CT	IO 420-525	10	7600	2	78700	90600
33	NITRO 3300 RACE	OP	OFF	FBG CT	IO 575-800	10	7600	2	109500	134500
35	NITRO 3500 RACE	OP	OFF	FBG CT	IO	10	7600	2	**	**
39 4	EXPRESS 39	OP	OFF	FBG CT	IO T900 HAWK	12	8500	2 6	**	**

LOA FT	LOA IN	NAME AND/ OR MODEL	TOP/ RIG	BOAT TYPE	-HULL- MTL	-HULL- TP	ENGINE TP	ENGINE # HP	ENGINE MFG	BEAM FT	BEAM IN	WGT LBS	DRAFT FT	DRAFT IN	RETAIL LOW	RETAIL HIGH
		1991 BOATS														
48		EXPRESS 48 PLEASURE	OP	OFF	FBG	CT	IO	T900	HAWK	11		10000	2	6	**	**
48		EXPRESS 48 PLEASURE	OP	OFF	FBG	CT	IO	R575	MRCR	11		10000	2	6	163500	180000
48		EXPRESS 48 PLEASURE	OP	OFF	FBG	CT	IO	R900	HAWK	11		10000	2	6	**	**
48		EXPRESS 48 RACE	OP	OFF	FBG	CT	IO	T		11		10000	2	6	**	**
48		EXPRESS 48 RACE	OP	OFF	FBG	CT	IO	R		11		10000	2	6	**	**
		1990 BOATS														
25	6	NITRO 2500	OP	OFF	FBG	CT	OB			8		1950		10	14900	16900
29		NITRO 2900	OP	OFF	FBG	CT	OB			8	11	2800		10	30300	33700
31		EXPRESS 3100 PLSR	OP	OFF	FBG	CT	IO	365	MRCR	8	11	6500	2		54300	59700
31		EXPRESS 3100 RACE	OP	OFF	FBG	CT	OB			8	11	6500	2		37000	41100
31		EXPRESS 3100 RACE	OP	OFF	FBG	CT	IO	365	MRCR	8	11	6500	2		54300	59700
33		EXPRESS 3100 PLSR	OP	OFF	FBG	CT	IO	420	MRCR	10		7600	2		73800	81100
33		NITRO 3300 RACE	OP	OFF	FBG	CT	IO	575	MRCR	10		7600	2		103000	113000
35		NITRO 3500 RACE	OP	OFF	FBG	CT	IO								**	**
39	4	EXPRESS 39	OP	OFF	FBG	CT	IO	T900		12		8500	2	6	**	**
48		EXPRESS 48 PLEASURE	OP	OFF	FBG	CT	IO	T900		11		10000	2	6	**	**
48		EXPRESS 48 PLEASURE	OP	OFF	FBG	CT	IO	R575		11		10000	2	6	154500	170000
48		EXPRESS 48 RACE	OP	OFF	FBG	CT	IO	T		11		10000	2	6	**	**
48		EXPRESS 48 RACE	OP	OFF	FBG	CT	IO	R		11		10000	2	6	**	**
		1985 BOATS														
39	4	SPORT CATAMARAN	OP	OFF	F/S	CT	IO	T330	MRCR	11	11	8500	1		54000	59400
		IO T370 MRCR 57400 63100, IO T400 MRCR 60800 66800, IO T440 MRCR 65900 72400														
		IO T511 75200 82700, IO T557 80500 88500														
		1984 BOATS														
39	4	EXPRESS 39		OFF	FBG		IB	T400		12		8500			82700	90900

EXPRESS YACHTING

MIDLAND ONTARIO CANADA

See inside cover to adjust price for area

LOA FT	LOA IN	NAME AND/ OR MODEL	TOP/ RIG	BOAT TYPE	-HULL- MTL	-HULL- TP	ENGINE TP	ENGINE # HP	ENGINE MFG	BEAM FT	BEAM IN	WGT LBS	DRAFT FT	DRAFT IN	RETAIL LOW	RETAIL HIGH
		1987 BOATS														
30		EXPRESS 30 SHOAL	SLP	SAIL	FBG	KL	IB	15D	YAN	10		8400	4	6	30800	34200
30		SCOUT 30		MY	FBG	DS	IB	43D	VLVO	9	6	10000	2	4	44900	49900
35		EXPRESS 35	SLP	SAIL	FBG	KL	IB	23D	YAN	11	6	14500	6	6	52500	57700
35		EXPRESS 35T	SLP	SAIL	FBG	KL	IB	20D	YAN	11	6	13100	6	8	47900	52600
		1986 BOATS														
29	7	EXPRESS 30-M	SLP	SA/RC	FBG	KL	IB	D		10		6200	5	4	21300	23700
30		EXPRESS 30-PC	SLP	SA/RC	FBG	KL	IB	D		10		8200	5	6	28300	31400
35		EXPRESS 35	SLP	SA/RC	FBG	KL	IB	D		11	6	11500	6	6	39500	43800
		1985 BOATS														
20		EXPRESS 20	SLP	SA/RC	FBG	KL				7	10	2000	4		5600	6450
29	7	EXPRESS 30 M	SLP	SAIL	FBG	KL	IB	8D	YAN	9	10	6200	5	4	20000	22200
30		EXPRESS 30	SLP	SA/RC	FBG	KL	IB	15D	YAN	10		8200	5	6	26600	29500
30		EXPRESS 30 SHOAL	SLP	SAIL	FBG	KL	IB	15D	YAN	10		8400	4	6	27200	30300
35		EXPRESS 35	SLP	SAIL	FBG	KL	IB	23D	YAN	11	6	11500	6	6	37100	41200
		1984 BOATS														
20		EXPRESS 20	SLP	SAIL	FBG	KL	OB			7	10	2000	3	11	5250	6050
26	8	NIAGARA 26	SLP	SAIL	FBG	KL	OB			8	4	4000	4		11300	12900
26	8	NIAGARA 26	SLP	SAIL	FBG	KL	SD		VLVO	8	4	4000	4		11700	13300
30		EXPRESS 30	SLP	SAIL	FBG	KL	IB	15D	YAN	10		8200	5	6	25000	27800
30		EXPRESS 30 M	SLP	SAIL	FBG	KL	OB			9	10	6200	5	4	18700	20800
30		EXPRESS 30 SHOAL	SLP	SAIL	FBG	KL	IB	15D	YAN	10		8400	4	6	25600	28500
35		EXPRESS 35	SLP	SAIL	FBG	KL	IB	23D	YAN	11	6	11200	5	6	34000	37800
35		EXPRESS 35	SLP	SAIL	FBG	KL	IB	23D	YAN	11	6	11200	6	6	34000	37800

....For earlier years, see the BUC Used Boat Price Guide, Volume 3

F L TRIPP & SONS

ANGLER
WESTPORT PT MA 02791 COAST GUARD MFG ID- TRP

See inside cover to adjust price for area

For more recent years, see the BUC Used Boat Price Guide, Volume 1

LOA FT	LOA IN	NAME AND/ OR MODEL	TOP/ RIG	BOAT TYPE	-HULL- MTL	-HULL- TP	ENGINE TP	ENGINE # HP	ENGINE MFG	BEAM FT	BEAM IN	WGT LBS	DRAFT FT	DRAFT IN	RETAIL LOW	RETAIL HIGH
		1996 BOATS														
18	3	TRIPP ANGLER 18	OP	CTRCN	FBG	SD	OB			7	2	1500	1		6050	6950
22	2	TRIPP ANGLER 22	OP	CTRCN	FBG	DS	IB	260	MRCR	7	10	3700	2	2	27400	30500
22	2	TRIPP ANGLER 22	OP	CTRCN	FBG	SD	OB			7	10	2200	1	2	7050	8100
22	2	TRIPP ANGLER 22	OP	CUD	FBG	DS	IB	260	MRCR	7	10	4400	2	2	31500	35000
22	2	TRIPP ANGLER 22	OP	CUD	FBG	SD	OB			7	10	2900	1	2	8650	9900
24		TRIPP ANGLER 24	OP	CTRCN	FBG	DS	IB	260	MRCR	9	6	4500	2		37200	41400
24		TRIPP ANGLER 24	ST	CUD	FBG	DS	IB	260	MRCR	9	6	4500	2		36800	40900
27	6	TRIPP ANGLER 27	ST	CUD	FBG	DS	IB	260	MRCR	9	10	7000	3		57600	63300
		1995 BOATS														
18	3	ANGLER 18	OP	OPFSH	FBG		OB			7	2	1500		10	5700	6550
22	2	COMPLEAT-ANGLER	ST	CUD	FBG		OB			7	10	2900		10	8250	9450
22	2	COMPLEAT-ANGLER	ST	CUD	FBG		IB	260	MRCR	7	10	4400	2	2	29300	32600
22	2	COMPLEAT-ANGLER	OP	OPFSH	FBG		OB			7	10	2200	1	2	6750	7750
22	2	COMPLEAT-ANGLER	OP	OPFSH	FBG		IB	260	MRCR	7	10	3700	2	2	26200	29100
24		ANGLER 24	OP	CUD	FBG	SV	IB	260	MRCR	9	6	4500	2		34100	37900
27	6	ANGLER 27	ST	CUD	FBG		IB	260	MRCR	9	10	7000	3		55100	60500
		1994 BOATS														
18	3	ANGLER 18	OP	OPFSH	FBG		OB			7	2	1500		10	5400	6200
22	2	COMPLEAT-ANGLER	ST	CUD	FBG		OB			7	10	2900		10	7850	9050
22	2	COMPLEAT-ANGLER	ST	CUD	FBG		IB	260	MRCR	7	10	4400	2	2	27700	30800
22	2	COMPLEAT-ANGLER	OP	OPFSH	FBG		OB			7	10	2200	1	2	6450	7400
22	2	COMPLEAT-ANGLER	OP	OPFSH	FBG		IB	260	MRCR	7	10	3700	2	2	24900	27700
24		ANGLER 24	OP	CUD	FBG	SV	IB	260	MRCR	9	6	4500	2		32200	35800
27	6	ANGLER 27	ST	CUD	FBG		IB	260	MRCR	9	10	7000	3		52400	57600
		1993 BOATS														
18	3	ANGLER 18	OP	OPFSH	FBG		OB			7	2	1500		10	5150	5950
22	2	COMPLEAT-ANGLER	ST	CUD	FBG		OB			7	10	2900		10	7550	8650
22	2	COMPLEAT-ANGLER	ST	CUD	FBG		IB	260	MRCR	7	10	4400	2	2	26200	29100
22	2	COMPLEAT-ANGLER	OP	OPFSH	FBG		OB			7	10	2200	1	2	6150	7100
22	2	COMPLEAT-ANGLER	OP	OPFSH	FBG		IB	260	MRCR	7	10	3700	2	2	23600	26200
24		ANGLER 24	OP	CUD	FBG	SV	IB	260	MRCR	9	6	4500	2		30400	33800
27	6	ANGLER 27	ST	CUD	FBG		IB	260	MRCR	9	10	7000	3		49600	54500
		1992 BOATS														
18	3	ANGLER 18	OP	OPFSH	FBG		OB			7	2	1500		10	4950	5700
22	2	COMPLEAT-ANGLER	ST	CUD	FBG		OB			7	10	2900		10	7250	8350
22	2	COMPLEAT-ANGLER	ST	CUD	FBG		IB	230	MRCR	7	10	4400	2	2	24600	27300
22	2	COMPLEAT-ANGLER	OP	OPFSH	FBG		OB			7	10	2200	1	2	5950	6800
22	2	COMPLEAT-ANGLER	OP	OPFSH	FBG		IB	230	MRCR	7	10	3700	2	2	22100	24600
24		ANGLER 24	OP	CUD	FBG	SV	IB	230	MRCR	9	6	4500	2		28600	31700
27	6	ANGLER 27	ST	CUD	FBG		IB	260	MRCR	9	10	7000	3		46900	51500
		1991 BOATS														
18	3	ANGLER 18	OP	OPFSH	FBG		OB			7	2	1500		10	4750	5450
22	2	COMPLEAT-ANGLER	ST	CUD	FBG		OB			7	10	2900		10	7000	8000
22	2	COMPLEAT-ANGLER	ST	CUD	FBG		IB	230	MRCR	7	10	4400		2	23300	25900
22	2	COMPLEAT-ANGLER	OP	OPFSH	FBG		OB			7	10	2200		2	5700	6550
22	2	COMPLEAT-ANGLER	OP	OPFSH	FBG		IB	230	MRCR	7	10	3700		2	21300	23600
27	6	ANGLER 27	ST	CUD	FBG		IB	260	MRCR	9	10	7000		3	43900	48800
		1990 BOATS														
18	3	ANGLER 18	OP	OPFSH	FBG		OB			7	2	1500		10	4500	5200
22	2	COMPLEAT-ANGLER	ST	CUD	FBG		OB			7	10	2900		10	6750	7750
22	2	COMPLEAT-ANGLER	ST	CUD	FBG		IB	230	MRCR	7	10	4400	2	2	22100	24500
22	2	COMPLEAT-ANGLER	OP	OPFSH	FBG		OB			7	10	2200	2	2	5500	6350
22	2	COMPLEAT-ANGLER	OP	OPFSH	FBG		IB	230	MRCR	7	10	3700	2	2	20200	22400
		1989 BOATS														
18	3	ANGLER 18	OP	OPFSH	FBG		OB			7	2	1500		10	4300	5000
22	2	COMPLEAT-ANGLER	ST	CUD	FBG		OB			7	10	2900		10	6500	7500
22	2	COMPLEAT-ANGLER	ST	CUD	FBG		IB	230	MRCR	7	10	4400	2	2	21400	23800
22	2	COMPLEAT-ANGLER	OP	OPFSH	FBG		OB			7	10	2200	2	2	5350	6100
22	2	COMPLEAT-ANGLER	OP	OPFSH	FBG		IB	230	MRCR	7	10	3700	2	2	19200	21300
		1988 BOATS														
18	3	ANGLER 18	OP	OPFSH	FBG		OB			7	2	1500		10	4100	4800
22	2	COMPLEAT-ANGLER	ST	CUD	FBG		OB			7	10	2900		10	6300	7250
22	2	COMPLEAT-ANGLER	ST	CUD	FBG		IB	230	MRCR	7	10	4400	2	2	20300	22600
22	2	COMPLEAT-ANGLER	OP	OPFSH	FBG		OB			7	10	2200	2	2	5150	5950
22	2	COMPLEAT-ANGLER	OP	OPFSH	FBG		IB	230	MRCR	7	10	3700	2	2	18400	20400
		1987 BOATS														
18	3	ANGLER 18	OP	OPFSH	FBG		OB			7	2	1500		10	3950	4600
22	2	COMPLEAT-ANGLER	ST	CUD	FBG		OB			7	10	2900		10	6100	7050
22	2	COMPLEAT-ANGLER	ST	CUD	FBG		IB	230	MRCR	7	10	4400	2	2	19400	21500
22	2	COMPLEAT-ANGLER	OP	OPFSH	FBG		OB			7	10	2200		10	5000	5750
22	2	COMPLEAT-ANGLER	OP	OPFSH	FBG		IB	230	MRCR	7	10	3700	2	2	17000	19400
		1986 BOATS														
18	3	ANGLER 18	OP	OPFSH	FBG		OB			7	2	1500		10	3800	4450
22	2	COMPLEAT-ANGLER	ST	CUD	FBG		OB			7	10	2500		10	5350	6150
22	2	COMPLEAT-ANGLER	ST	CUD	FBG		IB	230	MRCR	7	10	4200	2	2	17400	19700
22	2	COMPLEAT-ANGLER	OP	OPFSH	FBG		OB			7	10	2200		10	4850	5600
22	2	COMPLEAT-ANGLER	OP	OPFSH	FBG		IB	230	MRCR	7	10	3700	2	2	16200	18500
		1985 BOATS														
18	3	ANGLER 18	OP	OPFSH	FBG		OB			7	2	1500		10	3700	4300
22	2	COMPLEAT-ANGLER	ST	CUD	FBG		OB			7	10	2500		10	5200	6000
22	2	COMPLEAT-ANGLER	ST	CUD	FBG		IB	230	MRCR	7	10	4000	2	2	15900	18100
22	2	COMPLEAT-ANGLER	OP	OPFSH	FBG		OB			7	10	2200		10	4750	5450
22	2	COMPLEAT-ANGLER	OP	OPFSH	FBG		IB	230	MRCR	7	10	3700	2	2	15400	17600
22	2	COMPLEAT-ANGLER CABN	ST	CUD	FBG		OB			7	10	2600		10	5350	6150
22	2	COMPLEAT-ANGLER CABN	ST	CUD	FBG		IB	230	MRCR	7	10	4200	2	2	16600	18800

LOA FT IN	NAME AND/ OR MODEL	TOP/ RIG	BOAT TYPE	-HULL- MTL TP	----ENGINE--- TP # HP MFG	BEAM FT IN	WGT LBS	DRAFT FT IN	RETAIL LOW	RETAIL HIGH
---	--- 1984	BOATS	---							
18 3	ANGLER 18	OP	OPFSH	FBG	OB	7 2	1500	10	3600	4150
22 2	COMPLEAT-ANGLER	ST	CUD	FBG	OB	7 10	2500	10	5100	5850
22 2	COMPLEAT-ANGLER	ST	CUD	FBG	IB 230 MRCR	7 10	4000	2 2	15200	17200
22 2	COMPLEAT-ANGLER	OP	OPFSH	FBG	OB	7 10	2200	10	4650	5300
22 2	COMPLEAT-ANGLER	OP	OPFSH	FBG	IB 230 MRCR	7 10	3700	2 2	14700	16800

....For earlier years, see the BUC Used Boat Price Guide, Volume 3

FABOLA AB
GUSTAVSBERG SWEDEN   See inside cover to adjust price for area

LOA FT IN	NAME AND/ OR MODEL	TOP/ RIG	BOAT TYPE	-HULL- MTL TP	----ENGINE--- TP # HP MFG	BEAM FT IN	WGT LBS	DRAFT FT IN	RETAIL LOW	RETAIL HIGH
---	--- 1988	BOATS	---							
36	DIVA 35	SLP	SAIL	F/S KL IB	18D YAN	11	8690	6	46600	51200
38 7	DIVA 39	SLP	SAIL	F/S KL IB	18D YAN	10	9370	5 7	57500	63200
45 1	DIVA 45	SLP	SAIL	F/S KL IB	36D YAN	13 2	15159	7 7	124000	136500
---	--- 1987	BOATS	---							
36	DIVA 35	SLP	SAIL	F/S KL IB	18D YAN	11	8690	6	43400	48200
38 7	DIVA 39	SLP	SAIL	F/S KL IB	18D YAN	10	9370	5 7	54100	59400
45 1	DIVA 45	SLP	SAIL	F/S KL IB	36D YAN	13 2	15159	7 7	116500	128000
---	--- 1985	BOATS	---							
38 9	DIVA 39	SLP	SAIL	KL		9 10	9370	5 9	48200	53000

FAENOE YACHTYARDS LTD
FREDERICIA DENMARK   See inside cover to adjust price for area
FORMERLY SKAERBAEK BADEBYGGERI

LOA FT IN	NAME AND/ OR MODEL	TOP/ RIG	BOAT TYPE	-HULL- MTL TP	----ENGINE--- TP # HP MFG	BEAM FT IN	WGT LBS	DRAFT FT IN	RETAIL LOW	RETAIL HIGH
---	--- 1986	BOATS	---							
42	FAENO 42	SCH	MS	FBG KL IB	D	12 6	34000	6	194500	213500
47	FAENO 47	SCH	MS	FBG KL IB	D	14	42000	7	233500	256500

....For earlier years, see the BUC Used Boat Price Guide, Volume 3

FAIR WEATHER MARINE INC
SAN PEDRO CA 90731   See inside cover to adjust price for area

LOA FT IN	NAME AND/ OR MODEL	TOP/ RIG	BOAT TYPE	-HULL- MTL TP	----ENGINE--- TP # HP MFG	BEAM FT IN	WGT LBS	DRAFT FT IN	RETAIL LOW	RETAIL HIGH
---	--- 1991	BOATS	---							
38 10	FAIR WEATHER 39	SLP	SA/CR	FBG KL IB	59D PERK	11 10	19200	6	121500	133500
38 10	FAIR WEATHER 39 SHL	SLP	SA/CR	FBG KL IB	59D PERK	11 10	19200	4 10	121500	133500
---	--- 1990	BOATS	---							
38 10	FAIR WEATHER 39	SLP	SA/CR	FBG KL IB	59D PERK	11 10	19200	6	114500	125500
38 10	FAIR WEATHER 39	SLP	SA/CR	FBG KL IB	59D PERK	11 10	19200	4 10	114500	125500
---	--- 1989	BOATS	---							
38 10	FAIR WEATHER 39	SLP	SA/CR	FBG KL IB	59D PERK	11 10	19200	6	107500	118000
---	--- 1988	BOATS	---							
38 10	FAIR WEATHER 39	SLP	SA/CR	FBG KL IB	50D PERK	11 10	19200	6	101000	111000
---	--- 1987	BOATS	---							
37 10	FAIR WEATHER SN DK	FB	TRWL	FBG DV IB	T350 CRUS	12 10	17000	3 5	44300	49200
38 10	FAIR WEATHER 39	SLP	SA/CR	FBG KL IB	42D BENZ	11 10	19200	6	95300	104500
39 10	FAIR WEATHER SF	FB	SF	FBG DV IB	210D CAT	12 10	26800	3 10	69600	76500
41 10	FAIR WEATHER SP TRWL	FB	DCCPT	FBG DV IB	T200D PERK	13 8	22000	3 6	62000	68200
---	--- 1986	BOATS	---							
38 10	FAIR WEATHER 39	SLP	SA/CR	FBG KL IB	59D PERK	11 10	19200	6	89500	98400
---	--- 1985	BOATS	---							
28 7	LANCER POWERSAILER	SLP	SAIL	FBG KL OB		9 3	6800	5 3	26300	29300
38 10	FAIRWEATHER MARINER	SLP	SAIL	FBG IB	45D BENZ	11 10		6	84400	92700

....For earlier years, see the BUC Used Boat Price Guide, Volume 3

FAIRBANKS YACHTS INC
KENWOOD INVESTMENTS LTD   See inside cover to adjust price for area
RICHMOND BC CANADA V7B 1C1
formerly FAIRLINE SANGS

LOA FT IN	NAME AND/ OR MODEL	TOP/ RIG	BOAT TYPE	-HULL- MTL TP	----ENGINE--- TP # HP MFG	BEAM FT IN	WGT LBS	DRAFT FT IN	RETAIL LOW	RETAIL HIGH
---	--- 1992	BOATS	---							
30	SPORTSFISHER	FB	SF	FBG SV IO	T205 MRCR	10	8500	3	28000	31100
35 6	AFT CABIN	FB	TCMY	FBG SV IB	T267 VLVO	10 10	11200	3	62400	68600
35 6	SEDAN BRIDGE	FB	SF	FBG SV IO	T205 MRCR	10 10	10500	3	51200	56300
35 6	SEDAN BRIDGE	FB	SF	FBG SV IB	T267 VLVO	10 10	10500	3	56400	62000
---	--- 1987	BOATS	---							
30 7	FAIRBANKS 28	HT	SF	FBG DV IO	T165-T205	10	9000	3 1	19900	22700
30 7	FAIRBANKS 28	HT	SF	FBG DV IO	T130D VLVO	10	9000	3 1	28000	31100
32 2	FAIRBANKS 33	HT	SDNSF	FBG SV IO	T225-T230	10 10	12000	2 10	29800	33200
32 2	FAIRBANKS 33	HT	SDNSF	FBG SV IB	T200D VLVO	10 10	12000	2 10	39700	44100
---	--- 1986	BOATS	---							
30 7	FAIRLINE 28	HT	SF	FBG DV IB	T190 MRCR	10 2	9000	3 1	21700	24100
35 8	FAIRLINE 32	HT	SDN	FBG DV IB	T228 MRCR	10 10	12000	2 10	34700	38500

FAIRHAVEN MARINE INC
FAIRHAVEN MA 02719   COAST GUARD MFG ID- FHV See inside cover to adjust price for area
SEE SURF HUNTER CORP

LOA FT IN	NAME AND/ OR MODEL	TOP/ RIG	BOAT TYPE	-HULL- MTL TP	----ENGINE--- TP # HP MFG	BEAM FT IN	WGT LBS	DRAFT FT IN	RETAIL LOW	RETAIL HIGH
---	--- 1984	BOATS	---							
25	FISHERMAN		FSH	FBG DV IO	260	9 2	5000		11100	12700
25	FISHERMAN		FSH	FBG DV IO	260	9 2	5500		13900	15800
25	FISHERMAN		FSH	FBG DV IB	200D	9 2	6000		20500	22700
25	WEEKENDER		FSH	FBG DV IO	260	9 2	6000		12700	14400

....For earlier years, see the BUC Used Boat Price Guide, Volume 3

FAIRLINE BOATS PLC
HILTON HEAD NC 29925   COAST GUARD MFG ID- ZFA See inside cover to adjust price for area

FAIRLINE BOATS
OUNDLE ENGLAND PE8 5PA

For more recent years, see the BUC Used Boat Price Guide, Volume 1

LOA FT IN	NAME AND/ OR MODEL	TOP/ RIG	BOAT TYPE	-HULL- MTL TP	----ENGINE--- TP # HP MFG	BEAM FT IN	WGT LBS	DRAFT FT IN	RETAIL LOW	RETAIL HIGH
---	--- 1996	BOATS	---							
29 9	TARGA 28	OP	CR	FBG SV IO	205 MRCR	10 2	7600	3 2	47300	52000
29 9	TARGA 28	OP	CR	FBG SV IB	T150 MRCR	10 2	7600	3 2	63500	69800
29 9	TARGA 28	OP	CR	FBG SV IB	T150 VLVO	10 2	7600	3 2	73700	80900
32 5	TARGA 31	OP	CR	FBG SV IB	T280 MRCR	11 1	9000	3 2	69400	76300
32 5	TARGA 31	OP	CR	FBG SV IB	T200D VLVO	11 1	9000	3 2	91800	101000
32 5	TARGA 31	OP	CR	FBG SV IB	IOT220D-T230D	11 1	9000	3 2	80100	88800
34 1	TARGA 33	OP	CR	FBG SV IB	T280 MRCR	11 2	10000	3 2	94900	104500
	IO T200D VLVO 90600		99600,	IB T220D MRCR	109500 120500,	IO T230D VLVO			93400	102500
37 11	TARGA 37	OP	CR	FBG DV IB	T330 MRCR	11 8	13000	3 2	77300	85000
37 11	TARGA 37	OP	CR	FBG DV IB	T230D VLVO	11 8	13000	3 2	120000	132000
37 11	TARGA 37	OP	CR	FBG DV IB	T270D MRCR	11 8	13000	3 2	126000	138000
38 5	PHANTOM 37	FB	CR	FBG DV IB	T300D CAT	12 4	16500	3 2	150500	165500
38 5	PHANTOM 37	FB	CR	FBG DV IB	T310D VLVO	12 4	16500	3 2	145000	159500
38 5	PHANTOM 37	FB	CR	FBG DV IB	T370D CAT	12 4	16500	3 2	160000	175500
38 5	PHANTOM 37	FB	CR	FBG DV IB	T350D VLVO	12 4	16500	3 2	148500	163500
39 9	TARGA 39	OP	CR	FBG DV IB	T270D MRCR	12	15000	3	115000	126500
40 9	PHANTOM 40	FB	CR	FBG DV IB	T350D CAT	13 2	21000	3 3	198000	217500
40 9	PHANTOM 40	FB	CR	FBG DV IB	T370D VLVO	13 2	21000	3 3	190000	208500
40 9	TARGA 39	OP	CR	FBG DV IB	T330 MRCR	12	15000	3	97500	107000
40 9	TARGA 39	OP	CR	FBG DV IB	T230D VLVO	12	15000	3	149000	164000
44 5	SQUADRON 43	FB	MY	FBG SV IB	T420D CAT	13 7	31000	3 6	276500	304000
44 5	SQUADRON 43	FB	MY	FBG SV IB	T430D VLVO	13 7	31000	3 6	269000	296000
49 10	TARGA 48	OP	CR	FBG DV IB	T420D CAT	12 11	26000	3 7	237000	260500
51 10	SQUADRON 50	FB	MY	FBG SV IB	T550D GM	14 8	38000	3 8	339500	373500
	IO T600D CAT 354000		389000,	IB T600D MAN	353500 388500,	IB T600D VLVO			353500	388500
55 11	SQUADRON 55	FB	MY	FBG SV IB	T600D CAT	15 3	48000	3 8	408000	448000
55 11	SQUADRON 55	FB	MY	FBG SV IB	T600D VLVO	15 3	48000	3 8	408000	448000
59	SQUADRON 59	FB	MY	FBG SV IB	T600D MAN	15 6	49200	3 10	448500	493000
59	SQUADRON 59	FB	MY	FBG SV IB	T680D CAT	15 6	49200	3 10	478000	525000
59	SQUADRON 59	FB	MY	FBG SV IB	T600D CAT	15 6	49200	3 10	452000	497000
59 9	SQUADRON 59	FB	MY	FBG SV IB	T800D VLVO	15 6	49200	3 10	445000	489500
66 10	SQUADRON 65	OP	MY	FBG SV IB	T12CD MAN	17 4	67065	4 9	720000	791000
66 10	SQUADRON 65	FB	MY	FBG SV IB	T10CD MAN	17 4	60000	4 9	629500	692000
66 10	SQUADRON 65	FB	MY	FBG SV IB	T11CD MAN	17 4	60000	4 9	656500	721500
66 10	SQUADRON 65	FB	MY	FBG SV IB	T12CD CAT	17 4	60000	4 9	699000	768500

LOA FT	LOA IN	NAME AND/ OR MODEL	TOP/ RIG	BOAT TYPE	-HULL- MTL	-HULL- TP	ENGINE TP	ENGINE # HP	ENGINE MFG	BEAM FT	BEAM IN	WGT LBS	DRAFT FT	DRAFT IN	RETAIL LOW	RETAIL HIGH
		1995 BOATS														
29	9	TARGA 28	OP	CR	FBG	SV	IO	275-330		10	2	7600	3	2	46400	52700
29	9	TARGA 28	OP	CR	FBG	SV	IO	T205-T250		10	2	7600	3	2	49800	56900
29	9	TARGA 28	OP	CR	FBG	SV	IB	T150D	VLVO	10	2	7600	3	2	70000	76900
32	5	TARGA 31	OP	CR	FBG	SV	IO	T205-T275		11	1	9000	3	2	61300	71100
32	5	TARGA 31	OP	CR	FBG	SV	IB	T150D-T200D		11	1	9000	3	2	81900	95900
34	1	TARGA 33	OP	CR	FBG	SV	IO	T205-T235		11	2	10000	3	2	73200	82000
34	1	TARGA 33	OP	CR	FBG	SV	IB	T200D-T230D		11	2	10000	3	2	101500	115000
37		TARGA 36	OP	CR	FBG	DV	IO	T235	VLVO	11	8	12000	3	2	100500	110500
		IO T330 VLVO 107500 118000, IB T230D VLVO 137500 151000, IB T275D VLVO													142000	156000
38	5	PHANTOM 37	FB	CR	FBG	SV	IB	T230D	VLVO	12	4	16500	3	2	132000	145000
38	5	PHANTOM 37	FB	CR	FBG	SV	IB	T318D	CAT	12	4	16500	3	2	146500	161000
38	5	PHANTOM 37	FB	CR	FBG	SV	IB	T370D	CAT	12	4	16500	3	2	153000	168500
39	9	TARGA 39	OP	CR	FBG	DV	IO	T235	VLVO	12		13600	3	3	77100	84700
		IO T275 VLVO 78800 86500, IO T330 VLVO 83000 91300, IB T230D VLVO													128000	140500
40	9	PHANTOM 40	FB	CR	FBG	SV	IB	T318D	VLVO	13	2	20000	3	3	170000	187000
40	9	PHANTOM 40	FB	CR	FBG	SV	IB	T370D	VLVO	13	2	20000	3	3	176000	193500
44	5	SQUADRON 43	FB	MY	FBG	SV	IB	T430D	VLVO	13	7	28000	2	7	243500	267500
49	1	SQUADRON 50	FB	MY	FBG	SV	IB	T600D	VLVO	14	8	34000	3	8	308500	339000
58	10	SQUADRON 59	FB	MY	FBG	SV	IB	T600D	MAN	15	6	44000	3	10	392500	431000
58	10	SQUADRON 59	FB	MY	FBG	SV	IB	T680D	MAN	15	6	44000	3	10	420500	462000
66	10	SQUADRON 65	FB	MY	FBG	SV	IB	T820D	MAN	17	4	60000	4	9	559000	614000
66	10	SQUADRON 65	FB	MY	FBG	SV	IB	T10CD	MAN	17	4	60000	4	9	603000	662500
66	10	SQUADRON 65	FB	MY	FBG	SV	IB	T11CD	MAN	17	4	60000	4	9	628500	691000
		1994 BOATS														
29	9	TARGA 28	OP	CR	FBG	SV	IO	280		10	2	7600	3	2	42800	47900
		IB 270D MRCR 64200 70600, IO T145-T250 43800 53200, IB T150D VLVO													66600	73200
32	5	TARGA 31	OP	CR	FBG	SV	IO	T213-T280		11	1	9000	3	2	57600	66600
32	5	TARGA 31	OP	CR	FBG	SV	IB	T200D-T230D		11	1	9000	3	2	83000	94600
34	1	TARGA 33	OP	CR	FBG	SV	IO	T213-T280		11	2	10000	3	2	68700	78900
34	1	TARGA 33	OP	CR	FBG	SV	IB	T200D-T230D		11	2	10000	3	2	96600	109500
36	7	TARGA 35	OP	CR	FBG	DV	IO	T280	VLVO	11	5	12000	3	2	92400	101500
36	7	TARGA 35	OP	CR	FBG	DV	IO	T330	VLVO	11	5	12000	3	2	95900	105500
36	7	TARGA 35	OP	CR	FBG	DV	IB	T230D	VLVO	11	5	12000	3	2	126000	138500
37		BRAVA 36	FB	CR	FBG	DV	IB	T230D	VLVO	12		16000	2	11	151500	166000
37		BRAVA 36	FB	CR	FBG	DV	IB	T304D	CAT	12		16000	2	11	163500	180000
37		BRAVA 36	FB	CR	FBG	DV	IB	T355D	CAT	12		16000	2	11	170500	187500
38	5	PHANTOM 37	FB	CR	FBG	SV	IB	T230D	VLVO	12	4	16500	3	2	126500	139000
38	5	PHANTOM 37	FB	CR	FBG	SV	IB	T304D	CAT	12	4	16500	3	2	138500	152500
38	5	PHANTOM 37	FB	CR	FBG	SV	IB	T355D	CAT	12	4	16500	3	2	145000	159000
39	9	TARGA 38	OP	CR	FBG	DV	IO	T280	VLVO	12		13600	3	3	73800	81100
		IO T330 VLVO 77500 85200, IB T230D VLVO 122500 134500, IB T275D MRCR													129500	142500
42	3	PHANTOM 41	FB	CR	FBG	SV	IB	T304D	CAT	13	6	20000	3	4	173500	191000
		IB T306D VLVO 165500 182000, IB T340D VLVO 169500 186000, IB T355D CAT													180500	198500
		IB T380D VLVO 174000 191000, IB T430D VLVO 180000 198000														
43	2	TARGA 41	OP	CR	FBG	DV	IB	T430D	VLVO	13	6	22000	3	4	189500	208500
43	2	TARGA 41	OP	CR	FBG	DV	IB	T441D	CAT	13	6	22000	3	4	203000	223000
44	5	SQUADRON 43	FB	MY	FBG	SV	IB	T430D	VLVO	13	7	28000	2	7	233000	256500
44	5	SQUADRON 43	FB	MY	FBG	SV	IB	T441D	CAT	13	7	28000	2	7	244000	268500
49	1	SQUADRON 47	FB	MY	FBG	SV	IB	T480D	VLVO	14	8	34000	3	8	244500	269000
58	10	SQUADRON 56	FB	MY	FBG	SV	IB	T480D	VLVO	15	6	44000	3	10	329500	362000
58	10	SQUADRON 56	FB	MY	FBG	SV	IB	T550D	GM	15	6	44000	3	10	355500	390500
58	10	SQUADRON 56	FB	MY	FBG	SV	IB	T680D	MAN	15	6	44000	3	10	400500	440000
66	1	SQUADRON 62	FB	MY	FBG	SV	IB	T820D	MAN	17	4	60000	4	9	525500	577500
66	1	SQUADRON 62	FB	MY	FBG	SV	IB	T10CD	MAN	17	4	60000	4	9	575000	632000
66	1	SQUADRON 62	FB	MY	FBG	SV	IB	T11CD	MAN	17	4	60000	4	9	600000	659500
		1985 BOATS														
31	3	FAIRLINE 31	FB	CBNCR	FBG	DV	IO	T165D	BMW	11	7	9000	3	2	54300	59700
32	9	TARGA		CBNCR	FBG	DV	IO	T200D	VLVO	11	5		3		64700	71100

....For earlier years, see the BUC Used Boat Price Guide, Volume 3

FALES YACHTS INC

NEWPORT RI 02840

See inside cover to adjust price for area

LOA FT	LOA IN	NAME AND/ OR MODEL	TOP/ RIG	BOAT TYPE	-HULL- MTL	-HULL- TP	ENGINE TP	ENGINE # HP	ENGINE MFG	BEAM FT	BEAM IN	WGT LBS	DRAFT FT	DRAFT IN	RETAIL LOW	RETAIL HIGH
		1984 BOATS														
41	8	EXPLORER 38	KTH	SA/CR	FBG	KL	IB	85D		12		23500	5		77500	85100

....For earlier years, see the BUC Used Boat Price Guide, Volume 3

FALMOUTH BOAT CONST LTD

TUFNOL INDUSTRIES LTD
CORNWALL ENGLAND

See inside cover to adjust price for area

LOA FT	LOA IN	NAME AND/ OR MODEL	TOP/ RIG	BOAT TYPE	-HULL- MTL	-HULL- TP	ENGINE TP	ENGINE # HP	ENGINE MFG	BEAM FT	BEAM IN	WGT LBS	DRAFT FT	DRAFT IN	RETAIL LOW	RETAIL HIGH
		1985 BOATS														
35	11	BISCAY 36	SLP	SA/CR	FBG	KL	IB	51D	PERK	10	9	15680	5	6	66000	72500
35	11	BISCAY 36	KTH	SA/CR	FBG	KL	IB	51D	PERK	10	9	15680	5	6	67800	74500
		1984 BOATS														
35	11	BISCAY 36	SLP	SA/CR	FBG	KL	IB	50D	PERK	10	9	15680	5	6	62000	68100
35	11	BISCAY 36	KTH	SA/CR	FBG	KL	IB	50D	PERK	10	9	15680	5	6	63700	70000

....For earlier years, see the BUC Used Boat Price Guide, Volume 3

FALMOUTH MARINE SALES

FALMOUTH MA 02540

See inside cover to adjust price for area

LOA FT	LOA IN	NAME AND/ OR MODEL	TOP/ RIG	BOAT TYPE	-HULL- MTL	-HULL- TP	ENGINE TP	ENGINE # HP	ENGINE MFG	BEAM FT	BEAM IN	WGT LBS	DRAFT FT	DRAFT IN	RETAIL LOW	RETAIL HIGH
		1984 BOATS														
45	8	SEA 46	CUT	SA/CR	FBG	KL				13	6	33500	5	10	158500	174000
50	10	SEA 51	CUT	SA/RC	FBG	KL				14	3	38700	7		213500	234500
65		SEA 65	CUT	SA/RC	FBG	KC				16	4	55000	6		422000	464000

FAR EAST & ATLANTIC TRADING

DEFEVER
FT LAUDERDALE FL 33312 COAST GUARD MFG ID- FEF

See inside cover to adjust price for area

LOA FT	LOA IN	NAME AND/ OR MODEL	TOP/ RIG	BOAT TYPE	-HULL- MTL	-HULL- TP	ENGINE TP	ENGINE # HP	ENGINE MFG	BEAM FT	BEAM IN	WGT LBS	DRAFT FT	DRAFT IN	RETAIL LOW	RETAIL HIGH
		1994 BOATS														
44	4	CLASSIC 44.4 DEFEVER	FB	DCMY	FBG	SV	IB	T135D	LEHM	15	3	44000	4	10	265000	291500
		IB T210D CAT 272500 299000, IB T210D CUM 270500 297500, IB T375D CAT													297000	326500
48	8	CLASSIC 48.8 DEFEVER	FB	DCCPT	FBG	SV	IB	T135D	LEHM	15	4	48000	4	10	233500	256500
		IB T210D CAT 243000 267000, IB T210D CUM 240500 264500, IB T375D CAT													281500	309000
48	8	CLASSIC 48.8 DEFEVER	FB	TCMY	FBG	SV	IB	T135D	FORD	15	4	48000	4	10	303000	333000
		IB T210D CAT 314000 345000, IB T210D CUM 314000 345000, IB T375D CAT													350000	384500
		IB T450D GM 370000 406500														
49	10	CLASSIC 49.9 DEFEVER	FB	PH	FBG	SV	IB	T210D	CAT	15		50000	4	6	289000	317500
49	10	CLASSIC 49.9 DEFEVER	FB	PH	FBG	SV	IB	T210D	CUM	15		50000	4	6	289000	317500
49	10	CLASSIC 49.9 DEFEVER	FB	PH	FBG	SV	IB	T375D	CAT	15		50000	4	6	338000	371500
49	10	CLASSIC 49.9 DEVEVER	FB	PH	FBG	SV	IB	T135D	FORD	15		50000	4	6	278000	305500
50		CLASSIC 50 DEFEVER	FB	FDPH	FBG	SV	IB	T135D	FORD	15		52000	4	6	320000	351500
		IB T210D CAT 339000 372500, IB T210D CUM 338500 372000, IB T375D CAT													371500	408000
		1993 BOATS														
44	4	CLASSIC 44.4 DEFEVER	FB	DCMY	FBG	SV	IB	T135D	LEHM	15	3	44000	4	10	252500	277500
		IB T210D CAT 259500 285000, IB T210D CUM 257500 283000, IB T375D CAT													283000	311000
		IB T450D GM 294500 324000														
48	8	CLASSIC 48.8 DEFEVER	FB	DCCPT	FBG	SV	IB	T135D	LEHM	15	4	48000	4	10	222000	244000
		IB T210D CAT 231500 254000, IB T210D CUM 229000 252000, IB T375D CAT													268000	294500
		IB T450D GM 287500 316000														
48	8	CLASSIC 48.8 DEFEVER	FB	TCMY	FBG	SV	IB	T135D	FORD	15	4	48000	4	10	288500	317000
		IB T210D CAT 299000 329000, IB T210D CUM 299000 329000, IB T375D CAT													333500	366500
		IB T450D GM 352000 387000														
49	10	CLASSIC 49.9 DEFEVER	FB	PH	FBG	SV	IB	T210D	CAT	15		50000	4	6	275500	302500
49	10	CLASSIC 49.9 DEFEVER	FB	PH	FBG	SV	IB	T210D	CUM	15		50000	4	6	275500	302500
49	10	CLASSIC 49.9 DEFEVER	FB	PH	FBG	SV	IB	T375D	CAT	15		50000	4	6	322000	354000
49	10	CLASSIC 49.9 DEVEVER	FB	PH	FBG	SV	IB	T135D	FORD	15		50000	4	6	265000	291000
50		CLASSIC 50 DEFEVER	FB	FDPH	FBG	SV	IB	T135D	FORD	15		52000	4	6	305000	335000
		IB T210D CAT 323000 355000, IB T210D CUM 322500 354000, IB T375D CAT													354000	389000
		1992 BOATS														
44	4	CLASSIC 44.4 DEFEVER	FB	DCMY	FBG	SV	IB	T135D	LEHM	15	3	44000	4	10	240500	264500
		IB T210D CAT 247500 271500, IB T210D CUM 245500 270000, IB T375D CAT													270000	296500
		IB T450D GM 281000 308500														
48	8	CLASSIC 48.8 DEFEVER	FB	DCCPT	FBG	SV	IB	T135D	LEHM	15	4	48000	4	10	211500	232500

CONTINUED ON NEXT PAGE

LOA FT IN	NAME AND/ OR MODEL	TOP/ RIG	BOAT TYPE	-HULL- MTL TP TP #	----ENGINE--- HP MFG	BEAM FT IN	WGT LBS	DRAFT FT IN	RETAIL LOW	RETAIL HIGH
				1992 BOATS						
48 8	CLASSIC 48.8 DEFEVER	FB	DCCPT	FBG SV IB	T210D CAT	15 4	48000	4 10	220000	242000
	IB T210D CUM 218000 240000, IB T375D CAT 255500 280500, IB T450D GM 274000 301000									
48 8	CLASSIC 48.8 DEFEVER	FB	TCMY	FBG SV IB	T135D FORD	15 4	48000	4 10	275000	302500
	IB T210D CAT 285000 313500, IB T210D CUM 285000 313500, IB T375D CAT 318000 349500									
	IB T450D GM 335500 369000									
49 10	CLASSIC 49.9 DEFEVER	FB	PH	FBG SV IB	T210D CAT	15	50000	4 6	262500	288500
49 10	CLASSIC 49.9 DEFEVER	FB	PH	FBG SV IB	T210D CUM	15	50000	4 6	262500	288500
49 10	CLASSIC 49.9 DEFEVER	FB	PH	FBG SV IB	T375D CAT	15	50000	4 6	307000	337500
49 10	CLASSIC 49.9 DEVEVER	FB	PH	FBG SV IB	T135D FORD	15	50000	4 6	252500	277500
50	CLASSIC 50 DEFEVER	FB	FDPH	FBG SV IB	T135D FORD	15	52000	4 6	290500	319500
	IB T210D CAT 307500 338000, IB T210D CUM 307500 337500, IB T375D CAT 337500 370500									
				1991 BOATS						
44 4	CLASSIC 44.4 DEFEVER	FB	DCMY	FBG SV IB	T210D CUM	15 4	43000	4 6	230500	253500
48 8	CLASSIC 48.8 DEFEVER	FB	TCMY	FBG SV IB	T135D FORD	15 4	46000	4 6	255500	281000
48 8	CLASSIC 48.8 DEFEVER	FB	TCMY	FBG SV IB	T375D CAT	15 4	46000	4 6	293000	322000
49 9	CLASSIC 49 DEFEVER	FB	PH	FBG SV IB	T135D FORD	15	50000	4 6	252000	277000
49 9	CLASSIC 49 DEFEVER	FB	PH	FBG SV IB	T210D CAT	15	50000	4 6	266500	293000
50	CLASSIC 50 DEFEVER	FB	FDPH	FBG SV IB	T135D FORD	15	52000	4 6	277000	304500
50	CLASSIC 50 DEFEVER	FB	FDPH	FBG SV IB	T210D CAT	15	52000	4 6	293500	322500
				1990 BOATS						
44 4	CLASSIC 44.4 DEFEVER	FB	DCMY	FBG SV IB	T210D CUM	15 4	43000	4 6	220000	242000
48 8	CLASSIC 48.8 DEFEVER	FB	TCMY	FBG SV IB	T135D FORD	15 4	46000	4 6	244000	268000
48 8	CLASSIC 48.8 DEFEVER	FB	TCMY	FBG SV IB	T375D CAT	15 4	46000	4 6	279500	307500
49 9	CLASSIC 49 DEFEVER	FB	PH	FBG SV IB	T135D FORD	15	50000	4 6	240500	264500
49 9	CLASSIC 49 DEFEVER	FB	PH	FBG SV IB	T210D CAT	15	50000	4 6	254500	279500
50	CLASSIC 50 DEFEVER	FB	FDPH	FBG SV IB	T135D FORD	15	52000	4 6	264500	291000
50	CLASSIC 50 DEFEVER	FB	FDPH	FBG SV IB	T210D CAT	15	52000	4 6	280000	308000
				1989 BOATS						
44 4	CLASSIC 44.4 DEFEVER	FB	DCMY	FBG SV IB	T210D CUM	15 4	43000	4 6	210000	231000
48 8	CLASSIC 48.8 DEFEVER	FB	TCMY	FBG SV IB	T135D FORD	15 4	46000	4 6	233000	256000
48 8	CLASSIC 48.8 DEFEVER	FB	TCMY	FBG SV IB	T375D CAT	15 4	47000	4 6	271500	298500
49 9	CLASSIC 49 DEFEVER	FB	PH	FBG SV IB	T135D FORD	15	50000	4 6	229500	252500
49 9	CLASSIC 49 DEFEVER	FB	PH	FBG SV IB	T210D CAT	15	51600	4 6	248500	273000
50	CLASSIC 50 DEFEVER	FB	FDPH	FBG SV IB	T135D FORD	15	52000	4 6	252500	277500
50	CLASSIC 50 DEFEVER	FB	FDPH	FBG SV IB	T210D CAT	15	53500	4 6	275000	302000
				1988 BOATS						
44 4	CLASSIC 44.4 DEFEVER	FB	DCMY	FBG SV IB	T135D FORD	15 4		4 6	199500	219000
44 4	CLASSIC 44.4 DEVEFER	FB	PH	FBG SV IB	T135D FORD	15 4		4 6	199500	219000
48 8	CLASSIC 48.8 DEFEVER	FB	DCCPT	FBG SV IB	T135D FORD	15 4		4 6	182500	200500
48 8	CLASSIC 48.8 DEFEVER	FB	DCCPT	FBG SV IB	T210D CAT	15 4		4 6	209000	229500
48 8	CLASSIC 48.8 DEFEVER	FB	DCCPT	FBG SV IB	T375D CAT	15 4		4 6	229500	252500
48 8	CLASSIC 48.8 DEFEVER	FB	TCMY	FBG SV IB	T135D FORD	15 4		4 6	229500	252500
48 8	CLASSIC 48.8 DEFEVER	FB	TCMY	FBG SV IB	T210D CAT	15 4		4 6	235500	259000
48 8	CLASSIC 48.8 DEFEVER	FB	TCMY	FBG SV IB	T375D CAT	15 4		4 6	258000	283500
49 9	CLASSIC 49 DEFEVER	FB	PH	FBG SV IB	T135D FORD	15	50000	4 6	219500	241000
49 9	CLASSIC 49 DEFEVER	FB	PH	FBG SV IB	T210D CAT	15	51600	4 6	237500	261000
49 9	CLASSIC 49 DEFEVER	FB	PH	FBG SV IB	T375D CAT	15	52000	4 6	279500	307500
50	CLASSIC 50 DEFEVER	FB	FDPH	FBG SV IB	T135D FORD	15	52000	4 6	241500	265500
50	CLASSIC 50 DEFEVER	FB	FDPH	FBG SV IB	T210D CAT	15	53500	4 6	262500	288500
50	CLASSIC 50 DEFEVER	FB	FDPH	FBG SV IB	T375D CAT	15	54000	4 6	288500	317000
				1987 BOATS						
49 9	CLASSIC 49 DEFEVER	FB	TRWL	FBG DS IB	T135D LEHM	15	50000	4 6	213500	234500

FARR INTERNATIONAL
ANNAPOLIS MD 21403   See inside cover to adjust price for area

BRUCE FARR & ASSOCIATES
AUCKLAND NEW ZEALND

LOA FT IN	NAME AND/ OR MODEL	TOP/ RIG	BOAT TYPE	-HULL- MTL TP TP #	----ENGINE--- HP MFG	BEAM FT IN	WGT LBS	DRAFT FT IN	RETAIL LOW	RETAIL HIGH
				1994 BOATS						
35 10	MUMM 36	SLP	SAROD	FBG KL IB	18D VLVO	11 10	8150	7 4	40300	44800
				1993 BOATS						
30 10	FARR 31	SLP	SACAC	F/S SK OB		9 5	4800	6 4	19300	21500
33 11	FARR 34	SLP	SACAC	F/S KL IB	18D VLVO	10 6	8176	5 9	34300	38100
40	FARR 40	SLP	SACAC	F/S KL IB	43D VLVO	12 6	14500	6 6	81200	89200
				1992 BOATS						
30 10	FARR 31	SLP	SA/CR	F/S SK OB		9 5	4800	6 4	18100	20200
33 11	FARR 34	SLP	SA/CR	F/S KL IB	18D VLVO	10 6	8176	5 9	32100	35700
40	FARR 40	SLP	SA/CR	F/S KL IB	43D VLVO	12 6	14500	6 6	75800	83300
				1991 BOATS						
30 10	FARR 31	SLP	SA/CR	F/S SK OB		9 5	4800	6 4	16500	18800
33 11	FARR 34	SLP	SA/CR	F/S KL IB	18D VLVO	10 6	8176	5 9	29900	33200
40	FARR 40	SLP	SA/CR	F/S KL IB	43D VLVO	12 6	14500	6 6	70900	77900
				1990 BOATS						
30 10	FARR 31	SLP	SA/CR	F/S SK OB		9 5	4800	6 4	15500	17600
33 11	FARR 34	SLP	SA/CR	F/S KL IB	18D VLVO	10 6	8176	5 9	27900	31100
40	FARR 40	SLP	SA/CR	F/S KL IB	43D VLVO	12 6	14500	6 6	66200	72800
				1989 BOATS						
30 10	FARR 31	SLP	SA/RC	F/S SK OB		9 5	4800	6 4	14200	16100
33 11	FARR 34	SLP	SA/RC	F/S KL IB	18D VLVO	10 6	8176	5 9	26000	28900
40	FARR 40	SLP	SA/RC	F/S KL IB	43D VLVO	12 6	14500	6 6	61900	68000
				1988 BOATS						
30 10	FARR 31	SLP	SA/RC	F/S SK OB		9 5	4800	6 4	13200	15100
33 11	FARR 34	SLP	SA/RC	F/S KL IB	18D VLVO	10 6	8176	5 9	24300	27000
40	FARR 40	SLP	SA/RC	F/S KL IB	43D VLVO	12 6	14500	6 6	57800	63600
				1987 BOATS						
30 10	NOELEX 30	SLP	SA/RC	FBG KL OB		9 5	4125	6 4	10600	12000
33 11	FARR 1020	SLP	SA/RC	F/S KL SD	18D VLVO	10 6	8176	5 9	22600	25200
40	FARR 1220	SLP	SA/RC	F/S KL SD	D VLVO	12 6	14500	6 6	54000	59300
				1986 BOATS						
33 10	FARR 33	SLP	SA/RC	F/S KL IB	D	11 6	9239	6 9	23900	26500
44 1	FARR 44	SLP	SA/CR	F/S KL IB	D	13 1	16950	8 3	69700	76600
				1985 BOATS						
33 10		SLP	SA/RC	F/S KL IB	D	11 4	7239	6 7	17200	19500
40 2	FARR 136	SLP	SA/RC	F/S KL IB	D	13 3	13160	7 5	44200	49100
44 1		SLP	SA/RC	F/S KL IB	D	13 1	16950	5 6	65300	71600
44 1	FARR 137	SLP	SA/RC	F/S KC IB	D	13 1	16980	5 6	65300	71700
48 4	FARR 48	SLP	SA/RC	F/S KL IB	D	13 11	20111	8	92100	101000
				1984 BOATS						
40 2	FARR 136	SLP	SA/RC	F/S KL IB	D	13 3	13160	7 5	41300	45900
48 4	FARR 48	SLP	SA/RC	F/S KL IB	D	13 11	20111	8	86100	94700

FARRINGTON MARINE INC
SAN DIEGO CA 92127   COAST GUARD MFG ID- FDR See inside cover to adjust price for area

LOA FT IN	NAME AND/ OR MODEL	TOP/ RIG	BOAT TYPE	-HULL- MTL TP TP #	----ENGINE--- HP MFG	BEAM FT IN	WGT LBS	DRAFT FT IN	RETAIL LOW	RETAIL HIGH
				1986 BOATS						
52	FARRINGTON BASIC	SCH	SA/CR	FBG KL IB	88D BENZ	13 11	50000	6 6	203500	224000
52	FARRINGTON BASIC	KTH	SA/CR	FBG KL IB	88D BENZ	13 11	50000	5 6	211000	232000
				1985 BOATS						
52	FARRINGTON BASIC	SCH	SA/CR	FBG KL IB	88D BENZ	13 11	50000	5 6	190500	209500
52	FARRINGTON BASIC	SCH	SA/CR	FBG KL IB	88D BENZ	13 11	50000	6 6	190500	209500
52	FARRINGTON BASIC	KTH	SA/CR	FBG KL IB	88D BENZ	13 11	50000	5 6	197500	217000
52	FARRINGTON BASIC	KTH	SA/CR	FBG KL IB	88D BENZ	13 11	50000	6 6	197500	217000
52	FARRINGTON LIMITED	SCH	SA/CR	F/S KL IB	120D BENZ	13 11	50000	5 6	191000	210000
52	FARRINGTON LIMITED	SCH	SA/CR	F/S KL IB	120D BENZ	13 11	50000	6 6	191000	210000
52	FARRINGTON LIMITED	KTH	SA/CR	F/S KL IB	120D BENZ	13 11	50000	5 6	198000	218000
52	FARRINGTON LIMITED	KTH	SA/CR	F/S KL IB	120D BENZ	13 11	50000	6 6	198000	218000

....For earlier years, see the BUC Used Boat Price Guide, Volume 3

FAST BOATS
GLASCO NY 12432   See inside cover to adjust price for area
FORMERLY HUDSON RIVER BOAT BUILDING

LOA FT IN	NAME AND/ OR MODEL	TOP/ RIG	BOAT TYPE	-HULL- MTL TP TP #	----ENGINE--- HP MFG	BEAM FT IN	WGT LBS	DRAFT FT IN	RETAIL LOW	RETAIL HIGH
				1984 BOATS						
36 11	TRICE III	SLP	SA/RC	F/S TM OB		20	5240	2 6	54900	60300

FASTLANE MARINE
MOLENDINAR QUEENLD AUSTRALIA   See inside cover to adjust price for area

LOA FT IN	NAME AND/ OR MODEL	TOP/ RIG	BOAT TYPE	-HULL- MTL TP TP #	----ENGINE--- HP MFG	BEAM FT IN	WGT LBS	DRAFT FT IN	RETAIL LOW	RETAIL HIGH
				1992 BOATS						
40 7	FASTLANE 40	OP	EXP	FBG DV IO	T	9 5	10560	2 7	**	**
				1990 BOATS						
31 10	FASTLANE 32	OP	SPTCR	FBG DV IO	270 MRCR	8 6	8000	2 9	32800	36500
31 10	FASTLANE 32	OP	SPTCR	FBG DV IO	T270-T365 MRCR	8 6	8000	2 9	36400	44800
40 5	FASTLANE 40	OP	SPTCR	FBG DV IO	T365 MRCR	9 9	11000	1 9	64500	70800
				1989 BOATS						
31 10	FASTLANE 32	ST	SPTCR	FBG DV IO	T365 MRCR	8 6	8000	2 9	38000	42200
40 7	FASTLANE 40	ST	SPTCR	FBG DV IO	T365 MRCR	9 5	11000	3 4	64300	70700

FELT INDUSTRIES INC

MONMOUTH IL 61462 COAST GUARD MFG ID- FLI See inside cover to adjust price for area

LOA FT	LOA IN	NAME AND/ OR MODEL	TOP/ RIG	BOAT TYPE	-HULL- MTL	-HULL- TP	ENGINE TP	ENGINE # HP	ENGINE MFG	BEAM FT	BEAM IN	WGT LBS	DRAFT FT	DRAFT IN	RETAIL LOW	RETAIL HIGH
		1990 BOATS														
16	5	ECLIPSE MV650	OP	RNBT	FBG	DV	OB			7	2	1200			2250	2600
16	5	ECLIPSE MV650BR	OP	RNBT	FBG	DV	IO	120-175		7	2	2150			3350	3950
16	5	ECLIPSE MV650CB	OP	RNBT	FBG	DV	IO	120-175		7	2	2150			3350	3950
17	7	SPOILER MV850BR	OP	RNBT	FBG	DV	OB			7	4	1300			2450	2800
17	7	SPOILER MV850BR	OP	RNBT	FBG	DV	IO	120-260		7	4	2300			3750	4600
17	7	SPOILER MV850CB	OP	RNBT	FBG	DV	OB			7	4	1300			2450	2800
17	7	SPOILER MV850CB	OP	RNBT	FBG	DV	IO	120-260		7	4	2300			3750	4600
18	8	SATURN II MV19000BR	OP	RNBT	FBG	DV	IO	120-260		8		2650			4550	5400
19		METEOR MV950BR	OP	RNBT	FBG	DV	IO	120-235		7	4	2400			4100	5000
19		METEOR MV950BR	OP	RNBT	FBG	DV	IO	260		7	4	2400			6150	7050
19		METEOR MV950CB	OP	RNBT	FBG	DV	IO	120-260		7	4	2400			4100	5000
20	2	MARAUDER MV2000CC	OP	CUD	FBG	DV	IO	120-260		8		2750			5100	6050
20	9	COMMANDER MV2150BR	OP	RNBT	FBG	DV	IO	167-270		8		2900			5200	6150
20	9	COMMANDER MV2150BR	OP	RNBT	FBG	DV	IO	275	VLVO	8		2900			5650	6500
20	9	COMMANDER MV2150BR	OP	RNBT	FBG	DV	IO	330-340		8		2900			6000	7350
20	9	EXPLORER MV2100CC	OP	CUD	FBG	DV	IO	167-270		8		2900			5450	6450
20	9	EXPLORER MV2100CC	OP	CUD	FBG	DV	IO	275	VLVO	8		2900			5950	6800
20	9	EXPLORER MV2100CC	OP	CUD	FBG	DV	IO	330-340		8		2900			6300	7750
21	3	PLAYMATE MV2000CR	OP	SPTCR	FBG	DV	IO	167-260		8	6	4000			7050	8300
22	4	CONDOR MV2350CC	OP	SPTCR	FBG	DV	IO	200-270		8		3995			7150	8600
22	4	CONDOR MV2350CC	OP	SPTCR	FBG	DV	IO	275	VLVO	8		3995			7800	8950
22	4	CONDOR MV2350CC	OP	SPTCR	FBG	DV	IO	330-365		8		3995			8150	10100
23	8	MAGNUM MV2450CC	OP	SPTCR	FBG	DV	IO	200-275		8		4025			7700	9600
23	8	MAGNUM MV2450CC	OP	SPTCR	FBG	DV	IO	330-365		8		4025			8800	10700
26	7	CONCORDE MV2700CC	OP	SPTCR	FBG	DV	IO	330-364		8		5900			12800	15200
26	7	CONCORDE MV2700CC	OP	SPTCR	FBG	DV	IO	T229-T275		8		5900			13700	16500
26	7	CONCORDE MV2700CC	OP	SPTCR	FBG	DV	IO	T330-T340		8		5900			15400	18000
28	2	ENDEAVOR MV2900CC	OP	SPTCR	FBG	DV	IO	229-340		8		6200			12600	15600
		IO 365 MRCR 14000 15900, IO T230-T270 14400 17100, IO T330													16200	18400
28	5	CRUSADER MV2850CR	OP	CBNCR	FBG	DV	IO	260-365		8	6	6000			16300	19200
28	5	CRUSADER MV2850CR	OP	CBNCR	FBG	DV	IO	T120-T175		8	6	6000			16400	19000
		1989 BOATS														
16	5	ECLIPSE MV650	OP	RNBT	FBG	DV	OB			7	2	1250			2200	2600
16	5	ECLIPSE MV650	OP	RNBT	FBG	DV	IO	130-205		7	2	1950			2850	3450
17	7	SPOILER MV850	OP	RNBT	FBG	DV	OB			7	4	1300			2350	2750
17	7	SPOILER MV850	OP	RNBT	FBG	DV	IO	130-230		7	4	2300			3400	4100
17	7	SPOILER MV850	OP	RNBT	FBG	DV	IO	260		7	4	2300			3700	4300
18	8	CHALLENGER MV1900CC	OP	CUD	FBG	DV	IO	130-230		8		2550	2	4	4100	5150
18	8	CHALLENGER MV1900CC	OP	CUD	FBG	DV	IO	231-271		8		2550	2	4	4550	5500
18	8	SATURN II MV1900BR	OP	RNBT	FBG	DV	IO	130-230		8		2550			4000	4950
18	8	SATURN II MV1900BR	OP	RNBT	FBG	DV	IO	231-271		8		2550			4400	5350
19		METEOR MV950	OP	RNBT	FBG	DV	IO	130-205		7	4	2400			3750	4650
19		METEOR MV950	OP	RNBT	FBG	DV	IO	211-270		7	4	2400			4000	4750
19		METEOR MV950	OP	RNBT	FBG	DV	IO	271	VLVO	7	4	2400			4400	5050
20	2	MAURAUDER MV2000	OP	CUD	FBG	DV	IO	130-260		8		2750			4650	5750
20	2	MAURAUDER MV2000	OP	CUD	FBG	DV	IO	271	VLVO	8		2750			5250	6050
20	9	COMMANDER MV2150BR	OP	CR	FBG	DV	IO	165-270		8		2900	2	6	4950	6100
20	9	COMMANDER MV2150BR	OP	CR	FBG	DV	IO	271-340		8		2900	2	6	5550	6950
20	9	EXPLORER MV2100CC	OP	CUD	FBG	DV	IO	165-270		8		2950	2	6	5000	6150
20	9	EXPLORER MV2100CC	OP	CUD	FBG	DV	IO	271-340		8		2950	2	6	5600	7000
21	3	PLAYMATE MV2200CR	OP	SPTCR	FBG	DV	IO	165-260		8	6	4000	2	6	6500	7850
21	3	PLAYMATE MV2200CR	OP	SPTCR	FBG	DV	IO	271	VLVO	8	6	4000	2	6	7100	8150
22	4	CONDOR MV2350CC	OP	SPTCR	FBG	DV	IO	200-270		8		3360	2	8	5950	7200
22	4	CONDOR MV2350CC	OP	SPTCR	FBG	DV	IO	271-340		8		3360	2	8	6500	8050
22	4	CONDOR MV2350CC	OP	SPTCR	FBG	DV	IO	365	MRCR	8		3360	2	8	7550	8650
23	8	MAGNUM MV2450CC	OP	SPTCR	FBG	DV	IO	200-270		8		4025			7250	8700
23	8	MAGNUM MV2450CC	OP	SPTCR	FBG	DV	IO	330-365		8		4025			8200	10200
26	7	CONCORDE MV2700CC	OP	SPTCR	FBG	DV	IO	271-340		8		4750	2	9	10300	12500
		IO 365 MRCR 11400 13000, IO T205-T270 11300 13800, IO T271-T340													12500	15100
28	5	CRUSADER MV2850CR	OP	CBNCR	FBG	DV	IO	260-365		8	6	6000			15400	18100
28	5	CRUSADER MV2850CR	OP	CBNCR	FBG	DV	IO	T130-T205		8	6	6000			15600	17800
		1988 BOATS														
16	5	ECLIPSE MV650	OP	RNBT	FBG	DV	OB			7	2	1250			2100	2500
16	5	ECLIPSE MV650	OP	RNBT	FBG	DV	IO	130-205		7	2	1950			2700	3250
17	7	SPOILER MV850	OP	RNBT	FBG	DV	OB			7	4	1300			2250	2600
17	7	SPOILER MV850	OP	RNBT	FBG	DV	IO	130-230		7	4	2300			3200	3900
17	7	SPOILER MV850	OP	RNBT	FBG	DV	IO	260		7	4	2300			3500	4050
18	8	CHALLENGER MV1900CC	OP	CUD	FBG	DV	IO	130-230		8		2550	2	4	3900	4850
18	8	CHALLENGER MV1900CC	OP	CUD	FBG	DV	IO	231-271		8		2550	2	4	4250	5250
18	8	SATURN II MB1900BR	OP	RNBT	FBG	DV	IO	200	MRCR	8		2550			3850	4450
18	8	SATURN II MV1900BR	OP	RNBT	FBG	DV	IO	130-230		8		2550			3800	4700
18	8	SATURN II MV1900BR	OP	RNBT	FBG	DV	IO	231-271		8		2550			4100	5050
20	9	COMMANDER MV1250BR	OP	CR	FBG	DV	IO	340	OMC	8		2900	2	6	5700	6550
20	9	COMMANDER MV2150BR	OP	CR	FBG	DV	IO	165-270		8		2900	2	6	4700	5750
20	9	COMMANDER MV2150BR	OP	CR	FBG	DV	IO	271-330		8		2900	2	6	5250	6500
20	9	EXPLORER MV2100CC	OP	CUD	FBG	DV	IO	165-270		8		2950	2	6	4750	5800
20	9	EXPLORER MV2100CC	OP	CUD	FBG	DV	IO	271-340		8		2950	2	6	5300	6650
21	3	COMMODORE MV2200CR	OP	SPTCR	FBG	DV	IO	165-260		8	6	4000	2	6	6150	7450
21	3	COMMODORE MV2200CR	OP	SPTCR	FBG	DV	IO	271	VLVO	8	6	4000	2	6	6700	7700
22	4	CONDOR MV2350CC	OP	SPTCR	FBG	DV	IO	200-270		8		3360	2	8	5650	6800
22	4	CONDOR MV2350CC	OP	SPTCR	FBG	DV	IO	271-340		8		3360	2	8	6200	7600
22	4	CONDOR MV2350CC	OP	SPTCR	FBG	DV	IO	365	MRCR	8		3360	2	8	7150	8200
26	7	CONCORDE MV2700CC	OP	SPTCR	FBG	DV	IO	271-340		8		4750	2	9	9800	11800
		IO 365 MRCR 10800 12300, IO T205-T270 10700 13100, IO T271-T340													11800	14300
28	5	CRUSADER MV2850CR	OP	SPTCR	FBG	DV	IO	231-340		10		6000			11700	14500
28	5	CRUSADER MV2850CR	OP	SPTCR	FBG	DV	IO	365	MRCR	10		6000			13100	14900
28	5	CRUSADER MV2850CR	OP	SPTCR	FBG	DV	IO	T130-T205		10		6000			12100	14900
		1987 BOATS														
16	5	ECLIPSE MV650	OP	RNBT	FBG	DV	OB			7	2	1250			2000	2400
16	5	ECLIPSE MV650	OP	RNBT	FBG	DV	IO	120-205		7	2	1950			2600	3100
17	7	SPOILER MV850	OP	RNBT	FBG	DV	IO	120-230		7	4	2300			3050	3700
17	7	SPOILER MV850	OP	RNBT	FBG	DV	IO	260		7	4	2300			3300	3850
18	8	CHALLENGER MV1900CC	OP	CUD	FBG	DV	IO	130-230		8		2550	2	4	3700	4500
18	8	CHALLENGER MV1900CC	OP	CUD	FBG	DV	IO	260		8		2550	2	4	4000	4650
18	8	SATURN II MB1900BR	OP	RNBT	FBG	DV	IO	200	MRCR	8		2550			3650	4250
18	8	SATURN II MV1900 BR	OP	RNBT	FBG	DV	IO	180	MRCR	8		2550			3600	4200
18	8	SATURN II MV1900BR	OP	RNBT	FBG	DV	IO	130-260		8		2550			3600	4500
20	9	COMMANDER 2150BR	OP	CR	FBG	DV	IO		OMC	8		2900	2	6	**	**
20	9	COMMANDER 2150BR	OP	CR	FBG	DV	IO	165-260		8		2900	2	6	4450	5400
20	9	COMMANDER 2150BR	OP	CR	FBG	DV	IO	330-335		8		2900	2	6	5350	6150
20	9	EXPLORER MV2100	OP	CUD	FBG	DV	IO	200-260		8		2950	2	6	4800	5550
20	9	EXPLORER MV2100	OP	CUD	FBG	DV	IO	330-340		8		2950	2	6	5400	6300
20	9	EXPLORER MV2100	OP	RNBT	FBG	DV	IO	165	MRCR	8		2950	2	6	4250	4950
20	9	EXPLORER MV2100CC	OP	CUD	FBG	DV	IO	175-200		8		2950	2	6	4550	5200
21	3	COMMODORE MV2200	OP	SPTCR	FBG	DV	IO	165-260		8	6	4000	2	6	5850	7000
21	3	COMMODORE MV2200	OP	SPTCR	FBG	DV	IO	330-340		8	6	4000	2	6	6750	7850
22	4	CONDOR MV2350	OP	SPTCR	FBG	DV	IO	200-260		8		3360	2	8	5350	6400
22	4	CONDOR MV2350	OP	SPTCR	FBG	DV	IO	330-340		8		3360	2	8	6250	7250
22	4	CONDOR MV2350	OP	SPTCR	FBG	DV	IO	T165-T180		8		3360	2	8	6050	7000
26	7	CONCORDE MV2700	OP	SPTCR	FBG	DV	IO	330-340		8		4750	2	9	9800	11200
26	7	CONCORDE MV2700	OP	SPTCR	FBG	DV	IO	T205-T260		8		4750	2	9	10100	12300
26	7	CONCORDE MV2700	OP	SPTCR	FBG	DV	IO	T330-T350		8		4750	2	9	11800	13900
		1986 BOATS														
16	5	ECLIPSE MV650	OP	RNBT	FBG	DV	OB			7	2	1250			1950	2350
16	5	ECLIPSE MV650	OP	RNBT	FBG	DV	IO	120-205		7	2	1950			2450	2950
16	5	ECLIPSE MV650SD	OP	RNBT	FBG	DV	OB			7	2	1175			1850	2200
17	7	SPORTSTER MV800	OP	RNBT	FBG	DV	OB			7	4	1200			1950	2300
17	7	SPORTSTER MV800	OP	RNBT	FBG	DV	IO	120-230		7	4	2300			2900	3550
17	7	SPORTSTER MV800	OP	RNBT	FBG	DV	IO	260		7	4	2300			3150	3650
18	8	SATURN II MV1900	OP	RNBT	FBG	DV	IO	140-260		8		2550			3450	4300
19	11	BERMUDA MV2000	ST	RNBT	FBG	DV	IO	175-260		8		2850			3900	4800
20	9	EXPLORER MV2100	OP	CUD	FBG	DV	IO	175-260		8		2900			4200	5200
22	4	CONDOR MV2350	OP	SPTCR	FBG	DV	IO	200-260		8		3300			5050	6050
26	7	CONCORDE MV2650	OP	SPTCR	FBG	DV	IO	T205-T260		8		4750			9650	11700
		1985 BOATS														
16	5	ECLIPSE MV650	OP	RNBT	FBG	DV	OB			7	2	1250			1900	2250
16	5	ECLIPSE MV650	OP	RNBT	FBG	DV	IO	120-190		7	2	1950			2350	2800
17	7	SPORTSTER MV800	OP	RNBT	FBG	DV	OB			7	4	1200			1900	2250
17	7	SPORTSTER MV800	OP	RNBT	FBG	DV	IO	120-230		7	4	2300			2800	3400
17	7	SPORTSTER MV800	OP	RNBT	FBG	DV	IO	260		7	4	2300			3050	3500
19	11	BERMUDA MV2000	ST	RNBT	FBG	DV	IO	170-260		8		2850			3750	4600
20	9	EXPLORER MV2100	OP	CUD	FBG	DV	IO	170-260		8		2900			4050	5000
22	4	CONDOR MV2350	OP	SPTCR	FBG	DV	IO	200-260		8		3300			4850	5800
25	2	ENCOUNTER MK2500	ST	EXP	FBG	DV	IO	200-260		8		4700			7200	8600
		1984 BOATS														
17	7	MARK 7		RNBT	FBG	DV	IO	188		7	4				3250	3800
17	7	SPORTSTER		RNBT	FBG	DV	OB			7	4	1200			1850	2200
17	7	SPORTSTER		RNBT	FBG	DV	IO	188		7	4				2200	2600
19	11	BERMUDA		RNBT	FBG	DV	IO	198		8					3500	4050
19	11	FREEPORT		RNBT	FBG	DV	IO	198		8					3800	4400
22	4	CATALINA		RNBT	FBG	DV	IO	230		8					4700	5400
23	4	CONDOR		RNBT	FBG	DV	IO	228		8					4900	5600
25	2	ENCOUNTER		RNBT	FBG	DV	IO	260		8					6700	7700

FERRETTI YACHTS

47100 FORLI ITALY

See inside cover to adjust price for area

FERRETTI GROUP USA
MIAMI FL 33142

For more recent years, see the BUC Used Boat Price Guide, Volume 1

LOA FT	IN	NAME AND/ OR MODEL	TOP/ RIG	BOAT TYPE	HULL MTL	HULL TP	ENGINE TP	# HP	MFG	BEAM FT	IN	WGT LBS	DRAFT FT	IN	RETAIL LOW	RETAIL HIGH
		1996 BOATS														
51	2	50	FB	MY	FBG	DV	IB	T600	CAT	14	9	52920	4	2	410500	451500
55		FERRETTI 53	ST	MY	FBG	DV	IB	T770D		13	1	52920	3	3	530000	582500
57	5	57	FB	MY	FBG	DV	IB	T10CD		16	11	61740	4	11	617000	678000
60		FERRETTI 62	FB	MYCPT	FBG	DV	IB	T10CD	MTU	16	9	76734	5	2	802500	881500
65		65	OP	CRCPT	FBG	DV	IB	T11C	MTU	17	9	85664	5	7	878000	964500
73	6	FERRETTI 72	FB	MY	FBG	DV	IB	T12CD		20		97020	6	3	**	**
75		72	FB	MYCPT	FBG	DV	IB	T14CD	CAT	19	7	70T	5		**	**
		1995 BOATS														
48	7	47	FB	MYCPT	FBG	DV	IB	T435D	CAT	14		40131	4	4	309500	340000
55		53	ST	MYCPT	FBG	DV	IB	T770	MTU	16	2	52920	5	3	455000	500000
56		55	FB	MY	FBG	SV	IB	T10CD		5		61740	5	3	**	**
56	3	55	FB	MY	FBG	SV	IB	T770D	MTU	16	2	61740	5	3	528500	580500
64		FERRETTI 62	FB	MY	FBG	DV	IB	T10CD		17	11	76734	4	11	777000	854000
65		65	FB	MYCPT	FBG	SV	IB	T11CD	MTU	17	9	85664	4	11	924000	1.005M
74	7	225FLY	FB	MYFD	FBG	SV	IB	T12CD	CAT	19	8	97020	4	10	**	**
75		225 FLY	FB	MYCPT	FBG	DV	IB	T14CD	CAT	19	8	70T	4	11	**	**

FIBERGLASS FANTASTIC

FGF INC
EWA BEACH HI 96706 COAST GUARD MFG ID- FTS

See inside cover to adjust price for area

LOA FT	IN	NAME AND/ OR MODEL	TOP/ RIG	BOAT TYPE	HULL MTL	HULL TP	ENGINE TP	# HP	MFG	BEAM FT	IN	WGT LBS	DRAFT FT	IN	RETAIL LOW	RETAIL HIGH
		1986 BOATS														
22		DELUXE 2200	CAT	CANOE	FBG	OR				2	6	295		1	1900	2300
40		CHAMPIONSHIP 40	CAT	CANOE	FBG	OR				1	6	400		10	**	**
43	4	HAWAIIAN CLASS RACER	CAT	CANOE	FBG	OR				1	6	400		8	**	**
		1984 BOATS														
21		KAUAI SAMPAN	HT	FSH	FBG	FL	OB			7		2700		4	9200	10500
24		MOSQUITO 24	FB	SF	FBG	SV	OB			8		5500	1	8	17000	19300
24		MOSQUITO 24	FB	SF	FBG	SV	IO	260	CHRY	8		5800	2	4	12700	14400
		IO 260 MRCR 12700 14400, IO 260 VLVO 13000 14800, IB 260-330													13700	16100
		IB 200D-235D 19400 21600														
29	6	MOSQUITO 29	FB	SF	FBG	DV	IB	215D	J&T	9	6	9200	3	4	28600	31700
29	6	MOSQUITO 29	FB	SF	FBG	DV	IB	305D	CAT	9	6	10100	3	6	34800	38700
29	6	MOSQUITO 29	FB	SF	FBG	DV	IB	T200D	CHRY	9	6	9800			36300	40300

FIBERGLASS WORKS INC

ARIES BOATS
WHITE BLUFF TN 37187

See inside cover to adjust price for area

For more recent years, see the BUC Used Boat Price Guide, Volume 1

LOA FT	IN	NAME AND/ OR MODEL	TOP/ RIG	BOAT TYPE	HULL MTL	HULL TP	ENGINE TP	# HP	MFG	BEAM FT	IN	WGT LBS	DRAFT FT	IN	RETAIL LOW	RETAIL HIGH
		1996 BOATS														
16		160 BASS	OP	BASS	FBG	DV	OB			6	8	750			2200	2600
18	1	180T	OP	BASS	FBG	DV	OB			7	1	950			2950	3450
18	1	181XLT	OP	BASS	FBG	DV	OB			7	3	900			2800	3250
18	1	181XTE	OP	BASS	FBG	DV	OB			7	3	1000			3050	3550
19	2	200XLT	OP	BASS	FBG	DV	OB			7	8	1200			3500	4050
19	2	200XTE	OP	BASS	FBG	DV	OB			7	8	1200			3950	4600
		1995 BOATS														
16		160 BASS	OP	BASS	FBG	DV	OB			6	8	750			2050	2450
18	1	180SS FISH & SKI	OP	RNBT	FBG	DV	OB			7	1	900			2700	3100
18	1	180T	OP	BASS	FBG	DV	OB			7	1	950			2800	3250
18	1	181XFD	OP	BASS	FBG	DV	OB			7	3	900			2700	3150
18	1	181XLS FISH & SKI	OP	RNBT	FBG	DV	OB			7	3	950			2800	3250
18	1	181XLT	OP	BASS	FBG	DV	OB			7	3	900			2650	3100
19	2	200XFD	OP	BASS	FBG	DV	OB			7	8	1200			3550	4150
19	2	200XLT	OP	BASS	FBG	DV	OB			7	8	1200			3500	4100
		1994 BOATS														
18	1	180SS FISH & SKI	OP	RNBT	FBG	DV	OB			7	1	900			2550	3000
18	1	180T	OP	BASS	FBG	DV	OB			7	1	950			2700	3150
18	1	181XFD	OP	BASS	FBG	DV	OB			7	3	900			2600	3000
18	1	181XLS FISH & SKI	OP	RNBT	FBG	DV	OB			7	3	950			2700	3150
18	1	181XLT	OP	BASS	FBG	DV	OB			7	3	900			2550	2950
19	2	200XFD	OP	BASS	FBG	DV	OB			7	8	1200			3400	3950
19	2	200XLT	OP	BASS	FBG	DV	OB			7	8	1200			3350	3900
		1993 BOATS														
18	1	180SS FISH & SKI	OP	RNBT	FBG	DV	OB			7	1	900			2450	2850
18	1	180T	OP	BASS	FBG	DV	OB			7	1	950			2600	3000
18	1	181XLS FISH & SKI	OP	RNBT	FBG	DV	OB			7	3	900			2450	2850
18	1	181XLT	OP	BASS	FBG	DV	OB			7	3	950			2600	3000
19	2	200XLT	OP	BASS	FBG	DV	OB			7	8	1200			3250	3750
		1992 BOATS														
17		BASS 170	OP	BASS	FBG	SV	OB			7	1	850			2200	2550
18	1	FISH & SKI 180	OP	FSH	FBG	DV	OB			7	1	950			2450	2850
18	1	ST 180	OP	BASS	FBG	DV	OB			7	1	950			2450	2900
19	2	FD 1900	OP	BASS	FBG	DV	OB			7	8	1100			2900	3350
19	2	ST 1900	OP	BASS	FBG	DV	OB			7	8	1100			2900	3350
		1991 BOATS														
17		BASS 170	OP	BASS	FBG	SV	OB			7	1	850			2050	2450
17		FISH & SKI 170	OP	FSH	FBG	SV	OB			7	1	850			2050	2450
17		ST 170	OP	BASS	FBG	SV	OB			7	1	850			2050	2450
17	10	STS 180	OP	BASS	FBG	SV	OB			7	1	950			2350	2750
18	1	FISH & SKI 180	OP	FSH	FBG	DV	OB			7	1	950			2400	2750
18	1	ST 180	OP	BASS	FBG	DV	OB			7	1	950			2400	2750
19	2	ST 1900	OP	BASS	FBG	DV	OB			7	8	1100			2800	3250
		1990 BOATS														
17		170 BASS	OP	BASS	FBG	SV		140		7	1	850			**	**
17		170 FISH & SKI	OP	FSH	FBG	SV	OB			7	1	900			2100	2450
17		170 STS	OP	BASS	FBG	SV		150		7	1	850			**	**
17	10	180 FISH & SKI	OP	FSH	FBG	SV	OB			7	1	975			2350	2700
17	10	180 STS	OP	BASS	FBG	SV		150		7	1	975			**	**
		1989 BOATS														
16	7	BASS 167	OP	BASS	FBG	SV	OB			6	11	850			1900	2250
16	7	FISH-&-SKI 167	OP	BASS	FBG	DV	OB			6	11	900			2000	2350
16	8	MAGNUM 167 BASS	OP	BASS	FBG	DV	OB			7	1	850			1900	2250
16	8	MAGNUM 167 F/S	OP	BASS	FBG	DV	OB			7	1	900			2000	2350
17	6	FISH-&-SKI 176	OP	BASS	FBG	SV	OB			6	11	975			2250	2600
17	8	180 DTS	OP	BASS	FBG	SV	OB			7	1	975			2250	2650
17	8	BASS 180 STS	OP	BASS	FBG	SV	OB			7	1	975			2250	2650
		1988 BOATS														
16	7	BASS 167	OP	BASS	FBG	SV	OB			6	11	850			1800	2150
16	7	FISH-&-SKI 167	OP	BASS	FBG	DV	OB			6	11	900			1900	2300
16	8	MAGNUM 167 BASS	OP	BASS	FBG	DV	OB			7	1	850			1800	2150
16	8	MAGNUM 167 F/S	OP	BASS	FBG	DV	OB			7	1	900			1900	2300
17	6	BASS 176	OP	BASS	FBG	SV	OB			6	11	900			2000	2350
17	6	FISH-&-SKI 176	OP	BASS	FBG	SV	OB			6	11	975			2200	2550
		1987 BOATS														
16	7	BASS 167	OP	BASS	FBG	SV	OB			6	11	850			1750	2100
16	7	FISH-&-SKI 167	OP	BASS	FBG	DV	OB			6	11	900			1850	2200
16	8	MAGNUM 167 BASS	OP	BASS	FBG	DV	OB			7	1	850			1750	2100
16	8	MAGNUM 167 F/S	OP	BASS	FBG	DV	OB			7	1	900			1850	2200
17	6	BASS 176	OP	BASS	FBG	SV	OB			6	11	900			1900	2300
17	6	FISH-&-SKI 176	OP	BASS	FBG	SV	OB			6	11	975			2050	2450
		1986 BOATS														
16	7	BASS 167	OP	BASS	FBG	SV	OB			6	11	775			1550	1850
17	6	BASS 176	OP	BASS	FBG	SV	OB			6	11	880			1850	2200
17	6	FISH-&-SKI 176	OP	BASS	FBG	SV	OB			6	11	980			2000	2400
		1985 BOATS														
16	7	FISH-&-SKI 167	OP	BASS	FBG	SV	OB			6	6	775			1550	1800
17	6	BASS 176	OP	BASS	FBG	SV	OB			6	11	880			1800	2100
17	6	FISH-&-SKI 176	OP	BASS	FBG	SV	OB			6	11	980			1950	2350

....For earlier years, see the BUC Used Boat Price Guide, Volume 3

FIBERKING INC

BOMBER & COMMANDER BOATS
SMYRNA TN 37167 COAST GUARD MFG ID- FBK

See inside cover to adjust price for area

LOA FT	IN	NAME AND/ OR MODEL	TOP/ RIG	BOAT TYPE	HULL MTL	HULL TP	ENGINE TP	# HP	MFG	BEAM FT	IN	WGT LBS	DRAFT FT	IN	RETAIL LOW	RETAIL HIGH
		1993 BOATS														
16	7	BOMBER 166CF	OP	BASS	FBG	SV	OB			6	11	975			3150	3650
17	6	BOMBER 175	OP	BASS	FBG	SV	OB			7	3	985			3050	3550
17	6	BOMBER 175FS	OP	BASS	FBG	SV	OB			7	3	985			3500	4050
18		COMMANDER 180FS	OP	B/R	FBG	SV	IO	130-230		7	1	1900			4650	5600
18	4	COMMANDER 185	OP	B/R	FBG	SV	IO	130-200		7	1	1870			4700	5500
19	8	BOMBER 202 PRO	OP	BASS	FBG	SV	OB			7	6	1290			4450	5100
20		COMMANDER 2000FS	OP	B/R	FBG	SV	IO	150-260		7	7	2200			6400	7900
20		COMMANDER 200FS	OP	B/R	FBG	SV	IO	150-250		7	7	2200			6100	7600
20		COMMANDER 200FS	OP	B/R	FBG	SV	IO	260		7	7	2200			6850	7900
20	1	BOMBER 202FS	OP	BASS	FBG	SV	OB			7	10	1360			4900	5650

CONTINUED ON NEXT PAGE

LOA FT IN	NAME AND/ OR MODEL	TOP/ RIG	BOAT TYPE	MTL	-HULL- TP TP	----ENGINE--- # HP MFG	BEAM FT IN	WGT LBS	DRAFT FT IN	RETAIL LOW	RETAIL HIGH
--------------------- 1992 BOATS ---------------------											
16 7	BOMBER 166CF	OP	BASS	FBG	SV OB		6 11	975		3000	3500
17 6	BOMBER 175	OP	BASS	FBG	SV OB		7 3	985		3950	3450
17 6	BOMBER 175FS	OP	BASS	FBG	SV OB		7 3	985		3300	3850
18	COMMANDER 180FS	OP	B/R	FBG	SV IO	130-175	7 1	1900		4350	5050
18 4	COMMANDER 185	OP	B/R	FBG	SV IO	130-230	7 1	1870		4450	5350
19 8	BOMBER 202 PRO	OP	B/R	FBG	SV OB		7 6	1290		4200	4900
20	C2000FS	OP	B/R	FBG	SV IO	175	6 10	2200		5600	6400
20	COMMANDER 200FS	OP	B/R	FBG	SV OB	150-260	7 7	2200		5850	7300
20 1	B202FS	OP	B/R	FBG	SV OB		7 10	1360		4750	5450
--------------------- 1991 BOATS ---------------------											
16 4	BOMBER 165FS	OP	BASS	FBG	SV OB		6 8	975		2900	3350
16 7	BOMBER 166CF	OP	BASS	FBG	SV OB		6 11	975		2900	3400
17 3	COMMANDER 175	OP	B/R	FBG	SV IO	115-175	6 8	1800		3600	4250
17 6	BOMBER 175	OP	BASS	FBG	SV OB		7 3	985		2850	3300
17 6	BOMBER 175FS	OP	BASS	FBG	SV OB		7 3	985		3200	3700
18	COMMANDER 180FS	OP	B/R	FBG	SV IO	130-175	7 1	1900		4050	4750
18 4	BOMBER 185	OP	B/R	FBG	SV IO	130-230	7 1	1870		4100	5050
19 8	BOMBER 202 PRO	OP	B/R	FBG	SV OB		7 6	1290		4050	4750
20	COMMANDER 200FS	OP	B/R	FBG	SV OB	150-260	7 7	2200		5500	6850
21 2	COMMANDER 210BR	OP	B/R	FBG	SV IO	150-260	8	2500		6450	7950
21 2	COMMANDER 210CC	OP	CUD	FBG	SV IO	150-270	8	2500		6900	8550

....For earlier years, see the BUC Used Boat Price Guide, Volume 3

FIBRESPORT
PONTEJOS/CANTABRIA SPAIN   See inside cover to adjust price for area

LOA FT IN	NAME AND/ OR MODEL	TOP/ RIG	BOAT TYPE	MTL	-HULL- TP TP	----ENGINE--- # HP MFG	BEAM FT IN	WGT LBS	DRAFT FT IN	RETAIL LOW	RETAIL HIGH
--------------------- 1994 BOATS ---------------------											
17 10	ARTABAN 545	HT	FSH	FBG	SV IB	50D		2000	1 11	7200	8250
17 10	ARTABAN 560	HT	FSH	FBG	TR IB		7 1	1300	1 8	5700	6550
19 2	ARTABAN 585	HT	FSH	FBG	SV IB	70D	8 1	2900	1 1	10200	11600
22 5	ARTABAN 700	EPH	FSH	FBG	SV IB	140D	8 2	3200	2 1	12000	13700
--------------------- 1993 BOATS ---------------------											
24 6	ARTABAN 750	EPH	FSH	FBG	SV IB	T260D	9 2	6000	2 3	27600	30700

FIESTA BOATS INC
MESA AZ 85202   COAST GUARD MFG ID- SFQ See inside cover to adjust price for area

LOA FT IN	NAME AND/ OR MODEL	TOP/ RIG	BOAT TYPE	MTL	-HULL- TP TP	----ENGINE--- # HP MFG	BEAM FT IN	WGT LBS	DRAFT FT IN	RETAIL LOW	RETAIL HIGH
--------------------- 1986 BOATS ---------------------											
16 2	SKIPPER II	OP	RNBT	FBG	TR OB		6 4	950		1850	2200
16 2	SPORTSMAN	OP	BASS	FBG	TR OB		6	1000		1950	2300
16 6	V170	OP	RNBT	FBG	DV OB		7	1000		1950	2300
16 6	V170	OP	RNBT	FBG	DV IO	120-140	7	2000		2400	2800
16 6	V170 XL	OP	RNBT	FBG	DV IO	140-170	7	2000		2500	2950
--------------------- 1985 BOATS ---------------------											
16 2	SKIPPER II	OP	RNBT	FBG	TR OB		6 4	950		1800	2150
16 6	V170	OP	RNBT	FBG	DV OB		7	1000		1900	2250
16 6	V170	OP	RNBT	FBG	DV IO	120-140	7	2000		2350	2700

FINELINE INDUSTRIES INC
CENTURION BOATS   See inside cover to adjust price for area
MERCED CA 95340   COAST GUARD MFG ID- FIN
FOR OLDER MODELS SEE SKI CENTURION

For more recent years, see the BUC Used Boat Price Guide, Volume 1

LOA FT IN	NAME AND/ OR MODEL	TOP/ RIG	BOAT TYPE	MTL	-HULL- TP TP	----ENGINE--- # HP MFG	BEAM FT IN	WGT LBS	DRAFT FT IN	RETAIL LOW	RETAIL HIGH
--------------------- 1996 BOATS ---------------------											
20	LAPOINT ELITE	RNBT	FBG	DV	IB	250	7 4	2500		10800	12300
20	SPORT	RNBT	FBG	DV	IB	250	7 4	2500		10500	12000
20	SPORT BR	RNBT	FBG	DV	IB	250	7 2	2700		10900	12400
20	WARRIOR BAREFOOT	RNBT	FBG	DV	OB		6	1300		4800	5500
21 6	ELITE	RNBT	FBG	DV	VD	250	7 10	2900		12800	14500
21 6	ELITE BR	RNBT	FBG	DV	IB	250	7 10	2800		12500	14300
--------------------- 1995 BOATS ---------------------											
19	LAPOINT	RNBT	FBG	DV	IB	250	7 8	2500		9000	10200
20	FALCON	RNBT	FBG	DV	VD	250	7 3	2400		9700	11000
20	FALCON BAREFOOT	RNBT	FBG	DV	OB		7 2	1500		5150	5900
20	FALCON BAREFOOT BR	RNBT	FBG	DV	OB		7 2	1700		5650	6450
20	FALCON BR	RNBT	FBG	DV	IB	250	7 2	2500		9900	11300
20	FALCON SPORT	RNBT	FBG	DV	IB	250	7 4	2500		9900	11300
20	FALCON SPORT BR	RNBT	FBG	DV	IB	250	7 2	2700		10300	11700
20	HERITAGE BR	RNBT	FBG	DV	IB	250	7 4	2400		9750	11100
20	WARRIOR BAREFOOT	SKI	FBG	DV	OB		6	1300		4600	5300
--------------------- 1994 BOATS ---------------------											
16	WAVE	RNBT	FBG	DV	IB	140	6 9	1500		4750	5500
16	WAVE COMP	RNBT	FBG	DV	IB	225	6 9	1800		5550	6400
19	TRUTRAC	SKI	FBG	DV	IB	250	7 2	2400		7650	8800
19	TRUTRAC IV	SKI	FBG	DV	IB	250	7 2	2500		7850	9000
20	FALCON	RNBT	FBG	DV	IB	250	7 3	2400		9250	10500
20	FALCON	RNBT	FBG	DV	VD	250	7 3	2600		9600	10900
20	FALCON BAREFOOT	RNBT	FBG	DV	OB		7 2	1700		5400	6200
20	FALCON BAREFOOT BR	RNBT	FBG	DV	OB		7 2	1500		4900	5650
20	FALCON BR	RNBT	FBG	DV	IO	250	7 3	2550		7800	8950
20	FALCON BR XP	RNBT	FBG	DV	IB	250	7 3	2550		9500	10800
20	FALCON XP	RNBT	FBG	DV	IB	250	7 3	2500		9400	10700
20	WARRIOR BAREFOOT	SKI	FBG	DV	OB		6	1300		4400	5050
--------------------- 1993 BOATS ---------------------											
16	WAVE	RNBT	FBG	DV	IB	140	6 9	1500		4550	5200
16	WAVE COMP	RNBT	FBG	DV	IB	225	6 9	1800		5300	6050
19	TRUTRAC III	SKI	FBG	DV	IB	240	7 3	2300		7150	8200
19	TRUTRAC IV	SKI	FBG	DV	IB	240	7 2	2400		7250	8350
20	FALCON	RNBT	FBG	DV	IO	240	7 5	2500		7200	8300
20	FALCON	RNBT	FBG	DV	IB	240	7 5	2500		9050	10300
20	FALCON BAREFOOT	RNBT	FBG	DV	OB		7 2	1700		5150	5950
20	FALCON BAREFOOT BR	RNBT	FBG	DV	VD		7 2	1500		4700	5400
20	FALCON BR	RNBT	FBG	DV	IB	240	7 5	2750		9450	10800
20	FALCON BR XP	RNBT	FBG	DV	IB	240	7 3	2550		9000	10200
20	FALCON XP	RNBT	FBG	DV	IB	240	7 3	2500		8900	10100
20	WARRIOR BAREFOOT	SKI	FBG	DV	OB		6	1300		4150	4850
--------------------- 1992 BOATS ---------------------											
19	TRUTRAC III	SKI	FBG	DV	IB	250	7 3	2300		6800	7800
20	FALCON	RNBT	FBG	DV	IB	250	7 5	2500		8500	9750
20	FALCON	RNBT	FBG	DV	VD	250	7 5	2500		8500	9750
20	FALCON BAREFOOT	RNBT	FBG	DV	OB		7 2	1700		4950	5700
20	FALCON BAREFOOT BR	RNBT	FBG	DV	OB		7 2	1500		4550	5200
20	FALCON BR	RNBT	FBG	DV	VD	250	7 5	2900		9350	10600
20	FALCON BR XP	RNBT	FBG	DV	IB	250	7 3	2550		8500	9750
20	FALCON XP	RNBT	FBG	DV	IB	250	7 3	2500		8400	9650
20	WARRIOR BAREFOOT	RNBT	FBG	DV	OB		6	1300		4000	4650
--------------------- 1991 BOATS ---------------------											
19	TRUTRAC III	SKI	FBG	DV	IB	250	7 3	2300		6450	7400
20	FALCON	RNBT	FBG	DV	IB	250	7 5	2500		8050	9300
20	FALCON	RNBT	FBG	DV	VD	250	7 5	2800		8600	9900
20	FALCON BAREFOOT	RNBT	FBG	DV	OB		7 2	1700		4800	5500
20	FALCON BAREFOOT BR	RNBT	FBG	DV	OB		7 2	1500		4400	5050
20	FALCON BR	RNBT	FBG	DV	VD	250	7 5	2900		8900	10100
20	FALCON BR XP	RNBT	FBG	DV	IB	250	7 3	2550		8050	9250
20	FALCON XP	RNBT	FBG	DV	IO	250	7 3	2500		6350	7300
20	WARRIOR BAREFOOT	SKI	FBG	DV	OB		6	1300		3850	4500
--------------------- 1990 BOATS ---------------------											
19	WARRIOR BAREFOOT	SKI	FBG	DV	OB		6	1300		4150	4800
20	FALCON	RNBT	FBG	DV	IB	240	7 5	2500		7650	8800
20	FALCON BAREFOOT	RNBT	FBG	DV	OB		7 2	1500		4200	4850
20	FALCON BR	RNBT	FBG	DV	IB	240	7 5	2500		7650	8800
20	TRUTRAC III	SKI	FBG	DV	IB	240	7 3	2500		7050	8100
--------------------- 1989 BOATS ---------------------											
19	WARRIOR BAREFOOT	SKI	FBG	DV	OB		6	1300		4000	4650
20	FALCON	RNBT	FBG	DV	IB	240	7 5	2500		7300	8350
20	FALCON BR	RNBT	FBG	DV	IB	240	7 5	2500		7300	8350
20	TRUTRAC II	SKI	FBG	DV	IB	240	6 10	2500		6500	7450
--------------------- 1988 BOATS ---------------------											
19	TRUTRAC II	SKI	FBG	DV	IB	250	6 10	2300		5400	6200
20	FALCON	RNBT	FBG	DV	IB	260	6 10	2500		7000	8050
20	WARRIOR BAREFOOT	SKI	FBG	DV	OB		7 2	1500		3950	4550
20	WARRIOR BAREFT COMP	SKI	FBG	DV	OB		6	1300		3500	4100
21	HAWKE	RNBT	FBG	DV	IB	250	7 10	2900		8200	9400
21 6	CONCOURSE	RNBT	FBG	DV	IB	260	7 10	3200		9050	10300
24	DOMINATOR 24	RNBT	FBG	DV	IO	260	8	4000		9150	10400
24	DOMINATOR CAT	RNBT	FBG	DV	OB		8	4000		10000	11400
--------------------- 1987 BOATS ---------------------											
19	TRUTRAC II	SKI	FBG	DV	IB	250	6 10	2300		5150	5900
20	WARRIOR BAREFOOT	SKI	FBG	DV	OB		7 12	1500		3800	4450
20	WARRIOR BAREFT COMP	SKI	FBG	DV	OB		6	1300		3400	3950
21	HAWKE	RNBT	FBG	DV	IB	250	7 10	2900		7800	9000
21 6	CONCOURSE 22	RNBT	FBG	DV	IB	250	7 10	3200		8500	9800

LOA FT IN	NAME AND/ OR MODEL	TOP/ RIG	BOAT TYPE	-HULL- MTL TP	----ENGINE--- TP # HP MFG	BEAM FT IN	WGT LBS	DRAFT FT IN	RETAIL LOW	RETAIL HIGH
					1987 BOATS					
23	DOMINATOR		RNBT	FBG DV	IO 260	8	4000		8200	9450
					1986 BOATS					
16 6	16 SK		RNBT	FBG DV	OB	7	750		2050	2450
16 6	16 SK		RNBT	FBG DV	IO 140-170	7			3000	3500
16 6	16 SK		RNBT	FBG DV	JT 333 BERK	7			4850	5600
19	TRUTRAC		SKI	FBG DV	IB 250 PCM	6 10	2250		4850	5550
20	WARRIOR-BAREFOOT		SKI	FBG DV	OB	6 10	1350		3450	4000
20 8	SPORT 20		RNBT	FBG DV	IO 260 MRCR	7 10	2450		5200	6000
20 8	SPORT 20		RNBT	FBG DV	JT 333 BERK	7 10	2450		7450	8550
20 8	SPORT 20		RNBT	FBG DV	VD 405 CHEV	7 10	2450		7700	8850
23	CHIEFTAIN		RNBT	FBG DV	OB		1125		3100	3650
23	CHIEFTAIN		RNBT	FBG DV	IO 260 MRCR				7450	8550
					1985 BOATS					
16 6	16 SK		RNBT	FBG DV	OB	7	750		2000	2400
16 6	16 SK		RNBT	FBG DV	IO 140-170	7			2850	3350
16 6	16 SK		RNBT	FBG DV	JT 333 BERK	7			4650	5350
19	TRUTRAC		SKI	FBG DV	IB 250 PCM	6 10	2250		4650	5350
20	WARRIOR-BAREFOOT		SKI	FBG DV	OB	6 10	1350		3350	3900
20 8	SPORT 20		RNBT	FBG DV	IO 260 MRCR	7 10	2450		5000	5750
20 8	SPORT 20		RNBT	FBG DV	JT 333 BERK	7 10	2450		7100	8150
20 8	SPORT 20		RNBT	FBG DV	VD 405 CHEV	7 10	2450		7350	8450
23	CHIEFTAIN		RNBT	FBG DV	OB		1125		3050	3550
23	CHIEFTAIN		RNBT	FBG DV	IO 260 MRCR				7130	8200
					1984 BOATS					
17	16 SK		RNBT	FBG DV	OB				2050	2400
19	TRUTRAC		SKI	FBG DV	IB 351 PCM	6 10	2250		4850	5550
20 4	WARRIOR-BAREFOOT		SKI	FBG DV	OB	7 10	1350		3350	3850
20 8	SPORT 20		RNBT	FBG DV	OB	7 10	2450		5250	6050
20 8	SPORT 20		RNBT	FBG DV	IO 260 MRCR	7 10	2450		4850	5550
20 8	SPORT 20		RNBT	FBG DV	JT 320-333	7 10	2450		6800	7800
20 8	SPORT 20		RNBT	FBG DV	VD 360-405	7 10	2450		6650	8100

FINNGULF YACHTS
FIN 10211 INKOO FINLAND   See inside cover to adjust price for area

FINNGULF USA
NOANK CT 06340

For more recent years, see the BUC Used Boat Price Guide, Volume 1

LOA FT IN	NAME AND/ OR MODEL	TOP/ RIG	BOAT TYPE	-HULL- MTL TP	----ENGINE--- TP # HP MFG	BEAM FT IN	WGT LBS	DRAFT FT IN	RETAIL LOW	RETAIL HIGH
					1996 BOATS					
33 5	FINNGULF 335	SLP	SACAC	F/S KL	SD 20 VW	11 1	9020	9 4	81000	89000
35 8	FINNGULF 36	SLP	SACAC	F/S KL	SD 22 VW	11 7	12100	6 2	110500	121500
38 4	FINNGULF 38	SLP	SACAC	F/S KL	SD 28 VW	11 3	13200	6 2	131500	144500
39 3	FINNGULF 391	SLP	SACAC	F/S KL	SD 40 VW	11 7	14320	6 4	147000	161500
43 6	FINNGULF 44	SLP	SACAC	F/S KL	SD 50 VW	12 8	22660	7 2	241000	265000

FINNYACHT USA
BARNSTABLE MA 02630   See inside cover to adjust price for area

LOA FT IN	NAME AND/ OR MODEL	TOP/ RIG	BOAT TYPE	-HULL- MTL TP	----ENGINE--- TP # HP MFG	BEAM FT IN	WGT LBS	DRAFT FT IN	RETAIL LOW	RETAIL HIGH
					1989 BOATS					
24 7	TARGA	FB	FDPH	FBG SV	IO 200D VLVO	9 2	5511	2 7	19000	21100
27 3	H-BOAT	SLP	SA/OD	FBG KL	OB	7 2	3190	4 4	13500	15400
31 8	SIESTA 32	SLP	SA/RC	F/S KL	IB 18D YAN	9 2	7350	5 4	43500	48400
35 3	FINN 351	SLP	SA/RC	F/S KL	IB 28D VLVO	11 5	11464	5 10	73100	80400
38	SIRENA 38	SLP	SA/RC	F/S KL	IB 28D VLVO	10 2	10000	5 9	74200	81500
38 1	FINN 381	SLP	SA/RC	F/S KL	IB 28D VLVO	12 6	14330	6 3	100500	110500
44 3	SIRENA 44	SLP	SA/RC	F/S KL	IB 43D VLVO	12 4	18700	7 2	151000	166000
					1988 BOATS					
24 7	TARGA	FB	FDPH	FBG SV	IO 200D VLVO	9 2	5511	2 7	17600	20000
27 3	H-BOAT	SLP	SA/OD	FBG KL	OB	7 2	3190	4 4	12800	14500
31 8	SIESTA 32	SLP	SA/RC	F/S KL	IB 18D YAN	9 2	7350	5 4	40300	44800
35 3	FINN 351	SLP	SA/RC	F/S KL	IB 28D VLVO	11 5	11464	5 10	68400	75200
38	SIRENA 38	SLP	SA/RC	F/S KL	IB 28D VLVO	10 2	10000	5 9	69400	76300
38 1	FINN 381	SLP	SA/RC	F/S KL	IB 28D VLVO	12 6	14330	6 3	93900	103000
44 3	SIRENA 44	SLP	SA/RC	F/S KL	IB 43D VLVO	12 4	18700	7 2	141000	155000
					1987 BOATS					
24 7	TARGA	FB	FDPH	FBG SV	IO 200D VLVO	9 2	5511	2 7	16700	19000
27 3	H-BOAT	SLP	SA/OD	FBG KL	OB	7 2	3190	4 4	11800	13400
31 8	SIESTA 32	SLP	SA/RC	F/S KL	IB 18D YAN	9 2	7350	5 4	37800	42000
35 3	FINN 351	SLP	SA/RC	F/S KL	IB 28D VLVO	11 5	11464	5 10	64000	70300
38	SIRENA 38	SLP	SA/RC	F/S KL	IB 28D VLVO	10 2	10000	5 9	65000	71400
38 1	FINN 381	SLP	SA/RC	F/S KL	IB 28D VLVO	12 6	14330	6 3	87900	96600
44 3	SIRENA 44	SLP	SA/RC	F/S KL	IB 43D VLVO	12 4	18700	7 2	132000	145000
					1986 BOATS					
27	H-BOAT	SLP	SA/OD	FBG KL		7 2	3197	4 4	9350	10600
31 10	SIESTA	SLP	SA/RC	FBG KL		9 2	9261	5 5	33300	37000
32 4	H-BOAT 323	SLP	SA/RC	FBG KL		8 5	6174	4 9	27600	30700
34 6	H-BOAT 35	SLP	SA/RC	FBG KL		8 6	7718	5	39600	44000
					1985 BOATS					
27 3	H-BOAT	SLP	SA/OD	FBG KL	OB	7 2	3190	4 4	10300	11700
31 8	SIESTA 32	SLP	SA/RC	F/S KL	IB 15D YAN	9 2	7350	5 4	32600	36300
32 6	H-BOAT 323	SLP	SA/RC	F/S KL	IB 8D YAN	8 6	6160	4 9	27800	30900
32 9	ARTINA 33	SLP	SA/RC	FBG KL		10 3	9261	5 5	43500	48300
34 7	H-BOAT 35	SLP	SA/RC	FBG KL	IB 8D YAN	8 7	7700	4 11	36100	40100
35 3	FINN 351	SLP	SA/RC	F/S KL	IB 28D VLVO	11 5	11464	5 10	55900	61400
38	SIRENA 38	SLP	SA/RC	F/S KL	IB 23D VLVO	10 2	10000	5 9	56700	62400
44 3	SIRENA 44	SLP	SA/RC	F/S KL	IB 36D VLVO	12 4	18700	7 2	115500	126500
					1984 BOATS					
27 3	H-BOAT	SLP	SA/OD	FBG KL		7 2	3190	4 4	8250	9450
31 8	SIESTA 32	SLP	SA/RC	FBG KL		9 1	7350	5 4	22300	24800
32 6	H-BOAT 323	SLP	SA/RC	FBG KL	IB 8D YAN	8 6	6160	4 9	26200	29100
34 7	H-BOAT 35	SLP	SA/RC	FBG KL	IB 8D YAN	8 7	7700	4 11	34200	38000
38	SIRENA 38	SLP	SA/RC	F/S KL	SD 22D VLVO	10 2	10000	5 9	53500	58700
44 3	SIRENA 44	SLP	SA/RC	F/S KL	SD D VLVO	12 4	18700	7 2	109000	119500

....For earlier years, see the BUC Used Boat Price Guide, Volume 3

FINYA CUSTOM YACHTS
DIV OF CRUISING YACHTS INT'L   See inside cover to adjust price for area
HOUSTON TX 77077

LOA FT IN	NAME AND/ OR MODEL	TOP/ RIG	BOAT TYPE	-HULL- MTL TP	----ENGINE--- TP # HP MFG	BEAM FT IN	WGT LBS	DRAFT FT IN	RETAIL LOW	RETAIL HIGH
					1992 BOATS					
73 2	FINYA 75	CUT	SA/CR	F/S KL	IB 210D CAT	18 6	85000	8	**	**
					1991 BOATS					
73 2	FINYA 75	CUT	SA/CR	F/S KL	IB 210D CAT	18 6	85000	7 6	**	**
					1990 BOATS					
73 2	FINYA 75	CUT	SA/CR	F/S KL	IB 210D CAT	18 6	85000	7 6	**	**
					1989 BOATS					
73 2	FINYA 75	CUT	SA/CR	FBG KL	IB 210D CAT	18 6	75000	7 6	**	**
					1988 BOATS					
73 2	FINYA 75	CUT	SA/CR	FBG KL	IB 210D CAT	18 6	75000	7 6	**	**

FISCHER YACHTS
MIAMI FL 33168   See inside cover to adjust price for area

LOA FT IN	NAME AND/ OR MODEL	TOP/ RIG	BOAT TYPE	-HULL- MTL TP	----ENGINE--- TP # HP MFG	BEAM FT IN	WGT LBS	DRAFT FT IN	RETAIL LOW	RETAIL HIGH
					1988 BOATS					
56 9	FISCHER 57	HT	MY	AL DV	IB T10CD GM	17 6	66560	5	359500	395000
					1987 BOATS					
56 9	FISCHER 57	HT	MY	AL DV	IB T10CD GM	17 6	66560	5	344000	378000

FISHER CRAFT
BYRON CA 94514   COAST GUARD MFG ID- FSV See inside cover to adjust price for area

LOA FT IN	NAME AND/ OR MODEL	TOP/ RIG	BOAT TYPE	-HULL- MTL TP	----ENGINE--- TP # HP MFG	BEAM FT IN	WGT LBS	DRAFT FT IN	RETAIL LOW	RETAIL HIGH
					1984 BOATS					
28 9	FISHER-CRAFT	HT	HB	FBG SV	IO 138-260	11 10	7500	1 5	**	**
28 9	FISHER-CRAFT	HT	HB	FBG SV	IO 130D VLVO	11 10	7500	1 5	**	**
28 9	FISHER-CRAFT	FB	HB	FBG SV	IO 138-260	11 10	7500	1 5	**	**
28 9	FISHER-CRAFT	FB	HB	FBG SV	IO 130D VLVO	11 10	7500	1 5	**	**

....For earlier years, see the BUC Used Boat Price Guide, Volume 3

FISHER MARINE

DIV OF BRUNSWICK MARINE GROUP
TOPEKA IN 46571 COAST GUARD MFG ID- FMC

See inside cover to adjust price for area

LOA FT	LOA IN	NAME AND/ OR MODEL	TOP/ RIG	BOAT TYPE	HULL MTL	HULL TP	ENGINE TP	ENGINE # HP	ENGINE MFG	BEAM FT	BEAM IN	WGT LBS	DRAFT FT	DRAFT IN	RETAIL LOW	RETAIL HIGH
1996 BOATS																
16		1648	OP	JON	AL	FL	OB			5	7	264			930	1100
16		1650 MV	OP	JON	AL	FL	OB			6	3	327			1200	1450
16		DELUXE 1650 MV	OP	JON	AL	SV	OB			6	3	655			2300	2700
16	4	160 SC	OP	FSH	AL	SV	OB			6		510			2100	2500
16	4	GRIZZLY 16L	OP	UTL	AL	SV	OB			6		410			1550	1850
16	4	GRIZZLY 16S	OP	UTL	AL	SV	OB			6		410			1550	1850
16	4	SV 16 FS	OP	BASS	AL	SV	OB			6	5	825			3400	3950
16	6	HAWK 3V	OP	BASS	AL	SV	OB			6		995			4100	4750
16	6	SV 17 GT	OP	BASS	AL	SV	OB			6	9	1050			4300	5000
17	2	SV 17 FS	OP	BASS	AL	SV	OB			7		1095			4550	5250
17	2	SV 17 SC	OP	BASS	AL	SV	OB			7		1010			4200	4900
17	4	MARSH HAWK 3V	OP	BASS	AL	SV	OB			6	4	1076			4550	5200
18		1860 MV	OP	JON	AL	SV	OB			6	8	417			1300	1550
18	4	SV 18 DC	OP	FSH	AL	SV	OB			7	2	1170			4900	5650
19	6	SV 20 FS	OP	BASS	AL	SV	OB			7	4	1245			5450	6250
1995 BOATS																
16		1648	OP	JON	AL	FL	OB			5	7	264			880	1050
16		1650 MV	OP	JON	AL	FL	OB			6	3	327			1150	1350
16	2	SF 16 L	OP	UTL	AL	SV	OB			5	7	245			680	820
16	2	SF 16 S	OP	UTL	AL	FL	OB			5	7	245			860	1000
16	4	CAMP 16	OP	UTL	AL	FL	OB			5	7				1250	1500
16	4	SV 16 DC	OP	BASS	AL	SV	OB			6	5	825			3250	3750
16	4	SV 16 DC	OP	FSH	AL	SV	OB			6	5	965			3700	4300
16	4	SV 16 SC	OP	BASS	AL	FL	OB			6	5	800			3150	3650
16	4	SV 16 SC	OP	FSH	AL	SV	OB			6	5	933			3600	4200
16	4	SV 1600 SC	OP	BASS	AL	FL	OB			6	5	775			3150	3650
16	4	SV 1600 T	OP	BASS	AL	FL	OB			6	5	775			3000	3450
16	4	SV 1600 T	OP	FSH	AL	SV	OB			6	5	835			3250	3750
16	6	SV 17 GT	OP	BASS	AL	SV	OB			6	9	1050			4100	4750
16	6	SV 17 GT	OP	FSH	AL	DV	OB			6	9	1050			4050	4700
17	2	SV 17 FS	OP	BASS	AL	SV	OB			7		1095			4350	5000
17	2	SV 17 FS	OP	FSH	AL	SV	OB			7		1095			4250	4950
17	2	SV 17 SC	OP	BASS	AL	SV	OB			7		1010			4000	4650
17	2	SV 17 SC	OP	FSH	AL	SV	OB			7		1010			3950	4600
17	4	MARSH HAWK 3V	OP	BASS	AL	SV	OB			6	4	1076			4250	4950
18		1860 MV	OP	JON	AL	SV	OB			6	8	417			1250	1450
18	6	SV 19 GT	OP	BASS	AL	SV	OB			6	9	1117			4600	5300
19	6	SV 19 FS	OP	BASS	AL	SV	OB			7	5	1245			5150	5950
19	6	SV 19 FS	OP	FSH	AL	SV	OB			7	4	1245			5100	5850
1994 BOATS																
16		1648	OP	JON	AL	FL	OB			5	7	264			815	985
16		1650 MV	OP	JON	AL	FL	OB			6	3	327			1100	1300
16		HAWK 2V	OP	BASS	AL	SV	OB			6	4	895			3300	3850
16		HAWK 3V	OP	BASS	AL	SV	OB			6	4	915			3400	3950
16	2	SF 16	OP	UTL	AL	SV	OB			5	7	245			645	780
16	4	SV 16 DC	OP	FSH	AL	SV	OB			6	5	965			3500	4100
16	4	SV 16 SC	OP	FSH	AL	SV	OB			6	5	933			3400	3950
16	4	SV 16 T	OP	FSH	AL	SV	OB			6	5	835			3050	3550
16	6	SV 17 GT	OP	FSH	AL	DV	OB			6	9	1050			3850	4450
17	2	SV 17 FS	OP	FSH	AL	SV	OB			7		1095			4050	4700
17	2	SV 17 SC	OP	FSH	AL	SV	OB			7		1010			3750	4400
17	4	MARSH HAWK 3V	OP	BASS	AL	SV	OB			6	4	1085			4100	4750
18	6	SV 19 GT	OP	BASS	AL	SV	OB			6	9	1117			4400	5050
19	6	SV 19 FS	OP	FSH	AL	SV	OB			7	4	1245			4850	5550
1993 BOATS																
16		TUFFY 1619	OP	JON	AL	FL	OB			5	7	264			775	930
16		TUFFY 1619 LW	OP	JON	AL	FL	OB			5	7	264			855	1000
16		TUFFY 1624 MV	OP	JON	AL	SV	OB			5	9	327			985	1150
16	2	FISHER 16	OP	UTL	AL	SV	OB			5	7	245			760	915
16	2	FISHER 16 DLX C	OP	UTL	AL	SV	OB			5	7	455			1750	2100
16	2	FISHER 16 S/S	OP	UTL	AL	SV	OB			5	7	455			1150	1350
16	3	SV 17 GT	OP	BASS	AL	DV	OB			6	9	920			3250	3800
16	4	HAWK 2V	OP	BASS	AL	SV	OB			6	4	859			3100	3600
16	4	HAWK SS	OP	BASS	AL	SV	OB			6	4	975			3450	4000
16	4	SV 1	OP	FSH	AL	SV	OB			7		800			2800	3250
16	4	SV 2	OP	FSH	AL	SV	OB			7		880			3050	3550
17	4	MARSH HAWK 3V	OP	BASS	AL	SV	OB			6	4	1085			3900	4550
17	4	SV 3 FS	OP	FSH	AL	SV	OB			7	2	1020			3700	4300
17	4	SV 3 SC	OP	FSH	AL	SV	OB			7	2	1020			3550	4150
18	5	SV 19 GT	OP	BASS	AL	SV	OB			6	9	1100			4050	4700
19	4	SV 19 FISH	OP	FSH	AL	SV	OB			7	5	1250			4600	5300
19	6	SV 19 FISH	OP	FSH	AL	SV	OB			7	4	1245			4650	5300
1992 BOATS																
16		TUFFY 1619	OP	JON	AL	FL	OB			5	7	264			735	885
16		TUFFY 1619 LW	OP	JON	AL	FL	OB			5	7	264			795	960
16		TUFFY 1624 MV	OP	JON	AL	SV	OB			5	9	327			940	1100
16	2	FISHER 16	OP	UTL	AL	SV	OB			5	7	245			720	870
16	2	FISHER 16 DLX C	OP	UTL	AL	SV	OB			5	7	455			1650	2000
16	2	FISHER 16 S/S	OP	UTL	AL	SV	OB			5	7	455			1100	1350
16	3	SV 17 GT	OP	BASS	AL	DV	OB			6	9	920			3150	3650
16	4	HAWK 2V	OP	BASS	AL	SV	OB			6	4	859			2950	3400
16	4	HAWK 3V	OP	BASS	AL	SV	OB			6	4	975			3300	3850
16	4	SV 1	OP	FSH	AL	SV	OB			7		800			2700	3100
16	4	SV 2	OP	FSH	AL	SV	OB			7		880			2950	3400
17	4	MARSH HAWK 3V	OP	BASS	AL	SV	OB			6	4	1085			3750	4350
17	4	SV 3 FS	OP	FSH	AL	SV	OB			7	2	1020			3550	4150
17	4	SV 3 SC	OP	FSH	AL	SV	OB			7	2	1020			3350	3900
18	5	SV 19 GT	OP	BASS	AL	DV	OB			6	9	1100			3900	4500
19	4	SV 19 FISH	OP	FSH	AL	SV	OB			7	5	1250			4400	5050
1991 BOATS																
16		1624 MV	OP	JON	AL	SV	OB			5	9	248			685	825
16		HAWK 1V	OP	BASS	AL	SV	OB			5	9	418			1350	1600
16		HAWK 2V	OP	BASS	AL	SV	OB			5	9	500			1600	1900
16		HAWK 3V	OP	BASS	AL	SV	OB			5	9	500			1600	1900
16		HAWK CS	OP	BASS	AL	SV	OB			5	9	475			1550	1800
16		SV 16 GT	OP	BASS	AL	SV	OB			6	2	590			1900	2250
16		TUFFY 1619	OP	JON	AL	FL	OB			5	7	264			695	835
16		TUFFY 1619 LW	OP	JON	AL	FL	OB			5	7	264			760	915
17		MARSH HAWK 3V	OP	BASS	AL	SV	OB			6	1	750			2550	2950
17	10	SV 18 GT	OP	BASS	AL	SV	OB			6	10	845			2900	3350
18	3	SV 18 BT	OP	FSH	AL	DV	OB			7	2	980			3250	3800
18	3	SV 18 CC	OP	CTRCN	AL	DV	OB			7	2	980			3300	3850
18	3	SV 18 FS	OP	RNBT	AL	DV	OB			7	2	980			3400	3950
1989 BOATS																
16		MARSH-HAWK 2-V	OP	BASS	AL	SV	OB			5	9	453			1300	1600
16		MARSH-HAWK 3-V	OP	BASS	AL	SV	OB			5	9	500			1450	1750
16		NETTER 16	OP	JON	AL	FL	OB			5	9	248			630	760
16		NETTER 16 DLX	OP	BASS	AL	SV	OB			5	9	346			1000	1200
16		SV-16GT	OP	BASS	AL	SV	OB			6	2	600			1800	2100
16		SV-16GTC	OP	BASS	AL	SV	OB			6	2	590			1750	2050
16	2	SV-1			AL	SV	OB			6	3	525			1450	1750
16	2	SV-2	OP	FSH	AL	SV	OB			6	4	563			1600	1950
17	10	SV-18GT	OP	BASS	AL	SV	OB			6	10	715			2300	2700
18	2	SV-18FS	OP	RNBT	AL	SV	OB			7	1	850			2750	3200
18	3	SV-18CC	OP	CTRCN	AL	SV	OB			7		760			2450	2800
18	3	SV-18SC			AL	SV	OB			7		825			2550	3000
1988 BOATS																
16		MARSH-HAWK 2-V	OP	BASS	AL	SV	OB			5	9	453			1250	1500
16		MARSH-HAWK 3-V	OP	BASS	AL	SV	OB			5	9	500			1400	1650
16		NETTER 16	OP	JON	AL	FL	OB			5	9	248			605	725
16		NETTER 16 DLX	OP	BASS	AL	SV	OB			5	9	346			970	1150
16		SV-16GT	OP	BASS	AL	SV	OB			6	1	600			1700	2000
16		SV-16GTC	OP	BASS	AL	SV	OB			6	1	590			1650	2000
16	2	SV-2	OP	FSH	AL	SV	OB			6	4	563			1550	1850
16	2	SV-3	OP	FSH	AL	SV	OB			6	4	582			1600	1900
16	5	SV-16CC	OP	CTRCN	AL	SV	OB			6	1	700			2000	2350
16	5	SV-16FS	OP	RNBT	AL	SV	OB			6	1	710			2150	2500
17	10	SV-18GT	OP	BASS	AL	SV	OB			6	10	715			2250	2600
17	10	SV-18GTC	OP	BASS	AL	SV	OB			6	10	705			2200	2550
17	10	SV18GT/TC	OP	BASS	AL	SV	OB			6	10	735			2300	2650
18	2	SV-18FS	OP	RNBT	AL	SV	OB			7	3	850			2650	3050
18	3	SV-18CC	OP	CTRCN	AL	SV	OB			7		760			2350	2700
18	4	NETTER 18-V	OP	FSH	AL		OB			5	9	330			1000	1200
1987 BOATS																
16		MARSH-HAWK 2-V	OP	BASS	AL	SV	OB			5	9	453			1250	1450
16		MARSH-HAWK 3-V	OP	BASS	AL	SV	OB			5	9	500			1350	1600
16		NETTER 16-V	OP	JON	AL	SV	OB			5	9	248			575	690
16		NETTER DLX 16-V	OP	BASS	AL	SV	OB			5	9	346			935	1100
16		SV-16	OP	FSH	AL	SV	OB			5	7	261			655	790
16		SV-16 DLX	OP	FSH	AL	SV	OB			5	7	383			990	1200
16	3	SV-2	OP	FSH	AL	SV	OB			6	4	563			1450	1750
16	3	SV-3	OP	FSH	AL	SV	OB			6	4	582			1550	1850
17	4	TOURNEY-HAWK 17483V	OP	BASS	AL	SV	OB			5	9	522			1500	1750
18		SV-18GT	OP	BASS	AL	SV	OB			6	8	792			2350	2750
18	3	SV-18CC	OP	CTRCN	AL	SV	OB			7		760			2250	2600
18	3	SV-18FX	OP	RNBT	AL	SV	OB			7		840			2500	2950

CONTINUED ON NEXT PAGE

LOA FT	IN	NAME AND/ OR MODEL	TOP/ RIG	BOAT TYPE	-HULL- MTL	TP	ENGINE TP	# HP	MFG	BEAM FT	IN	WGT LBS	DRAFT FT	IN	RETAIL LOW	RETAIL HIGH
		1987 BOATS														
18	3	SV-18SC	OP	FSH	AL	SV	OB			7		720			2050	2450
18	3	SV-18TC	OP	FSH	AL	SV	OB			7		760			2250	2600
		1986 BOATS														
16		MARSH-HAWK 2-V	OP	BASS	AL	SV	OB			5	9	453			1200	1400
16		MARSH-HAWK 3-V	OP	BASS	AL	SV	OB			5	9	500			1300	1550
16		NETTER 16-V	OP	JON	AL	SV	OB			5	9	248			555	665
16		NETTER DLX 16-V	OP	BASS	AL	SV	OB			5	9	346			905	1100
16		SV-16	OP	FSH	AL	SV	OB			5	7	261			635	765
16		SV-16 DLX	OP	FSH	AL	SV	OB			5	7	383			965	1150
16	3	SV-2	OP	FSH	AL	SV	OB			6	4	563			1400	1700
16	3	SV-3	OP	FSH	AL	SV	OB			6	4	582			1450	1750
18	3	SV-18CC	OP	CTRCN	AL	SV	OB			7		750			2050	2450
18	3	SV-18SC	OP	FSH	AL	SV	OB			7		720			1950	2350
18	3	SV-18TC	OP	FSH	AL	SV	OB			7					2900	3400
18	3	SV-18TL	OP	RNBT	AL	SV	OB			7					2750	3200
		1985 BOATS														
16		MARSH-HAWK 2-V	OP	BASS	AL	SV	OB			5	9	460			1150	1400
16		MARSH-HAWK 3-PRO	OP	BASS	AL	SV	OB			5	9	540			1350	1600
16		MARSH-HAWK 3-V	OP	BASS	AL	SV	OB			5	9	550			1400	1650
16		NETTER 16-V	OP	JON	AL	SV	OB			5	9	310			650	785
16		NETTER DLX 16-V	OP	BASS	AL	SV	OB			5	9	370			935	1100
16		SV-16	OP	FSH	AL	SV	OB			5	7	370			900	1050
16		SWEET-16	OP	RNBT	AL	SV	OB			6	7	640			1650	1950
16	3	SV-1	OP	FSH	AL	SV	OB			6	4	485			1200	1400
16	3	SV-2	OP	FSH	AL	SV	OB			6	4	510			1250	1500
16	3	SV-3	OP	FSH	AL	SV	OB			6	4	550			1350	1600
17	4	TOURNEY-HAWK 17483V	OP	BASS	AL	SV	OB			5	9	534			1400	1700
		1984 BOATS														
16		MARSH-HAWK 1-V	OP	BASS	AL	SV	OB			5	9	442			1100	1300
16		MARSH-HAWK 2-V	OP	BASS	AL	SV	OB			5	9	460			1100	1350
16		MARSH-HAWK 2-V PLUS	OP	BASS	AL	SV	OB			5	9	456			1100	1300
16		MARSH-HAWK 3-PRO	OP	BASS	AL	SV	OB			5	9	540			1300	1550
16		MARSH-HAWK 3-V	OP	BASS	AL	SV	OB			5	9	550			1350	1600
16		NETTER 16-V	OP	JON	AL	SV	OB			5	9	310			630	760
16		NETTER DLX 16-V	OP	BASS	AL	SV	OB			5	9	370			910	1100
16		STRIDER DLX 16-V	OP	BASS	AL	SV	OB			5	4	345			845	1000
16		SWEET-16	OP	RNBT	AL	SV	OB			6	7	640			1600	1900
16		WATER-STRIDER 2-V	OP	BASS	AL	SV	OB			5	4	435			1050	1250
16		WATER-STRIDER 3-V	OP	BASS	AL	SV	OB			5	4	510			1250	1500
16	3	1675 UTC	OP	FSH	AL	SV	OB			6	4	389			925	1100
16	3	1675 UTILITY	OP	OPFSH	AL	SV	OB			6	4	340			735	885
16	3	1675 UTILITY PLUS	OP	FSH	AL	SV	OB			6	4	495			1050	1250
16	3	SV-1	OP	FSH	AL	SV	OB			6	4	485			1150	1350
16	3	SV-1C	OP	FSH	AL	SV	OB			6	4	495			1300	1550
16	3	SV-2	OP	FSH	AL	SV	OB			6	4	510			1200	1450
16	3	SV-3	OP	FSH	AL	SV	OB			6	4	550			1300	1550
16	3	SV-4	OP	CTRCN	AL	SV	OB			6	4	535			1300	1550

....For earlier years, see the BUC Used Boat Price Guide, Volume 3

FISHER YACHTS

DIST BY BRITISH YACHTS LTD
TAMPA BAY FL 33570

See inside cover to adjust price for area

LOA FT	IN	NAME AND/ OR MODEL	TOP/ RIG	BOAT TYPE	-HULL- MTL	TP	ENGINE TP	# HP	MFG	BEAM FT	IN	WGT LBS	DRAFT FT	IN	RETAIL LOW	RETAIL HIGH
		1984 BOATS														
25	3	FISHER 25 PH	KTH	SAIL	FBG	KL	IB	23D	VLVO	9	4	10500	3	9	37300	41400
25	3	FISHER POTTER PH	KTH	SAIL	FBG	KL	IB	23D	VLVO	9	4	10500	3	9	31300	34800
30		FISHER 30 PH	KTH	SAIL	FBG	KL	IB	36D	VLVO	9	6	15200	4	3	60300	66200
31	3	FISHER 31 PH	KTH	SAIL	FBG	KL	IB	36D	VLVO	10	4	15750	4	3	63500	69800
34	4	FISHER 34 PH	KTH	SAIL	FBG	KL	IB	60D	VLVO	11	3	25000	4	9	99800	109500
37		FISHER 37 AFT CABIN	KTH	SAIL	FBG	KL	IB	80D	FORD	12		33000	5	3	127000	139500
37		FISHER 37 PH	KTH	SAIL	FBG	KL	IB	80D	FORD	12		32000	5	3	124000	136500
46		FISHER 46 PH	KTH	SAIL	FBG	KL	IB	120D	FORD	15		54000	6	6	194000	213500

FISHIN' SKI-BARGE

KNOXVILLE AR 72845 COAST GUARD MFG ID- SKB See inside cover to adjust price for area

LOA FT	IN	NAME AND/ OR MODEL	TOP/ RIG	BOAT TYPE	-HULL- MTL	TP	ENGINE TP	# HP	MFG	BEAM FT	IN	WGT LBS	DRAFT FT	IN	RETAIL LOW	RETAIL HIGH
		1993 BOATS														
16	9	170 CC	OP	UTL	FBG	DV	OB			7	10	1025			3750	4350
17	2	FLATS FISHER 170	OP	UTL	FBG	SV	OB			6	10	800			2500	2900
17	2	FLATS FISHER 170SBSP	OP	UTL	FBG	SV	OB			6	10	800			3450	4000
17	5	FISHIN SKI 170	OP	UTL	FBG	SV	OB			7	4	785			2300	2700
17	5	FISHIN SKI 170 SS	OP	UTL	FBG	SV	OB			7	8	785			3000	3500
17	5	FISHIN SKI 170 W/LNR	OP	UTL	FBG	SV	OB			7	8	785			3200	3700
17	5	FISHIN SKI SPORT 170	OP	UTL	FBG	SV	OB			7	4	785			2800	3250
17	5	FISHIN SKI SPT DX170	OP	UTL	FBG	SV	OB			7	4	785			3250	3800
18	11	BARRACUDA	OP	UTL	FBG	SV	OB			7		860			3050	3550
18	11	BARRACUDA 190	OP	UTL	FBG	SV	OB			7		860			2500	2900
18	11	BARRACUDA 190 SS	OP	UTL	FBG	SV	OB			7		860			3650	4200
18	11	BARRACUDA FISHERMAN	OP	UTL	FBG	SV	OB			7		860			3300	3850
18	11	BARRACUDA IB JET	OP	UTL	FBG	SV	JT			7		860			**	**
18	11	BARRACUDA SS	OP	UTL	FBG	SV	OB			7		860			3250	3750
18	11	BARRACUDA STRIPPER	OP	UTL	FBG	SV	OB			7		860			3450	4000
19	2	FLATS FISHER	OP	UTL	FBG	SV	OB			7	10	1100			3250	3750
19	2	FLATS FISHER 192	OP	UTL	FBG	SV	OB					1100			3200	3700
19	2	FLATS FISHER 192 SS	OP	UTL	FBG	SV	OB					1100			4600	5250
19	2	FLATS FISHERMAN	OP	UTL	FBG	SV	OB			7	10	1100			4550	5200
19	8	MARLIN	OP	UTL	FBG	SV	OB			7	10	925			3250	3750
19	8	MARLIN DELUXE	OP	UTL	FBG	SV	OB			7	10	925			3700	4300
19	8	MARLIN FISHERMAN	OP	UTL	FBG	SV	OB			7	10	925			3250	3800
19	8	MARLIN IB JT	OP	UTL	FBG	SV	JT			7	10	925			**	**
19	8	MARLIN SS	OP	UTL	FBG	SV	OB			7	10	925			3450	4000
20	6	MARLIN 201	OP	UTL	FBG	SV	OB					925			2750	3200
20	6	MARLIN 201 PLAYTHING	OP	UTL	FBG	SV	OB			8		1300			4750	5500
20	6	MARLIN 201 SS	OP	UTL	FBG	SV	OB					925			3900	4550
21	7	210 PRO V	OP	UTL	FBG	SV	OB			8	6	1400			5100	5850
21	7	210 PRO V FISHIN PKG	OP	UTL	FBG	SV	OB			8	6	1400			5300	6100
		1992 BOATS														
16	9	170 CC	OP	UTL	FBG	DV	OB			7	10	1025			3550	4150
17	2	FLATS FISHER 170	OP	UTL	FBG	SV	OB			6	10	800			2400	2750
17	2	FLATS FISHER 170SBSP	OP	UTL	FBG	SV	OB			6	10	800			3300	3850
17	5	FISHIN SKI 170	OP	UTL	FBG	SV	OB			7	4	785			2250	2600
17	5	FISHIN SKI 170 SS	OP	UTL	FBG	SV	OB			7	8	785			2900	3350
17	5	FISHIN SKI 170 W/LNR	OP	UTL	FBG	SV	OB			7	8	785			3050	3550
17	5	FISHIN SKI SPORT 170	OP	UTL	FBG	SV	OB			7	4	785			2650	3100
17	5	FISHIN SKI SPT DX170	OP	UTL	FBG	SV	OB			7	4	785			3100	3650
18	11	BARRACUDA	OP	UTL	FBG	SV	OB			7		860			2950	3400
18	11	BARRACUDA 190	OP	UTL	FBG	SV	OB			7		860			2400	2800
18	11	BARRACUDA 190 SS	OP	UTL	FBG	SV	OB			7		860			3500	4050
18	11	BARRACUDA FISHERMAN	OP	UTL	FBG	SV	OB			7		860			3150	3700
18	11	BARRACUDA IB JET	OP	UTL	FBG	SV	JT			7		860			**	**
18	11	BARRACUDA SS	OP	UTL	FBG	SV	OB			7		860			3100	3600
18	11	BARRACUDA STRIPPER	OP	UTL	FBG	SV	OB			7		860			3300	3850
19	2	FLATS FISHER	OP	UTL	FBG	SV	OB			7	10	1100			3100	3600
19	2	FLATS FISHER 192	OP	UTL	FBG	SV	OB					1100			3050	3550
19	2	FLATS FISHER 192 SS	OP	UTL	FBG	SV	OB					1100			4400	5050
19	2	FLATS FISHERMAN	OP	UTL	FBG	SV	OB			7	10	1100			4350	5000
19	8	MARLIN	OP	UTL	FBG	SV	OB			7	10	925			3100	3600
19	8	MARLIN DELUXE	OP	UTL	FBG	SV	OB			7	10	925			3550	4100
19	8	MARLIN FISHERMAN	OP	UTL	FBG	SV	OB			7	10	925			3100	3600
19	8	MARLIN INBOARD JT 20	OP	UTL	FBG	SV	OB			7	10	925			3100	3600
19	8	MARLIN SS	OP	UTL	FBG	SV	OB			7	10	925			3300	3850
20	6	MARLIN 201	OP	UTL	FBG	SV	OB					925			2650	3100
20	6	MARLIN 201 PLAYTHING	OP	UTL	FBG	SV	OB			8		1300			4600	5300
20	6	MARLIN 201 SS	OP	UTL	FBG	SV	OB					925			3750	4350
21	7	210 PRO V	OP	UTL	FBG	SV	OB			8	6	1400			4900	5650
21	7	210 PRO V FISHIN PKG	OP	UTL	FBG	SV	OB			8	6	1400			5100	5850
		1991 BOATS														
16	9	170 CC	OP	UTL	FBG	DV	OB			7	10	1025			3450	4000
16	9	LEGACY 170	OP	RNBT	FBG	DV	OB			7	10	1025			3550	4100
17	2	FLATS FISHER 170	OP	UTL	FBG	SV	OB			6	10	800			2300	2700
17	2	FLATS FISHER 170SBSP	OP	UTL	FBG	SV	OB			6	10	800			3200	3700
17	5	FISHIN SKI 170	OP	UTL	FBG	SV	OB			7	4	785			2700	3150
17	5	FISHIN SKI 170 SPSPT	OP	UTL	FBG	SV	OB			7	8	785			2750	3200
17	5	FISHIN SKI 170 W/LNR	OP	UTL	FBG	SV	OB			7	8	785			2950	3450
17	5	FISHIN SKI SPORT 170	OP	UTL	FBG	SV	OB			7	4	785			2550	3000
17	5	FISHIN SKI SPT DX170	OP	UTL	FBG	SV	OB			7	4	785			3000	3500
18	11	BARRACUDA	OP	UTL	FBG	SV	OB			7		860			2850	3300
18	11	BARRACUDA 190	OP	UTL	FBG	SV	OB			7		860			2350	2700
18	11	BARRACUDA 190 SP SPT	OP	UTL	FBG	SV	OB			7		860			3350	3900
18	11	BARRACUDA FISHERMAN	OP	UTL	FBG	SV	OB			7		860			3050	3550
18	11	BARRACUDA IB JET	OP	UTL	FBG	SV	OB			7		860			2850	3300
18	11	BARRACUDA STRIPPER	OP	UTL	FBG	SV	OB			7		860			3150	3700
18	11	BARRACUDA SUPER SPT	OP	UTL	FBG	SV	OB			7		860			3000	3450

226 CONTINUED ON NEXT PAGE 96th ed. - Vol. II

LOA FT	LOA IN	NAME AND/ OR MODEL	TOP/ RIG	BOAT TYPE	-HULL- MTL	-HULL- TP	ENGINE TP	ENGINE # HP	ENGINE MFG	BEAM FT	BEAM IN	WGT LBS	DRAFT FT	DRAFT IN	RETAIL LOW	RETAIL HIGH
		1991 BOATS														
19	2	FLATS FISHER	OP	UTL	FBG	SV	OB			7	10	1100			3000	3450
19	2	FLATS FISHER 192	OP	UTL	FBG	SV	OB					1100			2950	3450
19	2	FLATS FISHER 192SPST	OP	UTL	FBG	SV	OB					1100			4200	4850
19	2	FLATS FISHERMAN	OP	UTL	FBG	SV	OB			7	10	1100			4150	4800
19	8	MARLIN	OP	UTL	FBG	SV	OB			7	10	925			3000	3450
19	8	MARLIN DELUXE	OP	UTL	FBG	SV	OB			7	10	925			3400	3950
19	8	MARLIN FISHERMAN	OP	UTL	FBG	SV	OB			7	10	925			3000	3500
19	8	MARLIN INBOARD JT 20	OP	UTL	FBG	SV	OB			7	10	925			3000	3450
19	8	MARLIN SUPER SPORT	OP	UTL	FBG	SV	OB			7	10	925			3150	3700
20	6	MARLIN 201	OP	UTL	FBG	SV	OB					925			2550	2950
20	6	MARLIN 201 SUP SPORT	OP	UTL	FBG	SV	OB					925			3600	4200
		1990 BOATS														
16	9	170 CC	OP	UTL	FBG	DV	OB			7	10	1025			3300	3850
16	9	LEGACY 170	OP	RNBT	FBG	DV	OB			7	10	1025			3400	3950
17	2	FLATS FISHER 170	OP	UTL	FBG	SV	OB			6	10	800			2250	2600
17	2	FLATS FISHER 170SBSP	OP	UTL	FBG	SV	OB			6	10	800			3100	3600
17	5	FISHIN SKI 170	OP	UTL	FBG	SV	OB			7	4	785			2000	2400
17	5	FISHIN SKI 170 SPSPT	OP	UTL	FBG	SV	OB			7	8	785			2700	3150
17	5	FISHIN SKI 170 W/LNR	OP	UTL	FBG	SV	OB			7	8	785			2850	3350
17	5	FISHIN SKI SPORT 170	OP	UTL	FBG	SV	OB			7	4	785			2500	2900
17	5	FISHING SKI SPORT DL	OP	UTL	FBG	SV	OB			7	4	785			2900	3350
17	5	FISHING SKIP SUPER S	OP	UTL	FBG	SV	OB			7	4	785			3000	3450
18	11	BARRACUDA	OP	UTL	FBG	SV	OB			7		860			2050	2400
18	11	BARRACUDA 190	OP	UTL	FBG	SV	OB			7		860			2250	2600
18	11	BARRACUDA 190 SP SPT	OP	UTL	FBG	SV	OB			7		860			3200	3750
18	11	BARRACUDA FISHERMAN	OP	UTL	FBG	SV	OB			7		860			2950	3400
18	11	BARRACUDA IB JET	OP	UTL	FBG	SV	OB			7		860			2750	3150
18	11	BARRACUDA STRIPPER	OP	UTL	FBG	SV	OB			7		860			3050	3550
18	11	BARRACUDA SUPER SPRT	OP	UTL	FBG	SV	OB			7		860			2850	3350
19	2	FLATS FISHER	OP	UTL	FBG	SV	OB			7	10	1100			2900	3350
19	2	FLATS FISHER 192	OP	UTL	FBG	SV	OB					1100			2850	3300
19	2	FLATS FISHER 192SPST	OP	UTL	FBG	SV	OB					1100			4050	4700
19	2	FLATS FISHERMAN	OP	UTL	FBG	SV	OB			7	10	1100			4000	4650
19	8	MARLIN	OP	UTL	FBG	SV	OB			7	10	925			2300	2700
19	8	MARLIN DELUXE	OP	UTL	FBG	SV	OB			7	10	925			3250	3800
19	8	MARLIN FISHERMAN	OP	UTL	FBG	SV	OB			7	10	925			2900	3350
19	8	MARLIN INBOARD JT20	OP	UTL	FBG	SV	OB			7	10	985			3050	3550
19	8	MARLIN SUPER SPORT	OP	UTL	FBG	SV	OB			7	10	925			3050	3550
20	6	MARLIN 201	OP	UTL	FBG	SV	OB					925			2450	2850
20	6	MARLIN 201 SUP SPORT	OP	UTL	FBG	SV	OB					925			3500	4050
		1989 BOATS														
17	5	FISHIN SKI 170	OP	UTL	FBG	SV	OB			7	4	785			1950	2300
17	5	FISHIN SKI SPORT 170	OP	UTL	FBG	SV	OB			7	4	785			2400	2800
17	5	FSHN SKI SPR SPT 170	OP	UTL	FBG	SV	OB			7	4	785			2900	3350
17	5	FSHN SKI SPT DLX 170	OP	UTL	FBC	SV	OB			7	4	785			2800	3250
18	11	BARRACUDA	OP	UTL	FBG	SV	OB			7		860			1950	2350
18	11	BARRACUDA FISHERMAN	OP	UTL	FBG	SV	OB			7		860			2850	3300
18	11	BARRACUDA IB JET	OP	UTL	FBG	SV	OB			7		860			2650	3050
18	11	BARRACUDA STRIPER	OP	UTL	FBG	SV	OB			7		860			2950	3450
18	11	BARRACUDA SUPER SPRT	OP	UTL	FBG	SV	OB			7		860			2800	3250
19	2	FLATS FISHER	OP	UTL	FBG	SV	OB			7	10	1100			2800	3250
19	2	FLATS FISHERMAN	OP	UTL	FBG	SV	OB			7	10	1100			3850	4500
19	8	MARLIN	OP	UTL	FBG	SV	OB			7	10	925			2250	2600
19	8	MARLIN DELUXE	OP	UTL	FBG	SV	OB			7	10	925			3150	3650
19	8	MARLIN FISHERMAN	OP	UTL	FBG	SV	OB			7	10	925			2800	3250
19	8	MARLIN INBOARD JT 20	OP	UTL	FBG	SV	OB			7	10	985			2950	3450
19	8	MARLIN SUPER SPORT	OP	UTL	FBG	SV	OB			7	10	925			2950	3450
		1988 BOATS														
18	11	BARRACUDA	OP	UTL	FBG	SV	OB			7		860			2100	2450
18	11	BARRACUDA FISHERMAN	OP	UTL	FBG	SV	OB			7		860			2650	3100
18	11	BARRACUDA IB JET	OP	UTL	FBG	SV	OB			7		860			2550	2950
18	11	BARRACUDA III	OP	UTL	FBG	SV	OB			7		860			2450	2800
18	11	BARRACUDA STRIPER	OP	UTL	FBG	SV	OB			7		860			3050	3550
19	2	FLATS FISHER	OP	UTL	FBG	SV	OB			7	10	1100			2750	3200
19	2	FLATS FISHERMAN	OP	UTL	FBG	SV	OB			7	10	1100			3700	4300
19	8	MARLIN	OP	UTL	FBG	SV	OB			7	10	925			2300	2650
19	8	MARLIN FISHERMAN	OP	UTL	FBG	SV	OB			7	10	925			2800	3250
19	8	MARLIN III	OP	UTL	FBG	SV	OB			7	10	925			2550	3000
19	8	MARLIN PARTY BARGE	OP	UTL	FBG	SV	OB			7	10	925			3150	3700
23	7	SPORTS FISHER	OP	UTL	FBG	SV	OB			8		1950			5550	6400
23	7	SPORTS FISHER SS	OP	UTL	FBG	SV	OB			8		1950			6950	7950
		1987 BOATS														
18	11	BARRACUDA	OP	UTL	FBG	SV	OB			7		855			2000	2350
18	11	BARRACUDA FSH	OP	UTL	FBG	SV	OB			7		855			2600	3000
18	11	BARRACUDA II	OP	UTL	FBG	SV	OB			7		855			2350	2750
18	11	BARRACUDA III	OP	UTL	FBG	SV	OB			7		855			2350	2750
18	11	BARRACUDA PLAYTHING	OP	UTL	FBG	SV	OB			7		855			3050	3550
19	2	FLATS FISHER	OP	UTL	FBG	RB	OB			7	10	920			3050	3550
19	2	FLATS FISHER WO/STR	OP	UTL	FBG	RB	OB			7	10	920			2250	2650
19	8	MARLIN	OP	UTL	FBG	RB	OB			7	10	985			2350	2700
19	8	MARLIN FSH	OP	UTL	FBG	RB	OB			7	10	985			2900	3400
19	8	MARLIN II	OP	UTL	FBG	RB	OB			7	10	985			2650	3100
19	8	MARLIN III	OP	UTL	FBG	RB	OB			7	10	985			2700	3100
19	8	MARLIN PLAYTHING	OP	UTL	FBG	RB	OB			7	10	985			3350	3900
23	7	SPORTS FISHER	OP	UTL	FBG	RB	OB			7	10	1700			5250	6050
		1986 BOATS														
18	11	BARRACUDA	OP	UTL	FBG	SV	OB			7		800			2300	2650
18	11	BARRACUDA FSH	OP	UTL	FBG	SV	OB			7		900			2550	2950
18	11	BARRACUDA I	OP	UTL	FBG	SV	OB			7		825			2350	2750
18	11	BARRACUDA I DELUXE	OP	UTL	FBG	SV	OB			7		830			2350	2700
18	11	BARRACUDA III	OP	UTL	FBG	SV	OB			7		825			2350	2700
18	11	BARRACUDA III DLX	OP	UTL	FBG	SV	OB			7		855			2400	2800
18	11	BARRACUDA PLAYTHING	OP	UTL	FBG	SV	OB			7		880			2500	2900
19	8	MARLIN	OP	UTL	FBG	RB	OB			7	10	900			2500	2900
19	8	MARLIN FSH	OP	UTL	FBG	RB	OB			7	10	1000			2750	3200
19	8	MARLIN II	OP	UTL	FBG	RB	OB			7	10	920			2550	2950
19	8	MARLIN II DELUXE	OP	UTL	FBG	RB	OB			7	10	935			2600	3000
19	8	MARLIN III	OP	UTL	FBG	RB	OB			7	10	925			2550	2950
19	8	MARLIN III DLX	OP	UTL	FBG	RB	OB			7	10	950			2600	3050
19	8	MARLIN PLAYTHING	OP	UTL	FBG	RB	OB			7	10	975			2700	3150
23	7	WORKMASTER 24	OP	UTL	FBG	RB	OB			7	10	1700			5150	5900
		1985 BOATS														
18	11	BARRACUDA	OP	UTL	FBG	SV	OB			7		800			2250	2600
18	11	BARRACUDA FSH	OP	UTL	FBG	SV	OB			7		900			2500	2900
18	11	BARRACUDA I	OP	UTL	FBG	SV	OB			7		825			2300	2650
18	11	BARRACUDA I DELUXE	OP	UTL	FBG	SV	OB			7		830			2300	2700
18	11	BARRACUDA III	OP	UTL	FBG	SV	OB			7		825			2300	2700
18	11	BARRACUDA III DLX	OP	UTL	FBG	SV	OB			7		855			2350	2750
18	11	BARRACUDA PLAYTHING	OP	UTL	FBG	SV	OB			7		880			2400	2800
19	8	MARLIN	OP	UTL	FBG	RB	OB			7	10	900			2400	2800
19	8	MARLIN FSH	OP	UTL	FBG	RB	OB			7	10	1000			2700	3150
19	8	MARLIN I	OP	UTL	FBG	RB	OB			7	10	920			2500	2900
19	8	MARLIN I DELUXE	OP	UTL	FBG	RB	OB			7	10	935			2500	2950
19	8	MARLIN III	OP	UTL	FBG	RB	OB			7	10	925			2500	2900
19	8	MARLIN III DLX	OP	UTL	FBG	RB	OB			7	10	950			2550	3000
19	8	MARLIN PLAYTHING	OP	UTL	FBG	RB	OB			7	10	975			2650	3050
23	7	WORKMASTER 24	OP	UTL	FBG	RB	OB			7	10	1700			5000	5750
		1984 BOATS														
18	11	BARRACUDA	OP	UTL	FBG	SV	OB			7		800			2200	2550
18	11	BARRACUDA FSH	OP	UTL	FBG	SV	OB			7		900			2400	2800
18	11	BARRACUDA I	OP	UTL	FBG	SV	OB			7		825			2250	2600
18	11	BARRACUDA I DELUXE	OP	UTL	FBG	SV	OB			7		830			2250	2650
18	11	BARRACUDA III	OP	UTL	FBG	SV	OB			7		825			2250	2650
18	11	BARRACUDA III DLX	OP	UTL	FBG	SV	OB			7		855			2350	2700
18	11	BARRACUDA PLAYTHING	OP	UTL	FBG	SV	OB			7		880			2350	2750
19	8	MARLIN	OP	UTL	FBG	RB	OB			7	10	900			2350	2750
19	8	MARLIN FSH	OP	UTL	FBG	RB	OB			7	10	1000			2650	3050
19	8	MARLIN I	OP	UTL	FBG	RB	OB			7	10	920			2450	2800
19	8	MARLIN I DELUXE	OP	UTL	FBG	RB	OB			7	10	935			2450	2850
19	8	MARLIN III	OP	UTL	FBG	RB	OB			7	10	925			2450	2850
19	8	MARLIN III DLX	OP	UTL	FBG	RB	OB			7	10	950			2500	2900
19	8	MARLIN PLAYTHING	OP	UTL	FBG	RB	OB			7	10	975			2550	3000

....For earlier years, see the BUC Used Boat Price Guide, Volume 3

FJORD PLAST LTD

FJORD PLAST (UK) LTD
HAMPSHIRE ENGLAND

See inside cover to adjust price for area

FJORD MOTOR SAILERS
ST PETERSBURG FL

LOA FT	LOA IN	NAME AND/ OR MODEL	TOP/ RIG	BOAT TYPE	-HULL- MTL	-HULL- TP	ENGINE TP	ENGINE # HP	ENGINE MFG	BEAM FT	BEAM IN	WGT LBS	DRAFT FT	DRAFT IN	RETAIL LOW	RETAIL HIGH
		1985 BOATS														
33	2	FJORD MS	SLP	MS	FBG	KL	IB		D	10	11	15400	4	5	72300	79400

 CONTINUED ON NEXT PAGE

```
     LOA   NAME AND/           TOP/ BOAT  -HULL- ----ENGINE--- BEAM  WGT  DRAFT RETAIL RETAIL
     FT IN OR MODEL            RIG  TYPE  MTL TP TP # HP  MFG  FT IN LBS  FT IN  LOW   HIGH
     ------------------ 1984 BOATS ---------------------------------------------------------
     33  2 FJORD MS            SLP  MS    FBG KL IB    D        4  5 15400 4  5 68000 74700
```

....For earlier years, see the BUC Used Boat Price Guide, Volume 3

FLETCHER INTL SPORTSBTS LTD

STAFFS ENGLAND   See inside cover to adjust price for area

```
     LOA   NAME AND/           TOP/ BOAT  -HULL- ----ENGINE--- BEAM  WGT  DRAFT RETAIL RETAIL
     FT IN OR MODEL            RIG  TYPE  MTL TP TP # HP  MFG  FT IN LBS  FT IN  LOW   HIGH
     ------------------ 1987 BOATS ---------------------------------------------------------
     16  5 ARROWSTREAK         RNBT FBG DV OB           6  6            1900  2250
     16  5 ARROWSTREAK         RNBT FBG DV IB 140  MRCR 6  6 1400       3300  3800
     17  4 ARROWBEAU           RNBT FBG DV OB           7              2850  3350
     17  4 ARROWBEAU           RNBT FBG DV IO 165  MRCR 7              3350  3900
     17  4 MALIBU FISH & SKI   OPFSH FBG DV OB          7              2800  3250
     18  2 FARO                SPTCR FBG DV OB          7              2850  3350
     18  2 VIGO 180CL          SPTCR FBG DV OB          7              2850  3350
     19  8 ARROWSHAFT          RNBT FBG DV OB           7              3900  4550
     21  4 BIMINI              OP   SF  FBG DV OB       7  5            5800  6700
     21  4 BIMINI              OP   SF  FBG DV IB 151  VLVO 7  5         8100  9300
     21  6 SUPERSPORT 21       OP   RNBT FBG DV OB 7  6 1200            4550  5200
     22    ARROWBOLT           RNBT FBG DV IB 260  MRCR 7  6 3200       8650  9950
     25    ZINGARO             SPTCR FBG DV ID 260  MRCR 8  2 5000     14400 16400
     ------------------ 1986 BOATS ---------------------------------------------------------
     16  5 ARROWSTREAK         RNBT FBG DV OB           6  6            1850  2200
     16  5 ARROWSTREAK         RNBT FBG DV IB 140  MRCR 6  6 1400       3150  3650
     17  4 ARROWBEAU           RNBT FBG DV OB           7              2800  3250
     17  4 ARROWBEAU           RNBT FBG DV IO 185  MRCR 7              3250  3750
     17  4 MALIBU FISH & SKI   OPFSH FBG DV OB          7              2700  3150
     18    FARO                SPTCR FBG DV OB          7              2800  3250
     18    VIGO 180CL          SPTCR FBG DV OB          7              2800  3250
     19  9 ARROWSHAFT          RNBT FBG DV OB           7              3800  4450
     20    VIGO 200CL          SPTCR FBG DV OB          7              4350  5000
     21  6 SUPERSPORT 21       OP   RNBT FBG DV IB      7  6 1200       4400  5050
     22    ARROWBOLT           RNBT FBG DV IB 260  MRCR 7  6 3200       8250  9500
     25    ZINGARO             SPTCR FBG DV IB 260  MRCR 8  2 5000     13800 15700
     ------------------ 1985 BOATS ---------------------------------------------------------
     16  5 ARROWSTREAK         RNBT FBG DV OB           6  6            1800  2150
     16  5 ARROWSTREAK         RNBT FBG DV IB 140  MRCR 6  6 1400       3000  3500
     17  4 ARROWBEAU           RNBT FBG DV OB           7              2700  3150
     17  4 ARROWBEAU           RNBT FBG DV IO 185  MRCR 7              3100  3600
     17  4 MALIBU FISH & SKI   OPFSH FBG DV OB          7              2650  3100
     18    FARO                SPTCR FBG DV OB          7              2700  3150
     18    VIGO 180CL          SPTCR FBG DV OB          7              2700  3150
     19  9 ARROWSHAFT          RNBT FBG DV OB           7              3750  4350
     20    VIGO 200CL          SPTCR FBG DV OB          7              4200  4900
     22    ARROWBOLT           RNBT FBG DV IB 260  MRCR 7  6 3200       7850  9050
     25    ZINGARO             SPTCR FBG DV IB 260  MRCR 8  2 5000     13200 15000
```

....For earlier years, see the BUC Used Boat Price Guide, Volume 3

FLORIDA BAY BOAT CO

MIAMI FL 33150   COAST GUARD MFG ID- FBQ See inside cover to adjust price for area

```
     LOA   NAME AND/           TOP/ BOAT  -HULL- ----ENGINE--- BEAM  WGT  DRAFT RETAIL RETAIL
     FT IN OR MODEL            RIG  TYPE  MTL TP TP # HP  MFG  FT IN LBS  FT IN  LOW   HIGH
     ------------------ 1987 BOATS ---------------------------------------------------------
     17    MUD-HEN             CAT  SAIL  FBG CB OB       6  3 650    6  3300  3850
     21    BAY-HEN             CAT  SAIL  F/S CB OB       6  3 900    10 4550  5200
     24    SAND-HEN            KTH  SAIL  FBG CB OB       8    3500   1  6 11300 12800
     ------------------ 1986 BOATS ---------------------------------------------------------
     17    MUD-HEN             CAT  SAIL  FBG CB OB       6  3 650    6  3150  3650
     21    BAY-HEN             CAT  SAIL  F/S CB OB       6  3 900    10 4200  4900
     24    SAND-HEN            KTH  SAIL  FBG CB OB       8    3500   1  6 10600 12000
     ------------------ 1985 BOATS ---------------------------------------------------------
     17    MARSH-HEN           CAT  SAIL  FBG CB OB       6    650    6  3200  3750
     17    MUD-HEN             CAT  SAIL  FBG CB OB       6    650    6  2650  3100
     17  3 PEKING-HEN MONO     CAT  SA/OD FBG CB          6  4         2950  3400
     21    BAY-HEN             CAT  SAIL  F/S CB OB       6    900    10 3500  4100
     21    BAY-HEN             YWL  SAIL  F/S CB OB       6    900    9  3950  4600
     21    BAY-HEN             KTH  SAIL  F/S CB OB       6    900    9  3950  4600
     21    LIGHT-FOOT          CAT  SAIL  F/S CB OB       6    900    10 4450  5150
     ------------------ 1984 BOATS ---------------------------------------------------------
     17    MARSH-HEN           CAT  SAIL  FBG CB OB       6    650    6  3000  3450
     17    MUD-HEN             CAT  SAIL  FBG CB OB       6    600    6  2650  3100
     17    MUD-HEN             CAT  SAIL  FBG CB OB       6    650    6  2550  2950
     17  3 PEKING-HEN-MONO     CAT  SA/OD FBG CB          6  4         2750  3200
     21    BAY-HEN             CAT  SAIL  F/S CB OB       6    900    10 3750  4350
     21    LIGHT-FOOT          CAT  SAIL  F/S CB OB       6    900    10 3750  4350
```

....For earlier years, see the BUC Used Boat Price Guide, Volume 3

FLORIDA BAY COASTER CO

GREEN COVE SPRINGS FL 3 COAST GUARD MFG ID- FBQ See inside cover to adjust price for area

```
     LOA   NAME AND/           TOP/ BOAT  -HULL- ----ENGINE--- BEAM  WGT  DRAFT RETAIL RETAIL
     FT IN OR MODEL            RIG  TYPE  MTL TP TP # HP  MFG  FT IN LBS  FT IN  LOW   HIGH
     ------------------ 1992 BOATS ---------------------------------------------------------
     45     COASTER 45         FB   TRWL  STL DS IB T 90D PERK 17   50T       **    **
     49     TRAWLER 49         FB   TRWL  STL DS IB  210D CUM  16    60000 4  6 **    **
     50     COASTER 50         FB   TRWL  STL DS IB T135D PERK 18   55T       **    **
     55     COASTER 55         FB   TRWL  STL DS IB T135D PERK 18   60T    4  **    **
     55     TRAWLER 55         FB   TRWL  STL DS IB T135D PERK 17    90000 4  6 **    **
     64 11  COASTER 65         FB   TRWL  STL DS IB T210D CUM  20   80T    4  6 **    **
     65     TRAWLER 65         FB   TRWL  STL DS IB  425D ALAS 19   70T    6    **    **
```

FLYE POINT MARINE

BROOKLIN ME 04616   See inside cover to adjust price for area

```
     LOA   NAME AND/           TOP/ BOAT  -HULL- ----ENGINE--- BEAM  WGT  DRAFT RETAIL RETAIL
     FT IN OR MODEL            RIG  TYPE  MTL TP TP # HP  MFG  FT IN LBS  FT IN  LOW   HIGH
     ------------------ 1995 BOATS ---------------------------------------------------------
     25     FLYE POINT 25      HT   BASS  FBG SV VD  170D YAN   9    6250  2  6 49700 54600
     25     FLYE POINT 25      HT   CBNCR FBG SV VD  170D YAN   9    6250  2  6 54500 59900
     28  4  FLYE POINT 28      HT   TRWL  FBG SV IB  240  CHRY 10  3 8500  3  3 57500 63100
     28  4  FLYE POINT 28      HT   TRWL  FBG SV IB      D     10  3 8500  3  3 **    **
     28  4  FLYE POINT 28      FB   TRWL  FBG SV IB 130D-200D 10  3 8500  3  3 70400 84300
     31  9  FLYE POINT 32 CRUISE FB TRWL  FBG SV IB      D     11  6 12500 3  6 **    **
     31  9  FLYE POINT 32 CRUISE FB TRWL  FBG SV IB 210D-300D 11  6 12500 3  6 115000 135000
     31  9  FLYE POINT 32 SPORT FB  TRWL  FBG SV IB      D     11  6 12500 3  6 **    **
     31  9  FLYE POINT 32 SPORT FB  TRWL  FBG SV IB 210D-300D 11  6 12500 3  6 111000 130500
     35 10  FLYE POINT 36      FB   TRWL  FBG SV IB      D     12  6 19000 3 11 **    **
            IB   210D CUM  162000 178000, IB  430D CAT  179000 196500, IB  433D CUM  175000 192500
            IB T210D CUM  175500 193000
     ------------------ 1994 BOATS ---------------------------------------------------------
     39  4  FLYE POINT 39      FB   TRWL  FBG SV IB      D     14  4 24000 4  3 **    **
     25     FLYE POINT 25      HT   BASS  FBG SV VD  170D YAN   9    6250  2  6 47500 52200
     25     FLYE POINT 25      HT   CBNCR FBG SV VD  170D YAN   9    6250  2  6 51800 56900
     28  4  FLYE POINT 28      HT   TRWL  FBG SV IB  240  CHRY 10  3 8500  3  3 54400 59800
     28  4  FLYE POINT 28      HT   TRWL  FBG SV IB      D     10  3 8500  3  3 **    **
     28  4  FLYE POINT 28      FB   TRWL  FBG SV IB 130D-200D 10  3 8500  3  3 67000 80200
     31  9  FLYE POINT 32 CRUISE FB TRWL  FBG SV IB      D     11  6 12500 3  6 **    **
     31  9  FLYE POINT 32 CRUISE FB TRWL  FBG SV IB 210D-300D 11  6 12500 3  6 109500 128500
     31  9  FLYE POINT 32 SPORT FB  TRWL  FBG SV IB      D     11  6 12500 3  6 **    **
     31  9  FLYE POINT 32 SPORT FB  TRWL  FBG SV IB 210D-300D 11  6 12500 3  6 105500 124000
     35 10  FLYE POINT 36      FB   TRWL  FBG SV IB      D     12  6 19000 3 11 **    **
            IB   210D CUM  154000 169500, IB  430D CAT  170000 187000, IB  433D CUM  166500 183000
            IB T210D CUM  167000 183500
     ------------------ 1993 BOATS ---------------------------------------------------------
     39  4  FLYE POINT 39      FB   TRWL  FBG SV IB      D     14  4 24000 4  3 **    **
     25     FLYE POINT 25      HT   BASS  FBG SV VD  170D YAN   9    6250  2  6 44800 49700
     25     FLYE POINT 25      HT   CBNCR FBG SV VD  170D YAN   9    6250  2  6 49400 54200
     28  4  FLYE POINT 28      HT   TRWL  FBG SV IB  240  CHRY 10  3 8500  3  3 51600 56700
     28  4  FLYE POINT 28      HT   TRWL  FBG SV IB      D     10  3 8500  3  3 **    **
     28  4  FLYE POINT 28      FB   TRWL  FBG SV IB 130D-200D 10  3 8500  3  3 63800 76400
     31  9  FLYE POINT 32 CRUISE FB TRWL  FBG SV IB      D     11  6 12500 3  6 **    **
     31  9  FLYE POINT 32 CRUISE FB TRWL  FBG SV IB 210D-300D 11  6 12500 3  6 104500 122500
     31  9  FLYE POINT 32 SPORT FB  TRWL  FBG SV IB      D     11  6 12500 3  6 **    **
     31  9  FLYE POINT 32 SPORT FB  TRWL  FBG SV IB 210D-300D 11  6 12500 3  6 100500 118000
     35 10  FLYE POINT 36      FB   TRWL  FBG SV IB      D     12  6 19000 3 11 **    **
            IB   210D CUM  147000 161500, IB  350D VLVO 153500 168500, IB  375D CAT  158000 173500
            IB T210D CUM  159500 175000
     ------------------ 1992 BOATS ---------------------------------------------------------
     39  4  FLYE POINT 39      FB   TRWL  FBG SV IB      D     14  4 24000 4  3 **    **
     25     FLYE POINT 25      HT   BASS  FBG SV VD  170D      9    6250  2  6 42500 47200
     25     FLYE POINT 25      HT   CBNCR FBG SV VD  170D      9    6250  2  6 47100 51800
     28  4  FLYE POINT 28      HT   TRWL  FBG SV IB  240  CHRY 10  3 8500  3  3 48900 53800
     28  4  FLYE POINT 28      HT   TRWL  FBG SV IB      D     10  3 8500  3  3 **    **
```

LOA FT IN	NAME AND/ OR MODEL	TOP/ RIG	BOAT TYPE	-HULL- MTL TP TP	----ENGINE--- # HP MFG	BEAM FT IN	WGT LBS	DRAFT FT IN	RETAIL LOW	RETAIL HIGH
			----------- 1992 BOATS -----------						
28 4	FLYE POINT 28	HT	TRWL	FBG SV IB	130D-200D	10	8500	3 3	60800	72900
31 9	FLYE POINT 32 CRUISE	FB	TRWL	FBG SV IB	D	11 6	12500	3 6	**	**
31 9	FLYE POINT 32 CRUISE	FB	TRWL	FBG SV IB	210D-300D	11 6	12500	3 6	99500	116500
31 9	FLYE POINT 32 SPORT	FB	TRWL	FBG SV IB	D	11 6	12500	3 6	**	**
31 9	FLYE POINT 32 SPORT	FB	TRWL	FBG SV IB	210D-300D	11 6	12500	3 6	96000	112500
35 10	FLYE POINT 36	FB	TRWL	FBG SV IB		12 6	19000	3 11	**	**
	IB 210D CUM 140000 154000, IB 350D VLVO 146000 160500, IB 375D CAT 150500 165500									
	IB T210D CUM 152000 167000									
			----------- 1989 BOATS -----------						
25	BHM 25	HT	CR	FBG DS IB		9		2 6	**	**
25	BHM 25 LOBSTER	HT	FSH	FBG DS IB		9		2 6	**	**
28	BHM 28	HT	CR	FBG DS IB		10 6		3	**	**
28	BHM 28 LOBSTER	HT	FSH	FBG DS IB		10 6		3	**	**
31 9	BHM 31	HT	CR	FBG DS IB		11 6		3 6	**	**
31 9	BHM 31 LOBSTER	HT	FSH	FBG DS IB		11 6		3 6	**	**
35 10	BHM 36	HT	CR	FBG DS IB		12 8	15000	3 11	**	**
35 10	BHM 36 LOBSTER	HT	FSH	FBG DS IB		12 8	15000	3 11	**	**
39 4	BHM 39	HT	FSH	FBG DS IB		14 4		4 9	**	**
			----------- 1988 BOATS -----------						
25	BHM 25	HT	CR	FBG DS IB		9		2 6	**	**
25	BHM 25 LOBSTER	HT	FSH	FBG DS IB		9		2 6	**	**
28	BHM 28	HT	CR	FBG DS IB		10 6		3	**	**
28	BHM 28 LOBSTER	HT	FSH	FBG DS IB		10 6		3	**	**
31 9	BHM 31	HT	CR	FBG DS IB		11 6		3 6	**	**
31 9	BHM 31 LOBSTER	HT	FSH	FBG DS IB		11 6		3 6	**	**
39 4	BHM 39	HT	FSH	FBG DS IB		14 4		4 9	**	**
			----------- 1987 BOATS -----------						
25	BHM 25	HT	CR	FBG DS IB		9		2 6	**	**
25	BHM 25 LOBSTER	HT	FSH	FBG DS IB		9		2 6	**	**
28	BHM 28	HT	CR	FBG DS IB		10 6		3	**	**
28	BHM 28 LOBSTER	HT	CR	FBG DS IB		10 6		3	**	**
31 9	BHM 31	HT	CR	FBG DS IB		11 6		3 6	**	**
31 9	BHM 31 LOBSTER	HT	FSH	FBG DS IB		11 6		3 6	**	**
39 4	BHM 39	HT	FSH	FBG DS IB		14 4		4 9	**	**
			----------- 1986 BOATS -----------						
25	BHM 25	HT	TRWL	F/W DS IB		9		2 6	**	**
25	BHM 25 LOBSTER	HT	FSH	FBG SV IB		9		2 6	**	**
28	BHM 28	HT	TRWL	F/W DS IB		10 6		3	**	**
28	BHM 28 LOBSTER	HT	PH	FBG SV IB		10 6		3	**	**
31 9	BHM 31	HT	TRWL	F/W DS IB		11 6		3 6	**	**
31 9	BHM 31 LOBSTER	HT	PH	FBG SV IB		11 6		3 6	**	**
39 4	BHM 39	HT	TRWL	F/W DS IB		14 4		4 9	**	**
			----------- 1985 BOATS -----------						
25	BHM 25	HT	TRWL	F/W DS IB		9		2 6	**	**
25	BHM 25 LOBSTER	HT	FSH	FBG SV IB		9		2 6	**	**
28	BHM 28	HT	TRWL	F/W DS IB		10 3		3	**	**
28	BHM 28 LOBSTER	HT	PH	FBG SV IB		10 3		3	**	**
31 9	BHM 31	HT	TRWL	F/W DS IB		11 6		3 6	**	**
31 9	BHM 31 LOBSTER	HT	PH	FBG SV IB		11 6		3 6	**	**
39 4	BHM 39	HT	TRWL	F/W DS IB		14 4		4 9	**	**

FLYING DUTCHMAN INTERNATL LTD
BELLEVUE WA 98004   See inside cover to adjust price for area

LOA FT IN	NAME AND/ OR MODEL	TOP/ RIG	BOAT TYPE	-HULL- MTL TP TP	----ENGINE--- # HP MFG	BEAM FT IN	WGT LBS	DRAFT FT IN	RETAIL LOW	RETAIL HIGH
			----------- 1989 BOATS -----------						
32	SUNDOWNER 32	PH		FBG SV IB	135D PERK	12	14600	3 8	96900	106500
			----------- 1988 BOATS -----------						
32	SUNDOWNER 32	PH		FBG SV IB	135D PERK	12	14600	3 8	92800	102000
			----------- 1987 BOATS -----------						
29 9	BABA 30	CUT		SA/CR FBG KL IB	27D YAN	10 3	11500	4 9	54500	59900
32	SUNDOWNER 32	TRWL		FBG SV IB	135D PERK	12	14600	3 8	92600	102000
34 11	BABA 35	CUT		SA/CR FBG KL IB	44D YAN	11 2	20000	5 6	91000	100000
34 11	BABA 35 PILOTHOUSE	CUT		SA/CR FBG KL IB	44D YAN	11 2	20000	5 6	93700	103000
38	FD380 SPORT SEDAN		SDNSF	FBG SV IB	T210D CUM	12 10	20000	3 10	134500	148000
38	FD380 SPORT SUNDECK	SF		FBG SV IB	T210D CUM	12 10	20000	3 10	134500	148000
			----------- 1985 BOATS -----------						
29 6	SUNDOWNER 30 TUG	UTL		FBG IB	100	11			39400	43800
29 9	BABA 30	CUT		SA/CR FBG KL SD	27D YAN	10 3	12500	4 9	52700	57900
34 11	BABA 35	CUT		SA/CR FBG KL VD	32D UNIV	11 2	20000	5 6	81500	89600
36	SUNDOWNER 36 TUG	UTL		FBG IB		12			**	**
			----------- 1984 BOATS -----------						
29 9	BABA 30	CUT		SA/CR FBG KL SD	23D YAN	10 3	12500	4 9	49500	54400
34 11	BABA 35	CUT		SA/CR FBG KL SD	33D YAN	11 2	20000	5 6	74400	81700
34 11	BABA 35 PH	CUT		SA/CR FBG KL SD	33D YAN	11 2	20000	5 6	79100	86900

FLYING SCOT INC
DEER PARK MD 21550   COAST GUARD MFG ID- GDB See inside cover to adjust price for area
                      FORMERLY GORDON DOUGLASS BOAT CO INC

For more recent years, see the BUC Used Boat Price Guide, Volume 1

LOA FT IN	NAME AND/ OR MODEL	TOP/ RIG	BOAT TYPE	-HULL- MTL TP TP	----ENGINE--- # HP MFG	BEAM FT IN	WGT LBS	DRAFT FT IN	RETAIL LOW	RETAIL HIGH
			----------- 1996 BOATS -----------						
19	FLYING SCOT	SLP	SAROD	F/S CB		6 9	850	4	7850	9050
			----------- 1995 BOATS -----------						
19	FLYING SCOT	SLP	SAROD	F/S CB		6 9	850	4	7350	8450
			----------- 1994 BOATS -----------						
19	FLYING SCOT	SLP	SAROD	F/S CB		6 9	850	4	6900	7950
			----------- 1993 BOATS -----------						
19	FLYING SCOT	SLP	SAROD	F/S CB		6 9	850	4	6500	7500
			----------- 1992 BOATS -----------						
19	FLYING SCOT	SLP	SA/OD	F/S CB		6 9	850	4	6150	7050
			----------- 1991 BOATS -----------						
19	FLYING SCOT	SLP	SA/OD	F/S CB		6 9	850	8	5750	6600
			----------- 1990 BOATS -----------						
19	FLYING SCOT	SLP	SA/OD	F/S CB		6 9	850	8	5400	6250
			----------- 1989 BOATS -----------						
19	FLYING-SCOT	SLP	SA/OD	F/S CB		6 9	850	8	5100	5850
			----------- 1988 BOATS -----------						
19	FLYING-SCOT	SLP	SA/OD	F/S CB		6 9	850	8	4800	5500
			----------- 1987 BOATS -----------						
19	FLYING-SCOT	SLP	SA/OD	F/S CB		6 9	850	8	4500	5200
			----------- 1986 BOATS -----------						
19	FLYING-SCOT	SLP	SA/OD	F/S CB		6 9	850	8	4200	4850
			----------- 1985 BOATS -----------						
19	FLYING-SCOT	SLP	SA/OD	F/S CB		6 9	850	8	3900	4550
			----------- 1984 BOATS -----------						
19	FLYING-SCOT	SLP	SA/OD	F/S CB		6 9	850	8	3700	4300

....For earlier years, see the BUC Used Boat Price Guide, Volume 3

FORCE MARINE INC
HILO HI 96720   See inside cover to adjust price for area

LOA FT IN	NAME AND/ OR MODEL	TOP/ RIG	BOAT TYPE	-HULL- MTL TP TP	----ENGINE--- # HP MFG	BEAM FT IN	WGT LBS	DRAFT FT IN	RETAIL LOW	RETAIL HIGH
			----------- 1994 BOATS -----------						
18	FORCE 18		OPFSH	F/S SV OB		7 11	2000	1	7200	8250
20	FORCE CAT 20	ST	FSH	F/S CT OB		8	1800	1 10	9150	10400
25	FORCE 25 FB	FB	FSH	FBG SV IO	200D VLVO	9	3700	1 8	26600	29500
25	FORCE 25 FB	FB	FSH	FBG SV IO	T140 VLVO	9	3700	1 8	21200	23500
25	FORCE 25 HARD TOP	HT	FSH	FBG SV IO	200D VLVO	9	3500	1 8	25800	28600
25	FORCE 25 HARD TOP	HT	FSH	FBG SV IO	T140 VLVO	9	3500	1 8	20600	22900
25	FORCE 25 SPT BRIDGE		FSH	FBG SV IO	200D VLVO	9	3500	1 8	25800	28600
25	FORCE 25 SPT BRIDGE		FSH	FBG SV IO	T140 VLVO	9	3500	1 8	20600	22900
27	FORCE 27 COMMERCIAL		FSH	FBG SV OB		10	6500	1 10	27300	30300
27	FORCE 27 COMMERCIAL		FSH	FBG SV IO	200D VLVO	10	6500	1 10	41000	45500
27	FORCE 27 COMMERCIAL		FSH	FBG SV IO	T130D VLVO	10	6500	1 10	46300	50900
30	FORCE 30 COMMERCIAL		FSH	FBG SV IO	T200D VLVO	10	7000	2	53600	58900
30	FORCE 30 FB	FB	FSH	FBG SV IB	300D CUM	10	8000	2	50200	55200
30	FORCE 30 FB	FB	FSH	FBG SV IB	T200D CUM	10	8000	2	56900	62500
30	FORCE 30 FB	FB	FSH	FBG SV IB	T210D CUM	10	8000	2	55500	61000
48	FORCE CAT 48		FSH	F/S CT IB	T300D CUM	18	12000	2 6	102500	112500
			----------- 1993 BOATS -----------						
18	FORCE 18		OPFSH	F/S SV OB		7 11	2000	1	6850	7900
20	FORCE CAT 20	ST	FSH	F/S CT OB		8	1800	1 10	8650	9950
22 8	FORCE 22 COMMERCIAL		FSH	FBG SV IO	D	8 10	3300	1 7	15500	17600
22 8	FORCE 22 COMMERCIAL		FSH	FBG SV IO	T D	8 10	3300	1 7	**	**
22 8	FORCE 22 FB	FB	FSH	FBG SV OB		8 10	3200	1 6	15200	17300
22 8	FORCE 22 FB	FB	FSH	FBG SV IO	D	8 10	3200	1 6	**	**
22 8	FORCE 22 FB	FB	FSH	FBG SV IO	T D	8 10	3200	1 6	**	**
22 8	FORCE 22 RECREATIONL		OPFSH	FBG SV OB		8 10	2900	1 5	14200	16600
22 8	FORCE 22 RECREATIONL		OPFSH	FBG SV IO	D	8 10	2900	1 5	**	**
22 8	FORCE 22 RECREATIONL		OPFSH	FBG SV IO	T D	8 10	2900	1 5	**	**
22 8	FORCE 22 SPORTBRIDGE		OPFSH	FBG SV OB		8 10	3000	1 6	14600	16600
22 8	FORCE 22 SPORTBRIDGE		OPFSH	FBG SV IO	D	8 10	3000	1 6	**	**
22 8	FORCE 22 SPORTBRIDGE		OPFSH	FBG SV IO	T D	8 10	3000	1 6	**	**

FORCE MARINE INC   -CONTINUED   See inside cover to adjust price for area

```
LOA   NAME AND/           TOP/ BOAT  -HULL- ----ENGINE--- BEAM  WGT  DRAFT RETAIL RETAIL
FT IN OR MODEL            RIG  TYPE  MTL TP  TP # HP MFG   FT IN LBS  FT IN LOW    HIGH
---------------------- 1993 BOATS -------------------------------------------------------
25    FORCE 25 FB         FB   FSH   FBG SV IO      D VLVO 9    3700  1 8   **     **
25    FORCE 25 FB         FB   FSH   FBG SV IO T      VLVO 9    3700  1 8   **     **
25    FORCE 25 HARD TOP   HT   FSH   FBG SV IO      D VLVO 9    3500  1 8   **     **
25    FORCE 25 HARD TOP   HT   FSH   FBG SV IO T      VLVO 9    3500  1 8   **     **
25    FORCE 25 SPT BRIDGE      FSH   FBG SV IO      D VLVO 9    3500  1 8   **     **
25    FORCE 25 SPT BRIDGE      FSH   FBG SV IO T      VLVO 9    3500  1 8   **     **
27    FORCE 27 COMMERCIAL      FSH   FBG SV OB            10    6500  1 10  26100  29000
27    FORCE 27 COMMERCIAL      FSH   FBG SV IO      D VLVO 10   6500  1 10  **     **
27    FORCE 27 COMMERCIAL      FSH   FBG SV IO T    D VLVO 10   6500  1 10  **     **
30    FORCE 30 COMMERCIAL      FSH   FBG SV IO      D VLVO 10   7000  2     **     **
30    FORCE 30 COMMERCIAL      FSH   FBG SV IO T    D VLVO 10   7000  2     **     **

30    FORCE 30 FB         FB   FSH   FBG SV IO      D VLVO 10   8000  2     **     **
      IB  D CUM  **  **, IO T  D VLVO  **  **, IB T  D CUM  **  **

48    FORCE-CAT-48        FB   FSH   F/S CT IB T    D CUM  18   12000 2 6   **     **
---------------------- 1992 BOATS -------------------------------------------------------
18    FORCE 18            OPFSH F/S  SV OB           7 11  2000  1     6600   7550
20    FORCE CAT 20        ST   FSH   F/S CT OB       8     1800    10  8300   9550
22  8 FORCE 22 COMMERCIAL      FSH   FBG SV IO       8 10  3300  1 7   14900  16900
22  8 FORCE 22 COMMERCIAL      FSH   FBG SV IO    D  8 10  3300  1 7   **     **
22  8 FORCE 22 COMMERCIAL      FSH   FBG SV IO T  D  8 10  3300  1 7   **     **
22  8 FORCE 22 FB         FB   FSH   FBG SV OB       8 10  3200  1 6   14600  16600
22  8 FORCE 22 FB         FR   FSH   FBG SV IO       8 10  3200  1 6   **     **
22  8 FORCE 22 FB         FB   FSH   FBG SV IO T  D  8 10  3200  1 6   **     **
22  8 FORCE 22 RECREATIONL OPFSH FBG SV OB          8 10  2900  1 5   13700  15900
22  8 FORCE 22 RECREATIONL OPFSH FBG SV IO       D  8 10  2900  1 5   **     **
22  8 FORCE 22 RECREATIONL OPFSH FBG SV IO T        8 10  2900  1 5   **     **
22  8 FORCE 22 SPORTBRIDGE OPFSH FBG SV OB          8 10  3000  1 6   14000  15900

22  8 FORCE 22 SPORTBRIDGE OPFSH FBG SV IO       D  8 10  3000  1 6   **     **
22  8 FORCE 22 SPORTBRIDGE OPFSH FBG SV IO T     D  8 10  3000  1 6   **     **
25    FORCE 25 FB         FB   FSH   FBG SV IO      D VLVO 9    3700  1 8   **     **
25    FORCE 25 FB         FB   FSH   FBG SV IO T      VLVO 9    3700  1 8   **     **
25    FORCE 25 HARD TOP   HT   FSH   FBG SV IO      D VLVO 9    3500  1 8   **     **
25    FORCE 25 HARD TOP   HT   FSH   FBG SV IO T      VLVO 9    3500  1 8   **     **
25    FORCE 25 SPT BRIDGE      FSH   FBG SV IO      D VLVO 9    3500  1 8   **     **
25    FORCE 25 SPT BRIDGE      FSH   FBG SV IO T      VLVO 9    3500  1 8   **     **
27    FORCE 27 COMMERCIAL      FSH   FBG SV OB            10    6500  1 10  25100  27900
27    FORCE 27 COMMERCIAL      FSH   FBG SV IO      D VLVO 10   6500  1 10  **     **
27    FORCE 27 COMMERCIAL      FSH   FBG SV IO T    D VLVO 10   6500  1 10  **     **

30    FORCE 30 COMMERCIAL      FSH   FBG SV IO      D VLVO 10   7000  2     **     **
30    FORCE 30 COMMERCIAL      FSH   FBG SV IO T    D VLVO 10   7000  2     **     **
30    FORCE 30 FB         FB   FSH   FBG SV IO      D VLVO 10   8000  2     **     **
      IB  D CUM  **  **, IO T  D VLVO  **  **, IB T  D CUM  **  **

48    FORCE-CAT-48        FB   FSH   F/S CT IB T    D CUM  18   12000 2 6   **     **
---------------------- 1991 BOATS -------------------------------------------------------
18    FORCE 18            OPFSH F/S  SV OB           7 11  2000  1     6300   7250
20    FORCE CAT 20        ST   FSH   F/S CT OB       8     1800    10  8000   9200
22  8 FORCE 22 COMMERCIAL      FSH   FBG SV IO       8 10  3300  1 7   14300  16300
22  8 FORCE 22 COMMERCIAL      FSH   FBG SV IO    D  8 10  3300  1 7   **     **
22  8 FORCE 22 COMMERCIAL      FSH   FBG SV IO T  D  8 10  3300  1 7   **     **
22  8 FORCE 22 FLYING BRG      FSH   FBG SV OB       8 10  3200  1 6   14100  16000
22  8 FORCE 22 FLYING BRG      FSH   FBG SV IO       8 10  3200  1 6   **     **
22  8 FORCE 22 FLYING BRG      FSH   FBG SV IO    D  8 10  3200  1 6   **     **
22  8 FORCE 22 RECREATIONL OPFSH FBG SV OB          8 10  2900  1 5   13200  15300
22  8 FORCE 22 RECREATIONL OPFSH FBG SV IO          8 10  2900  1 5   **     **
22  8 FORCE 22 RECREATIONL OPFSH FBG SV IO T        8 10  2900  1 5   **     **
22  8 FORCE 22 SPORT BRG   OPFSH FBG SV OB          8 10  3000  1 6   13500  15300

22  8 FORCE 22 SPORT BRG   OPFSH FBG SV IO          8 10  3000  1 6   **     **
22  8 FORCE 22 SPORT BRG   OPFSH FBG SV IO T        8 10  3000  1 6   **     **
27    FORCE 27 COMMERCIAL      FSH   FBG SV OB            10    6500  1 10  24100  26800
27    FORCE 27 COMMERCIAL      FSH   FBG SV IO      D VLVO 10   6500  1 10  **     **
27    FORCE 27 COMMERCIAL      FSH   FBG SV IO T    D VLVO 10   6500  1 10  **     **
30    FORCE 30 COMMERCIAL      FSH   FBG SV IO      D VLVO 10   7000  2     **     **
30    FORCE 30 COMMERCIAL      FSH   FBG SV IO T    D VLVO 10   7000  2     **     **
30    FORCE 30 FLYING BRG      FSH   FBG SV IO      D VLVO 10   8000  2     **     **
      IB  D CUM  **  **, IO T  D VLVO  **  **, IB T  D CUM  **  **

48    FORCE-CAT-48        FB   FSH   F/S CT IB T    D CUM  18   12000 2 6   **     **
---------------------- 1990 BOATS -------------------------------------------------------
18    FORCE 18            OPFSH F/S  SV OB           7 11  2000  1     6050   6950
20    FORCE-CAT-20        ST   FSH   F/S CT OB       8     1800    10  7700   8850
22  8 FORCE 22 COMMERCIAL      FSH   FBG SV IO       8 10  3300  1 7   13800  15700
22  8 FORCE 22 COMMERCIAL      FSH   FBG SV IO       8 10  3300  1 7   **     **
22  8 FORCE 22 COMMERCIAL      FSH   FBG SV IO T  D  8 10  3300  1 7   **     **
22  8 FORCE 22 FLYING BRG      FSH   FBG SV OB       8 10  3200  1 6   13600  15400
22  8 FORCE 22 FLYING BRG      FSH   FBG SV IO       8 10  3200  1 6   **     **
22  8 FORCE 22 FLYING BRG      FSH   FBG SV IO T  D  8 10  3200  1 6   **     **
22  8 FORCE 22 RECREATIONL OPFSH FBG SV OB          8 10  2900  1 5   12700  14800
22  8 FORCE 22 RECREATIONL OPFSH FBG SV IO          8 10  2900  1 5   **     **
22  8 FORCE 22 RECREATIONL OPFSH FBG SV IO T        8 10  2900  1 5   **     **
22  8 FORCE 22 SPORT BRG   OPFSH FBG SV OB          8 10  3000  1 6   13000  14800

22  8 FORCE 22 SPORT BRG   OPFSH FBG SV IO          8 10  3000  1 6   **     **
22  8 FORCE 22 SPORT BRG   OPFSH FBG SV IO T        8 10  3000  1 6   **     **
27    FORCE 22 COMMERCIAL      FSH   FBG SV OB            10    6500  1 10  23300  25900
27    FORCE 27 COMMERCIAL      FSH   FBG SV IO      D VLVO 10   6500  1 10  **     **
27    FORCE 27 COMMERCIAL      FSH   FBG SV IO T    D VLVO 10   6500  1 10  **     **
30    FORCE 30 COMMERCIAL      FSH   FBG SV IO      D VLVO 10   7000  2     **     **
30    FORCE 30 COMMERCIAL      FSH   FBG SV IO T    D VLVO 10   7000  2     **     **
30    FORCE 30 FLYING BRG      FSH   FBG SV IO      D VLVO 10   8000  2     **     **
      IB  D CUM  **  **, IO T  D VLVO  **  **, IB T  D CUM  **  **

48    FORCE-CAT-48        FB   FSH   F/S CT IB T    D CUM  18   12000 2 6   **     **
---------------------- 1989 BOATS -------------------------------------------------------
18    FORCE 18            OPFSH F/S  SV OB           7 11              5850   6700
22  8 FORCE 22 COMMERCIAL      FSH   FBG SV IO       8 10  3300  1 7   13400  15200
22  8 FORCE 22 COMMERCIAL      FSH   FBG SV IO T  D  8 10  3300  1 7   **     **
22  8 FORCE 22 FLYING BRG      FSH   FBG SV IO       8 10  3200  1 6   13100  14900
22  8 FORCE 22 FLYING BRG      FSH   FBG SV IO T  D  8 10  3200  1 6   **     **
22  8 FORCE 22 RECREATIONL OPFSH FBG SV IO          8 10  2900  1 5   12300  14300
22  8 FORCE 22 RECREATIONL OPFSH FBG SV IO T        8 10  2900  1 5   **     **
22  8 FORCE 22 SPORT BRG   OPFSH FBG SV IO          8 10  3000  1 6   12600  14300

22  8 FORCE 22 SPORT BRG   OPFSH FBG SV IO          8 10  3000  1 6   **     **
22  8 FORCE 22 SPORT BRG   OPFSH FBG SV IO T        8 10  3000  1 6   **     **
27    FORCE 27 COMMERCIAL      FSH   FBG SV OB            10    6500  1 10  22500  25000
27    FORCE 27 COMMERCIAL      FSH   FBG SV IO      D VLVO 10   6500  1 10  **     **
27    FORCE 27 COMMERCIAL      FSH   FBG SV IO T    D VLVO 10   6500  1 10  **     **
30    FORCE 30 COMMERCIAL      FSH   FBG SV IO      D VLVO 10   7000  2     **     **
30    FORCE 30 COMMERCIAL      FSH   FBG SV IO T    D VLVO 10   7000  2     **     **
30    FORCE 30 FLYING BRG      FSH   FBG SV IO      D VLVO 10   8000  2     **     **
30    FORCE 30 FLYING BRG      FSH   FBG SV IO T    D VLVO 10   8000  2     **     **
```

FORESTER BOATS
MORA MN 55051-1200   COAST GUARD MFG ID- FBT See inside cover to adjust price for area

```
LOA   NAME AND/             TOP/ BOAT  -HULL- ----ENGINE--- BEAM  WGT  DRAFT RETAIL RETAIL
FT IN OR MODEL              RIG  TYPE  MTL TP  TP # HP MFG   FT IN LBS  FT IN LOW    HIGH
---------------------- 1994 BOATS ---------------------------------------------------------
16    SPORT 1650            OP   RNBT  FBG DV OB 130    6 10 1875        3600   4450
16    TROLLER 16 DELUXE     OP   FSH   AL  DV OB        5 7  385         425    510
16  1 FISH 16               OP   FSH   AL  DV OB        5 6  220         235    285
16  2 CONQUEST 16           OP   FSH   AL  DV OB        6 3  570         655    790
16  2 CONTENDER 16 TILLER   OP   FSH   AL  DV OB        6 3  570         625    750
16  8 CLASSIC 1700          OP   RNBT  FBG DV IO        7 1  1000        1100   1300
16  8 CLASSIC 1750          OP   RNBT  FBG DV IO        7 1  2025        4000   4900
17    CHALLENGER 17         OP   FSH   AL  DV OB 175    7 6  870         975    1150
18    RIO 1800              OP   RNBT  FBG DV IO        7 3  1175        1300   1550
18    RIO 1800              OP   RNBT  FBG DV IO 150 TOHU 7 3 1175       3700   4300
18    RIO 1850              OP   RNBT  FBG DV IO 150 OMC  7 3 2200       4500   5200
18    RIO 1850              OP   RNBT  FBG DV IO 235    7 3  2200        4750   5850

19  6 RIO 1950              OP   RNBT  FBG DV IO 265    7 10 2550        6000   7250
20 10 DIVA 2150             OP   RNBT  FBG DV IO 265    7 10 2750        6450   7900
20 10 RIO 2150              OP   RNBT  FBG DV IO 265    7 10 2750        6850   8250
---------------------- 1993 BOATS ---------------------------------------------------------
16    DIVA 1600             OP   RNBT  FBG DV IO        6 6  950         990    1200
16    SPORT 160             OP   RNBT  FBG DV IO 125    6 6  1875        3350   3900
16  5 CONQUEST S/C V-165    OP   FSH   AL  DV OB        6 10            995    1200
16  5 CONTENDER V-165       OP   FSH   AL  DV OB        6 6  850         890    1000
16  8 CLASSIC 1700          OP   RNBT  FBG DV IO        7 1  1100        1150   1350
16  8 CLASSIC 1700          OP   RNBT  FBG DV IO 175    7 1  1100        3750   4350
17  6 CHALLENGER TC V-176   OP   FSH   AL  DV OB        6 6  925         985    1250
17  6 TERMINATOR S/C V-176  OP   FSH   AL  DV OB        6 10 1050        1050   1250
17  6 TERMINATOR V-176      OP   FSH   AL  DV OB        6 10 975         1050   1250
18    RIO 1800              OP   RNBT  FBG DV IO        7 3  2200        1900   2250
18    RIO 1800              OP   RNBT  FBG DV IO 130-200 7 3 2200        4200   4950
```

LOA		NAME AND/	TOP/	BOAT	-HULL-		----ENGINE---			BEAM		WGT	DRAFT		RETAIL	RETAIL
FT	IN	OR MODEL	RIG	TYPE	MTL	TP	TP	# HP	MFG	FT	IN	LBS	FT	IN	LOW	HIGH
		1993 BOATS														
19	6	RIO 1950	OP	RNBT	FBG	DV	IO	175-230		7	9	2550			5150	6150
20	10	DIVA 2100	OP	RNBT	FBG	DV	IO	155-265		7	9	2750			6050	7350
20	10	DIVA 2100	OP	RNBT	FBG	DV	IO	285	OMC	7	9	2750			6600	7600
		1992 BOATS														
16		DIVA 1600	OP	RNBT	FBG	DV	OB			6	5	950			945	1100
16		SPORT 160	OP	RNBT	FBG	DV	IO	130-150		6	9	1875			3100	3600
16	1	FISH V-16	OP	FSH	AL	DV	OB			5	5	220			190	230
16	5	CHALLENGER V-165	OP	FSH	AL	DV	OB			6	6	925			915	1100
16	5	CONTENDER S/C V-165	OP	FSH	AL	DV	OB			6	6	910			950	1150
16	5	PURSUIT S/C V-165	OP	FSH	AL	DV	OB			6	6	880			820	985
16	5	PURSUIT V-165	OP	FSH	AL	DV	OB			6	6	850			805	970
16	8	FISH-N-SKI 170	OP	RNBT	FBG	DV	OB			7	1	1100			1100	1300
16	8	PHANTOM 170	OP	RNBT	FBG	DV	OB			7	1	1995			1700	2050
16	8	PHANTOM 170	OP	RNBT	FBG	DV	IO	130-150		7	1	2025			3400	3950
16	8	SPORT 170	OP	RNBT	FBG	DV	OB			7	1	1100			1050	1250
16	8	SPORT 170	OP	RNBT	FBG	DV	IO	130-175		7	1	2025			3450	4050
16	8	TROLLER DELUXE V-16	OP	FSH	AL	DV	OB			6	2	765			855	1000
16	8	TROLLER V-16	OP	FSH	AL	DV	OB			6	2	730			735	885
17	6	CHALLENGER V-176	OP	FSH	AL	DV	OB			6	10	1025			1050	1200
17	6	PRO TERMINATOR V-176	OP	FSH	AL	DV	OB			6	10	1030			1050	1250
17	6	TERMINATOR S/C V-176	OP	FSH	AL	DV	OB			6	10	1030			1000	1200
17	6	TERMINATOR V-176	OP	FSH	AL	DV	OB			6	10	975			995	1200
18		DIVA 1800 F&S	OP	RNBT	FBG	DV	OB			7	3	1275			1250	1500
18		DIVA 1800 F&S	OP	RNBT	FBG	DV	IO	130-185		7	3	2300			4000	4700
18		DIVA 1800 GT	OP	RNBT	FBG	DV	OB			7	3	2200			1800	2150
18		DIVA 1800 GT	OP	RNBT	FBG	DV	IO	130-200		7	3	2200			3900	4650
18	6	ESCAPE 190	OP	RNBT	FBG	DV	IO	130-260		7	5	2500			4350	5400
19	6	RIO 1900 GT	OP	RNBT	FBG	DV	IO	175-235		7	9	2500			4750	5700
20	10	CASPIAN 2100 CC	OP	RNBT	FBG	DV	IO	175-235		7	9	2850			5750	6950
20	10	CASPIAN 2100 CC	OP	RNBT	FBG	DV	IO	275	OMC	7	9	2850			6250	7200
20	10	CASPIAN 2100 GT BR	OP	RNBT	FBG	DV	IO	130-260		7	9	2750			5600	6850
20	10	CASPIAN 2100 GT BR	OP	RNBT	FBG	DV	IO	285	OMC	7	9	2750			6150	7100
20	10	CASPIAN 2100 GT BR	OP	RNBT	FBG	DV	IO	330	OMC	7	9	2750			6850	7850
20	10	CASPIAN 2100 GT CC	OP	RNBT	FBG	DV	IO	175-260		7	9	2850			5800	7050
20	10	CASPIAN 2100 GT CC	OP	RNBT	FBG	DV	IO	285	OMC	7	9	2850			6400	7350
20	10	CASPIAN 2100 GT CC	OP	RNBT	FBG	DV	IO	330	OMC	7	9	2850			7050	8100
25	2	ESCAPE 252	OP	RNBT	FBG	DV	IO	130-200		8	5	3825			8450	10100
25	2	ESCAPE 252	OP	RNBT	FBG	DV	IO	260-330		8	5	3825			9300	11600
25	2	ESCAPE 252 GT	OP	RNBT	FBG	DV	IO	150-260		8	5	3825			8700	10800
25	2	ESCAPE 252 GT	OP	RNBT	FBG	DV	IO	285-330		8	5	3825			9800	11800
		1991 BOATS														
16		DIVA 1600	OP	RNBT	FBG	DV	OB			6	5	900			855	1000
16		PHANTOM 160	OP	RNBT	FBG	DV	IO	115-150		6	10	1775			2750	3250
16		SPORT 160	OP	RNBT	FBG	DV	IO	115-150		6	10	1775			2800	3300
16	5	CHALLENGER V-165	OP	FSH	AL	DV	OB			6	7	750			710	855
16	5	CONTENDER S/C V-165	OP	FSH	AL	DV	OB			6	7	725			720	870
16	5	CONTENDER V-165	OP	FSH	AL	DV	OB			6	7	725			710	855
16	5	PURSUIT S/C V-165	OP	FSH	AL	DV	OB			6	7	725			650	785
16	5	PURSUIT V-165	OP	FSH	AL	DV	OB			6	7	725			665	800
16	8	FISH-N-SKI 170	OP	RNBT	FBG	DV	OB			7	1	1050			990	1200
16	8	FISHERMAN V-16	OP	FSH	AL	DV	OB			6	2	665			575	690
16	8	PHANTOM 170	OP	RNBT	FBG	DV	OB			7	1	1950			1600	1900
16	8	PHANTOM 170	OP	RNBT	FBG	DV	IO	115-150		7	1	1995			3150	3650
16	8	SPORT 170	OP	RNBT	FBG	DV	OB			7	1	1950			1650	1950
16	8	SPORT 170	OP	RNBT	FBG	DV	IO	115-150		7	1	1995			3150	3700
16	8	TROLLER DELUXE V-16	OP	FSH	AL	DV	OB			6	2	665			705	850
16	8	TROLLER V-16	OP	FSH	AL	DV	OB			6	2	640			615	745
17	6	CHALLENGER V-176	OP	FSH	AL	DV	OB			6	11	850			840	1000
17	6	PRO TERMINATOR V-176	OP	FSH	AL	DV	OB			6	11	825			855	1000
17	6	TERMINATOR S/C V-176	OP	FSH	AL	DV	OB			6	11	825			775	935
17	6	TERMINATOR V-176	OP	FSH	AL	DV	OB			6	11	825			810	975
18		DIVA 1800	OP	RNBT	FBG	DV	IO	115-175		7	3	2100			3550	4200
18		DIVA 1800 F&S	OP	RNBT	FBG	DV	OB			7	3	1250			1200	1400
18		DIVA 1800 F&S	OP	RNBT	FBG	DV	IO	115-175		7	3	2200			3650	4300
18		DIVA 1800 GT	OP	RNBT	FBG	DV	OB			7	3	1175			1100	1350
18		DIVA 1800 GT	OP	RNBT	FBG	DV	IO	115-175		7	3	2100			3600	4250
18	6	ESCAPE 190	OP	RNBT	FBG	DV	IO	115-220		7	6	2400			4000	4750
18	6	OSPREY 190	OP	FSH	FBG	DV	OB			7	6	1475			1350	1600
18	6	PHANTOM 190	OP	RNBT	FBG	DV	IO	115-220		7	6	2280			3850	4650
18	6	SPORT 190	OP	RNBT	FBG	DV	IO	115-220		7	6	2280			3900	4650
20	10	CASPIAN 2100 BR	OP	RNBT	FBG	DV	IO	115-235		7	10	2650			5000	6000
20	10	CASPIAN 2100 BR	OP	RNBT	FBG	DV	IO	275	OMC	7	10	2650			5450	6300
20	10	CASPIAN 2100 CC	OP	RNBT	FBG	DV	IO	115-275		7	10	2650			5250	6500
20	10	CASPIAN 2100 GT BR	OP	RNBT	FBG	DV	IO	115-275		7	10	2750			5250	6550
20	10	CASPIAN 2100 GT CC	OP	RNBT	FBG	DV	IO	115-275		7	10	2650			5250	6550
25	2	ESCAPE 252	OP	RNBT	FBG	DV	IO	115-235		8	6	3675			7750	9550
25	2	ESCAPE 252	OP	RNBT	FBG	DV	IO	275	OMC	8	6	3675			8600	9900
25	2	ESCAPE 252 GT	OP	RNBT	FBG	DV	IO	115-235		8	6	3675			7850	9700
25	2	ESCAPE 252 GT	OP	RNBT	FBG	DV	IO	275	OMC	8	6	3675			8850	10100
		1990 BOATS														
16		PHANTOM 160	OP	RNBT	FBG	DV	IO	125-130		6	10	1595			2500	2900
16		SPORT 160	OP	RNBT	FBG	DV	IO	125-130		6	10	1595			2550	2950
16	4	OSPREY 166	ST	FSH	FBG	DV	OB			6	11	1050			925	1100
16	6	PHANTOM 166	OP	RNBT	FBG	DV	OB			6	11	1050			940	1100
16	6	PHANTOM 166	OP	RNBT	FBG	DV	IO	125-175		6	11	1950			2850	3450
16	6	SPORT 166	OP	RNBT	FBG	DV	OB			6	11	1050			965	1150
16	6	SPORT 166	OP	RNBT	FBG	DV	IO	125-175		6	11	1950			2900	3450
17	1	PHANTOM 171	OP	RNBT	FBG	DV	OB			7	3	1100			995	1200
17	1	PHANTOM 171	OP	RNBT	FBG	DV	IO	125-205		7	3	1630			2850	3400
17	1	SPORT 171	OP	RNBT	FBG	DV	OB			7	3	1100			1000	1200
17	1	SPORT 171	OP	RNBT	FBG	DV	IO	125-205		7	3	2025			3100	3750
18		DIVA 1800	OP	RNBT	FBG	DV	IO	125-205		7	3	2100			3350	4000
18		DIVA 1800 GT	OP	RNBT	FBG	DV	OB			7	3	1175			1100	1300
18		DIVA 1800 GT	OP	RNBT	FBG	DV	IO	125-205		7	3	1250			2800	3400
18		FISH 'N SKI 1800	OP	FSH	AL	DV	OB			7	3	1250			1100	1300
18	6	ESCAPE 190	OP	CUD	FBG	DV	IO	125-235		7	6	2400			3900	4700
18	6	ESCAPE 190	OP	CUD	FBG	DV	IO	260		7	6	2400			4200	4850
18	6	OSPREY 190	ST	FSH	FBG	DV	OB			7	6	1475			1250	1500
18	6	PHANTOM 190	ST	RNBT	FBG	DV	IO	125-235		7	6	2280			3650	4450
18	6	PHANTOM 190	ST	RNBT	FBG	DV	IO	260		7	6	2280			4050	4700
18	6	SPORT 190	ST	RNBT	FBG	DV	IO	125-200		7	6	2280			3700	4450
18	6	SPORT 190	ST	RNBT	FBG	DV	IO	205-260		7	6	2280			4200	4850
20	10	CASPIAN 2100	OP	CUD	FBG	DV	IO	125-270		7	10	2750			5200	6450
20	10	CASPIAN 2100	OP	CUD	FBG	DV	IO	340	OMC	7	10	2750			6400	7350
20	10	CASPIAN 2100	OP	CUD	FBG	DV	IO	365-370		7	10	2750			7050	8100
20	10	CASPIAN 2100 BR	OP	RNBT	FBG	SV	IO	125-270		8		2650			4950	6150
20	10	CASPIAN 2100 BR	OP	RNBT	FBG	SV	IO	340-360		8		2650			6100	7550
20	10	CASPIAN 2100 BR	OP	RNBT	FBG	SV	IO	370	OMC	8		2650			6700	7700
25	2	ESCAPE 252	OP	CUD	FBG	DV	IO	125-235		8	6	3675			7850	9650
25	2	ESCAPE 252	OP	CUD	FBG	DV	IO	260-270		8	6	3675			8600	10000
25	2	ESCAPE 252	OP	CUD	FBG	DV	IO	340-370		8	6	3675			9700	11600
		1989 BOATS														
16		PHANTOM 160	OP	RNBT	FBG	DV	IO	120-130		6	10	1595			2350	2800
16		SPORT 160	OP	RNBT	FBG	DV	IO	120-130		6	10	1595			2400	2850
16	4	OSPREY 164	ST	BASS	FBG	DV	OB			6	6	950			810	975
16	6	PHANTOM 166	OP	RNBT	FBG	DV	OB			6	11	850			735	885
16	6	PHANTOM 166	OP	RNBT	FBG	DV	IO	120-175		6	11	1650			2500	3000
16	6	SPORT 166	OP	RNBT	FBG	DV	OB			6	11	850			750	905
16	6	SPORT 166	OP	RNBT	FBG	DV	IO	120-175		6	11	1650			2500	3050
17	1	PHANTOM 171	OP	RNBT	FBG	DV	OB			7	3	925			810	975
17	1	PHANTOM 171	OP	RNBT	FBG	DV	IO	120-205		7	3	1630			2650	3200
17	1	PHANTOM 171	OP	RNBT	FBG	DV	IO	262	OMC	7	3	1630			2900	3400
17	1	SPORT 171	OP	RNBT	FBG	DV	OB			7	3	925			830	995
17	1	SPORT 171	OP	RNBT	FBG	DV	IO	120-205		7	3	1630			2700	3250
17	1	SPORT 171	OP	RNBT	FBG	DV	IO	262	OMC	7	3	1630			2950	3400
18		DIVA 1800	OP	RNBT	FBG	DV	IO	120-205		7	3	1735			2900	3500
18		DIVA 1800	OP	RNBT	FBG	DV	IO	262	OMC	7	3	1735			3150	3650
18		DIVA 1800 GT	OP	RNBT	FBG	DV	OB			7	3	1020			930	1100
18		DIVA 1800 GT	OP	RNBT	FBG	DV	IO	120-205		7	3	1735			2900	3600
18		DIVA 1800 GT	OP	RNBT	FBG	DV	IO	262	OMC	7	3	1735			3150	3700
18	6	ESCAPE 190	OP	CUD	FBG	DV	IO	128-235		7	6	2150			3400	4200
18	6	ESCAPE 190	OP	CUD	FBG	DV	IO	260-262		7	6	2150			3750	4400
18	6	OSPREY 190	ST	RNBT	FBG	DV	OB			7	6	1475			1250	1500
18	6	PHANTOM 190	ST	RNBT	FBG	DV	IO	128-235		7	6	2050			3250	4000
18	6	PHANTOM 190	ST	RNBT	FBG	DV	IO	260-262		7	6	2050			3650	4250
18	6	SPORT 190	ST	RNBT	FBG	DV	IO	128-235		7	6	2050			3250	4000
18	6	SPORT 190	ST	RNBT	FBG	DV	IO	260-262		7	6	2050			3700	4300
20	10	CASPIAN 2100	OP	RNBT	FBG	SV	IO	128-235		8		2260			4250	5150
20	10	CASPIAN 2100	OP	RNBT	FBG	SV	IO	260-270		8		2260			4650	5400
20	10	CASPIAN 2100	OP	RNBT	FBG	SV	IO	350	OMC	8		2260			5550	6400
22	7	ESCAPE 227	OP	CUD	FBG	DV	IO		MRCR	8	4	3250			**	**
		IO 128-262 6000 7300, IO 350 OMC 7400 8500, IO 460 OMC 10100 11500														
		1988 BOATS														
16		PHANTOM 160	OP	RNBT	FBG	DV	IO	120-130		6	10	1595			2200	2600
16		SPORT 160	OP	RNBT	FBG	DV	IO	120-130		6	10	1595			2250	2650
16	4	OSPREY 164	ST	BASS	FBG	DV	OB			6	6	950			780	940

CONTINUED ON NEXT PAGE

LOA FT	LOA IN	NAME AND/ OR MODEL	TOP/ RIG	BOAT TYPE	HULL MTL	HULL TP	ENGINE TP	ENGINE # HP	ENGINE MFG	BEAM FT	BEAM IN	WGT LBS	DRAFT FT	DRAFT IN	RETAIL LOW	RETAIL HIGH
1988 BOATS																
16	4	PHANTOM 164	OP	RNBT	FBG	DV	IO	120-165		6	6	1595			2200	2600
16	4	PHANTOM 164	ST	RNBT	FBG	DV	OB			6	6	750			625	750
16	4	PHANTOM 164	ST	RNBT	FBG	DV	IO	128-130		6	6	1595			2200	2600
16	4	SPORT 164	OP	RNBT	FBG	DV	IO	130-165		6	6	1595			2250	2600
16	4	SPORT 164	ST	RNBT	FBG	DV	OB			6	6	750			635	765
16	4	SPORT 164	ST	RNBT	FBG	DV	IO	120-128		6	6	1595			2200	2600
17	1	PHANTOM 171	OP	RNBT	FBG	DV	OB			7	3	925			775	935
17	1	PHANTOM 171	OP	RNBT	FBG	DV	IO	120-205		7	3	1630			2500	3050
17	1	SPORT 171	OP	RNBT	FBG	DV	OB			7	3	925			795	960
17	1	SPORT 171	OP	RNBT	FBG	DV	IO	120-165		7	3	1630			2550	2950
17	1	SPORT 171	OP	RNBT	FBG	DV	IO	175	MRCR	7	3	1630			2350	2750
17	1	SPORT 171	OP	RNBT	FBG	DV	IO	175-205		7	3	1630			3300	3800
17	7	PHANTOM 180	OP	RNBT	FBG	DV	IO	128-180		7	1	1845			2650	3200
17	7	PHANTOM 180	ST	RNBT	FBG	DV	OB			7	1	1090			925	1100
17	7	PHANTOM 180	ST	RNBT	FBG	DV	IO	120-205		7	1	1845			2700	3250
17	7	SPORT 180	OP	RNBT	FBG	DV	IO	130-180		7	1	1845			2750	3250
17	7	SPORT 180	ST	RNBT	FBG	DV	OB			7	1	1090			940	1100
17	7	SPORT 180	ST	RNBT	FBG	DV	IO	120-205		7	1	1845			2700	3300
18	6	ESCAPE 190	OP	CUD	FBG	DV	IO	120-230		7	6	2150			3250	3950
18	6	ESCAPE 190	OP	CUD	FBG	DV	IO	260		7	6	2150			3550	4150
18	6	OSPREY 190	ST	RNBT	FBG	DV	OB			7	6	1475			1200	1400
18	6	PHANTOM 190	OP	RNBT	FBG	DV	IO	130-200		7	6	2050			3100	3650
18	6	PHANTOM 190	ST	RNBT	FBG	DV	IO	120-230		7	6	2050			3050	3800
18	6	PHANTOM 190	ST	RNBT	FBG	DV	IO	260		7	6	2050			3100	4000
18	6	SPORT 190	OP	RNBT	FBG	DV	IO	130-200		7	6	2050			3100	3700
18	6	SPORT 190	ST	RNBT	FBG	DV	IO	120-230		7	6	2050			3100	3850
18	6	SPORT 190	ST	RNBT	FBG	DV	IO	260		7	6	2050			3450	4000
22	7	ESCAPE 227	OP	CUD	FBG	DV	IO	120-260		8	4	3250			5700	6900
1987 BOATS																
16	4	OSPREY 164	ST	BASS	FBG	DV	OB			6	6	950			750	900
16	4	PHANTOM 164	OP	RNBT	FBG	DV	IO	130-165		6	6	1545			2050	2450
16	4	PHANTOM 164	ST	RNBT	FBG	DV	OB			6	6	750			595	720
16	4	PHANTOM 164	ST	RNBT	FBG	DV	IO	120		6	6	1545			2050	2400
16	4	PHANTOM SPORT 164	OP	RNBT	FBG	DV	IO	130-165		6	6	1595			2050	2450
16	4	PHANTOM SPORT 164	ST	RNBT	FBG	DV	OB			6	6	750			615	740
16	4	PHANTOM SPORT 164	ST	RNBT	FBG	DV	IO	120		6	6	1595			2050	2450
17	1	PHANTOM 171	OP	RNBT	FBG	DV	OB			7	3	925			745	900
17	1	PHANTOM 171	OP	RNBT	FBG	DV	IO	120-205		7	3	1630			2350	2850
17	1	PHANTOM SPORT 171	OP	RNBT	FBG	DV	OB			7	3	925			765	920
17	1	PHANTOM SPORT 171	OP	RNBT	FBG	DV	IO	120-205		7	3	1630			2400	2850
17	7	PHANTOM 180	OP	RNBT	FBG	DV	IO	120-180		7	1	1795			2500	2950
17	7	PHANTOM 180	ST	RNBT	FBG	DV	OB			7	1	1090			885	1050
17	7	PHANTOM 180	ST	RNBT	FBG	DV	IO	120-205		7	1	1795			2500	2900
17	7	PHANTOM SPORT 180	OP	RNBT	FBG	DV	IO	130-180		7	1	1845			2550	3000
17	7	PHANTOM SPORT 180	ST	RNBT	FBG	DV	OB			7	1	1090			910	1100
17	7	PHANTOM SPORT 180	ST	RNBT	FBG	DV	IO	120-205		7	1	1795			2500	2950
18	6	ESCAPE 190	OP	CUD	FBG	DV	IO	130-200		7	6	2150			3050	3650
18	6	ESCAPE 190	ST	RNBT	FBG	DV	IO	120-230		7	1	2200			2900	3500
18	6	ESCAPE 190	ST	RNBT	FBG	DV	IO	260		7	1	2200			3150	3650
18	6	ESCAPE SPORT 190	OP	CUD	FBG	DV	IO	130-200		7	6	2200			3100	3650
18	6	ESCAPE SPORT 190	ST	RNBT	FBG	DV	IO	120-230		7	1	2200			2900	3550
18	6	ESCAPE SPORT 190	ST	RNBT	FBG	DV	IO	260		7	1	2200			3150	3700
18	6	OSPREY 190	ST	RNBT	FBG	DV	OB			7	6	1475			1150	1350
18	6	PHANTOM 190	OP	RNBT	FBG	DV	IO	130-200		7	6	2000			2900	3450
18	6	PHANTOM 190	ST	RNBT	FBG	DV	IO	120-230		7	6	2000			2900	3500
18	6	PHANTOM 190	ST	RNBT	FBG	DV	IO	260		7	6	2000			3150	3650
18	6	PHANTOM SPORT 190	OP	RNBT	FBG	DV	IO	130-200		7	6	2050			2900	3450
18	6	PHANTOM SPORT 190	ST	RNBT	FBG	DV	IO	120-230		7	6	2050			2900	3550
18	6	PHANTOM SPORT 190	ST	RNBT	FBG	DV	IO	260		7	6	2050			3200	3700
1986 BOATS																
16	2	PHANTOM	ST	RNBT	FBG	DV	IO	120		6	6	1120			1650	1950
16	2	PHANTOM 160	ST	RNBT	FBG	DV	OB			6	6	750			550	665
16	2	PHANTOM ANGLER 160	ST	FSH	FBG	DV	OB			6	6	750			570	685
16	2	PHANTOM SPORT	ST	RNBT	FBG	DV	IO	120		6	6	1120			1700	2050
16	2	PHANTOM SPORT 160	ST	RNBT	FBG	DV	OB			6	6	750			610	735
16	4	OSPREY 164	ST	BASS	FBG	DV	OB			6	6	950			720	870
16	4	PHANTOM 164	ST	RNBT	FBG	DV	OB			6	6	750			505	610
16	4	PHANTOM 164	ST	RNBT	FBG	DV	IO	120-170		6	6	1545			1950	2350
16	4	PHANTOM LE 164	ST	RNBT	FBG	DV	OB			6	6	750			665	805
16	4	PHANTOM LE 164	ST	RNBT	FBG	DV	IO	120-170		6	6	1595			2050	2500
16	4	PHANTOM SPORT 164	ST	RNBT	FBG	DV	OB			6	6	750			585	700
16	4	PHANTOM SPORT 164	ST	RNBT	FBG	DV	IO	120-170		6	6	1595			1900	2350
17	7	PHANTOM 180	ST	RNBT	FBG	DV	OB			7	1	1090			775	935
17	7	PHANTOM 180	ST	RNBT	FBG	DV	IO	120-205		7	1	1795			2400	2800
17	7	PHANTOM LE 180	ST	RNBT	FBG	DV	OB			7	1	1090			960	1150
17	7	PHANTOM LE 180	ST	RNBT	FBG	DV	IO	120-205		7	1	1200			2050	2550
17	7	PHANTOM SPORT 180	ST	RNBT	FBG	DV	OB			7	1	1090			850	1000
17	7	PHANTOM SPORT 180	ST	RNBT	FBG	DV	IO	120-205		7	1	1795			2400	2950
18	6	ESCAPE 190	ST	RNBT	FBG	DV	IO	120-230		7	1	2200			2650	3250
18	6	ESCAPE 190	ST	RNBT	FBG	DV	IO	260		7	1	2200			2900	3400
18	6	ESCAPE LE 190	ST	RNBT	FBG	DV	IO	120-260		7	1	2200			2900	3650
18	6	ESCAPE SPORT 190	ST	RNBT	FBG	DV	IO	120-230		7	1	2200			2750	3350
18	6	ESCAPE SPORT 190	ST	RNBT	FBG	DV	IO	260		7	1	2200			3000	3450
18	6	OSPREY 190	ST	RNBT	FBG	DV	OB			7	6	1475			1100	1300
18	6	PHANTOM 190	ST	RNBT	FBG	DV	IO	120-230		7	6	2000			2750	3350
18	6	PHANTOM 190	ST	RNBT	FBG	DV	IO	260		7	6	2000			3000	3500
18	6	PHANTOM LE 190	ST	RNBT	FBG	DV	IO	120-230		7	1	2050			2700	3250
18	6	PHANTOM LE 190	ST	RNBT	FBG	DV	IO	260		7	1	2050			2900	3400
18	6	PHANTOM SPORT 190	ST	RNBT	FBG	DV	IO	120-230		7	6	2050			2750	3350
18	6	PHANTOM SPORT 190	ST	RNBT	FBG	DV	IO	260		7	6	2050			3000	3500
1985 BOATS																
16	2	PHANTOM 160	ST	RNBT	FBG	DV	OB			6	6	750			535	640
16	2	PHANTOM 160	ST	RNBT	FBG	DV	IO	120		6	6	1120			1550	1850
16	2	PHANTOM SPORT 160	ST	RNBT	FBG	DV	OB			6	6	750			590	710
16	2	PHANTOM SPORT 160	ST	RNBT	FBG	DV	IO	120		6	6	1120			1650	1950
16	2	PHANTOM-ANGLER 160	ST	FSH	FBG	DV	OB			6	6	750			550	665
16	4	OSPREY 164	ST	BASS	FBG	DV	OB			6	6	950			695	840
16	4	PHANTOM 164	ST	RNBT	FBG	DV	OB			6	6	750			520	630
16	4	PHANTOM 164	ST	RNBT	FBG	DV	IO	120-170		6	6	1545			1850	2250
16	4	PHANTOM SPORT 164	ST	RNBT	FBG	DV	OB			6	6	750			610	735
16	4	PHANTOM SPORT 164	ST	RNBT	FBG	DV	IO	120-170		6	6	1595			1900	2250
17	7	PHANTOM 180	ST	RNBT	FBG	DV	OB			7	1	1090			795	960
17	7	PHANTOM 180	ST	RNBT	FBG	DV	IO	120-185		7	1	1795			2200	2650
17	7	PHANTOM ANGLER 180	ST	FSH	FBG	DV	OB			7	1	1090			815	980
17	7	PHANTOM SPORT 180	ST	RNBT	FBG	DV	OB			7	1	1090			865	1050
17	7	PHANTOM SPORT 180	ST	RNBT	FBG	DV	SE	115	OMC	7	1	1795			1250	1450
17	7	PHANTOM SPORT 180	ST	RNBT	FBG	DV	IO	120-185		7	1	1795			2350	2750
1984 BOATS																
16	2	PHANTOM 160	ST	RNBT	FBG	DV	OB			6	6	750			515	620
16	2	PHANTOM 160	ST	RNBT	FBG	DV	IO	120-140		6	6	1370			1650	1950
16	2	PHANTOM ANGLER 160	ST	FSH	FBG	DV	OB			6	6	750			535	645
16	2	PHANTOM SPORT 160	ST	RNBT	FBG	DV	OB			6	6	750			575	690
16	2	REBEL 1600	OP	SKI	FBG	DV	OB			6	5	695			500	600
16	2	SPORT 160	ST	RNBT	FBG	DV	IO	120-140		6	6	1370			1700	2050
17	7	PHANTOM 180	ST	RNBT	FBG	DV	OB			7	1	1090			775	935
17	7	PHANTOM 180	ST	RNBT	FBG	DV	IO	120-140		7	1	1710			2150	2500
17	7	PHANTOM ANGLER 180	ST	FSH	FBG	DV	OB			7	1	1090			790	950
17	7	PHANTOM SPORT 180	ST	RNBT	FBG	DV	OB			7	1	1090			825	990
17	7	SPORT 180	ST	RNBT	FBG	DV	IO	120-140		7	1	1710			2150	2500

....For earlier years, see the BUC Used Boat Price Guide, Volume 3

FORMAC YACHTING AMERIQUE INC

MONTREAL PQ CANADA

See inside cover to adjust price for area

LOA FT	LOA IN	NAME AND/ OR MODEL	TOP/ RIG	BOAT TYPE	HULL MTL	HULL TP	ENGINE TP	ENGINE # HP	ENGINE MFG	BEAM FT	BEAM IN	WGT LBS	DRAFT FT	DRAFT IN	RETAIL LOW	RETAIL HIGH
1984 BOATS																
17	8	JOUET 5.40 NG	SLP	SAIL	FBG	CB	OB			7	1	1056	1	5	3200	3700
20	7	JOUET 6.30 NG	SLP	SAIL	FBG	KL	OB			7	9	1760	2	7	4500	5150
20	7	JOUET 6.30 NG	SLP	SAIL	FBG	KL	IB	13D	VLVO	7	9	1760	2	7	6250	7150
21		JOUET 6.40	SLP	SAIL	FBG	CB	OB			7	8	1278		10	3850	4450
22		JOUET 6.80	SLP	SAIL	FBG	KC	OB			7	11	2800	3	6	6300	7250
22	4	JOUET 6.80	SLP	SAIL	FBG	KC	SD	8D	VLVO	7	11	2800	3	6	7650	8800
27		JOUET 8.20	SLP	SAIL	FBG	KC	OB			9	2	4800	5	3	13100	14900
27		JOUET 8.20	SLP	SAIL	FBG	KC	IB	8D	VLVO	9	2	4800	5	3	13700	15600
33		JOUET 10.00	SLP	SA/RC	FBG	KL	SD	25D	VLVO	10	10	7920	5	8	24800	27600
33		JOUET 10.00 NG	SLP	SA/CR	FBG	KL	IB	24D- 36D		10	11	9200	5		28800	32100
36		HARMONIE 11M	SLP	SA/RC	AL	KL	IB	35D	VLVO	12	2	15500	5	11	48600	53400
36	1	JOUET 11.00 NG	SLP	SA/CR	FBG	KL	SD	35D	VLVO	11	9	12260	5	3	39200	43600
37		POUVREAU 11.30M	SLP	SA/RC	AL	KL	IB	40D	PERK	11	9	12760	6	6	41500	46200
37	4	JOUET 11.40	SLP	SA/RC	FBG	KL	IB	24D	VLVO	12	2	11660	6	4	38900	43200
37	4	JOUET 11.40	SLP	SA/RC	FBG	KL	IB	36D	VLVO	12	2	11660	6	4	39100	43400
39	4	POUVREAU 12.00M	SLP	SA/RC	AL	KL	IB	40D	PERK	12	10	16100	7	3	55600	61100
43	2	JOUET 13.15	KTH	SA/CR	FBG	KL	SD	50D	PERK	13	10	19800	6	3	76400	83900
44	8	POUVREAU 13.80M	SLP	SA/CR	AL	CB	IB	40D	PERK	15	1	27500	3	3	96800	106500

FORMULA BOATWORKS LLC

NOANK CT 06340   COAST GUARD MFG ID- FMU See inside cover to adjust price for area
FORMERLY FORMULA YACHTS INC

For more recent years, see the BUC Used Boat Price Guide, Volume 1

LOA FT IN	NAME AND/ OR MODEL	TOP/ RIG	BOAT TYPE	-HULL- MTL TP	TP	ENGINE # HP	MFG	BEAM FT IN	WGT LBS	DRAFT FT IN	RETAIL LOW	RETAIL HIGH
	1996 BOATS											
24 9	EVELYN 25	SLP	SACAC	F/S KL	OB			8 8	2600	4 4	14100	16000
32 1	EVELYN 32	SLP	SACAC	F/S KL	OB			9 8	4500	6	28100	31300
42 2	EVELYN 42	SLP	SACAC	F/S KL	IB	30D	YAN	12 8	11800	7 4	110000	120500
	1995 BOATS											
24 9	EVELYN 25	SLP	SACAC	F/S KL	OB			8 8	2600	4 4	13300	15100
32 1	EVELYN 32	SLP	SACAC	F/S KL	OB			9 8	4500	6	26500	29400
42 2	EVELYN 42	SLP	SACAC	F/S KL	IB	30D	YAN	12 8	11800	7 4	103500	113500
	1994 BOATS											
24 9	EVELYN 25	SLP	SACAC	F/S KL				8 8		4 4	13000	14700
32 1	EVELYN 32	SLP	SACAC	F/S KL				9 8		6	34200	38000
42 2	EVELYN 42	SLP	SACAC	F/S KL	IB	D	YAN	12 8		7 4	135500	149000
	1993 BOATS											
24 9	EVELYN 25	SLP	SACAC	F/S KL				8 8		4 4	12200	13900
32 1	EVELYN 32	SLP	SACAC	F/S KL				9 8		6	32200	35700
42 2	EVELYN 42	SLP	SACAC	F/S KL	IB	D	YAN	12 8		7 4	127500	140000
	1992 BOATS											
24 9	EVELYN 25	SLP	SACAC	F/S KL	OB			8 8	2600	4 4	11000	12500
32 1	EVELYN 32	SLP	SACAC	F/S KL	OB			9 8	4500	6	22000	24500
42 2	EVELYN 42	SLP	SACAC	F/S KL	IB	30D	YAN	12 8	11800	7 4	85900	94400
	1991 BOATS											
25	EVELYN 25	SLP	SAIL	F/S KL	OB			8 8	2600	4 5	10500	11900
32	EVELYN 32	SLP	SAIL	F/S KL	OB			9 8	4500	6	20800	23100
42 2	EVELYN 42	SLP	SAIL	F/S KL	IB	30D	YAN	12 8	11800	7 4	80800	88800
	1990 BOATS											
25	EVELYN 25	SLP	SAIL	F/S KL	OB			8 8	2600	4 5	9900	11200
32	EVELYN 32	SLP	SAIL	F/S KL	OB			9 8	4500	6	19500	21700
42 2	EVELYN 42	SLP	SAIL	F/S KL	IB	30D	YAN	12 8	11800	7 4	76000	83500
	1989 BOATS											
25	EVELYN 25	SLP	SAIL	F/S KL	OB			8 8	2600	4 5	9350	10600
32	EVELYN 32	SLP	SAIL	F/S KL	OB			9 8	4500	6	18600	20700
42 2	EVELYN 42	SLP	SAIL	F/S KL	IB	30D	YAN	12 8	11800	7 4	71500	78600
	1988 BOATS											
25	EVELYN 25	SLP	SAIL	F/S KL	OB			8 8	2600	4 5	8700	10000
32	EVELYN 32	SLP	SAIL	F/S KL	OB			9 8	4500	6	17100	19400
42 2	EVELYN 42	SLP	SAIL	F/S KL	IB	30D	YAN	12 8	11800	7 4	67300	73900
	1987 BOATS											
25	EVELYN 25	SLP	SAIL	F/S KL	OB			8 8	2600	4 5	8150	9400
32	EVELYN 32	SLP	SAIL	F/S KL	OB			9 8	4500	6	16100	18300
42 2	EVELYN 42	SLP	SAIL	F/S KL	IB	30D	YAN	12 8	10800	7 4	60000	66000
	1986 BOATS											
25	EVELYN 25	SLP	SAIL	F/S KL	OB			8 8	2600	4 5	7700	8850
25 5	EVELYN 25.5	SLP	SAIL	F/S KL	OB			9	4300	4 5	12100	13800
25 5	EVELYN 25.5	SLP	SAIL	F/S KL	OB	D		9	4300	4 5	13100	14900
26	EVELYN 26	SLP	SA/OD	F/S KL	DB	OB		9 6	4500	1	13000	14800
26	EVELYN 26	SLP	SA/OD	F/S KL	OB			9 6	4500	4 6	12500	14200
32	EVELYN 32	SLP	SAIL	F/S KL	OB			9 8	4500	6	15100	17200
42 2	EVELYN 42	SLP	SAIL	F/S KL	IB	30D	YAN	12 8	10800	7 4	56500	62100
	1985 BOATS											
25	EVELYN 25	SLP	SAIL	F/S KL	OB			8 8	2600	4 5	7250	8300
25 5	EVELYN 25.5	SLP	SAIL	F/S KL	OB			9	4300	4 5	11400	13000
25 5	EVELYN 25.5	SLP	SAIL	F/S KL	OB	D		9	4300	4 5	12300	14000
26	EVELYN 26	SLP	SA/OD	F/S KL	DB			9 6	4500	1	12300	13900
26	EVELYN 26	SLP	SAIL	F/S KL	OB			9 6	4300	4 6	11700	13300
32	EVELYN 32	SLP	SAIL	F/S KL	OB			9 8	4500	6	14200	16200
42 2	EVELYN 42	SLP	SAIL	F/S KL	IB	30D	YAN	12 8	9800	7 4	50200	55100
	1984 BOATS											
25 5	EVELYN 25.5	SLP	SAIL	F/S KL	OB			9	4300	4 5	10700	12200
25 5	EVELYN 25.5	SLP	SAIL	F/S KL	OB	D		9	4300	4 5	11600	13200
26	EVELYN 26	SLP	SA/OD	F/S KL	DB			9 6	4500	1	11500	13100
26	EVELYN 26	SLP	SA/OD	F/S KL	OB			9 6	4300	4 6	11000	12600
32	EVELYN 32	SLP	SAIL	F/S KL	OB			9 8	4500	6	13400	15200

....For earlier years, see the BUC Used Boat Price Guide, Volume 3

FORT MYERS YHT & SHIPBLDG INC

FORT MYERS FL 33901   COAST GUARD MFG ID- FMW See inside cover to adjust price for area

LOA FT IN	NAME AND/ OR MODEL	TOP/ RIG	BOAT TYPE	-HULL- MTL TP	TP	ENGINE # HP	MFG	BEAM FT IN	WGT LBS	DRAFT FT IN	RETAIL LOW	RETAIL HIGH
	1986 BOATS											
24	CAPTIVA 24	OP	CTRCN	FBG SV	IB	240	CHRY	9 6	4200	2 2	15200	17300
24	CAPTIVA 24S	OP	CTRCN	FBG SV	IB	240	CHRY	9 6	4200	2 2	16300	18500
34 8	NIGHTWIND 35	SLP	SA/RC	FBG KC	IB	21D	UNIV	11 6	12500	2 9	75700	83200
42	BREWER 12.8	CUT	SA/CR	FBG KC	IB	61D	LEHM	13 6	23850	4 5	138500	152500
42	BREWER 12.8	CUT	SA/CR	FBG KL	IB	61D	LEHM	13 6	24000	5 2	139000	153000
42	BREWER 420	KTH	SA/CR	FBG KL	IB	61D	LEHM	13 6	25000	5	142500	156500
	1985 BOATS											
24	CAPTIVA 24	OP	CTRCN	FBG SV	IB	240	CHRY	9 6	4200	2 2	15000	17100
34 8	NIGHTWIND 35	SLP	SA/RC	FBG KC	IB	21D	UNIV	11 6	12500	2 9	71200	78200
42	BREWER 12.8	CUT	SA/CR	FBG KC	IB	61D	LEHM	13 6	23850	4	130500	143500
42	BREWER 12.8	CUT	SA/CR	FBG KL	IB	61D	LEHM	13 6	24000	5 2	131000	144000
42	BREWER 420	KTH	SA/CR	FBG KL	IB	61D	LEHM	13 6	25000	5	134000	147500
	1984 BOATS											
34 8	NIGHTWIND 35	SLP	SA/RC	FBG KC	IB	21D	UNIV	11 6	12500	2 9	66900	73500
42	BREWER 12.8	CUT	SA/CR	FBG KC	IB	61D	LEHM	13 6	25000	4 3	126000	138500
42	BREWER 12.8XL	KTH	SA/CR	FBG KC	IB	67D	LEHM	13 6	25000	5	126000	139000
42	BREWER 420	KTH	SA/CR	FBG KL	IB	61D	LEHM	13 6	25000	5	126000	138500

....For earlier years, see the BUC Used Boat Price Guide, Volume 3

FORTIER BOATS INC

SOMERSET MA 02725   COAST GUARD MFG ID- FDF See inside cover to adjust price for area

For more recent years, see the BUC Used Boat Price Guide, Volume 1

LOA FT IN	NAME AND/ OR MODEL	TOP/ RIG	BOAT TYPE	-HULL- MTL TP	TP	ENGINE # HP	MFG	BEAM FT IN	WGT LBS	DRAFT FT IN	RETAIL LOW	RETAIL HIGH
	1986 BOATS											
26 10	FORTIER 26	OP	CR	FBG DV	IB	185	VLVO	10	6500	2 2	29200	32500
26 10	FORTIER 26	OP	CR	FBG DV	IB	130D-200D		10	6500	2 6	35400	44000
33 5	FORTIER 33 BASS	OP	CR	FBG DV	IB			11 8		2 8	**	**
33 5	FORTIER 33 OFFSHORE	OP	CR	FBG DV	IB			11 8		2 8	**	**
33 5	FORTIER 33 SF	FB	CR	FBG DV	IB			11 8		2 8	**	**
	1985 BOATS											
26 10	FORTIER 26	OP	CR	FBG DV	IB	260	MRCR	10	6500	2 6	28900	32100
26 10	FORTIER 26	OP	CR	FBG DV	IB	158D-200D		10	6500	2 6	35100	42200
33 5	FORTIER 33	OP	CR	FBG DV	IB						**	**
33 5	FORTIER 33	FB	CR	FBG DV	IB						**	**
	1984 BOATS											
26 10	FORTIER 26	OP	CR	FBG DV	IB	260	MRCR	10	6500	2 6	27600	30700
26 10	FORTIER 26	OP	CR	FBG DV	IB	158D-200D		10	6500	2 6	33700	40500
33 5	FORTIER 33	OP	CR	FBG DV	IB						**	**
33 5	FORTIER 33	FB	CR	FBG DV	IB						**	**

....For earlier years, see the BUC Used Boat Price Guide, Volume 3

FOUNTAIN POWERBOATS INC

WASHINGTON NC 27889   COAST GUARD MFG ID- FGQ See inside cover to adjust price for area
FORMERLY FOUNTAIN & GARBRECHT INC

For more recent years, see the BUC Used Boat Price Guide, Volume 1

LOA FT IN	NAME AND/ OR MODEL	TOP/ RIG	BOAT TYPE	-HULL- MTL TP	TP	ENGINE # HP	MFG	BEAM FT IN	WGT LBS	DRAFT FT IN	RETAIL LOW	RETAIL HIGH
	1996 BOATS											
24	SPORT BOAT 24 CS	OP	CUD	F/S SV	IO	300-350		8 2	4000		18100	21700
24	SPORT BOAT 24 CS	OP	CUD	F/S SV	IO	385-415		8 2	4000		21100	25300
25	25CC	OP	CTRCN	F/S SV	OB			8 4	3900		19600	21800
25	25CC RIG	OP	CTRCN	F/S SV	OB			8 4	3900		20000	22200
25	SPORTFISH CR	OP	CUD	F/S SV	OB			8 4	4000		20000	22200
25	SPORTFISH CR RIG	OP	CUD	F/S SV	OB			8 4			21300	23700
27	FEVER 27	OP	OFF	F/S SV	IO	300-385		8 4	4800		25600	31500
27	FEVER 27	OP	OFF	F/S SV	IO	415	MRCR	8 4	4800		29600	32900
27	FEVER 27	OP	OFF	F/S SV	IO	525	MRCR	8 4	4800		34300	38200
29	29CC	OP	CTRCN	F/S SV	OB			8 4	4900		33200	36800
29	29CC RIG	OP	CTRCN	F/S SV	OB			8 4	4900		33600	37300
29	FEVER 29	OP	OFF	F/S SV	IO	300-415		8 4	6500		28400	34600
	IO 500-525 33500			37900, IO T300-T385		32800 40400,	IO T415		MRCR		37900	42100
	IO T525 MRCR 44100			49000								
29	SPORTFISH CR	OP	CUD	F/S SV	IO			8 4	5000		33200	36900
29	SPORTFISH CR	OP	CUD	F/S SV	IO	300-385		8 4	5000		25600	30800
29	SPORTFISH CR	OP	CUD	F/S SV	IO	415	MRCR	8 4	5000		28600	31800
29	SPORTFISH CR	OP	CUD	F/S SV	IO	415D	MRCR	8 4	5000		33300	37000
29	SPORTFISH CR RIG	OP	CUD	F/S SV	OB			8 4	5000		33600	37400
31	31CC	OP	CTRCN	F/S SV	OB			8 4	5500		40900	45000
31	31CC RIG	OP	CTRCN	F/S SV	OB			8 4	5500		40900	45400

FOUNTAIN POWERBOATS INC   -CONTINUED   See inside cover to adjust price for area

```
     LOA  NAME AND/         TOP/ BOAT  -HULL- ----ENGINE---  BEAM  WGT  DRAFT  RETAIL RETAIL
     FT IN OR MODEL         RIG  TYPE  MTL TP TP # HP  MFG    FT IN LBS  FT IN  LOW    HIGH
------------------------ 1996 BOATS ------------------------
31   SPORTFISH CR          OP CUD  F/S SV OB             8  4  5800            40600  45100
31   SPORTFISH CR RIG      OP CUD  F/S SV OB             8  4                  40900  45500
32   FEVER 32              OP OFF  F/S SV IO T300-T415   8  4  7200            43900  52500
32   FEVER 32              OP OFF  F/S SV IO T525  MRCR  8  4  7200            51100  56200
32   FEVER 32 SB           OP OFF  F/S SV IO T385  MRCR  8  4  7200            46800  51500
32   SPORTFISH CR          OP SF   F/S SV IO 300-415     8  4  8000            39100  45800
32   SPORTFISH CR          OP SF   F/S SV IO T300-T415   8  4  8000            44300  53100
35   LIGHTNING 35          OP OFF  F/S SV IO T300  MRCR  8  4  7500            62800  69000
        IO T350 MRCR 65200  71700, IO T385  MRCR 74000, IO T415 MRCR 69500  76400
        IO T525 MRCR 78000  85700, IO T600  MRCR 83300  91500

38   FEVER 38              OP OFF  F/S SV IO T300  MRCR  8  6  8200            61100  67200
        IO T350 MRCR 64100  70500, IO T385  MRCR 67100  73700, IO T415 MRCR 70100  77100
        IO T525 MRCR 82500  90700, IO T600  MRCR 89200  98000, IO T800 MRCR  **     **

38   SPORT CRUISER 38      OP OFF  F/S SV IO T300  MRCR  8  6  9500            65000  71400
        IO T350 MRCR 68000  74700, IO T385  MRCR 71000  78000, IO T415 MRCR 74000  81400
        IO T500 MRCR 83700  92000, IO T525  MRCR 86400  95000, IO T600 MRCR 93100 102500
        IO T800 MRCR  **     **

42   LIGHTNING 42          OP OFF  F/S SV IO T300  MRCR  8  6  8800            73700  80900
        IO T350 MRCR 78100  85800, IO T385  MRCR 81900  90000, IO T415 MRCR 85700  94100
        IO T525 MRCR 100500 110500, IO T600 MRCR 109000 119500, IO T800 MRCR  **     **
        IO R350 MRCR 83600  91800, IO R350 MRCR 86600  95200, IO R385 MRCR 97100 106500
        IO R415 MRCR 98000 107500, IO R525 MRCR 120000 132000

42   LIGHTNING 42 STAG     OP OFF  F/S SV IO T300  MRCR  8  4  9000            74900  82300
        IO T350 MRCR 79400  87200, IO T385  MRCR 83200  91500, IO T415 MRCR 86900  95500
        IO T525 MRCR 101500 111500, IO T600 MRCR 110000 121000

47   LIGHTNING 47          OP OFF  F/S SV IO R300  MRCR  8  6               94800 104000
        IO R350 MRCR 100500 110500, IO R385 MRCR 106000 116500, IO R415 MRCR 111500 122500
        IO R525 MRCR 132500 145500, IO R600 MRCR 145500 160000, IO R800 MRCR  **     **

47   SPORT CRUISER 47      OP OFF  F/S SV IO R300  MRCR                       95100 104500
        IO R350 MRCR 101000 110500, IO R385 MRCR 106000 116500, IO R415 MRCR 111000 122000
        IO R500 MRCR 127000 139500, IO R525 MRCR 131500 144500, IO R600 MRCR 143500 157500
        IO R800 MRCR  **     **
------------------------ 1995 BOATS ------------------------
24   SPORT BOAT 24 CS      OP CUD   F/S SV IO 300-350                         16800  20800
24   SPORT BOAT 24 CS      OP CUD   F/S SV IO 385-415                         20000  23900
25   25CC                  OP CTRCN F/S SV OB            8  4  3900            18500  21600
25   25CC RIG              OP CTRCN F/S SV OB            8  4  3900            19100  21200
25   SPORTFISH CR          OP CUD   F/S SV OB            8  4  4000            18800  20900
25   SPORTFISH CR          OP CUD   F/S SV IO 250-350    8  4  5000            19700  24500
25   SPORTFISH CR          OP CUD   F/S SV IO 385-415    8  4  5000            23500  27600
25   SPORTFISH CR RIG      OP CUD   F/S SV OB            8  4                  20400  22600
27   FEVER 27 SE           OP OFF   F/S SV IO 300-385    8  4  4800            22500  27700
27   FEVER 27 SE           OP OFF   F/S SV IO  415  MRCR 8  4  4800            26000  28900
27   FEVER 27 SE           OP OFF   F/S SV IO T525  MRCR 8  4  4800            41300  45900
29   29CC                  OP CTRCN F/S SV OB            8  4  4900            31100  34500

29   29CC RIG              OP CTRCN F/S SV OB            8  4  4900            32100  35700
29   FEVER 29 SB           OP OFF   F/S SV IO T300-T385  8  4  6500            29700  36600
29   FEVER 29 SB           OP OFF   F/S SV IO T415-T525  8  4  6500            36900  44400
29   FEVER 29 SE           OP OFF   F/S SV IO T415  MRCR 8  4  6500            31800  35300
29   SPORTFISH CR          OP CUD   F/S SV OB            8  4  5000            31200  34700
29   SPORTFISH CR          OP CUD   F/S SV IO 300-415    8  4  5000            23900  29700
29   SPORTFISH CR          OP CUD   F/S SV IO  240D MRCR 8  4  5000            24600  27300
29   SPORTFISH CR RIG      OP CUD   F/S SV OB            8  4  5000            32100  35700
31   31CC                  OP CTRCN F/S SV OB            8  4  5500            37900  42100
31   31CC RIG              OP CTRCN F/S SV OB            8  4  5500            39300  43700
31   SPORTFISH CR          OP CUD   F/S SV OB            8  4  5800            38300  42600
31   SPORTFISH CR RIG      OP CUD   F/S SV OB            8  4                  39000  43400

32   FEVER 32 SB           OP OFF   F/S SV IO T300-T415  8  4  7200            40900  49000
32   FEVER 32 SB           OP OFF   F/S SV IO T525  MRCR 8  4  7200            47900  52600
32   SPORT CRUISER 32      OP SF    F/S SV IO T350-T415  8  4  7650            42700  49700
32   SPORTFISH CR          OP CUD   F/S SV IO 300-415    8  4  8000            36500  42600
32   SPORTFISH CR          OP SF    F/S SV IO T250-T385  8  4  8000            39700  44800
32   SPORTFISH CR          OP SF    F/S SV IO T415  MRCR 8  4  8000            44800  49700
35   LIGHTNING 35 SB       OP OFF   F/S SV IO T300  MRCR 8  4  7500            60000  66000
        IO T350 MRCR 62300  68500, IO T385 MRCR 64400  70700, IO T415 MRCR 66400  72900
        IO T525 MRCR 74400  81700, IO T600 MRCR 79400  87200, IO T800 MRCR  **     **

38   FEVER 38 SB           OP OFF   F/S SV IO T300  MRCR 8  6  8200            57400  63000
        IO T350 MRCR 60200  66100, IO T385 MRCR 63000  69200, IO T415 MRCR 65800  72300
        IO T525 MRCR 77400  85000, IO T600 MRCR 83600  91900, IO T800 MRCR  **     **

38   SPORT CRUISER 38      OP OFF   F/S SV IO T350  MRCR 8  6  9500            63400  69700
        IO T385 MRCR 66200  72800, IO T415 MRCR 69100  75900, IO T500 MRCR 78100  85800
        IO T525 MRCR 80600  88600, IO T600 MRCR 86900  95500, IO T800 MRCR  **     **

42   LIGHTNING 42 SB       OP OFF   F/S SV IO T300  MRCR 8  6  8800            67400  74000
        IO T350 MRCR 71200  78300, IO T385 MRCR 74700  82100, IO T415 MRCR 78000  85700
        IO T525 MRCR 91200 100000, IO T600 MRCR 98800 108500, IO T800 MRCR  **     **

42   SIGNATURE 42 TE       OP OFF   F/S SV IO R300  MRCR 8  6 10200            76400  84000
        IO R350 MRCR 79000  86800, IO R385 MRCR 88400  97200, IO R415 MRCR 89200  98000
        IO R525 MRCR 109000 120000

47   SPORT CRUISER 47      OP OFF   F/S SV IO R385  MRCR                       98900 108500
        IO R415 MRCR 103500 114000, IO R500 MRCR 118500 130000, IO R525 MRCR 122500 134500
        IO R600 MRCR 134000 147000, IO R800 MRCR  **     **
------------------------ 1994 BOATS ------------------------
24   SPORT BOAT 24 CS      OP CUD   F/S SV IO 300-350                         15700  19400
24   SPORT BOAT 24 CS      OP CUD   F/S SV IO 385-415                         18900  22300
27   FEVER 27 SE           OP OFF   F/S SV IO 300-350    8  4  4800            21000  24700
        IO 415-465 24300  29000, IO  500  MRCR 27400  30500, IO T525 MRCR 41900  46500

27   FEVER 275 E           OP OFF   F/S SV IO  385  MRCR 8  4  4800            23300  25800
29   FEVER 29 SB           OP OFF   F/S SV IO T300-T385  8  4  6500            27700  34100
29   FEVER 29 SB           OP OFF   F/S SV IO T465-T525  8  4  6500            34300  41300
29   FEVER 29 SE           OP OFF   F/S SV IO T415  MRCR 8  4  6500            32000  35600
32   FEVER 32 SB           OP OFF   F/S SV IO T300-T465  8  4  7200            38100  47100
32   FEVER 32 SB           OP OFF   F/S SV IO T500-T525  8  4  7200            43500  49100
35   LIGHTNING 35 SB       OP OFF   F/S SV IO T300  MRCR 8  4  7500            56000  61600
        IO T350 MRCR 58200  63900, IO T385 MRCR 60100  66000, IO T415 MRCR 61900  68100
        IO T465 MRCR 65300  71800, IO T500 MRCR 67700  74400, IO T525 MRCR 69400  76300
        IO T600 MRCR 74100  81400, IO T800 MRCR  **     **

38   FEVER 38 SB           OP OFF   F/S SV IO T300  MRCR 8  6  8200            53600  58900
        IO T350 MRCR 56200  61700, IO T385 MRCR 58800  64600, IO T415 MRCR 61400  67500
        IO T465 MRCR 66400  72900, IO T500 MRCR 69900  76800, IO T525 MRCR 72200  79400
        IO T600 MRCR 78100  85800, IO T800 MRCR  **     **

38   SPORT CRUISER 38      OP OFF   F/S SV IO T385  MRCR 8  6  9500            59200  65100
        IO T385 MRCR 61800  67900, IO T415 MRCR 64500  70900, IO T465 MRCR 69400  76300
        IO T500 MRCR 72900  80100, IO T525 MRCR 75200  82700, IO T600 MRCR 81100  89100
        IO T800 MRCR  **     **

42   LIGHTNING 42 SB       OP OFF   F/S SV IO T300  MRCR 8  6  8800            67800  74500
        IO T385 MRCR 69700  76600, IO T415 MRCR 72800  80000, IO T465 MRCR 78500  86200
        IO T500 MRCR 82400  90600, IO T525 MRCR 85200  93600, IO T600 MRCR 92200 101500
        IO T800 MRCR  **     **

42   SIGNATURE 42 TE       OP OFF   F/S SV IO T415  MRCR 8  6 10200            75800  83300
        IO R350 MRCR 73700  81000, IO R385 MRCR 82600  90700, IO R465 MRCR 95900 105500
        IO R500 MRCR 97700 107500, IO R525 MRCR 101500 112000

47   SPORT CRUISER 47      OP OFF   F/S SV IO T  D SETK                        **     **
        IO R385 MRCR 92200 101500, IO R465 MRCR 105000 115000, IO R500 MRCR 110500 121500
        IO R525 MRCR 114500 125500, IO R600 MRCR 125000 137500, IO R800 MRCR  **     **
        IB R415D MRCR 189500 208000
------------------------ 1993 BOATS ------------------------
25   3 SPORTFISH 25        ST CTRCN F/S SV OB            8  4  3000            15200  17200
25   3 SPORTFISH CR 25     ST CUD   F/S SV OB            8  4  3300            15900  18100
27   FEVER 27 SE           OP OFF   F/S SV IO 300  MRCR  8  4  4800            19400  19800
        IO 365-390 20100  24100, IO 465-500 24400  28500, IO T525 MRCR 39100  43500

27   SPORTFISH 27          ST CTRCN F/S SV OB            8  4  3700            22100  24600
27   SPORTFISH CR 27       ST CUD   F/S SV OB            8  4  4800            22500  25000
29   FEVER 29 SB           OP OFF   F/S SV IO T300-T365  8  4  6500            25900  31000
29   FEVER 29 SB           OP OFF   F/S SV IO T390-T465  8  4  6500            33300  37000
29   FEVER 29 SB           OP OFF   F/S SV IO T500-T525  8  4  6500            40900  46500
29   FEVER 29 SE           OP OFF   F/S SV IO T390-T525  8  4  6500            24200  29500
31   SPORTFISH 31          ST CTRCN F/S SV OB            8  4  5700            31900  35400
31   SPORTFISH CR 31       ST CUD   F/S SV OB            8  4  5700            33100  35400
32   FEVER 32 SB           OP OFF   F/S SV IO T300-T365  8  4  7200            33100  39200
32   FEVER 32 SB           OP OFF   F/S SV IO T390-T525  8  4  7200            37400  45800

35   LIGHTNING 35 SB       OP OFF   F/S SV IO T300  MRCR 8  4  7500            48700  53500
        IO T365 MRCR 52300  57500, IO T390 MRCR 55800  61400, IO T465 MRCR 60100  66000
        IO T500 MRCR 62300  68500, IO T525 MRCR 64800  71300, IO T575 MRCR 67800  74500
```

 CONTINUED ON NEXT PAGE

LOA FT IN	NAME AND/ OR MODEL	TOP/ RIG	BOAT TYPE	HULL MTL TP TP	ENGINE # HP MFG	BEAM FT IN	WGT LBS	DRAFT FT IN	RETAIL LOW	RETAIL HIGH
1993 BOATS										
35	LIGHTNING 35 SB	OP	OFF	F/S SV	IO T600 MRCR	8	4 7500		73400	80600
38	FEVER 38 SB	OP	OFF	F/S SV	IO T300 MRCR	8	6 8200		47800	52500
	IO T365 MRCR 52700 57900, IO T390 MRCR 54800 60200, IO T465 MRCR 61100 67100									
	IO T500 MRCR 65300 71700, IO T525 MRCR 67500 74200, IO T575 MRCR 74100 81400									
	IO T600 MRCR 77300 85000									
38	SPORT CRUISER 38	OP	OFF	F/S SV	IO T390 MRCR	8	6 9500		57600	63300
	IO T465 MRCR 64900 71300, IO T500 MRCR 68100 74900, IO T525 MRCR 70300 77300									
	IO T575 MRCR 73100 80300, IO T600 MRCR 80300 88300									
42	LIGHTNING 42 SB	OP	OFF	F/S SV	IO T365 MRCR	8	6 8800		60200	66200
	IO T390 MRCR 65000 71400, IO T465 MRCR 73300 80600, IO T500 MRCR 77100 84700									
	IO T525 MRCR 79600 87500, IO T575 MRCR 87400 96000, IO T600 MRCR 91400 100500									
42	SIGNATURE 42 TE	OP	OFF	F/S SV	IO R365 MRCR	8	6 10200		68300	75000
	IO R390 MRCR 78700 86400, IO R465 MRCR 89700 98500, IO R500 MRCR 86700 95300									
	IO R525 MRCR 94100 103500									
47	SPORT CRUISER 47	OP	OFF	F/S SV	IO R390 MRCR				85900	94400
	IO R500 MRCR 103000 113500, IO R525 MRCR 107000 117500, IO R600 MRCR 125500 138000									
	IB R600D SETK 224500 246500									
1992 BOATS										
25	3 SPORTFISH 25	ST	CTRCN	F/S SV	OB	8	2 3400		14000	15900
27	FEVER 27 SE	OP	OFF	F/S SV	IO 300 MRCR	8	4 4800		16300	18500
27	FEVER 27 SE	OP	OFF	F/S SV	IO 350-390 MRCR	8	4 4800		18700	22500
27	FEVER 27 SE	OP	OFF	F/S SV	IO 445-490 MRCR	8	4 4800		22200	26300
29	FEVER 29 II	OP	OFF	F/S SV	IO T330-T350	8	4 6400		23200	27000
29	FEVER 29 II	OP	OFF	F/S SV	IO T390-T445	8	4 6400		26700	32300
31	SPORTFISH 31	ST	CTRCN	F/S SV	OB	8	4 5200		30600	34000
31	SPORTFISH CR 31	ST	CUD	F/S SV	OB	8	4 5700		30600	34000
32	FEVER 32	OP	OFF	F/S SV	IO T330-T390	8	4 7000		31500	38800
32	FEVER 32	OP	OFF	F/S SV	IO T445-T490	8	4 7000		36600	41900
35	LIGHTNING 35	OP	OFF	F/S SV	IO T330 MRCR	8	4 7300		44900	49900
	IO T350 MRCR 47100 51800, IO T390 MRCR 50800 55800, IO T400 MRCR 51100 56100									
	IO T445 MRCR 54400 59800, IO T465 MRCR 55600 61100, IO T490 MRCR 57100 62700									
	IO T525 MRCR 61400 67500, IO T540 MRCR 63600 69900									
38	FEVER 38	OP	OFF	F/S SV	IO T350 MRCR	8	4 8202		47400	52000
	IO T390 MRCR 51700 56800, IO T400 MRCR 52200 57400, IO T445 MRCR 56700 62300									
	IO T465 MRCR 58300 64300, IO T490 MRCR 60700 66700, IO T525 MRCR 66000 72500									
	IO T540 MRCR 68600 75400									
38	SPORT CRUISER 38	OP	OFF	F/S SV	IO T390 MRCR	8	6 9500		53900	59200
	IO T400 MRCR 54400 59800, IO T445 MRCR 59000 64800, IO T465 MRCR 60700 66700									
	IO T490 MRCR 62900 69100, IO T525 MRCR 68300 75100, IO T540 MRCR 71000 78000									
42	LIGHTNING 42	OP	OFF	F/S SV	IO T350 MRCR	8	4 8705		57000	62600
	IO T385 MRCR 62000 68100, IO T390 MRCR 62700 68900, IO T400 MRCR 63300 69600									
	IO T445 MRCR 68800 75600, IO T465 MRCR 70900 77900, IO T490 MRCR 73500 80700									
	IO T525 MRCR 79900 87700, IO T540 MRCR 83000 91300									
42	SIGNATURE 42	OP	OFF	F/S SV	IO R365 MRCR	8	4 9800		65300	71700
42	SIGNATURE 42	OP	OFF	F/S SV	IO R410 MRCR	8	4 9800		77500	85200
42	SIGNATURE 42	OP	OFF	F/S SV	IO R445 MRCR	8	4 9800		82700	90800
42	TRIPLE 42	OP	OFF	F/S SV	IO R350 MRCR	8	4 9800		62000	68100
	IO R390 MRCR 69600 76500, IO R445 MRCR 74700 82100, IO R490 MRCR 85200 93600									
47	SPORT CRUISER 47	OP	OFF	F/S SV	IO R390 MRCR				80300	88300
	IO R445 MRCR 88600 97400, IO R465 MRCR 91500 100500, IO R490 MRCR 95100 104500									
	IO R550 MRCR 111000 122000									
1991 BOATS										
27	FEVER 27	OP	OFF	F/S SV	IO 340-365	8	4 4800		18500	21200
27	FEVER 27	OP	OFF	F/S SV	IO 410-445	8	4 4800		21000	24500
29	FEVER 29	OP	OFF	F/S SV	IO T365-T410	8	4 6400		24300	29700
29	FEVER 29	OP	OFF	F/S SV	IO T445 MRCR	8	4 6400		28000	31200
31	SPORTFISH 31	OP	CTRCN	F/S SV	OB	8	4 4890		32400	36000
32	FEVER 32	OP	OFF	F/S SV	IO T365-T445	8	4 7000		31400	38100
35	LIGHTNING 35	OP	OFF	F/S SV	IO T365 MRCR	8	4 7300		45500	50000
	IO T385 MRCR 47300 52000, IO T410 MRCR 49100 54000, IO T445 MRCR 51000 56000									
	IO T465 MRCR 52100 57300, IO T525 MRCR 57500 63200									
38	FEVER 38	OP	OFF	F/S SV	IO T365 MRCR	8	4 8202		46000	50500
	IO T385 MRCR 47900 52700, IO T410 MRCR 50400 55400, IO T445 MRCR 53200 58500									
	IO T465 MRCR 54900 60300, IO T525 MRCR 61900 68000									
38	SPORT CRUISER 38	OP	OFF	F/S SV	IO T365 MRCR	8	6 9500		48000	52700
	IO T385 MRCR 50000 54900, IO T410 MRCR 52500 57700, IO T445 MRCR 55300 60800									
	IO T465 MRCR 57000 62600, IO T525 MRCR 64100 70400									
42	LIGHTNING 42	OP	OFF	F/S SV	IO T365 MRCR	8	4 8705		55400	60800
	IO T385 MRCR 58100 63900, IO T410 MRCR 61200 67300, IO T445 MRCR 64500 70900									
	IO T465 MRCR 66500 73100, IO T525 MRCR 74900 82300									
42	SIGNATURE 42	OP	OFF	F/S SV	IO R365 MRCR	8	4 9800		64500	70800
42	SIGNATURE 42	OP	OFF	F/S SV	IO R410 MRCR	8	4 9800		72700	79900
42	SIGNATURE 42	OP	OFF	F/S SV	IO R445 MRCR	8	4 9800		77500	85200
42	TRIPLE 42	OP	OFF	F/S SV	IO R365 MRCR	8	4 9800		57500	63200
42	TRIPLE 42	OP	OFF	F/S SV	IO R410 MRCR	8	4 9800		65100	71500
42	TRIPLE 42	OP	OFF	F/S SV	IO R445 MRCR	8	4 9800		70100	77000
1990 BOATS										
27	FEVER 27	OP	OFF	F/S SV	IO T270-T330	8	4 6300	2 0	20000	24800
27	FEVER 27	OP	OFF	F/S SV	IO T365 MRCR	8	4 6300	2 3	24500	27200
27	FEVER 27 II	OP	OFF	F/S SV	IO T270-T330	8	4 6400	2 2	19100	23500
27	FEVER 27 II	OP	OFF	F/S SV	IO T365 MRCR	8	4 6400	2 4	23200	25800
31	SPORT FISHERMAN 31	OP	CTRCN	F/S SV	OB	8	4 4200	2 4	35800	39800
33	LIGHTNING 33	OP	OFF	F/S SV	IO T330-T365	8	4 7600	3 2	33200	38200
33	LIGHTNING 33	OP	OFF	F/S SV	IO T420	8	4 7600	3 1	37200	41400
33	LIGHTNING 33	OP	OFF	F/S SV	IO T575 MRCR	8	4 7600	3 2	47500	52200
36	FEVER 36	OP	OFF	F/S SV	IO T330 MRCR	8	4 8200	3 2	31800	35300
	IO T365 MRCR 34100 37700, IO T420 MRCR 37700 41900, IO T420 MRCR 37700 41900									
	IO T575 MRCR 50400 55400									
40	LIGHTNING 40	OP	OFF	F/S SV	IO T365 MRCR	8	4 8500	3 3	49500	54300
	IO T420 MRCR 55200 60600, IO T575 MRCR 74700 82100, IO R365 MRCR 47900 52700									
	IO R420 MRCR 60900 66900									
40	SIGNATURE 40	OP	OFF	F/S SV	IO R365 MRCR	8	4 9700	3 11	61100	67100
1989 BOATS										
27	FEVER 27	OP	OFF	F/S SV	IO T260-T330	8	4 6300		18800	23400
27	FEVER 27	OP	OFF	F/S SV	IO T340-T365	8	4 6300		21500	23700
29	8.8 M SPORT BOAT	OP	CUD	F/S SV	IO T260-T320	8	4 6000		17000	21100
29	8.8 M SPORT BOAT	OP	CUD	F/S SV	IO T330-T370	8	4 6000		19300	23400
29	8.8 M SPORT BOAT	OP	CUD	F/S SV	IO T420	8	4 6000		22900	25400
33	LIGHTNING 33	OP	OFF	F/S SV	IO T330-T370	8	4 7600		30400	36300
33	LIGHTNING 33	OP	OFF	F/S SV	IO T420	8	4 7600		35500	39400
33	LIGHTNING 33	OP	OFF	F/S SV	IO T540-T800	8	4 7600		46000	55500
36	FEVER 36	OP	OFF	F/S SV	IO T330 MRCR	8	4 8200		30000	33300
	IO T340 OMC 30500 33800, IO T365 MRCR 32200 35700, IO T370 OMC 32400 36000									
	IO T420 MRCR 35600 39500, IO T540 FOUN 43600 48400, IO T575 MRCR 47800 52500									
	IO T800 FOUN ** **									
40	LIGHTNING 40	OP	OFF	F/S SV	IO T330 MRCR	8	4 8500		43100	47900
	IO T340 OMC 43800 48600, IO T365 MRCR 46900 51500, IO T370 OMC 47100 51800									
	IO T420 MRCR 52000 57200, IO T540 FOUN 64900 71300, IO T575 MRCR 70500 77400									
	IO T800 FOUN ** **									
1987 BOATS										
29	8.8M CENTER CONSOLE	OP	CTRCN	F/S SV	OB	8	4 6000	1 6	20900	23200
29	8.8M SPORT BOAT	OP	OFF	F/S SV	OB	8	4 3500	1 6	23600	26300
29	8.8M SPORT BOAT	OP	CUD	F/S SV	IO T		MRCR 8	4 6000	1 4	**	**
	IO T260-T320 15200 19000, IO T330-T370 MRCR 17100 21300, IO T420 MRCR 20500 22800									
33	10M SPORT BOAT	OP	OFF	F/S SV	OB	8	4 3000	1 6	25300	28100
33	10M SPORT BOAT	OP	OFF	F/S SV	IB T330-T375	8	4 7000	1 6	34400	41100
33	10M SPORT BOAT	OP	OFF	F/S SV	IB T420-T525	8	4 7000	1 6	39000	48300
33	10M SPORT BOAT	OP	OFF	F/S SV	IB T550-T650	8	4 7000	1 6	46200	56100
40	12M SPORT BOAT	OP	OFF	F/S SV	IB T330 MRCR	8	4 8200	1 6	62000	68100
	IB T370 MRCR 65600 72100, IB T375 KAAM 66100 72600, IB T420 MRCR 69200 76100									
	IB T425 KAAM 69400 76300, IB T475 MRCR 71400 78500, IB T525 MRCR 76500 84000									
	IB T550 KAAM 80400 88400, IB T575 MRCR 84500 92900, IB T580 MRCR 85400 93800									
	IB T650 MRCR 91300 100500, IB T650 MRCR 91300 100500									
1986 BOATS										
29	FEVER 29	OP	OFF	F/S SV	IO T260	8	4 6400		15000	17100
33	10M SPORT BOAT	OP	OFF	F/S SV	IO T330	8	4 3000		24600	27300
33	10M SPORT BOAT	OP	OFF	F/S SV	IO T330	8	4 7000		25900	28800
36	FEVER 36	OP	OFF	F/S SV	IO T330	8	4 8200		25800	28600
40	12M SPORT BOAT	OP	OFF	F/S SV	IO T330	8	4 8200		36600	40600
1985 BOATS										
22	9 FOUNTAIN 7M	OP	RACE	F/S SV	IO T260	8	4 4500		8700	10000
33	10M SPORT BOAT	OP	OFF	F/S SV	IO 330	8	4 7000		22400	24800
40	12M SPORT BOAT	OP	OFF	F/S SV	IO 330	8	4 8200		33100	36700
1984 BOATS										
33	10M SPORT BOAT	OP	OFF	F/S SV	IO 330	8	4 7000		21600	24000
33	10M SPORT BOAT	OP	OFF	F/S SV	IO 330	8	4 7000	1 8	24000	26600
40	12M SPORT BOAT	OP	OFF	F/S SV	IO 370	8	4 8200		34100	37900

....For earlier years, see the BUC Used Boat Price Guide, Volume 3

FOUNTAINE PAJOT

17290 AIGREFEUILLE FRANCE — See inside cover to adjust price for area

For more recent years, see the BUC Used Boat Price Guide, Volume 1

LOA FT	LOA IN	NAME AND/ OR MODEL	TOP/ RIG	BOAT TYPE	HULL MTL	HULL TP	ENGINE TP	ENGINE # HP	ENGINE MFG	BEAM FT	BEAM IN	WGT LBS	DRAFT FT	DRAFT IN	RETAIL LOW	RETAIL HIGH
		1996 BOATS														
35		TOBAGO 35	SLP	SACAC	F/S	CT	IB	T 10D	VLVO	19		8818	3		105500	116000
38		ATHENA 38	SLP	SACAC	F/S	CT	IB	T 18D	YAN	20	6	12125	3	3	142500	156500
42		VENEZIA 42	SLP	SACAC	F/S	CT	IB	T 28D	YAN	22	8	14991	3	9	197500	217000
56	3	MARQUISES 56	SLP	SACAC	F/S	CT	IB	T 48D	YAN	26	2	28660	4	4	543500	597500
		1995 BOATS														
35		TOBAGO 35	SLP	SACAC	F/S	CT	IB	T 10D	VLVO	19		8818	3		99400	109000
38		ATHENA 38	SLP	SACAC	F/S	CT	IB	T 18D	YAN	20	6	12125	3	3	134000	147500
42		VENEZIA 42	SLP	SACAC	F/S	CT	IB	T 28D	YAN	22	8	14991	3	9	186000	204500
56	3	MARQUISES 56	SLP	SACAC	F/S	CT	IB	T 48D	YAN	26	2	28660	4	4	510000	560500
		1994 BOATS														
32		MALDIVES 32	SLP	SACAC	F/S	CT	OB			17	5	6620	3		68000	74700
35		TOBAGO 35	SLP	SACAC	F/S	CT	IB	T 10D	VLVO	19		7725	3		90200	99200
37		ANTIGUA 37	SLP	SACAC	F/S	CT	IB	T 10D	YAN	19	6	9930	3	3	111000	122000
37		ANTIGUA 37 MAESTRO	SLP	SACAC	F/S	CT	IB	T 18D	YAN	19	6	9930	3	3	111000	122000
42		VENEZIA 42	SLP	SACAC	F/S	CT	IB	T 28D	YAN	22	8	15010	3	9	175000	192000
56	3	MARQUISES 56	SLP	SACAC	F/S	CT	IB	T 48D	YAN	26	2	29800	4	4	478500	526000
		1993 BOATS														
32		MALDIVES 32	SLP	SACAC	F/S	CT	OB			17	5	6620	3		63900	70300
37		ANTIGUA 37	SLP	SACAC	F/S	CT	IB	T 10D	YAN	19	6	9930	3	3	104500	115000
37		ANTIGUA 37 MAESTRO	SLP	SACAC	F/S	CT	IB	T 18D	YAN	19	6	9930	3	3	104500	115000
42		VENEZIA 42	SLP	SACAC	F/S	CT	IB	T 28D	YAN	22	8	15010	3	9	164500	181000
56	3	MARQUISES 56	SLP	SACAC	F/S	CT	IB	T 48D	YAN	26	2	29800	4	4	449000	493000

FOUR WINNS INC

CADILLAC MI 49601 — COAST GUARD MFG ID- GFN See inside cover to adjust price for area
FOR OLDER MODELS SEE SAF-T-MATE

For more recent years, see the BUC Used Boat Price Guide, Volume 1

LOA FT	LOA IN	NAME AND/ OR MODEL	TOP/ RIG	BOAT TYPE	HULL MTL	HULL TP	ENGINE TP	ENGINE # HP	ENGINE MFG	BEAM FT	BEAM IN	WGT LBS	DRAFT FT	DRAFT IN	RETAIL LOW	RETAIL HIGH
		1996 BOATS														
17	6	HORIZON 170	OP	RNBT	FBG	DV	OB			7		1760	2		3000	3500
17	6	HORIZON 170	OP	RNBT	FBG	DV	IO	135-160		7		2000	2	2	5000	5950
19		HORIZON 190	OP	RNBT	FBG	DV	OB			7	3	2050	2	2	3450	4000
19		HORIZON 190	OP	RNBT	FBG	DV	IO	160-220		7	3	2380	2	4	6150	7500
19		SUNDOWNER 195	OP	CUD	FBG	DV	IO	160-220		7	3	2560	2	6	6600	8050
20	2	HORIZON 200	OP	RNBT	FBG	DV	OB			8	1	2480	2	6	4950	5700
20	2	HORIZON 200	OP	RNBT	FBG	DV	IO	190-265		8	1	3170	2	6	9300	11300
20	2	HORIZON 203 CR	OP	SF	FBG	DV	OB			7	4	2620	2	3	5050	5800
20	4	CANDIA 214	OP	RNBT	FBG	TR	IO	190-265		8		3290	2	4	9650	11900
20	6	SUNDOWNER 205	OP	CUD	FBG	DV	OB			7	4	2650	2	3	5300	6100
20	6	SUNDOWNER 205	OP	CUD	FBG	DV	IO	160-220		8	1	3120	2	6	9850	11700
21	6	HORIZON 220	OP	RNBT	FBG	DV	IO	330	OMC	8	4	3630	2	11	13100	14900
21	9	HORIZON 220	OP	RNBT	FBG	DV	IO	220-265		8	4	3350	2	11	11000	13300
21	9	SUNDOWNER 225	OP	CUD	FBG	DV	IO	220	OMC	8	4	3220	2	11	11100	12600
21	9	SUNDOWNER 225	OP	CUD	FBG	DV	IO	265	OMC	8	4	3590	2	11	12300	14000
23	4	VISTA 238	OP	CR	FBG	DV	IO	190-265		8		4350	3		14600	17500
24	2	HORIZON 240	OP	RNBT	FBG	DV	IO	265	OMC	8	6	3930	2	11	13800	15700
24	2	HORIZON 240	OP	RNBT	FBG	DV	IO	330	OMC	8	6	4070	2	11	15400	17500
24	2	SUNDOWNER 245	OP	CUD	FBG	DV	IO	265-330		8	6	4330	3	1	15900	19800
25	4	VISTA 258	OP	CR	FBG	DV	IO	265-330		8	6	5120	3	3	18900	22500
27	2	VISTA 278	OP	CR	FBG	DV	IO	T190-T220		9	4	7420	3	3	27100	31000
		1995 BOATS														
17	6	FREEDOM 170	OP	RNBT	FBG	DV	OB			7		1620	2		2700	3150
17	6	FREEDOM 170	OP	RNBT	FBG	DV	IO	135-160		7		2040	2		4700	5750
19		HORIZON SE 190	OP	RNBT	FBG	DV	OB			7	3	2070	2		3300	3850
19		HORIZON SE 190	OP	RNBT	FBG	DV	IO	160-215		7	3	2620	2		6050	7250
19		SUNDOWNER 195	OP	CUD	FBG	DV	IO	160-215		7	3	2650	2	6	6300	7650
20	2	HORIZON 200	OP	RNBT	FBG	DV	OB			7	4	2320	2	3	4600	5250
20	2	HORIZON 200	OP	RNBT	FBG	DV	IO	160-215		7	4	2900	2	3	7650	9250
20	2	HORIZON 200	OP	RNBT	FBG	DV	IO	255	OMC	7	4	3130	2	3	8450	9750
20	2	HORIZON 203 CR	OP	SF	FBG	DV	OB			7	4	2620	2	3	4800	5500
20	2	SUNDOWNER 205	OP	CUD	FBG	DV	OB			7	4	2620	2	3	4850	5550
20	2	SUNDOWNER 205	OP	CUD	FBG	DV	IO	160-190		7	4	2920	2	6	8150	9450
20	2	SUNDOWNER 205	OP	CUD	FBG	DV	IO	215	OMC	7	4	3260	2	6	9050	10300
20	4	CANDIA 214	OP	RNBT	FBG	TR	IO	190-255		8		3290	2	4	9100	11000
21	6	HORIZON 220	OP	RNBT	FBG	DV	IO	190-270		7	9	3170	2	10	9400	11600
21	6	SUNDOWNER 225	OP	CUD	FBG	DV	IO	190-270		7	9	3410	2	11	10200	12600
23	4	VISTA 238	OP	CR	FBG	DV	IB	190	OMC	8		4240	3		16000	18200
23	4	VISTA 238	OP	CR	FBG	DV	IO	215-255		8		4280	3		13500	15900
23	8	HORIZON 240	OP	RNBT	FBG	DV	IO	255-270		8	4	3730	2	11	12000	14000
23	8	HORIZON 240	OP	RNBT	FBG	DV	IO	330	OMC	8	4	3830	2	11	13500	15300
23	8	SUNDOWNER 245	OP	CUD	FBG	DV	IO	255-270		8	4	3940	2	11	13300	15500
23	8	SUNDOWNER 245	OP	CUD	FBG	DV	IO	330	OMC	8	4	4060	2	11	14900	17000
25	4	VISTA 258	OP	CR	FBG	DV	IB	215	OMC	8	6	5010	3	3	19800	22000
25	4	VISTA 258	OP	CR	FBG	DV	IO	255-330		8	6	5100	3	3	17100	21200
27	2	VISTA 278	OP	CR	FBG	DV	IO	330	OMC	9	4	6650	3	3	23600	26200
27	2	VISTA 278	OP	CR	FBG	DV	IO	T190-T215		9	4	7380	3	3	25200	28800
		1994 BOATS														
17	6	FREEDOM 170	OP	RNBT	FBG	DV	OB			7		1620	2		2600	3000
17	6	FREEDOM 170	OP	RNBT	FBG	DV	IO	120-160		7		2040	2		4400	5350
19		HORIZON SE 180	OP	RNBT	FBG	DV	OB			7	3	2070	2		3150	3650
19		HORIZON SE 180	OP	RNBT	FBG	DV	IO	160-215		7	3	2620	2		5650	6750
19	8	CANDIA 194	OP	RNBT	FBG	TR	IO	160-215		7	8	2860	2	2	6350	7700
20	2	HORIZON 190	OP	RNBT	FBG	DV	OB			7	4	2320	2	3	4350	5000
20	2	HORIZON 190	OP	RNBT	FBG	DV	IO	160-215		7	4	2900	2	3	7150	8650
20	2	HORIZON 190	OP	RNBT	FBG	DV	IO	255	OMC	7	4	3130	2	3	7900	9100
20	2	SUNDOWNER 195	OP	CUD	FBG	DV	OB			7	4	2620	2	3	4600	5300
20	2	SUNDOWNER 195	OP	CUD	FBG	DV	IO	160-190		7	4	2920	2	6	7600	8850
20	2	SUNDOWNER 195	OP	CUD	FBG	DV	IO	215	OMC	7	4	3260	2	6	8350	9600
20	9	LIBERATOR 201	OP	CUD	FBG	DV	IO	270-300		7	8	3240	2	11	9300	11200
21	6	HORIZON 210	OP	RNBT	FBG	DV	IO	190-270		7	9	3170	2	10	8700	10800
21	6	SUNDOWNER 215	OP	CUD	FBG	DV	IO	190-270		7	9	3410	2	11	9500	11700
21	7	CANDIA 214	OP	RNBT	FBG	TR	IO	190-270		8		3100	2	4	8550	10700
23	3	LIBERATOR 221	OP	CUD	FBG	DV	IO	300	OMC	8	4	3990	2	10	12900	14700
23	3	LIBERATOR 221	OP	CUD	FBG	DV	IO	390	OMC	8	4	3990	2	10	15400	17500
23	4	VISTA 238	OP	CR	FBG	DV	IO	215	OMC	8		4280	3		12600	14300
23	4	VISTA 238	OP	CR	FBG	DV	IB	190D	OMC	8		4240	3		20600	22800
23	8	HORIZON 230	OP	RNBT	FBG	DV	IO	215-270		8	4	3650	2	11	10800	13000
23	8	HORIZON 230	OP	RNBT	FBG	DV	IO	300	OMC	8	4	3830	2	11	12000	13600
23	8	SUNDOWNER 235	OP	CUD	FBG	DV	IO	215-270		8	4	3850	2	11	12000	14400
23	8	SUNDOWNER 235	OP	CUD	FBG	DV	IO	300	OMC	8	4	4060	2	11	13300	15100
25	4	VISTA 258	OP	CR	FBG	DV	IO	255-300		8	6	5100	3	3	15900	19100
25	4	VISTA 278	OP	CR	FBG	DV	IB	215D	OMC	8	6	5010	3	3	24700	27400
27	2	VISTA 278	OP	CR	FBG	DV	IO	295	OMC	9	4	6650	3	3	21300	23700
27	2	VISTA 278	OP	CR	FBG	DV	IO	T190-T215		9	4	7380	3	3	23600	26900
		1993 BOATS														
18	6	FREEDOM 180	OP	RNBT	FBG	DV	OB			7	3	1790	2		2700	3150
18	6	FREEDOM 180	OP	RNBT	FBG	DV	IO	115-160		7	3	2230	2	2	4650	5550
19	8	CANDIA 190	OP	RNBT	FBG	TR	IO	160-200		7	8	2860	2	2	5950	7250
20	2	HORIZON 190	OP	RNBT	FBG	DV	OB			7	3	2320	2	3	4050	4700
20	2	HORIZON 190	OP	RNBT	FBG	DV	IO	160-200		7	3	2900	2	6	6650	7950
20	2	HORIZON 190	OP	RNBT	FBG	DV	IO	240	OMC	7	3	3130	2	3	7250	8300
20	2	HORIZON 190 LE	OP	RNBT	FBG	DV	IO	160-200		7	4				6900	8000
20	2	SUNDOWNER 195	OP	CUD	FBG	DV	OB			7	4	2630	2	3	4400	5050
20	2	SUNDOWNER 195	OP	CUD	FBG	DV	IO	160-190		7	4	2920	2	6	7100	8250
20	2	SUNDOWNER 195	OP	CUD	FBG	DV	IO	200	OMC	7	4	3260	2	6	7750	8900
20	9	HORIZON 200	OP	RNBT	FBG	DV	OB			7	8	2470	2	8	4450	5100
20	9	LIBERATOR 201	OP	CUD	FBG	DV	IO	260-295		7	8	3240	2	11	8500	10400
20	9	SUNDOWNER 205	OP	CUD	FBG	DV	OB			7	8	2730	2	10	4800	5850
21	6	HORIZON 210	OP	RNBT	FBG	DV	IO	190-260		7	9	3170	2	10	8100	10100
21	6	SUNDOWNER 215	OP	CUD	FBG	DV	IO	190-260		7	9	3410	2	11	8900	10900
21	7	CANDIA 210	OP	RNBT	FBG	TR	IO	190-260		8		3100	2	4	8000	9950
23	3	LIBERATOR 221	OP	CUD	FBG	DV	IO	295	OMC	8	4	3990	2	10	12000	13600
23	3	LIBERATOR 221	OP	CUD	FBG	DV	IO	375	OMC	8	4	3990	2	10	13900	15800
23	8	HORIZON 230	OP	RNBT	FBG	DV	IO	200-260		8	4	3650	2	11	10100	12100
23	8	HORIZON 230	OP	RNBT	FBG	DV	IO	295	OMC	8	4	3830	2	11	11200	12700
23	8	SUNDOWNER 235	OP	CUD	FBG	DV	IO	200-260		8	4	3850	2	11	11100	13400
23	8	SUNDOWNER 235	OP	CUD	FBG	DV	IO	295	OMC	8	4	4060	2	11	12400	14100
24	4	VISTA 245	OP	CR	FBG	DV	IO	200-295		8	6	4860	3		13800	17200
24	4	VISTA 245	OP	CR	FBG	DV	IB	187D	OMC	8	6	4900	3		22500	25000
26	2	VISTA 265	OP	CR	FBG	DV	IO	260-295		8	6	5690	3	3	17100	20200
26	2	VISTA 265	OP	CR	FBG	DV	IB	187D	OMC	8	6	5590	3	3	25200	28000
26	2	VISTA 265	OP	CR	FBG	DV	IO	T190	OMC	8	6	6500	3	3	20200	22400
27	2	VISTA 275	OP	CR	FBG	DV	IO	295	OMC						21900	24300
27	2	VISTA 275	OP	CR	FBG	DV	IO	T190-T200							22900	25600
28	11	EXPRESS CRUISER 285	OP	CR	FBG	SV	IB	T190	OMC	10	2	9230	3	3	33600	37400
28	11	EXPRESS CRUISER 285	OP	CR	FBG	SV	IO	T200-T250		10	2	9320	3	3	27900	32200
28	11	EXPRESS CRUISER 285	OP	CR	FBG	SV	IB	T187D	OMC	10	2	9320	3	3	46400	51000
30	6	EXPRESS CRUISER 315	OP	CR	FBG	SV	IO	T200-T295		11		11900	3	4	35600	40700
30	6	EXPRESS CRUISER 315	OP	CR	FBG	SV	IB	T187D	OMC	11		10600	3	4	52000	57200
30	6	EXPRESS CRUISER 325	OP	CR	FBG	SV	IO	T235-T320		11		10600	2	10	35800	41500
39		EXPRESS CRUISER 365	OP	CR	FBG	SV	IO	T320	CRUS	13	2	17500	3	2	58200	63900

 CONTINUED ON NEXT PAGE

LOA FT	LOA IN	NAME AND/ OR MODEL	TOP/ RIG	BOAT TYPE	-HULL- MTL	-HULL- TP	ENGINE TP	ENGINE # HP	ENGINE MFG	BEAM FT	BEAM IN	WGT LBS	DRAFT FT	DRAFT IN	RETAIL LOW	RETAIL HIGH
		1993 BOATS														
39		EXPRESS CRUISER 365	OP	CR	FBG	SV	IO	T380	CRUS	13	2	17500	3	2	62200	68300
39		EXPRESS CRUISER 365	OP	CR	FBG	SV	IO	T292D	CUM	13	2	17500	3	2	73100	80300
		1992 BOATS														
17	9	QUEST 187	OP	CTRCN	FBG	DV	OB			7	8	2150	2	3	2700	3150
17	9	QUEST 187 DLX	OP	CTRCN	FBG	DV	OB			7	8	2150	2	3	3000	3500
18	6	FREEDOM 180	OP	RNBT	FBG	DV	OB			7	3	1690	2		2500	2900
18	6	FREEDOM 180	OP	RNBT	FBG	DV	IO	115-150		7	3	2050	2	2	4150	4850
18	6	FREEDOM 180 CB	OP	RNBT	FBG	DV	OB			7	3	1690	2		2550	3000
18	6	FREEDOM 180 CB	OP	RNBT	FBG	DV	IO	115-150		7	3	2050	2	2	4250	5000
19	3	QUEST 207	OP	CTRCN	FBG	DV	OB			8	2	2760	2	6	3100	3600
19	3	QUEST 207 DLX	OP	CTRCN	FBG	DV	OB			8	2	2760	2	6	3450	4050
19	8	CANDIA 180	OP	RNBT	FBG	TR	IO	115-175		7	8	2800	2	2	5450	6650
19	8	HORIZON 190	OP	RNBT	FBG	DV	OB			7	3	2320	2	3	3200	3700
19	8	HORIZON 190	OP	RNBT	FBG	DV	IO	150-175		7	3	2640	2	6	5050	5950
19	8	SUNDOWNER 195	OP	CUD	FBG	DV	OB			7	3	2630	2	3	3400	3950
19	8	SUNDOWNER 195	OP	CUD	FBG	DV	IO	150-175		7	3	2920	2	6	5650	6550
20	1	QUEST 217	OP	CTRCN	FBG	DV	OB			8	6	3410	2	3	4000	4700
20	1	QUEST 217 DLX	OP	CTRCN	FBG	DV	OB			8	6	3700	2	8	4250	4900
20	9	HORIZON 200	OP	RNBT	FBG	DV	OB			7	8	2470	2	8	4300	5000
20	9	HORIZON 200	OP	RNBT	FBG	DV	IO	150-245		7	8	2870	2	10	6550	8000
20	9	HORIZON 200 CNV	OP	RNBT	FBG	DV	IO	150-245		7	8	2870	2	10	6800	8300
20	9	LIBERATOR 201	OP	CUD	FBG	DV	IO	215-275		7	8	3310	2	11	7800	9500
20	9	SUNDOWNER 205	OP	CUD	FBG	DV	OB			7	8	2730	2	10	4550	5250
20	9	SUNDOWNER 205	OP	CUD	FBG	DV	IO	150-245		7	8	3120	2	11	7350	9000
21	7	CANDIA 200	OP	RNBT	FBG	TR	IO	150-245		8		2850	2	4	7050	8650
22	6	QUEST 237	OP	CTRCN	FBG	DV	OB			9		4660	2	10	6250	7200
22	6	QUEST 237 DLX	OP	CTRCN	FBG	DV	OB			9		4660	2	10	6650	7650
23	3	HORIZON 220	OP	RNBT	FBG	DV	IO	215-275		8	4	3580	2	11	9250	11200
23	3	LIBERATOR 221	OP	CUD	FBG	DV	IO	245-275		8	4	3750	2	10	10200	12500
23	3	LIBERATOR 221	OP	CUD	FBG	DV	IO	375	OMC	8	4	3990	2	10	13000	14800
23	3	SUNDOWNER 225	OP	CUD	FBG	DV	IO	175-275		8	4	4020	2	11	10500	13100
24	4	VISTA 235	OP	CR	FBG	DV	IO	215-275		8	6	4800	3		12800	15600
24	4	VISTA 235	OP	CR	FBG	DV	IB	187D	OMC	8	6	4980	3		21700	24100
25		QUEST 257	OP	SF	FBG	DV	OB			9	5	6190	3		8400	9650
25		QUEST 257 DLX	OP	SF	FBG	DV	OB			9	5	6190	3		9050	10300
26	2	LIBERATOR 251	OP	CUD	FBG	DV	IO	275	OMC	8	6	4690	3	2	14600	16600
26	2	LIBERATOR 251	OP	CUD	FBG	DV	IO	T245	OMC	8	6	5380	3	2	18200	20200
26	2	LIBERATOR 251	OP	CUD	FBG	DV	IO	T375	OMC	8	6	5560	3	2	22200	24700
26	2	SUNDOWNER 255	OP	CUD	FBG	DV	IO	215-275		8	6	4860	3	2	14100	17200
26	2	SUNDOWNER 255	OP	CUD	FBG	DV	IO	T150	OMC	8	6	5550	3	2	16500	18800
26	2	VISTA 265	OP	CR	FBG	DV	IO	245-275		8	6	5690	3	3	15800	18700
26	2	VISTA 265	OP	CR	FBG	DV	IO	187D	OMC	8	6	5690	3	3	19100	21200
26	2	VISTA 265	OP	CR	FBG	DV	IO	T175-T200		8	6	6500	3	3	18900	21000
28	11	EXPRESS CRUISER 285	OP	CR	FBG	SV	IO	T215-T245		10	2	9320	3	3	26400	30100
28	11	EXPRESS CRUISER 285	OP	CR	FBG	SV	IO	T187D	OMC	10	2	9320	3	3	34200	38000
30	6	EXPRESS CRUISER 315	OP	CR	FBG	SV	IO	T215-T275		11		10600	3	4	32400	38900
30	6	EXPRESS CRUISER 315	OP	CR	FBG	SV	IO	T187D	OMC	11		10600	3	4	38600	42800
30	6	EXPRESS CRUISER 325	OP	CR	FBG	SV	IO	195D	VLVO	11		10600	2	10	34500	38300
30	6	EXPRESS CRUISER 325	OP	CR	FBG	SV	IO	T235-T300		11		10600	2	10	33500	38300
39		EXPRESS CRUISER 365	OP	CR	FBG	SV	IO	T300	CRUS	13	2	17500	3	2	53600	58900
39		EXPRESS CRUISER 365	OP	CR	FBG	SV	IO	T355	CRUS	13	2	17500	3	2	56400	62000
		1991 BOATS														
17	9	QUEST 187	OP	CTRCN	FBG	DV	OB			7	8	2150			2750	3200
18	6	FREEDOM 170	OP	RNBT	FBG	DV	OB			7	3	1690			2400	2800
18	6	FREEDOM 170	OP	RNBT	FBG	DV	IO	115-130		7	3	2050			3900	4550
18	6	FREEDOM 170 CB	OP	RNBT	FBG	DV	OB			7	3	1690			2500	2900
18	6	FREEDOM 170 CB	OP	RNBT	FBG	DV	IO	115-130		7	3	2050			4000	4700
18	6	HORIZON 180	OP	RNBT	FBG	DV	OB			7	3	2040			2650	3100
18	6	HORIZON 180	OP	RNBT	FBG	DV	IO	130-175		7	3	2420			4200	5200
18	6	HORIZON 180 CON	OP	RNBT	FBG	DV	OB			7	3	2040			2750	3200
18	6	HORIZON 180 CON	OP	RNBT	FBG	DV	IO	130-175		7	3	2420			4400	5350
19	3	QUEST 207	OP	CTRCN	FBG	DV	OB			8	2	2760			3150	3650
19	8	CANDIA 180	OP	RNBT	FBG	TR	OB			7	8	2390			3150	3650
19	8	CANDIA 180	OP	RNBT	FBG	TR	IO	130-175		7	8	2800			5150	6250
19	8	FREEDOM 190	OP	RNBT	FBG	DV	OB			7	3	1860			2750	3200
19	8	FREEDOM 190	OP	RNBT	FBG	DV	IO	115-150		7	3	2140			4300	5150
19	8	FREEDOM 195	OP	CUD	FBG	DV	OB			7	3	2580			3250	3800
19	8	FREEDOM 195	OP	CUD	FBG	DV	IO	130-150		7	3	2620			4950	5900
20	1	QUEST 217	OP	CTRCN	FBG	DV	OB			8	6	3350			4000	4650
20	9	HORIZON 200	OP	RNBT	FBG	DV	OB			7	8	2470			4100	4750
20	9	HORIZON 200	OP	RNBT	FBG	DV	IO	150-235		7	8	2870			6150	7600
20	9	HORIZON 200 CON	OP	RNBT	FBG	DV	IO	150-235		7	8	2870			6350	7850
20	9	LIBERATOR 201	OP	CUD	FBG	DV	IO	175-235		7	8	3240			7100	8550
20	9	SUNDOWNER 205	OP	CUD	FBG	DV	OB			7	8	2730			4400	5050
20	9	SUNDOWNER 205	OP	CUD	FBG	DV	IO	150-235		7	8	3120			6900	8500
21	7	CANDIA 200	OP	RNBT	FBG	TR	IO	150-235		8		2850			6650	8150
22	6	QUEST 237	OP	CTRCN	FBG	DV	OB			9					5350	6100
23	3	HORIZON 220	OP	RNBT	FBG	DV	IO	175-235		8	4	3510			8350	10000
23	3	HORIZON 220	OP	RNBT	FBG	DV	IO	275	OMC	8	4	3760			9350	10600
23	3	LIBERATOR 221	OP	CUD	FBG	DV	IO	210-275		8	4	3810			9550	11700
23	3	LIBERATOR 221	OP	CUD	FBG	DV	IO	310	OMC	8	4	3990			10800	12200
23	3	SUNDOWNER 225	OP	CUD	FBG	DV	IO	175-275		8	4	4020			9850	12300
24	4	VISTA 235	OP	CR	FBG	DV	IO	210-275		8	6	4800			12000	14600
25		QUEST 257	OP	SF	FBG	DV	OB			9	5	5860			8150	9350
26	2	LIBERATOR 251	OP	CUD	FBG	DV	IO	275-310		8	6	4690			13700	16100
26	2	LIBERATOR 251	OP	CUD	FBG	DV	IO	T175-T235		8	6	5380			15600	19000
26	2	SUNDOWNER 255	OP	CUD	FBG	DV	IO	210-275		8	6	4860			13200	16100
26	2	SUNDOWNER 255	OP	CUD	FBG	DV	IO	T150-T175		8	6	5550			15500	18400
26	2	VISTA 265	OP	CR	FBG	DV	IO	220-275		8	6	5690			14600	17600
26	2	VISTA 265	OP	CR	FBG	DV	IO	T150-T175		8	6	6300			16700	19700
28	11	EXPRESS CRUISER 285	OP	CR	FBG	SV	IO	275	OMC	10	2	8460			22200	24700
28	11	EXPRESS CRUISER 285	OP	CR	FBG	SV	IO	T150-T230		10	2	9320			23600	27900
30	6	EXPRESS CRUISER 315	OP	CR	FBG	SV	IO	T220-T275		11		10600			30500	36500
30	6	EXPRESS CRUISER 325	OP	CR	FBG	SV	IO	D	GM	11		10600			**	**
30	6	EXPRESS CRUISER 325	OP	CR	FBG	SV	IO	150D	VLVO	11		10600			32500	36100
30	6	EXPRESS CRUISER 325	OP	CR	FBG	SV	IO	T235-T300		11		10600			31400	35900
39		EXPRESS CRUISER 365	OP	CR	FBG	SV	IO			13	2	17500			**	**
		1990 BOATS														
18	6	FREEDOM 170	ST	RNBT	FBG	DV	OB			7	3	1700			2350	2750
18	6	FREEDOM 170	ST	RNBT	FBG	DV	IO	128-130		7	3	2050			3700	4300
18	6	FREEDOM 170 CB	ST	RNBT	FBG	DV	OB			7	3	1700			2400	2800
18	6	FREEDOM 170 CB	ST	RNBT	FBG	DV	IO	130	OMC	7	3	2050			3800	4400
18	6	HORIZON 180	ST	RNBT	FBG	DV	OB			7	3	1970			2550	2950
18	6	HORIZON 180	ST	RNBT	FBG	DV	IO	175-200		7	3	2480			4100	4950
18	6	HORIZON 180 CNV	ST	RNBT	FBG	DV	OB			7	3	1970			2600	3050
18	6	HORIZON 180 CNV	ST	RNBT	FBG	DV	IO	175-200		7	3	2420			4050	4750
19	8	CANDIA 180	ST	RNBT	FBG	TR	OB			7	8	2440			3100	3600
19	8	CANDIA 180	ST	RNBT	FBG	TR	IO	175-200		7	8	2860			4900	5850
19	8	FREEDOM 190	ST	RNBT	FBG	DV	OB			7	3	1860			2650	3100
19	8	FREEDOM 190	ST	RNBT	FBG	DV	IO	130-175		7	3	2140			4050	4900
19	8	FREEDOM 195	ST	CUD	FBG	DV	OB			7	3	2310			3000	3500
19	8	FREEDOM 195	ST	CUD	FBG	DV	IO	175	OMC	7	3	2740			4850	5550
19	10	QUEST 207 CC	ST	OPFSH	FBG	DV	OB			8	4	2390			3100	3600
19	10	QUEST 207 DC	ST	OPFSH	FBG	DV	OB			8	4	2390			3150	3650
20	9	HORIZON 200	ST	RNBT	FBG	DV	OB			7	8	2370			3850	4450
20	9	HORIZON 200	ST	RNBT	FBG	DV	IO	175-260		7	8	2770			5700	7050
20	9	HORIZON 200 CNV	ST	RNBT	FBG	DV	IO	175-260		7	8	2770			5900	7300
20	9	LIBERATOR 201	OP	CUD	FBG	DV	IO	260-270		7	8	3260			7050	8200
20	9	LIBERATOR 201 2+2	OP	CUD	FBG	DV	IO	270	OMC	7	8	3260			9700	11000
20	9	SUNDOWNER 205	ST	CUD	FBG	DV	OB			7	8	2540			4000	4650
20	9	SUNDOWNER 205	ST	CUD	FBG	DV	IO	175-260		7	8	2940			6250	7750
21	7	CANDIA 200	ST	RNBT	FBG	TR	IO	200-260		8		3240			6850	8300
23	3	HORIZON 220	ST	RNBT	FBG	DV	IO	200-260		8	4	3650			8100	9650
23	3	HORIZON 220	ST	RNBT	FBG	DV	IO	340	OMC	8	4	3990			10000	11400
23	3	LIBERATOR 221	OP	CUD	FBG	DV	IO	370	OMC	8	4	4140			11600	13200
23	3	LIBERATOR 221	ST	CUD	FBG	DV	IO	270	OMC	8	4	3990			9650	10900
23	3	LIBERATOR 221	ST	CUD	FBG	DV	IO	340	OMC	8	4	3990			10600	12100
23	3	SUNDOWNER 225	ST	CUD	FBG	DV	IO	200-260		8	4	4070			9400	11000
23	3	SUNDOWNER 225	ST	CUD	FBG	DV	IO	340	OMC	8	4	4370			11300	12900
23	8	SUNDOWNER 235	ST	CUD	FBG	DV	IO	260	OMC	8	6	4540			10800	12200
23	8	SUNDOWNER 235	ST	CUD	FBG	DV	IO	340	OMC	8	6	4540			11900	13500
23	8	VISTA 245	ST	CR	FBG	DV	IO	260	OMC	8	6	5470	3	2	12500	14200
23	8	VISTA 245	ST	CR	FBG	DV	IO	340	OMC	8	6	5720	3	2	14100	16000
23	8	VISTA 245	ST	CR	FBG	DV	IO	T175	OMC	8	6	6170	3	2	14500	16500
26		LIBERATOR 261	OP	CUD	FBG	DV	IO	T270	OMC	8		6180			17000	19300
26		LIBERATOR 261	OP	CUD	FBG	DV	IO	T340-T370		8		6800			20000	22500
26		QUEST 267	ST	SPTCR	FBG	DV	IO	260	OMC	8		5200	2	7	13100	14900
26		QUEST 267	ST	SPTCR	FBG	DV	IO	T140	OMC	8		5200	2	7	13700	15600
26	2	LIBERATOR 251	OP	CUD	FBG	DV	IO	340-370		8	6	4950			14200	16900
26	2	LIBERATOR 251	OP	CUD	FBG	DV	IO	T270	OMC	8	6	5860			16800	19100
26	2	SUNDOWNER 255	ST	CUD	FBG	DV	IO	260	OMC	8	6	5100			13300	15100
26	2	SUNDOWNER 255	ST	CUD	FBG	DV	IO	340	OMC	8	6	5340			14800	16800
26	2	SUNDOWNER 255	ST	CUD	FBG	DV	IO	T200	OMC	8	6	5900			15700	17900
26	2	VISTA 265	ST	CR	FBG	DV	IO	260	OMC	8	6	5470	3	3	13800	15700
26	2	VISTA 265	ST	CR	FBG	DV	IO	340	OMC	8	6	5980	3	3	15700	17900
26	2	VISTA 265	ST	CR	FBG	DV	IO	T200	OMC	8	6	6500	3	3	16600	18900

CONTINUED ON NEXT PAGE

LOA FT	IN	NAME AND/ OR MODEL	TOP/ RIG	BOAT TYPE	-HULL- MTL	TP	----ENGINE--- TP	# HP	MFG	BEAM FT	IN	WGT LBS	DRAFT FT	IN	RETAIL LOW	RETAIL HIGH
		1990 BOATS														
28	11	VISTA 285	ST	CR	FBG	TR	IO	T200-T260				9200	3	3	22900	26700
28	11	VISTA 285 SE	ST	CR	FBG	DV	IO	340	OMC	10		9670	2	9	23000	25600
28	11	VISTA 285 SE	ST	CR	FBG	DV	IO	T175	OMC	10		9670	2	9	23000	25500
30	6	VISTA 315	ST	CR	FBG	DV	IO	T260-T340		11		11000	3	4	29900	35600
		1989 BOATS														
16		FREEDOM 160	ST	RNBT	FBG	DV	OB			7	2	1825			2450	2850
16		FREEDOM 160	ST	RNBT	FBG	DV	IO	130	OMC	7	2	2090			3050	3550
18	6	FREEDOM 170	ST	RNBT	FBG	DV	OB			7	3	1670			2300	2650
18	6	FREEDOM 170	ST	RNBT	FBG	DV	IO	128	OMC	7	3	2010			3450	4050
18	6	HORIZON 180 CNV	ST	RNBT	FBG	DV	OB			7	3	1990			2500	2900
18	6	HORIZON 180 CNV	ST	RNBT	FBG	DV	IO	175-200		7	3	2420			3850	4600
19	8	FREEDOM 190	ST	RNBT	FBG	DV	OB			7	3	1670			2400	2800
19	8	FREEDOM 190	ST	RNBT	FBG	DV	IO	175	OMC	7	3	2105			3800	4450
19	10	QUEST 207	ST	OPFSH	FBG	DV	OB			8	4	2390			3000	3500
20	9	HORIZON 200	ST	RNBT	FBG	DV	OB			7	8	2370			3700	4300
20	9	HORIZON 200	ST	RNBT	FBG	DV	IO	175-260		7	8	2770			5350	6650
20	9	HORIZON 200 CNV	ST	RNBT	FBG	DV	IO	175-260		7	8	2770			5550	6850
20	9	LIBERATOR 201	OP	CUD	FBG	DV	IO	260-270		7	8	3060			6400	7450
20	9	SUNDOWNER 205	ST	CUD	FBG	DV	OB			7	8	2550			3850	4500
20	9	SUNDOWNER 205	ST	CUD	FBG	DV	IO	175-260		7	8	2940			5900	7350
21		HORIZON 210	ST	RNBT	FBG	DV	IO	200-260		8		3100			6100	7300
21		HORIZON 210	ST	RNBT	FBG	DV	IO	340	OMC	8		3400			7700	8850
21		LIBERATOR 211	OP	CUD	FBG	DV	IO	270	OMC	8		3260			6950	8000
21		LIBERATOR 211	OP	CUD	FBG	DV	IO	340	OMC	8		3560			8300	9550
21		SUNDOWNER 215	ST	CUD	FBG	DV	IO	200-260		8		3290			6650	7950
22	5	SUNDOWNER 225	ST	CUD	FBG	DV	IO	230-260		8		3540			7650	8850
22	5	SUNDOWNER 225	ST	CUD	FBG	DV	IO	340	OMC	8		3770			9300	10600
23	8	LIBERATOR 241	OP	CUD	FBG	DV	IO	340	OMC	8	6	5030			12100	13700
23	8	LIBERATOR 241	OP	CUD	FBG	DV	IO	T270	OMC	8	6	5640			13600	15400
23	8	SUNDOWNER 235	ST	CUD	FBG	DV	IO	260	OMC	8	6	4540			10200	11600
23	8	SUNDOWNER 235	ST	CUD	FBG	DV	IO	340	OMC	8	6	4840			11700	13300
23	8	VISTA 245	ST	CR	FBG	DV	IO	260	OMC	8	6	5470	2	7	11800	13400
23	8	VISTA 245	ST	CR	FBG	DV	IO	340	OMC	8	6	5770	2	7	13300	15200
23	8	VISTA 245	ST	CR	FBG	DV	IO	T175	OMC	8	6	6170	2	7	13700	15600
26		LIBERATOR 261	OP	CUD	FBG	DV	IO	T270	OMC	8		5900			15600	17800
26		LIBERATOR 261	OP	CUD	FBG	DV	IO	T340	OMC	8		6500			18700	20700
26		QUEST 267	ST	SPTCR	FBG	DV	IO	260	OMC	8		5200	2	7	12400	14100
26		QUEST 267	ST	SPTCR	FBG	DV	IO	T140	OMC	8		5320	2	7	13100	14900
26	2	SUNDOWNER 255	ST	CUD	FBG	DV	IO	235-260		8	6	5070			12200	14100
26	2	SUNDOWNER 255	ST	CUD	FBG	DV	IO	340	OMC	8	6	5300			13900	15800
26	2	SUNDOWNER 255	ST	CUD	FBG	DV	IO	T200	OMC	8	6	5900			14800	16900
26	2	VISTA 255	ST	CR	FBG	DV	IO	235-260		8	6	5820	3	1	13300	15300
26	2	VISTA 255	ST	CR	FBG	DV	IO	340	OMC	8	6	6050	3	1	14900	17000
26	2	VISTA 255	ST	CR	FBG	DV	IO	T200	OMC	8	6	6650	3	1	15900	18100
28	11	VISTA 285	ST	CR	FBG	DV	IO	T200-T260		10		9670	2	9	22100	25600
30	6	VISTA 315	ST	CR	FBG	DV	IO	T260-T340		11		11400	2	9	28500	34000
		1988 BOATS														
16		FREEDOM 160	ST	RNBT	FBG	DV	OB			7	2	1457			1900	2300
16		FREEDOM 160	ST	RNBT	FBG	DV	IO	130	OMC	7	2	1960			2800	3250
18	6	HORIZON 180	ST	RNBT	FBG	DV	OB			7	3	2006			2450	2850
18	6	HORIZON 180	ST	RNBT	FBG	DV	IO	130-205		7	3	2255			3450	4250
20	9	HORIZON 200	ST	RNBT	FBG	DV	OB			7	8	2255			3450	4000
20	9	HORIZON 200	ST	RNBT	FBG	DV	IO	175-260		7	8	2560			4950	6150
20	9	HORIZON 200	ST	RNBT	FBG	DV	IO	270	OMC	7	8	2661			5400	6250
20	9	LIBERATOR 201	OP	CUD	FBG	DV	IO	270	OMC	7	8	3060			6150	7050
20	9	SUNDOWNER 205	ST	CUD	FBG	DV	OB			7	8	2381			3550	4150
20	9	SUNDOWNER 205	ST	CUD	FBG	DV	IO	175-260		7	8	2740			5350	6650
21		HORIZON 210	ST	RNBT	FBG	DV	IO	175-270		8		2885			5500	6850
21		HORIZON 210	ST	RNBT	FBG	DV	IO	340	OMC	8		3320			7200	8250
21		LIBERATOR 211	OP	CUD	FBG	DV	IO	270	OMC	8		3260			6600	7550
21		LIBERATOR 211	OP	CUD	FBG	DV	IO	340	OMC	8		3260			7500	8600
21		SUNDOWNER 215	ST	CUD	FBG	DV	IO	175-260		8		3085			6000	7400
22	5	SUNDOWNER 225	ST	CUD	FBG	DV	IO	200-260		8		3519			7100	8450
23	8	LIBERATOR 241	OP	CUD	FBG	DV	IO	270-340		8	6	5640			11500	14100
23	8	LIBERATOR 241	OP	CUD	FBG	DV	IO	T205-T270		8	6	5640			12200	14600
23	8	SUNDOWNER 235	ST	CUD	FBG	DV	IO	230-260		8	6	4023			8600	10000
23	8	SUNDOWNER 235	ST	CUD	FBG	DV	IO	340	OMC	8	6	4317			10200	11600
23	8	SUNDOWNER 235	ST	CUD	FBG	DV	IO	T130-T205		8	6	4467			10100	12400
23	8	VISTA 245	ST	CR	FBG	DV	IO	260	OMC	8	6	4994			10400	11800
23	8	VISTA 245	ST	CR	FBG	DV	IO	340	OMC	8	6	5293			11800	13500
23	8	VISTA 245	ST	CR	FBG	DV	IO	T130-T205		8	6	5443			11700	14000
26		LIBERATOR 261	OP	CUD	FBG	DV	IO	340	OMC	8		6500			14600	16500
26		LIBERATOR 261	OP	CUD	FBG	DV	IO	T270	OMC	8		6500			15600	17700
26		LIBERATOR 261	OP	CUD	FBG	DV	IO	T340	OMC	8		6500			17300	19600
26		QUEST 267	ST	SPTCR	FBG	DV	IO	260	OMC	8		5054			11500	13100
28	11	VISTA 285	ST	CR	FBG	DV	IO	T175-T260		10		9470			20300	24300
28	11	VISTA 285	ST	CR	FBG	DV	IO	T340	OMC	10		10280			24000	26700
30	6	VISTA 315	ST	CR	FBG	DV	IO	T205-T340		11		10750			25500	31800
		1987 BOATS														
16		FREEDOM I	ST	RNBT	FBG	DV	OB			7	2	1200			1550	1850
16		FREEDOM I	ST	RNBT	FBG	DV	IO	130		7	2	1900			2650	3050
17		HORIZON 170	ST	RNBT	FBG	DV	OB			7	7	1400			1800	2150
17		HORIZON 170	ST	RNBT	FBG	DV	IO	165-205		7	7	1480			2650	3150
17		HORIZON 170	ST	RNBT	FBG	DV	IO	230		7	7	2100			3200	3700
18	8	HORIZON 190	ST	RNBT	FBG	DV	OB			7	7	1600			2050	2450
18	8	HORIZON 190	ST	RNBT	FBG	DV	IO	165-230		7	7	1580			3050	3700
18	8	HORIZON 190	ST	RNBT	FBG	DV	IO	260		7	7	2200			3700	4300
18	8	SUNDOWNER 195	ST	CUD	FBG	DV	OB			7	7	1600			2050	2450
18	8	SUNDOWNER 195	ST	CUD	FBG	DV	IO	260		7	7	2400			3950	4600
18	8	SUNDOWNER 195	ST	RNBT	FBG	DV	IO	165-230		7	7	1780			3150	3800
18	8	SUNDOWNER 195	ST	RNBT	FBG	DV	IO	260		7	7	1780			3400	4000
20		CANDIA 200	ST	RNBT	FBG	DV	IO	165-260		8		1805			4050	5050
21		HORIZON 210	ST	RNBT	FBG	DV	IO	165-260		8		2700			5050	6150
21		HORIZON 215	ST	CUD	FBG	DV	IO	260	OMC	8		2900			5750	6650
21		LIBERATOR 211	OP	CUD	FBG	DV	IO	350		8		2193			6250	7200
21		LIBERATOR 211	OP	RNBT	FBG	DV	IO	350	MRCR	8		3100			6850	7900
21		SUNDOWNER 215	ST	RNBT	FBG	DV	IO	165-260		8		2280			4700	5700
21		SUNDOWNER 215	ST	RNBT	FBG	DV	IO	T205	MRCR	8		2280			5650	6500
21		SUNDOWNER FISH 217	ST	CUD	FBG	DV	IO	260	OMC	8	8	3000			6150	7050
21		SUNDOWNER FISH 217	ST	RNBT	FBG	DV	IO	260	MRCR	8		3000			5650	6500
21		SUNDOWNER SPORT 212	ST	RNBT	FBG	DV	IO	260		8		2800			5450	6500
22	5	SUNDOWNER 225	ST	CUD	FBG	DV	IO	260	OMC	8	8	3415			7100	8150
22	5	SUNDOWNER 225	ST	RNBT	FBG	DV	IO	200-260		8		2613			5350	6450
23	8	SUNDOWNER 235	ST	CUD	FBG	DV	IO	260		8	6	3107			7050	8100
		IO 350 8200 9450, IO T130-T230 7600 9150, IO T260													8300	9550
23	8	VISTA 245	ST	CUD	FBG	DV	IO	350	MRCR	8	6	4093			9700	11000
23	8	VISTA 245	ST	CUD	FBG	DV	IO	T130-T205		8	6	4093			9150	10600
24	8	LIBERATOR 241	OP	CUD	FBG	DV	IO	454		8	6	4000			12700	14400
		IO T200-T230 9800 11400, IO T260 MRCR 8600 9850, IO T260-T350													13300	15100
24	8	SUNDOWNER 235	ST	CUD	FBG	DV	IO	T260		8	6	4000			9200	10400
24	8	VISTA 245	ST	CUD	FBG	DV	IO	260		8	6	5000			10400	11800
26		LIBERATOR 261	OP	CUD	FBG	DV	IO	T454		8		5500			19500	21700
26		QUEST 267	ST	SPTCR	FBG	DV	IO	260		8		5050			11000	12500
		1986 BOATS														
16		FREEDOM I	ST	RNBT	FBG	DV	OB			7	2	1200			1500	1800
16		FREEDOM I	ST	RNBT	FBG	DV	IO	140		7	2	1900			2500	2950
17		HORIZON 170	ST	RNBT	FBG	DV	OB			7	7	1400			1750	2100
17		HORIZON 170	ST	RNBT	FBG	DV	IO	230		7	7	2100			3050	3550
18	8	HORIZON 190	ST	RNBT	FBG	DV	OB			7	7	1600			2000	2400
18	8	HORIZON 190	ST	RNBT	FBG	DV	IO	260		7	7	2200			3550	4100
18	8	HORIZON CUDDY 195	ST	CUD	FBG	DV	OB			7	7	1600			2000	2400
18	8	HORIZON CUDDY 195	ST	CUD	FBG	DV	IO	260		7	7	2400			3800	4400
18	8	HORIZON CUDDY SP 196	ST	CUD	FBG	DV	OB			7	7	1700			2100	2500
18	8	HORIZON CUDDY SP 196	ST	CUD	FBG	DV	IO	260		7	7	2500			3850	4500
18	8	HORIZON SPORT 192	ST	RNBT	FBG	DV	OB			7	7	2300			2450	2900
18	8	HORIZON SPORT 192	ST	RNBT	FBG	DV	IO	260		7	7	2300			3600	4200
21		LIBERATOR 211	OP	CUD	FBG	DV	IO	300		8		3100			6150	7050
21		SANTARA 210	ST	RNBT	FBG	DV	IO	260		8		2700			5100	5850
21		SANTARA 215	ST	CUD	FBG	DV	IO	260	OMC	8		2900			5500	6350
21		SANTARA 215	ST	RNBT	FBG	DV	IO	260	MRCR	8	8	2900			5550	6350
21		SANTARA FISH 217	ST	CUD	FBG	DV	IO	260	OMC	8		3000			5650	6500
21		SANTARA FISH 217	ST	RNBT	FBG	DV	IO	260	MRCR	8		3000			5400	6250
21		SANTARA SPORT 212	ST	RNBT	FBG	DV	IO	260		8		2800			5200	6000
21		SANTARA SPORT 216	ST	CUD	FBG	DV	IO	260	OMC	8		3000			5600	6450
21		SANTARA SPORT 216	ST	RNBT	FBG	DV	IO	260	MRCR	8		3000			5400	6200
22	5	SUNDOWNER 225	ST	CUD	FBG	DV	IO	260	OMC	8		3415			6550	7550
22	5	SUNDOWNER 225	ST	RNBT	FBG	DV	IO	260	MRCR	8		3415			6250	7150
22	5	SUNDOWNER FISH 227	ST	CUD	FBG	DV	IO	260		8		3515			6750	7750
22	5	SUNDOWNER SPORT 226	ST	CUD	FBG	DV	IO	260		8		3515			6700	7700
24	8	LIBERATOR 241	OP	CUD	FBG	DV	IO	T260		8	6	4000			10200	11600
24	8	SUNDOWNER 235	ST	CUD	FBG	DV	IO	T260		8	6	4000			9600	10900
24	8	SUNDOWNER 245	ST	CUD	FBG	DV	IO	260		8	6	5000			9850	11200
24	8	SUNDOWNER SPORT 236	ST	CUD	FBG	DV	IO	T260		8	6	4100			10100	11500
26		LIBERATOR 261	OP	CUD	FBG	DV	IO	T300	MRCR	8		5500			13600	15500
26		QUEST 267	ST	SPTCR	FBG	DV	IO	260	MRCR	8		5050			10500	11900

 CONTINUED ON NEXT PAGE

LOA FT	LOA IN	NAME AND/ OR MODEL	TOP/ RIG	BOAT TYPE	-HULL- MTL	-HULL- TP	ENGINE TP	ENGINE # HP	ENGINE MFG	BEAM FT	BEAM IN	WGT LBS	DRAFT FT	DRAFT IN	RETAIL LOW	RETAIL HIGH
1985 BOATS																
17		HORIZON 170	ST	RNBT	FBG	DV	OB			7	7	1400			1700	2050
17		HORIZON 170	ST	RNBT	FBG	DV	IO	120-190		7	7	2000			2650	3100
17		HORIZON 170 BROUGHAM	ST	RNBT	FBG	DV	IO	120-190		7	7	2000			2750	3200
18	8	HORIZON 190	ST	RNBT	FBG	DV	OB			7	6	1600			1900	2250
18	8	HORIZON 190	ST	RNBT	FBG	DV	IO	120-230		7	6	2200			3050	3800
18	8	HORIZON 190 BROUGHAM	ST	RNBT	FBG	DV	IO	120-230		7	6	2200			3150	3800
18	8	HORIZON 192 SPORT	ST	RNBT	FBG	DV	OB			7	6	1600			2050	2450
18	8	HORIZON 195	ST	CUD	FBG	DV	OB			7	6	1600			1950	2350
18	8	HORIZON 195	ST	CUD	FBG	DV	IO	120-200		7	6	2400			3350	3900
18	8	HORIZON 196 SPORT	ST	CUD	FBG	DV	OB			7	6	1600			1950	2350
18	8	HORIZON 196 SPORT	ST	CUD	FBG	DV	IO	120-200		7	6	2500			3400	4000
18	8	HORIZON SPORT 192	ST	RNBT	FBG	DV	IO	120-140		7	6	2200			3050	3650
20	4	SEAJAUNT 217 WAR	ST	CUD	FBG	DV	IO	140-260		8		2990			4950	6050
21		LIBERATOR	OP	CUD	FBG	DV	IO	140-260		8		3000			5150	6250
21		SANTARA 210	ST	RNBT	FBG	DV	IO	140-260		8		2550			4500	5450
21		SANTARA 215	ST	CUD	FBG	DV	IO	140-260		8		2900			4900	6000
21		SANTARA 216 SPORT	ST	CUD	FBG	DV	IO	140-260		8		2900			5050	6150
21		SANTARA 217 FISH	ST	CUD	FBG	DV	IO	140-260		8		2900			5100	6250
22	5	SUNDOWNER 225	ST	CUD	FBG	DV	IO	170-200		8		3415			5600	6950
22	5	SUNDOWNER 225	ST	CUD	FBG	DV	IO	230-260		8		3415			6550	7550
22	5	SUNDOWNER 226 SPORT	ST	CUD	FBG	DV	IO	170-230		8		3415			5850	6900
22	5	SUNDOWNER 226 SPORT	ST	CUD	FBG	DV	IO	260		8		3415			6550	7550
22	5	SUNDOWNER 227 FISH	ST	CUD	FBG	DV	IO	170-260		8		3415			6400	7350
23		SEAJAUNT	ST	CUD	FBG	DV	IO	140		8		3000			5700	6550
26		LIBERATOR 260	OP	OFF	FBG	DV	IO	260		8		5200			10100	11500
26		QUEST 267	ST	SPTCR	FBG	DV	IO	260		8		4800			9800	11100
1984 BOATS																
16	7	MARQUISE 170	ST	RNBT	FBG	DV	OB			7	2	1100			1350	1600
16	7	MARQUISE 170	ST	RNBT	FBG	DV	IO	120-188		7	2	1780			2350	2750
16	7	MARQUISE 170 BROUGHM	ST	RNBT	FBG	DV	IO	120-185		7	2	1780			2350	2850
18	8	EXTASEA 190		CUD	FBG	DV	OB			7	6	1600			1850	2200
18	8	EXTASEA 190		CUD	FBG	DV	IO	120		7	6	2500			3200	3750
18	8	EXTASEA 190		RNBT	FBG	DV	OB			7	6	1250			1600	1900
18	8	EXTASEA 190		RNBT	FBG	DV	IO	120		7	6	2200			3000	3500
18	8	EXTASEA 190 SPORT		CUD	FBG	DV	OB			7	6	1600			1950	2350
18	8	EXTASEA 190 SPORT		CUD	FBG	DV	IO	120		7	6	2500			3350	3900
18	8	HORIZON 190	ST	RNBT	FBG	DV	OB			7	6	1600			1850	2200
18	8	HORIZON 190	ST	RNBT	FBG	DV	IO	120-230		7	6	2200			2950	3650
18	8	HORIZON 190 BROUGHAM	ST	RNBT	FBG	DV	IO	120-228		7	6	2200			3050	3700
18	8	HORIZON 192 SPORT	ST	RNBT	FBG	DV	OB			7	6	1600			2000	2350
18	8	HORIZON 195	ST	CUD	FBG	DV	OB			7	6	1600			1900	2300
18	8	HORIZON 195	ST	CUD	FBG	DV	IO	120-200		7	6	2400			3200	3800
18	8	HORIZON 196 SPORT	ST	CUD	FBG	DV	OB			7	6	1600			1900	2300
18	8	HORIZON 196 SPORT	ST	CUD	FBG	DV	IO	140-185		7	6	2400			3300	3850
20	4	LIBERATOR 201	OP	CUD	FBG	DV	IO	185-260		8		2838			4700	5650
20	4	SANTARA 200	ST	RNBT	FBG	DV	IO	140-260		8		2550			4150	5150
20	4	SANTARA 205	ST	CUD	FBG	DV	IO	140-260		8		2800			4450	5450
20	4	SANTARA 206 SPORT	ST	CUD	FBG	DV	IO	140-260		8		2800			4650	5650
20	4	SANTARA 207 FISH	ST	CUD	FBG	DV	IO	140-260		8		2800			4650	5700
20	4	SEAJAUNT 217 WAR	ST	CUD	FBG	DV	IO	140-260		8		2990			4750	5850
22	5	SUNDOWNER 225	ST	CUD	FBG	DV	IO	198-260		8		3415			5750	6900
22	5	SUNDOWNER 226 SPORT	ST	CUD	FBG	DV	IO	198-260		8		3415			5950	7100
22	5	SUNDOWNER 227 FISH	ST	CUD	FBG	DV	IO	170-260		8		3415			5850	7150

....For earlier years, see the BUC Used Boat Price Guide, Volume 3

FREEDOM YACHTS INC

MIDDLETOWN RI 02842 COAST GUARD MFG ID- FYC See inside cover to adjust price for area

For more recent years, see the BUC Used Boat Price Guide, Volume 1

LOA FT	LOA IN	NAME AND/ OR MODEL	TOP/ RIG	BOAT TYPE	-HULL- MTL	-HULL- TP	ENGINE TP	ENGINE # HP	ENGINE MFG	BEAM FT	BEAM IN	WGT LBS	DRAFT FT	DRAFT IN	RETAIL LOW	RETAIL HIGH
1996 BOATS																
24	5	FREEDOM 24	SLP	SA/CR	FBG	KL	OB			8		3250	4	5	15900	18000
35	3	FREEDOM 35	SLP	SACAC	FBG	KL	IB	27D	YAN	12		14611	4	6	101500	111500
40	4	FREEDOM 40	SLP	SACAC	FBG	KL	IB	45D	YAN	13	5	22500	5	2	165500	182000
44	6	FREEDOM 45 AFT	SLP	SACAC	FBG	KL	IB	75D	YAN	13	5	27000	4	10	219500	241500
44	6	FREEDOM 45 CC	SLP	SACAC	FBG	KL	IB	75D	YAN	13	6	27500	4	10	221500	243500
1995 BOATS																
24	5	FREEDOM 24	SLP	SA/CR	FBG	KL	OB			8		3250	4	5	14900	16900
35	3	FREEDOM 35	SLP	SACAC	FBG	KL	IB	27D	YAN	12		14611	4	6	95700	105000
40	4	FREEDOM 40	SLP	SACAC	FBG	KL	IB	45D	YAN	13	5	22500	5	2	155500	171000
44	6	FREEDOM 45 AFT	SLP	SACAC	FBG	KL	IB	75D	YAN	13	5	27000	4	10	206500	227000
44	6	FREEDOM 45 CC	SLP	SACAC	FBG	KL	IB	75D	YAN	13	6	27500	4	10	208500	229000
1994 BOATS																
24	5	FREEDOM 24	SLP	SA/CR	FBG	KL	OB			8		3250	4	5	14000	15900
35	3	FREEDOM 35	SLP	SACAC	FBG	KL	IB	27D	YAN	12		14611	4	6	90000	98900
40	4	FREEDOM 40	SLP	SACAC	FBG	KL	IB	45D	YAN	14	6	22500	5	2	146500	161000
44	6	FREEDOM 45 AFT	SLP	SACAC	FBG	KL	IB	75D	YAN	13	5	27000	4	10	194500	213500
44	6	FREEDOM 45 CC	SLP	SACAC	FBG	KL	IB	75D	YAN	13	6	27500	4	10	196000	215500
1993 BOATS																
31	6	FREEDOM 32	SLP	SACAC	FBG	KL	IB	18D	YAN	10	9	7660	4	6	44100	49000
31	6	FREEDOM 32 DEEP	SLP	SACAC	FBG	KL	IB	18D	YAN	10	9	7610	4	6	43800	48700
35	3	FREEDOM 35	SLP	SACAC	FBG	KL	IB	30D	PERK	12		14300	6	5	82700	90900
37	11	FREEDOM 38 DEEP	SLP	SACAC	FBG	KL	IB	27D	YAN	12	6	12000	6		76900	84500
37	11	FREEDOM 38 SHOAL	SLP	SACAC	FBG	KL	IB	27D	YAN	12	6	14000	4	6	87300	95900
37	11	FREEDOM 38 WING	SLP	SACAC	FBG	KL	IB	27D	YAN	12	6	14000	4		87300	95900
44	6	FREEDOM 45 AC	SLP	SACAC	FBG	KL	IB	75D	YAN	13	6	26000	4	11	183500	202000
44	6	FREEDOM 45 AFT	SLP	SACAC	FBG	KL	IB	75D	YAN	13	6	26000	6	6	178000	195500
44	6	FREEDOM 45 CC	SLP	SACAC	FBG	KL	IB	75D	YAN	13	6	26000	4	11	178000	195500
1992 BOATS																
31	6	FREEDOM 32	SLP	SA/CR	F/S	KL	IB	18D	YAN	10	9	7660	4	6	41500	46100
31	6	FREEDOM 32 DEEP	SLP	SA/CR	F/S	KL	IB	18D	YAN	10	9	7610	4	6	41200	45800
37	11	FREEDOM 38 DEEP	SLP	SA/CR	F/S	KL	IB	27D	YAN	12	6	12000	6		72300	79500
37	11	FREEDOM 38 SHOAL	SLP	SA/CR	F/S	KL	IB	27D	YAN	12	6	14000	4	6	82100	90300
37	11	FREEDOM 38 WING	SLP	SA/CR	F/S	KL	IB	27D	YAN	12	6	14000	4		82100	90300
44	6	FREEDOM 45 DEEP	SLP	SA/CR	F/S	KL	IB	75D	YAN	13	6	26000	6	6	169000	185500
44	6	FREEDOM 45 WING	SLP	SA/CR	F/S	KL	IB	75D	YAN	13	6	26000	4	11	169000	185500
1991 BOATS																
31	6	FREEDOM 32	SLP	SA/CR	F/S	KL	IB	18D	YAN	10	9	7660	4	6	39000	43400
31	6	FREEDOM 32 DEEP	SLP	SA/CR	F/S	KL	IB	18D	YAN	10	9	7610	4	6	38800	43100
37	11	FREEDOM 38 DEEP	SLP	SA/CR	F/S	KL	IB	27D	YAN	12	6	13400	6		74500	81900
37	11	FREEDOM 38 SHOAL	SLP	SA/CR	F/S	KL	IB	27D	YAN	12	6	14370	4	6	78900	86700
37	11	FREEDOM 38 WING	SLP	SA/CR	F/S	KL	IB	27D	YAN	12	6	14050	4		77500	85100
44	6	FREEDOM 45 DEEP	SLP	SA/CR	F/S	KL	IB	75D	YAN	13	6	26000	6	6	158500	174500
44	6	FREEDOM 45 WING	SLP	SA/CR	F/S	KL	IB	75D	YAN	13	6	26000	4	11	158500	174500
1990 BOATS																
31	6	FREEDOM 32	SLP	SA/CR	F/S	KL	IB	18D	YAN	10	9	7660	4	6	36700	40800
31	6	FREEDOM 32 DEEP	SLP	SA/CR	F/S	KL	IB	18D	YAN	10	9	7660	4	6	36700	40800
37	11	FREEDOM 38 DEEP	SLP	SA/CR	F/S	KL	IB	27D	YAN	12	6	14370	6		74200	81600
37	11	FREEDOM 38 SHOAL	SLP	SA/CR	F/S	KL	IB	27D	YAN	12	6	14370	4	6	74200	81600
37	11	FREEDOM 38 WING	SLP	SA/CR	F/S	KL	IB	27D	YAN	12	6	14370	4		74200	81600
44	6	FREEDOM 45 DEEP	SLP	SA/CR	F/S	KL	IB	74D	YAN	13	6	26000	6	6	149500	164000
44	6	FREEDOM 45 WING	SLP	SA/CR	F/S	KL	IB	74D	YAN	13	6	26000	4	11	149500	164000
1989 BOATS																
28	6	FREEDOM 28	SLP	SA/CR	F/S	KL	IB	18D	YAN	10	3	6370	4	6	26400	29400
31	6	FREEDOM 32	SLP	SA/CR	F/S	KL	IB	18D	YAN	10	9	7660	4	6	34500	38300
31	6	FREEDOM 32 DEEP	SLP	SA/CR	F/S	KL	IB	18D	YAN	10	9	7660	4	6	34600	38400
36	5	FREEDOM 38 SHOAL	SLP	SA/CR	F/S	KL	IB	27D	YAN	12	6	14370	4	6	66600	73100
37	11	FREEDOM 38 DEEP	SLP	SA/CR	F/S	KL	IB	27D	YAN	12	6	14370	6		69800	76700
44	6	FREEDOM 45 DEEP	SLP	SA/CR	F/S	KL	IB	66D	YAN	13	6	26000			140000	154000
44	6	FREEDOM 45 WING	SLP	SA/CR	F/S	KL	IB	66D	YAN	13	6	26000			140000	154000
1988 BOATS																
28	6	FREEDOM 28	SLP	SA/CR	F/S	KL	IB	18D	YAN	10	3	6370	4	6	24900	27600
29	11	FREEDOM 30	SLP	SA/CR	F/S	KL	IB	18D	YAN	10	9	7660	4	6	31200	34700
29	11	FREEDOM 30 DEEP	SLP	SA/CR	F/S	KL	IB	18D	YAN	10	9	7660	4	6	31300	34800
36	5	FREEDOM 36 DEEP	SLP	SA/CR	F/S	KL	IB	27D	YAN	12	6	14370	6		62400	68600
36	5	FREEDOM 36 SHOAL	SLP	SA/CR	F/S	KL	IB	27D	YAN	12	6	14370	4	6	62800	69000
42	3	FREEDOM 42 DEEP	SLP	SA/CR	F/S	KL	IB	66D	YAN	13	6	22600			110000	121000
42	3	FREEDOM 42 WING	SLP	SA/CR	F/S	KL	IB	66D	YAN	13	6	22600			110000	121000
1987 BOATS																
21	8	FREEDOM 21	SLP	SA/RC	F/S	KL	OB			8		1800	3	9	5250	6050
21	8	FREEDOM 21 SHOAL	SLP	SA/RC	F/S	KL	OB			8		2050	2		5700	6550
28	6	FREEDOM 28	SLP	SA/CR	F/S	KL	IB	18D	YAN	10	3	6370	4	6	23400	26000
29		FREEDOM 29 DEEP	SLP	SA/RC	F/S	KL	IB	D	YAN	10	2	7200	5	6	26900	29900
29		FREEDOM 29 SHOAL	SLP	SA/RC	F/S	KL	IB	D	YAN	10	2	7500	4	6	28100	31200
29	11	FREEDOM 30	SLP	SA/CR	F/S	KL	IB	18D	YAN	10	9	7660	4	6	29300	32600
29	11	FREEDOM 30 DEEP	SLP	SA/CR	F/S	KL	IB	18D	YAN	10	9	7660	4	6	29500	32800
32	9	FREEDOM 32 DEEP	SLP	SA/CR	F/S	KC	IB	23D	YAN	12	3	9000	6	1	36200	40200
32	9	FREEDOM 32 SHOAL	SLP	SA/CR	F/S	KL	IB	23D	YAN	12	3	9000	4	11	36200	40200
36	5	FREEDOM 36 DEEP	SLP	SA/CR	F/S	KL	IB	27D	YAN	12	6	14370	6		58600	64400
36	5	FREEDOM 36 DEEP	KTH	SA/CR	F/S	KL	IB	27D	YAN	12	6	13400	6		55200	60600
36	5	FREEDOM 36 SHOAL	SLP	SA/CR	F/S	KL	IB	27D	YAN	12	6	14370	4	6	59100	65000
36	5	FREEDOM 36 SHOAL	KTH	SA/CR	F/S	KL	IB	27D	YAN	12	6	13400	4	6	55600	61100
39		FREEDOM 39 EXPRESS	KTH	SA/CR	F/S	KC	IB	44D	YAN	12	10	18500	5	6	79200	87100
39		FREEDOM 39 PH	SCH	SA/CR	F/S	KL	IB	44D	YAN	12	10	18500	5	6	79000	86800
44		FREEDOM 44	KTH	SA/CR	F/S	KL	IB	50D	PERK	12		24000			115500	127000
44		FREEDOM 44 SHOAL	KTH	SA/CR	F/S	KL	IB	50D	PERK	12		24000	6		115500	127000

FREEDOM YACHTS INC   -CONTINUED   See inside cover to adjust price for area

LOA FT IN	NAME AND/ OR MODEL	TOP/ RIG	BOAT TYPE	HULL MTL TP	ENGINE TP	# HP MFG	BEAM FT IN	WGT LBS	DRAFT FT IN	RETAIL LOW	RETAIL HIGH
---	--- 1986 BOATS										
21 8	FREEDOM 21	SLP	SA/RC	F/S KL	OB	8		1800	3 9	4950	5700
21 8	FREEDOM 21 SHOAL	SLP	SA/RC	F/S KL	OB	8		2050	2	5350	6150
29	FREEDOM 29 DEEP	SLP	SA/RC	F/S KL IB	D YAN	10 2		7200	5 6	25300	28100
29	FREEDOM 29 SHOAL	SLP	SA/RC	F/S KL IB	D YAN	10 2		7500	4 6	26400	29300
30 6	ETCHELLS 22	SLP	SA/OD	FBG KL		6 11		3400	4 6	10900	12400
32 9	FREEDOM 32 DEEP	SLP	SA/CR	F/S KC IB	23D YAN	12 3		9000	6 1	34000	37800
32 9	FREEDOM 32 SHOAL	SLP	SA/CR	F/S KL IB	23D YAN	12 3		9000	4 11	34000	37800
36 5	FREEDOM 36 DEEP	SLP	SA/CR	F/S KL IB	27D YAN	12 6		14370	6	55400	60900
36 5	FREEDOM 36 DEEP	KTH	SA/CR	F/S KL IB	27D YAN	12 6		13400	6	52100	57300
36 5	FREEDOM 36 SHOAL	SLP	SA/CR	F/S KL IB	27D YAN	12 6		14370	4 6	55400	60900
36 5	FREEDOM 36 SHOAL	KTH	SA/CR	F/S KL IB	27D YAN	12 6		13400	4 6	52100	57300
39	FREEDOM 39 EXPRESS	KTH	SA/CR	F/S KC IB	44D YAN	12 10		18500	5 6	74500	81900
39	FREEDOM 39 PH	SCH	SA/CR	F/S KL IB	44D YAN	12 10		18500	5 6	74300	81600
44	FREEDOM 44	KTH	SA/CR	F/S KL IB	50D PERK	12		24000		108500	119500
44	FREEDOM 44 SHOAL	KTH	SA/CR	F/S KL IB	50D PERK	12		24000	6	108500	119500
---	--- 1985 BOATS										
21 8	FREEDOM 21	SLP	SA/RC	F/S KL	OB	8		1800	3 9	4650	5350
21 8	FREEDOM 21	KTH	SA/RC	F/S KL	OB	8		2000	3 9	4950	5700
21 8	FREEDOM 21 SHOAL	SLP	SA/RC	F/S KL	OB	8		2050	2	5050	5800
25 8	FREEDOM 25	KTH	SA/CR	F/S KL		8 6		3500	4 6	8850	10100
25 8	FREEDOM 25	SLP	SA/CR	F/S KC OB		8 6		3500	4 6	9450	10700
25 8	FREEDOM 25	SLP	SA/CR	F/S KC IB	8D YAN	8 6		3500	4 6	10200	11600
25 8	FREEDOM 25	SLP	SA/CR	F/S KL		8 6		3500	4 6	9450	10700
25 8	FREEDOM 25	SLP	SA/CR	F/S KL IB	8D YAN	8 6		3500	4 6	10200	11600
29	FREEDOM 28	SLP	SA/CR	F/S KL IB	D	10 1		7500	5 8	24800	27600
29	FREEDOM 28 SHOAL	SLP	SA/CR	F/S KL IB	D	10 1		7500	2	24800	27600
30 6	ETCHELLS 22	SLP	SA/OD	F/S KL		6 11			4 6	19800	22000
32 9	FREEDOM 32	SLP	SA/CR	F/S KC IB	23D YAN	12 3		9000	6 1	31800	35400
32 9	FREEDOM 32 SHOAL	SLP	SA/CR	F/S KL IB	23D YAN	12 3		9000	4 11	32100	35700
39	FREEDOM 39 EXPRESS	KTH	SA/CR	F/S KC IB	51D PERK	12 10		18000	5 6	68300	75100
39	FREEDOM 39 PH	SCH	SA/CR	F/S KL IB	51D PERK	12 10		18500	5 6	69500	76400
44	FREEDOM 44	KTH	SA/CR	F/S KL IB	51D PERK	12		24000	7 8	102000	112000
44	FREEDOM 44 SHOAL	KTH	SA/CR	F/S KL IB	51D PERK	12		24000	6	102000	112000
44 2	ALDEN 44	CUT	SA/RC	FBG KC IB	D	12 6		24000	4 11	103500	113500
---	--- 1984 BOATS										
21 8	FREEDOM 21	SLP	SA/RC	F/S KL	OB	8		1800	3 9	4400	5050
21 8	FREEDOM 21 SHOAL	SLP	SA/RC	F/S KL	OB	8		2050	2	4750	5450
25 8	FREEDOM 25	SLP	SA/CR	F/S KL		8 6		3500	4 6	8950	10100
25 8	FREEDOM 25	SLP	SA/CR	F/S KL IB	7D YAN	8 6		3500	4 6	9600	10900
28 4	FREEDOM 28	KTH	SA/CR	F/S KC IB	13D YAN	9 4		7000	4 5	21200	23600
32 9	FREEDOM 32	SLP	SA/CR	F/S KC IB	22D YAN	12 3		9000	6 1	29900	33300
32 9	FREEDOM 32 SHOAL	SLP	SA/CR	F/S KL IB	22D YAN	12 3		9000	4 11	30200	33600
39	FREEDOM 39 EXPRESS	KTH	SA/CR	F/S KL IB	50D PERK	12 10		18000	5 6	64200	70600
39	FREEDOM 39 PH	SCH	SA/CR	F/S KL IB	50D PERK	12 10		18500	5 6	65400	71800
44	FREEDOM 44 AFT CPT	KTH	SA/CR	F/S KL IB	50D PERK	12		24000	6	96000	105500

....For earlier years, see the BUC Used Boat Price Guide, Volume 3

FREELAND MANUFACTURERS
CAPE CORAL FL 33904   COAST GUARD MFG ID- FDX See inside cover to adjust price for area

LOA FT IN	NAME AND/ OR MODEL	TOP/ RIG	BOAT TYPE	HULL MTL TP	ENGINE TP	# HP MFG	BEAM FT IN	WGT LBS	DRAFT FT IN	RETAIL LOW	RETAIL HIGH
---	--- 1990 BOATS										
20 2	FREELAND 20		CTRCN	FBG DS OB				1450	11	3800	4400
24 6	FREELAND 24 SPORT		FSH	FBG SV OB		9		2660	15	7450	8550
26 2	FREELAND 26 CUDDY	OP	CUD	FBG SV OB		9		3485	15	11000	12500
26 2	FREELAND 26 FSHMAN	OP	FSH	FBG SV OB		9		3300	15	10900	12300
26 2	FREELAND 26 OPEN	OP	OPFSH	FBG SV OB		9		3125	15	10700	12200
---	--- 1989 BOATS										
24 6	FREELAND 24		CTRCN	FBG DV OB		9		2660	1 3	7200	8250
26 2	FREELAND FSHRMN 26		CTRCN	FBG DV OB		9		3250	1 3	10500	11900
26 2	FREELAND OPEN 26		OPFSH	FBG DV OB		9		3125	1 3	10400	11800
26 2	FREELAND WLKRND CUD		CTRCN	FBG DV OB		9		3485	1 3	10600	12100
---	--- 1986 BOATS										
20 4	ROOSTER 21	OP	RNBT	FBG TH OB		8		2650	1 3	5050	5800

FRERS AND CIBILS
BUENOS AIRES ARGENTINA   See inside cover to adjust price for area

LOA FT IN	NAME AND/ OR MODEL	TOP/ RIG	BOAT TYPE	HULL MTL TP	ENGINE TP	# HP MFG	BEAM FT IN	WGT LBS	DRAFT FT IN	RETAIL LOW	RETAIL HIGH
---	--- 1987 BOATS										
35 9	F&C 36'	SLP	SA/RC	F/S KL IB	18D VLVO	11 11		10350	6 3	58200	64000
35 9	F&C 36'	SLP	SA/RC	F/S KL IB	28D VLVO	11 11		10350	6 3	58400	64200
---	--- 1986 BOATS										
36 8	F&C 37V	SLP	SA/CR	FBG KL IB	D	11 8		12168	4 7	66100	72600
43 7	F&C 44	SLP	SA/RC	FBG KC IB	D	12 6		21400	7 6	136500	150000
---	--- 1985 BOATS										
36 8	F&C 37V	SLP	SA/CR	FBG KL IB	D	11 8		12168	4 7	62600	68800
43 7	F&C 44	SLP	SA/RC	FBG KL IB	D	12 6		21400	7 6	129000	142000
---	--- 1984 BOATS										
36 8	F&C 37V	SLP	SA/CR	FBG KL IB	D	11 8			4 7	59300	65200
40 4	F&C 40'	SLP	SA/CR	F/S KL IB	28D VLVO	12 6		14100	7 3	81000	89000
40 4	F&C 40'	SLP	SA/CR	F/S KL IB	28D VLVO	12 6		14100	7 3	81000	89000
40 4	F&C 40'	SLP	SA/CR	F/S KL IB	28D VLVO	12 6		14100	7 3	81000	89000
40 4	F&C 40'	SLP	SA/RC	F/S KL IB	28D VLVO	12 6		14100	6 3	81000	89000
40 4	F&C 40'	SLP	SA/RC	F/S KL IB	28D VLVO	12 6		14100	6 3	81000	89000
40 4	F&C 40'	SLP	SA/CR	F/S KL IB	28D VLVO	12 6		14100	7 3	81000	89000
43 7	F&C 44	SLP	SA/RC	FBG KC IB	D	12 6			7 6	122000	134500

....For earlier years, see the BUC Used Boat Price Guide, Volume 3

FRIENDSHIP
BALK NETHERLANDS 8560AA   See inside cover to adjust price for area

LOA FT IN	NAME AND/ OR MODEL	TOP/ RIG	BOAT TYPE	HULL MTL TP	ENGINE TP	# HP MFG	BEAM FT IN	WGT LBS	DRAFT FT IN	RETAIL LOW	RETAIL HIGH
---	--- 1993 BOATS										
26	FRIENDSHIP 25	SLP	SACAC	FBG KL OB		9 9		3111	3 3	14600	16600
---	--- 1992 BOATS										
24	FRIENDSHIP 22 S	SLP	SACAC	FBG KL OB		8 4		2889	3 7	11800	13400
26	FRIENDSHIP 26	SLP	SACAC	FBG KL SD	9 VLVO	8 3		4666	3 7	20700	23000
29	FRIENDSHIP 22	SLP	SACAC	FBG KL OB		8 4		3111	3 7	14700	16800
33 5	FRIENDSHIP 33 C	SLP	SACAC	F/S KL SD	18D VLVO	14 1		9555	4 3	48100	52800
---	--- 1991 BOATS										
39 5	FRIENDSHIP 38	SLP	SACAC	F/S KL SD	28D VLVO	13 10		15555	5 3	84400	92800
---	--- 1989 BOATS										
29	FRIENDSHIP 28	SLP	SACAC	FBG KL SD	18D VLVO	10		7777	3 10	31800	35300
---	--- 1985 BOATS										
33 5	FRIENDSHIP 33	SLP	SACAC	F/S KL SD	18D VLVO	14 5		9555	4 3	31100	34600

....For earlier years, see the BUC Used Boat Price Guide, Volume 3

FRIESLAND BOATING
8723 ER KOUDUM HOLLAND   See inside cover to adjust price for area

For more recent years, see the BUC Used Boat Price Guide, Volume 1

LOA FT IN	NAME AND/ OR MODEL	TOP/ RIG	BOAT TYPE	HULL MTL TP	ENGINE TP	# HP MFG	BEAM FT IN	WGT LBS	DRAFT FT IN	RETAIL LOW	RETAIL HIGH
---	--- 1996 BOATS										
31	FRIBO SKAW 930 AK	HT	MY	STL DS IB	36D BUKH	11		11000	2 4	43700	48600
31 2	FB 950	HT	HB	STL DS IB	36D BUKH	9		20000	2	36300	40300
31 2	FB 950	HT	HB	STL FL IB	36D BUKH	9		20000	2	36300	40300
35	FB 1050	HT	HB	STL DS IB	36D BUKH	10		28000	2	42300	47000
35	FB 1050	HT	HB	STL FL IB	36D BUKH	10		28000	2	42300	47000
38	FB 1150	HT	HB	STL DS IB	36D BUKH	10		32000	2	47700	52500
38	FB 1150	HT	HB	STL FL IB	36D BUKH	10		32000	2	47700	52500
41	FB 1250	HT	HB	STL DS IB	48D BUKH	11		38000	2	48700	53500
41	FB 1250	HT	HB	STL FL IB	48D BUKH	11		38000	2	48700	53500
49	FB 1500 AK	HT	HB	STL DS	120D DAF	13 3		48000	2 4	72500	79700
60	DUTCH BARGE REPLICA	HT	LNCH	STL DS	120D DAF	14		55000	3	102500	113000
60	DUTCH BARGE REPLICA	HT	LNCH	STL FL	120D DAF	14		55000	3	102500	113000
---	--- 1995 BOATS										
31	FRIBO SKAW 930 AK	HT	MY	STL DS IB	36D BUKH	11		11000	2 4	41500	46200
31 2	FB 950	HT	HB	STL DS IB	36D BUKH	9		20000	2	34300	38100
31 2	FB 950	HT	HB	STL FL IB	36D BUKH	9		20000	2	34300	38100
35	FB 1050	HT	HB	STL DS IB	36D BUKH	10		28000	2	40000	44400
35	FB 1050	HT	HB	STL FL IB	36D BUKH	10		28000	2	40000	44400
38	FB 1150	HT	HB	STL DS IB	36D BUKH	11		32000	2	44300	49200
38	FB 1150	HT	HB	STL FL IB	36D BUKH	11		32000	2	44300	49200
41	FB 1250	HT	HB	STL DS IB	48D BUKH	11		38000	2	45600	50200
41	FB 1250	HT	HB	STL FL IB	48D BUKH	11		38000	2	45600	50200
49	FB 1500 AK	HT	HB	STL DS IB	120D DAF	13		48000	2 4	71900	79000
60	DUTCH BARGE REPLICA	HT	LNCH	STL DS	120D DAF	14		55000	3	98100	108000
60	DUTCH BARGE REPLICA	HT	LNCH	STL FL	120D DAF	14		55000	3	98200	108000
---	--- 1994 BOATS										
31	FRIBO SKAW 930 AK	HT	MY	STL DS IB	36D BUKH	11		11000	2 4	39500	43900
31 2	FB 950	HT	HB	STL DS IB	36D BUKH	9		20000	2	32500	36200

LOA FT IN	NAME AND/ OR RIG	TOP/ RIG	BOAT TYPE	-HULL- MTL TP	ENGINE TP # HP MFG	BEAM FT IN	WGT LBS	DRAFT FT IN	RETAIL LOW	RETAIL HIGH
1994 BOATS										
31 2	FB 950	HT	HB	STL FL IB	36D BUKH 9	20000	2		32500	36200
35	FB 1050	HT	HB	STL DS IB	36D BUKH 10	28000	2		38000	42200
35	FB 1050	HT	HB	STL FL IB	36D BUKH 10	28000	2		38000	42200
38	FB 1150	HT	HB	STL DS IB	36D BUKH 10	32000	2		41300	45900
38	FB 1150	HT	HB	STL FL IB	36D BUKH 10	32000	2		41300	45900
41	FB 1250	HT	HB	STL DS IB	48D BUKH 11	38000	2		42100	46800
41	FB 1250	HT	HB	STL FL IB	48D BUKH 11	38000	2		42100	46800
49	FB 1500 AK	HT	HB	STL DS IB	120D DAF 13	48000	2 4		67500	74200
60	DUTCH BARGE REPLICA	HT	LNCH	STL DS IB	120D DAF 14	55000	3		85400	93900
60	DUTCH BARGE REPLICA	HT	LNCH	STL FL IB	120D DAF 14	55000	3		85500	94000
1993 BOATS										
31	FRIBO SKAW 930 AK	HT	MY	STL DS IB	36D BUKH 11	11000	2 4		37700	41800
31 2	FB 950	HT	HB	STL DS IB	36D BUKH 9	20000	2		31000	34500
31 2	FB 950	HT	HB	STL FL IB	36D BUKH 9	20000	2		31000	34500
35	FB 1050	HT	HB	STL DS IB	36D BUKH 10	28000	2		36200	40300
35	FB 1050	HT	HB	STL FL IB	36D BUKH 10	28000	2		36200	40300
38	FB 1150	HT	HB	STL DS IB	36D BUKH 10	32000	2		38700	43000
38	FB 1150	HT	HB	STL FL IB	36D BUKH 10	32000	2		38700	43000
41	FB 1250	HT	HB	STL DS IB	48D BUKH 11	38000	2		39500	43800
41	FB 1250	HT	HB	STL FL IB	48D BUKH 11	38000	2		39500	43800
49	FB 1500 AK	HT	HB	STL DS IB	120D DAF 13	48000	2 4		63800	70100
60	DUTCH BARGE REPLICA	HT	LNCH	STL DS IB	120D DAF 14	55000	3		81600	89700
60	DUTCH BARGE REPLICA	HT	LNCH	STL FL IB	120D DAF 14	55000	3		81600	89700
1992 BOATS										
31	FRIBO SKAW 930 AK	HT	MY	STL DS IB	36D BUKH 11	11000	2 4		35900	39900
31 2	FB 950	HT	HB	STL DS IB	36D BUKH 9	20000	2		29700	33000
31 2	FB 950	HT	HB	STL FL IB	36D BUKH 9	20000	2		29700	33000
35	FB 1050	HT	HB	STL DS IB	36D BUKH 10	28000	2		34700	38600
35	FB 1050	HT	HB	STL FL IB	36D BUKH 10	28000	2		34700	38600
38	FB 1150	HT	HB	STL DS IB	36D BUKH 10	32000	2		36500	40600
38	FB 1150	HT	HB	STL FL IB	36D BUKH 10	32000	2		36500	40600
41	FB 1250	HT	HB	STL DS IB	48D BUKH 11	38000	2		37500	41600
41	FB 1250	HT	HB	STL FL IB	48D BUKH 11	38000	2		37500	41600
49	FB 1500 AK	HT	HB	STL DS IB	120D DAF 13	48000	2 4		60700	66700
60	DUTCH BARGE REPLICA	HT	LNCH	STL DS IB	120D DAF 14	55000	3		77800	85500
60	DUTCH BARGE REPLICA	HT	LNCH	STL FL IB	120D DAF 14	55000	3		77900	85500
1991 BOATS										
31	FRIBO SKAW 930 AK	HT	MY	STL DS IB	36D BUKH 11	11000	2 4		34300	38100
31 2	FB 950	HT	HB	STL DS IB	36D BUKH 9	20000	2		28600	31700
31 2	FB 950	HT	HB	STL FL IB	36D BUKH 9	20000	2		28600	31700
35	FB 1050	HT	HB	STL DS IB	36D BUKH 10	28000	2		33300	37000
35	FB 1050	HT	HB	STL FL IB	36D BUKH 10	28000	2		33300	37000
38	FB 1150	HT	HB	STL DS IB	36D BUKH 10	32000	2		34700	38600
38	FB 1150	HT	HB	STL FL IB	36D BUKH 10	32000	2		34700	38600
41	FB 1250	HT	HB	STL DS IB	48D BUKH 11	38000	2		35400	39400
41	FB 1250	HT	HB	STL FL IB	48D BUKH 11	38000	2		35400	39400
49	FB 1500 AK	HT	HB	STL DS IB	120D DAF 13	48000	2 4		58000	63800
60	DUTCH BARGE REPLICA	HT	LNCH	STL DS IB	120D DAF 14	55000	3		74300	81600
60	DUTCH BARGE REPLICA	HT	LNCH	STL FL IB	120D DAF 14	55000	3		74300	81700
1990 BOATS										
31	FRIBO SKAW 930 AK	HT	MY	STL DS IB	36D BUKH 11	11000	2 4		32800	36400
31 2	FB 950	HT	HB	STL DS IB	36D BUKH 9	20000	2		27500	30500
31 2	FB 950	HT	HB	STL FL IB	36D BUKH 9	20000	2		27500	30500
35	FB 1050	HT	HB	STL DS IB	36D BUKH 10	28000	2		32100	35700
35	FB 1050	HT	HB	STL FL IB	36D BUKH 10	28000	2		32100	35700
38	FB 1150	HT	HB	STL DS IB	36D BUKH 10	32000	2		33200	36900
38	FB 1150	HT	HB	STL FL IB	36D BUKH 10	32000	2		33200	36900
41	FB 1250	HT	HB	STL DS IB	48D BUKH 11	38000	2		33900	37600
41	FB 1250	HT	HB	STL FL IB	48D BUKH 11	38000	2		33900	37600
60	DUTCH BARGE REPLICA	HT	LNCH	STL DS IB	120D DAF 14	55000	3		71000	78000
60	DUTCH BARGE REPLICA	HT	LNCH	STL FL IB	120D DAF 14	55000	3		71000	78000
1989 BOATS										
32	FB 950 HOUSEBOAT	HT	HB	STL FL IB	36D BUKH 8	21000	2		27200	30200
32	FRIBO SKAW 880 AK	HT	MY	STL DS IB	36D BUKH 11	12000	2 4		35400	39400
36	FB 1050 HOUSEBOAT	HT	HB	STL FL IB	36D BUKH 9	30000	2		31000	34500
39	FB 1150 HOUSEBOAT	HT	HB	STL FL IB	36D BUKH 9	36000	2		32400	36000
43	FB 1250 HOUSEBOAT	HT	HB	STL FL IB	48D BUKH 11	44000	2		41000	45600

FUZZY SPECIALTIES

LOA FT IN	NAME AND/ OR MODEL	TOP/ RIG	BOAT TYPE	-HULL- MTL TP	ENGINE TP # HP MFG	BEAM FT IN	WGT LBS	DRAFT FT IN	RETAIL LOW	RETAIL HIGH
1992 BOATS										
19	LIGHTNING	SLP	SA/OD F/S CB			6 6	700	5	5850	6700
1991 BOATS										
19	LIGHTNING	SLP	SA/OD F/S CB			6 6	700	5	5500	6300
1990 BOATS										
19	LIGHTNING	SLP	SA/OD F/S CB			6 6	700	5	5150	5950
1989 BOATS										
19	LIGHTNING	SLP	SA/OD F/S CB			6 6	700	5	4850	5600
1988 BOATS										
19	LIGHTNING	SLP	SA/OD F/S CB			6 6	700	5	4600	5300
1987 BOATS										
19	LIGHTNING	SLP	SA/OD F/S CB			6 6	700	5	4250	4950
1986 BOATS										
19	LIGHTNING	SLP	SA/OD F/S CB			6 6	700	5	4000	4650
1985 BOATS										
19	LIGHTNING	SLP	SA/OD F/S CB			6 6	700	5	3800	4400
1984 BOATS										
19	LIGHTNING	SLP	SA/OD F/S CB			6 6	700	5	3550	4150

....For earlier years, see the BUC Used Boat Price Guide, Volume 3

G W INVADER

LOA FT IN	NAME AND/ OR MODEL	TOP/ RIG	BOAT TYPE	-HULL- MTL TP	ENGINE TP # HP MFG	BEAM FT IN	WGT LBS	DRAFT FT IN	RETAIL LOW	RETAIL HIGH
1995 BOATS										
17 3	BRAVO 175 INDY	OP	B/R	FBG DV OB		7 4	1350	2 2	3200	3700
18 3	BRAVO 180 ES	OP	RNBT	FBG DV IO	160-275	7	2250	2 2	8900	10100
18 3	BRAVO 180 INDY	OP	RNBT	FBG DV IO	135-275	7 9	2000	2 2	8150	9300
19	RIVERA 190 LTD	OP	RNBT	FBG TR IO	135-275	8	2250	2 2	8650	10700
19	RIVERA 190 LTD	OP	RNBT	FBG TR IO	185 VLVO	8	2250	2 2	9750	11100
19	RIVERA 190 LTD	OP	RNBT	FBG TR IO	235 VLVO	8	2250	2 2	8850	10100
19	RIVERA 190 LTD	OP	RNBT	FBG TR IO	235 VLVO	8	2250	2 2	9200	10500
19 1	BRAVO 1900 COUPE	OP	RNBT	FBG DV IO	160-255	8 4	2600	2 6	9650	11700
19 1	BRAVO 1900 COUPE	OP	RNBT	FBG DV IO	275 VLVO	8 4	2600	2 6	10600	12100
20 4	BRAVO 200 ES	OP	RNBT	FBG DV IO	160-235	7 9	2400	2 6	10700	12600
20 4	BRAVO 200 ES	OP	RNBT	FBG DV IO	275 VLVO	8	2400	2 6	11800	13400
20 4	BRAVO 200 INDY	OP	RNBT	FBG DV IO	160-255	7 8	2400	2 6	10600	12900
20 4	BRAVO 200 INDY	OP	RNBT	FBG DV IO	275 VLVO	7 8	2400	2 6	11700	13300
20 6	RIVERA 206 SUPREME	OP	RNBT	FBG DV IO	160-275	8 6	2800	2 6	12200	15000
20 6	RIVERA 206 SUPREME	OP	RNBT	FBG DV IO	275 VLVO	8	2450	2 2	11000	13400
21	RIVERA 210 SPT DECK	OP	RNBT	FBG TR IO	160-275	8	2450	2 2	12200	13800
22	RIVERA 220 SUPREME	OP	RNBT	FBG TR IO	160-275	8 6	3000	2 4	12900	15900
22 6	RIVERA 226 SPT DECK	OP	RNBT	FBG TR IO	160-275	8	2750	2 2	12500	15400
23	RIVERA 230 SPT DECK	OP	RNBT	FBG TR IO	160-275	8 2	3400	2 4	14400	17600
23	RIVERA 230 SPT DECK	OP	RNBT	FBG TR IO	160-275	8 2	3400	2 4	14800	18100
1994 BOATS										
17 3	BRAVO 175 INDY	OP	B/R	FBG DV OB		7 2	1320		2950	3400
18 3	BRAVO 180 ES	OP	RNBT	FBG DV IO	160-185	8	2250	2 2	8200	9400
18 3	BRAVO 180 ESS	OP	RNBT	FBG DV IO	160-185	8	2250	2 2	8200	9400
18 3	BRAVO 180 INDY	OP	RNBT	FBG DV IO	160-185	8	2250	2 2	7050	8350
19	RIVERA 190 SILVER	OP	RNBT	FBG TR IO	160-185	8	2250	2 2	8100	9400
19 1	BRAVO 1900 COUPE	OP	RNBT	FBG DV IO	185-255	8 4	2600	2 6	9150	10900
20 4	BRAVO 200 ES	OP	RNBT	FBG DV IO	185-255	7 8	2400	2 6	10000	12000
20 4	BRAVO 200 ESC	OP	CUD	FBG DV IO	185-255	7 8	2400	2 6	10600	12700
20 6	BRAVO 2100 COUPE	OP	RNBT	FBG DV IO	185-255	8 6	2800	2 6	11500	13700
20 6	RIVERA 206 SUPREME	OP	RNBT	FBG DV IO	185-255	8	2250	2 6	11000	12100
21	RIVERA 210 SPT DECK	OP	RNBT	FBG TR IO	185-255	8 6	3300	2 6	12800	15200
22	RIVERA 220 GOLD SPT	OP	RNBT	FBG TR IO		PCM	8	3300	2	**	**
22	RIVERA 220 SUPREME	OP	RNBT	FBG TR IO	185-255	8	2750	2 6	11800	14000
23	RIVERA 230 SPT DECK	OP	RNBT	FBG TR IO	185-255	8	3300	2 6	13700	16200
1993 BOATS										
18 3	BRAVO 180 ES	OP	RNBT	FBG DV IO	175-185	8	2250		6800	7800
18 3	BRAVO 180 ESS	OP	RNBT	FBG DV IO	175-185	8	2250		7000	8050
18 3	BRAVO 180 SPECIAL	OP	RNBT	FBG DV IO	175-185	8	2250		6750	7750
19	RIVERA 190	OP	RNBT	FBG TR IO	175-185	8	2100		7300	8400
20	RIVERA 206	OP	RNBT	FBG TR IO	185 OMC	8	2500		9300	10600
20 4	BRAVO 200 ES	OP	RNBT	FBG DV IO	230 MRCR	8	2400		9600	10900
20 4	BRAVO 200 ES	OP	RNBT	FBG DV IO	240	7 7	2400		9250	10500
20 4	BRAVO 200 ESC	OP	CUD	FBG DV IO	230 MRCR	7 7	2600		9850	11200
20 4	BRAVO 200 ESC	OP	RNBT	FBG DV IO	240 OMC	7 7	2600		9550	10800
22	RIVERA 220 SILVER	OP	RNBT	FBG TR IO	230	8	2750		10600	12200
22 3	RIVERA 220 SPORT	OP	RNBT	FBG TR IB	230 PCM	8	3200		14500	16500
23 3	RIVERA 230 SPORT DK	OP	RNBT	FBG TR IO	200-205	8 2	3300		12600	14400
1992 BOATS										
18 3	BRAVO 180 ES	OP	RNBT	FBG DV IO	150-175	8	2100		6250	7300
18 3	BRAVO 180 ESS	OP	RNBT	FBG DV IO	150-175	8	2250		6450	7550

LOA FT IN	NAME AND/OR MODEL	TOP/RIG	BOAT TYPE	HULL MTL TP	ENGINE TP # HP MFG	BEAM FT IN	WGT LBS	DRAFT FT IN	RETAIL LOW	RETAIL HIGH
					1992 BOATS					
19	RIVERA 190	OP	RNBT	FBG TR	IO 150-175	8	2250		6750	7850
20 3	BRAVO 200	OP	RNBT	FBG DV	IO 230 MRCR	8	2450		8450	9700
20 4	BRAVO 200 ES	OP	RNBT	FBG DV	IO 230-240	7 7	2400		8400	9850
20 4	BRAVO 200 ESC	OP	RNBT	FBG DV	IO 230	7 7	2600		8950	10200
22	RIVERA 220 SILVER	OP	RNBT	FBG TR	IO 175-200	8	2750		9900	11400
22 3	RIVERA 220 SPORT	OP	RNBT	FBG TR	IB 230 PCM	8	3200		13700	15600
23	BRAVO 230	OP	RNBT	FBG DV	IO 365 MRCR	8 6	3600		15400	17500
					1991 BOATS					
18 3	BRAVO 180 ES		RNBT	FBG DV	IO MRCR	7 8	2100		**	**
19	RIVERA 190	OP	RNBT	FBG TR	IO MRCR	8	2250		**	**
20 3	BRAVO 200	OP	RNBT	FBG DV	IO 270 MRCR	7 6	2400		8250	9500
20 3	BRAVO 200 ES		RNBT	FBG DV	IO MRCR	7 6	2400		**	**
22	RIVERA 220		RNBT	FBG TR	IO 260 MRCR	8	2750		9800	11000
22 3	RIVERA 220 SPORT		RNBT	FBG TR	IB 260 MRCR	8	2750		12100	13800
23	BRAVO 230		RNBT	FBG DV	IO 365 MRCR	8 6	3600		14400	16400

G-CAT INTERNATIONAL INC
ST PETERSBURG FL 33705   COAST GUARD MFG ID- GAT   See inside cover to adjust price for area

LOA FT IN	NAME AND/OR MODEL	TOP/RIG	BOAT TYPE	HULL MTL TP	ENGINE TP # HP MFG	BEAM FT IN	WGT LBS	DRAFT FT IN	RETAIL LOW	RETAIL HIGH
					1986 BOATS					
16 8	G-CAT 5 METER	SLP	SAIL	FBG CT		8	360	8	2500	2900
16 8	G-CAT 5.0 DAY SAILER	SLP	SAIL	FBG CT		8	350	8	2450	2850
18 8	G-CAT 5.7 DAY SAILER	SLP	SAIL	FBG CT		8	380	8	2850	3350
18 8	G-CAT 5.7 METER	SLP	SAIL	FBG CT		8	390	8	2900	3400
					1985 BOATS					
16 8	G-CAT 5 METER	SLP	SAIL	FBG CT		8	360	8	2350	2700
16 8	G-CAT 5.0 DAY SAILER	SLP	SAIL	FBG CT		8	350	8	2300	2700
18 8	G-CAT 5.7 DAY SAILER	SLP	SAIL	FBG CT		8	380	8	2700	3150
18 8	G-CAT 5.7 METER	SLP	SAIL	FBG CT		8	390	8	2750	3200
					1984 BOATS					
16 8	G-CAT 5 METER	SLP	SAIL	FBG CT		8	360	8	2200	2600
16 8	G-CAT 5.0 DAY SAILER	SLP	SAIL	FBG CT		8	350	8	2200	2550
18 8	G-CAT 5.7 DAY SAILER	SLP	SAIL	FBG CT		8	380	8	2550	2950
18 8	G-CAT 5.7 METER	SLP	SAIL	FBG CT		8	390	8	2600	3000

....For earlier years, see the BUC Used Boat Price Guide, Volume 3

GALAXIE BOAT WORKS INC
JACKSONVILLE TX 75766   COAST GUARD MFG ID- GBW   See inside cover to adjust price for area

For more recent years, see the BUC Used Boat Price Guide, Volume 1

LOA FT IN	NAME AND/OR MODEL	TOP/RIG	BOAT TYPE	HULL MTL TP	ENGINE TP # HP MFG	BEAM FT IN	WGT LBS	DRAFT FT IN	RETAIL LOW	RETAIL HIGH
					1996 BOATS					
16 10	FISH & SKI 1700	ST	RNBT	FBG SV	IO 135	7 3	2200		6350	7600
16 10	ULTRA 1700	ST	RNBT	FBG DV	IO 135 MRCR	7 3	2200		6350	7300
16 10	ULTRA 1700	ST	RNBT	FBG DV	IO 135 VLVO	7 3	2200		6800	7850
17	171	ST	BASS	FBG DV	OB	7 1	1050		2550	3000
17	172	ST	BASS	FBG DV	OB	7 1	1175		2800	3300
17	173	ST	BASS	FBG DV	OB	7 1	1200		2850	3350
17 6	DECKBOAT 17	ST	RNBT	FBG DV	IO 160 MRCR	7 2	2295		6750	7750
17 6	DECKBOAT 17	ST	RNBT	FBG DV	IO 160 VLVO	7 2	2295		7100	8150
18 9	ULTRA 1900	ST	RNBT	FBG DV	IO 230-235	8	2560		8950	10200
19 7	DECKBOAT 2000	ST	RNBT	FBG SV	IO 205	7 1	2500		7950	9550
20 8	2050	ST	RNBT	FBG SV	IO 235-255	7 9	2545		10400	12600
20 8	2050 CC	ST	RNBT	FBG SV	IO 235-255	7 9	2565		10400	12600
22 1	DECKBOAT 22	ST	RNBT	FBG SV	IO 235-255	7 8	2920		11900	14200
22 9	ULTRA 2300	ST	RNBT	FBG DV	IO 255	8 6	3460		14200	16700
					1995 BOATS					
16 10	FISH & SKI	ST	RNBT	FBG SV	IO 135 MRCR	7 3	2200		5550	6350
16 10	FISH & SKI 1700	ST	RNBT	FBG SV	IO 135 VLVO	7 3	2200		5800	6700
16 10	ULTRA 1700	ST	RNBT	FBG SV	IO 135 MRCR	7 3	2200		5950	6850
16 10	ULTRA 1700	ST	RNBT	FBG SV	IO 135 VLVO	7 3	2200		7150	8200
17	171	ST	BASS	FBG DV	OB	7 1	1050		2450	2850
17	172	ST	BASS	FBG DV	OB	7 1	1175		2700	3150
17	173	ST	BASS	FBG DV	OB	7 1	1200		2750	3200
17 6	DECKBOAT 17	ST	RNBT	FBG DV	IO 160 MRCR	7 2	2295		6300	7200
17 6	DECKBOAT 17	ST	RNBT	FBG DV	IO 160 VLVO	7 2	2295		6600	7600
18 9	ULTRA 1900	ST	RNBT	FBG SV	IO 230-235	8	2560		8250	9450
19 7	DECKBOAT 19	ST	RNBT	FBG SV	IO 205	7 1	2500		7450	8950
20 8	2050	ST	RNBT	FBG SV	IO 235-255	7 9	2545		9700	11800
20 8	2050 CC	ST	RNBT	FBG SV	IO 235-255	7 9	2565		9700	11800
22 1	DECKBOAT 22	ST	RNBT	FBG SV	IO 235-255	7 8	2920		11100	13400
22 9	ULTRA 2300	ST	RNBT	FBG DV	IO 255	8 6	3460		13200	15500
					1994 BOATS					
16 10	ULTRA 1700	ST	RNBT	FBG DV	IO 175	7 3	2200		5600	6450
17	171	ST	BASS	FBG DV	OB	7 1	1050		2350	2700
17	172	ST	BASS	FBG DV	OB	7 1	1175		2550	3000
17	173	ST	BASS	FBG DV	OB	7 1	1200		2600	3050
17 6	DECKBOAT 17	ST	RNBT	FBG DV	IO 200 MRCR	7 2	2295		5950	6850
17 6	DECKBOAT 17	ST	RNBT	FBG DV	IO 200	7 2	2295		5900	7200
18 5	1800	ST	RNBT	FBG DV	OB	6 9	2350		4150	4800
18 5	1800	ST	RNBT	FBG DV	IO 175	6 9	2350		5950	7150
18 5	1800 CB	ST	RNBT	FBG DV	IO 175	6 9	2350		6300	7500
18 9	ULTRA 1900	ST	RNBT	FBG DV	IO 185	6 9	2560		7150	8200
19 6	1950	ST	RNBT	FBG SV	IO 235	7 9	2500		7400	8950
19 7	DECKBOAT 19	ST	RNBT	FBG SV	IO 205	7 1	2500		6450	8350
20 4	2000	ST	RNBT	FBG DV	IO 260	8	2800		9750	11600
20 8	2050	ST	RNBT	FBG SV	IO 260	7 9	2545		9350	11100
20 8	2050 CC	ST	RNBT	FBG SV	IO 260	7 9	2565		9350	11100
21 7	2200 CC	ST	RNBT	FBG DV	IO 260	8	3550		11800	13900
22 1	DECKBOAT 22	ST	RNBT	FBG SV	IO 260	7 8	2920		10600	12500
22 9	ULTRA 2300	ST	RNBT	FBG DV	IO 230-235	8 6	3460		12200	14300
					1993 BOATS					
16 10	ULTRA 1700	ST	RNBT	FBG DV	IO 175	7 3	2200		5250	6000
17	171	ST	BASS	FBG DV	OB	7 1	1050		2250	2650
17	172	ST	BASS	FBG DV	OB	7 1	1175		2450	2850
17	173	ST	BASS	FBG DV	OB	7 1	1200		2500	2900
17 6	DECKBOAT 17	ST	RNBT	FBG DV	IO 200 MRCR	7 2	2295		5550	6400
17 6	DECKBOAT 17	ST	RNBT	FBG DV	OB 200	7 2	2295		5550	6750
18 5	1800	ST	RNBT	FBG DV	OB	6 9	2350		3950	4600
18 5	1800	ST	RNBT	FBG DV	IO 175	6 9	2350		5550	6700
18 5	1800 CB	ST	RNBT	FBG DV	IO 175	6 9	2350		5850	7050
18 9	ULTRA 1900	ST	RNBT	FBG DV	IO 185	6 9	2560		6700	7700
19 6	1950	ST	RNBT	FBG SV	IO 235	7 9	2500		6950	8350
19 7	DECKBOAT 19	ST	RNBT	FBG SV	IO 205	7 1	2500		6500	7800
20 4	2000	ST	RNBT	FBG DV	IO 260	8	2800		9150	10900
20 8	2050	ST	RNBT	FBG SV	IO 260	7 9	2545		8650	10400
20 8	2050 CC	ST	RNBT	FBG SV	IO 260	7 9	2565		8650	10400
21 7	2200 CC	ST	RNBT	FBG DV	IO 260	8	3550		11000	13000
22 1	DECKBOAT 22	ST	RNBT	FBG SV	IO 260	7 8	2920		9950	11800
					1992 BOATS					
17	171	ST	BASS	FBG DV	OB	7 1	1050		2200	2550
17	172	ST	BASS	FBG DV	OB	7 1	1175		2350	2750
17	173	ST	BASS	FBG DV	OB	7 1	1200		2400	2800
17 6	DECKBOAT 17	ST	RNBT	FBG DV	IO 200 MRCR	7 2	2295		5200	6000
17 6	DECKBOAT 17	ST	RNBT	FBG DV	OB 200	7 2	2295		5150	6300
18 5	1800	ST	RNBT	FBG DV	OB	6 9	2350		3800	4450
18 5	1800	ST	RNBT	FBG DV	IO 175	6 9	2350		5200	6250
18 5	1800 CB	ST	RNBT	FBG DV	IO 175	6 9	2350		5500	6600
19 6	1950	ST	RNBT	FBG SV	IO 235	7 9	2500		6500	7800
19 7	DECKBOAT 19	ST	RNBT	FBG SV	IO 205	7 1	2500		6050	7300
20 4	2000	ST	RNBT	FBG DV	IO 260	8	2800		8450	10200
20 8	2050	ST	RNBT	FBG SV	IO 260	7 9	2545		8100	9750
20 8	2050 CC	ST	RNBT	FBG DV	IO 260	7 9	2565		8100	9750
21 7	2200	ST	RNBT	FBG DV	IO 260	8	3550		11000	12200
22 1	DECKBOAT 22	ST	RNBT	FBG SV	IO 260	7 8	2920		9300	11000
					1991 BOATS					
17	171	ST	BASS	FBG DV	OB	7 1	1050		2050	2450
17	172	ST	BASS	FBG DV	OB	7 1	1175		2300	2700
17	173	ST	BASS	FBG DV	OB	7 1	1200		2300	2700
17 6	DECKBOAT 17	ST	RNBT	FBG SV	IO 200 MRCR	7 2	2295		4900	5650
17 6	DECKBOAT 17	ST	RNBT	FBG SV	OB 200	7 2	2295		4850	5950
18 5	1800	ST	RNBT	FBG DV	OB	6 9	2350		3650	4250
18 5	1800	ST	RNBT	FBG DV	IO 175	6 9	2350		4900	5850
18 5	1800 CB	ST	RNBT	FBG DV	IO 175	6 9	2350		5150	6150
19 6	1950	ST	RNBT	FBG SV	IO 235	7 9	2500		6100	7350
19 7	DECKBOAT 19	ST	RNBT	FBG SV	IO 205	7 1	2500		5700	6850
20 4	2000	ST	RNBT	FBG DV	IO 260	8	2800		7950	9550
20 8	2050	ST	RNBT	FBG SV	IO 260	7 9	2545		7550	9100
20 8	2050 CC	ST	RNBT	FBG DV	IO 260	7 9	2565		7600	9150
21 7	2200	ST	RNBT	FBG DV	IO 260	8	3550		9700	11500
22 1	DECKBOAT 22	ST	RNBT	FBG SV	IO 260	7 8	2920		8650	10400

LOA FT IN	NAME AND/ OR MODEL	TOP/ RIG	BOAT TYPE	-HULL- MTL TP	----ENGINE--- TP # HP MFG	BEAM FT IN	WGT LBS	DRAFT FT IN	RETAIL LOW	RETAIL HIGH
				------ 1988 BOATS ------						
16 2	COMBO	ST	RNBT	FBG TR OB		6 6	960		1650	2000
16 11	XL1790V	ST	RNBT	FBG DV OB		7 1	2000		3650	4250
17 2	XL1800V	ST	RNBT	FBG DV OB	185	6 11	1125		1950	2350
17 2	XL1800V	ST	RNBT	FBG DV IO	185	6 11	2230		3850	4500
17 4	XL1850V	ST	RNBT	FBG DV OB		7 6	2400		4600	5250
19 4	XL1950V	ST	RNBT	FBG DV IO	260	7 6	2550		5200	5950
20 4	XL2000V	ST	RNBT	FBG DV IO	260	7 6	2650		6650	7650
21 7	XL2000V	ST	RNBT	FBG DV OB		8	2900		5000	5750
21 7	XL2200V	ST	RNBT	FBG DV IO	260	8	3500		8000	9200
				------ 1987 BOATS ------						
16 4	XL1790	ST	RNBT	FBG DV OB		7 1	2000		3050	3550
17 3	XL1800V	ST	RNBT	FBG DV OB		6 11	2200		3100	3650
17 3	XL1850V	ST	RNBT	FBG DV OB		7 6	2200		3100	3600
18 3	XL1900V	ST	RNBT	FBG DV OB		7 6	2600		3100	3850
19 4	XL1950V	ST	RNBT	FBG DV OB		7 6	2550		3500	4050
20 3	XL2000	ST	RNBT	FBG DV OB		8	2800		4150	4800
21 7	XL2200V	ST	RNBT	FBG DV OB		8	3500		5300	6100
				------ 1985 BOATS ------						
16 4	XL1700V	ST	RNBT	FBG DV OB		6 8	2000		2900	3350
17 2	XL1800V	ST	RNBT	FBG DV OB		6 11	2200		2950	3400
17 3	XL1850V	ST	RNBT	FBG DV OB		7 6	2200		2950	3400
18 3	XL1900V	ST	RNBT	FBG DV OB		6 11	2100		2900	3350
18 3	JET	ST	RNBT	FBG DV OB		7 6	2600		3100	3600
21 7	XL2200V	ST	RNBT	FBG DV OB		8	3500		5000	5750
				------ 1984 BOATS ------						
16 2	XL 1700	ST	RNBT	FBG TR OB		6 3	960		1500	1800
16 2	XL 1700 COMBO	ST	BASS	FBG TR OB		6 3	960		1500	1750
16 4	XL 1700V	ST	RNBT	FBG DV OB		7 3	1175		1800	2150
16 4	XL 1700V	ST	RNBT	FBG DV IO	120-170	7 3	2050		3000	3500
16 6	XL 1600 CONSOLE	ST	BASS	FBG TR OB		6 2	850		1350	1600
17 2	XL 1800V	ST	RNBT	FBG DV OB		6 11	1125		1750	2100
17 2	XL 1800V	ST	RNBT	FBG DV IO	120-200	6 11	2230		3200	3800
18 3	JET		RNBT	FBG DV IO	454				7300	8400
18 3	XL 1900V	ST	RNBT	FBG DV IO	170-260	7 6	2600		3850	4800
21 7	XL 2200	ST	RNBT	FBG DV IO	260	8	3550		6700	7700

....For earlier years, see the BUC Used Boat Price Guide, Volume 3

GALAXY BOAT MFG CO INC
COLUMBIA SC 29240   COAST GUARD MFG ID- GAL See inside cover to adjust price for area

LOA FT IN	NAME AND/ OR MODEL	TOP/ RIG	BOAT TYPE	-HULL- MTL TP	----ENGINE--- TP # HP MFG	BEAM FT IN	WGT LBS	DRAFT FT IN	RETAIL LOW	RETAIL HIGH
				------ 1990 BOATS ------						
18 6	CUDDY CABIN 1860	OP	RNBT	FBG SV IO	MRCR	7 10			**	**
18 8	DUAL CONSOLE 198	OP	FSH	FBG SV IO	MRCR	7			**	**
18 8	WALKAROUND 198	OP	RNBT	FBG SV IO	MRCR	7			**	**
18 9	BOW RIDER 190	OP	RNBT	FBG DV IO	MRCR	7 8			**	**
18 9	CUDDY CABIN 190	OP	RNBT	FBG SV IO	MRCR	7 8			**	**
18 11	CUDDY CABIN 195	OP	RNBT	FBG SV IO	MRCR	7 8			**	**
19 2	BOW RIDER 200	OP	RNBT	FBG DV IO	MRCR	7 9			**	**
20 5	SPORT 215 SL	OP	RNBT	FBG SV IO	MRCR	8			**	**
20 5	SPORT 215 SLC	OP	RNBT	FBG SV IO	MRCR	8			**	**
20 9	BOW RIDER 205	OP	RNBT	FBG DV IO	MRCR	7 8			**	**
20 9	CUDDY CABIN 205	OP	RNBT	FBG SV IO	MRCR	7 8			**	**
21 1	DUAL CONSOLE 228	OP	FSH	FBG SV IO	MRCR	8			**	**
21 1	WALKAROUND 228	OP	FSH	FBG SV IO	MRCR	8			**	**
22 5	SPORT 225	OP	RNBT	FBG SV IO	MRCR	7 8			**	**
22 6	WEEKENDER 225	OP	RNBT	FBG SV IO	MRCR	7 8			**	**
22 6	WEEKENDER EXP 225	OP	RNBT	FBG SV IO	MRCR	7 8			**	**
22 8	SPORT 235 SL	OP	RNBT	FBG SV IO	155 MRCR	8 2			5200	6000
22 8	SPORT 235 SLC	OP	RNBT	FBG SV IO	155 MRCR	8 2			5200	6000
26	SPORT 265 SLC	OP	RNBT	FBG SV IO	155 MRCR	8 2			7050	8100
				------ 1989 BOATS ------						
18 8	CENTER CONSOLE 198	OP	CTRCN	FBG SV IO		7			**	**
19 10	CUDDY CABIN 195	OP	RNBT	FBG SV IO		7 7			**	**
20 9	BOW RIDER 205	OP	RNBT	FBG SV IO		7 8			**	**
20 9	SUPER SPORT 205 CC	OP	RNBT	FBG SV IO		7 8			**	**
21 1	WALKAROUND 228	OP	RNBT	FBG SV IO		8			**	**
22 5	SUPER SPORT 225	OP	RNBT	FBG DV IO		7 10			**	**
22 6	WEEKENDER 225	OP	RNBT	FBG SV IO		7 10			**	**
24 5	SPORT EXPRESS 248	OP	CUD	FBG SV IO		8 6			**	**
				------ 1988 BOATS ------						
17 6	1760 B/R	OP	RNBT	FBG DV IO	130 MRCR	7 8	1775		2950	3450
17 6	1760 B/R	OP	RNBT	FBG DV IO	175-205 MRCR	7 8	1775		3000	3550
18 8	1860 B/R	ST	RNBT	FBG SV IO	130-205	7 8	1990		3350	4150
18 8	1860 CC		CUD	FBG SV IO	130-175	7 8	1990		3400	4200
18 8	1860 CC		CUD	FBG SV IO	205 MRCR	7 8	2230		3700	4300
18 9	190 B/R	OP	RNBT	FBG DV IO	130-205	7 8	2025		3350	4000
21	210 B/R	OP	RNBT	FBG SV IO	130-205	8			3900	4650
21	210 SPORT	OP	RNBT	FBG SV IO	130-205	8	2200		3700	4400
21	210 SPORT EXPRESS	OP	RNBT	FBG SV IO	130-205	8	2300		3800	4500
21 1	2100 B/R	ST	RNBT	FBG SV IO	MRCR	7 8	2265		**	**
21 1	2100 B/R	ST	RNBT	FBG SV IO	130-260	7 8	2265		3700	4600
21 1	2100 C/C	ST	CUD	FBG SV IO	130-260	7 8	2328		**	**
21 1	2100 C/C	ST	CUD	FBG SV IO		7 8	2328		3900	4850
21 1	2100 SPORT	ST	RNBT	FBG SV IO	MRCR	7 8	2385		**	**
21 1	2100 SPORT	ST	RNBT	FBG SV IO	130-260	7 8	2385		3750	4700
21 1	2100 WEEKENDER	ST	RNBT	FBG SV IO	MRCR	7 8	2499		**	**
21 1	2100 WEEKENDER	ST	RNBT	FBG SV IO	130-260	7 8	2499		3850	4800
21 1	228 FISH	OP	RNBT	FBG SV IO	MRCR	8	3500		**	**
21 1	228 FISH	OP	RNBT	FBG SV IO		8	3500		4900	5900
22 7	227 AFT CABIN		RNBT	FBG SV IO	175-260	8 6			**	**
22 7	227 AFT CABIN		RNBT	FBG SV IO	175-260	8 6			4750	5700
22 7	227 SPORT	OP	RNBT	FBG SV IO	175-260	8 6			**	**
22 7	227 SPORT	OP	RNBT	FBG SV IO	175-260	8 6			4750	5700
22 7	227 SPORT EXPRESS	OP	RNBT	FBG SV IO	MRCR	8 6	2830		**	**
22 7	227 SPORT EXPRESS	OP	RNBT	FBG SV IO	175-260	8 6	2830		4750	5700
24 8	248 AFT CABIN	OP	RNBT	FBG SV IO	MRCR	8 6	3595		**	**
24 8	248 AFT CABIN	OP	RNBT	FBG SV IO	175-260	8 6	3595		5950	7250
24 8	248 SPORT EXPRESS	OP	RNBT	FBG SV IO	MRCR	8 6			**	**
24 8	248 SPORT EXPRESS		RNBT	FBG SV IO	175-260	8 6			5950	7250
				------ 1987 BOATS ------						
16 6	176 B/R	OP	RNBT	FBG DV IO	120 MRCR	7	1825		2500	2950
17 6	189 B/R	OP	RNBT	FBG DV IO	120 MRCR	7 4	1870		2800	3250
18 8	1860 B/R	ST	RNBT	FBG SV IO	120 MRCR	7 8	2145		3250	3800
18 9	1900 B/R	ST	RNBT	FBG DV IO	120 MRCR	7 4	2000		3200	3700
18 11	ADMIRAL 199	OP	RNBT	FBG SV IO	120 MRCR	7 6	2130		3250	3800
18 11	ADMIRAL 199CC	OP	CUD	FBG DV IO	120 MRCR	7 6	2160		3350	3900
20 1	CLASSIC 226SE	OP	EXP	FBG DV IO	165 MRCR	8	2930		4000	4650
21 1	2100 B/R	ST	RNBT	FBG SV IO	165 MRCR	7 8	2328		3450	4050
21 1	2100 CCR	ST	RNBT	FBG SV IO	165 MRCR	7 8	2328		3500	4100
21 1	2100 SPORT	ST	RNBT	FBG SV IO	165 MRCR	7 8	2328		3650	4250
21 1	2100 WEEKENDER	ST	RNBT	FBG SV IO	165 MRCR	7 8	2582		3750	4350
21 3	213 CUDDY CABIN	ST	RNBT	FBG SV IO	165 MRCR	7 8	2480		3650	4250
				------ 1986 BOATS ------						
16 6	176 BR	OP	RNBT	FBG DV IO	MRCR	7 4	1230		**	**
17 6	185 BR	OP	RNBT	FBG DV IO	MRCR	7 4	1375		**	**
17 6	ADMIRAL 189	OP	RNBT	FBG DV IO	MRCR	7 6	1275		**	**
18 11	ADMIRAL 199	OP	RNBT	FBG DV IO	MRCR	7 6	1535		**	**
18 11	ADMIRAL 199CC	OP	CUD	FBG DV IO	MRCR	7 6	1565		**	**
18 11	ADMIRAL 201CC	OP	CUD	FBG DV IO	MRCR	7 6	1565		**	**
20 1	CLASSIC 226SE	OP	EXP	FBG DV IO	MRCR	8	2335		**	**
20 3	ADMIRAL 209	OP	RNBT	FBG DV IO	MRCR	7 6	1805		**	**
20 3	ADMIRAL 209CC	OP	CUD	FBG DV IO	MRCR	7 6	1835		**	**
20 3	ADMIRAL 211CC	OP	CUD	FBG DV IO	MRCR	7 6	1805		**	**
20 9	ADMIRAL 229AC	OP	CUD	FBG DV IO	MRCR	8	3020		**	**
20 9	ADMIRAL 229CC	OP	CUD	FBG DV IO	MRCR	8	2550		**	**
20 9	ADMIRAL 229FC	OP	CUD	FBG DV IO	MRCR	8	2550		**	**
25 5	CLASSIC 260DC	OP	DC	FBG DV IO	MRCR	8	4420		**	**

....For earlier years, see the BUC Used Boat Price Guide, Volume 3

GALLART SHIPYARDS
BARCELONA SPAIN   See inside cover to adjust price for area

LOA FT IN	NAME AND/ OR MODEL	TOP/ RIG	BOAT TYPE	-HULL- MTL TP	----ENGINE--- TP # HP MFG	BEAM FT IN	WGT LBS	DRAFT FT IN	RETAIL LOW	RETAIL HIGH
				------ 1984 BOATS ------						
36 6	GALLART 1050 MP	FB	DCMY	FBG DV IB	T250D VLVO	12 9	16250	3 6	62400	68500
36 6	GALLART 1050 SPORT	OP	SF	FBG SV IB	T235D VLVO	12 9	13670	3 6	54200	59500
44	GALLART 44	SLP MS		FBG KL IB	65D VLVO	14 2	25550	5 9	142500	156500
44	GALLART 44	SLP MS		FBG KL IB	T 65D VLVO	14 2	25550	5 9	146500	160500
44	GALLART 44	KTH MS		FBG KL IB	65D VLVO	14 2	25550	5 9	142500	156500
44	GALLART 44	KTH MS		FBG KL IB	T 65D VLVO	14 2	25550	5 9	146500	160500
44	GALLART 44	FB	TCMY	FBG DV IB	T320D VLVO	13 4	27780	3 9	117000	128500
54 5	GALLART 1750	FB	MY	FBG DV IB	T675D GM	17 1	52000	3 5	222000	244000

....For earlier years, see the BUC Used Boat Price Guide, Volume 3

GAMBLER MARINE
DEER PARK NY 11729   COAST GUARD MFG ID- GAN See inside cover to adjust price for area

LOA FT IN	NAME AND/ OR MODEL	TOP/ RIG	BOAT TYPE	-HULL- MTL TP	----ENGINE--- TP # HP MFG	BEAM FT IN	WGT LBS	DRAFT FT IN	RETAIL LOW	RETAIL HIGH
				---- 1984	BOATS					
16 5	DEALERS-CHOICE	OP	CTRCN	FBG SV	OB	6 9	1150	10	4000	4650
16 5	FISHERMAN	OP	CTRCN	FBG SV	OB	6 9	1050	10	3650	4250
20 8	GAMBLER-PLUS	OP	RACE	F/W DV	OB	7 3	1000	1 6	4200	4900

....For earlier years, see the BUC Used Boat Price Guide, Volume 3

GARRETT MARINE INC
LARGO FL 33541   See inside cover to adjust price for area

LOA FT IN	NAME AND/ OR MODEL	TOP/ RIG	BOAT TYPE	-HULL- MTL TP	----ENGINE--- TP # HP MFG	BEAM FT IN	WGT LBS	DRAFT FT IN	RETAIL LOW	RETAIL HIGH
				---- 1985	BOATS					
36 11	GARRETT 36	SLP	SA/CR	FBG KL	IB D	12 7	12000	7	38000	42200
40 1	GARRETT 40C	SLP	SA/CR	FBG KL	IB D	13 3	15000	8 5	54000	59400
40 1	GARRETT 40R	SLP	SA/RC	FBG KL	IB D	13 3	13100	7 7	49300	54100
				---- 1984	BOATS					
39 6	40R	SLP	SA/RC	FBG KL	IB D	13 3	13100	7 6	44300	49200
39 10	40C	SLP	SA/CR	FBG KL	IB D	13 3	14500	7 6	49000	53900

THE GARWOOD BOAT CO
ALGONAC MI   See inside cover to adjust price for area

LOA FT IN	NAME AND/ OR MODEL	TOP/ RIG	BOAT TYPE	-HULL- MTL TP	----ENGINE--- TP # HP MFG	BEAM FT IN	WGT LBS	DRAFT FT IN	RETAIL LOW	RETAIL HIGH
				---- 1990	BOATS					
22	GARWOOD STREAMLINER	OP	RNBT	MHG DV	IO 270 CRUS	7	3500	2	15100	17200
22	GARWOOD DELUXE	OP	RNBT	MHG DV	IO 350 CRUS	7 2	4600	2 7	26600	29600
33	BABY GAR	OP	RNBT	MHG DV	IO T270 CRUS	7 2	6050	2 6	54400	59800
33	GARWOOD DELUXE	OP	RNBT	MHG DV	IO 350 CRUS	7 2	4850	2 6	50400	55400

....For earlier years, see the BUC Used Boat Price Guide, Volume 3

GENERAL BOATS CORPORATION
EDENTON NC 27932   COAST GUARD MFG ID- GBX See inside cover to adjust price for area

For more recent years, see the BUC Used Boat Price Guide, Volume 1

LOA FT IN	NAME AND/ OR MODEL	TOP/ RIG	BOAT TYPE	-HULL- MTL TP	----ENGINE--- TP # HP MFG	BEAM FT IN	WGT LBS	DRAFT FT IN	RETAIL LOW	RETAIL HIGH
				---- 1988	BOATS					
22	RHODES 22	SLP	SAIL	FBG KC	OB	8	2500	1 8	6700	7700
				---- 1987	BOATS					
22	RHODES 22	SLP	SAIL	FBG KC	OB	8	2500	1 8	6300	7250
				---- 1986	BOATS					
22	RHODES 22	SLP	SAIL	FBG KC	OB	8	2500	1 8	6000	6800
26 7	RHODES 26	SLP	SAIL	FBG KC	IB 10	8 6	4000	2	11300	12800
				---- 1985	BOATS					
22	RHODES 22	SLP	SAIL	FBG KC	OB	8	2500	1 8	5550	6400
				---- 1984	BOATS					
22	RHODES 22	SLP	SAIL	FBG KC	OB	8	2500	1 8	5250	6000

....For earlier years, see the BUC Used Boat Price Guide, Volume 3

GENERAL MARINE INC
ARUNDEL ME 04043   COAST GUARD MFG ID- GMW See inside cover to adjust price for area

LOA FT IN	NAME AND/ OR MODEL	TOP/ RIG	BOAT TYPE	-HULL- MTL TP	----ENGINE--- TP # HP MFG	BEAM FT IN	WGT LBS	DRAFT FT IN	RETAIL LOW	RETAIL HIGH
				---- 1985	BOATS					
19 6	GM196		CTRCN	FBG FL	OB	7	1250	5	1900	2250
19 6	GM196 COMMERCIAL		UTL	FBG FL	OB	7	1250	5	1700	2000
19 6	GM196 CUDDY		CUD	FBG FL	OB	7	1350	5	2050	2450
24 9	GM 25		CTRCN	FBG SV	OB	9 6	3500	2	5650	6500
24 9	GM 25		CTRCN	FBG SV	IB 220 CRUS	9 6	4500	2	20800	23200
24 9	GM 25 BLUEWATER		CUD	FBG SV	IB 220 CRUS	9 6	4900	2	22100	24600
				---- 1984	BOATS					
19 6	GM196		CTRCN	FBG FL	OB	7	1250	5	1850	2200
19 6	GM196 COMMERCIAL		UTL	FBG FL	OB	7	1650	5	1950	
19 6	GM196 CUDDY		CUD	FBG FL	OB	7	1350	5	2000	2400

GENESIS POWERBOAT
UNITED MARINE CORPORATION
WATSEKA IL 60970   See inside cover to adjust price for area

For more recent years, see the BUC Used Boat Price Guide, Volume 1

LOA FT IN	NAME AND/ OR MODEL	TOP/ RIG	BOAT TYPE	-HULL- MTL TP	----ENGINE--- TP # HP MFG	BEAM FT IN	WGT LBS	DRAFT FT IN	RETAIL LOW	RETAIL HIGH
				---- 1996	BOATS					
18 10	GENESIS 1901	OP	B/R	FBG SV	IO 180 MRCR	7 8	2450		5650	6500
18 10	GENESIS 1901 F & S	OP	B/R	FBG SV	IO 180 MRCR	7 8	2450		5950	6850
20 1	GENESIS 2001	OP	B/R	FBG SV	IO 235 MRCR	8 5	2620		7450	8600
20 1	GENESIS 2002	OP	CUD	FBG SV	IO 235 MRCR	8 5	2620		8000	9150
25 2	GENESIS 2501	OP	B/R	FBG DV	IO 415 MRCR	8 6	4250		17000	19300
25 2	GENESIS 2502	OP	CUD	FBG DV	IO 415 MRCR	8 6	4250		18800	20900

GERAGHTY MARINE INC
EL CAJON CA 92020   See inside cover to adjust price for area

LOA FT IN	NAME AND/ OR MODEL	TOP/ RIG	BOAT TYPE	-HULL- MTL TP	----ENGINE--- TP # HP MFG	BEAM FT IN	WGT LBS	DRAFT FT IN	RETAIL LOW	RETAIL HIGH
				---- 1984	BOATS					
41	NELSON/MAREK 41	SLP	SA/RC	FBG KL		12 8	15300	7	47600	52300
44	FRERS 45		SA/RC	FBG KL		14	19000	8	59800	65700
54 5	NELSON/MAREK 55	SLP	SA/RC	FBG KL		12 6	17300	8	118000	130000
68	NELSON/MAREK 68		SA/RC	FBG KL		14 4	25413	9	151500	166500

GHOST INDUSTRIES
ISLAND PK NY 11558   COAST GUARD MFG ID- KKC See inside cover to adjust price for area

LOA FT IN	NAME AND/ OR MODEL	TOP/ RIG	BOAT TYPE	-HULL- MTL TP	----ENGINE--- TP # HP MFG	BEAM FT IN	WGT LBS	DRAFT FT IN	RETAIL LOW	RETAIL HIGH
				---- 1986	BOATS					
23	GHOST 23 SKI		OFF	FBG DV	OB	7 6	1400	1 6	6800	7850
23	GHOST 23 SPORT		OFF	FBG DV	OB	7 6	1800	1 6	8550	9800
28	GHOST 28 SPORT		OFF	FBG DV	OB	8	2800	2 6	19600	21800
				---- 1985	BOATS					
23	GHOST 23 SKI		OFF	FBG DV	OB	7 6	1400	1 6	6650	7650
23	GHOST 23 SPORT		OFF	FBG DV	OB	7 6	1800	1 6	8350	9600
28	GHOST 28 SPORT		OFF	FBG DV	OB	8	3100	2 6	19100	21300
				---- 1984	BOATS					
23	GHOST 23 SKI		OFF	FBG DV	OB	7 6	1400	1 6	6500	7450
23	GHOST 23 SPORT		OFF	FBG DV	OB	7 6	1800	1 6	8150	9400
28	GHOST 28 SPORT		OFF	FBG DV	OB	8	2800	2 6	18900	21000

GIACOMO COLOMBO
LAGO DI COMO ITALY   See inside cover to adjust price for area

LOA FT IN	NAME AND/ OR MODEL	TOP/ RIG	BOAT TYPE	-HULL- MTL TP	----ENGINE--- TP # HP MFG	BEAM FT IN	WGT LBS	DRAFT FT IN	RETAIL LOW	RETAIL HIGH
				---- 1996	BOATS					
20 9	SUPER-INDIOS 21	OP	RNBT	FBG DV	IO 280 MRCR	7 4			11300	12800
20 9	SUPER-INDIOS 21 GL	OP	RNBT	FBG DV	IO 230-280	7 4	3086		10800	12800
20 9	SUPER-INDIOS 21 GL	OP	RNBT	FBG DV	IO 130D VLVO	7 4	3086		13400	15200
24 4	RUNABOUT 24	OP	RNBT	FBG DV	IO 260-330	7 9			15800	19600
24 4	RUNABOUT 24	OP	RNBT	FBG DV	IO 365 MRCR	7 9			18900	21000
25 4	VANTAGE 25	OP	RNBT	FBG DV	IO 280 MRCR	8 1			16200	18500
25 4	VANTAGE 26	OP	SPTCR	FBG DV	IO 260-365	8 3			20800	25900
25 4	VANTAGE 26	OP	SPTCR	FBG DV	IO 200D-230D	8 3			24500	28100
25 4	VANTAGE 26	OP	SPTCR	FBG DV	IO T175-T205	8 3			22400	25500
26 6	ANTIBES 27	OP	RNBT	FBG DV	IO T280 MRCR	8 2			23900	26500
28 3	MAITE 28	OP	SPTCR	FBG DV	IO T230-T280	8 2			31900	37600
28 3	MAITE 28	OP	SPTCR	FBG DV	IOT200D-T230D	8 2			40100	45800
29 1	RACING 29	OP	RACE	FBG DV	IO T280 MRCR	9 2	7716		32100	35700
29 1	SIMILEGNO RACING 29	OP	RACE	FBG DV	IO T260-T270	9 2	7716		37100	46000
29 1	SIMILEGNO RACING 29	OP	RACE	FBG DV	IO T280-T365	9 2	7716		43300	48100
29 1	SIMILEGNO RACING 29	OP	RACE	FBG DV	IOT200D-T230D	9 2	7716		44000	50800
30 4	NOBLESSE 30	OP	SPTCR	FBG DV	IO T260-T330	9 1			34900	42100
30 4	NOBLESSE 30	OP	SPTCR	FBG DV	IO T365 MRCR	9 1			40400	44900
30 4	NOBLESSE 30	OP	SPTCR	FBG DV	IOT200D-T230D	9 1			42400	50100
30 9	SUPER-INDIOS 31	OP	RNBT	FBG DV	IO T260-T365	9 8	8598		38700	46700
30 9	SUPER-INDIOS 31	OP	RNBT	FBG DV	IOT200D-T230D	9 8	8598		45000	51800
31	COLOMBO 31 SF	OP	SPTCR	FBG DV	IO T260-T330	9 8			38600	46100
31	COLOMBO 31 SF	OP	SPTCR	FBG DV	IO T365 MRCR	9 8			44000	48900
31	COLOMBO 31 SF	OP	SPTCR	FBG DV	IOT200D-T230D	9 8			46600	54100

LOA FT	IN	NAME AND/ OR MODEL	TOP/ RIG	BOAT TYPE	-HULL- MTL	TP	ENGINE TP	# HP	MFG	BEAM FT	IN	WGT LBS	DRAFT FT IN	RETAIL LOW	RETAIL HIGH
		1996 BOATS													
32		ALIANTE 32	OP	SPTCR	FBG	DV	IO	T260-T365		9	1			34800	41600
32		ALIANTE 32	OP	SPTCR	FBG	DV	IO	T200D-T230D		9	1			37900	43800
34	5	VIRAGE 34	OP	SPTCR	FBG	DV	IO	T260-T365		9	8			66800	82800
34	5	VIRAGE 34	OP	SPTCR	FBG	DV	IO	T200D-T230D		9	8			89100	102000
38		ATLANTIC 38	OP	SPTCR	FBG	DV	IO	T280	MRCR	11				49600	54500
		IO T330 MRCR 51900 57000, IO T365 MRCR 54400 59800, IO T200D VLVO 71900 79000													
		IO T220D MRCR 74200 81500, IO T230D VLVO 72900 80100, IO T270D MRCR 76400 83900													
43		BLUE SHORE 43 SPORT	OP	SPTCR	FBG	DV	IO	T300D	CAT	10	6			108000	118500
		IO T440D CAT 119500 131500, IO R330 MRCR 81200 89300, IO R220D MRCR 102500 112500													
		IO R230D VLVO 101000 111000, IO R330D MRCR 111000 122000, IO R365D MRCR 114500 126000													
43	5	CAMRIDGE 42	OP	SPTCR	FBG	DV	IO	T420D	CUM	13	2			107000	118000
50		COLOMBO MIAMI 48	OP	SPTCR	FBG	DV	IO	T666D	MTU	13	2			203000	223000
		1995 BOATS													
20	9	SUPER-INDIOS 21 GL	OP	RNBT	FBG	DV	IO	230-270		7	4	3086		21900	25400
20	9	SUPER-INDIOS 21 GL	OP	RNBT	FBG	DV	IO	130D	VLVO	7	4	3086		27500	30500
24	4	RUNABOUT 24	OP	RNBT	FBG	DV	IO	270-330		7	9			33300	40100
24	4	RUNABOUT 24	OP	RNBT	FBG	DV	IO	365	MRCR	7	9			38700	42900
24	4	VANTAGE 25	OP	RNBT	FBG	DV	IO	270	MRCR	8	1			33600	37300
25	4	VANTAGE 26	OP	SPTCR	FBG	DV	IO	260-330		8	3			43100	51600
		IO 365 MRCR 49600 54500, IO 200D-230D 52800 60100, IO T205-T275 48300 57400													
26	6	ANTIBES 27	OP	RNBT	FBG	DV	IO	T270	MRCR	8	2			50200	55200
28	3	MAITE 28	OP	SPTCR	FBG	DV	IO	T230-T270		8	2			60100	69400
28	3	MAITE 28	OP	SPTCR	FBG	DV	IO	T200D-T230D		8	2			76200	87300
29	1	RACING 29	OP	RACE	FBG	DV	IO	T270	MRCR	9	2	7716		54600	60000
29	1	SIMILEGNO RACING 29	OP	RACE	FBG	DV	IO	T260-T365		9	2	7716		54100	66000
29	1	SIMILEGNO RACING 29	OP	RACE	FBG	DV	IO	T200D-T230D		9	2	7716		62300	71200
30	4	NOBLESSE 30	OP	SPTCR	FBG	DV	IO	T260-T365		9	1			69600	84300
30	4	NOBLESSE 30	OP	SPTCR	FBG	DV	IO	T200D-T230D		9	1			78800	90400
30	9	SUPER-INDIOS 31	OP	RNBT	FBG	DV	IO	T260-T365		9	8	8598		59000	70600
30	9	SUPER-INDIOS 31	OP	RNBT	FBG	DV	IO	T200D-T230D		9	8	8598		66500	75900
31		COLOMBO 31 SF	OP	SPTCR	FBG	DV	IO	T260-T365		9	8			76000	90900
31		COLOMBO 31 SF	OP	SPTCR	FBG	DV	IO	T200D-T230D		9	8			86000	98300
32		ALIANTE 32	OP	SPTCR	FBG	DV	IO	T260-T365		9	1			83000	98200
32		ALIANTE 32	OP	SPTCR	FBG	DV	IO	T200D-T230D		9	1			90600	103500
34	5	VIRAGE 34	OP	SPTCR	FBG	DV	IO	T260-T365		9	8			112500	133500
34	5	VIRAGE 34	OP	SPTCR	FBG	DV	IO	T420	MRCR	9	8			128000	141000
34	5	VIRAGE 34	OP	SPTCR	FBG	DV	IO	T200D-T230D		9	8			131500	148000
43		BLUE SHORE 43 SPORT	OP	SPTCR	FBG	DV	IO	T300D	CAT	10	6			192000	210500
		IO T425D CAT 227000 249500, IO R330 MRCR 189000 207500, IO R220D MRCR 198000 217500													
		IO R230D VLVO 198500 218500, IO R330D MRCR 236500 260000, IO R365D MRCR 249000 273500													
50		COLOMBO MIAMI 48	OP	SPTCR	FBG	DV	IO	T666D	MTU	13	2			322000	354000
		1994 BOATS													
20	9	SUPER-INDIOS 21 GL	OP	RNBT	FBG	DV	IO	230-270		7	4	3086		9450	11200
20	9	SUPER-INDIOS 21 GL	OP	RNBT	FBG	DV	IO	130D	VLVO	7	4	3086		11800	13400
24	4	RUNABOUT 24	OP	RNBT	FBG	DV	IO	270-330		7	9			13900	17100
24	4	RUNABOUT 24	OP	RNBT	FBG	DV	IO	365	MRCR	7	9			16100	18300
24	4	VANTAGE 25	OP	RNBT	FBG	DV	IO	270	MRCR	8	1			14000	15900
25	4	VANTAGE 26	OP	SPTCR	FBG	DV	IO	260-365		8	3			18500	23000
25	4	VANTAGE 26	OP	SPTCR	FBG	DV	IO	200D-230D		8	3			22100	24900
25	4	VANTAGE 26	OP	SPTCR	FBG	DV	IO	T205-T275		8	3			20300	24400
26	6	ANTIBES 27	OP	RNBT	FBG	DV	IO	T270	MRCR	8	2			20900	23200
28	3	MAITE 28	OP	SPTCR	FBG	DV	IO	T230-T270		8	2			27800	32700
28	3	MAITE 28	OP	SPTCR	FBG	DV	IO	T200D-T230D		8	2			34900	39900
29	1	RACING 29	OP	RACE	FBG	DV	IO	T270	MRCR	9	2	7716		27700	30800
29	1	SIMILEGNO RACING 29	OP	RACE	FBG	DV	IO	T260-T365		9	2	7716		32300	40000
29	1	SIMILEGNO RACING 29	OP	RACE	FBG	DV	IO	T200D-T230D		9	2	7716		38300	44200
30	4	NOBLESSE 30	OP	SPTCR	FBG	DV	IO	T260-T330		9	1			30400	36600
30	4	NOBLESSE 30	OP	SPTCR	FBG	DV	IO	T365	MRCR	9	1			35200	39100
30	4	NOBLESSE 30	OP	SPTCR	FBG	DV	IO	T200D-T230D		9	1			36900	43600
30	9	SUPER-INDIOS 31	OP	RNBT	FBG	DV	IO	T260-T365		9	8	8598		33700	40700
30	9	SUPER-INDIOS 31	OP	RNBT	FBG	DV	IO	T200D-T230D		9	8	8598		39100	45100
31		COLOMBO 31 SF	OP	SPTCR	FBG	DV	IO	T260-T330		9	8			33500	40100
31		COLOMBO 31 SF	OP	SPTCR	FBG	DV	IO	T365	MRCR	9	8			38300	42600
31		COLOMBO 31 SF	OP	SPTCR	FBG	DV	IO	T200D-T230D		9	8			40100	47100
32		ALIANTE 32	OP	SPTCR	FBG	DV	IO	T260-T365		9	1			30300	36200
32		ALIANTE 32	OP	SPTCR	FBG	DV	IO	T200D-T230D		9	1			33000	38100
34	5	VIRAGE 34	OP	SPTCR	FBG	DV	IO	T260-T365		9	8			58800	72100
34	5	VIRAGE 34	OP	SPTCR	FBG	DV	IO	T420	MRCR	9	8			72800	80000
34	5	VIRAGE 34	OP	SPTCR	FBG	DV	IO	T200D-T230D		9	8			77600	88600
37	6	COLOMBO 38	OP	SPTCR	FBG	DV	IO	T260	MRCR	10	6			42500	47200
		IO T270 MRCR 42700 47500, IO T330 MRCR 45500 50000, IO T365 MRCR 48100 52900													
		IO T200D VLVO 63600 69900, IO T220D MRCR 65600 72100, IO T230D VLVO 64500 70900													
43		BLUE SHORE 43 SPORT	OP	SPTCR	FBG	DV	IO	T300D	CAT	10	6			95100	104500
		IO T425D CAT 104000 114500, IO R330 MRCR 70700 77700, IO R220D MRCR 90200 99100													
		IO R230D VLVO 88800 97500, IO R330D MRCR 97900 107500, IO R365D MRCR 101000 111000													
50		COLOMBO MIAMI 48	OP	SPTCR	FBG	DV	IO	T666D	MTU	13	2			180000	197500
		1993 BOATS													
20	9	SUPER-INDIOS 21 GL	OP	RNBT	FBG	DV	IO	230-270		7	4	3086		8850	10500
20	9	SUPER-INDIOS 21 GL	OP	RNBT	FBG	DV	IO	130D	VLVO	7	4	3086		11100	12600
24	4	RUNABOUT 24	OP	RNBT	FBG	DV	IO	260-330		7	9			12900	15900
24	4	RUNABOUT 24	OP	RNBT	FBG	DV	IO	365	MRCR	7	9			15000	17100
24	4	VANTAGE 25	OP	RNBT	FBG	DV	IO	260-330		8	1			13000	16100
		IO 365 MRCR 15100 17200, IO 200D-230D 16300 19100, IO T180 MRCR 14300 16300													
		IO T205D MRCR 23100 25600													
26	6	ANTIBES 27	OP	RNBT	FBG	DV	IO	T230-T270		8	2			18900	22200
26	6	ANTIBES 27	OP	RNBT	FBG	DV	IO	T200D-T230D		8	2			26800	31000
28	3	COLOMBO 28	OP	SPTCR	FBG	DV	IO	T230-T270		8	2			25900	30500
28	3	COLOMBO 28	OP	SPTCR	FBG	DV	IO	T200D-T230D		8	2			32500	37200
29	1	RACING 29	OP	RACE	FBG	DV	IO	T260	MRCR	9	2	7716		24800	27500
		IO T270 MRCR 23800 26500, IO T270-T365 28300 31400, IOT200D-T230D 29700 34800													
29	1	SIMILEGNO RACING 29	OP	RACE	FBG	DV	IO	T260-T365		9	2	7716		35800	43300
29	1	SIMILEGNO RACING 29	OP	RACE	FBG	DV	IO	T200D-T230D		9	2	7716		41300	47600
30	4	COLOMBO 30	OP	SPTCR	FBG	DV	IO	T260-T330		9	1			28400	34200
30	4	COLOMBO 30	OP	SPTCR	FBG	DV	IO	T365	MRCR	9	1			32800	36500
30	4	COLOMBO 30	OP	SPTCR	FBG	DV	IO	T200D-T230D		9	1			34400	40700
30	9	SUPER-INDIOS 31	OP	RNBT	FBG	DV	IO	T260-T365		9	8	8598		31300	37800
30	9	SUPER-INDIOS 31	OP	RNBT	FBG	DV	IO	T200D-T230D		9	8	8598		36300	41900
31		COLOMBO 31 SF	OP	SPTCR	FBG	DV	IO	T260-T330		9	8			31300	37400
31		COLOMBO 31 SF	OP	SPTCR	FBG	DV	IO	T365	MRCR	9	8			35700	39700
31		COLOMBO 31 SF	OP	SPTCR	FBG	DV	IO	T200D-T220D		9	8			37400	43900
32		ALIANTE 32	OP	SPTCR	FBG	DV	IO	T260-T365		9	1			28200	33800
32		ALIANTE 32	OP	SPTCR	FBG	DV	IO	T200D-T230D		9	1			30800	35500
34	5	VIRAGE 34	OP	SPTCR	FBG	DV	IO	T260-T365		9	8			54900	67300
34	5	VIRAGE 34	OP	SPTCR	FBG	DV	IO	T420	MRCR	9	8			67900	74600
34	5	VIRAGE 34	OP	SPTCR	FBG	DV	IO	T200D-T230D		9	8			72300	82600
37	6	COLOMBO 38	OP	SPTCR	FBG	DV	IO	T260	MRCR	10	6			39600	44000
		IO T270 MRCR 39800 44200, IO T330 MRCR 42300 47000, IO T365 MRCR 44300 49300													
		IO T200D VLVO 59900 65900, IO T220D MRCR 61200 67300, IO T230D VLVO 60200 66100													
40	8	BLUE-SHORE 41 SPCL	OP	SPTCR	FBG	DV	IO	T425D	CAT	10	5			91700	101000
		IO R330 MRCR 56100 61600, IO R365 MRCR 59200 65100, IO R220D MRCR 78600 86300													
		IO R230D VLVO 77100 84700													
43		BLUE SHORE 43 SPORT	OP	SPTCR	FBG	DV	IO	T300D	CAT	10	6			89200	98100
		IO T425D CAT 97700 107500, IO R220D MRCR 84700 93000, IO R230D VLVO 83300 91600													
		IO R330D MRCR 91900 101000, IO R365D MRCR 94700 104000													
50		COLOMBO MIAMI 48	OP	SPTCR	FBG	DV	IO	T666D	MTU	13	2			169000	186000
		1991 BOATS													
19		SUPER-INDIOS 19	OP	RNBT	FBG	DV	IO	180-250		7	5			5050	6100
20	9	SUPER-INDIOS 21 GL	OP	RNBT	FBG	DV	IO	230-270		7	4	3086		7650	9150
20	9	SUPER-INDIOS 21 GL	OP	RNBT	FBG	DV	IO	130D	VLVO	7	4	3086		9800	11100
24	4	VANTAGE 25	OP	RNBT	FBG	DV	IO	260-330		8	1			11500	14300
		IO 365 MRCR 13300 15100, IO 200D VLVO 14200 16100, IO T180 MRCR 12700 14400													
		IO T205D MRCR 20500 22800													
26	6	ANTIBES 27	OP	RNBT	FBG	DV	IO	T230-T270		8	2			16100	19800
26	6	ANTIBES 27	OP	RNBT	FBG	DV	IO	T184D-T200D		8	2			24400	27100
29	1	RACING 29	OP	RACE	FBG	DV	IO	T260-T365		9	2	7716		26200	32200
29	1	RACING 29	OP	RACE	FBG	DV	IO	T200D-T220D		9	2	7716		31000	35500
30	9	SUPER-INDIOS 31	OP	RNBT	FBG	DV	IO	T260-T365		9	8	8598		27300	33000
30	9	SUPER-INDIOS 31	OP	RNBT	FBG	DV	IO	T200D-T220D		9	8	8598		32100	36400
31		COLOMBO 31 SF	OP	SPTCR	FBG	DV	IO	T260-T330		9	8			27300	32600
31		COLOMBO 31 SF	OP	SPTCR	FBG	DV	IO	T365	MRCR	9	8			31200	34600
31		COLOMBO 31 SF	OP	SPTCR	FBG	DV	IO	T200D-T220D		9	8			32600	38300
32		ALIANTE 32	OP	SPTCR	FBG	DV	IO	T260-T365		9	1			25000	29500
32		ALIANTE 32	OP	SPTCR	FBG	DV	IO	T200D	VLVO	9	1			26900	29900
33		COLOMBO 33	OP	SPTCR	FBG	DV	IO	T260-T330		9	8			42500	50800
33		COLOMBO 33	OP	SPTCR	FBG	DV	IO	T365	MRCR	9	8			49100	53900
33		COLOMBO 33	OP	SPTCR	FBG	DV	IO	T200D-T220D		9	8			62800	71500
35		COLOMBO 36	OP	SPTCR	FBG	DV	IO	T220	MRCR	10	4			46200	50800
		IO T260 MRCR 47100 51700, IO T270 MRCR 47400 52100, IO T330 MRCR 50400 55300													
		IO T365 MRCR 52900 58100, IO T200D VLVO 62300 68500, IO T220D 64800 71200													

CONTINUED ON NEXT PAGE

```
LOA  NAME AND/        TOP/ BOAT -HULL- ----ENGINE--- BEAM  WGT  DRAFT RETAIL RETAIL
FT IN OR MODEL        RIG TYPE MTL TP TP # HP  MFG   FT IN LBS  FT IN  LOW    HIGH
------------------- 1991 BOATS ------------------------------------------------
40  8 BLUE-SHORE 41 SPCL   OP  SPTCR FBG DV IO T380D CAT 10  5       79100  86900
      IO R330  MRCR 50800 55900, IO R365 MRCR 53400 58700, IO R200D VLVO 68000 74700

40  8 BLUE-SHORE 41 SPORT  OP  SPTCR FBG DV IO T380D CAT 10  3       79800  87600
      IO R330  MRCR 51300 56300, IO R365 MRCR 54000 59300, IO R200D VLVO 68500 75300

------------------- 1990 BOATS ------------------------------------------------
19    SUPER-INDIOS 19      OP  RNBT  FBG DV IO 180-205       7  5        4750   5500
20  9 SUPER-INDIOS 21 GL   OP  RNBT  FBG DV IO 230-270       7  4  3086  7150   8550
20  9 SUPER-INDIOS 21 GL   OP  RNBT  FBG DV IO 130D VLVO     7  4  3086  9150  10400
24  4 VANTAGE 25           OP  RNBT  FBG DV IO 260-330       8  1       10900  13400
      IO 365   MRCR 12600 14300, IO 200D VLVO 13400 15200, IO T180 MRCR 11900 13500
      IO T205D MRCR 19600 21800

26  6 ANTIBES 27           OP  RNBT  FBG DV IO T230-T270     8  2       15100  18600
26  6 ANTIBES 27           OP  RNBT  FBG DV IO IOT184D-T200D 8  2       22800  25300
29  1 RACING 29            OP  RACE  FBG DV IO T260-T365     9  2  7716 24500  30100
29  1 RACING 29            OP  RACE  FBG DV IO IOT184D-T200D 9  2  7716 28400  32200
30  9 SUPER-INDIOS 31      OP  RNBT  FBG DV IO T260-T365     9  8  8598 25500  30900
30  9 SUPER-INDIOS 31      OP  RNBT  FBG DV IO IOT184D-T200D 9  8  8598 29200  33300
31    COLOMBO 31 SF        OP  SPTCR FBG DV IO T260-T330     9  8       75600  91500
31    COLOMBO 31 SF        OP  SPTCR FBG DV IO T365 MRCR     9  8       29200  32400
31    COLOMBO 31 SF        OP  SPTCR FBG DV IO IOT184D-T700D 9  8       31200  34700
32    ALIANTE 32           OP  SPTCR FBG DV IO T260-T365     9  1       23900  28000
32    ALIANTE 32           OP  SPTCR FBG DV IO T200D VLVO    9  1       25500  28400

33    COLOMBO 33           OP  SPTCR FBG DV IO T260-T330     9  8       39800  47600
33    COLOMBO 33           OP  SPTCR FBG DV IO T365 MRCR     9  8       45900  50500
33    COLOMBO 33           OP  SPTCR FBG DV IO IOT184D-T200D 9  8       60100  66100
35    COLOMBO 36           OP  SPTCR FBG DV IO T260 MRCR 10  4       43500  48400
      IO T270  MRCR 43800 48700, IO T330 MRCR 47100 51800, IO T365 MRCR 49700 54700
      IO T184D MRCR 59900 65800, IO T200D VLVO 58900 64700, IO T220D 60600 66600

40  8 BLUE-SHORE 41 SPCL   OP  SPTCR FBG DV IO T380D CAT 10  5       75100  82500
      IO R330  MRCR 48300 53000, IO R365 MRCR 50800 55800, IO R200D VLVO 64500 70800

40  8 BLUE-SHORE 41 SPORT  OP  SPTCR FBG DV IO T380D CAT 10  3       75700  83200
      IO R330  MRCR 48700 53500, IO R365 MRCR 51300 56400, IO R200D VLVO 65000 71400

------------------- 1989 BOATS ------------------------------------------------
19    SUPER-INDIOS 19      OP  RNBT  FBG DV IO 180-205       7  5        4450   5150
20  9 SUPER-INDIOS 21 GL   OP  RNBT  FBG DV IO 230-270       7  4  3086  6750   8050
20  9 SUPER-INDIOS 21 GL   OP  RNBT  FBG DV IO 130D VLVO     7  4  3086  8500   9800
24  4 VANTAGE 25           OP  RNBT  FBG DV IO 260-330       8  1       10200  12700
      IO 365   MRCR 11800 13400, IO 200D VLVO 12700 14400, IO T180-T205 11200 12900

26  6 ANTIBES 27           OP  RNBT  FBG DV IO T230-T270     8  2       14400  17700
26  6 ANTIBES 27           OP  RNBT  FBG DV IO IOT184D-T200D 8  2       22400  24800
29  1 RACING 29            OP  RACE  FBG DV IO T260-T330     9  2  7716 20800  25200
29  1 RACING 29            OP  RACE  FBG DV IO T365 MRCR     9  2  7716 23800  26400
29  1 RACING 29            OP  RACE  FBG DV IO IOT184D-T200D 9  2  7716 26600  29600
30  9 SUPER-INDIOS 31      OP  RNBT  FBG DV IO T260-T365     9  8  8598 22500  27800
30  9 SUPER-INDIOS 31      OP  RNBT  FBG DV IO IOT184D-T200D 9  8  8598 26800  30300
31    COLOMBO 31 SF        OP  SPTCR FBG DV IO T260-T365     9  8       26000  32100
31    COLOMBO 31 SF        OP  SPTCR FBG DV IO IOT184D-T200D 9  8       31600  35100
32    ALIANTE 32           OP  SPTCR FBG DV IO T260-T365     9  1       29300  35000
32    ALIANTE 32           OP  SPTCR FBG DV IO T200D VLVO    9  1       35300  39200

33    COLOMBO 33           OP  SPTCR FBG DV IO T260-T330     9  8       34000  40600
      IO T365  MRCR 38500 42800, IB T184D MRCR 57900 63400, IO T200D VLVO 50400 55400

35    COLOMBO 36           OP  SPTCR FBG DV IO T260 MRCR 10  4       40200  44700
      IO T270  MRCR 40000 44500, IO T330 MRCR 42200 46900, IO T365 MRCR 43800 48600
      IO T184D MRCR 52800 58100, IO T200D VLVO 52700 57900, IO T220D 53900 59300

40  8 BLUE-SHORE 41 SPCL   OP  SPTCR FBG DV IO T380D CAT 10  5       71400  78400
      IO R330  MRCR 45000 49900, IO R365 MRCR 48300 53100, IO R300D VLVO 66000 72500

40  8 BLUE-SHORE 41 SPORT  OP  SPTCR FBG DV IO T380D CAT 10  3       72000  79100
      IO R330  MRCR 46300 50900, IO R365 MRCR 48800 53600, IO R200D VLVO 61800 67900

40  8 BLUE-SHORE 41 YACHT  OP  SPTCR FBG DV IB T380D CAT 10  6       91200 100000
      IO R330  MRCR 44800 49700, IB R330 MRCR 47300 52000, IO R365 MRCR 48100 52800

------------------- 1988 BOATS ------------------------------------------------
19    SUPER-INDIOS 19      OP  RNBT  FBG DV IO 180-205       7  5        4100   4850
20  9 SUPER-INDIOS 21 G.L. OP  RNBT  FBG DV IO 230-270       7  4  3086  6450   7650
20  9 SUPER-INDIOS 21 G.L. OP  RNBT  FBG DV IO 130D VLVO     7  4  3086  8050   9250
24  4 VANTAGE 25           OP  RNBT  FBG DV IO 260-330       8  1        9700  12000
      IO 365   MRCR 11300 12800, IO 200D VLVO 12000 13600, IO T175-T205 10600 12300

26  6 ANTIBES 27           OP  RNBT  FBG DV IO T200-T270     8         13600  16800
26  6 ANTIBES 27           OP  RNBT  FBG DV IO T350 MRCR     8         16400  18700
26  6 ANTIBES 27           OP  RNBT  FBG DV IO T184D BMW     8         21300  23700
29  1 RACING 29            OP  RACE  FBG DV IO T260-T330     9  2  7716 19500  23600
29  1 RACING 29            OP  RACE  FBG DV IO T365 MRCR     9  2  7716 22400  24800
29  1 RACING 29            OP  RACE  FBG DV IO IOT184D-T200D 9  2  7716 25100  27900
30  9 SUPER-INDIOS 31      OP  RNBT  FBG DV IO T260-T330     9  8  8598 21200  25400
30  9 SUPER-INDIOS 31      OP  RNBT  FBG DV IO T365 MRCR     9  8  8598 24200  26900
30  9 SUPER-INDIOS 31      OP  RNBT  FBG DV IO T200D VLVO    9  8  8598 25900  28800
31    COLOMBO 31 SF        OP  SPTCR FBG DV IO T200-T365     9  8       24400  30100

33    COLOMBO 33           OP  SPTCR FBG DV IO T270-T365     9  8       32300  40300
      IO T184D BMW  39400 43800, IO T200D VLVO 47600 52400, IB T260D MRCR 58700 64500
      IO T365D MRCR 56100 61600

35    COLOMBO 36           OP  SPTCR FBG DV IO T260 MRCR 10  4       37800  42200
      IO T270  MRCR 37600 41800, IO T330 MRCR 39700 44100, IO T365 MRCR 41100 45700
      IO T200D VLVO 49600 54500, IO T220D 50600 55600

40  8 BLUE-SHORE 41 SPORT  OP  SPTCR FBG DV IO 330 MRCR 10  4       39800  44200
      IO 365   MRCR 40700 45200, IO T330 43400 48200, IO T355D CAT 67300 73900
      IO T450D 70100 77100, IO R200D VLVO 59500 65300

40  8 BLUE-SHORE 41 YACHT  OP  SPTCR FBG DV IB 330 MRCR 10  6       42700  47500
      IO T330  MRCR 42500 47300, IO T365 MRCR 44300 49200, IB T355D CAT 85400 93800
      IB T450D 89100 97900

------------------- 1987 BOATS ------------------------------------------------
19    SUPER-INDIOS 19      OP  RNBT  FBG DV IO 175-205       7  5        3900   4550
20  9 SUPER-INDIOS 21      OP  RNBT  FBG DV IO 230-260       7  4  3086  6100   7200
20  9 SUPER-INDIOS 21      OP  RNBT  FBG DV IO 130D VLVO     7  4  3086  7600   8750
24  4 VANTAGE 25           OP  RNBT  FBG DV IO 260-330       8  1        9200  11300
24  4 VANTAGE 25           OP  RNBT  FBG DV IO T260-T330     8  1       11300  12800
24  4 VANTAGE 25           OP  RNBT  FBG DV IO T175-T205     8  1       10100  11600
26  6 ANTIBES 27           OP  RNBT  FBG DV IO T230-T260     8         13000  15300
26  6 ANTIBES 27           OP  RNBT  FBG DV IO T184D BMW     8         19900  22100
29  1 RACING 29            OP  RACE  FBG DV IO T260-T330     9  2  7716 18400  22300
29  1 RACING 29            OP  RACE  FBG DV IO IOT184D-T200D 9  2  7716 24100  26800
30  9 SUPER-INDIOS 31      OP  RNBT  FBG DV IO T260-T330     9  8  7716 19900  24400
30  9 SUPER-INDIOS 31      OP  RNBT  FBG DV IO T200D VLVO    9  8  8598 24500  27200

32    ALLANTE 32           OP  SPTCR FBG DV IO T200D VLVO    9         31300  34700
32    ALLANTE 32           OP  SPTCR FBG DV IB T260D MRCR    9         35400  39400
32    ALLANTE 32           OP  SPTCR FBG DV IO T330D-T370D   9         36100  42000
33    COLOMBO 33           OP  SPTCR FBG DV IO T330 MRCR     9  8       32400  36000
      IO T184D BMW  37100 41200, IO T200D VLVO 44100 49000, IB T260D MRCR 56800 62400
      IO T370D MRCR 53100 58300

35    COLOMBO 36           OP  SPTCR FBG DV IO T260 MRCR 10  4       35600  39600
      IO T330  MRCR 37400 41500, IO T370 MRCR 39000 43300, IO T200D VLVO 46600 51300
      IO T220D 47800 52600, IO T270D 45100 51700

36    COLOMBO 36           OP  SPTCR FBG DV IO T184D BMW 10  4       35200  39100
40  8 BLUE-SHORE 41 SPORT  OP  SPTCR FBG DV IO T330 MRCR 10  4       40700  45200
      IO T370  43000 47800, IO T355D CAT 63900 70200, IO T450D 66600 73200
      IO R330  40600 45200, IO R184D BMW 57200 62900, IO R200D VLVO 56500 62000

40  8 BLUE-SHORE 41 YACHT  OP  SPTCR FBG DV IO T330 MRCR 10  6       40200  44600
      IO T370  MRCR 42500 47200, IB T270D 75400 82900, IB T320D 77600 85300
      IB T355D CAT 81600 89600, IB T450D 85100 93500

41    BLUE-SHORE 41 SPORT  OP  SPTCR FBG DV IO T357D VLVO 10  4       61000  67000
------------------- 1986 BOATS ------------------------------------------------
19    SUPER-INDIOS 19      OP  RNBT  FBG DV IO 170-205       7  5        3650   4300
20  9 SUPER-INDIOS 21      OP  RNBT  FBG DV IO 230-260       7  4  3086  5800   6850
20  9 SUPER-INDIOS 21      OP  RNBT  FBG DV IO 118D VLVO     7  4  3086  7100   8150
22  5 SUPER-INDIOS 23      OP  RNBT  FBG DV IO 260 MRCR      8  4  3086  6450   7400
24  4 VANTAGE 25           OP  RNBT  FBG DV IO 260 MRCR      8  1        8600   9900
      IO 330   MRCR 9550 10800, IO 175D-220D 10600 13000, IO T170-T205 9600 11100

26  6 ANTIBES 27           OP  RNBT  FBG DV IO T230-T260     8         12400  14500
26  6 ANTIBES 27           OP  RNBT  FBG DV IO T190D BMW     8         19400  21600
29  1 RACING 29            OP  RACE  FBG DV IO T260-T330     9  2  7716 17000  21100
29  1 RACING 29            OP  RACE  FBG DV IO T175D VLVO    9  2  7716 21000  23400
30  9 SUPER-INDIOS 31      OP  RNBT  FBG DV IO T260-T330     9  8  8598 19000  23200
```

LOA FT IN	NAME AND/ OR MODEL		TOP/ RIG	BOAT TYPE	-HULL- MTL TP	----ENGINE--- TP # HP MFG	BEAM FT IN	WGT LBS	DRAFT FT IN	RETAIL LOW	RETAIL HIGH
		1986 BOATS									
30 9	SUPER-INDIOS 31		OP	RNBT	FBG DV	IO T175D VLVO	9 8	8598		22800	25300
33	COLOMBO 33		OP	SPTCR	FBG DV	IO T260 MRCR	9 8			31100	34600
33	COLOMBO 33		OP	SPTCR	FBG DV	IO T330 MRCR	9 8			30700	34100
33	COLOMBO 33		OP	SPTCR	FBG DV	IO T175D VLVO	9 8			40800	45400
35	COLOMBO 36		OP	SPTCR	FBG DV	IO T260 MRCR	10 4			33700	37400
	IO T330 MRCR 35300	39300, IO T370 MRCR 36800				40900, IO T175D VLVO				42900	47700
	IO T220D 44500	49500									
40 8	BLUE-SHORE 41 YACHT		OP	SPTCR	FBG DV	IO T270 MRCR	10 6			36700	40800
	IO T330 MRCR 38400	42600, IO T370 MRCR 40200				44600, IB T270D				72000	79100
	IB T320D 74100	81400, IB T355D CAT 77900				85600, IB T450D				81200	89300
		1985 BOATS									
19	SUPER-INDIOS 19		OP	RNBT	FBG DV	IO 170-185				3450	4050
20 9	SUPER-INDIOS 21		OP	RNBT	FBG DV	IO 230-260		3086		5550	6500
20 9	SUPER-INDIOS 21		OP	RNBT	FBG DV	IO 118D VLVO		3086		6800	7850
22 5	SUPER-INDIOS 23		OP	RNBT	FBG DV	IO 260 MRCR		3086		6150	7050
24	VANTAGE 25		OP	RNBT	FBG DV	IO 230 MRCR	8 1			8050	9250
	IO 330 MRCR 9100	10300, IO 165D VLVO				9950 11300, IO 220D				11000	12500
	IO T170-T185 9150	10500									
26 6	ANTIBES 27		OP	RNBT	FBG DV	IO T230-T260				11800	14000
26 6	ANTIBES 27		OP	RNBT	FBG DV	IO T150D				16900	19200
29 1	RACING 29		OP	RACE	FBG DV	IO T260-T330		7716		16100	20000
29 1	RACING 29		OP	RACE	FBG DV	IO T165D VLVO		7716		19700	21900
30 9	SUPER-INDIOS 31		OP	RNBT	FBG DV	IO T260-T330		8598		18000	21900
30 9	SUPER-INDIOS 31		OP	RNBT	FBG DV	IO T165D VLVO		8598		21800	24200
33	COLOMBO 33		OP	SPTCR	FBG DV	IB 220D				41600	46200
35	COLOMBO 36		OP	SPTCR	FBG DV	IO T260 MRCR	10 4			32000	35500
	IO T330 MRCR 33500	37300, IO T370 MRCR 34900				38800, IO T165D VLVO				40500	45000
	IO T220D 42200	46900									
40 8	BLUE-SHORE 41 YACHT		OP	SPTCR	FBG DV	IO T330 MRCR	10 6			36700	40800
	IO T370 MRCR 38400	42600, IB T270D				68500 75300, IB T355D CAT				74100	81400
		1984 BOATS									
20 9	SUPER-INDIOS 21		OP	RNBT	FBG DV	IO 198-260		3086		5250	6300
20 9	SUPER-INDIOS 21		OP	RNBT	FBG DV	IO 130D VLVO		3086		6600	7600
22 5	SUPER-INDIOS 23		OP	RNBT	FBG DV	IO 260 MRCR		3086		5900	6800
24 4	VANTAGE 25		OP	RNBT	FBG DV	IO 220-260	8 1			7650	9050
	IO 330 MRCR 8600	9900, IO 175D VLVO				9750 11100, IO T170-T185				8700	10000
26 6	ANTIBES 27		OP	RNBT	FBG DV	IO T198-T260				11100	13400
26 6	ANTIBES 27		OP	RNBT	FBG DV	IO T155D BMW				16300	18600
29 1	RACING 29		OP	RACE	FBG DV	IO T260-T330		7716		15300	19000
29 1	RACING 29		OP	RACE	FBG DV	IO T175D VLVO		7716		19100	21200
30 9	SUPER-INDIOS 31		OP	RNBT	FBG DV	IO T260 MRCR		8598		16600	18900
30 9	SUPER-INDIOS 31		OP	RNBT	FBG DV	IO T330 MRCR		8598		18800	20900
30 9	SUPER-INDIOS 31		OP	RNBT	FBG DV	IO T175D VLVO		8598		21100	23400
35	COLOMBO 36		OP	SPTCR	FBG DV	IO 260 MRCR	10 4			28400	31500
	IO 330 MRCR 29200	32400, IO 370 MRCR 29800				33100, IO 175D VLVO				36600	40700
	IO T270 MRCR 30700	34100									
40 8	BLUE-SHORE 41 YACHT		OP	SPTCR	FBG DV	IO T330 MRCR	10 6			34600	38400
40 8	BLUE-SHORE 41 YACHT		OP	SPTCR	FBG DV	IO T370 MRCR	10 6			36800	40800
40 8	BLUE-SHORE 41 YACHT		OP	SPTCR	FBG DV	IB T300D CAT	10 6			67900	74600

....For earlier years, see the BUC Used Boat Price Guide, Volume 3

GIBERT MARINE SA

For more recent years, see the BUC Used Boat Price Guide, Volume 1

LOA FT IN	NAME AND/ OR MODEL	TOP/ RIG	BOAT TYPE	-HULL- MTL TP	----ENGINE--- TP # HP MFG	BEAM FT IN	WGT LBS	DRAFT FT IN	RETAIL LOW	RETAIL HIGH
		1996 BOATS								
18 8	SERENITA 55	OP	RNBT	FBG SV	OB	8	1320	1 10	7300	8400
18 8	SERENITA 55	SLP	SACAC	FBG CB		8	1320	1 10	6900	7950
18 8	SERENITA 55	SLP	SACAC	FBG CB	9D YAN	8	1320	1 10	11000	12500
19	GIB 580	HT	CUD	FBG SV	OB	8	2100	2	10100	11400
19	GIB 580	HT	CUD	FBG SV	IB 27D- 48D	8	2100	2	16900	20600
20	GIB 600	HT	CUD	FBG SV	IB 48D- 85D	8 2	2900	1 8	24700	29400
21 8	GIB 660	HT	CUD	FBG SV	IB 85D-100D	8 2	3200	1 9	30000	33600
22 4	GIB 700	HT	CUD	FBG SV	IB 145D MRCR	8 2	3300	3 11	33500	37200
23 3	GIB'SEA 234	SLP	SACAC	FBG SK		8	2500	2 3	11700	13300
23 3	GIB'SEA 234	SLP	SACAC	FBG SK	IB 9D YAN	8	2500	2 3	14000	15900
26	GIB'SEA 264	SLP	SACAC	FBG KL		9 8	4500	4 9	21300	23700
26	GIB'SEA 264	SLP	SACAC	FBG KL	9D- 18D	9 8	4500	4 9	25600	28900
26 7	GIB 84	HT	CUD	FBG SV	IB 200D-220D	9 10	5512	2 9	55800	62900
27 1	JAMAICA 28	FB	CUD	FBG SV	IB 220D MRCR	9 8	6700	1 10	66300	72900
27 1	JAMAICA 28	FB	CUD	FBG SV	IB T145D MRCR	9 8	6700	1 10	74300	81600
29 10	GIB 900	HT	CUD	FBG SV	IB 200D-220D	9 10	5512	2 9	51000	57500
29 10	GIB'SEA 302	SLP	SACAC	FBG KL	IB 9D- 18D	10 7	7000	4 3	39000	43500
29 10	GIB'SEA 302	SLP	SACAC	FBG TK	IB 9D- 18D	10 7	7000	4 9	39000	43500
33	AMARANTHE 334	SLP	SACAC	FBG KL	IB 18D- 27D	11	10000	7 1	55700	61200
33	AMARANTHE 334	SLP	SACAC	FBG TK	IB 18D- 27D	11	8800	6 2	49000	53900
33	GIB'SEA 334	SLP	SACAC	FBG KL	IB 18D- 27D	11 3	8800	6 2	49000	54400
33	GIB'SEA 334	SLP	SACAC	FBG TK	IB 18D- 27D	11 3	8800	6 2	49000	53900
33	GIB'SEA 334 SHOAL	SLP	SACAC	FBG KL	IB 27D YAN	11 3	8800	5 2	50400	55400
33	GIB'SEA 334 SHOAL	SLP	SACAC	FBG TK	IB 27D YAN	11 3	8800	5 2	48600	53400
36 9	GIB'SEA 364	SLP	SACAC	FBG TK	IB 27D YAN	12	12000	4 9	67600	74300
37 6	JAMAICA 37	FB	CR	FBG SV	IB T290D MAN	12 8	19500	3 2	236500	260000
40 8	GIB'SEA 414 PLUS	SLP	SACAC	FBG TK	IB 48D YAN	13	15800	7 5	98500	108500
40 8	GIB'SEA 414 SHOAL	SLP	SACAC	FBG TK	IB 48D YAN	13	16500	6 1	101500	111500
45 7	GIB'SEA 444	SLP	SACAC	FBG TK	IB 48D YAN	13	21600	7 1	142500	156500
46 7	GIB'SEA 472	SLP	SACAC	FBG TK	IB 85D YAN	14	26000	7	160000	176000
46 7	GIB'SEA 472	SLP	SACAC	FBG TK	IB 85D YAN	14	26000	7	161000	177000
47 7	MASTER 48	SLP	SACAC	FBG TK	IB 85D YAN	14 4	28700	7 10	173000	190000
47 7	MASTER 48 PLUS	SLP	SACAC	FBG TK	IB 48D YAN	14 4	27600	7	169500	186500
47 7	MASTER 48 PLUS	SLP	SACAC	FBG TK	IB 85D YAN	14 4	27600	7	170500	187500
52 8	MASTER 52	SLP	SACAC	FBG TK	IB 85D YAN	15	35000	8 4	246500	271000
		1986 BOATS								
33 2	MASTER 33	SLP	SA/CR	FBG KC	IB 28D VLVO	10 10	8600	4 1	25800	28700
33 2	MASTER 33	SLP	SA/CR	FBG KL	IB 28D VLVO	10 10	8600	5 7	25800	28700
37 11	MASTER 38	SLP	SA/CR	FBG KC	IB 28D VLVO	11 10	10600	4	34100	37800
37 11	MASTER 38	SLP	SA/CR	FBG KL	IB 28D VLVO	11 10	10600	5 11	34100	37800
40 4	MASTER 40	SLP	SA/CR	FBG KL	IB 50D PERK	12	16500	6 5	54000	59300
44 8	MASTER 44	SLP	SA/CR	FBG KL	IB 50D PERK	13 4	19900	5 11	71100	78100
		1985 BOATS								
33 2	GIB'SEA 96	SLP	SA/CR	FBG KC	IB 28D VLVO	10 10	8600	4 1	24300	27000
33 2	GIB'SEA 96	SLP	SA/CR	FBG KL	IB 28D VLVO	10 10	8600	5 7	24300	27000
35 4	GIB'SEA 106	SLP	SA/CR	FBG KC	IB 28D VLVO	11 10	9800	4	29800	33100
35 4	GIB'SEA 106	SLP	SA/CR	FBG KL	IB 28D VLVO	11 10	10600	5 11	29800	33100
38 1	GIB'SEA 116 DEEP	SLP	SA/CR	FBG KL	IB 51D PERK	12	16500	6 5	46900	51600
38 1	GIB'SEA 116 SHOAL	SLP	SA/CR	FBG KL	IB 51D PERK	12	17300	5	48400	53200
42 8	GIB'SEA 126	SLP	SA/CR	FBG KL	IB 51D PERK	13 4	19900	5 11	61600	66700

GIBSON BOAT CO

LOA FT IN	NAME AND/ OR MODEL	TOP/ RIG	BOAT TYPE	-HULL- MTL TP	----ENGINE--- TP # HP MFG	BEAM FT IN	WGT LBS	DRAFT FT IN	RETAIL LOW	RETAIL HIGH
		1984 BOATS								
20 9	GBC 9080101	OP	UTL	KEV TR	IO 220D SAAB	6	2175	7	3300	3850
20 9	GBC 9080201	OP	OPFSH	KEV TR	IO 165 OMC	6	2090	7	1600	1900
21	GBC 9080601	OP	OPFSH	KEV TR	IO 160 OMC	7	2900	8	2050	2450
23	GBC 9080801	OP	UTL	KEV TR	IO 220D SAAB	7	3000	8	4350	5000
24	GBC 9080501	FB	UTL	KEV TR	IO 220D SAAB	7	3100	7	4700	5400
25	GBC 9080401	FB	UTL	KEV TR	IO 220D SAAB	7	3175	9	4800	5500
29	GBC 9080301	FB	UTL	KEV DV	IO T220D SAAB	8 9	6100	1	10800	12300
36	GBC 9080901	FB	HB	KEV DV	IO T220D SAAB	14	9600	2 9	46500	49500
49	GBC 9080901	FB	HB	KEV DV	IO T220D SAAB	16	10300	2 9	53800	59100
55	GBC 9090101	FB	MY	KEV DV	IB	16	14000	4	**	**

....For earlier years, see the BUC Used Boat Price Guide, Volume 3

GIBSON FIBERGLASS PROD INC

For more recent years, see the BUC Used Boat Price Guide, Volume 1

LOA FT IN	NAME AND/ OR MODEL	TOP/ RIG	BOAT TYPE	-HULL- MTL TP	----ENGINE--- TP # HP MFG	BEAM FT IN	WGT LBS	DRAFT FT IN	RETAIL LOW	RETAIL HIGH
		1996 BOATS								
37	SPORTS SERIES CR	FB	HB	FBG SV	IO 270 VLVO	14	12400	2 4	36500	40600
37	SPORTS SERIES CR	FB	HB	FBG SV	VD T260 CRUS	14	13000	2 4	41000	45500
41	SPORTS SERIES CR	FB	HB	FBG SV	VD T260 CRUS	14	14000	2 4	41700	46300
41	SPORTS SERIES CR	FB	HB	FBG SV	IO T200D VLVO	14	14900	2 4	53300	58600
42	SPORTS SERIES	FB	HB	FBG SV	JT 180 MPC	12	10000	1 3	27100	30100

LOA FT IN	NAME AND/ OR MODEL	TOP/ RIG	BOAT TYPE	-HULL- MTL	-HULL- TP	ENGINE TP	ENGINE # HP	ENGINE MFG	BEAM FT IN	WGT LBS	DRAFT FT	DRAFT IN	RETAIL LOW	RETAIL HIGH
	1996 BOATS													
42	SPORTS SERIES CR	FB	HB	FBG	SV	VD	T210	CRUS	12	10350	2	4	30600	34000
44	CABIN YACHT CR	FB	HB	FBG	SV	VD	T320	CRUS	14	20000	2	4	61500	67600
44	EXECUTIVE CR	FB	HB	FBG	SV	VD	T320	CRUS	14	21000	2	4	63700	70000
44	EXECUTIVE CR	FB	HB	FBG	SV	VD	T200D	VLVO	14	21000	2	4	74400	81700
44	STANDARD CR	FB	HB	FBG	SV	VD	T320	CRUS	14	20000	2	4	59500	65300
47	CABIN YACHT CR	FB	HB	FBG	SV	VD	T320	CRUS	14	19500	2	4	64600	71000
47	EXECUTIVE CR	FB	HB	FBG	SV	VD	T320	CRUS	14	20500	2	4	65200	71700
47	EXECUTIVE CR	FB	HB	FBG	SV	VD	T200D	VLVO	14	20500	2	4	76500	84100
47	SPORTS SERIES CR	FB	HB	FBG	SV	VD	T320	CRUS	14	19500	2	4	58200	63900
50	CABIN YACHT CR	FB	HB	FBG	SV	VD	T320	CRUS	14	23000	2	4	74900	82300
50	EXECUTIVE CR	FB	HB	FBG	SV	VD	T320	CRUS	14	24000	2	4	78800	86600
50	EXECUTIVE CR	FB	HB	FBG	SV	VD	T200D	VLVO	14	24000	2	4	90900	99900
50	STANDARD CR	FB	HB	FBG	SV	VD	T320	CRUS	14	22000	2	4	71000	78000
59	5900 SERIES CR	FB	HB	FBG	SV	VD	T360	CRUS	16	32000	2	8	126500	139000
	VD T380 CRUS 127500 140000, VD T280D PEN 147500 162500, VD T315D CUM 152000 167000													
	1994 BOATS													
37	GIBSON 37 SS	HT	HB	FBG		IO	245	VLVO	14	13000	2	4	34900	38800
	IO T210 CHMP 36600 40600, IO T210 CRUS 36600 40600, IO T235 CRUS 37100 41200													
	IO T245 VLVO 38700 43000, IO T250 CHMP 37500 41700, IO T300 VLVO 41700 46400													
41	GIBSON 41 CY	HT	HB	FBG		IO	245	VLVO	14	16350	2	4	39600	44000
	IO T210 CHMP 40800 45300, IO T210 CRUS 41400 46000, IO T235 CRUS 41500 46100													
	IO T245 VLVO 43000 47000, IO T250 CHMP 41900 46600, IO T300 VLVO 46300 50900													
41	GIBSON 41 SS	HT	HB	FBG		IO	245	VLVO	14	16350	2	4	38200	42400
	IO T210 CHMP 39500 43800, IO T210 CRUS 40100 44600, IO T235 CRUS 40200 44700													
	IO T245 VLVO 41600 46300, IO T250 CHMP 40600 45100, IO T300 VLVO 44400 49400													
44	GIBSON 44 STD	HT	HB	FBG		IO	245	VLVO	14	20000	2	4	47800	52600
	IO T210 CHMP 49200 54000, IO T210 CRUS 49200 54000, IO T235 CRUS 49600 54500													
	IO T245 VLVO 50500 55500, IO T250 CHMP 49900 54800, IO T300 VLVO 53000 58200													
	IO T320 CRUS 52700 57900													
47	GIBSON 47 CY	HT	HB	FBG		IO	245	VLVO	14	19500	2	4	50300	55200
	IO T210 CHMP 51100 56100, IO T210 CRUS 51700 56800, IO T235 CRUS 51700 56800													
	IO T245 VLVO 49800 54700, IO T250 CHMP 52100 57200, IO T300 VLVO 54600 60000													
	IO T320 CRUS 54400 59800													
47	GIBSON 47 SS	HT	HB	FBG		IO	245	VLVO	14	19500	2	4	43900	48700
	IO T210 CHMP 44900 49800, IO T210 CRUS 46200 50800, IO T235 CRUS 46300 50900													
	IO T245 VLVO 49800 54700, IO T250 CHMP 46500 51100, IO T300 VLVO 49700 54600													
	IO T320 CRUS 49300 54200													
50	GIBSON 50 CY	HT	HB	FBG		IO	245	VLVO	14	22000	2	4	54700	60100
	IO T210 CHMP 55600 61100, IO T210 CRUS 56200 61800, IO T235 CRUS 56200 61800													
	IO T245 VLVO 57300 63000, IO T250 CHMP 56600 62200, IO T300 VLVO 59400 65300													
	IO T320 CRUS 59200 65000													
50	GIBSON 50 CY EX	HT	HB	FBG		IO	245	VLVO	14	22000	2	4	56300	61800
	IO T210 CHMP 57100 62700, IO T210 CRUS 57700 63400, IO T235 CRUS 57700 63400													
	IO T245 VLVO 57300 63000, IO T250 CHMP 58100 63800, IO T300 VLVO 61000 67000													
	IO T320 CRUS 60700 66700													
50	GIBSON 50 STD	HT	HB	FBG		IO	245	VLVO	14	22000	2	4	53300	58500
	IO T210 CHMP 53800 59100, IO T210 CRUS 54400 59800, IO T235 CRUS 54500 59900													
	IO T245 VLVO 57300 63000, IO T250 CHMP 54800 60200, IO T300 VLVO 57800 63500													
	IO T320 CRUS 57500 63200													
	1993 BOATS													
37	GIBSON 37 SS	HT	HB	FBG		IO	245	VLVO	14	13000	2	4	33100	36800
	IO T210 CHMP 34700 38500, IO T210 CRUS 34700 38500, IO T235 CRUS 35200 39100													
	IO T245 VLVO 36700 40700, IO T250 CHMP 35600 39500													
41	GIBSON 41 CY	HT	HB	FBG		IO	245	VLVO	14	16350	2	4	36800	40900
	IO T210 CHMP 38300 42500, IO T210 CRUS 38300 42500, IO T235 CRUS 38700 43000													
	IO T245 VLVO 40100 44600, IO T250 CHMP 39100 43400													
42	GIBSON 42	HT	HB	FBG		IO	245	VLVO	12	14000	2	4	31700	35300
	IO T210 CHMP 33100 36800, IO T210 CRUS 33100 36800, IO T235 CRUS 33500 37300													
	IO T245 VLVO 34800 38700, IO T250 CHMP 33900 37700													
44	GIBSON 44 STD	HT	HB	FBG		IO	T210	CHMP	14	20000	2	4	46200	50800
	IO T210 CRUS 46200 50800, IO T235 CRUS 46700 51400, IO T250 CHMP 47100 51700													
	IO T320 CRUS 49900 54800													
47	GIBSON 47 CY	HT	HB	FBG		IO	T210	CHMP	14	19500	2	4	48400	53200
	IO T210 CRUS 49000 53900, IO T235 CRUS 49000 53900, IO T245 VLVO 50000 55000													
	IO T250 CHMP 49400 54200, IO T320 CRUS 51600 56800													
47	GIBSON 47 SS	HT	HB	FBG		IO	T210	CHMP	14	19500	2	4	42300	47000
	IO T210 CRUS 42900 47700, IO T235 CRUS 43000 47800, IO T245 VLVO 44100 49000													
	IO T250 CHMP 43200 48000, IO T320 CRUS 46300 50900													
50	GIBSON 50 CY	HT	HB	FBG		IO	T210	CHMP	14	22000	2	4	53900	59200
	IO T210 CRUS 54300 59700, IO T235 CRUS 54200 59500, IO T245 VLVO 54000 59300													
	IO T250 CHMP 54600 60000, IO T320 CRUS 57100 62800													
50	GIBSON 50 STD	HT	HB	FBG		IO	T210	CHMP	14	22000	2	4	51300	56400
	IO T210 CRUS 52000 57100, IO T235 CRUS 52100 57200, IO T250 CHMP 52200 57400													
	IO T320 CRUS 54400 59700													
	1992 BOATS													
36	GIBSON 36	HT	HB	FBG		IO	135	VLVO	12	10500	2	4	27000	30000
	IO 245 VLVO 27700 30800, IO T CHRY 29400 32700, IO T135 VLVO 29700 33000													
	IO T210 CRUS 29200 32500, IO T235 CRUS 29700 33000, IO T245 VLVO 31100 34600													
37	GIBSON 37 SS	HT	HB	FBG		IO	245	VLVO	14	13000	2	4	31500	35000
37	GIBSON 37 SS	HT	HB	FBG		IO	T210	CRUS	14	13000	2	4	33100	36700
41	GIBSON 41 CY	HT	HB	FBG		IO	T	CHRY	14	13000	2	4	30600	34000
	IO T210 CRUS 30400 33800, IO T235 CRUS 30800 34300, IO T245 VLVO 32100 35700													
42	GIBSON 42	HT	HB	FBG		IO	135	VLVO	12	14000	2	4	29600	32900
	IO 245 VLVO 30300 33600, IO T CHRY 31700 35200, IO T135 VLVO 31900 35500													
	IO T210 CRUS 31600 35100, IO T235 CRUS 32000 35500, IO T245 VLVO 33200 36900													
44	GIBSON 44 STD	HT	HB	FBG		IO	T235	CRUS	14	20000	2	4	43700	48600
44	GIBSON 44 STD	HT	HB	FBG		IO	T245	VLVO	14	20000	2	4	44800	49800
44	GIBSON 44 STD	HT	HB	FBG		IO	T320	CRUS	14	20000	2	4	47300	52000
50	GIBSON 50 CY	HT	HB	FBG		IO	T235	CRUS	14	22000	2	4	50400	55400
50	GIBSON 50 CY	HT	HB	FBG		IO	T245	VLVO	14	22000	2	4	51600	56700
50	GIBSON 50 CY	HT	HB	FBG		IO	T320	CRUS	14	22000	2	4	53300	58500
50	GIBSON 50 STD	HT	HB	FBG		IO	T235	CRUS	14	22000	2	4	50400	55400
50	GIBSON 50 STD	HT	HB	FBG		IO	T245	VLVO	14	22000	2	4	51600	56700
50	GIBSON 50 STD	HT	HB	FBG		IO	T320	CRUS	14	22000	2	4	53300	58500
	1991 BOATS													
36	GIBSON 36	HT	HB	FBG		IO	135	VLVO	12	10500	2	4	25800	28700
	IO 245 VLVO 26500 29500, IO T CHRY 28200 31300, IO T135 VLVO 28400 31600													
	IO T210 CRUS 28000 31100, IO T235 CRUS 28400 31600, IO T245 VLVO 29800 33100													
37	GIBSON 37 STD	HT	HB	FBG		IO	245	VLVO	14	13000	2	4	30200	33600
	IO T CHRY 31800 35400, IO T135 VLVO 32100 35700, IO T210 CRUS 31700 35200													
	IO T235 CRUS 32100 35700, IO T245 VLVO 33500 37200													
41	GIBSON 41 CY	HT	HB	FBG		IO	T	CHRY	14	13000	2	4	29300	32500
	IO T135 VLVO 29500 32800, IO T210 CRUS 29100 32400, IO T235 CRUS 29500 32800													
	IO T245 VLVO 30800 34200													
41	GIBSON 41 EX	HT	HB	FBG		IO	T	CHRY	14	16500	2	4	35400	39300
	IO T135 VLVO 35600 39500, IO T210 CRUS 35200 39100, IO T235 CRUS 35600 39600													
	IO T245 VLVO 36800 40900													
41	GIBSON 41 STD	HT	HB	FBG		IO	T	CHRY	14	13000	2	4	29300	32500
	IO T135 VLVO 29500 32800, IO T210 CRUS 29100 32400, IO T235 CRUS 29500 32800													
	IO T245 VLVO 30800 34200													
42	GIBSON 42 LC	HT	HB	FBG		IO	135	VLVO	12	14000	2	4	28400	31500
42	GIBSON 42 LC	HT	HB	FBG		IO	245	VLVO	12	14000	2	4	29000	32200
42	GIBSON 42 LC	HT	HB	FBG		IO	T135	VLVO	12	14000	2	4	30600	34000
42	GIBSON 42 STD	HT	HB	FBG		IO	135	VLVO	12	14000	2	4	28400	31500
	IO 245 VLVO 29000 32200, IO T CHRY 30400 33800, IO T135 VLVO 30600 34000													
	IO T210 CRUS 30300 33600, IO T235 CRUS 30600 34000, IO T245 VLVO 31800 35300													
44	GIBSON 44 EX	HT	HB	FBG		IO	T	CHRY	14	20000	2	4	41500	46100
	IO T235 CRUS 41700 46300, IO T245 VLVO 42700 47500, IO T320 CRUS 44600 49500													
44	GIBSON 44 STD	HT	HB	FBG		IO	T	CHRY	14	20000	2	4	41500	46100
	IO T235 CRUS 41700 46300, IO T245 VLVO 42700 47500, IO T320 CRUS 44600 49500													
47	GIBSON 47 CY	HT	HB	FBG		IO	T	CHRY	14	19500	2	4	41100	45700
	IO T235 CRUS 41300 45900, IO T245 VLVO 42300 47000, IO T320 CRUS 44000 48900													
47	GIBSON 47 EX	HT	HB	FBG		IO	T	CHRY	14	19500	2	4	41100	45700
	IO T235 CRUS 41300 45900, IO T245 VLVO 42300 47000, IO T320 CRUS 44000 48900													

 CONTINUED ON NEXT PAGE

```
        LOA   NAME AND/             TOP/ BOAT  -HULL-  ----ENGINE---   BEAM   WGT   DRAFT  RETAIL RETAIL
        FT IN OR MODEL              RIG  TYPE  MTL TP  TP # HP  MFG    FT IN  LBS   FT IN   LOW    HIGH
------------------------- 1991 BOATS -------------------------
 50     GIBSON 50 CY               HT  HB    FBG     IO  T     CHRY 14  22000  2  4  48400  53200
    IO T235  CRUS 48600  53400, IO T245 VLVO 49600 54500, IO T320  CRUS        50700  55700

 50     GIBSON 50 EX               HT  HB    FBG     IO  T     CHRY 14  22000  2  4  48400  53200
    IO T235  CRUS 48600  53400, IO T245 VLVO 49600 54500, IO T320  CRUS        50700  55700

 50     GIBSON 50 STD              HT  HB    FBG     IO  T     CHRY 14  22000  2  4  48400  53200
    IO T235  CRUS 48600  53400, IO T245 VLVO 49600 54500, IO T320  CRUS        50700  55700

------------------------- 1990 BOATS -------------------------
 36     GIBSON 36                  HT  HB    FBG     IO  135   VLVO 12  10500  2  4  24900  27600
    IO 245   VLVO 25500  28400, IO T    CHRY 27100 30100, IO T135  VLVO        27300  30400
    IO T210  CRUS 26900  29900, IO T235 CRUS 27400 30400, IO T245  VLVO        28700  31900

 37     GIBSON 37                  HT  HB    FBG     IO  135   VLVO 14  13000  2  4  28400  31600
    IO 245   VLVO 29100  32300, IO T    CHRY 30600 34000, IO T135  VLVO        30400  34300
    IO T210  CRUS 30500  33900, IO T235 CRUS 30900 34300, IO T245  VLVO        32200  35800

 41     GIBSON 41
    IO T     CHRY 28200  31300, IO T135 VLVO 28400 31500, IO T210  CRUS        26200  29100
    IO T235  CRUS 28400  31600, IO T245 VLVO 29600 32900                       28000  31200

 41     GIBSON 41 SPECIAL
    IO T     CHRY 28200  31300, IO T135 VLVO 28400 31500, IO T210  CRUS        26200  29100
    IO T235  CRUS 28400  31600, IO T245 VLVO 29600 32900                       28000  31200

 42     GIBSON 42 LC               HT  HB    FBG     IO  135   VLVO 12  14000  2  4  27300  30300
 42     GIBSON 42 LC               HT  HB    FBG     IO  245   VLVO 12  14000  2  4  29100  31000
 42     GIBSON 42 LC               HT  HB    FBG     IO  T135  VLVO 12  14000  2  4  29400  32700
 42     GIBSON 42 STD              HT  HB    FBG     IO  135   VLVO 12  14000  2  4  27300  30300
    IO 245   VLVO 27900  31000, IO T    CHRY 29200 32500, IO T135  VLVO        29400  32700
    IO T210  CRUS 29100  32300, IO T235 CRUS 29500 32800, IO T245  VLVO        30600  34000

 44     GIBSON 44                  HT  HB    FBG     IO  T     CHRY 12  14000  2  4  27200  30200
    IO T235  CRUS 27400  30400, IO T245 VLVO 28400 31500, IO T320  CRUS        30100  33400

 50     GIBSON 50                  HT  HB    FBG     IO  T     CHRY 14  22000  2  4  46400  50900
    IO T235  CRUS 46600  51200, IO T245 VLVO 47500 52200, IO T320  CRUS        49100  54000

------------------------- 1989 BOATS -------------------------
 36     GIBSON 36                  HT  HB    FBG     IO  146   VLVO 12  10500  2  4  24000  26700
    IO 270   VLVO 25100  27900, IO T146 VLVO 26400 29400, IO T210  VLVO        26000  28900
    IO 240   CHRY 26500  29500, IO T240 CRUS 26500 29500, IO T270  VLVO        28600  31700

 37     GIBSON 37                  HT  HB    FBG     IO  146   VLVO 14  13000  2  4  27400  30500
    IO 270   VLVO 28500  31700, IO T146 VLVO 29800 33200, IO T210  CRUS        29400  32700
    IO 240   CHRY 29900  33300, IO T240 CRUS 29900 33300, IO T270  VLVO        32000  35500

 41     GIBSON 41 EX              HT  HB    FBG     IO  146   VLVO 14  13000  2  4   25300  28100
    IO T146  VLVO 27400  30500, IO T210 CRUS 27100 30100, IO T240  CHRY        27500  30600
    IO T240  CRUS 27500  30600, IO T270 VLVO 29400 32600

 41     GIBSON 41 STD             HT  HB    FBG     IO  146   VLVO 14  13000  2  4   25300  28100
    IO T146  VLVO 27400  30500, IO T210 CRUS 27100 30100, IO T240  CHRY        27500  30600
    IO T240  CRUS 27500  30600, IO T270 VLVO 29400 32600

 42     GIBSON 42 LC              HT  HB    FBG     IO  146   VLVO 12  14000  2  4   26400  29300
 42     GIBSON 42 LC              HT  HB    FBG     IO  270   VLVO 12  14000  2  4   27300  30300
 42     GIBSON 42 LC              HT  HB    FBG     IO  T146  VLVO 12  14000  2  4   28500  31600
 42     GIBSON 42 STD             HT  HB    FBG     IO  146   VLVO 12  14000  2  4   26400  29300
    IO 270   VLVO 27300  30300, IO T146 VLVO 28500 31700, IO T210  CRUS        28100  31200
    IO 240   CHRY 28500  31700, IO T240 CRUS 28500 31700, IO T270  VLVO        30300  33700

 44     GIBSON 44 EX              HT  HB    FBG     IO  T240  CHRY 12  14000  2  4   26500  29400
    IO T240  CRUS 27100  30100, IO T270 CRUS 27100 30100, IO T330  CRUS        29600  32900

 44     GIBSON 44 STD             HT  HB    FBG     IO  T240  CHRY 12  14000  2  4   26500  29400
    IO T240  CRUS 26500  29400, IO T270 VLVO 28100 31200, IO T330  CRUS        29600  32800

 50     GIBSON 50 EX              HT  HB    FBG     IO  T240  CHRY 14  22000  2  4   44500  49400
    IO T240  CRUS 44500  49400, IO T270 VLVO 46400 51000, IO T330  CRUS        47800  52500

 50     GIBSON 50 STD             HT  HB    FBG     IO  T240  CHRY 12  22000  2  4   44500  49400
    IO T240  CRUS 44500  49400, IO T270 VLVO 46400 51000, IO T330  CRUS        47800  52500

------------------------- 1988 BOATS -------------------------
 36     GIBSON 36                 HT  HB    FBG     IO  146   VLVO 12  10500  2  4   23300  25900
    IO 270   VLVO 24300  27000, IO T146 VLVO 25600 28400, IO T210  CRUS        25200  28000
    IO 240   CHRY 25700  28600, IO T240 CRUS 25700 28600, IO T270  VLVO        27700  30800

 37     GIBSON 37                 HT  HB    FBG     IO  146   VLVO 14  13000  2  4   26600  29500
    IO 270   VLVO 27600  30700, IO T146 VLVO 28900 32100, IO T210  CRUS        28500  31700
    IO 240   CHRY 29000  32200, IO T240 CRUS 29000 32200, IO T270  VLVO        31000  34400
    IO T330  CRUS 32900  36500

 41     GIBSON 41 STD             HT  HB    FBG     IO  146   VLVO 14  13000  2  4   24500  27200
    IO T146  VLVO 26600  29500, IO T210 CRUS 26200 29100, IO T240  CHRY        26700  29600
    IO T240  CRUS 26700  29600, IO T270 VLVO 28400 31600, IO T330  CRUS        30100  33500

 42     GIBSON 42 LC              HT  HB    FBG     IO  146   VLVO 12  14000  2  4   25600  28400
 42     GIBSON 42 LC              HT  HB    FBG     IO  270   VLVO 12  14000  2  4   26400  29400
 42     GIBSON 42 LC              HT  HB    FBG     IO  T146  VLVO 12  14000  2  4   27600  30600
 42     GIBSON 42 STD             HT  HB    FBG     IO  146   VLVO 12  14000  2  4   25600  28400
    IO 270   VLVO 26400  29400, IO T146 VLVO 27600 30600, IO T210  CRUS        27200  30200
    IO 240   CHRY 27600  30700, IO T240 CRUS 27600 30700, IO T270  VLVO        29400  32600

 44     CLASSIC                   FB  HB    FBG SV VD  T270  CRUS 14  20000  2  4   **     **
 44     GIBSON 44 STD             HT  HB    FBG     IO  T240  CHRY 14  14000  2  4   25600  28500
    IO T240  CRUS 25600  28500, IO T270 CRUS 27200 30200, IO T330  CRUS        28600  31800

 50     GIBSON 50 STD             HT  HB    FBG     IO  T240  CHRY 12  22000  2  4   43000  47800
    IO T240  CRUS 43000  47800, IO T270 VLVO 44400 49400, IO T330  CRUS        46300  50800

------------------------- 1987 BOATS -------------------------
 36     GIBSON 36                 HT  HB    FBG     IO  210   VLVO 12  10500  2  4   22900  25400
    IO 210   VLVO 22900  25400, IO  225 VLVO 23000 25500, IO  270  VLVO        23600  26200
    IO 130D  VLVO 25500  28400, IO T146 VLVO 24900 27600, IO T210  VLVO        24500  27200
    IO T240  CHRY 25000  27700, IO T240 CRUS 25000 27700

 42     GIBSON 42 LC              HT  HB    FBG     IO  146   VLVO 12  14000  2  4   24800  27600
    IO 270   VLVO 25700  28500, IO  130D VLVO 28100 31300, IO T146 VLVO        26800  29700

 42     GIBSON 42 STD             HT  HB    FBG     IO  146   VLVO 12  14000  2  4   24800  27600
    IO 270   VLVO 25700  28500, IO  130D VLVO 28100 31300, IO T146 VLVO        26800  29700
    IO T210  CRUS 26400  29400, IO T240 CHRY 26900 29800, IO T240  CRUS        26900  29800

 44     GIBSON 44 EX              HT  HB    FBG     IO  T146  VLVO 14  14000  2  4   24800  27600
 44     GIBSON 44 EX              HT  HB    FBG     IO  T240  CRUS 14  14000  2  4   24900  27700
 44     GIBSON 44 EX              HT  HB    FBG     IO  T330  CRUS 14  14000  2  4   27800  30900
 44     GIBSON 44 STD             HT  HB    FBG     IO  146   VLVO 14  14000  2  4   23100  25600
    IO T146  VLVO 24800  27600, IO T240 CRUS 24900 27700, IO T330  CRUS        27800  30900

 50     GIBSON 50 EX              HT  HB    FBG     IO  T146  VLVO 12  22000  2  4   41700  46300
 50     GIBSON 50 EX              HT  HB    FBG     IO  T240  CRUS 12  22000  2  4   41800  46400
 50     GIBSON 50 EX              HT  HB    FBG     IO  T330  CRUS 12  22000  2  4   44400  49300
 50     GIBSON 50 STD             HT  HB    FBG     IO  146   VLVO 12  22000  2  4   40100  44600
    IO T146  VLVO 41700  46300, IO T240 CRUS 41800 46400, IO T330  CRUS        44400  49300

------------------------- 1986 BOATS -------------------------
 36     GIBSON 36                 HT  HB    FBG SV IO  145       12  10500  2  4   20800  23100
 36     GIBSON 36                 HT  HB    FBG SV IB  220       12  10500  2  4   22800  25300
 42     GIBSON 42                 HT  HB    FBG SV IO  145       12  14000  2  4   23000  25500
 42     GIBSON 42                 HT  HB    FBG SV IB  220       12  14000  2  4   24800  27500
 44     GIBSON 44                 HT  HB    FBG SV IO  145       14  18000  2  4   29200  32400
 44     GIBSON 44                 HT  HB    FBG SV IB  270       14  18000  2  4   30900  34300
 50     GIBSON 50                 HT  HB    FBG SV IO  145       14  20000  2  4   34300  38100
 50     GIBSON 50                 HT  HB    FBG SV IB  270       14  20000  2  4   35700  39700

------------------------- 1985 BOATS -------------------------
 36     GIBSON 36                 HT  HB    FBG SV IB  220       12  10500  2  4   22200  24700
 42     GIBSON 42                 HT  HB    FBG SV IO  145       12  14000  2  4   22700  25200
 42     GIBSON 42                 HT  HB    FBG SV IB  220       12  14000  2  4   24200  26900
 44     GIBSON 44                 HT  HB    FBG SV IB  270       14  18000  2  4   30200  33500
 50     GIBSON 50                 HT  HB    FBG SV IO  145       14  20000  2  4   33500  37200
 50     GIBSON 50                 HT  HB    FBG SV IB  270       14  20000  2  4   34900  38800

------------------------- 1984 BOATS -------------------------
 36     GIBSON 36                 HT  HB    FBG SV IO  138   VLVO 12  10500  2  4   20200  22400
    IO 200   VLVO 20300  22600, IO  225 VLVO 20500 22800, IO  270  VLVO        20900  23200
    IO T138  VLVO 21800  24300, VD T220 CRUS 22500 25100, VD T225  CHRY        21900  24300
    VD T270  CRUS 22800  25400

 42     GIBSON 42                 HT  HB    FBG SV IO  138   VLVO 12  14000  2  4   22500  25000
    IO T138  VLVO 24000  26600, VD T220 CRUS 24300 27000, VD T225  CHRY        23800  26400
    VD T270  CRUS 24600  27300

 42     GIBSON 42 LC              HT  HB    FBG SV IO  138   VLVO 12  12000  2  4   20000  22200
 42     GIBSON 42 LC              HT  HB    FBG SV IO  T138  VLVO 12  12000  2  4   21400  23800
```

GIBSON FIBERGLASS PROD INC   —CONTINUED   See inside cover to adjust price for area

LOA FT IN	NAME AND/ OR MODEL	TOP/ RIG	BOAT TYPE	-HULL- MTL TP	----ENGINE--- TP # HP MFG	BEAM FT IN	WGT LBS	DRAFT FT IN	RETAIL LOW	RETAIL HIGH
					----- 1984 BOATS -----					
44	GIBSON 44	HT	HB	FBG SV IO	138 VLVO 14		18000	2 4	28100	31200
	IO T138 VLVO 29700		33000, VD T270	CRUS	30000 33300, VD T330			CHRY	30000	33400
	VD T350 CRUS 31100		34500							
44	GIBSON 44 EXECUTIVE	HT	HB	FBG SV IO	T138 VLVO 14		19000	2 4	31400	34900
	VD T270 CRUS 31800		35300, VD T330	CHRY	31800 35300, VD T350			CRUS	32800	36500
50	GIBSON 50	HT	HB	FBG SV IO	138 VLVO 14		20000	2 4	33000	36700
	IO T138 VLVO 34500		38300, VD T270	CRUS	34500 38300, VD T330			CHRY	34500	38300
	VD T350 CRUS 35400		39400							
50	GIBSON 50 EXECUTIVE	HT	HB	FBG SV IO	T138 VLVO 14		20000	2 4	34500	38300
	VD T270 CRUS 34500		38300, VD T330	CHRY	34500 38300, VD T350			CRUS	35400	39400
50	GIBSON 50 LC	HT	HB	FBG SV IO	138 VLVO 14		20000	2 4	33000	36700
50	GIBSON 50 LC	HT	HB	FBG SV IO	T138 VLVO 14		20000	2 4	34500	38300

....For earlier years, see the BUC Used Boat Price Guide, Volume 3

GILBERT YACHTS LTD
OAKVILLE CANADA   See inside cover to adjust price for area

LOA FT IN	NAME AND/ OR MODEL	TOP/ RIG	BOAT TYPE	-HULL- MTL TP	----ENGINE--- TP # HP MFG	BEAM FT IN	WGT LDC	DRAFT FT IN	RETAIL LOW	RETAIL HIGH
					----- 1988 BOATS -----					
30 0	GILBERT 30+	SLP	SA/CR	KEV KL IB	18D VLVO 11 3		9000	4 11	35200	39100

GLANDER BOATS INC
TAVERNIER FL 33070   COAST GUARD MFG ID- GLB See inside cover to adjust price for area

LOA FT IN	NAME AND/ OR MODEL	TOP/ RIG	BOAT TYPE	-HULL- MTL TP	----ENGINE--- TP # HP MFG	BEAM FT IN	WGT LBS	DRAFT FT IN	RETAIL LOW	RETAIL HIGH
					----- 1986 BOATS -----					
33	TAVANA 33	SLP	SAIL	FBG KC IB	D	10	12000	3	21200	23600
					----- 1985 BOATS -----					
23	CAY 23	SLP	SAIL	FBG KL IB	D	8	6800	3	9850	11200
33	TAVANA 33	SLP	SAIL	FBG KC IB	D	10	12000	3	19900	22100
					----- 1984 BOATS -----					
23	CAY	SLP	SAIL	FBG KL IB	D	8	6800	3	9300	10600
33	TAVANA	SLP	SAIL	FBG KC IB	D	10	12900	3	20000	22200
33	TAVANA	YWL	SAIL	FBG KC IB	D	10	12900	3	20000	22200

....For earlier years, see the BUC Used Boat Price Guide, Volume 3

GLAS-PLY INC
KIRKLAND WA 98034   COAST GUARD MFG ID- GPL See inside cover to adjust price for area

LOA FT IN	NAME AND/ OR MODEL	TOP/ RIG	BOAT TYPE	-HULL- MTL TP	----ENGINE--- TP # HP MFG	BEAM FT IN	WGT LBS	DRAFT FT IN	RETAIL LOW	RETAIL HIGH
					----- 1986 BOATS -----					
16 1	1740		RNBT	FBG	OB	6 6	1060		2200	2550
16 1	1741		RNBT	FBG DV IO	120 MRCR	6 6	1835		2850	3300
16 1	1741		RNBT	FBG	IO 140	6 6	1740		2800	3250
16 10	L1800 IMPULSE		RNBT	FBG	OB	7 5	1300		2600	3050
16 10	L1801		RNBT	FBG	IO 120-190	7 5	1750		3150	3750
17 3	L1870		RNBT	FBG	OB	6 10	1095		2350	2700
17 3	L1871		RNBT	FBG	IO 120-170	6 10	1890		3200	3750
18 2	1910		RNBT	FBG DV IO		7	1360		2800	3250
18 2	1911		RNBT	FBG DV IO	190	7	1829		3400	4000
19 4	L2100		RNBT	FBG	IO	7 10	1515		3200	3700
19 4	L2101		RNBT	FBG	IO 120-190	7 10	2625		4600	5350
19 4	L2103C		CUD	FBG	IO 120-190	7 10	2785		4900	5700
19 4	L2104C		FSH	FBG	OB	7 10	1995		3800	4400
19 4	L2105C		FSH	FBG	IO 120-170	7 10	2785		5200	6000
21 4	L2211C		CUD	FBG	IO 170-260	8	3615		6800	8200
21 4	L2213C		CUD	FBG	IO 170-260	8	3615		6800	8200
24	L2511C		CUD	FBG	IO 170-260	8	3896		8300	9900
24	L2513C		OVNTR	FBG	IO 170-260	8	3996		8450	10100
24 4	L2213C		OVNTR	FBG	IO 190 MRCR	8	3615		8050	9200
26 4	2641		CR	FBG	IB 260	10	5600		13000	14800
26 4	GP-2643			FBG DV IO	260	10	5600		16400	18700
27 6	2969		CR	FBG DV IO	260	10 11	10000		19800	21900
27 7	GP-2967			FBG SV IB	260	10 11	10000		25100	27900
					----- 1985 BOATS -----					
16 1	GP-1700		RNBT	FBG DV OB		6 6	1060		2100	2500
16 1	GP-1740		RNBT	FBG DV OB	125	6 6	1740		2650	3100
16 10	GP-1875		RNBT	FBG DV IO	125	7 6	1750		3050	3550
17 3	GP-1800		FSH	FBG DV OB		6 10	1095		2250	2650
17 3	GP-1800		RNBT	FBG DV OB		6 10	1095		2250	2650
17 3	GP-1870		RNBT	FBG DV IO	125	6 10	1819		3000	3500
18 2	GP-1900		RNBT	FBG DV OB		7	1360		2750	3200
18 2	GP-1900		RNBT	FBG DV IO	125	7	1829		3250	3750
19 4	GP-2100		CUD	FBG DV OB		7 10	1995		3700	4300
19 4	GP-2100		FSH	FBG DV OB		7 10	1750		3450	4000
19 4	GP-2100		RNBT	FBG DV OB		7 10	1515		3100	3600
19 4	GP-2110		CUD	FBG DV IO	125	7 10	2540		4500	5200
19 4	GP-2110		RNBT	FBG DV IO	125	7 10	2440		4200	4900
21 4	GP-2200		CUD	FBG DV OB		8	2560		5350	6150
21 4	GP-2200		RNBT	FBG DV OB		8	2235		4900	5600
21 4	GP-2210		CUD	FBG DV IO	125	8	2820		5550	6350
21 4	GP-2210		RNBT	FBG DV IO	125	8	2600		5050	5800
23 2	GP-2400		CUD	FBG DV OB		8	2995		6650	7650
23 2	GP-2400		RNBT	FBG DV OB		8	2330		5450	6300
23 2	GP-2410		CUD	FBG DV IO	145	8	3506		7050	8100
23 2	GP-2410		RNBT	FBG DV IO	145	8	2900		5850	6750
24	GP-2510		CUD	FBG DV IO	145	8	3796		7800	8950
27 7	GP-2881		CR	FBG DV IO	260	10 11	7500		15800	18000
36	GP-3600		MY	FBG SV IB	150	12 3	18000		62400	68500
39	GP-3900		MY	FBG SV IB	150	12 3	20000		82200	90300
42	GP-4200		MY	FBG SV IB	150	12 3	22000		84100	92500
					----- 1984 BOATS -----					
16 1	GP-1700 SL	ST	RNBT	FBG SV OB		6 6	1060		2250	2650
16 1	GP-1700 SL	ST	RNBT	FBG DV IO	125	6 6	1740		2750	3200
16 1	GP-1740		RNBT	FBG SV OB		6 6	1060		2550	3000
16 1	GPRV-1700 X	ST	RNBT	FBG SV OB	117 VLVO	6 6	1060		1900	2250
16 10	1875		RNBT	FBG SV IO	117 VLVO	7 6	1750	1	3100	3600
16 10	GP-1875		RNBT	FBG DV IO	125	7 6	1750		2950	3400
17 3	GP-1800 FM	OP	FSH	FBG SV OB		6 10	1095		2200	2600
17 3	GP-1800 SL	ST	RNBT	FBG SV OB		6 10	1095		2350	2750
17 3	GP-1870		RNBT	FBG DV IO	125	6 10	1819		2900	3350
17 3	GP-1870 SL	OP	RNBT	FBG SV IO	117 VLVO	6 10	1890		3100	3600
17 3	GPV-1800 X	ST	RNBT	FBG DV IO		6 10	1095		2000	2400
18 2	GP-1900		SKI	FBG DV IO	125	7	1829		2950	3450
18 2	GP-1900 SL	OP	SKI	FBG SV OB		7	1360		2700	3100
18 2	GP-1900 SL	OP	SKI	FBG SV IO	117 VLVO	7	1900		3200	3700
19 4	GP-2100	ST	CUD	FBG SV OB		7 10	1995		3650	4250
19 4	GP-2100	ST	CUD	FBG SV IO	117 VLVO	7 10	2785		4750	5450
19 4	GP-2100	ST	RNBT	FBG SV OB		7 10	1515		3050	3550
19 4	GP-2100 FM	OP	FSH	FBG SV OB		7 10	1750		3350	3900
19 4	GP-2100 SL	ST	RNBT	FBG SV IO	117 VLVO	7 10	2625		4450	5100
19 4	GP-2110		CUD	FBG DV IO	125	7 10	2540		4300	5000
19 4	GP-2110		RNBT	FBG DV IO	125	7 10	2440		4050	4750
19 4	GPV-2100 X	ST	CUD	FBG SV OB		7 10	1700		3300	3850
19 4	GPV-2100 X	ST	CUD	FBG SV OB		7 10	1500		3000	3500
19 4	GPV-2181 SL	ST	CUD	FBG SV IO	117 VLVO	7 10	2800		4750	5450
19 4	GPV-2181 SL	ST	RNBT	FBG SV IO	117 VLVO	7 10	2650		4450	5150
21	GP-2200 FM	OP	FSH	FBG SV OB		8	2235		4700	5400
21	GPV-2210	ST	CUD	FBG SV IO		8	2560		5100	5900
21	GPV-2280 OV	ST	CUD	FBG SV IO		8	2758		5350	6150
21 4	GP-2200 SL	ST	RNBT	FBG SV OB		8	2235		4800	5500
21 4	GP-2200 SL	ST	RNBT	FBG SV IO	138 VLVO	8	3285		5750	6650
21 4	GP-2210		CUD	FBG SV IO	125	8	2820		5350	6150
21 4	GP-2210	ST	CUD	FBG SV IO	138 VLVO	8	3615		6050	6950
21 4	GP-2210		RNBT	FBG SV IO	125	8	2600		4850	5600
21 4	GP-2210 FB	FB	SPTCR	FBG SV IO	138 VLVO	8	3668		6550	7500
21 4	GP-2280 OV	ST	CUD	FBG SV IO	138 VLVO	8	3615		6900	7950
23 2	GP-2400	ST	RNBT	FBG SV OB		8	2330		5350	6150
23 2	GP-2400 SL	ST	RNBT	FBG SV IO	138 VLVO	8	3190		6150	7100
23 2	GP-2410		CUD	FBG SV IO	145	8	3506		6800	7800
23 2	GP-2410	ST	CUD	FBG SV IO	138 VLVO	8	3800		7350	8450
23 2	GP-2410		RNBT	FBG SV IO	145	8	2900		5650	6500
23 2	GP-2410 FB	FB	SPTCR	FBG SV IO	138 VLVO	8	3698		7250	8300
23 2	GPV-2400	ST	CUD	FBG SV OB		8	2330		5350	6150
24	GP-2510		CUD	FBG DV IO	145	8	3796		7500	8650
24	GP-2510	HT	CUD	FBG SV IO	138 VLVO	8	3896		7850	9050
24	GP-2580	HT	CUD	FBG SV IO	138 VLVO	8	3915		7850	9050
24	GPV-2500	ST	CUD	FBG SV OB		8	2990		6750	7750

LOA FT IN	NAME AND/ OR MODEL		TOP/ RIG	BOAT TYPE	-HULL- MTL TP	----ENGINE--- TP # HP MFG	BEAM FT IN	WGT LBS	DRAFT FT IN	RETAIL LOW	RETAIL HIGH
						1984 BOATS					
24	GPV-2580		ST	CUD	FBG SV OB		8	3050		6850	7900
26 4	GP-2600		HT	SDN	FBG SV IB	260 VLVO	10	7000	2 6	18800	20900
26 4	GP-2600		FB	SDN	FBG SV IB	260 VLVO	10	7400	2 6	19200	21400
27 7	GP-2800		FB	SDN	FBG SV IO	260 VLVO	10 11	9000	2 5	18600	20600
28	GP-2881	CRUISER	HT	SDN	FBG SV IO	260 VLVO	10 11	9500		19500	21700
28	GP-2881	SPORT FISH	HT	SDN	FBG DV IO	260 VLVO	10 11	8000		18200	20200
36	LRC 36		FB	TRWL	FBG SV IB	D	12 3	20000	4 11	**	**
39	LRC 39		FB	TRWL	FBG SV IB	D	12 3	22000	4 11	**	**
42	LRC 42		FB	TRWL	FBG SV IB	D	12 3	24000	4 11	**	**

....For earlier years, see the BUC Used Boat Price Guide, Volume 3

GLASS BOATWORKS INC
CAPE CHARLES VA 23310   See inside cover to adjust price for area

LOA FT IN	NAME AND/ OR MODEL		TOP/ RIG	BOAT TYPE	-HULL- MTL TP	----ENGINE--- TP # HP MFG	BEAM FT IN	WGT LBS	DRAFT FT IN	RETAIL LOW	RETAIL HIGH
						1990 BOATS					
18 3	CHINCOTEAGUE 18		OP	UTL	FBG SV OB		6 8	850	6	1750	2100
20 3	CHINCOTEAGUE 20		OP	UTL	FBG SV OB		7 1	1100	6	2250	2600
23 10	CHESAPEAKE 24		OP	UTL	FBG SV OB		9 2	2000	1	3400	3950
23 10	CHESAPEAKE 24 W/CBN		OP	UTL	FBG SV OB		9 2	2000	1	5100	5850
						1989 BOATS					
18 3	CHINCOTEAGUE 18		OP	UTL	FBG SV OB		6 8	850	6	1700	2050
20 3	CHINCOTEAGUE 20		OP	UTL	FBG SV OB		7 1	1100	6	2200	2550
23 10	CHESAPEAKE 24		OP	UTL	FBG SV OB		9 2	2000	1	3300	3850
23 10	CHESAPEAKE 24 W/CBN		OP	UTL	FBG SV OB		9 2	2000	1	4950	5650
						1988 BOATS					
18 3	CHINCOTEAGUE 18		OP	UTL	FBG SV OB		6 8	850	6	1650	1950
20 3	CHINCOTEAGUE 20		OP	UTL	FBG SV OB		7 1	1100	6	2050	2450
23 10	CLASSIC 24		OP	UTL	FBG SV OB		9 2	2000	1	3950	4600
						1987 BOATS					
18 3	CHINCOTEAGUE 18		OP	UTL	FBG SV OB		6 8	850	6	1600	1900
20 3	CHINCOTEAGUE 20		OP	UTL	FBG SV OB		7 1	1100	6	2000	2400
23 10	CLASSIC 24		OP	UTL	FBG SV OB		9 2	2000	1	3850	4500
						1986 BOATS					
18 3	CHINCOTEAGUE 18		OP	UTL	FBG SV OB		6 8	850	6	1550	1850
20 3	CHINCOTEAGUE 20		OP	UTL	FBG SV OB		7 1	1100	6	1950	2300
23 10	CLASSIC 24		OP	UTL	FBG SV OB		9 2	2000	1	3750	4400
						1985 BOATS					
18 3	CHINCOTEAGUE SCOW		OP	UTL	FBG	OB	6 4	850	7	1550	1800
20 3	CHINCOTEAGUE SCOW		OP	UTL	FBG	OB	6 10	1100	7	1900	2250
						1984 BOATS					
18 3	CHINCOTEAGUE SCOW		OP	UTL	FBG	OB	6 4	950	7	1650	1950
20 3	CHINCOTEAGUE SCOW		OP	UTL	FBG	OB	6 10	1250	7	2150	2500

GLASS MASTER'S INC
TULSA OK 74101   COAST GUARD MFG ID- GIN See inside cover to adjust price for area

LOA FT IN	NAME AND/ OR MODEL	TOP/ RIG	BOAT TYPE	-HULL- MTL TP	----ENGINE--- TP # HP MFG	BEAM FT IN	WGT LBS	DRAFT FT IN	RETAIL LOW	RETAIL HIGH
					1984 BOATS					
20 2	200	OP	OPFSH	FBG TR IO	165 MRCR	6 2	2990	10	3850	4500
21	210	OP	FSH	KEV DV IB	165 MRCR	6 2	2890		4700	5400
22	222	OP	FSH	KEV TR IO	260 OMC	6 2	2985	10	4650	5300
22	222-B	ST	RNBT	KEV DV IO	260 OMC	6 2	3165	10	4250	4950
26	226-C	FB	SDNSF	KEV DV IB T330		8 11	4220	1 2	12000	13600
36	236	FB	MY	KEV DV IB	440D GM	12 8	8990	1 4	43000	47800
44	244	FB	MY	KEV DV IB T570D GM		16	14700	1 6	96900	106500
66	266	FB	MY	KEV DV IB T500 SAAB		18	16880		237000	260500
75	275-CUSTOM	FB	MY	KEV DV IB T570D GM		22			**	**

....For earlier years, see the BUC Used Boat Price Guide, Volume 3

GLASSMASTER CO MARINE DIV
LEXINGTON SC 29072   COAST GUARD MFG ID- GPC See inside cover to adjust price for area

LOA FT IN	NAME AND/ OR MODEL	TOP/ RIG	BOAT TYPE	-HULL- MTL TP	----ENGINE--- TP # HP MFG	BEAM FT IN	WGT LBS	DRAFT FT IN	RETAIL LOW	RETAIL HIGH
					1987 BOATS					
16 5	SABRE 179BFS	ST	FSH	FBG SV OB		6 9	1050		5550	6400
16 5	SABRE 179BR	ST	RNBT	FBG DV IO		6 9	1050		5650	6500
16 5	SABRE 179BR	ST	RNBT	FBG DV IO	120-165	6 9	1800		2600	3150
17 5	SABRE 187CB	ST	RNBT	FBG DV IO	120 OMC	7 5	1960		3000	3500
17 6	SABRE 187 CUDDY	ST	CUD	FBG DV IO	120-165	7 5	2060		3150	3900
17 6	SABRE 187 CUDDY	ST	CUD	FBG DV IO	175	7 5	2460		3500	4100
17 6	SABRE 187BR	ST	RNBT	FBG DV IO	120-175	7 5	1960		3100	3850
17 6	SABRE 187CB	ST	RNBT	FBG DV IO	120-165	7 5	1960		2950	3500
17 6	SABRE 187CB	ST	RNBT	FBG DV IO	175	7 5	2200		3200	3700
17 6	SABRE 760 EPH	HT	FSH	FBG DV IO	130-165	7 5	2175		3450	4150
17 6	SABRE 760 EPH	HT	FSH	FBG DV IO	175	7 5	2470		3700	4300
18	SABRE 196CC	OP	FSH	FBG DV OB		7 6	1100		6100	7000
18	SABRE 196CC	OP	FSH	FBG DV SE		7 6	1500		**	**
18 5	SABRE 191BFS	ST	FSH	FBG DV OB	OMC	7 3	1370		7300	8400
18 5	SABRE 191BR	ST	RNBT	FBG DV IO	130-165	7 3	2150		3300	4000
18 5	SABRE 191BR	ST	RNBT	FBG DV IO	170-175	7 3	2650		3650	4300
18 5	SABRE 191BR	ST	RNBT	FBG DV IO	230	7 3	2950		4100	4750
21	SABRE 225 CUDDY	ST	CUD	FBG DV IO	165-230	7 9	2450		4750	5900
21	SABRE 225 CUDDY	ST	CUD	FBG DV IO	260	7 9	2650		5300	6100
21	SABRE 225BR	ST	RNBT	FBG DV IO	175-260	7 9	2950		5100	6350
21	SABRE 225EWF	ST	FSH	FBG DV IO	165-175	7 9	2900		5550	6700
21	SABRE 225EWF	ST	FSH	FBG DV IO	230-260	7 9	3300		6200	7300
21	SABRE WF	ST	FSH	FBG DV OB		7 9	2120		11000	12500
24 3	SABRE 258 AFT CABIN	ST	CUD	FBG DV IO	260-335	7 9	4720		9350	11500
24 3	SABRE 258 AFT CABIN	ST	CUD	FBG DV IO	T165-T175	7 9	4720		9950	11300
24 3	SABRE 258 AFT CABIN	ST	CUD	FBG DV IO	T330 MRCR	7 9	4720		12100	13800
24 3	SABRE 258 AFT CABIN	ST	FSH	FBG DV IO	T175 OMC	7 9	4720		10400	11900
24 3	SABRE 258CC	ST	CUD	FBG DV IO	230-260	7 9	4020		8050	9450
24 3	SABRE 258CC	ST	CUD	FBG DV IO	330-335	7 9	4020		9050	10400
24 3	SABRE 258CC	ST	CUD	FBG DV IO	T165 MRCR	7 9	4020		8950	10200
24 3	SABRE 258CCR	ST	CUD	FBG DV IO	230 OMC	7 9	4020		8000	9200
24 3	SABRE 258CCR	ST	CUD	FBG DV IO	T260	7 9	4020		9950	11300
					1986 BOATS					
16 5	SABRE 179	ST	RNBT	FBG DV OB		6 9	1050		5450	6300
16 5	SABRE 179	ST	RNBT	FBG DV IO	120-170	6 11	1800		2750	3200
16 5	SABRE-ONE 650ER			FBG IO	120-170	6 9	1800		2350	2750
16 5	STRIPER 650BFS	OP	FSH	FBG SV OB		6 9	1050		5350	6150
17 5	STRIPER 750BFS	OP	FSH	FBG DV OB		6 9	1150		6000	6850
17 6	SABRE 187	ST	CUD	FBG DV IO	120-190	7 4	2060		3000	3550
17 6	SABRE 187 B/R	ST	RNBT	FBG DV IO	120-190	7 4	1960		2900	3400
17 6	SABRE 187 CL BOW	ST	RNBT	FBG DV IO	120-190	7 4	1925		2850	3400
17 6	SABRE 760 EPH	HT	FSH	FBG DV IO	120-190	7 4	2060		3150	3750
18 5	SABRE 191	ST	RNBT	FBG DV IO	140-230	7 3	2150		3150	3850
18 5	STRIPER 850BFS	ST	FSH	FBG DV OB		7 3	1370		7050	8100
21	EGENCY 210EFSD	ST	CUD	FBG DV IO	170 OMC	7 9	2900		5000	5750
21	REGENCY 210EBS	ST	RNBT	FBG DV IO	140-200	7 9	2650		4550	5550
21	REGENCY 210EBS	ST	RNBT	FBG DV IO	260	7 9			5050	5800
21	REGENCY 210EFSD	ST	CUD	FBG DV IO	170-260	7 9	2900		5050	6150
21	REGENCY 210ESD	ST	FSH	FBG DV IO	170-260	7 9	2650		4500	5850
21	REGENCY 210FSD	ST	RNBT	FBG DV OB		7 9	2120		5300	6450
21	REGENCY 210WF	OP	FSH	FBG DV OB		7 9	2120		10600	12100
21	REGENCY EFRD	ST	CUD	FBG DV IO		7 9	2120		10600	12100
24 3	HERITAGE 244EFSD	ST	CUD	FBG DV IO	170-260	7 9	2875		4800	5800
24 3	HERITAGE 244EFSD	ST	CUD	FBG DV IO	260 OMC	7 9	4020		7800	9000
24 3	HERITAGE 244EFSD	ST	CUD	FBG DV IO	260 MRCR	7 9	4020		7850	9050
24 3	HERITAGE 244EFSD	ST	CUD	FBG DV IO	230	7 9	4020		7700	8850
24 3	HERITAGE 244ESD	ST	FSH	FBG DV IO	230-260	7 9	4020		8100	9550
24 3	HERITAGE 244ESD	ST	FSH	FBG DV IO	T170	7 9	4020		9050	10300
					1985 BOATS					
16 5	CADET 650BS	ST	RNBT	FBG TR OB		6 11	1050		5300	6100
16 5	CADET 650EBS	ST	RNBT	FBG DV SE	115 OMC	7 11	1800		8300	9550
16 5	CADET 650EBS	ST	RNBT	FBG DV IO	120-205	7 11	1800		2600	3150
16 5	SABRE-ONE 650 ER	ST		FBG SE	115 OMC	6 11	1800		8150	9400
16 5	SABRE-ONE 650 ER	ST		FBG IO	120-205	6 11	1800		2300	2750
17 5	CITATION 700EC	ST	RNBT	FBG DV SE	115 OMC	6 11	1890		8400	9650
17 5	CITATION 700EC	ST	RNBT	FBG DV IO	120-205	6 11	1890		2600	3100
17 5	DAYTONA		RNBT	FBG DV OB		6 11	1000		5250	6000
17 5	DAYTONA		RNBT	FBG DV IO	120	6 11	1810		2550	3000
17 5	PATRIOT 750BS	ST	RNBT	FBG DV OB		6 11	1150		5850	6700
17 5	PATRIOT 750EBS	ST	RNBT	FBG DV SE	115 OMC	6 11	1930		8500	9750
17 5	PATRIOT 750EBS	ST	RNBT	FBG DV IO	120-205	6 11	1930		2650	3150
17 6	SABRE 760EBS	ST	RNBT	FBG DV SE	115 OMC	7 5	1960		8600	9850
17 6	SABRE 760EBS	ST	RNBT	FBG DV IO	120-205	7 5	1960		2800	3350
17 6	SABRE 760ED	ST	RNBT	FBG DV SE	115 OMC	7 5	1925		8500	9750
17 6	SABRE 760ED	ST	RNBT	FBG DV IO	120-205	7 5	1925		2750	3300
17 6	SABRE 760ESD	ST	CUD	FBG DV SE	115 OMC	7 5	2060		8850	10100
17 6	SABRE 760ESD	ST	CUD	FBG DV IO	120-205	7 5	2060		2900	3450

LOA FT IN	NAME AND/ OR MODEL	TOP/ RIG	BOAT TYPE	-HULL- MTL TP	----ENGINE--- TP # HP MFG	BEAM FT IN	WGT LBS	DRAFT FT IN	RETAIL LOW	RETAIL HIGH
				1985 BOATS						
18 5	CHIEF 850EC	ST	RNBT	FBG TR	SE 115 OMC	7	2150		9200	10400
18 5	CHIEF 850EC	ST	RNBT	FBG TR	IO 120-230	7	2150		2950	3600
18 5	SUPREME 850BS	ST	RNBT	FBG DV	OB	7 3	1370		6850	7900
18 5	SUPREME 850EBS	ST	RNBT	FBG DV	SE 115 OMC	7 3	2150		9200	10400
18 5	SUPREME 850EBS	ST	RNBT	FBG DV	IO 120-230	7 3	2150		3000	3700
21	REGENCY 210EBS	ST	RNBT	FBG DV	IO 140-260	7 11	2875		4650	5650
21	REGENCY 210EFRD	ST	RNBT	FBG DV	IO 140-200	7 11	2875		4650	5400
21	REGENCY 210EFRD	ST	RNBT	FBG DV	SE 205 OMC	7 11	2875		12400	14100
21	REGENCY 210EFRD	ST	RNBT	FBG DV	IO 205-260	7 11	2875		4700	5650
21	REGENCY 210ESD	ST	CUD	FBG DV	IO 140-200	7 11	2650		4650	5400
21	REGENCY 210ESD	ST	CUD	FBG DV	SE 205 OMC	7 11	2650		11900	13500
21	REGENCY 210ESD	ST	CUD	FBG DV	IO 205-260	7 11	2650		4700	5650
21	REGENCY 210EWF	ST	FSH	FBG DV	IO 140-200	7 11	2900		5150	6000
21	REGENCY 210EWF	ST	FSH	FBG DV	SE 205 OMC	7 11	2900		12400	14100
21	REGENCY 210EWF	ST	FSH	FBG DV	IO 205-260	7 11	2900		5200	6250
21	REGENCY 210SD	ST	RNBT	FBG DV	OB	7 11	1870		9500	10800
21	REGENCY 210WF	OP	FSH	FBG DV	OB	7 11	2120		10300	11700
24 3	HERITAGE 244ESD	ST	FSH	FBG DV	IO 185-200	7 11	4020		7700	8850
24 3	HERITAGE 244ESD	ST	FSH	FBG DV	SE 205 OMC	7 11	4020		19500	21600
24 3	HERITAGE 244ESD	ST	FSH	FBG DV	IO 205-260	7 11	4020		7750	9200
24 3	HERITAGE 244ESD	ST	FSH	FBG DV	IO T120-T170	7 11	4020		8500	9900
				1984 BOATS						
16 5	CADET 650BS	OP	RNBT	FBG TR	OB	6 11	1050		5150	5900
16 5	CADET 650EBS	OP	RNBT	FBG DV	SE 115 OMC	6 11	1800		8050	9200
16 5	CADET 650EBS	OP	RNBT	FBG DV	IO 120-170	6 11	1800		2550	2950
17 5	CITATION 700EC	ST	RNBT	FBG DV	SE 115 OMC	6 11	1890		8150	9350
17 5	CITATION 700EC	ST	RNBT	FBG DV	IO 120-188	6 11	1890		2500	3000
17 5	DAYTONA		RNBT	FBG DV	OB	6 11	1000		5050	5800
17 5	DAYTONA		RNBT	FBG DV	IO 120	6 11	1810		2450	2900
17 5	PATRIOT 750BS	ST	RNBT	FBG DV	OB	6 11	1150		5650	6500
17 5	PATRIOT 750EBS	ST	RNBT	FBG DV	SE 115 OMC	6 11	1930		8250	9450
17 5	PATRIOT 750EBS	ST	RNBT	FBG DV	IO 120-188	6 11	1930		2550	3000
17 6	SABRE 760EBS	ST	RNBT	FBG DV	SE 115 OMC	7 5	1960		8350	9600
17 6	SABRE 760EBS	ST	RNBT	FBG DV	IO 120-188	7 5	1960		2700	3200
17 6	SABRE 760EBSS	ST	RNBT	FBG DV	SE 115 OMC	7 5	1960		8300	9500
17 6	SABRE 760EBSS	ST	RNBT	FBG DV	IO 120-188	7 5	1960		2700	3150
17 6	SABRE 760ESD	ST	CUD	FBG DV	SE 115 OMC	7 5	2060		8500	9750
17 6	SABRE 760ESD	ST	CUD	FBG DV	IO 120-188	7 5	2060		2800	3300
18 5	CHIEF 850EC	ST	RNBT	FBG TR	SE 115 OMC	7	2150		8900	10100
18 5	CHIEF 850EC	ST	RNBT	FBG TR	IO 120-230	7	2150		2850	3450
18 5	SUPREME 850BS	ST	RNBT	FBG DV	OB	7 3	1370		6650	7650
18 5	SUPREME 850EBS	ST	RNBT	FBG DV	SE 115 OMC	7 3	2150		8900	10100
18 5	SUPREME 850EBS	ST	RNBT	FBG DV	IO 120-230	7 3	2150		2900	3550
21	REGENCY 210EFRD	ST	RNBT	FBG DV	IO 140-260	7 11	2875		4500	5450
21	REGENCY 210ESD	ST	CUD	FBG DV	IO 140-260	7 11	2650		4500	5450
21	REGENCY 210EWF	ST	FSH	FBG DV	IO 140-260	7 11	2900		4950	6050
21	REGENCY 210SD	ST	RNBT	FBG DV	OB	7 11	1870		9200	10500
21	REGENCY 210WF	OP	FSH	FBG DV	OB	7 11	2120		10000	11400
24 3	HERITAGE 244ESD	ST	FSH	FBG DV	IO 185-260	7 11	4020		7400	8850
24 3	HERITAGE 244ESD	ST	FSH	FBG DV	IO T120-T170	7 11	4020		8200	9550

....For earlier years, see the BUC Used Boat Price Guide, Volume 3

GLASSTREAM BOATS
GENERAL MARINE IND
PANAMA CITY FL 32406   COAST GUARD MFG ID- GSY
See inside cover to adjust price for area

LOA FT IN	NAME AND/ OR MODEL	TOP/ RIG	BOAT TYPE	-HULL- MTL TP	----ENGINE--- TP # HP MFG	BEAM FT IN	WGT LBS	DRAFT FT IN	RETAIL LOW	RETAIL HIGH
				1993 BOATS						
16 6	165 SF	OP	BASS	FBG SV	OB	6 2	1255		1650	2000
17 2	INTRACOASTAL 1700	OP	CTRCN	FBG SV	OB	6 10	1283		1700	2050
17 5	180 SE BR	OP	B/R	FBG SV	IO 110	7 5	2192		4750	5450
17 5	180 SE CB	OP	RNBT	FBG SV	IO 110	7 5	2200		4950	5700
17 6	175 SF	OP	BASS	FBG SV	OB	6 10	1717		2300	2650
17 6	PRO 1750 DC	OP	BASS	FBG SV	OB	6 10	1727		2300	2650
18 3	REGATTA 192 BR	OP	B/R	FBG SV	IO 110				4900	5650
18 3	REGATTA 192 CC	OP	CUD	FBG SV	IO 110				5150	5900
18 8	190 SE BR	OP	B/R	FBG SV	IO 110	7 8	2382		5400	6200
18 8	190 SE CB	OP	RNBT	FBG SV	IO 110	7 8	2405		5650	6500
18 10	PRO 1850	OP	BASS	FBG SV	OB	7 8	1742		2350	2750
18 10	PRO 1850 DC	OP	BASS	FBG SV	OB	7 8	1792		2400	2800
20 5	PRO 2150	OP	BASS	FBG SV	OB	7 8	1817		2500	2950
20 5	PRO 2150 DC	OP	BASS	FBG SV	OB	7 8	1857		2550	3000
21 8	INTRACOASTAL 2100	OP	CTRCN	FBG SV	OB	7 4	2146		2950	3400
25 3	230 APT	OP	CUD	FBG SV	IO	8 9	4349		**	**
				1992 BOATS						
16 6	SPORT & FISH 166	OP	BASS	FBG SV	OB	6 4	1010		1250	1500
16 8	BASS & SKI 17V	OP	RNBT	FBG SV	OB	7 1	1085		1400	1650
16 8	FISH & SKI 17V	OP	BASS	FBG SV	OB	7 1	1085		1400	1650
16 8	HYDRABASS 17V	OP	BASS	FBG SV	OB	7 1	1085		1400	1650
17 2	172 GXL BR	OP	B/R	FBG SV	IO 120-130	6 10	1385		3550	4150
17 2	172 GXL CB	OP	RNBT	FBG SV	IO 115-130	6 10	1385		3550	4400
17 2	175	OP	BASS	FBG SV	OB	7 2	1500		1900	2300
17 2	175 CC	OP	CUD	FBG SV	IO 115-180	7 2	1540		3850	4750
17 5	180	OP	B/R	FBG SV	OB	7 5	1380		1750	2050
17 5	180 SE BR	OP	B/R	FBG SV	IO 115-180	7 5	1620		3800	4700
17 5	180 SE CB	OP	RNBT	FBG SV	IO 115-180	7 5	1620		4050	4950
17 6	BASS & SKI 1750	OP	BASS	FBG SV	OB	6 10	1360		1750	2050
17 6	HYDRABASS 1750	OP	BASS	FBG SV	OB	6 10	1335		1700	2050
18	COHO 19	OP	CTRCN	FBG SV	OB	7 6	1700		2150	2500
18 6	HYDRABASS 18V	OP	BASS	FBG SV	OB	7	1250		1650	1950
18 8	190 CC	OP	CUD	FBG SV	IO 115-180	7 8	1754		4750	5800
18 8	190 SE BR	OP	B/R	FBG SV	IO 115-180	7 8	1744		4450	5450
18 8	190 SE CB	OP	RNBT	FBG SV	IO 115-180	7 8	1744		4650	5600
19 3	192 CC	OP	CUD	FBG SV	IO 115-180	7 8	1960		5150	6200
19 3	192 GXL BR	OP	B/R	FBG SV	IO 115-180	7 8	1860		4750	5750
19 8	6.2 METER	OP	RNBT	FBG SV	IO	7 3	1225		1650	1950
19 8	COHO 21	OP	CTRCN	FBG SV	OB	8	1960		2450	2850
21 8	210 CC	OP	CUD	FBG SV	IO	8	2000		7000	8750
21 8	211 GXL BR	OP	B/R	FBG SV	IO 115-230	7 8	2300		6750	8400
21 8	FREE SPIRIT 21	OP	RNBT	FBG SV	IO 155-230	7 8	1830		6350	7600
21 8	FREE SPIRIT 21	OP	RNBT	FBG SV	IO 300	7 8	1830		7350	8450
22 5	230 CC	OP	CUD	FBG SV	IO 155-240	8 5	2800		8700	10300
	IO 300	9750	11100, IO	350 MRCR	10900 12400, IO		390 MRCR	12300	13900	
				1991 BOATS						
16 10	BASS & SKI 1700	OP	BASS	FBG SV	OB	7	875		1050	1250
16 10	FISH & SKI 1700	OP	RNBT	FBG DV	OB	7	875		1100	1300
16 10	HYDRA BASS 1700	OP	BASS	FBG SV	OB	7	875		1050	1250
17 1	GXL 172	OP	RNBT	FBG DV	OB	6 8	890		2950	3450
17 2	175 OB	OP	RNBT	FBG DV	OB	7 2	1500		1850	2200
17 5	180 SE CD	OP	RNBT	FBG SV	OB	7 5	2300		**	**
17 5	180 SE OB	OP	RNBT	FBG SV	OB	7 5	1554		1900	2250
17 5	ANGLER 176	OP	FSH	FBG SV	OB	6 10	990		1200	1400
17 6	BASS & SKI 1750	OP	BASS	FBG SV	OB	6 10	1360		1650	1950
18 8	175 CC	OP	CUD	FBG DV	IO	7 6	1540		**	**
18 2	CENTER CONSOLE 19	OP	CTRCN	FBG DV	IO	7 6	1700		2000	2350
18 4	BR 192	OP	RNBT	FBG DV	IO 230	7 7	1260		4100	4750
18 4	CUDDY CABIN 192	OP	CUD	FBG DV	IO 230	7 7	1260		4150	4850
18 4	GXL 192	OP	RNBT	FBG DV	IO 230	7 7	1260		4100	4750
18 4	SD GXL 192	OP	RNBT	FBG DV	IO 230	7 7	1260		4100	4750
18 6	HYDRA BASS 18	OP	BASS	FBG DV	IO	7	1250		1550	1850
18 8	190 SE	OP	B/R	FBG DV	IO	8	1744		**	**
18 8	190 SE CC	OP	CUD	FBG DV	IO	8	1744		**	**
18 8	190 SE CD	OP	RNBT	FBG DV	IO	8	1754		**	**
19 8	CUDDY CABIN GXL 192	OP	CUD	FBG DV	IO 230	7 7	1260		4600	5300
19 9	BMF 6.2	OP	FSH	FBG SV	OB	7 5	1225		1550	1850
19 10	CENTER CONSOLE 21	OP	CTRCN	FBG DV	IO	8	1960		2350	2750
20 9	CUDDY CABIN 211	OP	CUD	FBG DV	IO 271	7 9	1400		6250	7200
21 11	FREESPIRIT GXL21	OP	RNBT	FBG DV	IO 365	7 7	1430		8150	9400
22 1	CUDDY CABIN GXL 211	OP	CUD	FBG DV	IO 271	7 7	1400		6850	7850
25 2	SEAQUEST 23	OP	CNV	FBG DV	IO 365	7 3	3729		16500	18800
25 9	SEAQUEST 26	OP	CNV	FBG SV	IO 365	8 4	5350		25100	27900
				1990 BOATS						
16 2	CUTLASS 172	OP	RNBT	FBG DV	IO 140	6 8	890		2450	2850
16 2	GXL 162	OP	RNBT	FBG DV	OB 131	6 4	890		2300	2650
16 10	BASS & SKI 1700	OP	BASS	FBG SV	OB	7	875		1000	1150
16 10	CARAVELLE 182	OP	RNBT	FBG DV	OB 175	7	875		3000	3350
16 10	FISH & SKI 1700	OP	BASS	FBG SV	OB	7	875		1000	1200
16 10	HYDRA BASS 1700	OP	BASS	FBG SV	OB	7	875		1050	1250
17 1	GXL 172	OP	RNBT	FBG DV	IO 140	6 8	890		2750	3200
17 5	ANGLER 176	OP	FSH	FBG SV	OB	6 10	990		1150	1350
17 7	GXL 182	OP	RNBT	FBG DV	OB 175	7	1040		3150	3650
17 7	SD GXL 182	OP	RNBT	FBG DV	OB 175	7	1040		3150	3650
17 7	BOSS ELITE 180	OP	RNBT	FBG SV	OB	7	1100		1300	1550

LOA FT	IN	NAME AND/ OR MODEL	TOP/ RIG	BOAT TYPE	-HULL- MTL	TP	TP	----ENGINE--- # HP	MFG	BEAM FT	IN	WGT LBS	DRAFT FT	IN	RETAIL LOW	RETAIL HIGH
		1990 BOATS														
17	8	BOSS TE 180	OP	RNBT	FBG	SV	OB			7		1100			1300	1550
17	8	FISH & SKI 180	OP	RNBT	FBG	SV	OB			7		1100			1300	1550
18	1	FREESPIRIT 19	OP	RNBT	FBG	DV	IO	260		7	7	1270			3950	4600
18	2	CENTER CONSOLE 19	OP	CTRCN	FBG	SV	OB			7	6	1700			1900	2250
18	4	BR 192	OP	RNBT	FBG	DV	IO	230		7	7	1260			3850	4450
18	4	CUDDY CABIN 192	OP	CUD	FBG	DV	IO	230		7	7	1260			3900	4550
18	4	GXL 192	OP	RNBT	FBG	DV	IO	230		7	7	1260			3850	4450
18	4	SD GXL 192	OP	RNBT	FBG	DV	IO	230		7	7	1260			3850	4450
19	5	CUDDY CABIN GXL 192	OP	CUD	FBG	DV	IO	230		7	7	1260			4350	5000
19	9	BMF 6.2	OP	FSH	FBG	SV	OB			7	5	1225			1450	1750
19	10	CENTER CONSOLE 21	OP	CTRCN	FBG	SV	OB			8		1960			2250	2600
20	9	CUDDY CABIN 211	OP	CUD	FBG	DV	IO	271		7	9	1400			5850	6750
21	11	FREESPIRIT GXL21	OP	RNBT	FBG	DV	IO	365		7	7	1430			7650	8800
22		CUDDY CABIN GXL 211	OP	CUD	FBG	DV	IO	271		7	9	1400			6400	7350
25	2	SEAQUEST 23	OP	CNV	FBG	SV	IO	365		8	4	3720			15500	17700
27	9	SEAQUEST 26	OP	CNV	FBG	SV	IO	365		8	4	5350			23700	26300
		1989 BOATS														
16	3	CUTLASS 172	OP	B/R	FBG	DV	IO			6	8	1810			**	**
16	10	CARAVELLE 182	OP	B/R	FBG	DV	IO			6	11	1940			**	**
16	10	CARAVELLE 182	OP	B/R	FBG	DV	IO	165-175		6	11	1940			3200	3700
18	3	BOW RIDER 192	ST	B/R	FBG	DV	IO			7	8	2035			**	**
18	3	BOW RIDER 192	ST	B/R	FBG	DV	IO	165-205		7	8	2035			3800	4500
18	3	CUDDY CABIN 192	ST	CUD	FBG	DV	IO			7	8	2090			**	**
18	3	CUDDY CABIN 192	ST	CUD	FBG	DV	IO	165-205		7	8	2090			4150	4900
18	3	FREE SPIRIT 19	OP	RNBT	FBG	DV	IO	175-205		7	8	2710			4650	5400
20	8	CUDDY CABIN 211	OP	CUD	FBG	DV	IO	130-205		7	8	2495			5900	6900
20	8	FREE SPIRIT 21	OP	RNBT	FBG	DV	IO	260		7	8	2920			6550	7500
25	5	SEAQUEST 26	OP	CNV	FBG	DV	IO	260		8		5350			16200	18400
		1988 BOATS														
16	3	CUTLASS 172	OP	B/R		DV	IO			6	8	1810			**	**
16	10	CARAVELLE 182	OP	B/R		DV	IO			6	11	1940			**	**
16	10	CARAVELLE 182	OP	B/R		DV	IO	165-175		6	11	1940			3000	3500
18	3	BOW RIDER 192	ST	B/R		DV	IO			7	8	2035			**	**
18	3	BOW RIDER 192	ST	B/R		DV	IO	165-205		7	8	2035			3600	4300
18	3	CUDDY CABIN 192	ST	CUD		DV	IO			7	8	2090			**	**
18	3	CUDDY CABIN 192	ST	CUD		DV	IO	165-205		7	8	2090			3900	4600
18	3	FREE SPIRIT 19	OP	RNBT		DV	IO	175-260		7	8	2710			4400	5400
20	8	CUDDY CABIN 211	OP	CUD		DV	IO	120-205		7	8	2495			5550	6500
20	8	FREE SPIRIT 21	OP	RNBT		DV	IO			7	8	2920			**	**
20	8	FREE SPIRIT 21	OP	RNBT		DV	IO	260		7	8	2920			6200	7100
25	5	SEAQUEST 26	OP	CNV		DV	IO	260		8		5350			15300	17400
		1987 BOATS														
16	3	CUTLASS 172	OP	B/R		DV	IO			7		1810			**	**
16	10	CARAVELLE 182	OP	B/R		DV	IO			6	11	1940			**	**
16	10	CARAVELLE 182	OP	B/R		DV	IO	175		6	11	1940			2850	3350
16	10	HYDRA BASS 17V	OP	BASS		DV	OB			7		900			935	1100
17	6	ANGLER 176	OP	BASS		DV		150		7		990			**	**
17	9	BOSS 180TE	OP	BASS		DV	OB			7	3	1100			1150	1350
18	3	FREE SPIRIT 19	OP	RNBT		DV	IO	175-260		7	8	2710			4150	5150
18	3	REGATTA 192 CUD	ST	CUD		DV	IO			7	8	2090			**	**
18	3	REGATTA 192 CUD	ST	CUD		DV	IO	165-175		7	8	2090			3700	4300
18	3	REGATTA 192BR	ST	B/R		DV	IO			7	8	2035			**	**
18	3	REGATTA 192BR	ST	B/R	FBG	DV	IO			7	8	2035			**	**
18	3	REGATTA 192BR	ST	B/R		DV	IO	165-175		7	8	2035			3450	4000
20	4	ELIMINATOR 2000	OP	RNBT		DV	IO	175-260		7	3	2400			4750	5850
20	8	FREE SPIRIT 21	OP	RNBT		DV	IO			7	8	2920			**	**
20	8	FREE SPIRIT 21	OP	RNBT		DV	IO	260		7	8	2920			5900	6750
20	8	REGATTA 211 CR	OP	CR		DV	IO			7	8	2550			**	**
20	8	REGATTA 211 CR	OP	CR	FBG	DV	IO			7	8	2550			**	**
20	8	REGATTA 211 CR	OP	CR		DV	IO	165-260		7	8	2550			5400	6600
23	5	SEAQUEST	OP	CNV		DV	IO	260		8		3330			9000	10200
24	8	EAGLE 2500	OP	CR		DV	IO	260		8		3350			8600	9850
25	5	SEAQUEST	OP	CNV		DV	IO	260		8		5350			14600	16500

....For earlier years, see the BUC Used Boat Price Guide, Volume 3

GLASTRON BOATS

DIV OF GENMAR INDUSTRIES INC
LITTLE FALLS MN 56345 COAST GUARD MFG ID- GLA

See inside cover to adjust price for area

For more recent years, see the BUC Used Boat Price Guide, Volume 1

LOA FT	IN	NAME AND/ OR MODEL	TOP/ RIG	BOAT TYPE	-HULL- MTL	TP	TP	----ENGINE--- # HP	MFG	BEAM FT	IN	WGT LBS	DRAFT FT	IN	RETAIL LOW	RETAIL HIGH
		1996 BOATS														
17	1	SE 170	OP	RNBT	FBG	SV	OB			7	4	1125	2	4	1850	2250
17	1	SE 175	OP	RNBT	FBG	SV	IO	135		7	4	1650	2	7	4750	5650
17	1	SE 175 SKI & FISH	OP	RNBT	FBG	SV	IO	135		7	4	1750	2	7	5050	6300
17	1	SE 177	OP	RNBT	FBG	SV	IO	135		7	4	1650	2	7	4850	5750
17	11	GS 180	OP	RNBT	FBG	SV	OB			7	6	1300	2	5	2500	2900
17	11	GS 180 FISH & SKI	OP	RNBT	FBG	SV	OB			7	6	1425	2	5	2600	3050
18		GS 185	OP	RNBT	FBG	SV	IO	130-185		7	6	1950	2	7	5650	6500
18		GS 185 FISH & SKI	OP	RNBT	FBG	SV	IO	130-185		7	6	2050	2	8	5850	7100
18		GS 187	OP	RNBT	FBG	SV	IO	130-185		7	6	1950	2	7	5800	6650
19	11	GS 205	OP	RNBT	FBG	SV	IO	180-220		7	10	2349	2	8	6850	8400
19	11	GS 205	OP	RNBT	FBG	SV	IO	235-250		7	10	2599	2	8	7550	9050
19	11	GS 205 COLLECTOR ED	OP	RNBT	FBG	SV	IO	190-250		7	10	2499	2	8	7550	9100
21	2	GS 215	OP	RNBT	FBG	SV	IO	200-300		8	1	3050	2	8	8600	10700
23	3	GS 235	OP	RNBT	FBG	SV	IO	230-255		8	6	4100	2	11	11900	13900
23	3	GS 235	OP	RNBT	FBG	SV	IO	300		8	6	4165	2	11	12500	14900
24	10	GS 249	OP	CR	FBG	SV	IO	230-255		8	6	4515	2	11	14300	17000
24	10	GS 249	OP	CR	FBG	SV	IO	300		8	6	4600	2	11	15400	18100
		1995 BOATS														
17	1	SSV-170	OP	RNBT	FBG	SV	OB			7	4	1125	2	4	1900	2250
17	1	SSV-170 SE	OP	RNBT	FBG	SV	OB			7	4	1125	2	4	1750	2100
17	1	SSV-170 SKI & FISH	OP	RNBT	FBG	SV	OB			7	4	1125	2	4	2400	2800
17	1	SSV-175	OP	RNBT	FBG	SV	IO	135-160		7	4	1750	2	7	4450	5550
17	1	SSV-175 SE	OP	RNBT	FBG	SV	IO	135		7	4	1650	2	7	4500	5350
17	1	SSV-175 SKI & FISH	OP	RNBT	FBG	SV	IO	135		7	4	1750	2	7	4700	5900
17	1	SSV-175 SKI & FISH	OP	RNBT	FBG	SV	IO	160	MRCR	7	4	1925	2	7	4900	5650
17	1	SSV-175 SKI & FISH	OP	RNBT	FBG	SV	IO	160	VLVO	7	4	1950	2	7	5450	6250
17	1	SSV-177	OP	RNBT	FBG	SV	IO	135-160		7	4	1750	2	7	4450	5550
17	1	SSV-177 SE	OP	RNBT	FBG	SV	IO	135		7	4	1650	2	7	4500	5350
18	7	GS-195	OP	RNBT	FBG	SV	IO	205-215		7	7	2090	2	8	5700	6800
18	7	SSV-190	OP	RNBT	FBG	SV	OB			7	6	1200	2	5	2000	2350
18	7	SSV-190 SKI & FISH	OP	RNBT	FBG	SV	OB			7	6	1200	2	5	2450	2850
18	7	SSV-195	OP	RNBT	FBG	SV	IO	160-235		7	7	2000	2	8	5400	6750
18	7	SSV-195 SE	OP	RNBT	FBG	SV	IO	160		7	7	2000	2	8	5100	6150
18	7	SSV-195 SKI & FISH	OP	RNBT	FBG	SV	IO	160-235		7	7	2000	2	8	5600	6950
18	7	SSV-197	OP	RNBT	FBG	SV	IO	160-235		7	7	2000	2	8	5400	6750
18	7	SSV-199	OP	CUD	FBG	SV	IO	160-180		7	7	2000	2	8	5500	6650
18	7	SSV-199	OP	CUD	FBG	SV	IO	190-235		7	7	2150	2	8	6050	7000
21	2	SSV-215	OP	RNBT	FBG	SV	IO	190-255		8	1	3050	2	8	8000	9700
21	2	SSV-215	OP	RNBT	FBG	SV	IO	300	MRCR	8	1	3150	2	8	8850	10100
21	2	SSV-219	OP	CUD	FBG	SV	IO	190-255		8	1	3100	2	8	8500	10300
21	2	SSV-219	OP	CUD	FBG	SV	IO	300	MRCR	8	1	3200	2	9	9400	10700
23	3	SSV-235	OP	RNBT	FBG	SV	IO	205-255		8	6	3935	2	11	10400	13000
23	3	SSV-235	OP	RNBT	FBG	SV	IO	300		8	6	4165	2	11	11700	13900
24	10	SSV-249	OP	CR	FBG	SV	IO	205-255		8	6	4370	2	11	12800	15900
24	10	SSV-249	OP	CR	FBG	SV	IO	300		8	6	4600	2	11	14400	16900
		1994 BOATS														
17	1	SSV-170	OP	RNBT	FBG	SV	OB			7	4	1125	2	4	1800	2100
17	1	SSV-170 SE	OP	RNBT	FBG	SV	OB			7	4	1125	2	4	1700	2000
17	1	SSV-170 SKI & FISH	OP	RNBT	FBG	SV	OB			7	4	1125	2	4	2250	2650
17	1	SSV-175 ELITE	OP	RNBT	FBG	SV	IO	120-155		7	4	1650	2	7	4450	5300
17	1	SSV-175 SE	OP	RNBT	FBG	SV	IO	120-135		7	4	1650	2	7	4050	4750
17	1	SSV-175 SKI & FISH	OP	RNBT	FBG	SV	IO	120-155		7	4	1650	2	7	4800	5650
17	1	SSV-177 ELITE	OP	RNBT	FBG	SV	IO	120-155		7	4	1650	2	7	4450	5300
17	1	SSV-177 SE	OP	RNBT	FBG	SV	IO	120-135		7	4	1650	2	7	4050	4750
18	7	SSV-190	OP	RNBT	FBG	SV	OB			7	6	1200	2	5	1900	2250
18	7	SSV-190 SKI & FISH	OP	RNBT	FBG	SV	OB			7	6	1200	2	5	2300	2700
18	7	SSV-195 ELITE	OP	RNBT	FBG	SV	IO	120-205		7	7	1740	2	8	5000	6150
18	7	SSV-195 ELITE	OP	RNBT	FBG	SV	IO	225-250		7	7	2100	2	8	5750	6650
18	7	SSV-195 SE	OP	RNBT	FBG	SV	IO	135-175		7	7	1825	2	8	4700	5800
18	7	SSV-195 SKI & FISH	OP	RNBT	FBG	SV	IO	155-205		7	7	2000	2	8	5200	6450
18	7	SSV-195 SKI & FISH	OP	RNBT	FBG	SV	IO	225-230		7	7	2100	2	8	5950	6850
18	7	SSV-197 ELITE	OP	RNBT	FBG	SV	IO	120-230		7	7	1740	2	8	5000	6200
18	7	SSV-197 ELITE	OP	RNBT	FBG	SV	IO	250	VLVO	7	7	2100	2	8	5800	6650
18	7	SSV-197 SE	OP	RNBT	FBG	SV	IO	135-175		7	7	2100	2	8	5100	5900
18	7	SSV-199	OP	CUD	FBG	SV	IO	120-205		7	7	1875	2	8	5250	6500
18	7	SSV-199	OP	CUD	FBG	SV	IO	225-250		7	7	2150	2	8	5800	6900
21	2	SSV-215 ELITE	OP	RNBT	FBG	SV	IO	175-205		8	1	2900	2	8	7000	8600
21	2	SSV-215 ELITE	OP	RNBT	FBG	SV	IO	225-250		8	1	3050	2	8	7600	8950
21	2	SSV-215 ELITE	OP	RNBT	FBG	SV	IO	300		8	1	3150	2	8	8150	9900
21	2	SSV-215 SE	OP	RNBT	FBG	SV	IO	190-205		8	1	2755	2	8	7050	8100
21	2	SSV-219	OP	CUD	FBG	SV	IO	175-205		8	1	2950	2	9	7400	9100
21	2	SSV-219	OP	CUD	FBG	SV	IO	225-250		8	1	3100	2	9	8100	9500
21	2	SSV-219	OP	CUD	FBG	SV	IO	300		8	1	3200	2	9	8700	10500

GLASTRON BOATS -CONTINUED See inside cover to adjust price for area

LOA FT	IN	NAME AND/ OR MODEL	TOP/ RIG	BOAT TYPE	-HULL- MTL	TP	----ENGINE--- TP	# HP	MFG	BEAM FT	IN	WGT LBS	DRAFT FT	IN	RETAIL LOW	RETAIL HIGH
		1993 BOATS														
17	1	SSV-170	OP	RNBT	FBG	SV	OB			7	4	1125	2	4	1600	1900
17	1	SSV-170 SKI & FISH	OP	RNBT	FBG	SV	OB			7	4	1125	2	4	2000	2350
17	1	SSV-175 ELITE	OP	RNBT	FBG	SV	IO	110-155		7	4	1650	2	7	4150	5000
17	1	SSV-175 SKI & FISH	OP	RNBT	FBG	SV	IO	110-155		7	4	1650	2	7	4350	5200
17	1	SSV-175SE	OP	RNBT	FBG	SV	IO	110	VLVO	7	4	1650	2	7	3850	4450
17	1	SSV-177 ELITE	OP	RNBT	FBG	SV	IO	110-155		7	4	1650	2	7	4150	5000
17	1	SSV-177SE	OP	RNBT	FBG	SV	IO	110	VLVO	7	4	1650	2	7	3850	4450
18	7	SSV-190	OP	RNBT	FBG	SV	OB			7	6	1200	2	5	1800	2150
18	7	SSV-190 SKI & FISH	OP	RNBT	FBG	SV	OB			7	6	1200	2	5	2200	2550
18	7	SSV-195 ELITE	OP	RNBT	FBG	SV	IO	110-205		7	7	1740	2	8	4700	5800
18	7	SSV-195 ELITE	OP	RNBT	FBG	SV	IO	225-230		7	7	2100	2	8	5250	6050
18	7	SSV-195 SKI & FISH	OP	RNBT	FBG	SV	IO	155-205		7	7	2000	2	8	4700	5800
18	7	SSV-195 SKI & FISH	OP	RNBT	FBG	SV	IO	225-230		7	7	2100	2	8	5200	5950
18	7	SSV-195SE	OP	RNBT	FBG	SV	IO	155	VLVO	7	7	1990	2	8	4450	5150
18	7	SSV-197 ELITE	OP	RNBT	FBG	SV	IO	110-205		7	7	1740	2	8	4700	5800
18	7	SSV-197 ELITE	OP	RNBT	FBG	SV	IO	225-230		7	7	2100	2	8	5250	6050
18	7	SSV-197SE	OP	RNBT	FBG	SV	IO	155	VLVO	7	7	1990	2	8	4450	5150
20	1	SSV-205	OP	RNBT	FBG	SV	IO	155-205		8		2735	2	9	5950	7250
20	1	SSV-205	OP	RNBT	FBG	SV	IO	225-240		8		2835	2	9	6500	7450
20	1	SSV-209	OP	CUD	FBG	SV	IO	110-205		8		2390	2	9	5950	7450
20	1	SSV-209	OP	CUD	FBG	SV	IO	225-230		8		2750	2	9	6650	7650
22	5	SSV-225	OP	RNBT	FBG	SV	IO	180-240		8	2	3010	2	8	7100	8650
22	5	SSV-225	OP	RNBT	FBG	SV	IO	300		8	2	3230	2	8	8200	9700
22	5	SSV-225	OP	RNBT	FBG	SV	IO	360	MRCR	8	2	3230	2	8	9400	10700
23	5	SSV-239	OP	CUD	FBG	SV	IO	225-245		8	4	3450	2	8	9200	10600
23	5	SSV-239	OP	CUD	FBG	SV	IO	300		8	4	3670	2	8	9950	11500
23	5	SSV-239	OP	CUD	FBG	SV	IO	360	MRCR	8	4	3670	2	8	11200	12700
		1992 BOATS														
16	8	16 CSS	OP	RNBT	FBG	SV	OB			6	7	750	2	4	1150	1400
16	8	1700 EL	OP	RNBT	FBG	SV	IO	115-120		7	2	1900	2	8	3450	4200
16	8	GLASTRON 1700	OP	B/R	FBG	SV	OB			7	2	1900	2	8	2550	3000
16	8	GLASTRON 1700	OP	B/R	FBG	SV	IO	115-175		7	2	1900	2	8	3450	4250
16	8	SKI FISH 1700	OP	RNBT	FBG	SV	OB			7	2	1250	2	7	1850	2200
16	8	SKI FISH 1700	OP	RNBT	FBG	SV	IO	115-175		7	2	1900	2	8	3900	4750
18	2	18 CSS	OP	RNBT	FBG	SV	IO	175		7	7	1500	2	6	3900	4500
19	1	1900 EL	OP	RNBT	FBG	SV	IO	115-175		7	3	2050	2	7	4450	5350
19	2	GLASTRON 1900	OP	B/R	FBG	SV	IO	115-175		7	3	2050	2	7	4250	5200
19	2	GLASTRON 1900	OP	B/R	FBG	SV	IO	205-230		7	3	2050	2	7	4400	5350
19	4	CARLSON 19CSS	OP	RNBT	FBG	SV	IO	240	MRCR	7	2	2845			5550	6350
19	11	GLASTRON 2000	OP	CUD	FBG	SV	IO	115-230		7	11	2375	2	9	5400	6650
20	1	GLASTRON 20	OP	B/R	FBG	SV	IO	175-240		8		2825	2	8	5550	6700
20	1	GLASTRON 20	OP	B/R	FBG	SV	IO	275	VLVO	8		2825	2	8	6300	7250
22	5	GLASTRON 22	OP	B/R	FBG	SV	IO	205-240		8	2	3100	2	9	6800	7950
22	5	GLASTRON 22	OP	B/R	FBG	SV	IO	275-300			8	3100	2	9	7600	8700
22	5	GLASTRON 22	OP	B/R	FBG	SV	IO	330	VLVO	8	2	3100	2	9	8350	9600
23	5	GLASTRON 23	OP	CUD	FBG	SV	IO	230-300		8	4	3450	2	9	8300	10300
23	5	GLASTRON 23	OP	CUD	FBG	SV	IO	330-360		8	4	3450	2	9	9950	11500
23	8	24 CSS	OP	CUD	FBG	SV	IO	240-300		8	6	3550	2	8	8650	10600
23	8	24 CSS	OP	CUD	FBG	SV	IO	330		8	6	3550	2	8	9750	11600
		1991 BOATS														
16	8	GLASTRON 1700	OP	B/R	FBG	SV	OB			7	2	1900	3	4	2500	2900
16	8	GLASTRON 1700	OP	B/R	FBG	SV	IO	115-175		7	2	1900	3	4	3250	4000
19	2	GLASTRON 1900	OP	B/R	FBG	SV	IO	115-175		7	3	2050	3	9	4000	4850
19	2	GLASTRON 1900	OP	B/R	FBG	SV	IO	205-230		7	3	2050	3	9	4100	5000
19	4	CARLSON	OP	RNBT	FBG	SV	IO	240	MRCR	7	2	2845	4	8	5200	5950
19	11	GLASTRON 2000	OP	CUD	FBG	SV	IO	115-230		7	11	2375	4	6	5100	6250
20	1	GLASTRON 20	OP	B/R	FBG	SV	IO	175-240		8		2825	4	5	5200	6300
20	1	GLASTRON 20	OP	B/R	FBG	SV	IO	275	VLVO	8		2825	4	5	5950	6800
22	5	GLASTRON 22	OP	B/R	FBG	SV	IO	205-240		8	2	3100	4	6	6350	7450
22	5	GLASTRON 22	OP	B/R	FBG	SV	IO	275-300			8	3100	4	6	7100	8200
22	5	GLASTRON 22	OP	B/R	FBG	SV	IO	330	VLVO	8	2	3100	4	6	7850	9000
23	5	GLASTRON 23	OP	CUD	FBG	SV	IO	230-300		8	4	3450	4	11	7800	9650
23	5	GLASTRON 23	OP	CUD	FBG	SV	IO	330-360		8	4	3450	4	11	9400	10800
		1990 BOATS														
16	8	CARLSON 16CSS	OP	RNBT	FBG	SV	OB			6	6	750	2	4	1050	1300
16	8	SIERRA 175SS	OP	RNBT	FBG	SV	IO	125		7	2	1900	2	8	3250	3750
17	9	FUTURA 185SS	OP	RNBT	FBG	SV	IO	125		7	2	2025	2	8	3550	4100
18	2	CARLSON 18CSS	OP	RNBT	FBG	SV	OB			7	7	1500	2	6	2000	2400
19	1	SIERRA 195SS	OP	RNBT	FBG	SV	IO	125		7	3	1925	2	7	3800	4400
19	3	CARLSON 19CSS	OP	RNBT	FBG	SV	IO	200		7	2	2800	2	8	4650	5350
19	10	FUTURA 205SS	OP	RNBT	FBG	SV	IO	200		8		2850	2	10	5150	5950
19	10	SIERRA 199CC	OP	RNBT	FBG	SV	IO	125		7	10	2375	2	9	4600	5250
20	1	VENTURA 209	OP	CUD	FBG	SV	IO	200		8	6	4000	2	10	6850	7850
21	6	FUTURA 227SL	OP	RNBT	FBG	SV	IO	260		8		2875	2	10	5700	6550
22	7	FUTURA 237SL	OP	RNBT	FBG	SV	IO	260		8		3275	2	9	6450	7450
23	4	CARLSON 23CSS	OP	RNBT	FBG	SV	IO	200		7	7	2725	2	6	5700	6550
24	7	VENTURA 249	OP	CUD	FBG	SV	IO	200		9	5	6600	2	10	12800	14600
27	10	CARLSON 28CSS	OP	RNBT	FBG	DV	IO	T270		8	6	6900	3	2	15700	17800
32	9	CARLSON 33CSS	OP	OFF	FBG	DV	IO	T330		8	6	7800	3	2	29200	32400
		1989 BOATS														
16	2	SIERRA 160		RNBT	FBG	SV	OB			7	8	750			1000	1200
16	4	SIERRA 165SS		RNBT	FBG	SV	IO	130-146		6	8	1475			2550	3200
16	8	CARLSON 16CSS		RNBT	FBG	SV	OB			6	5	750			1050	1200
16	10	FUTURA 170		RNBT	FBG	SV	OB			7	3	1250			1600	1950
16	10	FUTURA 175SL		RNBT	FBG	SV	IO	130-175		7	3	1925			3150	3850
16	10	FUTURA 175SL		RNBT	FBG	SV	IO	205	VLVO	7	3	1925			3400	3950
16	10	FUTURA 175SS		RNBT	FBG	SV	IO	130-175		7	3	1925			3100	3800
16	10	FUTURA 175SS		RNBT	FBG	SV	IO	205	VLVO	7	3	1925			3350	3900
16	10	FUTURA 177SL		RNBT	FBG	SV	IO	130-175		7	3	1925			3150	3850
16	10	FUTURA 177SL		RNBT	FBG	SV	IO	205	VLVO	7	3	1925			3400	3950
17	1	SIERRA 170		RNBT	FBG	SV	OB			7	4	1200			1550	1850
17	2	SIERRA 175SL		RNBT	FBG	SV	IO	130-175		7	4	1875			3200	3950
17	2	SIERRA 175SL		RNBT	FBG	SV	IO	205	VLVO	7	4	1875			3500	4050
17	2	SIERRA 175SS		RNBT	FBG	SV	IO	130-175		7	4	1875			3150	3850
17	2	SIERRA 175SS		RNBT	FBG	SV	IO	205	VLVO	7	4	1875			3400	3950
17	2	SIERRA 177SL		RNBT	FBG	SV	IO	130-175							3300	4050
17	2	SIERRA 177SL		RNBT	FBG	SV	IO	205	VLVO						3600	4150
17	9	FUTURA 180		RNBT	FBG	SV	OB			7	3	1350			1750	2100
17	9	FUTURA 185SL		RNBT	FBG	SV	IO	130-175		7	3	2025			3400	4150
17	9	FUTURA 185SL		RNBT	FBG	SV	IO	205	VLVO	7	3	2025			3650	4250
17	9	FUTURA 185SS		RNBT	FBG	SV	IO	130-175		7	3	2025			3350	4100
17	9	FUTURA 185SS		RNBT	FBG	SV	IO	205	VLVO	7	3	2025			3600	4200
17	9	FUTURA 187SL		RNBT	FBG	SV	IO	130-175		7	3	2025			3400	4150
17	9	FUTURA 187SL		RNBT	FBG	SV	IO	205	VLVO	7	3	2025			3650	4250
18	11	SIERRA 199CC		RNBT	FBG	SV	IO	130-200		7	3	2080			3650	4450
18	11	SIERRA 199CC		RNBT	FBG	SV	IO	205-209		7	3	2080			3950	4600
19	1	SIERRA 195SL		RNBT	FBG	SV	IO	130-205		7	4	1975			3650	4600
19	1	SIERRA 195SL		RNBT	FBG	SV	IO	209	VLVO	7	4	1975			3950	4600
19	1	SIERRA 195SS		RNBT	FBG	SV	IO	130-200		7	4	1975			3600	4400
19	1	SIERRA 195SS		RNBT	FBG	SV	IO	205-209		7	4	1975			3900	4500
19	4	CARLSON 19CSS		RNBT	FBG	SV	IO	200-270		7	2	2675			4300	5350
19	4	CARLSON 19CSS		RNBT	FBG	SV	IO	275	VLVO	7	2	2675			4950	5650
19	11	FUTURA 200		RNBT	FBG	SV	OB			8		1900			2500	2900
19	11	FUTURA 205SL		RNBT	FBG	SV	IO	200-270		8		2850			4900	6000
19	11	FUTURA 205SL		RNBT	FBG	SV	IO	275	VLVO	8		2850			5550	6350
19	11	FUTURA 205SS		RNBT	FBG	SV	IO	200-270		8		2850			4800	5900
19	11	FUTURA 205SS		RNBT	FBG	SV	IO	275	VLVO	8		2850			5450	6250
19	11	FUTURA 207SL		RNBT	FBG	SV	IO	200-270		8		2850			4900	6000
19	11	FUTURA 207SL		RNBT	FBG	SV	IO	275	VLVO	8		2850			5550	6350
20	11	FUTURA 219CC		CUD	FBG	SV	IO	200-270		8		3350			5800	7000
20	11	FUTURA 219CC		CUD	FBG	SV	IO	275	VLVO	8		3350			6400	7400
21	6	FUTURA 225SL		RNBT	FBG	SV	IO	229-275		8		2925			5550	6750
21	6	FUTURA 225SL		RNBT	FBG	SV	IO	330	MRCR	8		2925			6150	7100
21	6	FUTURA 225SS		RNBT	FBG	SV	IO	229-275		8		2925			5450	6600
21	6	FUTURA 227SL		RNBT	FBG	SV	IO	229-275		8		2875			5450	6600
21	6	FUTURA 227SL		RNBT	FBG	SV	IO	330	MRCR	8		2875			6100	7000
22	8	FUTURA 235SL		RNBT	FBG	SV	IO	229-275		8		3275			5900	7100
22	8	FUTURA 235SL		RNBT	FBG	SV	IO	330	MRCR	8		3275			6550	7550
22	8	FUTURA 237SL		RNBT	FBG	SV	IO	229-275		8		3275			6450	7800
22	8	FUTURA 237SL		RNBT	FBG	SV	IO	330	MRCR	8		3275			7150	8200
23	4	FUTURA 239CC		CUD	FBG	SV	IO	229-275		8		3625			7250	8700
23	5	CARLSON 23CSS		RNBT	FBG	SV	IO	200-270		7	10	2725			5450	6600
23	5	CARLSON 23CSS		RNBT	FBG	SV	IO	275	VLVO	7	10	2725			6050	6950
		1986 BOATS														
16	2	HPV-165	OP	BASS	FBG	SV	OB			6	7	950			1100	1300
16	8	CVX16	OP	RACE	FBG	SV	OB			6	7	720			845	1000
17	1	SSV-176	ST	RNBT	FBG	SV	OB			6	11	955			1150	1400
17	1	SSV-178	ST	FSH	FBG	SV	OB			6	11	955			1150	1350
17	1	SSV-178	ST	RNBT	FBG	SV	IO	140-190		6	11	1100			2200	2600
17	6	SX180	ST	RNBT	FBG	SV	IO	170-230		7		1200			2350	2850
17	6	SX180	ST	RNBT	FBG	SV	IO	260		7		1200			2600	3050
17	7	CVX17	OP	RACE	FBG	SV	OB			6	6	875			1100	1300
17	10	HPV-175	OP	BASS	FBG	DV	OB			7	7	1115			1350	1600
18	1	CVX18	OP	RACE	FBG	SV	IO	200-230		7	8	950			2500	3000
18	1	CVX18	OP	RACE	FBG	SV	IO	260		7	8	950			2700	3150
18	8	SX-190	ST	RNBT	FBG	SV	IO	170-230		7	4	1250			2700	3300

 CONTINUED ON NEXT PAGE

LOA FT	LOA IN	NAME AND/ OR MODEL	TOP/ RIG	BOAT TYPE	HULL MTL	HULL TP	ENGINE TP	# HP	MFG	BEAM FT	BEAM IN	WGT LBS	DRAFT FT IN	RETAIL LOW	RETAIL HIGH
		1986 BOATS													
18	8	SX-190	ST	RNBT	FBG	SV	IO	260		7	4	1250		2950	3450
18	8	X-19	ST	RNBT	FBG	SV	IO	170-230		7	4	1230		2700	3300
18	8	X-19	ST	RNBT	FBG	SV	IO	260		7	4	1230		2950	3450
18	11	V195	ST	RNBT	FBG	SV	IO	170-230		7	3	1360		2750	3350
18	11	V195	ST	RNBT	FBG	SV	IO	260		7	3	1360		3050	3550
20	3	CVX-20	OP	RACE	FBG	DV	OB			7	6	1050		1550	1850
20	3	CVX-20	OP	SKI	FBG	DV	OB			7	6	1050		1550	1850
20	4	INTIMIDATOR CVX-20	OP	RACE	FBG	DV	IO	260		7	4	1400		3200	3700
20	7	V-219	ST	OPFSH	FBG	DV	IO	170-260		8		2030		3900	4850
23	4	V-232	ST	CUD	FBG	DV	IO	190-260		8		2500		4750	5750
23	4	V-233	ST	CUD	FBG	DV	IO	190-260		8		2650		4900	5900
24	4	V-243	ST	FSH	FBG	DV	OB			8		2650		3850	4450
24	4	V-243	ST	SF	FBG	DV	OB			8		2650		3850	4450
		1985 BOATS													
16	2	HPV-160	OP	BASS	FBG	SV	OB			6	7	950		1050	1250
16	2	HPV-165	OP	BASS	FBG	SV	OB			6	7	950		1100	1300
16	2	SSV-167	ST	RNBT	FBG	SV	OB			6	7	860		985	1200
16	8	CVX16	OP	RACE	FBG	SV	OB			6	7	720		810	975
17		SSV-176	ST	RNBT	FBG	SV	OB			6	11	955		1100	1350
17	1	SSV-177	ST	RNBT	FBG	SV	IO	140-190		6	11	1100		2050	2500
17	1	SSV-178	ST	FSH	FBG	SV	OB			6	11	955		1100	1300
17	6	SX180	ST	RNBT	FBG	SV	IO	170-230		7		1200		2300	2750
17	6	SX180	ST	RNBT	FBG	SV	IO	260		7		1200		2500	2900
17	7	CVX17	OP	RACE	FBG	SV	OB			6	6	875		1050	1250
17	10	HPV-175	OP	BASS	FBG	DV	OB			7	7	1115		1300	1550
18	2	CVX18	OP	RACE	FBG	SV	IO	200-230		7	8	950		2450	2900
18	2	CVX18	OP	RACE	FBG	SV	IO	260		7	8	950		2650	3050
18	8	SSV-194	ST	RNBT	FBG	SV	IO	170-230		7	4	1230		2600	3150
18	8	SSV-194	ST	RNBT	FBG	SV	IO	260		7	4	1230		2850	3300
18	8	SX-190	ST	RNBT	FBG	SV	IO	170-230		7	4	1250		2600	3150
18	8	SX-190	ST	RNBT	FBG	SV	IO	260		7	4	1250		2850	3300
18	9	V-192	ST	RNBT	FBG	DV	OB			7	3	1330		1550	1850
18	11	V195	ST	RNBT	FBG	SV	IO	170-230		7	3	1360		2650	3250
18	11	V195	ST	RNBT	FBG	SV	IO	260		7	3	1360		2900	3400
20	3	SKI-MACHINE	OP	SKI	FBG	DV	OB			7	6	1050		1500	1750
20	3	SPRINT	OP	RACE	FBG	DV	OB			7	6	1050		1500	1800
20	4	INTIMIDATOR CVX-20	OP	RACE	FBG	DV	IO	260		7	4	1400		3050	3550
20	7	SEA-FURY V-216	ST	OPFSH	FBG	DV	OB			8		2030		2550	3000
20	7	V-219	ST	OPFSH	FBG	DV	IO	170-260		8		2030		3750	4650
23	4	V-232	ST	CUD	FBG	DV	IO	190-260		8		2500		4600	5500
23	4	V-233	ST	CUD	FBG	DV	IO	190-260		8		2650		4700	5650
24	4	V-243	ST	FSH	FBG	DV	OB			8		2650		3700	4300
24	4	V-243	ST	SF	FBG	DV	OB			8		2650		3700	4300
		1984 BOATS													
16	2	HPV-165	OP	BASS	FBG	SV	OB			6	7	950		1050	1250
16	2	SSV-167	ST	RNBT	FBG	SV	OB			6	7	860		970	1150
16	4	SSV-168	OP	RNBT	FBG	SV	IO	120-140		6	7	880		1600	1950
16	4	SSV-168	ST	RNBT	FBG	SV	IO	120	MRCR	6	7	880		1650	1950
16	8	CVX16	OP	RACE	FBG	SV	OB					720		785	945
17	1	SSV-176	ST	RNBT	FBG	SV	OB			6	11	955		1100	1300
17	1	SSV-177	ST	RNBT	FBG	SV	IO	140-188		6	11	1100		2000	2400
17	1	SSV-178	ST	FSH	FBG	SV	OB			6	11			1400	1650
17	6	SX180	ST	RNBT	FBG	SV	IO	170-228		7		1200		2200	2700
17	6	SX180	ST	RNBT	FBG	SV	IO	260		7		1200		2400	2800
17	7	CVX17	OP	RACE	FBG	SV	OB			6	6	875		1000	1200
17	10	HPV-175	OP	BASS	FBG	DV	OB			7	7	1115		1250	1500
18	2	CVX 18	OP	RACE	FBG	SV	IO	198-228		7	8	950		2350	2800
18	2	CVX 18	OP	RACE	FBG	SV	IO	260	OMC	7	8	950		2550	2950
18	2	CVX18	OP	RACE	FBG	SV	IO	260	MRCR	7	8	950		2550	2950
18	8	SSV-194	ST	RNBT	FBG	SV	IO	170-228		7	4	1230		2500	3050
18	8	SSV-194	ST	RNBT	FBG	SV	IO	260		7	4	1230		2750	3200
18	8	SX-190	ST	RNBT	FBG	SV	IO	170-228		7	4	1250		2500	3050
18	8	SX-190	ST	RNBT	FBG	SV	IO	260		7	4	1250		2750	3200
18	8	V197	ST	CUD	FBG	SV	IO	140-188				1200		2600	3050
18	9	V-192	ST	RNBT	FBG	DV	OB			7	3	1330		1500	1750
18	10	V195	ST	RNBT	FBG	SV	IO	170-228				1360		2650	3200
18	10	V195	ST	RNBT	FBG	SV	IO	260	MRCR			1360		2900	3350
20	3	SKI-MACHINE	OP	SKI	FBG	DV	OB			7	6	1050		1450	1700
20	3	SPRINT	OP	RACE	FBG	DV	OB			7	6	1050		1450	1750
20	4	INTIMIDATOR CVX-20	OP	RACE	FBG	DV	IO	260		7	4	1400		2950	3450
20	7	SEA-FURY V-216	ST	OPFSH	FBG	DV	OB			8		2030		2500	2900
20	7	V-219	ST	OPFSH	FBG	DV	IO	188-260		8		2030		3650	4500
23	1	SCIMITAR	HT	RNBT	FBG	DV	IO	260		7	7	1850		3800	4400
23	5	CV-23	OP	RACE	FBG	DV	IO	260		7	8	1400		3800	4400
24	4	V-243	ST	SF	FBG	DV	OB			8		2650		3600	4150
24	4	V-243	ST	SF	FBG	DV	IB	270		8				7300	8400

....For earlier years, see the BUC Used Boat Price Guide, Volume 3

GLASWAY INC

TUFFY BOATS
LAKE MILLS WI 53551 COAST GUARD MFG ID- TUF

See inside cover to adjust price for area

LOA FT	LOA IN	NAME AND/ OR MODEL	TOP/ RIG	BOAT TYPE	HULL MTL	HULL TP	ENGINE TP	# HP	MFG	BEAM FT	BEAM IN	WGT LBS	DRAFT FT IN	RETAIL LOW	RETAIL HIGH
		1986 BOATS													
16	5	MUSKIE RAMPAGE		FSH	FBG	DV	OB			6	2	790		2050	2400
16	5	TUFFY 160		FSH	FBG	DV	OB			6	2	740		1900	2250
16	5	TUFFY 160 XT		FSH	FBG	DV	OB			6	2	700		1800	2150
16	9	BASS-N-MARAUDER		FSH	FBG	SV	OB			5	10	790		2050	2450
16	9	ESOX		FSH	FBG	DV	OB			5	10	740		2000	2400
16	9	ESOX LTD		FSH	FBG	DV	OB			5	10	700		1900	2300
16	9	MARAUDER SPORTSMAN		FSH	FBG	SV	OB			5	10	740		1850	2250
18		PIKE RAMPAGE		FSH	FBG	DV	OB			6	3	860		2350	2750
18		TUFFY 180		FSH	FBG	DV	OB			6	3	820		2300	2650
18		TUFFY 180 XT		FSH	FBG	DV	OB			6	3	780		2200	2550
		1985 BOATS													
16	5	MUSKIE RAMPAGE	OP	BASS	FBG	DV	OB			6	2	850		2200	2550
16	5	RAMPAGE 160 SPORTSMA	OP	FSH	FBG	DV	OB			6	2	750		1900	2250
16	5	RAMPAGE 160 XT	OP	FSH	FBG	DV	OB			6	2	700		1750	2100
16	9	BASS-N-MARAUDER	OP	BASS	FBG	SV	OB			5	10	850		2200	2550
16	9	MARAUDER	OP	FSH	FBG	SV	OB			5	10	700		1800	2150
16	9	MARAUDER SPORTSMAN	OP	FSH	FBG	SV	OB			5	10	750		1900	2300
18	1	PIKE RAMPAGE	OP	BASS	FBG	DV	OB			6	3	1000		2650	3050
18	1	RAMPAGE 180 SPORTSMA	OP	FSH	FBG	DV	OB			6	3	900		2400	2800
18	1	RAMPAGE 180 XT	OP	FSH	FBG	DV	OB			6	3	850		2300	2700

....For earlier years, see the BUC Used Boat Price Guide, Volume 3

GLOBAL MOTORBOAT CORP

COLUMBIA SC 29240-4185

See inside cover to adjust price for area

LOA FT	LOA IN	NAME AND/ OR MODEL	TOP/ RIG	BOAT TYPE	HULL MTL	HULL TP	ENGINE TP	# HP	MFG	BEAM FT	BEAM IN	WGT LBS	DRAFT FT IN	RETAIL LOW	RETAIL HIGH
		1993 BOATS													
18	8	GMC 198 WA	OP	B/R	FBG	DV	IO	115	MRCR	7	10	1575		3550	4100
18	9	GMC 190	OP	CUD	FBG	DV	IO	115-164		7	8	2200		4300	5250
18	9	GMC 195	OP	B/R	FBG	DV	IO	115-164		7	8	2150		4100	4900
20	5	GMC 215	OP	B/R	FBG	DV	IO	115-235		8	2	2400		4650	5800
20	5	GMC 215	OP	B/R	FBG	DV	IO	245-250		8	2	2400		5150	5900
20	5	GMC 215	OP	CUD	FBG	DV	IO	115-250		8	2	2700		5300	6550
20	5	GMC 215 SPORT	OP	RNBT	FBG	DV	IO	115-235		8	2	2700		5050	6250
20	5	GMC 215 SPORT	OP	RNBT	FBG	DV	IO	245-250		8	2	2700		5550	6400
21	10	GMC 228 DC	OP	CUD	FBG	SV	IO	115-235		8		2435		5300	6600
21	10	GMC 228 DC	OP	CUD	FBG	SV	IO	245-250		8		2435		5850	6700
21	10	GMC 228 WA	OP	CUD	FBG	SV	IO	115-235		8		2435		5400	6650
21	10	GMC 228 WA	OP	CUD	FBG	SV	IO	245-250		8		2435		5900	6800
22	1	WINNER 2280 130ME	OP	CUD	FBG	SV	IO	115-235		8		2485		5500	6750
22	1	WINNER 2280 130ME	OP	CUD	FBG	SV	IO	245-250		8		2485		6000	6900
22	6	GMC 225	OP	CUD	FBG	DV	IO	115-250		7	8	2750		5800	7250
22	6	GMC 225 WE	OP	CUD	FBG	DV	IO	115-250		7	10	2700		5800	7250
22	6	GMC 233 SPORT	OP	CUD	FBG	DV	IO	115-250		8	2	2900		6150	7650
22	6	GMC 233 SPORT	OP	CUD	FBG	DV	IO	300		8	2	2900		6900	8300
22	6	GMC 235 SPORT	OP	RNBT	FBG	DV	IO	115-250		8	2	2900		5800	7250
22	6	GMC 235 SPORT	OP	RNBT	FBG	DV	IO	300		8	2	2900		6500	7850
22	6	GMC 235 SPORT	OP	RNBT	FBG	DV	IO	350	MRCR	8	2	2900		7250	8350
22	9	GMC 230	OP	B/R	FBG	DV	IO	115-250		7	8	2650		5400	6750
24		GMC 258 WA	OP	CUD	FBG	SV	IO	115-250		8	4	3850		8050	9850
24		GMC 258 WA	OP	CUD	FBG	SV	IO	300-350		8	4	3850		8900	11000
24	1	BROUGHAM 2480	OP	CUD	FBG	DV	IO	245	VLVO	8	6	3995		8950	10200
24	1	BROUGHAM 2480	OP	CUD	FBG	SV	IO	115-250		8	6	3995		8300	10000
24	1	BROUGHAM 2480	OP	CUD	FBG	SV	IO	300		8	6	3995		9200	10800
24	1	WINNER 2480 WA/SP	OP	CUD	FBG	SV	IO	115-250		8	6	2995		6900	8550
24	1	WINNER 2480 WA/SP	OP	CUD	FBG	SV	IO	300		8	6	2995		7650	8800
26		GMC 263 SPORT	OP	CUD	FBG	DV	IO	T115-T164		8	2	3500		9700	12000
26		GMC 263 SPORT	OP	CUD	FBG	DV	IO	T180-T250		8	2	3500		10500	13100
26		GMC 263 SPORT	OP	CUD	FBG	DV	IO	T300		8	2	3500		11900	14000

CONTINUED ON NEXT PAGE

LOA FT IN	NAME AND/ OR MODEL	TOP/ RIG	BOAT TYPE	HULL MTL TP	TP	# HP	MFG	BEAM FT IN	WGT LBS	DRAFT FT IN	RETAIL LOW	RETAIL HIGH
					1993 BOATS							
26	GMC 265 SPORT	OP	CUD	FBG DV	IO	T115-T187		8 2	3500		9600	12000
26	GMC 265 SPORT	OP	CUD	FBG DV	IO	T190-T250		8 2	3500		10600	13000
26	GMC 265 SPORT	OP	CUD	FBG DV	IO	T300		8 2	3500		11800	13900
27 6	SUNCRUISER 280	OP	SPTCR	FBG DV	IO	115-206		8 6	5600		11800	14600
27 6	SUNCRUISER 280	OP	SPTCR	FBG DV	IO	225-300		8 6	5600		13100	15900
27 6	SUNCRUISER 280	OP	SPTCR	FBG DV	IO	350-390		8 6	5600		14500	17300
					1992 BOATS							
16	DC SEA PUP 160	OP	JON	FBG SV	OB			5 5	550		1400	1650
16 5	ALPHA II	OP	BASS	FBG SV	OB			6 8	630		1700	2050
16 5	ALPHA III	OP	BASS	FBG SV	OB			6 8	630		1700	2050
16 5	TOURNAMENT 1690	OP	BASS	FBG SV	OB			6 8	700		1900	2250
16 5	TOURNAMENT 1790	OP	BASS	FBG SV	OB			7 1	800		2200	2550
18	SKI 1850	OP	RNBT	FBG SV	OB			7 5	1000		2800	3250
18 1	CENTER CONSOLE 188	OP	CTRCN	FBG SV	OB			6 11	1400		3700	4300
18 3	FISH & SKI 1830	OP	CTRCN	FBG SV	OB			7 10	1900		4550	5250
18		OP	RNBT	FBG SV	OB			7 5	1000		2850	3300
18 9	GMC 190	OP	B/R	FBG DV	IO	135-175		7 8	2150		3650	4500
18 9	GMC 190	OP	CUD	FBG DV	IO	135-175		7 8	2200		4000	4950
18 9	GMC 195	OP	CUD	FBG DV	IO	135-175		7 8	2150		3750	4600
20 5	GMC 215	OP	B/R	FBG DV	IO	135-250		8 2	2400		4400	5450
20 5	GMC 215	OP	CUD	FBG DV	IO	135-250		8 2	2700		4950	6150
20 5	GMC 215 SPORT	OP	RNBT	FBG DV	IO	135-250		8 2	2700		4750	5850
21 10	GMC 228 DC	OP	CUD	FBG DV	IO	135-250		8	2435		4950	6150
21 10	GMC 228 DC	OP	CUD	FBG SV	IO	275	VLVO	8	7435		5650	6500
21 10	GMC 228 WA	OP	CUD	FBG SV	IO	135-250		8	2435		5100	6300
21 10	GMC 228 WA	OP	CUD	FBG SV	IO	275	VLVO	8	2435		5800	6650
22 1	WINNER 2280 130ME	OP	CUD	FBG DV	IO	135-250		8	2485		5150	6350
22 1	WINNER 2280 130ME	OP	CUD	FBG SV	IO	275	VLVO	8	2485		5850	6750
22 1	WINNER 2280 FT/WA	OP	CUD	FBG SV	OB			8	2485		6350	7300
22 6	GMC 225	OP	CUD	FBG DV	IO	135-250		7 8	2750		5450	6700
22 6	GMC 225 SPORT	OP	RNBT	FBG DV	IO	135-250		7 10	2900		5150	6300
22 6	GMC 235	OP	RNBT	FBG DV	IO	135-250		8 2	2900		5450	6700
22 6	GMC 235 SPORT	OP	RNBT	FBG DV	IO	275-300		8 2	2900		6100	7050
22 6	GMC 235 SPORT	OP	RNBT	FBG DV	IO	330-350		8 2	2900		6850	7900
22 6	TARGA 23	OP	CUD	FBG DV	IO	135-250		8 2	2900		5750	7050
22 6	TARGA 23	OP	CUD	FBG DV	IO	275-300		8 2	2900		6500	7450
22 6	TARGA 23	OP	CUD	FBG DV	IO	330-350		8 2	2900		7250	8350
22 9	GMC 230	OP	B/R	FBG DV	IO	135-250		7 8	2650		5050	6250
24	GMC 258 WA	OP	CUD	FBG SV	IO	135-175		8 4	3850		7550	9100
24	GMC 258 WA	OP	CUD	FBG SV	IO	275-350		8 4	3850		8250	9500
24	GMC 258 WA	OP	CUD	FBG SV	IO	330-350		8 4	3850		9150	10400
24 1	BROUGHAM 2480	OP	CUD	FBG SV	IO	135-250		8 6	2995		6450	7850
24 1	BROUGHAM 2480	OP	CUD	FBG SV	IO	275-300		8 6	2995		7150	8250
24 1	WINNER 2480 FT/WA	OP	CUD	FBG SV	OB			8 6	2995		8400	9650
24 1	WINNER 2480 WA/SP	OP	CUD	FBG SV	OB			8 6	2995		7650	8750
24 1	WINNER 2480 WA/SP	OP	CUD	FBG SV	IO	135-250		8 6	2995		6450	7900
24 1	WINNER 2480 WA/SP	OP	CUD	FBG SV	IO	275-300		8 6	2995		7200	8300
26	GMC 265 SPORT	OP	CUD	FBG DV	IO	T135-T205		8 2	3500		9200	11500
	IO T210-T275	10300	12400,	IO T330-T350		11300	13900,	IO T390	MRCR		13200	15000
26	TARGA 26	OP	CUD	FBG DV	IO	T135-T180		8 2	3500		9400	11400
26	TARGA 26	OP	CUD	FBG DV	IO	T205-T300		8 2	3500		10400	12800
26	TARGA 26	OP	CUD	FBG DV	IO	T330-T390		8 2	3500		12500	15300

GLOUCESTER YACHTS INC
GLOUCESTER VA 23061   COAST GUARD MFG ID- GYI   See inside cover to adjust price for area

LOA FT IN	NAME AND/ OR MODEL	TOP/ RIG	BOAT TYPE	HULL MTL TP	TP	# HP	MFG	BEAM FT IN	WGT LBS	DRAFT FT IN	RETAIL LOW	RETAIL HIGH
					1988 BOATS							
21 8	GLOUCESTER 22	SLP	SA/CR	FBG KC	OB			8	2400	1 8	4500	5200
					1987 BOATS							
19 3	GLOUCESTER 19 SHOAL	SLP	SA/CR	FBG KL	OB			7 6	1600	1 11	3100	3600
19 6	GLOUCESTER 20 SHOAL	SLP	SA/CR	FBG KL	OB			7 6	1600	1 11	3100	3600
21 4	CHESAPEAKE 22	OP	CTRCN	FBG DV	OB			8	1700	1 4	4100	4750
21 8	GLOUCESTER 22	SLP	SA/CR	FBG KC	OB			8	2400	1 8	4200	4850
					1986 BOATS							
18	BUCCANEER 18	SLP	SA/OD	FBG CB	OB			6	500	7	1600	1900
18	GLOUCESTER 18	SLP	SA/OD	FBG CB	OB			6	500	7	1600	1900
19 3	GLOUCESTER 19	SLP	SA/OD	FBG KC				7 6	1550	1	2800	3250
19 6	GLOUCESTER 20	SLP	SA/OD	FBG KC				7 6	1600	1	2850	3300
21 8	GLOUCESTER 22	SLP	SA/OD	FBG KC				8	2400	1 8	3800	4450
					1985 BOATS							
18	BUCCANEER 18	SLP	SA/OD	FBG CB	OB			6	500	7	1500	1750
19 3	GLOUCESTER 19	SLP	SA/CR	FBG KC	OB			7 6	1550	1	2700	3150
19 3	GLOUCESTER 19 SHOAL	SLP	SA/CR	FBG KL	OB			7 6	1600	1 11	2750	3200
19 6	GLOUCESTER 20	SLP	SA/CR	FBG KC	OB			7 6	1600	1	2850	3300
19 6	GLOUCESTER 20 SHOAL	SLP	SA/CR	FBG KL	OB			7 6	1600	1 11	2700	3100
21 8	GLOUCESTER 22	SLP	SA/CR	FBG KC	OB			8	2400	1 8	3700	4300
					1984 BOATS							
18	GLOUCESTER 18	SLP	SAIL	FBG CB				6 7	750	8	1650	1950
19 3	GLOUCESTER 19	SLP	SA/CR	FBG KC	OB			7 6	1550	1	2550	2950
19 3	GLOUCESTER 19 SHOAL	SLP	SA/CR	FBG KL	OB			7 6	1700	1 11	2600	3100
19 6	GLOUCESTER 20	SLP	SA/CR	FBG KC	OB			7 6	1600	1	2600	3000
19 6	GLOUCESTER 20 SHOAL	SLP	SA/CR	FBG KL	OB			7 6	1700	1 11	2700	3100
21 8	GLOUCESTER 22	SLP	SA/CR	FBG KC	OB			8	2300	1 8	3350	3900
26 8	GLOUCESTER 27	SLP	SA/CR	F/S KL				8	5500	3 8	8200	9450

....For earlier years, see the BUC Used Boat Price Guide, Volume 3

GODFREY MARINE
AQUA-PATIO HURRICANE & SANPAN   See inside cover to adjust price for area
ELKHART IN 46516   COAST GUARD MFG ID- GDY
FORMERLY GODFREY CONVEYOR COMPANY

For more recent years, see the BUC Used Boat Price Guide, Volume 1

LOA FT IN	NAME AND/ OR MODEL	TOP/ RIG	BOAT TYPE	HULL MTL TP	TP	# HP	MFG	BEAM FT IN	WGT LBS	DRAFT FT IN	RETAIL LOW	RETAIL HIGH
					1996 BOATS							
18 9	SUNDECK 185	OP	RNBT	FBG SV	IO	130-175		7 5	2585		7350	8550
20 8	SUNDECK 205	OP	RNBT	FBG SV	IB	175-235		8	2980		11900	13600
					1995 BOATS							
18 9	SUNDECK 185	OP	RNBT	FBG SV	IO	130-175		7 5	2585		6850	7950
20 8	SUNDECK 205	OP	RNBT	FBG SV	IB	175-235		8	2980		11300	12800
					1994 BOATS							
18 9	SUNDECK 185	OP	RNBT	FBG SV	IO	130-175		7 5	2585		6400	7450
20 8	SUNDECK 205	OP	RNBT	FBG SV	IB	175-235		8	2980		10700	12100
					1993 BOATS							
18 9	SUNDECK 185	OP	RNBT	FBG SV	IO	130-175		7 5	2585		6000	6950
20 8	SUNDECK 205	OP	RNBT	FBG SV	IB	175-235		8	2980		10100	11500
					1992 BOATS							
18 9	SUNDECK 185	OP	RNBT	FBG SV	IB	120-175		7 5	2585		7150	8750
20 8	SUNDECK 205	OP	RNBT	FBG SV	IB	175-235		8	2980		9600	10900
					1991 BOATS							
17 1	SUNDECK 176	OP	RNBT	FBG SV	OB			7 2	1670		2750	3200
18 9	SUNDECK 185	OP	RNBT	FBG SV	IB	120-175		7 5	2585		6800	8300
20 8	SUNDECK 205	OP	RNBT	FBG SV	IB	175-235		8	2980		9200	10400
21 10	SUNDECK 2200	OP	RNBT	FBG SV	IO	235-260		8	2375		6450	7600
					1990 BOATS							
16 8	CARLSON 16 CSS	OP	RNBT	FBG SV	OB			6 6	750	2 4	1350	1600
16 8	SIERRA 175 SS	OP	RNBT	FBG SV	OB	125		7 2	1900	2 8	3650	4250
17 1	SUNDECK 176	OP	RNBT	FBG SV	OB			7 2	1670		2650	3100
17 9	FUTURA 185SS	OP	RNBT	FBG SV	OB	125		7 2	2025	2 8	4050	4700
18 2	CARLSON 18CSS	OP	RNBT	FBG SV	OB			7 2	1500	2 6	2550	2950
18 9	SUNDECK 185	OP	RNBT	FBG SV	IO	130-175		7 5	2585		6550	7600
18 10	SUNDECK 196	OP	RNBT	FBG TR	IO	130-235		7 7	2825		5250	6300
19 1	SIERRA 19SS	OP	RNBT	FBG SV	IO	125		7 2	1925	2 7	4250	4950
19 3	CARLSON 19CSS	OP	RNBT	FBG SV	IO	200		7 2	2800	2 8	5300	6100
19 10	FUTURA 205SS	OP	RNBT	FBG SV	IO	200		8	2850	2 10	5850	6750
19 10	SIERRA 199SS	OP	RNBT	FBG SV	IO	125		7 10	2375	2 9	5200	5950
20 1	VENTURA 209	OP	CUD	FBG SV	IO	200		8 6	4000	2 10	8100	9300
20 8	SUNDECK 205	OP	RNBT	FBG SV	IB	175-235		8	2890		8500	9900
21 6	FUTURA 227SL	OP	RNBT	FBG SV	IO	260		8	2875	2 10	6750	7750
21 10	SUNDECK 2200	OP	RNBT	FBG SV	IO	235-260		8	2375		6050	7150
22 7	FUTURA 237SL	OP	RNBT	FBG SV	IO	260		8	3275	2 9	7650	8800
23 4	CARLSON 23CSS	OP	RNBT	FBG SV	IO	200		7 7	2725	2 6	6750	7750
24 7	VENTURA 249	OP	CUD	FBG SV	IO	260		8 6	6600	2 10	15200	17700
27 10	CARLSON 28CSS	OP	RNBT	FBG DV	IO	T270		8	5500	3 2	19000	21100
32 9	CARLSON 32SS	OP	RNBT	FBG DV	IO	T330		8	7800	3 2	36500	40600
					1989 BOATS							
17 1	CYPRUS SD176	OP	RNBT	FBG TR	OB			7 2	1070		1800	2150
17 1	CYPRUS SD176	OP	RNBT	FBG TR	OB	128-175		7 2	2070		3650	4300
17 1	FREEDOM	OP	RNBT	FBG TR	OB			8	1670		2550	3000
17 1	FREEDOM	OP	RNBT	FBG TR	IO	128		8	2450		4350	5050
18 10	CYPRUS SD196	OP	RNBT	FBG TR	IO	130-235		7 6	2500		4650	5500
18 10	GENEVA SD196	OP	RNBT	FBG TR	IO	130-235		8	2825		4950	5900
22	SUNDECK 2200	OP	RNBT	FBG TR	IO	200		8	2375		5700	6500

LOA FT	LOA IN	NAME AND/ OR MODEL	TOP/ RIG	BOAT TYPE	-HULL- MTL	-HULL- TP	ENGINE TP	ENGINE # HP	ENGINE MFG	BEAM FT	BEAM IN	WGT LBS	DRAFT FT	DRAFT IN	RETAIL LOW	RETAIL HIGH
		1988 BOATS														
17	1	CYPRUS SD176	OP	RNBT	FBG	TR	OB			7	2	1070			1750	2050
17	1	CYPRUS SD176	OP	RNBT	FBG	TR	IO	128-175		7	2	2070			3450	4100
18	10	CYPRUS SD196	OP	RNBT	FBG	TR	IO	130-230		7	6	2500			4400	5300
18	10	GENEVA SD196	OP	RNBT	FBG	TR	IO	130-230		7	6	2825			4700	5600
		1987 BOATS														
17	1	CYPRUS SD176	OP	RNBT	FBG	TR	OB			7	2	1070			1700	2000
17	1	CYPRUS SD176	OP	RNBT	FBG	TR	IO	120-175		7	2	2070			3350	3900
18	10	CYPRUS SD196	OP	RNBT	FBG	TR	IO	130-230		7	6	2500			4150	5000
18	10	GENEVA SD196	OP	RNBT	FBG	TR	IO	130-230		7	6	2500			4150	4950
		1986 BOATS														
17	1	CYPRES SD176	OP	RNBT	FBG	TR	IO	120-140		7	2	2070			3200	3700
17	1	CYPRUS SD176	OP	RNBT	FBG	TR	OB			7	2	1070			1650	1950
17	1	CYPRUS SD176	OP	RNBT	FBG	TR	IO	175		7	2	2070			3200	3750
18	10	CYPRUS SD196	OP	RNBT	FBG	TR	IO	140-230		7	6	2500			3950	4800
18	10	GENEVA SD196	OP	RNBT	FBG	TR	IO	140-230		7	6	2500			3950	4750
18	10	TAHOE SD196	OP	RNBT	FBG	TR	IO	140-230		7	6	2500			3950	4750
		1985 BOATS														
17	1	CYPRUS SD176	OP	RNBT	FBG	TR	OB			7	2	1070			1600	1900
17	1	CYPRUS SD176	OP	RNBT	FBG	TR	IO	120-170		7	2	2070			3050	3600
17	1	GENEVA SD176	OP	RNBT	FBG	TR	OB			7	2	1070			1600	1900
17	1	GENEVA SD176	OP	RNBT	FBG	TR	IO	120-170		7	2	2070			3050	3600
18	10	CYPRUS SD196	OP	RNBT	FBG	TR	IO	140-230		7	6	2500			3800	4550
18	10	GENEVA SD196	OP	RNBT	FBG	TR	IO	140-230		7	6	2500			3800	4550
18	10	TAHOE SD196	OP	RNBT	FBG	TR	IO	140-230		7	6	2500			3800	4550
		1984 BOATS														
17	1	CYPRUS SD176	OP	RNBT	FBG	TR	OB			7	2	1070			1550	1850
17	1	CYPRUS SD176	OP	RNBT	FBG	TR	IO	120-170		7	2	2070			2950	3450
17	1	GENEVA SD176	OP	RNBT	FBG	TR	OB			7	2	1070			1550	1850
17	1	GENEVA SD176	OP	RNBT	FBG	TR	IO	120-170		7	2	2070			2950	3450
18	10	CYPRUS SD196	OP	RNBT	FBG	TR	IO	140-230		7	6	2500			3650	4450
18	10	GENEVA SD196	OP	RNBT	FBG	TR	IO	140-230		7	6	2500			3650	4450
18	10	TAHOE SD196	OP	RNBT	FBG	TR	IO	140-230		7	6	2500			3650	4450

....For earlier years, see the BUC Used Boat Price Guide, Volume 3

GOLD COAST YACHTS INC

ST CROIX VI 00851

See inside cover to adjust price for area

For more recent years, see the BUC Used Boat Price Guide, Volume 1

LOA FT	LOA IN	NAME AND/ OR MODEL	TOP/ RIG	BOAT TYPE	-HULL- MTL	-HULL- TP	ENGINE TP	ENGINE # HP	ENGINE MFG	BEAM FT	BEAM IN	WGT LBS	DRAFT FT	DRAFT IN	RETAIL LOW	RETAIL HIGH
		1996 BOATS														
42		GC 42	SLP	SACAC	F/W	CT	OB			25		13600	4		**	**
44		GC 44C	SLP	SACAC	F/W	CT	IB	T 27D	YAN	26		15000	4	2	**	**
46		GC 46	SLP	SACAC	F/W	CT	OB			26		14600	4		285000	313500
53		GC 53	SLP	SACAC	F/W	CT	OB			28		19000	3	6	371500	408000
61		GC 62	SLP	SACAC	F/W	CT	OB			31	6	23000	4	6	415500	457000
61		GC 62	SLP	SACAC	F/W	CT	IB	T 85D	PERK	31	6	24000	4	6	415500	457000
62		GC 62 ECOD	SLP	SACAC	F/W	CT	IB	T 85D	PERK	31	6	24000	4	6	428000	470000
66		GC 66	SLP	SACAC	F/W	CT	IB	T100D	YAN	32		28000	4	6	490000	538500
70		GC 70	SLP	SACAC	F/W	CT	IB	T100D	YAN	32		32000	4	6	499500	548500
		1995 BOATS														
42		GC 42	SLP	SACAC	F/W	CT	OB			24		9000	3	6	**	**
42		GC 42	SLP	SACAC	F/W	CT	OB			25		13600	4		**	**
44		GC 44C	SLP	SACAC	F/W	CT	IB	T 27D	YAN	26		15000	4	2	**	**
46		GC 46	SLP	SACAC	F/W	CT	OB			26		14600	4		268500	295000
53		GC 53	SLP	SACAC	F/W	CT	OB			28		19000	3	6	349500	384000
61		GC 61	SLP	SACAC	F/W	CT	OB			31	6	23000	4	6	391000	429500
61		GC 61	SLP	SACAC	F/W	CT	IB	T 85D	PERK	31	6	24000	4	6	391000	429500
62		GC 62 ECOD	SLP	SACAC	F/W	CT	IB	T 85D	PERK	31	6	24000	4	6	402500	442500
		1994 BOATS														
42		GC 42	SLP	SACAC	F/W	CT	OB			24		9000	3	6	**	**
42		GC 42	SLP	SACAC	F/W	CT	OB			25		13500	4		**	**
44		GC 44C	SLP	SACAC	F/W	CT	IB	T 27D	YAN	26		15000	4	2	**	**
46		GC 46	SLP	SACAC	F/W	CT	OB			26		14600	4		252500	277500
53		GC 53	SLP	SACAC	F/W	CT	OB			28		19000	3	6	328500	361000
61		GC 61	SLP	SACAC	F/S	CT	OB			31	6	23000	4	6	367500	404000
61		GC 61	SLP	SACAC	F/S	CT	IB	T 85D	PERK	31	6	24000	4	6	367500	404000
		1993 BOATS														
42		GC 42	SLP	SACAC	F/W	CT	OB			24		9000	3	6	**	**
42		GC 42	SLP	SACAC	F/W	CT	OB			25		13500	4		**	**
44		GC 44C	SLP	SACAC	F/W	CT	IB	T 27D	YAN	26		15000	4	2	**	**
46		GC 46	SLP	SACAC	F/W	CT	OB			26		14600	4		237500	261000
53		GC 53	SLP	SACAC	F/W	CT	OB			28		19000	3	6	309000	339500
61		GC 61	SLP	SACAC	F/S	CT	IB	T 85D	PERK	31	6	24000	4	6	346000	380000
65		GC 65	SLP	SACAC	F/S	CT	OB			31	6	23000	4	6	393000	432000
		1992 BOATS														
42		GC 42		SAIL	F/W	CT	OB			24		9000	3	6	**	**
42		GC 42		SAIL	F/W	CT	OB			25		12000	4		**	**
42		GC 42C		SAIL	F/W	CT	OB			24		10000	3	6	**	**
44		GC 44C		SAIL	F/W	CT	IB	T 27D	YAN	26		13000	4	2	**	**
46		GC 46		SAIL	F/W	CT	OB			26		14000	4		223000	245500
53		GC 53		SAIL	F/W	CT	OB			28		18000	3	6	290500	319500
65		GC 65		SAIL	F/S	CT	OB			30	6	22000	4	6	369500	406000
		1991 BOATS														
42		GC 42		SAIL	F/W	CT	OB			24		9000	3	6	**	**
42		GC 42C		SAIL	FBG	CT	IB	T 18D	YAN	24		10000	3	6	**	**
44		GC 44C		SAIL	FBG	CT	IB	T 27D	YAN	26		13000	4	2	**	**
53		GC 53		SAIL	F/W	CT	OB			28		18000	3	6	273500	300500
53		GC 53C		SAIL	FBG	CT	IB	T 47D	YAN	30		22000	4	2	273500	300500
65		GC 65		SAIL	F/S	CT	OB			30	6	22000	4	6	347500	382000
		1990 BOATS														
42		GC 42		SAIL	F/W	CT	OB			24		9000	3	6	**	**
42		GC 42C		SAIL	F/S	CT	OB			25		9500	3	6	**	**
53		GC 53		SAIL	F/W	CT	OB			28		18000	3	6	257000	282500
65		GC 65		SAIL	F/S	CT	OB			30	6	22000	4	6	327000	359500
		1989 BOATS														
42		GC 42		SAIL	F/W	CT	OB			25		7000	3	6	**	**
42		GC 42C		SAIL	F/S	CT	OB			25		9500	3	6	**	**
50		GC 50		SAIL	F/W	CT	OB			28		16000	3	6	196000	215500
57		GC 57		SAIL	F/W	CT	OB			28		18000	4	2	262000	288000
65		GC 65		SAIL	F/S	CT	OB			30	6	22000	4	6	307500	338000
		1988 BOATS														
34		GC 34T CRUISER		SAIL	F/W	TM	OB			25		4200	3	4	**	**
42		GC 42		SAIL	F/W	CT	OB			25		7000	3	6	**	**
42		GC 42C		SAIL	F/S	CT	OB			25		9500	3	6	**	**
42		GC 42T		SAIL	F/S	TM	OB			28		7600	3	6	**	**
50		GC 50		SAIL	F/W	CT	OB			28		16000	4		184500	202500
57		GC 57		SAIL	F/W	CT	OB			28		16000	4	2	246500	270500
65		GC 65		SAIL	F/S	CT	OB			30	6	22000	4	6	289500	318000
		1987 BOATS														
42		GCY 42	SLP	SAIL	F/S	CT	OB			25		7000	3	6	**	**
		1986 BOATS														
34		GCY 34T CRUISER	CUT	SAIL	F/W	TM	OB			21		4200	3	4	**	**
57		GCY 57	SLP	SAIL	F/S	CT	OB			28		16000	4	2	218000	239500
65		GCY 65	SLP	SAIL	F/S	CT	OB			30	6	22000	4	6	256000	281500
		1985 BOATS														
42		GCY 42T	SLP	SAIL	F/S	TM	OB			28		7600	3	6	**	**

GOLD MINING & INVESTMENTS INC

GRAND JUNCTION CO 81501

See inside cover to adjust price for area

LOA FT	LOA IN	NAME AND/ OR MODEL	TOP/ RIG	BOAT TYPE	-HULL- MTL	-HULL- TP	ENGINE TP	ENGINE # HP	ENGINE MFG	BEAM FT	BEAM IN	WGT LBS	DRAFT FT	DRAFT IN	RETAIL LOW	RETAIL HIGH
		1986 BOATS														
44		VALHALLA BOATHOUSE	HT	HB	STL	PN	IO	T140	MRCR	14		19850	1	4	28500	31600

GOLDEN ERA BOATS INC

NOANK CT 06340 COAST GUARD MFG ID- GEB See inside cover to adjust price for area

LOA FT	LOA IN	NAME AND/ OR MODEL	TOP/ RIG	BOAT TYPE	-HULL- MTL	-HULL- TP	ENGINE TP	ENGINE # HP	ENGINE MFG	BEAM FT	BEAM IN	WGT LBS	DRAFT FT	DRAFT IN	RETAIL LOW	RETAIL HIGH
		1994 BOATS														
16		STONINGTON PULL	SLP	PRAM	KEV	KL				3	3	83			**	**
16		STONINGTON PULL A1	SLP	PRAM	FBG	KL				3	3	83			**	**
17		NOANK SMUGGLER	SLP	SAROD	FBG	KL				4	10	550			8500	9800
20	9	PETREL	SLP	SAROD	FBG	KL	IB	10D	YAN	7	2	3000	3	1	32700	36300
26	3	ORIANA	CUT	SACAC	FBG	KL	IB	12D	YAN	8	6	7100	3	11	87400	96000
		1993 BOATS														
16		STONINGTON PULL	SLP	PRAM	KEV	KL				3	3	83			**	**
16		STONINGTON PULL A1	SLP	PRAM	FBG	KL				3	3	83			**	**
16		STONINGTON PULL BOAT	SLP	SACAC	FBG	KL				3	3	83		3	**	**
17		NOANK SMUGGLER	SLP	SAROD	FBG	KL				4	10	550			7950	9150
20	9	PETREL	SLP	SAROD	FBG	KL	IB	10D	YAN	7	2	3000	3	1	30500	33900
26	3	ORIANA	CUT	SACAC	FBG	KL	IB	12D	YAN	8	6	7100	3	11	81700	89800
		1992 BOATS														
16		STONINGTON PULL BOAT	SLP	PRAM	FBG	KL				3	3	83		3	**	**
17		NOANK SMUGGLER	SLP	SA/OD	FBG	KL				4	10	550			7400	8500
20	9	PETREL	SLP	SA/OD	FBG	KL	IB	10D	YAN	7	2	3000	3	1	28600	31700
26	3	ORIANA	CUT	SA/CR	FBG	KL	IB	12D	YAN	8	6	7100	3	11	76800	84400

LOA FT	IN	NAME AND/ OR MODEL	TOP/ RIG	BOAT TYPE	HULL MTL	HULL TP	ENGINE TP	# HP	MFG	BEAM FT	IN	WGT LBS	DRAFT FT	IN	RETAIL LOW	RETAIL HIGH
		1986 BOATS														
17		NOANK-SMUGGLER	SLP	SAIL	FBG	RB				4	10	550	1	6	4850	5600
20	9	PETREL	GAF	SAIL	FBG	KL	OB			7	1	2850	3	1	13200	15000
20	9	PETREL	SLP	SAIL	FBG	KL	OB			7	1	2850	3	1	13600	15500
26	3	GOLDEN-ERA 26	SLP	SAIL	FBG	KL	IB	D		8	5	7100	3	11	51400	56500
		1985 BOATS														
17		NOANK-SMUGGLER	SLP	SAIL	FBG	KL				4		550	1	6	4550	5250
20	9	PETREL	SLP	SA/OD	FBG	KL				7	1	3000	3	1	13200	15000
21	9	PETREL	SLP	SAIL	FBG	KL	OB			7	1	3000	3	1	13800	15700
25	4	GOLDEN-ERA 25	CUT	SA/CR	FBG	KL	IB	D		8	7	6000	3	11	37800	42000
		1984 BOATS														
17		NOANK-SMUGGLER	SLP	SAIL	FBG	KL				4		550	1	3	4250	4950
20	9	PETREL	SLP	SA/OD	F/S	KL				7	2	2850	3	2	11900	13500
21	9	PETREL	SLP	SAIL	FBG	KL	OB			7	1	3000	3	1	13100	14900
23	11	ALLEGRA	CUT	SA/CR	FBG	KL	OB			8		6000	3	5	30200	33500

....For earlier years, see the BUC Used Boat Price Guide, Volume 3

GOLDEN STAR YACHTS

E TAGLIANETTE YACHT SALES INC
STATEN ISLAND NY 10309

See inside cover to adjust price for area

LOA FT	IN	NAME AND/ OR MODEL	TOP/ RIG	BOAT TYPE	HULL MTL	HULL TP	ENGINE TP	# HP	MFG	BEAM FT	IN	WGT LBS	DRAFT FT	IN	RETAIL LOW	RETAIL HIGH
		1992 BOATS														
34	8	CHAUSON 35 SD	FB	DCFD	FBG	SV	IB	T150D-T250D		12	9	18000	2	2	96700	112000
37		CHAUSON 37 SD	FB	DCFD	FBG	SV	IB	T150D	CUM	12	9	20000	2	2	103000	113000
37		CHAUSON 37 SD	FB	DCFD	FBG	SV	IB	T210D	CUM	12	9	20000	2	2	105500	116000
37		CHAUSON 37 SD	FB	DCFD	FBG	SV	IB	T250D	CUM	12	9	20000	2	2	107500	118000
37		CHAUSON 37 SF	FB	SF	FBG	SV	IB	T250D	CUM	12	9	20000	2	2	107500	118000
37		CHAUSON 37 SF	FB	SF	FBG	SV	IB	T260D	CAT	12	9	20000	2	2	111000	122000
37		CHAUSON 37 SF	FB	SF	FBG	SV	IB	T375D	CAT	12	9	21000	2	2	124500	136500
40		CHAUSON 40 YF	FB	YTFS	FBG	SV	IB	T210D	CUM	12	9	23000	2	2	135500	148500
40		CHAUSON 40 YF	FB	YTFS	FBG	SV	IB	T250D	CUM	12	9	23000	2	2	137500	151000
40		CHAUSON 40 YF	FB	YTFS	FBG	SV	IB	T260D	CAT	12	9	23000	2	2	142000	156000
42		CHAUSON 40 SF	FB	SF	FBG	SV	IB	T250D	CUM	12	9	26000	2	6	152000	167000
42		CHAUSON 40 SF	FB	SF	FBG	SV	IB	T260D	CAT	12	9	26000	2	6	156500	172000
42		CHAUSON 40 SF	FB	SF	FBG	SV	IB	T375D	CAT	12	9	27000	2	6	180000	197500
42	10	GOLDEN STAR 43 SD	FB	DCFD	FBG	SV	IB	T150D	VLVO	14	10	33000	3	4	170000	186500
		IB T200D PERK 166000 182500, IB T200D VLVO 163000 179000, IB T240D PERK 172000 189000														
		IB T260D CAT 175000 192500, IB T306D VLVO 178000 195500, IB T320D CAT 184000 202500														
		IB T355D LEHM 187000 205500, IB T357D VLVO 185000 203000, IB T375D CAT 193000 212000														
		IB T425D CAT 201000 220500														
47	6	GOLDEN STAR 48 PH	FB	DCFD	FBG	SV	IB	T150D	VLVO	14	10	37000	3	6	180000	198000
		IB T200D PERK 162500 178500, IB T200D VLVO 161500 177000, IB T240D PERK 171000 188000														
		IB T260D CAT 175500 193000, IB T306D VLVO 185500 203500, IB T320D CAT 188500 207500														
		IB T355D LEHM 195500 215000, IB T357D VLVO 196000 215500, IB T375D CAT 200000 219500														
		IB T425D CAT 209500 230000														
47	6	GOLDEN STAR 48 SD	FB	DCFD	FBG	SV	IB	T150D	VLVO	14	10	44000	3	6	183000	201500
		IB T200D PERK 186500 205000, IB T200D VLVO 186000 204500, IB T240D PERK 184500 202500														
		IB T260D CAT 188500 207000, IB T306D VLVO 196500 216000, IB T320D CAT 199500 219500														
		IB T355D LEHM 205500 226000, IB T357D VLVO 205500 226000, IB T375D CAT 209000 230000														
		IB T425D CAT 217500 239000														
47	6	GOLDEN STAR 48 YF	FB	DCFD	FBG	SV	IB	T150D	VLVO	14	10	37400	3	6	178500	196000
		IB T200D PERK 162000 178500, IB T200D VLVO 161000 177000, IB T240D PERK 170500 187000														
		IB T260D CAT 174500 192000, IB T306D VLVO 184000 202500, IB T320D CAT 187500 206000														
		IB T355D LEHM 194500 213500, IB T357D VLVO 194500 213500, IB T375D CAT 198500 218000														
		IB T425D CAT 208000 228500														
		1991 BOATS														
42	10	GOLDEN STAR 43 SD	FB	DCFD	FBG	RB	IB	T150D	VLVO	14	10	33000	3	4	163000	179000
		IB T200D PERK 159000 175000, IB T200D VLVO 156000 171500, IB T240D PERK 165000 181000														
		IB T260D CAT 168000 184500, IB T306D VLVO 170500 187500, IB T320D CAT 176500 194000														
		IB T355D LEHM 179500 197000, IB T357D VLVO 177500 195000, IB T375D CAT 185000 203000														
		IB T425D CAT 192500 211500														
47	6	GOLDEN STAR 48	FB	DCFD	FBG	RB	IB	T150D	VLVO	14	10	37000	3	6	175000	192500
		IB T200D PERK 157000 172500, IB T200D VLVO 156500 172000, IB T240D PERK 166000 182500														
		IB T260D CAT 170500 187500, IB T306D VLVO 180500 198000, IB T320D CAT 183500 202000														
		IB T355D LEHM 190500 209500, IB T357D VLVO 190500 209500, IB T375D CAT 194500 214000														
		IB T425D CAT 204000 224000														
47	6	GOLDEN STAR 48 SD	FB	DCFD	FBG	RB	IB	T150D	VLVO	14	10	44000	3	6	177000	194500
		IB T200D PERK 180000 198000, IB T200D VLVO 180000 198000, IB T240D PERK 178500 196000														
		IB T260D CAT 182000 200000, IB T306D VLVO 190000 209000, IB T320D CAT 193000 212000														
		IB T355D LEHM 199000 218500, IB T357D VLVO 199000 218500, IB T375D CAT 202500 222500														
		IB T425D CAT 210000 231000														
47	6	GOLDEN STAR 48 YF	FB	DCFD	FBG	RB	IB	T150D	VLVO	14	10	37400	3	6	172500	189500
		IB T200D PERK 156000 171500, IB T200D VLVO 155000 170500, IB T240D PERK 164500 180500														
		IB T260D CAT 168500 185500, IB T306D VLVO 178000 195500, IB T320D CAT 181500 199000														
		IB T355D LEHM 188000 206500, IB T357D VLVO 188000 206500, IB T375D CAT 192000 211000														
		IB T425D CAT 201000 221000														
		1990 BOATS														
41	2	VEGA SPORT FISH	FB	CNV	FBG	RB	IB	T200D	VLVO	15		24630	3	6	121000	133000
41	2	VEGA SPORT FISH	FB	CNV	FBG	RB	IB	T260D	CAT	15		24930	3	6	134500	147500
41	2	VEGA SPORT FISH	FB	CNV	FBG	RB	IB	T375D	CAT	15		25130	3	6	152000	167000
41	2	VEGA SUNDECK	FB	DCFD	FBG	RB	IB	T200D	VLVO	15		24630	3	6	123000	135000
41	2	VEGA SUNDECK	FB	DCFD	FBG	RB	IB	T260D	CAT	15		24930	3	6	135500	149000
41	2	VEGA SUNDECK	FB	DCFD	FBG	RB	IB	T375D	CAT	15		25130	3	6	151500	166500
42	6	GOLDEN STAR SUNDECK	FB	DCFD	FBG	SV	IB	T200D	VLVO	14	10		3	4	148500	163000
42	6	GOLDEN STAR SUNDECK	FB	DCFD	FBG	SV	IB	T260D	CAT	14	10	30800	3	4	151000	166000
44		GOLDEN STAR SPRT FSH	FB	CNV	FBG	SV	IB	T200D	VLVO	14	10	34500			149500	164500
44		GOLDEN STAR SPRT FSH	FB	CNV	FBG	SV	IB	T260D	CAT	14	10	34800	3	6	166500	183000
44		GOLDEN STAR SUNDECK	FB	DCFD	FBG	SV	IB	T200D	VLVO	14	10	34500	3	6	145000	159000
44		GOLDEN STAR SUNDECK	FB	DCFD	FBG	SV	IB	T260D	CAT	14	10	34800	3	6	157500	173000
48		GOLDEN STAR PILOTHS	FB	DCFD	FBG	SV	IB	T200D	VLVO	14	10	39600	3	6	153500	169000
48		GOLDEN STAR PILOTHSE	FB	DCFD	FBG	SV	IB	T260D	CAT	14	10	39900	3	6	163500	180000
48	6	GOLDEN STAR SUNDECK	FB	DCFD	FBG	SV	IB	T200D	VLVO	14	10	39600	3	6	165500	181500
48	6	GOLDEN STAR SUNDECK	FB	DCFD	FBG	SV	IB	T260D	CAT	14	10	39900	3	6	181500	199500
48	6	GOLDEN STAR YACHTFSH	FB	DCFD	FBG	SV	IB	T200D	VLVO	14	10	39600	3	6	141500	155500
		IB T260D CAT 153000 168500, IB T375D CAT 180500 198500, IB T425D CAT 192500 211500														
		1989 BOATS														
41	6	GOLDEN STAR SPRT FSH	FB	CNV	FBG	SV	IB	T200D	VLVO	14	10	34500	3	4	149500	164500
41	6	GOLDEN STAR SUNDECK	FB	DCFD	FBG	SV	IB	T200D	VLVO	14	10	30800	3	4	134000	147000
41	6	GOLDEN STAR SUNDECK	FB	DCFD	FBG	SV	IB	T260D	CAT	14	10	30800	3	4	143000	157500
44		GOLDEN STAR SPRT FSH	FB	CNV	FBG	SV	IB	T260D	CAT	14	10	34500	3	6	158000	173500
44		GOLDEN STAR SUNDECK	FB	DCFD	FBG	SV	IB	T200D	VLVO	14	10	34500	3	6	138500	152000
44		GOLDEN STAR SUNDECK	FB	DCFD	FBG	SV	IB	T260D	CAT	14	10	34500	3	6	149000	164000
48		GOLDEN STAR PILOTHS	FB	DCFD	FBG	SV	IB	T200D	VLVO	14	10	39600	3	6	147000	161500
48		GOLDEN STAR PILOTHSE	FB	DCFD	FBG	SV	IB	T260D	CAT	14	10	39600	3	6	155500	171000
48	6	GOLDEN STAR SUNDECK	FB	DCFD	FBG	SV	IB	T200D	VLVO	14	10	39600	3	6	158000	173500
48	6	GOLDEN STAR SUNDECK	FB	DCFD	FBG	SV	IB	T260D	CAT	14	10	39600	3	6	172500	189500
48	6	GOLDEN STAR YACHTFSH	FB	DCFD	FBG	SV	IB	T200D	VLVO	14	10	39600	3	6	135000	148500
		IB T260D CAT 145500 160000, IB T375D CAT 171500 188500, IB T425D CAT 180000 197500														
		1988 BOATS														
35		GOLDEN STAR SUNDECK	HT	DCFD	FBG	SV	IB	T135D	PERK	12		19800	3	4	89800	98700
35		GOLDEN STAR SUNDECK	FB	DCFD	FBG	DS	IB	T135D	PERK	12		19800	3	4	89900	98700
38	8	GOLDEN STAR SPRT FSH	FB	CNV	FBG	SV	IB	T135D	PERK	12		22000	3	4	106000	116500
38	8	GOLDEN STAR SUNDECK	HT	DCFD	FBG	SV	IB	T135D	PERK	12		22000	3	4	106000	116500
38	8	GOLDEN STAR SUNDECK	FB	DCFD	FBG	SV	IB	T135D	PERK	12		22000	3	4	106000	116500
38	8	GOLDEN STAR YCHT FSH	HT	YTFS	FBG	SV	IB	T135D	PERK	12		22000	3	4	106000	116500
41	6	GOLDEN STAR SUNDECK	HT	DCFD	FBG	SV	IB	T260D	CAT	14	10	30800	3	4	137000	150500
41	6	GOLDEN STAR SUNDECK	FB	DCFD	FBG	SV	IB	T260D	CAT	14	10	30800	3	4	137000	150500
44		GOLDEN STAR SUNDECK	FB	DCFD	FBG	SV	IB	T260D	CAT	14		34500	3	6	150500	165000
45		GOLDEN STAR PILOTHSE	FB	DCFD	FBG	SV	IB	T260D	CAT			38000	3	6	135000	148500
48		GOLDEN STAR PILOTHSE	FB	DCFD	FBG	SV	IB	T260D	CAT			39600	3	6	137000	151000
48	6	GOLDEN STAR SUNDECK	FB	DCFD	FBG	SV	IB	T260D	CAT	14	10	39600	3	6	159000	174500
48	6	GOLDEN STAR YACHTFSH	FB	DCFD	FBG	SV	IB	T260D	CAT			39600	3	6	137500	151000

GOLDEN WAVE SHIPYARD LTD

KOWLOON HONG KONG

See inside cover to adjust price for area

LOA FT	IN	NAME AND/ OR MODEL	TOP/ RIG	BOAT TYPE	HULL MTL	HULL TP	ENGINE TP	# HP	MFG	BEAM FT	IN	WGT LBS	DRAFT FT	IN	RETAIL LOW	RETAIL HIGH
		1989 BOATS														
38	4	GOLDEN-WAVE GW38	SLP	SA/CR	FBG	KL	VD	D	UNIV	11	10	19025	6		98200	108000
42		GOLDEN-WAVE GW42	SLP	SA/CR	FBG	KL	VD	51D	PERK	12	8	25000	6	2	132500	145500
47	10	GOLDEN-WAVE GW48	SLP	SA/CR	FBG	KC	IB	85D	PERK	15	11	34000	4	8	187000	205500
47	10	GOLDEN-WAVE GW48	SLP	SA/CR	FBG	KL	IB	85D	PERK	15	11	34000	6	6	187000	205500
47	10	GOLDEN-WAVE GW48	KTH	SA/CR	FBG	KC	IB	85D	PERK	15	11	34000	6	6	187000	205500
47	10	GOLDEN-WAVE GW48	KTH	SA/CR	FBG	KL	IB	85D	PERK	15	11	34000	6	6	187000	205500
55	9	GOLDEN-WAVE GW55	SLP	SA/CR	FBG	KL	IB	85D	PERK	16		48000	9	5	360500	396000
		1988 BOATS														
38	4	GOLDEN-WAVE GW38	SLP	SA/CR	FBG	KL	VD	D	UNIV	11	10	19025	6		92300	101500
42		GOLDEN-WAVE GW42	SLP	SA/CR	FBG	KL	VD	51D	PERK	12	8	25000	6	2	124500	136500
47	10	GOLDEN-WAVE GW48	SLP	SA/CR	FBG	KC	IB	85D	PERK	15	11	34000	4	8	176000	193500
47	10	GOLDEN-WAVE GW48	SLP	SA/CR	FBG	KL	IB	85D	PERK	15	11	34000	6	6	176000	193500

LOA FT	LOA IN	NAME AND/ OR MODEL	TOP/ RIG	BOAT TYPE	-HULL- MTL	-HULL- TP	ENGINE TP	ENGINE # HP	ENGINE MFG	BEAM FT	BEAM IN	WGT LBS	DRAFT FT	DRAFT IN	RETAIL LOW	RETAIL HIGH
		1988 BOATS														
47	10	GOLDEN-WAVE GW48	KTH	SA/CR	FBG	KC	IB	85D	PERK	15	11	34000	6	6	176000	193500
47	10	GOLDEN-WAVE GW48	KTH	SA/CR	FBG	KL	IB	85D	PERK	15	11	34000	6	6	176000	193500
55	9	GOLDEN-WAVE GW55	SLP	SA/CR	FBG	KL	IB	85D	PERK	16		48000	9	5	339000	372500
		1986 BOATS														
38	4	GOLDEN-WAVE GW38	SLP	SA/CR	FBG	KL	VD	D	UNIV	11	10	19025	6		81700	89800
42		GOLDEN-WAVE GW42	CUT	SA/CR	FBG	KL	VD	51D	PERK	12	8	25000	6	2	110000	121000
47	10	GOLDEN-WAVE GW48	SLP	SA/CR	FBG	KC	IB	62D	PERK	15	11	34000	4	8	155500	171000
47	10	GOLDEN-WAVE GW48	SLP	SA/CR	FBG	KL	IB	62D	PERK	15	11	34000	6	6	155500	171000
55	9	GOLDEN-WAVE GW55	SLP	SA/CR	FBG	KL	IB	85D	PERK	16		48000	9	5	299500	329000
		1985 BOATS														
38	4	GOLDEN-WAVE GW38	SLP	SA/CR	FBG	KL	VD	D	UNIV	11	10	19025	6		76900	84500
42		GOLDEN-WAVE GW42	SLP	SA/CR	FBG	KL	VD	51D	PERK	12	8	25000	6	2	103500	114000
42		GOLDEN-WAVE GW42	SLP	SA/RC	FBG	KL	IB			12	8	25000	6	2	102500	112500
47	10	GOLDEN-WAVE GW48	SLP	SA/CR	FBG	KC	IB	62D	PERK	15	11	34000	4	8	146000	160500
47	10	GOLDEN-WAVE GW48	SLP	SA/CR	FBG	KL	IB	62D	PERK	15	11	34000	6	6	146000	160500
55	9	GOLDEN-WAVE GW55	SLP	SA/CR	FBG	KL	IB	85D	PERK	16		48000	9	5	281500	309500
		1984 BOATS														
38	4	GOLDEN-WAVE GW38	SLP	SA/CR	FBG	KL	VD	D	UNIV	11	10	19025	6		72300	79400
42		GOLDEN-WAVE GW 42	SLP	SA/CR	FBG	KL				12	8	25000	6	2	95500	105000
42		GOLDEN-WAVE GW42	CUT	SA/CR	FBG	KL	VD	50D	PERK	12	8	25000	6	2	97400	107000
47	10	GOLDEN-WAVE GW48	SLP	SA/CR	FBG	KC	IB	62D	PERK	15	11	34000	4	8	137500	151000
47	10	GOLDEN-WAVE GW48	SLP	SA/CR	FBG	KL	IB	62D	PERK	15	11	34000	6	6	137500	151000
55	9	GOLDEN-WAVE GW55	SLP	SA/CR	FBG	KL	IB	85D	PERK	16		48000	9	5	264500	290500

....For earlier years, see the BUC Used Boat Price Guide, Volume 3

GOOD WOODEN BOATS

CAMDEN ME 04843

See inside cover to adjust price for area

LOA FT	LOA IN	NAME AND/ OR MODEL	TOP/ RIG	BOAT TYPE	-HULL- MTL	-HULL- TP	ENGINE TP	ENGINE # HP	ENGINE MFG	BEAM FT	BEAM IN	WGT LBS	DRAFT FT	DRAFT IN	RETAIL LOW	RETAIL HIGH
		1984 BOATS														
16	4	WHITEHALL	CAT	SAIL	WD	DB				4	4	160		4	2550	2950

GRADY-WHITE BOATS INC

GREENVILLE NC 27835-152 COAST GUARD MFG ID- NTL See inside cover to adjust price for area

For more recent years, see the BUC Used Boat Price Guide, Volume 1

LOA FT	LOA IN	NAME AND/ OR MODEL	TOP/ RIG	BOAT TYPE	-HULL- MTL	-HULL- TP	ENGINE TP	ENGINE # HP	ENGINE MFG	BEAM FT	BEAM IN	WGT LBS	DRAFT FT	DRAFT IN	RETAIL LOW	RETAIL HIGH
		1996 BOATS														
17	5	SPIRIT 175	OP	CTRCN	FBG	SV	OB			7	5	1500	1		6400	7350
19	2	TOURNAMENT 192	OP	RNBT	FBG	SV	OB			8		2075	1	2	8450	9700
20	4	ADVENTURE 208	OP	CUD	FBG	SV	OB			8	1	2650	1	2	12700	14400
20	4	ESCAPE 209	OP	CTRCN	FBG	SV	OB			8	1	2450	1	2	12200	13900
22	2	SEAFARER 226	OP	CUD	FBG	SV	OB			8		2875	1	3	16700	19000
22	2	SEAFARER 228G	OP	CUD	FBG	SV	OB			8		3000	1	3	17200	19500
22	2	TOURNAMENT 223	OP	RNBT	FBG	SV	OB			8		2875	1	3	15600	17700
22	2	TOURNAMENT 225G	OP	RNBT	FBG	SV	OB			8		3000	1	3	16000	18200
23	5	GULFSTREAM 232G	OP	CUD	FBG	SV	OB			9	3	4025	1	5	21300	23700
23	5	GULFSTREAM 232GT	OP	CUD	FBG	SV	OB			9	3	4092	1	5	21500	23900
24	9	STRIKE ADVANCE 247	OP	CTRCN	FBG	SV	OB			8	6	3500	1	3	20600	22900
24	9	VOYAGER 248	OP	CUD	FBG	SV	OB			8	6	4043	1	3	22600	25100
26	11	CHASE 263	OP	CTRCN	FBG	SV	OB			8	6	3975	1	3	24200	26900
26	11	ISLANDER 268	OP	RNBT	FBG	SV	OB			8	6	4660	1	3	28800	32000
27	10	SAILFISH 272	OP	CUD	FBG	SV	OB			9	6	5500	1	6	32800	36500
30	6	MARLIN 300	OP	CUD	FBG	SV	OB			10	7	7000	1	7	46500	51100
		1995 BOATS														
17	5	SPIRIT 175	OP	CTRCN	FBG	SV	OB			7	5	1500	1		6050	6950
19	2	TOURNAMENT 192	OP	RNBT	FBG	SV	OB			8		2075	1	2	8000	9200
20	4	ADVENTURE 208	OP	CUD	FBG	SV	OB			8	1	2650	1	2	12100	13700
20	4	ESCAPE 209	OP	CTRCN	FBG	SV	OB			8	1	2450	1	2	11600	13200
22	2	SEAFARER 226	OP	SF	FBG	SV	OB			8		2875	1	2	15800	18000
22	2	SEAFARER 227	OP	SF	FBG	SV	IO	235-250		8		3705	1	2	19300	21800
22	2	SEAFARER 228G	OP	SF	FBG	SV	OB			8		3000	1	2	16200	18400
22	2	TOURNAMENT 223	OP	RNBT	FBG	SV	OB			8		2875	1	3	14800	16800
22	2	TOURNAMENT 225G	OP	RNBT	FBG	SV	OB			8		3000	1	3	15200	17300
23	5	GULFSTREAM 232G	OP	SF	FBG	SV	OB			9	3	4025	1	5	20100	22400
23	5	GULFSTREAM 232GT	OP	SF	FBG	SV	OB			9	3	4092	1	5	20300	22600
24	1	EXPLORER 244	OP	SF	FBG	SV	OB			8	3	3400	1	3	18800	20900
24	1	EXPLORER 245	OP	SF	FBG	SV	IO	235-250		8	3	4500	1	3	24600	27700
24	1	EXPLORER 246G	OP	SF	FBG	SV	OB			8	3	3525	1	3	19300	21500
24	1	EXPLORER 246GT	OP	SF	FBG	SV	OB			8	3	3592	1	3	19500	21600
26	11	CHASE 263	OP	SF	FBG	SV	OB			8	6	3975	1	3	23000	25500
26	11	ISLANDER 268	OP	SF	FBG	SV	OB			8	6	4200	1	3	27100	30100
27	10	SAILFISH 272	OP	CUD	FBG	SV	OB			9	6	5500	1	6	31200	34600
30	6	MARLIN 300	OP	SF	FBG	SV	OB			10	7	7000	1	7	42300	47000
		1994 BOATS														
17	5	SPIRIT 175	OP	CTRCN	FBG	SV	OB			7	5	1500	1		5750	6650
19	2	TOURNAMENT 192	OP	RNBT	FBG	SV	OB			8		2075	1	2	7600	8700
20	4	ADVENTURE 208	OP	CUD	FBG	SV	OB			8	1	2650	1	2	11500	13100
20	4	ESCAPE 209	OP	CTRCN	FBG	SV	OB			8	1	2450	1	2	11100	12600
22	2	SEAFARER 226	OP	SF	FBG	SV	OB			8		2875	1	2	15100	17100
22	2	SEAFARER 227	OP	SF	FBG	SV	IO	205-250		8		3705	1	2	17000	20500
22	2	SEAFARER 228G	OP	SF	FBG	SV	OB			8		3000	1	2	15500	17600
22	2	TOURNAMENT 223	OP	RNBT	FBG	SV	OB			8		2875	1	3	14100	16000
22	2	TOURNAMENT 225G	OP	RNBT	FBG	SV	OB			8		3000	1	3	14500	16400
23	5	GULFSTREAM 230	OP	SF	FBG	SV	OB			9	3	3900	1	5	19000	21100
23	5	GULFSTREAM 231	OP	SF	FBG	SV	IO	225-300		9	3	5000	1	5	24700	29300
23	5	GULFSTREAM 231	OP	SF	FBG	SV	IO	185D-216D		9	3	5000	1	5	31900	36400
23	5	GULFSTREAM 232G	OP	SF	FBG	SV	OB			9	3	4025	1	5	19300	21500
23	5	GULFSTREAM 232GT	OP	SF	FBG	SV	OB			9	3	4092	1	5	19400	21500
24		CHASE 243	OP	SF	FBG	SV	OB			8	6	3975	1	3	19900	22100
24	1	EXPLORER 244	OP	SF	FBG	SV	OB			8	3	3400	1	3	17600	20000
24	1	EXPLORER 245	OP	SF	FBG	SV	IO	205-250		8	3	4500	1	3	22200	25800
24	1	EXPLORER 245	OP	SF	FBG	SV	IO	185D-216D		8	3	4500	1	3	30000	34300
24	1	EXPLORER 246G	OP	SF	FBG	SV	OB			8	3	3525	1	3	18400	20500
24	1	EXPLORER 246GT	OP	SF	FBG	SV	OB			8	3	3592	1	3	18700	20800
25	4	DOLPHIN 250	OP	SF	FBG	SV	OB			9	6	5125	1	6	22400	24800
25	4	DOLPHIN 251	OP	SF	FBG	SV	IO	235-300		9	6	6025	1	6	29200	35300
25	4	DOLPHIN 251	OP	SF	FBG	SV	IO	185D-216D		9	6	6025	1	6	38600	44200
25	4	DOLPHIN 253GT	OP	SF	FBG	SV	OB			9	6	5300	1	6	22700	25200
25	4	SAILFISH 252	OP	CUD	FBG	SV	OB			9	6	5500	1	6	24600	27300
28		MARLIN 280	OP	SF	FBG	SV	OB			10	7	7000	1	7	30800	34200
		1993 BOATS														
17	5	SPIRIT 175	OP	CTRCN	FBG	SV	OB			7	5	1500	1		5500	6350
18	11	TOURNAMENT 190	OP	RNBT	FBG	SV	OB			8		2075	1	2	7150	8200
20	4	ADVENTURE 208	OP	CUD	FBG	SV	OB			8	1	2650	1	2	11000	12500
20	4	ESCAPE 209	OP	CTRCN	FBG	SV	OB			8	1	2450	1	2	10600	12000
22		SEAFARER 226	OP	SF	FBG	SV	OB			8		2875	1	2	14200	16200
22		SEAFARER 227	OP	SF	FBG	SV	IO	205-245		8		3705	1	2	15800	19000
22		SEAFARER 228G	OP	SF	FBG	SV	OB			8		3000	1	2	14600	16600
22		TOURNAMENT 225G	OP	RNBT	FBG	SV	OB			8		3000	1	2	13700	15500
23	5	GULFSTREAM 230	OP	SF	FBG	SV	OB			9	3	3900	1	5	18100	20100
23	5	GULFSTREAM 231	OP	SF	FBG	SV	IO	225-300		9	3	5000	1	5	23100	27400
23	5	GULFSTREAM 231	OP	SF	FBG	SV	IO	185D-216D		9	3	5000	1	5	29800	34000
23	5	GULFSTREAM 232G	OP	SF	FBG	SV	OB			9	3	4025	1	5	18500	20500
23	5	GULFSTREAM 232GT	OP	SF	FBG	SV	OB			9	3	4092	1	5	18600	20700
24	1	EXPLORER 244	OP	SF	FBG	SV	OB			8	3	3400	1	4	16800	19100
24	1	EXPLORER 245	OP	SF	FBG	SV	IO	205-245		8	3	4500	1	4	20700	24000
24	1	EXPLORER 245	OP	SF	FBG	SV	IO	185D-216D		8	3	4500	1	4	28000	32000
24	1	EXPLORER 246G	OP	SF	FBG	SV	OB			8	3	3525	1	4	17300	19600
24	1	EXPLORER 246GT	OP	SF	FBG	SV	OB			8	3	3592	1	4	17500	19900
25	4	DOLPHIN 250	OP	SF	FBG	SV	OB			9	6	5125	1	7	21400	23800
25	4	DOLPHIN 251	OP	SF	FBG	SV	IO	230-300		9	6	6025	1	7	27200	32900
25	4	DOLPHIN 251	OP	SF	FBG	SV	IO	185D-216D		9	6	6025	1	7	36000	41300
25	4	DOLPHIN 253GT	OP	SF	FBG	SV	OB			9	6	5300	1	7	21700	24100
25	4	SAILFISH 252GT	OP	CUD	FBG	SV	OB			9	6	5300	1	7	23200	25700
25	4	SAILFISH 254	OP	CUD	FBG	SV	IO	230-300		9	6	6025	1	7	25100	30300
25	4	SAILFISH 254	OP	CUD	FBG	SV	IO	185D-216D		9	6	6025	1	7	30100	34400
25	4	SAILFISH 255	OP	CUD	FBG	SV	OB			9	6	5125	1	7	22900	25500
28		MARLIN 280	OP	SF	FBG	SV	OB			10	7	7000	1	6	29500	32800
		1992 BOATS														
17	5	SPIRIT 175	OP	CTRCN	FBG	SV	OB			7	5	1500	1		5250	6050
18	11	TOURNAMENT 190	OP	RNBT	FBG	SV	OB			8		2075	1	2	6800	7800
20	4	FISHERMAN 204	OP	CTRCN	FBG	SV	OB			8		2245	1	2	9650	11000
20	4	OVERNIGHTER 204C	OP	SF	FBG	SV	OB			8		2550	1	2	10300	11800
20	4	OVERNIGHTER 205	OP	SF	FBG	SV	IO	180	VLVO	8		3380	1	2	13000	14800
20	4	OVERNIGHTER 206G	OP	SF	FBG	SV	OB			8		2715	1	2	10600	12100
22		SEAFARER 226	OP	SF	FBG	SV	OB			8		2875	1	2	13600	15500
22		SEAFARER 227	OP	SF	FBG	SV	IO	180-245		8		3705	1	2	15100	17700
22		SEAFARER 228G	OP	SF	FBG	SV	OB			8		3000	1	2	14000	15900
22		TOURNAMENT 225G	OP	RNBT	FBG	SV	OB			8		3000	1	2	13100	14900
23	5	GULFSTREAM 230	OP	SF	FBG	SV	OB			9	3	3900	1	5	17000	19400
23	5	GULFSTREAM 231	OP	SF	FBG	SV	IO	230-300		9	3	5000	1	5	21200	25600
23	5	GULFSTREAM 231	OP	SF	FBG	SV	IO	200D-216D		9	3	5000	1	5	28300	31800

LOA FT	LOA IN	NAME AND/ OR MODEL	TOP/ RIG	BOAT TYPE	-HULL- MTL	-HULL- TP	ENGINE TP	ENGINE # HP	ENGINE MFG	BEAM FT	BEAM IN	WGT LBS	DRAFT FT	DRAFT IN	RETAIL LOW	RETAIL HIGH
		1992 BOATS														
23	5	GULFSTREAM 232G	OP	SF	FBG	SV	OB			9	3	4025	1	5	17400	19700
23	5	GULFSTREAM 232GT	OP	SF	FBG	SV	OB			9	3	4092	1	5	17500	19900
24	1	EXPLORER 244	OP	SF	FBG	SV	OB			8	3	3400	1	4	16100	18300
24	1	EXPLORER 245	OP	SF	FBG	SV	IO	205-245		8	3	4500	1	4	19400	22500
24	1	EXPLORER 245	OP	SF	FBG	SV	IO	200D-216D		8	3	4500	1	4	26600	30000
24	1	EXPLORER 246G	OP	SF	FBG	SV	OB			8	3	3525	1	4	16500	18800
24	1	EXPLORER 246GT	OP	SF	FBG	SV	OB			8	3	3592	1	4	16800	19100
25	4	DOLPHIN 250	OP	SF	FBG	SV	OB			9	6	5125	1	7	20500	22700
25	4	DOLPHIN 251	OP	SF	FBG	SV	IO	230-300		9	6	6025	1	7	25500	30900
25	4	DOLPHIN 251	OP	SF	FBG	SV	IO	200D-216D		9	6	6025	1	7	34300	38700
25	4	DOLPHIN 253GT	OP	SF	FBG	SV	OB			9	6	5300	1	7	20800	23100
25	4	SAILFISH 252GT	OP	CUD	FBG	SV	OB			9	6	5300	1	7	22200	24600
25	4	SAILFISH 254	OP	CUD	FBG	SV	IO	230-300		9	6	6025	1	7	23500	28300
25	4	SAILFISH 254	OP	CUD	FBG	SV	IO	200D-216D		9	6	6025	1	7	28600	32200
25	4	SAILFISH 255	OP	CUD	FBG	SV	OB			9	6	5125	1	7	22000	24400
26	11	ATLANTIC 260	FB	SF	FBG	SV	OB			9	3	5950	1	7	24200	26900
28		MARLIN 280	OP	SF	FBG	SV	OB			10	7	7000	1	6	28300	31500
		1991 BOATS														
18	11	TOURNAMENT 190	OP	RNBT	FBG	SV	OB			8		2075	1	2	6500	7500
20	4	FISHERMAN 204	OP	CTRCN	FBG	SV	OB			8		2245	1	2	9350	10600
20	4	FISHERMAN 204	ST	CTRCN	FBG	SV	OB			8		2245	1	2	9350	10600
20	4	FISHERMAN 204	TT	CTRCN	FBG	SV	OB			8		2245	1	2	9350	10600
20	4	OVERNIGHTER 204C	OP	FSH	FBG	SV	OB			8		2550	1	2	9950	11300
20	4	OVERNIGHTER 204C	HT	FSH	FBG	SV	OB			8		2550	1	2	9950	11300
20	4	OVERNIGHTER 205	OP	FSH	FBG	SV	IO	205	VLVO	8		3380	1	2	11400	13000
20	4	OVERNIGHTER 206G	OP	FSH	FBG	SV	OB			8		2715	1	2	10200	11600
20	4	OVERNIGHTER 206G	HT	FSH	FBG	SV	OB			8		2715	1	2	10200	11600
22		SEAFARER 226	OP	SF	FBG	SV	OB			8		2875	1	2	13100	14900
22		SEAFARER 226	HT	SF	FBG	SV	OB			8		2815	1	2	12900	14700
22		SEAFARER 227	OP	SF	FBG	SV	IO	205-275		8		3705	1	2	14300	17200
22		SEAFARER 227	HT	SF	FBG	SV	IO	205-275		8		3705	1	2	14300	17200
22		SEAFARER 228G	OP	SF	FBG	SV	OB			8		3000	1	2	13500	15300
22		SEAFARER 228G	HT	SF	FBG	SV	OB			8		3000	1	2	13500	15300
22		TOURNAMENT 225G	OP	FSH	FBG	SV	OB			8		3000	1	2	12600	14300
23	5	GULFSTREAM 230	ST	SF	FBG	SV	OB			9	3	3900	1	5	16400	18600
23	5	GULFSTREAM 230	HT	SF	FBG	SV	OB			9	3	3900	1	5	16400	18600
23	5	GULFSTREAM 231	ST	SF	FBG	SV	IO	260-330		9	3	5000	1	5	20200	25200
23	5	GULFSTREAM 231	HT	SF	FBG	SV	IO	260-330		9	3	5000	1	5	20200	25200
23	5	GULFSTREAM 232G	OP	SF	FBG	SV	OB			9	3	4025	1	5	16700	18900
23	5	GULFSTREAM 232G	HT	SF	FBG	SV	OB			9	3	4025	1	5	16700	18900
23	5	GULFSTREAM 232GT	OP	SF	FBG	SV	OB			9	3	4092	1	5	16800	19100
23	5	GULFSTREAM 232GT	HT	SF	FBG	SV	OB			9	3	4092	1	5	16800	19100
24	1	OFFSHORE 240	ST	SF	FBG	SV	OB			8	3	3200	1	4	14800	16800
24	1	OFFSHORE 240	HT	SF	FBG	SV	OB			8	3	3200	1	4	14800	16800
24	1	OFFSHORE 241	ST	SF	FBG	SV	IO	229-275		8	3	4300	1	4	18400	21200
24	1	OFFSHORE 241	HT	SF	FBG	SV	IO	229-275		8	3	4300	1	4	18400	21200
24	1	OFFSHORE 242G	ST	SF	FBG	SV	OB			8	3	3325	1	4	15200	17300
24	1	OFFSHORE 242G	HT	SF	FBG	SV	OB			8	3	3325	1	4	15200	17300
24	1	OFFSHORE 242GT	OP	SF	FBG	SV	OB			8	3	3392	1	4	15500	17600
24	1	OFFSHORE 242GT	HT	SF	FBG	SV	OB			8	3	3392	1	4	15500	17600
25	4	DOLPHIN 250	OP	SF	FBG	SV	OB			9	6	5125	1	7	20400	22600
25	4	DOLPHIN 250	HT	SF	FBG	SV	OB			9	6	5125	1	7	20400	22600
25	4	DOLPHIN 251	OP	SF	FBG	SV	IO	200-330		9	6	6025	1	7	24500	30300
25	4	DOLPHIN 251	HT	SF	FBG	SV	IO	200-330		9	6	6025	1	7	24500	29800
25	4	DOLPHIN 253GT	OP	SF	FBG	SV	OB			9	6	5300	1	7	20600	22900
25	4	DOLPHIN 253GT	HT	SF	FBG	SV	OB			9	6	5300	1	7	20600	22900
25	4	SAILFISH 252GT	ST	SF	FBG	SV	OB			9	6	5300	1	7	20600	22900
25	4	SAILFISH 252GT	HT	SF	FBG	SV	OB			9	6	5300	1	7	20600	22900
25	4	SAILFISH 254	ST	SF	FBG	SV	IO	260-330		9	6	6025	1	7	25000	30300
25	4	SAILFISH 254	ST	SF	FBG	SV	IO	T200	VLVO	9	6	6025	1	7	27600	30600
25	4	SAILFISH 254	HT	SF	FBG	SV	IO	260-330		9	6	6025	1	7	25600	31200
25	4	SAILFISH 254	HT	SF	FBG	SV	IO	T200	VLVO	9	6	6025	1	7	27600	30600
25	4	SAILFISH 255	OP	SF	FBG	SV	OB			9	6	5125	1	7	20400	22600
25	4	SAILFISH 255	HT	SF	FBG	SV	OB			9	6	5125	1	7	20400	22600
26	11	ATLANTIC 260FB	OP	SF	FBG	SV	OB			9	3	5900	1	7	23300	25900
28		MARLIN 280	ST	SF	FBG	SV	OB			10	7	7000	1	6	27300	30300
28		MARLIN 280	HT	SF	FBG	SV	OB			10	7	7000	1	6	27300	30300
		1990 BOATS														
18	11	TOURNAMENT 190	OP	RNBT	FBG	SV	OB			8		2075	1	2	6250	7200
20	4	FISHERMAN 204	OP	CTRCN	FBG	SV	OB			8		2245	1	2	9000	10200
20	4	FISHERMAN 204	ST	CTRCN	FBG	SV	OB			8		2245	1	2	9000	10200
20	4	FISHERMAN 204	TT	CTRCN	FBG	SV	OB			8		2245	1	2	9000	10200
20	4	OVERNIGHTER 204C	OP	FSH	FBG	SV	OB			8		2550	1	2	9600	10900
20	4	OVERNIGHTER 204C	HT	FSH	FBG	SV	OB			8		2550	1	2	9600	10900
20	4	OVERNIGHTER 205	OP	FSH	FBG	SV	IO	175-205		8		3380	1	2	10300	12200
20	4	OVERNIGHTER 205	HT	FSH	FBG	SV	IO	175-205		8		3380	1	2	10300	12200
20	4	OVERNIGHTER 206G	OP	FSH	FBG	SV	OB			8		2715	1	2	9850	11200
20	4	OVERNIGHTER 206G	HT	FSH	FBG	SV	OB			8		2715	1	2	9850	11200
22		SEAFARER 226	OP	SF	FBG	SV	OB			8		2875	1	2	12700	14400
22		SEAFARER 226	HT	SF	FBG	SV	OB			8		2875	1	2	12700	14400
22		SEAFARER 227	OP	SF	FBG	SV	IO	205-275		8		3705	1	2	13400	16200
22		SEAFARER 227	HT	SF	FBG	SV	IO	205-275		8		3705	1	2	13400	16200
22		SEAFARER 228G	OP	SF	FBG	SV	OB			8		3000	1	2	13000	14800
22		SEAFARER 228G	HT	SF	FBG	SV	OB			8		3000	1	2	13000	14800
23	5	GULFSTREAM 230	ST	SF	FBG	SV	OB			9	3	3900	1	5	15800	17900
23	5	GULFSTREAM 230	HT	SF	FBG	SV	OB			9	3	3900	1	5	15800	17900
23	5	GULFSTREAM 231	ST	SF	FBG	SV	IO	260-330		9	3	5000	1	5	19000	23700
23	5	GULFSTREAM 231	HT	SF	FBG	SV	IO	260-330		9	3	5000	1	5	19000	23700
23	5	GULFSTREAM 232G	ST	SF	FBG	SV	OB			9	3	4025	1	5	16100	18300
23	5	GULFSTREAM 232G	HT	SF	FBG	SV	OB			9	3	4092	1	5	16200	18400
24	1	OFFSHORE 240	ST	SF	FBG	SV	OB			8	3	3200	1	4	14300	16200
24	1	OFFSHORE 240	HT	SF	FBG	SV	OB			8	3	3200	1	4	14300	16200
24	1	OFFSHORE 241	ST	SF	FBG	SV	IO	229-330		8	3	4300	1	4	16900	20800
24	1	OFFSHORE 241	HT	SF	FBG	SV	IO	229-330		8	3	4300	1	4	16900	20800
24	1	OFFSHORE 242G	ST	SF	FBG	SV	OB			8	3	3325	1	4	14700	16700
24	1	OFFSHORE 242G	HT	SF	FBG	SV	OB			8	3	3325	1	4	14700	16700
25	4	SAILFISH 252G	ST	SF	FBG	SV	OB			9	6	4900	1	7	19300	21400
25	4	SAILFISH 252G	HT	SF	FBG	SV	OB			9	6	5625	1	7	20300	22600
25	4	SAILFISH 254	ST	SF	FBG	SV	IO	260-330		9	6	5625	1	7	22400	27300
25	4	SAILFISH 254	HT	SF	FBG	SV	IO	260-330		9	6	5625	1	7	22400	27300
25	4	SAILFISH 255	ST	SF	FBG	SV	OB			9	6	4725	1	7	19000	21100
25	4	SAILFISH 255	HT	SF	FBG	SV	OB			9	6	4725	1	7	19000	21100
25	4	TROPHY 257	ST	SF	FBG	SV	OB			9	6	4375	1	7	18600	20700
25	4	TROPHY 257	HT	SF	FBG	SV	OB			9	6	4375	1	7	18600	20700
25	4	TROPHY 258	ST	SF	FBG	SV	IO	260-330		9	6	5260	1	7	21400	26200
25	4	TROPHY 258	HT	SF	FBG	SV	IO	260-330		9	6	5260	1	7	21400	26200
25	4	TROPHY 259G	ST	SF	FBG	SV	OB			9	6	4530	1	7	18900	21000
25	4	TROPHY 259G	HT	SF	FBG	SV	OB			9	6	4530	1	7	18900	21000
28		MARLIN 28	ST	SF	FBG	SV	OB			10	7	7000	1	6	26300	29300
		1989 BOATS														
18	11	TOURNAMENT 190	ST	RNBT	FBG	SV	OB			8		2075	1	2	6050	6950
20	4	FISHERMAN 204	OP	CTRCN	FBG	SV	OB			8		2245	1	2	8600	9900
20	4	FISHERMAN 204	ST	CTRCN	FBG	SV	OB			8		2245	1	2	8600	9900
20	4	FISHERMAN 204	TT	CTRCN	FBG	SV	OB			8		2285	1	2	8800	10000
20	4	OVERNIGHTER 204C	ST	FSH	FBG	SV	OB			8		2550	1	2	9350	10600
20	4	OVERNIGHTER 204C	HT	FSH	FBG	SV	OB			8		2675	1	2	9500	10800
20	4	OVERNIGHTER 205	ST	FSH	FBG	SV	IO	180-260		8		3380	1	2	9700	11600
20	4	OVERNIGHTER 205	HT	FSH	FBG	SV	IO	180-260		8		3380	1	2	9700	11600
20	4	OVERNIGHTER 206G	ST	FSH	FBG	SV	OB			8		2715	1	2	9550	10900
20	4	OVERNIGHTER 206G	HT	FSH	FBG	SV	OB			8		2715	1	2	9550	10900
22		SEAFARER 226	ST	SF	FBG	SV	OB			8		2875	1	2	12200	13900
22		SEAFARER 226	HT	SF	FBG	SV	OB			8		2875	1	2	12200	13900
22		SEAFARER 227	ST	SF	FBG	SV	IO	180-260		8		3705	1	2	12200	14500
22		SEAFARER 227	HT	SF	FBG	SV	IO	180-260		8		3705	1	2	12200	14500
22		SEAFARER 228G	ST	SF	FBG	SV	OB			8		3000	1	2	12600	14300
22		SEAFARER 228G	HT	SF	FBG	SV	OB			8		3000	1	2	12600	14300
23	5	GULFSTREAM 230	ST	SF	FBG	SV	OB			9	3	3900	1	5	15300	17400
23	5	GULFSTREAM 231	ST	SF	FBG	SV	IO	260-330		9	3	5000	1	5	18100	21500
23	5	GULFSTREAM 231	HT	SF	FBG	SV	IO	260-330		9	3	5000	1	5	18100	21500
23	5	GULFSTREAM 232G	ST	SF	FBG	SV	OB			9	3	4025	1	5	15600	17700
23	5	GULFSTREAM 232G	HT	SF	FBG	SV	OB			9	3	4025	1	5	15600	17700
24	1	OFFSHORE 240	ST	SF	FBG	SV	OB			8	3	3200	1	4	13800	15700
24	1	OFFSHORE 240	HT	SF	FBG	SV	OB			8	3	3200	1	4	13800	15700
24	1	OFFSHORE 241	ST	SF	FBG	SV	IO	230-260		8	3	4300	1	4	15600	18000
24	1	OFFSHORE 241	HT	SF	FBG	SV	IO	230-260		8	3	4300	1	4	15600	18000
24	1	OFFSHORE 242G	ST	SF	FBG	SV	OB			8	3	3325	1	4	14200	16200
24	1	OFFSHORE 242G	HT	SF	FBG	SV	OB			8	3	3517	1	4	14800	16800
25	4	SAILFISH 252G	ST	SF	FBG	SV	OB			9	6	4530	1	7	18800	20900
25	4	SAILFISH 252G	HT	SF	FBG	SV	OB			9	6	4705	1	7	19100	21200
25	4	SAILFISH 254	ST	SF	FBG	SV	IO	260-330		9	6	5860	1	7	22200	26400
25	4	SAILFISH 254	ST	SF	FBG	SV	IO	T180	MRCR	9	6	5860	1	7	23200	25700
25	4	SAILFISH 254	HT	SF	FBG	SV	IO	260-330		9	6	5860	1	7	21700	25800
25	4	SAILFISH 255	ST	SF	FBG	SV	OB			9	6	4375	1	7	18600	20700
25	4	SAILFISH 255	HT	SF	FBG	SV	OB			9	6	4550	1	7	18900	21000
25	4	TROPHY 257	ST	SF	FBG	SV	OB			9	6	4375	1	7	17000	19300
25	4	TROPHY 257	HT	SF	FBG	SV	OB			9	6	4550	1	7	17400	19700

 CONTINUED ON NEXT PAGE

GRADY-WHITE BOATS INC -CONTINUED See inside cover to adjust price for area

LOA FT	IN	NAME AND/ OR MODEL	TOP/ RIG	BOAT TYPE	-HULL- MTL	TP	ENGINE TP	# HP	MFG	BEAM FT	IN	WGT LBS	DRAFT FT	IN	RETAIL LOW	RETAIL HIGH
		1989 BOATS														
25	4	TROPHY 258	ST	SF	FBG	SV	IO	260-330		9	6	5860	1	7	21200	25200
25	4	TROPHY 258	HT	SF	FBG	SV	IO	260-330		9	6	6219	1	7	22700	26800
25	4	TROPHY 259G	ST	SF	FBG	SV	OB			9	6	4530	1	7	17300	19700
25	4	TROPHY 259G	HT	SF	FBG	SV	OB			9	6	4705	1	7	18000	20000
28		MARLIN 28	ST	SF	FBG	SV	OB			10	7	7000	1	6	25500	28300
		1988 BOATS														
18	11	TOURNAMENT 190	ST	RNBT	FBG	SV	OB			8		2075	1	2	5850	6700
20	4	FISHERMAN 204	ST	CTRCN	FBG	SV	OB			8		2245	1	2	8350	9600
20	4	FISHERMAN 204	TT	CTRCN	FBG	SV	OB			8		2285	1	2	8450	9700
20	4	OVERNIGHTER 204C	ST	FSH	FBG	SV	OB			8		2550	1	2	9050	10300
20	4	OVERNIGHTER 204C	HT	FSH	FBG	SV	OB			8		2675	1	2	9250	10500
20	4	OVERNIGHTER 205	ST	FSH	FBG	SV	IO	175-260		8		3433	1	2	9250	11300
20	4	OVERNIGHTER 205	HT	FSH	FBG	SV	IO	175-260		8		3558	1	2	9450	11500
20	4	OVERNIGHTER 206G	ST	FSH	FBG	SV	OB			8		2715	1	2	9300	10600
20	4	OVERNIGHTER 206G	HT	FSH	FBG	SV	OB			8		2715	1	2	9300	10600
22		SEAFARER 226	ST	SF	FBG	SV	OB			8		2875	1	2	11900	13500
22		SEAFARER 226	HT	SF	FBG	SV	OB			8		2725	1	2	11500	13000
22		SEAFARER 227	ST	SF	FBG	SV	IO	230-260		8		3846	1	2	12100	14100
22		SEAFARER 227	HT	SF	FBG	SV	IO	180-260		8		3830	1	2	11800	13700
22		SEAFARER 228G	ST	SF	FBG	SV	OB			8		3000	1	2	12200	13900
22		SEAFARER 228G	HT	SF	FBG	SV	OB			8		3000	1	2	12200	13900
23	5	GULFSTREAM 230	ST	SF	FBG	SV	OB			9	3	3900	1	5	14800	16800
23	5	GULFSTREAM 231	ST	SF	FBG	SV	IO	260-340		9	3	5000	1	5	16800	20800
23	5	GULFSTREAM 232G	ST	SF	FBG	SV	OB			9	3	4092	1	5	15200	17300
24	1	FISHERMAN 249	ST	CTRCN	FBG	SV	OB			8	3	3260	1	4	13600	15500
24	1	FISHERMAN 249	TT	CTRCN	FBG	SV	OB			8	3	3300	1	4	13700	15600
24	1	FISHERMAN 249G	ST	CTRCN	FBG	SV	OB			8	3	3425	1	4	14100	16000
24	1	FISHERMAN 249G	TT	CTRCN	FBG	SV	OB			8	3	3532	1	4	14400	16400
24	1	OFFSHORE 240	ST	SF	FBG	SV	OB			8	3	3200	1	4	13400	15200
24	1	OFFSHORE 240	HT	SF	FBG	SV	OB			8	3	3325	1	4	13800	15700
24	1	OFFSHORE 241	ST	SF	FBG	SV	IO	230-260		8	3	4221	1	4	14500	16900
24	1	OFFSHORE 241	HT	SF	FBG	SV	IO	230-260		8	3	4346	1	4	14900	17300
24	1	OFFSHORE 242G	ST	SF	FBG	SV	OB			8	3	3325	1	4	13800	15700
24	1	OFFSHORE 242G	HT	SF	FBG	SV	OB			8	3	3450	1	4	14200	16100
25	4	SAILFISH 252G	ST	SF	FBG	SV	OB			9	6	4530	1	7	18200	20300
25	4	SAILFISH 252G	HT	SF	FBG	SV	OB			9	6	4705	1	7	18500	20600
25	4	SAILFISH 254	ST	SF	FBG	SV	OB			9	6	5447	1	7	19100	21200
25	4	SAILFISH 254	ST	SF	FBG	SV	IO	260		9	6	5263	1	7	19100	21200
25	4	SAILFISH 254	ST	SF	FBG	SV	IO	340	OMC	9	6	5620	1	7	21600	23900
25	4	SAILFISH 254	HT	SF	FBG	SV	IO	260-340		9	6	5438	1	7	19500	24400
25	4	SAILFISH 255	ST	SF	FBG	SV	OB			9	6	4375	1	7	18000	20000
25	4	SAILFISH 255	HT	SF	FBG	SV	OB			9	6	4550	1	7	18300	20300
25	4	TROPHY 257	ST	SF	FBG	SV	OB			9	6	4375	1	7	16500	18800
25	4	TROPHY 257	HT	SF	FBG	SV	OB			9	6	4550	1	7	16900	19200
25	4	TROPHY 258	ST	SF	FBG	SV	IO	260		9	6	5341	1	7	19300	21400
25	4	TROPHY 258	ST	SF	FBG	SV	IO	T175-T205		9	6	6044	1	7	22200	25200
25	4	TROPHY 258	HT	SF	FBG	SV	IO	260		9	6	5516	1	7	19700	21900
25	4	TROPHY 258	HT	SF	FBG	SV	IO	T175-T205		9	6	6219	1	7	22600	25600
25	4	TROPHY 259G	ST	SF	FBG	SV	OB			9	6	4530	1	7	16800	19100
25	4	TROPHY 259G	HT	SF	FBG	SV	OB			9	6	4705	1	7	17100	19500
		1987 BOATS														
18	11	TOURNAMENT 190	ST	RNBT	FBG	SV	OB			8		2075	1	2	5650	6500
20	4	FISHERMAN 204	ST	CTRCN	FBG	SV	OB			8		2245	1	2	8150	9350
20	4	FISHERMAN 204	TT	CTRCN	FBG	SV	OB			8		2285	1	2	8200	9450
20	4	OVERNIGHTER 204C	ST	FSH	FBG	SV	OB			8		2550	1	2	8800	10000
20	4	OVERNIGHTER 204C	HT	FSH	FBG	SV	OB			8		2675	1	2	9000	10200
20	4	OVERNIGHTER 205	ST	FSH	FBG	SV	IO	175-260		8		3433	1	2	8700	10700
20	4	OVERNIGHTER 205	HT	FSH	FBG	SV	IO	175-260		8		3558	1	2	9000	11000
20	4	OVERNIGHTER 206G	ST	FSH	FBG	SV	OB			8		2715	1	2	9050	10300
20	4	OVERNIGHTER 206G	HT	FSH	FBG	SV	OB			8		2715	1	2	9050	10300
22		SEAFARER 226	ST	SF	FBG	SV	OB			8		2875	1	2	11600	13100
22		SEAFARER 226	HT	SF	FBG	SV	OB			8		2875	1	2	11600	13100
22		SEAFARER 227	ST	SF	FBG	SV	IO	180-260		8		3705	1	2	11000	13400
22		SEAFARER 227	HT	SF	FBG	SV	IO	180-260		8		3830	1	2	11300	13700
22		SEAFARER 228G	ST	SF	FBG	SV	OB			8		3000	1	2	11900	13500
22		SEAFARER 228G	HT	SF	FBG	SV	OB			8		3000	1	2	11900	13500
23	5	GULFSTREAM 230	ST	SF	FBG	SV	OB			9	3	3900	1	5	14400	16400
23	5	GULFSTREAM 230	HT	SF	FBG	SV	OB			9	3	4075	1	5	14800	16800
23	5	GULFSTREAM 231	ST	SF	FBG	SV	IO	260		9	3	5000	1	5	16000	18100
23	5	GULFSTREAM 231	ST	SF	FBG	SV	IO	330-335		9	3	5181	1	5	18100	21200
23	5	GULFSTREAM 231	HT	SF	FBG	SV	IO	260		9	3	5175	1	5	16400	18600
23	5	GULFSTREAM 231	HT	SF	FBG	SV	IO	330-335		9	3	5356	1	5	18500	21700
23	5	GULFSTREAM 232G	ST	SF	FBG	SV	OB			9	3	4025	1	5	14700	16700
23	5	GULFSTREAM 232G	HT	SF	FBG	SV	OB			9	3	4200	1	5	15000	17100
24	1	FISHERMAN 249	ST	CTRCN	FBG	SV	OB			8		3260	1	4	13200	15000
24	1	FISHERMAN 249	TT	CTRCN	FBG	SV	OB			8		3300	1	4	13300	15200
24	1	FISHERMAN 249G	ST	CTRCN	FBG	SV	OB			8		3425	1	4	13700	15600
24	1	FISHERMAN 249G	TT	CTRCN	FBG	SV	OB			8		3532	1	4	14000	15900
24	1	OFFSHORE 240	ST	SF	FBG	SV	OB			8		3200	1	4	12200	13900
24	1	OFFSHORE 240	HT	SF	FBG	SV	OB			8		3325	1	4	12700	14400
24	1	OFFSHORE 241	ST	SF	FBG	SV	IO	230-260		8		4221	1	4	13300	15900
24	1	OFFSHORE 241	HT	SF	FBG	SV	IO	230-260		8		4346	1	4	13600	16200
24	1	OFFSHORE 242G	ST	SF	FBG	SV	OB			8		3392	1	4	13000	14800
24	1	OFFSHORE 242G	HT	SF	FBG	SV	OB			8		3517	1	4	13500	15300
24	1	OFFSHORE PRO 246	ST	SF	FBG	SV	OB			8		3200	1	4	13800	15700
24	1	OFFSHORE PRO 246	HT	SF	FBG	SV	OB			8		3325	1	4	14200	16100
24	1	OFFSHORE PRO 247	ST	SF	FBG	SV	IO	230-260		8		4221	1	4	14200	16500
24	1	OFFSHORE PRO 247	HT	SF	FBG	SV	IO	230-300		8		4346	1	4	14500	17000
24	1	OFFSHORE PRO 248G	ST	SF	FBG	SV	OB			8		3392	1	4	14200	16100
24	1	OFFSHORE PRO 248G	HT	SF	FBG	SV	OB			8		3450	1	4	14400	16300
25	4	SAILFISH 252G	ST	SF	FBG	SV	OB			9	6	4530	1	7	17100	19500
25	4	SAILFISH 252G	HT	SF	FBG	SV	OB			9	6	4705	1	7	17400	19800
25	4	SAILFISH 254	ST	SF	FBG	SV	IO	260-335		9	6	5263	1	7	18400	22600
25	4	SAILFISH 254	ST	SF	FBG	SV	IO	T175-T205		9	6	5966	1	7	20900	23700
25	4	SAILFISH 254	HT	SF	FBG	SV	IO	260-335		9	6	5438	1	7	18800	23100
25	4	SAILFISH 254	HT	SF	FBG	SV	IO	T175-T205		9	6	6141	1	7	21300	24200
25	4	SAILFISH 255	ST	SF	FBG	SV	OB			9	6	4375	1	7	16900	19300
25	4	SAILFISH 255	HT	SF	FBG	SV	OB			9	6	4550	1	7	17200	19600
25	4	TROPHY 257	ST	SF	FBG	SV	OB			9	6	4375	1	7	16300	18500
25	4	TROPHY 257	HT	SF	FBG	SV	OB			9	6	4550	1	7	16600	18800
25	4	TROPHY 258	ST	SF	FBG	SV	IO	260-335		9	6	5341	1	7	18600	22500
25	4	TROPHY 258	ST	SF	FBG	SV	IO	T175-T205		9	6	6044	1	7	21100	23900
25	4	TROPHY 258	HT	SF	FBG	SV	IO	260-335		9	6	5516	1	7	19000	22900
25	4	TROPHY 258	HT	SF	FBG	SV	IO	T175-T205		9	6	6219	1	7	21500	24400
25	4	TROPHY 259	ST	SF	FBG	SV	OB			9	6	4530	1	7	16600	18800
25	4	TROPHY 259	HT	SF	FBG	SV	OB			9	6	4705	1	7	16900	19200
		1986 BOATS														
18	11	TOURNAMENT 190	ST	RNBT	FBG	SV	OB			8		1900		1	5250	6050
18	11	TOURNAMENT 197	ST	RNBT	FBG	SV	IO	170-230		8		2800		1	5000	6050
18	11	TOURNAMENT 197	ST	RNBT	FBG	SV	IO	260		8		2800		1	5350	6450
18	11	TOURNAMENT 198	ST	RNBT	FBG	SV	SE	115	OMC	8		2450		1	5900	6750
18	11	TOURNAMENT 198G	ST	RNBT	FBG	SV	OB			8		2240	1	2	5700	6550
20	4	FISHERMAN 204	ST	FSH	FBG	SV	OB			8		1995		1	7350	8450
20	4	FISHERMAN 204	TT	FSH	FBG	SV	OB			8		2170		1	7750	8950
20	4	OVERNIGHTER 204C	ST	FSH	FBG	SV	OB			8		2300		1	8050	9250
20	4	OVERNIGHTER 204C	HT	FSH	FBG	SV	OB			8		2425		1	8300	9500
20	4	OVERNIGHTER 205	ST	FSH	FBG	SV	IO	170-230		8		3100		1	7800	9750
20	4	OVERNIGHTER 205	ST	FSH	FBG	SV	IO	260		8		3291		1	8550	10200
20	4	OVERNIGHTER 205	HT	FSH	FBG	SV	IO	170-230		8		3225		1	8000	9950
20	4	OVERNIGHTER 205	HT	FSH	FBG	SV	IO	260		8		3416		1	8850	10500
20	4	OVERNIGHTER 206	ST	FSH	FBG	SV	SE	205	OMC	8		3000		1	9150	10400
20	4	OVERNIGHTER 206	HT	FSH	FBG	SV	SE	205	OMC	8		3125		1	9250	10500
20	4	OVERNIGHTER 206G	ST	FSH	FBG	SV	OB			8		2715	1	2	8850	10000
20	4	OVERNIGHTER 206G	HT	FSH	FBG	SV	OB			8		2715	1	2	8850	10000
22		SEAFARER 226	ST	SF	FBG	SV	OB			8		2600		1	10500	12000
22		SEAFARER 226	HT	SF	FBG	SV	OB			8		2725		1	10900	12400
22		SEAFARER 227	ST	SF	FBG	SV	IO	170-230		8		3400		1	9850	12100
22		SEAFARER 227	ST	SF	FBG	SV	IO	260		8		3591		1	10700	12600
22		SEAFARER 227	HT	SF	FBG	SV	IO	170-230		8		3525		1	10100	12300
22		SEAFARER 227	HT	SF	FBG	SV	IO	260		8		3716		1	11000	12900
22		SEAFARER 228	ST	SF	FBG	SV	SE	205	OMC	8		3200		1	12000	13600
22		SEAFARER 228	ST	SF	FBG	SV	SE	T115	OMC	8		3700		1	12900	14600
22		SEAFARER 228	HT	SF	FBG	SV	SE	205	OMC	8		3325		1	12300	13900
22		SEAFARER 228	HT	SF	FBG	SV	SE	T115	OMC	8		3825		1	13000	14800
22		SEAFARER 228G	ST	SF	FBG	SV	OB			8		3000	1	2	11600	13100
22		SEAFARER 228G	HT	SF	FBG	SV	OB			8		3000	1	2	11600	13100
22		TOURNAMENT 223	ST	FSH	FBG	SV	OB			8		2400		1	9350	10600
22		TOURNAMENT 224	ST	FSH	FBG	SV	IO	170-230		8		3200		1	8800	10700
22		TOURNAMENT 224	ST	FSH	FBG	SV	IO	260		8		3391		1	9550	11300
22		TOURNAMENT 225	ST	FSH	FBG	SV	SE	205	OMC	8		3000		1	10800	12300
22		TOURNAMENT 225	ST	FSH	FBG	SV	SE	T115	OMC	8		3500		1	11700	13300
22		TOURNAMENT 225G	ST	FSH	FBG	SV	OB			8		2800	1	2	10400	11800
24	1	FISHERMAN 249	ST	CTRCN	FBG	SV	OB			8		2900		1	11800	13400
24	1	FISHERMAN 249	TT	CTRCN	FBG	SV	OB			8		3075		1	12300	14000
24	1	FISHERMAN 249G	ST	CTRCN	FBG	SV	OB			8		3425	1	4	13400	15200
24	1	FISHERMAN 249G	TT	CTRCN	FBG	SV	OB			8		3425	1	4	13400	15200

CONTINUED ON NEXT PAGE

GRADY-WHITE BOATS INC -CONTINUED See inside cover to adjust price for area

LOA FT	LOA IN	NAME AND/ OR MODEL	TOP/ RIG	BOAT TYPE	-HULL- MTL	-HULL- TP	ENGINE TP	ENGINE # HP	ENGINE MFG	BEAM FT	BEAM IN	WGT LBS	DRAFT FT	DRAFT IN	RETAIL LOW	RETAIL HIGH
		1986 BOATS														
24	1	FISHERMAN 249SD	ST	CTRCN	FBG	SV	SE		OMC	8		3960	1	4	**	**
24	1	FISHERMAN 249SD	ST	CTRCN	FBG	SV	SE	T	OMC	8			1	4	**	**
24	1	FISHERMAN 249SD	TT	CTRCN	FBG	SV	SE		OMC	8		3960	1	4	**	**
24	1	FISHERMAN 249SD	TT	CTRCN	FBG	SV	SE	T	OMC	8			1	4	**	**
24	1	OFFSHORE 240	ST	SF	FBG	SV	OB			8		2900		1	11000	12500
24	1	OFFSHORE 240	HT	SF	FBG	SV	OB			8		3025		1	12200	13800
24	1	OFFSHORE 241	ST	SF	FBG	SV	IO	230-260		8		4083		1	12800	15300
24	1	OFFSHORE 241	HT	SF	FBG	SV	IO	230-260		8		4208		1	13100	15600
24	1	OFFSHORE 242	ST	SF	FBG	SV	SE	205	OMC	8		3500		1	13100	14900
24	1	OFFSHORE 242	ST	SF	FBG	SV	SE	T115	OMC	8		4000		1	14500	16400
24	1	OFFSHORE 242	HT	SF	FBG	SV	SE	205	OMC	8		3625		1	13900	15800
24	1	OFFSHORE 242	HT	SF	FBG	SV	SE	T115	OMC	8		4125		1	15200	17200
24	1	OFFSHORE 242G	ST	SF	FBG	SV	OB			8		3325	1	4	12400	14100
24	1	OFFSHORE 242G	HT	SF	FBG	SV	OB			8		3325	1	4	12500	14200
24	1	OFFSHORE PRO 246	ST	SF	FBG	SV	OB			8		2900		1	12600	14300
24	1	OFFSHORE PRO 246	HT	SF	FBG	SV	OB			8		3075		1	12300	14000
24	1	OFFSHORE PRO 247	ST	SF	FBG	SV	IO	230-260		8		4010		1	12600	15100
24	1	OFFSHORE PRO 247	HT	SF	FBG	SV	IO	230-260		8		4135		1	12900	15400
24	1	OFFSHORE PRO 248	ST	SF	FBG		SE	205	OMC	8		3500		1	14000	15900
24	1	OFFSHORE PRO 248	ST	SF	FBG		SE	T115	OMC	8		4000		1	15300	17400
24	1	OFFSHORE PRO 248	HT	SF	FBG		SE	205	OMC	8		3500		1	13600	15400
24	1	OFFSHORE PRO 248	HT	SF	FBG		SE	T115	OMC	8		4000		1	14900	16900
24	1	OFFSHORE PRO 248G	ST	SF	FBG	SV	OB			8		3325	1	4	13700	15600
24	1	OFFSHORE PRO 248G	HT	SF	FBG	SV	OB			8		3325	1	4	13700	15500
25	4	SAILFISH 252	ST	SF	FBG	SV	SE	T205	OMC	9	6	5130		1	17500	19800
25	4	SAILFISH 252	HT	SF	FBG	SV	SE	T205	OMC	9	6	5305		1	18100	20100
25	4	SAILFISH 252	TT	SF	FBG	SV	SE	T205	OMC	9	6	5480		1	18300	20300
25	4	SAILFISH 254	ST	SF	FBG	SV	IO	260		9	6	5000		1	16900	19400
25	4	SAILFISH 254	ST	SF	FBG	SV	IO	T170-T205		9	6	5500		1	19300	21800
25	4	SAILFISH 254	HT	SF	FBG	SV	IO	260		9	6	5175		1	17300	19900
25	4	SAILFISH 254	HT	SF	FBG	SV	IO	T170-T205		9	6	5675		1	19700	22200
25	4	SAILFISH 254	TT	SF	FBG	SV	IO	260		9	6	5350		1	18000	20300
25	4	SAILFISH 254	TT	SF	FBG	SV	IO	T170-T205		9	6	5850		1	20000	22600
25	4	SAILFISH 255	ST	SF	FBG	SV	OB			9	6	4075		1	16000	18200
25	4	SAILFISH 255	HT	SF	FBG	SV	OB			9	6	4250		1	16300	18500
25	4	SAILFISH 255	TT	SF	FBG	SV	OB			9	6	4425		1	16500	18800
25	4	TROPHY 257	ST	SF	FBG	SV	OB			9	6	4075		1	15400	17400
25	4	TROPHY 257	HT	SF	FBG	SV	OB			9	6	4250		1	15700	17800
25	4	TROPHY 257	TT	SF	FBG	SV	OB			9	6	4425		1	16000	18200
25	4	TROPHY 258	ST	SF	FBG	SV	IO	260		9	6	5000		1	16300	18800
25	4	TROPHY 258	ST	SF	FBG	SV	IO	T170-T205		9	6	5500		1	18900	21200
25	4	TROPHY 258	HT	SF	FBG	SV	IO	260		9	6	5175		1	16700	19300
25	4	TROPHY 258	HT	SF	FBG	SV	IO	T170-T205		9	6	5675		1	19100	21700
25	4	TROPHY 258	TT	SF	FBG	SV	IO	260		9	6	5350		1	17100	19700
25	4	TROPHY 258	TT	SF	FBG	SV	IO	T170-T205		9	6	5850		1	19500	22100
25	4	TROPHY 259	ST	SF	FBG	SV	SE	T205	OMC	9	6	5130		1	17100	19400
25	4	TROPHY 259	HT	SF	FBG	SV	SE	T205	OMC	9	6	5305		1	17300	19700
25	4	TROPHY 259	TT	SF	FBG	SV	SE	T205	OMC	9	6	5480		1	17600	20000
		1985 BOATS														
18	11	TOURNAMENT 190	ST	RNBT	FBG	SV	OB			8		1900	1	2	5150	5900
18	11	TOURNAMENT 197	ST	RNBT	FBG	SV	IO	170-230		8		2800	1	2	4800	5850
18	11	TOURNAMENT 197	ST	RNBT	FBG	SV	IO	260		8		2800	1	2	5100	6200
18	11	TOURNAMENT 198	ST	RNBT	FBG	SV	SE	115	OMC	8		2450	1	2	5750	6600
20	4	FISHERMAN 204	ST	FSH	FBG	SV	OB			8		1995	1	2	7200	8250
20	4	FISHERMAN 204	TT	FSH	FBG	SV	OB			8		2170	1	2	7600	8700
20	4	OVERNIGHTER 204C	ST	FSH	FBG	SV	OB			8		2300	1	2	7850	9050
20	4	OVERNIGHTER 204C	HT	FSH	FBG	SV	OB			8		2425	1	2	8100	9300
20	4	OVERNIGHTER 205	ST	FSH	FBG	SV	IO	170-230		8		3100	1	2	7500	9350
20	4	OVERNIGHTER 205	ST	FSH	FBG	SV	IO	260		8		3291	1	2	8200	9850
20	4	OVERNIGHTER 205	HT	FSH	FBG	SV	IO	170-230		8		3225	1	2	7700	9550
20	4	OVERNIGHTER 205	HT	FSH	FBG	SV	IO	260		8		3416	1	2	8400	10100
20	4	OVERNIGHTER 206	ST	FSH	FBG	SV	SE	205	OMC	8		3000	1	2	8950	10100
20	4	OVERNIGHTER 206	HT	FSH	FBG	SV	SE	205	OMC	8		3125	1	2	9000	10200
22		SEAFARER 226	ST	SF	FBG	SV	OB			8		2600	1	2	10300	11700
22		SEAFARER 226	HT	SF	FBG	SV	OB			8		2725	1	2	10600	12100
22		SEAFARER 227	ST	SF	FBG	SV	IO	170-230		8		3400	1	2	9450	11600
22		SEAFARER 227	ST	SF	FBG	SV	IO	260		8		3591	1	2	10300	12100
22		SEAFARER 227	HT	SF	FBG	SV	IO	170-230		8		3525	1	2	9700	11800
22		SEAFARER 227	HT	SF	FBG	SV	IO	260		8		3716	1	2	10500	12400
22		SEAFARER 228	ST	SF	FBG	SV	SE	205	OMC	8		3200	1	2	11700	13300
22		SEAFARER 228	ST	SF	FBG	SV	SE	T115	OMC	8		3700	1	2	12600	14300
22		SEAFARER 228	HT	SF	FBG	SV	SE	205	OMC	8		3325	1	2	12000	13600
22		SEAFARER 228	HT	SF	FBG	SV	SE	T115	OMC	8		3825	1	2	12700	14500
22		TOURNAMENT 223	ST	FSH	FBG	SV	OB			8		2400	1	2	9150	10400
22		TOURNAMENT 224	ST	FSH	FBG	SV	IO	170-230		8		3200	1	2	8350	10400
22		TOURNAMENT 224	ST	FSH	FBG	SV	IO	260		8		3391	1	2	9200	10800
22		TOURNAMENT 225	ST	FSH	FBG	SV	SE	205	OMC	8		3000	1	2	10600	12000
22		TOURNAMENT 225	ST	FSH	FBG	SV	SE	T115	OMC	8		3500	1	2	11500	13000
22		TOURNAMENT 233	HT	FSH	FBG	SV	OB			8		2575	1	2	9550	10900
24	1	FISHERMAN 249	ST	CTRCN	FBG	SV	OB			8		2900	1	4	11500	13100
24	1	FISHERMAN 249	TT	CTRCN	FBG	SV	OB			8		3075	1	4	12000	13700
24	1	OFFSHORE 240	ST	SF	FBG	SV	OB			8		2900	1	4	10700	12200
24	1	OFFSHORE 240	HT	SF	FBG	SV	OB			8		3025	1	4	11900	13500
24	1	OFFSHORE 241	ST	SF	FBG	SV	IO	230-260		8		4083	1	4	12300	14700
24	1	OFFSHORE 241	HT	SF	FBG	SV	IO	230-260		8		4208	1	4	12600	15000
24	1	OFFSHORE 242	ST	SF	FBG	SV	SE	205	OMC	8		3500	1	4	12800	14600
24	1	OFFSHORE 242	ST	SF	FBG	SV	SE	T115	OMC	8		4000	1	4	14100	16100
24	1	OFFSHORE 242	HT	SF	FBG	SV	SE	205	OMC	8		3625	1	4	13600	15500
24	1	OFFSHORE 242	HT	SF	FBG	SV	SE	T115	OMC	8		4125	1	4	14800	16800
24	1	OFFSHORE PRO 246	ST	SF	FBG	SV	OB			8		2900	1	4	12300	14000
24	1	OFFSHORE PRO 246	HT	SF	FBG	SV	OB			8		3075	1	4	12000	13700
24	1	OFFSHORE PRO 247	ST	SF	FBG	SV	IO	230-260		8		4010	1	4	12100	14500
24	1	OFFSHORE PRO 247	HT	SF	FBG	SV	IO	230-260		8		4135	1	4	12400	14800
24	1	OFFSHORE PRO 248	ST	SF	FBG		SE	205	OMC	8		3500	1	4	13700	15600
24	1	OFFSHORE PRO 248	ST	SF	FBG		SE	T115	OMC	8		4000	1	4	14900	17000
24	1	OFFSHORE PRO 248	HT	SF	FBG		SE	205	OMC	8		3500	1	4	13300	15100
24	1	OFFSHORE PRO 248	HT	SF	FBG		SE	T115	OMC	8		4000	1	4	14500	16500
25	4	SAILFISH 252	ST	SF	FBG	SV	SE	T205	OMC	9	6	5130	1	7	17000	19300
25	4	SAILFISH 252	HT	SF	FBG	SV	SE	T205	OMC	9	6	5305	1	7	17200	19500
25	4	SAILFISH 252	TT	SF	FBG	SV	SE	T205	OMC	9	6	5480	1	7	17300	19700
25	4	SAILFISH 254	ST	SF	FBG	SV	IO	260		9	6	5000	1	7	16000	18500
25	4	SAILFISH 254	ST	SF	FBG	SV	IO	T170	MRCR	9	6	5500	1	7	14000	15900
25	4	SAILFISH 254	ST	SF	FBG	SV	IO	T170-T190		9	6	5500	1	7	18400	20800
25	4	SAILFISH 254	HT	SF	FBG	SV	IO	260		9	6	5175	1	7	16300	18900
25	4	SAILFISH 254	HT	SF	FBG	SV	IO	T170-T190		9	6	5675	1	7	18800	21200
25	4	SAILFISH 254	TT	SF	FBG	SV	IO	260		9	6	5350	1	7	16700	19300
25	4	SAILFISH 254	TT	SF	FBG	SV	IO	T170-T190		9	6	5850	1	7	19200	21400
25	4	SAILFISH 255	ST	SF	FBG	SV	OB			9	6	4075	1	7	15500	17600
25	4	SAILFISH 255	HT	SF	FBG	SV	OB			9	6	4250	1	7	15800	17900
25	4	SAILFISH 255	TT	SF	FBG	SV	OB			9	6	4425	1	7	16000	18200
25	4	TROPHY 257	ST	SF	FBG	SV	OB			9	6	4075	1	7	15200	17200
25	4	TROPHY 257	HT	SF	FBG	SV	OB			9	6	4250	1	7	15500	17600
25	4	TROPHY 257	TT	SF	FBG	SV	OB			9	6	4425	1	7	15800	17900
25	4	TROPHY 258	ST	SF	FBG	SV	IO	260		9	6	5000	1	7	15900	18400
25	4	TROPHY 258	ST	SF	FBG	SV	IO	T170		9	6	5500	1	7	13900	15800
25	4	TROPHY 258	ST	SF	FBG	SV	IO	T185-T190		9	6	5500	1	7	18500	20700
25	4	TROPHY 258	HT	SF	FBG	SV	IO	260		9	6	5175	1	7	16200	18800
25	4	TROPHY 258	HT	SF	FBG	SV	IO	T170-T190		9	6	5675	1	7	18700	21100
25	4	TROPHY 258	TT	SF	FBG	SV	IO	260		9	6	5350	1	7	16600	19200
25	4	TROPHY 258	TT	SF	FBG	SV	IO	T170-T190		9	6	5850	1	7	19100	21300
25	4	TROPHY 259	ST	SF	FBG	SV	SE	T205	OMC	9	6	5130	1	7	16800	19100
25	4	TROPHY 259	HT	SF	FBG	SV	SE	T205	OMC	9	6	5305	1	7	17000	19300
25	4	TROPHY 259	TT	SF	FBG	SV	SE	T205	OMC	9	6	5480	1	7	17300	19700
		1984 BOATS														
16	10	TOURNAMENT 170	ST	RNBT	FBG	SV	OB			6	9	1300	1		3650	4200
18	11	TOURNAMENT 190	ST	RNBT	FBG	SV	OB			8		1900	1	2	5000	5750
18	11	TOURNAMENT 197	ST	RNBT	FBG	SV	IO	170-230		8		2750	1	2	4650	5750
18	11	TOURNAMENT 197	ST	RNBT	FBG	SV	IO	260		8		2941	1	2	5100	6100
18	11	TOURNAMENT 198	ST	RNBT	FBG	SV	OB			8		2650	1	2	5750	6600
20	4	FISHERMAN 204	ST	FSH	FBG	SV	OB			8		1995	1	2	7050	8100
20	4	OVERNIGHTER 204C	ST	FSH	FBG	SV	OB			8		2300	1	2	7700	8850
20	4	OVERNIGHTER 204C	HT	FSH	FBG	SV	OB			8		2425	1	2	7900	9100
20	4	OVERNIGHTER 205	ST	FSH	FBG	SV	IO	170-175		8		3100	1	2	7250	8600
20	4	OVERNIGHTER 205	ST	FSH	FBG	SV	SE	185		8		3100	1	2	8800	10100
20	4	OVERNIGHTER 205	ST	FSH	FBG	SV	IO	188-230		8		3117	1	2	7300	9000
20	4	OVERNIGHTER 205	ST	FSH	FBG	SV	IO	260		8		3291	1	2	7950	9500
20	4	OVERNIGHTER 205	HT	FSH	FBG	SV	IO	170-228		8		3225	1	2	7400	9250
20	4	OVERNIGHTER 205	HT	FSH	FBG	SV	SE	230-260		8		3492	1	2	8900	10100
20	4	OVERNIGHTER 206	ST	FSH	FBG	SV	SE	155-205		8		3000	1	2	8650	9950
20	4	OVERNIGHTER 206	HT	FSH	FBG	SV	SE	155-205		8		3125	1	2	8850	10000
22		SEAFARER 226	ST	SF	FBG	SV	OB			8		2600	1	2	10100	11400
22		SEAFARER 226	HT	SF	FBG	SV	OB			8		2725	1	2	10400	11800
22		SEAFARER 227	ST	SF	FBG	SV	IO	170-230		8		3400	1	2	9200	11200
22		SEAFARER 227	ST	SF	FBG	SV	IO	260		8		3591	1	2	9950	11700
22		SEAFARER 227	ST	SF	FBG	SV	IO	130D-155D		8			1	2	12900	15000
22		SEAFARER 227	HT	SF	FBG	SV	SE	170		8		3525	1	2	12100	13900

 CONTINUED ON NEXT PAGE

LOA FT	LOA IN	NAME AND/ OR MODEL	TOP/ RIG	BOAT TYPE	-HULL- MTL	-HULL- TP	ENGINE TP	# HP	MFG	BEAM FT	BEAM IN	WGT LBS	DRAFT FT	DRAFT IN	RETAIL LOW	RETAIL HIGH
		1984 BOATS														
22		SEAFARER 227	HT	SF	FBG	SV	IO	175-198		8		3519	1	2	9650	11100
22		SEAFARER 227	HT	SF	FBG	SV	SE	200	OMC	8		3713	1	2	12300	14000
22		SEAFARER 227	HT	SF	FBG	SV	IO	200	VLVO	8		3705	1	2	10100	11400
22		SEAFARER 227	HT	SF	FBG	SV	SE	228	MRCR	8		3704	1	2	12300	14000
22		SEAFARER 227	HT	SF	FBG	SV	IO	230-260		8		3792	1	2	10000	11900
22		SEAFARER 227	HT	SF	FBG	SV	IO	130D-155D		8			1	2	12900	15000
22		SEAFARER 228	ST	SF	FBG	SV	SE	205	OMC	8		3200	1	2	11500	13000
22		SEAFARER 228	ST	SF	FBG	SV	SE	T115	OMC	8		3700	1	2	12300	14000
22		SEAFARER 228	HT	SF	FBG	SV	SE	205	OMC	8		3325	1	2	11700	13300
22		SEAFARER 228	HT	SF	FBG	SV	SE	T115	OMC	8		3825	1	2	12500	14200
22		TOURNAMENT 223	ST	FSH	FBG	SV	OB			8		2400	1	2	8950	10200
22		TOURNAMENT 224	ST	FSH	FBG	SV	IO	170-230		8		3200	1	2	8100	10000
22		TOURNAMENT 224	ST	FSH	FBG	SV	IO	260		8		3391	1	2	8900	10500
22		TOURNAMENT 224	ST	FSH	FBG	SV	IO	130D-155D		8			1	2	12900	15000
22		TOURNAMENT 224	HT	FSH	FBG	SV	IO	170-230		8		3375	1	2	8350	10400
22		TOURNAMENT 224	HT	FSH	FBG	SV	IO	260		8		3566	1	2	9200	10800
22		TOURNAMENT 224	HT	FSH	FBG	SV	IO	130D-155D		8			1	2	12900	15000
22		TOURNAMENT 225	ST	FSH	FBG	SV	SE	205	OMC	8		3000	1	2	10300	11700
22		TOURNAMENT 225	ST	FSH	FBG	SV	SE	T115	OMC	8		3500	1	2	11200	12800
22		TOURNAMENT 233	HT	FSH	FBG	SV	OB			8		2575	1	2	9400	10700
24	1	OFFSHORE 240	ST	SF	FBG	SV	OB			8		2900	1	4	11300	12800
24	1	OFFSHORE 240	HT	SF	FBG	SV	OB			8		3025	1	4	11600	13200
24	1	OFFSHORE 241	ST	SF	FBG	SV	IO	228-260		8		4083	1	4	11800	14100
24	1	OFFSHORE 241	ST	SF	FBG	SV	IO	130D-155D		8			1	4	18100	20400
24	1	OFFSHORE 241	HT	SF	FBG	SV	IO	228-260		8		4208	1	4	12100	14500
24	1	OFFSHORE 241	HT	SF	FBG	SV	IO	130D-155D		8			1	4	18000	20400
24	1	OFFSHORE 242	ST	SF	FBG	SV	SE	205	OMC	8		3500	1	4	13000	14800
24	1	OFFSHORE 242	ST	SF	FBG	SV	SE	T115	OMC	8		4000	1	4	14200	16200
24	1	OFFSHORE 242	HT	SF	FBG	SV	SE	205	OMC	8		3625	1	4	13300	15100
24	1	OFFSHORE 242	HT	SF	FBG	SV	SE	T115	OMC	8		4125	1	4	14500	16500
24	1	TOURNAMENT 243	ST	SF	FBG	SV	OB			8		2700	1	4	10600	12100
24	1	TOURNAMENT 243	HT	SF	FBG	SV	OB			8		2825	1	4	11000	12500
24	1	TOURNAMENT 244	ST	SF	FBG	SV	IO	198-260		8		3892	1	4	11300	13700
24	1	TOURNAMENT 244	ST	SF	FBG	SV	IO	130D-155D		8			1	4	16400	19000
24	1	TOURNAMENT 244	HT	SF	FBG	SV	IO	198-260		8		4067	1	4	11700	14100
24	1	TOURNAMENT 244	HT	SF	FBG	SV	IO	130D-155D		8			1	4	16400	19100
24	1	TOURNAMENT 245	ST	SF	FBG	SV	SE	205	OMC	8		3300	1	4	12400	14100
24	1	TOURNAMENT 245	ST	SF	FBG	SV	SE	T115	OMC	8		3800	1	4	13800	15600
25	4	SAILFISH 252	ST	SF	FBG	SV	SE	155	OMC	9	6	5130	1	7	16500	18800
25	4	SAILFISH 252	ST	SF	FBG	SV	SE	T205	OMC	9	6	5130	1	7	16700	18900
25	4	SAILFISH 252	HT	SF	FBG	SV	SE	T205	OMC	9	6	5305	1	7	16900	19200
25	4	SAILFISH 252	TT	SF	FBG	SV	SE	155	OMC	9	6	5480	1	7	16900	19200
25	4	SAILFISH 252	TT	SF	FBG	SV	SE	T205	OMC	9	6	5480	1	7	17000	19400
25	4	SAILFISH 254	ST	SF	FBG	SV	IO	260		9	6	5000	1	7	15500	17800
25	4	SAILFISH 254	ST	SF	FBG	SV	IO	T170-T188		9	6	5500	1	7	17500	20400
25	4	SAILFISH 254	HT	SF	FBG	SV	IO	260		9	6	5175	1	7	15800	18200
25	4	SAILFISH 254	HT	SF	FBG	SV	IO	T170-T188		9	6	5675	1	7	18200	20800
25	4	SAILFISH 254	TT	SF	FBG	SV	IO	260		9	6	5350	1	7	16200	18600
25	4	SAILFISH 254	TT	SF	FBG	SV	IO	T170-T188		9	6	5850	1	7	18600	21200
25	4	SAILFISH 255	ST	SF	FBG	SV	OB			9	6	4075	1	7	15200	17300
25	4	SAILFISH 255	HT	SF	FBG	SV	OB			9	6	4250	1	7	15500	17600
25	4	SAILFISH 255	TT	SF	FBG	SV	OB			9	6	4425	1	7	15700	17900
25	4	TROPHY 257	ST	SF	FBG	SV	OB			9	6	4075	1	7	14800	16800
25	4	TROPHY 257	HT	SF	FBG	SV	OB			9	6	4250	1	7	15100	17100
25	4	TROPHY 257	TT	SF	FBG	SV	OB			9	6	4425	1	7	15400	17500
25	4	TROPHY 258	ST	SF	FBG	SV	IO	260		9	6	5000	1	7	15300	17600
25	4	TROPHY 258	ST	SF	FBG	SV	IO	T170-T188		9	6	5500	1	7	17300	20200
25	4	TROPHY 258	HT	SF	FBG	SV	IO	260		9	6	5175	1	7	15700	18000
25	4	TROPHY 258	HT	SF	FBG	SV	IO	T170-T188		9	6	5675	1	7	18000	20600
25	4	TROPHY 258	TT	SF	FBG	SV	IO	260		9	6	5350	1	7	16000	18400
25	4	TROPHY 258	TT	SF	FBG	SV	IO	T170-T188		9	6	5850	1	7	18400	21000
25	4	TROPHY 259	ST	SF	FBG	SV	SE	T205	OMC	9	6	5130	1	7	16400	18600
25	4	TROPHY 259	HT	SF	FBG	SV	SE	T205	OMC	9	6	5305	1	7	16600	18900
25	4	TROPHY 259	TT	SF	FBG	SV	SE	T205	OMC	9	6	5480	1	7	16800	19100

....For earlier years, see the BUC Used Boat Price Guide, Volume 3

GRAMPIAN MARINE LTD INC

TORONTO ONTARIO CANADA COAST GUARD MFG ID- GRM See inside cover to adjust price for area

LOA FT	LOA IN	NAME AND/ OR MODEL	TOP/ RIG	BOAT TYPE	-HULL- MTL	-HULL- TP	ENGINE TP	# HP	MFG	BEAM FT	BEAM IN	WGT LBS	DRAFT FT	DRAFT IN	RETAIL LOW	RETAIL HIGH
		1989 BOATS														
26		STRIKE 26 CCOF		SF	FBG	SV	OB			8		5800	2	2	16500	18800
26		STRIKE 26 CCOF		SF	FBG	SV	IB	220-350		8		5800	2	2	16800	20500
26		STRIKE 26 CCOF		SF	FBG	SV	IB	200D-275D		8		5800	2	2	22800	26800
26		STRIKE 26 RB		SF	FBG	SV	OB			8		5800	2	2	16500	18800
26		STRIKE 26 RB		SF	FBG	SV	IB	220-350		8		5800	2	2	16200	19800
26		STRIKE 26 RB		SF	FBG	SV	IB	200D-275D		8		5800	2	2	21900	26200
29		STRIKE 29 CCOF		SF	FBG	SV	OB			10	11	11280			21900	24400
29		STRIKE 29 CCOF		SF	FBG	SV	IB	T220-T270		10	11	11280			37000	42200
29		STRIKE 29 CCOF		SF	FBG	SV	IB	T200D-T250D		10	11	11280			54100	61600
29		STRIKE 29 RB		SF	FBG	SV	OB			10	11	11280			21900	24400
29		STRIKE 29 RB		SF	FBG	SV	IB	T220-T270		10	11	11280			34500	39500
29		STRIKE 29 RB		SF	FBG	SV	IB	T200D-T275D		10	11	11280			50200	61100
		1987 BOATS														
20		GRAMPIAN 20	SLP	SAIL	FBG	SK	OB			7	6	2000	6		4100	4750
26		GRAMPIAN 26	SLP	SA/CR	FBG	KL	OB			8	4	5600	4	3	12900	14700
30		GRAMPIAN 30	SLP	SA/CR	FBG	KL	IB	D		9	6	9600	4	8	26400	29300
		1986 BOATS														
26		GRAMPIAN 26	SLP	SA/CR	FBG	KL	OB			8	4	5600	4	3	12100	13700
30		GRAMPIAN 30	SLP	SA/CR	FBG	KL	IB	D		9	6	9600	4	8	24600	27400
		1985 BOATS														
20		GRAMPIAN 20	SLP	SAIL	FBG	SK	OB			7	6	2000	6		3600	4150
26		GRAMPIAN 26	SLP	SA/CR	FBG	KL	OB			8	4	5600	4	3	11300	12800
30		GRAMPIAN 30	SLP	SA/CR	FBG	KL	IB	D		9	6	9600	4	8	23100	25600

....For earlier years, see the BUC Used Boat Price Guide, Volume 3

GRAND BANKS YACHTS LTD

GRAND BANKS
NEWPORT RI 02840 COAST GUARD MFG ID- GND
ALSO AMERICAN MARINE PTE
See inside cover to adjust price for area

For more recent years, see the BUC Used Boat Price Guide, Volume 1

LOA FT	LOA IN	NAME AND/ OR MODEL	TOP/ RIG	BOAT TYPE	-HULL- MTL	-HULL- TP	ENGINE TP	# HP	MFG	BEAM FT	BEAM IN	WGT LBS	DRAFT FT	DRAFT IN	RETAIL LOW	RETAIL HIGH
		1996 BOATS														
36	10	GRAND BANKS 36 CL	FB	TRTCC	FBG	DS	IB	210D	CUM	12	8	26000	4		195000	214500
36	10	GRAND BANKS 36 CL	FB	TRTCC	FBG	DS	IB	T210D	CUM	12	8	26000	4		207500	228000
36	10	GRAND BANKS 36 EU	FB	TRWL	FBG	DS	IB	210D	CUM	12	8	27000	4		205500	226000
36	10	GRAND BANKS 36 EU	FB	TRWL	FBG	DS	IB	T210D	CUM	12	8	27000	4		218000	239500
36	10	GRAND BANKS 36 MY	FB	TRWL	FBG	DS	IB	210D	CUM	12	8	26000	4		207500	228000
36	10	GRAND BANKS 36 MY	FB	TRWL	FBG	DS	IB	T210D	CUM	12	8	26000	4		221000	243000
36	10	GRAND BANKS 36 SE	FB	TRWL	FBG	DS	IB	210D	CUM	12	8	26000	4		193500	212500
36	10	GRAND BANKS 36 SE	FB	TRWL	FBG	DS	IB	T210D	CUM	12	8	26000	4		205500	226000
43	3	GRAND BANKS 42 CL	FB	TRTCC	FBG	DS	IB	210D	CUM	14	1	34000	4	2	268500	295500
43	3	GRAND BANKS 42 CL	FB	TRTCC	FBG	DS	IB	T210D	CUM	14	1	34000	4	2	283000	310500
43	3	GRAND BANKS 42 EU	FB	TRMY	FBG	DS	IB	210D	CUM	14	1	34000	4	2	280000	307500
43	3	GRAND BANKS 42 EU	FB	TRMY	FBG	DS	IB	T210D	CUM	14	1	34000	4	2	293500	322500
43	3	GRAND BANKS 42 MY	FB	TRWL	FBG	DS	IB	210D	CUM	14	1	34914	4	2	280000	308000
43	3	GRAND BANKS 42 MY	FB	TRWL	FBG	DS	IB	T210D	CUM	14	1	34914	4	2	292500	321000
47	1	GRAND BANKS 46 CL	FB	TRWL	FBG	DS	IB	T210D	CUM	14	9	39000	4	5	330500	363000
47	1	GRAND BANKS 46 EU	FB	TRWL	FBG	DS	IB	T210D	CUM	14	9	39000	4	5	357500	393000
47	1	GRAND BANKS 46 MY	FB	TRWL	FBG	DS	IB	T210D	CUM	14	9	39000	4	5	329000	361500
50	6	GRAND BANKS 49 CL	FB	TRWL	FBG	DS	IB	T210D	CAT	15	5	60000	5	1	394500	433500
50	6	GRAND BANKS 49 MY	FB	TRWL	FBG	DS	IB	T210D	CAT	15	5	60000	5	1	414500	455500
58	11	GRAND BANKS 58 MY	FB	MY	FBG	DS	IB	T460D	ALAS	17	6	95000	5	6	856000	940500
		1995 BOATS														
31	11	GRAND BANKS 32S	FB	TRWL	FBG	DS	IB	210D	CUM	11	6	17000	3	9	176500	194000
36	10	GRAND BANKS 36 CL	FB	TRTCC	FBG	DS	IB	210D	CUM	12	8	27000	4		195000	214500
36	10	GRAND BANKS 36 CL	FB	TRTCC	FBG	DS	IB	T210D	CUM	12	8	27000	4		207000	227500
36	10	GRAND BANKS 36 EU	FB	TRWL	FBG	DS	IB	210D	CUM	12	8	27000	4		200000	220000
36	10	GRAND BANKS 36 EU	FB	TRWL	FBG	DS	IB	T210D	CUM	12	8	27000	4		212000	233000
36	10	GRAND BANKS 36 MY	FB	TRWL	FBG	DS	IB	210D	CUM	12	8	27000	4		207500	228000
36	10	GRAND BANKS 36 MY	FB	TRWL	FBG	DS	IB	T210D	CUM	12	8	27000	4		221000	242500
36	10	GRAND BANKS 36 SE	FB	TRWL	FBG	DS	IB	210D	CUM	12	8	27000	4		193500	212500
36	10	GRAND BANKS 36 SE	FB	TRWL	FBG	DS	IB	T210D	CUM	12	8	27000	4		205500	225500
38		EASTBAY 38	ST	CRCPT	FBG	DS	IB	T300D	CAT	13	4	25000	3	11	219000	241000
43	3	GRAND BANKS 42 CL	FB	TRTCC	FBG	DS	IB	210D	CUM	14	1	34000	4	2	261500	287500
43	3	GRAND BANKS 42 CL	FB	TRTCC	FBG	DS	IB	T210D	CUM	14	1	34000	4	2	275500	303000
43	3	GRAND BANKS 42 MY	FB	TRWL	FBG	DS	IB	210D	CUM	14	1	34000	4	2	268000	294500
43	3	GRAND BANKS 42 MY	FB	TRWL	FBG	DS	IB	T210D	CUM	14	1	34000	4	2	279500	307000
47	1	GRAND BANKS 46 CL	FB	TRWL	FBG	DS	IB	T210D	CUM	14	9	39000	4	5	321500	353500
47	1	GRAND BANKS 46 EU	FB	TRWL	FBG	DS	IB	T210D	CUM	14	9	38000	4	5	343500	377000
47	1	GRAND BANKS 46 MY	FB	TRWL	FBG	DS	IB	T210D	CUM	14	9	39000	4	5	320500	352000

LOA FT	IN	NAME AND/ OR MODEL	TOP/ RIG	BOAT TYPE	-HULL- MTL	TP	----ENGINE--- TP	# HP	MFG	BEAM FT	IN	WGT LBS	DRAFT FT	IN	RETAIL LOW	RETAIL HIGH
		1995 BOATS														
50	6	GRAND BANKS 49 CL	FB	TRWL	FBG	DS	IB	T210D	CAT	15	5	60000	5	2	383500	421500
50	6	GRAND BANKS 49 MY	FB	TRWL	FBG	DS	IB	T210D	CAT	15	5	60000	5	2	404000	444000
58	11	GRAND BANKS 58 MY	FB	MY	FBG	DS	IB	T460D	ALAS	17	6	50T	5	6	864500	949500
		1994 BOATS														
31	11	GRAND BANKS 32S	FB	TRWL	FBG	DS	IB	135D	LEHM	11	6	17000	3	9	165500	181500
36	10	GRAND BANKS 36 CL	FB	TRTCC	FBG	DS	IB	135D	LEHM	12	8	27000	4		192500	211500
36	10	GRAND BANKS 36 CL	FB	TRTCC	FBG	DS	IB	T135D	LEHM	12	8	27000	4		199500	219500
36	10	GRAND BANKS 36 EU	FB	TRWL	FBG	DS	IB	135D	LEHM	12	8	27000	4		197500	217000
36	10	GRAND BANKS 36 EU	FB	TRWL	FBG	DS	IB	T135D	LEHM	12	8	27000	4		204000	224000
36	10	GRAND BANKS 36 SE	FB	TRWL	FBG	DS	IB	135D	LEHM	12	8	27000	4		190500	209000
36	10	GRAND BANKS 36 SE	FB	TRWL	FBG	DS	IB	T135D	LEHM	12	8	27000	4		197000	216500
43	3	GRAND BANKS 42 CL	FB	TRTCC	FBG	DS	IB	135D	LEHM	14	1	34000	4	2	251500	276500
43	3	GRAND BANKS 42 CL	FB	TRTCC	FBG	DS	IB	T135D	LEHM	14	1	34000	4	2	261500	287500
43	3	GRAND BANKS 42 MY	FB	TRWL	FBG	DS	IB	135D	LEHM	14	1	34000	4	2	257500	283000
43	3	GRAND BANKS 42 MY	FB	TRWL	FBG	DS	IB	T135D	LEHM	14	1	34000	4	2	266500	293000
47	1	GRAND BANKS 46 CL	FB	TRWL	FBG	DS	IB	T135D	LEHM	14	9	39000	4	5	304500	335000
47	1	GRAND BANKS 46 EU	FB	TRWL	FBG	DS	IB	T135D	LEHM	14	9	38000	4	5	325000	357500
47	1	GRAND BANKS 46 MY	FB	TRWL	FBG	DS	IB	T135D	LEHM	14	9	39000	4	5	304000	334000
50	6	GRAND BANKS 49 CL	FB	TRWL	FBG	DS	IB	T210D	CAT	15	5	60000	5	2	373500	410500
50	6	GRAND BANKS 49 MY	FB	TRWL	FBG	DS	IB	T210D	CAT	15	5	60000	5	2	392000	431000
58	11	GRAND BANKS 58 MY	FB	MY	FBG	DS	IB	T375D	CAT	17	6	50T	5	6	789000	867500
		1993 BOATS														
31	11	GRAND BANKS 32S	FB	TRWL	FBG	DS	IB	135D	LEHM	11	6	17000	3	9	160000	175500
36	10	GRAND BANKS 36 CL	FB	TRTCC	FBG	DS	IB	135D	LEHM	12	8	27000	4		186000	204500
36	10	GRAND BANKS 36 CL	FB	TRTCC	FBG	DS	IB	T135D	LEHM	12	8	27000	4		193000	212000
36	10	GRAND BANKS 36 EU	FB	TRWL	FBG	DS	IB	135D	LEHM	12	8	27000	4		191000	209500
36	10	GRAND BANKS 36 EU	FB	TRWL	FBG	DS	IB	T135D	LEHM	12	8	27000	4		197000	216500
36	10	GRAND BANKS 36 SE	FB	TRWL	FBG	DS	IB	135D	LEHM	12	8	27000	4		184000	202000
36	10	GRAND BANKS 36 SE	FB	TRWL	FBG	DS	IB	T135D	LEHM	12	8	27000	4		190500	209500
43	3	GRAND BANKS 42 CL	FB	TRTCC	FBG	DS	IB	135D	LEHM	14	1	34000	4	2	243000	267000
43	3	GRAND BANKS 42 CL	FB	TRTCC	FBG	DS	IB	T135D	LEHM	14	1	34000	4.	2	253000	278000
43	3	GRAND BANKS 42 MY	FB	TRWL	FBG	DS	IB	D	LEHM	14	1	34000	4	2	**	**
43	3	GRAND BANKS 42 MY	FB	TRWL	FBG	DS	IB	T D	LEHM	14	1	34000	4	2	**	**
47	1	GRAND BANKS 46 CL	FB	TRWL	FBG	DS	IB	T135D	LEHM	14	9	39000	4	5	294500	323500
47	1	GRAND BANKS 46 EU	FB	TRWL	FBG	DS	IB	T135D	LEHM	14	9	38000	4	5	314500	345500
47	1	GRAND BANKS 46 MY	FB	TRWL	FBG	DS	IB	T135D	LEHM	14	9	39000	4	5	293500	322500
50	6	GRAND BANKS 49 CL	FB	TRWL	FBG	DS	IB	T210D	CAT	15	5	60000	5	1	361000	396500
50	6	GRAND BANKS 49 MY	FB	TRWL	FBG	DS	IB	T210D	CAT	15	5	60000	5	1	379000	416500
58	11	GRAND BANKS 58 MY	FB	MY	FBG	DS	IB	T375D	CAT	17	6	50T	5	6	764500	840000
		1992 BOATS														
31	11	GRAND BANKS 32S	FB	TRWL	FBG	DS	IB	135D	LEHM	11	6	17000	3	9	154500	170000
36	10	GRAND BANKS 36 CL	FB	TRTCC	FBG	DS	IB	135D	LEHM	12	8	27000	4		179500	197500
36	10	GRAND BANKS 36 CL	FB	TRTCC	FBG	DS	IB	T135D	LEHM	12	8	27000	4		186000	204500
36	10	GRAND BANKS 36 EU	FB	TRWL	FBG	DS	IB	135D	LEHM	12	8	27000	4		184500	203000
36	10	GRAND BANKS 36 EU	FB	TRWL	FBG	DS	IB	T135D	LEHM	12	8	27000	4		190500	209500
36	10	GRAND BANKS 36 SE	FB	TRWL	FBG	DS	IB	135D	LEHM	12	8	27000	4		178000	195500
36	10	GRAND BANKS 36 SE	FB	TRWL	FBG	DS	IB	T135D	LEHM	12	8	27000	4		184000	202500
42	7	GRAND BANKS 42 EU	FB	TRMY	FBG	DS	IB	T135D	LEHM	13	7	34000	4	2	262000	288000
42	7	GRAND BANKS 42 SE	FB	TRWL	FBG	DS	IB	T135D	LEHM	13	7	34000	4	2	236500	260000
43	3	GRAND BANKS 42 CL	FB	TRTCC	FBG	DS	IB	135D	LEHM	14	1	34000	4	2	235000	258500
43	3	GRAND BANKS 42 CL	FB	TRTCC	FBG	DS	IB	T135D	LEHM	14	1	34000	4	2	244500	269000
43	3	GRAND BANKS 42 MY	FB	TRWL	FBG	DS	IB	135D	LEHM	14	1	34000	4	2	240500	264500
43	3	GRAND BANKS 42 MY	FB	TRWL	FBG	DS	IB	T135D	LEHM	14	1	34000	4	2	248500	273500
47	1	GRAND BANKS 46 CL	FB	TRWL	FBG	DS	IB	T135D	LEHM	14	9	39000	4	5	284500	313000
47	1	GRAND BANKS 46 MY	FB	TRWL	FBG	DS	IB	T135D	LEHM	14	9	39000	4	5	284000	312000
50	6	GRAND BANKS 49 CL	FB	TRWL	FBG	DS	IB	210D	CAT	15	5	60000	5	1	318500	350000
50	6	GRAND BANKS 49 MY	FB	TRWL	FBG	DS	IB	210D	CAT	15	5	60000	5	1	335000	368000
58	11	GRAND BANKS 58 MY	FB	MY	FBG	DS	IB	T375D	CAT	17	6	50T	5	6	739000	812000
		1991 BOATS														
31	11	GRAND BANKS 32S	FB	TRWL	FBG	DS	IB	135D	LEHM	11	6	17000	3	9	149500	164000
36	10	GRAND BANKS 36 CL	FB	TRTCC	FBG	DS	IB	135D	LEHM	12	8	27000	4		173500	190500
36	10	GRAND BANKS 36 CL	FB	TRTCC	FBG	DS	IB	T135D	LEHM	12	8	27000	4		180000	198000
36	10	GRAND BANKS 36 EU	FB	TRWL	FBG	DS	IB	135D	LEHM	12	8	27000	4		178500	196000
36	10	GRAND BANKS 36 EU	FB	TRWL	FBG	DS	IB	T135D	LEHM	12	8	27000	4		184000	202500
36	10	GRAND BANKS 36 SE	FB	TRWL	FBG	DS	IB	135D	LEHM	12	8	27000	4		172000	189000
36	10	GRAND BANKS 36 SE	FB	TRWL	FBG	DS	IB	T135D	LEHM	12	8	27000	4		178000	195500
42	7	GRAND BANKS 42 EU	FB	TRMY	FBG	DS	IB	T135D	LEHM	13	7	34000	4	2	253500	278500
42	7	GRAND BANKS 42 SE	FB	TRWL	FBG	DS	IB	T135D	LEHM	13	7	34000	4	2	228500	251500
43	3	GRAND BANKS 42 CL	FB	TRTCC	FBG	DS	IB	T135D	LEHM	14	1	34000	4	2	236500	260000
43	3	GRAND BANKS 42 MY	FB	TRWL	FBG	DS	IB	T135D	LEHM	14	1	34000	4	2	240500	264000
47	1	GRAND BANKS 46 CL	FB	TRWL	FBG	DS	IB	T135D	LEHM	14	9	39000	4	5	275000	302500
47	1	GRAND BANKS 46 MY	FB	TRWL	FBG	DS	IB	T135D	LEHM	14	9	39000	4	5	274500	301500
50	6	GRAND BANKS 49 CL	FB	TRWL	FBG	DS	IB	210D	CAT	15	5	60000	5	1	308000	338500
50	6	GRAND BANKS 49 MY	FB	TRWL	FBG	DS	IB	210D	CAT	15	5	60000	5	1	323500	355500
		1990 BOATS														
31	11	GRAND BANKS 32S	FB	TRWL	FBG	DS	IB	135D	LEHM	11	6	17000	3	9	144500	159000
36	10	GRAND BANKS 36 CL	FB	TRTCC	FBG	DS	IB	135D	LEHM	12	8	27000	4		169500	186000
36	10	GRAND BANKS 36 CL	FB	TRTCC	FBG	DS	IB	T135D	LEHM	12	8	27000	4		174500	192000
36	10	GRAND BANKS 36 EU	FB	TRWL	FBG	DS	IB	135D	LEHM	12	8	27000	4		171500	188500
36	10	GRAND BANKS 36 EU	FB	TRWL	FBG	DS	IB	T135D	LEHM	12	8	27000	4		177500	195000
36	10	GRAND BANKS 36 SE	FB	TRWL	FBG	DS	IB	135D	LEHM	12	8	27000	4		165000	181500
36	10	GRAND BANKS 36 SE	FB	TRWL	FBG	DS	IB	T135D	LEHM	12	8	27000	4		171500	188500
42	7	GRAND BANKS 42 EU	FB	TRMY	FBG	DS	IB	T135D	LEHM	13	7	34000	4	2	231500	254500
42	7	GRAND BANKS 42 SE	FB	TRWL	FBG	DS	IB	T135D	LEHM	13	7	34000	4	2	227000	249500
43	3	GRAND BANKS 42 CL	FB	TRTCC	FBG	DS	IB	T135D	LEHM	14	1	34000	4	2	238000	261500
43	3	GRAND BANKS 42 MY	FB	TRWL	FBG	DS	IB	T135D	LEHM	14	1	34000	4	2	229500	252000
47	1	GRAND BANKS 46 CL	FB	TRWL	FBG	DS	IB	T135D	LEHM	14	9	39000	4	5	272000	299000
47	1	GRAND BANKS 46 MY	FB	TRWL	FBG	DS	IB	T135D	LEHM	14	9	39000	4	5	259000	284500
50	6	GRAND BANKS 49 CL	FB	TRWL	FBG	DS	IB	210D	CAT	15	5	60000	5	1	304000	334500
50	6	GRAND BANKS 49 MY	FB	TRWL	FBG	DS	IB	210D	CAT	15	5	60000	5	1	306000	336000
		1989 BOATS														
31	11	GRAND BANKS 32	FB	TRWL	FBG	DS	IB	135D	LEHM	11	6	17000	3	9	139500	153500
36	10	GRAND BANKS 36 CL	FB	TRTCC	FBG	DS	IB	135D	LEHM	12	8	27000	4		163500	179500
36	10	GRAND BANKS 36 CL	FB	TRTCC	FBG	DS	IB	T135D	LEHM	12	8	27000	4		168500	185000
36	10	GRAND BANKS 36 EU	FB	TRWL	FBG	DS	IB	135D	LEHM	12	8	27000	4		165500	182000
36	10	GRAND BANKS 36 EU	FB	TRWL	FBG	DS	IB	T135D	LEHM	12	8	27000	4		171500	188500
36	10	GRAND BANKS 36 SE	FB	TRWL	FBG	DS	IB	135D	LEHM	12	8	27000	4		159000	175000
36	10	GRAND BANKS 36 SE	FB	TRWL	FBG	DS	IB	T135D	LEHM	12	8	27000	4		165500	182000
42	7	GRAND BANKS 42 EU	FB	TRMY	FBG	DS	IB	T135D	LEHM	13	7	34000	4	2	223500	246000
42	7	GRAND BANKS 42 SE	FB	TRWL	FBG	DS	IB	T135D	LEHM	13	7	34000	4	2	219000	241000
43	3	GRAND BANKS 42 CL	FB	TRTCC	FBG	DS	IB	T135D	LEHM	14	1	34000	4	2	229500	252500
43	3	GRAND BANKS 42 MY	FB	TRWL	FBG	DS	IB	T135D	LEHM	14	1	34000	4	2	221500	243500
47	1	GRAND BANKS 46 CL	FB	TRWL	FBG	DS	IB	T135D	LEHM	14	9	39000	4	5	262500	288500
47	1	GRAND BANKS 46 MY	FB	TRWL	FBG	DS	IB	T135D	LEHM	14	9	39000	4	5	250000	274500
50	6	GRAND BANKS 49 CL	FB	TRWL	FBG	DS	IB	135D	LEHM	15	5	60000	5	1	281500	309500
50	6	GRAND BANKS 49 MY	FB	TRWL	FBG	DS	IB	135D	LEHM	15	5	60000	5	1	283000	311000
		1988 BOATS														
31	11	GRAND BANKS 32	FB	TRWL	FBG	DS	IB	135D	LEHM	11	6	17000	3	9	135000	148000
36	10	GRAND BANKS 36 CL	FB	TRTCC	FBG	DS	IB	135D	LEHM	12	8	27000	4		157000	172500
36	10	GRAND BANKS 36 CL	FB	TRTCC	FBG	DS	IB	T135D	LEHM	12	8	27000	4		162500	178500
36	10	GRAND BANKS 36 EU	FB	TRWL	FBG	DS	IB	135D	LEHM	12	8	27000	4		157000	172500
36	10	GRAND BANKS 36 EU	FB	TRWL	FBG	DS	IB	T135D	LEHM	12	8	27000	4		162500	178500
36	10	GRAND BANKS 36 SE	FB	TRWL	FBG	DS	IB	135D	LEHM	12	8	27000	4		157000	172500
36	10	GRAND BANKS 36 SE	FB	TRWL	FBG	DS	IB	T135D	LEHM	12	8	27000	4		162500	178500
42	7	GRAND BANKS 42 EU	FB	TRMY	FBG	DS	IB	T135D	LEHM	13	7	34000	4	2	220500	242000
42	7	GRAND BANKS 42 SE	FB	TRWL	FBG	DS	IB	T135D	LEHM	13	7	34000	4	2	212500	233500
43	3	GRAND BANKS 42 CL	FB	TRTCC	FBG	DS	IB	T135D	LEHM	14	1	34000	4	2	220000	242000
43	3	GRAND BANKS 42 MY	FB	TRWL	FBG	DS	IB	T135D	LEHM	14	1	34000	4	2	209000	229500
47	1	GRAND BANKS 46 CL	FB	TRWL	FBG	DS	IB	T135D	LEHM	14	9	39000	4	5	253000	278000
47	1	GRAND BANKS 46 MY	FB	TRWL	FBG	DS	IB	T135D	LEHM	14	9	39000	4	5	241000	265000
50	6	GRAND BANKS 49 CL	FB	TRWL	FBG	DS	IB	135D	LEHM	15	5	60000	5	1	271500	298000
50	6	GRAND BANKS 49 MY	FB	TRWL	FBG	DS	IB	135D	LEHM	15	5	60000	5	1	272500	299500
		1987 BOATS														
31	11	GRAND BANKS 32	FB	TRWL	FBG	DS	IB	135D	LEHM	11	6	17000	3	9	130000	143000
36	10	GRAND BANKS 36 CL	FB	TRTCC	FBG	DS	IB	135D	LEHM	12	8	27000	4		151000	166000
36	10	GRAND BANKS 36 CL	FB	TRTCC	FBG	DS	IB	T135D	LEHM	12	8	27000	4		156500	172000
36	10	GRAND BANKS 36 EU	FB	TRWL	FBG	DS	IB	135D	LEHM	12	8	27000	4		151000	166000
36	10	GRAND BANKS 36 EU	FB	TRWL	FBG	DS	IB	T135D	LEHM	12	8	27000	4		156500	172000
36	10	GRAND BANKS 36 SE	FB	TRWL	FBG	DS	IB	135D	LEHM	12	8	27000	4		151000	166000
36	10	GRAND BANKS 36 SE	FB	TRWL	FBG	DS	IB	T135D	LEHM	12	8	27000	4		156500	172000
42	7	GRAND BANKS 42 EU	FB	TRMY	FBG	DS	IB	T135D	LEHM	13	7	34000	4	2	212000	233000
42	7	GRAND BANKS 42 SE	FB	TRWL	FBG	DS	IB	T135D	LEHM	13	7	34000	4	2	204500	225000
43	3	GRAND BANKS 42 CL	FB	TRTCC	FBG	DS	IB	T135D	LEHM	14	1	34000	4	2	211500	232500
43	3	GRAND BANKS 42 MY	FB	TRWL	FBG	DS	IB	T135D	LEHM	14	1	34000	4	2	201000	221000
47	1	GRAND BANKS 46 CL	FB	TRWL	FBG	DS	IB	T135D	LEHM	14	9	39000	4	5	243500	267500
47	1	GRAND BANKS 46 MY	FB	TRWL	FBG	DS	IB	T135D	LEHM	14	9	39000	4	5	232000	255000
50	6	GRAND BANKS 49 CL	FB	TRWL	FBG	DS	IB	135D	LEHM	15	5	60000	5	1	261000	287000
50	6	GRAND BANKS 49 MY	FB	TRWL	FBG	DS	IB	135D	LEHM	15	5	60000	5	1	262500	288500
		1986 BOATS														
31	11	GRAND BANKS 32	FB	TRWL	FBG	DS	IB	135D	LEHM	11	6	17000	3	8	125000	137500
31	11	GRAND BANKS 32 SPORT	FB	TRWL	FBG	DS	IB	165D	LEYL	11	6	17000	3	8	126500	139000
36	4	GRAND BANKS 36	FB	TRWL	FBG	DS	IB	135D	LEHM	12	2	23300	3	11	125500	138000
		IB 210D CAT 127000 139500, IB T135D LEHM 130500 143500, IB T165D LEYL 132000 145000														
41	10	GRAND BANKS 42 MY	FB	TRWL	FBG	DS	IB	120D	LEHM	13	7	34000	4	2	189500	208500
		IB 135D LEHM 210500 231000, IB T165D LEYL 199500 219000, IB T210D CAT 204500 224500														
		IB T320D CAT 214000 235000, IB T375D CAT 220000 242000														

CONTINUED ON NEXT PAGE

LOA FT IN	NAME AND/ OR MODEL	TOP/ RIG	BOAT TYPE	-HULL- MTL TP	----ENGINE--- TP # HP MFG	BEAM FT IN	WGT LBS	DRAFT FT IN	RETAIL LOW	RETAIL HIGH
---	--- 1986 BOATS ---									
41 10	GRAND BANKS CLASSIC	FB	TRWL	FBG DS IB	135D LEHM	13 7	34000	4 2	173500	190500
41 10	GRAND BANKS CLASSIC	FB	TRWL	FBG DS IB	T135D LEHM	13 7	34000	4 2	190500	209500
41 10	GRAND BANKS EUROPA	FB	TRWL	FBG DS IB	135D LEHM	13 7	34000	4 2	181000	199000
41 10	GRAND BANKS EUROPA	FB	TRWL	FBG DS IB	T135D LEHM	13 7	34000	4 2	198500	218500
41 10	GRAND BANKS EUROPA	FB	TRWL	FBG DS IB	T210D CAT	13 7	34000	4 2	201000	221000
46 7	GRAND BANKS 46	FB	TRWL	FBG DS IB	T135D LEHM	14 9	38000		199000	218500
	IB T210D CAT 206000 226500,			IB T320D CAT	216000 237000,		IB T375D CAT		220000	243500
50 6	GRAND BANKS 49	FB	TRWL	FBG DS IB	T135D LEHM	15 5	60000	5 2	244500	268500
	IB T210D CAT 256500 282000,			IB T320D CAT	274500 301500,		IB T375D CAT		283500	311500
---	--- 1985 BOATS ---									
31 11	GRAND BANKS 32	FB	TRWL	FBG DS IB	135D LEHM	11 6	17000	3 8	120000	132000
31 11	GRAND BANKS 32 SPORT	FB	TRWL	FBG DS IB	165D LEHM	11 6	17000	3 8	120500	133500
36 4	GRAND BANKS 36	FB	TRWL	FBG DS IB	135D LEHM	12 2	23300	3 11	120000	132000
	IB 165D LEYL 120000 131500,		IB	200D LEYL	120500 132500,		IB 210D CAT		121500	133500
41 10	GRAND BANKS 42 MY	FB	TRWL	FBG DS IB	120D LEHM	13 7	34000	4 2	181500	199500
	IB 135D LEHM 202500 222500,		IB	T165D LEYL	201000 221000,		IB T200D LEYL		202500	223000
	IB T210D CAT 204500 224500,		IB	T300D CAT	203000 223000					
41 10	GRAND BANKS CLASSIC	FB	TRWL	FBG DS IB	135D LEHM	13 7	34000	4 2	168000	184500
	IB T135D LEHM 182500 200500,		IB	T165D LEYL	180000 197500,		IB T200D LEYL		182500	200500
	IB T210D CAT 184500 202500									
41 10	GRAND BANKS EUROPA	FB	TRWL	FBG DS IB	135D LEHM	13 7	34000	4 2	171000	187500
	IB T135D LEHM 190500 209000,		IB	T165D LEYL	186500 205000,		IB T200D LEYL		188000	206500
50 6	GRAND BANKS 49	FB	TRWL	FBG DS IB	T135D LEHM	15 5	60000	5 2	234000	257000
	IB T200D LEYL 243000 267000,		IB	T210D CAT	245500 270000,		IB T300D CAT		259500	285500
	IB T355D CAT 268500 295000									
---	--- 1984 BOATS ---									
31 11	GRAND BANKS 32	FB	TRWL	FBG DS IB	120D LEHM	11 6	17000	3 8	114500	126000
31 11	GRAND BANKS 32 SPORT	FB	TRWL	FBG DS IB	165D LEYL	11 6	17000	3 8	116000	127500
36 4	GRAND BANKS 36	FB	TRWL	FBG DS IB	120D LEHM	12 2	23300	3 11	115000	126500
	IB 165D LEYL 114500 126000,		IB	200D LEHM	115000 126500,		IB T120D LEHM		118500	130500
	IB T165D LEYL 121000 133000									
41 10	GRAND BANKS 42	FB	TRWL	FBG DS IB	T120D	13 7	34000	4 2	170000	186500
41 10	GRAND BANKS 42 MY	FB	TRWL	FBG DS IB	120D LEHM	13 7	34000	4 2	176000	193500
	IB T120D LEHM 193000 212000,		IB	T165D LEYL	192000 211000,		IB T200D LEYL		193500	213000
41 10	GRAND BANKS CLASSIC	FB	TRWL	FBG DS IB	120D LEHM	13 7	34000	4 2	168500	185000
	IB T120D LEHM 171500 188500,		IB	T165D LEYL	172000 189000,		IB T200D LEYL		174500	191500
41 10	GRAND BANKS EUROPA	FB	TRWL	FBG DS IB	120D LEHM	13 7	34000	4 2	171000	188000
	IB T120D LEHM 178500 196500,		IB	T165D LEYL	178000 195500,		IB T200D LEYL		179500	197500
50 6	GRAND BANKS 49	FB	TRWL	FBG DS IB	T120D LEHM	15 5	60000	5 2	221500	243500
	IB T200D LEYL 232000 255000,		IB	T300D CAT	248000 272500,		IB T355D CAT		256000	281500

....For earlier years, see the BUC Used Boat Price Guide, Volume 3

GRAND CRAFT CORPORATION
HOLLAND MI 49423   COAST GUARD MFG ID- MBQ See inside cover to adjust price for area

For more recent years, see the BUC Used Boat Price Guide, Volume 1

LOA FT IN	NAME AND/ OR MODEL	TOP/ RIG	BOAT TYPE	-HULL- MTL TP	----ENGINE--- TP # HP MFG	BEAM FT IN	WGT LBS	DRAFT FT IN	RETAIL LOW	RETAIL HIGH
---	--- 1996 BOATS ---									
21	DOUBLE COCKPIT	OP	RNBT	MHG SV IB	250 CRUS	7 6	3000	1 8	**	**
21	SPORT	OP	RNBT	MHG SV IB	250 CRUS	7 6	3000	1 8	**	**
22	DOUBLE COCKPIT	OP	RNBT	MHG SV IB	250 CRUS	6 4	3300	2	**	**
24	LUXURY SPORT	OP	UTL	MHG SV IB	250 CRUS	8	5000	1 11	**	**
24	LUXURY SPORT	OP	UTL	MHG SV IB	T250 CRUS	8	5000	1 11	**	**
24	TRIPLE COCKPIT	OP	RNBT	MHG SV IB	250 CRUS	6 4	3700	2	**	**
26	LUXURY SPORT	OP	UTL	MHG SV IB	320 CRUS	8 6	4800	2 2	**	**
26	LUXURY SPORT	OP	UTL	MHG SV IB	T250 CRUS	8 6	5600	2 2	**	**
27	TRIPLE COCKPIT	OP	RNBT	MHG SV IB	320 CRUS	7 2	6000	2 4	**	**
28	LUXURY SPORT	HT	EXP	MHG SV IB	T250 CRUS	10	7900	2 1	**	**
30	TRIPLE COCKPIT	OP	RNBT	MHG SV IB	320 CRUS	8 6	7000	2 4	**	**
32	COMMUTER	HT	CBNCR	MHG SV IB	T140D YAN	9	7500	1 10	**	**
36	COMMUTER	HT	CBNCR	MHG SV IB	T170D YAN	9	8500	2 4	**	**
36	COMMUTER	HT	COMM	MHG SV IB	T170D YAN	9	8500	2 4	**	**
42	COMMUTER	HT	CBNCR	MHG SV IB		10			**	**
42	COMMUTER	HT	COMM	MHG SV IB		10			**	**
48	COMMUTER	HT	CBNCR	MHG SV IB		13			**	**
48	COMMUTER	HT	COMM	MHG SV IB		13			**	**
---	--- 1991 BOATS ---									
20	DOUBLE COCKPIT	OP	RNBT	WD SV IB	240 CHRY	7 6	3500	1 8	**	**
20	SPORT RUNABOUT	OP	UTL	WD SV IB	240 CHRY	7 6	3000	1 8	**	**
24	LUXURY SPORT	OP	UTL	WD SV IB	275 CHRY	8	4200	2	**	**
24	LUXURY SPORT	OP	UTL	WD SV IB	T275 CHRY	8	4200	2	**	**
27	RUNABOUT	OP	RNBT	WD SV IB	340 CHRY	7	4500	2 4	**	**
27	RUNABOUT	OP	RNBT	WD SV IB	T275 CHRY	7	4500	2 4	**	**
28	LUXURY SPORT	OP	UTL	WD SV IB	T300 CHRY	10	7900	2 4	**	**
---	--- 1990 BOATS ---									
20	DOUBLE COCKPIT	OP	RNBT	WD SV IB	240 CHRY	7 6	3500	1 8	**	**
20	SPORT RUNABOUT	OP	UTL	WD SV IB	240 CHRY	7 6	3000	1 8	**	**
24	LUXURY SPORT	OP	UTL	WD SV IB	275 CHRY	8	4200	2	**	**
24	LUXURY SPORT	OP	UTL	WD SV IB	T275 CHRY	8	4200	2	**	**
24	RUNABOUT	OP	RNBT	WD SV IB	240 CHRY	6 4	3500	2	**	**
27	RUNABOUT	OP	RNBT	WD SV IB	340 CHRY	7	4500	2 4	**	**
27	RUNABOUT	OP	RNBT	WD SV IB	T275 CHRY	7	4500	2 4	**	**
---	--- 1989 BOATS ---									
20	DOUBLE COCKPIT	OP	RNBT	WD SV IB	240 CHRY	7 6	3500	1 8	**	**
20	SPORT RUNABOUT	OP	UTL	WD SV IB	240 CHRY	7 6	3000	1 8	**	**
23	TAHOE	OP	UTL	WD SV IB	275 CHRY	8	4200	1 11	**	**
24	LUXURY SPORT	OP	UTL	WD SV IB	275 CHRY	8	4200	2	**	**
24	LUXURY SPORT	OP	UTL	WD SV IB	T275 CHRY	8	5200	2	**	**
24	RUNABOUT	OP	RNBT	WD SV IB	240 CHRY	6 4	3500	2 6	**	**
27	RUNABOUT	OP	RNBT	WD SV IB	340 CHRY	7	4500	2 4	**	**
27	RUNABOUT	OP	RNBT	WD SV IB	T275 CHRY	7	5500	1 10	**	**
---	--- 1988 BOATS ---									
20	DOUBLE COCKPIT	OP	RNBT	WD SV IB	240 CHRY	7 6	3500	1 8	**	**
20	SPORT RUNABOUT	OP	UTL	WD SV IB	240 CHRY	7 6	3000	1 8	**	**
23	TAHOE	OP	UTL	WD SV IB	275 CHRY	8	4200	1 11	**	**
24	RUNABOUT	OP	RNBT	WD SV IB	240 CHRY	6 4	3500	2	**	**
27	RUNABOUT	OP	RNBT	WD SV IB	340 CHRY	7	4500	2 4	**	**
27	RUNABOUT	OP	RNBT	WD SV IB	T240 CHRY	7	5500	1 10	**	**
---	--- 1987 BOATS ---									
20	DOUBLE COCKPIT	OP	RNBT	WD SV IB	240 CHRY	7 6	3500	1 8	**	**
20	SPORT RUNABOUT	OP	UTL	WD SV IB	240 CHRY	7 6	3000	1 8	**	**
23	TAHOE	OP	UTL	WD SV IB	275 CHRY	8	4200	1 11	**	**
24	RUNABOUT	OP	RNBT	WD SV IB	240 CHRY	6 4	3500	2	**	**
27	RUNABOUT	OP	RNBT	WD SV IB	340 CHRY	7	4500	2 4	**	**
27	RUNABOUT	OP	RNBT	WD SV IB	T240 CHRY	7	5500	1 10	**	**
---	--- 1986 BOATS ---									
20	GENEVA	OP	UTL	WD SV IB	235 CHRY	7	3000	1 6	**	**
20	TAHOE	OP	UTL	WD SV IB	235 CHRY	7	3000	1 6	**	**
23	GENEVA	OP	UTL	WD SV IB	350 CHRY	8	4000	1 8	**	**
23	TAHOE	OP	UTL	WD SV IB	350 CHRY	8	4000	1 8	**	**
24	RUNABOUT	OP	RNBT	WD SV IB	255 CHRY	6 8	3500	1 6	**	**
27	RUNABOUT	OP	RNBT	WD SV IB	330 CHRY	7	4500	1 10	**	**
---	--- 1985 BOATS ---									
20	GENEVA	OP	UTL	WD SV IB	240 CHRY	7	3000	1 6	**	**
20	TAHOE	OP	UTL	WD SV IB	240 CHRY	7	3000	1 6	**	**
23	GENEVA	OP	UTL	WD SV IB	350 CHRY	8	4000	1 8	**	**
23	TAHOE	OP	UTL	WD SV IB	350 CHRY	8	4000	1 8	**	**
24	RUNABOUT	OP	RNBT	WD SV IB	240 CHRY	6 8	3500	1 6	**	**
27	RUNABOUT	OP	RNBT	WD SV IB	350 CHRY	7	4500	1 10	**	**
27	RUNABOUT	OP	RNBT	WD SV IB	T240 CHRY	7	5500	1 10	**	**

GRAND SOLEIL OF AMERICA
CANTIERE DEL PARDO
CHICAGO IL 60611   See inside cover to adjust price for area

GRAND SOLEIL
FORLI 47100 ITALY

For more recent years, see the BUC Used Boat Price Guide, Volume 1

LOA FT IN	NAME AND/ OR MODEL	TOP/ RIG	BOAT TYPE	-HULL- MTL TP	----ENGINE--- TP # HP MFG	BEAM FT IN	WGT LBS	DRAFT FT IN	RETAIL LOW	RETAIL HIGH
---	--- 1996 BOATS ---									
35 7	GRAND SOLEIL 343	SLP	SARAC	FBG KL IB	29D VLVO	11 2	10253	5 9	82600	90700
39	GRAND SOLEIL 38	SLP	SARAC	FBG KL IB	29D VLVO	12	14332	6 9	127000	139500
42 3	GRAND SOLEIL 42	SLP	SARAC	FBG KL IB	40D VLVO	13 3	19845	6 7	180000	198000
45 7	GRAND SOLEIL 45	SLP	SARAC	FBG KL IB	62D YAN	13 6	24255	7 2	230500	253500
50 5	GRAND SOLEIL 50	SLP	SARAC	FBG KL IB	62D YAN	14 1	29326	7 2	321500	353500
63 9	GRAND SOLEIL MAXI OE	SLP	SARAC	FBG KL IB	125D YAN	17 5	50000	8 5	666000	732500

LOA FT IN	NAME AND/ OR MODEL	TOP/ RIG	BOAT TYPE	HULL MTL TP	ENGINE TP HP MFG	BEAM FT IN	WGT LBS	DRAFT FT IN	RETAIL LOW	RETAIL HIGH

-- 1985 BOATS ------

LOA FT IN	NAME AND/ OR MODEL	TOP/ RIG	BOAT TYPE	HULL MTL TP	ENGINE TP HP MFG	BEAM FT IN	WGT LBS	DRAFT FT IN	RETAIL LOW	RETAIL HIGH
37 3	GRAND-SOLEIL 35	SLP	SA/RC	FBG KL	IB 28D VLVO	11 6	12200	5 10	54400	59700
41	GRAND-SOLEIL 39	SLP	SA/RC	FBG KL	IB 51D PERK	12 4	18600	6 3	88500	97300
47 7	GRAND-SOLEIL 46	SLP	SA/RC	FBG KL	IB 65D VLVO	13 8	28660	6 6	148000	162500

GREAT MIDWEST YACHT CO
SUNBURY OH 43074   COAST GUARD MFG ID- GRU See inside cover to adjust price for area

LOA FT IN	NAME AND/ OR MODEL	TOP/ RIG	BOAT TYPE	HULL MTL TP	ENGINE TP # HP MFG	BEAM FT IN	WGT LBS	DRAFT FT IN	RETAIL LOW	RETAIL HIGH

-- 1994 BOATS ------
| 17 | THISTLE | SLP | SAROD | FBG CB | | 6 | 515 | 9 | 6950 | 7950 |

-- 1993 BOATS ------
| 17 | THISTLE | SLP | SAROD | FBG CB | | 6 | 500 | | 6450 | 7400 |

-- 1992 BOATS ------
| 17 | THISTLE | SLP | SA/OD | FBG CB | | 6 | 500 | | 6050 | 6950 |

-- 1991 BOATS ------
| 17 | THISTLE | SLP | SA/OD | FBG CB | | 6 | 500 | | 5700 | 6550 |

-- 1990 BOATS ------
| 17 | THISTLE | SLP | SA/OD | FBG CB | | 6 | 500 | 9 | 5350 | 6150 |

-- 1989 BOATS ------
| 17 | THISTLE | SLP | SA/OD | FBG CB | | 6 | 500 | 9 | 5050 | 5800 |

-- 1988 BOATS ------
| 17 | THISTLE | SLP | SA/OD | FBG CB | | 6 | 500 | 9 | 4750 | 5450 |

-- 1987 BOATS ------
| 17 | THISTLE | SLP | SA/OD | FBG CB | | 6 | 500 | 9 | 4500 | 5150 |

-- 1986 BOATS ------
| 17 | THISTLE | SLP | SA/OD | FBG CB | | 6 | 500 | 9 | 4150 | 4850 |

-- 1985 BOATS ------
| 17 | THISTLE | SLP | SA/OD | FBG CB | | 6 | 515 | 9 | 3950 | 4600 |

-- 1984 BOATS ------
| 17 | THISTLE | SLP | SA/OD | FBG CB | | 6 | 515 | 9 | 3750 | 4350 |

....For earlier years, see the BUC Used Boat Price Guide, Volume 3

GREGOR BOATS
FRESNO CA 93722   COAST GUARD MFG ID- GBC See inside cover to adjust price for area

For more recent years, see the BUC Used Boat Price Guide, Volume 1

LOA FT IN	NAME AND/ OR MODEL	TOP/ RIG	BOAT TYPE	HULL MTL TP	ENGINE TP # HP MFG	BEAM FT IN	WGT LBS	DRAFT FT IN	RETAIL LOW	RETAIL HIGH

-- 1996 BOATS ------
16	EAGLE AK-16	OP	FSH	AL	DV OB	6 4	450		1650	2000
16 5	GREGOR AK-16	OP	FSH	AL	DV OB	6 4	375		1400	1700
16 5	SEA HAWK V6-G4 FSHCC	OP	CTRCN	AL	DV OB	6 10	775		2950	3450
16 5	SEA HAWK V6-G4 FSHTC	OP	FSH	AL	DV OB	6 10	775		2950	3400
16 5	SEA HAWK V6-G4 FSHWT	OP	FSH	AL	DV OB	6 10	775		2650	3450
16 5	SEA HAWK V6-G4 SPTCC	OP	CTRCN	AL	DV OB	6 10	775		2950	3450
16 5	SEA HAWK V6-G4 SPTTC	OP	FSH	AL	DV OB	6 10	775		2950	3400
16 5	SEA HAWK V6-G4 SPTWT	OP	FSH	AL	DV OB	6 10	775		2950	3450
16 5	SEA HAWK V6-G4 SS CC	OP	CTRCN	AL	DV OB	6 10	775		2950	3450
16 5	SEA HAWK V6-G4 SS TC	OP	FSH	AL	DV OB	6 10	775		2950	3400
16 5	SEA HAWK V6-G4 SS WT	OP	FSH	AL	DV OB	6 10	775		2950	3400
16 6	GREGOR R-166J	OP	FSH	AL	OB	5 10	525		2000	2400
16 6	GREGOR R-166P	OP	FSH	AL	OB	5 10	505		1950	2300
17 2	GREGOR M-72L	OP	FSH	AL	OB	5 10	308		1250	1500
17 2	GREGOR MX-720	OP	FSH	AL	OB	5 10	440		1750	2100
18 5	SEA HAWK V8-G4 FSH	OP	CTRCN	AL	DV OB	6 10	855		3450	4000
18 5	SEA HAWK V8-G4 FSHTC	OP	FSH	AL	DV OB	6 10	855		3450	4000
18 5	SEA HAWK V8-G4 FSHWT	OP	FSH	AL	DV OB	6 10	855		3450	4000
18 5	SEA HAWK V8-G4 SPT	OP	CTRCN	AL	DV OB	6 10	855		3450	4000
18 5	SEA HAWK V8-G4 SPTTC	OP	FSH	AL	DV OB	6 10	855		3450	4000
18 5	SEA HAWK V8-G4 SPTWT	OP	FSH	AL	DV OB	6 10	855		3450	4000
18 5	SEA HAWK V8-G4 SS	OP	CTRCN	AL	DV OB	6 10	855		3450	4000
18 5	SEA HAWK V8-G4 SSTC	OP	FSH	AL	DV OB	6 10	855		3450	4000
18 5	SEA HAWK V8-G4 SSWT	OP	FSH	AL	DV OB	6 10	855		3450	4000
18 5	SEA HAWK V8-G5 CC	OP	CTRCN	AL	DV OB	6 10	835		3400	3950
18 5	SEA HAWK V8-G5 TC	OP	FSH	AL	DV OB	6 10	835		3400	3950
18 5	SEA HAWK V8-G5 WT	OP	FSH	AL	DV OB	6 10	835		3400	3950
18 6	GREGOR R-186	OP	FSH	AL	OB	7	795		3250	3800
20 6	GREGOR R-206	OP	FSH	AL	OB	7 6	860		3850	4450
20 6	SEA HAWK V10-G4 FSHC	OP	CTRCN	AL	DV OB	7	950		4200	4900
20 6	SEA HAWK V10-G4 FSHT	OP	FSH	AL	DV OB	7	950		4200	4900
20 6	SEA HAWK V10-G4 FSHW	OP	FSH	AL	DV OB	7	950		4200	4900
20 6	SEA HAWK V10-G4 SPTC	OP	CTRCN	AL	DV OB	7	950		4200	4900
20 6	SEA HAWK V10-G4 SPTT	OP	FSH	AL	DV OB	7	950		4200	4900
20 6	SEA HAWK V10-G4 SPTW	OP	FSH	AL	DV OB	7	950		4200	4900
20 6	SEA HAWK V10-G4 SSCC	OP	CTRCN	AL	DV OB	7	950		4200	4900
20 6	SEA HAWK V10-G4 SSTC	OP	FSH	AL	DV OB	7	950		4200	4900
20 6	SEA HAWK V10-G4 SSWT	OP	FSH	AL	DV OB	7	950		4200	4900
20 6	SEA HAWK V10-G5 CC	OP	CTRCN	AL	DV OB	7	960		4200	4900
20 6	SEA HAWK V10-G5 WC	OP	FSH	AL	DV OB	7	960		4200	4900
24 6	GREGOR R-246	OP	FSH	AL	OB	7 6	1050		8650	9950

-- 1995 BOATS ------
16	EAGLE AK-16 CC FSH	OP	FSH	AL	DV OB	6 4	450		1700	1700
16	EAGLE AK-16 CC SPT	OP	FSH	AL	DV OB	6 4	450		1700	2000
16	EAGLE AK-16 TC FSH	OP	FSH	AL	DV OB	6 4	450		1450	1750
16	EAGLE AK-16 TC SPT	OP	FSH	AL	DV OB	6 4	450		1750	2100
16 5	GREGOR AK-16-2	OP	FSH	AL	DV OB	6 4	375		1250	1450
16 5	GREGOR AK-16-5	OP	FSH	AL	DV OB	6 4	375		1400	1650
16 5	GREGOR AK-16-7	OP	FSH	AL	DV OB	6 4	375		1450	1700
16 5	SEA HAWK V6-G4 FSHCC	OP	CTRCN	AL	DV OB	6 10	775		2200	2600
16 5	SEA HAWK V6-G4 FSHTC	OP	FSH	AL	DV OB	6 10	775		2150	2550
16 5	SEA HAWK V6-G4 FSHWT	OP	FSH	AL	DV OB	6 10	775		2350	2700
16 5	SEA HAWK V6-G4 SPTCC	OP	CTRCN	AL	DV OB	6 10	775		2850	3300
16 5	SEA HAWK V6-G4 SPTTC	OP	FSH	AL	DV OB	6 10	775		2750	3200
16 5	SEA HAWK V6-G4 SPTWT	OP	FSH	AL	DV OB	6 10	775		2900	3350
16 5	SEA HAWK V6-G4 SS CC	OP	CTRCN	AL	DV OB	6 10	775		3350	3850
16 5	SEA HAWK V6-G4 SS TC	OP	FSH	AL	DV OB	6 10	775		3250	3750
16 5	SEA HAWK V6-G4 SS WT	OP	FSH	AL	DV OB	6 10	775		3350	3900
17 2	GREGOR M-72L	OP	FSH	AL	OB	5 10	308		1200	1400
17 2	GREGOR MX-720 FSH	OP	FSH	AL	OB	5 10	440		1400	1650
17 2	GREGOR MX-720 SPT	OP	FSH	AL	OB	5 10	440		1600	1900
17 2	GREGOR MX-720 SS	OP	FSH	AL	OB	5 10	440		2050	2450
18 5	SEA HAWK V8-G5 CC	OP	CTRCN	AL	DV OB	6 10	835		3200	3750
18 5	SEA HAWK V8-G5 TC	OP	FSH	AL	DV OB	6 10	833		3150	3650
18 5	SEA HAWK V8-G5 WT	OP	FSH	AL	DV OB	6 10	835		3300	3800
18 5	SEA HAWKS V8-G4 FSH	OP	CTRCN	AL	DV OB	6 10	855		2650	3100
18 5	SEA HAWKS V8-G4 FSHT	OP	FSH	AL	DV OB	6 10	855		2600	3050
18 5	SEA HAWKS V8-G4 FSHW	OP	FSH	AL	DV OB	6 10	855		2800	3250
18 5	SEA HAWKS V8-G4 SPT	OP	CTRCN	AL	DV OB	6 10	855		3350	3900
18 5	SEA HAWKS V8-G4 SPTT	OP	FSH	AL	DV OB	6 10	855		3250	3800
18 5	SEA HAWKS V8-G4 SPTW	OP	FSH	AL	DV OB	6 10	855		3400	3950
18 5	SEA HAWKS V8-G4 SS	OP	CTRCN	AL	DV OB	6 10	855		3850	4500
18 5	SEA HAWKS V8-G4 SSTC	OP	FSH	AL	DV OB	6 10	855		3800	4400
18 5	SEA HAWKS V8-G4 SSWT	OP	FSH	AL	DV OB	6 10	855		3900	4550
20 6	SEA HAWK V10-G4 FSHC	OP	CTRCN	AL	DV OB	7	950		3250	3800
20 6	SEA HAWK V10-G4 FSHT	OP	FSH	AL	DV OB	7	950		3200	3750
20 6	SEA HAWK V10-G4 FSHW	OP	FSH	AL	DV OB	7	950		3400	3950
20 6	SEA HAWK V10-G4 SPTC	OP	CTRCN	AL	DV OB	7	950		4050	4700
20 6	SEA HAWK V10-G4 SPTT	OP	FSH	AL	DV OB	7	950		3950	4600
20 6	SEA HAWK V10-G4 SPTW	OP	FSH	AL	DV OB	7	950		4100	4750
20 6	SEA HAWK V10-G4 SS T	OP	FSH	AL	DV OB	7	950		4600	5250
20 6	SEA HAWK V10-G4 SSCC	OP	CTRCN	AL	DV OB	7	950		4700	5400
20 6	SEA HAWK V10-G4 SSWT	OP	FSH	AL	DV OB	7	950		4700	5400
20 6	SEA HAWK V10-G5 CC	OP	CTRCN	AL	DV OB	7	960		4000	4700
20 6	SEA HAWK V10-G5 TC	OP	CTRCN	AL	DV OB	7	960		3950	4600
20 6	SEA HAWK V10-G5 WT	OP	FSH	AL	DV OB	7	960		4100	4750

-- 1994 BOATS ------
16 5	GREGOR AK-16-1	OP	FSH	AL	DV OB	6 4	375		1150	1400
16 5	GREGOR AK-16-2	OP	FSH	AL	DV OB	6 4	375		1200	1450
16 5	GREGOR AK-16-3	OP	FSH	AL	DV OB	6 4	375		1250	1500
16 5	GREGOR AK-16-4	OP	FSH	AL	DV OB	6 4	375		1300	1550
16 5	GREGOR AK-16-5	OP	FSH	AL	DV OB	6 4	375		1350	1600
16 5	GREGOR AK-16-6	OP	FSH	AL	DV OB	6 4	375		1400	1650
16 5	SEA HAWKS III 6/CC	OP	FSH	AL	DV OB	6 4	450		1500	1800
16 5	SEA HAWKS III 6/TC	OP	FSH	AL	DV OB	6 4	450		1550	1850
16 6	GREGOR R-166 PCC	OP	UTL	AL	OB	5 10	525		1700	2000
16 6	GREGOR R-166 PSC	OP	UTL	AL	OB	5 10	505		1700	2000
17	CUTLASS CP-170	OP	CTRCN	AL	DV OB	6	460		1650	1950
17 2	GREGOR F-17	OP	BASS	AL	DV IO 50	5 10	550		1700	2000
17 2	GREGOR M-72	OP	FSH	AL	DV OB	5 10	300		1100	1300
17 2	GREGOR M-72L	OP	FSH	AL	DV OB	5 10	308		1100	1350
17 2	GREGOR MX-720	OP	FSH	AL	DV OB	5 10	410		1500	1750
18 5	SEA HAWKS IV 8/CC	OP	FSH	AL	DV OB	5 10	590		2250	2600

LOA FT	LOA IN	NAME AND/ OR MODEL	TOP/ RIG	BOAT TYPE	-HULL- MTL	-HULL- TP	ENGINE TP	ENGINE # HP	ENGINE MFG	BEAM FT	BEAM IN	WGT LBS	DRAFT FT	DRAFT IN	RETAIL LOW	RETAIL HIGH
		1994 BOATS														
18	5	SEA HAWKS IV 8/TC	OP	FSH	AL	DV	OB			6	10	590			2300	2650
18	6	GREGOR R-186 CC	OP	UTL	AL		OB			7	6	795			2600	3050
18	6	GREGOR R-186 DASH	OP	UTL	AL		OB			7	6	795			2650	3050
18	6	GREGOR R-186 SC	OP	UTL	AL		OB			7	6	795			2600	3050
18	6	GREGOR R-186 TC	OP	UTL	AL		OB			7	6	795			2650	3100
18	6	GREGOR RJ-186	OP	UTL	AL		IB			7	6	1733			**	**
19		CUTLASS C-190	OP	CTRCN	AL	DV	OB			7		590			2350	2700
20	6	GREGOR R-206 CC	OP	UTL	AL		OB			7	6	860			2750	3200
20	6	GREGOR R-206 DASH	OP	UTL	AL		OB			7	6	860			2750	3200
20	6	GREGOR R-206 SC	OP	UTL	AL		OB			7	6	860			2750	3200
20	6	GREGOR R-206 TC	OP	UTL	AL		OB			7	6	860			2800	3250
20	6	GREGOR RJ-206	OP	UTL	AL		IB			7	6	1798			**	**
20	6	SEA HAWK V 10CC	OP	FSH	AL	DV	OB			7		785			3150	3650
20	6	SEA HAWK V 10TC	OP	FSH	AL	DV	OB			7		785			3300	3800
20	6	SEA HAWK V 8CC	OP	FSH	AL	DV	OB			7		700			2800	3300
20	6	SEA HAWK V 8TC	OP	FSH	AL	DV	OB			7		700			3000	3450
20	6	SEA HAWKS IV 10/TC	OP	FSH	AL	DV	IB	75		7		655			3800	4400
20	6	SEA HAWKS IV 10CC	OP	FSH	AL	DV	OB			7		655			2750	3200
24	6	GREGOR R-246 CC	OP	UTL	AL	SV	OB			7	6	1050			5000	5750
24	6	GREGOR R-246 DASH	OP	UTL	AL	SV	OB			7	6	1050			5000	5700
24	6	GREGOR R-246 SC	OP	UTL	AL	SV	OB			7	6	1050			5000	5700
24	6	GREGOR R-246 TC	OP	UTL	AL	SV	OB			7	6	1050			5050	5800
24	6	GREGOR RJ-246	OP	UTL	AL	SV	IB	120		7	6	2233			5450	6300
		1993 BOATS														
16	5	GREGOR AK-16-1	OP	FSH	AL	DV	OB			6	4	375			1100	1300
16	5	GREGOR AK-16-2	OP	FSH	AL	DV	OB			6	4	375			1150	1350
16	5	GREGOR AK-16-3	OP	FSH	AL	DV	OB			6	4	375			1200	1450
16	5	GREGOR AK-16-4	OP	FSH	AL	DV	OB			6	4	375			1250	1500
16	5	GREGOR AK-16-5	OP	FSH	AL	DV	OB			6	4	375			1300	1550
16	5	GREGOR AK-16-6	OP	FSH	AL	DV	OB			6	4	375			1300	1550
16	5	GREGOR AK-16-7	OP	FSH	AL	DV	OB			6	4	375			1300	1600
16	5	SEA HAWKS III 6/CC	OP	FSH	AL	DV	OB			6	4	450			1450	1750
16	5	SEA HAWKS III 6/TC	OP	FSH	AL	DV	OB			6	4	450			1500	1800
16	6	GREGOR R-166 PCC	OP	UTL	AL		OB			5	10	525			1700	2000
16	6	GREGOR R-166 PSC	OP	UTL	AL		OB			5	10	505			1650	1950
17		CUTLASS C-170	OP	CTRCN	AL	DV	OB			6	6	460			1550	1850
17	2	GREGOR F-17	OP	BASS	AL	DV	IO	50		5	10	550			1600	1900
17	2	GREGOR M-72	OP	FSH	AL	DV	OB			5	10	300			1050	1250
17	2	GREGOR M-72L	OP	FSH	AL	DV	OB			5	10	308			1050	1300
17	2	GREGOR MX-720	OP	FSH	AL	DV	OB			5	10	410			1400	1700
18	5	SEA HAWKS IV 8/CC	OP	FSH	AL	DV	OB			6	10	590			2100	2500
18	5	SEA HAWKS IV 8/TC	OP	FSH	AL	DV	OB			6	10	590			2200	2550
18	6	GREGOR R-186 CC	OP	UTL	AL		OB			7	6	795			2500	2900
18	6	GREGOR R-186 DASH	OP	UTL	AL		OB			7	6	795			2550	2950
18	6	GREGOR R-186 SC	OP	UTL	AL		OB			7	6	795			2500	2900
18	6	GREGOR R-186 TC	OP	UTL	AL		OB			7	6	795			2550	2950
18	6	GREGOR RJ-186	OP	UTL	AL		IB			7	6	1733			**	**
19		CUTLASS C-190	OP	CTRCN	AL	DV	OB			7		590			2250	2600
20	6	GREGOR R-206 CC	OP	UTL	AL		OB			7	6	860			2650	3050
20	6	GREGOR R-206 DASH	OP	UTL	AL		OB			7	6	860			2600	3050
20	6	GREGOR R-206 SC	OP	UTL	AL		OB			7	6	860			2600	3050
20	6	GREGOR R-206 TC	OP	UTL	AL		OB			7	6	860			2650	3100
20	6	GREGOR RJ-206	OP	UTL	AL		IB			7	6	1798			**	**
20	6	SEA HAWK V 10CC	OP	FSH	AL	DV	OB			7		785			3000	3500
20	6	SEA HAWK V 10TC	OP	FSH	AL	DV	OB			7		785			3150	3650
20	6	SEA HAWK V 8CC	OP	FSH	AL	DV	OB			7		700			2700	3150
20	6	SEA HAWK V 8TC	OP	FSH	AL	DV	OB			7		700			2850	3300
20	6	SEA HAWKS IV 10/TC	OP	FSH	AL	DV	IB	75		7		655			3550	4150
20	6	SEA HAWKS IV 10CC	OP	FSH	AL	DV	OB			7		655			2600	3050
24	6	GREGOR R-246 CC	OP	UTL	AL	SV	OB			7	6	1050			4850	5550
24	6	GREGOR R-246 DASH	OP	UTL	AL	SV	OB			7	6	1050			4800	5500
24	6	GREGOR R-246 SC	OP	UTL	AL	SV	OB			7	6	1050			4800	5500
24	6	GREGOR R-246 TC	OP	UTL	AL	SV	OB			7	6	1050			4900	5600
24	6	GREGOR RJ-246	OP	UTL	AL	SV	IB	120		7	6	2233			5150	5900
		1992 BOATS														
16	5	GREGOR AK-16-1	OP	FSH	AL	DV	OB			6	4	375			1050	1250
16	5	GREGOR AK-16-2	OP	FSH	AL	DV	OB			6	4	375			1100	1300
16	5	GREGOR AK-16-3	OP	FSH	AL	DV	OB			6	4	375			1150	1400
16	5	GREGOR AK-16-4	OP	FSH	AL	DV	OB			6	4	375			1200	1400
16	5	GREGOR AK-16-5	OP	FSH	AL	DV	OB			6	4	375			1250	1500
16	5	GREGOR AK-16-6	OP	FSH	AL	DV	OB			6	4	375			1250	1500
16	5	GREGOR AK-16-7	OP	FSH	AL	DV	OB			6	4	375			1250	1500
16	5	SEA HAWKS III 6/CC	OP	FSH	AL	DV	OB			6	4	450			1400	1650
16	5	SEA HAWKS III 6/TC	OP	FSH	AL	DV	OB			6	4	450			1450	1700
16	6	GREGOR R-166 CC	OP	UTL	AL		OB			5	10	525			1600	1950
16	6	GREGOR R-166 PSC	OP	UTL	AL		OB			5	10	505			1550	1850
17		CUTLASS C-170	OP	CTRCN	AL	DV	OB			6	6	460			1500	1800
17	2	GREGOR F-17	OP	BASS	AL	DV	IO	50		5	10	550			1500	1750
17	2	GREGOR F-17 SS	OP	BASS	AL	DV	IO	50		5	10	550			1900	2250
17	2	GREGOR M-72	OP	FSH	AL	DV	OB			5	10	300			1000	1200
17	2	GREGOR M-72L	OP	FSH	AL	DV	OB			5	10	308			1050	1250
17	2	GREGOR MX-720	OP	FSH	AL	DV	OB			5	10	410			1350	1600
17	2	GREGOR MX-720 SS	OP	FSH	AL	DV	OB			5	10	510			1700	2000
18	5	SEA HAWKS IV 8/CC	OP	FSH	AL	DV	OB			6	10	590			1600	1900
18	5	SEA HAWKS IV 8/TC	OP	FSH	AL	DV	OB			6	10	590			1650	1950
18	5	SEA HAWKS IV SS 8-1	OP	FSH	AL	DV	OB			6	10	590			2300	2650
18	5	SEA HAWKS IV SS 8-2	OP	FSH	AL	DV	OB			6	10	590			2300	2650
18	5	SEA HAWKS IV SS 8-3	OP	FSH	AL	DV	OB			6	10	590			2300	2700
18	5	SEA HAWKS IV SS 8-TC	OP	FSH	AL	DV	OB			6	10	590			2300	2650
18	6	GREGOR R-186 CC	OP	UTL	AL		OB			7	6	795			2400	2800
18	6	GREGOR R-186 DASH	OP	UTL	AL		OB			7	6	795			2400	2800
18	6	GREGOR R-186 SC	OP	UTL	AL		OB			7	6	795			2400	2800
18	6	GREGOR R-186 TC	OP	UTL	AL		OB			7	6	795			2450	2850
18	6	GREGOR RJ-186	OP	UTL	AL		IB			7	6	1733			**	**
19		CUTLASS C-190	OP	CTRCN	AL	DV	OB			7		590			2100	2500
20	6	GREGOR R-206 CC	OP	UTL	AL		OB			7	6	860			2500	2950
20	6	GREGOR R-206 DASH	OP	UTL	AL		OB			7	6	860			2500	2900
20	6	GREGOR R-206 SC	OP	UTL	AL		OB			7	6	860			2500	2900
20	6	GREGOR R-206 TC	OP	UTL	AL		OB			7	6	860			2550	2950
20	6	GREGOR RJ-206	OP	UTL	AL		IB			7	6	1798			**	**
20	6	SEA HAWKS IV 10/TC	OP	FSH	AL	DV	IB	75		7		655			3450	4000
20	6	SEA HAWKS IV 10CC	OP	FSH	AL	DV	OB			7		655			1950	2300
20	6	SEA HAWKS IV SS 10-1	OP	FSH	AL	DV	OB			7		655			2650	3050
20	6	SEA HAWKS IV SS 10-2	OP	FSH	AL	DV	OB			7		655			2650	3050
20	6	SEA HAWKS IV SS 10-3	OP	FSH	AL	DV	OB			7		655			2650	3100
20	6	SEA HAWKS IV SS 10TC	OP	FSH	AL	DV	OB			7		655			2650	3050
24	6	GREGOR R-246 CC	OP	UTL	AL		OB			7	6	1050			4500	5200
24	6	GREGOR R-246 DASH	OP	UTL	AL		OB			7	6	1050			4500	5150
24	6	GREGOR R-246 SC	OP	UTL	AL		OB			7	6	1050			4500	5150
24	6	GREGOR R-246 TC	OP	UTL	AL		OB			7	6	1050			4550	5250
24	6	GREGOR RJ-246	OP	UTL	AL		IB			7	6	2233			**	**
		1991 BOATS														
16	5	GREGOR AK-16-1	OP	FSH	AL	DV	OB			6	4	375			1050	1200
16	5	GREGOR AK-16-2	OP	FSH	AL	DV	OB			6	4	375			1050	1250
16	5	GREGOR AK-16-3	OP	FSH	AL	DV	OB			6	4	375			1100	1350
16	5	GREGOR AK-16-4	OP	FSH	AL	DV	OB			6	4	375			1150	1350
16	5	GREGOR AK-16-5	OP	FSH	AL	DV	OB			6	4	375			1200	1450
16	5	GREGOR AK-16-6	OP	FSH	AL	DV	OB			6	4	375			1200	1400
16	5	GREGOR AK-16-7	OP	FSH	AL	DV	OB			6	4	375			1200	1450
16	5	SEA HAWKS III 6/CC	OP	FSH	AL	DV	OB			6	4	450			1350	1600
16	5	SEA HAWKS III 6/TC	OP	FSH	AL	DV	OB			6	4	450			1400	1650
16	6	GREGOR R-166 CC	OP	UTL	AL		OB			5	10	525			1550	1850
16	6	GREGOR R-166 PSC	OP	UTL	AL		OB			5	10	505			1500	1800
17		CUTLASS C-170	OP	CTRCN	AL	DV	OB			6	6	460			1450	1750
17	2	GREGOR F-17	OP	BASS	AL	DV	IO	50		5	10	550			1400	1650
17	2	GREGOR F-17 SS	OP	BASS	AL	DV	IO	50		5	10	550			1750	2100
17	2	GREGOR M-72	OP	FSH	AL	DV	OB			5	10	300			965	1150
17	2	GREGOR M-72L	OP	FSH	AL	DV	OB			5	10	308			990	1200
17	2	GREGOR MX-720	OP	FSH	AL	DV	OB			5	10	410			1300	1550
17	2	GREGOR MX-720 SS	OP	FSH	AL	DV	OB			5	10	510			1600	1900
18	5	SEA HAWKS IV 8/CC	OP	FSH	AL	DV	OB			6	10	590			1550	1850
18	5	SEA HAWKS IV 8/TC	OP	FSH	AL	DV	OB			6	10	590			1600	1900
18	5	SEA HAWKS IV SS 8-1	OP	FSH	AL	DV	OB			6	10	590			2200	2550
18	5	SEA HAWKS IV SS 8-2	OP	FSH	AL	DV	OB			6	10	590			2200	2550
18	5	SEA HAWKS IV SS 8-3	OP	FSH	AL	DV	OB			6	10	590			2250	2600
18	5	SEA HAWKS IV SS 8-TC	OP	FSH	AL	DV	OB			6	10	590			2200	2550
18	6	GREGOR R-186 CC	OP	UTL	AL		OB			7	6	795			2350	2700
18	6	GREGOR R-186 DASH	OP	UTL	AL		OB			7	6	795			2350	2700
18	6	GREGOR R-186 SC	OP	UTL	AL		OB			7	6	795			2300	2700
18	6	GREGOR R-186 TC	OP	UTL	AL		OB			7	6	795			2350	2750
18	6	GREGOR RJ-186	OP	UTL	AL		IB			7	6	1733			**	**
19		CUTLASS C-190	OP	CTRCN	AL	DV	OB			7		590			2000	2400
20	6	GREGOR R-206 CC	OP	UTL	AL		OB			7	6	860			2400	2800
20	6	GREGOR R-206 DASH	OP	UTL	AL		OB			7	6	860			2400	2800
20	6	GREGOR R-206 SC	OP	UTL	AL		OB			7	6	860			2400	2800
20	6	GREGOR R-206 TC	OP	UTL	AL		OB			7	6	860			2450	2850
20	6	GREGOR RJ-206	OP	UTL	AL		IB			7	6	1798			**	**

CONTINUED ON NEXT PAGE

GREGOR BOATS -CONTINUED See inside cover to adjust price for area

LOA FT	LOA IN	NAME AND/ OR MODEL	TOP/ RIG	BOAT TYPE	HULL MTL	HULL TP	ENGINE TP	ENGINE # HP	ENGINE MFG	BEAM FT	BEAM IN	WGT LBS	DRAFT FT	DRAFT IN	RETAIL LOW	RETAIL HIGH
		1991 BOATS														
20	6	SEA HAWKS IV 10/TC	OP	FSH	AL	DV	IB	75		7		655			3250	3750
20	6	SEA HAWKS IV 10CC	OP	FSH	AL	DV	OB			7		655			1900	2250
20	6	SEA HAWKS IV SS 10-1	OP	FSH	AL	DV	OB			7		655			2550	2950
20	6	SEA HAWKS IV SS 10-2	OP	FSH	AL	DV	OB			7		655			2550	2950
20	6	SEA HAWKS IV SS 10-3	OP	FSH	AL	DV	OB			7		655			2550	2950
20	6	SEA HAWKS IV SS 10TC	OP	FSH	AL	DV	OB			7		655			2550	2950
24	6	GREGOR R-246 CC	OP	UTL	AL		OB			7	6	1050			4200	4900
24	6	GREGOR R-246 DASH	OP	UTL	AL		OB			7	6	1050			4200	4900
24	6	GREGOR R-246 SC	OP	UTL	AL		OB			7	6	1050			4200	4900
24	6	GREGOR R-246 TC	OP	UTL	AL		OB			7	6	1050			4250	4950
24	6	GREGOR RJ-246	OP	UTL	AL		IB			7	6	2233			**	**
		1990 BOATS														
16	5	GREGOR AK-16-1	OP	FSH	AL	DV	OB			6	4	375			990	1200
16	5	GREGOR AK-16-2	OP	FSH	AL	DV	OB			6	4	375			1050	1250
16	5	GREGOR AK-16-3	OP	FSH	AL	DV	OB			6	4	375			1100	1300
16	5	GREGOR AK-16-4	OP	FSH	AL	DV	OB			6	4	375			1100	1300
16	5	GREGOR AK-16-5	OP	FSH	AL	DV	OB			6	4	375			1150	1400
16	5	GREGOR AK-16-6	OP	FSH	AL	DV	OB			6	4	375			1150	1350
16	5	GREGOR AK-16-7	OP	FSH	AL	DV	OB			6	4	375			1200	1400
16	5	SEA HAWKS III 6/CC	OP	FSH	AL	DV	OB			6	4	450			1300	1550
16	5	SEA HAWKS III 6/TC	OP	FSH	AL	DV	OB			6	4	450			1350	1600
16	6	GREGOR R-166 JCC	OP	UTL	AL		OB			5	10	525			1500	1800
16	6	GREGOR R-166 JSC	OP	UTL	AL		OB			5	10	525			1500	1800
16	6	GREGOR R-166 PCC	OP	UTL	AL		OB			5	10	505			1450	1750
16	6	GREGOR R-166 PSC	OP	UTL	AL		OB			5	10	505			1450	1700
17	2	GREGOR F-17	OP	BASS	AL	DV	IO	50		5	10	550			1300	1550
17	2	GREGOR F-17 SS	OP	BASS	AL	DV	IO	50		5	10	550			1650	1950
17	2	GREGOR M-72	OP	FSH	AL	DV	OB			5	10	300			935	1100
17	2	GREGOR M-72L	OP	FSH	AL	DV	OB			5	10	308			955	1150
17	2	GREGOR MX-720	OP	FSH	AL	DV	OB			5	10	410			1250	1500
17	2	GREGOR MX-720 SS	OP	FSH	AL	DV	OB			5	10	510			1550	1850
18	5	SEA HAWKS IV 8/CC	OP	FSH	AL	DV	OB			6	10	590			1500	1750
18	5	SEA HAWKS IV 8/TC	OP	FSH	AL	DV	OB			6	10	590			1500	1800
18	5	SEA HAWKS IV SS 8-1	OP	FSH	AL	DV	OB			6	10	590			2100	2500
18	5	SEA HAWKS IV SS 8-2	OP	FSH	AL	DV	OB			6	10	590			2100	2500
18	5	SEA HAWKS IV SS 8-3	OP	FSH	AL	DV	OB			6	10	590			2150	2500
18	5	SEA HAWKS IV SS 8-TC	OP	FSH	AL	DV	OB			6	10	590			2100	2500
18	6	GREGOR R-186 CC	OP	UTL	AL		OB			7	6	795			2250	2650
18	6	GREGOR R-186 DASH	OP	UTL	AL		OB			7	6	795			2300	2650
18	6	GREGOR R-186 SC	OP	UTL	AL		OB			7	6	795			2250	2600
18	6	GREGOR R-186 TC	OP	UTL	AL		OB			7	6	795			2300	2650
18	6	GREGOR RJ-186	OP	UTL	AL		IB			7	6	1733			**	**
20	6	GREGOR R-206 CC	OP	UTL	AL		OB			7	6	860			2350	2700
20	6	GREGOR R-206 DASH	OP	UTL	AL		OB			7	6	860			2350	2750
20	6	GREGOR R-206 SC	OP	UTL	AL		OB			7	6	860			2350	2750
20	6	GREGOR R-206 TC	OP	UTL	AL		OB			7	6	860			2350	2750
20	6	GREGOR RJ-206	OP	UTL	AL		IB			7	6	1798			**	**
20	6	SEA HAWKS IV 10/TC	OP	FSH	AL	DV	OB			7		655			1900	2250
20	6	SEA HAWKS IV 10CC	OP	FSH	AL	DV	OB			7		655			1850	2200
20	6	SEA HAWKS IV SS 10-1	OP	FSH	AL	DV	OB			7		655			2550	2950
20	6	SEA HAWKS IV SS 10-2	OP	FSH	AL	DV	OB			7		655			2550	2950
20	6	SEA HAWKS IV SS 10-3	OP	FSH	AL	DV	OB			7		655			2550	3000
20	6	SEA HAWKS IV SS 10TC	OP	FSH	AL	DV	OB			7		655			2550	2950
24	6	GREGOR R-246 CC	OP	UTL	AL		OB			7	6	1050			3800	4400
24	6	GREGOR R-246 DASH	OP	UTL	AL		OB			7	6	1050			3750	4400
24	6	GREGOR R-246 SC	OP	UTL	AL		OB			7	6	1050			3750	4400
24	6	GREGOR R-246 TC	OP	UTL	AL		OB			7	6	1050			3800	4450
24	6	GREGOR RJ-246	OP	UTL	AL		IB			7	6	2233			**	**
		1986 BOATS														
16	5	V-6 I	OP	FSH	AL	SV	OB			6	4	375			905	1100
16	5	V-6 II	OP	FSH	AL	SV	OB			6	4	375			1050	1250
16	6	FISH-MASTER F-6	OP	BASS	AL	SV	OB			5	10	715			1850	2200
16	6	R-166 RIVER BOAT	OP	UTL	AL	SV	OB			5	10	505			1300	1550
17	2	FISH-MASTER F-7	OP	BASS	AL	SV	OB			5	10	542			1450	1750
17	2	M-72	OP	FSH	AL	SV	OB			5	10	300			825	995
17	2	M-72L	OP	FSH	AL	SV	OB			5	10	308			860	1000
18	5	V-8 I	OP	FSH	AL	SV	OB			6	10	470			1250	1500
18	5	V-8 II	OP	FSH	AL	SV	OB			6	10	470			1450	1750
18	6	R-186 RIVER BOAT	OP	UTL	AL	SV	OB			7	6	795			1950	2350
18	6	RJ-186 RIVER BOAT	OP	UTL	AL	SV	JT	215-235		7	6	1490			2650	3100
20	6	R-206 RIVER BOAT	OP	UTL	AL	SV	OB			7	6	860			2050	2450
20	6	RJ-206 RIVER BOAT	OP	UTL	AL	SV	JT	215-235		7	6	1555			3050	3550
24	6	R-246 RIVER BOAT	OP	UTL	AL	SV	OB			7	6	1050			3350	3900
24	6	RJ-246 RIVER BOAT	OP	UTL	AL	SV	JT	215-235		7	6	1990			4100	4800
		1985 BOATS														
16	5	V-6	OP	FSH	AL	SV	OB			6	4	375			885	1050
16	5	V-6 II	OP	FSH	AL	SV	OB			6	4	375			1050	1250
16	6	FISH-MASTER F-6	OP	BASS	AL	SV	OB			5	10	715			1800	2150
16	6	R-166 RIVER BOAT	OP	UTL	AL	SV	OB			5	10	505			1250	1500
17	2	FISH-MASTER F-7	OP	BASS	AL	SV	OB			5	10	542			1450	1700
17	2	M-72	OP	FSH	AL	SV	OB			5	10	300			805	970
17	2	M-72L	OP	FSH	AL	SV	OB			5	10	308			830	1000
18	5	V-8	OP	FSH	AL	SV	OB			6	10	470			1250	1500
18	5	V-8 II	OP	FSH	AL	SV	OB			6	10	470			1450	1700
18	6	R-186 RIVER BOAT	OP	UTL	AL	SV	OB			7	6	795			1950	2300
18	6	RJ-186 RIVER BOAT	OP	UTL	AL	SV	JT	215-235		7	6	1490			2550	2950
20	6	R-206 RIVER BOAT	OP	UTL	AL	SV	OB			7	6	860			2000	2400
20	6	RJ-206 RIVER BOAT	OP	UTL	AL	SV	JT	215-235		7	6	1555			2900	3400
24	6	R-246 RIVER BOAT	OP	UTL	AL	SV	OB			7	6	1050			3300	3800
24	6	RJ-246 RIVER BOAT	OP	UTL	AL	SV	JT	215-235		7	6	1990			3900	4600
		1984 BOATS														
16	5	V-6	OP	FSH	AL	SV	OB			6	4	375			935	1100
16	6	FISH-MASTER F-6	OP	BASS	AL	SV	OB			5	10	715			1750	2100
16	6	R-166 RIVER BOAT	OP	UTL	AL	SV	OB			5	10	505			1250	1450
16	6	R-166J	OP	UTL	AL	SV	JT	100		5	10	525			1200	1400
17	2	FISH-MASTER F-7	OP	BASS	AL	SV	OB			5	10	542			1400	1700
17	2	M-72	OP	FSH	AL	SV	OB			5	10	300			790	950
17	2	M-72L	OP	FSH	AL	SV	OB			5	10	308			810	975
18	5	V-8	OP	FSH	AL	SV	OB			6	10	470			1300	1550
18	6	R-186 RIVER BOAT	OP	UTL	AL	SV	OB			7	6	795			1900	2250
18	6	RJ-186	OP	UTL	AL	SV	JT	235		7	6	1490			2450	2850
18	6	RJ-186 RIVER BOAT	OP	UTL	AL	SV	JT	215	FORD	7	6	1490			2450	2800
20	6	R-206 RIVER BOAT	OP	UTL	AL	SV	OB			7	6	860			1950	2350
20	6	RJ-206	OP	UTL	AL	SV	JT	235		7	6	1555			2750	3200
20	6	RJ-206 RIVER BOAT	OP	UTL	AL	SV	JT	215	FORD	7	6	1555			2750	3200
24	6	R-246 RIVER BOAT	OP	UTL	AL	SV	OB			7	6	1050			3200	3750
24	6	RJ-246	OP	UTL	AL	SV	JT	235		7	6	1990			3750	4350
24	6	RJ-246 RIVER BOAT	OP	UTL	AL	SV	JT	215	FORD	7	6	1990			3700	4300

....For earlier years, see the BUC Used Boat Price Guide, Volume 3

AL GROVER'S

GROVER BUILT BOATS
FREEPORT NY 11520 COAST GUARD MFG ID- ALX

See inside cover to adjust price for area

LOA FT	LOA IN	NAME AND/ OR MODEL	TOP/ RIG	BOAT TYPE	HULL MTL	HULL TP	ENGINE TP	ENGINE # HP	ENGINE MFG	BEAM FT	BEAM IN	WGT LBS	DRAFT FT	DRAFT IN	RETAIL LOW	RETAIL HIGH
		1986 BOATS														
24		GROVERBUILT		FSH	FBG	RB	IB	100D		9					15800	17900
26		GROVERBUILT		FSH	FBG	RB	IB	100D		9					18900	21000
28		GROVERBUILT		FSH	FBG	RB	IB	100D		9					18400	20500

....For earlier years, see the BUC Used Boat Price Guide, Volume 3

GRUMMAN BOATS

DIV OF OMC ALUMINUM BOAT GROUP
LEBANON MO 65536 COAST GUARD MFG ID- GBM

See inside cover to adjust price for area

For more recent years, see the BUC Used Boat Price Guide, Volume 1

LOA FT	LOA IN	NAME AND/ OR MODEL	TOP/ RIG	BOAT TYPE	HULL MTL	HULL TP	ENGINE TP	ENGINE # HP	ENGINE MFG	BEAM FT	BEAM IN	WGT LBS	DRAFT FT	DRAFT IN	RETAIL LOW	RETAIL HIGH
		1996 BOATS														
16	1	V1666	OP	UTL	AL	SV	OB			5	8	235			920	1100
16	1	V1666P	OP	BASS	AL	SV	OB			5	8	500			2000	2400
16	1	V1666SP	OP	BASS	AL	SV	OB			5	8	530			2150	2550
16	1	V1666T	OP	UTL	AL	SV	OB			5	8	235			915	1100
16	1	V1666WT	OP	UTL	AL	SV	OB			5	8	395			1550	1850
17		1749B	OP	BASS	AL	SV	OB			5	8	675			2750	3200
17	6	V17SP	OP	FSH	AL	SV	OB			7	1	955			3950	4600
17	6	V17TC	OP	FSH	AL	SV	OB			7	1	1045			4300	5000
18		1848MT	OP	JON	AL	FL	OB			5	10	300			885	1050
19	1	V19TC	OP	FSH	AL	SV	OB			7	2	1120			4800	5550
		1995 BOATS														
16	9	V1784SP	OP	FSH	AL	SV	OB			7		840			3300	3800
16	9	V1784TC	OP	FSH	AL	SV	OB			7		890			3450	4000
17		1749B	OP	BASS	AL	SV	OB			5	8	675			2700	3150
18		1848MT	OP	JON	AL	FL	OB			5	10	300			845	1000

LOA FT	LOA IN	NAME AND/ OR MODEL	TOP/ RIG	BOAT TYPE	-HULL- MTL	-HULL- TP	ENGINE TP	ENGINE # HP	ENGINE MFG	BEAM FT	BEAM IN	WGT LBS	DRAFT FT IN	RETAIL LOW	RETAIL HIGH
		1995 BOATS													
19		V1987TC	OP	FSH	AL	SV	OB			7	3	1125		4600	5300
		1994 BOATS													
16	9	V1784SP	OP	FSH	AL	SV	OB			7		875		3250	3800
16	9	V1784TC	OP	FSH	AL	SV	OB			7		975		3600	4150
17		1748B	OP	BASS	AL	SV	OB			5	10	730		2800	3250
17		1749B	OP	BASS	AL	SV	OB			5	8	675		2600	3000
18		1848MT	OP	JON	AL	FL	OB			5	10	300		800	960
19		V1987SP	OP	FSH	AL	SV	OB			7	3	1125		4200	4900
19		V1987TC	OP	FSH	AL	SV	OB			7	3	1125		4550	5250
		1993 BOATS													
16	9	V1784SP	OP	FSH	AL	SV	OB			7		875		3100	3600
16	9	V1784TC	OP	FSH	AL	SV	OB			7		975		3450	4000
17		1748B	OP	BASS	AL	SV	OB			5	10	730		2700	3100
18		1848MT	OP	JON	AL	FL	OB			5	10	290		730	880
19		V1987SP	OP	FSH	AL	SV	OB			7	3	1125		4100	4750
19		V1987TC	OP	FSH	AL	SV	OB			7	3	1125		4250	4950
		1992 BOATS													
16		1666	OP	UTL	AL	SV	OB			5	8	250		815	980
16		1666TT	OP	UTL	AL	SV	OB			5	8	250		815	980
16		1666W	OP	UTL	AL	SV	OB			5	6			970	1150
16	9	LAKE 1784SC	OP	FSH	AL	DV	OB			7		875		3000	3500
16	9	LAKE 1784TC	OP	FSH	AL	DV	OB			7		1000		3350	3900
17		1748B	OP	BASS	AL	SV	OB			5	11	730		2550	3000
17	11	1849V	OP	JON	AL	SV	OB			5	11	286		705	845
		1991 BOATS													
16		4916	OP	JON	AL	FL	OB			5	11	284		930	1100
16		MASTERFISH 160 BASS	OP	BASS	AL	SV	OB			6	4	600		1950	2300
16		MASTERFISH 160 SD CN	OP	FSH	AL	SV	OB			6	4	461		1500	1750
16		MASTERFISH 160 TILLR	OP	FSH	AL	SV	OB			6	4	461		1500	1750
16	3	FISHERMAN	OP	FSH	AL	SV	OB			5	9	235		750	905
16	3	SPLIT SEAT	OP	FSH	AL	SV	OB			5	9	435		1400	1700
16	3	SUPER PRO FISHERMAN	OP	FSH	AL	SV	OB			5	9	434		1400	1700
16	4	RENEGADE 160 BASS	OP	BASS	AL	SV	OB			5	9	575		1900	2250
16	4	RENEGADE 160 FS	OP	BASS	AL	SV	OB			5	9	375		1250	1450
16	4	RENEGADE 160 SIDE CN	OP	BASS	AL	SV	OB			5	9	475		1550	1850
16	4	RENEGADE 160 TILLER	OP	BASS	AL	SV	OB			5	9	375		1250	1450
16	4	ULTRA 164 SIDE CON	OP	FSH	AL	SV	OB			7		840		2750	3150
16	4	ULTRA 164 SUPER FISH	OP	FSH	AL	SV	OB			7		840		2750	3150
16	4	ULTRA 164 TILLER	OP	FSH	AL	SV	OB			7		810		2650	3050
17	6	OUTLAW 170 BASS	OP	BASS	AL	SV	OB			5	9	610		2150	2500
17	9	MV1849	OP	JON	AL	SV	OB			5	11	286		705	850
18		4918	OP	JON	AL	FL	OB			5	11	312		740	895
18	4	ULTRA 184 CENTER CON	OP	FSH	AL	SV	OB			7		870		3050	3500
18	4	ULTRA 184 SIDE CON	OP	FSH	AL	SV	OB			7		870		3050	3500
18	4	ULTRA 184 SUPER FISH	OP	FSH	AL	SV	OB			7		870		3050	3500
18	4	ULTRA 184 TILLER	OP	FSH	AL	SV	OB			7		850		2950	3450
		1990 BOATS													
16		4916	OP	JON	AL	FL	OB			5	11	247		790	955
16		GMF 16 BASS	OP	BASS	AL	SV	OB			6	4	600		1850	2200
16		GMF 16 SC	OP	FSH	AL	SV	OB			6	4	461		1450	1700
16		GMF 16 TILLER	OP	FSH	AL	SV	OB			6	4	461		1450	1700
16		RENEGADE	OP	BASS	AL	SV	OB			5	9	575		1700	2050
16		RENEGADE AW	OP	BASS	AL	SV	OB			5	9	575		1850	2200
16	3	FISHERMAN	OP	FSH	AL	SV	OB			5	9	235		725	875
16	3	SPLIT SEAT	OP	FSH	AL	SV	OB			5	9	345		1100	1300
16	3	SPLIT SEAT DELUXE	OP	FSH	AL	SV	OB			5	9	320		1000	1200
16	4	GBT 164	OP	FSH	AL	SV	OB			7		765		2400	2800
16	4	GCC 164	OP	FSH	AL	SV	OB			7		840		2600	3000
16	4	GFF 164	OP	RNBT	AL	SV	OB			7		840		2650	3100
16	4	GSC 164	OP	FSH	AL	SV	OB			7		840		2650	3100
16	4	GSX 164 SKIDADDLE	OP	RNBT	AL	SV	OB			7		840		2650	3050
17		OUTLAW SX	OP	BASS	AL	SV	OB			6	4	610		1950	2300
17		OUTLAW SX-AW	OP	BASS	AL	SV	OB			6	4	610		2050	2450
17	9	MV1849	OP	JON	AL	SV	OB			5	11	286		680	820
18		4918	OP	JON	AL	FL	OB			5	11	277		610	735
18	4	GCC 184	OP	CTRCN	AL	SV	OB			7		870		2900	3400
18	4	GFF 184	OP	RNBT	AL	SV	OB			7		870		3000	3450
18	4	GSC 184	OP	FSH	AL	SV	OB			7		870		2750	3200
18	4	GSF 184	OP	FSH	AL	SV	OB			7		870		3050	3550
18	4	GSF 184I	OP	FSH	AL	SV	IO	130						3950	4550
18	4	GSX 184 SKIDADDLE	OP	RNBT	AL	SV	OB			7		870		2900	3350
18	4	GSX 184I SKIDADDLE	OP	RNBT	AL	SV	IO	130		7		1664		3350	3900
22	3	GBWI 223	OP	CUD	AL	SV	IO	130-175		8	5	2645		6150	7100
		1989 BOATS													
16		4916	OP	JON	AL	FL	OB			5	11	247		765	920
16		GMF 16 BASS	OP	BASS	AL	SV	OB			6	4	600		1800	2150
16		GMF 16 SC	OP	FSH	AL	SV	OB			6	4	461		1400	1650
16		GMF 16 TILLER	OP	FSH	AL	SV	OB			6	4	461		1400	1650
16		PANFISH II	OP	BASS	AL	SV	OB			5	9	575		1750	2100
16		RENEGADE	OP	BASS	AL	SV	OB			5	9	575		1650	1950
16		RENEGADE AW	OP	BASS	AL	SV	OB			5	9	575		1750	2100
16	3	FISHERMAN	OP	FSH	AL	SV	OB			5	9	235		700	845
16	3	PRO 16	OP	FSH	AL	SV	OB			5	9	415		1250	1500
16	3	SPLIT SEAT	OP	FSH	AL	SV	OB			5	9	345		1050	1250
16	3	SPLIT SEAT DELUXE	OP	FSH	AL	SV	OB			5	9	320		970	1150
16	4	GBT 164	OP	FSH	AL	SV	OB			7		765		2350	2700
16	4	GCC 164	OP	FSH	AL	SV	OB			7		840		2550	2950
16	4	GFF 164	OP	RNBT	AL	SV	OB			7		840		2550	2950
16	4	GSC 164	OP	FSH	AL	SV	OB			7		840		2550	2950
16	4	GSX 164 SKIDADDLE	OP	RNBT	AL	SV	OB			7		840		2550	3000
17		OUTLAW SX	OP	BASS	AL	SV	OB			6	4	610		1850	2200
17		OUTLAW SX-AW	OP	BASS	AL	SV	OB			6	4	610		2000	2350
17	9	MV1849	OP	JON	AL	SV	OB			5	11	286		655	790
18		4918	OP	JON	AL	FL	OB			5	11	277		590	710
18	4	GCC 184	OP	CTRCN	AL	SV	OB			7		870		2800	3300
18	4	GFF 184	OP	RNBT	AL	SV	OB			7		870		2900	3350
18	4	GSC 184	OP	FSH	AL	SV	OB			7		870		2650	3100
18	4	GSF 184	OP	FSH	AL	SV	OB			7		870		2950	3450
18	4	GSF 184I	OP	FSH	AL	SV	IO	120-130		7		1664		3400	3950
18	4	GSX 184 SKIDADDLE	OP	RNBT	AL	SV	OB			7		870		2800	3250
18	4	GSX 184I SKIDADDLE	OP	RNBT	AL	SV	IO	120-130		7		1664		3150	3650
22	3	GBW 223	OP	CUD	AL	SV	OB			8	5	1875		6400	7350
22	3	GBWI 223	OP	CUD	AL	SV	IO			8	5	2645		**	**
22	3	GBWI 223	OP	CUD	AL	SV	IO	130-175		8	5	2645		5800	6700
		1988 BOATS													
16		4916	OP	JON	AL	FL	OB			5	11	247		740	890
16		GMF 16 BASS	OP	BASS	AL	SV	OB			6	4	600		1750	2100
16		GMF 16 SC	OP	FSH	AL	SV	OB			6	4	461		1350	1600
16		GMF 16 TILLER	OP	FSH	AL	SV	OB			6	4	461		1350	1600
16		RENEGADE	OP	BASS	AL	SV	OB			5	9	575		1600	1900
16		RENEGADE AW	OP	BASS	AL	SV	OB			5	9	575		1700	2050
16		RENEGADE II	OP	BASS	AL	SV	OB			5	9	575		1750	2050
16	3	FISHERMAN	OP	FSH	AL	SV	OB			5	9	235		680	815
16	3	PRO 16	OP	FSH	AL	SV	OB			5	9	415		1200	1450
16	3	SPLIT SEAT	OP	FSH	AL	SV	OB			5	9	345		1000	1200
16	3	SPLIT SEAT DELUXE	OP	FSH	AL	SV	OB			5	9	320		940	1100
16	4	GBT 164	OP	FSH	AL	SV	OB			7		765		2300	2650
16	4	GCC 164	OP	FSH	AL	SV	OB			7		840		2450	2850
16	4	GFF 164	OP	RNBT	AL	SV	OB			7		840		2450	2900
16	4	GSC 164	OP	FSH	AL	SV	OB			7		840		2450	2850
16	4	GSX 164 SKIDADDLE	OP	RNBT	AL	SV	OB			7		840		2500	2900
17		OUTLAW SX	OP	BASS	AL	SV	OB			6	4	610		1800	2150
17		OUTLAW SX-AW	OP	BASS	AL	SV	OB			6	4	610		1900	2300
17	9	MV1849	OP	JON	AL	SV	OB			5	11	286		635	765
18		4918	OP	JON	AL	FL	OB			5	11	277		570	685
18	4	GCC 184	OP	CTRCN	AL	SV	OB			7		870		2700	3150
18	4	GFF 184	OP	RNBT	AL	SV	OB			7		870		2800	3250
18	4	GSC 184	OP	FSH	AL	SV	OB			7		870		2550	3000
18	4	GSF 184	OP	FSH	AL	SV	OB			7		870		2900	3350
18	4	GSF 184I	OP	FSH	AL	SV	IO	120-130		7		1664		3200	3750
18	4	GSX 184 SKIDADDLE	OP	RNBT	AL	SV	OB			7		870		2700	3150
18	4	GSX 184I SKIDADDLE	OP	RNBT	AL	SV	IO	120-130		7		1664		3000	3500
22	3	GBW 223	OP	CUD	AL	SV	OB			8	5	1875		6200	7100
22	3	GBWI 223	OP	CUD	AL	SV	OB			8	5	2645		8100	9300
22	3	GBWI 223	OP	CUD	AL	SV	IO	130-205		8	5	2645		5500	6400
22	3	GCB 223 CB	OP	RNBT	AL	SV	OB			8	5	1825		6050	6950
22	3	GCBI 223 CB	OP	RNBT	AL	SV	OB			8	5	2595		8000	9200
22	3	GCBI 223 CB	OP	RNBT	AL	SV	IO	130-205		8	5	2595		5150	6000
22	3	GCC 223	OP	CTRCN	AL	SV	OB			8	5	1825		6050	6950
		1987 BOATS													
16		GMF BASS	OP	BASS	AL	SV	OB			6	4	600		1700	2000
16		GMF SC	OP	FSH	AL	SV	OB			6	4	461		1300	1550
16		GMF TILLER	OP	FSH	AL	SV	OB			6	4	461		1300	1550
16		RENEGADE	OP	BASS	AL	SV	OB			5	9	575		1600	1950
16	3	16 SPLIT SEAT	OP	FSH	AL	SV	OB			5	9	345		980	1150
16	3	16 SPLIT SEAT DELUXE	OP	FSH	AL	SV	OB			5	9	320		910	1100
16	3	FISHERMAN	OP	FSH	AL	SV	OB			5	9	235		655	790
16	3	PRO 16	OP	FSH	AL	SV	OB			5	9	415		1200	1400
16	4	BACKTROLLER	OP	FSH	AL	SV	OB			7		765		2200	2550

CONTINUED ON NEXT PAGE

LOA FT	LOA IN	NAME AND/ OR MODEL	TOP/ RIG	BOAT TYPE	-HULL- MTL	-HULL- TP	ENGINE TP	ENGINE # HP	ENGINE MFG	BEAM FT	BEAM IN	WGT LBS	DRAFT FT	DRAFT IN	RETAIL LOW	RETAIL HIGH
		1987 BOATS														
16	4	CENTER CONSOLE	OP	FSH	AL	SV	OB			7		840			2450	2850
16	4	FISH-AND-FUN	OP	RNBT	AL	SV	OB			7		840			2400	2800
16	4	GSF 164	OP	FSH	AL	SV	OB			7		840			2400	2800
16	4	GSX 164I	OP	RNBT	AL	SV	IO	120		7		1620			2450	2850
16	4	SIDE CONSOLE	OP	FSH	AL	SV	OB			7		840			2300	2700
16	4	SKIDADDLE	OP	RNBT	AL	SV	OB			7		840			2400	2800
17		OUTLAW SX	OP	BASS	AL	SV	OB			6	4	610			1800	2150
17	9	MV1849	OP	JON	AL	SV	OB			5	11	286			615	740
18	4	GCC 184	OP	CTRCN	AL	SV	OB			7		870			2650	3050
18	4	GFF 184	OP	RNBT	AL	SV	OB			7		870			2700	3150
18	4	GSC 184	OP	FSH	AL	SV	OB			7		870			2500	2900
18	4	GSF 184	OP	FSH	AL	SV	OB			7		870			2800	3250
18	4	GSF 184I	OP	FSH	AL	SV	IO	120		7		1664			3050	3550
18	4	GSX 184	OP	RNBT	AL	SV	OB			7		870			2600	3050
18	4	GSX 184I	OP	RNBT	AL	SV	IO	120		7		1664			2850	3300
		1986 BOATS														
16		RENEGADE		BASS	AL	SV	OB			5	9	540			1500	1750
16	3	FISHERMAN 16		FSH	AL	SV	OB			5	9	235			635	770
16	3	PRO 16		FSH	AL	SV	OB			5	9	415			1150	1350
16	4	CENTER CONSOLE		FSH	AL	SV	OB			6	11	730			2000	2400
16	4	FISH-AND-FUN		RNBT	AL	SV	OB			6	11	840			2350	2700
16	4	SIDE CONSOLE		FSH	AL	SV	OB			6	11	760			2100	2450
16	4	SKIDADDLE		RNBT	AL	SV	OB			6	11	840			2350	2750
16	4	SUPER FISH		FSH	AL	SV	OB			6	11	840			2300	2700
16	4	TILLER STEER		FSH	AL	SV	OB			6	11	665			1850	2200
16	10	5.0 S/CON		BASS	AL	DV	OB			7	6	853			2400	2800
17		OUTLAW		BASS	AL	SV	OB			5	9	590			1700	2000
		1985 BOATS														
16	3	FISHERMAN	OP	FSH	AL	SV	OB			5	9	235			620	745
16	4	CENTER CONSOLE	OP	FSH	AL	SV	OB			7		730			1950	2300
16	4	FISH-AND-FUN	OP	RNBT	AL	SV	OB			7		840			2400	2750
16	4	SIDE CONSOLE	OP	FSH	AL	SV	OB			7		760			2000	2400
16	4	SKIDADDLE	OP	RNBT	AL	SV	OB			7		840			2200	2550
16	4	TILLER STEER	OP	FSH	AL	SV	OB			7		665			1800	2100
16	10	GRUMMAN 5.0 CTRCN	OP	BASS	AL	DV	OB			7	6	853			2350	2750
16	10	GRUMMAN 5.0 S/CON	OP	BASS	AL	DV	OB			7	6	853			2350	2700
17		OUTLAW	OP	BASS	AL	SV	OB			5	9	590			1650	1950
17	8	CORTEZ	OP	BASS	AL	SV	OB			6	1	620			1800	2100
17	9	1849	OP	JON	AL	FL	OB			6	2	282			570	690
		1984 BOATS														
16	3	FISHERMAN	OP	FSH	AL	SV	OB			5	6	235			605	725
16	4	CENTER CONSOLE	OP	FSH	AL	SV	OB			7		730			1900	2250
16	4	FISH-AND-FUN	OP	RNBT	AL	SV	OB			7		840			2250	2600
16	4	SIDE CONSOLE	OP	FSH	AL	SV	OB			7		760			1950	2350
16	4	TILLER STEER	OP	FSH	AL	SV	OB			7		665			1750	2050
16	10	GRUMMAN 5.0 CTRCN	OP	BASS	AL	DV	OB			7	6	853			2300	2700
16	10	GRUMMAN 5.0 S/CON	OP	BASS	AL	DV	OB			7	6	853			2300	2650

....For earlier years, see the BUC Used Boat Price Guide, Volume 3

GULFLINE BOATS

WAVELAND MS 39576 COAST GUARD MFG ID- GUF See inside cover to adjust price for area

For more recent years, see the BUC Used Boat Price Guide, Volume 1

LOA FT	LOA IN	NAME AND/ OR MODEL	TOP/ RIG	BOAT TYPE	-HULL- MTL	-HULL- TP	ENGINE TP	ENGINE # HP	ENGINE MFG	BEAM FT	BEAM IN	WGT LBS	DRAFT FT	DRAFT IN	RETAIL LOW	RETAIL HIGH
		1996 BOATS														
17	6	CHALLENGER I DLX	OP	CTRCN	FBG	DV	OB			7	6	1350			4100	4800
17	6	CHALLENGER I DLX DS	OP	OPFSH	FBG	DV	OB			7	6	1350			4050	4750
18		SEAHORSE	OP	OPFSH	FBG	DV	OB			8		1150			3600	4200
18		SEAHORSE I	OP	CTRCN	FBG	SV	OB			8		1150			3650	4250
18	6	CHALLENGER II DLX	OP	CTRCN	FBG	DV	OB			8		1500			4600	5250
18	6	CHALLENGER II DLX DS	OP	OPFSH	FBG	DV	OB			8		1500			4550	5250
18	6	GULF FLATS FISHER	OP	CTRCN	FBG	SV	OB			7		900			3000	3500
18	6	GULF SKIFF	OP	UTL	FBG	SV	OB			7		900			2700	3150
20	6	CHALLNGR III DLX DSC	OP	SF	FBG	DV	OB			8	5	2150			6500	7450
20	6	CHALLNGR III DLX VSF	OP	CTRCN	FBG	DV	OB			8	5	2150			6500	7450
		1995 BOATS														
17	6	CHALLENGER I DLX	OP	CTRCN	FBG	DV	OB			7	6	1350			3900	4500
17	6	CHALLENGER I DLX DS	OP	OPFSH	FBG	DV	OB			7	6	1350			3850	4500
18		SEAHORSE	OP	OPFSH	FBG	DV	OB			8		1150			3400	4000
18		SEAHORSE I	OP	CTRCN	FBG	SV	OB			8		1150			3450	4000
18	6	CHALLENGER II DLX	OP	CTRCN	FBG	DV	OB			8		1500			4300	5000
18	6	CHALLENGER II DLX DS	OP	OPFSH	FBG	DV	OB			8		1500			4250	4950
18	6	GULF FLATS FISHER	OP	CTRCN	FBG	SV	OB			7		900			2850	3300
18	6	GULFSKIFF	OP	UTL	FBG	SV	OB			7		900			2550	3000
20	6	CHALLNGR III DLX DSC	OP	SF	FBG	DV	OB			8	5	2150			6150	7050
20	6	CHALLNGR III DLX VSF	OP	CTRCN	FBG	DV	OB			8	5	2150			6150	7050
		1994 BOATS														
17	6	CHALLENGER I DLX	OP	CTRCN	FBG	DV	OB			7	6	1350			3650	4250
17	6	CHALLENGER I DLX DS	OP	OPFSH	FBG	DV	OB			7	6	1350			3650	4200
18		SEAHORSE	OP	OPFSH	FBG	DV	OB			8		1150			3250	3750
18		SEAHORSE I	OP	CTRCN	FBG	SV	OB			8		1150			3250	3800
18	6	CHALLENGER II DLX	OP	CTRCN	FBG	DV	OB			8		1500			4100	4750
18	6	CHALLENGER II DLX DS	OP	OPFSH	FBG	DV	OB			8		1500			4050	4750
18	6	GULFFLATS FISHER	OP	CTRCN	FBG	SV	OB			7		900			2700	3150
18	6	GULFSKIFF	OP	UTL	FBG	SV	OB			7		900			2450	2850
20	5	CHALLNGR III DLX DSC	OP	SF	FBG	DV	OB			8	5	2150			5800	6650
20	5	CHALLNGR III DLX VSF	OP	CTRCN	FBG	DV	OB			8	5	2150			5800	6650
		1993 BOATS														
17	6	CHALLENGER I DLX	OP	CTRCN	FBG	DV	OB			7	6	1350			3500	4050
17	6	CHALLENGER I DLX DS	OP	OPFSH	FBG	DV	OB			7	6	1350			3450	4000
18		SEAHORSE	OP	OPFSH	FBG	DV	OB			8		1150			3100	3600
18		SEAHORSE I	OP	CTRCN	FBG	SV	OB			8		1150			3100	3600
18	6	CHALLENGER II DLX	OP	CTRCN	FBG	DV	OB			8		1500			3900	4500
18	6	CHALLENGER II DLX DS	OP	OPFSH	FBG	DV	OB			8		1500			3850	4500
18	6	GULFSKIFF	OP	UTL	FBG	SV	OB			7		600			1500	1800
20	5	CHALLNGR III DLX DSC	OP	SF	FBG	DV	OB			8	5	2000			5250	6050
20	5	CHALLNGR III DLX VSF	OP	CTRCN	FBG	DV	OB			8	5	2000			5250	6050
		1992 BOATS														
17	4	CHALLENGER I DLX	OP	CTRCN	FBG	DV	OB			7	6	1350			3300	3850
17	4	CHALLENGER I DLX DS	OP	OPFSH	FBG	DV	OB			7	6	1350			3250	3800
18		SEAHORSE	OP	OPFSH	FBG	DV	OB			8		1150			2950	3400
18		SEAHORSE I	OP	CTRCN	FBG	SV	OB			8		1150			2950	3450
18	6	CHALLENGER II DLX	OP	CTRCN	FBG	DV	OB			8		1500			3650	4250
18	6	CHALLENGER II DLX DS	OP	B/R	FBG	DV	OB			8		1500			3750	4350
18	6	CHALLENGER II DLX DS	OP	OPFSH	FBG	DV	OB			8		1500			3650	4250
18	6	GULFSKIFF	OP	UTL	FBG	SV	OB			7		600			1450	1700
20	5	CHALLNGR III DLX DSC	OP	SF	FBG	DV	OB			8	5	1800			4650	5350
21	5	CHALLNGR III DLX VSF	OP	CTRCN	FBG	DV	OB			8	5	1800			4850	5600
		1991 BOATS														
17	4	CHALLENGER I DLX	OP	CTRCN	FBG	DV	OB			7	6	1350			3150	3650
17	4	CHALLENGER I DLX DS	OP	OPFSH	FBG	DV	OB			7	6	1350			3150	3650
18	6	CHALLENGER II DLX	OP	CTRCN	FBG	DV	OB			8		1500			3500	4050
18	6	CHALLENGER II DLX DS	OP	B/R	FBG	DV	OB			8		1500			3600	4150
18	6	CHALLENGER II DLX DS	OP	OPFSH	FBG	DV	OB			8		1500			3500	4050
20	5	CHALLNGR III DLX DSC	OP	SF	FBG	DV	OB			8	5	1800			4450	5100
20	5	CHALLNGR III DLX VSF	OP	CTRCN	FBG	DV	OB			8	5	1800			4450	5100
		1990 BOATS														
17	4	CHALLENGER I DLX	OP	CTRCN	FBG	DV	OB			7	6	1350			3000	3500
17	4	CHALLENGER I DLX DSC	OP	OPFSH	FBG	DV	OB			7	6	1350			3000	3500
18	6	CHALLENGER II DLX	OP	CTRCN	FBG	DV	OB			7	10	1500			3350	3900
18	6	CHALLENGER II DLX DS	OP	OPFSH	FBG	DV	OB			7	10	1500			3350	3900
18	6	CHALLENGER II STD	OP	CTRCN	FBG	DV	OB			7	10	1350			3100	3600
18	6	CHALLENGR II DLX DSC	OP	B/R	FBG	DV	OB			7	10	1400			3250	3800
20	5	CHALLNGR III DLX DSC	OP	SF	FBG	DV	OB			8	5	1800			4200	4900
20	5	CHALLNGR III DLX VSF	OP	CTRCN	FBG	DV	OB			8	5	1800			4200	4900
		1989 BOATS														
18	6	CHALLENGER II DLX	OP	CTRCN	FBG	DV	OB			7	10	1400			3350	3900
18	6	CHALLENGER II STD	OP	CTRCN	FBG	DV	OB			7	10	1400			2750	3200
18	6	CHALLENGR II DLX DSC	OP	B/R	FBG	DV	OB			7	10	1400			3100	3650
18	6	CHALLENGR II DLX DSC	OP	OPFSH	FBG	DV	OB			7	10	1400			3050	3550
20	5	CHALLNGR III DLX DSC	OP	SF	FBG	DV	OB			8	5	1800			4100	4750
20	5	CHALLNGR III DLX VSF	OP	SF	FBG	DV	OB			8	5	1800			4000	4650
		1988 BOATS														
16	8	1680 C/C	OP	CTRCN	FBG	DV	OB			6	8	700			1500	1800
17	8	1780 C/C	OP	UTL	FBG	TR	OB			7	4	950			2000	2400
17	8	1780 D/S/C	OP	UTL	FBG	TR	OB			7	4	950			2200	2550
17	8	1780 S/C	OP	UTL	FBG	TR	OB			7	4	950			1700	2050
18		FANTAIL 1800 C/C	OP	CTRCN	FBG	TR	OB			7	4	850			1900	2250
18		FANTAIL 1800 D/S/C	OP	OPFSH	FBG	TR	OB			7	4	850			2150	2500
18		FANTAIL 1800 S/C	OP	OPFSH	FBG	TR	OB			7	4	850			1650	2000
18	6	GULFSKIFF C/C	OP	FSH	FBG	SV	OB			7		650			1500	1800
18	6	GULFSKIFF S/C	OP	FSH	FBG	SV	OB			7		650			1600	1900
18	6	GULFSKIFF STD	OP	FSH	FBG	SV	OB			7		650			1500	1800
19	7	1970 C/C	OP	CTRCN	FBG	TR	OB			7	4	950			2250	2600
19	7	1970 D/S/C	OP	FSH	FBG	TR	OB			7	4	950			2450	2850
19	7	1970 S/C	OP	FSH	FBG	TR	OB			7	4	950			2000	2350
20	4	FANTAIL 2040 C/C	OP	CTRCN	FBG	TR	OB			7	4	1000			2400	2800
20	4	FANTAIL 2040 D/S/C	OP	OPFSH	FBG	TR	OB			7	4	1000			2600	3050
20	4	FANTAIL 2040 S/C	OP	OPFSH	FBG	TR	OB			7	4	1000			2150	2500
20	10	2100V C/C	OP	CTRCN	FBG	DV	SE			8	6	1500			**	**

LOA FT	LOA IN	NAME AND/ OR MODEL	TOP/ RIG	BOAT TYPE	-HULL- MTL	-HULL- TP	ENGINE TP	ENGINE # HP	ENGINE MFG	BEAM FT	BEAM IN	WGT LBS	DRAFT FT	DRAFT IN	RETAIL LOW	RETAIL HIGH
		1988 BOATS														
20	10	2100V D/S/C	OP	OPFSH	FBG	DV	SE	300		8	6	1500			3400	4000
22	8	FANTAIL 2280VF C/C	OP	OPFSH	FBG	DV	OB			8	3	1500			3000	3500
22	8	FANTAIL 2280VF C/C	OP	OPFSH	FBG	DV	SE	300		8	3	1500			3450	4050
22	8	FANTAIL 2280VF D/S/C	OP	OPFSH	FBG	DV	OB			8	3	1500			3200	3700
22	8	FANTAIL 2280VF D/S/C	OP	OPFSH	FBG	DV	SE	300		8	3	1500			3700	4300
22	8	FANTAIL 2280VF S/C	OP	OPFSH	FBG	DV	OB			8	3	1500			4600	5300
23	7	FANTAIL 2400VF C/C	OP	CTRCN	FBG	DV	SE	300		8	6	1700			4100	4750
23	7	FANTAIL 2400VF D/S/C	OP	OPFSH	FBG	DV	SE	300		8	6	1700			4100	4750
		1987 BOATS														
16	8	1680 C/C	OP	CTRCN	FBG	DV	OB			6	8	700			1450	1700
17	8	1780 C/C	OP	UTL	FBG	TR	OB			7	4	950			1950	2300
17	8	1780 D/S/C	OP	UTL	FBG	TR	OB			7	4	950			2050	2450
17	8	1780 S/C	OP	UTL	FBG	TR	OB			7	4	950			1650	1950
18		FANTAIL 1800 C/C	OP	CTRCN	FBG	TR	OB			7	4	850			1800	2150
18		FANTAIL 1800 D/S/C	OP	OPFSH	FBG	TR	OB			7	4	850			2050	2400
18		FANTAIL 1800 S/C	OP	OPFSH	FBG	TR	OB			7	4	850			1600	1900
18	6	GULFSKIFF C/C	OP	FSH	FBG		OB			7		650			1450	1750
18	6	GULFSKIFF S/C	OP	FSH	FBG		OB			7		650			1450	1750
18	6	GULFSKIFF STD	OP	FSH	FBG		OB			7		650			1450	1750
19	7	1970 C/C	OP	CTRCN	FBG	TR	OB			7	4	950			2150	2500
19	7	1970 D/S/C	OP	FSH	FBG	TR	OB			7	4	950			2400	2750
19	7	1970 S/C	OP	FSH	FBG	TR	OB			7	4	950			1900	2300
20	4	FANTAIL 2040 C/C	OP	CTRCN	FBG	TR	OB			7	4	1000			2300	2700
20	4	FANTAIL 2040 D/S/C	OP	OPFSH	FBG	TR	OB			7	4	1000			2500	2950
20	4	FANTAIL 2040 S/C	OP	OPFSH	FBG	TR	OB			7	4	1000			2050	2450
20	10	2100V C/C	OP	CTRCN	FBG	DV	SE			8	6	1500			**	**
20	10	2100V D/S/C	OP	OPFSH	FBG	DV	SE			8	6	1500			**	**
22	8	FANTAIL 2280VF C/C	OP	OPFSH	FBG	DV	SE			8	6	1500			**	**
22	8	FANTAIL 2280VF D/S/C	OP	OPFSH	FBG	DV	SE			8	6	1500			**	**
23	7	FANTAIL 2400VF C/C	OP	CTRCN	FBG	DV	SE	300		8	6	1700			3950	4600
23	7	FANTAIL 2400VF D/S/C	OP	OPFSH	FBG	DV	SE	300		8	6	1700			3950	4600
		1986 BOATS														
16	8	1680 C/C	OP	CTRCN	FBG	DV	OB			6	8	700			1400	1650
17	8	1780 C/C	OP	UTL	FBG	TR	OB			7	4	950			1900	2250
17	8	1780 D/S/C	OP	UTL	FBG	TR	OB			7	4	950			2000	2400
17	8	1780 S/C	OP	UTL	FBG	TR	OB			7	4	950			1600	1900
18		FANTAIL 1800 C/C	OP	CTRCN	FBG	TR	OB			7	4	850			1750	2100
18		FANTAIL 1800 D/S/C	OP	OPFSH	FBG	TR	OB			7	4	850			2000	2350
18		FANTAIL 1800 S/C	OP	OPFSH	FBG	TR	OB			7	4	850			1550	1850
18	6	GULFSKIFF	OP	CTRCN	FBG		OB			7		650			1400	1700
18	6	GULFSKIFF	OP	FSH	FBG		OB			7		650			1400	1700
18	6	GULFSKIFF	OP	FSH	FBG	TR	OB			7		650			1400	1700
19	7	1970 C/C	OP	CTRCN	FBG	TR	OB			7	4	950			2050	2450
19	7	1970 D/S/C	OP	FSH	FBG	TR	OB			7	4	950			2300	2700
19	7	1970 S/C	OP	FSH	FBG	TR	OB			7	4	950			1850	2200
20	4	FANTAIL 2040 C/C	OP	CTRCN	FBG	TR	OB			7	4	1000			2250	2600
20	4	FANTAIL 2040 D/S/C	OP	OPFSH	FBG	TR	OB			7	4	1000			2450	2850
20	4	FANTAIL 2040 S/C	OP	OPFSH	FBG	TR	OB			7	4	1000			2000	2350
20	10	2100V C/C	OP	CTRCN	FBG	DV	SE			8		1500			**	**
20	10	2100V D/S/C	OP	OPFSH	FBG	DV	SE			8		1500			**	**
23	7	FANTAIL 2400VF C/C	OP	CTRCN	FBG	DV	SE	300		8		1700			3800	4450
23	7	FANTAIL 2400VF D/S/C	OP	OPFSH	FBG	DV	SE	300		8		1700			3800	4450
		1985 BOATS														
16	8	1680 C/C	OP	CTRCN	FBG	DV	OB			6	8	700			1350	1600
17	8	1780 D/S/C	OP	UTL	FBG	TR	OB			7	4	950			1950	2350
17	8	1780 S/C	OP	UTL	FBG	TR	OB			7	4	950			1550	1850
18		FANTAIL 1800 D/S/C	OP	OPFSH	FBG	TR	OB			7	4	850			1700	2050
19	7	1970 C/C	OP	CTRCN	FBG	TR	OB			7	4	950			2000	2400
19	7	1970 D/S/C	OP	FSH	FBG	TR	OB			7	4	950			2000	2400
20	4	FANTAIL 2040 D/S/C	OP	OPFSH	FBG	TR	OB			7	4	1000			2150	2550
20	10	2100V C/C	OP	CTRCN	FBG	DV	SE			8		1500			**	**
23	7	FANTAIL 2400VF C/C	OP	CTRCN	FBG	DV	SE	300		8		1700			3700	4300
23	7	FANTAIL 2400VF D/S/C	OP	OPFSH	FBG	DV	SE	300		8		1700			3700	4300

GULFMASTER INC

BAY HAWK
MORRILTON AR 72110

See inside cover to adjust price for area

LOA FT	LOA IN	NAME AND/ OR MODEL	TOP/ RIG	BOAT TYPE	-HULL- MTL	-HULL- TP	ENGINE TP	ENGINE # HP	ENGINE MFG	BEAM FT	BEAM IN	WGT LBS	DRAFT FT	DRAFT IN	RETAIL LOW	RETAIL HIGH
		1995 BOATS														
17	2	BAY HAWK 172	OP	OPFSH	FBG	SV	OB			6	10	900		8	2800	3250
17	2	BAY HAWK 172 ST	OP	OPFSH	FBG	SV	OB			6	10	900		8	3000	3500
18	3	BAY HAWK V-190	OP	OPFSH	FBG	DV	OB			7	7	1070	1		3500	4050
18	6	BAY HAWK 186	OP	OPFSH	FBG	SV	OB			7	8	1150		8	3600	4150
18	6	BAY HAWK 186 ST	OP	OPFSH	FBG	SV	OB			7	8	1150		8	3850	4500
20	4	BAY HAWK 204	OP	OPFSH	FBG	SV	OB			7	8	1250		8	4250	4950
20	4	BAY HAWK 204 ST	OP	OPFSH	FBG	SV	OB			7	8	1250		8	4600	5300
22	6	BAY HAWK V-226	OP	OPFSH	FBG	DV	OB			8	6	1700	1		6100	7050
		1994 BOATS														
17	2	BAY HAWK 172	OP	FSH	FBG	FL	OB			6	10	900		8	2700	3150
17	2	BAY HAWK 172 ST	OP	FSH	FBG	TH	OB			6	10	900		9	2800	3300
18	3	BAY HAWK 190V	OP	FSH	FBG	SV	OB			7	7	1050		10	3300	3800
18	6	BAY HAWK 186	OP	FSH	FBG	SV	OB			7	8	1150		9	3500	4100
18	6	BAY HAWK 186 ST	OP	FSH	FBG	TH	OB			7	8	1150		10	3600	4200
20	4	BAY HAWK 204	OP	FSH	FBG	SV	OB			7	8	1300		8	4350	5000
20	4	BAY HAWK 204 ST	OP	FSH	FBG	SV	OB			7	8	1300		9	4450	5100
22	6	BAY HAWK 226	OP	FSH	FBG		OB			8	6	1700		11	5850	6700
		1993 BOATS														
17	2	BAY HAWK 172	OP	FSH	FBG	FL	OB			6	10	900		8	2600	3050
17	2	BAY HAWK 172 ST	OP	FSH	FBG	TH	OB			6	10	900		9	2700	3150
18	3	BAY HAWK 190V	OP	FSH	FBG	SV	OB			7	7	1050		10	3150	3650
18	6	BAY HAWK 186	OP	FSH	FBG	SV	OB			7	8	1150		9	3350	3900
18	6	BAY HAWK 186 ST	OP	FSH	FBG	TH	OB			7	8	1150		10	3450	4000
20	4	BAY HAWK 204	OP	FSH	FBG	SV	OB			7	8	1300		8	4150	4800
20	4	BAY HAWK 204 ST	OP	FSH	FBG	SV	OB			7	8	1300		9	4200	4900
22	6	BAY HAWK 226	OP	FSH	FBG		OB			8	6	1700		11	5600	6450
		1992 BOATS														
17	2	BAY HAWK 172	OP	FSH	FBG	FL	OB			6	10	900		8	2500	2950
17	2	BAY HAWK 172 ST	OP	FSH	FBG	TH	OB			6	10	900		9	2550	3000
18		BAY HAWK 180	OP	FSH	FBG	FL	OB			7	8	1150		9	3200	3700
18		BAY HAWK 180 ST	OP	FSH	FBG	TH	OB			7	8	1150		10	3250	3800
18	3	BAY HAWK 190V	OP	FSH	FBG	SV	OB			7	7	1050		10	3000	3500
18	6	BAY HAWK 186	OP	FSH	FBG	SV	OB			7	8	1150		9	3250	3800
18	6	BAY HAWK 186 ST	OP	FSH	FBG	TH	OB			7	8	1150		10	3300	3850
20	2	BAY HAWK 200	OP	FSH	FBG	FL	OB			7	8	1300		8	3800	4400
20	2	BAY HAWK 200 ST	OP	FSH	FBG	TH	OB			7	8	1300		9	4150	4850
20	4	BAY HAWK 204	OP	FSH	FBG	SV	OB			7	8	1300		8	4000	4600
20	4	BAY HAWK 204 ST	OP	FSH	FBG	SV	OB			7	8	1300		9	4050	4700
		1991 BOATS														
17	2	BAY HAWK 172	OP	FSH	FBG	FL	OB			6	10	750		8	2050	2450
17	2	BAY HAWK 172 ST	OP	FSH	FBG	TH	OB			6	10	750		9	2100	2500
18		BAY HAWK 180	OP	FSH	FBG	FL	OB			7	8	875		9	2450	2850
18		BAY HAWK 180 ST	OP	FSH	FBG	TH	OB			7	8	875		10	2500	2900
18	3	BAY HAWK 190V	OP	FSH	FBG	SV	OB			7	7	975		10	2750	3200
20	2	BAY HAWK 200	OP	FSH	FBG	FL	OB			7	8	975		8	2850	3350
20	2	BAY HAWK 200 ST	OP	FSH	FBG	TH	OB			7	8	975		9	3150	3650
20	4	BAY HAWK 204	OP	FSH	FBG	SV	OB			7	8	975		8	3000	3500
20	4	BAY HAWK 204 ST	OP	FSH	FBG	SV	OB			7	8	975		9	3050	3550

GULFSTAR INC

ST PETERSBURG FL 33714 COAST GUARD MFG ID- GFS See inside cover to adjust price for area

LOA FT	LOA IN	NAME AND/ OR MODEL	TOP/ RIG	BOAT TYPE	-HULL- MTL	-HULL- TP	ENGINE TP	ENGINE # HP	ENGINE MFG	BEAM FT	BEAM IN	WGT LBS	DRAFT FT	DRAFT IN	RETAIL LOW	RETAIL HIGH
		1988 BOATS														
43	9	GULFSTAR 44 MARK II	FB	MY	F/S	DS	IB	T375D	CAT	15		36400	3	6	199500	219000
43	9	OPEN AFT DECK MY	FB	MYDKH	F/S	DS	IB	T375D	CAT	15		36400	3	6	197000	216500
49		EXT AFT DECK MY	HT	MY	F/S	SV	IB	T435D	GM	15	1		3	10	207500	228000
49		MY MK IV	HT	MY	F/S	SV	IB	T435D	GM	15	1		3	10	207500	228000
55	7	MOTOR YACHT	HT	MY	FBG	SV	IB	T650D	GM	17	4	56000	4	5	344500	378500
62	6	COCKPIT MOTOR YACHT	HT	MYCPT	FBG	SV	IB	T735D	GM	17	4		4	9	455500	501000
62	6	MOTOR YACHT	HT	MY	FBG	DS	IB	T735D	GM	17	4	61500	4	9	464500	510500
69	6	MOTOR YACHT	HT	MY	FBG	SV	IB	T D	GM	17	4	73300	4	9	**	**
		1987 BOATS														
43	9	GULFSTAR 44 MARK II	FB	MY	F/S	DS	IB	T375D	CAT	15		36400	3	6	190500	209500
43	9	OPEN AFT DECK MY	FB	MYDKH	F/S	DS	IB	T375D	CAT	15		36400	3	6	188500	207000
49		EXT AFT DECK MY	HT	MY	F/S	SV	IB	T435D	GM	15	1		3	10	198500	218500
49		MY MK IV	HT	MY	F/S	SV	IB	T435D	GM	15	1		3	10	198500	218500
55	7	MOTOR YACHT	HT	MY	FBG	SV	IB	T650D	GM	17	4		4	5	259500	285500
62	6	COCKPIT MOTOR YACHT	HT	MYCPT	FBG	SV	IB	T735D	GM	17	4		4	9	433000	475500
62	6	MOTOR YACHT	HT	MY	FBG	SV	IB	T735D	GM	17	4		4	9	434500	477500
		1986 BOATS														
43	9	GULFSTAR 44 MARK II	FB	MY	FBG	DS	IB	T210D		15		36400	3	6	157000	172500
43	9	GULFSTAR 44 MARK II	FB	MY	FBG	DS	IB	T240D		15		36400	3	6	161500	177500
43	9	GULFSTAR 44 MARK II	FB	MY	FBG	DS	IB	T300D	CAT	15		36400	3	6	171500	188500
49		GULFSTAR 49 MKII		MY	FBG	DS	IB	T355D		15	2	42000	3	7	169500	186000
49		GULFSTAR 49 MKII		MY	FBG	DS	IB	T435D	GM	15	2	39000	3	7	174000	191500
60	6	GULFSTAR 60 MKII	SLP	SA/CR	FBG	KL	IB	135D	PERK	16		57500	6	6	349000	383500
		1985 BOATS														
36	1	GULFSTAR 36	SLP	SA/CR	FBG	KL	IB			12		15000	4	10	52700	57900
43	9	GULFSTAR 44 MARK II	FB	MY	FBG	DS	IB	T240D		15		36400	3	6	154500	170000

CONTINUED ON NEXT PAGE

GULFSTAR INC   -CONTINUED   See inside cover to adjust price for area

LOA FT IN	NAME AND/ OR MODEL	TOP/ RIG	BOAT TYPE	HULL MTL TP TP	ENGINE # HP MFG	BEAM FT IN	WGT LBS	DRAFT FT IN	RETAIL LOW	RETAIL HIGH
--------- 1985 BOATS ---------
43 9	GULFSTAR 44 MARK II	FB	MY	FBG DS IB	T300D CAT	15	36400	3 6	164500	180500
49	GULFSTAR 49 MK II		MY	FBG KL IB	T435D GM	15 2	39000	3 7	180000	198000
50	SAILMASTER 50	SLP	MS	FBG KL IB	D	14 6	42000	5 6	155500	171000
60 6	GULFSTAR 60 MK II	SLP	SA/CR	FBG KL IB	135D PERK	16	57500	6 6	331000	363500
62 10	SAILMASTER 62	SLP	MS	FBG KL IB	D	16 2	67500	6 9	385000	423500
--------- 1984 BOATS ---------
36 4	GULFSTAR 36	SLP	SA/CR	FBG KL IB	50D PERK	12	15000	4 10	50400	55400
38 4	GULFSTAR 38		MY	FBG SV IB	T 85D	12 5	20000	3 3	111000	122000
39 7	GULFSTAR 40 SAILMSTR	SLP	SA/CR	FBG SK IB	D	12 1	20000	4 10	72100	79300
44 8	GULFSTAR 44 MK II	SLP	SA/CR	FBG KL IB	50D PERK	13 2	26000	5 6	98000	107500
49	GULFSTAR 49		MY	FBG DS IB	T350D PERK	15 2	39000	3 7	161500	177500
50	GULFSTAR 50 SAILMSTR	SLP	SA/CR	FBG KL IB	135D PERK	14 6	42000	5 6	147500	162000
60 6	GULFSTAR 60	SLP	SA/CR	FBG KL IB	135D PERK	16	57500	6 6	313500	344500
62 10	GULFSTAR 62 SAILMSTR	SLP	SA/CR	FBG KL IB	135D PERK	16 3	67500	6 9	364000	400000

....For earlier years, see the BUC Used Boat Price Guide, Volume 3

GULFSTREAM BOATBUILDERS INC
OPA LOCKA FL 33054   See inside cover to adjust price for area

LOA FT IN	NAME AND/ OR MODEL	TOP/ RIG	BOAT TYPE	HULL MTL TP TP	ENGINE # HP MFG	BEAM FT IN	WGT LBS	DRAFT FT IN	RETAIL LOW	RETAIL HIGH
--------- 1991 BOATS ---------
20 9	PERFORMANCE 21	OP	FSH	FBG DV OB		7 8	1900	1 6	5300	6100
25	OPENFISH 250	OP	CTRCN	FBG DV OB		10	4500	2 6	11800	13400
25	OPENFISH 250	OP	CUD	FBG DV OB		10	4500	2 6	11800	13400
25	OPENFISH 250	OP	FSH	FBG DV OB		10	4500	2 6	11800	13400
25 8	PERFORMANCE 26	OP	FSH	FBG DV OB		8	3450	1 4	11100	12600
28 1	OPENFISH 281	OP	CTRCN	FBG DV OB		10	6000	2 6	15400	17500
28 1	OPENFISH 281	OP	CUD	FBG DV OB		10	6000	2 6	15500	17600
28 1	OPENFISH 281	OP	FSH	FBG DV OB		10	6000	2 6	15400	17500
28 1	TORUNAMENT 281	OP	FSH	FBG DV OB		10	6000	2 6	15400	17500
31	TORUNAMENT	TT	OPFSH	FBG SV IB	T300D	12		2 9	100000	110000
--------- 1990 BOATS ---------
20 9	PERFORMANCE 21	OP	FSH	FBG DV OB		7 8	1900	1 6	5150	5900
25	OPENFISH 250	OP	CTRCN	FBG DV OB		10	4500	2 6	11400	12900
25	OPENFISH 250	OP	CUD	FBG DV OB		10	4500	2 6	11400	12900
25	OPENFISH 250	OP	FSH	FBG DV OB		10	4500	2 6	11400	12900
25 8	PERFORMANCE 26	OP	FSH	FBG DV OB		8	3450	1 4	10700	12200
28 1	OPENFISH 281	OP	CTRCN	FBG DV OB		10	6000	2 6	14900	16900
28 1	OPENFISH 281	OP	CUD	FBG DV OB		10	6000	2 6	14900	16900
28 1	OPENFISH 281	OP	FSH	FBG DV OB		10	6000	2 6	13100	14900
28 1	TOURNAMENT 281	OP	FSH	FBG DV OB		10	6000	2 6	16600	18900
31	TOURNAMENT	TT	OPFSH	FBG SV IB	T300D	12		2 9	95500	105000
--------- 1989 BOATS ---------
20 9	PERFORMANCE 21	OP	FSH	FBG DV OB		7 8	1900	1 6	4950	5700
25	OPENFISH 250	OP	CTRCN	FBG DV OB		10	4500	2 6	11000	12500
25	OPENFISH 250	OP	CUD	FBG DV OB		10	4500	2 6	11000	12500
25	OPENFISH 250	OP	FSH	FBG DV OB		10	4500	2 6	11000	12500
25 8	PERFORMANCE 26	OP	FSH	FBG DV OB		8	3450	1 4	10400	11800
28 1	OPENFISH 281	OP	CTRCN	FBG DV OB		10	6000	2 6	14400	16300
28 1	OPENFISH 281	OP	CUD	FBG DV OB		10	6000	2 6	14400	16300
28 1	OPENFISH 281	OP	FSH	FBG DV OB		10	6000	2 6	14400	16300
28 1	TOURNAMENT 281	OP	FSH	FBG DV OB		10	6000	2 6	14400	16300
31	TOURNAMENT	TT	OPFSH	FBG SV IB	T300D	12		2 9	91400	100500

GULFSTREAM MARINE INTL
FT LAUDERDALE FL 33311   See inside cover to adjust price for area
FORMERLY COMPASS ISLAND YACHTS

LOA FT IN	NAME AND/ OR MODEL	TOP/ RIG	BOAT TYPE	HULL MTL TP TP	ENGINE # HP MFG	BEAM FT IN	WGT LBS	DRAFT FT IN	RETAIL LOW	RETAIL HIGH
--------- 1996 BOATS ---------
26	GULFSTREAM CLASSIC		FSH	FBG DV OB		8 6	4500	2 6	25500	28400
26	GULFSTREAM CLASSIC		FSH	FBG DV OB	260-330	8 6	5500	2 6	28800	33000
33	GULFSTREAM CLASSIC		FSH	FBG DV OB		9 6	6500	3	51700	56800
33	GULFSTREAM CLASSIC		FSH	FBG DV IB	375 VLVO	9 6	7500	3	65800	72300
33	GULFSTREAM CLASSIC		FSH	FBG DV IB	T180-T230	9 6	7500	3	65600	74400
--------- 1995 BOATS ---------
25 1	GULF-STREAM 25 XL	OP	CUD	FBG SV IB	200D VLVO	9 5		2	28000	31100
25 1	GULF-STREAM 25 XL	TT	CUD	FBG SV IB		9 5		2	**	**
25 1	GULF-STREAM 25 XL	TT	CUD	FBG SV IB	270 CRUS	9 5		2	25700	28500
25 1	GULF-STREAM 25 XL	TT	CUD	FBG SV IB	T140 YAN	9 5		2	26900	29900
26	CLASSIC	TT	FSH	FBG DV OB		8			24200	26900
26	CLASSIC SPORT		CUD	FBG DV OB		8			24300	27000
31	TOURNAMENT 31	OP	SF	FBG SV IB	T315 CRUS	12		2 10	58500	64200
31	TOURNAMENT 31	OP	SF	FBG SV IB	IBT230D-T325D	12		2 10	80000	86200
33	CLASSIC 33	OP	SF	FBG SV OB		9 6			35900	39900
33	CLASSIC 33	OP	SF	FBG SV IB	T170D YAN	9 6			75600	83000
33	CLASSIC 33	OP	SF	FBG SV IO	T230D DAY	9 6			70500	77500
--------- 1994 BOATS ---------
25 1	GULF-STREAM 25 XL	OP	CUD	FBG SV IB	270 CRUS	9 5		2	24300	26900
25 1	GULF-STREAM 25 XL	OP	CUD	FBG SV IB	200D VLVO	9 5		2	26600	29600
25 1	GULF-STREAM 25 XL	OP	CUD	FBG SV IB	T130D VLVO	9 5		2	31600	35100
25 1	GULF-STREAM 25 XL	TT	CUD	FBG SV IB	270 CRUS	9 5		2	24300	27000
25 1	GULF-STREAM 25 XL	TT	CUD	FBG SV IB	200D VLVO	9 5		2	26600	29600
25 1	GULF-STREAM 25 XL	TT	CUD	FBG SV IB	T130D VLVO	9 5		2	31600	35100
26	CLASSIC	TT	FSH	FBG DV OB		8			23000	25500
26	CLASSIC SPORT		CUD	FBG DV OB		8			23000	25600
31	TOURNAMENT 31	OP	SF	FBG SV IB	T245-T315	12		2 10	52800	60800
31	TOURNAMENT 31	OP	SF	FBG SV IB	IBT200D-T230D	12		2 10	64400	73200
31	TOURNAMENT 31	OP	SF	FBG SV IB	T325D DD	12		2 10	74700	82000
33	CLASSIC 33	OP	SF	FBG SV OB		9 10			34000	37800
33	CLASSIC 33	OP	SF	FBG SV IB	T235D VLVO	9 10			70200	77100
--------- 1993 BOATS ---------
25 1	GULF-STREAM 25 XL	OP	CUD	FBG SV IB	270 CRUS	9 5		2	22900	25500
25 1	GULF-STREAM 25 XL	OP	CUD	FBG SV IB	200D VLVO	9 5		2	25300	28100
25 1	GULF-STREAM 25 XL	OP	CUD	FBG SV IB	T130D VLVO	9 5		2	30000	33300
25 1	GULF-STREAM 25 XL	TT	CUD	FBG SV IB	270 CRUS	9 5		2	23000	25500
25 1	GULF-STREAM 25 XL	TT	CUD	FBG SV IB	200D VLVO	9 5		2	25300	28100
25 1	GULF-STREAM 25 XL	TT	CUD	FBG SV IB	T130D VLVO	9 5		2	30000	33300
26	CLASSIC	TT	FSH	FBG DV OB		8			21800	24200
26	CLASSIC SPORT		CUD	FBG DV OB		8			20100	24300
31	TOURNAMENT 31	OP	SF	FBG SV IB	T245-T315	12		2 10	50100	57600
31	TOURNAMENT 31	OP	SF	FBG SV IB	IBT200D-T230D	12		2 10	61400	69800
31	TOURNAMENT 31	OP	SF	FBG SV IB	T325D DD	12		2 10	71100	78200
33	CLASSIC 33	OP	SF	FBG SV OB		9 10			32300	35900
--------- 1992 BOATS ---------
25 1	GULF-STREAM 25 XL	OP	CUD	FBG SV IB	270 CRUS	9 5		2	21700	24200
	IB 200D VLVO 24100			26800, IB T200	CRUS	24200	26800,	IB T130D	VLVO	28600 31800
	IB T210D CUM 33600			37300						
25 1	GULF-STREAM 25 XL	TT	CUD	FBG SV IB	270 CRUS	9 5		2	21700	24200
	IB 200D-210D 24100			27800, IB T200	CRUS	24200	26800,	IB T130D	VLVO	28600 31800
26	CLASSIC	TT	FSH	FBG DV IB		8			**	**
31	TOURNAMENT 31	OP	SF	FBG SV IB	T245-T315	12		2 10	47800	54700
31	TOURNAMENT 31	OP	SF	FBG SV IB	IBT200D-T300D	12		2 10	58500	72100
31	TOURNAMENT 31	TT	SF	FBG SV IB	T245-T315	12		2 10	47800	54700
31	TOURNAMENT 31	TT	SF	FBG SV IB	IBT200D-T300D	12		2 10	58500	72100
--------- 1991 BOATS ---------
25 1	GULF-STREAM 25 XL	OP	CUD	FBG SV IB	270 CRUS	9 5		2	20600	22900
	IB 200D VLVO 23000			25500, IB T200	CRUS	22900	25500,	IB T130D	VLVO	27200 30300
	IB T210D CUM 32000			35600						
25 1	GULF-STREAM 25 XL	TT	CUD	FBG SV IB	200-270	9 5		2	20200	22900
25 1	GULF-STREAM 25 XL	TT	CUD	FBG SV IB	200D-210D	9 5		2	23000	26500
25 1	GULF-STREAM 25 XL	TT	CUD	FBG SV IB	T130D VLVO	9 5		2	27200	30300
31	TOURNAMENT 31	OP	SF	FBG SV IB	T245-T315	12		2 10	44900	52200
31	TOURNAMENT 31	OP	SF	FBG SV IB	IBT200D-T300D	12		2 10	55900	68900
31	TOURNAMENT 31	TT	SF	FBG SV IB	T245-T315	12		2 10	44900	52200
31	TOURNAMENT 31	TT	SF	FBG SV IB	IBT200D-T300D	12		2 10	55900	68900
--------- 1990 BOATS ---------
25 1	GULF-STREAM 25	OP	CUD	FBG SV IB	270 CRUS	9 5		2	19600	21800
	IB 200D VLVO 21900			24400, IB T200	CRUS	21800	24200,	IB T130D	VLVO	26000 28900
	IB T210D CUM 30600			34000						
25 1	GULF-STREAM 25	TT	CUD	FBG SV IB	270 CRUS	9 5		2	19600	21800
25 1	GULF-STREAM 25	TT	CUD	FBG SV IB	200D-210D	9 5		2	21800	24200
25 1	GULF-STREAM 25XL	TT	CUD	FBG SV IB	200D-210D	9 5		2	21900	24300
25 1	GULF-STREAM 25XL	TT	CUD	FBG SV IB	T130D VLVO	9 5		2	26000	28900
31	TOURNAMENT 31	OP	SF	FBG SV IB	T245-T315	12		2 10	42700	49700
31	TOURNAMENT 31	OP	SF	FBG SV IB	IBT200D-T300D	12		2 10	53400	65800
31	TOURNAMENT 31	TT	SF	FBG SV IB	T245-T315	12		2 10	42700	49700
31	TOURNAMENT 31	TT	SF	FBG SV IB	IBT200D-T300D	12		2 10	53400	65800
--------- 1989 BOATS ---------
25 1	GULF-STREAM 25CC	TT	CUD	FBG SV IB	270 CRUS	9 5		2	18700	20800
25 1	GULF-STREAM 25CC	TT	CUD	FBG SV IB	270 CRUS	9 5		2	20800	23100
25 1	GULF-STREAM 25F	OP	CUD	FBG SV IB	270 CRUS	9 5		2	18700	20800
	IB 200D-210D 21000			24100, IB T200	CRUS	20800	23100,	IB T130D	VLVO	24800 27600

LOA FT	LOA IN	NAME AND/ OR MODEL	TOP/ RIG	BOAT TYPE	HULL MTL	HULL TP	ENGINE TP	ENGINE # HP	ENGINE MFG	BEAM FT	BEAM IN	WGT LBS	DRAFT FT	DRAFT IN	RETAIL LOW	RETAIL HIGH
		1989 BOATS														
31		TOURNAMENT 31	OP	SF	FBG	SV	IB	T245-T315		12			2	10	40600	47300
31		TOURNAMENT 31	OP	SF	FBG	SV	IB	T200D-T250D		12			2	10	51100	59600
31		TOURNAMENT 31	TT	SF	FBG	SV	IB	T245-T315		12			2	10	40600	47300
31		TOURNAMENT 31	TT	SF	FBG	SV	IB	T200D-T250D		12			2	10	51100	59600
		1988 BOATS														
25	1	GULF-STREAM 25CC	TT	CUD	FBG	SV	IB	T200	CRUS	9	5		2		19800	22000
25	1	GULF-STREAM 25F	OP	CUD	FBG	SV	IB	270-275		9	5		2		17400	19800
25	1	GULF-STREAM 25F	OP	CUD	FBG	SV	IB	210D	CUM	9	5		2		20800	23100
25	1	GULF-STREAM 25F	OP	CUD	FBG	SV	IB	T150D	CUM	9	5		2		25400	28200
31		TOURNAMENT 31	OP	CUD	FBG	SV	IB	T245-T340		12			2	10	36600	43700
31		TOURNAMENT 31	OP	CUD	FBG	SV	IB	T210D	CUM	12			2	10	43100	47900
		1987 BOATS														
25	1	GULF-STREAM 25CC	TT	CUD	FBG	SV	IB	T200	CRUS	9	5		2		18900	21000
25	1	GULF-STREAM 25F	OP	CUD	FBG	SV	IB	270-275		9	5		2		16600	18900
25	1	GULF-STREAM 25F	OP	CUD	FBG	SV	IB	210D	CUM	9	5		2		19900	22100
25	1	GULF-STREAM 25F	OP	CUD	FBG	SV	IB	T150D	CUM	9	5		2		24300	27000
31		TOURNAMENT 31	OP	CUD	FBG	SV	IO	T245-T315		12			2	10	27300	32200
31		TOURNAMENT 31	OP	CUD	FBG	SV	IB	T340	CHRY	12			2	10	37500	41700
31		TOURNAMENT 31	OP	CUD	FBG	SV	IO	T210D	CUM	12			2	10	30200	33600
		1985 BOATS														
25	1	GULF-STREAM 25CC	OP	CUD	FBG	SV	IB	270	CRUS	9	5				15000	17000
		IB 165D-180D 16600 19800, IB T225 COMM 16700 19000, IB T120D													21400	23700
25	1	GULF-STREAM 25CC	TT	CUD	FBG	SV	IB	260	COMM	9	5				14800	16800
		IB 180D 17400 19800, IB T165 CRUS 16400 18700, IB T120D													21400	23800
		1984 BOATS														
22	1	GULF-STREAM 22F	OP	CTRCN	FBG	SV	OB			8			1	6	8100	9300
22	1	GULF-STREAM 22F	OP	CTRCN	FBG	SV	IB	165	CRUS	8			1	6	7350	8450
24	1	GULF-STREAM 24F	OP	OPFSH	FBG	SV	OB			9	5		2		12000	13600
24	1	GULF-STREAM 24F	OP	OPFSH	FBG	SV	IB	260-270		9	5		2		10900	12700
24	1	GULF-STREAM 24F	OP	OPFSH	FBG	SV	IB	T165-T225		9	5		2		12400	14100
24	1	GULF-STREAM 24F	TT	OPFSH	FBG	SV	IB	225-270		9	5		2		10800	12700
24	1	GULF-STREAM 24F	TT	OPFSH	FBG	SV	IB	T165-T225		9	5		2		12400	14100

GULFSTREAM YACHTS INC

VENTURA CA 93001 COAST GUARD MFG ID- GFQ See inside cover to adjust price for area
FORMERLY GULFSTREAM LTD

LOA FT	LOA IN	NAME AND/ OR MODEL	TOP/ RIG	BOAT TYPE	HULL MTL	HULL TP	ENGINE TP	ENGINE # HP	ENGINE MFG	BEAM FT	BEAM IN	WGT LBS	DRAFT FT	DRAFT IN	RETAIL LOW	RETAIL HIGH
		1990 BOATS														
41	11	VENTURA 42	FB	SF	FBG	SV	IB	T250D	GM	13	6	22000	3	1	107000	118000
41	11	VENTURA 42	FB	SF	FBG	SV	IB	T400D	GM	13	6	22000	3	1	123500	135500
		1989 BOATS														
39	8	VENTURA 37	FB	SF	FBG	SV	IB	T250D	GM	13		20000	2	8	94100	103500
41	11	GULFSTREAM 42	HT	DCCPT	FBG	SV	IB	T250D	GM	13	6	24500	3	6	112500	124000
41	11	VENTURA 42	FB	SF	FBG	SV	IB	T250D	GM	13	6	22000	3	1	102500	112500
41	11	VENTURA 42	FB	SF	FBG	SV	IB	T400D	GM	13	6	22000	3	1	118000	129500
45	11	GULFSTREAM 46	HT	DCCPT	FBG	SV	IB	T250D	GM	13	6	26500	3	6	122500	134500
		1988 BOATS														
39	8	VENTURA 37	FB	SF	FBG	SV	IB	T250D	GM	13		20000	2	8	89900	98800
39	8	VENTURA 37	FB	SF	FBG	SV	IB	T280D	GM	13		20000	2	8	91400	100500
		1987 BOATS														
39	8	VENTURA 37	FB	SF	FBG	SV	IB	T260D	GM	13		20000	2		86400	95000
39	8	VENTURA 37	FB	SF	FBG	SV	IB	T280D	GM	13		20000	2		87400	96100
		1986 BOATS														
39	8	VENTURA 37	FB	SF	FBG	SV	IB	T220D	GM	13		20000	2		81000	89000
39	8	VENTURA 37	FB	SF	FBG	SV	IB	T260D	GM	13		20000	2		82700	90900
		1985 BOATS														
39	8	VENTURA 37	FB	SF	FBG	SV	IB	T220D	GM	13		20000	2		77500	85200
39	8	VENTURA 37	FB	SF	FBG	SV	IB	T250D	GM	13		20000	2		78700	86500

H & H SAILCRAFT

DIV OF DYNAMIC PLASTICS INC See inside cover to adjust price for area
NEW PARIS OH 45347 COAST GUARD MFG ID- DYP

LOA FT	LOA IN	NAME AND/ OR MODEL	TOP/ RIG	BOAT TYPE	HULL MTL	HULL TP	ENGINE TP	ENGINE # HP	ENGINE MFG	BEAM FT	BEAM IN	WGT LBS	DRAFT FT	DRAFT IN	RETAIL LOW	RETAIL HIGH
		1992 BOATS														
16		CONTENDER	SLP	SAIL	FBG	CB				4	8	228			4750	5450
		1986 BOATS														
16		CONTENDER	CAT	SA/OD	FBG	CB				4	8	185		5	3000	3500
19	10	FLYING-DUTCHMAN	SLP	SA/OD	FBG	CB				5	11	365		8	5100	5900
		1985 BOATS														
16		CONTENDER	CAT	SA/OD	FBG	CB				4	8	185		5	2800	3250
19	10	FLYING-DUTCHMAN	SLP	SA/OD	FBG					5	11	365		8	4850	5550
		1984 BOATS														
16		CONTENDER	CAT	SA/OD	FBG	CB				4	8	185		5	2700	3100
19	10	FLYING-DUTCHMAN	SLP	SA/OD	FBG	CB				5	8	365		8	4550	5250

....For earlier years, see the BUC Used Boat Price Guide, Volume 3

HALLBERG-RASSY VARV A B

ELLOS SWEDEN SE-474 31 COAST GUARD MFG ID- HRV See inside cover to adjust price for area
FOR OLDER MODELS SEE XAX CORPORATION

LOA FT	LOA IN	NAME AND/ OR MODEL	TOP/ RIG	BOAT TYPE	HULL MTL	HULL TP	ENGINE TP	ENGINE # HP	ENGINE MFG	BEAM FT	BEAM IN	WGT LBS	DRAFT FT	DRAFT IN	RETAIL LOW	RETAIL HIGH
		1987 BOATS														
28	8	HALLBERG-RASSY 29	SLP	SA/CR	FBG	KL	IB	18D	VLVO	9	4	8360	4	11	51300	56300
30	10	HALLBERG-RASSY HR 94	SLP	MS	FBG	KL	IB	36D	VLVO	10	7	11440	3	9	71600	78700
30	11	HALLBERG-RASSY 312	SLP	SA/CR	FBG	KL	IB	28D	VLVO	10	1	10800	5	4	67500	74200
34	7	HALLBERG-RASSY 352	SLP	SA/CR	FBG	KL	IB	43D	VLVO	11	1	14800	5	4	91000	100000
38	1	HALLBERG-RASSY 382	SLP	SA/CR	FBG	KL	IB	65D	VLVO	11	11	19850	5	10	124500	137000
42		HALLBERG-RASSY 42	SLP	SA/CR	FBG	KL	IB	65D	VLVO	12	5	25368	6	9	166500	183000
42		HALLBERG-RASSY 42	KTH	SA/CR	FBG	KL	IB	65D	VLVO	12	5	25368	5	8	166500	183000
49	1	HALLBERG-RASSY 49	SLP	SA/CR	FBG	KL	IB	85D	VLVO	14	6	39700	7	3	267000	293500
49	1	HALLBERG-RASSY 49	KTH	SA/CR	FBG	KL	IB	85D	VLVO	14	6	39700	6	3	268000	294500
		1986 BOATS														
28	8	HALLBERG-RASSY 29	SLP	SA/CR	FBG	KL	IB	D		9	2	8360	4	10	48300	53000
30	6	HALLBERG-RASSY 94MS	SLP	MS	FBG	KL	IB	D		10	6	11440	3	9	67300	74000
30	11	HALLBERG-RASSY 312	SLP	SA/CR	FBG	KL	SD	D		10	1	10800	5	4	63500	69700
38		HALLBERG-RASSY 38	SLP	SA/CR	FBG	KL	IB	D		11	5	18750	5	9	111000	122000
42		HALLBERG-RASSY 42	KTH	SA/CR	FBG	KL	IB	D		12	5	25368	5	8	156000	171500
49	1	HALLBERG-RASSY 49	KTH	SA/CR	FBG	KL	IB	D		14	6	39700	6	3	252000	277000
		1985 BOATS														
28	8	HALLBERG-RASSY 29	SLP	SA/CR	FBG	KL	SD	D		9	2	8360	4	10	45600	50200
30	11	HALLBERG-RASSY 312	SLP	SA/CR	FBG	KL	SD	D		10	1	10800	5	4	59700	65600
34	7	HALLBERG-RASSY 352	SLP	SA/CR	FBG	KL	IB	D		11	1	14800	5	4	80400	88300
38		HALLBERG-RASSY 38	SLP	SA/CR	FBG	KL	IB	D		11	5	18750	5	9	104500	115000
42		HALLBERG-RASSY 42	KTH	SA/CR	FBG	KL	IB	D		12	5	25368	5	8	147000	161500
49	1	HALLBERG-RASSY 49	KTH	SA/CR	FBG	KL	IB	D		14	6	39700	7	3	237000	260500
		1984 BOATS														
28	8	HALLBERG-RASSY 29	SLP	SA/CR	FBG	KL	SD	15D	VLVO	9	2	8360	4	10	42400	47100
30	6	HALLBERG-RASSY 94 MS	SLP	SA/CR	FBG	KL	IB	36D	VLVO	10	6	11440	3	9	59700	65600
30	11	HALLBERG-RASSY 312	SLP	SA/CR	FBG	KL	SD	23D	VLVO	10	1	10800	5	4	56100	61700
34	7	HALLBERG-RASSY 352	SLP	SA/CR	FBG	KL	IB	61D	VLVO	11	1	14800	5	4	75900	83400
38		HALLBERG-RASSY 38	SLP	SA/CR	FBG	KL	IB	61D	VLVO	11	5	18750	5	9	98900	108500
42		HALLBERG-RASSY 42	KTH	SA/CR	FBG	KL	IB	61D	VLVO	12	5	25368	6	9	136000	149500
42		HALLBERG-RASSY 42 SH	KTH	SA/CR	FBG	KL	IB	61D	VLVO	12	5	25368	5	8	140500	154500
49	1	HALLBERG-RASSY 49	KTH	SA/CR	FBG	KL	IB	72D	VLVO	14	6	39700	7	3	220500	242500
49	1	HALLBERG-RASSY 49 SH	KTH	SA/CR	FBG	KL	IB	72D	VLVO	14	6	39700	6	3	224500	246500

....For earlier years, see the BUC Used Boat Price Guide, Volume 3

HALLETT BOATS

BARRON BOATS INC. See inside cover to adjust price for area
IRWINDALE CA 91706 COAST GUARD MFG ID- BAR

For more recent years, see the BUC Used Boat Price Guide, Volume 1

LOA FT	LOA IN	NAME AND/ OR MODEL	TOP/ RIG	BOAT TYPE	HULL MTL	HULL TP	ENGINE TP	ENGINE # HP	ENGINE MFG	BEAM FT	BEAM IN	WGT LBS	DRAFT FT	DRAFT IN	RETAIL LOW	RETAIL HIGH
		1996 BOATS														
20	11	CLOSED BOW 210		RNBT	FBG	SV	IO	260	MRCR	8		2600	3		11100	12600
20	11	OPEN BOW 210		W/T	FBG	SV	IO	260	MRCR	8		2600	3		11900	13500
21		VECTOR		RNBT	FBG	DV	IO	260	MRCR	8		2600	3		11100	12600
24	1	CLOSED BOW 240		CR	FBG	DV	IO	300	MRCR	8	6	3500	3	6	17100	19500
24	2	OPEN BOW 240		W/T	FBG	DV	IO	300	MRCR	8	6	3500	3	6	18400	20400
25	8	S-250		CR	FBG	DV	IO	300	MRCR	8	6	3300	3	6	20100	22300
26	8	PARTY CRUISER 260		UTL	FBG	DV	IO	300	MRCR	8	4	4600	3		26400	29400
27		S-270		CR	FBG	DV	IO	300	MRCR	8	6	4100	3	6	24400	27100
30	3	T-300		CR	FBG	DV	IO	T300	MRCR	8	6	6800	3	6	42200	46900
31	4	T-320		CR	FBG	DV	IO	T300	MRCR	8		7400	3	6	47600	52300
34		T-340		CR	FBG	DV	IO	T300	MRCR	8	6	8100	3	6	66400	72900
		1995 BOATS														
18		ELITE	OP	RNBT	FBG	DV	JT		CHEV	7	7	1900			**	**
18		ELITE	OP	RNBT	FBG	DV	IO	185		7	7	1900			7200	8300
18	6	MINI-CRUISER	OP	CR	FBG	DV	IB	320		7	7	2400			10400	11800
19	2	SPORT SKIER	OP	RNBT	FBG	DV	OB			6	9	1880			11500	13100
19	2	SPORT SKIER	OP	RNBT	FBG	DV	JT	320		6	9	1880			10300	11700

LOA FT IN	NAME AND/ OR MODEL	TOP/ RIG	BOAT TYPE	HULL MTL TP TP	ENGINE # HP	MFG	BEAM FT IN	WGT LBS	DRAFT FT IN	RETAIL LOW	RETAIL HIGH
1995 BOATS											
20 8	SUPER SPORT	OP	RNBT	FBG DV JT		CHEV	7 9	3150		**	**
20 8	SUPER SPORT	OP	RNBT	FBG DV JT	260	CHEV	7 9	3150		12400	14100
20 8	SUPER SPORT BR	OP	RNBT	FBG DV JT		CHEV	7 9	3150		**	**
20 8	SUPER SPORT BR	OP	RNBT	FBG DV JT	260		7 9	3150		12400	14100
21	VECTOR	OP	RNBT	FBG IO	340	MRCR	7 9	3200		14800	16800
23	DAY CRUISER	OP	CR	FBG DV JT		CHEV	8	3525		**	**
23	DAY CRUISER	OP	CR	FBG DV IO	290	VLVO	8	3525		17300	19600
26	OFFSHORE 7.9	OP	EXP	FBG DV IO	290	VLVO	7 9	3600		21400	23800
27	270-T	OP	OFF	FBG IO	T350	CHEV	8 4	5000		34600	38500
32	320-T	OP	OFF	FBG IO	T454	CHEV	8 2	6500		55400	60900
1988 BOATS											
18	ELITE	OP	RNBT	FBG DV JT		CHEV	7 7	1900		**	**
18	ELITE	OP	RNBT	FBG DV IO	185		7 7	1900		3900	4550
18 6	MINI-CRUISER	OP	CR	FBG DV IB	320		7 7	2400		5950	6850
19 2	SPORT SKIER	OP	RNBT	FBG DV OB			6 9	1880		8700	10000
19 2	SPORT SKIER	OP	RNBT	FBG DV JT	320		6 9	1880		5900	6800
20 8	SUPER SPORT	OP	RNBT	FBG DV JT		CHEV	7 9	3150		**	**
20 8	SUPER SPORT	OP	RNBT	FBG DV JT	260	CHEV	7 9	3150		7000	8050
20 8	SUPER SPORT BR	OP	RNBT	FBG DV JT		CHEV	7 9	3150		**	**
20 8	SUPER SPORT BR	OP	RNBT	FBG DV JT	260	CHEV	7 9	3150		7150	8200
21	VECTOR	OP	RNBT	FBG IO	340	MRCR	7 9	3200		8400	9650
23	DAY CRUISER	OP	CR	FBG DV JT		CHEV	8	3525		**	**
23	DAY CRUISER	OP	CR	FBG DV IO	290	CHEV	8	3525		9950	11300
26	OFFSHORE 7.9	OP	EXP	FBG DV IO	290	VLVO	7 9	3600		12200	13800
27	270-T	OP	OFF	FBG IO	T350	CHEV	8 4	5000		19900	22100
32	320-T	OP	OFF	FBG IO	T454	CHEV	8 2	6500		35400	39300
1987 BOATS											
18	ELITE	OP	RNBT	FBG DV JT		CHEV	7 7	1900		**	**
18	ELITE	OP	RNBT	FBG DV IO	185		7 7	1900		3700	4300
18 6	MINI-CRUISER	OP	CR	FBG DV IB	320		7 7	2400		5650	6500
19 2	SPORT SKIER	OP	RNBT	FBG DV OB			6 9	1880		8400	9650
19 2	SPORT SKIER	OP	RNBT	FBG DV JT	320		6 9	1880		5650	6450
20 8	SUPER SPORT	OP	RNBT	FBG DV JT		CHEV	7 9	3150		**	**
20 8	SUPER SPORT	OP	RNBT	FBG DV JT	260	CHEV	7 9	3150		6650	7600
20 8	SUPER SPORT BR	OP	RNBT	FBG DV JT		CHEV	7 9	3150		**	**
20 8	SUPER SPORT BR	OP	RNBT	FBG DV JT	260	CHEV	7 9	3150		6750	7800
21	VECTOR	OP	RNBT	FBG IO	340	MRCR	7 9	3200		7950	9150
23	DAY CRUISER	OP	CR	FBG DV JT		CHEV	8	3525		**	**
23	DAY CRUISER	OP	CR	FBG DV IO	290	VLVO	8	3525		9400	10700
26	OFFSHORE 7.9	OP	EXP	FBG DV IO	290	VLVO	7 9	3600		11500	13000
1986 BOATS											
18	ELITE	OP	RNBT	FBG DV JT		CHEV	7 7	1900		**	**
18	ELITE	OP	RNBT	FBG DV IO	185		7 7	1900		3500	4050
18 6	MINI-CRUISER	OP	CR	FBG DV IB	320		7 7	2400		5400	6200
19 2	SPORT SKIER	OP	RNBT	FBG DV OB			6 9	1880		8150	9400
19 2	SPORT SKIER	OP	RNBT	FBG DV JT	320		6 9	1880		5400	6200
20 8	SUPER SPORT	OP	RNBT	FBG DV JT		CHEV	7 9	3150		**	**
20 8	SUPER SPORT	OP	RNBT	FBG DV JT	260	CHEV	7 9	3150		6350	7300
20 8	SUPER SPORT BR	OP	RNBT	FBG DV JT		CHEV	7 9	3150		**	**
20 8	SUPER SPORT BR	OP	RNBT	FBG DV JT	260	CHEV	7 9	3150		6450	7400
23	DAY CRUISER	OP	CR	FBG DV JT		CHEV	8	3525		**	**
23	DAY CRUISER	OP	CR	FBG DV IO	290	VLVO	8	3525		8950	10200
26	OFFSHORE 7.9	OP	EXP	FBG DV IO	290	VLVO	7 9	3600		11000	12500
1984 BOATS											
18 6	MINI-CRUISER	OP	RNBT	FBG SV JT	260	OMC	7 7	2400		3800	4450
18 6	MINI-CRUISER	OP	RNBT	FBG SV JT	330	CHEV	7 7	2400		5550	6350
18 6	MINI-CRUISER	OP	RNBT	FBG SV VD	330	CHEV	7 7	2400		5200	6000
18 10	BUBBLE-DECK	OP	RNBT	FBG SV JT	330	CHEV	6 9	1880		4850	5550
18 10	JET-SPRINT	OP	RNBT	FBG SV JT	330	CHEV	6 9	1880		4850	5550
19 4	SPORTS-SKIER	OP	SKI	FBG SV VD	330	CHEV	6 9	1880		4500	5150
20 8	BOWRIDER	OP	RNBT	FBG SV JT	260	MRCR	7 10	3150		5950	6850
20 8	BOWRIDER	OP	RNBT	FBG SV JT	330	CHEV	7 10	3150		8300	9550
20 8	BOWRIDER	OP	RNBT	FBG SV VD	330	CHEV	7 10	3150		7900	9100
20 8	SUPER-SPORT	OP	RNBT	FBG SV JT	260	MRCR	7 10	3150		5850	6750
20 8	SUPER-SPORT	OP	RNBT	FBG SV JT	330	CHEV	7 10	3150		8100	9350
20 8	SUPER-SPORT	OP	RNBT	FBG SV VD	330	CHEV	7 10	3150		7700	8850
22 9	DAYCRUISER	OP	SPTCR	FBG SV IO	260	MRCR	8	3525		7650	8750
	JT 330 CHEV 10000 11300, IO 330 MRCR				8450	9750, VD 330		CHEV		9650	11000
30 3	OFFSHORE	OP	SPTCR	FBG IO	T330	MRCR	8	8500		21800	24200

....For earlier years, see the BUC Used Boat Price Guide, Volume 3

HALMAN MANUFACTURING COMPANY

DIV OF VORTEX PLASTICS LTD   See inside cover to adjust price for area
BEAMSVILLE ONTARIO CANA COAST GUARD MFG ID- ZHL

LOA FT IN	NAME AND/ OR MODEL	TOP/ RIG	BOAT TYPE	HULL MTL TP TP	ENGINE # HP	MFG	BEAM FT IN	WGT LBS	DRAFT FT IN	RETAIL LOW	RETAIL HIGH
1991 BOATS											
21 2	HALMAN 21	SLP	SA/CR	FBG KL			7 9	2500	2 10	6600	7550
23	BLUE JACKET 23	SLP	SA/CR	FBG KL IB	18D	YAN	10	6000	2 3	18200	20200
24	SHARK 24	SLP	SA/OD	FBG KL			6 10	2100	3 2	6650	7650
31 4	HORIZON CUTTER	CUT	SA/CR	FBG KL IB	18D	YAN	9 6	7200	4	25300	28100
1990 BOATS											
19 4	HENLEY 20	SLP	SAIL	FBG KL			8	1200	2 5	3900	4550
21 2	HALMAN 21	SLP	SA/CR	FBG KL			7 9	2500	2 10	6250	7200
23	BLUE JACKET 23	SLP	SA/CR	FBG KL IB	18D	YAN	10	6000	2 3	16800	19100
24	SHARK 24	SLP	SA/OD	FBG KL			6 10	2100	3 2	6300	7250
26 8	NIAGARA 26	SLP	SA/RC	FBG KL			8 4	4000	4	11200	12800
31 4	HORIZON CUTTER	CUT	SA/CR	FBG KL IB	18D	YAN	9 6	7200	4	24000	26600
1989 BOATS											
19 4	HENLEY 20	SLP	SAIL	FBG KL			8	1200	2 5	3700	4300
19 4	HALMAN 20	SLP	SA/CR	FBG KL			7 9	2500	2 10	5700	6550
21 2	HALMAN 21	SLP	SA/CR	FBG KL			7 9	2500	2 10	5900	6800
23	BLUE JACKET 23	SLP	SA/CR	FBG KL IB	18D	YAN	10	6000	2 3	15900	18100
24	SHARK 24	SLP	SA/OD	FBG KL			6 10	2100	3 2	6000	6900
26 8	NIAGARA 26	SLP	SA/RC	FBG KL			8 4	4000	4	10600	12100
31 4	HORIZON CUTTER	CUT	SA/CR	FBG KL IB	18D	YAN	9 6	7200	4	22700	25200
1988 BOATS											
19 4	HENLEY 20	SLP	SAIL	FBG KL			8	1200	2 5	3500	4100
19 4	HALMAN 20	SLP	SA/CR	FBG KL			7 9	2500	2 10	5400	6200
21 2	HALMAN 21	SLP	SA/CR	FBG KL			7 9	2500	2 10	5600	6450
23	BLUE JACKET 23	SLP	SA/CR	FBG KL IB	18D	YAN	10	6000	2 3	15100	17200
24	SHARK 24	SLP	SA/OD	FBG KL			6 10	2100	3 2	5650	6500
26 8	NIAGARA 26	SLP	SA/RC	FBG KL			8 4	4000	4	10100	11500
31 4	HORIZON CUTTER	CUT	SA/CR	FBG KL IB	18D	YAN	9 6	7200	4	21500	23900
1987 BOATS											
19 4	HENLEY 20	SLP	SAIL	FBG KL			7 10	1350	2 6	3550	4100
21 2	HALMAN 21	SLP	SA/CR	FBG KL			7 9	2500	2 10	5300	6100
24	SHARK 24	SLP	SA/OD	FBG KL			6 10	2100	3 2	5300	6150
26 8	NIAGARA 26	SLP	SA/RC	FBG KL			8 4	4000	4	9500	10900
31 4	HORIZON CUTTER	CUT	SA/CR	FBG KL IB	18D	YAN	9 6	7200	4	20400	22600
1986 BOATS											
19 8	NORDIC HALMAN 20	SLP	SA/CR	FBG KL			7 9	2500	2 10	4850	5550
24	SHARK	SLP	SA/OD	FBG CT			6 10	2100	3 2	9350	10600
27 4	HORIZON 27	SLP	SA/CR	FBG CT IB	D		9 6	7000	4	18100	20100
31 4	HORIZON	CUT	SA/CR	FBG KL IB	18D	YAN	9 6	7000	4	27300	30400
1985 BOATS											
24	SHARK	SLP	SA/OD	FBG KL			6 10	2200	3 2	4950	5700
27 4	HORIZON 27	SLP	SA/CR	FBG KL IB	18D	YAN	9 6	7000	4	16800	19100
31 4	HORIZON	CUT	SA/CR	FBG KL IB	18D	YAN	9 6	7000	4	17600	20000

....For earlier years, see the BUC Used Boat Price Guide, Volume 3

HALMATIC LIMITED

DIV OF HUNTING GROUP   See inside cover to adjust price for area
HAVANT HAMP ENGLAND   COAST GUARD MFG ID- HMT

LOA FT IN	NAME AND/ OR MODEL	TOP/ RIG	BOAT TYPE	HULL MTL TP TP	ENGINE # HP	MFG	BEAM FT IN	WGT LBS	DRAFT FT IN	RETAIL LOW	RETAIL HIGH
1988 BOATS											
29 6	HALMATIC 30	SLP	SA/CR	FBG KL IB	18D	VLVO	9 6	9000	4 6	38400	42700
34 6	WEYMOUTH 34	FB	MY	FBG DV IB	T120D		11 9	14000	2 10	97200	107000
41 5	WEYMOUTH 42	FB	MY	FBG DV IB	T180	FORD	11 11	18000	3 6	131000	144000
41 5	WEYMOUTH 42	FB	MY	FBG DV IB	T250	SABR	11 11	18000	3 6	132000	145000
43	WEYMOUTH 44	FB	MY	FBG DV IB	T180	FORD	13	28000	3 6	180500	198000
43	WEYMOUTH 44	FB	MY	FBG DV IB	T250	SABR	13	28000	3 6	182000	200000
48	AZURE 150	FB	MY	FBG DV IB	T		14 3	28000	3 3	**	**
48	AZURE 150	FB	MY	FBG DV IB	T300	SABR	14 3	28000	3 3	224000	246000
50	T50	FB	MY	FBG DV IB	T		15 3	34000	4 3	**	**
50	T50	FB	MY	FBG DV IB	T	D	CAT	15 3	34000	4 3	**	**
1987 BOATS											
29 6	HALMATIC 30	SLP	SA/CR	FBG KL IB	18D	VLVO	9 6	9000	4 6	35600	39500
34 6	WEYMOUTH 34	FB	MY	FBG DV IB	T120D		11 9	14000	2 10	91300	102500
41 5	WEYMOUTH 42	FB	MY	FBG DV IB	T180	FORD	11 11	18000	3 6	125000	137500
41 5	WEYMOUTH 42	FB	MY	FBG DV IB	T250	SABR	11 11	18000	3 6	126000	139000
43	WEYMOUTH 44	FB	MY	FBG DV IB	T180	FORD	13	28000	3 6	172500	189500
43	WEYMOUTH 44	FB	MY	FBG DV IB	T250	SABR	13	28000	3 6	174000	191000
48	AZURE 150	FB	MY	FBG DV IB	T		14 3	28000	3 3	**	**

LOA FT IN	NAME AND/ OR MODEL	TOP/ RIG	BOAT TYPE	-HULL- MTL TP	TP	---ENGINE--- # HP MFG	BEAM FT IN	WGT LBS	DRAFT FT IN	RETAIL LOW	RETAIL HIGH
	------------ 1987 BOATS										
48	AZURE 150	FB	MY	FBG DV	IB	T300 SABR	14 3	28000	3 3	213500	234500
50	T50	FB	MY	FBG DV	IB	T D	15 3	34000	4 3	**	**
50	T50	FB	MY	FBG DV	IB	T D CAT	15 3	34000	4 3	**	**
	------------ 1986 BOATS										
29 6	HALMATIC 30	SLP	SA/CR	FBG KL	IB	D	9 6	10300	4 6	38600	42900
	------------ 1985 BOATS										
29 6	HALMATIC 30	SLP	SA/CR	FBG KL	IB	D	9 6	10300	4 6	35800	39800
	------------ 1984 BOATS										
29 6	HALMATIC 30 MKII	SLP	SA/CR	FBG KL	SD	18D VLVO	9 6	10300	4 6	33100	36800

....For earlier years, see the BUC Used Boat Price Guide, Volume 3

J HAMILTON YACHT CO
ANNAPOLIS MD 21403

See inside cover to adjust price for area

For more recent years, see the BUC Used Boat Price Guide, Volume 1

LOA FT IN	NAME AND/ OR MODEL	TOP/ RIG	BOAT TYPE	-HULL- MTL TP	TP	---ENGINE--- # HP MFG	BEAM FT IN	WGT LBS	DRAFT FT IN	RETAIL LOW	RETAIL HIGH
	------------ 1996 BOATS										
17 5	SIMMONS SEA SKIFF	OP	FSH	L/P SV	OB		5 3	450	5	2600	3050
19 7	GUIDE BOAT	OP	FSH	L/P SV	OB			950	10	5500	6350
	------------ 1995 BOATS										
17 5	SIMMONS SEA SKIFF	OP	FSH	L/P SV	OB		5 3	450	5	2450	2900
	------------ 1994 BOATS										
17 1	SIMMONS SEA SKIFF	OP	FSH	L/P SV	OB		5 3	375	4	1900	2300

HAMMOND BOAT CO
AUSTIN TX 78762

COAST GUARD MFG ID- RRH See inside cover to adjust price for area

LOA FT IN	NAME AND/ OR MODEL	TOP/ RIG	BOAT TYPE	-HULL- MTL TP	TP	---ENGINE--- # HP MFG	BEAM FT IN	WGT LBS	DRAFT FT IN	RETAIL LOW	RETAIL HIGH
	------------ 1984 BOATS										
17	CORDOBA SL V1725	OP	RNBT	FBG DV	IO	120-170	7	2050		3200	3800
17	GRANADA V1750 SPORT	OP	RNBT	FBG DV	IO	120-170	7	2050		3350	3900
17	GRANADA V1750SL	OP	RNBT	FBG DV	IO	120-170	7	2050		3200	3800
17 6	CONTENDER V1850	OP	RNBT	FBG DV	IO	170-185	7 1	2000		3350	3950
19 4	EL-DORADO V1950SL	OP	RNBT	FBG DV	IO	198-260	7 6	2700		4400	5350
19 4	ST-TROPEZ V1940SPORT	OP	RNBT	FBG DV	IO	198-260	7 6	2700		4600	5550
19 4	ST-TROPEZ V1940XL	OP	RNBT	FBG DV	IO	198-260	7 6	2700		4700	5700
21	CHALLENGER 2150BR	OP	RNBT	FBG DV	IO	260	7 7			5800	6650
21	CHALLENGER MII V2150	OP	CUD	FBG DV	IB	260 MRCR	7 7	2700		5950	6850
21	CHALLENGER MII V2150	OP	CUD	FBG DV	IB	260 OMC	7 7	2700		7400	8500

....For earlier years, see the BUC Used Boat Price Guide, Volume 3

HAMPTON YACHTS INC
E HAMPTON NY 11937

See inside cover to adjust price for area

LOA FT IN	NAME AND/ OR MODEL	TOP/ RIG	BOAT TYPE	-HULL- MTL TP	TP	---ENGINE--- # HP MFG	BEAM FT IN	WGT LBS	DRAFT FT IN	RETAIL LOW	RETAIL HIGH
	------------ 1989 BOATS										
38 4	SYMBOL 39		CNV	FBG DV	IB	T270D CUM	14 8	22000	3 3	103500	113500
38 4	SYMBOL 39		CNV	FBG DV	IB	T306D VLVO	14 8	22000	3 3	104000	114000
38 4	SYMBOL 39		CNV	FBG DV	IB	T320D CAT	14 8	22000	3 3	110500	121500
38 4	SYMBOL 39		CR	FBG DV	IB	T270D CUM	14 8	22000	3 3	103000	113000
38 4	SYMBOL 39		CR	FBG DV	IB	T306D VLVO	14 8	22000	3 3	103500	113500
38 4	SYMBOL 39		CR	FBG DV	IB	T320D CAT	14 8	22000	3 3	110000	120500
40 10	SYMBOL 41		CNV	FBG DV	IB	T250D CUM	14 5	25500	3 8	126500	139000
40 10	SYMBOL 41		CNV	FBG DV	IB	T375D CAT	14 5	25500	3 8	144000	158000
40 10	SYMBOL 41		CR	FBG DV	IB	T250D CUM	14 5	25500	3 8	128000	140500
40 10	SYMBOL 41		CR	FBG DV	IB	T375D CAT	14 5	25500	3 8	141500	155500
44 2	SYMBOL 44		CNV	FBG DV	IB	T450D GM	14 9	27000	3 10	157500	173500
44 2	SYMBOL 44		CNV	FBG DV	IB	T450D GM	14 9	27000	3 10	171000	188000
44 2	SYMBOL 44		CR	FBG DV	IB	T375D CAT	14 9	27000	3 10	146000	160500
44 2	SYMBOL 44		CR	FBG DV	IB	T450D GM	14 9	27000	3 10	151000	166000
48 5	SYMBOL 48		YTFS	FBG DV	IB	T375D CAT	15	39600	3 9	169000	186000
48 5	SYMBOL 48		YTFS	FBG DV	IB	T450D J&T	15	39600	3 9	178500	196000
50 4	SYMBOL 51		MY	FBG DV	IB	T450D GM	15	40000	4 10	197000	216500
52 10	SYMBOL 52		YTFS	FBG DV	IB	T375D CAT	16 1	46800	3 9	203500	223500
52 10	SYMBOL 52		YTFS	FBG DV	IB	T450D GM	16 1	46800	3 9	222000	244000
57 7	SYMBOL 57		MY	FBG DV	IB	T485D J&T	17	52000	3 9	265000	291000
57 7	SYMBOL 57		MY	FBG DV	IB	T750D J&T	17	52000	3 9	329000	361500
57 7	SYMBOL 57		YTFS	FBG DV	IB	T485D J&T	17	52000	3 9	271500	298500
57 7	SYMBOL 57		YTFS	FBG DV	IB	T750D J&T	17	52000	3 9	335500	370500
58 8	SYMBOL 59		YTFS	FBG DV	IB	T710D GM	17 1	54000	4	341000	375000

CHARLES HANKINS
LAVALLETTE NJ 08735

COAST GUARD MFG ID- CHS See inside cover to adjust price for area

LOA FT IN	NAME AND/ OR MODEL	TOP/ RIG	BOAT TYPE	-HULL- MTL TP	TP	---ENGINE--- # HP MFG	BEAM FT IN	WGT LBS	DRAFT FT IN	RETAIL LOW	RETAIL HIGH
	------------ 1988 BOATS										
16 3	POWERSURF	OP	UTL	WD RB	OB		5 3	550		2950	3450
16 3	SEA-SKIFF	OP	ROW	WD RB	OB		5 3	350	1	**	**
16 3	SPIRIT RIGGED	GAF	SAIL	WD CB	OB		5 3	450	1 6	2500	2900
18	POWERSURF	OP	UTL	WD RB	OB		6 3	750		4000	4700
18	SEA-SKIFF	OP	ROW	WD RB	OB		6 3		1 3	**	**
18 4	SPIRIT RIGGED	GAF	SAIL	WD CB	OB		6 3	500	1 6	2850	3300
22	SEA-SKIFF CABIN	HT	CBNCR	WD RB	IB	170	8			8400	9650
22	SEA-SKIFF CABIN	HT	CBNCR	WD RB	IB	80D FORD	8	4000	2	11700	13300
22	SEA-SKIFF OPEN	OP	CR	WD	IO	77D YAN	8		2	9550	10800
22	SEA-SKIFF OPEN	OP	CR	WD	IB	80D FORD	8		2	12200	13900
22	SEA-SKIFF OPEN	OP	CR	WD RB	IB	130 VLVO	8			8650	9950
24	SEA-SKIFF CABIN	HT	CBNCR	WD RB	IB	130-225	8 6			10300	11800
24	SEA-SKIFF CABIN	HT	CBNCR	WD RB	IB	90D FORD	8 6	4200	2 1	12900	14700
24	SEA-SKIFF OPEN	OP	CR	WD RB	IB	80D FORD	8 6		2	13700	15500
24	SEA-SKIFF OPEN	OP	CR	WD	IB	130 VLVO	8 6			10900	12400
25 11	SEA-SKIFF CABIN	HT	CBNCR	WD RB	IB	120D LEHM	9 4	5500	2 6	20200	22500
25 11	SEA-SKIFF OPEN	OP	CR	WD	IB	120D LEHM	9 4		2 6	17300	19700
26	SEA-SKIFF CABIN	HT	CBNCR	WD RB	IB	225-270	9 4			14500	16500
26	SEA-SKIFF CABIN	HT	CBNCR	WD RB	IB	135D FORD	9 4			20500	22800
26	SEA-SKIFF OPEN	OP	CR	WD	IB	225	9 4			15800	18000
28	SEA-SKIFF CABIN	HT	CBNCR	WD RB	IB	225-270	9 6			19600	22100
28	SEA-SKIFF CABIN	HT	CBNCR	WD RB	IB	120D LEHM	9 6		2 6	23600	27000
28	SEA-SKIFF OPEN	OP	CR	WD	IB	120D LEHM	9 6		2 6	23600	26200
28	SEA-SKIFF OPEN	OP	CR	WD	IB	270 CHRY	9 6			17500	19900
30	SEA-SKIFF CABIN	HT	CBNCR	WD RB	IB	270 CHRY	10			25600	28500
32	SEA-SKIFF CABIN	HT	CBNCR	WD RB	IB	120D LEHM	10 6			31200	34700
32	SEA-SKIFF CABIN	HT	CBNCR	WD RB	IB	120D-135D	11		2 6	39700	44400
	------------ 1987 BOATS										
16 3	POWERSURF	OP	UTL	WD RB	OB		5 3	550		2900	3350
16 3	SEA-SKIFF	OP	ROW	WD RB	OB		5 3	350	1	**	**
16 3	SPIRIT RIGGED	GAF	SAIL	WD CB	OB		5 3	450	1 6	2350	2700
18	POWERSURF	OP	UTL	WD RB	OB		6 3	750		3900	4550
18	SEA-SKIFF	OP	ROW	WD RB	OB		6 3		1 3	**	**
18 4	SPIRIT RIGGED	GAF	SAIL	WD CB	OB		6 3	500	1 6	2700	3100
22	SEA-SKIFF CABIN	HT	CBNCR	WD RB	IB	170	8			8000	9200
22	SEA-SKIFF CABIN	HT	CBNCR	WD RB	IB	80D FORD	8	4000	2	11300	12800
22	SEA-SKIFF OPEN	OP	CR	WD	IO	185 MRCR	8		2	6850	7900
22	SEA-SKIFF OPEN	OP	CR	WD	IB	80D FORD	8		2	11700	13300
22	SEA-SKIFF OPEN	OP	CR	WD	IB	170	8			8300	9550
24	SEA-SKIFF CABIN	HT	CBNCR	WD RB	IB	170-225	8 6			9900	11300
24	SEA-SKIFF CABIN	HT	CBNCR	WD RB	IB	90D FORD	8 6	4200	2 1	12400	14200
24	SEA-SKIFF OPEN	OP	CR	WD RB	IB	80D FORD	8 6		2	13100	14900
24	SEA-SKIFF OPEN	OP	CR	WD	IB	170	8 6			10500	11900
25 11	SEA-SKIFF CABIN	HT	CBNCR	WD RB	IB	120D LEHM	9 4	5500	2 6	19400	21500
25 11	SEA-SKIFF OPEN	OP	CR	WD	IB	120D LEHM	9 4		2 6	16600	18800
26	SEA-SKIFF CABIN	HT	CBNCR	WD RB	IB	225 MRCR	9 4			13500	15700
26	SEA-SKIFF CABIN	HT	CBNCR	WD RB	IB	135D FORD	9 4			20100	22300
26	SEA-SKIFF OPEN	OP	CR	WD	IB	225	9 4			13800	15700
28	SEA-SKIFF OPEN	OP	CR	WD	IB	225	9 6			15100	17100
28	SEA-SKIFF CABIN	HT	CBNCR	WD RB	IB	225	9 6			18600	20700
28	SEA-SKIFF CABIN	HT	CBNCR	WD RB	IB	120D-135D	9 6		2 6	22600	25800
28	SEA-SKIFF OPEN	OP	CR	WD	IB	120D LEHM	9 6		2 6	22500	25000
28	SEA-SKIFF OPEN	OP	CR	WD	IB	225	9 6			16400	18600
30	SEA-SKIFF CABIN	HT	CBNCR	WD RB	IB	225	10			24100	26800
32	SEA-SKIFF CABIN	HT	CBNCR	WD RB	IB	120D LEHM	10			29900	33200
32	SEA-SKIFF CABIN	HT	CBNCR	WD RB	IB	225	10			30000	33300
32	SEA-SKIFF CABIN	HT	CBNCR	WD RB	IB	120D-135D	11		2 6	38000	42400
	------------ 1986 BOATS										
16 3	SEA-SKIFF	OP	ROW	WD RB	OB		5 3	350	1	**	**
16 3	SPIRIT RIGGED	GAF	SAIL	WD RB	OB		5 3	450	1 6	2200	2600
18	SPIRIT RIGGED	OP	ROW	WD RB	OB		6 3		1 3	**	**
18 4	SPIRIT RIGGED	GAF	SAIL	WD CB	OB		6 3	500	1 6	2500	2950
22	SEA-SKIFF CABIN	HT	CBNCR	WD RB	IB	80D FORD	8	4000	2	10800	12300

LOA FT	LOA IN	NAME AND/ OR MODEL	TOP/ RIG	BOAT TYPE	-HULL- MTL	-HULL- TP	ENGINE TP	ENGINE # HP	ENGINE MFG	BEAM FT	BEAM IN	WGT LBS	DRAFT FT	DRAFT IN	RETAIL LOW	RETAIL HIGH
		1986 BOATS														
22		SEA-SKIFF OPEN	OP	CR	WD		IO	185	MRCR	8			2		6500	7500
22		SEA-SKIFF OPEN	OP	CR	WD		IB	80D	FORD	8			2		11300	12800
24		SEA-SKIFF CABIN	HT	CBNCR	WD	RB	IB	230	MRCR	8		4200	2	1	9500	10800
24		SEA-SKIFF CABIN	HT	CBNCR	WD	RB	IB	80D	FORD	8		4200	2	1	11800	13500
24		SEA-SKIFF OPEN	OP	CR	WD		IB	80D	FORD	8	6		2		12700	14400
25	11	SEA-SKIFF CABIN	HT	CBNCR	WD	RB	IB	120D	LEHM	9	4	5500	2	6	18500	20600
25	11	SEA-SKIFF OPEN	OP	CR	WD		IB	120D	LEHM	9	4		2	6	15900	18000
28		SEA-SKIFF CABIN	HT	CBNCR	WD	RB	IB	120D	LEHM	9	6		2	6	22100	24500
28		SEA-SKIFF OPEN	OP	CR	WD		IB	120D	LEHM	9	6		2	6	22000	24500
30		SEA-SKIFF CABIN	HT	CBNCR	WD	RB	IB	120D	LEHM	10			2	6	28600	31800
32		SEA-SKIFF CABIN	HT	CBNCR	WD	RB	IB	120D	LEHM	11			2	6	36400	40400
		1985 BOATS														
16	3	SEA-SKIFF	OP	ROW	WD	RB	OB			5	3	350	1		**	**
16	3	SPIRIT RIGGED	GAF	SAIL	WD	CB	OB			5	3	450	1	6	2050	2450
18		SEA-SKIFF	OP	ROW	WD	RB	OB			6	3		1	3	**	**
18	4	SPIRIT RIGGED	GAF	SAIL	WD	CB	OB			6	3	500	1	6	2350	2750
22		SEA-SKIFF CABIN	HT	CBNCR	WD	RB	IB	170		8					7300	8350
22		SEA-SKIFF CABIN	HT	CBNCR	WD	RB	IB	80D	FORD	8		4000	2		10300	11800
22		SEA-SKIFF OPEN	OP	CR	WD		IO	185	MRCR	8			2		6250	7200
22		SEA-SKIFF OPEN	OP	CR	WD		IB	80D	FORD	8			2		10800	12300
22		SEA-SKIFF OPEN	OP	CR	WD	RB	IB	170		8					7550	8700
24		SEA-SKIFF CABIN	HT	CBNCR	WD	RB	IB	170-230		8	6				9100	10400
24		SEA-SKIFF CABIN	HT	CBNCR	WD	RB	IB	80D	FORD	8		4200	2	1	11400	12900
24		SEA-SKIFF OPEN	OP	CR	WD		IB	80D	FORD	8	6		2		12200	13800
24		SEA-SKIFF OPEN	OP	CR	WD	RB	IB	170		8	6				9650	11000
25	11	SEA-SKIFF CABIN	HT	CBNCR	WD	RB	IB	120D	LEHM	9	4	5500	2	6	17400	19700
25	11	SEA-SKIFF OPEN	OP	CR	WD		IB	120D	LEHM	9	4		2	6	15200	17300
26		SEA-SKIFF CABIN	HT	CBNCR	WD	RB	IB	225		9	4				12600	14400
26		SEA-SKIFF OPEN	OP	CR	WD	RB	IB	225		9	4				13700	15600
28		SEA-SKIFF CABIN	HT	CBNCR	WD	RB	IB	225		9	6				16600	18800
28		SEA-SKIFF CABIN	HT	CBNCR	WD	RB	IB	120D	LEHM	9	6		2	6	21200	23500
28		SEA-SKIFF OPEN	OP	CR	WD		IB	120D	LEHM	9	6		2	6	21100	23400
28		SEA-SKIFF OPEN	OP	CR	WD	RB	IB	225		9	6				14900	16900
30		SEA-SKIFF CABIN	HT	CBNCR	WD	RB	IB	225		10					22400	24900
30		SEA-SKIFF CABIN	HT	CBNCR	WD	RB	IB	120D	LEHM	10			2	6	27400	30400
32		SEA-SKIFF CABIN	HT	CBNCR	WD	RB	IB	225		10	6				27300	30300
32		SEA-SKIFF CABIN	HT	CBNCR	WD	RB	IB	120D	LEHM	11			2	6	34800	38700
		1984 BOATS														
16	3	SEA-SKIFF	OP	ROW	WD	RB	OB			5	3	350	1		**	**
16	3	SPIRIT RIGGED	GAF	SAIL	WD	CB	OB			5	3	450	1	6	1900	2300
18		SEA-SKIFF	OP	ROW	WD	RB	OB			6	3		1	3	**	**
18	4	SPIRIT RIGGED	GAF	SAIL	WD	CB	OB			6	3	500	1	6	2250	2650
22		SEA-SKIFF CABIN	HT	CBNCR	WD	RB	IB	80D	FORD	8		4000	2		10000	11400
22		SEA-SKIFF OPEN	OP	CR	WD		IO	185	MRCR	8			2		6000	6900
22		SEA-SKIFF OPEN	OP	CR	WD		IB	80D	FORD	8			2		10400	11800
24		SEA-SKIFF CABIN	HT	CBNCR	WD	RB	IB	225	MRCR	8		4200	2	1	8550	9850
24		SEA-SKIFF CABIN	HT	CBNCR	WD	RB	IB	80D	FORD	8		4200	2	1	11000	12500
24		SEA-SKIFF OPEN	OP	CR	WD		IB	80D	FORD	8	6		2		11700	13300
25	11	SEA-SKIFF CABIN	HT	CBNCR	WD	RB	IB	120D	LEHM	9	4	5500	2	6	16700	18900
25	11	SEA-SKIFF OPEN	OP	CR	WD		IB	120D	LEHM	9	4		2	6	14600	16600
28		SEA-SKIFF CABIN	HT	CBNCR	WD	RB	IB	120D	LEHM	9	6		2	6	20300	22600
28		SEA-SKIFF OPEN	OP	CR	WD		IB	120D	LEHM	9	6		2	6	20200	22500
30		SEA-SKIFF CABIN	HT	CBNCR	WD	RB	IB	120D	LEHM	10			2	6	26300	29200
32		SEA-SKIFF CABIN	HT	CBNCR	WD	RB	IB	120D	LEHM	11			2	6	33400	37100

....For earlier years, see the BUC Used Boat Price Guide, Volume 3

HARBOR CRAFT

DIV OF HOLIDAY RAMBLER CORP
NAPPANEE IN 46550 COAST GUARD MFG ID- HHD

See inside cover to adjust price for area

LOA FT	LOA IN	NAME AND/ OR MODEL	TOP/ RIG	BOAT TYPE	-HULL- MTL	-HULL- TP	ENGINE TP	ENGINE # HP	ENGINE MFG	BEAM FT	BEAM IN	WGT LBS	DRAFT FT	DRAFT IN	RETAIL LOW	RETAIL HIGH
		1987 BOATS														
17		HC 170		RNBT	FBG	TR	OB			7		1240	1	2	2450	2850
17	6	HC 180		RNBT	FBG	DV	OB			7		1260			2500	2900
18	7	HC 18		CTRCN	FBG	DV	OB			8		2250			3700	4250
20	2	HC 2000		RNBT	FBG	TR	IO	170		7	10	2050	1	3	4200	4900
20	2	HC 2001		RNBT	FBG	TR	IO	260		7	10	2050	1	3	4550	5250
20	2	HC 200C		CUD	FBG	DV	IO	140		7	7	1960	1	3	4150	4850
20	6	HC 210		CUD	FBG	DV	OB			8		2450			4750	5450
22		HC 220		CTRCN	FBG	DV	OB			8		2650			5550	6350
26	8	HC 250		SF	FBG	DV	IO	140		8		2900	1	3	9250	10500
27	10	HC 270		SF	FBG	DV	IO	140		8		3100	1	3	10700	12200
		1986 BOATS														
17	1	HARBOR-CRAFT 170		RNBT	FBG	TR	OB			7		1240			2400	2750
17	1	HARBOR-CRAFT 170		RNBT	FBG	TR	IO	140		7		1270			2350	2750
17	6	HARBOR-CRAFT 180		RNBT	FBG	SV	OB			7		1260			2400	2800
17	6	HARBOR-CRAFT 180		RNBT	FBG	SV	IO	140		7		1600			2600	3050
20	2	HARBOR-CRAFT 2000		RNBT	FBG	TR	IO	170		7	10	2050			4000	4650
20	2	HARBOR-CRAFT 2001		RNBT	FBG	TR	IO	260		7	10	2050			4250	4950
20	2	HARBOR-CRAFT 200C		CR	FBG	SV	IO	140		7	7	1960			4000	4650
22		HARBOR-CRAFT 18		CTRCN	FBG	SV	OB			8		2250			4750	5450
22		HARBOR-CRAFT 220		CTRCN	FBG	SV	OB			8		2650			5350	6150
26	8	HARBOR-CRAFT 250		SF	FBG	SV	IO	140		8		2900			8800	10000
27	10	HARBOR-CRAFT 270		SF	FBG	SV	IO	140		8		3100			10300	11700
		1985 BOATS														
17	6	HC V-180	ST	RNBT	FBG	SV	OB			7		1260	1	3	2350	2750
17	6	HC V-180	ST	RNBT	FBG	SV	SE	115	OMC	7		1600	1	3	2800	3250
17	6	HC V-180	ST	RNBT	FBG	SV	IO	120-185		7		1600	1	3	2700	3150
17	6	HC V-1800	ST	RNBT	FBG	SV	SE	115	OMC	7		1600	1	3	2800	3250
17	6	HC V-1800	ST	RNBT	FBG	SV	IO	120-185		7		1600	1	3	2700	3150
20	2	HC 200	ST	CUD	FBG	DV	SE	115	OMC	7	10	2050	1	3	3850	4500
20	2	HC 200	ST	CUD	FBG	DV	IO	120-260		7	10	2050	1	3	4150	4900
26	6	HC 250	ST	FSH	FBG	DV	SE	115	OMC	8		2900	1	3	9100	10400
26	6	HC 250	ST	FSH	FBG	DV	IO	165-195		8		2900	1	3	8350	9950
26	6	HC 250	ST	FSH	FBG	DV	SE	205	OMC	8		2900	1	3	9100	10400
26	6	HC 250	ST	FSH	FBG	DV	IO	230-260		8		2900	1	3	8900	10500
26	6	HC 250	ST	FSH	FBG	DV	SE	T115-T205		8		2900	1	3	9100	10400
27	10	HC 270	ST	FSH	FBG	DV	IO	260		8		3100	1	4	11200	12700
27	10	HC 270	ST	FSH	FBG	DV	SE	T115-T205		8		3100	1	4	11600	13200

....For earlier years, see the BUC Used Boat Price Guide, Volume 3

HARBOR MASTER BOATS

DIV OF E M G INC
GALLATIN TN 37066 COAST GUARD MFG ID- EVX
FORMERLY BOATING CORP OF AMERICA

See inside cover to adjust price for area

For more recent years, see the BUC Used Boat Price Guide, Volume 1

LOA FT	LOA IN	NAME AND/ OR MODEL	TOP/ RIG	BOAT TYPE	-HULL- MTL	-HULL- TP	ENGINE TP	ENGINE # HP	ENGINE MFG	BEAM FT	BEAM IN	WGT LBS	DRAFT FT	DRAFT IN	RETAIL LOW	RETAIL HIGH
		1996 BOATS														
40	2	HARBOR-MASTER 400	FB	HB	FBG	DV	VD	T270	CRUS	12		20000	2	6	94800	104000
40	2	HARBOR-MASTER 400	FB	HB	FBG	DV	VD	T350	CRUS	12		20000	2	6	96700	106500
40	2	HARBOR-MASTER 400	FB	HB	FBG	DV	VD	T350	MRCR	12		20000	2	6	95800	105000
44	3	STOLKRAFT	HT	HB	FBG	TM	JT	T420D	CUM	15	6	25000	2		218000	239500
45		HARBOR-MASTER 450	FB	HB	FBG	DV	VD	T350	CRUS	14		24000	3	2	119500	131500
45		HARBOR-MASTER 450	FB	HB	FBG	DV	VD	T400	CRUS	14		24000	3	2	121500	133500
46		HARBOR-MASTER 460WB	FB	HB	FBG	SV	IB	T270	CRUS	14		19500	2	4	70000	77000
46		HARBOR-MASTER 460WB	FB	HB	FBG	SV	VD	T350	CRUS	14		19500	2	4	72000	79100
46		HARBOR-MASTER 460WB	FB	HB	FBG	SV	VD	T400	CRUS	14		19500	2	4	74100	81500
51	11	HARBOR-MASTER 520	FB	HB	FBG	DV	VD	T350	CRUS	14		30000	2	6	156500	172000
51	11	HARBOR-MASTER 520	FB	HB	FBG	DV	VD	T400	CRUS	14		30000	2	6	158500	174000
51	11	HARBOR-MASTER 520	FB	HB	FBG	DV	VD	T315D	CUM	14		30000	2	6	176000	193500
52		HARBOR-MASTER 520WB	FB	HB	FBG	SV	VD	T270	CRUS	14		25000	2	4	117000	128500
52		HARBOR-MASTER 520WB	FB	HB	FBG	SV	VD	T350	CRUS	14		25000	2	4	119000	131000
52		HARBOR-MASTER 520WB	FB	HB	FBG	SV	VD	T400	CRUS	14		25000	2	4	121500	133500
		1995 BOATS														
40	2	HARBOR-MASTER 400	FB	HB	FBG	DV	VD	T225		12		20000	2	6	87600	96300
		VD T270 CRUS 88600 97300, VD T350 CRUS 90400 99300, VD T350 MRCR 89500 98400														
45		HARBOR-MASTER 450	FB	HB	FBG	DV	VD	T350	CRUS	14		24000	3	2	111500	122500
45		HARBOR-MASTER 450	FB	HB	FBG	DV	VD	T400	CRUS	14		24000	3	2	113500	125000
46		HARBOR-MASTER 460WB	FB	HB	FBG	SV	VD	T220	CRUS	14		19500	2	4	65100	71500
		IB T270 CRUS 65500 72000, VD T270 CRUS 65500 72000, VD T350 CRUS 67300 73900														
		VD T400 CRUS 69300 76200														
51	11	HARBOR-MASTER 520	FB	HB	FBG	DV	VD	T350	CRUS	14		30000	2	6	146000	160500
		VD T400 CRUS 148000 163000, VD T300D 164000 180500, VD T315D CUM 164500 181000														
52		HARBOR-MASTER 520WB	FB	HB	FBG	SV	VD	T270	CRUS	14		25000	2	4	110500	121500
		IB T350 CRUS 102000 112000, VD T350 CRUS 112500 123500, VD T400 CRUS 114500 126000														
		1994 BOATS														
34		MARINETTE 34	FB	CNV	AL	DV	IB	T229-T270		12	10	13500	2	8	65100	71700
34		MARINETTE 34	FB	DCMY	AL	DV	IB	T229-T270		12	10	13500	2	8	65400	72100

LOA FT	IN	NAME AND/ OR MODEL	TOP/ RIG	BOAT TYPE	-HULL- MTL	TP	TP	ENGINE # HP	MFG	BEAM FT	IN	WGT LBS	DRAFT FT	IN	RETAIL LOW	RETAIL HIGH
		1994 BOATS														
40	2	HARBOR-MASTER 400	FB	HB	FBG	DV	VD	T270	CRUS	12		20000	2	6	83300	91500
		VD T350 CRUS 85000 93400, VD T350 VLVO 85000 93400, VD T225D VLVO													93800	103000
41		MARINETTE 41	FB	CNV	AL	DV	IB	T330	VLVO	14		17000	3		84900	93300
41		MARINETTE 41	FB	CNV	AL	DV	IB	T350	CRUS	14		17000	3		86300	94800
41		MARINETTE 41	FB	CNV	AL	DV	IB	T350	CRUS	14		16000	3		83200	91400
41		MARINETTE 41	FB	DCMY	AL	DV	IB	T330	VLVO	14		18000	3		88600	97300
		IB T350 CRUS 89800 98700, IB T350 CRUS 83300 91600, IB T400 CRUS													93100	102500
44		MARINETTE 44	FB	DCMY	AL	DV	IB	T415D	CAT	14		22000	3		131500	144500
45		HARBOR-MASTER 450	FB	HB	FBG	DV	VD	T350	CRUS	14		24000	3	2	105000	115500
45		HARBOR-MASTER 450	FB	HB	FBG	DV	VD	T400	CRUS	14		24000	3	2	107000	117500
46		HARBOR-MASTER 460WB	FB	HB	FBG	SV	VD	T220	CRUS	14		19500	2	4	61200	67300
		IB T270 CRUS 61600 67700, VD T270 CRUS 61600 67700, VD T350 CRUS													63300	69600
		VD T400 CRUS 65200 71600														
51	11	HARBOR-MASTER 520	FB	HB	FBG	DV	VD	T350	CRUS	14		30000	2	6	126500	139000
		VD T400 CRUS 128500 141000, VD T300D CUM 141500 155500, VD T300D VLVO													140000	154000
52		HARBOR-MASTER 520WB	HT	HB	FBG	SV	VD	T270	CRUS	14		25000	2	4	105000	115000
52		HARBOR-MASTER 520WB	FB	HB	FBG	SV	IB	T350	CRUS	14		24000	2	4	96900	106500
52		HARBOR-MASTER 520WB	FB	HB	FBG	SV	VD	T350	CRUS	14		25000	2	4	106500	117000
52		HARBOR-MASTER 520WB	FB	HB	FBG	SV	VD	T400	CRUS	14		25000	2	4	109000	119500
		1993 BOATS														
34		MARINETTE 34	FB	CNV	AL	DV	IB	T229-T270		12	10	13500	2	8	61700	68000
34		MARINETTE 34	FB	DCMY	AL	DV	IB	T229-T270		12	10	13500	2	8	61900	68200
40	2	HARBOR-MASTER 400	FB	HB	FBG	DV	VD	T270	CRUS	12		20000	2	6	63100	69300
		VD T350 CRUS 64400 70700, VD T350 VLVO 64300 70700, VD T225D VLVO													71100	78100
41		MARINETTE 41	FB	CNV	AL	DV	IB	T330	VLVO	14		17000	3		80900	88900
41		MARINETTE 41	FB	CNV	AL	DV	IB	T350	CRUS	14		17000	3		82200	90300
41		MARINETTE 41	FB	CNV	AL	DV	IB	T350	CRUS	14		16000	3		79300	87100
41		MARINETTE 41	FB	DCMY	AL	DV	IB	T330	VLVO	14		18000	3		84400	92700
		IB T350 CRUS 85500 94000, IB T350 CRUS 79400 87200, IB T400 CRUS													88600	97400
45		HARBOR-MASTER 450	FB	HB	FBG	DV	VD	T350	CRUS	14		24000	3	2	86500	95100
45		HARBOR-MASTER 450	FB	HB	FBG	DV	VD	T400	CRUS	14		24000	3	2	88100	96800
46		HARBOR-MASTER 460WB	FB	HB	FBG	SV	VD	T220	CRUS	14		19500	2	4	58000	63700
		IB T270 CRUS 58300 64100, VD T270 CRUS 58300 64100, VD T350 CRUS													59900	65900
		VD T400 CRUS 61700 67800														
51	11	HARBOR-MASTER 520	FB	HB	FBG	DV	VD	T350	CRUS	14		30000	2	6	120000	131500
		VD T400 CRUS 121500 133500, VD T300D CUM 134000 147500, VD T300D VLVO													132500	146000
52		HARBOR-MASTER 520WB	HT	HB	FBG	SV	VD	T270	CRUS	14		25000	2	4	99900	110000
52		HARBOR-MASTER 520WB	FB	HB	FBG	SV	IB	T350	CRUS	14		24000	2	4	92400	101500
52		HARBOR-MASTER 520WB	FB	HB	FBG	SV	VD	T350	CRUS	14		25000	2	4	101500	112000
52		HARBOR-MASTER 520WB	FB	HB	FBG	SV	VD	T400	CRUS	14		25000	2	4	104000	114000
		1992 BOATS														
34		MARINETTE 34	FB	CNV	AL	DV	IB	T229-T235		12	10	13500	2	8	59000	65100
34		MARINETTE 34	FB	DC	AL	DV	IB	T229-T235		12	10	13500	2	8	56200	61800
40	2	HARBOR-MASTER 400	FB	HB	FBG	SV	VD	T270	CRUS	12		20000	2	6	60100	66000
		VD T350 CRUS 61300 67400, VD T350 VLVO 61300 67300, VD T225D VLVO													67700	74400
41		MARINETTE 41	FB	CNV	AL	DV	IB	T330	VLVO	14		17000	3		77100	84700
41		MARINETTE 41	FB	CNV	AL	DV	IB	T350	CRUS	14		17000	3		78300	86100
41		MARINETTE 41	FB	CNV	AL	DV	IB	T355	CRUS	14		17000	3		78600	86400
41		MARINETTE 41	FB	HB	AL	DV	IB	T330	VLVO	14		18000	3		58300	64100
41		MARINETTE 41	FB	HB	AL	DV	IB	T350	CRUS	14		18000	3		58900	64700
41		MARINETTE 41	FB	HB	AL	DV	IB	T400	CRUS	14		18000	3		61100	67200
45		HARBOR-MASTER 450	FB	HB	FBG	SV	VD	T350	CRUS	14		24000	3	2	82400	90600
45		HARBOR-MASTER 450	FB	HB	FBG	SV	VD	T400	CRUS	14		24000	3	2	83900	92200
45		HARBOR-MASTER 450	FB	HB	FBG	SV	VD	T300D	CUM	14		24000	3	2	94100	103500
46		HARBOR-MASTER WB460	HT	HB	FBG	SV	VD	T220	CRUS	14		17000	2	4	36800	40900
		VD T270 CRUS 37100 41300, VD T350 CRUS 38900 43200, VD T400 CRUS													40500	45000
46		HARBOR-MASTER WB460	FB	HB	FBG	SV	VD	T220	CRUS	14		17000	2	4	36800	40900
		VD T270 CRUS 37100 41300, VD T350 CRUS 38800 43200, VD T400 CRUS													40500	45100
51	11	HARBOR-MASTER 520	FB	HB	FBG	SV	VD	T350	CRUS	14		30000	2	6	114000	125500
51	11	HARBOR-MASTER 520	FB	HB	FBG	SV	VD	T400	CRUS	14		30000	2	6	115500	127000
51	11	HARBOR-MASTER 520	FB	HB	FBG	SV	VD	T300D	CUM	14		30000	2	6	128000	140500
52		HARBOR-MASTER WB520	HT	HB	FBG	SV	VD	T270	CRUS	14		25000	2	4	95600	105000
52		HARBOR-MASTER WB520	HT	HB	FBG	SV	VD	T350	CRUS	14		25000	2	4	97400	107000
52		HARBOR-MASTER WB520	HT	HB	FBG	SV	VD	T400	CRUS	14		25000	2	4	99400	109000
52		HARBOR-MASTER WB520	FB	HB	FBG	SV	VD	T270	CRUS	14		25000	2	4	95600	105000
52		HARBOR-MASTER WB520	FB	HB	FBG	SV	VD	T350	CRUS	14		25000	2	4	97400	107000
52		HARBOR-MASTER WB520	FB	HB	FBG	SV	VD	T400	CRUS	14		25000	2	4	99400	109000
		1991 BOATS														
40	2	HARBOR-MASTER 400	FB	HB	FBG	SV	VD	T270	CRUS	12		20000	2	6	57500	63200
		VD T270 VLVO 57500 63200, VD T350 CRUS 58700 64500, VD T350 VLVO													58700	64500
43		HARBOR-MASTER 430	HT	HB	FBG	SV	VD	T220	CRUS	13	6	17000	2	4	42500	47200
43		HARBOR-MASTER 430	HT	HB	FBG	SV	VD	T270	CRUS	13	6	17000	2	4	43000	47800
43		HARBOR-MASTER 430	HT	HB	FBG	SV	VD	T350	CRUS	13	6	17000	2	4	44800	49800
43		HARBOR-MASTER 430	FB	HB	FBG	SV	VD	T220	CRUS	13	6	17000	2	4	42600	47300
43		HARBOR-MASTER 430	FB	HB	FBG	SV	VD	T270	CRUS	13	6	17000	2	4	43200	48000
43		HARBOR-MASTER 430	FB	HB	FBG	SV	VD	T350	CRUS	13	6	17000	2	4	45500	50100
45		HARBOR-MASTER 450	FB	HB	FBG	SV	VD	T350	CRUS	14		24000	3	2	79000	86800
45		HARBOR-MASTER 450	FB	HB	FBG	SV	VD	T400	CRUS	14		24000	3	2	80400	88400
45		HARBOR-MASTER 450	FB	HB	FBG	SV	VD	T300D	CUM	14		24000	3	2	90100	99000
47		HARBOR-MASTER 470	HT	HB	FBG	SV	VD	T220	CRUS	14		19500	2	4	51200	56300
		VD T270 CRUS 51500 56600, VD T350 CRUS 53100 58300, VD T400 CRUS													54400	59700
47		HARBOR-MASTER 470	FB	HB	FBG	SV	VD	T220	CRUS	14		19500	2	4	51200	56300
		VD T270 CRUS 51500 56600, VD T350 CRUS 53100 58300, VD T400 CRUS													54300	59700
51	11	HARBOR-MASTER 520	FB	HB	FBG	SV	VD	T350	CRUS	14		30000	2	6	109500	120000
51	11	HARBOR-MASTER 520	FB	HB	FBG	SV	VD	T400	CRUS	14		30000	2	6	111000	122000
51	11	HARBOR-MASTER 520	FB	HB	FBG	SV	VD	T300D	CUM	14		30000	2	6	122500	134500
52		HARBOR-MASTER WB520	HT	HB	FBG	SV	VD	T270	CRUS	14		25000	2	4	91900	101000
52		HARBOR-MASTER WB520	HT	HB	FBG	SV	VD	T350	CRUS	14		25000	2	4	93600	103000
52		HARBOR-MASTER WB520	HT	HB	FBG	SV	VD	T400	CRUS	14		25000	2	4	95500	105000
52		HARBOR-MASTER WB520	FB	HB	FBG	SV	VD	T270	CRUS	14		25000	2	4	91900	101000
52		HARBOR-MASTER WB520	FB	HB	FBG	SV	VD	T350	CRUS	14		25000	2	4	93600	103000
52		HARBOR-MASTER WB520	FB	HB	FBG	SV	VD	T400	CRUS	14		25000	2	4	95500	105000
		1990 BOATS														
43		HARBOR-MASTER 430	HT	HB	FBG	SV	VD	T220	CRUS	13	8	17000	2	2	40900	45400
43		HARBOR-MASTER 430	HT	HB	FBG	SV	VD	T270	CRUS	13	8	17000	2	2	41300	45900
43		HARBOR-MASTER 430	HT	HB	FBG	SV	VD	T350	CRUS	13	8	17000	2	2	43100	47900
43		HARBOR-MASTER 430	FB	HB	FBG	SV	VD	T220	CRUS	13	8	17000	2	2	41000	45500
43		HARBOR-MASTER 430	FB	HB	FBG	SV	VD	T270	CRUS	13	8	17000	2	2	41500	46100
43		HARBOR-MASTER 430	FB	HB	FBG	SV	VD	T350	CRUS	13	8	17000	2	2	43200	48000
45		HARBOR-MASTER MY 450	FB	HB	FBG	DV	VD	T350	CRUS	14		25000	3	2	82200	90400
45		HARBOR-MASTER MY 450	FB	HB	FBG	DV	VD	T400	CRUS	14		25000	3	2	83600	91900
45		HARBOR-MASTER MY 450	FB	HB	FBG	DV	VD	T300D	CUM	14		25000	3	2	93300	102500
47		HARBOR-MASTER 470	FB	HB	FBG	SV	VD	T220	CRUS	14		19500	2	2	49700	54600
		VD T270 CRUS 50100 55000, VD T350 CRUS 51000 56100, VD T400 CRUS													52600	57800
52		HARBOR-MASTER MY 520	FB	HB	FBG	DV	VD	T350	CRUS	14		30000	2	6	121000	133000
52		HARBOR-MASTER MY 520	FB	HB	FBG	DV	VD	T400	CRUS	14		30000	2	6	123000	135000
52		HARBOR-MASTER MY 520	FB	HB	FBG	DV	VD	T300D	CUM	14		32500	2	6	149000	164000
52		HARBOR-MASTER WB 520	FB	HB	FBG	SV	VD	T270	CRUS	14		25000	2	2	88600	97400
52		HARBOR-MASTER WB 520	FB	HB	FBG	SV	VD	T350	CRUS	14		25000	2	2	90300	99200
52		HARBOR-MASTER WB 520	FB	HB	FBG	SV	VD	T400	CRUS	14		25000	2	2	92100	101000
		1989 BOATS														
37	2	HARBOR-MASTER 375	HT	HB	FBG	SV	VD	T220	CRUS	12		15000	2	4	38700	43000
37	2	HARBOR-MASTER 375	HT	HB	FBG	SV	VD	T270	CRUS	12		15000	2	4	39000	43300
37	2	HARBOR-MASTER 375	HT	HB	FBG	SV	VD	T350	CRUS	12		15000	2	4	40700	45200
37	2	HARBOR-MASTER 375	FB	HB	FBG	SV	VD	T220	CRUS	12		15500	2	4	42200	46900
37	2	HARBOR-MASTER 375	FB	HB	FBG	SV	VD	T270	CRUS	12		15500	2	4	42500	47200
37	2	HARBOR-MASTER 375	FB	HB	FBG	SV	VD	T350	CRUS	12		15500	2	4	44200	49100
43		HARBOR-MASTER 430	HT	HB	FBG	SV	VD	T220	CRUS	13	6	17000	2	4	39500	43800
43		HARBOR-MASTER 430	HT	HB	FBG	SV	VD	T270	CRUS	13	6	17000	2	4	39800	44200
43		HARBOR-MASTER 430	HT	HB	FBG	SV	VD	T350	CRUS	13	6	17000	2	4	41400	46000
43		HARBOR-MASTER 430	FB	HB	FBG	SV	VD	T220	CRUS	13	6	17500	2	4	43000	47800
43		HARBOR-MASTER 430	FB	HB	FBG	SV	VD	T270	CRUS	13	6	17500	2	4	43300	48100
43		HARBOR-MASTER 430	FB	HB	FBG	SV	VD	T350	CRUS	13	6	17500	2	4	44800	49800
45		COASTAL 450	FB	HB	FBG	DV	VD	T350	CRUS	14		25000	3	2	84000	92300
47		HARBOR-MASTER 470	HT	HB	FBG	SV	VD	T220	CRUS	14		19000	2	4	44000	48900
47		HARBOR-MASTER 470	HT	HB	FBG	SV	VD	T270	CRUS	14		19000	2	4	44400	49300
47		HARBOR-MASTER 470	HT	HB	FBG	SV	VD	T350	CRUS	14		19000	2	7	46300	50900
47		HARBOR-MASTER 470	FB	HB	FBG	SV	VD	T220	CRUS	14		19500	2	4	48000	52800
47		HARBOR-MASTER 470	FB	HB	FBG	SV	VD	T270	CRUS	14		19500	2	4	48300	53100
47		HARBOR-MASTER 470	FB	HB	FBG	SV	VD	T350	CRUS	14		19500	2	7	49700	54600
52		COASTAL 520	FB	HB	FBG	DV	VD	T350	CRUS	13	11	30000	2	7	117500	129000
52		COASTAL 520 EXEC	FB	HB	FBG	DV	VD	T350	CRUS	13	11	32500	2	7	136000	149000
52		HARBOR-MASTER 520	HT	HB	FBG	SV	VD	T220	CRUS	14		25000	2	4	85400	93900
52		HARBOR-MASTER 520	HT	HB	FBG	SV	VD	T270	CRUS	14		25000	2	4	85800	94200
52		HARBOR-MASTER 520	HT	HB	FBG	SV	VD	T350	CRUS	14		25000	2	4	87300	96000
52		HARBOR-MASTER 520	FB	HB	FBG	SV	VD	T220	CRUS	14		25000	2	4	85400	93900
		VD T270 CRUS 85800 94200, VD T350 CRUS 87300 96000, VD T300D VLVO													94800	104000

 CONTINUED ON NEXT PAGE

HARBOR MASTER BOATS   -CONTINUED   See inside cover to adjust price for area

LOA FT IN	NAME AND/ OR MODEL	TOP/ RIG	BOAT TYPE	HULL MTL TP TP	ENGINE # HP MFG	BEAM FT IN	WGT LBS	DRAFT FT IN	RETAIL LOW	RETAIL HIGH
—— 1988 BOATS ——										
37 2	HARBOR-MASTER 375	HT	HB	FBG SV VD	T220 CRUS	12	15000	2 4	37500	41600
37 2	HARBOR-MASTER 375	HT	HB	FBG SV VD	T270 CRUS	12	15000	2 4	37800	42000
37 2	HARBOR-MASTER 375	HT	HB	FBG SV VD	T350 CRUS	12	15000	2 4	39400	43700
37 2	HARBOR-MASTER 375	FB	HB	FBG SV VD	T220 CRUS	12	15500	2 4	40900	45500
37 2	HARBOR-MASTER 375	FB	HB	FBG SV VD	T270 CRUS	12	15500	2 4	41200	45800
37 2	HARBOR-MASTER 375	FB	HB	FBG SV VD	T350 CRUS	12	15500	2 4	42700	47400
43	HARBOR-MASTER 430	HT	HB	FBG SV VD	T220 CRUS	13 6	17000	2 4	38200	42500
43	HARBOR-MASTER 430	HT	HB	FBG SV VD	T270 CRUS	13 6	17000	2 4	38500	42800
43	HARBOR-MASTER 430	HT	HB	FBG SV VD	T350 CRUS	13 6	17000	2 4	39900	44400
43	HARBOR-MASTER 430	FB	HB	FBG SV VD	270 CRUS	13 6	17500	2 4	39900	44300
43	HARBOR-MASTER 430	FB	HB	FBG SV VD	T220 CRUS	13 6	17500	2 4	41600	46300
47	HARBOR-MASTER 470	HT	HB	FBG SV VD	T220 CRUS	14	19000	2 4	42600	47400
47	HARBOR-MASTER 470	HT	HB	FBG SV VD	T270 CRUS	14	19000	2 4	42900	47700
47	HARBOR-MASTER 470	HT	HB	FBG SV VD	T350 CRUS	14	19000		44300	49200
47	HARBOR-MASTER 470	FB	HB	FBG SV VD	T220 CRUS	14	19500	2 4	46500	51100
47	HARBOR-MASTER 470	FB	HB	FBG SV VD	T270 CRUS	14	19500	2 4	46800	51400
47	HARBOR-MASTER 470	FB	HB	FBG SV VD	T350 CRUS	14	19500		48200	52900
51 11	COASTAL 520	FB	HB	FBG DV VD	T350 CRUS	13 11	30000	2 6	98400	108000
51 11	COASTAL 520	FB	HB	FBG DV VD	T270D CUM	13 11	30000	2 6	109000	120000
52	COASTAL 520 EXECUTIV	FB	HB	FBG DV VD	T350 CRUS	13 11	32500	3	131500	145000
52	COASTAL 520 EXECUTIV	FB	HB	FBG DV VD	T270D CUM	13 11	32500	3	139000	152500
52	HARBOR-MASTER 520	HT	HB	FBG SV VD	T220 CRUS	14	25000	2 4	82900	91100
52	HARBOR-MASTER 520	HT	HB	FBG SV VD	T270 CRUS	14	25000	2 4	83200	91400
52	HARBOR-MASTER 520	HT	HB	FBG SV VD	T350 CRUS	14	25000	2 4	84700	93100
52	HARBOR-MASTER 520	FB	HB	FBG SV VD	T220 CRUS	14	25000	2 4	82900	91100
52	HARBOR-MASTER 520	FB	HB	FBG SV VD	T270 CRUS	14	25000	2 4	83200	91400
52	HARBOR-MASTER 520	FB	HB	FBG SV VD	T350 CRUS	14	25000	2 4	84700	93100
—— 1987 BOATS ——										
37 2	HARBOR-MASTER 375	HT	HB	FBG SV VD	T220 CRUS	12	15000	2 4	36400	40400
37 2	HARBOR-MASTER 375	HT	HB	FBG SV VD	T270 CRUS	12	15000	2 4	36700	40800
37 2	HARBOR-MASTER 375	HT	HB	FBG SV VD	T350 CRUS	12	15000	2 4	38100	42300
37 2	HARBOR-MASTER 375	FB	HB	FBG SV VD	T220 CRUS	12	15000	2 4	36400	40400
37 2	HARBOR-MASTER 375	FB	HB	FBG SV VD	T270 CRUS	12	15000	2 4	36700	40800
37 2	HARBOR-MASTER 375	FB	HB	FBG SV VD	T350 CRUS	12	15000	2 4	38100	42300
47	HARBOR-MASTER 470	HT	HB	FBG SV VD	T220 CRUS	14	16000	2 6	23100	25600
47	HARBOR-MASTER 470	HT	HB	FBG SV VD	T270 CRUS	14	16000	2 6	23200	25800
47	HARBOR-MASTER 470	HT	HB	FBG SV VD	T350 CRUS	14	16000	2 6	24800	27600
47	HARBOR-MASTER 470	FB	HB	FBG SV VD	T220 CRUS	14	16000	2 6	22700	25200
47	HARBOR-MASTER 470	FB	HB	FBG SV VD	T270 CRUS	14	16000	2 6	23800	26400
47	HARBOR-MASTER 470	FB	HB	FBG SV VD	T350 CRUS	14	16000	2 6	24800	27600
51 11	COASTAL 520	FB	HB	FBG DV VD	T350 CRUS	13 11	30000	2 6	95600	105000
51 11	COASTAL 520	FB	HB	FBG DV VD	T270D CUM	13 11	32000	3	118500	130500
52	COASTAL 520	FB	HB	FBG DV VD	T350 CRUS	13 11	30000	3	114000	125500
52	COASTAL 520	FB	HB	FBG DV VD	T270D CUM	13 11	32500	3	135500	148500
52	HARBOR-MASTER 520	HT	HB	FBG SV VD	T220 CRUS	14	25000	2 4	80600	88600
52	HARBOR-MASTER 520	HT	HB	FBG SV VD	T270 CRUS	14	25000	2 4	80900	89000
52	HARBOR-MASTER 520	HT	HB	FBG SV VD	T350 CRUS	14	25000	2 4	82400	90600
52	HARBOR-MASTER 520	FB	HB	FBG SV VD	T220 CRUS	14	25000	2 4	80600	88600
52	HARBOR-MASTER 520	FB	HB	FBG SV VD	T270 CRUS	14	25000	2 4	80900	89000
52	HARBOR-MASTER 520	FB	HB	FBG SV VD	T350 CRUS	14	25000	2 4	82400	90600

—————————— 1986 BOATS ——————————

```
37  2 HARBOR-MASTER 375   HT HB   FBG SV VD  200  VLVO         15000   2      34000  37700
    IO  260 VLVO 34500 38400,  IO  290 VLVO 35100 39000,  IO 165D VLVO 37100 41200
    VD T200 VLVO 36100 40100,  IO T200 VLVO 37200 41300,  IO T290 VLVO 38300 42500
    VD T158D VLVO 40600 45100,  IO T165D VLVO 40800 45300

37  2 HARBOR-MASTER 375   FB HB   FBG SV VD  200  VLVO         15000   2   4   34000  37700
    IO  260 VLVO 34500 38400,  IO  290 VLVO 35100 39000,  IO 165D VLVO 37100 41200
    IO T200 VLVO 36100 40100,  VD T260 CRUS 35400 39400,  IO T260 VLVO 37200 41300
    VD T270 CRUS 35700 39700,  IO T290 VLVO 38300 42500,  VD T350 CRUS 37100 41200
    VD T158D VLVO 40600 45100,  IO T165D VLVO 40800 45300

37  3 HARBOR-MASTER 375   HT HB   FBG SV VD  T220 CRUS  12     12000   2   4   17300  19600
37  3 HARBOR-MASTER 375   HT HB   FBG SV VD  T270 CRUS  12     12000   2   4   18500  20500
37  3 HARBOR-MASTER 375   HT HB   FBG SV VD  T350 CRUS  12     12000   2   4   19800  22100
47    HARBOR-MASTER 470   HT HB   FBG SV VD  260  VLVO  14     19500   2      42600  47300
    IO  290 VLVO 43100 47900,  IO 165D VLVO 46200 50700,  IO T200 VLVO 44100 49000
    VD T220 CRUS 22000 24500,  IO T260 VLVO 45700 50200,  VD T270 CRUS 22400 24800
    IO T290 VLVO 46800 51400,  VD T350 CRUS 23500 26100,  VD T158D VLVO 49700 54600
    IO T165D VLVO 49800 54800

47    HARBOR-MASTER 470   FB HB   FBG SV IO  260  VLVO  14     19500   2   4   42600  47300
    IO  290 VLVO 43100 47900,  IO 165D VLVO 46200 50700,  IO T200 VLVO 44100 49000
    VD T220 CRUS 43500 48400,  IO T260 VLVO 45700 50200,  VD T270 CRUS 43800 48600
    IO T290 VLVO 46800 51400,  VD T350 CRUS 45500 50100,  VD T158D VLVO 49700 54600
    IO T165D VLVO 49900 54800

52    COASTAL 520         FB HB   FBG DV VD  T200 VLVO  14     30000   3   4  106000 117000
52    COASTAL 520         FB HB   FBG DV VD  T350 CRUS  14     30000   3   4  108000 118500
52    HARBOR-MASTER 520   HT HB   FBG SV VD  T200 VLVO  14     25000   2      79300  87200
    VD T220 CRUS 56400 62000,  IO T260 VLVO 80600 88500,  VD T270 CRUS 56700 62400
    IO T290 VLVO 81800 89900,  VD T350 CRUS 58200 63900,  VD T158D VLVO 83100 91300
    IO T165D VLVO 83200 91500

52    HARBOR-MASTER 520   FB HB   FBG SV IO  T200 VLVO  14     25000   2   4   79300  87200
    VD T220 CRUS 78600 86400,  IO T260 VLVO 80600 88500,  VD T270 CRUS 78900 86700
    IO T290 VLVO 81800 89900,  VD T350 CRUS 80400 88300,  VD T158D VLVO 83100 91300
    IO T165D VLVO 83200 91500
```

—————————— 1985 BOATS ——————————

```
37  2 HARBOR-MASTER 375   HT HB   FBG SV IO  200  VLVO  12     15000   2   4   33200  36800
    IO  260 VLVO 33700 37400,  IO  290 VLVO 34200 38000,  IO 165D VLVO 36200 40300
    IO T200 VLVO 35200 39100,  VD T220 CRUS 34600 38400,  IO T260 VLVO 36300 40300
    VD T270 CRUS 34900 38700,  IO T290 VLVO 37300 41500,  VD T350 CRUS 36200 40200
    VD T158D VLVO 39700 44100,  IO T165D VLVO 39800 44200

37  2 HARBOR-MASTER 375   FB HB   FBG SV IO  200  VLVO  12     15000   2   4   33200  36800
    IO  260 VLVO 33700 37400,  IO  290 VLVO 34200 38000,  IO 165D VLVO 36200 40300
    IO T200 VLVO 35200 39100,  VD T220 CRUS 34600 38400,  IO T260 VLVO 36300 40300
    VD T270 CRUS 34900 38700,  IO T290 VLVO 37300 41500,  VD T350 CRUS 36100 40200
    VD T158D VLVO 39700 44100,  IO T165D VLVO 39800 44200

47    HARBOR-MASTER 470   HT HB   FBG SV IO  260  VLVO  14     19500   2   4   41600  46200
    IO  290 VLVO 42100 46800,  IO 165D VLVO 44600 49500,  IO T200 VLVO 43100 47800
    VD T220 CRUS 42500 47200,  IO T260 VLVO 44100 49000,  VD T270 CRUS 42700 47500
    IO T290 VLVO 45700 50200,  VD T350 CRUS 44000 48900,  VD T158D VLVO 48500 53300
    IO T165D VLVO 48700 53500

47    HARBOR-MASTER 470   FB HB   FBG SV IO  260  VLVO  14     19500   2   4   41600  46200
    IO  290 VLVO 42100 46800,  IO 165D VLVO 44600 49500,  IO T200 VLVO 43100 47800
    VD T220 CRUS 42500 47200,  IO T260 VLVO 44100 49000,  VD T270 CRUS 42700 47500
    IO T290 VLVO 45700 50200,  VD T350 CRUS 44000 48900,  VD T158D VLVO 48500 53300
    IO T165D VLVO 48700 53500

52    HARBOR-MASTER 520   HT HB   FBG SV IO  T200 VLVO  14     25000   2   4   77500  85200
    VD T220 CRUS 76800 84400,  IO T260 VLVO 78700 86500,  VD T270 CRUS 77100 84700
    IO T290 VLVO 79900 87800,  VD T350 CRUS 78500 86300,  VD T158D VLVO 81200 89200
    IO T165D VLVO 81400 89400

52    HARBOR-MASTER 520   FB HB   FBG SV IO  T200 VLVO  14     25000   2   4   77500  85200
    VD T220 CRUS 76800 84400,  IO T260 VLVO 78700 86500,  VD T270 CRUS 77100 84700
    IO T290 VLVO 79900 87800,  VD T350 CRUS 78500 86300,  VD T158D VLVO 81200 89200
    IO T165D VLVO 81400 89400
```

—————————— 1984 BOATS ——————————

```
34    HARBOR-MASTER 3400        CR  FBG DV IB  T270        13   16000          28800  32000
37  2 HARBOR-MASTER 375   HT HB     FBG SV IO  200         12                  30900  34300
    IO  200 VLVO 32400 36000,  IO  260 VLVO 33000 36600,  IO  290 VLVO 33500 37200
    IO 130D VLVO 35100 39000,  IO T200 VLVO 34400 38200,  IB T220 39600 44000
    VD T220 CRUS 33800 37600,  IO T260 VLVO 35500 39400,  VD T270 CRUS 34100 37900
    IO T290 VLVO 36500 40600,  VD T350 CRUS 35300 39300,  VD T124D VLVO 38100 42400
    IO T130D VLVO 38200 42500

37  2 HARBOR-MASTER 375   FB HB     FBG SV IO  200         12     15000   2   4   32400  36000
    IO  260 VLVO 33000 36600,  IO  290 VLVO 33500 37200,  IO 130D VLVO 35100 39000
    IO T200 VLVO 34400 38200,  VD T220 CRUS 33800 37600,  IO T260 VLVO 35500 39400
    VD T270 CRUS 34100 37900,  IO T290 VLVO 36500 40600,  VD T350 CRUS 35300 39300
    VD T124D VLVO 38100 42400,  IO T130D VLVO 38200 42500

47    HARBOR-MASTER 470   HT HB     FBG SV IO  260  VLVO  14     19500   2   4   40700  45200
    IO  290 VLVO 41200 45800,  IO 130D VLVO 43300 48100,  IO T200 VLVO 39900 44300
    IO  200 VLVO 42100 46800,  IB T220 39600 44000,  VD T220 CRUS 41500 46200
    IO T260 VLVO 42600 48000,  VD T270 CRUS 41800 46400,  IO T290 VLVO 43000 49100
    VD T350 CRUS 43000 47800,  IO T130D VLVO 46900 51500

47    HARBOR-MASTER 470   FB HB     FBG SV IO  260  VLVO  14     19500   2   4   40700  45200
    IO  290 VLVO 41200 45800,  IO 130D VLVO 43300 48100,  IO T200 VLVO 42100 46800
    VD T220 CRUS 41500 46200,  IO T260 VLVO 42600 48000,  VD T270 CRUS 41800 46400
    IO T290 VLVO 44200 49100,  VD T350 CRUS 43000 47800,  VD T124D VLVO 46800 51400
    IO T130D VLVO 46900 51500

52    HARBOR-MASTER 520   HT HB     FBG SV IO  T200 VLVO  14     25000   2   4   75900  83400
    IB T220 89100 97900,  VD T220 CRUS 75200 82600,  IO T260 90400 99400
```

LOA FT IN	NAME AND/ OR MODEL	TOP/ RIG	BOAT TYPE	-HULL- MTL TP TP	----ENGINE--- # HP MFG	BEAM FT IN	WGT LBS	DRAFT FT IN	RETAIL LOW	RETAIL HIGH

---- 1984 BOATS ----

52	HARBOR-MASTER 520	HT	HB	FBG SV IO	T260 VLVO	14	25000	2 4	77100	84700
	VD T270 CRUS 75500	83000, IO T290 VLVO		78300	86000, VD T350			CRUS	76900	84500
	VD T124D VLVO 78800	86600, IO T130D VLVO		78900	86700					

52	HARBOR-MASTER 520	FB	HB	FBG SV IO	T200 VLVO	14	25000	2 4	75900	83400
	VD T220 CRUS 75200	82600, IO T260	VLVO	77100	84700, VD T270			CRUS	75500	83000
	IO T290 VLVO 78300	86000, VD T350 CRUS		76900	84500, VD T124D VLVO				78800	86600
	IO T130D VLVO 78900	86700								

....For earlier years, see the BUC Used Boat Price Guide, Volume 3

HARLEY BOAT COMPANY
FIBERFLOAT CORPORATION
BARTOW FL 33830   COAST GUARD MFG ID- HDH   See inside cover to adjust price for area

LOA FT IN	NAME AND/ OR MODEL	TOP/ RIG	BOAT TYPE	-HULL- MTL TP TP	----ENGINE--- # HP MFG	BEAM FT IN	WGT LBS	DRAFT FT IN	RETAIL LOW	RETAIL HIGH

---- 1993 BOATS ----

26 7	MINI CUDDY 27		CUD	KEV DV OB		8 4	1800	2	4850	5550
26 7	RAISED CUDDY 27		CUD	KEV DV OB		8 4	2300	2	4850	5600
41 10	SUPERSTAR 42		SF	KEV DV IB	T400D	10 4	15000	2 6	115000	126500
50	SUPERSTAR 50		SF	KEV DV IB	T400D	14	25000	3	198000	217500
54 10	FLYBRIDGE 54	FB	SF	KEV DV IB	T735D	14	40000	3 3	318000	349500
54 10	SUPERSTAR 54		SF	KEV DV IB	T735D	14	32000	3	301500	331000
63 6	FLYBRIDGE 63	FB	SF	KEV DV IB	T10CD	18	54000	3 3	491000	539500
63 6	SPORTYACHT 63	FB	SF	KEV DV IB	T10CD	18	46000	3	426000	468000
70	MOTOR YACHT 70	FB	MY	KEV DV IB	T14CD	18	60000	3 4	673500	740000
70	SPORTYACHT 70	FB	SPTCR	KEV DV IB	T14CD	18	53000	3	677000	744000

---- 1992 BOATS ----

26 7	MINI CUDDY 27		CTRCN	KEV DV OB		8 4	1800	2	4450	5100
26 7	RAISED CUDDY 27		SF	KEV DV OB		8 4	2300	2	4550	5200
41 10	SUPERSTAR 42		SF	KEV DV IB	T400D	10 4	15000	2 6	109500	120000
48	SUPERSTAR 48		SF	KEV DV IB	T400D	14	25000	3	178000	195500
54 10	FLYBRIDGE 54	FB	SF	KEV DV IB	T735D	14	40000	3 3	304000	334000
54 10	SUPERSTAR 54		SF	KEV DV IB	T735D	14	32000	3	288000	316500
63 6	FLYBRIDGE 63	FB	SF	KEV DV IB	T10CD	18	54000	3 3	469500	516000
63 6	SPORTYACHT 63	FB	SF	KEV DV IB	T10CD	18	46000	3	406000	446000
70	MOTOR YACHT 70	FB	MY	KEV DV IB	T14CD	18	60000	3 4	643500	707000
70	SPORTYACHT 70	FB	SPTCR	KEV DV IB	T14CD	18	53000	3	647000	711000

---- 1987 BOATS ----

17 11	FREEDOM 18	OP	RNBT	KEV SV IO	170 OMC	6 11	1400		2500	2900
26 7	MINICUDDY	OP	CTRCN	KEV SV OB		8 5	1800	1	3750	4350
26 7	MINICUDDY	OP	CTRCN	KEV SV SE	225 OMC	8 5	2200	1 1	3800	4400
26 7	MINICUDDY	OP	CTRCN	KEV SV IO	260	8 5	2650	1 1	8650	9950
26 7	MINICUDDY	OP	CTRCN	KEV SV SE	T140-T225	8 5	2600	1 1	3850	4500
26 7	OPEN FISHERMAN	OP	CTRCN	KEV SV OB		8 5	1800		3750	4350
26 7	OPEN FISHERMAN	OP	CTRCN	KEV SV SE	225 OMC	8 5	2200	1	3800	4400
26 7	OPEN FISHERMAN	OP	CTRCN	KEV SV IO	260	8 5	2850	1 4	8850	10100
26 7	OPEN FISHERMAN	OP	CTRCN	KEV SV SE	T225 OMC	8 4	2700	1 1	3900	4500
26 7	RAISED CUDDY	ST	CUD	KEV SV OB		8 4	2300	1 1	3800	4450
26 7	RAISED CUDDY	ST	CUD	KEV SV SE	225 OMC	8 4	2650	1 2	3850	4450
26 7	RAISED CUDDY	ST	CUD	KEV SV IO	260	8 4	3150	1 4	8450	9700

26 7	RAISED CUDDY	ST	CUD	KEV SV SE	T140-T225	8 4	2900	1 4	3900	4600
34	HARLEY 34 SUPERSTAR	ST	SF	KEV DV IB	T260-T400	10 2	7000		28900	35300
34	HARLEY 34 SUPERSTAR	ST	SF	KEV DV IBT330D-T370D		10 2	8000		39000	45200
38		ST	RACE	KEV DV IB	T330 PCM	10 4	6000		56900	62600
38		ST	RACE	KEV DV IB	T370 PCM	10 4	6000		61300	67400
41 10	SUPERSTAR	ST	SF	KEV OB		10 4	10000		**	**
41 10	SUPERSTAR	ST	SF	KEV DV IB	T330 PCM	10 4	10000		55900	61400
42	SUPERSTAR	ST	SF	KEV DV IB	T400 PCM	10 4	10000		58900	64800
	IB T330D	71200	78300, IB T370D CAT		76700	84300, IB T375D CAT			79900	87800

63	SUPERSTAR		YTFS	KEV DV IB	T450D	10 4	12000		83600	91900
63	SUPERSTAR		YTFS	KEV DV IB	T750D	16 2	30000		264000	290000
63	SUPERSTAR		YTFS	KEV DV IB	T11CD	16 2	34000		304000	334000

---- 1986 BOATS ----

26 7	HARLEY 27		CUD	KEV DV OB		8 4	2300		3700	4350
26 7	HARLEY 27		SF	KEV DV OB		8 4	1800		3650	4200
34	SUPERSTAR		SF	KEV DV IB	T330	10	6500		28700	31900
38	SUPERSPORT		SF	KEV DV IB	T330	8	6000		47500	52200
42	SUPERSTAR		SF	KEV DV IB	T330	10 4	9000		52100	57200
42	SUPERSTAR		SF	KEV DV IB	T350D	10 4	10000		68300	75100

---- 1985 BOATS ----

17 11	FREEDOM 18	OP	RNBT	KEV SV IO	170 OMC	6 11	1400		2250	2650
26 7	MINICUDDY	OP	CTRCN	KEV SV OB		8 5	1800	1	3550	4100
26 7	MINICUDDY	OP	CTRCN	KEV SV SE	205 OMC	8 5	2200	1 1	3600	4200
26 7	MINICUDDY	OP	CTRCN	KEV SV IO	260	8 5	2650	1 1	7900	9050
26 7	MINICUDDY	OP	CTRCN	KEV SV SE	T115-T205	8 5	2600	1 1	3650	4250
26 7	OPEN FISHERMAN	OP	CTRCN	KEV SV OB		8 5	1800		3550	4100
26 7	OPEN FISHERMAN	OP	CTRCN	KEV SV SE	205 OMC	8 5	2200	1	3600	4200
26 7	OPEN FISHERMAN	OP	CTRCN	KEV SV IO	260	8 5	2850	1 4	8000	9200
26 7	OPEN FISHERMAN	OP	CTRCN	KEV SV SE	T205	8 4	2700	1 1	3650	4250
26 7	RAISED CUDDY	ST	CUD	KEV SV OB		8 4	2300	1 1	3650	4250
26 7	RAISED CUDDY	ST	CUD	KEV SV SE	205 OMC	8 4	2650	1 2	3700	4300
26 7	RAISED CUDDY	ST	CUD	KEV SV IO	260	8 4	3150	1 4	7700	8850

26 7	RAISED CUDDY	ST	CUD	KEV SV SE	T115-T205	8 4	2900	1 4	3700	4350
41 10	SUPERSTAR	ST	SF	KEV		10 4	5000		**	**
41 10	SUPERSTAR	ST	SF	KEV IB	T525	10 4	10000		59100	65000
41 10	SUPERSTAR	ST	SF	KEV IB	T400D	10 4	10000		68700	75400
41 10	SUPERSTAR	ST	SF	KEV DV IB	T330 PCM	10 4	10000		54600	60000
42	SUPERSTAR	ST	SF	KEV DV IB	T400 PCM	10 4	9500		53700	59000
42	SUPERSTAR	ST	SF	KEV DV IB	T330D	10 4	9500		63000	69200
42	SUPERSTAR	ST	SF	KEV DV IB	T355D CAT	10 4	9500		66900	73600
54	SUPERSTAR		YTFS	KEV IB	T485D				136500	150000
54	SUPERSTAR		YTFS	KEV IB	T565D				141500	155500
54	SUPERSTAR		YTFS	KEV IB	T710D				150500	165000

---- 1984 BOATS ----

17 11	FREEDOM 18	OP	RNBT	KEV SV IO	170 OMC	6 11	1350		2150	2500
26 7	MINICUDDY			KEV SV OB					2900	3350
26 7	MINICUDDY	OP	CTRCN	KEV SV SE	205 OMC	8 5	1750	1	3450	4000
26 7	MINICUDDY	OP	CTRCN	KEV SV SE	205 OMC	8 5	2200	1	3450	4100
26 7	MINICUDDY	OP	CTRCN	KEV SV IO	260 OMC	8 5	2650	1	7600	8750
26 7	MINICUDDY	OP	CTRCN	KEV SV IO	165D VLVO	8 5	2850	1 1	8450	9700
26 7	MINICUDDY	OP	CTRCN	KEV SV SE	T115-T205	8 5	2600	1 1	3550	4150
26 7	OPEN FISHERMAN			KEV SV OB					2900	3350
26 7	OPEN FISHERMAN	OP	CTRCN	KEV SV SE	205 OMC	8 5	1700	1	3450	4000
26 7	OPEN FISHERMAN	OP	CTRCN	KEV SV SE	205 OMC	8 5	2200	1	3500	4100
26 7	OPEN FISHERMAN	OP	CTRCN	KEV SV IO	260 OMC	8 5	2650	1	7600	8700
26 7	OPEN FISHERMAN	OP	CTRCN	KEV SV IO	165D VLVO	8 5	2850		8450	9700

26 7	OPEN FISHERMAN	OP	CTRCN	KEV SV SE	T205 OMC	8 4	2700	1 1	3600	4150
26 7	RAISED CUDDY			KEV SV OB					4200	4900
26 7	RAISED CUDDY	ST	CUD	KEV SV SE		8 4	2150	1	3550	4100
26 7	RAISED CUDDY	ST	CUD	KEV SV IO	115-205	8 4	2600		3600	4200
26 7	RAISED CUDDY	ST	CUD	KEV SV IO	260	8 4	3150	1 4	7450	8550
26 7	RAISED CUDDY	ST	CUD	KEV SV IO	165D VLVO	8 4	3250	1 4	7100	8150
26 7	RAISED CUDDY	ST	CUD	KEV SV SE	T115 OMC	8 4	2900	1 4	3650	4250
26 7	RAISED CUDDY	ST	CUD	KEV SV IO	T170	8 4	3450	1 4	8350	9600
26 7	RAISED CUDDY	ST	CUD	KEV SV SE	T205 OMC	8 4	3100		3650	4250
26 7	RAISED CUDDY	ST	CUD	KEV SV IO	T165D VLVO	8 4	4350	1 4	11600	13100
41 10	SUPERSTAR	ST	SF	KEV DV OB		10 4	10000		**	**

41 10	SUPERSTAR	ST	SF	KEV DV IB	T330 PCM	10	10000		52300	57500
	IB T400 PCM	51400	56500, IB T425 HARD		52500	57600, IB T500			55200	60700
	IB T550	57600	63300							

42	SUPERSTAR	ST	SF	KEV DV IB	T300D CAT	10 4	9500		59700	65700
42	SUPERSTAR	ST	SF	KEV DV IB	T355D CAT	10 4	9500		64000	70300
42	SUPERSTAR	ST	SF	KEV DV IB	T500D	10 4	9500		73400	80700

....For earlier years, see the BUC Used Boat Price Guide, Volume 3

HARMONIE SHIPYARD INC
MONTREAL PQ CANADA   See inside cover to adjust price for area

LOA FT IN	NAME AND/ OR MODEL	TOP/ RIG	BOAT TYPE	-HULL- MTL TP TP	----ENGINE--- # HP MFG	BEAM FT IN	WGT LBS	DRAFT FT IN	RETAIL LOW	RETAIL HIGH

---- 1984 BOATS ----

| 36 1 | HARMONIE 11M | SLP | SA/RC AL KL IB | | D | 12 2 | 15500 | 5 11 | 47000 | 51700 |
| 42 | HARMONIE 12.8M | SLP | SA/RC AL KL IB | | D | 12 3 | 18500 | 6 | 66000 | 72600 |

....For earlier years, see the BUC Used Boat Price Guide, Volume 3

HARRIS TAYLOR MARINE & IND LTD
PEGASUS YACHTS
SUFFOLK ENGLAND

See inside cover to adjust price for area

FORMERLY RYDGEWAY MARINE LTD

LOA FT IN	NAME AND/ OR MODEL	TOP/ RIG	BOAT TYPE	-HULL- MTL TP	----ENGINE--- TP # HP MFG	BEAM FT IN	WGT LBS	DRAFT FT IN	RETAIL LOW	RETAIL HIGH
			1994 BOATS							
19 3	PEGASUS 600	SLP	SARAC	FBG SK OB	6 10	6 10	2100	4 6	11700	13300
23 1	PANDORA 700	SLP	SARAC	FBG TK OB		6 11	2535	3 9	14900	17000
23 4	PEGASUS 700	SLP	SARAC	FBG WK IB	10D YAN	8 3	2865	3	19600	21700
25 9	PEGASUS 800	SLP	SARAC	FBG WK IB	20D YAN	8 9	4408	3 3	30200	33500
33 10	PEGASUS 1100	SLP	SARAC	FBG WK IB	40D YAN	11 4	8800	4	70800	77800
			1993 BOATS							
23 4	PEGASUS 700	SLP	SARAC	FBG WK IB	9D YAN	8 3	2865	3	18500	20500
25 9	PEGASUS 800	SLP	SARAC	FBG WK IB	18D YAN	8 9	4408	3 3	28200	31300
33 10	PEGASUS 1100	SLP	SARAC	FBG WK IB	28D VLVO	11 4	8270	4	62300	68500

....For earlier years, see the BUC Used Boat Price Guide, Volume 3

HARRISKAYOT
DIV OF HARRISKAYOT INC
FORT WAYNE IN 46808

COAST GUARD MFG ID- KAY
FORMERLY KAYOT

See inside cover to adjust price for area

For more recent years, see the BUC Used Boat Price Guide, Volume 1

LOA FT IN	NAME AND/ OR MODEL	TOP/ RIG	BOAT TYPE	-HULL- MTL TP	----ENGINE--- TP # HP MFG	BEAM FT IN	WGT LBS	DRAFT FT IN	RETAIL LOW	RETAIL HIGH
			1996 BOATS							
18	K-18	OP	RNBT	FBG TR IO	180-185	8	2930		6800	8150
21 6	ULTIMA	OP	RNBT	FBG TR IO	210-250	8	3400		8150	10100
21 6	ULTIMA	OP	RNBT	FBG TR IO	265 VLVO	8	3400		9000	10300
21 6	ULTRADECK	OP	RNBT	FBG TR IO	250 MRCR	8	4020		11100	12700
22 3	ULTRADECK	OP	RNBT	FBG TR IO	190-265	8	4500		12500	14900
23 11	ULTRACAT	OP	RNBT	FBG TR OB		8 6	4010		12900	14600
23 11	ULTRACAT	OP	RNBT	FBG TR IO	235-300	8 6	4900		14900	17500
			1995 BOATS							
18	K-18 DELUXE	OP	RNBT	FBG TR IO	180-185	8	2930		6350	7650
20	K200 LTD	OP	RNBT	FBG TR IO	190-275	7 9	3380		8400	10500
21 6	ULTIMA 2000	OP	RNBT	FBG TR IO	190-300	8	3400		9300	11300
21 6	ULTRADECK	OP	RNBT	FBG TR OB		8	3030		8600	9850
21 6	ULTRADECK	OP	RNBT	FBG TR IO	180-275	8	4020		10100	12600
23 11	ULTRACAT	OP	RNBT	FBG TR OB		8 6	3460		11100	12600
23 11	ULTRACAT	OP	RNBT	FBG TR IO	235-300	8 6	4350		12400	15000
			1994 BOATS							
18	K-18 DELUXE	OP	RNBT	FBG TR OB		8	2230		5200	5950
18	K-18 DELUXE	OP	RNBT	FBG TR IO	160-180	8	2230		5100	5900
18	K-18 STEP ON	OP	RNBT	FBG TR OB		8	2230		5200	5950
20	K200 LTD	OP	RNBT	FBG TR IO	180-255	7 9	2700		6600	7900
21 6	ULTIMA 2000	OP	RNBT	FBG TR IO	190-255	8	2750		7250	8700
21 6	ULTRADECK	OP	RNBT	FBG TR OB		8	2075		6400	7350
21 6	ULTRADECK	OP	RNBT	FBG TR IO	180-255	8	3015		7700	9250
23 11	ULTRACAT	OP	RNBT	FBG TR OB		8 6	3400		10500	11900
23 11	ULTRACAT	OP	RNBT	FBG TR IO	205-300	8 6	4300		11300	13800
			1993 BOATS							
18	K-18 DELUXE	OP	RNBT	FBG TR OB		8	2230		5000	5700
18	K-18 DELUXE	OP	RNBT	FBG TR IO	160-180	8	2230		4400	5500
20	K200 LTD	OP	RNBT	FBG TR OB	MRCR	7 9	2700		**	**
20	K200 LTD	OP	RNBT	FBG TR IO	180-260	7 9	2700		6150	7450
21 6	ULTIMA 2000	OP	RNBT	FBG TR IO	190-260	8	2750		6800	8200
21 6	ULTRADECK	OP	RNBT	FBG TR OB		8	2075		6150	7050
21 6	ULTRADECK	OP	RNBT	FBG TR IO	180-240	8	3015		7200	8500
			1992 BOATS							
18	K-18 DELUXE	OP	RNBT	FBG TR IO	175-205	8	2230		4500	5250
20	K200 LTD	OP	RNBT	FBG TR IO	200-260	7 9	2700		5750	7050
21 6	ULTIMA 2000	OP	RNBT	FBG TR IO	230-285	8	2750		6550	7950
21 6	ULTRADECK	OP	RNBT	FBG TR OB		8	2075		5900	6800
21 6	ULTRADECK	OP	RNBT	FBG TR IO	200-260	8	3015		6750	8150
			1991 BOATS							
18	K-18 DELUXE	OP	RNBT	FBG TR IO	175-205	8	2230		4200	4950
20	LIMITED 200	OP	RNBT	FBG TR IO	205-260	7 9	2700		5450	6600
21 6	ULTIMA 2000	OP	RNBT	FBG TR IO	230-260	8	2750		6150	7200
			1990 BOATS							
18	K-18 DELUXE	OP	RNBT	FBG TR IO	175-205	8	2230		3950	4650
20	LIMITED 200	OP	RNBT	FBG TR IO	205-260	7 9	2700		5150	6200
21 6	ULTIMA 2000	OP	RNBT	FBG TR IO	230-260	8	2750		5750	6800
			1989 BOATS							
18	KAYOT 180 DELUXE	OP	RNBT	FBG TR IO	165-205	8	2230		3700	4400
20	LIMITED 200	OP	RNBT	FBG TR OB		7 9	1400		3600	4200
20	LIMITED 200	OP	RNBT	FBG TR IO	185-260	7 9	2700		4800	5850
21 6	ULTIMA 2000	OP	RNBT	FBG TR IO	230-260	8	2750		5450	6450
			1985 BOATS							
16 7	CRUSADER K 167	OP	RNBT	FBG TR OB	140-190	7 3	1100		2300	2700
16 7	CRUSADER K 167	OP	RNBT	FBG TR OB		7 3	2000		2500	2950
17	REGENCY K 170	OP	RNBT	FBG TR OB		7 9	1250		2550	3000
17	REGENCY K 170	OP	RNBT	FBG TR IO	140-190	7 9	2200		2800	3300
20	CLASSIC K 200	OP	RNBT	FBG DV IO	200 MRCR	7 9	2700		3950	4600
20	CLASSIC K 200	OP	RNBT	FBG TR OB		7 9	1400		3200	3750
20	CLASSIC K 200	OP	RNBT	FBG TR IO	185-260	7 9	2700		3900	4800
20	LIMITED K 200	OP	RNBT	FBG TR IO	260	7 9	2700		4350	5000
			1984 BOATS							
16 7	CRUSADER K 167	OP	RNBT	FBG TR OB	120-188	7 3	1100		2250	2600
16 7	CRUSADER K 167	OP	RNBT	FBG TR OB		7 3	2000		2400	2850
17	REGENCY K 170	OP	RNBT	FBG TR OB		7 9	1250		2500	2900
17	REGENCY K 170	OP	RNBT	FBG TR IO	140-188	7 9	2200		2700	3200
17	REGENCY K 170	OP	RNBT	FBG TR IO	488 MRCR	7 9	2200		6500	7500
20	CLASSIC K 200	OP	RNBT	FBG DV IO	170-198	7 9	2700		3800	4450
20	CLASSIC K 200	OP	RNBT	FBG TR OB		7 9	1400		3150	3650
20	CLASSIC K 200	OP	RNBT	FBG TR IO	185-260	7 9	2700		3800	4550
20	CLASSIC K 200	OP	RNBT	FBG TR IO	488 MRCR	7 9	2700		7850	9000
20	LIMITED K 200	OP	RNBT	FBG TR IO	260	7 9	2700		4150	4800

....For earlier years, see the BUC Used Boat Price Guide, Volume 3

HARSTIL INDUSTRIES INC
FRASER MI 48026

COAST GUARD MFG ID- HRS See inside cover to adjust price for area

LOA FT IN	NAME AND/ OR MODEL	TOP/ RIG	BOAT TYPE	-HULL- MTL TP	----ENGINE--- TP # HP MFG	BEAM FT IN	WGT LBS	DRAFT FT IN	RETAIL LOW	RETAIL HIGH
			1986 BOATS							
31	KAULUA 31	CUT	SA/CR	F/S CT OB		14	6050	1 8	25500	28300
			1985 BOATS							
31	KAULUA 31	CUT	SA/CR	F/S CT OB		14	6050	1 8	24000	26600
			1984 BOATS							
31	KAULUA 31	CUT	SA/CR	F/S CT OB		14	6050	1 8	22500	25000

....For earlier years, see the BUC Used Boat Price Guide, Volume 3

HARTMANN-PALMER YACHTS INC
N MIAMI BEACH FL 33160

See inside cover to adjust price for area

LOA FT IN	NAME AND/ OR MODEL	TOP/ RIG	BOAT TYPE	-HULL- MTL TP	----ENGINE--- TP # HP MFG	BEAM FT IN	WGT LBS	DRAFT FT IN	RETAIL LOW	RETAIL HIGH
			1987 BOATS							
30 6	HP 31 TRAWLER	FB	TRWL	FBG DV IB	115D-135D	11 6	16000	3 6	60400	67000
37 11	HP 38 SUNDECK	FB	MY	FBG DV IB	115D CUM	12 10	22000	3	97200	107000
	IB T135D LEHM 98200 108000, IB T210D CUM 101000 111000, IB T225D LEHM 102000 112000									
	IB T275D LEHM 105000 115000									
38	HP 38	SLP	SA/CR	FBG KC VD	51D PERK	11 10	20600	4 6	63100	69300
40 10	HP 41 CONVERTIBLE	FB	MY	FBG DV IB	T210D CAT	14 5	25500	3 8	120000	132000
40 10	HP 41 CONVERTIBLE	FB	MY	FBG DV IB	T210D CUM	14 5	25500	3 8	116500	128000
40 10	HP 41 CONVERTIBLE	FB	MY	FBG DV IB	T375D CAT	14 5	25500	3 8	135500	149000
40 10	HP 41 SUNDECK	FB	MY	FBG DV IB	T210D CAT	14 5	25500	3 8	120000	132000
40 10	HP 41 SUNDECK	FB	MY	FBG DV IB	T210D CUM	14 5	25500	3 8	116500	128000
40 10	HP 41 SUNDECK	FB	MY	FBG DV IB	T375D CAT	14 5	25500	3 8	135500	149000
44 2	HP 44 SUNDECK MK II	FB	MY	FBG DV IB	T210D CAT	14 9	27000	3 10	144500	159000
	IB T210D CUM 143000 157000, IB T375D CAT 178500 196000, IB T450D GM 190500 209500									
45	HP 45 SUNDECK	FB	MY	FBG DV IB	T210D CUM				134000	147000
	IB T225D VLVO 133500 146500, IB T320D CUM 143500 157500, IB T375D CAT 153500 168500									
46	HP 46	SLP	MS	FBG KL IB	85D PERK	14 3	33000	5 10	106500	117000
48 3	HP 48 SPORTS SEDAN	FB	SDN	FBG DV IB	T255D VLVO	15 6		3 10	162500	178500
48 3	HP 48 SPORTS SEDAN	FB	SDN	FBG DV IB	T320D CUM	15 6		3	168500	185500
48 3	HP 48 SPORTS SEDAN	FB	SDN	FBG DV IB	T375D CAT	15 6		3	176500	194000
48 3	HP 48 YACHTFISH	FB	MY	FBG DV IB	T255D VLVO	15 6	38000	3 6	174500	192000
48 3	HP 48 YACHTFISH	FB	MY	FBG DV IB	T320D CUM	15 6	38000	3	182500	200500
48 3	HP 48 YACHTFISH	FB	MY	FBG DV IB	T375D CAT	15 6	38000	3	192000	211000
50 4	HP 51 CONVERTIBLE	FB	MY	FBG DV IB	T375D CAT	15	40000	4	201000	221000
50 4	HP 51 CONVERTIBLE	FB	MY	FBG DV IB	T375D GM	15	40000	4	216000	237000
50 4	HP 51 MOTORYACHT	FB	MY	FBG DV IB	T375D CAT	15	40000	4	198500	218000
50 4	HP 51 MOTORYACHT	FB	MY	FBG DV IB	T450D GM	15	40000	4	212500	234000
50 4	HP 51 YACHTFISH	FB	YTFS	FBG DV IB	T375D CAT	15	40000	4	197500	217000
50 4	HP 51 YACHTFISH	FB	YTFS	FBG DV IB	T450D GM	15	40000	4	217500	239000

LOA FT	LOA IN	NAME AND/ OR MODEL	TOP/ RIG	BOAT TYPE	-HULL- MTL	-HULL- TP	ENGINE TP	ENGINE # HP	ENGINE MFG	BEAM FT	BEAM IN	WGT LBS	DRAFT FT	DRAFT IN	RETAIL LOW	RETAIL HIGH
		1987 BOATS														
56	1	HP 56	FB	MY	FBG	DV	IB	T450D	J&T	17	1	57350	4	2	318000	349500
56	1	HP 56	FB	MY	FBG	DV	IB	T600D	GM	17	1	57350	4	2	359000	394500
56	1	HP 56ED	FB	MY	FBG	DV	IB	T450D	J&T	17	1	60850	4	2	336000	369500
56	1	HP 56ED	FB	MY	FBG	DV	IB	T600D	GM	17	1	60850	4	2	376000	413000
58	8	HP 59 MOTORYACHT	FB	MY	FBG	DV	IB	T550D	GM	17	1	54000	4		340000	373500
58	8	HP 59 MOTORYACHT	FB	MY	FBG	DV	IB	T710D	GM	17	1	54000	4		385000	423000
58	8	HP 59 YACHTFISH	FB	YTFS	FBG	DV	IB	T550D	GM	17	1	54000	4		347500	381500
58	8	HP 59 YACHTFISH	FB	YTFS	FBG	DV	IB	T710D	GM	17	1	54000	4		393500	432000
60		HP 60	FB	MY	FBG	DV	IB	T350D	GM	17	1	65025	4	6	336000	369000
60		HP 60	FB	MY	FBG	DV	IB	T600D	GM	17	1	65025	4	6	412500	453000
60		HP 60ED	FB	MY	FBG	DV	IB	T350D	GM	17	1	69025	4	6	361000	396500
60		HP 60ED	FB	MY	FBG	DV	IB	T600D	GM	17	1	69025	4	6	435000	478000
60	6	HP 61 YACHTFISH	FB	MY	FBG	DV	IB	T450D	J&T	17	1	61800	4	2	349500	384500
60	6	HP 61 YACHTFISH	FB	MY	FBG	DV	IB	T600D	GM	17	1	61800	4	2	398000	437000
68		HP 68 YACHTFISH	FB	MY	FBG	DV	IB	T600D	GM	17	1	69050	4	6	516500	567500
68		HP 68 YACHTFISH	FB	MY	FBG	DV	IB	T650D	J&T	17	1	69050	4	6	523000	574500
72		HP 72	FB	MY	FBG	DV	IB	T650D	J&T	17	1		5		**	**
75		HP 75	SLP	MS	FBG	KL	IB	D		18	5	59T	13	9	**	**
		1986 BOATS														
38		HP 38	SLP	SA/CR	FBG	KC	VD	51D	PERK	11	10	20600	4	6	59100	65000
46	2	HP 46	SLP	MS	FBG	KL	IB	85D	PERK	14	3	33000	5	10	100000	110000
56	1	HP 56	FB	MY	FBG	DV	IB	T450D	J&T	17	1	57350	4	2	304500	334500
56	1	HP 56	FB	MY	FBG	DV	IB	T600D	GM	17	1	57350	4	2	343500	377500
56	1	HP 56ED	FB	MY	FBG	DV	IB	T450D	J&T	17	1	60850	4	2	321500	353500
56	1	HP 56ED	FB	MY	FBG	DV	IB	T600D	GM	17	1	60850	4	2	359500	395000
60		HP 60	FB	MY	FBG	DV	IB	T350D	GM	17	1	65025	4	6	321500	353000
60		HP 60	FB	MY	FBG	DV	IB	T600D	GM	17	1	65025	4	6	394500	433500
60		HP 60ED	FB	MY	FBG	DV	IB	T350D	GM	17	1	69025	4	6	345500	379500
60		HP 60ED	FB	MY	FBG	DV	IB	T600D	GM	17	1	69025	4	6	416500	457500
60	6	HP 61 YACHTFISH	FB	MY	FBG	DV	IB	T450D	J&T	17	1	61800	4	2	334500	367500
60	6	HP 61 YACHTFISH	FB	MY	FBG	DV	IB	T600D	GM	17	1	61800	4	2	380500	418500
68		HP 68 YACHTFISH	FB	MY	FBG	DV	IB	T600D	GM	17	1	69050	4	6	494500	543500
68		HP 68 YACHTFISH	FB	MY	FBG	DV	IB	T650D	J&T	17	1	69050	4	6	500500	550000
72		HP 72	FB	MY	FBG	DV	IB	T650D	J&T	17	1		5		**	**
75		HP 75	SLP	MS	FBG	KC	IB	T135D	PERK	18	5	59T	6	1	**	**
		1985 BOATS														
46	2	HP 46	SLP	MS	FBG	KL	IB	85D	PERK	14	3	33000	5	10	93900	103000
56	1	HP 56	FB	MY	FBG	DV	IB	T450D	J&T	17	1	57350	4	2	291500	320500
56	1	HP 56	FB	MY	FBG	DV	IB	T600D	J&T	17	1	57350	4	2	329000	361500
60		HP 60	FB	MY	FBG	DV	IB	T398D	GM	17	1	65025	4	6	323000	354500
60		HP 60	FB	MY	FBG	DV	IB	T600D	GM	17	1	65025	4	6	378000	415000
60		HP 60	FB	MY	FBG	DV	IB	T675D		17	1	65025	4	6	391500	430000
61		HP 61		MY	FBG		IB	T600D	GM	17	1	62300	4	6	369000	405500
61		HP 61	FB	MY	FBG	DV	IB	T675D		17	1	61850	4	6	381500	419000
68		HP 68		MY	FBG		IB	T660D	GM	17	1	67800	4	6	479000	526500
		1984 BOATS														
38		HP 38	SLP	SA/CR	FBG	KC	VD	50D	PERK	11	10	20600	4	6	52100	57300
46	2	HP 46	SLP	MS	FBG	KL	IB	85D	PERK	14	3	33000	5	10	88400	97100
56	1	HP 56	FB	MY	FBG	DV	IB	T410D	J&T	17	1	57350	4	2	269000	295500
60		HP 60	FB	MY	FBG	DV	IB	T368D	GM	17	1	65025	4	6	300500	330000
75		HP 75	SLP	MS	FBG	KC	IB	135D	PERK	18	5	59T	6	1	**	**

HATTERAS YACHTS

DIV OF BRUNSWICK CORP
NEW BERN NC 28560 COAST GUARD MFG ID- HAT

See inside cover to adjust price for area

For more recent years, see the BUC Used Boat Price Guide, Volume 1

LOA FT	LOA IN	NAME AND/ OR MODEL	TOP/ RIG	BOAT TYPE	-HULL- MTL	-HULL- TP	ENGINE TP	ENGINE # HP	ENGINE MFG	BEAM FT	BEAM IN	WGT LBS	DRAFT FT	DRAFT IN	RETAIL LOW	RETAIL HIGH
		1996 BOATS														
39		CONVERTIBLE	FB	CNV	FBG	SV	IB	T420D	CAT	13	7	32000	4	8	233500	257000
39		CONVERTIBLE	FB	CNV	FBG	SV	IB	T465D	DD	13	7	32000	4	8	239000	262500
39		SPORT EXPRESS	FB	EXP	FBG	SV	IB	T420D	CAT	13	7	30000	4	8	224500	246500
39		SPORT EXPRESS	FB	EXP	FBG	SV	IB	T465D	DD	13	7	30000	4	8	229500	252500
40	10	MOTOR YACHT	FB	DCMY	FBG	SV	IB	T314D	DD	13	7	38000	4	9	258500	284500
		IB T340D CAT 263500 289500, IB T364D CAT 267000 293500, IB T388D DD 269000 295500														
		IB T417D VLVO 264500 290500														
42	10	COCKPIT MOTOR YACHT	FB	MYCPT	FBG	SV	IB	T364D	CAT	13	7	41000	4	9	295500	324500
42	10	COCKPIT MOTOR YACHT	FB	MYCPT	FBG	SV	IB	T388D	DD	13	7	41000	4	9	298500	328000
42	10	COCKPIT MY SE	FB	MYCPT	FBG	SV	IB	T314D	DD	13	7	41000	4	9	267500	294000
		IB T340D CAT 273500 300500, IB T364D CAT 259500 285000, IB T388D DD 263000 289000														
43	2	CONVERTIBLE	FB	CNV	FBG	SV	IB	T535D	DD	14	3	40000	4	5	296500	326000
43	2	SPORT EXPRESS 43	FB	EXP	FBG	SV	IB	T535D	DD	14	3	38000	4	5	292500	321000
46	10	CONVERTIBLE	FB	CNV	FBG	SV	IB	T720D	DD	15	7	52000	4	6	363500	399500
48	9	MOTOR YACHT	FB	MY	FBG	SV	IB	T720D	DD	16		63000	5	3	397500	436500
48	11	COCKPIT MOTOR YACHT	FB	MYCPT	FBG	SV	IB	T535D	DD	16		59000	5	6	358500	394000
50	10	CONVERTIBLE	FB	CNV	FBG	SV	IB	T720D	DD	16	1	60000	5	3	411000	452000
50	10	CONVERTIBLE	FB	CNV	FBG	SV	IB	T780D	MAN	16	1	60000	5	3	413000	454000
50	10	CONVERTIBLE	FB	CNV	FBG	SV	IB	T870D	DD	16	1	60000	5	3	438000	481500
50	10	SPORT DECK 50	FB	MY	FBG	SV	IB	T535D	DD	16		66000	5	6	386000	424500
52	9	MOTOR YACHT	FB	MY	FBG	SV	IB	T720D	DD	16		66000	5	2	461000	506500
52	11	COCKPIT MOTOR YACHT	FB	MYCPT	FBG	SV	IB	T720D	DD	16		66000	5	2	493500	542500
54	11	CONVERTIBLE	FB	CNV	FBG	SV	IB	T870D	DD	17	4	70000	5	4	557000	612000
		IB T10CD DD 592500 651000, IB T10CD MAN 593500 652500, IB T12CD CAT 624000 686000														
60	9	EXTENDED DECKHOUSE	FB	MYDKH	FBG	SV	IB	T870D	DD	18	2	87000	5	2	663500	729000
65	5	CONVERTIBLE	FB	CNV	FBG	SV	IB	T10CD	DD	18		51T	5	4	814500	895000
65	5	CONVERTIBLE	FB	CNV	FBG	SV	IB	T13CD	DD	18		51T	5	4	884000	971500
65	10	MOTOR YACHT	FB	MY	FBG	SV	IB	T870D	DD	18	2	99000	5	5	802000	881000
67	2	COCKPIT MOTOR YACHT	FB	MYCPT	FBG	SV	IB	T770D	DD	18	2	94000	5	1	743000	816500
67	2	EXT DECKHOUSE CKPT	FB	MYDKH	FBG	SV	IB	T870D	DD	18	2	95000	5	3	768500	844500
67	2	EXT DECKHOUSE CKPT	FB	MYDKH	FBG	SV	IB	T10CD	DD	18	2	95000	5	3	797000	876000
70	10	COCKPIT MOTOR YACHT	FB	MYCPT	FBG	SV	IB	T870D	DD	18	2	52T	5	6	904500	993500
70	10	COCKPIT MOTOR YACHT	FB	MYCPT	FBG	SV	IB	T10CD	DD	18	2	52T	5	6	949500	1.030M
70	10	SPORT DECK MY	FB	MY	FBG	SV	IB	T870D	DD	18	2	52T	5	6	923500	1.005M
70	10	SPORT DECK MY	FB	MY	FBG	SV	IB	T10CD	DD	18	2	52T	5	6	959000	1.045M
70	11	MOTOR YACHT	FB	MY	FBG	SV	IB	T870D	DD	18	2	54T	5	6	939500	1.020M
70	11	MOTOR YACHT	FB	MY	FBG	SV	IB	T10CD	DD	18	2	54T	5	6	969500	1.055M
74		SPORT DECK MY	FB	MY	FBG	SV	IB	T870D	DD	18	2	55T	5	6	**	**
74		SPORT DECK MY	FB	MY	FBG	SV	IB	T10CD	DD	18	2	55T	5	6	**	**
74	4	COCKPIT MY 74	FB	MY	FBG	SV	IB	T10CD	DD	18	2	55T	5	6	**	**
		1995 BOATS														
39		CONVERTIBLE	FB	CNV	FBG	SV	IB	T314D	DD	13	5	32000	4	8	209000	230000
		IB T340D CAT 213500 234500, IB T420D CAT 224500 247000, IB T465D DD 229500 252500														
39		SPORT EXPRESS	FB	EXP	FBG	SV	IB	T314D	DD	13	5	30000	4	8	200000	220000
		IB T340D CAT 204500 224500, IB T420D CAT 215500 237000, IB T465D DD 220500 242500														
40	10	MOTOR YACHT	FB	DCMY	FBG	SV	IB	T314D	DD	13	7	38000	4	9	247500	272000
		IB T340D CAT 252000 277000, IB T364D CAT 255500 280500, IB T388D DD 257500 283000														
		IB T417D VLVO 253000 278000														
42	10	COCKPIT MOTOR YACHT	FB	MYCPT	FBG	SV	IB	T364D	CAT	13	7	41000	4	9	282500	310500
42	10	COCKPIT MOTOR YACHT	FB	MYCPT	FBG	SV	IB	T388D	DD	13	7	41000	4	9	285500	314000
42	10	COCKPIT MOTOR YACHT	FB	MYCPT	FBG	SV	IB	T417D	VLVO	13	7	41000	4	9	267500	294000
42	10	COCKPIT MY SE	FB	MYCPT	FBG	SV	IB	T314D	DD	13	7	41000	4	9	256000	281000
		IB T340D CAT 261500 287500, IB T364D CAT 248000 272500, IB T388D DD 252000 276500														
43	2	CONVERTIBLE	FB	CNV	FBG	SV	IB	T535D	DD	14	3	40000	4	5	282500	310500
46	10	CONVERTIBLE	FB	CNV	FBG	SV	IB	T720D	DD	15	7	52000	4	6	344500	378500
46	10	CONVERTIBLE	FB	CNV	FBG	SV	IB	T780D	MAN	15	7	51000	4	6	333000	366000
48	9	MOTOR YACHT	FB	MY	FBG	SV	IB	T720D	DD	16		63000	5	3	376500	414000
48	11	COCKPIT MOTOR YACHT	FB	MYCPT	FBG	SV	IB	T535D	DD	16		59000	5	6	342500	376500
50	10	CONVERTIBLE	FB	CNV	FBG	SV	IB	T720D	DD	16	1	60000	5	3	390000	428500
50	10	CONVERTIBLE	FB	CNV	FBG	SV	IB	T780D	MAN	16	1	60000	5	3	392000	430500
50	10	CONVERTIBLE	FB	CNV	FBG	SV	IB	T870D	DD	16	1	60000	5	3	415500	456500
52	9	MOTOR YACHT	FB	MY	FBG	SV	IB	T720D	DD	16		66000	5	2	440500	484000
52	11	COCKPIT MOTOR YACHT	FB	MYCPT	FBG	SV	IB	T720D	DD	16		66000	5	2	473000	519500
54	11	CONVERTIBLE	FB	CNV	FBG	SV	IB	T870D	DD	17	4	70000	5	2	533500	586500
		IB T10CD DD 567500 623500, IB T10CD MAN 569000 625000, IB T12CD CAT 598000 657000														
60	9	EXTENDED DECKHOUSE	FB	MYDKH	FBG	SV	IB	T720D	DD	18	2	87000	5	2	603500	663000
60	9	EXTENDED DECKHOUSE	FB	MYDKH	FBG	SV	IB	T870D	DD	18	2	87000	5	2	636000	699000
65	5	CONVERTIBLE	FB	CNV	FBG	SV	IB	T10CD	DD	18		51T	5	4	781000	858000
65	5	CONVERTIBLE	FB	CNV	FBG	SV	IB	T13CD	DD	18		51T	5	4	844500	928000
65	10	MOTOR YACHT	FB	MY	FBG	SV	IB	T870D	DD	18	2	99000	5	5	769000	845000
67	2	COCKPIT MOTOR YACHT	FB	MYCPT	FBG	SV	IB	T770D	DD	18	2	94000	5	1	706500	776500
67	2	EXT DECKHOUSE CKPT	FB	MYDKH	FBG	SV	IB	T870D	DD	18	2	95000	5	3	735000	808000
67	2	EXT DECKHOUSE CKPT	FB	MYDKH	FBG	SV	IB	T10CD	DD	18	2	95000	5	3	759500	834500
70	10	COCKPIT MOTOR YACHT	FB	MYCPT	FBG	SV	IB	T870D	DD	18	2	52T	5	6	867000	953000
70	10	COCKPIT MOTOR YACHT	FB	MYCPT	FBG	SV	IB	T10CD	DD	18	2	52T	5	6	900500	989500
70	10	SPORT DECK MY	FB	MY	FBG	SV	IB	T870D	DD	18	2	52T	5	6	876000	962500
70	10	SPORT DECK MY	FB	MY	FBG	SV	IB	T10CD	DD	18	2	52T	5	6	910000	1.000M
70	11	MOTOR YACHT	FB	MY	FBG	SV	IB	T870D	DD	18	2	54T	5	6	891000	979000
70	11	MOTOR YACHT	FB	MY	FBG	SV	IB	T10CD	DD	18	2	54T	5	6	935000	1.015M
74		PORT DECK MYR YACHT	FB	MY	FBG	SV	IB	T870D	DD	18	2		5	6	**	**
74		PORT DECK MYR YACHT	FB	MY	FBG	SV	IB	T10CD	DD	18	2		5	6	**	**

CONTINUED ON NEXT PAGE

LOA FT	LOA IN	NAME AND/ OR MODEL	TOP/ RIG	BOAT TYPE	-HULL- MTL	-HULL- TP	TP	ENGINE # HP	ENGINE MFG	BEAM FT	BEAM IN	WGT LBS	DRAFT FT	DRAFT IN	RETAIL LOW	RETAIL HIGH
		1994 BOATS														
39		CONVERTIBLE	FB	CNV	FBG	SV	IB	T314D	DD	13	5	28000	4	8	181000	199000
39		CONVERTIBLE	FB	CNV	FBG	SV	IB	T465D	DD	13	5	28000	4	8	200500	220500
40	10	MOTOR YACHT	FB	DCMY	FBG	SV	IB	T314D	DD	13	7	38000	4	9	237000	260500
		IB T340D CAT 241500 265500, IB T363D CAT 244500 268500, IB T388D DD													246500	271000
		IB T417D VLVO 242500 266500														
42	10	COCKPIT MOTOR YACHT	FB	MYCPT	FBG	SV	IB	T314D	DD	13	7	41000	5	1	244000	268000
		IB T340D CAT 249500 274000, IB T363D CAT 253500 278500, IB T388D DD													257000	282500
		IB T417D VLVO 256500 281500														
43	2	CONVERTIBLE	FB	CNV	FBG	SV	IB	T535D	DD	14	3	40000	4	4	269500	296000
46	10	CONVERTIBLE	FB	CNV	FBG	SV	IB	T720D	DD	15	7	51000	4	11	324500	356500
46	10	CONVERTIBLE	FB	CNV	FBG	SV	IB	T780D	MAN	15	7	51000	4	11	316000	347500
48	9	MOTOR YACHT	FB	MY	FBG	SV	IB	T720D	DD	16		63000	5	3	357500	393000
48	11	COCKPIT MOTOR YACHT	FB	MYCPT	FBG	SV	IB	T535D	DD	16		59000	5	3	327500	360000
50	10	CONVERTIBLE	FB	CNV	FBG	SV	IB	T720D	DD	16	1	60000	5	9	370000	407000
50	10	CONVERTIBLE	FB	CNV	FBG	SV	IB	T780D	MAN	16	1	60000	5	9	372500	409500
50	10	CONVERTIBLE	FB	CNV	FBG	SV	IB	T870D	DD	16	1	60000	5	9	394500	433500
52	9	MOTOR YACHT	FB	MY	FBG	SV	IB	T720D	DD	16		66000	5		421500	463500
52	11	COCKPIT MOTOR YACHT	FB	MYCPT	FBG	SV	IB	T720D	DD	16		66000	5		454000	498500
54	9	EXTENDED DECK MY	FB	MYDKH	FBG	SV	IB	T720D	DD	17	6	76000	4	9	494000	543000
54	11	CONVERTIBLE	FB	CNV	FBG	SV	IB	T870D	DD	17	4	70000	5	6	512000	563000
54	11	CONVERTIBLE	FB	CNV	FBG	SV	IB	T10CD	DD	17	4	70000	5	6	537500	590500
60	9	EXTENDED DECKHOUSE	FB	MYDKH	FBG	SV	IB	T720D	DD	18	2	87000	5	2	578000	635000
60	9	EXTENDED DECKHOUSE	FB	MYDKH	FBG	SV	IB	T870D	DD	18	2	87000	5	2	609000	669500
65	5	CONVERTIBLE	FB	CNV	FBG	SV	IB	T10CD	DD	18		51T	5	11	740500	814000
65	5	CONVERTIBLE	FB	CNV	FBG	SV	IB	T13CD	DD	18		51T	5	11	797000	876000
65	10	MOTOR YACHT	FB	MY	FBG	SV	IB	T870D	DD	18	2	99000	5	5	736500	809500
67	2	COCKPIT MOTOR YACHT	FB	MYCPT	FBG	SV	IB	T870D	DD	18	2	94000	5	1	693500	762000
67	2	EXT DECKHOUSE CKPT	FB	MYDKH	FBG	SV	IB	T870D	DD	18	2	95000	5	3	702500	772000
67	2	EXT DECKHOUSE CKPT	FB	MYDKH	FBG	SV	IB	T10CD	DD	18	2	95000	5	3	725000	796500
70	10	COCKPIT MOTOR YACHT	FB	MYCPT	FBG	SV	IB	T870D	DD	18	2	52T	5	4	830500	912500
70	10	COCKPIT MOTOR YACHT	FB	MYCPT	FBG	SV	IB	T10CD	DD	18	2	52T	5	4	854000	938500
70	11	MOTOR YACHT	FB	MY	FBG	SV	IB	T870D	DD	18	2	54T	5	6	853500	938000
70	11	MOTOR YACHT	FB	MY	FBG	SV	IB	T10CD	DD	18	2	54T	5	6	877500	964000
		1993 BOATS														
38	10	CONVERTIBLE	FB	CNV	FBG	SV	IB	T465D	DD	13	5	32000	4	8	208000	229000
40	10	MOTOR YACHT	FB	DCMY	FBG	SV	IB	T375D	CAT	13	7	38000	4	9	234500	257500
40	10	MOTOR YACHT	FB	DCMY	FBG	SV	IB	T400D	DD	13	7	38000	4	9	236500	260000
42	10	COCKPIT MOTOR YACHT	FB	MYCPT	FBG	SV	IB	T375D	CAT	13	7	41000	4	9	243500	267500
42	10	COCKPIT MOTOR YACHT	FB	MYCPT	FBG	SV	IB	T400D	DD	13	7	41000	4	9	247000	271500
43	2	CONVERTIBLE	FB	CNV	FBG	SV	IB	T535D	DD	14	3	40000	4	4	256500	282000
46	10	CONVERTIBLE	FB	CNV	FBG	SV	IB	T720D	DD	15	7	51000	4	11	308000	338500
48	9	MOTOR YACHT	FB	MY	FBG	SV	IB	T720D	DD	16		63000	5	3	339500	373500
48	11	COCKPIT MOTOR YACHT	FB	MYCPT	FBG	SV	IB	T535D	DD	16		59000	5	3	312000	343000
50	10	CONVERTIBLE	FB	CNV	FBG	SV	IB	T720D	DD	16	1	60000	5	9	351500	386500
50	10	CONVERTIBLE	FB	CNV	FBG	SV	IB	T780D	MAN	16	1	60000	5	9	354000	389000
50	10	CONVERTIBLE	FB	CNV	FBG	SV	IB	T870D	DD	16	1	60000	5	9	375000	412000
52	9	MOTOR YACHT	FB	MY	FBG	SV	IB	T720D	DD	16		66000	5		402000	442000
52	11	COCKPIT MOTOR YACHT	FB	MYCPT	FBG	SV	IB	T720D	DD	16		66000	5		432500	475000
54	9	EXTENDED DECK MY	FB	MYDKH	FBG	SV	IB	T720D	DD	17	6	76000	4	9	470500	517500
54	11	CONVERTIBLE	FB	CNV	FBG	SV	IB	T870D	DD	17	4	70000	5	6	488000	536000
54	11	CONVERTIBLE	FB	CNV	FBG	SV	IB	T10CD	DD	17	4	70000	5	6	512000	562500
58	10	CONVERTIBLE	FB	CNV	FBG	SV	IB	T10CD	DD	17	9	92000	5	11	666000	731500
58	10	CONVERTIBLE	FB	CNV	FBG	SV	IB	T13CD	DD	17	9	92000	5	11	714500	785500
60	9	EXTENDED DECKHOUSE	FB	MYDKH	FBG	SV	IB	T720D	DD	18	2	87000	5	2	551000	605000
60	9	EXTENDED DECKHOUSE	FB	MYDKH	FBG	SV	IB	T870D	DD	18	2	87000	5	2	580500	638000
65	5	CONVERTIBLE	FB	CNV	FBG	SV	IB	T10CD	DD	18		51T	5	11	705500	775000
65	5	CONVERTIBLE	FB	CNV	FBG	SV	IB	T12CD	MTU	18		51T	5	11	763000	838500
65	5	CONVERTIBLE	FB	CNV	FBG	SV	IB	T13CD	DD	18		51T	5	11	759500	835000
65	10	MOTOR YACHT	FB	MY	FBG	SV	IB	T870D	DD	18	2	99000	5	5	702000	771000
67	2	COCKPIT MOTOR YACHT	FB	MYCPT	FBG	SV	IB	T870D	DD	18	2	94000	5	1	659000	724500
67	2	EXT DECKHOUSE CKPT	FB	MYDKH	FBG	SV	IB	T870D	DD	18	2	95000	5	3	670000	736000
67	2	EXT DECKHOUSE CKPT	FB	MYDKH	FBG	SV	IB	T10CD	DD	18	2	95000	5	3	692000	760500
70	10	COCKPIT MOTOR YACHT	FB	MYCPT	FBG	SV	IB	T870D	DD	18	2	52T	5	4	791000	869500
70	10	COCKPIT MOTOR YACHT	FB	MYCPT	FBG	SV	IB	T10CD	DD	18	2	52T	5	4	813500	894000
70	10	MOTOR YACHT	FB	MY	FBG	SV	IB	T870D	DD	18	2	54T	5	6	812000	892500
70	10	MOTOR YACHT	FB	MY	FBG	SV	IB	T10CD	DD	18	2	54T	5	6	835000	917500
		1992 BOATS														
38	10	CONVERTIBLE	FB	CNV	FBG	SV	IB	T465D	DD	13	5	32000	4	7	198500	218000
40	10	DOUBLE CABIN	FB	DCMY	FBG	SV	IB	T375D	CAT	13	7	38000	4	9	222500	244500
43	2	CONVERTIBLE	FB	CNV	FBG	SV	IB	T535D	DD	14	3	40000	4	4	244500	268500
45	8	CONVERTIBLE	FB	CNV	FBG	SV	IB	T535D	DD	14	6	45000	4	7	255500	281000
46	10	CONVERTIBLE	FB	CNV	FBG	SV	IB	T720D	DD	15	7	51000	4	10	293000	322000
48	9	MOTOR YACHT	FB	MY	FBG	SV	IB	T720D	DD	16		63000	5	3	323000	355000
50	10	CONVERTIBLE	FB	CNV	FBG	SV	IB	T720D	DD	16	1	60000	5	9	334500	367500
50	10	CONVERTIBLE	FB	CNV	FBG	SV	IB	T780D	MAN	16	1	60000	5	9	337000	370000
50	10	CONVERTIBLE	FB	CNV	FBG	SV	IB	T870D	DD	16	1	60000	5	9	356500	391500
52	9	COCKPIT MOTOR YACHT	FB	MYCPT	FBG	SV	IB	T720D	DD	16		66000	5		410000	450500
54	9	EXTENDED DECK MY	FB	MYDKH	FBG	SV	IB	T720D	DD	17	6	76000	4	9	448500	493000
54	11	CONVERTIBLE	FB	CNV	FBG	SV	IB	T870D	DD	17	4	70000	5	10	465000	511000
54	11	CONVERTIBLE	FB	CNV	FBG	SV	IB	T10CD	DD	17	4	70000	5	10	488000	536000
58	10	CONVERTIBLE	FB	CNV	FBG	SV	IB	T10CD	DD	17	9	92000	5	11	634500	697500
58	10	CONVERTIBLE	FB	CNV	FBG	SV	IB	T13CD	DD	17	9	92000	5	11	681000	748500
60	9	EXTENDED DECKHOUSE	FB	MYDKH	FBG	SV	IB	T720D	DD	18	2	87000	5	2	525000	577000
60	9	EXTENDED DECKHOUSE	FB	MYDKH	FBG	SV	IB	T870D	DD	18	2	87000	5	2	553500	608000
65	5	CONVERTIBLE	FB	CNV	FBG	SV	IB	T10CD	DD	18		51T	5	10	672500	739000
65	5	CONVERTIBLE	FB	CNV	FBG	SV	IB	T12CD	MTU	18		51T	5	10	726000	798000
65	5	CONVERTIBLE	FB	CNV	FBG	SV	IB	T13CD	DD	18		51T	5	10	723500	795000
65	10	MOTOR YACHT	FB	MY	FBG	SV	IB	T870D	DD	18	2	99000	5	5	669000	735000
67	2	COCKPIT MOTOR YACHT	FB	MYCPT	FBG	SV	IB	T870D	DD	18	2	94000	5	1	629000	691500
67	2	EXT DECKHOUSE COCKP	FB	MYDKH	FBG	SV	IB	T870D	DD	18	2	95000	5	3	627500	689500
67	2	EXT DECKHOUSE COCKP	FB	MYDKH	FBG	SV	IB	T10CD	DD	18	2	95000	5	3	648000	712000
70	10	COCKPIT MOTOR YACHT	FB	MYCPT	FBG	SV	IB	T870D	DD	18	2	52T	5	4	754000	829000
70	10	COCKPIT MOTOR YACHT	FB	MYCPT	FBG	SV	IB	T10CD	DD	18	2	52T	5	4	775500	852500
70	10	MOTOR YACHT	FB	MY	FBG	SV	IB	T870D	DD	18	2	54T	5	6	774500	851000
70	10	MOTOR YACHT	FB	MY	FBG	SV	IB	T10CD	DD	18	2	54T	5	6	796000	874500
72	8	MOTOR YACHT	FB	MY	FBG	SV	IB	T870D	DD	18	7	55T	5	3	**	**
77	9	COCKPIT MOTOR YACHT	FB	MYCPT	FBG	SV	IB	T870D	DD	18	7	70T	5	9	**	**
77	9	COCKPIT MOTOR YACHT	FB	MYCPT	FBG	SV	IB	T10CD	DD	18	7	70T	5	9	**	**
77	9	MOTOR YACHT	FB	MY	FBG	SV	IB	T870D	DD	18	7	70T	5	9	**	**
77	9	MOTOR YACHT	FB	MY	FBG	SV	IB	T10CD	DD	18	7	70T	5	9	**	**
		1991 BOATS														
38	10	CONVERTIBLE	FB	CNV	FBG	SV	IB	T465D	DD	13	5	28800	4	8	176000	193500
40	10	DOUBLE CABIN	FB	DCMY	FBG	SV	IB	T375D	CAT	13	7	29600	4	6	177500	195000
41	9	CONVERTIBLE	FB	CNV	FBG	SV	IB	T535D	DD	14	3	35400	4	4	216500	238000
43	1	DOUBLE CABIN	HT	DC	FBG	SV	IB	T310D	GM	14		34000	3	5	183000	201000
43	2	CONVERTIBLE	FB	CNV	FBG	SV	IB	T535D	DD	14	3	39000	4	2	229500	252000
48	9	MOTOR YACHT	FB	MY	FBG	SV	IB	T720D	DD	16		59000	5		301000	330500
50	10	CONVERTIBLE	FB	CNV	FBG	SV	IB	T720D	DD	16	1	62000	5	5	322500	354000
50	10	CONVERTIBLE	FB	CNV	FBG	SV	IB	T780D	MAN	16	1	62000	5	5	325000	357500
50	10	CONVERTIBLE	FB	CNV	FBG	SV	IB	T870D	DD	16	1	62000	5	5	343500	377500
52	9	COCKPIT MOTOR YACHT	FB	MYCPT	FBG	SV	IB	T720D	DD	16		60800	4	8	369000	405500
54	9	EXTENDED DECK MY	FB	MYDKH	FBG	SV	IB	T720D	DD	17	6	74300	4	10	434000	477000
54	11	CONVERTIBLE	FB	CNV	FBG	SV	IB	T870D	DD	17	4	72500	5	9	455000	500000
54	11	CONVERTIBLE	FB	CNV	FBG	SV	IB	T10CD	DD	17	4	72500	5	9	483000	530500
58	10	CONVERTIBLE	FB	CNV	FBG	SV	IB	T10CD	DD	17	9	92000	5	9	611500	672000
58	10	CONVERTIBLE	FB	CNV	FBG	SV	IB	T13CD	DD	17	9	92000	5	9	656500	721500
60	9	EXTENDED DECKHOUSE	FB	MY	FBG	SV	IB	T720D	DD	18	2	87000	5	1	510500	561000
60	9	EXTENDED DECKHOUSE	FB	MY	FBG	SV	IB	T870D	DD	18	2	87000	5	1	538000	591000
60	9	MOTOR YACHT	FB	MY	FBG	SV	IB	T720D	DD	18	2	75900	4	8	458000	503500
65	5	CONVERTIBLE	FB	CNV	FBG	SV	IB	T10CD	DD	18		51T	5	9	648000	712000
65	5	CONVERTIBLE	FB	CNV	FBG	SV	IB	T12CD	MTU	18		51T	5	9	701000	770500
65	5	CONVERTIBLE	FB	CNV	FBG	SV	IB	T13CD	DD	18		51T	5	9	700000	769500
65	10	MOTOR YACHT	FB	MY	FBG	SV	IB	T770D	DD	18	2	94300	5	8	597000	656000
65	10	MOTOR YACHT	FB	MY	FBG	SV	IB	T870D	DD	18	2	94300	5	8	614000	675000
67	2	COCKPIT MOTOR YACHT	FB	MYCPT	FBG	SV	IB	T870D	DD	18	2	86200	5	1	578500	636000
67	2	EXT DECKHOUSE COCKPT	FB	MY	FBG	SV	IB	T870D	DD	18	2	95000	5	2	580000	637500
70	10	COCKPIT MOTOR YACHT	FB	MYCPT	FBG	SV	IB	T870D	DD	18	2	52T	5	7	721500	792500
70	10	COCKPIT MOTOR YACHT	FB	MYCPT	FBG	SV	IB	T10CD	DD	18	2	52T	5	7	749000	823000
70	10	MOTOR YACHT	FB	MY	FBG	SV	IB	T870D	DD	18	2	53T	6	1	733000	805500
70	10	MOTOR YACHT	FB	MY	FBG	SV	IB	T10CD	DD	18	2	53T	6	1	761000	836000
72	8	MOTOR YACHT	FB	MY	FBG	SV	IB	T870D	DD	18	7	55T	5		**	**
77	8	COCKPIT MOTOR YACHT	FB	MYCPT	FBG	SV	IB	T870D	DD	18	7	70T	5		**	**
77	8	COCKPIT MOTOR YACHT	FB	MYCPT	FBG	SV	IB	T10CD	DD	18	7	70T	5		**	**
77	8	MOTOR YACHT	FB	MY	FBG	SV	IB	T870D	DD	18	7	70T	5		**	**
		1990 BOATS														
38	10	CONVERTIBLE	FB	CNV	FBG	SV	IB	T455D	GM	13	5	28800	4	8	163000	179500
40	10	DOUBLE CABIN	FB	DCMY	FBG	DV	IB	T350		13	7	29600	4	6	142500	157000
40	10	DOUBLE CABIN	FB	DCMY	FBG	DV	IB	T375D	CAT	13	7	29600	4	6	169500	186500
41	9	CONVERTIBLE	FB	CNV	FBG	DV	IB	T465D	GM	14	3	35400	4	4	194000	213500
41	9	CONVERTIBLE	FB	CNV	FBG	DV	IB	T535D	GM	14	3	35400	4	4	203500	224000
45	8	CONVERTIBLE	FB	CNV	FBG	SV	IB	T535D	GM	14	6	43800	4	7	225500	247500
48	8	CONVERTIBLE	FB	CNV	FBG	DV	IB	T720D	GM	16	1	51700	5	5	268500	295000
48	9	MOTOR YACHT	FB	MY	FBG	SV	IB	T535D	GM	16		59000	5		261000	287000
48	9	MOTOR YACHT	FB	MY	FBG	SV	IB	T720D	GM	16		59000	5		282000	310000
50	10	CONVERTIBLE	FB	CNV	FBG	DV	IB	T784D	MAN	16	1	62000	5	5	314500	345500
50	10	CONVERTIBLE	FB	CNV	FBG	DV	IB	T870D	GM	16	1	62000	5	5	327000	359500

CONTINUED ON NEXT PAGE

LOA FT	LOA IN	NAME AND/ OR MODEL	TOP/ RIG	BOAT TYPE	-HULL- MTL	-HULL- TP	ENGINE TP	ENGINE # HP	ENGINE MFG	BEAM FT	BEAM IN	WGT LBS	DRAFT FT	DRAFT IN	RETAIL LOW	RETAIL HIGH
		1990 BOATS														
52	9	COCKPIT MOTOR YACHT	FB	MYCPT	FBG	SV	IB	T720D	GM	16		60800	4	8	352000	386500
54	9	EXTENDED DECK MY	FB	MYDKH	FBG	SV	IB	T720D	GM	17	6	74300	4	10	413500	454500
54	9	MOTOR YACHT	FB	MY	FBG	DV	IB	T720D	GM	17	6	62500	4	2	358500	394000
58	10	CONVERTIBLE	FB	CNV	FBG	SV	IB	T10CD	GM	17	9	92000	5	6	588500	647000
58	10	CONVERTIBLE	FB	CNV	FBG	SV	IB	T13CD	GM	17	9	92000	5	6	632000	694500
60	9	EXTENDED DECKHOUSE	FB	MY	FBG	DV	IB	T870D	GM	18	2		5	1	445500	489500
60	9	MOTOR YACHT	FB	MY	FBG	DV	IB	T720D	GM	18	2	75900	5	1	444500	488500
65	5	CONVERTIBLE	FB	CNV	FBG	DV	IB	T10CD	GM	18		92800	5	9	579000	636500
65	5	CONVERTIBLE	FB	CNV	FBG	DV	IB	T12CD	MTU	18		51T	5	9	662000	727000
65	10	MOTOR YACHT		MY	FBG	SV	IB	T870D	GM	18	2	94300	5	8	595500	654500
67	2	COCKPIT MOTOR YACHT	FB	MYCPT	FBG	DV	IB	T870D	GM	18	2	86000	5	1	551500	606000
70	10	COCKPIT MOTOR YACHT	FB	MYCPT	FBG	DV	IB	T870D	GM	18	2	51T	5	11	680500	748000
70	10	MOTOR YACHT	FB	MY	FBG	DV	IB	T870D	GM	18	2	53T	6	1	696500	765500
72	8	MOTOR YACHT	FB	MY	FBG	DV	IB	T870D	GM	18	7	55T	5		**	**
77	8	COCKPIT MOTOR YACHT	FB	MYCPT	FBG	DV	IB	T870D	GM	18	7	70T	5		**	**
77	8	COCKPIT MOTOR YACHT	FB	MYCPT	FBG	DV	IB	T10CD	GM	18	7	70T	5		**	**
77	8	MOTOR YACHT	FB	MY	FBG	DV	IB	T870D	GM	18	7	70T	5		**	**
77	8	MOTOR YACHT	FB	MY	FBG	DV	IB	T10CD	GM	18	7	70T	5		**	**
		1989 BOATS														
38	10	CONVERTIBLE	FB	CNV	FBG	SV	IB	T455D	GM	13	7	30400	4	4	161000	177000
40	10	DOUBLE CABIN	FB	DCMY	FBG	DV	IB	T350		13	7	28000	4	4	130500	143000
40	10	DOUBLE CABIN	FB	DCMY	FBG	DV	IB	T375D	CAT	13	7	30000	4	4	163500	179500
41	9	CONVERTIBLE	FB	CNV	FBG	DV	IB	T455D	GM	14	3	32000	3	10	172500	189500
41	9	CONVERTIBLE	FB	CNV	FBG	DV	IB	T535D	GM	14	3	32000	3	10	183000	201000
45	8	CONVERTIBLE	FB	CNV	FBG	SV	IB	T535D	GM	14	6	39000	4	6	205000	225000
48	8	CONVERTIBLE	FB	MY	FBG	DV	IB	T720D	GM	16		51500	5		257000	282500
52		CONVERTIBLE	FB	CNV	FBG	SV	IB	T720D	GM	16	4	56000	5		300500	330000
52	11	YACHT FISHERMAN	FB	YTFS	FBG	DV	IB	T465D	GM	15	10	55000	4		260000	286000
53	1	EXTENDED DECKHOUSE	FB	MY	FBG	SV	IB	T465D	GM	15	10	57000	4		269000	295500
53	1	MOTOR YACHT	FB	MY	FBG	SV	IB	T465D	GM	15	10	55000	4		261500	287000
54	9	EXTENDED DECK MY	FB	MYDKH	FBG	SV	IB	T720D	GM	17	6	74300	4	2	395000	434500
54	9	MOTOR YACHT	FB	MY	FBG	DV	IB	T720D	GM	17	6	62500	4	2	343000	376500
55	8	CONVERTIBLE	FB	CNV	FBG	SV	IB	T870D	GM	17	6	70000	4	10	417000	458500
55	8	CONVERTIBLE	FB	CNV	FBG	SV	IB	T10CD	GM	17	6	70000	4	10	438000	481500
60	9	MOTOR YACHT	FB	MY	FBG	DV	IB	T720D	GM	18	2	80000	4	11	444500	488500
65		CONVERTIBLE	FB	CNV	FBG	DV	IB	T10CD	GM	18		51T	5	2	597000	656000
65		CONVERTIBLE	FB	CNV	FBG	DV	IB	T12CD	MTU	18		51T	5	2	630000	692000
65	10	MOTOR YACHT	FB	MY	FBG	SV	IB	T770D	GM	18	2	97000	5		566000	622000
67	8	COCKPIT MOTOR YACHT	FB	MYCPT	FBG	DV	IB	T770D	GM	18	2	51T	4	11	563500	619500
70	10	COCKPIT MOTOR YACHT	FB	MYCPT	FBG	DV	IB	T870D	GM	18	2	53T	5		615000	676000
70	10	MOTOR YACHT	FB	MY	FBG	DV	IB	T870D	GM	18	2	53T	5		706000	776000
72	8	MOTOR YACHT	FB	MY	FBG	DV	IB	T870D	GM	18	7	63T	5		**	**
77	8	COCKPIT MOTOR YACHT	FB	MYCPT	FBG	DV	IB	T870D	GM	18	7	67T	5		**	**
77	8	COCKPIT MOTOR YACHT	FB	MYCPT	FBG	DV	IB	T10CD	GM	18	7	67T	5		**	**
77	8	MOTOR YACHT	FB	MY	FBG	DV	IB	T870D	GM	18	7	67T	5		**	**
77	8	MOTOR YACHT	FB	MY	FBG	DV	IB	T10CD	GM	18	7	67T	5		**	**
		1988 BOATS														
36	6	SEDAN CRUISER	FB	SDN	FBG	DV	IB	T		13	7	25500	3	9	**	**
36	6	SEDAN CRUISER	FB	SDN	FBG	DV	IB	T320D	CAT	13	7	25500	3	9	112500	124000
38	10	CONVERTIBLE	FB	CNV	FBG	SV	IB	T350		13	7	30400	3	9	125500	138000
38	10	CONVERTIBLE	FB	CNV	FBG	SV	IB	T465D	GM	13	7	30400	3	9	155000	170000
40	10	DOUBLE CABIN	FB	DCMY	FBG	DV	IB	T		13	7	30000	2	9	**	**
40	10	DOUBLE CABIN	FB	DCMY	FBG	DV	IB	T320D	CAT	13	7	30000	2	9	150500	165500
41	9	CONVERTIBLE	FB	CNV	FBG	DV	IB	T465D	GM	14	3	32000	2	11	166000	182500
41	9	CONVERTIBLE	FB	CNV	FBG	DV	IB	T535D	GM	14	3	32000	2	11	174500	192000
43	1	MOTOR YACHT	FB	MY	FBG	SV	IB	T320D	CAT	14		34500	3	5	166000	182500
45	8	CONVERTIBLE	FB	CNV	FBG	SV	IB	T535D	GM	14	6	39000	4	2	195500	215000
48	8	CONVERTIBLE	FB	MY	FBG	DV	IB	T720D	GM	16		51500	4	7	245500	269500
52		CONVERTIBLE	FB	YTFS	FBG	SV	IB	T720D	GM	16	4	56000	4	6	283000	311000
52	11	YACHT FISHERMAN	FB	YTFS	FBG	DV	IB	T465D	GM	15	10	55000	4		248500	273500
53	1	EXTENDED DECKHOUSE	FB	MY	FBG	SV	IB	T465D	GM	15	10	57000	4		257500	283000
53	1	MOTOR YACHT	FB	MY	FBG	SV	IB	T465D	GM	15	10	55000	4		250500	275500
54	9	MOTOR YACHT	FB	MY	FBG	DV	IB	T650D	GM	17	6	62500	4	2	315000	346000
55	8	CONVERTIBLE	FB	CNV	FBG	SV	IB	T870D	GM	17	6	70000	4	10	399000	438000
55	8	CONVERTIBLE	FB	CNV	FBG	SV	IB	T10CD	GM	17	6	70000	4	10	418500	460000
60	9	MOTOR YACHT	FB	MY	FBG	DV	IB	T720D	GM	18	2	80000	4	11	425000	467000
65	5	CONVERTIBLE	FB	CNV	FBG	DV	IB	T10CD	GM	18		94000	5	2	534000	586500
65	5	CONVERTIBLE	FB	CNV	FBG	DV	IB	T12CD	MTU	18		94000	5	2	582000	639500
67	8	COCKPIT MOTOR YACHT	FB	MYCPT	FBG	DV	IB	T770D	GM	18	2	90000	4	11	510000	560000
70	10	COCKPIT MOTOR YACHT	FB	MYCPT	FBG	DV	IB	T870D	GM	18	2	97000	5		611500	672000
70	10	MOTOR YACHT	FB	MY	FBG	DV	IB	T870D	GM	18	2	50T	5		623500	685500
72	8	MOTOR YACHT	FB	MY	FBG	DV	IB	T840D	GM	18	7	60T	5		**	**
77	8	COCKPIT MOTOR YACHT	FB	MYCPT	FBG	DV	IB	T840D	GM	18	7	58T	5		**	**
77	8	COCKPIT MOTOR YACHT	FB	MYCPT	FBG	DV	IB	T935D	MTU	18	7	58T	5		**	**
77	8	COCKPIT MOTOR YACHT	FB	MYCPT	FBG	DV	IB	T975D	GM	18	7	58T	5		**	**
77	8	MOTOR YACHT	FB	MY	FBG	DV	IB	T840D	GM	18	7	58T	5		**	**
77	8	MOTOR YACHT	FB	MY	FBG	DV	IB	T935D	MTU	18	7	58T	5		**	**
77	8	MOTOR YACHT	FB	MY	FBG	DV	IB	T975D	GM	18	7	58T	5		**	**
		1987 BOATS														
32	8	FLYBRIDGE FISHERMAN	FB	SDNSF	FBG	DV	IB	T300	CRUS	12		18000	3	2	60000	65900
32	8	FLYBRIDGE FISHERMAN	FB	SDNSF	FBG	DV	IB	T320D	CAT	12		20000	3	2	90500	99400
36	6	CONVERTIBLE	FB	CNV	FBG	DV	IB	T300	CRUS	13	7	26500	3	9	90600	99600
36	6	CONVERTIBLE	FB	CNV	FBG	DV	IB	T375D	CAT	13	7	26500	3	9	115000	126500
36	6	CONVERTIBLE	FB	CNV	FBG	DV	IB	T430D	GM	13	7	26500	3	9	117000	128500
36	6	SEDAN CRUISER	FB	SDN	FBG	DV	IB	T300	CRUS	13	7	25500	3	9	88200	96900
36	6	SEDAN CRUISER	FB	SDN	FBG	DV	IB	T320D	CAT	13	7	25500	3	9	108000	118500
40	10	DOUBLE CABIN	FB	DCMY	FBG	DV	IB	T300	CRUS	13	7	30000	2	9	124500	137000
40	10	DOUBLE CABIN	FB	DCMY	FBG	DV	IB	T320D	CAT	13	7	30000	2	9	144000	158500
41	9	CONVERTIBLE	FB	CNV	FBG	DV	IB	T455D	GM	14	3	32000	2	11	157500	173000
43	1	MOTOR YACHT	FB	MY	FBG	SV	IB	T300	CRUS	14		34500	3	5	137500	151000
43	1	MOTOR YACHT	FB	MY	FBG	SV	IB	T320D	CAT	14		34500	3	5	158500	174000
43	1	MOTOR YACHT	FB	MY	FBG	SV	IB	T340D	GM	14		34500	3	5	158500	174000
45	8	CONVERTIBLE	FB	CNV	FBG	SV	IB	T500D	GM	14	6	39000	4	2	183000	201000
48	8	CONVERTIBLE	FB	MY	FBG	DV	IB	T720D	GM	16		51500	4	7	234500	257500
52		CONVERTIBLE	FB	YTFS	FBG	SV	IB	T675D	GM	16	4	56000	4	6	264000	290000
52	11	YACHT FISHERMAN	FB	YTFS	FBG	DV	IB	T465D	GM	15	10	55000	4		238000	261500
53	1	EXTENDED DECKHOUSE	FB	MY	FBG	SV	IB	T465D	GM	15	10	57000	4		247000	271500
53	1	MOTOR YACHT	FB	MY	FBG	SV	IB	T465D	GM	15	10	55000	4		240500	264500
54	9	MOTOR YACHT	FB	MY	FBG	DV	IB	T650D	GM	17	6	62500	4	2	301500	331000
55	8	CONVERTIBLE	FB	CNV	FBG	SV	IB	T875D	GM	17	6	70000	4	10	382000	420000
58	9	MOTOR YACHT	FB	MY	FBG	SV	IB	T650D	GM	18	2	79000	4	11	393000	432000
63	10	COCKPIT MOTOR YACHT	FB	MYCPT	FBG	DV	IB	T650D	GM	18	2	79000	4	11	411500	452000
63	10	MOTOR YACHT	FB	MY	FBG	DV	IB	T650D	GM	18	2	92000	5		477500	525000
65	4	SAIL YACHT	SLP	SA/CR	FBG	KL	IB	T175D	GM	17	2	56T	13	10	542500	596500
65	5	CONVERTIBLE	FB	CNV	FBG	DV	IB	T10CD	GM	18		94000	5	2	511000	561500
65	5	CONVERTIBLE	FB	CNV	FBG	DV	IB	T12CD	MTU	18		94000	5	2	558000	613000
68		COCKPIT MOTOR YACHT	FB	MYCPT	FBG	DV	IB	T775D	GM	18	2	96500	5		539500	592500
68	10	MOTOR YACHT	FB	MY	FBG	DV	IB	T775D	GM	18	2	50T	5		572500	629000
72	8	MOTOR YACHT	FB	MY	FBG	DV	IB	T840D	GM	18	7	60T	5		**	**
77	8	COCKPIT MOTOR YACHT	FB	MYCPT	FBG	DV	IB	T840D	GM	18	7	58T	5		**	**
77	8	COCKPIT MOTOR YACHT	FB	MYCPT	FBG	DV	IB	T935D	MTU	18	7	58T	5		**	**
77	8	COCKPIT MOTOR YACHT	FB	MYCPT	FBG	DV	IB	T975D	GM	18	7	58T	5		**	**
77	8	MOTOR YACHT	FB	MY	FBG	DV	IB	T840D	GM	18	7	58T	5		**	**
77	8	MOTOR YACHT	FB	MY	FBG	DV	IB	T935D	MTU	18	7	58T	5		**	**
77	8	MOTOR YACHT	FB	MY	FBG	DV	IB	T975D	GM	18	7	58T	5		**	**
		1986 BOATS														
32	8	FLYBRIDGE FISHERMAN	FB	SDNSF	FBG	DV	IB	T300	CRUS	12		18000	3	2	57200	62900
32	8	FLYBRIDGE FISHERMAN	FB	SDNSF	FBG	DV	IB	T300D-T305D		12		20000	3	2	85600	94100
32	8	SPORT FISHERMAN	OP	SF	FBG	DV	IB	T300	CRUS	12		17200	3	2	56200	61800
32	8	SPORT FISHERMAN	OP	SF	FBG	DV	IB	T300D-T305D		12		19100	3	2	83100	91300
36	6	CONVERTIBLE	FB	SDNSF	FBG	DV	IB	T300	CRUS	13	7	26500	3	9	85700	94200
36	6	CONVERTIBLE	FB	SDNSF	FBG	DV	IB	T355D	CAT	13	7	26500	3	9	106000	116500
36	6	CONVERTIBLE	FB	SDNSF	FBG	DV	IB	T390D	GM	13	7	26500	3	9	106500	117000
36	6	SEDAN CRUISER	FB	SDN	FBG	DV	IB	T350	CRUS	13	7	25500	3	9	85700	94200
36	6	SEDAN CRUISER	FB	SDN	FBG	DV	IB	T320D	CAT	13	7	25500	3	9	103000	113500
36	6	SPORT FISHERMAN	OP	SF	FBG	DV	IB	T300	CRUS	13	7	25000	3	9	82100	90200
36	6	SPORT FISHERMAN	OP	SF	FBG	DV	IB	T355D	CAT	13	7	25000	3	9	102000	112000
36	6	SPORT FISHERMAN	OP	SF	FBG	DV	IB	T390D	GM	13	7				79800	87700
41		CONVERTIBLE	FB	SDNSF	FBG	DV	IB	T450D	GM	14	3	32000	2	11	149500	164500
43	1	MOTOR YACHT	FB	MY	FBG	SV	IB	T300	CRUS	14		34500	3	5	131500	144500
43	1	MOTOR YACHT	FB	MY	FBG	SV	IB	T300D	CAT	14		34500	3	5	149500	164500
43	1	MOTOR YACHT	FB	MY	FBG	SV	IB	T340D	GM	14		34500	3	5	151500	166500
45	8	CONVERTIBLE	FB	CNV	FBG	SV	IB	T465D	GM	14	6	39000	4	2	171000	188000
45	8	CONVERTIBLE	FB	CNV	FBG	SV	IB	T500D	GM	14	6	39000	4	2	174500	192000
52		CONVERTIBLE	FB	YTFS	FBG	SV	IB	T585D	GM	16	4	56000	4	6	239500	263500
52		CONVERTIBLE	FB	YTFS	FBG	SV	IB	T675D	GM	16	4	56000	4	6	253000	278000
53	1	EXTENDED DECKHOUSE	FB	MY	FBG	SV	IB	T465D	GM	15	10	57000	4		237000	260500
53	1	MOTOR YACHT	FB	MY	FBG	SV	IB	T465D	GM	15	10	55000	4		231000	254000
54	9	MOTOR YACHT	FB	MY	FBG	DV	IB	T585D	GM	17	6	62500	4	2	277500	304500
54	9	MOTOR YACHT	FB	MY	FBG	DV	IB	T650D	GM	17	6	62500	4	2	288500	317000
55	8	CONVERTIBLE	FB	YTFS	FBG	SV	IB	T840D	GM	17	6	70000	4	10	361000	396500
58	9	MOTOR YACHT	FB	MY	FBG	SV	IB	T625D	GM	18	2	79000	4	11	372000	409000
60	11	CONVERTIBLE	FB	YTFS	FBG	SV	IB	T840D	GM	18		82000	4	11	404000	444000
60	11	CONVERTIBLE	FB	YTFS	FBG	SV	IB	T935D	GM	18		82000	4	11	417500	458500
60	11	CONVERTIBLE	FB	YTFS	FBG	SV	IB	T975D	GM	18		82000	4	11	423000	464500
63	10	COCKPIT MOTOR YACHT	FB	MYCPT	FBG	DV	IB	T840D	GM	18	2	79000	4	11	414500	455500

CONTINUED ON NEXT PAGE

LOA FT	LOA IN	NAME AND/ OR MODEL	TOP/ RIG	BOAT TYPE	-HULL- MTL	-HULL- TP	ENGINE TP	ENGINE # HP	ENGINE MFG	BEAM FT	BEAM IN	WGT LBS	DRAFT FT	DRAFT IN	RETAIL LOW	RETAIL HIGH
		1986 BOATS														
63	10	MOTOR YACHT	FB	MY	FBG	DV	IB	T840D	GM	18	2	92000	5		488500	537000
65		LONG RANGE CRUISER	FB	LRPH	FBG	SV	IB	T280D	GM	17	11	52T	4	10	457500	503000
65	4	SAIL YACHT	SLP	SA/CR	FBG	KC	IB	T175D	GM	17	2	56T	13	10	504500	554000
68		COCKPIT MOTOR YACHT	FB	MYCPT	FBG	DV	IB	T650D	GM	18	2	96500	5		501000	550500
68		COCKPIT MOTOR YACHT	FB	MYCPT	FBG	DV	IB	T775D	GM	18	2	96500	5		516000	567000
72	8	MOTOR YACHT	FB	MY	FBG	DV	IB	T650D	GM	18	7	60T	5		**	**
72	8	MOTOR YACHT	FB	MY	FBG	DV	IB	T840D	GM	18	7	60T	5		**	**
77	8	COCKPIT MOTOR YACHT	FB	MYCPT	FBG	DV	IB	T840D	GM	18	7	58T	5		**	**
77	8	COCKPIT MOTOR YACHT	FB	MYCPT	FBG	DV	IB	T975D	GM	18	7	58T	5		**	**
77	8	MOTOR YACHT	FB	MY	FBG	DV	IB	T840D	GM	18	7	58T	5		**	**
77	8	MOTOR YACHT	FB	MY	FBG	DV	IB	T975D	GM	18	7	58T	5		**	**
		1985 BOATS														
32	8	FLYBRIDGE FISHERMAN	FB	SDNSF	FBG	DV	IB	T300		12		18000	3	2	54600	60000
32	8	FLYBRIDGE FISHERMAN	FB	SDNSF	FBG	DV	IB	T300D-T305D		12		20000	3	2	82100	90300
32	8	SPORT FISHERMAN	OP	SF	FBG	DV	IB	T300		12		17200	3	2	53600	58900
32	8	SPORT FISHERMAN	OP	SF	FBG	DV	IB	T300D-T305D		12		19100	3	2	79700	87600
36	6	CONVERTIBLE	FB	SDNSF	FBG	DV	IB	T300		13	7	26500	3	9	81700	89700
36	6	CONVERTIBLE	FB	SDNSF	FBG	DV	IB	T355D	CAT	13	7	26500	3	9	101500	111500
36	6	CONVERTIBLE	FB	SDNSF	FBG	DV	IB	T375D	GM	13	7	26500	3	9	101000	111000
36	6	SEDAN CRUISER	FB	SDN	FBG	DV	IB	T350	MRCR	13	7	25500	3	9	81600	89700
36	6	SEDAN CRUISER	FB	SDN	FBG	DV	IB	T300D	CAT	13	7	25500	3	9	97400	107000
36	6	SPORT FISHERMAN	OP	SF	FBG	DV	IB	T300		13	7	25000	3	9	78200	85900
36	6	SPORT FISHERMAN	OP	SF	FBG	DV	IB	T355D	CAT	13	7	25000	3	9	97700	107500
36	6	SPORT FISHERMAN	OP	SF	FBG	DV	IB	T375D	GM	13	7				75400	82900
42	6	LONG RANGE CRUISER	FB	LRPH	FBG	DS	IB	T140D	GM	14	6	36000	3	10	135000	148000
43	1	DOUBLE CABIN	FB	DC	FBG	SV	IB	T300D		14		34000	3	5	138000	151500
43	1	MOTOR YACHT	FB	MY	FBG	SV	IB	T270	CRUS	14		34500	3	5	124000	136000
43	1	MOTOR YACHT	FB	MY	FBG	SV	IB	T300D	CAT	14		34500	3	5	143000	157000
43	1	MOTOR YACHT	FB	MY	FBG	SV	IB	T335D	GM	14		34500	3	5	144500	158500
43	8	CONVERTIBLE	FB	SDNSF	FBG	SV	IB	T450D		14	6	37000	4	2	156500	172000
45	8	CONVERTIBLE	FB	CNV	FBG	SV	IB	T450D		14	6	39000	4	2	161500	177500
45	8	CONVERTIBLE	FB	CNV	FBG	SV	IB	T475D	GM	14	6	39000	4	2	164000	180000
45	8	CONVERTIBLE	FB	CNV	FBG	SV	IB	T500D	GM	14	6	39000	4	2	166000	182500
46	2	CONVERTIBLE	FB	SF	FBG	SV	IB	T450D		14	9	41000	4	2	165500	181500
46	2	CONVERTIBLE	FB	SF	FBG	SV	IB	T650D	GM	14	9	41000	4	2	182500	201000
48	8	COCKPIT YACHT	FB	MYCPT	FBG	SV	IB	T280D	GM	15		47000	3	11	161000	177000
48	8	MOTOR YACHT	FB	MY	FBG	SV	IB	T280D	GM	15		49000	3	11	171500	188500
52		CONVERTIBLE	FB	YTFS	FBG	SV	IB	T550D	GM	16	4	56000	4	6	224500	247000
52		CONVERTIBLE	FB	YTFS	FBG	SV	IB	T650D	GM	16	4	56000	4	6	239500	263000
53	1	EXTENDED DECKHOUSE	FB	MY	FBG	SV	IB	T462D	GM	15	10	57000	4		227000	249500
53	1	MOTOR YACHT	FB	MY	FBG	SV	IB	T450D	S&S	15	10	55000	4		221500	243500
54	9	MOTOR YACHT	FB	MY	FBG	SV	IB	T500D	GM	17	6	62500	4	2	247500	272000
55	8	CONVERTIBLE	FB	YTFS	FBG	SV	IB	T840D		17	6	70000	4	10	346500	380500
55	8	CONVERTIBLE	FB	YTFS	FBG	SV	IB	T840D	GM	17	6	70000	4	10	345500	380000
56	3	MOTOR YACHT	HT	MY	FBG	SV	IB	T570D	GM	18	2	76000	4	11	326500	358500
58	9	MOTOR YACHT	FB	MY	FBG	SV	IB	T625D	GM	18	2	79000	4	11	356500	391500
60	11	CONVERTIBLE	FB	YTFS	FBG	SV	IB	T650D		18		82000	4	11	356000	391000
60	11	CONVERTIBLE	FB	YTFS	FBG	SV	IB	T840D	GM	18		82000	4	11	387000	425000
60	11	CONVERTIBLE	FB	YTFS	FBG	SV	IB	T975D	GM	18		82000	4	11	405000	445000
61	3	COCKPIT YACHT	HT	MYCPT	FBG	SV	IB	T650D	GM	18	2	85000	4	11	403500	443500
61	3	MOTOR YACHT	HT	MY	FBG	SV	IB	T650D	GM	18	2	88000	4	11	401000	441000
63	8	COCKPIT YACHT	HT	MYCPT	FBG	SV	IB	T650D	GM	18	2	79000	4	11	391000	429500
64	1	MOTOR YACHT	HT	MY	FBG	SV	IB	T650D	GM	18	4	95000	5		453500	498500
65		LONG RANGE CRUISER	FB	LRPH	FBG	SV	IB	T280D	GM	17	11	52T	4	10	438000	481500
65	4	SAIL YACHT	SLP	SA/CR	FBG	KC	IB	T175D	GM	17	2	56T	13	10	468500	515000
72	8	MOTOR YACHT	FB	MY	FBG	DV	IB	T840D	GM	18	7	60T	5		**	**
72	8	MOTOR YACHT	FB	MY	FBG	SV	IB	T650D		18	7	55T	7	5	**	**
77	8	COCKPIT MOTOR YACHT	FB	MYCPT	FBG	DV	IB	T840D	GM	18	7	58T	5		**	**
77	8	COCKPIT MOTOR YACHT	FB	MYCPT	FBG	DV	IB	T975D	GM	18	7	58T	5		**	**
77	8	MOTOR YACHT	FB	MY	FBG	DV	IB	T840D	GM	18	7	58T	5		**	**
77	8	MOTOR YACHT	FB	MY	FBG	DV	IB	T975D	GM	18	7	58T	5		**	**
		1984 BOATS														
32	8	FLYBRIDGE FISHERMAN	FB	SDNSF	FBG	DV	IB	T300		12		18000	3	2	52200	57400
32	8	FLYBRIDGE FISHERMAN	FB	SDNSF	FBG	DV	IB	T300D-T305D		12		20000	3	2	78800	86600
32	8	SPORT FISHERMAN	OP	SF	FBG	DV	IB	T300		12		17200	3	2	51300	56300
32	8	SPORT FISHERMAN	OP	SF	FBG	DV	IB	T300D-T305D		12		19100	3	2	76500	84100
36	6	CONVERTIBLE	FB	SDNSF	FBG	DV	IB	T300		13	7	26500	3	9	78200	86000
36	6	CONVERTIBLE	FB	SDNSF	FBG	DV	IB	T275D	CAT	13	7	26500	3	9	92700	102000
36	6	CONVERTIBLE	FB	SDNSF	FBG	DV	IB	T375D	GM	13	7	26500	3	9	96700	106500
36	6	SPORT FISHERMAN	OP	SF	FBG	DV	IB	T300		13	7	25000	3	9	74900	82300
36	6	SPORT FISHERMAN	OP	SF	FBG	DV	IB	T275D	CAT	13	7	25000	3	9	88900	97700
36	6	SPORT FISHERMAN	OP	SF	FBG	DV	IB	T375D	GM	13	7	25000	3	9	93000	102000
42	6	LONG RANGE CRUISER	FB	LRPH	FBG	DS	IB	T112D		14	6	36000	3	10	128000	140500
42	6	LONG RANGE CRUISER	FB	LRPH	FBG	DS	IB	T140D	GM	14	6	36000	3	10	129000	141500
43	1	DOUBLE CABIN	HT	DC	FBG	SV	IB	T280D	GM	14		34000	3	5	130500	143500
43	1	DOUBLE CABIN	HT	DC	FBG	SV	IB	T410D	GM	14		34000	3	5	142500	156500
43	1	DOUBLE CABIN	FB	DC	FBG	SV	IB	T280D	GM	14			3	5	145500	160000
43	1	DOUBLE CABIN	FB	DC	FBG	SV	IB	T410D	GM	14		34000	3	5	142000	156000
43	8	CONVERTIBLE HIGHPERF	FB	SF	FBG	SV	IB	T500D	GM	14	6	37000	4	2	153500	169000
46	2	CONVERTIBLE	FB	SF	FBG	SV	IB	T450D	S&S	14	9	41000	4	2	156000	171500
46	2	CONVERTIBLE	FB	SF	FBG	SV	IB	T650D	GM	14	9	41000	4	2	174000	191500
48	8	COCKPIT YACHT	FB	MYCPT	FBG	SV	IB	T280D	GM	15		47000	3	11	153500	168500
48	8	COCKPIT YACHT	FB	MYCPT	FBG	SV	IB	T425D	GM	15		45000	3	11	168500	185000
48	8	MOTOR YACHT	FB	MY	FBG	SV	IB	T280D	GM	15		49000	3	11	163500	179500
48	8	MOTOR YACHT	FB	MY	FBG	SV	IB	T425D	GM	15		45000	3	11	167500	184000
50		CONVERTIBLE	FB	YTFS	FBG	SV	IB	T570D	GM	16	4	54000	4	6	190500	209500
50		CONVERTIBLE HIGHPERF	FB	YTFS	FBG	SV	IB	T650D	GM	16	4	54000	4	6	197500	217000
52		CONVERTIBLE	FB	YTFS	FBG	SV	IB	T550D		16	4	56000	4	6	220500	242000
52		CONVERTIBLE	FB	YTFS	FBG	SV	IB	T650D		16	4	56000	4	6	234500	258000
53	1	EXTENDED DECKHOUSE	HT	MY	FBG	SV	IB	T462D	GM	15	10	57000	4		220000	242000
53	1	EXTENDED DECKHOUSE	FB	MY	FBG	SV	IB	T462D	GM	15	10	57000	4		218000	239500
53	1	MOTOR YACHT	FB	MY	FBG	SV	IB	T450D	S&S	15	10	55000	4		213000	234000
55	8	CONVERTIBLE	FB	YTFS	FBG	SV	IB	T650D		17	6	70000	4	10	304000	334000
55	8	CONVERTIBLE	FB	YTFS	FBG	SV	IB	T840D	GM	17	6	70000	4	10	331000	364000
55	8	CONVERTIBLE HIGHPERF	FB	YTFS	FBG	SV	IB	T825D	GM	17	6	68000	4	10	322000	354000
56	3	MOTOR YACHT	HT	MY	FBG	SV	IB	T570D	GM	18	2	76000	4	11	313000	344000
56	3	MOTOR YACHT	HT	MY	FBG	SV	IB	T625D		18	2	76000	4	11	325000	357000
56	3	MOTOR YACHT	FB	MY	FBG	SV	IB	T570D	GM	18	2	76000	4	11	307000	337500
60	11	CONVERTIBLE	FB	YTFS	FBG	SV	IB	T650D	GM	18		82000	4	11	344000	378000
60	11	CONVERTIBLE	FB	YTFS	FBG	SV	IB	T840D	GM	18		82000	4	11	370500	407500
60	11	CONVERTIBLE	FB	YTFS	FBG	SV	IB	T975D	GM	18		82000	4	11	388000	426500
61	3	COCKPIT YACHT	HT	MYCPT	FBG	SV	IB	T650D	GM	18	2	85000	4	11	387000	425000
61	3	COCKPIT YACHT	FB	MYCPT	FBG	SV	IB	T650D	GM	18	2	85000	4	11	383500	421500
61	3	MOTOR YACHT	HT	MY	FBG	SV	IB	T650D	GM	18	2	88000	4	11	384500	422500
61	3	MOTOR YACHT	FB	MY	FBG	SV	IB	T650D	GM	18	2	88000	4	11	381500	419000
64	1	MOTOR YACHT	HT	MY	FBG	SV	IB	T650D	GM	18	4	95000	5		434500	477500
64	1	MOTOR YACHT	FB	MY	FBG	SV	IB	T650D	GM	18	4	95000	5		434500	477500
65		LONG RANGE CRUISER	FB	LRPH	FBG	SV	IB	T174D		17	11	57T	4	10	436000	479000
65		LONG RANGE CRUISER	FB	LRPH	FBG	SV	IB	T280D	GM	17	11	52T	4	10	420000	461500
65	4	SAIL YACHT	SLP	SA/CR	FBG	KC	IB	T175D	GM	17	2	56T	13	10	436000	479000
72	8	MOTOR YACHT	FB	MY	FBG	DV	IB	T650D		18	7	55T	5		**	**
72	8	MOTOR YACHT	FB	MY	FBG	DV	IB	T840D	GM	18	7	63T	5		**	**
77	8	COCKPIT MOTOR YACHT	FB	MYCPT	FBG	DV	IB	T825D		18	7	58T	5		**	**
77	8	COCKPIT MOTOR YACHT	FB	MYCPT	FBG	DV	IB	T840D	GM	18	7	58T	5		**	**
77	8	COCKPIT MOTOR YACHT	FB	MYCPT	FBG	DV	IB	T975D	GM	18	7	58T	5		**	**
77	8	MOTOR YACHT	FB	MY	FBG	DV	IB	T825D		18	7	58T	5		**	**
77	8	MOTOR YACHT	FB	MY	FBG	DV	IB	T840D	GM	18	7	58T	5		**	**
77	8	MOTOR YACHT	FB	MY	FBG	DV	IB	T975D	GM	18	7	58T	5		**	**

....For earlier years, see the BUC Used Boat Price Guide, Volume 3

HAWKLINE BOAT COMPANY

NEWPORT RI 02840 COAST GUARD MFG ID- HAX See inside cover to adjust price for area

LOA FT	LOA IN	NAME AND/ OR MODEL	TOP/ RIG	BOAT TYPE	-HULL- MTL	-HULL- TP	ENGINE TP	ENGINE # HP	ENGINE MFG	BEAM FT	BEAM IN	WGT LBS	DRAFT FT	DRAFT IN	RETAIL LOW	RETAIL HIGH
		1985 BOATS														
20	3	LITTLE-RHODY		FSH	FBG	DS	OB			7	8	1600			4800	5550
20	3	LITTLE-RHODY		TRWL	FBG	DS	IO	120		7	8	1400			4100	4800
20	3	OPEN FISHERMAN	OP	UTL	FBG	DS	OB			7	8	1100			2950	3450
		1984 BOATS														
20	3	OPEN FISHERMAN					OB								3900	4550
20	3	OPEN FISHERMAN	OP	UTL	FBG	SV	OB			7	4	1200	1	2	3150	3700
42	3	LITTLE-RHODY					OB								**	**

....For earlier years, see the BUC Used Boat Price Guide, Volume 3

JACK A HELMS COMPANY

IRMO SC 29063 COAST GUARD MFG ID- JAH See inside cover to adjust price for area

LOA FT	LOA IN	NAME AND/ OR MODEL	TOP/ RIG	BOAT TYPE	-HULL- MTL	-HULL- TP	ENGINE TP	ENGINE # HP	ENGINE MFG	BEAM FT	BEAM IN	WGT LBS	DRAFT FT	DRAFT IN	RETAIL LOW	RETAIL HIGH
		1987 BOATS														
23	11	HELMS 24	SLP	SA/RC	FBG	KL	OB			8	10	4000	4		6750	7800
23	11	HELMS 24	SLP	SA/RC	FBG	KL	IB	D		8	10	4300	4		8050	9250

LOA FT	LOA IN	NAME AND/ OR MODEL	TOP/ RIG	BOAT TYPE	HULL MTL	HULL TP	ENGINE TP	ENGINE # HP	ENGINE MFG	BEAM FT	BEAM IN	WGT LBS	DRAFT FT	DRAFT IN	RETAIL LOW	RETAIL HIGH
		1987 BOATS														
26	10	HELMS 27	SLP	SA/RC	FBG	KL	IB	D		9	8	6200	4	3	12700	14500
32		HELMS 32	SLP	SA/RC	FBG	KL	IB	D		10	6	9500	4	10	21200	23600
		1986 BOATS														
23	11	HELMS 24	SLP	SA/CR	FBG	KL	OB			8	10	4000	4		6350	7300
23	11	HELMS 24	SLP	SA/CR	FBG	KL	IB	8D	YAN	8	10	4300	4		7500	8650
23	11	HELMS 24 SHOAL	SLP	SA/CR	FBG	KL	OB			8	10	4100	2	11	6500	7500
23	11	HELMS 24 SHOAL	SLP	SA/CR	FBG	KL	IB	8D	YAN	8	10	4400	2	11	7650	8800
26	10	HELMS 27	SLP	SA/CR	FBG	KL	OB			9	8	5800	4	3	10700	12200
26	10	HELMS 27	SLP	SA/CR	FBG	KL	IB	8D- 18D		9	8	6200	4	3	11900	13700
32		HELMS 32	SLP	SA/CR	FBG	KL	IB	15D- 23D		10	6	9500	4	10	19900	22200
		1985 BOATS														
23	11	HELMS 24	SLP	SA/CR	FBG	KL	OB			8	10	4000	4		6000	6900
23	11	HELMS 24	SLP	SA/CR	FBG	KL	IB	8D	YAN	8	10	4300	4		7050	8100
23	11	HELMS 24 SHOAL	SLP	SA/CR	FBG	KL	OB			8	10	4100	2	11	6150	7050
23	11	HELMS 24 SHOAL	SLP	SA/CR	FBG	KL	IB	8D	YAN	8	10	4400	2	11	7200	8300
26	10	HELMS 27	SLP	SA/CR	FBG	KL	IB	T 15D	YAN	9	8	6200	4	3	11800	13400
32		HELMS 32	SLP	SA/CR	FBG	KL	IB	15D- 23D		10	6	9500	4	10	19000	21100
		1984 BOATS														
23	11	HELMS 24	SLP	SA/CR	FBG	KL	OB			8	10	4000	4		5650	6450
23	11	HELMS 24	SLP	SA/CR	FBG	KL	IB	8D	YAN	8	10	4300	4		6650	7650
23	11	HELMS 24 SHOAL	SLP	SA/CR	FBG	KL	OB			8	10	4100	2	11	5750	6650
23	11	HELMS 24 SHOAL	SLP	SA/CR	FBG	KL	IB	8D	YAN	8	10	4400	2	11	6800	7800
26	10	HELMS 27	SLP	SA/CR	FBG	KL	IB	T 15D	YAN	9	8	6200	4	3	11100	12600
32		HELMS 32	SLP	SA/CR	FBG	KL	IB	15D- 22D		10	6	9500	4	10	17400	19800

....For earlier years, see the BUC Used Boat Price Guide, Volume 3

HENDERSON MFG CO INC

CLEARWATER FL 33522

See inside cover to adjust price for area

LOA FT	LOA IN	NAME AND/ OR MODEL	TOP/ RIG	BOAT TYPE	HULL MTL	HULL TP	ENGINE TP	ENGINE # HP	ENGINE MFG	BEAM FT	BEAM IN	WGT LBS	DRAFT FT	DRAFT IN	RETAIL LOW	RETAIL HIGH
		1985 BOATS														
21	7	BLASTER	SLP	SA/RC	FBG	KC	OB			7	11	1960	4	6	5650	6500

....For earlier years, see the BUC Used Boat Price Guide, Volume 3

HENRIQUES YACHTS INC

BAYVILLE NJ 08721 COAST GUARD MFG ID- HEH See inside cover to adjust price for area

For more recent years, see the BUC Used Boat Price Guide, Volume 1

LOA FT	LOA IN	NAME AND/ OR MODEL	TOP/ RIG	BOAT TYPE	HULL MTL	HULL TP	ENGINE TP	ENGINE # HP	ENGINE MFG	BEAM FT	BEAM IN	WGT LBS	DRAFT FT	DRAFT IN	RETAIL LOW	RETAIL HIGH
		1996 BOATS														
28	2	EXPRESS FISH 28	MT	EXP	FBG	SV	IB	300D		10	2	10500	2	6	79400	87200
28	2	EXPRESS FISH 28	MT	EXP	FBG	SV	IB	T150D-T200D		10	2	10500	2	6	79100	91400
35	4	ALASKA CRUISER	FB	TRLCP	FBG	DS	IB	350D	CAT	12	1	22000	3	4	147000	162000
35	4	ALASKA CRUISER	FB	TRLCP	FBG	DS	IB	420D	CUM	12	1	22000	3	4	148500	163000
35	4	MAINE COASTER	FB	SF	FBG	DS	IB	350D	CAT	12	1	22000	3	4	132500	145500
35	4	MAINE COASTER	FB	SF	FBG	DS	IB	420D	CUM	12	1	22000	3	4	133500	147000
35	4	MAINE COASTER	EPH	UTL	FBG	DS	IB	300D	CAT	12	1	18000	3	4	127500	140000
35	4	MAINE COASTER	EPH	UTL	FBG	DS	IB	350D	CAT	12	1	18000	3	4	129500	142000
38		EL BRAVO	TT	EXP	FBG	SV	IB	T375D	CAT	13	10	28000	3	10	201000	221000
38		EL BRAVO	TT	EXP	FBG	SV	IB	T420D	CAT	13	10	28000	3	10	208000	228500
38		SPORTFISH	FB	SF	FBG	SV	IB	T375D	CAT	13	10	28000	3	10	204000	224000
38		SPORTFISH	FB	SF	FBG	SV	IB	T420D	CAT	13	10	28000	3	10	210500	231500
44		SPORTFISH	FB	SF	FBG	SV	IB	T550D	DD	14	10	37000	3	8	281000	308500
44		SPORTFISH	FB	SF	FBG	SV	IB	T600D	MAN	14	10	37000	3	8	283000	311000
50		SPORTFISH	FB	SF	FBG	SV	IB	T725D	DD	16	6	48000	4	8	379500	417000
50		SPORTFISH	FB	SF	FBG	SV	IB	T840D	MAN	16	6	48000	4	8	404500	445000
		1995 BOATS														
28	4	HENRIQUES EXPRESS	TT	OPFSH	FBG	SV	IB	T200D	VLVO	10	2	11000	2	6	80100	88000
35	4	ALASKA CRUISER		TRWL	FBG	SV	IB	350D	CAT	12	1	22000	3	7	148500	163000
35	4	MAINE COASTER	FB	SF	FBG	SV	IB	T200D	VLVO	12	1	22000	3	1	126000	138000
35	4	MAINE COASTER	FB	SF	FBG	SV	IB	T250D	CUM	12	1	22000	3	1	129500	142500
35	4	MAINE COASTER	FB	SF	FBG	SV	IB	T250D	PERK	12	1	22000	3	1	131000	144000
35	4	MAINE COASTER WORK	FB	TRWL	FBG	SV	IB	250D	CUM	12	1	18000	3	3	126500	139000
		IB 250D DEER 126500 139000, IB 300D CAT 130000 143000, IB 300D CUM 129000 141500														
		IB 300D VLVO 128500 141000, IB 350D CAT 133000 146000, IB 400D CUM 134500 148000														
38		EL BRAVO	TT	OPFSH	FBG	SV	IB	T375D	CAT	13	10	28000	3	10	192500	211500
		IB T430D VLVO 189500 208500, IB T435D CAT 201500 221500, IB T450D MERL 198000 217500														
38		HENRIQUES	FB	SF	FBG	SV	IB	T375D	CAT	13	10	28000	3	10	193000	212000
38		HENRIQUES	FB	SF	FBG	SV	IB	T380D	VLVO	13	10	28000	3	10	184000	202500
38		HENRIQUES	FB	SF	FBG	SV	IB	T450D	MERL	13	10	28000	3	10	198000	218000
44		HENRIQUES	FB	SF	FBG	SV	IB	T550D	GM	14	10	37000	3	8	255500	281000
44		HENRIQUES	FB	SF	FBG	SV	IB	T600D	MERL	14	10	37000	3	8	264500	290500
44		HENRIQUES	FB	SF	FBG	SV	IB	T680D	MAN	14	10	37000	3	8	272000	299000
50		HENRIQUES	FB	SF	FBG	SV	IB	T725D	GM	16	2	50000	4		347500	382000
50		HENRIQUES	FB	SF	FBG	SV	IB	T735D	GM	16	2	50000	4		349500	384000
50		HENRIQUES	FB	SF	FBG	SV	IB	T840D	MAN	16	2	50000	4		371500	408000
		1994 BOATS														
28	4	HENRIQUES EXPRESS	TT	OPFSH	FBG	SV	IB	T200D	VLVO	10	2	11000	2	6	76200	83700
35	4	ALASKA CRUISER		TRWL	FBG	SV	IB	350D	CAT	12	1	22000	3	7	141000	155000
35	4	MAINE COASTER	FB	SF	FBG	SV	IB	T200D	VLVO	12	1	22000	3	1	119500	131500
35	4	MAINE COASTER	FB	SF	FBG	SV	IB	T250D	CUM	12	1	22000	3	1	123500	135500
35	4	MAINE COASTER	FB	SF	FBG	SV	IB	T250D	PERK	12	1	22000	3	1	125000	137000
35	4	MAINE COASTER WORK	FB	TRWL	FBG	SV	IB	250D	CUM	12	1	18000	3	3	120500	132500
		IB 250D DEER 120500 132500, IB 300D CAT 123500 136000, IB 300D CUM 122500 135000														
		IB 300D VLVO 122000 134000, IB 350D CAT 126500 139000, IB 400D CUM 128000 141000														
38		EL BRAVO	TT	OPFSH	FBG	SV	IB	T375D	CAT	13	10	28000	3	10	184500	203000
		IB T430D VLVO 181500 199500, IB T435D CAT 193000 212000, IB T450D MERL 189500 208500														
38		HENRIQUES	FB	SF	FBG	SV	IB	T375D	CAT	13	10	28000	3	10	185000	203000
38		HENRIQUES	FB	SF	FBG	SV	IB	T380D	VLVO	13	10	28000	3	10	176500	194000
38		HENRIQUES	FB	SF	FBG	SV	IB	T450D	MERL	13	10	28000	3	10	190000	208500
44		HENRIQUES	FB	SF	FBG	SV	IB	T550D	GM	14	10	37000	3	8	244500	269000
44		HENRIQUES	FB	SF	FBG	SV	IB	T600D	MERL	14	10	37000	3	8	253500	278500
44		HENRIQUES	FB	SF	FBG	SV	IB	T680D	MAN	14	10	37000	3	8	260500	286500
50		HENRIQUES	FB	SF	FBG	SV	IB	T725D	GM	16	2	50000	4		333000	365500
50		HENRIQUES	FB	SF	FBG	SV	IB	T735D	GM	16	2	50000	4		334500	368000
50		HENRIQUES	FB	SF	FBG	SV	IB	T840D	MAN	16	2	50000	4		355000	390500
		1993 BOATS														
35	4	MAINE COASTER	FB	SF	FBG	SV	IB	T200D	VLVO	12	1	22000	3	1	114000	125500
35	4	MAINE COASTER	FB	SF	FBG	SV	IB	T250D	CUM	12	1	22000	3	1	117500	129000
35	4	MAINE COASTER	FB	SF	FBG	SV	IB	T250D	PERK	12	1	22000	3	1	119000	130500
35	4	MAINE COASTER WORK	FB	TRWL	FBG	SV	IB	250D	CUM	12	1	18000	3	3	114500	126000
		IB 250D DEER 115000 126000, IB 300D CAT 118000 129500, IB 300D CUM 117000 128500														
		IB 300D VLVO 116500 128000, IB 350D CAT 120500 132500, IB 400D CUM 122000 134000														
38		EL BRAVO	TT	OPFSH	FBG	SV	IB	T375D	CAT	13	10	28000	3	10	176000	193000
		IB T430D VLVO 173000 190000, IB T435D CAT 184000 202000, IB T450D MERL 180500 198500														
38		HENRIQUES	FB	SF	FBG	SV	IB	T375D	CAT	13	10	28000	3	10	176000	193500
38		HENRIQUES	FB	SF	FBG	SV	IB	T380D	VLVO	13	10	28000	3	10	168000	185000
38		HENRIQUES	FB	SF	FBG	SV	IB	T450D	MERL	13	10	28000	3	10	181000	199000
44		HENRIQUES	FB	SF	FBG	SV	IB	T550D	GM	14	10	37000	3	8	233000	256000
44		HENRIQUES	FB	SF	FBG	SV	IB	T600D	MERL	14	10	37000	3	8	241500	265000
44		HENRIQUES	FB	SF	FBG	SV	IB	T680D	MAN	14	10	37000	3	8	248000	273000
50		HENRIQUES	FB	SF	FBG	SV	IB	T725D	GM	16	2	50000	4		317000	348500
50		HENRIQUES	FB	SF	FBG	SV	IB	T735D	GM	16	2	50000	4		319000	350500
50		HENRIQUES	FB	SF	FBG	SV	IB	T840D	MAN	16	2	50000	4		338000	371500
		1992 BOATS														
35	4	MAIN COASTER WKBOAT		TRWL	FBG	SV	IB	250D	CUM	12	1	18000	3	3	109500	120000
		IB 250D DEER 109500 120500, IB 300D CAT 112500 123500, IB 300D CUM 111500 122500														
		IB 300D VLVO 111000 122000, IB 350D CAT 115000 126500, IB 400D CUM 116500 128000														
35	4	MAINE COASTER	FB	SF	FBG	SV	IB	T200D	VLVO	12		22000	3	1	109000	119500
35	4	MAINE COASTER	FB	SF	FBG	SV	IB	T250D	CUM	12		22000	3	1	112000	123500
35	4	MAINE COASTER	FB	SF	FBG	SV	IB	T250D	PERK	12		22000	3	1	113500	125000
38		EL BRAVO	TT	OPFSH	FBG	SV	IB	T375D	CAT	13	10	28000	3	10	167500	184000
		IB T430D VLVO 165000 181500, IB T435D CAT 175000 192500, IB T450D MERL 172000 189500														
38		HENRIQUES	FB	SF	FBG	SV	IB	T375D	CAT	13	10	28000	3	10	168000	184500
38		HENRIQUES	FB	SF	FBG	SV	IB	T380D	VLVO	13	10	28000	3	10	160500	176000
38		HENRIQUES	FB	SF	FBG	SV	IB	T450D	MERL	13	10	28000	3	10	172500	189500
44		HENRIQUES	FB	SF	FBG	SV	IB	T550D	GM	14	10	37000	3	8	222000	244000
44		HENRIQUES	FB	SF	FBG	SV	IB	T600D	MERL	14	10	37000	3	8	230000	253000
44		HENRIQUES	FB	SF	FBG	SV	IB	T680D	MAN	14	10	37000	3	8	236500	260000
50		HENRIQUES	FB	SF	FBG	SV	IB	T725D	GM	16	2	50000	4		302000	332000
50		HENRIQUES	FB	SF	FBG	SV	IB	T735D	GM	16	2	50000	4		304000	334000
50		HENRIQUES	FB	SF	FBG	SV	IB	T840D	MAN	16	2	50000	4		322500	354000
		1989 BOATS														
35	4	MAINE-COASTER	FB	SF	FBG	SV	IB	T250D	GM	12		22000	3	1	98100	108000
38		HENRIQUES	FB	SF	FBG	DV	IB	T375D	CAT	13	10	28000	3	10	146000	160500
44		HENRIQUES	FB	SF	FBG	SV	IB	T440D		15		38000	4		180000	197500
44		HENRIQUES	FB	SF	FBG	SV	IB	T550D	GM	15		38000	4		196000	215000
		1988 BOATS														
35	4	MAINE-COASTER	FB	SF	FBG	SV	IB	T250D	GM	12		22000	3	1	93900	103000
38		HENRIQUES	FB	SF	FBG	DV	IB	T375D	CAT	13	10	28000	3	10	139500	153500

CONTINUED ON NEXT PAGE

LOA FT	IN	NAME AND/ OR MODEL	TOP/ RIG	BOAT TYPE	-HULL- MTL	TP	ENGINE TP	# HP	MFG	BEAM FT	IN	WGT LBS	DRAFT FT	IN	RETAIL LOW	RETAIL HIGH
		1988 BOATS														
38		HENRIQUES	FB	SF	FBG	DV	IB	T420D	GM	13	10	28000	3	10	140000	154000
44		HENRIQUES	FB	SF	FBG	SV	IB	T440D		15		38000	4		172000	189000
44		HENRIQUES	FB	SF	FBG	SV	IB	T550D	GM	15		38000	4		187000	205500
		1987 BOATS														
35	4	MAINE-COASTER	TT	OPFSH	FBG	SV	IB	T200D	VLVO	12		19000	3	1	87500	96200
35	4	MAINE-COASTER	TT	OPFSH	FBG	SV	IB	T250D	GM	12		19000	3	1	90600	99600
35	4	MAINE-COASTER	TT	OPFSH	FBG	SV	IB	T250D	VLVO	12		19000	3	1	89700	98600
35	4	MAINE-COASTER	FB	SF	FBG	SV	IB	T200D	VLVO	12		22000	3	1	87100	95700
35	4	MAINE-COASTER	FB	SF	FBG	SV	IB	T250D	GM	12		22000	3	1	89900	98800
35	4	MAINE-COASTER	FB	SF	FBG	SV	IB	T250D	VLVO	12		22000	3	1	89100	97900
38		HENRIQUES	FB	SF	FBG	DV	IB	T358D	VLVO	13	10	28000	3	10	126000	138500
38		HENRIQUES	FB	SF	FBG	DV	IB	T375D	CAT	13	10	28000	3	10	133500	146500
38		HENRIQUES	FB	SF	FBG	DV	IB	T420D	GM	13	10	28000	3	10	134000	147500
44		HENRIQUES	FB	SF	FBG	SV	IB	T375D	CAT	15		38000	4		158000	173500
		IB T440D 164500 180500, IB T450D CUM 165000 181500, IB T450D GM 165500 182000														
		IB T550D GM 179000 196500														
		1986 BOATS														
35	4	MAIN-COASTER OPFSH	OP	FSH	FBG	SV	IB	T220D	GM	12		14000	3	1	73200	80500
35	4	MAIN-COASTER OPFSH	OP	FSH	FBG	SV	IB	T250D	VLVO	12		14000	3	1	73900	81200
35	4	MAIN-COASTER SPT	FB	SF	FBG	SV	IB	T240D	CUM	12		15000	3	1	70400	77400
35	4	MAIN-COASTER SPT	FB	SF	FBG	SV	IB	T250D	VLVO	12		15000	3	1	68700	75500
35	4	MAINE-COASTER SPT	FB	SF	FBG	SV	IB	T165D	VLVO	12		15000	3	1	65300	71800
35	4	MAINE-COASTER SPT	FB	SF	FBG	SV	IB	T220D	GM	12		15000	3	1	68200	74900
35	4	MAINE-COASTER SPT	FB	SF	FBG	SV	IB	T240D	PERK	12		15000	3	1	68400	75200
44		MAINE-COASTER SPT	OP	FSH	FBG	SV	IB	T450D	GM	14	10	37000	4		149500	164000
44		MAINE-COASTER SPT	OP	FSH	FBG	SV	IB	T530D	GM	14	10	37000	4		158000	173500
44		MAINE-COASTER SPT	FB	SF	FBG	SV	IB	T300D	VLVO	14	10	37000	4		133500	147000
44		MAINE-COASTER SPT	FB	SF	FBG	SV	IB	T355D	CAT	14	10	37000	4		142500	156500
		1985 BOATS														
35	4	MAINE-COASTER CHARTR	OP	FSH	FBG	SV	IB	233D		12		14000	3	1	64900	71300
35	4	MAINE-COASTER CHARTR	OP	FSH	FBG	SV	IB	300D	VLVO	12		14000	3	1	65700	72200
35	4	MAINE-COASTER CHARTR	HT	FSH	FBG	SV	IB	300D	VLVO	12		14000	3	1	65700	72200
35	4	MAINE-COASTER CHARTR	FB	FSH	FBG	SV	IB	300D	VLVO	12		14000	3	1	65700	72200
35	4	MAINE-COASTER OPEN	TT	SF	FBG	SV	IB	T220D	GM	12		15000	3	1	72700	79800
35	4	MAINE-COASTER SPT	FB	SF	FBG	SV	IB	T165D	VLVO	12		15000	3	1	62700	68900
		IB T200D PERK 65300 71800, IB T220D GM 65400 71900, IB T240D CUM 66100 72600														
44		MAINE-COASTER SPORT	FB	FSH	FBG	SV	IB	T410D	J&T	14	10	37000	4		140000	153500
44		MAINE-COASTER SPT	FB	SF	FBG	SV	IB	T355D	CAT	14	10	37000	4		136000	149500
		1984 BOATS														
35	4	MAINE-COASTER CHARTR	HT	FSH	FBG	SV	IB	235D	VLVO	12		14000	3		64600	71000
		IB 286D VLVO 62800 69000, IB 300D CAT 66900 73500, IB 300D VLVO 64100 70500														
		IB 310D GM 64100 70400														
35	4	MAINE-COASTER CHARTR	FB	FSH	FBG	SV	IB	235D	VLVO	12		14000	3		61900	68000
		IB 286D VLVO 62800 69000, IB 300D CAT 64100 70400, IB 300D VLVO 63100 69300														
		IB 310D GM 63800 70100														
35	4	MAINE-COASTER COMM	HT	FSH	FBG	SV	IB	235D	VLVO	12		14000	3	2	59200	65000
35	4	MAINE-COASTER COMM	HT	FSH	FBG	SV	IB	300D	VLVO	12		14000	3	2	59400	65200
35	4	MAINE-COASTER COMM	HT	FSH	FBG	SV	IB	310D	GM	12		14000	3	2	63600	69900
35	4	MAINE-COASTER SPT	FB	SF	FBG	SV	IB	235D	VLVO	12		13500	3		54500	59900
		IB 300D VLVO 57800 63600, IB T165D VLVO 56900 62600, IB T215D J&T 60600 66600														
		IB T235D VLVO 61600 67700														
44		MAINE-COASTER CHARTR	FB	SF	FBG	DV	IB	T300D	VLVO	14	8	37000	4		127000	139500
44		MAINE-COASTER CHARTR	FB	SF	FBG	DV	IB	T355D	CAT	14	8	37000	4		136000	149500
44		MAINE-COASTER CNV	FB	SDNSF	FBG	SV	IB	T300D	VLVO	14	8	37000	4		125000	137500
44		MAINE-COASTER CNV	FB	SDNSF	FBG	SV	IB	T355D	CAT	14	8	37000	4		134000	147000
44		MAINE-COASTER CNV	FB	SDNSF	FBG	SV	IB	T410D	GM	14	8	37000	4		139000	152500

....For earlier years, see the BUC Used Boat Price Guide, Volume 3

HERITAGE BOAT WORKS INC

HOOD RIVER OR 47031 COAST GUARD MFG ID- HRG See inside cover to adjust price for area

LOA FT	IN	NAME AND/ OR MODEL	TOP/ RIG	BOAT TYPE	-HULL- MTL	TP	ENGINE TP	# HP	MFG	BEAM FT	IN	WGT LBS	DRAFT FT	IN	RETAIL LOW	RETAIL HIGH
		1990 BOATS														
20		BIG-WATER SKIFF		FSH	FBG	FL	IO	130		8		2250			7350	8450
20		BIG-WATER SKIFF		SF	FBG	SV	IO	130		8		2250			8000	9200
22		BIG-WATER SKIFF		FSH	FBG	FL	IO	130		8		2400			8550	9800
22		BIG-WATER SKIFF		SF	FBG	SV	IO	130		8		2600			9700	11000
26		YANKEE 26	SLP	SAIL	FBG		IB			8	9	5355	4	9	12100	13800
27	2	BIG-WATER 28		SDNSF	FBG	SV	IB	T150D	CUM	10		8500	2	6	48700	53500
29	6	SNOWBALL 29.5		FSH	FBG		IB	250D	CUM	10	6	9500	3		47100	51800
30		BIG-WATER 30		SDNSF	FBG	SV	IB	T210D	CUM	10		10500	2	6	54300	59700
30		YANKEE 30	SLP	SAIL	FBG		IB	18D	VLVO	9		10000	5		25100	27900
39		WINDFALL 39	SLP	SAIL	FBG		IB	D		12	4	23275	5		61600	67700
40		SNOWBALL 40		FSH	FBG		IB	375D	CAT	11	5	16000	4		124000	136000
		1989 BOATS														
20		BIG-WATER SKIFF		FSH	FBG	FL	IO	130		8		2250			6950	7950
20		BIG-WATER SKIFF		SF	FBG	SV	IO	130		8		2250			7500	8600
22		BIG-WATER SKIFF		FSH	FBG	FL	IO	130		8		2400			8100	9300
22		BIG-WATER SKIFF		SF	FBG	SV	IO	130		8		2600			9100	10400
26		YANKEE 26	SLP	SAIL	FBG		IB			8	9	5355	4	9	11400	12900
27	2	BIG-WATER 28		SDNSF	FBG	SV	IB	T150D	CUM	10		8500	2	6	46500	51100
29	6	SNOWBALL 29.5		FSH	FBG		IB	250D	CUM	10	6	9500	3		44500	49500
30		BENFORD 30	SLP	SAIL	FBG		IB			10	6	10975	4	6	25900	28700
30		BIG-WATER 30		SDNSF	FBG	SV	IB	T210D	CUM	10		10500	2	6	51900	57000
30		YANKEE 30	SLP	SAIL	FBG		IB	18D	VLVO	9		10000	5		23600	26200
39		WINDFALL 39	SLP	SAIL	FBG		IB			12	4	23275	5		56800	62400
40		SNOWBALL 40		FSH	FBG		IB	375D	CAT	11	5	16000	4		118500	130000
		1988 BOATS														
20		BIG-WATER SKIFF		FSH	FBG	FL	IO	130		8		2250			6550	7550
20		BIG-WATER SKIFF		SF	FBG	SV	IO	130		8		2250			7050	8150
22		BIG-WATER SKIFF		FSH	FBG	FL	IO	130		8		2400			7550	8700
22		BIG-WATER SKIFF		SF	FBG	SV	IO	130		8		2600			8500	9800
27	2	BIG-WATER 28		SDNSF	FBG	SV	IB	T150D	CUM	10		8500	2	6	44000	48900
30		BIG-WATER 30		SDNSF	FBG	SV	IB	T210D	CUM	10		10500	2	6	49700	54600
30		YANKEE 30		SAIL	FBG		IB	18D	VLVO	9		10500	5		23300	25900
40		SNOWBALL 40		FSH	FBG		IB	375D	CAT	11	5	16000	4		113000	124000
		1987 BOATS														
20		BIG-WATER 20		CUD	FBG	SV	OB			8		3100	1	5	7250	8350
20		BIG-WATER SKIFF		FSH	FBG	FL	IO	130		8		2250			6200	7150
20		BIG-WATER SKIFF		SF	FBG	SV	IO	130		8		2250			6700	7700
20		HERITAGE 20	CAT	SA/CR	FBG	KL				8		5250	3	6	8050	9250
22		BIG-WATER SKIFF		FSH	FBG	FL	OB			8		1260			4550	5200
22		BIG-WATER SKIFF		FSH	FBG	FL	IO	130		8		2400			7200	8250
22		BIG-WATER SKIFF		SF	FBG	SV	IO	130		8		2600			8150	9350
22		HERITAGE 22 KNOCKABT	SLP	SA/CR	FBG	KL				7		4000	3		6300	7250
26		YANKEE 26	SLP	SA/RC	FBG	KL				8	8	5335	4	6	9450	10700
27	2	BIG-WATER 28		SDNSF	FBG	SV	IB	T150D	CUM	10		8500	2	6	42400	47100
30		BENFORD 30	CUT	SA/CR	FBG	KL	IB	D		10	6	11000	4	6	23000	25500
30		BIG-WATER 30		SDNSF	FBG	SV	IB	T210D	CUM	10		10500	2	6	47600	52300
30		YANKEE 30	SLP	SA/RC	FBG	KL				9		10000	5		20800	23100
39		WINDFALL 39	CUT	SA/CR	FBG	KL	IB	D		12	4	23275	5		49800	54800
		1986 BOATS														
20		BIG WATER SKIFF		CUD	FBG	SV	OB			7	11	1200			4000	4600
20		BIG WATER SKIFF	FB	FSH	FBG	SV	IO	130		7	11	2200			5850	6700
20		HERITAGE 20		CR	FBG		IB	12D		8		5000			13800	15600
20		HERITAGE 20	CAT	SA/CR	FBG	KL				8		5250	3	6	7550	8700
20		KNOCKABOUT	SLP	SA/CR	FBG	KL	IB	D		7		4000	3		6350	7300
22		BIG WATER SKIFF		CTRCN	FBG	SV	OB			7	11	1800			6000	6900
22		BIG WATER SKIFF		CUD	FBG	SV	IO	130		7	11	3400			7950	9150
22		BIGWATER 22		CTRCN	FBG	SV	OB			8		3500	1	6	9550	10900
26		BIG WATER SKIFF		CBNCR	FBG	SV	OB			9	6	4000			13600	15500
26		BIG WATER SKIFF		CBNCR	FBG	SV	IO	220		9	6	6000			19200	21300
26		YANKEE 26	SLP	SA/RC	FBG	KL				8	8	5355	4	9	8950	10200
30		BENFORD 30	CUT	SA/CR	FBG	KL	IB	D		10	6	10975	4	6	21500	23900
30		BIG WATER SKIFF		CBNCR	FBG	SV	OB			9	11	4800			22000	24400
30		BIG WATER SKIFF		CBNCR	FBG	SV	IO	T220		9	11	10000			29600	32900
30		BIG WATER SKIFF	FB	SF	FBG	SV	IB	T220		9	11	10000			31800	35300
30		YANKEE 30	SLP	SA/RC	FBG	KL	IB	D		9		10000	5		19500	21700
39		WINDFALL 39	CUT	SA/CR	FBG	KL	IB	D		12	4	23275	5		46700	51300
		1985 BOATS														
16		HERITAGE 16	GAF	SA/OD	FBG	CB				4	6	250		8	955	1150
18	6	BIG-WATER SKIFF		SF	FBG	SV	IO	130		7		1100			3800	4450
20		BIG-WATER SKIFF		FSH	FBG	FL	IO	130		8		2250			5650	6500
20		BIG-WATER SKIFF		SF	FBG	SV	IO	130		8		2250			6150	7050
20		HERITAGE 20	CAT	SA/CR	FBG	KL				8		5250	3	6	7100	8200
22		BIG-WATER SKIFF		FSH	FBG	FL	OB			8		1260			4250	4950
22		BIG-WATER SKIFF		FSH	FBG	FL	IO	130		8		2400			6550	7550
22		BIG-WATER SKIFF		SF	FBG	SV	IO	130		8		2600			7350	8450
22		HERITAGE 22 KNOCKABT	SLP	SA/CR	FBG	KL				7		4000	3		5600	6400
26		YANKEE 26	SLP	SA/RC	FBG	KL				8	8	5335	4	6	8300	9550
30		BENFORD 30	CUT	SA/CR	FBG	KL	IB	D		10	6	11000	4	6	20300	22500
30		YANKEE 30	SLP	SA/RC	FBG	KL				9		10000	5		18600	20600
39		WINDFALL 39	CUT	SA/CR	FBG	KL	IB	D		12	4	23275	5		43300	48100

LOA FT IN	NAME AND/ OR MODEL	TOP/ RIG	BOAT TYPE	HULL MTL TP	TP	ENGINE # HP	MFG	BEAM FT IN	WGT LBS	DRAFT FT IN	RETAIL LOW	RETAIL HIGH
					1984 BOATS							
20	HERITAGE	OP	CR	FBG DV	IB	12D	BMW	8	5260	2 6	13200	15000
20	HERITAGE	SLP	SAIL	FBG CB	IB	12D	BMW	8	5260	2 6	7350	8450
20	HERITAGE	SLP	SAIL	FBG KL	IB	12D	BMW	8	5260	3 6	7350	8450
20	HERITAGE CRUISING	CAT	SA/CR	FBG KL	IB	12D	BMW	8	5260	3 6	7350	8450
22	BENFORD 22	SLP	SAIL	FBG KL	IB	7D	BMW	7	4000	3	5800	6650
26	YANKEE 26	SLP	SAIL	FBG	IB	6D	BMW	8 8	5335	4 9	8450	9700
30	BENFORD 30	MY		FBG SV	IO	35D	BMW	10	10975	4 6	34200	38000
30	BENFORD 30	SLP	SAIL	FBG KL	SD	35D	BMW	10 6	10975	4 6	19200	21300
30 1	YANKEE 30	SLP	SAIL	FBG KL	IB	10D	BMW	9	10000	5	17000	19300
39	WINDFALL 39	CUT	SAIL	F/S KL	IB	35D	BMW	12 4	23275	5	40100	44600

....For earlier years, see the BUC Used Boat Price Guide, Volume 3

HERITAGE YACHTS INTERNATIONAL
HUNTINGTON HABOR CA 926 COAST GUARD MFG ID- HTG See inside cover to adjust price for area

LOA FT IN	NAME AND/ OR MODEL	TOP/ RIG	BOAT TYPE	HULL MTL TP	TP	ENGINE # HP	MFG	BEAM FT IN	WGT LBS	DRAFT FT IN	RETAIL LOW	RETAIL HIGH
					1987 BOATS							
33 6	HERITAGE DC	FB	TRWL	FBG DV	IB	T120D	LEHM	11 9	17500	3 6	79600	87500
34 5	HERITAGE SUNDECK	FB	TRWL	FBG DV	IB	T120D	LEHM	12 6	18500	3 3	81300	89300
37 8	HERITAGE DC	FB	TRWL	FBG DV	IB	T120D	LEHM	12 10	21000	3 5	92000	101000
37 8	HERITAGE SUNDECK	FB	TRWL	FBG DV	IB	T120D	LEHM	12 10	21000	3 5	87300	95900
39 4	HERITAGE DC	FB	TRWL	FBG DV	IB	T170D	BENZ	13 3	32000	4 3	137000	150500
41 2	HERITAGE DC	FB	TRWL	FBG DV	IB	T170D	BENZ	13 9	28000	4 6	125500	138000
41 2	HERITAGE SDN	FB	TRWL	FBG DV	IB	T170D	BENZ	13	24000		117500	129000
44	HERITAGE SDN	FB	SF	FBG DV	IB	T410D	J&T	14 6	27000	3 10	148000	162500
47	HERITAGE DC	FB	TRWL	FBG DV	IB	T160D	LEHM	14	26000	3 10	127500	140000
48	HERITAGE	FB	TRWL	FBG DV	IB	T170D	BENZ	15	33000	3 10	152000	167000
48	HERITAGE 48	FB	YTFS	FBG DV	IB	T170D	BENZ	15	33000	3 10	134500	147500
48	HERITAGE FD	FB	TRWL	FBG DV	IB	T170D	BENZ	15	34000	3 10	141000	155000
56 1	HERITAGE	FB	TRWL	FBG DV	IB	T265D	GM	17 10	60000	4 4	213000	234000
					1986 BOATS							
33 6	HERITAGE DC	FB	TRWL	FBG DV	IB	T120D	LEHM	11 9	17500	3 6	76300	83800
34 5	HERITAGE SUNDECK	FB	TRWL	FBG DV	IB	T120D	LEHM	12 6	18500	3 3	**	**
34 5	HERITAGE SUNDECK	FB	TRWL	FBG DV	IB	T	D	12 6	18500	3 3	**	**
37 8	HERITAGE DC	FB	TRWL	FBG DV	IB	T	D	12 10	21000	3 5	**	**
37 8	HERITAGE SUNDECK	FB	TRWL	FBG DV	IB	T	D	12 10	21000	3 5	**	**
39 4	HERITAGE DC	FB	TRWL	FBG DV	IB	T170D	BENZ	13 3	32000	4 3	131000	144000
41 2	HERITAGE DC	FB	TRWL	FBG DV	IB	T170D	BENZ	13 9	28000	4 6	120000	132000
41 2	HERITAGE SDN	FB	TRWL	FBG DV	IB	T170D	BENZ	13	24000		112500	123500
44	HERITAGE SDN	FB	TRWL	FBG DV	IB	T410D	J&T	14 6	27000	3 10	137500	151500
47	HERITAGE DC	FB	TRWL	FBG DV	IB	T160D	LEHM	14 6	26000	3 10	122000	134000
48	HERITAGE	FB	TRWL	FBG DV	IB	T170D	BENZ	15	34000	3 10	149500	164500
48	HERITAGE 48	FB	YTFS	FBG DV	IB	T	D	15	34000	3 10	**	**
48	HERITAGE FD	FB	TRWL	FBG DV	IB	T170D	BENZ	15	34000	3 10	130500	143500
56 1	HERITAGE	FB	TRWL	FBG DV	IB	T265D	GM	17 10	60000	4 4	204000	224000
					1985 BOATS							
33 6	HERITAGE DC	FB	TRWL	FBG DV	IB	T120D	LEHM	11 9	17500	3 6	73200	80400
34 5	HERITAGE SUNDECK	FB	TRWL	FBG DV	IB	T120D	LEHM	12 6	18500	3 3	74800	82200
34 5	HERITAGE SUNDECK	FB	TRWL	FBG DV	IB	T120D		12 6	9500	3 3	52800	58000
34 5	HERITAGE SUNDECK	FB	TRWL	FBG DV	IB	T120D	LEHM	12 6	18500	3 3	77600	85300
39 4	HERITAGE DC	FB	TRWL	FBG DV	IB	T120D		13 3	23000	4	94900	104500
39 4	HERITAGE DC	FB	TRWL	FBG DV	IB	T170D	BENZ	13 3	32000	4	125500	137500
41 2	HERITAGE DC	FB	TRWL	FBG DV	IB	T170D	BENZ	13 9	28000	3 6	115000	126500
41 2	HERITAGE SDN	FB	TRWL	FBG DV	IB	T170D	BENZ	13	24000		107500	118500
44	HERITAGE SF	FB	SF	FBG DV	IB	T410D	J&T	14 6	27000	3 10	140000	154000
44 2	HERITAGE	FB	SF	FBG DV	IB	T310D		14	28000		115000	126500
46 7	HERITAGE SUNDECK	KTH	SA/CR	FBG KL	IB	120D		13 5	14000	5 3	139000	153000
47	HERITAGE DC	FB	TRWL	FBG DV	IB	T160D	LEHM	14	26000	3 10	116500	128000
47 8	HERITAGE FD	FB	TRWL	FBG DV	IB	T160D		15	40000	3 10	134500	148000
47 8	HERITAGE SUNDECK	FB	TRWL	FBG DV	IB	T170D	BENZ	15	40000	3 10	133000	146500
48	HERITAGE	FB	TRWL	FBG DV	IB	T170D	BENZ	15	34000	3 10	139000	153000
48	HERITAGE FD	FB	TRWL	FBG DV	IB	T170D	BENZ	15	34000	3 10	128000	140500
56 1	HERITAGE	FB	TRWL	FBG DV	IB	T265D	GM	17 10	60000	4 4	195000	214500

HALSEY C HERRESHOFF INC
BRISTOL RI 02809   See inside cover to adjust price for area

LOA FT IN	NAME AND/ OR MODEL	TOP/ RIG	BOAT TYPE	HULL MTL TP	TP	ENGINE # HP	MFG	BEAM FT IN	WGT LBS	DRAFT FT IN	RETAIL LOW	RETAIL HIGH
					1987 BOATS							
25	ALERION 25	SLP	SAIL	FBG KL				7 3	4800	3 7	19200	21300
33	BB 33	SLP	SAIL	FBG KL				8 6	6850	3 3	30900	34300
33	STREAKER	SLP	SA/RC	WD KL				8	5200	6	20900	23200
					1986 BOATS							
25	ALERION 25	SLP	SAIL	FBG KL				7 3	4800	3 7	18300	20300
33	BB 33	SLP	SA/OD	FBG KL				8 6	6850	3 3	29100	32300
33	STREAKER	SLP	SA/OD	WD KL				8	5200	6	19700	21900
					1985 BOATS							
25	ALERION 25	SLP	SAIL	FBG KL				7 3	4800	3 7	16800	19100
33	STREAKER	SLP	SA/RC	WD KL				8	5200	6	18700	20800
					1984 BOATS							
25	ALERION	SLP	SA/OD	FBG KL				7 3	4800	3 7	15800	17900
25	ALERION 25	SLP	SAIL	FBG KL				7 3	4800	3 7	15800	17900
33	STREAKER	SLP	SA/OD	FBG KL				8	5200	6	17200	19600
33	STREAKER	SLP	SA/RC	WD KL				8	5200	6	17200	19600

....For earlier years, see the BUC Used Boat Price Guide, Volume 3

HEWES MANUFACTURING CO INC
FT PIERCE FL 34946   COAST GUARD MFG ID- HMC See inside cover to adjust price for area
FORMERLY HEWES BOAT CO

For more recent years, see the BUC Used Boat Price Guide, Volume 1

LOA FT IN	NAME AND/ OR MODEL	TOP/ RIG	BOAT TYPE	HULL MTL TP	TP	ENGINE # HP	MFG	BEAM FT IN	WGT LBS	DRAFT FT IN	RETAIL LOW	RETAIL HIGH
					1996 BOATS							
16	BAYFISHER		CTRCN	FBG SV	OB			7	795	8	6200	7100
16	BONEFISHER		CTRCN	FBG SV	OB			7	795	8	6200	7100
18	BAYFISHER		CTRCN	FBG SV	OB			7	850	9	7100	8150
18	REDFISHER		CTRCN	FBG SV	OB			7	850	9	7100	8150
19 4	REDFISHER TUNNEL DR		CTRCN	FBG TU	OB			7	750	8	8200	9400
19 6	LIGHT TACKLE		CTRCN	FBG SV	OB			8	1100	10	9400	10700
19 6	REDFISHER		CTRCN	FBG TH	OB			7	1000		8600	9900
					1995 BOATS							
16	BAYFISHER		CTRCN	FBG SV	OB			7	795	8	5900	6750
16	BONEFISHER		CTRCN	FBG SV	OB			7	795	8	5900	6750
18	BAYFISHER		CTRCN	FBG SV	OB			7	850	9	6750	7750
18	LIMITED		CTRCN	KEV SV	OB			7	850	9	6750	7800
18	REDFISHER		CTRCN	FBG SV	OB			7	850	9	6750	7750
19 6	LIGHT TACKLE		CTRCN	FBG SV	OB			8	1100	10	8950	10200
					1994 BOATS							
16	BAYFISHER	OP	CTRCN	FBG SV	OB			7	795	8	5600	6450
16	TOURNAMENT	OP	CTRCN	FBG SV	OB			7	795	8	5600	6450
18	REDFISHER	OP	CTRCN	FBG SV	OB			7	825	9	6300	7200
19 6	LIGHT TACKLE	OP	CTRCN	FBG SV	OB			8	1100	10	8450	9700
					1993 BOATS							
16	TOURNAMENT	OP	CTRCN	FBG SV	OB			7	725	8	4900	5650
18	BONEFISHER 18	OP	CTRCN	FBG SV	OB			7	750	9	5500	6350
18	REDFISHER	OP	CTRCN	FBG SV	OB			7	790	9	5800	6650
19 6	HEWES	OP	CTRCN	FBG SV	OB			8	950		7150	8200
					1992 BOATS							
16	TOURNAMENT	OP	CTRCN	FBG SV	OB			7	725	8	4700	5400
18	BONEFISHER 18	OP	CTRCN	FBG SV	OB			7	750	9	5300	6100
18	REDFISHER	OP	CTRCN	FBG SV	OB			7	790	9	5550	6350
					1991 BOATS							
16	TOURNAMENT	OP	CTRCN	FBG SV	OB			7	725	8	4550	5250
18	BONEFISHER 18	OP	CTRCN	FBG SV	OB			7	750	9	5100	5850
18	REDFISHER	OP	CTRCN	FBG SV	OB			7	790	9	5350	6100
					1990 BOATS							
16	BONEFISHER 16		CTRCN	FBG SV	OB			7	700		4200	4900
18	BONEFISHER		CTRCN	FBG SV	OB			7	750		4900	5650
					1989 BOATS							
16	BONEFISHER	OP	FSH	FBG SV	OB			7	700		4050	4750
17 10	BONEFISHER	OP	FSH	FBG SV	OB			7	750	6 6	4300	5450
20 9	OCEANIC	OP	CTRCN	FBG SV	OB			8	2000	1 6	12300	13900
20 9	OPEN FISHERMAN		CTRCN	FBG SV	OB			8		1 3	8650	9950
25 9	BLUEWATER FISHERMAN		CTRCN	FBG SV	OB			8	3500		25000	27800
25 9	OPEN FISHERMAN	HT	CTRCN	FBG SV	OB			8	3200		24500	27200
					1988 BOATS							
16	BONEFISHER II SPCL	OP	CTRCN	FBG SV	OB			7	788	5	4450	5150
17 1	STALKER DELUXE	OP	CTRCN	FBG SV	OB			6 6	815	8	4800	5500
17 8	BONEFISHER	OP	CTRCN	FBG SV	OB			6 6	870	6	5200	6000
17 8	REDFISHER	OP	CTRCN	FBG SV	OB			7	810	8	4900	5600
17 10	BONEFISHER II	OP	CTRCN	FBG SV	OB			7	815	5	5200	6000
17 10	BONEFISHER II LTD	OP	CTRCN	KEV SV	OB			7	915	5	5750	6600

LOA FT IN	NAME AND/ OR MODEL	TOP/ RIG	BOAT TYPE	HULL MTL TP	ENGINE TP # HP MFG	BEAM FT IN	WGT LBS	DRAFT FT IN	RETAIL LOW	RETAIL HIGH
1987 BOATS										
16	BONEFISHER II SPCL	OP	CTRCN	FBG SV	OB	7	790	5	4350	5000
17 1	STALKER DELUXE	OP	CTRCN	FBG SV	OB	6 6	815	8	4650	5350
17 1	STALKER DELUXE	OP	CTRCN	KEV SV	OB	6 6	815	8	4650	5350
17 8	BONEFISHER	OP	CTRCN	FBG SV	OB	6 6	870	6	5050	5800
17 8	BONEFISHER	OP	CTRCN	KEV SV	OB	6 6	870	6	5050	5800
17 8	REDFISHER	OP	CTRCN	FBG SV	OB	6 6	810	6	4750	5450
17 8	REDFISHER	OP	CTRCN	KEV SV	OB	6 6	810	5	4750	5450
17 10	BONEFISHER II	OP	CTRCN	KEV SV	OB	7	915	5	5300	6100
1986 BOATS										
16	BONEFISHER II SPCL	OP	CTRCN	FBG SV	OB	7	790	5	4200	4900
17 1	STALKER DELUXE	OP	CTRCN	FBG SV	OB	6 6	815	8	4600	5250
17 1	STALKER DELUXE	OP	CTRCN	KEV SV	OB	6 6	815	8	4600	5250
17 8	BONEFISHER	OP	CTRCN	FBG SV	OB	6 6	870	6	4950	5700
17 8	BONEFISHER	OP	CTRCN	KEV SV	OB	6 6	870	6	4950	5700
17 8	REDFISHER	OP	CTRCN	FBG SV	OB	6 6	810	6	4650	5350
17 8	REDFISHER	OP	CTRCN	KEV SV	OB	6 6	810	5	4650	5350
17 10	BONEFISHER II	OP	CTRCN	KEV SV	OB	7	915	5	5200	5950
1985 BOATS										
16	BONEFISHER II SPCL	OP	CTRCN	FBG SV	OB	7	790	5	4100	4800
17 8	BONEFISHER	OP	CTRCN	FBG SV	OB	6 6	870	6	4800	5550
17 8	BONEFISHER	OP	CTRCN	KEV SV	OB	6 6	870	6	4800	5550
17 8	REDFISHER	OP	CTRCN	FBG SV	OB	6 6	810	6	4550	5250
17 8	REDFISHER	OP	CTRCN	KEV SV	OB	6 6	810	5	4550	5250
17 10	BONEFISHER II	OP	CTRCN	KEV SV	OB	7	915	5	4750	5450
17 10	BONEFISHER II SIGNTR	OP	CTRCN	KEV SV	OB	7	915		5400	6200
1984 BOATS										
17 8	BONEFISHER	OP	CTRCN	FBG SV	OB	6 6	870		4700	5450
17 8	BONEFISHER	OP	OPFSH	KEV SV	OB	6 6	870		4700	5400
17 8	REDFISHER	OP	CTRCN	KEV SV	OB	6 6	810		4450	5100
17 8	REDFISHER	OP	OPFSH	KEV SV	OB	6 6	810		4450	5100
17 10	BONEFISHER II	OP	CTRCN	KEV SV	OB	7	915		4950	5700
17 10	BONEFISHER II	OP	OPFSH	KEV SV	OB	7	915		4950	5700

....For earlier years, see the BUC Used Boat Price Guide, Volume 3

HEWES MARINE COMPANY INC

HEWESCRAFT
COLVILLE WA 99114   COAST GUARD MFG ID- HEW   See inside cover to adjust price for area

For more recent years, see the BUC Used Boat Price Guide, Volume 1

LOA FT IN	NAME AND/ OR MODEL	TOP/ RIG	BOAT TYPE	HULL MTL TP	ENGINE TP # HP MFG	BEAM FT IN	WGT LBS	DRAFT FT IN	RETAIL LOW	RETAIL HIGH
1996 BOATS										
16 8	SEA-RUNNER 17	OP	B/R	AL SV	OB	7 3	900	1 11	6350	7300
16 8	SEA-RUNNER 17	OP	RNBT	AL SV	OB	7 3	900	1 11	6350	7300
18 5	RIVER-RUNNER 18	OP	B/R	AL SV	OB	7 2	1050	1 11	7750	8950
18 5	RIVER-RUNNER 18	OP	RNBT	AL SV	OB	7 2	1050	1 11	7750	8950
18 11	SEA-RUNNER 19	OP	B/R	AL SV	OB	7 7	1300	2 1	9450	10700
18 11	SEA-RUNNER 19	OP	RNBT	AL SV	OB	7 7	1300	2 1	9450	10700
19 1	RIVER-RUNNER 19	OP	B/R	AL SV	OB	7 8	1300	2 1	9500	10800
19 1	RIVER-RUNNER 19	OP	RNBT	AL SV	OB	7 8	1300	2 1	9500	10800
19 1	RIVER-RUNNER 19E	OP	B/R	AL SV	OB	7 8	1300	2 1	9250	10500
19 1	RIVER-RUNNER 19E	OP	RNBT	AL SV	OB	7 8	1300	2 1	9250	10500
19 1	RIVER-RUNNER 19R	OP	B/R	AL SV	OB	7 8	1300	2 1	9750	11100
19 1	RIVER-RUNNER 19R	OP	RNBT	AL SV	OB	7 8	1300	2 1	9750	11100
20 11	SEA-RUNNER 21	OP	B/R	AL SV	OB	7 7	1400	2 1	10900	12400
20 11	SEA-RUNNER 21	OP	RNBT	AL SV	OB	7 7	1400	2 1	10800	12300
21 1	RIVER-RUNNER 21	OP	B/R	AL SV	OB	7 8	1400	2 1	11000	12500
21 1	RIVER-RUNNER 21	OP	B/R	AL SV	IB 216-285	7 8	1400	2 1	9050	10500
21 1	RIVER-RUNNER 21	OP	RNBT	AL SV	OB	7 8	1400	2 1	10900	12300
21 1	RIVER-RUNNER 21	OP	RNBT	AL SV	IB 216 FORD	7 8	1400	2 1	9250	10500
21 1	RIVER-RUNNER 21	OP	RNBT	AL SV	IB 285 FORD	7 8	2300	2 1	10600	12100
1995 BOATS										
16 8	SEA-RUNNER 17	OP	B/R	AL SV	OB	7 3	900	1 11	6000	6900
16 8	SEA-RUNNER 17	OP	RNBT	AL SV	OB	7 3	900	1 11	6000	6900
18 5	RIVER-RUNNER 18	OP	B/R	AL SV	OB	7 2	1050	1 11	7300	8350
18 5	RIVER-RUNNER 18	OP	RNBT	AL SV	OB	7 2	1050	1 11	7300	8350
18 11	SEA-RUNNER 19	OP	B/R	AL SV	OB	7 7	1300	2 1	8900	10100
18 11	SEA-RUNNER 19	OP	RNBT	AL SV	OB	7 7	1300	2 1	8900	10100
19 1	RIVER-RUNNER 19	OP	B/R	AL SV	OB	7 8	1300	2 1	9000	10200
19 1	RIVER-RUNNER 19	OP	RNBT	AL SV	OB	7 8	1300	2 1	9000	10200
20 11	SEA-RUNNER 21	OP	B/R	AL SV	OB	7 7	1400	2 1	10300	11700
20 11	SEA-RUNNER 21	OP	RNBT	AL SV	OB	7 7	1400	2 1	10200	11600
21 1	RIVER-RUNNER 21	OP	B/R	AL SV	OB	7 8	1400	2 1	10400	11800
21 1	RIVER-RUNNER 21	OP	B/R	AL SV	IB 216-300	7 8	1400	2 1	8450	10100
21 1	RIVER-RUNNER 21	OP	RNBT	AL SV	OB	7 8	1400	2 1	10300	11700
21 1	RIVER-RUNNER 21	OP	RNBT	AL SV	IB 216-300	7 8	1400	2 1	8650	10300
1994 BOATS										
16 8	SEA-RUNNER 16	OP	B/R	AL SV	OB	7 3	900	2 1	5700	6550
16 8	SEA-RUNNER 16	OP	RNBT	AL SV	OB	7 3	900	2 1	5700	6550
17 1	RIVER-RUNNER 17	OP	B/R	AL SV	OB	7 3	950	2 1	6050	6950
17 1	RIVER-RUNNER 17	OP	RNBT	AL SV	OB	7 3	950	2 1	6050	6950
18 11	SEA-RUNNER 19	OP	B/R	AL SV	OB	7 4	1200	2 1	7900	9100
18 11	SEA-RUNNER 19	OP	RNBT	AL SV	OB	7 4	1200	2 1	7900	9050
19 1	RIVER-RUNNER 19	OP	B/R	AL SV	OB	7 8	1200	2 1	7950	9150
19 1	RIVER-RUNNER 19	OP	RNBT	AL SV	OB	7 8	1200	2 1	7950	9150
20 11	SEA-RUNNER 21	OP	B/R	AL SV	OB	7 6	1300	2 1	9200	10500
20 11	SEA-RUNNER 21	OP	RNBT	AL SV	OB	7 6	1300	2 1	9150	10400
21 1	RIVER-RUNNER 21	OP	B/R	AL SV	OB	7 8	2300	2 1	14500	16400
21 1	RIVER-RUNNER 21	OP	B/R	AL SV	IB 216-300	7 8	2300	2 1	9150	10700
21 1	RIVER-RUNNER 21	OP	RNBT	AL SV	OB	7 8	2300	2 1	14300	16200
21 1	RIVER-RUNNER 21	OP	RNBT	AL SV	IB 216-300	7 8	2300	2 1	9350	10900
1993 BOATS										
16 2	RIVER-RUNNER 16	OP	B/R	AL SV	OB	7	900	1 11	5300	6100
16 2	RIVER-RUNNER 16	OP	RNBT	AL SV	OB	7	900	1 11	5300	6100
16 8	SEA-RUNNER 16	OP	B/R	AL SV	OB	7 1	900	1 11	5400	6200
16 8	SEA-RUNNER 16	OP	RNBT	AL SV	OB	7 1	900	1 11	5400	6200
18 2	RIVER-RUNNER 18	OP	B/R	AL SV	OB	7 1	1000	1 11	6250	7150
18 2	RIVER-RUNNER 18	OP	RNBT	AL SV	OB	7 1	1000	1 11	6250	7150
18 8	SEA-RUNNER 18	OP	B/R	AL SV	OB	7 2	1000	1 11	6350	7300
18 8	SEA-RUNNER 18	OP	RNBT	AL SV	OB	7 2	1000	1 11	6350	7300
20	RIVER-RUNNER 20	OP	B/R	AL SV	OB	7 2	1100	1 11	7250	8350
20	RIVER-RUNNER 20	OP	B/R	AL SV	IB 215-300	7 2	1100	1 11	6600	7900
20	RIVER-RUNNER 20	OP	RNBT	AL SV	OB	7 2	1100	1 11	7200	8300
20	RIVER-RUNNER 20	OP	RNBT	AL SV	IB 215-300	7 2	1100	1 11	6850	8150
20 7	SEA-RUNNER 20	OP	B/R	AL SV	OB	7 3	1100	1 11	7400	8500
20 7	SEA-RUNNER 20	OP	B/R	AL SV	IB 215-300	7 3	1100	1 11	7050	8450
20 7	SEA-RUNNER 20	OP	RNBT	AL SV	OB	7 3	1100	1 11	7300	8400
20 7	SEA-RUNNER 20	OP	RNBT	AL SV	IB 215-300	7 3	1100	1 11	7250	8650
1992 BOATS										
16 2	RIVER-RUNNER 16	OP	B/R	AL SV	OB	7	850	1 11	4800	5500
16 2	RIVER-RUNNER 16	OP	RNBT	AL SV	OB	7	850	1 11	4800	5500
16 3	SEA-RUNNER 16	OP	B/R	AL SV	OB	6 11	800	1 11	4550	5200
16 3	SEA-RUNNER 16	OP	RNBT	AL SV	OB	6 11	800	1 11	4550	5200
18 2	RIVER-RUNNER 18	OP	B/R	AL SV	OB	7 1	950	1 11	5700	6550
18 2	RIVER-RUNNER 18	OP	RNBT	AL SV	OB	7 1	950	1 11	5700	6550
18 3	SEA-RUNNER 18	OP	B/R	AL SV	OB	7	900	1 11	5450	6250
18 3	SEA-RUNNER 18	OP	RNBT	AL SV	OB	7	900	1 11	5450	6250
20	RIVER RUNNER 20	OP	B/R	AL SV	IB 215 FORD	7 2	1100	1 11	6250	7200
20	RIVER RUNNER 20	OP	RNBT	AL SV	IB 215 FORD	7 2	1100	1 11	6050	7450
20	RIVER RUNNER 20	OP	B/R	AL SV	OB	7	900	1 11	5800	6700
20	RIVER RUNNER 20	OP	RNBT	AL SV	OB	7	900	1 11	5750	6650
20 3	SEA RUNNER 20	OP	B/R	AL SV	OB	7 1	1050	1 11	6700	7700
20 3	SEA RUNNER 20	OP	RNBT	AL SV	OB	7 1	1050	1 11	6650	7650
1991 BOATS										
16 2	RIVER-RUNNER 16	OP	B/R	AL SV	OB	7	850	1 11	4550	5250
16 2	RIVER-RUNNER 16	OP	RNBT	AL SV	OB	7	850	1 11	4600	5250
18 2	RIVER-RUNNER 18	OP	B/R	AL SV	OB	7 2	950	1 11	5400	6250
18 2	RIVER-RUNNER 18	OP	RNBT	AL SV	OB	7 2	950	1 11	5400	6250
18 4	SEA-RUNNER 18	OP	B/R	AL SV	OB	7	900	1 11	5200	6000
18 4	SEA-RUNNER 18	OP	RNBT	AL SV	OB	7	900	1 11	5200	6000
20	RIVER-RUNNER 20	OP	B/R	AL SV	OB	7 2	1100	1 11	6600	7550
20	RIVER-RUNNER 20	OP	RNBT	AL SV	OB	7 2	1100	1 11	6550	7500
1990 BOATS										
17 11	KING-RUNNER 18	OP	FSH	AL SV	OB	6 6	425		2450	2800
18 2	RIVER-RUNNER 18	OP	B/R	AL SV	OB	7 2	800	2 1	4450	5150
18 2	RIVER-RUNNER 18	OP	RNBT	AL SV	OB	7 2	850	2	4700	5400
18 4	SEA-RUNNER 18	OP	B/R	AL SV	OB	6 10	725	2	4050	4750
18 4	SEA-RUNNER 18	OP	RNBT	AL SV	OB	6 10	725	2	4050	4750
1989 BOATS										
16 3	ROGUE-RUNNER 16	OP	B/R	AL SV	OB	7	700		3450	4000
16 3	ROGUE-RUNNER 16	OP	RNBT	AL SV	OB	7	700		3450	4000
17 11	KING-RUNNER 18	OP	FSH	AL SV	OB	6 6	425		2350	2700
18 2	ROGUE-RUNNER 18	OP	B/R	AL SV	OB	7 2	800	2 1	4250	4900
18 2	ROGUE-RUNNER 18	OP	RNBT	AL SV	OB	7 2	850	2	4500	5200
18 4	SEA-RUNNER 18	OP	B/R	AL SV	OB	6 10	725	2	3900	4550
18 4	SEA-RUNNER 18	OP	RNBT	AL SV	OB	6 10	725	2	3900	4550

LOA FT	LOA IN	NAME AND/ OR MODEL	TOP/ RIG	BOAT TYPE	HULL MTL	HULL TP	ENGINE TP	# HP	MFG	BEAM FT	BEAM IN	WGT LBS	DRAFT FT	DRAFT IN	RETAIL LOW	RETAIL HIGH
		1988 BOATS														
18	3	RIVER-RUNNER 18	OP	B/R	AL	SV	OB			7		800			4100	4750
18	3	RIVER-RUNNER 18	OP	RNBT	AL	SV	OB			7		800			4100	4750
18	4	SEA-RUNNER 18	OP	B/R	AL	SV	OB			6	10	725			3750	4350
18	4	SEA-RUNNER 18	OP	RNBT	AL	SV	OB			6	10	725			3750	4350
		1987 BOATS														
18	3	RIVER-RUNNER 18	OP	B/R	AL	SV	OB			7		800			3950	4600
18	3	RIVER-RUNNER 18	OP	RNBT	AL	SV	OB			7		800			3950	4600
18	4	SEA-RUNNER 18	OP	B/R	AL	SV	OB			6	10	725			3600	4200
18	4	SEA-RUNNER 18	OP	RNBT	AL	SV	OB			6	10	725			3600	4200
		1985 BOATS														
18	3	RIVER-RUNNER 18	OP	RNBT	AL	SV	OB			7		800			3650	4250
20	3	RIVER-RUNNER 20	OP	RNBT	AL	SV	OB			7	1	900			4400	5050
		1984 BOATS														
18	3	RIVER-RUNNER 18	OP	RNBT	AL	SV	OB			7		800			3550	4100
20	3	RIVER-RUNNER 20	OP	RNBT	AL	SV	OB			7	1	900			4200	4850

....For earlier years, see the BUC Used Boat Price Guide, Volume 3

HI-STAR MARINE LTD

KAOSIUNG TAIWAN See inside cover to adjust price for area

LOA FT	LOA IN	NAME AND/ OR MODEL	TOP/ RIG	BOAT TYPE	HULL MTL	HULL TP	ENGINE TP	# HP	MFG	BEAM FT	BEAM IN	WGT LBS	DRAFT FT	DRAFT IN	RETAIL LOW	RETAIL HIGH
		1991 BOATS														
42	3	HI-STAR 42	FB	CNV	FBG	SV	IB	T375D	CAT	14	9	30000	3	2	166000	182500
42	3	HI-STAR 42	FB	CR	FBG	SV	IB	T375D	CAT	14	9	30000	3	2	160000	176000
42	3	HI-STAR 42	FB	SDN	FBG	SV	IB	T375D	CAT	14	9	30000	3	2	167000	183500
43	9	HI-STAR 44	FB	CNV	FBG	SV	IB	T375D	CAT	15	2	33000	3	2	174500	192000
43	9	HI-STAR 44	FB	SDN	FBG	SV	IB	T375D	CAT	15	2	33000	3	2	177000	194500
47	9	HI-STAR 48	FB	CNV	FBG	SV	IB	T375D	CAT	15	2	35000	3	2	172500	189500
47	9	HI-STAR 48	FB	SDN	FBG	SV	IB	T375D	CAT	15	2	36000	3	3	204000	224500
47	9	HI-STAR 48	FB	YTFS	FBG	SV	IB	T375D	CAT	15	2	36000	3	3	184500	202500
51	9	HI-STAR 52	FB	CNV	FBG	SV	IB	T375D	CAT	15	2	38000	3	3	190500	209000
51	9	HI-STAR 52	FB	YTFS	FBG	SV	IB	T375D	CAT	15	2	38000	3	3	196500	216000
52		HI-STAR 52 MY	FB	MY	FBG	SV	IB	T550D	GM	16	5	45100	2	9	293000	322000
54	9	HI-STAR 55	FB	YTFS	FBG	SV	IB	T375D	CAT	15	2	39000	3	3	219500	241000
70		HI-STAR MY	FB	MY	FBG	SV	IB	T735D	GM	18	6	87000	3	10	591500	650000
		1990 BOATS														
42	3	HI-STAR 42	FB	CNV	FBG	SV	IB	T375D	CAT	14	9	30000	3	2	158500	174000
42	3	HI-STAR 42	FB	CR	FBG	SV	IB	T375D	CAT	14	9	30000	3	2	153000	168000
42	3	HI-STAR 42	FB	SDN	FBG	SV	IB	T375D	CAT	14	9	30000	3	2	159000	175000
43	9	HI-STAR 44	FB	CNV	FBG	SV	IB	T375D	CAT	15	2	33000	3	2	166500	183000
43	9	HI-STAR 44	FB	SDN	FBG	SV	IB	T375D	CAT	15	2	33000	3	2	169000	185500
47	9	HI-STAR 48	FB	CNV	FBG	SV	IB	T375D	CAT	15	2	35000	3	2	165000	181000
47	9	HI-STAR 48	FB	SDN	FBG	SV	IB	T375D	CAT	15	2	36000	3	3	195000	214000
47	9	HI-STAR 48	FB	YTFS	FBG	SV	IB	T375D	CAT	15	2	36000	3	3	176000	193500
51	9	HI-STAR 52	FB	CNV	FBG	SV	IB	T375D	CAT	15	2	38000	3	3	181500	199500
51	9	HI-STAR 52	FB	YTFS	FBG	SV	IB	T375D	CAT	15	2	38000	3	3	187500	206000
54	9	HI-STAR 55	FB	YTFS	FBG	SV	IB	T375D	CAT	15	2	39000	3	3	209500	230500
70		HI-STAR MY	FB	MY	FBG	SV	IB	T735D	GM	18	6	87000	3	10	564500	620500
		1989 BOATS														
42	3	HI-STAR 42		CNV	FBG	SV	IB	T375D	CAT	14	9	30000	3	2	151000	166000
42	3	HI-STAR 42		CR	FBG	SV	IB	T375D	CAT	14	9	30000	3	2	145500	160000
42	3	HI-STAR 42		SDN	FBG	SV	IB	T375D	CAT	14	9	30000	3	2	152000	167000
43	9	HI-STAR 44		CNV	FBG	SV	IB	T375D	CAT	15	2	33000	3	2	159000	174500
43	9	HI-STAR 44		SDN	FBG	SV	IB	T375D	CAT	15	2	33000	3	2	161000	177000
47	9	HI-STAR 48		CNV	FBG	SV	IB	T375D	CAT	15	2	36500	3	3	160000	175500
47	9	HI-STAR 48		SDN	FBG	SV	IB	T375D	CAT	15	2	37000	3	3	188500	207000
47	9	HI-STAR 48		YTFS	FBG	SV	IB	T375D	CAT	15	2	36500	3	3	168500	185000
51	9	HI-STAR 52		CNV	FBG	SV	IB	T375D	CAT	15	2	37500	3	3	171500	188000
51	9	HI-STAR 52		YTFS	FBG	SV	IB	T375D	CAT	15	2	38000	3	3	178000	195500
54	9	HI-STAR 55		YTFS	FBG	SV	IB	T375D	CAT	15	2	39000	3	3	199500	219000
66		HI-STAR MY		MY	FBG	SV	IB	T650D	GM	18	6	83000	3	10	517500	569000

HI-TECH CUSTOM BOATS

SIMI VALLEY CA 93065 COAST GUARD MFG ID- JHT See inside cover to adjust price for area

LOA FT	LOA IN	NAME AND/ OR MODEL	TOP/ RIG	BOAT TYPE	HULL MTL	HULL TP	ENGINE TP	# HP	MFG	BEAM FT	BEAM IN	WGT LBS	DRAFT FT	DRAFT IN	RETAIL LOW	RETAIL HIGH
		1987 BOATS														
20	4	HPM 206 TYPE I/O		CR	FBG	SV	IO	260	CHEV	7	1	3000	1	7	5550	6400
20	4	HPM 206 TYPE O		CR	FBG	SV	OB			7	1	2500	1	7	7500	8650
20	4	HPM 206 TYPE V		CR	FBG	SV	VD	260	CHRY			3000	1	7	6650	7650
20	4	HPM TYPE J		CR	FBG	SV	JT	330	CHEV	7	1	2800	1	7	7150	8200
24		CIERRA 24		CR	FBG	SV	OB			7	10	4000	2		13200	15000
24		CIERRA 24		CR	FBG	SV	IO	260	CHEV	7	10	4000	2		8550	9800
24		CIERRA 24		CR	FBG	SV	VD	330	CHEV	7	10	4000	2		10900	12400

HIDDEN HARBOR BOAT WORKS

BRADENTON FL 34203 COAST GUARD MFG ID- HHW See inside cover to adjust price for area

LOA FT	LOA IN	NAME AND/ OR MODEL	TOP/ RIG	BOAT TYPE	HULL MTL	HULL TP	ENGINE TP	# HP	MFG	BEAM FT	BEAM IN	WGT LBS	DRAFT FT	DRAFT IN	RETAIL LOW	RETAIL HIGH
		1985 BOATS														
36		VANCOUVER 36	CUT	SA/CR	F/S	KL	IB	D		11		18000	5		89100	97900
44		HIDDEN-HARBOR 44		MY	FBG	DS	IB	T 80D		14	6	48000			153500	168500
47	3	CYGNET 48	CUT	SA/CR	F/S	KC	IB	D		13	6	38000	4	8	164500	180500

....For earlier years, see the BUC Used Boat Price Guide, Volume 3

HIGH TECH MARINE AB

ETTERSTAD 0602 NORWAY See inside cover to adjust price for area

LOA FT	LOA IN	NAME AND/ OR MODEL	TOP/ RIG	BOAT TYPE	HULL MTL	HULL TP	ENGINE TP	# HP	MFG	BEAM FT	BEAM IN	WGT LBS	DRAFT FT	DRAFT IN	RETAIL LOW	RETAIL HIGH
		1989 BOATS														
49	5	HIGH TECH 5000		CR	FBG	DV	IB	R330	MRCR	9	4	11000			146000	160000
49	5	HIGH TECH 5000		CR	FBG	DV	IB	R200D	VLVO	9	4	11000			170000	187000

HIGH TECH YACHT & SHIP

FT LAUDERDALE FL 33316 See inside cover to adjust price for area
FORMERLY HIGH TECH MARINE

LOA FT	LOA IN	NAME AND/ OR MODEL	TOP/ RIG	BOAT TYPE	HULL MTL	HULL TP	ENGINE TP	# HP	MFG	BEAM FT	BEAM IN	WGT LBS	DRAFT FT	DRAFT IN	RETAIL LOW	RETAIL HIGH
		1993 BOATS														
42		EURO 42	FB	MY	F/S	SV	IB	T400D	DD	15		22500	3	7	167500	184500
56		EURO 56	FB	MY	F/S	SV	IB	T735D	DD	16		45000	3	11	314000	345500
65		EURO 65	FB	MY	F/S	SV	IB	T735D	DD	19		75000	4	11	503000	552500
		1992 BOATS														
50		EURO 50	FB	MY	F/S	SV	IB	T735D	DD	16		42000	4		257000	282000
55		EURO 55	FB	MY	F/S	SV	IB	T735D	DD	16		44000	4		295000	324000
59		EURO COCKPIT 59	FB	MY	F/S	SV	IB	T735D	DD	16		49000	4	4	328000	360500
63		EURO 63	FB	MY	F/S	SV	IB	T12CD	CAT	19		60000	4	6	475000	521500
70		EURO 70	FB	MY	F/S	SV	IB	T12CD	CAT	19		66000	4	7	549500	604000
		1991 BOATS														
44		CONVERTIBLE 44	FB	CNV	F/S	SV	IB	T425D	CAT	15		28000	3	10	150500	165500
50		EURO 50	FB	MY	F/S	SV	IB	T735D	DD	16		42000	4		245000	269000
50		FULLHOUSE 50	FB	MY	F/S	SV	IB	T485D	DD	16		41000	3	5	202500	222500
51		COCKPIT MY 51	FB	MYCPT	F/S	SV	IB	T425D	CAT	15		31000	4		177500	195000
55		EURO 55	FB	MY	F/S	SV	IB	T735D	DD	16		44000	4		282000	309500
57		EURO COCKPIT 57	FB	MY	F/S	SV	IB	T735D	DD	16		49000	4	4	299000	328500
63		EURO 63	FB	MY	F/S	SV	IB	T12CD	CAT	19		60000	4	6	452500	497500
70		EURO 70	FB	MY	F/S	SV	IB	T12CD	CAT	19		66000	4	7	524000	576000

HINCKLEY YACHTS

S W HARBOR ME 04679 COAST GUARD MFG ID- THC See inside cover to adjust price for area
FORMERLY HENRY R HINCKLEY & CO

For more recent years, see the BUC Used Boat Price Guide, Volume 1

LOA FT	LOA IN	NAME AND/ OR MODEL	TOP/ RIG	BOAT TYPE	HULL MTL	HULL TP	ENGINE TP	# HP	MFG	BEAM FT	BEAM IN	WGT LBS	DRAFT FT	DRAFT IN	RETAIL LOW	RETAIL HIGH
		1996 BOATS														
36	5	PICNIC BOAT	HT	MY	KEV	SV	JT	350D	YAN	10		10300	1	6	224000	246000
40	9	BERMUDA 40	SLP	SACAC	KEV	KC	IB	50D	YAN	11	9	20000	9	3	337500	371000
40	9	BERMUDA 40	YWL	SACAC	KEV	KC	ID	50D	YAN	11	9	20000	9	3	337500	371000
41	8	COMPETITION 42 MKII	SLP	SACAC	KEV	KL	IB	50D	YAN	12	6	23500	7		383500	421500
41	9	TALARIA 42	FB	CBNCR	KEV	DS	IB	300D	J&T	13	8	22000	4	4	320000	352000
42	9	SOU'WESTER 42 MKII	SLP	SACAC	KEV	KC	IB	50D	YAN	12	6	23500	9	2	397500	437000
42	9	SOU'WESTER 42 MKII	YWL	SACAC	KEV	KC	IB	50D	YAN	12	6	23500	9	2	397500	437000
43	10	SOU'WESTER 43	SLP	SACAC	KEV	KC	IB	50D	YAN	12	6	24000	9	2	419500	461000
43	10	SOU'WESTER 43	SLP	SACAC	KEV	KL	IB	50D	YAN	12	6	24000	7		419500	461000
51	3	SOU'WESTER 51	SLP	SACAC	KEV	KC	IB	88D	YAN	14		40000	5	11	734000	806500
51	3	SOU'WESTER 51	CUT	SACAC	KEV	KC	IB	88D	YAN	14		40000	5	11	732500	805000
51	3	SOU'WESTER 51	YWL	SACAC	KEV	KC	IB	88D	YAN	14		41000	5	11	738500	811500
51	3	SOU'WESTER 51	SLP	SARCC	KEV	KL	IB	88D	YAN	14		40000	9	4	734000	806500
51	3	SOU'WESTER 51	CUT	SARCC	KEV	KL	IB	88D	YAN	14		40000	9	4	733000	805500

LOA FT	LOA IN	NAME AND/ OR MODEL	TOP/ RIG	BOAT TYPE	-HULL- MTL	-HULL- TP	TP	ENGINE # HP	ENGINE MFG	BEAM FT	BEAM IN	WGT LBS	DRAFT FT	DRAFT IN	RETAIL LOW	RETAIL HIGH
		1996 BOATS														
51	3	SOU'WESTER 51	YWL	SARCC	KEV	KL	IB	88D	YAN	14		41000	9	4	738500	811500
51	6	SOU'WESTER 52	CUT	SACAC	KEV	KC	IB	88D	YAN	14		39000			740000	813000
59	3	SOU'WESTER 59	CUT	SARCC	KEV	KC	IB	135D	YAN	15	6	63000	8		1.050M	1.140M
59	3	SOU'WESTER 59	KTH	SARCC	KEV	KL	IB	135D	YAN	15	6	63000	12	6	1.050M	1.145M
70	3	HINCKLEY 70	CUT	SACAC	KEV	KC	IB	200D	PERK	17	6	90000	13		2.835M	3.080M
		1995 BOATS														
40	9	BERMUDA 40	SLP	SACAC	KEV	KC	IB	50D	YAN	11	9	20000	9	3	319500	351000
40	9	BERMUDA 40	YWL	SACAC	KEV	KC	IB	50D	YAN	11	9	20000	9	3	319500	351000
41	8	COMPETITION 42	SLP	SACAC	KEV	KL	IB	50D	YAN	12	6	23500	7		363000	399000
41	9	TALARIA 42	FB	CBNCR	KEV	DS	IB	300D	J&T	13	8	22000	4	4	307000	337500
42	9	SOU'WESTER 42 MKII	SLP	SACAC	KEV	KC	IB	50D	YAN	12	6	23500	9	2	376500	414000
42	9	SOU'WESTER 42 MKII	YWL	SACAC	KEV	KC	IB	50D	YAN	12	6	23500	9	2	376500	414000
43	10	SOU'WESTER 43	SLP	SACAC	KEV	KC	IB	50D	YAN	12	6	24000	9	2	397000	436500
43	10	SOU'WESTER 43	SLP	SACAC	KEV	KL	IB	50D	YAN	12	6	24000	7		397000	436500
51	3	SOU'WESTER 51	SLP	SACAC	KEV	KC	IB	88D	YAN	14		40000	5	11	695000	763500
51	3	SOU'WESTER 51	CUT	SACAC	KEV	KC	IB	88D	YAN	14		40000	5	11	693500	762000
51	3	SOU'WESTER 51	YWL	SACAC	KEV	KC	IB	88D	YAN	14		41000	5	11	699000	768500
51	3	SOU'WESTER 51	SLP	SARCC	KEV	KL	IB	88D	YAN	14		40000	9	4	695000	763500
51	3	SOU'WESTER 51	CUT	SARCC	KEV	KL	IB	88D	YAN	14		40000	9	4	693500	762500
51	3	SOU'WESTER 51	YWL	SARCC	KEV	KL	IB	88D	YAN	14		41000	9	4	699000	768500
51	6	SOU'WESTER 52	CUT	SACAC	KEV	KC	IB	88D	YAN	14		39000			700000	769500
59	3	SOU'WESTER 59	CUT	SARCC	KEV	KC	IB	135D	YAN	15	6	63000	8		992500	1.080M
59	3	SOU'WESTER 59	KTH	SARCC	KEV	KL	IB	135D	YAN	15	6	63000	12	6	999000	1.085M
70	3	HINCKLEY 70	CUT	SACAC	KEV	KC	IB	200D	PERK	17	6	90000	13		2.680M	2.915M
		1994 BOATS														
40	9	BERMUDA 40	SLP	SACAC	KEV	KC	IB	50D	YAN	11	9	20000	4	9	302500	332500
40	9	BERMUDA 40	YWL	SACAC	KEV	KC	IB	50D	YAN	11	9	20000	4	9	302500	332500
41	8	COMPETITION 42	SLP	SACAC	KEV	KL	IB	50D	YAN	12	6	21500	7		326000	358000
41	9	TALARIA 42	FB	CBNCR	KEV	DS	IB	300D	J&T	13	8	22000	4	4	294000	323000
41	9	TALARIA 42	FB	CBNCR	KEV	DS	IB	T300D	J&T	13	8	22000	4	4	327500	360000
42	9	SOU'WESTER 42	SLP	SACAC	KEV	KC	IB	50D	YAN	12	6	23000	9	2	352500	387000
42	9	SOU'WESTER 42	YWL	SACAC	KEV	KC	IB	50D	YAN	12	6	23000	9	2	352500	387000
43	10	SOU'WESTER 43	SLP	SACAC	KEV	KC	IB	50D	YAN	12	6	23000	9	2	368000	404500
43	10	SOU'WESTER 43	SLP	SACAC	KEV	KL	IB	50D	YAN	12	6	23000	7		368000	404500
51	3	SOU'WESTER 51	SLP	SACAC	KEV	KC	IB	88D	YAN	14		39000	11		654000	718500
51	3	SOU'WESTER 51	CUT	SACAC	KEV	KC	IB	70D	WEST	14		40000	5		655500	720000
51	3	SOU'WESTER 51	YWL	SACAC	KEV	KC	IB	88D	YAN	14		39000	11		654000	718500
51	3	SOU'WESTER 51	SLP	SARCC	KEV	KL	IB	88D	YAN	14		39000	8		654000	718500
51	3	SOU'WESTER 51	CUT	SARCC	KEV	KL	IB	88D	YAN	14		39000	8		652500	717000
51	3	SOU'WESTER 51	YWL	SARCC	KEV	KL	IB	88D	YAN	14		39000	8		654000	718500
51	6	SOU'WESTER 52	CUT	SACAC	KEV	KC	IB	88D	YAN	14		39000	11		662500	728000
59	3	SOU'WESTER 59	CUT	SARCC	KEV	KC	IB	135D	PERK	15	6	66000	12	6	966500	1.050M
59	3	SOU'WESTER 59	KTH	SARCC	KEV	KC	IB	135D	PERK	15	6	66000	12	6	972000	1.055M
70	3	HINCKLEY 70	CUT	SACAC	KEV	KC	IB	200D	PERK	17	6	90000	13		2.540M	2.760M
70	3	HINCKLEY 70	KTH	SACAC	KEV	KL	IB	200D	PERK	17	6	45000	13		958000	1.040M
		1993 BOATS														
40	9	BERMUDA 40	SLP	SACAC	KEV	KC	IB	50D	YAN	11	9	20000	4	9	286500	315000
40	9	BERMUDA 40	YWL	SACAC	FBG	KC	IB	50D	YAN	11	9	20000	4	9	286500	315000
41	8	COMPETITION 42	SLP	SACAC	KEV	KL	IB	500	YAN	12	6	21500	7		322000	353500
41	9	TALARIA 42	FB	CBNCR	FBG	DS	IB	320D	CAT	13	8	22000	3	10	285000	313000
41	9	TALARIA 42	FB	CBNCR	FBG	DS	IB	T320D	CAT	13	8	22000	3	10	321000	353000
42	9	SOU'WESTER 42	SLP	SACAC	KEV	KC	IB	50D	YAN	12	6	23000	9	2	333500	366500
42	9	SOU'WESTER 42	YWL	SACAC	FBG	KC	IB	50D	YAN	12	6	23000	9	2	333500	366500
43	10	SOU'WESTER 43	SLP	SACAC	KEV	KC	IB	50D	YAN	12	6	23000	9	1	348500	383000
51	3	SOU'WESTER 51	SLP	SACAC	KEV	KC	IB	88D	YAN	14		39000	11		619000	680500
51	3	SOU'WESTER 51	CUT	SACAC	KEV	KC	IB	70D	WEST	14		40000	5		620000	681500
51	3	SOU'WESTER 51	YWL	SACAC	FBG	KC	IB	88D	YAN	14		39000	11		619000	680500
51	6	SOU'WESTER 52	CUT	SACAC	KEV	KC	IB	88D	YAN	14		39000	11		627000	689000
59	3	SOU'WESTER 59	CUT	SACAC	KEV	KC	IB	135D	PERK	15	6	66000	12	6	907500	997000
59	3	SOU'WESTER 59	KTH	SACAC	FBG	KC	IB	135D	PERK	15	6	66000	12	6	923000	1.005M
70	3	HINCKLEY 70	CUT	SACAC	KEV	CB	IB	200D	PERK	17	6	90000	13		2.405M	2.615M
		1992 BOATS														
40	9	BERMUDA 40	SLP	SA/CR	KEV	KC	IB	46D	WEST	11	9	20000	4	9	271500	298000
40	9	BERMUDA 40	YWL	SA/CR	FBG	KC	IB	46D	WEST	11	9	20000	4	9	271500	298000
41	9	TALARIA 42	HT	CBNCR	FBG	DS	IB	300D	J&T	13	8	22000	4	4	267500	293500
41	9	TALARIA 42	FB	CBNCR	FBG	DS	IB	320D	CAT	13	8	22000	4	4	271500	298500
42	9	SOU'WESTER 42	SLP	SA/CR	KEV	KC	IB	46D	WEST	12	6	24000	5		323500	355500
42	9	SOU'WESTER 42	YWL	SA/CR	FBG	KC	IB	46D	WEST	12	6	24000	5		323500	355500
43	10	SOU'WESTER 43	SLP	SA/CR	KEV	KC	IB	46D	WEST	12	6	24000	5		337000	370500
51	3	SOU'WESTER 51	SLP	SA/CR	KEV	KC	IB	88D	YAN	14		40000	10	6	590000	648000
51	3	SOU'WESTER 51	CUT	SA/CR	KEV	KC	IB	70D	WEST	14		40000	5		586500	644500
51	3	SOU'WESTER 51	YWL	SA/CR	FBG	KC	IB	70D	WEST	14		41000	5		592500	651000
51	6	SOU'WESTER 52	CUT	SA/CR	KEV	KC	IB	88D	YAN	14		39000	5	11	593000	652000
59	3	SOU'WESTER 59	CUT	SA/CR	KEV	KC	IB	D	PERK	15	6	63000	6	6	834000	916500
59	3	SOU'WESTER 59	KTH	SA/CR	FBG	KC	IB	D	PERK	15	6	63000	6	6	839500	922500
		1991 BOATS														
40	9	BERMUDA 40	SLP	SA/CR	KEV	KC	IB	46D	WEST	11	9	20000	4	9	257000	282500
40	9	BERMUDA 40	YWL	SA/CR	FBG	KC	IB	46D	WEST	11	9	20000	4	9	257000	282500
41	9	TALARIA 42	HT	CBNCR	FBG	DS	IB	D	J&T	13	8	22000	4	4	**	**
41	9	TALARIA 42	FB	CBNCR	FBG	DS	IB	D	CAT	13	8	22000	4	4	**	**
42	9	SOU'WESTER 42	SLP	SA/CR	KEV	KC	IB	46D	WEST	12	6	24000	5		306500	337000
42	9	SOU'WESTER 42	YWL	SA/CR	FBG	KC	IB	46D	WEST	12	6	24000	5		306500	337000
43	10	SOU'WESTER 43	SLP	SA/CR	KEV	KC	IB	46D	WEST	12	6	24000	5		319500	351000
51	3	SOU'WESTER 51	SLP	SA/CR	KEV	KC	IB	88D	YAN	14		40000	10	6	558500	614000
51	3	SOU'WESTER 51	CUT	SA/CR	KEV	KC	IB	70D	WEST	14		40000	5		555000	610000
51	3	SOU'WESTER 51	YWL	SA/CR	FBG	KC	IB	70D	WEST	14		41000	5		561000	616500
51	6	SOU'WESTER 52	CUT	SA/CR	KEV	KC	IB	88D	YAN	14		39000	5	11	561000	616500
59	3	SOU'WESTER 59	CUT	SA/CR	KEV	KC	IB	D	PERK	15	6	63000	6	6	789000	867000
59	3	SOU'WESTER 59	KTH	SA/CR	FBG	KC	IB	D	PERK	15	6	63000	6	6	794500	873000
		1990 BOATS														
38	10	TALARIA 39	FB	CR	FBG	SV	IB	300D	J&T	13	8	19000	3	6	211000	232000
40	9	BERMUDA 40	SLP	SA/CR	FBG	KL	IB	46D	WEST	11	9	20000	4	9	243500	267500
42	9	SOU'WESTER 42	SLP	SA/CR	FBG	KL	IB	46D	WEST	12	6	24000	5		290500	319000
43	10	SOU'WESTER	SLP	SA/CR	FBG	KC	IB	46D	WEST	12	6	24000	5		302500	332500
51	3	SOU'WESTER	YWL	SA/CR	FBG	KC	IB	115D	YAN	14		41000	5	11	533500	586500
51	3	SOU'WESTER 51	SLP	SA/CR	FBG	KC	IB	70D	WEST	14		40000	5	11	528000	580000
51	3	SOU'WESTER 51	YWL	SA/CR	FBG	KC	IB	70D	WEST	14		41000	5	11	531000	584000
59	3	SOU'WESTER 59	CUT	SA/CR	KEV	KC	IB	D	PERK	15	6	63000	6	6	746500	820000
59	3	SOU'WESTER 59	KTH	SA/CR	FBG	KC	IB	D	PERK	15	6	63000	6	6	752000	826000
		1989 BOATS														
38	10	TALARIA 39	FB	CR	FBG	SV	IB	300D	J&T	13	8	19000	3	6	201500	221500
40	9	BERMUDA 40	SLP	SA/CR	FBG	KL	IB	46D	WEST	11	9	20000	4	9	230500	253500
42	9	SOU'WESTER	SLP	SA/CR	FBG	KC	IB	D		12	6	24000	5		275000	302000
51	3	SOU'WESTER	CUT	SA/CR	FBG	KC	IB	D		14		40000	5	11	497000	546000
59	3	SOU'WESTER 59	CUT	SA/CR	KEV	KC	IB	D	PERK	15	6	63000	6	6	706000	776000
59	3	SOU'WESTER 59	KTH	SA/CR	FBG	KC	IB	D	PERK	15	6	63000	6	6	711500	782000
		1988 BOATS														
40	9	BERMUDA	SLP	SA/CR	FBG	KC	IB	D		11	9	20000	4	3	218000	239500
40	9	BERMUDA	YWL	SA/CR	FBG	KC	IB	D		11	9	20000	4	3	218000	239500
42	9	SOU'WESTER	SLP	SA/CR	FBG	KC	IB	D		12	6	24000	5		260500	286500
42	9	SOU'WESTER	YWL	SA/CR	FBG	KC	IB	D		12	6	24000	5		260500	286500
51	3	SOU'WESTER	CUT	SA/CR	FBG	KC	IB	D		14		40000	5	11	470000	516500
59	3	SOU'WESTER	SLP	SA/CR	FBG	KC	IB	D		15	6	69000	6	6	712500	782500
		1987 BOATS														
40	9	BERMUDA	SLP	SA/CR	FBG	KC	IB	D		11	9	20000	4	3	206500	227000
40	9	BERMUDA	YWL	SA/CR	FBG	KC	IB	D		11	9	20000	4	3	206500	227000
42	9	SOU'WESTER 42	SLP	SA/CR	FBG	KC	IB	52D	WEST	12	6	24000	5		247500	272000
42	9	SOU'WESTER 42	YWL	SA/CR	FBG	KC	IB	52D	WEST	12	6	24000	5		247500	272000
51	3	MID-COCKPIT	CUT	SA/CR	FBG	KC	IB	D		14		40000	5	11	462500	508000
51	3	SOU'WESTER	CUT	SA/CR	FBG	KC	IB	D		14		40000	5	11	426500	469000
59	3	SOU'WESTER	SLP	SA/CR	FBG	KC	IB	D		15	6	63000	6	6	636000	698500
		1986 BOATS														
40	9	BERMUDA 40	SLP	SA/CR	FBG	KC	IB	40D	WEST	11	9	20000	4	3	196000	215500
42	9	COMPETITION 42	SLP	SA/CR	FBG	KL	IB	52D	WEST	12	6	24000	7		234500	257500
42	9	SOU'WESTER 42	SLP	SA/CR	FBG	KC	IB	52D	WEST	12	6	24000	5		234500	257500
42	9	SOU'WESTER 42	YWL	SA/CR	FBG	KC	IB	52D	WEST	12	6	24000	5		234500	257500
51	3	SOU'WESTER 51	CUT	SA/CR	FBG	KC	IB	85D		14		41000	5	11	422500	464500
59	3	SOU'WESTER 59	CUT	SA/CR	KEV	KC	IB	D	PERK	15	6	63000	6	6	597000	656000
59	3	SOU'WESTER 59	KTH	SA/CR	FBG	KC	IB	D	PERK	15	6	63000	6	6	602000	662000
		1985 BOATS														
40	9	BERMUDA 40	SLP	SA/CR	FBG	KC	IB	40D	WEST	11	9	20000	4	3	185500	204000
40	9	BERMUDA 40	YWL	SA/CR	FBG	KC	IB	40D	WEST	11	9	20000	4	3	185500	204000
42	9	SOU'WESTER 42	SLP	SA/CR	FBG	KC	IB	52D	WEST	12	6	24000	5		222000	244000
42	9	SOU'WESTER 42	YWL	SA/CR	FBG	KC	IB	52D	WEST	12	6	24000	5		222000	244000
51	3	SOU'WESTER 51	CUT	SA/CR	FBG	KC	IB	85D		14		41000	5	11	399500	439000
59	3	SOU'WESTER 59	SLP	SA/CR	FBG	KC	IB	D		15	6	63000	6	6	568500	625000
		1984 BOATS														
40	9	BERMUDA 40	SLP	SA/CR	FBG	KC	IB	40D	WEST	11	9	20000	4	3	176000	193500
40	9	BERMUDA 40	YWL	SA/CR	FBG	KC	IB	40D	WEST	11	9	20000	4	3	176000	193500
42	9	SOU'WESTER 42	SLP	SA/CR	FBG	KC	IB	52D	WEST	12	6	24000	5		210500	231500
42	9	SOU'WESTER 42	YWL	SA/CR	FBG	KC	IB	52D	WEST	12	6	24000	5		210500	231500
42	9	SOU'WESTER 42	YWL	SA/CR	FBG	KL	IB	52D	WEST	12	6	24000	7		210500	231500
59	3	SOU'WESTER 59	CUT	SA/CR	FBG	KC	IB	D		15	6	63000	6	6	536000	589500
59	3	SOU'WESTER 59	KTH	SA/CR	FBG	KC	IB	135D	PERK	15	6	63000	6	6	540000	593500

....For earlier years, see the BUC Used Boat Price Guide, Volume 3

HINTERHOELLER YACHTS

NIAGARA ON THE LAKE ONT COAST GUARD MFG ID- ZHY See inside cover to adjust price for area

LOA FT	LOA IN	NAME AND/ OR MODEL	TOP/ RIG	BOAT TYPE	-HULL- MTL	-HULL- TP	ENGINE TP	#	HP	MFG	BEAM FT	BEAM IN	WGT LBS	DRAFT FT	DRAFT IN	RETAIL LOW	RETAIL HIGH
		1995 BOATS															
26		NONSUCH 260	CAT	SACAC	FBG	KL	IB		18D	YAN	10	6	8500	3	10	63800	70100
32	4	NONSUCH 324	CAT	SACAC	FBG	KL	IB		28D	YAN	11	10	11500	4	4	88700	97500
35	1	NIAGARA 35 ENCORE	SLP	SACAC	FBG	KL	IB		39D	YAN	11	5	15000	5	2	112000	123000
35	1	NIAGARA 35 MARK I	SLP	SACAC	FBG	KL	IB		39D	YAN	11	5	15000	5	2	112000	123000
35	4	NONSUCH 354	CAT	SACAC	FBG	KL	IB		39D	YAN	12	6	15350	4	10	114000	125000
38	4	NONSUCH 384	CAT	SACAC	FBG	KL	IB		47D	YAN	12	8	17000	5	2	126500	139000
42	2	NIAGARA Y2	SLP	SACAC	FBG	KL	IB		51D	YAN	12	9	19800	5	8	175000	192500
42	2	NIAGARA Y2	CUT	SACAC	FBG	KL	IB		51D	YAN	12	9	19800	5	8	175000	192500
		1994 BOATS															
30	4	NONSUCH 30 CLASSIC	CAT	SACAC	FBG	KL	IB		30D	UNIV	11	2	11500	5		85100	93500
30	4	NONSUCH 30 ULTRA	CAT	SACAC	FBG	KL	IB		30D	UNIV	11	2	11500	5		85100	93500
30	4	NONSUCH 320	CAT	SACAC	FBG	KL	IB		30D	UNIV	11	2	11500	5		80300	88200
33	5	NONSUCH 33	CAT	SACAC	FBG	KL	IB		30D	UNIV	12	6	15350	5	4	107000	117500
35	1	NIAGARA 35 ENCORE	SLP	SACAC	FBG	KL	IB		30D	UNIV	11	5	15000	5	2	105000	115500
35	1	NIAGARA 35 MKI	SLP	SACAC	FBG	KL	IB		30D	UNIV	11	5	15000	5	2	97700	107500
36		NONSUCH 36	CAT	SACAC	FBG	KL	IB		44D	UNIV	12	8	17000	5	6	119000	130500
42	2	NIAGARA 42	SLP	SACAC	FBG	KL	IB		44D	UNIV	12	9	22000	5	8	162500	178500
		1993 BOATS															
22		NONSUCH 22	CAT	SACAC	FBG	KL	OB				8	6	5000	3	8	26400	29300
22		NONSUCH 22	CAT	SACAC	FBG	KL	IB		10D	UNIV	8	6	5000	3	8	28500	31700
25		NONSUCH 26 ULTRA	CAT	SACAC	FBG	KL	IB		21D	UNIV	10	6	8500	4	6	55500	60900
26		NONSUCH 26 CLASSIC	CAT	SACAC	FBG	KL	IB		21D	UNIV	10	6	8500	4	6	56500	62000
30	4	NONSUCH 30 CLASSIC	CAT	SACAC	FBG	KL	IB		30D	UNIV	11	2	11500	5		82100	90300
30	4	NONSUCH 30 NOVA	CAT	SACAC	FBG	KL	IB		30D	UNIV	11	2	11500	5		72700	79900
30	4	NONSUCH 30 ULTRA	CAT	SACAC	FBG	KL	IB		30D	UNIV	11	2	11500	5		80700	88700
31	3	NIAGARA 31	SLP	SACAC	FBG	KL	IB		21D	UNIV	10	4	8500	5		57300	63000
33	5	NONSUCH 33	CAT	SACAC	FBG	KL	IB		30D	UNIV	12	6	15350	5	4	100500	110500
35	1	NIAGARA 35	SLP	SACAC	FBG	KL	IB		30D	UNIV	11	5	15000	5	2	91900	101000
36		NONSUCH 36	CAT	SACAC	FBG	KL	IB		44D	UNIV	12	8	17000	5	6	112000	123000
42	2	NIAGARA 42	SLP	SACAC	FBG	KL	IB		44D	UNIV	12	9	22000	5	8	153000	168000
		1992 BOATS															
22		NONSUCH 22	CAT	SAIL	FBG	KL	OB				8	6	5000	3	8	24800	27600
22		NONSUCH 22	CAT	SAIL	FBG	KL	IB		10D	UNIV	8	6	5000	3	8	26800	29700
25		NONSUCH 26 VISTA	CAT	SAIL	FBG	KL	IB		21D	UNIV	10	6	8500	4	6	52200	57300
26		NONSUCH 26 CLASSIC	CAT	SAIL	FBG	KL	IB		21D	UNIV	10	6	8500	4	6	53100	58400
30	4	NONSUCH 30	CAT	SAIL	FBG	KL	IB		30D	UNIV	11	2	11500	5		73900	81200
31	3	NIAGARA 31	SLP	SAIL	FBG	KL	IB		21D	UNIV	10	4	8500	5		53900	59200
33	5	NONSUCH 33	CAT	SAIL	FBG	KL	IB		30D	UNIV	12	6	15350	5	4	94700	104000
35	1	NIAGARA 35	SLP	SAIL	FBG	KL	IB		30D	UNIV	11	5	15000	5	2	86400	95000
36		NONSUCH 36	CAT	SAIL	FBG	KL	IB		44D	UNIV	12	8	17000	5	6	105000	115500
42	2	NIAGARA 42	SLP	SAIL	FBG	KL	IB		44D	UNIV	12	9	22000	5	8	143500	158000
		1991 BOATS															
26		NONSUCH 26	CAT	SAIL	FBG	KL	IB		21D	UNIV	10	6	8500	4	6	50000	54900
30	4	NONSUCH 30	CAT	SAIL	FBG	KL	IB		30D	UNIV	11	10	11500	5		69500	76300
33	5	NONSUCH 33	CAT	SAIL	FBG	KL	IB		30D	UNIV	12	6	15350	5	4	89100	97900
35	1	NIAGARA 35	SLP	SAIL	FBG	KL	IB		30D	UNIV	11	5	15000	5	2	81300	89300
36		NONSUCH 36	CAT	SAIL	FBG	KL	IB		44D	UNIV	12	8	17000	5	6	98900	108500
42	2	NIAGARA 42	SLP	SAIL	FBG	KL	IB		44D	UNIV	12	9	22000	5	8	135000	148500
		1990 BOATS															
23	5	EXPRESS CRUISER 24		EXP	FBG	DV	IO		260	MRCR	9	6	5000	1	5	20800	23100
23	5	LIMESTONE 24		EXP	FBG	DV	IO		230	MRCR	9	6	4500	1	5	19100	21200
26		NONSUCH 26	CAT	SAIL	FBG	KL	IB		21D	UNIV	10	6	8500	4	6	47200	51800
30	4	NONSUCH 30	CAT	SAIL	FBG	KL	IB		30D	UNIV	11	10	11500	5		65300	71800
33	5	NONSUCH 33	CAT	SAIL	FBG	KL	IB		30D	UNIV	12	6	15350	5	4	83800	92100
35	1	NIAGARA 35	SLP	SAIL	FBG	KL	IB		30D	UNIV	11	5	15000	5	2	76500	84000
		1989 BOATS															
23	5	EXPRESS CRUISER 24		EXP	FBG	DV	IO		260	MRCR	9	6	5000	1	5	19600	21800
23	5	LIMESTONE 24		EXP	FBG	DV	IO		230	MRCR	9	6	4500	1	5	17600	20000
26		NONSUCH 26	CAT	SAIL	FBG	KL	IB		21D	UNIV	10	6	8500	4	6	43800	48700
30	4	NONSUCH 30	CAT	SAIL	FBG	KL	IB		30D	UNIV	11	10	11500	5		61500	67500
33	5	NONSUCH 33	CAT	SAIL	FBG	KL	IB		30D	UNIV	12	6	15350	5	4	78800	86600
35	1	NIAGARA 35	SLP	SAIL	FBG	KL	IB		30D	UNIV	11	5	15000	5	2	71900	79000
36		NONSUCH 36	CAT	SAIL	FBG	KL	IB	T	46D	WEST	12	8	17000	5	6	89400	98200
42	2	NIAGARA 42	SLP	SAIL	FBG	KL	IB		46D	WEST	12	9	22000	5	8	119500	131500
		1988 BOATS															
23	5	EXPRESS CRUISER 24		EXP	FBG	DV	IO		260	MRCR	9	6	5000	1	5	18800	20900
23	5	LIMESTONE 24		EXP	FBG	DV	IO		230	MRCR	9	6	4500	1	5	16700	18900
26		NONSUCH 26	CAT	SAIL	FBG	KL	IB		21D	UNIV	10	6	8500	4	6	41200	45800
30	4	NONSUCH 30	CAT	SAIL	FBG	KL	IB		30D	UNIV	11	10	11500	5		57800	63500
33	5	NONSUCH 33	CAT	SAIL	FBG	KL	IB		30D	UNIV	12	6	15350	5	4	74100	81500
35	1	NIAGARA 35	SLP	SAIL	FBG	KL	IB		30D	UNIV	11	5	15000	5	2	67700	74400
36		NONSUCH 36	CAT	SAIL	FBG	KL	IB		46D	WEST	12	8	17000	5	6	82400	90600
		1987 BOATS															
22		NONSUCH 22	CAT	SA/CR	FBG	KL	OB				8	6	5000	3	8	18200	20300
22		NONSUCH 22	CAT	SA/CR	FBG	KL	IB		D		8	6	5000	3	8	19900	22100
23	6	LIMESTONE 24		EXP	FBG	DV	IO		230		9		4700	1	5	16200	18400
26		NONSUCH 26	CAT	SA/CR	FBG	KL	IB		D		10	6	8500	4	6	38600	42900
26		NONSUCH ULTRA 26	CAT	SA/CR	FBG	KL	IB		D		10	6	8500	4	6	38600	42900
30	4	NONSUCH 30	CAT	SA/CR	F/S	KL	IB		D		11	10	11500	4	11	54300	59700
30	4	NONSUCH ULTRA 30	CAT	SA/CR	F/S	KL	IB		D		11	10	11500	4	11	54300	59700
35	1	NIAGARA 35	SLP	SA/CR	F/S	KL	IB		D		11	5	15000	5	2	63700	69900
35	1	NIAGARA ENCORE 35	SLP	SA/CR	F/S	KL	IB		D		11	5	15000	5	2	63700	69900
36		NONSUCH 36	CAT	SA/CR	F/S	KL	IB		D		12	8	17000	5	6	77400	85000
42	2	NIAGARA 42	SLP	SA/CR	F/S	KL	IB		D		12	9	20000	5	8	100000	110000
		1986 BOATS															
22		NONSUCH 22	CAT	SA/CR	FBG	KL	OB				8	6	5000	3	8	16700	19000
22		NONSUCH 22	CAT	SA/CR	FBG	KL	IB		10D-	13D	8	6	5000	3	8	18700	20900
26		NONSUCH 26	CAT	SA/CR	FBG	KL	IB		18D	WEST	10	6	8500	4	6	35200	39100
26		NONSUCH 26 SHOAL	CAT	SA/CR	FBG	KL	IB		18D	WEST	10	6	8500	3	9	35500	39500
26		NONSUCH ULTRA 26	CAT	SA/CR	FBG	KL	IB		18D	WEST	10	6	8500	4	6	36900	41000
26		NONSUCH ULTRA 26 SHL	CAT	SA/CR	FBG	KL	IB		18D	WEST	10	6	8500	3	9	37600	41800
30	4	NONSUCH 30	CAT	SA/CR	F/S	KL	IB		30D-	33D	11	10	11500	4	11	51000	56000
30	4	NONSUCH 30 SHOAL	CAT	SA/CR	F/S	KL	IB		30D	WEST	11	10	11500	3	11	51400	56500
30	4	NONSUCH ULTRA 30	CAT	SA/CR	F/S	KL	VD		29D-	33D	11	10	11500	4	11	51000	56300
30	4	NONSUCH ULTRA 30 SHL	CAT	SA/CR	F/S	KL	VD		29D	WEST	11	10	11500	3	11	51400	56500
30	4	NONSUCH UTLRA 30 SHL	CAT	SA/CR	F/S	KL	IB		33D	WEST	11	10	11500	3	11	53000	58300
35	1	NIAGARA 35	SLP	SA/CR	F/S	KL	VD		29D	WEST	11	5	15000	5	2	59900	65800
35	1	NIAGARA 35	SLP	SA/CR	F/S	KL	VD		33D	WEST	11	5	15000	5	2	59300	65200
35	1	NIAGARA ENCORE 35	SLP	SA/CR	F/S	KL	VD		27D	WEST	11	5	15000	5	2	59900	65800
35	1	NIAGARA ENCORE 35	SLP	SA/CR	F/S	KL	VD		33D	WEST	11	5	15000	5	2	60500	66500
36		NONSUCH 36	CAT	SA/CR	F/S	KL	VD		46D	WEST	12	8	16800	5	6	72200	79300
36		NONSUCH 36	CAT	SA/CR	F/S	KL	VD		58D	WEST	12	8	17000	5	6	73100	80300
36		NONSUCH 36	KTH	SA/CR	F/S	KL	VD		46D	WEST	12	8	17000	5	6	72900	80200
36		NONSUCH 36	KTH	SA/CR	F/S	KL	VD		58D	WEST	12	8	17000	5	6	73100	80300
36		NONSUCH 36 SHOAL	CAT	SA/CR	F/S	KL	VD		46D	WEST	12	8	17300	4	7	74100	81400
42	2	NIAGARA 42	SLP	SA/CR	F/S	KL	VD		46D	WEST	12	9	21000	5	8	96800	106500
42	2	NIAGARA 42	SLP	SA/CR	F/S	KL	VD		58D	WEST	12	9	21000	5	8	97200	107000
		1985 BOATS															
22		NONSUCH 22	CAT	SA/CR	FBG	KL	IB		8D		8	6	5000	3	8	17000	19300
26		NONSUCH 26	CAT	SA/CR	FBG	KL	IB		22D	WEST	10	6	8500	4	6	34000	37800
26		NONSUCH 26 SHOAL	CAT	SA/CR	FBG	KL	IB		22D	WEST	10	6	8500	3	9	34400	38200
30	4	NONSUCH 30	CAT	SA/CR	F/S	KL	IB		30D-	33D	11	10	11500	4	11	48000	52700
30	4	NONSUCH 30 SHOAL	CAT	SA/CR	F/S	KL	IB		30D	WEST	11	10	11500	3	11	48300	53100
30	4	NONSUCH ULTRA 30	CAT	SA/CR	F/S	KL	VD		29D-	33D	11	10	11500	4	11	48000	52900
30	4	NONSUCH ULTRA 30 SHL	CAT	SA/CR	F/S	KL	VD		29D	WEST	11	10	11500	3	11	48300	53000
30	4	NONSUCH UTLRA 30 SHL	CAT	SA/CR	F/S	KL	IB		33D	WEST	11	10	11500	3	11	49900	54800
35	1	NIAGARA 35	SLP	SA/CR	F/S	KL	VD		29D	WEST	11	5	15000	5	2	56300	61900
35	1	NIAGARA 35	SLP	SA/CR	F/S	KL	VD		33D	WEST	11	5	15000	5	2	55800	61300
35	1	NIAGARA ENCORE 35	SLP	SA/CR	F/S	KL	VD		27D	WEST	11	5	15000	5	2	56300	61900
35	1	NIAGARA ENCORE 35	SLP	SA/CR	F/S	KL	VD		33D	WEST	11	5	15000	5	2	56900	62600
36		NONSUCH 36	CAT	SA/CR	F/S	KL	VD		52D	WEST	12	8	16800	5	6	68000	74700
36		NONSUCH 36	CAT	SA/CR	F/S	KL	VD		58D	WEST	12	8	17000	5	6	68800	75600
36		NONSUCH 36 SHOAL	CAT	SA/CR	F/S	KL	VD		52D	WEST	12	8	17300	4	7	69700	76600
42	2	NIAGARA 42	SLP	SA/CR	F/S	KL	VD		46D	WEST	12	9	21000	5	8	91000	100000
42	2	NIAGARA 42	SLP	SA/CR	F/S	KL	VD		58D	WEST	12	9	21000	5	8	91300	100500
42	2	NIAGARA 42	CUT	SA/CR	F/S	KL	VD		46D	WEST	12	9	21000	5	8	90600	99500
		1984 BOATS															
22		NONSUCH 22	CAT	SA/CR	FBG	KL	IB		10D-	13D	8	6	5000	3	8	16200	18500
26		NONSUCH 26	CAT	SA/CR	FBG	KL	IB		21D	WEST	10	6	8500	4	6	32100	35600
26		NONSUCH 26 SHOAL	CAT	SA/CR	FBG	KL	IB		21D	WEST	10	6	8500	3	9	32200	35800
30	4	NONSUCH 30	CAT	SA/CR	F/S	KL	IB		29D-	33D	11	10	11500	4	11	44900	49900
30	4	NONSUCH 30 SHOAL	CAT	SA/CR	F/S	KL	IB		29D	WEST	11	10	11500	3	11	45700	50200
30	4	NONSUCH ULTRA 30	CAT	SA/CR	F/S	KL	VD		29D-	33D	11	10	11500	4	11	44900	50100
30	4	NONSUCH ULTRA 30 SHL	CAT	SA/CR	F/S	KL	VD		29D	WEST	11	10	11500	3	11	45700	50200
30	4	NONSUCH UTLRA 30 SHL	CAT	SA/CR	F/S	KL	IB		33D	WEST	11	10	11500	3	11	47200	51900
31	3	NIAGARA 31	SLP	SA/RC	FBG	KL	VD		21D	WEST	10	4	8500	5		31900	35400
35	1	NIAGARA 35	SLP	SA/CR	F/S	KL	VD		29D	WEST	11	5	15000	5	2	53000	58200
35	1	NIAGARA 35	SLP	SA/CR	F/S	KL	VD		33D	WEST	11	5	15000	5	2	53000	58300
36		NONSUCH 36	CAT	SA/CR	F/S	KL	VD		52D	WEST	12	8	16800	5	6	63900	70300
36		NONSUCH 36	CAT	SA/CR	F/S	KL	VD		58D	WEST	12	8	17000	5	6	64700	71100
36		NONSUCH 36	KTH	SA/CR	F/S	KL	VD		52D	WEST	12	8	17000	5	6	64600	71000
36		NONSUCH 36	KTH	SA/CR	F/S	KL	VD		58D	WEST	12	8	17000	5	6	64700	71100
36		NONSUCH 36 SHOAL	CAT	SA/CR	F/S	KL	VD		52D	WEST	12	8	17300	4	7	65600	72100
36	3	FRERS F3	SLP	SA/RC	F/S	KL	IB		29D	WEST	11	10	10900	6	9	43200	48000

....For earlier years, see the BUC Used Boat Price Guide, Volume 3

HIRSH SAILING YACHTS INC
BRADENTON FL 33507

See inside cover to adjust price for area

LOA FT IN	NAME AND/ OR MODEL	TOP/ RIG	BOAT TYPE	-HULL- MTL TP	TP #	--ENGINE--- HP MFG	BEAM FT IN	WGT LBS	DRAFT FT IN	RETAIL LOW	RETAIL HIGH
---------- 1987 BOATS ----------
44 8	HIRSH 45	SLP	SA/CR	FBG CB	IB	D PERK	13 2	26000	5 4	86900	95500
---------- 1986 BOATS ----------
44 8	HIRSH 45	SLP	SA/CR	FBG CB	IB	D PERK	13 2	26000	5 4	81800	89900
---------- 1985 BOATS ----------
37 9	HIRSH 38	SLP	SA/CR	FBG KL	IB	D PERK	12	15000	4 10	39400	43800
44 8	HIRSH 45	SLP	SA/CR	FBG KL	IB	D PERK	13 2	24500	5 4	74700	82100

HJB CUMULANT BV
HARLINGEN HOLLAND

See inside cover to adjust price for area

LOA FT IN	NAME AND/ OR MODEL	TOP/ RIG	BOAT TYPE	-HULL- MTL TP	TP #	--ENGINE--- HP MFG	BEAM FT IN	WGT LBS	DRAFT FT IN	RETAIL LOW	RETAIL HIGH
---------- 1990 BOATS ----------
36	HJB CUMULANT 36C	CUT	SA/CR	STL KL	IB	34D YAN	10 6	16800	5 7	122500	134500
36	HJB CUMULANT 36F	CUT	SA/CR	AL KL	IB	27D YAN	10 9	15000	5 3	110500	121500
36	HJB CUMULANT 36F	CUT	SA/CR	STL KL	IB	27D YAN	10 9	16800	6 2	122000	134500
38	HJB CUMULANT 38	CUT	SA/CR	AL KL	IB	34D YAN	11	16800	5 5	129000	142000
38	HJB CUMULANT 38	CUT	SA/CR	STL KL	IB	34D YAN	11	19000	6 6	142500	156500
41	HJB CUMULANT 41	CUT	SA/CR	AL KL	IB	44D YAN	13 7	19000	5 2	161000	177000
41	HJB CUMULANT 41	CUT	SA/CR	STL KL	IB	44D YAN	13 7	21000	6 6	171500	188500
45	HJB CUMULANT 45	CUT	SA/CR	AL KL	IB	60D YAN	13 7	22000	5 7	212000	233000
45	HJB CUMULANT 45	CUT	SA/CR	STL KL	IB	60D YAN	13 7	28000	5 7	237000	260500

HOBIE CAT COMPANY
HOBIE CATAMARANS
OCEANSIDE CA 92056

See inside cover to adjust price for area

COAST GUARD MFG ID- CCM
FORMERLY COAST CATAMARAN CORP

For more recent years, see the BUC Used Boat Price Guide, Volume 1

LOA FT IN	NAME AND/ OR MODEL	TOP/ RIG	BOAT TYPE	-HULL- MTL TP	TP #	--ENGINE--- HP MFG	BEAM FT IN	WGT LBS	DRAFT FT IN	RETAIL LOW	RETAIL HIGH
---------- 1996 BOATS ----------
16 7	HOBIE 16 SE	SLP	SACAC	F/S CT			7 11	320	10	4950	5700
17	HOBIE 17 SE	CAT	SACAC	F/S CT			8	340	1 6	5100	5850
17	HOBIE 17 SPORT	CAT	SACAC	F/S CT			8	340	1 6	5450	6250
18	HOBIE 18 SE	SLP	SACAC	F/S CT			8	400	2 6	5650	6500
18	HOBIE 18 SX	SLP	SACAC	F/S CT			8	400	2 6	6850	7850
19 6	HOBIE MIRACLE 20	SLP	SACAC	F/S CT			8 6	420	2 9	6950	8000
21	HOBIE SPORT CRUISER	SLP	SACAC	F/S CT			8 6	600	2 2	7450	8550
22	TRIFOILER	SLP	SACAC	F/S CT			19	340	2	**	**
24 6	MAGIC 25	SLP	SACAC	F/S CT			7 5	1870	5 6	24100	26800
---------- 1995 BOATS ----------
16 7	HOBIE 16	SLP	SACAC	F/S CT			7 11	320	10	4700	5400
17	HOBIE 17	CAT	SACAC	F/S CT			8	315	1 7	4700	5400
17	HOBIE 17 SPORT	CAT	SACAC	F/S CT			8	370	1 7	5350	6100
18	HOBIE 18	SLP	SACAC	F/S CT			8	400	2 6	5900	6800
18	HOBIE 18 SX	SLP	SACAC	F/S CT			8	445	2 6	6350	7300
19 6	HOBIE MIRACLE 20	SLP	SACAC	F/S CT			8 6	420	3	6600	7550
21	HOBIE SPORT CRUISER	SLP	SACAC	F/S CT			8 6	540	10	6700	7700
---------- 1994 BOATS ----------
16 7	HOBIE CAT 16	SLP	SACAC	F/S CT			7 11	320	10	4450	5100
17	HOBIE 17 SPORT	CAT	SACAC	F/S CT			8 6	370	1 7	5050	5800
17	HOBIE CAT 17	CAT	SACAC	F/S CT			8	315	1 7	4450	5150
18	HOBIE CAT 18	SLP	SACAC	F/S CT			8	400	2 6	5600	6450
18	HOBIE CAT 18 SX	SLP	SACAC	F/S CT			8	445	2 6	6000	6900
19 6	HOBIE CAT MIRACLE 20	SLP	SACAC	F/S CT			8 6	420	3	6250	7150
21	HOBIE SPORT CRUISER	SLP	SACAC	F/S CT			8 6	540	10	6350	7250
---------- 1993 BOATS ----------
16 7	HOBIE CAT 16	SLP	SACAC	F/S CT			7 11	320	10	4150	4850
17	HOBIE 17 SPORT	CAT	SACAC	F/S CT			8 6	370	1 7	4800	5500
17	HOBIE CAT 17	CAT	SACAC	F/S CT			8	315	1 7	4200	4850
18	HOBIE CAT 18	SLP	SACAC	F/S CT			8	400	2 6	5350	6150
18	HOBIE CAT 18 SX	SLP	SACAC	F/S CT			8	445	2 6	5700	6550
19 6	HOBIE CAT MIRACLE 20	SLP	SACAC	F/S CT			8 6	420	3	5900	6800
21	HOBIE SPORT CRUISER	SLP	SACAC	F/S CT			8 6	540	10	6000	6900
---------- 1992 BOATS ----------
16 7	HOBIE CAT 16	SLP	SAIL	F/S CT			7 11	320	10	3950	4600
17	HOBIE 17 SPORT	CAT	SAIL	F/S CT			8 6	370	1 7	4500	5200
17	HOBIE CAT 17	CAT	SAIL	F/S CT			8	315	1 7	3950	4600
18	HOBIE CAT 18	SLP	SAIL	F/S CT			8	400	2 6	5050	5800
18	HOBIE CAT 18 SX	SLP	SAIL	F/S CT			8	445	2 6	5400	6200
19 5	HOBIE CAT MIRACLE 20	SLP	SAIL	F/S CT			8 6	400	3	5400	6250
21 3	HOBIE CAT 21	SLP	SAIL	F/S CT			9 9	565	2 2	5900	6750
---------- 1991 BOATS ----------
16 7	HOBIE CAT 16	SLP	SAIL	F/S CT			7 11	320	10	3700	4350
17	HOBIE 17 SPORT	CAT	SAIL	F/S CT			8 6	370	1 7	4250	4900
17	HOBIE CAT 17	CAT	SAIL	F/S CT			8	315	1 7	3750	4350
18	HOBIE CAT 18	SLP	SAIL	F/S CT			8	400	2 6	4800	5500
18	HOBIE CAT 18 SX	SLP	SAIL	F/S CT			8	445	2 6	5100	5900
21 3	HOBIE CAT 21	SLP	SAIL	F/S CT			9 9	565	2 2	5550	6400
---------- 1990 BOATS ----------
16 7	HOBIE CAT 16	SLP	SAIL	F/S CT			7 11	320	10	3500	4100
17	HOBIE CAT 17	CAT	SAIL	F/S CT			8	315	1 7	3550	4100
18	HOBIE CAT 18	SLP	SAIL	F/S CT			8	400	2 6	4500	5200
18	HOBIE CAT 18 SX	SLP	SAIL	F/S CT			8	445	2 6	4850	5550
21 3	HOBIE CAT 21	SLP	SAIL	F/S CT			9 9	565	2 2	5300	6050
---------- 1989 BOATS ----------
16 7	HOBIE CAT 16	CAT	SAIL	F/S CT			7 11	800	10	3300	3850
17	HOBIE CAT 17	CAT	SAIL	F/S CT			8	350	1 5	3650	4200
18	HOBIE CAT 18	CAT	SAIL	F/S CT			8	400	2 6	4200	4900
21 3	DOMINATOR	CAT	SAIL	FBG CT			8 3	550	2 2	5200	5950
21	HOBIE CAT 21	CAT	SAIL	FBG CT			8 3	550	2 2	4650	5350
---------- 1988 BOATS ----------
16 7	HOBIE CAT 16	CAT	SAIL	F/S CT			7 11	800	10	3150	3650
17	HOBIE CAT 17	CAT	SAIL	F/S CT			8	350	1 6	3450	4000
18	HOBIE CAT 18	CAT	SAIL	F/S CT			8	400	2 6	3950	4600
21 3	DOMINATOR	CAT	SAIL	FBG CT			8 3	550	2 2	4800	5500
21	HOBIE CAT 21	CAT	SAIL	FBG CT			8 3	550	2 2	4600	5300
---------- 1986 BOATS ----------
16 7	HOBIE 16	SLP	SAIL	F/S CT			7 11	340	10	3000	3450
17	HOBIE 17	CAT	SAIL	F/S CT			8	300	1	3200	3700
18	HOBIE 18	SLP	SA/OD	FBG SK			8	400		3350	3900
18	HOBIE 18 MAGNUM	SLP	SA/OD	FBG SK			8	400		3800	4450
20 4	HOLDER 20	SLP	SA/OD	FBG DB	OB		7 10	1160	3 7	4900	5650
33	HOBIE 33	SLP	SA/OD	FBG SK	OB		8	4000	5 6	12000	13700
---------- 1985 BOATS ----------
16 7	HOBIE 16	SLP	SAIL	F/S CT			7 11	340	10	2850	3300
17	HOLDER 17	SLP	SA/OD	FBG SK			7 3	950	1 8	4000	4650
17	HOLDER 17 DS	SLP	SA/OD	FBG SK			7 3	925	1 8	3950	4600
18	HOBIE 18	SLP	SA/OD	F/S CT			8	400		3400	3950
18	HOBIE 18 MAGNUM	SLP	SA/OD	FBG SK			8	400		3400	3950
20 4	HOLDER 20	SLP	SA/OD	FBG DB			7 10	1160	3 7	4650	5350
33	HOBIE 33	SLP	SA/OD	FBG SK	OB		8	4000	5 6	11400	13000
---------- 1984 BOATS ----------
16 7	HOBIE 16	SLP	SAIL	F/S CT			7 11	340	10	2700	3150
17	HOLDER 17	SLP	SA/OD	FBG SK			7 3	950	1 8	3800	4400
17	HOLDER 17 DS	SLP	SA/OD	FBG SK			7 3	925	1 8	3750	4350
18	HOBIE 18	SLP	SA/OD	F/S CT			8	400		2950	3400
18	HOBIE 18 MAGNUM	SLP	SA/OD	FBG SK			8	400		3500	4100
20 4	HOLDER 20	SLP	SA/OD	FBG DB			7 10	1160	4 2	4450	5100
33	HOBIE 33	SLP	SA/OD	FBG SK			8	4000	5 5	7250	8300

....For earlier years, see the BUC Used Boat Price Guide, Volume 3

HOLBY MARINE CO
BRISTOL RI 02309

COAST GUARD MFG ID- HXY See inside cover to adjust price for area

For more recent years, see the BUC Used Boat Price Guide, Volume 1

LOA FT IN	NAME AND/ OR MODEL	TOP/ RIG	BOAT TYPE	-HULL- MTL TP	TP #	--ENGINE--- HP MFG	BEAM FT IN	WGT LBS	DRAFT FT IN	RETAIL LOW	RETAIL HIGH
---------- 1996 BOATS ----------
16	PT JUDE	SLP	DGY	FBG CB			5 11	525	3 4	**	**
17	BRISTOL SKIFF		OPFSH	FBG FL	OB		6 8	425		2000	2350
30	QUEST 30	SLP	SARAC	FBG KL			11 5	5750	6 9	72000	79100
---------- 1994 BOATS ----------
36 4	HOLBY		SACAC	F/S KC	IB	30D YAN	11 4	12400	3 8	94200	103500
---------- 1991 BOATS ----------
35 5	CLEARWATER	SLP	SA/CR	F/S KL	IB	30D YAN	12	12000	2	75700	83100
---------- 1990 BOATS ----------
28 3	ALERION-EXPRESS	SLP	SAIL	FBG KL	IB	9D YAN	8 2	4400	4 6	25400	28200
35 3	CLEARWATER 35	SLP	SAIL	FBG KL	IB	30D YAN	11 4	10000	5 11	60200	66200

For more recent years, see the BUC Used Boat Price Guide, Volume 1

```
      LOA   NAME AND/                 TOP/ BOAT  -HULL-  ----ENGINE---  BEAM   WGT   DRAFT  RETAIL  RETAIL
     FT IN  OR MODEL                  RIG  TYPE  MTL TP TP # HP  MFG    FT IN  LBS   FT IN  LOW     HIGH
---------------------------- 1996 BOATS -----------------------------------------------------------------
36   5 BARRACUDA 370                  FB   CR    FBG TR IO  135  VLVO 12   16000  2  6  35900   39900
36   5 BARRACUDA 370                  FB   CR    FBG TR IO  190  VLVO 12   16000  2  6  37200   41400
36   5 BARRACUDA 370                  FB   CR    FBG TR IO T185D VLVO 12   16000  2  6  47200   51800
37  11 COASTAL-BARRACUDA              FB   CR    FBG SV IO T190  VLVO 12   14000  2  6  38700   42900
37  11 COASTAL-BARRACUDA              FB   CR    FBG SV IO T185D VLVO 12   14000  2  6  47800   52600
39  11 AFT CABIN WA 390               FB   HB    FBG SV IO T180  VLVO 14   16000  2  7  45600   50100
39  11 AFT CABIN WA 390               FB   HB    FBG SV IO T245  VLVO 14   16000  2  7  47100   51700
40   7 MED-BARRACUDA                  FB   CR    FBG SV IO T190  VLVO 12   16000         49200   54100
40   7 MED-BARRACUDA                  FB   CR    FBG SV IO T185D VLVO 12   16000         59000   64800
42   3 AQUA HOME 420                  FB   HB    FBG SV IO T190  VLVO 14   24000  2  8  66100   72700
        IO T270 VLVO 67300  74000, IO T270 PCM 66900 73600, IO T300 VLVO 70300 77200
        IO T185D VLVO 71500 78500

45   3 COASTAL-COMMAND 450            FB   CR    FBG SV IO T300  VLVO 14   24000  2  8  73000   80200
46   3 AQUA HOME 460                  FB   HB    FBG SV IO T245  VLVO 14   24000  2  8  78500   86200
49   3 COASTAL-COMMAND 490            FB   CR    FBG SV IO T270  VLVO 14   24000  2  7  89500   98400
49   3 COASTAL-COMMAND 490            FB   CR    FBG SV IO T215D VLVO 14   24000  2  7  94900  104500
50   4 SANDPIPER                      FB   MY    FBG SV IB T318D CUM  14  1 28000  2 10 116000 127500
---------------------------- 1995 BOATS -----------------------------------------------------------------
36   5 BARRACUDA 370                  FB   CR    FBG TR IO  135  VLVO 12   16000  2  6  33500   37200
        IO 300 MRCR 34000 37700, IO T190 VLVO 34700 38600, IO T270 PCM 35400 39300
        IO T185D VLVO 43500 48300

37  11 COASTAL-BARRACUDA              FB   CR    FBG SV IO T190  VLVO 12   14000  2  6  36100   40100
        IO T270 PCM 36500 40600, IO T300 MRCR 37300 41400, IO T185D VLVO 44400 49300

39  11 AFT CABIN WA 390               FB   HB    FBG SV IO T180  VLVO 14   16000  2  7  42500   47200
39  11 AFT CABIN WA 390               FB   HB    FBG SV IO T245  VLVO 14   16000  2  7  43800   48700
40   7 MED-BARRACUDA                  FB   CR    FBG SV IO T190  VLVO 12   16000         46200   50700
        IO T270 PCM 47000 51600, IO T300 MRCR 47800 52500, IO T185D VLVO 55100 60500

42   3 AQUA HOME 420                  FB   HB    FBG SV IO T190  VLVO 14   24000  2  8  62300   68400
        IO T245 VLVO 63400 69700, IO T270 PCM 63100 69300, IO T300 VLVO 66200 72700
        IO T400 PCM 74300 81600, IO T185D VLVO 67500 74200

45   3 COASTAL-COMMAND 450            FB   CR    FBG SV IO T270  PCM  14   24000  2  8  66300   72900
45   3 COASTAL-COMMAND 450            FB   CR    FBG SV IO T300  VLVO 14   24000  2  8  68100   74800
45   3 COASTAL-COMMAND 450            FB   CR    FBG SV IO T400  PCM  14   24000  2  8  68900   75700
45   3 COASTAL-COMMANDER              FB   CR    FBG SV IO T400  PCM  14   24000  2  7  65700   72200
46   3 AQUA HOME 460                  FB   HB    FBG SV IO T190  VLVO 14   24000  2  8  72300   79500
        IO T245 VLVO 73400 80600, IO T270 PCM 73000 80200, IO T400 PCM 73200 91400
        IO T185D VLVO 82000 90100

49   3 COASTAL-COMMAND 490            FB   CR    FBG SV IO T270  PCM  14   24000  2  7  83500   91800
        IO T270 VLVO 83500 91800, IO T300 VLVO 85200 93600, IO T400 PCM 90400 99300
        IO T185D VLVO 86200 94700
---------------------------- 1994 BOATS -----------------------------------------------------------------
36   5 BARRACUDA 370                  FB   CR    FBG TR IO  135  VLVO 12   16000  2  6  31200   34700
        IO 300 MRCR 31700 35200, IO T190 VLVO 32400 36000, IO T270 PCM 33000 36700
        IO T185D VLVO 40600 45100

37  11 COASTAL-BARRACUDA              FB   CR    FBG SV IO T190  VLVO 12   14000  2  6  33500   37400
        IO T270 PCM 34100 37900, IO T300 MRCR 34800 38700, IO T185D VLVO 41400 46000

39  11 AFT CABIN WA                   FB   HB    FBG SV IO T180  VLVO 14   16000  2  7  40200   44700
39  11 AFT CABIN WA                   FB   HB    FBG SV IO T245  VLVO 14   16000  2  7  41500   46100
40   7 MED-BARRACUDA                  FB   CR    FBG SV IO T190  VLVO 12   16000         42600   47400
        IO T270 PCM 43400 48200, IO T300 MRCR 44200 49100, IO T185D VLVO 51400 56500

42   3 AQUA HOME 420                  FB   HB    FBG SV IO T190  VLVO 14   24000  2  8  59000   64800
        IO T245 VLVO 60000 66000, IO T270 PCM 59700 65600, IO T300 VLVO 62700 68900
        IO T400 PCM 70300 77300, IO T185D VLVO 64100 70500

45   3 COASTAL-COMMANDO               FB   CR    FBG SV IO T270  PCM  14   24000  2  8  53500   58800
45   3 COASTAL-COMMANDO               FB   CR    FBG SV IO T300  VLVO 14   24000  2  8  54900   60300
45   3 COASTAL-COMMANDO               FB   CR    FBG SV IO T400  PCM  14   24000  2  8  58800   64600
46   3 AQUA HOME 460                  FB   HB    FBG SV IO T190  VLVO 14   24000  2  8  67900   74700
        IO T245 VLVO 68900 75700, IO T270 PCM 68600 75400, IO T400 PCM 78100 85900
        IO T185D VLVO 77300 85000

49   3 COASTAL-COMMANDO               FB   CR    FBG SV IO T270  PCM  14   24000  2  7  67800   74500
        IO T270 VLVO 67800 74500, IO T300 VLVO 69200 76000, IO T400 PCM 73400 80700
        IO T185D VLVO 70100 77000
---------------------------- 1993 BOATS -----------------------------------------------------------------
36   5 BARRACUDA 370                  FB   CR    FBG TR IO  135  VLVO 12   16000  2  6  29200   32400
        IO 225 VLVO 29300 32600, IO 300 MRCR 29600 32900, IO T190 VLVO 30300 33700
        IO T225 VLVO 30600 34000, IO T270 PCM 30900 34300, IO T185D VLVO 38000 42200

37  11 COASTAL-BARRACUDA              FB   CR    FBG SV IO  135  VLVO 12   14000  2  6  30100   33500
        IO 225 VLVO 30300 33700, IO T190 VLVO 31500 35000, IO T225 VLVO 31700 35300
        IO T270 PCM 31900 35400, IO T300 MRCR 32500 36100, IO T185D VLVO 38700 43000

39      AQUA HOME AFT CABIN           FB   HB    FBG SV IO T150            20000  2  8  42200   46900
39      AQUA HOME AFT CABIN           FB   HB    FBG SV IO T245            20000  2  8  43400   48200
39  11 AFT CABIN WA                   FB   HB    FBG SV IO T180  VLVO 14   16000  2  7  38300   42500
39  11 AFT CABIN WA                   FB   HB    FBG SV IO T245  VLVO 14   16000  2  7  39500   43900
40   7 MED-BARRACUDA                  FB   CR    FBG SV IO  135  VLVO 12   16000         37800   42000
        IO 225 VLVO 38300 42500, IO T190 VLVO 39800 44300, IO T225 VLVO 40200 44700
        IO T270 PCM 40500 45000, IO T300 MRCR 41300 45900, IO T185D VLVO 48000 52800

42   3 AQUA HOME 420                  FB   HB    FBG SV IO  206  VLVO 14   24000  2  8  53700   59100
        IO T190 VLVO 56100 61700, IO T225 VLVO 56600 62200, IO T245 VLVO 57100 62800
        IO T270 PCM 56800 62400, IO T300 VLVO 59600 65500, IO T400 PCM 66900 73500
        IO T185D VLVO 61200 67300

42  11 COASTAL-COMMANDER              FB   CR    FBG SV IO T300  VLVO 14   16000  2  7  43700   48600
45   3 COASTAL-COMMANDO               FB   CR    FBG SV IO T270  PCM  14   24000  2  8  50000   54900
        IO T270 VLVO 51300 56400, IO T400 PCM 55000 60400, IO T185D VLVO 55100 60500

46   3 AQUA HOME 460                  FB   HB    FBG SV IO  206  VLVO 14   24000  2  8  62000   68100
        IO T190 VLVO 64200 70500, IO T225 VLVO 64700 71100, IO T245 VLVO 65100 71500
        IO T270 PCM 64800 71200, IO T300 VLVO 67300 74000, IO T400 PCM 73900 81200
        IO T185D VLVO 73300 80500

49   3 COASTAL-COMMANDO               FB   CR    FBG SV IO T270  PCM  14   24000  2  7  64600   71000
        IO T300 VLVO 66000 72500, IO T400 PCM 70000 76900, IO T185D VLVO 66800 73400
---------------------------- 1992 BOATS -----------------------------------------------------------------
29      BAYMASTER                     FB   HB    FBG SV IO  231  VLVO 12   11000  2  5  27700   30800
36   5 BARRACUDA FD                   FB   CR    FBG TR IO  271  VLVO 12   16000  2  6  27700   30800
36   5 BARRACUDA FD                   FB   CR    FBG TR IO  151  VLVO 12   16000  2  6  28100   31300
36   9 BARRACUDA AFT CABIN            FB   CR    FBG SV IO  260  VLVO 12   18000  1  7  30900   34300
        IB T270 CRUS 50900 55900, IO T271 VLVO 32500 36100, IO T200D VLVO 39600 44000

37  11 COASTAL-BARRACUDA              FB   CR    FBG SV IO T135D VLVO 12   15000  2  6  35000   38900
        IO T211 VLVO 31000 34400, IO T231 VLVO 31200 34600, IO T271 VLVO 31800 35300
        IO T130D VLVO 37000 41100

40   7 MED-BARRACUDA                  FB   CR    FBG SV VD T271  VLVO 12   16500         60400   66400
42   3 AQUA-HOME BARRACUDA            FB   HB    FBG SV VD T270  VLVO 14   24000  2  8  55500   61000
42   3 AQUA-HOME BARRACUDA            FB   HB    FBG SV VD T270  CRUS 14   24500  2  8  54800   60200
45   3 COASTAL-COMMANDER              FB   CR    FBG SV VD T350  CRUS 14   25500  2  8  73100   80300
46   3 AQUA-HOME BARRACUDA            FB   HB    FBG SV VD T270  CRUS 14   25000  2  8  65400   71800
46   3 AQUA-HOME BARRACUDA            FB   HB    FBG SV VD T350  CRUS 14   25500  2  8  66700   73300
49   3 COASTAL-COMMANDER              FB   CR    FBG SV VD T270  CRUS 14   25000  2  7  82000   90100
        VD T340 MRCR 86600 95200, VD T350 CRUS 87200 95800, VD T400 PCM 91100 100000
---------------------------- 1991 BOATS -----------------------------------------------------------------
36   5 BARRACUDA SUPER                FB   CR    FBG SV IO  130  VLVO 12          2  4  25500   28300
        IO 245 VLVO 25700 28500, IO 300 MRCR 25900 28700, IO T130 VLVO 26200 29100
        IO T187 VLVO 26400 29400, IO T245 VLVO 26900 29900, VD T270 PCM 42900 47700
        IO T185D VLVO 33100 36800

37  11 BARRACUDA AFT                  FB   CR    FBG SV IO  130  VLVO 12          2  4  29500   32800
        IO 245 VLVO 29600 32900, IO 300 MRCR 29800 33100, IO T130 VLVO 30100 33500
        IO T187 VLVO 30200 33500, IO T245 VLVO 30800 34200, VD T270 PCM 48800 53600
        IO T185D VLVO 36700 40800

37  11 BARRACUDA SUPER                FB   CR    FBG SV IO  130  VLVO 12          2  4  28100   31200
        IO 245 VLVO 28200 31400, IO 300 MRCR 28400 31500, IO T130 VLVO 28900 32100
        IO T187 VLVO 28900 32200, IO T245 VLVO 29300 33000, VD T270 PCM 47200 51900
        IO T185D VLVO 35800 39800

37  11 COASTAL-BARRACUDA              FB   CR    FBG SV IO  130  VLVO 12          2  4  23300   25800
        IO 245 VLVO 23700 26300, IO 300 MRCR 24000 26700, IO T130 VLVO 24600 27300
        IO T187 VLVO 24900 27600, IO T245 VLVO 25300 28100, VD T270 PCM 40000 44500
        IO T185D VLVO 32000 35500

37  11 MID-BARRACUDA                  FB   CR    FBG SV IO  130  VLVO 12          2  4  25400   28200
        IO 245 VLVO 25700 28600, IO 300 MRCR 26000 28900, IO T130 VLVO 26500 29400
```

```
      LOA  NAME AND/        TOP/ BOAT  -HULL-   ----ENGINE---   BEAM   WGT  DRAFT RETAIL RETAIL
     FT IN OR MODEL         RIG  TYPE  MTL TP TP #   HP   MFG   FT IN  LBS  FT IN  LOW    HIGH
-------------------- 1991 BOATS --------------------
37 11 MID-BARRACUDA        FB   CR   FBG SV IO T187  VLVO 12              2 4  26700 29700
      IO T245  VLVO 27000  30000, VD T270  PCM  42700 47400, IO T185D VLVO  33300 37000

42    AQUA HOME            FB   HB   FBG SV IO 204   VLVO 14              2 6  49000 53800
      IO  300  MRCR 49800  54700, IO T190  VLVO 51300 56400, IO T245  VLVO   52200 57400
      VD T270  PCM  50800  55900, IO T300  VLVO 54400 59700, VD T400  PCM    53600 58800
      IO T185D VLVO 55800  61300

45  3 COASTAL-COMMANDER    FB   CR   FBG SV VD T270  PCM  14              2 6  63400 69700
      IO T330  VLVO 42200  46900, VD T400  PCM  66300 72800, IO T185D VLVO  47400 52100

46    AQUA HOME            FB   HB   FBG SV IO 204   VLVO 14              2 6  59600 62200
      IO  300  MRCR 57300  63000, IO T190  VLVO 58600 64400, IO T245  VLVO   59500 65300
      VD T270  PCM  57900  63600, IO T300  VLVO 61500 67600, VD T400  PCM    60300 66300
      IO T185D VLVO 66800  73400

49  3 COASTAL-COMMANDER    FB   CR   FBG SV VD T270  PCM  14              2 6  76000 83600
      IO T330  VLVO 51100  56100, VD T400  PCM  79000 86800, IO T185D VLVO  53500 58800
-------------------- 1990 BOATS --------------------
29    BAY MASTER           FB   HB   FBG SV IO 231   VLVO 12    11000     2 5  25700 28600
36  5 BARRACUDA FD         FB   CR   FBG TR IO 271   VLVO 12    16000     2 6  24400 27100
36  5 BARRACUDA FD         FB   CR   FBG TR IO T151  VLVO 12    16000     2 6  24800 27600
36  9 BARRACUDA AFT CABIN  FB   CR   FBG SV IO 260   VLVO 12    18000     1 7  27200 30300
      IB T270  CRUS 46600  51200, IO T271  VLVO 28700 31900, IO T200D VLVO  34900 38800

37 11 COASTAL-BARRACUDA    FB   CR   FBG SV IO 135D  VLVO 12    15000     2 6  30900 34300
      IO T211  VLVO 27300  30400, IO T231  VLVO 27500 30600, IO T271  VLVO  31900 31100

40  7 MED-BARRACUDA        FB   CR   FBG SV VD T271  VLVO 12    16500     2 8  55000 60400
42  3 AQUA-HOME BARRACUDA  FB   HB   FBG SV VD T270  CRUS 14    24500     2 8  49300 54200
45  3 COASTAL COMMANDER    FB   HB   FBG SV VD T350  CRUS 14    25500     2 8  57500 63200
46  3 AQUA-HOME BARRACUDA  FB   HB   FBG SV VD T270  CRUS 14    25500     2 8  60100 66000
46  3 AQUA-HOME BARRACUDA  FB   HB   FBG SV VD T350  CRUS 14    25500     2 8  61300 67400
49  3 COASTAL-COMMANDER    FB   HB   FBG SV VD T270  CRUS 14    25000     2 7  74600 81900
      VD T340  MRCR 78800  86600, VD T350  CRUS 79400 87200, VD T400  PCM   82900 91100
-------------------- 1989 BOATS --------------------
36  5 BARRACUDA FD         HT   CR   FBG TR IO 271   VLVO 12    15000     2 6  22200 24600
36  5 BARRACUDA FD         FB   CR   FBG TR IO 231   VLVO 12    16000     2 6  22900 25400
      IO  271  VLVO 23000  25600, IO 130D  VLVO 28200 31400, IO T151  VLVO  23400 26000
      IO T231  VLVO 23000  26600, IO T270  CRUS 24000 26700, IO T130D VLVO  30200 32100
36  9 BARRACUDA AFT CBN    FB   CR   FBG SV IO 260   VLVO 12    18000     1 7  25700 28600
      IB T270  CRUS 44000  48900, IO T271  VLVO 27100 30100, IO T200D VLVO  33000 36600
37 11 COASTAL-BARRACUDA    FB   CR   FBG SV IO 135D  VLVO 12    15000     2 6  29200 32400
      IO 135D  VLVO 30400  33800, IO T211  VLVO 31600 35100, IO T231  VLVO  31900 35500
      IO T271  VLVO 33200  36900, IO T130D VLVO 33300 37000
40  7 MED-BARRACUDA        FB   CR   FBG SV VD T271  VLVO 12    16500     2 8  52500 57700
42  3 AQUA-HOME BARRACUDA  FB   HB   FBG SV VD T270  CRUS 14    24500     2 8  49300 54200
45  3 COASTAL COMMANDER    FB   HB   FBG SV VD T350  CRUS 14    25500     2 8  57500 63200
46  3 AQUA-HOME BARRACUDA  FB   HB   FBG SV VD T270  CRUS 14    25500     2 8  60300 63700
46  3 AQUA-HOME BARRACUDA  FB   HB   FBG SV VD T350  CRUS 14    25500     2 8  59200 65100
49  3 COASTAL-COMMANDER    FB   HB   FBG SV VD T270  CRUS 14    25000     2 7  56600 62200
      VD T340  MRCR 59800  65700, VD T350  CRUS 57900 63600, VD T400  PCM   61200 67300
-------------------- 1988 BOATS --------------------
35  3 BARRACUDA FD         HT   CR   FBG TR IO 271   VLVO 12    15000     2 6  25200 28000
35  3 BARRACUDA FD         FB   CR   FBG TR IO 231   VLVO 12    16000     2 6  25800 28700
      IO  271  VLVO 26000  28800, IO 130D  VLVO 29200 32400, IO T151  VLVO  26300 29200
      IO T231  VLVO 27000  30100, IO T270  CRUS 27300 30400, IO T130D VLVO  29000 32200
36  9 BARRACUDA AFT CBN    FB   CR   FBG SV IO 260   VLVO 12    18000     1 7  24300 27000
      IB T270  CRUS 42100  46700, IO T271  VLVO 25600 28500, IO T200D VLVO  31200 34700
36  9 COASTAL-BARRACUDA    FB   HB   FBG SV IO 231   VLVO 12    15000     1 7  28300 31400
      IO 135D  VLVO 29600  32800, IO T211  VLVO 30600 34000, IO T231  VLVO  31000 34400
      IO T271  VLVO 32200  35700, IO T130D VLVO 32400 36000
46  3 AQUA-HOME BARRACUDA  FB   HB   FBG SV VD T270  CRUS 14    25500     2 8  56200 61700
46  3 AQUA-HOME BARRACUDA  FB   HB   FBG SV VD T350  CRUS 14    25500     2 8  57400 63100
49  3 COASTAL-COMMANDER    FB   HB   FBG SV VD T270  CRUS 14    25000     2 7  55100 60600
      VD T340  MRCR 57900  63700, VD T350  CRUS 56000 61600, VD T400  PCM   59300 65200
-------------------- 1987 BOATS --------------------
35  3 BARRACUDA FD         HT   CR   FBG TR SE 205   OMC  12    15000     2 6  50800 55800
35  3 BARRACUDA FD         HT   CR   FBG TR IO 225   VLVO 12    15000     2 6  23800 26400
      IO  260  VLVO 23900  26600, IO 130D  VLVO 26600 29600, IO T151  VLVO  24300 27000
      IO  200  VLVO 24700  27500, IB T228  MRCR 31700 35200, IO T130D VLVO  26500 29400
35  3 BARRACUDA FD         FB   CR   FBG TR SE 205   OMC  12    16000     2 6  50800 55800
35  3 BARRACUDA FD         FB   CR   FBG TR IO 225   VLVO 12    16000     2 6  24600 27300
      IO  260  VLVO 24600  27400, IO 130D  VLVO 27800 30800, IO T151  VLVO  25000 27800
      IO  200  VLVO 25400  28200, IB T228  MRCR 32600 36200, IO T130D VLVO  26500 30600
36  9 BARRACUDA AFT CBN    HT   CR   FBG SV SE 205   OMC  12    17000     1 7  65700 72200
36  9 BARRACUDA AFT CBN    FB   CR   FBG SV IO 225   VLVO 12    18000     1 7  23000 25500
      IO  260  VLVO 23100  25700, IO 130D  VLVO 28100 31200, IO T151  VLVO  22700 25200
      IO  200  VLVO 22900  26400, VD T220  CRUS 39900 44300, IO T260  VLVO  24200 26900
      IO T130D VLVO 29000  32200
36  9 BARRACUDA AFT CBN    FB   CR   FBG SV SE 205   OMC  12    18000     1 7  65700 72200
36  9 BARRACUDA AFT CBN    FB   CR   FBG SV IO 225   VLVO 12    18000     1 7  23000 25600
      IO  260  VLVO 23100  25700, IO 130D  VLVO 28100 31200, IO T151  VLVO  23500 26100
      IO  200  VLVO 23700  26400, IB T220  CRUS 39900 44300, IO T260  VLVO  24200 26900
      IO T130D VLVO 29000  32200
36  9 COASTAL-BARRACUDA    HT   HB   FBG SV SE 205   OMC  12    15000     1 7  27400 30400
      IO  225  VLVO 27400  30500, IO  260  VLVO 27900 31000, IO 130D  VLVO  28700 31900
      IO T151  VLVO 29300  32500, IO  200  VLVO 29600 32900, VD T228  MRCR  29300 32500
      IO T130D VLVO 31500  35000
36  9 COASTAL-BARRACUDA    FB   HB   FBG SV SE 205   OMC  12    15000     1 7  27400 30400
      IO  225  VLVO 27400  30500, IO  260  VLVO 27900 31000, IO 130D  VLVO  28700 31900
      IO T151  VLVO 29300  32500, IO  200  VLVO 29600 32900, IB T228  MRCR  29000 32200
      IO T130D VLVO 31500  35000
46  3 AQUA-HOME BARRACUDA  FB   HB   FBG SV IO 225   VLVO 14    24000     2 6  49900 54900
46  3 AQUA-HOME BARRACUDA  FB   HB   FBG SV VD T270  CRUS 14    25500     2 8  54900 60300
49  3 COASTAL-COMMANDER    FB   HB   FBG SV VD T270  CRUS 14    25000     2 7  53600 58900
49  3 COASTAL-COMMANDER    FB   HB   FBG SV VD T350  CRUS 14    25000     2 7  54700 60100
49  3 COASTAL-COMMANDER    FB   HB   FBG SV IO T185D VLVO 14    26000     2 8  63900 70200
-------------------- 1986 BOATS --------------------
35  3 BARRACUDA FD         HT   CR   FBG TR SE 205   OMC  12    15000     2 6  49500 54400
35  3 BARRACUDA FD         HT   CR   FBG TR IO 225   VLVO 12    15000     2 6  22700 25300
      IO  260  VLVO 22800  25400, IO 130D  VLVO 25400 28200, IO T140  VLVO  23100 25700
      IO  200  VLVO 23600  26200, IB T228  MRCR 30300 33600, IO T130D VLVO  25500 28100
35  3 BARRACUDA FD         FB   CR   FBG TR SE 205   OMC  12    16000     2 6  49500 54400
35  3 BARRACUDA FD         FB   CR   FBG TR IO 225   VLVO 12    16000     2 6  23400 26100
      IO  260  VLVO 23500  26100, IO 130D  VLVO 26500 29400, IO T140  VLVO  23800 26400
      IO  200  VLVO 24300  27000, IB T228  MRCR 31100 34500, IO T130D VLVO  26300 29200
36  9 BARRACUDA AFT CBN    HT   CR   FBG SV SE 205   OMC  12    17000     1 7  64100 70400
36  9 BARRACUDA AFT CBN    HT   CR   FBG SV IO 225   VLVO 12    18000     1 7  22000 24400
      IO  260  VLVO 22100  24500, IO 130D  VLVO 26900 29800, IO T200  VLVO  21800 24300
      VD T220  CRUS 38200  42400, IO T260  VLVO 23100 25700, IO T130D VLVO  27700 30700
36  9 BARRACUDA AFT CBN    FB   CR   FBG SV SE 205   OMC  12    18000     1 7  64100 70400
36  9 BARRACUDA AFT CBN    FB   CR   FBG SV IO 225   VLVO 12    18000     1 7  22000 24400
      IO  260  VLVO 22100  24500, IO 130D  VLVO 26900 29800, IO T140  VLVO  21800 24300
      IO  200  VLVO 22600  25200, IB T220  CRUS 38200 42400, IO T260  VLVO  23100 25700
      IO T130D VLVO 27700  30700
36  9 BARRACUDA AFTCBN     HT   CR   FBG SV IO T140  VLVO 12    17000     1 7  21600 24000
36  9 COASTAL-BARRACUDA    HT   HB   FBG SV SE 205   OMC  12    15000     1 7  26700 29600
      IO  225  VLVO 26700  29700, IO  260  VLVO 27200 30200, IO 130D  VLVO  28000 31100
      IO T140  VLVO 28500  31700, IO  200  VLVO 28900 32100, VD T228  MRCR  28500 31700
      IO T130D VLVO 30700  34100
36  9 COASTAL-BARRACUDA    FB   HB   FBG SV SE 205   OMC  12    15000     1    26700 29600
      IO  225  VLVO 26700  29700, IO  260  VLVO 27200 30200, IO 130D  VLVO  28000 31100
      IO T140  VLVO 28500  31700, IO  200  VLVO 28900 32100, IB T228  MRCR  28300 31400
      IO T130D VLVO 30700  34100
-------------------- 1985 BOATS --------------------
35  3 BARRACUDA FD         HT   CR   FBG TR IO 225   VLVO 12    15000     2 6  21800 24200
      IO  230  OMC  20800  23100, IO  260  VLVO 21900 24300, IO T140  VLVO  22200 24700
35  3 BARRACUDA FD         FB   CR   FBG TR SE 205   OMC  12    16000     2 6  48400 53100
35  3 BARRACUDA FD         FB   CR   FBG TR IO 225   VLVO 12    16000     2 6  22500 25000
      IO  260  VLVO 22600  25100, IO  330  MRCR 23300 25900, IO T200  VLVO  23300 25900
      IO T260  VLVO 24500  27200, IB T270  CRUS 31800 35300, IO T290  VLVO  24300 27000
36  9 BARRACUDA AFT CBN    HT   CR   FBG SV IO T200  VLVO 12    17000     1 7  21000 23300
36  9 BARRACUDA AFT CBN    FB   CR   FBG SV OB            VLVO       16000           **    **
36  9 BARRACUDA AFT CBN    FB   CR   FBG SV IO T140  VLVO 12    18000     1 7  21500 23900
```

LOA FT IN	NAME AND/ OR MODEL	TOP/ RIG	BOAT TYPE	-HULL- MTL TP	----ENGINE--- TP # HP MFG	BEAM FT IN	WGT LBS	DRAFT FT IN	RETAIL LOW	RETAIL HIGH
					------ 1985 BOATS ------					
36 9	BARRACUDA AFT CBN	FB	CR	FBG SV IO	T260 VLVO	12	18000	1 7	22200	24600
36 9	BARRACUDA AFT CBN	FB	CR	FBG SV IO	T270 CRUS		18000	1 7	40800	45400
36 9	COASTAL-BARRACUDA	HT	HB	FBG SV IO	260 VLVO	12	15000	1 7	26500	29500
36 9	COASTAL-BARRACUDA	FB	HB	FBG SV SE	205 OMC	12	15000	1 7	26000	28900
	IO 225 VLVO 26100	29000, IO	260	VLVO	26500 29500,	IO T140	VLVO		27800	30900
	IO T200 VLVO 28200	31300, IO	T225	VLVO	28500 31700,	IB T270	CRUS		28900	32100
	IO T130D VLVO 30000	33400								
37 9	BARRACUDA FD	HT	CR	FBG SV IO		12	14000		**	**
37 9	BARRACUDA FD	HT	CR	FBG SV IB	225	12	14000		32100	35700
39 3	BARRACUDA AFT CBN	HT	CR	FBG SV IO	225	12	18000		25100	27900
39 3	BARRACUDA AFT CBN	HT	CR	FBG SV IO	225	12	18000		42200	46900
39 3	COASTAL-BARRACUDA	HT	HB	FBG SV IO	225	12	15000		25500	28400
39 3	COASTAL-BARRACUDA	HT	HB	FBG SV IO	225	12	15000		25700	28600
					------ 1984 BOATS ------					
35 3	BARRACUDA FD	HT	CR	FBG TR IO	225 VLVO	12	15000	2 6	21100	23400
	IO 260 VLVO 21100	23500, IO	T200	VLVO	21900 24300,	IB T230	CRUS		27700	30800
35 3	BARRACUDA FD	FB	CR	FBG TR IO	T200 VLVO	12	15000	2 6	21900	24300
36 9	BARRACUDA AFT CBN	HT	CR	FBG SV SE	205 OMC	12	17000	1 7	61200	67200
36 9	BARRACUDA AFT CBN	FB	CR	FBG SV IO	T200 VLVO	12	17000	1 7	22000	22500
36 9	BARRACUDA AFT CBN	FB	CR	FBG SV SE	205 OMC	12	18000	1 7	61200	67200
36 9	BARRACUDA AFT CBN	FB	CR	FBG SV IO	225 VLVO	12	18000	1 7	20300	22600
	IO 260 VLVO 20400	22700, IO	130D	VLVO	24900 27600,	VD T220	CRUS		35000	38900
	IO 260 VLVO 21400	23800, IO	T130D	VLVO	25600 28500					
36 9	COASTAL-BARRACUDA	FB	CR	FBG SV IO	T260 VLVO	12	15000	1 7	19200	21300
36 9	COASTAL-BARRACUDA	HT	HB	FBG SV IO	225 VLVO	12	15000	1 7	25600	28400
	IO 260 VLVO 26000	28800, IO	T200	VLVO	27600 30600,	VD T228	MRCR		27300	30300
36	COASTAL-BARRACUDA	FB	HB	FBG SV SE	205 OMC	12	15000	1 7	25500	28300
	IO 225 VLVO 25600	28400, IO	T200	VLVO	26000 28800,	IO 330	MRCR		27700	29900
	IO T200 VLVO 27600	30600, IO	T225	VLVO	27900 31000,	IO T130D	VLVO		29400	32700
37 9	BARRACUDA FD	HT	CR	FBG SV IB	225	12	14000		30800	34200
39 3	BARRACUDA AFT CBN	HT	CR	FBG SV IB	225	12	18000		40500	45000
39 3	COASTAL-BARRACUDA	HT	HB	FBG SV IB	225	12	15000		25200	27900

....For earlier years, see the BUC Used Boat Price Guide, Volume 3

HONNOR MARINE UK LTD

DARTINGTON
TOTNES DEVON ENGLAND TQ COAST GUARD MFG ID- HNR   See inside cover to adjust price for area

LOA FT IN	NAME AND/ OR MODEL	TOP/ RIG	BOAT TYPE	-HULL- MTL TP	----ENGINE--- TP # HP MFG	BEAM FT IN	WGT LBS	DRAFT FT IN	RETAIL LOW	RETAIL HIGH
					------ 1995 BOATS ------					
18 9	LUGGER	YWL	SACAC	FBG SK	OB	6 3	748	4	8900	10100
21 9	COASTER	YWL	SACAC	FBG SK	OB	6 7	1060	3 10	12500	14200
21 9	LONGBOAT	YWL	SACAC	FBG SK	OB	6 7	880	4 2	11800	13400
25	GIG	YWL	SACAC	FBG SK	OB	7	1760	5 1	19300	21500
					------ 1994 BOATS ------					
18 9	DRASCOMBE LUGGER	YWL	SACAC	FBG SK	OB	6 3	748	4	8250	9500
21 9	DRASCOMBE COASTER	YWL	SACAC	FBG SK	OB	6 7	1060	4 2	11800	13400
21 9	DRASCOMBE LONGBOAT	YWL	SACAC	FBG SK	OB	6 7	880	4 2	11100	12600
25	DRASCOMBE GIG	YWL	SACAC	FBG SK	OB	7	1760	5 1	18400	20400
					------ 1993 BOATS ------					
18 9	DRASCOMBE LUGGER	YWL	SACAC	FBG SK	OB	6 3	748	4	7800	8950
21 9	DRASCOMBE COASTER	YWL	SACAC	FBG SK	OB	6 7	1060	4 2	11100	12600
21 9	DRASCOMBE LONGBOAT	YWL	SACAC	FBG SK	OB	6 7	880	4 2	10400	11800
25	DRASCOMBE GIG	YWL	SACAC	FBG SK	OB	7	1760	5 1	16900	19200
					------ 1985 BOATS ------					
18 9	LUGGER	YWL	SAIL	FBG CB	OB	6 3	850	10	5000	5750
21 6	DRIFTER	YWL	SAIL	FBG BB	OB	7 3	2000	2	9050	10300
21 6	DRIFTER	YWL	SAIL	FBG IB	6D BMW	7 3	2000	2	11300	12900
21 9	COASTER	YWL	SAIL	FBG CB	OB	6 7	1060	1	6750	7750
21 9	LONGBOAT	YWL	SAIL	FBG CB	OB	6 7	880	1	6350	7300
25	GIG	YWL	SAIL	FBG CB	OB	7	2155		11700	13300
					------ 1984 BOATS ------					
18 9	LUGGER	YWL	SAIL	FBG CB	OB	6 3	850	10	4400	9650
21 6	DRIFTER	YWL	SAIL	FBG BB	OB	7 3	2000	2	8400	9650
21 6	DRIFTER	YWL	SAIL	FBG IB	6D BMW	7 3	2000	2	10700	12100
21 9	COASTER	YWL	SAIL	FBG CB	OB	6 7	1060	1	6350	7300
21 9	LONGBOAT	YWL	SAIL	FBG CB	OB	6 7	880	1	5950	6850
25	GIG	YWL	SAIL	FBG CB	OB	7	2155		11000	12500

....For earlier years, see the BUC Used Boat Price Guide, Volume 3

TED HOOD YACHT BUILDERS

PORTSMOUTH RI 02871   See inside cover to adjust price for area

For more recent years, see the BUC Used Boat Price Guide, Volume 1

LOA FT IN	NAME AND/ OR MODEL	TOP/ RIG	BOAT TYPE	-HULL- MTL TP	----ENGINE--- TP # HP MFG	BEAM FT IN	WGT LBS	DRAFT FT IN	RETAIL LOW	RETAIL HIGH
					------ 1996 BOATS ------					
51 11	TED HOOD PH 51	CUT	SACAC	FBG KC IB	105D YAN	15 2	49440	5 11	402000	441500

HOOG BOATS INC

MIAMI FL 33197-1502   COAST GUARD MFG ID- HOG See inside cover to adjust price for area

LOA FT IN	NAME AND/ OR MODEL	TOP/ RIG	BOAT TYPE	-HULL- MTL TP	----ENGINE--- TP # HP MFG	BEAM FT IN	WGT LBS	DRAFT FT IN	RETAIL LOW	RETAIL HIGH
					------ 1995 BOATS ------					
16 8	HOOG 16	OP	FSH	FBG SV	OB	6	800	9	5450	6250
17 3	HOOG 17	OP	FSH	FBG SV	OB	6 2	1050	11	7100	8150
19 6	HOOG 19 LONG DECK	OP	FSH	FBG SV	OB	7	1050	8	7900	9100
19 6	HOOG 19 SHORT DECK	OP	FSH	FBG SV	OB	7	1050	8	7400	8500
23	HOOG 23	OP	FSH	FBG SV	OB	8	2500	1 6	13300	15100
23	HOOG 23 SINGLE BRCKT	OP	FSH	FBG SV	OB	8	2500	1 6	14600	16500
23	HOOG 23 TWIN BRCKT	OP	FSH	FBG SV	OB	8	2500	1 6	16400	18700
					------ 1994 BOATS ------					
16 8	HOOG 16	OP	FSH	FBG	OB	6	800	9	5200	6000
17 3	HOOG 17	OP	FSH	FBG	OB	6 2	1050	11	6800	7800
19 6	HOOG 19 LONG DECK	OP	FSH	FBG	OB	7	1050	8	7550	8700
19 6	HOOG 19 SHORT DECK	OP	FSH	FBG	OB	7	1050	8	7050	8100
23	HOOG 23	OP	FSH	FBG	OB	8	2500	1 6	12300	13900
23	HOOG 23 BRCKT	OP	FSH	FBG	OB	8	2500	1 6	14100	16000
					------ 1993 BOATS ------					
16 8	HOOG 16	OP	FSH	FBG	OB	6	800	9	5000	5750
17 3	HOOG 17	OP	FSH	FBG	OB	6 2	1050	11	6500	7500
19 6	HOOG 19 LONG DECK	OP	FSH	FBG	OB	7	1050	8	7250	8350
19 6	HOOG 19 SHORT DECK	OP	FSH	FBG	OB	7	1050	8	6750	7800
23	HOOG 23	OP	FSH	FBG	OB	8	2500	1 6	11800	13400
23	HOOG 23 BRCKT	OP	FSH	FBG	OB	8	2500	1 6	13500	15400
23 10	HOOG 24	OP	FSH	FBG	OB	8	2500	1 6	13900	15800
					------ 1992 BOATS ------					
16 8	HOOG 16	OP	FSH	FBG	OB	6	800	9	4800	5500
17 3	HOOG 17	OP	FSH	FBG	OB	6 2	1050	11	6250	7200
23	HOOG 23	OP	FSH	FBG	OB	8	2500	1 6	13000	14800
23	HOOG 23 BRCKT	OP	FSH	FBG	OB	8	2500	1 6	13400	15300
23 10	HOOG 24	OP	FSH	FBG	OB	8	2500	1 6	13400	15200
					------ 1991 BOATS ------					
16 8	HOOG 16	OP	FSH	FBG	OB	6	800	9	4650	5350
17 3	HOOG 17	OP	FSH	FBG	OB	6 2	1050	10	6050	6950
23	HOOG 23	OP	FSH	FBG	OB	8 3	2000	1 8	10400	11800
23	HOOG 23 BRCKT	OP	FSH	FBG	OB	8 3	2500	1 8	11900	13500
24	EURO TRANSOM	OP	FSH	FBG	OB	8 3	2400	1 8	12500	14200
26	EURO TRANSOM	OP	FSH	FBG	OB	8 3	3000	1 8	19600	21800
					------ 1990 BOATS ------					
16 8	HOOG 16	OP	FSH	FBG	OB	6	800	9	4500	5150
17 3	HOOG 17	OP	FSH	FBG	OB	6 2	1050	10	5800	6700
23	HOOG 23	OP	FSH	FBG	OB	8	2000	1 8	10000	11400
23	HOOG 23 BRCKT	OP	FSH	FBG	OB	8	2500	1 8	11500	13000
					------ 1989 BOATS ------					
16 8	HOOG 16	OP	FSH	FBG	OB	6	800	9	4350	5000
17 3	HOOG 17	OP	FSH	FBG	OB	6 2	1050	10	5650	6500
23	HOOG 23	OP	FSH	FBG	OB	8	2000	1 8	9700	11000
23	HOOG 23 BRCKT	OP	FSH	FBG	OB	8	2500	1 8	12100	13800
					------ 1988 BOATS ------					
16 8	HOOG 16	OP	FSH	FBG	OB	6	800	9	4150	4850
17 3	HOOG 17	OP	FSH	FBG	OB	6 2	1050	10	5450	6300
					------ 1987 BOATS ------					
16 8	HOOG 16	OP	FSH	FBG	OB	6	800	9	4050	4700
17 3	HOOG 17	OP	FSH	FBG	OB	6 2	1050	10	5300	6100

HOPWOOD YACHTS USA INC
ALAMEDA CA 94501   COAST GUARD MFG ID- HPW   See inside cover to adjust price for area

LOA FT IN	NAME AND/ OR MODEL	TOP/ RIG	BOAT TYPE	HULL MTL TP	TP	ENGINE # HP	MFG	BEAM FT IN	WGT LBS	DRAFT FT IN	RETAIL LOW	RETAIL HIGH
--- 1986 BOATS ---
25 7	ROSS 780	SLP	SA/RC	F/S DB	OB			8 1	2490	5 11	12900	14600
27 3	ROSS 830	SLP	SA/RC	F/S DB	OB			8 8	2500	5	13800	15700
30 6	ROSS 930	SLP	SA/RC	F/S KL	IB	9D	YAN	9 3	3800	5 6	22900	25400
35	ROSS 35	SLP	SA/RC	F/S KL	IB	18D	YAN	11	7800	6	48400	53200
40 8	ROSS 40	SLP	SA/RC	F/S KL	IB	27D	YAN	12	10600	7	83800	92100
--- 1985 BOATS ---
25 7	ROSS 780	SLP	SA/RC	F/S DB	OB			8 1	2490	5 11	12200	13800
27 3	ROSS 830	SLP	SA/RC	F/S DB	OB			8 8	2500	5	13000	14800
30 6	ROSS 930	SLP	SA/RC	F/S KL	IB	7D	BMW	9 3	3800	5 6	21700	24100
35	ROSS 35	SLP	SA/RC	F/S KL	IB	18D	VLVO	11	7800	6	44800	49800
40 8	ROSS 40	SLP	SA/RC	F/S KL	IB	28D	VLVO	12	9800	7	74200	81600

HORIZON YACHT & MARINE CO
CLEARWATER FL 33520   COAST GUARD MFG ID- HXY   See inside cover to adjust price for area

LOA FT IN	NAME AND/ OR MODEL	TOP/ RIG	BOAT TYPE	HULL MTL TP	TP	ENGINE # HP	MFG	BEAM FT IN	WGT LBS	DRAFT FT IN	RETAIL LOW	RETAIL HIGH
--- 1984 BOATS ---
26	HORIZON 26	SLP	SA/CR	FBG KL	OB			8	4450	2 1	8550	9850
26	HORIZON 26	SLP	SA/CR	FBG KL	IB	8D	YAN	8	4550	2 1	9400	10700
38 7	HORIZON 39	SLP	SA/CR	FBG KC	IB	50D	PERK	11 2	18700	4	46700	51300
38 7	HORIZON 39	SLP	SA/CR	FBG KL	IB	50D	PERK	11 2	19000	4 4	47300	51900
39 7	HORIZON 39	KTH	SA/CR	FBG KC	IB	50D	PERK	11 2	18700	4	48700	53500
39 7	HORIZON 39	KTH	SA/CR	FBG KL	IB	50D	PERK	11 2	19000	5 4	49300	54100

....For earlier years, see the BUC Used Boat Price Guide, Volume 3

HOTFOOT BOATS
SAANICHTON BC CANADA   COAST GUARD MFG ID- ZHV   See inside cover to adjust price for area

LOA FT IN	NAME AND/ OR MODEL	TOP/ RIG	BOAT TYPE	HULL MTL TP	TP	ENGINE # HP	MFG	BEAM FT IN	WGT LBS	DRAFT FT IN	RETAIL LOW	RETAIL HIGH
--- 1987 BOATS ---
27	HOTFOOT 27	SLP	SA/RC	F/S KL	OB			9 4	3600	5 5	13200	15000
29 10	HOTFOOT 30	SLP	SA/RC	F/S KL	IB	D		10 4	4600	6	20200	22400
31 6	HOTFOOT 31	SLP	SA/RC	F/S KL	IB	D		10 6	5000	6	22900	25400
--- 1986 BOATS ---
20	HOTFOOT 20	SLP	SA/RC	F/S SK	OB			8 4	1000	5 5	3900	4500
27	HOTFOOT 27	SLP	SA/RC	F/S KL	OB			9 4	3600	5 5	12400	14100
31 6	HOTFOOT 31	SLP	SA/RC	F/S KL	IB	D		10 6	5000	5 9	21400	23800
--- 1985 BOATS ---
27	HOTFOOT 27	SLP	SA/RC	F/S KL	OB			9 4	3500	5 5	11300	12900
31 6	HOTFOOT 31	SLP	SA/RC	F/S KL	IB	15D	YAN	10 6	5000	5 9	20000	22300

....For earlier years, see the BUC Used Boat Price Guide, Volume 3

HOUSEBOAT SALES
RTM ASSOCIATES   See inside cover to adjust price for area
HOLLAND MI 49423

LOA FT IN	NAME AND/ OR MODEL	TOP/ RIG	BOAT TYPE	HULL MTL TP	TP	ENGINE # HP	MFG	BEAM FT IN	WGT LBS	DRAFT FT IN	RETAIL LOW	RETAIL HIGH
--- 1984 BOATS ---
18	HOBO	HT	CAMPR	FBG CT	OB				1800		5150	5900
18	HOBO RENTAL	HT	CAMPR	FBG CT	OB				1800		5750	6600

HOWIE CRAFT INC
LAKE OSWEGO OR   COAST GUARD MFG ID- HWC   See inside cover to adjust price for area

LOA FT IN	NAME AND/ OR MODEL	TOP/ RIG	BOAT TYPE	HULL MTL TP	TP	ENGINE # HP	MFG	BEAM FT IN	WGT LBS	DRAFT FT IN	RETAIL LOW	RETAIL HIGH
--- 1986 BOATS ---
20	HERITAGE MORC	SLP	SA/CR	FBG KL	IB	7D	YAN	6	3500	2 10	16100	18300
--- 1984 BOATS ---
20	HERITAGE MORC	SLP	SA/RC	FBG KL	IB	7D	REN	6 6	3500	2 11	14100	16000

....For earlier years, see the BUC Used Boat Price Guide, Volume 3

HUCKINS YACHT CORP
FAIRFORM-FLYER   See inside cover to adjust price for area
JACKSONVILLE FL 32210   COAST GUARD MFG ID- HNS

For more recent years, see the BUC Used Boat Price Guide, Volume 1

LOA FT IN	NAME AND/ OR MODEL	TOP/ RIG	BOAT TYPE	HULL MTL TP	TP	ENGINE # HP	MFG	BEAM FT IN	WGT LBS	DRAFT FT IN	RETAIL LOW	RETAIL HIGH
--- 1995 BOATS ---
44 10	SPORTSMAN 44	EPH	YTFS	F/S SV	IB	T350D	CAT	13 9	18000	2 6	292500	321500
44 10	SPORTSMAN 44	EPH	YTFS	F/S SV	IB	T350D	CUM	13 9	18000	2 6	288000	316500
--- 1987 BOATS ---
58	LINWOOD	FB	TCMY	F/S FL	IB	T350D	GM	16 3	45000	4	337500	371000
60	KIRKLINE 60	FB	SF	F/S DV	IB	T450D	CUM	16 3	40000	3 6	313500	344500
60	KIRKLINE 60	FB	SF	F/S SV	IB	T760D		16 11	42000	4 6	397000	436000
74	FAIRFORM FLYER	FB	YTFS	F/S FL	IB	T675D	GM	17 4	80000	4 7	**	**
78	FAIRFORM FLYER	FB	YTFS	F/S SV	IB	T760D		20 1	96000	3 4	**	**
--- 1986 BOATS ---
51	FAIRFORM FLYER	FB	SF	FBG SV	IB	T460D		16	40000		321500	353500
60	KIRKLINE 60	FB	SF	F/S DV	IB	T450D	CUM	16 3	40000	3 6	301500	331000
60	KIRKLINE 60	FB	SF	F/S DV	IB	T500D	J&T	16 3	40000	3 6	318000	349500
60	KIRKLINE 60	FB	SF	F/S DV	IB	T675D	MPC	16 3	40000	3 6	363000	398500
74	FAIRFORM FLYER	HT	SPTCR	F/S FL	IB	T100D	J&T	17 6	80000	4 4	**	**
74	FAIRFORM FLYER	FB	YTFS	F/S SV	IB	T675D	J&T	17 6		4 4	**	**
--- 1985 BOATS ---
51	FAIRFORM FLYER	FB	SF	FBG SV	IB	T460D		16	40000		308000	338500
60	KIRKLINE 60	FB	SF	F/S DV	IB	T450D	CUM	16 3	40000	3 6	289500	318000
60	KIRKLINE 60	FB	SF	F/S DV	IB	T500D	J&T	16 3	40000	3 6	306000	336000
60	KIRKLINE 60	FB	SF	F/S DV	IB	T675D	MPC	16 3	40000	3 6	331500	364500
77	FAIRFORM FLYER	FB	YTFS	FBG SV	IB	T650D		19 6	88000		**	**
--- 1984 BOATS ---
58	KIRKLINE 58	FB	SF	F/S DV	IB	T450D	CUM	16 3	40000	3 6	294000	323000
58	KIRKLINE 58	FB	SF	F/S DV	IB	T500D	J&T	16 3	41000	3 6	319000	350500
58	KIRKLINE 58	FB	SF	F/S DV	IB	T675D	J&T	16 3	42000	3 6	390000	428500
74	FAIRFORM FLYER	HT	SPTCR	F/S FL	IB	T10CD		17 6	80000	4 4	**	**
74	FAIRFORM FLYER	FB	YTFS	F/S SV	IB	T675D	J&T	17 6		4 6	**	**

....For earlier years, see the BUC Used Boat Price Guide, Volume 3

HUDSON BOAT LTD
RANCHO PALOS VERDE CA 90732   See inside cover to adjust price for area

LOCUST HILL CORP
WINCHESTER VA 22601

LOA FT IN	NAME AND/ OR MODEL	TOP/ RIG	BOAT TYPE	HULL MTL TP	TP	ENGINE # HP	MFG	BEAM FT IN	WGT LBS	DRAFT FT IN	RETAIL LOW	RETAIL HIGH
--- 1987 BOATS ---
44	SEA-WOLF 44	KTH	SA/RC	FBG KL	IB	D		13	30000	6	93400	102500
45	HUDSON 450	KTH	SA/RC	FBG KL	IB	D		13 3	27000	6 8	92700	102000
50 10	FORCE 50 PH	KTH	SA/RC	FBG KL	IB	D		14 2	52000	6	161000	177000
59 10	FORCE 60 PH	KTH	SA/RC	FBG KL	IB	D		16 6	60000	6	347000	381500
65	SEA-WOLF 65 PH	KTH	SA/RC	FBG KL	IB	D		17 6	75000	5 11	487000	535000
67	SEA-WOLF 67 PH	KTH	SA/RC	FBG KL	IB	D		17 6	78000	5 11	507500	558000
70	SEA-WOLF 70 PH	KTH	SA/RC	FBG KL	IB	D		18 3	80000	6 6	532000	584500
--- 1986 BOATS ---
44	SEA-WOLF 44	KTH	SA/RC	FBG KL	IB	D		13	30000	6	87900	96600
45	HUDSON 450	KTH	SA/RC	FBG KL	IB	D		13 3	27000	6 8	87200	95900
50 10	FORCE 50 PH	KTH	SA/RC	FBG KL	IB	D		14 2	52000	6	151500	166500
59 10	FORCE 60 PH	KTH	SA/RC	FBG KL	IB	D		16 6	60000	6	325500	357500
65	SEA-WOLF 65 PH	KTH	SA/RC	FBG KL	IB	D		17 6	75000	5 11	455500	500500
67	SEA-WOLF 67 PH	KTH	SA/RC	FBG KL	IB	D		17 6	78000	5 11	475000	522000
--- 1985 BOATS ---
44	SEA-WOLF 44	KTH	SA/RC	FBG KL	IB	D		13	30000	6	82700	90800
45	HUDSON 450	KTH	SA/RC	FBG KL	IB	D		13 3	27000	6 8	82000	90200
50 10	FORCE 50 PH	KTH	SA/RC	FBG KL	IB	D		14 2	52000	6	142500	156500
59 10	FORCE 60 CTR CPT	KTH	SA/RC	FBG KL	IB	D		16 6	60000	6	305500	335500
59 10	FORCE 60 PH	KTH	SA/RC	FBG KL	IB	D		16 6	60000	6	305500	335500
63	SEA-WOLF 63	CUT	SA/RC	FBG KL	IB	D		17	75000	6	405500	445500
--- 1984 BOATS ---
44	SEA-WOLF 44	KTH	SA/RC	FBG KL	IB	D		13	30000	6	77700	85400
45	HUDSON 450	KTH	SA/RC	FBG KL	IB	D		13 3	27000	6 8	77200	84800
50 10	FORCE 50 CTR CPT	KTH	SA/RC	FBG KL	IB	D		14 2	52000	6	135000	148500
50 10	FORCE 50 PH	KTH	SA/RC	FBG KL	IB	D		14 2	52000	6	135000	146000
59 10	FORCE 60 CTR CPT	KTH	SA/RC	FBG KL	IB	D		16 6	60000	6	287000	315000
59 10	FORCE 60 PH	KTH	SA/RC	FBG KL	IB	D		16 6	60000	6	287000	315000

....For earlier years, see the BUC Used Boat Price Guide, Volume 3

HUMBOLT BAY YACHTS INC

EUREKA CA 95501 See inside cover to adjust price for area

LOA FT	IN	NAME AND/ OR MODEL	TOP/ RIG	BOAT TYPE	-HULL- MTL	TP	TP	----ENGINE--- # HP	MFG	BEAM FT	IN	WGT LBS	DRAFT FT	IN	RETAIL LOW	RETAIL HIGH
		1984 BOATS														
30		HB30	SLP	SA/RC	FBG	CB				10	6	5050		9	18600	20700

HUNT-LEE YACHTS LTD

IMPORTER FOR LAVER SPA
NEWPORT BEACH CA 92660 COAST GUARD MFG ID- LHL See inside cover to adjust price for area

LOA FT	IN	NAME AND/ OR MODEL	TOP/ RIG	BOAT TYPE	-HULL- MTL	TP	TP	----ENGINE--- # HP	MFG	BEAM FT	IN	WGT LBS	DRAFT FT	IN	RETAIL LOW	RETAIL HIGH
		1986 BOATS														
41	3	LAVER		MY	FBG	SV	IB	T355D	CAT	13	6	22000	2	3	88600	97400
		IB T435D GM 91500 100500, IB T475D GM 94400 104000, IB T530D IF													98800	108500
41	3	LAVER	FB	MY	FBG	SV	IB	T355D	CAT	13	6	22000	2	3	89000	97800
		IB T435D GM 91800 101000, IB T475D GM 94800 104000, IB T530D IF													99200	109000
		1985 BOATS														
41	3	LAVER		EXP	FBG	SV	IB	T355D	CAT	13	6	22000	2	3	85800	94300
41	3	LAVER		EXP	FBG	SV	IB	T475D	GM	13	6	22000	2	3	91500	100500
41	3	LAVER		EXP	FBG	SV	IB	T530D	IF	13	6	22000	2	3	95800	105000
41	3	LAVER	FB	SDN	FBG	SV	IB	T355D	CAT	13	6	22000	2	3	82300	90400
41	3	LAVER	FB	SDN	FBG	SV	IB	T475D	GM	13	6	22000	2	3	87700	96400
41	3	LAVER	FB	SDN	FBG	SV	IB	T530D	IF	13	6	22000	2	3	91800	101000

HUNTER MARINE CORP

ST AUGUSTINE FL 32084 COAST GUARD MFG ID- HUN See inside cover to adjust price for area

For more recent years, see the BUC Used Boat Price Guide, Volume 1

LOA FT	IN	NAME AND/ OR MODEL	TOP/ RIG	BOAT TYPE	-HULL- MTL	TP	TP	----ENGINE--- # HP	MFG	BEAM FT	IN	WGT LBS	DRAFT FT	IN	RETAIL LOW	RETAIL HIGH
		1996 BOATS														
23	8	HUNTER 23.5	SLP	SACAC	FBG	KL	OB			8	4	3000	5	6	10700	12100
25	9	HUNTER 26	SLP	SACAC	FBG	KL	OB			9		2700	6		10900	12400
29	6	HUNTER 29.5	SLP	SACAC	FBG	WK	IB	18D	YAN	10	6	7000	4	6	31600	35100
33	6	HUNTER 336	SLP	SACAC	FBG	WK	IB	27D	YAN	11	8	11030	4	6	51200	56300
37	6	HUNTER 376	SLP	SACAC	FBG	WK	IB	36D	YAN	12	10	16400	6	6	78800	86600
40	2	HUNTER 40.5	SLP	SACAC	FBG	WK	IB	50D	VLVO	13	5	20000	4	10	102500	112500
42	6	HUNTER 430	SLP	SACAC	FBG	WK	IB	50D	VLVO	14		23800	4	11	125000	137500
42	6	PASSAGE 42	SLP	SACAC	FBG	WK	IB	62D	YAN	14		24000	4	11	126500	139000
		1995 BOATS														
19		HUNTER 19	SLP	SACAC	FBG	KL	OB			7	9	2100	4	6	7250	8350
23	8	HUNTER 23.5	SLP	SACAC	FBG	KL	OB			8	4	3000	5	6	9950	11300
25	9	HUNTER 26	SLP	SACAC	FBG	KL	OB			9		2700	6		10200	11600
29	6	HUNTER 29.5	SLP	SACAC	FBG	WK	IB	18D	YAN	10	6	7000	4	6	29500	32800
33	6	HUNTER 336	SLP	SACAC	FBG	WK	IB	27D	YAN	11	8	11030	4	6	47800	52500
35	7	HUNTER 35.5	SLP	SACAC	FBG	WK	IB	27D	YAN	11	9	13000	4	6	57100	62800
37	6	HUNTER 37.5	SLP	SACAC	FBG	WK	IB	36D	YAN	12	10	16400	4	11	73600	80900
40	2	HUNTER 40.5	SLP	SACAC	FBG	WK	IB	50D	YAN	13	5	20000	4	10	95700	105000
42	6	HUNTER 430	SLP	SACAC	FBG	WK	IB	50D	YAN	14		23800	4	11	117000	128500
42	6	PASSAGE 42	SLP	SACAC	FBG	WK	IB	62D	YAN	14		24000	4	11	118000	129500
		1994 BOATS														
19	8	HUNTER 19	SLP	SACAC	FBG	KL	OB			7	1	1550	1	2	5700	6550
23	5	HUNTER 23.5	SLP	SACAC	FBG	KL	OB			8		2000	4	8	7000	8050
25	9	HUNTER 26	SLP	SACAC	FBG	KL	OB			9		2700	6		9500	10800
26	7	HUNTER 27	SLP	SACAC	FBG	KL	IB	9D	YAN	9		5000	3	6	18500	20600
29	6	HUNTER 29.5	SLP	SACAC	FBG	KL	IB	18D	YAN	10	6	7000	4		27600	30600
30	1	HUNTER 30	SLP	SACAC	FBG	KL	IB	18D	YAN	11		10500	4	3	42000	46600
32		VISION 32	SLP	SACAC	FBG	KL	IB	27D	YAN	11	4	11400	4	3	46300	50900
33	4	HUNTER 33.5	SLP	SACAC	FBG	KL	IB	27D	YAN	10	11	11000	4	6	44200	49200
35	7	LEGEND 35.5	SLP	SACAC	FBG	KL	IB	27D	YAN	11	9	13000	4	6	53400	58600
36		VISION 36	SLP	SACAC	FBG	KL	IB	34D	YAN	12	9	16400	4	9	66300	72800
37	6	LEGEND 37.5	SLP	SACAC	FBG	KL	IB	34D	YAN	12	10	16400	4	11	68700	75500
40	4	LEGEND 40.5	SLP	SACAC	FBG	KL	IB	50D	YAN	13	5		4	10	89900	98800
42	6	LEGEND 43	SLP	SACAC	FBG	KL	IB	50D	YAN	14		23800	4	11	109500	120000
42	6	PASSAGE 42	SLP	SACAC	FBG	KL	IB	62D	YAN	14		24000	4	11	121000	133000
		1993 BOATS														
19	8	HUNTER 19	SLP	SACAC	FBG	KL	OB			7	1	1550	1	2	5300	6100
23	5	HUNTER 23.5	SLP	SACAC	FBG	KL	OB			8		2000	4	8	6550	7550
26	7	HUNTER 27	SLP	SACAC	FBG	KL	OB			9		4850	3	6	15600	17700
26	7	HUNTER 27	SLP	SACAC	FBG	KL	IB	9D	YAN	9		5000	3	6	16900	19200
28		HUNTER 28	SLP	SACAC	FBG	KL	IB	18D	YAN	10	6	7400	3	9	26500	29500
30	1	HUNTER 30	SLP	SACAC	FBG	KL	IB	18D	YAN	11		10500	4	3	39200	43600
32		VISION 32	SLP	SACAC	FBG	KL	IB	27D	YAN	11	4	11400	4	3	42800	47500
33	4	HUNTER 33.5	SLP	SACAC	FBG	KL	IB	27D	YAN	10	11	11000	4	6	41300	45900
35	7	LEGEND 35.5	SLP	SACAC	FBG	KL	IB	27D	YAN	11	9	13000	4	6	49800	54800
36		VISION 36	SLP	SACAC	FBG	KL	IB	34D	YAN	12	9	16400	4	9	61900	68000
37	6	LEGEND 37.5	SLP	SACAC	FBG	KL	IB	34D	YAN	12	10	16400	4	11	64200	70500
40	4	LEGEND 40.5	SLP	SACAC	FBG	KL	IB	50D	YAN	13	5		4	10	84000	92300
42	6	LEGEND 43	SLP	SACAC	FBG	KL	IB	50D	YAN	14		23800	4	11	102000	112000
42	6	PASSAGE 42	SLP	SACAC	FBG	KL	IB	62D	YAN	14		24000	4	11	113000	124500
		1992 BOATS														
18	5	HUNTER 18.5	SLP	SAIL	FBG	KL	OB			7	1	1600	2		5050	5800
23	3	HUNTER 23	SLP	SAIL	FBG	KL	OB			8		2450	2	3	6900	7900
26	7	HUNTER 27	SLP	SAIL	FBG	KL	OB			9		4850	3	6	14600	16600
26	7	HUNTER 27	SLP	SAIL	FBG	KL	IB	9D	YAN	9		5000	3	6	15800	18000
28		HUNTER 28	SLP	SAIL	FBG	KL	IB	18D	YAN	10	6	7400	3	9	24800	27500
30	1	HUNTER 30	SLP	SAIL	FBG	KL	IB	18D	YAN	11		10500	4	3	36600	40700
32		VISION 32	SLP	SAIL	FBG	KL	IB	27D	YAN	11	4	11400	4	3	40000	44400
33	4	HUNTER 33.5	SLP	SAIL	FBG	KL	IB	27D	YAN	10	11	11000	4	6	38600	42900
35	7	LEGEND 35.5	SLP	SAIL	FBG	KL	IB	27D	YAN	11	9	13000	4	6	46800	51400
36		VISION 36	SLP	SAIL	FBG	KL	IB	34D	YAN	12	9	16400	4	9	57800	63500
37	6	LEGEND 37.5	SLP	SAIL	FBG	KL	IB	34D	YAN	12	10	16400	4	11	59900	65900
42	6	LEGEND 43	SLP	SAIL	FBG	KL	IB	50D	YAN	14		23800	4	11	95400	105000
42	6	PASSAGE 42	SLP	SAIL	FBG	KL	IB	63D	YAN	14		24000	4	11	105500	116000
		1991 BOATS														
18	5	HUNTER 18.5	SLP	SAIL	FBG	KL	OB			7	1	1600	2		4700	5400
23	3	HUNTER 23	SLP	SAIL	FBG	KL	OB			8		2450	2	3	6450	7400
26	7	HUNTER 27 IB	SLP	SAIL	FBG	KL	IB	9D	YAN	9		5000	3	6	14800	16800
26	7	HUNTER 27 OB	SLP	SAIL	FBG	KL	OB			9		4850	3	6	13600	15500
28		HUNTER 28	SLP	SAIL	FBG	KL	IB	18D	YAN	10	6	7400	3	9	23200	25700
30	1	HUNTER 30	SLP	SAIL	FBG	KL	IB	18D	YAN	11		10500	4	3	34200	38000
32		VISION 32	SLP	SAIL	FBG	KL	IB	27D	YAN	11	4	11400	4	3	37300	41500
33	4	HUNTER 33.5	SLP	SAIL	FBG	KL	IB	27D	YAN	10	11	11000	4	6	36100	40100
35	7	LEGEND 35.5	SLP	SAIL	FBG	KL	IB	27D	YAN	11	9	13000	4	6	43300	48100
36		VISION 36	SLP	SAIL	FBG	KL	IB	34D	YAN	12	9	16400	4	9	54000	59400
37	6	LEGEND 37.5	SLP	SAIL	FBG	KL	IB	34D	YAN	12	10	16400	4	11	56000	61500
42	6	LEGEND 43	SLP	SAIL	FBG	KL	IB	50D	YAN	14		23800	4	11	89100	97900
42	6	PASSAGE 42	SLP	SAIL	FBG	KL	IB	55D	YAN	14		24000	4	10	98600	108500
		1990 BOATS														
18	5	HUNTER 18.5	SLP	SAIL	FBG	KL	OB			7	1	1600	2		4400	5100
23	3	HUNTER 23	SLP	SAIL	FBG	KL	OB			8		2450	2	3	6000	6900
26	7	HUNTER 27	SLP	SAIL	FBG	KL	OB			9		4850	3	6	12700	14500
26	7	HUNTER 27	SLP	SAIL	FBG	KL	IB	9D	YAN	9		5000	3	6	13800	15700
28		HUNTER 28	SLP	SAIL	FBG	KL	IB	18D	YAN	10	6	7400	3	9	21600	24000
31		HUNTER 30	SLP	SAIL	FBG	KL	IB	18D	YAN	11		9500	4	3	29000	32300
32		VISION 32	SLP	SAIL	FBG	KL	IB	27D	YAN	11	4	11400	4	3	34900	38800
33	4	HUNTER 33.5	SLP	SAIL	FBG	KL	IB	18D	YAN	11		10800	4	6	33100	36700
35	7	LEGEND 35.5	SLP	SAIL	FBG	KL	IB	27D	YAN	11	9	13000	4	6	40400	44900
37	6	LEGEND 37	SLP	SAIL	FBG	KL	IB	34D	YAN	12	10	15600	4	9	50200	55200
39	8	LEGEND 40	SLP	SAIL	FBG	KL	IB	44D	YAN	13	5	19800	5		66000	72500
39	8	LEGEND 40	SLP	SAIL	FBG	KL	IB	44D	YAN	13	5	19800	6	6	66000	72500
42	6	PASSAGE 42	SLP	SAIL	FBG	KL	IB	55D	YAN	14		24000	4	10	92100	101000
		1989 BOATS														
18	5	HUNTER 18.5	SLP	SAIL	FBG	KL	OB			7	1	1600	2		4050	4700
23	3	HUNTER 23	SLP	SA/CR	FBG	KL	OB			8		2450	2	3	5600	6450
26	7	HUNTER 26.5 SHOAL	SLP	SA/CR	FBG	KL	OB			9		4400	3	6	10800	12300
26	7	HUNTER 27	SLP	SA/CR	FBG	KL	IB	9D	YAN	9		5000	3	6	12900	14700
28		HUNTER 28	SLP	SA/CR	FBG	KL	IB	18D	YAN	10	6	7400	3	9	20200	22500
28	5	HUNTER 28.5 DEEP	SLP	SA/CR	FBG	KL	IB	18D	YAN	10	6	7000	5	2	19300	21400
28	5	HUNTER 28.5 SHOAL	SLP	SA/CR	FBG	KL	IB	18D	YAN	10	6	7100	4		19500	21700
30	1	HUNTER 30	SLP	SA/CR	FBG	KL	IB	18D	YAN	11		9500	4	3	27000	30000
32		VISION 32	SLP	SA/CR	FBG	KL	IB	18D	YAN	11	4	11400	4	3	32600	36200
33	4	HUNTER 33.5	SLP	SA/CR	FBG	KL	IB	18D	YAN	11		10800	4	6	30900	34300
35	7	LEGEND 35 DEEP	SLP	SA/CR	FBG	KL	IB	27D	YAN	11	9	12400	6	6	36200	40200
35	7	LEGEND 35 SHOAL	SLP	SA/CR	FBG	KL	IB	27D	YAN	11	9	12600	4	6	36700	40800
35	7	LEGEND 35.5	SLP	SA/CR	FBG	KL	IB	27D	YAN	11	9	12600	4	6	36700	40800
37	6	LEGEND 37 DEEP	SLP	SA/CR	FBG	KL	IB	34D	YAN	12	10	14700	6	8	44500	49400
37	6	LEGEND 37 SHOAL	SLP	SA/CR	FBG	KL	IB	34D	YAN	12	10	14900	4	9	45000	49900
39	8	LEGEND 40 DEEP	SLP	SA/CR	FBG	KL	IB	44D	YAN	13	5	17400	6	6	56400	62000
39	8	LEGEND 40 SHOAL	SLP	SA/CR	FBG	KL	IB	44D	YAN	13	5	17900	5		57500	63200
46	8	LEGEND 45 DEEP	SLP	SA/CR	FBG	KL	IB	55D	YAN	13	10	25300	6	6	99200	109000
46	8	LEGEND 45 SHOAL	SLP	SA/CR	FBG	KL	IB	55D	YAN	13	10	25600	5	7	99700	109500
		1988 BOATS														
18	5	HUNTER 18.5	SLP	SAIL	FBG	KL	OB			7	1	1600	2		3750	4400
23	3	HUNTER 23	SLP	SA/CR	FBG	KL	OB			8		2450	2	3	5250	6000
26	7	HUNTER 26.5 SHOAL	SLP	SA/CR	FBG	KL	OB			9		4400	3	6	10100	11500

 CONTINUED ON NEXT PAGE

LOA FT	LOA IN	NAME AND/ OR MODEL	TOP/ RIG	BOAT TYPE	-HULL- MTL	-HULL- TP	TP	ENGINE # HP	ENGINE MFG	BEAM FT	BEAM IN	WGT LBS	DRAFT FT	DRAFT IN	RETAIL LOW	RETAIL HIGH
		1988 BOATS														
28	5	HUNTER 28.5 DEEP	SLP	SA/CR	FBG	KL	IB	18D	YAN	10	6	7000	5	2	18200	20200
28	5	HUNTER 28.5 SHOAL	SLP	SA/CR	FBG	KL	IB	18D	YAN	10	6	7100	4		18500	20500
30	1	HUNTER 30	SLP	SA/CR	FBG	KL	IB	18D	YAN	11			4	3	19000	21100
33	4	HUNTER 33.5	SLP	SA/CR	FBG	KL	IB	18D	YAN	11		10800	4	6	28900	32100
35	7	LEGEND 35 DEEP	SLP	SA/CR	FBG	KL	IB	27D	YAN	11	9	12400	6	6	33800	37600
35	7	LEGEND 35 SHOAL	SLP	SA/CR	FBG	KL	IB	27D	YAN	11	9	12600	4	6	34300	38100
37	6	LEGEND 37 DEEP	SLP	SA/CR	FBG	KL	IB	34D	YAN	12	10	14700	6	8	41600	46200
37	6	LEGEND 37 SHOAL	SLP	SA/CR	FBG	KL	IB	34D	YAN	12	10	14900	4	9	42000	46700
39	8	LEGEND 40 DEEP	SLP	SA/CR	FBG	KL	IB	44D	YAN	13	5	17400	6	6	52700	57900
39	8	LEGEND 40 SHOAL	SLP	SA/CR	FBG	KL	IB	44D	YAN	13	5	17900	5		53800	59100
46	8	LEGEND 45 DEEP	SLP	SA/CR	FBG	KL	IB	55D	YAN	13	10	25300	6	6	92700	102000
46	8	LEGEND 45 SHOAL	SLP	SA/CR	FBG	KL	IB	55D	YAN	13	10	25600	5	7	93200	102500
		1987 BOATS														
23	3	HUNTER 23	SLP	SA/CR	FBG	SK	OB			8		2450			4900	5650
26	7	HUNTER 26.5 SHOAL	SLP	SA/CR	FBG	KL	OB			9		4400	3	6	9450	10700
28	5	HUNTER 28.5	SLP	SA/CR	FBG	KL	IB	18D	YAN	10	6	7000	5	2	16600	18900
28	5	HUNTER 28.5 SHOAL	SLP	SA/CR	FBG	KL	IB	18D	YAN	10	6	7100	4		16900	19200
31	4	HUNTER 31 DEEP	SLP	SA/CR	FBG	KL	IB	18D	YAN	10	11	9700	5	6	24300	27000
31	4	HUNTER 31 SHOAL	SLP	SA/CR	FBG	KL	IB	18D	YAN	10	11	9900	4		24800	27500
34	5	HUNTER 34	SLP	SA/CR	FBG	KL	IB	25D	YAN	11	7	11920	5	6	29900	33200
34	5	HUNTER 34 SHOAL	SLP	SA/CR	FBG	KL	IB	25D	YAN	11	7	11920	4	3	29900	33200
35	7	LEGEND 35 DEEP	SLP	SA/CR	FBG	KL	IB	27D	YAN	11	9	12100	6	6	30900	34300
35	7	LEGEND 35 SHOAL	SLP	SA/CR	FBG	KL	IB	27D	YAN	11	9	12300	4	6	31400	34900
37	6	LEGEND 37 DEEP	SLP	SA/CR	FBG	KL	IB	34D	YAN	12	10	13700	6	8	36600	40700
37	6	LEGEND 37 SHOAL	SLP	SA/CR	FBG	KL	IB	34D	YAN	12	10	13900	4	9	37100	41200
39	8	LEGEND 40	SLP	SA/CR	FBG	KL	IB	44D	YAN	13	5	17400	6	6	49300	54200
39	8	LEGEND 40 SHOAL	SLP	SA/CR	FBG	KL	IB	44D	YAN	13	5	17900	5		50300	55200
46	8	LEGEND 45 DEEP	SLP	SA/CR	FBG	KL	IB	55D	YAN	13	10	25300	6	6	86600	95200
46	8	LEGEND 45 SHOAL	SLP	SA/CR	FBG	KL	IB	55D	YAN	13	10	25600	5	7	87000	95700
		1986 BOATS														
23	3	HUNTER 23	SLP	SA/CR	FBG	SK	OB			8		2450			4600	5300
23	3	HUNTER 23 SHOAL	SLP	SA/CR	FBG	KL	OB			8		2450	2	3	4600	5300
25	7	HUNTER 25.5	SLP	SA/CR	FBG	KL	IB	D		9	1	4500	4	6	9300	10500
25	7	HUNTER 25.5 SHOAL	SLP	SA/CR	FBG	KL	IB	D		9	1	4500	3	3	9300	10500
28	5	HUNTER 28.5	SLP	SA/CR	FBG	KL	IB	15D	YAN	10	6	6950	5	1	15400	17500
28	5	HUNTER 28.5 SHOAL	SLP	SA/CR	FBG	KL	IB	15D	YAN	10	6	7030	3	11	15600	17700
34	5	HUNTER 34	SLP	SA/CR	FBG	KL	IB	25D	YAN	11	7	11920	5	6	28000	31100
34	5	HUNTER 34 SHOAL	SLP	SA/CR	FBG	KL	IB	25D	YAN	11	7	11920	4	3	28000	31100
39	8	HUNTER 40	SLP	SA/CR	FBG	KL	IB	44D	YAN	13	5	17400	6	6	46400	50900
39	8	HUNTER 40 SHOAL	SLP	SA/CR	FBG	KL	IB	44D	YAN	13	5	17900	5		47300	51900
		1985 BOATS														
22	3	HUNTER 22	SLP	SA/CR	FBG	KL	OB			7	11	3400	3	2	5300	6050
22	3	HUNTER 22	SLP	SA/CR	FBG	SK	OB			7	11	3200	1	11	5050	5800
25	7	HUNTER 25.5	SLP	SA/CR	FBG	KL	IB	D		9	1	4500	4	6	8550	9850
25	7	HUNTER 25.5 SHOAL	SLP	SA/CR	FBG	KL	IB	D		9	1	4500	3	3	8550	9850
28	5	HUNTER 28.5	SLP	SA/CR	FBG	KL	IB	D		10	6	6950	5	1	14400	16400
28	5	HUNTER 28.5 SHOAL	SLP	SA/CR	FBG	KL	IB	D		10	6	7030	3	11	14600	16600
31	4	HUNTER 31	SLP	SA/CR	FBG	KL	IB	15D	YAN	10	11	9700	5	3	21200	23600
31	4	HUNTER 31 SHOAL	SLP	SA/CR	FBG	KL	IB	15D	YAN	10	11	9900	4		21600	24100
34	5	HUNTER 34	SLP	SA/CR	FBG	KL	IB	23D	YAN	11	7	11820	5	6	26000	28800
34	5	HUNTER 34 SHOAL	SLP	SA/CR	FBG	KL	IB	23D	YAN	11	7	11920	4	3	26200	29100
37		HUNTER 37	SLP	SA/CR	FBG	KL	IB	D		11	10	17800	5	1	39200	43600
37		HUNTER 37 SHOAL	SLP	SA/CR	FBG	KL	IB	D		11	10	17800	4		39200	43600
39	8	HUNTER 40	SLP	SA/CR	FBG	KL	IB	44D	YAN	13	5	17400	6	6	42900	47600
39	8	HUNTER 40 SHOAL	SLP	SA/CR	FBG	KL	IB	44D	YAN	13	5	17900	5		43700	48600
45	5	HUNTER 45	SLP	SA/CR	FBG	KL	IB	D		13	6	21950	6	6	66500	73100
45	5	HUNTER 45 SHOAL	SLP	SA/CR	FBG	KL	IB	D		13	6	22450	5		67200	73900
		1984 BOATS														
19	8	HUNTER 20	SLP	SA/CR	FBG	CB	OB			7	6	1700	1	3	3000	3500
22	3	HUNTER 22	SLP	SA/CR	FBG	KL	OB			7	11	3400	3	2	4950	5700
22	3	HUNTER 22	SLP	SA/CR	FBG	SK	OB			7	11	3200	1	11	4700	5400
25	7	HUNTER 25.5 DEEP	SLP	SA/CR	FBG	KL	IB	D		9	1	3700	4	6	6750	7750
25	7	HUNTER 25.5 SHOAL	SLP	SA/CR	FBG	KL	IB	D		9	1	3700	3	3	6750	7750
27	2	HUNTER 27	SLP	SA/CR	FBG	KL	IB	10D	WEST	9	3	7000	4	3	13200	15000
27	2	HUNTER 27 SHOAL	SLP	SA/CR	FBG	KL	IB	10D	WEST	9	3	7000	3	3	13200	15000
31	4	HUNTER 31	SLP	SA/CR	FBG	KL	IB	15D	YAN	10	11	9000	5	3	18600	20700
31	4	HUNTER 31 SHOAL	SLP	SA/CR	FBG	KL	IB	15D	YAN	10	11	9000			18600	20700
34	5	HUNTER 34	SLP	SA/CR	FBG	KL	IB	20D	YAN	11	7	10900	5	6	22400	24900
34	5	HUNTER 34 SHOAL	SLP	SA/CR	FBG	KL	IB	20D	YAN	11	7	11120	4	3	22900	25400
37		HUNTER 37	SLP	SA/CR	FBG	KL	IB	D		11	11	17800	5	1	36700	40800
37		HUNTER 37 SHOAL	SLP	SA/CR	FBG	KL	IB	D		11	11	17800	4		36700	40800
39	4	HUNTER 39	SLP	SA/CR	FBG	KL	IB	D		13	5	16500	6	6	37800	42000
39	8	HUNTER 40 DEEP	SLP	SA/CR	FBG	KL	IB	44D	YAN	13	5	17400	6	6	40100	44600
39	8	HUNTER 40 SHOAL	SLP	SA/CR	FBG	KL	IB	44D	YAN	13	5	17900	5		40900	45500
53	10	HUNTER 54	SLP	SA/CR	FBG	KL	IB	50D	PERK	11	4	20500	6		109500	120500

....For earlier years, see the BUC Used Boat Price Guide, Volume 3

HUSTLER POWERBOATS

GLOBAL MARINE PERFORMANCE INC
CALVERTON NY 11933 COAST GUARD MFG ID- HUX
ALSO HUSTLER INDUSTRIES

See inside cover to adjust price for area

For more recent years, see the BUC Used Boat Price Guide, Volume 1

LOA FT	LOA IN	NAME AND/ OR MODEL	TOP/ RIG	BOAT TYPE	-HULL- MTL	-HULL- TP	TP	ENGINE # HP	ENGINE MFG	BEAM FT	BEAM IN	WGT LBS	DRAFT FT	DRAFT IN	RETAIL LOW	RETAIL HIGH
		1988 BOATS														
21		HUSTLER 21	OP	RNBT	FBG	DV	OB			7	10	1250			9250	10500
21		HUSTLER 21	OP	RNBT	FBG	DV	IO	260	MRCR	7	10	2500			7000	8050
26		HUSTLER 26	OP	RNBT	FBG	DV	IO		MRCR	8		4500			**	**
26		HUSTLER 26	OP	RNBT	FBG	DV	IO	311-320		8		4500			14000	15900
26		HUSTLER 26	OP	RNBT	FBG	DV	IO	T	MRCR	8		4500			**	**
31	10	HUSTLE LIMITED 32	OP	SPTCR	FBG	DV	IO	T	MRCR	8		6500			**	**
31	10	HUSTLE LIMITED 32	OP	SPTCR	FBG	DV	IO	T405-T450		8		6500			33000	37000
31	10	HUSTLE LIMITED 32	OP	SPTCR	FBG	DV	IO	T600-T850		8		6500			36300	44600
31	10	HUSTLER SPORT 32	OP	SPTCR	FBG	DV	IO	T	MRCR	8		6500			**	**
31	10	HUSTLER SPORT 32	OP	SPTCR	FBG	DV	IO	T270-T450		8		6500			29500	34800
31	10	HUSTLER SPORT 32	OP	SPTCR	FBG	DV	IO	T600-T850		8		6500			35200	43600
39	11	HUSTLER 40	OP	SPTCR	FBG	DV	IO	T	MRCR	8	8	9000			**	**
		IO T405 KAAM 54600 60000, IO T420 MRCR 54900 60400, IO T450 KAAM													58500	64300
		IO T575 MRCR 67000 73700, IO T600 68500 75200, IO T600 KAAM													70400	77400
		IO T675 71700 78700, IO T775 59400 65300, IO T850													**	**
		IO T330D 63300 69500, IO T450D 70000 76900														
		1987 BOATS														
21		SPORT 21	OP	RNBT	FBG	DV	OB			7	10	2500			15100	17200
21		SPORT 21	OP	RNBT	FBG	DV	IB	260	MRCR	7	10	2500			8550	9850
26		SPORT 26	OP	RNBT	FBG	DV	IO	T	MRCR	8		4500			**	**
		IO T260-T300 15500 19100, IO T320 MRCR 17200 19500, IO T400													20500	22800
26		SPORT 26 W/BRKT	OP	RNBT	FBG	DV	OB			8		4500			29000	32200
31	10	HUSTLER SPORT ED	OP	SPTCR	FBG	DV	OB			8		6500			49400	54300
31	10	HUSTLER SPORT ED	OP	SPTCR	FBG	DV	IO	T	MRCR	8		6500			**	**
31	10	HUSTLER SPORT ED	OP	SPTCR	FBG	DV	IO	T330-T500		8		6500			26700	32900
31	10	HUSTLER SPORT ED	OP	SPTCR	FBG	DV	IO	T550-T720		8		6500			31900	35900
31	10	SPORT 32 LE	OP	SPTCR	FBG	DV	IO	T	MRCR	8		6500			**	**
31	10	SPORT 32 LE	OP	SPTCR	FBG	DV	IO	T330-T425		8		6500			30900	36000
31	10	SPORT 32 LE	OP	SPTCR	FBG	DV	IO	T500-T720		8		6500			35000	39300
39	11	SPORT 39	OP	SPTCR	FBG	DV	IO	T370	MRCR	8	8	9000			48700	53600
		IO T375 49000 53900, IO T375 KAAM 49700 54600, IO T420 MRCR													52200	57400
		IO T425 KAAM 53500 58800, IO T500 58600 64300, IO T500 KAAM													59900	65900
		IO T550 KAAM 63800 70100, IO T575 63700 70000, IO T575 KAAM													65500	71900
		IO T575 MRCR 63700 70000, IO T650 67200 73900, IO T720													69300	76200
		1986 BOATS														
21		SPORT 21	OP	RNBT	FBG	DV	IB	260	MRCR	7	10	2500			8150	9400
24		SPORT 21	OP	RNBT	FBG	DV	OB			7	10	1250			9050	10300
24		SPORT 21	OP	RNBT	FBG	DV	IB	300	MRCR	7	10	2500			9700	11000
26		HUSTLER S-26	OP	CUD	FBG	DV	IO	330	MRCR	8		4400	3		13800	15700
26		SPORT 26	OP	RNBT	FBG	DV	OB			8					26100	29100
26		SPORT 26	OP	RNBT	FBG	DV	IO		OMC	8		4500			**	**
		IO 330-375 13400 16300, IO 400-440 15000 18300, IO T OMC													**	**
		IO T260-T300 14700 17900, IO T330 MRCR 16700 19000, IO T375-T425													19000	23700
31	10	HUSTLER SPORT ED	OP	SPTCR	FBG	DV	OB			8		6500			43100	47900
31	10	HUSTLER SPORT ED	OP	SPTCR	FBG	DV	IO	T	MRCR	8		6500			**	**
		IO T OMC ** ** , IO T300-T570 25200 31200, IO T650													28700	31900
		IO R MRCR ** **														
31	10	SPORT 32 LE	OP	SPTCR	FBG	DV	OB			8		6500			53500	58800
31	10	SPORT 32 LE	OP	SPTCR	FBG	DV	IO	T	MRCR	8		6500			**	**
		IO T OMC ** ** , IO T300-T375 27800 34000, IO T400-T700													29700	36700
		IO R MRCR ** **														
31	10	SPORT 32 SE	OP	SPTCR	FBG	DV	OB			8		4000			43800	48600
31	10	SPORT 32 SE	OP	SPTCR	FBG	DV	IO	T	MRCR	8		6500			**	**
		IO T OMC ** ** , IO T300-T375 24000 29900, IO T400-T650													28300	33400
		IO T725 32100 35700, IO R MRCR ** **														
		1985 BOATS														
24		SPORT 21	OP	RNBT	FBG	DV	OB								19800	22000
24		SPORT 21	OP	RNBT	FBG	DV	IO	260-300							9550	11300

LOA FT	LOA IN	NAME AND/ OR MODEL	TOP/ RIG	BOAT TYPE	HULL MTL	HULL TP	ENGINE TP	ENGINE # HP	ENGINE MFG	BEAM FT	BEAM IN	WGT LBS	DRAFT FT	DRAFT IN	RETAIL LOW	RETAIL HIGH
		1985 BOATS														
26		HUSTLER S-26	OP	CUD	FBG	DV	IO	330	MRCR	8		4400	3		13200	15000
26		HUSTLER S-260	OP	CUD	FBG	DV	OB			8		2500	1	6	23400	26000
26		SPORT 26	OP	RNBT	FBG	DV	OB			8					25300	28100
26		SPORT 26	OP	RNBT	FBG	DV	IO	330-375		8		4500			12800	15600
		IO 400-440 14300 17500, IO 599-650 19600 22700, IO T260-T300													14200	17200
		IO T330 MRCR 16000 18200														
31	10	HUSTLER LE	OP	SPTCR	FBG	DV	OB					4000			54100	59400
31	10	HUSTLER LE	OP	SPTCR	FBG	DV	IO	T300-T375				6500			28000	34400
31	10	HUSTLER LE	OP	SPTCR	FBG	DV	IO	T400-T725				6500			32000	37900
31	10	HUSTLER SE	OP	SPTCR	FBG	DV	OB					4000			47300	52000
31	10	HUSTLER SE	OP	SPTCR	FBG	DV	IO	T300-T370				6500			24200	30100
31	10	HUSTLER SE	OP	SPTCR	FBG	DV	IO	T375-T570				6500			27300	33600
31	10	HUSTLER SE	OP	SPTCR	FBG	DV	IO	T650-T725				6500			31200	34600
31	10	HUSTLER SE-32	OP	OFF	FBG	DV	IO	T330	MRCR	8		7100	3		26600	29500
31	10	HUSTLER SE-320	OP	OFF	FBG	DV	OB			8		3500	1	6	46000	50600
31	10	HUSTLER SPORT	OP	SPTCR	FBG	DV	IO	T225-T440				6500			24500	29500
31	10	HUSTLER SPORT	OP	SPTCR	FBG	DV	IO	T475				6500			25000	27800
31	10	HUSTLER SPORT	OP	SPTCR	FBG	DV	IO	T475-T650				6500			28700	31900
31	10	HUSTLER SS-32	OP	OFF	FBG	DV	IO	T330	MRCR	8		6700	3		26400	29400
31	10	HUSTLER SS-320	OP	OFF	FBG	DV	OB			8		3100	1	6	46000	50600
39	6	HUSTLER SE-40	OP	OFF	FBG	DV	IO	T370	MRCR	8	8	9000	3	2	43400	48200
		1984 BOATS														
26		HUSTLER S-26	OP	CUD	FBG	DV	IO	330	MRCR	8		4400	3		12800	14500
26		HUSTLER S-260	OP	CUD	FBG	DV	OB			8		2500	1	6	22700	25300
31	10	HUSTLER SE-32	OP	OFF	FBG	DV	IO	T330	MRCR	8		7100	3		25600	28400
31	10	HUSTLER SE-320	OP	OFF	FBG	DV	OB			8		3500	1	6	44200	49100
31	10	HUSTLER SS-32	OP	OFF	FBG	DV	IO	T330	MRCR	8		6700	3		25600	28400
31	10	HUSTLER SS-320	OP	OFF	FBG	DV	OB			8		3100	1	6	44200	49100
39	2	HUSTLER 40	OP	OFF	FBG	DV	IO	T330		9		9000			38100	42300
39	6	HUSTLER 40	OP	EXP	FBG	DV	OB			8	8	5500			**	**
39	6	HUSTLER SE-40	OP	OFF	FBG	DV	IO	T370	MRCR	8	8	9000	3	2	41900	46500

....For earlier years, see the BUC Used Boat Price Guide, Volume 3

HUTCHINS CO INC

CLEARWATER FL 33765 COAST GUARD MFG ID- ABV See inside cover to adjust price for area

For more recent years, see the BUC Used Boat Price Guide, Volume 1

LOA FT	LOA IN	NAME AND/ OR MODEL	TOP/ RIG	BOAT TYPE	HULL MTL	HULL TP	ENGINE TP	ENGINE # HP	ENGINE MFG	BEAM FT	BEAM IN	WGT LBS	DRAFT FT	DRAFT IN	RETAIL LOW	RETAIL HIGH
		1996 BOATS														
16	11	COM-PAC 16	SLP	SCFAC	FBG	KC				6		1100	1	6	6100	7050
16	11	RAVEN	SLP	SCFAC	FBG	KC				6		1100	1	6	7750	8900
20	1	COM-PAC 19XL	SLP	SCFAC	FBG	KL				7		2000	2		9650	11000
23	11	COM-PAC 23/3	SLP	SCFAC	FBG	KL				7	10	3000	2	3	12100	13800
23	11	COM-PAC 23D	SLP	SCFAC	FBG	KL	IB	9D	YAN	7	10	3300	2	3	17200	19500
28	2	COM-PAC 25	SLP	SCFAC	FBG	KL				8	6	4800	2	6	20300	22600
29	7	COM-PAC 27/2	SLP	SCFAC	FBG	KL	IB	18D	WEST	9	6	6000	3	6	40000	44400
36	9	COM-PAC 35	SLP	SCFAC	FBG	KL	IB	27D	WEST	11	10	12500	4		82800	91000
		1995 BOATS														
16	11	COM-PAC 16XL	SLP	SAROD	FBG	KL	OB			6		1100	1	6	6000	6900
20	1	COM-PAC 19XL	SLP	SACAC	FBG	KL	OB			7		2000	2		9150	10400
23	11	COM-PAC 23/3	SLP	SACAC	FBG	KL	OB			7	10	3000	2	3	11400	13000
23	11	COM-PAC 23D	SLP	SACAC	FBG	KL	IB	10D	YAN	7	10	3300	2	3	16200	18500
28	2	COM-PAC 25	SLP	SACAC	FBG	KL	OB			8	6	4800	2	6	19700	21800
29	7	COM-PAC 27/2	SLP	SACAC	FBG	KL	IB	18D	WEST	9	6	6000	3	6	37600	41800
30		C-CAT 3014	SLP	SACAC	FBG	CT	IB	35		14	9	6000	2	10	51400	56500
36	9	COM-PAC 35	SLP	SACAC	FBG	KL	IB	27D	WEST	11	10	12500	4		77900	85600
		1994 BOATS														
16	11	COM-PAC 16XL	SLP	SAROD	FBG	KL	OB			6		1100	1	6	5650	6500
20	1	COM-PAC 19XL	SLP	SACAC	FBG	KL	OB			7		2000	2		8500	9750
23	11	COM-PAC 23/3	SLP	SACAC	FBG	KL	OB			7	10	3000	2	3	10700	12200
23	11	COM-PAC 23D	SLP	SACAC	FBG	KL	IB	9D	YAN	7	10	3300	2	3	15200	17300
29	7	COM-PAC 27/2	SLP	SACAC	FBG	KL	IB	18D	WEST	9	6	6000	3	6	35400	39300
30		C-CAT 3014	CAT	SACAC	FBG	CT	OB			14	9	6000	2	10	48400	53200
36	9	COM-PAC 35	SLP	SACAC	FBG	KL	IB	27D	WEST	11	10	12500	4		73200	80500
		1993 BOATS														
16	11	COM-PAC 16XL	SLP	SAROD	FBG	KL	OB			6		1100	1	6	5350	6150
20	1	COM-PAC 19XL	SLP	SACAC	FBG	KL	OB			7		2000	2		8000	9150
23	11	COM-PAC 23/3	SLP	SACAC	FBG	KL	OB			7	10	3000	2	3	10100	11500
23	11	COM-PAC 23/D	SLP	SACAC	FBG	KL	IB	10D	YAN	7	10	3300	2	3	15300	17300
29	7	COM-PAC 27/2	SLP	SACAC	FBG	KL	IB	18D	WEST	9	6	6000	3	6	33300	36900
34	9	COM-PAC 33	SLP	SACAC	FBG	KL	IB	25D	WEST	11	10	11000	4		65300	71700
36	9	COM-PAC 35	SLP	SACAC	FBG	KL	IB	27D	WEST	11	10	12500	4		68900	75700
		1992 BOATS														
16	11	COM-PAC 16/1XL	SLP	SAIL	FBG	KL	OB			6		1100	1	6	5500	6300
20	1	COM-PAC 19/3	SLP	SA/CR	FBG	KL	OB			7		2000	2		7700	8850
23	11	COM-PAC 23/3	SLP	SA/CR	FBG	KL	OB			7	10	3000	2	3	9500	10800
23	11	COM-PAC 23/D	SLP	SA/CR	FBG	KL	IB	10D	YAN	7	10	3300	2	3	14400	16300
29	7	COM-PAC 27/2	SLP	SA/CR	FBG	KL	IB	12D	UNIV	9	6	6000	3	6	31000	34500
34	9	COM-PAC 33	SLP	SA/CR	FBG	KL	IB	25D	UNIV	11	10	11000	4		61300	67400
		1991 BOATS														
16	11	COM-PAC 16/3	SLP	SAIL	FBG	KL	OB			6		1100	1	6	4600	5250
20	1	COM-PAC 19/3	SLP	SA/CR	FBG	KL	OB			7		2000	2		7200	8300
23	11	COM-PAC 23/3	SLP	SA/CR	FBG	KL	OB			7	10	3000	2	3	8950	10200
23	11	COM-PAC 23/D	SLP	SA/CR	FBG	KL	IB	9D	YAN	7	10	3300	2	3	13500	15300
29	7	COM-PAC 27/2	SLP	SA/CR	FBG	KL	IB	12D	UNIV	9	6	6000	3	6	29200	32400
34	9	COM-PAC 33	SLP	SA/CR	FBG	KL	IB	25D	UNIV	11	10	11000	4		57700	63400
		1990 BOATS														
16	11	COM-PAC 16/3	SLP	SAIL	FBG	KL	OB			6		1100	1	6	4300	4950
20	1	COM-PAC 19/3	SLP	SA/CR	FBG	KL	OB			7		2000	2		6800	7800
23	11	COM-PAC 23/3	SLP	SA/CR	FBG	KL	OB			7	10	3000	2	3	8350	9600
23	11	COM-PAC 23/D	SLP	SA/CR	FBG	KL	IB	9D	YAN	7	10	3300	2	3	12700	14400
29	7	COM-PAC 27/2	SLP	SA/CR	FBG	KL	IB	12D	UNIV	9	6	6000	3	6	27400	30500
34	9	COM-PAC 33	SLP	SA/CR	FBG	KL	IB	25D	UNIV	11	10	11000	4		54300	59600
		1989 BOATS														
16	11	COM-PAC 16/3	SLP	SAIL	FBG	KL	OB			6		1100	1	6	4000	4650
20	1	COM-PAC 19/3	SLP	SA/CR	FBG	KL	OB			7		2000	2		6400	7350
23	11	COM-PAC 23/3	SLP	SA/CR	FBG	KL	OB			7	10	3000	2	3	7850	9000
29	7	COM-PAC 27/2	SLP	SA/CR	FBG	KL	IB	12D		9	6	6000	3	6	25800	28600
		1988 BOATS														
16	11	COM-PAC 16/3	SLP	SAIL	FBG	KL	OB			6		1100	1	6	3800	4400
20	1	COM-PAC 19/3	SLP	SA/CR	FBG	KL	OB			7		2000	2		6000	6900
23	11	COM-PAC 23/3	SLP	SA/CR	FBG	KL	OB			7	10	3000	2	3	7400	8500
29	7	COM-PAC 27/2	SLP	SA/CR	FBG	KL	IB	10D		9	6	6000	3	6	24200	26900
		1987 BOATS														
16	11	COM-PAC	SLP	SAIL	FBG	KL	OB			6		1100	1	6	3850	4500
20	1	COM-PAC	SLP	SA/CR	FBG	KL	OB			7		2000	2		5500	6300
23	11	COM-PAC	SLP	SA/CR	FBG	KL	OB			7	10	3000	2	3	7800	9000
29	7	COM-PAC	SLP	SA/CR	FBG	KL	IB	10D		9	6	6000	3	6	20200	22400
		1986 BOATS														
16		COM-PAC	SLP	SAIL	FBG	KL	OB			6		1100	1	6	3650	4250
20	1	COM-PAC II	SLP	SA/CR	FBG	KL	OB			7		2000	2		5400	6200
23	11	COM-PAC II	SLP	SA/CR	FBG	KL	OB			7	10	3000	2	3	7200	8300
29	7	COM-PAC 27	SLP	SA/CR	FBG	KL	IB	10D		9	6	6000	3	6	18600	20700
		1985 BOATS														
16		COM-PAC	SLP	SAIL	FBG	KL	OB			6		1100	1	8	3400	3950
19		COM-PAC	SLP	SA/OD	FBG	KL				7		2000	2		4800	5550
20	2	COM-PAC II	SLP	SA/CR	FBG	KL	OB			7		2100	2		5250	6000
22	9	COM-PAC	SLP	SA/OD	FBG	KL				7	10	3000	2	3	6650	7650
23	11	COM-PAC II	SLP	SA/CR	FBG	KL	OB			7	10	3000	2	3	6800	7800
28	9	COM-PAC	SLP	SA/CR	FBG	KL	IB	10D		9	10	6000	3	6	17300	19700
		1984 BOATS														
16		COM-PAC	SLP	SAIL	FBG	KL	OB			6		1100	1	6	3200	3750
16		COM-PAC COMM ED	SLP	SAIL	FBG	KL	OB			6		1100	1	6	3300	3850
19		COM-PAC	SLP	SA/CR	FBG	KL	OB			7		2000	2		4550	5250
20	2	COM-PAC II	SLP	SA/CR	FBG	KL	OB			7		2100	2		4900	5650
22	9	COM-PAC	SLP	SA/CR	FBG	KL	OB			7	10	3000	2	3	6300	7200
23	11	COM-PAC II	SLP	SA/CR	FBG	KL	OB			7	10	3000	2	3	6400	7350

....For earlier years, see the BUC Used Boat Price Guide, Volume 3

W C HYATT YACHTS LTD INC

NEW ALBANY IN 47150

See inside cover to adjust price for area

For more recent years, see the BUC Used Boat Price Guide, Volume 1

LOA FT	LOA IN	NAME AND/ OR MODEL	TOP/ RIG	BOAT TYPE	HULL MTL	HULL TP	ENGINE TP	ENGINE # HP	ENGINE MFG	BEAM FT	BEAM IN	WGT LBS	DRAFT FT	DRAFT IN	RETAIL LOW	RETAIL HIGH
		1996 BOATS														
42		RESORT CRUISER 42	FB	CR	FBG	SV	IB	T300D	CAT	14		28000	3		284000	312000
42		RESORT CRUISER 42	FB	CR	FBG	SV	IB	T420D	CAT	14		28000	3		307000	337000
47		COCKPIT MY 47	FB	YTFS	FBG	SV	IB	T300D	CAT	14		32000	3		197000	216500
47		COCKPIT MY 47	FB	YTFS	FBG	SV	IB	T420D	CAT	14		32000	3		214500	235500
51		MOTOR YACHT 51	FB	MY	FBG	SV	IB	T375D	CAT	15	6	40000	4		249000	273500
51		MOTOR YACHT 51	FB	MY	FBG	SV	IB	T435D	CAT	15	6	40000	4		260500	286000
57		COCKPIT MY 57	FB	MYCPT	FBG	SV	IB	T375D	CAT	15	6	40000	4		224000	246000
57		COCKPIT MY 57	FB	MYCPT	FBG	SV	IB	T435D	CAT	15	6	40000	4		247000	271500
		1995 BOATS														
40		SUNDECK 40	FB	MY	FBG	SV	IB	T300D	CAT	14	6	26000	3		173000	190000
40		SUNDECK 40	FB	MY	FBG	SV	IB	T375D	CAT	14	6	26000	3		182000	200000

CONTINUED ON NEXT PAGE

LOA FT	IN	NAME AND/ OR MODEL	TOP/ RIG	BOAT TYPE	-HULL- MTL	TP	TP	---ENGINE--- # HP	MFG	BEAM FT	IN	WGT LBS	DRAFT FT	IN	RETAIL LOW	RETAIL HIGH
		1995 BOATS														
42		RESORT CRUISER 42	FB	CR	FBG	SV	IB	T300D	CAT	14		28000	3		272000	299000
42		RESORT CRUISER 42	FB	CR	FBG	SV	IB	T350D	CAT	14		28000	3		280500	308500
45		SUNDECK 45	FB	MY	FBG	SV	IB	T300D	CAT	14	6	33000	3		191000	209500
45		SUNDECK 45	FB	MY	FBG	SV	IB	T375D	CAT	14	6	33500	3		201500	221500
47		COCKPIT MY 47	FB	YTFS	FBG	SV	IB	T300D	CAT	14		32000	3		186500	205000
47		COCKPIT MY 47	FB	YTFS	FBG	SV	IB	T375D	CAT	14		32000	3		196500	215500
47		MOTOR YACHT 47	FB	MY	FBG	SV	IB	T375D	CAT						223500	245500
47		MOTOR YACHT 47	FB	MY	FBG	SV	IB	T435D	CAT						231000	253500
47		MOTOR YACHT 47	FB	MY	FBG	SV	IB	T485D	DD						236000	259500
49		MOTOR YACHT 49	FB	MY	FBG	SV	IB	T375D	CAT	16		40000	3		233000	256000
56		COCKPIT MY 56	FB	MYCPT	FBG	SV	IB	T375D	CAT	15	6	40000	4		217000	238500
56		COCKPIT MY 56	FB	MYCPT	FBG	SV	IB	T435D	CAT	15	6	40000	4		239500	263000
		1994 BOATS														
40		SUNDECK 40	FB	MY	FBG	SV	IB	T250D	CUM	14	6	26000	3		157000	173000
		IB T300D CAT 165500 182000, IB T300D CUM 161000 177000, IB T375D CAT													174500	191500
42		RESORT CRUISER 42	FB	CR	FBG	SV	IB	T300D	CAT	14		28000	3		260500	286500
42		RESORT CRUISER 42	FB	CR	FBG	SV	IB	T300D	CUM	14		28000	3		255500	280500
42		RESORT CRUISER 42	FB	CR	FBG	SV	IB	T375D	CAT	14		28000	3		273000	300000
45		SUNDECK 45	FB	MY	FBG	SV	IB	T250D	CUM	14	6	33000	3		173500	191000
		IB T300D CAT 181500 199000, IB T300D CUM 178000 196000, IB T375D CAT													191500	210500
47		COCKPIT MY 47	FB	YTFS	FBG	SV	IB	T300D	CAT	14		32000	3		177000	194500
47		COCKPIT MY 47	FB	YTFS	FBG	SV	IB	T375D	CAT	14		32000	3		186500	205000
47		MOTOR YACHT 47	FB	MY	FBG	SV	IB	T375D	CAT						211500	232500
47		MOTOR YACHT 47	FB	MY	FBG	SV	IB	T425D	CAT						217500	239000
47		MOTOR YACHT 47	FB	MY	FBG	SV	IB	T485D	DD						224000	246000
49		MOTOR YACHT 49	FB	MY	FBG	SV	IB	T375D	CAT	16		40000	3		221000	242500
53		COCKPIT MY 53	FB	MYCPT	FBG	SV	IB	T375D	CAT	15	6	40000	4		195000	214500
53		COCKPIT MY 53	FB	MYCPT	FBG	SV	IB	T425D	CAT	15	6	40000	4		209000	229500
53		COCKPIT MY 53	FB	MYCPT	FBG	SV	IB	T485D	DD	15	6	40000	4		225500	247500
		1993 BOATS														
40		SUNDECK 40	FB	MY	FBG	SV	IB	T250D	CUM	14	6	26000	3		150000	164500
		IB T300D CAT 158000 173500, IB T300D CUM 153500 168500, IB T375D CAT													166000	182500
41	10	RESORT CRUISER 42	FB	CR	FBG	SV	IB	T375D	CAT	14		28000	3	4	174000	191000
42		RESORT CRUISER 42	FB	CR	FBG	SV	IB	T300D	CAT	14		28000	3		248500	273000
42		RESORT CRUISER 42	FB	CR	FBG	SV	IB	T300D	CUM	14		28000	3		243500	267500
45		COCKPIT MY 45	FB	MYCPT	FBG	SV	IB	T300D	CAT	14	6	33500	3		166500	183000
45		COCKPIT MY 45	FB	MYCPT	FBG	SV	IB	T375D	CAT	14	6	33500	3		175000	192000
45		SUNDECK 45	FB	MY	FBG	SV	IB	T250D	CUM	14	6	33000	3		165000	181000
		IB T300D CAT 172000 189500, IB T300D CUM 169500 186000, IB T375D CAT													184500	202500
47		COCKPIT MY 47	FB	YTFS	FBG	SV	IB	T300D	CAT	14		32000	3		168000	184500
47		COCKPIT MY 47	FB	YTFS	FBG	SV	IB	T375D	CAT	14		32000	3		177500	195000
47		MOTOR YACHT 47	FB	MY	FBG	SV	IB	T375D	CAT						201000	221000
47		MOTOR YACHT 47	FB	MY	FBG	SV	IB	T425D	CAT						206500	227000
47		MOTOR YACHT 47	FB	MY	FBG	SV	IB	T485D	DD						212500	233500
53		COCKPIT MY 53	FB	MYCPT	FBG	SV	IB	T375D	CAT	15	6	40000	4		186000	204500
53		COCKPIT MY 53	FB	MYCPT	FBG	SV	IB	T425D	CAT	15	6	40000	4		199000	218500
53		COCKPIT MY 53	FB	MYCPT	FBG	SV	IB	T485D	DD	15	6	40000	4		214500	236000
		1992 BOATS														
40		SUNDECK 40	FB	MY	FBG	SV	IB	T250D	CUM	14	6	26000	3		143000	157000
		IB T300D CAT 150500 165500, IB T300D CUM 146500 161000, IB T375D CAT													158500	174000
41	10	RESORT CRUISER 42	FB	CR	FBG	SV	IB	T300D	CAT	14		28000	3	4	158500	174000
41	10	RESORT CRUISER 42	FB	CR	FBG	SV	IB	T300D	CUM	14		28000	3	4	155000	170500
45		COCKPIT MY 45	FB	MYCPT	FBG	SV	IB	T250D	CUM	14	6	33500	3		148500	163000
		IB T300D CAT 154500 170000, IB T300D CUM 145500 160000, IB T375D CAT													162500	179000
45		SUNDECK 45	FB	MY	FBG	SV	IB	T250D	CUM	14	6	33500	3		161000	177000
		IB T300D CAT 173000 190000, IB T300D CUM 169500 186000, IB T375D CAT													179000	197000
47		MOTOR YACHT 47	FB	MY	FBG	SV	IB	T375D	CAT						191000	210000
47		MOTOR YACHT 47	FB	MY	FBG	SV	IB	T425D	CAT						196500	216000
47		MOTOR YACHT 47	FB	MY	FBG	SV	IB	T485D	DD						202000	222000
53		COCKPIT MY 53	FB	MYCPT	FBG	SV	IB	T375D	CAT	15	6	40000	4		177500	195000
53		COCKPIT MY 53	FB	MYCPT	FBG	SV	IB	T425D	CAT	15	6	40000	4		190000	208500
53		COCKPIT MY 53	FB	MYCPT	FBG	SV	IB	T485D	DD	15	6	40000	4		204500	225000
		1991 BOATS														
37		SUNDECK 37	FB	MY	FBG	SV	IB	T210D	CUM	14	6	25000	3		114500	125500
37		SUNDECK 37	FB	MY	FBG	SV	IB	T250D	CUM	14	6	25000	3		116500	128000
37		SUNDECK 37	FB	MY	FBG	SV	IB	T300D	CUM	14	6	25000	3		120000	131500
40		SUNDECK 40	FB	MY	FBG	SV	IB	T210D	CUM	14	6	26000	3		134000	147000
		IB T250D CUM 136000 149500, IB T300D CUM 139500 153500, IB T375D CAT													151000	166000
44		MEDITERRANEAN 44	FB	MY	FBG	SV	IB	T210D	CUM	14	6	33500	3		143000	157000
		IB T250D CUM 145500 160000, IB T300D CUM 149500 164000, IB T375D CAT													159500	175000
45		SUNDECK	FB	MY	FBG	SV	IB	T210D	CUM	14	6	33500	3		147500	162000
45		SUNDECK	FB	MY	FBG	SV	IB	T250D	CUM	14	6	33500	3		150000	165000
45		SUNDECK	FB	MY	FBG	SV	IB	T300D	CUM	14	6	33500	3		153500	169000
45		SUNDECK 45	FB	MY	FBG	SV	IB	T375D	CAT	14	6	33500	3		165000	181500
45		YACHTFISH 45	FB	YTFS	FBG	SV	IB	T210D	CUM	14	6	33500	3		138000	152000
		IB T250D CUM 140500 154500, IB T300D CUM 144500 159000, IB T375D CAT													155000	170500
53		YACHTFISH 53	FB	YTFS	FBG	SV	IB	T375D	CAT	15	6	40000	4		160000	176000
		1990 BOATS														
37		SUNDECK 37	FB	MY	FBG	DV	IB	T260D	CAT	14	6	25000	3		114500	125500
40		SUNDECK 40	FB	MY	FBG	DV	IB	T300D	J&T	14	6	26000	3		134500	148000
43		SUNDECK 43	FB	MY	FBG	DV	IB	T300D	CUM	14	6	33500	3		157500	173000
44		SUNDECK 44 MED	FB	MY	FBG	DV	IB	T375D	CAT	14	6	33500	3		156000	171000
45		SUNDECK 45	FB	MY	FBG	DV	IB	T375D	CAT	14	6	33500	3		174000	191000
45		YACHTFISHER 45	FB	MY	FBG	DV	IB	T375D	CAT	14	6	33500	3		142500	156500
53		YACHTFISHER 53	FB	MY	FBG	DV	IB	T425D	J&T	14	6	40000	3		172000	189000

HYDRA-SPORTS INC

DIV OF GENMAR
SARASOTA FL 34243 COAST GUARD MFG ID- HSX

See inside cover to adjust price for area

For more recent years, see the BUC Used Boat Price Guide, Volume 1

LOA FT	IN	NAME AND/ OR MODEL	TOP/ RIG	BOAT TYPE	-HULL- MTL	TP	TP	---ENGINE--- # HP	MFG	BEAM FT	IN	WGT LBS	DRAFT FT	IN	RETAIL LOW	RETAIL HIGH
		1996 BOATS														
16	4	HYDRA SPORT X260	OP	FSH	FBG	SV	OB			6	9	990			2800	3250
16	4	HYDRA SPORT Z260	OP	FSH	FBG	SV	OB			6	9	850			2450	2850
16	4	KEY LARGO 1650 FLATS	OP	FSH	FBG	SV	OB			6	10	976		10	2750	3200
16	8	HYDRA SPORT 265 F/S	OP	RNBT	FBG	SV	OB			6	11	1040			3150	3650
16	9	HYDRA SKIFF 17	OP	CTRCN	FBG	SV	OB			7	4	1290			3650	4250
17	5	HYDRA SPORT 171	OP	CTRCN	FBG	SV	OB			7	1	1000			3000	3450
17	6	HYDRA SPORT 1750CC	OP	CTRCN	FBG	SV	OB			7	6	1500	1	2	4150	4850
17	9	175E	OP	BASS	FBG	SV	OB			7		1150			3350	3900
17	9	175EDC	OP	BASS	FBG	SV	OB			7		1150			3350	3900
17	9	HYDRA SPORT 175EFS	OP	RNBT	FBG	SV	OB			7	3	1220			3700	4350
17	9	HYDRA SPORT LS175DC	OP	BASS	FBG	SV	OB			7		1150			3600	4200
17	9	LS175	OP	BASS	FBG	SV	OB			7		1150			3600	4200
18	6	BLUEWATER 1900CC	OP	CTRCN	FBG	SV	OB			7	9	1720	1	4	4700	5400
18	9	185 F/S	OP	BASS	FBG	SV	OB					1670			4800	5500
18	9	185E	OP	BASS	FBG	SV	OB			7	5	1450			4300	5000
18	9	HYDRA SPORT LS185	OP	FSH	FBG	SV	OB			7	5	1450			4150	4800
18	9	HYDRA SPORT LS185DC	OP	FSH	FBG	SV	OB			7	5	1450			4150	4850
19		HYDRA SKIFF 19	OP	CTRCN	FBG	SV	OB			8		1624			4600	5300
20	1	HYDRA SPORT 2150 WAH	OP	CUD	FBG	DV	OB			8	6		1	6	8400	9650
20	1	HYDRA SPORT LS205DC	OP	FSH	FBG	SV	OB			7	9	1525			5550	6400
20	1	LS205	OP	BASS	FBG	SV	OB			7	8	1525			5650	6500
20	2	BLUEWATER 2000CC	OP	CTRCN	FBG	SV	OB			8		2300	1	6	7400	8500
20	2	BLUEWATER 2000DC	OP	B/R	FBG	SV	OB			8		2300	1	4	7700	8850
21	8	HYDRA SKIFF 21	OP	CTRCN	FBG	SV	OB			8		1880			7000	8050
22	6	BLUEWATER 2350WA	OP	CUD	FBG	SV	OB			9	4	4200	1	4	12700	14500
24	3	HYDRA SPORT 2350CC	OP	CTRCN	FBG	DV	OB			9	4	3000			11400	12900
25		BLUEWATER 2500CC	OP	CTRCN	FBG	SV	OB			8		3500	1	10	13200	15000
25	5	BLUEWATER 2750WA	OP	CUD	FBG	SV	OB			9	5	5100	1	9	16800	19100
30	1	BLUEWATER 3100SF	OP	SF	FBG	SV	OB			10	7	10180	2	3	32300	35900
		1995 BOATS														
16	4	HYDRA SPORT 1600	OP	CTRCN	FBG	SV	OB			6	10	820			2300	2650
16	4	HYDRA SPORT X260	OP	FSH	FBG	SV	OB			6	9	990			2650	3100
16	4	HYDRA SPORT Z260	OP	FSH	FBG	SV	OB			6	9	850			2300	2700
16	4	KEY LARGO 1650 FLATS	OP	FSH	FBG	SV	OB			6	10	976		10	2600	3050
16	8	HYDRA SPORT 265 F/S	OP	RNBT	FBG	SV	OB			6	11	1040			3000	3450
16	9	HYDRA SKIFF 17	OP	CTRCN	FBG	SV	OB			7	4	1290			3450	4050
17	5	HYDRA SPORT 171	OP	CTRCN	FBG	SV	OB			7	1	1000			2800	3300
17	6	HYDRA SPORT 1750CC	OP	CTRCN	FBG	SV	OB			7	6	1500	1	2	3950	4600
17	6	HYDRA SPORT VS-150T	OP	FSH	FBG	SV	OB			7	1	1095			3000	3500
17	9	175E	OP	BASS	FBG	SV	OB			7		1150			3150	3700
17	9	175EDC	OP	BASS	FBG	SV	OB			7		1150			3050	3550
17	9	HYDRA SPORT 175EFS	OP	RNBT	FBG	SV	OB			7	3	1220			3500	4100
17	9	HYDRA SPORT LS175DC	OP	BASS	FBG	SV	OB			7		1150			3650	4200
17	9	LS175	OP	BASS	FBG	SV	OB			7		1150			3200	3750
18	6	BLUEWATER 1900CC	OP	CTRCN	FBG	SV	OB			7	9	1720	1	4	4450	5100
18	9	185 F/S	OP	BASS	FBG	SV	OB					1670			4500	5200

 CONTINUED ON NEXT PAGE

LOA FT	LOA IN	NAME AND/ OR MODEL	TOP/ RIG	BOAT TYPE	-HULL- MTL	-HULL- TP	TP	#	HP	MFG	BEAM FT	BEAM IN	WGT LBS	DRAFT FT	DRAFT IN	RETAIL LOW	RETAIL HIGH
		1995 BOATS															
18	9	185E	OP	BASS	FBG	SV	OB				7	5	1450			4050	4700
18	9	HYDRA SPORT LS185	OP	FSH	FBG	SV	OB				7	5	1450			3900	4550
18	9	HYDRA SPORT LS185DC	OP	FSH	FBG	SV	OB				7	5	1450			3950	4600
19		HYDRA SKIFF 19	OP	CTRCN	FBG	SV	OB				8		1624			4300	5000
20	1	HYDRA SPORT 2150 WAH	OP	CUD	FBG	DV	OB				8	6		1	6	7950	9150
20	1	HYDRA SPORT LS205DC	OP	FSH	FBG	SV	OB				7	9	1525			5300	6100
20	1	LS205	OP	BASS	FBG	SV	OB				7	8	1525			5350	6150
20	2	BLUEWATER 2000CC	OP	CTRCN	FBG	SV	OB				8		2300	1	6	7050	8100
20	2	BLUEWATER 2000DC	OP	B/R	FBG	SV	OB				8		2300	1	4	7300	8400
21	8	BLUEWATER 2200CC	OP	CTRCN	FBG	SV	OB				8		2325	1	10	7850	9050
21	8	HYDRA SKIFF 21	OP	CTRCN	FBG	SV	OB				8		1880			6700	7700
22	6	BLUEWATER 2350WA	OP	CUD	FBG	SV	OB				9	4	4200	1	4	12100	13700
24	3	HYDRA SPORT 2350CC	OP	CTRCN	FBG	DV	OB				9	4	3000			10800	12300
25		BLUEWATER 2500CC	OP	CTRCN	FBG	SV	OB				8		3500	1	10	12600	14300
25	5	BLUEWATER 2750WA	OP	CUD	FBG	SV	OB				9	5	5100	1	9	15800	18000
30	1	BLUEWATER 3100SF	OP	SF	FBG	SV	OB				10	7	10180	2	3	30800	34200
		1994 BOATS															
16	4	HYDRA SPORT 1600	OP	CTRCN	FBG	SV	OB				6	10	820			2150	2500
16	4	HYDRA SPORT X260	OP	FSH	FBG	SV	OB				6	9	990			2500	2950
16	4	HYDRA SPORT Z260	OP	FSH	FBG	SV	OB				6	9	850			2200	2550
16	4	KEY LARGO 1650 FLATS	OP	FSH	FBG	SV	OB				6	10	976		10	2500	2900
16	8	HYDRA SPORT 265 F/S	OP	RNBT	FBG	SV	OB				6	11	1040			2800	3300
16	11	HYDRA SPORT 17 SKIFF	OP	CTRCN	FBG	SV	OB				6	11	1350		10	3400	4000
17	5	HYDRA SPORT 171	OP	CTRCN	FBG	SV	OB				7	1	1000			2650	3100
17	5	HYDRA SPORT X270	OP	FSH	FBG	SV	OB				6	9	1050			2750	3200
17	6	BLUEWATER 175CC	OP	CTRCN	FBG	SV	OB				7	5	1500	1	2	3700	4300
17	6	HYDRA SPORT 1750CC	OP	CTRCN	FBG	SV	OB				7	6	1500	1	2	3700	4300
17	6	HYDRA SPORT VS-150T	OP	FSH	FBG	SV	OB				7	1	1095			2850	3300
17	9	HYDRA SPORT 175FS	OP	RNBT	FBG	SV	OB				7	3	1220			3350	3900
17	9	HYDRA SPORT LS175DC	OP	BASS	FBG	SV	OB				7		1150			3100	3600
18	3	HYDRA SPORT 180FS	OP	RNBT	FBG	SV	OB				7	2	1215			3350	3900
18	6	BLUEWATER 1850CC	OP	CTRCN	FBG	SV	OB				7	9	1720	1	4	4150	4850
18	8	SKIFF 1900	OP	CTRCN	FBG	DV	OB				8		1740		11	4200	4900
18	9	HYDRA SPORT LS185	OP	FSH	FBG	SV	OB				7	5	1450			3700	4300
18	9	HYDRA SPORT LS185DC	OP	FSH	FBG	SV	OB				7	5	1450			3700	4300
19	1	KEY LARGO 1900 FLATS	OP	CTRCN	FBG	SV	OB				7	3	1145		11	3100	3600
19	4	CCM 1900	OP	CTRCN	FBG	DV	OB				7	1				5400	6200
20	1	HYDRA SPORT 2150 WAH	OP	CUD	FBG	DV	OB				8	6		1	6	7550	8700
20	1	HYDRA SPORT LS205DC	OP	FSH	FBG	SV	OB				7	9	1525			5050	5800
20	2	BLUEWATER 2000CC	OP	CTRCN	FBG	SV	OB				8		2300	1	6	6700	7700
20	2	BLUEWATER 2000DC	OP	B/R	FBG	SV	OB				8		2300	1	4	6900	7950
20	8	BLUEWATER 2100WA	OP	CUD	FBG	SV	OB				8	6	3100	1	3	8200	9450
20	8	BLUEWATER 2100WA	OP	CUD	FBG	SV	IO		260		8	6	3100	1	3	11400	12900
21	8	BLUEWATER 2200CC	OP	CTRCN	FBG	SV	OB				8		2325	1	10	7500	8650
21	8	HYDRA SPORT 21 SKIFF	OP	CTRCN	FBG	SV	OB				7	6	2030		11	6800	7800
22	6	BLUEWATER 2300WA	OP	CUD	FBG	SV	OB				9	4	4200	1	4	11500	13100
22	6	BLUEWATER 2300WA	OP	CUD	FBG	SV	IO		260		9	4	4200	1	4	15700	17800
24	3	HYDRA SPORT 2300CC	OP	CTRCN	FBG	DV	OB				9	4	3000			10300	11700
25		BLUEWATER 2500CC	OP	CTRCN	FBG	SV	OB				8		3500	1	10	12000	13600
25		BLUEWATER 2500WA	OP	CUD	FBG	SV	OB				8		3900	1	10	13000	14800
25	5	BLUEWATER 2550WA	OP	CUD	FBG	SV	OB				9	5	5100	1	9	15100	17200
25	5	BLUEWATER 2550WA	OP	CUD	FBG	SV	IO		300		9	5	5100	1	9	21400	23800
30	1	BLUEWATER 2800SF	OP	SF	FBG	SV	OB				10	7	10180	2	3	29400	32700
		1993 BOATS															
16	4	HYDRA SPORT X260	OP	FSH	FBG	SV	OB				6	9	990			2400	2800
16	4	HYDRA SPORT Z260	OP	FSH	FBG	SV	OB				6	9	850			2050	2400
17	5	HYDRA SPORT X270	OP	FSH	FBG	SV	OB				6	9	1050			2600	3050
17	6	BLUEWATER 1750DC	OP	CTRCN	FBG	SV	OB				7	5	1500	1	2	3550	4100
17	6	BLUEWATER 175CC	OP	CTRCN	FBG	SV	OB				7	5	1500	1	2	3550	4100
17	6	HYDRA SPORT VS-150T	OP	FSH	FBG	SV	OB				7	1	1095			2700	3150
17	9	HYDRA SPORT 175FS	OP	RNBT	FBG	SV	OB				7	3	1220			3150	3650
18	3	HYDRA SPORT 180FS	OP	RNBT	FBG	SV	OB				7	2	1215			3150	3700
18	6	BLUEWATER 1850CC	OP	CTRCN	FBG	SV	OB				7	9	1720	1	4	3950	4600
18	9	HYDRA SPORT LS180	OP	FSH	FBG	SV	OB				7	5	1450			3500	4050
18	9	HYDRA SPORT LS180DC	OP	FSH	FBG	SV	OB				7	5	1450			3550	4150
20	1	HYDRA SPORT LS200DC	OP	FSH	FBG	SV	OB				7	9	1525			4850	5550
20	2	BLUEWATER 2000CC	OP	CTRCN	FBG	SV	OB				8		2300	1	6	6400	7400
20	2	BLUEWATER 2000DC	OP	B/R	FBG	SV	OB				8		2300	1	4	6600	7550
20	8	BLUEWATER 2100WA	OP	CUD	FBG	SV	OB				8	6	3100	1	3	7850	9000
20	8	BLUEWATER 2100WA	OP	CUD	FBG	SV	IO		260		8	6	3100	1	3	10600	12100
21	8	BLUEWATER 2200CC	OP	CTRCN	FBG	SV	OB				8		2325	1	10	7200	8250
22	6	BLUEWATER 2300WA	OP	CUD	FBG	SV	OB				9	4	4200	1	4	11000	12500
22	6	BLUEWATER 2300WA	OP	CUD	FBG	SV	IO		260		9	4	4200	1	4	14600	16600
25		BLUEWATER 2500CC	OP	CTRCN	FBG	SV	OB				8		3500	1	10	11500	13000
25		BLUEWATER 2500WA	OP	CUD	FBG	SV	OB				8		3900	1	10	12400	14100
25	5	BLUEWATER 2550WA	OP	CUD	FBG	SV	OB				9	5	5100	1	9	14300	16200
25	5	BLUEWATER 2550WA	OP	CUD	FBG	SV	IO		300		9	5	5100	1	9	20000	22200
30	1	BLUEWATER 2800SF	OP	SF	FBG	SV	OB				10	7	10180	2	3	28200	31300
		1992 BOATS															
17	6	1750 CC	OP	CTRCN	FBG	DV	OB				7	5	1500			3400	3950
17	6	1750 DC	OP	FSH	FBG	DV	OB				7	5	1500			3300	3850
18	6	1850 CC	OP	CTRCN	FBG	SV	OB				8		1600			3600	4150
20	2	2000 CC	OP	CTRCN	FBG	DV	OB				8		2300			6150	7100
20	2	2000 DC	OP	FSH	FBG	DV	OB				8		2300			6150	7100
20	8	2100 WA	OP	FSH	FBG	DV	OB				8	7	3100			7450	8550
21	8	2200 CC	OP	CTRCN	FBG	DV	OB				8		2300			6850	7900
24	5	2300 WA	OP	FSH	FBG	DV	OB				9	2	3600			10900	12400
25		2500 CC	OP	CTRCN	FBG	DV	OB				8		3500			11000	12500
25		2500 WA	OP	FSH	FBG	DV	OB				8		3900			11700	13300
27	3	2550 WA	OP	FSH	FBG	DV	OB				9	9	6000			16000	18200
30	2	2800 SF	OP	FSH	FBG	DV	OB				10	8	10180			27400	30500
32	11	3300 SF	TT	SF	FBG	DV	OB				9	6	10500			34100	37800
		1991 BOATS															
16	4	1650 CC	OP	CTRCN	FBG	SV	OB				6	10	1500			3200	3700
17	6	1750 CC	OP	CTRCN	FBG	DV	OB				7	5	1500			3200	3700
17	6	1750 DC	OP	FSH	FBG	DV	OB				7	5	1500			3150	3650
18	6	1850 CC	OP	CTRCN	FBG	SV	OB				8		1600			3450	4000
20	2	2000 CC	OP	CTRCN	FBG	DV	OB				8		2300			5950	6850
20	2	2000 DC	OP	FSH	FBG	DV	OB				8		2300			5950	6850
20	8	2100 WA	OP	FSH	FBG	DV	OB				8	7	3100			7150	8250
21	8	2200 CC	OP	CTRCN	FBG	DV	OB				8		2300			6600	7600
24	5	2300 WA	OP	FSH	FBG	DV	OB				9	2	3600			10500	11900
25		2500 CC	OP	CTRCN	FBG	DV	OB				8		3500			10600	12100
25		2500 WA	OP	FSH	FBG	DV	OB				8		3900			11300	12800
27	3	2550 WA	OP	FSH	FBG	DV	OB				9	9	6000			15400	17500
30	2	2800 SF	OP	FSH	FBG	DV	OB				10	8	10180			26400	29300
32	11	3300 SF	TT	SF	FBG	DV	OB				9	6	10500			32600	36200
		1990 BOATS															
17	6	1750 CC	OP	CTRCN	FBG	DV	OB				7	5	1400			2900	3400
17	6	1750 DC	OP	FSH	FBG	DV	OB				7	5	1400			2850	3350
20	2	2000 CC	OP	CTRCN	FBG	SV	OB				8		2000			5300	6050
20	2	2000 DC	OP	FSH	FBG	DV	OB				8		2000			5300	6050
20	2	2000 DC	OP	FSH	FBG	SV	OB				8		2000			5300	6050
21	6	2200 WA	OP	FSH	FBG	SV	OB				8		2900			7350	8450
21	8	2200 CC	OP	FSH	FBG	SV	OB				8		2300			6400	7350
21	8	2200 DC	OP	CTRCN	FBG	SV	OB				8		2300			6400	7350
25		2500 CC	OP	FSH	FBG	SV	OB				8		3400			10100	11500
25		2500 WA	OP	FSH	FBG	SV	OB				8		3400			10100	11500
32	11	3300 SF	TT	SF	FBG	DV	OB				9	6	10500			31200	34700
		1989 BOATS															
16	3	X260	OP	BASS	FBG	TR	OB				6	9	810			1700	2000
17	5	X270	OP	BASS	FBG	TR	OB				6	4	895			1950	2300
17	6	1750 CC	OP	CTRCN	FBG	DV	OB				7	5	1400			2800	3250
17	6	1750 DC	OP	FSH	FBG	DV	OB				7	5	1400			2750	3200
17	6	VEESTAR 150FF	OP	BASS	FBG	TR	OB				7	1	950			2050	2400
17	6	VEESTAR 150T	OP	BASS	FBG	TR	OB				7	1	950			2050	2400
18	3	DIAMOND VEE 180	OP	BASS	FBG	TR	OB				7	2	1125			2450	2850
18	3	DIAMOND VEE 180SX	OP	BASS	FBG	TR	OB				7	2	1075			2350	2750
18	10	DIAMOND VEE DVFF	OP	BASS	FBG	TR	OB				7	3	1300			2800	3250
18	10	DIAMOND VEE DVTS	OP	BASS	FBG	TR	OB				7	3	1300			2800	3250
19	3	DIAMOND VEE 200	OP	BASS	FBG	TR	OB				7	11	1150			2550	3000
19	3	DIAMOND VEE 200FF	OP	BASS	FBG	TR	OB				7	11	1165			2600	3000
20	2	2000 CC	OP	CTRCN	FBG	SV	OB				8		2000			5100	5850
20	2	2000 DC	OP	FSH	FBG	SV	OB				8		2000			5100	5850
20	2	2000 DC	OP	FSH	FBG	SV	IO				8		2000			**	**
21	1	2200 WA	OP	FSH	FBG	SV	OB				8		2900			6850	7850
21	8	2200 CC	OP	FSH	FBG	SV	OB				8		2300			6200	7100
21	8	2200 DC	OP	CTRCN	FBG	SV	OB				8		2300			6200	7100
25		2500 CC	OP	FSH	FBG	SV	OB				8		3400			9800	11100
25		2500 WA	OP	FSH	FBG	SV	OB				8		3500			9950	11300
32	11	3000 SF	TT	SF	FBG	DV	OB				9	6	10500			30100	33400
		1984 BOATS															
16		265-SX	OP	BASS	FBG	SV	OB				6	4	750			1300	1550
16		X-260	OP	BASS	FBG	SV	OB				6	4	700			1200	1450
16	9	PLAYMATE PL 120	OP	RNBT	FBG	SV	OB				6	9	800			1450	1700
17	5	275-SX	OP	BASS	FBG	SV	OB				6	9	850			1550	1850
17	5	X-270	OP	BASS	FBG	SV	OB				6	9	800			1450	1750
17	5	XK-270	OP	RNBT	FBG	SV	OB				6	9	850			1550	1850
17	6	STRIPER 1800 SS	OP	CTRCN	FBG	SV	OB				7	5	1320			2300	2650

CONTINUED ON NEXT PAGE

LOA FT	IN	NAME AND/ OR MODEL	TOP/ RIG	BOAT TYPE	-HULL- MTL	TP	----ENGINE--- TP	# HP	MFG	BEAM FT	IN	WGT LBS	DRAFT FT	IN	RETAIL LOW	RETAIL HIGH
		1984 BOATS														
17	6	VL-475	OP	BASS	FBG	SV	OB			7	1				3250	3750
17	6	VL-475	OP	BASS	KEV	SV	OB			7	1				3600	4200
17	9	PLAYMATE PL 150	OP	RNBT	FBG	SV	OB			6	9	850			1600	1900

....For earlier years, see the BUC Used Boat Price Guide, Volume 3

HYDRO-TECHNOLOGY

GROSSE ILE MI 48138 COAST GUARD MFG ID- HTQ See inside cover to adjust price for area

LOA FT	IN	NAME AND/ OR MODEL	TOP/ RIG	BOAT TYPE	-HULL- MTL	TP	----ENGINE--- TP	# HP	MFG	BEAM FT	IN	WGT LBS	DRAFT FT	IN	RETAIL LOW	RETAIL HIGH
		1989 BOATS														
21	1	RAM-WING	OP	OFF	FBG	CT	OB			8			1		4450	5150
21	1	RAM-WING	OP	OFF	FBG	CT	IO	205-270		8			1	3	6950	8500
21	1	RAM-WING-X	OP	RACE	FBG	CT	OB			8			1		4100	4800
21	1	RAM-WING-X	OP	RACE	FBG	CT	IO	365	MRCR	8			1	4	9000	10200
21	6	HUNTER F-22	OP	FSH	FBG	DV	OB			8	6		1		4550	5250
24	3	SABER 25-X	OP	OFF	F/S	CT	IO	270	MRCR	8			1		11000	12500
24	3	SABER 25-X	OP	OFF	F/S	CT	IO	365	MRCR	8			1		12800	14500
24	3	SABER 250	OP	SPTCR	F/S	CT	IO	230-270		8			1		10800	12700
24	3	SABER 250	OP	SPTCR	F/S	CT	IO	320-365		8			1		11900	14800
24	8	CUDA 250	OP	SPTCR	FBG	DV	IO	T175-T260		7			1	4	10900	13500
25	8	HUNTER F-26	OP	FSH	FBG	DV	OB			9			1	5	8550	9850
26	6	TWISTER	OP	OFF	FBG	CT	OB			8	4		1		9750	11100
26	6	TWISTER	OP	OFF	FBG	CT	IO	T260-T330		8	4		1	4	16000	19600
27	6	ANIMAL 28	OP	OFF	FBG	DV	OB			8			2		12300	14000
27	6	ANIMAL 28	OP	OFF	FBG	DV	IO	T260-T320		8			2		19500	23300
27	6	ANIMAL 28	OP	OFF	FBG	DV	IO	T420	MRCR	8			2		24800	27600
29	2	SABER 300	OP	SPTCR	F/S	CT	IO	T260-T365		8			1	2	19100	23800
29	2	SABER 300	OP	SPTCR	F/S	CT	IO	T420	MRCR	8			1	2	23100	25700
29	2	SABER 30X	OP	OFF	F/S	CT	IO	T365-T420		8			1	2	24900	30000
29	6	SPEARFISH	OP	SF	STL	DV	IO	260-340		8			1	6	16000	18600
31	8	HUNTER F-32	OP	FSH	FBG	DV	OB			9	6		2		17100	19400
32	7	CUDA 33-S	OP	RACE	FBG	CT	IO	T420-T475		9	4		1		51300	63100
32	7	CUDA 33-S	OP	RACE	FBG	CT	IO	T575-T630		9	4		1		68500	79700
32	7	CUDA 330	OP	SPTCR	FBG	CT	IO	T260-T365		9	4		1	2	37300	46000
32	7	CUDA 330	OP	SPTCR	FBG	CT	IO	T425	PCM	9	4		1	2	45600	50100
32	7	CYCLONE	OP	OFF	FBG	CT	IO	T270-T365		9	4		1	2	45800	54800
32	7	CYCLONE	OP	OFF	FBG	CT	IO	T420	MRCR	9	4		1	2	52400	57600
32	7	CYCLONE	OP	OFF	FBG	CT	IO	T575	MRCR	9	4		1	2	68800	75600
32	7	PHANTOM	OP	LNCH	FBG	CT	IB								**	**
35		TORNADO	OP	SPTCR	FBG	DV	IO	T330	MRCR	8		8200	1	5	51400	56500
		IO T420 MRCR 56000 61600, IO T575 MRCR 64500 70900, IO T630 MRCR													67100	73700
38		INFERNO	OP	OFF	FBG	DV	IO	T320	MRCR	8	6		1	6	58900	64700
		IO T330 MRCR 59400 65300, IO T420 MRCR 66400 72900, IO T575 MRCR													80900	88900
38	6	CUDA 39-X	OP	OFF	F/S	CT	IO	T500		10			1	4	93600	103000
38	6	CUDA 39-X	OP	OFF	F/S	CT	IO	T600		10			1	4	105000	115500
38	6	CUDA 390	OP	SPTCR	FBG	CT	IO	T330	MRCR	10			1	4	70700	77700
		IO T365 MRCR 73700 81000, IO T420 MRCR 80100 88100, IB T215D GM													131000	144000
42		FURY	OP	OFF	FBG	DV	IO	T420	MRCR	9	6		1	9	62700	68900
42		FURY	OP	OFF	FBG	DV	IO	T575	MRCR	9	6		1	9	77500	85200
46	6	VINDICATOR	FB	SPTCR	F/S	CT	IB	T500D	S&S	13	11				235000	258000
46	6	VINDICATOR	FB	SPTCR	F/S	CT	IB	T600D	S&S	13	11				251500	276500
46	6	VINDICATOR	FB	SPTCR	F/S	CT	IO	Q420	MRCR	13	11				186000	204500
46	6	VINDICATOR-X	OP	OFF	C/S	CT	IO	Q600		13	11				169000	185500
63		TALLADEGA	OP	OFF	FBG	DV	OB			12			2	6	**	**
63		TALLADEGA	OP	OFF	FBG	DV	IO	T575	MRCR	12			3	9	**	**
		IO T630 MRCR ** **, IO T330D FORD ** **, IO T370D FORD													**	**
		1988 BOATS														
21	1	RAM-WING	OP	OFF	FBG	CT	OB			8			1		4250	4950
21	1	RAM-WING	OP	OFF	FBG	CT	IO	200-260		8			1	3	6500	7900
21	1	RAM-WING	OP	OFF	FBG	CT	IO	300	MRCR	8			1	3	7350	8450
21	1	RAM-WING X	OP	RACE	FBG	CT	OB			8			1		3950	4600
21	1	RAM-WING X	OP	RACE	FBG	CT	IO	400	MRCR	8			1	4	9600	10900
21	6	HUNTER F-22	OP	FSH	FBG	DV	OB			8	6		1		4400	5050
24	3	SABER 250	OP	SPTCR	F/S	CT	IO	260-300		8			1		10400	12400
		IB 340 MRCR 12900 14700, IO 350 PCM 11900 13500, IO 425 PCM													14400	16400
24	3	SABER 25X	OP	OFF	F/S	CT	IO	350		8			1		12000	13700
24	3	SABER 25X	OP	OFF	F/S	CT	IO	400		8			1		13500	15300
24	8	CUDA 250	OP	SPTCR	FBG	DV	IO	T185-T260		7			1	4	10400	12700
25	8	HUNTER F-26	OP	FSH	FBG	DV	OB			9			1	5	8250	9500
26	6	TWISTER	OP	OFF	FBG	CT	OB			8	4		1		9400	10700
26	6	TWISTER	OP	OFF	FBG	CT	IO	T260-T300		8	4		1	4	14700	17700
26	6	TWISTER	OP	OFF	FBG	CT	IO	T330	MRCR	8	4		1	7	16400	18600
27	6	ANIMAL 28	OP	OFF	FBG	DV	OB			8			2		11900	13600
27	6	ANIMAL 28	OP	OFF	FBG	DV	IO	T260	MRCR	8			2		18400	20400
27	6	ANIMAL 28	OP	OFF	FBG	DV	IO	T400	MRCR	8			2	4	22600	25100
27	6	ANIMAL 28	OP	OFF	FBG	DV	IO	T575	MRCR	8			2	4	30400	33800
29	2	SABER 300	OP	SPTCR	F/S	CT	IO	T260-T300		8			1	2	17500	20700
29	2	SABER 300	OP	SPTCR	F/S	CT	IO	T350		8			1	2	19800	21900
29	2	SABER 300	OP	SPTCR	F/S	CT	IO	T440		8			1	2	22300	24800
29	2	SABER 30X	OP	OFF	F/S	CT	IO	T440		8			1	2	26300	29200
29	2	SABER 30X	OP	OFF	F/S	CT	IO	T575		8			1	2	31700	35300
29	6	SPEARFISH	OP	SF	STL	DV	IO	260-340		8			1	6	14700	17600
31	8	HUNTER F-32	OP	FSH	FBG	DV	OB			9	6		2		16500	18700
32	7	CUDA 33-S	OP	RACE	FBG	CT	IO	T350-T370		9	4		1		40400	47100
32	7	CUDA 33-S	OP	RACE	FBG	CT	IO	T400-T440		9	4		1	4	46100	55400
32	7	CUDA 33-S	OP	RACE	FBG	CT	IO	T575-T600		9	4		1	6	64300	72700
32	7	CUDA 330	OP	SPTCR	FBG	CT	IO	T260-T370		9	4		1	2	34900	43000
32	7	CUDA 330	OP	SPTCR	FBG	CT	IO	T425	PCM	9	4		1		42400	47100
32	7	CYCLONE	OP	OFF	FBG	CT	IO	T300-T425		9	4		1	6	43700	54300
32	7	PHANTOM	OP	LNCH	FBG	CT	IB								**	**
38		INFERNO	OP	OFF	FBG	DV	IO	T330	MRCR	8	6		1	6	56000	61500
		IO T400 MRCR 60800 66800, IO T440 MRCR 64400 70800, IO T575 MRCR													76200	83800
38	6	CUDA 390	OP	SPTCR	FBG	CT	IB	T340	MRCR	10			1	4	104500	114500
		IO T350 PCM 68100 74900, IO T425 PCM 76200 83700, IB T215D GM													125000	137500
38	6	CUDA 39X	OP	OFF	F/S	CT	IO	T500		10					88200	96900
38	6	CUDA 39X	OP	OFF	F/S	CT	IO	T600		10					99100	109000
42		FURY	OP	OFF	FBG	DV	IO	T400	MRCR	9	6		1	9	57300	62900
42		FURY	OP	OFF	FBG	DV	IO	T440	MRCR	9	6		1	9	61000	67000
42		FURY	OP	OFF	FBG	DV	IO	T575	MRCR	9	6		1	9	73100	80300
46	6	VINDICATOR	FB	SPTCR	F/S	CT	IB	T500D	S&S	13	11				224500	246500
46	6	VINDICATOR	FB	SPTCR	F/S	CT	IB	T600D	S&S	13	11				240000	264000
46	6	VINDICATOR	FB	SPTCR	F/S	CT	IO	Q425	PCM	13	11				179000	196500
46	6	VINDICATOR-X	OP	OFF	C/S	CT	IO	Q600		13	11				159500	175000
63		TALLADEGA	OP	OFF	FBG	DV	OB			12			2	6	**	**
63		TALLADEGA	OP	OFF	FBG	DV	IO	T440	MRCR	12			3	9	**	**
		IO T575 MRCR ** **, IO T330D FORD ** **, IO T370D FORD													**	**
		1987 BOATS														
21	1	RAM-WING	OP	OFF	FBG	CT	OB			8			1		4100	4800
21	1	RAM-WING	OP	OFF	FBG	CT	IO	200-260		8			1	3	6150	7400
21	1	RAM-WING	OP	OFF	FBG	CT	IO	300	MRCR	8			1	3	6950	8000
21	1	RAM-WING X	OP	RACE	FBG	CT	OB			8			1		3850	4450
21	1	RAM-WING X	OP	RACE	FBG	CT	IO	400	MRCR	8			1	4	9100	10300
24	3	SABER 250	OP	SPTCR	F/S	CT	IO	260-300		8			1		9850	11700
		IB 340 MRCR 12300 14000, IO 350 PCM 11200 12800, IO 425 PCM													13400	15200
24	3	SABER 25X	OP	OFF	F/S	CT	IO	350		8			1		11400	12900
24	3	SABER 25X	OP	OFF	F/S	CT	IO	400		8			1		12800	14500
24	8	CUDA 250	OP	SPTCR	FBG	DV	IO	185-188		7		3400	1	4	7550	8700
		IO 260 MRCR 8500 9750, IO T185-T198 10200 11700, IO T260 MRCR													11600	13200
26	6	TWISTER	OP	OFF	FBG	CT	OB			8	4		1		9150	10400
26	6	TWISTER	OP	OFF	FBG	CT	IO	T260-T300		8	4		1	4	13700	16700
26	6	TWISTER	OP	OFF	FBG	CT	IO	T330	MRCR	8	4		1	7	15500	17600
29	2	SABER 300	OP	SPTCR	F/S	CT	IO	T260-T350		8			1	2	16800	20700
29	2	SABER 300	OP	SPTCR	F/S	CT	IO	T440		8			1	2	21100	23400
29	2	SABER 30X	OP	OFF	F/S	CT	IO	T400		8			1	2	23300	25900
29	2	SABER 30X	OP	OFF	F/S	CT	IO	T575		8			1	2	30000	33300
29	6	SPEARFISH	OP	SF	STL	DV	IO	260		8			1	6	13600	15500
29	6	SPEARFISH	OP	SF	STL	DV	IB	340	MRCR	8			1	6	16100	18300
32	7	CUDA 33-S	OP	RACE	FBG	CT	IO	T350-T370		9	4		1		38200	44400
32	7	CUDA 33-S	OP	RACE	FBG	CT	IO	T400-T425		9	4		1	4	43000	50500
32	7	CUDA 330	OP	SPTCR	FBG	CT	IO	T260-T350		9	4	6650	1	2	32700	39200
32	7	CUDA 330	OP	SPTCR	FBG	CT	IO	T370-T425		9	4	7800	1	4	37500	44700
32	7	CYCLONE	OP	OFF	FBG	CT	IO	T300-T425		9	4		1	6	41200	51200
32	7	CYCLONE	OP	OFF	FBG	CT	IB	T250D-T360D		9	4		1	6	65200	80600
32	7	CYCLONE	OP	OFF	FBG	CT	IB	T450D-T500D		9	4		1	8	82200	96600
32	7	PHANTOM	OP	LNCH	FBG	CT	IB	T360D	GM	9	4	7200	1	6	49700	54600
32	7	PHANTOM	OP	LNCH	FBG	CT	IB	T450D	GM	9	4	8300	1	8	58000	63800
38		INFERNO	OP	OFF	FBG	DV	IO	T330	MRCR	8	6		1	6	52900	58200
		IO T400 MRCR 57500 63200, IO T440 MRCR 60900 66900, IO T575 MRCR													72100	79200
38	6	CUDA 390	OP	SPTCR	FBG	CT	IB	T340	MRCR	10			1	4	99600	109500

 CONTINUED ON NEXT PAGE

LOA FT	LOA IN	NAME AND/ OR MODEL	TOP/ RIG	BOAT TYPE	HULL MTL	HULL TP	ENGINE TP	# HP	MFG	BEAM FT	BEAM IN	WGT LBS	DRAFT FT	DRAFT IN	RETAIL LOW	RETAIL HIGH
		1987 BOATS														
38	6	CUDA 390	OP	SPTCR	FBG	CT	IO	T350	PCM	10			1	4	64400	70800
38	6	CUDA 390	OP	SPTCR	FBG	CT	IO	T425	PCM	10			1	4	72000	79100
38	6	CUDA 390	OP	SPTCR	FBG	CT	IB	T215D	GM	10			1	4	119500	131500
38	6	CUDA 39X	OP	OFF	F/S	CT	IO	T500		10					83400	91700
38	6	CUDA 39X	OP	OFF	F/S	CT	IO	T600		10					93700	103000
42		FURY	OP	OFF	FBG	DV	IO	T400	MRCR	9	6		1	9	54200	59500
42		FURY	OP	OFF	FBG	DV	IO	T440	MRCR	9	6		1	9	57700	63400
42		FURY	OP	OFF	FBG	DV	IO	T575	MRCR	9	6		1	9	69100	75900
46	6	VINDICATOR	FB	SPTCR	F/S	CT	IB	T500D	S&S	13	11				214000	235500
46	6	VINDICATOR	FB	SPTCR	F/S	CT	IB	T600D	S&S	13	11				229500	252000
46	6	VINDICATOR	FB	SPTCR	F/S	CT	IO	Q425	PCM	13	11				170000	187000
46	6	VINDICATOR-X	OP	OFF	C/S	CT	IO	Q600		13	11				151000	166000
63		TALLADEGA	OP	OFF	FBG	DV	OB						2	6	**	**
63		TALLADEGA	OP	OFF	FBG	DV	IO	T440	MRCR	11	6		2	9	**	**
		IO T575 MRCR ** ** , IO T330D FORD ** ** , IO T370D FORD													**	**
		1986 BOATS														
21	1	RAM-WING	OP	OFF	FBG	CT	OB			8			1		3950	4600
21	1	RAM-WING	OP	OFF	FBG	CT	IO	200-260		8			1	3	5850	7050
21	1	RAM-WING	OP	OFF	FBG	CT	IO	300	MRCR	8			1	3	6550	7500
21	1	RAM-WING X	OP	RACE	FBG	CT	OB			8			1		3700	4300
21	1	RAM-WING X	OP	RACE	FBG	CT	IO	400	MRCR	8			1	4	8550	9800
24	3	SABER 250	OP	SPTCR	F/S	CT	IO	260-300		8			1		9350	11100
		IB 340 MRCR 11700 13300, IO 350 PCM 10700 12100, IO 425 PCM													12700	14400
24	3	SABER 25X	OP	OFF	F/S	CT	IO	350		8			1		10800	12300
24	3	SABER 25X	OP	OFF	F/S	CT	IO	400		8			1		12100	13800
24	8	CUDA 250	OP	SPTCR	FBG	DV	IO	185-188		7		3400	1	4	7150	8250
		IO 260 MRCR 8100 9300, IO T185-T188 9700 11000, IO T260 MRCR													11000	12500
26	6	TWISTER	OP	OFF	FBG	CT	OB			8	4		1		8900	10100
26	6	TWISTER	OP	OFF	FBG	CT	IO	T260-T300		8	4		1	4	12900	15600
26	6	TWISTER	OP	OFF	FBG	CT	IO	T330	MRCR	8	4		1	7	14700	16700
29	2	SABER 300	OP	SPTCR	F/S	CT	IO	T260-T350		8			1	2	16200	19700
29	2	SABER 300	OP	SPTCR	F/S	CT	IO	T400		8			1	2	18900	21000
29	2	SABER 30X	OP	OFF	F/S	CT	IO	T350-T400		8			1	2	20700	24600
32	7	CUDA 33-S	OP	RACE	FBG	CT	IO	T350-T370		9	4		1		35800	41900
32	7	CUDA 33-S	OP	RACE	FBG	CT	IO	T400-T425		9	4		1	4	41100	47800
32	7	CUDA 330	OP	SPTCR	FBG	CT	IO	T260-T350		9	4	6650	1	2	31000	37000
32	7	CUDA 330	OP	SPTCR	FBG	CT	IO	T370-T425		9	4	7800	1	4	35100	42200
32	7	CYCLONE	OP	OFF	FBG	CT	IO	T300-T425		9	4		1	6	38900	48400
32	7	CYCLONE	OP	OFF	FBG	CT	IB	T250D-T360D		9	4		1	6	62600	77400
32	7	CYCLONE	OP	OFF	FBG	CT	IB	T450D-T500D		9	4		1	8	79000	92800
32	7	PHANTOM	OP	LNCH	FBG	CT	IB	T360D	GM	9	4	7200	1	6	47700	52400
32	7	PHANTOM	OP	LNCH	FBG	CT	IB	T450D	GM	9	4	8300	1	8	55600	61100
38	6	CUDA 390	OP	SPTCR	FBG	CT	IB	T340	MRCR	10			1	4	94800	104000
		IO T350 PCM 61200 67200, IO T425 PCM 68400 75100, IB T215D GM													113500	125000
38	6	CUDA 39X	OP	OFF	F/S	CT	IO	T500		10					79200	87000
38	6	CUDA 39X	OP	OFF	F/S	CT	IO	T600		10					88900	97700
46	6	VINDICATOR	FB	SPTCR	F/S	CT	IB	T500D	S&S	13	11				204000	224000
46	6	VINDICATOR	FB	SPTCR	F/S	CT	IB	T600D	S&S	13	11				218000	240000
46	6	VINDICATOR	FB	SPTCR	F/S	CT	IO	Q425	PCM	13	11				162500	178500
46	6	VINDICATOR-X	OP	OFF	C/S	CT	IO	Q600		13	11				143500	157500
		1985 BOATS														
24	3	SABER 250	OP	SPTCR	F/S	CT	IO	260-300		8			1		8950	10600
		IB T340 MRCR 13200 15000, IO T350 PCM 13000 14800, IO T425 PCM													17100	19400
24	3	SABER 25X	OP	OFF	F/S	CT	IO	T350		8			1		13300	15100
24	3	SABER 25X	OP	OFF	F/S	CT	IO	T400		8			1		16200	18400
24	8	CUDA 250	OP	SPTCR	FBG	DV	IO	185-188		7		3400	1	4	6800	7850
		IO 260 MRCR 7750 8900, IO T185-T188 9250 10500, IO T260 MRCR													10500	11900
29	2	SABER 300	OP	SPTCR	F/S	CT	IO	T260-T350		8			1	2	15200	18900
29	2	SABER 300	OP	SPTCR	F/S	CT	IO	T400		8			1	2	18000	20000
29	2	SABER 30X	OP	OFF	F/S	CT	IO	T350-T400		8			1	2	19700	23400
32	7	CUDA 33-S	OP	RACE	FBG	CT	IO	T350-T370		9	4		1		33800	39600
32	7	CUDA 33-S	OP	RACE	FBG	CT	IO	T400-T425		9	4		1	4	38700	45800
32	7	CUDA 330	OP	SPTCR	FBG	CT	IO	T260-T370		9	4	6650	1	2	29400	36800
32	7	CUDA 330	OP	SPTCR	FBG	CT	IO	T425	PCM	9	4	7000	1		35400	39300
32	7	CYCLONE	OP	OFF	FBG	CT	IO	T300-T400		9	4		1	6	36400	44800
		IO T425 PCM 41400 46000, IBT250D-T360D 60200 74400, IBT450D-T500D													75900	89200
32	7	PHANTOM	OP	LNCH	FBG	CT	IB	T360D	GM	9	4				46000	50500
32	7	PHANTOM	OP	LNCH	FBG	CT	IB	T450D	GM	9	4				53100	58300
38	6	CUDA 390	OP	SPTCR	FBG	CT	IB	T340	MRCR	10			1	4	90200	99200
		IO T350 PCM 58300 64100, IO T425 PCM 65200 71600, IB T215D GM													108000	119000
38	6	CUDA 39X	OP	OFF	F/S	CT	IO	T500		10					75500	83000
38	6	CUDA 39X	OP	OFF	F/S	CT	IO	T600		10					84800	93200
46	6	VINDICATOR	FB	SPTCR	F/S	CT	IB	T500D	S&S	13	11				194000	213000
46	6	VINDICATOR	FB	SPTCR	F/S	CT	IB	T600D	S&S	13	11				207500	228500
46	6	VINDICATOR	FB	SPTCR	F/S	CT	IO	Q425	PCM	13	11				156000	171000
46	6	VINDICATOR-X	OP	OFF	C/S	CT	IO	Q600		13	11				137000	150500
		1984 BOATS														
24	3	SABER 250	OP	SPTCR	F/S	CT	IO	260-300		8			1		8450	10200
24	3	SABER 250	OP	SPTCR	F/S	CT	IO	340-350		8			1		9550	11100
24	3	SABER 250	OP	SPTCR	F/S	CT	IO	425	PCM	8			1		11600	13200
24	3	SABER 25X	OP	OFF	F/S	CT	IO	350		8			1		9900	11200
24	3	SABER 25X	OP	OFF	F/S	CT	IO	400		8			1		11100	12600
24	8	CUDA 250	OP	SPTCR	FBG	DV	IO	185-188		7		3400	1	4	6450	7450
		IO 260 MRCR 7400 8500, IO T185-T188 8850 10100, IO T260 MRCR													10100	11400
29	2	SABER 300	OP	SPTCR	F/S	CT	IO	T260-T350		8			1	2	14500	18100
29	2	SABER 300	OP	SPTCR	F/S	CT	IO	T400		8			1	2	16900	19200
29	2	SABER 30X	OP	OFF	F/S	CT	IO	T350-T400		8			1	2	18900	22400
32	7	CUDA 33-S	OP	RACE	FBG	CT	IB	T350	PCM	9	4		1		51400	56500
32	7	CUDA 33-S	OP	RACE	FBG	CT	IO	T370-T400		9	4		1	4	33800	40400
32	7	CUDA 33-S	OP	RACE	FBG	CT	IB	T425	PCM	9	4		1		62200	68400
32	7	CUDA 330	OP	SPTCR	FBG	CT	IO	T260	MRCR	9	4	6650	1	2	28100	31300
		IB T280-T300 35600 40100, IO T330 MRCR 30000 33400, IB T350 PCM													38300	42500
		IO T370 MRCR 31600 35200, IB T425 PCM 40400 44900														
38	6	CUDA 390	OP	SPTCR	FBG	CT	IB	T340	MRCR	10			1	4	86000	94500
		IB T350 PCM 86300 94900, IB T425 PCM 89800 98700, IB T215D GM													103000	113500
38	6	CUDA 39X	OP	OFF	F/S	CT	IO	T500		10					72400	79500
38	6	CUDA 39X	OP	OFF	F/S	CT	IO	T600		10					81300	89300
46	6	VINDICATOR	FB	SPTCR	F/S	CT	IO	T425	PCM	13	11				99100	109000
46	6	VINDICATOR	FB	SPTCR	F/S	CT	IO	T500		13	11				113000	124500
46	6	VINDICATOR	FB	SPTCR	F/S	CT	IO	T600		13	11				130000	143000
46	6	VINDICATOR-X	OP	OFF	C/S	CT	IO	Q600		13	11				131000	144000

....For earlier years, see the BUC Used Boat Price Guide, Volume 3

HYDRODYNE BOATS CO INC

NEW PARIS IN 46553 COAST GUARD MFG ID- THI See inside cover to adjust price for area

LOA FT	LOA IN	NAME AND/ OR MODEL	TOP/ RIG	BOAT TYPE	HULL MTL	HULL TP	ENGINE TP	# HP	MFG	BEAM FT	BEAM IN	WGT LBS	DRAFT FT	DRAFT IN	RETAIL LOW	RETAIL HIGH
		1996 BOATS														
20	2	HYDRODYNE COMP XP	OP	SKI	FBG	SV	IB	310	PCM	7	6	2450	1	9	13900	15800
20	2	HYDRODYNE GRAND SPRT	OP	SKI	FBG	SV	IB	310	PCM	7	6	2550	1	9	13900	15800
20	2	HYDRODYNE GS ELITE	OP	SKI	FBG	SV	IB	310	PCM	7	6	2550	1	9	14500	16500
		1995 BOATS														
20	2	COMP XP CB		SKI	F/S	SV	IB	310	PCM	7	6	2450	1	9	13200	15000
20	2	GRAND SPORT BR		SKI	F/S	SV	IB	310	PCM	7	6	2550	1	9	13400	15300
		1994 BOATS														
20	2	COMP XP CB		SKI	F/S	SV	IB	310	PCM	7		2450	1	6	12000	13600
20	2	GRAND SPORT BR		SKI	F/S	SV	IB	310	PCM	7		2550	1	6	12300	13900
		1993 BOATS														
20	2	INBOARD COMP	OP	SKI	F/S		IB	285		7	6	2450	1	9	11600	13200
		1992 BOATS														
20		DYNE COMP		SKI	F/S	SV	OB			7		1185			6250	7200
20	2	INBOARD COMP	OP	SKI	F/S		IB	285		7	6	2450	1	9	11000	12500
		1991 BOATS														
20		DYNE COMP		SKI	F/S	SV	OB			7		1185			6000	6900
20		DYNE COMP	OP	SKI	F/S		OB			7		1100	1	7	5850	6700
20		FAMILY SKIER		SKI	F/S	SV	OB			7		1185			6400	7400
20	2	LEGACY		SKI	F/S	SV	IB	330		7	6	2450			10800	12300
20	2	LEGACY	OP	SKI	F/S		IB	285		7	6	2450	1	9	10500	11900
		1990 BOATS														
17	6	176 XB	OP	SKI	FBG	SV	OB			7		900	1	5	4250	4950
17	6	176 XB	OP	SKI	FBG	SV	IO	175-205		7		1760	1	7	4600	5350
20		DYNE	OP	SKI	FBG	SV	OB			7		1100	1	7	5450	6250
20		DYNE	OP	SKI	FBG	SV	IO	175-260		7		2235	1	11	6600	8150
20		FAMILY SKIER	OP	SKI	FBG	SV	OB			7		1100	1	7	5850	6700
		1989 BOATS														
17	6	176 XB	OP	SKI	FBG	SV	OB			7		900	1	5	4100	4800
17	6	176 XB	OP	SKI	FBG	SV	IO	175-205		7		1760	1	7	4350	5150
20		DYNE	OP	SKI	FBG	SV	OB			7		1100	1	7	5300	6050
20		DYNE	OP	SKI	FBG	SV	IO	175-260		7		2235	1	11	6250	7700
20		FAMILY SKIER	OP	SKI	FBG	SV	OB			7		1100	1	7	5600	6450

HYDRODYNE BOATS CO INC — CONTINUED
See inside cover to adjust price for area

LOA FT IN	NAME AND/ OR MODEL	TOP/ RIG	BOAT TYPE	HULL MTL TP	TP	ENGINE # HP	MFG	BEAM FT IN	WGT LBS	DRAFT FT IN	RETAIL LOW	RETAIL HIGH
				— 1988 BOATS —								
17 6	176 XB	OP	SKI	FBG SV OB				7	900	1 5	4000	4650
17 6	176 XB	OP	SKI	FBG SV IO		130-205		7	1760	1 7	4050	4900
20	DYNE	OP	SKI	FBG SV OB				7	1100	1 7	5150	5900
20	DYNE	OP	SKI	FBG SV IO		175-260		7	2235	1 11	5900	7300
20	FAMILY SKIER	OP	SKI	FBG SV OB				7	1100	1 7	5400	6200
				— 1987 BOATS —								
17 6	176 XB	OP	SKI	FBG SV OB				7	900	1 5	3850	4500
17 6	176 XB	OP	SKI	FBG SV IO		130-205		7	1760	1 7	3850	4650
20	DYNE	OP	SKI	FBG SV OB				7	1100	1 7	5000	5750
20	DYNE	OP	SKI	FBG SV IO		175-260		7	2235	1 11	5600	6950
20	FAMILY SKIER	OP	SKI	FBG SV OB				7	1100	1 7	5250	6050
				— 1985 BOATS —								
17 6	176 XB	OP	SKI	FBG SV OB				7 1	983		4000	4600
20	DYNE	OP	SKI	FBG SV OB				7 1	1575	1 10	6550	7500
20	DYNE	OP	SKI	FBG SV IO		170-260		7 1	2648	2	5650	6950
20	FAMILY SKIER	OP	SKI	FBG SV OB				7 1	1475		6200	7150
				— 1984 BOATS —								
20	DYNE	OP	SKI	FBG SV OB				6 11	1010	1 10	4500	5150
20	DYNE	OP	SKI	FBG SV IO		170-200		6	2800	2 4	5250	6500
20	DYNE	OP	SKI	FBG SV IO		260		6 11	2800	2 4	5950	6850

....For earlier years, see the BUC Used Boat Price Guide, Volume 3

HYDROSTREAM
DIV OF W E PIPKORN MFG CO
NEW BRGHTN MN 55112   COAST GUARD MFG ID- HSP   See inside cover to adjust price for area

LOA FT IN	NAME AND/ OR MODEL	TOP/ RIG	BOAT TYPE	HULL MTL TP	TP	ENGINE # HP	MFG	BEAM FT IN	WGT LBS	DRAFT FT IN	RETAIL LOW	RETAIL HIGH
				— 1985 BOATS —								
16 6	VAMP	OP	RNBT	FBG DV OB				7			2700	3150
16 6	VENTURA	OP	RNBT	FBG DV OB				7			2350	2700
17 1	VARMINT	OP	FSH	FBG DV OB				7 4			2200	2600
17 1	VECTOR	OP	RNBT	FBG DV OB				7 5			2550	2950
17 9	V-KING	OP	RNBT	FBG DV OB				7 5			2900	3350
17 9	VALERO	OP	RNBT	FBG DV OB				7 5			3000	3450
20	VEGAS	OP	RNBT	FBG DV OB				7 5			3500	4100
20	VENUS	OP	CUD	FBG DV OB				7 5			3850	4500
20	VOYAGER	OP	RNBT	FBG DV OB				7 5			4550	5250
20	VULTURE	OP	RNBT	FBG DV OB				7 5			3400	3950

....For earlier years, see the BUC Used Boat Price Guide, Volume 3

I M P BOATS
INTERNATIONAL MARINE PRODUCTS
IOLA KS 66749   COAST GUARD MFG ID- XMP   See inside cover to adjust price for area

LOA FT IN	NAME AND/ OR MODEL	TOP/ RIG	BOAT TYPE	HULL MTL TP	TP	ENGINE # HP	MFG	BEAM FT IN	WGT LBS	DRAFT FT IN	RETAIL LOW	RETAIL HIGH
				— 1991 BOATS —								
20 3	EUROPA BOW RIDER 205		RNBT	FBG SV IO		175	OMC	8	2800	2 7	4950	5700
21 4	SPORTSMAN 220		FSH	FBG DV IO		185	OMC	8	3400	2 8	6550	7550
23 6	ELEGANZA 235		RACE	FBG DV IO		330	MRCR	8	2900	2 8	6950	8000
23 6	EUROPA BOW RIDER 235		RNBT	FBG DV IO		260	MRCR	8	2900	2 8	6150	7050
23 6	EUROPA SPORT CUD 235		RNBT	FBG DV IO		260	MRCR	8	2900	2 8	6300	7250
25 4	ELEGANZA 255		RACE	FBG DV IO		330	MRCR	8	5600	2 8	11400	12900
30 4	ELEGANZA 310		RACE	FBG DV IO		T330	MRCR	8	7500	2 10	19700	21900
				— 1990 BOATS —								
17 6	ASHANTI 180 BR	OP	B/R	FBG DV IO		107-175		7	1900	2 8	3000	3500
18 6	ASHANTI 190 BR	OP	B/R	FBG DV IO		107-260		7 7	2600	2 8	3900	4750
18 6	ASHANTI 190 BR	OP	B/R	FBG SV IO		275	VLVO	7 7	2600	2 8	4450	5100
18 6	ASHANTI 190 SC	OP	CUD	FBG DV IO		107-260		7 7	2600	2 8	4150	5100
18 6	ASHANTI 190 SC	OP	CUD	FBG SV IO		275	VLVO	7 7	2600	2 8	4700	5400
20 3	EUROPA 205 BR	OP	B/R	FBG DV IO		107-260		8	2800		4700	5650
21 4	SPORTSMAN 220	OP	CUD	FBG DV IO		107-260		8	3400	2 8	6000	7150
21 4	SPORTSMAN 220	OP	CUD	FBG SV IO		275	VLVO	8	3400	2 8	6550	7500
21 4	SPORTSMAN 220 W/BRCK	OP	CUD	FBG DV IO				8	3400	2 8	3650	4250
23 2	SPORTSMAN 245	OP	CUD	FBG DV IO			OMC	8	3600	2 8	**	**
23 2	SPORTSMAN 245	OP	CUD	FBG DV IO		235-275		8	3600	2 8	6850	8500
23 2	SPORTSMAN 245	OP	CUD	FBG DV IO		307-360		8	3600	2 8	7800	9550
23 6	ELEGANZA 235	OP	CUD	FBG DV IO		240-270		8	2900	2 8	6450	7600
23 6	ELEGANZA 235	OP	CUD	FBG DV IO		275-320		8	2900	2 8	7050	8450
23 6	ELEGANZA 235	OP	CUD	FBG DV IO		330-370		8	2900	2 8	7900	9100
23 6	EUROPA 235 BR	OP	B/R	FBG DV IO		229-275		8	2900		5900	7150
23 6	EUROPA 235 BR	OP	B/R	FBG DV IO		307-360		8	2900		6550	8100
23 6	EUROPA 235 BR	OP	B/R	FBG DV IO		370	OMC	8	2900		7150	8200
23 6	EUROPA 235 SC	OP	CUD	FBG DV IO		229-320		8	2900		6300	7650
23 6	EUROPA 235 SC	OP	CUD	FBG DV IO		330-360		8	2900		6900	8150
23 6	EUROPA 235 SC	OP	CUD	FBG DV IO		370	OMC	8	2900		7750	8950
25 4	ELEGANZA 255	OP	CUD	FBG DV IO		330-370		8	5600	2 8	11900	13800
	IO 410-420	13100	15100,	IO T240-T275		12100	14800,	IO T320	MRCR		13600	15400
26 9	EXPRESS 270	OP	EXP	FBG DV IO		150-260		8	6000	2 10	11100	13600
	IO 275-360	12300	15000,	IO T107-T205		12200	15100,	IO T229-T260			13700	15800
30 4	ELEGANZA 310	OP	CUD	FBG DV IO		T240-T340		8	7500	2 10	17400	20600
30 4	ELEGANZA 310	OP	CUD	FBG DV IO		T360-T420		8	7500	2 10	19600	23300
34 8	ELANTE 320	OP	EXP	FBG DV IO		T240-T370		11	10500		34600	42000
				— 1989 BOATS —								
17 6	ASHANTI 180 BR	OP	B/R	FBG DV IO		128-131		7	1900	2 8	2650	3300
17 6	ASHANTI 180 BR	OP	B/R	FBG DV IO		151-180		7	1900	2 8	2850	3300
18 6	ASHANTI 190 BR	OP	B/R	FBG DV IO		128-230		7 7	2600	2 8	3850	4300
18 6	ASHANTI 190 BR	OP	B/R	FBG DV IO		231-260		7 7	2600	2 8	3850	4500
18 6	ASHANTI 190 SC	OP	CUD	FBG DV IO		128-200		7 7	2600	2 8	3750	4600
18 6	ASHANTI 190 SC	OP	CUD	FBG DV IO		205-260		7 7	2600	2 8	3850	4800
20 2	ASHANTI 200 BR	OP	RNBT	FBG DV IO			OMC	7 8	2800	2 8	**	**
20 2	ASHANTI 200 BR	OP	RNBT	FBG DV IO		260-270		7 8	2800	2 8	4600	5350
20 2	ASHANTI 200 BR	OP	RNBT	FBG SV IO		311	VLVO	7 8	2800	2 8	5300	6100
21 4	SPORTSMAN 220	OP	CUD	FBG DV IO		130-260		8	3400	2 8	5500	6750
21 4	SPORTSMAN 220 W/BRCK	OP	CUD	FBG DV OB				8	3400	2 8	1350	1600
22 3	ASHANTI 230 BR	OP	RNBT	FBG DV IO		260-270	MRCR 8		3800	2 8	**	**
	IO OMC	**	**,	IO		6200	7200,	IO 311	VLVO		6950	7950
23 2	SPORTSMAN 245	OP	CUD	FBG DV IO		200-270	MRCR 8		3600	2 8	**	**
	IO OMC	**	**,	IO		6150	7450,	IO 271	VLVO		6750	7750
23 2	SPORTSMAN 245 LTD	OP	CUD	FBG DV IO		200-270	MRCR 8		3600	2 8	**	**
	IO OMC	**	**,	IO		6600	7950,	IO 271-311			7200	8500
23 6	ELEGANZA 235	OP	CUD	FBG DV IO		260-270	MRCR 8		3200	2 8	**	**
	IO OMC	**	**,	IO		6550	7600,	IO 311-365			7350	9050
23 6	EUROPA 235	OP	CUD	FBG DV IO		230-271	MRCR 8		3200	2 8	**	**
	IO OMC	**	**,	IO		6100	7550,	IO 311-365			6650	8300
25 4	ELEGANZA 255	OP	CUD	FBG DV IO		260-320	MRCR 8		5600	2 8	**	**
	IO OMC	**	**,	IO		10200	12400,	IO 365-420			11400	14300
	IO T OMC	**	**,	IO T260-T320		11700	14500					
26 9	EXPRESS 270	OP	EXP	FBG DV IO		230-271	MRCR 8		6200	2 10	**	**
	IO OMC	**	**,	IO		11300	13300,	IO T128-T230			11700	14600
	IO T231-T260	13100	15100'									
30 4	ELEGANZA 310	OP	CUD	FBG DV IO T		T260-T320	MRCR 8		6800	2 10	**	**
	IO T OMC	**	**,	IO T260-T320		16400	19700,	IO T365-T420			18600	21600
				— 1988 BOATS —								
17 6	BOW RIDER 175	OP	B/R	FBG SV OB				7	2100	2 8	1950	2300
17 6	BOW RIDER 175	OP	B/R	FBG SV IO		120-131		7	2100	2 8	2650	3250
18 6	BOW RIDER 190	OP	B/R	FBG SV OB				7 7	2800	2 8	2350	2750
18 6	BOW RIDER 190	OP	B/R	FBG SV IO		130-211		7 7	2800	2 8	3500	4350
18 6	SPORT CUDDY 190	OP	CUD	FBG SV OB				7 7	2800	2 8	2350	2750
18 6	SPORT CUDDY 190	OP	CUD	FBG SV IO		130-211		7 7	2800	2 8	3700	4650
21 4	FISH 22	OP	CUD	FBG DV OB				8	3400	2 8	3100	3600
21 4	FISH 22	OP	CUD	FBG DV IO		130-211		8	3400	2 8	5200	6300
21 4	FISH 22 W/BRACKET	OP	CUD	FBG DV OB				8	3400	2 8	1350	1650
23 2	FISH 245	OP	CUD	FBG DV OB				8	3600	2 8	3800	4450
23 2	FISH 245	OP	CUD	FBG DV IO		200-271	MRCR 8		3600	2 8	**	**
	IO OMC	**	**,	IO		5750	7150,	IO 311	VLVO		6650	7650
	IO T130-T180	6400	7500'									
23 2	FISH PLUS 245	OP	CUD	FBG DV OB				8	3600	2 8	4200	4900
23 2	FISH PLUS 245	OP	CUD	FBG DV IO		200-271	MRCR 8		3600	2 8	**	**
	IO OMC	**	**,	IO		6300	7850,	IO 311	VLVO		7250	8350
	IO T130-T180	6950	8050'									
23 2	SPORTS CUDDY 245	OP	CUD	FBG DV OB				8	3600	2 8	4150	4800
23 2	SPORTS CUDDY 245	OP	CUD	FBG DV IO		200-271	MRCR 8		3600	2 8	**	**
	IO OMC	**	**,	IO		6150	7650,	IO 311	VLVO		7100	8150
	IO T130-T180	6800	7900'									
23 6	ELEGANZA 235	OP	CUD	FBG DV OB				8	3450	2 8	1600	1900

CONTINUED ON NEXT PAGE

LOA FT	LOA IN	NAME AND/ OR MODEL	TOP/ RIG	BOAT TYPE	-HULL- MTL	-HULL- TP	ENGINE TP	ENGINE # HP	ENGINE MFG	BEAM FT	BEAM IN	WGT LBS	DRAFT FT	DRAFT IN	RETAIL LOW	RETAIL HIGH
		1988 BOATS														
23	6	ELEGANZA 235	OP	CUD	FBG	DV	IO		MRCR	8		3450	2	8	**	**
		IO OMC ** ** , IO 260-271 6200 7450, IO 311 VLVO													6950	7950
23	8	EUROPA 230	OP	B/R	FBG	SV	IO			8		3600	2	6	**	**
23	8	EUROPA 230	OP	CUD	FBG	SV	IO			8		3600	2	6	**	**
25	4	ELEGANZA 255	OP	CUD	FBG	DV	OB			8		5600	2	8	4800	5550
25	4	ELEGANZA 255	OP	CUD	FBG	DV	IO		MRCR	8		5600	2	8	**	**
		IO OMC ** ** , IO 260-311 9600 11700, IO T OMC													**	**
		IO T200-T270 10400 12900, IO T271-T311 11600 14100														
26	9	SPORTS EXPRESS 270	OP	EXP	FBG	SV	OB			8		6000	2	10	6800	7850
26	9	SPORTS EXPRESS 270	OP	EXP	FBG	SV	IO		MRCR	8		6000	2	10	**	**
		IO OMC ** ** , IO 260-311 10700 12900, IO T130-T230													10900	13600
		IO T231-T270 12200 14400, IO T311 VLVO 13600 15500														
30	4	ELEGANZA 310	OP	CUD	FBG	DV	OB			8		6600	2	10	10600	12000
30	4	ELEGANZA 310	OP	CUD	FBG	DV	IO	T	MRCR	8		6600	2	10	**	**
		IO T OMC ** ** , IO T260-T311 15400 18600, IO T365 MRCR													17200	19500
33	10	SPORT EXPRESS 300	OP	EXP	FBG	SV	IO			10		8200	3	3	**	**
34		CONSTITUTION 360		CR	FBG	SV	IB	275	CHRY	13	1	16000	2		39000	43300
		1987 BOATS														
17	4	X180 BR	ST	RNBT	FBG		IO	130		7	2	2150			2700	3150
17	4	X180 BR	ST	RNBT	FBG	SV	IO	165-180		7	2	2150			2700	3200
18	6	X190 BR	ST	RNBT	FBG	SV	IO	165-260		7	7	2960			3550	4400
18	6	X190 SC	ST	RNBT	FBG	SV	IO	165-260		7	7	2960			3600	4450
20	2	X200 BR	ST	RNBT	FBG	DV	IO	200-260		7	8	3140			4150	5050
20	4	X215 BR	ST	RNBT	FBG	DV	IO		MRCR	7	8	3300			**	**
20	4	X215 BR	ST	RNBT	FBG	DV	IO	180-260		7	8	3300			4150	5100
20	4	X215 SC	ST	RNBT	FBG	DV	IO		MRCR	7	8	3300			**	**
20	4	X215 SC	ST	RNBT	FBG	DV	IO	180-260		7	8	3300			4550	5400
21	4	22 FISH	ST	CUD	FBG		IO	130-260							4950	6000
21	4	FISH O/B	ST	FSH	FBG	DV	OB					2100	2	4	965	1150
22	3	X230 SC	ST	CUD	FBG	DV	IO		MRCR	8		3900			**	**
22	3	X230 SC	ST	CUD	FBG	DV	IO	200-260		8		3900			5800	6900
22	3	X230 SC	ST	CUD	FBG	DV	IO	330	MRCR	8		3900			6650	7650
23	2	245 FISH	ST	CUD	FBG		IO		MRCR						**	**
23	2	245 FISH	ST	CUD	FBG		IO	230-260							6150	7100
23	2	245 SC	ST	CUD	FBG		IO		MRCR						**	**
23	2	245 SC	ST	CUD	FBG		IO	260-335							6550	7950
23	2	245 SC	ST	CUD	FBG	DV	IO	340	OMC						7000	8050
23	3	X230 BR	ST	CUD	FBG	DV	IO		MRCR	8		4110			**	**
23	3	X230 BR	ST	CUD	FBG	DV	IO	200-260		8		4110			6350	7550
23	3	X230 BR	ST	CUD	FBG	DV	IO	330-340		8		4110			7200	8350
25	4	X255 SC	ST	SPTCR	FBG	DV	IO		MRCR	8		5210			**	**
		IO 330 MRCR 8250 9450, IO 335-340 9450 10700, IO T260													10100	11400
26	9	X270 SE	ST	EXP	FBG	DV	IO	260-340		8		5700			9850	12100
26	9	X270 SE	ST	EXP	FBG	DV	IO	T165-T260		8		6700			11400	14100
31		X310	ST	SPTCR	FBG		IO	340	OMC	8		6250			15300	17400
31		X310	ST	SPTCR	FBG		IO	T320-T420		8		6250			18000	21300
34		360	ST	CR	FBG		IB	T270	CHRY						35600	39600
		1985 BOATS														
17	4	X180 BR	ST	RNBT	FBG		IO	140		7	2	2150			2500	2900
17	4	X180 BR	ST	RNBT	FBG	SV	OB			7	2	1300			1000	1200
17	4	X180 BR	ST	RNBT	FBG	SV	IO	117-190		7	2	2150			2600	3050
17	6	X175 BR	ST	RNBT	FBG	DV	IO	117-190		7		2200			2600	3100
18	6	X190 BR	ST	RNBT	FBG		IO	140		7	6	2960			3200	3750
18	6	X190 BR	ST	RNBT	FBG	SV	IO	138-230		7	7	2960			3400	4100
		IO 260 3450 4250, IO 290-330 3850 4650, IO 370 MRCR													4650	5350
18	6	X190 SC	ST	RNBT	FBG		IO	140		7	6	2960			3250	3800
18	6	X190 SC	ST	RNBT	FBG	SV	IO	138-230		7	7	2960			3400	4100
		IO 260 3500 4250, IO 290-330 3850 4700, IO 370 MRCR													4600	5300
20	2	X200 BR	ST	RNBT	FBG	DV	IO	138-260		7	8	3140			3900	4850
20	2	X200 BR	ST	RNBT	FBG	DV	IO	290-330		7	8	3140			4450	5300
20	2	X200 BR	ST	RNBT	FBG	DV	IO	370	MRCR	7	8	3140			5150	5900
20	2	X200 SC	ST	RNBT	FBG	DV	IO	138-260		7	8	3140			3900	4850
20	2	X200 SC	ST	RNBT	FBG	DV	IO	290-330		7	8	3140			4450	5250
20	2	X200 SC	ST	RNBT	FBG	DV	IO	370	MRCR	7	8	3140			5100	5850
20	2	X200 SC	HT	RNBT	FBG	DV	IO	138-260		7	8	3290			4000	5000
20	2	X200 SC	HT	RNBT	FBG	DV	IO	290-330		7	8	3290			4550	5400
20	2	X200 SC	HT	RNBT	FBG	DV	IO	370	MRCR	7	8	3290			5250	6050
20	4	X215 BR	ST	RNBT	FBG		IO	140		7	7	2950			3600	4200
20	4	X215 BR	ST	RNBT	FBG	DV	OB			7	8	2100			1750	2100
20	4	X215 BR	ST	RNBT	FBG	DV	IO	138-260		7	8	3300			4050	5050
20	4	X215 BR	ST	RNBT	FBG	DV	IO	290-330		7	8	3300			4600	5400
20	4	X215 BR	ST	RNBT	FBG	DV	IO	370	MRCR	7	8	3300			5250	6050
20	4	X215 SC	ST	RNBT	FBG		IO	140		7	7	2950			3650	4250
20	4	X215 SC	ST	RNBT	FBG	DV	OB			7	8	2100			1850	2200
20	4	X215 SC	ST	RNBT	FBG	DV	IO	138-260		7	8	3300			4050	5050
20	4	X215 SC	ST	RNBT	FBG	DV	IO	290-330		7	8	3300			4600	5450
20	4	X215 SC	ST	RNBT	FBG	DV	IO	370	MRCR	7	8	3300			5300	6100
22	3	X230 SC	ST	CUD	FBG	DV	IO	138-260		8		3900			5400	6550
22	3	X230 SC	ST	CUD	FBG	DV	IO	290-330		8		3900			5950	7000
22	3	X230 SC	ST	CUD	FBG	DV	IO	370	MRCR	8		3900			6700	7650
22	3	X230 SC	ST	SPTCR	FBG		IO	140		8		3900			5250	6050
23	2	X230 Z	ST	CUD	FBG	DV	IO	138-260		8		4110			5900	7100
		IO 290-330 6400 7550, IO 370 MRCR 7150 8250, IO T138-T230													6700	8000
		IO T260 6900 8400, IO T290-T330 7750 9300, IO T370 MRCR													9350	10600
23	2	X230 Z	ST	CUD	FBG	SV	IO	T170	OMC	8		4110			6400	7350
23	2	X230 Z	HT	CUD	FBG	DV	IO	138-290		8		4260			6050	7550
		IO 330-370 6750 8400, IO T138-T260 6850 8550, IO T290-T330													7900	9450
		IO T370 MRCR 9450 10700														
23	2	X230 Z	ST	SPTCR	FBG	DV	IO	140		8		4110			5750	6600
24	10	X250 SE	ST	CR	FBG		IO	140		8		4500			6550	7550
24	10	X250 SE	ST	EXP	FBG	DV	IO	138-260		8		4500			6650	8250
24	10	X250 SE	ST	EXP	FBG	DV	IO	290-330		8		4500			7400	8750
24	10	X250 SE	ST	EXP	FBG	DV	IO	370	MRCR	8		4500			8150	9350
25	4	X255	ST	SPTCR	FBG		IO	140		8		4210			6350	7300
25	4	X255 SC	ST	SPTCR	FBG	DV	IO	138-230		8		4210			6450	7850
		IO 260-290 6950 8400, IO 330-370 7550 9300, IO T138-T230													8500	10400
		IO T260-T290 9300 11400, IO T330 MRCR 10300 11800, IO T370 VLVO													11900	13500
26	9	X270 SE	ST	CR	FBG		IO	140		8		5700			8250	9500
26	9	X270 SE	ST	EXP	FBG	DV	IO	138-230		8		5700			8300	10200
		IO 260-330 9100 11000, IO 370 MRCR 10200 11500, IO T138-T230													10400	12700
		IO T260-T330 11400 14200, IO T370 MRCR 13400 15200														
31		X310	ST	SPTCR	FBG		IO	T330		8		6250			16300	18500
		1984 BOATS														
16		X160 BR	ST	RNBT	FBG	SV	OB			6	11	1150			845	1000
16		X160 BR	ST	RNBT	FBG	SV	IO	117-188		6	11	1900			2200	2550
17	4	X180 BR	ST	RNBT	FBG	SV	OB			7	2	1300			970	1150
17	4	X180 BR	ST	RNBT	FBG	SV	IO	117-188		7	2	2150			2500	2950
17	6	X175 BR	ST	RNBT	FBG	DV	IO	117-188		7		2200			2550	2950
18	6	X190 BR	ST	RNBT	FBG	SV	IO	138-260		7	7	2960			3250	4000
18	6	X190 BR	ST	RNBT	FBG	SV	IO	290-340		7	7	2960			3750	4500
18	6	X190 BR	ST	RNBT	FBG	SV	IO	370	MRCR	7	7	2960			4450	5100
18	6	X190 SC	ST	RNBT	FBG	SV	IO	138-260		7	7	2960			3300	4050
18	6	X190 SC	ST	RNBT	FBG	SV	IO	290-340		7	7	2960			3750	4550
18	6	X190 SC	ST	RNBT	FBG	SV	IO	370	MRCR	7	7	2960			4450	5150
20		W200	OP	BASS	FBG	SV	OB			8		1400			1100	1300
20	2	X200 BR	ST	RNBT	FBG	DV	IO	138-260		7	8	3140			3800	4650
20	2	X200 BR	ST	RNBT	FBG	DV	IO	290-340		7	8	3140			4250	5150
20	2	X200 BR	ST	RNBT	FBG	DV	IO	370	MRCR	7	8	3140			4950	5700
20	2	X200 SC	ST	RNBT	FBG	DV	IO	138-260		7	8	3140			3750	4600
20	2	X200 SC	ST	RNBT	FBG	DV	IO	290-340		7	8	3140			4200	5100
20	2	X200 SC	ST	RNBT	FBG	DV	IO	370	MRCR	7	8	3140			4900	5650
20	2	X200 SC	HT	RNBT	FBG	DV	IO	138-260		7	8	3290			3850	4800
20	2	X200 SC	HT	RNBT	FBG	DV	IO	290-340		7	8	3290			4400	5250
20	2	X200 SC	HT	RNBT	FBG	DV	IO	370	MRCR	7	8	3290			5050	5800
20	4	X215 BR	ST	RNBT	FBG	DV	OB			7	8	2100			1650	1950
20	4	X215 BR	ST	RNBT	FBG	DV	IO	138-260		7	8	3300			3900	4750
20	4	X215 BR	ST	RNBT	FBG	DV	IO	290-340		7	8	3300			4400	5250
20	4	X215 BR	ST	RNBT	FBG	DV	IO	370	MRCR	7	8	3300			5050	5850
20	4	X215 SC	ST	RNBT	FBG	DV	OB			7	8	2100			1700	2000
20	4	X215 SC	ST	RNBT	FBG	DV	IO	138-260		7	8	3300			3950	4850
20	4	X215 SC	ST	RNBT	FBG	DV	IO	290-340		7	8	3300			4500	5300
20	4	X215 SC	ST	RNBT	FBG	DV	IO	370	MRCR	7	8	3300			5150	5900
22	3	X230 SC	ST	CUD	FBG	DV	IO	138-260		8		3900			5200	6350
22	3	X230 SC	ST	CUD	FBG	DV	IO	290-340		8		3900			5750	6750
22	3	X230 SC	ST	CUD	FBG	DV	IO	370	MRCR	8		3900			6450	7400
23	2	X230 Z	ST	CUD	FBG	DV	IO	138-260		8		4110			5700	6850
		IO 290-340 6200 7300, IO 370 MRCR 6900 7950, IO T138-T255													6450	7750
		IO T260 6650 8100, IO T290-T340 7500 8950, IO T370 MRCR													9000	10200

 CONTINUED ON NEXT PAGE

LOA FT IN	NAME AND/ OR MODEL		TOP/ RIG	BOAT TYPE	-HULL- MTL TP	----ENGINE--- TP # HP MFG	BEAM FT IN	WGT LBS	DRAFT FT IN	RETAIL LOW	RETAIL HIGH
				---- 1984 BOATS							
23	2 X230 Z		ST	CUD	FBG SV IO	T170-T185	8	4110		6150	7200
23	2 X230 Z		HT	CUD	FBG DV IO	138-290	8	4260		5850	7300
	IO 330-370	6500	8100,	IO	138-260	6600	8250, IO	T290-T340		7650	9150
	IO T370 MRCR	9150	10400								
24	10 X250 SE		ST	EXP	FBG DV IO	138-260	8	4500		6450	7950
	IO 290-340	7150	8450,	IO	370 MRCR	7850	9050, IO	T138-T255		7350	9000
	IO T260	7850	9400,	IO	T290-T340	8600	10200, IO	T370 MRCR		9900	11200
25	4 X255 SC		ST	SPTCR	FBG DV IO	138-255	8	4210		6250	7600
	IO 260-290	6700	8150,	IO	330-370	7300	9000, IO	T138-T255		8200	10100
	IO T260-T290	8950	11000,	IO	T330-T340	10400	11900, IO	T370 VLVO		11500	13100
26	9 X270 SE		ST	EXP	FBG DV IO	138-255	8	5700		8000	9900
	IO 260-340	8700	10700,	IO	370 MRCR	9800	11100, IO	T138-T255		10000	12300
	IO T260-T340	11000	13700,	IO	T370 MRCR	12900	14600				

....For earlier years, see the BUC Used Boat Price Guide, Volume 3

IMAGE BOAT COMPANY
LK HOPATCNG NJ 07849   COAST GUARD MFG ID- KRG See inside cover to adjust price for area

LOA FT IN	NAME AND/ OR MODEL	TOP/ RIG	BOAT TYPE	-HULL- MTL TP	----ENGINE--- TP # HP MFG	BEAM FT IN	WGT LBS	DRAFT FT IN	RETAIL LOW	RETAIL HIGH
			---- 1985 BOATS							
21	SHADOW 21	OP	RNBT	FBG DV OB		7 7	1350		4500	5150
21	SHADOW 21	OP	RNBT	FBG DV IO	260 MRCR	7 7	2500		6850	7900
21	SHADOW 21	OP	RNBT	FBG DV IB	260	7 7			8900	10100
21	SHADOW 21 AFT	OP	RNBT	FBG DV OB		7 7	1500		4900	5600
30	SHADOW 30 RAMWING	OP	RNBT	FBG CT OB		8	2800		31900	35400
30	SHADOW 30 RAMWING	OP	RNBT	FBG CT IO	T330-T440	8	3000		20100	24200
			---- 1984 BOATS							
21	SHADOW 21			OB					4500	5150
21	SHADOW 21	OP	RNBT	FBG DV OB		7 7	1350		4400	5050
21	SHADOW 21	OP	RNBT	FBG DV IO	260 MRCR	7 7	2500		6650	7600
21	SHADOW 21 AFT	OP	RNBT	FBG DV OB		7 7	1500		4800	5500
30	SHADOW 30 RAMWING	OP	RNBT	FBG CT OB		8	2800		19100	21200
30	SHADOW 30 RAMWING	OP	RNBT	FBG CT IO		8	3000		**	**
30	SHADOW 30 RAMWING	OP	RNBT	FBG CT IB	T330	8			30400	33800

....For earlier years, see the BUC Used Boat Price Guide, Volume 3

IMPULSE MARINE INC
DALLAS TX 75230   COAST GUARD MFG ID- IMM See inside cover to adjust price for area

LOA FT IN	NAME AND/ OR MODEL	TOP/ RIG	BOAT TYPE	-HULL- MTL TP	----ENGINE--- TP # HP MFG	BEAM FT IN	WGT LBS	DRAFT FT IN	RETAIL LOW	RETAIL HIGH
			---- 1993 BOATS							
21	IMPULSE 21	SLP	SAROD	F/S KL		8	1300	3 3	6300	7250
			---- 1992 BOATS							
21	IMPULSE 21	SLP	SA/OD	F/S KL		8	1300	3 4	6000	6900
			---- 1991 BOATS							
21	IMPULSE 21	SLP	SA/OD	F/S KL		8	1300	3 4	5650	6500
			---- 1990 BOATS							
21	IMPULSE 21	SLP	SA/OD	F/S KL		8	1300	3 4	5350	6150
			---- 1989 BOATS							
21	IMPULSE 21	SLP	SA/OD	F/S KL		8 6	1300	3 4	5100	5850
21	IMPULSE 21	SLP	SAROD	F/S KL		8 6	1300	3 4	5100	5850
			---- 1987 BOATS							
26	IMPULSE 26	SLP	SA/OD	F/S KL		8 6	2730	4 9	8800	10000
			---- 1986 BOATS							
21	IMPULSE-EAGLE	SLP	SA/RC	KL		8	1200	3 9	4150	4850
26	IMPULSE 26	SLP	SA/OD	F/S KL		8 6	2730	4 9	8250	9500
			---- 1985 BOATS							
26	IMPULSE 26	SLP	SA/OD	F/S KL IB	9D YAN	8 6	2750	4 9	8900	10100

INACE SHIPYARD
FT LAUDERDALE FL 33316   See inside cover to adjust price for area

For more recent years, see the BUC Used Boat Price Guide, Volume 1

LOA FT IN	NAME AND/ OR MODEL	TOP/ RIG	BOAT TYPE	-HULL- MTL TP	----ENGINE--- TP # HP MFG	BEAM FT IN	WGT LBS	DRAFT FT IN	RETAIL LOW	RETAIL HIGH
			---- 1996 BOATS							
78	INACE	FB	MY	AL DS IB	T900D DD	19		4 6	**	**

INDEPENDENCE BOAT WORKS
INDEPENDNCE WI 54747   See inside cover to adjust price for area

LOA FT IN	NAME AND/ OR MODEL		TOP/ RIG	BOAT TYPE	-HULL- MTL TP	----ENGINE--- TP # HP MFG	BEAM FT IN	WGT LBS	DRAFT FT IN	RETAIL LOW	RETAIL HIGH
				---- 1986 BOATS							
36	LIBERTY-BELL		HT	HB	STL	IO	MRCR 14			17400	19800
	IO VLVO	18100	20100, IO	T	MRCR	19400	21600, IO T		VLVO	20100	22300
40	LIBERTY-BELL		HT	HB	STL	IO	MRCR 14			19100	21200
	IO VLVO	19400	21600, IO	T	MRCR	20400	22600, IO T		VLVO	21000	23300
44	LIBERTY-BELL		HT	HB	STL	IO	MRCR 14			21000	23300
	IO VLVO	21300	23600, IO	T	MRCR	22200	24700, IO T		VLVO	22800	25300
				---- 1985 BOATS							
36	LIBERTY-BELL		HT	HB	STL	IO	MRCR 14			17000	19300
	IO VLVO	17300	19700, IO	T	MRCR	19000	21100, IO T		VLVO	19600	21800
40	LIBERTY-BELL		HT	HB	STL	IO	MRCR 14			18700	20700
	IO VLVO	19000	21100, IO	T	MRCR	20300	22500, IO T		VLVO	20500	22800
44	LIBERTY-BELL		HT	HB	STL	IO	MRCR 14			20500	22700
	IO VLVO	20800	23100, IO	T	MRCR	21700	24100, IO T		VLVO	22300	24700

INDEPENDENCE CHERUBINI CO
ANNAPOLIS MD 21403-1328 COAST GUARD MFG ID- CVJ See inside cover to adjust price for area
FORMERLY CHERUBINI BOAT CO INC

For more recent years, see the BUC Used Boat Price Guide, Volume 1

LOA FT IN	NAME AND/ OR MODEL	TOP/ RIG	BOAT TYPE	-HULL- MTL TP	----ENGINE--- TP # HP MFG	BEAM FT IN	WGT LBS	DRAFT FT IN	RETAIL LOW	RETAIL HIGH
			---- 1991 BOATS							
44	CHERUBINI 44 CRUISE	KTH	SAIL	FBG KL IB	66D YAN	12	28000	4 10	324000	356000
48	CHERUBINI STAYSAIL	SCH	SAIL	FBG KL IB	88D YAN	13	37500	5	394000	433000
62	CHERUBINI STAYSAIL	SCH	SAIL	FBG KL IB	170D YAN	14 6	65000	6	1.025M	1.115M
62	CHERUBINI STAYSAIL	SCH	SAIL	FBG KL IB	170D YAN	14 6	65000	6	1.040M	1.130M
			---- 1986 BOATS							
44	CHERUBINI 44	SCH	SA/CR FBG KL IB		72D BENZ	12	28000	4 10	219500	241000
44	CHERUBINI 44	KTH	SA/CR FBG KL IB		72D BENZ	12	28000	4 10	232500	255500
48	9 CHERUBINI 48	SCH	SA/CR FBG KL IB		88D BENZ	13	37000	5	289500	318000
48	9 CHERUBINI 48	KTH	SA/CR FBG KL IB		88D BENZ	13	37000	5	307500	338000
			---- 1985 BOATS							
44	CHERUBINI 44 CUST	KTH	SA/CR FBG KL IB		72D BENZ	12	28000	4 10	228000	250500
44	CHERUBINI 44 STD	KTH	SA/CR FBG KL IB		72D BENZ	12	28000	4 10	207000	227500
48	9 CHERUBINI 48 CUST	SCH	SA/CR FBG KL IB		88D BENZ	13	37000	5	288500	317000
48	9 CHERUBINI 48 STD	SCH	SA/CR FBG KL IB		88D BENZ	13	37000	5	252500	277500
			---- 1984 BOATS							
44	CHERUBINI 44 CUST	KTH	SA/CR FBG KC IB		50D BMW	12	28000	4 10	214000	235000
44	CHERUBINI 44 STD	KTH	SA/CR FBG KC IB		50D BMW	12	28000	4 10	194000	213500
48	9 CHERUBINI 48 CUST	SCH	SA/CR FBG KL IB		75D BMW	13	37000	5	271500	298500
48	9 CHERUBINI 48 STD	SCH	SA/CR FBG KL IB		75D BMW	13	37000	5	238000	261500

....For earlier years, see the BUC Used Boat Price Guide, Volume 3

INDIAN RIVER BOAT MFG CO
DIV OF DAYTONA MARINE IND INC   See inside cover to adjust price for area
NEW SMYRNA BEACH FL 321 COAST GUARD MFG ID- JHR

LOA FT IN	NAME AND/ OR MODEL	TOP/ RIG	BOAT TYPE	-HULL- MTL TP	----ENGINE--- TP # HP MFG	BEAM FT IN	WGT LBS	DRAFT FT IN	RETAIL LOW	RETAIL HIGH
			---- 1984 BOATS							
16	V-16	OP	OFF	FBG SV OB		6 8	950		1700	2000
16	VB-16	OP	RNBT	FBG SV OB		6 8	1000		1800	2100
18	10 V-18	OP	OFF	FBG SV OB		7 2	1100		2150	2500

....For earlier years, see the BUC Used Boat Price Guide, Volume 3

INFINITY POWER BOATS
COLUMBIA SC 29260   See inside cover to adjust price for area

LOA FT IN	NAME AND/ OR MODEL	TOP/ RIG	BOAT TYPE	-HULL- MTL TP	----ENGINE--- TP # HP MFG	BEAM FT IN	WGT LBS	DRAFT FT IN	RETAIL LOW	RETAIL HIGH
			--------- 1994	BOATS						
18 1	CENTER CONSOLE 1860	OP	CTRCN	FBG SV	OB	8	1800		3900	4550
24 11	258 WA	OP	CUD	FBG SV	IO 235 MRCR	8 2	4400		9350	10600
26	CIGARETTE 26	OP	RNBT	FBG SV	IO T300 MRCR	8 2			11900	13500

INFINITY YACHTS
DEERFIELD BEACH FL 3344 COAST GUARD MFG ID- IYI See inside cover to adjust price for area

For more recent years, see the BUC Used Boat Price Guide, Volume 1

LOA FT IN	NAME AND/ OR MODEL	TOP/ RIG	BOAT TYPE	-HULL- MTL TP	----ENGINE--- TP # HP MFG	BEAM FT IN	WGT LBS	DRAFT FT IN	RETAIL LOW	RETAIL HIGH
			--------- 1992	BOATS						
56 6	SPORT YACHT	OP	SPTCR	FBG SV	IB T760D GM	14 6	30000	3 1	351500	386500
75	MOTOR YACHT	FB	MY	FBG SV	IB T15CD GM	21 3	80000	3 6	**	**
			--------- 1991	BOATS						
56 6	SPORT YACHT	OP	SPTCR	FBG SV	IB T760D GM	14 6	30000	3 1	335500	368500
74	MOTOR YACHT	FB	MY	FBG SV	IB T15CD GM	21 3	80000	3 6	**	**
			--------- 1988	BOATS						
50	COMMUTER	FB		FBG SV	IO R330D FORD	14	22000	3	180500	198000
67	SPORT FISHERMAN	FB	SF	FBG SV	IO T450D GM	21	33000	3	407500	448000
67	SPORT YACHT	FB		FBG SV	IO T450D GM	21	33000	3	407500	448000
75	YACHT FISHERMAN	FB	YTFS	FBG	JT T960D MWM	21 3	80000	3 6	**	**
76	INFINITY MOTOR YACHT	FB	MY	FBG DV	JT Q11CD MWM	21 3	72000	3 3	**	**
76	INFINITY MOTOR YACHT	FB	MY	FBG SV	JT T800D MAN	21 3	65000	3 1	**	**
			--------- 1987	BOATS						
50	COMMUTER	FB		FBG SV	IO R350D FORD	14	22000	3	173500	191000
67	SPORT FISHERMAN	FB	SF	FBG SV	IO T450D GM	21	33000	3	387500	426000
67	SPORT YACHT	FB		FBG SV	IO T450D GM	21	33000	3	387500	426000
76	INFINITY MOTOR YACHT	FB	MY	FBG DV	JT Q13CD FORD	23	42000	4	**	**
76	INFINITY MOTOR YACHT	FB	MY	FBG SV	JT T11CD FORD	23	42000	4	**	**

INITIAL MARINE CORP INC
SANFORD FL 32771   COAST GUARD MFG ID- VMP See inside cover to adjust price for area
FORMERLY VELOCITY MARINE INC

For more recent years, see the BUC Used Boat Price Guide, Volume 1

LOA FT IN	NAME AND/ OR MODEL	TOP/ RIG	BOAT TYPE	-HULL- MTL TP	----ENGINE--- TP # HP MFG	BEAM FT IN	WGT LBS	DRAFT FT IN	RETAIL LOW	RETAIL HIGH
			--------- 1986	BOATS						
21 8	TUNA-TEASER 22	OP	RNBT	F/S DV	OB	7 10	1850		11600	13200
21 8	VELOCITY 22	OP	RNBT	F/S DV	OB	7 10	1580		10200	11600
21 8	VELOCITY 22	OP	RNBT	F/S DV	IO 260 MRCR	7 10	2540		5000	5700
21 8	VELOCITY 22	OP	RNBT	F/S DV	IO 290-300 MRCR	7 10	2540		5500	6300
21 8	VELOCITY 22	OP	RNBT	F/S DV	IO 400 MRCR	7 10	2540		7150	8200
30	SPORT CRUISER	OP	CR	F/S DV	OB	8	4200		42600	47300
30	SPORT CRUISER	OP	CR	F/S DV	IO 370 MRCR	8	6100		16200	18400
30	SPORT CRUISER	OP	CR	F/S DV	IO T260-T330	8	6100		16900	20800
30	SPORT CRUISER	OP	CR	F/S DV	IO T400-T440	8	6100		20700	24400
30	TUNA-TEASER 30	OP	CR	F/S DV	OB	8	4500		42600	47300
30	TUNA-TEASER 30	TT	CR	F/S DV	OB	8	4500		42700	47400
39 2	SPORT CRUISER	OP	CR	F/S DV	OB	8	6800		**	**
39 2	SPORT CRUISER	OP	CR	F/S DV	IO T370 MRCR	8	9700		42900	47700
	IO T375 KAAM 43700 48600, IO T400 MRCR 44600 49500, IO T440 MRCR 47600 52300									
	IO T525 53100 58400									
			--------- 1985	BOATS						
21 8	VELOCITY 22	OP	RNBT	F/S DV	OB	7 10	1580		9900	11300
21 8	VELOCITY 22	OP	RNBT	F/S DV	IO 260 MRCR	7 10	2540		4750	5450
30	VELOCITY 30		SPTCR	F/S DV	OB	8	4200		41500	46100
30	VELOCITY 30		SPTCR	F/S DV	IO T330	8	6800		18500	20500
38	VELOCITY 40		SPTCR	F/S DV	OB	8 2	6200		51100	56200
38	VELOCITY 40		SPTCR	F/S DV	IO T330	8 2	8200		35100	39000
42	VELOCITY 42		SF	F/W DV	IB T400	14	23000		81300	89300
			--------- 1984	BOATS						
21 8	VELOCITY 22	OP	RNBT	F/S DV	OB	7 10	1511	11	9300	10600
21 8	VELOCITY 22	OP	RNBT	F/S DV	IO 260 MRCR	7 10	2600	1 2	4600	5250
30	VELOCITY SPTCR	ST	OFF	F/S DV	OB	8	4200	1 4	40800	45300
30	VELOCITY SPTCR	ST	OFF	F/S DV	IO T330 MRCR	8	7100	1 7	18000	20000
38 10	VELOCITY SPTCR	ST	OFF	F/S DV	IO T370 MRCR	8	8200	2 1	37600	41700
42	CUSTOM	FB	SF	F/W DV	IB T300D VLVO	14	18000	3	79500	87400

....For earlier years, see the BUC Used Boat Price Guide, Volume 3

INTER CATAMARANS
SANTA ANA CA 92705   See inside cover to adjust price for area

For more recent years, see the BUC Used Boat Price Guide, Volume 1

LOA FT IN	NAME AND/ OR MODEL	TOP/ RIG	BOAT TYPE	-HULL- MTL TP	----ENGINE--- TP # HP MFG	BEAM FT IN	WGT LBS	DRAFT FT IN	RETAIL LOW	RETAIL HIGH
			--------- 1996	BOATS						
18	INTER 18	SLP	SAROD	F/S CT		8 6	374		7700	8850

INTER-SERVICE INC
HIGH POINT NC 27260   See inside cover to adjust price for area

LOA FT IN	NAME AND/ OR MODEL	TOP/ RIG	BOAT TYPE	-HULL- MTL TP	----ENGINE--- TP # HP MFG	BEAM FT IN	WGT LBS	DRAFT FT IN	RETAIL LOW	RETAIL HIGH
			--------- 1987	BOATS						
16 9	FLYING-CRUISER-JOLLE	SLP	SAIL	FBG CB		6 7	440	8	3200	3700
16 9	FLYING-CRUISER-S	SLP	SAIL	FBG CB		6 7	550	8	3550	4100
			--------- 1986	BOATS						
16 9	FLYING-CRUISER-JOLLE	SLP	SAIL	FBG CB		6 7	550	8	3300	3850
16 9	FLYING-CRUISER	SLP	SAIL	FBG CB		6 7	440	8	3000	3450
			--------- 1985	BOATS						
16 9	FLYING-CRUISER-JOLLE	SLP	SAIL	FBG CB		6 7	440	8	2800	3250
16 9	FLYING-CRUISER-S	SLP	SAIL	FBG CB		6 7	550	8	3100	3650

INTERCANTIERI OF FLORIDA
MIAMI FL 33131   See inside cover to adjust price for area

LOA FT IN	NAME AND/ OR MODEL	TOP/ RIG	BOAT TYPE	-HULL- MTL TP	----ENGINE--- TP # HP MFG	BEAM FT IN	WGT LBS	DRAFT FT IN	RETAIL LOW	RETAIL HIGH
			--------- 1986	BOATS						
55	MAIORA 55		MY	FBG SV	IB T710D	15	41800		241000	265000
57	MAIORA 57		MY	FBG SV	IB T710D	17 6	61600		302000	332000
77	MAIORA 77		MY	FBG SV	IB T870D	20 6	83600		**	**
			--------- 1985	BOATS						
53	MAIORA 50		MY	FBG SV	IB T575D	17	45000		219500	241500
53	MAIORA 53		OFF	FBG SV	IB T650D	15	38000		206000	226500
63	MAIORA 60		MY	FBG SV	IB T700D	18	59000		310500	341500

INTERNATIONAL CATAMARAN INC
NEW SMYRNA BEACH FL   See inside cover to adjust price for area

LOA FT IN	NAME AND/ OR MODEL	TOP/ RIG	BOAT TYPE	-HULL- MTL TP	----ENGINE--- TP # HP MFG	BEAM FT IN	WGT LBS	DRAFT FT IN	RETAIL LOW	RETAIL HIGH
			--------- 1990	BOATS						
28	INTERCAT 1500 SHOAL	SLP	SA/CR	FBG CT	OB	14 4	5800	2 10	33330	37000
35	NEW WORLD 35	SLP	SA/CR	FBG CT	IB T 18D	16 3	12000	2 8	75800	83300

INTERNATIONAL CENTER
PT CLINTON OH 43452   See inside cover to adjust price for area

LOA FT IN	NAME AND/ OR MODEL	TOP/ RIG	BOAT TYPE	-HULL- MTL TP	----ENGINE--- TP # HP MFG	BEAM FT IN	WGT LBS	DRAFT FT IN	RETAIL LOW	RETAIL HIGH
			--------- 1985	BOATS						
31 9	UNION 32		TRWL	DS IB	25D VLVO	10 10	11500	4 10	36800	40800
39 6	KHA-SHING 40		TRWL	DS IB	T165D VLVO	14 1	23000	4 1	86800	95400

INTERNATIONAL MARINE INC
INGLEWOOD CA 90302   COAST GUARD MFG ID- HMS See inside cover to adjust price for area
FORMERLY H M S MARINE INC

For more recent years, see the BUC Used Boat Price Guide, Volume 1

LOA FT IN	NAME AND/ OR MODEL	TOP/ RIG	BOAT TYPE	-HULL- MTL TP	----ENGINE--- TP # HP MFG	BEAM FT IN	WGT LBS	DRAFT FT IN	RETAIL LOW	RETAIL HIGH
			--------- 1996	BOATS						
18 9	WESTWIGHT POTTER 19	SLP	SACAC	FBG KL	OB	7 6	1225	3 7	8200	9450
			--------- 1995	BOATS						
18 9	WESTWIGHT POTTER 19	SLP	SACAC	FBG KL		7 6	1225	3 7	7800	8950
			--------- 1994	BOATS						
19	WESTWIGHT POTTER	SLP	SACAC	FBG KL		7 6	1200	10	7350	8450

LOA FT IN	NAME AND/ OR MODEL	TOP/ RIG	BOAT TYPE	HULL MTL TP	TP	ENGINE # HP	MFG	BEAM FT IN	WGT LBS	DRAFT FT IN	RETAIL LOW	RETAIL HIGH
						1993 BOATS						
19	WESTWIGHT POTTER	SLP	SACAC	FBG	KL			7 6	1200	10	6950	8000
						1988 BOATS						
19	WEST WIGHT POTTER 19	SLP	SAIL	FBG	CB OB			7 6	1250	3 7	5400	6200
						1987 BOATS						
19	WEST WIGHT POTTER 19	SLP	SAIL	FBG	CB OB			7 6	1250	3 7	5150	5900
						1986 BOATS						
19	WEST-WIGHT-POTTER	SLP	SA/CR	FBG	SK OB			7 6	1250	3 7	4850	5600
						1985 BOATS						
19	WEST WIGHT POTTER 19	SLP	SAIL	FBG	CB OB			7 6	1250	3 7	4650	5300
						1984 BOATS						
19	WEST-WIGHT-POTTER 19	SLP	SAIL	FBG	CB OB			7 6	1250	6	4400	5050

....For earlier years, see the BUC Used Boat Price Guide, Volume 3

INTREPID POWERBOATS INC
LARGO FL 33773

See inside cover to adjust price for area

For more recent years, see the BUC Used Boat Price Guide, Volume 1

LOA FT IN	NAME AND/ OR MODEL	TOP/ RIG	BOAT TYPE	HULL MTL TP	TP	ENGINE # HP	MFG	BEAM FT IN	WGT LBS	DRAFT FT IN	RETAIL LOW	RETAIL HIGH
						1996 BOATS						
26	26 WALKAROUND	HT	EXPSF	FBG	DV OB			9 1	3000	2	30700	34100
28 9	289	OP	CUD	FBG	DV OB			9 1	4200	2	44200	49100
32 2	322	TT	CUD	FBG	SV OB			9 1	4500	2	58900	64700
32 2	CUDDY 322	OP	CUD	FBG	DV OB			9 1	4500	2	58900	64700
33 9	CENTER CONSOLE 339	OP	CTRCN	FBG	DV OB			10	6000	2	68700	75500
33 9	WALKAROUND 339	OP	CUD	FBG	DV OB			10	6500	2	68700	75500
33 9	WALKAROUND 339	TH	CUD	FBG	DV OB			10	6500	2	68700	75500
35 6	CUDDY 356	HT	CUD	KEV	DV OB			10 6	6500	2	81100	89100
35 6	MODEL 356	OP	CUD	FBG	DV OB			10 6	6500	2	81100	89100
						1995 BOATS						
20 6	INTREPID 20	OP	CTRCN	F/S	DV OB			8 6	950	9	7600	8750
24 6	INTREPID 23	OP	CUD	F/S	DV OB			8 6	2500	2	20400	22700
24 6	INTREPID 23	OP	OPFSH	F/S	DV OB			8 6	2200	2	18800	20900
28 4	INTREPID 26	OP	CUD	F/S	DV OB			8 6	2900	2	40100	44600
28 4	INTREPID 26	OP	OPFSH	F/S	DV OB			8 6	2600	2	39700	44100
32 1	INTREPID 30	OP	CUD	F/S	DV OB			8 6	3300	2	54200	59600
33	INTREPID 31	OP	CUD	F/S	DV OB			10	5000	2	63300	69500
33	INTREPID 33	OP	CUD	KEV	DV OB			10	5500	2	75400	82900
35 6	INTREPID 35	OP	SF	KEV	DV OB			10 7	8500	2 2	76500	84100
37 6	INTREPID 37	OP	SF	KEV	DV IB	T900		12	14000	2 6	128000	141000
						1994 BOATS						
20 6	INTREPID 20	OP	CTRCN	F/S	DV OB			8 6	950	9	7250	8350
24 6	INTREPID 23	OP	CUD	F/S	DV OB			8 6	2500	2	19500	21700
24 6	INTREPID 23	OP	OPFSH	F/S	DV OB			8 6	2200	2	17600	20300
28 4	INTREPID 26	OP	CUD	F/S	DV OB			8 6	2900	2	38400	42600
28 4	INTREPID 26	OP	OPFSH	F/S	DV OB			8 6	2600	2	37800	42000
32 1	INTREPID 30	OP	CUD	F/S	DV OB			8 6	3300	2	51800	57000
35	INTREPID 33	OP	CUD	F/S	DV OB			10 6	5500	2	72100	79300
36 6	INTREPID 35	OP	SF	KEV	DV OB			10 7	8500	2	73100	80400
						1993 BOATS						
23	INTREPID VIPER 23	OP	CUD	F/S	DV IO	215	MRCR	8 6	3500	2	13800	15700
24 6	INTREPID 23	OP	CUD	F/S	DV OB			8 6	2500	2	18900	21000
24 6	INTREPID 23	OP	OPFSH	F/S	DV OB			8 6	2200	2	16800	19100
28 4	INTREPID 26	OP	CUD	F/S	DV OB			8 6	2900	2	36800	40900
28 4	INTREPID 26	OP	OPFSH	F/S	DV OB			8 6	2600	2	36100	40100
32 1	INTREPID 30	OP	CUD	F/S	DV OB			8 6	3300	2	43700	48600
34 6	INTREPID 35	OP	CUD	F/S	DV OB			10 6	5500	2	61900	68000
36 6	INTREPID 35	OP	SF	KEV	DV IB	T700D		10 7	8500	2 2	118000	129500
37 4	INTREPID 36X	OP	SF	KEV	DV IB	T300D		10 8	12000	3 1	66700	73300
41 8	EURO 39	OP	EXP	F/S	DV OB	465	MRCR	8 6			97800	107500
41	EURO 39	OP	EXP	F/S	DV IB	T600D	SETK	8 6			198500	218000
						1992 BOATS						
24 6	INTREPID 23	OP	CUD	F/S	DV OB			8 6	2500	2	18200	20200
24 6	INTREPID 23	OP	OPFSH	F/S	DV OB			8 6	2175	2	16000	18200
26 4	INTREPID 26	OP	CUD	F/S	DV OB			8 6	2900	2	27100	30000
26 4	INTREPID 26	OP	CUD	F/S	DV IO	300	MRCR	8 6	3000	2 6	17400	19800
26 4	INTREPID 26	OP	CUD	F/S	DV IO	230D	VLVO	8 6	3200	2 6	19200	21300
26 4	INTREPID 26	OP	OPFSH	F/S	DV OB			8 6	2400	2	25900	28800
29 11	INTREPID 30	OP	CUD	F/S	DV OB			8 4	2900	2	42000	46700
37 6	EVOLUTION 38	TT	EXP	F/S	DV IB	T450D	CAT	12	14000	2 6	119000	131000
37 6	EVOLUTION 38	TT	EXP	F/S	DV IB	T450D	MERL	12	14000	2 6	114500	126000
						1991 BOATS						
24 6	INTREPID 23	OP	CUD	F/S	DV OB			8 6	2500	2	17100	19500
24 6	INTREPID 23	OP	OPFSH	F/S	DV OB			8 6	2175	2	15400	17500
26 4	INTREPID 26	OP	CUD	F/S	DV OB			8 6	2600	2	26100	29000
26 4	INTREPID 26	OP	OPFSH	F/S	DV OB			8 6	2400	2	24800	27600
29 11	INTREPID 30	OP	CUD	F/S	DV OB			8 4	2900	2	40500	45000
37 6	EVOLUTION	TT	EXP	F/S	DV IB	T450D	CAT	12	14000	2 6	113500	125000
37 6	EVOLUTION	TT	EXP	F/S	DV IB	T450D	CUM	12	14000	2 6	108000	119000
						1990 BOATS						
24 6	INTREPID 23	OP	CUD	F/S	DV OB			8 6	2500	2	16500	18800
24 6	INTREPID 23	OP	OPFSH	F/S	DV OB			8 6	2175	2	14900	16900
26 4	INTREPID 26	OP	CUD	F/S	DV OB			8 6	2600	2	25200	28000
26 4	INTREPID 26	OP	OPFSH	F/S	DV OB			8 6	2400	2	23800	26400
29 11	INTREPID 30	OP	CUD	F/S	DV OB			8 4	2900	2	39100	43400
						1989 BOATS						
24 6	INTREPID 23	OP	CUD	F/S	DV OB			8 6	2500	2	16000	18200
24 6	INTREPID 23	OP	OPFSH	F/S	DV OB			8 6	2175	2	14400	16300
26 4	INTREPID 26	OP	CUD	F/S	DV OB			8 6	2600	2	24300	27000
26 4	INTREPID 26	OP	OPFSH	F/S	DV OB			8 6	2400	2	23000	25600
29 11	INTREPID 30	OP	CUD	F/S	DV OB			8 4	2900	2	37800	41900
						1988 BOATS						
26 4	INTREPID 26	OP	CUD	F/S	DV OB			8 6	2600	2	23500	26100
26 4	INTREPID 26	OP	OPFSH	F/S	DV OB			8 6	2400	2	22100	24600
29 11	INTREPID 30	OP	CUD	F/S	DV OB			8 4	2900	2	36500	40600
						1987 BOATS						
26 4	INTREPID 26	OP	OPFSH	F/S	DV OB			8 4	2400	2	21600	24000
29 11	INTREPID 30	OP	CUD	F/S	DV OB			8 4	2900	2	35400	39400
						1985 BOATS						
30	INTREPID 30	OP	CUD	F/S	DV OB			8 4	2400	8 4	33700	37500
30	INTREPID 30	OP	CUD	F/S	DV IB	260	VLVO	8 4	3700	8 4	20600	22900

INTREPID YACHTS
E TAUNTON MA 02718   COAST GUARD MFG ID- CPD See inside cover to adjust price for area

LOA FT IN	NAME AND/ OR MODEL	TOP/ RIG	BOAT TYPE	HULL MTL TP	TP	ENGINE # HP	MFG	BEAM FT IN	WGT LBS	DRAFT FT IN	RETAIL LOW	RETAIL HIGH
						1986 BOATS						
40	INTREPID 40 AFT CPT	SLP	SA/CR	FBG	KL IB	51D	PERK	12 7	20000	5 8	86400	94900
40	INTREPID 40 CTR CPT	SLP	SA/CR	FBG	KL IB	51D	PERK	12 7	20000	5 8	91900	101000
						1985 BOATS						
40	INTREPID 40 AFT CPT	SLP	SA/CR	FBG	KL IB	51D	PERK	12 7	20000	5 8	81500	89500
40	INTREPID 40 CTR CPT	SLP	SA/CR	FBG	KL IB	51D	PERK	12 7	20000	5 8	85300	93700
						1984 BOATS						
40	INTREPID 40 AFT CPT	SLP	SA/CR	FBG	KL IB	46D	PERK	12 7	20000	5 8	75700	83200
40	INTREPID 40 CTR CPT	SLP	SA/CR	FBG	KL IB	46D	PERK	12 7	20000	5 8	80400	88300

....For earlier years, see the BUC Used Boat Price Guide, Volume 3

INVADER MARINE INC
GIDDINGS TX 78942   COAST GUARD MFG ID- ILP See inside cover to adjust price for area
FORMERLY INVADER BOATS INC

LOA FT IN	NAME AND/ OR MODEL	TOP/ RIG	BOAT TYPE	HULL MTL TP	TP	ENGINE # HP	MFG	BEAM FT IN	WGT LBS	DRAFT FT IN	RETAIL LOW	RETAIL HIGH
						1995 BOATS						
16 5	VIRADA V164	OP	B/R	FBG	DV OB			7 2	1500		2350	2750
16 5	VIRADA V165	OP	B/R	FBG	DV OB	135	MRCR	7 2	1920		4850	5550
16 6	REEFRUNNER V161	OP	FSH	FBG	DV OB			7 2	1250		1950	2300
16 6	REEFRUNNER V171	OP	FSH	FBG	DV OB			7 2	1500		2300	2650
17 3	REEFRUNNER V183	OP	CTRCN	FBG	DV OB			7 1	1800		2650	3050
18 6	VIRADA V180	OP	B/R	FBG	DV OB			8	2000		2950	3400
18 6	VIRADA V185	OP	B/R	FBG	DV IO	180	MRCR	8	2500		6850	7900
18 8	ALPHA V196	OP	CUD	FBG	DV OB			7 7	2000		2950	3400
18 8	ALPHA V197	OP	CUD	FBG	DV IO	180	MRCR	7 7	2700		7500	8650
19 6	REEFRUNNER V191	OP	FSH	FBG	DV OB			8	2000		3050	3550
20 6	ALPHA V210	OP	CUD	FBG	DV IO	180	MRCR	7 6	3000		8300	9550
20 6	VIRADA V214	OP	B/R	FBG	DV OB			8	2100		6850	7850
20 6	VIRADA V216	OP	B/R	FBG	DV IO	205	MRCR	8	2800		7800	8950
20 7	VIRADA V204	OP	CUD	FBG	DV IO	205	MRCR	8	2700		8200	9400
20 7	VIRADA V215	OP	CUD	FBG	DV IO	205	MRCR	8	2785		8350	9550
21	REEFRUNNER V212	OP	FSH	FBG	DV OB			8	2700		8250	9500
21	REEFRUNNER V213	OP	FSH	FBG	DV OB			8	2700		7950	9100
23 2	REEFRUNNER V244	OP	FSH	FBG	DV OB			8	3500		11500	13000
23 2	REEFRUNNER V245	OP	FSH	FBG	DV IO	205	MRCR	8	3300		12500	14200
23 2	REEFRUNNER V245B	OP	FSH	FBG	DV OB			8	3300		11000	12500
23 7	VIRADA V240 AC	OP	SPTCR	FBG	DV IO	235	MRCR	8 6	6300		17000	19400
25 10	VIRADA V265 AC	OP	SPTCR	FBG	DV IO	300	MRCR	8 6	6300		20900	23200
29 6	VIRADA V300	OP	SPTCR	FBG	DV IO	T180	MRCR	10	8000		28900	32200

CONTINUED ON NEXT PAGE

INVADER MARINE INC -CONTINUED See inside cover to adjust price for area

LOA FT	LOA IN	NAME AND/ OR MODEL	TOP/ RIG	BOAT TYPE	HULL MTL	HULL TP	ENGINE TP	ENGINE # HP	ENGINE MFG	BEAM FT	BEAM IN	WGT LBS	DRAFT FT IN	RETAIL LOW	RETAIL HIGH
		1994 BOATS													
16	5	VIRADA V164	OP	B/R	FBG	DV	OB			7	2	1500		2250	2600
16	5	VIRADA V165	OP	B/R	FBG	DV	IO	115	MRCR	7	2	1920		4550	5200
16	6	REEFRUNNER V161	OP	FSH	FBG	DV	OB			6	2	1250		1850	2200
16	9	REEFRUNNER V171	OP	FSH	FBG	DV	OB			7	2	1500		2200	2550
17	3	REEFRUNNER V183	OP	CTRCN	FBG	DV	OB			7	1	1800		2500	2900
17	6	CLASSIC 18	OP	CR	FBG	DV	IO	250	MRCR	7	3	2200		6050	6950
18	6	VIRADA V180	OP	B/R	FBG	DV	OB			8		2000		2800	3250
18	6	VIRADA V185	OP	B/R	FBG	DV	IO	180	MRCR	8		2500		6400	7350
18	8	ALPHA V196	OP	CUD	FBG	DV	OB			7	7	2000		2800	3250
18	8	ALPHA V197	OP	CUD	FBG	DV	IO	115	MRCR	7	7	2700		6900	7950
19	4	REEFRUNNER V191	OP	FSH	FBG	DV	OB			8		2000		2850	3350
20	6	ALPHA V210	OP	CUD	FBG	DV	IO	190	MRCR	7	6	3000		7750	8950
20	6	VIRADA V214	OP	B/R	FBG	DV	OB			8		2100		6500	7450
20	6	VIRADA V216	OP	B/R	FBG	DV	IO	115	MRCR	8		2800		7150	8200
20	7	VIRADA V204	OP	CUD	FBG	DV	IO	190	MRCR	8		2700		7600	8750
20	7	VIRADA V215	OP	CUD	FBG	DV	IO	190	MRCR	8		2785		7750	8900
21		REEFRUNNER V212	OP	FSH	FBG	DV	OB			8		2700		7850	9050
21		REEFRUNNER V213	OP	FSH	FBG	DV	OB			8		2500		7450	8550
23	2	REEFRUNNER V244	OP	FSH	FBG	DV	OB			8		3500		10900	12400
23	2	REEFRUNNER V245	OP	FSH	FBG	DV	IO	190	MRCR	8		3800		11600	13200
23	2	REEFRUNNER V245B	OP	FSH	FBG	DV	OB			8		3300		10500	11900
23	7	VIRADA V240 AC	OP	SPTCR	FBG	DV	IO	250	MRCR	8	6	5700		16000	18200
25		VIRADA V250	OP	CUD	FBG	DV	IO	300	MRCR	8		4500		14700	16700
25	10	VIRADA V265 AC	OP	SPTCR	FBG	DV	IO	250	MRCR	8	6	6300		18900	21000
29	6	VIRADA V300	OP	SPTCR	FBG	DV	IO	T180	MRCR	10		8000		27000	30000
		1993 BOATS													
16	5	ALPHA V164	OP	B/R	FBG	DV	OB			7	6	1150		1650	1950
16	5	VIRADA V165	OP	B/R	FBG	DV	IO	115	MRCR	7	6	1775		4150	4800
17	3	FISHERMAN V183	OP	CTRCN	FBG	DV	OB			6	5	1200		1700	2050
17	4	VIRADA V177	OP	B/R	FBG	DV	IO	115	MRCR	7	6	2250		5000	5750
17	6	CLASSIC 18	OP	CR	FBG	DV	IO	200	MRCR	7	3	1920		5000	5750
18	3	ALPHA V186	OP	B/R	FBG	DV	OB			7	1	1200		1800	2100
18	4	ALPHA V187	OP	B/R	FBG	DV	IO	200	MRCR	7	1	2400		5450	6250
18	6	FISH & SKI V184	OP	RNBT	FBG	SV	OB			7	2	1400		2050	2450
18	8	ALPHA V196	OP	CUD	FBG	DV	OB			7	7	1730		2400	2800
18	8	ALPHA V197	OP	CUD	FBG	DV	IO	115	MRCR	7	7	2750		6550	7500
18	8	ALPHA V198	OP	B/R	FBG	DV	IO	115	MRCR	7	6	2500		5750	6600
19	2	VIRADA V190	OP	B/R	FBG	DV	IO	115	MRCR	7	6	2210		5550	6400
20	3	ALPHA V210	OP	CUD	FBG	DV	IO	115	MRCR	7	8	3000		7150	8200
20	3	FISHERMAN V211	OP	CTRCN	FBG	DV	OB			7	8	1950		5700	6550
20	7	VIRADA V203	OP	B/R	FBG	DV	IO	115	MRCR	8	1	2750		6650	7650
20	7	VIRADA V204	OP	RNBT	FBG	DV	IO	115	MRCR	8	1	2850		6950	8000
20	7	VIRADA V215	OP	CUD	FBG	DV	IO	115	MRCR	8	1	2750		7100	8200
23		FISHERMAN V244	OP	FSH	FBG	DV	OB			8		2650		8300	9550
23		FISHERMAN V245	OP	FSH	FBG	DV	IO	115	MRCR	8		3500		10000	11400
24	7	VIRADA V240 AC	OP	SPTCR	FBG	DV	IO	230	MRCR	8	6	4750		13300	15100
26	1	VIRADA V265 AC	OP	SPTCR	FBG	DV	IO	230	MRCR	8	6	5600		15900	18100
		1992 BOATS													
16	5	ALPHA V164	OP	B/R	FBG	DV	OB			7	6	1150		1550	1850
16	5	VIRADA V165	OP	B/R	FBG	DV	IO	115	MRCR	7	6	1775		3900	4500
17	3	FISHERMAN V183	OP	CTRCN	FBG	DV	OB			6	5	1200		1600	1950
17	4	VIRADA V177	OP	B/R	FBG	DV	IO	115	MRCR	7	6	2250		4700	5400
17	6	CLASSIC 18	OP	CR	FBG	DV	IO	200	MRCR	7	3	1920		4700	5400
18	3	ALPHA V186	OP	B/R	FBG	DV	OB			7	1	1200		1700	2050
18	4	ALPHA V187	OP	B/R	FBG	DV	IO	200	MRCR	7	1	2400		5100	5850
18	6	FISH & SKI V184	OP	RNBT	FBG	SV	OB			7	2	1400		1950	2350
18	8	ALPHA V196	OP	CUD	FBG	DV	OB			7	7	1730		2300	2700
18	8	ALPHA V197	OP	CUD	FBG	DV	IO	115	MRCR	7	7	2750		6100	7050
18	8	ALPHA V198	OP	B/R	FBG	DV	IO	115	MRCR	7	6	2500		5350	6200
19	2	VIRADA V190	OP	B/R	FBG	DV	IO	115	MRCR	7	6	2210		5200	5950
20	3	ALPHA V210	OP	CUD	FBG	DV	IO	115	MRCR	7	8	3000		6700	7700
20	3	FISHERMAN V211	OP	CTRCN	FBG	DV	OB			7	8	1950		5450	6250
20	7	VIRADA V203	OP	B/R	FBG	DV	IO	115	MRCR	8	1	2750		6250	7200
20	7	VIRADA V204	OP	RNBT	FBG	DV	IO	115	MRCR	8	1	2850		6500	7500
20	7	VIRADA V215	OP	CUD	FBG	DV	IO	115	MRCR	8	1	2750		6650	7650
23		FISHERMAN V244	OP	FSH	FBG	DV	OB			8		2650		7950	9150
23		FISHERMAN V245	OP	FSH	FBG	DV	IO	115	MRCR	8		3500		9400	10700
24	7	VIRADA V240 AC	OP	SPTCR	FBG	DV	IO	230	MRCR	8	6	4750		12500	14200
26	1	VIRADA V265 AC	OP	SPTCR	FBG	DV	IO	230	MRCR	8	6	5600		14900	16900
		1991 BOATS													
16	5	ALPHA V164	OP	B/R	FBG	DV	OB			7	6	1150		1500	1750
16	5	VIRADA V165	OP	B/R	FBG	DV	IO	115	MRCR	7	6	1775		3650	4250
17	3	FISHERMAN V183	OP	CTRCN	FBG	DV	OB			6	5	1200		1550	1850
17	4	VIRADA V177	OP	B/R	FBG	DV	IO	115	MRCR	7	6	2250		4400	5050
18	3	ALPHA V186	OP	B/R	FBG	DV	OB			7	1	1200		1600	1950
18	4	ALPHA V187	OP	B/R	FBG	DV	IO	115	MRCR	7	1	2400		4700	5400
18	6	FISH & SKI V184	OP	RNBT	FBG	SV	OB			7	2	1400		1850	2200
18	8	ALPHA V196	OP	CUD	FBG	DV	OB			7	7	1730		2200	2550
18	8	ALPHA V197	OP	CUD	FBG	DV	IO	115	MRCR	7	7	2750		5750	6600
18	8	ALPHA V198	OP	B/R	FBG	DV	IO	115	MRCR	7	6	2500		5050	5800
19	2	VIRADA V190	OP	B/R	FBG	DV	IO	115	MRCR	7	6	2210		4900	5600
20	3	ALPHA V210	OP	CUD	FBG	DV	IO	115	MRCR	7	8	3000		6300	7200
20	3	FISHERMAN V211	OP	CTRCN	FBG	DV	OB			7	8	1950		5200	5950
20	7	VIRADA V203	OP	B/R	FBG	DV	IO	115	MRCR	8	1	2750		5850	6750
20	7	VIRADA V204	OP	RNBT	FBG	DV	IO	115	MRCR	8	1	2850		6100	7000
20	7	VIRADA V215	OP	CUD	FBG	DV	IO	115	MRCR	8	1	2750		6250	7200
23		FISHERMAN V244	OP	FSH	FBG	DV	OB			8		2650		7500	8650
23		FISHERMAN V245	OP	FSH	FBG	DV	IO	115	MRCR	8		3500		8850	10000
24	7	VIRADA V240 AC	OP	SPTCR	FBG	DV	IO	115	MRCR	8	6	4750		11200	12700
26	1	VIRADA V265 AC	OP	SPTCR	FBG	DV	IO	115	MRCR	8	6	5600		13000	14700
		1990 BOATS													
16	1	V170	ST	RNBT	FBG	SV	OB			6	4	1050		1300	1550
16	1	V170 SP	OP	RNBT	FBG	SV	IO	125-145		6	5	1790		3300	3850
16	1	VADER-PAK V170	OP	RNBT	FBG	SV	OB			6	5	1050		1300	1550
16	6	FISHERMAN V172	OP	FSH	FBG	TR	OB			6	2	750		950	1150
16	6	VADER-PAK V172	OP	FSH	FBG	TR	OB			6	2	750		950	1150
17	1	V180	ST	RNBT	FBG	SV	OB			7	7	1250		1550	1850
17	1	V181 SP	OP	RNBT	FBG	SV	OB			7	6	2190		2350	2750
17	1	VADER-PAK V180	OP	RNBT	FBG	SV	OB			7	7	1250		1550	1850
17	3	FISHERMAN V182	OP	FSH	FBG	SV	OB			6	2	1200		1500	1750
17	3	VAKER-PAK V182	OP	FSH	FBG	SV	OB			6	2	1200		1500	1750
17	4	ELAN SPORT V177	OP	RNBT	FBG	SV	IO	125-145		7	6	2150		4200	4900
18	3	ELAN SPORT V187	OP	SKI	FBG	SV	IO	125-260		7	1	2400		4400	5500
18	3	SPORT V186	OP	RNBT	FBG	SV	OB			7	1	1200		1550	1850
18	3	VADER-PAK V186	OP	RNBT	FBG	SV	OB			7	1	1200		1550	1850
18	8	V196 CC	OP	CUD	FBG	SV	OB			7	4	1730		2050	2450
18	8	V197 CC	ST	CUD	FBG	SV	IO	125-260		7	4	2750		5300	6550
18	8	V198 SP	ST	RNBT	FBG	SV	IO	125-260		7	6	2500		4950	6100
18	8	VADER-PAK V196	OP	CUD	FBG	SV	OB			7	4	1730		2050	2450
19		ELAN SPORT V190	OP	RNBT	FBG	SV	IO	125-175		7	7	2210		4750	5500
20	3	FISHERMAN V210	OP	FSH	FBG	SV	OB			7	8	1970		5000	5750
20	3	V210 CC	ST	CUD	FBG	DV	IO	125-271		7	8	3000		5900	7350
20	7	ELAN SPORT V203	OP	RNBT	FBG	SV	IO	125-271		8	1	2800		5700	7050
23	3	FISHERMAN V244	OP	FSH	FBG	SV	OB			8		2607		7150	8250
23	4	FISHERMAN V245	OP	FSH	FBG	SV	IO	125-260		8		3500		8400	10100
23	7	ELAN AC V239	OP	CUD	FBG	DV	IO	125	MRCR	8	6	4750		10300	11700
23	7	ELAN AC V239	OP	CUD	FBG	DV	IO	T145	MRCR	8	6	4750		11300	12900
23	7	ELAN AC V240	OP	RNBT	FBG	DV	IO	125	MRCR	8	6	4750		9700	11000
23	7	ELAN AC V240	OP	RNBT	FBG	DV	IO	T145	MRCR	8	6	4750		10700	12100
25	10	ELAN AC V265	OP	RNBT	FBG	DV	IO	125-260		8	6	5600		11300	13900
		1989 BOATS													
16	1	V170	ST	RNBT	FBG	SV	OB			6	4	1050		1250	1500
16	1	V171 SP	OP	RNBT	FBG	SV	IO	131-165		6	5	1790		3300	3850
16	1	VADER-PAK V170	OP	RNBT	FBG	SV	OB			6	5	1050		1250	1500
16	6	FISHERMAN V172	OP	FSH	FBG	TR	OB			6	2	750		915	1100
16	6	VADER-PAK V172	OP	FSH	FBG	TR	OB			6	2	750		915	1100
17	1	V180	ST	RNBT	FBG	SV	OB			7	7	1250		1500	1750
17	1	V181 SP	OP	RNBT	FBG	SV	IO	131-175		7	6	2190		4150	4850
17	1	VADER-PAK V180	OP	RNBT	FBG	SV	OB			7	7	1250		1500	1750
17	3	FISHERMAN V182	OP	FSH	FBG	SV	OB			6	2	1200		1400	1700
17	3	VADER-PAK V182	OP	FSH	FBG	SV	OB			6	2	1200		1400	1700
17	4	ELAN SPORT V177	OP	RNBT	FBG	SV	IO	131-165		7	6	2150		4200	4850
18	3	V186 SPORT	OP	RNBT	FBG	SV	OB			7	1	1200		1500	1750
18	3	V187 ELAN SPORT	OP	SKI	FBG	SV	IO	131-260		7	1	2400		4350	5200
18	3	VADER-PAK V186	OP	RNBT	FBG	SV	OB			7	1	1200		1500	1750
18	8	V196 CC	OP	CUD	FBG	SV	OB			7	4	1730		2000	2350
18	8	V197 CC	ST	CUD	FBG	SV	IO	131-260		7	4	2750		5200	6200
18	8	V198 SP	ST	RNBT	FBG	SV	IO	131-260		7	6	2500		4850	5750
18	8	VADER-PAK V196	OP	CUD	FBG	SV	OB			7	4	1730		2000	2350
19		ELAN SPORT V190	OP	RNBT	FBG	SV	IO	131-175		7	7	2210		4700	5400
20	3	FISHERMAN V210	OP	FSH	FBG	SV	OB			7	8	1970		4800	5500
20	3	V210 CC	ST	CUD	FBG	DV	IO	131-271		7	8	3000		5800	6950
20	7	ELAN SPORT V203	OP	RNBT	FBG	SV	IO	131-271		8	1	2800		5550	6650
23	3	FISHERMAN V244	OP	FSH	FBG	SV	OB			8		2607		6850	7900
23	4	FISHERMAN V245	OP	FSH	FBG	SV	IO	131-260		8		3500		8100	9500
23	7	ELAN AC V239	OP	CUD	FBG	DV	IO	131-260		8	6	4750		9900	11500
23	7	ELAN AC V240	OP	RNBT	FBG	DV	IO	131-260		8	6	4750		9350	10800

 CONTINUED ON NEXT PAGE

LOA FT	IN	NAME AND/ OR MODEL	TOP/ RIG	BOAT TYPE	-HULL- MTL	TP	----ENGINE--- TP	# HP	MFG	BEAM FT	IN	WGT LBS	DRAFT FT	IN	RETAIL LOW	RETAIL HIGH
		1989 BOATS														
25	10	ELAN AC V265	OP	RNBT	FBG	DV	IO	131-260		8	6	5600			10800	13100
		1988 BOATS														
16	1	V170	ST	RNBT	FBG	SV	OB			6	4	1050			1200	1450
16	1	V171	ST	RNBT	FBG	SV	IO	120-170		6	4	1790			2900	3600
16	1	V171 SP	OP	RNBT	FBG	SV	IO	120	OMC	6	5	1790			2900	3350
16	1	V171 SP	OP	RNBT	FBG	SV	IO	120-131		6	5	1790			3100	3650
17	1	V181	ST	RNBT	FBG	SV	IO	120-185		7	7	1970			3600	4400
17	1	V181 SP	OP	RNBT	FBG	SV	IO	131-175		7	6	1970			3750	4350
17	3	V180	ST	RNBT	FBG	DV	OB			6	4	1150			1350	1600
17	3	V182	OP	CTRCN	FBG	DV	OB			7		1200			1350	1650
18	3	V186 SPORT	OP	SKI	FBG	SV	OB			7	1	1300			1500	1800
18	3	V187	OP	SKI	FBG	SV	IO	120-205		7	1	2200			3700	4550
18	3	V187	OP	SKI	FBG	SV	IO	225-260		7	1	2200			4100	5050
18	8	V195	ST	RNBT	FBG	DV	OB			7	7	1250			1500	1800
18	8	V197 CC	OP	CUD	FBG	DV	IO	131	VLVO	7	4	2750			4950	5650
18	8	V198	ST	RNBT	FBG	DV	IO	170-260		7	7	2500			4500	5500
18	8	V198	ST	RNBT	FBG	SV	IO	120-185		7	7	2500			4450	5350
18	8	V198	ST	RNBT	FBG	SV	IO	260	VLVO	7	7	2500			5050	5800
20	3	V210 B/R	ST	RNBT	FBG	DV	IO	120-230		7	8	3000			5050	6250
20	3	V210 B/R	ST	RNBT	FBG	DV	IO	260		7	8	3000			5400	6450
20	3	V210 CC	ST	CUD	FBG	DV	IO	120-230		7	8	3000			5300	6500
20	3	V210 CC	ST	CUD	FBG	DV	IO	260		7	8	3000			5650	6750
20	3	V210 FISHERMAN		CTRCN	FBG	DV	OB			7	8	2000			4650	5350
24		AFT CABIN V250	OP	DC	FBG	DV	IO	T130	OMC	8	5	4999			12100	13800
24		AFT CABIN V265	OP	DC	FBG	DV	IO	230	MRCR	8	5	4999			11300	12900
		1987 BOATS														
16	1	V170	ST	RNBT	FBG	SV	OB			6	5	1050			1150	1400
16	1	V171	ST	RNBT	FBG	SV	IO	120-170		6	5	1790			2800	3450
16	1	V171 USA	OP	RNBT	FBG	SV	IO	120		6	5	1790			2800	3450
16	6	V172	OP	CTRCN	FBG	TR	OB			6	2	750			850	1000
17	1	V181	ST	RNBT	FBG	SV	IO	120-185		7	7	1970			3400	4150
17	1	V181 USA	OP	RNBT	FBG	SV	IO	120		7	7	1970			3400	4150
17	3	V180	ST	RNBT	FBG	DV	OB			6	4	1150			1300	1550
17	3	V182	OP	CTRCN	FBG	DV	OB			7		1200			1300	1550
18	3	V186 SPORT	OP	SKI	FBG	SV	OB			7	1	1300			1450	1700
18	3	V187	OP	SKI	FBG	SV	IO	120-205		7	1	2200			3500	4300
18	3	V187	OP	SKI	FBG	SV	IO	225-260		7	1	2200			3900	4750
18	8	V195	ST	RNBT	FBG	DV	OB			7	7	1250			1450	1700
18	8	V197 CC	OP	CUD	FBG	DV	IO	131	VLVO	7	4	2750			4700	5400
18	8	V198	ST	RNBT	FBG	DV	IO	170-260		7	7	2500			4200	5250
18	8	V198	ST	RNBT	FBG	SV	IO	120-185		7	7	2500			4200	5050
18	8	V198	ST	RNBT	FBG	SV	IO	260	VLVO	7	7	2500			4800	5500
20	3	V210 B/R	ST	RNBT	FBG	DV	IO	120-230		7	8	3000			4800	5900
20	3	V210 B/R	ST	RNBT	FBG	DV	IO	260		7	8	3000			5100	6150
20	3	V210 CC	ST	CUD	FBG	DV	IO	120-230		7	8	3000			5000	6200
20	3	V210 CC	ST	CUD	FBG	DV	IO	260		7	8	3000			5350	6450
20	3	V210 FISHERMAN		CTRCN	FBG	DV	OB			7	8	2000			4450	5150
24		AFT CABIN V250	OP	DC	FBG	DV	IO	230	MRCR	8	5	4999			10800	12300
24		AFT CABIN V250	OP	DC	FBG	DV	IO	T130	OMC	8	5	5500			12400	14100
24		V250 AFT CABIN	OP	DC	FBG	DV	IO	120		8	5				10500	11900
		1986 BOATS														
16	1	V170		RNBT	FBG	SV	OB			6	5	1050			1100	1350
16	1	V171		RNBT	FBG	DV	IO	131		6	5				2750	3200
16	1	V171 USA		RNBT	FBG	DV	IO	131		6	5				2550	3000
17	1	V180		RNBT	FBG	DV	OB			7	7	1150			1250	1500
17	1	V181		RNBT	FBG	DV	IO	131		7	7				3500	4100
17	1	V181 USA		RNBT	FBG	DV	IO	131		7	7				3300	3850
18	2	V182		CTRCN	FBG	DV	OB			7		1200			1300	1550
18	3	V186		RNBT	FBG	DV	OB			7	1	1200			1350	1600
18	8	V195		RNBT	FBG	DV	OB			7	7	1275			1400	1700
18	8	V197		CUD	FBG	DV	IO	131		7	4				4250	4950
18	8	V198		RNBT	FBG	DV	IO	131		7	7				3850	4500
20	3	V210		CTRCN	FBG	DV	OB			7	8	1850			4050	4700
20	3	V210		CUD	FBG	DV	IO	131		7	8				4800	5500
		1985 BOATS														
16	1	V170	ST	RNBT	FBG	SV	OB			6	5	1050			1100	1300
16	1	V170 USA	OP	RNBT	FBG	SV	OB			6	5	1050			1100	1300
16	1	V171	ST	RNBT	FBG	SV	IO	120-170		6	5	1790			2550	3150
16	1	V171 USA	OP	RNBT	FBG	SV	IO	120		6	5	1790			2550	3150
16	6	V172	OP	CTRCN	FBG	TR	OB			6	2	750			790	955
17	1	V181	ST	RNBT	FBG	SV	IO	120-185		7	7	1970			3100	3800
17	1	V181 USA	OP	RNBT	FBG	SV	IO	120		7	7	1970			3100	3800
17	3	V180	ST	RNBT	FBG	DV	OB			6	4	1150			1200	1450
17	3	V182	OP	CTRCN	FBG	DV	OB			7		1200			1250	1500
18	3	V186 SPORT	OP	SKI	FBG	SV	OB			7	1	1300			1350	1600
18	3	V187	OP	SKI	FBG	SV	IO	120-205		7	1	2200			3200	3950
18	3	V187	OP	SKI	FBG	SV	IO	225-260		7	1	2200			3550	4350
18	8	V195	ST	RNBT	FBG	DV	OB			7	7	1250			1350	1600
18	8	V198	ST	RNBT	FBG	DV	IO	170-260		7	7	2500			3850	4800
18	8	V198	ST	RNBT	FBG	SV	IO	120-185		7	7	2500			3850	4650
18	8	V198	ST	RNBT	FBG	DV	IO	225-260		7	7	2500			4150	5050
18	8	V198 USA	OP	RNBT	FBG	DV	IO	120		7	7	2500			3850	4650
20	3	V210 B/R	ST	RNBT	FBG	DV	IO	120-230		7	8	3000			4450	5450
20	3	V210 B/R	ST	RNBT	FBG	DV	IO	260		7	8	3000			4700	5650
20	3	V210 CC	ST	CUD	FBG	DV	IO	120-230		7	8	3000			4600	5650
20	3	V210 CC	ST	CUD	FBG	DV	IO	260		7	8	3000			4900	5900
20	3	V210 FISHERMAN		CTRCN	FBG	DV	OB			7	8	2000			4100	4800
		1984 BOATS														
16	1	INVADER 16V B/R	ST	RNBT	FBG	SV	OB			6	5	1050			1050	1250
16	1	INVADER 16V B/R	ST	RNBT	FBG	SV	IO	120-140		6	5	1790			2450	2850
16	6	INVADER I-16	OP	CTRCN	FBG	TR	OB			6	2	750			770	930
17	1	INVADER 17 SPORT	ST	RNBT	FBG	SV	IO	117	VLVO	7	7	1900			3100	3650
17	3	17V B/R SPORT	ST	RNBT	FBG	DV	OB			6	4	1075			1100	1300
17	3	INVADER 17 B/R	ST	RNBT	FBG	DV	OB			7		1530			1450	1750
17	3	INVADER 17 FISH	OP	CTRCN	FBG	DV	OB			7		1200			1200	1450
17	3	INVADER 17V B/R	ST	RNBT	FBG	DV	IO	140-200		7		2500			3300	3900
17	3	INVADER 17V C/B	ST	RNBT	FBG	DV	IO	138	VLVO	7		2500			3450	4000
18	8	INVADER 19 B/R	ST	RNBT	FBG	DV	OB			7	7	1250			1300	1550
18	8	INVADER 19 B/R	ST	RNBT	FBG	DV	IO	170-260		7	7	2800			3950	4900
20	3	INVADER 20 B/R	ST	RNBT	FBG	DV	IO	170-260		7	8	3000			4250	5250
20	3	INVADER 20 CC	ST	CUD	FBG	DV	IO	170-260		7	8	3000			4500	5450
20	3	V210 FISHERMAN		CTRCN	FBG	DV	OB			7	8	2000			4000	4650

....For earlier years, see the BUC Used Boat Price Guide, Volume 3

INVADER MARINE LLC

HESPERIA CA 92345 COAST GUARD MFG ID- SKP See inside cover to adjust price for area
FORMERLY SKIPJACK INTERNATIONAL

For more recent years, see the BUC Used Boat Price Guide, Volume 1

LOA FT	IN	NAME AND/ OR MODEL	TOP/ RIG	BOAT TYPE	-HULL- MTL	TP	----ENGINE--- TP	# HP	MFG	BEAM FT	IN	WGT LBS	DRAFT FT	IN	RETAIL LOW	RETAIL HIGH
		1996 BOATS														
20	5	OPEN CRUISER 20	OP	RNBT	FBG	SV	IO	225-250		7	10	3200	2	6	13800	16100
20	5	OPEN CRUISER 20	OP	RNBT	FBG	SV	IO	140D	VLVO	7	10	3200	2	6	16700	19000
23	10	OPEN CRUISER 24	OP	RNBT	FBG	SV	IO	250	VLVO	8		4000	2	6	19500	21700
23	10	OPEN CRUISER 24	OP	RNBT	FBG	SV	IO	185D-216D		8		4000	2	6	23300	26700
23	10	OPEN CRUISER 24	OP	RNBT	FBG	SV	IO	T135	VLVO	8		4000	2	6	21300	23600
25		FISHERMAN 25	OP	FSH	FBG	SV	IO	250-300		8		5000	3	3	27200	31800
25		FISHERMAN 25	OP	FSH	FBG	SV	IO	185D-216D		8		5000	3	3	37300	42900
25		FISHERMAN 25	OP	FSH	FBG	SV	IO	T135	VLVO	8		5000	3	3	29100	32300
25		SPORT CRUISER 25	OP	SPTCR	FBG	SV	IO	250-300		8		5000	2	6	25700	30100
25		SPORT CRUISER 25	OP	SPTCR	FBG	SV	IO	185D-216D		8		5000	2	6	29900	34400
25		SPORT CRUISER 25	OP	SPTCR	FBG	SV	IO	T135	VLVO	8		5000	2	6	27400	30500
26		FISHERMAN 26	OP	FSH	FBG	SV	IO	250-300		8	1	6000	2	6	33500	39000
		IO 185D-216D 46600 52700, IO T187 VLVO 36700 40800, IO T140D VLVO													54200	59600
26		FLY BRIDGE 26	FB	SF	FBG	SV	IO	250-300		8	1	6000	2	6	36500	42600
		IO 185D-216D 47000 53500, IO T187 VLVO 40300 44800, IO T140D VLVO													55300	60800
26		SPORTSMAN 26	OP	CUD	FBG	SV	IO	250-300		8	1	6000	2	6	31800	37000
		IO 185D-216D 36900 42500, IO T187 VLVO 34700 38600, IO T140D VLVO													43100	47800
28		FLY BRIDGE 28	FB	SF	FBG	SV	IO	300	VLVO	8		6600	2	7	40100	44600
		IO 216D VLVO 48700 53500, IO T250 VLVO 44700 49700, IO T140D VLVO													54000	59300
		1995 BOATS														
20	5	OPEN CRUISER 20	OP	RNBT	FBG	SV	IO	225-250		7	10	3200	2	6	12900	15000
20	5	OPEN CRUISER 20	OP	RNBT	FBG	SV	IO	140D	VLVO	7	10	3200	2	6	15600	17700
23	10	OPEN CRUISER 24	OP	RNBT	FBG	SV	IO	250	VLVO	8		4000	2	6	18400	20400
23	10	OPEN CRUISER 24	OP	RNBT	FBG	SV	IO	185D-216D		8		4000	2	6	21800	24900
23	10	OPEN CRUISER 24	OP	RNBT	FBG	SV	IO	T135	VLVO	8		4000	2	6	19800	22000
25		FISHERMAN 25	OP	FSH	FBG	SV	IO	250-300		8		5000	3	3	25300	29700
25		FISHERMAN 25	OP	FSH	FBG	SV	IO	185D-216D		8		5000	3	3	34800	40100
25		FISHERMAN 25	OP	FSH	FBG	SV	IO	T135	VLVO	8		5000	3	3	27100	30100
25		SPORT CRUISER 25	OP	SPTCR	FBG	SV	IO	250-300		8		5000	2	6	24000	28100
25		SPORT CRUISER 25	OP	SPTCR	FBG	SV	IO	185D-216D		8		5000	2	6	27900	32100
25		SPORT CRUISER 25	OP	SPTCR	FBG	SV	IO	T135	VLVO	8		5000	2	6	25600	28400

LOA FT	LOA IN	NAME AND/ OR MODEL	TOP/ RIG	BOAT TYPE	-HULL- MTL	-HULL- TP	ENGINE TP	ENGINE # HP	ENGINE MFG	BEAM FT	BEAM IN	WGT LBS	DRAFT FT	DRAFT IN	RETAIL LOW	RETAIL HIGH
		1995 BOATS														
26		FISHERMAN 26	OP	FSH	FBG	SV	IO	250-300		8	1	6000	2	6	31300	36400
		IO 185D-216D 43000 49400, IO T187 VLVO 34300 38100, IO T115D VLVO 48400 53200														
26		FLY BRIDGE 26	FB	SF	FBG	SV	IO	250-300		8	1	6000	2	6	34000	39600
		IO 185D-216D 43400 49900, IO T187 VLVO 37500 41600, IO T115D VLVO 49500 54400														
26		SPORTSMAN 26	OP	CUD	FBG	SV	IO	250-300		8	1	6000	2	6	29700	34500
		IO 185D-216D 34400 39600, IO T187 VLVO 32400 36000, IO T115D VLVO 38400 42700														
28		FLY BRIDGE 28	FB	SF	FBG	SV	IO	300	VLVO	8		6600	2	7	37400	41500
		IO 216D VLVO 45000 50000, IO T250 VLVO 41600 46200, IO T140D VLVO 50300 55300														
		1994 BOATS														
20	5	OPEN CRUISER 20	OP	RNBT	FBG	SV	IO	225-245		7	10	3200	2	6	12100	14000
20	5	OPEN CRUISER 20	OP	RNBT	FBG	SV	IO	115D	VLVO	7	10	3200	2	6	14200	16100
23	10	OPEN CRUISER 24	OP	RNBT	FBG	SV	IO	245	VLVO	8		4000	2	6	16700	19000
23	10	OPEN CRUISER 24	OP	RNBT	FBG	SV	IO	185D-216D		8		4000	2	6	20300	23300
23	10	OPEN CRUISER 24	OP	RNBT	FBG	SV	IO	T135	VLVO	8		4000	2	6	18700	20800
25		FISHERMAN 25	OP	FSH	FBG	SV	IO	245-300		8		5000	3	3	23600	27700
25		FISHERMAN 25	OP	FSH	FBG	SV	IO	185D-216D		8		5000	3	3	32500	37400
25		FISHERMAN 25	OP	FSH	FBG	SV	IO	T135	VLVO	8		5000	3	3	25300	28100
25		SPORT CRUISER 25	OP	SPTCR	FBG	SV	IO	245-300		8		5000	2	6	22300	26200
25		SPORT CRUISER 25	OP	SPTCR	FBG	SV	IO	185D-216D		8		5000	2	6	26000	29900
25		SPORT CRUISER 25	OP	SPTCR	FBG	SV	IO	T135	VLVO	8		5000	2	6	23900	26500
26		FISHERMAN 26	OP	FSH	FBG	SV	IO	245-300		8	1	6000	2	6	29100	34000
		IO 185D-216D 40100 46100, IO T135-T187 30700 35500, IO T115D VLVO 44900 49900														
26		FLY BRIDGE 26	FB	SF	FBG	SV	IO	245-300		8	1	6000	2	6	31600	36900
		IO 185D-216D 40400 46400, IO T135-T187 33600 38900, IO T115D VLVO 46200 50800														
26		SPORTSMAN 26	OP	CUD	FBG	SV	IO	245-300		8	1	6000	2	6	27600	32200
		IO 185D-216D 32200 37000, IO T135-T187 29000 33600, IO T115D VLVO 35900 39900														
28		FLY BRIDGE 28	FB	SF	FBG	SV	IO	300	VLVO	8		6600	2	7	34900	38700
		IO 216D VLVO 41800 46500, IO T187-T245 36500 42900, IO T115D VLVO 44600 49500														
		1993 BOATS														
20	5	FISHERMAN 20	OP	FSH	FBG	SV	IO	229-265		7		3200	2	6	11900	14100
20	5	FISHERMAN 20	OP	FSH	FBG	SV	IO	130D	VLVO	7		3200	2	6	16900	19200
20	5	OPEN CRUISER 20	OP	RNBT	FBG	SV	IO	229-265		7	10	3200	2	6	11300	13400
20	5	OPEN CRUISER 20	OP	RNBT	FBG	SV	IO	130D	VLVO	7	10	3200	2	6	13500	15300
23	10	OPEN CRUISER 24	OP	RNBT	FBG	SV	IO	265	VLVO	8		4000	2	6	15900	18100
23	10	OPEN CRUISER 24	OP	RNBT	FBG	SV	IO	150D	VLVO	8		4000	2	6	18600	20700
23	10	OPEN CRUISER 24	OP	RNBT	FBG	SV	IO	T146	VLVO	8		4000	2	6	17100	19500
25		FISHERMAN 25	OP	FSH	FBG	SV	IO	265-330		8		5000	3	3	22400	27000
25		FISHERMAN 25	OP	FSH	FBG	SV	IO	150D	VLVO	8		5000	3	3	29200	32500
25		FISHERMAN 25	OP	FSH	FBG	SV	IO	T146	VLVO	8		5000	3	3	23800	26400
25		FLY BRIDGE 25	FB	SF	FBG	SV	IO	265-330		8		5000	2	6	24800	30000
25		FLY BRIDGE 25	FB	SF	FBG	SV	IO	150D	VLVO	8		5000	2	6	30000	33400
25		FLY BRIDGE 25	FB	SF	FBG	SV	IO	T146	VLVO	8		5000	2	6	26700	29600
25		SPORT CRUISER 25	OP	SPTCR	FBG	SV	IO	265-330		8		5000	2	6	21200	25600
25		SPORT CRUISER 25	OP	SPTCR	FBG	SV	IO	150D	VLVO	8		5000	2	6	23400	26000
25		SPORT CRUISER 25	OP	SPTCR	FBG	SV	IO	T146	VLVO	8		5000	2	6	22500	24900
25		SPORTSMAN 25	OP	CUD	FBG	SV	IO	265-330		8		5000	2	6	21200	25600
25		SPORTSMAN 25	OP	CUD	FBG	SV	IO	150D	VLVO	8		5000	2	6	23400	26000
25		SPORTSMAN 25	OP	CUD	FBG	SV	IO	T146	VLVO	8		5000	2	6	22400	24900
26		FISHERMAN 26	OP	FSH	FBG	SV	IO	265-330		8	1	6000	2	6	27600	32900
		IO 150D VLVO 36000 40000, IO T146-T229 28900 34500, IO T130D VLVO 43000 47800														
26		FLY BRIDGE 26	FB	SF	FBG	SV	IO	265-330		8	1	6000	2	6	30000	35700
		IO 150D VLVO 36200 40200, IO T146-T229 31700 37700, IO T130D VLVO 43800 48700														
26		SPORTSMAN 26	OP	CUD	FBG	SV	IO	265-330		8	1	6000	2	6	26200	31200
		IO 150D VLVO 28800 32100, IO T146-T229 27300 32700, IO T130D VLVO 34400 38300														
28		FLY BRIDGE 28	FB	SF	FBG	SV	IO	330	VLVO	8		6600	2	7	33500	37200
28		FLY BRIDGE 28	FB	SF	FBG	SV	IO	T229-T265		8		6600	2	7	35500	41000
28		FLY BRIDGE 28	FB	SF	FBG	SV	IO	T130D	VLVO	8		6600	2	7	42800	47500
		1992 BOATS														
20	5	OPEN CRUISER 20	OP	RNBT	FBG	SV	IO	230-270		7	10	3200	2	6	10600	12600
20	5	OPEN CRUISER 20	OP	RNBT	FBG	SV	IO	130D	VLVO	7	10	3200	2	6	12600	14300
23	10	FLY BRIDGE 24	FB	SF	FBG	SV	IO	230-270		8		4600	2	6	20600	23600
23	10	FLY BRIDGE 24	FB	SF	FBG	SV	IO	130D	VLVO	8		4600	2	6	25800	28700
23	10	OPEN CRUISER 24	OP	RNBT	FBG	SV	IO	270	VLVO	8		4000	2	6	15000	17000
23	10	OPEN CRUISER 24	OP	RNBT	FBG	SV	IO	150D	VLVO	8		4000	2	6	17100	19400
23	10	OPEN CRUISER 24	OP	RNBT	FBG	SV	IO	T150	VLVO	8		4000	2	6	16000	18200
24		FISHERMAN 24	OP	FSH	FBG	SV	IO	270	VLVO	8			2	6	17000	19300
24		FISHERMAN 24	OP	FSH	FBG	SV	IO	150D	VLVO	8			2	6	23200	25800
24		FISHERMAN 24	OP	FSH	FBG	SV	IO	T150	VLVO	8			2	6	18700	20800
25		FISHERMAN 25	OP	FSH	FBG	SV	IO	270-330		8		5000	3	3	21100	25300
25		FISHERMAN 25	OP	FSH	FBG	SV	IO	150D	VLVO	8		5000	3	3	27400	30400
25		FISHERMAN 25	OP	FSH	FBG	SV	IO	T150	VLVO	8		5000	3	3	22300	24800
25		FLY BRIDGE 25	FB	SF	FBG	SV	IO	270-330		8		5000	2	6	23300	28000
25		FLY BRIDGE 25	FB	SF	FBG	SV	IO	150D	VLVO	8		5000	2	6	28100	31200
25		FLY BRIDGE 25	FB	SF	FBG	SV	IO	T150	VLVO	8		5000	2	6	25000	27800
25		SPORT CRUISER 25	OP	SPTCR	FBG	SV	IO	270-330		8		5000	2	6	19900	23900
25		SPORT CRUISER 25	OP	SPTCR	FBG	SV	IO	150D	VLVO	8		5000	2	6	21900	24300
25		SPORT CRUISER 25	OP	SPTCR	FBG	SV	IO	T150	VLVO	8		5000	2	6	21100	23400
25		SPORTSMAN 25	OP	CUD	FBG	SV	IO	270-330		8		5000	2	6	19900	23900
25		SPORTSMAN 25	OP	CUD	FBG	SV	IO	150D	VLVO	8		5000	2	6	21900	24300
25		SPORTSMAN 25	OP	CUD	FBG	SV	IO	T150	VLVO	8		5000	2	6	21000	23300
26		FISHERMAN 26	OP	FSH	FBG	SV	IO	150-270		8	1	6000	2	6	23900	28900
26		FISHERMAN 26	OP	FSH	FBG	SV	IO	330	VLVO	8	1	6000	2	6	27700	30800
26		FISHERMAN 26	OP	FSH	FBG	SV	IO	T150	VLVO	8	1	6000	2	6	27100	30100
26		FLY BRIDGE 26	FB	SF	FBG	SV	IO	270-330		8	1	6000	2	6	28200	33400
26		FLY BRIDGE 26	FB	SF	FBG	SV	IO	150D	VLVO	8	1	6000	2	6	33900	37600
26		FLY BRIDGE 26	FB	SF	FBG	SV	IO	T150	VLVO	8	1	6000	2	6	29700	33000
28		FLY BRIDGE 28	FB	SF	FBG	SV	IO	330	VLVO	8		6600	2	7	31400	34800
28		FLY BRIDGE 28	FB	SF	FBG	SV	IO	T230-T270		8		6600	2	7	33200	38600
28		FLY BRIDGE 28	FB	SF	FBG	SV	IO	T130D	VLVO	8		6600	2	7	39900	44400
40		FLY BRIDGE 35	FB	SF	FBG	SV	IO	T250D	CUM	12		17000	3	6	110000	121000
		1991 BOATS														
20	5	OPEN CRUISER 20	OP	RNBT	FBG	SV	IO	230-270		7	10	3200	2	6	9950	11800
20	5	OPEN CRUISER 20	OP	RNBT	FBG	SV	IO	130D	VLVO	7	10	3200	2	6	11800	13400
23	10	FLY BRIDGE 24	FB	SF	FBG	SV	IO	270	VLVO	8		4600	2	6	19900	22100
23	10	FLY BRIDGE 24	FB	SF	FBG	SV	IO	200D	VLVO	8		4600	2	6	25600	28400
23	10	FLY BRIDGE 24	FB	SF	FBG	SV	IO	T150	VLVO	8		4600	2	6	21600	24000
23	10	OPEN CRUISER 24	OP	RNBT	FBG	SV	IO	270	VLVO	8		4000	2	6	14100	16000
23	10	OPEN CRUISER 24	OP	RNBT	FBG	SV	IO	200D	VLVO	8		4000	2	6	16700	19000
23	10	OPEN CRUISER 24	OP	RNBT	FBG	SV	IO	T150	VLVO	8		4000	2	6	15000	17100
25		FISHERMAN 25	OP	FSH	FBG	SV	IO	270	VLVO	8		5000	2	6	19800	22000
25		FISHERMAN 25	OP	FSH	FBG	SV	IO	200D	VLVO	8		5000	2	6	27100	30100
25		FISHERMAN 25	OP	FSH	FBG	SV	IO	T150	VLVO	8		5000	2	6	20900	23200
25		FLY BRIDGE 25	FB	SF	FBG	SV	IO	270	VLVO	8		5000	2	6	21900	24300
25		FLY BRIDGE 25	FB	SF	FBG	SV	IO	200D	VLVO	8		5000	2	6	27800	30900
25		FLY BRIDGE 25	FB	SF	FBG	SV	IO	T150	VLVO	8		5000	2	6	23400	26000
25		SPORT CRUISER 25	OP	SPTCR	FBG	SV	IO	270	VLVO	8		5000	2	6	18900	21000
25		SPORT CRUISER 25	OP	SPTCR	FBG	SV	IO	200D	VLVO	8		5000	2	6	21700	24100
25		SPORT CRUISER 25	OP	SPTCR	FBG	SV	IO	T150	VLVO	8		5000	2	6	19800	21900
28		FLY BRIDGE 28	FB	SF	FBG	SV	IO	T230-T270		8		6600	2	7	31200	36100
28		FLY BRIDGE 28	FB	SF	FBG	SV	IO	T130D	VLVO	8		6600	2	7	37400	41500
40		FLY BRIDGE 35	FB	SF	FBG	SV	IO	T250D	CUM	12		17000			103500	113500
		1990 BOATS														
20	5	OPEN CRUISER 20	OP	RNBT	FBG	SV	IO	230-270		7	10	3200	2	6	9400	11100
20	5	OPEN CRUISER 20	OP	RNBT	FBG	SV	IO	130D	VLVO	7	10	3200	2	6	11100	12600
23	10	FLY BRIDGE 24	FB	SF	FBG	SV	IO	270	VLVO	8		4600	2	6	18800	20900
23	10	FLY BRIDGE 24	FB	SF	FBG	SV	IO	200D	VLVO	8		4600	2	6	24000	26700
23	10	FLY BRIDGE 24	FB	SF	FBG	SV	IO	T150	VLVO	8		4600	2	6	20300	22500
23	10	OPEN CRUISER 24	OP	RNBT	FBG	SV	IO	270	VLVO	8		4000	2	6	13200	15000
23	10	OPEN CRUISER 24	OP	RNBT	FBG	SV	IO	T150	VLVO	8		4000	2	6	14200	16100
23	10	OPEN CRUISER 24	OP	RNBT	FBG	SV	IO	T200D	VLVO	8		4000	2	6	20900	23200
25		FISHERMAN 25	OP	FSH	FBG	SV	IO	270	VLVO	8		5000	2	6	18800	20900
25		FISHERMAN 25	OP	FSH	FBG	SV	IO	200D	VLVO	8		5000	2	6	25500	28300
25		FISHERMAN 25	OP	FSH	FBG	SV	IO	T150	VLVO	8		5000	2	6	19700	21900
25		FLY BRIDGE 25	FB	SF	FBG	SV	IO	270	VLVO	8		5000	2	6	20600	22800
25		FLY BRIDGE 25	FB	SF	FBG	SV	IO	200D	VLVO	8		5000	2	6	26100	29000
25		FLY BRIDGE 25	FB	SF	FBG	SV	IO	T150	VLVO	8		5000	2	6	22000	24400
25		SPORT CRUISER 25	OP	SPTCR	FBG	SV	IO	270	VLVO	8		5000	2	6	17400	19800
25		SPORT CRUISER 25	OP	SPTCR	FBG	SV	IO	200D	VLVO	8		5000	2	6	20400	22700
25		SPORT CRUISER 25	OP	SPTCR	FBG	SV	IO	T150	VLVO	8		5000	2	6	18800	20800
28		FLY BRIDGE 28	FB	SF	FBG	SV	IO	T230-T270		8		6600	2	7	29300	34000
28		FLY BRIDGE 28	FB	SF	FBG	SV	IO	T130D	VLVO	8		6600	2	7	35100	39000
40		FLY BRIDGE 35	FB	SF	FBG	SV	IO	T250D	CUM	12		17000			97100	106500
		1984 BOATS														
20	5	SKIPJACK 20	OP	CR	FBG	DV	IO	225-260		7	10	3200			7300	8700
20	5	SKIPJACK 20	OP	CR	FBG	DV	IO	110D	VLVO	7	10	3200			8550	9800
23	10	SKIPJACK 24	OP	CR	FBG	DV	IO	225-260		8		4000			10200	11900
23	10	SKIPJACK 24	OP	CR	FBG	DV	IO	165D	VLVO	8		4000			12200	13900
23	10	SKIPJACK 24	OP	CR	FBG	DV	IO	T138	VLVO	8		4000			11300	12900
23	10	SKIPJACK 24	FB	CR	FBG	DV	IO	225-260		8		4600			11300	13200

 CONTINUED ON NEXT PAGE

INVADER MARINE LLC -CONTINUED See inside cover to adjust price for area

LOA FT	LOA IN	NAME AND/ OR MODEL	TOP/ RIG	BOAT TYPE	HULL MTL	HULL TP	ENGINE TP	ENGINE # HP	ENGINE MFG	BEAM FT	BEAM IN	WGT LBS	DRAFT FT	DRAFT IN	RETAIL LOW	RETAIL HIGH
		1984 BOATS														
23	10	SKIPJACK 24	FB	CR	FBG	DV	IO	165D	VLVO	8		4600			13300	15200
23	10	SKIPJACK 24	FB	CR	FBG	DV	IO	T138	VLVO	8		4600			12400	14100
25		SKIPJACK 25	HT	CBNCR	FBG	DV	IO	225-330		8		5200	2	6	15500	18600
25		SKIPJACK 25	HT	CBNCR	FBG	DV	IO	165D	VLVO	8		5200	2	6	20200	22400
25		SKIPJACK 25	HT	CBNCR	FBG	DV	IO	T138	VLVO	8		5200	2	6	16500	18800
25		SKIPJACK 25	HT	SPTCR	FBG	DV	IO	225-330		8		5000	2	6	12600	15600
25		SKIPJACK 25	HT	SPTCR	FBG	DV	IO	165D	VLVO	8		5000	2	6	14600	16600
25		SKIPJACK 25	HT	SPTCR	FBG	DV	IO	T138	VLVO	8		5000	2	6	13700	15500
25		SKIPJACK 25 PH	HT	FSH	FBG	DV	IO	225-330		8		5000	2	6	13300	16400
25		SKIPJACK 25 PH	HT	FSH	FBG	DV	IO	165D	VLVO	8		5000	2	6	18600	20700
25		SKIPJACK 25 PH	HT	FSH	FBG	DV	IO	T138	VLVO	8		5000	2	6	14400	16400
28		SKIPJACK 28	FB	PH	FBG	DV	IO	T170-T260		8		6600	2	9	19300	23800
28		SKIPJACK 28	FB	PH	FBG	DV	IO	T165D	VLVO	8		6600	2	9	25400	28300
28		SKIPJACK 28	FB	SPTCR	FBG	DV	IO	T170-T260		8		6600	2	9	18100	21900
28		SKIPJACK 28	FB	SPTCR	FBG	DV	IO	T165D	VLVO	8		6600	2	9	22300	24700

....For earlier years, see the BUC Used Boat Price Guide, Volume 3

INVERNESS MARINE
OSTERVILLE MA 02655

See inside cover to adjust price for area

LOA FT	LOA IN	NAME AND/ OR MODEL	TOP/ RIG	BOAT TYPE	HULL MTL	HULL TP	ENGINE TP	ENGINE # HP	ENGINE MFG	BEAM FT	BEAM IN	WGT LBS	DRAFT FT	DRAFT IN	RETAIL LOW	RETAIL HIGH
		1984 BOATS														
34	7	INVERNESS 35		TRWL	FBG	SV	IB	T 42D	VW	11	3	21000	4	9	90000	98900

....For earlier years, see the BUC Used Boat Price Guide, Volume 3

INVERTED CHINE BOATS INC
TOMS RIVER NJ 08753 COAST GUARD MFG ID- NVC

See inside cover to adjust price for area

LOA FT	LOA IN	NAME AND/ OR MODEL	TOP/ RIG	BOAT TYPE	HULL MTL	HULL TP	ENGINE TP	ENGINE # HP	ENGINE MFG	BEAM FT	BEAM IN	WGT LBS	DRAFT FT	DRAFT IN	RETAIL LOW	RETAIL HIGH
		1984 BOATS														
24		CUDDY FLYBRIDGE 24	FB	CUD	FBG	SV	IO	240	OMC	7	10	4900	2	4	8900	10100
24		CUDDY HARDTOP 24	HT	CUD	FBG	SV	IO	240	OMC	7	10	4300	2	4	7950	9150
24		FISHING 24		CUD	FBG	SV	IO	240	OMC	7	10	4400	2	4	8100	9300
24		OPEN CUDDY 24	OP	CUD	FBG	SV	IO	240	OMC	7	10	4200	2	4	7800	8950

....For earlier years, see the BUC Used Boat Price Guide, Volume 3

IROQUOIS
REG WHITE LTD
BRIGHTLING SEA ENGLAND

See inside cover to adjust price for area

WORLD CATAMARANS
FT LAUDERDALE FL

LOA FT	LOA IN	NAME AND/ OR MODEL	TOP/ RIG	BOAT TYPE	HULL MTL	HULL TP	ENGINE TP	ENGINE # HP	ENGINE MFG	BEAM FT	BEAM IN	WGT LBS	DRAFT FT	DRAFT IN	RETAIL LOW	RETAIL HIGH
		1989 BOATS														
32		CHIEFTAIN	SLP	SA/CR	F/S	CT	OB			13	6	6800	1	6	90600	99500

IRWIN YACHTS INTERNATIONAL INC
IRWIN YACHTS
TREASURE ISLAND FL 3370 COAST GUARD MFG ID- XYM
FORMERLY IRWIN YACHT & MARINE CORP

See inside cover to adjust price for area

For more recent years, see the BUC Used Boat Price Guide, Volume 1

LOA FT	LOA IN	NAME AND/ OR MODEL	TOP/ RIG	BOAT TYPE	HULL MTL	HULL TP	ENGINE TP	ENGINE # HP	ENGINE MFG	BEAM FT	BEAM IN	WGT LBS	DRAFT FT	DRAFT IN	RETAIL LOW	RETAIL HIGH
		1990 BOATS														
40	1	IRWIN 39 MKII SHOAL	SLP	SA/CR	FBG	KL	IB	44D		12	3	20000	4	6	86100	94600
40	2	IRWIN 39 MKII FIN	SLP	SA/CR	FBG	KL	IB	44D		12	3	20000	6	3	86300	94800
45	6	IRWIN 43 MKIII	SLP	SA/CR	FBG	KL	IB	66D		13	7	26000	4	11	110500	121500
55	8	IRWIN 52	SLP	SA/CR	FBG	KL	IB	77D	YAN	15	4	46000	5	6	201500	221500
57	2	IRWIN 54	SLP	SA/CR	FBG	CB	IB	77D	YAN	15	4	46000	12	6	225000	247500
57	2	IRWIN 54	SLP	SA/CR	FBG	KL	IB	77D	YAN	15	4	46000	5	6	225000	247500
58	4	IRWIN 54	KTH	SA/CR	FBG	KL	IB	77D	YAN	15	4	46000	5	6	226000	248500
73		IRWIN 68	SLP	SA/CR	FBG	CB	IB	T165D	PERK	17	4	78500	14	6	**	**
73		IRWIN 68 DEEP	KTH	SA/CR	FBG	KL	IB	T165D	PERK	17	4	78500	14	6	**	**
73		IRWIN 68 SHOAL	SLP	SA/CR	FBG	KL	IB	T165D	PERK	17	4	78500	6	1	**	**
73		IRWIN 68 SHOAL	KTH	SA/CR	FBG	KL	IB	T165D	PERK	17	4	78500	6	1	**	**
		1989 BOATS														
40	2	IRWIN 38 MKII FIN	SLP	SA/CR	FBG	KL	IB	44D		12	3	20000	6	3	74300	81700
40	2	IRWIN 38 MKII SHOAL	SLP	SA/CR	FBG	KL	IB	44D		12	3	20000	4	6	74300	81700
45	6	IRWIN 43 MKIII	SLP	SA/CR	FBG	KL	IB	66D		13	7	26000	4	11	103500	114000
55	8	IRWIN 52	SLP	SA/CR	FBG	KL	IB	77D	YAN	15	4	46000	5	6	189500	208000
57	2	IRWIN 54	SLP	SA/CR	FBG	CB	IB	77D	YAN	15	4	46000	12	6	211500	232000
57	2	IRWIN 54	SLP	SA/CR	FBG	KL	IB	77D	YAN	15	4	46000	5	6	211500	232000
58	4	IRWIN 54	KTH	SA/CR	FBG	KL	IB	77D	YAN	15	4	46000	5	6	212500	233500
73		IRWIN 68	KTH	SA/CR	FBG	CB	IB	130D		17	4	78500	14	6	**	**
73		IRWIN 68 DEEP	KTH	SA/CR	FBG	KL	IB	130D		17	4	78500	8	10	**	**
73		IRWIN 68 SHOAL	KTH	SA/CR	FBG	KL	IB	130D		17	4	78500	6	1	**	**
76		IRWIN 68 SHOAL	KTH	SA/CR	FBG	KL	IB	T140D		17	4	78500	6	1	**	**
		1988 BOATS														
32	3	CITATION 32 FIN	SLP	SA/RC	FBG	KL	IB	18D	YAN	11	1	10500	6		35000	38800
32	3	CITATION 32 SHOAL	SLP	SA/RC	FBG	KL	IB	18D	YAN	11	1	10500	4	2	34600	38400
35	5	CITATION 35 FIN	SLP	SA/RC	FBG	KL	IB	27D	YAN	11	6	11500	6	6	39800	44200
35	5	CITATION 35 SHOAL	SLP	SA/RC	FBG	KL	IB	27D	YAN	11	6	11500	4	8	39400	43800
38		CITATION 38 FIN	SLP	SA/RC	FBG	KL	IB	27D	YAN	12	6	15000	6	11	55500	60900
38		CITATION 38 SHOAL	SLP	SA/RC	FBG	KL	IB	27D	YAN	12	6	15000	4	11	55000	60500
40	2	IRWIN 38 MKII FIN	SLP	SA/CR	FBG	KL	IB	44D		12	3	20000	6	3	69900	76800
40	2	IRWIN 38 MKII SHOAL	SLP	SA/CR	FBG	KL	IB	44D		12	3	20000	4	6	69900	76800
43	6	IRWIN 44	SLP	SA/CR	FBG	KL	IB	44D		13	4	25000	4	11	90900	99900
45	6	IRWIN 43 MKIII	SLP	SA/CR	FBG	KL	IB	66D		13	7	26000			97500	107000
55	8	IRWIN 52	SLP	SA/CR	FBG	KL	IB	77D	YAN	15	4	46000	5	6	178000	195500
57	2	IRWIN 54	SLP	SA/CR	FBG	CB	IB	77D	YAN	15	4	46000	12	6	198500	218000
57	2	IRWIN 54	SLP	SA/CR	FBG	KL	IB	77D	YAN	15	4	46000	5	6	198500	218000
58	4	IRWIN 54	KTH	SA/CR	FBG	KL	IB	77D	YAN	15	4	46000	5	6	200000	219500
73		IRWIN 68	KTH	SA/CR	FBG	CB	IB	130D		17	4	78500	14	6	**	**
73		IRWIN 68 DEEP	KTH	SA/CR	FBG	KL	IB	130D		17	4	78500	8	10	**	**
73		IRWIN 68 SHOAL	KTH	SA/CR	FBG	KL	IB	130D		17	4	78500	6	1	**	**
		1987 BOATS														
32	4	IRWIN 32	SLP	SA/RC	FBG	KL	IB	18D		11	1	10500	4		32700	36400
34	7	IRWIN 34	SLP	SA/RC	FBG	KL	IB	D		11	3	11500	4		36500	40600
35	5	IRWIN 35	SLP	SA/RC	FBG	KL	IB	27D		11	5	11500	4	8	37200	41300
40	2	IRWIN 38	SLP	SA/RC	FBG	KL	IB	27D		12	6	20000	4	11	65500	71900
40	2	IRWIN 38 MKII	SLP	SA/CR	FBG	KL	IB	27D		12	3	20000	4	6	65500	71900
43	6	IRWIN 44	SLP	SA/CR	FBG	KL	IB	44D		13	4	25000	5	5	85500	93900
45	6	IRWIN 43 MKIII	SLP	SA/CR	FBG	KL	IB	66D		13	7	26000	4	11	91600	100500
52	6	IRWIN 53	SLP	SA/CR	FBG	KL	IB	77D	YAN	15	4	48000	5	9	173000	190000
55	8	IRWIN 52 MKIV	KTH	SA/CR	FBG	KL	IB	77D	YAN	15	4	50000	5	9	171500	188500
59	6	IRWIN 60	KTH	SA/CR	FBG	KL	IB	D		16		58000	5	9	196500	216000
65	6	IRWIN 65	KTH	SA/CR	FBG	KL	IB	130D	YAN	17	4	78500	5	9	392500	431500
73		IRWIN 68	KTH	SA/CR	FBG	KL	IB	130D		17	4	78500	5	9	**	**
		1986 BOATS														
32	3	CITATION 32	SLP	SA/RC	FBG	KC	IB	18D	YAN	11	1	10500	4		30800	34200
32	3	CITATION 32	SLP	SA/RC	FBG	KL	IB	18D	YAN	11	1	10500	6		30800	34200
35	5	CITATION 35	SLP	SA/RC	FBG	KC	IB	27D	YAN	11	5	11500	4	8	35000	38900
35	5	CITATION 35	SLP	SA/RC	FBG	KL	IB	27D	YAN	11	5	11500	6	6	35000	38900
38		CITATION 38	SLP	SA/RC	FBG	KC	IB	27D	YAN	12	6	15000	4	11	48900	53700
38		CITATION 38	SLP	SA/RC	FBG	KL	IB	27D	YAN	12	6	15000	6	11	48900	53700
40	2	IRWIN 38	SLP	SA/CR	FBG	KC	IB	50D	YAN	12	3	20000	4	6	62700	68900
40	2	IRWIN 38	SLP	SA/CR	FBG	KL	IB	50D	YAN	12	3	20000	6	3	62200	68400
40	2	IRWIN 38 SHOAL	SLP	SA/CR	FBG	KL	IB	50D	YAN	12	3	20000	4	6	61300	67400
45	6	IRWIN 43	SLP	SA/CR	FBG	KC	IB	62D	YAN	13	7	26000	4	10	86800	95400
45	6	IRWIN 43	SLP	SA/CR	FBG	KL	IB	62D	YAN	13	7	26000	6	3	86500	95100
45	6	IRWIN 43 SHOAL	SLP	SA/CR	FBG	KL	IB	62D	YAN	13	7	26000	4	11	85300	93800
55	8	IRWIN 52	SLP	SA/CR	FBG	KC	IB	85D	YAN	15	4	55000	5	6	165500	182000
55	8	IRWIN 52	SLP	SA/CR	FBG	KL	IB	85D	YAN	15	4	55000	7	1	164500	180500
55	8	IRWIN 52 SHOAL	SLP	SA/CR	FBG	KL	IB	85D	YAN	15	4	55000	5	6	162500	179000
64	8	IRWIN 65 SHOAL	SLP	SA/CR	FBG	KL	IB	130D	YAN	17	4	78500	5	9	369500	406000
65	6	IRWIN 65	SLP	SA/CR	FBG	KC	IB	130D	YAN	17	4	78500	5	9	369500	406000
65	6	IRWIN 65	SLP	SA/CR	FBG	KL	IB	130D	YAN	17	4	78500	8	6	369500	406000
65	6	IRWIN 65	KTH	SA/CR	FBG	KL	IB	130D	PERK	17	4	78500	5	9	368500	405000
		1985 BOATS														
31	3	CITATION 31	SLP	SA/RC	FBG	KC	IB	15D	YAN	11		9300	4		25800	28600
31	3	CITATION 31	SLP	SA/RC	FBG	KL	IB	15D	YAN	11		9300	6		25700	28600
31	3	CITATION 31 SHOAL	SLP	SA/RC	FBG	KL	IB	15D	YAN	11		9300	4		25200	28000
34	7	CITATION 34	SLP	SA/RC	FBG	KC	IB	15D- 23D		11	3	11500	4		32600	36300
34	7	CITATION 34	SLP	SA/RC	FBG	KL	IB	15D- 23D		11	3	11500	5	4	32400	36100
34	7	CITATION 34 SHOAL	SLP	SA/RC	FBG	KL	IB	15D- 23D		11	3	11500	4		31800	35400
40	2	IRWIN 38	SLP	SA/CR	FBG	KC	IB	51D	PERK	12	3	20000	4		58600	64400
40	2	IRWIN 38	SLP	SA/CR	FBG	KL	IB	51D	PERK	12	3	20000	6	3	58200	63900
40	2	IRWIN 38 SHOAL	SLP	SA/CR	FBG	KL	IB	51D	PERK	12	3	20000	4	6	57200	62900
41	8	IRWIN 41	KTH	SA/CR	FBG	KC	IB	62D	PERK	13	4	25000	4	6	76800	84400
41	8	IRWIN 41	KTH	SA/CR	FBG	KL	IB	62D	PERK	13	4	25000			76600	84200

LOA FT	IN	NAME AND/ OR MODEL	TOP/ RIG	BOAT TYPE	-HULL- MTL	TP	TP	ENGINE #	HP	MFG	BEAM FT	IN	WGT LBS	DRAFT FT	IN	RETAIL LOW	RETAIL HIGH
		1985 BOATS															
41	8	IRWIN 41 SHOAL	KTH	SA/CR	FBG	KL	IB		62D	PERK	13	4	25000	4	6	75500	82900
45	6	IRWIN 43	SLP	SA/CR	FBG	KC	IB		62D	PERK	13	7	26000	4	10	80400	88400
45	6	IRWIN 43	SLP	SA/CR	FBG	KL	IB		62D	PERK	13	7	26000	4	11	80400	88400
45	6	IRWIN 46	KTH	SA/CR	FBG	KC	IB		D		13	6	33000	4	8	101500	111500
55	8	IRWIN 52	KTH	SA/CR	FBG	KC	IB		85D	PERK	15	5	44500	5	6	147000	161500
55	8	IRWIN 52	KTH	SA/CR	FBG	KC	IB		135D	PERK	15	5	44500	5	6	147000	161500
55	8	IRWIN 52	KTH	SA/CR	FBG	KL	IB		85D	PERK	15	5	46500	7	1	149000	164000
55	8	IRWIN 52	KTH	SA/CR	FBG	KL	IB		135D	PERK	15	5	46500	7	1	149000	164000
55	8	IRWIN 52 SHOAL	KTH	SA/CR	FBG	KL	IB		85D	PERK	15	5	46500	5	6	147500	162500
55	8	IRWIN 52 SHOAL	KTH	SA/CR	FBG	KL	IB		135D	PERK	15	5	46500	5	6	147500	162500
65	8	IRWIN 65	KTH	SA/CR	FBG	KL	IB		135D	PERK	17	4	78500	8	6	348000	382000
65	8	IRWIN 65	KTH	SA/CR	FBG	KL	IB		200D	PERK	17	4	78500	8	6	348000	382500
65	8	IRWIN 65 SHOAL	KTH	SA/CR	FBG	KL	IB		135D	PERK	17	4	78500	5	9	345000	379000
65	8	IRWIN 65 SHOAL	KTH	SA/CR	FBG	KL	IB		200D	PERK	17	4	78500	5	9	346000	380000
		1984 BOATS															
31	3	CITATION 31	SLP	SA/RC	FBG	KC	IB		15D	YAN	11		9300	4		24300	26900
31	3	CITATION 31	SLP	SA/RC	FBG	KL	IB		15D	YAN	11		9300	6		24200	26900
31	3	CITATION 31 SHOAL	SLP	SA/RC	FBG	KL	IB		15D	YAN	11		9300	4		23700	26300
34	7	CITATION 34	SLP	SA/RC	FBG	KC	IB		15D-	23D	11	3	11500	4		30700	34100
34	7	CITATION 34	SLP	SA/RC	FBG	KL	IB		15D-	23D	11	3	11500	5	4	30500	34000
34	7	CITATION 34 SHOAL	SLP	SA/RC	FBG	KL	IB		15D-	23D	11	3	11500	4		29900	33300
34	8	IRWIN 34	SLP	SA/CR	FBG	KL	IB		15D	YAN	11	3	11500	4		30400	33800
37		IRWIN 37	SLP	SA/CR	FBG	KC	IB		D		11	6	20000		4	52800	58100
40	2	IRWIN 38	SLP	SA/CR	FBG	KC	IB		50D	PERK	12	3	20000	4		55100	60500
40	2	IRWIN 38	SLP	SA/CR	FBG	KL	IB		50D	PERK	12	3	20000	6	3	54700	60100
40	2	IRWIN 38 SHOAL	SLP	SA/CR	FBG	KL	IB		50D	PERK	12	3	20000	4	6	53800	59200
41	8	IRWIN 41	KTH	SA/CR	FBG	KC	IB		62D	PERK	13	4	25000	4	6	72300	79400
41	8	IRWIN 41	KTH	SA/CR	FBG	KL	IB		62D	PERK	13	4	25000			72100	79200
41	8	IRWIN 41 SHOAL	KTH	SA/CR	FBG	KL	IB		62D	PERK	13	4	25000	4	6	71000	78000
45	6	IRWIN 46	KTH	SA/CR	FBG	KC	IB		D		13	6	33000	4	8	95300	104500
55	8	IRWIN 52	KTH	SA/CR	FBG	KC	IB		85D	PERK	15	5	44500	5	6	138000	151500
55	8	IRWIN 52	KTH	SA/CR	FBG	KC	IB		135D	PERK	15	5	44500	5	6	171500	188500
55	8	IRWIN 52	KTH	SA/CR	FBG	KL	IB		85D	PERK	15	5	46500	7	1	140000	154000
55	8	IRWIN 52	KTH	SA/CR	FBG	KL	IB		135D	PERK	15	5	46500	7	1	140000	154000
55	8	IRWIN 52 SHOAL	KTH	SA/CR	FBG	KL	IB		85D	PERK	15	5	46500	5	6	139000	152500
55	8	IRWIN 52 SHOAL	KTH	SA/CR	FBG	KL	IB		135D	PERK	15	5	46500	5	6	139000	152500
65	8	IRWIN 65	KTH	SA/CR	FBG	KL	IB		135D	PERK	17	4	78500	8	6	327000	359500
65	8	IRWIN 65	KTH	SA/CR	FBG	KL	IB		200D	PERK	17	4	78500	8	6	327500	359500
65	8	IRWIN 65 SHOAL	KTH	SA/CR	FBG	KL	IB		135D	PERK	17	4	78500	5	9	324500	356500
65	8	IRWIN 65 SHOAL	KTH	SA/CR	FBG	KL	IB		200D	PERK	17	4	78500	5	9	325500	357500

....For earlier years, see the BUC Used Boat Price Guide, Volume 3

ISLAND CREEK BOAT SERVICE

ST LEONARD MD 20685 COAST GUARD MFG ID- GSA See inside cover to adjust price for area

LOA FT	IN	NAME AND/ OR MODEL	TOP/ RIG	BOAT TYPE	-HULL- MTL	TP	TP	ENGINE #	HP	MFG	BEAM FT	IN	WGT LBS	DRAFT FT	IN	RETAIL LOW	RETAIL HIGH
		1988 BOATS															
18		ISLAND-CREEK 18	SLP	SAIL	FBG	CB					5	4	450	1		4250	4950
		1987 BOATS															
18		ISLAND-CREEK 18	SLP	SAIL	FBG	CB					5	4	450	1		4000	4650
		1986 BOATS															
18		ISLAND-CREEK 18	SLP	SAIL	FBG	CB					5	4	450	1		3750	4400
		1985 BOATS															
18		ISLAND-CREEK 18	SLP	SAIL	FBG	CB					5	4	450	1		3550	4150

....For earlier years, see the BUC Used Boat Price Guide, Volume 3

ISLAND PACKET YACHTS

LARGO FL 34641 COAST GUARD MFG ID- TDL See inside cover to adjust price for area
FORMERLY TRADITIONAL

For more recent years, see the BUC Used Boat Price Guide, Volume 1

LOA FT	IN	NAME AND/ OR MODEL	TOP/ RIG	BOAT TYPE	-HULL- MTL	TP	TP	ENGINE #	HP	MFG	BEAM FT	IN	WGT LBS	DRAFT FT	IN	RETAIL LOW	RETAIL HIGH
		1996 BOATS															
32		ISLAND PACKET 29	SLP	SACAC	FBG	KL	IB		27D	YAN	10	10	10900	4	3	94500	104000
35		ISLAND PACKET 32	CUT	SACAC	FBG	KL	IB		27D	YAN	11	6	12900	4	4	108000	118500
35		PACKET CAT 35	SLP	SACAC	FBG	CT	IB	T	27D	YAN	15		11900	2	6	134000	147000
38	5	ISLAND PACKET 37	CUT	SACAC	FBG	KL	IB		35D	YAN	12	2	18500	4	6	150000	165000
41	6	ISLAND PACKET 40	CUT	SACAC	FBG	KL	IB		50D	YAN	12	11	22800	4	8	187500	206500
45	3	ISLAND PACKET 45	CUT	SACAC	FBG	KL	IB		62D	YAN	13	4	26000	4	10	242500	266500
		1995 BOATS															
32		ISLAND PACKET 29	SLP	SACAC	FBG	KL	IB		27D	YAN	10	10	10900	4	3	90400	99300
35		ISLAND PACKET 32	CUT	SACAC	FBG	KL	IB		27D	YAN	11	6	12900	4	4	103000	113500
35		PACKET CAT 35	SLP	SACAC	FBG	CT	IB	T	27D	YAN	15		11900	2	6	128000	140500
38	5	ISLAND PACKET 37	CUT	SACAC	FBG	KL	IB		35D	YAN	12	2	18500	4	6	143500	157500
41	6	ISLAND PACKET 40	CUT	SACAC	FBG	KL	IB		50D	YAN	12	11	22800	4	8	179500	197500
44	6	ISLAND PACKET 44	CUT	SACAC	FBG	KL	IB		62D	YAN	13	1	27500	5	7	232000	254500
		1994 BOATS															
32		ISLAND PACKET 29	SLP	SACAC	FBG	KL	IB		27D	YAN	10	10	10900	4	3	86300	94900
35		ISLAND PACKET 32	CUT	SACAC	FBG	KL	IB		27D	YAN	11	6	12900	4	4	98500	108500
35		PACKET CAT 35	SLP	SACAC	FBG	CT	IB	T	27D	YAN	15		11900	2	6	122500	134500
38		ISLAND PACKET 35	CUT	SACAC	FBG	KL	IB		35D	YAN	12		17500	4	6	130000	142500
41	6	ISLAND PACKET 40	CUT	SACAC	FBG	KL	IB		50D	YAN	12	11	22800	4	8	171500	188500
44	6	ISLAND PACKET 44	CUT	SACAC	FBG	KL	IB		62D	YAN	13	1	27500	5	7	221500	243500
		1993 BOATS															
32		ISLAND PACKET 29	SLP	SACAC	FBG	KL	IB		18D	YAN	10	10	10900	4	3	82200	90300
35		ISLAND PACKET 32	CUT	SACAC	FBG	KL	IB		27D	YAN	11	6	12900	4	4	94000	103500
35		PACKET CAT 35	SLP	SACAC	FBG	CT	IB	T	27D	YAN	15		11900	2	6	116500	128000
38		ISLAND PACKET 35	CUT	SACAC	FBG	KL	IB		35D	YAN	12		17500	4	6	124000	136000
41	6	ISLAND PACKET 38	CUT	SACAC	FBG	KL	IB		50D	YAN	12	8	21500	5		151500	166500
44	6	ISLAND PACKET 44	CUT	SACAC	FBG	KL	IB		62D	YAN	13	1	27500	5	7	211000	232000
		1992 BOATS															
30		ISLAND PACKET 27	SLP	SA/CR	FBG	KL	IB		18D	YAN	10	6	8000	3	8	50900	55900
32		ISLAND PACKET 29	SLP	SA/CR	FBG	KL	IB		18D	YAN	10	10	10900	4	3	78200	86000
35		ISLAND PACKET 32	CUT	SA/CR	FBG	KL	IB		27D	YAN	11	6	12900	4	4	89500	98400
38		ISLAND PACKET 35	CUT	SA/CR	FBG	KL	IB		35D	YAN	12		17500	4	6	118000	129500
41	6	ISLAND PACKET 38	CUT	SA/CR	FBG	KL	IB		50D	YAN	12	8	21500	5		144500	158500
44	6	ISLAND PACKET 44	CUT	SA/CR	FBG	KL	IB		62D	YAN	13	1	27500	5	7	201000	221000
		1991 BOATS															
30		ISLAND PACKET 27	SLP	SA/CR	FBG	KL	IB		18D	YAN	10	6	8000	3	8	48400	53200
32		ISLAND PACKET 29	SLP	SA/CR	FBG	KL	IB		18D	YAN	10	10	10900	4	3	74400	81800
35		ISLAND PACKET 32	SLP	SA/CR	FBG	KL	IB		27D	YAN	11	6	12900	4	4	85100	93500
38		ISLAND PACKET 35	CUT	SA/CR	FBG	KL	IB		35D	YAN	12		17500	4	6	112000	123000
41	6	ISLAND PACKET 38	CUT	SA/CR	FBG	KL	IB		50D	YAN	12	8	21500	5		137500	151000
		1990 BOATS															
30		ISLAND PACKET 27	SLP	SA/CR	FBG	KL	IB		18D	YAN	10	6	8000	3	8	46200	50700
35		ISLAND PACKET 32	SLP	SA/CR	FBG	KL	IB		27D	YAN	11	6	12900	4	4	80800	88800
38		ISLAND PACKET 35	CUT	SA/CR	FBG	KL	IB		35D	YAN	12		17500	4	6	106500	117000
41	6	ISLAND PACKET 38	CUT	SA/CR	FBG	KL	IB		44D	YAN	12	8	21500	5		130000	143000
		1989 BOATS															
30		ISLAND PACKET 27	CUT	SA/CR	FBG	KC	IB		18D	YAN	10	6	8000	3	8	43300	48100
30		ISLAND PACKET 27	CUT	SA/CR	FBG	KL	IB		18D	YAN	10	6	8000	3	8	43300	48100
34	4	ISLAND PACKET 31	CUT	SA/CR	FBG	KC	IB		27D	YAN	11	6	11000	4		65400	71900
34	4	ISLAND PACKET 31	CUT	SA/CR	FBG	KL	IB		27D	YAN	11	6	11000	4		65400	71900
35	4	ISLAND-PACKET 35	CUT	SA/CR	FBG	KC	IB		35D	YAN	12		17500	3	8	101000	111000
35	4	ISLAND-PACKET 35	CUT	SA/CR	FBG	KL	IB		35D	YAN	12		17500	4	6	101000	111000
38		ISLAND-PACKET 38	CUT	SA/CR	FBG	KC	IB		44D	YAN	12	8	21500	4		123500	135500
38		ISLAND-PACKET 38	CUT	SA/CR	FBG	KL	IB		44D	YAN	12	8	21500	5		123500	135500
		1988 BOATS															
30		ISLAND PACKET 27	CUT	SA/CR	FBG	KC	IB		18D	YAN	10	6	8000	3	8	41000	45500
30		ISLAND PACKET 27	CUT	SA/CR	FBG	KL	IB		18D	YAN	10	6	8000	3	8	41000	45500
34	4	ISLAND PACKET 31	CUT	SA/CR	FBG	KC	IB		27D	YAN	11	6	11000	4		61900	68100
34	4	ISLAND PACKET 31	CUT	SA/CR	FBG	KL	IB		27D	YAN	11	6	11000	4		61900	68100
38		ISLAND-PACKET 38	CUT	SA/CR	FBG	KC	IB		44D	YAN	12	8	21500	4		117000	128500
38		ISLAND-PACKET 38	CUT	SA/CR	FBG	KL	IB		44D	YAN	12	8	21500	5		117000	128500
		1987 BOATS															
30		ISLAND PACKET 27	CUT	SA/CR	FBG	KC	IB		18D	YAN	10	6	8000	3	8	38700	43100
30		ISLAND PACKET 27	CUT	SA/CR	FBG	KL	IB		18D	YAN	10	6	8000	3	8	38700	43100
34	4	ISLAND PACKET 31	CUT	SA/CR	FBG	KC	IB		27D	YAN	11	6	11000	4		58500	64300
34	4	ISLAND PACKET 31	CUT	SA/CR	FBG	KL	IB		27D	YAN	11	6	11000	4		58500	64300
38		ISLAND-PACKET 38	CUT	SA/CR	FBG	KC	IB		44D	YAN	12	8	21500	4		110500	121500
38		ISLAND-PACKET 38	CUT	SA/CR	FBG	KL	IB		44D	YAN	12	8	21500	5		110500	121500
		1986 BOATS															
30		ISLAND PACKET 27	CUT	SA/CR	FBG	KC	IB		18D	YAN	10	6	8000	3	8	36600	40600
30		ISLAND PACKET 27	CUT	SA/CR	FBG	KL	IB		18D	YAN	10	6	8000	3	8	36600	40600
34	4	ISLAND PACKET 31	CUT	SA/CR	FBG	KC	IB		27D	YAN	11	6	11000	4		55300	60700
34	4	ISLAND PACKET 31	CUT	SA/CR	FBG	KL	IB		27D	YAN	11	6	11000	4		55300	60700
38		ISLAND-PACKET 38	CUT	SA/CR	FBG	KC	IB		44D	YAN	12	8	21000	4		102500	112500
38		ISLAND-PACKET 38	CUT	SA/CR	FBG	KL	IB		44D	YAN	12	8	21000	5		102500	112500
		1985 BOATS															
30		ISLAND PACKET 27	CUT	SA/CR	FBG	KC	IB		17D	YAN	10	6	8000	3	8	34400	38300
30		ISLAND PACKET 27	CUT	SA/CR	FBG	KL	IB		17D	YAN	10	6	8000	3	8	34400	38300
34	4	ISLAND PACKET 31	CUT	SA/CR	FBG	KC	IB		27D	YAN	11	6	11000	4		52100	57200
34	4	ISLAND PACKET 31	CUT	SA/CR	FBG	KL	IB		27D	YAN	11	6	11000	4		52100	57200
		1984 BOATS															
30		ISLAND PACKET 26MKII	CUT	SA/CR	FBG	KC	IB		15D	YAN	10	6	8000	3	8	32000	35600
30		ISLAND PACKET 26MKII	CUT	SA/CR	FBG	KL	IB		15D	YAN	10	6	8000	3	8	32000	35600

LOA FT	IN	NAME AND/ OR MODEL	TOP/ RIG	BOAT TYPE	-HULL- MTL	TP	----ENGINE--- TP	# HP	MFG	BEAM FT	IN	WGT LBS	DRAFT FT	IN	RETAIL LOW	RETAIL HIGH
		1984 BOATS														
30		ISLAND PACKET 27	CUT	SA/CR	FBG	KC	IB	15D	YAN	10	6	8000	3	8	32300	35900
30		ISLAND PACKET 27	CUT	SA/CR	FBG	KL	IB	15D	YAN	10	6	8000	3	8	32300	35900
34	4	ISLAND PACKET 31	CUT	SA/CR	FBG	KC	IB	22D	YAN	11	6	11000	4		49000	53800
34	4	ISLAND PACKET 31	CUT	SA/CR	FBG	KL	IB	22D	YAN	11	6	11000	4		49000	53800

....For earlier years, see the BUC Used Boat Price Guide, Volume 3

ISLAND RUNNER LLC

DIV OF OFFSHORE TECHNOLOGIES
RIVIERA BEACH FL 33404 COAST GUARD MFG ID- INT

See inside cover to adjust price for area

SARASOTA MARINE CORP
BRADENTON FL 34203

For more recent years, see the BUC Used Boat Price Guide, Volume 1

LOA FT	IN	NAME AND/ OR MODEL	TOP/ RIG	BOAT TYPE	-HULL- MTL	TP	----ENGINE--- TP	# HP	MFG	BEAM FT	IN	WGT LBS	DRAFT FT	IN	RETAIL LOW	RETAIL HIGH
		1987 BOATS														
35	6	ISLAND-RUNNER 35 M/S	KTH	MS	FBG	CB	IB	110D	VLVO	12	1	19832	4	5	81000	89000
		1986 BOATS														
35	6	ISLAND-RUNNER 35	KTH	MS	FBG	CB	IB	110D	VLVO	12	1	19832	4	5	75800	83300

ISLANDER YACHTS

IRVINE CA 92714 COAST GUARD MFG ID- XLY See inside cover to adjust price for area

LOA FT	IN	NAME AND/ OR MODEL	TOP/ RIG	BOAT TYPE	-HULL- MTL	TP	----ENGINE--- TP	# HP	MFG	BEAM FT	IN	WGT LBS	DRAFT FT	IN	RETAIL LOW	RETAIL HIGH
		1986 BOATS														
27	11	ISLANDER 28	SLP	SA/RC	FBG	KL	IB	D		9	10	7000	5		21900	24400
29	11	ISLANDER 30	SLP	SA/RC	FBG	KL	IB	D		10		8230	5		26000	28800
36	1	ISLANDER 36	SLP	SA/RC	FBG	KL	IB	D		11	2	13450	6		43300	48100
38		ISLANDER 38	SLP	SA/CR	FBG	KL	IB	D		12		17000	5	3	56900	62500
39	6	ISLANDER 40	SLP	SA/RC	FBG	KL	IB	D		11	10	17000	7	2	61200	67300
41		ISLANDER 41	KTH	SA/CR	FBG	KL	IB	D		13	2	22000	5		78400	86100
		1985 BOATS														
27	11	ISLANDER 28	SLP	SA/CR	FBG	KL	IB	15D	YAN	9	11	7000	5		20800	23100
29	11	ISLANDER 30	SLP	SA/CR	FBG	KL	IB	15D	YAN	10		8230	5		24600	27300
29	11	ISLANDER 30 SHOAL	SLP	SA/CR	FBG	KL	IB	15D	YAN	10		8320	4		24900	27600
34	4	ISLANDER 34	SLP	SA/CR	FBG	KL	IB	23D	YAN	11		9656	6	2	28800	32000
34	4	ISLANDER 34 SHOAL	SLP	SA/CR	FBG	KL	IB	23D	YAN	11		9656	4	10	28800	32000
36	1	ISLANDER 36	SLP	SA/CR	FBG	KL	IB	30D	YAN	11	2	13450	6		41100	45600
36	1	ISLANDER 36 SHOAL	SLP	SA/CR	FBG	KL	IB	30D	YAN	11	2	13600	4	9	41500	46100
38		ISLANDER 38C	SLP	SA/CR	FBG	KL	IB	42D	PATH	12		17000	5	3	53900	59200
39	7	ISLANDER 40	SLP	SA/CR	FBG	KL	IB	44D	YAN	11	10	17000	7	2	58500	64300
39	7	ISLANDER 40 SHOAL	SLP	SA/CR	FBG	KL	IB	44D	YAN	11	10	17000	5	1	58500	64300
41		ISLANDER 41C	KTH	SA/CR	FBG	KL	IB	82D	PATH	13	2	22000	5		74700	82100
47	6	ISLANDER 48	CUT	SA/CR	FBG	KL	IB	82D		13	10	29125	5	11	115000	126500
47	6	ISLANDER 48C	SLP	SA/CR	FBG	KL	IB	82D	PATH	13	10	29125	5	11	115000	126500
		1984 BOATS														
27	11	ISLANDER 28	SLP	SA/RC	FBG	KL	IB	15D	YAN	9	11	7000	5		19700	21900
29	11	ISLANDER 30	SLP	SA/RC	FBG	KL	SD	15D	YAN	10		8230	5		23300	25900
29	11	ISLANDER 30 SHOAL	SLP	SA/RC	FBG	KL	SD	15D	YAN	10		8320	4		23600	26200
35	9	ISLANDER 36 CTR CPT	SLP	SA/RC	FBG	KL	IB	D		12		17000	5	3	47800	52500
36	1	ISLANDER 36	SLP	SA/RC	FBG	KL	IB	30D	YAN	11	2	13450	6		38900	43200
36	1	ISLANDER 36 SHOAL	SLP	SA/RC	FBG	KL	IB	30D	YAN	11	2	13600	4	9	39300	43700
38		ISLAND CRUISING 38	SLP	SA/CR	FBG	KL	IB	42D	PATH	12		17000	5	3	51100	56100
39	7	ISLANDER 40	SLP	SA/RC	FBG	KL	IB	44D	YAN	11	10	17000	7	2	55400	60900
39	7	ISLANDER 40 SHOAL	SLP	SA/RC	FBG	KL	IB	44D	YAN	11	10	17000	5	1	55400	60900
41		ISLANDER CRUISING 41	KTH	SA/CR	FBG	KL	IB	82D	PATH	13	2	22000	5		70800	77800
47	6	ISLANDER 48	CUT	SA/CR	FBG	KL	IB	82D		13	10	29125	5	11	109000	120000
47	6	ISLANDER CRUISING 48	SLP	SA/CR	FBG	KL	IB	82D	PATH	13	10	29125	5	11	109000	120000

....For earlier years, see the BUC Used Boat Price Guide, Volume 3

J & J NASH IND LTD

STRATHROY ONTARIO CANAD COAST GUARD MFG ID- ZJN See inside cover to adjust price for area

LOA FT	IN	NAME AND/ OR MODEL	TOP/ RIG	BOAT TYPE	-HULL- MTL	TP	----ENGINE--- TP	# HP	MFG	BEAM FT	IN	WGT LBS	DRAFT FT	IN	RETAIL LOW	RETAIL HIGH
		1986 BOATS														
26		NASH 26	SLP	SA/CR	FBG	KL	SD	15	OMC	8	6	5200	3	6	10200	11600
26		NASH 26	SLP	SA/CR	FBG	KL	SD	8D	BUKH	8	6	5200	3	6	10500	11900
33		NASH 33	SLP	SA/CR	FBG	KL	SD	15D	BUKH	11	1	10000	4	6	21500	23900
		1985 BOATS														
26		NASH 26	SLP	SA/CR	FBG	KL	SD	15	OMC	8	6	5200	3	6	9550	10900
26		NASH 26	SLP	SA/CR	FBG	KL	SD	8D	BUKH	8	6	5200	3	6	9850	11200
33		NASH 33	SLP	SA/CR	FBG	KL	IB			11	1	10000	4	6	20200	22400
		1984 BOATS														
26		NASH 26	SLP	SA/CR	FBG	KL	SD	15	OMC	8	6	5200	3	6	9050	10300
26		NASH 26	SLP	SA/CR	FBG	KL	SD	15D	VLVO	8	6	5200	3	6	9400	10700

....For earlier years, see the BUC Used Boat Price Guide, Volume 3

J BOATS INC

TPI INC
NEWPORT RI 02840 COAST GUARD MFG ID- PCX

See inside cover to adjust price for area

For more recent years, see the BUC Used Boat Price Guide, Volume 1

LOA FT	IN	NAME AND/ OR MODEL	TOP/ RIG	BOAT TYPE	-HULL- MTL	TP	----ENGINE--- TP	# HP	MFG	BEAM FT	IN	WGT LBS	DRAFT FT	IN	RETAIL LOW	RETAIL HIGH
		1996 BOATS														
22	6	J/22	SLP	SAROD	F/S	KL	OB			8		1790	3	8	12600	14300
24		J/24	SLP	SAROD	F/S	KL	OB			8	9	3100	4		19700	21800
26		J/80	SLP	SAROD	F/S	KL	OB			8		2900	4	9	21200	23600
30		J/92	SLP	SAROD	F/S	KL	IB	9D	YAN	10		5500	5	9	47300	52000
34	5	J/105 DEEP	SLP	SAROD	F/S	KL	IB	20D	YAN	11		7750	6	5	69500	76400
34	5	J/105 SHOAL	SLP	SAROD	F/S	KL	IB	20D	YAN	11		7850	5	5	70500	77400
36		J/110 AL MAST	SLP	SAROD	F/S	KL	IB	28D	YAN	11		12200	5	9	107500	118500
36		J/110 CF MAST	SLP	SAROD	F/S	KL	IB	28D	YAN	11		12200	5	9	115500	126500
40		J/120 AL DEEP	SLP	SAROD	F/S	KL	IB	38D	YAN	12		13000	7		139000	152500
40		J/120 AL SHOAL	SLP	SAROD	F/S	KL	IB	38D	YAN	12		13000	6		140000	154000
40		J/120 CF DEEP	SLP	SAROD	F/S	KL	IB	38D	YAN	12		13000	7		147500	162500
40		J/120 CF SHOAL	SLP	SAROD	F/S	KL	IB	38D	YAN	12		13000	6		149000	163500
42		J/42 DEEP	SLP	SAROD	F/S	KL	IB	47D	YAN	12	1	18000	6		194000	213000
42		J/42 SHOAL	SLP	SAROD	F/S	KL	IB	47D	YAN	12	1	18000	5	3	195000	214500
42	7	J/130 AL DEEP	SLP	SAROD	F/S	KL	IB	47D	YAN	12	8	18000	8	5	194000	213000
42	7	J/130 CF DEEP	SLP	SAROD	F/S	KL	IB	47D	YAN	12	8	18000	8	5	206000	226000
52	7	J/160	SLP	SAROD	F/S	KL	IB	88D	YAN	14	5	26200	8	8	422000	463500
		1995 BOATS														
22	5	J/22	SLP	SAROD	F/S	KL	OB			8		1790	3	8	11700	13300
24		J/24	SLP	SAROD	F/S	KL	OB			8	9	3100	4		18600	20600
26	1	J/80	SLP	SAROD	F/S	KL	OB			8		2900	4	9	19900	22100
30		J/92	SLP	SAROD	F/S	KL	IB	9D	YAN	10		5500	5	9	43800	48700
34	5	J/105 DEEP	SLP	SAROD	F/S	KL	IB	20D	YAN	11		7750	6	5	65100	71500
36		J/110 AL MAST	SLP	SAROD	F/S	KL	IB	28D	YAN	11		12200	5	9	97000	106500
36		J/110 CF MAST	SLP	SAROD	F/S	KL	IB	28D	YAN	11		12200	5	9	104000	114500
40		J/120 AL MAST	SLP	SAROD	F/S	KL	IB	38D	YAN	12		12900	7		129500	142500
40		J/120 CF MAST	SLP	SAROD	F/S	KL	IB	38D	YAN	12		12900	7		138500	152000
40	3	J/40 DEEP	SLP	SAROD	F/S	KL	IB	47D	YAN	12	1	21000	6	5	188500	207000
40	3	J/40 SHOAL	SLP	SAROD	F/S	KL	IB	47D	YAN	12	1	21000	5		188500	207000
42	7	J/130 AL MAST	SLP	SAROD	F/S	KL	IB	47D	YAN	12	8	15000	8	5	169000	185500
42	7	J/130 CF MAST	SLP	SAROD	F/S	KL	IB	47D	YAN	12	8	14000	8	5	162500	178500
		1994 BOATS														
22	5	J/22	SLP	SAROD	F/S	KL	OB			8		1790	3	8	11000	12500
24		J/24	SLP	SAROD	F/S	KL	OB			8	9	3100	4		17000	19300
26	1	J/80	SLP	SAROD	F/S	KL	OB			8		2900	4	9	18900	21000
30		J/92	SLP	SAROD	F/S	KL	IB	9D	YAN	10		5500	5	9	41000	45500
34	5	J/105 DEEP	SLP	SAROD	F/S	KL	IB	20D	YAN	11		7750	6	5	60900	66900
35	2	J/35C DEEP	SLP	SAROD	F/S	KL	IB	30D	YAN	11	1	11800	5	5	93100	102500
35	5	J/35 DEEP	SLP	SAROD	F/S	KL	IB	28D	YAN	12		10500	6	9	83800	92100
39	5	J/39	SLP	SAROD	F/S	KL	IB	28D	YAN	12	4	12500	7	2	117000	128500
40		J/120 AL MAST	SLP	SAROD	F/S	KL	IB	38D	YAN	12		12900	7		121500	133500
40		J/120 CF MAST	SLP	SAROD	F/S	KL	IB	38D	YAN	12		12900	7		129000	142000
40	3	J/40 DEEP	SLP	SAROD	F/S	KL	IB	47D	YAN	12	1	21000	6	5	176500	194000
40	3	J/40 SHOAL	SLP	SAROD	F/S	KL	IB	47D	YAN	12	1	21000	5		176500	194000
42	7	J/130 AL MAST	SLP	SAROD	F/S	KL	IB	47D	YAN	12	8	15000	8	5	158000	173500
42	7	J/130 CF MAST	SLP	SAROD	F/S	KL	IB	47D	YAN	12	8	14000	8	5	152000	167000
44	9	J/44 DEEP	SLP	SAROD	F/S	KL	IB	62D	YAN	13	8	22000	8	1	216500	238000
52	5	J/160	SLP	MS	F/S	KL	IB	88D	YAN	14		25200	8	8	362500	398500
		1993 BOATS														
22	6	J/22	SLP	SAROD	F/S	KL	OB			8		1750	3	11	10200	11600
24		J/24	SLP	SAROD	F/S	KL	OB			8	9	3100	4		15900	18000
30		J/92 DEEP	SLP	SAROD	F/S	KL	IB	9D		10		5500	5	9	38300	42600
30		J/92 SHOAL	SLP	SAROD	F/S	KL	IB	9D		10		5500	5	9	38300	42600
34	5	J/105 DEEP	SLP	SAROD	F/S	KL	IB	20D	YAN	11		7300	6	5	53600	58900

LOA FT	LOA IN	NAME AND/ OR MODEL	TOP/ RIG	BOAT TYPE	HULL MTL	HULL TP	ENGINE TP	# HP	ENGINE MFG	BEAM FT	BEAM IN	WGT LBS	DRAFT FT	DRAFT IN	RETAIL LOW	RETAIL HIGH
		1993 BOATS														
35	5	J/35 DEEP	SLP	SAROD	F/S	KL	IB	23D	YAN	11	9	10000	6	11	66100	72600
35	5	J/35C DEEP	SLP	SAROD	F/S	KL	IB	23D	YAN	11	9	10000	5	9	83400	91700
39	5	J/39	SLP	SARAC	F/S	KL	IB	28D		12	4	12500	7	2	109000	120000
40		J/40 DEEP	SLP	SAROD	F/S	KL	IB	43D	VLVO	12	2	15500	6	6	163500	180000
40		J/40 SHOAL	SLP	SAROD	F/S	KL	IB	43D	VLVO	12	2	15500	5		163500	180000
42	7	J/130 DEEP	SLP	SACAC	F/S	KL	IB	47D		12	8	15000	8	5	147500	162000
42	7	J/130 SHOAL	SLP	SACAC	F/S	KL	IB	47D		12	8	15000	6	5	147500	162000
44	9	J/44 DEEP	SLP	SAROD	F/S	KL	IB	55D	VLVO	13	7	22000	8		202000	222000
		1992 BOATS														
22	6	J/22	SLP	SA/OD	F/S	KL	OB			8		1750	3	11	9550	10800
24		J/24	SLP	SA/OD	F/S	KL	OB			8	9	3100	4		14800	16900
27	5	J/27	SLP	SA/OD	F/S	KL	OB			8	5	3800	4	9	22200	24700
33	5	J/33 DEEP	SLP	SA/OD	F/S	KL	IB	18D	VLVO	10	3	7500	6	1	51100	56200
34	5	J/105 DEEP	SLP	SA/OD	F/S	KL	IB	20D	YAN	11		7300	6	5	50100	55100
35	5	J/35 DEEP	SLP	SA/OD	F/S	KL	IB	23D	YAN	11	9	10000	6	11	61300	67300
35	5	J/35C DEEP	SLP	SA/OD	F/S	KL	IB	23D	YAN	11	9	10000	5	9	78600	86400
37	5	J/37C DEEP	SLP	SA/OD	F/S	KL	IB	28D	VLVO	12	4	14500	7		103500	114000
37	5	J/37C SHOAL	SLP	SA/OD	F/S	KL	IB	28D	VLVO	12	4	14500	5		103500	114000
40		J/40 DEEP	SLP	SA/OD	F/S	KL	IB	43D	VLVO	12	2	15500	6	6	153000	168500
40		J/40 SHOAL	SLP	SA/OD	F/S	KL	IB	43D	VLVO	12	2	15500	5		153000	168500
44	9	J/44 DEEP	SLP	SA/OD	F/S	KL	IB	55D	VLVO	13	7	22000	8		189000	207500
		1991 BOATS														
22	6	J/22	SLP	SA/OD	F/S	KL	OB			8		1750	3	11	8950	10200
24		J/24	SLP	SA/OD	F/S	KL	OB			8	9	3100	4		13900	15800
27	5	J/27	SLP	SA/OD	F/S	KL	OB			8	5	3800	4	9	20800	23100
33	5	J/33 DEEP	SLP	SA/OD	F/S	KL	IB	18D	VLVO	10	3	7500	6	1	47800	52600
35	5	J/35 DEEP	SLP	SA/OD	F/S	KL	IB	23D	YAN	11	9	10000	6	11	57900	63600
35	5	J/35C DEEP	SLP	SA/OD	F/S	KL	IB	23D	YAN	11	9	10000	5	9	73000	80200
37	5	J/37C DEEP	SLP	SA/OD	F/S	KL	IB	28D	VLVO	12	4	14500	7		96900	106500
37	5	J/37C SHOAL	SLP	SA/OD	F/S	KL	IB	28D	VLVO	12	4	14500	5		96900	106500
40		J/40 DEEP	SLP	SA/OD	F/S	KL	IB	43D	VLVO	12	2	15500	5		149000	163500
40		J/40 SHOAL	SLP	SA/OD	F/S	KL	IB	43D	VLVO	12	2	15500	6	6	137500	151500
44	9	J/44 DEEP A	SLP	SA/OD	F/S	KL	IB	55D	VLVO	13	7	22000	8		170000	186500
44	9	J/44 DEEP B	SLP	SA/OD	F/S	KL	IB	55D	VLVO	13	7	22000	8		183500	202000
44	9	J/44 SHOAL A	SLP	SA/OD	F/S	KL	IB	55D	VLVO	13	7	22000	6		170000	186500
44	9	J/44 SHOAL B	SLP	SA/OD	F/S	KL	IB	55D	VLVO	13	7	22000	6		183500	202000
		1990 BOATS														
22	6	J/22	SLP	SA/OD	F/S	KL	OB			8		1750	3	11	8300	9500
24		J/24	SLP	SA/OD	F/S	KL	OB			8	9	3100	4		13000	14700
27	5	J/27	SLP	SA/OD	F/S	KL	OB			8	5	3800	4	9	19400	21600
29	11	J/30	SLP	SA/OD	F/S	KL	IB	15D	YAN	11	3	7000	5	3	40100	44500
33	5	J/33 DEEP	SLP	SA/OD	F/S	KL	IB	18D	VLVO	10	3	7500	6	1	44500	49500
34	5	J/34C SHOAL	SLP	SA/OD	F/S	KL	IB	28D	VLVO	11	1	10000	5		60300	66200
35	5	J/35C DEEP	SLP	SA/OD	F/S	KL	IB	23D	YAN	11	9	10000	6	11	55500	61000
35	5	J/35C SHOAL	SLP	SA/OD	F/S	KL	IB	23D	YAN	11	9	10000	5	9	67000	73600
37	5	J/37C DEEP	SLP	SA/OD	F/S	KL	IB	28D	VLVO	12	4	14500	7		90700	99700
37	5	J/37C SHOAL	SLP	SA/OD	F/S	KL	IB	28D	VLVO	12	4	14500	5		90700	99700
40		J/40 DEEP	SLP	SA/OD	F/S	KL	IB	43D	VLVO	12	2	15500	6	6	134000	147500
40		J/40 SHOAL	SLP	SA/OD	F/S	KL	IB	43D	VLVO	12	2	15500	5		134000	147500
44	9	J/44 DEEP	SLP	SA/OD	F/S	KL	IB	55D	VLVO	13	7	22000	8		165500	182000
44	9	J/44 SHOAL	SLP	SA/OD	F/S	KL	IB	55D	VLVO	13	7	22000	6		165500	182000
		1989 BOATS														
22	6	J/22	SLP	SA/OD	F/S	KL	OB			8		1750	3	11	7750	8900
24		J/24	SLP	SA/OD	F/S	KL	OB			8	11	3100	4		12100	13800
27	6	J/27	SLP	SA/OD	F/S	KL	OB			8	6	3800	4	9	18500	20500
28	6	J/28 DEEP	SLP	SA/OD	F/S	KL	IB	18D	YAN	10		7900	5		41000	45500
28	6	J/28 SHOAL	SLP	SA/OD	F/S	KL	IB	18D	YAN	10		7900	3	11	41000	45500
29	11	J/30	SLP	SA/OD	F/S	KL	IB	15D	YAN	11	3	7000	5	3	37500	41700
33	5	J/33 DEEP	SLP	SA/OD	F/S	KL	IB	18D	VLVO	10	3	7500	6	1	41700	46300
34	5	J/34C SHOAL	SLP	SA/OD	F/S	KL	IB	28D	VLVO	11	1	10000	5		56400	62000
35	5	J/35 DEEP	SLP	SA/OD	F/S	KL	IB	23D	YAN	11	9	10000	6	11	57300	63000
35	5	J/35 SHOAL	SLP	SA/OD	F/S	KL	IB	23D	YAN	11	9	10000	5	9	57300	63000
37	6	J/37 DEEP	SLP	SA/OD	F/S	KL	IB	28D	VLVO	12	3	13500	7		80200	88100
37	6	J/37 SHOAL	SLP	SA/OD	F/S	KL	IB	28D	VLVO	12	3	13500	6		80200	88100
40		J/40 DEEP	SLP	SA/OD	F/S	KL	IB	43D	VLVO	12	2	15500	6	6	125500	138000
40		J/40 SHOAL	SLP	SA/OD	F/S	KL	IB	43D	VLVO	12	2	15500	5		125500	138000
44		J/44 DEEP	SLP	SA/OD	F/S	KL	IB	55D	VLVO	13	10	20600	8		144500	159000
44		J/44 SHOAL	SLP	SA/OD	F/S	KL	IB	55D	VLVO	13	10	21000	6		146000	160500
		1988 BOATS														
22	6	J/22	SLP	SA/OD	F/S	KL	OB			8		1750	3	11	7250	8300
24		J/24	SLP	SA/OD	F/S	KL	OB			8	11	3100	4		11300	12900
27	6	J/27	SLP	SA/OD	F/S	KL	OB			8	6	3800	4	9	16900	19200
28	6	J/28 DEEP	SLP	SA/OD	F/S	KL	IB	18D	YAN	10		7900	5		38300	42600
28	6	J/28 SHOAL	SLP	SA/OD	F/S	KL	IB	18D	YAN	10		7900	3	11	38300	42600
29	11	J/30	SLP	SA/OD	F/S	KL	IB	15D	YAN	11	3	7000	5	3	35100	39000
33	5	J/33 DEEP	SLP	SA/OD	F/S	KL	IB	18D	VLVO	10	3	7500	6	1	39000	43300
34	5	J/34C SHOAL	SLP	SA/OD	F/S	KL	IB	28D	VLVO	11	1	10000	5		52800	58000
35	5	J/35 DEEP	SLP	SA/OD	F/S	KL	IB	23D	YAN	11	9	10000	6	11	53600	58900
35	5	J/35 SHOAL	SLP	SA/OD	F/S	KL	IB	23D	YAN	11	9	10000	5	9	53600	58900
37	6	J/37 DEEP	SLP	SA/OD	F/S	KL	IB	28D	VLVO	12	3	13500	7		75000	82500
37	6	J/37 SHOAL	SLP	SA/OD	F/S	KL	IB	28D	VLVO	12	3	13500	6		75000	82500
40		J/40 DEEP	SLP	SA/OD	F/S	KL	IB	43D	VLVO	12	2	15500	6	6	117500	129000
40		J/40 SHOAL	SLP	SA/OD	F/S	KL	IB	43D	VLVO	12	2	15500	5		117500	129000
		1987 BOATS														
22	6	J/22	SLP	SA/OD	F/S	KL	OB			8		1750	3	11	6750	7800
24		J/24	SLP	SA/OD	F/S	KL	OB			8	11	3100	4		10600	12100
27	6	J/27	SLP	SA/OD	F/S	KL	OB			8	6	3800	4	9	15800	18000
28	6	J/28 DEEP	SLP	SA/OD	F/S	KL	IB	18D	YAN	10		7900	5		35900	39800
28	6	J/28 SHOAL	SLP	SA/OD	F/S	KL	IB	18D	YAN	10		7900	3	11	35900	39800
29	6	J/29	SLP	SA/OD	F/S	KL	OB			11		6000	5	7	27300	30300
29	6	J/29	SLP	SA/OD	F/S	KL	IB	8D	YAN	11		6000	5	7	27700	30800
29	11	J/30	SLP	SA/OD	F/S	KL	IB	15D	YAN	11	3	7000	5	3	32900	36500
34		J/34	SLP	SA/OD	F/S	KL	IB	30D	YAN	11	2	8100	6	2	39700	44100
35	5	J/35 DEEP	SLP	SA/OD	F/S	KL	IB	23D	YAN	11	9	10000	6	11	50200	55100
35	5	J/35 SHOAL	SLP	SA/OD	F/S	KL	IB	23D	YAN	11	9	10000	5	9	50200	55100
36		J/36	SLP	SA/OD	F/S	KL	IB			11	9	11000	6	7	55000	60500
37	6	J/37 DEEP	SLP	SA/OD	F/S	KL	IB	28D	VLVO	12	3	13500	7		70200	77200
37	6	J/37 SHOAL	SLP	SA/OD	F/S	KL	IB	28D	VLVO	12	3	13500	6		70200	77200
40		J/40 DEEP	SLP	SA/OD	F/S	KL	IB	43D	VLVO	12	2	15500	6	6	110000	121000
40		J/40 SHOAL	SLP	SA/OD	F/S	KL	IB	43D	VLVO	12	2	15500	5		110000	121000
40	10	J/41	SLP	SA/OD	F/S	KL	IB	30D	YAN	13	3	15500	7	5	92100	101000
		1986 BOATS														
22	6	J/22	SLP	SA/OD	F/S	KL	OB			8		1750	3	9	6350	7250
24		J/24	SLP	SA/OD	F/S	KL	OB			8	11	3100	4		9950	11300
27	6	J/27	SLP	SA/OD	F/S	KL	OB			8	6	3800	4	9	14800	16800
29	6	J/29	SLP	SA/OD	F/S	KL	OB			11		6000	5	7	25500	28400
29	6	J/29	SLP	SA/OD	F/S	KL	IB	8D	YAN	11		6000	5	7	26000	28800
29	11	J/30	SLP	SA/OD	F/S	KL	IB	15D	YAN	11	3	7000	5	3	30700	34200
34		J/34	SLP	SA/OD	F/S	KL	IB	30D	YAN	11	2	8100	6	2	37200	41300
35	5	J/35	SLP	SA/OD	F/S	KL	IB	23D	YAN	11	9	10000	6	11	47200	51900
36		J/36	SLP	SA/RC	F/S	KL	IB			11	9	11000	6	7	51500	56600
40		J/40	SLP	SA/OD	F/S	KL	IB	D		12	2	15500	5		103000	113000
40	10	J/41	SLP	SA/OD	F/S	KL	IB	30D	YAN	13	3	15500	7	5	86200	94700
		1985 BOATS														
22	6	J/22	SLP	SA/OD	F/S	KL	OB			8		1750	3	9	5900	6800
24		J/24	SLP	SA/OD	F/S	KL	OB			8	11	3100	4		9350	10600
27	6	J/27	SLP	SA/OD	F/S	KL	OB			8	6	3800	4	9	13800	15700
29	6	J/29	SLP	SA/OD	F/S	KL	OB			11		6000	5	7	23900	26600
29	6	J/29	SLP	SA/OD	F/S	KL	IB	8D	YAN	11		6000	5	7	24300	27000
29	11	J/30	SLP	SA/OD	F/S	KL	IB	15D	YAN	11	3	7000	5	3	28800	32000
34		J/34	SLP	SA/OD	F/S	KL	IB	30D	YAN	11	2	8100	6	2	34800	38700
35	5	J/35	SLP	SA/OD	F/S	KL	IB	23D	YAN	11	9	10000	6	11	43700	48600
35	11	J/36	SLP	SA/OD	F/S	KL	IB	23D	YAN	11	10	10700	6	7	47700	52400
40	10	J/41	SLP	SA/OD	F/S	KL	IB	30D	YAN	13	3	15500	7	5	80700	88600
		1984 BOATS														
22	6	J/22	SLP	SA/OD	F/S	KL	OB			8		1750	3	9	5550	6350
24		J/24	SLP	SA/OD	F/S	KL	OB			8	11	2700	4		7800	8950
27	6	J/27	SLP	SA/OD	F/S	KL	OB			8	6	3800	4	9	13000	14700
29	6	J/29	SLP	SA/OD	F/S	KL	OB			11		6000	5	7	22400	24800
29	6	J/29	SLP	SA/OD	F/S	KL	IB	8		11		6000	5	7	22500	25000
29	11	J/30	SLP	SA/OD	F/S	KL	IB	15D	YAN	11	3	7000	5	3	26900	29900
35	5	J/35	SLP	SA/OD	F/S	KL	IB	23D	YAN	11	9	10000	6	11	40900	45400
36		J/36	SLP	SA/OD	F/S	KL	IB	23D	YAN	11	10	10700	6	7	44200	49200
40	10	J/41	SLP	SA/OD	F/S	KL	IB	30D	YAN	13	5	15500	7	5	75500	82900

....For earlier years, see the BUC Used Boat Price Guide, Volume 3

J C CUSTOM BOATS INC

HOLLIS NH 03049

COAST GUARD MFG ID- JCA See inside cover to adjust price for area
FORMERLY J C BOAT WORKS

LOA FT	LOA IN	NAME AND/ OR MODEL	TOP/ RIG	BOAT TYPE	HULL MTL	HULL TP	ENGINE TP	# HP	ENGINE MFG	BEAM FT	BEAM IN	WGT LBS	DRAFT FT	DRAFT IN	RETAIL LOW	RETAIL HIGH
		1992 BOATS														
31	4	BASIC 31 WORKBOAT	HT	FSH	F/S	DS	IB	150		11	2	11370	3		46900	51500
31	4	BASIC 31 WORKBOAT	HT	FSH	F/S	DS	IB	210D-425D		11	2	11370	3		57200	70400
31	4	CASCO BAY 31	FB	CR	F/S	DS	IB	150		11	2	11370	3		46900	51500
31	4	CASCO BAY 31	FB	CR	F/S	DS	IB	210D-425D		11	2	11370	3		57100	70300
31	4	CHESAPEAKE 31	FB	FSH	F/S	DS	IB	150		11	2	11370	3		46900	51500
31	4	CHESAPEAKE 31	FB	FSH	F/S	DS	IB	210D-425D		11	2	11370	3		57200	70400

LOA FT	LOA IN	NAME AND/ OR MODEL	TOP/ RIG	BOAT TYPE	HULL MTL	HULL TP	TP	ENGINE # HP	ENGINE MFG	BEAM FT	BEAM IN	WGT LBS	DRAFT FT	DRAFT IN	RETAIL LOW	RETAIL HIGH
		1992 BOATS														
31	4	PROVINCETOWN 31	TT	SF	F/S	DS	IB	150		11	2	11370	3		46900	51500
31	4	PROVINCETOWN 31	TT	SF	F/S	DS	IB	210D-425D		11	2	11370	3		57100	70300
35		CASCO BAY 35	HT	CR	F/S	DS	IB	250		12		14000	3	6	71000	78100
		IB 210D CUM 81300 89300, IB 250D CUM 81300 89400, IB 250D GM													81500	89500
		IB 270D IVCO 82000 90100, IB 300D CUM 82700 90900, IB 306D VLVO													82500	90600
		IB 320D CAT 84100 92400, IB 375D CAT 86100 94700, IB 425D CAT													88200	96900
35		PROVINCETOWN 35		SF	F/S	DS	IB	250		12		14000	3	6	71000	78000
		IB 210D CUM 81200 89200, IB 250D CUM 81300 89300, IB 250D GM													81400	89500
		IB 270D IVCO 81900 90000, IB 300D CUM 82700 90900, IB 306D VLVO													82400	90600
		IB 320D CAT 84100 92400, IB 375D CAT 86100 94600, IB 425D CAT													88200	96900
35		STD 35 WORKBOAT	HT	FSH	F/S	DS	IB	250		12		14000	3	6	71000	78100
		IB 210D CUM 81200 89200, IB 250D CUM 81300 89400, IB 250D GM													81400	89500
		IB 270D IVCO 82000 90100, IB 300D CUM 82700 90900, IB 306D VLVO													82500	90600
		IB 320D CAT 84100 92400, IB 375D CAT 86100 94700, IB 425D CAT													88200	96900
		1988 BOATS														
26	11	CASCO-BAY	HT	SF	F/S	DS	IB	340	CHRY	10		8000	2	10	29300	32500
26	11	CASCO-BAY	HT	SF	F/S	DS	IB	T275	CHRY	10		8900	2	10	33900	37600
26	11	ISLANDER	OP	SF	F/S	DS	IB	340	CHRY	10			2	10	26200	29100
26	11	PROVINCETOWN II	OP	SF	F/S	DS	IB	340	CHRY	10			2	10	33200	36900
26	11	PROVINCETOWN II	OP	SF	F/S	DS	IB	T275	CHRY	10		7500	2	10	31000	34400
26	11	WORKBOAT	HT	FSH	F/S	DS	IB	340	CHRY	10			2	10	29900	33300
31	4	CASCO-BAY	FB	SF	F/S	DS	IB	250D	GM	11	2		3	4	42600	47400
31	4	CASCO-BAY	FB	SF	F/S	DS	IB	T200D	VLVO	11	2		3	4	46600	51200
31	4	CHESAPEAKE	HT	FSH	F/S	DS	IB	250D	GM	11	2		3	4	42700	47400
31	4	OPEN FISH	OP	FSH	F/S	DS	IB	250D	GM	11	2		3	4	42700	47400
31	4	PROVINCETOWN	OP	SF	F/S	DS	IB	250D	GM	11	2		3	4	42400	47100
31	4	PROVINCETOWN	OP	SF	F/S	DS	IB	T200D	VLVO	11	2		3	4	46300	50900
31	4	PROVINCETOWN II	OP	SF	F/S	DS	IB	250D	GM	11	2		3	3	42800	47600
31	4	PROVINCETOWN II	OP	SF	F/S	DS	IB	T200D	VLVO	11	2		3	3	46700	51300
31	4	WORKBOAT	HT	FSH	F/S	DS	IB	250D	GM	11	2		3	2	42700	47400
35		CASCO-BAY	FB	SF	F/S	DS	IB	320D	CAT	12			3	6	64200	70500
35		CASCO-BAY	FB	SF	F/S	DS	IB	T250D	GM	12			3	6	68400	75200
35		CHESAPEAKE	HT	FSH	F/S	DS	IB	320D	CAT	12			3	6	64200	70500
35		OPEN FISH	OP	FSH	F/S	DS	IB	320D	CAT	12			3	6	64200	70500
35		PROVINCETOWN II	OP	SF	F/S	DS	IB	320D	CAT	12			3	6	64100	70500
35		PROVINCETOWN II	OP	SF	F/S	DS	IB	T250D	GM	12			3	6	68400	75200
35		WORK BOAT	HT	FSH	F/S	DS	IB	320D	CAT	12			3	6	64200	70500
40		WORK BOAT	HT	FSH	F/S	DS	IB	375D	CAT	13	3		4	6	87900	96500
		1987 BOATS														
26	11	ISLANDER	OP	SF	F/S	DS	IB	240	CHRY	10			2	10	27200	30200
26	11	PROVINCETOWN II	OP	SF	F/S	DS	IB	260	CHRY	10			2	10	27400	30400
26	11	WORKBOAT	HT	FSH	F/S	DS	IB	240	CHRY	10			2	10	27400	30400
31	4	CASCO-BAY	FB	SF	F/S	DS	IB	240	CHRY	11	2		3	4	30900	34300
31	4	CASCO-BAY	FB	SF	F/S	DS	IB	T240	CHRY	11	2		3	4	33700	37500
31	4	CHESAPEAKE	HT	FSH	F/S	DS	IB	240	CHRY	11	2		3	4	30900	34300
31	4	OPEN FISH	OP	FSH	F/S	DS	IB	240	CHRY	11	2		3	4	30900	34300
31	4	PROVINCETOWN	OP	SF	F/S	DS	IB	240	CHRY	11	2		3	4	30700	34100
31	4	PROVINCETOWN	OP	SF	F/S	DS	IB	T240	CHRY	11	2		3	4	33600	37300
31	4	PROVINCETOWN II	OP	SF	F/S	DS	IB	240	CHRY	11	2		3	3	31000	34500
31	4	PROVINCETOWN II	OP	SF	F/S	DS	IB	T240	CHRY	11	2		3	3	33900	37600
31	4	WORKBOAT	HT	FSH	F/S	DS	IB	240	CHRY	11	2		3	2	30900	34300
35		CASCO-BAY	FB	SF	F/S	DS	IB	240	CHRY	12			3	6	48600	53400
35		CASCO-BAY	FB	SF	F/S	DS	IB	T240	CHRY	12			3	6	51200	56300
35		CHESAPEAKE	HT	FSH	F/S	DS	IB	240	CHRY	12			3	6	49700	54600
35		OPEN FISH	OP	FSH	F/S	DS	IB	240	CHRY	12			3	6	48600	53400
35		PROVINCETOWN II	OP	SF	F/S	DS	IB	240	CHRY	12			3	6	52600	57800
35		PROVINCETOWN II	OP	SF	F/S	DS	IB	T240	CHRY	12			3	6	51200	56300
35		WALKAROUND	OP	SF	F/S	DS	IB	240	CHRY	12			3	6	44300	49200
35		WORK BOAT	HT	FSH	F/S	DS	IB	240	CHRY	12			3	6	47800	52500
40		WORK BOAT	HT	FSH	F/S	DS	IB	320	CAT	13	3		4	6	**	**
		1986 BOATS														
31	4	CASCO-BAY	FB	SF	F/S	DS	IB			11	2		3	4	**	**
31	4	CASCO-BAY	FB	SF	F/S	DS	IB	T		11	2		3	4	**	**
31	4	CHESAPEAKE	HT	FSH	F/S	DS	IB			11	2		3	4	**	**
31	4	OPEN FISH	OP	FSH	F/S	DS	IB			11	2		3	4	**	**
31	4	PROVINCETOWN	OP	SF	F/S	DS	IB			11	2		3	4	**	**
31	4	WORKBOAT	HT	FSH	F/S	DS	IB			11	2		3	2	**	**
35		CASCO-BAY	FB	SF	F/S	DS	IB	440		12			3	6	48800	53600
35		CASCO-BAY	FB	SF	F/S	DS	IB	T440		12			3	6	53700	59000
35		CHESAPEAKE	HT	FSH	F/S	DS	IB			12			3	6	**	**
35		OPEN FISH	OP	FSH	F/S	DS	IB			12			3	6	**	**
35		PROVINCETOWN	OP	SF	F/S	DS	IB			12			3	6	**	**
35		WALKAROUND	OP	SF	F/S	DS	IB			12			3	6	**	**
35		WORK BOAT	HT	FSH	F/S	DS	IB			12			3	6	**	**
40		WORK BOAT	HT	FSH	F/S	DS	IB			13	3		4	6	**	**

....For earlier years, see the BUC Used Boat Price Guide, Volume 3

JACHTBOUW P VALK

FRANEKER HOLLAND

See inside cover to adjust price for area

LOA FT	LOA IN	NAME AND/ OR MODEL	TOP/ RIG	BOAT TYPE	HULL MTL	HULL TP	TP	ENGINE # HP	ENGINE MFG	BEAM FT	BEAM IN	WGT LBS	DRAFT FT	DRAFT IN	RETAIL LOW	RETAIL HIGH
		1989 BOATS														
46	6	VALK VLET		MY		RB	IB	155D		13	7				144000	158000
46	6	VALK VLET		MY		RB	IB	T155D		13	7				151500	166500

JACHTBOUW PEDRO-BOAT BV

ZUIDBROEK HOLLAND

See inside cover to adjust price for area

LOA FT	LOA IN	NAME AND/ OR MODEL	TOP/ RIG	BOAT TYPE	HULL MTL	HULL TP	TP	ENGINE # HP	ENGINE MFG	BEAM FT	BEAM IN	WGT LBS	DRAFT FT	DRAFT IN	RETAIL LOW	RETAIL HIGH
		1995 BOATS														
31	6	PEDRO 30	HT	MY	STL	DS	IB	100D	VLVO	10	6	12141	3		55900	61400
32	9	PEDRO 33 DONKY	HT	MY	STL	DS	IB	100D	VLVO	10	6	11039	3		56800	62500
32	9	PEDRO 33 SOLANO	HT	MY	STL	DS	IB	100D	VLVO	10	6	15011	3		70100	77100
34	9	PEDRO 34	HT	MY	STL	DS	IB	100D	VLVO	10	6	15011	3		81000	89000
34	9	PEDRO 34 BORA	FB	MY	STL	DS	IB	100D	VLVO	12	2	19067	3	3	95700	105000
34	9	PEDRO 35 ASPRE	HT	MY	STL	DS	IB	59	VLVO	10	6	14000			66600	73200
37	2	PEDRO 36	HT	MY	STL	DS	IB	100D	VLVO	11	2	15894	3	3	88000	96700
38	5	PEDRO 38 BORA	FB	MY	STL	DS	IB	150D	VLVO	12	6	22075	3	6	113000	124000
40	5	PEDRO 40	HT	MY	STL	DS	IB	150D	VLVO	11	6	19867	3	7	119500	131500
41	8	PEDRO 41 BORA	FB	MY	STL	DS	IB	150D	VLVO	12	1	26490	3	6	146000	160500
42		PEDRO SOLANO 42	HT	MY	STL	DS	IB	200D	VLVO	13		22000	3		126500	139000
43	1	PEDRO 43	HT	MY	STL	DS	IB	150D	VLVO	11	1	20971	3		136000	149500
47	7	PEDRO 47	HT	MY	STL	DS	IB	200D	VLVO	14	2	33112	4	3	192000	211000
47	7	PEDRO 47 BORA	FB	MY	STL	DS	IB	200D	VLVO	14	6	33112	4		191500	210500
47	7	PEDRO 47 BORA AK	FB	MY	STL	DS	IB	200D	VLVO	14	6	34216	4		194000	213000
60	9	PEDRO 60 BORA	FB	MY	STL	DS	IB	306D	VLVO	17	2	52980	4		265500	291500
		1994 BOATS														
31	6	PEDRO 30	HT	MY	STL	DS	IB	100D	VLVO	10	6	12141	3		53600	58900
32	9	PEDRO 33 DONKY	HT	MY	STL	DS	IB	100D	VLVO	10	6	11039	3		54500	59900
32	9	PEDRO 33 SOLANO	HT	MY	STL	DS	IB	100D	VLVO	10	6	15011	3		66600	73200
34	9	PEDRO 34	HT	MY	STL	DS	IB	100D	VLVO	10	6	15011	3		76900	84500
34	9	PEDRO 34 BORA	FB	MY	STL	DS	IB	100D	VLVO	12	2	19067	3	3	90900	99900
34	9	PEDRO 35 ASPRE	HT	MY	STL	DS	IB	59	VLVO	10	6	14000			62900	69200
37	2	PEDRO 36	HT	MY	STL	DS	IB	100D	VLVO	11	2	15894	3	3	83400	91700
38	5	PEDRO 38 BORA	FB	MY	STL	DS	IB	150D	VLVO	12	6	22075	3	6	107000	117500
40	5	PEDRO 40	HT	MY	STL	DS	IB	150D	VLVO	11	6	19867	3	7	113500	124500
41	8	PEDRO 41 BORA	FB	MY	STL	DS	IB	150D	VLVO	12	1	26490	3	6	138500	152000
42		PEDRO SOLANO 42	HT	MY	STL	DS	IB	200D	VLVO	13		22000	3		120000	132000
43	1	PEDRO 43	HT	MY	STL	DS	IB	150D	VLVO	11	1	20971	3		129000	142000
47	7	PEDRO 47	HT	MY	STL	DS	IB	200D	VLVO	14	2	33112	4	3	182000	200000
47	7	PEDRO 47 BORA	FB	MY	STL	DS	IB	200D	VLVO	14	6	33112	4		181500	199500
47	7	PEDRO 47 BORA AK	FB	MY	STL	DS	IB	200D	VLVO	14	6	34216	4		184000	202000
60	9	PEDRO 60 BORA	FB	MY	STL	DS	IB	306D	VLVO	17	2	52980	4		254000	279000
		1993 BOATS														
31	6	PEDRO 30	HT	MY	STL	DS	IB	62D	VLVO	10	6	12141	3		50900	56000
32	9	PEDRO 33 DONKY	HT	MY	STL	DS	IB	62D	VLVO	10	6	11039	3		51800	56900
32	9	PEDRO 33 SOLANO	HT	MY	STL	DS	IB	62D	VLVO	10	6	15011	3		63300	69500
34	9	PEDRO 34	HT	MY	STL	DS	IB	62D	VLVO	10	6	15011	3		72900	80100
34	9	PEDRO 34 BORA	FB	MY	STL	DS	IB	100D	VLVO	12	2	19067	3	3	86500	95000
37	2	PEDRO 36	HT	MY	STL	DS	IB	100D	VLVO	11	2	15894	3	3	79200	87100
38	5	PEDRO 38 BORA	FB	MY	STL	DS	IB	150D	VLVO	12	6	22075	3	6	101500	112000
40	5	PEDRO 40	HT	MY	STL	DS	IB	150D	VLVO	11	6	19867	3	7	107500	118500
41	8	PEDRO 41 BORA	FB	MY	STL	DS	IB	150D	VLVO	12	1	26490	3	6	131500	144500
42		PEDRO SOLANO 42	HT	MY	STL	DS	IB	230D	VLVO	13		22000	3		115000	126500
43	1	PEDRO 43	HT	MY	STL	DS	IB	150D	VLVO	11	1	20971	3		122500	134500
47	7	PEDRO 47	HT	MY	STL	DS	IB	200D	VLVO	14	2	33112	4	3	173000	190500
47	7	PEDRO 47 BORA	FB	MY	STL	DS	IB	200D	VLVO	14	6	33112	4		172500	189500
47	7	PEDRO 47 BORA AK	FB	MY	STL	DS	IB	200D	VLVO	14	6	34216	4		175000	192000
60	9	PEDRO 60 BORA	FB	MY	STL	DS	IB	306D	VLVO	17	2	52980	4		242000	266000
		1992 BOATS														
31	6	PEDRO 30	HT	MY	STL	DS	IB	62D	VLVO	10	6	12141	3		49000	53800
32	9	PEDRO 33	HT	MY	STL	DS	IB	62D	VLVO	10	6	15011	3		60600	66600

JACHTBOUW PEDRO-BOAT BV — CONTINUED

See inside cover to adjust price for area

1992 BOATS

LOA	Name and/or Model	Top/Rig	Type	Hull	Eng HP	Eng MFG	Beam	Wgt	Draft	Retail Low	Retail High
32 9	PEDRO 33 DONKY	HT	MY	STL DS IB	62D	VLVO	10 6	11039	3	49800	54700
34 9	PEDRO 34	HT	MY	STL DS IB	62D	VLVO	10 6	15011	3	69400	76300
34 9	PEDRO 34 BORA	FB	MY	STL DS IB	100D	VLVO	12	19067	3 3	82300	90500
37 2	PEDRO 36	HT	MY	STL DS IB	100D	VLVO	11 2	15894	3	75400	82800
38 5	PEDRO 38 BORA	FB	MY	STL DS IB	150D	VLVO	12 6	22075	3 6	96800	106500
40 5	PEDRO 40	HT	MY	STL DS IB	150D	VLVO	11 6	19867	3 7	102500	112500
41 8	PEDRO 41 BORA	HT	MY	STL DS IB	150D	VLVO	12 1	26490	3 6	125000	137500
42	PEDRO SOLANO 42	HT	MY	STL DS IB	230D	VLVO	13	22000		109500	120000
43 1	PEDRO 43	HT	MY	STL DS IB	150D	VLVO	11 1	20971	3	116500	128000
47 7	PEDRO 47	HT	MY	STL DS IB	200D	VLVO	14 2	33112	4 3	164500	181000
47 7	PEDRO 47 BORA	FB	MY	STL DS IB	200D	VLVO	14 6	33112	4	160000	180500
47 7	PEDRO 47 BORA AK	FB	MY	STL DS IB	200D	VLVO	14 6	34216	4	166000	182500
60 9	PEDRO 60 BORA	FB	MY	STL DS IB	306D	VLVO	17 2	52980	4	231000	253500

1991 BOATS

LOA	Name and/or Model	Top/Rig	Type	Hull	Eng HP	Eng MFG	Beam	Wgt	Draft	Retail Low	Retail High
29	PEDRO 29 DONKY	HT	MY	STL DS IB	62D	VLVO	9 2	8830	2 8	32400	36000
31 6	PEDRO 30	HT	MY	STL DS IB	62D	VLVO	10 6	12141	3	46700	51300
32 9	PEDRO 33	HT	MY	STL DS IB	62D	VLVO	10 6	15011	3	58300	64100
32 9	PEDRO 33 DONKY	HT	MY	STL DS IB	62D	VLVO	10 6	11039	3	47500	52200
34 9	PEDRO 34	HT	MY	STL DS IB	62D	VLVO	10 6	15011	3	66200	72700
34 9	PEDRO 34 BORA	FB	MY	STL DS IB	100D	VLVO	12 3	19067	3 3	78500	86300
37 2	PEDRO 36	HT	MY	STL DS IB	100D	VLVO	11 2	15894	3	71800	78900
38 5	PEDRO 38 BORA	FB	MY	STL DS IB	150D	VLVO	12 6	22075	3 6	92100	101500
40 5	PEDRO 40	HT	MY	STL DS IB	150D	VLVO	11 6	19867	3 7	97500	107000
41 8	PEDRO 41 BORA	HT	MY	STL DS IB	150D	VLVO	12 1	26490	3 6	119000	131000
43 1	PEDRO 43	HT	MY	STL DS IB	150D	VLVO	11 1	20971	3	111000	122000
47	PEDRO 47	HT	MY	STL DS IB	200D	VLVO	14 2	33112	4 3	154000	169000
47 7	PEDRO 47 BORA	FB	MY	STL DS IB	200D	VLVO	14 6	33112	4	156500	172000
47 7	PEDRO 47 BORA AK	FB	MY	STL DS IB	200D	VLVO	14 6	34216	4	158500	174000
60 9	PEDRO 60 BORA	FB	MY	STL DS IB	306D	VLVO	17 2	52980	4	220000	242000

1990 BOATS

LOA	Name and/or Model	Top/Rig	Type	Hull	Eng HP	Eng MFG	Beam	Wgt	Draft	Retail Low	Retail High
29	PEDRO 29 DONKY	HT	MY	STL DS IB	62D	VLVO	9 2	8830	2 8	30900	34300
31 6	PEDRO 30	HT	MY	STL DS IB	62D	VLVO	10 6	12141	3	44100	49000
32 9	PEDRO 33	HT	MY	STL DS IB	62D	VLVO	10 6	15011	3	55700	61200
32 9	PEDRO 33 DONKY	HT	MY	STL DS IB	62D	VLVO	10 6	11039	3	44800	49800
34 9	PEDRO 34	HT	MY	STL DS IB	62D	VLVO	10 6	15011	3	63200	69500
34 9	PEDRO 34 BORA	HT	MY	STL DS IB	100D	VLVO	12 3	19067	3 3	74800	82200
37 2	PEDRO 36	HT	MY	STL DS IB	100D	VLVO	11 2	15894	3	68400	75200
38 5	PEDRO 38 BORA	FB	MY	STL DS IB	150D	VLVO	12 6	22075	3 6	87800	96500
40 5	PEDRO 40	HT	MY	STL DS IB	150D	VLVO	11 6	19867	3 7	93000	102000
41 8	PEDRO 41 BORA	HT	MY	STL DS IB	150D	VLVO	12 1	26490	3 6	113500	125000
43 1	PEDRO 43	HT	MY	STL DS IB	150D	VLVO	11 1	20971	3	106000	116500
47	PEDRO 47	HT	MY	STL DS IB	200D	VLVO	14 2	33112	4 3	146500	161000
47 7	PEDRO 47 BORA	FB	MY	STL DS IB	200D	VLVO	14 6	33112	4	149000	163500
47 7	PEDRO 47 BORA AL	FB	MY	STL DS IB	200D	VLVO	14 6	34216	4	151000	166000
60 9	PEDRO 60 BORA	FB	MY	STL DS IB	306D	VLVO	17 2	52980	4	210000	231000

JACHTWERF VAN RYNSOEVER B V

TELEFOON 1444 HOLLAND See inside cover to adjust price for area

1991 BOATS

LOA	Name and/or Model	Top/Rig	Type	Hull	Eng HP	Eng MFG	Draft	Retail Low	Retail High
23 3	STAVERSE JOL 7.00M	SLP	SAIL	STL KL IB	D	VLVO	2 7	22000	24500
26	STAVERSE JOL 7.80M	SLP	SAIL	STL KL IB	D	VLVO	3 2	30500	33900
30 3	LEMSTERAAK 9.10M	SLP	SAIL	STL KL IB	D	VLVO	2 8	58200	63900
33 3	LEMSTERAAK 10M	SLP	SAIL	STL KL IB	D	VLVO	3 2	80300	88300
36 2	SCHOENER 10.85M	SLP	SAIL	STL KL IB	D	VLVO	3 2	101500	111500
38 3	LEMSTERAAK 11.50M	SLP	SAIL	STL KL IB	D	VLVO	3 1	129500	142500
51 7	LEMSTERAAK 15M	SLP	SAIL	STL KL IB	D	VLVO	3 7	283000	311000

1990 BOATS

LOA	Name and/or Model	Top/Rig	Type	Hull	Eng HP	Eng MFG	Draft	Retail Low	Retail High
23 3	STAVERSE JOL 7.00M	SLP	SAIL	STL KL IB	D	VLVO	2 7	20600	22900
26	STAVERSE JOL 7.80M	SLP	SAIL	STL KL IB	D	VLVO	3 2	28500	31700
30 3	LEMSTERAAK 9.10M	SLP	SAIL	STL KL IB	D	VLVO	2 8	54800	60300
33 3	LEMSTERAAK 10M	SLP	SAIL	STL KL IB	D	VLVO	3 2	75300	82800
36 2	SCHOENER 10.85M	SLP	SAIL	STL KL IB	D	VLVO	3 2	95300	104500
38 3	LEMSTERAAK 11.50M	SLP	SAIL	STL KL IB	D	VLVO	3 1	121500	133500
51 7	LEMSTERAAK 15M	SLP	SAIL	STL KL IB	D	VLVO	3 7	266500	292500

1989 BOATS

LOA	Name and/or Model	Type	Hull	Eng HP	Eng MFG	Draft	Retail Low	Retail High
23 3	STAVERSE JOL 7.00M	SAIL	STL KL IB	D	VLVO	2 7	19700	21900
26	STAVERSE JOL 7.80M	SAIL	STL KL IB	D	VLVO	3 2	26700	29600
30 3	LEMSTERAAK 9.10M	SAIL	STL KL IB	D	VLVO	2 7	51300	56400
33 3	LEMSTERAAK 10M	SAIL	STL KL IB	D	VLVO	2 8	70600	77600
36 2	SCHOENER 10.85M	SAIL	STL KL IB	D	VLVO	3 2	89300	98100
38 3	LEMSTERAAK 11.50M	SAIL	STL KL IB	D	VLVO	3 1	114000	125000
51 7	LEMSTERAAK 15M	SAIL	STL KL IB	D	VLVO	3 7	250500	275500

JAEGER YACHTS

BRITISH COLUMBIA CANADA COAST GUARD MFG ID- ZJY See inside cover to adjust price for area

1984 BOATS

LOA	Name and/or Model	Top/Rig	Type	Hull	Eng HP	Beam	Wgt	Draft	Retail Low	Retail High
37 4	C-37	CUT	SA/CR	FBG CT HD	38D	20	13000	2	40400	44900

....For earlier years, see the BUC Used Boat Price Guide, Volume 3

JAGUAR YACHTS LTD

DIV OF RUSSELL MARINE LTD
ESSEX ENGLAND See inside cover to adjust price for area

JAGUAR YACHTS USA
PUNTAGORDA FL 33950

1987 BOATS

LOA	Name and/or Model	Top/Rig	Type	Hull	Eng HP	Eng MFG	Beam	Wgt	Draft	Retail Low	Retail High
17 9	EXPLORER	CAT	SAIL	FBG KC OB			6 8	1200	1 11	4550	5200
21 5	JAGUAR 21	SLP	SAIL	FBG KC OB			8 2	2500	10	7100	8200
26 6	JAGUAR 27	SLP	SAIL	FBG KL IB	10D	YAN	9	4560	3 3	15000	17100
28	JAGUAR 28	SLP	SAIL	FBG KL IB	17D	VLVO	9 1	6600	3 9	22200	24700

1985 BOATS

LOA	Name and/or Model	Top/Rig	Type	Hull	Eng HP	Eng MFG	Beam	Wgt	Draft	Retail Low	Retail High
17 9	EXPLORER	CAT	SAIL	FBG KC OB			6 8	1200	1 11	3950	4600
21 5	JAGUAR 21	SLP	SAIL	FBG KC OB			8 2	2500	10	6300	7250
23	JAGUAR 23	SLP	SAIL	FBG KC OB			8	3200	2	7950	9100
26 6	JAGUAR 27	SLP	SAIL	FBG KL IB	10D	YAN	9	4560	3 3	13500	15100
28	JAGUAR 28	SLP	SAIL	FBG KL IB	17D	VLVO	9 1	6600	3 9	19700	21900

1984 BOATS

LOA	Name and/or Model	Top/Rig	Type	Hull	Eng HP	Beam	Wgt	Draft	Retail Low	Retail High
21 6	JAGUAR 21 C/R	SLP	SA/CR	FBG KL SD		8	2550	10	6600	7600
23	JAGUAR 23	SLP	SA/CR	FBG KL SD		8	3150	1	7950	9150
28	JAGUAR 28 SHOAL	SLP	SA/CR	FBG KL SD	8D-17D	9 1	6600	3 11	18600	20800

....For earlier years, see the BUC Used Boat Price Guide, Volume 3

JAMESTOWNER HOUSEBOATS

DIV MEDARIS MARINE INC
RUSSELL SPRINGS KY 4264 COAST GUARD MFG ID- MWC See inside cover to adjust price for area

For more recent years, see the BUC Used Boat Price Guide, Volume 1

1996 BOATS

LOA	Name and/or Model	Type	Hull	Eng HP	Eng MFG	Beam	Draft	Retail Low	Retail High
54	VETERAN	HB	AL SV IO	135	MRCR	14	2 4	53800	59100
54	VETERAN WIDEBODY	HB	AL SV IO	135	MRCR	14	2 4	56700	62300
60	VETERAN	HB	AL SV IO	135	MRCR	16	2 4	51600	56700
60	VETERAN WIDEBODY	HB	AL SV IO	135	MRCR	16	2 4	52200	57400
63	AMERICANA WIDEBODY	HB	AL SV IO	135	MRCR	14	2 4	55700	61200
64	VETERAN	HB	AL SV IO	135	MRCR	16	2 4	55900	61400
64	VETERAN WIDEBODY	HB	AL SV IO	135	MRCR	16	2 4	59200	65000
68	AMERICANA	HB	AL SV IO	T135	MRCR	16	2 4	**	**
68	AMERICANA WIDEBODY	HB	AL SV IO	T135	MRCR	16	2 4	**	**

1995 BOATS

LOA	Name and/or Model	Type	Hull	Eng HP	Eng MFG	Beam	Draft	Retail Low	Retail High
47	VETERAN	HB	AL SV IO	135	MRCR	14	1 3	34100	37900
54	VETERAN	HB	AL SV IO	135	MRCR	14	1 3	51600	56700
56	AMERICANA	HB	AL SV IO	135	MRCR	16	1 3	50200	55100
60	VETERAN	HB	AL SV IO	135	MRCR	16	1 3	48500	53300
62	AMERICANA WIDEBODY	HB	AL SV IO	135	MRCR	16	1 3	51800	56800
64	VETERAN	HB	AL SV IO	135	MRCR	16	1 3	53800	58800
67	AMERICANA	HB	AL SV IO	135	MRCR	16	1 3	54000	59300
67	AMERICANA WIDEBODY	HB	AL SV IO	135	MRCR	16	1 3	56900	62500

1994 BOATS

LOA	Name and/or Model	Type	Hull	Eng HP	Eng MFG	Beam	Draft	Retail Low	Retail High
47	VETERAN	HB	AL SV IO	115	MRCR	14	1 3	32000	35600
54	VETERAN	HB	AL SV IO	115	MRCR	14	1 3	48400	53200
56	AMERICANA	HB	AL SV IO	115	MRCR	16	1 3	46900	51400
60	VETERAN	HB	AL SV IO	115	MRCR	16	1 3	44600	49000
62	AMERICANA WIDEBODY	HB	AL SV IO	115	MRCR	16	1 3	48700	53500
64	VETERAN	HB	AL SV IO	115	MRCR	16	1 3	50400	55400
67	AMERICANA	HB	AL SV IO	115	MRCR	16	1 3	50900	55900
67	AMERICANA WIDEBODY	HB	AL SV IO	115	MRCR	16	1 3	53600	59000

LOA FT IN	NAME AND/ OR MODEL	TOP/ RIG	BOAT TYPE	-HULL- MTL	-HULL- TP	ENGINE TP	ENGINE # HP	ENGINE MFG	BEAM FT IN	WGT LBS	DRAFT FT	DRAFT IN	RETAIL LOW	RETAIL HIGH
	1993 BOATS													
47	VETERAN		HB	AL	SV	IO	115	MRCR	14		1	3	30300	33700
54	VETERAN		HB	AL	SV	IO	115	MRCR	14		1	3	45600	50100
56	AMERICANA		HB	AL	SV	IO	115	MRCR	14		1	3	43400	48200
60	VETERAN		HB	AL	SV	IO	115	MRCR	16		1	3	42000	46700
62	AMERICANA WIDEBODY		HB	AL	SV	IO	115	MRCR	14		1	3	45600	50100
64	VETERAN		HB	AL	SV	IO	115	MRCR	16		1	3	47700	52400
67	AMERICANA		HB	AL	SV	IO	115	MRCR	16		1	3	47400	52000
67	AMERICANA WIDEBODY		HB	AL	SV	IO	115	MRCR	16		1	3	51200	56300
72	AMERICANA WIDEBODY		HB	AL	SV	IO	115	MRCR	16		1	3	**	**
	1992 BOATS													
47	VETERAN		HB	AL	SV	IO	115	MRCR	14		1	3	28800	32000
54	VETERAN		HB	AL	SV	IO	115	MRCR	14		1	3	42700	47400
56	AMERICANA		HB	AL	SV	IO	115	MRCR	14		1	3	40700	45300
60	VETERAN		HB	AL	SV	IO	115	MRCR	16		1	3	39700	44100
64	VETERAN		HB	AL	SV	IO	115	MRCR	16		1	3	44500	49500
67	AMERICANA		HB	AL	SV	IO	115	MRCR	16		1	3	46800	51400
72	AMERICANA		HB	AL	SV	IO	115	MRCR	16		1	3	**	**
	1986 BOATS													
40	JAMESTOWNER 40-A	HT	HB	AL	SV	IO	140	OMC	14	21000	1	3	23200	25800
40	JAMESTOWNER 40-A	HT	HB	STL	SV	IO	140	OMC	14	24000	1	3	21800	24200
40	JAMESTOWNER 40-B	HT	HB	AL	SV	IO	140	OMC	14	21000	1	3	23200	25800
40	JAMESTOWNER 40-B	HT	HB	STL	SV	IO	140	OMC	14	24000	1	3	21800	24200
46	JAMESTOWNER 40-A	HT	HB	AL	SV	IO	140	OMC	14	24000	1	3	25100	27900
46	JAMESTOWNER 40-A+B	HT	HB	AL	SV	IO	230	OMC	14	24000	1	3	25300	28200
46	JAMESTOWNER 40-B	HT	HB	STL	SV	IO	140	OMC	14	28000	1	3	24500	27200
46	JAMESTOWNER 40-B+A	HT	HB	STL	SV	IO	230	OMC	14	28000	1	3	24700	27400
50	JAMESTOWNER 46-A	HT	HB	AL	SV	IO	140	OMC	14	26000	1	3	27600	30600
50	JAMESTOWNER 46-A	HT	HB	STL	SV	IO	140	OMC	14	30000	1	3	26600	29500
50	JAMESTOWNER 46-B	HT	HB	AL	SV	IO	140	OMC	14	26000	1	3	27600	30600
50	JAMESTOWNER 46-B	HT	HB	STL	SV	IO	140	OMC	14	30000	1	3	26600	29500
53	JAMESTOWNER 46-A	HT	HB	AL	SV	IO	230	OMC	14	28000	1	3	32900	36500
53	JAMESTOWNER 46-A	HT	HB	STL	SV	IO	230	OMC	14	32000	1	3	31400	34900
53	JAMESTOWNER 46-B	HT	HB	AL	SV	IO	230	OMC	14	28000	1	3	32900	36500
53	JAMESTOWNER 46-B	HT	HB	STL	SV	IO	230	OMC	14	32000	1	3	31400	34900
53	JAMESTOWNER 53-A	HT	HB	AL	SV	IO	140	OMC	14	28000	1	3	32600	36200
53	JAMESTOWNER 53-A	HT	HB	STL	SV	IO	140	OMC	14	32000	1	3	31200	34600
53	JAMESTOWNER 53-B	HT	HB	AL	SV	IO	140	OMC	14	28000	1	3	32600	36200
53	JAMESTOWNER 53-B	HT	HB	STL	SV	IO	140	OMC	14	32000	1	3	31200	34600
57	JAMESTOWNER 50-B	HT	HB	AL	SV	IO	230	OMC	14	29000	1	3	34800	38600
58	JAMESTOWNER 50-A	HT	HB	AL	SV	IO	140	OMC	14	30000	1	3	35300	39200
58	JAMESTOWNER 50-A	HT	HB	STL	SV	IO	140	OMC	14	35000	1	3	33800	37500
58	JAMESTOWNER 50-A	HT	HB	AL	SV	IO	230	OMC	14	30000	1	3	35500	39500
58	JAMESTOWNER 50-A	HT	HB	STL	SV	IO	230	OMC	14	35000	1	3	34000	37800
58	JAMESTOWNER 50-A	HT	HB	AL	SV	IO	T140	OMC	14	30000	1	3	36600	40700
58	JAMESTOWNER 50-A	HT	HB	STL	SV	IO	T140	OMC	14	35000	1	3	34900	38800
58	JAMESTOWNER 50-B	HT	HB	AL	SV	IO	140	OMC	14	30000	1	3	35300	39200
58	JAMESTOWNER 50-B	HT	HB	AL	SV	IO	230	OMC	14	30000	1	3	35500	39500
58	JAMESTOWNER 50-B	HT	HB	STL	SV	IO	230	OMC	14	35000	1	3	34000	37800
58	JAMESTOWNER 50-B	HT	HB	STL	SV	IO	T140	OMC	14	35000	1	3	35100	39000
58	JAMESTOWNER 50-B	HT	HB	STL	SV	IO	T230	OMC	14	35000	1	3	35500	39400
60	JAMESTOWNER 1660-A+B	HT	HB	AL	SV	IO	140	OMC	16	36000	1	3	33100	36800
60	JAMESTOWNER 1660-A+B	HT	HB	AL	SV	IO	230	OMC	16	36000	1	3	33400	37100
60	JAMESTOWNER 1660-A+B	HT	HB	STL	SV	IO	230	OMC	16	41000	1	3	31500	35000
60	JAMESTOWNER 1660-A+B	HT	HB	AL	SV	IO	T140	OMC	16	36000	1	3	34300	38200
60	JAMESTOWNER 1660-A+B	HT	HB	STL	SV	IO	T140	OMC	16	41000	1	3	32400	36000
60	JAMESTOWNER 1660-A+B	HT	HB	AL	SV	IO	T230	OMC	16	36000	1	3	34800	38700
60	JAMESTOWNER 1660-A+B	HT	HB	STL	SV	IO	T230	OMC	16	41000	1	3	32800	36500
60	JAMESTOWNER 52-A	HT	HB	AL	SV	IO	140	OMC	14	31000	1	3	31800	35300
60	JAMESTOWNER 52-A	HT	HB	STL	SV	IO	140	OMC	14	36000	1	3	30300	33700
60	JAMESTOWNER 52-A	HT	HB	AL	SV	IO	230	OMC	14	31000	1	3	32000	35600
60	JAMESTOWNER 52-A	HT	HB	STL	SV	IO	230	OMC	14	36000	1	3	30500	33900
60	JAMESTOWNER 52-B	HT	HB	AL	SV	IO	140	OMC	14	31000	1	3	31800	35300
60	JAMESTOWNER 52-B	HT	HB	STL	SV	IO	140	OMC	14	36000	1	3	30300	33700
60	JAMESTOWNER 52-B	HT	HB	AL	SV	IO	230	OMC	14	31000	1	3	32000	35600
60	JAMESTOWNER 52-B	HT	HB	STL	SV	IO	230	OMC	14	36000	1	3	30500	33900
62	JAMESTOWNER 54-A	HT	HB	AL	SV	IO	T140	OMC	14	32000	1	3	33900	37700
62	JAMESTOWNER 54-B	HT	HB	AL	SV	IO	140	OMC	14	32000	1	3	32700	36300
62	JAMESTOWNER 62-A	HT	HB	AL	SV	IO	230	OMC	14	32000	1	3	32900	36600
62	JAMESTOWNER 62-A	HT	HB	STL	SV	IO	230	OMC	14	37000	1	3	31300	34800
62	JAMESTOWNER 62-B	HT	HB	AL	SV	IO	T230	OMC	14	32000	1	3	34300	38200
62	JAMESTOWNER 62-B	HT	HB	STL	SV	IO	T230	OMC	14	37000	1	3	32600	36200
63	JAMESTOWNER 63-A	HT	HB	AL	SV	IO	230	OMC	14	33000	1	3	33500	37200
63	JAMESTOWNER 63-A	HT	HB	STL	SV	IO	230	OMC	14	38000	1	3	31800	35300
63	JAMESTOWNER 63-A	HT	HB	AL	SV	IO	T230	OMC	14	33000	1	3	34900	38800
63	JAMESTOWNER 63-A	HT	HB	STL	SV	IO	T230	OMC	14	38000	1	3	33100	36800
63	JAMESTOWNER 63-B	HT	HB	AL	SV	IO	230	OMC	14	33000	1	3	33500	37200
63	JAMESTOWNER 63-B	HT	HB	STL	SV	IO	230	OMC	14	33000	1	3	30600	34100
63	JAMESTOWNER 63-B	HT	HB	AL	SV	IO	T230	OMC	14	33000	1	3	34900	38800
63	JAMESTOWNER 63-B	HT	HB	STL	SV	IO	T230	OMC	14	38000	1	3	33100	36800
64	JAMESTOWNER 1664-A+B	HT	HB	AL	SV	IO	230	OMC	16	38000	1	3	35000	38900
64	JAMESTOWNER 1664-A+B	HT	HB	STL	SV	IO	230	OMC	16	44000	1	3	33100	36800
64	JAMESTOWNER 1664-A+B	HT	HB	AL	SV	IO	T140	OMC	16	38000	1	3	36000	40000
64	JAMESTOWNER 1664-A+B	HT	HB	STL	SV	IO	T140	OMC	16	44000	1	3	34000	37800
64	JAMESTOWNER 1664-A+B	HT	HB	AL	SV	IO	T230	OMC	16	38000	1	3	36500	40500
64	JAMESTOWNER 1664-A+B	HT	HB	STL	SV	IO	T230	OMC	16	44000	1	3	34400	38200
64	JAMESTOWNER 64-A+B	HT	HB	AL	SV	IO	140	OMC	14	33000	1	3	33600	37300
64	JAMESTOWNER 64-A+B	HT	HB	STL	SV	IO	T140	OMC	14	39000	1	3	33100	36800
64	JAMESTOWNER 64-B+A	HT	HB	STL	SV	IO	140	OMC	14	39000	1	3	32000	35600
64	JAMESTOWNER 64-B+A	HT	HB	AL	SV	IO	T140	OMC	14	33000	1	3	34800	38600
	1985 BOATS													
40	JAMESTOWNER 40-A	HT	HB	AL	SV	IO	140	OMC	14				19100	21200
40	JAMESTOWNER 40-A	HT	HB	STL	SV	IO	140	OMC	14				16200	18400
40	JAMESTOWNER 40-B	HT	HB	AL	SV	IO	140	OMC	14				19100	21200
40	JAMESTOWNER 40-B	HT	HB	STL	SV	IO	140	OMC	14				16200	18400
45	JAMESTOWNER 40-B	HT	HB	AL	SV	IO	140	OMC	14		1	3	19800	22000
50	JAMESTOWNER 40-B	HT	HB	AL	SV				14		1	3	19800	21900
50	JAMESTOWNER 46-A	HT	HB	AL	SV	IO	140	OMC	14	14000	1		20200	22500
50	JAMESTOWNER 46-A	HT	HB	STL	SV	IO	140	OMC	14	20000	1	3	22200	24700
50	JAMESTOWNER 46-B	HT	HB	AL	SV	IO	140	OMC	14	14000	1		20200	22500
50	JAMESTOWNER 46-B	HT	HB	STL	SV	IO	140	OMC	14	20000	1	3	22200	24700
51	JAMESTOWNER 45-B	HT	HB	AL	SV				14		1	3	20100	22400
52	JAMESTOWNER 45-B	HT	HB	STL	SV				14		1	3	22900	25400
53	JAMESTOWNER 46-A	HT	HB	AL	SV	IO	230	OMC	14	14000	1		23200	25800
53	JAMESTOWNER 46-A	HT	HB	STL	SV	IO	230	OMC	14	20000	1	3	25700	28500
53	JAMESTOWNER 46-B	HT	HB	AL	SV	IO	230	OMC	14	14000	1		23200	25800
53	JAMESTOWNER 46-B	HT	HB	STL	SV	IO	230	OMC	14	20000	1	3	25700	28500
53	JAMESTOWNER 53-A	HT	HB	AL	SV	IO	140	OMC	14				28500	31700
53	JAMESTOWNER 53-A	HT	HB	STL	SV	IO	140	OMC	14				26100	29000
53	JAMESTOWNER 53-B	HT	HB	AL	SV	IO	140	OMC	14				28500	31700
53	JAMESTOWNER 53-B	HT	HB	STL	SV	IO	140	OMC	14				26100	29000
57	JAMESTOWNER 50-B	HT	HB	AL	SV	IO	230	OMC	14	16000	1		26600	29500
58	JAMESTOWNER 45-B	HT	HB	AL	SV				14		1	3	30500	33800
58	JAMESTOWNER 45-B	HT	HB	STL	SV				14		1	3	27900	31000
58	JAMESTOWNER 45-B	HT	HB	AL	SV	IO	140	MRCR	14		1	3	33900	37600
58	JAMESTOWNER 50-A	HT	HB	AL	SV	IO	140	OMC	14	16000	1		26700	29600
58	JAMESTOWNER 50-A	HT	HB	STL	SV	IO	140	OMC	14	22000	1	3	28200	31300
58	JAMESTOWNER 50-A	HT	HB	AL	SV	IO	230	OMC	14				34100	37900
58	JAMESTOWNER 50-A	HT	HB	STL	SV	IO	230	OMC	14				31200	34600
58	JAMESTOWNER 50-A	HT	HB	AL	SV	IO	T140	OMC	14	16000	1		28000	31100
58	JAMESTOWNER 50-A	HT	HB	STL	SV	IO	T140	OMC	14	22000	1	3	29400	32700
58	JAMESTOWNER 50-B	HT	HB	AL	SV	IO	140	OMC	14	16000	1		26700	29600
58	JAMESTOWNER 50-B	HT	HB	AL	SV	IO	230	OMC	14				34100	37900
58	JAMESTOWNER 50-B	HT	HB	STL	SV	IO	230	OMC	14				31200	34600
58	JAMESTOWNER 50-B	HT	HB	STL	SV	IO	230	OMC	14	22000	1	3	28400	31600
58	JAMESTOWNER 50-B	HT	HB	STL	SV	IO	T140	OMC	14	22000	1	3	29400	32700
60	JAMESTOWNER 52-A	HT	HB	AL	SV	IO	140	OMC	14				31200	34600
60	JAMESTOWNER 52-A	HT	HB	STL	SV	IO	140	OMC	14				28500	31700
60	JAMESTOWNER 52-A	HT	HB	AL	SV	IO	230	OMC	14				31100	34600
60	JAMESTOWNER 52-A	HT	HB	STL	SV	IO	230	OMC	14				28700	31900
60	JAMESTOWNER 52-B	HT	HB	STL	SV				14		1	3	19700	21900
60	JAMESTOWNER 52-B	HT	HB	AL	SV	IO	140	OMC	14				31200	34600
60	JAMESTOWNER 52-B	HT	HB	STL	SV	IO	140	OMC	14				28500	31700
60	JAMESTOWNER 52-B	HT	HB	AL	SV	IO	230	OMC	14				31600	35100
60	JAMESTOWNER 52-B	HT	HB	STL	SV	IO	230	OMC	14				28700	31900
62	JAMESTOWNER 54-A	HT	HB	AL		IO	T140	OMC	14				36200	40200
62	JAMESTOWNER 54-B	HT	HB	AL		IO	140	OMC	14				35000	38900
62	JAMESTOWNER 55-B	HT	HB	AL	SV	IO	T230	OMC	17		1	3	35100	39000
62	JAMESTOWNER 62-A	HT	HB	AL	SV	IO	230	OMC	14				33700	37400
62	JAMESTOWNER 62-A	HT	HB	STL	SV	IO	230	OMC	14				30800	34300
62	JAMESTOWNER 62-B	HT	HB	AL	SV	IO	230	OMC	14				33700	37400
62	JAMESTOWNER 62-B	HT	HB	STL	SV	IO	230	OMC	14				30800	34300
63	JAMESTOWNER 55-B	HT	HB	AL	SV				16		1	3	24900	27700
63	JAMESTOWNER 63-A	HT	HB	AL		IO	230	OMC	14				35500	39500
63	JAMESTOWNER 63-A	HT	HB	STL		IO	230	OMC	14				32500	36100
63	JAMESTOWNER 63-A	HT	HB	AL		IO	T230	OMC	14				37000	41100
63	JAMESTOWNER 63-A	HT	HB	STL		IO	T230	OMC	14				33800	37600
63	JAMESTOWNER 63-B	HT	HB	AL		IO	230	OMC	14				35500	39500

CONTINUED ON NEXT PAGE

LOA FT IN	NAME AND/OR MODEL	TOP/RIG	BOAT TYPE	HULL MTL	HULL TP	ENGINE TP	# HP	MFG	BEAM FT IN	WGT LBS	DRAFT FT IN	RETAIL LOW	RETAIL HIGH
1985 BOATS													
63	JAMESTOWNER 63-B	HT	HB	STL		IO	230	OMC	14			32500	36100
63	JAMESTOWNER 63-B	HT	HB	AL		IO	T230	OMC	14			37000	41100
63	JAMESTOWNER 63-B	HT	HB	STL		IO	T230	OMC	14			33800	37600
64	JAMESTOWNER 55-B	HT	HB	AL	SV	IO	230	OMC	16		1 3	35100	39000
1984 BOATS													
40	JAMESTOWNER 40-A	HT	HB	AL		IO	140	OMC	14			18600	20700
40	JAMESTOWNER 40-A	HT	HB	STL	SV	IO	140	OMC	14			15800	18000
40	JAMESTOWNER 40-B	HT	HB	AL	SV	IO	140	OMC	14			18600	20700
40	JAMESTOWNER 40-B	HT	HB	STL	SV	IO	140	OMC	14			15800	18000
50	JAMESTOWNER 46-A	HT	HB	AL	SV	IO	140	OMC	14	14000	1	20200	22400
50	JAMESTOWNER 46-A	HT	HB	STL	SV	IO	140	OMC	14	20000	1 3	21700	24200
50	JAMESTOWNER 46-B	HT	HB	AL	SV	IO	140	OMC	14	14000	1	20200	22400
50	JAMESTOWNER 46-B	HT	HB	STL	SV	IO	140	OMC	14	20000	1 3	21700	24200
53	JAMESTOWNER 46-A	HT	HB	AL	SV	IO	230	OMC	14	14000	1	22700	25200
53	JAMESTOWNER 46-A	HT	HB	STL	SV	IO	230	OMC	14	20000	1 3	24700	27500
53	JAMESTOWNER 46-B	HT	HB	AL	SV	IO	230	OMC	14	14000	1	22900	25500
53	JAMESTOWNER 46-B	HT	HB	STL	SV	IO	230	OMC	14	20000	1 3	25400	28300
53	JAMESTOWNER 53-A	HT	HB	AL	SV	IO	140	OMC	14			27900	30900
53	JAMESTOWNER 53-A	HT	HB	STL	SV	IO	140	OMC	14			25500	28300
53	JAMESTOWNER 53-B	HT	HB	AL	SV	IO	140	OMC	14			27900	30900
53	JAMESTOWNER 53-B	HT	HB	STL	SV	IO	140	OMC	14			25500	28300
58	JAMESTOWNER 50-A	HT	HB	AL	SV	IO	140	OMC	14	16000	1	26100	29000
58	JAMESTOWNER 50-A	HT	HB	STL	SV	IO	140	OMC	14	22000	1 3	27600	30700
58	JAMESTOWNER 50-A	HT	HB	AL	SV	IO	230	OMC	14	16000	1	29700	33000
58	JAMESTOWNER 50-A	HT	HB	STL	SV	IO	T140	OMC	14	22000	1 3	27400	30400
58	JAMESTOWNER 50-A	HT	HB	AL	SV	IO	T140	OMC	14	16000	1	28800	32000
58	JAMESTOWNER 50-B	HT	HB	STL	SV	IO	140	OMC	14	22000	1	26100	29000
58	JAMESTOWNER 50-B	HT	HB	AL	SV	IO	140	OMC	14	16000		26300	29300
58	JAMESTOWNER 50-B	HT	HB	STL	SV	IO	230	OMC	14	22000	1 3	27800	30900
58	JAMESTOWNER 50-B	HT	HB	STL	SV	IO	T140	OMC	14	22000	1 3	28800	32000
60	JAMESTOWNER 52-A	HT	HB	AL	SV	IO	140	OMC	14			30500	33800
60	JAMESTOWNER 52-A	HT	HB	STL	SV	IO	140	OMC	14			27900	31000
60	JAMESTOWNER 52-A	HT	HB	AL	SV	IO	230	OMC	14			30700	34100
60	JAMESTOWNER 52-A	HT	HB	STL	SV	IO	230	OMC	14			28100	31200
60	JAMESTOWNER 52-B	HT	HB	AL	SV	IO	140	OMC	14			30500	33800
60	JAMESTOWNER 52-B	HT	HB	STL	SV	IO	140	OMC	14			27900	31000
60	JAMESTOWNER 52-B	HT	HB	AL	SV	IO	230	OMC	14			30700	34100
60	JAMESTOWNER 52-B	HT	HB	STL	SV	IO	230	OMC	14			28100	31200
62	JAMESTOWNER 54-A	HT	HB	AL		IO	140	OMC	14			34200	38000
62	JAMESTOWNER 54-B	HT	HB	AL		IO	140	OMC	14			34200	38000
62	JAMESTOWNER 62-A	HT	HB	AL	SV	IO	230	OMC	14			32900	36600
62	JAMESTOWNER 62-B	HT	HB	STL	SV	IO	230	OMC	14			30100	33500
62	JAMESTOWNER 62-B	HT	HB	AL	SV	IO	230	OMC	14			32900	36600
62	JAMESTOWNER 62-B	HT	HB	STL	SV	IO	230	OMC	14			30100	33500
63	JAMESTOWNER 63-A	HT	HB	AL		IO	230	OMC	14			34700	38600
63	JAMESTOWNER 63-A	HT	HB	STL		IO	230	OMC	14			31800	35300
63	JAMESTOWNER 63-A	HT	HB	AL		IO	T230	OMC	14			36200	40200
63	JAMESTOWNER 63-B	HT	HB	STL		IO	T230	OMC	14			33100	36800
63	JAMESTOWNER 63-B	HT	HB	AL		IO	230	OMC	14			34700	38600
63	JAMESTOWNER 63-B	HT	HB	STL		IO	230	OMC	14			31800	35300
63	JAMESTOWNER 63-B	HT	HB	AL		IO	T230	OMC	14			36200	40200
63	JAMESTOWNER 63-B	HT	HB	STL		IO	T230	OMC	14			33100	36800

....For earlier years, see the BUC Used Boat Price Guide, Volume 3

JARMADA MARINE SERVICES INC

JAMES A RYDER CO
COCONUT GROVE FL 33133   COAST GUARD MFG ID- HDA   See inside cover to adjust price for area

LOA FT IN	NAME AND/OR MODEL	TOP/RIG	BOAT TYPE	HULL MTL	HULL TP	ENGINE TP	# HP	MFG	BEAM FT IN	WGT LBS	DRAFT FT IN	RETAIL LOW	RETAIL HIGH
1984 BOATS													
17 11	RYDER CRAFT	OP	UTL	FBG	TM	OB			7 10	1250	8	3750	4350

....For earlier years, see the BUC Used Boat Price Guide, Volume 3

JAVELIN BOATS INC

DIV OF OMC FISHING GROUP
MURFREESBORO TN 37130   COAST GUARD MFG ID- BNZ   See inside cover to adjust price for area

For more recent years, see the BUC Used Boat Price Guide, Volume 1

LOA FT IN	NAME AND/OR MODEL	TOP/RIG	BOAT TYPE	HULL MTL	HULL TP	ENGINE TP	# HP	MFG	BEAM FT IN	WGT LBS	DRAFT FT IN	RETAIL LOW	RETAIL HIGH
1996 BOATS													
16 8	360FS	OP	BASS	FBG	SV	OB			6 9	1597		2250	2650
16 8	369FS	OP	BASS	FBG	SV	OB			6 11	1926		2550	2950
16 8	369SE	OP	BASS	FBG	SV	OB			6 11	1425		2000	2400
17 9	379F/S	OP	BASS	FBG	SV	OB			6 11	2260		2700	3150
17 9	379T	OP	BASS	FBG	SV	OB			7 1	2071		2600	3050
17 9	379TDC	OP	BASS	FBG	SV	OB			7 1	2141		2650	3100
18 9	389FS	OP	BASS	FBG	SV	OB			7 5	2355		2800	3250
18 9	389DC	OP	BASS	FBG	SV	OB			7 5	2302		2800	3250
18 9	389T/TS	OP	BASS	FBG	SV	OB			7 5	2302		2800	3250
19 1	320A	OP	BASS	FBG	SV	OB			7 7	2295		2550	3300
19 9	400T/E	OP	BASS	FBG	SV	OB			7 7	1652		2500	2950
19 9	400TDC	OP	BASS	FBG	SV	OB			7 7	1652		2500	2900
20 1	409FS	OP	BASS	FBG	SV	OB			7 9	2666		3550	4150
20 1	409T	OP	BASS	FBG	SV	OB			7 9	2525		3500	4050
20 1	409TDC	OP	BASS	FBG	SV	OB			7 9	2550		3500	4100
1995 BOATS													
16 8	360FS	OP	BASS	FBG	SV	OB			6 9	1597		2100	2500
16 8	367A	OP	BASS	FBG	SV	OB			6 11	1425		1900	2300
16 8	367FS	OP	BASS	FBG	SV	OB			6 11	1926		2450	2850
17 9	379DC	OP	BASS	FBG	SV	OB			7 1	2141		2500	2950
17 9	379F/S	OP	BASS	FBG	SV	OB			6 11	2260		2600	3000
17 9	379T	OP	BASS	FBG	SV	OB			7 1	2071		2500	2900
18 9	389DC	OP	BASS	FBG	SV	OB			7 5	2337		2650	3100
18 9	389FS	OP	BASS	FBG	SV	OB			7 5	2355		2700	3100
18 9	389T/TS	OP	BASS	FBG	SV	OB			7 5	2302		2650	3100
19 1	320A	OP	BASS	FBG	SV	OB			7 7	2295		2700	3150
19 9	400D	OP	BASS	FBG	SV	OB			7 7	1652		2400	2800
19 9	400T/E	OP	BASS	FBG	SV	OB			7 7	1652		2400	2750
20 1	409DC	OP	BASS	FBG	SV	OB			7 9	2550		3300	3850
20 1	409FS	OP	BASS	FBG	SV	OB			7 9	2666		3400	3950
20 1	409T	OP	BASS	FBG	SV	OB			7 9	2525		3300	3850
1994 BOATS													
16 8	360A	OP	BASS	FBG	SV	OB			6 9	1425		1800	2150
16 8	360FS	OP	BASS	FBG	SV	OB			6 9	1597		2000	2350
16 8	361A	OP	BASS	FBG	SV	OB			6 11	1425		1800	2150
16 8	363B	OP	BASS	FBG	SV	OB			6 11	1826		2250	2600
16 8	363DC	OP	BASS	FBG	SV	OB			6 11	1876		2300	2650
16 8	363FS	OP	BASS	FBG	SV	OB			6 11	1926		2350	2700
17 5	310TA	OP	BASS	FBG	SV	OB			7 1	1922		2300	2700
17 9	379DC	OP	BASS	FBG	SV	OB			7 1	2141		2450	2850
17 9	379F/S	OP	BASS	FBG	SV	OB			6 11	2260		2500	2900
17 9	379T	OP	BASS	FBG	SV	OB			7 1	2071		2400	2800
18 9	389DC	OP	BASS	FBG	SV	OB			7 5	2337		2550	2950
18 9	389FS	OP	BASS	FBG	SV	OB			7 5	2355		2550	2950
18 9	389T/TS	OP	BASS	FBG	SV	OB			7 5	2302		2500	2900
19 1	320A	OP	BASS	FBG	SV	OB			7 7	2295		2550	3000
19 9	400D	OP	BASS	FBG	SV	OB			7 7	1652		2250	2650
19 9	400T/E	OP	BASS	FBG	SV	OB			7 7	1652		2250	2650
20 1	409DC	OP	BASS	FBG	SV	OB			7 9	2550		3150	3650
20 1	409FS	OP	BASS	FBG	SV	OB			7 9	2666		3200	3700
20 1	409T	OP	BASS	FBG	SV	OB			7 9	2525		3150	3650
1993 BOATS													
16 8	360A	OP	BASS	FBG	SV	OB			6 9	1425		1700	2050
16 8	360FS	OP	BASS	FBG	SV	OB			6 9	1597		1900	2250
16 8	363B	OP	BASS	FBG	SV	OB			6 11	1826		2100	2500
16 8	363DC	OP	BASS	FBG	SV	OB			6 11	1876		2150	2550
16 8	363FS	OP	BASS	FBG	SV	OB			6 11	1926		2200	2550
17 5	310TA	OP	BASS	FBG	SV	OB			7 1	1922		2200	2550
17 9	379DC	OP	BASS	FBG	SV	OB			7 1	2141		2300	2700
17 9	379F/S	OP	BASS	FBG	SV	OB			6 11	2260		2400	2750
17 9	379T	OP	BASS	FBG	SV	OB			7 1	2071		2300	2650
18 9	389DC	OP	BASS	FBG	SV	OB			7 5	2337		2450	2850
18 9	389FS	OP	BASS	FBG	SV	OB			7 5	2355		2450	2850
18 9	389T/TS	OP	BASS	FBG	SV	OB			7 5	2302		2450	2850
19 1	320A	OP	BASS	FBG	SV	OB			7 7	2295		2500	2900
20 1	409DC	OP	BASS	FBG	SV	OB			7 9	2550		3000	3450
20 1	409FS	OP	BASS	FBG	SV	OB			7 9	2666		3050	3550
20 1	409T	OP	BASS	FBG	SV	OB			7 9	2525		2950	3450
1992 BOATS													
16 8	363 BASS	OP	BASS	F/W	SV	OB			6 11	1120		1350	1600
16 8	363 FISH/SKI	OP	SKI	F/W	SV	OB			6 11	1120	11	1300	1550

LOA FT	LOA IN	NAME AND/ OR MODEL	TOP/ RIG	BOAT TYPE	HULL MTL	HULL TP	ENGINE TP	# HP	MFG	BEAM FT	BEAM IN	WGT LBS	DRAFT FT	DRAFT IN	RETAIL LOW	RETAIL HIGH
		1992 BOATS														
17	5	310T ANGLER	OP	FSH	F/W	SV	OB			7	1		1		1650	1950
17	9	373 BASS	OP	BASS	F/W	SV	OB			7		1225	1		1500	1750
17	9	373 FISH/SKI	OP	SKI	F/W	SV	OB			7		1225	1		1450	1750
18	9	389 DC BASS	OP	BASS	F/W	SV	OB			7	5	1475	1	3	1750	2100
18	9	389 FISH/SKI	OP	SKI	F/W	SV	OB			7	5	1500	1	3	1750	2100
18	9	389T BASS	OP	BASS	F/W	SV	OB			7	5	1475	1	3	1750	2100
19	1	320 ANGLER	OP	FSH	F/W	SV	OB			7	7		1	3	1900	2250
19	6	396 FISH/SKI	OP	SKI	F/W	SV	OB			7	7	1615	1	4	1900	2300
20	1	409 DC BASS	OP	BASS	F/W	SV	OB			7	9	1580	1	4	2150	2550
20	1	409 FISH/SKI	OP	SKI	F/W	SV	OB			7	9	1700	1	4	2300	2650
20	1	409T BASS	OP	BASS	F/W	SV	OB			7	9	1575	1	4	2150	2500

....For earlier years, see the BUC Used Boat Price Guide, Volume 3

JAY BEE BOATS

JAY BEE ENTERPRISES INC
LANCASTER KY 40444 COAST GUARD MFG ID- JBE

See inside cover to adjust price for area

LOA FT	LOA IN	NAME AND/ OR MODEL	TOP/ RIG	BOAT TYPE	HULL MTL	HULL TP	ENGINE TP	# HP	MFG	BEAM FT	BEAM IN	WGT LBS	DRAFT FT	DRAFT IN	RETAIL LOW	RETAIL HIGH
		1987 BOATS														
16		BASS-PRO 160SV	OP	BASS	FBG	SV	OB			6	6				2250	2600
16		BASS-SKIER DLX 16	OP	BASS	FBG	DV	OB			6	6				2250	2600
16		BASSMASTER 160SV	OP	BASS	FBG	SV	OB			6	8				2250	2600
16		HORNET	OP	RNBT	FBG	DV	IO	115		6	6				2600	3000
17		BASS-MASTER 169SV	OP	BASS	FBG	DV	OB			7					2850	3350
17		BASS-PRO 170SV	OP	BASS	FBG	SV	OB			7	3				2650	3050
17		BASS-SKIER DLX 17	OP	BASS	FBG	DV	OB			7					2850	3350
17		CRAPPIE MASTER 17	OP	BASS	FBG	DV	OB			7					2200	2550
17		DRONE	OP	RNBT	FBG	DV	IO	120		7					2900	3400
18		QUEEN-BEE	OP	RNBT	FBG	DV	IO	120		7	3				3600	4150
18	6	BASS-MASTER 186SV	OP	BASS	FBG	DV	OB			7	3				3850	4450
19	3	BASS-MASTER 193	OP	BASS	FBG	DV	OB			7	8				3950	4600
		1985 BOATS														
16		680V	OP	RNBT	FBG	DV	OB			6	8	850			2100	2500
16		680V	OP	RNBT	FBG	DV	IO	120	OMC	6	8				2400	2750
16		BASS-PRO 160SV	OP	BASS	FBG	SV	OB			6	8				2250	2650
16		BASS-SKIER 680V	OP	SKI	FBG	DV	OB			6	8	850			1950	2350
16		BASS-SKIER 680V DLX	OP	SKI	FBG	DV	OB			6	8	850			2200	2600
16		BASSMASTER 160SV	OP	BASS	FBG	SV	OB			6	8				1950	2300
16	3	675	OP	RNBT	FBG	TR	OB			6	3	850			2100	2500
16	3	675	OP	RNBT	FBG	TR	IO	120	MRCR	6	3	1500			2300	2650
16	3	679	OP	RNBT	FBG	TR	IO	120-140		6	7	1750			2500	2900
17		784	OP	SKI	FBG	DV	IO	120-185		7		1700			2500	3000
17		BASS-PRO 170SV	OP	BASS	FBG	SV	OB			7					2500	2900
17		BASS-SKIER 784	OP	SKI	FBG	DV	OB			7		990			2500	2900
18		888	OP	RNBT	FBG	DV	IO	120-170		7	4	2100			3200	3850
18		888	OP	RNBT	FBG	DV	IO	185-198		7	4	2400			3500	4050
		1984 BOATS														
16		680V	OP	RNBT	FBG	DV	OB			6	8	850			2050	2400
16		680V	OP	RNBT	FBG	DV	IO	120	OMC	6	8				2300	2700
16		BASS-PRO 160SV	OP	BASS	FBG	SV	OB			6	8				2200	2550
16		BASS-SKIER 680V	OP	SKI	FBG	DV	OB			6	8	850			1900	2300
16		BASS-SKIER 680V DLX	OP	SKI	FBG	DV	OB			6	8	850			2150	2500
16		BASSMASTER 160SV	OP	BASS	FBG	SV	OB			6	8				1900	2250
16	3	675	OP	RNBT	FBG	TR	OB			6	3	850			2050	2450
16	3	675	OP	RNBT	FBG	TR	IO	120	MRCR	6	3	1500			2200	2550
16	3	679	OP	RNBT	FBG	TR	IO	120-140		6	7	1750			2400	2800
17		784	OP	SKI	FBG	DV	IO	120-185		7		1700			2450	2900
17		BASS-PRO 170SV	OP	BASS	FBG	SV	OB			7					2450	2850
17		BASS-SKIER 784	OP	SKI	FBG	DV	OB			7		990			2450	2850
18		888	OP	RNBT	FBG	DV	IO	120-170		7	4	2100			3100	3700
18		888	OP	RNBT	FBG	DV	IO	185-198		7	4	2400			3350	3950

....For earlier years, see the BUC Used Boat Price Guide, Volume 3

JEANNEAU

DIV OF GROUPE BENETEAU
ANNAPOLIS MD 21403 COAST GUARD MFG ID- IRI

See inside cover to adjust price for area

For more recent years, see the BUC Used Boat Price Guide, Volume 1

LOA FT	LOA IN	NAME AND/ OR MODEL	TOP/ RIG	BOAT TYPE	HULL MTL	HULL TP	ENGINE TP	# HP	MFG	BEAM FT	BEAM IN	WGT LBS	DRAFT FT	DRAFT IN	RETAIL LOW	RETAIL HIGH
		1996 BOATS														
34	6	LAGOON 35 CCC	SLP	SACAC	FBG	CT	IB	T 10D	YAN	15	9	9500	3	3	86100	94600
34	11	SUN ODYSSEY 35.1	SLP	SACAC	FBG	KL	IB	27D	YAN	12	2	11000	6	3	65700	72200
36	9	LAGOON 37	SLP	SACAC	FBG	CT	IB	T 18D	PERK	20	2	11883	3	4	103000	113500
37	5	SUN ODYSSEY 37.1	SLP	SACAC	FBG	KL	IB	27D	YAN	12	9	13230	6	2	82000	90100
42	6	LAGOON 42	SLP	SACAC	FBG	CT	IB	T 27D	PERK	20	2	16550	4	5	167000	183000
46	3	LAGOON 47	SLP	SACAC	FBG	CT	IB	T 38D	YAN	24	11	19842	3	11	223000	245000
46	5	SUN ODYSSEY 45.1	SLP	SACAC	FBG	KL	IB	60D	YAN	14	8	21208	6	7	170000	187000
47	3	SUN ODYSSEY 47 CC	SLP	SACAC	FBG	KL	IB	85D	YAN	14	7	27560	6	11	196500	216000
55	6	LAGOON 57	SLP	SACAC	FBG	CT	IB	T 48D	YAN	30	2	28660	3	11	393000	432000
67	7	LAGOON 67	SLP	SACAC	FBG	CT	IB	T100D	YAN	35		39000	5	3	1.070M	1.165M
		1995 BOATS														
28	6	SUN ODYSSEY 28.1	SLP	SCFAC	FBG			18D	YAN	9	10		4	11	**	**
29		SUN WAY 29	SLP	SCFAC	FBG	KL	IB	D	YAN	9	9	9105	3	8	57500	63200
30		MERRY FISHER 900 CR	SLP	SCFAC	FBG	KL	IB	T185D		11	7	9105	2	7	59700	65600
32	1	SUN ODYSSEY	SLP	SCFAC	FBG	KL	IB	18D	YAN	10	8	3020	6	3	15900	18100
33	10	SUN ODYSSEY 33.1	SLP	SACAC	FBG	KL	IB	28D	YAN	11	6	11000	6	5	62200	68300
36	9	LAGOON 37	SLP	SCFAC	FBG	CT	IB	T 18D	PERK	20	2	11883	3	4	97000	106500
37	5	SUN ODYSSEY 37.1	SLP	SACAC	FBG	KL	IB	48D	YAN	12	9	13230	6	2	77700	85400
42		SUN ODYSSEY 42.1	SLP	SACAC	FBG	KL	IB	50D		13	1	18519	6	3	113000	124000
42	6	LAGOON 42	SLP	SCFAC	FBG	CT	IB	T 30D	PERK	20	2	16550	4	5	157000	172500
46	5	SUN ODYSSEY 45.1	SLP	SCFCC	FBG	KL	IB	60D	YAN	14	8	21208	6	7	160000	176000
47	3	SUN ODYSSEY 47 CC	SLP	SCFCC	FBG	WK	IB	88D	YAN	14	7	27560	6	11	185000	203500
50	6	INTERNATIONAL 50	SLP	SCFAC	FBG	KL	IB	85D	PERK	15	11	33000	5	11	213000	234000
51		SUN ODYSSEY 51	SLP	SCFAC	FBG	KL	IB	80D		16		33000	6	6	213500	235000
55	6	LAGOON 57	SLP	SCFAC	FBG	CT	IB	T 48D	YAN	30	2	28660	3	11	370000	406500
		1985 BOATS														
24	7	EOLIA 25	SLP	SA/CR	FBG	KC	IB	8D	YAN	9	2	3750	2	7	10500	12000
24	7	EOLIA 25	SLP	SA/CR	FBG	KL	IB	8D	YAN	9	2	3750	4	9	10500	12000
27	3	FANTASIA 27	SLP	SA/CR	FBG	KC	IB	8D	YAN	9	6	4704	2	7	14100	16000
27	3	FANTASIA 27	SLP	SA/CR	FBG	KL	IB	8D	YAN	9	6	4704	5		14000	16000
29	6	ARCADIA 30	SLP	SA/CR	FBG	KC	IB	8D	YAN	10	4	6835	4	3	21000	23300
29	6	ARCADIA 30	SLP	SA/CR	FBG	KL	IB	8D	YAN	10	4	6175	5	4	19200	21300
31	10	ATTALIA 32	SLP	SA/CR	FBG	KC	IB	15D	YAN	10	5	7616	3	7	23200	25800
31	10	ATTALIA 32	SLP	SA/CR	FBG	KL	IB	15D	YAN	10	5	7616	5	8	23200	25800
34	7	SUN-RISE 34	SLP	SA/CR	FBG	KC	IB	15D	YAN	11	5	10361	3	7	31300	34700
34	7	SUN-RISE 34	SLP	SA/CR	FBG	KL	IB	15D	YAN	11	5	10361	5	11	31300	34700
36	5	SUNSHINE 36	SLP	SA/CR	FBG	KC	IB	23D	YAN	12	7	11872	4	1	36600	40700
36	5	SUNSHINE 36	SLP	SA/CR	FBG	KL	IB	23D	YAN	12	7	11872	6	3	36600	40700
37	3	SELECTION 37	SLP	SA/CR	FBG	KL	IB	15D	YAN	10	8	7616	6	3	25000	27800
45	1	SUN-KISS 45	SLP	SA/CR	FBG	KC	IB	50D	PERK	14	5	25312	5		87400	96000
45	1	SUN-KISS 45	SLP	SA/CR	FBG	KL	IB	50D	PERK	14	5	25312	6	6	87400	96000
47	7	TRINIDAD 48	SLP	SA/CR	FBG	KC	IB	80D	PERK	15	1	28000	4	7	101500	111500
47	7	TRINIDAD 48	SLP	SA/CR	FBG	KL	IB	80D	PERK	15	1	28000	7	5	101500	111500
		1984 BOATS														
20	4	ESPACE 620	SLP	SAIL	FBG	KC				8	2	2640	2	3	5500	6300
20	4	ESPACE 620	SLP	SAIL	FBG	KL				8	2	2640	3	7	5500	6300
22	9	BAHIA	SLP	SAIL	FBG	CB				7	11	1853	1	5	4900	5600
27	3	FANTASIA	SLP	SA/RC	FBG	KC	IB	8D		9	6	4200	2	7	11900	13500
27	3	FANTASIA	SLP	SA/RC	FBG	KL	IB	8D		9	6	4200	5		11900	13500
31	10	ATTALIA	SLP	SAIL	FBG	KC	IB	15D		10	6	7616	3	7	21800	24300
31	10	ATTALIA	SLP	SAIL	FBG	KL	IB	15D		10	6	7616	5	9	21800	24300
36	5	SUNSHINE	SLP	SAIL	FBG	KC	IB	D	YAN	12	7	10600	4	1	31200	34700
36	5	SUNSHINE	SLP	SAIL	FBG	KL	IB	D	YAN	12	7	10600	6	3	31200	34700
45	1	SUN-KISS	SLP	SAIL	FBG	KC	IB	50D		14	5	25300	5		82500	90700
45	1	SUN-KISS	SLP	SAIL	FBG	KL	IB	50D		14	5	25300	7	5	82500	90700
45	1	SUN-KISS SHOAL	SLP	SAIL	FBG	KL	IB	50D		14	5	25300	6	6	82500	90700
47	6	TRINIDAD	SLP	SA/RC	FBG	KC	IB	D		15	1	25000	4	6	91600	100500
47	6	TRINIDAD	SLP	SA/RC	FBG	KL	IB	D		15	1	25000	7	4	91600	100500
47	6	TRINIDAD	KTH	SA/RC	FBG	KC	IB	D		15	1	25000	4	6	91600	100500
47	6	TRINIDAD	KTH	SA/RC	FBG	KL	IB	D		15	1	25000	7	4	91600	100500

....For earlier years, see the BUC Used Boat Price Guide, Volume 3

JEFFERSON YACHTS INC

JEFFERSONVILLE IN 47130

See inside cover to adjust price for area

For more recent years, see the BUC Used Boat Price Guide, Volume 1

LOA FT	LOA IN	NAME AND/ OR MODEL	TOP/ RIG	BOAT TYPE	HULL MTL	HULL TP	ENGINE TP	# HP	MFG	BEAM FT	BEAM IN	WGT LBS	DRAFT FT	DRAFT IN	RETAIL LOW	RETAIL HIGH
		1996 BOATS														
41	8	CONVERTIBLE 43	FB	CNV	FBG	DV	IB	T315D	CUM	14	5	26000	3	7	168000	184500
41	8	CONVERTIBLE 43	FB	CNV	FBG	DV	IB	T375D	CAT	14	5	28000	3	7	190500	209000

LOA FT	IN	NAME AND/ OR MODEL	TOP/ RIG	BOAT TYPE	-HULL- MTL	TP	TP	----ENGINE--- # HP	MFG	BEAM FT	IN	WGT LBS	DRAFT FT	IN	RETAIL LOW	RETAIL HIGH
		1996 BOATS														
41	8	CONVERTIBLE 43	FB	CNV	FBG	DV	IB	T420D	CUM	14	5	30000	3	7	201000	221000
41	8	VISCOUNT 42 SD	FB	MY	FBG	DV	IB	T315D	CUM	14	5	28000	3	7	180000	198000
41	8	VISCOUNT 42 SD	FB	MY	FBG	DV	IB	T375D	CAT	14	5	30000	3	7	202000	222000
42	10	MARLAGO SUNDECK 43FB	FB	MY	FBG	DV	IB	T315D	CUM	15		30000	3	10	186500	205000
		IB T375D CAT 209000 229500, IB T420D CUM 212500 233500, IB T435D CAT													219500	241500
44	8	VISCOUNT 45 CPT	FB	MY	FBG	DV	IB	T315D	CUM	14	5	28000	3	7	164500	181000
44	8	VISCOUNT 45 CPT	FB	MY	FBG	DV	IB	T375D	CAT	14	5	30000	3	7	183500	201500
45	10	MARLAGO 46 CPT	FB	MY	FBG	DV	IB	T315D	CUM	15		34000	3	10	182000	200000
		IB T375D CAT 196000 215500, IB T420D CUM 200500 220000, IB T435D CAT													205500	225500
45	10	MARLAGO 46 SUNDECK	FB	MY	FBG	DV	IB	T315D	CUM	15		36000	3	10	186000	204000
		IB T375D CAT 199500 219000, IB T420D CUM 202500 223000, IB T435D CAT													208000	228500
48	4	CONVERTIBLE 48	FB	CNV	FBG	DV	IB	T550D	DD	16		46000	4		240000	264000
48	4	RIVANNA 48 CPT	FB	DCMY	FBG	DV	IB	T315D	CUM	16		40000	4		196000	215500
		IB T375D CAT 213000 234000, IB T420D CUM 216500 238000, IB T435D CAT													221500	243000
		IB T550D DD 242500 266500														
48	4	RIVANNA 48 SD	FB	MY	FBG	DV	IB	T315D	CUM	16		42000	4		205500	226000
		IB T375D CAT 219000 240500, IB T420D CUM 221500 243000, IB T435D CAT													227000	249500
		IB T550D DD 247000 271500														
52	4	CONVERTIBLE 52	FB	CNV	FBG	DV	IB	T550D	DD	16		54000	4		304000	334000
52	4	CONVERTIBLE 52	FB	CNV	FBG	DV	IB	T735D	DD	16		54000	4		344000	378000
52	4	MARQUESSA 52 EXT DK	FB	MYDKH	FBG	DV	IB	T550D	DD	16		54000	4		304500	334500
52	4	MARQUESSA 52 STD DK	FB	MY	FBG	DV	IB	T550D	DD	16		54000	4		305000	335000
52	4	RIVANNA 52 CPT	FB	MY	FBG	DV	IB	T315D	CUM	16		44000	4		218000	239500
		IB T375D CAT 235500 258500, IB T420D CUM 241500 265500, IB T435D CAT													247500	272000
		IB T550D DD 277000 304000														
52	4	RIVANNA 52 SD	FB	MY	FBG	DV	IB	T315D	CUM	16		44000	4		229500	252500
		IB T375D CAT 247500 272000, IB T420D CUM 255000 280500, IB T435D CAT													260500	286000
		IB T550D DD 291000 320000														
56	4	MARQUESSA 56 CPT	FB	MYDKH	FBG	DV	IB	T550D	DD	16		58000	4		337500	371000
56	4	MARQUESSA 56 EXT	FB	MY	FBG	DV	IB	T550D	DD	16		56000	4		338000	371500
56	4	RIVANNA 56 CPT	FB	MY	FBG	DV	IB	T315D	CUM	16		46000	4		220000	242000
		IB T375D CUM 253000 278000, IB T420D CUM 268500 295000, IB T435D CAT													273000	300000
		IB T550D DD 317500 348500														
56	4	RIVANNA 56 SD	FB	MY	FBG	DV	IB	T315D	CUM	16		46000	4		227500	250500
		IB T375D CAT 244000 268000, IB T420D CUM 259000 284500, IB T435D CAT													264000	290000
		IB T550D DD 300000 329500														
60	4	MARQUESSA 60 CPT	FB	MY	FBG	DV	IB	T550D	DD	16		60000	4		352000	386500
60	4	MARQUESSA 60 CPT	FB	MY	FBG	DV	IB	T735D	DD	16		60000	4		399500	439000
60	4	RIVANNA 60 CPT	FB	MY	FBG	DV	IB	T375D	CAT	16		50000	4		267000	293000
		IB T420D CUM 269500 296500, IB T435D CAT 275500 302500, IB T550D DD													290500	319500
		IB T735D DD 319500 351000														
64	4	MARQUESSA 64 CPT	FB	MY	FBG	DV	IB	T550D	DD	16		63900	4		380000	417500
64	4	MARQUESSA 64 CPT	FB	MY	FBG	DV	IB	T735D	DD	16		63900	4		406000	446500
		1995 BOATS														
35		MARLAGO FS 35	OP	CTRCN	FBG	DV	OB			9	2	4700	2	3	42900	47700
41	8	CONVERTIBLE 43	FB	CNV	FBG	DV	IB	T300D	CUM	14	5	26000	3	7	159000	175000
41	8	CONVERTIBLE 43	FB	CNV	FBG	DV	IB	T375D	CAT	14	5	28000	3	7	182500	200500
41	8	CONVERTIBLE 43	FB	CNV	FBG	DV	IB	T400D	CUM	14	5	30000	3	7	190000	208500
41	8	PISCOUNT 42 SD	FB	MY	FBG	DV	IB	T375D	CAT	14	5	30000	3	7	193500	212500
41	8	VISCOUNT 42 SD	FB	MY	FBG	DV	IB	T300D	CUM	14	5	28000	3	7	171000	188000
42	10	MARLAGO SUNDECK 43FB	FB	MY	FBG	DV	IB	T300D	CUM	15		30000	3	10	177000	194500
		IB T375D CAT 200500 220500, IB T400D CUM 200500 220500, IB T435D CAT													210500	231500
44	8	VISCOUNT 45 CPT	FB	MY	FBG	DV	IB	T300D	CUM	14	5	28000	3	7	155500	171000
44	8	VISCOUNT 45 CPT	FB	MY	FBG	DV	IB	T375D	CAT	14	5	30000	3	7	176000	193000
45	10	MARLAGO 46 CPT	FB	MY	FBG	DV	IB	T300D	CUM	15		34000	3	10	172000	189000
		IB T375D CAT 187500 206000, IB T400D CUM 189000 207500, IB T435D CAT													196500	216000
45	10	MARLAGO 46 SUNDECK	FB	MY	FBG	DV	IB	T375D	CAT	15		36000	3	10	190000	209000
45	10	MARLAGO 46 SUNDECK	FB	MY	FBG	DV	IB	T400D	CUM	15		36000	3	10	191000	210000
45	10	MARLAGO 46 SUNDECK	FB	MY	FBG	DV	IB	T435D	CAT	15		36000	3	10	198500	218500
48	4	CONVERTIBLE 48	FB	CNV	FBG	DV	IB	T550D	DD	16		46000	4		228500	251000
48	4	RIVANNA 48 CPT	FB	DCMY	FBG	DV	IB	T300D	CUM	16		40000	4		185000	203500
		IB T375D CAT 203000 223500, IB T400D CUM 204000 224000, IB T435D CAT													211000	232000
		IB T550D DD 232000 255000														
48	4	RIVANNA 48 SD	FB	MY	FBG	DV	IB	T300D	CUM	16		42000	4		194500	213500
		IB T375D CAT 208500 229000, IB T400D CUM 208500 229000, IB T435D CAT													216000	237500
		IB T550D DD 236000 259000														
52	4	CONVERTIBLE 52	FB	CNV	FBG	DV	IB	T550D	DD	16		54000	4		291500	320500
52	4	CONVERTIBLE 52	FB	CNV	FBG	DV	IB	T735D	DD	16		54000	4		329500	362000
52	4	MARQUESSA 52 EXT DK	FB	MYDKH	FBG	DV	IB	T550D	DD	16		54000	4		291500	320500
52	4	MARQUESSA 52 STD DK	FB	MY	FBG	DV	IB	T550D	DD	16		54000	4		292000	321000
52	4	RIVANNA 52 CPT	FB	MY	FBG	DV	IB	T300D	CUM	16		44000	4		205500	226000
		IB T375D CAT 224500 247000, IB T400D CUM 227000 249500, IB T435D CAT													236500	260000
		IB T550D DD 264500 291000														
52	4	RIVANNA 52 SD	FB	MY	FBG	DV	IB	T300D	CUM	16		44000	4		216500	238000
		IB T375D CAT 236500 260000, IB T400D CUM 239500 263500, IB T435D CAT													249000	273500
		IB T550D DD 279000 306500														
56	4	MARQUESSA 56 CPT	FB	MYDKH	FBG	DV	IB	T550D	DD	16		58000	4		323500	355500
56	4	MARQUESSA 56 EXT	FB	MY	FBG	DV	IB	T550D	DD	16		56000	4		324000	356000
56	4	RIVANNA 56 CPT	FB	MY	FBG	DV	IB	T300D	CUM	16		46000	4		206000	226500
		IB T375D CUM 242500 266500, IB T400D CUM 251000 275500, IB T435D CAT													262000	287500
		IB T550D DD 304000 334500														
56	4	RIVANNA 56 SD	FB	MY	FBG	DV	IB	T300D	CUM	16		46000	4		213500	234500
		IB T375D CAT 233500 257000, IB T400D CUM 241500 265500, IB T435D CAT													253000	278000
		IB T550D DD 287500 316000														
60	4	MARQUESSA 60 CPT	FB	MY	FBG	DV	IB	T550D	DD	16		60000	4		337500	371000
60	4	MARQUESSA 60 CPT	FB	MY	FBG	DV	IB	T735D	DD	16		60000	4		383000	421000
60	4	RIVANNA 60 CPT	FB	MY	FBG	DV	IB	T375D	CAT	16		50000	4		254500	280000
		IB T400D CUM 255000 280000, IB T435D CAT 263000 289000, IB T550D DD													277500	305000
		IB T735D DD 305000 335500														
64	4	MARQUESSA 64 CPT	FB	MY	FBG	DV	IB	T550D	DD	16		63900	4		363000	399000
64	4	MARQUESSA 64 CPT	FB	MY	FBG	DV	IB	T735D	DD	16		63900	4		389000	427500
		1994 BOATS														
36	10	CONVERTIBLE 37	FB	CNV	FBG	DV	IB	T300D	CUM	14	5	22000	3	5	119500	131000
36	10	VISCOUNT 37 SD	FB	MY	FBG	DV	IB	T300D	CUM	14	5	22000	3	5	119000	131000
36	10	VISCOUNT 37 SD	FB	MY	FBG	DV	IB	T375D	CAT	14	5	24000	3	5	137500	151000
39	10	CONVERTIBLE 40	FB	CNV	FBG	DV	IB	T300D	CUM	14	5	24000	3	5	143500	157500
39	10	CONVERTIBLE 40	FB	CNV	FBG	DV	IB	T375D	CAT	14	5	26000	3	5	165000	181000
39	10	VISCOUNT 40 CPT	FB	MY	FBG	DV	IB	T300D	CUM	14	5	24000	3	5	143500	157500
39	10	VISCOUNT 40 CPT	FB	MY	FBG	DV	IB	T375D	CAT	14	5	26000	3	5	164500	181000
41	8	CONVERTIBLE 43	FB	CNV	FBG	DV	IB	T300D	CUM	14	5	26000	3	7	152500	167500
41	8	CONVERTIBLE 43	FB	CNV	FBG	DV	IB	T375D	CAT	14	5	28000	3	7	175000	192500
41	8	CONVERTIBLE 43	FB	CNV	FBG	DV	IB	T400D	CUM	14	5	30000	3	7	182000	200000
41	8	SPECIAL EDITION 42	FB	MY	FBG	DV	IB	T300D	CUM	14	5	28000	3	7	160000	176000
41	8	SPECIAL EDITION 43	FB	CNV	FBG	DV	IB	T300D	CUM	14	5	28000	3	5	163000	179500
41	8	VISCOUNT 42 SD	FB	MY	FBG	DV	IB	T300D	CUM	14	5	28000	3	7	166500	183000
41	8	VISCOUNT 42 SD	FB	MY	FBG	DV	IB	T375D	CAT	14	5	30000	3	7	186000	204000
42	10	MARLAGO SUNDECK 43	FB	MY	FBG	DV	IB	T300D	CUM	15		30000	3	10	167000	183500
		IB T320D CAT 181000 198500, IB T375D CAT 189000 208000, IB T425D CAT													197000	216500
44	8	SPECIAL EDITION 85	FB	MY	FBG	DV	IB	T300D	CUM	15		28000	3	7	146500	161000
44	8	VISCOUNT 45 CPT	FB	MY	FBG	DV	IB	T300D	CUM	14	5	28000	3	7	149000	163500
44	8	VISCOUNT 45 CPT	FB	MY	FBG	DV	IB	T375D	CAT	14	5	30000	3	7	168500	185000
45	10	MARLAGO 46 CPT	FB	MY	FBG	DV	IB	T300D	CUM	15		34000	3	10	162000	178000
		IB T375D CAT 179500 197000, IB T400D CUM 181000 199000, IB T425D CAT													186500	205000
45	10	MARLAGO 46 SUNDECK	FB	MY	FBG	DV	IB	T300D	CUM	15		34000	3	10	165500	182000
		IB T375D CAT 182000 200000, IB T400D CUM 182500 200500, IB T425D CAT													188500	207500
48	4	CONVERTIBLE 48	FB	CNV	FBG	DV	IB	T550D	DD	16		46000	4		218500	240000
48	4	RIVANNA 48 CPT	FB	DCMY	FBG	DV	IB	T300D	CUM	16		40000	4		177000	194500
		IB T375D CAT 194500 213500, IB T400D CUM 195000 214500, IB T425D CAT													200500	220500
		IB T550D DD 222000 244000														
48	4	RIVANNA 48 SD	FB	MY	FDG	DV	IB	T300D	CUM	16		42000	4		185500	204000
		IB T375D CAT 199500 219000, IB T400D CUM 199500 219000, IB T425D CAT													205500	226000
		IB T550D DD 225500 248000														
52	4	CONVERTIBLE 52	FB	CNV	FBG	DV	IB	T550D	DD	16		54000	4		279500	307000
52	4	CONVERTIBLE 52	FB	CNV	FBG	DV	IB	T735D	DD	16		54000	4		316000	347000
52	4	MARQUESSA 52 EXT DK	FB	MYDKH	FBG	DV	IB	T550D	DD	16		54000	4		279500	307000
52	4	MARQUESSA 52 STD DK	FB	MY	FBG	DV	IB	T550D	DD	16		54000	4		280000	307500
52	4	MONTICELLO 52 FDFB	FB	MY	FBG	DV	IB	T425D	CAT	16		50000	4		237000	260500
52	4	MONTICELLO 52 FDFB	FB	MY	FBG	DV	IB	T550D	DD	16		52000	4		267000	293000
52	4	RIVANNA 52 CPT	FB	MY	FBG	DV	IB	T300D	CUM	16		44000	4		198500	218000
		IB T375D CAT 216500 238000, IB T400D CUM 219000 241000, IB T425D CAT													226000	248500
		IB T550D DD 255500 280500														

CONTINUED ON NEXT PAGE

```
      LOA  NAME AND/            TOP/ BOAT  -HULL- ----ENGINE--- BEAM    WGT  DRAFT RETAIL RETAIL
      FT IN OR MODEL            RIG  TYPE  MTL TP TP # HP  MFG  FT IN   LBS  FT IN LOW    HIGH
---------------------------- 1994 BOATS ---------------------------------------------------------
52  4 RIVANNA 52 SD            FB  MY   FBG DV IB T300D CUM  16      44000 4     206000 226500
      IB T375D CAT 225000 247000, IB T400D CUM 228000 250500, IB T425D CAT 234500 258000
      IB T550D DD  265500 292000

56  4 MARQUESSA 56             FB MYDKH FBG DV IB T550D DD   16      58000 4     330500 363000
56  4 MARQUESSA 56 CPT         FB  MY   FBG DV IB T550D DD   16      56000 4     323000 355000
56  4 MONTICELLO 56            FB  MY   FBG DV IB T425D CAT  16      56000 4     301500 331500
56  4 MONTICELLO 56            FB  MY   FBG DV IB T550D DD   16      56000 4     330000 362500
56  4 MONTICELLO 56 CPT        FB  MY   FBG DV IB T425D CAT  16      52000 4     282500 310500
56  4 MONTICELLO 56 CPT        FB  MY   FBG DV IB T550D DD   16      54000 4     327500 360000
56  4 RIVANNA 56 CPT           FB  MY   FBG DV IB T300D CUM  16      46000 4     201000 221000
      IB T375D CAT 232500 255500, IB T400D CUM 240500 264500, IB T425D CAT 248000 272500
      IB T550D DD  291500 320500

59 10 GRAND MARQUESSA 60       FB  MY   FBG DV IB T735D DD   17  6   88000 4  7  506000 556000
60  4 GRAND MARQUESSA 60 CPT   FB  MY   FBG DV IB T550D DD   16      60000 4     334000 367000
60  4 MARQUESSA 60 EXT         FB  MY   FBG DV IB T550D DD   16      60000 4     311500 342500
60  4 RIVANNA 60 CPT           FB  MY   FBG DV IB T375D CAT  16      50000 4     244000 268500
      IB T400D CUM 244500 268500, IB T425D CAT 250500 275500, IB T550D DD  266000 292000

64 10 GRAND MARQUESSA 65       FB  MY   FBG DV IB T735D DD   17  6   98000 4  7  450000 494500
64 10 GRAND MARQUESSA 65       FB  MY   FBG DV IB T900D DD   17  6     51T 4  7  475000 522000
64 10 GRAND MARQUESSA CPT      FB  MY   FBG DV IB T735D DD   17  6   94000 4  7  440000 488000
64 10 GRAND MARQUESSA CPT      FB  MY   FBG DV IB T900D DD   17  6   98000 4  7  469000 515500
---------------------------- 1993 BOATS ---------------------------------------------------------
36 10 CONVERTIBLE 37           FB  CNV  FBG DV IB T300D CUM  14  5   22000 3  5  113500 125000
36 10 VISCOUNT 37 SD           FB  MY   FBG DV IB T300D CUM  14  5   22000 3  5  113500 125000
36 10 VISCOUNT 37 SD           FB  MY   FBG DV IB T375D CAT  14  5   24000 3  5  131000 143500
39 10 CONVERTIBLE 40           FB  CNV  FBG DV IB T300D CUM  14  5   24000 3  5  136500 150000
39 10 CONVERTIBLE 40           FB  CNV  FBG DV IB T375D CAT  14  5   26000 3  5  157000 172500
39 10 VISCOUNT 40 CPT          FB  MY   FBG DV IB T300D CUM  14  5   24000 3  5  136500 150000
39 10 VISCOUNT 40 CPT          FB  MY   FBG DV IB T375D CAT  14  5   26000 3  5  157000 172500
41  8 CONVERTIBLE 43           FB  CNV  FBG DV IB T300D CUM  14  5   26000 3  7  145500 159500
41  8 CONVERTIBLE 43           FB  CNV  FBG DV IB T375D CAT  14  5   28000 3  7  166500 183000
41  8 CONVERTIBLE 43           FB  CNV  FBG DV IB T400D CUM  14  5   30000 3  7  173500 190500
41  8 SPECIAL EDITION          FB  MY   FBG DV IB T300D CUM  14  5   28000 3  7  153500 168500
41  8 SPECIAL EDITION 43       FB  CNV  FBG DV IB T300D CUM  14  5   28000 3  5  155500 171000

41  8 VISCOUNT 42 SD           FB  MY   FBG DV IB T300D CUM  14  5   28000 3  7  159000 174500
41  8 VISCOUNT 42 SD           FB  MY   FBG DV IB T375D CAT  14  5   30000 3  7  177000 194500
42 10 MARLAGO SUNDECK 43       FB  MY   FBG DV IB T300D CUM  15      30000 3 10  159000 175000
      IB T320D CAT 172000 189000, IB T375D CAT 180000 198000, IB T425D CAT 187500 206000

44  8 SPECIAL EDITION CPT      FB  MY   FBG DV IB T300D CUM  15      28000 3  7  141500 155000
44  8 VISCOUNT 45 CPT          FB  MY   FBG DV IB T300D CUM  14  5   28000 3  7  142000 156000
44  8 VISCOUNT 45 CPT          FB  MY   FBG DV IB T375D CAT  14  5   30000 3  7  160500 176000
45 10 MARLAGO 46 CPT           FB  MY   FBG DV IB T300D CUM  15      34000 3 10  154000 169500
      IB T375D CAT 171000 188000, IB T400D CUM 172500 189500, IB T425D CAT 178000 195500

45 10 MARLAGO 46 SUNDECK       FB  MY   FBG DV IB T300D CUM  15      34000 3 10  158000 173500
      IB T375D CAT 173500 190500, IB T400D CUM 174000 191500, IB T425D CAT 180000 197500

48  4 CONVERTIBLE 48           FB  CNV  FBG DV IB T550D J&T  16      46000 4     207000 227500
48  4 RIVANNA 48 CPT           FB DCMY  FBG DV IB T300D CUM  16      40000 4     169000 185500
      IB T375D CAT 185500 203500, IB T400D CUM 186000 204500, IB T425D CAT 191500 210000
      IB T550D J&T 211000 232000

48  4 RIVANNA 48 SD            FB  MY   FBG DV IB T300D CUM  16      42000 4     177000 194500
      IB T375D CAT 190000 209000, IB T400D CUM 190000 209000, IB T425D CAT 196000 215500
      IB T550D J&T 214500 235500

52  4 CONVERTIBLE 52           FB  CNV  FBG DV IB T550D J&T  16      54000 4     266500 293000
52  4 CONVERTIBLE 52           FB  CNV  FBG DV IB T735D J&T  16      54000 4     301500 331000
52  4 MARQUESSA 52 EXT DK      FB MYDKH FBG DV IB T550D J&T  16      54000 4     268000 294500
52  4 MARQUESSA 52 STD DK      FB  MY   FBG DV IB T550D J&T  16      50000 4     267500 294000
52  4 MONTICELLO 52 FDFB       FB  MY   FBG DV IB T425D CAT  16      52000 4     226500 248500
52  4 MONTICELLO 52 FDFB       FB  MY   FBG DV IB T550D J&T  16      52000 4     256500 281500
52  4 RIVANNA 52 CPT           FB  MY   FBG DV IB T300D CUM  16      44000 4     189500 208000
      IB T375D CAT 207000 227000, IB T400D CUM 209000 230000, IB T425D CAT 216000 237000
      IB T550D J&T 245500 270000

52  4 RIVANNA 52 SD            FB  MY   FBG DV IB T300D CUM  16      44000 4     197000 216500
      IB T375D CAT 215000 236000, IB T400D CUM 217500 239000, IB T425D CAT 224000 246500
      IB T550D J&T 255000 280000

56  4 MARQUESSA 56             FB MYDKH FBG DV IB T550D J&T  16      58000 4     316000 347000
56  4 MARQUESSA 56 CPT         FB  MY   FBG DV IB T550D J&T  16      56000 4     308500 339000
56  4 MONTICELLO 56            FB  MY   FBG DV IB T425D CAT  16      56000 4     287500 316000
56  4 MONTICELLO 56            FB  MY   FBG DV IB T550D J&T  16      56000 4     315000 346000
56  4 MONTICELLO 56 CPT        FB  MY   FBG DV IB T425D CAT  16      52000 4     269000 296000
56  4 MONTICELLO 56 CPT        FB  MY   FBG DV IB T550D J&T  16      54000 4     313000 344000
56  4 RIVANNA 56 CPT           FB  MY   FBG DV IB T300D CUM  16      46000 4     192000 211000
      IB T375D CAT 221500 243500, IB T400D CUM 229000 251500, IB T425D CAT 236000 259500
      IB T550D J&T 278000 305500

59 10 GRAND MARQUESSA 60       FB  MY   FBG DV IB T735D J&T  17  6   88000 4  7  484000 531500
60  4 MARQUESSA 60 CPT         FB  MY   FBG DV IB T550D J&T  16      60000 4     319500 351000
60  4 MARQUESSA 60 EXT         FB  MY   FBG DV IB T550D J&T  16      60000 4     298000 327500
60  4 RIVANNA 60 CPT           FB  MY   FBG DV IB T375D CAT  16      50000 4     233500 256500
      IB T400D CUM 233500 256500, IB T425D CAT 239500 263000, IB T550D J&T 259000 284500

64 10 GRAND MARQUESSA 65       FB  MY   FBG DV IB T735D J&T  17  6   98000 4  7  428000 470500
64 10 GRAND MARQUESSA 65       FB  MY   FBG DV IB T900D J&T  17  6     51T 4  7  452000 496500
64 10 GRAND MARQUESSA CPT      FB  MY   FBG DV IB T735D J&T  17  6   94000 4  7  422500 464000
64 10 GRAND MARQUESSA CPT      FB  MY   FBG DV IB T900D J&T  17  6   98000 4  7  446500 490500
---------------------------- 1992 BOATS ---------------------------------------------------------
36 10 CONVERTIBLE 37           FB  CNV  FBG DV IB T250D CUM  14  5   22000 3  5  105000 115500
36 10 CONVERTIBLE 37           FB  CNV  FBG DV IB T260D CAT  14  5   22000 3  5  108000 118500
36 10 CONVERTIBLE 37           FB  CNV  FBG DV IB T300D CUM  14  5   22000 3  5  108500 119000
36 10 VISCOUNT 37 SD           FB  MY   FBG DV IB T250D CUM  14  5   22000 3  5  105000 115500
      IB T260D CAT 115000 126000, IB T300D CUM 108500 119000, IB T375D CAT 124500 137000

39 10 CONVERTIBLE 40           FB  CNV  FBG DV IB T250D CUM  14  5   24000 3  5  127000 139500
      IB T260D CAT 139000 153000, IB T300D CUM 130000 143000, IB T375D CAT 149500 164500

39 10 VISCOUNT 40 CPT          FB  MY   FBG DV IB T250D CUM  14  5   24000 3  5  126500 139500
      IB T260D CAT 131000 143500, IB T300D CUM 130000 143000, IB T375D CAT 149500 164500

41  8 SPECIAL EDITION          FB  MY   FBG DV IB T300D CUM  14  5   28000 3  7  146000 160500
41  8 VISCOUNT 42 SD           FB  MY   FBG DV IB T250D CUM  14  5   28000 3  7  143500 157500
      IB T260D CAT 147500 162000, IB T300D CUM 151500 166500, IB T375D CAT 169000 185500

42 10 MARLAGO SUNDECK 43       FB  MY   FBG DV IB T250D CUM  15      30000 3 10  145500 160000
      IB T260D CAT 156500 171500, IB T300D CUM 151500 166500, IB T320D CAT 164000 180500
      IB T375D CAT 171500 188500, IB T425D CAT 179000 196500

44  8 VISCOUNT 45 CPT          FB  MY   FBG DV IB T250D CUM  14  5   28000 3  7  129000 141500
      IB T260D CAT 137500 151000, IB T300D CUM 135000 148500, IB T375D CAT 153000 168000

45 10 MARLAGO 46 CPT           FB  MY   FBG DV IB T250D CUM  15      34000 3 10  142000 156000
      IB T260D CAT 147500 162000, IB T300D CUM 147000 161500, IB T320D CAT 153500 169000
      IB T375D CAT 163000 179000, IB T425D CAT 169500 186500

45 10 MARLAGO 46 SUNDECK       FB  MY   FBG DV IB T250D CUM  15      34000 3 10  146500 161000
      IB T260D CAT 147000 161500, IB T300D CUM 150500 165000, IB T320D CAT 156500 172000
      IB T375D CAT 165000 181500, IB T425D CAT 171500 188500

48  4 CONVERTIBLE 48           FB  CNV  FBG DV IB T550D J&T  16      46000 4     197000 216500
48  4 CONVERTIBLE 48           FB  CNV  FBG DV IB T735D J&T  16      46000 4     215000 236000
48  4 RIVANNA 48 CPT           FB DCMY  FBG DV IB T300D CUM  16      40000 4     161000 176500
      IB T320D CAT 171000 187500, IB T375D CAT 176500 194000, IB T425D CAT 182000 200500
      IB T550D J&T 201500 221000

48  4 RIVANNA 48 SD            FB  MY   FBG DV IB T300D CUM  16      42000 4     168500 185500
      IB T320D CAT 175500 193000, IB T375D CAT 181000 199000, IB T425D CAT 186500 205000
      IB T550D J&T 204500 224500

52  4 MARQUESSA 52 EXT DK      FB MYCPT FBG DV IB T550D J&T  16      54000 4     272500 299500
52  4 MARQUESSA 52 EXT DK      FB MYDKH FBG DV IB T550D J&T  16      54000 4     255500 281000
52  4 MARQUESSA 52 STD DK      FB  MY   FBG DV IB T550D J&T  16      54000 4     255000 280500
52  4 MONTICELLO 52 FDFB       FB  MY   FBG DV IB T425D CAT  16      50000 4     216000 237500
52  4 MONTICELLO 52 FDFB       FB  MY   FBG DV IB T425D CAT  16      52000 4     217500 239000
52  4 MONTICELLO 52 FDFB       FB  MY   FBG DV IB T550D J&T  16      52000 4     244500 268500
52  4 RIVANNA 52 CPT           FB  MY   FBG DV IB T300D CUM  16      44000 4     181000 198500
      IB T320D CAT 188500 207500, IB T375D CAT 197500 217000, IB T425D CAT 206000 226000
      IB T550D J&T 234000 257000

52  4 RIVANNA 52 SD            FB  MY   FBG DV IB T300D CUM  16      44000 4     188000 206500
      IB T320D CAT 196500 216500, IB T375D CAT 205000 225500, IB T425D CAT 214000 235000
      IB T550D J&T 243500 267500

56  4 MARQUESSA 56             FB MYDKH FBG DV IB T550D J&T  16      58000 4     301000 331000
56  4 MARQUESSA 56 CPT         FB  MY   FBG DV IB T550D J&T  16      56000 4     293500 322500
56  4 MONTICELLO 56            FB  MY   FBG DV IB T425D CAT  16      56000 4     274000 301000
56  4 MONTICELLO 56            FB  MY   FBG DV IB T550D J&T  16      56000 4     274500 301500
56  4 MONTICELLO 56            FB  MY   FBG DV IB T550D J&T  16      56000 4     301000 330500
```

LOA FT IN	NAME AND/ OR MODEL	TOP/ RIG	BOAT TYPE	HULL MTL	HULL TP	ENGINE TP	ENGINE #	HP	MFG	BEAM FT IN	WGT LBS	DRAFT FT IN	RETAIL LOW	RETAIL HIGH

1992 BOATS

56 4	MONTICELLO 56 CPT	FB	MY	FBG	DV	IB	T425D	CAT	16		52000	4	257000	282000
56 4	MONTICELLO 56 CPT	FB	MY	FBG	DV	IB	T425D	J&T	16		52000	4	257500	282500
56 4	MONTICELLO 56 CPT	FB	MY	FBG	DV	IB	T550D	J&T	16		54000	4	298500	328000
56 4	RIVANNA 56 CPT	FB	MY	FBG	DV	IB	T300D	CUM	16		46000	4	183000	201000

IB T320D CAT 195000 214500, IB T375D CAT 211000 232000, IB T425D CAT 225000 247500
IB T550D J&T 265000 291000

59 10	GRAND MARQUESSA 60	FB	MY	FBG	DV	IB	T735D	J&T	17	6 8	88000	4 7	461000	507000
64 10	GRAND MARQUESSA 65	FB	MY	FBG	DV	IB	T735D	J&T	17	6 9	94000	4 7	401500	441000
64 10	GRAND MARQUESSA 65	FB	MY	FBG	DV	IB	T900D	J&T	17	6 9	98000	4 7	423000	464500

1991 BOATS

36 10	CONVERTIBLE 37	FB	CNV	FBG	DV	IB	T260D	CUM	14	5 2	23700	3 5	102500	112500
36 10	CONVERTIBLE 37	FB	CNV	FBG	DV	IB	T260D	CAT	14	5 2	23700	3 5	108500	119500
36 10	CONVERTIBLE 37	FB	CNV	FBG	DV	IB	T300D	CUM	14	5 2	23700	3 5	105500	116000
36 10	VISCOUNT 37 SD	FB	MY	FBG	DV	IB	T250D	CUM	14	5 2	23000	3 5	103500	113500

IB T260D CAT 109500 120500, IB T300D CUM 106500 117000, IB T375D CAT 122000 134500

| 39 10 | CONVERTIBLE 40 | FB | CNV | FBG | DV | IB | T250D | CUM | 14 | 5 2 | 25000 | 3 5 | 125000 | 137000 |

IB T260D CAT 132500 145500, IB T300D CUM 128000 140500, IB T375D CAT 146500 161000

39 10	VISCOUNT 40 CPT	FB	MY	FBG	DV	IB	T250D	CUM	14	5 2	24000	3 5	121000	133000
39 10	VISCOUNT 40 CPT	FB	MY	FBG	DV	IB	T260D	CAT	14	5 2	25000	3 5	128500	141500
39 10	VISCOUNT 40 CPT	FB	MY	FBG	DV	IB	T300D	CUM	14	5 2	24000	3 5	125000	136500
41 8	VISCOUNT 42 SD	FB	MY	FBG	DV	IB	T250D	CUM	14	5 2	28000	3 7	137000	150500

IB T260D CAT 144000 158500, IB T300D CUM 142000 156000, IB T375D CAT 161000 177000

| 42 10 | MARLAGO SUNDECK 43 | FB | MY | FBG | DV | IB | T250D | CUM | 15 | | 31000 | 3 10 | 142000 | 156000 |

IB T260D CAT 149000 164000, IB T300D CUM 148000 162500, IB T320D CUM 158500 174000
IB T375D CAT 167500 184000, IB T425D CAT 176000 193000

44 8	VISCOUNT 45 CPT	FB	MY	FBG	DV	IB	T260D	CAT	14	5 3	30500	3 7	132500	145500
44 8	VISCOUNT 45 CPT	FB	MY	FBG	DV	IB	T300D	CUM	14	5 2	29500	3 7	133000	146000
44 8	VISCOUNT 45 CPT	FB	MY	FBG	DV	IB	T375D	J&T	14	5 3	31500	3 7	150000	164500
44 8	VOSCPIMT 45 CPT	FB	MY	FBG	DV	IB	T250D	CUM	14	5 2	29500	3 7	126000	138500
45 10	MARLAGO 46 CPT	FB	MY	FBG	DV	IB	T250D	CUM	15		34000	3 10	138000	151500

IB T260D CAT 142500 157000, IB T300D CUM 142500 156500, IB T320D CUM 150000 164500
IB T375D CAT 158000 173500, IB T425D CAT 165500 182000

| 45 10 | MARLAGO 46 SUNDECK | FB | MY | FBG | DV | IB | T250D | CUM | 15 | | 34700 | 3 10 | 138500 | 152000 |

IB T260D CAT 143500 157500, IB T300D CUM 142500 156500, IB T320D CUM 150000 164500
IB T375D CAT 157000 172500, IB T425D CAT 164000 180000

48 4	CONVERTIBLE 48	FB	MY	FBG	DV	IB	T550D	J&T	16		46300	4	188000	207000
48 4	CONVERTIBLE 48	FB	CNV	FBG	DV	IB	T735D	J&T	16		47500	4	207000	227500
48 4	RIVANNA 48 CPT	FB	DCMY	FBG	DV	IB	T300D	CUM	16		41000	4	154500	170000

IB T320D CAT 163000 179000, IB T375D CAT 169000 186000, IB T425D CAT 175500 193000

| 48 4 | RIVANNA 48 SD | FB | MY | FBG | DV | IB | T300D | CUM | 16 | | 44000 | 4 | 163500 | 180000 |

IB T260D CAT 168000 185000, IB T375D CAT 174500 191500, IB T425D CAT 179500 197500

52 4	MARQUESSA 52 EXT DK	MYCPT		FBG	DV	IB	T550D	J&T	16		55800	4	266500	293000
52 4	MARQUESSA 52 EXT DK	FB	MYDKH	FBG	DV	IB	T550D	J&T	16		55800	4	249000	273500
52 4	MARQUESSA 52 STD DK	FB	MY	FBG	DV	IB	T550D	J&T	16		55800	4	249000	273500
52 4	MONTICELLO 52 FDFB	FB	MY	FBG	DV	IB	T425D	CAT	16		51000	4	208500	229000
52 4	MONTICELLO 52 FDFB	FB	MY	FBG	DV	IB	T425D	CAT	16		51000	4	210000	230500
52 4	MONTICELLO 52 FDFB	FB	MY	FBG	DV	IB	T550D	J&T	16		52500	4	234500	258000
52 4	RIVANNA 52 CPT	FB	MY	FBG	DV	IB	T300D	CUM	16		44500	4	177000	194500

IB T320D CAT 184000 202000, IB T375D CAT 193000 212000, IB T425D CAT 202000 222000

56 4	MARQUESSA 56	FB	MYDKH	FBG	DV	IB	T550D	J&T	16		59000	4	291000	320000
56 4	MARQUESSA 56 CPT	FB	MY	FBG	DV	IB	T550D	J&T	16		57500	4	290000	319000
56 4	MONTICELLO 56	FB	MY	FBG	DV	IB	T425D	CAT	16		56000	4	261500	287000
56 4	MONTICELLO 56	FB	MY	FBG	DV	IB	T425D	CAT	16		56000	4	262000	287500
56 4	MONTICELLO 56	FB	MY	FBG	DV	IB	T550D	J&T	16		57500	4	288500	317000
56 4	MONTICELLO 56 CPT	FB	MY	FBG	DV	IB	T425D	CAT	16		52500	4	247500	271500
56 4	MONTICELLO 56 CPT	FB	MY	FBG	DV	IB	T425D	CAT	16		52500	4	247500	272000
56 4	RIVANNA 56 CPT	FB	MY	FBG	DV	IB	T300D	CUM	16		47000	4	177500	195000

IB T320D CAT 188000 206500, IB T375D CAT 205000 225000, IB T425D CAT 220000 242000

| 59 10 | GRAND MARQUESSA 60 | FB | MY | FBG | DV | IB | T735D | J&T | 17 | 6 8 | 88000 | 4 7 | 440000 | 483500 |
| 64 10 | GRAND MARQUESSA 65 | FB | MY | FBG | DV | IB | T735D | J&T | 17 | 6 9 | 94000 | 4 7 | 383000 | 421000 |

1990 BOATS

| 36 10 | CONVERTIBLE 37 | FB | CNV | FBG | DV | IB | T210D | CUM | 14 | 5 2 | 22700 | 3 5 | 95700 | 105000 |

IB T250D CUM 97800 107500, IB T260D CUM 100500 110500, IB T300D CAT 103500 113500

| 36 10 | VISCOUNT 37 SD | FB | MY | FBG | DV | IB | T210D | CUM | 14 | 5 2 | 23000 | 3 5 | 96600 | 106000 |

IB T250D CUM 98700 108500, IB T260D CUM 101500 111500, IB T300D CAT 104000 114500
IB T375D CAT 110500 121500

| 39 10 | CONVERTIBLE 40 | FB | CNV | FBG | DV | IB | T210D | CUM | 14 | 5 2 | 25000 | 3 5 | 117000 | 128500 |

IB T250D CUM 119000 131000, IB T260D CUM 123000 135000, IB T300D CUM 122000 134500
IB T375D CAT 132500 145500

| 39 10 | VISCOUNT 40 CPT | FB | MY | FBG | DV | IB | T210D | CUM | 14 | 5 2 | 24000 | 3 5 | 113500 | 124500 |

IB T250D CUM 115500 127000, IB T260D CUM 119000 131000, IB T300D CUM 118500 130000

| 41 8 | VISCOUNT 42 SD | FB | MY | FBG | DV | IB | T210D | CUM | 14 | 5 2 | 28000 | 3 7 | 127000 | 139500 |

IB T250D CUM 130500 143500, IB T260D CUM 134000 147500, IB T300D CAT 138500 152000
IB T375D CAT 147000 161500

| 42 10 | MARLAGO SUNDECK 43 | FB | MY | FBG | DV | IB | T210D | CUM | 15 | | 31000 | 3 10 | 131500 | 144500 |

IB T250D CUM 135500 149000, IB T260D CUM 139000 152500, IB T300D CUM 141500 155500
IB T320D CAT 146000 160500, IB T375D CAT 153000 168000, IB T425D CAT 159500 175500

| 44 8 | VISCOUNT 45 CPT | FB | MY | FBG | DV | IB | T210D | CUM | 14 | 5 2 | 29500 | 3 7 | 117000 | 128500 |

IB T250D CUM 121000 133000, IB T260D CUM 123500 136000, IB T300D CUM 128500 141000
IB T380D CAT 151500

| 45 10 | MARLAGO 46 CPT | FB | MY | FBG | DV | IB | T210D | CUM | 15 | | 34000 | 3 10 | 128500 | 141500 |

IB T250D CUM 131500 144500, IB T260D CUM 134000 147500, IB T300D CUM 136000 149000
IB T320D CAT 139500 153500, IB T375D CAT 146000 160500, IB T425D CAT 152000 167000

| 45 10 | MARLAGO 46 SUNDECK | FB | MY | FBG | DV | IB | T210D | CUM | 15 | | 34700 | 3 10 | 129500 | 142500 |

IB T250D CUM 132000 145000, IB T260D CUM 135000 148000, IB T300D CUM 136000 149500
IB T320D CAT 140000 153500, IB T375D CAT 145500 159500, IB T425D CAT 151000 165500

48 4	CONVERTIBLE 48	FB	MY	FBG	DV	IB	T550D	J&T	16		46300	4	179500	197000
48 4	CONVERTIBLE 48	FB	CNV	FBG	DV	IB	T735D	J&T	16		46300	4	196000	215500
48 4	RIVANNA 48 CPT	FB	DCMY	FBG	DV	IB	T260D	CUM	16		41000	4	144000	158500

IB T375D CAT 156000 171500, IB T300D CUM 147500 162000, IB T320D CAT 151000 166000
IB T425D CAT 161000 176500

| 48 4 | RIVANNA 48 SD | FB | MY | FBG | DV | IB | T250D | CUM | 16 | | 42500 | 4 | 150500 | 166500 |

IB T260D CAT 153500 168500, IB T300D CUM 154000 169000, IB T320D CAT 157500 173500
IB T375D CAT 162500 178500, IB T425D CAT 167500 184000

52 4	MARQUESSA 52	FB	MY	FBG	DV	IB	T550D	J&T	16		55800	4	228500	251000
52 4	MARQUESSA 52	FB	MYCPT	FBG	DV	IB	T550D	J&T	16		55800	4	242000	266000
52 4	MARQUESSA 52	FB	MYDKH	FBG	DV	IB	T550D	J&T	16		55800	4	231500	254500
52 4	MONTICELLO 52 FDFB	FB	MY	FBG	DV	IB	T425D	CAT	16		51000	4	199000	219000
52 4	MONTICELLO 52 FDFB	FB	MY	FBG	DV	IB	T425D	CAT	16		51000	4	200500	220500
52 4	MONTICELLO 52 FDFB	FB	MY	FBG	DV	IB	T550D	J&T	16		51000	4	221000	242500
52 4	RIVANNA 52 CPT	FB	MY	FBG	DV	IB	T250D	CUM	16		44500	4	163500	180000

IB T260D CAT 166500 183000, IB T300D CUM 169000 186000, IB T320D CAT 173500 190500
IB T375D CAT 181000 199000, IB T425D CAT 188000 207500

56 4	MARQUESSA 56	FB	MYDKH	FBG	DV	IB	T550D	J&T	16		59000	4	278000	305500
56 4	MARQUESSA 56 CPT	FB	MY	FBG	DV	IB	T550D	J&T	16		57500	4	268000	294500
56 4	MONTICELLO 56	FB	MY	FBG	DV	IB	T425D	CAT	16		56000	4	249500	274000
56 4	MONTICELLO 56	FB	MY	FBG	DV	IB	T425D	CAT	16		56000	4	250000	274500
56 4	MONTICELLO 56	FB	MY	FBG	DV	IB	T550D	J&T	16		56000	4	279500	307000
56 4	MONTICELLO 56 CPT	FB	MY	FBG	DV	IB	T425D	CAT	16		52500	4	235500	259000
56 4	MONTICELLO 56 CPT	FB	MY	FBG	DV	IB	T425D	CAT	16		52500	4	236000	259500
56 4	MONTICELLO 56 CPT	FB	MY	FBG	DV	IB	T550D	J&T	16		52500	4	266500	293000
56 4	RIVANNA 56 CPT	FB	MY	FBG	DV	IB	T250D	CUM	16		47000	4	159000	174500

IB T260D CAT 162000 178000, IB T300D CUM 169500 186500, IB T320D CAT 174500 192000
IB T375D CAT 189000 207500, IB T425D CAT 202000 222000

| 59 10 | GRAND MARQUESSA 60 | FB | MY | FBG | DV | IB | T735D | J&T | 17 | 6 8 | 88000 | 4 7 | 420000 | 461500 |
| 64 10 | GRAND MARQUESSA 65 | FB | MY | FBG | DV | IB | T735D | J&T | 17 | 6 9 | 94000 | 4 7 | 366000 | 402000 |

1989 BOATS

| 36 10 | CONVERTIBLE 37 | FB | CNV | FBG | DV | IB | T210D | CUM | 14 | 5 2 | 22700 | 3 | 91400 | 100500 |

IB T250D CUM 93400 102500, IB T260D CAT 96000 105500, IB T320D CAT 100000 110000
IB T375D CAT 104500 115000

| 36 10 | SUNDECK 37 | FB | MY | FBG | DV | IB | T210D | CUM | 14 | 5 2 | 22700 | 3 | 91400 | 100500 |

IB T250D CUM 93300 102500, IB T260D CAT 96000 105500, IB T320D CAT 100000 110000

| 39 8 | JEFFERSON 40 CNV | FB | CNV | FBG | DV | IB | T210D | CUM | 14 | 5 2 | 27000 | 3 | 118000 | 130000 |

IB T250D CUM 120000 132000, IB T260D CAT 123500 136000, IB T320D CAT 128000 140500
IB T375D CAT 133000 146000

| 39 10 | JEFFERSON 40 CPT | FB | MY | FBG | DV | IB | T210D | CUM | 14 | 5 2 | 24000 | 3 | 108500 | 119000 |

IB T250D CUM 110000 121000, IB T260D CAT 113500 125000, IB T320D CAT 118000 130000
IB T375D CAT 123000 135000

```
        LOA  NAME AND/       TOP/ BOAT  -HULL- ----ENGINE--- BEAM    WGT  DRAFT RETAIL RETAIL
        FT IN  OR MODEL       RIG TYPE  MTL TP TP # HP MFG   FT IN   LBS  FT IN  LOW    HIGH
--------------------------- 1989 BOATS --------------------------------------------------------
41  8 SUNDECK 42            FB  MY    FBG DV IB T210D CUM  14  3 29574 3  7 123500 136000
      IB T250D CUM  126500 139000, IB T260D CAT 130000 142500, IB T320D CAT 135500 148500
      IB T375D CAT  141000 155000

45  3 JEFFERSON 45          FB  MY    FBG DV IB T210D CUM  15  2       4  5 115000 126000
      IB T250D CUM  120500 132000, IB T260D CAT 123000 135000, IB T320D CAT 132500 145500
      IB T375D CAT  141000 155000

45  8 JEFFERSON 46 CPT      FB  MY    FBG DV IB T210D CUM  14  3       3  7 135000 148500
      IB T250D CUM  142000 156000, IB T260D CAT 144500 159000, IB T320D CAT 154500 169500
      IB T375D CAT  162500 178500

45  8 SUNDECK 46            FB  MY    FBG DV IB T210D CUM  14  3       3  7 139000 153000
      IB T250D CUM  146000 160500, IB T260D CAT 148500 163000, IB T320D CAT 158000 173500
      IB T375D CAT  166500 183000

47  3 JEFFERSON 48 CNV      FB  CNV   FBG DV IB T550D J&T  16    46300      168500 185000
47  3 JEFFERSON 48 CNV      FB  CNV   FBG DV IB T650D J&T  16    46300      176000 193500
47  3 JEFFERSON 48 CNV      FB  CNV   FBG DV IB T735D J&T  16    46300      182500 200500
47  6 JEFFERSON 48          FB  MY    FBG DV IB T210D CUM  15  4       3  7 145000 159500
      IB T250D CUM  151500 166500, IB T260D CAT 153500 169000, IB T320D CAT 164000 180000
      IB T375D CAT  173000 190000

47  6 JEFFERSON 48 CPT      FB  MY    FBG DV IB T210D CUM  15  4       3  7 141000 155000
      IB T250D CUM  147500 162000, IB T260D CAT 149500 164500, IB T320D CAT 160000 175500
      IB T375D CAT  169000 185500

51  6 JEFFERSON 52 CPT      FB  MY    FBG DV IB T210D CUM  15  4       3  7 173500 190500
      IB T250D CUM  169500 186500, IB T260D CAT 171000 188000, IB T320D CAT 179500 197500
      IB T375D CAT  186500 205000

51  6 MONTICELLO 52         FB  TCMY  FBG DV IB T425D J&T  15  4       3  7 223000 245000
51  6 MONTICELLO 52         FB  TCMY  FBG DV IB T550D J&T  15  4       3  7 238500 262500
52  5 MARQUESSA 52 CPT EDH  FB  MY    FBG DV IB T550D J&T  16    55800      223000 245000
52  5 MARQUESSA 52          FB  MY    FBG DV IB T550D J&T  16    55800      223000 245000
52  5 MARQUESSA 52 SDH      FB  MY    FBG DV IB T550D J&T  16    55800      215000 236500
59 10 JEFFERSON 60          FB  MY    FBG DV IB T550D J&T  17  6 88000 4  7 411500 452500
59 10 JEFFERSON 60          FB  MY    FBG DV IB T650D J&T  17  6 88000 4  7 429500 472000
59 10 JEFFERSON 60          FB  MY    FBG DV IB T735D J&T  17  6 88000 4  7 445000 489000
64 10 JEFFERSON 65 CPT      FB  MY    FBG DV IB T550D J&T  17  6 94000      465500 512500
64 10 JEFFERSON 65 CPT      FB  MY    FBG DV IB T650D J&T  17  6 94000      480000 527000
64 10 JEFFERSON 65 CPT      FB  MY    FBG DV IB T735D J&T  17  6 94000      489500 538000

64 10 JEFFERSON 65 MY       FB  MY    FBG DV IB T550D J&T  17  6 98000      480500 528000
64 10 JEFFERSON 65 MY       FB  MY    FBG DV IB T650D J&T  17  6 98000      491500 540500
64 10 JEFFERSON 65 MY       FB  MY    FBG DV IB T735D J&T  17  6 98000      500500 550000
--------------------------- 1988 BOATS --------------------------------------------------------
41  8 JEFFERSON 42 SF       FB  YTFS  FBG DV IB T210D CUM  14  3 29574 3  7 117000 129000
      IB T240D PERK 122000 134000, IB T260D CAT 124000 136000, IB T320D CAT 130000 142500
      IB T375D CAT  136000 149000

41  8 SUNDECK 42            FB  MY    FBG DV IB T210D CUM  14  3 29574 3  7 118000 130000
      IB T240D PERK 122500 134500, IB T260D CAT 124000 136500, IB T320D CAT 129500 142000
      IB T375D CAT  134500 148000

45  3 JEFFERSON 45          FB  MY    FBG DV IB T210D CUM  15  2       4  5 109500 120500
      IB T240D PERK 114500 126000, IB T260D CAT 117500 129000, IB T320D CAT 126500 139000
      IB T375D CAT  135000 148000

45  8 JEFFERSON 46          FB  SF    FBG DV IB T210D CUM  14  3       3  7 119500 131500
      IB T240D PERK 125500 138000, IB T260D CAT 129500 142000, IB T320D CAT 141000 154500
      IB T375D CAT  151000 165500

45  8 JEFFERSON 46 CPT      FB  MY    FBG DV IB T210D CUM  14  3       3  7 129500 142500
      IB T240D PERK 135500 149000, IB T260D CAT 139000 152500, IB T320D CAT 148000 162500
      IB T375D CAT  156000 171500

45  8 SUNDECK 46            FB  MY    FBG DV IB T210D CUM  14  3       3  7 132500 145500
      IB T240D PERK 138000 151500, IB T260D CAT 141500 155000, IB T320D CAT 150500 165500
      IB T375D CAT  158500 174500

47  6 JEFFERSON 48          FB  TCMY  FBG DV IB T210D CUM  15  4       3  7 163500 179500
      IB T240D PERK 170500 187000, IB T260D CAT 174500 192000, IB T320D CAT 181500 199500
      IB T375D CAT  191000 210000

47  6 JEFFERSON 48 CPT      FB  DCMY  FBG DV IB T210D CUM  15  4       3  7 142000 156000
      IB T240D PERK 148000 163000, IB T260D CAT 152000 167000, IB T320D CAT 162500 178500
      IB T375D CAT  171500 188500

47  6 MONTICELLO 48         FB  TCMY  FBG DV IB T320D CAT  15  4       3  7 191500 210500
47  6 MONTICELLO 48         FB  TCMY  FBG DV IB T375D CAT  15  4       3  7 200500 220500
51  6 JEFFERSON 52          FB  TCMY  FBG DV IB T210D CUM  15  4       3  7 191000 210500
      IB T240D PERK 186000 204500, IB T260D CAT 189500 208000, IB T320D CAT 194500 213500
      IB T375D CAT  202000 222000

51  6 JEFFERSON 52          FB  YTFS  FBG DV IB T210D CUM  15  4       3  7 158500 174000
      IB T240D PERK 164000 180000, IB T260D CAT 167500 184000, IB T320D CAT 177500 195500
      IB T375D CAT  186000 204500

51  6 JEFFERSON 52 CPT      FB  MY    FBG DV IB T210D CUM  15  4       3  7 166000 182000
      IB T240D PERK 160500 176500, IB T260D CAT 163500 180000, IB T320D CAT 171500 188500
      IB T375D CAT  178500 196000

51  6 MONTICELLO 52         FB  TCMY  FBG DV IB T320D CAT  15  4       3  7 202500 223000
51  6 MONTICELLO 52         FB  TCMY  FBG DV IB T375D CAT  15  4       3  7 210500 231500
59 10 JEFFERSON 60          FB  MY    FBG DV IB T550D J&T  17  6 88000 4  7 404500 433000
59 10 JEFFERSON 60          FB  MY    FBG DV IB T650D J&T  17  6 88000 4  7 411500 452000
59 10 JEFFERSON 60          FB  MY    FBG DV IB T750D J&T  17  6 88000 4  7 428500 471000
--------------------------- 1987 BOATS --------------------------------------------------------
42  1 JEFFERSON 42 SF       FB  YTFS  FBG DV IB T200D PERK 14  1 29574 3  7 111500 122500
      IB T240D PERK 115500 127000, IB T260D CAT 117500 129000, IB T320D CAT 123500 136000
      IB T375D CAT  129500 142500

42  1 SUNDECK 42            FB  MY    FBG DV IB T200D PERK 14  1 29574 3  7 113500 125000
      IB T210D CAT  110500 121500, IB T240D CUM 109000 119500, IB T240D PERK 116500 128500
      IB T260D CAT  118500 130000, IB T320D CAT 123500 136000, IB T375D CAT 128500 141500

45  3 JEFFERSON 45          FB  MY    FBG DV IB T200D PERK 15  2       4  5 105000 115500
      IB T240D PERK 109500 120500, IB T260D CAT 112500 123500, IB T320D CAT 121000 133000
      IB T375D CAT  129000 141500

45  8 JEFFERSON 46          FB  SF    FBG DV IB T200D PERK 14  1       3  7 114000 125500
      IB T240D PERK 120000 132000, IB T260D CAT 124000 136000, IB T320D CAT 135000 148000
      IB T375D CAT  144500 158500

45  8 JEFFERSON 46 CPT      FB  MY    FBG DV IB T200D PERK 14  1       3  7 125000 137500
      IB T210D CUM  126000 138500, IB T240D PERK 131500 144500, IB T260D CAT 134500 148000
      IB T320D CAT  134500 158000, IB T375D CAT 151500 166500

45  8 SUNDECK 46            FB  MY    FBG DV IB T200D PERK 14  1       3  7 127000 139500
      IB T210D CUM  128000 140500, IB T240D PERK 133500 146500, IB T260D CAT 136500 150000
      IB T320D CAT  145500 159500, IB T375D CAT 153000 168500

47  6 JEFFERSON 48          FB  TCMY  FBG DV IB T200D PERK 15  2       4  5 175000 192000
      IB T240D PERK 165500 181500, IB T260D CAT 169500 186000, IB T320D CAT 175000 192500
      IB T375D CAT  183500 202000

47  6 JEFFERSON 48 CPT      FB  DCMY  FBG DV IB T200D PERK 15  2       4  5 153500 168500
      IB T240D PERK 143500 158000, IB T260D CAT 147500 162000, IB T320D CAT 157500 173000
      IB T375D CAT  166000 182500

47  6 MONTICELLO 48         FB  TCMY  FBG DV IB T320D CAT  15  2       3  7 185500 204000
47  6 MONTICELLO 48         FB  TCMY  FBG DV IB T375D CAT  15  2       3  7 194000 213500
51  6 JEFFERSON 52          FB  TCMY  FBG DV IB T200D PERK 15  2       3  7 182000 200000
      IB T240D PERK 179000 197000, IB T260D CAT 182500 200500, IB T320D CAT 186500 204500
      IB T375D CAT  192000 211000

51  6 JEFFERSON 52          FB  YTFS  FBG DV IB T200D PERK 15  2       3  7 149500 164500
      IB T240D PERK 157000 172500, IB T260D CAT 160500 176000, IB T320D CAT 170000 186500
      IB T375D CAT  178000 195500

51  6 JEFFERSON 52 CPT      FB  MY    FBG DV IB T200D PERK 15  2       3  7 158000 173500
      IB T240D PERK 155000 170000, IB T260D CAT 157500 173500, IB T320D CAT 165500 181500
      IB T375D CAT  172000 189000

51  6 MONTICELLO 52         FB  TCMY  FBG DV IB T320D CAT  15  2       3  7 196000 215500
51  6 MONTICELLO 52         FB  TCMY  FBG DV IB T375D CAT  15  2       3  7 202000 222000
59 10 JEFFERSON 60          FB  MY    FBG DV IB T550D J&T  17  6       4  7 256000 281000
59 11 JEFFERSON 60              MY    FBG SV IB T565D      17  6 88000      380000 417500
--------------------------- 1986 BOATS --------------------------------------------------------
42  1 JEFFERSON 42 CNV      FB  SDNSF FBG DV IB T200D PERK 14  1 29574 3  7 106500 117000
      IB T260D CAT  111500 123000, IB T270D CUM 110500 121500, IB T320D CAT 117500 129000
      IB T320D CAT  123000 135500

42  1 JEFFERSON 42 SDN      FB  MY    FBG DV IB T200D PERK 14  1 29574 3  7 108000 118500
      IB T260D CAT  112000 123500, IB T270D CUM 111000 122000, IB T320D CAT 117000 128500
```

```
                              TOP/ BOAT  -HULL-  ----ENGINE---    BEAM   WGT  DRAFT RETAIL RETAIL
LOA  NAME AND/               RIG  TYPE   MTL TP TP #   HP   MFG   FT IN  LBS  FT IN  LOW   HIGH
FT IN  OR MODEL
------------------------- 1986 BOATS -------------------------------------------------------------
42  1 JEFFERSON 42 SDN        FB   MY    FBG DV IB T375D CAT  14  1 29574  3  7 122000 134000
42  1 JEFFERSON 42 SF         FB   YTFS  FBG DV IB T200D PERK 14  1 29574  3  7 107000 117500
     IB T260D CAT 112500 123500, IB T270D CUM 111500 122500, IB T320D CAT 118500 130000
     IB T375D CAT 124000 136500

42  1 SUNDECK 42              FB   MY    FBG DV IB T200D PERK 14  1 29574  3  7 108500 119500
     IB T260D CAT 113000 124500, IB T270D CUM 112000 123000, IB T320D CAT 118000 130000
     IB T375D CAT 123000 135500

45  3 JEFFERSON 45            FB   MY    FBG DV IB T200D PERK 15  2        4  5 100500 110500
     IB T260D CAT 107500 118000, IB T270D CUM 108000 118500, IB T320D CAT 116000 127500
     IB T375D CAT 123500 135500

45  8 JEFFERSON 46            FB   SF    FBG DV IB T200D PERK 14  1          109000 120000
     IB T260D CAT 118500 130000, IB T270D CUM 119500 131000, IB T320D CAT 129000 141500
     IB T375D CAT 138000 152000

45  8 JEFFERSON 46            FB   YTFS  FBG DV IB T200D PERK 14  1        3  7 110000 120500
     IB T260D CAT 122000 134000, IB T270D CUM 123000 135000, IB T320D CAT 133000 146000
     IB T375D CAT 142500 156500

45  8 JEFFERSON 46 CPT        FB   MY    FBG DV IB T200D PERK 14  1        3  7 119000 130500
     IB T260D CAT 128000 140500, IB T270D CUM 128500 141500, IB T320D CAT 136500 150000
     IB T375D CAT 144000 158000

45  8 SUNDECK 46              FB   MY    FBG DV IB T200D PERK 14  1        3  7 122500 134500
     IB T260D CAT 131500 144500, IB T270D CUM 132500 145500, IB T320D CAT 140000 154000
     IB T375D CAT 147500 162000

47  6 JEFFERSON 48            FB   DCMY  FBG DV IB T200D PERK 15  2        4  5 147000 161500
     IB T260D CAT 141000 155000, IB T270D CUM 142500 156500, IB T320D CAT 150500 165500
     IB T375D CAT 159000 174500

47  6 JEFFERSON 48            FB   TCMY  FBG DV IB T200D PERK 15  2        4  5 167000 184000
     IB T260D CAT 162000 178000, IB T270D CUM 163500 180000, IB T320D CAT 167500 184000
     IB T375D CAT 175500 193000

47  6 MONTICELLO 48           FB   TCMY  FBG DV IB T320D CAT  15  2        3  7 177500 195000
     IB T375D CAT 185500 204000, IB T410D J&T 184000 202500, IB T450D J&T 189000 207500

51  6 JEFFERSON 52            FB   TCMY  FBG DV IB T200D PERK 15  2        3  7 174000 191500
     IB T260D CAT 174500 192000, IB T270D CUM 176000 193500, IB T320D CAT 178000 195500
     IB T375D CAT 185000 203500

51  6 JEFFERSON 52            FB   YTFS  FBG DV IB T200D PERK 15  2        3  7 143000 157000
     IB T260D CAT 153500 168500, IB T270D CUM 155000 170500, IB T320D CAT 162500 178500
     IB T375D CAT 170500 187000

51  6 JEFFERSON 52 CPT        FB   MY    FBG DV IB T200D PERK 15  2        3  7 151000 166000
     IB T260D CAT 151000 166000, IB T270D CUM 152000 167000, IB T320D CAT 158500 174000
     IB T375D CAT 164500 180500

51  6 MONTICELLO 52           FB   TCMY  FBG DV IB T320D CAT  15  2        3  7 188000 206500
     IB T375D CAT 195000 214500, IB T410D J&T 194500 213500, IB T450D J&T 199000 219000

------------------------- 1985 BOATS -------------------------------------------------------------
42  1 JEFFERSON 42 CNV        FB   SDNSF FBG DV IB T200D PERK 14  1 29574  3  7 102000 112000
     IB T210D CAT 102500 112500, IB T300D CAT 110500 121500, IB T305D GM 109500 120000
     IB T350D PERK 115500 127000, IB T355D CAT 116000 127500

42  1 JEFFERSON 42 SDN        FB   MY    FBG DV IB T200D PERK 14  1 29574  3  7 103000 113500
     IB T210D CAT 104000 114000, IB T300D CAT 110500 121500, IB T305D GM 109000 120000
     IB T350D PERK 114500 126000, IB T355D CAT 115000 126500

42  1 JEFFERSON 42 SF         FB   YTFS  FBG DV IB T200D PERK 14  1 29574  3  7 102500 112500
     IB T210D CAT 103000 113500, IB T300D CAT 111500 122500, IB T305D GM 110000 121000
     IB T350D PERK 116500 128000, IB T355D CAT 117000 128500

42  1 SUNDECK 42              FB   MY    FBG DV IB T200D PERK 14  1 29574  3  7 104000 114500
     IB T210D CAT 104500 115000, IB T300D CAT 111500 122500, IB T305D GM 110000 121000
     IB T350D PERK 116000 127500, IB T355D CAT 116000 127500

45  3 JEFFERSON 45            FB   MY    FBG DV IB T200D PERK 15  2        4  5 96200 105500
     IB T210D CAT 97100 106500, IB T300D CAT 108000 119000, IB T310D J&T 109000 119500
     IB T350D PERK 115000 126500, IB T355D CAT 115500 127000

47  6 JEFFERSON 48            FB   DCMY  FBG DV IB T200D PERK 15  2        4  5 140500 154500
     IB T210D CAT 126500 139000, IB T300D CAT 141500 155000, IB T305D GM 142000 156000
     IB T350D PERK 150500 163500, IB T355D CAT 149500 164000

47  6 JEFFERSON 48            FB   TCMY  FBG DV IB T200D PERK 15  2        4  5 160000 176000
     IB T210D CAT 145500 160000, IB T300D CAT 162000 178000, IB T305D GM 162500 178500
     IB T350D PERK 169500 186500, IB T355D CAT 170000 187000

51  6 JEFFERSON 52            FB   TCMY  FBG DV IB T200D PERK 15  2        4  5 166500 183000
     IB T210D CAT 167500 184000, IB T300D CAT 172500 189500, IB T305D GM 173000 190000
     IB T350D PERK 179000 196500, IB T355D CAT 179500 197500

51  6 JEFFERSON 52            FB   YTFS  FBG DV IB T200D PERK 15  2        4  5 137000 150500
     IB T210D CAT 138500 152500, IB T300D CAT 153000 168000, IB T305D GM 153500 168500
     IB T350D PERK 160000 175500, IB T355D CAT 160500 176500

------------------------- 1984 BOATS -------------------------------------------------------------
45  3 JEFFERSON 45            FB   MY    FBG DV IB T200D PERK 15  2        4  5 92100 101500
     IB T210D CAT 92900 102000, IB T300D CAT 103500 114000, IB T305D GM 103500 114000
     IB T350D PERK 110000 121000

46  1 JEFFERSON 42 CNV        FB   SDNSF FBG DV IB T200D PERK 14  1 29574  3  7 91200 100000
     IB T210D CAT 91600 100500, IB T300D CAT 95900 105500, IB T305D GM 94700 104000
     IB T350D PERK 98900 108500

46  1 JEFFERSON 42 SF         FB   YTFS  FBG DV IB T200D PERK 14  1 29574  3  7 87200 95800
     IB T210D CAT 87600 96200, IB T300D CAT 92100 101000, IB T305D GM 91200 100000
     IB T350D PERK 95900 105500

46  1 JEFFERSOON 42 SDN       FB   MY    FBG DV IB T200D PERK 14  1 29574  3  7 93900 103000
     IB T210D CAT 94300 103500, IB T300D CAT 98500 108500, IB T305D GM 97300 107000
     IB T350D PERK 101500 111500

46  1 SUNDECK 42              FB   MY    FBG DV IB T200D PERK 14  1 29574  3  7 94000 103500
     IB T210D CAT 94400 103500, IB T300D CAT 98700 108500, IB T305D GM 97500 107000
     IB T350D PERK 101500 112000

47  6 JEFFERSON 48            FB   MY    FBG DV IB T200D PERK 15  2        4  5 129000 141500
     IB T210D CAT 116000 127500, IB T300D CAT 129000 141500, IB T305D GM 129500 142000
     IB T350D PERK 135500 149000

51  6 JEFFERSON 52            FB   YTFS  FBG DV IB T200D PERK 15  2        4  5 131500 144500
     IB T210D CAT 133000 146000, IB T300D CAT 146500 161000, IB T305D GM 147000 161500
     IB T350D PERK 153000 168500
```

....For earlier years, see the BUC Used Boat Price Guide, Volume 3

JERSEY YACHTS
LUMBERTON NJ 08048   COAST GUARD MFG ID- NJB See inside cover to adjust price for area
                      FORMERLY JERSEY BOATS INC

```
                              TOP/ BOAT  -HULL-  ----ENGINE---    BEAM   WGT  DRAFT RETAIL RETAIL
LOA  NAME AND/               RIG  TYPE   MTL TP TP #   HP   MFG   FT IN  LBS  FT IN  LOW   HIGH
FT IN  OR MODEL
------------------------- 1989 BOATS -------------------------------------------------------------
36  4 JERSEY DAWN III         SF        FBG SV IB T350  CRUS 13  4 23000  3  2 87500 96200
36  4 JERSEY DAWN III         SF        FBG SV IB T320D CAT  13  4 23000  3  2 105000 115000
42  4 JERSEY DAWN III         SF        FBG SV IB T375D CAT  15  8 30500  3  6 158000 173500
42  4 JERSEY DAWN III         SF        FBG SV IB T485D GM   15  8 30500  3  6 171500 188500
47  4 JERSEY DAWN III         SF        FBG SV IB T485D GM   15  8 36000  3 10 195500 215000
------------------------- 1988 BOATS -------------------------------------------------------------
36  4 JERSEY DAWN III         SF        FBG SV IB T350  CRUS 13  4 23000  3  2 83700 91900
36  4 JERSEY DAWN III         SF        FBG SV IB T320D CAT  13  4 23000  3  2 100000 110000
42  4 JERSEY DAWN III         SF        FBG SV IB T375D CAT  15  8 30500  3  6 151000 166000
42  4 JERSEY DAWN III         SF        FBG SV IB T485D GM   15  8 30500  3  6 163500 180000
47  4 JERSEY DAWN III         SF        FBG SV IB T485D GM   15  8 36000  3 10 187000 205500
------------------------- 1987 BOATS -------------------------------------------------------------
36    JERSEY DAWN 36          SF        FBG SV IB T350  CRUS 14  4 22000  2  6 75400 82900
     IB T200D VLVO 82700 90900, IB T250D J&T 86000 94500, IB T250D VLVO 84600 93000
     IB T320D CAT 90800 99700

40    JERSEY DAWN PLAN A      SF        FBG SV IB T350  CRUS 14  6 26000  3  5 105000 115000
     IB T250D VLVO 113000 124000, IB T320D CAT 125500 138000, IB T450D J&T 138000 151500

40    JERSEY DAWN PLAN B      SF        FBG SV IB T350  CRUS 14  6 26000  3  5 105000 115000
     IB T250D VLVO 118500 130500, IB T320D CAT 131500 144500, IB T450D J&T 144000 158000
```

JERSEY YACHTS   -CONTINUED   See inside cover to adjust price for area

LOA FT IN	NAME AND/ OR MODEL	TOP/ RIG	BOAT TYPE	HULL MTL TP	TP	ENGINE TP # HP MFG	BEAM FT IN	WGT LBS	DRAFT FT IN	RETAIL LOW	RETAIL HIGH
						1986 BOATS					
36	JERSEY DAWN 36	SF	FBG SV	IB T350 CRUS	13	4 19000	2 6	66300		72900	
	IB T210D CUM 72700 79900,	IB T245D J&T	74700 82000,	IB T250D VLVO	75500	83000					
	IB T320D CAT 86800 95400										
40	JERSEY DAWN PLAN A	SF	FBG SV	IB T350 CRUS	14	6 26000	3 5	103000		113000	
	IB T250D VLVO 108000 118500,	IB T320D CAT	120000 132000,	IB T450D J&T	132000	145000					
40	JERSEY DAWN PLAN B	SF	FBG SV	IB T350 CRUS	14	6 26000	3 5	97700		107500	
	IB T250D VLVO 113500 125000,	IB T320D CAT	126000 138500,	IB T450D J&T	137500	151500					
						1985 BOATS					
40	DAWN PLAN A	FB	SDN	FBG SV	IB T235D VLVO	14	6 26000	3 5	99600	109500
40	DAWN PLAN A	FB	SDN	FBG SV	IB T300D CAT	14	6 26000	3 5	107500	118000
40	DAWN PLAN A	FB	SDN	FBG SV	IB T450D J&T	14	6 26000	3 5	117000	128500
40	DAWN PLAN B	FB	SDN	FBG SV	IB T235D VLVO	14	6 26000	3 5	105000	115500
40	DAWN PLAN B	FB	SDN	FBG SV	IB T300D CAT	14	6 26000	3 5	113000	124000
40	DAWN PLAN B	FB	SDN	FBG SV	IB T450D J&T	14	6 26000	3 5	122500	134500
44	DEVIL PLAN A	FB	SDNSF	FBG SV	IB T300D CAT	14	6 34800	3 10	130500	143500
44	DEVIL PLAN A	FB	SDNSF	FBG SV	IB T300D VLVO	14	6 34800	3 10	123500	136000
44	DEVIL PLAN A	FB	SDNSF	FBG SV	IB T410D J&T	14	6 34800	3 10	144500	159000
44	DEVIL PLAN B	FB	SDNSF	FBG SV	IB T300D CAT	14	6 34800	3 10	135000	148000
44	DEVIL PLAN B	FB	SDNSF	FBG SV	IB T300D VLVO	14	6 34800	3 10	128000	140500
44	DEVIL PLAN B	FB	SDNSF	FBG SV	IB T410D J&T	14	6 34800	3 10	149500	164000
44	DEVIL PLAN C	FB	SDNSF	FBG SV	IB T300D CAT	14	6 34800	3 10	139000	152500
44	DEVIL PLAN C	FB	SDNSF	FBG SV	IB T300D VLVO	14	6 34800	3 10	132000	145000
44	DEVIL PLAN C	FB	SDNSF	FBG SV	IB T420D GM	14	6 34800	3 10	147500	162000
47 10	JERSEY 480	FB	YTFS	FBG SV	IB T300D CAT	14	9 40200	3 5	137500	151000
47 10	JERSEY 480	FB	YTFS	FBG SV	IB T300D VLVO	14	9 40200	3 5	135500	148500
47 10	JERSEY 480	FB	YTFS	FBG SV	IB T410D J&T	14	9 40200	3 5	151500	166500
						1984 BOATS					
40	DAWN PLAN A	FB	SDN	FBG SV	IB T235D VLVO	14	6 26000	3 5	94100	103500
	IB T300D CAT 103000 113500,	IB T300D VLVO	94800 104000,	IB T410D J&T	107500	118000					
40	DAWN PLAN B	FB	SDN	FBG SV	IB T235D VLVO	14	6 26000	3 5	98100	108000
	IB T300D CAT 107000 117500,	IB T300D VLVO	98400 108000,	IB T410D J&T	111500	122500					
40	DAWN PLAN C	FB	SDN	FBG SV	IB T235D VLVO	14	6 26000	3 5	102000	112000
	IB T300D CAT 112500 123500,	IB T300D VLVO	104000 114000,	IB T410D J&T	115000	126000					
44	DEVIL PLAN A	FB	SDNSF	FBG SV	IB T300D CAT	14	6 34800	3 10	125000	137500
44	DEVIL PLAN A	FB	SDNSF	FBG SV	IB T300D VLVO	14	6 34800	3 10	118500	130500
44	DEVIL PLAN A	FB	SDNSF	FBG SV	IB T410D J&T	14	6 34800	3 10	138500	152500
44	DEVIL PLAN B	FB	SDNSF	FBG SV	IB T300D CAT	14	6 34800	3 10	129000	142000
44	DEVIL PLAN B	FB	SDNSF	FBG SV	IB T300D VLVO	14	6 34800	3 10	122500	135000
44	DEVIL PLAN B	FB	SDNSF	FBG SV	IB T410D J&T	14	6 34800	3 10	143000	157500
44	DEVIL PLAN C	FB	SDNSF	FBG SV	IB T300D CAT	14	6 34800	3 10	133000	146500
44	DEVIL PLAN C	FB	SDNSF	FBG SV	IB T300D VLVO	14	6 34800	3 10	126500	139500
44	DEVIL PLAN C	FB	SDNSF	FBG SV	IB T420D GM	14	6 34800	3 10	141500	155500
47 10	JERSEY 480	FB	YTFS	FBG SV	IB T300D CAT	14	9 40200	3 5	132000	145000
47 10	JERSEY 480	FB	YTFS	FBG SV	IB T300D VLVO	14	9 40200	3 5	129500	142500
47 10	JERSEY 480	FB	YTFS	FBG SV	IB T410D J&T	14	9 40200	3 5	145500	159500

....For earlier years, see the BUC Used Boat Price Guide, Volume 3

JET SET MARINE
PALMYRA NJ 08065   COAST GUARD MFG ID- FUF See inside cover to adjust price for area
    FORMERLY OFFSHORE UNLIMITED

LOA FT IN	NAME AND/ OR MODEL	TOP/ RIG	BOAT TYPE	HULL MTL TP	TP	ENGINE # HP MFG	BEAM FT IN	WGT LBS	DRAFT FT IN	RETAIL LOW	RETAIL HIGH
						1987 BOATS					
22	AVANTI 22	EXP	FBG DV	IO		260	7 2			7400	8500
22 2	AVANTI 22	EXP	FBG DV	OB			7	1700		5150	5950
22 2	AVANTI 22	EXP	FBG DV	IB			7			**	**
27	AVANTI 27	EXP	FBG DV	IO			7	2600		14100	16000
27	AVANTI 27	EXP	FBG DV	IB			7			**	**
27	AVANTI 27	EXP	FBG DV	OB		330	7			12800	14600
33	AVANTI 33	EXP	FBG DV	IO			8	3500		20600	22900
33	AVANTI 33	EXP	FBG DV	IB		T330	8			39300	43600
39	AVANTI 39	EXP	FBG DV	IB			8			**	**
39	AVANTI 39	EXP	FBG DV	IB		T330	8			71800	78800
40 10	AVANTI 41	EXP	FBG DV	IO			9			**	**
40 10	AVANTI 41	EXP	FBG DV	IO		T330	8			76100	83700
						1986 BOATS					
27	AVANTI 27	EXP	FBG DV	IB			7	4200		**	**

....For earlier years, see the BUC Used Boat Price Guide, Volume 3

JETCRAFT INC
TACOMA WA 98408   COAST GUARD MFG ID- JCI See inside cover to adjust price for area

LOA FT IN	NAME AND/ OR MODEL	TOP/ RIG	BOAT TYPE	HULL MTL TP	TP	ENGINE TP # HP MFG	BEAM FT IN	WGT LBS	DRAFT FT IN	RETAIL LOW	RETAIL HIGH
						1987 BOATS					
16 8	UNICRAFT 200	RNBT	AL SV	OB			7			4700	5400
18 3	UNICRAFT 1860	UTL	AL SV	OB			7 4			4650	5350
						1986 BOATS					
16 8	UNICRAFT 200	RNBT	AL SV	OB			7		1400		4550	5250
16 8	UNICRAFT SS200	RNBT	AL SV	IB		140	7	3000		3500	
18 3	UNICRAFT 1860	RNBT	AL SV	OB			7 4			4900	5650
18 3	UNICRAFT 1860	RNBT	AL SV	IB		235	7 4	1850		4100	4750
20 3	UNICRAFT 2066	RNBT	AL SV	IB		340	7 9	2150		5900	6750
						1985 BOATS					
17	UNICRAFT 17	UTL	AL SV	OB			7	1150	9	5000	5750
17	UNICRAFT 17	UTL	AL SV	IB		100	7	1200	9	2400	2750
						1984 BOATS					
17	UNICRAFT 17	ST	UTL	AL SV	OB		6 6	800	9	3500	4100
17	UNICRAFT 17	ST	UTL	AL SV	IB	100D FORD	6 6	1200	9	4450	5100
18	UNICRAFT 18	ST	UTL	AL SV	OB		6 6	1000	9	4350	5000
18	UNICRAFT 18	ST	UTL	AL SV	IB	215D FORD	6 6	1600	9	6200	7100
19	UNICRAFT 19	ST	CUD	AL SV	IB	215D FORD	8	1800	9	7250	8300

JOHNSON BOAT WORKS INC
WHITE BEAR LAKE MN 5511 COAST GUARD MFG ID- JBW See inside cover to adjust price for area

For more recent years, see the BUC Used Boat Price Guide, Volume 1

LOA FT IN	NAME AND/ OR MODEL	TOP/ RIG	BOAT TYPE	HULL MTL TP	TP	ENGINE TP # HP MFG	BEAM FT IN	WGT LBS	DRAFT FT IN	RETAIL LOW	RETAIL HIGH
						1996 BOATS					
16	CLASS M SCOW	SLP	SAROD	FBG BB			5 8	440	3	6350	7300
16	CLASS MC SCOW	CAT	SAROD	FBG BB			5 8	420	3	6900	7900
16	CLASS X	SLP	SAROD	FBG CB			6 1	470	3	6500	7500
16	J SAILOR	CAT	SAROD	FBG BB			5 8	420	3	5800	6650
18	JOHNSON 18	SLP	SAROD	FBG BB			6 7	480 4 6		7200	8300
20	CLASS C SCOW	CAT	SAROD	FBG BB			7	650 3 3		9350	10600
28	CLASS E SCOW	SLP	SAROD	FBG BB			6 9	965 3 9		18200	20200
						1986 BOATS					
16	JOHNSON DAYSAILER	SLP	SAIL	FBG CB			6 1	500 1 7		3550	4100
16	JOHNSON J-SCOW	CAT	SA/OD	FBG BB			5 8			3400	3950
16	JOHNSON M-16 SCOW	SLP	SA/OD	FBG BB			5 8			3300	3850
16	JOHNSON MC SCOW	CAT	SA/OD	FBG BB			5 8			3400	3950
16	JOHNSON X-BOAT	SLP	SA/OD	FBG BB			6 1	500 1 7		3550	4100
18	JOHNSON WEEKENDER	SLP	SAIL	FBG SK			7 6	800 1 7		4750	5450
20	JOHNSON C-SCOW	CAT	SA/OD	FBG BB			6 10			6500	7450
20	JOHNSON M-20 SCOW	SLP	SA/OD	FBG BB			5 10			6450	7450
28	JOHNSON E-SCOW	SLP	SA/OD	FBG BB			6 9			25800	28700
						1985 BOATS					
16	JOHNSON DAYSAILER 16	SLP	SA/OD	FBG CB			6 1			3150	3650
16	JOHNSON J-SCOW	CAT	SA/OD	FBG BB			5 8	420		3150	3700
16	JOHNSON M-16 SCOW	SLP	SA/OD	FBG BB			5 8	440		3150	3700
19	JOHNSON DAYSAILER 19	SLP	SA/OD	FBG CB			6 7			5900	6800
20	JOHNSON C-SCOW	CAT	SA/OD	FBG BB			6 10	650		4600	5300
20	JOHNSON M-20 SCOW	SLP	SA/OD	FBG BB			5 10	595		4400	5050
28	JOHNSON E-SCOW	SLP	SA/OD	FBG BB			6 9	965		8850	10000
						1984 BOATS					
16	JOHNSON DAYSAILER 16	SLP	SAIL	FBG CB			6 1			3000	3450
16	JOHNSON J-SCOW	CAT	SA/OD	FBG BB			5 8			2900	3350
16	JOHNSON M-16 SCOW	SLP	SA/OD	FBG BB			5 8			3000	3450
16	JOHNSON MC SCOW	CAT	SA/OD	FBG BB			5 8			3200	3750
16	JOHNSON X-BOAT	SLP	SA/OD	FBG CB			6 1			3000	3450
19	JOHNSON DAYSAILER 19	SLP	SAIL	FBG CB			6 7			3700	4300
20	JOHNSON C-SCOW	CAT	SA/OD	FBG BB			6 10			5750	6600
20	JOHNSON M-20 SCOW	SLP	SA/OD	FBG BB			5 10			5650	6500
28	JOHNSON E-SCOW	SLP	SA/OD	FBG BB			6 9		3 9	23200	25800

....For earlier years, see the BUC Used Boat Price Guide, Volume 3

JONES BOATS

TUCKAHOE NJ 08250   COAST GUARD MFG ID- JNF   See inside cover to adjust price for area

LOA FT IN	NAME AND/ OR MODEL	TOP/ RIG	BOAT TYPE	HULL MTL	TP	TP	ENGINE #	HP	MFG	BEAM FT IN	WGT LBS	DRAFT FT IN	RETAIL LOW	RETAIL HIGH

----- 1985 BOATS -----

17	TUCKAHOE-CATBOAT	SLP	SA/CR	F/S	KL					7 8	1500	2 4	3950	4600
21	PILOT GAF	SLP	SA/CR	P/C	TK	IB	5		HOND	7 4	2200	1 9	5700	6550
28 6	DRAGONFLY 28	SLP	SA/CR	P/P	TM					17 8	2400	1 8	21700	24100

JONGERT

DAHM INTERNATIONAL
MEDEMBLIK NETHERLANDS 1670 AC   See inside cover to adjust price for area

LOA FT IN	NAME AND/ OR MODEL	TOP/ RIG	BOAT TYPE	HULL MTL	TP	TP	ENGINE #	HP	MFG	BEAM FT IN	WGT LBS	DRAFT FT IN	RETAIL LOW	RETAIL HIGH

----- 1988 BOATS -----

57 5	JONGERT 1700S	SLP	SA/RC	STL	KL	IB	117D		BENZ	15 9		9 6	712000	782500
58	JONGERT 17S	KTH	SA/RC	STL	KL	IB	117D		BENZ	15 9		8 6	777000	854000
66	JONGERT 2000S	SLP	SA/RC	AL	KL	IB	204D		BENZ	17 7		9 8	813500	894000
67 9	JONGERT 20DS	KTH	SA/CR	STL	KL	IB	204D		BENZ	17 3		8 3	1.195M	1.300M
67 9	JONGERT 20S	KTH	SA/CR	STL	KL	IB	204D		BENZ	17 3		8 3	1.040M	1.130M
72 5	JONGERT 2200S	SLP	SA/RC	AL	KL	IB	220D		BENZ	18 9		8 8	**	**
74 2	JONGERT 21S	KTH	SA/CR	STL	KL	IB	237D		BENZ	18 9		10	**	**
76 2	JONGERT 22D	KTH	SA/CR	STL	KL	IB	237D		BENZ	19		9 2	**	**
78 8	JONGERT 2400S	SLP	SA/RC	STL	KL	IB	240D		BENZ	21 4		11 6	**	**

----- 1987 BOATS -----

57 5	JONGERT 1700S	SLP	SA/RC	STL	KL	IB	117D		BENZ	15 9		9 6	666500	732500
58	JONGERT 17S	KTH	SA/CR	STL	KL	IB	117D		BENZ	15 9		8 6	728000	800000
62 3	JONGERT 1900S	KTH	SA/CR	STL	KL	IB	117D		BENZ	16 5		10	794500	873000
66	JONGERT 2000S	SLP	SA/RC	AL	KL	IB	204D		BENZ	17 7		9 8	762500	838000
67 9	JONGERT 20DS	KTH	SA/CR	STL	KL	IB	204D		BENZ	17 3		8 3	1.095M	1.190M
67 9	JONGERT 20S	KTH	SA/CR	STL	KL	IB	204D		BENZ	17 3		8 3	1.015M	1.100M
72 5	JONGERT 2200S	SLP	SA/RC	AL	KL	IB	220D		BENZ	18 9		8 8	**	**
74 2	JONGERT 21S	KTH	SA/CR	STL	KL	IB	237D		BENZ	18 9		10	**	**
76 2	JONGERT 22D	KTH	SA/CR	STL	KL	IB	237D		BENZ	19		9 2	**	**
78 8	JONGERT 2400S	SLP	SA/CR	STL	KL	IB	240D		BENZ	21 4		11 6	**	**

----- 1986 BOATS -----

57 5	JONGERT 1200S	SLP	SA/RC	STL	KL	IB	117D		BENZ	15 9		9 6	624000	685500
58	JONGERT 17S	KTH	SA/CR	STL	KL	IB	117D		BENZ	15 9		8 6	681500	749000
62 3	JONGERT 1900S	KTH	SA/CR	STL	KL	IB	117D		BENZ	16 5		10	744500	818000
67 9	JONGERT 20DS	KTH	SA/CR	STL	KL	IB	204D		BENZ	17 3		8 3	1.035M	1.125M
67 9	JONGERT 20S	KTH	SA/CR	STL	KL	IB	204D		BENZ	17 3		8 3	942000	1.025M
72 5	JONGERT 2200S	SLP	SA/RC	AL	KL	IB	220D		BENZ	18 9		8 8	**	**
74 2	JONGERT 21S	KTH	SA/CR	STL	KL	IB	237D		BENZ	18 9		10	**	**
76 2	JONGERT 22D	KTH	SA/CR	STL	KL	IB	237D		BENZ	19		9 2	**	**
78 8	JONGERT 2400S	KTH	SA/CR	STL	KL	IB	240D		BENZ	21 4		11 6	**	**
78 8	JONGERT 2400S	KTH	SA/RC	AL	KL	IB	240D		BENZ	21 4		11 6	**	**

----- 1985 BOATS -----

57 3	JONGERT 1700	SLP	SA/CR	AL	KL	IB		D	BENZ	15 9		9 4	590500	649000
58	JONGERT 17S	KTH	SA/CR	AL	KL	IB	117D		BENZ	15 9		8 6	638000	701000
58 2	JONGERT 17S	KTH	SA/CR	AL	KL	IB		D	BENZ	15 6		9 2	641000	704500
62 3	JONGERT 1900	KTH	SA/CR	AL	KL	IB		D	BENZ	16 5		9 7	699000	768000
62 3	JONGERT 1900S	KTH	SA/CR	AL	KL	IB	117D		BENZ	16		10	698000	767000
67 7	JONGERT 20D	KTH	SA/CR	STL	KL	IB		D	BENZ	17 6		9 7	927500	1.010M
67 9	JONGERT 20DS	KTH	SA/CR	STL	KL	IB	204D		BENZ	17 3		8 3	971000	1.055M
67 9	JONGERT 20S	KTH	SA/CR	STL	KL	IB	204D		BENZ	17 3		8 3	878500	965500
72	JONGERT 2200S	KTH	SA/CR	AL	KL	IB	220D		BENZ	18 8		8 8	**	**
72 3	JONGERT 2200	SLP	SA/CR	AL	KL	IB		D	BENZ	18 7		12	**	**
74 2	JONGERT 21SP	KTH	SA/CR	STL	KL	IB	237D		BENZ	18 9		10	**	**
76	JONGERT 22D	KTH	SA/CR	STL	KL	IB		D	BENZ	19		9 2	**	**
76 2	JONGERT 22D	KTH	SA/CR	STL	KL	IB	237D		BENZ	19		9 2	**	**

KAARINA YACHTS

KAARINA FINLAND   See inside cover to adjust price for area

ESKIL TRADING INC
W PALM BCH FL 33407

LOA FT IN	NAME AND/ OR MODEL	TOP/ RIG	BOAT TYPE	HULL MTL	TP	TP	ENGINE #	HP	MFG	BEAM FT IN	WGT LBS	DRAFT FT IN	RETAIL LOW	RETAIL HIGH

----- 1986 BOATS -----

32 2	ALBATROSS 32	CUT	MS	FBG	KL	IB	78D		PERK	10 10	14994	5 1	58900	64800
36 3	SEA-CAT 37	CUT	MS	FBG	KL	IB	48D		PERK	11	13670	4 9	55400	60800
40 8	SEAFINN 41	KTH	MS	FBG	KL	IB	78D		PERK	11 10	25350	5 1	107500	118000

----- 1985 BOATS -----

| 40 8 | SEAFINN | YWL | MS | FBG | KL | IB | 85D | | PERK | 11 10 | 25350 | 5 1 | 92400 | 101500 |
| 40 8 | SEAFINN | YWL | MS | FBG | KL | IB | 135D | | PERK | 11 10 | 25350 | 5 1 | 93100 | 102500 |

KADEY-KROGEN YACHTS INC

STUART FL 34994   COAST GUARD MFG ID- CBK   See inside cover to adjust price for area

For more recent years, see the BUC Used Boat Price Guide, Volume 1

LOA FT IN	NAME AND/ OR MODEL	TOP/ RIG	BOAT TYPE	HULL MTL	TP	TP	ENGINE #	HP	MFG	BEAM FT IN	WGT LBS	DRAFT FT IN	RETAIL LOW	RETAIL HIGH

----- 1996 BOATS -----

42 4	KROGEN	FB	TRWL	F/S	DS	IB	135D		PERK	15		4 7	294000	323000
48 5	KROGEN	FB	TRWL	F/S	DS	IB	210D		CAT	16 8		5	485500	533500
48 5	WHALEBACK	EPH	TRWL	F/S	DS	IB	210D		CAT	16 8		5	454500	499500

----- 1995 BOATS -----

42 4	TRAWLER	FB	TRWL	F/S	DS	IB	135D		PERK	15	39500	4 7	314000	345000
48 5	KROGEN	EPH	TRWL	F/S	DS	IB	210D		CAT	16 8		5	454000	499000
48 5	WHALEBACK	EPH	TRWL	F/S	DS	IB	210D		CAT	16 8		5	435500	478500

----- 1994 BOATS -----

38 2	CUTTER	CUT	SACAC	F/S	KL	IB	50D		WEST	12 8	24000	3 2	165500	182000
42 4	TRAWLER	FB	TRWL	F/S	DS	IB	135D		PERK	15	39500	4 7	301000	330500
48 5	TRAWLER	EPH	TRWL	F/S	DS	IB	210D		CAT	16 8		5	316500	348000

----- 1993 BOATS -----

38 2	CUTTER	CUT	SACAC	F/S	KL	IB	50D		WEST	12 8	24000	3 2	156500	172000
42 4	TRAWLER	FB	TRWL	F/S	DS	IB	135D		PERK	15	39500	4 7	286500	315000
48 5	TRAWLER	EPH	TRWL	F/S	DS	IB	210D		CAT	16 8		5	302500	332500

----- 1992 BOATS -----

| 38 2 | CUTTER | CUT | SA/CR | F/S | KL | IB | 50D | | WEST | 12 8 | 24000 | 3 2 | 148500 | 163000 |
| 42 4 | TRAWLER | FB | TRWL | F/S | DS | IB | 135D | | PERK | 15 | 39500 | 4 7 | 273000 | 300000 |

----- 1991 BOATS -----

36 4	MANATEE TRAWLER	FB	TRWL	F/S	DS	IB	100D		WEST	13 8	23000	3 2	166000	182500
38 2	CUTTER	CUT	SA/CR	F/S	KL	IB	50D		WEST	12 8	24000	3 2	140500	154500
42	TRAWLER	FB	TRWL	F/S	DS	IB	135D		PERK	15	39500	4 7	260500	286500

----- 1988 BOATS -----

36 4	MANATEE 36	FB	TRWL	F/S	DS	IB	100D		VLVO	13 8	23000	3 4	144500	159000
38 2	KROGEN 38 SHOAL	CUT	SAIL	F/S	CB	IB	46D		WEST	12 8	24000	3 2	119500	131500
42 4	KROGEN 42	FB	TRWL	F/S	DS	IB	135D		LEHM	15	39500	4 7	213500	235000
54 5	KROGEN 54	FB	TRWL	F/S	DS	IB	225D		LEHM	17	70000	5 6	355500	391000

----- 1987 BOATS -----

36 4	MANATEE 36	FB	TRWL	F/S	DS	IB	100D		VLVO	13 8	23000	3 4	138000	152000
36 4	MANATEE 36	FB	TRWL	F/S	DS	IB	110D		VLVO	13 8	23000	3	143000	157500
38 2	KROGEN 38	CUT	SA/CR	FBG	KC	IB	50D		PERK	12 8	21700	5	104500	114500
42 4	KROGEN 42	FB	TRWL	F/S	DS	IB	135D		LEHM	15	39500	4 7	204500	224500
54 5	KROGEN 54	FB	TRWL	FBG	DS	IB	225D			17	67800	5 6	332000	364500
54 5	KROGEN 54	FB	TRWL	F/S	DS	IB	225D		LEHM	17	70000	5 6	341000	374500

----- 1986 BOATS -----

| 36 4 | MANATEE 36 | FB | TRWL | F/S | DS | IB | 90D | | VLVO | 13 8 | 18000 | 3 4 | 132000 | 145000 |
| 42 | KROGEN 42 | FB | TRWL | F/S | DS | IB | 135D | | LEHM | 15 | 39000 | 4 7 | 193500 | 212500 |

----- 1985 BOATS -----

36 4	MANATEE 36	FB	TRWL	F/S	DS	IB	85D		VLVO	13 8	18000	3 4	126000	138500
38 2	KROGEN 38	CUT	SA/CR	FBG	KC	IB	50D		PERK	12 8	21700	3	93700	103000
42 4	KROGEN 42	FB	TRWL	FBG	DS	IB	135D			15	39500		187500	206000

----- 1984 BOATS -----

36 4	MANATEE 36	FB	TRWL	F/S	DS	IB	90D		VLVO	13 8	18000	3 4	121000	133000
38 2	KROGEN 38	CUT	SA/CR	KC	KC	IB	50D		PERK	12 8	21700	3	88800	97500
38 2	KROGEN 38	CUT	SA/CR	F/S	KL	IB	50D		PERK	12 8	21700	5	88800	97500
42 4	KROGEN 42	FB	TRWL	F/S	DS	IB	135D		LEHM	15	39000	4 7	177500	195000

....For earlier years, see the BUC Used Boat Price Guide, Volume 3

JOHN KAISER ASSOC INC

WILMINGTON DE 19807-098 COAST GUARD MFG ID- JRK See inside cover to adjust price for area

LOA FT IN	NAME AND/ OR MODEL	TOP/ RIG	BOAT TYPE	HULL MTL	TP	TP	ENGINE #	HP	MFG	BEAM FT IN	WGT LBS	DRAFT FT IN	RETAIL LOW	RETAIL HIGH

----- 1986 BOATS -----

| 34 | GALE-FORCE PILOT | CUT | SA/CR | FBG | KL | IB | | D | | 10 6 | 20000 | 5 3 | 107500 | 118500 |

----- 1985 BOATS -----

| 34 | GALE-FORCE PILOT | CUT | SA/CR | FBG | KL | IB | | D | | 10 6 | 20000 | 5 3 | 101500 | 111500 |

....For earlier years, see the BUC Used Boat Price Guide, Volume 3

KAMPER KRAFT MFG
HOLLAND MI 49423

See inside cover to adjust price for area

LOA FT IN	NAME AND/ OR MODEL	TOP/ RIG	BOAT TYPE	-HULL- MTL TP	----ENGINE--- TP # HP MFG	BEAM FT IN	WGT LBS	DRAFT FT IN	RETAIL LOW	RETAIL HIGH
---	--- 1985 BOATS ---									
19	HOBO		CAMPR	FBG OB		8	1600		4550	5250
21	GREAT-LAKES KAMPER		CAMPR	FBG OB		8	1900		5950	6850
21	GREAT-LAKES KAMPER		CAMPR	FBG IO	140	8	1900		3900	4550
24	GREAT-LAKES KAMPER		CAMPR	FBG OB		8	2400		8050	9250
24	GREAT-LAKES KAMPER		CAMPR	FBG IO	190	8	2400		5150	5900

KANTER YACHTS
ST THOMAS ONTARIO CANADA

See inside cover to adjust price for area

For more recent years, see the BUC Used Boat Price Guide, Volume 1

LOA FT IN	NAME AND/ OR MODEL	TOP/ RIG	BOAT TYPE	-HULL- MTL TP	----ENGINE--- TP # HP MFG	BEAM FT IN	WGT LBS	DRAFT FT IN	RETAIL LOW	RETAIL HIGH
---	--- 1987 BOATS ---									
44 9	KANTER-ATLANTIC 45	CUT	SA/RC	AL KL	IB 92D VLVO	13 10	36000	6 6	183000	201000
48	EMPACHER 48	CUT	SA/RC	AL CB	IB D	14 6	37000	4 10	200000	219500
55 2	EMPACHER 55	CUT	SA/RC	AL CB	IB D	16 2	51000	5 5	310000	340500
---	--- 1986 BOATS ---									
44 9	KANTER-ATLANTIC 45	CUT	SA/CR	STL KL	IB 92D VLVO	13 10	36000	6 6	172000	189000
44 9	KANTER-ATLANTIC 45	KTH	SA/CR	STL KL	IB 92D VLVO	13 10	36000	6 6	172000	189000
---	--- 1985 BOATS ---									
44 9	KANTER-ATLANTIC 45	CUT	SA/CR	STL KL	IB 92D VLVO	13 11	36000	6 6	161500	177500
49	KANTER-ATLANTIC 49	CUT	SA/CR	STL KL	IB 92D VLVO	13 11	42000	6 6	192500	211500
---	--- 1984 BOATS ---									
44 9	KANTER-ATLANTIC 45	CUT	SA/CR	STL KL	IB 92D VLVO	13 11	36000	6 6	152000	167000
44 9	KANTER-ATLANTIC 45	KTH	SA/CR	STL KL	IB 96D VLVO	13 11	36000	6 6	152500	167500
49	KANTER-ATLANTIC 49	CUT	SA/CR	STL KL	IB 92D VLVO	13 11	42000	6 6	181500	199500

....For earlier years, see the BUC Used Boat Price Guide, Volume 3

KAUFMAN DESIGN INC
BERMUDA LTD
SEVERNA PARK MD 21146   COAST GUARD MFG ID- KDB
FORMERLY KAUFMAN & ASSOCIATES

See inside cover to adjust price for area

LOA FT IN	NAME AND/ OR MODEL	TOP/ RIG	BOAT TYPE	-HULL- MTL TP	----ENGINE--- TP # HP MFG	BEAM FT IN	WGT LBS	DRAFT FT IN	RETAIL LOW	RETAIL HIGH
---	--- 1990 BOATS ---									
43	KAUFMAN 43	CUT	SA/CR	FBG KC	IB 60D LEHM	12 6	25000	4 9	114500	126000
43	KAUFMAN 43	CUT	SA/CR	FBG KL	IB 60D LEHM	12 6	24000	5 10	112000	123000
49	KAUFMAN 49	CUT	SA/CR	FBG KC	IB 70D WEST	13 9	33000	4 10	162000	178500
49	KAUFMAN 49	CUT	SA/CR	FBG KL	IB 70D WEST	13 9	33000	7	162000	178500
---	--- 1987 BOATS ---									
43	KAUFMAN 43	CUT	SA/CR	FBG KC	IB 60D LEHM	12 6	25000	4 9	95400	105000
43	KAUFMAN 43	CUT	SA/CR	FBG KL	IB 60D LEHM	12 6	24000	5 10	93300	102500
47	KAUFMAN 47	CUT	SA/CR	FBG KC	IB 70D WEST	13 9	33000	4 10	124000	136500
47	KAUFMAN 47	CUT	SA/CR	FBG KL	IB 70D WEST	13 9	33000	7	124000	136500
49	KAUFMAN 49	CUT	SA/CR	FBG KC	IB 70D WEST	13 9	33000	4 10	135000	148000
49	KAUFMAN 49	CUT	SA/CR	FBG KL	IB 70D WEST	13 9	33000	7	135000	148000
---	--- 1986 BOATS ---									
47	KAUFMAN 47	CUT	SA/CR	FBG KC	IB 70D WEST	13 9	33000	4 10	116500	128000
47	KAUFMAN 47	CUT	SA/CR	FBG KL	IB 70D WEST	13 9	33000	7	116500	128000
---	--- 1985 BOATS ---									
43	KAUFMAN 43	CUT	SA/CR	FBG KC	IB 60D FORD	12 6	25000	4 9	84400	92800
43	KAUFMAN 43	CUT	SA/CR	FBG KL	IB 60D FORD	12 6	24000	5 11	82500	90700
47	KAUFMAN 47	CUT	SA/CR	FBG KC	IB 70D WEST	13 9	33000	4 10	109500	120500
47	KAUFMAN 47	CUT	SA/CR	FBG KL	IB 70D WEST	13 9	33000	7	109500	120500

KAVALK BOATS LTD
BURNABY BC CANADA V3J7N COAST GUARD MFG ID- ZKV See inside cover to adjust price for area

LOA FT IN	NAME AND/ OR MODEL	TOP/ RIG	BOAT TYPE	-HULL- MTL TP	----ENGINE--- TP # HP MFG	BEAM FT IN	WGT LBS	DRAFT FT IN	RETAIL LOW	RETAIL HIGH
---	--- 1991 BOATS ---									
19	CLASSIC	OP	RNBT	FBG DV	IO 240 MRCR	6 3	2500	1 8	12000	13700
19	CONTINENTAL	OP	RNBT	FBG DV	IO 240 MRCR	6 3	2500	1 8	12000	13700
29 2	SPORT CRUISER	OP	SPTCR	FBG DV	IO T330-T410	8 6	7000	2 2	62200	75800
---	--- 1988 BOATS ---									
19	CLASSIC	OP	RNBT	F/S DV	IO 260 MRCR	6 3	2300	1 7	9950	11300
19	CONTINENTAL 3 SEAT	OP	RNBT	F/S DV	IO 260 MRCR	6 3	2400	1 8	10200	11500
19	CONTINENTAL 5 SEAT	OP	RNBT	F/S DV	IO 260 MRCR	6 3	2450	1 8	10300	11700
---	--- 1987 BOATS ---									
19	MISTRAL	OP	RNBT	MHG DV	IO 260 MRCR	6 3	2450	1 7	9700	11000
19	MISTRAL L	OP	RNBT	F/S DV	IO 260 MRCR	6 3	2450	1 7	9750	11100
19	MISTRAL S	OP	RNBT	F/S DV	IO 260 MRCR	6 3	2400	1 8	9650	10900
19	MISTRAL	OP	RNBT	MHG DV	IO 260 MRCR	6 3	2400	1 8	9600	10900
---	--- 1985 BOATS ---									
18 7	KAVALK 570	OP	SPTCR	F/S DV	IO MRCR	5 9	2200	1	**	**
18 7	KAVALK 570	OP	SPTCR	F/S DV	IO VLVO	5 9	2200	1	**	**
18 7	KAVALK 570	OP	SPTCR	F/S DV	IO D BMW	5 9	2200	1	**	**
18 7	MISTRAL	OP	SPTCR	F/S DV	IO MRCR	5 9	2200	1	**	**
18 7	MISTRAL	OP	SPTCR	F/S DV	IO D BMW	5 9	2200	1	**	**
25 5	KAVALK 770	OP	SPTCR	F/S DV	IO 260-330	10 2		1 6	23400	28000
25 5	KAVALK 770	OP	SPTCR	F/S DV	IO 165D-190D	10 2		1 6	28800	32800
25 5	KAVALK 770	OP	SPTCR	F/S DV	IO T145-T190	10 2		1 6	25100	28800

....For earlier years, see the BUC Used Boat Price Guide, Volume 3

JACK KELLY YACHT SALES INC
SAN DIEGO CA 92106   COAST GUARD MFG ID- JKY See inside cover to adjust price for area

LOA FT IN	NAME AND/ OR MODEL	TOP/ RIG	BOAT TYPE	-HULL- MTL TP	----ENGINE--- TP # HP MFG	BEAM FT IN	WGT LBS	DRAFT FT IN	RETAIL LOW	RETAIL HIGH
---	--- 1987 BOATS ---									
46 3	KELLY/PETERSON 46	CUT	SA/CR	F/S KL	IB 82D PATH	13 4	33300	6 8	174000	191500
---	--- 1986 BOATS ---									
46 3	KELLY/PETERSON 46	CUT	SA/CR	F/S KL	IB 82D PATH	13 5	33300	6 8	165000	181500
---	--- 1985 BOATS ---									
46 3	KELLY/PETERSON 46	CUT	SA/CR	F/S KL	IB 82D PATH	13 4	33300	6 8	156500	172000
---	--- 1984 BOATS ---									
46 3	KELLY/PETERSON 46	CUT	SA/CR	F/S KL	IB 82D PATH	13 4	33300	6 8	148000	163000

....For earlier years, see the BUC Used Boat Price Guide, Volume 3

KELT MARINE INC
56000 VANNES FRANCE

See inside cover to adjust price for area

LOA FT IN	NAME AND/ OR MODEL	TOP/ RIG	BOAT TYPE	-HULL- MTL TP	----ENGINE--- TP # HP MFG	BEAM FT IN	WGT LBS	DRAFT FT IN	RETAIL LOW	RETAIL HIGH
---	--- 1986 BOATS ---									
28 4	KELT 29	SLP	SA/RC	FBG KL	IB D	10 2	6394	5 4	21500	23900
31 2	KELT 31	SLP	SA/RC	FBG KL	IB D	10 2	7276	5 11	26500	29500
39	KELT 39	SLP	SA/RC	FBG KL	IB D	12 6	15400	7 2	64600	71000
---	--- 1985 BOATS ---									
27 3	KELT 7.60	SLP	SA/RC	FBG KL	IB D	9 5	4190	4 3	12700	14400
28 4	KELT 8.50	SLP	SA/RC	FBG KL	IB D	10 2	6394	5 3	20300	22500
31	KELT 9.00	SLP	SA/RC	FBG KL	IB D	10 2	7276	5 11	24900	27600
---	--- 1984 BOATS ---									
24 11	KELT 7.60	SLP	SA/CR	FBG KC	OB	9 5	4500	2 5	10500	11900
SD 8	VLVO 10800	12300, SD		10D VLVO	11300 12900,	IB	10D VLVO	11300	12900	
24 11	KELT 7.60	SLP	SA/CR	FBG KL	OB	9 5	4500	4 3	10500	11900
SD 8	VLVO 10800	12300, SD		10D VLVO	11300 12900,	IB	10D VLVO	11300	12900	

....For earlier years, see the BUC Used Boat Price Guide, Volume 3

KENNER MFG CO INC
SPRINGFIELD MO 65803   COAST GUARD MFG ID- KEN See inside cover to adjust price for area

For more recent years, see the BUC Used Boat Price Guide, Volume 1

LOA FT IN	NAME AND/ OR MODEL	TOP/ RIG	BOAT TYPE	-HULL- MTL TP	----ENGINE--- TP # HP MFG	BEAM FT IN	WGT LBS	DRAFT FT IN	RETAIL LOW	RETAIL HIGH
---	--- 1996 BOATS ---									
16 4	KENNER 16		CTRCN	FBG SV	OB	7 4	900	9	4350	5000
16 4	KENNER 16 KST		CTRCN	FBG TH	OB	7 4	900	9	4400	5100
16 5	KENNER 16-V		CTRCN	FBG FL	OB	6 10	600	10	3000	3450
16 10	KENNER 17 SKIFF		UTL	FBG FL	OB	6 7	490	5	2200	2550
16 10	KENNER 17 SKIFF TUN		UTL	FBG FL	OB	6 7	490	5	2300	2700
18 4	KENNER 18		CTRCN	FBG SV	OB	8	1100	10	5400	6200
18 4	KENNER 18 KST		CTRCN	FBG TH	OB	8	1100	10	5550	6350
18 5	KENNER 18-V		CTRCN	FBG SV	OB	7 7	950	11	4850	5550
18 5	KENNER 18VT-90		CTRCN	FBG SV	OB	7 7	950	11	4850	5550
18 5	KENNER 18VT-130	OP	CTRCN	FBG SV	OB	7 7	950		4850	5550
18 5	KENNER 18VT-90	OP	CTRCN	FBG SV	OB	7 7	950		4850	5550
19 2	KENNER 19 SKIFF		UTL	FBG FL	OB	6 7	625	5	2750	3200
21 2	KENNER 21		CTRCN	FBG SV	OB	8	1300	10	6650	7600

CONTINUED ON NEXT PAGE

LOA FT	LOA IN	NAME AND/ OR MODEL	TOP/ RIG	BOAT TYPE	HULL MTL	HULL TP	ENGINE TP	# HP	MFG	BEAM FT	BEAM IN	WGT LBS	DRAFT FT	DRAFT IN	RETAIL LOW	RETAIL HIGH
		1996 BOATS														
21	2	KENNER 21 KST		CTRCN	FBG	TH	OB			8		1300		10	6750	7800
21	6	KENNER 21VT-130	OP	CTRCN	FBG	SV	OB			7	7	1300			6750	7750
21	6	KENNER 21VT-200	OP	CTRCN	FBG	SV	OB			7	7	1300			6750	7750
21	7	KENNER 21-V		CTRCN	FBG	SV	OB			7	7	1300	1	2	6750	7750
21	7	KENNER 21V-130		CTRCN	FBG	SV	OB			7	7	1250	1	2	6550	7500
		1995 BOATS														
16	4	KENNER 16	OP	CTRCN	FBG	SV	OB			7	4	900			4050	4700
16	4	KENNER 16 KST	OP	CTRCN	FBG	TH	OB			7	4	900			4150	4850
16	5	KENNER 16-V	OP	CTRCN	FBG	SV	OB			6	10	600			2850	3350
16	10	KENNER 17 SKIFF	OP	UTL	FBG	FL	OB			6	6	490			2100	2500
16	10	KENNER 17 TUN	OP	UTL	FBG	TH	OB			6	6	490			2200	2550
18	2	KENNER 18	OP	CTRCN	FBG	SV	OB			8		1100			5100	5850
18	2	KENNER 18 KST	OP	CTRCN	FBG	TH	OB			8		1100			5200	6000
18	5	KENNER 18-V	OP	CTRCN	FBG	SV	OB			7	7	950			4550	5250
19	2	KENNER 19 SKIFF	OP	UTL	FBG	FL	OB			6	6	625			2600	3050
21	2	KENNER 21	OP	CTRCN	FBG	SV	OB			8		1300			6250	7200
21	2	KENNER 21 KST	OP	CTRCN	FBG	TH	OB			8		1300			6400	7350
21	2	KENNER 21-V	OP	CTRCN	FBG	SV	OB			7	7	1300			6300	7250
		1994 BOATS														
16	4	KENNER 16	OP	CTRCN	FBG	SV	OB			7	4	900			3850	4450
16	4	KENNER 16 KST	OP	CTRCN	FBG	TH	OB			7	4	900			3950	4600
16	5	KENNER 16-V	OP	CTRCN	FBG	SV	OB			6	10	600			2750	3200
16	10	KENNER 17 SKIFF	OP	UTL	FBG	FL	OB			6	6	490			2000	2400
18	2	KENNER 18	OP	CTRCN	FBG	SV	OB			8		1100			4950	5650
18	2	KENNER 18 KST	OP	CTRCN	FBG	TH	OB			8		1100			4800	5550
18	5	KENNER 18-V	OP	CTRCN	FBG	SV	OB			7	7	950			4300	5000
19	2	KENNER 19 SKIFF	OP	UTL	FBG	FL	OB			6	6	625			2450	2900
21	2	KENNER 21	OP	CTRCN	FBG	SV	OB			8		1300			5950	6850
21	2	KENNER 21 KST	OP	CTRCN	FBG	TH	OB			8		1300			6050	6950
21	2	KENNER 21-V	OP	CTRCN	FBG	SV	OB			7	7	1300			6000	6900
		1993 BOATS														
16	4	KENNER 16	OP	CTRCN	FBG	SV	OB			7	4	900			3550	4150
16	4	KENNER 16 KST	OP	CTRCN	FBG	TH	OB			7	4	900			3700	4300
16	5	KENNER 16 V	OP	CTRCN	FBG	SV	OB			6	10	600			2600	3000
18	2	KENNER 18	OP	CTRCN	FBG	SV	OB			8		1100			4750	5450
18	2	KENNER 18 KST	OP	CTRCN	FBG	TH	OB			8		1100			4450	5100
18	5	KENNER 18 V	OP	CTRCN	FBG	SV	OB			7	7	950			4050	4700
21	2	KENNER 21	OP	CTRCN	FBG	SV	OB			8		1300			5700	6550
21	2	KENNER 21 KST	OP	CTRCN	FBG	TH	OB			8		1300			5700	6550
21	7	KENNER 21 V	OP	CTRCN	FBG	SV	OB			8		1300			5700	6550
		1992 BOATS														
16	4	KENNER 16	OP	CTRCN	FBG	SV	OB			7	4	900			3350	3900
16	4	KENNER 16 KST	OP	CTRCN	FBG	TH	OB			7	4	900			3450	4050
16	5	KENNER 16-V	OP	CTRCN	FBG	SV	OB			6	10	600			2450	2850
18	2	KENNER 18	OP	CTRCN	FBG	SV	OB			8		1100			4250	4950
18	2	KENNER 18 KST	OP	CTRCN	FBG	TH	OB			8		1100			4350	5050
18	5	KENNER 18-V	OP	CTRCN	FBG	SV	OB			7	7	950			3800	4450
21	2	KENNER 21	OP	CTRCN	FBG	SV	OB			8		1300			5450	6300
21	2	KENNER 21 KST	OP	CTRCN	FBG	TH	OB			8		1300			5350	6150
21	7	KENNER 21-V	OP	CTRCN	FBG	SV	OB			7	7	1300			5450	6300
		1991 BOATS														
16	4	KENNER 16	OP	CTRCN	FBG	SV	OB			7	4	825			2950	3450
16	4	KENNER 16 EC	OP	CTRCN	FBG	SV	OB			7	4	800			2900	3350
16	4	KENNER 16 EC KST	OP	CTRCN	FBG	TH	OB			7	4	800			3000	3450
16	4	KENNER 16 KST	OP	CTRCN	FBG	TH	OB			7	4	825			3050	3550
18	2	KENNER 18	OP	CTRCN	FBG	SV	OB			8		1025			3850	4450
18	2	KENNER 18 EC	OP	CTRCN	FBG	SV	OB			8		1000			3650	4250
18	2	KENNER 18 EC KST	OP	CTRCN	FBG	TH	OB			8		1000			3800	4400
18	2	KENNER 18 KST	OP	CTRCN	FBG	TH	OB			8		1025			3850	4450
21	2	KENNER 21	OP	CTRCN	FBG	SV	OB			8		1300			5050	5850
21	2	KENNER 21 KST	OP	CTRCN	FBG	TH	OB			8		1300			5150	5950
		1989 BOATS														
16	4	KENNER 16		CTRCN	FBG	SV	OB			7	4	750		7	2500	2950
16	4	KENNER 16KST		CTRCN	FBG	SV	OB			7	4	750		7	2600	3000
18	5	KENNER 18		CTRCN	FBG	SV	OB			8		920		8	3100	3600
18	5	KENNER 18KST		CTRCN	FBG	SV	OB			8		920		8	3150	3700
21	3	KENNER 21		CTRCN	FBG	SV	OB			8		1100		8	3600	4200
21	3	KENNER 21KST		CTRCN	FBG	SV	OB			8		1100		8	4350	5000
32		QUEST SPORT CRUISER		SPTCR	FBG	SV	SE		OMC	9					**	**
47		SUWANEE 47		HB	FBG	SV	SE		VLVO	13	10	18000	1	4	**	**
		IO T230 MRCR 47700 52400, IO T230 OMC 47400 52100, IO T230 VLVO 48900 53800														
		SE T270 48400 53200, VD T270 44400 49300, SE T330 50100 55000														
		JT T330 47600 52300, VD T330 46000 50500, IO T200D VLVO 53500 58800														
		1988 BOATS														
16	4	KENNER 16		CTRCN	FBG	SV	OB			7	4	750		7	2450	2800
18	5	KENNER 18		CTRCN	FBG	SV	OB			8		920		8	3000	3500
21	3	KENNER 21		CTRCN	FBG	SV	OB			8		1100		8	3750	4400
32		QUEST SPORT CRUISER		SPTCR	FBG	SV	SE		OMC	9					**	**
47		SUWANEE 47		HB	FBG	SV		T		13	10	18000	1	4	37800	42000
		1987 BOATS														
25		KENNER 25		CTRCN	FBG	SV	OB			8		1800			8050	9250
28		KENNER 28		UTL	FBG	SV	OB			8		1800			15700	17900
32		KENNER 32		UTL	FBG	SV	OB			10		3500			24300	27000
45		SKIPJACK 35	KTH	SA/CR	FBG	KC	IB	30D		11	10	12000	2	4	62600	68800
47		SUWANEE 47		HB	FBG	SV	IB			13	8	18000	1	4	39100	43500
		1986 BOATS														
26		UTILITY 26		UTL	FBG	SV	OB			8	3	1600			9450	10800
26		UTILITY 26		UTL	FBG	SV	IO	260		8	3	1600			4700	5400
28		UTILITY 28		UTL	FBG	SV	OB			8		1800			15300	17400
32		HOUSEBOAT	HT	HB	FBG	SV	OB			12		6500			20000	22200
47		SKIPJACK	KTH	SA/CR	FBG	KC	IB	30D		11	8	14000	2	4	73700	81000
		1985 BOATS														
25		SUWANEE 25		CTRCN	FBG	SV	OB			8		1800			7300	8400
28		KENNER		UTL	FBG	SV	OB			8		1800			15000	17000
32		SUWANEE 32		OVNTR	FBG	SV	OB			10		3500			23200	25800
32		SUWANEE 32		OVNTR	FBG	SV	IO			10					**	**
45		SKIPJACK 35	KTH	SA/CR	FBG	KC	IB	30D		11	10	12000	2	4	55000	60500

....For earlier years, see the BUC Used Boat Price Guide, Volume 3

KEYS KRAFT BOATS

MARATHON FL 33050 COAST GUARD MFG ID- KEK See inside cover to adjust price for area

LOA FT	LOA IN	NAME AND/ OR MODEL	TOP/ RIG	BOAT TYPE	HULL MTL	HULL TP	ENGINE TP	# HP	MFG	BEAM FT	BEAM IN	WGT LBS	DRAFT FT	DRAFT IN	RETAIL LOW	RETAIL HIGH
		1993 BOATS														
27		OPEN FISHERMAN	OP	FSH	FBG	SV	IB	250D		10		6500	3	3	20200	23000
		1992 BOATS														
27		FISHERMAN	ST	CTRCN	FBG	SV	IB	250D	CUM	10		6500	2	10	19300	21400
27		FISHERMAN	HT	CUD	FBG	SV	IB	225D	CUM	10		6500	2	10	19000	21100
		1991 BOATS														
27		FISHERMAN	ST	CTRCN	FBG	SV	OB					6500	2	10	22100	24500
27		FISHERMAN	ST	CUD	FBG	SV	OB					6500	2	10	22100	24600

KHA SHING ENTERPRISES

KAOHSIUNG TAIWAN See inside cover to adjust price for area

LOA FT	LOA IN	NAME AND/ OR MODEL	TOP/ RIG	BOAT TYPE	HULL MTL	HULL TP	ENGINE TP	# HP	MFG	BEAM FT	BEAM IN	WGT LBS	DRAFT FT	DRAFT IN	RETAIL LOW	RETAIL HIGH
		1986 BOATS														
49		KAUFMAN 49	CUT	SARAC	FBG	KL	IB	70D	YAN	13	9		7		158500	174500

KINGS CRAFT INC

FLORENCE AL 35630 COAST GUARD MFG ID- KCR See inside cover to adjust price for area

LOA FT	LOA IN	NAME AND/ OR MODEL	TOP/ RIG	BOAT TYPE	HULL MTL	HULL TP	ENGINE TP	# HP	MFG	BEAM FT	BEAM IN	WGT LBS	DRAFT FT	DRAFT IN	RETAIL LOW	RETAIL HIGH
		1987 BOATS														
35		KINGS-CRAFT HOMECRUI	HT	HB	AL	SV	IB	225		12		8000			25000	27800
36		KINGS-CRAFT SALON		CR	AL	SV	IB	T215D		13		12000			55600	61100
40		KINGS-CRAFT HOMECRUI	HT	HB	AL	SV	IB	225		12		10500			27900	31000
44		KINGS-CRAFT HOMECRUI	HT	HB	AL	SV	IB	T225		15		14000			36800	40900
45		KINGS-CRAFT SALON		CR	AL	SV	IB	T235D		15		16000			99100	109000
52		KINGS-CRAFT SALON		CR	AL	SV	IB	T300D		16		20000			137000	150500
55		KINGS-CRAFT HOMECRUI	HT	HB	AL	SV	IB	T225		15		18500			56300	61800
60		KINGS-CRAFT HOMECRUI	HT	HB	AL	SV	IB	T250		15		20500			59900	65800
		1986 BOATS														
35		KINGS-CRAFT HOMECRUI	HT	HB	AL	SV	IB	225		12		8000			24400	27100
36		KINGS-CRAFT SALON		CR	AL	SV	IB	T215D		13		12000			52900	58200
40		KINGS-CRAFT HOMECRUI	HT	HB	AL	SV	IB	225		12		10500			27200	30200
45		KINGS-CRAFT SALON		CR	AL	SV	IB	T235D		15		16000			94300	103500
52		KINGS-CRAFT SALON		CR	AL	SV	IB	T300D		16		20000			132000	145000
55		KINGS-CRAFT HOMECRUI	HT	HB	AL	SV	IB	T225		15		18500			54900	60300
60		KINGS-CRAFT HOMECRUI	HT	HB	AL	SV	IB	T250		15		20500			58000	63700
		1985 BOATS														
35		KINGS-CRAFT HOMECRUI	HT	HB	AL	SV	IB	225		12		8000	2	6	23900	26500
36		KINGS-CRAFT SALON		CR	AL	SV	IB	T215D		13		12000			50500	55500
40		KINGS-CRAFT HOMECRUI	HT	HB	AL	SV	IB	225		12		10500	2	7	26500	29500
44		KINGS-CRAFT HOMECRUI	HT	HB	AL	SV	IB	T225		15		14000	2	8	35000	38900
45		KINGS-CRAFT SALON		CR	AL	SV	IB	T235D		15		16000			89800	98600
52		KINGS-CRAFT SALON		CR	AL	SV	IB	T300D		16		20000			127000	139500
55		KINGS-CRAFT HOMECRUI	HT	HB	AL	SV	IB	T225		15		18500	2	10	53700	59000

....For earlier years, see the BUC Used Boat Price Guide, Volume 3

KIRIE
LES SABLES D'OLONNE CEDEX

See inside cover to adjust price for area

For more recent years, see the BUC Used Boat Price Guide, Volume 1

LOA FT IN	NAME AND/OR MODEL	TOP/RIG	BOAT TYPE	HULL MTL	HULL TP	ENG TP	ENG #	HP	MFG	BEAM FT IN	WGT LBS	DRAFT FT IN	RETAIL LOW	RETAIL HIGH
								1996 BOATS						
28 4	FEELING 29 DI	SLP	SACAC	FBG	SK	IB		18D	YAN	10 2	7716	2 3	44200	49100
29 6	FEELING 286 DEEP	SLP	SACAC	FBG	KL	IB		18D	YAN	10	6393	5 6	37400	41600
29 7	FEELING 286 SHOAL	SLP	SACAC	FBG	KL	IB		18D	YAN	10	6613	3 8	38700	43000
32	FEELING 326 DEEP	SLP	SACAC	FBG	KL	IB		27D	YAN	11 1	8047	5 3	48700	53500
32	FEELING 326 DI	SLP	SACAC	FBG	SK	IB		27D	YAN	11 1	8378	2 1	50800	55800
32	FEELING 326 SHOAL	SLP	SACAC	FBG	KL	IB		27D	YAN	11 1	8400	4 3	50800	55800
34 1	FEELING 346 DEEP	SLP	SACAC	FBG	KL	IB		27D	YAN	11 4	9700	6 1	58300	64000
34 1	FEELING 346 DI	SLP	SACAC	FBG	SK	IB		27D	YAN	11 4	10803	2 4	64800	71200
34 1	FEELING 346 SHOAL	SLP	SACAC	FBG	KL	IB		27D	YAN	11 4	10900	4 4	65300	71800
36 5	FEELING 1090 DEEP	SLP	SACAC	FBG	KL	IB		27D	YAN	11 4	11905	5 9	72600	79700
36 5	FEELING 1090 SHOAL	SLP	SACAC	FBG	KL	IB		27D	YAN	11 1	12235	4 6	74400	81700
38 6	FEELING 396 DEEP	SLP	SACAC	FBG	KL	IB		38D	YAN	12 6	15470	5 11	93700	103000
38 6	FEELING 396 DI	SLP	SACAC	FBG	SK	IB		38D	YAN	12 6	17680	7 4	104500	115000
41 3	FEELING 416 DEEP	SLP	SACAC	FBG	KL	IB		50D	YAN	13 8	16535	6 4	110500	121500
41 3	FEELING 416 DI	SLP	SACAC	FBG	SK	IB		50D	YAN	13 8	18519	2 6	119000	131000
47 6	FEELING 486 DEEP	SLP	SACAC	FBG	KL	IB		62D	YAN	14 6	22000	6 7	161500	177500
47 6	FEELING 486 SHOAL	SLP	SACAC	FBG	KL	IB		62D	YAN	14 6	22220	5 3	162000	178000
55 5	FEELING 546 DEEP	SLP	SACAC	FBG	KL	IB		110D	YAN	17 1	39683	8 8	325000	357000
55 5	FEELING 546 SHOAL	SLP	SACAC	FBG	KL	IB		110D	YAN	17 1	39683	6 7	325000	357000

KLAMATH BOAT CO INC
VALLEJO CA 94592

COAST GUARD MFG ID- KLO See inside cover to adjust price for area
FORMERLY TRAILORBOAT CO

For more recent years, see the BUC Used Boat Price Guide, Volume 1

LOA FT IN	NAME AND/OR MODEL	TOP/RIG	BOAT TYPE	HULL MTL	HULL TP	ENG TP	HP	MFG	BEAM FT IN	WGT LBS	DRAFT FT IN	RETAIL LOW	RETAIL HIGH
							1996 BOATS						
16 1	KLAMATH ALASKAN	OP	UTL	AL	SV	OB			6 5	460		1300	1500
16 1	KLAMATH EXPLORER	OP	FSH	AL	SV	OB			6 5	460		1300	1550
17	XL-17	OP	FSH	AL	SV	OB			6 8	700		2050	2450
18 1	KLAMATH OFFSHORE	OP	FSH	AL	SV	OB			7	495		1500	1800
18 1	KLAMATH OFFSHORE S	OP	FSH	AL	SV	OB			7	510		1650	1950
18 1	KLAMATH OPEN	OP	FSH	AL	SV	OB			7	590		1800	2150
19 11	KT-200	OP	FSH	AL	SV	OB			7 2	785		2500	2950
							1995 BOATS						
16 1	KLAMATH ALASKAN	OP	UTL	AL	SV	OB			6 5	460		1200	1450
16 1	KLAMATH EXPLORER	OP	FSH	AL	SV	OB			6 5	460		1250	1450
16 1	KLAMATH OPEN	OP	FSH	AL	SV	OB			6 5	585		1550	1850
17	XL-17	OP	FSH	AL	SV	OB			6 8	700		1950	2300
18 1	KLAMATH OFFSHORE	OP	FSH	AL	SV	OB			7	495		1400	1700
18 1	KLAMATH OPEN	OP	FSH	AL	SV	OB			7	510		1550	1850
18 1	KLAMATH OPEN	OP	FSH	AL	SV	OB			7	590		1700	2050
19 11	KT-200	OP	FSH	AL	SV	OB			7 2	785		2450	2850
							1994 BOATS						
16 1	KLAMATH ALASKAN	OP	UTL	AL	SV	OB			6 5	335		840	1000
16 1	KLAMATH OPEN	OP	FSH	AL	SV	OB			6 5	370		950	1150
17	XL-17	OP	FSH	AL	SV	OB			6 8	700		1850	2200
18 1	KLAMATH OFFSHORE	OP	FSH	AL	SV	OB			7	450		1200	1450
18 1	KLAMATH OFFSHORE S	OP	FSH	AL	SV	OB			7	450		1300	1550
18 1	KLAMATH OPEN	OP	FSH	AL	SV	OB			7	525		1450	1750
19 11	KT-200	OP	FSH	AL	SV	OB			7 2	785		2300	2700
							1993 BOATS						
16 1	KLAMATH ALASKAN	OP	UTL	AL	SV	OB			6 5	335		790	950
16 1	KLAMATH OPEN	OP	FSH	AL	SV	OB			6 5	370		900	1050
17	XL-17	OP	FSH	AL	SV	OB			6 8	700		1750	2050
18 1	KLAMATH OFFSHORE	OP	FSH	AL	SV	OB			7	450		1150	1350
18 1	KLAMATH OFFSHORE S	OP	FSH	AL	SV	OB			7	450		1300	1500
18 1	KLAMATH OPEN	OP	FSH	AL	SV	OB			7	450		1400	1650
19 11	KT-200	OP	FSH	AL	SV	OB			7 2	785		2200	2550
							1992 BOATS						
16 1	KLAMATH ALASKAN	OP	UTL	AL	SV	OB			6 5	335		750	905
16 1	KLAMATH OPEN	OP	FSH	AL	SV	OB			6 5	370		855	1000
17	XL-17	OP	FSH	AL	SV	OB			6 8	700		1650	1950
18 1	KLAMATH OFFSHORE	OP	FSH	AL	SV	OB			7	450		1100	1300
18 1	KLAMATH OFFSHORE S	OP	FSH	AL	SV	OB			7	450		1200	1450
18 1	KLAMATH OPEN	OP	FSH	AL	SV	OB			7	525		1300	1600
19 11	KT-200	OP	FSH	AL	SV	OB			7 2	785		2050	2400
							1991 BOATS						
16 1	KLAMATH ALASKAN	OP	UTL	AL	SV	OB			6 5	335		720	865
18 1	KLAMATH OFFSHORE	OP	FSH	AL	SV	OB			7	450		805	970
18 1	KLAMATH OFFSHORE S	OP	FSH	AL	SV	OB			7	450		1050	1250
18 1	KLAMATH OPEN	OP	FSH	AL	SV	OB			7	525		1250	1500
							1990 BOATS						
16 1	KLAMATH ALASKAN	OP	UTL	AL	SV	OB			6 5	335		685	825
16 1	KLAMATH OPEN	OP	FSH	AL	SV	OB			6 5	370		770	930
18 1	KLAMATH OFFSHORE	OP	FSH	AL	SV	OB			7	450		995	1200
18 1	KLAMATH OFFSHORE S	OP	FSH	AL	SV	OB			7	450		1100	1300
18 1	KLAMATH OPEN	OP	FSH	AL	SV	OB			7	525		1200	1450
							1989 BOATS						
16 1	KLAMATH ALASKAN		UTL	AL	SV	OB			6 5	335		655	790
16 1	KLAMATH OPEN		FSH	AL	SV	OB			6 5	370		740	890
18 1	KLAMATH OFFSHORE		FSH	AL	SV	OB			7	450		965	1150
18 1	KLAMATH OFFSHORE S		FSH	AL	SV	OB			7	450		1050	1250
18 1	KLAMATH OPEN		FSH	AL	SV	OB			7	525		1150	1400
							1988 BOATS						
16 1	KLAMATH ALASKAN		UTL	AL	SV	OB			6 5	335		630	760
16 1	KLAMATH OPEN		FSH	AL	SV	OB			6 5	370		710	855
18 1	KLAMATH OFFSHORE		FSH	AL	SV	OB			7	450		975	1150
18 1	KLAMATH OPEN		FSH	AL	SV	OB			7	525		1100	1300
							1987 BOATS						
16 1	KALMATH OPEN		FSH	AL	SV	OB			6 9	370		685	825
16 1	KLAMATH ALASKAN		UTL	AL	SV	OB			6 9	335		610	735
18 1	KLAMATH OFFSHORE		FSH	AL	SV	OB			7	450		940	1100
18 1	KLAMATH OPEN		FSH	AL	SV	OB			7	525		1050	1300
							1985 BOATS						
16 1	KLAMATH DELUXE		UTL	AL	SV	OB			6 9	335		570	685
18	TRAILORBOAT OFFSHORE		FSH	AL	SV	OB			7	450		870	1050
							1984 BOATS						
16 1	KLAMATH DELUXE	OP	UTL	AL	SV	OB			6 9	335		550	665

....For earlier years, see the BUC Used Boat Price Guide, Volume 3

HANS KLEPPER CORP
NEW YORK NY 10003

COAST GUARD MFG ID- HNK See inside cover to adjust price for area

LOA FT IN	NAME AND/OR MODEL	TOP/RIG	BOAT TYPE	HULL MTL	HULL TP	BEAM FT IN	WGT LBS	RETAIL LOW	RETAIL HIGH
					1984 BOATS				
16	MISSOURI	SLP	KAYAK	FBG	LB	2 7	88	**	**
17 1	AERIUS II FOLDING	SLP	KAYAK	WD	LB	2 10	90	1200	1400

....For earlier years, see the BUC Used Boat Price Guide, Volume 3

KMV BOATS LTD
NEW LOWELL CANADA L0M 1N0

See inside cover to adjust price for area

LOA FT IN	NAME AND/OR MODEL	BOAT TYPE	HULL TP	ENG TP	BEAM FT IN	WGT LBS	RETAIL LOW	RETAIL HIGH
				1987 BOATS				
17 4	KMV 1700	CAMPR	SV	OB	6 8	902	2600	3050
17 4	KMV 528			OB	6 8	860	2500	2900
				1986 BOATS				
17 4	1700	CAMPR	SV	OB	6 8	902	2550	2950
17 4	528	CTRCN	SV	OB	6 8	860	2450	2850

KNOWLES BOATS
STUART FL 34997-6523

See inside cover to adjust price for area

LOA FT IN	NAME AND/OR MODEL	TOP/RIG	BOAT TYPE	HULL MTL	HULL TP	ENG TP	HP	MFG	BEAM FT IN	WGT LBS	DRAFT FT IN	RETAIL LOW	RETAIL HIGH
							1994 BOATS						
37 6	SPORT FISHERMAN	SF		FBG	SV	IB	T300D	CUM	12 2	12000	3 2	229500	252500
37 6	SPORT FISHERMAN WA	SF		FBG	SV	IB	T300D	CUM	12 2	12000	3 2	229500	252500
							1993 BOATS						
37 6	SPORT FISHERMAN	SF		FBG	SV	IB	T300D	CUM	12 2	12000	3 2	219000	240500

....For earlier years, see the BUC Used Boat Price Guide, Volume 3

KORHONEN VENEVEISTAMO T
VARKAUS 85 FINLAND

See inside cover to adjust price for area

LOA FT IN	NAME AND/ OR MODEL	TOP/ RIG	BOAT TYPE	-HULL- MTL TP	----ENGINE--- TP # HP MFG	BEAM FT IN	WGT LBS	DRAFT FT IN	RETAIL LOW	RETAIL HIGH
			1985 BOATS							
28 5	TRISTAN 870	CR	FBG	IB		9 6	6800		**	**
29 6	TRISTAN 301	CR	FBG	IB		9 8	9680		**	**

KUKJI AMERICA CORP
LARSEN YACHTS
ANNAPOLIS MD 21404

See inside cover to adjust price for area

LOA FT IN	NAME AND/ OR MODEL	TOP/ RIG	BOAT TYPE	-HULL- MTL TP	----ENGINE--- TP # HP MFG	BEAM FT IN	WGT LBS	DRAFT FT IN	RETAIL LOW	RETAIL HIGH
			1986 BOATS							
33	SWIFT AC	SLP	SA/CR FBG KL	IB	D	11 3	14720	5 3	42500	47200
36	SWIFT CC	KTH	SA/CR FBG KL	IB	D	11 9	19000	5 7	56200	61800
40	SWIFT CC	KTH	SA/CR FBG SK	IB	D	13 4	24300	5 3	78200	86000
			1985 BOATS							
33	SWIFT AC	SLP	SA/CR FBG KL	IB	D	11 3	14720	5 3	40000	44400
36	SWIFT CC	KTH	SA/CR FBG KL	IB	D	11 9	19000	5 7	52900	58100
40	SWIFT CC	KTH	SA/CR FBG SK	IB	D	13 4	24300	5 3	73600	80900

L & M MANUFACTURING CO INC
MARYSVILLE WA 98270

COAST GUARD MFG ID- LMM See inside cover to adjust price for area

LOA FT IN	NAME AND/ OR MODEL	TOP/ RIG	BOAT TYPE	-HULL- MTL TP	----ENGINE--- TP # HP MFG	BEAM FT IN	WGT LBS	DRAFT FT IN	RETAIL LOW	RETAIL HIGH
			1984 BOATS							
16 9	170B	OP	BASS	FBG SV	OB	6 3	1175		3200	3700
16 9	P170	OP	CTRCN	FBG SV	OB	6 3	1100		3000	3500
16 9	S170	OP	LNCH	FBG SV	OB	6 3	1025		**	**
17 6	P180	OP	CTRCN	FBG SV	OB	7	1275		3450	4050

L B I INC
GROTON CT 06340

COAST GUARD MFG ID- LBK See inside cover to adjust price for area

LOA FT IN	NAME AND/ OR MODEL	TOP/ RIG	BOAT TYPE	-HULL- MTL TP	----ENGINE--- TP # HP MFG	BEAM FT IN	WGT LBS	DRAFT FT IN	RETAIL LOW	RETAIL HIGH
			1987 BOATS							
20	MYSTIC 20	SLP	SA/CR FBG CB	IB	D	18 6	3000	2 1	11200	12800
33 8	MYSTIC 30	CUT	SA/CR FBG KL	IB	D	10 3	9500	4 4	39900	44300
35	LEGNOS L35C	FSH	F/S SV	IB	200	12	12500		55000	60500
35	LEGNOS L35S	SF	F/S SV	IB	200	12	12500		55300	60800
			1986 BOATS							
20	MYSTIC 20	CAT	SA/CR FBG CB			8	3000	4 3	7750	8950
33	MYSTIC 30	CUT	SA/CR FBC KL	IB	D	10 3	9500	4 4	37300	41500
			1985 BOATS							
20 3	MYSTIC 20	CAT	SA/CR FBG CB	IB	7D BMW	8	3000	4 3	9400	10700
20 3	MYSTIC 20	SLP	SA/CR FBG CB	IB	7D BMW	8	3000	4 3	9400	10700
33 5	MYSTIC 10-3	CUT	SA/CR FBG KL	IB	13D VLVO	10 3	9000	4 4	32700	36300
33 8	MYSTIC 30	CUT	SA/CR FBG KL	IB	15D YAN	10 3	9500	4 4	34700	38600
35	FISHERMAN 35	FB	SF	F/S SV	IB	300D VLVO	12	12800	3	61000	67000
35	FISHERMAN 35	FB	SF	F/S SV	IB	T215D GM	12	13500	3	67000	73600

....For earlier years, see the BUC Used Boat Price Guide, Volume 3

LA FITTE YACHTS INC
ANNAPOLIS MD 21403

COAST GUARD MFG ID- PKE See inside cover to adjust price for area

LA FITTE YACHTS INC
NEWPORTBCH CA 92663

FORMERLY PACIFIC FAR EAST INDUSTRIES

LOA FT IN	NAME AND/ OR MODEL	TOP/ RIG	BOAT TYPE	-HULL- MTL TP	----ENGINE--- TP # HP MFG	BEAM FT IN	WGT LBS	DRAFT FT IN	RETAIL LOW	RETAIL HIGH
			1986 BOATS							
44 4	LAFITTE 44	CUT	SA/CR FBG KL	IB	D	12 8	28000	6 4	132500	145500
44 4	LAFITTE 44	CUT	SA/CR FBG KL	IB	60D PERK	12 8	28000	6 4	132000	145000
66	LAFITTE 66	KTH	SA/CR FBG KL	IB	D	16 4	67000	6 9	452000	496500
			1985 BOATS							
44 4	LAFITTE 44	CUT	SA/CR FBG KL	IB	60D PERK	12 8	28000	6 4	124000	136000
44 4	LAFITTE 44	CUT	SA/CR FBG KL	IB	62D PERK	12 8	28000	6 4	124000	136000
66	LAFITTE 66	KTH	SA/CR FBG KL	IB	135D PERK	16 4	67000	6 9	423000	465000
			1984 BOATS							
44 4	LAFITTE 44	CUT	SA/CR FBG KL	IB	60D PERK	12 8	28000	6 4	116500	128000

....For earlier years, see the BUC Used Boat Price Guide, Volume 3

LA PIERRE INTL YACHTS
VANCOUVER BC CANADA

See inside cover to adjust price for area

LOA FT IN	NAME AND/ OR MODEL	TOP/ RIG	BOAT TYPE	-HULL- MTL TP	----ENGINE--- TP # HP MFG	BEAM FT IN	WGT LBS	DRAFT FT IN	RETAIL LOW	RETAIL HIGH
			1987 BOATS							
39 11	CREALA 40	CUT	SA/CR FBG KL	IB	44D YAN	12	24000		100000	110000
			1985 BOATS							
35 11	CREALA 36	CUT	SA/CR FBG KL	IB	33D YAN	11 2	18800	5 9	65800	72300

LACE YACHTS
FT LAUDERDALE FL 33315

FORMERLY REX LACE

See inside cover to adjust price for area

For more recent years, see the BUC Used Boat Price Guide, Volume 1

LOA FT IN	NAME AND/ OR MODEL	TOP/ RIG	BOAT TYPE	-HULL- MTL TP	----ENGINE--- TP # HP MFG	BEAM FT IN	WGT LBS	DRAFT FT IN	RETAIL LOW	RETAIL HIGH
			1994 BOATS							
40 3	LACE 40	FB	MY	FBG SV	IB	300D CUM	13 6	23500	3 8	151500	166500
55 6	LACE 556 MY	FB	MY	FBG SV	IB	465D DD	17 6	62500	3 8	352000	386500
60	LACE 60 CMY	FB	MY	FBG SV	IB	465D DD	17 6	65600	3 8	414000	454500
64 2	LACE 58/63	FB	MY	FBG SV	IB	425D CAT	17	65000	3 9	543000	596500
73 6	LACE 73	FB	MY	FBG SV	IB	550D DD	20 6	75000	3 9	**	**
73 6	LACE 73 CMY	FB	MY	FBG SV	IB	550D DD	20 6	75000	3 9	**	**
76	LACE 76 SF	FB	SF	FBG SV	IB	14CD DD	20 6	77000	3 9	**	**
			1993 BOATS							
40 3	LACE 40	FB	MY	FBG SV	IB	300D CUM	13 6	23500	3 8	144000	158500
55 6	LACE 556 MY	FB	MY	FBG SV	IB	465D DD	17 6	62500	3 8	335000	368500
60	LACE 60 CMY	FB	MY	FBG SV	IB	465D DD	17 6	65600	3 8	395500	434500
64 2	LACE 58/63	FB	MY	FBG SV	IB	425D CAT	17	65000	3 9	519000	570500
73 6	LACE 73	FB	MY	FBG SV	IB	550D DD	20 6	75000	3 9	**	**
73 6	LACE 73 CMY	FB	MY	FBG SV	IB	550D DD	20 6	75000	3 9	**	**
76	LACE 76 SF	FB	SF	FBG SV	IB	14CD DD	20 6	77000	3 9	**	**
			1990 BOATS							
44	MIDNIGHT LACE 44		EXP	FBG DS	IB	T260D J&T	11	15900	2 10	138000	152000
44	MIDNIGHT LACE 44	FB	EXP	FBG DS	IB	T260D J&T	11	15900	2 10	138500	152500
52	MIDNIGHT LACE 52		EXP	FBG DS	IB	T260D	13	19850	3	201500	221000
52 6	MIDNIGHT LACE 52	FB	EXP	FBG DS	IB	T260D	13	19850	3	202500	222500
			1989 BOATS							
44	MIDNIGHT LACE 44		EXP	FBG DS	IB	T260D J&T	11	15900	2 10	132000	145000
44	MIDNIGHT LACE 44	FB	EXP	FBG DS	IB	T260D J&T	11	15900	2 10	132500	145500
52	MIDNIGHT LACE 52		EXP	FBG DS	IB	T260D	13	19850	3	192500	211500
52 6	MIDNIGHT LACE 52	FB	EXP	FBG DS	IB	T260D	13	19850	3	193500	212500
			1988 BOATS							
37 5	MIDNIGHT LACE 37		EXP	FBG DS	IB	T220D J&T	13 3	16000	3 2	81800	89900
37 5	MIDNIGHT LACE 37	FB	EXP	FBG DS	IB	T220D J&T	13 3	16000	3 2	81900	90000
44	MIDNIGHT LACE 44		EXP	FBG DS	IB	T220D	11	15900	2 10	121500	133500
44	MIDNIGHT LACE 44	FB	EXP	FBG DS	IB	T220D	11	15900	2 10	122000	134000
52	MIDNIGHT LACE 52		EXP	FBG DS	IB	T260D	13	19850	3	184000	202000
52 6	MIDNIGHT LACE 52	FB	EXP	FBG DS	IB	T260D	13	19850	3	185000	203000
65 4	MIDNIGHT LACE 66	FB	EXP	FBG DS	IB	T375D CAT	18 6	48000	4 2	457500	503000
			1987 BOATS							
37 5	MIDNIGHT LACE 37	HT	EXP	FBG DS	IB	T220D J&T	13 3	16000	3 2	78200	86000
37 5	MIDNIGHT LACE 37	FB	EXP	FBG DS	IB	T220D J&T	13 3	16000	3 2	78300	86100
44	MIDNIGHT LACE 44	HT	EXP	FBG DS	IB	T220D	11	15900	2 10	117000	128500
44	MIDNIGHT LACE 44	FB	EXP	FBG DS	IB	T220D	11	15900	2 10	121000	133000
44	MIDNIGHT LACE 44	HT	EXP	FBG DS	IB	T220D	11	15900	2 10	116500	128000
44	MIDNIGHT LACE 44	FB	EXP	FBG DS	IB	T260D	11	15900	2 10	120500	132500
52	MIDNIGHT LACE 52	HT	EXP	FBG DS	IB	T260D	13	19850	3	178500	196000
52 6	MIDNIGHT LACE 52	FB	EXP	FBG DS	IB	T260D	13	19850	3	177000	194500
65 4	MIDNIGHT LACE 66	FB	EXP	FBG DS	IB	T375D CAT	18 6	48000	4 2	438500	481500
			1986 BOATS							
44	MIDNIGHT-LACE 44	HT	EXP	F/S SV	IB	T250D J&T	11	15400	2 10	112000	123000
44	MIDNIGHT-LACE 44	FB	EXP	F/S SV	IB	T250D J&T	11	15400	2 10	147000	161500
52	MIDNIGHT-LACE 52	HT	EXP	F/S SV	IB	T220D J&T	13 2	19850	3	168000	185000
52 6	MIDNIGHT-LACE 52	FB	EXP	F/S SV	IB	T220D J&T	13 2	19850	3	166500	183000
65 4	MIDNIGHT-LACE 66	FB	EXP	F/S SV	IB	T550D J&T	17 6	40000	2 9	418500	460000
			1985 BOATS							
36	MIDNIGHT-LACE 36		EXP	FBG DS	IB	T D	11			**	**
44	MIDNIGHT-LACE 44		EXP	FBG DS	IB	T210D	11	15400		102000	112000
44	MIDNIGHT-LACE 44	HT	EXP	FBG DS	IB	T250D J&T	11	15400	2 10	107000	118000
44	MIDNIGHT-LACE 44		EXP	FBG DS	IB	T220D	11	15400		103500	114000
44	MIDNIGHT-LACE 44	FB	EXP	F/S SV	IB	T250D J&T	11	15900	2 10	140500	154500

96th ed. - Vol. II

CONTINUED ON NEXT PAGE

LOA FT IN	NAME AND/ OR MODEL	TOP/ RIG	BOAT TYPE	-HULL- MTL TP	TP	-ENGINE- # HP	MFG	BEAM FT IN	WGT LBS	DRAFT FT IN	RETAIL LOW	RETAIL HIGH
			------ 1985 **BOATS**									
52 6	MIDNIGHT-LACE 52	HT	EXP	F/S SV	IB	T250D	J&T	13 2	19850	3	167500	184000
52 6	MIDNIGHT-LACE 52	FB	EXP	F/S SV	IB	T250D	J&T	13 2	20950	3	166000	182500
			------ 1984 **BOATS**									
44	MIDNIGHT-LACE 44	HT	EXP	F/S SV	IB	T250D	J&T	11	15400	2 10	102500	113000
44	MIDNIGHT-LACE 44	FB	EXP	F/S SV	IB	T250D	J&T	11	15400	2 10	102000	112500
52	MIDNIGHT-LACE 52	HT	EXP	F/S SV	IB	T250D	J&T	13 2	19850	3	160500	176500
52 6	MIDNIGHT-LACE 52	FB	EXP	F/S SV	IB	T250D	J&T	13 2	19850	3	159000	174500

TOM LACK CATAMARANS LTD
DORSET ENGLAND   COAST GUARD MFG ID- TLC See inside cover to adjust price for area

LOA FT IN	NAME AND/ OR MODEL	TOP/ RIG	BOAT TYPE	-HULL- MTL TP	TP	-ENGINE- # HP	MFG	BEAM FT IN	WGT LBS	DRAFT FT IN	RETAIL LOW	RETAIL HIGH
			---------- 1986 **BOATS**									
27	CATALAC 8M	SLP	SAIL	FBG CT	OB			13 6	6720	2 4	39400	43800
27	CATALAC 8M	SLP	SAIL	FBG CT	IB	T 9D	YAN	13 6	6800	2 4	40500	45000
29 3	CATALAC 9M MKII	SLP	SAIL	FBG CT	IB	T 9D	YAN	14	8960	2 6	55300	60700
34	CATALAC 10M	SLP	SAIL	FBG CT	IB	T 18D	YAN	15 3	12320	2 9	90300	99300
40 10	CATALAC 12M	SLP	SAIL	FBG CT	IB	T 34D	YAN	17 3	17920	3	158500	174000
			---------- 1985 **BOATS**									
27	CATALAC 8M	SLP	SAIL	FBG CT	OB			13 6	6720	2 4	37000	41100
27	CATALAC 8M	SLP	SAIL	FBG CT	IB	T 9D	YAN	13 6	6800	2 4	38000	42200
29 3	CATALAC 9M MKII	SLP	SAIL	FBG CT	IB	T 9D	YAN	14	8960	2 6	52000	57100
34	CATALAC 10M	SLP	SAIL	FBG CT	IB	T 18D	YAN	15 3	12320	2 9	85000	93400
40 10	CATALAC 12M	SLP	SAIL	FBG CT	IB	T 35D	YAN	17 3	17920	3	149000	164000
			---------- 1984 **BOATS**									
27 1	CATALAC 8M	SLP	SAIL	FBG CT	OB			13	6720	2 3	35100	39000
27	CATALAC 8M	SLP	SAIL	FBG CT	IB	T 8D	YAN	13	6800	2 3	36100	40100
29 3	CATALAC 9M MKII	SLP	SAIL	FBG CT	IB	T 8D	YAN	14	8960	2 6	48900	53700
40 10	CATALAC 12M	SLP	SAIL	FBG CT	IB	T 30D	YAN	17 3	17920	3	140000	154000

....For earlier years, see the BUC Used Boat Price Guide, Volume 3

LAGER YACHTS INC
PORT WASHINGTON NY 11050   See inside cover to adjust price for area

For more recent years, see the BUC Used Boat Price Guide, Volume 1

LOA FT IN	NAME AND/ OR MODEL	TOP/ RIG	BOAT TYPE	-HULL- MTL TP	TP	-ENGINE- # HP	MFG	BEAM FT IN	WGT LBS	DRAFT FT IN	RETAIL LOW	RETAIL HIGH
			---------- 1996 **BOATS**									
45 3	LAGER 45 STD	SLP	SACAC	F/S KL	IB	D		13 6	18900	5 2	208500	229000
45 3	LAGER 45 WING	SLP	SACAC	F/S WK	IB	D		13 6	18900	7 2	208500	229000
60 8	LAGER 60 STD	SLP	SACAC	F/S KL	IB	140D	YAN	16 6	50000	9 8	753500	828000
60 8	LAGER 60 WING	SLP	SACAC	F/S WK	IB	140D	YAN	16 6	50000	8	753500	828000
65 9	LAGER 65 STD	SLP	SACAC	F/S KL	IB	140D	YAN	17 3	57500	10 5	835000	917500
65 9	LAGER 65 WING	SLP	SACAC	F/S WK	IB	140D	YAN	17 3	57500	6 10	835000	917500
76	LAGER 76 DEEP	SLP	SACAC	F/S KL	IB	175D	YAN	19 2	72000	11	**	**
76	LAGER 76 STD	SLP	SACAC	F/S KL	IB	175D	YAN	19 2	72000	8 6	**	**
			---------- 1995 **BOATS**									
44 11	LAGER 44	SLP	SACAC	F/S KL	IB	66D	YAN	13 4	21500	6	204500	225000
49 7	LAGER 49	SLP	SACAC	F/S KL	IB	77D	YAN	14 4	31000	6	295000	324500
52 6	LAGER 53	SLP	SACAC	F/S KL	IB	110D	YAN	15 6	36000	7	385000	423000
60 9	LAGER 60	SLP	SACAC	F/S KL	IB	140D	YAN	17 3	50000	8	710000	780000
65 9	LAGER 65	SLP	SACAC	F/S KL	IB	140D	YAN	17 3	57500	8	785000	862500
76	LAGER 75	SLP	SACAC	F/S KL	IB	200D	YAN	19 2	72000	8 6	**	**
			---------- 1994 **BOATS**									
44 11	LAGER 44	SLP	SACAC	F/S KL	IB	66D	YAN	13 4	21500	6	192500	211500
49 7	LAGER 49	SLP	SACAC	F/S KL	IB	75D	YAN	14 4	31000	6	276500	303500
52 6	LAGER 53	SLP	SACIS	F/S KL	IB	110D	YAN	15 6	36000	7	361000	396500
60 9	LAGER 60	SLP	SACAC	F/S KL	IB	140D	YAN	17 3	50000	8	667500	733500
65 9	LAGER 65	SLP	SACIS	F/S KL	IB	170D	YAN	17 3	57900	8	744000	817500
			---------- 1993 **BOATS**									
44 11	LAGER 44	SLP	SARAC	F/S KL	IB	55D	YAN	13 4	21500		180500	198500
48 9	LAGER 48	SLP	SARAC	F/S KL	IB	66D	YAN	14 4	27500		234500	257500
60	LAGER 60	SLP	SARAC	F/S KL	IB	140D	YAN	16 6	50000		617000	678000
65 9	LAGER 65	SLP	SARAC	F/S KL	IB	140D	YAN	17 3	57500		693500	762500

LAGUNA YACHTS INC
STANTON CA 90680   COAST GUARD MFG ID- LAY See inside cover to adjust price for area

LOA FT IN	NAME AND/ OR MODEL	TOP/ RIG	BOAT TYPE	-HULL- MTL TP	TP	-ENGINE- # HP	MFG	BEAM FT IN	WGT LBS	DRAFT FT IN	RETAIL LOW	RETAIL HIGH
			---------- 1987 **BOATS**									
23 7	LAGUNA 24	SLP	SA/CR	FBG SK				8 4	2600	2 11	4950	5700
25 9	LAGUNA 26	SLP	SA/CR	FBG SK				8 4	3900	3 1	7450	8600
30	LAGUNA 30	SLP	SA/CR	FBG SK				10 8	9040	4	19800	22000
32 8	LAGUNA 33	SLP	SA/CR	FBG SK				10 8	9400	4	19600	21800
			---------- 1986 **BOATS**									
16	LAGUNA 16	SLP	SAIL	FBG KL	OB			7 5	1000	2 5	2100	2500
18	LAGUNA 18	SLP	SAIL	FBG KL	OB			8	1500	2 3	2900	3400
18	LAGUNA 18 DAYSAILOR	SLP	SAIL	FBG KL	OB			8	1500	2 3	2450	3850
18	LAGUNA DAYSAILOR	SLP	SAIL	FBG KL	OB			8	1400	2 3	2600	3000
21 7	LAGUNA 22	SLP	SAIL	FBG KL	OB			8	2280	2 11	3850	4450
21 7	LAGUNA 22S	SLP	SAIL	FBG KL	OB			8	2280	2 11	3850	4450
23 7	LAGUNA 24	SLP	SA/CR	FBG KL	OB			8 4	2600	2 11	4700	5350
23 7	LAGUNA 24S	SLP	SA/CR	FBG KL	OB			8 4	2800	2 11	4950	5650
25 9	LAGUNA 26	SLP	SA/CR	FBG KL	OB			8 4	3900	3 1	7200	8250
25 9	LAGUNA 26S	SLP	SA/CR	FBG KL	OB			8 4	3900	3 1	7200	8250
29 11	LAGUNA 30	SLP	SA/CR	FBG KL	IB	15D	YAN	10 8	9040	4	19200	21300
29 11	LAGUNA 30S	SLP	SAIL	FBG KL	IB	15D	YAN	10 8	8700	4	18400	20500
			---------- 1985 **BOATS**									
16	LAGUNA 16	SLP	SAIL	FBG KL	OB			7 5	1000	2 5	1950	2350
18	LAGUNA 18 SC	SLP	SAIL	FBG KL	OB			8	1500	2 3	2500	2950
18	LAGUNA DAYSAILER-S	SLP	SAIL	FBG KL	OB			8	1500	2 3	2250	2650
21 7	LAGUNA 22 SF	SLP	SAIL	FBG KL	OB			8	2280	2 11	3600	4200
21 7	LAGUNA 22 SR	SLP	SAIL	FBG KL	OB			8	2280	2 11	3600	4200
23 7	LAGUNA 24	SLP	SAIL	FBG KL	OB			8 4	2600	2 11	4400	5100
25 9	LAGUNA 26	SLP	SA/CR	FBG KL	OB			8 4	3900	3 1	6750	7750
25 9	LAGUNA 26	SLP	SA/CR	FBG KL	IB	10D	YAN	8 4	3900	3 1	7350	8450
29 11	LAGUNA 30	SLP	SA/CR	FBG KL	IB	15D	YAN	10 10	8700	4	17000	19300
			---------- 1984 **BOATS**									
16	LAGUNA 16	SLP	SAIL	FBG KL	OB			7 5	1000	2 5	1850	2200
18	LAGUNA 18 SC	SLP	SAIL	FBG KL	OB			8	1500	2 3	2350	2750
18	LAGUNA DAYSAILER-S	SLP	SAIL	FBG KL	OB			8	1200	2 3	2100	2500
21 7	LAGUNA 22 RF	SLP	SAIL	FBG SK	OB			8	1980	1 3	3000	3500
21 7	LAGUNA 22 RS	SLP	SAIL	FBG SK	OB			8	1980	1 3	3200	3750
21 7	LAGUNA 22 SF	SLP	SAIL	FBG KL	OB			8	2280	2 11	3400	3950
21 7	LAGUNA 22 SR	SLP	SAIL	FBG KL	OB			8	2280	2 11	3400	3950
23 7	LAGUNA 24	SLP	SAIL	FBG KL	OB			8 4	2600	2 11	4100	4800
25 9	LAGUNA 26	SLP	SA/CR	FBG KL	OB			8 4	3900	3 1	6350	7300
29 11	LAGUNA 30	SLP	SA/CR	FBG KL		D		10 10	8700	4	15500	17700

....For earlier years, see the BUC Used Boat Price Guide, Volume 3

LAKE RAIDER
CAMDENTON MO 65020   See inside cover to adjust price for area

For more recent years, see the BUC Used Boat Price Guide, Volume 1

LOA FT IN	NAME AND/ OR MODEL	TOP/ RIG	BOAT TYPE	-HULL- MTL TP	TP	-ENGINE- # HP	MFG	BEAM FT IN	WGT LBS	DRAFT FT IN	RETAIL LOW	RETAIL HIGH
			---------- 1996 **BOATS**									
16	JON 1656	OP	JON	AL FL	OB			4 8			1300	1500
16	JON 1670	OP	JON	AL FL	OB			5 10	275		1000	1200
16	JON 1670 OPEN	OP	JON	AL FL	OB			5 10	275		1100	1300
16	JON 1670 W/T	OP	JON	AL FL	OB			5 10	275		1100	1300
16	JON 1685	OP	JON	AL FL	OB			7 1	430		1550	1850
16	JON 1685 OPEN	OP	JON	AL FL	OB			7 1	430		1600	1950
17	BASS 1770	OP	BASS	AL FL	OB			5 10	645		2600	3000
18	JON 1870	OP	JON	AL FL	OB			5 10			1500	1800
18	JON 1870 OPEN	OP	JON	AL FL	OB			5 10			1600	1900
18	JON 1870 W/T	OP	JON	AL FL	OB			5 10			1600	1900
18	JON 1885	OP	JON	AL FL	OB			7 1	500		1550	1850
18	JON 1885 OPEN	OP	JON	AL FL	OB			7 1	500		1600	1900
			---------- 1995 **BOATS**									
16	JON 1656	OP	JON	AL FL	OB			4 8			1200	1450
16	JON 1670	OP	JON	AL FL	OB			5 10	275		975	1150
16	JON 1670 OPEN	OP	JON	AL FL	OB			5 10	275		1050	1250
16	JON 1670 W/T	OP	JON	AL FL	OB			5 10	275		1050	1250
16	JON 1685	OP	JON	AL FL	OB			7 1	430		1500	1750
16	JON 1685 OPEN	OP	JON	AL FL	OB			7 1	430		1550	1850
17	BASS 1770	OP	BASS	AL FL	OB			5 10	645		2500	2900
18	JON 1870	OP	JON	AL FL	OB			5 10			1400	1700
18	JON 1870 OPEN	OP	JON	AL FL	OB			5 10			1550	1850
18	JON 1870 W/T	OP	JON	AL FL	OB			5 10			1500	1800
18	JON 1885	OP	JON	AL FL	OB			7 1	500		1450	1750
18	JON 1885 OPEN	OP	JON	AL FL	OB			7 1	500		1500	1800

LAMINEX IND OF CANADA LTD
DUNCAN BC CANADA See inside cover to adjust price for area

LOA FT IN	NAME AND/ OR MODEL	TOP/ RIG	BOAT TYPE	-HULL- MTL TP	----ENGINE--- TP # HP MFG	BEAM FT IN	WGT LBS	DRAFT FT IN	RETAIL LOW	RETAIL HIGH
					1984 BOATS					
22	POCKET-ROCKET	SLP	SA/OD	FBG KL	OB	9 6	2400	5	6450	7400

....For earlier years, see the BUC Used Boat Price Guide, Volume 3

LANCER BOATS
ADEL GA 31620 COAST GUARD MFG ID- LNB See inside cover to adjust price for area

For more recent years, see the BUC Used Boat Price Guide, Volume 1

LOA FT IN	NAME AND/ OR MODEL	TOP/ RIG	BOAT TYPE	-HULL- MTL TP	----ENGINE--- TP # HP MFG	BEAM FT IN	WGT LBS	DRAFT FT IN	RETAIL LOW	RETAIL HIGH
					1996 BOATS					
16 10	KINGFISHER 1778 CTR	OP	CTRCN	FBG TR	OB	6 6	850		2050	2450
16 10	KINGFISHER 1778DBL	OP	OPFSH	FBG TR	OB	6 6	875		2150	2500
16 10	KINGFISHER 1778SGL	OP	OPFSH	FBG TR	OB	6 6	850		2050	2450
					1995 BOATS					
16 10	KINGFISHER 1778 CTR	OP	CTRCN	FBG TR	OB	6 6	850		1950	2350
16 10	KINGFISHER 1778DBL	OP	OPFSH	FBG TR	OB	6 6	875		2000	2400
16 10	KINGFISHER 1778SGL	OP	OPFSH	FBG TR	OB	6 6	850		1950	2350
					1994 BOATS					
16 10	KINGFISHER 1778	OP	CTRCN	FBG TR	OB	6 6	850		1900	2250
16 10	KINGFISHER 1778DBL	OP	OPFSH	FBG TR	OB	6 6	850		1950	2300
16 10	KINGFISHER 1778SGL	OP	OPFSH	FBG TR	OB	6 6	850		1900	2250
					1993 BOATS					
16 10	KINGFISHER 1778	OP	CTRCN	FBG TR	OB	6 6	850		1800	2150
16 10	KINGFISHER 1778DBL	OP	OPFSH	FBG TR	OB	6 6	850		1850	2200
16 10	KINGFISHER 1778SGL	OP	OPFSH	FBG TR	OB	6 6	850		1800	2150
					1992 BOATS					
16 8	BASS 1786	OP	BASS	FBG DV	OB	7 2	875		1750	2100
16 10	KINGFISHER 1778	OP	CTRCN	FBG TR	OB	6 6	875		1750	2050
16 10	KINGFISHER 1778CNSLE	OP	OPFSH	FBG TR	OB	6 6	850		1800	2100
					1991 BOATS					
16 8	BASS 1786	OP	BASS	FBG DV	OB	7 2	875		1700	2050
16 10	KINGFISHER 1778	OP	CTRCN	FBG TR	OB	6 6	850		1650	2000
16 10	KINGFISHER DBL CNSLE	OP	OPFSH	FBG TR	OB	6 6	875		1700	2050
					1990 BOATS					
16 8	BASS 1786	OP	BASS	FBG DV	OB	7 2	875		1650	1950
16 10	KINGFISHER 1778	OP	CTRCN	FBG TR	OB	6 6	850		1600	1900
16 10	KINGFISHER DBL CNSLE	OP	OPFSH	FBG TR	OB	6 6	875		1650	1950
					1989 BOATS					
16 8	BASS 1786	OP	BASS	FBG DV	OB	7 2	875		1600	1900
16 10	KINGFISHER 1778	OP	CTRCN	FBG TR	OB	6 6	850		1550	1850
16 10	KINGFISHER DBL CNSLE	OP	OPFSH	FBG TR	OB	6 6	875		1600	1900
					1988 BOATS					
16 10	KINGFISHER 1778	OP	CTRCN	FBG TR	OB	6 6	850		1500	1800
16 10	KINGFISHER DBL CNSLE	OP	OPFSH	FBG TR	OB	6 6	875		1550	1850
16 10	KINGFISHER SIDE CNSLE	OP	OPFSH	FBG TR	OB	6 6	850		1500	1800
					1987 BOATS					
16 10	KINGFISHER 1778	OP	CTRCN	FBG TR	OB	6 6	850		1450	1750
16 10	KINGFISHER DBL CNSLE	OP	OPFSH	FBG TR	OB	6 6	875		1500	1800
16 10	KINGFISHER SIDE CNSL	OP	OPFSH	FBG TR	OB	6 6	850		1450	1750
					1986 BOATS					
16 10	KINGFISHER 1778	OP	CTRCN	FBG TR	OB	6 6	850		1450	1700
16 10	KINGFISHER DBL CNSLE	OP	OPFSH	FBG TR	OB	6 6	875		1450	1750
16 10	KINGFISHER SIDE CNSL	OP	OPFSH	FBG TR	OB	6 6	850		1450	1700
					1985 BOATS					
16 10	KINGFISHER 1778	OP	CTRCN	FBG TR	OB	6 6	850		1400	1650
16 10	KINGFISHER 1778	OP	OPFSH	FBG TR	OB	6 6	850		1400	1650

LANCER YACHT CORP
IRVINE CA 92714 COAST GUARD MFG ID- LYP See inside cover to adjust price for area
SEE ALSO WILLARD COMPANY INC

LOA FT IN	NAME AND/ OR MODEL	TOP/ RIG	BOAT TYPE	-HULL- MTL TP	----ENGINE--- TP # HP MFG	BEAM FT IN	WGT LBS	DRAFT FT IN	RETAIL LOW	RETAIL HIGH
					1986 BOATS					
44 7	LANCER 45	SLP	MS	FBG KL IB	D	13 9	24000	6	88000	96700
65 4	LANCER 65	SLP	MS	FBG KL IB	D	17 11	55000	6 11	248000	272500
					1985 BOATS					
24 8	POWERSAILER	SLP	SAIL	FBG KL OB		8	3500	3 4	5950	6850
26 7	POWERSAILER	SLP	SAIL	FBG KL SD		8 6	4600	4 3	8850	10100
26 7	POWERSAILER	SLP	SAIL	FBG KL SD	15 OMC	8 6	4600	4 3	9100	10300
26 7	POWERSAILER	SLP	SAIL	FBG KL IB	8D- 15D	8 6	4600	4 3	9350	10700
26 7	POWERSAILER SHOAL	SLP	SAIL	FBG KL OB		8 6	4600	3 3	8850	10100
26 7	POWERSAILER SHOAL	SLP	SAIL	FBG KL SD	15 OMC	8 6	4600	3 3	9100	10300
26 7	POWERSAILER SHOAL	SLP	SAIL	FBG KL IB	8D- 15D	8 6	4600	3 3	9350	10700
28 7	POWERSAILER	SLP	SAIL	FBG KL OB		9 3	6800	5 3	14500	16500
29 6	LANCER 30	SLP	SAIL	FBG KL OB		10	8200	5 2	18700	20800
29 6	LANCER 30	SLP	SAIL	FBG KL SD	15 OMC	10	8200	5 2	18800	20900
29 6	LANCER 30	SLP	SAIL	FBG KL IB	15D YAN	10	8200	5 2	19000	21100
29 6	LANCER 30 SHOAL	SLP	SAIL	FBG KL OB		10	8200	4 2	18700	20800
29 6	LANCER 30 SHOAL	SLP	SAIL	FBG KL SD	15 OMC	10	8200	4 2	18800	20900
29 6	LANCER 30 SHOAL	SLP	SAIL	FBG KL IB	15D YAN	10	8200	4 2	19000	21100
36 2	LANCER 36	SLP	SA/RC	FBG KL IB	D	11 9	10500	6 2	29200	32400
39 6	LANCER 40 AC	SLP	SAIL	FBG KL SD	23D VLVO	12	16000	6 3	51700	56900
39 6	LANCER 40 AC	SLP	SAIL	FBG KL SD	35D VLVO	12	16000	6 3	50800	55900
39 6	LANCER 40 AC	SLP	SAIL	FBG KL IB	61D VLVO	12	16000	6 3	52400	57600
39 6	LANCER 40 AC SHOAL	SLP	SAIL	FBG KL SD	23D VLVO	12	16000	4 11	51700	56900
39 6	LANCER 40 AC SHOAL	SLP	SAIL	FBG KL SD	35D VLVO	12	16000	4 11	52000	57100
39 6	LANCER 40 AC SHOAL	SLP	SAIL	FBG KL IB	61D VLVO	12	16000	4 11	52400	57600
39 6	LANCER 40 MC	SLP	SAIL	FBG KL SD	23D VLVO	12	16000	6 3	51700	56900
39 6	LANCER 40 MC	SLP	SAIL	FBG KL SD	35D VLVO	12	16000	6 3	53100	58400
39 6	LANCER 40 MC	SLP	SAIL	FBG KL SD	61D VLVO	12	16000	6 3	52400	57600
39 6	LANCER 40 MC SHOAL	SLP	SAIL	FBG KL SD	23D VLVO	12	16000	4 11	51700	56900
39 6	LANCER 40 MC SHOAL	SLP	SAIL	FBG KL SD	35D VLVO	12	16000	4 11	52000	57100
39 6	LANCER 40 MC SHOAL	SLP	SAIL	FBG KL IB	61D VLVO	12	16000	4 11	52400	57600
39 6	POWERSAILER	SLP	MS	FBG KL IB	62D PERK 12	16000		6 3	52000	57200
	IB 85D PERK 52300	57500,	IB	115D PERK	52600 57800, IB T 51D PERK				53300	58600
	IB T 62D PERK 53600	58900,	IB T	85D PERK	54100 59500, IB T115D PERK				54800	60200
39 6	POWERSAILER SHOAL	SLP	MS	FBG KL IB	62D PERK 12	16000		4 11	52000	57200
	IB 85D PERK 52300	57500,	IB	115D PERK	52600 57800, IB T 51D PERK				53300	58600
	IB T 62D PERK 53600	58900,	IB T	85D PERK	54100 59500, IB T115D PERK				54800	60200
44 7	LANCER 45 AC	SLP	SAIL	FBG KL IB	62D PERK 13	9 24000		6	82400	90600
	IB 85D PERK 81200	89200,	IB	135D PERK	83200 91400, IB 200D PERK				83800	92100
	IB T 51D PERK 83700	92000								
44 7	LANCER 45 AC SHOAL	SLP	SAIL	FBG KL IB	62D PERK 13	9 24000		4 11	82400	90600
	IB 85D PERK 82700	90900,	IB	135D PERK	83200 91400, IB 200D PERK				83800	92100
	IB T 51D PERK 83700	92000								
44 7	LANCER 45 MC	SLP	SAIL	FBG KL IB	62D PERK 13	9 24000		6	82400	90600
	IB 85D PERK 84200	92500,	IB	135D PERK	83200 91400, IB 200D PERK				83800	92100
44 7	LANCER 45 MC SHOAL	SLP	SAIL	FBG KL IB	62D PERK 13	9 24000		4 11	82400	90600
	IB 85D PERK 82700	90900,	IB	135D PERK	83200 91400, IB 200D PERK				83800	92100
44 7	POWERSAILER	SLP	MS	FBG KL IB	85D PERK 13	9 24000		6	82700	90900
	IB 135D PERK 83200	91400,	IB	200D PERK	83800 92100, IB T 51D PERK				83700	92000
	IB T 62D PERK 84000	92300,	IB T	85D PERK	84500 92900, IB T135D PERK				85600	94100
	IB T200D PERK 86800	95400								
44 7	POWERSAILER SHOAL	SLP	MS	FBG KL IB	85D PERK 13	9 24000		4 11	82700	90900
	IB 135D PERK 83200	91400,	IB	200D PERK	83800 92100, IB T 51D PERK				83700	92000
	IB T 62D PERK 84000	92300,	IB T	85D PERK	84500 92900, IB T135D PERK				85600	94100
	IB T200D PERK 86800	95400								
65 4	LANCER 65	SLP	MS	FBG KL IB	135D PERK 17	11 60000		6 11	250500	275000
	IB 200D PERK 251000	275500,	IB	240D PERK	251500 276000, IB 350D PERK				252500	277500
	IB T135D PERK 252500	277500,	IB	T200D PERK	253500 279000, IB T240D PERK				254500	279500
	IB T350D PERK 238500	262000								
65 4	LANCER 65 FB	SLP	MS	FBG KL IB	135D PERK 17	11 55000		6 11	232000	255000
	IB 200D PERK 232500	255500,	IB	240D PERK	233000 256000, IB 350D PERK				234000	257500
	IB T135D PERK 234000	257500,	IB	T200D PERK	235500 258500, IB T240D PERK				236000	259500
	IB T350D PERK 238500	262000								
65 4	LANCER 65 FB SHOAL	SLP	MS	FBG KL IB	135D PERK 17	11 55000		5 8	232000	255000
	IB 200D PERK 232500	255500,	IB	240D PERK	233000 256000, IB 350D PERK				234000	257500
	IB T135D PERK 234000	257500,	IB	T200D PERK	235500 258500, IB T240D PERK				236000	259500
	IB T350D PERK 238500	262000								
65 4	LANCER 65 PH	SLP	MS	FBG KL IB	135D PERK 17	11 55000		6 11	232000	255000
	IB 200D PERK 232500	255500,	IB	240D PERK	233000 256000, IB 350D PERK				234000	257500
	IB T135D PERK 234000	257500,	IB	T200D PERK	235500 258500, IB T240D PERK				236000	259500
	IB T350D PERK 238500	262000								
65 4	LANCER 65 PH SHOAL	SLP	MS	FBG KL IB	135D PERK 17	11 55000		5 8	232000	255000
	IB 200D PERK 232500	255500,	IB	240D PERK	233000 256000, IB 350D PERK				234000	257500

LOA FT IN	NAME AND/ OR MODEL	TOP/ RIG	BOAT TYPE	HULL MTL TP TP	ENGINE # HP MFG	BEAM FT IN	WGT LBS	DRAFT FT IN	RETAIL LOW	RETAIL HIGH
	1985 BOATS									
65 4	LANCER 65 PH SHOAL	SLP	MS	FBG KL IB	135D PERK	17 11	55000	5 8	234000	257500
	IB T200D PERK 235500 258500, IB T240D PERK 236000 259500, IB T350D PERK 238500 262000									
65 4	LANCER 65 SHOAL	SLP	MS	FBG KL IB	135D PERK	17 11	60000	5 8	250500	275000
	IB 200D PERK 251000 275500, IB 240D PERK 251500 276000, IB 350D PERK 252500 277500									
	IB T135D PERK 252500 277500, IB T200D PERK 253500 279000, IB T240D PERK 254500 279500									
	IB T350D PERK 238500 262000									
	1984 BOATS									
24 8	LANCER 25	SLP	SAIL	FBG KL OB		8	3600	3	6650	7600
24 8	LANCER 25 MKV	SLP	SAIL	FBG KL IB		8	3600	3	4900	5600
24 8	LANCER 25 MKV	SLP	SAIL	FBG KL SD		8	3600	3	6050	6950
24 8	LANCER 25 POWERSAILR	SLP	MS	FBG KL	15 OMC	8	3500	3 4	5450	6250
26 7	LANCER POWERSAILER	SLP	SAIL	FBG KL OB		8 6	4600	3 3	8250	9500
26 7	LANCER POWERSAILER	SLP	SAIL	FBG KL IB	15	8 6	4600	3 3	8450	9750
26 7	LANCER POWERSAILER	SLP	SAIL	FBG KL SD	8D- 15D	8 6	4600	3 3	8700	10100
27 8	LANCER 28T MKV	SLP	SAIL	FBG KL OB		8	5200	3	9950	11300
27 8	LANCER 28T MKV	SLP	SAIL	FBG KL IB	15 OMC	8	5200	3	10100	11500
27 8	LANCER 28T MKV	SLP	SAIL	FBG KL IB	8D YAN	8	5200	3	10300	11700
29 6	LANCER 30 MKV	SLP	SAIL	FBG KL IB		10	8200	5 2	16600	18800
29 6	LANCER 30 MKV	SLP	SAIL	FBG KL SD	15 OMC	10	8200	5 2	16700	19000
29 6	LANCER 30 MKV	SLP	SAIL	FBG KL IB	15D YAN	10	8200	5 2	16900	19200
29 6	LANCER 30 MKV SHOAL	SLP	SAIL	FBG KL IB		10	8200	4 2	18200	20200
29 6	LANCER 30 MKV SHOAL	SLP	SAIL	FBG KL SD	15 OMC	10	8200	4 2	18200	20300
29 6	LANCER 30 MKV SHOAL	SLP	SAIL	FBG KL IB	15D YAN	10	8200	4 2	18400	20400
36 2	LANCER 36	SLP	SAIL	FBG KL IB	15D YAN	11 9	10500	6 2	26700	29700
36 2	LANCER 36	SLP	SAIL	FBG KL IB	22D YAN	11 9	10500	6 2	26800	29800
36 2	LANCER 36	SLP	SAIL	FBG KL IB	30D YAN	11 9	10500	6 2	26900	29900
36 2	LANCER 36 SHOAL	SLP	SAIL	FBG KL IB	15D YAN	11 9	10500	4 11	28000	31100
36 2	LANCER 36 SHOAL	SLP	SAIL	FBG KL IB	22D YAN	11 9	10500	4 11	28100	31200
36 2	LANCER 36 SHOAL	SLP	SAIL	FBG KL IB	30D YAN	11 9	10500	4 11	28100	31300
39 6	LANCER 40 AC	SLP	SAIL	FBG KL SD	23D VLVO	12	15500	6 3	45900	50400
39 6	LANCER 40 AC	SLP	SAIL	FBG KL SD	35D VLVO	12	15500	6 3	46100	50600
39 6	LANCER 40 AC	SLP	SAIL	FBG KL SD	61D VLVO	12	15500	6 3	46600	51200
39 6	LANCER 40 AC SHOAL	SLP	SAIL	FBG KL SD	23D VLVO	12	15500	4 11	47100	51800
39 6	LANCER 40 AC SHOAL	SLP	SAIL	FBG KL SD	35D VLVO	12	15500	4 11	47300	52000
39 6	LANCER 40 AC SHOAL	SLP	SAIL	FBG KL SD	61D VLVO	12	15500	4 11	47800	52500
39 6	LANCER 40 MC	SLP	SAIL	FBG KL SD	23D VLVO	12	15500	6 3	48300	53100
39 6	LANCER 40 MC	SLP	SAIL	FBG KL SD	35D VLVO	12	15500	6 3	48500	53300
39 6	LANCER 40 MC	SLP	SAIL	FBG KL SD	61D VLVO	12	15500	6 3	48900	53800
39 6	LANCER 40 MC SHOAL	SLP	SAIL	FBG KL SD	23D VLVO	12	15500	4 11	49500	54400
39 6	LANCER 40 MC SHOAL	SLP	SAIL	FBG KL SD	35D VLVO	12	15500	4 11	49800	54700
39 6	LANCER 40 MC SHOAL	SLP	SAIL	FBG KL SD	61D VLVO	12	15500	4 11	50100	55100
39 6	LANCER 40 MS	SLP	MS	FBG KL IB	62D PERK	12	16000	6 3	48400	53100
	IB 85D PERK 48600 53400, IB 115D PERK 49000 53800, IB T 50D PERK 49600 54500									
	IB T 62D PERK 49900 54800, IB T 85D PERK 50400 55400, IB T115D PERK 51000 56000									
39 6	LANCER 40 MS SHOAL	SLP	MS	FBG KL IB	62D PERK	12	16000	4 11	49500	54400
	IB 85D PERK 49800 54700, IB 115D PERK 50000 55000, IB T 50D PERK 50700 55700									
	IB T 62D PERK 50900 55900, IB T 85D PERK 51400 56500, IB T115D PERK 52000 57200									
44 7	LANCER 45 AC	SLP	SAIL	FBG KL IB	62D PERK	13 9	24000	6	74400	81800
	IB 85D PERK 74700 82100, IB 135D PERK 75200 82700, IB 200D PERK 75900 83400									
	IB T 50D PERK 77300 84900									
44 7	LANCER 45 AC SHOAL	SLP	SAIL	FBG KL IB	62D PERK	13 9	24000	4 11	77500	85100
	IB 85D PERK 77700 85400, IB 135D PERK 78200 85900, IB 200D PERK 78800 86600									
	IB T 50D PERK 80100 88100									
44 7	LANCER 45 MC	SLP	SAIL	FBG KL IB	62D PERK	13 9	24000	6	77600	85300
	IB 85D PERK 77900 85600, IB 135D PERK 78400 86100, IB 200D PERK 78900 86800									
44 7	LANCER 45 MC SHOAL	SLP	SAIL	FBG KL IB	62D PERK	13 9	24000	4 11	80600	88600
	IB 85D PERK 80900 88900, IB 135D PERK 81300 89400, IB 200D PERK 81900 90000									
44 7	LANCER 45 MS	SLP	MS	FBG KL IB	85D PERK	13 9	24000	6	76400	83900
	IB 135D PERK 76900 84500, IB 200D PERK 77400 85100, IB T 50D PERK 77400 85000									
	IB T 62D PERK 77700 85300, IB T 85D PERK 78200 85900, IB T135D PERK 79200 87100									
	IB T200D PERK 80500 88400									
44 7	LANCER 45 MS SHOAL	SLP	MS	FBG KL IB	85D PERK	13 9	24000	4 11	79200	87000
	IB 135D PERK 79700 87600, IB 200D PERK 80300 88200, IB T 50D PERK 80100 88000									
	IB T 62D PERK 80400 88300, IB T 85D PERK 80900 88900, IB T135D PERK 81800 89900									
	IB T200D PERK 82900 91100									
65 4	LANCER 65	SLP	MS	FBG KL IB	135D PERK	17 11	55000	6 11	210500	231000
	IB 200D PERK 211000 231500, IB 240D PERK 211500 232500, IB 350D PERK 212500 233500									
	IB T135D PERK 213000 234000, IB T200D PERK 214000 235000, IB T240D PERK 215000 236000									
	IB T350D PERK 217500 238500									
65 4	LANCER 65 FB	SLP	MS	FBG KL IB	135D PERK	17 11	55000	6 11	219000	240500
	IB 200D PERK 219500 241500, IB 240D PERK 220000 241500, IB 350D PERK 221000 243000									
	IB T135D PERK 221000 243000, IB T200D PERK 222000 244000, IB T240D PERK 223000 245000									
	IB T350D PERK 225000 247500									
65 4	LANCER 65 FB SHOAL	SLP	MS	FBG KL IB	135D PERK	17 11	55000	5 8	222500	244500
	IB 200D PERK 223000 245000, IB 240D PERK 223500 245500, IB 350D PERK 224500 246500									
	IB T135D PERK 224500 246500, IB T200D PERK 225500 248000, IB T240D PERK 226000 248500									
	IB T350D PERK 228500 251000									
65 4	LANCER 65 PH	SLP	MS	FBG KL IB	135D PERK	17 11	55000	6 11	220000	241500
	IB 200D PERK 220500 242500, IB 240D PERK 221000 242500, IB 350D PERK 222000 244000									
	IB T135D PERK 222000 244000, IB T200D PERK 223000 245000, IB T240D PERK 223500 246000									
	IB T350D PERK 226000 248500									
65 4	LANCER 65 PH SHOAL	SLP	MS	FBG KL IB	135D PERK	17 11	55000	5 8	223500	245500
	IB 200D PERK 224000 246000, IB 240D PERK 224500 246500, IB 350D PERK 225500 247500									
	IB T135D PERK 225500 247500, IB T200D PERK 226500 249000, IB T240D PERK 227000 249500									
	IB T350D PERK 229000 252000									
65 4	LANCER 65 SHOAL	SLP	MS	FBG KL IB	135D PERK	17 11	55000	5 8	214000	235000
	IB 200D PERK 214500 235500, IB 240D PERK 215000 236000, IB 350D PERK 216000 237500									
	IB T135D PERK 216000 237500, IB T200D PERK 217500 239000, IB T240D PERK 218000 239500									
	IB T350D PERK 220500 242500									

....For earlier years, see the BUC Used Boat Price Guide, Volume 3

LAND N' SEA WEST
OAKLAND CA 94606   See inside cover to adjust price for area

LOA FT IN	NAME AND/ OR MODEL	TOP/ RIG	BOAT TYPE	HULL MTL TP TP	ENGINE # HP MFG	BEAM FT IN	WGT LBS	DRAFT FT IN	RETAIL LOW	RETAIL HIGH
	1986 BOATS									
28	LAND-N-SEA	HT	HB	FBG TR OB		8 6	7000		**	**
	1985 BOATS									
28	LAND-N-SEA	HT	HB	FBG TR OB		8 6	7000		**	**

....For earlier years, see the BUC Used Boat Price Guide, Volume 3

LANDAU BOATS INC
LEBANON MO 65536   COAST GUARD MFG ID- LBO See inside cover to adjust price for area
FORMERLY LANDAU MANUFACTURING CO

For more recent years, see the BUC Used Boat Price Guide, Volume 1

LOA FT IN	NAME AND/ OR MODEL	TOP/ RIG	BOAT TYPE	HULL MTL TP TP	ENGINE # HP MFG	BEAM FT IN	WGT LBS	DRAFT FT IN	RETAIL LOW	RETAIL HIGH
	1996 BOATS									
16	1650AW FLAT	OP	UTL	AL FL OB		5 11	413		2150	2500
16	1656	OP	JON	AL FL OB		4 8	160		805	970
16	1669V	OP	UTL	AL SV OB		5 10			1950	2300
16	1670	OP	JON	AL FL OB		5 10	260		1300	1550
16	1670 OPEN	OP	JON	AL FL OB		6 8	260		1400	1650
16	BASS 160	OP	BASS	AL SV OB		5 10			2600	3000
16	BRUTE 1680	OP	JON	AL FL OB		6 8	400		1950	2300
16	MV1650AW	OP	UTL	AL FL OB		5 9	413		2150	2500
16	MV1670	OP	JON	AL FL OB		5 10	260		1400	1700
16	MV1670 OPEN	OP	JON	AL FL OB		6 8	260		1050	1300
16	MV1680	OP	JON	AL FL OB		6 8	400		2050	2450
16	V16 GUIDE	OP	JON	AL SV OB		6 2			1500	1800
17	MV1752AW	OP	UTL	AL SV OB		6 4	453		2400	2750
17	PRO 17 BASS	OP	BASS	AL SV OB		6 4			2300	2700
17	PRO 17 BASS AWH	OP	BASS	AL SV OB		6 4			2450	2850
18	BRUTE 1880	OP	JON	AL FL OB		6 8	440		1850	2200
18	BRUTE MV1880	OP	JON	AL FL OB		7 3	420		1700	2000
18	HAWG 1894	OP	JON	AL FL OB		7 10	575		2500	2900
18	MV1860AW	OP	UTL	AL FL OB		7 3	555		2800	3250
18	PRO 18 BASS AWH	OP	BASS	AL SV OB		7 3			4350	5050
19	HAWG 1994	OP	JON	AL FL OB		7 10	640		2700	3150

LOA FT IN	NAME AND/ OR MODEL	TOP/ RIG	BOAT TYPE	HULL MTL	HULL TP	ENGINE TP	#	HP	MFG	BEAM FT IN	WGT LBS	DRAFT FT IN	RETAIL LOW	RETAIL HIGH
						1995 BOATS								
16	1650AW FLAT	OP	UTL	AL		OB				5 11			1800	2150
16	1656	OP	JON	AL	FL	OB				4 8	160		765	920
16	1669V	OP	UTL	AL		OB				5 10			1800	2150
16	1670	OP	JON	AL	FL	OB				5 10	260		1250	1500
16	BASS 160	OP	BASS	AL	SV	OB				5 10			2650	3050
16	BASS 160 TILLER	OP	BASS	AL	SV	OB				5 10			2300	2700
16	BRUTE 1670	OP	JON	AL	FL	OB				6 8	260		1350	1600
16	BRUTE 1670/15	OP	JON	AL	FL	OB				6 8	260		1250	1500
16	BRUTE 1680	OP	JON	AL	FL	OB				6 8	400		2050	2400
16	BRUTE MV1680	OP	JON	AL	FL	OB				6 8	400		1450	1750
16	BRUTE MV1680LW	OP	JON	AL	FL	OB				6 8	400		2200	2600
16	MV1650AW	OP	UTL	AL		OB				5 8			1800	2150
16	MV1670	OP	JON	AL	FL	OB				5 10	260		1350	1600
17	MV1752AW	OP	UTL	AL		OB				6 4			2200	2550
18	BRUTE 1880	OP	JON	AL	FL	OB				6 8	440		1750	2050
18	BRUTE MV1880	OP	JON	AL	FL	OB				6 8	420		1600	1900
18	HAWG 1894	OP	JON	AL	FL	OB				7 10	500		2000	2400
18	MV1860AW	OP	UTL	AL		OB				7 3			2500	2900
19	HAWG 1994	OP	JON	AL	FL	OB				7 10	550		2200	2550
						1994 BOATS								
16	1656	OP	JON	AL	FL	OB				4 8	160		720	870
16	1656LW	OP	JON	AL	FL	OB				4 8	160		845	1000
16	1670	OP	JON	AL	FL	OB				5 10	260		1100	1300
16	1670LW	OP	JON	AL	FL	OB				5 10	260		1200	1450
16	BRUTE 1670	OP	JON	AL	FL	OB				6 8	260		1850	2200
16	BRUTE 1670LW	OP	JON	AL	FL	OB				6 8	260		1200	1450
16	BRUTE 1680	OP	JON	AL	FL	OB				6 8	400		1650	2000
16	BRUTE 1680LW	OP	JON	AL	FL	OB				6 8	400		1800	2150
16	BRUTE MV 1680LW	OP	JON	AL	FL	OB				6 8	400		1900	2250
16	BRUTE MV1670	OP	JON	AL	FL	OB				6 8	260		1200	1400
16	BRUTE MV1670LW	OP	JON	AL	FL	OB				6 8	260		1300	1550
16	BRUTE MV1680	OP	JON	AL	FL	OB				6 8	400		1800	2150
16	MV1656	OP	JON	AL	FL	OB				4 8	160		825	990
16	MV1656LW	OP	JON	AL	FL	OB				4 8	160		950	1150
16	MV1670	OP	JON	AL	FL	OB				5 10	260		1200	1450
16	MV1670-20	OP	JON	AL	FL	OB				5 10	260		1250	1500
16	MV1670LW	OP	JON	AL	FL	OB				5 10	260		1350	1600
16 8	SUPER HAWK 10	OP	BASS	AL	FL	OB				6 8	677		3250	3800
18	1870	OP	JON	AL	FL	OB				5 10	280		855	1000
18	1870LW	OP	JON	AL	FL	OB				5 10	280		940	1100
18	BASS 80	OP	BASS	AL	FL	OB				6 8	820		4050	4700
18	BRUTE 1870	OP	JON	AL	FL	OB				6 8	280		875	1050
18	BRUTE 1870LW	OP	JON	AL	FL	OB				6 8	280		945	1150
18	BRUTE 1880	OP	JON	AL	FL	OB				6 8	440		1650	1950
18	BRUTE 1880LW	OP	JON	AL	FL	OB				6 8	420		1500	1800
18	BRUTE 1894	OP	JON	AL	FL	OB				7 10	500		1900	2250
18	BRUTE 1894LW	OP	JON	AL	FL	OB				7 10	500		1950	2300
18	BRUTE MV1870	OP	JON	AL	FL	OB				6 8	280		940	1100
18	BRUTE MV1870LW	OP	JON	AL	FL	OB				6 8	280		995	1200
18	BRUTE MV1880	OP	JON	AL	FL	OB				6 8	420		1500	1800
18	BRUTE MV1880LW	OP	JON	AL	FL	OB				6 8	420		1650	1950
18	MV1870	OP	JON	AL	FL	OB				5 10	280		935	1100
18	MV1870-20	OP	JON	AL	FL	OB				5 10	280		970	1150
18	MV1870LW	OP	JON	AL	FL	OB				5 10	280		1000	1200
19	BRUTE 1994	OP	JON	AL	FL	OB				7 10	550		1950	2300
19	BRUTE 1994LW	OP	JON	AL	FL	OB				7 10	550		2050	2450
						1993 BOATS								
16	1656	OP	JON	AL	FL	OB				4 8	160		785	950
16	16680	OP	FSH	AL	SV	OB				5 8	244		1050	1250
16	1670	OP	JON	AL	FL	OB				5 10	260		1050	1250
16	BRUTE 1670	OP	JON	AL	FL	OB				6 8	400		1750	2100
16	BRUTE 1680	OP	JON	AL	FL	OB				6 8	400		1700	2000
16 8	SUPER HAWK 10	OP	BASS	AL	FL	OB				6 8	677		3100	3600
18	1870	OP	JON	AL	FL	OB				5 10	280		895	1050
18	BASS 80	OP	BASS	AL	FL	OB				6 8	820		3850	4500
18	BRUTE 1870	OP	JON	AL	FL	OB							1350	1600
18	BRUTE 1880	OP	JON	AL	FL	OB				6 8	440		1550	1850
18	BRUTE 1894	OP	JON	AL	FL	OB				7 10	500		1800	2150
19	BRUTE 1994	OP	JON	AL	FL	OB				7 10	550		1900	2300
						1992 BOATS								
16	1656FP	OP	JON	AL	FL	OB				4 8	160		750	905
16	16680	OP	FSH	AL	SV	OB				5 8	244		1000	1200
16	1670 TUNNEL	OP	JON	AL	FL	OB				5 10	260		1200	1450
16	1670FP	OP	JON	AL	FL	OB				5 10	260		1000	1200
16	1680 BRUTE	OP	JON	AL	FL	OB				6 8	400		1650	2000
16	1680FP	OP	JON	AL	FL	OB				6 8	400		1600	1900
16	NATURAL	OP	BASS	AL		OB				5 10	510		2250	2600
16 8	SUPER HAWK 10	OP	BASS	AL	FL	OB				6 8	677		2950	3400
18	1870FP	OP	JON	AL	FL	OB				5 10	280		850	1000
18	1880 BRUTE	OP	JON	AL	FL	OB				6 8	440		1500	1750
18	1880FP	OP	JON	AL	FL	OB				6 8	400		1300	1550
18	NATURAL	OP	BASS	AL		OB				5 10	680		3100	3600
						1991 BOATS								
16	1656FP	OP	JON	AL	FL	OB				4 8	160		715	860
16	1668V	OP	FSH	AL	SV	OB				5 8	244		970	1150
16	1670 TUNNEL	OP	JON	AL	FL	OB				5 10	260		1150	1400
16	1670FP	OP	JON	AL	FL	OB				5 10	260		975	1150
16	1680 BRUTE	OP	JON	AL	FL	OB				6 8	400		1550	1850
16	1680FP	OP	JON	AL	FL	OB				6 8	400		1500	1800
16	CRAPPIE CATCHER	OP	BASS	AL	FL	OB				6 2	380		1550	1850
16	HANDLER DX	OP	BASS	AL	FL	OB				6 2	560		2350	2750
16	SCOUT 16	OP	FSH	AL	DV	OB				5 8	480		1900	2300
16 8	SUPER HAWK 10	OP	BASS	AL	FL	OB				6 7	677		2800	3250
17	GUIDE 17	OP	FSH	AL	DV	OB				6 2	640		2650	3100
17	MASTER GUIDE 17	OP	FSH	AL	DV	OB				6 2	730		3000	3500
18	1870FP	OP	JON	AL	FL	OB				5 10	280		800	965
18	1880 BRUTE	OP	JON	AL	FL	OB				6 8	440		1450	1700
18	1880FP	OP	JON	AL	FL	OB				6 8	440		1400	1650
18 8	GUIDE 19	OP	FSH	AL	DV	OB				6 4	740		3250	3750
18 8	MASTER GUIDE 19	OP	FSH	AL	DV	OB				6 4	842		3600	4200
						1990 BOATS								
16	1656FP	OP	JON	AL	FL	OB				4 8	157		675	810
16	1666VP	OP	FSH	AL	SV	OB				5 8	244		930	1100
16	1670FP	OP	JON	AL	FL	OB				5 10	271		1050	1250
16	1670FPMV	OP	JON	AL	FL	OB				5 10	271		1050	1250
16	1676VP	OP	FSH	AL	FL	OB				6 4	450		1700	2050
16	1680FP	OP	JON	AL	FL	OB				6 8	311		1200	1400
16	1680FPAW	OP	JON	AL	FL	OB				6 8	311		1200	1400
16	HANDLER	OP	BASS	AL	FL	OB				5 2	395		1550	1850
16 5	SUPER-HAWK 10	OP	BASS	AL	FL	OB				5 9	530		2150	2500
16 9	1676 GUIDE	OP	FSH	AL	SV	OB				5 4	580		2350	2750
16 9	CHEROKEE 1650	OP	OPFSH	AL	SV	OB				5 4	740		2850	3300
17	MAGNUM TR	OP	BASS	AL	TR	OB				6	550		2300	2700
18	1870FP	OP	JON	AL	FL	OB				5 10	287		790	955
18	1876FP	OP	FSH	AL	FL	OB				6 4	575		2450	2850
18	1880FPAW	OP	JON	AL	FL	OB				6 8	340		990	1200
18	1880FPCO	OP	JON	AL	FL	OB				6 8	340		990	1200
18 9	1876 GUIDE	OP	FSH	AL	SV	OB				5 6	690		2900	3400
18 9	CHEROKEE 1850	OP	FSH	AL	DV	OB				5 4	880		3600	4200
						1989 BOATS								
16	1656FP	OP	JON	AL	FL	OB				4 8	157		645	780
16	1664VP	OP	FSH	AL	SV	OB				5 4	244		890	1050
16	1670FP	OP	JON	AL	FL	OB				5 10	271		1000	1200
16	1670FP VEE	OP	FSH	AL	FL	OB				5 10	271		995	1200
16	1676FP	OP	FSH	AL	FL	OB				6 4	450		1650	1950
16	1680FP	OP	JON	AL	FL	OB				6 8	311		1050	1200
16	1680FP COMMERCIAL	OP	JON	AL	FL	OB				6 8	311		1250	1500
16	HANDLER	OP	BASS	AL	FL	OB				5 2	395		1450	1700
16	HANDLER DIX	OP	BASS	AL	FL	OB				5 2	395		1500	1800
16 6	CHEROKEE 1650 SE	OP	OPFSH	AL	DV	OB				6 4	650		2450	2800
16 6	CHEROKEE 1650 SS	OP	CTRCN	AL	DV	OB				6 4	650		2500	2900
16	SUPER-HAWK	OP	BASS	AL	FL	OB				5 8	530		1950	2350
16 6	SUPER-HAWK 10	OP	BASS	AL	FL	OB				5 8	530		2100	2500
17	MAGNUM TR	OP	BASS	AL	TR	OB				6	500		1950	2350
17 4	BOW RIDER	OP	RNBT	AL	DV	IO		140-185		7 1	1982		4250	5000
18	1870FP	OP	JON	AL	FL	OB				5 10	287		760	915
18	1876VP	OP	FSH	AL	FL	OB				6 4	575		2350	2750
18	1880FP	OP	JON	AL	FL	OB				6 8	340		850	1000
18	1880FP COMMERCIAL	OP	JON	AL	FL	OB				6 8	340		1050	1200
18	CHEROKEE 1850SC	OP	FSH	AL	DV	OB				6 2	700		2700	3150
18	CHEROKEE 1850SXs	OP	FSH	AL	DV	OB				6 2	700		2700	3250
21 3	BOW RIDER	OP	RNBT	AL	DV	IO		205-260		7 9	3320		7950	9500
22 3	C223V CUDDY	OP	CUD	AL	DV	IO		230-260		8	2681		8000	9450
22 4	CUDDY 224	OP	CUD	AL	DV	IO			MRCR	8	4420		**	**
22 4	CUDDY 224	OP	CUD	AL	DV	IO			OMC	8	4420		**	***
22 4	CUDDY 224	OP	CUD	AL	DV	IO		260		8	4420		11500	13000
22 4	OPEN BOW 224	OP	RNBT	AL	DV	IO		230-260		8	3740		9450	10900
40	LANDAU 40	HT	HB	AL	PN	OB				10			12600	14300

IO 120 MRCR 21100, 23400, IO 120 OMC 21000 23300, IO 140 MRCR 21100 23400

LOA FT	IN	NAME AND/ OR MODEL	TOP/ RIG	BOAT TYPE	-HULL- MTL	TP	ENGINE TP	# HP	MFG	BEAM FT	IN	WGT LBS	DRAFT FT	IN	RETAIL LOW	RETAIL HIGH
		1989 BOATS														
40		LANDAU 40	HT	HB	AL	PN	IO	140	OMC	10					21000	23300
		1988 BOATS														
16		1656FP	OP	JON	AL	FL	OB			4	8	157			620	745
16		1664VP	OP	FSH	AL	SV	OB			5	4	244			855	1000
16		1670FP	OP	JON	AL	FL	OB			5	10	271			980	1150
16		1670FP VEE	OP	FSH	AL	FL	OB			5	10	271			955	1150
16		1676VP	OP	FSH	AL	FL	OB			6	4	450			1600	1900
16		1680FP	OP	JON	AL	FL	OB			6	8	311			990	1200
16		1680FP COMMERCIAL	OP	JON	AL	FL	OB			6	8	311			1200	1400
16		HANDLER	OP	BASS	AL	FL	OB			5	2	395			1400	1650
16		HANDLER DIX	OP	BASS	AL	FL	OB			5	2	395			1450	1700
16	6	CHEROKEE 1650 SE	OP	OPFSH	AL	DV	OB			6	4	650			2350	2750
16	6	CHEROKEE 1650 SS	OP	CTRCN	AL	DV	OB			6	4	650			2400	2800
16	6	SUPER-HAWK	OP	BASS	AL	FL	OB			5	8	530			1900	2250
16	6	SUPER-HAWK 10	OP	BASS	AL	FL	OB			5	8	530			2000	2400
17		MAGNUM TR	OP	BASS	AL	TR	OB			6		500			1900	2250
17	4	BOW RIDER	OP	RNBT	AL	DV	IO	140-185		7	1	1982			4000	4700
18		1870FP	OP	JON	AL	FL	OB			5	10	287			730	880
18		1876VP	OP	FSH	AL	FL	OB			6	4	575			2250	2650
18		1880FP	OP	JON	AL	FL	OB			6	8	340			810	975
18		1880FP COMMERCIAL	OP	JON	AL	FL	OB			6	8	340			1000	1200
18		CHEROKEE 1850SC	OP	FSH	AL	DV	OB			6	2	700			2600	3050
18		CHEROKEE 1850SXS	OP	FSH	AL	DV	OB			6	2	700			2700	3150
21	3	BOW RIDER	OP	RNBT	AL	DV	IO	205-260		7	9	3320			7550	9000
22	3	C223V CUDDY	OP	CUD	AL	DV	IO	230-260		8		2681			7550	8950
22	4	CUDDY 224	OP	CUD	AL	DV	IO		MRCR	8		4420			**	**
22	4	CUDDY 224	OP	CUD	AL	DV	IO		OMC	8		4420			**	**
22	4	CUDDY 224	OP	CUD	AL	DV	IO	260		8		4420			10900	12300
22	4	OPEN BOW 224	OP	RNBT	AL	DV	IO	230-260		8		3740			8950	10400
28		LANDAU 28	HT	HB	AL	PN	OB			8		2975			**	**
40		LANDAU 40	HT	HB	AL	PN	OB			10					12200	13800
		IO 120 MRCR 20300 22600, IO 120 OMC 20300 22500, IO 140 MRCR 20400 22600														
		IO 140 OMC 20300 22600														
		1987 BOATS														
16		1656FP	OP	JON	AL	FL	OB			4	8	157			595	720
16		1664VP	OP	FSH	AL	SV	OB			5	4	244			810	980
16		1670FP	OP	JON	AL	FL	OB			5	10	271			945	1150
16		1680FP	OP	JON	AL	FL	OB			6	8	311			960	1150
16		1680FP COMMERCIAL	OP	JON	AL	FL	OB			6	8	311			1150	1350
16		HANDLER	OP	BASS	AL	FL	OB			5	2	395			1350	1600
16	6	CHEROKEE 1650 CC	OP	CTRCN	AL	DV	OB			6	4	650			2300	2700
16	6	CHEROKEE 1650 SC	OP	OPFSH	AL	DV	OB			6	4	650			2250	2650
16	6	SUPER-HAWK	OP	BASS	AL	FL	OB			5	8	530			1800	2150
16	6	SUPER-HAWK 10	OP	BASS	AL	FL	OB			5	8	530			1950	2300
17		MAGNUM TR	OP	BASS	AL	TR	OB			6		500			1800	2150
18		1870FP	OP	JON	AL	FL	OB			5	10	287			700	845
18		1880FP	OP	JON	AL	FL	OB			6	8	340			775	935
18		1880FP COMMERCIAL	OP	JON	AL	FL	OB			6	8	340			985	1150
22	3	C223V CUDDY	OP	CUD	FBG	DV	IO	230-260		8		2681			7200	8500
28		LANDAU 28	HT	HB	AL	PN	OB			8		2975			**	**
40		LANDAU 40	HT	HB	AL	PN	OB			10					11800	13400
		1986 BOATS														
16		1656FP	OP	JON	AL	FL	OB			4	8	157			575	695
16		1664VP	OP	FSH	AL	SV	OB			5	4	244			785	945
16		1670FP	OP	JON	AL	FL	OB			5	10	271			910	1100
16		1680FP	OP	JON	AL	FL	OB			6	8	311			930	1100
16		1680FP COMMERCIAL	OP	JON	AL	FL	OB			6	8	311			1100	1300
16		HANDLER	OP	BASS	AL	FL	OB			5	2	395			1300	1550
16	6	CHEROKEE 1650 CC	OP	CTRCN	AL	DV	OB			6	4	650			2250	2600
16	6	CHEROKEE 1650 SC	OP	OPFSH	AL	DV	OB			6	4	650			2200	2550
16	6	SUPER-HAWK	OP	BASS	AL	FL	OB			5	8	530			1750	2100
16	6	SUPER-HAWK 10	OP	BASS	AL	FL	OB			5	8	530			1850	2200
17		MAGNUM TR	OP	BASS	AL	TR	OB			6		500			1750	2100
17	7	RUNABOUT 18	OP	RNBT	FBG	DV	IO	120		7	2	1616			3400	3950
18		1870FP	OP	JON	AL	FL	OB			5	10	287			675	815
18		1880FP	OP	JON	AL	FL	OB			6	8	340			750	905
18		1880FP COMMERCIAL	OP	JON	AL	FL	OB			6	8	340			950	1150
22	3	C223V CUDDY	OP	CUD	FBG	DV	IO	170-260		8		2681			6700	8100
28		LANDAU 28	HT	HB	AL	PN	OB			8		2975			**	**
40		LANDAU 40	HT	HB	AL	PN	OB			10					11500	13100
		1985 BOATS														
16		1656FP	OP	JON	AL	FL	OB			4	8	157			555	670
16		1664VP	OP	FSH	AL	SV	OB			5	4	244			755	910
16		1670FP	OP	JON	AL	FL	OB			5	10	271			880	1050
16		1680FP	OP	JON	AL	FL	OB			6	8	311			900	1050
16		1680FP COMMERCIAL	OP	JON	AL	FL	OB			6	8	311			1100	1300
16		HANDLER	OP	BASS	AL	FL	OB			5	2	395			1250	1500
16	6	CHEROKEE 1650 CC	OP	CTRCN	AL	DV	OB			6	4	650			2150	2500
16	6	CHEROKEE 1650 SC	OP	OPFSH	AL	DV	OB			6	4	650			2050	2450
16	6	SUPER-HAWK	OP	BASS	AL	FL	OB			5	8	530			1700	2000
16	6	SUPER-HAWK 10	OP	BASS	AL	FL	OB			5	8	530			1800	2150
17		MAGNUM TR	OP	BASS	AL	TR	OB			6		500			1700	2000
17	7	RUNABOUT 18	OP	RNBT	FBG	DV	IO	120		7	2	1616			3250	3800
18		1870FP	OP	JON	AL	FL	OB			5	10	287			655	790
18		1880FP	OP	JON	AL	FL	OB			6	8	340			725	875
18		1880FP COMMERCIAL	OP	JON	AL	FL	OB			6	8	340			920	1100
22	3	C223V CUDDY	OP	CUD	FBG	DV	IO	170-260		8		2681			6450	7800
28		LANDAU 28	HT	HB	AL	PN	OB			8		2975			**	**
40		LANDAU 40	HT	HB	AL	PN	OB			10					11200	12700
		1984 BOATS														
16		1656FP	OP	JON	AL	FL	OB			4	8	157			540	655
16		1664V	OP	FSH	AL	SV	OB			5	4	244			735	885
16		1670FP	OP	JON	AL	FL	OB			5	10	271			855	1000
16		1680FP	OP	JON	AL	FL	OB			6	8	311			870	1050
16		1680FP COMMERCIAL	OP	JON	AL	FL	OB			6	8	311			1050	1250
16		HANDLER	OP	BASS	AL	FL	OB			5	2	395			1250	1450
16	6	CHEROKEE 1650 CC	OP	CTRCN	AL	DV	OB			6	4	650			2050	2450
16	6	CHEROKEE 1650 SC	OP	OPFSH	AL	DV	OB			6	4	650			2000	2400
16	6	CHEROKEE 1650 SKI	OP	RNBT	AL	DV	OB			6	4	700			2300	2700
16	6	HAWK STD	OP	BASS	AL	FL	OB			5	8	485			1550	1850
16	6	SUPER-HAWK	OP	BASS	AL	FL	OB			5	8	530			1650	1950
16	6	SUPER-HAWK 10	OP	BASS	AL	FL	OB			5	8	530			1750	2050
17		MAGNUM TR	OP	BASS	AL	TR	OB			6		500			1650	1950
18		1870FP	OP	JON	AL	FL	OB			5	10	287			635	765
18		1880FP	OP	JON	AL	FL	OB			6	8	340			700	845
18		1880FP COMMERCIAL	OP	JON	AL	FL	OB			6	8	340			890	1050

....For earlier years, see the BUC Used Boat Price Guide, Volume 3

THE LANDING SCHOOL

KENNEBNKPRT ME 04046 COAST GUARD MFG ID- LKS See inside cover to adjust price for area
ALSO LANDING SCHOOL OF BOAT BLDG

For more recent years, see the BUC Used Boat Price Guide, Volume 1

LOA FT	IN	NAME AND/ OR MODEL	TOP/ RIG	BOAT TYPE	-HULL- MTL	TP	ENGINE TP	# HP	MFG	BEAM FT	IN	WGT LBS	DRAFT FT	IN	RETAIL LOW	RETAIL HIGH
		1995 BOATS														
17		SWAMPSCOTT DORY	SLP	ROW	P/P	CB				4					13700	15600
18	8	BUZZARDS BAY 19	SLP	SACAC	P/P	CB				6	8	2300	2		14100	16100
26		LS 26	SLP	SACAC	CDR	KL	IB	10D	YAN	7	6	4630	4	3	33700	37500
		1987 BOATS														
16		CROCKER-CAT	CAT	SAIL	WD	CB				7	6	2500	1	10	9300	10600
16		HAVEN CLASS	SLP	SAIL	WD					6	1		1	6	6900	7950
17		SWAMPSCOTT-DORY	GAF	SAIL	WD	CB				4	6	250		6	2900	3350
17	2	BUZZARDS-BAY	SLP	SAIL	WD	CB				5	1	1200	1	6	6000	6900
17	8	CONCORDIA SLOOP	GAF	SAIL	WD	CB				5	6	1200	1	6	6000	6850
18	1	ALDEN-O-BOAT	SLP	SAIL	WD	CB				6	8	1800	1	1	7450	8550
18	4	CARTER CATBOAT	CAT	SAIL	WD	CB				8	6	4200	2		13300	15100
18	8	BUZZARDS-BAY SLOOP	GAF	SAIL	WD	KC				6	4	1800	2	3	7450	8550
18	8	CAPE-COD-CAT	GAF	SAIL	MHG	CB	OB			9		4250	2		13600	15400
18	8	CAPE-COD-CAT	GAF	SAIL	MHG	CB	IB			9		4250	2		14500	16500
26		JOHN HACKER MISS		RNBT	CDR	SV	IB	400	CRUS	5	11	2800	1		17100	19400
34	3	BUTLER CUTTER	CUT	SAIL	CDR	KL				10	3	14800	5	6	70100	77000
		1986 BOATS														
16		CROCKER-CAT	CAT	SAIL	WD	CB	OB			7	6	2600	1	10	8950	10200
18	8	BUZZARDS-BAY SLOOP	GAF	SAIL	WD	CB	OB			6	8	2300	2	6	8100	9300
18	8	CARTER CATBOAT	GAF	SAIL	WD	CB	OB			9	5	4250	2	3	12800	14500
		1985 BOATS														
16		CROCKER-CAT	CAT	SAIL	WD	CB				7	6	2500	1	10	8150	9350
17		SWAMPSCOTT-DORY	GAF	SAIL	WD	CB				4	6	250		6	2550	2950
17	2	BUZZARDS-BAY	SLP	SAIL	WD	CB				5	1	1200	1	6	5300	6100
17	8	CONCORDIA SLOOP	GAF	SAIL	WD	CB				5	6	1200	1	6	5300	6100
18		CATBOAT	CAT	SAIL	P/M	CB				8	6	4000	2	8	11000	12500
18	1	ALDEN-O-BOAT	SLP	SAIL	WD	CB				6	8	1800	1	1	6600	7600
18	4	CARTER CATBOAT	CAT	SAIL	WD	CB				8	6	4200	2		11800	13400
18	8	BUZZARDS-BAY SLOOP	GAF	SAIL	WD	KC				6	4	1800	2	3	6550	7550
18	8	CAPE-COD-CAT	GAF	SAIL	MHG	CB	OB			9		4250	2		12000	13700
18	8	CAPE-COD-CAT	GAF	SAIL	MHG	CB	IB			9		4250	2		12800	14600

 CONTINUED ON NEXT PAGE

LOA FT	IN	NAME AND/ OR MODEL	TOP/ RIG	BOAT TYPE	-HULL- MTL	TP	ENGINE TP	# HP	MFG	BEAM FT	IN	WGT LBS	DRAFT FT	IN	RETAIL LOW	RETAIL HIGH
		1985 BOATS														
34	3	BUTLER CUTTER	CUT	SAIL	CDR	KL				10	3	14800	5	6	62000	68200
		1984 BOATS														
17		SWAMPSCOTT-DORY	GAF	SAIL	WD	CB				4	3	250		6	2400	2800
17	8	CONCORDIA SLOOP	GAF	SAIL	WD	CB				5	6	1200	1	6	5000	5700
18		CATBOAT	CAT	SAIL	P/M	CB				8	6	4000	2	8	10400	11800
18	1	O-BOAT	SLP	SAIL	WD	CB				6	8	1200	1	6	5000	5750
18	8	BUZZARDS-BAY SLOOP	GAF	SAIL	WD	KC				6		2000	2	6	6550	7550

....For earlier years, see the BUC Used Boat Price Guide, Volume 3

LANG YACHTS LTD

NORFOLD VA 23505

See inside cover to adjust price for area

For more recent years, see the BUC Used Boat Price Guide, Volume 1

LOA FT	IN	NAME AND/ OR MODEL	TOP/ RIG	BOAT TYPE	-HULL- MTL	TP	ENGINE TP	# HP	MFG	BEAM FT	IN	WGT LBS	DRAFT FT	IN	RETAIL LOW	RETAIL HIGH
		1996 BOATS														
28		FLY BRIDGE 280	FB	SF	FBG	SV	IB	400D	CUM	11					61400	67500
28		SUPERFISH 280	OP	SF	FBG	SV	IB	T230D	VLVO	11					58200	63900
28		TRUNK CABIN 280	OP	SF	FBG	SV	IB	T230D	VLVO	11					58000	63700
32		FLY BRIDGE	FB	SF	FBG	SV	IB	T350D	CAT	10					76500	84000
32		SUPERFISH	OP	SF	FBG	SV	IB	T350D	CAT	10					76500	84000
35		FLY BRIDGE	FB	SF	FBG	SV	IB	T400D	CUM	12					127000	140000
35		SUPERFISH	OP	SF	FBG	SV	IB	T400D	CUM	12					122500	134500
39		FLY BRIDGE	FB	SF	FBG	SV	IB	T800D	PERK	14					234000	257000
39		SUPERFISH	OP	SF	FBG	SV	IB	T800D	PERK	14					225500	247500
47		FLYBRIDGE	FB	SF	FBG	SV	IB	T10CD	MAN	14					145000	159500
47		SUPERFISH	OP	SF	FBG	SV	IB	T10CD	MAN	14					143500	157500
52		FLY BRIDGE	FB	SF	FBG	SV	IB	T10CD	MAN	16					153500	168500
52		SUPERFISH	OP	SF	FBG	SV	IB	T10CD	MAN	16					151500	166000
57		ENC FLY BRIDGE	FB	SF	FBG	SV	IB	T14CD	DD	18					169500	186000
57		SUPERFISH	OP	SF	FBG	SV	IB	T14CD	DD	18					167000	183500
70		ENC FLY BRIDGE	FB	SF	FBG	SV	IB	T24CD	DD	22					1.215M	1.320M
		1995 BOATS														
28		FLY BRIDGE 280	FB	SF	FBG	SV	IB	400D	CUM	11					58200	63900
28		SUPERFISH 280	OP	SF	FBG	SV	IB	T230D	VLVO	11					55200	60600
28		TRUNK CABIN 280	OP	SF	FBG	SV	IB	T230D	VLVO	11					55000	60400
32		FLY BRIDGE	FB	SF	FBG	SV	IB	T350D	CAT	10					72500	79700
32		SUPERFISH	OP	SF	FBG	SV	IB	T350D	CAT	10					72500	79700
35		FLY BRIDGE	FB	SF	FBG	SV	IB	T400D	CUM	12					120500	132500
35		SUPERFISH	OP	SF	FBG	SV	IB	T400D	CUM	12					116000	127500
39		FLY BRIDGE	FB	SF	FBG	SV	IB	T800D	PERK	14					223000	245000
39		SUPERFISH	OP	SF	FBG	SV	IB	T800D	PERK	14					214500	236000
47		FLYBRIDGE	FB	SF	FBG	SV	IB	T10CD	MAN	14					139000	153000
47		SUPERFISH	OP	SF	FBG	SV	IB	T10CD	MAN	14					137500	151000
52		FLY BRIDGE	FB	SF	FBG	SV	IB	T10CD	MAN	16					147000	161500
52		SUPERFISH	OP	SF	FBG	SV	IB	T10CD	MAN	16					145000	159000
57		ENC FLY BRIDGE	FB	SF	FBG	SV	IB	T14CD	DD	18					162000	178500
57		SUPERFISH	OP	SF	FBG	SV	IB	T14CD	DD	18					160000	175500
70		ENC FLY BRIDGE	FB	SF	FBG	SV	IB	T24CD	DD	22					1.160M	1.260M
		1994 BOATS														
28		FLY BRIDGE 280	FB	SF	FBG	SV	IB	400D	CUM	11					55200	60700
28		SUPERFISH 280	OP	SF	FBG	SV	IB	T230D	VLVO	11					52400	57600
28		TRUNK CABIN 280	OP	SF	FBG	SV	IB	T230D	VLVO	11					52200	57400
32		FLY BRIDGE	FB	SF	FBG	SV	IB	T350D	CAT	10					68900	75700
32		SUPERFISH	OP	SF	FBG	SV	IB	T350D	CAT	10					68900	75700
35		FLY BRIDGE	FB	SF	FBG	SV	IB	T400D	CUM	12					114500	125500
35		SUPERFISH	OP	SF	FBG	SV	IB	T400D	CUM	12					110000	121000
39		FLY BRIDGE	FB	SF	FBG	SV	IB	T800D	PERK	14					212500	233500
39		SUPERFISH	OP	SF	FBG	SV	IB	T800D	PERK	14					205000	225000
47		FLYBRIDGE	FB	SF	FBG	SV	IB	T10CD	MAN	14					133500	146500
47		SUPERFISH	OP	SF	FBG	SV	IB	T10CD	MAN	14					131500	144500
52		FLY BRIDGE	FB	SF	FBG	SV	IB	T10CD	MAN	16					141000	155000
52		SUPERFISH	OP	SF	FBG	SV	IB	T10CD	MAN	16					139000	153000
57		ENC FLY BRIDGE	FB	SF	FBG	SV	IB	T14CD	DD	18					156000	171500
57		SUPERFISH	OP	SF	FBG	SV	IB	T14CD	DD	18					153500	169000
70		ENC FLY BRIDGE	FB	SF	FBG	SV	IB	T24CD	DD	22					1.105M	1.205M
		1993 BOATS														
28		FLY BRIDGE 280	FB	SF	FBG	SV	IB	400D	CUM	11					52500	57700
28		SUPERFISH 280	OP	SF	FBG	SV	IB	T230D	VLVO	11					49800	54800
28		TRUNK CABIN 280	OP	SF	FBG	SV	IB	T230D	VLVO	11					49700	54600
32		FLY BRIDGE	FB	SF	FBG	SV	IB	T350D	CAT	10					65500	72000
32		SUPERFISH	OP	SF	FBG	SV	IB	T350D	CAT	10					65500	72000
35		FLY BRIDGE	FB	SF	FBG	SV	IB	T400D	CUM	12					109000	119500
35		SUPERFISH	OP	SF	FBG	SV	IB	T400D	CUM	12					105000	115000
39		FLY BRIDGE	FB	SF	FBG	SV	IB	T800D	PERK	14					202500	222500
39		SUPERFISH	OP	SF	FBG	SV	IB	T800D	PERK	14					195000	214500
47		FLYBRIDGE	FB	SF	FBG	SV	IB	T10CD	MAN	14					127000	139500
47		SUPERFISH	OP	SF	FBG	SV	IB	T10CD	MAN	14					125500	138000
52		FLY BRIDGE	FB	SF	FBG	SV	IB	T10CD	MAN	16					134500	148000
52		SUPERFISH	OP	SF	FBG	SV	IB	T10CD	MAN	16					132500	145500
57		ENC FLY BRIDGE	FB	SF	FBG	SV	IB	T14CD	DD	18					148500	163000
57		SUPERFISH	OP	SF	FBG	SV	IB	T14CD	DD	18					146500	161000
70		ENC FLY BRIDGE	FB	SF	FBG	SV	IB	T24CD	DD	22					1.060M	1.150M
		1992 BOATS														
28		CANYON RUNNER	HT	CR	FBG	SV	IB	T300D	CUM	11			2	1	53400	58700
28		SUPERFISH	OP	CR	FBG	SV	IB	T200D	VLVO	11			2		46800	51400
32		SUPERFISH	OP	CR	FBG	SV	IB	T300D	CUM	10			2	6	64400	70700
34		CANYON RUNNER	FB	CNV	FBG	SV	IB	T300D	CUM	10			2	6	112500	123500
35		SUPERFISH	OP	CR	FBG	SV	IB	T400D	CUM	12			3		91900	101000
39		SUPERFISH	OP	CR	FBG	SV	IB	T700D	FIAT	14			3		167500	184000
43		CANYON RUNNER	FB	SDNSF	FBG	SV	IB	T700D	FIAT	14			3		217000	238000
47		SUPERFISH	OP	CR	FBG	SV	IB	T820D	MAN	14			3	6	232500	255500
52		CANYON RUNNER	FB	SDNSF	FBG	SV	IB	T820D	MAN	14			3	6	356000	391000
57		SUPERFISH	OP	CR	FBG	SV	IB	T11CD	MAN	18			4		129000	141500
62		CANYON RUNNER	FB	SDNSF	FBG	SV	IB	T14CD	DD	18			4		573500	630000
		1991 BOATS														
28		CANYON RUNNER	HT	CR	FBG	SV	IB	T300D	CUM	11			2	1	50900	55900
28		SUPERFISH	OP	CR	FBG	SV	IB	T200D	VLVO	11			2		44100	49000
32		SUPERFISH	OP	CR	FBG	SV	IB	T300D	CUM	10			2	6	61400	67400
34		CANYON RUNNER	FB	CNV	FBG	SV	IB	T300D	CUM	10			2	6	107000	117500
35		CANYON RUNNER	FB	CNV	FBG	SV	IB	T400D	CUM	12			3		103000	113500
35		SUPERFISH	OP	CR	FBG	SV	IB	T400D	CUM	12			3		87600	96300
39		SUPERFISH	OP	CR	FBG	SV	IB	T700D	FIAT	14			3		159500	175500
43		CANYON RUNNER	FB	SDNSF	FBG	SV	IB	T700D	FIAT	14			3		206500	227000
47		SUPERFISH	OP	CR	FBG	SV	IB	T820D	MAN	14			3	6	221500	243500
52		CANYON RUNNER	FB	SDNSF	FBG	SV	IB	T820D	MAN	14			3	6	340500	374000
57		SUPERFISH	OP	CR	FBG	SV	IB	T11CD	MAN	18			4		123000	135000
62		CANYON RUNNER	FB	SDNSF	FBG	SV	IB	T14CD	DD	18			4		548500	603000
		1990 BOATS														
27		SUPERFISH	OP	CR	FBG	SV	IB	T210D	CUM	11			2		35900	39900
30		CANYON RUNNER	HT	CR	FBG	SV	IB	T210D	CUM	11			2	1	45800	50300
31		SUPERFISH	OP	CR	FBG	SV	IB	T250D	CUM	10			2	6	48100	52800
34		CANYON RUNNER	FB	CNV	FBG	SV	IB	T250D	CUM	10			2	6	99000	108500
35		CANYON RUNNER	FB	CNV	FBG	SV	IB	T300D	CUM	12			3		90400	99300
35		SUPERFISH	OP	CR	FBG	SV	IB	T300D	CUM	12			3		76000	83500
39		SUPERFISH	OP	CR	FBG	SV	IB	T400D	CUM	14			3	6	115500	126500
43		CANYON RUNNER	FB	SDNSF	FBG	SV	IB	T400D	CUM	14			3	6	158000	174000
47		SUPERFISH	OP	CR	FBG	SV	IB	T450D	GM	14			4		175500	193000
52		CANYON RUNNER	FB	SDNSF	FBG	SV	IB	T450D	GM	14			4		255000	280500
57		SUPERFISH	OP	CR	FBG	SV	IB	T735D	GM	18			4	6	279000	306500
62		CANYON RUNNER	FB	SDNSF	FBG	SV	IB	T735D	GM	18			4	6	391000	429500
		1989 BOATS														
28		CANYON RUNNER	HT	CR	FBG	SV	IB	T210D	CUM	11			2	1	41300	45900
28		SUPERFISH	OP	CR	FBG	SV	IB	250D	CUM	11			2		35200	39100
31		LANG CANYON RUNNER	FB	CNV	FBG	SV	IB	T250D	CUM	10			2	6	54000	59300
31		SUPERFISH	OP	CR	FBG	SV	IB	T250D	CUM	10			2	6	45900	50500
32		LANG CANYON RUNNER	FB	CNV	FBG	SV	IB	T300D	CUM	12			3		65900	72400
39		SUPERFISH	OP	CR	FBG	SV	IB	T300D	CUM	14			3	6	101500	111500
47		CANYON RUNNER	FB	SDNSF	FBG	SV	IB	T700D	FIAT	14			4		204000	224000
57		CANYON RUNNER	FB	SDNSF	FBG	SV	IB	T11CD	GM	18			4	6	113500	125000
		1988 BOATS														
28		SPORTFISHER 280 CR	OP	SF	FBG	SV	IB	T260		11			2	2	24000	26600
30	4	SPORTFISHER 300 CR	HT	SF	FBG	SV	IB	T260		11			2	2	27600	30600
31	3	SUPER FISH 31 CR	OP	SF	FBG	SV	IB	T340		10			2	2	31900	35500
34		FLYBRIDGE 31	FB	SDNSF	FBG	SV	IB	T340		10			2	2	57600	63300
35		FLYBRIDGE 35 CR	FB	SDNSF	FBG	SV	IB	358D		12			2	6	67200	73900
35		SUPER FISH 35 CR	OP	SF	FBG	SV	IB	T358D		12			2	6	79600	87500
43		FLYBRIDGE 43 CR	FB	SDNSF	FBG	SV	IB	T485D		12			3	2	162000	178000
43		SUPER FISH 43 CR	TT	SF	FBG	SV	IB	T485D		12			3	2	165000	181500
52		ENCLOSED FLYBRIDGE	FB	SDNSF	FBG	SV	IB	T735D		12			3	4	288500	317000
52		SUPER FISH 52 CR	TT	SF	FBG	SV	IB	T735D		12			3	2	269500	296000
62		ENCLOSED FLYBRIDGE	FB	SDNSF	FBG	SV	IB	T11CD		18			4	3	413000	454000
62		WC MOTOR YACHT 62	FB	TCMY	FBG	SV	IB	T13CD		18			4	6	447500	492000
		1987 BOATS														
28		BEACH-RUNNER 280	OP	SF	FBG	SV	IB	T260		11			2	2	20600	22900
28		SUPER FISH 280	OP	SF	FBG	SV	IB	T260		11			2	2	25000	27800
34		FLYBRIDGE 31	FB	SDNSF	FBG	SV	IB	T350		10	2	12400	2	2	49300	54200
35		FLYBRIDGE 35	FB	SDNSF	FBG	SV	IB	340		12		16080	2	6	54100	59400
35		SUPER FISH 35	OP	SF	FBG	SV	IB	T340		12			2	6	47000	51700

LOA FT	LOA IN	NAME AND/ OR MODEL	TOP/ RIG	BOAT TYPE	-HULL- MTL	-HULL- TP	ENGINE TP	ENGINE # HP	ENGINE MFG	BEAM FT	BEAM IN	WGT LBS	DRAFT FT	DRAFT IN	RETAIL LOW	RETAIL HIGH
		1987 BOATS														
43		FLYBRIDGE	FB	SDNSF	FBG	SV	IB	T350D		14			3	2	134000	147000
43		SUPER FISH 43	TT	SF	FBG	SV	IB	T350D		14			3	2	136000	149500
52		ENCLOSED FLYBRIDGE	FB	SDNSF	FBG	SV	IB	T750D		14			3	4	279500	307000
62		ENCLOSED FLYBRIDGE	FB	SDNSF	FBG	SV	IB	T11CD		18			4	3	396500	436000
		1986 BOATS														
17	7	LANG 170		CTRCN	FBG	SV	IB	100		7	7	1700			3600	4200
17	7	LANG 170 CANYON RUN		CTRCN	FBG	SV	IO	100		7	7	1700			3400	3950
29		LANG 260 CANYON RUN	FB	SF	FBG	SV	IO	T140		10		7800			21200	23500
31		LANG 280 CANYON RUN		SF	FBG	SV	IB	T260		11		8900			26700	29700
35		LANG 310 CANYON RUN		SF	FBG	SV	IB	T225		12		12580			47600	52300
35		LANG 310 CANYON RUN	FB	SF	FBG	SV	IB	T260		12		16080			53800	59100
43		LANG 380 CANYON RUN		SF	FBG	SV	IB	T350		13	8	20500			108000	118500
43		LANG 380 CANYON RUN	FB	SF	FBG	SV	IB	T350D		13	8	23500			138000	151500
52		LANG 460 CANYON RUN		SF	FBG	SV	IB	T375D		14		27700			171500	188500
52		LANG 460 CANYON RUN	FB	SF	FBG	SV	IB	T375D		14		30500			176500	194000
62		LANG 550 CANYON RUN		SF	FBG	SV	IB	T750D		18		35800			291500	320500
62		LANG 550 CANYON RUN	FB	SF	FBG	SV	IB	T10CD		18		43900			333000	366000
		1985 BOATS														
26		LANG 26 CANYON RUNNR		CTRCN	FBG		IB	260		10		6200			16400	18600
26		LANG 26 CANYON RUNNR		CUD	FBG		IB	260		10		5300			14400	16300
27	8	LANG 28 CANYON RUNNR		CUD	FBG		IB	T225		11		8900			24600	27400
30	6	LANG 30 CANYON RUNNR	FB	CR	FBG		IB	425		11	6	12500			31400	34900
34		LANG 34 CANYON RUNNR	FB	CR	FBG		IB	T350		12	6	14300			47600	52300
38		LANG 38 CANYON RUNNR	FB	CR	FBG		IB	T425		13		16100			71800	78900
71	8	LANG 71 CANYON RUNNR	FB	CR	FBG		IB	T870D		20	6	53000			418500	460000

LARSON BOATS

DIV OF GENMAR INDUSTRIES
LITTLE FALLS MN 56345

COAST GUARD MFG ID- LAR
FORMERLY LUND AMERICAN

See inside cover to adjust price for area

For more recent years, see the BUC Used Boat Price Guide, Volume 1

LOA FT	LOA IN	NAME AND/ OR MODEL	TOP/ RIG	BOAT TYPE	-HULL- MTL	-HULL- TP	ENGINE TP	ENGINE # HP	ENGINE MFG	BEAM FT	BEAM IN	WGT LBS	DRAFT FT	DRAFT IN	RETAIL LOW	RETAIL HIGH
		1996 BOATS														
16	1	ALL AMERICAN 160	OP	B/R	FBG	DV	OB			6	11	1025			3050	3550
17	5	LEI 174	OP	B/R	FBG	DV	IO	180	MRCR	7	6	1760			3750	4350
17	5	LEI 174	OP	B/R	FBG	DV	IO	185	VLVO	7	6	1760			4750	5450
17	5	LXI 174	OP	B/R	FBG	DV	IO	135		7	6	1760			4750	5700
17	5	LXI 174	OP	B/R	FBG	DV	IO	180	MRCR	7	6	1760			4150	4850
17	5	LXI 174	OP	B/R	FBG	DV	IO	180-185		7	6	1760			5150	5950
17	5	SEI 174	OP	B/R	FBG	DV	OB			7	6	1487			4250	4950
17	5	SEI 174	OP	B/R	FBG	DV	IO	135		7	6	1760			4100	4950
17	5	SEI 174	OP	B/R	FBG	DV	IO	180	MRCR	7	6	1760			4200	4900
17	5	SEI 174	OP	B/R	FBG	DV	IO	180-185		7	6	1760			4700	5400
17	5	SEI 174 F+S	OP	B/R	FBG	DV	OB			7	6	1487			4250	4950
19	5	LXI 194	OP	B/R	FBG	DV	IO	180	MRCR	8		2300			5700	6550
19	5	LXI 194	OP	B/R	FBG	DV	IO	180-250		8		2300			6850	8100
19	5	SEI 194	OP	B/R	FBG	DV	OB			8		1797			5200	5950
19	5	SEI 194	OP	B/R	FBG	DV	IO	180	MRCR	8		2300			5100	5900
19	5	SEI 194	OP	B/R	FBG	DV	IO	180-250		8		2300			6200	7400
20	9	LXI 215	OP	B/R	FBG	DV	IO	190-210		8	6	2840			8350	9600
20	9	LXI 215	OP	B/R	FBG	DV	IO	220-265		8	6	2840			9200	10500
20	9	SEI 215	OP	B/R	FBG	DV	IO	190-210		8	6	2840			7650	8800
20	9	SEI 215	OP	B/R	FBG	DV	IO	220-265		8	6	2840			8500	9750
20	9	SEI 215	OP	B/R	FBG	DV	IO	300		8	6	2840			9400	11300
23	1	HAMPTON 235	OP	CUD	FBG	DV	IO	190-300		8	6	4200			13400	16600
23	1	SEI 235	OP	B/R	FBG	DV	IO	190-300		8	6	4200			12500	15600
24	2	HAMPTON 240	OP	CUD	FBG	DV	IO	235-300		8	6	4260			14500	17600
26	1	CABRIO 260	OP	OVNTR	FBG	DV	IO	235-300		9		6000			20700	24300
26	1	CABRIO 260	OP	OVNTR	FBG	DV	IO	138D	VLVO	9		6000			22900	25400
28	11	CABRIO 280	OP	OVNTR	FBG	SV	IO	300		10		7200			28500	31800
28	11	CABRIO 280	OP	OVNTR	FBG	SV	IO	240D	MRCR	10		7200			32200	35800
28	11	CABRIO 280	OP	OVNTR	FBG	SV	IO	T180-T220		10		7200			29400	34200
32	6	CABRIO 310	OP	OVNTR	FBG	SV	IO	T210-T250		10	6	9500			43000	49200
32	6	CABRIO 310	OP	OVNTR	FBG	SV	IO	T216D	VLVO	10	6	9500			51100	56200
		1995 BOATS														
16	1	ALL AMERICAN 160	OP	B/R	FBG	DV	OB			6	11	1025			2900	3350
17	5	LXI 174	OP	B/R	FBG	DV	IO	180	MRCR	7	6	1760	2	8	4250	4950
17	5	LXI 174	OP	B/R	FBG	DV	IO	185	VLVO	7	6	1760	2	8	4900	5600
17	5	SEI 174	OP	B/R	FBG	DV	OB			7	6	1487			4050	4700
17	5	SEI 174	OP	B/R	FBG	DV	IO	135-185		7	6	1760			4000	4950
17	5	SEI 174 CB	OP	RNBT	FBG	DV	IO	135-180		7	6	1760	2	8	4250	5250
17	5	SEI 174 CB	OP	RNBT	FBG	DV	IO	185	VLVO	7	6	1760	2	8	4600	5300
19	5	LXI 194	OP	B/R	FBG	DV	IO	180-235		8		2300			5700	7000
19	5	SEI 194	OP	B/R	FBG	DV	OB			7	5	1797			4950	5700
19	5	SEI 194	OP	B/R	FBG	DV	IO	180-185		8		2300			5300	6350
19	5	SEI 194	OP	B/R	FBG	DV	IO	190-235		8		2300			5750	6650
19	5	SEI 194 CB	OP	RNBT	FBG	DV	IO	180-235		8		2300	2	9	5700	7000
21	1	HAMPTON 200	OP	CUD	FBG	DV	IO	180-190		7	11	2700			7500	9100
21	6	LXI 214	OP	B/R	FBG	DV	IO	190-255		8	6	2840			8450	10000
21	6	SEI 214	OP	B/R	FBG	DV	IO	190-255		8	6	2840			7700	9500
21	6	SEI 214 CB	OP	RNBT	FBG	DV	IO	190-255		8	6	2840	2	9	8250	9950
23	1	ESCAPADE 220	OP	CUD	FBG	SV	IO	235-255		8	6	3430			10200	12200
23	1	ESCAPADE 220	OP	CUD	FBG	SV	IO	300		8	6	3430			11000	13000
23	3	HAMPTON 220	OP	CUD	FBG	SV	IO	205-255		8	6	3300	2	9	9800	11900
25	5	ESCAPADE 240	OP	CUD	FBG	SV	IO	235-300		8	6	4260			13200	16400
27		CABRIO 250	OP	OVNTR	FBG	DV	IO	235-300		8	6	4900	2	10	17100	20600
27		CABRIO 250	OP	OVNTR	FBG	DV	IO	T140D	VLVO	8	6	4900	2	10	22500	25100
28	11	CABRIO 280	OP	OVNTR	FBG	SV	IO	300	MRCR	10		7200	2	10	26600	29500
28	11	CABRIO 280	OP	OVNTR	FBG	SV	IO	T180-T220		10		7200	2	10	27400	31800
32	6	CABRIO 310	OP	OVNTR	FBG	SV	IO	T205-T250		10	6	9500	2	10	39900	45800
32	6	CABRIO 310	OP	OVNTR	FBG	SV	IO	T185D	VLVO	10	6	9500	2	10	46300	50800
		1994 BOATS														
16	1	ALL AMERICAN 160	OP	B/R	FBG	DV	OB			6	11	1025			2750	3200
17	5	SEI 174	OP	B/R	FBG	DV	IO	115-164		7	8	1760			3800	4700
17	5	SEI 174	OP	B/R	FBG	DV	IO	185	VLVO	7	8	1760			4100	4750
17	8	ALL AMERICAN 180	OP	B/R	FBG	DV	OB			7	4	1160			3150	3650
19	5	LXI 194	OP	B/R	FBG	DV	IO	160-255		8		2300			5300	6600
19	5	SEI 194	OP	B/R	FBG	DV	IO	160-205		8		2300			4900	5950
19	5	SEI 194	OP	B/R	FBG	DV	IO	225-235		8		2300			5350	6150
20		ALL AMERICAN 200	OP	B/R	FBG	DV	OB			7	5	2010			5050	5800
21	1	ESCAPADE 200	OP	CUD	FBG	SV	IO	160-235		7	11	2840			7400	9150
21	1	ESCAPADE 200	OP	CUD	FBG	SV	IO	255	VLVO	7	11	2840			8150	9400
21	1	HAMPTON 200	OP	CUD	FBG	DV	IO	160-235		7	11	2700			6950	8650
21	1	HAMPTON 200	OP	CUD	FBG	DV	IO	255	VLVO	7	11	2700			7850	9000
21	6	LXI 214	OP	B/R	FBG	DV	IO	185-255		8	6	2840			7800	9250
21	6	SEI 214	OP	B/R	FBG	DV	IO	185-250		8	6	2840			7250	9000
23	1	ESCAPADE 220	OP	CUD	FBG	SV	IO	185-255		8	6	3430			9600	11400
23	1	ESCAPADE 220	OP	CUD	FBG	SV	IO	300		8	6	3430			10200	12200
23	3	HAMPTON 220	OP	CUD	FBG	SV	IO	185-255		8	6	3300	2	9	9400	11100
23	3	HAMPTON 220	OP	CUD	FBG	SV	IO	300		8	6	3300	2	9	10000	11900
25	5	ESCAPADE 240	OP	CUD	FBG	SV	IO	185-300		8	6	4260			12300	15300
25	5	HAMPTON 240 MC	OP	SPTCR	FBG	DV	IO	185-300		8	6	4660	3	1	13200	16300
28	11	CABRIO 280	OP	OVNTR	FBG	SV	IO	250-300		10		7152	2	10	23900	27700
28	11	CABRIO 280	OP	OVNTR	FBG	SV	IO	T180-T190		10		7152	2	10	25600	28900
28	11	CABRIO 280	OP	OVNTR	FBG	SV	IO	T135D	VLVO	10		7152	2	10	29200	32400
29	11	CABRIO 300	OP	OVNTR	FBG	SV	IO	T225-T300		10	6	9500	2	10	33300	39300
		1993 BOATS														
17		ALL AMERICAN 170	OP	B/R	FBG	DV	OB			7	4	1160			3000	3450
17		ALL AMERICAN 170	OP	B/R	FBG	DV	IO	110-155		7	4	1760			3700	4350
17		ALL AMERICAN 170 CB	OP	RNBT	FBG	DV	IO	110-155		7	4	1775			3850	4750
17		SENZA 170 BR	OP	B/R	FBG	DV	OB			7	3	1380			3450	4000
18	4	SEI 180	OP	B/R	FBG	DV	IO	155-175		7	3	1925			4050	5050
18	4	SEI 180	OP	B/R	FBG	DV	IO	180	MRCR	7	3	1925			4100	4800
18	4	SEI 180	OP	B/R	FBG	DV	IO	180-205		7	3	1925			4500	5150
19		ALL AMERICAN 190	OP	B/R	FBG	DV	IO	110-230		7	5	2300			4700	5800
19		SENZA 190 CB	OP	RNBT	FBG	DV	IO	155-190		7	4	2450			4900	5950
20		HAMPTON 200	OP	CUD	FBG	DV	IO	155-205		7	11	2700			6500	7950
20		HAMPTON 200	OP	CUD	FBG	DV	IO	225-230		7	11	2700			7100	8150
20		SEI 200	OP	B/R	FBG	DV	IO	155-205		7	11	2350			5550	6850
20		SEI 200	OP	B/R	FBG	DV	IO	225-230		7	11	2350			6100	7000
20		SEI 200 S	OP	B/R	FBG	DV	IO	155-230		7	11	2500			5750	7150
20	10	SENZA 210	OP	CUD	FBG	DV	IO	180-250		8		2975			7200	8950
20	10	SENZA 210	OP	CUD	FBG	DV	IO	300		8		2975			8100	9800
22		HAMPTON 220	OP	CUD	FBG	SV	IO	155-250		8	6	3300	2	9	8400	10400
22		HAMPTON 220	OP	CUD	FBG	SV	IO	300		8	6	3300	2	9	9400	11100
22		HAMPTON 220 MC	OP	SPTCR	FBG	DV	IO	155-250		8	6	3900	2	9	9450	11500
22		HAMPTON 220 MC	OP	SPTCR	FBG	DV	IO	300		8	6	3900	2	9	10400	12300
24	2	HAMPTON 240 MC	OP	SPTCR	FBG	DV	IO	180-250		8	6	4660	3	1	12100	14400
24	2	HAMPTON 240 MC	OP	SPTCR	FBG	DV	IO	300		8	6	4660	3	1	13000	15200
25	1	HAMPTON 250	OP	OVNTR	FBG	SV	IO	180-250		8	6	4900	2	10	12900	15400
25	1	HAMPTON 250	OP	OVNTR	FBG	SV	IO	300		8	6	4900	2	10	14000	16300
25	2	SENZA SPECTRE 250	OP	RNBT	FBG	DV	IO	245-300		8	3	4000			11000	13400
25	2	SENZA SPECTRE 250	OP	RNBT	FBG	DV	IO	350-390		8	3	4000			12400	15200
27	2	CABRIO 260	OP	OVNTR	FBG	DV	IO	205-230		9	6	4900	2	10	15700	18300
27	2	CABRIO 260	OP	OVNTR	FBG	DV	IO	300		9	6	4900	2	10	17100	19700

CONTINUED ON NEXT PAGE

LOA FT	LOA IN	NAME AND/ OR MODEL	TOP/ RIG	BOAT TYPE	-HULL- MTL	-HULL- TP	TP	ENGINE # HP	ENGINE MFG	BEAM FT	BEAM IN	WGT LBS	DRAFT FT	DRAFT IN	RETAIL LOW	RETAIL HIGH
		1993 BOATS														
27	3	CABRIO 270	OP	OVNTR	FBG	SV	IO	T155-T235		9		7800	2	10	22300	26500
27	3	CABRIO 270	OP	OVNTR	FBG	SV	IO	T115D	VLVO	9		7800	2	10	27700	30700
29	11	CABRIO 300	OP	OVNTR	FBG	SV	IO	T155-T230		10	6	9500	2	10	29300	34500
29	11	CABRIO 300	OP	OVNTR	FBG	SV	IO	T185D	VLVO	10	6	9500	2	10	36100	40100
		1992 BOATS														
17		ALL AMERICAN 170	OP	B/R	FBG	DV	OB			7	4	1160			2850	3300
17		ALL AMERICAN 170	OP	B/R	FBG	DV	IO	110-155		7	4	1785			3500	4050
17		ALL AMERICAN 170 CB	OP	RNBT	FBG	DV	IO	110-155		7	4	1800			3650	4450
17		ALL AMERICAN 170 SE	OP	B/R	FBG	DV	IO	110-155		7	4	1825			3500	4100
17		ALL AMERICAN 170 SPT	OP	B/R	FBG	DV	IO	110-155		7	4	1785			3600	4200
17		ALL AMERICAN 170 SPT	OP	RNBT	FBG	DV	IO	110-115		7	4	1785			3650	4250
17		ALL AMERICAN 170 XLT	OP	B/R	FBG	DV	IO	110-115		7	4	1785			3300	3850
17		ALL AMERICAN 170 XLT	OP	RNBT	FBG	DV	IO	110-115		7	4	1785			3700	4300
17		SENZA 170	OP	B/R	FBG	DV	OB			7	3	1380			3250	3800
17		SENZA 170 CB	OP	RNBT	FBG	DV	OB			7	3	1220			2950	3450
18	4	LAZER 180	OP	B/R	FBG	DV	IO	155-175		7	3	1925			3800	4700
18	4	LAZER 180	OP	B/R	FBG	DV	IO	180	MRCR	7	3	1925			3850	4500
18	4	LAZER 180	OP	B/R	FBG	DV	IO	180-205		7	3	1925			4150	4800
18	4	LAZER 180 XLT SPORT	OP	B/R	FBG	DV	IO	115-180		7	3	1925			3750	4350
18	4	LEGACY 180 XLT	OP	B/R	FBG	DV	IO	115-180		7	3	1925			3650	4250
19		ALL AMERICAN 190	OP	B/R	FBG	DV	IO	115-190		7	5	2300			4200	5250
19		ALL AMERICAN 190	OP	B/R	FBG	DV	IO	205-230		7	5	2300			4300	5300
19		ALL AMERICAN 190	OP	B/R	FBG	DV	IO	245	VLVO	7	5	2300			4750	5450
19		ALL AMERICAN 190	OP	CUD	FBG	DV	OB			7	5	1750			4100	4800
19		ALL AMERICAN 190	OP	CUD	FBG	DV	IO	110-230		7	5	2485			4850	5950
19		ALL AMERICAN 190	OP	CUD	FBG	DV	IO	245	VLVO	7	5	2485			5300	6100
19		ALL AMERICAN 190 SE	OP	B/R	FBG	DV	IO	110-245		7	5	2350			4550	5600
19		ALL AMERICAN 190 SPT	OP	B/R	FBG	DV	IO	110-245		7	5	2300			4550	5600
19		SENZA 190	OP	B/R	FBG	DV	IO	155-190		7	4	2772			4750	5850
19		SENZA 190 CB	OP	B/R	FBG	DV	IO	190	VLVO	7	4	2772			4950	5650
19		SENZA 190 CB	OP	RNBT	FBG	DV	IO	155-180		7	4	2450			4600	5550
20		LAZER 200	OP	B/R	FBG	DV	IO	150-245		7	11	2350			5450	6600
20		LAZER 200 S	OP	B/R	FBG	DV	IO	155-230		7	11	2500			5400	6700
20		LAZER 200 S	OP	B/R	FBG	DV	IO	245	VLVO	7	11	2500			6000	6900
20		LAZER 2000 SPORT	OP	B/R	FBG	DV	IO	155-230		7	11	2350			5300	6500
20		LAZER 2000 SPORT	OP	B/R	FBG	DV	IO	245	VLVO	7	11	2350			5850	6700
20		LEGACY 200 SE	OP	B/R	FBG	DV	IO	150-245		7	11	2500			5650	6850
20	4	INTERNATIONAL DC204	OP	CTRCN	FBG	DV	OB			7	6	2000			6750	7750
20	10	SENZA 210	OP	B/R	FBG	DV	IO	180-245		8		2950			6300	7850
20	10	SENZA 210	OP	B/R	FBG	DV	IO	300	MRCR	8		2950			7050	8100
20	10	SENZA 210	OP	CUD	FBG	DV	IO	180-245		8		2975			6750	8400
20	10	SENZA 210	OP	CUD	FBG	DV	IO	300		8		2975			7550	9200
21		ALL AMERICAN 210	OP	CUD	FBG	DV	IO	155-245		8	4	2850			6750	8450
21	8	DELTA 215	OP	SPTCR	FBG	DV	IO	150-245		8		2900	2	9	7150	8650
22		HAMPTON 220	OP	CUD	FBG	SV	IO	155-245		8	6	3300	2	9	7850	9700
22		IIAMPTON 220	OP	CUD	FBG	SV	IO	300	MRCR	8	6	3300	2	9	8800	10000
22		HAMPTON 220 MC	OP	SPTCR	FBG	DV	IO	155-245		8	6	3900	2	9	8900	10600
22		HAMPTON 220 MC	OP	SPTCR	FBG	DV	IO	300		8	6	3900	2	9	9700	11500
22		INTERNATIONAL DC228	OP	CUD	FBG	SV	OB			8		2800			9500	10800
25		INTERNATIONAL DC258	OP	CUD	FBG	SV	OB			9		4070			14100	16000
25	1	HAMPTON 250	OP	OVNTR	FBG	SV	IO	175-245		8	6	4900	2	10	12000	14500
25	1	HAMPTON 250	OP	OVNTR	FBG	SV	IO	300		8	6	4900	2	10	13100	15300
25	2	SENZA SPECTRE	OP	RNBT	FBG	DV	IO	225-300		8	3	4000			10200	12500
25	2	SENZA SPECTRE	OP	RNBT	FBG	DV	IO	330	MRCR	8	3	4000			11200	12700
27	2	CABRIO 260	OP	OVNTR	FBG	DV	IO	180-245		9	6	6000	2	10	15900	19200
27	2	CABRIO 260	OP	OVNTR	FBG	DV	IO	300		9	6	6000	2	10	17500	20100
27	3	CABRIO 270	OP	OVNTR	FBG	SV	IO	T155-T245		9		7800	2	10	20900	25300
29	11	CABRIO 300	OP	OVNTR	FBG	SV	IO	T155-T245		10	6	9500	2	10	27400	32800
		1991 BOATS														
16		ANGLER 160	OP	FSH	FBG	SV	OB			6	5	1000			2350	2700
17		ALL AMERICAN 170	OP	B/R	FBG	DV	OB			7	4	1160			2700	3150
17		ALL AMERICAN 170	OP	B/R	FBG	DV	IO	110-155		7	4	1785			3250	3850
17		ALL AMERICAN 170 CB	OP	RNBT	FBG	DV	IO	110-155		7	4	1825			3450	4150
17		ALL AMERICAN 170 SE	OP	B/R	FBG	DV	IO	110-155		7	4	1825			3300	3850
17		ALL AMERICAN 170 SPT	OP	B/R	FBG	DV	IO	110-155		7	4	1785			3300	3950
17		ALL AMERICAN 170CBSE	OP	RNBT	FBG	DV	IO	110-155		7	4	1825			3500	4100
17		FISH N SKI 170	OP	B/R	FBG	DV	OB			7	4	1250			2900	3350
17		SENZA 170	OP	B/R	FBG	DV	OB			7	3	1380			3100	3600
17		SENZA 170 CB	OP	RNBT	FBG	DV	OB			7	3	1220			2850	3300
18		INTERNATIONAL DC-184	OP	CTRCN	FBG	DV	OB					1850			3850	4450
18	4	LEGACY 180	OP	B/R	FBG	DV	IO	110-180		7	3	1925			3600	4400
18	4	LEGACY 180 SE	OP	B/R	FBG	DV	IO	110-180		7	3	2100			3800	4500
18	4	LEGACY 180 SPORT	OP	B/R	FBG	DV	IO	110-180		7	3	1925			3700	4450
19		ALL AMERICAN 190	OP	B/R	FBG	DV	OB			7	5	1490			3400	3950
19		ALL AMERICAN 190	OP	B/R	FBG	DV	IO	110-230		7	5	2300			4150	5050
19		ALL AMERICAN 190	OP	CUD	FBG	DV	OB			7	5	1750			3900	4550
19		ALL AMERICAN 190	OP	CUD	FBG	DV	IO	110-230		7	5	2485			4600	5550
19		ALL AMERICAN 190 SE	OP	B/R	FBG	DV	IO	110-230		7	5	2350			4200	5050
19		ALL AMERICAN 190 SE	OP	CUD	FBG	DV	IO	110-230		7	5	2485			4750	5750
19		ALL AMERICAN 190 SPT	OP	B/R	FBG	DV	IO	110-230		7	5	2300			4200	5100
19		ALL AMERICAN 190 SPT	OP	CUD	FBG	DV	IO	110-230		7	5	2455			4650	5650
19		FISH N SKI 190	OP	B/R	FBG	DV	OB			7	5	1490			3700	4350
19		SENZA 190 LX	OP	B/R	FBG	DV	IO	150-180							4700	5450
19		SENZA 190 LX CB	OP	RNBT	FBG	DV	IO	150-180		7	4	2450			4500	5200
20		LEGACY 200 S	OP	B/R	FBG	DV	IO	150-245		7	11	2500			5250	6400
20		LEGACY 200 SE	OP	B/R	FBG	DV	IO	150-245		7	11	2500			5300	6450
20		LEGACY 2000	OP	B/R	FBG	DV	IO	150-245		7	11	2350			5100	6200
20		LEGACY 2000 SPORT	OP	B/R	FBG	DV	IO	150-245		7	11	2350			5150	6300
20	4	INTERNATIONAL DC204	OP	CTRCN	FBG	DV	OB			7	6	2000			6500	7450
20	10	SENZA 210 LX	OP	B/R	FBG	DV	IO	180-245		8		2950			5900	7350
20	10	SENZA 210 LX	OP	B/R	FBG	DV	IO	300	MRCR	8		2950			6650	7600
20	10	SENZA 210 LX	OP	CUD	FBG	DV	IO	180-245		8		2975			6350	7900
20	10	SENZA 210 LX	OP	CUD	FBG	DV	IO	300	MRCR	8		2975			7100	8150
21		ALL AMERICAN 210	OP	CUD	FBG	DV	IO	150-245		8	4	2850			6350	7900
21	8	DELTA 215	OP	SPTCR	FBG	DV	IO	150-245		8		2900	2	9	6700	8100
22		HAMPTON 220	OP	SPTCR	FBG	SV	IO	150-300		8	6	3300	2	9	7600	9400
22		INTERNATIONAL DC228	OP	CUD	FBG	SV	OB			8		2800			9150	10400
25		INTERNATIONAL DC258	OP	CUD	FBG	SV	OB			9		4070			13500	15300
25	1	SAN MARINO	OP	OVNTR	FBG	SV	IO	175-300		8	6	4900	2	10	11300	14000
25	1	SAN MARINO	OP	OVNTR	FBG	SV	IO	185D	VLVO	8	6	4900	2	10	13900	15800
25	2	SENZA SPECTRE	OP	RNBT	FBG	DV	IO	230-300		8	3	4000			9450	11800
25	2	SENZA SPECTRE	OP	RNBT	FBG	DV	IO	360	MRCR	8	3	4000			11100	12600
27	3	MIRADO	OP	OVNTR	FBG	SV	IO	300		9		7800	2	10	18400	20700
27	3	MIRADO	OP	OVNTR	FBG	SV	IO	T155-T245		9		7800	2	10	18600	22200
27	3	MIRADO	OP	OVNTR	FBG	SV	IO	T120D	VLVO	9		7800	2	10	23000	25500
29	11	CABRIO	OP	OVNTR	FBG	SV	IO	T155-T245		10	6	9500	2	10	25700	30800
29	11	CABRIO	OP	OVNTR	FBG	SV	IO	T185D	VLVO	10	6	9500	2	10	31700	35200
		1990 BOATS														
16		LAKER 160	OP	RNBT	FBG	DV	OB			6	6	760			1700	2050
16	2	SENZA 165	OP	B/R	FBG	DV	OB			7	1	1000			2300	2650
16	2	SENZA 165 C/B	OP	RNBT	FBG	DV	OB			7	1	1050			2400	2800
16	11	SENZA 170	OP	B/R	FBG	DV	IO	125-175		7	1	1725			2750	3250
17		ALL AMERICAN 170	OP	B/R	FBG	DV	OB			7	4	1160			2600	3000
17		ALL AMERICAN 170	OP	B/R	FBG	DV	IO	120-175		7	4	1785			3050	3600
17		ALL AMERICAN 170 CB	OP	RNBT	FBG	DV	IO	120-175		7	4	1800			3250	3800
17		ALL AMERICAN 170 SPD	OP	B/R	FBG	DV	IO	120-175		7	4	1825			3100	3650
17	1	LAKER 170	OP	RNBT	FBG	DV	OB			7	4	1125			2550	2950
18		INTERNATIONAL DC-184	OP	CTRCN	FBG	DV	OB			7	6	1850			3650	4250
18	4	LAZER 180	OP	B/R	FBG	DV	IO	125-205		7	3	1925			3250	3900
18	4	LAZER 180 SPED	OP	B/R	FBG	DV	IO	125-205		7	3	2100			3400	4050
19		ALL AMERICAN 190	OP	B/R	FBG	DV	OB			7	5	1490			3400	3950
19		ALL AMERICAN 190	OP	B/R	FBG	DV	IO	120-260		7	5	2300			3950	4800
19		ALL AMERICAN 190 CC	OP	CUD	FBG	DV	IO	120-260		7	5	2485			4400	5300
19		ALL AMERICAN 190 SPD	OP	B/R	FBG	DV	IO	120-260		7	5	2350			3950	4850
19		ALL AMERICAN 190CUD	OP	CUD	FBG	DV	OB			7	5	1750			3750	4350
19		SENZA 190 LX	OP	B/R	FBG	DV	IO	167-209		7	4	2590			4200	4950
20		LAZER 200	OP	B/R	FBG	DV	IO	167-260		7	11	2350			4850	5800
20		LAZER 200	OP	B/R	FBG	DV	IO	275	VLVO	7	11	2350			5400	6200
20		LAZER 200 CC SP ED	OP	CUD	FBG	DV	IO	167-260		7	11	2550			5400	6400
20		LAZER 200 CC SP ED	OP	CUD	FBG	DV	IO	275	VLVO	7	11	2550			5950	6850
20		LAZER 200 SP ED	OP	B/R	FBG	DV	IO	167-260		7	11	2500			5000	5950
20		LAZER 200 SP ED	OP	B/R	FBG	DV	IO	275	VLVO	7	11	2500			5500	6350
20	4	INTERNATIONAL DC-204	OP	CTRCN	FBG	DV	OB			7	6	2000			6250	7150
20	10	SENZA 210 LX	OP	B/R	FBG	DV	IO	200-260		8		2950			5600	6800
20	10	SENZA 210 LX	OP	B/R	FBG	DV	IO	275-330		8		2950			6250	7650
20	10	SENZA 210 LX CUD	OP	CUD	FBG	DV	IO	200-260		8		2975			6000	7300
20	10	SENZA 210 LX CUD	OP	CUD	FBG	DV	IO	275-330		8		2975			6700	8200
21		ALL AMERICAN 210 CC	OP	CUD	FBG	DV	IO	167-260		8	3	2850			6150	7300
21		ALL AMERICAN 210 CC	OP	CUD	FBG	DV	IO	275	VLVO	8	3	2850			6700	7700
21	8	DELTA 215	OP	SPTCR	FBG	DV	IO	167-260		8		2900			6350	7500
21	8	DELTA 215	OP	SPTCR	FBG	DV	IO	275	VLVO	8		2900			6900	7900
22		HAMPTON 220	OP	SPTCR	FBG	SV	IO	167-275		8	6	3300			7150	8850
22		INTERNATIONAL DC-228	OP	CUD	FBG	DV	OB			8		2800			8800	10000
22		INTERNATIONAL DC-228	OP	CUD	FBG	DV	IO	200-260		8		3650			7300	8800
22		INTERNATIONAL DC-228	OP	CUD	FBG	DV	IO	275	VLVO	8		3650			8000	9200
25	1	SAN MARINO	OP	OVNTR	FBG	SV	IO	200-275		8	6	4900			10700	13100

CONTINUED ON NEXT PAGE

LOA FT	LOA IN	NAME AND/ OR MODEL	TOP/ RIG	BOAT TYPE	-HULL- MTL	-HULL- TP	TP	ENGINE # HP	ENGINE MFG	BEAM FT	BEAM IN	WGT LBS	DRAFT FT	DRAFT IN	RETAIL LOW	RETAIL HIGH
		1990 BOATS														
25	1	SAN MARINO	OP	OVNTR	FBG	SV	IO	200D	VLVO	8	6	4900			13300	15100
25	2	SENZA SPECTRE	OP	RNBT	FBG	DV	IO		MRCR	8	3	4000			**	**
25	2	SENZA SPECTRE	OP	RNBT	FBG	DV	IO	240-275		8	3	4000			8950	10700
25	2	SENZA SPECTRE	OP	RNBT	FBG	DV	IO	330		8	3	4000			9900	11600
27	3	MIRADO	OP	OVNTR	FBG	SV	IO	330		9		7800			17300	20000
27	3	MIRADO	OP	OVNTR	FBG	SV	IO	T175-T275		9		7800			17400	21600
27	3	MIRADO	OP	OVNTR	FBG	SV	IO	T130D	VLVO	9		7800			21900	24400
29	11	COMTEMPRA	OP	OVNTR	FBG	SV	IO	200-275		10	6	9500			22800	26400
29	11	COMTEMPRA	OP	OVNTR	FBG	SV	IO	200D	VLVO	10	6	9500			26400	29300
29	11	COMTEMPRA	OP	OVNTR	FBG	SV	IO	T175	MRCR	10	6	9500			24600	27300
		1989 BOATS														
16	2	SENZA V-165 B/R	OP	RNBT	FBG	SV	OB			7	11	1000			2200	2550
16	2	SENZA V-165 C/B	OP	RNBT	FBG	SV	OB			7	1	1050			2300	2700
16	6	CITATION DC-170 B/R	OP	RNBT	FBG	DV	OB			6	6	950	2	2	2050	2450
17		ALL AMER ANV DC-170		RNBT	FBG	SV	IO	130	MRCR	7	11	1785			3050	3550
17		ALL AMER DC-170 B/R		RNBT	FBG	SV	IO	130	MRCR	7	4	1785			2900	3350
17	5	CITATION DC-175 B/R	OP	RNBT	FBG	SV	OB			6	11	1100	2	4	2500	2900
18		INTERNATIONAL DC-184		OFF	FBG	DV	OB			7	6	1800			3450	4000
18	4	LAZER DC-180 B/R		RNBT	FBG	DV	IO	130-175		7	3	1925	2	4	3200	3800
18	11	ALL AM DC-190 CUDDY		RNBT	FBG	SV	IO	130	MRCR	9		2485			4400	5050
18	11	ALL AMER DC-190 B/R		RNBT	FBG	SV	IO	130	MRCR	7	5	2300			3650	4250
20		LAZER DC-200 ANV B/R		RNBT	FBG	SV	IO	230	MRCR	8		2400			4700	5450
20		LAZER DC-200 B/R		RNBT	FBG	DV	IO	165-230		8		2350	2	6	4550	5400
20		LAZER DC-200 CUDDY		CUD	FBG	DV	IO	165-230		8		2550	2	6	4900	5800
20	4	INTERNATIONAL DC-204		OFF	FBG	DV	OB			7	6	1950			5900	6800
20	10	SENZA V-210 B/R LX		RNBT	FBG	DV	IO	200	MRCR	8		2800			5200	6000
20	10	SENZA V-210 CUDDY LX		RNBT	FBG	DV	IO	200	MRCR	8		2650			5050	5800
21	8	DELTA DC-215 CBN CR		CBNCR	FBG	DV	IO	165-230		8		3575	2	9	7300	8550
21	8	DELTA-SPORT DC-215	ST	SPTCR	FBG	DV	IO	165-230		8		2900	2	8	5800	6800
21	11	HAMPTON DC-220		CR	FBG	SV	IO	165-230		8	6	3700			7050	8250
22		INTERNATIONAL DC-224		OFF	FBG	DV	OB			8		2220			7100	8150
22		INTERNATIONAL DC-228		OFF	FBG	DV	OB			8		2800			8400	9650
22	1	SENZA V-220 CUDDY		CUD	FBG	SV	IO	230-260		8		2875	2	9	6050	7100
22	1	SENZA V-220 CUDDY		CUD	FBG	SV	IO	330	MRCR	8		2875	2	9	7000	8050
23	9	DELTA DC-230	ST	SPTCR	FBG	DV	IO	200-260		8		3575	2	9	7450	8850
23	9	DELTA DC-230 B/R		RNBT	FBG	DV	IO	200-260		8		3400			6750	8050
25	1	SAN MARINO DC-250		CR	FBG	SV	IO	200-260		8	6	4850			10000	11900
26		INTERNATIONAL DC-264		OFF	FBG	DV	OB			8		3200	1	2	12900	14600
26		INTERNATIONAL DC-265		OFF	FBG	DV	OB			8		3650			13300	15100
27	3	MILANO DC-270		CR	FBG	SV	IO	330	MRCR	9		7750			16300	18500
27	3	MILANO DC-270		CR	FBG	SV	IO	T165-T260		9		7750			16200	19900
29	11	CONTEMPRA DC-300 CBC		CBNCR	FBG	DV	IO	T165-T260		10	6	9500	2	10	27500	32100
		1988 BOATS														
16	1	CITATION DC-170 B/R	OP	RNBT	FBG	DV	OB			6	2	920	2	2	1900	2250
16	1	CITATION DC-170 B/R	OP	RNBT	FBG	DV	IO	120-130		6	2	1650	2	2	2300	2650
16	1	SENZA V-165 B/R	OP	RNBT	FBG	SV	OB			7	1	950			1950	2350
16	1	SENZA V-165 C/B	OP	RNBT	FBG	SV	OB			6	6	750			1550	1850
17	2	CITATION DC-175 B/R	OP	RNBT	FBG	SV	OB			6	11	1100	2	4	2350	2750
17	2	CITATION DC-175 B/R	OP	RNBT	FBG	SV	IO	120-175		6	11	1850	2	4	2700	3200
17	2	CITATION DC-175 C/B	OP	RNBT	FBG	SV	IO	120-175		6	11	1800	2	4	2700	3150
17	2	SENZA V-175 B/R	OP	RNBT	FBG	DV	OB			6	11	1250	2	4	2550	3000
17	2	SENZA V-175 B/R	OP	RNBT	FBG	DV	IO	120-205		6	11	2000	2	4	2800	3350
17	2	SENZA V-175 C/B	OP	RNBT	FBG	DV	IO	120-205		6	11	1950	2	4	2800	3300
17	5	CITATION DC-175 B/R	OP	RNBT	FBG	DV	OB			6	11	1100			2400	2750
17	10	LAZER DC-180 B/R		RNBT	FBG	DV	IO	120-205		7	2	1920	2	4	2950	3500
18	8	CITATION DC-190 B/R	OP	RNBT	FBG	DV	IO	120-230		7	6	2250	2	6	3400	4100
18	8	CITATION DC-190 B/R	OP	RNBT	FBG	DV	IO	260		7	6	2250	2	6	3700	4300
18	8	CITATION DC-205 CUD		CUD	FBG	DV	IO	120-230		7	6	2400	2	8	3600	4400
18	8	CITATION DC-205 CUD		CUD	FBG	DV	IO	260		7	6	2400	2	8	3900	4550
19	5	SENZA V-195 CUDDY	OP	CUD	FBG	DV	IO	120-230		7	8	2500	2	6	3900	4750
19	5	SENZA V-195 CUDDY	OP	CUD	FBG	DV	IO	260-270		7	8	2500	2	6	4200	5000
20		LAZER DC-200 B/R		RNBT	FBG	DV	IO	120-260		7	10	2325	2	6	4150	5200
20		LAZER DC-200 CUDDY		CUD	FBG	DV	IO	120-260		7	10	2550	2	6	4600	5600
20	4	INTERNATIONAL DC-204		OFF	FBG	DV	OB			7	6	1890			5600	6400
21	3	DELTA DC-215 CBN CR		CBNCR	FBG	DV	IO	165-260		8		3675	2	9	6850	8250
21	3	DELTA-SPORT DC-215	ST	SPTCR	FBG	DV	IO	165-260		8		2900	2	8	5350	6500
22		INTERNATIONAL DC-224		OFF	FBG	DV	OB			8		2200			6800	7800
22		INTERNATIONAL DC-224		OFF	FBG	DV	SE		OMC	8		2200			**	**
22		INTERNATIONAL DC-225		OFF	FBG	DV	OB			8		2800			8100	9300
22		INTERNATIONAL DC-225		OFF	FBG	DV	SE		OMC	8		2800			**	**
22		INTERNATIONAL DC-226		OFF	FBG	DV	OB			8		2575			7650	8800
22		INTERNATIONAL DC-226		OFF	FBG	DV	SE		OMC	8		2575			**	**
22		INTERNATIONAL DC-226		OFF	FBG	DV	IO	165-205		8		2575			5200	6050
22		SENZA V-220 CUDDY		CUD	FBG	SV	IO	165-270		8		2875	2	9	5550	6800
22		SENZA V-220 CUDDY		CUD	FBG	SV	IO	330-335		8		2875	2	9	6600	7600
23	4	CITATION DC-230 B/R		RNBT	FBG	DV	IO	165-270		8		3400	2	9	6200	7550
23	4	CITATION DC-230 B/R		RNBT	FBG	DV	IO	330-335		8		3400	2	9	7200	8300
23	4	DELTA DC-230	ST	SPTCR	FBG	DV	IO	165-260		8		3550	2	9	6800	8150
24	7	DELTA DC-250	ST	SPTCR	FBG	DV	IO	165-260		8		4250	2	10	8200	9950
24	7	DELTA DC-250 CBN CR	ST	CBNCR	FBG	DV	IO	165-260		8		4400	2	10	10000	11800
26		INTERNATIONAL DC-264		OFF	FBG	DV	OB			8		3200			12400	14100
26		INTERNATIONAL DC-264		OFF	FBG	DV	SE		OMC	8		3200			**	**
26		INTERNATIONAL DC-264		OFF	FBG	DV	SE	T	OMC	8		3200			**	**
26		INTERNATIONAL DC-265		OFF	FBG	DV	OB			8					12900	14600
26		INTERNATIONAL DC-265		OFF	FBG	DV	SE		OMC	8		3550			**	**
26		INTERNATIONAL DC-265		OFF	FBG	DV	SE	T	OMC	8		3550			**	**
26		INTERNATIONAL DC-267		OFF	FBG	DV	OB			8		4000			13100	14900
26		INTERNATIONAL DC-267		OFF	FBG	DV	SE		OMC	8		4000			**	**
26		INTERNATIONAL DC-267		OFF	FBG	DV	IO	165-260		8		4000			8350	10400
26		INTERNATIONAL DC-267		OFF	FBG	DV	SE	T	OMC	8		4000			**	**
26		INTERNATIONAL DC-269		OFF	FBG	DV	OB			8		4580			13600	15500
26		INTERNATIONAL DC-269		OFF	FBG	DV	SE		OMC	8		4580			**	**
26		INTERNATIONAL DC-269		OFF	FBG	DV	IO	165-260		8		4580			9200	11100
26		INTERNATIONAL DC-269		OFF	FBG	DV	SE	T	OMC	8		4580			**	**
29	11	CONTEMPRA DC-300 CBC		CBNCR	FBG	DV	IO	205-260		10	6	9200	2	10	22500	26100
29	11	CONTEMPRA DC-300 CBC		CBNCR	FBG	DV	IO	T165-T205		10	6	9200	2	10	24700	28400
		1987 BOATS														
16	1	CITATION DC-165 B/R	OP	RNBT	FBG	DV	OB			6	2	920			1850	2200
16	1	CITATION DC-165 B/R	OP	RNBT	FBG	DV	IO	120		6	2	1570			2050	2450
16	1	SENZA V-165 B/R	OP	RNBT	FBG	DV	OB			7	1	950			1900	2250
16	1	SENZA V-165 C/B	OP	RNBT	FBG	SV	OB			6	6	700			1400	1700
17	2	CITATION DC-175 B/R	OP	RNBT	FBG	SV	OB			6	11	1150			2350	2750
17	2	CITATION DC-175 B/R	OP	RNBT	FBG	SV	IO	120-205		6	11	1950			2600	3150
17	2	CITATION DC-175 C/B	OP	RNBT	FBG	SV	IO	120-205		6	11	1850			2600	3100
17	2	SENZA V-175 B/R	OP	RNBT	FBG	DV	OB			6	11	1250			2500	2900
17	2	SENZA V-175 B/R	OP	RNBT	FBG	DV	IO	120-205		6	11	2000			2650	3200
17	2	SENZA V-175 C/B	OP	RNBT	FBG	DV	IO	120-205		6	11	1950			2650	3150
18	8	CITATION DC-190 B/R	OP	RNBT	FBG	DV	IO	120-230		7	6	2235			3200	3900
18	8	CITATION DC-190 B/R	OP	RNBT	FBG	DV	IO	260		7	6	2235			3500	4050
18	8	DELTA DC-190 CUDDY	ST	CUD	FBG	DV	IO	120-230		7	6	2290			3350	4050
18	8	DELTA DC-190 CUDDY	ST	CUD	FBG	DV	IO	260		7	6	2290			3650	4250
19	5	SENZA V-195 C/B	OP	CUD	FBG	DV	IO	120-230		7	8	2600			3800	4600
19	5	SENZA V-195 C/B	OP	CUD	FBG	DV	IO	260		7	8	2600			4100	4750
20	4	INTERNATIONAL DC204	OP	CTRCN	FBG	DV	OB			7	5	1925		9	5450	6300
21	3	DELTA-SPORT DC-215	ST	SPTCR	FBG	DV	IO	165-260		8			2	8	5350	6150
22		INTERNATIONAL DC-224	OP	CTRCN	FBG	DV	OB			8		2200		10	6600	7550
22		INTERNATIONAL DC-225	OP	CTRCN	FBG	DV	OB			8		2500		10	7250	8300
22		INTERNATIONAL DC-226	OP	CUD	FBG	DV	OB			8		3360		10	8800	10000
22		INTERNATIONAL DC-226	OP	CUD	FBG	DV	IO	250		8		3360		10	6050	6950
22		NANTUCKET EXP V-220	ST	EXP	FBG	DV	IO	170-260		7	11	3500			5950	7150
22		SENZA V-220 CUDDY	OP	RNBT	FBG	DV	IO	165		8		2875			5000	5750
23	4	DELTA AFT CAB DC-230	ST	CR	FBG	DV	IO	165-205		8			2	9	7000	8750
23	4	DELTA AFT CAB DC-230	ST	CR	FBG	DV	IO	230-260		8		4350	3	6	7650	9000
23	4	DELTA DC-230 B/R	OP	RNBT	FBG	DV	IO	170	MRCR	8		3179			5650	6500
23	4	DELTA SPORT DC-230	ST	SPTCR	FBG	DV	IO	170-260		8		3560			6500	7800
24	7	DELTA DC-250	ST	SPTCR	FBG	DV	IO	170-260		8		4250			7800	9450
24	7	DELTA DC-250	ST	SPTCR	FBG	SV	IO	165		8			2	10	9950	11300
24	7	DELTA DC-250 AFT CAB	ST	CR	FBG	DV	IO	165-260		8			2	11	9950	11300
26		INTERNATIONAL DC-265	OP	CTRCN	FBG	DV	OB			8		3625	2		12300	14000
26		INTERNATIONAL DC-265	OP	CTRCN	FBG	DV	IO	T400		8		4525	2	6	15100	17100
26		INTERNATIONAL DC-267	OP	CUD	FBG	DV	OB			8		4000	2		12700	14400
26		INTERNATIONAL DC-267	OP	CUD	FBG	DV	IO	T400		8		4900	2	6	14800	16800
29	11	CONTEMPRA DC-300	OP	CR	FBG	DV	IO	T165		10	6	8600	2	10	18400	20500
		1986 BOATS														
16	1	CITATION DC-165 B/R	OP	RNBT	FBG	DV	OB			6	2	920			1750	2100
16	1	SENZA V-165 B/R	OP	RNBT	FBG	DV	OB			7	1	950			1800	2150
16	1	SENZA V-165 CB	OP	RNBT	FBG	SV	OB			6	6	700			1350	1600
17	2	CITATION DC-175 B/R	OP	RNBT	FBG	SV	OB			6	11	1150			2250	2650
17	2	CITATION DC-175 B/R	OP	RNBT	FBG	SV	IO	120-205		6	11	1950			2500	3000
17	2	CITATION DC-175 C/B	OP	RNBT	FBG	SV	IO	120-205		6	11	1850			2450	2950
17	2	SENZA V-175 B/R	OP	RNBT	FBG	DV	OB			6	11	1250			2450	2850
17	2	SENZA V-175 B/R	OP	RNBT	FBG	DV	IO	120-205		6	11	2000			2550	3050
17	2	SENZA V-175 C/B	OP	RNBT	FBG	DV	IO	120-205		6	11	1950			2550	3000
18	8	CITATION DC-190 B/R	OP	RNBT	FBG	DV	IO	120-230		7	6	2235			3100	3700
18	8	CITATION DC-190 B/R	OP	RNBT	FBG	DV	IO	260		7	6	2235			3350	3900
18	8	DELTA DC-190 CUDDY	ST	CUD	FBG	DV	IO	120-230		7	6	2290			3200	3900
18	8	DELTA DC-190 CUDDY	ST	CUD	FBG	DV	IO	260		7	6	2290			3450	4050

CONTINUED ON NEXT PAGE

LOA FT IN	NAME AND/ OR MODEL	TOP/ RIG	BOAT TYPE	HULL MTL TP TP #	ENGINE HP MFG	BEAM FT IN	WGT LBS	DRAFT FT IN	RETAIL LOW	RETAIL HIGH
					1986 BOATS					
19 5	SENZA V-195 C/B	OP	CUD	FBG DV	120-230	7 8	2600		3650	4400
19 5	SENZA V-195 C/B	OP	CUD	FBG DV	260	7 8	2600		4200	4550
21 3	DELTA-SPORT DC-215	ST	SPTCR	FBG DV	170-260	8	2900		4850	5900
22	NANTUCKET EXP V-220	ST	EXP	FBG DV IO	170-260	7 11	3500		5700	6850
23 4	DELTA AFT CAB DC-230	ST	CR	FBG DV IO	170-260	8	4350	3 6	7200	8600
23 4	DELTA SPORT DC-230	ST	SPTCR	FBG DV IO	170-260	8	3560		6200	7700
24 7	DELTA DC-250	ST	SPTCR	FBG DV IO	170-260	8	4250		7450	9050
24 7	DELTA DC-250 AFT CAB	ST	CR	FBG DV IO	170-260	8	4350		7600	9150
					1985 BOATS					
16 1	MIRADO V-165 B/R	OP	RNBT	FBG DV OB		7 1	900		1650	2000
16 1	SENZA V-165	OP	RNBT	FBG SV OB		7	700		1300	1550
16 2	ALL-AMERICAN V165B/R	OP	RNBT	FBG DV OB		6 8	1000		1850	2200
16 2	ALL-AMERICAN V165B/R	OP	RNBT	FBG SV OB		6 8	1700		2050	2550
17 2	CITATION 5500 C/B	OP	RNBT	FBG DV IO	120-170	6 11	1850		2350	2800
17 2	CITATION DC-175 C/B	OP	RNBT	FBG DV OB		6 11	1950		2200	2550
17 2	CITATION DC-175 C/B	OP	RNBT	FBG SV IO	120-190	6 11	1950		2400	2850
17 2	SENZA V-175 B/R	OP	RNBT	FBG DV OB		6 11	1250		2350	2750
17 2	SENZA V-175 C/B	OP	RNBT	FBG DV IO	120-190	6 11	2000		2450	2900
17 2	SENZA V-175 C/B	OP	RNBT	FBG DV IO	120-190	6 11	1950		2450	2900
18 8	CITATION DC-190 B/R	OP	RNBT	FBG DV IO	120-230	7 6	2235		2950	3550
18 8	CITATION DC-190 B/R	OP	RNBT	FBG DV IO	260	7 6	2235		3200	3700
18 8	DELTA DC-190 CUDDY	ST	CUD	FBG DV IO	120-230	7 6	2290		3050	3750
18 8	DELTA DC-190 CUDDY	ST	CUD	FBG DV IO	260	7 6	2290		3350	3900
19 5	NANTUCKET EXP V-195	ST	EXP	FBG DV IO	170-260	7 8	2800		3650	4550
19 5	SENZA V-195 C/B	ST	CUD	FBG DV IO	120-230	7 8	2600		3500	4200
19 5	SENZA V-195 C/B	ST	CUD	FBG DV IO	260	7 8	2600		3750	4350
21 3	DELTA-SPORT DC-215	ST	SPTCR	FBG DV IO	170-260	8	2900		4700	5650
22	NANTUCKET EXP V-220	ST	EXP	FBG DV IO	170-260	7 11	3500		5450	6550
23 4	DELTA AFT CAB DC-230	ST	CR	FBG DV IO	170-260	8	4350	3 6	6900	8250
23 4	DELTA SPORT DC-230	ST	SPTCR	FBG DV IO	170-260	8	3560		6950	7150
24 7	DELTA DC-250	ST	SPTCR	FBG DV IO	170-260	8	4250		7150	8650
					1984 BOATS					
16 1	MIRADO 5000 B/R	OP	RNBT	FBG DV OB		7 1	900		1650	1950
16 1	MIRADO 5000 C/B	OP	RNBT	FBG DV OB		7 1	900		1600	1900
16 1	SCRAMBLER	OP	RNBT	FBG SV OB		6 6	950		1700	2050
16 1	WILDFIRE	OP	RNBT	FBG SV OB		6 6	700		1250	1500
16 2	ALL-AMERICAN 5000 SE	OP	RNBT	FBG DV OB		6 8	1000		1950	2300
16 2	ALL-AMERICAN 5000 SE	OP	RNBT	FBG DV IO	117-170	6 8	1700		2250	2650
16 2	ALL-AMERICAN 5000B/R	OP	RNBT	FBG SV OB		6 8	1000		1650	1950
16 2	ALL-AMERICAN 5000B/R	OP	RNBT	FBG SV IO	117-170	6 8	1700		2050	2450
17 2	CITATION 5500 B/R	OP	RNBT	FBG DV OB		6 11	1150		1900	2250
17 2	CITATION 5500 C/B	OP	RNBT	FBG DV OB		6 11	1950		2350	2800
17 2	CITATION 5500 C/B	OP	RNBT	FBG SV OB		6 11	1100		2000	2400
17 2	CITATION 5500 C/B	OP	RNBT	FBG SV IO	117-188	6 11	1850		2400	2850
17 2	CITATION 5500 SE	OP	RNBT	FBG DV OB		6 11	1150		2300	2700
17 2	CITATION 5500 SE	OP	RNBT	FBG DV IO	117-188	6 11	1950		2550	3050
17 2	MACH I B/R	OP	RNBT	FBG DV OB		6 11	1250		2300	2650
17 2	MACH I B/R	OP	RNBT	FBG DV IO	117-188	6 11	2000		2500	2950
17 2	MACH I C/B	OP	RNBT	FBG DV OB		6 11	1220		2300	2600
17 2	MACH I C/B	OP	RNBT	FBG DV IO	120-140	6 11	1950		2350	2900
	IO 170 MRCR	2350	2700, IO	170 OMC	2350	2700, IO	170-188		2550	2950
18 8	CITATION 6000 B/R	OP	RNBT	FBG DV IO	117-230	7 6	2235		3000	3600
18 8	CITATION 6000 B/R	OP	RNBT	FBG DV IO	260	7 6	2235		3100	3800
18 8	CITATION 6000 B/R SE	OP	RNBT	FBG DV IO	117-230	7 6	2280		3000	3650
18 8	CITATION 6000 B/R SE	OP	RNBT	FBG DV IO	260	7 6	2280		3100	3850
19 5	CONCORDE B/R	OP	RNBT	FBG DV IO	117-230	7 8	2500		3300	4100
19 5	CONCORDE B/R	OP	RNBT	FBG DV IO	260 MRCR	7 8	2600		3500	4050
19 5	CONCORDE C/B	OP	CUD	FBG DV IO	117-230	7 8	2600		3500	4400
19 5	CONCORDE C/B	OP	CUD	FBG DV IO	260	7 8	3060		3750	4400
19 5	CONCORDE C/B	OP	CUD	FBG DV SE	115 OMC	7 8	2600		3600	4450
19 5	NANTUCKET EXP 6500	OP	EXP	FBG DV IO	117-230	7 8	2800		3700	4350
19 5	NANTUCKET EXP 6500	OP	EXP	FBG DV IO	260	7 8	2800		3550	4400
19 5	NANTUCKET EXP 6500	OP	EXP	FBG DV IO	260	7 8	2800		3750	4600
21 3	DELTA-SPORT 7000	OP	SPTCR	FBG DV IO	170-230	8	2900		4550	5500
21 3	DELTA-SPORT 7000	OP	SPTCR	FBG DV IO	260	8	2900		4750	5700
22	NANTUCKET EXP 7500	OP	EXP	FBG DV IO	170-230	7 11	3500		5250	6350
22	NANTUCKET EXP 7500	OP	EXP	FBG DV IO	260	7 11	3500		5500	6600
23 2	ADMIRAL DAY 8000	OP	CR	FBG DV IO	170-230	8	3000		5100	6150
23 2	ADMIRAL DAY 8000	OP	CR	FBG DV IO	260	8	3000		5350	6400
24 7	DELTA 8500	OP	SPTCR	FBG DV IO	170-260	8	4250		6900	8600

....For earlier years, see the BUC Used Boat Price Guide, Volume 3

LASER INTERNATIONAL
HAWKESBURY ONTARIO CANA COAST GUARD MFG ID- PSL See inside cover to adjust price for area
FORMERLY PERFORMANCE SAILCRAFT INC

LOA FT IN	NAME AND/ OR MODEL	TOP/ RIG	BOAT TYPE	HULL MTL TP TP #	ENGINE HP MFG	BEAM FT IN	WGT LBS	DRAFT FT IN	RETAIL LOW	RETAIL HIGH
					1989 BOATS					
26 10	MERRIMACK 27		LNCH	FBG SV IO		9 6	11050	1 5	**	**
26 10	MERRIMACK 27		LNCH	FBG SV IB		9 6	11050	1 5	**	**
28 5	LASER 28 RACER/CR	SLP	SA/OD	FBG KL SD	8D BUKH	9 6	3950	5	23200	25800
29 10	MERRIMACK 30		LNCH	FBG SV IO		9 6	12100	1 3	**	**
29 10	MERRIMACK 30		LNCH	FBG SV IB		9 6	12100	1 3	**	**
					1988 BOATS					
28 5	LASER 28 RACER/CR	SLP	SA/OD	FBG KL SD	8D BUKH	9 6	3950	5	21800	24200
					1987 BOATS					
28 5	LASER 28 RACER	SLP	SA/OD	FBG KL SD	8D BUKH	9 6	3950	5	20500	22800
					1986 BOATS					
28 5	LASER 28 CRUISER	SLP	SA/OD	FBG KL SD	8D BUKH	9 6	3950	5	18100	20100
28 5	LASER 28 RACER	SLP	SA/OD	FBG KL SD	8D BUKH	9 6	3950	5	20700	23000
					1985 BOATS					
28 5	LASER 28	SLP	SA/OD	FBG KL SD	8D BUKH	9 6	3950	5	18300	20400
					1984 BOATS					
28 4	LASER 28	SLP	SAIL	FBG KL		9 4	4000	4 9	16300	18500

....For earlier years, see the BUC Used Boat Price Guide, Volume 3

LAVEY CRAFT INC
CITY OF INDUSTRY CA 91715   See inside cover to adjust price for area

LOA FT IN	NAME AND/ OR MODEL	TOP/ RIG	BOAT TYPE	HULL MTL TP TP #	ENGINE HP MFG	BEAM FT IN	WGT LBS	DRAFT FT IN	RETAIL LOW	RETAIL HIGH
					1990 BOATS					
16	SPRITE		RNBT	FBG SV OB		6 6	860		5250	6050
18 2	INTERCEPTOR		B/R	FBG SV OB		7 2	900		5900	6800
18 2	INTERCEPTOR		B/R	FBG SV IB	272	7 2	900		8350	9600
18 2	INTERCEPTOR		RNBT	FBG SV OB		7 2	900		5900	6800
18 2	INTERCEPTOR		RNBT	FBG SV IB	272	7 2	900		7350	8450
18 10	SEBRING MOD V.P.			FBG TH OB		7	570		4050	4700
20 2	SEBRING MOD V.P.		B/R	FBG TH OB		8	950		7100	8200
20 2	SEBRING MOD V.P.		RACE	FBG TH OB		7 2	650		5150	5900
21	SUPER INTERCEPTER		B/R	FBG SV IB		8	950		**	**
22 10	TURBO CRUISER		B/R	FBG SV IB		8	950		**	**
22 10	TURBO CRUISER		CR	FBG SV IB		8	950		**	**
22 10	TURBO SEBRING			FBG TH OB		8	950		7400	8500
22 10	TURBO SEBRING		B/R	FBG TH IB		8	950		**	**
22 10	TURBO SEBRING		CR	FBG TH OB		8	950		7300	8400
22 10	TURBO SEBRING		CR	FBG TH IB		8	950		**	**

LAZY DAYS MFG CO INC
BUFORD GA 30518   COAST GUARD MFG ID- LDM See inside cover to adjust price for area

For more recent years, see the BUC Used Boat Price Guide, Volume 1

LOA FT IN	NAME AND/ OR MODEL	TOP/ RIG	BOAT TYPE	HULL MTL TP TP #	ENGINE HP MFG	BEAM FT IN	WGT LBS	DRAFT FT IN	RETAIL LOW	RETAIL HIGH
					1995 BOATS					
63	HIGH BOW CUSTOM	FB	HB	AL SV VD	T330 MRCR	15		3	139000	153000
63	SOUTHERN NIGHTS LB	FB	HB	AL SV IO	T250 MRCR	15		3	142500	156500
64	LOW BOW SPORTSMAN	FB	HB	AL SV IO	T250 MRCR	16		3	147000	161500
74	LOW BOW SPORTSMAN	FB	HB	AL SV IO	T300 MRCR	16		3	**	**
					1987 BOATS					
50	SPORTSMAN	HT	HB	AL TR IO	T200	14 6		3	69900	76900
50	SPORTSMAN	HT	HB	AL TR IB	T130D	14 6		3	80000	87900
52	HIGH BOW SPORTSMAN	HT	HB	AL TR IO	T200	14 6		3	73100	80300
52	HIGH BOW SPORTSMAN	HT	HB	AL TR IB	T130D	14 6		3	80600	88500
58	SPORTSMAN	HT	HB	AL TR IO	T200	14 6		3	80100	88000
58	SPORTSMAN	HT	HB	AL TR IB	T130D	14 6		3	86200	94700
60	HIGH BOW SPORTSMAN	HT	HB	AL TR IO	T200	14 6		3	95900	105500
60	HIGH BOW SPORTSMAN	HT	HB	AL TR IB	T130D	14 6		3	**	**
					1986 BOATS					
50 2	SPORTSMAN	HT	HB	AL TR IO	225 VLVO	14 6		3	66000	72600
	IO T200 VLVO	69800	76700, IO	T260 VLVO	72000 79100,	IO T290	VLVO	74200	81500	
	IO T330 MRCR	75700	83200, IO	T130D VLVO	76400 83900,	IO T165D	VLVO	77800	85400	
50 2	SPORTSMAN	FB	HB	AL TR IO	T200 VLVO	14 6		3	69800	76700

LOA FT IN	NAME AND/ OR MODEL	TOP/ RIG	BOAT TYPE	-HULL- MTL TP TP	----ENGINE--- # HP MFG	BEAM FT IN	WGT LBS	DRAFT FT IN	RETAIL LOW	RETAIL HIGH

———————— 1986 BOATS ————————

50	2 SPORTSMAN	FB	HB	AL TR IO	T225 VLVO	14 6		3	70500	77400
	IO T260 VLVO 72000,	79100, IO T290 VLVO 74200 81500, IO T330 MRCR 75700 83200
	IO T130D VLVO 76400	83900, IO T165D VLVO 77800 85400
52	HIGH BOW SPORTSMAN	HT	HB	AL TR IO	T130 VLVO	14 6		3	70700	77700
	IO T190 VLVO 71100,	78200, IO T200 VLVO 71700 78800, IO T225 VLVO 72000 79100
	IO T260 VLVO 73500	80700, IO T330 MRCR 77300 85000, IO T165D VLVO 79900 87800
52	HIGH BOW SPORTSMAN	FB	HB	AL TR IO	T200 VLVO	14 6		3	71800	78900
	IO T225 VLVO 72100,	79300, IO T260 VLVO 73600 80900, IO T290 VLVO 75400 82800
	IO T330 MRCR 77200	84900, IO T130D VLVO 79200 87100, IO T165D VLVO 80800 88800
57	SPORTSMAN	HT	HB	AL TR IO	T200 VLVO	14 6		3	80500	88500
	IO T225 VLVO 81100,	89100, IO T260 VLVO 82600 90800, IO T290 VLVO 84600 93000
	IO T330 MRCR 86200	94700, IO T130D VLVO 80100 88000, IO T165D VLVO 81500 89500
57	SPORTSMAN	FB	HB	AL TR IO	T200 VLVO	14 6		3	80800	88800
	IO T225 VLVO 81900,	90000, IO T260 VLVO 83000 91200, IO T290 VLVO 85300 93700
	IO T330 MRCR 86700	95300, IO T130D VLVO 80100 88000, IO T165D VLVO 81500 89600
59	HIGH BOW SPORTSMAN	HT	HB	AL TR IO	T200 VLVO	14 6		3	80600	88600
	IO T225 VLVO 81500,	89500, IO T260 VLVO 83000 91200, IO T290 VLVO 84900 93300
	IO T330 MRCR 86700	95300, IO T130D VLVO 84700 93100, IO T165D VLVO 86400 94900
59	HIGH BOW SPORTSMAN	FB	HB	AL TR IO	T130 VLVO	14 6		3	80800	88800
	IO T225 VLVO 83100,	91300, IO T260 VLVO 84400 92700, IO T290 VLVO 86200 94700
	IO T330 MRCR 88400	97200, IO T165D VLVO 86500 95100
62	2 CUSTOM	HT	HB	AL SV IO	T200 VLVO	14 6		3	99200	109000
	IO T225 VLVO 99900	110000, IO T260 VLVO 101500 111500, IO T290 VLVO 104000 114000
	IO T330 MRCR 105500	116000, IO T130D VLVO ** **, IO T165D VLVO ** **
62	2 CUSTOM	FB	HB	AL SV IO	T200 VLVO	14 6		3	99200	109000
	IO T225 VLVO 99900	110000, IO T260 VLVO 101500 111500, IO T290 VLVO 104000 114000
	IO T330 MRCR 105500	116000, IO T130D VLVO ** **, IO T165D VLVO ** **

———————— 1985 BOATS ————————

50	SPORTSMAN	HT	HB	AL TR IO	T200	14 6		3	76300	83900
52	HIGH BOW SPORTSMAN	HT	HB	AL TR IO	T130D	14 6		3	68300	75100
52	HIGH BOW SPORTSMAN	HT	HB	AL TR IO	T200	14 6		3	76800	84400
52	HIGH BOW SPORTSMAN	HT	HB	AL TR IB	T130D	14 6		3	76400	83900
57	SPORTSMAN	HT	HB	AL TR IO	T200	14 6		3	77300	85000
57	SPORTSMAN	HT	HB	AL TR IO	T130D	14 6		3	79200	87000
57	SPORTSMAN	HT	HB	AL TR IB	T130D	14 6		3	77700	85400
59	HIGH BOW SPORTSMAN	HT	HB	AL TR IO	T200	14 6		3	77500	85200
59	HIGH BOW SPORTSMAN	HT	HB	AL TR IO	T130D	14 6		3	83500	91700
59	HIGH BOW SPORTSMAN	HT	HB	AL TR IB	T130D	14 6		3	82500	90700

———————— 1984 BOATS ————————

50	2 SPORTSMAN	HT	HB	AL TR IO	T200 VLVO	14 6		3	66900	73500
	VD T220 CRUS 65700	72200, IO T225 VLVO 67500 74200, IO T260 VLVO 69000 75800
	IO T290 VLVO 71000	78100, IO T330 MRCR 72500 79700, IO T130D VLVO 73200 80400
	VD T158D VLVO 74200	81500, IO T165D VLVO 74500 81800
50	2 SPORTSMAN	FB	HB	AL TR IO	T200 VLVO 14			3	66900	73500
	VD T220 CRUS 65700	72200, IO T225 VLVO 67500 74200, IO T260 VLVO 69000 75800
	IO T290 VLVO 71000	78100, IO T330 MRCR 72500 79700, IO T130D VLVO 73200 80400
	VD T158D VLVO 74200	81500, IO T165D VLVO 74500 81800
52	HIGH BOW SPORTSMAN	HT	HB	AL TR IO	T200 VLVO 14			3	67800	74500
	VD T220 CRUS 66600	73200, IO T225 VLVO 68200 75000, IO T260 VLVO 69800 76700
	IO T290 VLVO 71600	78700, IO T330 MRCR 73100 80300, IO T130D VLVO 73200 80500
	VD T158D VLVO 74400	81700, IO T165D VLVO 74900 82400
52	HIGH BOW SPORTSMAN	FB	HB	AL TR IO	T200 VLVO 14			3	67700	74400
	VD T220 CRUS 66800	73400, IO T225 VLVO 68400 75100, IO T260 VLVO 69800 76700
	IO T290 VLVO 71700	78800, IO T330 MRCR 73100 80300, IO T130D VLVO 75000 82400
	VD T158D VLVO 74800	82200, IO T165D VLVO 76600 84200
57	SPORTSMAN	HT	HB	AL TR IO	T200 VLVO 14			3	77000	84700
	VD T220 CRUS 76000	83500, IO T225 VLVO 77600 85300, IO T260 VLVO 79000 86900
	IO T290 VLVO 81000	89000, IO T330 MRCR 82400 90600, IO T130D VLVO 75700 83200
	VD T158D VLVO 75400	82900, IO T165D VLVO 77300 84900
57	SPORTSMAN	FB	HB	AL TR IO	T200 VLVO 14			3	77100	84700
	VD T220 CRUS 76000	83500, IO T225 VLVO 77700 85400, IO T260 VLVO 79200 87000
	IO T290 VLVO 81100	89100, IO T330 MRCR 82500 90600, IO T130D VLVO 76200 83700
	VD T158D VLVO 75400	82900, IO T165D VLVO 77600 85200
59	HIGH BOW SPORTSMAN	HT	HB	AL TR IO	T200 VLVO 14			3	77000	84600
	VD T220 CRUS 75900	83500, IO T225 VLVO 77600 85300, IO T260 VLVO 79000 86800
	IO T290 VLVO 81000	89000, IO T330 MRCR 82400 90600, IO T130D VLVO 80300 88200
	VD T158D VLVO 80100	88000, IO T165D VLVO 81600 89700
59	HIGH BOW SPORTSMAN	FB	HB	AL TR IO	T200 VLVO 14			3	77700	85400
	VD T220 CRUS 76400	83900, IO T225 VLVO 78000 85700, IO T260 VLVO 79400 87300
	IO T290 VLVO 81500	89500, IO T330 MRCR 82900 91000, IO T130D VLVO 80300 88200
	VD T158D VLVO 80100	88000, IO T165D VLVO 81900 90000
62	2 CUSTOM	HT	HB	AL SV IO	T200 VLVO 14			3	94200	103500
	VD T220 CRUS 89700	98600, IO T225 VLVO 95000 104500, IO T260 VLVO 96600 106000
	IO T290 VLVO 99000	109000, IO T330 MRCR 100500 110500, VD T330 MRCR 90800 99800
	IO T130D VLVO **	**, VD T158D VLVO ** **, IO T165D VLVO ** **
	VD T310D J&T **	**
62	2 CUSTOM	FB	HB	AL SV IO	T200 VLVO 14			3	94400	103500
	VD T220 CRUS 89700	98500, IO T225 VLVO 95000 104500, IO T260 VLVO 96500 106000
	IO T290 VLVO 99000	108500, IO T330 MRCR 100500 110500, VD T330 MRCR 91300 100500
	IO T130D VLVO **	**, VD T158D VLVO ** **, IO T165D VLVO ** **
	VD T310D J&T **	**

....For earlier years, see the BUC Used Boat Price Guide, Volume 3

LAZZARA YACHT CORP
TAMPA FL 33611   See inside cover to adjust price for area

For more recent years, see the BUC Used Boat Price Guide, Volume 1

LOA FT IN	NAME AND/ OR MODEL	TOP/ RIG	BOAT TYPE	-HULL- MTL TP TP	----ENGINE--- # HP MFG	BEAM FT IN	WGT LBS	DRAFT FT IN	RETAIL LOW	RETAIL HIGH

———————— 1996 BOATS ————————

| 76 | GRAND SALON | FB | MY | FBG SV IB | T11CD MTU | 19 2 | | 8 6 | ** | ** |

———————— 1995 BOATS ————————

| 76 | WALK AROUND | FB | MY | FBG | IB | T11CD MTU | 19 2 | | 8 6 | ** | ** |

A LE COMTE COMPANY INC
NEW ROCHELL NY 10803   COAST GUARD ID- LCH See inside cover to adjust price for area

LOA FT IN	NAME AND/ OR MODEL	TOP/ RIG	BOAT TYPE	-HULL- MTL TP TP	----ENGINE--- # HP MFG	BEAM FT IN	WGT LBS	DRAFT FT IN	RETAIL LOW	RETAIL HIGH

———————— 1986 BOATS ————————

26 5	A-L-C 800		UTL	FBG	IB	110D	12 9	6850		14800	16800
33 3	A-L-C 1000		UTL	FBG	IB	110D	12 9	7770		20100	22400
39 11	A-L-C 1200		UTL	FBG	IB	110D	12 9	8690		23400	26000
45 7	A-L-C 46	SLP	SA/CR	FBG KL IB	D	12 3	25000	6 9	168500	185000
45 7	A-L-C 46	KTH		FBG KL IB	D	12 3	25000	6 9	173500	190500
46 6	A-L-C 1400		UTL	FBG	IB	110D	12 9			**	**
53 2	A-L-C 1600		UTL	FBG	IB	110D	12 9			173500	191000
59 9	A-L-C 1800		UTL	FBG	IB	110D	12 9	11450		**	**
66 4	A-L-C 2000		UTL	FBG	IB	110D	12 9	12370		123500	136000

———————— 1985 BOATS ————————

45 10	A-L-C 46	SLP	SA/CR	FBG KL IB	51D PERK	12 3	25000	6 9	158500	174000
45 10	A-L-C 46	KTH	SA/CR	FBG KL IB	51D PERK	12 3	25000	6 9	163000	179500
45 10	A-L-C 46 TALL RIG	KTH	SA/CR	FBG KL IB	51D PERK	12 3	25000	6 9	164000	180000

———————— 1984 BOATS ————————

45 10	A-L-C 46	SLP	SA/CR	FBG KL IB	50D PERK	12 3	25000	6 9	148500	163000
45 10	A-L-C 46	KTH	SA/CR	FBG KL IB	50D PERK	12 3	25000	6 9	153000	168000
45 10	A-L-C 46 TALL RIG	KTH	SA/CR	FBG KL IB	50D PERK	12 3	25000	6 9	153500	169000

....For earlier years, see the BUC Used Boat Price Guide, Volume 3

LES VOILIERS EVASION
ANJOU QUEBEC CANADA   See inside cover to adjust price for area

LOA FT IN	NAME AND/ OR MODEL	TOP/ RIG	BOAT TYPE	-HULL- MTL TP TP	----ENGINE--- # HP MFG	BEAM FT IN	WGT LBS	DRAFT FT IN	RETAIL LOW	RETAIL HIGH

———————— 1987 BOATS ————————

| 27 7 | EVASION 27 | SLP | SA/RC | FBG KL IB | D | 9 6 | 5050 | 4 6 | 22000 | 24400 |

———————— 1986 BOATS ————————

| 27 7 | EVASION 27 | SLP | SA/OD | FBG KL IB | D | 9 6 | 5050 | 4 6 | 20700 | 23000 |
| 27 7 | EVASION 27 | SLP | SA/RC | FBG KL IB | D | 9 6 | 5050 | 4 6 | 20700 | 23000 |

———————— 1985 BOATS ————————

| 27 7 | EVASION 27 | SLP | SA/CR | FBG KL IB | D | 9 6 | 5050 | 4 6 | 19400 | 21600 |
| 27 7 | EVASION 27 | SLP | SA/OD | | KL IB | D | 9 6 | | 4 6 | 19400 | 21600 |

LIBERTY YACHT CORPORATION
LELAND NC 28451 COAST GUARD MFG ID- LYH See inside cover to adjust price for area

LOA FT IN	NAME AND/OR MODEL	TOP/RIG	BOAT TYPE	HULL MTL TP	ENGINE TP #HP MFG	BEAM FT IN	WGT LBS	DRAFT FT IN	RETAIL LOW	RETAIL HIGH
1987 BOATS										
27 9	PIED-PIPER 28 MKIII	SLP	SA/CR	FBG KL	IB 18D VLVO	8 9	8400	4	22800	25400
1986 BOATS										
28 6	PIED-PIPER 28	SLP	SA/CR	FBG KC	IB 18D VLVO	8 9	8300	3 3	21400	23800
1985 BOATS										
28	LIBERTY 28	SLP	SA/CR	FBG KL	IB 18D VLVO	8 7	8400	4	20300	22500
28 9	PIED-PIPER	SLP	SAIL	FBG KC	IB 18D VLVO	8 9	8300	3 3	20200	22400

....For earlier years, see the BUC Used Boat Price Guide, Volume 3

LIBERTY YACHTS INC
RIVIERA BEACH FL 33404 COAST GUARD MFG ID- LBN See inside cover to adjust price for area

LOA FT IN	NAME AND/OR MODEL	TOP/RIG	BOAT TYPE	HULL MTL TP	ENGINE TP #HP MFG	BEAM FT IN	WGT LBS	DRAFT FT IN	RETAIL LOW	RETAIL HIGH
1994 BOATS										
38 9	LIBERTY 38 SF	FB	SF	F/S DV	IB T375D CAT	14 10	26000	3 8	198000	217500
38 9	LIBERTY 38 SF	FB	SF	F/S DV	IB T435D CAT	14 10	26000	3 8	208000	228500
38 9	LIBERTY 38 SF	FB	SF	F/S DV	IB T550D GM	14 10	26000	3 8	221000	242500
1993 BOATS										
38 9	LIBERTY 38 SF	FB	SF	F/S DV	IB T375D CAT	14 10	26000	3 8	188500	207500
38 9	LIBERTY 38 SF	FB	SF	F/S DV	IB T425D CAT	14 10	26000	3 8	196500	216000
38 9	LIBERTY 38 SF	FB	SF	F/S DV	IB T550D GM	14 10	26000	3 8	210500	231500
1992 BOATS										
38 9	LIBERTY 38 SF	FB	SF	F/S DV	IB T550D GM	14 10	26000	3 11	200500	220500
1991 BOATS										
38 9	LIBERTY 38 SF	FB	SF	F/S DV	IB T425D CAT	14 10	25000	2 11	173500	191000
1990 BOATS										
28	LIBERTY 28	CUT	SA/CR	FBG KL	IB 25D PERK	9	12000	4	32600	36200
38	FENNELL 38	CUT	SA/CR	FBG KL	IB 50D PERK	11 6	22000	5	83700	92000
1988 BOATS										
28	LIBERTY 28	CUT	SA/CR	FBG KL	IB 21D	9 7	12000	4	28900	32100
38	LIBERTY 38	CUT	SA/CR	FBG KL	IB 50D	11 6	21500	5	73100	80400
1987 BOATS										
28	LIBERTY 28	CUT	SA/CR	FBG KL	IB 21D	9 7	12000	4	27200	30200
38	LIBERTY 38	CUT	SA/CR	FBG KL	IB 40D	11 6	21500	5	68500	75400
38	LIBERTY 38	KTH	SA/CR	FBG KL	IB D	11 6	20000	4 9	65100	71500
1986 BOATS										
28	ALLEGRA 24	CUT	SA/CR	FBG KL	IB D	8	6500	3 6	13200	15000
31 6	ALLEGRA 28	CUT	SA/CR	FBG KL	IB D	9 7	12000	4	25800	28700
38	LIBERTY 38	CUT	SA/CR	FBG KL	IB D	11 6		4 9	65200	71700
38	LIBERTY 38	KTH	SA/CR	FBG KL	IB D	11 6	20000	4 9	61200	67200
1985 BOATS										
28	ALLEGRA 24	CUT	SA/CR	FBG KL	IB D	8	6500	3 6	12400	14100
28	LIBERTY 28	CUT	SA/CR	FBG KL SD	15D	9 7	12000	4	24000	26700
38	LIBERTY 38	CUT	SA/CR	FBG KL	IB 40D	11 6	21500	5	60700	66700
1984 BOATS										
28	LIBERTY 28	CUT	SA/CR	FBG KL SD	15D	9 7	12000	4	22600	25100
38	LIBERTY 38	CUT	SA/CR	FBG KL	IB 40D	11 6	21500	4 11	55600	61100
38	LIBERTY 38 PH	CUT	SA/CR	FBG KL	IB 40D	11 6	21500	4 11	58600	64400

....For earlier years, see the BUC Used Boat Price Guide, Volume 3

LIBERTY YACHTS INC
SEATTLE WA 98109 See inside cover to adjust price for area

LOA FT IN	NAME AND/OR MODEL	TOP/RIG	BOAT TYPE	HULL MTL TP	ENGINE TP #HP MFG	BEAM FT IN	WGT LBS	DRAFT FT IN	RETAIL LOW	RETAIL HIGH
1987 BOATS										
38 9	GATSBY 39	MS		FBG	IB 66D YAN	12 3	24800	5	115500	127000
38 9	GATSBY 39	MY		FBG	IB 66D YAN	12 3	24800	5	136500	150000
45 8	LIBERTY 458	CUT	SA/CR	FBG KL	IB 90D LEHM	12 11	31000	6 4	167000	183500
48 9	LIBERTY 49	CUT	SA/CR	FBG KL	IB 90D LEHM	14	38000	6 4	206000	226500
1986 BOATS										
45 8	LIBERTY 458	CUT	SA/CR	FBG KL	IB 90D LEHM	12 11	31000	6 4	158500	174000
48 8	LIBERTY 49	CUT	SA/CR	FBG KL	IB 90D LEHM	14	38000	6 4	195500	214500
1984 BOATS										
45 8	LIBERTY 458	CUT	SA/CR	FBG KL	IB				138500	152500
45 8	LIBERTY 458	CUT	SA/CR	FBG KL	IB 90D LEHM	12 11	31000	6 4	142000	156000

....For earlier years, see the BUC Used Boat Price Guide, Volume 3

LINDENBERG YACHTS INC
COCOA FL 32922 COAST GUARD MFG ID- LDB See inside cover to adjust price for area

LOA FT IN	NAME AND/OR MODEL	TOP/RIG	BOAT TYPE	HULL MTL TP	ENGINE TP #HP MFG	BEAM FT IN	WGT LBS	DRAFT FT IN	RETAIL LOW	RETAIL HIGH
1987 BOATS										
28	LINDENBERG 28	SLP	SA/RC	FBG KL	IB D	9 6	4000	5 3	13700	15600
1986 BOATS										
28	LINDENBERG 28	SLP	SA/RC	FBG KL	IB D	9 6	4000	5 3	12900	14700
1985 BOATS										
28	LINDENBERG 28	SLP	SA/OD	FBG KL	IB D	9 6	4000	5 3	12200	13800
28	LINDENBERG 28	SLP	SA/OD	FBG KL	IB D	9 6	4000	5 3	12200	13800
1984 BOATS										
28	LINDENBERG 28	SLP	SA/OD	FBG KL	IB D	9 6	4000	5 4	11400	13000

....For earlier years, see the BUC Used Boat Price Guide, Volume 3

LINDMARK YACHT SALES LTD
DESPLAINES IL 60018 COAST GUARD MFG ID- LDR See inside cover to adjust price for area

LOA FT IN	NAME AND/OR MODEL	TOP/RIG	BOAT TYPE	HULL MTL TP	ENGINE TP #HP MFG	BEAM FT IN	WGT LBS	DRAFT FT IN	RETAIL LOW	RETAIL HIGH
1985 BOATS										
30	LINDMARK Q31 SDN	FB	TRWL	FBG DS	IB 230	11 6	16000	3 6	41100	45700
34 4	LINDMARK G35 DC	FB	TRWL	FBG DS	IB 120D	12	18000	3	73000	80200
35 8	LINDMARK SR-36 GC	FB	TRWL	FBG DS	IB 120D	13 4	19000	3	77700	85400
38 3	LINDMARK SR-39 GC	FB	TRWL	FBG DS	IB 120D	13	23000	3	95800	105000
41	LINDMARK Q41 DC	FB	TRWL	FBG DS	IB 120D	14	30000	4	122000	134000
44 10	LINDMARK Q45 SDN	FB	TRWL	FBG DS	IB T120D	15	30000	4	126500	139000
45 6	LINDMARK Q46 SUNDK	FB	CR	FBG DS	IB T145D	14	30000	4	116500	128000
47 3	LINDMARK SR-47 PH	FB	PH	FBG DS	IB T120D	14 8	27000	4	144500	159000
48	LINDMARK Q48	FB		FBG DS	IB T120D	15			109000	120000
51	LINDMARK SR-51 FD	FB	MY	FBG DS	IB T210D	16	50000	4 8	177500	195000
55	LINDMARK SR-55 PH	FB	MY	FBG DS	IB T310D	18 7	64900	4	241500	265500
60	LINDMARK SR-60 FD	FB	MY	FBG DS	IB T	19	72000	4	334500	367500
65	LINDMARK SR-65 FD	FB	MY	FBG DS	IB T460D	19	79400	4 9	413000	454000
1984 BOATS										
30	LINDMARK Q31 SDN	FB	TRWL	FBG DS	IB T 85D LEHM	11 6	16000	3 6	59300	65100
34 4	LINDMARK G35	FB	TRWL	FBG DS	IB 135D LEHM	12	18000	3	69800	76700
34 4	LINDMARK G35 DC	FB	TRWL	FBG DS	IB T 85D LEHM	12	18000	3	71400	78500
35 8	LINDMARK SR-36 GC	FB	TRWL	FBG DS	IB 135D LEHM	13 4	19000	3	74200	81600
35 8	LINDMARK SR-36 GC	FB	TRWL	FBG DS	IB T135D LEHM	13 4	19000	3	78500	86300
35 8	LINDMARK SR-36 SEDAN	FB	TRWL	FBG DS	IB 135D LEHM	13 4	19000	3	74200	81600
35 8	LINDMARK SR-36 SEDAN	FB	TRWL	FBG DS	IB T135D LEHM	13 4	19000	3	78500	86300
38 3	LINDMARK SR-39 GC	FB	TRWL	FBG DS	IB 135D LEHM	13	23000	3	86400	95000
38 3	LINDMARK SR-39 GC	FB	TRWL	FBG DS	IB T135D LEHM	13	23000	3	92000	101000
38 3	LINDMARK SR-39 SEDAN	FB	TRWL	FBG DS	IB 135D LEHM	13	23000	3	86400	95000
38 3	LINDMARK SR-39 SEDAN	FB	TRWL	FBG DS	IB T135D LEHM	13	23000	3	92000	101000
41	LINDMARK Q41	FB	TRWL	FBG DS	IB 135D LEHM	14	30000	4	116500	128000
41	LINDMARK Q41	FB	TRWL	FBG DS	IB T135D LEHM	14	30000	4	123000	135000
44 10	LINDMARK Q45 PH	FB	TRWL	FBG DS	IB T135D PERK	15	30000	4	122500	134500
44 10	LINDMARK Q45 SDN	FB	TRWL	FBG DS	IB T135D PERK	15	30000	4	117000	128500
45	LINDMARK SR-45 GC	FB	TRWL	FBG DS	IB T135D LEHM	15		4	143500	157500
45	LINDMARK SR-45 GC	FB	TRWL	FBG DS	IB T158D VLVO	15 3		4	143500	158000
45	LINDMARK SR-45 GC	FB	TRWL	FBG DS	IB T235D VLVO	15 3		4	147500	162000
45 6	LINDMARK Q46 SUNDK	FB		FBG DS	IB T145D ISUZ	14 3	30000	4 2	120000	132000
45 6	LINDMARK Q46 SUNDK	FB		FBG DS	IB T200D PERK	14 4	30000	4 2	125500	137500
47 3	LINDMARK SR-47 PH	FB PH		FBG DS	IB T124D VLVO	14 8	27000	4	138000	152000
	IB T160D LEHM 107500 118000; IB T180D SABR 112500 123500; IB T240D PERK 128500 141000									
	IB T270D CUM 134500 147500; IB T300D CAT 141500 155500									
51	LINDMARK SR-51 FD	FB	MY	FBG DS	IB T235D VLVO	16 8	50000	4	174000	191000
51	LINDMARK SR-51 FD	FB	MY	FBG DS	IB T310D GM	16	50000	4 3	175500	193000
51	LINDMARK SR-51 FD	FB	MY	FBG DS	IB T425D CUM	16	50000	4 3	197000	216500
55	LINDMARK SR-55 FD	FB	MY	FBG DS	IB T310D GM	18 7	64900	4	225000	247500
55	LINDMARK SR-55 PHS	FB	MY	FBG DS	IB T310D GM	18 7	64900	4	219000	240500
60	LINDMARK SR-60	FB	MY	FBG DS	IB T462D GM	19	72000	4	318500	350000
65 6	LINDMARK SR-65	FB	MY	FBG DS	IB T462D GM	19	79400	4 9	408500	449000

....For earlier years, see the BUC Used Boat Price Guide, Volume 3

LITTLE HARBOR CUSTOM YACHTS

PORTSMOUTH RI 02871 COAST GUARD MFG ID- LHB See inside cover to adjust price for area
FORMERLY OCEAN RANGER YACHTS

For more recent years, see the BUC Used Boat Price Guide, Volume 1

LOA FT	LOA IN	NAME AND/ OR MODEL	TOP/ RIG	BOAT TYPE	HULL MTL	HULL TP	ENGINE TP	# HP	MFG	BEAM FT	BEAM IN	WGT LBS	DRAFT FT	DRAFT IN	RETAIL LOW	RETAIL HIGH
		1996 BOATS														
40	2	LITTLE HARBOR 40	ST	EXP	FBG	SV	IB	T300D	CUM	11		18000	3		293500	322500
52	3	LITTLE HARBOR 52	CUT	SACAC	FBG	CB	IB	100D	WEST	15	3	48650	4	8	779000	856500
53	11	LITTLE HARBOR 54	CUT	SACAC	FBG	KC	IB	100D	WEST	15	1	51450	5	8	876500	963500
60	5	LITTLE HARBOR 60	CUT	SACAC	FBG	CB	IB	135D	PERK	16	2	70500	5		1.540M	1.675M
67	6	LITTLE HARBOR 68	CUT	SACAC	FBG	KC	IB	185D	PERK	18	4	56T	6		2.740M	2.980M
71	2	LITTLE HARBOR 70	CUT	SACAC	FBG		IB	185D	PERK	18	4	56T	6		2.540M	2.760M
		1995 BOATS														
40	2	LITTLE HARBOR 40	ST	EXP	FBG	SV	IB	T250D	CUM	11		18000	3		273500	300500
52	3	LITTLE HARBOR 52	CUT	SACAC	FBG	CB	IB	100D	WEST	15	3	48650	4	8	706500	776500
53	11	LITTLE HARBOR 54	CUT	SACAC	FBG	KC	IB	100D	WEST	15	1	51450	5	8	798000	877000
60	5	LITTLE HARBOR 60	CUT	SACAC	FBG	CB	IB	135D	PERK	16	2	70500	5		1.440M	1.565M
67	6	LITTLE HARBOR 68	CUT	SACAC	FBG	KC	IB	185D	PERK	18	4	56T	6		2.560M	2.780M
		1994 BOATS														
36	2	LITTLE HARBOR 36	ST	EXP	FBG	SV	IB	T250D	CUM	11		16000	3		190000	208500
40	2	LITTLE HARBOR 40	ST	EXP	FBG	SV	IB	T250D	CUM	11		18000	3		262000	288000
42	8	LITTLE HARBOR 42	CUT	SACAC	FBG	KC	IB	52D	WEST	13	1	29450	4	11	354000	389000
45	8	LITTLE HARBOR 46	CUT	SACAC	FBG	KC	IB	70D	WEST	13	8	37500	5	4	450500	495500
50	7	LITTLE HARBOR 51	CUT	SACAC	FBG	CB	IB	100D	WEST	15	3	48650	4	8	615500	676500
52	3	LITTLE HARBOR 52	CUT	SACAC	FBG	CB	IB	100D	WEST	15	3	48650	4	8	678000	745000
53	11	LITTLE HARBOR 54	CUT	SACAC	FBG	KC	IB	100D	WEST	15	1	51450	5	8	763000	838500
60	5	LITTLE HARBOR 60	CUT	SACAC	FBG	CB	IB	135D	PERK	16	2	70500	5		1.345M	1.460M
67	6	LITTLE HARBOR 68	CUT	SACAC	FBG	KC	IB	185D	PERK	18	4	56T	6		2.390M	2.600M
		1993 BOATS														
36	2	LITTLE HARBOR 36	ST	EXP	FBG	SV	IB	T250D	CUM	11		16000	3		180500	198500
40	2	LITTLE HARBOR 40	ST	EXP	FBG	SV	IB	T250D	CUM	11		18000	3		250000	274500
42	8	LITTLE HARBOR 42	CUT	SACAC	FBG	KC	IB	52D	WEST	13	1	29450	4	11	331000	363500
45	8	LITTLE HARBOR 46	CUT	SACAC	FBG	KC	IB	70D	WEST	13	8	37500	5	4	420500	462000
50	7	LITTLE HARBOR 51	CUT	SACAC	FBG	CB	IB	100D	WEST	15	3	48650	4	8	574000	630500
52	3	LITTLE HARBOR 52	CUT	SACAC	FBG	CB	IB	100D	WEST	15	3	48650	4	8	632500	695000
53	11	LITTLE HARBOR 54	CUT	SACAC	FBG	KC	IB	100D	WEST	15	1	51450	5	8	712000	782500
60	5	LITTLE HARBOR 60	CUT	SACAC	FBG	CB	IB	135D	PERK	16	2	70500	5		1.255M	1.365M
67	6	LITTLE HARBOR 68	CUT	SACAC	FBG	KC	IB	185D	PERK	18	4	56T	6		2.230M	2.425M
		1989 BOATS														
42	8	LITTLE-HARBOR 42 AFT	SLP	SA/CR	F/S	KC	IB	52D	WEST	13	1	28450	4	7	247500	272000
44	3	LITTLE-HARBOR 44 AFT	SLP	SA/CR	F/S	KC	IB	58D	WEST	13	8	32500	5		283500	311500
45	8	LITTLE-HARBOR 46 AFT	SLP	SA/CR	F/S	KC	IB	70D	WEST	13	8	32500	5		283000	311000
45	8	LITTLE-HARBOR 46 MID	SLP	SA/CR	F/S	KC	IB	70D	WEST	13	8	32500	5		319500	351000
50	9	LITTLE-HARBOR 50 AFT	SLP	SA/CR	F/S	KC	IB	100D	WEST	15	1	43200	5	6	428000	470000
52	8	LITTLE-HARBOR 53 MID	SLP	SA/CR	F/S	KC	IB	100D	WEST	15	1	43200	5	6	483000	531000
58	8	LITTLE-HARBOR 58 MID	SLP	SA/CR	F/S	KC	IB	135D	PERK	16	2	56720	4	11	800000	879000
63	6	LITTLE-HARBOR 63 MID	SLP	SA/CR	F/S	KC	IB	130D	PERK	17	3	65000	6		951500	1.035M
		1988 BOATS														
42	8	LITTLE-HARBOR 42 AFT	SLP	SA/CR	F/S	KC	IB	52D	WEST	13	1	28450	4	7	231000	254000
44	3	LITTLE-HARBOR 44 AFT	SLP	SA/CR	F/S	KC	IB	58D	WEST	13	8	32500	5		265000	291000
45	8	LITTLE-HARBOR 46 AFT	SLP	SA/CR	F/S	KC	IB	70D	WEST	13	8	32500	5		255500	280500
45	8	LITTLE-HARBOR 46 MID	SLP	SA/CR	F/S	KC	IB	70D	WEST	13	8	32500	5		297000	326500
50	9	LITTLE-HARBOR 50 AFT	SLP	SA/CR	F/S	KC	IB	100D	WEST	15	1	43200	5	6	399500	439000
52	8	LITTLE-HARBOR 53 MID	SLP	SA/CR	F/S	KC	IB	100D	WEST	15	1	43200	5	6	451000	495500
58	8	LITTLE-HARBOR 58 MID	SLP	SA/CR	F/S	KC	IB	135D	PERK	16	2	56720	4	11	747500	821500
63	6	LITTLE-HARBOR 63 MID	SLP	SA/CR	F/S	KC	IB	130D	PERK	17	3	65000	6		880000	967000
		1987 BOATS														
42	8	LITTLE-HARBOR 42	SLP	SA/CR	F/S	KC	IB	52D	WEST	13	1	27450	4	8	212000	233000
44	3	LITTLE-HARBOR 44 AFT	SLP	SA/CR	F/S	KC	IB	58D	WEST	13	8	32500	5		247500	272000
45	8	LITTLE-HARBOR 46 AFT	SLP	SA/CR	F/S	KC	IB	70D	WEST	13	8	32500	5		253000	278000
45	8	LITTLE-HARBOR 46 AFT	KTH	SA/CR	F/S	KC	IB	70D	WEST	13	8	32500	5		264000	290000
45	8	LITTLE-HARBOR 46 CTR	SLP	SA/CR	F/S	KC	IB	70D	WEST	13	8	32500	5		273500	300500
45	8	LITTLE-HARBOR 46 CTR	KTH	SA/CR	F/S	KC	IB	70D	WEST	13	8	32500	5		264000	290000
50	9	LITTLE-HARBOR 50 AFT	SLP	SA/CR	F/S	KC	IB	100D	WEST	15	1	43200	5	6	373000	409500
52	8	LITTLE-HARBOR 53	SLP	SA/CR	F/S	KC	IB	100D	WEST	15	1	43200	5	6	421500	463000
52	8	LITTLE-HARBOR 53	KTH	SA/CR	F/S	KC	IB	100D	WEST	15	1	43200	5	6	423500	465500
63	6	LITTLE-HARBOR 63	SLP	SA/CR	F/S	KC	IB	130D	PERK	17	3	65000	6		822500	904000
		1986 BOATS														
42	8	LITTLE-HARBOR 42	SLP	SA/CR	F/S	KC	IB	52D	WEST	13	1	27450	4	8	198000	217500
44	3	LITTLE-HARBOR 44 AFT	SLP	SA/CR	F/S	KC	IB	58D	WEST	13	8	32500	5		224500	247000
44	3	LITTLE-HARBOR 44 CTR	SLP	SA/CR	F/S	KC	IB	58D	WEST	13	8	32500	5		238500	262000
45	8	LITTLE-HARBOR 46 AFT	KTH	SA/CR	F/S	KC	IB	70D	WEST	13	8	32500	5		239500	263500
45	8	LITTLE-HARBOR 46 CTR	KTH	SA/CR	F/S	KC	IB	70D	WEST	13	8	32500	5		254000	279000
50	9	LITTLE-HARBOR 50 AFT	SLP	SA/CR	F/S	KC	IB	100D	WEST	15	1	43200	5	6	336500	370000
50	9	LITTLE-HARBOR 50 CTR	SLP	SA/CR	F/S	KC	IB	100D	WEST	15	1	43200	5	6	359500	395000
52	8	LITTLE-HARBOR 53	SLP	SA/CR	F/S	KC	IB	100D	WEST	15	1	43200	5	6	393500	432500
52	8	LITTLE-HARBOR 53	KTH	SA/CR	F/S	KC	IB	100D	WEST	15	1	43200	5	6	396000	435000
		1985 BOATS														
44	3	LITTLE-HARBOR 44	SLP	SA/CR	FBG	KC	IB	62D	PERK	13	8	30700	5		209500	230000
50	9	LITTLE-HARBOR 50	SLP	SA/CR	FBG	KC	IB	85D	PERK	15	1	43200	5	6	323000	355000
		1984 BOATS														
38		LITTLE-HARBOR 38	SLP	SA/RC	FBG	KC	IB	50D	PERK	11	10	20000	4	6	118000	129500
44	3	LITTLE-HARBOR 44 AFT	SLP	SA/RC	FBG	KC	IB	62D	PERK	13	8	30700	5		196000	215000
44	3	LITTLE-HARBOR 44 CTR	SLP	SA/CR	FBG	KC	IB	62D	PERK	13	8	30700	5		196000	215000
50	9	LITTLE-HARBOR 50	SLP	SA/CR	FBG	KC	IB	85D	PERK	15	1	43200	5	6	302500	332000
61	7	LITTLE-HARBOR 62	SLP	SA/CR	FBG	KC	IB	T135D	PERK	16	4	91000	6		895500	984000
77		LITTLE-HARBOR 75	SLP	SA/CR	FBG	KC	IB	T135D	PERK	18	5	64T	6	6	**	**

....For earlier years, see the BUC Used Boat Price Guide, Volume 3

LOGIC BOATS

DIV OF GENMAR
DURHAM NC 27705

See inside cover to adjust price for area

For more recent years, see the BUC Used Boat Price Guide, Volume 1

LOA FT	LOA IN	NAME AND/ OR MODEL	TOP/ RIG	BOAT TYPE	HULL MTL	HULL TP	ENGINE TP	# HP	MFG	BEAM FT	BEAM IN	WGT LBS	DRAFT FT	DRAFT IN	RETAIL LOW	RETAIL HIGH
		1996 BOATS														
17	2	LOGIC 17	OP	FSH		SV	OB			6	6	1125		9	2400	2800
17	2	LOGIC 17 CC	OP	CTRCN		SV	OB			6	6	1150		9	2450	2850
17	2	LOGIC 17 TILLER	OP	FSH		SV	OB			6	6	1125		9	2400	2800

LOGICAL BOAT COMPANY

AMITYVILLE NY 11701

See inside cover to adjust price for area

LOA FT	LOA IN	NAME AND/ OR MODEL	TOP/ RIG	BOAT TYPE	HULL MTL	HULL TP	ENGINE TP	# HP	MFG	BEAM FT	BEAM IN	WGT LBS	DRAFT FT	DRAFT IN	RETAIL LOW	RETAIL HIGH
		1987 BOATS														
46		LOGICAL 46		CR	F/S	CT	IB	T165D	VLVO	23	10	26000	3	3	142000	156000
46		LOGICAL 46	SLP	SA/CR	F/S	CT	IB	T125D	VLVO	23	10	26000	3	3	206500	227000
		1986 BOATS														
46		LOGICAL 46	FB	MY	F/S	CT	IB	T165D	VLVO	23	10	26000	3	3	190500	209000
		1985 BOATS														
46		LOGICAL 46	SLP	MS	F/S	CT	IB	T165D	VLVO	23	10	26000	3	3	183500	201500
46		LOGICAL 46	FB	MY	F/S	CT	IB	T165D	VLVO	23	10	26000	3	3	182000	200500
46		LOGICAL 46	SLP	SA/CR	F/S	CT	IB	T125D	VLVO	23	10	26000	3	6	182500	200500

LOVFALD MARINE

TARPON SPRINGS FL 33589 COAST GUARD MFG ID- LVF See inside cover to adjust price for area

LOA FT	LOA IN	NAME AND/ OR MODEL	TOP/ RIG	BOAT TYPE	HULL MTL	HULL TP	ENGINE TP	# HP	MFG	BEAM FT	BEAM IN	WGT LBS	DRAFT FT	DRAFT IN	RETAIL LOW	RETAIL HIGH
		1987 BOATS														
16		SKIMMER 16	CAT	SAIL	FBG	CT				8			2		4050	4750
18		SKIMMER 18	CAT	SAIL	FBG	CT				8			2		6300	7250
30		SKIMMER 30	SLP	SA/CR	FBG	CT	OB			19		3200	2		43000	47800
31		SKIMMER 31		SF	FBG	CT	OB			14		6000			37600	41800
40		SKIMMER 40	CUT	SA/CR	FBG	CT	OB			25		6600	2		115000	126500
		1986 BOATS														
26		SKIMMER 26	SLP	SA/RC	FBG	TM	OB			16		2400	3		18200	20200
30		SKIMMER 30	SLP	SA/RC	FBG	CT	OB			19		3200	3		40500	45000
31		SKIMMER 31		SF	FBG	CT	OB			14		6000			36200	40300
40		SKIMMER 40	CUT	SA/RC	FBG	CT	OB			25		6600	4		108000	119000
46		SKIMMER 46		SF	AL	CT	IB	T250		20		34000			109500	120000
		1985 BOATS														
16		SKIMMER 16	CAT	SAIL	FBG	CT				8			2		3600	4200
18		SKIMMER 18	CAT	SAIL	FBG	CT				8			2		5600	6400
18		SKIMMER 18 SQ	CAT	SAIL	FBG	CT				12					5600	6400
26		SKIMMER 26	SLP	SA/RC	FBG	TM				16		2400	3		16700	19000
30		SKIMMER 30	SLP	SA/CR	FBG	CT				19		3200	3		38100	42300
31		SKIMMER 31		SF	FBG	CT	OB			14		6000			34900	38800
40		SKIMMER 40	CUT	SA/CR	FBG	CT				25		6600	4		101500	112000
46		SKIMMER 46		SF	AL	CT	IB	T250		20		34000			104500	115000
		1984 BOATS														
16		SKIMMER 16	CAT	SA/OD	FBG	CT				8			2		2050	2400
18		SKIMMER 18	CAT	SA/OD	FBG	CT				8			2		3250	3750

....For earlier years, see the BUC Used Boat Price Guide, Volume 3

LOWE BOATS

DIV OF OMC ALUMINUM BOAT GROUP
LEBANON MO 65536   COAST GUARD MFG ID- LWN
          FORMERLY LOWE INDUSTRIES & LOWE ALUMINUM BOATS

See inside cover to adjust price for area

For more recent years, see the BUC Used Boat Price Guide, Volume 1

LOA FT IN	NAME AND/ OR MODEL	TOP/ RIG	BOAT TYPE	HULL MTL	TP	TP	ENGINE #	HP	MFG	BEAM FT IN	WGT LBS	DRAFT FT IN	RETAIL LOW	RETAIL HIGH
						1996 BOATS								
16 1	JUMBO V1666	OP	UTL	AL	SV	OB				5 8	235		455	550
16 1	JUMBO V1666T	OP	UTL	AL	SV	OB				5 8	250		485	585
16 1	JUMBO V1666WT	OP	UTL	AL	SV	OB				5 8	395		775	935
16 9	BASS STRIKER 1700	OP	BASS	AL	SV	OB				6 8	900		2050	2450
17	1705PL	OP	BASS	AL	SV	OB					400		915	1100
17	1752VCT COMBO	OP	JON	AL	FL	OB				6 2	330		570	685
17	HUSKY JON 1760MT	OP	JON	AL	FL	OB				6 11	460		800	965
17	JON BASS 170	OP	BASS	AL	SV	OB				6 2	715		1650	1950
17 2	BACKTROLLER 1710	OP	FSH	AL	SV	OB				7	1050		2350	2750
17 2	FISH N SKI 1730	OP	FSH	AL	DV	OB				7	1080		2500	2900
17 2	FISH PRO 1720	OP	FSH	AL	DV	OB				7	1050		2200	2600
17 11	JUMBO 1880T	OP	UTL	AL	SV	OB				6 8	470		885	1050
18	BIG JON 1848	OP	JON	AL	FL	OB				5 10	300		515	620
18	OLYMPIC 1852 COM	OP	JON	AL	FL	OB				6 3	345		590	710
18	OLYMPIC JON 1852MT	OP	JON	AL	FL	OB				6 3	345		605	725
18	OLYMPIC JON 1852T	OP	JON	AL	FL	OB				6 3	345		565	685
18	TUNNEL JON 1852MTNN	OP	JON	AL	FL	OB				6 3	385		650	780
18 4	BASS STRIKER 1800	OP	BASS	AL	SV	OB				6 8	1230		2800	3250
19	HUSKY JON 1960MT	OP	JON	AL	FL	OB				6 11	500		765	920
19 1	BACKTROLLER 1910	OP	FSH	AL	SV	OB				7 2	1150		2600	3000
19 1	FISH N SKI 1930	OP	FSH	AL	DV	OB				7 2	1250		2750	3200
19 1	FISH PRO 1920	OP	FSH	AL	DV	OB				7 2	1150		2600	3000
22 1	SILHOUETTE 2200	ST	BASS	AL	SV	OB				8	1800		3750	4350
22 1	SILHOUETTE 2220	ST	BASS	AL	SV	OB				8	1800		3750	4400
24	SILHOUETTE 2400	ST	BASS	AL	SV	OB				8 6	2420		5150	5900
						1995 BOATS								
16 1	JUMBO V1666	OP	UTL	AL	SV	OB				5 8	235		425	515
16 1	JUMBO V1666T	OP	UTL	AL	SV	OB				5 8	250		455	550
16 1	JUMBO V1666WT	OP	UTL	AL	SV	OB				5 8	395		730	880
16 1	JUMBO V1672T	ST	UTL	AL	SV	OB				5 8	330		605	725
16 9	BASS STRIKER 1700	OP	BASS	AL	SV	OB				6 8	900		1900	2300
17	1752V COMBO	OP	JON	AL	FL	OB				6 2	330		535	645
17	HUSKY JON 1760MT	OP	JON	AL	FL	OB				6 11	460		740	890
17	JON BASS 170	OP	BASS	AL	SV	OB				6 2	715		1500	1800
17	JON BASS 170	OP	BASS	AL	SV	JT	50- 70			6 2	715		5000	6150
17 2	BACKTROLLER 1710	OP	FSH	AL	SV	OB				7	1050		2200	2550
17 2	FISH N SKI 1730	OP	FSH	AL	DV	OB				7	1080		2400	2750
17 2	FISH N SKI 1730	OP	FSH	AL	DV	OB				7	1080		2350	2700
17 2	FISH PRO 1720	OP	FSH	AL	DV	OB				7	1050		2000	2400
17 2	FISH PRO 1720	OP	FSH	AL	DV	OB				7	1050		2050	2450
17 11	JUMBO 1880T	OP	UTL	AL	SV	OB				6 8	470		820	985
18	BIG JON 1848	OP	JON	AL	FL	OB				5 10	300		465	565
18	OLYMPIC 1852 COM	OP	JON	AL	FL	OB				6 3	345		540	650
18	OLYMPIC JON 1852MT	OP	JON	AL	FL	OB				6 3	345		545	655
18	OLYMPIC JON 1852T	OP	JON	AL	FL	OB				6 3	345		535	645
18	TUNNEL JON 1852MTNN	OP	JON	AL	FL	OB				6 3	385		605	730
18 4	BASS STRIKER 1800	OP	BASS	AL	SV	OB				6 8	1230		2600	3050
19	HUSKY JON 1960MT	OP	JON	AL	FL	OB				6 11	500		700	840
19	SILHOUETTE 1900	ST	BASS	AL	SV	OB				8	1500		3100	3600
19 1	BACKTROLLER 1910	OP	FSH	AL	DV	OB				7 2	1150		2450	2850
19 1	BACKTROLLER 1910	OP	FSH	AL	SV	OB				7 2	1150		2450	2850
19 1	FISH N SKI 1930	OP	FSH	AL	DV	OB				7 2	1250		2600	3000
19 1	FISH N SKI 1930	OP	FSH	AL	DV	OB				7 2	1250		2600	3000
19 1	FISH PRO 1920	OP	FSH	AL	DV	OB				7 2	1150		2450	2850
19 1	FISH PRO 1920	OP	FSH	AL	DV	OB				7 2	1150		2450	2850
22 1	SILHOUETTE 2200	ST	BASS	AL	SV	OB				8	1800		3550	4150
22 1	SILHOUETTE 2220	ST	BASS	AL	SV	OB				8	1800		3550	4150
22 1	SILHOUETTE 2220 SD	ST	BASS	AL	SV	IO	175			8	2605		13500	15400
24	SILHOUETTE 2400	ST	BASS	AL	SV	OB				8 6	2420		4900	5650
						1994 BOATS								
16 9	1700	OP	BASS	AL	DV	OB				6 8	900		1750	2100
16 9	1700	OP	BASS	AL	DV	OB				6 8	900		1750	2100
17	170	OP	JON	AL	FL	OB				6 2	715		1400	1700
17	1752 6V COMBO	OP	JON	AL	FL	OB				6 2	330		510	615
17	HUSKY JON	OP	JON	AL	FL	OB				6 11	460		710	855
17	HUSKY JON SC	OP	JON	AL	FL	OB				6 11	460		735	885
17 2	1710	OP	FSH	AL	SV	OB				7	1050		2000	2350
17 2	1720	OP	FSH	AL	DV	OB				7	1050		1850	2250
17 2	1720	OP	FSH	AL	DV	OB				7	1050		1900	2300
17 2	1730	OP	FSH	AL	DV	OB				7	1050		2150	2500
17 2	1730	OP	FSH	AL	SV	OB				7	1050		2050	2450
18	BIG JON	OP	JON	AL	FL	OB				5 10	300		455	545
18	BIG JON SC	OP	JON	AL	FL	OB				5 10	300		465	560
18	OLYMPIC 1852 COM	OP	JON	AL	FL	OB				6 3	345		505	605
18	OLYMPIC 1852 COM SC	OP	JON	AL	FL	OB				6 3	345		520	625
18	OLYMPIC JON	OP	JON	AL	FL	OB				6 3	345		495	595
18	OLYMPIC JON MVB	OP	JON	AL	FL	OB				6 3	345		515	620
18	OLYMPIC JON MVB SC	OP	JON	AL	FL	OB				6 3	345		525	630
18	OLYMPIC JON SC	OP	JON	AL	FL	OB				6 3	345		515	625
18	TUNNEL JON MVB	OP	JON	AL	FL	OB				6 3	345		500	605
18	TUNNEL JON MVB SC	OP	JON	AL	FL	OB				6 3	345		520	625
18	HUSKY JON	OP	JON	AL	FL	OB				6 11	500		675	815
18	HUSKY JON SC	OP	JON	AL	FL	OB				6 11	500		695	840
19 1	1910	OP	FSH	AL	DV	OB				7 2	1150		2300	2700
19 1	1910	OP	FSH	AL	SV	OB				7 2	1150		2300	2700
19 1	1920	OP	FSH	AL	DV	OB				7 2	1150		2300	2700
19 1	1920	OP	FSH	AL	SV	OB				7 2	1150		2300	2700
19 1	1930	OP	FSH	AL	DV	OB				7 2	1250		2450	2850
19 1	1930	OP	FSH	AL	SV	OB				7 2	1250		2450	2850
						1993 BOATS								
16	BIG JON MVB/WT	OP	JON	AL	FL	OB				5 10	275		455	550
16 6	1700	OP	BASS	AL	DV	OB				6 8	920		1750	2050
17	170	OP	BASS	AL	DV	OB				6 1	670		1250	1500
17	1710	OP	FSH	AL	DV	OB				7	840		1500	1900
17	1720	OP	FSH	AL	DV	OB				7	875		1600	1900
17	1730	OP	FSH	AL	DV	OB				7	1050		1900	2250
17	1752 6V COMBO	OP	JON	AL	FL	OB				6 2	370		545	655
18	BIG JON	OP	JON	AL	FL	OB				5 10	290		455	545
18	OLYMPIC 1852 COM	OP	JON	AL	FL	OB				6 3	325		495	595
18	OLYMPIC JON	OP	JON	AL	FL	OB				6 3	325		495	595
18	OLYMPIC JON MVB	OP	JON	AL	FL	OB				6 3	330		505	610
18 10	1910	OP	FSH	AL	SV	OB				7	1150		2100	2500
18 10	1920	OP	FSH	AL	SV	OB				7	1100		2000	2400
18 10	1930	OP	FSH	AL	SV	OB				7	1200		2250	2600
18 10	1940	OP	FSH	AL	DV	OB				7	995		1800	2150
						1992 BOATS								
16	BIG JON MVB/WT	OP	JON	AL	FL	OB				5 10	275		430	520
16 3	V1670	OP	UTL	AL	SV	OB				5 10	250		380	465
16 3	V1670TT	OP	UTL	AL	SV	OB				5 10	250		380	465
16 6	1700	OP	BASS	AL	DV	OB				6 8	920		1650	1950
17	170	OP	BASS	AL	SV	OB				6 1	670		1200	1400
17	1710	OP	FSH	AL	DV	OB				7	840		1400	1700
17	1720	OP	FSH	AL	DV	OB				7	875		1450	1700
17	1730	OP	FSH	AL	DV	OB				7	1050		1750	2100
17	1740	OP	FSH	AL	DV	OB				7	875		1450	1750
17	1752 6V COMBO	OP	JON	AL	FL	OB				6 2	370		515	620
18	HUSKY JON MVB	OP	JON	AL	FL	OB				6 11	422		585	705
18	BIG JON	OP	JON	AL	FL	OB				5 10	290		430	515
18	OLYMPIC JON	OP	JON	AL	FL	OB				6 3	325		465	560
18	OLYMPIC JON MVB	OP	JON	AL	FL	OB				6 3	330		475	570
18 10	1910	OP	FSH	AL	SV	OB				7	1150		1950	2350
18 10	1920	OP	FSH	AL	SV	OB				7	1100		1900	2250
18 10	1930	OP	FSH	AL	DV	OB				7	1200		2050	2450
18 10	1940	OP	FSH	AL	DV	OB				7	995		1700	2050
19	HULK MVB	OP	JON	AL	FL	OB				6 11	600		770	925
19	HUSKY JON MVB	OP	JON	AL	FL	OB				6 11	440		510	615
						1991 BOATS								
16	160	OP	BASS	AL	SV	OB				6	600		1000	1200
16	1600	OP	BASS	AL	SV	OB				6	720		1200	1450
16	1605	OP	FSH	AL	SV	OB				5 7	360		585	705
16	1610	OP	FSH	AL	DV	OB				5 7	360		550	665
16	1615	OP	FSH	AL	DV	OB				6 1	525		860	1000
16	1620	OP	FSH	AL	DV	OB				6 1	620		1000	1200
16	1625	OP	FSH	AL	DV	OB				6 1	525		860	1000
16	1648	OP	JON	AL	FL	OB				5 10	282		415	500
16	165	OP	BASS	AL	SV	OB				5 10	475		800	960
16	1652 MVB	OP	JON	AL	FL	OB				6 3	280		410	500
16	BIG JON	OP	JON	AL	FL	OB				5 10	275		375	455
16	BIG JON MVB 16T	OP	JON	AL	FL	OB				5 10	275		395	480
16	BIG JON MVB 21T	OP	JON	AL	FL	OB				5 10	275		395	480
16	BIG JON MVB/WT	OP	JON	AL	FL	OB				5 10	275		415	505

LOA FT	LOA IN	NAME AND/ OR MODEL	TOP/ RIG	BOAT TYPE	-HULL- MTL	-HULL- TP	ENGINE TP	ENGINE # HP MFG	BEAM FT	BEAM IN	WGT LBS	DRAFT FT IN	RETAIL LOW	RETAIL HIGH
		1991 BOATS												
16		JUMBO 16T	OP	UTL	AL	SV	OB		5	7	250		360	440
16		JUMBO 21T	OP	UTL	AL	SV	OB		5	7	250		370	450
16		OLYMPIC JON	OP	JON	AL	FL	OB		6	3	280		410	500
16		OLYMPIC JON MVB	OP	JON	AL	FL	OB		6	3	285		420	505
16		ROVER JON MVB	OP	JON	AL	FL	OB		5		207		315	385
16		TUNNEL JON	OP	JON	AL	FL	OB		5	10	275		450	540
16	6	1700	OP	BASS	AL	DV	OB		6	8	920		1550	1800
16	6	1701	OP	BASS	AL	DV	OB		6	8	940		1600	1900
17		170	OP	BASS	AL	SV	OB		6	1	670		1150	1350
17		1720	OP	FSH	AL	DV	OB		7		875		1400	1650
17		1730	OP	FSH	AL	DV	OB		7		1200		1900	2250
17		1740	OP	FSH	AL	DV	OB		7		875		1400	1650
17		1752	OP	JON	AL	FL	OB		6	2	370		495	595
17		HUSKY JON MVB	OP	JON	AL	FL	OB		6	11	422		560	675
17	1	1710	OP	FSH	AL	DV	OB		7		840		1350	1600
18		BIG JON	OP	JON	AL	FL	OB		5	10	290		395	480
18		OLYMPIC JON	OP	JON	AL	FL	OB		6	3	325		435	525
18		OLYMPIC JON MVB	OP	JON	AL	FL	OB		6	3	330		450	540
18		OLYMPIC JON MVB/COMM	OP	JON	AL	FL	OB		6	3	325		450	540
18	10	1930	OP	FSH	AL	DV	OB		7		1050		1700	2000
18	10	1940	OP	FSH	AL	DV	OB		7		995		1600	1950
19		1960 MVB	OP	JON	AL	FL	OB		6	11	587		705	850
19		HUSKY JON MVB	OP	JON	AL	FL	OB		6	11	440		490	590
		1990 BOATS												
16		ANGLER PRO	OP	BASS	AL	SV	OB		6		600		975	1150
16		BACKTROLLER V	OP	BASS	AL	SV	OB		6	2	590		960	1150
16		BASS V	OP	BASS	AL	SV	OB		6	2	720		1150	1400
16		BIG-JON	OP	JON	AL	FL	OB		5	10	278		390	475
16		BIG-JON LW	OP	JON	AL	FL	OB		5	10	280		390	475
16		BIG-JON MVB	OP	JON	AL	FL	OB		5	10	275		360	440
16		BIG-JON MVB/WT	OP	JON	AL	FL	OB		5	10	280		390	475
16		COMBO JON MVB	OP	JON	AL		OB		6	3	280		390	475
16		FALCON	OP	BASS	AL	FL	OB		6		475		760	915
16		FISH N PRO	OP	FSH	AL	DV	OB		6	2	620		960	1150
16		JUMBO V 16T	OP	FSH	AL	SV	OB		5	5	250		370	450
16		JUMBO V 20T	OP	JON	AL	SV	OB		5	5	265		370	455
16		JUMBO V DELUXE	OP	JON	AL	SV	OB		5	5	360		495	595
16		OLYMPIC-JON	OP	JON	AL	FL	OB		6	3	280		390	475
16		OLYMPIC-JON MVB/LW	OP	JON	AL	FL	OB		6	3	285		395	485
16		ROVER-JON MVB/LW	OP	JON	AL	FL	OB		5		207		300	365
16		TUNNEL JON 16T	OP	JON	AL		OB		5	10	275		405	495
16	6	BASS V	OP	BASS	AL	SV	OB		6	8	920		1400	1700
16	6	BASS V TWIN	OP	BASS	AL	SV	OB		6	8	920		1500	1750
17		BACKTROLLER V	OP	BASS	AL	SV	OB		6	10	840		1350	1600
17		CENTER CONSOLE V	OP	CTRCN	AL	DV	OB		7		875		1350	1600
17		COMMANDER	OP	BASS	AL	TR	OB		6	2	670		1050	1300
17		FISH-N-PRO V	OP	BASS	AL		OB		6	10	1000		1500	1800
17		FISH-N-PRO V TWIN	OP	BASS	AL		OB		6	10	1000		1600	1950
17		HULK TUNNEL CC	OP	JON	AL	FL	OB		6	11	440		555	670
17		HUSKY-JON MVB	OP	JON	AL	FL	OB		6	11	422		535	640
17		PADDLE JON	OP	JON	AL	FL	OB		3	10	135		175	215
17		TOURNAMENT SPECIAL V	OP	FSH	AL	DV	OB		7		925		1400	1650
18		BIG-JON	OP	JON	AL	FL	OB		5	10	290		375	455
18		OLYMPIC-JON	OP	JON	AL	FL	OB		6	3	325		400	490
18		OLYMPIC-JON MVB/COM	OP	JON	AL	FL	OB		6	3	325		420	505
18		OLYMPIC-JON MVB/LW	OP	JON	AL	FL	OB		6	3	330		420	505
19		CENTER CONSOLE	OP	CTRCN	AL	DV	OB		7	2	995		1550	1850
19		FISH N SKI	OP	RNBT	AL	DV	OB		7	2	1050		1700	2050
19		HULK MVB	OP	JON	AL	FL	OB		6	11	587		675	810
		1989 BOATS												
16		ANGLER PRO	OP	BASS	AL	SV	OB		6		600		935	1100
16		BACKTROLLER V	OP	BASS	AL	SV	OB		6	2	590		920	1100
16		BASS V	OP	BASS	AL	SV	OB		6	2	720		1100	1300
16		BIG-JON	OP	JON	AL	FL	OB		5	10	278		370	450
16		BIG-JON LW	OP	JON	AL	FL	OB		5	10	280		370	450
16		BIG-JON MVB	OP	JON	AL	FL	OB		5	10	275		345	420
16		BIG-JON MVB/LW	OP	JON	AL	FL	OB		5	10	280		375	460
16		BIG-JON MVB/LW 20T	OP	JON	AL	FL	OB		5	10	282		375	460
16		BIG-JON MVB/WT	OP	JON	AL	FL	OB		5	10	280		370	455
16		COMBO JON MVB	OP	JON	AL		OB		6	3	280		375	455
16		CRAPPIE V	OP	BASS	AL	SV	OB		6	2	690		1050	1250
16		FALCON	OP	BASS	AL	FL	OB		6		475		725	875
16		FISHERMAN	OP	FSH	AL		OB		6		430		625	750
16		JUMBO V 16T	OP	FSH	AL	SV	OB		5	5	250		350	425
16		JUMBO V 20T	OP	JON	AL	SV	OB		5	5			495	595
16		JUMBO V DELUXE	OP	JON	AL	SV	OB		5	5	360		470	570
16		OLYMPIC-JON	OP	JON	AL	FL	OB		6	3	280		375	455
16		OLYMPIC-JON MVB/LW	OP	JON	AL	FL	OB		6	3	285		380	465
16		OPEN-JON MVB 20T	OP	JON	AL		OB		5	10	350		460	555
16		PIKE V	OP	BASS	AL	SV	OB		6	2	620		965	1150
16		ROVER-JON MVB	OP	JON	AL	SV	OB		5		207		290	350
16		ROVER-JON MVB/LW	OP	JON	AL	FL	OB		5		211		295	360
16		TUNNEL JON 16T	OP	JON	AL		OB		5	10	275		390	475
16		TUNNEL JON 20T	OP	JON	AL	FL	OB		5	10	300		395	480
16		TUNNEL JON OLY 20T	OP	JON	AL	FL	OB		6	3	305		405	490
16	6	BASS V	OP	BASS	AL	SV	OB		6	8	920		1400	1650
17		BACKTROLLER V	OP	BASS	AL	SV	OB		6	10	840		1250	1500
17		COMMANDER	OP	BASS	AL	TR	OB		6	2	670		1050	1200
17		FISH-N-SKI V	OP	BASS	AL		OB		6	10	1000		1500	1750
17		HUSKY-JON	OP	JON	AL	FL	OB		6	11	422		510	615
17		HUSKY-JON MVB	OP	JON	AL	FL	OB		6	11	422		510	615
17		PIKE V	OP	BASS	AL	SV	OB		6	10	875		1300	1550
17		TUNNEL HUSKY 20T	OP	JON	AL	FL	OB		6	11	440		530	640
18		BIG-JON	OP	JON	AL	FL	OB		5	10	290		350	430
18		OLYMPIC-JON	OP	JON	AL	FL	OB		6	3	325		380	465
18		OLYMPIC-JON MVB/COM	OP	JON	AL	FL	OB		6	3	325		395	480
18		OLYMPIC-JON MVB/LW	OP	JON	AL	FL	OB		6	3	330		390	480
19		HULK MVB	OP	JON	AL	FL	OB		6	11	587		645	775
19		HUSKY-JON MVB	OP	JON	AL	FL	OB		6	11	440		445	535
		1988 BOATS												
16		ANGLER PRO	OP	BASS	AL	SV	OB		5	10	560		800	965
16		ANGLER PRO (PTD)	OP	BASS	AL	FL	OB		5	10	560		855	1000
16		BIG-JON	OP	JON	AL	FL	OB		5	10	268		345	420
16		COMBO JON	OP	JON	AL								**	**
16		FALCON	OP	BASS	AL	FL	OB		5	10	475		690	830
16		FAMILY-JON	OP	JON	AL	FL	OB		5	10	280		360	435
16		FISHERMAN	OP	FSH	AL		OB		5	10	428		590	715
16		HUSKY-JON	OP	JON	AL	FL	OB		6	11	422		515	625
16		JUMBO V	OP	FSH	AL	SV	OB		5	5	250		335	410
16		JUMBO V-WT	OP	FSH	AL	SV	OB		5	5	280		380	465
16		LAKE-JON	OP	JON	AL	FL	OB		4	9	198		265	325
16		LUNKER I-WT	OP	FSH	AL	SV	OB		6		300		410	500
16		LUNKER II	OP	FSH	AL	SV	OB		6		565		790	950
16		LUNKER III	OP	FSH	AL	SV	OB		6	1	623		885	1050
16		LUNKER III (PTD)	OP	FSH	AL	SV	OB		6	1	623		885	1050
16		LUNKER V	OP	FSH	AL	SV	OB		6		280		380	465
16		OLYMPIC-JON	OP	JON	AL	FL	OB		6	3	280		360	435
16		OPEN-JON MVB	OP	JON	AL		OB		5	10	348		440	530
16		ROVER-JON MVB	OP	JON	AL	SV	OB		5		210		280	340
16		SUPERIOR V	OP	FSH	AL	SV	OB		5	2	225		300	365
16		TUNNEL JON	OP	JON	AL								**	**
17		COMMANDER	OP	BASS	AL	TR	OB		6	2	620		920	1100
17		PADDLE-JON	OP	JON	AL		OB						560	675
18		BIG-JON	OP	JON	AL	FL	OB		5	10	294		335	410
18		HULK	OP	JON	AL	FL	OB		6	11	587		660	795
18		HUSKY-JON	OP	JON	AL	FL	OB		6	11	440		490	595
18		OLYMPIC-JON	OP	JON	AL	FL	OB		6	3	326		370	450
18	5	CONDOR	OP	BASS	AL	SV	OB		6	11	820		1200	1400
20		HUSKY-JON	OP	JON	AL	FL	OB		6	11	460		445	535
20		OLYMPIC-JON MVB	OP	JON	AL	SV	OB		6	3	375		325	395
		1987 BOATS												
16		1648 COMMERCIAL	OP	JON	AL	FL	OB		5	10	390		480	575
16		1648 WELDED	OP	JON	AL	FL	OB		5	10	390		455	550
16		ANGLER PRO	OP	BASS	AL	SV	OB		5	10	560		770	925
16		ANGLER PRO (PTD)	OP	BASS	AL	FL	OB		5	10	560		800	965
16		BIG-JON	OP	JON	AL	FL	OB		5	10	268		330	405
16		FALCON	OP	BASS	AL	FL	OB		5	10	475		665	800
16		FAMILY JON	OP	JON	AL	FL	OB		5	10	280		345	420
16		FISHERMAN	OP	FSH	AL		OB		5	10	368		490	595
16		HUSKY-JON	OP	JON	AL	FL	OB		6	11	422		495	600
16		JUMBO V	OP	FSH	AL	SV	OB		5	5	260		335	410
16		JUMBO V-WT	OP	FSH	AL	SV	OB		5	5	285		370	455
16		LAKE-JON	OP	JON	AL	FL	OB		4	9	198		255	310
16		LUNKER II	OP	FSH	AL	SV	OB		6		565		755	910
16		LUNKER III	OP	FSH	AL	SV	OB		6	1	623		845	1000
16		LUNKER V	OP	FSH	AL	SV	OB		6		280		365	445
16		LUNKER V-WT	OP	FSH	AL	SV	OB						960	1150

 CONTINUED ON NEXT PAGE

LOA FT IN	NAME AND/ OR MODEL	TOP/ RIG	BOAT TYPE	HULL MTL TP	TP	ENGINE # HP MFG	BEAM FT IN	WGT LBS	DRAFT FT IN	RETAIL LOW	RETAIL HIGH
--- 1987 BOATS ---											
16	OLYMPIC-JON	OP	JON	AL	FL OB		6 3	280		345	420
16	OPEN-JON	OP	JON	AL	OB		5 10	348		420	510
16	ROVER JON MVB	OP	JON	AL	SV OB		5	210		270	330
16	SUPERIOR V	OP	FSH	AL	SV OB		5 2	238		305	375
17	COMMANDER	OP	BASS	AL	TR OB		6 1	640		910	1100
17	PADDLE JON	OP	JON	AL	OB					540	650
18	1852 WELDED	OP	JON	AL	FL OB		6 3	462		495	595
18	1860 WELDED	OP	JON	AL	FL OB		6 11	500		535	640
18	BIG-JON	OP	JON	AL	FL OB		5 10	294		320	390
18	HULK	OP	JON	AL	FL OB		6 11	587		630	760
18	HUSKY-JON	OP	JON	AL	FL OB		6 11	440		470	570
18	OLYMPIC-JON	OP	JON	AL	FL OB		6 3	326		350	425
18 6	CONDOR	OP	BASS	AL	SV OB		6 11	820		1150	1350
20	HUSKY-JON	OP	JON	AL	SV OB		6 11	460		430	520
20	OLYMPIC-JON	OP	JON	AL	SV OB		6 3	375		315	385
--- 1986 BOATS ---											
16	1648 COMMERCIAL	OP	JON	AL	FL OB		5 10	390		460	555
16	1648 WELDED	OP	JON	AL	FL OB		5 10	390		440	530
16	ANGLER	OP	BASS	AL	SV OB		5 10	515		690	830
16	ANGLER PRO	OP	BASS	AL	SV OB		5 10	560		755	910
16	BIG-JON	OP	JON	AL	FL OB		5 10	268		320	390
16	FAMILY JON	OP	JON	AL	FL OB		5 10	280		330	405
16	HUSKY-JON	OP	JON	AL	FL OB		6 11	422		485	585
16	JUMBO V	OP	FSH	AL	SV OB		5 5	260		325	395
16	LAKE-JON	OP	JON	AL	FL OB		4 9	198		245	300
16	LAKEMASTER	OP	BASS	AL	SV OB		5 10	428		570	690
16	LUNKER I	OP	FSH	AL	SV OB		6	300		380	460
16	LUNKER II	OP	FSH	AL	SV OB		6	565		730	880
16	LUNKER III	OP	FSH	AL	SV OB		6 1	623		805	965
16	LUNKER V	OP	FSH	AL	SV OB		6	280		350	425
16	OLYMPIC-JON	OP	JON	AL	FL OB		6 3	280		330	405
16	OPEN-JON V	OP	JON	AL	OB		5 10	348		400	490
16	ROVER JON MVB	OP	JON	AL	SV OB		5	210		260	315
16	SUPERIOR V	OP	FSH	AL	SV OB		5 2	238		295	355
17	COMMANDER	OP	BASS	AL	TR OB		6 1	640		875	1050
18	1852 WELDED	OP	JON	AL	FL OB		6 3	462		475	570
18	1860 WELDED	OP	JON	AL			6 11	500		510	615
18	BIG-JON	OP	JON	AL	FL OB		5 10	294		305	370
18	HULK	OP	JON	AL	FL OB		6 11	587		605	725
18	HUSKY-JON	OP	JON	AL	FL OB		6 11	440		450	545
18	OLYMPIC-JON	OP	JON	AL	FL OB		6 3	326		330	405
18 6	CONDOR	OP	BASS	AL	SV OB		6 11	820		1100	1300
20	HUSKY-JON	OP	JON	AL	FL OB		6 11	460		410	500
20	OLYMPIC-JON V	OP	JON	AL	SV OB		6 3	375		305	370
--- 1985 BOATS ---											
16	1648	OP	JON	AL	FL OB		5 10	390		435	525
16	BASS-CATCHER	OP	BASS	AL	TR OB		5 6	484		630	755
16	BASS-CATCHER PRO	OP	BASS	AL	TR OB		5 6	530		670	810
16	BASS-CATCHER PRO PTD	OP	BASS	AL	TR OB		5 6	530		700	840
16	BIG-JON	OP	JON	AL	FL OB		5 10	268		310	375
16	HUSKY-JON	OP	JON	AL	FL OB		6 11	422		465	565
16	JUMBO V	OP	FSH	AL	SV OB		5 5	260		315	380
16	LAKE-JON	OP	JON	AL	FL OB		4 9	198		240	290
16	LUNKER II	OP	FSH	AL	SV OB		6	565		695	840
16	LUNKER III	OP	FSH	AL	SV OB		6	623		775	930
16	LUNKER V	OP	FSH	AL	SV OB		6	280		335	410
16	OLYMPIC-JON	OP	JON	AL	FL OB		6 3	280		320	390
16	OPEN-JON V	OP	JON	AL	OB		5 10	348		390	475
16	SUPERIOR V	OP	FSH	AL	SV OB		5 2	238		285	345
17	COMMANDER	OP	BASS	AL	TR OB		6 1	640		830	1000
17	EXPLORER	OP	BASS	AL	OB		6 8	651		860	1000
17	FISH-N-SKI	OP	BASS	AL	FL OB		6 1	660		870	1050
17	PADDLE-JON	OP	JON	AL	FL OB		3 10	142		150	180
18	1848	OP	JON	AL	FL OB		5 10	412		400	485
18	1852	OP	JON	AL	FL OB		6 3	462		455	550
18	1860 WELDED	OP	JON	AL	FL OB		6 11	500		495	595
18	BIG-JON	OP	JON	AL	FL OB		5 10	294		285	350
18	HULK	OP	JON	AL	FL OB		6 11	587		585	700
18	HUSKY-JON	OP	JON	AL	FL OB		6 11	440		430	520
18	OLYMPIC-JON	OP	JON	AL	FL OB		6 3	326		320	390
18 5	BIG-BASS-BOAT	OP	BASS	AL	FL OB		7	715		950	1150
20	2052	OP	JON	AL	FL OB		6 3	533		490	595
20	2060 WELDED	OP	JON	AL	FL OB		6 11	565		525	635
20	HUSKY-JON	OP	JON	AL	FL OB		6 11	460		395	485
20	OLYMPIC-JON	OP	JON	AL	FL OB		6 3	375		295	355
--- 1984 BOATS ---											
16	1648	OP	JON	AL	FL OB		5 10	385		415	500
16	BASS-CATCHER	OP	BASS	AL	TR OB		5 4	484		610	730
16	BASS-CATCHER PRO	OP	BASS	AL	TR OB		5 5	530		655	785
16	BASS-CATCHER PRO PTD	OP	BASS	AL	TR OB		5 5	530		675	810
16	BIG-JON	OP	JON	AL	FL OB		5 10	268		300	365
16	HUSKY-JON	OP	JON	AL	FL OB		6 11	422		450	545
16	JUMBO V	OP	FSH	AL	SV OB		5 5	260		305	370
16	LAKE-JON	OP	JON	AL	FL OB		4 9	198		230	285
16	LUNKER II	OP	FSH	AL	SV OB		6	530		635	765
16	LUNKER III	OP	FSH	AL	SV OB		6	623		745	900
16	LUNKER V	OP	FSH	AL	SV OB		6	280		325	400
16	OLYMPIC-JON	OP	JON	AL	FL OB		6 3	280		310	375
16	SUPERIOR V	OP	FSH	AL	SV OB		5 2	238		275	335
17	COMMANDER	OP	BASS	AL	TR OB		6	640		800	965
17	FISH-N-SKI	OP	BASS	AL	FL OB		6	660		825	995
17	HUSTLER PRO	OP	BASS	AL	TR OB		5 5	615		770	930
17	PADDLE-JON	OP	JON	AL	FL OB		3 10	142		145	175
18	1848	OP	JON	AL	FL OB		5 10	412		385	470
18	1852	OP	JON	AL	FL OB		6 3	462		440	530
18	BIG-JON	OP	JON	AL	FL OB		5 10	294		275	335
18	HULK	OP	JON	AL	FL OB		6 11	560		535	645
18	HUSKY-JON	OP	JON	AL	FL OB		6 11	440		415	500
18	OLYMPIC-JON	OP	JON	AL	FL OB		6 3	326		305	370
20	2052	OP	JON	AL	FL OB		6 3	533		475	570
20	HUSKY-JON	OP	JON	AL	FL OB		6 11	460		385	470
20	OLYMPIC-JON	OP	JON	AL	FL OB		6 3	375		285	345

....For earlier years, see the BUC Used Boat Price Guide, Volume 3

PERT LOWELL CO INC
NEWBURY MA 01951

For more recent years, see the BUC Used Boat Price Guide, Volume 1

LOA FT IN	NAME AND/ OR MODEL	TOP/ RIG	BOAT TYPE	HULL MTL TP	TP	ENGINE # HP MFG	BEAM FT IN	WGT LBS	DRAFT FT IN	RETAIL LOW	RETAIL HIGH
--- 1996 BOATS ---											
16 6	PR DORY SKIFF	SLP	SACAC	WD	KL OB		6 6	300	8	3700	4300
16 6	TOWNCLASS	SLP	SACAC	FBG	KL		5 9	800	8	12000	13700
16 6	TOWNCLASS	SLP	SACAC	WD	KL		5 9	750	7	11600	13200
17	SWAMPSCOTT DORY	SLP	SACAC	WD	KL		4 8	400	6	8850	10000
17 9	FLEET O WING	SLP	SACAC	WD	KL		6	1200	3	14900	16900
--- 1995 BOATS ---											
16 6	PR DORY SKIFF	SLP	SACAC	WD	KL OB		6 6	300	8	3450	4050
16 6	TOWNCLASS	SLP	SACAC	FBG	KL		5 9	800	8	11300	12800
16 6	TOWNCLASS	SLP	SACAC	WD	KL		5 9	750	7	10900	12400
17	SWAMPSCOTT DORY	SLP	SACAC	WD	KL		4 8	400	6	8200	9400
17 9	FLEET O WING	SLP	SACAC	WD	KL		6	1200	3	13900	15800
--- 1994 BOATS ---											
16 6	PR DORY SKIFF	SLP	SACAC	WD	KL OB		6 6	300	8	3250	3800
16 6	TOWNCLASS	SLP	SACAC	FBG	KL		5 9	750	2 4	10300	11700
16 6	TOWNCLASS	SLP	SACAC	WD	KL		5 9	750	2 4	10300	11700
17	SWAMPSCOTT DORY	SLP	SACAC	WD	KL		4 8	400	1 8	7700	8850
17 9	FLEET O WING	SLP	SACAC	WD	KL		6	1200	3	13100	14900
--- 1993 BOATS ---											
16 6	PR DORY SKIFF	SLP	SACAC	WD	KL OB		6 6	300	8	3050	3550
16 6	TOWNCLASS	SLP	SACAC	FBG	KL		5 9	750	2 4	9650	11000
16 6	TOWNCLASS	SLP	SACAC	WD	KL		5 9	750	2 4	9650	11000
17	SWAMPSCOTT DORY	SLP	SACAC	WD	KL		4 8	400	1 8	7200	8300
17 9	FLEET O WING	SLP	SACAC	WD	KL		6	1200	3	12300	14000
--- 1992 BOATS ---											
16 6	TOWNCLASS	SLP	SAIL	FBG	KL		5 9	750	2 4	9100	10300
16 6	TOWNCLASS	SLP	SAIL	WD	KL		5 9	750	2 4	9100	10300
17	SWAMPSCOTT DORY	SLP	SAIL	WD	KL		4 8	400	1 8	6750	7750
17 9	FLEET O WING	SLP	SAIL	WD	KL		6	1200	3	11600	13200
--- 1988 BOATS ---											
16 6	TOWNCLASS	SLP	SA/OD	FBG	CB OB		5 10	800	7	7350	8450
16 6	TOWNCLASS	SLP	SA/OD	WD	CB OB		5 10	630	7	6550	7500
17	SWAMPSCOTT-DORY	SLP	SA/OD	WD	CB		4 8	500	6	5800	6700
17 9	FLEET-O-WING	SLP	SA/OD	WD	KL OB		6	1200	3	9200	10400

LOA FT IN	NAME AND/ OR MODEL	TOP/ RIG	BOAT TYPE	-HULL- MTL TP	----ENGINE--- TP # HP MFG	BEAM FT IN	WGT LBS	DRAFT FT IN	RETAIL LOW	RETAIL HIGH
--------------- 1987 BOATS ---------------										
16 6	TOWNCLASS	SLP	SA/OD	FBG CB	OB	5 10	800	7	6900	7900
16 6	TOWNCLASS	SLP	SA/OD	WD CB	OB	5 10	630	7	6150	7050
17	SWAMPSCOTT-DORY	SLP	SAIL	WD CB		4 8	500	6	5500	6300
17 9	FLEET-O-WING	SLP	SA/OD	WD KL	OB	6	1200	3	8550	9850
--------------- 1986 BOATS ---------------										
16 6	TOWNCLASS	SLP	SA/OD	FBG CB	OB	5 10	800	7	6450	7450
16 6	TOWNCLASS	SLP	SA/OD	WD CB	OB	5 10	630	7	5850	6650
17	SWAMPSCOTT-DORY	SLP	SAIL	WD CB		4 8		6	5850	6700
17 9	FLEET-O-WING	SLP	SA/OD	WD KL	OB	6	1200	3	8000	9200
--------------- 1985 BOATS ---------------										
16 6	TOWNCLASS	SLP	SA/OD	WD KL	OB	5 3	630	7	5400	6200
17 9	FLEET-O-WING	SLP	SA/OD	WD KL	OB	6	1400	3 6	8150	9350

....For earlier years, see the BUC Used Boat Price Guide, Volume 3

LOWELL'S BOAT SHOP INC
AMESBURY MA 01913   COAST GUARD MFG ID- LMR See inside cover to adjust price for area

LOA FT IN	NAME AND/ OR MODEL	TOP/ RIG	BOAT TYPE	-HULL- MTL TP	----ENGINE--- TP # HP MFG	BEAM FT IN	WGT LBS	DRAFT FT IN	RETAIL LOW	RETAIL HIGH
--------------- 1987 BOATS ---------------										
16	AMESBURY SKIFF	OP	UTL	WD	OB	6 5	300		1750	2100
16	SPORT SURF DORY	OP	ROW	WD	OB	5 3	330		**	**
18	AMESBURY SKIFF	OP	UTL	WD	OB	6 9	375		2150	2500
18	SPORT SURF DORY	OP	ROW	WD	OB	5 6	380		**	**
20	SPORT SURF DORY	OP	ROW	WD	OB	6 6	430		**	**
--------------- 1986 BOATS ---------------										
16	AMESBURY SKIFF	OP	UTL	WD	OB	6 5	300		1700	2050
16	SPORT SURF DORY	OP	ROW	WD	OB	5 3	330		**	**
18	AMESBURY SKIFF	OP	UTL	WD	OB	6 9	375		2050	2450
18	SPORT SURF DORY	OP	ROW	WD	OB	5 6	380		**	**
20	SPORT SURF DORY	OP	ROW	WD	OB	6 6	430		**	**
--------------- 1985 BOATS ---------------										
16	AMESBURY SKIFF	OP	UTL	WD	OB	6 5	300		1650	1950
16	SAILING SURF	SLP	SAIL	WD	CB	6 9		5	3650	4250
16	SPORT SURF DORY	OP	ROW	WD	OB	5 3	330		**	**
17	SAILING SURF	CAT	SAIL	WD	CB	3 8		4	4800	5550
18	AMESBURY SKIFF	OP	UTL	WD	OB	6 9	375		2000	2350
18	SAILING SURF	SLP	SAIL	WD	CB	5 6		5	5700	6550
18	SPORT SURF DORY	OP	ROW	WD	OB	6 10	380		**	**
20	SAILING SURF	SLP	SAIL	WD	CB	6 6		6	4150	4850
20	SPORT SURF DORY	OP	ROW	WD	OB	6 6	430		**	**

....For earlier years, see the BUC Used Boat Price Guide, Volume 3

LUCAT MARINE LTD
HENRYVILLE PQ CANADA   See inside cover to adjust price for area

LOA FT IN	NAME AND/ OR MODEL	TOP/ RIG	BOAT TYPE	-HULL- MTL TP	----ENGINE--- TP # HP MFG	BEAM FT IN	WGT LBS	DRAFT FT IN	RETAIL LOW	RETAIL HIGH
--------------- 1990 BOATS ---------------										
19	TWISTER 5.8 BR	OP	UTL	FBG SV	IO 205 OMC	7 4	2600		5450	6250
19	TWISTER 5.8 BR	OP	RNBT	FBG SV	IO 205 MRCR	7 4	2550		4800	5550
21	TWISTER 6.4	OP	CUD	FBG SV	IO 270 MRCR	8	2900		6900	7900
21	TWISTER 6.4 BR	OP	UTL	FBG SV	IO 205 OMC	8	3000		7150	8200
27 1	SIGNATURE II	OP	SPTCR	FBG SV	IO 270 OMC	9	5200		14900	17000
32 10	SIGNATURE III	OP	SPTCR	FBG SV	IO T205 MRCR	11 1	9200		33400	37100

LUGER BOATS INC
ST JOSEPH MO 64502   COAST GUARD MFG ID- LUG See inside cover to adjust price for area
FORMERLY LUGER INDUSTRIES

LOA FT IN	NAME AND/ OR MODEL	TOP/ RIG	BOAT TYPE	-HULL- MTL TP	----ENGINE--- TP # HP MFG	BEAM FT IN	WGT LBS	DRAFT FT IN	RETAIL LOW	RETAIL HIGH
--------------- 1988 BOATS ---------------										
16	LEEWARD	SLP	SAIL	FBG CB	OB	6 3	650	3 9	1550	1850
16 1	SEABREEZE	SLP	SAIL	FBG SK	OB	6 4	700	4 2	1600	1900
20	SOUTHWIND	SLP	SA/CR	FBG SK	OB	7	1850	5 1	3050	3550
21 7	WINDSONG	SLP	SA/CR	FBG SK	OB	7	2500	2	4000	4650
25 6	PILOTHOUSE	HT	PH	FBG RB	OB	8	1800	2	8900	10100
25 6	SPORT FISHERMAN	OP	CTRCN	FBG RB	OB	8	1700	2	8650	9900
25 7	TRADEWINDS	SLP	SA/CR	FBG SK	OB	8	2600	5 6	5050	5800
26 11	FAIRWINDS	SLP	SA/CR	FBG SK	OB	8	2800	5	5500	6350
29 9	ADVENTURER	SLP	MS	FBG KC	IB 40	8	7300	3	14700	16700
29 9	ADVENTURER	KTH	MS	FBG KC	IB 40	8	7300	3	14700	16700
29 11	VOYAGER	SLP	SA/CR	FBG KC	OB	8	7000	3	13900	15800
29 11	VOYAGER	KTH	SA/CR	FBG KC	OB	8	7000	3	13900	15800
--------------- 1987 BOATS ---------------										
16	LEEWARD	SLP	SAIL	FBG CB	OB	6 3	650	3 9	1450	1750
16 1	SEABREEZE	SLP	SAIL	FBG SK	OB	6 4	700	4 2	1500	1800
20	SOUTHWIND	SLP	SA/CR	FBG SK	OB	7	1850	5 1	2850	3350
21 7	WINDSONG	SLP	SA/CR	FBG SK	OB	7	2500	2	3750	4350
25 6	PILOTHOUSE	HT	PH	FBG RB	OB	8	1800	2	8550	9850
25 6	SPORT FISHERMAN	OP	CTRCN	FBG RB	OB	8	1700	2	8400	9650
25 7	TRADEWINDS	SLP	SA/CR	FBG SK	OB	8	2600	5	5450	5950
26 11	FAIRWINDS	SLP	SA/CR	FBG SK	OB	8	2800	5 8	5300	6100
29 9	ADVENTURER	SLP	MS	FBG KC	IB 40	8	7300	3	13800	15700
29 9	ADVENTURER	KTH	MS	FBG KC	IB 40	8	7300	3	13800	15700
29 11	VOYAGER	SLP	SA/CR	FBG KC	OB	8	7000	3	13100	14900
29 11	VOYAGER	KTH	SA/CR	FBG KC	OB	8	7000	3	13100	14900
--------------- 1986 BOATS ---------------										
16	LEEWARD	SLP	SAIL	FBG CB	OB	6 3	650	3 9	1350	1600
16 1	SEABREEZE	SLP	SAIL	FBG SK	OB	6 4	700	4 2	1400	1700
20	SOUTHWIND	SLP	SA/CR	FBG SK	OB	7	1850	5 1	2700	3150
25 6	PILOTHOUSE	HT	PH	FBG RB	OB	8	1800	2	8350	9550
25 6	SPORT FISHERMAN	OP	CTRCN	FBG RB	OB	8	1700	2	8150	9400
25 7	TRADEWINDS	SLP	SA/CR	FBG SK	OB	8	2600	5	4900	5200
26 11	FAIRWINDS	SLP	SA/CR	FBG SK	OB	8	2800	5 8	4900	5600
29 9	ADVENTURER	SLP	MS	FBG KC	IB 40	8	7300	3	13000	14700
29 9	ADVENTURER	KTH	MS	FBG KC	IB 40	8	7300	3	13000	14700
29 11	VOYAGER	SLP	SA/CR	FBG KC	OB	8	7000	3	12300	14000
29 11	VOYAGER	KTH	SA/CR	FBG KC	OB	8	7000	3	12300	14000
--------------- 1985 BOATS ---------------										
16	LEEWARD	SLP	SAIL	FBG CB	OB	6 3	650	3 9	1300	1550
16 1	SEABREEZE	SLP	SAIL	FBG SK	OB	6 4	700	4 2	1350	1600
20	SOUTHWIND	SLP	SA/CR	FBG SK	OB	7	1850	5 1	2550	2950
20 6	BAHAMA	FB	CR	FBG SV	OB	8	3500		6700	7700
20 6	BIMINI	OP	UTL	FBG SV	OB	8	3600		6150	7050
23 8	MONTE-CARLO	FB	CR	FBG SV	OB	7 9	2300		6700	7700
25 6	PILOTHOUSE	HT	PH	FBG RB	OB	8	1800	2	8150	9350
25 6	SPORT FISHERMAN	OP	CTRCN	FBG RB	OB	8	1700	2	7950	9150
25 7	TRADEWINDS	SLP	SA/CR	FBG SK	OB	8	2600	5	4200	4850
26 11	FAIRWINDS	SLP	SA/CR	FBG SK	OB	8	2800	5 8	4600	5300
29 9	ADVENTURER	SLP	MS	FBG KC	IB 40	8	7300	3	12200	13900
29 9	ADVENTURER	KTH	MS	FBG KC	IB 40	8	7300	3	12200	13900
29 11	VOYAGER	SLP	SA/CR	FBG KC	OB	8	7000	3	11600	13200
29 11	VOYAGER	KTH	SA/CR	FBG KC	OB	8	7000	3	11600	13200
30	HOLIDAY	OP	CR	FBG SV	IB 400	10 3	9000	2 6	20700	23000
30	VACATIONER	FB	CR	FBG SV	IB 400	10 3	9000	2 6	20700	23000
30	VAGABOND	FB	TRWL	FBG SV	IB 400	10 4	9000	2 6	22800	25400
--------------- 1984 BOATS ---------------										
16	LEEWARD	SLP	SAIL	FBG CB	OB	6 3	650	3 9	1200	1450
16 1	SEA-BREEZE	SLP	SAIL	FBG SK	OB	6 4	700	4 2	1250	1500
20	SOUTHWIND	SLP	SA/CR	FBG SK	OB	7	1850	5 1	2400	2800
25 6	PILOTHOUSE	OP	PH	FBG RB	OB	8	1800	2	7950	9150
25 6	SPORT FISHERMAN	OP	CTRCN	FBG RB	OB	8	1700	2	7800	8950
25 7	TRADEWINDS	SLP	SA/CR	FBG SK	OB	8	2600	5	3950	4600
26 11	FAIRWINDS 2702	SLP	SA/CR	FBG SK	OB	8	2800	5 8	4300	5000
29 9	ADVENTURER	SLP	MS	FBG KC	IB D	8	7300	3	11600	13200
29 9	ADVENTURER	KTH	MS	FBG KC	IB D	8	7300	3	11600	13200
29 11	VOYAGER	SLP	SA/CR	FBG KC	OB	8	7000	3	10900	12400
29 11	VOYAGER	KTH	SA/CR	FBG KC	OB	8	7000	3	10900	12400

....For earlier years, see the BUC Used Boat Price Guide, Volume 3

LUHRS CORPORATION
ST AUGUSTINE FL 32086   COAST GUARD MFG ID- LHR See inside cover to adjust price for area
For more recent years, see the BUC Used Boat Price Guide, Volume 1

LOA FT IN	NAME AND/ OR MODEL	TOP/ RIG	BOAT TYPE	-HULL- MTL TP	----ENGINE--- TP # HP MFG	BEAM FT IN	WGT LBS	DRAFT FT IN	RETAIL LOW	RETAIL HIGH
--------------- 1996 BOATS ---------------										
25 1	TOURNAMENT 250	HT	FSH	FBG SV	IB T270 MPC	9 3	8300	2 3	39900	44400
25 1	TOURNAMENT 250	HT	FSH	FBG SV	IB T170D YAN	9 3	8300	2 3	55500	61000
25 1	TOURNAMENT 250 CC	HT	CTRCN	FBG SV	IB T270 MPC	9 3	8000	2 3	38900	43200
25 1	TOURNAMENT 250 CC	HT	CTRCN	FBG SV	IB T170D YAN	9 3	8000	2 3	54100	59400
31 10	TOURNAMENT 290	TT	OPFSH	FBG SV	IB T270 MPC	11 6	10000	2 8	57300	63000
31 10	TOURNAMENT 290	TT	OPFSH	FBG SV	IB T170D YAN	11 6	10000	2 8	66600	73200
31 10	TOURNAMENT 290	TT	OPFSH	FBG SV	IB T315D YAN	11 6	10000	2 8	78000	85700

LOA FT	LOA IN	NAME AND/ OR MODEL	TOP/ RIG	BOAT TYPE	HULL MTL	HULL TP	ENGINE TP	ENGINE # HP	ENGINE MFG	BEAM FT	BEAM IN	WGT LBS	DRAFT FT	DRAFT IN	RETAIL LOW	RETAIL HIGH
		1996 BOATS														
34	6	TOURNAMENT 300	TT	OPFSH	FBG	SV	IB	T270	MPC	10	9	11000	2	6	66600	73200
34	6	TOURNAMENT 300	TT	OPFSH	FBG	SV	IB	T170D-T315D		10	9	11000	2	6	89600	111000
34	8	TOURNAMENT 320 CNV	FB	CNV	FBG	SV	IB	T340	MPC	13		15000	3	1	86700	95300
34	8	TOURNAMENT 320 CNV	FB	CNV	FBG	SV	IB	T315D	YAN	13		15000	3	1	127500	140000
34	8	TOURNAMENT 320 OPEN	TT	SF	FBG	SV	IB	T340	MPC	13		15000	3	1	84200	92500
34	8	TOURNAMENT 320 OPEN	TT	SF	FBG	SV	IB	T300D-T315D		13		15000	3	1	104000	115500
38	6	TOURNAMENT 350 CNV	FB	CNV	FBG	SV	IB	T370	MPC	12	10	20000	3	4	85600	94000
		IB T425 MPC 88200 96900, IB T315D YAN 137500 151000, IB T350D CAT													142000	156000
40	10	TOURNAMENT 380 CNV	FB	CNV	FBG	SV	IB	T420D	CAT	14	11	30000	3	7	185000	203000
40	10	TOURNAMENT 380 OP	TT	SF	FBG	SV	IB	T420D	CAT	14	11	30000	3	7	183500	201500
		1995 BOATS														
25	1	TOURNAMENT 250	HT	FSH	FBG	SV	IB	T270	MPE	9	3	8300	2	3	37700	41900
25	1	TOURNAMENT 250	HT	FSH	FBG	SV	IB	T170D	YAN	9	3	8300	2	3	52700	58000
25	1	TOURNAMENT 250 CC	HT	CTRCN	FBG	SV	IB	T270	MPE	9	3	8000	2	3	36700	40800
25	1	TOURNAMENT 250 CC	HT	CTRCN	FBG	SV	IB	T170D	YAN	9	3	8000	2	3	51400	56500
31	10	TOURNAMENT 290	TT	OPFSH	FBG	SV	IB	T270-T310		11	6	10000	2		54200	61100
31	10	TOURNAMENT 290	TT	OPFSH	FBG	SV	IB	T170D-T230D		11	6	10000	2		63300	73500
31	10	TOURNAMENT 290	TT	OPFSH	FBG	SV	IB	T315D	YAN	11	6	10000	2		74100	81400
34	6	TOURNAMENT 300	TT	OPFSH	FBG	SV	IB	T270-T310		10	9	11000	2	6	63000	70900
34	6	TOURNAMENT 300	TT	OPFSH	FBG	SV	IB	T170D-T230D		10	9	11000	2	6	69700	81000
34	8	TOURNAMENT 320 CNV	FB	CNV	FBG	SV	IB	T340-T370		13		15000	3	1	81900	91800
34	8	TOURNAMENT 320 CNV	FB	CNV	FBG	SV	IB	T315D	YAN	13		15000	3	1	97000	106500
34	8	TOURNAMENT 320 OPEN	TT	SF	FBG	SV	IB	T340-T370		13		15000	3	1	79600	88900
34	8	TOURNAMENT 320 OPEN	TT	SF	FBG	SV	IB	T300D-T315D		13		15000	3	1	90400	100500
38	6	TOURNAMENT 350	FB	SF	FBG	SV	IB	T370	MPE	12	10	19000	3	4	74500	81900
		IB T425 MPE 76600 84100, IB T315D YAN 118000 129500, IB T350D CAT													121500	133500
		IB T370D VLVO 121000 133000														
40	10	TOURNAMENT 380 CNV	FB	CNV	FBG	SV	IB	T420D	CAT	14	11	30000	3	7	177000	195000
		IB T420D YAN 173000 190500, IB T485D DD 184500 203000, IB T490D ALAS													187000	205500
40	10	TOURNAMENT 380 OP	TT	SF	FBG	SV	IB	T420D	CAT	14	11	30000	3	7	176000	193500
		IB T420D YAN 172000 189000, IB T485D DD 183500 201500, IB T490D ALAS													186000	204000
		1994 BOATS														
25	1	TOURNAMENT 250	HT	FSH	FBG	SV	IB	320	MPE	9	3	8300	2	3	33400	37200
		IB 315D YAN 47600 52300, IB T245 MPE 35400 39300, IB T170D YAN													50200	55200
25	1	TOURNAMENT 250 CC	HT	CTRCN	FBG	SV	IB	320	MPE	9	3	8000	2	3	32500	36100
25	1	TOURNAMENT 250 CC	HT	CTRCN	FBG	SV	IB	T245	MPE	9	3	8000	2	3	34400	38300
25	1	TOURNAMENT 250 CC	HT	CTRCN	FBG	SV	IB	T170D	YAN	9	3	8000	2	3	48900	53800
31	10	TOURNAMENT 290	TT	OPFSH	FBG	SV	IB	T245-T270		11	6	10000	2		50500	56400
31	10	TOURNAMENT 290	TT	OPFSH	FBG	SV	IB	T170D-T230D		11	6	10000	2		60200	69900
31	10	TOURNAMENT 290	TT	OPFSH	FBG	SV	IB	T315D	YAN	11	6	10000	2		70500	77500
34	6	TOURNAMENT 300	TT	OPFSH	FBG	SV	IB	T245-T270		10	9	12000	2	6	60000	66900
34	6	TOURNAMENT 300	TT	OPFSH	FBG	SV	IB	T170D-T230D		10	9	12000	2	6	69900	80800
34	8	TOURNAMENT 320	FB	SF	FBG	SV	IB	T320-T365		13		15000	3	1	70700	79600
34	8	TOURNAMENT 320	FB	SF	FBG	SV	IB	T315D	YAN	13		15000	3	1	82400	90500
34	8	TOURNAMENT 320	TT	SF	FBG	SV	IB	T320-T365		13		15000	3	1	74500	83900
34	8	TOURNAMENT 320	TT	SF	FBG	SV	IB	T300D-T315D		13		15000	3	1	86100	95500
35	5	TOURNAMENT 350	FB	SF	FBG	SV	IB	T320	MPE	12	10	19000	3	4	101500	111500
		IB T385 MPE 104000 114500, IB T315D YAN 126000 138500, IB T350D CAT													130500	143500
40	10	TOURNAMENT 380 CNV	FB	CNV	FBG	SV	IB	T420D	YAN	14	11	28000	3	7	157500	173000
40	10	TOURNAMENT 380 CNV	FB	CNV	FBG	SV	IB	T485D	DD	14	11	28000	3	7	168500	185000
40	10	TOURNAMENT 380 CNV	FB	CNV	FBG	SV	IB	T490D	ALAS	14	11	28000	3	7	171000	188000
40	10	TOURNAMENT 380 OP	TT	SF	FBG	SV	IB	T420D	YAN	14	11	28000	3	7	156500	172000
40	10	TOURNAMENT 380 OP	TT	SF	FBG	SV	IB	T485D	J&T	14	11	28000	3	7	165000	181000
40	10	TOURNAMENT 380 OP	TT	SF	FBG	SV	IB	T490D	ALAS	14	11	28000	3	7	169500	186500
		1993 BOATS														
31	10	TOURNAMENT 290	TT	OPFSH	FBG	SV	IB	T260-T310		11	6	10000	2	9	48300	54800
31	10	TOURNAMENT 290	TT	OPFSH	FBG	SV	IB	T170D-T230D		11	6	10000	2	9	57400	66600
34	6	TOURNAMENT 300	TT	OPFSH	FBG	SV	IB	T260-T310		10	9	12000	2	6	70300	78900
34	6	TOURNAMENT 300	TT	OPFSH	FBG	SV	IB	T170D-T230D		10	9	12000	2	6	80200	91000
34	8	TOURNAMENT 320	FB	SF	FBG	SV	IB	T320-T365		12	8	15000	3	1	66800	75100
34	8	TOURNAMENT 320	FB	SF	FBG	SV	IB	T300D	J&T	12	8	15000	3	1	77300	84900
35	5	TOURNAMENT 350	FB	SF	FBG	SV	IB	T320	MPC	12	10	19000	3	4	96100	105500
		IB T365 MPC 97800 107500, IB T502 MPC 105000 115000, IB T300D CAT													120000	132000
		IB T300D J&T 119000 130500														
37	9	TOURNAMENT 380 CNV	FB	CNV	FBG	SV	IB	T425D	J&T	14	11	28000	3	7	173500	191000
37	9	TOURNAMENT 380 CNV	FB	CNV	FBG	SV	IB	T485D	J&T	14	11	28000	3	7	182000	200000
37	9	TOURNAMENT 380 OP	TT	SF	FBG	SV	IB	T485D	J&T	14	11	28000	3	7	180500	198500
		1992 BOATS														
30		ALURA 30	OP	FSH	FBG	SV	IB	T260	CRUS	10	3	7800	2	11	37100	41200
30		ALURA 30	OP	FSH	FBG	SV	IB	T210D	CUM	10	3	7800	2	11	46100	50700
34		MOTOR YACHT 3400	FB	MY	FBG	SV	IB	T320	CRUS	12	6	13500	3	2	81500	89600
34		MOTOR YACHT 3400	FB	MY	FBG	SV	IB	T300D	CUM	12	6	13500	3	2	97300	107000
34		MOTOR YACHT 3420	FB	MY	FBG	SV	IB	T320	CRUS	12	6	13500	3	2	73300	80600
34		MOTOR YACHT 3420	FB	MY	FBG	SV	IB	T250D	J&T	12	6	13500	3	2	93200	102500
34	6	TOURNAMENT 300	TT	OPFSH	FBG	SV	IB	T260-T310		10	9	12000	2	6	66700	74900
34	6	TOURNAMENT 300	TT	OPFSH	FBG	SV	IB	T170D	YAN	10	9	12000	2	6	76500	84000
34	8	TOURNAMENT 320	FB	SF	FBG	SV	IB	T320-T365		12	8	15000	3	1	63400	71300
34	8	TOURNAMENT 320	FB	SF	FBG	SV	IB	T300D	J&T	12	8	15000	3	1	73700	81000
35	5	TOURNAMENT 350	FB	SF	FBG	SV	IB	T320	CRUS	12	10	19000	3	4	91600	100500
		IB T365 MPC 92800 102000, IB T465 CRUS 98200 108000, IB T300D CAT													114500	125500
		IB T300D J&T 113500 124500, IB T330D ALAS 117000 128500														
37	9	TOURNAMENT 380 CNV	FB	CNV	FBG	SV	IB	T425D	J&T	14	11	28000	3	7	165500	182000
37	9	TOURNAMENT 380 CNV	FB	CNV	FBG	SV	IB	T440D	ALAS	14	11	28000	3	7	171000	188000
37	9	TOURNAMENT 380 CNV	FB	CNV	FBG	SV	IB	T485D	J&T	14	11	28000	3	7	173500	190500
37	9	TOURNAMENT 380 OP	TT	SF	FBG	SV	IB	T440D	ALAS	14	11	28000	3	7	170000	186500
37	9	TOURNAMENT 380 OP	TT	SF	FBG	SV	IB	T485D	J&T	14	11	28000	3	7	172000	189000
		1991 BOATS														
30		ALURA 30	OP	FSH	FBG	SV	IB	T240	CRUS	10	3	7800	2	11	34700	38600
30		ALURA 30	OP	FSH	FBG	SV	IB	T210D	CUM	10	3	7800	2	11	43500	48400
34		MOTOR YACHT 3400	FB	MY	FBG	SV	IB	T320	CRUS	12	6	13500	3	2	74900	82400
34		MOTOR YACHT 3400	FB	MY	FBG	SV	IB	T300D	CUM	12	6	13500	3	2	92800	102000
34		MOTOR YACHT 3420	FB	MY	FBG	SV	IB	T320	CRUS	12	6	13500	3	2	72200	79300
34		MOTOR YACHT 3420	FB	MY	FBG	SV	IB	T250D	J&T	12	6	13500	3	2	88900	97700
34	6	TOURNAMENT 300	TT	OPFSH	FBG	SV	IB	T240	CRUS	10	9	12000	2	6	63100	69400
34	6	TOURNAMENT 300	TT	OPFSH	FBG	SV	IB	T170D	YAN	10	9	12000	2	6	73000	80200
34	8	TOURNAMENT 320	FB	SF	FBG	SV	IB	T320-T365		12	8	15000	3	1	60200	67800
34	8	TOURNAMENT 320	FB	SF	FBG	SV	IB	T300D	J&T	12	8	15000	3	1	70400	77300
35	5	TOURNAMENT 350	FB	SF	FBG	SV	IB	T320	CRUS	12	10	19000	3	4	87000	95600
35	5	TOURNAMENT 350	FB	SF	FBG	SV	IB	T365	MPC	12	10	19000	3	4	88200	96900
35	5	TOURNAMENT 350	FB	SF	FBG	SV	IB	T300D	J&T	12	10	19000	3	4	108000	119000
37	9	OPEN 380	OP	SF	FBG	SV	IB	T485D	J&T	14	11	24000	3	7	147500	162000
37	9	TOURNAMENT 380	FB	SF	FBG	SV	IB	T425D	J&T	14	11	28000	3	7	157000	172500
37	9	TOURNAMENT 380	FB	SF	FBG	SV	IB	T460D	ALAS	14	11	28000	3	7	164500	181000
37	9	TOURNAMENT 380	FB	SF	FBG	SV	IB	T485D	J&T	14	11	28000	3	7	164000	180500
40		MOTOR YACHT 4000	FB	MY	FBG	SV	IB	T320	CRUS			20000	3	7	111000	122000
		1990 BOATS														
29	6	TOURNAMENT 290	TT	OPFSH	FBG	SV	IB	T240	CRUS	11	6	10000	2	5	39900	44400
29	6	TOURNAMENT 290	TT	OPFSH	FBG	SV	IB	T140D	YAN	11	6	10000	2	5	48100	52800
30		TOURNAMENT ALURA 30	OP	CUD	FBG	SV	IB	240	CRUS	10	3	7800	2	11	29400	32600
30		TOURNAMENT ALURA 30	OP	CUD	FBG	SV	IB	T215	CRUS	10	3	7800	2	11	32400	36000
30		TOURNAMENT ALURA 30	OP	CUD	FBG	SV	IB	T210D	CUM	10	3	7800	2	11	41600	46200
34		TOURNAMENT 342	FB	SF	FBG	SV	IB	T240-T320		12	6	15000	3	2	65700	74700
34		TOURNAMENT 342	FB	SF	FBG	SV	IB	T250D	J&T	12	6	15000	3	2	81800	89900
34	8	TOURNAMENT 320	FB	SF	FBG	SV	IB	T240-T320		12	8	15000	3	1	54900	62900
34	8	TOURNAMENT 320	FB	SF	FBG	SV	IB	T300D	J&T	12	8	15000	3	1	67200	73900
35	5	TOURNAMENT ALURA 35	OP	CR	FBG	SV	IB	T240	CRUS	12	2	12800	2	11	69300	76100
35	5	TOURNAMENT ALURA 35	OP	CR	FBG	SV	IB	T320	CRUS	12	2	12800	2	11	71500	78600
39	10	TOURNAMENT 400	FB	SF	FBG	SV	IB	T320	CRUS	14		25500	3	6	114500	126000
39	10	TOURNAMENT 400	FB	SF	FBG	SV	IB	T320D	CAT	14		25500	3	6	134000	147000
		1989 BOATS														
29	6	TOURNAMENT 290	TT	OPFSH	FBG	SV	IB	140D	YAN	10	9	10000	2	5	43100	47800
29	6	TOURNAMENT 290	TT	OPFSH	FBG	SV	IB	T240	CRUS	10	9	10000	2	5	37600	41800
30		ALURA 30	OP	CUD	FBG	RB	IB	240	CRUS	10	3	7800	2	11	28000	31100
30		ALURA 30	OP	CUD	FBG	RB	IB	210D	CUM	10	3	7800	2	11	33100	36800
30		ALURA 30	OP	CUD	FBG	RB	IB	T215	CRUS	10	3	7800	2	11	30800	34200
34		TOURNAMENT 342	FB	SF	FBG	SV	IB	T240	CRUS	12	6	13500	3	2	60400	66400
34		TOURNAMENT 342	FB	SF	FBG	SV	IB	T320	CRUS	12	6	13500	3	2	62600	68800
34		TOURNAMENT 342	FB	SF	FBG	SV	IB	T250D	J&T	12	6	13500	3	2	74300	81700
34	6	TOURNAMENT 320	FB	SF	FBG	SV	IB	T300D	J&T	12	8	15000	3	1	64300	70700
34	6	TOURNAMENT 320	TT	SF	FBG	SV	IB	T240-T320		12	8	15000	3	1	55100	63200
35	5	ALURA 35 TW BIG BLCK	OP	CR	FBG	RB	IB	T320	CRUS	12	2	12800	2	11	68100	74800
35	5	ALURA 35 TW SML BLCK	OP	CR	FBG	RB	IB	T240	CRUS	12	2	12800	2	11	66000	72500
39	10	TOURNAMENT 400	FB	SF	FBG	SV	IB	T320	CRUS	14		25500	3	6	109500	120500
39	10	TOURNAMENT 400	FB	SF	FBG	SV	IB	T320D	CAT	14		25500	3	6	128000	140500
		1988 BOATS														
26	2	ALURA 27	OP	EXP	FBG	SV	IB	240	CHRY	10		5370	2	6	18500	20500
29	6	TOURNAMENT 290	TT	OPFSH	FBG	SV	IB	T270	CRUS	10	9	9000	2	5	32100	35700
30		ALURA 30	OP	CUD	FBG	RB	IB	240	CHRY	10	3	7800	2	11	26600	29500
30		ALURA 30	OP	CUD	FBG	RB	IB	T240	CHRY	10	3	7800	2	11	29800	33100
34		TOURNAMENT 342	FB	SF	FBG	SV	IB	T350	CRUS	12	6	13500	3	2	60600	66600
34	6	TOURNAMENT 320	TT	SF	FBG	SV	IB	T350	CRUS	12	8	15000	3	1	55700	61200
35	5	ALURA 35	OP	EXP	FBG	RB	IB	T240	CHRY	12	2	12800	2	11	62500	68700

 CONTINUED ON NEXT PAGE

LOA FT IN	NAME AND/ OR MODEL	TOP/ RIG	BOAT TYPE	-HULL- MTL TP	----ENGINE--- TP # HP MFG	BEAM FT IN	WGT LBS	DRAFT FT IN	RETAIL LOW	RETAIL HIGH
					1988 BOATS					
39 10	TOURNAMENT 400	FB	SF	FBG SV	IB T320 CRUS	14	25500	3 6	104500	115000
					1987 BOATS					
29 10	TOURNAMENT 290	TT	OPFSH	FBG SV	IB T270 CRUS	11 6	10000	2 6	36000	40000
34	TOURNAMENT 340	OP	SF	FBG SV	IB T350 CRUS	12 6	15000	3 4	59600	65500
34	TOURNAMENT 340	OP	SF	FBG SV	IB T300D J&T	12 6	15000	3 4	74500	81900
34	TOURNAMENT 342	FB	SF	FBG SV	IB T350 CRUS	12 6	15000	3 4	59600	65500
34	TOURNAMENT 342	FB	SF	FBG SV	IB T250D J&T	12 6	15000	3 4	71700	78800
40	TOURNAMENT 400	FB	SF	FBG SV	IB T350 CRUS	14	25000	3 4	101000	111000
40	TOURNAMENT 400	FB	SF	FBG SV	IB T375D CAT	14	25000	3 4	121000	133000
					1986 BOATS					
29 10	TOURNAMENT 290	TT	OPFSH	FBG SV	IB T270 CRUS	11 6	10000	2 9	34300	38100
34	TOURNAMENT 340	OP	SF	FBG SV	IB T350 CRUS	12 6	15000	3 4	56900	62600
34	TOURNAMENT 342	FB	SF	FBG SV	IB T350 CRUS	12 6	15000	3 4	56900	62600

....For earlier years, see the BUC Used Boat Price Guide, Volume 3

LUND BOAT COMPANY

DIV OF GENMAR INDUSTRIES INC   See inside cover to adjust price for area
N Y MILLS MN 56567   COAST GUARD MFG ID- LUN
FORMERLY LUND AMERICAN INC

For more recent years, see the BUC Used Boat Price Guide, Volume 1

LOA FT IN	NAME AND/ OR MODEL	TOP/ RIG	BOAT TYPE	-HULL- MTL TP	----ENGINE--- TP # HP MFG	BEAM FT IN	WGT LBS	DRAFT FT IN	RETAIL LOW	RETAIL HIGH
					1996 BOATS					
16	LAKER 16	OP	UTL	AL SV	OB	6	451		2050	2450
16	REBEL 16	OP	FSH	AL SV	OB	6 1	455		2050	2450
16	REBEL 16 DELUXE	OP	FSH	AL SV	OB	6 1	520		2400	2750
16	WC-16	OP	UTL	AL SV	OB	5 5	268		1200	1400
16 2	SV-16	OP	UTL	AL SV	OB	5 11	321		1450	1700
16 3	ANGLER 1650	OP	FSH	AL DV	OB	6 8	770		3550	4100
16 3	ANGLER 1650 DLX	OP	FSH	AL DV	OB	6 8	802		3650	4250
16 3	EXPLORER 1600	OP	FSH	AL SV	OB	6 1	542		2500	2900
16 3	EXPLORER 1600 DELUXE	OP	FSH	AL SV	OB	6 1	610		2800	3300
16 3	PRO ANGLER 1600	OP	FSH	AL SV	OB	6 2	712		3250	3800
16 3	PRO ANGLER 1600 DLX	OP	FSH	AL SV	OB	6 2	752		3450	4000
16 3	PRO V 1660	OP	FSH	AL SV	OB	6 7	830		3550	4150
16 3	PRO V 1660 DELUXE	OP	FSH	AL SV	OB	6 7	860		3700	4300
16 3	PRO V 1660 SE	OP	FSH	AL SV	OB	6 7	830		4000	4650
16 3	PRO V 1660 SE DLX	OP	FSH	AL SV	OB	6 7	860		4100	4800
16 3	TYEE 1650	OP	RNBT	AL DV	OB	6 8	975		4450	5100
16 10	PRO ANGLER 1700	OP	FSH	AL SV	OB	7	776		3650	4250
16 10	PRO ANGLER 1700 DLX	OP	FSH	AL SV	OB	7	825		3850	4500
17 2	FISHERMAN 1700	OP	FSH	AL SV	OB	7 1	1033		4800	5500
17 2	PRO BASS 1790	OP	BASS	AL DV	OB	7 11	905		4250	4950
17 3	PRO SPORT 1700	OP	RNBT	AL DV	OB	7 1	1102		5050	5800
17 3	PRO GUIDE 1700	OP	UTL	AL SV	OB	6 3	676		3100	3600
17 3	PRO GUIDE 1700 DLX	OP	UTL	AL SV	OB	6 3	704		3250	3750
17 3	TYEE 1750	OP	RNBT	AL SV	OB	6 11	1195		4900	5650
17 3	TYEE 1750	OP	RNBT	AL SV	IO	6 11	2015		6100	7400
17 3	TYEE 1750 GS	OP	RNBT	AL SV	IO 135	6 11	1195		5950	6800
17 3	TYEE 1750 GS	OP	RNBT	AL SV	IO 135	6 11	2015		6750	8200
17 6	PRO V 1775	OP	FSH	AL SV	OB	7 2	1085		4650	5350
17 6	PRO V 1775 DELUXE	OP	FSH	AL SV	OB	7 2	1085		4500	5200
17 6	PRO V 1775 SE	OP	FSH	AL SV	OB	7 2	1085		5250	6000
17 6	PRO V 1775 SE DLX	OP	FSH	AL SV	OB	7 2	1085		5300	6050
17 6	PRO V 1775 SIG	OP	FSH	AL SV	OB	7 2	1085		5350	6100
17 6	PRO V 1775 SIG DLX	OP	FSH	AL SV	OB	7 2	1085		5350	6150
18	ALASKAN 18V	OP	FSH	AL SV	OB	6 3	602		3050	3500
18	PRO V 1800 SE BASS	OP	BASS	AL SV	OB	7 4	1295		5900	6800
18	SV-18	OP	UTL	AL SV	OB	6 3	436		1950	2300
18 1	GRAN SPORT 1800 LE	OP	FSH	AL DV	OB	7 4	1490		6600	7550
18 3	FISHERMAN 1800	OP	FSH	AL DV	OB	7 3	1360		6200	7100
18 3	FISHERMAN 1800	OP	FSH	AL DV	IO 135 MRCR	7 3	1915		7350	8450
18 3	FISHERMAN 1800	OP	FSH	AL DV	IO 135 VLVO	7 3	1915		7750	8900
18 3	FISHERMAN 1800	OP	FSH	AL DV	IO 180-185	7 3	1915		7450	9050
18 3	TYEE 1850	OP	RNBT	AL SV	OB	7 4	1342		5550	6350
18 3	TYEE 1850	OP	RNBT	AL SV	IO 135-185	7 4	2396		7250	8750
18 3	TYEE 1850 GS	OP	RNBT	AL SV	OB	7 4	1342		6700	7700
18 3	TYEE 1850 GS	OP	RNBT	AL SV	IO 135	7 4	2396		8050	9700
18 3	TYEE 1850 GS	OP	RNBT	AL SV	IO 180-185	7 4	2396		7800	9400
18 3	TYEE 1850 GS SIG	OP	RNBT	AL SV	OB	7 4	2396		8600	9850
18 3	TYEE 1850 GS SIG	OP	RNBT	AL SV	IO 180-185	7 4	2396		8300	10000
18 11	PRO 1890 V	OP	FSH	AL DV	OB	7 8	1225		5200	6000
18 11	PRO 1890 V DLX	OP	FSH	AL DV	OB	7 8	1250		5350	6150
18 11	PRO V 1890 LE	OP	FSH	AL DV	OB	7 8	1480		6750	7750
18 11	PRO V 1890 SE	OP	FSH	AL DV	OB	7 8	1225		5900	6800
18 11	PRO V 1890 SE DLX	OP	FSH	AL DV	OB	7 8	1250		6000	6900
18 11	PRO V 1890 SIG	OP	FSH	AL DV	OB	7 8	1225		6400	7350
18 11	PRO V 1890 SIG DLX	OP	FSH	AL DV	OB	7 8	1250		6450	7400
19 8	TYEE 1950 MAGNUM GS	OP	RNBT	AL DV	OB	8 6	1650		7250	8350
19 8	TYEE 1950 MAGNUM GS	OP	RNBT	AL DV	IO 180-250	8 6	2840		9800	12200
19 8	TYEE 1950 MAGNUM SIG	OP	RNBT	AL DV	OB	8 6	1650		7850	9000
19 8	TYEE 1950 MAGNUM SIG	OP	RNBT	AL DV	IO 180-250	8 6	2840		10300	12700
20 1	ALASKAN 20	OP	FSH	AL SV	OB	7 1	760		3500	4050
20 1	ALASKAN 20 DLX	OP	FSH	AL SV	OB	7 1	760		3800	4450
20 3	BARON 2100	ST	CUD	AL DV	OB	7 5	1705		7250	8350
20 3	BARON 2100	ST	CUD	AL DV	IO 180-250	7 5	2700		9500	11300
20 3	BARON 2100	OP	RNBT	AL DV	IO 250 VLVO	7 5	2710		9500	10800
20 3	BARON 2100	OP	RNBT	AL DV	IO 250 MRCR	7 5	2710		9550	10900
20 3	BARON 2100 MAGNUM	OP	RNBT	AL DV	OB	7 5	1702		7250	8350
20 3	BARON 2100 MAGNUM GS	OP	RNBT	AL DV	IO 180-210	7 5	2710		9200	10800
20 3	BARON 2100 MAGNUM GS	OP	RNBT	AL DV	IO 250 VLVO	7 5	2710		10500	12000
24	GENMAR 2450	HT	CUD	AL DV	IO MRCR	8 6	4150		**	**
24	GENMAR 2450	HT	CUD	AL DV	IO VLVO	8 6	4150		**	**
					1995 BOATS					
16	LAKER 16	OP	UTL	AL SV	OB	6	451		1950	2300
16	REBEL 16	OP	FSH	AL SV	OB	6 1	455		1950	2350
16	REBEL 16 DELUXE	OP	FSH	AL SV	OB	6 1	520		2300	2650
16 2	SV-16	OP	UTL	AL SV	OB	5 11	321		1400	1650
16 3	EXPLORER 1600	OP	FSH	AL SV	OB	6 1	542		2400	2800
16 3	EXPLORER 1600 DELUXE	OP	FSH	AL SV	OB	6 1	610		2700	3150
16 3	PRO V 1660	OP	FSH	AL SV	OB	6 7	830		3600	4200
16 3	PRO V 1660 DELUXE	OP	FSH	AL SV	OB	6 7	860		3750	4350
16 10	PRO ANGLER 1700	OP	FSH	AL SV	OB	7	776		3450	4050
16 10	PRO ANGLER 1700 DLX	OP	FSH	AL SV	OB	7	825		3700	4250
17 2	FISHERMAN 1700	OP	FSH	AL SV	OB	7 1	1033		4600	5300
17 2	PRO BASS 1790	OP	BASS	AL SV	OB	6 11	905		4050	4700
17 2	PRO SPORT 1700	OP	RNBT	AL DV	OB	7 1	1102		4850	5550
17 3	TYEE 1750 GS	OP	RNBT	AL SV	OB	6 11	1195		5200	5950
17 3	TYEE 1750 GS	OP	RNBT	AL SV	IO 120-135	6 11	2015		6300	7250
17 3	TYEE 1750 GS	OP	RNBT	AL SV	IO 160-205	6 11	2015		6000	7400
17 3	TYEE 1750 GS	OP	RNBT	AL SV	IO 225-235	6 11	2015		6650	7650
17 6	PRO V 1775 DELUXE	OP	FSH	AL SV	OB	7 2	1085		4800	5550
18	SV-18	OP	UTL	AL SV	OB	6 3	436		1850	2200
18 3	FISHERMAN 1800	OP	FSH	AL DV	OB	7 3	1360		5900	6800
18 3	FISHERMAN 1800	OP	FSH	AL DV	OB 120 VLVO	7 3	1915		7250	8300
	IO 135 MRCR 6850		7900, IO 135 VLVO 7250 8300, IO 160-205						6900	8500
	IO 225-235 7600		8750							
18 3	TYEE 1850 F/S	OP	RNBT	AL SV	IO 120-235	7 4	2396		7450	8700
18 3	TYEE 1850 F/S	OP	RNBT	AL SV	IO 335 VLVO	7 4	2396		10100	11500
18 3	TYEE 1850 GS	OP	RNBT	AL SV	IO 120 VLVO	7 4	1342		5850	6700
18 3	TYEE 1850 GS	OP	RNBT	AL SV	IO	7 4	2396		7450	8550
	IO 135 7150		8600, IO 160-205 7150 8700, IO 225-235						7800	8950
18 10	PRO 1890 V	OP	FSH	AL DV	OB	7 7	1225		5550	6350
20 3	BARON 2100	ST	CUD	AL DV	OB	7 5	1705		6950	7950
20 3	BARON 2100	ST	CUD	AL DV	IO 120-205	7 5	2700		9150	10600
20 3	BARON 2100	OP	RNBT	AL DV	IO 225-235	7 5	2710		9150	10400
22	GENMAR 2250	HT	CUD	AL DV	IO 120-225	8 6	3550		12600	14700
22	GENMAR 2250	HT	CUD	AL DV	IO 235 MRCR	8 6	3550		12600	14400
24	GENMAR 2450	HT	CUD	AL DV	IO 160-235	8 6	4010		14800	17500
					1994 BOATS					
16	LAKER 16	OP	UTL	AL SV	OB	6	451		1850	2200
16	REBEL 16	OP	FSH	AL SV	OB	6 1	455		1900	2250
16	REBEL 16 DELUXE	OP	FSH	AL SV	OB	6 1	520		2200	2550
16	WS-16	OP	UTL	AL SV	OB	6 1	430		1750	2050
16 2	SV-16	OP	UTL	AL SV	OB	5 11	321		1300	1550
16 3	ANGLER II 1600	OP	FSH	AL SV	OB	6 1	712		3000	3450
16 3	ANGLER II 1600 DXL	OP	FSH	AL SV	OB	6 1	752		3150	3650
16 3	EXPLORER 1600	OP	FSH	AL SV	OB	6 1	542		2300	2700
16 3	EXPLORER 1600 DELUXE	OP	FSH	AL SV	OB	6 1	610		2550	3000
16 3	PRO V 1660	OP	FSH	AL SV	OB	6 7	830		3450	4000
16 3	PRO V 1660 DELUXE	OP	FSH	AL SV	OB	6 7	860		3550	4150
16 3	TYEE 1650 II F/S	OP	RNBT	AL DV	OB	6 8	975		4000	4650
16 10	PRO ANGLER 1700	OP	FSH	AL SV	OB	7	776		3300	3850

LOA FT	LOA IN	NAME AND/ OR MODEL	TOP/ RIG	BOAT TYPE	HULL MTL	HULL TP	ENGINE TP	ENGINE # HP	ENGINE MFG	BEAM FT	BEAM IN	WGT LBS	DRAFT FT IN	RETAIL LOW	RETAIL HIGH
		1994 BOATS													
16	10	PRO ANGLER 1700 DLX	OP	FSH	AL	SV	OB			7		825		3500	4100
17	2	FISHERMAN 1700	OP	FSH	AL	SV	OB			7	1	1033		4400	5050
17	2	PRO BASS 1790	OP	BASS	AL	SV	OB			6	11	905		3850	4500
17	2	PRO SPORT 1700	OP	RNBT	AL	DV	OB			7	1	1102		4650	5350
17	3	TYEE 1750 F/S	OP	RNBT	AL	SV	OB			6	11	1195		4550	5200
17	3	TYEE 1750 F/S	OP	RNBT	AL	SV	IO	120-235		6	11	2015		5650	6900
17	3	TYEE 1750 GS	OP	RNBT	AL	SV	OB			6	11	1195		5400	6200
17	3	TYEE 1750 GS	OP	RNBT	AL	SV	IO	120-135		6	11	2015		6100	7000
17	3	TYEE 1750 GS	OP	RNBT	AL	SV	IO	160-205		6	11	2015		5850	7150
17	3	TYEE 1750 GS	OP	RNBT	AL	SV	IO	225-235		6	11	2015		6400	7350
17	6	PRO V 1775	OP	RNBT	AL	SV	OB			7	2	1085		4650	5350
17	6	PRO V 1775 DELUXE	OP	FSH	AL	SV	OB			7	2	1085		4650	5350
18		ALASKAN 18	OP	FSH	AL	SV	OB			6	3	602		2750	3200
18		SV-18	OP	UTL	AL	SV	OB			6	3	436		1750	2100
18	3	FISHERMAN 1800	OP	FSH	AL	DV	OB			7	3	1360		5650	6500
18	3	FISHERMAN 1800	OP	FSH	AL	DV	IO	120	VLVO	7	3	1915		6750	7750
		IO 135 MRCR 6400 7350, IO 135 VLVO 6750 7750, IO 160-205 6450 7900													
		IO 225-235 7100 8150													
18	3	TYEE 1850 F/S	OP	RNBT	AL	SV	OB			7	4	1342		5150	5900
18	3	TYEE 1850 F/S	OP	RNBT	AL	SV	IO	120-235		7	4	2396		6750	7900
18	3	TYEE 1850 F/S	OP	RNBT	AL	SV	IO	335	VLVO	7	4	2396		9450	10700
18	3	TYEE 1850 GS	OP	RNBT	AL	SV	OB			7	4	1342		6000	6900
18	3	TYEE 1850 GS	OP	RNBT	AL	SV	IO	120	VLVO	7	4	2396		7200	8250
18	3	TYEE 1850 GS	OP	RNBT	AL	SV	IO	135		7	4	2396		6850	8250
18	3	TYEE 1850 GS	OP	RNBT	AL	SV	IO	160-235		7	4	2396		6900	8350
18	10	PRO 1890 V	OP	FSH	AL	DV	OB			7	7	1225		5300	6100
18	10	PRO 1890 V DELUXE	OP	FSH	AL	DV	OB			7	7	1250		5400	6200
20	3	BARON 2100	ST	CUD	AL	DV	OB			7	5	1705		6650	7600
20	3	BARON 2100	ST	CUD	AL	DV	IO	120-205		7	5	2700		8450	9850
20	3	BARON 2100	OP	RNBT	AL	DV	IO	225-235		7	5	2710		8200	9450
20	3	BARON 2100 GS	OP	RNBT	AL	DV	OB			7	5	1702		6600	7600
20	3	BARON 2100 GS	OP	RNBT	AL	DV	IO	135-205		7	5	2710		7850	9500
20	3	BARON 2100 GS	OP	RNBT	AL	DV	IO	225-235		7	5	2710		8650	9950
22		GENMAR 2250	ST	CUD	AL	DV	IO	120-225		8	6	3550		11800	13800
22		GENMAR 2250	ST	CUD	AL	DV	IO	235	MRCR	8	6	3550		11800	13400
22		GENMAR 2250	HT	CUD	AL	DV	IO	120-225		8	6	3550		11800	13800
22		GENMAR 2250	HT	CUD	AL	DV	IO	235	MRCR	8	6	3550		11800	13400
24		GENMAR 2450	ST	CUD	AL	DV	IO	160-235		8	6	4010		13800	16500
24		GENMAR 2450	HT	CUD	AL	DV	IO	160-235		8	6	4010		13800	16400
		1993 BOATS													
16		PIKE REBEL 16	OP	FSH	AL	SV	OB			6	1	455		1800	2150
16		S-16	OP	UTL	AL	SV	OB			5	5	300		1200	1400
16		WS-16	OP	UTL	AL	SV	OB			6	1	430		1700	2000
16	3	ANGLER 1600	OP	FSH	AL	DV	OB			6	1	712		2850	3350
16	3	ANGLER 1600 DELUXE	OP	FSH	AL	DV	OB			6	1	752		3000	3500
16	3	EXPLORER 1600	OP	FSH	AL	SV	OB			6	1	542		2200	2600
16	3	EXPLORER 1600 DELUXE	OP	FSH	AL	SV	OB			6	1	610		2450	2850
16	3	MV 1648	OP	JON	AL	SV	OB			5	9	306		1200	1450
16	3	PRO V 1660	OP	FSH	AL	SV	OB			6	7	830		3300	3850
16	3	PRO V 1660 DELUXE	OP	FSH	AL	SV	OB			6	7	860		3400	4000
16	3	TYEE 1650 II F/S	OP	RNBT	AL	DV	OB			6	8	975		3850	4450
16	5	XLT 17	OP	FSH	AL	SV	OB			6	2	760		3050	3550
16	10	PRO ANGLER 1700	OP	FSH	AL	SV	OB			7		776		3200	3700
16	10	PRO ANGLER 1700 DLX	OP	FSH	AL	SV	OB			7		800		3300	3800
17	2	PRO BASS 1790	OP	BASS	AL	SV	OB			6	11	905		3700	4300
17	2	PRO SPORT 1700	OP	RNBT	AL	DV	OB			7	1	1070		4300	5000
17	3	TYEE 1750 F/S	OP	RNBT	AL	SV	OB			6	11	1195		4400	5050
17	3	TYEE 1750 F/S	OP	RNBT	AL	SV	IO	110-135		6	11	2015		5250	6050
17	3	TYEE 1750 GS	OP	RNBT	AL	SV	OB			6	11	1195		5150	5900
17	3	TYEE 1750 GS	OP	RNBT	AL	SV	IO	110-135		6	11	2015		5750	6600
17	6	PRO V 1775	OP	RNBT	AL	SV	OB			7	2	1100		4500	5150
17	6	PRO V 1775 DELUXE	OP	FSH	AL	SV	OB			7	2	1085		4450	5100
18		ALASKAN 18	OP	FSH	AL	SV	OB			6	3	578		2550	2950
18		S-18	OP	UTL	AL	SV	OB			6	1	430		1650	2000
18	3	FISHERMAN 1800	OP	FSH	AL	DV	OB			7	3	1360		5400	6200
18	3	FISHERMAN 1800	OP	FSH	AL	DV	IO	110-180		7	3	1915		6300	7350
18	3	TYEE 1850 F/S	OP	FSH	AL	SV	IO	135	VLVO	7	4	2396		7050	8100
18	3	TYEE 1850 F/S	OP	RNBT	AL	SV	OB			7	4	1342		4950	5700
18	3	TYEE 1850 F/S	OP	RNBT	AL	SV	IO	110-180		7	4	2396		6300	7350
18	3	TYEE 1850 GS	OP	RNBT	AL	SV	OB			7	4	1342		5750	6600
18	3	TYEE 1850 GS	OP	RNBT	AL	SV	IO	110-180		7	4	2396		6700	7800
18	10	PRO 1890 V	OP	FSH	AL	DV	OB			7	7	1225		5100	5850
18	10	PRO 1890 V DELUXE	OP	FSH	AL	DV	OB			7	7	1250		5150	5950
20	3	BARON 2100	ST	CUD	AL	DV	OB			7	5	1705		6350	7300
20	3	BARON 2100	ST	CUD	AL	DV	IO	110-225		7	5	2700		7900	9450
20	3	BARON 2100	OP	RNBT	AL	DV	IO	205		7	5	2710		7250	8700
20	3	BARON 2100 GS	OP	RNBT	AL	DV	OB			7	5	1702		6350	7300
20	3	BARON 2100 GS	OP	RNBT	AL	DV	IO	110-235		7	5	2710		7600	9150
22		GENMAR 2250	OP	CUD	AL	DV	IO	205-235		8	6	3550		10900	12700
22		GENMAR 2250	ST	CUD	AL	DV	IO	110-225		8	6	3550		11000	12900
22		GENMAR 2250	HT	CUD	AL	DV	IO	110-135		8	6	3550		11000	12500
		IO 155-180 10700 12600, IO 205 10900 12700, IO 225 VLVO 11300 12900													
		IO 235 MRCR 11000 12500													
24		GENMAR 2450	OP	CUD	AL	DV	IO	205-235		8	6	4010		13000	15200
24		GENMAR 2450	ST	CUD	AL	DV	IO	155-225		8	6	4010		12900	15400
24		GENMAR 2450	HT	CUD	AL	DV	IO	155-235		8	6	4010		12900	15300
		1992 BOATS													
16		PIKE REBEL 16	OP	FSH	AL	SV	OB			6	11	445		1700	2000
16		S-16	OP	FSH	AL	SV	OB			5	5	265		995	1200
16		WS-16	OP	UTL	AL	SV	OB			5	11	480		1800	2150
16	3	ANGLER 1600	OP	FSH	AL	DV	OB			6	1	670		2600	3000
16	3	ANGLER 1600 DELUXE	OP	FSH	AL	DV	OB			6	1	695		2700	3150
16	3	BASS ANGLER 1600	OP	BASS	AL	DV	OB			6	1	745		2850	3350
16	3	CRAPPIE 16	OP	FSH	AL	SV	OB					485		1850	2250
16	3	CRAPPIE 16 DELUXE	OP	FSH	AL	SV	OB					520		2000	2400
16	3	CRAPPIE 16 SS	OP	FSH	AL	SV	OB					502		1950	2300
16	3	EXPLORER 1600	OP	FSH	AL	SV	OB			6	1	542		2100	2500
16	3	EXPLORER 1600 DELUXE	OP	FSH	AL	SV	OB			6	1	573		2250	2600
16	3	MV 1648	OP	JON	AL	SV	OB					306		1150	1400
16	3	PRO V 1600	OP	FSH	AL	SV	OB			6	7	830		3200	3700
16	3	PRO V 1600 DELUXE	OP	FSH	AL	SV	OB			6	7	860		3300	3800
16	3	TYEE 1650 II F/S	OP	RNBT	AL	DV	OB			6	8	975		3700	4300
17	3	BASS 17	OP	BASS	AL	SV	OB					705		2850	3300
17	3	TYEE 1750 F/S	OP	RNBT	AL	SV	OB			7		1185		4550	5250
17	3	TYEE 1750 F/S	OP	RNBT	AL	SV	IO	110-135		7		2015		5200	5950
17	3	TYREE 1750	OP	RNBT	AL	SV	IO	135	VLVO	7		2015		5200	5950
17	6	PRO V 1775	OP	FSH	AL	SV	OB			7	2	1100		4250	4950
17	6	PRO V 1775 DELUXE	OP	FSH	AL	SV	OB			7	2	1085		4200	4900
18		ALASKAN 18	OP	UTL	AL	SV	OB			7	1	575		2250	2600
18		S-18	OP	FSH	AL	SV	OB			5	11	340		1450	1750
18	3	TYEE 1850 F/S	OP	RNBT	AL	SV	OB			7	4	1200		4700	5400
18	3	TYEE 1850 F/S	OP	RNBT	AL	SV	IO	110-180		7	4	2140		5750	6700
18	10	PRO 1890 V	OP	FSH	AL	DV	OB			7	7	1225		4900	5600
18	10	PRO 1890 V DELUXE	OP	FSH	AL	DV	OB			7	7	1250		4950	5700
20	3	BARON 2100 F/S	ST	RNBT	AL	DV	OB			7	5	1580		5750	6650
20	3	BARON 2100 F/S	ST	RNBT	AL	DV	IO	110-230		7	5	2595		6950	8250
20	3	BARON 2100 G/D	ST	RNBT	AL	DV	IO	175	MRCR	7	5	2595		6750	7750
21	6	GENMAR 2150	ST	CUD	AL	DV	IO	110-230		8	6	3141		9350	10800
22		SPORT FISHERMAN 2250	ST	CUD	AL	DV	IO	155-230		8	6	3550		10100	12000
24		GENMAR 2450	ST	CUD	AL	DV	IO	155-230		8	6	4010		12100	14300
		1991 BOATS													
16		PIKE REBEL 16	OP	FSH	AL	SV	OB			6	11	445		1650	1950
16		PREDATOR 1650 II	OP	FSH	AL	DV	OB			6	7	795		2900	3400
16		RENEGADE 1650 II	OP	FSH	AL	DV	OB			6	7	820		3000	3500
16		S-16	OP	FSH	AL	SV	OB			5	5	265		955	1150
16		WS-16	OP	UTL	AL	DV	OB			5	11	480		1750	2100
16	3	ANGLER 1600	OP	FSH	AL	DV	OB			6	1	670		2500	2900
16	3	ANGLER 1600 DELUXE	OP	FSH	AL	DV	OB			6	1	695		2600	3000
16	3	BASS ANGLER 1600	OP	BASS	AL	DV	OB			6	1	745		2750	3200
16	3	CHALLENGER 1600	OP	FSH	AL	DV	OB			6	1	555		2050	2450
16	3	CRAPPIE 16	OP	FSH	AL	SV	OB					485		1800	2150
16	3	CRAPPIE 16 DELUXE	OP	FSH	AL	SV	OB					520		1950	2300
16	3	CRAPPIE 16 SS	OP	FSH	AL	SV	OB					502		1850	2200
16	3	MV 1648	OP	JON	AL	SV	OB					306		1100	1350
16	3	SCOUT 1600	OP	FSH	AL	SV	OB			6	1	520		1950	2300
16	3	TYEE 1650 II F/S	OP	RNBT	AL	DV	OB			6	8	975		3550	4150
16	4	V-16-DELUXE	OP	FSH	AL	DV	OB			5	8	430		1600	1900
16	6	PRO V 1700	OP	FSH	AL	SV	OB			6	9	950		3500	4050
16	6	PRO V 1700 DELUXE	OP	FSH	AL	SV	OB			6	9	985		3600	4200
17	3	BASS 17	OP	BASS	AL	SV	OB					705		2750	3200
17	3	TYEE 1750 F/S	OP	RNBT	AL	SV	OB			7		1185		4400	5050
17	3	TYEE 1750 F/S	OP	RNBT	AL	SV	IO	130	MRCR	7		2015		4650	5350
17	10	PRO 1800 V	OP	FSH	AL	DV	OB			7	2	1045		4000	4650
17	10	PRO 1800 V DELUXE	OP	FSH	AL	DV	OB			7	2	1075		4100	4750
18		ALASKAN 18	OP	UTL	AL	SV	OB			7	1	575		2150	2500

 CONTINUED ON NEXT PAGE

LOA FT	LOA IN	NAME AND/ OR MODEL	TOP/ RIG	BOAT TYPE	-HULL- MTL	-HULL- TP	ENGINE TP	ENGINE # HP	ENGINE MFG	BEAM FT	BEAM IN	WGT LBS	DRAFT FT	DRAFT IN	RETAIL LOW	RETAIL HIGH
		1991 BOATS														
18		S-18	OP	FSH	AL	SV	OB			5	11	340			1400	1700
18	3	NEWPORT 1850	ST	CTRCN	AL	DV	OB			7	4	1100			4200	4900
18	3	TYEE 1850 F/S	OP	RNBT	AL	SV	OB			7	4	1200			4550	5250
18	3	TYEE 1850 F/S	OP	RNBT	AL	SV	IO	125-205		7	4	2020			5050	5900
20	3	BARON 2100 F/S	ST	RNBT	AL	DV	OB			7	5	1580			5550	6400
20	3	BARON 2100 F/S	ST	RNBT	AL	DV	IO	130-260		7	5	2475			6100	7550
20	3	NEWPORT 2100	ST	CTRCN	AL	DV	OB			7	5	1550			5450	6300
20	4	GENMAR 2100	ST	CUD	AL	DV	IO	130-260		8		3105			7600	9300
20	4	SPORT FISHERMAN 2100	ST	CUD	AL	DV	IO	130-260		8		2900			7300	8950
22		SPORT FISHERMAN 225	ST	CUD	AL	DV	IO			8	6	3550			**	**
24		GENMAR 2450	ST	CUD	AL	DV	IO	175-260		8	6	4010			11400	13400
		1990 BOATS														
16		MR-PIKE REBEL 16	OP	FSH	AL	SV	OB			6	11	610			2200	2550
16		PIKE REBEL 16	OP	FSH	AL	SV	OB			6	11	445			1550	1850
16		PREDATOR 1650 II	OP	FSH	AL	DV	OB			6	7	795			2800	3300
16		PRO-ANGLER REBEL 16	OP	FSH	AL	SV	OB			6	11	570			2000	2400
16		RENEGADE 1650 II	OP	FSH	AL	DV	OB			6	7	820			2900	3350
16		S-16	OP	FSH	AL	SV	OB			5	5	265			925	1100
16		TYEE REBEL 16	OP	FSH	AL	SV	OB			6	5	910			3200	3750
16		WS-16	OP	UTL	AL	SV	OB			5	11	480			1700	2000
16	3	CHALLENGER 1600	OP	FSH	AL	DV	OB			6	1	555			2000	2350
16	3	FURY 1600	OP	FSH	AL	DV	OB			5	11	660			2400	2750
16	3	SCOUT 1600	OP	FSH	AL	DV	OB			6	1	520			1850	2200
16	3	STINGER 1600	OP	FSH	AL	DV	OB			5	11	630			2300	2700
16	3	TYEE 1650 F/S	OP	RNBT	AL	SV	OB			6	5	910			3250	3750
16	4	V-16-DELUXE	OP	FSH	AL	DV	OB			5	8	430			1550	1850
16	6	PRO V 1700	OP	FSH	AL	SV	OB			6	9	950			3400	3950
16	6	PRO V 1700 DELUXE	OP	FSH	AL	SV	OB			6	9	985			3500	4050
17		TYEE REBEL 17	OP	FSH	AL	SV	OB			6	8	1030			3700	4300
17	3	TYEE 1750 F/S	OP	RNBT	AL	SV	OB			7		1185			4200	4850
17	3	TYEE 1750 F/S	OP	RNBT	AL	SV	IO	130	MRCR	7		2015			4350	5000
17	10	PRO 1800 V	OP	FSH	AL	DV	OB			7	2	1045			3850	4450
17	10	PRO 1800 V DELUXE	OP	FSH	AL	DV	OB			7	2	1075			3950	4600
18		ALASKAN 18	OP	UTL	AL	SV	OB			7	1	575			2050	2400
18		S-18	OP	FSH	AL	SV	OB			5	11	340			1350	1650
18	3	NEWPORT 1850	ST	CTRCN	AL	DV	OB			7	4	1100			4050	4750
18	3	TYEE 1850 F/S	OP	RNBT	AL	SV	OB			7	4	1200			4400	5050
18	3	TYEE 1850 F/S	OP	RNBT	AL	SV	IO	130-205		7	4	2020			4750	5550
20	3	BARON 2100 F/S	ST	RNBT	AL	DV	OB			7	5	1580			5350	6150
20	3	BARON 2100 F/S	ST	RNBT	AL	DV	IO	130-260		7	5	2475			5750	7100
20	3	NEWPORT 2100	ST	CTRCN	AL	DV	OB			7	5	1550			5300	6100
20	4	GENMAN 2100	ST	CUD	AL	DV	IO	130-260		8		3105			7150	8750
20	4	GENMAR 2100	HT	CUD	AL	DV	IO	130-260		8		3245			7350	9000
20	4	SPORT FISHERMAN 2100	ST	CUD	AL	DV	OB			8		2100			6600	7600
20	4	SPORT FISHERMAN 2100	ST	CUD	AL	DV	IO	130-260		8		2900			6850	8400
22		SPORT FISHERMAN 2250	ST	CUD	AL	DV	IO			8	6	3550			**	**
22		SPORTFISHERMAN 2250	HT	CUD	AL	DV	IO			8	6	3690			**	**
24		GENMAR 2450	ST	CUD	AL	DV	IO	165-260		8	6	4010			10700	12600
24		GENMAR 2450	HT	CUD	AL	DV	IO	165-260		8	6	4015			10700	12600
		1989 BOATS														
16		MR-PIKE REBEL 16	OP	FSH	AL	SV	OB			6	11	610			2100	2500
16		PIKE 16D	OP	FSH	AL	SV	OB			5	11	480			1650	1950
16		PIKE REBEL 16	OP	FSH	AL	SV	OB			6	11	445			1500	1800
16		PRO-ANGLER REBEL 16	OP	FSH	AL	SV	OB			6	11	570			1950	2300
16		S-16	OP	FSH	AL	SV	OB			5	5	265			900	1050
16		S-16 DELUXE	OP	FSH	AL	SV	OB			5	5	305			1050	1250
16		TYEE REBEL 16	OP	FSH	AL	SV	OB			6	5	910			3100	3600
16		WS-16	OP	UTL	AL	SV	OB			5	11	480			1650	1950
16	1	PREDATOR 1650	OP	FSH	AL	DV	OB			6	7	695			2400	2800
16	1	RENEGADE 1650	OP	FSH	AL	DV	OB			6	7	720			2500	2900
16	3	FURY 1600	OP	FSH	AL	DV	OB			5	11	660			2350	2700
16	3	STINGER 1600	OP	FSH	AL	DV	OB			5	11	630			2250	2600
16	3	TYEE 1650 F/S	OP	RNBT	AL	SV	OB			6	5	910			3100	3650
16	6	PRO V 1700	OP	FSH	AL	SV	OB			6	9	950			3300	3800
16	6	PRO V 1700 DELUXE	OP	FSH	AL	SV	OB			6	9	985			3400	3950
17		TYEE REBEL 17	OP	FSH	AL	SV	OB			6	8	1030			3600	4150
17	3	TYEE 1750 F/S	OP	RNBT	AL	SV	OB			7		1185			4050	4700
17	3	TYEE 1750 F/S	OP	RNBT	AL	SV	IO	130	MRCR	7		2015			4050	4750
18		ALASKAN 18	OP	UTL	AL	SV	OB			7	1	575			1950	2350
18		S-18	OP	FSH	AL	SV	OB			5	11	340			1350	1600
18	3	NEWPORT 1850	ST	CTRCN	AL	DV	OB			7	4	1100			3950	4600
18	3	TYEE 1850 F/S	OP	RNBT	AL	SV	OB			7	4	1200			4200	4900
18	3	TYEE 1850 F/S	OP	RNBT	AL	SV	IO	130-205		7	4	2020			4500	5300
20	3	BARON 2100 F/S	ST	RNBT	AL	DV	OB			7	5	1580			5200	5950
20	3	BARON 2100 F/S	ST	RNBT	AL	DV	IO	130-260		7	5	2475			5450	6700
20	3	NEWPORT 2100	ST	CTRCN	AL	DV	OB			7	5	1550			5100	5900
20	4	GENMAR 2100	ST	CUD	AL	DV	IO	130-260		8		3105			6750	8250
20	4	GENMAR 2100	HT	CUD	AL	DV	IO	130-260		8		3245			6950	8500
20	4	SPORT FISHERMAN 2100	ST	CUD	AL	DV	OB			8		2100			6400	7350
20	4	SPORT FISHERMAN 2100	ST	CUD	AL	DV	IO	130-260		8		2900			6500	8100
24		GENMAR 2450	ST	CUD	AL	DV	IO	165-260		8	6	4010			10100	11900
24		GENMAR 2450	HT	CUD	AL	DV	IO	165-260		8	6	4015			10100	11900
		1988 BOATS														
16		ALASKAN 16	OP	UTL	AL	SV	OB			5	11	450			1500	1800
16		MR-PIKE REBEL 16	OP	FSH	AL	SV	OB			6	11	610			2000	2400
16		PIKE 16D	OP	FSH	AL	SV	OB			5	11	480			1600	1900
16		PIKE REBEL 16	OP	FSH	AL	SV	OB			6	11	445			1500	1750
16		PRO-ANGLER REBEL 16	OP	FSH	AL	SV	OB			6	11	570			1900	2250
16		PRO-PIKE 16	OP	FSH	AL	SV	OB			5	5	415			1400	1650
16		S-16	OP	FSH	AL	SV	OB			5	5	265			875	1050
16		S-16 DELUXE	OP	FSH	AL	SV	OB			5	5	305			1000	1200
16		TYEE REBEL 16	OP	FSH	AL	SV	OB			6	5	910			3000	3500
16		WS-16	OP	UTL	AL	SV	OB			5	11	480			1600	1900
16	1	PREDATOR 1650	OP	FSH	AL	DV	OB			6	7	695			2350	2700
16	1	RENEGADE 1650	OP	FSH	AL	DV	OB			6	7	720			2400	2800
16	2	NISSWA V-16	OP	FSH	FBG	SV	OB			7	5	795			2650	3100
16	2	NISSWA V-16 DELUXE	OP	FSH	FBG	SV	OB			7	5	825			2750	3200
16	3	FURY 1600	OP	FSH	AL	DV	OB			5	11	660			2250	2650
16	3	STINGER 1600	OP	FSH	AL	DV	OB			5	11	630			2150	2500
16	3	TYEE 4.9	OP	FSH	AL	SV	OB			6	5	910			3050	3500
16	6	PRO V 1700	OP	FSH	AL	SV	OB			6	9	950			3200	3700
16	6	PRO V 1700 DELUXE	OP	FSH	AL	SV	OB			6	9	985			3300	3800
17		TYEE REBEL 17	OP	FSH	AL	SV	OB			6	8	1030			3450	4050
17	2	CHEROKEE V-17	OP	FSH	FBG	SV	OB			6	7	1190			3950	4600
17	4	TYEE 5.3	OP	FSH	AL	SV	OB			6	8	1030			3500	4100
18		ALASKAN 18	OP	UTL	AL	SV	OB			7	1	575			1900	2250
18		S-18	OP	FSH	AL	SV	OB			5	11	340			1300	1550
18	3	NEWPORT 1800	ST	CTRCN	AL	DV	OB			7	4	1100			3800	4450
18	3	TYEE 5.5	OP	FSH	AL	SV	OB			7	4	1200			4100	4750
18	3	TYEE 5.5	OP	FSH	AL	SV	IO	130-205		7	4	2020			4600	5350
20	3	BARON 2100 F/S	ST	RNBT	AL	DV	OB			7	5	1580			5050	5800
20	3	BARON 2100 F/S	ST	RNBT	AL	DV	IO	130-260		7	5	2475			5150	6350
20	3	NEWPORT 2100	ST	CTRCN	AL	DV	OB			7	5	1550			4950	5700
20	4	GENMAR 2100	ST	CUD	AL	DV	IO	130-230		8					6100	7250
20	4	GENMAR 2100	ST	CUD	AL	DV	IO	260		8		3105			6800	7800
20	4	SPORT FISHERMAN 2100	ST	CUD	AL	DV	OB			8		2100			6200	7150
20	4	SPORT FISHERMAN 2100	ST	CUD	AL	DV	IO	130-260		8		2900			6150	7650
		1987 BOATS														
16		ALASKAN 16	OP	UTL	AL	SV	OB			6	1	450			1450	1750
16		MR-PIKE 16	OP	FSH	AL	SV	OB			6		690			2250	2650
16		PIKE 16D	OP	FSH	AL	SV	OB			5	11	480			1550	1850
16		PRO-ANGLER 16	OP	FSH	AL	SV	OB			6	1	570			1850	2200
16		WS-16	OP	UTL	AL	SV	OB			6	1	480			1550	1850
16	1	PREDATOR	OP	FSH	AL	DV	OB			6	7	695			2300	2650
16	1	RENEGADE	OP	FSH	AL	DV	OB			6	7	720			2350	2750
16	2	NISSWA-GUIDE			FBG	SV	OB			6	7	880			2850	3300
16	3	TYEE 4.9	OP	FSH	AL	SV	OB			6	7	910			2950	3450
17	2	CHEROKEE-GUIDE			FBG	SV	OB			6	9	1170			3800	4400
17	4	TYEE 5.3	OP	FSH	AL	SV	OB			6	10	1030			3400	3950
18		ALASKAN	OP	UTL	AL	SV	OB			6	3	575			1850	2200
18		MR-PIKE 18	OP	FSH	AL	SV	OB			6	3	795			2800	3250
18		PRO-ANGLER 18	OP	FSH	AL	SV	OB			6	3	755			2650	3100
18		S-18	OP	FSH	AL	SV	OB			5	10	390			1450	1700
18		TYEE 5.5	OP	FSH	AL	SV	OB			7	4	1200			3950	4600
18		TYEE 5.5	OP	FSH	AL	SV	IO	120		7	4	1450			3750	4350
18	3	NEWPORT 1800	ST	CTRCN	AL	DV	OB			7	4	1100			3700	4300
20	3	BARON 2100 F/S	ST	RNBT	AL	DV	OB			7	5	1580			4900	5650
20	3	BARON 2100 F/S	ST	RNBT	AL	DV	IO	170-205		7	5	2300			4750	5750
20	3	NEWPORT 2100	ST	CTRCN	AL	DV	OB			7	5	1550			4850	5550
20	3	SPORTFISHERMAN 2100V	ST	CUD	AL	DV	OB			8		1800			5400	6200
20	3	SPORTFISHERMAN 2100V	ST	CUD	AL	DV	IO	170		8		2400			5250	6050
20	3	SPORTFISHERMAN 2100V	ST	CUD	AL	DV	IO	205		8		2900			5900	6800
		1986 BOATS														
16		ALASKAN	OP	UTL	AL	SV	OB			6	1	450			1400	1700
16		MR-PIKE 16	OP	FSH	AL	SV	OB			6		690			2200	2600
16		PIKE 16D	OP	FSH	AL	SV	OB			5	11	480			1500	1800
16		PRO-ANGLER 16	OP	FSH	AL	SV	OB			6	1	570			1800	2150
16	2	NISSWA DLX					OB			6	7	900			2850	3300

 CONTINUED ON NEXT PAGE

LOA FT IN	NAME AND/OR MODEL	TOP/RIG	BOAT TYPE	HULL MTL TP	ENGINE TP # HP MFG	BEAM FT IN	WGT LBS	DRAFT FT IN	RETAIL LOW	RETAIL HIGH
					1986 BOATS					
16 2	NISSWA-GUIDE			SV OB		6 7	880		2800	3250
16 3	PREDATOR			AL SV OB		6 7	695		2250	2600
16 3	RENEGADE			AL SV OB		6 7	720		2350	2700
16 3	TYEE 4.9	OP	FSH	AL SV OB		6 7	910		2850	3350
16 3	XRF 4.9	OP	UTL	AL SV OB		6 7	830		2600	3050
17 2	CHEROKEE-GUIDE			SV OB		6 9	1170		3700	4300
17 4	TYEE 5.3			SV OB		6 10	1030		3350	3850
18	ALASKAN 18	OP	FSH	AL SV OB		6 3	575		1800	2150
18	MR-PIKE 18	OP	FSH	AL SV OB		6 3	795		2700	3150
18	PIKE 18	OP	FSH	AL SV OB		6 3	590		2050	2450
18	PRO-ANGLER 18	OP	FSH	AL SV OB		6 3	755		2600	3000
18	S-18	OP	FSH	AL SV OB		5 10	390		1400	1650
18	TYEE 5.5	OP	FSH	AL SV OB		7 4	1200		3850	4500
18	TYEE 5.5	OP	FSH	AL SV IO	120	7 4	1450		3550	4150
20 3	2100			AL SV IO	170	7 5	2300		4500	5200
20 3	BARON 2100 F/S	OP	FSH	AL SV OB		7 5	1580		4800	5500
					1985 BOATS					
16	MR-BASS	OP	FSH	AL SV OB		6	690		2050	2400
16	MR-PIKE 16	OP	FSH	AL SV OB		6	690		2250	2600
16	PIKE 160	OP	FSH	AL SV OB		5 11	480		1500	1750
16	PRO-ANGLER 16	OP	FSH	AL SV OB		6 1	570		1750	2100
16	WS-16	OP	FSH	AL SV OB		6 1	480		1500	1750
16 2	NISSWA-GUIDE			FBG SV OB		6 1	480		1500	1750
16 3	TYEE 4.9	OP	FSH	AL SV OB		6 7	880		2700	3150
16 3	XRF 4.9	OP		AL SV OB		6 7	910		2800	3250
16 3	XRV SPORT	OP	RNBT	AL DV OB		6 7	830		2600	3000
17 2	CHEROKEE-GUIDE			FBG SV OB		6 7	890		2750	3200
17 2	CHIPPEWA-GUIDE			FBG SV OB		6 9	1170		3600	4200
17 4	TYEE 5.3	OP	FSH	SV OB		6 10	1030		3250	3800
18	ALASKAN	OP		AL		6 3	575		1950	2350
18	MR-PIKE 18	OP	FSH	AL SV OB		6 3	795		2650	3100
18	PIKE 18	OP	FSH	AL SV OB		6 3	590		2000	2400
18	PRO-ANGLER 18	OP	FSH	AL SV OB		6 3	755		2550	2950
18	S-18	OP	FSH	AL SV OB		5 10	390		1350	1600
18	TYEE	OP	FSH	AL SV OB		7 4	1200		3900	4500
18	TYEE 5.5	OP	FSH	AL SV OB		7 4	1200		3650	4250
18	TYEE 5.5	OP	FSH	AL SV IO	120	7 4	1450		3450	4000
18	XRV	OP	RNBT	AL DV OB		7 4	1017		3300	3850
18	XRV	OP	RNBT	AL DV IO	120	7 4	1450		3200	3750

....For earlier years, see the BUC Used Boat Price Guide, Volume 3

LYDIA YACHT IMPORT CORP
GLEN COVE NY 11542   FORMERLY LYDIA YACHTS   See inside cover to adjust price for area

LOA FT IN	NAME AND/OR MODEL	TOP/RIG	BOAT TYPE	HULL MTL TP	ENGINE TP # HP MFG	BEAM FT IN	WGT LBS	DRAFT FT IN	RETAIL LOW	RETAIL HIGH
					1995 BOATS					
43	LYDIA GLASSADE	FB	MY	FBG	IB T375D CAT	15 6	38000	4 6	254000	279000
48	LYDIA GLASSADE	FB	MY	FBG	IB T375D CAT	15 6	43000	4 6	271000	297500
					1994 BOATS					
43	LYDIA GLASSADE	FB	MY	FBG	IB T375D CAT	15 6	38000	4 6	243500	267500
48	LYDIA GLASSADE	FB	MY	FBG	IB T375D CAT	15 6	43000	4 6	259500	285000
					1993 BOATS					
43	LYDIA GLASSADE	FB	MY	FBG	IB T375D CAT	15 6	38000	4 6	233000	256000
48	LYDIA GLASSADE	FB	MY	FBG	IB T375D CAT	15 6	43000	4 6	247500	272000
					1992 BOATS					
43	LYDIA GLASSADE	FB	MY	FBG	IB T375D CAT	15 6	38000	4 6	222000	244000
48	LYDIA GLASSADE	FB	MY	FBG	IB T375D CAT	15 6	43000	4 6	236000	259000
					1991 BOATS					
43	LYDIA GLASSADE	FB	MY	FBG	IB T375D CAT	15 6	38000	4 6	211500	232500
48	LYDIA GLASSADE	FB	MY	FBG	IB T375D CAT	15 6	43000	4 6	225000	247000
					1990 BOATS					
43	LYDIA GLASSADE	FB	MY	FBG	IB T320 CUM	15 6	38000	4 6	169500	186500
48	LYDIA GLASSADE	FB	MY	FBG	IB T320 CUM	15 6	43000	4 6	187000	206000
					1989 BOATS					
43	LYDIA GLASSADE	FB	MY	FBG	IB T320D CUM	15 6	38000	4 6	183000	201500
48	LYDIA GLASSADE	FB	MY	FBG	IB T320D CUM	15 6	43000	4 6	196000	215500
					1987 BOATS					
43	LYDIA 43	FB	MY	FBG SV	IB T350	15	35000	4 6	141000	155000
	IB T270D CUM 164000 180500, IB T320D CUM 168000 184500, IB T375D CAT 176500 194000									
48	LYDIA 48 COCKPIT	FB	MYCPT	FBG SV	IB T320D CUM	15		4 6	170000	186500
48	LYDIA 48 COCKPIT	FB	MYCPT		IB T375D CAT	15		4 6	177500	195000

LYMAN-MORSE BOATBUILDING CO
THOMASTON ME 04861   COAST GUARD MFG ID- MJE   See inside cover to adjust price for area

LOA FT IN	NAME AND/OR MODEL	TOP/RIG	BOAT TYPE	HULL MTL TP	ENGINE TP # HP MFG	BEAM FT IN	WGT LBS	DRAFT FT IN	RETAIL LOW	RETAIL HIGH
					1993 BOATS					
44 6	SEGUIN 44	SLP	SARAC	F/S KC	IB 50D WEST	12 8	25000	6	342500	376500
49 6	SEGUIN 49	SLP	SARAC	F/S CB	IB 35D PERK	15 6	49000	5	525000	577000
52	LYMAN-HUNT	FB	MY	F/S DV	IB T225D CAT	16	30000		318500	350000
					1992 BOATS					
37	LYMAN-HUNT	HT	MY	F/S DV	IB T D	13	22000	3 6	**	**
39 8	SEGUIN 40	CUT	SA/RC	F/S CB	IB D	12 3	17200	2 4	216000	237000
42 6	LYMAN-HUNT	HT	MY	F/S DV	IB T D	13 1	28000	3 9	**	**
44 6	SEGUIN 44	CUT	SA/RC	F/S KC	IB D	12 9	25000	3	322000	354000
46	LYMAN-NEWMAN	FB	MY	F/S DS	IB D	15 1	36000	4 6	**	**
47 3	LYMAN-HUNT	HT	TCMY	F/S DV	IB D	15 2	35000	4	**	**
48 3	LYMAN-LINCOLN	FB	TCMY	F/S DS	IB D	17 4	39000	5	**	**
48 6	ACADIA 49	CAT	SA/RC	F/S KC	IB D	14	28000	6 6	397000	436000
48 6	MONHEGAN 48	CUT	SA/RC	F/S KC	IB D	13 9	26000	4 6	390000	428500
50 10	SEGUIN 49	CUT	SA/RC	F/S CB	IB D	15 6	47200	3 10	514000	565000
51 8	LYMAN-HUNT	FB	TCMY	F/S DV	IB T D	15 4	47000	4	**	**
54 11	LYMAN-HOOD 55	KTH	SA/RC	F/S KC	IB D	16	52000	5 9	629000	691000
61	LYMAN-HUNT	FB	TCMY	F/S DV	IB T D	16 9	65000	5 2	**	**
					1989 BOATS					
40	SEGUIN 40	SLP	SA/RC	FBG CB	IB D	12 2	17200	2 3	183000	201000
44 1	SEGUIN 44	SLP	SA/RC	FBG KC	IB D	12 9	26000	3	269500	296000
49	SEGUIN 49	SLP	SA/RC	FBG CB	IB D	15 6	42000	3 10	388000	426000
50 6	SEGUIN 51	CUT	SA/RC	FBG CB	IB 85D	15 6	44000	4 4	427000	469000
54 11	HOOD/LYMAN 55	SLP	SA/CR	FBG KC	IB D	16	52000	5 9	523500	575000
					1988 BOATS					
40	SEGUIN 40	SLP	SA/RC	FBG CB	IB D	12 2	17200	2 3	172000	189000
44 1	SEGUIN 44	SLP	SA/RC	FBG KC	IB D	12 9	26000	3	253500	278500
54 11	HOOD/LYMAN 55	SLP	SA/CR	FBG KC	IB D	16	52000	5 9	365000	401000
					1987 BOATS					
40	SEGUIN 40	SLP	SA/RC	FBG CB	IB D	12 2	16000	2 3	154000	169500
44 1	SEGUIN 44	SLP	SA/RC	FBG KC	IB D	12 6	26000	3	238000	262000
49	SEGUIN 49	SLP	SA/RC	FBG CB	IB D	15 6	42000	3 10	343000	377000
54 11	HOOD/LYMAN 55	SLP	SA/CR	FBG KC	IB D	16	52000	5 9	463000	509000
					1986 BOATS					
40	SEGUIN 40	SLP	SA/RC	FBG CB	IB D	12 2	16000	2 3	145000	159000
44 1	SEGUIN 44	SLP	SA/RC	FBG KC	IB D	12 6	26000	3	224000	246000
					1985 BOATS					
40	SEGUIN 40	SLP	SA/RC	FBG CB	IB D	12 2	16000	2 3	136500	150000
44 1	SEGUIN 44	SLP	SA/RC	FBG KC	IB D	12 6	26000	3	211000	231500
					1984 BOATS					
39 8	SEGUIN 40	SLP	SA/RC	FBG KC	IB 22D YAN	12 3	17200	2 4	131500	144500

MACGREGOR YACHT CORP
COSTA MESA CA 92627   COAST GUARD MFG ID- MAC   to adjust price for area

For more recent years, see the BUC Used Boat Price Guide, Volume 1

LOA FT IN	NAME AND/OR MODEL	TOP/RIG	BOAT TYPE	HULL MTL TP	ENGINE TP # HP MFG	BEAM FT IN	WGT LBS	DRAFT FT IN	RETAIL LOW	RETAIL HIGH
					1996 BOATS					
25 10	MACGREGOR 26	SLP	SACAC	FBG DB OB		7 10	2350	5 6	9750	11100
					1995 BOATS					
18 10	MACGREGOR 19	SLP	SACAC	FBG CB OB		7 5	2250	5 1	7500	8650
25 10	MACGREGOR 26	SLP	SACAC	FBG CB OB		7 11	2350	5 6	9200	10500
65	MACGREGOR 65 SHOAL	SLP	SACAC	FBG KL IB	150D MRCR	12	32000	6	181500	199500
					1994 BOATS					
18 10	MACGREGOR 19	SLP	SACAC	FBG CB OB		7 5	2050	5 1	6700	7650
25 10	MACGREGOR 26	SLP	SACAC	FBG CB OB		7 11	2850	5 6	10000	11400
65	MACGREGOR 65 SHOAL	SLP	SACAC	FBG KL IB	150D MRCR	12	32000	6	170000	187000
					1993 BOATS					
18 10	MACGREGOR 19	SLP	SACAC	FBG CB OB		7 5	2050	5 1	6300	7200
25 10	MACGREGOR 26	SLP	SACAC	FBG CB OB		7 11	2850	5 6	9450	10700
65	MACGREGOR 65	SLP	SACAC	FBG KL IB	150D VLVO	12	35000	8 6	159000	175000
65	MACGREGOR 65 SHOAL	SLP	SACAC	FBG KL IB	150D VLVO	12	35000	6	159000	175000
					1992 BOATS					
18 10	MACGREGOR 19	SLP	SAIL	FBG KL OB		7 5	1900	5	5650	6500
25 10	MACGREGOR 26	SLP	SAIL	FBG KL OB		7 11	2850	4 8	8950	10200
65	MACGREGOR 65	SLP	SA/RC	FBG KL IB	150D VLVO	12	35000	8 6	149000	163500

LOA FT	LOA IN	NAME AND/ OR MODEL	TOP/ RIG	BOAT TYPE	HULL MTL	HULL TP	ENGINE TP	ENGINE # HP	ENGINE MFG	BEAM FT	BEAM IN	WGT LBS	DRAFT FT	DRAFT IN	RETAIL LOW	RETAIL HIGH
		1992 BOATS														
65		MACGREGOR 65 SHOAL	SLP	SA/RC	FBG	KL	IB	150D	VLVO	12		35000	6		149000	163500
		1990 BOATS														
25	10	MACGREGOR 26	SLP	SAIL	FBG	KL	IB	10		7	11	2850	6	4	8150	9350
65		MACGREGOR 65	SLP	SA/RC	FBG	KL	IB	110D	YAN	12		30000	8	6	130000	143000
65		MACGREGOR 65 SHOAL	SLP	SA/RC	FBG	KL	IB	110D	YAN	12		30000	6		130000	143000
		1986 BOATS														
21		MAC-GREGOR 21	SLP	SA/CR	FBG	SK	OB			6	10	1175	1		3050	3550
22		MAC-GREGOR 22	SLP	SA/CR	FBG	SK	OB			7	4	1800	1		3800	4400
24	11	MAC-GREGOR 25	SLP	SA/CR	FBG	SK	OB			5	8	2100	1	10	4650	5300
65		MAC-GREGOR 65	CUT	SA/CR	FBG	SK	IB	80D	PATH	11	8	21000	8	6	99400	109000
		1985 BOATS														
21		MAC-GREGOR 21	SLP	SA/RC	FBG	SK	OB			6	10	1175	1	1	2850	3350
22		MAC-GREGOR 22	SLP	SA/RC	FBG	SK	OB			7	4	1800	1	1	3550	4150
24	11	MAC-GREGOR 25	SLP	SA/RC	FBG	SK	OB			5	8	2100	1	10	4350	5000
65		MACGREGOR 65	CUT	SA/RC	FBG	KL	IB	D		11	9	22000	8	6	93100	102500
		1984 BOATS														
21		MAC-GREGOR 21	SLP	SA/CR	FBG	SK	OB			6	10	1175	1		2700	3150
22		MAC-GREGOR 22	SLP	SA/CR	FBG	SK	OB			7	4	1800	1		3350	3900
24	11	MAC-GREGOR 25	SLP	SA/CR	FBG	SK	OB			5	8	2100	1	10	4050	4700
65		MAC-GREGOR 65	SLP	SA/RC	FBG	KL	IB	D		11	8	21000	8	6	87400	96000

....For earlier years, see the BUC Used Boat Price Guide, Volume 3

MACH 1 BOATS

BY FREEDOM BOATS INC
MONMOUTH IL 61462 COAST GUARD MFG ID- FLI

See inside cover to adjust price for area

LOA FT	LOA IN	NAME AND/ OR MODEL	TOP/ RIG	BOAT TYPE	HULL MTL	HULL TP	ENGINE TP	ENGINE # HP	ENGINE MFG	BEAM FT	BEAM IN	WGT LBS	DRAFT FT	DRAFT IN	RETAIL LOW	RETAIL HIGH
		1994 BOATS														
18		SPITFIRE 1800	OP	B/R	FBG	DV	IO	180		8		2100	3		4100	5050
20	9	COMMANDER 2150	OP	B/R	FBG	DV	IO	295-300		8		2900	2	10	6400	7900
21	3	PLAYMATE 2200	OP	CR	FBG	DV	IO	170-235		8	6	4000	3		8050	9500
21	3	PLAYMATE 2200	OP	CR	FBG	DV	IO	300	VLVO	8	6	4000	3		9350	10600
22	4	CONDOR 2350	OP	CUD	FBG	DV	IO	300	VLVO	8		3995	3	3	9550	10900
22	4	CONDOR 2350	OP	CUD	FBG	DV	IO	375-390		8		3995	3	3	10600	12600
23	8	MARAUDER 2450	OP	B/R	FBG	DV	IO	300	VLVO	8		4025	3	3	9550	10900
23	8	MARAUDER 2450	OP	B/R	FBG	DV	IO	390-420		8		4025	3	3	11000	13300
23	8	MARAUDER 2450	OP	CUD	FBG	DV	IO	300	VLVO	8		4025	3	3	10200	11600
23	8	MARAUDER 2450	OP	CUD	FBG	DV	IO	390-420		8		4025	3	3	11800	14200
26	7	CONCORDE 2700	OP	B/R	FBG	DV	IO	300-375		8		4720	3	5	12200	14900
		IO 390 MRCR 13500 15300, IO T300-T350 16200 19500, IO T375 OMC 18300 20400														
26	7	CONCORDE 2700	OP	CUD	FBG	DV	IO	300-375		8		4720	3	5	13300	16300
26	7	CONCORDE 2700	OP	CUD	FBG	DV	IO	390	MRCR	8		4720	3	5	14800	16800
26	7	CONCORDE 2700	OP	CUD	FBG	DV	IO	T300-T375		8		5900	3	5	18100	21800
28	2	ENDEAVOR 2900	OP	B/R	FBG	DV	IO	300	VLVO	8		5020	3	5	12100	13700
28	2	ENDEAVOR 2900	OP	B/R	FBG	DV	IO	375-390		8		5020	3	5	12800	14900
28	2	ENDEAVOR 2900	OP	B/R	FBG	DV	IO	T300-T375		8		6200	3	5	15500	19100
28	2	ENDEAVOR 2900	OP	CUD	FBG	DV	IO	300-390		8		5020	3	5	15200	18800
28	2	ENDEAVOR 2900	OP	CUD	FBG	DV	IO	T300-T375		8		6200	3	5	19600	23700
28	5	CRUSADER 2850	OP	CR	FBG	DV	IO	300-390		8	5	6000	3	10	16600	20300
28	5	CRUSADER 2850	OP	CR	FBG	DV	IO	T160-T180		8	5	6700	3	10	17400	20200
28	5	CRUSADER 2850	OP	CR	FBG	DV	IO	T185D	VLVO	8	5	6700	3	10	22600	25100
34	2	SOVEREIGN 3400	OP	CUD	FBG	DV	IO	T295-T350		9	8	8800	3	2	34000	39600
		1993 BOATS														
18		SPITFIRE 1800	OP	B/R	FBG	DV	IO	180		8		2100	3		3850	4700
20	9	COMMANDER 2150	OP	B/R	FBG	DV	IO	300-330		8		2900	2	10	6100	7400
21	3	PLAYMATE 2200	OP	CR	FBG	DV	IO	235-260		8	6	4000	3		7750	9000
21	3	PLAYMATE 2200	OP	CR	FBG	DV	IO	300	VLVO	8	6	4000	3		8650	9950
22	4	CONDOR 2350	OP	CUD	FBG	DV	IO	300-370		8		3995	3	3	9000	11100
22	4	CONDOR 2350	OP	CUD	FBG	DV	IO	390	MRCR	8		3995	3	3	10400	11800
23	8	MARAUDER 2450	OP	B/R	FBG	DV	IO	300	VLVO	8		4025	3	3	9000	10200
23	8	MARAUDER 2450	OP	B/R	FBG	DV	IO	390-420		8		4025	3	3	10300	12500
23	8	MARAUDER 2450	OP	CUD	FBG	DV	IO	300	VLVO	8		4025	3	3	9550	10800
23	8	MARAUDER 2450	OP	CUD	FBG	DV	IO	390-420		8		4025	3	3	11000	13300
26	7	CONCORDE 2700	OP	B/R	FBG	DV	IO	300	VLVO	8		4720	3	5	11400	12900
		IO 390-420 12600 14900, IO T300-T350 15200 18200, IO T420 OMC 18800 20900														
26	7	CONCORDE 2700	OP	CUD	FBG	DV	IO	300	VLVO	8		4720	3	5	12400	14100
		IO 390-420 13800 16300, IO T300-T350 16600 19900, IO T420 OMC 19900 22100														
28	2	ENDEAVOR 2900	OP	B/R	FBG	DV	IO	300	VLVO	8		5020	3	5	11300	12800
		IO 390-420 12300 14400, IO T300-T350 14400 17200, IO T420 OMC 16900 19200														
28	2	ENDEAVOR 2900	OP	CUD	FBG	DV	IO	300-390		8		5020	3	5	14200	17600
		IO 420 OMC 16000 18200, IO T300-T350 18500 21500, IO T420 OMC 21000 23400														
28	5	CRUSADER 2850	OP	CR	FBG	DV	IO	300-390		8	5	6000	3	10	15500	19000
		IO 420 OMC 17200 19600, IO T175-T180 16500 18800, IO T185D VLVO 21100 23400														
34	2	SOVEREIGN 3400	OP	CUD	FBG	DV	IO	T300-T350		9	8	8800	3	2	32200	37000
		1992 BOATS														
16	5	ECLIPSE 650	OP	RNBT	FBG	DV	IO	205		7	2	2150			3300	4050
18		SPITFIRE 1800	OP	RNBT	FBG	DV	IO	205		8		2100			3800	4650
20	9	COMMADER 2150	OP	RNBT	FBG	DV	IO	330		8		2900			6200	7600
21	3	PLAYMATE 2200	OP	CR	FBG	DV	IO	260		8	6	4000			7400	8800
22	4	CONDOR 2350	OP	CUD	FBG	DV	IO	365		8		3995			9150	11000
22	8	FIESTA 2250	OP	RNBT	FBG	DV	IO	365		8		3000			7400	9150
23	8	MARAUDER 2450	OP	CUD	FBG	DV	IO	420		8		4025			11100	13600
26	7	CONCORDE 2700	OP	CUD	FBG	DV	IO	T420		8		5900			19000	22000
28	2	ENDEAVOR 2900	OP	CR	FBG	DV	IO	T420		8		6200			19800	22800
28	5	CRUSADER 2850	OP	CR	FBG	DV	IO	T420		8	6	6000			20000	22900
34	2	SOVEREIGN 3400	OP	OFF	FBG	DV	IO	T420		9	8	8800			36800	41600
		1991 BOATS														
18		SPITFIRE 1800	OP	RNBT	FBG	DV	IO	205	MRCR			2100	1	9	3550	4150
20	9	COMMANDER 2150	OP	RNBT	FBG	DV	IO	270	MRCR			2900	1	11	5200	5950
21	3	PLAYMATE 2200	OP	CR	FBG	DV	IO	260	MRCR			4000	3		6950	7950
22	4	CONDOR 2350	OP	CUD	FBG	DV	IO	365	MRCR			3995	2	10	8500	9800
23	8	MAGNUM 2450	OP	CUD	FBG	DV	IO	365	MRCR			4025	2	10	9150	10400
26	7	CONCORDE 2700	OP	CUD	FBG	DV	IO	T365	MRCR			5900	2	10	16000	18200
28	2	ENDEAVOR 2900	OP	CR	FBG	DV	IO	T365	MRCR			6200	2	10	18000	20000
28	5	CRUSADER 2850	OP	CR	FBG	DV	IO	T230	MRCR			6000	3		15100	17100
34	2	SOVEREIGN 3400	OP	OFF	FBG	DV	IO	T465	MRCR			8800	3		37200	41300

MAGIC BOATS INC

MAGIC BOATS
LAKE HAVASU CITY AZ 864 COAST GUARD MFG ID- MGE
FORMERLY LAKE HAVASU BOAT MFG

See inside cover to adjust price for area

LOA FT	LOA IN	NAME AND/ OR MODEL	TOP/ RIG	BOAT TYPE	HULL MTL	HULL TP	ENGINE TP	ENGINE # HP	ENGINE MFG	BEAM FT	BEAM IN	WGT LBS	DRAFT FT	DRAFT IN	RETAIL LOW	RETAIL HIGH
		1994 BOATS														
33	9	OFFSHORE WARRIOR	OP	OFF	FBG	DV	IO	T300-T415		8		7500	3	6	44300	53600
33	9	OFFSHORE WARRIOR	OP	OFF	FBG	DV	IO	T465-T500		8		7500	3	6	51100	58000
40		VOODOO 39	OP	OFF	FBG	DV	IO	T300	MRCR	8		10500	3	6	47300	52000
		IO T415 MRCR 52800 58100, IO T465 MRCR 56500 62000, IO T500 MRCR 59000 64800														
		IO T525 MRCR 60700 66700														
		1993 BOATS														
33	9	OFFSHORE MAGNUM	OP	OFF	FBG	DV	IO	T300-T415		8		7500	3	6	41400	50400
33	9	OFFSHORE MAGNUM	OP	OFF	FBG	DV	IO	T465-T500		8		7500	3	6	47800	54200
40		VOODOO 38	OP	OFF	FBG	DV	IO	T300	MRCR	8		10500	3	6	43800	48600
		IO T350 MRCR 46100 50600, IO T390 MRCR 47900 52600, IO T415 MRCR 49400 54300														
		IO T465 MRCR 52800 58000, IO T500 MRCR 55100 60600, IO T525 MRCR 56700 62400														
		1991 BOATS														
20	6	SPORT 206 SS		RACE	F/S	SV	IO	230-270		8		2365			5800	7050
23		OPEN BOW SPORT 230LE		RACE	F/S	SV	IO	260-270		8		2650			7200	8400
23		OPEN BOW SPORT 230LE		RACE	F/S	SV	IO	330	MRCR	8		2850			8400	9650
23		OPEN BOW SPORT 230LE		RACE	F/S	SV	IO	365	MRCR	8		2850			9250	10500
23		SPORT 230 SS		RACE	F/S	SV	IO	260-270		8		2575			7100	8250
		IO 330 MRCR 8300 9500, IO 365 MRCR 9150 10400, IO 420 MRCR 10800 12300														
		1990 BOATS														
20	6	206SS SPORT		RACE	F/S	SV	IO	260	MRCR	8		2395			5650	6500
23		230LE OPEN BOW SPORT		RACE	F/S	SV	IO	260-270		8		2650			6750	7900
23		230LE OPEN BOW SPORT		RACE	F/S	SV	IO	330	MRCR	8		2850			7900	9050
23		230SS SPORT		RACE	F/S	SV	IO	260-270		8		2575			6650	7800
23		230SS SPORT		RACE	F/S	SV	IO	330	MRCR	8		2775			7800	8950
23		230SS SPORT		RACE	F/S	SV	IO	365	MRCR	8		2775			8500	9800
		1989 BOATS														
23		M23CD SPORT		RACE	F/S	SV	IO	260-270		8		2575			6300	7350
23		M23CD SPORT		RACE	F/S	SV	IO	320-330		8		2600			6950	8450
23		M23CD SPORT		RACE	F/S	SV	IO	365	MRCR	8		2775			8050	9250
23		M23OB SPORT		RACE	F/S	SV	IO	260-270		8		2650			6350	7450
23		M23OB SPORT		RACE	F/S	SV	IO	320-330		8		2680			7050	8550
		1988 BOATS														
23		MAGIC 23		RACE	F/S	SV	IO	260-270		8		2575			5950	6950
23		MAGIC 23		RACE	F/S	SV	IO	320-330		8		2600			6600	8000
23		MAGIC 23		RACE	F/S	SV	IO	365	MRCR	8		2775			7600	8750
23		MAGIC 23 OPEN BOW		RACE	F/S	SV	IO	260-270		8		2650			6050	7050
23		MAGIC 23 OPEN BOW		RACE	F/S	SV	IO	320-330		8		2680			6700	8100

 CONTINUED ON NEXT PAGE

LOA FT	LOA IN	NAME AND/ OR MODEL	TOP/ RIG	BOAT TYPE	-HULL- MTL	-HULL- TP	ENGINE TP	ENGINE # HP	ENGINE MFG	BEAM FT	BEAM IN	WGT LBS	DRAFT FT	DRAFT IN	RETAIL LOW	RETAIL HIGH
1987 BOATS																
23		MAGIC 23		RACE	F/S	SV	IO	260	MRCR	8		2575			5650	6500
23		MAGIC 23		RACE	F/S	SV	IO	330	MRCR	8		2740			6550	7550
23		MAGIC 23 OPEN BOW		RACE	F/S	SV	IO	260	MRCR	8		2650			5750	6600

MAGNUM MARINE CORPORATION

N MIAMI BEACH FL 33180 COAST GUARD MFG ID- MAG See inside cover to adjust price for area

For more recent years, see the BUC Used Boat Price Guide, Volume 1

LOA FT	LOA IN	NAME AND/ OR MODEL	TOP/ RIG	BOAT TYPE	-HULL- MTL	-HULL- TP	ENGINE TP	ENGINE # HP	ENGINE MFG	BEAM FT	BEAM IN	WGT LBS	DRAFT FT	DRAFT IN	RETAIL LOW	RETAIL HIGH
1996 BOATS																
27	4	MAGNUM 27 FISH	OP	CTRCN	FBG	DV	OB			7	10	5200	2	5	47800	52500
27	4	MAGNUM 27 FISH	OP	CTRCN	FBG	DV	IO	T200	MRCR	7	10	5600	2	5	33500	37300
27	4	MAGNUM 27 SDN	OP	CR	FBG	DV	IO	T330	MRCR	7	10	5600	2	5	37300	41500
27	4	STARFIRE 27	OP	SPTCR	FBG	DV	IO	T365	MRCR	7	10	5200	2	4	38000	42200
40		MAGNUM 40 SPORT	OP	SPTCR	FBG	DV	IB	T425D	CAT	12	3	25500	3	4	323000	355000
50		MAGNUM 50 SPORT	OP	SPTCR	FBG	DV	IB	T736D	DD	13	8	46200	3	6	496000	545000
52	11	MAGNUM 53 CRUISER	ST	CR	FBG	DV	IB	T735D	DD	15	10	54500	4		638000	701000
52	11	MAGNUM 53 SPORT	OP	SPTCR	FBG	DV	IB	T800D	DD	15	9	54500	4		666000	732000
56		MAGNUM 56 SPORT	OP	SPTCR	FBG	DV	IB	T800D	DD	15	9	60000	3		720000	791000
63		MAGNUM 63 BIMINI	F+T	CR	KEV	DV	IB	T14CD	DD	17		75000	6		1.120M	1.220M
63		MAGNUM 63 SPORT	OP	CR	KEV	DV	IB	T14CD	DD	17		75000	6		1.120M	1.220M
71		MAGNUM 71 FLYBRIDGE	FB	CR	KEV	DV	IB	T14CD	DD	17		90000	6		1.415M	1.535M
71		MAGNUM 71 SPORT	OP	MY	KEV	DV	IB	T14CD	DD	17		90000	6		1.365M	1.485M
1995 BOATS																
27	4	MAGNUM 27 FISH	OP	CTRCN	FBG	DV	OB			7	10	5200			45600	50100
27	4	MAGNUM 27 SDN	OP	CR	FBG	DV	IO	T330	MRCR	7	10	5600	2	5	34800	38700
27	4	STARFIRE 27	OP	SPTCR	FBG	DV	IO	T365		7	10	5200	2	4	35400	39300
40		MAGNUM 40 SPORT	OP	SPTCR	FBG	DV	IB	T425D	CAT	12	3	25500	3	4	310000	340500
50		MAGNUM 50 SPORT	OP	SPTCR	FBG	DV	IB	T736D	DD	13	8	46200	3	6	473500	520500
52	11	MAGNUM 53 CRUISER	ST	CR	FBG	DV	IB	T735D	DD	15	10	54500	4		608500	668500
52	11	MAGNUM 53 SPORT	OP	SPTCR	FBG	DV	IB	T800D	DD	15	9	54500	4		635500	698500
56		MAGNUM 56 SPORT	OP	SPTCR	FBG	DV	IB	T800D	DD	15	9	60000	3		686000	754000
63		MAGNUM 63 BIMINI	F+T	CR	KEV	DV	IB	T14CD	DD	17		75000	6		1.070M	1.165M
63		MAGNUM 63 SPORT	OP	CR	KEV	DV	IB	T14CD	DD	17		75000	6		1.070M	1.165M
71		MAGNUM 71 FLYBRIDGE	FB	CR	KEV	DV	IB	T14CD	DD	17		90000	6		1.345M	1.465M
71		MAGNUM 71 SPORT	OP	MY	KEV	DV	IB	T14CD	DD	17		90000	6		1.300M	1.415M
71		SUPERFAST 71	ST	EXP	KEV	DV	IB	T40CD	LYC	17		90000	6		2.870M	3.120M
1994 BOATS																
27	4	MAGNUM 27 FISH	OP	CTRCN	FBG	DV	OB			7	10	5200			43000	47800
27	4	MAGNUM 27 SDN	OP	CR	FBG	DV	IO	T330	MRCR	7	10	5600	2	5	32500	36100
27	4	STARFIRE 27	OP	SPTCR	FBG	DV	IO	T365		7	10	5200	2	4	33000	36700
40		MAGNUM 40 SPORT	OP	SPTCR	FBG	DV	IB	T425D	CAT	12	3	25500	3	4	297000	326500
50		MAGNUM 50 SPORT	OP	SPTCR	FBG	DV	IB	T735D	GM	13	8	46200	3	6	445000	489500
52	11	MAGNUM 53 BIMINI	ST	SPTCR	FBG	DV	IB	T735D	GM	15	10	54500	4		599500	658500
52	11	MAGNUM 53 CRUISER	ST	CR	FBG	DV	IB	T735D	GM	15	10	54500	4		571500	628000
52	11	MAGNUM 53 SPORT	OP	SPTCR	FBG	DV	IB	T735D	GM	15	10	54500	3		572000	628500
63		MAGNUM 63 BIMINI	F+T	CR	KEV	DV	IB	T14CD	GM	17		75000	6		1.005M	1.090M
63		MAGNUM 63 SPORT	OP	CR	KEV	DV	IB	T14CD	GM	17		75000	6		1.005M	1.090M
70		MAGNUM 70	OP	SPTCR	KEV	DV	IB	T14CD	GM	17		90000	6		1.230M	1.340M
70		MAGNUM 70 SPORT	FB	MY	KEV	DV	IB	T17CD		17		90000	6		1.340M	1.455M
70		SUPERFAST 70	ST	EXP	KEV	DV	IB	T40CD	LYC	17		90000	6		2.685M	2.920M
1993 BOATS																
27	4	MAGNUM 27 FISH	OP	CTRCN	FBG	DV	OB			7	10	5200			41200	45800
27	4	MAGNUM 27 SDN	OP	CR	FBG	DV	IO	T330	MRCR	7	10	5600	2	5	30400	33800
27	4	STARFIRE 27	OP	SPTCR	FBG	DV	IO	T365		7	10	5200	2	4	30900	34300
40		MAGNUM 40 SPORT	OP	SPTCR	FBG	DV	IB	T425D	CAT	12	3	25500	3	4	283000	311000
44	7	MAGNUM 45 BIMINI	FB	SF	FBG	DV	IB	T735D		13	8	41000	3	6	450000	494500
44	7	MAGNUM 45 SPORT	OP	SPTCR	FBG	DV	IB	T735D	GM	13	8	40500	3	6	377000	414000
52	11	MAGNUM 53 BIMINI	ST	SPTCR	FBG	DV	IB	T735D	GM	15	10	54500	4		572000	629000
52	11	MAGNUM 53 CRUISER	ST	CR	FBG	DV	IB	T735D	GM	15	10	54500	4		546000	600000
52	11	MAGNUM 53 SPORT	OP	SPTCR	FBG	DV	IB	T735D	GM	15	10	54500	3		546000	600000
63		MAGNUM 63 BIMINI	F+T	CR	KEV	DV	IB	T14CD	GM	17		75000	6		957500	1.040M
63		MAGNUM 63 SPORT	OP	CR	KEV	DV	IB	T14CD	GM	17		75000	6		957500	1.040M
70		MAGNUM 70	OP	SPTCR	KEV	DV	IB	T14CD	GM	17		90000	6		1.175M	1.280M
70		MAGNUM 70 SPORT	FB	MY	KEV	DV	IB	T17CD		17		90000	6		1.280M	1.390M
70		SUPERFAST 70	ST	EXP	KEV	DV	IB	T40CD	LYC	17		90000	6		2.565M	2.790M
1992 BOATS																
27	4	MAGNUM 27 FISH	OP	CTRCN	FBG	DV	OB			7	10	5200			39600	44000
27	4	MAGNUM 27 SDN	OP	CR	FBG	DV	IO	T330	MRCR	7	10	5600	2	5	28400	31600
27	4	STARFIRE 27	OP	SPTCR	FBG	DV	IO	T365		7	10	5200	2	4	28900	32100
40		MAGNUM 40 SPORT	OP	SPTCR	FBG	DV	IB	T425D	CAT	12	3	25500	3	4	269500	296500
44	7	MAGNUM 45 BIMINI	FB	SF	FBG	DV	IB	T735D		13	8	41000	3	6	428500	471000
44	7	MAGNUM 45 SPORT	OP	SPTCR	FBG	DV	IB	T735D	GM	13	8	40500	3	6	359000	394500
52	11	MAGNUM 53 BIMINI	ST	SPTCR	FBG	DV	IB	T735D	GM	15	10	54500	4		546500	600500
52	11	MAGNUM 53 CRUISER	ST	CR	FBG	DV	IB	T735D	GM	15	10	54500	4		521500	573000
52	11	MAGNUM 53 SPORT	OP	SPTCR	FBG	DV	IB	T735D	GM	15	10	54500	3		521500	573000
63		MAGNUM 63 BIMINI	F+T	CR	KEV	DV	IB	T14CD	GM	17		75000	6		905500	995000
63		MAGNUM 63 SPORT	OP	CR	KEV	DV	IB	T14CD	GM	17		75000	6		905500	995000
70		MAGNUM 70	OP	SPTCR	KEV	DV	IB	T14CD	GM	17		90000	6		1.135M	1.235M
70		MAGNUM 70 SPORT	FB	MY	KEV	DV	IB	T17CD		17		90000	6		1.225M	1.335M
70		SUPERFAST 70	ST	EXP	KEV	DV	IB	T40CD	LYC	17		90000	6		2.450M	2.665M
1991 BOATS																
27	4	MAGNUM 27 FISH	OP	CTRCN	FBG	DV	OB			7	10	5200			38100	42400
27	4	MAGNUM 27 SDN	OP	CR	FBG	DV	IO	T330	MRCR	7	10	5600	2	5	26700	29700
27	4	STARFIRE 27	OP	SPTCR	FBG	DV	IO	T365		7	10	5200	2	4	27100	30100
40		MAGNUM 40	OP	SPTCR	FBG	DV	IB	T425D	CAT	12	3	25500	3	4	257500	282500
44	7	MAGNUM 45	FB	SF	FBG	DV	IB	T735D		13	8	41000			408500	448500
44	7	MAGNUM 45	OP	SPTCR	FBG	DV	IB	T735D	GM	13	8	40500			339500	373000
52	11	MAGNUM 53	OP	SPTCR	FBG	DV	IB	T735D	GM	15	9	54500	5		499500	549000
63		MAGNUM 63	OP	CR	KEV	DV	IB	T14CD	GM	17		75000			866500	952000
70		MAGNUM 70	FB	MY	KEV	DV	IB	T17CD		17					1.175M	1.275M
70		MAGNUM 70	OP	SPTCR	KEV	DV	IB	T14CD	GM	17		90000			1.085M	1.180M
1990 BOATS																
27	4	MAGNUM 27 FISH	OP	CTRCN	FBG	DV	OB			7	10	5200			36800	40900
27	4	MAGNUM 27 SDN	OP	CR	FBG	DV	IO	T340	MRCR	7	10	5600	2	5	25500	28400
27	4	STARFIRE 27	OP	SPTCR	FBG	DV	IO	T370		7	10	5200	2	4	25700	28500
40		MAGNUM 40	OP	SPTCR	FBG	DV	IB	T375D	CAT	12	3	22000	3	4	216000	237000
44	7	MAGNUM 45	FB	SF	FBG	DV	IB	T735D		13	8	36000			369000	405500
44	7	MAGNUM 45	OP	SPTCR	FBG	DV	IB	T735D	GM	13	8	36000			306500	337000
52	11	MAGNUM 53	FB	CR	FBG	DV	IB	T735D	GM	15	9	44000	5		434500	477500
52	11	MAGNUM 53	FB	CR	FBG	DV	IB	T11CD	GM	15	9	44000	5		555500	610500
52	11	MAGNUM 53	OP	SPTCR	FBG	DV	IB	T735D	GM	15	9	44000	5		450500	495000
52	11	MAGNUM 53	OP	SPTCR	FBG	DV	IB	T11CD	GM	15	9	44000	5		589500	648000
63		MAGNUM 63	OP	CR	KEV	DV	IB	T13CD	GM	17		53000			734000	806500
63		MAGNUM 63	HT	MY	FBG	DV	IB	T13CD	GM	17		53000			746000	819500
70		MAGNUM 70	OP	CR	KEV	DV	IB	T14CD	DD	17		70000			1.015M	1.100M
70		MAGNUM 70	FB	MY	KEV	DV	IB	T17CD	GM	17		70000			1.085M	1.180M
1989 BOATS																
27	4	MAGNUM 27 FISH	OP	CTRCN	FBG	DV	OB			7	10	5200			35600	39600
27	4	MAGNUM 27 SDN	OP	CR	FBG	DV	IO	T340	MRCR	7	10	5600	2	5	24100	26700
27	4	STARFIRE 27	OP	SPTCR	FBG	DV	IO	T370		7	10	5200	2	4	24200	26900
40		MAGNUM 40	OP	SF	FBG	DV	IB	T375D	CAT	12	3	22000	3	4	206000	226500
40		MAGNUM 40	OP	SF	FBG	DV	IB	T380D	GM	12	3	22000	3	4	201000	221000
40		MAGNUM 40	OP	SF	FBG	DV	IB	T550D	GM	12	3	22000	3	4	229000	252000
44	7	MAGNUM 45	FB	SF	FBG	DV	IB	T735D		13	8	36000			352000	387000
44	7	MAGNUM 45	OP	SPTCR	FBG	DV	IB	T735D	GM	13	8	36000			292500	321500
52	11	MAGNUM 53	FB	CR	FBG	DV	IB	T735D	GM	15	9	44000	5		416000	457500
52	11	MAGNUM 53	FB	CR	FBG	DV	IB	T11CD	GM	15	9	44000	5		530500	583000
52	11	MAGNUM 53	ST	SF	FBG	DV	IB	T735D	GM	15	9	44000	5		462000	507500
52	11	MAGNUM 53	ST	SF	FBG	DV	IB	T11CD	GM	15	9	44000	5		593500	652000
52	11	MAGNUM 53	OP	SPTCR	FBG	DV	IB	T735D	GM	15	9	44000	5		431000	473500
52	11	MAGNUM 53	OP	SPTCR	FBG	DV	IB	T11CD	GM	15	9	44000	5		563000	618500
63		MAGNUM 63	OP	CR	KEV	DV	IB	T13CD	GM	17		53000			703500	773000
63		MAGNUM 63	HT	MY	FBG	DV	IB	T13CD	GM	17		53000			715000	786000
63		MAGNUM 63	FB	MY	FBG	DV	IB	T13CD	GM	17		53000			715000	786000
70		MAGNUM 70	OP	CR	KEV	DV	IB	T D	GM	17		70000			**	**
70		MAGNUM 70	FB	MY	KEV	DV	IB	T17CD	GM	17		70000			1.055M	1.145M
1988 BOATS																
27	4	MAGNUM 27 FISH	OP	CTRCN	FBG	DV	OB			7	10	5200			34600	38400
27	4	MAGNUM 27 SDN	OP	CR	FBG	DV	IO	T340	MRCR	7	10	5600	2	5	22800	25300
27	4	STARFIRE 27	OP	SPTCR	FBG	DV	IO	T370		7	10	5200	2	4	22900	25500
40		MAGNUM 40	OP	SF	FBG	DV	IB	T375D	CAT	12	3	22000	3	4	197000	216500
40		MAGNUM 40	OP	SF	FBG	DV	IB	T380D	GM	12	3	22000	3	4	192000	211000
40		MAGNUM 40	OP	SF	FBC	DV	ID	T550D	GM	12	3	22000	3	4	219000	240500
44	7	MAGNUM 45	FB	SF	FBG	DV	IB	T735D		13	8	36000			336000	369500
44	7	MAGNUM 45	OP	SPTCR	FBG	DV	IB	T735D	GM	13	8	36000			279500	307000
52	11	MAGNUM 53	FB	CR	FBG	DV	IB	T735D	GM	15	9	44000	5		398500	438000
52	11	MAGNUM 53	FB	CR	FBG	DV	IB	T11CD	GM	15	9	44000	5		507000	557000
52	11	MAGNUM 53	ST	SF	FBG	DV	IB	T735D	GM	15	9	44000	5		442500	486500
52	11	MAGNUM 53	ST	SF	FBG	DV	IB	T11CD	GM	15	9	44000	5		567000	623000
52	11	MAGNUM 53	OP	SPTCR	FBG	DV	IB	T735D	GM	15	9	44000	5		413000	454000
52	11	MAGNUM 53	OP	SPTCR	FBG	DV	IB	T11CD	GM	15	9	44000	5		538000	591500
63		MAGNUM 63	OP	CR	KEV	DV	IB	T13CD	GM	17		53000			675000	742000
63		MAGNUM 63	HT	MY	FBG	DV	IB	T13CD	GM	17		53000			686000	754000
63		MAGNUM 63	FB	MY	FBG	DV	IB	T13CD	GM	17		53000			686000	754000

 CONTINUED ON NEXT PAGE

LOA FT	LOA IN	NAME AND/ OR MODEL	TOP/ RIG	BOAT TYPE	-HULL- MTL	-HULL- TP	ENGINE TP	ENGINE # HP	ENGINE MFG	BEAM FT	BEAM IN	WGT LBS	DRAFT FT	DRAFT IN	RETAIL LOW	RETAIL HIGH
		1988 BOATS														
70		MAGNUM 70	FB	MY	KEV	DV	IB	T17CD	GM	17		70000			1.010M	1.095M
		1987 BOATS														
27	4	MAGNUM 27 FISH	OP	CTRCN	FBG	DV	OB			7	10	5200			33600	37300
27	4	MAGNUM 27 SDN	OP	CR	FBG	DV	IO	T340	MRCR	7	10	5600	2	5	21700	24100
27	4	STARFIRE	OP	SPTCR	FBG	DV	IO	T370		7	10	5200	2	4	21800	24200
27	6	MALTESE	OP	RNBT	FBG	DV	IO	T340		7	11	5200	2	4	19600	21700
40		MAGNUM 40	OP	SF	FBG	DV	IB	T375D	CAT	12	3	22000	3	4	188500	207000
40		MAGNUM 40	OP	SF	FBG	DV	IB	T380D	GM	12	3	22000	3	4	184000	202000
40		MAGNUM 40	OP	SF	FBG	DV	IB	T570D	GM	12	3	22000	3	4	213000	234000
44	7	MAGNUM 45	FB	SF	FBG	DV	IB	T650D		13	8	36000			309000	339500
44	7	MAGNUM 45	OP	SPTCR	FBG	DV	IB	T650D	GM	13	8	36000			257500	283000
52	11	MAGNUM 53	FB	CR	FBG	DV	IB	T650D	GM	15	9	44000	5		361500	397500
52	11	MAGNUM 53	FB	CR	FBG	DV	IB	T11CD	GM	15	9	44000	5		485000	533000
52	11	MAGNUM 53	ST	SF	FBG	DV	IB	T650D	GM	15	9	44000	5		400000	439500
52	11	MAGNUM 53	ST	SF	FBG	DV	IB	T11CD	GM	15	9	44000	5		542500	596000
52	11	MAGNUM 53	OP	SPTCR	FBG	DV	IB	T650D	GM	15	9	44000	5		373500	410000
52	11	MAGNUM 53	OP	SPTCR	FBG	DV	IB	T11CD	GM	15	9	44000	5		514500	565500
63		MAGNUM 63	OP	CR	KEV	DV	IB	T13CD	GM	17		53000			648500	712500
63		MAGNUM 63	HT	MY	FBG	DV	IB	T13CD	GM	17		53000			659000	724000
63		MAGNUM 63	FB	MY	FBG	DV	IB	T13CD	GM	17		53000			659000	724000
70		MAGNUM 70	FB	MY	KEV	DV	IB	T17CD	GM	17		70000			977000	1.060M
		1986 BOATS														
27	4	MAGNUM 27 SDN		CR	FBG	DV	IO	T340		7	10	5600	2	5	20700	23000
27	4	MAGNUM 27 SPORT		RNBT	FBG	DV	IO	T260		7	10	5200	2	4	16200	18400
27	4	STARFIRE		SPTCR	FBG	DV	IO	T340		7	10	5200	2	4	20000	22200
27	6	MAGNUM 28		SPTCR	FBG	DV	IO	T340		7	11	5200	2	4	20300	22600
38		MAGNUM 38		SPTCR	FBG	DV	IB	T340		12	3	16500	3	4	107500	118000
40		MAGNUM 40		SF	FBG	DV	IB	T340		12	3	22000	3	4	147500	162000
52	11	MAGNUM 53	OP	SPTCR	FBG	DV	IB	T570D		15	9	44000	5		345000	379500
63		MAGNUM 63	OP	CR	KEV	DV	IB	T12CD		17		53000			600500	660000
		1985 BOATS														
27	4	MAGNUM 27 SDN		CR	FBG	DV	IO	T340		7	10	5600	2	5	19900	22100
27	4	MAGNUM 27 SPORT		RNBT	FBG	DV	IO	T260		7	10	5200	2	4	15600	17700
27	4	STARFIRE		SPTCR	FBG	DV	IO	T340		7	10	5200	2	4	19200	21400
27	6	MALTESE		RNBT	FBG	DV	IO	T340		7	11	5200	2	4	18100	20200
38		MAGNUM 38		SPTCR	FBG	DV	IB	T340		12	3	16500	3	4	102500	113000
40		MAGNUM 40		SPTCR	FBG	DV	IB	T340		12	3	22000	3	4	141000	155000
44	7	MAGNUM 45		SPTCR	FBG	DV	IB	T570D		13	8	36000			250000	275000
52	11	MAGNUM 53	OP	SPTCR	FBG	DV	IB	T570D		15	9	44000	5		331000	363500
63		MAGNUM 63	OP	CR	KEV	DV	IB	T12CD		17		53000			577500	634500
		1984 BOATS														
27		SEDAN	OP	CR	FBG	DV	IO	T340	MRCR	7	10	5600	2	5	19000	21100
27		SPORT	OP	RNBT	FBG	DV	IO	T260	MRCR	7	10	5200	2	4	14600	16600
27	4	STARFIRE	OP	SPTCR	FBG	DV	IO	T340	MRCR	7	10	5200	2	4	18800	20800
27	4	STARFIRE	OP	SPTCR	FBG	DV	IB	T450	BPM	7	10	5200	2	4	23700	26300
27	6	MALTESE	OP	RNBT	FBG	DV	IO	T340	MRCR	7	11	5200	2	4	17100	19500
38		FLYBRIDGE CRUISER	FB	SDN	FBG	DV	IO	T340	MRCR	12	3	19000	3	4	68200	74900
		IB T460 MRCR 115000 126500, IB T320D CUM 129000 141500, IB T350D GM													132500	145500
		IB T435D GM 142000 156000														
38		FLYBRIDGE FISHERMAN	FB	SDNSF	FBG	DV	IO	T340	MRCR	12	3	19000	3	4	88400	97100
		IB T460 MRCR 114500 125500, IB T320D CUM 128000 140500, IB T350D GM													131500	144500
		IB T435D GM 141000 154500														
38		HARDTOP	HT	SPTCR	FBG	DV	IO	T340	MRCR	12	3	18000	3	4	65700	72300
		IB T460 MRCR 111000 122000, IB T320D CUM 124000 136000, IB T350D GM													127500	140000
		IB T435D GM 137000 150500														
38		HARDTOP CRUISER	HT	SDN	FBG	DV	IO	T340	MRCR	12	3	18000	3	4	65600	72100
		IB T460 MRCR 111000 122000, IB T320D CUM 124500 137000, IB T350D GM													128000	141000
		IB T435D GM 137500 151500														
38		SPORT	OP	SPTCR	FBG	DV	IO	T340	MRCR	12	3	16500	3	4	61900	68000
		IB T460 MRCR 104500 115000, IB T320D CUM 117000 128500, IB T350D GM													120500	132500
		IB T435D GM 130000 143000														
40		SPORT	OP	SPTCR	FBG	DV	IB	320D	CUM	12	3	22000	3	4	141000	155000
		IB 435D GM 147500 162500, IO T340 MRCR 78500 86300, IB T460 MRCR													132000	145000
		IB T350D GM 158000 174000														
44	7	SPORT	OP	SPTCR	FBG	DV	IB	T570D	GM	13	8	36000			236000	259500
44	7	SPORT	OP	SPTCR	FBG	DV	IB	T640D	S&S	13	8	36000			241000	264500
52	11	FLYBRIDGE CRUISER	FB	CR	FBG	DV	IB	T640D	S&S	15	9	44000	5		320000	351500
52	11	FLYBRIDGE CRUISER	FB	CR	FBG	DV	IB	T975D	S&S	15	9	44000	5		404000	444000
52	11	HARDTOP	HT	SPTCR	FBG	DV	IB	T640D	S&S	15	9	44000	5		336500	369500
52	11	HARDTOP	HT	SPTCR	FBG	DV	IB	T975D	S&S	15	9	44000	5		442000	485500
52	11	SPORT	OP	SPTCR	FBG	DV	IB	T640D	S&S	15	9	44000	5		324500	357000
52	11	SPORT	OP	SPTCR	FBG	DV	IB	T975D	S&S	15	9	44000	5		410500	451000
63		PININFARINA FB CRUIS	FB	MY	FBG	DV	IB	T12CD	S&S	17		58000			564000	620000
63		PININFARINA HARDTOP	HT	MY	FBG	DV	IB	T12CD	S&S	17		58000			564000	620000
63		PININFARINA SPORT	OP	CR	FBG	DV	IB	T12CD	S&S	17		53000			546500	600500

....For earlier years, see the BUC Used Boat Price Guide, Volume 3

MAINE CAT

BREMEN ME 04551

See inside cover to adjust price for area

For more recent years, see the BUC Used Boat Price Guide, Volume 1

LOA FT	LOA IN	NAME AND/ OR MODEL	TOP/ RIG	BOAT TYPE	-HULL- MTL	-HULL- TP	ENGINE TP	ENGINE # HP	ENGINE MFG	BEAM FT	BEAM IN	WGT LBS	DRAFT FT	DRAFT IN	RETAIL LOW	RETAIL HIGH
		1996 BOATS														
22		MAINE CAT 22	SLP	SARAC	F/S	CT	OB			13		1100		11	**	**
30		MARINE CAT 30	SLP	SACAC	F/S	CT	OB			16		3600	3		79800	87700
		1995 BOATS														
22		MAINE CAT 22	SLP	SARAC	F/S	CT	OB			13		1100		11	**	**
		1994 BOATS														
22		MAINE CAT 22	SLP	SARAC	F/S	CT	OB			13		1000		11	**	**

MAINSHIP CORPORATION

LUHRS MARINE GROUP
ST AUGUSTINE FL 32086 COAST GUARD MFG ID- MPT

See inside cover to adjust price for area

For more recent years, see the BUC Used Boat Price Guide, Volume 1

LOA FT	LOA IN	NAME AND/ OR MODEL	TOP/ RIG	BOAT TYPE	-HULL- MTL	-HULL- TP	ENGINE TP	ENGINE # HP	ENGINE MFG	BEAM FT	BEAM IN	WGT LBS	DRAFT FT	DRAFT IN	RETAIL LOW	RETAIL HIGH
		1996 BOATS														
33	3	SEDAN BRIDGE 31	FB	SDN	FBG	SV	IB	T270	MPC	11	10	16000	2	10	75100	82500
36	5	MOTOR YACHT 34	FB	MY	FBG	SV	IB	T340	MPC	13	8	18500	3	2	91200	100500
39	6	MOTOR YACHT 37	FB	MY	FBG	SV	IB	T340	MPC	13	5	21000	3	7	107500	118000
43	2	SEDAN BRIDGE 40	FB	SDN	FBG	SV	IB	T340	MPC	13	4	20000	3	5	116500	128000
46	10	MOTOR YACHT 47	FB	MY	FBG	SV	IB	T485D	DD	15	5	44000	3	10	240000	264000
		1995 BOATS														
33	3	SEDAN BRIDGE 31	FB	SDN	FBG	SV	IB	T270-T370		11	10	16000	2	10	71000	82900
33	3	SEDAN BRIDGE 31	FB	SDN	FBG	SV	IB	T275D-T315D		11	10	16000	2	10	101500	115500
39	6	MOTOR YACHT 37	FB	MY	FBG	SV	IB	T340	MPC	13	5	21000	3	7	103000	113000
		IB T370 MPC 104000 114500, IB T275D MPC 119000 130500, IB T315D YAN													121500	133500
		IB T350D CAT 127500 140500														
43	2	SEDAN BRIDGE 40	FB	SDN	FBG	SV	IB	T340	MPC	13	4	20000	3	5	112000	123000
43	2	SEDAN BRIDGE 40	FB	SDN	FBG	SV	IB	T370	MPC	13	4	20000	3	5	113000	124000
43	2	SEDAN BRIDGE 40	FB	SDN	FBG	SV	IB	T315D	YAN	13	4	20000	3	5	130000	143000
46	10	MOTOR YACHT 47	FB	MY	FBG	SV	IB	T485D	DD	15	5	44000	3	10	230000	253000
		1994 BOATS														
33	3	SEDAN BRIDGE 31	FB	SDN	FBG	SV	IB	T245	MPC	11	10	16000	2	10	66100	72700
33	3	SEDAN BRIDGE 31	FB	SDN	FBG	SV	IB	T270-T365		11	10	16000	2	10	76800	84400
33	3	SEDAN BRIDGE 31	FB	SDN	FBG	SV	IB	T315D	YAN	11	10	16000	2	10	100000	110000
34	11	CONVERTIBLE 35	FB	CNV	FBG	SV	IB	T320-T365		12	8	16000	2	10	76300	85800
34	11	CONVERTIBLE 35	FB	CNV	FBG	SV	IB	T315D	YAN	12	8	16000	2	10	96400	106000
40	7	SEDAN BRIDGE 40	FB	SDN	FBG	SV	IB	T320	MPC	13	6	20000	3	6	105500	116000
40	7	SEDAN BRIDGE 40	FB	SDN	FBG	SV	IB	T365	MPC	13	6	20000	3	6	107000	117500
40	7	SEDAN BRIDGE 40	FB	SDN	FBG	SV	IB	T315D	YAN	13	6	20000	3	6	124000	136000
46	10	MOTOR YACHT 47	FB	MY	FBG	SV	IB	T485D	DD	15	5	44000	3	6	220500	242500
		1993 BOATS														
34	11	CONVERTIBLE 35	FB	CNV	FBG	SV	IB	T320	CRUS	12	8	16000	2	10	72600	79800
34	11	CONVERTIBLE 35	FB	CNV	FBG	SV	IB	T300D	J&T	12	8	16000	2	10	90800	99800
36	5	EXPRESS 36	OP	EXP	FBG	SV	IB	T320	CRUS	12	5	13500	2	8	69400	76300
36	5	EXPRESS 36	OP	EXP	FBG	SV	IB	T300D	J&T	12	5	14400	2	8	84000	92300
39	2	EXPRESS 39	OP	EXP	FBG	SV	IB	T380	CRUS	14	1	16000	3	4	80000	87900
39	2	EXPRESS 39	OP	EXP	FBG	SV	IB	T300D	J&T	14	1	16900	3	4	96900	106500
40	6	SEDAN BRIDGE 40	FB	SDN	FBG	SV	IB	T320	CRUS	13	6	20000	3	6	101000	111000
40	6	SEDAN BRIDGE 40	FB	SDN	FBG	SV	IB	T300D	J&T	13	6	20000	3	6	117000	128500
		1992 BOATS														
34	11	CONVERTIBLE 35	FB	CNV	FBG	SV	IB	T320	CRUS	12	8	16000	2	10	68900	75700
34	11	CONVERTIBLE 35	FB	CNV	FBG	SV	IB	T300D	J&T	12	8	16900	2	10	88700	97500
36	5	EXPRESS 36	OP	EXP	FBG	SV	IB	T320	CRUS	12	5	13500	2	8	66200	72700
36	5	EXPRESS 36	OP	EXP	FBG	SV	IB	T300D	J&T	12	5	14400	2	8	80100	88000
36	5	SEDAN BRIDGE 36	FB	SDN	FBG	SV	IB	T320	CRUS	12	5	16750	2	8	75800	83300
36	5	SEDAN BRIDGE 36	FB	SDN	FBG	SV	IB	T300D	J&T	12	5	17650	2	8	92300	101500
39	2	EXPRESS 39	OP	EXP	FBG	SV	IB	T380	CRUS	14	1	16000	3	4	76300	83800
39	2	EXPRESS 39	OP	EXP	FBG	SV	IB	T300D	J&T	14	1	16900	3	4	92400	101500
40	6	SEDAN BRIDGE 40	FB	SDN	FBG	SV	IB	T320	CRUS	13	6	20000	3	6	96400	106000

LOA FT	LOA IN	NAME AND/ OR MODEL	TOP/ RIG	BOAT TYPE	-HULL- MTL	-HULL- TP	TP	# HP	MFG	BEAM FT	BEAM IN	WGT LBS	DRAFT FT	DRAFT IN	RETAIL LOW	RETAIL HIGH
		1992 BOATS														
40	6	SEDAN BRIDGE 40	FB	SDN	FBG	SV	IB	T300D	J&T	13	6	20000	3	6	111500	122500
40	11	CONVERTIBLE 41	FB	CNV	FBG	SV	IB	T320	CRUS	14	5	22000	3	6	100500	110500
40	11	CONVERTIBLE 41	FB	CNV	FBG	SV	IB	T380	CRUS	14	5	22000	3	6	104500	114500
40	11	CONVERTIBLE 41	FB	CNV	FBG	SV	IB	T425D	CAT	14	5	23000	3	6	136500	150000
46	10	MOTOR YACHT 47	HT	MY	FBG	SV	IB	T485D	J&T	15	5	44000	3	10	201500	221500
		1991 BOATS														
34	11	COCKPIT 35	FB	SDN	FBG	SV	IB	T315	CRUS	12	8	16000	2	10	65300	71700
34	11	COCKPIT 35	FB	SDN	FBG	SV	IB	T300D	J&T	12	8	16000	2	10	82700	90900
36		OPEN 35	OP	EXP	FBG	SV	IB	T315	CRUS	12	5	13500	2	8	61900	68100
36	5	OPEN 35	OP	EXP	F/S	SV	IB	T300D	GM	12	10	14000	2	8	73500	80800
36	5	OPEN BRIDGE 35	FB	SDN	F/S	SV	IB	T310	CRUS	12	10	16750	2	8	70700	77700
36	5	OPEN BRIDGE 35	FB	SDN	F/S	SV	IB	T300D	GM	12	10	17000	2	8	84600	92900
39	2	OPEN 39	FB	EXP	FBG	SV	IB	T360	CRUS	14	1	18000	3	4	79000	86800
39	2	OPEN 39	FB	EXP	FBG	SV	IB	T300D	J&T	14	1	18000	3	4	92000	101000
40	11	COCKPIT 41	FB	SDN	FBG	SV	IB	T375D	CAT	14	1	22000	3	6	122000	134000
		1990 BOATS														
34	11	COCKPIT 35	FB	SDN	FBG	SV	IB	T315	CRUS	12	8	16000	2	10	62100	68200
34	11	COCKPIT 35	FB	SDN	FBG	SV	IB	T300D	J&T	12	8	16000	2	10	79000	86800
36		OPEN 35	OP	EXP	FBG	SV	IB	T315	CRUS	12	5	13500	2	8	59100	65000
39	2	OPEN 39	FB	EXP	FBG	SV	IB	T360	CRUS	14	1	18000	3	4	75400	82800
39	2	OPEN 39	FB	EXP	FBG	SV	IB	T300D	J&T	14	1	18000	3	4	87900	96500
40	11	COCKPIT 41	FB	SDN	FBG	SV	IB	T315	CRUS	14	1	22000	3	6	94200	103500
40	11	COCKPIT 41	FB	SDN	FBG	SV	IB	T375D	CAT	14	1	22000	3	6	116000	127500
40	11	DOUBLE CABIN 41	FB	DC	FBG	SV	IB	T315	CRUS	14	1	23000	3	6	96600	106000
40	11	DOUBLE CABIN 41	FB	DC	FBG	SV	IB	T375D	CAT	14	1	23000	3	6	120500	132500
40	11	GRAND SALON 41	FB	MY	FBG	SV	IB	T315	CRUS	14	1	23000	3	6	96500	106000
40	11	GRAND SALON 41	FB	MY	FBG	SV	IB	T375D	CAT	14	1	23000	3	6	120500	132500
46	10	MOTOR YACHT 47	FB	MY	FBG	SV	IB	T465D	J&T	15	5	44000	4	10	179500	197500
		1989 BOATS														
34	11	COCKPIT 35	FB	SDN	FBG	SV	IB	T350	CRUS	12	8	16000	2	10	60200	66100
34	11	COCKPIT 35	FB	SDN	FBG	SV	IB	T300D	J&T	12	8	16000	2	10	75600	83000
36	2	DOUBLE CABIN	FB	DC	FBG	DS	IB	T270	CRUS	13		20000	3		67500	74200
39	2	OPEN 39	FB	EXP	FBG	SV	IB	T400	CRUS	14	1	18000	3	4	73500	80800
39	2	OPEN 39	FB	EXP	FBG	SV	IB	T300D	J&T	14	1	18000	3	4	83900	92200
40	11	COCKPIT 41	FB	SDN	FBG	SV	IB	T350	CRUS	14	1	22000	3	6	91200	100000
40	11	COCKPIT 41	FB	SDN	FBG	SV	IB	T375D	CAT	14	1	22000	3	6	111000	122000
40	11	DOUBLE CABIN 41	FB	DC	FBG	SV	IB	T375D	CAT	14	1	23000	3	6	115000	126500
40	11	DOUBLE CABIN 41	FB	SDN	FBG	SV	IB	T350	CRUS	14	1	23000	3	6	94700	104000
40	11	GRAND SALON 41	FB	MY	FBG	SV	IB	T350	CRUS	14	1	23000	3	6	93800	103000
40	11	GRAND SALON 41	FB	MY	FBG	SV	IB	T375D	CAT	14	1	23000	3	6	115000	126500
		1988 BOATS														
34	11	MEDITERRANEAN 35	FB	CR	FBG	DS	IB	T350	CRUS	12	9	16000	2	10	54700	60100
36	2	NANTUCKET 36 DC	FB	TRWL	FBG	DS	IB	T270	CRUS	13		20000	3		66900	73500
36	2	NANTUCKET 36 DC	FB	TRWL	FBG	DS	IB	T250D	J&T	13		20000	3		79200	87000
36	2	NANTUCKET 36 SDN	FB	SDN	FBG	DS	IB	T270	CRUS	13		20000	3		65800	72300
36	2	NANTUCKET 36 SDN	FB	SDN	FBG	DS	IB	T250D	J&T	13		20000	3		77000	84600
40		NANTUCKET 40	FB	TRWL	FBG	DS	IB	T350	CRUS	14		23400	3	4	88800	97600
40		NANTUCKET 40	FB	TRWL	FBG	DS	IB	T250D	J&T	14		23400	3	4	98100	108000
		1987 BOATS														
34		MAINSHIP 34 III	FB	TRWL	FBG	DS	IB	220D	J&T	11	11	14000	2	10	56400	61900
36		MAINSHIP 36	FB	TRWL	FBG	DS	IB	T270	CRUS	13		19700	2	3	62800	69000
36		MAINSHIP 36	FB	TRWL	FBG	DS	IB	T220D	J&T	13		19700	2	3	73100	80400
40		MAINSHIP 40	FB	TRWL	FBG	DS	IB	T350	CRUS	14		23400	3	4	85000	93400
40		MAINSHIP 40	FB	TRWL	FBG	DS	IB	T220D	J&T	14		23400	3	4	92500	101500
		1986 BOATS														
34		MAINSHIP 34 III	FB	TRWL	FBG	DS	IB	220D	J&T	11	11	14000	2	10	59400	65300
36		MAINSHIP 36 DC	FB	TRWL	FBG	DS	IB	T270	CRUS	13		19700	2	3	63100	69400
36		MAINSHIP 36 DC	FB	TRWL	FBG	DS	IB	T220D	J&T	13		19700	2	3	73500	80700
36	2	MAINSHIP 36	FB	TRWL	FBG	DV	IB	T270	CRUS	13		19700	2	3	60700	66700
36	2	MAINSHIP 36	FB	TRWL	FBG	DV	IB	T220D	J&T	13		19700	2	3	70400	77400
40		MAINSHIP 40	FB	TRWL	FBG	DV	IB	T200D	PERK	14		23400	3	4	89000	97800
40		MAINSHIP 40 DC	FB	TRWL	FBG	DS	IB	T350	CRUS	14		23400	3	4	85400	93800
40		MAINSHIP 40 DC	FB	TRWL	FBG	DS	IB	T220D	J&T	14		23400	3	4	92900	102000
		1985 BOATS														
34		MAINSHIP 34 III	FB	TRWL	FBG	DS	IB	270	CRUS	11	11	14000	2	10	46200	50700
34		MAINSHIP 34 III	FB	TRWL	FBG	DS	IB	200D	PERK	11	11	14000	2	10	56600	62200
36		MAINSHIP 36 DC	FB	TRWL	FBG	DS	IB	T270	CRUS	13		19700	2	3	60400	66400
36		MAINSHIP 36 DC	FB	TRWL	FBG	DS	IB	T200D	PERK	13		19700	2	3	70100	77000
40		MAINSHIP 40 DC	FB	TRWL	FBG	DS	IB	T350	CRUS	14		23400	3	4	81700	89800
40		MAINSHIP 40 DC	FB	TRWL	FBG	DS	IB	T200D	PERK	14		23400	3	4	89500	98300
		1984 BOATS														
34		MAINSHIP 34 III	FB	TRWL	FBG	DS	IB	200D	PERK	11	11	14000	2	10	54300	59700
34		MAINSHIP 34 III	FB	TRWL	FBG	DS	IB	T270	CRUS	11	11	14000	2	10	48300	53100
36		MAINSHIP 36 DC	FB	TRWL	FBG	DS	IB	T270	CRUS	13		19700	2	3	57900	63600
36		MAINSHIP 36 DC	FB	TRWL	FBG	DS	IB	T200D	PERK	13		19700	2	3	67200	73800
40		MAINSHIP 40 DC	FB	TRWL	FBG	DS	IB	T350	CRUS	14		23400	3	4	78300	86100
40		MAINSHIP 40 DC	FB	TRWL	FBG	DS	IB	T200D	PERK	14		23400	3	4	85700	94200

....For earlier years, see the BUC Used Boat Price Guide, Volume 3

MAJEK BOATS

CORPUS CHRISTI TX 78414 COAST GUARD MFG ID- MJK See inside cover to adjust price for area

For more recent years, see the BUC Used Boat Price Guide, Volume 1

LOA FT	LOA IN	NAME AND/ OR MODEL	TOP/ RIG	BOAT TYPE	-HULL- MTL	-HULL- TP	TP	# HP	MFG	BEAM FT	BEAM IN	WGT LBS	DRAFT FT	DRAFT IN	RETAIL LOW	RETAIL HIGH
		1996 BOATS														
16		TEXAS SKIFF TUNNEL		CTRCN	FBG		OB			7	6	750			2300	2700
18		18 REDFISH TUNNEL		CTRCN	FBG		OB			7	6	850			2750	3250
18		18 SKIFF FLAT BOTTOM		CTRCN	FBG		OB			6	8	950			3050	3550
20		20 V TUNNEL		CTRCN	FBG		OB			7	11	1300			4500	5150
21		21 REDFISH TUNNEL		CTRCN	FBG		OB			7	10	1150			4150	4800
23		23 SKIFF FLAT BOTTOM		CTRCN	FBG		OB			8		1800			6450	7400
		1995 BOATS														
16		TEXAS SKIFF TUNNEL		CTRCN	FBG		OB			7	6	750			2200	2550
18		18 REDFISH TUNNEL		CTRCN	FBG		OB			7	6	850			2650	3100
18		18 SKIFF		CTRCN	FBG		OB			6	8	950			2900	3400
20		20 V TUNNEL		CTRCN	FBG		OB			7	11	1300			4250	4950
21		21 REDFISH TUNNEL		CTRCN	FBG		OB			7	10	1150			3950	4600
23		23 SKIFF FLAT BOTTOM		CTRCN	FBG		OB			8		1800			6150	7050
		1994 BOATS														
16		TEXAS SKIFF TUNNEL		CTRCN	FBG		OB			7	6	750			2050	2450
17		17.5 REDFISH TUNNEL		CTRCN	FBG		OB			7	6	950			2700	3150
18		18 REDFISH TUNNEL		CTRCN	FBG		OB			7	6	850			2550	2950
18		18 SKIFF		CTRCN	FBG		OB			6	8	950			2800	3250
20		20V TUNNELL		CTRCN	FBG		OB			7	11	1300			4050	4700
21		21 REDFISH TUNNEL		CTRCN	FBG		OB			7	10	1150			3750	4400
23		23 SKIFF FLAT BOTTOM		CTRCN	FBG		OB			8		1800			5850	6750
		1993 BOATS														
16		TEXAS SKIFF TUNNEL		CTRCN	FBG		OB			7	6	750			1950	2350
17		17.5 REDFISH TUNNEL		CTRCN	FBG		OB			7	6	950			2600	3000
18		18 REDFISH TUNNEL		CTRCN	FBG		OB			7	6	850			2400	2800
18		18 SKIFF		CTRCN	FBG		OB			6	8	950			2650	3100
20		20 V		CTRCN	FBG		OB			7	11	1300			3900	4500
21		21 REDFISH TUNNEL		CTRCN	FBG		OB			7	10	1150			3600	4200
23		23 SKIFF FLAT BOTTOM		CTRCN	FBG		OB			8		1800			5650	6450
		1992 BOATS														
16		TEXAS SKIFF TUNNEL		CTRCN	FBG		OB			7	6	750			1900	2250
17		17.5 REDFISH TUNNEL		CTRCN	FBG		OB			7	6	950			2500	2900
18		18 REDFISH TUNNEL		CTRCN	FBG		OB			7	6	850			2350	2700
18		18 SKIFF		CTRCN	FBG		OB			6	8	950			2550	3000
21		21 REDFISH TUNNEL		CTRCN	FBG		OB			7	10	1150			3450	4050
23		23 SKIFF FLAT BOTTOM		CTRCN	FBG		OB			8		1800			5400	6200

MAJESTIC YACHTS INC

FT LAUDERDALE FL 33008 See inside cover to adjust price for area

For more recent years, see the BUC Used Boat Price Guide, Volume 1

LOA FT	LOA IN	NAME AND/ OR MODEL	TOP/ RIG	BOAT TYPE	-HULL- MTL	-HULL- TP	TP	# HP	MFG	BEAM FT	BEAM IN	WGT LBS	DRAFT FT	DRAFT IN	RETAIL LOW	RETAIL HIGH
		1996 BOATS														
38	3	DOUBLE CABIN	FB	DCMY	FBG	SV	IB	220D	CAT	12	8	20000	3	4	233000	256000
41	10	DOUBLE CABIN	FB	DCMY	FBG	SV	IB	T220D	CAT	13	8	24000	3	6	324000	356000
46	3	AFT COCKPIT	FB	DCMY	FBG	SV	IB	T375D	CAT	14	6	35000	3	10	366500	403000
46	3	PILOTHOUSE	FB	PH	FBG	SV	IB	T375D	CAT	14	6	35000	3	10	380000	417500
46	3	WIDE AFT DECK	FB	DCMY	FBG	SV	IB	T375D	CAT	14	6	35000	3	10	366500	403000
56	4	DOUBLE CABIN	FB	PH	FBG	SV	IB	T650D	GM	17	3	64000	3	6	553000	607500
58		MAJESTIC 58 PH	FB	TCMY	FBG	SV	IB	T650D	GM	17	6	64000	3	7	554500	609500
65		MOTORYACHT	FB	TCMY	FBG	SV	IB	T770D	GM	17	8	85000	4	10	518500	569500
66		MAJESTIC 66 PH	FB	TCMY	FBG	SV	IB	T770D	GM	17	6	84000	3	7	528000	580500
72		AFT COCKPIT	FB	TCMY	FBG	SV	IB	T770D	GM	17	8	86000	4	10	**	**
		1995 BOATS														
38	3	DOUBLE CABIN	FB	DCMY	FBG	SV	IB	220D	CAT	12	8	20000	3	4	219500	241000
41	10	DOUBLE CABIN	FB	DCMY	FBG	SV	IB	T220D	CAT	13	8	24000	3	6	305000	335500
46	3	AFT COCKPIT	FB	DCMY	FBG	SV	IB	T375D	CAT	14	6	35000	3	10	347000	381000
46	3	PILOTHOUSE	FB	PH	FBG	SV	IB	T375D	CAT	14	6	35000	3	10	359500	395000
46	3	WIDE AFT DECK	FB	DCMY	FBG	SV	IB	T375D	CAT	14	6	35000	3	10	347000	381000
56	4	DOUBLE CABIN	FB	PH	FBG	SV	IB	T650D	GM	17	3	64000	3	6	521500	573000
65		MOTORYACHT	FB	TCMY	FBG	SV	IB	T770D	GM	17	8	85000	4	10	483000	530500
72		AFT COCKPIT	FB	TCMY	FBG	SV	IB	T770D	GM	17	8	86000	4	10	**	**

CONTINUED ON NEXT PAGE

LOA FT	IN	NAME AND/ OR MODEL	TOP/ RIG	BOAT TYPE	-HULL- MTL	TP	----ENGINE--- TP	# HP	MFG	BEAM FT	IN	WGT LBS	DRAFT FT	IN	RETAIL LOW	RETAIL HIGH
		1994 BOATS														
38	3	DOUBLE CABIN	FB	DCMY	FBG	SV	IB	220D	CAT	12	8	20000	3	4	207500	228000
41	10	DOUBLE CABIN	FB	DCMY	FBG	SV	IB	T220D	CAT	13	8	24000	3	6	288000	316500
46	3	AFT COCKPIT	FB	DCMY	FBG	SV	IB	T375D	CAT	14	6	35000	3	10	328000	360500
46	3	PILOTHOUSE	FB	PH	FBG	SV	IB	T375D	CAT	14	6	35000	3	10	340000	373500
46	3	WIDE AFT DECK	FB	DCMY	FBG	SV	IB	T375D	CAT	14	6	35000	3	10	328000	360500
56	4	DOUBLE CABIN	FB	PH	FBG	SV	IB	T650D	GM	17	3	64000	3	6	481500	529000
65		MOTORYACHT	FB	TCMY	FBG	SV	IB	T770D	GM	17	8	85000	4	10	453500	498500
72		AFT COCKPIT	FB	TCMY	FBG	SV	IB	T770D	GM	17	8	86000	4	10	**	**
		1993 BOATS														
38	3	DOUBLE CABIN	FB	DCMY	FBG	SV	IB	220D	CAT	12	8	20000	3	4	196000	215000
41	10	DOUBLE CABIN	FB	DCMY	FBG	SV	IB	T220D	CAT	13	8	24000	3	6	272000	298500
46	3	AFT COCKPIT	FB	DCMY	FBG	SV	IB	T375D	CAT	14	6	35000	3	10	310000	340500
46	3	PILOTHOUSE	FB	PH	FBG	SV	IB	T375D	CAT	14	6	35000	3	10	321000	353000
46	3	WIDE AFT DECK	FB	DCMY	FBG	SV	IB	T375D	CAT	14	6	35000	3	10	310000	340500
56	4	DOUBLE CABIN	FB	PH	FBG	SV	IB	T650D	GM	17	3	64000	3	6	450000	494500
65		MOTORYACHT	FB	TCMY	FBG	SV	IB	T770D	GM	17	8	85000	4	10	419000	460500
72		AFT COCKPIT	FB	TCMY	FBG	SV	IB	T770D	GM	17	8	86000	4	10	**	**
		1992 BOATS														
46	3	AFT COCKPIT	FB	DCMY	FBG	SV	IB	T375D	CAT	14	6	35000	3	10	293000	322000
46	3	PILOTHOUSE	FB	PH	FBG	SV	IB	T375D	CAT	14	6	35000	3	10	303000	333000
46	3	WIDE AFT DECK	FB	DCMY	FBG	SV	IB	T375D	CAT	14	6	35000	3	10	293000	322000
65		MOTORYACHT	FB	TCMY	FBG	SV	IB	T770D	GM	17	8	85000	4	10	391000	430000
72		AFT COCKPIT	FB	TCMY	FBG	SV	IB	T770D	GM	17	8	86000	4	10	**	**
		1991 BOATS														
46	3	M46-AFT COCKPIT	FB	YTFS	FBG	SV	IB	T375D	CAT	14	6	35000	3	10	223500	246000
46	3	M46-WIDE AFT DECK	FB	MY	FBG	SV	IB	T375D	CAT	14	6	35000	3	10	224000	246000
46	3	M46P-PILOTHOUSE	FB	PH	FBG	SV	IB	T375D	CAT	14	6	35000	3	10	236000	259500
65	10	MOTORYACHT	FB	MY	FBG	SV	IB	T770D	GM	17	8	85000	4	10	366500	403000
70	10	AFT COCKPIT	FB	YTFS	FBG	SV	IB	T770D	GM	17	8	88000	4	10	450000	494500
		1990 BOATS														
46	3	M46-AFT COCKPIT	FB	YTFS	FBG	SV	IB	T375D	CAT	14	6	35000	3	10	213500	234500
46	3	M46-WIDE AFT DECK	FB	MY	FBG	SV	IB	T375D	CAT	14	6	35000	3	10	213500	235000
		1989 BOATS														
46	3	M46-AFT COCKPIT	FB	YTFS	FBG	SV	IB	T375D	CAT	14	6	35000	3	10	204000	224000
46	3	M46-WIDE AFT DECK	FB	MY	FBG	SV	IB	T375D	CAT	14	6	35000	3	10	204000	224500
		1988 BOATS														
46	3	M46-AFT COCKPIT	FB	YTFS	FBG	SV	IB	T375D	CAT	14	6	35000	3	10	195000	214000
46	3	M46-WIDE AFT DECK	FB	MY	FBG	SV	IB	T375D	CAT	14	6	35000	3	10	195000	214500
		1987 BOATS														
46	3	M46-AFT COCKPIT	FB	YTFS	FBG	SV	IB	T375D	CAT	14	6	35000	3	10	186500	205000
46	3	M46-WIDE AFT DECK	FB	MY	FBG	SV	IB	T375D	CAT	14	6	35000	3	10	186500	205000
		1986 BOATS														
46	3	M46-AFT COCKPIT	FB	YTFS	FBG	SV	IB	T375D	CAT	14	6	35000	3	10	178500	196000
46	3	M46-WIDE AFT DECK	FB	MY	FBG	SV	IB	T375D	CAT	14	6	35000	3	10	178500	196000
		1984 BOATS														
39		MAJESTIC 39	SLP	SA/CR	FBG	KL	IB	50D		12		19500	5		114500	126000

MAKO BOATS

SPRINGFIELD MO 65803 COAST GUARD MFG ID- MRK See inside cover to adjust price for area

For more recent years, see the BUC Used Boat Price Guide, Volume 1

LOA FT	IN	NAME AND/ OR MODEL	TOP/ RIG	BOAT TYPE	-HULL- MTL	TP	----ENGINE--- TP	# HP	MFG	BEAM FT	IN	WGT LBS	DRAFT FT	IN	RETAIL LOW	RETAIL HIGH
		1996 BOATS														
16	9	MAKO 171 FLATS	OP	CTRCN	FBG	SV	OB			7	3	850		6	3700	4300
17		MAKO 171 ANGLER	OP	CTRCN	FBG	SV	OB			7		1250		9	5250	6050
17	3	MAKO 17 CC	OP	CTRCN	FBG	SV	OB			7	2	1250		9	5300	6100
17	10	MAKO 181 FLATS	OP	CTRCN	FBG	SV	OB			8		995		7	4450	5100
19		MAKO 19 CC	OP	CTRCN	FBG	SV	OB			8		1900		9	7350	8450
19	10	MAKO 205 DELUXE	OP	B/R	FBG	SV	OB			8		2000	1	1	8600	9900
20	4	MAKO 201 DELUXE	OP	CTRCN	FBG	DV	OB			8		2150		11	9200	10400
20	4	MAKO 201 DELUXE	OP	CTRCN	FBG	SV	OB			8		2150		11	9200	10400
21	9	MAKO 223 WA	OP	CUD	FBG	SV	OB			8		2700	1	1	12200	13900
21	10	MAKO 22 CC	OP	CTRCN	FBG	SV	OB			8		2600	1	1	11500	13000
21	10	MAKO 225 DELUXE	OP	B/R	FBG	SV	OB			8		2400	1	1	11700	13300
22	8	MAKO 231 DELUXE	OP	CTRCN	FBG	SV	OB			8		2600	1	1	11400	12900
22	8	MAKO 232 DELUXE	OP	CTRCN	FBG	SV	OB			8		2600	1	1	12400	14100
22	9	MAKO 232 DELUXE	OP	CTRCN	FBG	SV	OB			8		2600	1	1	12400	14100
23		MAKO 236 DELUXE	OP	CTRCN	FBG	SV	IB	260		8		3800	2		22500	25000
23		MAKO 236 DELUXE	OP	CTRCN	FBG	SV	IB	170D-210D		8		3800	2		30200	34400
23	11	MAKO 243 DELUXE	OP	CUD	FBG	SV	OB			8	6	3000	1	2	14800	16800
24	4	MAKO 241 DELUXE	OP	CTRCN	FBG	SV	OB			8	6	3800	1	4	17200	19500
24	6	MAKO 243 WA	OP	CUD	FBG	SV	OB			8	6	3000	1	4	15200	17300
24	10	MAKO 231 DELUXE	OP	CTRCN	FBG	SV	OB			8		2600	1	1	11200	12700
25	7	MAKO 251 DELUXE	OP	CTRCN	FBG	SV	OB			8		3400	1	2	17500	19900
26		MAKO 261 DELUXE	OP	CTRCN	FBG	SV	OB			8	6	3900	1	4	19500	21700
26	2	MAKO 262 DELUXE	OP	CTRCN	FBG	SV	OB			8	6	3800	1	4	19700	21900
27	9	MAKO 263 DELUXE	OP	CUD	FBG	SV	OB			8	6	4000	1	4	21500	23800
28	1	MAKO 282 DELUXE	OP	CTRCN	FBG	SV	OB			8	6	4100	1	4	26400	29300
28	5	MAKO 286 DELUXE	OP	CUD	FBG	SV	IB	T250-T260		9	10	8000	2	6	50500	56200
28	5	MAKO 286 DELUXE	OP	CUD	FBG	SV	IB	T170D-T250D		9	10	8000	2	6	63200	77000
30	10	MAKO 293 DELUXE	OP	CUD	FBG	SV	OB			9	6	5000	1	7	28600	31800
33	3	MAKO 295 CC	OP	CUD	FBG	SV	OB			10		6800	1	9	37400	41500
33	3	MAKO 295 FD	OP	CUD	FBG	SV	OB			10		6800	1	9	37700	41900
		1995 BOATS														
16	9	MAKO 171 FLATS	OP	CTRCN	FBG	SV	OB			7	3	850		6	3500	4100
17		MAKO 171 ANGLER	OP	CTRCN	FBG	SV	OB			7		1250		9	4900	5650
17	3	MAKO 17 CC	OP	CTRCN	FBG	SV	OB			7	2	1250		9	4950	5700
17	10	MAKO 181 FLATS	OP	CTRCN	FBG	SV	OB			8		995		7	4150	4800
19		MAKO 19 CC	OP	CTRCN	FBG	SV	OB			8		1900		9	6850	7900
19	10	MAKO 205 DELUXE	OP	B/R	FBG	SV	OB			8		2000	1	1	8000	9200
20	4	MAKO 201 DELUXE	OP	CTRCN	FBG	DV	OB			8		2150		11	8650	9950
20	4	MAKO 201 DELUXE	OP	CTRCN	FBG	SV	OB			8		2150		11	8650	9950
21	9	MAKO 223 WA	OP	CUD	FBG	SV	OB			8		2700	1	1	11600	13100
21	10	MAKO 22 CC	OP	CTRCN	FBG	SV	OB			8		2200	1	1	9600	10900
21	10	MAKO 225 DELUXE	OP	B/R	FBG	SV	OB			8		2400	1	1	11000	12500
22	8	MAKO 231 DELUXE	OP	CTRCN	FBG	SV	OB			8		2600	1	1	10600	12100
22	8	MAKO 232 DELUXE	OP	CTRCN	FBG	SV	OB			8		2600	1	1	12000	13600
23		MAKO 236 DELUXE	OP	CTRCN	FBG	SV	IB	260		8		3800	2		21300	23700
23		MAKO 236 DELUXE	OP	CTRCN	FBG	SV	IB	170D-210D		8		3800	2		28700	32700
23	11	MAKO 243 DELUXE	OP	CUD	FBG	SV	OB			8	6	3000	1	2	14000	15900
24	4	MAKO 241 DELUXE	OP	CTRCN	FBG	SV	OB			8	6	3800	1	4	16200	18400
25	4	MAKO 251 DELUXE	OP	CTRCN	FBG	SV	OB			8		3400	1	2	15900	18100
25	7	MAKO 251 DELUXE	OP	CTRCN	FBG	SV	OB			8		3400	1	2	16500	18800
26		MAKO 261 DELUXE	OP	CTRCN	FBG	SV	OB			8	6	3900	1	4	18500	20500
26	2	MAKO 262 DELUXE	OP	CTRCN	FBG	SV	OB			8	6	3800	1	4	18800	20900
26	2	MAKO 263 DELUXE	OP	CUD	FBG	SV	OB			8	6	4000	1	4	20300	22500
28	1	MAKO 282 DELUXE	OP	CTRCN	FBG	SV	OB			8	6	4100	1	4	25000	27800
28	5	MAKO 286 DELUXE	OP	CUD	FBG	SV	IB	T250-T260		9	10	8000	2	6	47700	53100
28	5	MAKO 286 DELUXE	OP	CUD	FBG	SV	IB	T170D-T250D		9	10	8000	2	6	60000	73200
28	7	MAKO 293 DELUXE	OP	CUD	FBG	SV	OB			9	6	5000	1	7	27100	30200
31	3	MAKO 295 CC	OP	CUD	FBG	SV	OB			10		6800	1	9	35400	39400
31	3	MAKO 295 FD	OP	CUD	FBG	SV	OB			10		6800	1	9	35400	39400
		1994 BOATS														
16	9	MAKO 161 FLATS		CTRCN	FBG	SV	OB			7	3	850		6	3350	3850
17	3	MAKO 171 CLASSIC		CTRCN	FBG	SV	OB			7	2	1250		9	4750	5450
17	10	MAKO 171 ANGLER		CTRCN	FBG	SV	OB			7		1250		9	4800	5500
17	10	MAKO 181 FLATS		CTRCN	FBG	SV	OB			8		995		7	4000	4650
19	10	MAKO 191 CLASSIC		CTRCN	FBG	SV	OB			8		1900		9	6900	7950
19	10	MAKO 195 DUAL CONSLE		B/R	FBG	DV	OB			8		2000		10	7650	8800
20	4	MAKO 201 DELUXE		CTRCN	FBG	DV	OB			8		2150		11	8200	9450
21	9	MAKO 213 CLASSIC		CUD	FBG	DV	OB			8		2700	1	1	11000	12400
21	10	MAKO 211 CLASSIC		CTRCN	FBG	DV	OB			8		2200	1	1	9200	10400
21	10	MAKO 215 DUAL CONSLE		B/R	FBG	DV	OB			8		2300	1	1	10100	11500
22	8	MAKO 221 DELUXE		CTRCN	FBG	DV	OB			8		2600	1	1	10800	12300
22	8	MAKO 221B DLX W/BRK		CTRCN	FBG	DV	OB			8		2600	1	1	10800	12300
23		MAKO 236		FSH	FBG	SV	IB	260		8		3800	2		19800	22000
24	4	MAKO 241 DELUXE		CTRCN	FBG	DV	OB			8	6	3800	1	4	15200	17300
24	9	MAKO 233 WALKAROUND		CBNCR	FBG	DV	OB			8	6	3800	1	4	15700	17900
25	7	MAKO 251 DELUXE		CTRCN	FBG	DV	OB			8		3400	1	2	15600	17800
25	8	MAKO 253B WALKAROUND		CBNCR	FBG	DV	OB			8	6	4000	1	6	17500	19800
26		MAKO 261 DELUXE		CTRCN	FBG	DV	OB			8	6	3900	1	4	17400	19800
27	8	MAKO 273B WALKAROUND		CUD	FBG	DV	OB			8	6	4750	1	6	24200	26900
28	3	MAKO 290 RD CABIN		SF	FBG	SV	OB			10		7500	1	11	24200	26900
28	3	MAKO 295 FD CABIN		SF	FBG	SV	OB			10		6800	1	11	24200	26900
28	4	MAKO 261B DLX W/BRK		CTRCN	FBG	DV	OB			8	6	3900	1	4	24600	27300
28	5	MAKO 286		FSH	FBG	SV	IB	T520		9	10	8000	2	6	55700	61200
		1993 BOATS														
16	9	MAKO 161 FLATS		CTRCN	FBG	SV	OB			7	3	850		6	3150	3700
17		MAKO 171 ANGLER		CTRCN	FBG	SV	OB			7	2	1050		9	3850	4500
17	3	MAKO 171 CLASSIC		CTRCN	FBG	SV	OB			7	2	1250		9	4500	5200
17	10	MAKO 181 FLATS		CTRCN	FBG	SV	OB			8		995		7	3750	4350
19	10	MAKO 191 CLASSIC		CTRCN	FBG	SV	OB			8		1900		9	6600	7550
19	10	MAKO 195 DUAL CONSOL		B/R	FBG	DV	OB			8		2000		10	7250	8350
20	4	MAKO 201		CTRCN	FBG	DV	OB			8		2150		11	7800	8950
21	9	MAKO 213 CLASSIC		CUD	FBG	DV	OB			8		2700	1	1	10400	11800
21	10	MAKO 211 CLASSIC		CTRCN	FBG	DV	OB			8		2200	1	1	8700	10000
21	10	MAKO 215 DUAL CONSLE		B/R	FBG	DV	OB			8		2300	1	1	9650	10900
22	8	MAKO 221		B/R	FBG	DV	OB			8		2600	1	1	11000	12500

LOA FT	LOA IN	NAME AND/ OR MODEL	TOP/ RIG	BOAT TYPE	-HULL- MTL	-HULL- TP	ENGINE TP	ENGINE # HP	ENGINE MFG	BEAM FT	BEAM IN	WGT LBS	DRAFT FT	DRAFT IN	RETAIL LOW	RETAIL HIGH
		1993 BOATS														
22	8	MAKO 221B		CTRCN	FBG	DV	OB			8		2600	1	1	10300	11700
23		MAKO 236		FSH	FBG	SV	IB	260		8		3800	2		19000	21100
24	4	MAKO 241		CTRCN	FBG	DV	OB			8	6	3800	1	4	14500	16500
24	9	MAKO 233 WALKAROUND		CBNCR	FBG	DV	OB			8	6	3800	1	4	14900	17000
25	7	MAKO 251		CTRCN	FBG	DV	OB			8		3400	1	2	14900	16900
25	8	MAKO 253B WALKAROUND		CBNCR	FBG	DV	OB			8	6	4000	1	6	16600	18800
26		MAKO 261		CTRCN	FBG	DV	OB			8	6	3900	1	4	15500	17600
26		MAKO 261B		CTRCN	FBG	DV	OB			8	6	3900	1	4	17600	20000
27	8	MAKO 273B WALKAROUND		CUD	FBG	DV	OB			8	6	4750	1	6	23000	25600
28	3	MAKO 290		SF	FBG	SV	OB			10		7500	1	11	23100	25700
28	3	MAKO 295		SF	FBG	SV	OB			10		6800	1	11	23100	25700
28	5	MAKO 286		FSH	FBG	SV	IB	T520		9	10	8000	2	6	52800	58000
		1992 BOATS														
17	3	MAKO 171 ANGLER	OP	CTRCN	FBG	SV	OB			7	2	1250		9	5500	6350
17	3	MAKO 171 SPECIAL	OP	CTRCN	FBG	SV	OB			7	2	1250		9	3050	3550
17	10	MAKO 181 FLATS BOAT	OP	FSH	FBG	DV	OB			8		900		9	3250	3800
19		MAKO 191	OP	CTRCN	FBG	DV	OB			8		1900		9	5950	6850
20	3	MAKO 201	OP	CTRCN	FBG	SV	OB			8		2150		9	7400	8500
21	9	MAKO 210 WALKAROUND	OP	CUD	FBG	DV	OB			8		2700	1	1	9950	11300
21	10	MAKO 211	OP	CTRCN	FBG	DV	OB			8		2200	1	1	8300	9550
21	10	MAKO 215 DUAL CONSL	OP	B/R	FBG	DV	OB			8		2600	1	1	10000	11400
22	8	MAKO 221	OP	CTRCN	FBG	DV	OB			8		2600	1	1	9800	11100
22	8	MAKO 221B CTRCN	OP	CTRCN	FBG	DV	OB			8		2600	1	1	9800	11100
23		MAKO 230 WALKAROUND	OP	CUD	FBG	DV	OB			8		3100	1	2	11800	13400
23		MAKO 230B WALKAROUND	OP	CUD	FBG	DV	OB			8		3100	1	2	11800	13400
23		MAKO 236	OP	CTRCN	FBG	DV	IB	260	MRCR	8		3800	2		18000	20000
24	4	MAKO 241	OP	CTRCN	FBG	DV	OB			8	6	3800	1	4	13900	15700
25	7	MAKO 251	OP	CTRCN	FBG	DV	OB			8		3400	1	2	14200	16200
25	8	MAKO 250 WALKAROUND	OP	CUD	FBG	DV	OB			8	6	4000	1	6	15400	17500
25	8	MAKO 250B WALKAROUND	OP	CUD	FBG	DV	OB			8	6	4000	1	6	17100	19400
26		MAKO 261	OP	CTRCN	FBG	DV	OB			8	6	3900	1	4	14900	16900
26		MAKO 261B CC W/BRKT	OP	CTRCN	FBG	DV	OB			8	6	3900	1	4	16800	19100
27	8	MAKO 270B WA W/BRKT	OP	CUD	FBG	DV	OB			8	6	5100	1	4	21900	24300
		1991 BOATS														
17	3	MAKO 171 ANGLER	OP	CTRCN	FBG	SV	OB			7	2	1250		9	5250	6000
17	3	MAKO 171 SPECIAL	OP	CTRCN	FBG	SV	OB			7	2	1250		9	2950	3400
19		MAKO 191	OP	CTRCN	FBG	DV	OB			8		1900		9	5700	6550
20	3	MAKO 201	OP	CTRCN	FBG	SV	OB			8		2150		9	7100	8150
21	9	MAKO 210 WALKAROUND	OP	CUD	FBG	DV	OB			8		2700	1	1	9500	10800
21	10	MAKO 211	OP	CTRCN	FBG	DV	OB			8		2200	1	1	7950	9100
22	8	MAKO 221	OP	CTRCN	FBG	DV	OB			8		2600	1	1	9450	10700
23		MAKO 230 WALKAROUND	OP	CUD	FBG	DV	OB			8		3100	1	2	11200	12800
23		MAKO 230B WALKAROUND	OP	CUD	FBG	DV	OB			8		3100	1	2	11200	12800
23		MAKO 236	OP	CTRCN	FBG	DV	IB	260	MRCR	8		3800	2		16700	19000
23	2	MAKO 231	OP	CTRCN	FBG	DV	OB			8		2880	1	1	10400	11800
24	4	MAKO 241	OP	CTRCN	FBG	DV	OB			8	6	3800	1	4	13300	15100
25	7	MAKO 251	OP	CTRCN	FBG	DV	OB			8		3400	1	2	13700	15500
25	8	MAKO 250 WALKAROUND	OP	CUD	FBG	DV	OB			8	6	4000	1	6	14900	16900
25	8	MAKO 250B WALKAROUND	OP	CUD	FBG	DV	OB			8	6	4000	1	6	16100	18300
26		MAKO 261	OP	CTRCN	FBG	DV	OB			8	6	3900	1	4	15100	17200
27	8	MAKO 260 WALKAROUND	OP	CUD	FBG	DV	OB			8	6	4750	1	2	20200	22500
27	8	MAKO 260B WALKAROUND	OP	CUD	FBG	DV	OB			8	6	4750	1	2	21600	24000
28	5	MAKO 281	OP	CUD	FBG	DV	OB			9	10	6000	2		21500	23900
28	5	MAKO 285 TWN CONSOLE	OP	CUD	FBG	DV	OB			9	10	6000	1	8	22700	25200
28	5	MAKO 286 TWN CONSOLE	OP	CUD	FBG	DV	IB	T260	MRCR	9	10	8000	2	6	38700	43000
		1990 BOATS														
17	3	MAKO 171 ANGLER	OP	CTRCN	FBG	SV	OB			7	2	1250		7	4200	4850
17	3	MAKO 171 SPECIAL	OP	CTRCN	FBG	SV	OB			7	2	1250		7	3650	4200
19		MAKO 191	OP	CTRCN	FBG	DV	OB			8		1900		9	5450	6300
20	3	MAKO 201	OP	CTRCN	FBG	SV	OB			8		2150		9	6800	7850
21	6	MAKO 211	OP	CTRCN	FBG	DV	OB			8		2400	1	1	7950	9150
21	9	MAKO 210 WALKAROUND	OP	CUD	FBG	DV	OB			8		2500	1	1	8600	9900
22	8	MAKO 221	OP	CTRCN	FBG	DV	OB			8		2480	1	1	8700	10000
23		MAKO 230	OP	CUD	FBG	DV	OB			8		2800	1	2	10000	11400
23		MAKO 230B WALKAROUND	OP	CUD	FBG	DV	OB			8		2800	1	2	10000	11400
23		MAKO 230 WALKAROUND	OP	CUD	FBG	DV	IB	260	MRCR	8		3800	2		15900	18100
23	2	MAKO 231	OP	CTRCN	FBG	DV	OB			8		2880	1	1	10000	11300
24	4	MAKO 241	OP	CTRCN	FBG	DV	OB			8	6	3500	1	3	12100	13700
25	7	MAKO 251	OP	CTRCN	FBG	DV	OB			8		3200	1	6	12800	14600
25	8	MAKO 250 WALKAROUND	OP	CUD	FBG	DV	OB			8	6	4000	1	6	13800	15600
25	8	MAKO 250B WALKAROUND	OP	CUD	FBG	DV	OB			8	6	4000	1	6	15700	17900
26		MAKO 261	OP	CTRCN	FBG	DV	OB			8	6	3600	1	4	14300	16200
27	8	MAKO 260 WALKAROUND	OP	CUD	FBG	DV	OB			8	6	4750	1	2	18700	20800
27	8	MAKO 260B WALKAROUND	OP	CUD	FBG	DV	OB			8	6	4750	1	2	21500	23900
28	5	MAKO 281	OP	CUD	FBG	DV	OB			9	10	6000	1	8	20900	23300
28	5	MAKO 285 TWN CONSOLE	OP	CUD	FBG	DV	OB			9	10	6000	1	8	21600	24000
28	5	MAKO 286 TWN CONSOLE	OP	CUD	FBG	DV	IB	T260	MRCR	9	10	8000	2	6	36800	40900
		1989 BOATS														
17		MAKO 171 ANGLER	OP	CTRCN	FBG	SV	OB			7	2	1250		7	3750	4350
17	3	MAKO 171 SPECIAL	OP	CTRCN	FBG	SV	OB			7	2	1250		7	3750	4350
19	3	MAKO 191	OP	CTRCN	FBG	SV	OB			8		1900		9	5350	6100
20	2	MAKO 201	OP	CTRCN	FBG	SV	OB			8		2150		9	6500	7500
21	3	MAKO 210	OP	CUD	FBG	DV	OB			8		2620	1	1	8250	9500
21	5	MAKO 211	OP	CTRCN	FBG	DV	OB			8		2400	1	1	7650	8800
22	7	MAKO 220	OP	CUD	FBG	DV	OB			8		2500	1	1	8650	9950
22	7	MAKO 221	OP	CTRCN	FBG	DV	OB			8		2480	1	1	8350	9600
23	2	MAKO 231	OP	CTRCN	FBG	DV	OB			8		2880	1	1	9650	11000
23	2	MAKO 236	OP	CTRCN	FBG	DV	IB	260	MRCR	8		3800	2		15300	17400
24	6	MAKO 240	OP	CUD	FBG	DV	OB			8	6	3600	1	2	12300	14000
25	6	MAKO 251	OP	CTRCN	FBG	DV	OB			8		3200	1	6	12200	13900
25	7	MAKO 250	OP	CUD	FBG	DV	OB			8		3200	1	6	12900	14600
26		MAKO 230	OP	CUD	FBG	DV	OB			8		2800	1	2	13500	15300
26		MAKO 261	OP	CTRCN	FBG	DV	OB			8	6	3600	1	4	13800	15700
28	5	MAKO 281	OP	CTRCN	FBG	DV	OB			9	10	6000	1	8	20400	22600
28	5	MAKO 285 TWIN CONSLE	OP	CUD	FBG	DV	OB			9	10	6000	1	8	20500	22800
28	5	MAKO 286	OP	CUD	FBG	DV	IB	T260	MRCR	9	10	8000	2	6	35000	38900
30		MAKO 260	OP	CUD	FBG	DV	OB			8	6	3750	1	2	24300	27000
		1988 BOATS														
17		MAKO 171 ANGLER	OP	CTRCN	FBG	SV	OB			7	2	1250		7	3600	4200
17		MAKO 171 STANDARD	OP	CTRCN	FBG	SV	OB			7	2	1250		7	3550	4150
20	2	MAKO 201	OP	CTRCN	FBG	SV	OB			8		2150		9	6300	7250
21	5	MAKO 211	OP	CTRCN	FBG	DV	OB			8		2400	1	1	7400	8500
22	7	MAKO 220	OP	CUD	FBG	DV	OB			8		2500	1	1	8300	9550
22	7	MAKO 221	OP	CTRCN	FBG	DV	OB			8		2480	1	1	8050	9250
23	2	MAKO 231	OP	CTRCN	FBG	DV	OB			8		2880	1	1	9350	10600
23	2	MAKO 236	OP	CTRCN	FBG	DV	IB	260	MRCR	8		3800	2		14600	16600
24	6	MAKO 240	OP	CUD	FBG	DV	OB			8	6	3600	1	2	11800	13500
25	6	MAKO 251	OP	CTRCN	FBG	DV	OB			8		3200	1	6	11800	13500
25	7	MAKO 250	OP	CUD	FBG	DV	OB			8		3200	1	6	12400	14100
26		MAKO 230	OP	CUD	FBG	DV	OB			8		2800	1	2	13000	14800
26		MAKO 261	OP	CTRCN	FBG	DV	OB			8	6	3600	1	4	13300	15200
28	5	MAKO 281	OP	CTRCN	FBG	DV	OB			9	10	6000	1	8	19800	22000
28	5	MAKO 281	OP	CUD	FBG	DV	OB			9	10	6000	1	8	19500	21700
28	5	MAKO 285 TWIN CONSLE	OP	CUD	FBG	DV	OB			9	10	6000	1	8	20100	22400
28	5	MAKO 286	OP	CUD	FBG	DV	IB	T260	MRCR	9	10	8000	2	6	33400	37100
30		MAKO 260	OP	CUD	FBG	DV	OB			8	6	3750	1	2	23600	26200
		1987 BOATS														
17		MAKO 171 ANGLER	OP	CTRCN	FBG	SV	OB			7	2	1200		7	3400	3950
17		MAKO 172 STANDARD	OP	CTRCN	FBG	SV	OB			7	2	1200		7	3300	3850
20		MAKO 20C	OP	CTRCN	FBG	SV	OB			8		1775		9	5350	6100
21		MAKO 21B	OP	CTRCN	FBG	DV	OB			8		2100	1		6150	7050
21		MAKO 21C	OP	CTRCN	FBG	DV	OB			8		2100	1		6600	7600
22	6	MAKO 224	OP	CTRCN	FBG	DV	OB			8		2300	1	1	7350	8400
22	6	MAKO 228	OP	CUD	FBG	DV	OB			8		2300	1	1	7500	8600
23		MAKO 235	OP	CTRCN	FBG	DV	OB			8		2300	1		7450	8600
23		MAKO 236	OP	CTRCN	FBG	DV	IB	260	MRCR	8		3800	2		13800	15700
23		MAKO 236	OP	CTRCN	FBG	DV	IB	140D-165D		8		4000	2		19100	23500
23		MAKO 236	OP	CTRCN	FBG	DV	IB	200D	PERK	8		4000	2		22000	24400
23		MAKO 238	OP	CBNCR	FBG	DV	OB			8		2500	1	2	8050	9250
23	2	MAKO 231	OP	CTRCN	FBG	DV	OB			8		2880	1		9100	10300
24	6	MAKO 248	OP	CBNCR	FBG	DV	OB			8	6	2960	1		9850	11200
25	6	MAKO 254	OP	CTRCN	FBG	DV	OB			8		3000	1	2	11200	12700
25	6	MAKO 258	OP	CUD	FBG	DV	OB			8		3200	1	6	11800	13400
26	4	MAKO 261	OP	CTRCN	FBG	DV	OB			8	6	3600	1	4	13700	15600
28	5	MAKO 284	OP	CTRCN	FBG	DV	OB			9	10	6000	1	8	19200	21400
28	5	MAKO 285 TWIN CONSOL	OP	CUD	FBG	DV	OB			9	10	6000	1	8	19300	21400
28	5	MAKO 286 TWIN CONSLE	OP	CUD	FBG	DV	IB	T260	MRCR	9	10	6000	1	8	28900	32200
28	5	MAKO 286 TWIN CONSLE	OP	CUD	FBG	DV	IB	T 40D	VLVO	9	10	6000	1	8	24300	27000
		1986 BOATS														
17		MAKO 171 ANGLER	OP	CTRCN	FBG	SV	OB			7	2	1200		7	3250	3750
17		MAKO 172 STANDARD	OP	CTRCN	FBG	SV	OB			7	2	1200		7	3250	3750
20		MAKO 20B	OP	CTRCN	FBG	SV	OB			8		1775		9	5200	5950
21		MAKO 21	OP	CTRCN	FBG	DV	OB			8		2100	1		6200	7150
22	6	MAKO 224	OP	CTRCN	FBG	DV	OB			8		2300	1	1	7150	8200
22	6	MAKO 228	OP	CUD	FBG	DV	OB			8		2300	1	1	7250	8350
23		MAKO 235	OP	CTRCN	FBG	DV	OB			8		2300	1		7250	8350
23		MAKO 236	OP	CTRCN	FBG	DV	IB	260	MRCR	8		3800	2		13200	14900
23		MAKO 236	OP	CTRCN	FBG	DV	IB	140D-165D		8		4000	2		18300	22500
23		MAKO 236	OP	CTRCN	FBG	DV	IB	200D	PERK	8		4000	2		21100	23400
23		MAKO 238	OP	CBNCR	FBG	DV	OB			8		2500	1	2	7800	9000

CONTINUED ON NEXT PAGE

LOA FT	LOA IN	NAME AND/ OR MODEL	TOP/ RIG	BOAT TYPE	-HULL- MTL	-HULL- TP	ENGINE TP	ENGINE # HP	ENGINE MFG	BEAM FT	BEAM IN	WGT LBS	DRAFT FT	DRAFT IN	RETAIL LOW	RETAIL HIGH
		1986 BOATS														
23	2	MAKO 231	OP	CTRCN	FBG	DV	OB			8		2880	1		8850	10000
24	6	MAKO 248	OP	CTRCN	FBG	DV	OB			8	6	2960	1		9500	10800
25	6	MAKO 254	OP	CTRCN	FBG	DV	OB			8		3000	1	2	10900	12400
25	6	MAKO 258	OP	CUD	FBG	DV	OB			8		3200	1	6	11500	13000
26	4	MAKO 261	OP	CTRCN	FBG	DV	OB			8	6	3600	1	4	13400	15200
28	5	MAKO 284	OP	CTRCN	FBG	DV	OB			9	10	6000	1	8	18900	21100
28	5	MAKO 285 TWIN CONSOL	OP	CUD	FBG		OB			9	10	6000	1	8	19000	21100
		1985 BOATS														
17		MAKO 171 ANGLER	OP	CTRCN	FBG	SV	OB			7	2	1200		7	3150	3650
17		MAKO 172	OP	CTRCN	FBG	SV	OB			7	2	1200		7	3150	3650
20		MAKO 20C	OP	FSH	FBG	SV	OB			8		1775			5050	5800
21	3	MAKO 21B	OP	FSH	FBG	DV	OB			8		2100			6150	7050
22	6	MAKO 224	OP	CTRCN	FBG	DV	OB			8		2200	1	1	6700	7700
22	6	MAKO 228	OP	CUD	FBG	DV	OB			8		2300	1	1	7050	8100
23		MAKO 235	OP	CTRCN	FBG	DV	OB			8		2500	1		7600	8700
23		MAKO 236	OP	CTRCN	FBG	SV	IB	260		8		3800	2		12600	14300
23		MAKO 238	OP	CBNCR	FBG	DV	OB			8		2500	1	2	7600	8750
25	6	MAKO 254	OP	CTRCN	FBG	DV	OB			8		2800	1	2	10400	11800
25	6	MAKO 258	OP	CUD	FBG	DV	OB			8		3200	1	6	11100	12600
28	5	MAKO 284		CUD	FBG	DV	OB			9	10	6000	1	8	18500	20600
28	5	MAKO 285	OP	CUD	FBG	DV	OB			9	10	6000	1	8	18500	20600
		1984 BOATS														
17		MAKO 171 ANGLER	OP	CTRCN	FBG	SV	OB			7	2	1200		7	3100	3600
17		MAKO 172 STANDARD	OP	CTRCN	FBG	SV	OB			7	2	1200		7	3050	3550
20		MAKO 20B	OP	CTRCN	FBG	SV	OB			8		1775		9	4950	5700
21		MAKO 21	OP	CTRCN	FBG	DV	OB			8		2100	1		5900	6800
22	6	MAKO 224	OP	CTRCN	FBG	DV	OB			8		2300	1	1	6800	7800
22	6	MAKO 228	OP	CUD	FBG	DV	OB			8		2300	1	1	6850	7900
23		MAKO 235	OP	CTRCN	FBG	DV	OB			8		2300	1		6900	7950
23		MAKO 236	OP	CTRCN	FBG	DV	IB	260	MRCR	8		3800	2		12000	13600
23		MAKO 236	OP	CTRCN	FBG	DV	IB	140D	VLVO	8		4000	2		16500	18800
23		MAKO 236	OP	CTRCN	FBG	DV	IB	165D-200D		8		4000	2		18900	21600
23		MAKO 238	OP	CBNCR	FBG	DV	OB			8		2500	1	2	7450	8550
25	6	MAKO 254	OP	CTRCN	FBG	DV	OB			8		3000	1	2	10400	11900
25	6	MAKO 258	OP	CUD	FBG	DV	OB			8		3200	1	6	10800	12300
28	5	MAKO 284	OP	CTRCN	FBG	DV	OB			9	10	6000	1	8	18100	20100
28	5	MAKO 285 TWIN CONSOL	OP	CUD	FBG		OB			9	10	6000	1	8	18100	20100

....For earlier years, see the BUC Used Boat Price Guide, Volume 3

MALIBU BOATS INC

MERCED CA 95340-8463 COAST GUARD MFG ID- MB2 See inside cover to adjust price for area

For more recent years, see the BUC Used Boat Price Guide, Volume 1

LOA FT	LOA IN	NAME AND/ OR MODEL	TOP/ RIG	BOAT TYPE	-HULL- MTL	-HULL- TP	ENGINE TP	ENGINE # HP	ENGINE MFG	BEAM FT	BEAM IN	WGT LBS	DRAFT FT	DRAFT IN	RETAIL LOW	RETAIL HIGH
		1996 BOATS														
20		FLIGHTCRAFT BAREFOOT	OP	SKI	FBG	SV	OB			6	8	1805			10000	11400
20		MALIBU ECHELON	OP	SKI	FBG	SV	IB	265	MRCR	7	6	2500	1	4	12400	14100
20		MALIBU ECHELON LX	OP	SKI	FBG	SV	IB	265	MRCR	7	6	2600	1	4	12700	14400
20		MALIBU RESPONSE		SKI	FBG	SV	IB	265	MRCR	7	6	2450	1	6	12300	14000
20		MALIBU RESPONSE LX		SKI	FBG	SV	IB	265	MRCR	7	6	2450	1	6	12300	14000
20		MALIBU TANTRUM		SKI	FBG	SV	IB	265	MRCR	7	3	2100	1	6	9000	10200
21		MALIBU SUNSETTER		SKI	FBG	SV	IB	265	MRCR	7	9	2800	1	8	14300	16200
21		MALIBU SUNSETTER VLX		SKI	FBG	SV	IB	265	MRCR	7	9	2850	1	8	14400	16400
		1995 BOATS														
20		FLIGHTCRAFT BAREFOOT	OP	SKI	FBG	SV	OB			6	8	1805			9550	10800
20		FLIGHTCRAFT SPORT	OP	SKI	FBG	SV	IB	265	MRCR	6	8	2200	1	6	10300	11700
20		MALIBU ECHELON	OP	SKI	FBG	SV	IB	265	MRCR	7	6	2500	1	4	11700	13300
20		MALIBU ECHELON LX	OP	SKI	FBG	SV	IB	265	MRCR	7	6	2600	1	4	12000	13600
20		MALIBU RESPONSE		SKI	FBG	SV	IB	260	MRCR	7	6	2450	1	6	11600	13200
21		MALIBU SUNSETTER		SKI	FBG	SV	IB	260	MRCR	7	9	2800	1	8	13500	15300
		1994 BOATS														
19	6	EURO SKIER	OP	SKI	FBG	SV	IB	260	MRCR	7	2	2400	1	3	9450	10800
19	6	MALIBU SKIER	OP	SKI	FBG	SV	IB	260	MRCR	7	2	2350	1	3	9400	10700
20		ECHELON PRES LTD ED	OP	SKI	FBG	SV	IB	395	MRCR	7	6	2650	1	4	13000	14800
20		FLIGHTCRAFT BAREFOOT	OP	SKI	FBG	SV	OB			6	8	1805			9200	10400
20		FLIGHTCRAFT SPORT	OP	SKI	FBG	SV	IB	265	MRCR	6	8	2200	1	6	9750	11100
20		MALIBU ECHELON	OP	SKI	FBG	SV	IB	265	MRCR	7	6	2500	1	4	11100	12600
20		MALIBU ECHELON LX	OP	SKI	FBG	SV	IB	265	MRCR	7	6	2600	1	4	11300	12900
20	2	EURO SUNSETTER OPEN	OP	SKI	FBG	SV	IB	260	MRCR	7	6	2800	1	6	11900	13600
		1993 BOATS														
19	6	EURO SKIER	OP	SKI	FBG	SV	IB	260	MRCR	7	2	2400	1	3	9050	10300
19	6	MALIBU SKIER	OP	SKI	FBG	SV	IB	260	MRCR	7	2	2350	1	3	8950	10100
20		FLIGHTCRAFT BAREFOOT	OP	SKI	FBG	SV	OB			6	8	1805			8700	10000
20		FLIGHTCRAFT SPORT	OP	SKI	FBG	SV	IB	265	MRCR	6	8	2200	1	6	9300	10600
20		MALIBU ECHELON	OP	SKI	FBG	SV	IB	265	MRCR	7	6	2500	1	4	10500	12000
20		MALIBU ECHELON LX	OP	SKI	FBG	SV	IB	265	MRCR	7	6	2600	1	4	10800	12200
20	2	EURO SUNSETTER OPEN	OP	SKI	FBG	SV	IB	260	MRCR	7	6	2800	1	6	11300	12900
		1992 BOATS														
19	6	EURO SKIER	OP	SKI	FBG	SV	IB	260	MRCR	7	2	2400	1	3	8450	9750
19	6	MALIBU SKIER	OP	SKI	FBG	SV	IB	260	MRCR	7	2	2350	1	3	8400	9650
20		FLIGHTCRAFT 18XLT	OP	SKI	FBG	SV	IB	265	MRCR	6	8	2200	1	6	8850	10000
20		FLIGHTCRAFT 20XLOB	OP	SKI	FBG	SV	OB			6	8	1805			8350	9600
20	2	EURO SUNSETTER OPEN	OP	SKI	FBG	SV	IB	260	MRCR	7	6	2800	1	6	10700	12200
20	2	MALIBU SUNSETTER OPN	OP	SKI	FBG	SV	OB			7	6	2750	1	6	10800	12200
21	6	MYSTERE	OP	SKI	FBG	DV	IB	260	MRCR	7	4	2800	1	7	11200	12800
21	6	MYSTERE LX	OP	SKI	FBG	DV	IB	260	MRCR	7	4	2800	1	7	11700	13300
		1985 BOATS														
16	6	SPRINT 16.6	OP	SKI	FBG	SV	OB			7		950			3400	3950
16	6	SPRINT 16.6	OP	SKI	FBG	SV	IO	120-140		7		1750			3000	3500
18	6	SEBRING 18.6	OP	SKI	FBG	SV	OB			7		1050			3950	4600
18	6	SEBRING 18.6	OP	SKI	FBG	SV	IO	140-185		7		1750			3450	4100
19	6	MALIBU SKIER	OP	SKI	FBG	SV	IB	250		7	2	2300	2		5900	6750
20	3	SPORTSTER 20.6	OP	SKI	FBG	SV	IO	170-260		7	4	2300			4950	6050
		1984 BOATS														
18	6	BUBBLE 18.6		SKI	FBG	SV	IO	185	OMC	5	9	2100			3300	3850
19	6	MALIBU SKIER		SKI	FBG	SV	IB	250	PCM	7		2300	1	11	5550	6400

MANATEE BOATS INC

PALMETTO FL 33561 COAST GUARD MFG ID- MNT See inside cover to adjust price for area
FORMERLY MANATEE MARINE PROD INC

LOA FT	LOA IN	NAME AND/ OR MODEL	TOP/ RIG	BOAT TYPE	-HULL- MTL	-HULL- TP	ENGINE TP	ENGINE # HP	ENGINE MFG	BEAM FT	BEAM IN	WGT LBS	DRAFT FT	DRAFT IN	RETAIL LOW	RETAIL HIGH
		1989 BOATS														
17		CLASSIC 170VBR	ST	RNBT	FBG	DV	OB			6	9	1175			1000	1200
18	2	CLASSIC 182VBR	ST	RNBT	FBG	DV	OB			7	4	1370			1250	1450
18	2	CLASSIC 182VC	ST	CUD	FBG	DV	OB			7	4	1500			1300	1500
20	7	CLASSIC 207VC	ST	CUD	FBG	DV	OB			7	4	1520			1950	2300
20	7	CLASSIC 207VJ	ST	RNBT	FBG	DV	OB			7	4	1575			2000	2350
21		CLASSIC 210VC	ST	CUD	FBG	DV	IO	170-200		8		3600			5950	6900
22		SUNFISH 22VC	OP	FSH	FBG	DV	OB			8		2150			2750	3200
		1988 BOATS														
17		CLASSIC 170VBR	ST	RNBT	FBG	DV	OB			6	9	1175			965	1150
17	10	SUNFISH 1710VC	OP	FSH	FBG	DV	OB			7	2	1240			940	1100
18	2	CLASSIC 182VBR	ST	RNBT	FBG	DV	OB			7	4	1370			1150	1400
18	2	CLASSIC 182VBR	ST	RNBT	FBG	DV	IO	120-200		7	4	2225			3300	3950
18	2	CLASSIC 182VC	ST	CUD	FBG	DV	OB			7	4	1500			1200	1450
20	7	CLASSIC 207VC	ST	CUD	FBG	DV	OB			7	4	1520			1900	2250
20	7	CLASSIC 207VJ	ST	RNBT	FBG	DV	OB			7	4	1575			1950	2300
21		CLASSIC 210VC	ST	CUD	FBG	DV	IO	170-200		8		3600			5650	6550
22		SUNFISH 22VC	OP	FSH	FBG	DV	OB			8		2150			2650	3100
		1987 BOATS														
17		CLASSIC 170VBR	ST	RNBT	FBG	DV	OB			6	9	1175			900	1050
17	10	SUNFISH 1710VC	OP	FSH	FBG	DV	OB			7	2	1240			895	1050
18	2	CLASSIC 182VBR	ST	RNBT	FBG	DV	OB			7	4	1370			1100	1300
18	2	CLASSIC 182VBR	ST	RNBT	FBG	DV	IO	120-200		7	4	2225			3150	3750
18	2	CLASSIC 182VC	ST	CUD	FBG	DV	OB			7	4	1500			1150	1400
20	7	CLASSIC 207VC	ST	CUD	FBG	DV	OB			7	4	1520			1850	2200
20	7	CLASSIC 207VJ	ST	RNBT	FBG	DV	OB			7	4	1575			1900	2250
21		CLASSIC 210VC	ST	CUD	FBG	DV	IO	170-200		8		3600			5350	6200
22		SUNFISH 22VC	OP	FSH	FBG	DV	OB			8		2150			2600	3000
		1986 BOATS														
17		CLASSIC 170VBR	ST	RNBT	FBG	DV	OB			6	9	1175			860	1000
17	10	SUNFISH 1710VC	OP	FSH	FBG	DV	OB			7	2	1240			855	1000
18	2	CLASSIC 182V	ST	RNBT	FBG	DV	OB			7	4	1300			980	1150
18	2	CLASSIC 182VBR	ST	RNBT	FBG	DV	OB			7	4	1370			1050	1250
18	2	CLASSIC 182VBR	ST	RNBT	FBG	DV	IO	120-228		7	4	2225			3000	3650
18	2	CLASSIC 182VC	ST	CUD	FBG	DV	OB			7	4	1500			1100	1300
20	7	CLASSIC 207VC	ST	CUD	FBG	DV	OB			7	4	1520			1800	2100
21		CLASSIC 210VC	ST	CUD	FBG	DV	IO	170-260		8		3600			5150	6200
22		SUNFISH 22VC	OP	FSH	FBG	DV	OB			8		2150			2500	2900
		1985 BOATS														
17		CLASSIC 170VBR	ST	RNBT	FBG	DV	OB			6	9	1175			810	980
17	10	SUNFISH 1710VC	OP	FSH	FBG	DV	OB			7	2	1240			790	955
17	10	SUNFISH 1710VD	ST	FSH	FBG	DV	OB			7	2	1240			790	955
18	2	CLASSIC 182V	ST	RNBT	FBG	DV	OB			7	4	1300			920	1100
18	2	CLASSIC 182VBR	ST	RNBT	FBG	DV	OB			7	4	1370			980	1150
18	2	CLASSIC 182VBR	ST	RNBT	FBG	DV	IO	120-228		7	4	2225			2900	3500
18	2	CLASSIC 182VC	ST	CUD	FBG	DV	OB			7	4	1500			1050	1250

LOA FT	LOA IN	NAME AND/ OR MODEL	TOP/ RIG	BOAT TYPE	HULL MTL	HULL TP	ENGINE TP	ENGINE # HP MFG	BEAM FT	BEAM IN	WGT LBS	DRAFT FT	DRAFT IN	RETAIL LOW	RETAIL HIGH
		1985 BOATS													
18	7	FANTAIL 187TFC	OP	FSH	FBG	TR	OB		7	4	1200			820	985
18	7	FANTAIL 187TFD	ST	FSH	FBG	TR	OB		7	4	1200			775	935
18	7	FANTAIL 187TFS	OP	FSH	FBG	TR	OB		7	4	1200			750	900
20	7	CLASSIC 207VC	ST	CUD	FBG	DV	OB		7	4	1520			1750	2050
21		CLASSIC 210VC	ST	CUD	FBG	DV	IO	170-260	8		3600			4900	5950
22		SUNFISH 22VC	OP	FSH	FBG	DV	OB		8		2150			2450	2850
		1984 BOATS													
16	11	SUNFISH 1611TC	OP	FSH	FBG	TR	OB		7	4	1125			715	860
16	11	SUNFISH 1611TD	ST	FSH	FBG	TR	OB		7	4	1125			660	795
16	11	SUNFISH 1611TS	OP	FSH	FBG	TR	OB		7	4	1125			625	755
16	11	SUNFISH 1611VC	OP	FSH	FBG	DV	OB		7	4	900			520	630
17		CLASSIC 170VBR	ST	RNBT	FBG	DV	OB		6	9	1175			765	920
17	10	SUNFISH 1710VC	OP	FSH	FBG	DV	OB		7	2	1240			760	915
17	10	SUNFISH 1710VD	ST	FSH	FBG	DV	OB		7	2	1240			760	915
18	2	CLASSIC 182V	ST	RNBT	FBG	DV	OB		7	4	1300			885	1050
18	2	CLASSIC 182VBR	ST	RNBT	FBG	DV	OB		7	4	1370			920	1100
18	2	CLASSIC 182VBR	ST	RNBT	FBG	DV	IO	120-228	7	4	2225			2800	3350
18	2	CLASSIC 182VC	ST	CUD	FBG	DV	OB		7	4	1500			985	1150
18	4	SUNFISH 184TC	OP	FSH	FBG	TR	OB		7	4	1235			810	975
18	4	SUNFISH 184TD	ST	FSH	FBG	TR	OB		7	4	1235			760	915
18	4	SUNFISH 184TS	OP	FSH	FBG	TR	OB		7	4	1235			730	875
18	7	FANTAIL 187TFC	OP	FSH	FBG	TR	OB		7	4	1200			770	925
18	7	FANTAIL 187TFD	ST	FSH	FBG	TR	OB		7	4	1200			745	895
18	7	FANTAIL 187TFS	OP	FSH	FBG	TR	OB		7	4	1200			720	865
20	4	FANTAIL 204TFC	OP	FSH	FBG	TR	OB		7	5	1200			1400	1650
20	4	FANTAIL 204TFD	ST	FSH	FBG	TR	OB		7	5	1200			1400	1650
20	4	FANTAIL 204TFD	ST	FSH	FBG	TR	IO	117-170	7	5	1200			3200	3700
20	4	FANTAIL 204TTS	OP	FSH	FBG	TR	OB		7	5	1200			1350	1650
20	5	FANTAIL 205TFC	OP	FSH	FBG	TR	OB		7	3	1150			1350	1600
20	5	FANTAIL 205TFD	ST	FSH	FBG	TR	OB		7	3	1150			1350	1600
20	7	CLASSIC 207VC	ST	CUD	FBG	DV	OB		7	4	1520			1700	2000
21		CLASSIC 210VC	ST	CUD	FBG	DV	IO	170-260	8		3600			4750	5750
22		SUNFISH 22VC	OP	FSH	FBG	DV	OB		8		2150			2400	2800
23	7	CLASSIC 240VC	ST	CUD	FBG	DV	IO	170-260	8		4050			5950	7100

....For earlier years, see the BUC Used Boat Price Guide, Volume 3

MANSON BOAT WORKS INC

SALISBURY MA 01950 COAST GUARD MFG ID- MBN See inside cover to adjust price for area

LOA FT	LOA IN	NAME AND/ OR MODEL	TOP/ RIG	BOAT TYPE	HULL MTL	HULL TP	ENGINE TP	ENGINE # HP MFG	BEAM FT	BEAM IN	WGT LBS	DRAFT FT	DRAFT IN	RETAIL LOW	RETAIL HIGH
		1985 BOATS													
34		MANSON		SF	WD		IB	T225	12	2				26100	29100
41		MANSON		SF	WD		IB	T300D	14	2				68000	74700
45		MANSON		SF	WD		IB	T330	15	6				69600	76500
50		MANSON	HT	MYDKH	WD		IB	T310D	15	6				113500	124500

....For earlier years, see the BUC Used Boat Price Guide, Volume 3

MANTA RACING INC

HOLLYWOOD FL 33023 COAST GUARD MFG ID- MNN See inside cover to adjust price for area
FORMERLY MANTA MARINE INC

For more recent years, see the BUC Used Boat Price Guide, Volume 1

LOA FT	LOA IN	NAME AND/ OR MODEL	TOP/ RIG	BOAT TYPE	HULL MTL	HULL TP	ENGINE TP	ENGINE # HP MFG	BEAM FT	BEAM IN	WGT LBS	DRAFT FT	DRAFT IN	RETAIL LOW	RETAIL HIGH
		1996 BOATS													
28	2	MANTA 28	OP	OFF	FBG	DV	OB		8		4000	1	6	54700	60100
28	2	MANTA 28 CC/SF	OP	OPFSH	FBG	DV	OB		8		4800	1	6	54600	60000
28	2	MANTA 28 SM	OP	OFF	FBG	DV	IO	T270-T330	8		5900	1	6	34000	40500
28	2	MANTA 28 SM	OP	OFF	FBG	DV	IO	T365-T420	8		5900	1	6	38400	46500
30		MANTA PRO 30	OP	OPFSH	FBG	DV	OB		9		4000	1	6	66700	73200
30		MANTA PRO 30	OP	SF	FBG	DV	OB		9		4000	1	6	66900	73500
32	10	MANTA 32 CC/SF	OP	OPFSH	FBG	DV	OB		8		4800	1	6	69700	76600
32	10	MANTA 32 SM	OP	RACE	FBG	DV	OB		8		4800	1	6	108500	119500
32	10	MANTA 32 SM	OP	RACE	FBG	DV	IO	T350-T415	8		8000	1	6	48900	59100
32	10	MANTA 32 SM	OP	RACE	FBG	DV	IO	T459-T500	8		8000	1	6	58200	69300
32	10	MANTA 32 SM	OP	RACE	FBG	DV	IO	T600 MRCR	8		8000	1	6	75300	82700
38	6	MANTA 38	OP	OPFSH	FBG	DV	OB		8	8	6500	1	6	102000	112500
38	6	MANTA 38	OP	RACE	FBG	DV	IO	T365 MRCR	8	8	9800	1	6	60600	66600
		IO T415 MRCR 63900 70300, IO T450 MRCR 66700 73300, IO T500 MRCR 71200 78200													
		IO T525 MRCR 73500 80800, IO T600 MRCR 80700 88700, IO T800 MRCR ** **													
		IO T230D VLVO 66600 73200													
		1995 BOATS													
28	2	MANTA 28		RNBT	FBG	DV	OB		8		5400	1	6	52100	57300
28	2	MANTA 28	OP	RNBT	FBG	DV	OB		8		4000	1	6	52100	57300
28	2	MANTA 28 CC/SF	OP	OPFSH	FBG	DV	OB		8		4800	1	6	52000	57100
28	2	MANTA 28 SM		RNBT	FBG	DV	IO	T270-T330	8		5900	1	6	25500	30500
28	2	MANTA 28 SM		RNBT	FBG	DV	IO	T365-T420	8		5900	1	6	28900	35100
30		MANTA 30 SPORT PRO	OP	SF	FBG	DV	OB		9					63700	70000
30		MANTA PRO 30	OP	OPFSH	FBG	DV	OB		9		4000	1	6	63500	69700
32	10	MANTA 32 CC/SF	OP	OPFSH	FBG	DV	OB		8		4800	1	6	66400	73000
32	10	MANTA 32 SM		RNBT	FBG	DV	OB		8		4800	1	6	103500	114000
32	10	MANTA 32 SM		RNBT	FBG	DV	IO	T350-T459	8		8000	1	6	41900	51000
32	10	MANTA 32 SM		RNBT	FBG	DV	IO	T500-T600	8		8000	1	6	47800	56200
32	10	MANTA 32 SM	OP	RNBT	FBG	DV	OB		8		4800	1	6	103500	114000
38	6	MANTA 38	OP	OPFSH	FBG	DV	OB		8	8	6500	1	6	97300	107000
38	6	MANTA 38		RNBT	FBG	DV	IO	T365 MRCR	8	8	9800	1	6	62100	68200
		IO T415 MRCR 66400 73000, IO T450 MRCR 70000 76900, IO T500 MRCR 75200 82600													
		IO T525 MRCR 77600 85300, IO T600 MRCR 83700 92000, IO T800 MRCR ** **													
		IO T230D VLVO 64900 71300													
		1994 BOATS													
22	8	MANTA 23		RNBT	FBG	DV	OB		7	8	3600	1	6	28600	31800
22	8	MANTA 23 OF	OP	OPFSH	FBG	DV	OB		7	8	2500	1	6	22400	24900
22	8	MANTA 23 SM		RNBT	FBG	DV	IO	270 MRCR	7	8	2500	1	6	9200	10500
		IO 330 MRCR 10300 11700, IO 365 MRCR 11300 12900, IO 420 MRCR 13600 15400													
28	2	MANTA 28		RNBT	FBG	DV	OB		8		5400	1	6	49800	54700
28	2	MANTA 28 CC/SF	OP	OPFSH	FBG	DV	OB		8		4800	1	6	49600	54500
28	2	MANTA 28 SM		RNBT	FBG	DV	IO	T270-T330	8		5900	1	6	23800	28500
28	2	MANTA 28 SM		RNBT	FBG	DV	IO	T365-T420	8		5900	1	6	27000	32800
32		MANTA 32		RNBT	FBG	DV	OB		8			1	6	73000	80200
32		MANTA 32 CC/SF	OP	OPFSH	FBG	DV	OB		8		4500	1	6	66700	73300
32		MANTA 32 SM		RNBT	FBG	DV	IO	T330-T425	8		8000	1	6	33600	39800
32		MANTA 32 SM		RNBT	FBG	DV	IO	T575 MRCR	8		8000	1	6	39500	43900
38	6	MANTA 38	OP	OPFSH	FBG	DV	OB		8	8	6500	1	6	92900	102000
38	6	MANTA 38		RNBT	FBG	DV	IO	T365 MRCR	8	8	9800	1	6	57900	63700
		IO T390 MRCR 59800 65800, IO T425 MRCR 62900 69200, IO T465 MRCR 66800 73400													
		IO T525 MRCR 72500 79600, IO T575 MRCR 76400 84000, IO T800 MRCR ** **													
		IO T230D VLVO 60600 66500													
		1993 BOATS													
22	8	MANTA 23	OP	CUD	FBG	DV	OB		7	8	3600	1	6	27400	30400
22	8	MANTA 23 OF	OP	RNBT	FBG	DV	OB		7	8	2500	1	6	21400	23800
22	8	MANTA 23 SM	OP	CUD	FBG	DV	IO	270 MRCR	7	8	2500	1	6	9100	10400
		IO 330 MRCR 10200 11600, IO 365 MRCR 11200 12800, IO 420 MRCR 13400 15300													
28	2	MANTA 28	OP	CUD	FBG	DV	OB		8		5400	1	6	47800	52500
28	2	MANTA 28 CC/SF	OP	RNBT	FBG	DV	OB		8		4800	1	6	47700	52400
28	2	MANTA 28 SM	OP	CUD	FBG	DV	IO	T270-T330	8		5900	1	6	28200	33800
28	2	MANTA 28 SM	OP	CUD	FBG	DV	IO	T365-T420	8		5900	1	6	31900	37700
32		MANTA 32	OP	RNBT	FBG	DV	OB		8			1	6	69900	76800
32		MANTA 32 CC/SF	OP	OPFSH	FBG	DV	OB		8		4500	1	6	63800	70100
32		MANTA 32 SM	OP	OFF	FBG	DV	IO	T330-T425	8		8000	1	6	41800	49300
32		MANTA 32 SM	OP	OFF	FBG	DV	IO	T575 MRCR	8		8000	1	6	49200	54000
38	6	MANTA 38	OP	OFF	FBG	DV	IO	T365 MRCR	8	8	9800	1	6	61600	67600
		IO T390 MRCR 63600 69900, IO T425 MRCR 66900 73500, IO T465 MRCR 71000 78000													
		IO T525 MRCR 77000 84600, IO T575 MRCR 81200 89300, IO T800 MRCR ** **													
		IO T230D VLVO 69600 76500													
		1992 BOATS													
22	8	MANTA 23	OP	CUD	FBG	DV	OB		7	8	3600	1	6	26300	29200
22	8	MANTA 23 OF	OP	RNBT	FBG	DV	OB		7	8	2500	1	6	20500	22800
22	8	MANTA 23 SM	OP	CUD	FBG	DV	IO	270 MRCR	7	8	2500	1	6	8450	9700
		IO 330 MRCR 9550 10800, IO 365 MRCR 10500 12000, IO 420 MRCR 12600 14300													
28	2	MANTA 28	OP	CUD	FBG	DV	OB		8		5400	1	6	46100	50600
28	2	MANTA 28 CC/SF	OP	RNBT	FBG	DV	OB		8		4800	1	6	46000	50500
28	2	MANTA 28 SM	OP	CUD	FBG	DV	IO	T270-T330	8		5900	1	6	26400	31600
28	2	MANTA 28 SM	OP	CUD	FBG	DV	IO	T365-T420	8		5900	1	6	29800	35300
32		MANTA 32	OP	RNBT	FBG	DV	OB		8			1	6	67000	73600
32		MANTA 32 CC/SF	OP	OPFSH	FBG	DV	OB		8		4500	1	6	61100	67100
32		MANTA 32 SM	OP	OFF	FBG	DV	IO	T330-T425	8		8000	1	6	39200	46100
32		MANTA 32 SM	OP	OFF	FBG	DV	IO	T575 MRCR	8		8000	1	6	46300	50900
38	4	MANTA 38 SM	OP	OFF	FBG	DV	IO	T365 MRCR	8	6	9000			56500	62100
38	4	MANTA 38 SM	OP	OFF	FBG	DV	IO	T425 MRCR	8	6	9000			61500	67600
38	4	MANTA 38 SM	OP	OFF	FBG	DV	IO	T575 MRCR	8	6	9000			74800	82200

LOA FT IN	NAME AND/ OR MODEL	TOP/ RIG	BOAT TYPE	HULL MTL TP TP	ENGINE # HP MFG	BEAM FT IN	WGT LBS	DRAFT FT IN	RETAIL LOW	RETAIL HIGH
--- 1991 **BOATS** ---
22 8	MANTA 23	OP	CUD	FBG DV OB		7 8	3600	1 6	25200	28000
22 8	MANTA 23 OF	OP	RNBT	FBG DV OB		7 8	2500	1 6	19800	22900
22 8	MANTA 23 SM	OP	CUD	FBG DV IO	270 MRCR	7 8	2500	1 6	7900	9100
22 8	MANTA 23 SM	OP	CUD	FBG DV IO	330-365	7 8	2500	1 6	9000	11200
22 8	MANTA 23 SM	OP	CUD	FBG DV IO	420 MRCR	7 8	2500	1 6	11800	13400
28 2	MANTA 28	OP	CUD	FBG DV OB		8	5400	1 6	43800	48700
28 2	MANTA 28	OP	RNBT	FBG DV OB		8	4800	1 6	43700	48500
28 2	MANTA 28 CC/SF	OP	CUD	FBG DV IO	T270-T330	8	5900	1 6	24700	29700
28 2	MANTA 28 SM	OP	CUD	FBG DV IO	T365-T420	8	5900	1 6	28000	33100
32	MANTA 32	OP	RNBT	FBG DV OB		8			64300	70700
32	MANTA 32 CC/SF	OP	OPFSH	FBG DV OB		8	4500	1 6	58700	64500
32	MANTA 32 SM	OP	OFF	FBG DV IO	T330-T425	8	8000		36700	43300
32	MANTA 32 SM	OP	OFF	FBG DV IO	T575 MRCR	8	8000		42900	47700
38 4	MANTA 38 SM	OP	OFF	FBG DV IO	T365 MRCR	8 6	9000		53000	58300
38 4	MANTA 38 SM	OP	OFF	FBG DV IO	T420 MRCR	8 6	9000		57300	62900
38 4	MANTA 38 SM	OP	OFF	FBG DV IO	T575 MRCR	8 6	9000		70200	77200
--- 1990 **BOATS** ---
22 8	MANTA 23	OP	CUD	FBG DV IO	320-330	7 8	2500	1 6	8150	9600
22 8	MANTA 23	OP	CUD	FBG DV IO	365 MRCR	7 8	2500	1 6	9350	10600
22 8	MANTA 23	OP	CUD	FBG DV IO	420 MRCR	7 8	2500	1 6	11100	12600
22 8	MANTA 23	OP	RNBT	FBG DV OB		7 8	3600	1 6	24300	27000
22 8	MANTA 23 OF	OP	SF	FBG DV OB		7 8	2500	1 6	19100	21200
22 8	MANTA 23 SM	OP	CUD	FBG DV IO	260 MRCR	7 8	2500	1 6	7350	8450
28 2	MANTA 28	OP	OFF	FBG DV IO	T330-T365	8	5900	1 6	22900	26700
28 2	MANTA 28	OP	OFF	FBG DV IO	T420 MRCR	8	5900	1 6	26300	29300
28 2	MANTA 28	OP	RNBT	FBG DV OB		8	5400	1 6	42000	46700
28 2	MANTA 28	OP	SF	FBG DV OB		8	4800	1 6	41900	46500
28 2	MANTA 28 CC/SF	OP	CUD	FBG DV IO	T260-T320	8	5900	1 6	23000	27500
28 2	MANTA 28 SM	OP	RNBT	FBG DV OB		8			61800	67900
32	MANTA 32	OP	OPFSH	FBG DV IO		8	4500	1 6	56400	61900
32	MANTA 32 CC/SF	OP	OFF	FBG DV IO	T330-T420	8	8000		34500	40600
32	MANTA 32 SM	OP	OFF	FBG DV IO	T575 MRCR	8	8000		40400	44900
32	MANTA 32 SM	OP	OFF	FBG DV IO	T365 MRCR	8	8000		49900	54800
38 4	MANTA 38 SM	OP	OFF	FBG DV IO	T420 MRCR	8 6	9000		53900	59200
38 4	MANTA 38 SM	OP	OFF	FBG DV IO	T575 MRCR	8 6	9000		66000	72600
--- 1989 **BOATS** ---
22 8	MANTA 23	OP	RNBT	FBG DV OB		7 8	3600	1 6	23400	26000
22 8	MANTA 23 OF	OP	SF	FBG DV OB		7 8	2500	1 6	18600	20600
22 8	MANTA 23 SM	OP	CUD	FBG DV IO	260 MRCR	7 8	2500	1 6	6950	8000
	IO 320-330	7700	9050, IO	365	MRCR	8800	10000, IO	420	MRCR	10500 11900
28 2	MANTA 28	OP	RNBT	FBG DV OB		8	5400	1 6	40500	45000
28 2	MANTA 28 CC/SF	OP	SF	FBG DV OB		8	4800	1 6	40300	44800
28 2	MANTA 28 SM	OP	CUD	FBG DV IO	T260-T330	8	5900	1 6	21700	26300
28 2	MANTA 28 SM	OP	CUD	FBG DV IO	T365-T420	8	5900	1 6	24800	29400
32	MANTA 32	OP	RNBT	FBG DV OB		8			59600	65400
32	MANTA 32 CC/SF	OP	CUD	FBG DV OB		8	4500	1 6	54500	59900
32	MANTA 32 SM	OP	CUD	FBG DV IO	T330-T420	8	8000		28700	34000
32	MANTA 32 SM	OP	CUD	FBG DV IO	T575 MRCR	8	8000		32800	36500
38 4	MANTA 38 SM	OP	CUD	FBG DV IO	T365 MRCR		9000		46800	51400
38 4	MANTA 38 SM	OP	CUD	FBG DV IO	T420 MRCR		9000		50300	55300
38 4	MANTA 38 SM	OP	CUD	FBG DV IO	T575 MRCR		9000		61800	67900
--- 1986 **BOATS** ---
19	MANTA 19	OP	FSH	FBG DV OB					8600	9850
22 8	MANTA 23	OP	FSH	FBG DV OB		7 8	3600		21100	23500
22 8	MANTA 23	OP	RNBT	FBG DV OB		7 8	3600		21100	23500
22 8	MANTA 23 SM	OP	RNBT	FBG DV IO	260 MRCR	7 8	4000		7500	8600
	IO 330 MRCR	8250	9500, IO	370	MRCR	9150	10400, IO	T170	MRCR	8100 9300
28 2	MANTA 28	OP	CR	FBG DV OB		8	5400	1 6	37100	41300
28 2	MANTA 28 CC/SF	OP	CTRCN	FBG DV OB		8	4800	1 6	36400	40500
28 2	MANTA 28 SM	OP	CR	FBG DV OB		8	4800	1 6	37100	41300
28 2	MANTA 28 SM	OP	CR	FBG DV IO	T185-T260	8		1 6	17000	20900
28 2	MANTA 28 SM	OP	CR	FBG DV IO	T300-T370	8		1 6	19500	23800
32	MANTA 32 SM	OP	CR	FBG DV IO	T330-T370	8	7800		49500	54400
32	MANTA 32 SM	OP	CR	FBG DV IO		8	7800		26500	30300

....For earlier years, see the BUC Used Boat Price Guide, Volume 3

MAO TA YACHT CORP
KAOHSIUNG TAIWAN ROC

See inside cover to adjust price for area

KAUFMAN & ASSOC
ANNAPOLIS MD 21403

LOA FT IN	NAME AND/ OR MODEL	TOP/ RIG	BOAT TYPE	HULL MTL TP TP	ENGINE # HP MFG	BEAM FT IN	WGT LBS	DRAFT FT IN	RETAIL LOW	RETAIL HIGH
--- 1989 **BOATS** ---
51	KAUFMAN 51/53	CUT	SA/RC	FBG KL IB	85D PERK	14 3	40000	7	165000	181500
51	KAUFMAN 51/53	KTH	SA/RC	FBG KL IB	85D PERK	14 3	40000	7	170500	187500
51	MAO TA 51/53	CUT	SA/RC	FBG KL IB	85D PERK	14 3	40000	7	165000	181500
--- 1988 **BOATS** ---
51	KAUFMAN 51/53	CUT	SA/RC	FBG KL IB	85D PERK	14 3	40000	7	155000	170500
51	KAUFMAN 51/53	KTH	SA/RC	FBG KL IB	85D PERK	14 3	40000	7	159500	175500
51	MAO TA 51/53	CUT	SA/RC	FBG KL IB	85D PERK	14 3	40000	7	155000	170500
--- 1985 **BOATS** ---
36 2	MAO-TA 36	CUT	SA/CR	FBG KL IB	35D	11 2	22000	5 10	52900	58100
41 9	BREWER 42	KTH	SA/RC	FBG KL IB	50D	12 11	24750	5 9	70000	76900
50 10	MAO-TA 51	CUT	SA/RC	FBG KL IB	85D	14 3	38708	6 10	126500	139000

MARADA POWERBOATS
MARADA BOATS
IRVINE KY 40336

See inside cover to adjust price for area

FORMERLY ARMADA MANUFACTURING

For more recent years, see the BUC Used Boat Price Guide, Volume 1

LOA FT IN	NAME AND/ OR MODEL	TOP/ RIG	BOAT TYPE	HULL MTL TP TP	ENGINE # HP MFG	BEAM FT IN	WGT LBS	DRAFT FT IN	RETAIL LOW	RETAIL HIGH
--- 1996 **BOATS** ---
17 10	MX-1 EXECUTIVE	ST	RNBT	FBG SV IO	135 MRCR	7 3	2200		4850	5550
17 10	MX-1 FISH & SKI	ST	RNBT	FBG SV IO	135 MRCR	7 3	2200		4950	5650
17 10	MX-1 SPORT	ST	RNBT	FBG SV IO	135 MRCR	7 3	2200		4000	4650
17 10	MX-1 SPORT BB	ST	RNBT	FBG SV IO	135 MRCR	7 3	2200		4100	4800
17 10	MX-1 ULTIMA	ST	RNBT	FBG SV IO	135 MRCR	7 3	2200		5300	6100
19	MX-2 EXECUTIVE	ST	RNBT	FBG SV IO	190 MRCR	8	2650		5850	6750
19	MX-2 SPORT	ST	RNBT	FBG SV IO	190 MRCR	8	2650		5100	5850
19	MX-2 ULTIMA	ST	RNBT	FBG SV IO	190 MRCR	8	2650		6350	7250
20 5	MX-3 CUDDY	ST	RNBT	FBG SV IO	190 MRCR	8	2950		7150	8200
20 5	MX-3 EXECUTIVE	ST	RNBT	FBG SV IO	190 MRCR	8	2950		6950	8000
20 5	MX-3 FISH & SKI	ST	FSH	FBG SV IO	190 MRCR	8	2950		7550	8650
20 5	MX-3 SPORT	ST	RNBT	FBG SV IO	190 MRCR	8	2950		6100	7000
20 5	MX-3 ULTIMA	ST	RNBT	FBG SV IO	190 MRCR	8	2950		7450	8600
20 10	2100 MVB	ST	RNBT	FBG SV IO	190 MRCR	7 10	2850		6750	7750

MARATHON BOAT CO INC
KERSHAW SC 29067

See inside cover to adjust price for area

LOA FT IN	NAME AND/ OR MODEL	TOP/ RIG	BOAT TYPE	HULL MTL TP TP	ENGINE # HP MFG	BEAM FT IN	WGT LBS	DRAFT FT IN	RETAIL LOW	RETAIL HIGH
--- 1989 **BOATS** ---
19 2	EAGLE 2001	OP	RNBT	FBG DV IB	175-260	7 8	2400		3950	4700
19 2	FALCON 2001	OP	B/R	FBG DV IB	130-175	7 8	2400		3600	4350
19 2	FALCON 2001 XL	OP	B/R	FBG DV IB	130-260	7 8	2400		3750	4550
20	VIVA 2001	OP	CUD	FBG DV IB	130-175		2650		4050	4900
20 3	WEEKENDER 2100	OP	CBNCR	FBG DV IB	130-230	8	3400		5000	5950
21 6	SPORTFISH 2200	OP	CUD	FBG DV IB	130-260	8	3300		5250	6300
21 6	STARFISH 2200	OP	CUD	FBG DV IB	130-260	8	3300		5250	6300
21 6	SUPER SPORT 2200	OP	CUD	FBG DV IB	130-260	8	3300		5250	6300
23	SUNBLAZER 2400	OP	CBNCR	FBG DV IB	230-260	8	4100		7100	8200
23 8	EAGLE 2450	OP	RNBT	FBG DV IB	260-330	8	4000		7100	8400
23	SPORTFISH 2450	OP	CUD	FBG DV IB	260-365	8	4000		7100	8600
24 6	BERMUDA 2550 EXPRESS	OP	CBNCR	FBG DV IB	260	8 4	4600		8600	9900
24 6	BERMUDA 2550 EXPRESS	OP	CBNCR	FBG DV IB	T130-T165	8 4	4600		9050	10600
24 6	BERMUDA 2550 SPORT	OP	CBNCR	FBG DV IB	260-330	8 4	4600		8600	10100
24 6	BERMUDA 2550 SPORT	OP	CBNCR	FBG DV IB	T130-T165	8 4	4600		9050	10600
27	RIVIERA 2700	FB	CBNCR	FBG DV IB	260	9 2	5500		13600	15400
27	RIVIERA 2700	FB	CBNCR	FBG DV IB	T130-T165	9 2	5500		13800	15800
27 6	SPORTFISH 2750	OP	CBNCR	FBG DV IB	260	9 2	5500		13600	15400
27 6	SPORTFISH 2750	OP	CBNCR	FBG DV IB	T130-T165	9 2	5500		13800	15800
31 6	EAGLE 3200	OP	CBNCR	FBG DV IB	T330-T365	9 2	7000		21000	23900
--- 1988 **BOATS** ---
19 2	EAGLE 2001	OP	RNBT	FBG DV IB	120-230	7 8	2400		3550	4400
19 2	EAGLE 2001	OP	RNBT	FBG DV IB	260	7 8	2400		3850	4600
19 2	FALCON 2001	OP	B/R	FBG DV IB	120-230	7 8	2400		3350	4200
19 2	FALCON 2001	OP	B/R	FBG DV IB	260	7 8	2400		3650	4350
19 2	FALCON 2001 XL	OP	B/R	FBG DV IB	120-230	7 8	2400		3500	4350
19 2	FALCON 2001 XL	OP	B/R	FBG DV IB	260	7 8	2400		3800	4500
20	VIVA 2001	OP	CUD	FBG DV IB	120-230	7 8	2650		3800	4700

LOA FT IN	NAME AND/ OR MODEL	TOP/ RIG	BOAT TYPE	-HULL- MTL TP	----ENGINE--- TP # HP MFG	BEAM FT IN	WGT LBS	DRAFT FT IN	RETAIL LOW	RETAIL HIGH
			--- 1988	**BOATS**						
20	VIVA 2001	OP	CUD	FBG DV	IB 260	7 8	2650		4100	4900
20 3	WEEKENDER 2100	OP	CBNCR	FBG DV	IB 140-180	8	3400		4800	5650
21 6	SPORTFISH 2200	OP	CUD	FBG DV	IB 120-260	8	3300		5050	6200
21 6	STARFISH 2200	OP	CUD	FBG DV	IB 120-170	8	3300		5050	5900
21 6	STARFISH 2200	OP	CUD	FBG DV	IO 175-180	8	3300		4050	4750
21 6	STARFISH 2200	OP	CUD	FBG DV	IB 230-260	8	3300		5250	6200
21 6	SUPER SPORT 2200	OP	CUD	FBG DV	IB 120-260	8	3300		5950	5950
23 6	SUNBLAZER 2400	OP	CBNCR	FBG DV	IB 225-260	8	4100		6850	7900
23 9	EAGLE 2450	OP	RNBT	FBG DV	IB 175-365	8	4000		6650	8200
23 9	SPORTFISH 2450	OP	CUD	FBG DV	IB 175-365	8	4000		6650	8150
24 6	BERMUDA 2550 EXPRESS	OP	CBNCR	FBG DV	IB 260 MRCR	8	3900		6900	7950
	IB 260 VLVO 8300	9550, IB T		MRCR	** **	, IB T140	MRCR		8600	9900
24 6	BERMUDA 2550 SPORT	OP	CBNCR	FBG DV	IB 260	8 4	4600		8250	9550
24 6	BERMUDA 2550 SPORT	OP	CBNCR	FBG DV	IB T MRCR	8 4	4600		**	**
24 6	BERMUDA 2550 SPORT	OP	CBNCR	FBG DV	IB T140 MRCR	8 4	4600		8600	9900
26	SEA BLAZER 2750	OP	CBNCR	FBG DV	IB 260	10 2	8000		14200	16200
26	SEA BLAZER 2750	OP	CBNCR	FBG DV	IB T MRCR	10 2	8000		**	**
26	SEA BLAZER 2750	OP	CBNCR	FBG DV	IB T140 MRCR	10 2	8000		14600	16600
27 6	RIVIERA 2700	FB	CBNCR	FBG DV	IB 260	9 2	5500		12900	14800
27 6	RIVIERA 2700	FB	CBNCR	FBG DV	IB T MRCR	9 2	5500		**	**
27 6	RIVIERA 2700	FB	CBNCR	FBG DV	IB T140 MRCR	9 2	5500		13100	14900
27 6	SPORTFISH 2750	OP	CBNCR	FBG DV	IB 260	9 2	5500		12900	14800
27 6	SPORTFISH 2750	OP	CBNCR	FBG DV	IB T MRCR	9 2	5500		**	**
27 6	SPORTFISH 2750	OP	CBNCR	FBG DV	IB T140 MRCR	9 2	5500		13100	14900
31 6	EAGLE 3200	OP	RNBT	FBG DV	IB T260-T365	9 7	7000		19200	22800
			--- 1987	**BOATS**						
19 2	EAGLE 2001	OP	RNBT	FBG DV	IB	7 8	1600		**	**
19 2	EAGLE 2001	OP	RNBT	FBG DV	IB 120-200	7 8	1600		2900	3600
19 2	EAGLE 2001	OP	RNBT	FBG DV	IB 230-260	7 8	1600		3100	3650
19 2	FALCON 2001	OP	B/R	FBG DV	IB MRCR	7 8	1600		**	**
19 2	FALCON 2001	OP	B/R	FBG DV	IB 120-180	7 8	1600		2700	3400
19 2	FALCON 2001	OP	B/R	FBG DV	IB 200-260	7 8	1600		2950	3500
19 2	FALCON 2001 XL	OP	B/R	FBG DV	IB MRCR	7 8	1600		**	**
19 2	FALCON 2001 XL	OP	B/R	FBG DV	IB 120-200	7 8	1600		2800	3500
19 2	FALCON 2001 XL	OP	B/R	FBG DV	IB 230-260	7 8	1600		3050	3550
20	VIVA 2001	OP	CUD	FBG DV	IB MRCR	7 8	1850		**	**
20	VIVA 2001	OP	CUD	FBG DV	IB 120-200	7 8	1850		3050	3800
20 3	2100 WEEKENDER	OP	CBNCR	FBG DV	IB MRCR	8	2600		**	**
20 3	2100 WEEKENDER	OP	CBNCR	FBG DV	IB 165-180	8	2600		3900	4600
22 6	2200 SPORTFISH II	OP	CUD	FBG DV	IB MRCR	8	2500		**	**
22 6	2200 SPORTFISH II	OP	CUD	FBG DV	IB 120-260	8	2500		4300	5300
22 6	2200 SPORTFISH II	OP	CUD	FBG DV	IB 350 MRCR	8	2500		4850	5550
22 6	2200 SUPER FISH	OP	CUD	FBG DV	IB TR	8	2500		**	**
22 6	2200 SUPER FISH	OP	CUD	FBG DV	IB 120-260	8	2500		4250	5200
22 6	2200 SUPER FISH	OP	CUD	FBG DV	IB 350 MRCR	8	2500		4800	5500
22 6	2200 SUPER SPORT	OP	CUD	FBG DV	IB MRCR	8	2500		**	**
22 6	2200 SUPER SPORT	OP	CUD	FBG DV	IB 120-260	8	2500		4000	5000
22 6	2200 SUPER SPORT	OP	CUD	FBG DV	IB 350 MRCR	8	2500		4650	5300
22 6	STARFISH 2200	OP	CUD	FBG DV	IB	8			**	**
	IB 120-165 4250	5100, IO 175-180			3450 4050, IB	200-350			4500	5500
23 6	SUNBLAZER 2350	OP	CBNCR	FBG DV	IB 180-260	8	3100		5250	6100
24 6	2550 COMMAND BRIDGE	FB	TCMY	FBG DV	IB 260 MRCR	8 4	4200		7050	8100
24 6	2550 COMMAND BRIDGE	FB	TCMY	FBG DV	IB T MRCR	8 4	4200		**	**
24 6	2550 COMMAND BRIDGE	FB	TCMY	FBG DV	IB T165	8 4	4200		7650	8800
24 6	BERMUDA 2550 EXP	OP	CBNCR	FBG DV	IB 230-260	8 4	3600		6550	7550
24 6	BERMUDA 2550 EXP	OP	CBNCR	FBG DV	IB T MRCR	8 4	3600		**	**
24 6	BERMUDA 2550 EXP	OP	CBNCR	FBG DV	IB T165	8 4	3600		7100	8150
24 6	BERMUDA 2550 SPORT	OP	CBNCR	FBG DV	IB 230-260	8 4	3600		6550	7550
24 6	BERMUDA 2550 SPORT	OP	CBNCR	FBG DV	IB T MRCR	8 4	3600		**	**
24 6	BERMUDA 2550 SPORT	OP	CBNCR	FBG DV	IB T165	8 4	3600		7100	8150
26	2750 COMMAND BRIDGE	FB	CBNCR	FBG DV	IB OMC	10	9000		**	**
	IB 260-454 14600	18000, IB T		MRCR	** **	, IB T165-T180			15300	17600
31 6	EAGLE 3200	OP	RNBT	FBG DV	IB T OMC	9 7	7000		**	**
31 6	EAGLE 3200	OP	RNBT	FBG DV	IB T260 MRCR	9 7	7000		18300	20300
31 6	EAGLE 3200	OP	RNBT	FBG DV	IB T454 MRCR	9 7	7000		20900	23200
			--- 1986	**BOATS**						
19 2	EAGLE		RNBT	FBG DV	IO 120	7 8	2500		2650	3050
19 2	FALCON		RNBT	FBG DV	IO 120	7 8	2500		2600	3000
19 2	FISH & SKI		RNBT	FBG DV	IO 120	7 8	2500		2650	3100
19 2	SPECIAL		RNBT	FBG DV	IO 120	7 8	2500		2450	2850
20	VIVA 2001		CR	FBG DV	IO 120	7 8	2700		2900	3400
20 3	MARATHON 2100		WKNDR	FBG DV	IO 120	8	3600		3650	4250
			--- 1984	**BOATS**						
20 3	WEEKENDER	OP	WKNDR	FBG DV	IO 170 MRCR	7 11	3350		3350	3900
21 3	STARFISH	OP	FSH	FBG DV	IO 140 MRCR	7 11	3100		3600	4200
22 3	SUNBLAZER	OP	EXP	FBG DV	IO 228 MRCR	8	3600		3600	4200
24 3	BERMUDA AFT CABIN	OP	CR	FBG DV	IO T120 MRCR	8	4950		4950	5700
24 3	BERMUDA EXPRESS	HT	EXP	FBG DV	IO 228 MRCR	8	4600		4600	5250
25 9	SEA-BLAZER	FB	CBNCR	FBG DV	IO T120 MRCR	10	10900		10900	12300

MARES YACHT INC

For more recent years, see the BUC Used Boat Price Guide, Volume 1

LOA FT IN	NAME AND/ OR MODEL	TOP/ RIG	BOAT TYPE	-HULL- MTL TP	----ENGINE--- TP # HP MFG	BEAM FT IN	WGT LBS	DRAFT FT IN	RETAIL LOW	RETAIL HIGH
			--- 1996	**BOATS**						
38	PERFORMANCE CAT 38	OP	OFF	F/S CT	IO T415 MRCR	11 4	9300	1 9	67500	74100
	IO T465 MRCR 74000	81300, IO T500		MRCR	78600 86400, IB	T230D VLVO	91000		100000	
	IB T420D CAT 117500	129000								
40	SPORTFISH 40	FB	SF	F/S CT	IB T370D VLVO 15		33000	2 5	206000	226500
	IB T375D CUM 210000	230500, IB T420D CAT			222500 244500, IB	T420D CUM	215500		236500	
	IB T430D VLVO 212500	233500								
50	EXPRESS CAT 50	OP	EXP	F/S CT	IB T10CD MAN	17 4	30000	3	482000	529500
54	MOTOR YACHT 54	FB	MY	F/S CT	IB T760D GM	17 4	38000	3	463500	509000
54	MOTOR YACHT 54	FB	MY	F/S CT	IB T800D CAT	17 4	38000	3	481500	529500
54	MOTOR YACHT 54	FB	MY	F/S CT	IB T820D MAN	17 4	38000	3	484000	531500
			--- 1992	**BOATS**						
46	LUXURY CAT	FB	SDN	FBG CT	IB T450D DD	17 2	25800	2 6	235500	258500
48	SPORT CAT		EXP	FBG CT	IB T600D SETK	17 2	24300	2 6	266500	292500
50	LUXURY CAT	FB	SDN	FBG CT	IB T600D SETK	17 2	26800	2 6	327000	359000

MARIAH BOATS INC

For more recent years, see the BUC Used Boat Price Guide, Volume 1

LOA FT IN	NAME AND/ OR MODEL	TOP/ RIG	BOAT TYPE	-HULL- MTL TP	----ENGINE--- TP # HP MFG	BEAM FT IN	WGT LBS	DRAFT FT IN	RETAIL LOW	RETAIL HIGH
			--- 1996	**BOATS**						
18	SHABAH 180	OP	RNBT	FBG SV	IO 135 MRCR	7 8	2125	2 3	5700	6550
18	SHABAH 180 SS	OP	RNBT	FBG SV	IO 135 MRCR	7 8	2125	2 3	5900	6750
18	SHABAH 183	OP	RNBT	FBG SV	IO 135 MRCR	7 8	2125	2 3	5700	6550
18	SHABAH 183 SS	OP	RNBT	FBG SV	IO 135 MRCR	7 8	2125	2 3	5900	6750
18 10	SHABAH 190	OP	RNBT	FBG SV	IO 135-205	7 10	2450	2 3	6100	7400
18 10	SHABAH 190 SS	OP	RNBT	FBG SV	IO 135-205	7 10	2450	2 3	6300	7550
18 10	SHABAH Z190	OP	RNBT	FBG SV	IO 135-190	7 10	2450	2 3	6850	7900
18 10	SHABAH Z190 SS	OP	RNBT	FBG SV	IO 135-190	7 10	2450	2 3	7100	8200
18 10	TALARI 191	OP	RNBT	FBG SV	IO 135-205	7 10	2450	2 3	6100	7400
18 10	TALARI 191 SS	OP	RNBT	FBG SV	IO 135-205	7 10	2450	2 3	6300	7550
18 10	TALARI Z191	OP	RNBT	FBG SV	IO 135-190	7 10	2450	2 3	6850	7900
18 10	TALARI Z191 SS	OP	RNBT	FBG SV	IO 135-190	7 10	2450	2 3	7100	8200
20 1	SHABAH 200	OP	RNBT	FBG SV	IO 135-205	8	2550	2 4	7300	8500
20 1	SHABAH 200 SS	OP	RNBT	FBG SV	IO 135-205	8	2550	2 4	7500	8700
20 1	SHABAH 203	OP	RNBT	FBG SV	IO 135-205	8	2550	2 4	7300	8500
20 1	SHABAH 203 SS	OP	RNBT	FBG SV	IO 135-205	8	2550	2 4	7500	8700
20 1	SHABAH Z200	OP	RNBT	FBG SV	IO 135-205	8	2550	2 4	8200	9500
20 1	SHABAH Z200 SS	OP	RNBT	FBG SV	IO 135-205	8	2550	2 4	8450	9800
20 1	SHABAH Z203	OP	RNBT	FBG SV	IO 135-205	8	2550	2 4	8200	9800
20 1	SHABAH Z203 SS	OP	RNBT	FBG SV	IO 135-205	8	2550	2 4	8450	9800
20 1	TALARI 201	OP	RNBT	FBG SV	IO 135-205	8	2550	2 4	7300	8500
20 1	TALARI 201 SS	OP	RNBT	FBG SV	IO 135-205	8	2550	2 4	7500	8700
20 1	TALARI 209	OP	RNBT	FBG SV	IO 135-250	8	2800	2 3	8300	10100
20 1	TALARI 209	OP	RNBT	FBG SV	IO 280-300	8	2800	2 3	9250	10800
20 1	TALARI Z201	OP	RNBT	FBG SV	IO 135-205	8	2550	2 4	8200	9500
20 1	TALARI Z201 SS	OP	RNBT	FBG SV	IO 135-205	8	2550	2 4	8450	9800
20 9	SHABAH 210	OP	RNBT	FBG SV	IO 135-250	8 4	2800	2 3	8100	9450
20 9	SHABAH 210	OP	RNBT	FBG SV	IO 280-300	8 4	2800	2 3	9000	10600
20 9	SHABAH 210 SS	OP	RNBT	FBG SV	IO 135-280	8 4	2800	2 3	8350	10400
20 9	SHABAH 210 SS	OP	RNBT	FBG SV	IO 300 MRCR	8 4	2800	2 3	9400	10700
20 9	SHABAH Z210	OP	RNBT	FBG SV	IO 135-300	8 4	2800	2 3	9150	11400

                  CONTINUED ON NEXT PAGE

LOA FT	IN	NAME AND/ OR MODEL	TOP/ RIG	BOAT TYPE	-HULL- MTL	TP	----ENGINE--- TP	# HP	MFG	BEAM FT	IN	WGT LBS	DRAFT FT	IN	RETAIL LOW	RETAIL HIGH
		1996 BOATS														
20	9	SHABAH Z210 SS	OP	RNBT	FBG	SV	IO	135-300		8	4	2800	2	3	9400	11600
20	9	TALARI 209 SS	OP	RNBT	FBG	SV	IO	135-280		8	4	2800	2	3	8350	10400
20	9	TALARI 209 SS	OP	RNBT	FBG	SV	IO	300	MRCR	8	4	2800	2	3	9400	10700
20	9	TALARI Z209	OP	RNBT	FBG	SV	IO	135-300		8	4	2800	2	3	9150	11400
20	9	TALARI Z209 SS	OP	RNBT	FBG	SV	IO	135-300		8	4	2800	2	3	9400	11600
21		TALARI 215	OP	RNBT	FBG	SV	IO	135-280		8	5	3400	2	6	9500	11600
21		TALARI 215	OP	RNBT	FBG	SV	IO	300	MRCR	8	5	3400	2	6	10600	12000
21		TALARI 215 SS	OP	RNBT	FBG	SV	IO	135-280		8	5	3400	2	6	9700	11800
21		TALARI 215 SS	OP	RNBT	FBG	SV	IO	300	MRCR	8	5	3400	2	6	10700	12200
21		TALARI Z215	OP	RNBT	FBG	SV	IO	135-300		8	5	3400	2	6	10500	12900
21		TALARI Z215 SS	OP	RNBT	FBG	SV	IO	135-300		8	5	3400	2	6	10800	13100
21	2	SHABAH 211	OP	RNBT	FBG	SV	IO	135-250		7	8	2850	2	5	8150	9400
21	2	SHABAH 211	OP	RNBT	FBG	SV	IO	280-300		7	8	2850	2	5	8950	10600
21	2	SHABAH 211 SS	OP	RNBT	FBG	SV	IO	135-280		7	8	2850	2	5	8350	10400
21	2	SHABAH 211 SS	OP	RNBT	FBG	SV	IO	300	MRCR	7	8	2850	2	5	9400	10700
21	2	SHABAH 212	OP	RNBT	FBG	SV	IO	135-250		7	8	2850	2	5	8150	9400
21	2	SHABAH 212	OP	RNBT	FBG	SV	IO	280-300		7	8	2850	2	5	8950	10600
21	2	SHABAH 212 SS	OP	RNBT	FBG	SV	IO	135-280		7	8	2850	2	5	8350	10400
21	2	SHABAH 212 SS	OP	RNBT	FBG	SV	IO	300	MRCR	7	8	2850	2	5	9400	10700
21	2	SHABAH Z211 SS	OP	RNBT	FBG	SV	IO	135-300		7	8	2850	2	5	9400	11600
21	2	SHABAH Z212	OP	RNBT	FBG	SV	IO	135-300		7	8	2850	2	5	9150	11300
21	2	SHABAH Z212 SS	OP	RNBT	FBG	SV	IO	135-300		7	8	2850	2	5	9400	11600
21	10	TALARI 220	OP	RNBT	FBG	SV	IO	135-300		8	6	3700	2	7	11000	13500
21	10	TALARI 220	OP	RNBT	FBG	SV	IO	330-350		8	6	3700	2	7	12300	14600
21	10	TALARI 220	OP	RNBT	FBG	SV	IO	385	MRCR	8	6	3700	2	7	14000	15900
21	10	TALARI 220 SS	OP	RNBT	FBG	SV	IO	135-300		8	6	3700	2	7	11300	13800
21	10	TALARI 220 SS	OP	RNBT	FBG	SV	IO	330-350		8	6	3700	2	7	12500	14800
21	10	TALARI 220 SS	OP	RNBT	FBG	SV	IO	385	MRCR	8	6	3700	2	7	14200	16100
21	10	TALARI 225	OP	RNBT	FBG	SV	IO	135-300		8	6	3850	2	7	11400	14000
21	10	TALARI 225	OP	RNBT	FBG	SV	IO	330-350		8	6	3850	2	7	12700	15100
21	10	TALARI 225	OP	RNBT	FBG	SV	IO	385	MRCR	8	6	3850	2	7	14500	16500
21	10	TALARI 225 SS	OP	RNBT	FBG	SV	IO	135-300		8	6	3850	2	7	11600	14300
21	10	TALARI 225 SS	OP	RNBT	FBG	SV	IO	330-350		8	6	3850	2	7	12900	15300
21	10	TALARI 225 SS	OP	RNBT	FBG	SV	IO	385	MRCR	8	6	3850	2	7	14700	16700
21	10	TALARI Z220	OP	RNBT	FBG	SV	IO	190-280		8	6	3700	2	7	11300	13700
21	10	TALARI Z220	OP	RNBT	FBG	SV	IO	300-350		8	6	3700	2	7	12800	15600
21	10	TALARI Z220	OP	RNBT	FBG	SV	IO	385-415		8	6	3700	2	7	14900	18000
21	10	TALARI Z220 SS	OP	RNBT	FBG	SV	IO	190-280		8	6	3700	2	7	11600	14100
21	10	TALARI Z220 SS	OP	RNBT	FBG	SV	IO	300-350		8	6	3700	2	7	13100	15900
21	10	TALARI Z220 SS	OP	RNBT	FBG	SV	IO	385-415		8	6	3700	2	7	15200	18300
21	10	TALARI Z225	OP	RNBT	FBG	SV	IO	190-280		8	6	3850	2	7	11700	14200
21	10	TALARI Z225	OP	RNBT	FBG	SV	IO	300-350		8	6	3850	2	7	13200	16100
21	10	TALARI Z225	OP	RNBT	FBG	SV	IO	385	MRCR	8	6	3850	2	7	15400	17500
21	10	TALARI Z225 SS	OP	RNBT	FBG	SV	IO	190-280		8	6	3850	2	7	11500	14000
21	10	TALARI Z225 SS	OP	RNBT	FBG	SV	IO	300-350		8	6	3850	2	7	13000	15900
21	10	TALARI Z225 SS	OP	RNBT	FBG	SV	IO	385	MRCR	8	6	3850	2	7	15200	17200
23	4	TALARI 235	OP	CUD	FBG	SV	IO	190-280		8	6	4150	2	7	12800	15700
23	4	TALARI 235	OP	CUD	FBG	SV	IO	300-350		8	6	4150	2	7	14500	17600
23	4	TALARI 235	OP	CUD	FBG	SV	IO	385-415		8	6	4150	2	7	16800	20700
23	4	TALARI 235 SS	OP	CUD	FBG	SV	IO	190-280		8	6	4150	2	7	13000	15900
23	4	TALARI 235 SS	OP	CUD	FBG	SV	IO	300-350		8	6	4150	2	7	14700	17900
23	4	TALARI 235 SS	OP	CUD	FBG	SV	IO	385-415		8	6	4150	2	7	17100	20900
23	4	TALARI 240	OP	RNBT	FBG	SV	IO	190-300		8	6	4000	2	7	11600	14400
		IO 330-350 13500 15800, IO 385 MRCR 15100 17200, IO 415 MRCR 16900 19100														
23	4	TALARI 240 SS	OP	RNBT	FBG	SV	IO	190-280		8	6	4000	2	7	11900	14600
		IO 300-350 13400 16000, IO 385 MRCR 15300 17400, IO 415 MRCR 17100 19400														
23	4	TALARI Z235	OP	CUD	FBG	SV	IO	190-280		8	6	4150			14000	16900
23	4	TALARI Z235	OP	CUD	FBG	SV	IO	300-350		8	6	4150			15600	18800
23	4	TALARI Z235	OP	CUD	FBG	SV	IO	385-415		8	6	4150			18300	21700
23	4	TALARI Z235 SS	OP	CUD	FBG	SV	IO	190-280		8	6	4150			14300	17200
23	4	TALARI Z235 SS	OP	CUD	FBG	SV	IO	300-350		8	6	4150			15900	19200
23	4	TALARI Z235 SS	OP	CUD	FBG	SV	IO	385-415		8	6	4150			18600	22000
23	4	TALARI Z240	OP	RNBT	FBG	SV	IO	190-280		8	6	4000	2	7	12800	15600
23	4	TALARI Z240	OP	RNBT	FBG	SV	IO	300-330		8	6	4000	2	7	14200	17000
23	4	TALARI Z240	OP	RNBT	FBG	SV	IO	350-385		8	6	4000	2	7	16200	19800
23	4	TALARI Z240 SS	OP	RNBT	FBG	SV	IO	190-280		8	6	4000	2	7	13100	15900
		IO 300-350 14500 17200, IO 385 MRCR 16400 18600, IO 415 MRCR 18600 20700														
25		SHABAH Z252	OP	CUD	FBG	DV	IO	205-300		8	6	4800	2	7	16900	20800
25		SHABAH Z252	OP	CUD	FBG	DV	IO	330-385		8	6	4800	2	7	19200	23400
25		SHABAH Z252	OP	CUD	FBG	DV	IO	415	MRCR	8	6	4800	2	7	22300	24800
25		SHABAH Z255	OP	CUD	FBG	DV	IO	205-300		8	6	4900			17200	21100
25		SHABAH Z255	OP	CUD	FBG	DV	IO	330-385		8	6	4900			19500	23800
25		SHABAH Z255	OP	CUD	FBG	DV	IO	415	MRCR	8	6	4900			22700	25200
27	2	SHABAH Z272	OP	CUD	FBG	DV	IO	205-300		8	6	6100	2	7	19300	24000
27	2	SHABAH Z272	OP	CUD	FBG	DV	IO	330-415		8	6	6100	2	7	21900	27200
27	2	SHABAH Z275	OP	CUD	FBG	DV	IO	205-330		8	6	6100	2	7	24200	29700
27	2	SHABAH Z275	OP	CUD	FBG	DV	IO	350-415		8	6	6100	2	7	27300	32500
		1995 BOATS														
18	2	BARCHETTA 181	OP	RNBT	FBG	SV	IO	135-180		7	8	2250	2	3	5600	6550
18	2	BARCHETTA 182	OP	RNBT	FBG	SV	IO	135-180		7	8	2250	2	3	5600	6550
18	2	TALARI 180	OP	RNBT	FBG	SV	IO	135-180		7	8	2250	2	3	5600	6550
18	10	BARCHETTA 192	OP	RNBT	FBG	SV	IO	135-180		7	8	2450	2	3	5600	6900
18	10	BARCHETTA Z192	OP	RNBT	FBG	SV	IO	135-180		7	8	2450	2	3	6300	7450
18	10	TALARI 190	OP	RNBT	FBG	SV	IO	135-180		7	8	2450	2	3	5600	6900
18	10	TALARI Z190	OP	RNBT	FBG	SV	IO	135-180		7	8	2450	2	3	6300	7450
19	10	TALARI 200	OP	RNBT	FBG	SV	IO	180-250		7	8	2650	2	4	6300	7700
19	10	TALARI Z200	OP	RNBT	FBG	SV	IO	135-250		7	8	2650	2	4	7200	8600
20	2	SHABAH 202	OP	RNBT	FBG	SV	IO	180-250		7	8	2800	2	5	7150	8700
20	2	SHABAH Z202	OP	RNBT	FBG	SV	IO	135-250		7	8	2800	2	5	8050	9450
20	3	DAVANTI 205	OP	CUD	FBG	SV	IO	180-250		8		3050	2	6	8200	9900
20	3	TALARI 210	OP	RNBT	FBG	SV	IO	180-250		8		3000	2	6	7700	9350
20	3	TALARI Z210	OP	RNBT	FBG	SV	IO	135-250		8		3000	2	6	8650	10100
21		DAVANTI 215	OP	CUD	FBG	SV	IO	180-250		8	5	3400	2	7	9450	11200
21		DAVANTI Z215	OP	CUD	FBG	SV	IO	180-250		8	5	3400	2	7	10500	12300
21	2	SHABAH 212	OP	RNBT	FBG	SV	IO	180-250		7	8	2850	2	5	7400	9000
21	2	SHABAH Z211	OP	RNBT	FBG	SV	IO	180-250		7	8	2850	2	5	8650	10300
21	2	SHABAH Z212	OP	RNBT	FBG	SV	IO	180-250		7	8	2850	2	5	8400	10000
21	10	DAVANTI 225	OP	CUD	FBG	SV	IO	180-250		8	6	3850	2	7	10800	13000
21	10	DAVANTI Z225	OP	CUD	FBG	SV	IO	180-300		8	6	3850	2	7	11900	14200
21	10	TALARI 220	OP	RNBT	FBG	SV	IO	180-250		8	6	3700	2	7	9900	11700
21	10	TALARI Z220	OP	RNBT	FBG	SV	IO	180-250		8	6	3700	2	7	11100	12900
23	4	DAVANTI 235	OP	CUD	FBG	SV	IO	190-250		8	6	4150	2	7	12300	14400
23	4	DAVANTI 235	OP	CUD	FBG	SV	IO	385	MRCR	8	6	4150	2	7	17300	19700
23	4	DAVANTI Z235	OP	CUD	FBG	SV	IO	190-300		8	6	4150	2	7	13700	15900
23	4	TALARI 240	OP	RNBT	FBG	SV	IO	205-250		8	6	4000	2	7	10900	12800
23	4	TALARI 240	OP	RNBT	FBG	SV	IO	385	MRCR	8	6	4000	2	7	14400	16400
23	4	TALARI Z240	OP	RNBT	FBG	SV	IO	190-300		8	6	4000	2	7	12100	14100
27	2	BARCHETTA Z272	OP	RNBT	FBG	SV	IO	300-385		8	6	5650	2	9	19000	23100
27	2	BARCHETTA Z272	OP	RNBT	FBG	SV	IO	415	MRCR	8	6	5650	2	9	21500	23900
27	2	DAVANTI Z275	OP	CUD	FBG	SV	IO	300-385		8	6	4950	2	9	20400	25100
27	2	DAVANTI Z275	OP	CUD	FBG	SV	IO	415	MRCR	8	6	4950	2	9	23700	26300
		1994 BOATS														
18	1	DIABIO 183	OP	RNBT	FBG	SV	OB			7	6	1650	2	3	4700	5400
18	2	BARCHETTA 181	OP	RNBT	FBG	SV	IO	115-180		7	6	2200	2	3	5150	5950
18	2	BARCHETTA 182	OP	RNBT	FBG	SV	IO	115-180		7	6	2200	2	3	5150	5950
18	2	TALARI 180	OP	RNBT	FBG	SV	IO	115-180		7	6	2200	2	3	5150	5950
18	10	BARCHETTA Z192	OP	RNBT	FBG	SV	IO	135-180		7	8	2350	2	3	5900	6800
18	10	TALARI 190	OP	RNBT	FBG	SV	IO	135-180		7	8	2350	2	3	5250	6300
18	10	TALARI 192	OP	RNBT	FBG	SV	IO	135-180		7	8	2350	2	3	5250	6300
18	10	TALARI Z190	OP	RNBT	FBG	SV	IO	135-180		7	8	2350	2	3	5900	6800
19	10	SHABAH 202	OP	RNBT	FBG	SV	IO	135-240		7	8	2550	1		5700	6950
19	10	SHABAH Z202	OP	RNBT	FBG	SV	IO	135-240		7	8	2550	1		6500	7700
19	10	TALARI 200	OP	RNBT	FBG	SV	IO	135-240		7	8	2550	1		5700	6950
19	10	TALARI Z200	OP	RNBT	FBG	SV	IO	135-240		7	8	2550	1		6600	7850
20	3	DAVANTI 205	OP	RNBT	FBG	SV	IO	135-240		8		2900	1	1	7050	8500
20	3	DAVANTI Z205	OP	RNBT	FBG	SV	IO	135-240		8		2900	1	1	7850	9350
20	3	TALARI 210	OP	RNBT	FBG	SV	IO	135-240		8		2850	1	1	6950	8400
20	3	TALARI Z210	OP	RNBT	FBG	SV	IO	135-240		8		2850	1	1	7850	9300
21	2	SHABAH 211	OP	RNBT	FBG	SV	IO	135-240		7	8	2700	1	1	6800	8300
21	2	SHABAH 212	OP	RNBT	FBG	SV	IO	135-240		7	8	2700	1	1	6800	8300
21	2	SHABAH Z211	OP	RNBT	FBG	SV	IO	135-240		7	8	2700	1	1	7850	9250
21	2	SHABAH Z212	OP	RNBT	FBG	SV	IO	135-240		7	8	2700	1	1	7850	9250
21	10	DAVANTI 225	OP	RNBT	FBG	SV	IO	180-240		8	6	3400	2	7	9300	10800
21	10	DAVANTI 225	OP	RNBT	FBG	SV	IO	350	MRCR	8	6	3400	2	7	11300	12800
21	10	DAVANTI Z225	OP	RNBT	FBG	SV	IO	180-300		8		3400	2	7	9050	11300
21	10	TALARI 220	OP	RNBT	FBG	SV	IO	180-240		8	6	3250	2	7	9050	10600
21	10	TALARI 220	OP	RNBT	FBG	SV	IO	350	MRCR	8	6	3250	2	7	11000	12500
21	10	TALARI Z220	OP	RNBT	FBG	SV	IO	180-240		8		3250	2	7	8700	10300
21	10	TALARI Z220	OP	RNBT	FBG	SV	IO	350	MRCR	8		3250	2	7	10800	12200
23	4	DAVANTI 235	OP	RNBT	FBG	SV	IO	190-240		8	6	3800	2	7	11400	13100
23	4	DAVANTI 235	OP	RNBT	FBG	SV	IO	385	MRCR	8	6	3800	2	7	14500	16400
23	4	DAVANTI Z235	OP	RNBT	FBG	SV	IO	190-300		8	6	3950	2	7	11000	13500
23	4	DAVANTI Z241	OP	RNBT	FBG	SV	IO	205-300		8	6	3850	2	7	10800	13300
23	4	TALARI 240	OP	RNBT	FBG	SV	IO	190-240		8	6	3800	2	7	9800	11500
23	4	TALARI 240	OP	RNBT	FBG	SV	IO	385	MRCR	8	6	3800	2	7	13100	14800

 CONTINUED ON NEXT PAGE

LOA FT	LOA IN	NAME AND/ OR MODEL	TOP/ RIG	BOAT TYPE	-HULL- MTL	-HULL- TP	ENGINE TP	ENGINE # HP	ENGINE MFG	BEAM FT	BEAM IN	WGT LBS	DRAFT FT	DRAFT IN	RETAIL LOW	RETAIL HIGH
		1994 BOATS														
23	4	TALARI Z240	OP	RNBT	FBG	SV	IO	190-300		8	6	3800	2	7	10900	13200
27	2	BARCHETTA Z272	OP	RNBT	FBG	SV	IO	250-300		8	6	4950	2	9	15600	18600
27	2	BARCHETTA Z272	OP	RNBT	FBG	SV	IO	385	MRCR	8	6	4950	2	9	18600	20700
27	2	DAVANTI Z275	OP	RNBT	FBG	SV	IO	250-300		8	6	4950	2	9	16500	19600
27	2	DAVANTI Z275	OP	RNBT	FBG	SV	IO	385	MRCR	8	6	4950	2	9	19300	21400
		1993 BOATS														
18	1	DIABLO	OP	RNBT	FBG	SV	OB			7	6	1600	2	3	4400	5050
18	1	DIABLO	OP	RNBT	FBG	SV	IO	125-175		7	6	2200	2	3	4750	5650
18	7	1900 Z	OP	RNBT	FBG	SV	IO	145-205		7	7	2280	2	3	5300	6500
18	7	1900 ZS	OP	RNBT	FBG	SV	IO	145-205		7	6	2280	2	3	5000	5850
18	7	MX 19	OP	RNBT	FBG	SV	IO	145-205		7	7	2250	2	3	5000	5950
18	7	MX 19 S	OP	RNBT	FBG	SV	IO	145-205		7	7	2280	2	3	4800	5950
18	10	BARCHETTA	OP	RNBT	FBG	SV	IO	145-205		7	6	2500	2	3	5050	5950
18	10	BARCHETTA Z	OP	RNBT	FBG	SV	IO	145-205		7	6	2500	2	3	5550	6500
19	8	SHABAH MX 198	OP	RNBT	FBG	SV	IO	175-260							5600	6900
19	8	SHABAH Z 198	OP	RNBT	FBG	SV	IO	175-260							6250	7600
19	10	TALARI MX 200	OP	RNBT	FBG	SV	IO	175-260		7	6	2550	2	3	5400	6650
19	10	TALARI Z 200	OP	RNBT	FBG	SV	IO	175-260		7	6	2550	2	3	6000	7300
20	3	2000 Z	OP	RNBT	FBG	SV	IO	175-260		8		2760	2	6	6800	8450
20	3	2000 Z C	OP	RNBT	FBG	SV	IO	175-260		8		2860	2	6	6950	8600
20	3	MX 20	OP	RNBT	FBG	SV	IO	175-260		8		2760	2	6	6800	8450
20	3	MX 20 C	OP	RNBT	FBG	SV	IO	175-260		8		2860	2	6	6950	8600
21	2	SHABAH MX 212	OP	RNBT	FBG	SV	IO	175-260		7	8	2650	2	6	6400	7850
21	2	SHABAH MX 212S	OP	RNBT	FBG	SV	IO	175-260		7	6	2650	2	6	6350	7800
21	2	SHABAH Z 212	OP	RNBT	FBG	SV	IO	175-260		7	8	2650	2	6	7250	8700
21	2	SHABAH ZS 212	OP	RNBT	FBG	SV	IO	175-260		7	6	2650	2	6	7150	8650
21	6	2200 Z	OP	RNBT	FBG	SV	IO	200-260		8		3150	2	7	7900	9450
21	6	2200 Z	OP	RNBT	FBG	SV	IO	270	MRCR	8		3380	2	7	8950	10200
21	6	2200 Z C	OP	RNBT	FBG	SV	IO	200-260		8		3250	2	7	8050	9650
21	6	2200 Z C	OP	RNBT	FBG	SV	IO	270	MRCR	8		3380	2	7	9350	10600
21	6	MX 22	OP	RNBT	FBG	SV	IO	200-270		8		3150	2	7	7900	9450
21	6	MX 22 C	OP	RNBT	FBG	SV	IO	200-260		8		3250	2	7	8050	9650
21	6	MX 22 C	OP	RNBT	FBG	SV	IO	270	MRCR	8		3480	2	7	8950	10200
23	4	2350 Z	OP	RNBT	FBG	SV	IO	200-330		8	6	3900	2	7	10200	12700
23	4	2350 Z C	OP	RNBT	FBG	SV	IO	200-260		8	6	3800	2	7	10000	12000
23	4	2350 Z C	OP	RNBT	FBG	SV	IO	330	MRCR	8	6	3900	2	7	11600	13100
23	4	240 Z	OP	RNBT	FBG	SV	IO	200-260		8	6	3900	2	7	10200	12000
23	4	240 Z	OP	RNBT	FBG	SV	IO	330	MRCR	8	6	3900	2	7	12000	13600
		1992 BOATS														
18	1	DIABLO MX 18	OP	RNBT	FBG	SV	OB			7	6	1600	2	3	4200	4850
18	1	DIABLO MX 18	OP	RNBT	FBG	SV	IO	125-175		7	6	2200	2	3	4500	5350
18	7	1900 Z	OP	RNBT	FBG	SV	IO	145-205		7	7	2280	2	3	4950	6100
18	7	MX 19	OP	RNBT	FBG	SV	IO	145-205		7	7	2250	2	3	4700	5550
18	7	MX 19 S	OP	RNBT	FBG	SV	IO	145-205		7	7	2280	2	3	4500	5550
19	8	SHABAH MX 198	OP	RNBT	FBG	SV	IO	175-260							5300	6450
19	8	SHABAH MX 198	OP	RNBT	FBG	SV	IO	330	MRCR						6500	7450
19	8	SHABAH Z 198	OP	RNBT	FBG	SV	IO	175-260							5850	7100
19	8	SHABAH Z 198	OP	RNBT	FBG	SV	IO	330	MRCR						7100	8200
20	3	2000 Z	OP	RNBT	FBG	SV	IO	175-260		8		2760	2	6	6400	7900
20	3	2000 Z C	OP	RNBT	FBG	SV	IO	175-260		8		2860	2	6	6500	8050
20	3	MX 20	OP	RNBT	FBG	SV	IO	175-260		8		2760	2	6	6400	7900
20	3	MX 20 C	OP	RNBT	FBG	SV	IO	175-260		8		2860	2	6	6500	8050
21	2	SHABAH MX 212	OP	RNBT	FBG	SV	IO	175-260		7	8	2650	2	6	5950	7250
21	2	SHABAH Z 212	OP	RNBT	FBG	SV	IO	175-260		7	8	2650	2	6	6850	8250
21	6	2200 Z	OP	RNBT	FBG	SV	IO	200-260		8		3150	2	7	7400	8850
21	6	2200 Z	OP	RNBT	FBG	SV	IO	330	MRCR	8		3380	2	7	9100	10300
21	6	2200 Z C	OP	RNBT	FBG	SV	IO	200-260		8		3250	2	7	7550	9000
21	6	2200 Z C	OP	RNBT	FBG	SV	IO	330	MRCR	8		3380	2	7	10100	11500
21	6	MX 22	OP	RNBT	FBG	SV	IO	200-330		8		3150	2	7	7400	9200
21	6	MX 22 C	OP	RNBT	FBG	SV	IO	200-260		8		3250	2	7	7550	9000
21	6	MX 22 C	OP	RNBT	FBG	SV	IO	330	MRCR	8		3480	2	7	9250	10500
23	4	2350 Z	OP	RNBT	FBG	SV	IO	200-260		8	6	3900	2	7	9550	11200
23	4	2350 Z	OP	RNBT	FBG	SV	IO	330	MRCR	8	6	3900	2	7	10800	12300
23	4	2350 Z C	OP	RNBT	FBG	SV	IO	200-260		8	6	3800	2	7	9400	11200
23	4	2350 Z C	OP	RNBT	FBG	SV	IO	330	MRCR	8	6	3900	2	7	10800	12300
23	4	240 Z	OP	RNBT	FBG	SV	IO	200-260		8	6	3900	2	7	9550	11200
23	4	240 Z	OP	RNBT	FBG	SV	IO	330	MRCR	8	6	3900	2	7	10800	12300
		1991 BOATS														
18	1	DIABLO MX 18	OP	RNBT	FBG	SV	IO	130-175		7	6	2200	2	3	4150	5000
18	7	1900 Z	OP	RNBT	FBG	SV	IO	145-205		7	7	2280	2	3	4600	5600
18	7	1900 Z S	OP	RNBT	FBG	SV	IO	145-205		7	7	2280	2	3	4600	5600
18	7	MX 19	OP	RNBT	FBG	SV	IO	145-205		7	7	2250	2	3	4400	5150
18	7	MX 19 S	OP	RNBT	FBG	SV	IO	145-175		7	7	2280	2	3	4100	5100
18	7	MX 19 S	OP	RNBT	FBG	SV	IO	205	MRCR	7	7	2450	2	3	4500	5150
20	3	2000 Z	OP	RNBT	FBG	SV	IO	175-260		8		2760	2	6	6000	7400
20	3	2000 Z C	OP	RNBT	FBG	SV	IO	175-260		8		2860	2	6	6100	7550
20	3	MX 20	OP	RNBT	FBG	SV	IO	175-260		8		2760	2	6	6000	7400
20	3	MX 20 C	OP	RNBT	FBG	SV	IO	175-260		8		2860	2	6	6100	7550
21	6	2150 Z C	OP	RNBT	FBG	SV	IO	200-260		8		3250	2	7	6950	8300
21	6	2150 Z C	OP	RNBT	FBG	SV	IO	330	MRCR	8		3380	2	7	9050	10300
21	6	2200 Z	OP	RNBT	FBG	SV	IO	200-260		8		3150	2	7	6950	8300
21	6	2200 Z	OP	RNBT	FBG	SV	IO	330	MRCR	8		3380	2	7	8250	9500
21	6	2200 Z C	OP	RNBT	FBG	SV	IO	200-260		8		3250	2	7	7150	8650
21	6	2200 Z C	OP	RNBT	FBG	SV	IO	330	MRCR	8		3380	2	7	9350	10600
21	6	MX 22	OP	RNBT	FBG	SV	IO	200-330		8		3150	2	7	6950	8450
21	6	MX 22 C	OP	RNBT	FBG	SV	IO	200-260		8		3250	2	7	7050	8450
21	6	MX 22 C	OP	RNBT	FBG	SV	IO	330	MRCR	8		3480	2	7	8600	9900
23	4	2350 Z C	OP	RNBT	FBG	SV	IO	260	MRCR	8	6	3800	2	7	9150	10400
23	4	2350 Z C	OP	RNBT	FBG	SV	IO	330-365		8	6	3900	2	7	10200	12400
		1990 BOATS														
18	6	1850 XL	OP	RNBT	FBG	SV	IO	130-205		7	6	2270	2	3	4050	5050
20		2000 XL	OP	RNBT	FBG	SV	IO	175-260		8		2760	2	6	5550	6900
20		2000 XLC	OP	CUD	FBG	SV	IO	175-260		8		2860	2	6	5900	7350
21	6	2150 XL	OP	RNBT	FBG	SV	IO	200-260		8		3150	2	7	6500	7800
21	6	2150 XL	OP	RNBT	FBG	SV	IO	330	MRCR	8		3380	2	7	7950	9150
21	6	2150 XLC	OP	CUD	FBG	SV	IO	200-260		8		3250	2	7	7000	8400
21	6	2150 XLC	OP	CUD	FBG	SV	IO	330	MRCR	8		3480	2	7	8550	9800

MARIEHOLMS PLAST AB

HILLERSTORP SWEDEN COAST GUARD MFG ID- MHM See inside cover to adjust price for area

ATKINS YACHT SALES
ANNAPOLIS MD 21403

LOA FT	LOA IN	NAME AND/ OR MODEL	TOP/ RIG	BOAT TYPE	-HULL- MTL	-HULL- TP	ENGINE TP	ENGINE # HP	ENGINE MFG	BEAM FT	BEAM IN	WGT LBS	DRAFT FT	DRAFT IN	RETAIL LOW	RETAIL HIGH
		1984 BOATS														
25	9	INTERNATL-FOLKBOAT	SLP	SA/OD	FBG	KL	OB			7	5				11800	13400
25	9	INTERNATL-FOLKBOAT	SLP	SA/OD	FBG	KL	IB	8D	VLVO	7	5				12700	14400
26		MARIEHOLM 261	SLP	SA/CR	FBG	KL	IB	7D	VLVO						14200	16200

....For earlier years, see the BUC Used Boat Price Guide, Volume 3

MARIN YACHT SALES

SAN RAFAEL CA 94901 COAST GUARD MFG ID- MYA See inside cover to adjust price for area

LOA FT	LOA IN	NAME AND/ OR MODEL	TOP/ RIG	BOAT TYPE	-HULL- MTL	-HULL- TP	ENGINE TP	ENGINE # HP	ENGINE MFG	BEAM FT	BEAM IN	WGT LBS	DRAFT FT	DRAFT IN	RETAIL LOW	RETAIL HIGH
		1989 BOATS														
36		PT 36	FB	SF	FBG	DV	IB	T150D	CUM	12	6	20000	3		71000	78000
36		PT 36	FB	SF	FBG	DV	IB	T210D	CUM	12	6	20000	3		72500	79600
36		PT 36	FB	SF	FBG	DV	IB	T250D	CUM	12	6	20000	3		74000	81300
39		PT 35	FB	SF	FBG	DV	IB	T150D	CUM	12	6	20000			84700	93000
39		PT 35	FB	SF	FBG	DV	IB	T210D	CUM	12	6	20000			86700	95300
39		PT 35	FB	SF	FBG	DV	IB	T250D	CUM	12	6	20000			88400	97100
41	5	PT 38	FB	YTFS	FBG	SV	IB	T150D	CUM	13	7	23000	3	6	89500	98400
41	5	PT 38	FB	YTFS	FBG	SV	IB	T210D	CUM	13	7	23000	3	6	96000	105500
41	5	PT 38	FB	YTFS	FBG	SV	IB	T250D	CUM	13	7	23000	3	6	100000	110000
45	6	PT 42	FB	YTFS	FBG	SV	IB	T150D	CUM	13	7	23000	3	6	76200	83800
45	6	PT 42	FB	YTFS	FBG	SV	IB	T210D	CUM	13	7	23000	3	6	80900	88900
45	6	PT 42	FB	YTFS	FBG	SV	IB	T250D	CUM	13	7	23000	3	6	88400	97100
46	4	PT 46	FB	YTFS	FBG	SV	IB	T300D	CUM	15	9	31500	3	8	110000	120500
46	4	PT 46	FB	YTFS	FBG	SV	IB	T375D	CAT	15	9	31500	3	8	123500	136000
51	10	PT 52	FB	YTFS	FBG	SV	IB	T300D	CUM	15	9	31500	3	8	104500	115000
51	10	PT 52	FB	YTFS	FBG	SV	IB	T375D	CAT	15	9	31500	3	8	120000	132000
		1985 BOATS														
35	4	SUNDECK P/T 35	FB	TRWL	FBG	SV	IB	135D	PERK	12	6	19000	3		48900	53700
		IB 200D PERK 49700 54600, IB 350D PERK 52600 57800, IB T135D PERK 51700 56800														
		IB T200D PERK 54000 59300														
37	6	P/T 38	FB	TRWL	FBG	DS	IB	135D	PERK	13	6	21000	3	6	62300	68500
		IB 200D PERK 63200 69400, IB 350D CAT 66700 73300, IB T135D PERK 66700 73300														
		IB T200D PERK 68900 75700, IB T350D CAT 76400 84000														
38	6	SUNDECK P/T 38/2	FB	TRWL	FBG	DS	IB	135D	PERK	13	6	21000	3	6	64800	71200
		IB 200D PERK 65700 72200, IB 350D CAT 69400 76300, IB T135D PERK 69500 76400														
		IB T200D PERK 71700 78800, IB T350D CAT 79300 87100														

CONTINUED ON NEXT PAGE

LOA FT IN	NAME AND/ OR MODEL		TOP/ RIG	BOAT TYPE	-HULL- MTL TP TP	----ENGINE--- # HP MFG	BEAM FT IN	WGT LBS	DRAFT FT IN	RETAIL LOW	RETAIL HIGH
						1985 BOATS					
41	P/T 41		FB	TRWL	FBG DS IB	135D PERK 13	6	26000	3 6	81200	89200
	IB 200D PERK	82200	90400, IB		350D CAT	85800 94300,	IB T135D PERK	85900		94400	
	IB T200D PERK	88000	96700, IB		T350D CAT	95200 104500					
42	SUNDECK P/T 42		FB	TRWL	FBG DS IB	135D PERK 13	6	27000	3 6	81700	89800
	IB 200D PERK	82800	91000, IB		350D PERK	86200 94200,	IB T135D PERK	86000		94500	
	IB T200D PERK	88100	96900, IB		T350D PERK	95000 104500					
46	SUNDECK P/T 46		FB	TRWL	FBG SV IB	T225D 15		31000	4	80300	88300
	IB T250D	81200	89200, IB		T270D	81900 89900,	IB T355D PERK	85200		93600	

....For earlier years, see the BUC Used Boat Price Guide, Volume 3

MARINE CONCEPTS
TARPON SPRINGS FL 34689 COAST GUARD MFG ID- MHC See inside cover to adjust price for area

For more recent years, see the BUC Used Boat Price Guide, Volume 1

LOA FT IN	NAME AND/ OR MODEL	TOP/ RIG	BOAT TYPE	-HULL- MTL TP TP	----ENGINE--- # HP MFG	BEAM FT IN	WGT LBS	DRAFT FT IN	RETAIL LOW	RETAIL HIGH
					1996 BOATS					
21	SEA-PEARL 21	KTH	SACAC	F/S LB OB		5 6	650	6	8250	9450
21	SEA-PEARL TRI-21	KTH	SACAC	F/S TM		14	950	6	11300	12900
27 8	SEA-PEARL 28	KTH	SACAC	F/S CB OB		8	4200	1 7	32300	35900
					1995 BOATS					
21	SEA-PEARL 21	KTH	SACAC	F/S LB OB		5 6	650	6	7800	8950
21	SEA-PEARL TRI-21	KTH	SACAC	F/S TM		14	950	6	10700	12200
27 8	SEA-PEARL 28	KTH	SACAC	F/S CB OB		8	4200	1 7	30600	34000
					1994 BOATS					
21	SEA-PEARL 21	KTH	SACAC	F/S LB OB		5 6	650	6	7400	8500
21	SEA-PEARL TRI-21	KTH	SACAC	F/S TM		14	950	6	10200	11500
27 8	SEA-PEARL 28	KTH	SACAC	F/S CB OB		8	4200	1 7	29000	32200
28 8	ROB-ROY 23	YWL	SACAC	F/S CB OB		6 11	2650	1 6	15300	17400
					1993 BOATS					
21	SEA-PEARL 21	KTH	SACAC	F/S LB OB		5 6	650	6	7000	8050
27 8	SEA-PEARL 28	KTH	SACAC	F/S CB OB		8	3750	1 7	24600	27400
28 8	ROB-ROY 23	YWL	SACAC	F/S CB OB		6 11	2650	1 6	14500	16500
					1992 BOATS					
21	SEA-PEARL 21	KTH	SAIL	F/S LB OB		5 6	650	6	6650	7600
21	SEA-PEARL 21	KTH	SAIL	F/S CB OB		5 6	650	6	6650	7600
27 8	SEA-PEARL 28	KTH	SAIL	F/S CB OB		8	3750	1 7	23300	25900
28 8	ROB-ROY 23	YWL	SAIL	F/S CB OB		6 11	2650	1 6	13700	15600
					1991 BOATS					
16	SEA-PEARL 16	CAT	SAIL	F/S CB OB		5 6	450	5	4200	4900
21	SEA-PEARL 21	KTH	SAIL	F/S CB OB		5 6	550	6	6000	6900
21	SEA-PEARL 21	KTH	SAIL	F/S LB OB		5 6	550	6	6000	6900
23	SUNSEEKER 23 SLOOP	SLP	SAIL	F/S CB OB		6 11	2400	1 6	12300	14000
27 8	SEA-PEARL 28	KTH	SAIL	F/S CB OB		8	3750	1 6	22100	24600
28 8	ROB-ROY 23	YWL	SAIL	F/S CB OB		6 11	2600	1 6	12800	14600
					1990 BOATS					
16	SEA-PEARL 16	CAT	SAIL	F/S CB OB		5 6	450	5	4000	4650
21	SEA-PEARL 21	KTH	SAIL	F/S CB OB		5 6	550	6	5700	6550
21	SEA-PEARL 21	KTH	SAIL	F/S LB OB		5 6	550	6	5700	6550
23	SUNSEEKER 23 SLOOP	SLP	SAIL	F/S CB OB		6 11	2400	1 6	11700	13300
27 8	SEA-PEARL 28	KTH	SAIL	F/S CB OB		8	3750	1 6	20900	23300
28 8	ROB-ROY 23	YWL	SA/CR	F/S CB OB		6 11	2600	1 6	12100	13800
					1989 BOATS					
16	SEA-PEARL 16	CAT	SAIL	F/S CB OB		5 6	450	5	3750	4400
21	SEA-PEARL 21	KTH	SAIL	F/S CB OB		5 6	550	6	5400	6200
21	SEA-PEARL 21	KTH	SAIL	F/S LB OB		5 6	550	6	5400	6200
23	SUNSEEKER 23 SLOOP	SLP	SAIL	F/S CB OB		6 11	2400	1 6	11100	12600
24	SEA-PEARL 24	KTH	SAIL	FBG CB OB		7	2500	1 6	12000	13600
24	SEA-PEARL 24	KTH	SAIL	FBG LB OB		7	1700	8	9600	10900
27 8	SEA-PEARL 28	KTH	SAIL	FBG CB OB		8	3750	1 6	19800	22000
28 8	ROB-ROY 23	YWL	SA/CR	F/S CB OB		6 11	2600	1 6	11500	13100
					1988 BOATS					
16	SEA-PEARL	CAT	SAIL	FBG CB OB		5 6	400	5	3350	3900
21	SEA-PEARL MARCONI	KTH	SAIL	FBG CB OB		5 6	550	6	5100	5900
21	SEA-PEARL MARCONI	KTH	SAIL	FBG LB OB		5 6	550	6	5100	5900
23	SUNSEEKER 23 SLOOP	SLP	SAIL	F/S CB OB		6 11	2400	1 6	10500	11900
28 8	ROB-ROY 23	YWL	SA/CR	F/S CB OB		6 11	2600	1 8	10900	12400
					1987 BOATS					
16	SEA-PEARL	CAT	SAIL	FBG CB OB		5 6	400	5	3200	3700
21	SEA-PEARL LUG	KTH	SAIL	FBG CB OB		5 6	550	6	4900	5600
21	SEA-PEARL LUG	KTH	SAIL	FBG LB OB		5 6	550	6	5050	5800
21	SEA-PEARL MARCONI	KTH	SAIL	FBG CB OB		5 6	550	6	4650	5350
21	SEA-PEARL MARCONI	KTH	SAIL	FBG LB OB		5 6	550	6	4800	5500
28 8	ROB-ROY 23	YWL	SA/CR	F/S CB OB		6 11	2600	1 8	10300	11700
28 8	ROB-ROY 23	YWL	SA/CR	F/S CB IB	6D BMW	6 11	2600	1 8	12200	13900
					1986 BOATS					
16	SEA-PEARL	KTH	SAIL	FBG CB OB		5 6	400	5	3000	3500
21	SEA-PEARL LUG	KTH	SAIL	FBG CB OB		5 6	550	6	4600	5300
21	SEA-PEARL LUG	KTH	SAIL	FBG LB OB		5 6	550	6	4750	5500
21	SEA-PEARL MARCONI	KTH	SAIL	FBG CB OB		5 6	550	6	4450	5100
21	SEA-PEARL MARCONI	KTH	SAIL	FBG LB OB		5 6	550	6	4600	5300
28 8	ROB-ROY 23	YWL	SA/CR	F/S CB OB		6 11	2600	1 7	9800	11100
28 8	ROB-ROY 23	YWL	SA/CR	F/S CB IB	6D BMW	6 11	2600	1 7	11600	13200
					1985 BOATS					
21	SEA-PEARL LUG	KTH	SAIL	FBG CB OB		5 6	550	6	4400	5050
21	SEA-PEARL LUG	KTH	SAIL	FBG LB OB		5 6	550	6	4550	5250
21	SEA-PEARL MARCONI	KTH	SAIL	FBG CB OB		5 6	550	6	4150	4850
21	SEA-PEARL MARCONI	KTH	SAIL	FBG LB OB		5 6	550	6	4400	5050
28 8	ROB-ROY 23	YWL	SA/CR	F/S CB OB		6 11	2500	1 6	9100	10300
28 8	ROB-ROY 23	YWL	SA/CR	F/S CB SD	8 VLVO	6 11	2500	1 6	9650	11000
28 8	ROB-ROY 23	YWL	SA/CR	F/S CB IB	6D BMW	6 11	2500	1 6	10700	12200
					1984 BOATS					
21	SEA-PEARL 21	KTH	SAIL	FBG LB		5 6	550	6	4100	4750
28 8	ROB-ROY 23	YWL	SA/CR	F/S CB OB		6 11	2200	1 6	7850	9000

....For earlier years, see the BUC Used Boat Price Guide, Volume 3

MARINE GROUP INC
DIV OF TRACKER MARINE   See inside cover to adjust price for area
SPRINGFIELD MO 65803   COAST GUARD MFG ID- MGI

LOA FT IN	NAME AND/ OR MODEL		TOP/ RIG	BOAT TYPE	-HULL- MTL TP TP	----ENGINE--- # HP MFG	BEAM FT IN	WGT LBS	DRAFT FT IN	RETAIL LOW	RETAIL HIGH
						1988 BOATS					
16	ASTROGLASS-BASS 160		OP	BASS	FBG SV OB		5 10	1050		2250	2600
16	ASTROGLASS-COMBO 160		OP	BASS	FBG SV OB		5 10	1050		2350	2700
16	ASTROGLASS-CRAPPIE		OP	BASS	FBG SV OB		5 10	1050		2050	2450
16	PROCRAFT F-&-S 1600		OP	BASS	FBG SV OB		5 10	1050		2350	2700
16	PROCRAFT-BASS 1600		OP	BASS	FBG SV OB		5 10	1050		2250	2600
16	PROCRAFT-CRAPPIE		OP	UTIL	FBG SV OB		5 10	1050		2250	2650
16 6	ASTROGLASS-BASS 166		OP	BASS	FBG SV OB		6 10	1100		2300	2650
16 6	ASTROGLASS-COMBO 166		OP	BASS	FBG SV OB		6 10	1100		2350	2750
16 6	ASTROGLASS-RIVAL 166		OP	BASS	FBG SV OB		6 10	1100		2450	2850
16 6	FABUGLAS-BAHAMA		ST	RNBT	FBG DV OB		6 9	1100		2350	2750
16 6	FABUGLAS-BAHAMA SF		OP	RNBT	FBG DV OB		6 9	1100		2350	2750
16 6	FABUGLAS-BIMINI		ST	RNBT	FBG DV IO		6 9	1600		2350	2700
16 6	FABUGLAS-BUCCANEER		ST	RNBT	FBG DV IO	130	6 7	1600		2350	2700
16 6	FABUGLAS-TEMPEST		ST	RNBT	FBG DV OB	130	6 7	1000		2200	2550
16 6	PROCRAFT-BASS 1660		OP	BASS	FBG SV OB		6 10	1100		2300	2650
16 6	PROCRAFT-COMPETITOR		OP	BASS	FBG SV OB		6 10	1100		2450	2850
16 6	PROCRAFT-F-&-S 1660		OP	BASS	FBG SV OB		6 10	1100		2350	2750
17 3	FABUGLAS-CAYMAN		ST	RNBT	FBG DV IO	205	7 1	2200		3000	3500
17 8	ASTROGLASS-BASS 178		OP	BASS	FBG SV OB		7 2	1200		2650	3950
17 8	ASTROGLASS-COMBO 178		OP	BASS	FBG SV OB		7 2	1200		2550	3000
17 8	ASTROGLASS-RIVAL 178		OP	BASS	FBG SV OB		7 2	1200		2750	3200
17	PROCRAFT-BASS 1780		OP	BASS	FBG SV OB		7 2	1200		2550	2950
17	PROCRAFT-COMPETITOR		OP	BASS	FBG SV OB		7 2	1200		2750	3200
17	PROCRAFT-F-&-S 1780		OP	BASS	FBG SV OB		7 2	1200		2550	3000
18 9	FABUGLAS-JAMAICAN		OP	RNBT	FBG DV IO	260	7 4	2400		3750	4350
19	ASTROGLASS-BASS 195		OP	BASS	FBG SV OB		7 4	1550		3300	3850
19	ASTROGLASS-COMBO 195		OP	BASS	FBG SV OB		7 4	1550		3400	3950
19	ASTROGLASS-RIVAL 195		OP	BASS	FBG SV OB		7 4	1550		3500	4050
19	PROCRAFT-BASS 1950		OP	BASS	FBG SV OB		7 4	1550		3300	3850
19	PROCRAFT-COMPETITOR		OP	BASS	FBG SV OB		7 4	1550		3500	4050
19	PROCRAFT-F-&-S 1950		OP	BASS	FBG SV OB		7 4	1550		3400	3950
						1987 BOATS					
16	ASTROGLASS-BASS 160			BASS	FBG OB		6 8	1050		2200	2550
16	ASTROGLASS-COMBO 160			BASS	FBG OB		6 8	1050		2350	2700
16	ASTROGLASS-CRAPPIE			BASS	FBG OB		6 8	1050		2050	2400
16	PROCRAFT-BASS 1600			BASS	FBG OB		6 8	1050		2200	2550
16	PROCRAFT-CRAPPIE			BASS	FBG OB		6 8	1050		2050	2400
16	PROCRAFT-F-&-S 1600			BASS	FBG OB		6 8	1050		2350	2700
16 6	ASTROGLASS-BASS 166			BASS	FBG SV OB		6 10	1100		2200	2550
16 6	ASTROGLASS-BASS 166V	OP		BASS	FBG SV OB		6 10	1100		2250	2650
16 6	ASTROGLASS-COMBO 166			BASS	FBG OB		6 10	1100		2300	2700
16 6	ASTROGLASS-COMBO 166	OP		BASS	FBG SV OB		6 10	1100		2350	2750
16 6	ASTROGLASS-RIVAL 166			BASS	FBG OB		6 10	1100		2400	2800
16 6	FABUGLAS-BAHAMA			RNBT	FBG OB		6 9	1100		2200	2600

LOA FT	LOA IN	NAME AND/ OR MODEL	TOP/ RIG	BOAT TYPE	HULL MTL	HULL TP	ENGINE TP	ENGINE # HP	ENGINE MFG	BEAM FT	BEAM IN	WGT LBS	DRAFT FT	DRAFT IN	RETAIL LOW	RETAIL HIGH
		1987 BOATS														
16	6	FABUGLAS-BAHAMA SF		RNBT	FBG		OB			6	9	1100			2400	2800
16	6	FABUGLAS-BUCCANEER		RNBT	FBG		IO	130		6	7	1600			2200	2600
16	6	FABUGLAS-BUCCANEER	ST	RNBT	FBG	DV	IO	120		6	7	1600			2200	2600
16	6	FABUGLAS-TEMPEST		RNBT	FBG		OB			6	7	1000			2100	2500
16	6	FABUGLAS-TEMPEST	ST	RNBT	FBG	DV	OB			6	7	1000			2100	2500
16	6	PROCRAFT-BASS 1660		BASS	FBG		OB			6	10	1100			2200	2550
16	6	PROCRAFT-BASS 166OV	OP	BASS	FBG	SV	OB			6	10	1100			2250	2650
16	6	PROCRAFT-COMPETITOR		BASS	FBG		OB			6	10	1100			2400	2800
16	6	PROCRAFT-F-&-S 1660		BASS	FBG		OB			6	10	1100			2300	2700
16	6	PROCRAFT-F-&-S 166OV	OP	BASS	FBG	SV	OB			6	10	1100			2350	2750
17	2	FABUGLAS-CUTLASS	ST	RNBT	FBG	DV	OB			7	4	1600			3150	3650
17	3	FABUGLAS-CAYMAN		RNBT	FBG		IO	205		7	1	2200			2850	3300
17	3	FABUGLAS-CAYMAN	ST	RNBT	FBG	DV	IO	120		7	1	2200			2800	3250
17	8	ASTROGLASS-BASS 178		BASS	FBG		OB			7	2	1200			2450	2850
17	8	ASTROGLASS-BASS 178V	OP	BASS	FBG	SV	OB			7	2	1200			2400	2800
17	8	ASTROGLASS-COMBO 178		BASS	FBG		OB			7	2	1200			2500	2900
17	8	ASTROGLASS-COMBO 178	OP	BASS	FBG	SV	OB			7	2	1200			2500	2950
17	8	ASTROGLASS-RIVAL 178		BASS	FBG		OB			7	2	1200			2700	3100
17	8	ASTROGLASS-RIVAL 178	OP	BASS	FBG	SV	OB			7	2	1200			2700	3150
17	8	FABUGLAS-CRUSADER	ST	RNBT	FBG	DV	IO	120		7	4	2400			3050	3550
17	8	PROCRAFT-BASS 1780		BASS	FBG		OB			7	2	1200			2450	2850
17	8	PROCRAFT-BASS 178OV	OP	BASS	FBG	SV	OB			7	2	1200			2400	2800
17	8	PROCRAFT-COMPETITOR		BASS	FBG		OB			7	2	1200			2700	3100
17	8	PROCRAFT-COMPETITOR	OP	BASS	FBG	SV	OB			7	2	1200			2500	2950
17	8	PROCRAFT-F-&-S 1780		BASS	FBG		OB			7	2	1200			2500	2900
17	8	PROCRAFT-F-&-S 178OV	OP	BASS	FBG	SV	OB			7	2	1200			2700	3150
18	8	FABUGLAS-COMMODORE	ST	RNBT	FBG	DV	IO	120		7	5	2500			3300	3850
18	9	FABUGLAS-JAMAICAN		RNBT	FBG		IO	260		7	7	2400			3550	4150
19	6	ASTROGLASS-BASS 195		BASS	FBG		OB			7	4	1550			3200	3750
19	6	ASTROGLASS-BASS 195V	OP	BASS	FBG	SV	OB			7	4	1550			3200	3750
19	6	ASTROGLASS-COMBO 195		BASS	FBG		OB			7	4	1550			3300	3850
19	6	ASTROGLASS-COMBO 195	OP	BASS	FBG	SV	OB			7	4	1550			3300	3850
19	6	ASTROGLASS-RIVAL 195		BASS	FBG		OB			7	4	1550			3400	3950
19	6	ASTROGLASS-RIVAL 195	OP	BASS	FBG	SV	OB			7	4	1550			3400	3950
19	6	PROCRAFT F-&-S 1950V	OP	BASS	FBG	SV	OB			7	4	1550			3300	3850
19	6	PROCRAFT-BASS 1950		BASS	FBG		OB			7	4	1550			3200	3750
19	6	PROCRAFT-BASS 1950V	OP	BASS	FBG	SV	OB			7	4	1550			3200	3750
19	6	PROCRAFT-COMPET 1950	OP	BASS	FBG	SV	OB			7	4	1550			3400	3950
19	6	PROCRAFT-COMPETITOR		BASS	FBG		OB			7	4	1550			3400	3950
19	6	PROCRAFT-F-&-S 1950		BASS	FBG		OB			7	4	1550			3300	3850
		1986 BOATS														
16	6	ASTROGLASS-BASS 165V	OP	BASS	FBG	SV	OB			6	8	1075			2200	2550
16	6	ASTROGLASS-COMBO 165	OP	BASS	FBG	SV	OB			6	8	1075			2200	2600
16	6	FABUGLAS-BUCCANEER	ST	RNBT	FBG	DV	IO	120		6	7	1600			2050	2450
16	6	FABUGLAS-TEMPEST	ST	RNBT	FBG	DV	OB			6	7	1000			2050	2400
16	6	PROCRAFT-BASS 1650V	OP	BASS	FBG	SV	OB			6	8	1075			2200	2550
16	6	PROCRAFT-F-&-S 1650V	OP	BASS	FBG	SV	OB			6	8	1075			2200	2600
17	2	FABUGLAS-CUTLASS	ST	RNBT	FBG	DV	OB			7	4	1600			3050	3550
17	6	ASTROGLASS-BASS 175V	OP	BASS	FBG	SV	OB			7		1175			2300	2700
17	6	ASTROGLASS-COMBO 175	OP	BASS	FBG	SV	OB			7		1175			2350	2700
17	6	ASTROGLASS-RIVAL 175	OP	BASS	FBG	SV	OB			7		1175			2650	3100
17	6	PROCRAFT-BASS 1750V	OP	BASS	FBG	SV	OB			7		1175			2300	2700
17	6	PROCRAFT-COMPETITOR	OP	BASS	FBG	SV	OB			7		1175			2650	3100
17	6	PROCRAFT-F-&-S 1750V	OP	BASS	FBG	SV	OB			7		1175			2350	2700
17	8	FABUGLAS-CRUSADER	ST	RNBT	FBG	DV	IO	120		7	4	2400			2900	3400
18	8	FABUGLAS-COMMODORE	ST	RNBT	FBG	DV	IO	120		7	5	2500			3150	3650
19	6	ASTROGLASS-BASS 195V	OP	BASS	FBG	SV	OB			7	4	1550			3150	3650
19	6	ASTROGLASS-COMBO 195	OP	BASS	FBG	SV	OB			7	4	1550			3250	3800
19	6	ASTROGLASS-RIVAL 195	OP	BASS	FBG	SV	OB			7	4	1550			3250	3800
19	6	PROCRAFT F-&-S 1950V	OP	BASS	FBG	SV	OB			7	4	1550			3250	3800
19	6	PROCRAFT-BASS 1950V	OP	BASS	FBG	SV	OB			7	4	1550			3150	3650
19	6	PROCRAFT-COMPET 1950	OP	BASS	FBG	SV	OB			7	4	1550			3250	3800
		1985 BOATS														
16	6	ASTROGLASS-BASS 165	OP	BASS	FBG	SV	OB			6	8	1000			1900	2250
16	6	ASTROGLASS-COMBO 165	OP	BASS	FBG	SV	OB			6	8	1000			2050	2450
16	6	FABUGLAS-BUCCANEER	ST	RNBT	FBG	DV	IO	120		6	7	1900			2200	2550
16	6	FABUGLAS-TEMPEST	ST	RNBT	FBG	DV	OB			6	7	1200			2350	2750
16	6	PROCRAFT-BASS 1650V	OP	BASS	FBG	SV	OB			6	8	1000			1900	2250
16	6	PROCRAFT-FISH-&-SKI	OP	BASS	FBG	SV	OB			6	8	1000			2050	2450
17	2	FABUGLAS-CUTLASS	ST	RNBT	FBG	DV	OB			7	4	1600			3000	3450
17	6	ASTROGLASS-BASS 175	OP	BASS	FBG	SV	OB			7		1050			1950	2350
17	6	ASTROGLASS-COMBO 175	OP	BASS	FBG	SV	OB			7		1050			2200	2550
17	6	ASTROGLASS-RIVAL 175	OP	BASS	FBG	SV	OB			7		1050			2350	2700
17	6	PROCRAFT-BASS 1750V	OP	BASS	FBG	SV	OB			7		1050			1950	2350
17	6	PROCRAFT-COMPETITOR	OP	BASS	FBG	SV	OB			7		1050			2350	2700
17	6	PROCRAFT-FISH-&-SKI	OP	BASS	FBG	SV	OB			7		1050			2200	2550
17	8	FABUGLAS-CRUSADER	ST	RNBT	FBG	DV	IO	120		7	4	2400			2800	3250
18	8	FABUGLAS-COMMODORE	ST	RNBT	FBG	DV	IO	120		7	5	2500			3050	3500
		1984 BOATS														
16	6	FABUGLAS-BUCCANEER	ST	RNBT	FBG	DV	IO	120		6	7	1800			2050	2400
16	6	FABUGLAS-TEMPEST	ST	RNBT	FBG	DV	OB			6	7	1200			2300	2700
16	6	FISH-&-SKI 1650V	OP	BASS	FBG	SV	OB			6	8				2050	2450
16	6	PROCRAFT 1650V	OP	BASS	FBG	SV	OB			6	8				2050	2450
17	6	FISH-&-SKI 1750V	OP	BASS	FBG	SV	OB			7					2350	2700
17	6	PROCRAFT 1750V	OP	BASS	FBG	SV	OB			7					2300	2650
17	6	PROCRAFT-COMPETITOR	OP	BASS	FBG	SV	OB			7		1200			2350	2750
17	9	FABUGLAS-LANCER	ST	RNBT	FBG	DV	OB			7	2	1500			2800	3250
17	9	FABUGLAS-LANCER	ST	RNBT	FBG	DV	IO	120		7	2	2100			2500	2900

....For earlier years, see the BUC Used Boat Price Guide, Volume 3

MARINE PERFORMANCE

MARCUS HOOK PA 19061 COAST GUARD MFG ID- MPP See inside cover to adjust price for area

For more recent years, see the BUC Used Boat Price Guide, Volume 1

LOA FT	LOA IN	NAME AND/ OR MODEL	TOP/ RIG	BOAT TYPE	HULL MTL	HULL TP	ENGINE TP	ENGINE # HP	ENGINE MFG	BEAM FT	BEAM IN	WGT LBS	DRAFT FT	DRAFT IN	RETAIL LOW	RETAIL HIGH
		1991 BOATS														
16		BAY-SKIFF	OP	UTL	FBG	FL	OB			6	5	700	2	5	3250	3800
16		BAY-SKIFF 16	OP	OPFSH	FBG		IB	90	MRCR	6	5	1650	2	5	5200	5950
16		COMPETITION 16	OP	RACE	FBG	FL	IB	230	MRCR	6	5	1760	2	5	6900	7900
17		K-CRAFT	OP	OPFSH	FBG	DV	OB			6	6	900	2	2	4300	5000
17		K-CRAFT	OP	OPFSH	FBG	DV	IB	90	MRCR	6	6	1850	2	2	6000	6900
18		BAY-GARVEY	OP	UTL	FBG	FL	OB			6	5	750	1	6	3500	4050
18		BAY-GARVEY	OP	UTL	FBG	FL	IB	90	MRCR	6	5	1750	1	6	6150	7050
18		SPEED-GARVEY	OP	RACE	FBG	FL	IB	230	MRCR	6	5	1625	1	6	7400	8550
		1990 BOATS														
16		BAY-SKIFF	OP	UTL	FBG	FL	OB			6	5	700	2	5	3150	3650
16		BAY-SKIFF 16	OP	OPFSH	FBG		IB	90	MRCR	6	5	1650	2	5	5000	5700
16		COMPETITION 16	OP	RACE	FBG	FL	IB	230	MRCR	6	5	1760	2	5	6550	7500
17		K-CRAFT	OP	OPFSH	FBG	DV	OB			6	6	900	2	2	4100	4800
17		K-CRAFT	OP	OPFSH	FBG	DV	IB	90	MRCR	6	6	1850	2	2	5700	6550
18		BAY-GARVEY	OP	UTL	FBG	FL	OB			6	6	750	1	6	3350	3900
18		BAY-GARVEY	OP	UTL	FBG	FL	IB	90	MRCR	6	5	1750	1	6	5850	6700
18		SPEED-GARVEY	OP	RACE	FBG	FL	IB	230	MRCR	6	5	1625	1	6	7050	8100
		1989 BOATS														
16		BAY-SKIFF	OP	UTL	FBG	FL	OB			6	5	700	2	5	3000	3500
16		BAY-SKIFF 16	OP	OPFSH	FBG		IB	90	MRCR	6	5	1650	2	5	4750	5450
16		COMPETITION 16	OP	RACE	FBG	FL	IB	230	MRCR	6	5	1760	2	5	6300	7250
17		K-CRAFT	OP	OPFSH	FBG	DV	OB			6	6	900	2	2	3950	4600
17		K-CRAFT	OP	OPFSH	FBG	DV	IB	90	MRCR	6	6	1850	2	2	5450	6250
18		BAY-GARVEY	OP	UTL	FBG	FL	OB			6	5	750	1	6	3250	3750
18		BAY-GARVEY	OP	UTL	FBG	FL	IB	90	MRCR	6	5	1750	1	6	5600	6450
18		SPEED-GARVEY	OP	RACE	FBG	FL	IB	230	MRCR	6	5	1625	1	6	6750	7750
		1988 BOATS														
16		BAY-SKIFF	OP	UTL	FBG	FL	OB			6	5	700	2	5	2900	3350
16		BAY-SKIFF 16	OP	OPFSH	FBG		IB	90	MRCR	6	5	1650	2	5	4500	5150
16		COMPETITION 16	OP	RACE	FBG	FL	IB	230	MRCR	6	5	1760	2	5	6000	6900
17		K-CRAFT	OP	OPFSH	FBG	DV	OB			6	6	900	2	2	3800	4450
17		K-CRAFT	OP	OPFSH	FBG	DV	IB	90	MRCR	6	6	1850	2	2	5200	5950
18		BAY-GARVEY	OP	UTL	FBG	FL	OB			6	5	750	1	6	3100	3600
18		BAY-GARVEY	OP	UTL	FBG	FL	IB	90	MRCR	6	5	1750	1	6	5350	6150
18		SPEED-GARVEY	OP	RACE	FBG	FL	IB	230	MRCR	6	5	1625	1	6	6500	7450
		1987 BOATS														
16		BAY SKIFF	OP	UTL	FBG	FL	OB			6	5	700	2	5	2800	3250
16		BAY-SKIFF 16	OP	OPFSH	FBG		IB	90	MRCR	6	5	1650	2	5	4250	4950
16		COMPETITION 16	OP	RACE	FBG	FL	IB	230	MRCR	6	5	1760	2	5	5700	6550
17		K-CRAFT	OP	OPFSH	FBG	DV	OB			6	6	900	2	2	3650	4250
17		K-CRAFT	OP	OPFSH	FBG	DV	IB	90	MRCR	6	6	1850	2	2	5000	5750
18		BAY-GARVEY	OP	UTL	FBG	FL	OB			6	5	750	1	6	3000	3500
18		BAY-GARVEY	OP	UTL	FBG	FL	IB	90	MRCR	6	5	1750	1	6	5100	5850
18		SPEED-GARVEY	OP	RACE	FBG	FL	IB	230	MRCR	6	5	1625	1	6	6150	7100
		1986 BOATS														
16		BAY-SKIFF 16	OP	OPFSH	FBG		IB	170	MRCR	6	5	1650	2	5	4800	5500
16		COMPETITION 16	OP	RACE	FBG	FL	IB	260	MRCR	6	5	1760	2	5	5550	6400
17		K-CRAFT	OP	OPFSH	FBG	DV	OB			6	6	1300	2	2	4900	5650
17		K-CRAFT	OP	OPFSH	FBG	DV	IB	170	MRCR	6	6	1850	2	2	5400	6200
17	6	BAY-GARVEY	OP	UTL	FBG	FL	OB			6	5	1200	1	6	4500	5150
17	6	BAY-GARVEY	OP	UTL	FBG	FL	IB	170	MRCR	6	5	1750	1	6	5350	6150

LOA FT	IN	NAME AND/ OR MODEL	TOP/ RIG	BOAT TYPE	-HULL- MTL	TP	TP	ENGINE # HP	MFG	BEAM FT	IN	WGT LBS	DRAFT FT	IN	RETAIL LOW	RETAIL HIGH
		1986 BOATS														
17	6	SPEED-GARVEY	OP	RACE	KEV	FL	IB	260	MRCR	6	5	1625	1	6	5700	6550
		1985 BOATS														
16		BAY-SKIFF 16	OP	OPFSH	FBG		IB	125	MRCR	6	5	1650	2	5	4200	4850
16		COMPETITION 16	OP	RACE	FBG	FL	IO	165	MRCR	6	5	1760	2	5	3850	4500
17		K-CRAFT	OP	OPFSH	FBG	DV	OB			6	6	1300	2	2	4750	5450
17		K-CRAFT	OP	OPFSH	FBG	DV	IB	200D		6	6	1850	2	2	10200	11600
17	6	BAY-GARVEY	OP	UTL	FBG	FL	OB			6	5	1200	1	6	4300	5000
17	6	BAY-GARVEY	OP	UTL	FBG	FL	IB	125	MRCR	6	5	1750	1	6	4850	5550
17	6	SPEED-GARVEY	OP	RACE	KEV	FL	IB	330		6	5	1625	1	6	5800	6700
		1984 BOATS														
16		BAY-SKIFF 16	OP	OPFSH	FBG		IB	125	MRCR	6	5	1650	2	5	4000	4650
16		COMPETITION 16	OP	RNBT	FBG	FL	IO	165	MRCR	6	5	1760	2	5	3450	4050
17		K-CRAFT	OP	OPFSH	FBG	DV	OB			6	6	1850	2	2	5900	6800
17		K-CRAFT	OP	OPFSH	FBG	DV	IB	200D		6	6	1850	2	2	9900	11300
17	6	BAY-GARVEY	OP	UTL	FBG	FL	IB	125	MRCR	6	5	1750	1	6	4600	5300

....For earlier years, see the BUC Used Boat Price Guide, Volume 3

MARINE PROJECTS (PLYMOUTH) LTD

PLYMOUTH DEVON ENGLAND PL1 3QG See inside cover to adjust price for area

EASTERN YACHT SALES
HINGHAM MA 02043

For more recent years, see the BUC Used Boat Price Guide, Volume 1

LOA FT	IN	NAME AND/ OR MODEL	TOP/ RIG	BOAT TYPE	-HULL- MTL	TP	TP	ENGINE # HP	MFG	BEAM FT	IN	WGT LBS	DRAFT FT	IN	RETAIL LOW	RETAIL HIGH
		1992 BOATS														
27	8	RIVIERA 266	OP	SPTCR	FBG	SV	IB	330	VLVO	10		6000	2	9	34300	38200
		IB 200D VLVO 38000 42200, IB T120-T205 32900 40400, IB T130D VLVO 42500 47200														
31		PRINCESS 315	FB	CBNCR	FBG	SV	IO	T130D	VLVO	11	2	10000	2	11	64500	70900
		IBT150D-T200D 83600 99500, IO T210D VLVO 73200 80500, IB T230D VLVO 92000 101000														
33	8	PRINCESS 330	FB	CBNCR	FBG	SV	IB	T150D	VLVO	11	9	11000	2	7	97500	107000
		IO T200D VLVO 81400 89400, IB T200D VLVO 104000 114000, IO T210D VLVO 82400 90500														
		IB T230D VLVO 107500 118500														
35	3	PRINCESS 35	FB	SDN	FBG	SV	IB	T150D	VLVO	12	1	12600	3	3	102500	112500
		IO T200D VLVO 83800 92100, IB T200D VLVO 106500 117000, IO T210D VLVO 84500 92800														
		IB T230D VLVO 109500 120000, IB T250D CUM 112000 123000														
35	11	RIVIERA 346	OP	SPTCR	FBG	SV	IB	T229	VLVO	11	6	11900	2	11	86700	95300
35	11	RIVIERA 346	OP	SPTCR	FBG	SV	IB	T200D	VLVO	11	6	11900	2	11	101000	111000
35	11	RIVIERA 346	OP	SPTCR	FBG	SV	IB	T230D	VLVO	11	6	11900	2	11	103000	113000
38	1	PRINCESS 368	FB	MY	FBG	DS	IB	T230D	VLVO	12	1	16800	3	9	118000	129500
		IB T250D CUM 121000 133000, IB T300D CUM 125000 137500, IB T306D VLVO 123500 135500														
40	8	PRINCESS 398	FB	MY	FBG	DS	IB	T250D	CUM	13	7	17800	3	1	130000	143000
40	8	PRINCESS 398	FB	MY	FBG	DS	IB	T306D	VLVO	13	7	17800	3	1	133500	147000
40	8	PRINCESS 415	FB	MY	FBG	DS	IB	T306D	VLVO	13	11	23000	3	9	155000	170500
40	8	PRINCESS 415	FB	MY	FBG	DS	IB	T380D	VLVO	13	11	23000	3	9	163000	179500
40	8	RIVIERA 406	OP	SPTCR	FBG	SV	IB	T306D	VLVO	13	1	16600	2	11	130000	143000
40	8	RIVIERA 406	OP	SPTCR	FBG	SV	IB	T380D	VLVO	13	1	16600	2	11	139500	153000
43	8	PRINCESS 435	FB	MY	FBG	DS	IB	T306D	VLVO	13	11	24000	3	1	179000	196500
43	8	PRINCESS 435	FB	MY	FBG	DS	IB	T380D	VLVO	13	11	24000	3	1	193500	212500
45	4	PRINCESS 45	FB	MY	FBG	DS	IB	T306D	VLVO	14	1	28000	3	9	193000	212000
45	4	PRINCESS 45	FB	MY	FBG	DS	IB	T380D	VLVO	14	1	28000	3	9	207500	228000
45	4	PRINCESS 45	FB	MY	FBG	DS	IB	T430D	VLVO	14	1	28000	3	9	217500	239000
46	6	RIVIERA 46	OP	SPTCR	FBG	SV	IB	T380D	VLVO	14		22800	2	11	187000	205500
46	6	RIVIERA 46	OP	SPTCR	FBG	SV	IB	T425D	CAT	14		22800	2	11	202500	222500
46	6	RIVIERA 46	OP	SPTCR	FBG	SV	IB	T430D	VLVO	14		22800	2	11	201000	221000
49	6	PRINCESS 48	FB	MY	FBG	DS	IB	T380D	VLVO	14	7	28000	3	6	221500	243500
49	6	PRINCESS 48	FB	MY	FBG	DS	IB	T425D	CAT	14	7	28000	3	6	235500	259000
49	6	PRINCESS 48	FB	MY	FBG	DS	IB	T430D	VLVO	14	7	28000	3	6	231500	254500
55	5	PRINCESS 55	FB	MY	FBG	DS	IB	T380D	VLVO	15	8	31000	3	6	221500	243500
		IB T425D CAT 239500 263000, IB T430D VLVO 237000 260500, IB T480D VLVO 254500 280000														
66	3	PRINCESS 65	FB	MY	FBG	DS	IB	T612D	VLVO	17	2	56000	5		484500	532500
66	3	PRINCESS 65	FB	MY	FBG	DS	IB	T820D	MAN	17	2	56000	5		525500	577500
66	3	PRINCESS 65	FB	MY	FBG	DS	IB	T10CD	MTU	17	2	56000	5		596000	655000
		1987 BOATS														
32	6	SIGMA 33	SLP	SA/RC	FBG	KL	IB	D		10	6	9500	5	9	47400	52100
32	6	SIGMA 33 OOD	SLP	SA/RC	FBG	KL	IB	D		10	6	9200	5	9	46000	50600
36		SIGMA 362	SLP	SA/RC	FBG	KL	IB	D		11	6	12800	6	1	63000	69200
38		SIGMA 38	SLP	SA/RC	FBG	KL	IB	D		12	2	13750	6	8	70700	77700
		1986 BOATS														
29		SIGMA 292	SLP	SA/RC	FBG	KL	IB	D		10	1	6600	5	1	28200	31300
32	6	SIGMA 33	SLP	SA/OD	FBG	KL	IB	D		10	6	9500	5	9	44100	48900
32	6	SIGMA 33	SLP	SA/RC	FBG	KL	IB	D		10	6	9500	5	9	44100	48900
36		SIGMA 36	SLP	SA/RC	FBG	KL	IB	D		11	6	12500	6	1	57900	63700
41	9	SIGMA 41	SLP	SA/RC	FBG	KL	IB	D		12	10	19000	6	10	97500	107000
		1985 BOATS														
29		SIGMA 292	SLP	SA/RC	FBG	KL	IB	D		10	1	6600	5	1	26400	29300
30		PRINCESS-RIVIERA 286	HT	CR	FBG	DV	IO	165		11		6945			21000	23300
30	5	PRINCESS 30DS	HT	CR	FBG	DV	IO	165D		11		9038			27700	30800
30	5	PRINCESS 30DS	HT	CR	FBG	DV	IB	165D		11		9038			37900	42100
32	6	SIGMA 33	SLP	SA/OD	FBG	KL	IB	D		10	6	9200	5	9	40000	44400
32	6	SIGMA 33	SLP	SA/RC	FBG	KL	IB	D		10	6	9500	5	9	41300	45900
33		PRINCESS 33	FB	CR	FBG	DV	IO	T125		11	3	11462			38100	42400
33		PRINCESS 33	FB	CR	FBG	DV	IB	T165D		11	3	11462			60200	66100
35	3	PRINCESS 35	FB	CR	FBG	DV	IB	T165D	VLVO	12	1		3	3	71700	78800
36		SIGMA 36	SLP	SA/RC	FBG	KL	IB	D		11	6	12500	6	1	54600	60000
41	2	PRINCESS 412-2	FB	MY	FBG	DV	IB	T255D		13		19839			108000	119000
41	2	PRINCESS 414	FB	MY	FBG	DV	IB	T165D		13		19839			100500	110500
41	9	SIGMA 41	SLP	SA/RC	FBG	KL	IB	D		12	10	19000	6	10	91600	100500
45		PRINCESS 45	FB	MY	FBG	DV	IB								**	**
		1984 BOATS														
30		PRINCESS 30DS	HT	CR	FBG	DV	IO	T200	VLVO						24100	26800
30		PRINCESS 30DS	HT	CR	FBG	DV	IO	T130D	VLVO						27700	30700
30		PRINCESS 30DS	HT	CR	FBG	DV	IB	T158D	VLVO						39200	43500
33		PRINCESS 33	FB	CR	FBG	DV	IB	T158D	VLVO						57900	63600
33		PRINCESS 33	FB	CR	FBG	DV	IO	T165D	VLVO						42400	47200
38	1	PRINCESS 38	FB	SDN	FBG	DV	IB	T235D	VLVO	13		16400	3		77100	84700
40	9	SIGMA 41	SLP	SA/RC	FBG	KL	IB	36D	BUKH	12	10	18000	6	10	80300	88200
41		PRINCESS 412	FB	MY	FBG	DV	IB	T235D	VLVO						102000	112500
41		PRINCESS 414	FB	MY	FBG	DV	IB	T235D	VLVO						106000	116500
45		PRINCESS 45	FB	MY	FBG	DV	IB	T306D	VLVO						127500	140000

....For earlier years, see the BUC Used Boat Price Guide, Volume 3

MARINE TRADING INTERNATIONAL

TOMS RIVER NJ 08754 See inside cover to adjust price for area

For more recent years, see the BUC Used Boat Price Guide, Volume 1

LOA FT	IN	NAME AND/ OR MODEL	TOP/ RIG	BOAT TYPE	-HULL- MTL	TP	TP	ENGINE # HP	MFG	BEAM FT	IN	WGT LBS	DRAFT FT	IN	RETAIL LOW	RETAIL HIGH
		1996 BOATS														
33	6	MARINE-TRADER DC	FB	TRWL	FBG	DS	IB	135D	LEHM	11	9		3	6	98000	107500
33	6	MARINE-TRADER SDN	FB	TRWL	FBG	DS	IB	135D	LEHM	11	9		3	6	98000	107500
38		MARINE-TRADER DC	FB	TRWL	FBG	DS	IB	135D	LEHM	12	10		4		125500	138000
38		MARINE-TRADER DC	FB	TRWL	FBG	DS	IB	T135D	LEHM	12	10		4		133000	146000
38		MARINE-TRADER SDN	FB	TRWL	FBG	DS	IB	135D	LEHM	12	10		4	4	125500	138000
38		MARINE-TRADER SDN	FB	TRWL	FBG	DS	IB	T135D	LEHM	12	10		4	4	133000	146000
39	4	MARINE-TRADER SUNDK	FB	TRWL	FBG	DS	IB	135D	LEHM	12	11		4		152000	167000
39	4	MARINE-TRADER SUNDK	FB	TRWL	FBG	DS	IB	T135D	LEHM	12	11		4		159500	175500
42	6	TRADEWINDS 43	FB	MY	FBG	SV	IB	T135D	LEHM	14	11		3	6	172500	189500
43	4	MARINE-TRADER 40/44	FB	TRWL	FBG	DS	IB	135D	LEHM	12	11		4		155500	171000
43	4	MARINE-TRADER 40/44	FB	TRWL	FBG	DS	IB	T135D	LEHM	12	11		4		161000	177000
46	2	MARINE-TRADER DC	FB	TRWL	FBG	DS	IB	T135D	LEHM	14	7		3	8	205500	226000
46	6	TRADEWINDS 43/47 FSH	FB	YTFS	FBG	SV	IB	T135D	LEHM	14	11		3	6	178000	195500
46	6	TRADEWINDS 47	FB	MY	FBG	SV	IB	T135D	LEHM	14	11		3	6	205500	225500
		1995 BOATS														
33	6	MARINE-TRADER DC	FB	TRWL	FBG	DS	IB	135D	LEHM	11	9		3	6	93100	102500
33	6	MARINE-TRADER SDN	FB	TRWL	FBG	DS	IB	135D	LEHM	11	9		3	6	93100	102500
35	6	MARINE-TRADER SDN	FB	TRWL	FBG	DS	IB	135D	LEHM	12	8		3	4	118000	129500
35	6	MARINE-TRADER SDN	FB	TRWL	FBG	DS	IB	T135D	LEHM	12	8		3	4	123000	135000
35	6	MARINE-TRADER SUNDK	FB	TRWL	FBG	DS	IB	135D	LEHM	12	8		3	4	122500	134500
35	6	MARINE-TRADER SUNDK	FB	TRWL	FBG	DS	IB	T135D	LEHM	12	8		3	4	127000	139500
38		MARINE-TRADER DC	FB	TRWL	FBG	DS	IB	135D	LEHM	12	10		4		120500	132500
38		MARINE-TRADER DC	FB	TRWL	FBG	DS	IB	T135D	LEHM	12	10		4		127500	140000
38		MARINE-TRADER SDN	FB	TRWL	FBG	DS	IB	135D	LEHM	12	10		4	4	120500	132500
38		MARINE-TRADER SDN	FB	TRWL	FBG	DS	IB	T135D	LEHM	12	10		4	4	127500	140000
39	4	ISLAND TRADER T R S	SLP	MS	FBG	KL	IB	135D	LEHM	13	4	34400	4	9	155000	170500
39	4	MARINE-TRADER SUNDK	FB	TRWL	FBG	DS	IB	135D	LEHM	12	11		4		145500	160000
39	4	MARINE-TRADER SUNDK	FB	TRWL	FBG	DS	IB	T135D	LEHM	12	11		4		153000	168000
42	6	TRADEWINDS 43	FB	MY	FBG	SV	IB	T135D	LEHM	14	11		3	6	165000	181500
43	4	MARINE-TRADER 40/44	FB	TRWL	FBG	DS	IB	135D	LEHM	12	11		4		149000	164000

LOA FT	LOA IN	NAME AND/ OR MODEL	TOP/ RIG	BOAT TYPE	HULL MTL	HULL TP	ENGINE TP	ENGINE # HP	ENGINE MFG	BEAM FT	BEAM IN	WGT LBS	DRAFT FT	DRAFT IN	RETAIL LOW	RETAIL HIGH
		1995 BOATS														
43	4	MARINE-TRADER 40/44	FB	TRWL	FBG	DS	IB	T135D	LEHM	12	11		4		154500	170000
45	6	ISLANDE TRADER T R S	KTH	MS	FBG	KL	IB	135D	LEHM	15	2	48360	5	6	207500	228000
46	2	MARINE-TRADER DC	FB	TRWL	FBG	DS	IB	T135D	LEHM	14	7		3	8	197000	216500
46	6	TRADEWINDS 43/47 FSH	FB	YTFS	FBG	SV	IB	T135D	LEHM	14	11		3	6	169000	186000
46	6	TRADEWINDS 47	FB	MY	FBG	SV	IB	T135D	LEHM	14	11		3	6	196000	215000
		1994 BOATS														
33	6	MARINE-TRADER DC	FB	TRWL	FBG	DS	IB	135D	LEHM	11	9		3	6	88600	97300
33	6	MARINE-TRADER SDN	FB	TRWL	FBG	DS	IB	135D	LEHM	11	9		3	6	88600	97300
36		MARINE-TRADER SDN	FB	TRWL	FBG	DS	IB	135D	LEHM	12	2		3	6	97100	106500
36		MARINE-TRADER SDN	FB	TRWL	FBG	DS	IB	T135D	LEHM	12	2		3	6	101500	111500
36		MARINE-TRADER SUNDK	FB	TRWL	FBG	DS	IB	135D	LEHM	12	2		3	6	100500	110500
36		MARINE-TRADER SUNDK	FB	TRWL	FBG	DS	IB	T135D	LEHM	12	2		3	6	105000	115500
38		MARINE-TRADER DC	FB	TRWL	FBG	DS	IB	135D	LEHM	12	10		4		115500	127000
38		MARINE-TRADER DC	FB	TRWL	FBG	DS	IB	T135D	LEHM	12	10		4		122000	134500
38		MARINE-TRADER SDN	FB	TRWL	FBG	DS	IB	135D	LEHM	12	10		4	4	115500	127000
38		MARINE-TRADER SDN	FB	TRWL	FBG	DS	IB	T135D	LEHM	12	10		4	4	122000	134500
39	4	IS TRAD TRAWL R SAIL	SLP	MS	FBG	KL	IB	135D	LEHM	13	4	34400	4	9	146000	160500
39	4	MARINE-TRADER SUNDK	FB	TRWL	FBG	DS	IB	135D	LEHM	12	11		4		139500	153500
39	4	MARINE-TRADER SUNDK	FB	TRWL	FBG	DS	IB	T135D	LEHM	12	11		4		146500	161000
42		MARINE-TRADER 42 SDN	FB	TRWL	FBG	DS	IB	135D	LEHM	12	10		4		165000	181000
42		MARINE-TRADER 42 SDN	FB	TRWL	FBG	DS	IB	T135D	LEHM	12	10		4		172000	189000
42	6	TRADEWINDS 43	FB	MY	FBG	SV	IB	T135D	LEHM	14	11		3	6	158000	174000
43	4	MARINE-TRADER 40/44	FB	TRWL	FBG	DS	IB	135D	LEHM	12	11		4		143000	157000
43	4	MARINE-TRADER 40/44	FB	TRWL	FBG	DS	IB	T135D	LEHM	12	11		4		148000	163000
45	6	IS TRAD TRAWL R SAIL	KTH	MS	FBG	KL	IB	135D	LEHM			48360	5	6	195000	214500
46	2	MARINE-TRADER DC	FB	TRWL	FBG	DS	IB	T135D	LEHM	14	7		3	8	189000	207500
46	6	TRADEWINDS 43/47 FSH	FB	YTFS	FBG	SV	IB	T135D	LEHM	14	11		3	6	161000	177000
46	6	TRADEWINDS 47	FB	MY	FBG	SV	IB	T135D	LEHM	14	11		3	6	187000	205500
		1993 BOATS														
33	6	MARINE-TRADER DC	FB	TRWL	FBG	DS	IB	135D	LEHM	11	9		3	6	84300	92700
33	6	MARINE-TRADER SDN	FB	TRWL	FBG	DS	IB	135D	LEHM	11	9		3	6	84300	92700
36		MARINE-TRADER DC	FB	TRWL	FBG	DS	IB	135D	LEHM	12	2		3	6	92800	102000
36		MARINE-TRADER DC	FB	TRWL	FBG	DS	IB	T135D	LEHM	12	2		3	6	97100	106500
36		MARINE-TRADER SDN	FB	TRWL	FBG	DS	IB	135D	LEHM	12	2		3	6	92800	102000
36		MARINE-TRADER SDN	FB	TRWL	FBG	DS	IB	T135D	LEHM	12	2		3	6	97100	106500
36		MARINE-TRADER SUNDK	FB	TRWL	FBG	DS	IB	135D	LEHM	12	2		3	6	97000	106500
36		MARINE-TRADER SUNDK	FB	TRWL	FBG	DS	IB	T135D	LEHM	12	2		3	6	101000	111000
38		MARINE-TRADER DC	FB	TRWL	FBG	DS	IB	135D	LEHM	12	10		4		110000	121000
38		MARINE-TRADER DC	FB	TRWL	FBG	DS	IB	T135D	LEHM	12	10		4		116500	128000
38		MARINE-TRADER SDN	FB	TRWL	FBG	DS	IB	135D	LEHM	12			4	6	115000	126500
38		MARINE-TRADER SDN	FB	TRWL	FBG	DS	IB	T135D	LEHM	12			4		121500	133500
38	10	TRADEWINDS 39	FB	MY	FBG	SV	IB	T135D	LEHM	14	4		3	1	112000	123000
39	4	ISLAND-TRADER	SLP	MS	FBG	KL	IB	135D	LEHM	13	4	34400	4	9	137500	151000
39	4	MARINE-TRADER SUNDK	FB	TRWL	FBG	DS	IB	135D	LEHM	12	11		4		133000	146000
39	4	MARINE-TRADER SUNDK	FB	TRWL	FBG	DS	IB	T135D	LEHM	12	11		4		140000	153500
42		MARINE-TRADER 42 SDN	FB	TRWL	FBG	DS	IB	135D	LEHM	12	10		4		157000	172500
42		MARINE-TRADER 42 SDN	FB	TRWL	FBG	DS	IB	T135D	LEHM	12	10		4		163500	180000
42		TRADEWINDS 38/42 FSH	FB	YTFS	FBG	SV	IB	135D	LEHM	12	10		3	5	87600	96200
42		TRADEWINDS 38/42 FSH	FB	YTFS	FBG	SV	IB	T135D	LEHM	12	10		3	5	81300	89300
42	6	TRADEWINDS 43	FB	MY	FBG	SV	IB	T135D	LEHM	14	11		5	7	150500	165500
43	4	MARINE-TRADER 40/44	FB	TRWL	FBG	DS	IB	135D	LEHM	12	11		4		136000	149500
43	4	MARINE-TRADER 40/44	FB	TRWL	FBG	DS	IB	T135D	LEHM	12	11		4		141000	155000
45	6	ISLAND-TRADER	SLP	MS	FBG	KL	IB	135D	LEHM	15	2	48363	5	6	182500	200500
46	2	MARINE-TRADER DC	FB	TRWL	FBG	DS	IB	T135D	LEHM	14	7		3	8	180000	197500
46	6	TRADEWINDS 43/47 FSH	FB	YTFS	FBG	SV	IB	T135D	LEHM	14	6		3	10	153500	169000
46	6	TRADEWINDS 47	FB	MY	FBG	SV	IB	T135D	LEHM	14	6		3	10	178500	196000
48	6	MARINE-TRADER PH	FB	TRWL	FBG	DS	IB	T135D	LEHM	15		46000	4	6	238000	261500
48	6	MARINE-TRADER PH SDK	FB	TRWL	FBG	DS	IB	T135D	LEHM	15			4	6	209500	230000
50		MARINE-TRADER MY	FB	TRWL	FBG	DS	IB	T135D	LEHM	15	5	47500	4	8	237500	261000
50		MARINE-TRADER WIDE	FB	MY	FBG	DS	IB	T135D	LEHM	15	5		4	6	187500	206000
		1992 BOATS														
33	6	MARINE-TRADER DC	FB	TRWL	FBG	DS	IB	135D	LEHM	11	9		3	6	80400	88400
33	6	MARINE-TRADER SDN	FB	TRWL	FBG	DS	IB	135D	LEHM	11	9		3	6	80400	88400
36		MARINE-TRADER DC	FB	TRWL	FBG	DS	IB	135D	LEHM	12	2		3	6	87200	95800
36		MARINE-TRADER DC	FB	TRWL	FBG	DS	IB	T135D	LEHM	12	2		3	6	92600	101500
36		MARINE-TRADER SDN	FB	TRWL	FBG	DS	IB	135D	LEHM	12	2		3	6	91100	100000
36		MARINE-TRADER SDN	FB	TRWL	FBG	DS	IB	T135D	LEHM	12	2		3	6	92500	101500
36		MARINE-TRADER SUNDK	FB	TRWL	FBG	DS	IB	135D	LEHM	12	2		3	6	91100	100000
36		MARINE-TRADER SUNDK	FB	TRWL	FBG	DS	IB	T135D	LEHM	12	2		3	6	96300	106000
38		MARINE-TRADER DC	FB	TRWL	FBG	DS	IB	135D	LEHM	12	10		4		105000	115500
38		MARINE-TRADER DC	FB	TRWL	FBG	DS	IB	T135D	LEHM	12	10		4		111000	122000
38		MARINE-TRADER SDN	FB	TRWL	FBG	DS	IB	135D	LEHM	12			4	6	110000	120500
38		MARINE-TRADER SDN	FB	TRWL	FBG	DS	IB	T135D	LEHM	12			4	6	116000	127500
38	10	TRADEWINDS 39	FB	MY	FBG	SV	IB	T135D	LEHM	14	4		3	1	106500	117000
39	4	ISLAND-TRADER	SLP	MS	FBG	KL	IB	135D	LEHM	13	4	34400	4	9	129000	142000
39	4	MARINE-TRADER SUNDK	FB	TRWL	FBG	DS	IB	135D	LEHM	12	11		4		127000	139500
39	4	MARINE-TRADER SUNDK	FB	TRWL	FBG	DS	IB	T135D	LEHM	12	11		4		133000	146500
42		MARINE-TRADER 42 SDN	FB	TRWL	FBG	DS	IB	135D	LEHM	12	10		4		149500	164500
42		MARINE-TRADER 42 SDN	FB	TRWL	FBG	DS	IB	T135D	LEHM	12	10		4		156000	171500
42		TRADEWINDS 38/42 FSH	FB	YTFS	FBG	SV	IB	135D	LEHM	12	10		3	5	83500	91700
42		TRADEWINDS 38/42 FSH	FB	YTFS	FBG	SV	IB	T135D	LEHM	12	10		3	5	77500	85200
42	6	TRADEWINDS 43	FB	MY	FBG	SV	IB	T135D	LEHM	14	11		5	7	143500	158000
43	4	MARINE-TRADER 40/44	FB	TRWL	FBG	DS	IB	135D	LEHM	12	11		4		130000	142500
43	4	MARINE-TRADER 40/44	FB	TRWL	FBG	DS	IB	T135D	LEHM	12	11		4		134500	148000
45	6	ISLAND-TRADER	SLP	MS	FBG	KL	IB	135D	LEHM	15	2	48363	5	6	171500	188500
46	2	MARINE-TRADER DC	FB	TRWL	FBG	DS	IB	T135D	LEHM	14	7		3	8	171500	188500
46	6	TRADEWINDS 43/47 FSH	FB	YTFS	FBG	SV	IB	T135D	LEHM	14	6		3	10	146500	160500
46	6	TRADEWINDS 47	FB	MY	FBG	SV	IB	T135D	LEHM	14	6		3	10	170000	187000
48	6	MARINE-TRADER PH	FB	TRWL	FBG	DS	IB	T135D	LEHM	15		46000	4	6	226500	249000
48	6	MARINE-TRADER PH SDK	FB	TRWL	FBG	DS	IB	T135D	LEHM	15			4	6	199500	219500
50		MARINE-TRADER MY	FB	TRWL	FBG	DS	IB	T135D	LEHM	15	5	47500	4	8	226500	249000
50		MARINE-TRADER WIDE	FB	MY	FBG	DS	IB	T135D	LEHM	15	5		4	6	179000	196500
		1991 BOATS														
33	6	MARINE-TRADER DC	FB	TRWL	FBG	DS	IB	135D	LEHM	11	9		3	6	76700	84300
33	6	MARINE-TRADER SDN	FB	TRWL	FBG	DS	IB	135D	LEHM	11	9		3	6	76700	84300
36		MARINE-TRADER DC	FB	TRWL	FBG	DS	IB	135D	LEHM	12	2		3	6	84400	92700
36		MARINE-TRADER DC	FB	TRWL	FBG	DS	IB	T135D	LEHM	12	2		3	6	88200	96900
36		MARINE-TRADER SDN	FB	TRWL	FBG	DS	IB	135D	LEHM	12	2		3	6	84400	92700
36		MARINE-TRADER SDN	FB	TRWL	FBG	DS	IB	T135D	LEHM	12	2		3	6	88200	96900
36		MARINE-TRADER SNDK	FB	TRWL	FBG	DS	IB	135D	LEHM	12	2		3	6	88300	97000
36		MARINE-TRADER SNDK	FB	TRWL	FBG	DS	IB	T135D	LEHM	12	2		3	6	92000	101000
38		MARINE-TRADER DC	FB	TRWL	FBG	DS	IB	135D	LEHM	12	10		4		100000	110000
38		MARINE-TRADER DC	FB	TRWL	FBG	DS	IB	T135D	LEHM	12	10		4		106000	116500
38		MARINE-TRADER SDN	FB	TRWL	FBG	DS	IB	135D	LEHM	12			4	6	104500	115000
38		MARINE-TRADER SDN	FB	TRWL	FBG	DS	IB	T135D	LEHM	12			4	6	110500	121500
38	10	TRADEWINDS 39	FB	MY	FBG	SV	IB	T135D	LEHM	14	4		3	1	101500	112000
39	4	ISLAND-TRADER	SLP	MS	FBG	KL	IB	135D	LEHM	13	4	34400	4	9	121500	133500
39	4	MARINE-TRADER SUNDCK	FB	TRWL	FBG	DS	IB	135D	LEHM	12	11		4		121000	133000
39	4	MARINE-TRADER SUNDCK	FB	TRWL	FBG	DS	IB	T135D	LEHM	12	11		4		127000	139500
42		MARINE-TRADER 42 SDN	FB	TRWL	FBG	DS	IB	135D	LEHM	12	10		4		143000	157000
42		MARINE-TRADER 42 SDN	FB	TRWL	FBG	DS	IB	T135D	LEHM	12	10		4		149000	163500
42		TRADEWINDS 38/42 FSH	FB	YTFS	FBG	SV	IB	135D	LEHM	12	10		3	5	79600	87500
42		TRADEWINDS 38/42 FSH	FB	YTFS	FBG	SV	IB	T135D	LEHM	12	10		3	5	73900	81200
42	6	TRADEWINDS 43	FB	MY	FBG	SV	IB	T135D	LEHM	14	11		5	7	137000	150500
43	4	MARINE-TRADER 40/44	FB	TRWL	FBG	DS	IB	135D	LEHM	12	11		4		124000	136000
43	4	MARINE-TRADER 40/44	FB	TRWL	FBG	DS	IB	T135D	LEHM	12	11		4		128500	141000
45	6	ISLAND-TRADER	SLP	MS	FBG	KL	IB	135D	LEHM	15	2	48363	5	6	161000	177000
46	2	MARINE-TRADER DC	FB	TRWL	FBG	DS	IB	T135D	LEHM	14	7		3	8	163500	179500
46	6	TRADEWINDS 43/47 FSH	FB	YTFS	FBG	SV	IB	T135D	LEHM	14	6		3	10	139500	153000
46	6	TRADEWINDS 47	FB	MY	FBG	SV	IB	T135D	LEHM	14	6		3	10	162000	178000
48	6	MARINE-TRADER PH	FB	TRWL	FBG	DS	IB	T135D	LEHM	15		46000	4	6	216500	237500
48	6	MARINE-TRADER PH SDK	FB	TRWL	FBG	DS	IB	T135D	LEHM	15			4	6	190500	209000
50		MARINE-TRADER MY	FB	TRWL	FBG	DS	IB	T135D	LEHM	15	5	47500	4	8	216000	237500
50		MARINE-TRADER WIDE	FB	MY	FBG	DS	IB	T135D	LEHM	15	5		4	6	170500	187500
		1990 BOATS														
33	6	MARINE-TRADER DC	FB	TRWL	FBG	DS	IB	135D	LEHM	11	9		3	6	73300	80600
33	6	MARINE-TRADER SDN	FB	TRWL	FBG	DS	IB	135D	LEHM	11	9		3	6	73300	80600
36		MARINE-TRADER DC	FB	TRWL	FBG	DS	IB	135D	LEHM	12	2		3	6	80400	88300
36		MARINE-TRADER DC	FB	TRWL	FBG	DS	IB	T135D	LEHM	12	2		3	6	84100	92400
36		MARINE-TRADER SDN	FB	TRWL	FBG	DS	IB	135D	LEHM	12	2		3	6	80400	88300
36		MARINE-TRADER SDN	FB	TRWL	FBG	DS	IB	T135D	LEHM	12	2		3	6	84100	92400
36		MARINE-TRADER SNDK	FB	TRWL	FBG	DS	IB	135D	LEHM	12	2		3	6	84500	92800
36		SUNDECK 36	FB	TRWL	FBG	DS	IB	T135D	LEHM	12	2		3	6	87900	96600
38		MARINE-TRADER DC	FB	TRWL	FBG	DS	IB	135D	LEHM	12	10		4		95500	105000
38		MARINE-TRADER DC	FB	TRWL	FBG	DS	IB	T135D	LEHM	12	10		4		101000	111000
38		MARINE-TRADER SDN	FB	TRWL	FBG	DS	IB	135D	LEHM	12			4	6	99900	110000
38		MARINE-TRADER SDN	FB	TRWL	FBG	DS	IB	T135D	LEHM	12			4	6	105500	116000
38	10	TRADEWINDS 39	FB	MY	FBG	SV	IB	T135D	LEHM	14	4		3	1	97100	106500
39	4	ISLAND-TRADER	SLP	MS	FBG	KL	IB	135D	LEHM	13	4	34400	4	9	114000	125500
39	4	MARINE-TRADER SUNDCK	FB	TRWL	FBG	DS	IB	135D	LEHM	12	11		4		115500	127000
39	4	MARINE-TRADER SUNDCK	FB	TRWL	FBG	DS	IB	T135D	LEHM	12	11		4		121500	133500
42		MARINE-TRADER 42 SDN	FB	TRWL	FBG	DS	IB	135D	LEHM	12	10		4		136500	150000
42		MARINE-TRADER 42 SDN	FB	TRWL	FBG	DS	IB	T135D	LEHM	12	10		4		142000	156000
42		TRADEWINDS 38/42 FSH	FB	YTFS	FBG	SV	IB	135D	LEHM	12	10		3	5	76000	83500
42		TRADEWINDS 38/42 FSH	FB	YTFS	FBG	SV	IB	T135D	LEHM	12	10		3	5	70500	77500
42	6	TRADEWINDS 43	FB	MY	FBG	SV	IB	T135D	LEHM	14	11		5	7	131000	143500
43	4	MARINE-TRADER 40/44	FB	TRWL	FBG	DS	IB	135D	LEHM	12	11		4		118000	130000
43	4	MARINE-TRADER 40/44	FB	TRWL	FBG	DS	IB	T135D	LEHM	12	11		4		122500	134500

CONTINUED ON NEXT PAGE

LOA FT	LOA IN	NAME AND/ OR MODEL	TOP/ RIG	BOAT TYPE	-HULL- MTL	-HULL- TP	ENGINE TP	ENGINE # HP	ENGINE MFG	BEAM FT	BEAM IN	WGT LBS	DRAFT FT	DRAFT IN	RETAIL LOW	RETAIL HIGH
		1990 BOATS														
45	6	ISLAND-TRADER	SLP	MS	FBG	KL	IB	135D	LEHM	15	2	48363	5	6	151000	166000
46	2	MARINE-TRADER DC	FB	TRWL	FBG	DS	IB	T135D	LEHM	14	7		3	8	156000	171500
46	6	TRADEWINDS 43/47 FSH	FB	YTFS	FBG	SV	IB	T135D	LEHM	14	6		3	10	133000	146000
46	6	TRADEWINDS 47	HT	MY	FBG	SV	IB	T135D	LEHM	14	6		3	10	155500	171000
48	6	MARINE-TRADER PH	FB	TRWL	FBG	DS	IB	T135D	LEHM	15		46000	4	6	206500	227000
48	6	MARINE-TRADER PH SDK	FB	TRWL	FBG	DS	IB	T135D	LEHM	15			4	6	181500	199500
50		MARINE-TRADER MY	FB	TRWL	FBG	DS	IB	T135D	LEHM	15	5	47500	4	8	206500	226500
50		MARINE-TRADER WIDE	FB	MY	FBG	DS	IB	T135D	LEHM	15	5		4	6	162500	179000
		1989 BOATS														
33	6	MARINE-TRADER DC	FB	TRWL	FBG	DS	IB	135D	LEHM	11	9		3	6	70100	77000
33	6	MARINE-TRADER DC	FB	TRWL	FBG	DS	IB	T 90D		11	9		3	6	71800	79000
33	6	MARINE-TRADER SDN	FB	TRWL	FBG	DS	IB	135D	LEHM	11	9		3	6	70100	77000
33	6	MARINE-TRADER SDN	FB	TRWL	FBG	DS	IB	T 90D		11	9		3	6	71800	79000
36		MARINE-TRADER DC	FB	TRWL	FBG	DS	IB	135D	LEHM	12	2		3	6	76800	84400
36		MARINE-TRADER DC	FB	TRWL	FBG	DS	IB	T 90D		12	2		3	6	78800	86500
36		MARINE-TRADER SDN	FB	TRWL	FBG	DS	IB	135D	LEHM	12	2		3	6	76800	84400
36		MARINE-TRADER SDN	FB	TRWL	FBG	DS	IB	T 90D	LEHM	12	2		3	6	78800	86500
36		MARINE-TRADER SNDK	FB	TRWL	FBG	DS	IB	135D	LEHM	12	2		3	6	80700	88600
36		SUNDECK 36	FB	TRWL	FBG	DS	IB	T 90D	LEHM	12	2		3	6	82400	90500
38		MARINE-TRADER DC	FB	TRWL	FBG	DS	IB	135D	LEHM	12	10		4		91200	100500
38		MARINE-TRADER DC	FB	TRWL	FBG	DS	IB	T135D	LEHM	12	10		4		96500	106000
38		MARINE-TRADER SDN	FB	TRWL	FBG	DS	IB	135D	LEHM	12			4	6	95500	105000
38		MARINE-TRADER SDN	FB	TRWL	FBG	DS	IB	T135D	LEHM	12			4	6	100500	110500
38	10	TRADEWINDS 39	FB	MY	FBG	SV	IB	T135D	LEHM	14	4		3	1	92700	102000
39	4	ISLAND-TRADER	SLP	MS	FBG	KL	IB	135D	LEHM	13	4	34400	4	9	107500	118000
39	4	MARINE-TRADER SUNDCK	FB	TRWL	FBG	DS	IB	135D	LEHM	12	11		4		110000	121000
39	4	MARINE-TRADER SUNDCK	FB	TRWL	FBG	DS	IB	T135D	LEHM	12	11		4		116000	127500
42		MARINE-TRADER 42 SDN	FB	TRWL	FBG	DS	IB	135D	LEHM	12	10		4		130000	143000
42		MARINE-TRADER 42 SDN	FB	TRWL	FBG	DS	IB	T135D	LEHM	12	10		4		135500	149000
42		TRADEWINDS 38/42 FSH	FB	YTFS	FBG	SV	IB	135D	LEHM	12	10		3	5	72600	79700
42		TRADEWINDS 38/42 FSH	FB	YTFS	FBG	SV	IB	T135D	LEHM	12	10		3	5	67400	74000
42	6	TRADEWINDS 43	FB	MY	FBG	SV	IB	T135D	LEHM	14	11		5	7	125000	137000
43	4	MARINE-TRADER 40/44	FB	TRWL	FBG	DS	IB	135D	LEHM	12	11		4		113000	124000
43	4	MARINE-TRADER 40/44	FB	TRWL	FBG	DS	IB	T135D	LEHM	12	11		4		117000	128500
45	6	ISLAND-TRADER	SLP	MS	FBG	KL	IB	135D	LEHM	15	2	48363	5	6	142000	156000
46	6	TRADEWINDS 43/47 FSH	FB	YTFS	FBG	SV	IB	T135D	LEHM	14	6		3	10	127000	139500
46	6	TRADEWINDS 47	HT	MY	FBG	SV	IB	T135D	LEHM	14	6		3	10	148500	163000
48	6	MARINE-TRADER PH	FB	TRWL	FBG	DS	IB	T135D	LEHM	15		46000	4	6	197000	216500
48	6	MARINE-TRADER PH SDK	FB	TRWL	FBG	DS	IB	T135D	LEHM	15			4	6	173500	190500
50		MARINE-TRADER MY	FB	TRWL	FBG	DS	IB	T135D	LEHM	15	5	47500	4	8	197000	216500
50		MARINE-TRADER WIDE	FB	MY	FBG	DS	IB	T135D	LEHM	15	5		4	6	155500	170500
		1988 BOATS														
33	6	MARINE-TRADER DC	FB	TRWL	FBG	DS	IB	135D	LEHM	11	9		3	6	67000	73700
33	6	MARINE-TRADER DC	FB	TRWL	FBG	DS	IB	T 90D		11	9		3	6	68800	75600
33	6	MARINE-TRADER PH	FB	TRWL	FBG	DS	IB	135D	LEHM	11	9		3	6	67000	73700
33	6	MARINE-TRADER SDN	FB	TRWL	FBG	DS	IB	135D	LEHM	11	9		3	6	67000	73700
33	6	MARINE-TRADER SDN	FB	TRWL	FBG	DS	IB	T 90D		11	9		3	6	68800	75600
36		MARINE-TRADER DC	FB	TRWL	FBG	DS	IB	135D	LEHM	12	2		3	6	72800	80000
36		MARINE-TRADER DC	FB	TRWL	FBG	DS	IB	T 90D		12	2		3	6	74700	82100
36		MARINE-TRADER SDN	FB	TRWL	FBG	DS	IB	135D	LEHM	12	2		3	6	74600	82000
36		MARINE-TRADER SDN	FB	TRWL	FBG	DS	IB	T 90D	LEHM	12	2		3	6	76400	84000
36		SUNDECK 36	FB	TRWL	FBG	DS	IB	135D	LEHM	12	2		3	6	76400	84000
36		SUNDECK 36	FB	TRWL	FBG	DS	IB	T 90D	LEHM	12	2		3	6	78100	85800
37	4	ISLAND-TRADER	KTH	SA/CR	FBG	KL	IB	D		12		26400	4	6	80600	88600
37	10	TRADEWINDS 38	HT	MY	FBG	DV	IB	135D	LEHM	12	10		3	5	87600	96300
37	10	TRADEWINDS 38	HT	MY	FBG	DV	IB	T135D	LEHM	12	10		3	5	92100	101000
38		MARINE-TRADER DC	FB	TRWL	FBG	DS	IB	135D	LEHM	12	10		4		87200	95800
38		MARINE-TRADER DC	FB	TRWL	FBG	DS	IB	T135D	LEHM	12	10		4		92200	101500
38		MARINE-TRADER SDN	FB	TRWL	FBG	DS	IB	135D	LEHM	12			4	6	91200	100500
38		MARINE-TRADER SDN	FB	TRWL	FBG	DS	IB	T135D	LEHM	12			4	6	96200	106000
39	4	ISLAND-TRADER	SLP	MS	FBG	KL	IB	135D	LEHM	13	4	34400	4	9	101000	111000
39	4	MARINE-TRADER SUNDCK	FB	TRWL	FBG	DS	IB	135D	LEHM	12	11		4		105500	116000
39	4	MARINE-TRADER SUNDCK	FB	TRWL	FBG	DS	IB	T135D	LEHM	12	11		4		110500	121500
40	3	ISLAND-TRADER AFTCPT	KTH	SA/CR	FBG	KL	IB	D		12		29000	6		88600	97400
40	3	ISLAND-TRADER CTRCPT	KTH	SA/CR	FBG	KL	IB	D		12		29000	6		93000	102000
42		MARINE-TRADER 42 SDN	FB	TRWL	FBG	DS	IB	135D	LEHM	12	10		4		124500	136500
42		MARINE-TRADER 42 SDN	FB	TRWL	FBG	DS	IB	T135D	LEHM	12	10		4		129500	142500
42		TRADEWINDS 38/42 FSH	FB	YTFS	FBG	DS	IB	135D	LEHM	12	10		3	5	69300	76200
42		TRADEWINDS 38/42 FSH	FB	YTFS	FBG	DS	IB	T135D	LEHM	12	10		3	5	64700	71100
42	6	TRADEWINDS 43	FB	MY	FBG	DS	IB	T135D	LEHM	14	11		5	7	120500	132500
43	4	MARINE-TRADER 40/44	FB	TRWL	FBG	DS	IB	135D	LEHM	12	11		4		108000	118500
43	4	MARINE-TRADER 40/44	FB	TRWL	FBG	DS	IB	T135D	LEHM	12	11		4		112000	123000
43	6	MARINE-TRADER 2 STRM	FB	TRWL	FBG	DS	IB	135D	LEHM	14	4		4	2	142000	156000
43	6	MARINE-TRADER 2 STRM	FB	TRWL	FBG	DS	IB	T135D	LEHM	14	4		4	2	147000	161500
43	6	MARINE-TRADER 3 STRM	FB	TRWL	FBG	DS	IB	135D	LEHM	14	4		4	2	142000	156000
43	6	MARINE-TRADER 3 STRM	FB	TRWL	FBG	DS	IB	T135D	LEHM	14	4		4	2	147000	161500
43	6	MARINE-TRADER SUNDK	FB	TRWL	FBG	DS	IB	135D	LEHM	14	4		4	2	148000	162500
43	6	MARINE-TRADER SUNDK	FB	TRWL	FBG	DS	IB	T135D	LEHM	14	4		4	2	153000	168000
45	6	ISLAND-TRADER	SLP	MS	FBG	KL	IB	135D	LEHM	15	2	48363	5	6	133000	146500
46	6	TRADEWINDS 43/47 FSH	FB	YTFS	FBG	DS	IB	T135D	LEHM	14	6		3	10	121000	133000
46	6	TRADEWINDS 47	HT	MY	FBG	DV	IB	T135D	LEHM	14	6		3	10	144000	158500
48	6	MARINE-TRADER PH	FB	TRWL	FBG	DS	IB	T135D	LEHM	15		46000	4	6	188500	207000
48	6	MARINE-TRADER PH SDK	FB	TRWL	FBG	DS	IB	T135D	LEHM	15			4	6	166000	182500
50		MARINE-TRADER MY	FB	TRWL	FBG	DS	IB	T135D	LEHM	15	5	47500	4	8	188500	207000
50		MARINE-TRADER WIDE	FB	MY	FBG	DS	IB	T135D	LEHM	15	5		4	6	148500	163000
50	10	ISLAND-TRADER CTRCPT	KTH	SA/CR	FBG	KL	IB	135D	LEHM	14	1	52000	6	2	165500	182000
50	10	ISLAND-TRADER PH	KTH	SA/CR	FBG	KL	IB	135D	LEHM	14	1	52000	6	2	157000	172500
		1987 BOATS														
33	6	MARINE-TRADER DC	FB	TRWL	FBG	DS	IB	135D	LEHM	11	9		3	6	64200	70600
33	6	MARINE-TRADER DC	FB	TRWL	FBG	DS	IB	T 90D		11	9		3	6	65900	72400
33	6	MARINE-TRADER PH	FB	TRWL	FBG	DS	IB	135D	LEHM	11	9		3	6	64200	70600
33	6	MARINE-TRADER SDN	FB	TRWL	FBG	DS	IB	135D	LEHM	11	9		3	6	64200	70600
33	6	MARINE-TRADER SDN	FB	TRWL	FBG	DS	IB	T 90D		11	9		3	6	65900	72400
36		MARINE-TRADER DC	FB	TRWL	FBG	DS	IB	135D	LEHM	12	2		3	6	70200	77200
36		MARINE-TRADER DC	FB	TRWL	FBG	DS	IB	T 90D		12	2		3	6	72000	79100
36		MARINE-TRADER SDN	FB	TRWL	FBG	DS	IB	135D	LEHM	12	2		3	6	70200	77200
36		MARINE-TRADER SDN	FB	TRWL	FBG	DS	IB	T 90D	LEHM	12	2		3	6	72000	79100
36		MARINE-TRADER SUNDCK	FB	TRWL	FBG	DS	IB	135D	LEHM	12	2		3	6	73700	81000
36		MARINE-TRADER SUNDCK	FB	TRWL	FBG	DS	IB	T 90D	LEHM	12	2		3	6	75300	82700
37	4	ISLAND-TRADER	KTH	SA/CR	FBG	KL	IB	D		12		26400	4	6	75800	83300
37	10	TRADEWINDS 38	HT	MY	FBG	DV	IB	135D	LEHM	12	10		3	5	83800	92100
38		MARINE-TRADER DC	FB	TRWL	FBG	DS	IB	135D	LEHM	12	10		4		83400	91600
38		MARINE-TRADER DC	FB	TRWL	FBG	DS	IB	T135D	LEHM	12	10		4		88200	96900
38		MARINE-TRADER SDN	FB	TRWL	FBG	DS	IB	135D	LEHM	12			4	6	87200	95900
38		MARINE-TRADER SDN	FB	TRWL	FBG	DS	IB	T135D	LEHM	12			4	6	92000	101000
39	4	ISLAND-TRADER	SLP	MS	FBG	KL	IB	120D	LEHM	13	4	34400	4	9	94800	104000
39	4	MARINE-TRADER SUNDCK	FB	TRWL	FBG	DS	IB	135D	LEHM	12	11		4		100500	110500
39	4	MARINE-TRADER SUNDCK	FB	TRWL	FBG	DS	IB	T135D	LEHM	12	11		4		106000	116500
40	3	ISLAND-TRADER AFTCPT	KTH	SA/CR	FBG	KL	IB	D		12		29000	6		83400	91600
40	3	ISLAND-TRADER CTRCPT	KTH	SA/CR	FBG	KL	IB	D		12		29000	6		87500	96100
42		MARINE-TRADER 42 SDN	FB	TRWL	FBG	DS	IB	135D	LEHM	12	10		4		119000	131000
42		MARINE-TRADER 42 SDN	FB	TRWL	FBG	DS	IB	T135D	LEHM	12	10		4		124000	136500
42		TRADEWINDS 38/42 FSH	FB	YTFS	FBG	DS	IB	T135D	LEHM	12	10		3	5	61900	68000
42	6	TRADEWINDS 43	FB	MY	FBG	DS	IB	T135D	LEHM	14	11		5	7	115500	127000
43	4	MARINE-TRADER 40/44	FB	TRWL	FBG	DS	IB	135D	LEHM	12	11		4		103000	113500
43	4	MARINE-TRADER 40/44	FB	TRWL	FBG	DS	IB	T135D	LEHM	12	11		4		107000	117500
43	6	MARINE-TRADER 2 STRM	FB	TRWL	FBG	DS	IB	135D	LEHM	14	4		4	2	136000	149000
43	6	MARINE-TRADER 2 STRM	FB	TRWL	FBG	DS	IB	T135D	LEHM	14	4		4	2	140500	154500
43	6	MARINE-TRADER 3 STRM	FB	TRWL	FBG	DS	IB	135D	LEHM	14	4		4	2	136000	149000
43	6	MARINE-TRADER 3 STRM	FB	TRWL	FBG	DS	IB	T135D	LEHM	14	4		4	2	140500	154500
43	6	MARINE-TRADER SUNDCK	FB	TRWL	FBG	DS	IB	135D	LEHM	14	4		4	2	141500	155500
43	6	MARINE-TRADER SUNDCK	FB	TRWL	FBG	DS	IB	T135D	LEHM	14	4		4	2	146000	160500
45	6	ISLAND-TRADER	KTH	MS	FBG	KL	IB	120D	LEHM	15	2	48363	5	6	126500	139000
46	6	TRADEWINDS 43/47 FSH	FB	YTFS	FBG	DS	IB	T135D	LEHM	14	6		3	10	116000	127000
46	6	TRADEWINDS 47	HT	MY	FBG	DV	IB	T200D	VLVO	14	6		3	10	135000	148500
48	6	MARINE-TRADER PH	FB	TRWL	FBG	DS	IB	T135D	LEHM	15		46000	4	6	180000	198000
48	6	MARINE-TRADER PH SD	FB	TRWL	FBG	DS	IB	T135D	LEHM	15			4	6	158500	174500
50		MARINE-TRADER MY	FB	TRWL	FBG	DS	IB	T135D	LEHM	15	5	47500	4	8	180000	198000
50		MARINE-TRADER WIDE	FB	MY	FBG	DS	IB	T135D	LEHM	15	5		4	6	142000	156000
50	10	ISLAND-TRADER CTRCPT	KTH	SA/CR	FBG	KL	IB	120D	LEHM	14	1	52000	6	2	155000	170500
50	10	ISLAND-TRADER PH	KTH	SA/CR	FBG	KL	IB	120D	LEHM	14	1	52000	6	2	147000	161500
		1986 BOATS														
32		RETRIEVER TUG		TRWL	FBG	DS	IB	90D		11	6	17000	3	5	61400	67500
33	6	MARINE-TRADER DC	FB	TRWL	FBG	DS	IB	120D	LEHM	11	9		3	6	61300	67400
33	6	MARINE-TRADER DC	FB	TRWL	FBG	DS	IB	T 90D		11	9		3	6	63100	69400
33	6	MARINE-TRADER PH	FB	TRWL	FBG	DS	IB	120D	LEHM	11	9		3	6	61300	67400
33	6	MARINE-TRADER SDN	FB	TRWL	FBG	DS	IB	120D	LEHM	11	9		3	6	61300	67400
33	6	MARINE-TRADER SDN	FB	TRWL	FBG	DS	IB	T 90D		11	9		3	6	63100	69400
36		MARINE-TRADER DC	FB	TRWL	FBG	DS	IB	120D	LEHM	12	2		3	6	67500	74200
36		MARINE-TRADER DC	FB	TRWL	FBG	DS	IB	T 90D		12	2		3	6	68900	75800
36		MARINE-TRADER SDN	FB	TRWL	FBG	DS	IB	120D	LEHM	12	2		3	6	67500	74200
36		MARINE-TRADER SDN	FB	TRWL	FBG	DS	IB	T 90D	LEHM	12	2		3	6	68900	75800
36		MARINE-TRADER SUNDCK	FB	TRWL	FBG	DS	IB	120D	LEHM	12	2		3	6	70600	77600
36		MARINE-TRADER SUNDCK	FB	TRWL	FBG	DS	IB	T 90D	LEHM	12	2		3	6	71900	79000
37	4	ISLAND-TRADER	KTH	SA/CR	FBG	KL	IB	D		12		26400	4	6	71300	78400
37	10	TRADEWINDS 38	HT	MY	FBG	DV	IB	120D	LEHM	12	10		3	5	80100	88000

 CONTINUED ON NEXT PAGE

LOA FT	LOA IN	NAME AND/ OR MODEL	TOP/ RIG	BOAT TYPE	-HULL- MTL	-HULL- TP	ENGINE TP	ENGINE # HP	ENGINE MFG	BEAM FT	BEAM IN	WGT LBS	DRAFT FT	DRAFT IN	RETAIL LOW	RETAIL HIGH
		1986 BOATS														
38		MARINE-TRADER DC	FB	TRWL	FBG	DS	IB	120D	LEHM	12	10		4		79700	87600
38		MARINE-TRADER DC	FB	TRWL	FBG	DS	IB	T120D	LEHM	12	10		4		83900	92200
39	4	ISLAND-TRADER	SLP	MS	FBG	KL	IB	120D	LEHM	13	4	34400	4	9	89200	98000
39	4	MARINE-TRADER SUNDCK	FB	TRWL	FBG	DS	IB	120D	LEHM	12	11		4		96200	105500
39	4	MARINE-TRADER SUNDCK	FB	TRWL	FBG	DS	IB	T120D	LEHM	12	11		4		101000	111000
39	8	MARINE-TRADER SDN	FB	TRWL	FBG	DS	IB	120D	LEHM	13	8		4		98300	108000
39	8	MARINE-TRADER SDN	FB	TRWL	FBG	DS	IB	T120D	LEHM	13	8		4		103000	113000
40		LA-BELLE 40	FB	MY	FBG	SV	IB	T165D	VLVO	13	6		3	6	94500	104000
40	3	ISLAND-TRADER AFTCPT	KTH	SA/CR	FBG	KL	IB	D		12		29000	6		78300	86000
40	3	ISLAND-TRADER CTRCPT	KTH	SA/CR	FBG	KL	IB	D		12		29000	6		82400	90600
43		LA-BELLE 43	FB	MY	FBG	SV	IB	T165D	VLVO	14	2		4	2	106000	116500
43	4	MARINE-TRADER 40/44	FB	TRWL	FBG	DS	IB	120D	LEHM	12	11		4		98400	108000
43	4	MARINE-TRADER 40/44	FB	TRWL	FBG	DS	IB	T120D	LEHM	12	11		4		102000	112000
43	6	MARINE-TRADER 2 STRM	FB	TRWL	FBG	DS	IB	120D	LEHM	14	4		4	2	129500	142500
43	6	MARINE-TRADER 2 STRM	FB	TRWL	FBG	DS	IB	T120D	LEHM	14	4		4	2	134000	147500
43	6	MARINE-TRADER 3 STRM	FB	TRWL	FBG	DS	IB	120D	LEHM	14	4		4	2	129500	142500
43	6	MARINE-TRADER 3 STRM	FB	TRWL	FBG	DS	IB	T120D	LEHM	14	4		4	2	134000	147500
43	6	MARINE-TRADER SUNDCK	FB	TRWL	FBG	DS	IB	120D	LEHM	14	4		4	2	135000	148500
43	6	MARINE-TRADER SUNDCK	FB	TRWL	FBG	DS	IB	T120D	LEHM	14	4		4	2	139000	153000
45	6	ISLAND-TRADER	KTH	MS	FBG	KL	IB	120D	LEHM	15	2	48363	5	6	119000	131000
46	6	TRADEWINDS 47	HT	MY	FBG	DV	IB	T165D	VLVO	14	6		3	10	132500	145500
48	6	MARINE-TRADER PH	FB	TRWL	FBG	DS	IB	T120D	LEHM	15		46000	4	6	171000	188000
48	6	MARINE-TRADER PH	FB	TRWL	FBG	DS	IB	T200D	PERK	15			4	6	176000	193500
48	6	MARINE-TRADER PH SD	FB	TRWL	FBG	DS	IB	T120D	LEHM	15			4	6	151000	166000
48	6	MARINE-TRADER PH SD	FB	TRWL	FBG	DS	IB	T200D	LEHM	15			4	6	156500	172000
50		MARINE-TRADER MY	FB	TRWL	FBG	DS	IB	T120D	LEHM	15	5	47500	4	8	170000	187000
50		MARINE-TRADER MY	FB	TRWL	FBG	DS	IB	T200D	LEHM	15	5	47500	4	6	181000	199000
50		MARINE-TRADER WDE	FB	MY	FBG	DS	IB	T120D	LEHM	15	5		4	6	134500	148000
50		MARINE-TRADER WDE	FB	MY	FBG	DS	IB	T200D	LEHM	15	5		4	6	132500	146000
50	10	ISLAND-TRADER CTRCPT	KTH	SA/CR	FBG	KL	IB	120D	LEHM	14	1	52000	6	2	146000	160000
50	10	ISLAND-TRADER PH	KTH	SA/CR	FBG	KL	IB	120D	LEHM	14	1	52000	6	2	137500	151000
56	1	MARINE-TRADER MY	FB	TRWL	FBG	DS	IB	T165D	PERK	17	1		4	4	148500	163500
		1985 BOATS														
32		RETRIEVER TUG		TRWL	FBG	DS	IB	D		11	6	17000	3	5	**	**
33	6	MARINE-TRADER DC	FB	TRWL	FBG	DS	IB	120D	LEHM	11	9		3	6	58800	64600
33	6	MARINE-TRADER DC	FB	TRWL	FBG	DS	IB	T 90D	LEHM	11	9		3	6	60500	66500
33	6	MARINE-TRADER PH	FB	TRWL	FBG	DS	IB	120D	LEHM	11	9		3	6	58800	64600
33	6	MARINE-TRADER SDN	FB	TRWL	FBG	DS	IB	120D	LEHM	11	9		3	6	58800	64600
33	6	MARINE-TRADER SDN	FB	TRWL	FBG	DS	IB	T 90D	LEHM	11	9		3	6	60500	66500
36		MARINE-TRADER DC	FB	TRWL	FBG	DS	IB	120D	LEHM	12	2		3	6	64600	71000
36		MARINE-TRADER DC	FB	TRWL	FBG	DS	IB	T 90D	LEHM	12	2		3	6	65500	72000
36		MARINE-TRADER SDN	FB	TRWL	FBG	DS	IB	120D	LEHM	12	2		3	6	64600	71000
36		MARINE-TRADER SDN	FB	TRWL	FBG	DS	IB	T 90D	LEHM	12	2		3	6	68400	75100
36		MARINE-TRADER SUNDCK	FB	TRWL	FBG	DS	IB	120D	LEHM	12	2		3	6	67600	74300
36		MARINE-TRADER SUNDCK	FB	TRWL	FBG	DS	IB	T 90D		12	2		3	6	68400	75100
37	4	ISLAND-TRADER	KTH	SA/CR	FBG	KL	IB	D		12		26400	4	6	67100	73700
37	10	TRADEWINDS SUNDECK	FB	MY	FBG	SV	IB	120D	LEHM	12	10		3	5	76700	84300
38		MARINE-TRADER DC	FB	TRWL	FBG	DS	IB	120D	LEHM	12	10		4		76300	83800
38		MARINE-TRADER DC	FB	TRWL	FBG	DS	IB	T120D	LEHM	12	10		4		80300	88300
39	4	MARINE-TRADER DC SDK	FB	TRWL	FBG	DS	IB	120D	LEHM	12	11		4		92100	101000
39	4	MARINE-TRADER DC SDK	FB	TRWL	FBG	DS	IB	T120D	LEHM	12	11		4		96800	106500
39	4	MARINE-TRADER SUNDCK	FB	TRWL	FBG	DS	IB	120D	LEHM	12	11		4		92100	101000
39	4	MARINE-TRADER SUNDCK	FB	TRWL	FBG	DS	IB	T120D	LEHM	12	11		4		96400	106000
39	8	MARINE-TRADER SDN	FB	TRWL	FBG	DS	IB	120D	LEHM	13	8		4		94100	103500
39	8	MARINE-TRADER SDN	FB	TRWL	FBG	DS	IB	T120D	LEHM	13	8		4		98600	108500
39	9	ISLAND-TRADER	SLP	MS	FBG	KL	IB	120D	LEHM	13	4	34400	4	9	84400	92700
40		LA-BELLE CRUISER	FB	MY	FBG	SV	IB	T165D	VLVO	13	6		3	6	90500	99500
40	3	ISLAND-TRADER AFTCPT	KTH	SA/CR	FBG	KL	IB	D		12		29000	6		73600	80900
40	3	ISLAND-TRADER CTRCPT	KTH	SA/CR	FBG	KL	IB	D		12		29000	6		77500	85200
43		LA-BELLE CRUISER	FB	MY	FBG	SV	IB	T165D	VLVO	14	2		4	2	101500	111500
43	6	MARINE-TRADER 2 STRM	FB	TRWL	FBG	DS	IB	120D	LEHM	14	4		4	2	124500	137000
43	6	MARINE-TRADER 2 STRM	FB	TRWL	FBG	DS	IB	T120D	LEHM	14	4		4	2	128000	140500
43	6	MARINE-TRADER 3 STRM	FB	TRWL	FBG	DS	IB	120D	LEHM	14	4		4	2	124500	137000
43	6	MARINE-TRADER 3 STRM	FB	TRWL	FBG	DS	IB	T120D	LEHM	14	4		4	2	128000	140500
43	6	MARINE-TRADER MK II	FB	TRWL	FBG	DS	IB	120D	LEHM	14	4		4	2	124500	137000
43	6	MARINE-TRADER MK II	FB	TRWL	FBG	DS	IB	T120D	LEHM	14	4		4	2	128000	140500
43	6	MARINE-TRADER SUNDCK	FB	TRWL	FBG	DS	IB	120D	LEHM	14	4		4	2	125500	138000
43	6	MARINE-TRADER SUNDCK	FB	TRWL	FBG	DS	IB	T120D	LEHM	14	4		4	2	132500	146000
45	6	ISLAND-TRADER	KTH	MS	FBG	KL	IB	120D	LEHM	15	2	48363	5	6	112000	123000
46	6	TRADEWINDS SUNDECK	FB	MY	FBG	SV	IB	T165D	VLVO	14	6		3	10	124000	136000
46	6	TRADEWINDS SUNDECK	FB	MY	FBG	SV	IB	T225D	VLVO	14	6		3	10	123500	136000
48	6	MARINE-TRADER PH	FB	TRWL	FBG	DS	IB	T120D	LEHM	15		46000	4	6	164000	180000
48	6	MARINE-TRADER PH	FB	TRWL	FBG	DS	IB	T200D	LEHM	15			4	6	168500	185000
48	6	MARINE-TRADER PH SDK	FB	TRWL	FBG	DS	IB	T120D	LEHM	15			4	6	144500	159000
48	6	MARINE-TRADER PH SDK	FB	TRWL	FBG	DS	IB	T160D	LEHM	15			4	6	146500	161000
48	6	MARINE-TRADER PH SDK	FB	TRWL	FBG	DS	IB	T200D	LEHM	15			4	6	149500	164500
50		MARINE-TRADER MY	FB	TRWL	FBG	DS	IB	T120D		15	5	47500	4	6	163000	179000
50		MARINE-TRADER MY	FB	TRWL	FBG	DS	IB	T120D	LEHM	15	5	47500	4	8	163000	179000
50		MARINE-TRADER WDE	FB	MY	FBG	DS	IB	T200		15	5		4	6	120500	132500
50		MARINE-TRADER WDE	FB	MY	FBG	DS	IB	T120D	LEHM	15	5		4	6	129000	141500
50	10	ISLAND-TRADER CTRCPT	KTH	SA/CR	FBG	KL	IB	120D	LEHM	14	1	52000	6	2	136500	150000
50	10	ISLAND-TRADER PH	KTH	SA/CR	FBG	KL	IB	120D	LEHM	14	1	52000	6	2	128500	141500
56	1	MARINE-TRADER MY	FB	TRWL	FBG	DS	IB	T D		17	1		4	4	**	**
		1984 BOATS														
32		MARINE-TRADER SDN	FB	TRWL	FBG	DS	IB	80D		11	4	14000	3	4	48200	52900
33	6	MARINE-TRADER DC	FB	TRWL	FBG	DS	IB	120D	LEHM	11	9		3	6	56400	62000
33	6	MARINE-TRADER DC	FB	TRWL	FBG	DS	IB	T 65D		11	9		3	6	57100	62700
33	6	MARINE-TRADER PH	FB	TRWL	FBG	DS	IB	120D	LEHM	11	9		3	6	56400	62000
33	6	MARINE-TRADER SDN	FB	TRWL	FBG	DS	IB	120D	LEHM	11	9		3	6	56400	62000
33	6	MARINE-TRADER SDN	FB	TRWL	FBG	DS	IB	T 65D		11	9		3	6	57100	62700
36		MARINE-TRADER DC	FB	TRWL	FBG	DS	IB	120D	LEHM	12	2		3	6	62900	69100
36		MARINE-TRADER DC	FB	TRWL	FBG	DS	IB	T 65D		12	2		3	6	64000	70300
36		MARINE-TRADER SDN	FB	TRWL	FBG	DS	IB	120D	LEHM	12	2		3	6	62900	69100
36		MARINE-TRADER SDN	FB	TRWL	FBG	DS	IB	T 65D		12	2		3	6	64000	70300
37	4	ISLAND-TRADER	KTH	SA/CR	FBG	KL	IB	D		12		26400	4	6	63100	69300
38		MARINE-TRADER DC	FB	TRWL	FBG	DS	IB	120D	LEHM	12	10		4		73100	80300
38		MARINE-TRADER DC	FB	TRWL	FBG	DS	IB	T120D	LEHM	12	10		4		77000	84600
39	4	MARINE-TRADER DC SDK	FB	TRWL	FBG	DS	IB	120D	LEHM	12	11		4		88300	97000
39	4	MARINE-TRADER DC SDK	FB	TRWL	FBG	DS	IB	T120D	LEHM	12	11		4		92500	101500
39	8	MARINE-TRADER DC	FB	TRWL	FBG	DS	IB	120D	LEHM	13	8		4		90200	99100
39	8	MARINE-TRADER DC	FB	TRWL	FBG	DS	IB	T120D	LEHM	13	8		4		94500	104000
39	8	MARINE-TRADER SDN	FB	TRWL	FBG	DS	IB	120D	LEHM	13	8		4		90200	99100
39	8	MARINE-TRADER SDN	FB	TRWL	FBG	DS	IB	T120D	LEHM	13	8		4		94500	104000
39	9	ISLAND-TRADER	SLP	MS	FBG	KL	IB	120D	LEHM	13	4	34400	4	9	79300	87200
40		LA-BELLE CRUISER	FB	MY	FBG	SV	IB	T165D	VLVO	13	6		3	6	86700	95300
40	3	ISLAND-TRADER AFTCPT	KTH	SA/CR	FBG	KL	IB	D		12		29000	6		69300	76200
40	3	ISLAND-TRADER CTRCPT	KTH	SA/CR	FBG	KL	IB	D		12		29000	6		72900	80100
43		LA-BELLE CRUISER	FB	MY	FBG	SV	IB	T165D	VLVO	14	2		4	2	97100	106500
43	6	MARINE-TRADER 2 STRM	FB	TRWL	FBG	DS	IB	120D	LEHM	14	4		4	2	119500	131000
43	6	MARINE-TRADER 2 STRM	FB	TRWL	FBG	DS	IB	T120D	LEHM	14	4		4	2	123000	135500
43	6	MARINE-TRADER 3 STRM	FB	TRWL	FBG	DS	IB	120D	LEHM	14	4		4	2	119500	131000
43	6	MARINE-TRADER 3 STRM	FB	TRWL	FBG	DS	IB	T120D	LEHM	14	4		4	2	123000	135500
43	6	MARINE-TRADER MK II	FB	TRWL	FBG	DS	IB	120D	LEHM	14	4		4	2	119500	131000
43	6	MARINE-TRADER MK II	FB	TRWL	FBG	DS	IB	T120D	LEHM	14	4		4	2	123000	135500
43	6	MARINE-TRADER SUNDCK	FB	TRWL	FBG	DS	IB	120D	LEHM	14	4		4	2	124500	136500
43	6	MARINE-TRADER SUNDCK	FB	TRWL	FBG	DS	IB	T120D	LEHM	14	4		4	2	128000	140500
44	10	ISLAND TRADER	KTH	SA/CR	FBG	KL	IB	D		13	6	31600	5	2	84400	92700
45	6	ISLAND-TRADER	KTH	MS	FBG	KL	IB	120D	LEHM	15	2	48363	5	6	105000	115500
48	6	MARINE-TRADER PH	FB	TRWL	FBG	DS	IB	T120D	LEHM	15			4	6	158000	173500
48	6	MARINE-TRADER PH	FB	TRWL	FBG	DS	IB	T165D	PERK	15			4	6	160500	176500
48	6	MARINE-TRADER PH SDK	FB	TRWL	FBG	DS	IB	T120D	LEHM	15			4	6	138500	152500
48	6	MARINE-TRADER PH SDK	FB	TRWL	FBG	DS	IB	T160D	LEHM	15			4	6	140500	154500
50		MARINE-TRADER MY	FB	TRWL	FBG	DS	IB	T120D	LEHM	15	5	47500	4	6	156000	171500
50		MARINE-TRADER MY	FB	TRWL	FBG	DS	IB	T160D	LEHM	15	5	47500	4	6	161500	177000
50	10	ISLAND-TRADER CTRCPT	KTH	SA/CR	FBG	KL	IB	120D	LEHM	14	1	52000	6	2	130500	143500
50	10	ISLAND-TRADER PH	KTH	SA/CR	FBG	KL	IB	120D	LEHM	14	1	52000	6	2	118500	130000
56	1	MARINE-TRADER MY	FB	TRWL	FBG	DS	IB	T165D	PERK	17	1		4	4	137000	150500

....For earlier years, see the BUC Used Boat Price Guide, Volume 3

MARINER BOAT WORKS INC

NAPLES FL 33941 COAST GUARD MFG ID- MZB See inside cover to adjust price for area

LOA FT	LOA IN	NAME AND/ OR MODEL	TOP/ RIG	BOAT TYPE	-HULL- MTL	-HULL- TP	ENGINE TP	ENGINE # HP	ENGINE MFG	BEAM FT	BEAM IN	WGT LBS	DRAFT FT	DRAFT IN	RETAIL LOW	RETAIL HIGH
		1986 BOATS														
24		OLDFIELD 240	OP	CTRCN	FBG	SV	OB			9	6	3700	2		10000	12100
24		OLDFIELD 240	OP	CTRCN	FBG	SV	IB	270	CRUS	9	6	4000	2	4	12500	14200
		1985 BOATS														
24		OLDFIELD 240	OP	CTRCN	FBG	SV	IB	270	CRUS	9	6	4000	2	4	12000	13600

MARITEC INDUSTRIES INC

GAMBLER BASS BOATS
GROVELAND FL 34736   COAST GUARD MFG ID- SDE   See inside cover to adjust price for area

For more recent years, see the BUC Used Boat Price Guide, Volume 1

LOA FT IN	NAME AND/ OR MODEL	TOP/ RIG	BOAT TYPE	-HULL- MTL TP	--ENGINE--- TP # HP MFG	BEAM FT IN	WGT LBS	DRAFT FT IN	RETAIL LOW	RETAIL HIGH
					1996 BOATS					
17 5	VICTORY SKIFF 175	OFF		FBG	OB	6 6	1300		4050	4700
19 3	INTIMIDATOR I	BASS		FBG SV	OB	7 6	1550		10000	11400
19 3	INTIMIDATOR IIB	BASS		FBG SV	OB	7 6	1550		10200	11600
20 6	GT206SS	SKI		FBG SV	OB	7 4	1500		11600	13200
20 9	GT209GE	BASS		FBG SV	OB	7 6	1650		12500	14200
20 9	GT209TE	BASS		FBG SV	OB	7 6	1650		12900	14600
20 9	VICTORY 21	OFF		FBG	OB	7 9	1950		14400	16300
					1995 BOATS					
17 5	VICTORY SKIFF 175	OFF		FBG	OB	6 6	1300		7750	8900
19 3	INTIMIDATOR I	BASS		FBG SV	OB	7 6	1550		9450	10700
19 3	INTIMIDATOR IIB	BASS		FBG SV	OB	7 6	1550		9650	11000
20 6	GT206SS	SKI		FBG SV	OB	7 4	1500		11000	12500
20 9	GT209GE	BASS		FBG SV	OB	7 6	1650		11800	13400
20 9	GT209TE	BASS		FBG SV	OB	7 6	1650		12200	13800
20 9	VICTORY 21	OFF		FBG	OB	7 9	1950		13600	15500
					1994 BOATS					
19 3	INTIMIDATOR I	BASS		FBG SV	OB	7 6	1550		8950	10200
19 3	INTIMIDATOR II	BASS		FBG SV	OB	7 6	1550		9100	10300
19 3	INTIMIDATOR IIB	BASS		FBG SV	OB	7 6	1550		9100	10300
20 6	GT206DL	BASS		FBG SV	OB	7 4	1500		10500	11900
20 6	GT206SL	BASS		FBG SV	OB	7 4	1500		10400	11800
20 6	GT206SS	SKI		FBG SV	OB	7 4	1500		10400	11800
20 9	GT209GE	BASS		FBG SV	OB	7 6	1650		11200	12700
20 9	GT209TE	BASS		FBG SV	OB	7 6	1650		11500	13100
					1993 BOATS					
18 3	GT183GS	BASS		FBG SV	OB	7 4	1250		6950	7950
18 3	GT183TE	BASS		FBG SV	OB	7 4	1250		6950	7950
19 3	INTIMIDATOR I	BASS		FBG SV	OB	7 6	1200		6900	7900
19 3	INTIMIDATOR II	BASS		FBG SV	OB	7 6	1200		6950	8000
19 3	INTIMIDATOR IIB	BASS		FBG SV	OB	7 6	1200		6950	8000
20 6	GT206CC	BASS		FBG SV	OB	7 4	1400		9350	10600
20 6	GT206DL	BASS		FBG SV	OB	7 4	1500		10200	11600
20 6	GT206GS	BASS		FBG SV	OB	7 4	1500		9650	11000
20 6	GT206SL	BASS		FBG SV	OB	7 4	1500		10000	11300
20 6	GT206SS	SKI		FBG SV	OB	7 4	1300		8700	10000
20 6	GT206TE	BASS		FBG SV	OB	7 4	1500		9750	11100
					1992 BOATS					
18 3	GT183	BASS		FBG SV	OB	7 4	1250		6300	7250
18 3	GT183CC	BASS		FBG SV	OB	7 4	1150		6200	7100
18 3	GT183DL	BASS		FBG SV	OB	7 4	1250		6850	7900
18 3	GT183DT/ST	BASS		FBG SV	OB	7 4	1250		6600	7600
18 3	GT183GS	BASS		FBG SV	OB	7 4	1250		6500	7500
18 3	GT183SL	BASS		FBG SV	OB	7 4	1250		6750	7750
18 3	GT183TE	BASS		FBG SV	OB	7 4	1250		6550	7500
19 3	INTIMIDATOR I	BASS		FBG SV	OB	7 5	1200		6600	7600
19 3	INTIMIDATOR II	BASS		FBG SV	OB	7 5	1200		6600	7600
20 6	GT206CC	BASS		FBG SV	OB	7 4	1400		8900	10100
20 6	GT206DL	BASS		FBG SV	OB	7 4	1500		9700	11000
20 6	GT206DT/ST	BASS		FBG SV	OB	7 4	1500		9400	10700
20 6	GT206GS	BASS		FBG SV	OB	7 4	1500		9250	10500
20 6	GT206SL	BASS		FBG SV	OB	7 4	1500		9550	10800
20 6	GT206SS	SKI		FBG SV	OB	7 4	1300		8250	9500
20 6	GT206TE	BASS		FBG SV	OB	7 4	1500		9250	10500
					1991 BOATS					
18 3	GT183	BASS		FBG SV	OB	7 4	1250		6050	6950
18 3	GT183CC	BASS		FBG SV	OB	7 4	1150		5900	6750
18 3	GT183DL	BASS		FBG SV	OB	7 4	1250		6550	7550
18 3	GT183DT/ST	BASS		FBG SV	OB	7 4	1250		6300	7250
18 3	GT183GS	BASS		FBG SV	OB	7 4	1250		6200	7150
18 3	GT183SL	BASS		FBG SV	OB	7 4	1250		6450	7400
18 3	GT183TE	BASS		FBG SV	OB	7 4	1250		6250	7150
19 3	INTIMIDATOR 193	BASS		FBG SV	OB	7 5	1200		6300	7200
20 6	GT206CC	BASS		FBG SV	OB	7 4	1400		8400	9650
20 6	GT206DL	BASS		FBG SV	OB	7 4	1500		9250	10500
20 6	GT206DT/ST	BASS		FBG SV	OB	7 4	1500		8950	10200
20 6	GT206GS	BASS		FBG SV	OB	7 4	1500		8850	10000
20 6	GT206SL	BASS		FBG SV	OB	7 4	1500		9100	10300
20 6	GT206SS	SKI		FBG SV	OB	7 4	1300		7950	9100
20 6	GT206TE	BASS		FBG SV	OB	7 4	1500		8850	10100
					1990 BOATS					
18 3	GAMBLER GT-183	OP	BASS	FBG DV	OB	7 4	1300		6100	7000
18 3	GAMBLER GT-183CC	OP	BASS	FBG DV	OB		1400		6550	7550
18 3	GAMBLER GT-183DL	OP	BASS	FBG DV	OB		1300		6350	7300
18 3	GAMBLER GT-183SL	OP	BASS	FBG DV	OB	7 4	1300		6350	7300
18 3	GAMBLER GT-183TE	OP	BASS	FBG DV	OB		1300		6100	7000
20 6	GAMBLER GT-206CC	OP	BASS	FBG DV	OB	7 4	1500		8850	10100
20 6	GAMBLER GT-206DL	OP	BASS	FBG DV	OB	7 4	1600		9050	10300
20 6	GAMBLER GT-206GS	OP	BASS	FBG DV	OB		1500		8300	9500
20 6	GAMBLER GT-206SL	OP	BASS	FBG DV	OB		1600		9050	10300
20 6	GAMBLER GT-206SS	OP	RNBT	FBG DV	OB	7 4	1500		8500	9800
20 6	GAMBLER GT-206TE	OP	BASS	FBG DV	OB	7 4	1550		8850	10000
					1989 BOATS					
18 3	GAMBLER GT-183		BASS	FBG DV	OB	7 4	1300		5800	6650
18 3	GAMBLER GT-183CC		BASS	FBG DV	OB		1400		6300	7250
18 3	GAMBLER GT-183DL		BASS	FBG DV	OB		1300		6050	6950
18 3	GAMBLER GT-183SL		BASS	FBG DV	OB	7 4	1300		6100	7000
18 3	GAMBLER GT-183TE		BASS	FBG DV	OB		1300		5850	6700
20 6	GAMBLER GT-206CC		BASS	FBG DV	OB	7 4	1400		8400	9650
20 6	GAMBLER GT-206DL		BASS	FBG DV	OB	7 4	1500		8600	9850
20 6	GAMBLER GT-206GS		BASS	FBG DV	OB		1500		7950	9150
20 6	GAMBLER GT-206SL		BASS	FBG DV	OB		1600		8600	9850
20 6	GAMBLER GT-206TE		BASS	FBG DV	OB	7 4	1550		8350	9600
					1988 BOATS					
18 3	GAMBLER GT-183		BASS	FBG DV	OB	7 6	1150		5200	5950
20 6	GAMBLER GT-206DL		BASS	FBG DV	OB	7 4	1600		8300	9500
20 6	GAMBLER GT-206GS		BASS	FBG DV	OB	7 4	1500		7850	9050
20 6	GAMBLER GT-206SL		BASS	FBG DV	OB	7 4	1575		8200	9400
20 6	GAMBLER GT-206TE		BASS	FBG DV	OB	7 4	1550		8100	9300

MARITIME INDUSTRIES INC

CORPUS CHRISTI TX 78415 COAST GUARD MFG ID- MIE See inside cover to adjust price for area

LOA FT IN	NAME AND/ OR MODEL	TOP/ RIG	BOAT TYPE	-HULL- MTL TP	--ENGINE--- TP # HP MFG	BEAM FT IN	WGT LBS	DRAFT FT IN	RETAIL LOW	RETAIL HIGH
					1985 BOATS					
16 10	SEA-VENTURE	OP	CTRCN	FBG TR	OB	7 6	740	1	1700	2000

....For earlier years, see the BUC Used Boat Price Guide, Volume 3

MARK LINDSAY BOAT BUILDERS

EAST BOSTON MA 02128-2800   See inside cover to adjust price for area
FORMERLY MARK LINDSAY BOATBUILDERS LTD

LOA FT IN	NAME AND/ OR MODEL	TOP/ RIG	BOAT TYPE	-HULL- MTL TP	--ENGINE--- TP # HP MFG	BEAM FT IN	WGT LBS	DRAFT FT IN	RETAIL LOW	RETAIL HIGH
					1995 BOATS					
39 3	FARR 39ML	SLP	SARAC	FBG KL	SD D YAN	12 1	10251	8 4	90800	99700
					1994 BOATS					
38 4	TAYLOR 38	SLP	SACAC	F/S KL	SD 27D YAN	11 11	13750	5 10	99900	110000
39 7	TAYLOR 40	SLP	SARAC	F/S KL	IB 27D YAN	12 6	13600	7 6	108500	119000
40 5	SCHUMACHER 40	SLP	SARAC	F/S KL	IB 27D YAN	10 6	12246	6 6	106500	117000
41 1	TAYLOR 41	SLP	SARAC	F/S KL	SD 35D YAN	13	15392	7 11	128500	141500
					1989 BOATS					
19 10	OLYMPIC FLYING DUTCH	SLP	SA/OD	KEV	CB	5 11	276	3 8	2900	3350
38	LINDSAY/TRIPP 38	SLP	SA/RC	F/S KL	IB 27D YAN	11 10	11000	6 11	60000	66000
39 7	LINDSAY/TAYLOR 40	SLP	SA/RC	F/S KL	IB 27D YAN	12 6	13600	7 6	79700	87600
					1987 BOATS					
20	OLYMPIC-FLYING-DUTCH	SLP	SA/OD		CB	6	275	8	2600	3050
27	GRAHAM-&-SCHLAGETER	SLP	SA/RC	FBG KL	IB D	9	4800	5	16400	18700
27	MARIAH 27	SLP	SA/RC	KL	IB D	9	4800	5	16400	18700
32	PARIS 32	SLP	SAIL	FBG	IB D	8	6000	8	23600	26200
38 3	DOBROTH 38	SLP	SAIL	FBG	IB D	11 6	12000	11 6	58000	63700
					1986 BOATS					
16 6	INTERNATIONAL 505	SLP	SA/OD		CB	6 3		6	2150	2500
19 10	FLYING-DUTCHMAN	SLP	SA/OD		CB	5 11	365	8	2550	3000
20	OLYMPIC-TORNADO	SLP	SA/OD		CT	10	375	8	2650	3000
27	GRAHAM & SCHLAGETER	SLP	SA/RC	FBG KL	IB D	9	4800	3 5	15400	17600
32	PARIS 32	SLP	SAIL	KL	IB D	8	6000	8	22100	24600
37 5	FARR 1.5 METER	SLP	SA/OD		KL IB D	14 9		6 8	51700	56800
					1985 BOATS					
19 10	FLYING-DUTCHMAN	SLP	SA/OD		CB	5 11	365	8	2400	2800
20	OLYMPIC-TORNADO	SLP	SA/OD		CT	10	300	8	2150	2500
27	GRAHAM-&-SCHLAGETER	SLP	SA/RC	FBG KL	IB D	9	4800	3 5	14500	16500
37 5	FARR 11.5 METER	SLP	SA/OD		KL IB D	14 9		6 8	48600	53400
					1984 BOATS					
19 10	OLYMPIC-FLYING-DUTCH	SLP	SA/OD		CB	5 11			2600	3000
20	OLYMPIC-TORNADO	CAT	SAIL		CT	10		2 6	2400	2800

MARK LINDSAY BOAT BUILDERS -CONTINUED

See inside cover to adjust price for area

LOA FT IN	NAME AND/OR MODEL	TOP/RIG	BOAT TYPE	HULL MTL	HULL TP	TP#	ENGINE HP	MFG	BEAM FT IN	WGT LBS	DRAFT FT IN	RETAIL LOW	RETAIL HIGH
1984 BOATS													
27	MORC 27	SLP	SA/RC	KL	IB		D		9		5	16700	19000
37 5	FARR 11.5 METER	SLP	SA/OD	KL	IB		D		14 8		6 8	45900	50500

....For earlier years, see the BUC Used Boat Price Guide, Volume 3

MARK O'CUSTOM BOATS
COLOGNE NJ 08213   COAST GUARD MFG ID- MKU See inside cover to adjust price for area

LOA FT IN	NAME AND/OR MODEL	TOP/RIG	BOAT TYPE	HULL MTL	HULL TP	TP#	ENGINE HP	MFG	BEAM FT IN	WGT LBS	DRAFT FT IN	RETAIL LOW	RETAIL HIGH
1987 BOATS													
21 3	ATLANTIC CITY KITTY	CAT	SAIL	FBG	CB	IB	18D	YAN	9 6	5200	2	14400	16300
24	ATLANTIC CITY CAT	CAT	SAIL	FBG	CB	IB	18D	YAN	11	8000	2	24200	26900
1985 BOATS													
21 3	ATLANTIC-CITY-KITTY	CAT	SAIL	FBG	CB	IB	D		9 6	5300	2	12700	14500
24	ATLANTIC-CITY	CAT	SAIL	FBG	CB	IB	D		11	8000	2	21400	23800
1984 BOATS													
24	ATLANTIC-CITY	CAT	SA/CR	FBG	KC				11	8000	2	18900	21000

....For earlier years, see the BUC Used Boat Price Guide, Volume 3

MARK TWAIN MARINE IND INC
BOCA RATON FL 33487-160 COAST GUARD MFG ID- MTM See inside cover to adjust price for area

LOA FT IN	NAME AND/OR MODEL	TOP/RIG	BOAT TYPE	HULL MTL	HULL TP	TP#	ENGINE HP	MFG	BEAM FT IN	WGT LBS	DRAFT FT IN	RETAIL LOW	RETAIL HIGH
1985 BOATS													
16	160BR	OP	RNBT	FBG	DV	OB			6 8	1100		3050	3550
16	160BR	OP	RNBT	FBG	DV	IO	120-185		6 8	1700		1700	2100
17 1	170BR	OP	RNBT	FBG	DV	OB			7 2	1650		4350	5000
17 1	170BR	OP	RNBT	FBG	DV	SE	115	OMC	7 2	2050		5000	5750
17 1	170BR	OP	RNBT	FBG	DV	IO	120-205		7 2	2250		5250	5700
17 1	170S	OP	RNBT	FBG	DV	IO	120-205		7 2	2350		2300	2750
18 8	190BR	OP	RNBT	FBG	DV	OB			7 10	1850		4800	5500
18 8	190BR	OP	RNBT	FBG	DV	IO	120-200		7 10	2500		2700	3200
18 8	190BR	OP	RNBT	FBG	DV	SE	205	OMC	7 10	2500		5500	6300
18 8	190BR	OP	RNBT	FBG	DV	IO	205-260		7 10	2500		2750	3350
18 8	190S	OP	RNBT	FBG	DV	IO	120-230		7 10	2600		2750	3300
18 8	190S	OP	RNBT	FBG	DV	IO	260		7 10	2600		2950	3450
21	210 SF CUDDY	OP	FSH	FBG	DV	OB			7 11	2650		7700	8850
21	210 SF CUDDY	OP	FSH	FBG	DV	IO	140-200		7 11	3500		4550	5300
21	210 SF CUDDY	OP	FSH	FBG	DV	SE	205	OMC	7 11	3500		8600	9900
21	210BR	OP	FSH	FBG	DV	IO	205-260		7 11	3500		4600	5450
21	210BR	OP	RNBT	FBG	DV	IO	140-205		7	3700		4000	4700
21	210XL	OP	CUD	FBG	DV	IO	230-260		7 11	3700		4350	5150
21	ESCAPE 210	OP	CR	FBG	DV	IO	140-260		7 11	4300		4450	5400
24 1	240 SF CUDDY	OP	FSH	FBG	DV	IO	170-260		8	3900		5000	6000
24 1	240 SF CUDDY	OP	FSH	FBG	DV	IO	170-200		8	3900		5800	6750
24 1	240 SF CUDDY	OP	FSH	FBG	DV	SE	205	OMC	8	3900		12200	13800
24 1	240 SF CUDDY	OP	FSH	FBG	DV	SE	T115	OMC	8	3900		12200	13800
24 1	240 SF CUDDY	OP	FSH	FBG	DV	IO	T120-T190		8	3900		6500	7600
24 1	240 SF CUDDY	OP	FSH	FBG	DV	IO	T205	OMC	8	3900		12200	13800
25 1	COSTA-BRAVA 250	OP	CR	FBG	DV	IO	260		8	5150		7350	8450
25 1	COSTA-BRAVA 250	OP	CR	FBG	DV	IO	T120-T190		8	5150		7600	9150
1984 BOATS													
16	160BR	OP	RNBT	FBG	DV	OB			6 8	1100		3000	3500
16	160BR	OP	RNBT	FBG	DV	IO	120-140		6 8	1700		1650	1950
17 1	170BR	OP	RNBT	FBG	DV	OB			7 2	1650		4200	4900
17 1	170BR	OP	RNBT	FBG	DV	SE	115	OMC	7 2	2050		4900	5600
17 1	170BR	OP	RNBT	FBG	DV	IO	120-188		7 2	2250		2150	2550
17 1	170S	OP	RNBT	FBG	DV	SE	115	OMC	7 2	2050		4900	5600
17 1	170S	OP	RNBT	FBG	DV	IO	120-188		7 2	2350		2200	2600
17 3	175BR	OP	RNBT	FBG	DV	OB			7	1400		3750	4350
17 3	175BR	OP	RNBT	FBG	DV	IO	120-200		7	2100		2050	2450
18 8	190BR	OP	RNBT	FBG	DV	OB			7 10	1850		4700	5400
18 8	190BR	OP	RNBT	FBG	DV	IO	120-230		7 10	2500		2600	3150
18 8	190BR	OP	RNBT	FBG	DV	IO	260		7 10	2500		2800	3250
18 8	190S	OP	RNBT	FBG	DV	IO	120-230		7 10	2600		2650	3200
18 8	190S	OP	RNBT	FBG	DV	IO	260		7 10	2600		2850	3300
18 8	190XL	OP	CUD	FBG	DV	IO	140-260		7 10	2800		2850	3550
21	210 SF CUDDY	OP	FSH	FBG	DV	OB			7 11	2650		7550	8650
21	210 SF CUDDY	OP	FSH	FBG	DV	IO	140-260		7 11	3500		4400	5300
21	210XL	OP	CUD	FBG	DV	IO	140-260		7 11	3700		4250	5200
21	ESCAPE 210	OP	CR	FBG	DV	IO	170-260		7 11	4300		4800	5800
25 1	COSTA-BRAVA 250	OP	CR	FBG	DV	IO	260		8	5150		7100	8150

....For earlier years, see the BUC Used Boat Price Guide, Volume 3

MARLIN BOAT COMPANY
SEATTLE WA 98178-2951 COAST GUARD MFG ID- MBD See inside cover to adjust price for area

For more recent years, see the BUC Used Boat Price Guide, Volume 1

LOA FT IN	NAME AND/OR MODEL	TOP/RIG	BOAT TYPE	HULL MTL	HULL TP	TP#	ENGINE HP	MFG	BEAM FT IN	WGT LBS	DRAFT FT IN	RETAIL LOW	RETAIL HIGH
1996 BOATS													
16	SKI	OP	SKI	FBG	FL	VD						**	**
18 2	SKI JET	OP	SKI	FBG	SV	JT						**	**
21	DAY CRUISER	OP	SPTCR	FBG	SV	IO	260					14100	16000
21	DAY CRUISER	OP	SPTCR	FBG	SV	JT	330					17000	19300
1995 BOATS													
16	SKI	OP	SKI	FBG	FL	VD						**	**
18 2	SKI JET	OP	SKI	FBG	SV	JT						**	**
21	DAY CRUISER	OP	SPTCR	FBG	SV	IO	260					13100	14900
21	DAY CRUISER	OP	SPTCR	FBG	SV	JT	330					16000	18200
1993 BOATS													
16	SKI	OP	SKI	FBG	FL	VD						**	**
18 2	SKI JET	OP	SKI	FBG	SV	JT						**	**
21	DAY CRUISER	OP	SPTCR	FBG	SV	IO	260					11400	13000
21	DAY CRUISER	OP	SPTCR	FBG	SV	JT	330					14400	16300
1992 BOATS													
16	SKI	OP	SKI	FBG	FL	VD						**	**
18 2	SKI JET	OP	SKI	FBG	SV	JT						**	**
21	DAY CRUISER	OP	SPTCR	FBG	SV	IO	260					10700	12200
21	DAY CRUISER	OP	SPTCR	FBG	SV	JT	330					13600	15500
1991 BOATS													
16	SKI	OP	SKI	FBG	FL	VD						**	**
18 2	SKI JET	OP	SKI	FBG	SV	JT						**	**
21	DAY CRUISER	OP	SPTCR	FBG	SV	IO	260					10000	11400
21	DAY CRUISER	OP	SPTCR	FBG	SV	JT	330					13000	14700
1990 BOATS													
16	SKI	OP	SKI	FBG	FL	VD						**	**
18 2	SKI JET	OP	SKI	FBG	SV	JT						**	**
21	DAY CRUISER	OP	SPTCR	FBG	SV	IO	260					9450	10700
21	DAY CRUISER	OP	SPTCR	FBG	SV	JT	330					12300	14000
1989 BOATS													
16	SKI	OP	SKI	FBG	FL	VD						**	**
18 2	SKI JET	OP	SKI	FBG	SV	JT						**	**
21	DAY CRUISER	OP	SPTCR	FBG	SV	IO	260					8950	10200
21	DAY CRUISER	OP	SPTCR	FBG	SV	JT	330					11700	13300
1988 BOATS													
16	SKI	OP	SKI	FBG	FL	VD						**	**
18 2	SKI JET	OP	SKI	FBG	SV	JT						**	**
21	DAY CRUISER	OP	SPTCR	FBG	SV	IO	260					8400	9650
21	DAY CRUISER	OP	SPTCR	FBG	SV	JT	330					11200	12700
1987 BOATS													
16	SKI	OP	SKI	FBG	FL	VD						**	**
18 2	SKI JET	OP	SKI	FBG	SV	JT						**	**
21	DAY CRUISER	OP	SPTCR	FBG	SV	IO	260					7950	9150
21	DAY CRUISER	OP	SPTCR	FBG	SV	JT	330					10700	12100
1985 BOATS													
16	SKI	OP	SKI	FBG	FL	VD						**	**
18 2	SKI JET	OP	SKI	FBG	SV	JT						**	**
21	DAY CRUISER	OP	SPTCR	FBG	SV	JT	330					9700	11000
21	DAY CRUISER	OP	SPTCR	FBG	SV	VD	440					10500	12000
1984 BOATS													
16	SKI	OP	SKI	FBG	FL	VD						**	**
18 2	SKI JET	OP	SKI	FBG	SV	JT						**	**
21	DAY CRUISER	OP	SPTCR	FBG	SV	JT	330					9350	10600
21	DAY CRUISER	OP	SPTCR	FBG	SV	VD	440					10100	11400

....For earlier years, see the BUC Used Boat Price Guide, Volume 3

MARLIN BOATS INC

WHITE CITY OR 97503 COAST GUARD MFG ID- EKW See inside cover to adjust price for area

LOA FT	IN	NAME AND/ OR MODEL	TOP/ RIG	BOAT TYPE	-HULL- MTL	TP	ENGINE TP	# HP	MFG	BEAM FT	IN	WGT LBS	DRAFT FT IN	RETAIL LOW	RETAIL HIGH
		1990 BOATS													
16		BASS 16	OP	BASS	FBG	DV	OB							2500	2950
16		BOWRIDER 171 BR	OP	B/R	FBG	DV	OB							3000	3500
16	7	RAMPAGE 176 BR	OP	B/R	FBG	DV	OB			6	6	2110		5850	6700
16	7	RAMPAGE 176 BR	OP	B/R	FBG	DV	SE			6	6	2110		**	**
16	7	RAMPAGE 176 BR	OP	B/R	FBG	DV	IO	125-155		6	6	2110		3900	4600
16	7	RAMPAGE 176 BR	OP	B/R	FBG	DV	IO	205	VLVO	6	6	2110		4350	5000
17		CENTER CONSOLE 17	OP	CTRCN	FBG	DV	OB							4550	5200
17		MINICRUISER	OP	SKI	FBG	DV	IO	125	MRCR					4050	4700
17		SKIFF 17	OP	FSH	FBG	DV	OB							4500	5200
17		SLANT 17	OP	SKI	FBG	DV	OB							4500	5150
17		SLANT DECK	OP	SKI	FBG	DV	OB							4500	5150
17	6	CONQUEST 188 BR	OP	B/R	FBG	DV	SE			6	6	2210		**	**
17	6	CONQUEST 188 BR	OP	B/R	FBG	DV	IO	125-200		6	6	2210		4250	5050
17	6	CONQUEST 188 BR	OP	B/R	FBG	DV	IO	205-260		6	6	2210		4650	5450
17	6	CUDDY 188	HT	CUD	FBG	DV	SE			7	2	2610		**	**
17	6	CUDDY 188	HT	CUD	FBG	DV	IO	125-230		7	2	2610		5300	6400
18	6	CUDDY 198	OP	CUD	FBG	DV	IO	155-205		8		2690		6150	7500
18	6	ISLANDER 198 BR	OP	B/R	FBG	DV	SE			8		2440		**	**
18	6	ISLANDER 198 BR	OP	B/R	FBG	DV	IO	155-260		8		2440		5450	6750
18	6	ISLANDER 198 BR	OP	B/R	FBG	DV	IO	270-271		8		2440		6000	7300
18	11	SUNFISH 202	OP	FSH	FBG	DV	OB			7	6	1520		4700	5400
19	2	MARLIN SKIER DD	OP	SKI	FBG	DV	IO	350	MRCR	6	6	2260		6700	7750
19	5	SIDEWINDER	OP	RNBT	FBG	DV	IO	175		7	1	2120		5200	6250
19	5	SIDEWINDER	OP	RNBT	FBG	DV	JT	454		7	1	2120		7900	9050
20		ARIES	OP	SKI	FBG	DV	OB							4150	4850
20		BASS 20	OP	BASS	FBG	DV	OB							4650	5350
20		CENTER CONSOLE 202	OP	CTRCN	FBG	DV	OB							4650	5350
20	1	ELITE BR/DD	OP	B/R	FBG	DV	IO	350	MRCR	7	7	2770		7950	9150
20	1	ELITE CP DD	OP	CUD	FBG	DV	IO	350	MRCR	7	7	2770		8500	9800
20	2	ARIES BR	OP	B/R	FBG	DV	OB			7	4			4700	5400
20	2	ARIES BR	OP	B/R	FBG	DV	IO	175-270		7	4	2380		5550	6950
20	2	ARIES BR	OP	B/R	FBG	DV	JT	350	MRCR	7	4	2380		8400	9650
20	2	ARIES CD	OP	RNBT	FBG	DV	OB			7	4	1150		4150	4850
20	2	ARIES CD	OP	RNBT	FBG	DV	IO	175-270		7	4			5700	7100
20	2	ARIES CD	OP	RNBT	FBG	DV	IO	430	VLVO	7	4			11300	12900
20	2	ARIES CD	OP	RNBT	FBG	DV	JT	454		7	4			8550	9850
20	2	SPORTFISHER 213	HT	FSH	FBG	DV	SE			7	7	3040		**	**
20	2	SPORTFISHER 213	HT	FSH	FBG	DV	IO	155-230		7	7	3040		7350	8900
20	10	RAVEN 210 BR	OP	B/R	FBG	DV	SE			8		3350		**	**
20	10	RAVEN 210 BR	OP	B/R	FBG	DV	IO	200-270		8		3350		7500	9050
20	10	RAVEN 210 BR	OP	B/R	FBG	DV	IO	271	VLVO	8		3350		8250	9500
20	10	RAVEN 210 BR	OP	B/R	FBG	DV	IO	330-350		8		3350		9450	11300
20	10	RAVEN 210 CD	OP	CUD	FBG	DV	SE			8		3350		**	**
20	10	RAVEN 210 CD	OP	CUD	FBG	DV	IO	200-270		8		3350		8000	9700
20	10	RAVEN 210 CD	OP	CUD	FBG	DV	IO	271	VLVO	8		3350		8900	10100
20	10	RAVEN 210 CD	OP	CUD	FBG	DV	IO	330-350		8		3350		10000	12000
21	2	COBRA BR	OP	B/R	FBG	DV	IO	260-275		7	9	3060		7400	9050
21	2	COBRA BR	OP	B/R	FBG	DV	IO	350-360		7	9	3060		8950	10500
21	2	COBRA BR	OP	B/R	FBG	DV	JT	454		7	9	3060		10400	11800
21	2	COBRA CD	OP	CUD	FBG	DV	IO	260-275		7	9	3060		7900	9700
21	2	COBRA CD	OP	CUD	FBG	DV	IO	350-360		7	9	3060		9500	11100
21	2	COBRA CD	OP	CUD	FBG	DV	JT	454		7	9	3060		10400	11800
22		BILLFISH 22	OP	FSH	FBG	DV	SE							**	**
22		BILLFISH 22	OP	FSH	FBG	DV	IO		VLVO					**	**
22		BILLFISH 22	OP	FSH	FBG	DV	IO	260-271						9700	11600
22		BILLFISH 22	OP	FSH	FBG	DV	IO	454	MRCR					15200	17300
22		BILLFISH 22	OP	FSH	FBG	DV	SE	T						**	**
22		EMPRESS 230	OP	OVNTR	FBG	DV	IO	260-270		8		3620		9400	10700
		IO 350-360 10900 12700, JT 454 12200 13800, IO 570 VLVO												21500	23900
22		MARIAH 220	OP	CR	FBG	DV	SE			8		3550		**	**
22		MARIAH 220	OP	CR	FBG	DV	IO	230-271		8		3550		9050	11000
22		MARIAH 220	OP	CR	FBG	DV	IO	330-350		8		3550		10900	13000
23	4	CEAERO 240	OP	OFF	FBG	DV	IO	260-275		6	10	3800		9950	11900
23	4	CEAERO 240	OP	OFF	FBG	DV	IO	350-360		6	10	3800		11500	13300
24		ESCORT 240	HT	OVNTR	FBG	DV	SE			8		4400		**	**
24		ESCORT 240	HT	OVNTR	FBG	DV	IO	230-271		8		4400		11700	14100
24		ESCORT 240	HT	OVNTR	FBG	DV	IO	330	VLVO	8		4400		13500	15400
24		ESCORT 240	HT	OVNTR	FBG	DV	IO	454		8		4400		17100	21000
24		ESCORT 240	FB	OVNTR	FBG	DV	SE			8		4800		**	**
24		ESCORT 240	FB	OVNTR	FBG	DV	IO	230-271		8		4800		12500	15000
24		ESCORT 240	FB	OVNTR	FBG	DV	IO	330	VLVO	8		4800		14400	16300
24		ESCORT 240	FB	OVNTR	FBG	DV	IO	454		8		4800		18300	21700
24		ESCORT CUDDY	OP	CUD	FBG	DV	SE			8		3300		**	**
24		ESCORT CUDDY	OP	CUD	FBG	DV	IO	260-271		8		3300		9750	11600
24		ESCORT CUDDY	OP	CUD	FBG	DV	IO	454		8		3300		14900	18600
24		ESCORT CUDDY	OP	CUD	FBG	DV	SE	T		8		3300		**	**
24	8	BILLFISH 265	OP	CBNCR	FBG	DV	SE			8	6	5650		**	**
24	8	BILLFISH 265	OP	CBNCR	FBG	DV	IO	260	MRCR	8	6	5650		17600	20000
24	8	BILLFISH 265	OP	CBNCR	FBG	DV	IO	271	VLVO	8	6	5650		18500	20500
24	8	BILLFISH 265	OP	CBNCR	FBG	DV	IO	454		8	6	5650		23000	27200
24	8	BILLFISH 265	OP	CBNCR	FBG	DV	SE	T		8	6	5650		**	**
24	8	RAVEN 265	OP	OVNTR	FBG	DV	SE			8	6	5650		**	**
24	8	RAVEN 265	OP	OVNTR	FBG	DV	IO	260-271		8	6	5650		15000	17500
		IO 330 VLVO 16600 18800, IO 454 20200 23800, IO T175 MRCR												15900	18100
		IO T430 VLVO 27100 30100													
28		CEAERO 280	OP	OFF	FBG	DV	IO	360-454		7	6	4700		18100	22400
28		CEAERO 280	OP	OFF	FBG	DV	IO	T260-T270		7	6	4700		19200	21600
30	6	CEAERO 310	OP	OFF	FBG	DV	IO	T270-T360		8		6120		26800	32300
30	6	CEAERO 310	OP	OFF	FBG	DV	IO	T454	MRCR	8		6120		32000	35600
		1989 BOATS													
16	7	RAMPAGE 176BR	OP	RNBT	FBG	SV	OB			7	2	2110		5600	6450
16	7	RAMPAGE 176BR	OP	RNBT	FBG	SV	SE			7	2	2110		**	**
16	7	RAMPAGE 176BR	OP	RNBT	FBG	SV	IO	120-175		7	2	2110		4150	4850
16	7	RAMPAGE 176BR	OP	RNBT	FBG	SV	JT	350		7	2	2110		6550	7550
17	6	188 CUDDY	HT	CBNCR	FBG	DV	OB			7	2	2610		5750	6650
17	6	188 CUDDY	HT	CBNCR	FBG	DV	SE			7	2	2610		**	**
17	6	188 CUDDY	HT	CBNCR	FBG	DV	IO	128-235		7	2	2610		5100	6200
17	6	CONQUEST 188BR	OP	RNBT	FBG	DV	OB			7	2	2210		5550	6400
17	6	CONQUEST 188BR	OP	RNBT	FBG	DV	SE			7	2	2210		**	**
17	6	CONQUEST 188BR	OP	RNBT	FBG	DV	IO	120-260		7	2	2210		4500	5600
17	6	CONQUEST 188BR	OP	RNBT	FBG	DV	JT	350		7	2	2210		7000	8050
18	6	198 CUDDY	OP	RNBT	FBG	DV	OB			8		2690		5950	6800
18	6	198 CUDDY	OP	RNBT	FBG	DV	SE			8		2690		**	**
18	6	198 CUDDY	OP	RNBT	FBG	DV	IO	165-270		8		2690		5650	7000
18	6	198 CUDDY	OP	RNBT	FBG	DV	IO	271	VLVO	8		2690		6450	7400
18	6	198 CUDDY	OP	RNBT	FBG	DV	JT	350		8		2690		8550	9800
18	6	ISLANDER 198BR	OP	RNBT	FBG	DV	OB			8		2440		5800	6650
18	6	ISLANDER 198BR	OP	RNBT	FBG	DV	SE			8		2440		**	**
18	6	ISLANDER 198BR	OP	RNBT	FBG	DV	IO	165-235		8		2440		5350	6550
		IO 260-271 5850 7100, JT 350 8150 9350, IO 350 OMC												7000	8050
18	6	ISLANDER 198SD	OP	RNBT	FBG	DV	OB			8		2440		5800	6650
18	6	ISLANDER 198SD	OP	RNBT	FBG	DV	SE			8		2440		**	**
18	6	ISLANDER 198SD	OP	RNBT	FBG	DV	IO		OMC	8		2440		**	**
		IO 165-235 5350 6550, IO 260-271 5850 7100, JT 350												8150	9350
18	6	ISLANDRE 198SD	OP	RNBT	FBG	DV	IO	175-185		8		2440		5250	6150
18	6	ISLANDRE 198SD	OP	RNBT	FBG	DV	IO	270	MRCR	8		2440		5850	6700
18	11	SUNFISH 202	OP	CTRCN	FBG	SV	OB			7	6	1520		4500	5150
19	2	MARLIN SKIER	OP	SKI	FBG	DV	IO	350	MRCR	6	8	2260		6400	7350
19	5	SIDEWINDER	OP	SKI	FBG	SV	OB			7	1	2120		5650	6500
19	5	SIDEWINDER	OP	SKI	FBG	SV	IO	175-205		7	1	2120		4750	5800
19	5	SIDEWINDER	OP	SKI	FBG	SV	JT	454		7	1	2120		7300	8350
20	1	ELITE	OP	SKI	FBG	DV	IO	350	MRCR	7	1	2120		6600	7550
20	2	ARIES BR	OP	SKI	FBG	DV	OB			7	4	1150		4000	4650
20	2	ARIES BR	OP	SKI	FBG	DV	IO		OMC	7	4	2380		**	**
20	2	ARIES BR	OP	SKI	FBG	DV	IO	175-270		7	4	2380		5350	6600
20	2	ARIES BR	OP	SKI	FBG	DV	JT	454		7	4	2380		8000	9200
20	2	ARIES SPORTDECK	OP	SKI	FBG	SV	OB			7	4	1150		4000	4650
20	2	ARIES SPORTDECK	OP	SKI	FBG	SV	IO		OMC	7	4	2380		**	**
20	2	ARIES SPORTDECK	OP	SKI	FBG	SV	IO	175-270		7	4	2380		5350	6600
20	2	ARIES SPORTDECK	OP	SKI	FBG	SV	JT	454		7	4	2380		8000	9200
20	2	SPORTFISHER 213	HT	CBNCR	FBG	DV	OB			7	7	3040		7450	8600
20	2	SPORTFISHER 213	HT	CBNCR	FBG	DV	SE			7	7	3040		**	**
20	2	SPORTFISHER 213	HT	CBNCR	FBG	DV	IO	130-205		7	7	3040		7000	8550
20	10	RAVEN 210	OP	CR	FBG	DV	OB			8		3350		8500	9750
20	10	RAVEN 210	OP	CR	FBG	DV	SE			8		3350		**	**
20	10	RAVEN 210	OP	CR	FBG	DV	IO		OMC	8		3350		**	**
		IO 165-270 7450 9200, IO 271 VLVO 8300 9550, IO 350-365												9400	11100
20	10	RAVEN 210BR	OP	CR	FBG	DV	OB			8		3350		8500	9750
20	10	RAVEN 210BR	OP	CR	FBG	DV	SE			8		3350		**	**
20	10	RAVEN 210BR	OP	CR	FBG	DV	IO		OMC	8		3350		**	**
		IO 165-270 7450 9200, IO 271 VLVO 8300 9550, IO 350-365												9400	11100

CONTINUED ON NEXT PAGE

MARLIN BOATS INC -CONTINUED See inside cover to adjust price for area

LOA FT	LOA IN	NAME AND/ OR MODEL	TOP/ RIG	BOAT TYPE	-HULL- MTL	-HULL- TP	ENGINE TP	ENGINE # HP	ENGINE MFG	BEAM FT	BEAM IN	WGT LBS	DRAFT FT IN	RETAIL LOW	RETAIL HIGH
		1989 BOATS													
21	2	COBRA BR	OP	SKI	FBG	DV	OB			7	9	3060		8550	9800
21	2	COBRA BR	OP	SKI	FBG	DV	IO		OMC	7	9	3060		**	**
		IO 185-270 6600 8100, IO 350-365 8350 10000, JT 454												9900	11200
21	2	COBRA SPORTDECK	OP	SKI	FBG	DV	OB			8		3350		8950	10200
21	2	COBRA SPORTDECK	OP	SKI	FBG	DV	IO		OMC	8		3350		**	**
		IO 185-270 7100 8700, IO 271 VLVO 7900 9100, IO 350-365												8950	10600
		JT 454 10600 12000													
22		EMPRESS 230	OP	CR	FBG	DV	OB			8		3620		10200	11600
22		EMPRESS 230	OP	CR	FBG	DV	IO		OMC	8		3620		**	**
		IO 260-271 8850 10600, IO 350-365 10300 12100, JT 454												11600	13100
22		MARIAH 220	OP	CR	FBG	DV	OB			8		3550		10100	11500
22		MARIAH 220	OP	CR	FBG	DV	SE			8		3550		**	**
22		MARIAH 220	OP	CR	FBG	DV	IO		OMC	8		3550		**	**
		IO 165-270 8250 10100, IO 271 VLVO 9200 10500, IO 350-365												10200	12000
24		ESCORT 240	HT	OVNTR	FBG	DV	OB			8		4400		13400	15300
24		ESCORT 240	HT	OVNTR	FBG	DV	SE			8		4400		**	**
24		ESCORT 240	HT	OVNTR	FBG	DV	IO		OMC	8		4400		**	**
		IO 230-271 11000 13300, IO 365 MRCR 13100 14900, IO 454 MRCR												16100	18300
24		ESCORT 240	FB	OVNTR	FBG	DV	OB			8		4800		14000	16000
24		ESCORT 240	FB	OVNTR	FBG	DV	SE			8		4800		**	**
24		ESCORT 240	FB	OVNTR	FBG	DV	IO		OMC	8		4800		**	**
		IO 230-271 11800 14200, IO 365 MRCR 13900 15800, IO 454 MRCR												16900	19200
24		ESCORT CUDDY	OP	CR	FBG	DV	OB			8		3300		11100	12600
24		ESCORT CUDDY	OP	CR	FBG	DV	SE			8		3300		**	**
24		ESCORT CUDDY	OP	CR	FBG	DV	IO		OMC	8		3300		**	**
24		ESCORT CUDDY	OP	CR	FBG	DV	IO	185-271		8		3300		8800	10900
24		ESCORT CUDDY	OP	CR	FBG	DV	IO	365	MRCR	8		3300		11000	12500
24	8	BILLFISH 265	OP	CBNCR	FBG	DV	OB			8	6	4200		13200	15000
24	8	BILLFISH 265	OP	CBNCR	FBG	DV	SE			8	6	4200		**	**
24	8	BILLFISH 265	OP	CBNCR	FBG	DV	IO			8	6	4200		**	**
24	8	BILLFISH 265	OP	CBNCR	FBG	DV	IO	260-271		8	6	4200		13400	15700
24	8	BILLFISH 265	OP	CBNCR	FBG	DV	IO	365	MRCR	8	6	4200		15200	17300
24	8	BILLFISH 265	OP	CBNCR	FBG	DV	SE	T		8	6	4200		**	**
24	8	BILLFISH 265	OP	CBNCR	FBG	DV	IO	T	VLVO	8	6	4200		**	**
24	8	RAVEN 265	OP	OVNTR	FBG	DV	SE			8	6	5650		**	**
24	8	RAVEN 265	OP	OVNTR	FBG	DV	IO		OMC	8	6	5650		**	**
		IO 260-271 14100 16600, IO 365 MRCR 16000 18100, IO 454 MRCR												19000	21100
		IO T165-T205 15000 17900													
24	10	CEAERO 240	OP	OFF	FBG	DV	OB							13200	15000
24	10	CEAERO 240	OP	OFF	FBG	DV	IO			6	10	3800		**	**
		IO OMC ** **, IO 260-271 10200 12100, IO 454												14800	16800
29	6	CEAERO 280	OP	OFF	FBG	DV	OB			8		4200		18200	20200
29	6	CEAERO 280	OP	OFF	FBG	DV	IO	365-454		8		4200		19600	23700
29	6	CEAERO 280	OP	OFF	FBG	DV	IO	T	OMC	8		4200		**	**
29	6	CEAERO 280	OP	OFF	FBG	DV	IO	T260-T270		8		4200		21100	23700
30	6	CEAERO 310	OP	OFF	FBG	DV	OB			8		6120		20100	22300
30	6	CEAERO 310	OP	OFF	FBG	DV	IO	T	OMC	8		6120		**	**
30	6	CEAERO 310	OP	OFF	FBG	DV	IO	T270-T365		8		6120		25300	30600
30	6	CEAERO 310	OP	OFF	FBG	DV	IO	T454	MRCR	8		6120		30200	33600
		1988 BOATS													
16	7	RAMPAGE 176BR	OP	RNBT	FBG	SV	OB			7	2			3950	4600
16	7	RAMPAGE 176BR	OP	RNBT	FBG	SV	IO	120-175		7	2	2110		3900	4600
16	7	RAMPAGE 176BR	OP	RNBT	FBG	SV	JT	350-460		7	2	2110		6250	7200
17	6	CONQUEST 188BR	OP	RNBT	FBG	DV	OB			7	2			4650	5350
17	6	CONQUEST 188BR	OP	RNBT	FBG	DV	IO	120-230		7	2	2210		4200	5150
17	6	CONQUEST 188BR	OP	RNBT	FBG	DV	IO	260		7	2	2210		4650	5350
17	6	CONQUEST 188BR	OP	RNBT	FBG	DV	JT	350-460		7	2	2210		6700	7650
17	6	CUDDY 188	HT	CBNCR	FBG	DV	OB			7	2			5000	5750
17	6	CUDDY 188	HT	CBNCR	FBG	DV	SE			7	2	2610		**	**
17	6	CUDDY 188	HT	CBNCR	FBG	DV	IO	120-230		7	2	2610		4850	5850
17	6	RAMPAGE 188BR	OP	RNBT	FBG	SV	IO	175		7	2	2210		4250	4950
18	6	195BR	OP	RNBT	FBG	DV	IO			7	6	2530		**	**
18	6	198BR & SPORT	OP	RNBT	FBG	DV	OB			8		2350		5500	6350
18	6	198BR & SPORT	OP	RNBT	FBG	DV	IO	165-260		8		2350		5000	6150
18	6	198BR & SPORT	OP	RNBT	FBG	DV	JT	350-460		8		2350		7650	8800
18	6	CUDDY 198	OP	RNBT	FBG	DV	OB			8				5450	6250
18	6	CUDDY 198	OP	RNBT	FBG	DV	IO	175-260		8		2690		5300	6550
18	6	CUDDY 198	OP	RNBT	FBG	DV	JT	350-460		8		2690		8150	9350
18	6	RAMPAGE 195BR	OP	RNBT	FBG	SV	IO	260		7	6	2530		5300	6100
18	11	SUNFISH 202	OP	CTRCN	FBG	SV	OB			7	6	1520		4250	4950
19	2	MAGNUM	OP	SKI	FBG	SV	IO	350	MRCR	6	8	2260		6050	6950
19	5	SIDEWINDER	OP	SKI	FBG	SV	OB			7	1			5450	6250
19	5	SIDEWINDER	OP	SKI	FBG	SV	IO		MRCR	7	1	2120		**	**
		IO 175-260 4500 5550, IO 320 MRCR 5550 6400, JT 454												6950	8000
20	2	ARIES	OP	SKI	FBG	SV	OB			7	4			3900	4500
20	2	ARIES	OP	SKI	FBG	SV	IO		MRCR	7	4	2610		**	**
		IO 175-260 5250 6400, IO 320 MRCR 6300 7200, JT 454												7950	9150
20	2	FOOTER	OP	SKI	FBG	SV	OB			7	4	1150		3850	4450
20	2	SPORTFISHER 213	HT	CBNCR	FBG	DV	OB			7	7			7200	8250
20	2	SPORTFISHER 213	HT	CBNCR	FBG	DV	SE			7	7	3040		**	**
20	2	SPORTFISHER 213	HT	CBNCR	FBG	DV	IO	130-175		7	7	3040		6650	7700
20	10	RAVEN 210	OP	CR	FBG	DV	OB			8				8200	9400
20	10	RAVEN 210	OP	CR	FBG	DV	IO		MRCR	8		3150		**	**
20	10	RAVEN 210	OP	CR	FBG	DV	IO		OMC	8		3150		**	**
20	10	RAVEN 210	OP	CR	FBG	DV	IO	165-260		8		3150		6800	8250
21	2	COBRA BR	OP	SKI	FBG	DV	OB			7	9			8350	9600
21	2	COBRA BR	OP	SKI	FBG	DV	IO		MRCR	7	9	3060		**	**
		IO OMC ** **, IO 260 6600 7600, IO 320 MRCR												7300	8400
		JT 454 9400 10700													
22		EMPRESS 230	OP	CR	FBG	DV	OB			8				8950	10100
22		EMPRESS 230	OP	CR	FBG	DV	IO			8		3620		**	**
		IO MRCR ** **, IO OMC ** **, IO 260												8300	9550
		IO 320 MRCR 9150 10400, JT 350 MRCR 11000 12500													
22		MARIAH 220	OP	CR	FBG	DV	OB			8				10500	12000
22		MARIAH 220	OP	CR	FBG	DV	IO		MRCR	8		3550		**	**
22		MARIAH 220	OP	CR	FBG	DV	IO		OMC	8		3550		**	**
22		MARIAH 220	OP	CR	FBG	DV	IO	165-260		8		3550		7800	9400
24		ESCORT 240	HT	OVNTR	FBG	DV	OB			8				13200	15000
24		ESCORT 240	HT	OVNTR	FBG	DV	IO		MRCR	8		4000		**	**
24		ESCORT 240	HT	OVNTR	FBG	DV	IO		OMC	8		4000		**	**
24		ESCORT 240	HT	OVNTR	FBG	DV	IO	230-260		8		4000		9700	11300
24		ESCORT 240	FB	OVNTR	FBG	DV	OB			8				13200	15000
24		ESCORT 240	FB	OVNTR	FBG	DV	IO		MRCR	8		4400		**	**
24		ESCORT 240	FB	OVNTR	FBG	DV	IO		OMC	8		4400		**	**
24		ESCORT 240	FB	OVNTR	FBG	DV	IO	230-260		8		4400		10400	12100
24		ESCORT CUDDY	OP	CR	FBG	DV	OB			8				10700	12100
24		ESCORT CUDDY	OP	CR	FBG	DV	JT			8		3300		**	**
		IO MRCR ** **, IO OMC ** **, IO 200-260												8350	9950
24	8	BILLFISH 265	OP	CBNCR	FBG	DV	OB			8	6			12700	14400
24	8	BILLFISH 265	OP	CBNCR	FBG	DV	JT			8	6	3600		**	**
		IO ** **, IO 260 11400 13000, IO 454												16100	18300
		IO T165-T175 12200 13800													
24	8	RAVEN 265	OP	OVNTR	FBG	DV	IO		MRCR	8	6	4800		**	**
		IO OMC ** **, IO 260 11900 13500, IO T165-T175												12600	14400
24	10	CEAERO 240	OP	OFF	FBG	DV	IO			6	10	3300		**	**
		IO MRCR ** **, IO OMC ** **, IO 260-320												8950	11000
		JT 454 12200 13900, IO 454 13300 15100													
30	6	CEAERO 310	OP	OFF	FBG	DV	OB			8				19300	21400
30	6	CEAERO 310	OP	OFF	FBG	DV	IO	T		8		6120		**	**
		IO T OMC ** **, IO T320 MRCR 25000 27800, IO T454 MRCR												28600	31800
		1987 BOATS													
16		RENEGADE 161	OP	BASS	FBG	DV	OB			6	6	770		2100	2450
16	2	SATELLITE 171BR	OP	B/R	FBG	DV	OB			6	7	970		2650	3100
16	2	SATELLITE 171BR	OP	B/R	FBG	DV	IO	102-175		6	7	1620		2800	3350
16	2	SATELLITE 171CD	OP	RNBT	FBG	DV	OB			6	7	970		2700	3150
16	2	SATELLITE 171CD	OP	RNBT	FBG	DV	IO	120-175		6	7	1620		3050	3550
16	5	AURORA	OP	SKI	FBG	SV	OB			7	1	870		2400	2750
16	5	AURORA	OP	SKI	FBG	SV	IO	130		7	1			3000	3500
16	7	CHALLENGER 176BR	OP	RNBT	FBG	DV	IO	130-175		7	2	1750		3400	4000
16	7	RALLY 176	OP	RNBT	FBG	DV	OB			7	2	1830		4700	5400
16	7	RALLY 176	OP	RNBT	FBG	DV	IO	130-205		7	2	1830		3450	4150
17	6	188	HT	CUD	FBG	DV	IO	130-205		7	6	1520		3550	4250
17	6	188BR	OP	B/R	FBG	DV	IO	130-205		7	2	1820		3450	4150
18	6	198 CUDDY	OP	CUD	FBG	DV	IO	165-260		8		2690		5250	6450
18	6	198BR	OP	B/R	FBG	DV	IO	165-260		8		2350		4600	5650
18	6	198CD	OP	RNBT	FBG	DV	IO	165-260		8		2350		4750	5850

96th ed. - Vol. II
CONTINUED ON NEXT PAGE
375

LOA FT	LOA IN	NAME AND/ OR MODEL	TOP/ RIG	BOAT TYPE	-HULL- MTL	-HULL- TP	ENGINE TP	ENGINE # HP	ENGINE MFG	BEAM FT	BEAM IN	WGT LBS	DRAFT FT IN	RETAIL LOW	RETAIL HIGH
		1987 BOATS													
18	6	RALLY 195 MAGNUM	OP	RNBT	FBG	DV	IO	165-260		7	6	2640		4850	5950
18	6	RALLY 195 MAGNUM	OP	RNBT	FBG	DV	IO	350	MRCR	7	6	2640		6450	7400
18	11	SUNFISH 202	OP	CTRCN	FBG	SV	OB			7	6	1520		4100	4800
19		NAKED	OP	SKI	FBG	SV	IO	350	MRCR					5650	6500
19	2	MAGNUM	OP	SKI	FBG	SV	IO	350	MRCR	6	8	2260		5750	6650
19	2	SPORTFISHER 203	HT	SF	FBG	DV	IO	130-205		7	4	2890		6100	7150
19	5	SIDEWINDER	OP	SKI	FBG	SV	IO	175-205		7	1	1800		3950	4700
20	2	ARIES	OP	SKI	FBG	SV	OB			7	4	1970		5650	6450
20	2	ARIES	OP	SKI	FBG	SV	IO		MRCR	7	4	1970		**	**
20	2	ARIES	OP	SKI	FBG	SV	IO	175-260		7	4	1970		4400	5400
20	2	FOOTER	OP	SKI	FBG	SV	OB			7	4	1150		3650	4250
20	10	RAVEN 21	OP	CR	FBG	DV	IO	230-260		8		3350		6900	8100
21	2	COBRA	OP	SKI	FBG	DV	IO		MRCR	7	9	2310		**	**
21	2	COBRA	OP	SKI	FBG	DV	IO		OMC	7	9	2310		**	**
21	2	COBRA	OP	SKI	FBG	DV	IO	230-260		7	9	2310		5250	6250
21	2	COBRA 21BR	OP	SKI	FBG	DV	IO		MRCR	7	9	2460		**	**
21	2	COBRA 21BR	OP	SKI	FBG	DV	IO		OMC	7	9	2460		**	**
21	2	COBRA 21BR	OP	SKI	FBG	DV	IO	230-260		7	9	2460		5400	6400
21	2	COBRA 21EXP	OP	SKI	FBG	DV	IO		MRCR	7	9	2460		**	**
21	2	COBRA 21EXP	OP	SKI	FBG	DV	IO		OMC	7	9	2460		**	**
21	2	COBRA 21EXP	OP	SKI	FBG	DV	IO	230-260		7	9	2460		5400	6400
22		EMPRESS	OP	SKI	FBG	DV	IO		MRCR	8		3300		**	**
22		EMPRESS	OP	SKI	FBG	DV	IO		OMC	8		3300		**	**
22		EMPRESS	OP	SKI	FBG	DV	IO	260		8		3300		6950	8000
22		MARIAH 22	OP	CR	FBG	DV	IO	230-260		8		3550		7600	8950
24		ESCORT CUDDY	OP	CUD	FBG	DV	IO		MRCR	8		3300		**	**
24		ESCORT CUDDY	OP	CUD	FBG	DV	IO	230-260		8		3300		8050	9450
24		ESCORT FB24	FB	CR	FBG	DV	IO		MRCR	8		4400		**	**
24		ESCORT FB24	FB	CR	FBG	DV	IO	230-260		8		4400		9950	11500
24		ESCORT HT24	HT	CR	FBG	DV	IO		MRCR	8		4190		**	**
24		ESCORT HT24	HT	CR	FBG	DV	IO	230-260		8		4190		9550	11100
26		EMPEROR	OP	SKI	FBG	DV	IO		MRCR	8		3800		**	**
26		EMPEROR	OP	SKI	FBG	DV	IO		OMC	8		3800		**	**
26		EMPEROR	OP	SKI	FBG	DV	IO	260		8		3800		10000	11300
26	5	RAVEN 265	OP	CR	FBG	DV	IO		MRCR	8	6	4800		**	**
26	5	RAVEN 265	OP	CR	FBG	DV	IO	230-260		8	6	4800		12200	14200
		1986 BOATS													
16	2	160 BR	ST	RNBT	F/W	DV	OB			6	7	970		2600	3050
16	2	160 BR	ST	RNBT	F/W	DV	IO	140		6	7	1620		2950	3400
16	2	160 CD	ST	RNBT	F/W	DV	OB			6	7	970		2500	2950
16	2	160 CD	ST	RNBT	F/W	DV	IO	140		6	7	1620		2850	3350
16	5	AURORA	OP	SKI	F/W	SV	OB			7	1	840		2200	2600
16	5	AURORA	OP	SKI	F/W	SV	IO	140		7	1	1595		2850	3300
16	7	170 BR	ST	RNBT	F/W	DV	IO	170		7		1740		3200	3750
16	7	170 RALLY BR	ST	RNBT	F/W	DV	OB			7		1060		2800	3250
16	7	170 RALLY BR	ST	RNBT	F/W	DV	IO	170		7		1830		3300	3850
17	6	180 BR	ST	RNBT	F/W	DV	IO	185-190		7	2	1820		3550	4150
17	6	180 CUDDY	OP	CUD	F/W	DV	IO	170		7	2	2160		3900	4500
17	11	TIGERSHARK	OP	SKI	F/W	SV	OB			7	2	870		2450	2850
18		BARRACUDA	OP	SKI	F/W	SV	JT	460		6	7	1865		5350	6150
18		RENEGADE BB	OP	BASS	F/W		OB			6	3	690		1950	2350
18		RENEGADE BB	OP	BASS	F/W		JT	460		6	3	1480		4800	5550
18	6	190 BR	ST	RNBT	F/W	DV	IO	185-190		7	6	2530		4550	5250
18	6	190 RALLY BR	ST	RNBT	F/W	DV	IO	230		7	6	2530		4650	5350
18	6	198 BR	ST	RNBT	F/W	DV	IO	230		8		2350		4700	5400
18	6	198 CD	ST	RNBT	F/W	DV	IO	230		8		2350		4700	5400
18	6	198 CUDDY	ST	RNBT	F/W	DV	IO	260		8		2870		5350	6150
18	6	MAGNUM 190 RALLY	OP	SKI	F/W	DV	IB	255D		7	6	2530		11000	12500
18	11	192 SUNFISH	ST	CTRCN	F/W	DV	OB			7	6	1530		4000	4650
19	2	MAGNUM SKIER	OP	SKI	F/W	DV	IB	255D		6	8	2260		10600	12000
19	2	SPORTFISHER	HT	CBNCR	F/W	DV	IO	170		7	8	2890		5600	6400
20	2	ARIES B/R	OP	SKI	F/W	SV	OB			7	4	1010		3150	3650
20	2	ARIES B/R	OP	SKI	F/W	SV	IO	230		7	4	1970		4300	5000
20	2	ARIES B/R	OP	SKI	F/W	SV	JT	460		7	4	1970		6450	7400
20	2	LUNAR	OP	SKI	F/W	SV	OB			7	4	1010		3150	3650
20	2	LUNAR	OP	SKI	F/W	SV	IO	230		7	4	2000		4350	5000
20	2	LUNAR	OP	SKI	F/W	SV	JT	460		7	4	2000		6450	7450
20	4	LIBRA	OP	CR	F/W	DV	JT	460		7	7	2250		6950	8000
20	4	LIBRA	OP	SKI	F/W	DV	IO	230		7	7	2250		4700	5400
20	10	RAVEN	OP	CR	F/W	DV	IO	260		8		3250		6600	7600
22		EMPRESS	ST	CR	F/W	SV	IO	260		8		2940		6600	7600
22		EMPRESS	ST	CR	F/W	SV	JT	460		8		2940		8900	10100
22		MARIAH	ST	CR	F/W	DV	IO	260		8		3550		7450	8550
24		ESCORT	OP	CUD	F/W	DV	IO	260		7	11	3300		7850	9000
24		ESCORT	FB	OVNTR	F/W	DV	IO	260		7	11	4400		9650	11000
26		EMPEROR	ST	OVNTR	F/W	DV	IO	260		8		3800		10200	11600
26		EMPEROR	ST	OVNTR	F/W	DV	JT	460		8		3800		14600	16600
		1985 BOATS													
16	2	160 BR	OP	RNBT	FBG		OB			6	7	970		2500	2900
16	2	160 BR	OP	RNBT	FBG		IO	140		6	7	1620		2800	3250
16	2	160 CD		RNBT	FBG		OB			6	7	970		2500	2900
16	2	160 CD		RNBT	FBG		IO	140		6	7	1620		2800	3250
16	2	SATELLITE		RNBT	F/W	DV	OB			6	7	970		2450	2850
16	2	SATELLITE		RNBT	F/W	DV	IO	140		6	7	1690		2850	3300
16	2	SATELLITE BR		RNBT	F/W	DV	OB			6	7	970		2550	2950
16	3	VENUS		RNBT	F/W	TR	IO	140		6	5	1750		2850	3350
16	5	AURORA	OP	SKI	F/W	SV	OB			7	1	840		2100	2500
16	5	AURORA	OP	SKI	F/W	SV	IO	140		7	1	1595		2750	3200
16	7	170 BR	OP	RNBT	FBG		IO	170		7		1740		3100	3600
16	7	170 RALLY BR	OP	RNBT	FBG		OB			7		1060		2750	3200
16	7	170 RALLY BR	OP	RNBT	FBG		IO	170		7		1830		3150	3650
16	7	CHALLENGER		RNBT	F/W	DV	IO	170		7		1830		3150	3650
16	7	MARLIN 170		RNBT	F/W	DV	OB			7		1060		2700	3150
16	7	MARLIN 170		RNBT	F/W	DV	IO	170		7				3250	3750
17	6	180 BR	OP	RNBT	FBG		IO	185-190		7	2	1820		3400	3950
17	6	MERCURY BR		RNBT	F/W	DV	IO	170		7	2	1820		3400	3950
17	8	JUPITER		RNBT	F/W	TR	IO	170		7		1425		3100	3600
17	11	TIGERSHARK	OP	SKI	F/W	SV	OB			7	2	870		2350	2750
17	11	TIGERSHARK	OP	SKI	F/W	SV	IO	170		7	2	1730		3250	3750
18		BARRACUDA	OP	RNBT	F/W	SV	JT	460		6	7	1865		5300	6100
18	6	190 BR	OP	RNBT	FBG		IO	185-190		7	6	2530		4350	5050
18	6	190 RALLY BR	OP	RNBT	FBG		IO	230		7	6	2530		4500	5150
18	6	198 BR	OP	RNBT	FBG		IO	230		8		2350		4500	5200
18	6	198 CD	OP	RNBT	FBG		IO	230		8		2350		4500	5200
18	6	198 CUDDY	OP	RNBT	FBG		IO	260		8		2870		5150	5900
18	6	ISLANDER CUDDY		CUD	F/W	DV	IO	230		8		2850		5100	5900
18	6	ISLANDER SPORT		RNBT	F/W	DV	IO	228		8		2350		4500	5200
18	6	MARLIN 190		RNBT	F/W	DV	IO	228		7	6			4450	5100
18	11	MARLIN 192		RNBT	F/W	DV	OB			7	6	1530		3950	4550
18	11	SUNFISH 192	OP	CTRCN	FBG		OB			7	6	1530		3850	4500
19	2	SPORTFISHER	HT	CBNCR	F/W	DV	IO	170		7	8	2890		5350	6150
20	2	ARIES B/R	OP	SKI	F/W	SV	OB			7	4	1010		3050	3550
20	2	ARIES B/R	OP	SKI	F/W	SV	IO	230		7	4	1970		4100	4800
20	2	ARIES B/R	OP	SKI	F/W	SV	JT	460		7	4	1970		6150	7050
20	2	LUNAR	OP	SKI	F/W	SV	OB			7	4	1010		3050	3550
20	2	LUNAR	OP	SKI	F/W	SV	IO	230		7	4	2000		4150	4800
20	2	LUNAR	OP	SKI	F/W	SV	JT	460		7	4	2000		6200	7100
20	4	LIBRA	OP	CR	F/W	DV	JT	460		7	7	2250		6650	7600
20	4	LIBRA	OP	SKI	F/W	DV	IO	230		7	7	2250		4500	5200
22		EMPRESS	ST	CR	F/W	SV	IO	260		8		2940		6350	7300
22		EMPRESS	ST	CR	F/W	SV	JT	460		8		2940		8400	9650
22		MARIAH	ST	CR	F/W	DV	IO	260		8		3550		7150	8200
24		ESCORT	OP	CUD	F/W	DV	IO	260		7	11	3300		7500	8650
24		ESCORT	FB	OVNTR	F/W	DV	IO	260		7	11	4400		9300	10600
26		EMPEROR	ST	OVNTR	F/W	DV	IO	260		8		3800		9750	11100
26		EMPEROR	ST	OVNTR	F/W	DV	JT	460		8		3800		13900	15900
		1984 BOATS													
16	2	SATELLITE	ST	RNBT	F/W	DV	OB			6	7	970		2350	2750
16	2	SATELLITE	ST	RNBT	F/W	DV	IO	120-170		6	7	1690		2750	3200
16	2	SATELLITE B/R	ST	RNBT	F/W	DV	OB			6	7	970		2450	2850
16	2	SATELLITE B/R	ST	RNBT	F/W	DV	IO	170	MRCR	6	7	1690		2800	3250
16	3	VENUS B/R	ST	RNBT	F/W	TR	OB			6	5	790		1950	2350
16	3	VENUS B/R	ST	RNBT	F/W	TR	IO	120-140		6	5	1750		2750	3200
16	5	AURORA	OP	SKI	F/W	SV	OB			7	1	870		2150	2500
16	5	AURORA	OP	SKI	F/W	SV	IO	140		7	1	1600		2650	3100
16	7	CHALLENGER	ST	RNBT	F/W	DV	IO	140-170		7		1830		3000	3550
16	7	CHALLENGER	ST	RNBT	F/W	DV	IO	350		7		1830		4500	5200
17	6	MERCURY	ST	RNBT	F/W	DV	OB			7	2	1270		3150	3650
17	6	MERCURY B/R	ST	RNBT	F/W	DV	IO	140-188		7	2	1820		3250	3800
17	6	MERCURY B/R	ST	RNBT	F/W	DV	IO	350	CHEV	7	2	1820		4700	5400
17	8	JUPITER	OP	RNBT	F/W	TR	IO	140-170		7		1425		2950	3450
17	11	TIGERSHARK	OP	SKI	F/W	SV	OB			7	2	870		2300	2650
18		BARRACUDA	OP	RNBT	F/W	SV	JT	260-330		6	7	850		4500	5150
18		CAPRI	ST	CBNCR	F/W	SV	OB			6	8	1490		3550	4100
18		CAPRI	ST	CBNCR	F/W	SV	IO	120-140		6	8	2270		3750	4350
18		RENEGADE	OP	RNBT	F/W	TH	JT	320-330		6	3	550		4550	5250
18	6	ISLANDER B/R	ST	RNBT	F/W	DV	IO	228	MRCR	8		2350		4300	5000

CONTINUED ON NEXT PAGE

LOA FT IN	NAME AND/ OR MODEL		TOP/ RIG	BOAT TYPE	HULL MTL	TP	TP	ENGINE # HP	MFG	BEAM FT IN	WGT LBS	DRAFT FT IN	RETAIL LOW	RETAIL HIGH
		1984 BOATS												
18 6	ISLANDER CUDDY		ST	CUD	F/W	DV	IO	185-260		8	2850		4800	5850
18 6	ISLANDER SPORT		ST	RNBT	F/W	DV	IO	185-260		8	2350		4200	5200
19 2	SPORTFISHER		HT	CBNCR	F/W	DV	IO	140-188		7 8	2890		5150	5950
20 2	ARIES B/R		OP	SKI	F/W	SV	OB			7 4	1100		3200	3700
20 2	ARIES B/R		OP	SKI	F/W	SV	IO	185-260		7 4	2000		3900	4850
20 2	ARIES B/R		OP	SKI	F/W	SV	JT	350-460		7 4	2000		5900	6800
20 2	LUNAR		OP	SKI	F/W	SV	OB			7 4	1100		3200	3700
20 2	LUNAR		OP	SKI	F/W	SV	JT		FORD	7 4	2000		**	**
	IO 185-230	3900	4600,	JT	260			CHEV	5900	6800,	IO	260	4150	4850
	JT 330 CHEV	5900	6800											
20 4	LIBRA		OP	SKI	F/W	DV	IO		FORD	7 7	2250		**	**
20 4	LIBRA		OP	SKI	F/W	DV	IO	228-260		7 7	2250		4300	5200
20 4	LIBRA		OP	SKI	F/W	DV	JT	330	CHEV	7 7	2250		6350	7300
22	MARIAH		ST	CR	F/W	DV	IO	228-260		8	3550		6700	7900
24	ESCORT		OP	CUD	F/W	DV	IO	228-260		7 11	3300		7100	8350
24	ESCORT		HT	SDN	F/W	DV	IO	228-260		7 11	4000		8100	9500
24	ESCORT		FB	SDN	F/W	DV	IO	228-260		7 11	4400		8800	10200
26	EMPEROR		ST	OVNTR	F/W	DV	JT		FORD	8	3800		**	**
26	EMPEROR		ST	OVNTR	F/W	DV	IO	260		8	3800		9450	10700
26	EMPEROR		ST	OVNTR	F/W	DV	IO	330	CHEV	8	3800		12600	14300
31 7	LUNAR		OP	SKI	F/W	SV	IO	228	MRCR	7 4	2800		12000	13600

MARLIN YACHT MFG INC
MIAMI FL 33179-4510   See inside cover to adjust price for area

For more recent years, see the BUC Used Boat Price Guide, Volume 1

LOA FT IN	NAME AND/ OR MODEL		TOP/ RIG	BOAT TYPE	HULL MTL	TP	TP	ENGINE # HP	MFG	BEAM FT IN	WGT LBS	DRAFT FT IN	RETAIL LOW	RETAIL HIGH
		1996 BOATS												
35 6	MARLIN 350D		CTRCN	FBG	DV	OB		370D		9 4	4500	1 6	63500	69700
35 6	MARLIN 350FM		CTRCN	F/S	DV	OB				9 4	4500	1 6	37400	41600
35 6	MARLIN 350SF		CTRCN	F/S	DV	OB				9 4	4500	1 6	37400	41600
		1995 BOATS												
35 6	MARLIN 350FM		CTRCN	F/S	DV	OB				9 4	4500	1 6	35400	39300
35 6	MARLIN 350SF		CUD	F/S	DV	OB				9 4	4500	1 6	35900	39900

MARQUE YACHTS INC
MARQUE INVESTMENTS
EAGAN MN 55120-1127   COAST GUARD MFG ID- MQE   See inside cover to adjust price for area

LOA FT IN	NAME AND/ OR MODEL		TOP/ RIG	BOAT TYPE	HULL MTL	TP	TP	ENGINE # HP	MFG	BEAM FT IN	WGT LBS	DRAFT FT IN	RETAIL LOW	RETAIL HIGH
		1984 BOATS												
46	SEA-CONDO			MY	FBG	SV	IB	T305D	GM	14 6	39000	3 6	149500	164000

MARSHALL MARINE CORP
S DARTMOUTH MA 02748   COAST GUARD MFG ID- MMC See inside cover to adjust price for area

For more recent years, see the BUC Used Boat Price Guide, Volume 1

LOA FT IN	NAME AND/ OR MODEL		TOP/ RIG	BOAT TYPE	HULL MTL	TP	TP	ENGINE # HP	MFG	BEAM FT IN	WGT LBS	DRAFT FT IN	RETAIL LOW	RETAIL HIGH
		1996 BOATS												
18 2	SANDERLING		CAT	SAROD	FBG	CB	OB			8 6	2200	4 4	18400	20500
18 2	SANDERLING		CAT	SAROD	FBG	CB	IB	9D	YAN	8 6	2200	4 4	26700	29600
22 2	MARSHALL 22		CAT	SACAC	FBG	CB	IB	18D	YAN	10 2	5660	5 5	40800	45300
22 2	MARSHALL 22		SLP	SACAC	FBG	CB	IB	18D	YAN	10 2	5660	5 5	40800	45300
		1995 BOATS												
18 2	SANDERLING		CAT	SAROD	FBG	CB	OB			8 6	2200	4 4	17000	19400
18 2	SANDERLING		CAT	SAROD	FBG	CB	IB	9D	YAN	8 6	2200	4 4	25300	28100
22 2	MARSHALL 22		CAT	SACAC	FBG	CB	IB	18D	YAN	10 2	5660	5 5	38600	42900
22 2	MARSHALL 22		SLP	SACAC	FBG	CB	IB	18D	YAN	10 2	5660	5 5	38600	42900
		1994 BOATS												
18 2	SANDERLING		CAT	SAROD	FBG	CB	OB			8 6	2200	4 4	16100	18300
18 2	SANDERLING		CAT	SAROD	FBG	CB	IB	9D	YAN	8 6	2200	4 4	23900	26600
22 2	MARSHALL 22		CAT	SACAC	FBG	CB	IB	18D	YAN	10 2	5660	5 5	36500	40600
22 2	MARSHALL 22		SLP	SACAC	FBG	CB	IB	18D	YAN	10 2	5660	5 5	36500	40600
		1993 BOATS												
18 2	SANDERLING		CAT	SAROD	FBG	CB	OB			8 6	2200	1 7	15300	17400
18 2	SANDERLING		CAT	SAROD	FBG	CB	IB	9D	YAN	8 6	2200	1 7	22700	25200
22 2	MARSHALL 22		CAT	SACAC	FBG	CB	IB	18D	YAN	10 2	5660	2	34500	38400
22 2	MARSHALL 22		SLP	SACAC	FBG	CB	IB	18D	YAN	10 2	5660	2	34500	38400
		1992 BOATS												
18 2	SANDERLING		CAT	SA/OD	FBG	CB	OB			8 6	2200	1 7	14500	16500
18 2	SANDERLING		CAT	SA/OD	FBG	CB	IB	9D	YAN	8 6	2200	1 7	21500	23800
22 2	MARSHALL 22		CAT	SA/CR	FBG	CB	IB	18D	YAN	10 2	5660	2	32700	36300
22 2	MARSHALL 22		SLP	SA/CR	FBG	CB	IB	18D	YAN	10 2	5660	2	32700	36300
		1991 BOATS												
18 2	SANDERLING		CAT	SA/OD	FBG	CB	OB			8 6	2200	1 7	13700	15600
18 2	SANDERLING		CAT	SA/OD	FBG	CB	IB	9D	YAN	8 6	2200	1 7	20300	22600
22 2	MARSHALL 22		CAT	SA/CR	FBG	CB	IB	18D	YAN	10 2	5660	2	30900	34400
22 2	MARSHALL 22		SLP	SA/CR	FBG	CB	IB	18D	YAN	10 2	5660	2	30900	34400
		1990 BOATS												
18 2	SANDERLING		CAT	SA/OD	FBG	CB	OB			8 6	2200	1 7	13000	14800
18 2	SANDERLING		CAT	SA/OD	FBG	CB	IB	9D	YAN	8 6	2200	1 7	19300	21400
22 2	MARSHALL 22		CAT	SA/CR	FBG	CB	IB	18D	YAN	10 2	5660	2	29300	32600
22 2	MARSHALL 22		SLP	SA/CR	FBG	CB	IB	18D	YAN	10 2	5660	2	29300	32600
		1989 BOATS												
18 2	SANDERLING		CAT	SA/OD	FBG	CB	OB			8 6	2200	1 7	12300	14000
18 2	SANDERLING		CAT	SA/OD	FBG	CB	IB	9D	YAN	8 6	2200	1 7	18500	20500
22 2	MARSHALL 22		CAT	SA/CR	FBG	CB	IB	18D	YAN	10 2	5660	2	27700	30800
22 2	MARSHALL 22		SLP	SA/CR	FBG	CB	IB	18D	YAN	10 2	5660	2	27700	30800
		1988 BOATS												
18 2	SANDERLING		CAT	SA/OD	FBG	CB	OB			8 6	2200	1 7	11700	13300
18 2	SANDERLING		CAT	SA/OD	FBG	CB	IB	9D	YAN	8 6	2200	1 7	17100	19400
22 2	MARSHALL 22		CAT	SA/CR	FBG	CB	IB	18D	YAN	10 2	5660	2	26300	29200
22 2	MARSHALL 22		SLP	SA/CR	FBG	CB	IB	18D	YAN	10 2	5660	2	26300	29200
		1987 BOATS												
18 2	SANDERLING		CAT	SA/OD	FBG	CB	OB			8 6	2200	1 7	11100	12600
18 2	SANDERLING		CAT	SA/OD	FBG	CB	IB	9D	YAN	8 6	2200	1 7	16200	18400
22 2	MARSHALL 22		CAT	SA/CR	FBG	CB	IB	18D	YAN	10 2	5660	2	24900	27700
22 2	MARSHALL 22		SLP	SA/CR	FBG	CB	IB	18D	YAN	10 2	5660	2	24900	27700
		1986 BOATS												
18 2	SANDERLING		CAT	SA/OD	FBG	CB	OB			8 6	2200	1 7	10500	11900
18 2	SANDERLING		CAT	SA/OD	FBG	CB	IB	9D	YAN	8 6	2200	1 7	15400	17400
22 2	MARSHALL 22		CAT	SA/OD	FBG	CB	IB	18D	YAN	10 2	5660	2	23600	26200
22 2	MARSHALL 22		SLP	SA/CR	FBG	CB	IB	18D	YAN	10 2	5660	2	23600	26200
		1985 BOATS												
18 2	SANDERLING		CAT	SA/OD	FBG	CB	OB			8 6	2200	1 7	9950	11300
18 2	SANDERLING		CAT	SA/OD	FBG	CB	IB	8D	YAN	8 6	2200	1 7	14500	16400
22 2	MARSHALL 22		CAT	SA/OD	FBG	CB	IB	23D	YAN	10 2	5660	2	22500	25000
22 2	MARSHALL 22		SLP	SA/CR	FBG	CB	IB	23D	YAN	10 2	5660	2	22500	25000
		1984 BOATS												
18 2	SANDERLING		CAT	SA/OD	FBG	CB	OB			8 6	2200	1 6	9400	10700
18 2	SANDERLING		CAT	SA/OD	FBG	CB	IB	7D	YAN	8 6	2200	1 6	13600	15500
22 2	MARSHALL 22		CAT	SA/CR	FBG	CB	IB	22D	YAN	10 2	5660	2	21400	23800
22 2	MARSHALL 22		SLP	SA/CR	FBG	CB	IB	22D	YAN	10 2	5660	2	21400	23800

....For earlier years, see the BUC Used Boat Price Guide, Volume 3

MARTHAS VINEYARD SHIPYD INC
VINEYARD HVN MA 02568   COAST GUARD MFG ID- MVS See inside cover to adjust price for area

LOA FT IN	NAME AND/ OR MODEL		TOP/ RIG	BOAT TYPE	HULL MTL	TP	TP	ENGINE # HP	MFG	BEAM FT IN	WGT LBS	DRAFT FT IN	RETAIL LOW	RETAIL HIGH
		1986 BOATS												
34 4	VIXEN 34		SLP	SA/CR	FBG	KL	IB	50D	PATH	10 6	12500	5 2	69900	76800
		1985 BOATS												
29 7	OVERNIGHTER		SLP	SA/CR	FBG	KL	IB	D		8 6	7800	4 3	39100	43500
29 7	VIXEN		SLP	SA/CR	FBG	KL	IB	D		8 6	8600	4 6	43200	48100
34 4	VIXEN 34		SLP	SA/CR	FBG	KL	IB	50D	PATH	10 6	12500	5 2	65500	72000
		1984 BOATS												
29 7	VIXEN 29 OVNTR		SLP	SA/CR	FBG	KL	SD	15D	VLVO	8 6	8600	4 6	40500	45000
34 4	VIXEN 34		SLP	SA/CR	FBG	KL	IB	42D	PATH	10 6	12500	5 2	61400	67400

....For earlier years, see the BUC Used Boat Price Guide, Volume 3

MASCOT BOATS A/S
GESDEN DENMARK   See inside cover to adjust price for area

LOA FT IN	NAME AND/ OR MODEL		TOP/ RIG	BOAT TYPE	HULL MTL	TP	TP	ENGINE # HP	MFG	BEAM FT IN	WGT LBS	DRAFT FT IN	RETAIL LOW	RETAIL HIGH
		1992 BOATS												
27 10	MASCOT 28		SLP	MS	FBG	KL	IB	18D	VLVO	9 7	8800	4 3	51400	56500
29 10	MASCOT 910		SLP	MS	FBG	KL	IB	18D	VLVO	9 9	9200	4 5	55900	61400
32 8	MASCOT 1110		SLP	MS	FBG	KL	IB	28D	VLVO	11 2	13670	4 9	83900	92200
32 8	MASCOT 33		SLP	MS	FBG	KL	IB	28D	VLVO	11 2	13228	4 11	81300	89300

LOA FT IN	NAME AND/ OR MODEL	TOP/ RIG	BOAT TYPE	-HULL- MTL TP	----ENGINE--- HP MFG	BEAM FT IN	WGT LBS	DRAFT FT IN	RETAIL LOW	RETAIL HIGH
					1992 BOATS					
36 5	MASCOT 35 DS	SLP	MS	FBG KL IB	43D VLVO 11	2	13620	4 11	87600	96200
45 4	MASCOT 43 DS	SLP	MS	FBG KL IB	43D VLVO 13	6	22000	5 7	178500	196500
					1991 BOATS					
27 10	MASCOT 28	SLP	MS	FBG KL IB	18D VLVO 9	7	8800	4 3	48400	53100
29 10	MASCOT 910	SLP	MS	FBG KL IB	18D VLVO 9	8	9200	4 3	52600	57800
32 8	MASCOT 33	SLP	MS	FBG KL IB	28D VLVO 11	2	13228	4 11	76300	83900
32 8	MASCOT 35	SLP	MS	FBG KL IB	43D VLVO 11	2	13620	4 11	78500	86300
36 5	MASCOT 1110	SLP	MS	FBG KL IB	28D VLVO 11	2	13670	4 11	82200	90300
					1990 BOATS					
27 10	MASCOT 28	SLP	MS	FBG KL IB	18D VLVO 9	7	8800	4 3	45000	50000
29 10	MASCOT 910	SLP	MS	FBG KL IB	18D VLVO 9	8	9200	4 3	49300	54200
32 8	MASCOT 33	SLP	MS	FBG KL IB	28D VLVO 11	2	13228	4 11	71700	78700
32 8	MASCOT 35	SLP	MS	FBG KL IB	43D VLVO 11	2	13620	4 11	73700	81000
36 5	MASCOT 1110	SLP	MS	FBG KL IB	28D VLVO 11	2	13670	4 11	77100	84800
					1989 BOATS					
27 10	MASCOT 28	SLP	MS	FBG KL IB	18D VLVO 9	7	8800	4 3	42100	46800
29 10	MASCOT 910	SLP	MS	FBG KL IB	18D VLVO 9	8	9200	4 3	46500	51100
32 8	MASCOT 33	SLP	MS	FBG KL IB	28D VLVO 11	2	13228	4 11	67300	73900
35 2	MASCOT 35	SLP	MS	FBG KL IB	43D VLVO 11	2	13620	4 11	70500	77400
36 5	MASCOT 1110	SLP	MS	FBG KL IB	28D VLVO 11	2	13670	4 11	72400	79500
					1988 BOATS					
27 10	MASCOT 28	SLP	MS	FBG KL IB	18D VLVO 9	7	8800	4 3	39500	43900
29 10	MASCOT 910	SLP	MS	FBG KL IB	18D VLVO 9	8	9200	4 3	43200	48000
32 8	MASCOT 33	SLP	MS	FBG KL IB	28D VLVO 11	2	13228	4 11	63100	69400
35 2	MASCOT 35	SLP	MS	FBG KL IB	43D VLVO 11	2	13620	4 11	66100	72700
36 5	MASCOT 1110	SLP	MS	FBG KL IB	28D VLVO 11	2	13670	4 11	67900	74600
					1987 BOATS					
27 10	MASCOT 28	SLP	MS	FBG KL IB	18D VLVO 9	7	8800	4 3	37000	41100
29 10	MASCOT 910	SLP	MS	FBG KL IB	18D VLVO 9	8	9200	4 3	40500	45000
32 8	MASCOT 33	SLP	MS	FBG KL IB	28D VLVO 11	2	13228	4 11	59300	65100
					1986 BOATS					
27 10	MASCOT 28	SLP	MS	FBG KL IB	18D VLVO 9	7	8800	4 3	34700	38500
32 8	MASCOT 33	SLP	MS	FBG KL IB	28D VLVO 11	2	13228	4 11	55900	61400
					1985 BOATS					
27 10	MASCOT 28	SLP	MS	FBG KL IB	18D VLVO 9	7	8800	4 3	32500	36100
32 8	MASCOT 33	SLP	MS	FBG KL IB	28D VLVO 11	2	12100	4 11	48300	53100

MASON BOATS LTD
SMITHS FALLS ONTARIO CA COAST GUARD MFG ID- MAS See inside cover to adjust price for area

LOA FT IN	NAME AND/ OR MODEL	TOP/ RIG	BOAT TYPE	-HULL- MTL TP	TP #	----ENGINE--- HP MFG	BEAM FT IN	WGT LBS	DRAFT FT IN	RETAIL LOW	RETAIL HIGH
						1988 BOATS					
16 6	CCF17	OP	CTRCN	FBG TR	OB		6 8	1100	2 4	3400	4000
22 2	CC238	OP	CUD	FBG DV	IO		8	3500	3	**	**
22 2	CF220	OP	FSH	FBG DV	IO	205 MRCR	8	3060	3	7200	8300
26 9	MX284	OP	CR	FBG DV	IO	260 MRCR	8	4635	3	12500	14200
						1986 BOATS					
16 6	CCF17	ST	CTRCN	FBG TR	OB		6 8	1100	2	3200	3750
22	CC238	ST	CR	FBG DV	IO	140	8	3327	3	6400	7350
22	CF220	ST	FSH	FBG DV	IO	140	8	3200	3	6600	7550
22	CR220	ST	CUD	FBG DV	IO	140	8	3200	3	6250	7150
22 2	CC238	ST	CR	FBG DV	IO	330 MRCR	8	3500	3	7850	9000
22 2	CF220	ST	FSH	FBG DV	OB		8	2500	3	7400	8550
22 2	CR220	ST	FSH	FBG DV	IO	330 MRCR	8	3500	3	8250	9500
22 2	CR220	ST	CR	FBG DV	IO	330 MRCR	8	3200	3	7450	8550
22 2	CR220	ST	CUD	FBG DV	IO	330 MRCR	8	3200	3	7450	8550
26 9	MX284	ST	DCCPT	FBG DV	IO	198 MRCR	8 6	4500	3	11700	13300
26 9	MX284	ST	DCCPT	FBG DV	IO	370 MRCR	8 6	4600	3	13900	15800
						1985 BOATS					
16 6	CCF17		FSH	FBG TR	OB		6 8	1100		3100	3650
22	CC238		CUD	FBG DV	OB	140	8	3327		6150	7050
22	CF220		CUD	FBG DV	IO		8	2500		7150	8200
22	CR220		CUD	FBG DV	IO	140	8	3200		6000	6900
22	CR220		CUD	FBG DV	IO	140	8	3200		6000	6900
26 8	MX284		CBNCR	FBG DV	IO	198	8	4500		12900	14600
						1984 BOATS					
16 6	CCF17	OP	CTRCN	FBG SV	OB		6 8	1100	10	3050	3550
22	CF220	OP	OPFSH	FBG DV	IO	170-260	8	3300	1 6	6200	6450
22	CF220	OP	OPFSH	FBG DV	IO	170-260	8	3300	1 6	6200	7550
22	CR220	OP	RNBT	FBG DV	IO	170-260	8	3300	1 6	5550	6650
22	CR220S	OP	RNBT	FBG DV	IO	OMC	8	3300	1 6	**	**
22	CR220S	OP	RNBT	FBG DV	IO	170-260	8	3300	1 6	5550	6950
22 2	CC222		CUD	FBG DV	IO	170-260	8	3300		5950	7200
26 9	MARDI-GRAS MX2786		CUD	FBG DV	IO	228-260	8 6	4600		10200	11900
26 9	MARDI-GRAS MX2786		CUD	FBG DV	IO	330 MRCR	8 6	4600		11300	12900

....For earlier years, see the BUC Used Boat Price Guide, Volume 3

MASTER FABRICATORS
REDDING CA 96001   COAST GUARD MFG ID- HLR See inside cover to adjust price for area

MASTER FABRICATORS
RUSSELLVLE AR 72801

LOA FT IN	NAME AND/ OR MODEL	TOP/ RIG	BOAT TYPE	-HULL- MTL TP	TP #	----ENGINE--- HP MFG	BEAM FT IN	WGT LBS	DRAFT FT IN	RETAIL LOW	RETAIL HIGH
						1985 BOATS					
39	MODEL A	HT	HB	STL PN	OB	14	14		2 6	14200	16200
	IO 140 OMC 14800	16800,	IO	185 OMC	14800	16900, IO T140		OMC		15900	18000
	IO T185 OMC 16000	18100									
47	MODEL B	HT	HB	STL PN	OB	14	14		2 6	15300	17300
	IO 140 OMC 16600	18800,	IO	185 OMC	16600	18900, IO T140		OMC		17600	20000
	IO T185 OMC 18100	20100									
47	MODEL C	HT	HB	STL PN	OB	14	14		2 6	15900	18000
	IO 140 OMC 18300	20300,	IO	185 OMC	18300	20400, IO T140		OMC		19300	21500
	IO T185 OMC 19400	21600									
55	MODEL D	HT	HB	STL PN	OB	14	14		2 6	24000	26700
	IO 140 OMC 24000	26700,	IO	185 OMC	24100	26800, IO T140		OMC		25200	28000
	IO T185 OMC 25300	28100									
55	MODEL E	HT	HB	STL PN	OB	14	14		2 6	23600	26200
	IO 140 OMC 27800	30800,	IO	185 OMC	27800	30900, IO T140		OMC		28900	32100
	IO T185 OMC 29000	32300									
						1984 BOATS					
39	MODEL A	HT	HB	STL PN	OB	14	14		2 6	13900	15800
	IO 140 OMC 14500	16400,	IO	185 OMC	14500	16500, IO T140		OMC		15500	17600
	IO T185 OMC 15600	17700									
47	MODEL B	HT	HB	STL PN	OB	14	14		2 6	14900	17000
	IO 140 OMC 16200	18400,	IO	185 OMC	16200	18500, IO T140		OMC		17200	19500
	IO T185 OMC 17300	19700									
47	MODEL C	HT	HB	STL PN	OB	14	14		2 6	15500	17600
	IO 140 OMC 17500	19900,	IO	185 OMC	17500	19900, IO T140		OMC		18900	21000
	IO T185 OMC 19000	21100									
55	MODEL D	HT	HB	STL PN	OB	14	14		2 6	23500	26100
	IO 140 OMC 23500	26100,	IO	185 OMC	23600	26200, IO T140		OMC		24600	27400
	IO T185 OMC 24800	27500									
55	MODEL E	HT	HB	STL PN	OB	14	14		2 6	23000	25600
	IO 140 OMC 27100	30200,	IO	185 OMC	27200	30200, IO T140		OMC		28300	31400
	IO T185 OMC 28400	31600									

....For earlier years, see the BUC Used Boat Price Guide, Volume 3

MASTER MARINERS CORP
NEWPORT BEACH CA 92663   See inside cover to adjust price for area

LOA FT IN	NAME AND/ OR MODEL	TOP/ RIG	BOAT TYPE	-HULL- MTL TP	----ENGINE--- HP MFG	BEAM FT IN	WGT LBS	DRAFT FT IN	RETAIL LOW	RETAIL HIGH
					1985 BOATS					
36	MARINER-POLARIS MKII	SLP	SA/CR	FBG KL IB	50D	11 4	18200	5 6	62700	68900
41	MARINER-NEPTUNE	SLP	SA/CR	FBG KL IB	61D	14	26000	6	94000	103500
47 11	MARINER-MERCURY MKII	SLP	SA/CR	FBG KL IB	85D	13 6	37500	6 5	145500	160000

....For earlier years, see the BUC Used Boat Price Guide, Volume 3

MASTER MOLDERS INC
KINGFISHER BOATS   See inside cover to adjust price for area
CLARKSVLLE TX 75426   COAST GUARD MFG ID- KNG

LOA FT IN	NAME AND/ OR MODEL	TOP/ RIG	BOAT TYPE	-HULL- MTL TP	TP	----ENGINE--- HP MFG	BEAM FT IN	WGT LBS	DRAFT FT IN	RETAIL LOW	RETAIL HIGH
						1993 BOATS					
16 9	KINGFISHER 169DC		BASS	FBG SV	OB		6 4	1175		3700	4300
16 9	KINGFISHER 169FS		BASS	FBG SV	OB		6 4	1065		3400	3950
16 9	KINGFISHER 169SC		BASS	FBG SV	OB		6 4	1080		3400	4000

LOA FT	LOA IN	NAME AND/ OR MODEL	TOP/ RIG	BOAT TYPE	-HULL- MTL	-HULL- TP	ENGINE TP	# HP	MFG	BEAM FT	BEAM IN	WGT LBS	DRAFT FT	DRAFT IN	RETAIL LOW	RETAIL HIGH
		1993 BOATS														
17		KINGFISHER 170		BASS	FBG	DV	OB			7	8	1050			3350	3900
17		KINGFISHER 170T		BASS	FBG	DV	OB			7	8	1050			3350	3900
17	9	KINGFISHER 179DC		BASS	FBG	SV	OB			7	4	1415			4450	5100
17	9	KINGFISHER 179FS		BASS	FBG	SV	OB			7	4	1390			4350	5000
17	9	KINGFISHER 179SC		BASS	FBG	SV	OB			7	4	1345			4200	4900
19	6	KINGFISHER 196DC		BASS	FBG	SV	OB			7	8	1575			5050	5850
19	6	KINGFISHER 196FS		BASS	FBG	SV	OB			7	8	1545			5000	5750
19	6	KINGFISHER 196SC		BASS	FBG	SV	OB			7	8	1375			4600	5300
		1992 BOATS														
16	9	KINGFISHER 169DC		BASS	FBG	SV	OB			6	4	1175			3550	4100
16	9	KINGFISHER 169FS		BASS	FBG	SV	OB			6	4	1065			3250	3800
16	9	KINGFISHER 169SC		BASS	FBG	SV	OB			6	4	1080			3300	3800
17		KINGFISHER 170		BASS	FBG	DV	OB			7	8	1050			3250	3750
17		KINGFISHER 170T		BASS	FBG	DV	OB			7	8	1050			3250	3750
17	9	KINGFISHER 179DC		BASS	FBG	SV	OB			7	4	1415			4200	4900
17	9	KINGFISHER 179FS		BASS	FBG	SV	OB			7	4	1390			4150	4850
17	9	KINGFISHER 179SC		BASS	FBG	SV	OB			7	4	1345			4050	4700
19	6	KINGFISHER 196DC		BASS	FBG	SV	OB			7	8	1575			4850	5600
19	6	KINGFISHER 196FS		BASS	FBG	SV	OB			7	8	1545			4800	5500
19	6	KINGFISHER 196SC		BASS	FBG	SV	OB			7	8	1375			4450	5100
		1991 BOATS														
16	9	KINGFISHER 169DC		BASS	FBG	SV	OB			6	4	1175			3400	3950
16	9	KINGFISHER 169FS		BASS	FBG	SV	OB			6	4	1065			3150	3650
16	9	KINGFISHER 169SC		BASS	FBG	SV	OB			6	4	1080			3150	3700
17		KINGFISHER 170		BASS	FBG	DV	OB			7	8	1050			3100	3600
17		KINGFISHER 170T		BASS	FBG	DV	OB			7	8	1050			3100	3600
17	9	KINGFISHER 179DC		BASS	FBG	SV	OB			7	4	1415			4050	4700
17	9	KINGFISHER 179FS		BASS	FBG	SV	OB			7	4	1390			4000	4650
17	9	KINGFISHER 179SC		BASS	FBG	SV	OB			7	4	1345			3900	4550
19	6	KINGFISHER 196DC		BASS	FBG	SV	OB			7	8	1575			4700	5400
19	6	KINGFISHER 196FS		BASS	FBG	SV	OB			7	8	1545			4650	5350
19	6	KINGFISHER 196SC		BASS	FBG	SV	OB			7	8	1375			4200	4900
		1990 BOATS														
16	9	169 DC	OP	BASS	F/S	DV	OB			6	6	1175			3450	4050
16	9	169 FS	OP	BASS	F/S	DV	OB			6	6	1175			3300	3850
16	9	169 SC	OP	BASS	F/S	DV	OB			6	6	1175			3100	3600
17	9	179 DC	OP	BASS	F/S	DV	OB			7	4	1415			3900	4550
17	9	179 FS	OP	BASS	F/S	DV	OB			7	4	1390			3850	4500
17	9	179 SC	OP	BASS	F/S	DV	OB			7	4	1345			3750	4400
19	6	196 DC	OP	BASS	F/S	DV	OB			7	8	1575			4550	5250
19	6	196 FS	OP	BASS	F/S	DV	OB			7	8	1545			4500	5150
19	6	196 SC	OP	BASS	F/S	DV	OB			7	8	1375			4050	4750
		1989 BOATS														
16		16HPV	OP	BASS	FBG	DV	OB			6	6	940			2550	3000
16		16HPV FS	OP	BASS	FBG	DV	OB			6	6	1030			2800	3250
16	9	169DC	OP	BASS	FBG	DV	OB			6	6	970			2700	3150
16	9	169FS	OP	BASS	FBG	DV	OB			6	6	950			2650	3100
16	9	169SC	OP	BASS	FBG	DV	OD			6	6	940			2600	3050
17	9	179DC	OP	BASS	FBG	DV	OB			7	4	1140			3200	3700
17	9	179FS	OP	BASS	FBG	DV	OB			7	4	1120			3150	3650
17	9	179SC	OP	BASS	FBG	DV	OB			7	4	1100			3100	3600
19	6	196DC	OP	BASS	FBG	DV	OB			7	8	1340			3850	4500
19	6	196FS	OP	BASS	FBG	DV	OB			7	8	1320			3800	4450
19	6	196SC	OP	BASS	FBG	DV	OB			7	8	1300			3750	4400
		1988 BOATS														
16		16HPV	OP	BASS	FBG	SV	OB			6	6	940			2500	2900
16		16HPV-F/S	OP	BASS	FBG	SV	OB			6	6	990			2600	3050
17		17HPV	OP	BASS	FBG	SV	OB			7	4	1100			2950	3400
17		17HPV-F/S	OP	BASS	FBG	SV	OB			7	4	1120			3000	3450
19	1	19HPV	OP	BASS	FBG	SV	OB			7	8	1300			3600	4200
		1987 BOATS														
16		16HPV	OP	BASS	FBG	SV	OB			6	6	940			2400	2800
17		17HPV	OP	BASS	FBG	SV	OB			7	4	1100			2850	3300
17		17HPV-F/S	OP	BASS	FBG	SV	OB			7	4	1120			2900	3350
19	1	19HPV	OP	BASS	FBG	SV	OB			7	8	1300			3500	4050
		1986 BOATS														
16		16HPV	OP	BASS	FBG	SV	OB			6	6	940			2350	2750
17		170	OP	BASS	FBG	TR	OB			6		880			2300	2700
17		171	OP	BASS	FBG	TR	OB			6		940			2450	2850
17		17HPV	OP	BASS	FBG	SV	OB			7	4	1100			2800	3250
17		17HPV-F/S	OP	BASS	FBG	SV	OB			7	4	1120			2800	3300
		1985 BOATS														
16		16HPV	OP	BASS	FBG	SV	OB			6	6	940			2300	2700
16		KING-FISHER 16V	OP	FSH	FBG	DV	OB			7	5	1000			2450	2800
17		170	OP	BASS	FBG	TR	OB			6		880			2250	2650
17		171	OP	BASS	FBG	TR	OB			6		940			2350	2750
17		17HPV	OP	BASS	FBG	SV	OB			7	4	1100			2700	3150
17		17HPV-F/S	OP	BASS	FBG	SV	OB			7	4	1120			2750	3200
		1984 BOATS														
16		16V	OP	BASS	FBG	DV	OB			7	5	1000			2400	2750
17		170	OP	BASS	FBG	TR	OB			6		880			2200	2550
17		171	OP	BASS	FBG	TR	OB			6		1000			2450	2850
17		17HPV	OP	BASS	FBG		OB			7	4	1100			2650	3100

....For earlier years, see the BUC Used Boat Price Guide, Volume 3

MASTERCRAFT BOAT CO INC

VONORE TN 37885 COAST GUARD MFG ID- MBC See inside cover to adjust price for area

For more recent years, see the BUC Used Boat Price Guide, Volume 1

LOA FT	LOA IN	NAME AND/ OR MODEL	TOP/ RIG	BOAT TYPE	-HULL- MTL	-HULL- TP	ENGINE TP	# HP	MFG	BEAM FT	BEAM IN	WGT LBS	DRAFT FT	DRAFT IN	RETAIL LOW	RETAIL HIGH
		1996 BOATS														
19	5	PROSTAR 190	OP	SKI	FBG	SV	IB	275-328		7	2	2450	1	10	12100	14400
19	5	SAMMY DUVAL 190	OP	SKI	FBG	SV	IB	275-328		7	2	2450	1	10	12100	14400
19	11	MARISTAR 200 VRS	OP	RNBT	FBG	SV	VD	275-328		7	10	2900	1	10	14800	17400
20	1	BAREFOOT 200	OP	SKI	FBG	SV	OB			6	8	1550	1	9	2900	3350
20	5	PROSTAR 205	OP	SKI	FBG	SV	IB	275-328		7	3	2660	1	10	13700	16100
20	5	SAMMY DUVAL 205	OP	SKI	FBG	SV	IB	275-328		7	3	2660	1	10	13700	16100
22	6	MARISTAR 225 VRS	OP	RNBT	FBG	SV	VD	275-328		8		3000	1	10	17400	20400
		1995 BOATS														
19	5	PROSTAR 190	OP	SKI	FBG	SV	IB	275-310		7	2	2450	1	10	11000	12900
19	5	SAMMY DUVAL SERIES	OP	SKI	FBG	SV	IB	275-310		7	2	2450	1	10	11900	13900
19	11	MARISTAR 200	OP	RNBT	FBG	SV	IB	275-310		7	10	2700	1	10	13000	15200
19	11	MARISTAR 200 VRS	OP	RNBT	FBG	SV	IB	275-310		7	10	2700	1	10	13900	16100
20	1	BAREFOOT 200	OP	SKI	FBG	SV	OB			6	8		1	9	3350	3900
20	5	PROSTAR 205	OP	SKI	FBG	SV	IB	275-310		7	1	2650	1	10	12700	14800
22	6	MARISTAR 225	OP	RNBT	FBG	SV	IB	275-310		8		3000	1	10	15900	18500
22	6	MARISTAR 225 VRS	OP	RNBT	FBG	SV	IB	275-310		8		3000	1	10	17000	19600
		1994 BOATS														
19	5	PROSTAR 190	OP	SKI	FBG	SV	IB	250	CHEV	7	1	2450	1	10	10700	12200
19	11	MARISTAR 200	OP	RNBT	FBG	SV	IB	250	CHEV	7	10	2700	1	10	11800	13400
19	11	MARISTAR 200 CB	OP	RNBT	FBG	SV	IB	250	CHEV	7	10	2700	1	10	11500	13100
20	1	BAREFOOT 200	OP	SKI	FBG	SV	OB			6	8	1550	2	2	2550	3000
20	5	PROSPORT 205	OP	RNBT	FBG	SV	IB	250	CHEV	7	1	2650	1	10	12300	14000
20	5	PROSTAR 205	OP	RNBT	FBG	SV	IB	250	CHEV	7	1	2550	1	10	12000	13700
22	6	MARISTAR 225	OP	RNBT	FBG	SV	IB	250	CHEV	8		3000	1	10	14300	16200
22	6	MARISTAR 225 VRS	OP	RNBT	FBG	SV	IB	250	CHEV	8		3000	1	10	15000	17100
		1993 BOATS														
19	5	PROSTAR 190	OP	SKI	FBG	SV	IB	250	CHEV	7	1	2450	1	10	10200	11600
		IB 250 FORD 10200 11600, IB 285-330 10300 12200, IB 400 CHEV 11900 13500														
20	1	BAREFOOT 200	OP	SKI	FBG	SV	OB			6	8	1550	2	2	2400	2800
20	5	PROSPORT 205	OP	RNBT	FBG	SV	IB	250-330		7	1	2600	1	10	11400	13600
20	5	PROSPORT 205	OP	RNBT	FBG	SV	IB	400	CHEV	7	1	2600	1	10	13000	14800
20	5	PROSTAR 205	OP	RNBT	FBG	SV	IB	250	CHEV	7	1	2600	1	10	11400	12900
		IB 250 FORD 11500 13100, IB 285 CHEV 10800 12300, IB 285-400 12000 14800														
22	6	MARISTAR 225	OP	RNBT	FBG	SV	IB	250-330		7	10	3000	2		14600	17300
22	6	MARISTAR 225	OP	RNBT	FBG	SV	IB	400	CHEV	7	10	3000	2		16300	18500
		1992 BOATS														
19	5	PROSTAR 190	OP	SKI	FBG	SV	IB	240	INDM	7	1	2400	1	7	9450	10800
20	2	BAREFOOT 200	OP	SKI	FBG	SV	OB			6	8	1550	2	2	2300	2650
20	5	PROSTAR 205	OP	RNBT	FBG	SV	IB	240	INDM						11200	12700
21		MARISTAR 210 S	OP	RNBT	FBG	SV	IB	240	INDM	7	6	3100	1	7	12800	14500
21		MARISTAR 210 W/T	OP	RNBT	FBG	SV	IB	240	INDM	7	6	3200	1	7	13100	14800
24	10	MARISTAR 240	OP	RNBT	FBG	SV	IB	240	INDM	8		3500	1	10	17300	19700
24	10	MARISTAR 240 SC	OP	RNBT	FBG	SV	IB	240	INDM	8		3500	1	10	18200	20200
		1991 BOATS														
19		PROSTAR 190	OP	SKI	FBG	SV	IB	240	INDM	7	1	2400	1	7	8800	10000
19		TRI-STAR 190	OP	RNBT	FBG	SV	IB	240	INDM	7	6	2660		11	9900	11300
20	2	BAREFOOT 200	OP	SKI	FBG	SV	OB			6	8	1550	2	2	2150	2500
20	2	PROSTAR 200	OP	SKI	FBG	SV	OB			6	8	1395	2	2	1950	2300
21		MARISTAR 210 S	OP	RNBT	FBG	SV	IB	240	INDM	7	6	3100	1	7	12200	13800
21		MARISTAR 210 W/T	OP	RNBT	FBG	SV	IB	240	INDM	7	6	3200	1	7	12400	14100
22		TRI-STAR 220	OP	RNBT	FBG	SV	IB	240	INDM	8		2700		11	12100	13800
24	10	MARISTAR 240	OP	RNBT	FBG	SV	IB	240	INDM	8		3500	1	10	16400	18700
24	10	MARISTAR 240 SC	OP	RNBT	FBG	SV	IB	240	INDM	8		3500	1	10	16900	19200
		1990 BOATS														
19		PROSTAR 190	OP	SKI	FBG	SV	IB	240	INDM	6	8	2200	1	7	7650	8800
19		TRI-STAR 190	OP	RNBT	FBG	SV	IB	240	INDM	7	6	2400	1	10	9000	10200
20	2	PROSTAR 200	OP	SKI	FBG	SV	OB			6	8	1250	2	2	1750	2050
22		TRI-STAR 220	OP	RNBT	FBG	SV	IB	240	INDM	8		2700	1	10	11500	13100
24	10	MARISTAR 240	OP	RNBT	FBG	SV	IB	351	INDM	8		3500	2		16800	19100

LOA FT	LOA IN	NAME AND/ OR MODEL	TOP/ RIG	BOAT TYPE	-HULL- MTL	-HULL- TP	ENGINE TP	ENGINE # HP	ENGINE MFG	BEAM FT	BEAM IN	WGT LBS	DRAFT FT	DRAFT IN	RETAIL LOW	RETAIL HIGH
		1990 BOATS														
24	10	MARISTAR 240 SC	OP	RNBT	FBG	SV	IB	351	INDM	8		3500	2		17200	19600
		1989 BOATS														
19		PROSTAR 190	OP	SKI	FBG	SV	IB	240	INDM	6	8	2200	1	7	7300	8350
19		TRI-STAR 190	OP	RNBT	FBG	SV	IB	240	INDM	7	6	2400	1	10	8450	9700
20	2	PROSTAR 200	OP	SKI	FBG	SV	OB			6	8	1250	2	2	1650	2000
22		TRI-STAR 220	OP	RNBT	FBG	SV	IB	240	INDM	8		2700	1	10	11000	12500
24	10	MARISTAR 240	OP	RNBT	FBG	SV	IB	425	INDM	8		3500	2		17400	19800
		1988 BOATS														
19		PROSTAR 190	OP	SKI	FBG	SV	IB	240	INDM	6	8	2200	1	7	6950	7950
19		TRI-STAR 190	OP	RNBT	FBG	SV	IB	240	INDM	7	6	2400	1	10	8050	9250
20	2	PROSTAR 200	OP	SKI	FBG	SV	OB			6	8	1250	2	2	1550	1850
22		TRI-STAR 220	OP	RNBT	FBG	SV	IB	240	INDM	8		2700	1	10	10500	11900
		1987 BOATS														
19		PROSTAR 190	OP	SKI	FBG	SV	IB	240	INDM	6	8	2200	1	7	6600	7600
19		TRI-STAR 190	OP	RNBT	FBG	SV	IB	240	INDM	7	6	2400	1	10	7700	8800
20	2	PROSTAR 200	OP	SKI	FBG	SV	OB			6	8	1250	2	2	1550	1800
22		TRI-STAR 220	OP	RNBT	FBG	SV	IB	240	INDM	8		2700	1	10	10000	11400
		1986 BOATS														
19		TOURNAMENT SKIER	OP	SKI	FBG	SV	IB	255		6	8	2200	1	9	6400	7350
22		TRISTAR	OP	RNBT	FBG	SV	IB	255		8		2700	1	10	9600	10900
		1985 BOATS														
19		TOURNAMENT SKIER DLX	OP	SKI	FBG	SV	IB	250		6	9	2200	1	7	6150	7050
19		TOURNAMENT SKIER DLX	OP	SKI	FBG	SV	IB	350		6	9	2200	1	7	6700	7700
		1984 BOATS														
19		TOURNAMENT SKIER DLX	OP	SKI	FBG	SV	IB	250-255		6	9	2200	1	7	5850	6750
19		TOURNAMENT SKIER DLX	OP	SKI	FBG	SV	IB	350		6	9	2200	1	7	6400	7350

....For earlier years, see the BUC Used Boat Price Guide, Volume 3

MASTERCRAFTERS CAJUN BOATS

WEST MONROE LA 71291-52 COAST GUARD MFG ID- MBV See inside cover to adjust price for area
FORMERLY MASTERCRAFTERS CORP

For more recent years, see the BUC Used Boat Price Guide, Volume 1

LOA FT	LOA IN	NAME AND/ OR MODEL	TOP/ RIG	BOAT TYPE	-HULL- MTL	-HULL- TP	ENGINE TP	ENGINE # HP	ENGINE MFG	BEAM FT	BEAM IN	WGT LBS	DRAFT FT	DRAFT IN	RETAIL LOW	RETAIL HIGH
		1996 BOATS														
16	4	RAGIN CAJUN 164	OP	BASS	FBG	SV	OB			6	9	1030			2850	3300
16	4	RAGIN CAJUN 164 DC	OP	BASS	FBG	SV	OB			6	9	1050			2900	3400
16	6	FISHMASTER 1550	OP	UTL	FBG	FL	OB			6	2	900			2350	2700
16	10	FISHMASTER 1650	OP	CTRCN	FBG	FL	OB			7	3	1200			3150	3650
17		ESPIRIT 170 SE	OP	BASS	FBG	SV	OB			7		1200			3150	3700
17		ESPIRIT 1700	OP	BASS	FBG	SV	OB			7		1200			3450	4000
17	4	RAGIN CAJUN 171	OP	BASS	FBG	SV	OB			7	5	1150			3200	3750
17	11	RAGIN CAJUN 180	OP	BASS	FBG	SV	OB			7	5	1225			3450	4000
17	11	RAGIN CAJUN 180 DC	OP	BASS	FBG	SV	OB			7	5	1245			3500	4050
18		ESPIRIT 180 SE	OP	BASS	FBG	SV	OB			7	6	1400			3650	4250
18		ESPIRIT 1800	OP	BASS	FBG	SV	OB			7	6	1400			3950	4600
18	8	FISHMASTER 1850	OP	CTRCN	FBG	FL	OB			7	8	1650			4150	4800
18	8	RAGIN CAJUN 185	OP	BASS	FBG	SV	OB			7	5	1390			3850	4500
18	8	RAGIN CAJUN 185 DC	OP	BASS	FBG	SV	OB			7	5	1410			3900	4550
18	9	FISHMASTER 1850 V	OP	CTRCN	FBG	SV	OB			7	8	1600			4100	4750
19		RAGIN CAJUN 190	OP	BASS	FBG	SV	OB			7	2	1300			3700	4350
19		RAGIN CAJUN 190 DC	OP	BASS	FBG	SV	OB			7	2	1320			3750	4350
20	2	ESPIRIT 2000	OP	BASS	FBG	SV	OB			7	9	1500			4200	4900
20	8	RAGIN CAJUN 210	OP	BASS	FBG	SV	OB			7	8	1450			4200	4900
20	8	RAGIN CAJUN 210 DC	OP	BASS	FBG	SV	OB			7	8	1470			4250	4950
21	9	FISHMASTER 2100	OP	CTRCN	FBG	FL	OB			7	8	1850			2250	2600
21	9	FISHMASTER 2100 V	OP	CTRCN	FBG	SV	OB			7	8	1850			2250	2650
24	2	FISHMASTER 2300	OP	CTRCN	FBG	FL	OB			7	10	2500			7400	8550
		1995 BOATS														
16	6	FISHMASTER 1650	OP	CTRCN	FBG	FL	OB			7	2	1050			2350	2750
16	6	PRO SPORT 160	OP	BASS	FBG	SV	OB			6	10	750			1700	2000
17		ADVENTURE 170	OP	BASS	FBG	KL	OB			6	8	850			**	**
17		ESPIRIT 1700	OP	BASS	FBG	SV	OB			6	8	750			1700	2050
17	1	PRO ADVENTURE 171	OP	BASS	FBG	SV	OB			7	2	900			2050	2450
17	9	RAGIN CAJUN X DC	OP	BASS	FBG	SV	OB			7	7	1250			2800	3250
17	9	RAGIN CAJUN X SC	OP	BASS	FBG	SV	OB			7	7	900			2100	2500
18		ADVENTURE 180	OP	BASS	FBG	KL	OB			6	8	1100			**	**
18		ANGLER 1800	OP	BASS	FBG	DV	OB			7	8	1400			3100	3600
18		ESPIRIT 1800	OP	BASS	FBG	SV	OB			6	8	900			2100	2500
18	6	FISHMASTER 1850	OP	CTRCN	FBG	FL	OB			7	10	1250			2750	3200
18	6	FISHMASTER 1850 V	OP	CTRCN	FBG	DV	OB			7	10	1600			3750	4400
18	6	RAGIN CAJUN XL DC	OP	BASS	FBG	SV	OB			7	2	1315			2950	3400
18	6	RAGIN CAJUN XL SC	OP	BASS	FBG	SV	OB			7	4	1000			2400	2750
19		ESPIRIT 1900	OP	BASS	FBG	SV	OB			7	4	1175			2700	3150
20		ESPRIT 2000	OP	BASS	FBG	SV	OB			7	10	1375			2750	3200
20		RAGIN CAJUN XXL	OP	BASS	FBG	SV	OB			7	7	1250			2600	3000
20		RAGIN CAJUN XXL DC	OP	BASS	FBG	SV	OB			7	7	1420			3750	4350
21		FISHMASTER 2100	OP	CTRCN	FBG	FL	OB			8		1350			1600	1900
21		FISHMASTER 2100 V	OP	CTRCN	FBG	DV	OB			8		1885			2050	2450
23		FISHMASTER 2300	OP	CTRCN	FBG	FL	OB			8		1885			2250	2600
		1994 BOATS														
16	6	FISHMASTER 1650	OP	CTRCN	FBG	FL	OB			7	2	1050			2250	2600
16	6	PRO SPORT 160	OP	BASS	FBG	SV	OB			6	10	750			1600	1900
17		ADVENTURE 170	OP	BASS	FBG	SV	OB			6	8	850			1850	2200
17		ESPIRIT 1700	OP	BASS	FBG	SV	OB			6	8	750			1600	1900
17	1	RAGIN CAJUN MVP	OP	BASS	FBG	SV	OB			7	2	900			1950	2300
17	9	RAGIN CAJUN X	OP	BASS	FBG	SV	OB			7	7	900			1950	2350
18		ADVENTURE 180	OP	BASS	FBG	SV	OB			6	8	1100			2400	2800
18		ANGLER 1800	OP	BASS	FBG	DV	OB			7	8	1400			2900	3350
18		ESPIRIT 1800	OP	BASS	FBG	SV	OB			6	8	900			1950	2350
18	6	FISHMASTER 1850	OP	CTRCN	FBG	FL	OB			7	10	1250			2650	3050
18	6	RAGIN CAJUN XL	OP	BASS	FBG	SV	OB			7	4	1000			2250	2600
19		ESPIRIT 1900	OP	BASS	FBG	SV	OB			7	4	1175			2600	3000
19		FISHMASTER 1900	OP	CTRCN	FBG	DV	OB			7	2	1150			2500	2900
19	6	FISHMASTER 1950	OP	CTRCN	FBG	FL	OB			8		1400			2850	3350
20		ANGLER 2000	OP	BASS	FBG	SV	OB			7	10	1400			2650	3050
20		ESPRIT 2000	OP	BASS	FBG	SV	OB			7	10	1375			2600	3000
20		RAGIN CAJUN XXL	OP	BASS	FBG	SV	OB			7	7	1250			2450	2850
21		ANGLER 2100	OP	BASS	FBG	SV	OB			8		1350			1550	1850
21		FISHMASTER 2100	OP	CTRCN	FBG	FL	OB			8		1350			1500	1800
		1993 BOATS														
16	1	162 ZS	OP	BASS	FBG	SV	OB			6	5	650			1200	1450
16	1	162 ZW	OP	BASS	FBG	SV	OB			6	5	650			1350	1600
16	6	FISHMASTER 1650	OP	CTRCN	FBG	FL	OB			7	2	1050			2050	2400
16	6	PRO SPORT 168	OP	BASS	FBG	SV	OB			7	1	750			1500	1750
16	8	165 ZW	OP	BASS	FBG	SV	OB			6	8	750			1500	1800
17		ESPIRIT 1700	OP	BASS	FBG	SV	OB			6	8	750			1500	1800
17	1	RAGIN CAJUN MVP	OP	BASS	FBG	SV	OB			7	2	900			1800	2150
17	1	RAGIN CAJUN X	OP	BASS	FBG	SV	OB			7	2	900			1800	2150
17	4	174 ZW	OP	BASS	FBG	SV	OB			6	8	750			1500	1800
17	6	178 ZW	OP	BASS	FBG	SV	OB			7	4	900			1850	2200
17	6	PRO SPORT 178	OP	BASS	FBG	SV	OB			7	4	800			1600	1900
18		ANGLER	OP	BASS	FBG	DV	OB			7	8	1400			2700	3150
18		ANGLER SPORT	OP	BASS	FBG	DV	OB			7	8	1400			2750	3200
18		ESPIRIT 1800	OP	BASS	FBG	SV	OB			6	8	900			1850	2200
18	6	FISHMASTER 1850	OP	CTRCN	FBG	FL	OB			7	10	1250			2500	2900
18	6	RAGIN CAJUN XL	OP	BASS	FBG	SV	OB			7	4	1000			2050	2450
19		ESPIRIT 1900	OP	BASS	FBG	SV	OB			7	4	1175			2450	2800
19		FISHMASTER 1900	OP	CTRCN	FBG	DV	OB			7	2	1150			2350	2750
19	6	PRO SPORT 190	OP	BASS	FBG	SV	OB			7	10	1350			2700	3100
20		ESPIRIT 2000	OP	BASS	FBG	SV	OB			7	10	1375			2500	2900
21		FISHMASTER 2100	OP	CTRCN	FBG	FL	OB			8		1350			1400	1700
		1992 BOATS														
16		FISHMASTER 1550	OP	OPFSH	FBG	TR	OB			6		650			1350	1600
16	1	162RB	OP	RNBT	AL	SV	OB			6	5	800			1700	2050
16	1	162ZS	OP	RNBT	AL	SV	OB			6	5	800			1800	2150
16	1	162ZW	OP	RNBT	AL	SV	OB			6	5	800			1950	2350
16	6	FISHMASTER 1650	OP	BASS	FBG	FL	OB			7	2	1050			1950	2300
16	6	PRO SPORT 168	OP	FSH	AL	SV	OB			7	1	750			1700	2050
17	1	RAGIN CAJUN	OP	FSH	AL	SV	OB			7	6	900			2100	2450
17	1	RAGIN CAJUN SPORT	OP	RNBT	AL	SV	OB			7	6	900			2150	2500
17	4	174ZW	OP	RNBT	AL	DV	OB			6	8	850			2000	2400
17	6	ESPIRIT 1750	OP	RNBT	AL	DV	OB			7	4	1100			2550	2950
17	6	PRO SPORT 178	OP	FSH	AL	SV	OB			7	4	1100			2500	2900
17	8	TOURNAMENT 1780	OP	BASS	FBG	SV	OB			7	4	1100			2550	2950
18		PT 1800	OP	BASS	FBG	SV	OB			7	4	1100			2100	2500
18	6	ESPIRIT 1850	OP	RNBT	AL	DV	OB			7	4	1200			2800	3250
18	6	FISHMASTER 1850	OP	OPFSH	FBG	TR	OB			7	10	1200			2500	2900
19		FISHMASTER 1900	OP	BASS	FBG	SV	OB			7	2	1150			2250	2600
19	6	ESPIRIT 1950	OP	RNBT	AL	SV	IO	200		7	10	1500			4450	5150
19	6	PRO SPORT 190	OP	BASS	FBG	SV	OB			7	10	1300			3050	3550
19	6	TOURNAMENT 1900	OP	BASS	FBG	SV	OB			7	10	1350			3150	3650
21		FISHMASTER 2100	OP	BASS	FBG	FL	OB			7	8	1450			1500	1800
		1991 BOATS														
16		FISHMASTER 1550	OP	OPFSH	FBG	TR	OB			6		650			1250	1500
16	1	162RB	OP	RNBT	AL	SV	OB			6	5	800			1650	1950
16	1	162ZS	OP	RNBT	AL	SV	OB			6	5	800			1750	2050

LOA FT	LOA IN	NAME AND/ OR MODEL	TOP/ RIG	BOAT TYPE	HULL MTL	HULL TP	ENGINE TP	ENGINE # HP	ENGINE MFG	BEAM FT	BEAM IN	WGT LBS	DRAFT FT	DRAFT IN	RETAIL LOW	RETAIL HIGH
		1991 BOATS														
16	1	162ZW	OP	RNBT	AL	SV	OB			6	5	800			1900	2250
16	6	PRO SPORT 168	OP	FSH	AL	SV	OB			7	1	750			1650	1950
17	1	RAGIN CAJUN	OP	RNBT	AL	SV	OB			7	6	900			2200	2550
17	1	RAGIN CAJUN SPORT	OP	RNBT	AL	SV	OB			7	6	900			1900	2250
17	4	174ZW	OP	RNBT	AL	DV	OB			6	8	850			1900	2300
17	6	ESPIRIT 1750	OP	RNBT	AL	DV	OB			7	4	1100			2450	2850
17	6	PRO SPORT 178	OP	FSH	AL	SV	OB			7	4	1100			2400	2800
17	8	TOURNAMENT 1780	OP	BASS	FBG	SV	OB			7	4	1100			2450	2850
18	6	ESPIRIT 1850	OP	RNBT	AL	DV	OB			7	4	1200			2650	3100
18	6	FISHMASTER 1850	OP	OPFSH	FBG	TR	OB			7	10	1200			2350	2750
19	6	ESPIRIT 1950	OP	FSH	AL	SV	IO	230		7	10	2300			5350	6150
19	6	ESPIRIT 1950	OP	RNBT	AL	SV	IO	200		7	10	1500			4150	4800
19	6	GRAND PRIX TX	OP	BASS	FBG	SV	OB			7	10	1300			3350	3900
19	6	PRO SPORT 190	OP	BASS	FBG	SV	OB			7	10	1300			2450	2850
19	6	TOURNAMENT 1900	OP	BASS	FBG	SV	OB			7	10	1350			3000	3450
19	6	TOURNAMENT GRAND PRX	OP	FSH	AL	SV	OB			7	10	1500			3200	3750
20		PONTOON 2000	OP	FSH	FBG	PN	OB			8		1300			2600	3050
24		PONTOON 2400	OP	FSH	FBG	PN	OB			8		1450			1450	1700
		1990 BOATS														
16		PRO SPORT 160	OP	FSH	AL	SV	OB			6		650			1350	1600
16	1	162RB	OP	RNBT	AL	SV	OB			6	5	800			1550	1850
16	1	162ZD	OP	FSH	AL	SV	OB			6	5	800			1650	1950
16	1	162ZS	OP	RNBT	AL	SV	OB			6	5	800			1650	2000
16	1	162ZW	OP	RNBT	AL	DV	OB			6	5	800			1800	2150
16	6	PRO SPORT 168	OP	FSH	AL	SV	OB			7	1	750			1550	1850
17	1	RAGIN CAJUN COMBO	OP	RNBT	AL	SV	OB			7	6	900			1950	2300
17	1	RAGIN CAJUN PRO	OP	RNBT	AL	SV	OB			7	6	900			1850	2200
17	1	RAGIN CAJUN SPORT	OP	RNBT	AL	SV	OB			7	6	900			2000	2400
17	4	174ZW	OP	RNBT	AL	DV	OB			6	8	850			1850	2200
17	6	ESPIRIT 1750	OP	RNBT	AL	DV	OB			7	4	1100			2350	2750
17	6	PRO SPORT 178	OP	FSH	AL	SV	OB			7	4	1100			2300	2650
18	6	ELIAS EDITION	OP	FSH	AL	SV	OB			7	4	1200			2550	3000
18	6	ESPIRIT 1850	OP	RNBT	AL	DV	OB			7	4	1200			2550	2950
18	6	FISHING MACHINE 1850	OP	FSH	AL	SV	OB			7	4	1200			2400	2750
18	6	PRO STAFF 1850	OP	FSH	AL	SV	OB			7	4	1200			2550	3000
18	6	RICKY GREEN	OP	FSH	AL	SV	OB			7	4	1200			2500	2900
19	6	1950 FISHIN MACHINE	OP	FSH	AL	SV	OB			7	10	1500			3050	3550
19	6	ESPIRIT 1950	OP	FSH	AL	SV	IO	230		7	10	2300			5000	5750
19	6	ESPIRIT 1950	OP	RNBT	AL	SV	OB			7	10	1500			3150	3650
19	6	ESPIRIT GRAND PRIX	OP	RNBT	AL	SV	IO	200		7	10	1500			3900	4550
19	6	TOURNAMENT GRAND PRX	OP	FSH	AL	SV	OB			7	10	1500			3050	3550
		1986 BOATS														
16	1	ESPIRIT 165	OP	BASS	FBG	SV	OB			6	8	750			1400	1650
16	1	ESPIRIT ENCORE	OP	BASS	FBG	SV	OB			6	8	750			1200	1450
16	4	MAVERICK I	OP	BASS	FBG	SV	OB			7	1	750			1250	1500
16	4	MAVERICK II	OP	BASS	FBG	SV	OB			7	1	750			1350	1600
16	4	PURSUIT I	OP	BASS	FBG	SV	OB			7	1				1050	1250
16	4	PURSUIT II	OP	BASS	FBG	SV	OB			7	1				1100	1300
16	4	PURSUIT III	OP	BASS	FBG	SV	OB			7	1				1100	1300
17	1	RAGIN-CAJUN I	OP	BASS	FBG	SV	OB			7	2	950			1600	1950
17	1	RAGIN-CAJUN II	OP	BASS	FBG	SV	OB			7	2				1250	1500
17	6	DEUX-VOIE	OP	BASS	FBG	SV	OB			6	11				1600	1900
17	6	ESPIRIT 175	OP	BASS	FBG	SV	OB			7	3	1100			1850	2200
17	6	FISHING-MACHINE 175D	OP	BASS	FBG	SV	OB			7	4	1100			1950	2300
17	6	FISHING-MACHINE 175S	OP	BASS	FBG	SV	OB			7	4	1100			1800	2100
18	5	ESPIRIT 185	OP	BASS	FBG	SV	OB			7	4	1100			1900	2250
18	5	FISHING-MACHINE 185	OP	BASS	FBG	SV	OB			7	4				1600	1900
18	5	RICKY-GREEN MACHINE	OP	BASS	FBG	SV	OB			7	4	1150			1950	2350
20	1	GRANDE-BATEAU	OP	BASS	FBG	SV	OB			7	6	1200			1950	2350
		1985 BOATS														
16	1	ENCORE COMBO	OP	BASS	FBG	SV	OB			6	8				1050	1300
16	1	ENCORE II	OP	BASS	FBG	SV	OB			6	8				990	1200
16	4	PURSUIT I	OP	BASS	FBG	SV	OB			7	1				1050	1250
16	4	PURSUIT II	OP	BASS	FBG	SV	OB			7	1				1150	1350
16	4	PURSUIT III	OP	BASS	FBG	SV	OB			7	1				1100	1300
16	4	PURSUIT ONE SPECIAL	OP	BASS	FBG	SV	OB			7	1				880	1050
16	8	ESPIRIT	OP	BASS	FBG	SV	OB			7	2	950			1550	1850
17	1	RAGIN-CAJUN I	OP	BASS	FBG	SV	OB			7	2	950			1550	1850
17	1	RAGIN-CAJUN II	OP	BASS	FBG	SV	OB			7	2				1250	1450
17	1	RAGIN-CAJUN III	OP	BASS	FBG	SV	OB			7	2				1200	1400
17	6	DEUX-VOIE	OP	BASS	FBG	SV	OB			6	11				1500	1800
18	5	FISHING-MACHINE II	OP	BASS	FBG	SV	OB			7	4				1550	1850
18	5	FISHING-MACHINE III	OP	BASS	FBG	SV	OB			7	4				1500	1800
18	5	RICKY-GREEN MACHINE	OP	BASS	FBG	SV	OB			7	4	1150			1850	2250
20	1	GRANDE-BATEAU II	OP	BASS	FBG	SV	OB			7	6	1200			1900	2300
20	1	GRANDE-BATEAU III	OP	BASS	FBG	SV	OB			7	6	1200			1800	2150
		1984 BOATS														
16	8	DEUX-VOIE I	OP	BASS	FBG	SV	OB			6	8	900			1400	1700
16	8	ESPIRIT	OP	BASS	FBG		OB			7	2	950			1500	1750
16	8	RAGIN-CAJUN	OP	BASS	FBG	DV	OB			7	2	950			1450	1700
16	8	SCRAMBLER I	OP	BASS	FBG	SV	OB			6	4	850		5	1300	1550
16	8	SCRAMBLER II	OP	BASS	FBG	SV	OB			6	4	850		5	1400	1650
16	8	SCRAMBLER III	OP	BASS	FBG	SV	OB			6	4	850		5	1300	1550
17	6	BRUTE I	OP	BASS	FBG	DV	OB			6	11	1000		7	1500	1800
17	6	BRUTE II	OP	BASS	FBG	DV	OB			6	11	1000		7	1550	1850
17	6	BRUTE III	OP	BASS	FBG	DV	OB			6	11	1000			1550	1800
17	6	DEUX-VOIE II	OP	BASS	FBG	DV	OB			6	11	1000		7	1550	1800
18	5	RICKY-GREEN MACHINE	OP	BASS	FBG		OB			7	4	1150			1750	2100
20	1	GRANDE-BATEAU COMB	OP	BASS	FBG		OB			7	6	1200			1750	2050
20	1	GRANDE-BATEAU I	OP	BASS	FBG	DV	OB			7	2	1200			1750	2100
20	1	GRANDE-BATEAU WEST	OP	BASS	FBG		OB			7	6	1200			1800	2150

....For earlier years, see the BUC Used Boat Price Guide, Volume 3

MATRIX MARINE

HUNGARIAN MARINE ENGINEERING
VENTURA CA 93001 COAST GUARD MFG ID- HUK

See inside cover to adjust price for area

LOA FT	LOA IN	NAME AND/ OR MODEL	TOP/ RIG	BOAT TYPE	HULL MTL	HULL TP	ENGINE TP	ENGINE # HP	ENGINE MFG	BEAM FT	BEAM IN	WGT LBS	DRAFT FT	DRAFT IN	RETAIL LOW	RETAIL HIGH
		1987 BOATS														
24	3	ALLEGRA 24	CUT	SA/CR	F/S	KL	IB	9D	YAN	8	2	6500	3	9	20900	23200
27		MATRIX 27	SLP	SA/RC	F/S	KL	SD	9D	YAN	8	5	6400	3	1	21100	23500
31	5	MOBIUS 31	SLP	SA/CR	F/S	KL	IB	23D	YAN	10	9	13500	5		43500	48400
38	5	TORUS 38	SLP	SA/RC	F/S	KL	IB	30D	YAN	12	4	15500	5	3	56700	62300
41	2	MANTISSA 41	SLP	SA/RC	F/S	KL	IB	44D	YAN	12		17750	5		72500	79600
44		MATRIX 44	SLP	SA/RC	F/S	KL	IB	60D	YAN	13		24000	6		99200	109000
		1986 BOATS														
24	3	ALLEGRA 24	CUT	SA/CR	F/S	KL	IB	9D	YAN	8		6500	3	9	19600	21800
27		MATRIX 27	SLP	SA/RC	F/S	KL	SD	9D	YAN	8		6400	3	1	19900	22100
31	5	MOBIUS 31	SLP	SA/CR	F/S	KL	IB	23D	YAN	10	9	13500	5		40900	45500
38	5	TORUS 38	SLP	SA/RC	F/S	KL	IB	30D	YAN	12	4	15500	5	3	53300	58600
41	2	MANTISSA 41	SLP	SA/RC	F/S	KL	IB	44D	YAN	12		17750	5		68200	74900
42	11	MATRIX 42/43	CUT	SA/CR	F/S	KL	IB	44D	YAN	13		31500	5	8	102500	112500
44		MATRIX 44	SLP	SA/RC	F/S	KL	IB	60D	YAN	13		24000	6		93300	102500
55		MATRIX 55	CUT	SA/CR	F/S	KL	IB	60D	YAN	15	6	43000	6	6	213000	234000
		1985 BOATS														
24		ALLEGRA 24	CUT	SA/CR	F/S	KL	IB	9D	YAN	8		6500	3	6	18600	20700
27		MATRIX 27	SLP	SA/RC	F/S	KL	SD	9D	YAN	8		6400	3	5	18900	21000
31	5	MOBIUS 31	SLP	SA/CR	F/S	KL	IB	23D	YAN	10	9	13500	5		38500	42800
38	5	TORUS 38	SLP	SA/RC	F/S	KL	IB	30D	YAN	12	4	15500	5	3	50200	55100
41	2	MANTISSA 41	SLP	SA/RC	F/S	KL	IB	44D	YAN	12		17750	5		64100	70500
44		MATRIX 44	SLP	SA/RC	F/S	KL	IB	60D	YAN	13		24000	6		87700	96400

MAURELL PRODUCTS INC

OWOSSO MI 48867 COAST GUARD MFG ID- MAU See inside cover to adjust price for area

For more recent years, see the BUC Used Boat Price Guide, Volume 1

LOA FT	LOA IN	NAME AND/ OR MODEL	TOP/ RIG	BOAT TYPE	HULL MTL	HULL TP	ENGINE TP	ENGINE # HP	ENGINE MFG	BEAM FT	BEAM IN	WGT LBS	DRAFT FT	DRAFT IN	RETAIL LOW	RETAIL HIGH
		1990 BOATS														
35		3514	HT	HB	AL	PN	OB					5000			10000	11400
41		4114 DELUXE	HT	HB	AL	PN	OB					7000			10700	12100
41		4114 STANDARD	HT	HB	AL	PN	OB					7000			9600	10900
		1989 BOATS														
29		MODEL 3514		HB	AL	PN	OB					5000			9800	11100
29		MODEL 4114 DELUXE		HB	AL	PN	OB					7000			15000	17000
29		MODEL 4114 STANDARD		HB	AL	PN	OB					7000			13400	15200
		1988 BOATS														
38		DELUXE 4114		HB	AL	PN	OB			14		7000			12300	14000
38		STANDARD 4114		HB	AL	PN	OB			14		7000			11200	12700
		1987 BOATS														
38		4114 DELUXE		HB	AL	PN	OB			10					14500	16500
38		STANDARD 4114		HB	AL	PN	OB			10					13100	14900
		1986 BOATS														
35		3510	HT	HB	AL	PN	OB			10		7200			13300	15200
35		3514 PLAN A	HT	HB	AL	PN	OB			12		7600			13400	15200
35		3514 PLAN B	HT	HB	AL	PN	OB			12		7600			14600	16600

CONTINUED ON NEXT PAGE

LOA FT IN	NAME AND/ OR MODEL	TOP/ RIG	BOAT TYPE	HULL MTL TP TP	# HP	ENGINE MFG	BEAM FT IN	WGT LBS	DRAFT FT IN	RETAIL LOW	RETAIL HIGH
			1985 BOATS								
35	3510	HT	HB	AL PN	OB		10	7200		13000	14800
35	3514	HT	HB	AL PN	OB		12	7600		13700	15600
			1984 BOATS								
35	3510	HT	HB	AL PN	OB		10	7200		12700	14500
35	3514	HT	HB	AL PN	OB		12	7600		13400	15200

....For earlier years, see the BUC Used Boat Price Guide, Volume 3

MAVERICK BOAT COMPANY INC
FT PIERCE FL 34946   COAST GUARD MFG ID- MVI See inside cover to adjust price for area

For more recent years, see the BUC Used Boat Price Guide, Volume 1

LOA FT IN	NAME AND/ OR MODEL	TOP/ RIG	BOAT TYPE	HULL MTL TP TP	# HP	ENGINE MFG	BEAM FT IN	WGT LBS	DRAFT FT IN	RETAIL LOW	RETAIL HIGH
			1996 BOATS								
16 5	MIRAGE 16	OP	OPFSH	F/S SV	OB		6 6	675	10	6850	7850
17	MASTER ANGLER	OP	OPFSH	F/S SV	OB		7 6	800	10	8400	9650
18 5	MASTER ANGLER	OP	OPFSH	F/S SV	OB		7 6	900	10	10300	11700
18 5	MASTER ANGLER RL	OP	OPFSH	FBG SV	OB		7 6	950	10	10800	12300
			1995 BOATS								
16 5	MIRAGE 16	OP	OPFSH	F/S SV	OB		6 6	675	10	6450	7450
17	MASTER ANGLER	OP	OPFSH	F/S SV	OB		7 6	800	10	7950	9150
18 5	MASTER ANGLER	OP	OPFSH	F/S SV	OB		7 6	900	10	9750	11100
			1994 BOATS								
16 5	MIRAGE 16	OP	OPFSH	F/S SV	OB		6 6	675	10	6150	7050
17 10	MASTER ANGLER	OP	OPFSH	F/S SV	OB		7 6	800	10	7950	9150
18 5	MASTER ANGLER	OP	OPFSH	F/S SV	OB		7 6	900	10	9200	10500
			1993 BOATS								
16 10	DELUXE 16	OP	OPFSH	F/S SV	OB		7 4	800	9	7100	8150
16 10	MIRAGE 16	OP	OPFSH	F/S SV	OB		6 6	675	10	6000	6900
18 3	DELUXE 18	OP	OPFSH	F/S SV	OB		7 4	875	10	8350	9600
18 5	MASTER ANGLER	OP	OPFSH	F/S SV	OB		7 6	900	10	8650	9950
			1992 BOATS								
16 10	DELUXE 16	OP	OPFSH	F/S SV	OB		7 4	800	9	6700	7750
16 10	MIRAGE 16	OP	OPFSH	F/S SV	OB		6 6	675	10	5750	6600
18 3	DELUXE 18	OP	OPFSH	F/S SV	OB		7 4	875	10	7950	9150
18 5	MASTER ANGLER	OP	OPFSH	F/S SV	OB		7 6	900	10	8250	9500
			1991 BOATS								
16 10	DELUXE 16	OP	OPFSH	F/S SV	OB		7 4	800	9	6450	7400
18 3	DELUXE 18	OP	OPFSH	F/S SV	OB		7 4	875	10	7550	8700
18 5	MASTER ANGLER	OP	OPFSH	F/S SV	OB		7 6	900	10	7850	9050
			1990 BOATS								
16 10	DELUXE 16	OP	OPFSH	F/S SV	OB			800	9	6200	7100
18 3	DELUXE 18	OP	OPFSH	F/S SV	OB			875	10	7250	8350
18 5	MASTER ANGLER	OP	OPFSH	F/S SV	OB			900	10	7500	8600
			1989 BOATS								
16 10	DELUXE 16		OPFSH	FBG SV	OB		7 4	730	10	5500	6350
18 3	DELUXE 18		OPFSH	FBG SV	OB		7 4	875	10	7000	8050
18 5	MASTER ANGLER		OPFSH	FBG SV	OB		7 4	900	10	7200	8300
			1987 BOATS								
16	MAVERICK XL	OP	CTRCN	FBG DV	OB					4400	5050
18 3	MAVERICK DELUXE	OP	CTRCN	FBG DV	OB		7 4	875	10	7300	8400
18 3	MAVERICK XL	OP	CTRCN	FBG DV	OB		7 4	875	10	6000	6900

MAXUM BOATS
DIV OF BRUNSWICK
EVERETT WA 98209   See inside cover to adjust price for area

ALSO MAXUM MARINE

For more recent years, see the BUC Used Boat Price Guide, Volume 1

LOA FT IN	NAME AND/ OR MODEL	TOP/ RIG	BOAT TYPE	HULL MTL TP TP	# HP	ENGINE MFG	BEAM FT IN	WGT LBS	DRAFT FT IN	RETAIL LOW	RETAIL HIGH
			1996 BOATS								
17 3	1700 SR	OP	RNBT	FBG SV	IO	135 MRCR	7 5	1850	2 6	5050	5850
17 3	1700 XR	OP	RNBT	FBG SV	OB		7 5	1574	2 7	3250	3800
18 5	1900 XR	OP	RNBT	FBG SV	OB		8	1885	2 9	3750	4350
18 7	1800 SR2	OP	RNBT	FBG SV	IO	180 MRCR	8	2225	2 9	6350	7300
18 7	1900 SR	OP	RNBT	FBG SV	IO	135-180	8	2215	2 9	6100	7200
18 7	1900 SR2	OP	RNBT	FBG SV	IO	135 MRCR	8	2225	2 9	6900	7150
19 7	2000 SB	OP	RNBT	FBG SV	IO	135-235	7 6	2700	2 10	7200	8550
19 7	2000 SC	OP	CUD	FBG SV	IO	135-235	7 6	2700	2 10	7250	8700
19 7	2000 SR	OP	RNBT	FBG SV	IO	135-235	7 6	2700	2 10	6800	8200
20 8	2100 SC	OP	CUD	FBG SV	IO	180-250	8 3	3150	3 4	9400	11100
20 8	2100 SR	OP	RNBT	FBG SV	IO	180-250	8 6	3035	3 4	8850	10800
20 8	2100 SR	OP	RNBT	FBG SV	IO	300 MRCR	8 6	3350	3 4	10300	11700
20 8	2100 SR2	OP	RNBT	FBG SV	IO	180-250	8 6	3035	3 4	9100	11000
20 8	2100 SR2	OP	RNBT	FBG SV	IO	300 MRCR	8 6	3350	3 4	10500	11900
21 5	210 SS	OP	RNBT	FBG DV	IO	235-250	8	4200	2 5	11400	13100
23 7	2300 SC	OP	CUD	FBG SV	IO	300 MRCR	8 4	4700	3 1	15700	17800
23 7	2300 SC	OP	CUD	FBG SV	IO	235-300	8 4	4700	4 1	14800	17800
23 7	2300 SR	OP	RNBT	FBG SV	IO	235-300	8 4	4700	4 1	13900	15800
25 3	2400 SCR	OP	CR	FBG SV	IO	180-250	8 6	5000	2 11	16200	19300
28 9	2700 SCR	OP	CR	FBG SV	IO	250-300	9 8	6450	3 3	25700	29600
28 9	2700 SCR	OP	CR	FBG SV	IO	240D MRCR	9 8	6550	3 3	29700	33100
28 9	2700 SCR	OP	CR	FBG SV	IO	T250 MRCR	9 8	6450	3 3	29700	33000
34 9	3200 SCR	OP	CR	FBG SV	IO	T250-T300	11	10800	3 8	46800	53500
34 9	3200 SCR	OP	CR	FBG SV	IO	T240D MRCR	11	11500	3 8	55300	60800
43 7	3900 SCR	OP	CR	FBG SV	IO	T300 MRCR	13 6	18000	3 6	74900	82300
	IO T400 MRCR 82200	90300, IO T315D CUM	90900	99900, IO T420D CUM						98500	108000
			1995 BOATS								
17 3	1700 SR	OP	RNBT	FBG SV	IO	135 MRCR	7 5	1850	2 6	4750	5450
17 3	1700 XR	OP	RNBT	FBG SV	OB		7 5	1574	1 11	3100	3600
18 1	1800 SB	OP	RNBT	FBG SV	IO	135-180	7 7	2190	2 9	5650	6450
18 1	1800 SR	OP	RNBT	FBG SV	IO	135-180	7 7	2190	2 9	5300	6500
18 1	1800 SR2	OP	RNBT	FBG SV	IO	135-180	7 7	2190	2 9	5400	6600
18 1	1800 XR	OP	RNBT	FBG SV	OB		7 7	1820	2 9	3450	4050
19 6	2000 SC	OP	CUD	FBG SV	IO	135-205	7 10	2575	2 9	6750	8300
19 6	2000 SR	OP	RNBT	FBG SV	IO	135-180	7 10	2400	2 9	6150	7500
19 6	2000 SR	OP	RNBT	FBG SV	IO	190-205	7 10	2759	2 9	6750	7750
19 6	2000 SR2	OP	RNBT	FBG SV	IO	180-205	7 10	2600	2 9	6650	7950
19 6	2000 SRB	OP	RNBT	FBG SV	IO	180 MRCR	7 10	2577	2 9	6550	7550
20 8	2100 SR	OP	RNBT	FBG SV	IO	180-235	8 6	3035	3 4	8200	10000
20 8	2100 SR	OP	RNBT	FBG SV	IO	300 MRCR	8 6	3350	3 4	9550	10800
20 8	2100 SRB	OP	RNBT	FBG SV	IO	180-235	8 6	3035	3 4	8350	10200
20 8	2100 SRB	OP	RNBT	FBG SV	IO	300 MRCR	8 6	3350	3 4	9700	11000
22 8	2300 SD	OP	RNBT	FBG TH	IO	180-205	8	3450	2 8	9600	11400
23 7	2300 SC	OP	CUD	FBG DV	IO	205-300	8 4	4300	3 1	12600	15700
23 7	2300 SC	OP	CUD	FBG SV	IO	205-235	8	4300	3 1	12800	14700
23 7	2300 SC	OP	CUD	FBG SV	IO	300	8 6	4520	3	14300	16200
23 7	2300 SR	OP	RNBT	FBG DV	IO	205-300	8 4	4100	3 1	11600	14500
23 7	2300 SR	OP	RNBT	FBG SV	IO	205-235	8	4100	3 1	11600	13300
23 7	2300 SR	OP	RNBT	FBG SV	IO	300	8 6	4496	3	13300	15200
25	2400 SCR	OP	CR	FBG SV	IO	180-250	8 6	4600	3 4	14200	17300
28 9	2700 SCR	OP	CR	FBG SV	IO	250-300	9 8	6450	3 3	24000	27800
28 9	2700 SCR	OP	CR	FBG SV	IO	T180 MRCR	9 8	6692	3 3	26100	29000
34 9	3200 SCR	OP	CR	FBG SV	IO	T250-T300	11	10800	3	43200	50200
34 9	3200 SCR	OP	CR	FBG SV	IO	T238D MRCR	11	11500	3	51500	56600
			1994 BOATS								
17 3	1700 SR	OP	RNBT	FBG SV	IO	135	7 5	1850		4450	5100
17 3	1700 XR	OP	RNBT	FBG SV	OB		7 5	1675		3100	3600
18 1	1800 SR	OP	RNBT	FBG SV	IO	135-205	7 7	2190	2 9	5000	6100
18 1	1800 SR2	OP	RNBT	FBG SV	IO	135-205	7 7	2190	2 9	5200	6300
18 1	1800 XR	OP	RNBT	FBG SV	OB		7 7	1855	2 9	3350	3900
19 6	2000 SC	OP	CUD	FBG SV	IO	135-205	7 10	2400		6050	7350
19 6	2000 SC	OP	CUD	FBG SV	IO	230 MRCR	7 10	2668		6650	7650
19 6	2000 SR	OP	RNBT	FBG SV	IO	135-205	7 10	2400		5750	7000
19 6	2000 SR	OP	RNBT	FBG SV	IO	230 MRCR	7 10	2668		6300	7250
19 6	2000 SR2	OP	RNBT	FBG SV	IO	205-230	7 10	2577		6250	7450
19 6	2000 SRB	OP	RNBT	FBG SV	IO	205-230	7 10	2577		6200	7350
22 6	2300 SC	OP	CUD	FBG SV	IO	230-260	8 6	3580		10100	11800
22 6	2300 SR	OP	RNBT	FBG SV	IO	230-260	8 6	3500		9450	10900
22 6	2300 SR	OP	RNBT	FBG SV	IO	330 MRCR	8 6	3732		11100	12600
22 6	2300 SR2	OP	RNBT	FBG SV	IO	260 MRCR	8 6	3775		11100	11500
22 6	2300 SR2	OP	RNBT	FBG SV	IO	330 MRCR	8 6	3993		11500	13100
25	2400 SD	OP	CR	FBG SV	IO	205-260	8 6	4600	3 4	13800	16600
28 9	2700 SD	OP	CR	FBG SV	IO	260-330	9 8	6365	3 3	21200	25200
28 9	2700 SD	OP	CR	FBG SV	IO	T205 MRCR	9 8	6900	3 3	23800	26500
34 9	3200 SD	OP	CR	FBG SV	IO	T260-T330	11	10800	3 4	46800	54400
			1993 BOATS								
16 7	1700 SR	OP	RNBT	FBG SV	OB	130	5 10	1850		3500	4050
16 7	1700 XR	OP	RNBT	FBG SV	OB		5 10	1250		2350	2750
17 4	QUANTUM 1700 XB	OP	BASS	FBG SV	OB	130	7 7	1650		2950	3400
18 1	1800 SR	OP	RNBT	FBG SV	IO	130-205	7 7	1820		3200	3700
18 1	1800 SR	OP	RNBT	FBG SV	IO	205	7 7	2190		4750	5800
18 3	QUANTUM 1800 XB	OP	BASS	FBG SV	OB		7 7	1900		3250	3800
19 6	1900 SC	OP	CUD	FBG SV	IO	130-205	7 10	2400		5650	6900
19 6	1900 SC	OP	CUD	FBG SV	IO	230	7 10	2668		6200	7150

LOA FT IN	NAME AND/ OR MODEL	TOP/ RIG	BOAT TYPE	HULL MTL TP	TP	# HP	ENGINE MFG	BEAM FT IN	WGT LBS	DRAFT FT IN	RETAIL LOW	RETAIL HIGH
			---- 1993 BOATS									
19 6	1900 SR	OP	RNBT	FBG SV	IO	130-205		7 10	2400		5350	6550
19 6	1900 SR	OP	RNBT	FBG SV	IO	230		7 10	2668		5900	6800
19 6	1900 SR2	OP	RNBT	FBG SV	IO	130-205		7 10	2400		5550	6750
19 6	1900 SR2	OP	RNBT	FBG SV	IO	230		7 10	2668		6050	7000
19 6	1900 SRB	OP	RNBT	FBG SV	IO	205-230		7 10	2580		5800	6900
19 6	1900 SSL	OP	RNBT	FBG SV	IO	205-230		7 10	2480		5650	6750
19 6	1900 XR	OP	RNBT	FBG SV	OB			7 10	2100		3700	4250
20 7	QUANTUM 2100 SB	OP	RNBT	FBG SV	IO	130-205		7 4	2280		5650	6850
22 6	2200 SC	OP	CUD	FBG SV	IO	230-260		8 6	3580		9400	11000
22 6	2200 SR	OP	RNBT	FBG SV	IO	230-260		8 6	3500		8800	10300
22 6	2200 SR	OP	RNBT	FBG SV	IO	330		8 6	3732		10300	11700
22 6	2200 SR2	OP	RNBT	FBG SV	IO	260		8 6	3775		9400	10700
22 6	2200 SR2	OP	RNBT	FBG SV	IO	330		8 6	3993		10800	12200
23	2300 SCR	OP	CR	FBG SV	IO	205-260		8 6	4400		11100	13200
26 9	2700 SCR	OP	CR	FBG SV	IO	270-330		9 8	6450		19000	23100
26 9	2700 SCR	OP	CR	FBG SV	IO	T205		9 8	7046		21300	23700
			---- 1992 BOATS									
16 7	1700 XR	OP	RNBT	FBG SV	OB			5 10	1215		2250	2600
17 4	QUANTUM 1700 XB	OP	BASS	FBG SV	OB			7 3	1650		2800	3300
17 10	QUANTUM 1800 XB	OP	BASS	FBG SV	OB			7 3	1625		2800	3300
18	1800 XR	OP	RNBT	FBG SV	OB			7 2	1820		3050	3550
18 1	1800 SR	OP	RNBT	FBG SV	IO	130-205		7 7	2190		4450	5450
19 6	1900 SC	OP	CUD	FBG SV	IO	230	MRCR	7 10	2670		5800	6700
19 6	1900 SR	OP	RNBT	FBG SV	IO	130	MRCR	7 10	2400		5000	5800
19 6	1900 SR	OP	RNBT	FBG SV	IO	205-230		7 10	2575		5400	6450
19 6	1900 SR2	OP	RNBT	FBG SV	IO	130-205		7 10	2400		5200	6450
19 6	1900 SRB	OP	RNBT	FBG SV	IO	205-230		7 10	2577		5400	6450
19 6	1900 SSL	OP	RNBT	FBG SV	IO	205-230		7 10	2480		5300	6300
19 6	1900 XR	OP	RNBT	FBG SV	OB			7 10	2100		3550	4100
19 7	2000 XB	OP	BASS	FBG SV	IO			8	2050		3500	4050
20 7	2100 LDC	OP	CUD	FBG SV	IO	120	FRCE	7 4	1975		5200	5950
20 7	2100 SB	OP	RNBT	FBG SV	IO	130-205		7 4	2280		5200	6400
20 7	2100 SC	OP	RNBT	FBG SV	IO	205-230		7 4	2570		5950	7100
20 7	2100 SR	OP	RNBT	FBG SV	IO	205-230		7 4	2460		5600	6650
20 7	2100 SSL	OP	RNBT	FBG SV	IO	205-260		7 4	2345		5450	6750
23	2300 SCR	OP	CR	FBG SV	IO	205-260		8 6	3750		9250	11000
23 7	2400 SC	OP	CUD	FBG SV	IO	260	MRCR	8 6	3450		9400	10700
23 7	2400 SC	OP	CUD	FBG SV	IO	330	MRCR	8 6	3700		10700	12200
23 7	2400 SSL	OP	CUD	FBG SV	IO	330	MRCR	8 6	3740		10700	12200
25 5	2500 SCR	OP	CR	FBG SV	IO	230-260		8 6	4450		12700	14900
27	2700 SCR	OP	CR	FBG SV	IO	260-330		9 6	5800		16500	20400
27	2700 SCR	OP	CR	FBG SV	IO	180D	MRCR	9 6	6045		19300	21400
			---- 1991 BOATS									
16 7	1700 XR	OP	RNBT	FBG SV	OB			5 10	1215		2100	2500
17 8	1800 XR	OP	RNBT	FBG SV	IO	130	MRCR	7 2	1940		3700	4300
17 8	1800 XR	OP	RNBT	FBG SV	OB			7 2	1550		2600	3050
17 10	1800 XB	OP	BASS	FBG SV	OB			7 3	1625		2700	3150
19 7	2000 XB	OP	BASS	FBG SV	OB			8	2050		3350	3900
20 7	2100 LDC	OP	CUD	FBG SV	IO			7 4	1975		3700	4300
20 7	2100 LDR	OP	RNBT	FBG SV	IO			7 4	1850		3500	4100
20 7	2100 SR	OP	RNBT	FBG SV	IO	175-230		7 4	2460		5150	6250
20 7	2100 SSL	OP	RNBT	FBG SV	IO	260	MRCR	7 4	2555		5600	6450
20 7	2100 XC	OP	CUD	FBG SV	IO			7 4	1980		3700	4300
20 7	2100 XC	OP	CUD	FBG SV	IO	175-230		7 4	2570		5500	6550
20 7	2100 XR	OP	RNBT	FBG SV	OB			7 4	1830		3500	4050
23	2300 SCR	OP	CR	FBG SV	IO	175-260		8 6	3750		8550	10400
23 7	2400 SC	OP	CUD	FBG SV	IO	230	MRCR	8 6	3490		8500	9800
23 7	2400 SC	OP	CUD	FBG SV	IO	330	MRCR	8 6	3708		10000	11400
23 7	2400 SSL	OP	CUD	FBG SV	IO	330	MRCR	8 6	3740		10100	11400
25 5	2500 SCR	OP	CR	FBG SV	IO	230-260		8 6	4450		11900	13900
27	2700 SCR	OP	CR	FBG SV	IO	260-330		9 6	5800		15500	19200

MC LAUGHLIN BOAT WORKS
CHATANOOGA TN 37343   COAST GUARD MFG ID- MGH See inside cover to adjust price for area

For more recent years, see the BUC Used Boat Price Guide, Volume 1

LOA FT IN	NAME AND/ OR MODEL	TOP/ RIG	BOAT TYPE	HULL MTL TP	TP	# HP	ENGINE MFG	BEAM FT IN	WGT LBS	DRAFT FT IN	RETAIL LOW	RETAIL HIGH
			---- 1996 BOATS									
19	LIGHTNING		SAROD	FBG				7	700	4	6650	7650
			---- 1995 BOATS									
19	LIGHTNING		SAROD	FBG				7	700	4	6250	7200
			---- 1994 BOATS									
19	LIGHTNING		SAROD	FBG				7	700	4	5900	6800
			---- 1993 BOATS									
19	LIGHTNING		SAROD	FBG				7	700	4	5550	6400
			---- 1985 BOATS									
19	LIGHTNING		SLP	SA/OD	CB			6 6	700	5	3400	3950
			---- 1984 BOATS									
17	THISTLE		SLP	SA/OD	CB			6	515	9	2600	3000

....For earlier years, see the BUC Used Boat Price Guide, Volume 3

DAMIAN MC LAUGHLIN JR CO
N FALMOUTH MA 02556   COAST GUARD MFG ID- DAM See inside cover to adjust price for area

LOA FT IN	NAME AND/ OR MODEL	TOP/ RIG	BOAT TYPE	HULL MTL TP	TP	# HP	ENGINE MFG	BEAM FT IN	WGT LBS	DRAFT FT IN	RETAIL LOW	RETAIL HIGH
			---- 1985 BOATS									
29	NEWICK 30		SAIL	FBG TM				25	4000		24800	27600
35	AMA 35		SAIL	FBG TM				25	5400		44700	49600
			---- 1984 BOATS									
18	CAPE-COD-KNOCKABOUT		SLP	SA/OD FBG	CB			6 2	1300	9	3750	4350

....For earlier years, see the BUC Used Boat Price Guide, Volume 3

MC YACHTS CORP
STAMFORD CT 06905   COAST GUARD MFG ID- TLI See inside cover to adjust price for area

LOA FT IN	NAME AND/ OR MODEL	TOP/ RIG	BOAT TYPE	HULL MTL TP	TP	# HP	ENGINE MFG	BEAM FT IN	WGT LBS	DRAFT FT IN	RETAIL LOW	RETAIL HIGH
			---- 1988 BOATS									
42 5	BLUEOCEAN 42		CUT	SA/CR AL	KL IB		42D PATH	12 10	21800	5 9	77500	85200
42 5	BLUEOCEAN 42 AFTCPT		CUT	SA/CR AL	KL IB		42D PATH	12 10	21800	5 9	72700	79900
50 1	FIREISLAND 50		CUT	SA/CR AL	KC IB		100D WEST	16 2	4400		88100	96900
			---- 1987 BOATS									
42 5	BLUEOCEAN 42		CUT	SA/CR AL	KL IB		42D PATH	12 10	21800	5 9	72900	80100
42 5	BLUEOCEAN 42 AFTCPT		CUT	SA/CR AL	KL IB		42D PATH	12 10	21800	5 9	68400	75200
50 1	FIREISLAND 50		CUT	SA/CR AL	KC IB		100D WEST	16 2	4400		82900	91100
			---- 1986 BOATS									
42 5	BLUEOCEAN 42		CUT	SA/CR AL	KL IB		D	12 10	21800	5 9	66600	73200
			---- 1985 BOATS									
42 5	BLUEOCEAN 42		CUT	SA/CR AL	KL IB		42D PATH	12 10	21800	5 9	64500	70900
42 5	BLUEOCEAN 42 AFTCPT		CUT	SA/CR AL	KL IB		42D PATH	12 10	21800	5 9	60500	66500
			---- 1984 BOATS									
42 5	BLUEOCEAN 42		CUT	SA/CR AL	KL IB		42D PATH	12 10	21800	5 9	58800	64600

MCKEE CRAFT
MC KEE CRAFT
FAIRMONT NC 28340   COAST GUARD MFG ID- MKC   See inside cover to adjust price for area
     FORMERLY LANNESS K MCKEE & CO

For more recent years, see the BUC Used Boat Price Guide, Volume 1

LOA FT IN	NAME AND/ OR MODEL	TOP/ RIG	BOAT TYPE	HULL MTL TP	TP	# HP	ENGINE MFG	BEAM FT IN	WGT LBS	DRAFT FT IN	RETAIL LOW	RETAIL HIGH
			---- 1996 BOATS									
16	CAPE FEAR 16	OP	CTRCN	FBG TR	OB			6 5	1170	9	3200	3700
16	WACCAMAW 16	OP	W/T	FBG TR	OB			6 5	1170	9	3150	3700
16 11	PULSE 1700 CC	OP	CTRCN	FBG DV	OB			7	1260	1	3450	4000
16 11	PULSE 1700 WT	OP	W/T	FBG DV	OB			7	1260	1	3400	3950
17 4	OFFSHORE FISHERMN 17	OP	CTRCN	FBG TR	OB			7 2	1480	10	3900	4550
17 4	SOUTHPORTER 17	OP	W/T	FBG TR	OB			7 2	1480	10	3850	4500
18 3	PULSE 1800 CC	OP	CTRCN	FBG DV	OB			7	1500	1 5	4000	4650
18 3	PULSE 1800 WT	OP	W/T	FBG DV	OB			7	1500	1 5	3950	4600
19 8	HAMMERHEAD 198 CC	OP	CTRCN	FBG DV	OB			8	2200	1	5350	6150
19 8	HAMMERHEAD 198 WT	OP	W/T	FBG DV	OB			8	2200	1	5450	6250
23 11	HAMMERHEAD 220 CC	OP	CTRCN	FBG DV	OB			8	2865	1	10100	11400
23 11	HAMMERHEAD 220 WA	OP	CUD	FBG DV	OB			8	3100	1	10700	12100
23 11	HAMMERHEAD 220 WT	OP	W/T	FBG DV	OB			8	2865	1	10100	11400
			---- 1995 BOATS									
16	CAPE FEAR	OP	RNBT	FBG TR	OB			6 4	1170		3050	3550
16	WACCAMAW	OP	RNBT	FBG TR	OB			6 4	1170		3200	3700
16 9	PULSE 1700 CC	OP	RNBT	FBG TR	OB			7	1300	1	3450	4000
16 9	PULSE 1700 WT	OP	RNBT	FBG TR	OB			7	1300	1	3450	4000

LOA FT	LOA IN	NAME AND/ OR MODEL	TOP/ RIG	BOAT TYPE	-HULL- MTL	-HULL- TP	ENGINE TP	#	HP	MFG	BEAM FT	BEAM IN	WGT LBS	DRAFT FT	DRAFT IN	RETAIL LOW	RETAIL HIGH
		1995 BOATS															
17	4	OFFSHORE FISHERMAN	OP	RNBT	FBG	TR	OB				7		1480		10	3900	4550
17	4	SOUTHPORTER	OP	RNBT	FBG	TR	OB				7		1480		10	3800	4400
18	3	PULSE 1800 CC	OP	RNBT	FBG	TR	OB				7	10	1500	1	5	3950	4600
18	3	PULSE 1800 WT	OP	RNBT	FBG	TR	OB				7	10	1500	1	5	3950	4600
19	8	HAMMERHEAD 198 CC	OP	RNBT	FBG	TR	OB				8		2400		10	5500	6300
19	8	HAMMERHEAD 198 WT	OP	RNBT	FBG	TR	OB				8		2400		10	5550	6400
22		HAMMERHEAD 220 CC	OP	RNBT	FBG	TR	OB				12		2865	1		8350	9600
22		HAMMERHEAD 220 WA	OP	RNBT	FBG	TR	OB				12		2865	1		9200	10500
22		HAMMERHEAD 220 WT	OP	RNBT	FBG	TR	OB				12		2865	1		8450	9700
		1994 BOATS															
16		CAPE FEAR	OP	RNBT	FBG	TR	OB				6	4	1170		9	2900	3350
16		WACCAMAW	OP	RNBT	FBG	TR	OB				6	4	1170		9	3000	3500
16	9	PULSE 1700 CC	OP	RNBT	FBG	TR	OB				7		1300	1		3250	3800
16	9	PULSE 1700 WT	OP	RNBT	FBG	TR	OB				7		1300	1		3250	3800
17	4	OFFSHORE FISHERMAN	OP	RNBT	FBG	TR	OB				7		1480		10	3650	4250
17	4	SOUTHPORTER	OP	RNBT	FBG	TR	OB				7		1480		10	3550	4150
18	3	PULSE 1800 CC	OP	RNBT	FBG	TR	OB				7	10	1500	1	5	3700	4300
18	3	PULSE 1800 WT	OP	RNBT	FBG	TR	OB				7	10	1500	1	5	3700	4300
19	8	HAMMERHEAD 198 CC	OP	RNBT	FBG	TR	OB				8		2400		10	5200	6000
19	8	HAMMERHEAD 198 WT	OP	RNBT	FBG	TR	OB				8		2400		10	5250	6050
22		HAMMERHEAD 220 CC	OP	RNBT	FBG	TR	OB				12		2865	1		7900	9050
22		HAMMERHEAD 220 WA	OP	RNBT	FBG	TR	OB				12		2865	1		8650	9950
22		HAMMERHEAD 220 WT	OP	RNBT	FBG	TR	OB				12		2865	1		8000	9200
		1993 BOATS															
16		CAPE FEAR	OP	RNBT	FBG	TR	OB				6	5	1170		9	2850	3300
16		WACCAMAW	OP	RNBT	FBG	TR	OB				6	5	1170		9	2700	3150
16	9	PULSE 1700 CC	OP	RNBT	FBG	DV	OB				7		1300	1		3050	3550
16	9	PULSE 1700 WT	OP	RNBT	FBG	DV	OB				7		1300	1		3050	3550
17	4	OFFSHORE FISHERMAN	OP	RNBT	FBG	TR	OB				7	2	1480	1		3450	4050
17	4	SOUTHPORTER	OP	RNBT	FBG	TR	OB				7	2	1480	1		3400	3950
18	3	PULSE 1800 CC	OP	CTRCN	FBG	DV	OB				7	10	1500	1	5	3400	3950
18	3	PULSE 1800 WT	OP	RNBT	FBG	DV	OB				7	10	1500	1	5	3500	4100
19	8	HAMMERHEAD 198 CC	OP	OFF	FBG	DV	OB				8		2400	1		4700	5450
19	8	HAMMERHEAD 198 WT	OP	OFF	FBG	DV	OB				8		2400	1		4750	5450
23	11	HAMMERHEAD 220 CC	OP	OFF	FBG	DV	OB				8		2865	1	2	8550	9850
23	11	HAMMERHEAD 220 WA	OP	CUD	FBG	DV	OB				8		2865	1	2	8600	9850
23	11	HAMMERHEAD 220 WT	OP	OFF	FBG	DV	OB				8		2865	1	2	8550	9850
		1992 BOATS															
16		CAPE FEAR	OP	RNBT	FBG	TR	OB				6	5	1170	9		2700	3150
16		CC FISHER	OP	RNBT	FBG	TR	OB				6	5	1100	9		2500	2900
16		SANTEE DELUXE	OP	RNBT	FBG	TR	OB				6	5	1170	9		2450	2850
16		WACCAMAW	OP	RNBT	FBG	TR	OB				6	5	1170	9		2800	3300
16	7	PULSE 1670 CC	OP	RNBT	FBG	DV	OB				7		1250	1		2800	3250
16	7	PULSE 1670 WT	OP	RNBT	FBG	DV	OB				7		1250	1		2800	3250
17	4	OFFSHORE FISHERMAN	OP	RNBT	FBG	TR	OB				7	2	1480	1		3300	3800
17	4	SOUTHPORTER	OP	RNBT	FBG	TR	OB				7	2	1480	1		3200	3750
18	3	PULSE 1800 CC	OP	CTRCN	FBG	DV	OB				7	10	1500	1	5	3150	3700
18	3	PULSE 1800 WT	OP	RNBT	FBG	DV	OB				7	10	1500	1	5	3350	3900
19	8	HAMMERHEAD 198 CC	OP	OFF	FBG	DV	OB				8		2400	1		4450	5150
19	8	HAMMERHEAD 198 WT	OP	OFF	FBG	DV	OB				8		2400	1		4500	5200
23	11	HAMMERHEAD 220 CC	OP	OFF	FBG	DV	OB				8		2865	1	2	8150	9350
23	11	HAMMERHEAD 220 WA	OP	CUD	FBG	DV	OB				8		2865	1	2	8150	9400
23	11	HAMMERHEAD 220 WA	OP	CUD	FBG	DV	IO		200	VLVO	8		4200	1	4	14800	16800
23	11	HAMMERHEAD 220 WT	OP	OFF	FBG	DV	OB				8		2865	1	2	8150	9350
23	11	HAMMERHEAD 220 WT	OP	OFF	FBG	DV	IO		200	VLVO	8		4200	1	4	14800	16800
		1991 BOATS															
16		CAPE FEAR	OP	RNBT	FBG	TR	OB				6	5	1170		9	2600	3000
16		CC FISHER	OP	RNBT	FBG	TR	OB				6	5	1100		9	2400	2800
16		SANTEE DELUXE	OP	RNBT	FBG	TR	OB				6	5	1170		9	2300	2700
16		WACCAMAW	OP	RNBT	FBG	TR	OB				6	5	1170		9	2700	3100
17	4	OFFSHORE FISHERMAN	OP	RNBT	FBG	TR	OB				7	2	1480		10	3100	3600
17	4	SOUTHPORTER	OP	RNBT	FBG	TR	OB				7	2	1480		10	3050	3550
18	3	PULSE 1800 CC	OP	CTRCN	FBG	DV	OB				7	10	1500	1	5	3000	3500
18	3	PULSE 1800 WT	OP	RNBT	FBG	DV	OB				7	10	1500	1	5	3150	3650
19	8	HAMMERHEAD 198CC	OP	OFF	FBG	DV	OB				8		2400	1		4150	4850
19	8	HAMMERHEAD 198WT	OP	OFF	FBG	DV	OB				8		2400	1		4200	4900
23	11	HAMMERHEAD 220 WA	OP	CUD	FBG	DV	IO		200D	VLVO	8		4200	1	4	17200	19500
23	11	HAMMERHEAD 220 WT	OP	OFF	FBG	DV	IO		200D	VLVO	8		4200	1	4	17200	19500
23	11	HAMMERHEAD 220CC	OP	OFF	FBG	DV	OB				8		2865	1	2	7650	8800
23	11	HAMMERHEAD 220WA	OP	CUD	FBG	DV	OB				8		2865	1	2	7800	8950
23	11	HAMMERHEAD 220WT	OP	OFF	FBG	DV	OB				8		2865	1	2	7900	9050
		1990 BOATS															
16		CAPE FEAR	OP	RNBT	FBG	TR	OB				6	5	1170		9	2550	2950
16		CC FISHER	OP	RNBT	FBG	TR	OB				6	5	1100		9	2300	2650
16		SANTEE DELUXE	OP	RNBT	FBG	TR	OB				6	5	1170		9	2100	2500
16		WACCAMAW	OP	RNBT	FBG	TR	OB				6	5	1170		9	2500	2900
17	4	OFFSHORE FISHERMAN	OP	RNBT	FBG	TR	OB				7	2	1480		10	3050	3550
17	4	OFFSHOREMAN	OP	RNBT	FBG	TR	OB				7	2	1480		10	2800	3300
17	4	SOUTHPORTER	OP	RNBT	FBG	TR	OB				7	2	1480		10	2900	3350
19	8	HAMMERHEAD 198CC	OP	OFF	FBG	DV	OB				8		2400	1		3950	4600
19	8	HAMMERHEAD 198WT	OP	OFF	FBG	DV	OB				8		2400	1		4000	4700
23	11	HAMMERHEAD 220 WA	OP	OFF	FBG	DV	OB				8		2865	1	2	7950	9150
23	11	HAMMERHEAD 220CC	OP	OFF	FBG	DV	OB				8		2865	1	2	7100	8150
23	11	HAMMERHEAD 220WT	OP	OFF	FBG	DV	OB				8		2865	1	2	7300	8400
		1989 BOATS															
16		CAPE FEAR	OP	RNBT	FBG	TR	OB				6	5	1170		9	2450	2850
16		CC FISHER	OP	RNBT	FBG	TR	OB				6	5	1100		9	2200	2550
16		SANTEE DELUXE	OP	RNBT	FBG	TR	OB				6	5	1170		9	2000	2350
16		WACCAMAW	OP	RNBT	FBG	TR	OB				6	5	1170		9	2450	2850
17	4	OFFSHORE FISHERMAN	OP	RNBT	FBG	TR	OB				7	2	1480		10	2900	3400
17	4	OFFSHOREMAN	OP	RNBT	FBG	TR	OB				7	2	1480		10	2700	3100
17	4	SOUTHPORTER	OP	RNBT	FBG	TR	OB				7	2	1480		10	2750	3200
19	8	HAMMERHEAD 198CC	OP	OFF	FBG	DV	OB				8		2400	1		3750	4350
19	8	HAMMERHEAD 198WT	OP	OFF	FBG	DV	OB				8		2400	1		3850	4450
23	11	HAMMERHEAD 220 WA	OP	OFF	FBG	DV	OB				8		2865	1	2	7600	8750
23	11	HAMMERHEAD 220CC	OP	OFF	FBG	DV	OB				8		2865	1	2	6800	7800
23	11	HAMMERHEAD 220WT	OP	OFF	FBG	DV	OB				8		2865	1	2	7000	8050
		1988 BOATS															
16		CAPE FEAR	OP	RNBT	FBG	TR	OB				6	5	1170		9	2350	2750
16		CC FISHER	OP	RNBT	FBG	TR	OB				6	5	1100		9	2050	2400
16		SANTEE DELUXE	OP	RNBT	FBG	TR	OB				6	5	1170		9	1900	2250
16		WACCAMAW	OP	RNBT	FBG	TR	OB				6	5	1170		9	2300	2700
17	4	OFFSHORE FISHERMAN	OP	RNBT	FBG	TR	OB				7	2	1480		10	2800	3250
17	4	OFFSHOREMAN	OP	RNBT	FBG	TR	OB				7	2	1480		10	2550	3000
17	4	SOUTHPORTER	OP	RNBT	FBG	TR	OB				7	2	1480		10	2650	3050
19	8	HAMMERHEAD 198CC	OP	OFF	FBG	DV	OB				8		2400	1		3550	4150
19	8	HAMMERHEAD 198WT	OP	OFF	FBG	DV	OB				8		2400	1		3650	4250
23	11	HAMMERHEAD 220CC	OP	OFF	FBG	DV	OB				8		2865	1	2	6750	7750
23	11	HAMMERHEAD 220WT	OP	OFF	FBG	DV	OB				8		2865	1	2	6950	8000
		1987 BOATS															
16		CAPE FEAR	OP	RNBT	FBG	TR	OB				6	5	1170		9	2200	2600
16		SANTEE DELUXE	OP	RNBT	FBG	TR	OB				6	5	1170		9	1800	2150
16		WACCAMAW	OP	RNBT	FBG	TR	OB				6	5	1170		9	2250	2600
17	4	OFFSHORE FISHERMAN	OP	RNBT	FBG	TR	OB				7	2	1480		10	2650	3100
17	4	OFFSHOREMAN	OP	RNBT	FBG	TR	OB				7	2	1480		10	2500	2900
17	4	SOUTHPORTER	OP	RNBT	FBG	TR	OB				7	2	1480		10	2500	2900
23	11	HAMMERHEAD 220CC	OP	OFF	FBG	DV	OB				8		2865	1	2	6550	7500
23	11	HAMMERHEAD 220WT	OP	OFF	FBG	DV	OB				8		2865	1	2	6650	7650
		1986 BOATS															
16		CAPE FEAR	OP	RNBT	FBG	TR	OB				6	5	1170		9	2050	2450
16		SANTEE DELUXE	OP	RNBT	FBG	TR	OB				6	5	1170		9	1750	2050
16		WACCAMAW	OP	RNBT	FBG	TR	OB				6	5	1170		9	2150	2500
17	4	OFFSHORE FISHERMAN	OP	RNBT	FBG	TR	OB				7	2	1480		10	2550	2950
17	4	OFFSHOREMAN	OP	RNBT	FBG	TR	OB				7	2	1480		10	2400	2800
17	4	SOUTHPORTER	OP	RNBT	FBG	TR	OB				7	2	1480		10	2450	2850
		1985 BOATS															
16		CAPE FEAR	OP	RNBT	FBG	TR	OB				6	5	1170		9	2100	2500
16		SANTEE	OP	RNBT	FBG	TR	OB				6	5	1170		9	1600	1900
16		SANTEE DELUXE	OP	RNBT	FBG	TR	OB				6	5	1170		9	1700	2050
16		WACCAMAW	OP	RNBT	FBG	TR	OB				6	5	1170		9	2250	2600
17	4	OFFSHOREMAN	OP	RNBT	FBG	TR	OB				7	2	1480		10	2350	2750
17	4	SOUTHPORTER	OP	RNBT	FBG	TR	OB				7	2	1480		10	2400	2800
20		BREAKERS	OP	RNBT	FBG	TR	OB				6	9	1705	1		3500	4100
20		OFFSHOREMAN	OP	RNBT	FBG	TR	OB				6	9	1705	1		3400	4000
		1984 BOATS															
16		CAPE-FEAR	OP	RNBT	FBG	TR	OB				6	6	1170		9	1950	2350
16		SANTEE	OP	RNBT	FBG	TR	OB				6	6	1170		9	1450	1750
16		WACCAMAW	OP	RNBT	FBG	TR	OB				6	6	1170		9	2050	2400
17	4	OFFSHOREMAN	OP	RNBT	FBG	TR	OB				7	4	1480		10	2250	2650
17	4	SOUTHPORTER	OP	RNBT	FBG	TR	OB				7	4	1480		10	2350	2700
20		BREAKERS	OP	RNBT	FBG	TR	OB				7		1705	1	2	3400	4000
20		OFFSHOREMAN	OP	RNBT	FBG	TR	OB				7		1705	1	2	3300	3850

....For earlier years, see the BUC Used Boat Price Guide, Volume 3

MED YACHTS INTERNATIONAL

TOMS RIVER NJ 08754

See inside cover to adjust price for area

For more recent years, see the BUC Used Boat Price Guide, Volume 1

LOA FT	LOA IN	NAME AND/ OR MODEL	TOP/ RIG	BOAT TYPE	-HULL- MTL	-HULL- TP	TP	ENGINE # HP	ENGINE MFG	BEAM FT	BEAM IN	WGT LBS	DRAFT FT	DRAFT IN	RETAIL LOW	RETAIL HIGH
		1996 BOATS														
41	3	MED 12.6 METER	FB	SDN	FBG	SV	IB	T300D	CUM	14	8	26400	3	2	182000	200000
48	6	MED 14 METER	FB	MY	FBG	DV	IB	T300D	CUM	14	5	26450	3	11	194500	214000
56	6	MED 17 METER	FB	MY	FBG	DV	IB	T550D	CUM	16	7	52900	4	3	399000	438500
59	5	MED 18 METER	FB	MY	FBG	DV	IB	T550D	GM	16	7	52900	4	6	402000	442000
		1995 BOATS														
41	3	MED 12.6 METER	FB	DC	FBG	SV	IB	T300D	CUM	14	8	26400	3	2	173000	190000
41	3	MED 12.6 METER	FB	SDN	FBG	SV	IB	T300D	CUM	14	8	26400	3	2	174500	191500
48	6	MED 14 METER	FB	MY	FBG	DV	IB	T300D	CUM	14	5	26450	3	11	185000	203500
56	6	MED 17 METER	FB	MY	FBG	DV	IB	T550D	CUM	16	7	52900	4	3	382500	420500
59	5	MED 18 METER	FB	MY	FBG	DV	IB	T550D	GM	16	7	52900	4	6	385500	423500
		1994 BOATS														
42	9	MED 12 METER	FB	MY	FBG	DV	IB	T250D	CUM	13	7	16500	3	7	140000	154000
48	6	MED 14 METER	FB	MY	FBG	DV	IB	T300D	CUM	14	5	26450	3	11	176500	194000
56	6	MED 17 METER	FB	MY	FBG	DV	IB	T550D	CUM	16	7	52900	4	3	366500	403000
59	5	MED 18 METER	FB	MY	FBG	DV	IB	T550D	GM	16	7	52900	4	6	369500	406000
		1993 BOATS														
42	9	MED 12 METER	FB	MY	FBG	DV	IB	T250D	CUM	13	7	16500	3	7	133500	146500
43		SPORTFISHERMAN	FB	SF	FBG	DV	IB	T210D	CUM	15			4	6	153000	168000
43		ST MORITZ SD	FB	MY	FBG	DV	IB	T210D	CUM	15			4	6	166500	183000
43		ST TROPEZ	FB	MY	FBG	DV	IB	T210D	CUM	15			4	6	160000	176000
45		CANNES	FB	MY	FBG	DV	IB	T210D	CUM	15			4	6	148500	163000
48		MARSEILLE	FB	MY	FBG	DV	IB	T210D	CUM	15			4	7	150000	165000
48		MONACO	FB	MY	FBG	DV	IB	T210D	CUM	15			4	7	161500	177000
48		MOROCCO	FB	MY	FBG	DV	IB	T210D	CUM	15			4	7	171500	188500
48	6	MED 14 METER	FB	MY	FBG	DV	IB	T300D	CUM	14	5	26450	3	11	168500	185000
50		MALLORCA	FB	MY	FBG	DV	IB	T210D	CUM	15	1		4	7	185500	204000
55		GIBRALTAR	FB	MY	FBG	DV	IB	T210D	CUM	15			4	7	203500	223500
56		MONTE CRISTO	FB	MY	FBG	DV	IB	T210D	CUM	16			4	7	233500	257000
56	6	MED 17 METER	FB	MY	FBG	DV	IB	T550D	CUM	16	7	52900	4	3	349500	384000
59	5	MED 18 METER	FB	MY	FBG	DV	IB	T550D	GM	16	7	52900	4	6	352000	386500
		1992 BOATS														
42	9	MED 12 METER	FB	MY	FBG	DV	IB	T250D	CUM	13	7	16500	3	7	127000	139500
43		SPORTFISHERMAN	FB	SF	FBG	DV	IB	T210D	CUM	15			4	6	146000	160500
43		ST MORITZ SD	FB	MY	FBG	DV	IB	T210D	CUM	15			4	6	155500	171000
45		CANNES	FB	MY	FBG	DV	IB	T210D	CUM	15			4	6	141000	155000
48		MARSEILLE	FB	MY	FBG	DV	IB	T210D	CUM	15			4	7	143000	157000
48		MONACO	FB	MY	FBG	DV	IB	T210D	CUM	15			4	7	153500	168500
48		MOROCCO	FB	MY	FBG	DV	IB	T210D	CUM	15			4	7	163000	179500
48	6	MED 14 METER	FB	MY	FBG	DV	IB	T300D	CUM	14	5	26450	3	11	160000	176000
50		MALLORCA	FB	MY	FBG	DV	IB	T210D	CUM	15	1		4	7	176500	194000
55		GIBRALTAR	FB	MY	FBG	DV	IB	T210D	CUM	15			4	7	194000	213000
56		MONTECRISTO	FB	MY	FBG	DV	IB	T210D	CUM	16			4	7	223000	245000
56	6	MED 17 METER	FB	MY	FBG	DV	IB	T550D	CUM	16	7	52900	4	3	333000	366000
59	5	MED 18 METER	FB	MY	FBG	DV	IB	T550D	GM	16	7	52900	4	6	335500	368500
		1991 BOATS														
42	9	MED 12 METER	FB	MY	FBG	DV	IB	T250D	CUM	13	7	16500	3	7	121500	133500
43		SPORTFISHERMAN	FB	SF	FBG	DV	IB	T210D	CUM	15			4	6	139000	153000
43		ST MORITZ SD	FB	MY	FBG	DV	IB	T210D	CUM	15			4	6	148500	163000
45		CANNES	FB	MY	FBG	DV	IB	T210D	CUM	15			4	6	134500	148000
48		MARSEILLE	FB	MY	FBG	DV	IB	T210D	CUM	15			4	7	135500	149000
48		MONACO	FB	MY	FBG	DV	IB	T210D	CUM	15			4	7	146500	160500
48		MOROCCO	FB	MY	FBG	DV	IB	T210D	CUM	15			4	7	156000	171500
48	6	MED 14 METER	FB	MY	FBG	DV	IB	T300D	CUM	14	5	26450	3	11	152500	168000
50		MALLORCA	FB	MY	FBG	DV	IB	T210D	CUM	15	1		4	7	168500	185000
55		GIBRALTAR	FB	MY	FBG	DV	IB	T210D	CUM	15			4	7	185000	203000
56		MONTECRISTO	FB	MY	FBG	DV	IB	T210D	CUM	16			4	7	212500	233500
56	6	MED 17 METER	FB	MY	FBG	DV	IB	T550D	CUM	16	7	52900	4	3	317500	349000
59	5	MED 18 METER	FB	MY	FBG	DV	IB	T550D	GM	16	7	52900	4	6	320000	351500
		1990 BOATS														
43		SPORTFISHERMAN	FB	SF	FBG	DV	IB	T210D	CUM	15			4	6	132500	146000
43		ST MORITZ SD	FB	MY	FBG	DV	IB	T210D	CUM	15			4	6	144500	158500
43		ST TROPEZ	FB	MY	FBG	DV	IB	T210D	CUM	15			4	6	138500	152500
45		CANNES	FB	MY	FBG	DV	IB	T210D	CUM	15			4	6	128500	141000
48		MARSEILLE	FB	MY	FBG	DV	IB	T210D	CUM	15			4	7	129500	142000
48		MONACO	FB	MY	FBG	DV	IB	T210D	CUM	15			4	7	139500	153500
48		MOROCCO	FB	MY	FBG	DV	IB	T210D	CUM	15			4	7	149000	163500
50		MALLORCA	FB	MY	FBG	DV	IB	T210D	CUM	15	1		4	7	160500	176500
55		GIBRALTAR	FB	MY	FBG	DV	IB	T210D	CUM	15			4	7	176500	194000
56		MONTECRISTO	FB	MY	FBG	DV	IB	T210D	CUM	16			4	7	203000	223000
61		MED 58	FB	MY	FBG	DV	IB	T485D	CUM	17	6		5	3	329000	361500
65	6	MED 62	FB	MY	FBG	DV	IB	T485D	CUM	17	6		5	3	550000	604000
65	6	MED 62 W/COCKPIT	FB	MYCPT	FBG	DV	IB	T485D	CUM	17	6		5	3	402500	442500
		1989 BOATS														
43		SPORTFISHERMAN	FB	SF	FBG	DV	IB	T210D	CUM	15			4	6	126500	139000
43		ST MORITZ SNDK	FB	MY	FBG	DV	IB	T210D	CUM	15			4	6	138000	152000
43		ST TROPEZ SDN	FB	MY	FBG	DV	IB	T210D	CUM	15			4	6	132000	145500
45		CANNES SNDK	FB	MY	FBG	DV	IB	T210D	CUM	15			4	6	122500	134500
48		MARSEILLE 48 SNDK	FB	MY	FBG	DV	IB	T210D	CUM	15			4	7	122000	134500
48		MONACO 48 SNDK	FB	MY	FBG	DV	IB	T210D	CUM	15			4	7	132000	145000
48		MOROCCO 48 MY	FB	MY	FBG	DV	IB	T210D	CUM	15			4	7	144000	158500
49	6	MALLORCA 50	FB	MY	FBG	DV	IB	T210D	CUM	15	1		4	7	152500	167500
55		GIBRALTAR 55 SNDK	FB	MY	FBG	DV	IB	T210D	CUM	15	1		4	7	168500	185500
55	6	MONTECRISTO MED 56	FB	MY	FBG	DV	IB	T210D	CUM	16			4	7	191500	210500
57	2	MED-YACHT 58	FB	MY	FBG	DV	IB	T485D		17	6		5	3	259000	284500
65	6	MED-YACHT 62	FB	MY	FBG	DV	IB	T485D		17	6		5	3	510000	560000
65	6	MED-YACHT 62 FSH	FB	MY	FBG	DV	IB	T485D		17	6		5	3	492500	541500
		1988 BOATS														
43		SPORTFISHERMAN	FB	SF	FBG	DV	IB	T210D	CUM	15			4	6	121000	133000
43		ST MORITZ SNDK	FB	MY	FBG	DV	IB	T210D	CUM	15			4	6	132500	145500
43		ST TROPEZ SDN	FB	MY	FBG	DV	IB	T210D	CUM	15			4	6	126000	138500
45		CANNES SNDK	FB	MY	FBG	DV	IB	T210D	CUM	15			4	6	117000	128500
48		MARSEILLE 48 SNDK	FB	MY	FBG	DV	IB	T210D	CUM	15			4	7	117000	128500
48		MONACO 48 SNDK	FB	MY	FBG	DV	IB	T210D	CUM	15			4	7	126000	138500
48		MOROCCO 48 MY	FB	MY	FBG	DV	IB	T210D	CUM	15			4	7	137500	151000
49	6	MALLORCA 50	FB	MY	FBG	DV	IB	T210D	CUM	15	1		4	7	145500	160000
55		GIBRALTAR 55 SNDK	FB	MY	FBG	DV	IB	T210D	CUM	15	1		4	7	161000	177000
55	6	MONTECRISTO MED 56	FB	MY	FBG	DV	IB	T210D	CUM	16			4	7	183000	201000
57	2	MED-YACHT 58	FB	MY	FBG	DV	IB	T375D	GM	17	6		5	3	232500	255500
65	6	MED-YACHT 62	FB	MY	FBG	DV	IB	T375D	GM	17	6		5	3	439500	483000
65	6	MED-YACHT 62 FSH	FB	MY	FBG	DV	IB	T375D	GM	17	6		5	3	486000	534000
		1987 BOATS														
43		ST MORITZ SNDK	FB	MY	FBG	DV	IB	T210D	CUM	15			4	6	126000	138500
43		ST TROPEZ SDN	FB	MY	FBG	DV	IB	T210D	CUM	15			4	6	121000	133000
45		CANNES SNDK	FB	MY	FBG	DV	IB	T210D	CUM	15			4	6	112000	123000
48		MARSEILLE 48 SNDK	FB	MY	FBG	DV	IB	T210D	CUM	15			4	7	118000	130000
48		MONACO 48 SNDK	FB	MY	FBG	DV	IB	T210D	CUM	15			4	7	124000	136500
49	6	MALLORCA 50	FB	MY	FBG	DV	IB	T210D	CUM	15	1		4	7	139000	153000
55		GIBRALTAR 55 SNDK	FB	MY	FBG	DV	IB	T210D	CUM	15	1		4	7	154000	169500
55	6	MONTECRISTO MED 56	FB	MY	FBG	DV	IB	T210D	CUM	16			4	7	175000	192500
57	2	MED-YACHT 58	FB	MY	FBG	DV	IB	T375D	GM	17	6		5	3	222500	244500
65	6	MED-YACHT 62	FB	MY	FBG	DV	IB	T375D	GM	17	6		5	3	453500	498500
65	6	MED-YACHT 62 FSH	FB	MY	FBG	DV	IB	T375D	GM	17	6		5	3	431500	474500
		1986 BOATS														
43		SPORTFISHERMAN	FB	SF	FBG	DV	IB	T200D	VLVO	15			4	6	108500	119000
43		ST MORITZ SNDK	FB	MY	FBG	DV	IB	T200D	VLVO	15			4	6	118500	130000
43		ST TROPEZ SEDAN	FB	MY	FBG	DV	IB	T200D	VLVO	15			4	6	114000	125000
48		MARSEILLE 48 SNDK	FB	MY	FBG	DV	IB	T200D	VLVO	15			4	7	111000	122000
48		MONACO 48 SNDK	FB	MY	FBG	DV	IB	T200D	VLVO	15			4	7	117000	128500
48		MONTE-CARLO 48	FB	MY	FBG	DV	IB	T200D	VLVO	15			4	7	115000	126500
49	6	MALLORCA 50	FB	MY	FBG	DV	IB	T200D	VLVO	15	1		4	7	131000	144000
55		GIBRALTAR 55 SNDK	FB	MY	FBG	DV	IB	T200D	VLVO	15	1		4	7	146500	161000
57	2	MED-YACHT 58	FB	MY	FBG	DV	IB	T210D	CAT	17	6		5	3	190000	209000
57	2	MED-YACHT 58	FB	MY	FBG	DV	IB	T355D		17	6		6	5	210500	231500
65	6	MED-YACHT 62	FB	MY	FBG	DV	IB	T135D		17	6		5		360000	396000
		1985 BOATS														
43		ST MORITZ 43 SNDK	FB	MY	FBG	SV	IB	T165D	VLVO	15			4	6	110000	121000
43		ST TROPEZ 43	FB	MY	FBG	SV	IB	T165D	VLVO	15			4	6	103500	114000
48		MONACO 48 SNDK	FB	MY	FBG	SV	IB	T165D	VLVO	15			4	7	108500	119500
48		MONTE-CARLO 48	FB	MY	FBG	SV	IB	T165D	VLVO	15			4	7	107000	117500
49	6	MALLORCA 50	FB	MY	FBG	SV	IB	T165D	VLVO	15	1		4	7	123000	135000
57	2	MED-YACHT 58	FB	MY	FBG	SV	IB	T355D	CAT	17	6		5	3	198500	218500

MEDITERRANEAN YACHTS

CASSOPOLIS MI 49031-938 COAST GUARD MFG ID- WHI See inside cover to adjust price for area
FORMERLY INTERNATIONAL OFFSHORE MARINE

For more recent years, see the BUC Used Boat Price Guide, Volume 1

LOA FT	LOA IN	NAME AND/ OR MODEL	TOP/ RIG	BOAT TYPE	-HULL- MTL	-HULL- TP	TP	ENGINE # HP	ENGINE MFG	BEAM FT	BEAM IN	WGT LBS	DRAFT FT	DRAFT IN	RETAIL LOW	RETAIL HIGH
		1996 BOATS														
38	4	MEDITERRANEAN 38	FB	SF	FBG	DV	IB	T270	CRUS	12	8	24000	3	4	119000	131000
53	7	MEDITERRANEAN 54	FB	SF	FBG	DV	IB	T485D	DD	16	8	55000	4	6	319000	350500

CONTINUED ON NEXT PAGE

MEDITERRANEAN YACHTS   –CONTINUED   See inside cover to adjust price for area

LOA FT IN	NAME AND/ OR MODEL	TOP/ RIG	BOAT TYPE	–HULL– MTL TP	TP	––ENGINE–– # HP MFG	BEAM FT IN	WGT LBS	DRAFT FT IN	RETAIL LOW	RETAIL HIGH
	–––––––––––––– 1995 BOATS ––––––––––––––										
38 4	MEDITERRANEAN 38	FB	SF	FBG DV	IB	T270 CRUS	12 8	24000	3 4	114000	125500
53 7	MEDITERRANEAN 54	FB	SF	FBG DV	IB	T485D DD	16 8	55000	4 6	306000	336000
	–––––––––––––– 1994 BOATS ––––––––––––––										
38 4	MEDITERRANEAN 38	FB	SF	FBG DV	IB	T270 CRUS	12 6	25000	3 2	114000	125500
38 4	MEDITERRANEAN 38	FB	SF	FBG DV	IB	T375D CAT	12 6	25000	3 2	140500	154000
53 7	MEDITERRANEAN 54	FB	SF	FBG SV	IB	T760D DD	16 6	55000	4 6	346500	380500
	–––––––––––––– 1993 BOATS ––––––––––––––										
38 4	MEDITERRANEAN 38	FB	SF	FBG DV	IB	T270 CRUS	12 6	25000	3 2	108500	119500
38 4	MEDITERRANEAN 38	FB	SF	FBG DV	IB	T375D CAT	12 6	25000	3 2	133500	147000
	–––––––––––––– 1992 BOATS ––––––––––––––										
38 4	MEDITERRANEAN 38	FB	SF	FBG DV	IB	T270 CRUS	12 6	25000	3 2	103500	114000
38 4	MEDITERRANEAN 38	FB	SF	FBG DV	IB	T375D CAT	12 6	25000	3 2	127500	140000

....For earlier years, see the BUC Used Boat Price Guide, Volume 3

MEIJER YACHTS
BB BALK NETHERLANDS   See inside cover to adjust price for area

SAILSPIRIT
MIAMI FL 33114

LOA FT IN	NAME AND/ OR MODEL	TOP/ RIG	BOAT TYPE	–HULL– MTL TP	TP	––ENGINE–– # HP MFG	BEAM FT IN	WGT LBS	DRAFT FT IN	RETAIL LOW	RETAIL HIGH
	–––––––––––––– 1984 BOATS ––––––––––––––										
29 9	FRIENDSHIP 30	SLP	SA/CR	FBG	SD	35D VLVO	9 7	8377	5 4	26800	29800
35	FRIENDSHIP 35 SHOAL	SLP	SA/CR	FBG KC	SD	17D VLVO	9 7	8350	3 8	27900	31000
35	FRIENDSHIP 35	SLP	SA/CR	FBG KL	SD	25D VLVO	11 5	13250	6 2	43600	48400
35	FRIENDSHIP 35 SHOAL	SLP	SA/CR	FBG KC	SD	25D VLVO	11 5	13250	3 11	43700	48600
35	FRIENDSHIP 35 SHOAL	SLP	SA/CR	FBG KL	SD	25D VLVO	11 5	13250	5 8	43600	48400

....For earlier years, see the BUC Used Boat Price Guide, Volume 3

MEL-HART PRODUCTS INC
BARETTA & SUCCESS BOATS   See inside cover to adjust price for area
CONWAY 32 AR 72032   COAST GUARD MFG ID– MHP

LOA FT IN	NAME AND/ OR MODEL	TOP/ RIG	BOAT TYPE	–HULL– MTL TP	TP	––ENGINE–– # HP MFG	BEAM FT IN	WGT LBS	DRAFT FT IN	RETAIL LOW	RETAIL HIGH
	–––––––––––––– 1987 BOATS ––––––––––––––										
16 2	BARETTA SS	OP	RNBT	FBG DV	IO	120-130	6 11	1875		1300	1600
16 2	BARETTA SS	OP	RNBT	FBG DV	IO	131-151	6 11	1875		1450	1700
16 2	BARETTA SUCCESS	OP	RNBT	FBG DV	IO	120-131	6 11	1875		1450	1800
16 2	BARETTA SUCCESS	OP	RNBT	FBG DV	IO	151 VLVO	6 11	1875		1500	1800
17 3	BARETTA SS	OP	RNBT	FBG DV	IO	120-130	7 7	2030		1550	1850
17 3	BARETTA SS	OP	RNBT	FBG DV	IO	131-180	7 7	2030		1650	2000
17 3	BARETTA SUCCESS	OP	RNBT	FBG DV	IO	120-130	7 7	2030		1700	2000
17 3	BARETTA SUCCESS	OP	RNBT	FBG DV	IO	131-180	7 7	2030		1800	2150
18 9	BARETTA SS	OP	B/R	FBG DV	IO	120-131	7 7	2115		1650	2050
18 9	BARETTA SS	OP	B/R	FBG DV	IO	151-180	7 7	2115		1750	2150
18 9	BARETTA SS	OP	CUD	FBG DV	IO	120-165	7 7	2645		2050	2600
18 9	BARETTA SS	OP	CUD	FBG DV	IO	171-260	7 7	2645		2250	2700
18 9	BARETTA SS	OP	CUD	FBG DV	IO	271 VLVO	7 7	2645		2450	2850
18 9	BARETTA SS	OP	RNBT	FBG DV	IO	200-205	7 7	2115		1900	2250
18 9	BARETTA SS	OP	RNBT	FBG DV	IO	211-260	7 7	2115		2000	2400
18 9	BARETTA SS	OP	RNBT	FBG DV	IO	271 VLVO	7 7	2115		2200	2550
18 9	BARETTA SUCCESS	OP	B/R	FBG DV	IO	120-130	7 7	2115		1800	2100
	IO 131-230 1900 2250, IO 260 MRCR 1900 2250, IO 260-271									2450	2850
18 9	BARETTA SUCCESS	OP	CUD	FBG DV	IO	120-211	7 7	2645		2250	2800
18 9	BARETTA SUCCESS	OP	CUD	FBG DV	IO	225-271	7 7	2645		2400	3000
18 9	BARETTA SUCCESS	OP	RNBT	FBG DV	IO	175 MRCR	7 7	2115		1850	2200
20 4	BARETTA SUCCESS	OP	B/R	FBG DV	IO	120-260	8	3020		2650	3300
20 4	BARETTA SUCCESS	OP	B/R	FBG DV	IO	271 VLVO	8	3020		3000	3500
20 4	FISHERMAN 205	OP	CUD	FBG DV	IO	120-260				2950	3650
20 4	FISHERMAN 205	OP	CUD	FBG DV	IO	271 VLVO				3350	3900
20 4	FISHERMAN 223	OP	CUD	FBG DV	IO	120-260				3150	3900
20 4	FISHERMAN 223	OP	CUD	FBG DV	IO	271 VLVO				3500	4100
20 4	SUCCESS 205	OP	CUD	FBG DV	IO	120-260	8	3250		3000	3750
20 4	SUCCESS 205	OP	CUD	FBG DV	IO	271 VLVO	8	3250		3400	3950
20 4	SUCCESS 210	OP	CUD	FBG DV	IO	120-260	8	3283		3050	3750
20 4	SUCCESS 210	OP	CUD	FBG DV	IO	271 VLVO	8	3283		3400	4000
22 3	BARETTA SUCCESS	OP	CUD	FBG DV	IO	120 MRCR	8	2690		2950	3450
22 3	BARETTA SUCCESS	OP	CUD	FBG DV	IO	120-260	8	3690		3600	4500
22 3	BARETTA SUCCESS	OP	CUD	FBG DV	IO	271 VLVO	8	3690		4050	4700
	–––––––––––––– 1986 BOATS ––––––––––––––										
16 2	LEGEND B/R		RNBT	FBG DV	IO	120-140	6 11			1300	1550
16 3	CAMPAIGNER B/R		RNBT	FBG DV	IO	120-140	7 1			1300	1550
16 3	CAMPAIGNER B/R		RNBT	FBG DV	IO	120-170	7 1			1450	1700
17 3	BARETTA B/R		RNBT	FBG DV	IO	120-185	7 7			1550	1850
17 3	SUCCESS B/R		RNBT	FBG DV	IO	120-175	7 5			1500	1800
17 11	CAMPAIGNER B/R		RNBT	FBG DV	IO	120-230	7 7			1650	2050
17 11	CAMPAIGNER B/R		RNBT	FBG DV	IO	260	7 7			1800	2150
18 9	BARETTA B/R		RNBT	FBG DV	IO	120-185	7 7			1600	1950
18 9	BARETTA B/R		RNBT	FBG DV	IO	190-260	7 7			1750	2100
18 9	BARETTA CC		CUD	FBG DV	IO	120-230	7 7			1950	2400
18 9	BARETTA CC		CUD	FBG DV	IO	260	7 7			2100	2500
18 9	CAMPAIGNER B/R	ST	RNBT	FBG DV	IO	120-230	7 7			1700	2100
18 9	CAMPAIGNER B/R	ST	RNBT	FBG DV	IO	260	7 7			1900	2250
18 9	CAMPAIGNER CC		CUD	FBG DV	IO	120-205	7 7			2000	2500
18 9	CAMPAIGNER CC		CUD	FBG DV	IO	230-260	7 7			2150	2600
18 9	LEGEND		RNBT	FBG DV	IO	120-205	7 6			1700	2050
18 9	SUCCESS		CUD	FBG DV	IO	120-260	7 7			2150	2650
18 9	SUCCESS B/R		RNBT	FBG DV	IO	120-205	7 7			1800	2200
18 9	SUCCESS B/R		RNBT	FBG DV	IO	230-260	7 7			1850	2300
20 4	BARETTA CC		CUD	FBG DV	IO	120-260	8			3100	3700
20 4	BARETTA SPORTSMAN		CUD	FBG DV	IO	120-205	8			2750	3450
20 4	BARETTA SPORTSMAN		CUD	FBG DV	IO	230-260	8			3000	3500
	–––––––––––––– 1985 BOATS ––––––––––––––										
16 2	LEGEND B/R		RNBT	FBG DV	IO	120-140	6 11			1250	1450
16 3	ADVANTAGE B/R		RNBT	FBG DV	IO	120 MRCR	7 1			1250	1500
16 3	BARETTA B/R		RNBT	FBG DV	IO	120-140	7 1			1250	1500
16 9	BARETTA B/R		RNBT	FBG DV	IO	120-175	7 1			1350	1650
17 11	BARETTA B/R		RNBT	FBG DV	IO	120-205	7 1			1550	1950
18 9	BARETTA B/R		RNBT	FBG DV	IO	120-190	7 7			1550	1900
18 9	LEGEND B/R	ST	RNBT	FBG DV	IO	200-205	7 7			1600	1950
18 9	SUCCESS		CUD	FBG DV	IO	120-205	7 7			1900	2350
18 9	SUCCESS B/R		RNBT	FBG DV	IO	120-205	7 7			1700	2050
	–––––––––––––– 1984 BOATS ––––––––––––––										
16 2	LEGEND B/R		RNBT	FBG DV	IO	120-140	6 11			1200	1400
16 3	ADVANTAGE B/R		RNBT	FBG DV	IO	120-140	7 1			1150	1400
16 3	BARETTA B/R		RNBT	FBG DV	IO	120-140	7 1			1250	1500
16 4	BARETTA B/R		RNBT	FBG DV	TR	120-140	6 4			1200	1450
16 4	BARETTA B/R		RNBT	FBG DV	TR	120-140	6 4			1200	1450
16 9	BARETTA B/R		RNBT	FBG DV	IO	120-170	7 1			1250	1500
16 9	SUCCESS B/R		RNBT	FBG DV	IO	120-170	7 1			1350	1650
17 4	LEGEND		RNBT	FBG DV	IO	185-188	6 11			1300	1650
17 4	LEGEND		RNBT	FBG DV	IO	120-188	7 3			1400	1650
17 11	BARETTA B/R		RNBT	FBG DV	IO	120-188	7 7			1500	1800
18 4	SUCCESS B/R		RNBT	FBG DV	IO	140-230	8			1650	2050
18 9	ADVANTAGE B/R	ST	RNBT	FBG DV	SE	115 OMC	7 7			**	**
18 9	ADVANTAGE B/R	ST	RNBT	FBG DV	IO	120-188	7 7			1550	1850
18 9	BARETTA B/R		RNBT	FBG DV	SE	115 OMC	7 7			**	**
18 9	BARETTA B/R		RNBT	FBG DV	IO	120-200	7 7			1500	1800
18 9	BARETTA C/D		RNBT	FBG DV	SE	115 OMC	7 7			**	**
18 9	BARETTA C/D		RNBT	FBG DV	IO	120-200	7 7			1600	1900
18 9	SUCCESS		CUD	FBG DV	SE	115 OMC	7 7			**	**
18 9	SUCCESS		CUD	FBG DV	IO	120-200	7 7			1850	2200
18 9	SUCCESS B/R		RNBT	FBG DV	SE	115 OMC	7 7			**	**
18 9	SUCCESS B/R		RNBT	FBG DV	IO	120-200	7 7			1600	1900
20 4	BARETTA		CUD	FBG DV	IO	140-260	8			2650	3250
20 4	BARETTA B/R		RNBT	FBG DV	IO	140-260	8			2400	2950

....For earlier years, see the BUC Used Boat Price Guide, Volume 3

MELGES BOAT WORKS INC
ZENDA WI 53195   COAST GUARD MFG ID– MEB See inside cover to adjust price for area

For more recent years, see the BUC Used Boat Price Guide, Volume 1

LOA FT IN	NAME AND/ OR MODEL	TOP/ RIG	BOAT TYPE	–HULL– MTL TP	TP	––ENGINE–– # HP MFG	BEAM FT IN	WGT LBS	DRAFT FT IN	RETAIL LOW	RETAIL HIGH
	–––––––––––––– 1996 BOATS ––––––––––––––										
16	M-16 SCOW	SLP	SAROD	FBG BB			5 8	440		7550	8700
16	MC-SCOW	CAT	SAROD	FBG BB			5 8	420		6000	6900
16	X-BOAT	SLP	SAROD	FBG CB			6 1	470		5450	6300
20	C-SCOW	CAT	SAROD	FBG BB			7	650		11000	12500
22	STAR OF THE 90'S	SLP	SARAC	FBG KL			7	2250		21500	23800
24	MELGES 24	SLP	SARAC	FBG KL			8	1750		20900	23200

LOA FT	LOA IN	NAME AND/ OR MODEL	TOP/ RIG	BOAT TYPE	-HULL- MTL	-HULL- TP	ENGINE TP	ENGINE # HP	ENGINE MFG	BEAM FT	BEAM IN	WGT LBS	DRAFT FT	DRAFT IN	RETAIL LOW	RETAIL HIGH
		1996 BOATS														
28		E-SCOW	SLP	SAROD	FBG	BB				6	9	965			21900	24300
31	6	5.5 METER	SLP	SARAC	FBG	KL				7	6	3500			43200	48000
		1995 BOATS														
16		M-16 SCOW	SLP	SAROD	FBG	BB				5	8	440			7050	8100
16		MC-SCOW	CAT	SAROD	FBG	BB				5	8	420			6900	7950
16		X-BOAT	SLP	SAROD	FBG	CB				6	1	470			7300	8400
20		C-SCOW	CAT	SAROD	FBG	BB				7		650			10200	11600
20		M-20 SCOW	SLP	SAROD	FBG	BB				5	8	595			9950	11300
22		STAR OF THE 90'S	SLP	SARAC	FBG	KL				7		2250			20000	22300
24		MELGES 24	SLP	SARAC	FBG	KL				8		1750			19500	21700
28		E-SCOW	SLP	SAROD	FBG	BB				6	9	965			20500	22700
31	6	5.5 METER	SLP	SARAC	FBG	KL				7	6	3500			40300	44800
38		A-SCOW	SLP	SAROD	FBG	BB									**	**
		1994 BOATS														
16		M-16 SCOW	SLP	SAROD	FBG	BB				5	8	440			6600	7600
16		MC-SCOW	CAT	SAROD	FBG	BB				5	8	420			5200	6000
16		X-BOAT	SLP	SAROD	FBG	CB				6	1	470			4750	5500
20		C-SCOW	CAT	SAROD	FBG	BB				7		650			9550	10900
20		M-20 SCOW	SLP	SAROD	FBG	BB				5	8	595			9350	10600
22		STAR OF THE 90'S	SLP	SARAC	FBG	KL				7		2250			18900	21000
24		MELGES 24	SLP	SARAC	FBG	KL				8		1750			18400	20400
28		E-SCOW	SLP	SAROD	FBG	BB				6	9	965			24900	27700
31	6	5.5 METER	SLP	SARAC	FBG	KL				7	6	3500			37600	41800
		1993 BOATS														
16		M-16 SCOW	SLP	SAROD	FBG	BB				5	8	440			6150	7100
16		MC-SCOW	CAT	SAROD	FBG	BB				5	8	420			4850	5600
16		X-BOAT	SLP	SAROD	FBG	CB				6	1	470			4500	5150
20		C-SCOW	CAT	SAROD	FBG	BB				7		650			9000	10200
20		M-20 SCOW	SLP	SAROD	FBG	BB				5	8	595			8650	9950
28		E-SCOW	SLP	SAROD	FBG	BB				6	9	965			23300	25900
38		A-SCOW	SLP	SAROD	FBG	BB									**	**
		1992 BOATS														
16		M-16 SCOW	SLP	SA/OD	FBG	BB				5	8	440			5750	6600
16		MC-SCOW	CAT	SA/OD	FBG	BB				5	8	420			4600	5250
16		X-BOAT	SLP	SA/OD	FBG	CB				6	1	470			4150	4800
20		C-SCOW	CAT	SA/OD	FBG	BB				7		650			8300	9550
20		M-20 SCOW	SLP	SA/OD	FBG	BB				5	8	595			8050	9300
28		E-SCOW	SLP	SA/OD	FBG	BB				6	9	965			21800	24200
38		A-SCOW	SLP	SA/OD	FBG	BB									107500	118500
		1990 BOATS														
16		M-16-SCOW	SLP	SA/OD	FBG	BB				5	8	440	3		5000	5750
16		M-C-SCOW	CAT	SA/OD	FBG	BB				5	8	420	3		3950	4600
16		X-BOAT	SLP	SA/OD	FBG	BB				6		500	3	3	3750	4350
20		C-SCOW	CAT	SA/OD	FBG	BB				6	6	650	3	9	7250	8350
20		M-20-SCOW	SLP	SA/OD	FBG	BB				5	8	595	3	6	7050	8100
22	6	STAR	SLP	SA/OD	FBG	KL				5	6	1470	3	3	11500	13100
28		E-SCOW	SLP	SA/OD	FBG	BB				6	9	965			19000	21100
31	6	5.5 METRE	SLP	SA/OD	FBG	KL				6	6	4500	5		34400	38300
38		A-SCOW	SLP	SA/OD	FBG	BB				8	6	1850	6	4	3850	4500
		1989 BOATS														
16		M-16-SCOW	SLP	SA/OD	FBG	BB				5	8	440	3		4700	5400
16		M-C-SCOW	CAT	SA/OD	FBG	BB				5	8	420	3		3700	4300
16		X-SCOW	SLP	SA/OD	FBG	BB				6		500	3	3	3500	4050
20		C-SCOW	CAT	SA/OD	FBG	BB				6	6	650	3	9	6750	7800
20		M-20-SCOW	SLP	SA/OD	FBG	BB				5	8	595	3	6	6600	7550
28		E-SCOW	SLP	SA/OD	FBG	BB	OB			6	9	965			16400	18600
38		A-SCOW	SLP	SA/OD	FBG	BB				8	6	1850	6	4	3600	4200
		1988 BOATS														
16		M-16-SCOW	SLP	SA/OD	FBG	BB				5	8	440	3		4400	5050
16		M-C-SCOW	CAT	SA/OD	FBG	BB				5	8	420	3		3450	4000
16		X-SCOW	SLP	SA/OD	FBG	BB				6		500	3	3	3250	3800
20		C-SCOW	CAT	SA/OD	FBG	BB				6	6	650	3	9	6350	7300
20		M-20-SCOW	SLP	SA/OD	FBG	BB				5	8	595	3	6	6150	7050
28		E-SCOW	SLP	SA/OD	FBG	BB				6	9	965	6		12600	14300
38		A-SCOW	SLP	SA/OD	FBG	BB				8	6	1850	6	4	3400	3950
		1987 BOATS														
16		M-16-SCOW	SLP	SA/OD	FBG	BB				5	8	440	3		4100	4750
16		M-C-SCOW	CAT	SA/OD	FBG	BB				5	8	420	3		3250	3750
16		X-SCOW	SLP	SA/OD	FBG	BB				6		500	3	3	3050	3550
20		C-SCOW	CAT	SA/OD	FBG	BB				6	6	650	3	9	5900	6800
20		M-20-SCOW	SLP	SA/OD	FBG	BB				5	8	595	3	6	5750	6600
28		E-SCOW	SLP	SA/OD	FBG	BB				6	9	965	6		11700	13300
38		A-SCOW	SLP	SA/OD	FBG	BB				8	6	1850	6	4	3150	3650
		1986 BOATS														
16		M-16-SCOW	SLP	SA/OD	FBG	BB				5	8	440	3		3800	4450
16		M-C-SCOW	CAT	SA/OD	FBG	BB				5	8	420	3		3000	3500
16		X-SCOW	SLP	SA/OD	FBG	BB				6		500	3	3	2850	3300
20		C-SCOW	CAT	SA/OD	FBG	BB				6	6	650	3	9	5550	6350
20		M-20-SCOW	SLP	SA/OD	FBG	BB				5	8	595	3	6	5400	6200
28		E-SCOW	SLP	SA/OD	FBG	BB				6	9	965	6		11000	12500
38		A-SCOW	SLP	SA/OD	FBG	BB				8	6	1850	6	4	2950	3450
		1985 BOATS														
16		M-16-SCOW	SLP	SA/OD	FBG	BB				5	8	440		3	3550	4150
16		M-C-SCOW	CAT	SA/OD	FBG	BB				5	8	420		6	2800	3300
16		X-SCOW	SLP	SA/OD	FBG	BB				6		500		2	2650	3100
20		C-SCOW	CAT	SA/OD	FBG	BB				6	6	650	3	9	5200	5950
20		M-20-SCOW	SLP	SA/OD	FBG	BB				5	8	595	3	6	5050	5800
22		STAR	SLP	SA/OD	FBG	KL				5	4		3	4	12100	13800
28		E-SCOW	SLP	SA/OD	FBG	BB				6	9	965	6		10300	11700
38		A-SCOW	SLP	SA/OD	FBG	BB				8	6	1850	6	4	2750	3200
		1984 BOATS														
16		M-16-SCOW	SLP	SA/OD	FBG	BB				5	8	440		3	3350	3900
16		M-C-SCOW	CAT	SA/OD	FBG	BB				5	8	420		6	2650	3050
16		X-SCOW	SLP	SA/OD	FBG	BB				6		500		2	2500	2900
20		C-SCOW	CAT	SA/OD	FBG	BB				6	6	650	3	9	4850	5550
20		M-20-SCOW	SLP	SA/OD	FBG	BB				5	8	595	3	9	4700	5400
22		STAR	SLP	SA/OD	FBG	KL				5			3	4	11300	12800
28		E-SCOW	SLP	SA/OD	FBG	BB				6	9	965	6		9600	10900
38		A-SCOW	SLP	SA/OD	FBG	BB				8	6	1850	6	4	2600	3000

....For earlier years, see the BUC Used Boat Price Guide, Volume 3

MENARD FIBERGLASS BOAT

LATROBE PA 15650

See inside cover to adjust price for area

FORMERLY M F G LINE

LOA FT	LOA IN	NAME AND/ OR MODEL	TOP/ RIG	BOAT TYPE	-HULL- MTL	-HULL- TP	ENGINE TP	ENGINE # HP	ENGINE MFG	BEAM FT	BEAM IN	WGT LBS	DRAFT FT	DRAFT IN	RETAIL LOW	RETAIL HIGH
		1990 BOATS														
16	11	CAPRICE 17 BR	OP	CUD	FBG	DV	OB			6	5	1100			3200	3700
16	11	CAPRICE 17 BR	OP	RNBT	FBG	DV	IO	120-130		6	5	1100			3050	3650
16	11	CAPRICE 17 BR	OP	RNBT	FBG	DV	IO	131-175		6	5	1100			3350	3900
16	11	CAPRICE 17 CLASSIC	OP	RNBT	FBG	DV	IO	130-205		6	5	1800			3750	4650
18	10	CAPRICE 19	OP	CUD	FBG	DV	OB			7	6	1600			4950	5650
18	10	CAPRICE 19	OP	CUD	FBG	DV	IO	130-205		7	6	2650			5750	6900
18	10	CAPRICE 19 BR	OP	CUD	FBG	DV	OB			7	6	1600			4100	4800
18	10	CAPRICE 19 BR	OP	RNBT	FBG	SV	IO	130-230		7	6	2500			5550	6700
18	10	CAPRICE 19 CB	OP	CUD	FBG	DV	OB			7	6	1600			3600	4150
18	10	CAPRICE 19 CB	OP	RNBT	FBG	SV	IO	120-205		7	6	2500			5400	6450
18	10	CAPRICE 19 W/BRKTS	OP	CUD	FBG	DV	OB			7	6	1600			5500	6300
18	10	CAPRICE 19BR W/BRKTS	OP	RNBT	FBG	DV	OB			7	6	1600			4850	5550
18	10	CAPRICE 19CB W/BRKTS	OP	RNBT	FBG	DV	OB			7	6	1600			4250	4900
22	3	CAPRICE 22	OP	SF	FBG	DV	IO	175-230		8		3500			10400	12100
22	3	CAPRICE 22 ELITE	OP	RNBT	FBG	DV	OB			8		3500			9900	11300
22	3	CAPRICE 22 ELITE	OP	RNBT	FBG	DV	IO	205-260		8		3500			8700	10700
22	3	CAPRICE 22 W/BRKTS	OP	SF	FBG	DV	OB			8		3500			9900	11300
		1989 BOATS														
16	11	CAPRICE 17 BR	ST	RNBT	FBG	DV	OB			6	5	1100			3100	3600
16	11	CAPRICE 17 BR	ST	RNBT	FBG	DV	IO	130-175		6	5	1800			3550	4150
17	4	CAPRICE CLASSIC 17	ST	RNBT	FBG	DV	IO	130-205		7	2	2000			4050	4850
18	10	CAPRICE 19	ST	CUD	FBG	DV	OB			7	6	1907			4650	5350
18	10	CAPRICE 19	ST	CUD	FBG	DV	IO		OMC	7	6	2650			**	**
18	10	CAPRICE 19	ST	CUD	FBG	DV	IO	130-205		7	6	2650			5400	6350
18	10	CAPRICE 19 BR	ST	RNBT	FBG	DV	OB			7	6	1600			4150	4850
18	10	CAPRICE 19 BR	ST	RNBT	FBG	DV	IO	130-230		7	6	2500			5100	6050
18	10	CAPRICE 19 BR W/BRAC	ST	RNBT	FBG	DV	OB			7	6	1600			4650	5350
18	10	CAPRICE 19 CB	ST	RNBT	FBG	DV	OB			7	6	1600			4150	4800
18	10	CAPRICE 19 CB	ST	RNBT	FBG	DV	IO	130-205		7	6	2300			4850	5700
18	10	CAPRICE 19 CB W/BRAC	ST	RNBT	FBG	DV	OB			7	6	1600			4650	5350
18	10	CAPRICE 19 W/BRAC	ST	CUD	FBG	DV	OB			7	6	1907			5150	5950
22	3	CAPRICE 22	ST	FSH	FBG	DV	IO	175-230		8		3500			9150	10600
22	3	CAPRICE 22 ELITE	ST	CUD	FBG	DV	IO	205-260		8		3500			8650	10300
22	3	CAPRICE 22 ELITE W/B	ST	CUD	FBG	DV	OB			8					9600	10900
22	3	CAPRICE 22 W/BRAC	ST	FSH	FBG	DV	OB			8					9600	10900
		1988 BOATS														
16	11	CAPRICE 17 BR	ST	RNBT	FBG	DV	OB			6	5	1100			3000	3500
16	11	CAPRICE 17 BR	ST	RNBT	FBG	DV	IO	120-130		6	5	1800			3300	3900
16	11	CAPRICE 17 BR	ST	RNBT	FBG	DV	IO	131-175		6	5	1800			3550	4150
17	4	CAPRICE CLASSIC 17	ST	RNBT	FBG	DV	IO	130-205		7	2	2000			3850	4700
18	10	CAPRICE 19	ST	CUD			OB					1907			4750	5450
18	10	CAPRICE 19	ST	CUD	FBG	DV	OB			7	6	1907			4750	5450
18	10	CAPRICE 19	ST	CUD	FBG	DV	IO	130-205		7	6	2650			5100	6150
18	10	CAPRICE 19 BR	ST	RNBT	FBG	DV	IO	130-230		7	6	2500			4800	5800

CONTINUED ON NEXT PAGE

MENARD FIBERGLASS BOAT —CONTINUED

See inside cover to adjust price for area

LOA FT IN	NAME AND/ OR MODEL	TOP/ RIG	BOAT TYPE	HULL MTL TP	TP #	HP	MFG	BEAM FT IN	WGT LBS	DRAFT FT IN	RETAIL LOW	RETAIL HIGH
1988 BOATS												
18 10	CAPRICE 19 CB	ST	RNBT	FBG DV	OB			7 6	1600		4250	4950
18 10	CAPRICE 19 CB	ST	RNBT	FBG DV	IO	120-205		7 6	2300		4650	5550
22 3	CAPRICE 22	ST	CUD	FBG DV	IO	260	VLVO	8	3500		8900	10100
22 3	CAPRICE 22	ST	FSH	FBG DV	IO	175-230		8	3500		8600	10100
22 3	CAPRICE 22 ELITE	ST	CUD	FBG DV	IO	205-260		8	3500		8200	10100
1987 BOATS												
16 11	CAPRICE 17 BR	ST	RNBT	FBG DV	OB			6 5	1100		2950	3400
16 11	CAPRICE 17 BR	ST	RNBT	FBG DV	IO	120-130		6 5	1800		3150	3700
16 11	CAPRICE 17 BR	ST	RNBT	FBG DV	IO	131-175		6 5	1800		3400	3950
17 4	CAPRICE CLASSIC 17	ST	RNBT	FBG DV	IO	120-151		7 2	2000		3600	4500
17 4	CAPRICE CLASSIC 17	ST	RNBT	FBG DV	IO	171-211		7 2	2000		3850	4550
18 10	CAPRICE 19	ST	CUD	FBG DV	IO	130-205		7 6	2650		4850	5850
18 10	CAPRICE 19 BR	ST	RNBT	FBG DV	IO	120-230		7 6	2500		4550	5500
18 10	CAPRICE 19 CB	ST	RNBT	FBG DV	OB			7 6			4150	4800
18 10	CAPRICE 19 CB	ST	RNBT	FBG DV	IO	120-205		7 6	2300		4350	5300
22 3	CAPRICE 22	ST	CUD	FBG DV	IO	260	VLVO	8	3500		8400	9650
22 3	CAPRICE 22	ST	FSH	FBG DV	IO	175-230		8	3500		8150	9550
22 3	CAPRICE 22 ELITE	ST	CUD	FBG DV	IO	205-260		8	3500		7800	9350
1986 BOATS												
16 11	CAPRICE 17 BR	ST	RNBT	FBG DV	OB			6 5	1100		2850	3300
16 11	CAPRICE 17 BR	ST	RNBT	FBG DV	IO	120-175		6 5	1800		3050	3750
17 4	CAPRICE CLASSIC 17	ST	RNBT	FBG DV	IO	120-205		7 2	2000		3450	4250
18 10	CAPRICE 19	ST	CUD	FBG DV	OB			7 6	1600		4000	4700
18 10	CAPRICE 19	ST	CUD	FBG DV	IO	140-205		7 6	2500		4550	5300
18 10	CAPRICE 19 BR	ST	RNBT	FBG DV	OB			7 6			4000	4700
18 10	CAPRICE 19 BR	ST	RNBT	FBG DV	IO	120-230		7 6	2500		4400	5250
18 10	CAPRICE 19 CB	ST	RNBT	FBG DV	OB			7 6			4000	4700
18 10	CAPRICE 19 CB	ST	RNBT	FBG DV	IO	120-190		7 6	2300		4150	5050
22 3	CAPRICE 22	ST	CUD	FBG DV	IO	200-260		8	3500		7450	9200
22 3	CAPRICE 22	ST	FSH	FBG DV	IO	170-230		8	3500		7800	9150
1985 BOATS												
16 11	CAPRICE 17 BR	ST	RNBT	FBG DV	OB			6 5	1100		2800	3250
16 11	CAPRICE 17 BR	ST	RNBT	FBG DV	IO	120-185		6 5	1800		3150	3650
17 4	CAPRICE CLASSIC 17	ST	RNBT	FBG DV	IO	120-230		7 2	2000		3600	4300
18 10	CAPRICE 19 BR	ST	RNBT	FBG DV	OB			7 6			4150	4850
18 10	CAPRICE 19 BR	ST	RNBT	FBG DV	IO	120-230		7 6	2500		4450	5250
18 10	CAPRICE 19 CB	ST	RNBT	FBG DV	OB			7 6			3700	4300
18 10	CAPRICE 19 CB	ST	RNBT	FBG DV	IO	120-185		7 6	2300		4250	4950
22 3	CAPRICE 22	ST	CUD	FBG DV	IO	165-260		8	3500		7350	8800

MENGER BOATWORKS INC
OYSTER BAY NY 11771-151 COAST GUARD MFG ID- MEN See inside cover to adjust price for area
FORMERLY MENGER ENTERPRISES INC

For more recent years, see the BUC Used Boat Price Guide, Volume 1

LOA FT IN	NAME AND/ OR MODEL	TOP/ RIG	BOAT TYPE	HULL MTL TP	TP #	HP	MFG	BEAM FT IN	WGT LBS	DRAFT FT IN	RETAIL LOW	RETAIL HIGH
1996 BOATS												
19	MENGER CAT 19	CAT	SACAC	FBG CB	OB			8	2900	1 10	14100	16000
19	MENGER CAT 19	CAT	SACAC	FBG CB	OB	9D	YAN	8	2900	1 10	19400	21500
22 6	MENGER CAT 23	CAT	SACAC	FBG CB	IB	18D	YAN	10	6500	2 6	34600	38400
1995 BOATS												
19	MENGER CAT 19	CAT	SACAC	FBG CB	OB			8	2900	1 10	13200	15000
19	MENGER CAT 19	CAT	SACAC	FBG CB	OB	9D	YAN	8	2900	1 10	18400	20500
22 6	MENGER CAT 23	CAT	SACAC	FBG CB	IB	18D	YAN	10	6500	2 6	32500	36100
1994 BOATS												
19	MENGER CAT 19	CAT	SACAC	FBG CB	OB			8	2900	1 10	12400	14100
19	MENGER CAT 19	CAT	SACAC	FBG CB	OB	9D	YAN	8	2900	1 10	16900	19200
22 6	MENGER CAT 23	CAT	SACAC	FBG CB	IB	18D	YAN	10	6500	2 6	30600	34000
1993 BOATS												
19	MENGER CAT 19	GAF	SACAC	FBG CB	IB	8D	YAN	8	2900	1 10	15800	18000
22 6	MENGER CAT 23	GAF	SACAC	FBG CB	IB	18D	YAN	10	5500	2 6	24100	26800
1992 BOATS												
19	MENGER CAT 19	GAF	SAIL	FBG CB	IB	8D	YAN	8	2900	1 10	14900	16900
22 6	MENGER CAT 23	GAF	SAIL	FBG CB	IB	18D	YAN	10	5500	2 6	22700	25200
1986 BOATS												
17	MENGER CAT	CAT	SA/CR	FBG CB	OB			8	2200	1 8	6550	7550
17	MENGER CAT	CAT	SA/CR	FBG CB	OB	9D	YAN	8	2200	1 8	10000	11300
31 3	OYSTERMAN 23	SLP	SA/CR	FBG CB	OB			8	2800	1 8	9250	10400
31 3	OYSTERMAN 23	SLP	SA/CR	FBG CB	SD	15	OMC	8	2800	1 8	9250	10500
31 3	OYSTERMAN 23	SLP	SA/CR	FBG CB	IB	9D		8	2800	1 8	9200	10400
31 3	OYSTERMAN 23	KTH	SA/CR	FBG CB	OB			8	2800	1 8	9300	10600
31 3	OYSTERMAN 23	KTH	SA/CR	FBG CB	SD	15	OMC	8	2800	1 8	9250	10500
31 3	OYSTERMAN 23	KTH	SA/CR	FBG CB	IB	9D		8	2800	1 8	9300	10600
1985 BOATS												
17	MENGER CAT	CAT	SA/CR	FBG CB	OB			8	2200	1 8	6150	7100
17	MENGER CAT	CAT	SA/CR	FBG CB	OB	9D	YAN	8	2200	1 8	9400	10700
31 3	OYSTERMAN 23	SLP	SA/CR	FBG CB	OB			8	2800	1 8	8550	9800
31 3	OYSTERMAN 23	SLP	SA/CR	FBG CB	IB	9D		8	2800	1 8	8650	9950
31 3	OYSTERMAN 23	KTH	SA/CR	FBG CB	OB			8	2800	1 8	8550	9800
31 3	OYSTERMAN 23	KTH	SA/CR	FBG CB	IB	9D		8	2800	1 8	8650	9950

....For earlier years, see the BUC Used Boat Price Guide, Volume 3

MERIT MARINE
PACOIMA CA 91331

See inside cover to adjust price for area

LOA FT IN	NAME AND/ OR MODEL	TOP/ RIG	BOAT TYPE	HULL MTL TP	TP #	HP	MFG	BEAM FT IN	WGT LBS	DRAFT FT IN	RETAIL LOW	RETAIL HIGH
1986 BOATS												
22	MERIT 22	SLP	SA/OD	F/S KC				8	2000	4	3800	4400
22	MERIT 22	SLP	SA/RC	F/S DB				8	2000	4	3800	4400
25	MERIT 25	SLP	SA/OD	F/S KL				8	3000	4	5750	6600
25	MERIT 25	SLP	SA/RC	F/S KL				8	2600	4	5200	5950
1985 BOATS												
22	MERIT 22	SLP	SA/RC	F/S KC	OB			8	2000	4	3550	4150
22 6	MERIT 23 SPRINT	SLP	SA/RC	F/S KC	OB			8 2	1700	2	3350	3850
25	MERIT 25	SLP	SA/RC	F/S KC	OB			8	3000	4	5500	6300
30	MERIT 30 MAGNUM	SLP	SA/RC	F/S KC	IO	110D	VLVO	9 6	4800	2	10600	12100
1984 BOATS												
22	MERIT 22	SLP	SA/RC	F/S	OB			8	2000	4	3350	3900
25	MERIT 25	SLP	SA/RC	F/S KL	OB			8	3000	4	5150	5950

....For earlier years, see the BUC Used Boat Price Guide, Volume 3

MERRITT BOAT & ENG WORKS
POMPANO BEACH FL 33062 COAST GUARD MFG ID- MBN See inside cover to adjust price for area

LOA FT IN	NAME AND/ OR MODEL	TOP/ RIG	BOAT TYPE	HULL MTL TP	TP #	HP	MFG	BEAM FT IN	WGT LBS	DRAFT FT IN	RETAIL LOW	RETAIL HIGH
1996 BOATS												
58 6			SF	KEV	IB	T130D	CAT	18 4	65000	4 6	642500	706000

....For earlier years, see the BUC Used Boat Price Guide, Volume 3

METAL CRAFT MARINE INC
KINGSTON ONTARIO CANADA COAST GUARD MFG ID- QME See inside cover to adjust price for area

LOA FT IN	NAME AND/ OR MODEL	TOP/ RIG	BOAT TYPE	HULL MTL TP	TP #	HP	MFG	BEAM FT IN	WGT LBS	DRAFT FT IN	RETAIL LOW	RETAIL HIGH
1991 BOATS												
16 4	KINGFISHER 5.0	OP	CTRCN	AL	DV	OB		6 8	750	10	4350	5000
18	KINGFISHER 5.5	OP	CTRCN	AL	DV	OB		7	850	1	5200	6000
18	KINGFISHER 5.5	OP	CTRCN	AL	DV	JT	200	7	850	1	4400	6050
18	KINGFISHER 5.5	OP	CTRCN	AL	DV	IO	200	7	850	1	3150	3700
19 8	KINGFISHER 6.0	OP	CTRCN	AL	DV	OB		7 4	950	1 2	6050	7000
19 8	KINGFISHER 6.0	OP	CTRCN	AL	DV	JT	260	7 4	950	1 2	5400	6200
19 8	KINGFISHER 6.0	OP	CTRCN	AL	DV	IO	260	7 4	950	1 2	4300	5000
20 6	KINGSTON 20	OP	CUD	AL	DV	JT	260	8 6	2800	1 2	10200	11600
20 6	KINGSTON 20	OP	CUD	AL	DV	IO	260	8 6	2800	1 2	7850	9000
24 4	KINGSTON 24	HT	FSH	AL	DV	JT	330	9 4	5100	1 6	18700	20800
24 4	KINGSTON 24	HT	FSH	AL	DV	IO	330	9 4	5100	1 6	16300	18500
31 5	DELTA 315	FB	SPTCR	AL	DV	JT	T260	11 6	7500	1 8	42200	46900
31 5	DELTA 315	FB	SPTCR	AL	DV	IO	T260	11 6	7500	1 8	33900	37700

METALMAST MARINE INC
PUTNAM CT 06260 COAST GUARD MFG ID- MET See inside cover to adjust price for area

LOA FT IN	NAME AND/ OR MODEL	TOP/ RIG	BOAT TYPE	HULL MTL TP	TP #	HP	MFG	BEAM FT IN	WGT LBS	DRAFT FT IN	RETAIL LOW	RETAIL HIGH
1984 BOATS												
29 11	METALMAST 30	SLP	SA/CR	FBG KL	IB	8D	YAN	10 2	7100	5 4	21900	24400
35 6	METALMAST 36	SLP	SA/CR	FBG KL	IB	15D	YAN	11 2	13000	6 4	41000	45600

....For earlier years, see the BUC Used Boat Price Guide, Volume 3

METANAV INC

LASSOMPTION QUE CANADA

See inside cover to adjust price for area

LOA FT IN	NAME AND/ OR MODEL	TOP/ RIG	BOAT TYPE	HULL MTL	HULL TP	ENG TP	ENG #	ENG HP	ENG MFG	BEAM FT IN	WGT LBS	DRAFT FT IN	RETAIL LOW	RETAIL HIGH
1987 BOATS														
33 8	E-G-VANDESTADT 34	SLP	SAIL	STL	KL	IB		20D		10 10	11905	4 3	43600	48400
34 5	A-P-231	CUT	SAIL	STL	KL	IB		33D		10 6	16800	4 3	59800	65700
40 3	CORTEN 40	CUT	SAIL	STL	KL	IB		62D		12 4	30000	5 6	102500	113000
1986 BOATS														
28 7	SEA-DOG 29	SLP	SAIL	STL	KL	IB		20D		9 6	8378	5 1	26400	29300
28 7	SEA-DOG 29	SLP	SAIL	STL	KL	IB		20D		9 6	8378	5 1	26400	29300
33 8	E-G-VANDESTADT 34	SLP	SAIL	STL	KL	IB		20D		10 10	11905	4 3	34100	37900
33 8	E-G-VANDESTADT 34	SLP	SAIL	STL	KL	IB		20D		10 10	11905	4 3	40700	45300
34 5	A-P-231	CUT	SAIL	STL	KL	IB		33D		10 6	16800	5 3	56500	62100
38 1	TRIADE 38	SLP	SAIL	STL	KL	IB		33D		12	18900	6 6	66000	72500
40 3	CORTEN 40	CUT	SAIL	STL	KL	IB		62D		12 4	30000	5 6	96000	105500
1985 BOATS														
28 7	SEA-DOG 29	SLP	SAIL	STL	KL	IB		20D		9 6	8378	5 1	24700	27400
32 10	NAUTILUS 33	SLP	SAIL	STL	KL	IB		20D		9 10	13000	5 4	41500	46100
33 8	VAN-DE-STADT 34	SLP	SAIL	STL	KL	IB		20D		10 10	11905	5 11	38100	42300

MEYERS BOAT COMPANY INC

ADRIAN MI 49221 — COAST GUARD MFG ID- MEY See inside cover to adjust price for area

FORMERLY MEYERS INDUSTRIES

For more recent years, see the BUC Used Boat Price Guide, Volume 1

LOA FT IN	NAME AND/ OR MODEL	TOP/ RIG	BOAT TYPE	HULL MTL	HULL TP	ENG TP	ENG #	ENG HP	ENG MFG	BEAM FT IN	WGT LBS	DRAFT FT IN	RETAIL LOW	RETAIL HIGH
1986 BOATS														
16	RUNABOUT 16-CB	OP	RNBT	AL	SV	OB				6	580		1350	1600
1985 BOATS														
16	RUNABOUT 16-CB	OP	RNBT	AL	SV	OB				6	610		1400	1650
1984 BOATS														
16	RUNABOUT	OP	RNBT	AL	SV	OB				6	610		1350	1600

....For earlier years, see the BUC Used Boat Price Guide, Volume 3

MICHI-CRAFT

ADRIAN MI 49221 — COAST GUARD MFG ID- MEY See inside cover to adjust price for area

For more recent years, see the BUC Used Boat Price Guide, Volume 1

LOA FT IN	NAME AND/ OR MODEL	TOP/ RIG	BOAT TYPE	HULL MTL	HULL TP	ENG TP	ENG #	ENG HP	ENG MFG	BEAM FT IN	WGT LBS	DRAFT FT IN	RETAIL LOW	RETAIL HIGH
1986 BOATS														
16	HURON H-16		FSH	AL	FL	OB				5 11	290		815	980
1985 BOATS														
16	SP-16	OP	RNBT	AL	DV	OB				6	280		765	925

....For earlier years, see the BUC Used Boat Price Guide, Volume 3

MID OCEAN BOATS

OPA LOCKA FL 33054

See inside cover to adjust price for area

LOA FT IN	NAME AND/ OR MODEL	TOP/ RIG	BOAT TYPE	HULL MTL	HULL TP	ENG TP	ENG #	ENG HP	ENG MFG	BEAM FT IN	WGT LBS	DRAFT FT IN	RETAIL LOW	RETAIL HIGH
1988 BOATS														
19 6	TOURNAMENT LITETACKL	OP	RNBT	FBG	SV	OB				7 4	980	1	3300	3800
20 3	SPORT 20	OP	RNBT	FBG	SV	OB				7 3	1200	1	4150	4850
20 9	PERFORMANCE FISHERMN	OP	CTRCN	FBG	DV	OB				7 8	1600	1 6	5400	6250
20 9	SPORT 21	OP	RNBT	FBG	DV	OB				7 8	1400	1 6	4850	5600
25 8	MID OCEAN 26	OP	CTRCN	FBG	DV	OB				8	2200	1 4	11100	12600
25 8	TOURNAMENT	OP	CTRCN	FBG	DV	OB				8	2800	1 4	12000	13600
33	PERFORMANCE FISHERMN	OP	CTRCN	FBG	DV	OB				9 6	5000	1 8	28200	31300
40	OPEN SPORT 40	OP	CTRCN	FBG	DV	OB				9 6	6000	1 8	**	**

MID-JET MFG

PORTLAND OR 97206 — COAST GUARD MFG ID- MJG See inside cover to adjust price for area

LOA FT IN	NAME AND/ OR MODEL	TOP/ RIG	BOAT TYPE	HULL MTL	HULL TP	ENG TP	ENG #	ENG HP	ENG MFG	BEAM FT IN	WGT LBS	DRAFT FT IN	RETAIL LOW	RETAIL HIGH
1988 BOATS														
16	MID-JET 16	OP	FSH	AL	SV	OB				7	610		1900	2250
16	MID-JET 16	OP	FSH	AL	SV	IB		122	FORD	7	1100		3550	4100
16	MID-JET 16	OP	FSH	AL	SV	IB		213	FORD	7	1450		4600	5300
16	MID-JET 16WS	OP	FSH	AL	SV	OB				7	730		2300	2700
16	MID-JET 16WS	OP	FSH	AL	SV	IB		122	FORD	7	1250		3800	4400
16	MID-JET 16WS	OP	FSH	AL	SV	IB		213	FORD	7	1600		4800	5500
17	MID-JET 17	OP	FSH	AL	SV	OB				7	640		2100	2500
17	MID-JET 17	OP	FSH	AL	SV	IB		122	FORD	7	1300		4400	5050
17	MID-JET 17	OP	FSH	AL	SV	IB		213	FORD	7	1650		5300	6050
17	MID-JET 17WS	OP	FSH	AL	SV	OB				7	760		2500	2900
17	MID-JET 17WS	OP	FSH	AL	SV	IB		122	FORD	7	1450		4550	5250
17	MID-JET 17WS	OP	FSH	AL	SV	IB		213	FORD	7	1800		5500	6300
18	MID-JET 18	OP	FSH	AL	SV	OB				7	670		2350	2700
18	MID-JET 18	OP	FSH	AL	SV	IB		122	FORD	7	1500		5050	5800
18	MID-JET 18	OP	FSH	AL	SV	IB		213	FORD	7	1850		5950	6850
18	MID-JET 18WS	OP	FSH	AL	SV	OB				7	790		2650	3100
18	MID-JET 18WS	OP	FSH	AL	SV	IB		122	FORD	7	1650		5250	6050
18	MID-JET 18WS	OP	FSH	AL	SV	IB		213	FORD	7	2000		6200	7100
1987 BOATS														
17 2	MID-JET 17	OP	FSH	AL	SV	JT		122-185	FORD	6 9	1400	11	5150	6400
17 2	MID-JET 17	OP	FSH	AL	SV	JT		215	FORD	6 9	1400	11	5650	6500
18 2	MID-JET 18	OP	FSH	AL	SV	JT		215-250		6 9	1600	11	5950	7050

MIDNIGHT EXPRESS

OPA LOCKA FL 33054

See inside cover to adjust price for area

FOR MORE RECENT YEARS SEE GOLDEN WAVE SHIPYARD

LOA FT IN	NAME AND/ OR MODEL	TOP/ RIG	BOAT TYPE	HULL MTL	HULL TP	ENG TP	ENG #	ENG HP	ENG MFG	BEAM FT IN	WGT LBS	DRAFT FT IN	RETAIL LOW	RETAIL HIGH
1988 BOATS														
26	SPORT		OFF	FBG	DV	OB				8	2400	1	24000	26700
32	CENTER CONSOLE	OP	OFF	FBG	DV	OB				8	5500	1 6	48600	53500
32	SPORT		OFF	FBG	DV	OB				8	5100	1	48600	53500
32	SPORT/RACE		OFF	FBG	DV	IO	T600		MRCR	8	5300	1 6	50600	55600
37	CENTER CONSOLE	OP	OFF	FBG	DV	OB				9 6	8500	1 6	60200	66200
37	CENTER CONSOLE	OP	OFF	FBG	DV	OB				9 6	8500	1 6	60000	65900
37	CENTER CONSOLE	OP	OFF	FBG	DV	OB				9 6	8500	1 10	60000	65900
37	CENTER CONSOLE	OP	OFF	FBG	DV	IO	T420		MRCR	9 6	8500	2	62300	68500
37	CENTER CONSOLE	OP	OFF	FBG	DV	IO	T600		MRCR	9 6	8500	2	79000	86800
37	MIDNIGHT CATAMARAN		OFF	FBG	CT	OB				12	8500	1 6	104500	115000
37	MIDNIGHT CATAMARAN		OFF	FBG	CT	IO	T600		MRCR	12	8500	1 10	70600	77600
37	MIDNIGHT SPECIAL		OFF	FBG	DV	OB				9 6	8000	1 6	60000	65900
37	MIDNIGHT SPECIAL		OFF	FBG	DV	IO	T850			9 6	8000	1 8	**	**
37	SPORT		OFF	FBG	DV	OB				9 6	8300	1 6	60200	66200
37	SPORT		OFF	FBG	DV	OB				9 6	8300	1 8	60000	65900
37	SPORT		OFF	FBG	DV	OB				9 6	8300	1 10	60000	65900
37	SPORT		OFF	FBG	DV	IO	T420		MRCR	9 6	8300	2	63500	69800
37	SPORT		OFF	FBG	DV	IO	T850			9 6	8300	2	**	**
47	SPORT		OFF	FBG	DV	IB	T550		GM	12	18000	3	233500	256500
47	SPORT		OFF	FBG	DV	IB	T750		GM	12	18900	3	258000	283500

....For earlier years, see the BUC Used Boat Price Guide, Volume 3

MIKELSON YACHTS INC

SAN DIEGO CA 92106

See inside cover to adjust price for area

For more recent years, see the BUC Used Boat Price Guide, Volume 1

LOA FT IN	NAME AND/ OR MODEL	TOP/ RIG	BOAT TYPE	HULL MTL	HULL TP	ENG TP	ENG #	ENG HP	ENG MFG	BEAM FT IN	WGT LBS	DRAFT FT IN	RETAIL LOW	RETAIL HIGH
1996 BOATS														
48 6	MIKELSON 48	FB	SDNSF	F/S	SV	VD	T435D		CAT	16 8	38000	4 4	307500	338000
50 6	MIKELSON 50	FB	SDNSF	F/S	SV	VD	T435D		CAT	16 8	45000	3 10	329500	362000
56 2	MIKELSON 56	FB	SDNSF	F/S	SV	IB	T735D		GM	17 2	49000	5	517000	568000
56 2	MIKELSON 56	FB	YTFS	F/S	SV	IB	T735D		GM	17 2	49000	5	523000	575000
59 1	MIKELSON 60	FB	SDNSF	F/S	SV	IB	T735D		GM	17 2	52000	5	491000	539500
59 1	MIKELSON 60	FB	SDNSF	F/S	SV	IB	T735D		GM	17 2	52000	5	539500	592500
72 6	MIKELSON 72	FB	SDNSF	F/S	SV	IB	T11CD		GM	20 6	85000	5 6	**	**
77 7	MIKELSON 78	FB	SDNSF	F/S	SV	IB	T11CD		MTU	20 6	91000	5 6	**	**
1995 BOATS														
48 6	MIKELSON 48	FB	SDNSF	F/S	SV	VD	T435D		CAT	16 8	38000	4 4	294000	323000
50 6	MIKELSON 50	FB	SDNSF	F/S	SV	VD	T435D		CAT	16 8	45000	3 10	315500	346500
56 2	MIKELSON 56	FB	SDNSF	F/S	SV	IB	T735D		GM	17 2	49000	5	427500	470000
56 2	MIKELSON 56	FB	SDNSF	F/S	SV	IB	T735D		GM	17 2	49000	5	496000	545000
56 2	MIKELSON 56	FB	SDNSF	F/S	SV	IB	T10CD		MTU	17 2	49000	5	580500	637500
56 2	MIKELSON 56	FB	SDNSF	F/S	SV	IB	T550D		GM	17 2	49000	5	431000	474000
56 2	MIKELSON 56	FB	YTFS	F/S	SV	IB	T735D		GM	17 2	49000	5	501000	550500
56 2	MIKELSON 56	FB	YTFS	F/S	SV	IB	T10CD		MTU	17 2	49000	5	592500	651500

LOA FT	IN	NAME AND/ OR MODEL	TOP/ RIG	BOAT TYPE	-HULL- MTL	TP	TP	----ENGINE--- # HP	MFG	BEAM FT	IN	WGT LBS	DRAFT FT	IN	RETAIL LOW	RETAIL HIGH
		1995 BOATS														
59	1	MIKELSON 60	FB	SDNSF	F/S	SV	IB	T550D	GM	17	2	52000	5		407000	447500
59	1	MIKELSON 60	FB	SDNSF	F/S	SV	IB	T735D	GM	17	2	52000	5		471000	517500
59	1	MIKELSON 60	FB	SDNSF	F/S	SV	IB	T10CD	MTU	17	2	52000	5		547000	601000
59	1	MIKELSON 60	FB	YTFS	F/S	SV	IB	T550D	GM	17	2	52000	5		446500	490500
59	1	MIKELSON 60	FB	YTFS	F/S	SV	IB	T735D	GM	17	2	52000	5		517500	568500
59	1	MIKELSON 60	FB	YTFS	F/S	SV	IB	T10CD	MTU	17	2	52000	5		602000	661500
72	6	MIKELSON 72	FB	SDNSF	F/S	SV	IB	T11CD	GM	20	6	85000	5	6	**	**
77	7	MIKELSON 78	FB	SDNSF	F/S	SV	IB	T11CD	MTU	20	6	91000	5	6	**	**
		1994 BOATS														
48	6	MIKELSON 48	FB	SDNSF	F/S	SV	VD	T435D	CAT	16	8	38000	4	4	281500	309000
50	5	MIKELSON 50	FB	SDNSF	F/S	SV	IB	T435D	CAT	16	8	45000	3	10	306500	336500
56	2	MIKELSON 56	FB	SDNSF	F/S	SV	IB	T550D	GM	17	2	49000	5		409500	450000
56	2	MIKELSON 56	FB	SDNSF	F/S	SV	IB	T735D	GM	17	2	49000	5		475000	522000
56	2	MIKELSON 56	FB	SDNSF	F/S	SV	IB	T10CD	MTU	17	2	49000	5		556000	611000
56	2	MIKELSON 56	FB	YTFS	F/S	SV	IB	T550D	GM	17	2	49000	5		413000	454000
56	2	MIKELSON 56	FB	YTFS	F/S	SV	IB	T735D	GM	17	2	49000	5		480000	527500
56	2	MIKELSON 56	FB	YTFS	F/S	SV	IB	T10CD	MTU	17	2	49000	5		567500	624000
59	1	MIKELSON 60	FB	SDNSF	F/S	SV	IB	T550D	GM	17	2	52000	5		390000	428500
59	1	MIKELSON 60	FB	SDNSF	F/S	SV	IB	T735D	GM	17	2	52000	5		451000	495500
59	1	MIKELSON 60	FB	SDNSF	F/S	SV	IB	T10CD	MTU	17	2	52000	5		524000	576000
59	1	MIKELSON 60	FB	YTFS	F/S	SV	IB	T550D	GM	17	2	52000	5		427500	470000
59	1	MIKELSON 60	FB	YTFS	F/S	SV	IB	T735D	GM	17	2	52000	5		495500	544500
59	1	MIKELSON 60	FB	YTFS	F/S	SV	IB	T10CD	MTU	17	2	52000	5		576500	633500
72	6	MIKELSON 72	FB	SDNSF	F/S	SV	IB	T10CD	GM	20	6	85000	5	6	**	**
77	7	MIKELSON 78	FB	SDNSF	F/S	SV	IB	T11CD	MTU	20	6	91000	5	6	**	**
		1993 BOATS														
48	6	MIKELSON 48	FB	SDNSF	F/S	SV	VD	T435D	CAT	16	8	35000	3	6	259500	285000
50	5	MIKELSON 50	FB	SDNSF	F/S	SV	IB	T435D	CAT	17		49000	3	6	296500	326000
56	2	MIKELSON 56	FB	SDNSF	F/S	SV	IB	T550D	GM	17		49000	3	6	390000	429000
56	2	MIKELSON 56	FB	SDNSF	F/S	SV	IB	T735D	GM	17		49000	3	6	452500	497500
56	2	MIKELSON 56	FB	SDNSF	F/S	SV	IB	T10CD	MTU	17		49000	3	6	529500	582000
56	2	MIKELSON 56	FB	YTFS	F/S	SV	IB	T550D	GM	17		49000	3	6	394000	433000
56	2	MIKELSON 56	FB	YTFS	F/S	SV	IB	T735D	GM	17		49000	3	6	458000	503000
56	2	MIKELSON 56	FB	YTFS	F/S	SV	IB	T10CD	MTU	17		49000	3	6	541000	594500
59	1	MIKELSON 60	FB	SDNSF	F/S	SV	IB	T550D	GM	17	2	49000	3	6	355000	390000
59	1	MIKELSON 60	FB	SDNSF	F/S	SV	IB	T735D	GM	17	2	48000	4	6	408500	449000
59	1	MIKELSON 60	FB	SDNSF	F/S	SV	IB	T10CD	MTU	17	2	49000	4	6	485500	533500
59	1	MIKELSON 60	FB	YTFS	F/S	SV	IB	T550D	GM	17	2	49000	3	6	390500	429000
59	1	MIKELSON 60	FB	YTFS	F/S	SV	IB	T735D	GM	17	2	48000	3	6	452500	497500
59	1	MIKELSON 60	FB	YTFS	F/S	SV	IB	T10CD	MTU	17	2	49000	3	6	537000	590000
72		MIKELSON 72	FB	SDNSF	F/S	SV	IB	T10CD	GM	20		65000	4	6	**	**
		1992 BOATS														
41	9	MIKELSON 42	FB	SDNSF	F/S	SV	VD	T300D	J&T	13		24000	3		166000	182500
47	1	MIKELSON 47	OP	EXP	F/S	SV	TD	T425D	CAT	15	6	29000	3		204500	225000
		TD T485D J&T 210000 231000, TD T550D J&T 219500 241000, TD T750D J&T 237000 260500														
48	6	MIKELSON 48	FB	SDNSF	F/S	SV	VD	T425D	CAT	16	8	35000	3	6	244500	268500
		VD T485D J&T 258500 284000, VD T550D J&T 274500 301500, VD T750D J&T 322500 354500														
50	5	MIKELSON 50	FB	SDNSF	F/S	SV	IB	T425D	CAT	17		49000	3	6	285000	313000
		IB T485D J&T 299500 329000, IB T550D J&T 315000 346000, IB T750D J&T 358500 394000														
56	2	MIKELSON 56	FB	YTFS	F/S	SV	IB	T485D	J&T	17		49000	3	6	356000	391500
		1991 BOATS														
41	9	MIKELSON 42	FB	SDNSF	F/S	SV	VD	T260D	J&T	13		24000	3		152000	167500
41	9	MIKELSON 42	FB	SDNSF	F/S	SV	VD	T300D	J&T	13		24000	3		158500	174000
47	1	MIKELSON 47	OP	EXP	F/S	SV	TD	T425D	CAT	15	6	29000	3		195000	214500
		TD T485D J&T 200500 220000, TD T550D J&T 209500 230000, TD T750D J&T 226000 248500														
48	6	MIKELSON 48	FB	SDNSF	F/S	SV	VD	T375D	CAT	16	8	35000	3	6	219500	241500
48	6	MIKELSON 48	FB	SDNSF	F/S	SV	VD	T425D	CAT	16	8	35000	3	6	233000	256000
48	6	MIKELSON 48	FB	SDNSF	F/S	SV	VD	T485D	J&T	16	8	35000	3	6	246000	270500
56	2	MIKELSON 56	FB	YTFS	F/S	SV	IB	T425D	CAT	17		49000	3	6	317000	348500
		IB T485D J&T 339500 373500, IB T550D J&T 362500 398000, IB T750D J&T 424500 466500														
		1990 BOATS														
41	9	MIKELSON SPORT SEDAN	FB	CNV	F/S	SV	IB	T260D	J&T	13		24000	3		145000	159500
48	6	MIKELSON SEDAN SF	FB	CNV	F/S	SV	IB	T375D	CAT	16	8	35000	3	6	201000	221000
50	10	MIKELSON PILOTHOUSE	CUT	SAIL	FBG	KL	IB	135D	LEHM	14	2	50000	6	2	277000	304500
56	2	MIKELSON YACHTFISH	FB	YTFS	F/S	SV	IB	T565D	J&T	17		50000	4		356000	391000

MILLAR MARINE

ONTARIO CA 91764 COAST GUARD MFG ID- RNN See inside cover to adjust price for area

LOA FT	IN	NAME AND/ OR MODEL	TOP/ RIG	BOAT TYPE	-HULL- MTL	TP	TP	----ENGINE--- # HP	MFG	BEAM FT	IN	WGT LBS	DRAFT FT	IN	RETAIL LOW	RETAIL HIGH
		1984 BOATS														
21		REYNOLDS 21	SLP	SAIL	F/S	CT				11	3	900		8	6650	7650

....For earlier years, see the BUC Used Boat Price Guide, Volume 3

REID MILLER

SANTA BARBARA CA 93105 See inside cover to adjust price for area

LOA FT	IN	NAME AND/ OR MODEL	TOP/ RIG	BOAT TYPE	-HULL- MTL	TP	TP	----ENGINE--- # HP	MFG	BEAM FT	IN	WGT LBS	DRAFT FT	IN	RETAIL LOW	RETAIL HIGH
		1986 BOATS														
36		ROLAND 36		SAIL		CT	IB	D		20		2050	4	5	26900	29900
		1985 BOATS														
36		ROLAND 36		SAIL		CT	IB	D		20		2050			25200	27900

MIRAGE MANFACTURING LLC

MIRAGE HOLDING INC See inside cover to adjust price for area
SEATTLE WA 98107 COAST GUARD MFG ID- MCJ
FORMERLY MIRAGE MARINE CORPORATION

For more recent years, see the BUC Used Boat Price Guide, Volume 1

LOA FT	IN	NAME AND/ OR MODEL	TOP/ RIG	BOAT TYPE	-HULL- MTL	TP	TP	----ENGINE--- # HP	MFG	BEAM FT	IN	WGT LBS	DRAFT FT	IN	RETAIL LOW	RETAIL HIGH
		1996 BOATS														
18	2	TROVARE 182 BR	ST	RNBT	FBG	DV	IO	190-205		7	9	2300			7800	9050
20	2	TROVARE 202 BR	ST	RNBT	FBG	DV	IO	210-250		8	6	2620			10800	12700
20	2	TROVARE 202 CUDDY	ST	CUD	FBG	DV	IO	210-250		8	6	2850			11800	13900
21	1	TROVARE 211 BR	ST	RNBT	FBG	DV	IO	250-300		8		3100			12300	15000
21	1	TROVARE 211 CUDDY	ST	CUD	FBG	DV	IO	250-300		8		3100			13000	15800
21	7	INTRUDER 217	ST	OFF	FBG	DV	IO	250-300		8		3850			15300	18500
21	7	INTRUDER 217	ST	OFF	FBG	DV	IO	330-350		8		3850			17200	20400
21	7	INTRUDER 217	ST	OFF	FBG	DV	IO	385-415		8		3850			19900	24100
23	2	TROVARE 232 CUDDY	ST	CUD	FBG	DV	IO	250-300		8		3850			16600	20000
23	2	TROVARE 232 CUDDY	ST	CUD	FBG	DV	IO	350-385		8		3850			19500	23500
23	2	TROVARE 232 CUDDY	ST	CUD	FBG	DV	IO	415	MRCR	8		3850			22900	25500
25	7	TROVARE 257 BR	ST	RNBT	FBG	DV	IO	300-350		8		4300			20300	24300
25	7	TROVARE 257 BR	ST	RNBT	FBG	DV	IO	415	MRCR	8		4300			24600	27400
25	7	TROVARE 257 CUDDY	ST	CUD	FBG	DV	IO	300-350		8		4300			22100	26400
25	7	TROVARE 257 CUDDY	ST	CUD	FBG	DV	IO	385-415		8		4300			25300	29800
		1995 BOATS														
18	2	TROVARE 182 BR	ST	RNBT	FBG	DV	IO	135-180		7	9	2300			7200	8350
20	2	TROVARE 202 BR	ST	RNBT	FBG	DV	IO	180-250		8	6	2620			10000	11900
20	2	TROVARE 202 CUDDY	ST	CUD	FBG	DV	IO	180-250		8	6	2850			10900	12900
21	1	TROVARE 211 BR	ST	RNBT	FBG	DV	IO	190-250		8		3100			11100	13100
21	1	TROVARE 211 BR	ST	RNBT	FBG	DV	IO	300	MRCR	8		3100			12300	14000
21	1	TROVARE 211 CUDDY	ST	CUD	FBG	DV	IO	190-250		8		3100			11600	13700
21	1	TROVARE 211 CUDDY	ST	CUD	FBG	DV	IO	300	MRCR	8		3100			13000	14700
21	7	INTRUDER 217	ST	OFF	FBG	DV	IO	250-300		8		3850			14300	17300
21	7	INTRUDER 217	ST	OFF	FBG	DV	IO	350-385		8		3850			16800	20900
21	7	INTRUDER 217	ST	OFF	FBG	DV	IO	415	MRCR	8		3850			20200	22500
23	2	TROVARE 232 CUDDY	ST	CUD	FBG	DV	IO	250-300		8		3850			15500	18600
23	2	TROVARE 232 CUDDY	ST	CUD	FBG	DV	IO	350-385		8		3850			18400	22000
23	2	TROVARE 232 CUDDY	ST	CUD	FBG	DV	IO	415	MRCR	8		3850			21400	23800
25	7	TROVARE 257 BR	ST	RNBT	FBG	DV	IO	300-350		8		4300			19200	22700
25	7	TROVARE 257 BR	ST	RNBT	FBG	DV	IO	415	MRCR	8		4300			23000	25600
25	7	TROVARE 257 CUDDY	ST	CUD	FBG	DV	IO	300-350		8		4300			20600	24600
25	7	TROVARE 257 CUDDY	ST	CUD	FBG	DV	IO	385-415		8		4300			23600	27800
27		INTIMIDATOR 270	ST	OFF	FBG	DV	IO	T300-T350		8		6100			31300	37600
27		INTIMIDATOR 270	ST	OFF	FBG	DV	IO	T385-T415		8		6100			36100	42500
		1994 BOATS														
18	2	TROVARE 180 BR	ST	RNBT	FBG	DV	IO	185	MRCR	7	9	2300			6700	7700
18	2	TROVARE 182 BR	ST	RNBT	FBG	DV	OB			7	9	2300			6350	7300
18	2	TROVARE 182 BR	ST	RNBT	FBG	DV	IO	135-185		7	9	2300			6700	8300
20	2	TROVARE 202 BR	ST	RNBT	FBG	DV	IO	180-250		8	6	2620			9350	11600
20	2	TROVARE 202 CUDDY	ST	CUD	FBG	DV	IO	180-250		8	6	2850			10200	12600
21	1	TROVARE 211 BR	ST	RNBT	FBG	DV	IO	190-250		8		3100			10400	12700
21	1	TROVARE 211 BR	ST	RNBT	FBG	DV	IO	300		8		3100			11500	13800
21	1	TROVARE 211 CUDDY	ST	CUD	FBG	DV	IO	190-250		8		3100			10900	13400
21	1	TROVARE 211 CUDDY	ST	CUD	FBG	DV	IO	300		8		3100			12100	14500
21	7	INTRUDER 217	ST	OFF	FBG	DV	IO	300		8		3850			14200	16800
21	7	INTRUDER 217	ST	OFF	FBG	DV	IO	350-385		8		3850			15700	19500
21	7	INTRUDER 217	ST	OFF	FBG	DV	IO	390-415		8		3850			19100	21200

LOA FT	IN	NAME AND/ OR MODEL	TOP/ RIG	BOAT TYPE	-HULL- MTL	TP	----ENGINE--- TP	# HP	MFG	BEAM FT	IN	WGT LBS	DRAFT FT	IN	RETAIL LOW	RETAIL HIGH
		1994 BOATS														
23	2	TROVARE 232 CUDDY	ST	CUD	FBG	DV	IO	300-350		8		3850			15300	19100
23	2	TROVARE 232 CUDDY	ST	CUD	FBG	DV	IO	385-415		8		3850			18700	22200
25	7	TROVARE 257 BR	ST	RNBT	FBG	DV	IO	300-350		8		4300			17500	21200
25	7	TROVARE 257 BR	ST	RNBT	FBG	DV	IO	385	MRCR	8		4300			20300	22500
25	7	TROVARE 257 BR	ST	RNBT	FBG	DV	IO	390-415		8		5310			23700	26300
25	7	TROVARE 257 CUDDY	ST	CUD	FBG	DV	IO	300-350		8		4300			19200	23000
25	7	TROVARE 257 CUDDY	ST	CUD	FBG	DV	IO	390-415		8		5310			25600	28500
25	7	TROVARE C257 CUDDY	ST	CUD	FBG	DV	IO	385	MRCR	8		4300			22000	24500
27		INTIMIDATOR 270	ST	OFF	FBG	DV	IO	350-415		8		6100			26300	31700
		IO T250-T300 27600 32500, IO T350 MRCR 31600 35100, IO T415 MRCR													35700	39700
		1993 BOATS														
17		VIKING 170 FISHERMAN	OP	CUD	FBG	DV	IO	115-180		6	10	2225			5450	6700
18	2	TROVARE 180 BR	ST	RNBT	FBG	DV	IO	160	MRCR	7	9	2300			6300	7250
18	2	TROVARE 182 BR	ST	RNBT	FBG	DV	OB			7	9	2300			6050	7000
18	2	TROVARE 182 BR	ST	RNBT	FBG	DV	IO	115-187		7	9	2300			6250	7650
18	2	TROVARE 182 CUDDY	ST	CUD	FBG	DV	OB			7	9				6050	7000
18	2	TROVARE 182 CUDDY	ST	CUD	FBG	DV	IO	115-187		7	9				6450	7850
18	9	VIKING 190 FISHERMAN	ST	CUD	FBG	DV	OB			8		1900			5650	6500
18	9	VIKING 190 FISHERMAN	ST	CUD	FBG	DV	IO	115-190		8		2800			7550	9200
19	10	VIKING WALKAROUND	OP	CUD	FBG	DV	OB			7	8	1800			5800	6700
20	2	TROVARE 202 BR	ST	RNBT	FBG	DV	IO	180-235							8650	10400
20	2	TROVARE 202 CB	ST	RNBT	FBG	DV	IO	180-235							8650	10400
20	2	TROVARE 202 CUDDY	ST	CUD	FBG	DV	IO	180-235							9500	11200
21	1	TROVARE 211 BR	ST	RNBT	FBG	DV	IO	190-250		8		3100			9700	11800
21	1	TROVARE 211 BR	ST	RNBT	FBG	DV	IO	300	MRCR	8		3100			10800	12200
21	1	TROVARE 211 CUDDY	ST	CUD	FBG	DV	IO	190-250		8		3100			10200	12400
21	1	TROVARE 211 CUDDY	ST	CUD	FBG	DV	IO	300	MRCR	8		3100			11300	12900
21	7	INTRUDER 217	ST	OFF	FBG	DV	IO	235-250		8		3850			12300	14600
		IO 300 13200 15700, IO 350 MRCR 14600 16600, IO 390-415													16200	19800
23	2	TROVARE 232 CUDDY	ST	CUD	FBG	DV	IO	235-250		8		3850			13400	15800
23	2	TROVARE 232 CUDDY	ST	CUD	FBG	DV	IO	300-350		8		3850			14300	17800
23	2	TROVARE 232 CUDDY	ST	CUD	FBG	DV	IO	390	MRCR	8		3850			17300	19600
25	7	TROVARE 257 BR	ST	RNBT	FBG	DV	IO	300-350		8		4300			16400	20000
25	7	TROVARE 257 BR	ST	RNBT	FBG	DV	IO	390-415		8		4300			19100	22300
25	7	TROVARE 257 BR	ST	RNBT	FBG	DV	IO	T245-T250		8		5310			21200	23500
25	7	TROVARE 257 CUDDY	ST	CUD	FBG	DV	IO	300-350		8		4300			18200	21500
25	7	TROVARE 257 CUDDY	ST	CUD	FBG	DV	IO	415	MRCR	8		4300			21800	24200
25	7	TROVARE 257 CUDDY	ST	CUD	FBG	DV	IO	T240-T245		8		5310			22200	25500
25	7	TROVARE C257 CUDDY	ST	CUD	FBG	DV	IO	390	MRCR	8		4300			20800	23100
27		INTIMIDATOR 270	ST	OFF	FBG	DV	IO	390-415		8		5900			25400	29100
27		INTIMIDATOR 270	ST	OFF	FBG	DV	IO	T300-T350		8		5900			26900	32300
27		INTIMIDATOR 270	ST	OFF	FBG	DV	IO	T390-T415		8		5900			31400	36700
		1992 BOATS														
17		VIKING FISHERMAN	OP	CUD	FBG	DV	IO	115-180		6	10	2225			5100	6300
18	2	TROVARE BOWRIDER	ST	RNBT	FBG	DV	IO	115-180		7	9	2300			5850	7150
18	9	VIKING FISHERMAN	ST	CUD	FBG	DV	OB			8		1900			5400	6200
18	9	VIKING FISHERMAN	ST	CUD	FBG	DV	IO	115-190		8		2800			7100	8600
19	10	VIKING WALKAROUND	OP	CUD	FBG	DV	OB			7	8	1800			5600	6400
21	1	TROVARE BOATRIDER	ST	RNBT	FBG	DV	IO	180-240		8		3100			9100	10700
21	1	TROVARE BOWRIDER	ST	RNBT	FBG	DV	IO	225-245		8		3100			9550	11100
21	1	TROVARE CUDDY	ST	CUD	FBG	DV	IO	180-245		8		3100			9500	11600
21	7	INTRUDER	ST	OFF	FBG	DV	IO	230-245		8		3850			11500	13700
		IO 300 12400 14700, IO 350 MRCR 13700 15600, IO 390 MRCR													15200	17300
23	2	TROVARE CUDDY	ST	CUD	FBG	DV	IO	230-245		8		3850			12500	14800
23	2	TROVARE CUDDY	ST	CUD	FBG	DV	IO	300-350		8		3850			13400	16700
23	2	TROVARE CUDDY	ST	CUD	FBG	DV	IO	390	MRCR	8		3850			16200	18400
25	7	TROVARE BOWRIDER	ST	RNBT	FBG	DV	IO	300-350		8		4300			15300	18700
25	7	TROVARE BOWRIDER	ST	RNBT	FBG	DV	IO	390	MRCR	8		4300			18100	20100
25	7	TROVARE BOWRIDER	ST	RNBT	FBG	DV	IO	T230-T245		8		5300			19200	22000
25	7	TROVARE CUDDY	ST	CUD	FBG	DV	IO	300-350		8		4310			16700	20400
25	7	TROVARE CUDDY	ST	CUD	FBG	DV	IO	390	MRCR	8		4310			19500	21600
25	7	TROVARE CUDDY	ST	CUD	FBG	DV	IO	T230-T245		8		5310			20600	24100
27		INTIMIDATOR	ST	OFF	FBG	DV	IO	300-390		8		5900			21800	26400
27		INTIMIDATOR	ST	OFF	FBG	DV	IO	T240-T300		8		5900			23500	28700
27		INTIMIDATOR	ST	OFF	FBG	DV	IO	T350-T390		8		5900			27300	32700
		1991 BOATS														
17		MAGNA BOWRIDER	ST	RNBT	FBG	DV	IO	155-180		6	10	2250			4750	5850
17		MAGNA CUDDY	ST	RNBT	FBG	DV	IO	155-180		6	10	2380			4900	6000
18	9	RAMPAGE BOWRIDER	ST	RNBT	FBG	DV	IO	180-190		8		2800			6250	7750
18	9	RAMPAGE BOWRIDER	ST	RNBT	FBG	DV	IO	205-240		8		2800			6300	7850
18	9	RAMPAGE BOWRIDER	ST	RNBT	FBG	DV	IO	245	VLVO	8		2800			6950	8000
18	9	RAMPAGE CUDDY	ST	RNBT	FBG	DV	IO	180-190		8		2800			6450	8000
18	9	RAMPAGE CUDDY	ST	RNBT	FBG	DV	IO	205-240		8		2800			6500	8100
18	9	RAMPAGE CUDDY	ST	RNBT	FBG	DV	IO	245	VLVO	8		2800			7150	8250
18	9	RAMPAGE FISHERMAN	ST	RNBT	FBG	DV	IO	180-190		8		2800			6450	8000
18	9	RAMPAGE FISHERMAN	ST	RNBT	FBG	DV	IO	205-240		8		2800			6500	8100
18	9	RAMPAGE FISHERMAN	ST	RNBT	FBG	DV	IO	245	VLVO	8		2800			7150	8250
21	1	TROVARE CUDDY	ST	CUD	FBG	DV	IO	180-245		8		3150			9050	11000
21	1	TROVARE SP CUDDY	OP	CUD	FBG	DV	IO	180-245		8		3100			8950	10900
21	7	INTRUDER	ST	OFF	FBG	DV	IO	230-245		8		3850			10800	12800
		IO 300 11600 13800, IO 350 MRCR 12900 14600, IO 390 MRCR													14300	16200
21	7	INTRUDER SP CUDDY	OP	CUD	FBG	DV	IO	230-245		8		3850			10800	12800
		IO 300 11600 13800, IO 350 MRCR 12900 14600, IO 390 MRCR													14300	16200
23	2	TROVARE CUDDY	ST	CUD	FBG	DV	IO	230-245		8		3850			11700	13900
23	2	TROVARE CUDDY	ST	CUD	FBG	DV	IO	300-350		8		3850			12600	15600
23	2	TROVARE CUDDY	ST	CUD	FBG	DV	IO	390	MRCR	8		3850			15200	17200
23	2	TROVARE SP CUDDY	OP	CUD	FBG	DV	IO	230-245		8		3850			11700	13900
23	2	TROVARE SP CUDDY	OP	CUD	FBG	DV	IO	300-350		8		3850			12600	15600
23	2	TROVARE SP CUDDY	OP	CUD	FBG	DV	IO	390	MRCR	8		3850			15200	17200
25	7	TROVARE BOWRIDER	ST	RNBT	FBG	DV	IO	300-350		8		4300			14400	17600
		IO 390 MRCR 16600 18900, IO T460-T480 28000 32600, IO T490 VLVO													32800	36400
25	7	TROVARE CUDDY	ST	CUD	FBG	DV	IO	300-350		8		4300			15600	19100
		IO 390 MRCR 18500 20500, IO T460-T480 29900 34800, IO T490 VLVO													35200	39100
25	7	TROVARE SP CUDDY	OP	CUD	FBG	DV	IO	300-350		8		4300			15600	19100
		IO 390 MRCR 18500 20500, IO T460-T480 29900 34800, IO T490 VLVO													35000	38900
27		INTIMIDATOR	ST	OFF	FBG	DV	IO	390	MRCR	8		5900			22300	24800
		IO T390 MRCR 27600 30600, IO T480-T490 33100 39800, IO T600-T700													39400	47300
		1990 BOATS														
17		MAGNA BOWRIDER	ST	RNBT	FBG	DV	IO	175-205		6	6	2200		8	4400	5400
17		MAGNA CUDDY	ST	RNBT	FBG	DV	IO	175-205		6	6	2380		8	4550	5600
18	9	RAMPAGE BOWRIDER	ST	RNBT	FBG	DV	IO	205-270		8		2490		8	5800	7150
18	9	RAMPAGE BOWRIDER	ST	RNBT	FBG	DV	IO	275	VLVO	8		2490		8	6600	7600
18	9	RAMPAGE CUDDY	ST	RNBT	FBG	DV	IO	205-270		8		2640		8	6000	7350
18	9	RAMPAGE CUDDY	ST	RNBT	FBG	DV	IO	275	VLVO	8		2640		8	6800	7800
18	9	RAMPAGE FISHERMAN	ST	RNBT	FBG	DV	IO	205-270		8		2375		8	5650	7000
18	9	RAMPAGE FISHERMAN	ST	RNBT	FBG	DV	IO	275	VLVO	8		2375		8	6500	7450
21	1	TROVARE BOWRIDER	ST	B/R	FBG	DV	IO	260-275		8		3120			8250	10100
21	1	TROVARE CUDDY	ST	CUD	FBG	DV	IO	260-275		8		3120			8900	10300
21	7	INTRUDER OFFSHORE	ST	OFF	FBG	DV	IO	260-270		8		3750		9	10200	12200
21	7	INTRUDER OFFSHORE	ST	OFF	FBG	DV	IO	330-365		8		3750		9	11400	14000
22		ANTIGUA SUNBRIDGE	ST	CNV	FBG	DV	IO	270-275		8	6	4600			14200	16800
22		ANTIGUA SUNBRIDGE	ST	CNV	FBG	DV	IO	330		8	6	4600			15400	18300
23	2	TROVARE BOWRIDER	ST	B/R	FBG	DV	IO	260-275		8		3900			10700	12700
23	2	TROVARE BOWRIDER	ST	B/R	FBG	DV	IO	330-365		8		3900			11700	14400
23	2	TROVARE CUDDY	ST	CUD	FBG	DV	IO	260-275		8		3900			11400	13600
23	2	TROVARE CUDDY	ST	CUD	FBG	DV	IO	330-365		8		3900			12500	15300
25	7	TROVARE BOWRIDER	ST	B/R	FBG	DV	IO	330-365		8		4290			14100	16900
		IO 420 MRCR 16500 18800, IO T205-T270 14400 17700, IO T275 VLVO													16200	18500
25	7	TROVARE CUDDY	ST	CUD	FBG	DV	IO	330-365		8		4290			15300	18400
		IO 420 MRCR 18400 20400, IO T205-T270 15700 19300, IO T275 VLVO													18000	20000
27		INTIMIDATOR OFFSHORE	ST	OFF	FBG	DV	IO	270-365		8		5600			18200	22000
27		INTIMIDATOR OFFSHORE	ST	OFF	FBG	DV	IO	420	MRCR	8		5600			21300	23700
27		INTIMIDATOR OFFSHORE	ST	OFF	FBG	DV	IO	T320-T330		8		5600			23000	26000
		1989 BOATS														
17		MAGNA BOWRIDER	ST	RNBT	FBG	DV	IO	165-205		6	8	2200		8	4100	4900
17		MAGNA CUDDY	ST	RNBT	FBG	DV	IO	165-205		6	8	2250		8	4150	4950
18	9	RAMPAGE BOWRIDER	ST	RNBT	FBG	DV	IO	175-270		8		2450		8	5350	6700
18	9	RAMPAGE CUDDY	ST	RNBT	FBG	DV	IO	165-260		8		2375		8	5250	6500
18	9	RAMPAGE CUDDY	ST	RNBT	FBG	DV	IO	270	MRCR	8		2375		8	5750	6600
18	9	RAMPAGE FISHERMAN	ST	RNBT	FBG	DV	IO	165-260		8		2375		8	5250	6500
21	7	INTRUDER OFFSHORE	ST	OFF	FBG	DV	IO	230-270		8		3480		9	8250	9850
21	7	INTRUDER OFFSHORE	ST	OFF	FBG	DV	IO	330	MRCR	8		3480		9	9600	10900
21	7	INTRUDER OFFSHORE LE	ST	OFF	FBG	DV	IO	230-270		8		3480		9	9550	11200
21	7	INTRUDER OFFSHORE LE	ST	OFF	FBG	DV	IO	330-365		8		3480		9	10900	12700
22		ANTIGUA SUNBRIDGE	ST	CNV	FBG	DV	IO	205-270		8	6	4600			12900	15200
22		ANTIGUA SUNBRIDGE	ST	CNV	FBG	DV	IO	330	MRCR	8	6	4600			14500	16500
27		INTIMIDATOR OFFSHORE		OFF	FBG	DV	IO	365	MRCR	8		5600			18900	21000
27		INTIMIDATOR OFFSHORE		OFF	FBG	DV	IO	T270-T330		8		5600			19700	23900
27		INTIMIDATOR OFFSHORE		OFF	FBG	DV	IO	T365	MRCR	8		5600			22900	25400

 CONTINUED ON NEXT PAGE

LOA FT	IN	NAME AND/ OR MODEL	TOP/ RIG	BOAT TYPE	-HULL- MTL	TP	----ENGINE--- TP	# HP	MFG	BEAM FT	IN	WGT LBS	DRAFT FT	IN	RETAIL LOW	RETAIL HIGH
		1988 BOATS														
17		MAGNA BOWRIDER	ST	RNBT	FBG	DV	IO	165-205		6	8	2200		8	3900	4600
17		MAGNA CUDDY	ST	RNBT	FBG	DV	IO	165-205		6	8	2250		8	3950	4700
18	9	RAMPAGE BOWRIDER	ST	RNBT	FBG	DV	IO	175-270		8		2450		8	5050	6300
18	9	RAMPAGE CUDDY	ST	RNBT	FBG	DV	IO	165-260		8		2375		8	5000	6150
18	9	RAMPAGE CUDDY	ST	RNBT	FBG	DV	IO	270	MRCR	8		2375		8	5400	6250
21	7	INTRUDER OFFSHORE	ST	OFF	FBG	DV	IO	230-260		8		3480		9	7800	9250
21	7	INTRUDER OFFSHORE	ST	OFF	FBG	DV	IO	270-330		8		3480			8800	10400
21	7	INTRUDER OFFSHORE LE	ST	OFF	FBG	DV	IO	230-270		8		3480		9	9100	10600
21	7	INTRUDER OFFSHORE LE	ST	OFF	FBG	DV	IO	330-365		8		3480		9	10300	12000
22		ANTIGUA SUNBRIDGE	ST	CNV	FBG	DV	IO	205-270		8	6	4600			12200	14400
22		ANTIGUA SUNBRIDGE	ST	CNV	FBG	DV	IO	330	MRCR	8	6	4600			13800	15600
27		ANTIGUA		OFF	FBG	DV	IO	T320	MRCR	8		5600			20000	22200
27		INTIMIDATOR OFFSHORE		OFF	FBG	DV	IO	365	MRCR	8		5600			17500	19900
27		INTIMIDATOR OFFSHORE		OFF	FBG	DV	IO	T270	MRCR	8		5600			18900	21000
27		INTIMIDATOR OFFSHORE		OFF	FBG	DV	IO	T640-T730		8		5600			33700	39600
		1987 BOATS														
17		MAGNA BOWRIDER	ST	RNBT	FBG	DV	OB			6	10	1285		8	3150	3650
17		MAGNA BOWRIDER	ST	RNBT	FBG	DV	IO	130-205		6	10	1875		8	3300	4000
17		MAGNA CUDDY	ST	RNBT	FBG	DV	OB			6	10	1285		8	3500	4050
17		MAGNA CUDDY	ST	RNBT	FBG	DV	IO	130-205		6	10	1875		8	3500	4200
18	9	RAMPAGE BOWRIDER	ST	RNBT	FBG	DV	OB			8		1785		8	4150	4850
18	9	RAMPAGE BOWRIDER	ST	RNBT	FBG	DV	IO	165-200		8		2375		8	4650	5400
18	9	RAMPAGE BOWRIDER	ST	RNBT	FBG	DV	SE	205	OMC	8		2375		8	4950	5700
18	9	RAMPAGE BOWRIDER	ST	RNBT	FBG	DV	IO	205-260		8		2375		8	4700	5700
18	9	RAMPAGE CUDDY	ST	RNBT	FBG	DV	OB			8		1785		8	4830	5550
18	9	RAMPAGE CUDDY	ST	RNBT	FBG	DV	IO	165-200		8		2375		8	4850	5600
18	9	RAMPAGE CUDDY	ST	RNBT	FBG	DV	SE	205	OMC	8		2375		8	5150	5950
18	9	RAMPAGE CUDDY	ST	RNBT	FBG	DV	IO	205-260		8		2375		8	4900	5900
21	7	INTRUDER OFFSHORE	ST	OFF	FBG	DV	IO	230-260		8		3400		9	7250	8600
21	7	INTRUDER OFFSHORE	ST	OFF	FBG	DV	IO	320-350		8		3400			8950	10200
21	7	INTRUDER OFFSHORE LE	ST	OFF	FBG	DV	IO	230-320		8		3400		9	8400	10200
21	7	INTRUDER OFFSHORE LE	ST	OFF	FBG	DV	IO	335-350		8		3400			9700	11600
22		ANTIQUA SUNBRIDGE	ST	CNV	FBG	DV	IO	165-260		8	6	3900			10200	12100
25	6	ROYALE SUNBRIDGE	ST	SPTCR	FBG	DV	IO	230-260		8	6	4350		10	11800	13700
27		INTIMIDATOR OFFSHORE		OFF	FBG	DV	IO	T260		8		5000			16600	18800
27		INTIMIDATOR OFFSHORE		OFF	FBG	DV	IO	T320-T350		8					19500	21700
27		INTIMIDATOR OFFSHORE		OFF	FBG	DV	IO	T454	MRCR	8		5000			24000	26600
27	7	INTRUDER OFFSHORE	ST	OFF	FBG	DV	IO	340	OMC	8		3400			14300	16200
		1986 BOATS														
17		MAGNA BOWRIDER	ST	RNBT	FBG	DV	OB			6	10	1285		8	3050	3550
17		MAGNA BOWRIDER	ST	RNBT	FBG	DV	IO	140-205		6	10	1875		8	3200	3850
17		MAGNA CUDDY	ST	RNBT	FBG	DV	OB			6	10	1285		8	3400	3950
17		MAGNA CUDDY	ST	RNBT	FBG	DV	IO	140-205		6	10	1875		8	3350	4000
18	6	RAMPAGE BOWRIDER	ST	RNBT	FBG	DV	OB			8		1785		8	4000	4650
18	6	RAMPAGE BOWRIDER	ST	RNBT	FBG	DV	IO	170-200		8		2375		8	4400	5100
18	6	RAMPAGE BOWRIDER	ST	RNBT	FBG	DV	SE	205	OMC	8		2375		8	4800	5500
18	6	RAMPAGE BOWRIDER	ST	RNBT	FBG	DV	IO	205-260		8		2375		8	4450	5400
18	6	RAMPAGE CUDDY	ST	RNBT	FBG	DV	OB			8		1785		8	4500	5150
18	6	RAMPAGE CUDDY	ST	RNBT	FBG	DV	IO	170-200		8		2375		8	4600	5450
18	6	RAMPAGE CUDDY	ST	RNBT	FBG	DV	SE	205	OMC	8		2375		8	4950	5700
18	6	RAMPAGE CUDDY	ST	RNBT	FBG	DV	IO	205-260		8		2375		8	4650	5600
21		INTRUDER BOWRIDER	ST	RNBT	FBG	DV	OB			8				9	5200	6000
21		INTRUDER BOWRIDER	ST	RNBT	FBG	DV	IO	170-200		8		3200		9	6500	7550
21		INTRUDER BOWRIDER	ST	RNBT	FBG	DV	SE	205	OMC	8		3200		9	7300	8400
21		INTRUDER BOWRIDER	ST	RNBT	FBG	DV	IO	205-260		8		3200		9	6600	7900
21		INTRUDER BOWRIDER	ST	RNBT	FBG	DV	IO	300	MRCR	8		3200		9	7250	8350
21		INTRUDER OFFSHORE	ST	OFF	FBG	DV	OB			8				9	4550	5200
21		INTRUDER OFFSHORE	ST	OFF	FBG	DV	IO	170-200		8		3200		9	6850	7950
21		INTRUDER OFFSHORE	ST	OFF	FBG	DV	SE	205	OMC	8		3200		9	7300	8400
21		INTRUDER OFFSHORE	ST	OFF	FBG	DV	IO	205-260		8		3200		9	6900	8300
21		INTRUDER OFFSHORE	ST	OFF	FBG	DV	IO	300	MRCR	8		3200		9	7650	8800
21		INTRUDER OFFSHORE LE	ST	OFF	FBG	DV	OB			8				9	5950	6800
21		INTRUDER OFFSHORE LE	ST	OFF	FBG	DV	IO	230-260		8				9	6900	8150
21		INTRUDER OFFSHORE LE	ST	OFF	FBG	DV	IO	300	MRCR	8				9	7500	8650
21		RENEGADE SUNBRIDGE	ST	SPTCR	FBG	DV	IO	170-200		8	6	3900		10	8050	9350
21		RENEGADE SUNBRIDGE	ST	SPTCR	FBG	DV	SE	205	OMC	8	6	3900		10	7600	8700
21		RENEGADE SUNBRIDGE	ST	SPTCR	FBG	DV	IO	205-260		8	6	3900		10	8150	9700
24		ROYALE SUNBRIDGE	ST	SPTCR	FBG	DV	IO	230-300		8	6	4350		10	10400	12500
27		INTIMIDATOR		OFF	FBG	DV	IO	T260-T300		8		4000			14700	17700
27		INTIMIDATOR		OFF	FBG	DV	IO	T330-T370		8		4000			16500	20300
		1985 BOATS														
16		BAJA BOWRIDER	ST	RNBT	FBG	DV	OB			6	10	955		6	2400	2750
16		BAJA BOWRIDER	ST	RNBT	FBG	DV	IO	120-140		6	10	1775		7	3150	3650
17		MAGNA BOWRIDER	ST	RNBT	FBG	DV	OB			6	10	1285		8	3050	3550
17		MAGNA BOWRIDER	ST	RNBT	FBG	DV	IO	120-190		6	10	1875		8	3350	3850
17		MAGNA CUDDY	ST	RNBT	FBG	DV	OB			6	10	1285		8	3250	3750
17		MAGNA CUDDY	ST	RNBT	FBG	DV	IO	120-190		6	10	1875		8	3450	4050
18	6	RAMPAGE BOWRIDER	ST	RNBT	FBG	DV	OB			8		1785		8	4000	4650
18	6	RAMPAGE BOWRIDER	ST	RNBT	FBG	DV	IO	165-200		8		2375		8	4500	5250
18	6	RAMPAGE BOWRIDER	ST	RNBT	FBG	DV	SE	205	OMC	8		2375		8	4650	5350
18	6	RAMPAGE BOWRIDER	ST	RNBT	FBG	DV	IO	230-260		8		2375		8	4400	5250
18	6	RAMPAGE CUDDY	ST	RNBT	FBG	DV	OB			8		1785		8	4200	4900
18	6	RAMPAGE CUDDY	ST	RNBT	FBG	DV	IO	165-200		8		2375		8	4650	5400
18	6	RAMPAGE CUDDY	ST	RNBT	FBG	DV	SE	205	OMC	8		2375		8	4800	5550
18	6	RAMPAGE CUDDY	ST	RNBT	FBG	DV	IO	205-260		8		2375		8	4350	5400
21		INTRUDER BOWRIDER	ST	RNBT	FBG	DV	IO	165-200		8		3200		9	6550	7600
21		INTRUDER BOWRIDER	ST	RNBT	FBG	DV	SE	205	OMC	8		3200		9	7100	8200
21		INTRUDER BOWRIDER	ST	RNBT	FBG	DV	IO	205-260		8		3200		9	6300	7550
21		INTRUDER OFFSHORE	ST	OFF	FBG	DV	IO	165-200		8		3200		9	6850	7950
21		INTRUDER OFFSHORE	ST	OFF	FBG	DV	SE	205	OMC	8		3200		9	7100	8150
21		INTRUDER OFFSHORE	ST	OFF	FBG	DV	IO	205-260		8		3200		9	6650	7950
21		RENEGADE SUNCRUISER	ST	SPTCR	FBG	DV	IO	170-200		8	6	3900		10	7750	9300
21		RENEGADE SUNCRUISER	ST	SPTCR	FBG	DV	SE	205	OMC	8	6	3900		10	7350	8500
21		RENEGADE SUNCRUISER	ST	SPTCR	FBG	DV	IO	205-260		8	6	3900		10	7800	9300
24		ROYALE SUNCRUISER	ST	SPTCR	FBG	DV	IO	230-260		8	6	4350		10	9950	11500
27		INTIMIDATOR		OFF	FBG	DV	IO	260-330		8		4000			11700	14400
27		INTIMIDATOR		OFF	FBG	DV	IO	T260		8		4000			14100	16000
27		INTIMIDATOR		OFF	FBG	DV	IO	T330	MRCR	8		4000			15800	17900

MIRAGE MANUFACTURING CO

GAINESVILLE FL 32609 COAST GUARD MFG ID- MGY See inside cover to adjust price for area

For more recent years, see the BUC Used Boat Price Guide, Volume 1

LOA FT	IN	NAME AND/ OR MODEL	TOP/ RIG	BOAT TYPE	-HULL- MTL	TP	----ENGINE--- TP	# HP	MFG	BEAM FT	IN	WGT LBS	DRAFT FT	IN	RETAIL LOW	RETAIL HIGH
		1988 BOATS														
20		MIRAGE 5.5	SLP	SA/RC	FBG	SK				8		1200	1	4	3800	4450
23	6	MIRAGE 236	SLP	SA/RC	FBG	KL				9		2800	4	6	7200	8300
27	5	MIRAGE 28	SLP	SA/RC	FBG	KL				9	2	4150	5		11600	13200
27	5	MIRAGE 28	SLP	SA/RC	FBG	KL	IB	D		9	2	4150	5		13900	15800
33	8	MIRAGE 338	SLP	SA/RC	FBG	KL				10	8	4480	6		12500	14200
33	8	MIRAGE 338	SLP	SA/RC	FBG	KL	IB	D		10	8	4480	6		15800	18000
		1987 BOATS														
20		MIRAGE 5.5	SLP	SA/RC	FBG	SK				8		1200		1	3600	4150
23	6	MIRAGE 236	SLP	SA/RC	FBG	KL				9		2800	4	6	6750	7750
27	6	MIRAGE 28	SLP	SA/RC	FBG	KL				9	2	4150	5		10900	12400
27	6	MIRAGE 28	SLP	SA/RC	FBG	KL	IB	D		9	2	4150	5		13100	14900
33	8	MIRAGE 338	SLP	SA/RC	FBG	KL				10	8	4480	6		11800	13400
33	8	MIRAGE 338	SLP	SA/RC	FBG	KL	IB	D		10	8	4480	6		14900	17000
		1986 BOATS														
20		MIRAGE 5.5	SLP	SA/RC	FBG	SK				8		1200		1	3350	3900
23	6	MIRAGE 236	SLP	SA/RC	FBG	KL				9		2800	4	6	6300	7250
27	6	MIRAGE 28	SLP	SA/RC	FBG	KL				9	2	4150	5		10200	11600
27	6	MIRAGE 28	SLP	SA/RC	FBG	KL	IB	D		9	2	4150	5		12300	14000
33	8	MIRAGE 338	SLP	SA/RC	FBG	KL				10	8	4480	6		11100	12600
33	8	MIRAGE 338	SLP	SA/RC	FBG	KL	IB	D		10	8	4480	6		13900	15800
		1985 BOATS														
20		MIRAGE 5.5	SLP	SA/RC	FBG	SK				8		1200	1	4	3150	3650
23	6	MIRAGE 236	SLP	SA/RC	FBG	KL				9		2800	4	6	5950	6800
27	6	MIRAGE 28	SLP	SA/RC	FBG	KL				9	2	4150	5		9600	10900
27	6	MIRAGE 28	SLP	SA/RC	FBG	KL	IB	D		9	2	4150	5		11500	13100
33	8	MIRAGE 338	SLP	SA/RC	FBG	KL				10	8	4480	6		10400	11800
33	8	MIRAGE 338	SLP	SA/RC	FBG	KL	IB	D		10	8	4480	6		13100	14900
		1984 BOATS														
20		MIRAGE 5.5	SLP	SA/RC	FBG	CB	OB			7	11	1200	1	4	2950	3450
23	6	MIRAGE 236	SLP	SA/RC	FBG	KL	OB			9		2950	4	6	5800	6650
27	5	MIRAGE 28	SLP	SA/RC	FBG	KL	IB	8D	YAN	9	2	5580	5		14500	16500
33	8	MIRAGE 338	SLP	SA/RC	FBG	KL	OB			10	8	4580	6		12400	14100

....For earlier years, see the BUC Used Boat Price Guide, Volume 3

MIRROCRAFT BOATS

NORTHPORT CORP OF ST CLAIR
GILLETT WI 54124

COAST GUARD MFG ID- MRR
FORMERLY NORTHPORT INC

See inside cover to adjust price for area

For more recent years, see the BUC Used Boat Price Guide, Volume 1

LOA FT	LOA IN	NAME AND/ OR MODEL	TOP/ RIG	BOAT TYPE	-HULL- MTL	-HULL- TP	ENGINE TP	ENGINE # HP	ENGINE MFG	BEAM FT	BEAM IN	WGT LBS	DRAFT FT	DRAFT IN	RETAIL LOW	RETAIL HIGH
		1996 BOATS														
16		DEEP FISH 4656	OP	UTL	AL	SV	OB			5	4	243			505	605
16		DEEP FISH 4656-24	OP	FSH	AL	SV	OB			5	4	243			505	610
16		DEEP FISH II 3696	OP	FSH	AL	SV	OB			5	4	343			725	875
16		DEEP FISH II 3696-24	OP	FSH	AL	SV	OB			5	4	343			725	875
16		STRIKER LTD 1615	OP	UTL	AL	SV	OB			5	7	355			745	900
16		TROLLER LTD 1660	OP	FSH	AL	DV	OB			5	6	385			820	985
16		TROLLER LTD 1661	OP	FSH	AL	DV	OB			5	6	430			925	1100
16		TROLLER XL 1628	OP	RNBT	AL	SV	OB			5	7	510			1100	1350
16	2	AGGRESSOR 1625	OP	FSH	AL	SV	OB			6	3	570			1250	1450
16	2	OUTFITTER 1600	OP	BASS	AL	SV	OB			6	3	550			1200	1450
16	2	PRO FISHERMAN 1630	OP	FSH	AL	SV	OB			6	3	630			1350	1600
16	7	DUAL IMPACT 1745	OP	FSH	AL	SV	OB			6	8	985			2150	2500
16	7	GUIDE IMPACT 1735	OP	FSH	AL	SV	OB			6	8	760			1650	1950
16	7	GUIDE IMPACT 1736	OP	FSH	AL	SV	OB			6	8	720			1550	1850
17		AGGRESSOR MAG 1757	OP	FSH	AL	SV	OB			6	8	1025			2250	2600
17		AGGRESSOR XL 1755	OP	FSH	AL	SV	OB			6	8	900			1950	2350
17		OUTFITTER XL 1756	OP	BASS	AL	SV	OB			6	8	840			1850	2200
17		PRO FISHERMAN 1730	OP	FSH	AL	SV	OB			7	2	870			1900	2250
18		MV860-20T	OP	FSH	AL	SV	OB			7	2	450			995	1200
18		MV860F/D-20T	OP	FSH	AL	SV	OB			7	2	450			1150	1400
18	6	PRO FISHERMAN 1930	OP	FSH	AL	SV	OB			7	8	1185			2700	3150
19	6	MV2060-20T	OP	FSH	AL	SV	OB			7	2	560			1400	1700
20	4	STRIPER IMPACT 2095	OP	FSH	AL	SV	OB			8		990			2500	2900
		1995 BOATS														
16		DEEP FISH 4656	OP	UTL	AL	SV	OB			5	4	243			480	575
16		DEEP FISH 4656-24	OP	FSH	AL	SV	OB			5	4	243			480	580
16		DEEP FISH II 3696	OP	FSH	AL	SV	OB			5	4	343			690	830
16		DEEP FISH II 3696-24	OP	FSH	AL	SV	OB			5	4	343			690	830
16		STRIKER LTD 1615	OP	UTL	AL	SV	OB			5	7	355			710	855
16		STRIKER XL 1612	OP	FSH	AL	SV	OB			5	7	340			685	825
16		TROLLER LTD 1660	OP	FSH	AL	DV	OB			5	6	385			780	935
16		TROLLER LTD 1661	OP	FSH	AL	DV	OB			5	6	430			880	1050
16		TROLLER XL 1628	OP	RNBT	AL	SV	OB			5	7	510			1050	1250
16	2	AGGRESSOR 1625	OP	FSH	AL	SV	OB			6	3	570			1150	1400
16	2	OUTFITTER 1600	OP	BASS	AL	SV	OB			6	3	550			1150	1350
16	2	PRO FISHERMAN 1630	OP	FSH	AL	SV	OB			6	3	630			1300	1550
16	7	DUAL IMPACT 1745	OP	FSH	AL	SV	OB			6	8	985			2000	2400
16	7	GUIDE IMPACT 1735	OP	FSH	AL	SV	OB			6	8	760			1550	1850
16	7	GUIDE IMPACT 1736	OP	FSH	AL	SV	OB			6	8	720			1500	1800
17		AGGRESSOR XL 1755	OP	FSH	AL	SV	OB			6	8	900			1850	2200
17		OUTFITTER XL 1756	OP	BASS	AL	SV	OB			6	8	840			1750	2100
17		PRO FISHERMAN 1730	OP	FSH	AL	SV	OB			7	2	870			1800	2150
18		MV860-20T	OP	FSH	AL	SV	OB			7	2	450			930	1100
18		MV860F/D-20T	OP	FSH	AL	SV	OB			7	2	450			1100	1350
18	6	PRO FISH 1930	OP	FSH	AL	SV	OB			7	8	1185			2550	3000
19		MAGNUM IMPACT 1935	OP	BASS	AL	SV	OB			8		1175			2550	2950
		1994 BOATS														
16		DEEP FISH 4656	OP	UTL	AL	SV	OB			5	4	243			455	550
16		DEEP FISH 4656-24	OP	FSH	AL	SV	OB			5	4	243			460	555
16		DEEP FSH II 3696	OP	FSH	AL	SV	OB			5	4	343			660	795
16		DEEP FSH II 3696-24	OP	FSH	AL	SV	OB			5	4	343			660	795
16		STRIKER LTD 1615	OP	UTL	AL	SV	OB			5	7	355			680	820
16		STRIKER XL 1612	OP	FSH	AL	SV	OB			5	7	340			650	785
16		TROLLER LTD 1660	OP	FSH	AL	DV	OB			5	6	385			740	890
16		TROLLER LTD 1661	OP	FSH	AL	DV	OB			5	6	430			830	1000
16		TROLLER XL1628	OP	RNBT	AL	SV	OB			5	7	510			1000	1200
16	2	AGGRESSOR 1625	OP	FSH	AL	SV	OB			6	3	570			1100	1350
16	2	OUTFITTER 1600	OP	BASS	AL	SV	OB			6	3	550			1100	1300
16	2	PRO FISHERMAN 1630	OP	FSH	AL	SV	OB			6	3	630			1250	1450
16	3	SIERRA 165V	OP	RNBT	FBG	DV	OB			6	7	960			1850	2200
16	3	SIERRA 165V	OP	RNBT	FBG	DV	IO			6	7	1650			**	**
16	7	GUIDE IMPACT 1735	OP	FSH	AL	SV	OB			6	8	760			1500	1800
16	7	ULTRA PRO 1700	OP	FSH	AL	DV	OB			7		942			1850	2150
16	7	ULTRA PRO 1701	OP	FSH	AL	DV	OB			7		985			1900	2250
17		PRO FISHERMAN 1730	OP	FSH	AL	SV	OB			7	2	870			1700	2050
17		ULTRA PRO AL 1702	OP	FSH	AL	SV	OB			6	10	810			1600	1950
17		ULTRA PRO AL 1703	OP	FSH	AL	SV	OB			6	10	865			1700	2050
17	11	SIERRA 180	OP	RNBT	FBG	DV	IO			7	6	1935			**	**
18		MV860-20T	OP	FSH	AL	SV	OB			7	2	450			890	1050
18		MV860F/D-20T	OP	FSH	AL	SV	OB			7	2	450			1050	1250
18		SIERRA F185	OP	RNBT	FBG	SV	OB			7	6	1185			2400	2800
18	6	PRO FSH 1930	OP	FSH	AL	SV	OB			7	8	1185			2450	2850
18	6	ULTRA PRO CL 1902	OP	FSH	F/S	SV	OB			7	6	1620			3150	3650
19		MAGNUM IMPACT 1935	OP	BASS	AL	SV	OB			8		1175			2450	2850
19	4	SIERRA 195V	OP	SKI	FBG	DV	IO			7	6	1978			**	**
20	4	TROPHY STRIPER 2095	OP	FSH	AL	SV	OB			8		990			2300	2700
		1993 BOATS														
16		DEEP FISH 4656	OP	UTL	AL	SV	OB			5	4	243			440	530
16		DEEP FISH 4656-24	OP	FSH	AL	SV	OB			5	4	243			440	530
16		DEEP FSH II 3696	OP	FSH	AL	SV	OB			5	4	343			630	760
16		DEEP FSH II 3696-24	OP	FSH	AL	SV	OB			5	4	343			630	760
16		STRIKER XL 1612	OP	FSH	AL	SV	OB			5	7	340			625	750
16		TROLLER LTD 1660	OP	FSH	AL	DV	OB			5	6	385			710	855
16		TROLLER LTD 1661	OP	FSH	AL	DV	OB			5	6	430			795	955
16		TROLLER XL1628	OP	RNBT	AL	SV	OB			5	7	510			965	1150
16	2	AGGRESSOR 1625	OP	FSH	AL	SV	OB			6	3	570			1050	1250
16	2	OUTFITTER 1600	OP	BASS	AL	SV	OB			6	3	550			1050	1250
16	2	PRO FISHERMAN 1630	OP	FSH	AL	SV	OB			6	3	650			1200	1450
16	3	SIERRA 165V	OP	RNBT	FBG	DV	OB			6	7	960			1750	2100
16	3	SIERRA 165V	OP	RNBT	FBG	DV	IO	110-115		6	7	1650			3450	4050
16	7	GUIDE IMPACT 1735	OP	FSH	AL	SV	OB			6	8	600			1150	1350
16	7	ULTRA PRO 1700	OP	FSH	AL	DV	OB			7		942			1750	2100
16	7	ULTRA PRO 1701	OP	FSH	AL	DV	OB			7		985			1800	2150
17		PRO FISHERMAN 1730	OP	FSH	AL	SV	OB			7	2	800			1550	1800
17		ULTRA PRO AL 1703	OP	FSH	AL	SV	OB			6	10	865			1650	1950
17		ULTRA PRO AL 1704	OP	FSH	AL	SV	OB			6	10	810			1550	1850
18		MV860-20T	OP	FSH	AL	SV	OB			7	2	440			920	1100
18		MV860F/D-20T	OP	FSH	AL	SV	OB			7	2	450			935	1100
18		SIERRA F185	OP	RNBT	FBG	SV	OB			7	5	1185			2300	2650
18	6	PRO FSH 1930	OP	FSH	AL	SV	OB			7	8	1185			2350	2700
18	6	STRIPER 1835	OP	FSH	AL	SV	OB			7	8	745			1500	1800
18	6	ULTRA PRO CL 1902	OP	FSH	F/S	SV	OB			7	6	1620			3000	3500
19	4	SIERRA 195V	OP	SKI	FBG	DV	IO	110-180		7	6	2740			5600	6500
20		TROPHY STRIPER 2095	OP	FSH	AL	SV	OB			8		1350			2800	3250
		1992 BOATS														
16		DEEP FISH 4656	OP	UTL	AL	SV	OB			5	4	243			425	510
16		DEEP FSH II 3696	OP	FSH	AL	SV	OB			5	4	343			605	730
16		DEEP FSH II 3696-24	OP	FSH	AL	SV	OB			5	4	343			605	730
16		TROLLER LTD 1660	OP	FSH	AL	DV	OB			5	6	385			680	820
16		TROLLER LTD 1661	OP	FSH	AL	DV	OB			5	6	430			760	915
16		TROLLER XL1628	OP	RNBT	AL	SV	OB			5	7	510			925	1100
16	2	AGGRESSOR 1625	OP	FSH	AL	SV	OB			6	3	570			1000	1200
16	2	OUTFITTER 1600	OP	BASS	AL	SV	OB			6	3	550			995	1200
16	2	PRO FISHERMAN 1630	OP	FSH	AL	SV	OB			6	3	650			1150	1400
16	3	SIERRA 165V	OP	RNBT	FBG	DV	OB			6	7	960			1700	2000
16	3	SIERRA 165V	OP	RNBT	FBG	DV	IO	110-115		6	7	1650			3250	3750
16	7	ULTRA PRO 1700	OP	FSH	AL	DV	OB			7		942			1700	2000
16	7	ULTRA PRO 1701	OP	FSH	AL	DV	OB			7		985			1750	2100
16	9	SIERRA SX1700	OP	BASS	FBG	SV	OB			7	2	1180			2050	2450
17		ANGLER 1725	OP	FSH	AL	SV	OB			7	2				1600	1900
17		PRO FISHERMAN 1730	OP	FSH	AL	SV	OB			7	2				1600	1900
17		ULTRA PRO AL 1703	OP	FSH	AL	SV	OB			6	10	865			1600	1900
17		ULTRA PRO AL 1704	OP	FSH	AL	SV	OB			6	10	810			1500	1750
17	11	SIERRA 180V	OP	RNBT	FBG	SV	OB			7	5	1135			2050	2450
17	11	SIERRA 180V	OP	RNBT	FBG	SV	IO	110-180		7	5	1935			4150	4900
18		SIERRA F185	OP	RNBT	FBG	SV	OB			7	5	1185			2200	2550
18	6	PRO FSH 1930	OP	FSH	AL	SV	OB			7	8	1185			2300	2650
18	6	ULTRA PRO CL 1902	OP	FSH	F/S	SV	OB			7	6	1620			2900	3350
19	4	SIERRA 195V	OP	SKI	FBG	DV	IO	110-180		7	6	2740			5250	6100
20		TROPHY STRIPER 2095	OP	FSH	AL	SV	OB								2400	2800
20	4	VOYAGEUR 2096	OP	FSH	AL	DV	OB			8		1350			2750	3150
20	9	SIERRA 210V	OP	CUD	FBG	DV	IO	110-180		8	4	3100			7600	8800
		1991 BOATS														
16		DEEP FISH 4656	OP	UTL	AL	SV	OB			5	4	243			405	490
16		DEEP FSH II 3696	OP	FSH	AL	SV	OB			5	4	343			580	700
16		DEEP FSH II 3696-24	OP	FSH	AL	SV	OB			5	4	343			580	700
16		STRIKER 1606	OP	FSH	AL	SV	OB			5	6	370			625	755
16		TROLLER LTD 1660	OP	FSH	AL	DV	OB			5	6	385			655	790
16		TROLLER LTD 1661	OP	FSH	AL	DV	OB			5	6	430			730	880
16		TROLLER XL1628	OP	RNBT	AL	SV	OB			5	7	510			890	1050
16	2	COMPETITOR 1680	OP	BASS	AL	DV	OB			6	3	725			1250	1500
16	2	MUSKY 1625	OP	FSH	AL	SV	OB			6	3	570			985	1150

CONTINUED ON NEXT PAGE

LOA FT	IN	NAME AND/ OR MODEL	TOP/ RIG	BOAT TYPE	-HULL- MTL	TP	----ENGINE--- TP	# HP	MFG	BEAM FT	IN	WGT LBS	DRAFT FT	IN	RETAIL LOW	RETAIL HIGH
		1991 BOATS														
16	2	NORTHPORT ANGLR 1620	OP	BASS	AL	SV	OB			6	3	610			1050	1250
16	2	OUTFITTER 1600	OP	BASS	AL	SV	OB			6	3	550			955	1150
16	2	PRO FISHERMAN 1630	OP	FSH	AL	SV	OB			6	3	650			1100	1350
16	3	SIERRA 165V	OP	RNBT	FBG	DV	OB			6	7	960			1650	1950
16	3	SIERRA 165V	OP	RNBT	FBG	DV	IO	110-115		6	7	1650			3050	3550
16	4	GUIDE-CLASSIC 1675	OP	BASS	AL	FL	OB			6	4	650			1150	1350
16	7	ULTRA PRO 1700	OP	FSH	AL	DV	OB			7		942			1600	1900
16	7	ULTRA PRO 1701	OP	FSH	AL	DV	OB			7		985			1700	2000
16	9	SIERRA SX1700	OP	BASS	FBG	SV	OB			7	2	1180			2000	2350
17		ULTRA PRO AL 1703	OP	FSH	AL	SV	OB			6	10	865			1500	1800
17		ULTRA PRO AL 1704	OP	FSH	AL	SV	OB			6	10	810			1450	1700
17	11	SIERRA 180V	OP	RNBT	FBG	SV	OB			7	5	1135			2000	2350
17	11	SIERRA 180V	OP	RNBT	FBG	SV	IO	110-180		7	5	1935			3900	4600
18		SIERRA F185	OP	RNBT	FBG	SV	OB			7	5	1185			2050	2450
18	2	SIERRA SX1800	OP	BASS	FBG	SV	OB			7	8	1350			2350	2700
18	6	KING FSH 1950	OP	FSH	AL	SV	OB			7	8	1185			2050	2400
18	6	PRO FSH 1930	OP	FSH	AL	SV	OB			7	8	1185			2200	2550
18	6	ULTRA PRO CL 1901	OP	FSH	F/S	SV	OB			7	6	1620			2550	2950
18	6	ULTRA PRO CL 1902	OP	FSH	F/S	SV	OB			7	6	1620			2800	3250
18	6	ULTRA PRO CL 1905	OP	CTRCN	F/S	SV	OB			7	6	1670			2700	3150
19	4	SIERRA 195V	OP	SKI	FBG	DV	IO	110-180		7	6	2740			4900	5700
20	4	NAVIGATOR 2090	OP	FSH	AL	DV	OB			8		1305			2550	2950
20	4	NAVIGATOR 2090	OP	FSH	AL	DV	IO	110-180		8		2205			6000	6950
20	4	VOYAGEUR 2096	OP	FSH	AL	DV	OB			8		1350			2600	3050
20	4	VOYAGEUR 2096	OP	FSH	AL	DV	IO	110-180		8		2265			6050	7000
20	9	SIERRA 210V	OP	CUD	FBG	DV	IO	110-180		8	4	3100			7100	8250
		1990 BOATS														
16		DEEP FSH II 3696	OP	FSH	AL	SV	OB			5	4	343			560	675
16		DEEP FSH II 3696-24	OP	FSH	AL	SV	OB			5	4	343			560	675
16		STRIKER 1606	OP	FSH	AL	DV	OB			5	6	370			605	730
16		TROLLER LTD. 1660	OP	FSH	AL	DV	OB			5	6	385			630	760
16		TROLLER LTD. 1661	OP	FSH	AL	DV	OB			5	6	430			705	850
16	2	COMPETITOR 1680	OP	BASS	AL	DV	OB			6	3	725			1200	1450
16	2	MUSKY 1625	OP	FSH	AL	SV	OB			6	3	570			950	1150
16	2	NORTHPORT ANGLR 1620	OP	BASS	AL	SV	OB			6	3	610			1000	1200
16	2	OUTFITTER 1600	OP	BASS	AL	SV	OB			6	3	550			925	1100
16	2	PRO FISHERMAN 1630	OP	FSH	AL	SV	OB			6	3	650			1100	1300
16	3	SIERRA 165V	OP	RNBT	FBG	DV	OB			6	7	960			1550	1850
16	3	SIERRA 165V	OP	RNBT	FBG	DV	IO	110-128		6	7	1650			2850	3350
16	4	GUIDE-CLASSIC 1675	OP	BASS	AL	FL	OB			6	4	650			1100	1300
16	7	ULTRA PRO 1700	OP	FSH	AL	DV	OB			7		942			1550	1850
16	7	ULTRA PRO 1701	OP	FSH	AL	DV	OB			7		985			1600	1950
16	9	SIERRA SX1700	OP	BASS	FBG	SV	OB			7	2	1180			1900	2250
17	11	SIERRA 180V	OP	RNBT	FBG	SV	OB			7	5	1135			1900	2300
17	11	SIERRA 180V	OP	RNBT	FBG	SV	IO	110-205		7	5	1935			3650	4350
18		SIERRA F185	OP	RNBT	FBG	SV	OB			7	5	1185			2000	2350
18	2	SIERRA SX1800	OP	BASS	FBG	SV	OB			7	8	1350			2250	2650
18	6	KING FSH 1950	OP	FSH	AL	SV	OB			7	8	1185			1950	2350
18	6	PRO FSH 1930	OP	FSH	AL	SV	OB			7	8	1185			2050	2450
19	4	SIERRA 195V	OP	SKI	FBG	DV	IO	110-205		7	6	2740			4650	5450
20	4	NAVIGATOR 2090	OP	FSH	AL	DV	OB			8		1305			2450	2850
20	4	NAVIGATOR 2090	OP	FSH	AL	DV	IO	110-180		8		2205			5600	6550
20	4	VOYAGEUR 2096	OP	FSH	AL	DV	OB			8		1350			2550	2950
20	4	VOYAGEUR 2096	OP	FSH	AL	DV	IO	110-180		8		2265			5700	6600
20	9	SIERRA 210V	OP	CUD	FBG	DV	IO	110-205		8	4	3100			6700	7800
		1989 BOATS														
16		DEEP FSH II 3696	OP	FSH	AL	SV	OB			5	4	343			545	655
16		DEEP FSH II 3696-24	OP	FSH	AL	SV	OB			5	4	348			550	665
16		NORTHPORT TROL F3636	OP	FSH	AL	SV	OB			5	4	390			650	785
16		NORTHPORT TROL F3666	OP	FSH	AL	SV	OB			5	4	390			590	710
16	2	MUSKY 1625	OP	FSH	AL	SV	OB			6	3	570			920	1100
16	2	NORTHPORT ANGLR 1620	OP	BASS	AL	SV	OB			6	3	610			985	1150
16	2	OUTFITTER 1600	OP	BASS	AL	SV	OB			6	3	550			895	1050
16	2	PRO FISHERMAN 1630	OP	FSH	AL	SV	OB			6	3	650			1050	1250
16	3	SIERRA 165V	OP	RNBT	FBG	DV	OB			6	7	960			1500	1800
16	3	SIERRA 165V	OP	RNBT	FBG	DV	IO	120-205		6	7	1650			2700	3250
16	3	SIERRA 166V	OP	FSH	FBG	SV	OB			6	7	940			1500	1750
16	4	GUIDE-CLASSIC 1675	OP	BASS	AL	FL	OB			6	4	650			1050	1250
16	10	SIERRA 178V	OP	FSH	FBG	SV	OB			7	2	1175			1850	2200
17	11	SIERRA 180V	OP	RNBT	FBG	SV	OB			7	5	1135			1850	2200
17	11	SIERRA 180V	OP	RNBT	FBG	SV	IO	120-205		7	5	1935			3450	4150
18	6	KING FSH 1950	OP	FSH	AL	SV	OB			7	8	1185			1950	2300
18	6	PRO FSH 1930	OP	FSH	AL	SV	OB			7	8	1185			1950	2350
19	4	SIERRA 195V	OP	SKI	FBG	DV	IO	120-205		7	6	2740			4400	5150
20	4	NAVIGATOR 2090	OP	FSH	AL	DV	OB			8		1305			2400	2750
20	4	NAVIGATOR 2090	OP	FSH	AL	DV	IO	120-175		8		2205			5300	6150
20	4	VOYAGEUR 2096	OP	FSH	AL	DV	OB			8		1350			2450	2850
20	4	VOYAGEUR 2096	OP	FSH	AL	DV	IO	120-175		8		2265			5350	6200
20	9	SIERRA 210V	OP	CUD	FBG	DV	IO	120-205		8	4	3100			6300	7400
		1988 BOATS														
16		DEEP FSH II 3696	OP	FSH	AL	SV	OB			5	4	343			525	635
16		DEEP FSH II 3696-24	OP	FSH	AL	SV	OB			5	4	348			535	645
16		DEEP FSH III 3696-24	OP	UTL	AL	SV	OB			5	4	348			535	645
16		NORTHPORT TROL F3636	OP	FSH	AL	SV	OB			5	4	390			600	725
16		NORTHPORT TROL F3666	OP	UTL	AL	SV	OB			5	4	365			560	675
16	2	MUSKY 1625	OP	FSH	AL	SV	OB			6	3	625			975	1150
16	2	NORTHPORT ANGLR 1620	OP	BASS	AL	SV	OB			6	3	610			955	1150
16	2	OUTFITTER 1600	OP	BASS	AL	SV	OB			6	3	550			865	1050
16	2	PRO FISHERMAN 1630	OP	FSH	AL	SV	OB			6	3	650			1000	1200
16	4	GUIDE-CLASSIC 1675	OP	BASS	AL	FL	OB			6	4	650			1000	1200
16	4	TROPHY CLASSIC 1670	OP	FSH	AL	SV	OB			6	2	590			930	1100
18	4	KING-FISHERMAN 1840	OP	CTRCN	AL	DV	OB			6	10	830			1400	1650
18	4	PRO-FISHERMAN 1820	OP	FSH	AL	DV	OB			6	10	775			1300	1550
20	4	NAVIGATOR 2090	OP	FSH	AL	DV	OB			8		1305			2350	2700
20	4	NAVIGATOR 2090	OP	FSH	AL	DV	IO	120	MRCR	8		2205			5050	5800
20	4	VOYAGEUR 2096	OP	FSH	AL	DV	OB			8		1350			2400	2750
20	4	VOYAGEUR 2096	OP	FSH	AL	DV	IO	120	MRCR	8		2265			5100	5850
		1987 BOATS														
16		DEEP FSH F-4656	OP	FSH	AL	SV	OB			5	4	243			355	435
16		DEEP FSH F-4656-24	OP	FSH	AL	SV	OB			5	4	248			365	445
16		DEEP FSH III 3696	OP	UTL	AL	SV	OB			5	4	343	2	6	510	615
16		DEEP FSH III 3696-24	OP	UTL	AL	SV	OB			5	4	348	2	6	520	625
16		NORTHPORT DLX F-3636	OP	FSH	AL	SV	OB			5	4	390			585	705
16		NORTHPORT F-3666	OP	UTL	AL	SV	OB			5	4	365	2	6	545	655
16	2	LAKE III F-3616-20	OP	FSH	AL	SV	OB			6	2	435			660	795
16	2	LAKE-FISHER F-3616	OP	FSH	AL	SV	OB			6	2	308	2	10	465	560
16	2	MISTER-MUSKY F-3646	OP	BASS	AL	SV	OB			6	2	620	2	10	940	1100
16	2	NORTHPORT 1620	OP	BASS	AL	SV	OB			6	3	610	2	9	925	1100
16	2	OUTFITTER 1600	OP	BASS	AL	SV	OB			6	3	550	2	9	845	1000
16	2	PRO FISHERMAN 1630	OP	FSH	AL	SV	OB			6	3	650			985	1150
16	4	GUIDE-CLASSIC 1675	OP	BASS	AL	FL	OB			6	4	650			995	1200
16	10	OFFSHORE CC 6740	OP	CTRCN	FBG	DV	OB			7	2	1130			1700	2000
16	10	OFFSHORE GL 6720	OP	FSH	FBG	DV	OB			7	2	1130	3	2	1700	2000
16	10	SUNSPORT 17 6710	OP	RNBT	FBG	DV	OB			7	2	1050			1600	1900
18	4	KING-FISHERMAN 18	OP	CTRCN	AL	DV	OB			6	10	830			1350	1600
18	4	PRO-FISHERMAN 18	OP	FSH	AL	DV	OB			6	10	775			1300	1500
20	4	VOYAGEUR	OP	CUD	AL	DV	OB			8		1350			2350	2700
		1986 BOATS														
16		DEEP FSH F-3656	OP	FSH	AL	SV	OB			5	4	323	2	6	470	565
16		DEEP FSH F-3656-24	OP	FSH	AL	SV	OB			5	4	328	2	6	475	575
16		DEEP FSH F-4656	OP	FSH	AL	SV	OB			5	4	243			345	425
16		DEEP FSH F-4656-24	OP	FSH	AL	SV	OB			5	4	248			355	430
16		DEEP FSH III 3696	OP	UTL	AL	SV	OB			5	4	343	2	6	500	600
16		DEEP FSH III 3696-24	OP	UTL	AL	SV	OB			5	4	348	2	6	505	610
16		NORTHPORT DLX F-3636	OP	FSH	AL	SV	OB			5	4	390			570	685
16		NORTHPORT F-3666	OP	UTL	AL	SV	OB			5	4	365	2	6	530	640
16	2	LAKE II F-3616-16	OP	FSH	AL	SV	OB			6	2	400	2	10	590	710
16	2	LAKE III F-3616-20	OP	FSH	AL	SV	OB			6	2	435			645	775
16	2	LAKE-FISHER F-3616	OP	FSH	AL	SV	OB			6	2	308	2	10	455	550
16	2	MISTER-MUSKY F-3646	OP	BASS	AL	SV	OB			6	2	620	2	10	915	1100
16	2	NORTHPORT 1620	OP	BASS	AL	SV	OB			6	3	610	2	9	910	1100
16	2	OUTFITTER 1600	OP	BASS	AL	SV	OB			6	3	550	2	9	810	980
16	2	TOURNAMENT F-3626	OP	BASS	AL	SV	OB			6	2	778	2	10	1150	1350
16	10	OFFSHORE CC 6740	OP	FSH	FBG	DV	OB			7	2	1130			1650	1950
16	10	OFFSHORE GL 6720	OP	BASS	FBG	DV	OB			7	2	1130	3	2	1650	1950
16	10	SUNSPORT 17 6710	OP	RNBT	FBG	DV	OB			7	2	1050			1550	1850
17	6	KING-FISH F-1740	OP	CTRCN	AL	SV	OB			6	6	780	3	2	1200	1450
17	6	PRO-FISH F-1720	OP	FSH	AL	SV	OB			6	6	700	3	2	1100	1300
18	4	KING-FISHERMAN 18	OP	CTRCN	AL	DV	OB			6	10	830			1300	1550
18	4	PRO-FISHERMAN 18	OP	FSH	AL	DV	OB			6	10	775			1250	1500
		1985 BOATS														
16		DEEP FSH F-3656	OP	FSH	AL	SV	OB			5	4	323	2	6	460	555
16		DEEP FSH F-3656-24	OP	FSH	AL	SV	OB			5	4	328	2	6	465	560
16		DEEP FSH F-4656	OP	FSH	AL	SV	OB			5	4	243			340	415
16		DEEP FSH F-4656-24	OP	FSH	AL	SV	OB			5	4	248			345	420
16		NORTHPORT DLX F-3636	OP	FSH	AL	SV	OB			5	4	390			555	670
16		NORTHPORT F-3666	OP	UTL	AL	SV	OB			5	4	365	2	6	520	625
16	2	LAKE II F-3616-16	OP	FSH	AL	SV	OB			6	2	400	2	10	580	695

 CONTINUED ON NEXT PAGE

LOA FT IN	NAME AND/OR MODEL	TOP/RIG	BOAT TYPE	HULL MTL TP	TP #	ENGINE HP	MFG	BEAM FT IN	WGT LBS	DRAFT FT IN	RETAIL LOW	RETAIL HIGH
	**1985 BOATS**
16 2	LAKE III F-3616-20	OP	FSH	AL SV	OB			6 2	435		625	755
16 2	LAKE-FISHER F-3616	OP	FSH	AL SV	OB			6 2	308	2 10	445	535
16 2	MISTER-MUSKY F-3646	OP	BASS	AL SV	OB			6 2	620	2 10	900	1050
16 2	TOURNAMENT F-3626-26	OP	BASS	AL SV	OB			6 2	778	2 10	1100	1350
16 10	OFFSHORE 17	OP	FSH	FBG DV	OB			7 2	1130		1600	1900
16 10	SUNSPORT 17	OP	RNBT	FBG DV	OB			7 2	1050		1500	1800
17 6	BREAKAWAY F-1710	OP	RNBT	AL SV	OB			6 6	769	3 2	1150	1400
17 6	DAYBREAK II F-1715	OP	FSH	AL SV	OB			6 6	795	3 2	1200	1450
17 6	KING-FISH F-1740	OP	CTRCN	AL SV	OB			6 6	780	3 2	1200	1400
17 6	PRO-FISH F-1720	OP	FSH	AL SV	OB			6 6	700	3 2	1050	1300
18 4	KING-FISHERMAN 18	OP	CTRCN	AL DV	OB			6 10	830		1300	1550
18 4	PRO-FISHERMAN 18	OP	FSH	AL DV	OB			6 10	775		1300	1450
	**1984 BOATS**
16	FISHERMAN F-3656	OP	FSH	AL SV	OB			5 4	323	2 6	450	545
16	FISHERMAN F-3656-24	OP	FSH	AL SV	OB			5 4	328	2 6	455	550
16	FISHERMAN F-4656	OP	FSH	AL SV	OB			5 4	243		330	405
16	FISHERMAN F-4656-24	OP	FSH	AL SV	OB			5 4	248		340	415
16	NORTHPORT DLX F-3636	OP	FSH	AL SV	OB			5 4	390		545	615
16	NORTHPORT F-3666	OP	UTL	AL SV	OB			5 4	365	2 6	510	655
16 2	FISHERMAN F-3676	OP	BASS	AL SV	OB			6 2	482	2 10	680	820
16 2	LAKE II F-3616-16	OP	FSH	AL SV	OB			6 2	400	2 10	565	680
16 2	LAKE III F-3616-20	OP	FSH	AL SV	OB			6 2	435		615	740
16 2	LAKE-FISHER F-3616	OP	FSH	AL SV	OB			6 2	308	2 10	435	525
16 2	MISTER-MUSKY F-3646	OP	BASS	AL SV	OB			6 2	620	2 10	885	1050
16 2	TOURNAMENT F-3626-26	OP	BASS	AL SV	OB			6 2	778	2 10	1100	1300
17 6	BREAKAWAY F-1710	OP	RNBT	AL SV	OB			6 6	769	3 2	1150	1350
17 6	DAYBREAK II F-1715	OP	FSH	AL SV	OB			6 6	795	3 2	1200	1400
17 6	KING-FISH F-1740	OP	CTRCN	AL SV	OB			6 6	780	3 2	1150	1400
17 6	PRO FISH DLX F-1720	OP	FSH	AL DV	OB			6 6	720	3 2	1100	1300
17 6	PRO-FISH F-1720	OP	FSH	AL SV	OB			6 6	700	3 2	1050	1250

....For earlier years, see the BUC Used Boat Price Guide, Volume 3

MISTRAL SAILBOAT INC
MISTAL INC
LONGUEUIL QU CANADA   COAST GUARD MFG ID- ZMI   See inside cover to adjust price for area

LOA FT IN	NAME AND/OR MODEL	TOP/RIG	BOAT TYPE	HULL MTL TP	TP #	ENGINE HP	MFG	BEAM FT IN	WGT LBS	DRAFT FT IN	RETAIL LOW	RETAIL HIGH
	**1986 BOATS**
16	MISTRAL	SLP	SA/RC	FBG CB				6 1	365	3 10	1400	1650
16	MISTRAL 16 CABIN	SLP	SAIL	FBG CB				6 2	640	4	1900	2250
20	MISTRAL EQUIPE	SLP	SA/RC	FBG SK	OB			8	1200	4 11	2950	3400
21	MISTRAL T-21	SLP	SA/RC	FBG SK	OB			8 2	2500	5 1	4700	5400
	**1985 BOATS**
16	MISTRAL 16 CABIN	SLP	SAIL	FBG CB				6 2	640	4	1750	2100
16	MISTRAL 16 COMP	SLP	SA/RC	FBG CB				6 1	365	3 10	1300	1500
16	MISTRAL 16 STD	SLP	SAIL	FBG CB				6 1	365	3 10	1300	1500
21	MISTRAL T-21	SLP	SA/RC	FBG SK	OB			8 2	2500	5 1	4400	5050
	**1984 BOATS**
16	MISTRAL 16 CABIN	SLP	SAIL	FBG CB				6 2	640	3 10	1650	1950
16	MISTRAL 16 COMP	SLP	SA/RC	FBG CB				6 1	365	3 10	1200	1450
16	MISTRAL 16 STANDARD	SLP	SAIL	FBG CB				6 1	365	3 10	1200	1450
21	MISTRAL T-21	SLP	SAIL	FBG CB				8 2	2700	5 1	4350	5000

....For earlier years, see the BUC Used Boat Price Guide, Volume 3

MITCHELL FISHING BOATS INC
SARASOTA FL 33577   See inside cover to adjust price for area

LOA FT IN	NAME AND/OR MODEL	TOP/RIG	BOAT TYPE	HULL MTL TP	TP #	ENGINE HP	MFG	BEAM FT IN	WGT LBS	DRAFT FT IN	RETAIL LOW	RETAIL HIGH
	**1986 BOATS**
16	MITCHELL 160	OP	FSH	FBG TR	OB			6 4			735	885
16 6	MITCHELL 170	OP	FSH	FBG SV	OB			6 8	605		815	980
	**1985 BOATS**
16	MITCHELL 160	OP	FSH	FBG TR	OB			6 4			710	855
16 6	MITCHELL 170	OP	FSH	FBG SV	OB			6 8	605		790	950

MITCHELL MOULDINGS LTD
NR ROCHFORD ENGLAND   See inside cover to adjust price for area

LOA FT IN	NAME AND/OR MODEL	TOP/RIG	BOAT TYPE	HULL MTL TP	TP #	ENGINE HP	MFG	BEAM FT IN	WGT LBS	DRAFT FT IN	RETAIL LOW	RETAIL HIGH
	**1991 BOATS**
23	MITCHELL FF 700	HT	SPTCR	FBG DV	IO	130D	VLVO	8	4000	2 9	17200	19600
31	MARK II 31	HT	MY	FBG SV	IB	90D	SABR 11		8000	2 7	41300	45900
	IB 125D-225D 48200		59300, IB T 80D SABR 48600 53400, IBT150D-T160D								58100	64900
31	MITCHELL 31 MK III	HT	MY	FBG SV	IB	90D	SABR 11		8500	2 7	42700	47400
31	MITCHELL 31 MK III	HT	MY	FBG SV	IB	125D-225D	11		8500	2 7	48600	59000
31	MITCHELL 31 MK III	HT	MY	FBG SV	IB	T90D-T160D	11		8500	2 7	51900	64100
31	MITCHELL AFT CABIN	HT	MY	FBG SV	IB	125D	SABR 11		8000	2 7	48200	53000
31	MITCHELL AFT CABIN	HT	MY	FBG SV	IB	T 80D	SABR 11		8000	2 7	52900	58100
31	SEA ANGLER 31	HT	FSH	FBG SV	IB	90D	SABR 11		8000	2 7	37700	44800
31	SEA ANGLER 31	HT	FSH	FBG SV	IB	125D-225D	11		8000	2 7	38600	43600
31	SEA ANGLER 31	HT	FSH	FBG SV	IB	T150D-T160D	11		8000	2 7	43500	48800
	**1990 BOATS**
23	MITCHELL FF 700	HT	CR	FBG DV	IO	130D	VLVO	8	4000	2 9	15700	17900
31	MARK II 31	HT	TRWL	FBG DS	IB	90D	SABR 11		8000	2 7	40500	45000
	IB 125D-225D 47500		58900, IB T 80D SABR 44200 49200, IBT150D-T160D								55000	60700
31	MITCHELL AFT CABIN	HT	TRWL	FBG DS	IB	T 80D		11		8000	2 7	49200	54100
31	SEA ANGLER 31	HT	TRWL	FBG DS	IB	90D	SABR 11		8000	2 7	34300	38100
	IB 125D-190D 40100		49300, IB 225D SABR 46900 51600, IB T 80D SABR								46800	51500
	IBT150D-T160D 55000		60700										
	**1989 BOATS**
23	MITCHELL FF 700	HT	CR	FBG DV	IO	130D	VLVO	8 3	4480	3	16000	18200
23	MITCHELL FF 700	HT	CR	FBG DV	IO	130D	VLVO	8 3	4480	3	20700	23000
31	31 MK II	HT	TRWL	FBG DS	IB	255D	FORD 11		8960	2 7	51200	56300
31	31 MK II	HT	TRWL	FBG DS	IB	T160D	SABR 11		8960	2 7	54600	60000
31	MARK II 31	HT	TRWL	FBG DS	IB	90D	SABR 11		8000	2 7	35700	39700
31	MARK II 31	HT	TRWL	FBG DS	IB	125D-190D	11		8000	2 7	41600	50700
31	MARK II 31	HT	TRWL	FBG DS	IB	225D	SABR 11		8000	2 7	48200	53000
31	SEA ANGLER	HT	TRWL	FBG DS	IB	255D	FORD 11		8960	2 7	51200	56300
31	SEA ANGLER	HT	TRWL	FBG DS	IB	T160D	SABR 11		8960	2 7	54600	60000
31	SEA ANGLER 31	HT	TRWL	FBG DS	IB	90D	SABR 11		8000	2 7	35700	39700
31	SEA ANGLER 31	HT	TRWL	FBG DS	IB	125D-190D	11		8000	2 7	41600	50700
31	SEA ANGLER 31	HT	TRWL	FBG DS	IB	225D	SABR 11		8000	2 7	48200	53000

MOBJACK SALES CORP
GLEN ALLEN VA 23059-7128   See inside cover to adjust price for area

For more recent years, see the BUC Used Boat Price Guide, Volume 1

LOA FT IN	NAME AND/OR MODEL	TOP/RIG	BOAT TYPE	HULL MTL TP	TP #	ENGINE HP	MFG	BEAM FT IN	WGT LBS	DRAFT FT IN	RETAIL LOW	RETAIL HIGH
	**1996 BOATS**
17	MOBJACK	SLP	SAROD	FBG CB	OB			6 6	400	9	6000	6900
	**1995 BOATS**
17	MOBJACK	SLP	SAROD	FBG CB	OB			6 6	400	9	5650	6500
	**1994 BOATS**
17	MOBJACK	SLP	SAROD	FBG CB	OB			6 6	400	9	5350	6100
	**1993 BOATS**
17	MOBJACK	SLP	SAROD	FBG CB	OB			6 6	400	9	5000	5750
	**1992 BOATS**
17	MOBJACK	SLP	SA/OD	FBG CB	OB			6 6	400	9	4700	5400
	**1991 BOATS**
17	MOBJACK	SLP	SA/OD	FBG CB	OB			6 6	400	9	4450	5150
	**1990 BOATS**
17	MOBJACK	SLP	SA/OD	FBG CB	OB			6 6	400	9	4150	4800
	**1989 BOATS**
17	MOBJACK	SLP	SA/OD	FBG CB	OB			6 6	400	9	3900	4550
	**1988 BOATS**
17	MOBJACK	SLP	SA/OD	FBG CB	OB			6 6	400	9	3650	4250
	**1987 BOATS**
17	MOBJACK	SLP	SA/OD	FBG CB	OB			6 6	400	9	3450	4000
	**1986 BOATS**
17	MOBJACK	SLP	SA/OD	FBG CB	OB			6 6	400	9	3250	3800
	**1985 BOATS**
17	MOBJACK	SLP	SA/OD	FBG CB	OB			6 6	400	9	3050	3550
	**1984 BOATS**
17	MOBJACK	SLP	SA/OD	FBG CB	OB			6 6	400	9	2850	3350

....For earlier years, see the BUC Used Boat Price Guide, Volume 3

MOCHI CRAFT
FERRETTI GROUP
ITALY

See inside cover to adjust price for area

For more recent years, see the BUC Used Boat Price Guide, Volume 1

LOA FT IN	NAME AND/ OR MODEL	TOP/ RIG	BOAT TYPE	-HULL- MTL TP	----ENGINE--- TP # HP MFG	BEAM FT IN	WGT LBS	DRAFT FT IN	RETAIL LOW	RETAIL HIGH
---------------- 1984 BOATS ----------------
36 8	DOMINATOR	FB	OFF	FBG DV	IB T235D VLVO 11 10	15850	3 6	63400	69600
	IB T270D FIAT 66000	72500,	IB T300D CAT	68900 75700,	IB T320D CUM	67900	74600
	IB T355D CAT 72100	79200,	IB T500D CUM	79100 86900
40 11	DOMINATOR	FB	OFF	FBG DV	IB T270D FIAT 12 8	21600	3 7	98100	108000
	IB T300D CAT 102000	112000,	IB T300D VLVO	97700 107500,	IB T320D CUM	100500	110500
	IB T350D IF 103000	113000,	IB T355D CAT	106000 116500,	IB T400D IF	106500	117000
	IB T500D CUM 114500	125500

MOLLYS COVE BOAT WORKS
MATTAPOISTT MA 02739

See inside cover to adjust price for area

LOA FT IN	NAME AND/ OR MODEL	TOP/ RIG	BOAT TYPE	-HULL- MTL TP	----ENGINE--- TP # HP MFG	BEAM FT IN	WGT LBS	DRAFT FT IN	RETAIL LOW	RETAIL HIGH
---------------- 1985 BOATS ----------------
38	GALATEA	KTH	SA/CR	F/S KL	IB 27D WEST 11	24000	5 3	71800	78900

....For earlier years, see the BUC Used Boat Price Guide, Volume 3

MONARK MARINE
TOPEKA IN 46571

COAST GUARD MFG ID- MAK See inside cover to adjust price for area
FORMERLY MONARK BOAT CO

For more recent years, see the BUC Used Boat Price Guide, Volume 1

LOA FT IN	NAME AND/ OR MODEL	TOP/ RIG	BOAT TYPE	-HULL- MTL TP	----ENGINE--- TP # HP MFG	BEAM FT IN	WGT LBS	DRAFT FT IN	RETAIL LOW	RETAIL HIGH
---------------- 1996 BOATS ----------------
16	1648	OP	JON	AL FL	OB	5 7	264		605	725
16	1650 MV	OP	JON	AL FL	OB	7 1	327		760	915
16	SKIFF 16	OP	UTL	AL SV	OB	5 6	400		935	1100
16 2	SF 16 L	OP	UTL	AL SV	OB	5 7	245		560	670
16 2	SF 16 S	OP	UTL	AL SV	OB	5 7	245		560	670
16 4	CLASSIC 1600 SC	OP	BASS	AL SV	OB	6 2	687		1500	1750
16 4	CLASSIC 1600 T	OP	BASS	AL SV	OB	6 2	750		1950	2300
16 4	SF 16 CAMP	OP	UTL	AL SV	OB	6 2	520		1200	1450
16 6	PRO 1650	OP	BASS	AL SV	OB	6 9	915		2750	3200
16 9	PRO 170	OP	BASS	AL SV	OB	6	870		2300	2700
17	PRO 1700	OP	BASS	AL SV	OB	7 1	1000		2650	3100
18	1860 MV	OP	JON	AL FL	OB	7 6	417		790	955
18	PRO 1800	OP	BASS	FBG SV	OB	6 11	1335		3450	4000
18	PRO 1800 DC	OP	BASS	FBG SV	OB	6 11	1415		3600	4200
18	PRO 1800 FS	OP	BASS	FBG SV	OB	6 11	1415		3600	4200
18 9	PRO 1900	OP	BASS	AL SV	OB	7 6	1183		3150	3700
20 1	SUNDECK 20	ST	RNBT	AL SV	OB	8 4	1870		5250	6050
21 5	DACOTAH 2101	OP	CUD	AL SV	IO 135-180	8	1550		7250	8450
---------------- 1995 BOATS ----------------
16	1648	OP	JON	AL FL	OB	5 7	264		575	690
16	1650 MV	OP	JON	AL FL	OB	7 1	327		725	870
16 2	SF 16 L	OP	UTL	AL SV	OB	5 7	245		530	640
16 2	SF 16 S	OP	UTL	AL SV	OB	5 7	245		530	640
16 4	1600 SC	OP	BASS	AL SV	OB	6 2	687		1400	1650
16 4	1600 T	OP	BASS	AL SV	OB	6 2	611		1450	1750
16 4	PRO 170	OP	BASS	AL SV	OB	6	870		2150	2500
16 6	PRO 1650 SC	OP	BASS	AL SV	OB	6 9	915		2600	3050
17	PRO 1700	OP	BASS	AL SV	OB	7 1	1000		2500	2900
18	1860 MV	OP	JON	AL FL	OB	7 6	417		750	900
18 9	PRO 1900	OP	BASS	AL SV	OB	7 6	1183		3000	3500
---------------- 1994 BOATS ----------------
16	1648	OP	JON	AL FL	OB	5 7	264		545	660
16	1650 MV	OP	JON	AL FL	OB	6 3	327		690	830
16 2	SF 16	OP	UTL	AL SV	OB	5 7	520		935	1100
16 2	1600 T	OP	BASS	AL SV	OB	5 7	245		510	610
16 4	1600 SC	OP	BASS	AL SV	OB	6 2	687		1300	1550
16 4	1600 T	OP	BASS	AL SV	OB	6 2	537		1200	1450
16 6	1650 SC	OP	BASS	AL SV	OB	6 9	960		2550	3000
17	1700 DC	OP	BASS	AL SV	OB	7 1	1034		2400	2800
17	PRO BASS 170	OP	BASS	AL SV	OB	6	902		2100	2500
18 9	1900 DC	OP	BASS	AL SV	OB	7 6	1155		2750	3200
---------------- 1993 BOATS ----------------
16	1648	OP	JON	AL FL	OB	5 7	264		520	625
16	1648 LW	OP	JON	AL FL	OB	5 7	264		565	685
16	1650 MV	OP	JON	AL FL	OB	6 3	327		655	795
16	CRAPPIE 160 LX	OP	BASS	AL SV	OB	6 1	795		1750	2100
16 2	BP 16	OP	UTL	AL SV	OB	5 7	245		485	585
16 2	BP 16SS	OP	UTL	AL SV	OB	5 7	455		780	940
16 2	CLASSIC BP 16 DLX C	OP	UTL	AL SV	OB	5 7	455		1100	1300
16 5	CLASSIC 1600 SC	OP	BASS	AL SV	OB	6 2	510		930	1100
16 5	CLASSIC 1600 T	OP	BASS	AL SV	OB	6 2	600		1300	1500
16 6	PRO 1650 SC	OP	BASS	AL SV	OB	6 8	891		2250	2650
16 8	PRO 1650 DC	OP	BASS	AL SV	OB	6 8	912		2000	2350
17	PRO 1700 DC	OP	BASS	AL SV	OB	7 1	1050		2350	2700
17	PRO 1700 SC	OP	BASS	AL SV	OB	7 1	1030		2300	2650
17	PRO BASS 170	OP	BASS	AL SV	OB	6 2	890		1950	2350
18 9	PRO 1900 DC	OP	BASS	AL SV	OB	7 6	1300		2850	3350
18 9	PRO 1900 SS	OP	BASS	AL SV	IO 115-155	7 6	1235		4050	4700
---------------- 1992 BOATS ----------------
16	CRAPPIE 160 LX	OP	BASS	AL SV	OB	6 1	790		1650	2000
16	CRAPPIE PRO 160	OP	BASS	AL SV	OB	6 1	770		1450	1750
16	LEGEND 1648	OP	JON	AL FL	OB	5 7	264		495	600
16	LEGEND 1648 LW	OP	JON	AL FL	OB	5 7	264		535	645
16	LEGEND 1650 MV	OP	JON	AL FL	OB	6 3	325		620	750
16	LEGEND BASS 160	OP	BASS	AL SV	OB	6 1	550		1600	1900
16 2	LEGEND BP 16	OP	UTL	AL SV	OB	5 7	245		465	560
16 2	LEGEND BP 16 DLX C	OP	UTL	AL SV	OB	5 7	455		1050	1250
16 2	LEGEND BP 16 LW	OP	UTL	AL SV	OB	5 7	455		720	870
16 3	LEGEND 1600 FS	OP	RNBT	AL SV	OB	7 5	675		1400	1650
16 3	LEGEND 1600 XT	OP	RNBT	AL SV	OB	6 8	675		1400	1650
16 3	LEGEND 1650 SC	OP	BASS	AL SV	OB	6 8	675		1550	1850
16 5	LEGEND 1600 SC	OP	BASS	AL SV	OB	6 2	510		895	1050
16 5	LEGEND 1600 T	OP	BASS	AL SV	OB	6 2	600		1200	1450
17	PRO BASS 170	OP	BASS	AL SV	OB	6 1	890		1850	2200
17 6	PRO BASS 180 V	OP	BASS	AL SV	OB	6 2	900		1900	2250
18 3	BLUEWATER 1800	OP	RNBT	AL SV	IO 115 MRCR	6 7	950		3050	3550
18 3	LEGEND 1800 CC	OP	CTRCN	AL SV	OB	6 7	975		1450	1750
18 3	LEGEND 1800 FS	OP	RNBT	AL SV	OB	6 7	950		2050	2450
18 3	LEGEND 1800 XT	OP	RNBT	AL SV	OB	6 7	950		2050	2400
18 3	LEGEND 1850 SC	OP	BASS	AL SV	OB	6 8	935		2000	2400
---------------- 1991 BOATS ----------------
16	CRAPPIE 160 LX	OP	BASS	AL SV	OB	6 1	540		1100	1300
16	CRAPPIE PRO 160	OP	BASS	AL SV	OB	6 1	540		975	1150
16	LEGEND 1648	OP	JON	AL FL	OB	5 7	264		470	570
16	LEGEND 1648 LW	OP	JON	AL FL	OB	5 7	264		510	610
16	LEGEND 1648 MV	OP	JON	AL FL	OB	5 9	248		465	560
16	LEGEND BASS 160	OP	BASS	AL SV	OB	6 1	550		1050	1250
16 1	LEGEND 1600 FS	OP	RNBT	AL SV	OB	7 5	650		1250	1500
16 2	LEGEND BP 16	OP	UTL	AL SV	OB	5 7	245		450	540
16 2	LEGEND BP 16 DLX C	OP	UTL	AL SV	OB	5 7	455		950	1150
16 2	LEGEND BP 16 WILL	OP	UTL	AL SV	OB	5 7	455		765	920
16 5	LEGEND 1600 SC	OP	BASS	AL SV	OB	6 2	650		1100	1300
16 5	LEGEND 1600 T	OP	BASS	AL SV	OB	6 2	625		1200	1450
16 5	LEGEND 1600 XT	OP	RNBT	AL SV	OB	7 5	650		1250	1500
16 5	LEGEND 1650 SC	OP	BASS	AL SV	OB	6 2	650		1450	1700
17	PRO BASS 170	OP	BASS	AL SV	OB	6 1	745		1500	1750
17 6	PRO BASS 180 V	OP	BASS	AL SV	OB	6 2	800		1600	1900
18 4	LEGEND 1800 CC	OP	CTRCN	AL SV	OB	6 7	850		1750	2050
18 4	LEGEND 1800 FS	OP	RNBT	AL SV	OB	6 7	900		1850	2250
18 4	LEGEND 1800 XT	OP	RNBT	AL SV	OB	6 7	900		1850	2200
---------------- 1990 BOATS ----------------
16	155C	OP	BASS	AL SV	OB	6	535		980	1150
16	160	OP	BASS	AL SV	OB	6	515		940	1100
16	160C	OP	BASS	AL SV	OB	6	540		985	1200
16	160PF	OP	FSH	AL SV	OB	6	540		985	1150
16	1648	OP	JON	AL FL	OB	5 7	248		440	530
16	1648LW	OP	JON	AL FL	OB	5 7	248		450	545
16	1652	OP	JON	AL FL	OB	5 7	349		585	700
16	1652LW	OP	JON	AL FL	OB	6 1	349		620	745
17	170	OP	BASS	AL SV	OB	6	700		1350	1600
17	180XT	OP	RNBT	AL SV	OB	6	745		1400	1700
18	1852	OP	JON	AL FL	OB	6 1	410		595	711
18	1852LW	OP	JON	AL FL	OB	6 1	430		630	755
---------------- 1989 BOATS ----------------
16	1648	OP	JON	AL FL	OB	5 7	248		415	500
16	1648A	OP	JON	AL FL	OB	5 7	290		480	580
16	1648ALW	OP	JON	AL FL	OB	5 7	315		520	630

LOA FT IN	NAME AND/OR MODEL	TOP/RIG	BOAT TYPE	HULL MTL	HULL TP	ENG TP	ENG #	ENG HP	ENG MFG	BEAM FT IN	WGT LBS	DRAFT FT IN	RETAIL LOW	RETAIL HIGH
1989 BOATS														
16	1648LW	OP	JON	AL	FL	OB				5 7	248		435	520
16	1652	OP	JON	AL	FL	OB				6 1	349		555	665
16	1652LW	OP	JON	AL	FL	OB				6 1	349		590	710
16	BASSFINDER 1650V	OP	BASS	AL	SV	OB				6	515		915	1100
16	BASSFINDER 1650VC	OP	BASS	AL	SV	OB				6	535		945	1150
16	BASSFINDER 1650VDS	OP	BASS	AL	SV	OB				6	540		955	1150
17	1750MVA	OP	FSH	AL	SV	OB		3		6 3	338		630	760
17	BASSFINDER 1750VA	OP	BASS	AL	SV	OB				6	700		1300	1550
17	BASSFINDER 1750VAF	OP	BASS	AL	SV	OB				6	745		1350	1650
18	1852	OP	JON	AL	FL	OB				6 1	410		575	690
18	1852LW	OP	JON	AL	FL	OB				6 1	430		605	730
1988 BOATS														
16	1644MV	OP	JON	AL	FL	OB				5 8	260		420	505
16	1648	OP	JON	AL	FL	OB				5 7	248		310	380
16	1648LW	OP	JON	AL	FL	OB				5 7	248		485	585
16	1648X	OP	FSH	AL	FL	OB				5 7	320		460	555
16	1648XL	OP	FSH	AL	FL	OB				5 7	320		615	740
16	1652	OP	JON	AL	FL	OB				6 1	349		515	625
16	1652LW	OP	JON	AL	FL	OB				6 1	349		570	690
16	BASSFINDER 1650V	OP	BASS	AL	SV	OB				6	515		890	1050
16	BASSFINDER 1650VDS	OP	BASS	AL	SV	OB				6	515		890	1050
16 2	16V LUNKER I	OP	BASS	AL	DV	OB				6 7	680		1150	1400
16 2	16V LUNKER II	OP	BASS	AL	DV	OB				6 7	695		1200	1450
16 2	16V LUNKER III	OP	BASS	AL	DV	OB				6 7	720		1250	1450
16 6	16VCC	OP	BASS	AL	DV	OB				6 10	800		1400	1650
17	BASSFINDER 1750VA	OP	BASS	AL	DV	OB				6	750		1350	1600
17 10	SILVER SHADOW 180SS	OP	BASS	AL	DV	OB				7 3	950		1700	2050
18	18VCC	OP	BASS	AL	DV	OB				6 10	950		1700	2050
1987 BOATS														
16	1644J	OP	FSH	AL	SV	OB				5 8	260		420	505
16	1644JAW	OP	JON	AL	SV	OB				5 8	285		435	525
16	1648	OP	JON	AL	FL	OB				5 7	248		360	440
16	1648D	OP	JON	AL	FL	OB				5 7	248		400	485
16	1652	OP	JON	AL	FL	OB				6 1	274		420	505
16	1652D	OP	JON	AL	FL	OB				6 1	289		440	530
16	BASSFINDER 1644V	OP	BASS	AL	SV	OB				5 8	540		905	1100
16 1	160 BASS	OP	BASS	FBG	DV	OB				6 3			1100	1300
16 1	FIERO 161	OP	RNBT	FBG	DV	OB				6 3			720	865
16 1	VSF-16	OP	BASS	FBG	DV	OB				6 5	800		1300	1600
16 6	171	ST	RNBT	FBG	DV	OB				6 9			1250	1450
16 6	171	ST	RNBT	FBG	DV	IO		120		6 9			2450	2850
16 6	171 CC	OP	CTRCN	FBG	DV	OB				6 9			1250	1450
16 6	171 RD	OP	CTRCN	FBG	DV	OB				6 9			1250	1450
17	1748V	OP	BASS	FBG	DV	OB				5 9	620		1100	1350
17	BASSFINDER 1748VAW	OP	BASS	AL	SV	OB				5 11	640		1100	1350
17 2	V-172SF	OP	FSH	FBG	SV	OB				7	1050		1750	2100
17 2	V-172SF	OP	FSH	FBG	SV	IO		170		7 1	1750		2550	3000
17 2	V172 PRO	OP	BASS	FBG	SV	OB				7			1700	2000
18 8	181	ST	RNBT	FBG	DV	IO		175		7 2	2200		2850	3300
19 1	191	ST	RNBT	FBG	DV	IO		200		7 8	2670		3600	4200
19 1	190 BASS	OP	BASS	FBG	SV	OB				7 9	1120		1900	2300
19 1	190FS	OP	BASS	FBG	SV	OB				7 8	1120		2050	2450
19 1	191	ST	RNBT	FBG	SV	OB				7 9	1565		2600	3000
19 1	191CC	OP	CTRCN	FBG	DV	OB				7 9	1775		2800	3250
19 1	MANTA 2000	ST	RNBT	FBG	DV	IO		260		7 9			3800	4450
19 1	TARGA	ST	RNBT	FBG	DV	IO		200		7 8	2670		2850	3300
1986 BOATS														
16	1644J	OP	FSH	AL	SV	OB				5 8	260		400	485
16	1648	OP	JON	AL	FL	OB				5 7	248		360	440
16	1649	OP	JON	AL	FL	OB				5 7	278		400	490
16	1652	OP	JON	AL	FL	OB				6 1	274		395	480
16	3029	OP	UTL	AL	SV	OB				4 9	194		275	335
16	BASSFINDER 1644V	OP	BASS	AL	SV	OB				5 8	540		880	1050
16 1	160 BASS	OP	BASS	FBG	DV	OB				6 3			1100	1300
16 1	FIERO 161	OP	RNBT	FBG	DV	OB				6 3			700	845
16 1	V-16	OP	BASS	FBG	DV	OB				6 5	740		1200	1400
16 1	VSF-16	OP	BASS	FBG	DV	OB				6 5	800		1300	1550
16 6	171	OP	RNBT	FBG	DV	OB				6 9			1200	1450
16 6	171	OP	RNBT	FBG	DV	IO		120-190		6 9			2300	2750
16 6	171 CC	OP	CTRCN	FBG	DV	OB				6 9			1200	1400
16 6	171 RD	OP	CTRCN	FBG	DV	OB				6 9			1200	1400
16 10	171 XK	OP	CTRCN	FBG	DV	OB				6 9			1200	1400
16	BASSFINDER 1750V	OP	BASS	AL	SV	OB				5 9	680		1150	1350
17	1748V	OP	BASS	FBG	DV	OB				5 9	620		1050	1250
17 2	17SF	OP	FSH	FBG	SV	OB				6 3	890		1450	1750
17 2	MC-FAST 17	OP	FSH	FBG	SV	OB				6 3	870		1450	1700
17 2	PRO V-172	OP	FSH	FBG	SV	OB				7 1	1010		1650	1950
17 2	ROCKET II	OP	RNBT	FBG	DV	OB				7			1500	1500
17 2	ROCKET II	OP	RNBT	FBG	DV	OB				7 1	1010		1650	2000
17 2	V-172	OP	FSH	FBG	SV	OB				7 1	1100		1800	2100
17 2	V-172SF	OP	FSH	FBG	SV	OB				7 1	1050		1700	2050
17 2	V-172SF	OP	FSH	FBG	SV	IO		170-185		7 1	1750		2400	2800
17 2	V172 PRO	OP	BASS	FBG	SV	IO				7 1	1750		1650	1950
18	1852	OP	JON	AL	FL	OB				6 1	313		375	455
18	1860	OP	JON	AL	FL	OB				7 2	413		520	625
19 1	191	OP	RNBT	FBG	DV	IO		170-230		7 9	2670		3350	4050
19 1	191	OP	RNBT	FBG	DV	IO		140-200		7 8			2250	2600
19 1	191 CC	OP	CTRCN	FBG	DV	OB				7 8			2650	3150
19 1	191CC	OP	CTRCN	FBG	DV	OB				7 9	1775		2200	2600
19 1	TARGA	OP	RNBT	FBG	DV	IO		140-230		7 9			2750	3200
19 1	TARGA CUDDY	OP	EXP	FBG	DV	IO		140-260		7 9	2998		3550	4400
20	2060	OP	JON	AL	FL	OB				7 2	428		500	605
1985 BOATS														
16	1644J	OP	FSH	AL	SV	OB				5 8	260		385	465
16	1648	OP	JON	AL	FL	OB				5 7	248		345	420
16	1649	OP	JON	AL	FL	OB				5 7	278		385	470
16	1652	OP	JON	AL	FL	OB				6 1	274		380	460
16	3029	OP	UTL	AL	SV	OB				4 9	194		265	325
16	3530	OP	UTL	AL	SV	OB				6 11	378		550	660
16	BASSFINDER 1644V	OP	BASS	AL	SV	OB				5 8	540		855	1000
16	BASSFINDER 16SV	OP	BASS	AL	FL	OB				5 7	535		850	1000
16 1	MC-FAST V-16	OP	BASS	FBG	DV	OB				6 5	740		1150	1400
16 1	MC-FAST VSF-16	OP	BASS	FBG	DV	OB				6 5	800		1250	1500
16 1	ROCKET ONE	OP	RNBT	FBG	DV	OB				6 5	835		1300	1550
16 7	S-1 CC	OP	FSH	FBG	DV	OB				7	1030		1600	1900
16 7	S-1 XK	OP	FSH	FBG	DV	OB				7	960		1500	1800
16 7	S-1 XK	OP	RNBT	FBG	DV	OB				7	960		1500	1800
16 7	SEA-DRIVE S-1	OP	RNBT	FBG	DV	SE				7	1520		**	**
16 7	SPORTBOAT S1	OP	RNBT	FBG	DV	OB				7	1150		1800	2100
16 10	SPORTBOAT S1	OP	RNBT	FBG	DV	IO		120-185		7	1900		2200	2600
16	BASSFINDER 1750V	OP	BASS	AL	SV	OB				6 3	680		1100	1350
17 2	MC-FAST 17	OP	FSH	FBG	SV	OB				6 3	870		1400	1650
17 2	MC-FAST 17SF	OP	FSH	FBG	SV	OB				6 3	890		1400	1700
17 2	MC-FAST V-172	OP	FSH	FBG	SV	OB				7 1	1100		1700	2050
17 2	MC-FAST V-172SF	OP	FSH	FBG	SV	OB				7 1	1050		1650	1950
17 2	MC-FAST V-172SF	OP	FSH	FBG	SV	IO		170-185		7 1	1750		2300	2700
17 2	PRO V-172	OP	FSH	FBG	SV	OB				7 1	1010		1600	1900
17 2	ROCKET II	OP	RNBT	FBG	SV	OB				7 1	1010		1600	1950
18	1852	OP	JON	AL	FL	OB				6 1	313		365	445
18	1860	OP	JON	AL	FL	OB				7 2	413		510	615
18	3532	OP	UTL	AL	SV	OB				6 11	419		585	705
19 1	191	OP	RNBT	FBG	DV	IO		170-230		7 9	2670		3200	3850
19 1	191	OP	RNBT	FBG	DV					7 9	1565		2450	2800
19 1	191CC	OP	CTRCN	FBG	DV	OB				7 9	1775		2700	3100
19 1	TARGA CUDDY	OP	EXP	FBG	DV	IO		140-260		7 9	2998		3350	4200
20	2060	OP	JON	AL	FL	OB				7 2	428		490	590
1984 BOATS														
16	1642	OP	JON	AL	FL	OB				5 1	263		355	430
16	1643	OP	JON	AL	FL	OB				5 1	279		370	450
16	1644J	OP	FSH	AL	SV	OB				5 8	260		370	450
16	1644V	OP	BASS	AL	SV	OB				5 7	540		825	995
16	1644VSF	OP	BASS	AL	SV	OB				5 7	570		880	1050
16	1648	OP	JON	AL	FL	OB				5 7	248		335	405
16	1649	OP	JON	AL	FL	OB				5 7	278		370	450
16	1652	OP	JON	AL	FL	OB				6 1	274		365	445
16	16SV	OP	BASS	AL	FL	OB				5 7	535		820	985
16	3029	OP	UTL	AL	SV	OB				4 9	194		255	310
16	3525	OP	UTL	AL	SV	OB				5 1	243		315	395
16	3530	OP	FSH	AL	SV	OB				6 11	378		555	670
16 1	MC-FAST V-16	OP	BASS	FBG	FL	OB				6 5	740		1150	1350
16 1	MC-FAST VSF-16	OP	BASS	FBG	FL	OB				6 5	800		1200	1450
16 7	ROCKET ONE	OP	RNBT	FBG	DV	OB				7	835		1300	1500
16 7	S-1 CC	OP	FSH	FBG		OB				7	1030		1300	1850
16 7	S-1 XK	OP	FSH	FBG		OB				7	960		1450	1700
16 7	SPORTBOAT S1	OP	RNBT	FBG	DV	OB				7	1150		1750	2100
16 7	SPORTBOAT S1	OP	RNBT	FBG	SV	IO		120-185		7	1900		2050	2500
16 10	1750V	OP	BASS	AL	SV	OB				6 3	680		1100	1300

LOA FT	LOA IN	NAME AND/ OR MODEL	TOP/ RIG	BOAT TYPE	-HULL- MTL	-HULL- TP	ENGINE TP	ENGINE # HP	ENGINE MFG	BEAM FT	BEAM IN	WGT LBS	DRAFT FT	DRAFT IN	RETAIL LOW	RETAIL HIGH
		1984 BOATS														
17	2	MC-FAST 17SF	OP	FSH	FBG	FL	OB			7	1	890			1350	1650
17	2	MC-FAST V-172	OP	FSH	FBG	FL	OB			7	1	1100			1650	1950
17	2	MC-FAST V-172	OP	FSH	FBG	FL	IO	170	OMC	7	1	1750			2200	2550
17	2	MC-FAST V-172SF	OP	FSH	FBG	FL	IO	165-185		7	1	1750			2200	2600
18		1852	OP	JON	AL	FL	OB			6	1	313			330	405
18		1860	OP	JON	AL	FL	OB			7	2	413			495	595
18		3532	OP	UTL	AL	SV	OB			6	11	419			565	680
20		2060	OP	JON	AL	FL	OB			7	2	428			475	575

....For earlier years, see the BUC Used Boat Price Guide, Volume 3

MONTE FINO CUSTOM YACHTS

FINO YACHTS LTD
FT LAUDERDALE FL 33315-2220

See inside cover to adjust price for area

For more recent years, see the BUC Used Boat Price Guide, Volume 1

LOA FT	LOA IN	NAME AND/ OR MODEL	TOP/ RIG	BOAT TYPE	-HULL- MTL	-HULL- TP	ENGINE TP	ENGINE # HP	ENGINE MFG	BEAM FT	BEAM IN	WGT LBS	DRAFT FT	DRAFT IN	RETAIL LOW	RETAIL HIGH
		1995 BOATS														
51	10	MONTE FINO 52	FB	MY	FBG	DS	IB	T435D	CAT	15	1	44150	4		298500	328000
64	6	MONTE FINO 65	FB	MY	FBG	DS	IB	T600D	MTU	16	9	64960	4	5	488500	536500
67		MONTE FINO 67	FB	MY	FBG	DS	IB	T800D	CAT	18	6	50T	4	9	669500	736000
71	6	MONTE FINO 72	FB	MY	FBG	DS	IB	T800D	CAT	18	6	54T	4	9	875500	962500
77	6	MONTE FINO 78	FB	MY	FBG	DS	IB	T12CD	CAT	18	6	57T	4	9	**	**

MONTEREY BOATS

WILLISTON FL 32696

COAST GUARD MFG ID- RGF See inside cover to adjust price for area
FORMERLY SEABRING MARINE IND

For more recent years, see the BUC Used Boat Price Guide, Volume 1

LOA FT	LOA IN	NAME AND/ OR MODEL	TOP/ RIG	BOAT TYPE	-HULL- MTL	-HULL- TP	ENGINE TP	ENGINE # HP	ENGINE MFG	BEAM FT	BEAM IN	WGT LBS	DRAFT FT	DRAFT IN	RETAIL LOW	RETAIL HIGH
		1996 BOATS														
18	6	MONTURA 186	OP	B/R	FBG	SV	IO	135-180		7	10	2200	3	1	5900	7150
19	6	MONTURA 196	OP	B/R	FBG	SV	IO	135-250		8	2	2700	3	1	7400	8800
20	10	MONTURA 210	OP	B/R	FBG	SV	IO	180-250		8	4	3000	2	6	9300	11400
20	10	MONTURA 210	OP	CUD	FBG	SV	IO	180-250		8	4	3000	2	6	9850	12100
23	2	EXPLORER 230	OP	RNBT	FBG	SV	IO	180-250		8	6	4100	2	9	13000	15600
23	6	MONTURA 236	OP	B/R	FBG	SV	IO	190-300		8	6	3850	3	2	12900	16100
23	6	MONTURA 236	OP	CUD	FBG	SV	IO	190-300		8	6	3950	3	2	14000	17400
24	10	CRUISER 256	OP	CR	FBG	SV	IO	190-300		8	6	4500	2	10	16200	20200
24	10	CRUISER 256	OP	CR	FBG	SV	IO	185D-216D		8	6	4500	2	10	19800	23100
29		CRUISER 276	OP	CR	FBG	SV	IO	300		9	6	6500	3		25600	28800
29		CRUISER 276	OP	CR	FBG	SV	IO	200D-216D		9	6	6500	3		29400	32700
29		CRUISER 276	OP	CR	FBG	SV	IO	T180-T185		9	6	6500	3		26500	29900
31	6	CRUISER 296	OP	CR	FBG	SV	IO	300		10		8000	3	1	33900	37900
31	6	CRUISER 296	OP	CR	FBG	SV	IO	T135-T250		10		8000	3	1	33600	41600
31	6	CRUISER 296	OP	CR	FBG	SV	IO	T200D-T300D		10		8000	3	1	46500	57400
		1995 BOATS														
18	6	MONTURA 186	OP	B/R	FBG	SV	IO	135-180		7	10	2200	3	1	5500	6700
19	6	MONTURA 196	OP	B/R	FBG	SV	IO	135-250		8	2	2700	3	1	6900	8200
20	10	MONTURA 210	OP	B/R	FBG	SV	IO	180-250		8	4	3000	2	6	8550	10700
20	10	MONTURA 210	OP	CUD	FBG	SV	IO	180-250		8	4	3000	2	6	9250	11300
23	2	EXPLORER 230	OP	RNBT	FBG	SV	IO	180-250		8	6	4100	2	9	12100	14600
23	6	MONTURA 236	OP	B/R	FBG	SV	IO	190-300		8	6	3850	3	2	12000	15000
23	6	MONTURA 236	OP	CUD	FBG	SV	IO	190-300		8	6	3950	3	2	13000	16300
24	10	CRUISER 256	OP	CR	FBG	SV	IO	190-300		8	6	4500	2	10	15100	18900
24	10	CRUISER 256	OP	CR	FBG	SV	IO	185D-216D		8	6	4500	2	10	18600	21600
29		CRUISER 276	OP	CR	FBG	SV	IO	300		9	6	6500	3		23900	26800
29		CRUISER 276	OP	CR	FBG	SV	IO	200D-216D		9	6	6500	3		27500	30600
29		CRUISER 276	OP	CR	FBG	SV	IO	T180-T185		9	6	6500	3		24700	27900
31	6	CRUISER 296	OP	CR	FBG	SV	IO	300		10		8000	3	1	31700	35400
31	6	CRUISER 296	OP	CR	FBG	SV	IO	T135-T250		10		8000	3	1	31300	38800
31	6	CRUISER 296	OP	CR	FBG	SV	IO	T200D-T300D		10		8000	3	1	42900	53500
		1994 BOATS														
18	6	BOWRIDER 180	ST	RNBT	FBG	DV	OB			7	2	2000	1	8	2750	3200
18	6	BOWRIDER 180	ST	RNBT	FBG	DV	IO	115-185		7	2	2000	1	8	4800	5900
19	2	BOWRIDER 190	ST	RNBT	FBG	DV	OB			8		2200	1	8	2950	3450
19	2	BOWRIDER 190	ST	RNBT	FBG	DV	IO	110-215		8		2200	1	8	5600	6900
19	2	CUDDY 192	ST	CUD	FBG	DV	IO	110-215		8		2400	1	8	6000	7450
20	6	BOWRIDER 206	ST	RNBT	FBG	DV	IO	180-240		8		2650	1	10	7300	9000
20	6	BOWRIDER 206	ST	RNBT	FBG	DV	IO	250-255		8		2650	1	10	7650	9250
20	6	CUDDY 206	ST	CUD	FBG	DV	IO	180-240		8		2850	1	9	7950	9750
20	6	CUDDY 206	ST	CUD	FBG	DV	IO	250-255		8		2850	1	9	8300	10000
22	8	BOWRIDER 225	ST	RNBT	FBG	DV	IO	180-255		8	6	3650	1	9	10200	12400
22	8	BOWRIDER 225	ST	RNBT	FBG	DV	IO	300		8	6	3650	1	9	11100	13100
22	8	CUDDY 225	ST	CUD	FBG	DV	IO	180-255		8	6	3750	1	9	11000	13400
22	8	CUDDY 225	ST	CUD	FBG	DV	IO	300		8	6	3750	1	9	12000	14200
23	2	EXPLORER 230	OP	RNBT	FBG		IO	180-255		8	6	4100	1	5	11300	13600
24	10	CRUISER 246	ST	CUD	FBG	DV	IO	180-255		8	6	4500	1	6	13800	16700
24	10	CRUISER 246	ST	CUD	FBG	DV	IO	300		8	6	4500	1	6	15100	17600
26	10	CRUISER 265	ST	SPTCR	FBG	DV	IO	225-300		9	6	6500	1	8	20400	24000
26	10	CRUISER 265	ST	SPTCR	FBG	DV	IO	T180-T185		9	6	6500	1	8	22100	25000
31	6	CRUISER 286	ST	SPTCR	FBG	DV	IO	225-300		10		8000	1	9	31900	36900
31	6	CRUISER 286	ST	SPTCR	FBG	DV	IO	T180-T225		10		8000	1	9	34100	39400
		1993 BOATS														
18		BOWRIDER 180	ST	RNBT	FBG		OB			7		2000			2650	3100
18		BOWRIDER 180	ST	RNBT	FBG		IO	115-120		7		2000			4300	5250
18	11	BOWRIDER 190	ST	RNBT	FBG		OB			7	10	2200			2850	3300
18	11	BOWRIDER 190	ST	RNBT	FBG		IO	115-205		7	10	2200			5100	6250
19	2	CUDDY 192	ST	CUD	FBG		IO	115-205		8		2400			5600	6900
20	6	BOWRIDER 206	ST	RNBT	FBG		IO	155-230		8		2500			6600	8150
		IO 240 MRCR 6850 7900, IO 240 YAMA 6850 7900, IO 275 VLVO													7550	8650
20	6	CUDDY 206	ST	CUD	FBG		IO	155-240		8		2650			7100	8750
20	6	CUDDY 206	ST	CUD	FBG		IO	275-300		8		2650			8100	9800
22	8	BOWRIDER 225	ST	RNBT	FBG		IO	155-275		8	6	3750			9650	12000
22	8	BOWRIDER 225	ST	RNBT	FBG		IO	300		8	6	3750			10500	12500
22	8	BOWRIDER 225	ST	RNBT	FBG		IO	330	VLVO	8	6	3750			11700	13300
22	8	CUDDY 225	ST	CUD	FBG		IO	155-300		8	6	3750			10200	12800
22	8	CUDDY 225	ST	CUD	FBG		IO	330	VLVO	8	6	3750			12400	14100
24	10	CRUISER 246	ST	CUD	FBG		IO	155-240		8	6	4500			12700	15300
24	10	CRUISER 246	ST	CUD	FBG		IO	275-330		8	6	4500			14000	17300
27	4	CRUISER 250	ST	SPTCR	FBG		IO	240-330		9		5250			17200	21400
27	4	CRUISER 250	ST	SPTCR	FBG		IO	T120-T175		9		5250			18400	21500
28	8	CRUISER 270	ST	CBNCR	FBG		IO	300-330		9	6	6500			28900	32600
28	8	CRUISER 270	ST	CBNCR	FBG		IO	T135-T300		9	6	6500			28800	33400
31	6	CRUISER 286	ST	SPTCR	FBG		IO	300-330		10	2				31100	35100
31	6	CRUISER 286	ST	SPTCR	FBG		IO	T155-T229		10	2				31200	37100
31	6	CRUISER 286	ST	SPTCR	FBG		IO	T300	YAMA	10	2				35200	39100
		1992 BOATS														
18		BOWRIDER 179	ST	RNBT	FBG		OB			7		2000			2500	2900
18		BOWRIDER 179	ST	RNBT	FBG		IO	115-140		7		2000			4000	4900
18	11	BOWRIDER 189	ST	RNBT	FBG		IO	115-175		7	10	2200			4750	5750
18	11	LTD 189	ST	RNBT	FBG		IO	115-120		7	10	2200			4750	5700
18	11	OUTBOARD 189	ST	RNBT	FBG		OB			7	10				2500	2950
19	2	CUDDY 192	ST	CUD	FBG		IO	115-205		8		2400			5250	6450
20	6	BOWRIDER 206	ST	RNBT	FBG		IO	155-240		8		2500			6150	7650
20	6	BOWRIDER 206	ST	RNBT	FBG		IO	275	VLVO	8		2500			7050	8100
20	6	CUDDY 206	ST	CUD	FBG		IO	155-240		8		2650			6650	8200
20	6	CUDDY 206	ST	CUD	FBG		IO	275-300		8		2650			7600	9200
22	8	BOWRIDER 225	ST	RNBT	FBG		IO		MRCR	8	6	3750			**	**
		IO 155-275 9050 11300, IO 300 9900 11700, IO 330 VLVO													10900	12400
22	8	CUDDY 225	ST	CUD	FBG		IO	155-300		8	6	3750			9550	12000
22	8	CUDDY 225	ST	CUD	FBG		IO	330	VLVO	8	6	3750			11600	13200
24	10	CRUISER 236	ST	CUD	FBG		IO	155-240		8	6	4500			11900	14300
24	10	CRUISER 236	ST	CUD	FBG		IO	275-330		8	6	4500			13200	16200
27	4	CRUISER 250	ST	SPTCR	FBG		IO	240-300		9		5250			16100	19600
27	4	CRUISER 250	ST	SPTCR	FBG		IO	330	VLVO	9		5250			18200	20300
27	4	CRUISER 250	ST	SPTCR	FBG		IO	T120-T175		9		5250			16800	20300
28	8	CRUISER 270	ST	SPTCR	FBG		IO	300-330		9	6	6500			22000	24400
28	8	CRUISER 270	ST	SPTCR	FBG		IO	T135-T205		9	6	6500			21700	26100
28	8	CRUISER 270	ST	SPTCR	FBG		IO	T300	YAMA	9	6	6500			25700	28600
		1991 BOATS														
18	11	BOWRIDER 189	ST	RNBT	FBG		IO	130-250		9	4	2200			5100	5850
18	11	CUDDY 190	ST	CUD	FBG		IO	130-205		7	10	2650			5050	6100
18	11	CUDDY 190	ST	CUD	FBG		IO	230-250		7	10	2650			5500	6500
20	1	SPORT 2000	ST	RNBT	FBG		IO	200-260		8		2600			5850	7100
20	1	SPORT 2000	ST	RNBT	FBG		IO	350	MRCR	8		2600			7500	8600
20	1	SS 2000	ST	RNBT	FBG		IO	210-265		8		2600			6150	7500
20	6	BOWRIDER 206	ST	RNBT	FBG		IO	175-260		8		2500			5800	7150
20	6	CUDDY 206	ST	CUD	FBG		IO	175-260		8		2650			6250	7700
22	8	BOWRIDER 220	ST	RNBT	FBG		IO	200-260		8	6	3750			8500	10100
22	8	BOWRIDER 220	ST	RNBT	FBG		IO	275-350		8	6	3750			9350	11600
22	8	CUDDY 220	ST	CUD	FBG		IO	200-300		8	6	3750			9100	11200
22	8	CUDDY 220	ST	CUD	FBG		IO	330-350		8	6	3750			10900	12400

 CONTINUED ON NEXT PAGE

MONTEREY BOATS — CONTINUED

LOA FT IN	NAME AND/ OR MODEL	TOP/ RIG	BOAT TYPE	-HULL- MTL TP	----ENGINE--- TP # HP MFG	BEAM FT IN	WGT LBS	DRAFT FT IN	RETAIL LOW	RETAIL HIGH
1991 BOATS										
23	BOWRIDER 230	ST	RNBT	FBG	IO 200-265	8	3250		7650	9550
23	BOWRIDER 230	ST	RNBT	FBG	IO 300 MRCR	8	3250		8400	9650
23	BOWRIDER 230	ST	RNBT	FBG	IO 330-350	8	3250		9400	10700
23	CUDDY 230	ST	CUD	FBG	IO 200-300	8	3950		9400	11500
23	CUDDY 230	ST	CUD	FBG	IO 330-350	8	3950		11200	12700
27 4	CRUISER 250	ST	SPTCR	FBG	IO 260 MRCR	9	5250		**	**
					IO 260 MRCR 15400 17500, IO 740 VLVO 25700 28600, IO T130-T205 15700 19400					
					IO T430 VLVO 24400 27200					
****										
27 4	CRUISER 250C	ST	SPTCR	FBG	IO 570 VLVO	9	5250		23400	26000
28 8	CRUISER 270	ST	SPTCR	FBG	IO VLVO	9 6	6500		**	**
					IO 300 MRCR 20600 22900, IO 740 VLVO 28800 32000, IO T130-T200 20200 24200					
					IO T430-T431 29200 32400, IO T254D MRCR 30000 33300					
28 8	SPTISER 270	ST	CR	FBG	IO T205 MRCR	9 6	6500		21800	24300
1990 BOATS										
18 11	BOWRIDER 1800	ST	RNBT	FBG	IO 125 MRCR	9 4	2200		4800	5500
18 11	BOWRIDER 1800	ST	RNBT	FBG	IO 145-175	9 4	2200		4800	5550
18 11	BOWRIDER 1900	ST	RNBT	FBG	IO 125-260	7 10	2450		4450	5450
18 11	CUDDY 1900	ST	CUD	FBG	IO 125-260	7 10	2550		4700	5750
18 11	OUTBOARD 1900	ST	RNBT	FBG	OB	7 10	1640		2100	2500
20 1	SPORT 2000	ST	RNBT	FBG	IO 200-260	8	2600		5500	6650
20 1	SPORT 2000	ST	RNBT	FBG	IO 350 MRCR	8	2600		5800	8100
20 6	BOWRIDER 2000	ST	RNBT	FBG	IO 175-260	9 6	2500		6150	7400
21	CUDDY 2100	ST	CUD	FBG	IO 175-260	8 2	3900		7800	9400
21	CUDDY 2100	ST	CUD	FBG	IO 350 MRCR	8 2	3900		9550	10900
23	BOWRIDER 2300	ST	RNBT	FBG	IO MRCR	8	3250		**	**
23	BOWRIDER 2300	ST	RNBT	FBG	IO 200-260	8	3250		7200	8600
23	BOWRIDER 2300	ST	RNBT	FBG	IO 350 MRCR	8	3250		8850	10000
23	CUDDY 2300	ST	CUD	FBG	IO MRCR	8 2	3950		**	**
23	CUDDY 2300	ST	CUD	FBG	IO 200-260	8 2	3950		8900	10500
23	CUDDY 2300	ST	CUD	FBG	IO 350 MRCR	8 2	3950		10500	11900
28 8	CRUISER 2700	ST	SPTCR	FBG	IO MRCR	9 6	6500		**	**
					IO 350 MRCR 20200 22400, IO T175-T260 20000 24100, IOT183D-T219D 25100 29600					
1989 BOATS										
18 11	BOWRIDER 1900	ST	RNBT	FBG	OB	7 10	1640		2000	2400
18 11	BOWRIDER 1900	ST	RNBT	FBG	IO 165-200	7 10	2450		4150	5150
18 11	BOWRIDER 1900	ST	RNBT	FBG	IO 230	7 10	2680		4550	5250
18 11	CUDDY 1900	ST	CUD	FBG	IO 165-230	7 10	2550		4450	5500
20 1	SPORT 2000	ST	RNBT	FBG	IO 200-260	8	2600		5200	6300
20 1	SPORT 2000	ST	RNBT	FBG	IO 350 MRCR	8	2600		6650	7650
23	BOWRIDER 2300	ST	RNBT	FBG	IO 230-260	8	3160		6750	8100
23	BOWRIDER 2300	ST	RNBT	FBG	IO 350	8	3250		8250	9450
23	CUDDY 2300	ST	CUD	FBG	IO 200-260	8 2	3950		8300	9900
23	CUDDY 2300	ST	CUD	FBG	IO 350	8 2	3950		9900	11300
27	CRUISER 2700	ST	CR	FBG	IO 260-350	8	6500		14600	18000
27	CRUISER 2700	ST	CR	FBG	IO 454	8	6500		18400	20400
27	CRUISER 2700	ST	CR	FBG	IO T165-T260	8	6500		15400	19100
1988 BOATS										
18 11	BOWRIDER 1900	ST	RNBT	FBG	OB	7 10	1640		1950	2300
18 11	BOWRIDER 1900	ST	RNBT	FBG	IO 165-200	7 10	2450		3950	4850
18 11	BOWRIDER 1900	ST	RNBT	FBG	IO 230	7 10	2680		4250	4950
18 11	CUDDY 19	ST	CUD	FBG	IO 165-200	7 10	2550		4150	5150
18 11	CUDDY 19	ST	CUD	FBG	IO 230	7 10	2780		4550	5250
23	BOWRIDER 2300	ST	RNBT	FBG	IO 230-260	8	3160		6400	7700
23	BOWRIDER 2300	ST	RNBT	FBG	IO 350	8	3250		7800	8950
1987 BOATS										
18 11	CUDDY 19	ST	CUD	FBG	IO 260	7 10	2800		4500	5200
18 11	SPORTABOUT 19	OP	RNBT		OB	7 10	1750		1950	2350
18 11	SPORTABOUT 19	OP	RNBT		IO 260	7 10	2600		4150	4800

MONTGOMERY MARINE PROD

COSTA MESA CA 92627   COAST GUARD MFG ID- MMP See inside cover to adjust price for area

LOA FT IN	NAME AND/ OR MODEL	TOP/ RIG	BOAT TYPE	-HULL- MTL TP	----ENGINE--- TP # HP MFG	BEAM FT IN	WGT LBS	DRAFT FT IN	RETAIL LOW	RETAIL HIGH
1986 BOATS										
17 2	MONTGOMERY 17	SLP	SAIL	FBG KC		7 4	1550	1 9	7450	8600
23	MONTGOMERY 23	SLP	SAIL	FBG KC		8	3600	2 5	16100	18300
1985 BOATS										
17 2	MONTGOMERY 17	SLP	SAIL	FBG KC		7 4	1550	1 9	7000	8050
23	MONTGOMERY 23	SLP	SAIL	FBG KC		8	3600	2 5	15100	17100

....For earlier years, see the BUC Used Boat Price Guide, Volume 3

MONZA MARINE INC

MIAMI FL 33142   COAST GUARD MFG ID- MXU See inside cover to adjust price for area
FORMERLY MONZA MARINE CORP

For more recent years, see the BUC Used Boat Price Guide, Volume 1

LOA FT IN	NAME AND/ OR MODEL	TOP/ RIG	BOAT TYPE	-HULL- MTL TP	----ENGINE--- TP # HP MFG	BEAM FT IN	WGT LBS	DRAFT FT IN	RETAIL LOW	RETAIL HIGH
1992 BOATS										
22 6	FISHMASTER 2300	OP	CTRCN	FBG DV	OB	8	2100	1 3	7850	9000
26 4	BOW RUNNER 2700	OP	OPFSH	FBG DV	OB	8	3200	1 6	15300	17400
26 4	COMBI 2700	ST	CTRCN	FBG DV	OB	8	3400	1 6	15600	17800
26 4	FISHMASTER 2700	OP	CTRCN	FBG DV	OB	8	3100	1 6	15400	17500
26 4	SPORT FAMILY 2700	OP	CUD	FBG DV	OB	8	3600	1 6	15800	18000
26 4	SPORT FAMILY 2700	OP	CUD	FBG DV	IO 230-300	8	3600	1 6	19300	22800
26 4	SPORT FAMILY 2700	OP	CUD	FBG DV	IO 254D MRCR	8	3600	1 6	23400	26000
30 6	FISHMASTER 3000	ST	CTRCN	FBG DV	OB	8	4100	1 8	24300	27000
39 6	SUPER SPORT 40	OP	OFF	FBG DV		8 6			**	**
39 6	SUPER SPORT 40	OP	OFF	FBG DV	IO T350 MRCR	8 6			87600	96200
					IO T390 MRCR 92900 102000, IO T425 MRCR 99600 109500, IO T465 MRCR 106500 117000					
1991 BOATS										
22 6	FISHMASTER 2300	OP	CTRCN	FBG DV	OB	8	2100	1 3	7500	8600
26 4	COMBI	ST	CTRCN	FBG DV	OB	8			15000	17000
26 4	FISHMASTER 2700	OP	CTRCN	FBG DV	OB	8	3100	1 6	14700	16700
26 4	SPORT FAMILY		CBNCR	FBG DV	IO 300	8			23900	26500
26 4	SUPER SPORT 2700	OP	CTRCN	FBG DV	OB	8			15000	17000
26 4	SUPER SPORT 2700	OP	CTRCN	FBG DV	IO 300-390	8			25400	28300
26 4	SUPER SPORT 2700	OP	CTRCN	FBG DV	IO T240-T300	8			25400	30300
30	FISHMASTER 3000	ST	CTRCN	FBG DV	OB	8	4100	1 8	23400	25900
39 6	SUPER SPORT 40	OP	OFF	FBG DV		8 6			**	**
39 6	SUPER SPORT 40	OP	OFF	FBG DV	IO T350 MRCR	8 6			82200	90300
					IO T390 MRCR 87100 95700, IO T425 MRCR 93600 103000, IO T465 MRCR 100500 110500					
1990 BOATS										
22 6	FISHMASTER 2300	OP	CTRCN	FBG DV	OB	8	2100	1 3	7200	8250
26 4	FISHMASTER 2700	OP	CTRCN	FBG DV	OB	8	3100	1 6	14100	16000
26 4	SPORT CRUISER 2700	OP	CBNCR	FBG DV	SE T300 OMC	8			15000	17000
26 4	SUPER SPORT 2700	OP	CTRCN	FBG DV	OB	8			14300	16300
26 4	SUPER SPORT 2700	OP	CTRCN	FBG DV	IO 300-410	8			22000	27400
26 4	SUPER SPORT 2700	OP	CTRCN	FBG DV	IO T240-T300	8			24300	28700
30	FISHMASTER 3000	ST	CTRCN	FBG DV	OB	8		1 8	22500	25000
39 6	SUPER SPORT 40	OP	OFF	FBG DV		8 6			**	**
39 6	SUPER SPORT 40	OP	OFF	FBG DV	IO T360 MRCR	8 6			78400	86200
					IO T410 MRCR 85600 94100, IO T425 MRCR 88400 97100, IO T465 MRCR 94900 104500					
					IO T500 MRCR 99600 109500, IO T575 MRCR 108000 118500					
1989 BOATS										
22 6	STEP BOTTOM 2240OF	OP	OPFSH	FBG DV	OB	8			9100	10300
26 4	MONZA 2600SS	OP	OPFSH	FBG DV	OB	8			12900	14700
26 4	MONZA 2640CC	OP	OPFSH	FBG DV	OB	8			13600	15500
26 4	MONZA 2640CC	OP	OPFSH	FBG DV	IO MRCR	8			**	**
26 4	MONZA 2640CC	OP	OPFSH	FBG DV	IO 260-311	8			20000	23500
26 4	MONZA 2700SS	OP	OFF	FBG DV	IO	8	2600		13200	15000
26 4	MONZA 2700SS	OP	OFF	FBG DV	IO 365-420	8			19800	23700
26 4	MONZA 2700SS	OP	OFF	FBG DV	IO T260-T270	8			20500	23900
26 4	MONZA 2700SS	OP	OFF	FBG DV	IO T365 MRCR	8			24600	27300
26 4	SPORT CRUISER 2700	OP	CBNCR	FBG DV	IO	8	4200		14300	16200
26 4	SPORT CRUISER 2700	OP	CBNCR	FBG DV	IO 260-330	8	3700		19500	22400
26 4	SPORT CRUISER 2700	OP	CBNCR	FBG DV	SE T300 OMC	8	3700		15400	15900
26 4	SPORT FISH 2700	OP	CTRCN	FBG DV	IO 260-330	8			20200	23800
26 4	SPORT FISH 2700	OP	SF	FBG DV	IO	8			13800	15600
26 4	SPORT FISH 2700	OP	SF	FBG DV	SE	8			**	**
26 4	SPORT FISH 2700	OP	SF	FBG DV	SE 270 OMC MRCR	8			22200	24700
29 10	FISH 3140CCO	OP	OPFSH	FBG DV	OB	8			21200	23500
31	SUPER SPORT 3100	OP	OFF	FBG DV	IO	8			24100	26900
31	SUPER SPORT 3100	OP	OFF	FBG DV	IO T270-T365	8			33300	40300
39 6	SUPER SPORT 40	OP	OFF	FBG DV	IO	8 6	9500		**	**
39 6	SUPER SPORT 40	OP	OFF	FBG DV	SE T OMC	8 6	9500		**	**
39 6	SUPER SPORT 40	OP	OFF	FBG DV	IO T420 MRCR	8 6	9500		82900	91000
39 6	SUPER SPORT 40	OP	OFF	FBG DV	IO T575 MRCR	8 6	9500		96500	106000
1988 BOATS										
22 6	OPEN FISH 3200CC	OP	OPFSH	FBG DV	OB	8			8650	9950
22 6	STEP BOTTOM 2240OF	OP	OPFSH	FBG DV	OB	8			8650	9950
26 4	MONZA 2600 OF	OP	OPFSH	FBG DV	OB	8			12400	14100
26 4	MONZA 2640CC	OP	RACE	FBG DV	OB	8			13300	15100
26 4	MONZA 2640CC	OP	RACE	FBG DV	IO 260-330	8			17200	21100
26 4	MONZA 2700SS	OP	RACE	FBG DV	IO	8	2600		12700	14400
26 4	MONZA 2700SS	OP	RACE	FBG DV	IO 365-420	8			19900	23600

LOA FT	IN	NAME AND/ OR MODEL	TOP/ RIG	BOAT TYPE	-HULL- MTL	TP	----ENGINE--- TP	# HP	MFG	BEAM FT	IN	WGT LBS	DRAFT FT	IN	RETAIL LOW	RETAIL HIGH
		1988 BOATS														
26	4	MONZA 2700SS	OP	RACE	FBG	DV	IO	T260-T270		8					20400	23700
26	4	MONZA 2700SS	OP	RACE	FBG	DV	IO	T365	MRCR	8					24200	26900
26	4	SPORT CRUISER 2700	OP	CBNCR	FBG	DV	OB			8		4200			13700	15600
26	4	SPORT CRUISER 2700	OP	CBNCR	FBG	DV	IO	260-330		8		3700			18400	21500
26	4	SPORT CRUISER 2700	OP	CBNCR	FBG	DV	SE	T300	OMC	8		3700			13400	15300
26	4	SPORT FISH 2700	OP	CTRCN	FBG	DV	IO	260-330		8					19000	22400
26	4	SPORT FISH 2700	OP	SF	FBG	DV	OB			8					13200	15000
26	4	SPORT FISH 2700	OP	SF	FBG	DV	SE		OMC	8					**	**
26	4	SPORT FISH 2700	OP	SF	FBG	DV	IO	270	MRCR	8					21400	23700
31		SUPER SPORT 3100		RNBT	FBG	DV	OB			8					23000	25600
31		SUPER SPORT 3100		RNBT	FBG	DV	IO	T270-T365		8					27300	34100
39	6	SUPER SPORT 40	OP	RNBT	FBG	DV	OB			8	6				**	**
39	6	SUPER SPORT 40	OP	RNBT	FBG	DV	SE	T	OMC	8	6				**	**
39	6	SUPER SPORT 40	OP	RNBT	FBG	DV	IO	T420	MRCR	8	6				58500	64300
39	6	SUPER SPORT 40	OP	RNBT	FBG	DV	IO	T575	MRCR	8	6				72700	79900
		1987 BOATS														
22	6	STEPBOTOM 2240	OP	FSH	FBG	DV	OB			8					8200	9450
26		MONZA 2600 OF	OP	OPFSH	FBG	DV	OB			8					12000	13600
26	4	MONZA 2640CC	OP	CTRCN	FBG	DV	OB			8					12200	13800
26	4	MONZA 2640CC	OP	CTRCN	FBG	DV	IO		MRCR	8					**	**
26	4	MONZA 2640CC	OP	CTRCN	FBG	DV	IO	260-320		8					17400	21200
26	4	MONZA 2700SS	OP	RACE	FBG	DV	OB			8		2600			12200	13900
26	4	MONZA 2700SS	OP	RACE	FBG	DV	IO		MRCR	8		4800			**	**
26	4	MONZA 2700SS	OP	RACE	FBG	DV	IO	260-320		8		4800			15800	19100
26	4	MONZA 2700SS	OP	RACE	FBG	DV	IO	370	MRCR	8		4800			18400	20500
26	4	SPORT CRUISER 2700	OP	CBNCR	FBG	DV	OB			8		4200			13200	15000
26	4	SPORT CRUISER 2700	OP	CBNCR	FBG	DV	IO		MRCR	8		3700			**	**
26	4	SPORT CRUISER 2700	OP	CBNCR	FBG	DV	IO	260-370		8		3700			17000	21200
26	4	SPORT FISH 2700	OP	CTRCN	FBG	DV	OB			8					13400	15200
26	4	SPORT FISH 2700	OP	CTRCN	FBG	DV	IO		MRCR	8					**	**
26	4	SPORT FISH 2700	OP	CTRCN	FBG	DV	IO	260-320		8					18200	21500
39	6	FINO 39.5	OP	RNBT	FBG	DV	OB			8	6	9500			**	**
39	6	FINO 39.5	OP	RNBT	FBG	DV	IO	T420	MRCR	8	6	9500			62400	68600
39	6	FINO 39.5	OP	RNBT	FBG	DV	IO	T575	MRCR	8	6	9500			76000	83500
		1986 BOATS														
23	8	MONZA 24SS		RNBT	FBG	DV	IB	260		7					13900	15800
26	4	ASTRO 26CC	OP	CTRCN	FBG	DV	IO	225-260		8					16300	19000
26	4	ASTRO 26CC	OP	CTRCN	FBG	DV	IO	165D	VLVO	8					24700	27500
26	4	ASTRO 26CC	OP	CTRCN	FBG	DV	IO	T125	VLVO	8					18000	20100
26	4	ASTRO CUDDY CABIN	OP	CTRCN	FBG	DV	IO	225-260		8					16700	19500
26	4	ASTRO CUDDY CABIN	OP	CTRCN	FBG	DV	IO	165D	VLVO	8					24700	27500
26	4	ASTRO CUDDY CABIN	OP	CTRCN	FBG	DV	IO	T125	VLVO	8					18400	20500
26	4	MONZA 27SS	OP	RACE	FBG	DV	OB			8		2600			11800	13400
26	4	MONZA 27SS	OP	RACE	FBG	DV	IO	330-370		8		4800			16200	19400
		IO 400 MRCR 18300 20400, IO T260-T330 18300 22300, IO T370-T400													22000	25700
26	4	SPORT CRUISER 2700	OP	CBNCR	FBG	DV	OB			8		4200			12800	14500
26	4	SPORT CRUISER 2700	OP	CBNCR	FBG	DV	IO	290-330		8		3700			16700	19200
26	4	SPORT CRUISER 2700	OP	CBNCR	FBG	DV	IO	T170-T260		8		3700			17000	20700
26	4	SPORT CRUISER 2700	OP	CBNCR	FBG	DV	IO	T290-T330		8		3700			19300	22000
26	4	SPORT FISHERMAN 2640	OP	CTRCN	FBG	DV	OB			8		3900			12600	14300
39	6	FINO 39.5	OP	OFF	FBG	DV	IO	T370	MRCR	8	6	9500			62600	68800
		IO T400 MRCR 65700 72200, IO T440 MRCR 70100 77000, IO T480													74300	81600
		IB T300D CAT 92400 101500														
		1985 BOATS														
23	8	MONZA 24SS		RNBT	FBG	DV	IB	260		7					13300	15100
23	8	MONZA MX24		SPTCR	FBG	DV	IB	330		7					14200	16100
23	8	SPORT 24S	OP	RACE	FBG	DV	IO	260-300		7					10100	12400
23	8	SPORT 24S	OP	RACE	FBG	DV	IO	330-370		7					11200	13900
26	4	MONZA 27SS	OP	RACE	FBG	DV	OB			8		2600			11400	13000
26	4	MONZA 27SS	OP	RACE	FBG	DV	IO	330-370		8		4800			15400	18500
		IO 400 MRCR 17100 19400, IO T260-T290 17100 20800, IO T330-T370													19500	23200
		IO T400 MRCR 22100 24500														
26	4	SPORT CRUISER 2700	OP	CBNCR	FBG	DV	OB			8					12000	13600
26	4	SPORT CRUISER 2700	OP	CBNCR	FBG	DV	IO	290-330		8		3700			15900	18300
26	4	SPORT CRUISER 2700	OP	CBNCR	FBG	DV	IO	T170-T260		8		3700			16200	19700
26	4	SPORT CRUISER 2700	OP	CBNCR	FBG	DV	IO	T290	VLVO	8		3700			18400	20400
26	4	SPORT FISHERMAN 2640	OP	CTRCN	FBG	DV	OB			8		2600			11400	12900
39	6	FINO 39.5		OFF	FBG	DV	OB			8	6				**	**
39	6	FINO 39.5	OP	OFF	FBG	DV	IO	T370	MRCR	8	8	8700			57700	63400
		IO T400 MRCR 60500 66500, IO T440 MRCR 64600 70900, IO T480													68600	75300
		IB T300D CAT 84400 92700														
		1984 BOATS														
26	4	CONCORD 2700	OP	RACE	FBG	DV	OB			8					11600	13200
26	4	CONCORD 2700	OP	RACE	FBG	DV	IO	T330-T370		8		5100			19200	22700
26	4	CONCORD 2700	OP	RACE	FBG	DV	IO	T400	MRCR	8		5100			22000	24500
26	4	CONCORD 2700	OP	RACE	FBG	DV	IO	T475	MRCR	8		5100			25400	28200
26	4	FAMILY CRUISER 2700	OP	CBNCR	FBG	DV	OB			8					11600	13200
26	4	FAMILY CRUISER 2700	OP	CBNCR	FBG	DV	IO	290-330		8		3700			15300	17600
26	4	FAMILY CRUISER 2700	OP	CBNCR	FBG	DV	IO	T170-T260		8		3700			15500	18900
26	4	FAMILY CRUISER 2700	OP	CBNCR	FBG	DV	IO	T290	VLVO	8		3700			17200	19600
26	4	MONZA 27SS	OP	RACE	FBG	DV	OB			8		2600			11100	12600
26	4	MONZA 27SS	OP	RACE	FBG	DV	IO	330-370		8		4800			14800	17700
		IO 400 MRCR 16400 18600, IO T260-T290 16300 20000, IO T330-T370													18700	22200
		IO T400 MRCR 21500 23900														
26	4	SPORT FISHERMAN 2640	OP	SF	FBG	DV	OB			8		2600			11000	12500
39	6	FINO 39	OP	OFF	FBG	DV	IO	T370	MRCR	8	8				59400	65300
39	6	FINO 39	OP	OFF	FBG	DV	IO	T400	MRCR	8	8				62900	69100
39	6	FINO 39	OP	OFF	FBG	DV	IO	T440	MRCR	8	8				68000	74700

....For earlier years, see the BUC Used Boat Price Guide, Volume 3

A H MOODY & SON LTD

S HAMPTON HANTS ENGLAND

See inside cover to adjust price for area

IMPEX ENTERPRISES LTD
READING PA 19603

LOA FT	IN	NAME AND/ OR MODEL	TOP/ RIG	BOAT TYPE	-HULL- MTL	TP	----ENGINE--- TP	# HP	MFG	BEAM FT	IN	WGT LBS	DRAFT FT	IN	RETAIL LOW	RETAIL HIGH
		1987 BOATS														
46	5	MOODY 47	SLP	SA/CR	FBG	KL	IB	60D		14	8	27500	6	9	141500	155500
57	6	MOODY 58	CUT	SA/CR	FBG	KL	IB	725D	PERK	16	3	50000	7	1	449500	494000
		1985 BOATS														
27	8	MOODY 27	SLP	SA/CR	FBG	KL	IB	D		9	8	5750	4	8	21200	23500
30	8	MOODY 31	SLP	SA/CR	FBG	KL	IB	D		10	5	8750	5		34200	38000
33	6	MOODY 34	SLP	SA/CR	FBG	KL	IB	D		11	6	11200	5		43500	48400
41		MOODY 41	SLP	SA/CR	FBG	KL	IB	D		13	2	20600	6		85900	94400
46	5	MOODY 47	SLP	SA/CR	FBG	KL	IB	D		14	6	28500	6	7	127500	140000
60		MOODY 60	KTH	SA/CR	FBG	KL	IB	D		16	3	70100	8		496500	545500

....For earlier years, see the BUC Used Boat Price Guide, Volume 3

MOONEY MARINE INC

DELTAVILLE VA 23043

COAST GUARD MFG ID- MYH See inside cover to adjust price for area
FORMERLY MOONEY BROS BOATBUILDING

LOA FT	IN	NAME AND/ OR MODEL	TOP/ RIG	BOAT TYPE	-HULL- MTL	TP	----ENGINE--- TP	# HP	MFG	BEAM FT	IN	WGT LBS	DRAFT FT	IN	RETAIL LOW	RETAIL HIGH
		1985 BOATS														
35		DEPARTURE 35	CUT	SA/CR	STL	KL	IB	D		11		16480	5		35800	39800
40		DEPARTURE 40	CUT	SA/CR	STL	KL	IB	D		13		20400	6	7	44700	49700
42		DEPARTURE 42	CUT	SA/CR	STL	KL	IB	D		12	5	24800	5	9	54300	59700
42		DEPARTURE 42	KTH	SA/CR	STL	KL	IB	D		12	5	24800	5	9	54700	60100
		1984 BOATS														
30		DEPARTURE 30	SLP	SA/CR	STL	KL	IB	D		10		11640	4	6	25300	28100
35		DEPARTURE 35	CUT	SA/CR	STL	KL	IB	18D	SAAB	11		16480	5		33600	37300
35		DEPARTURE 35	CUT	SA/CR	STL	KL	SD	23D	VLVO	11		16480	5		33600	37300
35		DEPARTURE 35	KTH	SA/CR	STL	KL	IB	18D	SAAB	11		16480	5		33600	37300
35		DEPARTURE 35	KTH	SA/CR	STL	KL	SD	23D	VLVO	11		16480	5		33600	37300
40	4	DEPARTURE 40	CUT	SA/CR	STL	KL	IB	D		13		20384	6	7	42400	47100
42		WITTHOLZ 42	CUT	SA/CR	STL	KL	SD	35D	VLVO	12	5	24800	5	9	50900	55900

....For earlier years, see the BUC Used Boat Price Guide, Volume 3

MOORE SAILBOATS

WATSONVILLE CA 95076

COAST GUARD MFG ID- MSS See inside cover to adjust price for area

For more recent years, see the BUC Used Boat Price Guide, Volume 1

LOA FT	IN	NAME AND/ OR MODEL	TOP/ RIG	BOAT TYPE	-HULL- MTL	TP	----ENGINE--- TP	# HP	MFG	BEAM FT	IN	WGT LBS	DRAFT FT	IN	RETAIL LOW	RETAIL HIGH
		1996 BOATS														
17	6	WYLIE CAT 17	CAT	SAROD	F/S	KL				6	1	390	4	2	5400	6200
18		MERCURY	SLP	SAROD	F/S	KL				5	4	1100	3	1	8850	10100
24		MOORE 24	SLP	SAROD	F/S	KL				7	2	2050	4	1	17600	20000
30	5	WYLIE CAT 30	CAT	SACAC	F/S	KL				9	6	5500	5	3	47900	52700
39	4	WYLIE CAT 39	CAT	SACAC	F/S	KL				11	5	12000	6	6	175000	192000

LOA FT IN	NAME AND/OR MODEL	TOP/RIG	BOAT TYPE	HULL MTL TP	ENGINE TP #HP MFG	BEAM FT IN	WGT LBS	DRAFT FT IN	RETAIL LOW	RETAIL HIGH
1995 BOATS										
18	MERCURY	SLP	SAROD	F/S KL		5 4	1100	3 1	8200	9450
24	MOORE 24	SLP	SARCC	F/S KL	OB	7 2	2050	4 1	16500	18700
30 10	ANTRIM 30+	SLP	SARCC	F/S TM	OB	24 5	3900	5	79800	87700
1994 BOATS										
18	MERCURY	SLP	SAROD	F/S KL		5 4	1100	3 1	7700	8850
24	MOORE 24	SLP	SARCC	F/S KL	OB	7 2	2050	4 1	15400	17500
30 10	ANTRIM 30+	SLP	SARCC	F/S TM	OB	24 5	3900	5	74800	82200
1993 BOATS										
18	MERCURY	SLP	SAROD	F/S KL		5 4	1100	3 1	7250	8300
24	MOORE 24	SLP	SARCC	F/S KL		7 2	2050	4 1	14300	16300
1992 BOATS										
18	MERCURY	SLP	SA/OD	F/S KL		5 4	1200	3 1	7100	8150
24	MOORE 24	SLP	SA/RC	F/S KL		7 2	2050	4 1	13500	15300
1986 BOATS										
23 9	MOORE 24	SLP	SAIL	F/S KL	OB	7 2	2100	4 1	9250	10500
29 10	MOORE 30	SLP	SAIL	KEV KL	OB	14	2000	6 6	10300	11700
1985 BOATS										
23 9	MOORE 24	SLP	SA/OD	FBG KL	OB	7 2	2050	4 2	8450	9750
30	MOORE 30	SLP	SA/RC	KEV KL	OB	14	2000	6 6	9650	11000
1984 BOATS										
23 9	MOORE 24	SLP	SA/OD	FBG KL	OB	7 2	2050	4 3	7950	9150
37 5	MOORE 37	SLP	SA/RC	FBG KL	OB	11	7000	6 2	37500	41700

....For earlier years, see the BUC Used Boat Price Guide, Volume 3

MORETTES LTD
ERIN ONTARIO CANADA   COAST GUARD MFG ID- ZMT   See inside cover to adjust price for area

LOA FT IN	NAME AND/OR MODEL	TOP/RIG	BOAT TYPE	HULL MTL TP	ENGINE TP #HP MFG	BEAM FT IN	WGT LBS	DRAFT FT IN	RETAIL LOW	RETAIL HIGH
1985 BOATS										
18	CHASER-CAT	CAT	SAIL	FBG KC		7 6	1300	4	4850	5550
1984 BOATS										
18	CHASER CAT	CAT	SAIL	FBG KC OB		7 6	1300	4	4550	5250
39 11	CHASER 39 PH	SLP	SAIL	F/S KL IB	36D PERK	12	17500	5 10	79000	86800

....For earlier years, see the BUC Used Boat Price Guide, Volume 3

MORGAN MARINE
BY CATALINA YACHTS
WOODLAND HILLS CA 91367 COAST GUARD MFG ID- MRY   See inside cover to adjust price for area

For more recent years, see the BUC Used Boat Price Guide, Volume 1

LOA FT IN	NAME AND/OR MODEL	TOP/RIG	BOAT TYPE	HULL MTL TP TP	ENGINE #HP MFG	BEAM FT IN	WGT LBS	DRAFT FT IN	RETAIL LOW	RETAIL HIGH
1996 BOATS										
38 5	MORGAN 38 CC FIN	SLP	SACAC	FBG KL IB	37D WEST	12 4	17500	6	91600	100500
38 5	MORGAN 38 CC WING	SLP	SACAC	FBG WK IB	37D WEST	12 4	18000	5	93600	103000
45 3	MORGAN 45 CC FIN	SLP	SACAC	FBG KL IB	50D YAN	13 9	25225	6 6	159000	175000
45 3	MORGAN 45 CC WING	SLP	SACAC	FBG KL IB	50D YAN	13 9	25225	5 7	159000	175000
1995 BOATS										
38 5	MORGAN 38 CC FIN	SLP	SACAC	FBG KL IB	37D WEST	12 4	17500	6	86800	95300
38 5	MORGAN 38 CC WING	SLP	SACAC	FBG WK IB	37D WEST	12 4	18000	5	88600	97400
45 3	MORGAN 45 CC FIN	SLP	SACAC	FBG KL IB	50D YAN	13 9	25225	6 6	150500	165500
45 3	MORGAN 45 CC WING	SLP	SACAC	FBG KL IB	50D YAN	13 9	25225	5 7	150500	165500
50 5	CATALINA 50-3 AFT	SLP	SACAC	FBG WK IB	75D YAN	14 9	36000	5 7	221500	243000
50 5	CATALINA 50-4 AFT	SLP	SACAC	FBG WK IB	75D YAN	14 9	36000	5 7	224500	246500
50 5	CATALINA 50-4+1 AFT	SLP	SACAC	FBG WK IB	75D YAN	14 9	36000	5 7	229000	251500
1994 BOATS										
38 5	MORGAN 38 CC	SLP	SACAC	FBG KL IB	38D WEST	12 4	17500	6 6	82200	90300
38 5	MORGAN 38 CC	SLP	SACAC	FBG KL IB	38D WEST	12 4	17500	6 6	82200	90300
45 3	MORGAN 45 CC	SLP	SACAC	FBG KL IB	50D YAN	13 6	25000	5 7	142000	156000
45 3	MORGAN 45 CC	SLP	SACAC	FBG KL IB	50D YAN	13 6	25450	6 6	143500	157500
50 5	CATALINA 50-3 AFT	SLP	SACAC	FBG KL IB	75D YAN	14 9	36000	5 7	209500	230500
50 5	CATALINA 50-4 AFT	SLP	SACAC	FBG KL IB	75D YAN	14 9	36000	5 7	212500	233500
50 5	CATALINA 50-4+1 AFT	SLP	SACAC	FBG KL IB	75D YAN	14 9	36000	5 7	216500	238000
1993 BOATS										
38 5	MORGAN 38	SLP	SACAC	FBG KL IB	35D YAN	12 4	17500	6 6	77700	85400
38 5	MORGAN 38	SLP	SACAC	FBG KL IB	35D YAN	12 4	17500	6 6	77700	85400
45 5	MORGAN 45	SLP	SACAC	FBG KL IB	50D YAN	13 6	25450	6 6	135500	149000
45 5	MORGAN 45	SLP	SACAC	FBG KL IB	50D YAN	13 6	25000	5 7	134500	148000
50 5	CATALINA 50-3	SLP	SACAC	FBG WK IB	75D YAN	14 9	36000	5 7	202500	222500
1992 BOATS										
45 3	MORGAN 45	SLP	SA/CR	FBG KL IB	50D YAN	13 6	25450	6 6	128500	141500
45 3	MORGAN 45	SLP	SA/CR	FBG WK IB	50D YAN	13 6	25000	5 7	127500	140000
50 5	CATALINA 50-2	SLP	SA/CR	FBG WK IB	75D YAN	14 9	36000	5 7	190000	209000
50 5	CATALINA 50-3	SLP	SA/CR	FBG WK IB	75D YAN	14 9	36000	5 7	191500	210500
1991 BOATS										
29 11	CATALINA 30	SLP	SA/CR	FBG KL IB	D	10 10	10200	5 3	30500	33900
29 11	CATALINA 30	SLP	SA/CR	FBG KL IB	D	10 10	10300	5 3	30400	34300
41 3	MORGAN CLASSIC 41	SLP	SAIL	FBG KL IB	D YAN	13 10	23000	4 10	97100	107000
45 3	MORGAN 45	SLP	SA/CR	FBG KL IB	50D YAN	13 9	25000	5 7	121000	133250
50 5	CATALINA 50 2 CABIN	SLP	SA/CR	FBG WK IB	75D YAN	14 9	36000	5 7	179500	197500
50 5	CATALINA 50 3 CABIN	SLP	SA/CR	FBG WK IB	75D YAN	14 9	36000	5 7	182000	200000
1990 BOATS										
41 3	MORGAN CLASSIC 41	SLP	SAIL	FBG KL IB	D	13 10	23000	4 10	92000	101000
44	MORGAN 44	SLP	SAIL	FBG KL IB	D	13 6	23500	5 5	104500	115000
1986 BOATS										
31 11	MORGAN 32	SLP	SA/CR	FBG KL IB	21D UNIV	11 6	11000	4	27600	30600
36	MORGAN 36	SLP	SA/RC	FBG KC IB	21D UNIV	11 10	11900	4 6	33500	37300
36	MORGAN 36	SLP	SA/RC	FBG KL IB	21D UNIV	11 10	11900	4 6	33500	37300
38 4	MORGAN 384 DEEP	SLP	SA/RC	FBG KL IB	51D PERK	12	18000	6 8	54300	59700
38 4	MORGAN 384 STD	SLP	SA/RC	FBG KL IB	51D PERK	12	18000	5	53700	59000
43	MORGAN 43 SHOAL	SLP	SA/CR	FBG KL IB	51D PERK	13 6	23500	5	80100	88000
43	MORGAN 43 SHOAL	SLP	SA/RC	FBG KL IB	62D PERK	13 6	23500	5	80400	88300
43	MORGAN 43 STD	SLP	SA/CR	FBG KL IB	51D PERK	13 6	23500	6 6	79700	87600
43	MORGAN 43 STD	SLP	SA/RC	FBG KL IB	62D PERK	13 6	23500	6 6	79700	87600
45 7	MORGAN 46	SLP	SA/RC	FBG KC IB	51D PERK	13 6	22500	5 4	89200	98000
45 7	MORGAN 46 FIN	SLP	SA/RC	FBG KL IB	51D PERK	13 6	22500	8 7	88900	97200
45 7	MORGAN 46 SHOAL	SLP	SA/RC	FBG KC IB	51D PERK	13 6	21000	5	86400	94900
60 1	MORGAN 60	SCH	SA/CR	FBG KL IB	135D PERK	15 8	60000	5 10	287500	316000
62	MORGAN 62	SCH	SA/CR	FBG KL IB	135D PERK	15 10		5 10	276500	304000
1985 BOATS										
31 11	MORGAN 32	SLP	SA/CR	FBG KL IB	21D UNIV	11 6	11000	4	26100	29000
36	MORGAN 36	SLP	SA/RC	FBG KC IB	21D UNIV	11 10	11900	4 6	31800	35300
36	MORGAN 36	SLP	SA/RC	FBG KL IB	21D UNIV	11 10	11900	4 6	31800	35300
38 4	MORGAN 384 DEEP	SLP	SA/RC	FBG KL IB	51D PERK	12	18000	6 8	51500	56600
38 4	MORGAN 384 STD	SLP	SA/RC	FBG KL IB	51D PERK	12	18000	5	50900	55900
43	MORGAN 43 SHOAL	SLP	SA/CR	FBG KL IB	51D PERK	13 6	23500	5	75900	83400
43	MORGAN 43 SHOAL	SLP	SA/RC	FBG KL IB	62D PERK	13 6	23500	5	76200	83700
43	MORGAN 43 STD	SLP	SA/CR	FBG KL IB	51D PERK	13 6	23500	6 6	75600	83000
43	MORGAN 43 STD	SLP	SA/RC	FBG KL IB	62D PERK	13 6	23500	6 6	75600	83000
45 7	MORGAN 46	SLP	SA/RC	FBG KC IB	51D PERK	13 6	22500	5 4	84600	92900
45 7	MORGAN 46 FIN	SLP	SA/RC	FBG KL IB	51D PERK	13 6	22500	8 7	84200	92500
45 7	MORGAN 46 SHOAL	SLP	SA/CR	FBG KC IB	51D PERK	13 6	21000	5	81900	90000
60 1	MORGAN 60	SCH	SA/CR	FBG KL IB	135D PERK	15 8	60000	5 10	272500	299000
62	MORGAN 62	SCH	SA/CR	FBG KL IB	135D PERK	15 10		5 10	262000	288000
1984 BOATS										
31 11	MORGAN 323	SLP	SA/CR	FBG KL IB	23D YAN	11 6	11000	4	24800	27500
36	MORGAN 36	SLP	SA/RC	FBG KC IB	21D UNIV	11 10	11900	4 6	30100	33500
36	MORGAN 36	SLP	SA/RC	FBG KL IB	21D UNIV	11 10	11900	4 6	30100	33500
38 4	MORGAN 384	SLP	SA/RC	FBG KL IB	50D PERK	12	18000	5	48500	53300
41 3	OUT-ISLAND 416	KTH	SA/RC	FBG KL IB	44D UNIV	13 10	27000	4 2	73100	80300
45	MORGAN 45	SLP	SA/RC	FBG KC IB	44D UNIV	13 5	22500	7 11	77800	85500
45	MORGAN 45	SLP	SA/RC	FBG KL IB	44D UNIV	13 5	22500	7 11	77800	85500
45	MORGAN 45	SLP	SA/RC	FBG KL IB	44D UNIV	13 5	21000	7 11	75400	82800
45	MORGAN 45	SLP	SA/RC	FBG KL IB	44D UNIV	13 5	21000	7 11	75400	82800
60 1	MORGAN 60	SCH	SA/RC	FBG KL IB	135D PERK	15 8	60000	5 10	258000	283500
62	MORGAN 62	SCH	SA/RC	FBG KL IB	135D PERK	15 10		5 10	248500	273000

....For earlier years, see the BUC Used Boat Price Guide, Volume 3

ALAN MORGAN YACHTING
BRIGHTON E SUSSEX ENGLAND   See inside cover to adjust price for area

LOA FT IN	NAME AND/OR MODEL	TOP/RIG	BOAT TYPE	HULL MTL TP TP	ENGINE #HP MFG	BEAM FT IN	WGT LBS	DRAFT FT IN	RETAIL LOW	RETAIL HIGH
1995 BOATS										
50 8	FRERS 51	SLP	SARAC	F/S KL IB	80D YAN	15 5	35000	8 2	228500	251000
54	MYSTIC 54	SLP	SARAC	F/S KL IB	80D YAN	15 7	36500	8 4	280000	308000
60	MYSTIC 60	CUT	SARAC	F/S KL IB	135D PERK	16 3	55400	8 6	504000	553500
1991 BOATS										
50 8	FRERS 51 AC	SLP	SARAC	F/S KL IB	80D YAN	15 5	35000	8 2	175000	192000
1989 BOATS										
43	KAUFMAN 43	CUT	SA/RC	FBG KL IB	40D	12 6	25000	4 9	96200	105500
43	KAUFMAN 43	CUT	SA/RC	FBG KL IB	40D	12 6	25000	4 9	96200	105500
49	KAUFMAN 49	CUT	SA/RC	FBG KL IB	65D WEST	13 9	34000	4 10	135000	148500
49	KAUFMAN 49	CUT	SA/RC	FBG KL IB	65D WEST	13 9	34000		135000	148500
51	KAUFMAN 51/53	CUT	SA/RC	FBG KL IB	85D PERK	14 3	40000	7	155500	171000
51	KAUFMAN 51/53	KTH	SA/RC	FBG KL IB	85D PERK	14 3	40000	7	165000	181500

LOA FT	IN	NAME AND/ OR MODEL	TOP/ RIG	BOAT TYPE	-HULL- MTL	TP	----ENGINE--- TP	#	HP	MFG	BEAM FT	IN	WGT LBS	DRAFT FT	IN	RETAIL LOW	RETAIL HIGH
		1988 BOATS															
43		KAUFMAN 43	CUT	SA/RC	FBG	KL	IB		40D		12	6	25000	4	9	90000	98900
43		KAUFMAN 43	CUT	SA/RC	FBG	KL	IB		40D		12	6	25000	5	10	90000	98900
49		KAUFMAN 49	CUT	SA/RC	FBG	KL	IB		65D	WEST	13	9	34000	4	10	126500	139000
49		KAUFMAN 49	CUT	SA/RC	FBG	KL	IB		65D	WEST	13	9	34000	7		126500	139000

MORRIS YACHTS

BASS HARBOR ME 04653-03 COAST GUARD MFG ID- TMY See inside cover to adjust price for area

For more recent years, see the BUC Used Boat Price Guide, Volume 1

LOA FT	IN	NAME AND/ OR MODEL	TOP/ RIG	BOAT TYPE	-HULL- MTL	TP	----ENGINE--- TP	#	HP	MFG	BEAM FT	IN	WGT LBS	DRAFT FT	IN	RETAIL LOW	RETAIL HIGH
		1996 BOATS															
28	1	MORRIS 28	SLP	SACAC	FBG	KL	IB		18D	VLVO	9	2	8300	4	4	108000	118500
32	6	MORRIS 32	SLP	SACAC	FBG	KL	IB		18D	VLVO	10	5	11400	4	3	160000	175500
36	3	MORRIS 36	SLP	SACAC	FBG	KL	IB		28D	VLVO	11	7	15600	4	6	225500	247500
37	6	MORRIS 38	SLP	SACAC	FBG	KL	IB		36D	YAN	11	7	15600	4	6	235500	258500
40	5	MORRIS 40	SLP	SACAC	FBG	KL	IB		50D	YAN	12	7	19000	5	3	303000	333000
40	5	MORRIS 40 2HD	SLP	SACAC	FBG	KL	IB		50D	YAN	12	7	19000	5	3	323000	354500
44	6	MORRIS 44	SLP	SACAC	FBG	KL	IB		50D	YAN	13	1	23500	5	9	409000	449500
45	11	MORRIS 46	SLP	SACAC	FBG	KL	IB		50D	YAN	13	1	23500	5	9	426500	468500
45	11	MORRIS 46 CUSTOM	SLP	SACAC	FBG	KL	IB		50D	YAN	13	1	23500	5	9	440000	484000
		1995 BOATS															
28	1	MORRIS 28	SLP	SACAC	FBG	KL	IB		18D	VLVO	9	2	8300	4	4	101500	111500
32	6	MORRIS 32	SLP	SACAC	FBG	KL	IB		18D	VLVO	10	5	11400	4	3	150500	165500
36	3	MORRIS 36	SLP	SACAC	FBG	KL	IB		28D	VLVO	11	7	15600	4	6	211500	232500
37	6	MORRIS 38	SLP	SACAC	FBG	KL	IB		36D	YAN	11	7	15600	4	6	220500	242500
40	5	MORRIS 40	SLP	SACAC	FBG	KL	IB		50D	YAN	12	7	19000	5	3	289500	318000
44	5	MORRIS 44	SLP	SACAC	FBG	KL	IB		50D	YAN	13	1	23500	5	9	371500	408500
		1994 BOATS															
28	1	MORRIS 28	SLP	SACAC	FBG	KL	IB		18D	VLVO	9	2	8300	4	4	95600	105000
32	6	MORRIS 32	SLP	SACAC	FBG	KL	IB		18D	VLVO	10	5	11400	4	3	141500	155500
36	3	MORRIS 36	SLP	SACAC	FBG	KL	IB		28D	VLVO	11	7	15600	4	6	199500	219000
37	6	MORRIS 38	SLP	SACAC	FBG	KL	IB		36D	YAN	11	7	15600	4	6	208000	228500
40	5	MORRIS 40	SLP	SACAC	FBG	KL	IB		50D	YAN	12	7	19000	5	3	276000	303500
44	5	MORRIS 44	SLP	SACAC	FBG	KL	IB		50D	YAN	13	1	23500	5	9	359000	394500
		1993 BOATS															
28	1	MORRIS 28 LINDA	CAT	SARAC	FBG	KL	IB		28D	VLVO	9	2	8300	4	4	90300	99200
28	1	MORRIS 28 LINDA	SLP	SARAC	FBG	KL	IB		28D	VLVO	9	2	8300	4	4	90300	99200
32	6	MORRIS 32	CAT	SARAC	FBG	KL	IB		28D	VLVO	10	5	11400	4	3	133000	146500
32	6	MORRIS 32	SLP	SARAC	FBG	KL	IB		28D	VLVO	10	5	11400	4	3	133000	146500
36	3	MORRIS 36	CAT	SARAC	FBG	KL	IB		43D	VLVO	11	7	15100	4	3	201500	221500
36	3	MORRIS 36	SLP	SARAC	FBG	KL	IB		43D	VLVO	11	7	15100	5	6	201500	221500
37	6	MORRIS 38	SLP	SARAC	FBG	KL	IB	T	43D	VLVO	11	7	15800	5	6	201500	221500
39	11	MORRIS 40	SLP	SARAC	FBG	KL	IB		50D	YAN	12	7	19000	4	11	256500	281500
44	5	MORRIS 44	CAT	SACAC	FBG	KL	IB		50D	YAN	13	1	23500	5	9	374500	411500
44	5	MORRIS 44	SLP	SARAC	FBG	KL	IB		50D	YAN	13	1	23500	5	9	372000	409000
		1992 BOATS															
28	1	MORRIS 28 LINDA	CAT	SARAC	FBG	KL	IB		28D	VLVO	9	2	8300	4	4	84900	93300
28	1	MORRIS 28 LINDA	SLP	SARAC	FBG	KL	IB		28D	VLVO	9	2	8300	4	4	84900	93300
32	6	MORRIS 32	CAT	SARAC	FBG	KL	IB		28D	VLVO	10	5	11400	4	3	125000	137500
32	6	MORRIS 32	SLP	SARAC	FBG	KL	IB		28D	VLVO	10	5	11400	4	3	125000	137500
36	3	MORRIS 36	CAT	SARAC	FBG	KL	IB		43D	VLVO	11	7	15100	4	3	189500	208000
36	3	MORRIS 36	SLP	SARAC	FBG	KL	IB		43D	VLVO	11	7	15100	5	6	189500	208000
44	5	MORRIS 44	CAT	SACAC	FBG	KL	IB		50D	YAN	13	1	23500	5	9	352000	386500
44	5	MORRIS 44	SLP	SARAC	FBG	KL	IB		50D	YAN	13	1	23500	5	9	349000	384000
		1989 BOATS															
26		MORRIS 26 FRANCES	SLP	SA/CR	FBG	KL	IB		10D	VLVO	8	2	6800	3	10	57200	62800
26		MORRIS 26 VICTORIA	SLP	SA/CR	FBG	KL	IB		10D	YAN	8	2	6800	3	10	48500	53300
26		MORRIS 26 VICTORIA	CUT	SA/CR	FBG	KL	IB		10D	YAN	8	2	6800	3	10	52900	58100
28	1	MORRIS 28 LINDA	SLP	SA/CR	FBG	KL	IB		18D	VLVO	9	2	8300	4	4	70400	77300
29	8	MORRIS 30 LEIGH	SLP	SA/CR	FBG	KL	IB		13D	VLVO	9	7	9100	4	7	80200	88200
29	8	MORRIS 30 LEIGH	CUT	SA/CR	FBG	KL	IB		13D	VLVO	9	7	9100	4	7	80200	88200
29	8	MORRIS 30 VICTORIA	SLP	SA/CR	FBG	KL	IB		15D	YAN	9	7	9010	4	7	79500	87400
29	8	MORRIS 30 VICTORIA	CUT	SA/CR	FBG	KL	IB		15D	YAN	9	7	9010	4	7	79500	87400
32	3	MORRIS 32 FLEET	SLP	SA/CR	FBG	KL	IB		18D	VLVO	10	5	11225	4	3	113000	124000
34	3	VICTORIA 34	SLP	SA/CR	FBG	KL	IB		27D	YAN	10	8	12719	4	10	117500	129000
36	3	MORRIS 36 JUSTINE	SLP	SA/CR	FBG	KL	IB		23D	VLVO	11	7	15600	5	6	161000	177000
36	3	MORRIS 36 JUSTINE	CUT	SA/CR	FBG	KL	IB		23D	VLVO	11	7	15600	5	6	161000	177000
36	3	MORRIS 36S JUSTINE	SLP	SA/CR	FBG	KL	IB		23D	VLVO	11	7	15600	4	6	161000	177000
36	3	MORRIS 36S JUSTINE	CUT	SA/CR	FBG	KL	IB		23D	VLVO	11	7	15600	4	6	161000	177000
42	3	MORRIS 42	SLP	SA/CR	FBG	KL	IB		33D	WEST	12	9	22000	5	4	256000	281500
		1988 BOATS															
26		MORRIS 26 FRANCES	SLP	SA/CR	FBG	KL	IB		10D	VLVO	8	2	6800	3	10	53800	59100
26		MORRIS 26 VICTORIA	SLP	SA/CR	FBG	KL	IB		10D	YAN	8	2	6800	3	10	45900	50400
26		MORRIS 26 VICTORIA	CUT	SA/CR	FBG	KL	IB		10D	YAN	8	2	6800	3	10	49800	54700
28	1	MORRIS 28 LINDA	SLP	SA/CR	FBG	KL	IB		18D	VLVO	9	2	8300	4	4	66200	72700
29	8	MORRIS 30 LEIGH	SLP	SA/CR	FBG	KL	IB		13D	VLVO	9	7	9100	4	7	75500	82900
29	8	MORRIS 30 LEIGH	CUT	SA/CR	FBG	KL	IB		13D	VLVO	9	7	9100	4	7	75500	82900
29	8	MORRIS 30 VICTORIA	SLP	SA/CR	FBG	KL	IB		15D	YAN	9	7	9010	4	7	74800	82200
29	8	MORRIS 30 VICTORIA	CUT	SA/CR	FBG	KL	IB		15D	YAN	9	7	9010	4	7	74800	82200
32	3	MORRIS 32 FLEET	SLP	SA/CR	FBG	KL	IB		18D	VLVO	10	5	11225	4	3	96400	106000
34	3	VICTORIA 34	SLP	SA/CR	FBG	KL	IB		27D	YAN	10	8	12719	4	10	110500	121500
36	3	MORRIS 36 JUSTINE	SLP	SA/CR	FBG	KL	IB		23D	VLVO	11	7	15600	5	6	150500	165500
36	3	MORRIS 36 JUSTINE	CUT	SA/CR	FBG	KL	IB		23D	VLVO	11	7	15600	5	6	151000	166000
36	3	MORRIS 36S JUSTINE	SLP	SA/CR	FBG	KL	IB		23D	VLVO	11	7	15600	4	6	153000	168000
36	3	MORRIS 36S JUSTINE	CUT	SA/CR	FBG	KL	IB		23D	VLVO	11	7	15600	4	6	152000	167000
42	3	MORRIS 42	SLP	SA/CR	FBG	KL	IB		33D	WEST	12	9	22000	5	4	240500	264500
		1987 BOATS															
26		MORIS 26 FRANCES	SLP	SA/CR	FBG	KL	IB		10D	VLVO	8	2	6800	3	10	53400	58600
26		MORRIS 26 VICTORIA	SLP	SA/CR	FBG	KL	IB		10D	YAN	8	2	6800	3	10	39900	44300
26		MORRIS 26 VICTORIA	CUT	SA/CR	FBG	KL	IB		10D	YAN	8	2	6800	3	10	47100	51700
28	1	MORRIS 28 LINDA	SLP	SA/CR	FBG	KL	IB		18D	VLVO	9	2	8300	4	4	62300	68400
29	8	MORRIS 30 LEIGH	SLP	SA/CR	FBG	KL	IB		13D	VLVO	9	7	9100	4	7	71000	78000
29	8	MORRIS 30 LEIGH	CUT	SA/CR	FBG	KL	IB		13D	VLVO	9	7	9100	4	7	71000	78000
29	8	MORRIS 30 VICTORIA	SLP	SA/CR	FBG	KL	IB		15D	YAN	9	7	9010	4	7	70300	77300
29	8	MORRIS 30 VICTORIA	CUT	SA/CR	FBG	KL	IB		15D	YAN	9	7	9010	4	7	70300	77300
32	3	MORRIS 32 FLEET	SLP	SA/CR	FBG	KL	IB		18D	VLVO	10	5	11225	4	3	90700	99700
34	3	VICTORIA 34	SLP	SA/CR	FBG	KL	IB		27D	YAN	10	8	12719	4	10	104000	114000
36	3	MORRIS 36 JUSTINE	SLP	SA/CR	FBG	KL	IB		23D	VLVO	11	7	15600	5	6	142000	156000
36	3	MORRIS 36 JUSTINE	CUT	SA/CR	FBG	KL	IB		23D	VLVO	11	7	15600	5	6	142000	156000
36	3	MORRIS 36S JUSTINE	SLP	SA/CR	FBG	KL	IB		23D	VLVO	11	7	15600	4	6	143500	157500
36	3	MORRIS 36S JUSTINE	CUT	SA/CR	FBG	KL	IB		23D	VLVO	11	7	15600	4	6	143000	157500
		1986 BOATS															
26		MORRIS 26 VICTORIA	SLP	SAIL	FBG	KL	IB		10D		8	2	6800	3	10	43600	48500
26		MORRIS 26 VICTORIA	CUT	SAIL	FBG	KL	IB		10D		8	2	6800	3	10	43600	48500
28	1	MORRIS 28 LINDA	SLP	SA/CR	FBG	KL	IB		18D	VLVO	9	2	8300	4	4	58600	64400
29	6	MORRIS 30 ANNIE	SLP	SA/CR	FBG	KL	SD		18D	VLVO	9	6	11027	4	6	81300	89400
29	8	MORRIS 30 LEIGH	SLP	SA/CR	FBG	KL	IB		13D	VLVO	9	7	9100	4	7	66800	73400
29	8	MORRIS 30 LEIGH	CUT	SA/CR	FBG	KL	IB		13D	VLVO	9	7	9100	4	7	66800	73400
29	8	MORRIS 30 VICTORIA	SLP	SA/CR	FBG	KL	IB		15D		9	7	9100	4	7	66800	73400
29	8	MORRIS 30 VICTORIA	CUT	SA/CR	FBG	KL	IB		15D		9	7	9100	4	7	66800	73400
34	3	VICTORIA 34	SLP	SA/CR	FBG	KL	IB		D	YAN	10	8	12719	4	10	97800	107500
36	3	MORRIS 36 JUSTINE	SLP	SA/CR	FBG	KL	IB		23D	VLVO	11	7	15500	5	4	132000	145000
36	3	MORRIS 36 JUSTINE	CUT	SA/CR	FBG	KL	IB		23D	VLVO	11	7	15500	5	4	131500	144500
36	3	MORRIS 36S JUSTINE	SLP	SA/CR	FBG	KL	IB		23D	VLVO	11	7	15500	4	4	135000	148500
36	3	MORRIS 36S JUSTINE	CUT	SA/CR	FBG	KL	IB		23D	VLVO	11	7	15500	4	4	135000	148000
		1985 BOATS															
26		MORRIS 26 FRANCES	SLP	SAIL	FBG	KL	IB		10D	BMW	8	2	6800	3	10	43400	48200
26		MORRIS 26 FRANCES	CUT	SAIL	FBG	KL	IB		10D	BMW	8	2	6800	3	10	42900	47600
26		MORRIS 26 VICTORIA	SLP	SAIL	FBG	KL	IB		10D		8	2	6800	3	10	38800	43100
26		MORRIS 26 VICTORIA	CUT	SAIL	FBG	KL	IB		10D		8	2	6800	3	10	39200	43600
28	1	MORRIS 28 LINDA	SLP	SA/CR	FBG	KL	IB		18D	VLVO	9	2	8300	4	4	55100	60500
29	6	MORRIS 30 ANNIE	SLP	SA/CR	FBG	KL	SD		18D	VLVO	9	6	11027	4	6	76500	84100
29	8	MORRIS 30 LEIGH	SLP	SA/CR	FBG	KL	IB		13D	VLVO	9	7	9100	4	7	62800	69000
29	8	MORRIS 30 LEIGH	CUT	SA/CR	FBG	KL	IB		13D	VLVO	9	7	9100	4	7	62800	69000
29	8	MORRIS 30 VICTORIA	SLP	SA/CR	FBG	KL	IB		15D		9	7	9100	4	7	62800	69000
29	8	MORRIS 30 VICTORIA	CUT	SA/CR	FBG	KL	IB		15D		9	7	9100	4	7	62800	69000
36	3	MORRIS 36 JUSTINE	SLP	SA/CR	FBG	KL	IB		28D	VLVO	11	7	15500	5	4	124000	136500
36	3	MORRIS 36 JUSTINE	CUT	SA/CR	FBG	KL	IB		28D	VLVO	11	7	15500	5	4	124000	136500
36	3	MORRIS 36S JUSTINE	SLP	SA/CR	FBG	KL	IB		28D	VLVO	11	7	15500	4	4	127000	139500
36	3	MORRIS 36S JUSTINE	CUT	SA/CR	FBG	KL	IB		28D	VLVO	11	7	15500	4	4	127000	139500
		1984 BOATS															
26		FRANCES 26	SLP	SAIL	FBG	KL	IB		10D	BMW	8		6800	3	10	38600	42900
26		FRANCES 26	CUT	SAIL	FBG	KL	IB		10D	BMW	8		6800	3	10	38600	42900
29	5	ANNIE	SLP	SAIL	FBG	KL	SD		15D	VLVO	9	4	11027	4	6	71800	78900
29	8	LEIGH 30	SLP	SA/CR	FBG	KL	IB		13D	WEST	9	7	9100	4	7	59100	65000
29	8	LEIGH 30	CUT	SAIL	FBG	KL	IB		13D	WEST	9	2	9100	4	7	59100	65000
36		JUSTINE 36	SLP	SAIL	FBG	KL	IB		22D	VLVO	11	7	15500	5	6	116000	127500
36		JUSTINE 36	CUT	SAIL	FBG	KL	IB		22D	VLVO	11	7	15500	5	6	116500	128000
36		JUSTINE 36 SHOAL	SLP	SAIL	FBG	KL	IB		22D	VLVO	11	7	15500	4	4	119000	130500
36		JUSTINE 36 SHOAL	CUT	SAIL	FBG	KL	IB		22D	VLVO	11	7	15500	4	4	118000	130000

....For earlier years, see the BUC Used Boat Price Guide, Volume 3

SAM L MORSE CO
COSTA MESA CA 92627   COAST GUARD MFG ID- SFJ See inside cover to adjust price for area

For more recent years, see the BUC Used Boat Price Guide, Volume 1

LOA FT IN	NAME AND/ OR MODEL	TOP/ RIG	BOAT TYPE	-HULL- MTL TP TP	----ENGINE--- # HP MFG	BEAM FT IN	WGT LBS	DRAFT FT IN	RETAIL LOW	RETAIL HIGH
\-\-\- 1996 BOATS										
30 6	FALMOUTH CUTTER	CUT	CUT	SACAC FBG KL IB	10D YAN	8	7400	3 6	67400	74000
37	BRISTOL CHANNEL CUT	CUT	SACAC FBG KL IB	27D YAN	10 1	14000	4 10	141500	155500
\-\-\- 1995 BOATS										
30 6	FALMOUTH CUTTER	CUT	CUT	SACAC FBG KL IB	10D YAN	8	7400	3 6	63700	70000
37	BRISTOL CHANNEL CUT	CUT	SACAC FBG KL IB	27D YAN	10 1	14000	4 10	134000	147000
\-\-\- 1994 BOATS										
30 6	FALMOUTH CUTTER	CUT	SA/CR FBG KL IB	10D YAN	8	7400	3 6	60300	66200
37 9	BRISTOL-CHANNEL	CUT	SA/CR FBG KL IB	27D YAN	10 1	14000	4 10	127000	139500
\-\-\- 1992 BOATS										
22	FALMOUTH CUTTER	CUT	SA/CR FBG KL IB	10D YAN	8	7400	3 6	54000	59400
28 1	BRISTOL-CHANNEL	CUT	SA/CR FBG KL IB	18D VLVO	10 1	14000	4 10	113000	124500
\-\-\- 1991 BOATS										
22	FALMOUTH CUTTER	CUT	SA/CR FBG KL IB	10D YAN	8	7400	3 6	51300	56400
28 1	BRISTOL-CHANNEL	CUT	SA/CR FBG KL IB	18D VLVO	10 1	14000	4 10	107000	117500
\-\-\- 1990 BOATS										
22	FALMOUTH CUTTER	CUT	SA/CR FBG KL IB	8D YAN	8	7400	3 6	48500	53300
28 1	BRISTOL-CHANNEL	CUT	SA/CR FBG KL IB	18D VLVO	10 1	14000	4 10	101000	111500
\-\-\- 1989 BOATS										
28 1	BRISTOL-CHANNEL	CUT	SA/CR FBG KL IB	18D VLVO	10 1	14000	4 10	95800	105000
\-\-\- 1988 BOATS										
22	FALMOUTH CUTTER	CUT	SA/CR FBG KL IB	8D YAN	8	7400	3 6	42800	47600
28 1	BRISTOL-CHANNEL	CUT	SA/CR FBG KL IB	18D VLVO	10 1	14000	4 10	90600	99500
\-\-\- 1987 BOATS										
22	FALMOUTH CUTTER	CUT	SA/CR FBG KL IB	8D YAN	8	7400	3 6	40400	44900
28 1	BRISTOL-CHANNEL	CUT	SA/CR FBG KL IB	18D VLVO	10 1	14000	4 10	85600	94100
\-\-\- 1986 BOATS										
22	FALMOUTH CUTTER	CUT	SA/CR FBG KL IB	8D YAN	8	7400	3 6	38200	42400
28 1	BRISTOL-CHANNEL	CUT	SA/CR FBG KL IB	18D VLVO	10 1	14000	4 10	81000	89000
\-\-\- 1985 BOATS										
22	FALMOUTH CUTTER	CUT	SA/CR FBG KL IB	8D YAN	8	7400	3 6	36000	40000
28 1	BRISTOL-CHANNEL	CUT	SA/CR FBG KL IB	18D VLVO	10 1	14000	4 10	76500	84100
\-\-\- 1984 BOATS										
22	FALMOUTH CUTTER	CUT	SA/CR FBG KL IB	8D YAN	8	7400	3 6	34100	37900
28 1	BRISTOL-CHANNEL	CUT	SA/CR FBG KL IB	15D VLVO	10 1	14000	4 10	72400	79600

....For earlier years, see the BUC Used Boat Price Guide, Volume 3

MUELLER BOAT COMPANY
LORAIN OH 44052   COAST GUARD MFG ID- JWM See inside cover to adjust price for area

LOA FT IN	NAME AND/ OR MODEL	TOP/ RIG	BOAT TYPE	-HULL- MTL TP TP	----ENGINE--- # HP MFG	BEAM FT IN	WGT LBS	DRAFT FT IN	RETAIL LOW	RETAIL HIGH
\-\-\- 1985 BOATS										
19	LIGHTNING	SLP	SA/OD FBG CB			6 6	700	5	4100	4750

....For earlier years, see the BUC Used Boat Price Guide, Volume 3

MULTIHULL CARIBBEAN YACHTS
ARECIBO PR 00613   See inside cover to adjust price for area

LOA FT IN	NAME AND/ OR MODEL	TOP/ RIG	BOAT TYPE	-HULL- MTL TP TP	----ENGINE--- # HP MFG	BEAM FT IN	WGT LBS	DRAFT FT IN	RETAIL LOW	RETAIL HIGH
\-\-\- 1986 BOATS										
26 6	HEAVENLY-TWINS	KTH	SA/CR FBG CT OB		13 9	3000	2 3	27700	30700
26 6	HEAVENLY-TWINS	KTH	SA/CR FBG CT IB	9D YAN	13 9	3000	2 3	27700	30700
\-\-\- 1985 BOATS										
26 6	HEAVENLY-TWINS	KTH	SA/CR FBG CT OB		13 9	3000	2 3	26000	28900
26 6	HEAVENLY-TWINS	KTH	SA/CR FBG CT IB	9D YAN	13 9	3000	2 3	26000	28900

MULTIHULL CONSTRUCTORS
LYNNWOOD WA 98037   See inside cover to adjust price for area

LOA FT IN	NAME AND/ OR MODEL	TOP/ RIG	BOAT TYPE	-HULL- MTL TP TP	----ENGINE--- # HP MFG	BEAM FT IN	WGT LBS	DRAFT FT IN	RETAIL LOW	RETAIL HIGH
\-\-\- 1986 BOATS										
30	TURISSIMO 9		SAIL	CT		20	2200	5 1	30500	33800
\-\-\- 1985 BOATS										
30	TURISSIMO 9		SAIL	CT		20	2200		28700	31800

MURPHY BOAT WORKS
LA GROSSE WI 54601   COAST GUARD MFG ID- MOF See inside cover to adjust price for area

LOA FT IN	NAME AND/ OR MODEL	TOP/ RIG	BOAT TYPE	-HULL- MTL TP TP	----ENGINE--- # HP MFG	BEAM FT IN	WGT LBS	DRAFT FT IN	RETAIL LOW	RETAIL HIGH
\-\-\- 1989 BOATS										
21 2	CROWN-LAKER	ST	RNBT	WD SV IB	190 CRUS	8	2136		**	**
21 2	CROWN-LAKER	ST	RNBT	WD IO	205 OMC	8	2136		**	**
24	ROYAL-LAKER	ST	RNBT	WD IB	230 CHRY	8	3610		**	**
24	ROYAL-LAKER	ST	RNBT	WD IO	230-350	8	4170		**	**
24 2	LEXINGTON	ST	CBNCR	WD IO	200-230	8	3960		**	**
24 5	CONCORD	ST	SF	WD IO	230-240	8	4260		**	**
\-\-\- 1988 BOATS										
18 2	CROWN-LAKER	ST	RNBT	WD IB	190 CRUS	8	2136		**	**
18 2	CROWN-LAKER	ST	RNBT	WD IO	205 OMC	8	2136		**	**
24	ROYAL-LAKER	ST	RNBT	WD IB	230 CHRY	8	3610		**	**
24	ROYAL-LAKER	ST	RNBT	WD IB	230-350	8	4170		**	**
24 2	LEXINGTON	ST	CBNCR	WD IO	200-230	8	3960		**	**
24 5	CONCORD	ST	SF	WD IO	230-240	8	4260		**	**
\-\-\- 1987 BOATS										
18 2	CROWN-LAKER	ST	RNBT	WD IB	190 CRUS	8	2136		**	**
18 2	CROWN-LAKER	ST	RNBT	WD IO	205 OMC	8	2136		**	**
21 9	CLASSIC 21	ST	RNBT	WD IB	200 OMC	8	2950		**	**
21 9	CLASSIC LAKER	ST	RNBT	WD IB	200 CHRY	8	2950		**	**
24	ROYAL-LAKER	ST	RNBT	WD IB	215-230	8	3610		**	**
24 2	LEXINGTON	ST	CBNCR	WD IO	185-230	8			**	**
24 2	VICTORIA	ST	SPTCR	WD IO	200-230	8	3750		**	**
24 5	CONCORD	ST	SF	WD IO	230-240	8	4260		**	**
24 5	CONCORD	ST	SF	WD IO	T120	8			**	**
\-\-\- 1986 BOATS										
18	CROWN-LAKER		RNBT	WD SV IO	170	7 10	2136		**	**
21 2	CLASSIC 2100		RNBT	WD SV IO	120	8			**	**
21 8	CLASSIC-LAKER		RNBT	WD SV IO	215	8			**	**
24	ROYAL-LAKER		RNBT	WD SV IO	260	8			**	**
24 6	LEXINGTON		CR	WD SV IO	185	8			**	**
\-\-\- 1985 BOATS										
18	SPORTSTER	ST	CTRCN	WD SV OB		7 6	1400		4700	5450
18	SPORTSTER	ST	RNBT	WD SV OB		7 6	1400		4750	5450
18 2	CROWN-LAKER	ST	RNBT	WD SV IO	120 OMC	7	2136		**	**
18 2	CROWN-LAKER	ST	RNBT	WD SV IB	190 CRUS	8	2136		**	**
18 2	VICTORIA	ST	RNBT	WD SV IO	120	7			**	**
21 9	CLASSIC 21	ST	RNBT	WD SV IO	200 OMC	8	2950		**	**
21 9	CLASSIC LAKER	ST	RNBT	WD SV IB	200 CHRY	8	2950		**	**
24	CENTURION	ST	RNBT	WD SV IO	140	8			**	**
24	ROYAL-LAKER	ST	RNBT	WD SV IB	215-230	8	3610		**	**
24 2	LEXINGTON	ST	CBNCR	WD SV IO	185-230	8			**	**
24 2	VICTORIA	ST	SPTCR	WD SV IO	200-230	8	3750		**	**
24 5	CONCORD	ST	SF	WD IO	230-240	8	4260		**	**
24 5	CONCORD	ST	SF	WD IO	T120	8			**	**
\-\-\- 1984 BOATS										
18 3	GRAND LAKER	ST	RNBT	L/P SV OB		7	1900	1 9	5700	6550
21	CLASSIC 2100	ST	RNBT	L/P SV IO		7 10	2950		**	**
21	CLASSIC 2100	ST	RNBT	L/P SV IO	185	8	2950		**	**
24	CENTURION	ST	SPTCR	L/P SV IO	200	8	3700		**	**
24 2	CENTURION	ST	RNBT	L/P SV IO	225D	8	3750		**	**
24 2	LEXINGTON	HT	CBNCR	L/P SV IO	230D	8	4000		**	**
24 2	LEXINGTON	HT	CBNCR	L/P SV IO	250D	8	3900		**	**
24 6	CONCORD	FB	SF	L/P SV IO	230D	8	4200		**	**
24 6	CONCORD	FB	SF	L/P SV IO	225D	8	4200		**	**

....For earlier years, see the BUC Used Boat Price Guide, Volume 3

MURRAY BOATS
ONTARIO CANADA   COAST GUARD MFG ID- ZDZ See inside cover to adjust price for area

LOA FT IN	NAME AND/ OR MODEL	TOP/ RIG	BOAT TYPE	-HULL- MTL TP TP	----ENGINE--- # HP MFG	BEAM FT IN	WGT LBS	DRAFT FT IN	RETAIL LOW	RETAIL HIGH
\-\-\- 1985 BOATS										
33			CUT	SA/CR STL KL IB	13D VLVO	11	15000	5 6	24100	26700
33			CUT	SA/CR STL KL SD	20D BUKH	11	15000	5 6	24100	26800
33			CUT	SA/CR STL KL VD	35D YAN	11	15000	5 6	24100	26800
33	SHOAL		SLP	SA/CR STL KL IB	13D VLVO	11	15000	4 10	24100	26700
33	SHOAL		SLP	SA/CR STL KL SD	20D BUKH	11	15000	4 10	24100	26800
33	SHOAL		SLP	SA/CR STL KL VD	35D YAN	11	15000	4 10	24100	26800
33	SHOAL		CUT	SA/CR STL KL IB	13D VLVO	11	15000	4 10	24100	26700
33	SHOAL		CUT	SA/CR STL KL SD	20D BUKH	11	15000	4 10	24100	26800
33	SHOAL		CUT	SA/CR STL KL VD	35D YAN	11	15000	4 10	24100	26800

....For earlier years, see the BUC Used Boat Price Guide, Volume 3

MUSTANG BOAT COMPANY
MELISSA TX 75454-0299   COAST GUARD MFG ID- MNG See inside cover to adjust price for area

LOA FT IN	NAME AND/ OR MODEL	TOP/ RIG	BOAT TYPE	-HULL- MTL TP	----ENGINE--- TP # HP MFG	BEAM FT IN	WGT LBS	DRAFT FT IN	RETAIL LOW	RETAIL HIGH
			——— 1993 BOATS ———							
16 8	MUSTANG SUPER SEA SL	RNBT		F/S	OB	6 8	600		3350	3850
17 2	BRONCO	RACE		F/S SV	OB		480		2900	3350
18	LIGHTNING SUPER V	RNBT		F/S DV	OB		600		3550	4100
18 2	LIGHTNING SUPER V	SKI		F/S DV	OB		650		3850	4450
20 2	MUSTANG SUPER SEA SL	RNBT		F/S	OB	8	920		5050	5800
			——— 1992 BOATS ———							
16 8	MUSTANG SUPER SEA SL	RNBT		F/S	OB	6 8	600		3200	3750
17 2	LIGHTNING SUPER V	RNBT		F/S DV	OB		480		2650	3100
18	LIGHTNING SUPER V	RNBT		F/S DV	OB		600		3400	3950
18 2	LIGHTNING SUPER V	SKI		F/S DV	OB		650		3700	4300
20 2	MUSTANG SUPER SEA SL	RNBT		F/S	OB	8	920		4850	5550

....For earlier years, see the BUC Used Boat Price Guide, Volume 3

MYSTERE INTERNATIONAL
BLAINVILLE QUE CANADA J COAST GUARD MFG ID- ZVB See inside cover to adjust price for area

For more recent years, see the BUC Used Boat Price Guide, Volume 1

LOA FT IN	NAME AND/ OR MODEL	TOP/ RIG	BOAT TYPE	-HULL- MTL TP	----ENGINE--- TP # HP MFG	BEAM FT IN	WGT LBS	DRAFT FT IN	RETAIL LOW	RETAIL HIGH
			——— 1996 BOATS ———							
14 5	MYSTERE 5.0M	SLP	SARAC	F/S	CT	7 7	300	9	4000	4650
16 5	MYSTERE 5.0M	SLP	SARAC	FBG	CT	0 6	315	9	4400	5100
16 5	MYSTERE 5.0M XLC	SLP	SARAC	FBG	CT	8 6	315	9	4400	4650
18 3	MYSTERE 5.5M	SLP	SARAC	F/S	CT	8 6	400	2 4	5550	6350
18 3	MYSTERE 5.5M FUN	SLP	SARAC	F/S	CT	8 6	390	1 10	5450	6250
19 8	MYSTERE 6.0M	SLP	SARAC	F/S	CT	8 6	430	2 4	6200	7150
19 8	MYSTERE 6.0M C	SLP	SARAC	F/S	CT	8 6	430	2 4	6250	7200
19 8	MYSTERE 6.0M XL	SLP	SARAC	F/S	CT	10	440	2 4	6300	7250
19 8	MYSTERE 6.0M XLC	SLP	SARAC	F/S	CT	10	440	2 4	6350	7300
			——— 1995 BOATS ———							
16 5	MYSTERE 5.0M	SLP	SARAC	F/S	CT	7 7	300	9	3750	4400
16 5	MYSTERE 5.0M XL	SLP	SARAC	FBG	CT	8 6	315	9	4100	4800
16 5	MYSTERE 5.0M XLC	SLP	SARAC	FBG	CT	8 6	315	9	3750	4350
18 3	MYSTERE 5.5M	SLP	SARAC	F/S	CT	8 6	400	2 4	5200	6000
18 3	MYSTERE 5.5M FUN	SLP	SARAC	F/S	CT	8 6	390	1 10	5100	5900
19 8	MYSTERE 6.0M	SLP	SARAC	F/S	CT	8 6	430	2 4	5850	6700
19 8	MYSTERE 6.0M C	SLP	SARAC	F/S	CT	8 6	430	2 4	5850	6750
19 8	MYSTERE 6.0M XL	SLP	SARAC	F/S	CT	10	440	2 4	5900	6800
19 8	MYSTERE 6.0M XLC	SLP	SARAC	F/S	CT	10	440	2 4	5950	6850
			——— 1994 BOATS ———							
16 5	MYSTERE 5.0M	SLP	SARAC	F/S	CT	7 7	300	9	3550	4100
16 5	MYSTERE 5.0M XL	SLP	SARAC	FBG	CT	8 6	315	9	3850	4500
16 5	MYSTERE 5.0M XLC	SLP	SARAC	F/S	CT	8 6	315	9	3500	4100
18 3	MYSTERE 5.5M	SLP	SARAC	F/S	CT	8 6	400	2 4	4900	5600
18 3	MYSTERE 5.5M FUN	SLP	SARAC	F/S	CT	8 6	390	1 10	4800	5550
19 8	MYSTERE 6.0M	SLP	SARAC	F/S	CT	8 6	430	2 4	5500	6300
19 8	MYSTERE 6.0M C	SLP	SARAC	F/S	CT	8 6	430	2 4	5500	6350
19 8	MYSTERE 6.0M XL	SLP	SARAC	F/S	CT	10	440	2 4	5550	6400
19 8	MYSTERE 6.0M XLC	SLP	SARAC	F/S	CT	10	440	2 4	5600	6450
			——— 1993 BOATS ———							
16 5	MYSTERE 5.0M ST	SLP	SARAC	F/S	CT	7 7	300	9	3350	3850
16 5	MYSTERE 5.0M XL	SLP	SARAC	FBG	CT	8 6	315	9	3450	4050
19 8	MYSTERE 6.0M SX	SLP	SARAC	F/S	CT	8 6	420	2 4	5100	5850
19 8	MYSTERE 6.0M XL	SLP	SARAC	F/S	CT	10	425	2 4	5150	5900
			——— 1992 BOATS ———							
16 5	MYSTERE 5.0M ST	SLP	SA/RC	F/S	CT	7 7	305	8	3200	3700
16 5	MYSTERE 5.0M XL	SLP	SA/RC	F/S	CT	8 6	315	8	3300	3800
19 8	MYSTERE 6.0M SX	SLP	SA/RC	F/S	CT	8 6	415	2	4750	5500
19 8	MYSTERE 6.0M XL	SLP	SA/RC	F/S	CT	10	420	2	4800	5500
			——— 1991 BOATS ———							
16 5	MYSTERE 5.0 METERS	SLP	SAIL	F/S	CT	7 7	275		2700	3150
19 8	MYSTERE 6.0 METERS	SLP	SAIL	F/S	CT	8 6	390		4300	5000

MYSTIC YACHT LIMITED
BRIGHTON EAST SUSSEX ENGLAND   See inside cover to adjust price for area

LOA FT IN	NAME AND/ OR MODEL	TOP/ RIG	BOAT TYPE	-HULL- MTL TP	----ENGINE--- TP # HP MFG	BEAM FT IN	WGT LBS	DRAFT FT IN	RETAIL LOW	RETAIL HIGH
			——— 1996 BOATS ———							
50 8	FRERS 51	CUT	SARAC	F/S KL	IB	80D YAN	15 5	36000	8 2	426500 469000
55 2	MYSTIC 55	CUT	SARAC	F/S KL	IB	90D PERK	15 10	40235	6 3	596500 655500
55 2	MYSTIC 55	CUT	SARAC	KEV KL	IB	90D PERK	15 10	40235	8 2	596500 655500
60	MYSTIC 60	CUT	SARAC	F/S KL	IB	130D PERK	16 3	55400	8 6	898000 987000
60	MYSTIC 60	KTH	SARAC	F/S KL	IB	130D PERK	16 3	55400	9 6	920500 1.000M
			——— 1987 BOATS ———							
60	MYSTIC 60	CUT	SARAC	F/S KL	IB	110D YAN	16 3	55400	8 6	492500 541000

NACRA
NORTH AMERICAN CAT RACING ASC   See inside cover to adjust price for area
PERFORMANCE CATAMARANS INC
SANTA ANA CA 92705   COAST GUARD MFG ID- NAC

For more recent years, see the BUC Used Boat Price Guide, Volume 1

LOA FT IN	NAME AND/ OR MODEL	TOP/ RIG	BOAT TYPE	-HULL- MTL TP	----ENGINE--- TP # HP MFG	BEAM FT IN	WGT LBS	DRAFT FT IN	RETAIL LOW	RETAIL HIGH
			——— 1996 BOATS ———							
16 8	NACRA 5.0	SLP	SAROD	F/S	CT		8	340		6500	7500
18	NACRA 5.5SL	SLP	SAROD	F/S	CT		8 6	375		7500	8650
18	NACRA 5.5UNI	SLP	SAROD	F/S	CT		8 6	340		7000	8050
18 6	NACRA 5.7	SLP	SAROD	F/S	CT		8	360		7500	8600
19	NACRA 5.8NA	SLP	SAROD	F/S	CT		8	410		8400	9650
20	NACRA 6.0NA	SLP	SAROD	F/S	CT		8 6	420		7900	9100
			——— 1995 BOATS ———							
16 8	NACRA 5.0	CAT	SAROD	F/S	CT			340		6050	6950
18	NACRA 5.5 SL	CAT	SAROD	F/S	CT			375		6950	8000
18	NACRA 5.5 UNI	CAT	SAROD	F/S	CT			340		6500	7450
18 6	NACRA 5.7	CAT	SAROD	F/S	CT			360		6950	8000
19	NACRA 5.8	CAT	SAROD	F/S	CT			410		7800	8950
20	NACRA 6.0	CAT	SAROD	F/S	CT			420		7350	8450
			——— 1994 BOATS ———							
16 8	NACRA 5.0	CAT	SAROD	F/S	CT		8 6	320	2 3	6500	6300
18	NACRA 5.5 SL	SLP	SAROD	F/S	CT		8 6	375	2 10	6650	7650
18	NACRA 5.5 UNI	CAT	SAROD	F/S	CT		8 6	340	2 10	6100	7000
18 6	NACRA 5.7	SLP	SAROD	F/S	CT		8	360	2 3	6650	7600
19	NACRA 5.8	SLP	SAROD	F/S	CT		8 6	410	3 2	7400	8550
20	NACRA 6.0 NA	SLP	SAROD	F/S	CT		8 6	420	3 2	7000	8050
			——— 1993 BOATS ———							
16 8	NACRA 5.0	CAT	SAROD	F/S	CT		8 6	320	2 3	5150	5950
18	NACRA 5.5 SL	SLP	SAROD	F/S	CT		8 6	375	2 10	6250	7200
18	NACRA 5.5 UNI	CAT	SAROD	F/S	CT		8 6	340	2 10	5800	6650
18 6	NACRA 5.7	SLP	SAROD	F/S	CT		8	360	2 3	6250	7150
19	NACRA 5.8	SLP	SAROD	F/S	CT		8 6	410	3 2	7000	8000
20	NACRA 6.0	SLP	SAROD	F/S	CT		8 6	420	3 2	6550	7550
			——— 1992 BOATS ———							
16 8	NACRA 5.0	CAT	SA/OD	F/S	CT		8 6	320	2 3	4900	5650
18	NACRA 5.5 SL	SLP	SA/OD	F/S	CT		8 6	375	2 10	5900	6800
18	NACRA 5.5 UNI	CAT	SA/OD	F/S	CT		8 6	340	2 10	5500	6300
18 6	NACRA 5.7	SLP	SA/OD	F/S	CT		8	360	2 3	5900	6750
19	NACRA 5.8	SLP	SA/OD	F/S	CT		8 6	410	3 2	6550	7550
20	NACRA 6.0	SLP	SA/OD	F/S	CT		8 6	420	3 2	6200	7100
			——— 1991 BOATS ———							
16 8	NACRA 5.0	CAT	SA/OD	FBG	CT		8 6	340	2 10	5100	5850
18	NACRA 5.5 SL	CAT	SA/OD	FBG	CT		8 6	375	2 10	5800	6650
19	NACRA 5.8	CAT	SA/OD	FBG	CT		8 6	410	3 2	6450	7400
20	NACRA 6.0	CAT	SA/OD	FBG	CT		8 6	425	3 2	6100	7000
			——— 1986 BOATS ———							
18	INTERNATIONAL 18.2	CAT	SA/OD	FBG	CT		11	330	4	3900	4550
			——— 1985 BOATS ———							
18	INTERNATIONAL 18.2	CAT	SA/OD	FBG	CT		11	370	4	4000	4650
18	INTERNATIONAL 5.5	CAT	SA/OD	FBG	CT		8	350	4	3800	4450
18 6	INTERNATIONAL 5.7	SLP	SA/OD	FBG	CT		8	385	4	4250	4950
19	INTERNATIONAL 5.8	SLP	SA/OD	FBG	CT		8	410	6	4600	5300
			——— 1984 BOATS ———							
16 8	INTERNATIONAL 5.0	SLP	SA/OD	FBG			8	335	8	2850	3300
17	INTERNATIONAL 5.2	SLP	SA/OD	FBG	CT		8	350	4	3450	4000
18	INTERNATIONAL 18.2	CAT	SA/OD	FBG	CT		11	330	4	3450	4000
18	INTERNATIONAL 5.5	SLP	SA/OD	FBG	CT		8	330	4	3450	4000
18 6	INTERNATIONAL 5.7	SLP	SA/OD	FBG	CT		8	330	4	3600	4150
19	INTERNATIONAL 5.8	SLP	SA/OD	FBG	CT		8	410	6	4300	5000
36	ROLAND 36		SA/RC	FBG	CT		20		8	62800	69000

....For earlier years, see the BUC Used Boat Price Guide, Volume 3

NAJAD

INTERNATIONAL MARINE CORP NA
SE-473 31 HENAN SWEDEN

See inside cover to adjust price for area

For more recent years, see the BUC Used Boat Price Guide, Volume 1

LOA FT	IN	NAME AND/ OR MODEL	TOP/ RIG	BOAT TYPE	-HULL- MTL	TP	ENGINE TP	# HP	MFG	BEAM FT	IN	WGT LBS	DRAFT FT	IN	RETAIL LOW	RETAIL HIGH
		1986 BOATS														
31	10	NAJAD 320	SLP	SA/CR	FBG	KL	SD	28D	VLVO	10	4	10582	5	3	57900	63600
33	6	NAJAD 343	SLP	SA/CR	FBG	KL	IB	36D	VLVO	10	11	14330	5	5	76600	84100
35	3	NAJAD 360	SLP	SA/RC	FBG	KL	IB	43D	VLVO	10	11	15400	5	7	82500	90700
37	1	NAJAD 371	SLP	SA/CR	FBG	KL	IB	45D	VLVO	11	6	19841	5	9	106000	116500
38	7	NAJAD 390	SLP	SA/RC	FBG	KL	IB	62D	VLVO	11	6	20900	6	2	115000	126500
		1985 BOATS														
31	10	NAJAD 320	SLP	SA/CR	FBG	KL	SD	28D	VLVO	10	4	10582	5	3	54500	59900
33	6	NAJAD 343	SLP	SA/CR	FBG	KL	IB	36D	VLVO	10	11	14330	5	5	71600	78700
37	1	NAJAD 371	SLP	SA/CR	FBG	KL	IB	45D	VLVO	11	6	19841	5	9	99000	109000
39		NAJAD 390	SLP	SA/RC	FBG	KL	IB	62D	VLVO	11	6	20900	6	2	109000	120000
		1984 BOATS														
31	10	NAJAD 320	SLP	SA/CR	FBG	KL	IB	28D	VLVO	10	4	10582	5	3	51200	56300
33	6	NAJAD 343	SLP	SA/CR	FBG	KL	IB	36D	VLVO	10	11	14330	5	5	67300	73900
37	1	NAJAD 371	SLP	SA/CR	FBG	KL	IB	61D	VLVO	11	6	19841	5	9	93300	102500

NATIONAL ONE DESIGN RACING

SO BEND IN 46615

See inside cover to adjust price for area

For more recent years, see the BUC Used Boat Price Guide, Volume 1

LOA FT	IN	NAME AND/ OR MODEL	TOP/ RIG	BOAT TYPE	-HULL- MTL	TP	ENGINE TP	# HP	MFG	BEAM FT	IN	WGT LBS	DRAFT FT	IN	RETAIL LOW	RETAIL HIGH
		1996 BOATS														
17		NATIONAL ONE DESIGN	SLP	SAROD	FBG	CB				5	8	400	3	4	3450	4050
		1994 BOATS														
17		NATIONAL OD	SLP	SAROD	FBG	CB				5	8	400	3	4	3050	3550
		1990 BOATS														
17		NATIONAL-ONE DESIGN	SLP	SAIL	FBG	CB				5	8	400	3	4	2400	2800
		1986 BOATS														
17		NATIONAL-ONE-DESIGN	SLP	SA/OD	FBG	CB				5	8	400	3	4	1850	2200
		1985 BOATS														
17		NATIONAL-ONE-DESIGN	SLP	SA/OD	FBG	CB				5	8	400	3	4	1750	2100
		1984 BOATS														
17		NATIONAL-ONE-DESIGN	SLP	SA/OD	FBG	CB				5	8	400	3	4	1650	1950

....For earlier years, see the BUC Used Boat Price Guide, Volume 3

NAUSET MARINE INC

ORLEANS MA 02653

COAST GUARD MFG ID- ACJ See inside cover to adjust price for area

For more recent years, see the BUC Used Boat Price Guide, Volume 1

LOA FT	IN	NAME AND/ OR MODEL	TOP/ RIG	BOAT TYPE	-HULL- MTL	TP	ENGINE TP	# HP	MFG	BEAM FT	IN	WGT LBS	DRAFT FT	IN	RETAIL LOW	RETAIL HIGH
		1996 BOATS														
24	9	NAUSET 25 SPT CONV		CNV	FBG	DS	IB	225	CHRY	10		4000	2		30000	33300
28		NAUSET 28 BRIDGEDECK		CBNCR	FBG	DS	IB	260	CHRY	10	8		2	9	59700	65600
28		NAUSET 28 BRIDGEDECK		CBNCR	FBG	DS	IB	310D		10	8		2	9	77700	85400
28		NAUSET 28 EXPRESS		CNV	FBG	DS	IB	260		10	8		2	9	56600	62200
28		NAUSET 28 EXPRESS		CNV	FBG	DS	IB	310D		10	8		2	9	86100	94700
28		NAUSET 28 HARDTOP	HT	CBNCR	FBG	DS	IB	260		10	8		2	9	59700	65600
28		NAUSET 28 HARDTOP	HT	CBNCR	FBG	DS	IB	310D		10	8		2	9	77700	85400
36		NAUSET 36 SDN CR		SDN	FBG	DS	IB	340		12	6		3	2	121000	133000
		IB 300D 148000 162500, IB 375D 152000 167000, IB 425D													155000	170500
		1995 BOATS														
24	9	NAUSET 25 SPT CONV		CNV	FBG	DS	IB	225	CHRY	10		4000	2		28200	31300
28		NAUSET 28 BRIDGEDECK		CBNCR	FBG	DS	IB	260	CHRY	10	8		2	9	56400	62000
28		NAUSET 28 BRIDGEDECK		CBNCR	FBG	DS	IB	310D		10	8		2	9	73700	81000
28		NAUSET 28 EXPRESS		CNV	FBG	DS	IB	260		10	8		2	9	53500	58800
28		NAUSET 28 EXPRESS		CNV	FBG	DS	IB	310D		10	8		2	9	81800	89900
28		NAUSET 28 HARDTOP	HT	CBNCR	FBG	DS	IB	260		10	8		2	9	56500	62000
28		NAUSET 28 HARDTOP	HT	CBNCR	FBG	DS	IB	310D		10	8		2	9	73700	81000
35		NAUSET 35 SPT CR		SPTCR	FBG	DS	IB	340		12			3		104000	114000
35		NAUSET 35 SPT CR		SPTCR	FBG	DS	IB	300D		12			3		106500	117000
36		NAUSET 36 SDN CR		SDN	FBG	DS	IB	340		12	6		3	2	116000	127500
		IB 300D 141500 155500, IB 375D 145500 160000, IB 425D													148500	163000
		1994 BOATS														
18	6	ISLANDER 18	OP	CTRCN	FBG	SV	OB			8		1200		10	5300	6100
21	4	NAUSET 21		CTRCN	FBG	SV	OB			8		1700	1	2	8200	9450
21	4	NAUSET 21		CUD	FBG	SV	OB			8		2100	1	2	9750	11100
24	9	NAUSET 25		CNV	FBG	SV	IB	260	MRCR	10		4000	2		27200	30200
28		NAUSET 28		CR	FBG	SV	IB	260	MRCR	10	6	9600	2	10	47800	52500
35		NAUSET 35	FB	CR	FBG	SV	IB	340		12		14500	3		100500	110500
35		NAUSET 35	FB	CR	FBG	SV	IB	T340		12		17000	3		114500	126000
36		NAUSET 36		CBNCR	FBG	SV	IB	340	MRCR	12	6	18000	3	2	118000	129500
42	3	NAUSET 42		CBNCR	FBG	SV	IB			14		22000	3	10	**	**
		1993 BOATS														
18	2	AMERICA	CAT	SACAC	FBG	CB	OB			8		2500	1	10	11400	12900
18	2	AMERICA	CAT	SACAC	FBG	CB	IB	7D		8		2500	1	10	15800	18000
22		NAUSET 22		CTRCN	FBG	SV	OB			7	6	2000			7350	8450
22		NAUSET 22		CUD	FBG	SV	OB			7	6	2000			9300	10600
24	9	NAUSET 249		CNV	FBG	SV	IB	250D	CUM	10		4000	2		36900	41000
28		NAUSET 28		CR	FBG	SV	IB	260	MRCR	10	6	9600	2	10	44800	49800
36		NAUSET 36		CBNCR	FBG	SV	IB	340	MRCR	12	6	18000	3	2	112500	123500
42	3	NAUSET 42		CBNCR	FBG	SV	IB			14		19340	4		**	**
		1992 BOATS														
18	2	AMERICA	CAT	SAIL	FBG	CB	OB			8		2500	1	10	10700	12100
18	2	AMERICA	CAT	SAIL	FBG	CB	IB	7D		8		2500			14900	16900
18	2	HARBOR PILOT		UTL	FBG	SV	IB	15D	YAMA	8		2200	1	10	10900	12400
22		NAUSET 22		CTRCN	FBG	SV	OB			7	6	2000			7100	8150
22		NAUSET 22		CUD	FBG	SV	OB			7	6	2000			8950	10200
24	9	NAUSET 249		CNV	FBG	SV	IB	260	MRCR	10		4000	2		24500	27200
24	9	NAUSET 249		CNV	FBG	SV	IB	250D	CUM	10		4000	2		35200	39100
28		NAUSET 28		CBNCR	FBG	SV	IB	260	MRCR	10	6	9600	2	10	48000	52700
35		NAUSET 35		CBNCR	FBG	SV	IB	340	MRCR	12		14500	3		96400	106000
36		NAUSET 36		CBNCR	FBG	SV	IB	340	MRCR	12	6	18000	3	2	107000	117500
42	3	NAUSET 42		CBNCR	FBG	SV	IB			14		19340	4		**	**
		1986 BOATS														
18		PILOT 18 CLUB		UTL	FBG	DS	IB	46D		8		2500			9900	11200
18		SEA-OTTER	OP	CTRCN	FBG	SV	IO	120-170		7	10	1800	1		5200	6050
18	2	AMERICA II	GAF	SA/CR	FBG	CB	OB			8		2500	1	10	7350	8450
18	2	AMERICA II	GAF	SA/CR	FBG	CB	SD		OMC	8		2500	1	10	8200	9450
18	2	AMERICA II	GAF	SA/CR	FBG	CB	IB	7D	YAN	8		2500	1	10	10400	11800
18	2	NAUSET CAT-KETCH	KTH	SA/OD	FBG	CB	OB			8		2000	1	10	6400	7350
18	2	NAUSET HBR PILOT	HT	PH	FBG	DS	IB	15D	YAN	8		2200	1	10	8350	9600
18	2	PILOT 18	OP	LNCH			IB	46D	WEST	8		2600	1	10	14700	16700
20	2	NAUSET 20	OP	CUD	FBG	SV	OB			8		2200	1		7000	8050
21	1	NAUSET 21 POACHER	SLP	SA/CR	FBG	CB	OB			7	6	1792	1		6400	7400
21	1	NAUSET 21 POACHER	KTH	SA/CR	FBG	CB	OB			7	6	1792	1		6400	7400
24		DOWNEASTER	GAF	SA/OD	FBG	CB	OB			8		2500	1	10	9100	10300
24		NAUSET 24	ST	CUD	FBG	SV	OB			9	6	4000	2		13800	15700
24		NAUSET 24	ST	CUD	FBG	SV	IB	165-260		9	6	4000	2		16100	18700
24		NAUSET 24	ST	CUD	FBG	SV	IB	85D-158D		9	6	4000	2		22000	24400
24		NAUSET 24 CTRCN	ST	CUD	FBG	SV	OB			9	6	4000	2		13000	14800
24		NAUSET 24 CTRCN	ST	CUD	FBG	SV	SE	170		9	6	4000	2		13400	15300
24		NAUSET 24 CTRCN	ST	CUD	FBG	SV	IO	185	MRCR	9	6	4000	2		12600	14300
24		NAUSET 24 CTRCN	ST	CUD	FBG	SV	IB	230-340		9	6	4000	2		15700	18900
24		NAUSET 24 CTRCN	ST	CUD	FBG	SV	IB	85D-215D		9	6	4000	2		21200	26200
24		NAUSET 24 WORKBOAT	OP	FSH	FBG	SV	IB	165-260		9	6		2		16100	18300
24		NAUSET 24 WORKBOAT	OP	FSH	FBG	SV	IB	85D-165D		9	6		2		23800	27700
24		NAUSET 24 WORKBOAT	HT	FSH	FBG	SV	IB	165-260		9	6		2		16100	18300
24		NAUSET 24 WORKBOAT	HT	FSH	FBG	SV	IB	85D-165D		9	6		2		23800	27700
24		NAUSET 24 WORKBOAT	FB	FSH	FBG	SV	IB	165-260		9	6		2		16100	18300
24		NAUSET 24 WORKBOAT	FB	FSH	FBG	SV	IB	85D-165D		9	6		2		23800	27700
24	1	NAUSET 24	OP	LNCH	FBG	SV	IB	165		9	6		2		18200	20200
24	1	NAUSET 24	OP	LNCH	FBG	SV	IB	80D		9	6		2		22600	25100
25	7	NAUSET 26S SHOAL	SLP	SA/CR	FBG	KL	OB			8		5700	2	3	19100	21200
25	7	NAUSET 26S SHOAL	SLP	SA/CR	FBG	KL	SD	15	OMC	8		5700	2	3	19800	22000
25	7	NAUSET 26S SHOAL	SLP	SA/CR	FBG	KL	IB	8D	YAN	8		5700	2	3	20400	22700
25	7	NAUSET 26S SWING	SLP	SA/CR	FBG	SK	OB			8		5700	1	8	22500	25000
25	7	NAUSET 26S SWING	SLP	SA/CR	FBG	SK	SD	15	OMC	8		5700	1	8	22900	25500
25	7	NAUSET 26S SWING	SLP	SA/CR	FBG	SK	IB	8D	YAN	8		5700	1	8	23500	26100
27	6	NAUSET 27	HT	CBNCR	FBG	DS	IB	230-260		9	10		3		37300	42200
27	6	NAUSET 27	HT	CBNCR	FBG	DS	IB	124D-165D		9	10		3		40100	47500
27	6	NAUSET 27	FB	CBNCR	FBG	DS	IB	230-260		9	10		3		37300	42200
27	6	NAUSET 27	FB	CBNCR	FBG	DS	IB	124D-165D		9	10		3		40100	47500
27	6	NAUSET 27 WORKBOAT	ST	FSH	FBG	DS	IB	165-260		9	10		3		33000	38000
27	6	NAUSET 27 WORKBOAT	ST	FSH	FBG	DS	IB	85D-165D		9	10		3		30500	36800
30		NAUSET 30	ST	SPTCR	FBG	DS	IB	230-260		10	4		2	6	32600	36800
30		NAUSET 30	ST	SPTCR	FBG	DS	IB	124D-215D		10	4		2	6	43500	48900
30		NAUSET 30	HT	SPTCR	FBG	DS	IB	230-260		10	4		2	6	32600	36800
30		NAUSET 30	HT	SPTCR	FBG	DS	IB	124D-215D		10	4		2	6	43500	48900
35		NAUSET 35	HT	CBNCR	FBG	DS	IB	260	MRCR	12		14000	2	10	69100	76000
		IB 340 MRCR 71000 78100, IB 210D CAT 83500 91700, IB 215D GM													83300	91500
		IB 235D VLVO 83600 91900, IB 240D PERK 84700 93100, IB 275D CAT													86300	94800
		IB T230 MRCR 77000 84700, IB T340 MRCR 81100 89100, IB T165D VLVO													93600	103000

CONTINUED ON NEXT PAGE

LOA FT	LOA IN	NAME AND/ OR MODEL	TOP/ RIG	BOAT TYPE	HULL MTL	HULL TP	ENGINE TP	# HP	MFG	BEAM FT	BEAM IN	WGT LBS	DRAFT FT	DRAFT IN	RETAIL LOW	RETAIL HIGH
		1986 BOATS														
35		NAUSET 35	HT	CBNCR	FBG	DS	IB	T200D	PERK	12		14000	2	10	92800	102000
35		NAUSET 35	HT	CBNCR	FBG	DS	IB	T215D	GM	12		16000	2	10	98200	108000
35		NAUSET 35	FB	CBNCR	FBG	DS	IB	260	MRCR	12			2	10	70800	77800
		IB 340 MRCR 72500 79700, IB 210D CAT 87100 95700, IB 215D GM 86900 95500														
		IB 235D VLVO 87200 95800, IB 240D PERK 88300 97000, IB 275D CAT 89700 98600														
		IB T230 MRCR 75000 82400, IB T340 MRCR 79100 86900, IB T165D VLVO 91800 101000														
		IB T200D PERK 96100 105500, IB T215D GM 96500 106000														
35		NAUSET 35 CHART/SPRT	HT	FSH	FBG	DS	IB	230	VLVO	11	11	14000	2	10	65200	71700
		IB 260 MRCR 65500 71900, IB 340 MRCR 66700 73300, IB 135D PERK 78500 86300														
		IB 140D GM 78000 85700, IB 165D PERK 77800 85500, IB 175D GM 77300 84900														
		IB 200D PERK 77300 85000, IB 210D CAT 77200 84900, IB 215D GM 76800 84400														
		IB 235D VLVO 76300 83800, IB 240D PERK 77200 84800, IB 275D CAT 78100 85800														
35		NAUSET 35 WORKBOAT	HT	FSH	FBG	DS	IB	230	MRCR	11	10	12000	2	11	61500	67600
		IB 260 MRCR 62000 68100, IB 340 MRCR 63200 69500, IB 135D PERK 71600 78700														
		IB 140D GM 71100 78200, IB 165D PERK 71000 78000, IB 200D PERK 70600 77600														
		IB 210D CAT 70600 77600, IB 210D GM 70200 77200, IB 215D GM 70300 77300														
		IB 235D VLVO 70400 77400, IB 240D PERK 71400 78500, IB 275D CAT 72400 79600														
		1985 BOATS														
18		SEA-OTTER	OP	CTRCN	FBG	SV	IO	120-170		7	10	1800	1		5000	5800
18	2	NAUSET AMERICA II	GAF	SA/CR	FBG	CB	OB			8		2500	1	10	6900	7950
18	2	NAUSET AMERICA II	GAF	SA/CR	FBG	CB	SD		OMC	8		2500	1	10	7700	8900
18	2	NAUSET AMERICA II	GAF	SA/CR	FBG	CB	IB	8D	YAN	8		2500	1	10	9850	11200
18	2	NAUSET CAT-KETCH	KTH	SA/OD	FBG	CB	OB			8		2000	1	10	6050	6950
18	2	NAUSET HBR PILOT	HT	PH	FBG	DS	IB	15D- 30D		8		2200	1	10	8000	9850
18	2	NAUSET HBR PILOT	HT	PH	FBG	DS	IB	45D	BMW	8		2200	1	10	9100	10300
18	2	PILOT 18	OP	LNCH			IB	45D	BMW	8		2600	1	10	13900	15700
20	2	NAUSET 20	OP	CUD	FBG	SV	OB			8		2200	1		6800	7800
24		DOWNEASTER	GAF	SA/OD	FBG	CB	OB			8		2500	1	10	8450	9700
24		DOWNEASTER	GAF	SA/OD	FBG	CB	IB	8D	YAN	8		2500	1	10	9850	11200
24		NAUSET 24	ST	CUD	FBG	SV	OB			9	6	4000	2		13100	14800
24		NAUSET 24	ST	CUD	FBG	SV	IB	165	CRUS	9	6	4000	2		15400	17500
		IO 170 14300 16200, IB 170-260 15200 17500, IB 85D-158D 20700 23000														
24		NAUSET 24 WORKBOAT	OP	FSH	FBG	SV	IB	165-260		9	6		2		15400	17500
24		NAUSET 24 WORKBOAT	OP	FSH	FBG	SV	IB	85D-165D		9	6		2		22800	26600
24		NAUSET 24 WORKBOAT	HT	FSH	FBG	SV	IB	165-260		9	6		2		15400	17500
24		NAUSET 24 WORKBOAT	HT	FSH	FBG	SV	IB	85D-165D		9	6		2		22800	26600
24		NAUSET 24 WORKBOAT	FB	FSH	FBG	SV	IB	165-260		9	6		2		15400	17500
24		NAUSET 24 WORKBOAT	FB	FSH	FBG	SV	IB	85D-165D		9	6		2		22800	26600
25	7	NAUSET 26AC SHOAL	SLP	SA/CR	FBG	KL	OB			8		5700	2	3	18100	20100
25	7	NAUSET 26AC SHOAL	SLP	SA/CR	FBG	KL	SD	15	OMC	8		5700	2	3	18800	20900
25	7	NAUSET 26AC SHOAL	SLP	SA/CR	FBG	KL	IB	8D	YAN	8		5700	2	3	19200	21400
25	7	NAUSET 26AC SWING	SLP	SA/CR	FBG	SK	OB			8		5700	1	8	21200	23600
25	7	NAUSET 26AC SWING	SLP	SA/CR	FBG	SK	SD	15	OMC	8		5700	1	8	21500	23900
25	7	NAUSET 26AC SWING	SLP	SA/CR	FBG	SK	IB	8D	YAN	8		5700	1	8	22100	24500
27	6	NAUSET 27	HT	CBNCR	FBG	DS	IB	165-260		9	10		3		34200	40300
27	6	NAUSET 27	HT	CBNCR	FBG	DS	IB	124D-165D		9	10		3		38500	45600
27	6	NAUSET 27	FB	CBNCR	FBG	DS	IB	165-260		9	10		3		34200	40300
27	6	NAUSET 27	FB	CBNCR	FBG	DS	IB	124D-165D		9	10		3		38500	45600
30		NAUSET 30	ST	SPTCR	FBG	DS	IB	230-260		10	4		2	6	31200	35100
30		NAUSET 30	ST	SPTCR	FBG	DS	IB	124D-158D		10	4		2	6	41700	46300
30		NAUSET 30	HT	SPTCR	FBG	DS	IB	230-260		10	4		2	6	31200	35100
30		NAUSET 30	HT	SPTCR	FBG	DS	IB	124D-158D		10	4		2	6	41700	46300
35		NAUSET 35	HT	CBNCR	FBG	DS	IB	260	MRCR	12		14000	2	10	66000	72500
		IB 340 MRCR 67800 74500, IB 200D PERK 79700 87600, IB 210D CAT 80100 88000														
		IB 215D GM 79900 87800, IB 235D VLVO 80200 88200, IB 240D PERK 81300 89300														
		IB 300D CAT 83900 92200, IB T230 MRCR 73600 80800, IB T340 MRCR 77500 85100														
		IB T165D VLVO 89800 98700, IB T215D GM 94200 103500														
35		NAUSET 35	FB	CBNCR	FBG	DS	IB	260	MRCR	12			2	10	67600	74300
		IB 340 MRCR 69300 76100, IB 200D PERK 83200 91400, IB 210D CAT 83600 91800														
		IB 215D GM 83300 91600, IB 235D VLVO 83700 91900, IB 240D PERK 84700 93100														
		IB 300D CAT 87100 95800, IB T230 MRCR 71700 78700, IB T340 MRCR 75500 83000														
		IB T165D VLVO 88000 96700, IB T215D GM 92500 101500														
35		NAUSET 35 WORKBOAT	HT	FSH	FBG	DS	IB	230	MRCR	11	10	12000	2	11	58700	64600
		IB 260 MRCR 59200 65000, IB 340 MRCR 60400 66400, IB 135D PERK 68700 75500														
		IB 165D PERK 68100 74800, IB 200D PERK 67700 74400, IB 210D CAT 67800 74500														
		IB 235D VLVO 67500 74200, IB 240D PERK 68500 75300, IB 275D CAT 69500 76400														
		1984 BOATS														
18		SEA-OTTER	OP	CTRCN	FBG	SV	IO	120-170		7	10	1800	1		4850	5600
18	2	NAUSET AMERICA II	GAF	SA/CR	FBG	CB	OB			8		2500	1	10	6500	7500
18	2	NAUSET AMERICA II	GAF	SA/CR	FBG	CB	SD		OMC	8		2500	1	10	7250	8350
18	2	NAUSET AMERICA II	GAF	SA/CR	FBG	CB	IB	7D	YAN	8		2500	1	10	9250	10500
18	2	NAUSET BAY FISH	OP	FSH	FBG	DS	IB	15D	YAN	8		2100	1	10	7550	8700
18	2	NAUSET BAY FISH	OP	FSH	FBG	DS	IB	35D- 45D		8		2100	1	10	8200	9750
18	2	NAUSET CAT-KETCH	KTH	SA/OD	FBG	CB	OB			8		2000	1	10	5700	6500
18	2	NAUSET HBR PILOT	HT	PH	FBG	DS	IB	15D- 35D		8		2200	1	10	7700	9600
18	2	NAUSET HBR PILOT	HT	PH	FBG	DS	IB	45D	BMW	8		2200	1	10	8650	9950
20	2	NAUSET 20	OP	CUD	FBG	SV	OB			8		2200	1		6650	7600
21	1	NAUSET 21CK	KTH	SA/CR	FBG	CB	OB			7	6	1792	1		5700	6550
21	1	NAUSET 21SL	SLP	SA/CR	FBG	CB	OB			7	6	1792	1		5700	6550
24		DOWNEASTER	GAF	SA/OD	FBG	CB	OB			8		2500	1	10	7950	9150
24		NAUSET 24	ST	CUD	FBG	SV	IB	165-260		9	6	4000	2		14700	16900
24		NAUSET 24	ST	CUD	FBG	SV	IB	50D-158D		9	6	4000	2		18600	21900
24		NAUSET 24	OP	FSH	FBG	SV	IB	165-230		9	6		2		14700	16900
24		NAUSET 24	OP	FSH	FBG	SV	IB	85D-158D		9	6		2		21900	25500
24		NAUSET 24	HT	FSH	FBG	SV	IB	165-230		9	6		2		14700	16900
24		NAUSET 24	HT	FSH	FBG	SV	IB	85D-158D		9	6		2		21900	25500
25	7	NAUSET 26AC	SLP	SA/CR	FBG	CB	OB			8		5700	1	8	18600	20700
25	7	NAUSET 26AC	SLP	SA/CR	FBG	CB	IB		OMC	8		5700	1	8	19000	21100
25	7	NAUSET 26AC	SLP	SA/CR	FBG	CB	IB	7D	YAN	8		5700	1	8	19400	21500
27	6	NAUSET 27	HT	CBNCR	FBG	DS	IB	165-260		9	10		3		32700	38500
27	6	NAUSET 27	HT	CBNCR	FBG	DS	IB	124D-158D		9	10		3		37000	43300
27	6	NAUSET 27	FB	CBNCR	FBG	DS	IB	165-260		9	10		3		32700	38500
27	6	NAUSET 27	FB	CBNCR	FBG	DS	IB	124D-158D		9	10		3		37000	43300
27	6	NAUSET 27	ST	FSH	FBG	DS	IB	170-340		9	10		3		30100	35800
27	6	NAUSET 27	ST	FSH	FBG	DS	IB	85D-165D		9	10		3		28100	34800
27	6	NAUSET 27	ST	FSH	FBG	DS	IB	200D-210D		9	10		3		32600	36600
30		NAUSET 30	ST	SPTCR	FBG	DS	IB	165-260		10	4		2	6	28800	33600
30		NAUSET 30	ST	SPTCR	FBG	DS	IB	85D-158D		10	4		2	6	38000	44500
30		NAUSET 30	HT	SPTCR	FBG	DS	IB	165-260		10	4		2	6	28800	33600
30		NAUSET 30	HT	SPTCR	FBG	DS	IB	85D-158D		10	4		2	6	38000	44500
35		NAUSET 35	HT	CBNCR	FBG	DS	IB	230	MRCR	11	11		2	10	64200	70500
		IB 260 MRCR 64800 71200, IB 340 MRCR 66300 72900, IB 135D PERK 78000 85700														
		IB 165D PERK 78900 86700, IB 200D PERK 80000 87900, IB 210D CAT 80300 88300														
		IB 225D CRUS 80400 88400, IB 235D VLVO 80400 88400, IB 275D CAT 82700 90900														
		IB 350D PERK 85900 94400														
35		NAUSET 35	FB	CBNCR	FBG	DS	IB	230	MRCR	11	11		2	10	64200	70600
		IB 260 MRCR 64800 71200, IB 340 MRCR 66300 72900, IB 135D PERK 78000 85700														
		IB 165D PERK 78900 86700, IB 200D PERK 80000 87900, IB 210D CAT 80300 88300														
		IB 225D CRUS 80500 88400, IB 235D VLVO 80400 88400, IB 275D CAT 82800 90900														
		IB 350D PERK 85900 94400														
35		NAUSET 35	HT	FSH	FBG	DS	IB	230	MRCR	11	11		2	10	56900	62500
		IB 260 MRCR 56900 62500, IB 340 MRCR 57600 63400, IB 135D PERK 63500 69800														
		IB 140D GM 63100 69300, IB 165D PERK 63000 69200, IB 200D PERK 62700 68900														
		IB 210D CAT 62600 68800, IB 210D GM 62200 68400, IB 215D GM 62200 68400														
		IB 225D CRUS 62200 68300, IB 235D VLVO 62000 68100, IB 240D PERK 62900 69100														
		IB 275D CAT 63700 70000, IB 286D VLVO 63100 69300														

....For earlier years, see the BUC Used Boat Price Guide, Volume 3

NAUTICAL DEVELOPMENT CORP

LARGO FL 33541 COAST GUARD MFG ID- NDV See inside cover to adjust price for area

LOA FT	LOA IN	NAME AND/ OR MODEL	TOP/ RIG	BOAT TYPE	HULL MTL	HULL TP	ENGINE TP	# HP	MFG	BEAM FT	BEAM IN	WGT LBS	DRAFT FT	DRAFT IN	RETAIL LOW	RETAIL HIGH
		1986 BOATS														
55	9	NAUTICAL 56	KTH	MS	FBG	KL	IB	135D	LEHM	15	7	51000	5	6	270000	296500
59	6	NAUTICAL 60	KTH	MS	FBG	KL	IB	135D	LEHM	15	7	52000	5	6	334500	367500
61	6	NAUTICAL 62	KTH	MS	FBG	KC	IB	135D	LEHM	15	7	55000	5	10	353500	388500
		1985 BOATS														
55	9	NAUTICAL 56	KTH	MS	FBG	KL	IB	135D	LEHM	15	7	51000	5	6	255500	281000
59	6	NAUTICAL 60	KTH	MS	FBG	KL	IB	135D	LEHM	15	7	52000	5	6	317000	348000
61	6	NAUTICAL 62	KTH	MS	FBG	KC	IB	135D	LEHM	15	7	55000	5	10	335000	368000
		1984 BOATS														
55	9	NAUTICAL 56	SLP	SA/CR	FBG	KL	IB	135D	LEHM	15	7	51000	5	6	241000	265000
55	9	NAUTICAL 56	CUT	SA/CR	FBG	KL	IB	135D	LEHM	15	7	51000	5	6	238500	262000
55	9	NAUTICAL 56	KTH	SA/CR	FBG	KL	IB	120D	LEHM	15	7	51000	5	6	242000	266000
55	9	NAUTICAL 56	KTH	SA/CR	FBG	KL	IB	135D	LEHM	15	7	51000	5	6	242000	266000
55	9	NAUTICAL CUSTOM 56	KTH	SA/CR	FBG	KL	IB	120D	LEHM	15	7	50000	5	6	241000	265000
59	6	NAUTICAL 60	SLP	SA/CR	FBG	KL	IB	135D	LEHM	15	7	52000	5	6	300000	330000
59	6	NAUTICAL 60	CUT	SA/CR	FBG	KL	IB	135D	LEHM	15	7	52000	5	6	300000	329500

 CONTINUED ON NEXT PAGE

LOA FT	LOA IN	NAME AND/ OR MODEL	TOP/ RIG	BOAT TYPE	-HULL- MTL	-HULL- TP	ENGINE TP	# HP	MFG	BEAM FT	BEAM IN	WGT LBS	DRAFT FT	DRAFT IN	RETAIL LOW	RETAIL HIGH
		1984 BOATS														
59	6	NAUTICAL 60	KTH	SA/CR	FBG	KL	IB	120D	LEHM	15	7	52000	5	6	300000	329500
59	6	NAUTICAL 60	KTH	SA/CR	FBG	KL	IB	135D	LEHM	15	7	52000	5	6	300500	330000
61	6	NAUTICAL 62	SLP	SA/CR	FBG	KC	IB	135D	LEHM	15	7	55000	5	10	317500	348500
61	6	NAUTICAL 62	CUT	SA/CR	FBG	KC	IB	135D	LEHM	15	7	55000	5	10	317500	348500
61	6	NAUTICAL 62	KTH	SA/CR	FBG	KC	IB	120D	LEHM	15	7	60000	5	11	333500	366000
61	6	NAUTICAL 62	KTH	SA/CR	FBG	KC	IB	135D	LEHM	15	7	55000	5	10	317500	349000
61	6	NAUTICAL 62	KTH	SA/CR	FBG	KC	IB	T 50D	LEHM	15	7	60000	5	11	334500	367500

....For earlier years, see the BUC Used Boat Price Guide, Volume 3

NAUTICAT YACHTS

RIIHIKOSKI FINLAND FIN- COAST GUARD MFG ID- SLT See inside cover to adjust price for area
ALSO SILTALA YACHTS

For more recent years, see the BUC Used Boat Price Guide, Volume 1

LOA FT	LOA IN	NAME AND/ OR MODEL	TOP/ RIG	BOAT TYPE	-HULL- MTL	-HULL- TP	ENGINE TP	# HP	MFG	BEAM FT	BEAM IN	WGT LBS	DRAFT FT	DRAFT IN	RETAIL LOW	RETAIL HIGH
		1996 BOATS														
32	1	NAUTICAT 32	SLP	MS	FBG	KL	IB	27D	YAN	10	5	12230	5	3	106500	117500
33	1	NAUTICAT 33/1.25	KTH	MS	FBG	KL	IB	88D	YAN	10	8	17650	4	1	152500	167500
33	1	NAUTICAT 33/1.55	KTH	MS	FBG	KL	IB	88D	YAN	10	8	18120	5	1	156000	171500
34	11	NAUTICAT 35/1.52	SLP	MS	FBG	KL	IB	50D	YAN	11	4	17650	4	11	154000	169000
34	11	NAUTICAT 35/1.70	SLP	MS	FBG	KL	IB	50D	YAN	11	4	17650	5	7	154000	169000
37	5	NAUTICAT 38	KTH	MS	FBG	KL	IB	110D	YAN	11		25880	5	11	222500	244500
38	10	NAUTICAT 39	SLP	MS	FBG	KL	IB	50D	YAN	11	6	18820	6		181000	198500
41	6	NAUTICAT 42	SLP	MS	FBG	KL	IB	110D	YAN	13	1	31760	6	4	283500	311500
42	7	NAUTICAT 43	KTH	MS	FBG	KL	IB	140D	YAN	13	9	35290	6	3	311500	342500
43	7	NAUTICAT 44	KTH	MS	FBG	KL	IB	140D	YAN	12	1	34120	5	11	316000	347000
50	8	NAUTICAT 515	KTH	MS	FBG	KL	IB	135D	PERK	15	1	48000	7	2	478000	525500
51	1	NAUTICAT 521	KTH	MS	FBG	KL	IB	135D	PERK	15	1	56470	7	2	511000	562000
		1995 BOATS														
32		NAUTICAT 32	SLP	MS	FBG	KL	IB	D	YAN	10	4		5	3	101000	111000
33	2	NAUTICAT 33	KTH	MS	FBG	KL	IB	110D		10	8	16500	4	1	135500	153500
34	11	NAUTICAT 35	SLP	MS	FBG	KL	IB	50D	YAN	11	4	16500	5	7	137000	150500
37	6	NAUTICAT 38	KTH	MS	FBG	KL	IB	110D	YAN	11	2	24200	5	11	200000	220000
39	5	NAUTICAT 39	SLP	MS	FBG	KL	IB	50D	YAN	11	7	15200	5	9	151500	166500
39	5	NAUTICAT 42	SLP	MS	FBG	KL	IB	110D	YAN	13	1	29800	6	3	245000	269000
42	8	NAUTICAT 43	KTH	MS	FBG	KL	IB	110D	YAN	13	10	33080	6	3	284000	312500
43	8	NAUTICAT 44	KTH	MS	FBG	KL	IB	150D	YAN	12	2	32000	6	3	290500	319500
51	2	NAUTICAT 521	KTH	MS	FBG	KL	IB	150D	YAN	15	1	56470	7	3	489000	537500
		1994 BOATS														
32		NAUTICAT 32	SLP	MS	FBG	KL	IB	D	YAN	10	4		5	3	95700	105000
33	2	NAUTICAT 33	KTH	MS	FBG	KL	IB	110D		10	8	16500	4	1	128500	145000
34	11	NAUTICAT 35	SLP	MS	FBG	KL	IB	50D	YAN	11	4	16500	5	7	130000	142500
37	6	NAUTICAT 38	KTH	MS	FBG	KL	IB	110D	VLVO	11	2	24200	5	11	189500	208000
39	5	NAUTICAT 39	SLP	MS	FBG	KL	IB	50D	YAN	11	7	15200	5	9	143500	157500
39	5	NAUTICAT 42	SLP	MS	FBG	KL	IB	110D	VLVO	13	1	29800	6	3	231500	254500
42	8	NAUTICAT 43	KTH	MS	FBG	KL	IB	110D	VLVO	13	10	33080	6	3	268500	295000
43	8	NAUTICAT 44	KTH	MS	FBG	KL	IB	150D	VLVO	12	2	32000	6	3	275000	302000
51	2	NAUTICAT 521	KTH	MS	FBG	KL	IB	150D	VLVO	15	1	52900	7	3	454500	499500
		1993 BOATS														
33	2	NAUTICAT 33	KTH	MS	FBG	KL	IB	90D		10	8	16500	4	1	121500	137500
34	11	NAUTICAT 35	SLP	MS	FBG	KL	IB	43D	VLVO	11	4	16500	5	7	123000	135000
37	6	NAUTICAT 38	KTH	MS	FBG	KL	IB	90D	LEHM	11	2	24200	5	11	178500	196500
39	5	NAUTICAT 39	KTH	MS	FBG	KL	IB	50D	YAN	11	7	15200	5	9	136000	149500
39	5	NAUTICAT 40	KTH	MS	FBG	KL	IB	90D	LEHM	13	1	29800	5	9	218500	240000
42	8	NAUTICAT 43	KTH	MS	FBG	KL	IB	90D	LEHM	13	10	33080	6	3	253500	278500
43	8	NAUTICAT 44	KTH	MS	FBG	KL	IB	135D	LEHM	12	2	32000	6	3	259500	285500
51	2	NAUTICAT 521	KTH	MS	FBG	KL	IB	135D	LEHM	15	1	52900	7	3	429500	472000
		1990 BOATS														
33	2	NAUTICAT 33	KTH	MS	FBG	KL	IB	90D		10	8	16500	4	1	103500	116500
34	11	NAUTICAT 35	SLP	MS	FBG	KL	IB	43D	VLVO	11	4	16500	5	7	104500	114500
37	6	NAUTICAT 38	KTH	MS	FBG	KL	IB	90D	LEHM	11	2	24200	5	11	152000	167000
39	5	NAUTICAT 40	KTH	MS	FBG	KL	IB	90D	LEHM	13	1	29800	5	9	185500	204000
42	8	NAUTICAT 43	KTH	MS	FBG	KL	IB	90D	LEHM	13	10	33080	6	3	215500	237000
43	8	NAUTICAT 44	KTH	MS	FBG	KL	IB	135D	LEHM	12	2	32000	6	3	220500	242500
51	2	NAUTICAT 521	KTH	MS	FBG	KL	IB	135D	LEHM	15	1	52900	7	3	365000	401500
		1989 BOATS														
33	2	NAUTICAT 33	KTH	MS	FBG	KL	IB	90D		10	8	16500	4	1	97800	110500
34	11	NAUTICAT 35	SLP	MS	FBG	KL	IB	43D	VLVO	11	4	16500	5	7	98900	108500
37	6	NAUTICAT 38	KTH	MS	FBG	KL	IB	90D	LEHM	11	2	24200	5	11	144000	158000
39	5	NAUTICAT 40	KTH	MS	FBG	KL	IB	90D	LEHM	13	1	29800	5	9	176000	193000
42	8	NAUTICAT 43	KTH	MS	FBG	KL	IB	90D	LEHM	13	10	33080	6	3	204000	224500
43	8	NAUTICAT 44	KTH	MS	FBG	KL	IB	135D	LEHM	12	2	32000	6	3	209000	230000
51	2	NAUTICAT 521	KTH	MS	FBG	KL	IB	135D	LEHM	15	1	52900	7	3	346000	380000
		1988 BOATS														
33	2	NAUTICAT 33	KTH	MS	FBG	KL	IB	90D		10	8	16500	4	1	92700	105000
34	11	NAUTICAT 35	SLP	MS	FBG	KL	IB	43D	VLVO	11	4	16500	5	7	93700	103000
37	6	NAUTICAT 38	KTH	MS	FBG	KL	IB	90D	LEHM	11	2	24200	5	11	136500	150000
39	5	NAUTICAT 40	KTH	MS	FBG	KL	IB	90D	LEHM	13	1	29800	5	9	166500	183000
42	8	NAUTICAT 43	KTH	MS	FBG	KL	IB	90D	LEHM	13	10	33080	6	3	193500	212500
43	8	NAUTICAT 44	KTH	MS	FBG	KL	IB	135D	LEHM	12	2	32000	6	3	198000	217500
51	2	NAUTICAT 521	KTH	MS	FBG	KL	IB	135D	LEHM	15	1	52900	7	3	328000	360000
		1987 BOATS														
33	2	NAUTICAT 33	KTH	MS	FBG	KL	IB	90D		10	8	16980	4	1	90200	99200
34	11	NAUTICAT 35	SLP	MS	FBG	KL	IB	43D		11	4		4	11	94300	103500
35	5	NAUTICAT 36	KTH	MS	FBG	KL	IB	90D	LEHM	10	10	17640	4	11	95500	105000
35	5	NAUTICAT 36	KTH	MS	FBG	KL	IB	90D	LEHM	10	10	17640	5	3	95500	105000
37	6	NAUTICAT 38	KTH	MS	FBG	KL	IB	90D	LEHM	11	2	24260	5	11	129500	142000
39	5	NAUTICAT 40	KTH	MS	FBG	KL	IB	90D	LEHM	12	2	29770	5	9	158000	173500
42	8	NAUTICAT 43	KTH	MS	FBG	KL	IB	90D	LEHM	13	2	33075	6	3	183500	201500
43	8	NAUTICAT 44	KTH	MS	FBG	KL	IB	135D	LEHM	13	9	31980	6	3	187500	206000
51	2	NAUTICAT 52	KTH	MS	FBG	KL	IB	135D	LEHM	15	1	52920	7	3	310500	341500
		1986 BOATS														
33	2	NAUTICAT 33	KTH	MS	FBG	KL	IB	90D		10	8	16980	4	1	85500	94000
35	5	NAUTICAT 36	KTH	MS	FBG	KL	IB	90D	LEHM	10	10	17640	4	11	90500	99400
35	5	NAUTICAT 36	KTH	MS	FBG	KL	IB	90D	LEHM	10	10	17640	5	3	90500	99400
37	6	NAUTICAT 38	KTH	MS	FBG	KL	IB	90D	LEHM	11	2	24260	5	11	122500	135000
39	5	NAUTICAT 40	KTH	MS	FBG	KL	IB	90D	LEHM	12	2	29770	5	9	149500	164500
42	8	NAUTICAT 43	KTH	MS	FBG	KL	IB	90D	LEHM	13	2	33075	6	3	173500	191000
43	8	NAUTICAT 44	KTH	MS	FBG	KL	IB	135D	LEHM	13	9	31980	6	3	178000	195500
51	2	NAUTICAT 52	KTH	MS	FBG	KL	IB	135D	LEHM	15	1	52920	7	3	294500	323500
		1985 BOATS														
33	1	NAUTICAT 33	KTH	MS	FBG	KL	IB	80D	FORD	10	6	15430	5	3	74000	81300
35	6	NAUTICAT 36	KTH	MS	FBG	KL	IB	85D	PERK	10	9	17640	5	3	85500	93900
42	8	MAUTICAT 43	KTH	MS	FBG	KL	IB	80D	FORD	13	10	35270	6	3	170500	187000
43	4	NAUTICAT 44	KTH	MS	FBG	KL	IB	120D	FORD	12	1	37480	5	11	180500	198500
51	2	NAUTICAT 52	CUT	SA/CR	FBG	KC	IB	80D	FORD	15		59520	7	3	287000	315500
51	2	NAUTICAT 52	YWL	SA/CR	FBG	KC	IB	120D	FORD	15		59520	7	3	288000	316500
		1984 BOATS														
33		NAUTICAT 33	KTH	SAIL	FBG	KL	IB	80D	FORD	10	8	15200	5	8	69100	75900
36		NAUTICAT 36	KTH	SAIL	FBG	KL	IB	85D	FORD	10	9	16000	5	3	75500	82900
38		NAUTICAT 38	KTH	SAIL	FBG	KL	IB	80D	FORD	11	2	24000	5	11	110500	121500
43		NAUTICAT 43	KTH	SAIL	FBG	KL	IB	80D	FORD	13	10	35280	6	3	163000	179500
44		NAUTICAT 44	KTH	SAIL	FBG	KL	IB	120D	FORD	12	1	39700	6		180000	198000
52		NAUTICAT 52	KTH	SAIL	FBG	KL	IB	120D	FORD	15		54000	7	2	277000	304500
52		NAUTICAT 52	KTH	SAIL	FBG	KL	IB	T 80D	FORD	15		54000	7	2	280000	307500

....For earlier years, see the BUC Used Boat Price Guide, Volume 3

NAUTIQUE YACHT

See inside cover to adjust price for area

LOA FT	LOA IN	NAME AND/ OR MODEL	TOP/ RIG	BOAT TYPE	-HULL- MTL	-HULL- TP	ENGINE TP	# HP	MFG	BEAM FT	BEAM IN	WGT LBS	DRAFT FT	DRAFT IN	RETAIL LOW	RETAIL HIGH
		1985 BOATS														
38	2	NAUTIQUE 38 SUNDECK	FB	TRWL	FBG	SV	IB	T210D	CAT	13	2	21000	3	9	88500	97200
38	2	NAUTIQUE 38 SUNDECK	FB	TRWL	FBG	SV	IB	T225D	LEHM	13	2	21000	3	9	87400	96100

NAUTOR AB

PIETARSAARI FINLAND FIN COAST GUARD MFG ID- NAJ See inside cover to adjust price for area

NAUTOR AB
PIETARSAARI FINDLAND 68601

LOA FT	LOA IN	NAME AND/ OR MODEL	TOP/ RIG	BOAT TYPE	-HULL- MTL	-HULL- TP	ENGINE TP	# HP	MFG	BEAM FT	BEAM IN	WGT LBS	DRAFT FT	DRAFT IN	RETAIL LOW	RETAIL HIGH
		1994 BOATS														
36	7	SWAN 36	SLP	SACAC	FBG	KL	IB	28D	VLVO	11	10	14800	6	9	160000	176000
40	2	SWAN 40	SLP	SACAC	FBG	KL	IB	35D	NANN	12	9	18100	7	1	218000	239500
43	10	SWAN 44	SLP	SACAC	FBG	KL	IB	50D	PERK	13	1	24500	8	2	300000	329500
47	2	SWAN 46	SLP	SACAC	FBG	KL	IB	53D	PERK	14	5	31300	8	9	384000	422000
52	7	SWAN 53	SLP	SACAC	FBG	KL	IB	87D	VLVO	15	5	44100	10	2	565000	621000
54	10	SWAN 55	SLP	SACAC	FBG	KL	IB	116D	PERK	15	9	52000	8	5	666500	732500
61	8	SWAN 60 C/R	SLP	SACAC	FBG	KL	IB	120D		17	5	63900	11	5	1.040M	1.130M
61	8	SWAN 60 R	SLP	SACAC	FBG	KL	IB	100D	YAN	17	5	51800	11	5	924000	1.005M
67	7	SWAN 68	SLP	SACAC	FBG	KL	IB	182D	PERK	17	8	88200	11	6	1.520M	1.650M
76	10	SWAN 77	SLP	SACAC	FBG	KL	IB	220D	PERK	19	6	56T	11	2	**	**
		1993 BOATS														
36	7	SWAN 36	SLP	SACAC	FBG	KL	IB	28D	VLVO	11	10	14800	6	9	151500	166500
43	10	SWAN 44	SLP	SACAC	FBG	KL	IB	50D	PERK	13	1	24500	8	2	284000	312000
47	2	SWAN 46	SLP	SACAC	FBG	KL	IB	53D	PERK	14	5	31300	8	9	364000	400000
52	7	SWAN 53	SLP	SACAC	FBG	KL	IB	87D	VLVO	15	5	44100	10	2	535000	588000

LOA FT	IN	NAME AND/ OR MODEL	TOP/ RIG	BOAT TYPE	-HULL- MTL	TP	----ENGINE--- TP	# HP	MFG	BEAM FT	IN	WGT LBS	DRAFT FT	IN	RETAIL LOW	RETAIL HIGH
		1993 BOATS														
54	10	SWAN 55	SLP	SACAC	FBG	KL	IB	116D	PERK	15	9	52000	8	5	631000	693500
58	8	SWAN 59	SLP	SACAC	FBG	KL	IB	87D	VLVO	16	4	60000	10	2	884500	972000
60	5	SWAN 61	SLP	SACAC	FBG	KL	IB	114D	VLVO	16	4	60000	9	8	931500	1.010M
67	7	SWAN 68	SLP	SACAC	FBG	KL	IB	182D	PERK	17	8	88200	11	6	1.435M	1.560M
76	10	SWAN 77	SLP	SACAC	FBG	KL	IB	220D	PERK	19	6	56T	11	2	**	**
		1992 BOATS														
36	7	SWAN 36	SLP	SA/CR	FBG	KL	IB	28D	VLVO	11	10	14800	6	9	143500	158000
43	10	SWAN 44	SLP	SA/CR	FBG	KL	IB	50D	PERK	13	1	24500	8	2	269000	295500
47	2	SWAN 46	SLP	SA/CR	FBG	KL	IB	53D	PERK	14	5	31300	8	9	344500	378500
52	7	SWAN 53	SLP	SA/CR	FBG	KL	IB	87D	VLVO	15	5	44100	10	2	507000	557000
54	10	SWAN 55	SLP	SA/CR	FBG	KL	IB	116D	PERK	15	9	52000	8	5	597500	656500
58	8	SWAN 59	SLP	SA/CR	FBG	KL	IB	87D	VLVO	16	4	60000	10	2	838000	920500
60	5	SWAN 61	SLP	SA/CR	FBG	KL	IB	114D	VLVO	16	4	60000	9	8	872500	959000
67	7	SWAN 68	SLP	SA/CR	FBG	KL	IB	182D	PERK	17	8	88200	11	6	1.360M	1.480M
76	10	SWAN 77	SLP	SA/CR	FBG	KL	IB	220D	PERK	19	6	56T	11	2	**	**
		1986 BOATS														
36	8	SWAN 371	SLP	SA/CR	FBG	KL	IB	20D	BUKH	11	3	16100	6	9	112000	123000
39	10	SWAN 391	SLP	SA/CR	FBG	KL	IB	40D	PERK	12	5	20000	7	4	149000	163500
41	10	SWAN 42	SLP	SA/CR	FBG	KL	IB	40D	PERK	13		24000	7	9	178000	195500
42	11	SWAN 43	SLP	SA/CR	FBG	KL	IB	45D	VLVO	13	1	23400	7	6	183500	201500
47	1	SWAN 46	SLP	SA/CR	FBG	KL	IB	58D	PERK	14	5	31300	8	2	248500	273000
47	1	SWAN 46	SLP	SA/RC	FBG	KL	IB	58D	PERK	14	5	31300	8	9	248500	273000
47	2	SWAN 46	SLP	SA/RC	FBG	KC	IB	58D	PERK	14	5	31300	5	6	249500	274000
47	8	SWAN 47	SLP	SA/CR	FBG	KC	SD	61D	VLVO	13	8	34100	5	9	264000	290000
47	8	SWAN 47	SLP	SA/CR	FBG	KL	SD	61D	VLVO	13	8	32400	7	8	258500	284500
51	3	SWAN 51	SLP	SA/CR	FBG	KC	IB	73D	PERK	14	7	41000	5	9	334500	367500
51	3	SWAN 51	SLP	SA/CR	FBG	KL	IB	73D	PERK	14	7	41900	8	9	334500	367500
57	5	SWAN 57	SLP	SA/CR	FBG	KC	IB	73D	PERK	15	9	51500	6	4	544000	598000
57	5	SWAN 57	SLP	SA/CR	FBG	KL	IB	73D	PERK	15	9	49500	9	1	535500	588500
57	5	SWAN 57	KTH	SA/CR	FBG	KC	IB	73D	PERK	15	9	51500	6	4	544000	598000
57	5	SWAN 57	KTH	SA/CR	FBG	KL	IB	73D	PERK	15	9	49500	9	1	535500	588500
58	8	SWAN 59	SLP	SA/CR	FBG	KC	IB	86D	VLVO	16	5	61000	7	2	611000	671500
58	10	SWAN 59	SLP	SA/RC	FBG	KL	IB	86D	VLVO	16	5	62400	11	2	621500	683000
60	6	SWAN 61	SLP	SA/CR	FBG	KC	IB	110D	VLVO	16	5	61000	7	2	638000	701000
60	6	SWAN 61	SLP	SA/CR	FBG	KL	IB	110D	VLVO	16	5	61000	9	8	638000	701000
64	6	SWAN 65	SLP	SA/CR	FBG	KL	IB	115D	PERK	16	3	70000	9	6	739500	812500
64	6	SWAN 65	KTH	SA/CR	FBG	KL	IB	115D	PERK	16	3	70000	9	6	739500	812500
65	6	SWAN 651	SLP	SA/CR	FBG	KC	IB	115D	PERK	17	5	79300	7	2	849500	933500
65	6	SWAN 651	SLP	SA/CR	FBG	KL	IB	115D	PERK	17	5	79300	11	5	849500	933500
65	6	SWAN 651	KTH	SA/CR	FBG	KC	IB	115D	PERK	17	5	79300	7	2	849500	933500
65	6	SWAN 651	KTH	SA/CR	FBG	KL	IB	115D	PERK	17	5	79300	11	5	849500	933500
76	3	SWAN 76	SLP	SA/CR	FBG	KC	IB	200D	BENZ	19		53T	7	8	**	**
76	3	SWAN 76	SLP	SA/CR	FBG	KL	IB	200D	BENZ	19		98700	12		**	**
76	3	SWAN 76	KTH	SA/CR	FBG	KC	IB	200D	BENZ	19		53T	7	8	**	**
76	3	SWAN 76	KTH	SA/CR	FBG	KL	IB	200D	BENZ	19		98700	12		**	**
		1985 BOATS														
36	8	SWAN 371	SLP	SA/RC	FBG	KL	IB	20D	BUKH	11	3	13700	6	6	92200	101500
39	10	SWAN 391	SLP	SA/CR	FBG	KL	IB	51D	PERK	12	5	18000	7	2	131500	144500
41	10	SWAN 42	SLP	SA/CR	FBG	KL	IB	51D	PERK	13		22000	7	9	160500	176500
42	11	SWAN 43	SLP	SA/CR	FBG	KL	IB	40D	VLVO	13	1	23370	7	7	173500	190500
42	11	SWAN 43	SLP	SA/RC	FBG	KL	IB	40D	VLVO	13	1	23370	7	7	173500	190500
47	1	SWAN 46	SLP	SA/RC	FBG	KC	IB	62D	PERK	14	6	31300	5	6	235500	259000
47	1	SWAN 46	SLP	SA/RC	FBG	KL	IB	62D	PERK	14	6	27700	8	2	224500	246500
47	9	SWAN 47	SLP	SA/RC	FBG	KC	SD	61D	VLVO	13	9	34100	5	9	250500	275500
47	9	SWAN 47	SLP	SA/RC	FBG	KL	SD	61D	VLVO	13	9	32400	7	9	246000	270000
51	3	SWAN 51	SLP	SA/RC	FBG	KC	IB	85D	PERK	14	7	39600	5	11	312500	343500
51	3	SWAN 51	SLP	SA/RC	FBG	KL	IB	85D	PERK	14	7	39600	8	9	312500	343500
57	5	SWAN 57	SLP	SA/RC	FBG	KC	IB	85D	PERK	15	9	51500	6	4	516000	567000
57	5	SWAN 57	SLP	SA/RC	FBG	KL	IB	85D	PERK	15	9	47600	9	1	500000	549500
57	5	SWAN 57	KTH	SA/RC	FBG	KC	IB	85D	PERK	15	9	51500	6	4	516000	567000
57	5	SWAN 57	KTH	SA/RC	FBG	KL	IB	85D	PERK	15	9	47600	9	1	500000	549500
58	10	SWAN 59	SLP	SA/CR	FBG	KC	IB	92D	VLVO	16	5	60000	7	2	576500	633500
58	10	SWAN 59	SLP	SA/RC	FBG	KL	IB	92D	VLVO	16	5	62400	11	2	589000	647500
60	6	SWAN 61	SLP	SA/CR	FBG	KC	IB	105D	VLVO	16	5	61000	7	2	604500	664000
60	6	SWAN 61	SLP	SA/CR	FBG	KL	IB	105D	VLVO	16	5	61000	9	10	604500	664000
60	6	SWAN 61	KTH	SA/CR	FBG	KC	IB	105D	VLVO	16	5	61000	7	2	604500	664000
60	6	SWAN 61	KTH	SA/CR	FBG	KL	IB	105D	VLVO	16	5	61000	9	10	604500	664000
64	6	SWAN 65	SLP	SA/RC	FBG	KL	IB	124D	VLVO	16	4	70000	9	6	702000	771500
64	6	SWAN 65	KTH	SA/RC	FBG	KL	IB	124D	VLVO	16	4	70000	9	6	702000	771500
65	6	SWAN 651	SLP	SA/RC	FBG	KC	IB	135D	PERK	17	5	75000	11	5	760500	836000
65	6	SWAN 651	SLP	SA/RC	FBG	KL	IB	135D	PERK	17	5	75000	11	5	760500	836000
65	6	SWAN 651	KTH	SA/RC	FBG	KC	IB	135D	PERK	17	5	75000	11	5	760500	836000
65	6	SWAN 651	KTH	SA/RC	FBG	KL	IB	135D	PERK	17	5	75000	11	5	760500	836000
76	3	SWAN 76	SLP	SA/RC	FBG	KC	IB	200D	BENZ	19		50T	7		**	**
76	3	SWAN 76	SLP	SA/RC	FBG	KL	IB	200D	BENZ	19		50T	12		**	**
76	3	SWAN 76	KTH	SA/RC	FBG	KC	IB	200D	BENZ	19		50T	7		**	**
76	3	SWAN 76	KTH	SA/RC	FBG	KL	IB	200D	BENZ	19		50T	12		**	**
		1984 BOATS														
36	8	SWAN 371	SLP	SA/RC	FBG	KL	IB	20D	BUKH	11	3	13700	6	6	87400	96100
39	10	SWAN 391	SLP	SA/CR	FBG	KL	IB	50D	PERK	12	5	18000	7	2	124500	137000
41	10	SWAN 42	SLP	SA/RC	FBG	KL	IB	40D	PERK	13		22000	7	9	151500	166500
47	1	SWAN 46	SLP	SA/RC	FBG	KC	IB	62D	PERK	14	6	31300	5	6	223500	245500
47	1	SWAN 46	SLP	SA/RC	FBG	KL	IB	62D	PERK	14	6	31300	8	2	223500	245500
47	9	SWAN 47	SLP	SA/RC	FBG	KC	SD	61D	VLVO	13	9	34100	5	9	237500	261000
47	9	SWAN 47	SLP	SA/RC	FBG	KL	SD	61D	VLVO	13	9	32400	7	9	233000	256000
51	3	SWAN 51	SLP	SA/RC	FBG	KC	IB	85D	PERK	14	7	39600			296000	325500
51	3	SWAN 51	SLP	SA/RC	FBG	KL	IB	85D	PERK	14	7	39600	8	9	296000	325500
57	5	SWAN 57	SLP	SA/RC	FBG	KC	IB	85D	PERK	15	9	51500	6	4	488500	537000
57	5	SWAN 57	SLP	SA/RC	FBG	KL	IB	85D	PERK	15	9	47600	9	1	474000	520500
57	5	SWAN 57	KTH	SA/RC	FBG	KC	IB	85D	PERK	15	9	51500	6	4	489000	537500
57	5	SWAN 57	KTH	SA/RC	FBG	KL	IB	85D	PERK	15	9	47600	9	1	474000	521000
58	10	SWAN 59	SLP	SA/CR	FBG	KC	IB	92D	VLVO	16	5	60000	7	2	546500	600500
58	10	SWAN 59	SLP	SA/RC	FBG	KL	IB	92D	VLVO	16	5	62400	11	2	558500	613500
64	6	SWAN 65	SLP	SA/RC	FBG	KL	IB	124D	VLVO	16	4	70000	9	6	665500	731500
64	6	SWAN 65	KTH	SA/RC	FBG	KL	IB	124D	VLVO	16	4	70000	9	6	665500	731500
65	6	SWAN 651	SLP	SA/RC	FBG	KC	IB	135D	PERK	17	5	75000	11	5	721000	792000
65	6	SWAN 651	SLP	SA/RC	FBG	KL	IB	135D	PERK	17	5	75000	11	5	721000	792000
65	6	SWAN 651	KTH	SA/RC	FBG	KC	IB	135D	PERK	17	5	75000	11	5	721000	792000
65	6	SWAN 651	KTH	SA/RC	FBG	KL	IB	135D	PERK	17	5	75000	11	5	721000	792000
76	3	SWAN 76	SLP	SA/RC	FBG	KC	IB	200D	BENZ	19		50T	7		**	**
76	3	SWAN 76	SLP	SA/RC	FBG	KL	IB	200D	BENZ	19		50T	12		**	**
76	3	SWAN 76	KTH	SA/RC	FBG	KC	IB	200D	BENZ	19		50T	7		**	**
76	3	SWAN 76	KTH	SA/RC	FBG	KL	IB	200D	BENZ	19		50T	12		**	**

....For earlier years, see the BUC Used Boat Price Guide, Volume 3

NAVIGATOR YACHTS INC

PERRIS CA 92570 COAST GUARD MFG ID- NVY See inside cover to adjust price for area

For more recent years, see the BUC Used Boat Price Guide, Volume 1

LOA FT	IN	NAME AND/ OR MODEL	TOP/ RIG	BOAT TYPE	-HULL- MTL	TP	----ENGINE--- TP	# HP	MFG	BEAM FT	IN	WGT LBS	DRAFT FT	IN	RETAIL LOW	RETAIL HIGH
		1996 BOATS														
42		CLASSIC 42	FB	MY	FBG	SV	IB	T318D		15		30000			171000	187500
46		CLASSIC 46	FB	MYPH	FBG	SV	IB	T318D		15		34000			190500	209000
50		CLASSIC 50	FB	MYPH	FBG	SV	IB	T370D		15		40000			225500	247500
53		CLASSIC 53	FB	MYPH	FBG	SV	IB	T370D		15		42500			232500	255500
53		SUNDANCE 5300	FB	MYPH	FBG	SV	IB	T370D		15		46000			247500	272000
56		SUNDANCE 5600	FB	MYPH	FBG	SV	IB	T430D		15		50000			277500	305000
		1995 BOATS														
42		CLASSIC 42	FB	MY	FBG	SV	IB	T318D		15		30000			164000	180000
46		CLASSIC 46	FB	MYPH	FBG	SV	IB	T318D		15		34000			182500	200500
50		CLASSIC 50	FB	MYPH	FBG	SV	IB	T370D		15		40000			216000	237500
53		SUNDANCE 5300	FB	MYPH	FBG	SV	IB	T370D		15		46000			237500	261000
		1994 BOATS														
33		NAVIGATOR 3300 FE		MY	FBG	SV	IB	T318D		15		27000			105000	115500
43		NAVIGATOR 4300 FE	FB	MYPH	FBG	SV	IB	T318D		15		31600			168500	185000
48		NAVIGATOR 4800 FE	FB	MYPH	FBG	SV	IB	T318D		15		36000			183500	202000
50		NAVIGATOR 5000	FB	MYPH	FBG	SV	IB	T370D		15		40000			207000	227500
52		SUNDANCE 5200	FB	MYPH	FBG	SV	IB	T370D		15		44000			221500	243500
56		SUNDANCE 5600	FB	MYPH	FBG	SV	IB	T430D		15		50000			255500	280500
		1993 BOATS														
33		NAVIGATOR 3300 FE		MY	FBG	SV	IB	T318D		15		27000			99900	110000
43		NAVIGATOR 4300 FE	FB	MYPH	FBG	SV	IB	T318D		15		31000			158000	174000
48		NAVIGATOR 4800 FE	FB	MYPH	FBG	SV	IB	T318D		15		36000			175000	192000
50		NAVIGATOR 5000	FB	MYPH	FBG	SV	IB	T370D		15		40000			197500	217000
52		SUNDANCE 5200	FB	MYPH	FBG	SV	IB	T370D		15		44000			211000	232000
56		SUNDANCE 5600	FB	MYPH	FBG	SV	IB	T430D		15		50000			243000	267000
		1992 BOATS														
33	6	NAVIGATOR 336		MY	FBG	SV	IB	T318D		15		27000			95200	104500
43		NAVIGATOR 43 SE	FB	MYPH	FBG	SV	IB	T318D		15		31000			151000	165500
		1991 BOATS														
33	6	NAVIGATOR 336		MY	FBG	SV	IB	T420		15		27000			64700	71100
33	6	NAVIGATOR 336		MY	FBG	SV	IB	T318D		15		27000			90900	99900
43		NAVIGATOR 43 SE	FB	MYPH	FBG	SV	IB	T318D		15		31000			144000	158000
53		NAVIGATOR 53 SE	FB	MYPH	FBG	SV	IB	T370D		15		45000			193500	212500

408 CONTINUED ON NEXT PAGE 96th ed. - Vol. II

LOA FT IN	NAME AND/OR MODEL	TOP/RIG	BOAT TYPE	HULL MTL TP TP	ENGINE # HP MFG	BEAM FT IN	WGT LBS	DRAFT FT IN	RETAIL LOW	RETAIL HIGH
1990 BOATS										
33 6	NAVIGATOR 336		MY	FBG SV IB	T300 CHRY	11 11	16000	2 10	48300	53100
43	NAVIGATOR 43 SE	FB	MYPH	FBG SV IB	T318D	15	31000		137500	151000

LORD NELSON YACHTS
SUN VALLEY ID 83353

See inside cover to adjust price for area

LOA FT IN	NAME AND/OR MODEL	TOP/RIG	BOAT TYPE	HULL MTL TP TP	ENGINE # HP MFG	BEAM FT IN	WGT LBS	DRAFT FT IN	RETAIL LOW	RETAIL HIGH
1986 BOATS										
41	LORD-NELSON 41	CUT		SA/CR FBG KL IB	D	12 10	30500	5 8	132500	145500
1985 BOATS										
35	LORD-NELSON 35	CUT		SA/CR FBG KL IB	D	11 10	20500	5 4	82500	90600
36 11	VICTORY TUG	TUG		FBG DS IB	130D	13 2	20825	3 6	**	**
41	LORD-NELSON 41	CUT		SA/CR FBG KL IB	D	12 10	30500	5 8	125500	137500
1984 BOATS										
36 11	VICTORY TUG	PH		FBG IB		13 2	20585	3 6	**	**
41	LORD-NELSON 41	CUT		SA/RC FBG KL IB	D BMW	12 10	30500	5 8	119000	130500

NEPTUNUS YACHTS
NEPTUNUS CANADA LTD
DANIA FL 33004

See inside cover to adjust price for area

For more recent years, see the BUC Used Boat Price Guide, Volume 1

LOA FT IN	NAME AND/OR MODEL	TOP/RIG	BOAT TYPE	HULL MTL TP TP	ENGINE # HP MFG	BEAM FT IN	WGT LBS	DRAFT FT IN	RETAIL LOW	RETAIL HIGH
1996 BOATS										
50	50 AFT CABIN		MY	FBG SV IB	T420D CAT	14 7	32000	4	249000	273500
55	51 SEDAN		SDN	FBG SV IB	T550D DD	15 7	52000	4 5	326000	358500
63	60 SEDAN		SDN	FBG SV IB	T735D DD	17	72000	5	508500	559000
65 4	65 SEDAN		SDN	FBG SV IB	T11CD DD	18 11	84000	4 6	812500	893000
70 4	70 SEDAN		SDN	FBG SV IB	T14CD DD	18 11	96000	5	862500	948000
1995 BOATS										
43	129/43 AFT CABIN	FB	MY	FBG SV IB	T300D CAT	14	28000	4	179000	197000
43	129/43 EXPRESS		DCMY	FBG SV IB	T300D CAT	14	28000	4	176500	194000
43	129/43 SEDAN		SDN	FBG SV IB	T300D CAT	14	28000	4	179000	196500
50	141/47 SEDAN		SDN	FBG SV IB	T375D CAT	14 7	32000	4	193000	212000
55	156/51 SEDAN		SDN	FBG SV IB	T550D DD	15 7	52000	4 5	300500	330500
63	174/58 SEDAN		SDN	FBG SV IB	T735D DD	17	72000	5	473500	520500
65 4	195/65 SEDAN		SDN	FBG SV IB	T11CD DD	18 11	84000	4 6	765500	841000
73	218/72 SEDAN		SDN	FBG SV IB	T14CD DD	19 6	96000	5 3	**	**

NEREIA YACHTS
WILMINGTON NC 28405

COAST GUARD MFG ID- KAT   See inside cover to adjust price for area

LOA FT IN	NAME AND/OR MODEL	TOP/RIG	BOAT TYPE	HULL MTL TP TP	ENGINE # HP MFG	BEAM FT IN	WGT LBS	DRAFT FT IN	RETAIL LOW	RETAIL HIGH
1988 BOATS										
21 2	INDIAN	SLP		SA/OD FBG KC OB		6 4	1200	1 6	2900	3350
38	NEREIA	KTH		SA/CR FBG KL IB	51D PERK	11	23000	5 3	57600	63300
1987 BOATS										
21 2	INDIAN	SLP		SA/OD FBG KC OB		6 4	1200	1 6	2700	3150
38	NEREIA	KTH		SA/CR FBG KL IB	51D PERK	11	23000	5 3	54200	59500
1986 BOATS										
21	INDIAN	SLP		SA/OD FBG KC		6 4	1100	1 6	2450	2850
38	NEREIA	KTH		SA/CR FBG KL IB	51D PERK	11	23000	5 3	50900	56000
1985 BOATS										
21 2	INDIAN	SLP		SA/OD FBG KC OB		6 4	1200	1 6	2400	2800
38	NEREIA	KTH		SA/CR FBG KL IB	51D PERK	11	23000	5 3	47900	52600
1984 BOATS										
21 2	INDIAN	SLP		SA/OD FBG KC OB		6 4	1200	1 6	2300	2650
38	NEREIA	KTH		SA/CR FBG KL IB	51D PERK	11	23000	5 3	44800	49800

....For earlier years, see the BUC Used Boat Price Guide, Volume 3

NETH SHIPS B A
HOGE RIJNDIJK 211 NETHERLANDS

See inside cover to adjust price for area

LOA FT IN	NAME AND/OR MODEL	TOP/RIG	BOAT TYPE	HULL MTL TP TP	ENGINE # HP MFG	BEAM FT IN	WGT LBS	DRAFT FT IN	RETAIL LOW	RETAIL HIGH
1988 BOATS										
46 2	LOWLAND-TRAWLER 462		MY	STL DS IB		13 10		4 1	**	**
47 5	LOWLAND-CUTTER 471		MY	STL DS IB		15	50600		**	**
47 5	LOWLAND-CUTTER 472		MY	STL DS IB		15	50600		**	**
47 5	LOWLAND-CUTTER 473		MY	STL DS IB		15		5 1	**	**
50 10	LOWLAND-TRAWLER 501		MY	STL DS IB		15 1		4 11	**	**
52	LOWLAND-CUTTER 521		MY	STL DS IB		16 6		5 1	**	**
52	LOWLAND-CUTTER 522		MY	STL DS IB		16 6	57200		**	**
52 10	NETH-SHIP 52		MY	STL DS IB T		16 7	94600		**	**
57	NETH-SHIP 57		MY	STL DS IB		17	58T		**	**
57 4	LOWLAND-TRAWLER 571		MY	STL DS IB		16		4 11	**	**
59 6	NETH-SHIP 60		MY	AL DS IB		16 11		4 8	**	**
60 8	NETH-SHIP 61		MY	STL DS IB T		17 9	64T		**	**
61	NETH-SHIP 611		MY	STL DS IB		19		6	**	**
63 6	NETH-SHIP 64		MY	STL DS IB		19	75T		**	**
63 7	NETH-SHIP 58		MY	AL DS IB		18 6		4 4	**	**
64 7	NETH-SHIP 641		MY	AL DS IB		19 1		5 6	**	**
65 7	NETH-SHIP 66		MY	STL DS IB		19	85T		**	**
67 1	NETH-SHIP 67		MY	STL DS IB		19		6 1	**	**
70	LOWLAND 701		MY	STL DS IB		20		6 7	**	**
73 6	NETH-SHIP 74		MY	AL DS IB		19		4 11	**	**
74 10	NETH-SHIP 75		MY	STL DS IB		19	96T		**	**
77 6	NETH-SHIP 80		MY	STL DS IB		17 5		5 9	**	**
1987 BOATS										
46 2	LOWLAND-TRAWLER 462		MY	STL DS IB		13 10		4 1	**	**
47 5	LOWLAND-CUTTER 471		MY	STL DS IB		15	50600		**	**
47 5	LOWLAND-CUTTER 472		MY	STL DS IB		15	50600		**	**
47 5	LOWLAND-CUTTER 473		MY	STL DS IB		15		5 1	**	**
50 10	LOWLAND-TRAWLER 501		MY	STL DS IB		15 1		4 11	**	**
52	LOWLAND-CUTTER		MY	STL DS IB		16 6		5 1	**	**
52	LOWLAND-CUTTER 522		MY	STL DS IB		16 6	57200		**	**
52 10	NETH-SHIP 52		MY	STL DS IB T		16 7	94600		**	**
57	NETH-SHIP 57		MY	STL DS IB		17	58T		**	**
57 4	LOWLAND-TRAWLER 571		MY	STL DS IB		16		4 11	**	**
59 6	NETH-SHIP 60		MY	AL DS IB		16 11		4 8	**	**
60 8	NETH-SHIP 61		MY	STL DS IB T		17 9	64T		**	**
61	NETH-SHIP 611		MY	STL DS IB		19		6	**	**
63 6	NETH-SHIP 64		MY	STL DS IB		19	75T		**	**
63 7	NETH-SHIP 58		MY	AL DS IB		18 6		4 4	**	**
64 7	NETH-SHIP 641		MY	AL DS IB		19 1		5 6	**	**
65 7	NETH-SHIP 66		MY	STL DS IB		19	85T		**	**
67 1	NETH-SHIP 67		MY	STL DS IB		19		6 1	**	**
70	LOWLAND 701		MY	STL DS IB		20		6 1	**	**
73 6	NETH-SHIP 74		MY	AL DS IB		19		4 11	**	**
74 10	NETH-SHIP 75		MY	STL DS IB		19	96T		**	**
77 6	NETH-SHIP 80		MY	STL DS IB		17 5		5 9	**	**
1986 BOATS										
37 9	LOWLAND-CUTTER 1150		MY	STL DS IB	85D	12 5	28600		97200	107000
42 4	LOWLAND-TRAWLER 1290		MY	STL DS IB	117D	13 10	35275		125500	137500
45 5	LOWLAND-TRAWLER 1350		MY	STL DS IB	141D	13 10	40785		139000	152500
45 5	LOWLAND-CUTTER 1385		MY	STL DS IB	T141D	15 1	50700		160000	175500
46 3	LOWLAND-PRINCESS		MY	STL DS IB	141D	13 10	44100		157500	172500
47 5	LOWLAND-CUTTER 471		MY	STL DS IB	184D	15	50600		162500	178500
47 5	LOWLAND-CUTTER 472		MY	STL DS IB	184D	15	50600		162500	178500
50 2	LOWLAND-PRINCESS 150		MY	STL DS IB	T184D	14 7	52920		172500	189500
52	LOWLAND-CUTTER 522		MY	STL DS IB	184D	16 6	57200		177500	195000
52 10	LOWLAND-PRINCESS		MY	STL DS IB	T184D	14 7	59525		186000	204000
52 10	NETH-SHIP 52		MY	STL DS IB	T184D	16 7	94600		225500	247500
57	NETH-SHIP 57		MY	STL DS IB	T184D	17	58T		313500	344500
60 8	NETH-SHIP 61		MY	STL DS IB	T207D	17 9	63T		387000	425500
65 7	NETH-SHIP 66		MY	STL DS IB	T209D	19	84T		519000	570000
74 10	NETH-SHIP 75		MY	STL DS IB	T229D	19	95T		**	**
1985 BOATS										
37 9	LOWLAND-CUTTER 1150		MY	STL DS IB	85D	12 5	28600		92500	101500
41	LOWLAND-CUTTER 1250		MY	STL DS IB	117D	13	38580		129500	142000
42 4	LOWLAND-TRAWLER 1290		MY	STL DS IB	117D	13 10	35275		119500	131000
44 4	LOWLAND-TRAWLER 1350		MY	STL DS IB	141D	13 10	40785		132000	145000
45 5	LOWLAND-CUTTER 1385		MY	STL DS IB	184D	15 1	50700		152500	167500
46 3	LOWLAND-PRINCESS		MY	STL DS IB	141D	13 10	44100		142500	156500
47 5	LOWLAND-CUTTER 471		MY	STL DS IB	184D	15	50600		154500	170000
47 5	LOWLAND-CUTTER 472		MY	STL DS IB	184D	15	50600		154500	170000
48 5	LOWLAND-CUTTER 1485		MY	STL DS IB	184D	15 1	63925		169500	186500
50 2	LOWLAND-PRINCESS		MY	STL DS IB	T184D	14 7	52920		164500	180500
52	LOWLAND-CUTTER 522		MY	STL DS IB	T184D	16	57200		171000	188000
52 10	LOWLAND-PRINCESS		MY	STL DS IB	T184D	14 7	59525		179000	196500
52 10	NETH-SHIP 52		MY	STL DS IB	T184D	16 7	94600		217000	238500
57	NETH-SHIP 57		MY	STL DS IB	T184D	17	58T		303000	332500
60 8	NETH-SHIP 61		MY	STL DS IB	T207D	17 9	64T		375000	412000

LOA FT IN	NAME AND/ OR MODEL	TOP/ RIG	BOAT TYPE	-HULL- MTL TP	----ENGINE--- TP # HP MFG	BEAM FT IN	WGT LBS	DRAFT FT IN	RETAIL LOW	RETAIL HIGH
					1985 BOATS					
63 8	NETH-SHIP 64	MY	STL DS	IB 209D		19	75T		453500	498000
65 7	NETH-SHIP 66	MY	STL DS	IB 209D		19	85T		496000	545000
74 10	NETH-SHIP 75	MY	STL DS	IB 279D		19	96T		**	**
					1984 BOATS					
37 9	LOWLAND-CUTTER	MY	STL DS	IO 85D		12 5	28600		69500	76300
41	LOWLAND-CUTTER	MY	STL DS	IO 117D		13	38580		97200	107000
42 4	LOWLAND-TRAWLER	MY	STL DS	IO 117D		13 10	35275		89600	98400
44 4	LOWLAND-TRAWLER	MY	STL DS	IO 141D		13 10	40785		99200	109000
45 5	LOWLAND-CUTTER	MY	STL DS	IO 184D		15 1	50700		114500	125500
46 3	LOWLAND-PRINCESS	MY	STL DS	IO T141D		13 10	44100		112500	123500
47 5	LOWLAND-CUTTER	MY	STL DS	IO 184D		15	50600		116000	127500
48 9	LOWLAND-CUTTER	MY	STL DS	IO 184D		15 1	63925		128500	141000
50 2	LOWLAND-CUTTER	MY	STL DS	IO T184D		14 7	52920		126500	139000
52	LOWLAND-PRINCESS	MY	STL DS	IO 184D		16 6	57200		126500	139000
52 10	LOWLAND-PRINCESS	MY	STL DS	IO 184D		14 7	59525		129000	141500
52 10	NETH-SHIP 52	MY	STL DS	IO T184D		16 7	94600		163000	179500
55 10	LOWLAND-PRINCESS	MY	STL DS	IO T207D		15 4	63935		137000	150500
57	NETH-SHIP 57	MY	STL DS	IO T184D		17	58T		212000	233000
60 8	NETH-SHIP 61	MY	STL DS	IO T207D		17 9	64T		264000	290000
63 8	NETH-SHIP 64	MY	STL DS	IO T209D		19	75T		322500	354500
65 7	NETH-SHIP 66	MY	STL DS	IO T209D		19	85T		352500	387500
74 10	NETH-SHIP 75	MY	STL DS	IO T279D		19	96T		**	**

NEW ENGLAND PERFORMANCE YACHT
MARBLEHEAD MA 04519   See inside cover to adjust price for area

LOA FT IN	NAME AND/ OR MODEL	TOP/ RIG	BOAT TYPE	-HULL- MTL TP TP	----ENGINE--- # HP MFG	BEAM FT IN	WGT LBS	DRAFT FT IN	RETAIL LOW	RETAIL HIGH
					1985 BOATS					
41 10	ANSA 42	SLP	SA/RC	FBG KL IB	28D VLVO	10 2	12127	6 4	44000	48900

NEW ORLEANS MARINE INC
NEW OLEANS LA 70115   See inside cover to adjust price for area

LOA FT IN	NAME AND/ OR MODEL	TOP/ RIG	BOAT TYPE	-HULL- MTL TP TP	----ENGINE--- # HP MFG	BEAM FT IN	WGT LBS	DRAFT FT IN	RETAIL LOW	RETAIL HIGH
					1985 BOATS					
37 11	FRERS 38	SLP	SA/RC	FBG KL IB	D	12 3	13000	6 6	33600	37300
42 6	PETERSON 43	SLP	SA/RC	FBG KL IB	D	13 3	17500	7 5	53200	58500
					1984 BOATS					
37 11	FRERS 38	SLP	SA/RC	FBG KL IB	D	12 3	13000	6 6	31600	35100
42 6	PETERSON 43	SLP	SA/RC	FBG KL IB	D	13 3	17500		50100	55000

....For earlier years, see the BUC Used Boat Price Guide, Volume 3

NEW WAVE MARKETING
NEWPORT RI 02840   See inside cover to adjust price for area

LOA FT IN	NAME AND/ OR MODEL	TOP/ RIG	BOAT TYPE	-HULL- MTL TP TP	----ENGINE--- # HP MFG	BEAM FT IN	WGT LBS	DRAFT FT IN	RETAIL LOW	RETAIL HIGH
					1986 BOATS					
36 3	7-3C	SLP	SA/RC	FBG KL IB	D	11 11	10900	6 9	51000	56000
					1985 BOATS					
36 3	F-3	SLP	SA/RC	FBG KL IB	D	11 10	10900	6 9	48000	52700
					1984 BOATS					
36 3	F-3	SLP	SA/RC	FBG KL IB	D	11 10	10900	6 9	44900	49900

NEW ZEALAND MARINE VENTURES
BIRKENHEAD AUCKLAND 10   See inside cover to adjust price for area
FORMERLY SOUTH PACIFIC ASSOCIATES LTD

LOA FT IN	NAME AND/ OR MODEL	TOP/ RIG	BOAT TYPE	-HULL- MTL TP TP	----ENGINE--- # HP MFG	BEAM FT IN	WGT LBS	DRAFT FT IN	RETAIL LOW	RETAIL HIGH
					1988 BOATS					
41 11	SOUTH PACIFIC 42	CUT	SA/CR	F/S KL IB	44D YAN	13 3	18500	5 8	147500	162500
					1987 BOATS					
41 11	SOUTH PACIFIC 42	CUT	SA/CR	F/S KL IB	44D YAN	13 3	18500	5 9	138000	152000
					1986 BOATS					
40	DAVIDSON 40	SLP	SA/RC	WD KL IB	D	12 5	13500	7 7	99800	109500
42	SOUTH-PACIFIC 42	SLP	SA/RC	F/S KL IB	D	12 8	18500	6 5	132000	145000
					1985 BOATS					
40	DAVIDSON 40	SLP	SA/RC	WD KL IB	D	12 5	13500	7 7	93300	102500
					1984 BOATS					
36 6	DAVIDSON 36	SLP	SA/RC	FBG KL IB	D	11 4	7800	5 4	44900	49900
40	DAVIDSON 40	SLP	SA/RC	WD KL IB	D	12 4	14000	7 4	89900	98800
40 6	ANTARES 41	SLP	SA/RC	WD KL IB	D	12 6	13200	6 9	87900	96600

NEWMAN FINE BOATS INC
VELVET FLEET   COAST GUARD MFG ID- NEW   See inside cover to adjust price for area
MIAMI OK 74354

LOA FT IN	NAME AND/ OR MODEL	TOP/ RIG	BOAT TYPE	-HULL- MTL TP TP	----ENGINE--- # HP MFG	BEAM FT IN	WGT LBS	DRAFT FT IN	RETAIL LOW	RETAIL HIGH
					1984 BOATS					
16 2	CAM II	ST	RNBT	FBG TR OB		6 1	925		2400	2750
16 2	CAM II	ST	RNBT	FBG TR IO	140 MRCR	6 1	1580		3400	3950
16 2	CAM II FS	OP	RNBT	FBG TR OB		6 1	925		2550	2950
17	BASS-MATE	OP	BASS	FBG TR OB		6 1	860		2350	2750
17	BASS-MATE	OP	BASS	FBG TR IO	140 MRCR	6 1	1770		3800	4450
17	SCORPION F/S	OP	BASS	FBG OB					2350	2750
17 6	MACH I	ST	RNBT	FBG TR OB		6 10	1260		3350	3900
17 6	MACH II	ST	RNBT	FBG TR IO	140-228	6 10	2190		4550	5450
18	PLA-VILLE	ST	RNBT	FBG DV OB	140-230	7 1	2360		4950	5850
18	SCORPION	OP	BASS	FBG DV OB		7 2	1020		2800	3250
18	SCORPION FS	OP	BASS	FBG DV OB		7 2	1020		2900	3400
20	PLA-BUOY	ST	RNBT	FBG DV IO	170-260	7 7	2670		6450	7850
22 4	ISLANDER	ST	RNBT	FBG DV IO	170-260	8	3030		7900	9550

....For earlier years, see the BUC Used Boat Price Guide, Volume 3

JARVIS NEWMAN MARINE BROKERS
NE HARBOR ME 04662-0331 COAST GUARD MFG ID- JNY See inside cover to adjust price for area

LOA FT IN	NAME AND/ OR MODEL	TOP/ RIG	BOAT TYPE	-HULL- MTL TP TP	----ENGINE--- # HP MFG	BEAM FT IN	WGT LBS	DRAFT FT IN	RETAIL LOW	RETAIL HIGH
					1986 BOATS					
25	PEMAGUID	SLP	SA/CR	FBG KL IB	D	8 8		4 3	18600	20600
26	HINCKLEY 26		LNCH	FBG DS IB	46D	8 2	3500		19800	22100
30 6	NEWMAN 30		SF	FBG DS IB	46D	10 8		5	71000	78000
31	DICTATOR	GAF	SA/CR	FBG KL IB	D	10 8			55100	60500
32	NEWMAN 32	HT	MYDKH	FBG DS IB	D	11	14000		**	**
36	NEWMAN 36	HT	MYDKH	FBG DS IB	D	11	16000		**	**
38	NEWMAN 38	HT	MYDKH	FBG DS IB	D	13 4	22000		**	**
46	NEWMAN 46	HT	MYDKH	FBG DS IB	D	15	30000		**	**
					1985 BOATS					
25	PEMAGUID	SLP	SA/CR	FBG KL IB	D	8 8		4 3	17000	19300
30 6	NEWMAN 30	MY	FBG	RB IB	D	10 8			51700	56800
31	DICTATOR	GAF	SA/CR	FBG KL IB	D	10 8		5	**	**
32	NEWMAN 32	HT	MYDKH	FBG DS IB	D	11	14000	3 6	**	**
36	NEWMAN 36	HT	MYDKH	FBG DS IB	D	11	16000	3 5	**	**
38	NEWMAN 38	HT	MYDKH	FBG DS IB	D	13 4	22000	4 5	**	**
46	NEWMAN 46	HT	MYDKH	FBG DS IB	D	15	30000	4 6	**	**

....For earlier years, see the BUC Used Boat Price Guide, Volume 3

NEXUS MARINE CORPORATION
EVERETT WA 98201   COAST GUARD MFG ID- RAK See inside cover to adjust price for area
ALSO NEXUS MARINE CONST

LOA FT IN	NAME AND/ OR MODEL	TOP/ RIG	BOAT TYPE	-HULL- MTL TP TP	----ENGINE--- # HP MFG	BEAM FT IN	WGT LBS	DRAFT FT IN	RETAIL LOW	RETAIL HIGH
					1993 BOATS					
16	SAN JUAN DORY	OP	UTL	WD FL OB		5 6	300	4	995	1200
17 6	PORT MOLLER SKIFF	OP	UTL	WD FL OB		6 11	475	6	1550	1850
18	BEACH SKIFF 18	OP	UTL	WD FL OB		6 8	480	6	1550	1850
18 4	SEA SKIFF 18V	OP	OPFSH	WD SV OB		6 8	800	10	2850	3300
20 9	ALASKAN SKIFF 20	OP	UTL	WD FL OB		7 2	600	6	1750	2100
20 11	NEXUS DORY 21	OP	FSH	WD FL OB		6 6	600		2200	2550
23	CHINOOK 23	OP	OVNTR	WD SV OB		8	2000	1	7450	8550
23	NEXUS DORY 23	OP	FSH	WD FL OB		7 8	1900		7100	8200
24 8	NUSHAGAK SKIFF 24	OP	UTL	WD FL OB		8 10	1000	10	6600	7600
24 8	TYEE	OP	OVNTR	WD SV IO	200	8 8	3500	1	19400	21600
27 1	ST-PIERRE DORY 27	HT	WKNDR	WD FL OB		8 9	2700	1	19300	21400
					1988 BOATS					
16	NEXUS DORY 16	OP	UTL	WD FL OB		5 6	300	4	785	945
17	PORT MOLLER SKIFF	OP	UTL	WD FL OB		7	450	2 3	1200	1400
18	SEA SKIFF	OP	UTL	WD SV OB		6 8	475	9	1250	1450

LOA FT	LOA IN	NAME AND/ OR MODEL	TOP/ RIG	BOAT TYPE	HULL MTL	HULL TP	ENGINE TP	# HP	MFG	BEAM FT	BEAM IN	WGT LBS	DRAFT FT	DRAFT IN	RETAIL LOW	RETAIL HIGH
		1988 BOATS														
18	2	BEACH SKIFF	OP	UTL	WD	FL	OB			6	9	440		3	1150	1350
20	9	ALASKAN SKIFF 20	OP	UTL	WD	FL	OB			7	2	600		6	1400	1700
20	11	NEXUS DORY 21	OP	UTL	WD	FL	OB			6	6	500		3	1100	1300
21		CHINOOK	HT	CR	WD	SV	OB			8		2000	1	10	5550	6350
22	3	BAY SKIFF 22	OP	UTL	WD	FL	OB			8		800		6	1900	2300
22	11	CHINOOK 23	HT	CR	WD	SV	OB			8		2430	1	10	7000	8050
23		NEXUS DORY 23	HT	UTL	WD	FL	OB			7	8	1300	1	6	3350	3850
24	8	NUSHAGAK SKIFF	OP	UTL	WD	SV	OB			8	10	1000	2	7	4500	5150
27		ST-PIERRE DORY	HT	CUD	WD	DS	IB	30D	YAN	9		3500	2	8	15800	17900
28		CARGO SKIFF	OP	UTL	WD	FL	OB			10		1500		4	15200	17200
28	6	GULF-ISLANDER 29	HT	CBNCR	WD	SV	IB	130	VLVO	9	10	6700	2	11	22600	25100
		1987 BOATS														
16		NEXUS DORY 16	OP	UTL	WD	FL	OB			5	6	300		4	755	910
17		PORT MOLLER SKIFF	OP	UTL	WD	FL	OB			7		450	2	3	1150	1350
18		BEACH SKIFF	OP	UTL	WD	FL	OB			6	6	440		3	1100	1300
20	9	ALASKAN SKIFF 20	OP	UTL	WD	FL	OB			7	2	600		6	1350	1600
20	11	NEXUS DORY 21	OP	UTL	WD	FL	OB			6	6	500		3	1100	1300
22	3	ALASKAN SKIFF 22	OP	UTL	WD	FL	OB			8		800		6	1850	2200
22	11	CHINPOOK 23	HT	CR	WD	SV	OB			8		2430	1	10	6750	7750
23		NEXUS DORY 23	HT	UTL	WD	FL	OB			7	8	1300	1	6	3200	3750
27		ST-PIERRE DORY	HT	CUD	WD	DS	IB	30D	YAN	9		3500	2	8	15100	17200
28		CARGO SKIFF	OP	UTL	WD	FL	OB			10		1500		4	14600	16600
28	6	GULF-ISLANDER 29	HT	CBNCR	WD	SV	IB	130	VLVO	9	10	6700	2	11	21600	24000
		1986 BOATS														
16		SAN-JUAN DORY	OP	UTL	WD	FL	OB			5	6	300		4	730	880
18		BEACH SKIFF	OP	UTL	WD	FL	OB			6	6	440		3	1050	1250
20	11	ROBERTS DORY	OP	UTL	WD	FL	OB			6	6	500		3	1050	1250
23		AUKE-BAY	OP	UTL	WD	FL	OB			7	8	1300	1	6	3100	3600
27		ST-PIERRE DORY	HT	CUD	WD	DS	IB	30D	YAN	9		3500	2	8	14500	16500
28		CARGO SKIFF	OP	UTL	WD	FL	OB			10		1500		4	14100	16000
		1984 BOATS														
18		BEACH SKIFF	OP	UTL	WD	FL	OB			6	6	440		3	1000	1200
20	7	CAROLINA DORY	OP	UTL	WD	FL	OB			6		485		3	965	1150
22		ALASKAN SKIFF	OP	UTL	WD	FL	OB			8		875	1	6	1850	2200
27		ST-PIERRE DORY	HT	CUD	WD	DS	IB	30D	BMW	9		3500	2	8	13300	15100
28		CARGO SKIFF	OP	UTL	WD	FL	OB			10		1500		4	13200	15000

....For earlier years, see the BUC Used Boat Price Guide, Volume 3

NIAGARA NAUTIC INC

NIAGARA LAKE ONTARIO CA COAST GUARD MFG ID- ZNN See inside cover to adjust price for area

LOA FT	LOA IN	NAME AND/ OR MODEL	TOP/ RIG	BOAT TYPE	HULL MTL	HULL TP	ENGINE TP	# HP	MFG	BEAM FT	BEAM IN	WGT LBS	DRAFT FT	DRAFT IN	RETAIL LOW	RETAIL HIGH
		1984 BOATS														
36	9	NAUTILUS 36	SLP	SA/CR	FBG	KL	IB	D		11	6	15000	5		67200	73900
39	9	NAUTILUS 40	SLP	SA/CR	FBG	KL	IB	D		11	10	18000	5	9	88100	96800

....For earlier years, see the BUC Used Boat Price Guide, Volume 3

NICKELS BOAT WORKS INC

FENTON MI 48430 COAST GUARD MFG ID- NBI See inside cover to adjust price for area
FORMERLY NICKELS & HOLMAN LTD

LOA FT	LOA IN	NAME AND/ OR MODEL	TOP/ RIG	BOAT TYPE	HULL MTL	HULL TP	ENGINE TP	# HP	MFG	BEAM FT	BEAM IN	WGT LBS	DRAFT FT	DRAFT IN	RETAIL LOW	RETAIL HIGH
		1994 BOATS														
16		REBEL SAILBOAT	SLP	SAROD	F/S	CB	IB			6	3	700	3	6	4350	5050
19		LIGHTNING SAILBOAT	SLP	SAROD	F/S	CB	SD			6	6	700	4	11	4850	5600
		1993 BOATS														
16		REBEL SAILBOAT	SLP	SAROD	F/S	CB	IB			6	3	700	3	6	4050	4750
19		LIGHTNING SAILBOAT	SLP	SAROD	F/S	CB	SD			6	6	700	4	11	4600	5300
		1985 BOATS														
19		LIGHTNING	SLP	SA/OD	F/S	CB				6	6	700	4	11	2300	2700
		1984 BOATS														
19		LIGHTNING	SLP	SA/OD	FBG	CB				6	6	700	4	11	2200	2550

....For earlier years, see the BUC Used Boat Price Guide, Volume 3

NIMBLE BOATS INC

ODESSA FL 33556-0386 See inside cover to adjust price for area

For more recent years, see the BUC Used Boat Price Guide, Volume 1

LOA FT	LOA IN	NAME AND/ OR MODEL	TOP/ RIG	BOAT TYPE	HULL MTL	HULL TP	ENGINE TP	# HP	MFG	BEAM FT	BEAM IN	WGT LBS	DRAFT FT	DRAFT IN	RETAIL LOW	RETAIL HIGH
		1996 BOATS														
20	3	VAGABOND STD	HT	TRWL	FBG	DS	OB			8		2600	1		13400	15200
20	3	VAGABOND TROPICAL	HT	TRWL	FBG	DS	OB			8		2600	1		13900	15800
20	10	NIMBLE 20 TROPICAL	SLP	SACAC	FBG	KL	OB			7	9	2200		11	13400	15200
24	2	NIMBLE 24 TROPICAL	SLP	SACAC	FBG	KL	IB	D		8	3	2900	2	10	19400	21500
24	7	NOMAD STD	HT	TRWL	FBG	DS	OB			8	6	3250	1	3	20000	22200
24	7	NOMAD TROPICAL	HT	TRWL	FBG	DS	OB			8	6	3250	1	3	23700	26300
26	4	KODIAK SPECIAL	SLP	SACAC	FBG	CB	OB			8	6	3950	2	10	25200	28000
26	4	KODIAK SPECIAL	SLP	SACAC	FBG	KL	OB			8	6	3950	2	10	25000	27800
26	4	KODIAK SPECIAL	YWL	SACAC	FBG	CB	OB			8	6	3950	2	10	25200	28000
26	4	KODIAK SPECIAL	YWL	SACAC	FBG	KL	OB			8	6	3950	2	10	25100	27900
26	4	KODIAK SPECIAL	EPH	TRWL	FBG	DS	IB	10D		8	6	3250	2	10	22900	25500
26	4	KODIAK TROPICAL	SLP	SACAC	FBG	CB	OB			8	6	3950	2	10	28700	31900
26	4	KODIAK TROPICAL	SLP	SACAC	FBG	CB	IB	10		8	6	3950	2	10	27100	30100
26	4	KODIAK TROPICAL	SLP	SACAC	FBG	KL	OB			8	6	3950	2	10	28800	32000
26	4	KODIAK TROPICAL	SLP	SACAC	FBG	KL	IB	10D		8	6	3950	2	10	24900	27700
26	4	KODIAK TROPICAL	YWL	SACAC	FBG	CB	OB			8	6	3950	2	10	28600	31800
26	4	KODIAK TROPICAL	YWL	SACAC	FBG	CB	IB	10		8	6	3950	2	10	27100	30100
26	4	KODIAK TROPICAL	YWL	SACAC	FBG	KL	OB			8	6	3950	2	10	28700	31900
26	4	KODIAK TROPICAL	YWL	SACAC	FBG	KL	IB	10D		8	6	3950	2	10	28000	31100
26	4	KODIAK TROPICAL	EPH	TRWL	FBG	DS	IB	18D		8	6	3250	2	10	23700	26300
30	9	NIMBLE 30 EXPRESS	SLP	SACAC	FBG	KL	IB	18D		9	4	7400	4	6	60200	66200
32	5	WANDERER	HT	TRWL	FBG	DS	IB	10D		8	6	8800	2	10	60600	66600
32	5	WANDERER TROPICAL	SLP	SACAC	FBG	KL	IB	18D		8	6	8800	2	10	72700	79800
33	2	NIMBLE 30	SLP	SACAC	FBG	KL	IB	18D		9	4	7000	4	6	55900	61500
33	2	NIMBLE 30	YWL	SACAC	FBG	KL	IB	18D		9	4	7000	4	6	55900	61500
		1994 BOATS														
20	10	NIMBLE 20 OFF	SLP	SACAC	FBG	KL	OB			7	9	2200	4	3	12500	14200
20	10	NIMBLE 20 STD	SLP	SACAC	FBG	KL	OB			7	9	2200	4	1	11200	12700
20	10	NIMBLE 20 TROPICAL	SLP	SACAC	FBG	KL	OB			7	9	2200	4	1	11900	13500
24	2	NIMBLE 24 D	SLP	SACAC	FBG	KL	IB	D		8	3	2900	2	6	19900	22100
24	2	NIMBLE 24 OFF	SLP	SACAC	FBG	KL	IB	D		8	3	2900	2	8	17100	19400
24	2	NIMBLE 24 STD	SLP	SACAC	FBG	CB	IB	D		8	3	2900	4	2	14700	16700
24	2	NIMBLE 24 STD	SLP	SACAC	FBG	KL	IB	D		8	3	2900	2	6	15900	18100
24	2	NIMBLE 24 TROPICAL	SLP	SACAC	FBG	CB	IB	D		8	3	2900	4	2	15400	17500
24	2	NIMBLE 24 TROPICAL	SLP	SACAC	FBG	KL	IB	D		8	3	2900	2	6	16600	18800
24	2	NIMBLE 25 ARCTIC D	SLP	SACAC	FBG	KL	IB	D		8	3	2900	2	6	17600	20000
24	7	NOMAD MAPLE LEAF	HT	TRWL	FBG	DS	OB			8	6	2450	1	2	16900	19200
24	7	NOMAD STD	HT	TRWL	FBG	DS	OB			8	6	3250	1	2	18400	20400
24	7	NOMAD TROPICAL	HT	TRWL	FBG	DS	OB			8	6	3250	1	2	21500	23900
25	2	VAGABOND STD	HT	TRWL	FBG	DS	OB			8	6	2900	1	2	18900	21000
25	2	VAGABOND TROPICAL	HT	TRWL	FBG	DS	OB			8	6	2900	1	2	19600	21800
26	4	KODIAK	SLP	SACAC	FBG	CB	IB	10D		8	6	3640	2	10	25400	28200
26	4	KODIAK	SLP	SACAC	FBG	KL	IB	10D		8	6	3640	2	10	24300	27000
26	4	KODIAK TRAWLER		TRWL	FBG	DS	OB			8	6	3640	2	10	25200	28000
26	4	KODIAK TRAWLER DP		TRWL	FBG	DS	IB	18D		8	6	3640	2	10	24000	26700
26	4	KODIAK WP	SLP	SACAC	FBG	CB	IB	10D		8	6	3640	2	10	22000	24400
26	4	KODIAK WP	SLP	SACAC	FBG	KL	IB	10D		8	6	3640	2	10	20900	23200
29	11	NIMBLE 30	SLP	SACAC	FBG	CB	IB	18D	YAN	9	4	7000	5	6	49600	54500
29	11	NIMBLE 30	SLP	SACAC	FBG	KL	IB	18D	YAN	9	4	7000	4	6	49500	54400
29	11	NIMBLE 30	YWL	SACAC	FBG	KL	IB	18D	YAN	9	4	7000	4	6	49500	54400
		1993 BOATS														
20	10	NIMBLE 20 OFF	SLP	SACAC	FBG	KL	OB			7	9	2200	4	3	11900	13500
20	10	NIMBLE 20 STD	SLP	SACAC	FBG	KL	OB			7	9	2200	4	1	10400	11800
20	10	NIMBLE 20 TROPICAL	SLP	SACAC	FBG	KL	OB			7	9	2200	4	1	11100	12700
24	2	NIMBLE 24 D	SLP	SACAC	FBG	KL	IB	D		8	3	2900	2	6	17100	19500
24	2	NIMBLE 24 OFF	SLP	SACAC	FBG	KL	IB	D		8	3	2900	2	8	14900	16900
24	2	NIMBLE 24 STD	SLP	SACAC	FBG	CB	IB	D		8	3	2900	4	2	17500	19800
24	2	NIMBLE 24 STD	SLP	SACAC	FBG	KL	IB	D		8	3	2900	2	6	16500	18700
24	2	NIMBLE 24 TROPICAL	SLP	SACAC	FBG	CB	IB	D		8	3	2900	4	2	16500	18700
24	2	NIMBLE 24 TROPICAL	SLP	SACAC	FBG	KL	IB	D		8	3	2900	2	6	16500	18700
24	2	NIMBLE 25 ARCTIC	SLP	SACAC	FBG	CB	IB	D		8	3	2900	4	2	17500	19800
24	2	NIMBLE 25 ARCTIC	SLP	SACAC	FBG	KL	IB	D		8	3	2900	2	6	16500	18700
24	2	NIMBLE 25 ARCTIC D	SLP	SACAC	FBG	KL	IB	D		8	3	2900	2	6	16500	18700
24	7	NOMAD MAPLE LEAF	HT	TRWL	FBG	DS	OB			8	6	2450	1	2	14700	16700
24	7	NOMAD STD	HT	TRWL	FBG	DS	OB			8	6	3250	1	2	17200	19500
24	7	NOMAD TROPICAL	HT	TRWL	FBG	DS	OB			8	6	3250	1	2	19700	21900
25	2	VAGABOND STD	HT	TRWL	FBG	DS	OB			8	6	2900	1	2	18000	20000
25	2	VAGABOND TROPICAL	HT	TRWL	FBG	DS	OB			8	6	2900	1	2	18900	21000
26	4	KODIAK	SLP	SACAC	FBG	CB	IB	10D		8	6	3640	2	10	24300	27000
26	4	KODIAK	SLP	SACAC	FBG	KL	IB	10D		8	6	3640	2	10	23400	26000
26	4	KODIAK TRAWLER		TRWL	FBG	DS	OB			8	6	3640	2	10	24100	26800
26	4	KODIAK TRAWLER DP		TRWL	FBG	DS	IB	18D		8	6	3640	2	10	22900	25400

LOA FT	LOA IN	NAME AND/ OR MODEL	TOP/ RIG	BOAT TYPE	-HULL- MTL	-HULL- TP	ENGINE TP	ENGINE # HP	ENGINE MFG	BEAM FT	BEAM IN	WGT LBS	DRAFT FT	DRAFT IN	RETAIL LOW	RETAIL HIGH
		1993 BOATS														
26	4	KODIAK WP	SLP	SACAC	FBG	CB	IB	10D		8	6	3640	2	10	20500	22800
26	4	KODIAK WP	SLP	SACAC	FBG	KL	IB	10D		8	6	3640	2	10	19800	22000
28	7	WANDERER STD	SLP	SACAC	FBG	KL	IB	12D		8	6	6400	4	9	40000	44400
28	7	WANDERER TROPICAL	SLP	SACAC	FBG	KL	IB	18D		8	6	6400	4	9	40100	44600
29	11	NIMBLE 30	SLP	SACAC	FBG	CB	IB	18D	YAN	9	4	7000	5	6	46300	50900
29	11	NIMBLE 30	SLP	SACAC	FBG	KL	IB	18D	YAN	9	4	7000	4	6	46300	50800
29	11	NIMBLE 30	YWL	SACAC	FBG	KL	IB	18D	YAN	9	4	7000	4	6	46300	50800
30	5	VOYAGER 26 STD	SLP	SACAC	FBG	KL	IB	12D		8	3	6700	3	4	42100	46800
30	5	VOYAGER 26 TROPICAL	SLP	SACAC	FBG	KL	IB	12D		8	3	6700	3	4	46800	51500
		1992 BOATS														
20	10	NIMBLE 20 OFF	SLP	SAIL	FBG	KL	OB			7	9	2200	4	3	11100	12600
20	10	NIMBLE 20 STD	SLP	SAIL	FBG	KL	OB			7	9	2200	4	1	9800	11100
20	10	NIMBLE 20 TROPICAL	SLP	SAIL	FBG	KL	OB			7	9	2200	4	1	10400	11800
24	2	NIMBLE 24 D	SLP	SAIL	FBG	KL	IB	D		8	3	2900	2	6	16000	18200
24	2	NIMBLE 24 OFF	SLP	SAIL	FBG	KL	IB	D		8	3	2900	2	8	14000	15900
24	2	NIMBLE 24 STD	SLP	SAIL	FBG	CB	IB	D		8	3	2900	4	2	16300	18600
24	2	NIMBLE 24 STD	SLP	SAIL	FBG	KL	IB	D		8	3	2900	2	6	15400	17500
24	2	NIMBLE 24 TROPICAL	SLP	SAIL	FBG	CB	IB	D		8	3	2900	4	2	15400	17500
24	2	NIMBLE 24 TROPICAL	SLP	SAIL	FBG	KL	IB	D		8	3	2900	2	6	15400	17500
24	2	NIMBLE 25 ARCTIC	SLP	SAIL	FBG	CB	IB	D		8	3	2900	4	2	16300	18600
24	2	NIMBLE 25 ARCTIC	SLP	SAIL	FBG	KL	IB	D		8	3	2900	2	6	15400	17500
24	2	NIMBLE 25 ARCTIC D	SLP	SAIL	FBG	KL	IB	D		8	3	2900	2	6	15400	17500
24	7	NOMAD MAPLE LEAF	HT	TRWL	FBG	DS	OB			8	6	2450	1	2	14100	16000
24	7	NOMAD STD	HT	TRWL	FBG	DS	OB			8	6	3250	1	2	16400	18700
24	7	NOMAD TROPICAL	HT	TRWL	FBG	DS	OB			8	6	3250	1	2	19000	21100
25	2	VAGABOND STD	HT	TRWL	FBG	DS	OB			8	6	2900	1	2	16900	19200
25	2	VAGABOND TROPICAL	HT	TRWL	FBG	DS	OB			8	6	2900	1	2	18200	20200
28	7	WANDERER STD	SLP	SAIL	FBG	KL	IB	12D		8	6	6400	4	9	37700	41900
28	7	WANDERER TROPICAL	SLP	SAIL	FBG	KL	IB	18D		8	6	6400	4	9	37800	42000
29	11	NIMBLE 30	SLP	SAIL	FBG	CB	IB	18D	YAN	9	4	7000	5	6	43300	48100
29	11	NIMBLE 30	SLP	SAIL	FBG	KL	IB	18D	YAN	9	4	7000	4	6	43200	48000
29	11	NIMBLE 30	YWL	SAIL	FBG	KL	IB	18D	YAN	9	4	7000	4	6	43200	48000
30	5	VOYAGER 26 STD	SLP	SAIL	FBG	KL	IB	12D		8	3	6700	3	4	40500	45000
30	5	VOYAGER 26 TROPICAL	SLP	SAIL	FBG	KL	IB	12D		8	3	6700	3	4	43100	47900
		1988 BOATS														
20	11	NIMBLE 20 OFFSHORE	YWL	SA/CR	F/S	KC	OB			7	9	2200		11	8150	9400
20	11	NIMBLE 20 STANDARD	YWL	SA/CR	F/S	KC	OB			7	9	2200		11	8150	9400
20	11	NIMBLE 20 TROPICAL	YWL	SA/CR	F/S	KC	OB			7	9	2200		11	8150	9400
26	2	NIMBLE 24 ARCTIC	SLP	SAIL	F/S	KC	OB			7	9	2600	2		10100	11500
26	2	NIMBLE 24 ARCTIC	SLP	SAIL	F/S	KC	IB	10D		7	9	2600	2		11100	12600
27	2	NIMBLE 24 STANDARD	YWL	SA/CR	F/S	KC	OB			7	9	2400	1	4	9700	11000
27	2	NIMBLE 24 STANDARD	YWL	SA/CR	F/S	KC	IB	10D		7	9	2400	1	4	10600	12100
29	11	NIMBLE 30	SLP	SA/CR	F/S	KC	IB	10D	YAN	9	4	7000	2	6	33200	36900
29	11	NIMBLE 30	SLP	SA/CR	F/S	KL	IB	10D	YAN	9	4	7000	4	6	32800	36400
33	2	NIMBLE 30	YWL	SA/CR	F/S	KC	IB	10D	YAN	9	4	7000	2	6	33200	36900
33	2	NIMBLE 30	YWL	SA/CR	F/S	KL	IB	10D	YAN	9	4	7000	4	6	32800	36400
		1987 BOATS														
20	11	NIMBLE 20 OFFSHORE	YWL	SA/CR	F/S	KC	OB			7	9	2200		11	7650	8750
20	11	NIMBLE 20 STANDARD	YWL	SA/CR	F/S	KC	OB			7	9	2200		11	7650	8750
20	11	NIMBLE 20 TROPICAL	YWL	SA/CR	F/S	KC	OB			7	9	2200		11	7650	8750
29	11	NIMBLE 30	SLP	SA/CR	F/S	KC	IB	10D	YAN	9	4	7000	2	6	31000	34500
29	11	NIMBLE 30	SLP	SA/CR	F/S	KL	IB	10D	YAN	9	4	7000	4	6	30700	34100
33	2	NIMBLE 30	YWL	SA/CR	F/S	KC	IB	10D	YAN	9	4	7000	2	6	31000	34500
33	2	NIMBLE 30	YWL	SA/CR	F/S	KL	IB	10D	YAN	9	4	7000	4	6	30700	34100
		1986 BOATS														
20	10	NIMBLE 20	YWL	SAIL	FBG	KC	OB			7	9	2200	4		6650	7650
29	11	NIMBLE 30	YWL	SA/RC	FBG	KL	IB	10D	YAN	9	4	7000	4	6	28800	32000
		1985 BOATS														
29	11	NIMBLE 30	YWL	SA/RC	FBG	KL	IB	10D	YAN	8	10	7000	6	11	26900	29900

NISSAN MARINE & POWER PROD

MARENGO IL 60152-3235

See inside cover to adjust price for area

LOA FT	LOA IN	NAME AND/ OR MODEL	TOP/ RIG	BOAT TYPE	-HULL- MTL	-HULL- TP	ENGINE TP	ENGINE # HP	ENGINE MFG	BEAM FT	BEAM IN	WGT LBS	DRAFT FT	DRAFT IN	RETAIL LOW	RETAIL HIGH
		1990 BOATS														
16		SP16BR	OP	RNBT	FBG	DV	OB			6	4	650			3250	3750
16		SP16VFS	OP	FSH	FBG	DV	OB			6	4	775			3650	4250
16		WANB160BA	OP	BASS	AL	SV	OB			5	7	570			2850	3350
16	6	SR17BR	OP	RNBT	FBG	DV	OB			7		1225			5550	6400
16	6	SR17SS DLX	OP	RNBT	FBG	DV	OB			7		1225			5800	6700
16	9	SP17BA	OP	BASS	FBG	SV	OB			7	2	1100			5150	5900
16	10	SP17CC	OP	CTRCN	FBG	DV	OB			7	4	1200			5450	6250
18		WA18BR	OP	RNBT	AL	SV	OB			6	8	750			4000	4650
18		WA18CC	OP	CTRCN	AL	SV	OB			6	8	750			3850	4500
18		WA18FS	OP	FSH	AL	SV	OB			6	8	750			3850	4450
19		TT19CC	OP	CTRCN	FBG	DV	OB			7	10	1550			6800	7800

NOR'SEA MARINE

DANA POINT CA 92629

See inside cover to adjust price for area

LOA FT	LOA IN	NAME AND/ OR MODEL	TOP/ RIG	BOAT TYPE	-HULL- MTL	-HULL- TP	ENGINE TP	ENGINE # HP	ENGINE MFG	BEAM FT	BEAM IN	WGT LBS	DRAFT FT	DRAFT IN	RETAIL LOW	RETAIL HIGH
		1986 BOATS														
27		NOR'SEA 27	SLP	SA/CR	FBG	KL	IB	15D		8		8000	3	6	34300	38100
35	6	NOR'SEA 35	SLP	SA/CR	FBG	KL	IB	35D	YAN	11	8	20000	5	6	89500	98400
		1985 BOATS														
27		NOR'SEA 27	SLP	SA/CR	FBG	KL	IB	15D		8		8000	3	6	32500	36100
35	6	NOR'SEA 35	SLP	SA/CR	FBG	KL	IB	22D	SABB	11	8	20000	5	6	84600	92900

NORD YACHTS

DIV OF RECREATIONAL EQUIP CO
BUENA PARK CA 90621 COAST GUARD MFG ID- NRD
SEE ALSO OY FISKARS A/B

See inside cover to adjust price for area

LOA FT	LOA IN	NAME AND/ OR MODEL	TOP/ RIG	BOAT TYPE	-HULL- MTL	-HULL- TP	ENGINE TP	ENGINE # HP	ENGINE MFG	BEAM FT	BEAM IN	WGT LBS	DRAFT FT	DRAFT IN	RETAIL LOW	RETAIL HIGH
		1986 BOATS														
52	6	NORD	SCH	SA/CR	STL	KL	IB	120D	LEHM	15	1	48400	7		219500	241500
54		NORD	SCH	SA/CR	STL	KL	IB	120D	LEHM	15	5	63000	7	4	253000	278000
60	6	NORD	SCH	SA/CR	STL	KL	IB	120D	LEHM	17		72750	7	6	448500	492500
		1985 BOATS														
47		SEA-ROVER 47	SCH	SA/CR	STL	KL	IB	D		13	6	35850	5	9	147000	161500
52	6	NORD	SCH	SA/CR	STL	KL	IB	120D	LEHM	15	1	48400	7		205500	225500
54		NORD	SCH	SA/CR	STL	KL	IB	120D	LEHM	15	5	63000	7	4	236500	260000
60	6	NORD	SCH	SA/CR	STL	KL	IB	120D	LEHM	17		72750	7	6	419000	460500
		1984 BOATS														
31		FINN-FLYER 31	SLP	SA/RC	FBG	KL	IB	D		10	6	7275	5	8	28900	32100
54		SEA-ROVER 54	SCH	SA/CR	STL	KL	IB	D		14	9	46300	6	6	209000	229500
60		SEA-ROVER 60	SCH	SA/CR	STL	KL	IB	D		15	1	55875	7	4	328000	360500

....For earlier years, see the BUC Used Boat Price Guide, Volume 3

NORDIC BOATS INC

LAKE HAVASU CITY AZ 864 COAST GUARD MFG ID- NDC See inside cover to adjust price for area

For more recent years, see the BUC Used Boat Price Guide, Volume 1

LOA FT	LOA IN	NAME AND/ OR MODEL	TOP/ RIG	BOAT TYPE	-HULL- MTL	-HULL- TP	ENGINE TP	ENGINE # HP	ENGINE MFG	BEAM FT	BEAM IN	WGT LBS	DRAFT FT	DRAFT IN	RETAIL LOW	RETAIL HIGH
		1996 BOATS														
22		SUNRUNNER		CTRCN	FBG	SV	IO	300	MRCR	8		2900			26800	29700
22	2	SPRINT		RNBT	FBG	SV	IO	300	MRCR	7	10	3300			24800	27500
22	2	SPRINT BOWRIDER		RNBT	FBG	SV	IO	300	MRCR	7	10	3300			26000	28900
22	7	SUNRUNNER II		CTRCN	FBG	SV	IO	300	MRCR	8	4	3550			31800	35300
23	2	VENTURE		CUD	FBG	SV	IO	300	MRCR	8		3550			29400	32600
23	2	VENTURE OPEN BOW		B/R	FBG	SV	IO	300	MRCR	8		3550			27500	30600
24	5	SCANDIA 25		CUD	FBG	SV	IO	300	MRCR	8		3700			32600	36200
24	5	SCANDIA 25 OPEN BOW		B/R	FBG	SV	IO	300	MRCR	8		3700			30500	33900
26		VIKING 26		CUD	FBG	SV	IO	300	MRCR	8		3800			38300	42500
26		VIKING 26 OPEN BOW		CUD	FBG	SV	IO	300	MRCR	8		3800			39900	44300
28	1	NORDIC 28		OFF	FBG	DV	IO	385	MRCR	8	4	4900			55200	60700
28	1	NORDIC 28 OPEN BOW		OFF	FBG	DV	IO	385	MRCR	8	4	4900			56800	62400
28	9	NORDIC 29		OFF	FBG	DV	IO	365	MRCR	8	2	5100			56700	62300
28	9	NORDIC 29 OPEN BOW		OFF	FBG	DV	IO	T385	MRCR	8	2	6225			81000	89000
32	6	NORDIC 32		OFF	FBG	DV	IO	T300	MRCR	8	6	7900			108000	118500
32	6	NORDIC 32 OPEN BOW		OFF	FBG	DV	IO	T300	MRCR	8	6	7900			110000	121000
		1995 BOATS														
22		SUNRUNNER		CTRCN	FBG	SV	IO	300	MRCR	8		2900			24900	27600
22	2	SPRINT		RNBT	FBG	SV	IO	300	MRCR	7	10	3300			23100	25700
22	2	SPRINT BOWRIDER		RNBT	FBG	SV	IO	300	MRCR	7	10	3300			24200	26900
22	7	SUNRUNNER II		CTRCN	FBG	SV	IO	300	MRCR	8	4	3550			29600	32900
23	2	VENTURE		CUD	FBG	SV	IO	300	MRCR	8		3550			27300	30300
23	2	VENTURE OPEN BOW		B/R	FBG	SV	IO	300	MRCR	8		3550			25600	28500
24	5	SCANDIA 25		CUD	FBG	SV	IO	300	MRCR	8		3700			30300	33600
24	5	SCANDIA 25 OPEN BOW		B/R	FBG	SV	IO	300	MRCR	8		3700			28500	31700
26		VIKING 26		CUD	FBG	SV	IO	300	MRCR	8		3800			35400	39300
26		VIKING 26 OPEN BOW		CUD	FBG	SV	IO	300	MRCR	8		3800			37200	41400
28	1	NORDIC 28		OFF	FBG	DV	IO	385	MRCR	8	4	4900			51500	56600
28	1	NORDIC 28 OPEN BOW		OFF	FBG	DV	IO	385	MRCR	8	4	4900			53000	58300

CONTINUED ON NEXT PAGE

LOA FT	IN	NAME AND/ OR MODEL	TOP/ RIG	BOAT TYPE	-HULL- MTL	TP	TP	ENGINE # HP	MFG	BEAM FT	IN	WGT LBS	DRAFT FT	IN	RETAIL LOW	RETAIL HIGH
		1995 BOATS														
28	9	NORDIC 29		OFF	FBG	DV	IO	365	MRCR	8	2	5100			52900	58100
28	9	NORDIC 29 OPEN BOW		OFF	FBG	DV	IO	T385	MRCR	8	2	6225			75400	82900
32	6	NORDIC 32		OFF	FBG	DV	IO	T300	MRCR	8	6	7900			112500	123500
32	6	NORDIC 32 OPEN BOW		OFF	FBG	DV	IO	T300	MRCR	8	6	7900			114500	126000
		1994 BOATS														
22		SUNRUNNER		CTRCN	FBG	SV	IO	330	MRCR	8		2900			24700	27400
22	2	SPRINT		RNBT	FBG	SV	IO	330	MRCR	7	10	3300			22800	25400
22	2	SPRINT BOWRIDER		RNBT	FBG	SV	IO	330	MRCR	7	10	3300			24000	26600
22	7	SUNRUNNER II		CTRCN	FBG	SV	IO	330	MRCR	8	4	3550			29100	32300
23	2	VENTURE		CUD	FBG	SV	IO	330	MRCR	8		3550			26900	29800
23	2	VENTURE OPEN BOW		B/R	FBG	SV	IO	330	MRCR	8		3550			25200	28000
24	5	SCANDIA 25		CUD	FBG	SV	IO	330	MRCR	8		3700			29700	33000
24	5	SCANDIA 25 OPEN BOW		B/R	FBG	SV	IO	330	MRCR	8		3700			27800	30900
26		VIKING 26		CUD	FBG	SV	IO	330	MRCR	8		3800			34400	38200
26		VIKING 26 OPEN BOW		CUD	FBG	SV	IO	330	MRCR	8		3800			35800	39700
28	1	NORDIC 28		OFF	FBG	DV	IO	415	MRCR	8	4	4900			50600	55600
28	1	NORDIC 28 OPEN BOW		OFF	FBG	DV	IO	415	MRCR	8	4	4900			52000	57200
28	9	NORDIC 29		OFF	FBG	DV	IO	365	MRCR	8	2	5100			49300	54200
28	9	NORDIC 29 OPEN BOW		OFF	FBG	DV	IO	T415	MRCR	8	2	6225			75600	83100
32	6	NORDIC 32		OFF	FBG	DV	IO	T330	MRCR	8	6	7900			96900	106500
32	6	NORDIC 32 OPEN BOW		OFF	FBG	DV	IO	T330	MRCR	8	6	7900			98900	108500
		1993 BOATS														
22		SUNRUNNER		CTRCN	FBG	SV	IO	330-365		8		2900			23000	28000
22	2	SPRINT		RNBT	FBG	SV	IO	330-365		7	10	3300			21800	26400
23	2	VENTURE		CUD	FBG	SV	IO	330-365		8		3550			24900	30000
23	2	VENTURE		CUD	FBG	SV	IO	390	MRCR	8		3550			29000	32200
23	2	VENTURE OPEN BOW		B/R	FBG	SV	IO	330-365		8		3550			23500	28300
23	2	VENTURE OPEN BOW		B/R	FBG	SV	IO	390	MRCR	8		3550			27200	30200
24	5	SCANDIA 25		CUD	FBG	SV	IO	330-365		8		3700			27400	32800
24	5	SCANDIA 25		CUD	FBG	SV	IO	390-415		8		3700			31400	37400
24	5	SCANDIA 25 OPEN BOW		B/R	FBG	SV	IO	330-365		8		3700			25900	30900
24	5	SCANDIA 25 OPEN BOW		B/R	FBG	SV	IO	390-415		8		3700			29600	35100
26		VIKING 26		CUD	FBG	SV	IO	330-390		8		3800			32300	40400
28	1	NORDIC 27		OFF	FBG	DV	IO	365-390		8	4	4900			43000	49900
28	9	NORDIC 29		OFF	FBG	DV	IO	365-390		8	2	5100			45700	52400
28	9	NORDIC 29		OFF	FBG	DV	IO	T330-T365		8	2	6225			57700	68400
32	6	NORDIC 32		OFF	FBG	DV	IO	T330-T390		8	6	7900			90300	111500
		1992 BOATS														
22		SUNRUNNER		CTRCN	FBG	SV	IO	330-365		8		2900			21400	26100
22	2	SPRINT		RNBT	FBG	SV	IO	330-365		7	10	3300			20400	24700
23	2	VENTURE		CUD	FBG	SV	IO	330-365		8		3550			23300	28100
23	2	VENTURE		CUD	FBG	SV	IO	415	MRCR	8		3550			29000	32300
23	2	VENTURE OPEN BOW		B/R	FBG	SV	IO	330-365		8		3550			21900	26400
23	2	VENTURE OPEN BOW		B/R	FBG	SV	IO	415	MRCR	8		3550			27200	30200
26		VIKING 26		CUD	FBG	SV	IO	330-365		8		3800			30200	35700
26		VIKING 26		CUD	FBG	SV	IO	415	MRCR	8		3800			35600	39600
28	1	NORDIC 27		OFF	FBG	DV	IO	365-415		8	4	4900			40000	49100
28	9	NORDIC 29		OFF	FBG	DV	IO	365-415		8	2	5100			42300	51300
28	9	NORDIC 29		OFF	FBG	DV	IO	T330-T365		8	2	6225			54100	64000
32	6	NORDIC 32		OFF	FBG	DV	IO	T330-T415		8	6	7900			94100	112000

....For earlier years, see the BUC Used Boat Price Guide, Volume 3

NORDIC TUGS INC

BURLINGTON WA 98233 COAST GUARD MFG ID- NTK See inside cover to adjust price for area

For more recent years, see the BUC Used Boat Price Guide, Volume 1

LOA FT	IN	NAME AND/ OR MODEL	TOP/ RIG	BOAT TYPE	-HULL- MTL	TP	TP	ENGINE # HP	MFG	BEAM FT	IN	WGT LBS	DRAFT FT	IN	RETAIL LOW	RETAIL HIGH
		1996 BOATS														
26	4	NORDIC TUG 2-26	EPH	MY	FBG	DS	IB	62D	YAN	9	6	7500	2	9	80100	88000
32	2	NORDIC TUG 32	EPH	MY	FBG	DS	IB	210D	CUM	11		13500	3	6	130000	142500
42		NORDIC TUG 42	EPH	MY	FBG	DS	IB	300D	CUM	13	10	29000	4		240000	263500
		1995 BOATS														
26	4	NT 2-26		TUG	FBG	DS	IB	62D	YAN	9	6	6900	2	9	67100	73700
32	2	NT-32		TUG	FBG	DS	IB	210D	CUM	11		13500	3	6	114500	126000
42		NT 42		TUG	FBG	DS	IB	300D	DEER	13	10	25000	4		133000	146000
		1994 BOATS														
26	4	CRUISER		TUG	FBG	DS	IB	62D	YAN	9	6	6500	2		57500	63200
32		CRUISER		TUG	FBG	DS	IB	210D	CUM	11		13500	3		108500	119000
		1993 BOATS														
26	4	CRUISER		TUG	FBG	DS	IB	62D	YAN	9	6	6500	2		54800	60200
32		CRUISER		TUG	FBG	DS	IB	210D	CUM	11		13500	3		103500	113500
		1992 BOATS														
26	4	NORDIC BASIC TUG	HT	PH	FBG	DS	IB	50D	YAN	9	6	6000	2		51400	56500
26	4	NORDIC CRUISE TUG	HT	PH	FBG	DS	IB	62D	YAN	9	6	6750	2		58800	64600
32		NORDIC BASIC TUG	HT	PH	FBG	DS	IB	115D	CUM	11		13000	3		100500	110500
32		NORDIC CRUISE TUG	HT	PH	FBG	DS	IB	115D	CUM	11		13500	3		103500	114000
36		NORDIC BASIC TUG	HT	TUG	FBG	DS	IB	115D	CUM	11		16000	3		**	**
36		NORDIC CRUISE TUG	HT	TUG	FBG	DS	IB	210D	CUM	11		16500	3		**	**
		1991 BOATS														
26	4	NORDIC BASIC TUG	HT	PH	FBG	DS	IB	50D	YAN	9	6	6000	2		49100	54000
26	4	NORDIC CRUISE TUG	HT	PH	FBG	DS	IB	62D- 88D		9	6	6750	2		56200	62600
32		NORDIC BASIC TUG	HT	PH	FBG	DS	IB	115D	CUM	11		13000	3		96100	105500
32		NORDIC CRUISE TUG	HT	PH	FBG	DS	IB	115D-210D		11		13500	3		99000	109000
36		NORDIC BASIC TUG	HT	TUG	FBG	DS	IB	115D	CUM	11		16000	3		**	**
36		NORDIC CRUISE TUG	HT	TUG	FBG	DS	IB	210D	CUM	11		16500	3		**	**
		1990 BOATS														
26	4	NORDIC CRUISE TUG	HT	PH	FBG	DS	IB	55D- 77D		9	6	6750	2		53400	59400
32		NORDIC CRUISE TUG	HT	PH	FBG	DS	IB	115D-210D		11		13500	3		94600	104000
		1989 BOATS														
26	4	NORDIC CRUISE TUG	HT	PH	FBG	DS	IB	55D- 77D		9	6	6750	2		51200	57000
32		NORDIC CRUISE TUG	HT	PH	FBG	DS	IB	115D-210D		11		13500	3		90500	99400
		1988 BOATS														
26	4	NORDIC CRUISE TUG	HT	PH	FBG	DS	IB	55D- 77D		9	6	6750	2		49100	54600
32		NORDIC CRUISE TUG	HT	PH	FBG	DS	IB	115D-210D		11		13500	3		86600	95200
		1987 BOATS														
26	4	NORDIC CRUISE TUG	HT	PH	FBG	DS	IB	44D- 77D		9	6	6750	2		46900	55300
26	4	NORDIC SPORT TUG	HT	PH	FBG	DS	IB	44D- 77D		9	6	6100	2		41600	51800
32		NORDIC CRUISE TUG	HT	PH	FBG	DS	IB	120D-175D		11	2	11000	3		70400	77300
32		NORDIC SPORT TUG	HT	PH	FBG	DS	IB	120D	YAN	11	2	10500	3		67900	74600
		1986 BOATS														
26	4	NORDIC CRUISE TUG	HT	PH	FBG	DS	IB	33		9	6	6000	2		32000	35600
26	4	NORDIC CRUISE TUG	HT	PH	FBG	DS	IB	44D	YAN	9	6	6750	2		44500	49400
26	4	NORDIC CRUISE TUG	HT	PH	FBG	DS	IB	55D-100D		9	6		2		53600	59700
26	4	NORDIC SPORT TUG	HT	PH	FBG	DS	IB	33		9	6	5600	2		30300	33700
26	4	NORDIC SPORT TUG	HT	PH	FBG	DS	IB	44D	YAN	9	6	6100	2		39900	44300
26	4	NORDIC SPORT TUG	HT	PH	FBG	DS	IB	55D-100D		9	6		2		45800	51500
26	4	NORDIC WORK TUG	HT	PH	FBG	DS	IB	33		9	6	5200	2		28600	31800
26	4	NORDIC WORK TUG	HT	PH	FBG	DS	IB	44D	YAN	9	6	5200	2		33400	37200
26	4	NORDIC WORK TUG	HT	PH	FBG	DS	IB	55D-100D		9	6		2		40400	46400
32		NORDIC CRUISE TUG	HT	PH	FBG	DS	IB	120D-175D		11		11000	3		67300	73900
32		NORDIC SPORT TUG	HT	PH	FBG	DS	IB	120D	YAN	11		10500	3		64900	71300
		1985 BOATS														
26		NORDIC CRUISE TUG	HT	PH	FBG	DS	IB	66D- 85D		9	6	6750			43400	49400
26		NORDIC SPORT TUG	HT	PH	FBG	DS	IB	66D	YAN	9	6	5300			33700	37500
26	4	NORDIC CRUISE TUG	HT	PH	FBG	DS	IB			9	6	6000	2		**	**
26	4	NORDIC CRUISE TUG	HT	PH	FBG	DS	IB	44D-100D		9	6	6750	2		42600	50600
32		NORDIC CRUISE TUG	HT	PH	FBG	DS	IB	145D-175D		11		11100	3		63800	70200
		1984 BOATS														
26	4	NORDIC CRUISE TUG	HT	PH	FBG	DS	IB	33D	YAN	9	6	6750	2		40500	45000
26	4	NORDIC CRUISE TUG	HT	PH	FBG	DS	IB	50D- 85D		9	6		2		48900	55300
26	4	NORDIC SPORT TUG	HT	PH	FBG	DS	IB	33D	YAN	9	6	6100	2		36300	40400
26	4	NORDIC SPORT TUG	HT	PH	FBG	DS	IB	50D- 85D		9	6		2		41400	47700
26	4	NORDIC WORK TUG	HT	PH	FBG	DS	IB	33D	YAN	9	6	5200	2		30400	33800
26	4	NORDIC WORK TUG	HT	PH	FBG	DS	IB	50D- 85D		9	6		2		37100	43000

NORDIC YACHTS INC

BELLINGHAM WA 98227 COAST GUARD MFG ID- NYA See inside cover to adjust price for area

LOA FT	IN	NAME AND/ OR MODEL	TOP/ RIG	BOAT TYPE	-HULL- MTL	TP	TP	ENGINE # HP	MFG	BEAM FT	IN	WGT LBS	DRAFT FT	IN	RETAIL LOW	RETAIL HIGH
		1990 BOATS														
34	4	NORDIC 34	SLP	SA/CR	FBG	KL	IB	25D	UNIV	11		10656	6	2	63400	69700
34	4	NORDIC 34	SLP	SA/CR	FBG	WK	IB	25D	UNIV	11		10656	4	9	63400	69700
39	9	NORDIC 40SE DEEP	SLP	SA/CR	FBG	KL	IB	40D	UNIV	12	5	18000	6	6	111000	121500
39	9	NORDIC 40SE SHOAL	SLP	SA/CR	FBG	KL	IB	40D	UNIV	12	5	18000	5	6	111000	121500
39	9	NORDIC CUSTOM 40 DP	SLP	SA/CR	FBG	KL	IB	40D	UNIV	12	5	18000	6	6	124500	137000
39	9	NORDIC CUSTOM 40 SHL	SLP	SA/CR	FBG	KL	IB	40D	UNIV	12	5	18000	5	6	124500	137000
43	10	NORDIC 44SE DEEP	SLP	SA/CR	FBG	KL	IB	50D	UNIV	12	11	24000	7		157500	173000
43	10	NORDIC 44SE SHOAL	SLP	SA/CR	FBG	KL	IB	50D	UNIV	12	11	24000	5	11	157500	173000
43	10	NORDIC CUSTOM 44 DP	SLP	SA/CR	FBG	KL	IB	50D	UNIV	12	11	24000	7		176000	193500
43	10	NORDIC CUSTOM 44 SHL	SLP	SA/CR	FBG	KL	IB	50D	UNIV	12	11	24000	5	11	176000	193500
45	4	NORDIC 45 DEEP	SLP	SA/CR	FBG	KL	IB	D		12	11	25000	7		183000	201000
45	4	NORDIC 45 SHOAL	SLP	SA/CR	FBG	KL	IB	D		12	11	25000	5	10	183000	201000
48		NORDIC 480	FB	MY	FBG	SV	IB	T375D	CAT	15	8	39500	3	11	267000	293500
48		NORDIC 480	FB	MY	FBG	SV	IB	T425D	CAT	15	8	39500	3	11	276500	304000
48		NORDIC 480	FB	MY	FBG	SV	IB	T485D	GM	15	8	39500	3	11	286000	314500
50		NORDIC 500	FB	MY	FBG	SV	IB	T375D	CAT	15	8	39500	3	11	275500	302500
50		NORDIC 500	FB	MY	FBG	SV	IB	T425D	CAT	15	8	39500	3	11	289000	318000

CONTINUED ON NEXT PAGE

LOA FT	LOA IN	NAME AND/ OR MODEL	TOP/ RIG	BOAT TYPE	-HULL- MTL	-HULL- TP	TP	# HP	MFG	BEAM FT	BEAM IN	WGT LBS	DRAFT FT	DRAFT IN	RETAIL LOW	RETAIL HIGH
		1990 BOATS														
50		NORDIC 500	FB	MY	FBG	SV	IB	T485D	GM	15	8	39500	3	11	305500	335500
56		NORDIC 560	FB	MY	FBG	SV	IB	T550D	GM	18		55000	3	10	443500	487500
56		NORDIC 560	FB	MY	FBG	SV	IB	T650D	GM	18		55000	3	10	478000	525500
56		NORDIC 560	FB	MY	FBG	SV	IB	T735D	GM	18		55000	3	10	505500	555500
		1989 BOATS														
34	4	NORDIC 34	SLP	SA/CR	FBG	KL	IB	25D	UNIV	11		10656	6	2	60100	66000
34	4	NORDIC 34	SLP	SA/CR	FBG	WK	IB	25D	UNIV	11		10656	4	9	60100	66000
39	9	NORDIC 40SE DEEP	SLP	SA/CR	FBG	KL	IB	40D	UNIV	12	5	18000	6	6	104500	115000
39	9	NORDIC 40SE SHOAL	SLP	SA/CR	FBG	KL	IB	40D	UNIV	12	5	18000	5	6	104500	115000
39	9	NORDIC CUSTOM 40 DP	SLP	SA/CR	FBG	KL	IB	40D	UNIV	12	5	18000	6	6	118500	130500
39	9	NORDIC CUSTOM 40 SHL	SLP	SA/CR	FBG	KL	IB	40D	UNIV	12	5	18000	5	6	118500	130500
43	10	NORDIC 44SE DEEP	SLP	SA/CR	FBG	KL	IB	50D	UNIV	12	11	24000	7		147000	161500
43	10	NORDIC 44SE SHOAL	SLP	SA/CR	FBG	KL	IB	50D	UNIV	12	11	24000	5	11	147000	161500
43	10	NORDIC CUSTOM 44 DP	SLP	SA/CR	FBG	KL	IB	50D	UNIV	12	11	24000	7		169000	186000
43	10	NORDIC CUSTOM 44 SHL	SLP	SA/CR	FBG	KL	IB	50D	UNIV	12	11	24000	5	11	169000	186000
44	10	NORDIC 45 DEEP	SLP	SA/CR	FBG	KL	IB	D		12	11	25000	7		169000	186000
44	10	NORDIC 45 SHOAL	SLP	SA/CR	FBG	KL	IB	D		12	11	25000	5	10	169000	186000
48		NORDIC 480	FB	MY	FBG	SV	IB	T350	CRUS	15	8	39500	3	11	228000	251000
		IB T250D GM 235000 258500, IB T320D CAT 246500 271000, IB T375D CAT													255000	280500
		IB T440D 264500 290500, IB T485D GM 273500 300500, IB T550D GM													286000	314500
		IB T735D GM 319500 351500														
50		NORDIC 500	FB	MY	FBG	SV	IB	T350	CRUS	15	8	39500	3	11	233500	256500
		IB T250D GM 234000 257000, IB T320D CAT 250000 274500, IB T375D CAT													263000	289000
		IB T440D 280000 307500, IB T485D GM 291500 320500, IB T550D GM													308500	339000
52		NORDIC 520	FB	MY	FBG	SV	IB	T350	CRUS	15	8	39500	3	11	252500	277500
		IB T250D GM 250000 275000, IB T320D CAT 267500 294000, IB T375D CAT													280000	308000
		IB T440D 298500 328000, IB T485D GM 306500 337000, IB T550D GM													325500	358000
		IB T735D GM 377000 414000														
		1986 BOATS														
39	9	NORDIC 40 DEEP	SLP	SA/CR	FBG	KL	VD	32D	UNIV	12	5	18000	6	4	93900	103000
39	9	NORDIC 40 SHOAL	SLP	SA/CR	FBG	KL	VD	32D	UNIV	12	5	18000	5	6	95400	105000
43	10	NORDIC 44 DEEP	SLP	SA/CR	FBG	KL	VD	44D	UNIV	12	11	23500	7		135000	148000
43	10	NORDIC 44 SHOAL	SLP	SA/CR	FBG	KL	VD	44D	UNIV	12	11	23500	5	11	130500	143500
48		NORDIC 480	FB	MY	FBG	SV	IB	T250D	GM	15	8	39500	3	11	204000	224500
52		NORDIC 520	FB	MY	FBG	SV	IB	T320D	CAT	15	8	41500	3	11	240000	264000
		1985 BOATS														
39	9	NORDIC 40	SLP	SA/CR	FBG	KL	VD	32D	UNIV	12	5	18000	6	6	88900	97700
39	9	NORDIC 40 SHOAL	SLP	SA/CR	FBG	KL	VD	32D	UNIV	12	5	18000	5	2	90400	99300
43	10	NORDIC 44	SLP	SA/CR	FBG	KL	VD	44D	UNIV	12	11	24000	7		126000	138500
43	10	NORDIC 44 SHOAL	SLP	SA/CR	FBG	KL	VD	44D	UNIV	12	11	24000	5	11	128000	141000
44		NORDIC 440	FB	MY	FBG	SV	IB	T125D		15	8				160000	176000
48		NORDIC 480	FB	MY	FBG	SV	IB	T215D	GM	15	8	39500	3	11	191500	210500
48		NORDIC 480	FB	MY	FBG	SV	IB	T250D		15	8		3	11	194500	213500
52		NORDIC 520	FB	MY	FBG	SV	IB	T300D	CAT	15	8	41000	3	11	226000	248000
		1984 BOATS														
39	9	NORDIC 40	SLP	SA/CR	FBG	KL	VD	32D	UNIV	12	5	18000	6	6	84200	92500
39	9	NORDIC 40 SHOAL	SLP	SA/CR	FBG	KL	VD	32D	UNIV	12	5	18000	5	2	85700	94200
43	10	NORDIC 44	SLP	SA/CR	FBG	KL	VD	44D	UNIV	12	11	24000	7		119500	131500
43	10	NORDIC 44 SHOAL	SLP	SA/CR	FBG	KL	VD	44D	UNIV	12	11	24000	5	11	121500	133500

....For earlier years, see the BUC Used Boat Price Guide, Volume 3

NORSEMAN SHIPBLDG CORP

MIAMI FL 33136 COAST GUARD MFG ID- NSM See inside cover to adjust price for area

LOA FT	LOA IN	NAME AND/ OR MODEL	TOP/ RIG	BOAT TYPE	-HULL- MTL	-HULL- TP	TP	# HP	MFG	BEAM FT	BEAM IN	WGT LBS	DRAFT FT	DRAFT IN	RETAIL LOW	RETAIL HIGH
		1984 BOATS														
52			FB	SF	FBG	SV	IB	T630D	S&S	16	6	52000	4	3	235000	258000

....For earlier years, see the BUC Used Boat Price Guide, Volume 3

NORSEMAN YACHTS

MARINA DEL REY CA 90292 See inside cover to adjust price for area

LOA FT	LOA IN	NAME AND/ OR MODEL	TOP/ RIG	BOAT TYPE	-HULL- MTL	-HULL- TP	TP	# HP	MFG	BEAM FT	BEAM IN	WGT LBS	DRAFT FT	DRAFT IN	RETAIL LOW	RETAIL HIGH
		1990 BOATS														
40		NORSEMAN 400	SLP	SAIL	FBG	KL	IB	D	YAN						129000	142000
45		NORSEMAN 447	SLP	SAIL	FBG	KL	IB	D	YAN						185500	204000
45		NORSEMAN 447 SHOAL	SLP	SAIL	FBG	KL	IB	D	YAN				5	4	185500	204000
54		NORSEMAN 535	SLP	SAIL	FBG	KL	IB	85D	YAN						351500	386000
54		NORSEMAN 535	CUT	SAIL	FBG	KL	IB	85D	YAN						351000	386000
54		NORSEMAN 535 SHOAL	SLP	SAIL	FBG	KL	IB	85D	YAN				5	4	351500	386000

NORTH AMERICAN FIBERGLASS INC

SEA OX BOATS
GREENVILLE NC 27834-904 COAST GUARD MFG ID- XNA
See inside cover to adjust price for area

For more recent years, see the BUC Used Boat Price Guide, Volume 1

LOA FT	LOA IN	NAME AND/ OR MODEL	TOP/ RIG	BOAT TYPE	-HULL- MTL	-HULL- TP	TP	# HP	MFG	BEAM FT	BEAM IN	WGT LBS	DRAFT FT	DRAFT IN	RETAIL LOW	RETAIL HIGH
		1995 BOATS														
21		SEA CAT 2100-SL1	OP	CTRCN	FBG	CT	OB			8	6	2550		11	8300	9550
25	4	SEA CAT 2550-SL5	OP	CTRCN	FBG	CT	OB			8	6	3500	1		13500	15300
25	4	SEA CAT 2550-SL5 WA	OP	CUD	FBG	CT	OB			8	6	4250	1	1	14700	16700
		1994 BOATS														
18	3	SEA OX 180	OP	CTRCN	FBG	SV	OB			7	4	1850		11	4850	5600
18	3	SEA OX 180D W/T	OP	FSH	FBG	SV	OB			7	4	1850		11	4850	5550
20	3	SEA OX 200	OP	CTRCN	FBG	DV	OB			8		2550	1	2	7350	8450
20	3	SEA OX 200 BRKT	OP	CTRCN	FBG	DV	OB			8		2550	1	2	7350	8450
20	3	SEA OX 200C W/A	OP	CUD	FBG	DV	OB			8		2950	1	2	7400	8500
20	3	SEA OX 200C W/A	OP	CUD	FBG	DV	IO	155-180		8		3100	1	2	9200	10500
20	3	SEA OX 200C W/A BRKT	OP	CUD	FBG	DV	OB			8		2950	1	2	8200	9450
20	3	SEA OX 200D W/T	OP	FSH	FBG	DV	OB			8		2550	1	2	6900	7900
20	3	SEA OX 200D W/T BRKT	OP	FSH	FBG	DV	OB			8		2550	1	2	7850	9050
21		SEA CAT S1	OP	CTRCN	FBG	CT	OB			8	6	2000		11	6700	7750
21		SEA CAT SL2	OP	CTRCN	FBG	CT	OB			8	6	2500		11	7800	9000
23		SEA OX 230	OP	CTRCN	FBG	DV	OB			8		2750	1	4	9450	10800
23		SEA OX 230C W/A	OP	CUD	FBG	DV	OB			8		3300	1	4	10300	11700
23		SEA OX 230C W/A	OP	CUD	FBG	DV	IO	155	VLVO	8		3450	1	4	11300	12800
		IO 205-230 11400 13200, IO 245-300 11700 14300, IO 120D VLVO													13600	15400
23		SEA OX 230C W/A BRKT	OP	CUD	FBG	DV	OB			8		3300	1	4	11200	12800
25		BLUE WATER 250C	OP	CUD	FBG	DV	IO	250	MRCR	8	6	4200	1	5	15000	17000
25		BLUE WATER 250C	OP	CUD	FBG	DV	IO	150D-216D		8	6	4200	1	7	16700	20900
25		BLUE WATER 250C BRKT	OP	CUD	FBG	DV	OB			8	6	4200	1	7	13700	15600
25		BLUE WATER 250C W/A	OP	CUD	FBG	DV	OB			8	6	4100	1	7	13500	15400
25		BLUE WATER 250C W/A	OP	CUD	FBG	DV	IO	230-300		8	6	4200	1	7	15000	18500
25		SEA OX 250	OP	CTRCN	FBG	DV	IO	230-300		8	6	3550	1	5	14500	17900
25		SEA OX 250 BRKT	OP	CTRCN	FBG	DV	OB			8	6	3550	1	5	12500	14200
25	6	SEA CAT 2550-SL5	OP	CTRCN	FBG	CT	OB			8	9	3500	1		13100	14900
26		BLUE WATER 260C	OP	CUD	FBG	DV	IO	216D	VLVO	10		7300	1	7	29700	32900
26		BLUE WATER 260C	OP	CUD	FBG	DV	IO	T205-T230		10		7300	1	7	26600	30100
26		BLUE WATER 260C BRKT	OP	CUD	FBG	DV	OB			10		7300	1	7	16900	19200
26		BLUE WATER 260C W/A	OP	CUD	FBG	DV	IO	300	VLVO	10		7300	1	9	25000	27800
26		BLUE WATER 260C W/A	OP	CUD	FBG	DV	IO	T260	VLVO	10		7300	1	9	27900	31000
26		BLUE WATER 260C W/A	OP	CUD	FBG	DV	IO	T130D-T200D		10		7300	1	9	32700	39800
		1993 BOATS														
18	3	SEA OX 180	OP	CTRCN	FBG	SV	OB			7	4	1850		11	4600	5300
18	3	SEA OX 180D W/T	OP	FSH	FBG	SV	OB			7	4	1850		11	4600	5300
20	3	SEA OX 200	OP	CTRCN	FBG	DV	OB			8		2400	1	2	6850	7850
20	3	SEA OX 200 BRKT	OP	CTRCN	FBG	DV	OB			8		2400	1	2	6850	7850
20	3	SEA OX 200C W/A	OP	CUD	FBG	DV	OB			8		2750	1	2	6900	7950
20	3	SEA OX 200C W/A	OP	CUD	FBG	DV	IO	155-180		8		2750	1	2	7950	9200
20	3	SEA OX 200C W/A BRKT	OP	CUD	FBG	DV	OB			8		2750	1	2	7650	8800
20	3	SEA OX 200D BRKT	OP	FSH	FBG	DV	OB			8		2400	1	2	7300	8400
20	3	SEA OX 200D W/T	OP	FSH	FBG	DV	OB			8		2400	1	2	6400	7350
21		SEA CAT S	OP	CTRCN	FBG	DV	OB			8	6	1800		11	5950	6850
21		SEA CAT S2	OP	CTRCN	FBG	DV	OB			8	6	2000		11	6450	7400
23		SEA OX 230	OP	CTRCN	FBG	DV	OB			8		2600	1	4	8600	9900
23		SEA OX 230C W/A	OP	CUD	FBG	DV	OB			8		3100	1	4	9450	10800
23		SEA OX 230C W/A	OP	CUD	FBG	DV	IO	155	VLVO	8		3100	1	4	9850	11200
		IO 205-230 10000 11500, IO 245-300 10300 12600, IO 120D VLVO													12000	13600
23		SEA OX 230C W/A BRKT	OP	CUD	FBG	DV	OB			8		3100	1	4	10300	11700
25		BLUE WATER 250C	OP	CUD	FBG	DV	IO	250	MRCR	8		4100	1	5	13500	15300
25		BLUE WATER 250C	OP	CUD	FBG	DV	IO	150D-200D		8	6	4100	1	7	15300	18600
25		BLUE WATER 250C	OP	CUD	FBG	DV	IO	216D	VLVO	8	6	4100	1	5	16900	19200
25		BLUE WATER 250C BRKT	OP	CUD	FBG	DV	OB			8	6	4100	1	7	12900	14700
25		BLUE WATER 250C W/A	OP	CUD	FBG	DV	OB			8	6	4100	1	7	12900	14700
25		BLUE WATER 250C W/A	OP	CUD	FBG	DV	IO	275-300		8	6	4100	1	7	14500	17000
25		BLUE WATER 250C W/A	OP	CUD	FBG	DV	IO	T230	VLVO	8	6	4100	1	7	16700	19000
25		SEA OX 250	OP	CTRCN	FBG	DV	IO	230-275		8	6	3400	1	5	13100	15700
25		SEA OX 250	OP	CTRCN	FBG	DV	IO	300	VLVO	8	6	3400	1	5	14500	16500
25		SEA OX 250	OP	CTRCN	FBG	DV	IO	130D-150D		8	6	3400	1	5	16700	19600

NORTH AMERICAN FIBERGLASS INC -CONTINUED See inside cover to adjust price for area

LOA FT	IN	NAME AND/ OR MODEL	TOP/ RIG	BOAT TYPE	-HULL- MTL	TP	----ENGINE--- TP	# HP	MFG	BEAM FT	IN	WGT LBS	DRAFT FT	IN	RETAIL LOW	RETAIL HIGH
		1993 BOATS														
25		SEA OX 250 BRKT	OP	CTRCN	FBG	DV	OB			8	6	3400	1	5	11700	13300
26		BLUE WATER 260C	OP	CUD	FBG	DV	IO	216D	VLVO	10		7300	1	7	27700	30800
26		BLUE WATER 260C	OP	CUD	FBG	DV	IO	T205-T230		10		7300	1	7	24800	28100
26		BLUE WATER 260C BRKT	OP	CUD	FBG	DV	OB			10		6600	1	7	15900	18000
26		BLUE WATER 260C W/A	OP	CUD	FBG	DV	IO	300	VLVO	10		7300	1	9	23400	26000
26		BLUE WATER 260C W/A	OP	CUD	FBG	DV	IO	T260	VLVO	10		7300	1	9	26100	29000
26		BLUE WATER 260C W/A	OP	CUD	FBG	DV	IO	T130D-T200D		10		7300	1	9	30500	37100
		1992 BOATS														
18	3	SEA OX 180	OP	CTRCN	FBG	SV	OB			7	4	1850		11	4400	5100
18	3	SEA OX 180D W/T	OP	FSH	FBG	SV	OB			7	4	1850		11	4400	5050
20	3	SEA OX 200	OP	CTRCN	FBG	DV	OB			8		2400		11	6550	7550
20	3	SEA OX 200 BRKT	OP	CTRCN	FBG	DV	OB			8		2400		11	6550	7550
20	3	SEA OX 200C W/A	OP	CUD	FBG	DV	OB			8		2750		11	6600	7600
20	3	SEA OX 200C W/A	OP	CUD	FBG	DV	IO	155-180		8		2750		11	7400	8600
20	3	SEA OX 200C W/A BRKT	OP	CUD	FBG	DV	OB			8		2750		11	7350	8450
20	3	SEA OX 200D BRKT	OP	FSH	FBG	DV	OB			8		2400		11	7000	8050
20	3	SEA OX 200D W/T	OP	FSH	FBG	DV	OB			8		2400		11	6150	7050
23		SEA OX 230	OP	CTRCN	FBG	DV	OB			8		2600		11	8250	9500
23		SEA OX 230C W/A	OP	CUD	FBG	DV	OB			8		3100		11	9150	10400
23		SEA OX 230C W/A	OP	CUD	FBG	DV	IO	155	VLVO	8		3100		11	9250	10500
		IO 205-230 9350 10800, IO 245-300 9600 11800, IO 120D VLVO 11200 12700														
23		SEA OX 230C W/A BRKT	OP	CUD	FBG	DV	OB			8		3100		11	9900	11200
25		BLUE WATER 250C	OP	CUD	FBG	DV	IO	150D-200D		8	6	4100	1	7	14100	17400
25		BLUE WATER 250C BRKT	OP	CUD	FBG	DV	OB			8	6	4100	1	7	12400	14100
25		BLUE WATER 250C W/A	OP	CUD	FBG	DV	IO	275-300		8	6	4100	1	7	13400	15700
25		BLUE WATER 250C W/A	OP	CUD	FBG	DV	IO	T230	VLVO	8	6	4100	1	7	15400	17500
25		BLUEWATER 250C	OP	CUD	FBG	DV	OB			8		3400	1	5	11200	12700
25		BLUEWATER 250C	OP	CUD	FBG	DV	IO	216D	VLVO	8	6	4100	1	5	15600	17800
25		SEA OX 250	OP	CTRCN	FBG	DV	IO	230-300		8	6	3400	1	5	12300	15200
25		SEA OX 250	OP	CTRCN	FBG	DV	IO	130D-150D		8	6	3400	1	5	15400	18300
25		SEA OX 250 BRKT	OP	CTRCN	FBG	DV	OB			8	6	3400	1	5	11200	12700
26		BLUE WATER 260C	OP	CUD	FBG	DV	IO	T205-T230		10		7300	1	7	23200	26300
26		BLUE WATER 260C BRKT	OP	CUD	FBG	DV	OB			10		6600	1	7	15200	17300
26		BLUE WATER 260C W/A	OP	CUD	FBG	DV	IO	300	VLVO	10		7300	1	9	21800	24300
26		BLUE WATER 260C W/A	OP	CUD	FBG	DV	IO	T260	VLVO	10		7300	1	9	24400	27100
26		BLUE WATER 260C W/A	OP	CUD	FBG	DV	IO	T130D-T200D		10		7300	1	9	28600	34700
26		BLUEWATER 260C	OP	CUD	FBG	DV	IO	216D	VLVO	10		7300	1	7	25900	28800
		1991 BOATS														
18	3	SEA OX 180	OP	CTRCN	FBG	SV	OB			7	4	1850		11	4200	4850
18	3	SEA OX 180D W/T	OP	FSH	FBG	SV	OB			7	4	1850		11	4200	4850
20	3	SEA OX 200	OP	CTRCN	FBG	DV	OB			8		2400		11	6350	7250
20	3	SEA OX 200C WA	OP	CUD	FBG	DV	OB			8		2750		11	6750	7750
20	3	SEA OX 200C WA	OP	CUD	FBG	DV	IO		OMC	8		2750		11	**	**
20	3	SEA OX 200C WA BRKT	OP	CUD	FBG	DV	OB			8		2750		11	6750	7750
20	3	SEA OX 200D BRKT	OP	FSH	FBG	DV	OB			8		2400		11	6850	7850
20	3	SEA OX 200D W/T	OP	FSH	FBG	DV	OB			8		2400		11	5800	6700
23		SEA OX 230	OP	CTRCN	FBG	DV	OB			8		2600		11	7950	9150
23		SEA OX 230C WA	OP	CUD	FBG	DV	OB			8		3100		11	9200	10400
23		SEA OX 230C WA	OP	CUD	FBG	DV	IO		OMC	8		3100		11	**	**
23		SEA OX 230C WA	OP	CUD	FBG	DV	IO	205-235		8		3100		11	8400	10100
23		SEA OX 230C WA BRKT	OP	CUD	FBG	DV	OB			8		3100		11	9200	10400
25		BLUE WATER 250C	OP	CUD	FBG	DV	IO	130D-150D		8	6		1	7	12900	15100
25		BLUE WATER 250C	OP	CUD	FBG	DV	IO	200D	VLVO	8	6		1	7	14200	16200
25		BLUE WATER 250C BRKT	OP	CUD	FBG	DV	OB			8	6	4100	1	7	11900	13600
25		BLUE WATER 250C WA	OP	CUD	FBG	DV	IO		OMC	8	6	4100	1	7	**	**
		IO 240-300 11800 14800, IO 130D-150D 13100 15400, IO 200D VLVO 14600 16600														
		IO T OMC ** **, IO T225-T230 13800 16600														
25		SEA OX 250	OP	CTRCN	FBG	DV	IO		OMC	8	6	3400	1	7	**	**
		IO 230-275 11300 13700, IO 300 12200 14300, IO 130D-150D 14500 17100														
		IO 200D VLVO 16400 18600, IO T OMC ** **														
25		SEA OX 250 BRKT	OP	CTRCN	FBG	DV	OB			8	6	3400	1	7	10800	12300
26		BLUE WATER 260C	OP	CUD	FBG	DV	IO	235	OMC	10		7300	1	9	19300	21500
26		BLUE WATER 260C	OP	CUD	FBG	DV	IO	T205-T230		10		7300	1	9	21400	24600
26		BLUE WATER 260C	OP	SF	FBG	DV	SE	T		10		6600	1	9	**	**
26		BLUE WATER 260C BRKT	OP	CUD	FBG	DV	OB			10		6600	1	9	14600	16600
26		BLUE WATER 260C WA	OP	CUD	FBG	DV	IO	240-300		10		7300	1	9	19400	22700
26		BLUE WATER 260C WA	OP	CUD	FBG	DV	IO	130D-200D		10		7300	1	9	22600	26600
26		BLUE WATER 260C WA	OP	CUD	FBG	DV	IO	T260		10		7300	1	9	22300	25400
		1990 BOATS														
18	3	SEA OX 180	OP	CTRCN	FBG	SV	OB			7	4	1850		11	4050	4700
18	3	SEA OX 180 DUAL	OP	FSH	FBG	SV	OB			7	4	1850		11	4000	4700
18	3	SEA OX 180 DUAL	ST	FSH	FBG	SV	OB			7	4	1850		11	4000	4700
20	3	SEA OX 200	OP	CTRCN	FBG	DV	OB			8		2400		11	6100	7000
20	3	SEA OX 200 DUAL	OP	FSH	FBG	DV	OB			8		2400		11	5600	6450
20	3	SEA OX 200 DUAL	ST	FSH	FBG	DV	OB			8		2400		11	6100	7000
20	3	SEA OX 200 DUAL W/BK	OP	FSH	FBG	DV	OB			8		2400		11	6600	7600
20	3	SEA OX 200C WA	OP	CUD	FBG	DV	OB			8		2750		11	6050	6950
20	3	SEA OX 200C WA	OP	CUD	FBG	DV	IO		OMC	8		2750		11	**	**
20	3	SEA OX 200C WA BRK	OP	CUD	FBG	DV	OB			8		2750		11	6950	7950
23		SEA OX 230	OP	CTRCN	FBG	DV	OB			8		2600		11	7700	8850
23		SEA OX 230C WA	OP	CUD	FBG	DV	OB			8		3100		11	8300	9550
23		SEA OX 230C WA	OP	CUD	FBG	DV	IO		OMC	8		3100		11	**	**
23		SEA OX 230C WA	OP	CUD	FBG	DV	IO	205-235		8		3100		11	7850	9500
23		SEA OX 230C WA	HT	CUD	FBG	DV	OB			8		3100	1		8350	9600
23		SEA OX 230C WA	HT	CUD	FBG	DV	IO		OMC	8		3100	1		**	**
23		SEA OX 230C WA	HT	CUD	FBG	DV	IO	205-235		8		3100	1		7850	9500
23		SEA OX 230C WA BRKT	OP	CUD	FBG	DV	OB			8		3100		11	9350	10600
23		SEA OX 230C WA BRKT	HT	CUD	FBG	DV	OB			8		3100	1		9250	10500
23		SEA OX 230C WA W/BRK	OP	CUD	FBG	DV	OB			8		3100		11	8850	10100
23		SEA OX 230C WA W/BRK	HT	CUD	FBG	DV	OB			8		3100	1		8850	10100
25		BLUE WATER 250C	OP	CUD	FBG	DV	IO			8	6	4100	1	7	**	**
		IO MRCR ** **, IO 260-275 11300 13400, IO T ** **														
25		BLUE WATER 250C	ST	CUD	FBG	DV	IO			8	6	4100	1	7	**	**
		IO MRCR ** **, IO 260-275 11300 13400, IO T ** **														
25		BLUE WATER 250C	HT	CUD	FBG	DV	IO			8	6	4100	1	7	**	**
		IO MRCR ** **, IO 260-275 11300 13400, IO T ** **														
25		BLUE WATER 250C BRKT	OP	CUD	FBG	DV	OB			8	6	4100	1	7	11500	13100
25		BLUE WATER 250C BRKT	ST	CUD	FBG	DV	OB			8	6	4100	1	7	11500	13100
25		BLUE WATER 250C BRKT	HT	CUD	FBG	DV	OB			8	6	4100	1	7	11500	13100
25		BLUE WATER 250C W/BR	OP	CUD	FBG	DV	OB			8	6	4100	1	7	11500	13100
25		BLUE WATER 250C W/BR	ST	CUD	FBG	DV	OB			8	6	4100	1	7	11500	13100
25		BLUE WATER 250C W/BR	HT	CUD	FBG	DV	OB			8	6	4100	1	7	11500	13100
25		SEA OX 250	OP	CTRCN	FBG	DV	IO		MRCR	8	6	3400	1	7	**	**
		IO OMC ** **, IO 260-275 10900 12900, IO T OMC ** **														
25		SEA OX 250 BRKT	OP	CTRCN	FBG	DV	OB			8	6	3400	1	7	10400	11800
25		SEA OX 250 W/BRKT	OP	CTRCN	FBG	DV	OB			8	6	3400	1	7	10400	11800
26		BLUE WATER 260C	OP	CUD	FBG	DV	SE	T		10		7300	1	9	**	**
26		BLUE WATER 260C	OP	CUD	FBG	DV	IO	T205-T230		10		7300	1	9	20100	23100
26		BLUE WATER 260C	ST	CUD	FBG	DV	SE	T		10		6600	1	9	**	**
26		BLUE WATER 260C	ST	CUD	FBG	DV	IO	T205-T230		10		7300	1	9	20100	23100
26		BLUE WATER 260C	HT	CUD	FBG	DV	SE	T		10		6600	1	9	**	**
26		BLUE WATER 260C	HT	CUD	FBG	DV	IO	T205-T230		10		7300	1	9	20100	23100
26		BLUE WATER 260C BRKT	OP	CUD	FBG	DV	OB			10		6600	1	9	14100	16000
26		BLUE WATER 260C BRKT	ST	CUD	FBG	DV	OB			10		7300	1	9	14400	16300
26		BLUE WATER 260C BRKT	HT	CUD	FBG	DV	OB			10		6600	1	9	14100	16100
		1989 BOATS														
18	3	SEA OX 180	OP	CTRCN	FBG	SV	OB			7	4	1900		11	3950	4600
18	3	SEA OX 180D	OP	FSH	FBG	SV	OB			7	4	1900		11	3950	4550
20	3	SEA OX 200	OP	CTRCN	FBG	SV	OB			8		2200		11	5650	6450
20	3	SEA OX 200C	OP	CUD	FBG	SV	OB			8		2200		11	5650	6450
20	3	SEA OX 200D	OP	FSH	FBG	SV	OB			8		2200		11	5650	6450
23		SEA OX 230	OP	CTRCN	FBG	SV	OB			8		2600		11	7450	8550
23		SEA OX 230C	OP	CUD	FBG		IO	175	OMC	8		3100	1		7350	8450
23		SEA OX 230C	OP	CUD	FBG	SV	OB			8		3100	1		8500	9750
23		SEA OX 230C	OP	CUD	FBG	SV	IO		OMC	8		3100	1		**	**
23		SEA OX 230C	OP	CUD	FBG	SV	IO	171-211		8		3100	1		7600	8850
25		BLUE WATER 250C	OP	CUD	FBG	SV	OB			8	6	4100	1	9	11200	12700
25		BLUE WATER 250C	OP	CUD	FBG	SV	IO			8	6	4100	1	9	**	**
25		BLUE WATER 250C	OP	CUD	FBG	SV	IO	230-260		8	6	4100	1	9	10400	12200
25		BLUE WATER 250C	OP	CUD	FBG	SV	IO	T		8	6	4100	1	9	**	**
26		BLUE WATER 260C	OP	CUD	FBG	SV	OB			10		6600	1	7	13700	15500
26		BLUE WATER 260C	OP	CUD	FBG	SV	IO	T		10		7300	1	7	**	**
26		BLUE WATER 260C	OP	CUD	FBG	SV	IO	T171-T211		10		7300	1	7	18900	21600
		1988 BOATS														
18	3	SEA OX 180	OP	CTRCN	FBG	SV	OB			7	4	1900		11	3800	4400
18	3	SEA OX 180D	OP	FSH	FBG	SV	OB			7	4	1900		11	3800	4400
20	3	SEA OX 200	OP	CTRCN	FBG	SV	OB			8		2200		11	5450	6300
20	3	SEA OX 200C	OP	CUD	FBG	SV	OB			8		2200		11	5450	6300
20	3	SEA OX 200D	OP	FSH	FBG	SV	OB			8		2200		11	5450	6300
23		SEA OX 230	OP	CTRCN	FBG	SV	OB			8		2600		11	7200	8300
23		SEA OX 230C	OP	CUD	FBG	SV	OB			8		2600	1		7200	8300
23		SEA OX 230C	OP	CUD	FBG	SV	IO		OMC	8		3100	1		**	**
23		SEA OX 230C	OP	CUD	FBG	SV	IO	171-211		8		3100	1		7200	8400
25		BLUE WATER 250C	OP	CUD	FBG	SV	OB			8	6	4100	1	9	10800	12300

 CONTINUED ON NEXT PAGE

LOA FT IN	NAME AND/ OR MODEL	TOP/ RIG	BOAT TYPE	-HULL- MTL TP	----ENGINE--- TP # HP MFG	BEAM FT IN	WGT LBS	DRAFT FT IN	RETAIL LOW	RETAIL HIGH
					---- 1988 BOATS ----					
25	BLUE WATER 250C	OP	CUD	FBG SV	IO	8 6	4100	1 9	**	**
25	BLUE WATER 250C	OP	CUD	FBG SV	IO 211-260	8 6	4100	1 9	9900	11500
25	BLUE WATER 250C	OP	CUD	FBG SV	IO T	8 6	4100	1 9	**	**
26	BLUE WATER 260C	OP	CUD	FBG SV	IO	10	6600	1 7	13300	15100
26	BLUE WATER 260C	OP	CUD	FBG SV	IO T	10	7300	1 7	**	**
26	BLUE WATER 260C	OP	CUD	FBG SV	IO T175-T200	10	7300	1 7	17200	19900
					---- 1986 BOATS ----					
18 3	SEA-OX 180	OP	CTRCN	FBG SV	OB	7 4	1900	11	3600	4150
18 3	SEA-OX 180	OP	CTRCN	FBG SV	SE T115 OMC	7 4	1900	11	3600	4150
18 3	SEA-OX 180D	OP	UTL	FBG SV	OB	7 4	1900	11	3400	3950
18 3	SEA-OX 180D	OP	UTL	FBG SV	SE T115 OMC	7 4	1900	11	3400	3950
18 3	SEA-OX 200	OP	CTRCN	FBG SV	OB	7 4	2250	10	3900	4500
20 3	SEA-OX 200	OP	CTRCN	FBG SV	OB	8	2200	10	5200	5950
20 3	SEA-OX 200	OP	CTRCN	FBG SV	SE T205 OMC	8	2250	10	5250	6050
20 3	SEA-OX 200C	OP	CUD	FBG SV	OB	8	2550	10	5600	6450
20 3	SEA-OX 200C	OP	CUD	FBG SV	SE T115-T205	8	2600	10	5650	6500
20 3	SEA-OX 200C	HT	CUD	FBG SV	OB	8	2550	10	5600	6450
20 3	SEA-OX 200C	HT	CUD	FBG SV	SE T115-T205	8	2600	10	5650	6500
20 3	SEA-OX 200D	OP	UTL	FBG SV	OB	8	2200	10	4700	5400
20 3	SEA-OX 200D	OP	UTL	FBG SV	SE T115-T205	8	2200	10	4700	5400
22 7	SEA-OX 2300	OP	PH	FBG SV	OB	8	1875	11	5150	5900
22 7	SEA-OX 2300	OP	PH	FBG SV	IO 165-200	8	1875	11	5350	6150
22 7	SEA-OX 2300	OP	PH	FBG SV	IO 165D BMW	8	1875	11	7600	8750
22 7	SEA-OX 2300	HT	UTL	FBG SV	OB	8	1875	11	4550	5200
22 7	SEA-OX 2300	HT	UTL	FBG SV	IO 170-200	8	1875	11	5250	6050
22 9	SEA-OX 230	OP	CTRCN	FBG SV	OB	8	2400	11	6350	7300
22 9	SEA-OX 230C	OP	CUD	FBG SV	OB	8	2400	11	6350	7300
22 9	SEA-OX 230C	OP	CUD	FBG SV	IO 170 MRCR	8	2800	11	5850	6700
22 9	SEA-OX 230C	OP	CUD	FBG SV	IO 175 OMC	8	2800	11	7150	8250
22 9	SEA-OX 230C	OP	CUD	FBG SV	IO 200 VLVO	8	2800	11	6100	7000
22 9	SEA-OX 230C	OP	CUD	FBG SV	SE 205 OMC	8	2800	11	7150	8250
22 9	SEA-OX 230C	OP	CUD	FBG SV	IO 155D OMC	8	2800	11	8100	9350
22 9	SEA-OX 230C	OP	CUD	FBG SV	IO 190D	8		11	9100	10300
22 9	SEA-OX 230C	HT	CUD	FBG SV	OB	8	2700	11	6950	8000
22 9	SEA-OX 230C	HT	CUD	FBG SV	IO 155 OMC	8	2800	11	7150	8250
22 9	SEA-OX 230C	HT	CUD	FBG SV	IO 170 MRCR	8	2800	11	5850	6700
22 9	SEA-OX 230C	HT	CUD	FBG SV	SE 175 OMC	8	2800	11	7150	8250
22 9	SEA-OX 230C	HT	CUD	FBG SV	IO 195-200	8	2800	11	6150	7100
23	SEA-OX 230C	OP	SF	FBG SV	SE 170	8	3100	11	7800	8950
26	SEA-OX 260C	OP	CUD	FBG SV	OB	10	7000	1	12700	14400
26	SEA-OX 260C	OP	CUD	FBG SV	SE T155 OMC	10	7000	1	12700	14400
26	SEA-OX 260C	OP	CUD	FBG SV	IO T170 MRCR	10	7000	1	15000	17000
26	SEA-OX 260C	OP	CUD	FBG SV	IO T175 OMC	10	7000	1	12700	14400
26	SEA-OX 260C	OP	CUD	FBG SV	IO T200 VLVO	10	7000	1	15500	17600
26	SEA-OX 260C	OP	CUD	FBG SV	SE T205 OMC	10	7000	1	12700	14400
26	SEA-OX 260C	HT	CUD	FBG SV	OB	10	7000	1	12700	14400
26	SEA-OX 260C	HT	CUD	FBG SV	SE T155 OMC	10	7000	1	12700	14400
26	SEA-OX 260C	HT	CUD	FBG SV	IO T170 MRCR	10	7000	1	15000	17000
26	SEA-OX 260C	HT	CUD	FBG SV	IO T175 OMC	10	7000	1	12700	14400
26	SEA-OX 260C	HT	CUD	FBG SV	IO T200 VLVO	10	7000	1	15500	17600
26	SEA-OX 260C	HT	CUD	FBG SV	SE T205 OMC	10	7000	1	12700	14400
26	SEA-OX 260C	TT	CUD	FBG SV	OB	10	7000	1	12700	14400
26	SEA-OX 260C	TT	CUD	FBG SV	IO T120 MRCR	10	7000	1	14500	16500
26	SEA-OX 260C	TT	CUD	FBG SV	SE T155 OMC	10	7000	1	12700	14400
26	SEA-OX 260C	TT	CUD	FBG SV	IO T200 VLVO	10	7000	1	15500	17600
26	SEA-OX 260C	TT	CUD	FBG SV	SE T205 OMC	10	7000	1	12700	14400
					---- 1985 BOATS ----					
18 3	SEA-OX 180	OP	CTRCN	FBG SV	OB	7 4	1900	11	3500	4050
18 3	SEA-OX 180	OP	CTRCN	FBG SV	SE T115 OMC	7 4	1900	11	3500	4050
18 3	SEA-OX 180D	OP	UTL	FBG SV	OB	7 4	1900	11	3300	3850
18 3	SEA-OX 180D	OP	UTL	FBG SV	SE T115 OMC	7 4	1900	11	3300	3850
20 3	SEA-OX 200	OP	CTRCN	FBG SV	OB	8	2200	10	5050	5800
20 3	SEA-OX 200C	OP	CUD	FBG SV	OB	8	2550	10	5500	6300
20 3	SEA-OX 200C	OP	CUD	FBG SV	SE T115 OMC	8	2600	10	5500	6350
20 3	SEA-OX 200C	HT	CUD	FBG SV	OB	8	2550	10	5500	6300
20 3	SEA-OX 200C	HT	CUD	FBG SV	SE T115 OMC	8	2600	10	5500	6350
20 3	SEA-OX 200D	OP	UTL	FBG SV	OB	8	2200	10	4600	5300
20 3	SEA-OX 200D	OP	UTL	FBG SV	SE T115 OMC	8	2200	10	4600	5300
22 7	SEA-OX 2300	OP	PH	FBG SV	OB	8	1875	11	5050	5800
22 7	SEA-OX 2300	OP	PH	FBG SV	IO 165-200	8	1875	11	5100	5850
22 7	SEA-OX 2300	OP	PH	FBG SV	IO 165D BMW	8	1875	11	7300	8400
22 7	SEA-OX 2300	HT	UTL	FBG SV	OB	8	1875	11	4450	5100
22 7	SEA-OX 2300	HT	UTL	FBG SV	IO 170-200	8	1875	11	5000	6150
22 7	SEA-OX 2300	HT	UTL	FBG SV	IO 165D BMW	8	1875	11	8900	10100
22 9	SEA-OX 230	OP	CTRCN	FBG SV	OB	8	2400	11	6200	7150
22 9	SEA-OX 230C	OP	CUD	FBG SV	OB	8	2400	11	6200	7150
22 9	SEA-OX 230C	OP	CUD	FBG SV	IO 170-200	8	2800	11	6000	6800
22 9	SEA-OX 230C	OP	CUD	FBG SV	SE 205 OMC	8	2800	11	7000	8050
22 9	SEA-OX 230C	OP	CUD	FBG SV	IO 165D BMW	8	2800	11	7850	9000
22 9	SEA-OX 230C	HT	CUD	FBG SV	OB	8	2700	11	6800	7850
22 9	SEA-OX 230C	HT	CUD	FBG SV	IO 170-195	8	2800	11	5600	6800
22 9	SEA-OX 230C	HT	CUD	FBG SV	SE 205 OMC	8	2800	11	7000	8050
22 9	SEA-OX 230C	HT	CUD	FBG SV	IO 165D BMW	8	2800	11	7850	9000
26	SEA-OX 260C	OP	CUD	FBG SV	OB	10	7000	1 9	12400	14100
26	SEA-OX 260C	OP	CUD	FBG SV	SE T155 OMC	10	7000	1 9	12400	14100
26	SEA-OX 260C	OP	CUD	FBG SV	IO T170-T200	10	7000	1 9	14200	17000
26	SEA-OX 260C	OP	CUD	FBG SV	SE T205 OMC	10	7000	1 9	12400	14100
26	SEA-OX 260C	HT	CUD	FBG SV	OB	10	7000	1 9	12400	14100
26	SEA-OX 260C	HT	CUD	FBG SV	SE T155 OMC	10	7000	1 9	12400	14100
26	SEA-OX 260C	HT	CUD	FBG SV	IO T170-T200	10	7000	1 9	14200	17000
26	SEA-OX 260C	HT	CUD	FBG SV	SE T205 OMC	10	7000	1 9	12400	14100
26	SEA-OX 260C	TT	CUD	FBG SV	OB	10	7000	1 9	12400	14100
26	SEA-OX 260C	TT	CUD	FBG SV	IO T120	10	7000	1 9	13800	15600
26	SEA-OX 260C	TT	CUD	FBG SV	SE T155 OMC	10	7000	1 9	12400	14100
26	SEA-OX 260C	TT	CUD	FBG SV	SE T195-T200	10	7000	1 9	14900	17000
26	SEA-OX 260C	TT	CUD	FBG SV	SE T205 OMC	10	7000	1 9	12400	14100
					---- 1984 BOATS ----					
18 3	SEA-OX 180		CTRCN	FBG SV	OB	7 3	1900		3400	3950
18 3	SEA-OX 180D		CTRCN	FBG SV	OB	7 3	1900		3400	3950
20 3	SEA-OX 200	OP	CTRCN	FBG SV	OB	8	1725	9	4200	4850
20 3	SEA-OX 200C	OP	CUD	FBG SV	OB	8	2500	9	5300	6100
20 3	SEA-OX 200C	OP	CUD	FBG SV	SE T115 OMC	8	2600	9	5400	6200
22 7	SEA-OX 2300	OP	PH	FBG SV	OB	8	1875	9	4950	5650
22 7	SEA-OX 2300	OP	PH	FBG SV	IO 170-190	8	1875	9	4700	5700
22 7	SEA-OX 2300	OP	PH	FBG SV	IO 150D BMW	8	1875	9	6850	7900
22 7	SEA-OX 2300	HT	UTL	FBG SV	OB	8	1875	9	4300	5000
22 7	SEA-OX 2300	HT	UTL	FBG SV	IO 170-190	8	1875	9	4850	5900
22 7	SEA-OX 2300	HT	CTRCN	FBG SV	IO 150D BMW	8	2350	9	8300	9500
22 9	SEA-OX 230C			FBG SV	OB	8		9	6000	6850
22 9	SEA-OX 230C	OP	CUD	FBG SV	OB	8	2700	9	6650	7650
22 9	SEA-OX 230C	OP	CUD	FBG SV	SE 155 OMC	8	2700	9	6650	7650
22 9	SEA-OX 230C	OP	CUD	FBG SV	IO 170-190	8	2700	9	5300	6400
22 9	SEA-OX 230C	OP	CUD	FBG SV	SE 205 OMC	8	2700	9	6650	7650
22 9	SEA-OX 230C	OP	CUD	FBG SV	IO 150D BMW	8	2700	9	7350	8400
22 9	SEA-OX 230C	TT	CUD	FBG SV	SE T115 OMC	8	2700	9	6650	7650
22 9	SEA-OX 230C	TT	CUD	FBG SV	OB	8	2700	9	6650	7650
22 9	SEA-OX 230C	TT	CUD	FBG SV	IO 170-190	8	2700	9	5300	6400
22 9	SEA-OX 230C	TT	CUD	FBG SV	SE 205 OMC	8	2700	9	6650	7650
22 9	SEA-OX 230C	TT	CUD	FBG SV	IO 150D BMW	8	2700	9	7350	8400

....For earlier years, see the BUC Used Boat Price Guide, Volume 3

NORTH CASTLE MARINE LTD
GODERICH ON CANADA N7A 4C6   See inside cover to adjust price for area

GOZZARD YACHTS
GODERICH ONTARIO CANADA

For more recent years, see the BUC Used Boat Price Guide, Volume 1

LOA FT IN	NAME AND/ OR MODEL	TOP/ RIG	BOAT TYPE	-HULL- MTL TP	----ENGINE--- TP # HP MFG	BEAM FT IN	WGT LBS	DRAFT FT IN	RETAIL LOW	RETAIL HIGH
					---- 1996 BOATS ----					
36 2	GOZZARD 31	CUT	SACAC	FBG KL	IB 35D WEST	11	10500	4 4	143500	157500
42	GOZZARD 36	CUT	SACAC	FBG KL	IB 63D WEST	12	18150	4 6	278500	306000
42	GOZZARD-MS 36	CUT	SACAC	FBG KL	IB 52D WEST	12	18000	4 9	276000	303500
50	GOZZARD 44	CUT	SACAC	FBG KL	IB 82D WEST	13 8	29850	5 6	497000	546500
					---- 1990 BOATS ----					
23	CLASSIC 23	ST	LNCH	F/S DS	IB 18D WEST	8	1800	1 6	14500	16500
36	H-T-GOZZARD 31	CUT	SA/CR	FBG KL	IB 30D WEST	11	12000	4 4	111500	123000
40	PILGRIM	MY		FBG SV	IB 100D WEST	14	22000	3 9	108500	119000
42	H-T-GOZZARD 36	CUT	SA/CR	FBG KL	IB 46D WEST	12	18000	4 9	187500	206500
42	H-T-GOZZARD-MS 36	CUT	SA/CR	FBG KL	IB 52D WEST	12	18000	4 4	188000	206500
42 9	PILGRIM 43	FB	MY	F/S SV	IB 140D CUM	14	26000	3 9	127500	140000
					---- 1989 BOATS ----					
23	CLASSIC 23	ST	LNCH	F/S DS	IB 18D WEST	8	1800	1 6	13800	15700
40	PILGRIM	MY		FBG SV	IB 100D WEST	14	22000	3 9	103500	114000

LOA FT IN	NAME AND/ OR MODEL	TOP/ RIG	BOAT TYPE	-HULL- MTL TP	----ENGINE--- TP # HP MFG	BEAM FT IN	WGT LBS	DRAFT FT IN	RETAIL LOW	RETAIL HIGH
					1989 BOATS					
42	H-T-GOZZARD	CUT	SA/CR	FBG KL	IB 46D WEST	12	17000	4 9	170000	187000
42	H-T-GOZZARD-MS	CUT	SA/CR	FBG KL	IB 52D WEST	12	17000	4 9	170500	187500
					1988 BOATS					
40	PILGRIM	MY	FBG SV	IB 100D WEST		14	22000	3 9	98900	108500
42	H-T-GOZZARD	CUT	SA/CR	FBG KL	IB 46D WEST	12	17000	4 9	159500	175500
42	H-T-GOZZARD-MS	CUT	SA/CR	FBG KL	IB 52D WEST	12	17000	4 9	160000	175500
					1987 BOATS					
40	PILGRIM	MY	FBG SV	IB 100D WEST		14	22000	3 9	94600	104000
42	H-T-GOZZARD	CUT	SA/CR	FBG KL	IB 46D WEST	12	17000	4 9	149500	164500
42	H-T-GOZZARD-MS	CUT	SA/CR	FBG KL	IB 52D WEST	12	17000	4 9	150000	164500
					1986 BOATS					
40	PILGRIM 40	FB MY	F/S DS	IB 100D WEST		14	24000	3 6	97400	107000

NORTH COAST MARINE
SAG HARBOR NY 11963   See inside cover to adjust price for area

LOA FT IN	NAME AND/ OR MODEL	TOP/ RIG	BOAT TYPE	-HULL- MTL TP	----ENGINE--- TP # HP MFG	BEAM FT IN	WGT LBS	DRAFT FT IN	RETAIL LOW	RETAIL HIGH
					1984 BOATS					
23 9	WABBIT	SLP	SA/OD	FBG KL		5 7	875	3 6	5200	5950
28	HAWKFARM 28	SLP	SA/OD	FBG KL		9 10	5700	5	19100	21200

....For earlier years, see the BUC Used Boat Price Guide, Volume 3

NORTH COAST YACHTS INC
HYANNIS MA 02601   COAST GUARD MFG ID- NEH See inside cover to adjust price for area
FORMERLY NORTH COAST BOAT WORKS

LOA FT IN	NAME AND/ OR MODEL	TOP/ RIG	BOAT TYPE	-HULL- MTL TP	----ENGINE--- TP # HP MFG	BEAM FT IN	WGT LBS	DRAFT FT IN	RETAIL LOW	RETAIL HIGH
					1992 BOATS					
32 4	NORTH COAST 33	OP	SF	FBG DV	IB T375D CAT	12 2	13500	3 4	105500	116000
					1991 BOATS					
24 2	NORTH COAST 24	OP	CUD	FBG DV	OB	9 2	3850	2 9	20300	22500
24 2	NORTH COAST 24	OP	CUD	FBG DV	IB T220 CRUS	9 2	6500	2 9	26600	29500
24 2	NORTH COAST 24	OP	CUD	FBG DV	IB T130D VLVO	9 2	6500	2 9	34700	38600
30 8	NORTH COAST 31	OP	SF	FBG DV	IB T315 CRUS	11	11300	3 1	61300	67300
30 8	NORTH COAST 31	OP	SF	FBG DV	IBT250D-T375D	12	12000	3 1	79600	99300
32 4	NORTH COAST 33	OP	SF	FBG DV	IB T375D CAT	12 2	13500	3 4	100000	110000
					1990 BOATS					
24 2	NORTH COAST 24	OP	CUD	FBG DV	OB	9 2	3850	2 9	19500	21600
24 2	NORTH COAST 24	OP	CUD	FBG DV	IB T220 CRUS	9 2	6500	2 9	25300	28100
24 2	NORTH COAST 24	OP	CUD	FBG DV	IB T130D VLVO	9 2	6500	2 9	33200	36800
30 8	NORTH COAST 31	OP	SF	FBG DV	IB T315 CRUS	11	11300	3 1	58300	64000
30 8	NORTH COAST 31	OP	SF	FBG DV	IBT250D-T375D	12	12000	3 1	76100	94900
					1989 BOATS					
24 2	NORTH COAST 24	OP	CUD	FBG DV	OB	9 2	3850	2 9	18900	21000
24 2	NORTH COAST 24	OP	CUD	FBG DV	IB T150 YAMA	9 2	4900	2 9	20900	23200
24 2	NORTH COAST 24	OP	CUD	FBG DV	IB T220	9 2	6500		24100	28300
24 2	NORTH COAST 24	OP	SF	FBG DV	OB	9 2	3850	2 9	18800	20900
24 2	NORTH COAST 24	OP	SF	FBG DV	IB T220 CRUS	9 2	6500	2 9	24000	26700
30 8	NORTH COAST 31	OP	SF	FBG DV	IB T315 CRUS	11 11	11700	3 1	56000	61500
30 8	NORTH COAST 31	OP	SF	FBG DV	IBT250D-T300D	11 11	12000	3 7	72700	83000
					1988 BOATS					
24 2	NORTH COAST 24	OP	CUD	FBG DV	OB	9 2	3850		18300	20300
24 2	NORTH COAST 24	OP	CUD	FBG DV	IB T220 CRUS	9 2	7500		25600	28500
24 2	NORTH COAST 24	OP	SF	FBG DV	OB	9 2	3850	2 2	18300	20300
24 2	NORTH COAST 24	OP	SF	FBG DV	IB T220 CRUS	9 2	7500	2 2	25600	28400
30 8	NORTH COAST 31	OP	SF	FBG DV	IB T315 PCM	11 11	11300	3 1	52700	57900
32 4	NORTH COAST 33	OP	SF	FBG DV	IB T250D CUM	12 2		3 4	63900	76100
					1987 BOATS					
23 10	NORTH COAST 24	OP	CUD	FBG DV	OB	9	3850		17100	19400
23 10	NORTH COAST 24	OP	SF	FBG DV	OB	9	7500		24100	26700
32 4	NORTH COAST 33	OP	SF	FBG DV	IB T250D CUM	12 2		3 4	66300	72900

NORTH RIVER BOATWORKS
SCHENECTADY NY 12309-61 COAST GUARD MFG ID- NRM See inside cover to adjust price for area

LOA FT IN	NAME AND/ OR MODEL	TOP/ RIG	BOAT TYPE	-HULL- MTL TP	----ENGINE--- TP # HP MFG	BEAM FT IN	WGT LBS	DRAFT FT IN	RETAIL LOW	RETAIL HIGH
					1989 BOATS					
18	ST LAWRENCE SKIFF		SAIL	WD CB		3 6	185	7	5650	6450
19 2	MADRIGAL	SLP	SAIL	WD KC	OB	6 10	2700	2 2	19500	21600
					1988 BOATS					
17 2	SWAMPSCOTT DORY	SLP	SAIL	WD CB		4 6	150	6	4550	5200
18	ST LAWRENCE SKIFF		SAIL	WD CB		3 6	185	7	5300	6100
19 2	MADRIGAL	SLP	SAIL	WD KC	OB	6 10	2700	2 2	18500	20600
					1987 BOATS					
17 2	SWAMPSCOTT DORY	SLP	SAIL	WD CB		4 6	150	6	4200	4900
19 2	MADRIGAL	SLP	SAIL	WD KC	OB	6 10	2700	2 2	17000	19300
					1986 BOATS					
17 2	SWAMPSCOTT DORY	SLP	SAIL	WD CB		4 6	150	6	3950	4600
19 2	MADRIGAL	SLP	SAIL	WD KC	OB	6 10	2700	2 2	16000	18200

NORTHERN YACHT LTD
AJAX ONTARIO CANADA   COAST GUARD MFG ID- ZYT See inside cover to adjust price for area

LOA FT IN	NAME AND/ OR MODEL	TOP/ RIG	BOAT TYPE	-HULL- MTL TP	----ENGINE--- TP # HP MFG	BEAM FT IN	WGT LBS	DRAFT FT IN	RETAIL LOW	RETAIL HIGH
					1986 BOATS					
25 2	NORTHERN 25	SLP	SAIL	FBG KL	OB	8 2	5300	4 3	12400	14100
25 2	NORTHERN 25	SLP	SAIL	FBG KL	IB 8D YAN	8 2	5300	4 3	13200	15000
29 1	NORTHERN 29	SLP	SAIL	FBG KL	IB 14D UNIV	9	8250	4 2	22000	24400
36 10	NORTHERN 37	KTH	SAIL	FBG KL	IB 51D PERK	11 1	14950	5 8	42200	46900
					1985 BOATS					
25 2	NORTHERN 25	SLP	SAIL	FBG KL	OB	8 2	5300	4 3	11600	13200
25 2	NORTHERN 25	SLP	SAIL	FBG KL	IB 8D YAN	8 2	5300	4 3	12400	14100
29 1	NORTHERN 29	SLP	SAIL	FBG KL	IB 14D UNIV	9	8250	4 2	20700	23000
36 10	NORTHERN 37	KTH	SAIL	FBG KL	IB 51D PERK	11 1	14950	5 8	39500	43900

NORTHSHORE YACHTS LTD
CHICHESTER W SUSSEX UK COAST GUARD MFG ID- NRS See inside cover to adjust price for area

For more recent years, see the BUC Used Boat Price Guide, Volume 1

LOA FT IN	NAME AND/ OR MODEL	TOP/ RIG	BOAT TYPE	-HULL- MTL TP	----ENGINE--- TP # HP MFG	BEAM FT IN	WGT LBS	DRAFT FT IN	RETAIL LOW	RETAIL HIGH
					1996 BOATS					
25 3	VANCOUVER 25	KTH	SCPAC	FBG KL	IB 27D YAN	9 4	10080	3 9	65700	72200
28	VANCOUVER 28	SLP	SACAC	FBG KL	IB 18D YAN	8 8	8960	4 3	284500	312500
31 3	FISHER 31	SLP	SCPAC	FBG KL	IB 38D YAN	10 4	15680	4 3	130000	143000
32	SOUTHERLY 100	SLP	SACIS	FBG SK	IB 18D YAN	9 11	9500	1 10	80700	88900
32 6	SIGMA 33	SLP	SARAC	FBG KL	IB 18D YAN	10 6	9200	5 9	79100	86900
33 9	SOUTHERLY 101	SLP	SACIS	FBG SK	IB 27D YAN	10 3	9950	1 10	88200	97000
34 1	FISHER 34	KTH	SCPAC	FBG KL	IB 75D YAN	11	25760	4 11	216000	237500
34 3	VANCOUVER 34	SLP	SACAC	FBG KL	IB 27D YAN	10 6	14000	4 9	124000	136500
34 3	VANCOUVER 34 PILOT	SLP	SACIS	FBG KL	IB 27D YAN	10 6	14000	4 9	124000	136500
34 4	MG 346	SLP	SARAC	FBG KL	IB 27D YAN	11 3	8900	4 3	80500	88500
36	SWORDFISH 36	ST	MY	FBG SV	IB T275D SABR	12 3		3 6	179000	196500
36	VANCOUVER 36	SLP	SACAC	FBG KL	IB 44D YAN	12	20494	5 7	184000	202000
36 10	SOUTHERLY 115	SLP	SACIS	FBG SK	IB 38D YAN	11 11	15215	2 6	147500	162500
38	SIGMA 38	SLP	SARAC	FBG KL	IB 27D YAN	12 2	13750	6 8	144500	159000
38	VANCOUVER 38 PILOT	SLP	SACIS	FBG KL	IB 44D YAN	12	22378	6 7	212500	233500
40 3	SIGMA 400	SLP	SARAC	FBG KL	IB 38D YAN	12 9	16540	7 6	195000	214000
42 6	FISHER 37	KTH	SCPAC	FBG KL	IB 82D PERK	12	31360	5 2	268000	294500
44	SOUTHERLY 135	SLP	SACIS	FBG KL	IB 44D YAN	13 3	23100	2 6	290000	318500
50	FREEBIRD 50	SLP	SACAC	FBG CT	IB T 38D YAN	25	27500	3 6	561500	617000
51 6	FISHER 46	KTH	SCPAC	FBG KL	IB 120D SABR	15	56000	6 6	479500	527000
					1995 BOATS					
25 3	FISHER 25	KTH	SCPAC	FBG KL	IB 27D YAN	9 4	10080	3 9	61800	67900
28	VANCOUVER 28	SLP	SACAC	FBG KL	IB 18D YAN	8 8	8960	4 3	961500	1.045M
31 3	FISHER 31	SLP	SCPAC	FBG KL	IB 38D YAN	10 4	15680	4 3	122500	134500
32	SOUTHERLY 100	SLP	SACIS	FBG SK	IB 18D YAN	9 11	9500	1 10	76100	83600
32 6	SIGMA 33	SLP	SARAC	FBG KL	IB 18D YAN	10 6	9200	5 9	74400	81800
33 9	SOUTHERLY 101	SLP	SACIS	FBG SK	IB 27D YAN	10 3	9950	1 10	83000	91200
34 1	FISHER 34	KTH	SCPAC	FBG KL	IB 75D YAN	11	25760	4 11	203500	223500
34 3	VANCOUVER 34	SLP	SACAC	FBG KL	IB 27D YAN	10 6	14000	4 9	116500	128000
34 3	VANCOUVER 34 PILOT	SLP	SACIS	FBG KL	IB 27D YAN	10 6	14000	4 9	116500	128000
34 4	MG 346	SLP	SARAC	FBG KL	IB 27D YAN	11 3	8900	6 3	75700	83200
36	SWORDFISH 36	ST	MY	FBG SV	IB T275D SABR	12 3		3 6	171500	188500
36	VANCOUVER 36	SLP	SACAC	FBG KL	IB 44D YAN	12	20494	5 7	173000	190000
36 10	SOUTHERLY 115	SLP	SACIS	FBG SK	IB 38D YAN	11 11	15215	2 6	139000	152500
38	SIGMA 38	SLP	SARAC	FBG KL	IB 27D YAN	12 2	13750	6 8	136000	149500
38	VANCOUVER 38 PILOT	SLP	SACIS	FBG KL	IB 44D YAN	12	22378	6 7	200000	220000
40 3	SIGMA 400	SLP	SARAC	FBG KL	IB 38D YAN	12 9	16540	7 6	183200	201500
42 6	FISHER 37	KTH	SCPAC	FBG KL	IB 82D PERK	12	31360	5 2	252000	277000
44	SOUTHERLY 135	SLP	SACIS	FBG KL	IB 44D YAN	13 3	23100	2 6	290000	318500
50	FREEBIRD 50	SLP	SACAC	FBG CT	IB T 38D YAN	25	27500	3 6	526500	578500
51 6	FISHER 46	KTH	SCPAC	FBG KL	IB 120D SABR	15	56000	6 6	450500	495000

LOA FT	LOA IN	NAME AND/ OR MODEL	TOP/ RIG	BOAT TYPE	-HULL- MTL	-HULL- TP	ENGINE TP	ENGINE # HP	ENGINE MFG	BEAM FT	BEAM IN	WGT LBS	DRAFT FT	DRAFT IN	RETAIL LOW	RETAIL HIGH
		1987 BOATS														
25	3	FISHER 25	KTH	SCPAC	F/S	KL	IB	27D	YAN	9	4	10058	3	9	37500	41700
28		VANCOUVER 28	SLP	SA/CR	F/S	KL	IB	18D	YAN	8	8	8960	4	3	37500	41700
30		FISHER 30	KTH	SCPAC	F/S	KL	IB	36D	VLVO	9	6	14525	4	3	67200	73800
31	3	FISHER 31	SLP	SCPAC	F/S	KL	IB	35D	VLVO	10	4	15100	4	3	72200	79400
32		SOUTHERLY 100	SLP	SA/CR	FBG	SK	IB	18D	YAN	9	11	9500	1	10	46900	51500
32		VANCOUVER 32	SLP	SA/CR	F/S	KL	IB	27D	YAN	10	7	14000	4	9	68100	74800
34	4	FISHER 34	KTH	SCPAC	F/S	KL	IB	46D	VLVO	11	3	23469	4	9	114500	126000
36	10	SOUTHERLY 115	SLP	SA/CR	FBG	SK	IB	34D	YAN	11	11	14600	2	3	82100	90200
38		VANCOUVER 38	CUT	SA/CR	STL	KL	IB	48D		11	8	23000	5	6	125000	137500
41	6	FISHER 37	KTH	SCPAC	F/S	KL	IB	80D	FORD	12		31046	5	3	177000	194500
44		SOUTHERLY 135	SLP	SA/CR	FBG	SK	IB	44D	YAN	13	11	28000	2	4	180500	198000
45	8	FISHER 46	KTH	SCPAC	F/S	KL	IB	120D	FORD	15		55882	6	6	269500	296500
50	8	SOUTHERLY 145	KTH	SA/CR	FBG	SK	IB	62D	VLVO	13	11	26500	2	6	253500	278500
		1986 BOATS														
25	3	FISHER 25	KTH	SCPAC	FBG	KL	IB	22D	YAN	9	4	10000	3	9	34900	38800
30		FISHER 30	KTH	SCPAC	FBG	KL	IB	36D	VLVO	9	6	14525	4	3	63200	69500
32		SOUTHERLY 100	SLP	SA/CR	FBG	SK	IB	20D	BUKH	9	11	9500	1	10	43600	48400
34	4	FISHER 34	KTH	SCPAC	FBG	KL	IB	62D	VLVO	11	3	23500	4	9	108000	119000
36	10	SOUTHERLY 115	SLP	SA/CR	FBG	SK	IB	36D	BUKH	11	11	14600	2	3	77300	85000
37		FISHER 37	KTH	SCPAC	FBG	KL	IB	80D	SABR	12		31360	5	3	145500	159500
45	8	FISHER 46	KTH	SCPAC	FBG	KL	IB	120D	SABR	15		56000	6	6	253000	278000
50	8	SOUTHERLY 145	KTH	SA/CR	FBG	SK	IB	65D	VLVO	13	11	26500	2	6	237500	261000
		1985 BOATS														
25	3	FISHER 25	KTH	SCPAC	FBG	KL	IB	22D	YAN	9	4	10000	3	9	32800	36500
30		FISHER 30	KTH	SCPAC	FBG	KL	IB	36D	VLVO	9	6	14525	4	3	59400	65300
32		SOUTHERLY 100	SLP	SA/CR	FBG	SK	IB	20D	BUKH	9	11	9500	1	10	41000	45600
34	4	FISHER 34	KTH	SCPAC	FBG	KL	IB	61D	VLVO	11	3	23500	4	9	102000	112000
36	10	SOUTHERLY 115	SLP	SA/CR	FBG	SK	IB	36D	BUKH	11	11	14600	2	3	72700	79900
37		FISHER 37	KTH	SCPAC	FBG	KL	IB	80D	SABR	12		31360	5	3	136500	150000
44		SOUTHERLY 135	SLP	SAIL	FBG	KC	IB	61D	VLVO	13	11	28000	2	6	159000	174500
45	8	FISHER 46	KTH	SCPAC	FBG	KL	IB	120D	SABR	15		56000	6	6	237000	260500
50	8	SOUTHERLY 145	KTH	SA/CR	FBG	SK	IB	65D	VLVO	13	11	26500	2	6	222500	244500
		1984 BOATS														
27	6	SOUTHERLY 28	SLP	SAIL	FBG	SK	IB	20D	BUKH	9		8500	2	6	28900	32100
31	8	SOUTHERLY 95	SLP	SAIL	FBG	SK	IB	20D	BUKH	9	11	9500	1	10	38200	42400
35	7	SOUTHERLY 105	SLP	SAIL	FBG	SK	IB	36D	BUKH	11	11	13000	2	3	58300	64100
36	10	SOUTHERLY 115	SLP	SAIL	FBG	SK	IB	36D	BUKH	11	11	14600	2	3	68400	75200
44		SOUTHERLY 135	SLP	SAIL	FBG	SK	IB	47D	PERK	13	11	28000	2	6	148000	162500
44		SOUTHERLY 135	SLP	SAIL	FBG	SK	IB	61D	VLVO	13	11	28000	2	6	149000	164000
50	8	SOUTHERLY 145	SLP	SAIL	FBG	SK	IB	80D	VLVO	13	11	26500	2	6	202500	222500

....For earlier years, see the BUC Used Boat Price Guide, Volume 3

NOVA MARINE CO LTD

CLEARWATER FL 33515

See inside cover to adjust price for area

HERITAGE EAST YACHTS INC
CLEARWATER FL

LOA FT	LOA IN	NAME AND/ OR MODEL	TOP/ RIG	BOAT TYPE	-HULL- MTL	-HULL- TP	ENGINE TP	ENGINE # HP	ENGINE MFG	BEAM FT	BEAM IN	WGT LBS	DRAFT FT	DRAFT IN	RETAIL LOW	RETAIL HIGH
		1988 BOATS														
35	9	SUNDECK 36	HT	MY	FBG	DS	IB	T150D	VLVO	12	7	14400	3	6	89500	98400
38	8	SUNDECK 40	HT	MY	FBG	DS	IB	T150D	VLVO	13	6	20000	3	7	101000	111000
42		SUNDECK 42	HT	MY	FBG	DS	IB	T150D	VLVO	13	8	24000	3	8	120500	132500
43	3	FISHING COCKPIT 44	HT	MY	FBG	DS	IB	T150D	VLVO	13	6	22000	3	7	114500	126000
43	5	SUNDECK 44	HT	MY	FBG	DS	IB	T150D	VLVO	13	8	24400	3	10	121500	134000
46		FISHING COCKPIT	HT	YTFS	FBG	DS	IB	T150D	VLVO	13	8	25500	3	8	106000	116500
46		SUNDECK MOTOR YACHT	FB	MY	FBG	SV	IB	T150D	VLVO	13	8	27000	3	10	116500	128000
48		COCKPIT MOTOR YACHT	FB	YTFS	FBG	SV	IB	T150D	VLVO	13	8	27000	3	8	116000	127500
		1987 BOATS														
35	9	SUNDECK 36	HT	MY	FBG	DS	IB	T150D	VLVO	12	7	14400	3	6	85700	94200
38	8	SUNDECK 40	HT	MY	FBG	DS	IB	T150D	VLVO	13	6	20000	3	7	96600	106000
42		SUNDECK 42	HT	MY	FBG	DS	IB	T150D	VLVO	13	8	24000	3	8	115000	126500
43	3	FISHING COCKPIT 44	HT	MY	FBG	DS	IB	T150D	VLVO	13	6	22000	3	7	109500	120500
43	5	SUNDECK 44	HT	MY	FBG	DS	IB	T150D	VLVO	13	8	24400	3	10	116500	128000
46		FISHING COCKPIT	HT	YTFS	FBG	DS	IB	T150D	VLVO	13	8	25500	3	8	101000	111000

NYE YACHTS

ALLAN NYE SCOTT ENT LTD
BLOOMFIELD ONTARIO CANA COAST GUARD MFG ID- ZSG

See inside cover to adjust price for area

LOA FT	LOA IN	NAME AND/ OR MODEL	TOP/ RIG	BOAT TYPE	-HULL- MTL	-HULL- TP	ENGINE TP	ENGINE # HP	ENGINE MFG	BEAM FT	BEAM IN	WGT LBS	DRAFT FT	DRAFT IN	RETAIL LOW	RETAIL HIGH
		1988 BOATS														
22		ALBERG 22	SLP	SA/CR	FBG	KL	OB			7		3200	3	1	7650	8800
29	3	ALBERG 29	SLP	SA/CR	FBG	KL	IB	20D	YAN	9	2	9000	4	6	28100	31200
34	1	ALBERG 34	SLP	SA/CR	FBG	KL	IB	30D	YAN	10	1	14000	5	3	42500	47200
34	1	ALBERG PILOT 34	SLP	SA/CR	FBG	KL	IB	30D	YAN	10	1	15000	5	3	45800	50300
		1987 BOATS														
22		ALBERG 22	SLP	SA/CR	FBG	KL	OB			7		3200	3	1	7200	8250
29	3	ALBERG 29	SLP	SA/CR	FBG	KL	IB	20D	YAN	9	2	9000	4	6	26400	29300
34	1	ALBERG 34	SLP	SA/CR	FBG	KL	IB	30D	YAN	10	1	14000	5	3	40000	44400
34	1	ALBERG PILOT 34	SLP	SA/CR	FBG	KL	IB	30D	YAN	10	1	15000	5	3	42600	47400
		1986 BOATS														
22		ALBERG 22	SLP	SA/CR	FBG	KL	OB			7		3200	3	1	6750	7800
29	3	ALBERG 29	SLP	SA/CR	FBG	KL	IB	20D	YAN	9	2	9000	4	6	24800	27600
34	1	ALBERG 34	SLP	SA/CR	FBG	KL	IB	30D	YAN	10	1	14000	5	3	37600	41800
34	1	ALBERG PILOT 34	SLP	SA/CR	FBG	KL	IB	30D	YAN	10	1	15000	5	3	40100	44500
		1985 BOATS														
22		ALBERG 22	SLP	SA/CR	FBG	KL	OB			7		3200	3	1	6350	7300
29	3	ALBERG 29	SLP	SA/CR	FBG	KL	IB	15D	YAN	9	2	9000	4	6	23300	25900
34	1	ALBERG 34	SLP	SA/CR	FBG	KL	IB	23D	YAN	10	1	14000	5	3	34100	37900
34	1	ALBERG PILOT 34	SLP	SA/CR	FBG	KL	IB	23D	YAN	10	1	14000	5	3	36500	40600
		1984 BOATS														
22		ALBERG 22	SLP	SA/CR	FBG	KL	OB			7		3200	3	1	6000	6900
29	3	ALBERG 29	SLP	SA/CR	FBG	KL	IB	15D	YAN	9	2	9000	4	6	21900	24400
34	1	ALBERG 34	SLP	SA/CR	FBG	KL	IB	20D	YAN	10	1	14000	5	3	33200	36900
34	1	ALBERG PILOT 34	SLP	SA/CR	FBG	KL	IB	22D	YAN	10	1	14000	5	3	33200	36900

....For earlier years, see the BUC Used Boat Price Guide, Volume 3

O'DAY

PEARSON YACHT CORP
ASSONET MA 02702

See inside cover to adjust price for area

COAST GUARD MFG ID- XDY
formerly LEAR SIEGLER MARINE

LOA FT	LOA IN	NAME AND/ OR MODEL	TOP/ RIG	BOAT TYPE	-HULL- MTL	-HULL- TP	ENGINE TP	ENGINE # HP	ENGINE MFG	BEAM FT	BEAM IN	WGT LBS	DRAFT FT	DRAFT IN	RETAIL LOW	RETAIL HIGH
		1991 BOATS														
16	9	DAY SAILER 3	SLP	SAIL	FBG	CB	OB			6	3	1268	3	9	4100	4800
24	7	O'DAY 240 LE	SLP	SAIL	FBG	WK	OB			8	3	3600	2	8	10300	11800
28	9	O'DAY 290	SLP	SAIL	FBG	KL	IB	12D	WEST	10	5	7450	3	11	25900	28700
32	2	O'DAY 322	SLP	SAIL	FBG	KL	IB	18D	YAN	10	9	10250	4	2	36300	40400
		1990 BOATS														
16	9	DAY SAILER 3	SLP	SAIL	FBG	CB	OB			6	3	1268	3	9	3850	4500
24	7	O'DAY 240 LE	SLP	SAIL	FBG	WK	OB			8	3	3600	2	8	9750	11100
32	2	O'DAY 322	SLP	SAIL	FBG	KL	IB	18D	YAN	10	9	10250	4	2	34200	38000
		1989 BOATS														
16	9	DAY SAILER 3	SLP	SA/OD	FBG	CB	OB			6	3	1268		7	3650	4250
18	7	O'DAY 192	SLP	SAIL	FBG	KC	OB			7	1	1400	1	5	3900	4500
24	7	O'DAY 24 OLE	SLP	SA/CR	FBG	KL	OB			8	3	3600	2	8	9400	10700
24	7	O'DAY 240	SLP	SA/CR	FBG	KL	OB			8	3	3600	2	8	8950	10200
26	11	O'DAY 272	SLP	SA/CR	FBG	KL	OB			9		5025	2	11	14000	15900
26	11	O'DAY 272	SLP	SA/CR	FBG	KL	IB	12D	WEST	9		5375	2	11	14600	16600
26	11	O'DAY 272 LE	SLP	SA/CR	FBG	KL	IB	12D	WEST	9		5375	2	11	16800	19100
29	7	O'DAY 302	SLP	SA/CR	FBG	KL	IB	18D	YAN	10		7200	3	11	22000	24400
29	7	O'DAY 302 MK II	SLP	SA/CR	FBG	KL	IB	18D	YAN	10		7200	3	11	22800	25300
32	2	O'DAY 322	SLP	SA/CR	FBG	KL	IB	18D	YAN	10	8	10250	4	2	32100	35700
34	11	O'DAY 35 DEEP	SLP	SA/CR	FBG	KL	IB	21D	UNIV	11	3	11500	5	7	35700	39600
34	11	O'DAY 35 SHOAL	SLP	SA/CR	FBG	KL	IB	21D	UNIV	11	3	11500	4	5	35700	39600
39	7	O'DAY 40 DEEP	SLP	SA/CR	FBG	KL	IB	46D	WEST	12	8	18000	6	4	59600	65500
39	7	O'DAY 40 SHOAL	SLP	SA/CR	FBG	KL	IB	46D	WEST	12	8	18500	4	11	60800	66800
		1988 BOATS														
16	9	DAY SAILER 3	SLP	SA/OD	FBG	CB	OB			6	3	1268		7	3400	3950
18	7	O'DAY 192	SLP	SAIL	FBG	KC	OB			7	1	1400	1	5	3650	4250
21	9	O'DAY 222	SLP	SA/CR	FBG	KC	OB			7	11	2200	1	8	5150	5950
24	7	O'DAY 240	SLP	SA/CR	FBG	KL	OB			8	3	3600	2	8	8550	9850
26	11	O'DAY 272	SLP	SA/CR	FBG	KL	OB			9		5025	2	11	13100	14900
26	11	O'DAY 272	SLP	SA/CR	FBG	KL	IB	12D	WEST	9		5375	2	11	13800	15700
26	11	O'DAY 272 LE	SLP	SA/CR	FBG	KL	IB	12D	WEST	9		5375	2	11	15800	17900
29	7	O'DAY 302	SLP	SA/CR	FBG	KL	IB	18D	YAN	10		7200	3	11	21000	23400
32	2	O'DAY 322	SLP	SA/CR	FBG	KL	IB	18D	YAN	10	8	10250	4	2	30200	33600
34	11	O'DAY 35 DEEP	SLP	SA/CR	FBG	KL	IB	21D	UNIV	11	3	11500	5	7	33500	37300
34	11	O'DAY 35 SHOAL	SLP	SA/CR	FBG	KL	IB	21D	UNIV	11	3	11500	4	5	33500	37300
39	7	O'DAY 40 DEEP	SLP	SA/CR	FBG	KL	IB	46D	WEST	12	8	18000	6	4	56100	61600
39	7	O'DAY 40 SHOAL	SLP	SA/CR	FBG	KL	IB	46D	WEST	12	8	18500	4	11	57100	62800
		1987 BOATS														
16	9	DAY SAILER 3	SLP	SA/OD	FBG	CB	OB			6	3	1268		7	3200	3750
18	7	O'DAY 192	SLP	SAIL	FBG	KC	OB			7	1	1400	1	5	3450	4000

LOA FT	IN	NAME AND/ OR MODEL	TOP/ RIG	BOAT TYPE	-HULL- MTL	TP	ENGINE TP	# HP	MFG	BEAM FT	IN	WGT LBS	DRAFT FT	IN	RETAIL LOW	RETAIL HIGH
		1987 BOATS														
21	9	O'DAY 222	SLP	SA/CR	FBG	KC	OB			7	11	2200	1	8	4850	5600
26	11	O'DAY 272	SLP	SA/CR	FBG	KL	OB			9		5025	2	11	12400	14100
26	11	O'DAY 272	SLP	SA/CR	FBG	KL	IB	10		9		5375	2	11	13500	15300
26	11	O'DAY 272 LE	SLP	SA/CR	FBG	KL	IB	10D	WEST	9		5375	2	11	13900	15800
29	7	O'DAY 302	SLP	SA/CR	FBG	KL	IB	18D	YAN	10		7200	3	11	19800	22000
32	2	O'DAY 322	SLP	SA/CR	FBG	KL	IB	18D	YAN	10	8	10250	4	2	28400	31600
34	11	O'DAY 35 DEEP	SLP	SA/CR	FBG	KL	IB	21D	UNIV	11	3	11500	5	7	31500	35100
34	11	O'DAY 35 SHOAL	SLP	SA/CR	FBG	KL	IB	21D	UNIV	11	3	11500	4	5	31500	35100
39	7	O'DAY 40 DEEP	SLP	SA/CR	FBG	KL	IB	46D	WEST	12	8	18000	6	4	52700	58000
39	7	O'DAY 40 SHOAL	SLP	SA/CR	FBG	KL	IB	46D	WEST	12	8	18500	4	11	53800	59100
		1986 BOATS														
16	9	DAY SAILER 3	SLP	SA/OD	FBG	CB	OB			6	3	1268		7	3000	3500
18	7	O'DAY 192	SLP	SAIL	FBG	KC	OB			7	1	1400	1	5	3250	3750
21	9	O'DAY 222	SLP	SA/CR	FBG	KC	OB			7	11	2200	1	8	4600	5300
25	9	O'DAY 26	SLP	SA/CR	FBG	CB	OB			8		4800	2	6	10600	12000
25	9	O'DAY 26	SLP	SA/CR	FBG	CB	IB	D		8		4800	2	6	11300	12800
26	11	O'DAY 272	SLP	SA/CR	FBG	KL	OB			9		4870	2	11	11300	12800
26	11	O'DAY 272	SLP	SA/CR	FBG	KL	IB	9D	YAN	9		4870	2	11	11800	13500
28	3	O'DAY 28 DEEP	SLP	SA/CR	FBG	KL	IB	10D	UNIV	10	3	7300	4	8	18700	20700
28	3	O'DAY 28 SHOAL	SLP	SA/CR	FBG	KC	IB	10D	UNIV	10	3	7700	3	8	19500	21700
31		O'DAY 31 DEEP	SLP	SA/CR	FBG	KL	IB	14D	UNIV	10	9	10100	5	3	26400	29400
31		O'DAY 31 SHOAL	SLP	SA/CR	FBG	KL	IB	14D	UNIV	10	9	10400	4		27200	30200
34	11	O'DAY 35 DEEP	SLP	SA/CR	FBG	KL	IB	21D	UNIV	11	3	11500	5	7	29700	33000
34	11	O'DAY 35 SHOAL	SLP	SA/CR	FBG	KL	IB	21D	UNIV	11	3	11500	4	5	29700	33000
39	7	O'DAY 40 DEEP	SLP	SA/CR	FBG	KL	IB	46D	WEST	12	8	18000	6	4	49600	54500
39	7	O'DAY 40 SHOAL	SLP	SA/CR	FBG	KL	IB	46D	WEST	12	8	18500	4	11	50600	55600
		1985 BOATS														
16	9	DAY SAILER	SLP	SA/OD	FBG	CB	OB			6	3	575		7	1850	2250
18	7	O'DAY 192	SLP	SAIL	FBG	KC	OB			7	1	1400	1	5	3050	3550
19		O'DAY 19	SLP	SA/OD	FBG	CB				7	9	1350	1		3000	3500
21	9	O'DAY 222	SLP	SA/CR	FBG	KC	OB			7	11	2200	1	8	4250	4950
22	9	O'DAY 23	SLP	SA/CR	FBG	KC	OB			8		3000	2	3	5550	6400
25	9	O'DAY 26	SLP	SA/CR	FBG	CB	OB			8		4800	2	6	9950	11300
28	3	O'DAY 28	SLP	SA/CR	FBG	KL	IB	10D	UNIV	10	3	7300	4	8	17200	19500
28	3	O'DAY 28 SHOAL	SLP	SA/CR	FBG	KC	IB	10D	UNIV	10	3	7700	3	8	18600	20600
31	1	O'DAY 31 DEEP	SLP	SA/CR	FBG	KL	IB	14D	UNIV	10	9	10100	5	3	24900	27600
31	1	O'DAY 31 SHOAL	SLP	SA/CR	FBG	KL	IB	14D	UNIV	10	9	10400	4		25600	28400
34	11	O'DAY 35 DEEP	SLP	SA/CR	FBG	KL	IB	21D	UNIV	11	3	11500	5	7	27900	31000
34	11	O'DAY 35 SHOAL	SLP	SA/CR	FBG	KL	IB	21D	UNIV	11	3	11500	4	5	27900	31000
38	7	O'DAY 39 DEEP	SLP	SA/CR	FBG	KL	IB	44D	UNIV	12	8	18000	6	4	44500	49500
38	7	O'DAY 39 SHOAL	SLP	SA/CR	FBG	KL	IB	44D	UNIV	12	8	18000	4	11	44500	49500
39	7	O'DAY 40 DEEP	SLP	SA/CR	FBG	KL	IB	46D	WEST	12	7	18000	6	4	46900	51600
39	7	O'DAY 40 SHOAL	SLP	SA/CR	FBG	KL	IB	46D	WEST	12	7	18500	4	11	47800	52500
		1984 BOATS														
16	9	DAY SAILER	SLP	SA/OD	FBG	CB	OB			6	3	575		7	1750	2100
19		O'DAY 19	SLP	SAIL	FBG	CB	OB			7	9	1350	1		2800	3300
21	9	O'DAY 222	SLP	SA/CR	FBG	KC	OB			7	11	2200	1	8	4000	4650
22	9	O'DAY 23	SLP	SA/CR	FBG	KC	OB			8		3000	2	3	5250	6000
25	9	O'DAY 26	SLP	SA/CR	FBG	CB	OB			8		5280	2	6	10300	11700
28	3	O'DAY 28 DEEP	SLP	SA/CR	FBG	KL	IB	10D	UNIV	10	3	7300	4	8	16200	18400
28	3	O'DAY 28 SHOAL	SLP	SA/CR	FBG	KL	IB	10D	UNIV	10	3	7700	3	8	17100	19400
29	11	O'DAY 30	SLP	SA/RC	FBG	KC	IB	14D	UNIV	10	9	10600	3	6	24500	27200
29	11	O'DAY 30	SLP	SA/RC	FBG	KL	IB	14D	UNIV	10	9	10150	4	11	23400	26000
30	2	O'DAY 31 DEEP	SLP	SA/CR	FBG	KL	IB	14D	UNIV	10	9	10100	5	4	23300	25900
30	2	O'DAY 31 SHOAL	SLP	SA/CR	FBG	KL	IB	14D	UNIV	10	9	10400	4	2	24100	26700
34		O'DAY 34 DEEP	SLP	SA/CR	FBG	KL	IB	21D	UNIV	11	3	11500	5	7	26200	29100
34		O'DAY 34 SHOAL	SLP	SA/CR	FBG	KL	IB	21D	UNIV	11	3	11500	4	5	26200	29100
35		O'DAY 35 DEEP	SLP	SA/CR	FBG	KL	IB	21D	UNIV	11	3	11500	5	7	26300	29200
35		O'DAY 35 SHOAL	SLP	SA/CR	FBG	KL	IB	21D	UNIV	11	3	11500	4	5	26300	29200
37		O'DAY 37	SLP	SA/CR	FBG	KL	IB	32D	UNIV	11	2	14000	4	9	32500	36100
38	7	O'DAY 39	SLP	SA/CR	FBG	KL	IB	44D	UNIV	12	8	18000	6	4	41900	46500
38	7	O'DAY 39 SHOAL	SLP	SA/CR	FBG	KL	IB	44D	UNIV	12	8	18000	4	11	41900	46500

....For earlier years, see the BUC Used Boat Price Guide, Volume 3

OCEAN ALEXANDER

81203 KAOHSIUNG TAIWAN

See inside cover to adjust price for area

OCEAN ALEXANDER OF FLORDA
FT LAUDERDALE FL 33316

FORMERLY ALEXANDER MARINE

For more recent years, see the BUC Used Boat Price Guide, Volume 1

LOA FT	IN	NAME AND/ OR MODEL	TOP/ RIG	BOAT TYPE	-HULL- MTL	TP	ENGINE TP	# HP	MFG	BEAM FT	IN	WGT LBS	DRAFT FT	IN	RETAIL LOW	RETAIL HIGH
		1996 BOATS														
39	3	390 MOTOR YACHT	FB	MY	FBG	DS	IB	T210D	CAT	13	11	24800	3	2	179000	196500
39	3	390 MOTOR YACHT	FB	MY	FBG	DS	IB	T300D	CAT	13	11	24800	3	2	188000	206500
39	3	390 MOTOR YACHT	FB	MY	FBG	DS	IB	T375D	CAT	13	11	24800	3	2	198000	217500
42		42 SEDAN	FB	SDN	FBG	DS	IB	T375D	CAT	14	4	23000	3	1	199500	219000
42		42 SEDAN	FB	SDN	FBG	DS	IB	T435D	CAT	14	4	22000	3	1	204500	224500
42	3	420 COCKPIT MY	FB	MYCPT	FBG	DS	IB	T210D	CAT	13	11	27000	3	2	190000	209000
42	3	420 COCKPIT MY	FB	MYCPT	FBG	DS	IB	T300D	CAT	13	11	27000	3	2	210000	230500
42	3	420 COCKPIT MY	FB	MYCPT	FBG	DS	IB	T375D	CAT	13	11	27000	3	2	226500	249000
42	6	CLASSICCO 423 MY	FB	MY	FBG	DS	IB	T210D	CAT	14	8	34200	3	10	228000	250500
42	6	CLASSICCO 423 MY	FB	MY	FBG	DS	IB	T300D	CAT	14	8	34200	3	10	244000	268000
42	6	CLASSICCO 423 S	FB	SDN	FBG	DS	IB	T210D	CAT	14	8	33800	3	10	228500	251500
42	6	CLASSICCO 423 S	FB	SDN	FBG	DS	IB	T300D	CAT	14	8	33800	3	10	239000	262500
43	9	440 COCKPIT MY	FB	MYCPT	FBG	DS	IB	T210D	CAT	13	11	28000	3	2	189500	208000
43	9	440 COCKPIT MY	FB	MYCPT	FBG	DS	IB	T300D	CAT	13	11	28000	3	2	214500	235500
43	9	440 COCKPIT MY	FB	MYCPT	FBG	DS	IB	T375D	CAT	13	11	28000	3	2	235000	258500
45	6	456 TRAWLER	FB	TRWL	FBG	DS	IB	T210D	CAT	15	8	40000	4		228500	251000
45	6	456 TRAWLER	FB	TRWL	FBG	DS	IB	T300D	CAT	15	8	40000	4		236000	259500
45	6	456 TRAWLER	FB	TRWL	FBG	DS	IB	T375D	CAT	15	8	40000	4		243500	268000
45	9	460 COCKPIT MY	FB	MYCPT	FBG	DS	IB	T210D	CAT	13	11	28000	3	2	184000	202500
45	9	460 COCKPIT MY	FB	MYCPT	FBG	DS	IB	T300D	CAT	13	11	28000	3	2	204500	224500
45	9	460 COCKPIT MY	FB	MYCPT	FBG	DS	IB	T375D	CAT	13	11	28000	3	2	229000	251500
46		46 SEDAN	FB	SDN	FBG	DS	IB	T375D	CAT	14	4	33400	3	1	235500	259000
46		46 SEDAN	FB	SDN	FBG	DS	IB	T435D	CAT	14	4	36400	3	1	256000	281500
46		46 SEDAN	FB	SDN	FBG	DS	IB	T485D	GM	14	4	36400	3	1	260000	285500
48		486 PILOTHOUSE	FB	PH	FBG	DS	IB	T375D	CAT	15	8	48000	4		280500	308500
48		486 PILOTHOUSE	FB	PH	FBG	DS	IB	T400D	GM	15	8	48000	4		283000	311000
48		486 PILOTHOUSE	FB	PH	FBG	DS	IB	T435D	CAT	15	8	48000	4		291000	320000
48	6	480 SEDAN	FB	SDN	FBG	DS	IB	T375D	CAT	15	6	36000	2	9	262000	288000
		IB T400D GM 265500 291500, IB T435D CAT 270000 296500, IB T485D GM 276000 303000														
		IB T550D GM 283500 311500														
51	1	51 SEDAN	FB	SDN	FBG	DS	IB	T400D	GM	16	4	44500	3	2	302000	332000
		IB T435D CAT 310000 340500, IB T485D GM 320500 352000, IB T550D GM 333500 366500														
		IB T735D GM 367000 403500														
52	5	520 PILOTHOUSE	FB	PH	FBG	DS	IB	T400D	GM	15	6	41500	4		320500	352000
52	5	520 PILOTHOUSE	FB	PH	FBG	DS	IB	T435D	CAT	15	6	41500	4		334500	368000
52	5	520 PILOTHOUSE	FB	PH	FBG	DS	IB	T485D	GM	15	6	41500	4		354000	389000
53		53 SEDAN	FB	SDN	FBG	DS	IB	T400D	GM	16	4	44500	3	2	330500	363000
		IB T435D CAT 342000 376000, IB T485D GM 358000 393500, IB T550D GM 377500 414500														
		IB T735D GM 427000 469000														
54		540 PILOTHOUSE	FB	PH	FBG	DS	IB	T400D	GM	15	6	41500	4		330500	363500
54		540 PILOTHOUSE	FB	PH	FBG	DS	IB	T435D	CAT	15	6	41500	4		347000	381000
54		540 PILOTHOUSE	FB	PH	FBG	DS	IB	T485D	GM	15	6	41500	4		368500	405000
60		60 MOTOR YACHT	FB	MY	FBG	DS	IB	T550D	GM	18		65000	4	10	546500	600500
60		60 MOTOR YACHT	FB	MY	FBG	DS	IB	T735D	GM	18		65000	4	10	612000	672500
63		63 COCKPIT MY	FB	MYCPT	FBG	DS	IB	T550D	GM	18		62500	4	10	561500	617000
63		63 COCKPIT MY	FB	MYCPT	FBG	DS	IB	T735D	GM	18		62500	4	10	636500	699500
63		630 MOTOR YACHT	FB	MY	FBG	DS	IB	T735D	GM	17	6	68000	4	4	718000	789000
66		66 MOTOR YACHT	FB	MY	FBG	DS	IB	T550D	GM	18		71000	4	10	714500	785000
66		66 MOTOR YACHT	FB	MY	FBG	DS	IB	T735D	GM	18		71000	4	10	778000	855000
69	6	70 COCKPIT MY	FB	MYCPT	FBG	DS	IB	T735D	GM	18		72000	5		813500	894000
69	6	70 MOTOR YACHT	FB	MY	FBG	DS	IB	T735D	GM	18		77000	5		842500	926000
		1995 BOATS														
39	3	390 MOTOR YACHT	FB	MY	FBG	DS	IB	T210D	CAT	13	11	24800	3	2	171500	188500
39	3	390 MOTOR YACHT	FB	MY	FBG	DS	IB	T300D	CAT	13	11	24800	3	2	180500	198000
39	3	390 MOTOR YACHT	FB	MY	FBG	DS	IB	T375D	CAT	13	11	24800	3	2	190000	209000
42		42 SEDAN	FB	SDN	FBG	DS	IB	T375D	CAT	14	4	23000	3	1	191000	210000
42		42 SEDAN	FB	SDN	FBG	DS	IB	T435D	CAT	14	4	22000	3	1	196000	215500
42	3	420 COCKPIT MY	FB	MYCPT	FBG	DS	IB	T210D	CAT	13	11	27000	3	2	182000	200500
42	3	420 COCKPIT MY	FB	MYCPT	FBG	DS	IB	T300D	CAT	13	11	27000	3	2	201000	221000
42	3	420 COCKPIT MY	FB	MYCPT	FBG	DS	IB	T375D	CAT	13	11	27000	3	2	217500	239000
42	6	CLASSICCO 423 MY	FB	MY	FBG	DS	IB	T210D	CAT	14	8	34200	3	10	218500	240000
42	6	CLASSICCO 423 MY	FB	MY	FBG	DS	IB	T300D	CAT	14	8	34200	3	10	234000	257000
42	6	CLASSICCO 423 S	FB	SDN	FBG	DS	IB	T210D	CAT	14	8	33800	3	10	219500	241000
42	6	CLASSICCO 423 S	FB	SDN	FBG	DS	IB	T300D	CAT	14	8	33800	3	10	229000	252000
43	9	440 COCKPIT MY	FB	MYCPT	FBG	DS	IB	T210D	CAT	13	11	28000	3	2	181500	199500
43	9	440 COCKPIT MY	FB	MYCPT	FBG	DS	IB	T300D	CAT	13	11	28000	3	2	205500	226000
43	9	440 COCKPIT MY	FB	MYCPT	FBG	DS	IB	T375D	CAT	13	11	28000	3	2	225500	248000
45	6	456 TRAWLER	FB	TRWL	FBG	DS	IB	T210D	CAT	15	8	40000	4		218500	240000

CONTINUED ON NEXT PAGE

LOA FT	IN	NAME AND/ OR MODEL	TOP/ RIG	BOAT TYPE	-HULL- MTL	TP	TP	----ENGINE--- # HP	MFG	BEAM FT	IN	WGT LBS	DRAFT FT	IN	RETAIL LOW	RETAIL HIGH
		1995 BOATS														
45	6	456 TRAWLER	FB	TRWL	FBG	DS	IB	T300D	CAT	15	8	40000	4		226000	248500
45	6	456 TRAWLER	FB	TRWL	FBG	DS	IB	T375D	CAT	15	8	40000	4		233500	256500
45	9	460 COCKPIT MY	FB	MYCPT	FBG	DS	IB	T210D	CAT	13	11	28000	3	2	176000	193500
45	9	460 COCKPIT MY	FB	MYCPT	FBG	DS	IB	T300D	CAT	13	11	28000	3	2	196000	215500
45	9	460 COCKPIT MY	FB	MYCPT	FBG	DS	IB	T375D	CAT	13	11	28000	3	2	219500	241000
46		46 SEDAN	FB	SDN	FBG	DS	IB	T375D	CAT	14	4	33400	3	1	226000	248000
46		46 SEDAN	FB	SDN	FBG	DS	IB	T435D	CAT	14	4	36400	3	1	245500	270000
46		46 SEDAN	FB	SDN	FBG	DS	IB	T485D	GM	14	4	36400	3	1	249500	274000
48		486 PILOTHOUSE	FB	PH	FBG	DS	IB	T375D	CAT	15	8	48000	4		268500	295000
48		486 PILOTHOUSE	FB	PH	FBG	DS	IB	T400D	GM	15	8	48000	4		271000	297500
48		486 PILOTHOUSE	FB	PH	FBG	DS	IB	T435D	CAT	15	8	48000	4		278500	306500
48	6	480 SEDAN	FB	SDN	FBG	DS	IB	T375D	CAT	15	6	36000	2	9	251500	276000
		IB T400D GM 254500 279500, IB T435D CAT 259000 284500, IB T485D GM													264500	290500
		IB T550D GM 271500 298500														
51	1	51 SEDAN	FB	SDN	FBG	DS	IB	T400D	GM	16	4	44500	3	2	289500	318500
		IB T435D CAT 297000 326500, IB T485D GM 307500 338000, IB T550D GM													320000	351500
		IB T735D GM 352000 387000														
52	5	520 PILOTHOUSE	FB	PH	FBG	DS	IB	T400D	GM	15	6	41500	4		307500	337500
52	5	520 PILOTHOUSE	FB	PH	FBG	DS	IB	T435D	CAT	15	6	41500	4		321000	352500
52	5	520 PILOTHOUSE	FB	PH	FBG	DS	IB	T485D	GM	15	6	41500	4		339500	373000
53		53 SEDAN	FB	SDN	FBG	DS	IB	T400D	GM	16	4	44500	3	2	317000	348500
		IB T435D CAT 328000 360500, IB T485D GM 343000 377000, IB T550D GM													362000	397500
		IB T735D GM 409500 450000														
54		540 PILOTHOUSE	FB	PH	FBG	DS	IB	T400D	GM	15	6	41500	4		317000	348500
54		540 PILOTHOUSE	FB	PH	FBG	DS	IB	T435D	CAT	15	6	41500	4		332500	365500
54		540 PILOTHOUSE	FB	PH	FBG	DS	IB	T485D	GM	15	6	41500	4		353500	388500
60		60 MOTOR YACHT	FB	MY	FBG	DS	IB	T550D	GM	18		65000	4	10	524000	576000
60		60 MOTOR YACHT	FB	MY	FBG	DS	IB	T735D	GM	18		65000	4	10	587000	645000
63		63 COCKPIT MY	FB	MYCPT	FBG	DS	IB	T550D	GM	18		62500	4	10	538500	591500
63		63 COCKPIT MY	FB	MYCPT	FBG	DS	IB	T735D	GM	18		62500	4	10	610000	670500
63		630 MOTOR YACHT	FB	MY	FBG	DS	IB	T735D	GM	17	6	68000	4	4	688000	756000
66		66 MOTOR YACHT	FB	MY	FBG	DS	IB	T550D	GM	18		71000	4	10	685500	753000
66		66 MOTOR YACHT	FB	MY	FBG	DS	IB	T735D	GM	18		71000	4	10	746000	820000
69	6	70 COCKPIT MY	FB	MYCPT	FBG	DS	IB	T735D	GM	18		72000	5		780500	857500
69	6	70 MOTOR YACHT	FB	MY	FBG	DS	IB	T735D	GM	18		77000	5		808500	888500
		1994 BOATS														
39	3	390 MOTOR YACHT	FB	MY	FBG	DS	IB	T210D	CAT	13	11	24800	3	2	164500	180500
39	3	390 MOTOR YACHT	FB	MY	FBG	DS	IB	T300D	CAT	13	11	24800	3	2	172500	190000
39	3	390 MOTOR YACHT	FB	MY	FBG	DS	IB	T375D	CAT	13	11	24800	3	2	182000	200000
42		42 SEDAN	FB	SDN	FBG	DS	IB	T375D	CAT	14	4	23000	3	1	183000	201000
42		42 SEDAN	FB	SDN	FBG	DS	IB	T435D	CAT	14	4	22000	3	1	188000	206500
42	3	420 COCKPIT MY	FB	MYCPT	FBG	DS	IB	T210D	CAT	13	11	27000	3	2	174500	192000
42	3	420 COCKPIT MY	FB	MYCPT	FBG	DS	IB	T300D	CAT	13	11	27000	3	2	192500	212000
42	3	420 COCKPIT MY	FB	MYCPT	FBG	DS	IB	T375D	CAT	13	11	27000	3	2	208000	229000
42	6	CLASSICCO 423 MY	FB	MY	FBG	DS	IB	T210D	CAT	14	8	34200	3	10	209500	230000
42	6	CLASSICCO 423 MY	FB	MY	FBG	DS	IB	T300D	CAT	14	8	34200	3	10	224000	246500
42	6	CLASSICCO 423 S	FB	SDN	FBG	DS	IB	T210D	CAT	14	8	33800	3	10	210000	231000
42	6	CLASSICCO 423 S	FB	SDN	FBG	DS	IB	T300D	CAT	14	8	33800	3	10	219500	241500
43	9	440 COCKPIT MY	FB	MYCPT	FBG	DS	IB	T210D	CAT	13	11	28000	3	2	174000	191000
43	9	440 COCKPIT MY	FB	MYCPT	FBG	DS	IB	T300D	CAT	13	11	28000	3	2	197000	216500
43	9	440 COCKPIT MY	FB	MYCPT	FBG	DS	IB	T375D	CAT	13	11	28000	3	2	216000	237500
45	6	456 TRAWLER	FB	TRWL	FBG	DS	IB	T210D	CAT	15	8	40000	4		215500	237000
45	6	456 TRAWLER	FB	TRWL	FBG	DS	IB	T300D	CAT	15	8	40000	4		223000	245000
45	6	456 TRAWLER	FB	TRWL	FBG	DS	IB	T375D	CAT	15	8	40000	4		231000	254000
45	9	460 COCKPIT MY	FB	MYCPT	FBG	DS	IB	T210D	CAT	13	11	28000	3	2	177000	194500
45	9	460 COCKPIT MY	FB	MYCPT	FBG	DS	IB	T300D	CAT	13	11	28000	3	2	190500	209500
45	9	460 COCKPIT MY	FB	MYCPT	FBG	DS	IB	T375D	CAT	13	11	28000	3	2	210500	231500
46		46 SEDAN	FB	SDN	FBG	DS	IB	T375D	CAT	14	4	33400	3	1	218000	239500
46		46 SEDAN	FB	SDN	FBG	DS	IB	T435D	CAT	14	4	36400	3	1	236000	259500
46		46 SEDAN	FB	SDN	FBG	DS	IB	T485D	GM	14	4	36400	3	1	239500	263500
48		486 PILOTHOUSE	FB	PH	FBG	DS	IB	T375D	CAT	15	8	48000	4		267000	293500
48		486 PILOTHOUSE	FB	PH	FBG	DS	IB	T400D	GM	15	8	48000	4		267500	294000
48		486 PILOTHOUSE	FB	PH	FBG	DS	IB	T435D	CAT	15	8	48000	4		276000	303500
48	6	480 SEDAN	FB	SDN	FBG	DS	IB	T375D	CAT	15	6	36000	2	9	241500	265500
		IB T400D GM 244000 268500, IB T435D CAT 249000 273500, IB T485D GM													254000	279000
		IB T550D GM 261500 287000														
51	1	51 SEDAN	FB	SDN	FBG	DS	IB	T400D	GM	16	4	44500	3	2	278000	305000
		IB T435D CAT 285500 313500, IB T485D GM 294500 324000, IB T550D GM													307000	337000
		IB T735D GM 338000 371500														
52	5	520 PILOTHOUSE	FB	PH	FBG	DS	IB	T400D	GM	15	6	41500	4		297000	326500
52	5	520 PILOTHOUSE	FB	PH	FBG	DS	IB	T435D	CAT	15	6	41500	4		311000	341500
52	5	520 PILOTHOUSE	FB	PH	FBG	DS	IB	T485D	GM	15	6	41500	4		326000	358000
53		53 SEDAN	FB	SDN	FBG	DS	IB	T400D	GM	16	4	44500	3	2	304500	334500
		IB T435D CAT 316000 347500, IB T485D GM 329500 362000, IB T550D GM													347000	381500
		IB T735D GM 393000 432000														
54		540 PILOTHOUSE	FB	PH	FBG	DS	IB	T400D	GM	15	6	41500	4		304500	334500
54		540 PILOTHOUSE	FB	PH	FBG	DS	IB	T435D	CAT	15	6	41500	4		319500	351500
54		540 PILOTHOUSE	FB	PH	FBG	DS	IB	T485D	GM	15	6	41500	4		339000	372500
60		60 MOTOR YACHT	FB	MY	FBG	DS	IB	T550D	GM	18		65000	4	10	502000	551500
60		60 MOTOR YACHT	FB	MY	FBG	DS	IB	T735D	GM	18		65000	4	10	562500	618500
63		63 COCKPIT MY	FB	MYCPT	FBG	DS	IB	T550D	GM	18		62500	4	10	516500	567500
63		63 COCKPIT MY	FB	MYCPT	FBG	DS	IB	T735D	GM	18		62500	4	10	585000	643000
63		630 MOTOR YACHT	FB	MY	FBG	DS	IB	T735D	GM	17	6	68000	4	4	661500	727000
66		66 MOTOR YACHT	FB	MY	FBG	DS	IB	T550D	GM	18		71000	4	10	657000	722000
66		66 MOTOR YACHT	FB	MY	FBG	DS	IB	T735D	GM	18		71000	4	10	714500	785500
69	6	70 COCKPIT MY	FB	MYCPT	FBG	DS	IB	T735D	GM	18		72000	5		747500	821500
69	6	70 MOTOR YACHT	FB	MY	FBG	DS	IB	T735D	GM	18		77000	5		774000	850500
		1993 BOATS														
39	3	390 MOTOR YACHT	FB	MY	FBG	DS	IB	T250D	CUM	13	11	24800	3	2	156000	171500
		IB T300D CAT 164500 181000, IB T300D CUM 160000 175500, IB T375D CAT													173500	190500
42		42 SEDAN	FB	SDN	FBG	DS	IB	T250D	CUM	14	4	23000	3	1	156500	172000
		IB T300D CAT 165000 181500, IB T300D CUM 161500 177500, IB T375D CAT													174500	191500
		IB T400D GM 174000 191000, IB T425D CAT 177500 195000														
42	3	420 COCKPIT MY	FB	MYCPT	FBG	DS	IB	T250D	CUM	13	11	27000	3	2	171000	188000
		IB T300D CAT 183500 202000, IB T300D CUM 180000 198000, IB T375D CAT													198500	218000
43	9	440 COCKPIT MY	FB	MYCPT	FBG	DS	IB	T250D	CUM	13	11	28000	3	2	173000	190000
		IB T300D CAT 187500 206000, IB T300D CUM 185000 203500, IB T375D CAT													206000	226000
45	6	456 TRAWLER	FB	TRWL	FBG	DS	IB	T210D	CUM	15	8	40000	4		203000	223000
		IB T250D CUM 205500 226000, IB T300D CAT 212500 233500, IB T300D CUM													209500	230000
		IB T375D CAT 219500 241500														
45	9	460 COCKPIT MY	FB	MYCPT	FBG	DS	IB	T250D	CUM	13	11	28000	3	2	170500	187000
		IB T300D CAT 181500 199500, IB T300D CUM 179500 197000, IB T375D CAT													200500	220500
46		46 SEDAN	FB	SDN	FBG	DS	IB	T250D	CUM	14	4	33400	3	1	192500	211500
		IB T300D CAT 199500 219000, IB T300D CUM 197500 217500, IB T375D CAT													207500	228000
		IB T400D GM 219500 241500, IB T425D CAT 224000 246000, IB T485D GM													228000	251000
48		486 PILOTHOUSE	FB	PH	FBG	DS	IB	T300D	CAT	15	8	48000	4		245000	269000
		IB T300D CUM 242000 265500, IB T375D CAT 254500 279500, IB T400D CUM													254000	279000
		IB T400D GM 254500 280000, IB T430D VLVO 256000 281500														
48	6	480 SEDAN	FB	SDN	FBG	DS	IB	T375D	CAT	15	6	36000	2	9	230000	253000
		IB T400D GM 232500 255500, IB T425D CAT 236000 259500, IB T485D GM													242000	266000
		IB T550D GM 249000 273500														
51	1	51 SEDAN	FB	SDN	FBG	DS	IB	T400D	GM	16	4	44500	3	2	264500	291000
		IB T485D GM 281000 308500, IB T550D GM 292500 321000, IB T735D GM													322000	353500
52	5	520 PILOTHOUSE	FB	PH	FBG	DS	IB	T400D	GM	15	6	41500	4		283500	311500
52	5	520 PILOTHOUSE	FB	PH	FBG	DS	IB	T425D	CAT	15	6	41500	4		293500	322500
52	5	520 PILOTHOUSE	FB	PH	FBG	DS	IB	T485D	GM	15	6	41500	4		310500	341500
53		53 SEDAN	FB	SDN	FBG	DS	IB	T400D	GM	16	4	44500	3	2	290500	319000
		IB T485D GM 314000 345000, IB T550D GM 331000 363500, IB T735D GM													374500	411500
54		540 PILOTHOUSE	FB	PH	FBG	DS	IB	T400D	GM	15	6	41500	4		290500	319000
54		540 PILOTHOUSE	FB	PH	FBG	DS	IB	T425D	CAT	15	6	41500	4		301000	330500
54		540 PILOTHOUSE	FB	PH	FBG	DS	IB	T485D	GM	15	6	41500	4		323000	355000
60		60 MOTOR YACHT	FB	MY	FBG	DS	IB	T550D	GM	18		65000	4	10	478000	525500
60		60 MOTOR YACHT	FB	MY	FBG	DS	IB	T735D	GM	18		65000	4	10	536000	589000
60		60 MOTOR YACHT	FB	MY	FBG	DS	IB	T900D	GM	18		65000	4	10	581500	639000
63		63 COCKPIT MY	FB	MYCPT	FBG	DS	IB	T550D	GM	18		62500	4	10	492000	541000
63		63 COCKPIT MY	FB	MYCPT	FBG	DS	IB	T735D	GM	18		62500	4	10	557000	612500
63		63 COCKPIT MY	FB	MYCPT	FBG	DS	IB	T900D	GM	18		62500	4	10	608500	669000
63		630 MOTOR YACHT	FB	MY	FBG	DS	IB	T735D	GM	17	6	68000	4	4	630500	693000
63		630 MOTOR YACHT	FB	MY	FBG	DS	IB	T900D	GM	17	6	68000	4	4	677500	744500
66		66 MOTOR YACHT	FB	MY	FBG	DS	IB	T550D	GM	18		71000	4	10	626000	688000
66		66 MOTOR YACHT	FB	MY	FBG	DS	IB	T735D	GM	18		71000	4	10	681000	748000
66		66 MOTOR YACHT	FB	MY	FBG	DS	IB	T900D	GM	18		71000	4	10	726500	798500
69	6	70 COCKPIT MY	FB	MYCPT	FBG	DS	IB	T735D	GM	18		72000	5		712000	782500

CONTINUED ON NEXT PAGE

LOA FT	IN	NAME AND/ OR MODEL	TOP/ RIG	BOAT TYPE	-HULL- MTL	TP	---ENGINE--- TP	# HP	MFG	BEAM FT	IN	WGT LBS	DRAFT FT	IN	RETAIL LOW	RETAIL HIGH
		1993 BOATS														
69	6	70 COCKPIT MY	FB	MYCPT	FBG	DS	IB	T900D	GM	18		72000	5		743000	816500
69	6	70 MOTOR YACHT	FB	MY	FBG	DS	IB	T735D	GM	18		77000	5		737500	810500
69	6	70 MOTOR YACHT	FB	MY	FBG	DS	IB	T900D	GM	18		77000	5		768500	844500
		1992 BOATS														
39	3	390 MOTOR YACHT	FB	MY	FBG	DS	IB	T250D	CUM	13	11	24800	3	2	148500	163500
39	3	390 MOTOR YACHT	FB	MY	FBG	DS	IB	T300D	CUM	13	11	24800	3	2	152500	167500
39	3	390 MOTOR YACHT	FB	MY	FBG	DS	IB	T375D	CAT	13	11	24800	3	2	165500	181500
42		42 SEDAN	FB	SDN	FBG	DS	IB	T250D	CUM	14	4	23000	3	1	149000	164000
		IB T300D CUM 154000 169000, IB T375D CAT 166500 183000, IB T400D GM 165500 182000														
		IB T425D CAT 169000 186000														
42	3	420 COCKPIT MY	FB	MYCPT	FBG	DS	IB	T250D	CUM	13	11	27000	3	2	163000	179000
42	3	420 COCKPIT MY	FB	MYCPT	FBG	DS	IB	T300D	CUM	13	11	27000	3	2	171500	188500
42	3	420 COCKPIT MY	FB	MYCPT	FBG	DS	IB	T375D	CAT	13	11	27000	3	2	189000	208000
43	9	440 COCKPIT MY	FB	MYCPT	FBG	DS	IB	T250D	CUM	13	11	27000	3	2	161500	177500
43	9	440 COCKPIT MY	FB	MYCPT	FBG	DS	IB	T300D	CUM	13	11	27000	3	2	173000	190000
43	9	440 COCKPIT MY	FB	MYCPT	FBG	DS	IB	T375D	CAT	13	11	27000	3	2	193000	212000
45	6	456 TRAWLER	FB	TRWL	FBG	DS	IB	T210D	CUM	15	8	39000	4		190500	209500
45	6	456 TRAWLER	FB	TRWL	FBG	DS	IB	T250D	CUM	15	8	39000	4		193000	212500
45	6	456 TRAWLER	FB	TRWL	FBG	DS	IB	T300D	CUM	15	8	39000	4		197000	216500
45	9	460 COCKPIT MY	FB	MYCPT	FBG	DS	IB	T250D	CUM	13	11	28000	3	2	162000	178000
45	9	460 COCKPIT MY	FB	MYCPT	FBG	DS	IB	T300D	CUM	13	11	28000	3	2	171000	187500
45	9	460 COCKPIT MY	FB	MYCPT	FBG	DS	IB	T375D	CAT	13	11	28000	3	2	191000	210000
46		46 SEDAN	FB	SDN	FBG	DS	IB	T250D	CUM	14	4	26000	3	1	161000	176500
		IB T300D CUM 166000 182500, IB T375D CAT 176000 193500, IB T400D CAT 179000 196500														
		IB T400D GM 177000 194500, IB T485D GM 186000 204500														
51		51 SEDAN	FB	SDN	FBG	DS	IB	T400D	GM	16	4	44500	3	2	251500	276000
		IB T425D CAT 256000 281500, IB T485D GM 266500 293000, IB T550D GM 277000 304500														
		IB T735D GM 305000 335000														
52	5	520 PILOTHOUSE	FB	PH	FBG	DS	IB	T400D	GM	15	6	41500	4		270500	297000
52	5	520 PILOTHOUSE	FB	PH	FBG	DS	IB	T425D	CAT	15	6	41500	4		280000	307500
52	5	520 PILOTHOUSE	FB	PH	FBG	DS	IB	T485D	GM	15	6	41500	4		296000	325500
53		53 SEDAN	FB	SDN	FBG	DS	IB	T400D	GM	16	4	44500	3	2	277000	304000
		IB T425D CAT 285000 313000, IB T485D GM 299500 329000, IB T550D GM 315500 346500														
		IB T735D GM 357000 392500														
54		540 PILOTHOUSE	FB	PH	FBG	DS	IB	T400D	GM	15	6	41500	4		277000	304000
54		540 PILOTHOUSE	FB	PH	FBG	DS	IB	T425D	CAT	15	6	41500	4		287000	315500
54		540 PILOTHOUSE	FB	PH	FBG	DS	IB	T485D	GM	15	6	41500	4		308000	338000
60		60 MOTOR YACHT	FB	MY	FBG	DS	IB	T550D	GM	18		65000	4	10	456000	501000
60		60 MOTOR YACHT	FB	MY	FBG	DS	IB	T735D	GM	18		65000	4	10	511000	561500
63		63 COCKPIT MY	FB	MYCPT	FBG	DS	IB	T550D	GM	18		62500	4	10	469500	515500
63		63 COCKPIT MY	FB	MYCPT	FBG	DS	IB	T735D	GM	18		62500	4	10	531000	583500
63		63 MOTOR YACHT	FB	MY	FBG	DS	IB	T550D	GM	18		62500	4	10	481000	528500
63		63 MOTOR YACHT	FB	MY	FBG	DS	IB	T735D	GM	17	6	68000	4		582000	639500
63		63 MOTOR YACHT	FB	MY	FBG	DS	IB	T735D	GM	18		62500	4	10	545000	599000
66		66 MOTOR YACHT	FB	MY	FBG	DS	IB	T550D	GM	18		71000	4	10	596500	655500
66		66 MOTOR YACHT	FB	MY	FBG	DS	IB	T735D	GM	18		71000	4	10	649000	713000
66		66 MOTOR YACHT	FB	MY	FBG	DS	IB	T900D	GM	18		71000	4	10	692500	761000
69	6	70 COCKPIT MY	FB	MYCPT	FBG	DS	IB	T735D	GM	18		72000	4	10	679000	746000
69	6	70 COCKPIT MY	FB	MYCPT	FBG	DS	IB	T900D	GM	18		72000	4	10	708000	778000
69	6	70 MOTOR YACHT	FB	MY	FBG	DS	IB	T735D	GM	18		77000	4	10	703000	772500
69	6	70 MOTOR YACHT	FB	MY	FBG	DS	IB	T900D	GM	18		76000	4	10	729000	801000
		1991 BOATS														
39	3	390 MOTOR YACHT	FB	MY	FBG	DS	IB	T250D	CUM	13	11	24800	3	2	141500	156000
39	3	390 MOTOR YACHT	FB	MY	FBG	DS	IB	T300D	CUM	13	11	24800	3	2	145500	160000
39	3	390 MOTOR YACHT	FB	MY	FBG	DS	IB	T375D	CAT	13	11	24800	3	2	157500	173500
42		42 SEDAN	FB	SDN	FBG	DS	IB	T250D	CUM	14	4	23000	3	1	142500	156500
		IB T300D CUM 147000 161500, IB T375D CAT 158500 174500, IB T400D GM 158000 173500														
42	3	420 COCKPIT MY	FB	MYCPT	FBG	DS	IB	T250D	CUM	13	11	27000	3	2	155500	171000
42	3	420 COCKPIT MY	FB	MYCPT	FBG	DS	IB	T300D	CUM	13	11	27000	3	2	164000	180000
42	3	420 COCKPIT MY	FB	MYCPT	FBG	DS	IB	T375D	CAT	13	11	27000	3	2	180500	198000
43	9	440 COCKPIT MY	FB	MYCPT	FBG	DS	IB	T250D	CUM	13	11	27000	3	2	154000	169000
43	9	440 COCKPIT MY	FB	MYCPT	FBG	DS	IB	T300D	CUM	13	11	27000	3	2	165000	181000
43	9	440 COCKPIT MY	FB	MYCPT	FBG	DS	IB	T375D	CAT	13	11	27000	3	2	184000	202000
45	6	456 TRAWLER	FB	TRWL	FBG	DS	IB	T210D	CUM	15	8		4		173500	191000
45	6	456 TRAWLER	FB	TRWL	FBG	DS	IB	T250D	CUM	15	8		4		176500	193500
45	6	456 TRAWLER	FB	TRWL	FBG	DS	IB	T300D	CUM	15	8		4		179500	197500
45	9	460 COCKPIT MY	FB	MYCPT	FBG	DS	IB	T250D	CUM	13	11	28000	3	2	154500	169500
45	9	460 COCKPIT MY	FB	MYCPT	FBG	DS	IB	T300D	CUM	13	11	28000	3	2	163000	179000
45	9	460 COCKPIT MY	FB	MYCPT	FBG	DS	IB	T375D	CAT	13	11	28000	3	2	182500	200500
46		46 SEDAN	FB	SDN	FBG	DS	IB	T250D	CUM	14	4	26000	3	1	153500	168500
		IB T300D CUM 158000 174000, IB T375D CAT 168000 184500, IB T485D GM 177500 195000														
48		YACHTSMAN COCKPIT	FB	MYCPT	FBG	DS	IB	T375D	CAT	15	6	40000	4	6	204500	224500
48		YACHTSMAN COCKPIT	FB	MYCPT	FBG	DS	IB	T400D	GM	15	6	40000	4	6	207000	227500
48		YACHTSMAN COCKPIT	FB	MYCPT	FBG	DS	IB	T485D	CAT	15	6	40000	4	6	224500	246500
51		51 SEDAN	FB	SDN	FBG	DS	IB	T400D	GM	16	4	44500	3	2	239500	263500
		IB T425D CAT 244500 268500, IB T485D GM 254000 279500, IB T550D GM 264500 290500														
		IB T735D GM 291000 319500														
52	5	520 PILOTHOUSE	FB	PH	FBG	DS	IB	T400D	GM	15	6	41500	4		258000	283500
52	5	520 PILOTHOUSE	FB	PH	FBG	DS	IB	T425D	CAT	15	6	41500	4		267500	294000
52	5	520 PILOTHOUSE	FB	PH	FBG	DS	IB	T485D	GM	15	6	41500	4		282500	310500
53		53 SEDAN	FB	SDN	FBG	DS	IB	T400D	GM	16	4	44500	3	2	264000	290500
		IB T425D CAT 272000 299000, IB T485D GM 285500 314000, IB T550D GM 301000 330500														
		IB T735D GM 340500 374500														
54		540 PILOTHOUSE	FB	PH	FBG	DS	IB	T400D	GM	15	6	41500	4		264000	290500
54		540 PILOTHOUSE	FB	PH	FBG	DS	IB	T425D	CAT	15	6	41500	4		274000	301000
54		540 PILOTHOUSE	FB	PH	FBG	DS	IB	T485D	GM	15	6	41500	4		293500	322500
56		56 MOTOR YACHT	FB	MY	FBG	DS	IB	T550D	GM	18		61500	4	10	393500	432500
56		56 MOTOR YACHT	FB	MY	FBG	DS	IB	T735D	GM	18		61500	4	10	441500	485000
56		56 MOTOR YACHT WB	FB	MY	FBG	DS	IB	T550D	GM	18		61500	4	10	408000	448500
56		56 MOTOR YACHT WB	FB	MY	FBG	DS	IB	T735D	GM	18		61500	4	10	456500	502000
56		56 PILOTHOUSE	FB	PH	FBG	DS	IB	T735D	GM	18		55000	4	10	447500	492000
60		60 MOTOR YACHT	FB	MY	FBG	DS	IB	T550D	GM	18		65000	4	10	435000	478000
60		60 MOTOR YACHT	FB	MY	FBG	DS	IB	T735D	GM	18		65000	4	10	487500	535500
60		60 PILOTHOUSE	FB	PH	FBG	DS	IB	T550D	GM	18		60000	4	10	406500	447000
60		60 PILOTHOUSE	FB	PH	FBG	DS	IB	T735D	GM	18		60000	4	10	461000	506500
63		63 COCKPIT MY	FB	MYCPT	FBG	DS	IB	T550D	GM	18		62500	4	10	425000	467000
63		63 COCKPIT MY	FB	MYCPT	FBG	DS	IB	T735D	GM	18		62500	4	10	482000	529500
63		63 MOTOR YACHT	FB	MY	FBG	DS	IB	T550D	GM	18		62500	4	10	482500	530000
63		63 MOTOR YACHT	FB	MY	FBG	DS	IB	T735D	GM	18		62500	4	10	545500	599500
66		66 MOTOR YACHT	FB	MY	FBG	DS	IB	T550D	GM	18		71000	4	10	569000	625500
66		66 MOTOR YACHT	FB	MY	FBG	DS	IB	T735D	GM	18		71000	4	10	619000	680500
69	6	70 COCKPIT MY	FB	MYCPT	FBG	DS	IB	T735D	GM	18		72000	4	10	647500	711500
69	6	70 MOTOR YACHT	FB	MY	FBG	DS	IB	T735D	GM	18		77000	4	10	670500	737000
		1985 BOATS														
38	4	OCEAN 38 DC	FB	DC	FBG		IB	T135D	LEHM	13	4	20500	3	2	88200	96900
39	4	OCEAN 40 DC	FB	TRWL	FBG	SV	IB	120D	LEHM	13	4	21000	3	6	88300	97100
		IB T135D LEHM 94900 104500, IB T215D GM 99100 109000, IB T225D LEHM 99600 109500														
39	4	OCEAN 40 S	FB	TRWL	FBG	SV	IB	120D	LEHM	13	4	19800	3	6	84200	92600
		IB T135D LEHM 94900 104500, IB T215D GM 99100 109000, IB T225D LEHM 99600 109500														
42	6	OCEAN 43 DC	FB	TRWL	FBG	SV	IB	T215D	GM	14	6	27500	3	6	115000	126000
42	6	OCEAN 43 DC	FB	TRWL	FBG	SV	IB	T270D	CUM	14	6	29000	3	6	121500	133500
42	8	OCEAN 43 DC	FB	TRWL	FBG	DS	IB	T135D	LEHM	14	6	30000	3	10	119500	131500
42	8	OCEAN 43 FD	FB	TRWL	FBG	DS	IB	T135D	LEHM	14	6	28000	3	10	113000	124500
42	8	OCEAN 43 S	FB	TRWL	FBG	DS	IB	T135D	LEHM	14	6	28000	3	10	113000	124500
46		OCEAN AFT CPT	FB	FD	FBG		IB	T D		15	4				**	**
46		OCEAN AFT CPT FD	FB	MY	FBG		IB	T D		15	4				**	**
48	7	OCEAN SDN	FB	MY	FBG		IB	T135D	LEHM	15	6	43500	3	10	147500	162000
48	7	OCEAN SDN	FB	MY	FBG		IB	T135D	PERK	15	6	43500	3	10	148500	163000
48	7	OCEAN SDN	FB	MY	FBG		IB	T260D	J&T	15	6	43500	3	10	155000	170000
50		OCEAN	FB	FD	FBG		IB	T D		15	6	40000	4	5	**	**
50		OCEAN FD	FB	MY	FBG		IB	T D		15	6	40000	4	5	**	**
50		OCEAN RAID PH	FB	MY	FBG		IB	T D		15	6	40000	4	5	**	**
50		OCEAN RAIDED PH	FB	MY	FBG		IB	T D		15	6	40000	4	5	**	**
54		OCEAN 54 MY	FB	MY	FBG	SV	IB	T220D	GM	15	5	46500	4	6	169000	186000
54		OCEAN FISH CPT	FB	FD	FBG		IB	T D		15	6	40000	4	5	**	**
54		OCEAN FISH CPT FD	FB	MY	FBG		IB	T D		15	6	40000	4	5	**	**
56		OCEAN 56 MY	FB	MY	FBG	SV	IB	T320D	CUM	17	9	55000	4	6	221000	242500
56		OCEAN 56 PH	FB	PH	FBG	SV	IB	T320D	CUM	18		54000	4	10	232000	255000
59	5	OCEAN 60 MY	FB	MY	F/S	SV	IB	T530D	J&T	18		59000	4	10	306000	336000
59	5	OCEAN 60 PH	FB	PH	FBG	SV	IB	T530D	J&T	18		56000	4	10	305500	335500
69	5	OCEAN 70 MY W/COCKPT	FB	MY	FBG	SV	IB	T675D	GM	18		70000	4	10	481000	528500
70		OCEAN 70 MY	FB	MY	FBG	SV	IB	T675D	J&T	18		77000	5		509500	559500
		1984 BOATS														
37	8	OCEAN 38 DC	FB	TRWL	FBG	SV	IB	T135D	PERK	13	4	19000	3	6	79500	87400
39	4	OCEAN 40 DC	FB	TRWL	FBG	SV	IB	120D	LEHM	13	4	21000	3	6	84600	93000
39	4	OCEAN 40 DC	FB	TRWL	FBG	SV	IB	T135D	LEHM	13	4	21200	3	6	90900	99900
39	4	OCEAN 40 DC	FB	TRWL	FBG	SV	IB	T215D	GM	13	4	21500	3	6	94900	104500
39	4	OCEAN 40 S	FB	TRWL	FBG	SV	IB	120D	LEHM	13	4	19800	3	6	80700	88700
39	4	OCEAN 40 S	FB	TRWL	FBG	SV	IB	T135D	LEHM	13	4	21200	3	6	90900	99900
39	4	OCEAN 40 S	FB	TRWL	FBG	SV	IB	T215D	GM	13	4	21500	3	6	94900	104500
42	6	OCEAN 43 DC	FB	TRWL	FBG	SV	IB	T215D	GM	14	6	27500	3	6	110000	121000

CONTINUED ON NEXT PAGE

OCEAN ALEXANDER -CONTINUED See inside cover to adjust price for area

LOA FT	IN	NAME AND/ OR MODEL	TOP/ RIG	BOAT TYPE	-HULL- MTL	TP	TP	----ENGINE--- # HP	MFG	BEAM FT	IN	WGT LBS	DRAFT FT	IN	RETAIL LOW	RETAIL HIGH
		1984 BOATS														
42	6	OCEAN 43 DC	FB	TRWL	FBG	SV	IB	T270D	CUM	14	6	29000	3	6	116500	128000
42	8	OCEAN 43 DC	FB	TRWL	FBG	DS	IB	T135D	LEHM	14	6	30000	3	10	114500	126000
42	8	OCEAN 43 FD	FB	TRWL	FBG	DS	IB	T135D	LEHM	14	6	28000	3	10	108500	119000
42	8	OCEAN 43 S	FB	TRWL	FBG	DS	IB	T135D	FORD	14	6	28000	3	10	108500	119000
43	8	OCEAN 43 FD	FB	TRWL	FBG	DS	IB	T215D	GM	14	6	28000	3	10	111000	122000
50	3	OCEAN 50 MY	FB	TRWL	FBG	SV	IB	T270D	CUM	15	6	50500	4	6	155000	170500
50	3	OCEAN 50 MY	FB	TRWL	FBG	SV	IB	T310D	GM	15	6	51000	4	6	159000	175000
50	3	OCEAN 50 PH	FB	PH	FBG	SV	IB	T270D	CUM	15	6	46500	4	6	154000	169500
50	3	OCEAN 50 PH	FB	TRWL	FBG	SV	IB	T320D	CUM	15	6	46500	4	6	153000	168000
59	5	OCEAN 60 MY	FB	MY	F/S	SV	IB	T425D	CUM	18		58600	4	10	268500	295000
59	5	OCEAN 60 MY	FB	MY	F/S	SV	IB	T530D	GM	18		59000	4	10	294500	324000
59	5	OCEAN 60 PH	FB	PH	F/S	SV	IB	T425D	CUM	18		52000	4	10	256500	282000
59	5	OCEAN 60 PH	FB	PH	FBG	SV	IB	T530D	GM	18		56000	4	10	292500	321000
69	5	OCEAN 70 MY	FB	MY	FBG	SV	IB	T D	GM	18		70000	4	10	**	**

....For earlier years, see the BUC Used Boat Price Guide, Volume 3

OCEAN CRUISING YTS INC

BAR HARBOR ME 04609 COAST GUARD MFG ID- XYG See inside cover to adjust price for area

LOA FT	IN	NAME AND/ OR MODEL	TOP/ RIG	BOAT TYPE	-HULL- MTL	TP	TP	----ENGINE--- # HP	MFG	BEAM FT	IN	WGT LBS	DRAFT FT	IN	RETAIL LOW	RETAIL HIGH
		1984 BOATS														
39	2	OC-39	CUT	SA/RC	FBG	KL	IB	30D	WEST	12	[illegible]	10000	6	6	103500	114000
40	2	OC-40	SLP	SA/CR	FBG	KC	IB	37D	WEST	12	3	20200	4	4	118000	130000
40	2	OC-40	CUT	SA/CR	FBG	KC	IB	37D	WEST	12	3	20200	4	4	118000	130000
42	3	OC-42 AFT COCKPIT	SLP	SA/CR	FBG	KC	IB	51D		12	4	24800	4	8	144500	159000
42	3	OC-42 AFT COCKPIT	SLP	SA/CR	FBG	KL	IB	51D		12	4	24800	5	8	144500	159000
42	3	OC-42 AFT COCKPIT	KTH	SA/CR	FBG	KC	IB	51D		12	4	24800	4	8	144500	159000
42	3	OC-42 AFT COCKPIT	KTH	SA/CR	FBG	KL	IB	51D		12	4	24800	5	8	144500	159000
42	3	OC-42 MID COCKPIT	SLP	SA/CR	FBG	KC	IB	51D		12	4	24800	4	8	144500	159000
42	3	OC-42 MID COCKPIT	SLP	SA/CR	FBG	KL	IB	51D		12	4	24800	5	8	144500	159000
47	7	OC-48 AFT COCKPIT	SLP	SA/CR	FBG	KC	IB	58D	WEST	13	9	34000	4	10	211000	232000
47	7	OC-4A AFT-COCKPIT	KTH	SA/CR	FBG	KC	IB	58D	WEST	13	9	34000	4	10	211500	232500
52		OC-52 AFT-COCKPIT	SLP	SA/CR	FBG	KC	IB	85D		14	8	44000	5	6	280500	308500
52		OC-52 AFT-COCKPIT	KTH	SA/CR	FBG	KC	IB	85D		14	8	44000	5	6	282500	310500
52		OC-52 MID COCKPIT	SLP	SA/CR	FBG	KC	IB	85D		14	8	44000	5	6	280500	308500
52		OC-52 MID COCKPIT	KTH	SA/CR	FBG	KC	IB	85D		14	8	44000	5	6	282500	310500

....For earlier years, see the BUC Used Boat Price Guide, Volume 3

OCEAN MASTER MARINE INC

RIVIERA BEACH FL 33404 COAST GUARD MFG ID- OMB See inside cover to adjust price for area

For more recent years, see the BUC Used Boat Price Guide, Volume 1

LOA FT	IN	NAME AND/ OR MODEL	TOP/ RIG	BOAT TYPE	-HULL- MTL	TP	TP	----ENGINE--- # HP	MFG	BEAM FT	IN	WGT LBS	DRAFT FT	IN	RETAIL LOW	RETAIL HIGH
		1996 BOATS														
24		OCEAN MASTER 24 C/C	OP	CTRCN	FBG	DV	OB			8	6	3600	1	5	19200	21400
26	11	OCEAN MASTER 27 C/C	OP	CTRCN	FBG	DV	OB			8	6	4000	1	5	26200	29100
26	11	OCEAN MASTER 27 W/A	OP	CTRCN	FBG	DV	OB			8	6	4400	1	5	26400	29300
30	7	OCEAN MASTER 31 C/C	OP	CTRCN	FBG	SV	OB			10	3	5140	1	4	42400	47100
30	7	OCEAN MASTER 31 S/C	OP	CTRCN	FBG	SV	OB			10	3	5240	1	4	42400	47100
30	7	OCEAN MASTER 31 W/A	OP	CTRCN	FBG	SV	OB			10	3	5440	1	4	42400	47100
34		OCEAN MASTER 34 C/C	OP	FSH	FBG	SV	OB			11	6	8000	1	6	74300	81700
34		OCEAN MASTER 34 W/A	OP	FSH	FBG	SV	OB			11	6	9000	1	6	74300	81700
		1995 BOATS														
24		OCEAN MASTER 24 C/C	OP	CTRCN	FBG	DV	OB			8	6	3600	1	5	18400	20400
26	11	OCEAN MASTER 27 C/C	OP	CTRCN	FBG	DV	OB			8	6	4000	1	5	25000	27800
26	11	OCEAN MASTER 27 W/A	OP	CTRCN	FBG	DV	OB			8	6	4400	1	5	25100	27900
30	7	OCEAN MASTER 31 C/C	OP	CTRCN	FBG	SV	OB			10	3	5140	1	4	39900	44400
30	7	OCEAN MASTER 31 S/C	OP	CTRCN	FBG	SV	OB			10	3	5240	1	4	39900	44400
30	7	OCEAN MASTER 31 W/A	OP	CTRCN	FBG	SV	OB			10	3	5440	1	4	39900	44400
34		OCEAN MASTER 34 C/C	OP	FSH	FBG	SV	OB			11	6	8000	1	6	70300	77200
34		OCEAN MASTER 34 W/A	OP	FSH	FBG	SV	OB			11	6	9000	1	6	70300	77200
		1994 BOATS														
24		OCEAN MASTER 24 C/C	OP	CTRCN	FBG	DV	OB			8	6	3600	1	5	17100	19500
26	11	OCEAN MASTER 27 C/C	OP	CTRCN	FBG	DV	OB			8	6	4000	1	5	23900	26500
26	11	OCEAN MASTER 27 W/A	OP	CTRCN	FBG	DV	OB			8	6	4400	1	5	24000	26700
30	7	OCEAN MASTER 31 C/C	OP	CTRCN	FBG	SV	OB			10	3	5140	1	4	37900	42200
30	7	OCEAN MASTER 31 S/C	OP	CTRCN	FBG	SV	OB			10	3	5240	1	4	37900	42200
30	7	OCEAN MASTER 31 W/A	OP	CTRCN	FBG	SV	OB			10	3	5440	1	4	37900	42200
34		OCEAN MASTER 34 C/C	OP	FSH	FBG	SV	OB			11	6	8000	1	6	66600	73200
34		OCEAN MASTER 34 W/A	OP	FSH	FBG	SV	OB			11	6	9000	1	6	66600	73200
		1993 BOATS														
23	11	OCEAN MASTER 24 C/C	OP	CTRCN	FBG	DV	OB			8	6	3600	1	5	16300	18500
26	11	OCEAN MASTER 27 C/C	OP	CTRCN	FBG	DV	OB			8	6	4000	1	5	22900	25400
26	11	OCEAN MASTER 27 W/A	OP	CTRCN	FBG	DV	OB			8	6	4200	1	5	23000	25500
30	7	OCEAN MASTER 31 C/C	OP	CTRCN	FBG	SV	OB			10	3	5140	1	4	36100	40200
30	7	OCEAN MASTER 31 S/C	OP	CTRCN	FBG	SV	OB			10	3	5200	1	4	36100	40200
30	7	OCEAN MASTER 31 W/A	OP	CTRCN	FBG	SV	OB			10	3	5400	1	4	36100	40200
34		OCEAN MASTER 34 C/C	OP	FSH	FBG	SV	OB			11	6	7500	1	6	63200	69500
34		OCEAN MASTER 34 W/A	OP	FSH	FBG	SV	OB			11	6	8500	1	6	63200	69500
		1992 BOATS														
23		OCEAN MASTER CE	OP	OPFSH	FBG	DV	OB			8	6	3600	1	5	14800	16800
26	11	OCEAN MASTER CE 27	OP	OPFSH	FBG	DV	OB			8	6	3800	1	5	21800	24200
26	11	OCEAN MASTER CE 27	TT	OPFSH	FBG	DV	OB			8	6	3800	1	5	21900	24400
30	7	OCEAN MASTER 31 W/A	OP	OPFSH	FBG	SV	OB			10	3	5440	1	4	33900	37600
30	7	OCEAN MASTER 31 W/A	TT	OPFSH	FBG	SV	OB			10	3	5440	1	4	34600	38400
30	7	OCEAN MASTER CE 31	OP	OPFSH	FBG	SV	OB			10	3	5140	1	4	33900	37600
30	7	OCEAN MASTER CE 31	TT	OPFSH	FBG	SV	OB			10	3	5140	1	4	34600	38400
34		OCEAN MASTER CEFH 34	OP	OPFSH	FBG	SV	OB			11	6	6500	1	6	60200	66200
34		OCEAN MASTER CEFH 34	TT	OPFSH	FBG	SV	IB	T300D		11	6	6500	1	6	88500	97200
34		OCEAN MASTER EXP	OP	OPFSH	FBG	SV	OB			11	6	8500	1	6	60200	66200
34		OCEAN MASTER EXP	TT	OPFSH	FBG	SV	IB	T300D		11	6	8500	1	6	97700	107500
34		OCEAN MSTR 34 LH/ES	OP	OPFSH	FBG	SV	OB			11	6	8500	1	6	60200	66200
34		OCEAN MSTR 34 LH/ES	TT	OPFSH	FBG	SV	IB	T300D		11	6	8500	1	6	92100	101000
		1991 BOATS														
23		OCEAN MASTER CE	OP	OPFSH	FBG	DV	OB			8	6	3600	1	5	14200	16200
26	11	OCEAN MASTER CE 27	OP	OPFSH	FBG	DV	OB			8	6	3800	1	5	21100	23400
26	11	OCEAN MASTER CE 27	TT	OPFSH	FBG	DV	OB			8	6	3800	1	5	21100	23500
30	7	OCEAN MASTER 31 W/A	OP	OPFSH	FBG	SV	OB			10	3	5440	1	4	32600	36200
30	7	OCEAN MASTER 31 W/A	TT	OPFSH	FBG	SV	OB			10	3	5440	1	4	33100	36800
30	7	OCEAN MASTER CE 31	OP	OPFSH	FBG	SV	OB			10	3	5140	1	4	32600	36200
30	7	OCEAN MASTER CE 31	TT	OPFSH	FBG	SV	OB			10	3	5140	1	4	33100	36800
34		OCEAN MASTER CEFH 34	OP	OPFSH	FBG	SV	OB			11	6	6500	1	6	57500	63200
34		OCEAN MASTER CEFH 34	TT	OPFSH	FBG	SV	IB	T300D		11	6	6500	1	6	84400	92700
34		OCEAN MASTER EXP	OP	OPFSH	FBG	SV	OB			11	6	8500	1	6	57500	63200
34		OCEAN MASTER EXP	TT	OPFSH	FBG	SV	IB	T300D		11	6	8500	1	6	93000	102000
34		OCEAN MDYT 34 LH/ES	OP	OPFSH	FBG	SV	OB			11	6	8500	1	6	57500	63200
34		OCEAN MSTR 34 LH/ES	TT	OPFSH	FBG	SV	IB	T300D		11	6	8500	1	6	87700	96300
		1990 BOATS														
26	11	OCEAN MASTER 27 CE	OP	OPFSH	FBG	DV	OB			8	6	3800	1	5	20300	22500
26	11	OCEAN MASTER 27 CE	TT	OPFSH	FBG	DV	OB			8	6	3800	1	5	20400	22700
30	7	OCEAN MASTER 31 CE	OP	OPFSH	FBG	SV	OB			10	3	5140	1	4	31500	35000
30	7	OCEAN MASTER 31 CE	TT	OPFSH	FBG	SV	OB			10	3	5140	1	4	31800	35400
30	7	OCEAN MASTER 31 W/A	OP	OPFSH	FBG	SV	OB			10	3	5440	1	4	31500	35000
30	7	OCEAN MASTER 31 W/A	TT	OPFSH	FBG	SV	OB			10	3	5440	1	4	31800	35400
34		OCEAN MASTER 34 CEFH	OP	OPFSH	FBG	SV	OB			11	6	6500	1	6	55000	60500
34		OCEAN MASTER 34 CEFH	TT	OPFSH	FBG	SV	IB	T300		11	6	6500	1	6	65600	72100
34		OCEAN MASTER 34 EXP	OP	EXP	FBG	SV	OB			11	6	8500	1	6	55000	60500
34		OCEAN MASTER 34 EXP	TT	EXP	FBG	SV	IB	T300		11	6	8500	1	6	76900	84500
34		OCEAN MSTR 34 LG/WA	OP	OPFSH	FBG	SV	OB			11	6	8500	1	6	55000	60500
34		OCEAN MSTR 34 LG/WA	TT	OPFSH	FBG	SV	IB	T300		11	6	8500	1	6	68300	75100
34		OCEAN MSTR 34 SM/WA	OP	OPFSH	FBG	SV	OB			11	6	7500	1	6	55000	60500
34		OCEAN MSTR 34 SM/WA	TT	OPFSH	FBG	SV	IB	T300		11	6	7500	1	6	66800	73400

....For earlier years, see the BUC Used Boat Price Guide, Volume 3

OCEAN VOYAGER CORPORATION

CLEARWATER FL 33520 COAST GUARD MFG ID- OVC See inside cover to adjust price for area

LOA FT	IN	NAME AND/ OR MODEL	TOP/ RIG	BOAT TYPE	-HULL- MTL	TP	TP	----ENGINE--- # HP	MFG	BEAM FT	IN	WGT LBS	DRAFT FT	IN	RETAIL LOW	RETAIL HIGH
		1988 BOATS														
30	5	VOYAGER 26 MKII	CUT	SA/CR	FBG	KL	IB	12D	UNIV	8	3	6700	3	4	29100	32300
		1987 BOATS														
30	5	VOYAGER 26 MKII	CUT	SA/CR	FBG	KL	IB	12D	UNIV	8	3	6700	3	4	27300	30400
		1986 BOATS														
30	5	VOYAGER 26 MKII	CUT	SA/CR	FBG	KL	IB	12D- 18D		8	3	6700	3	4	25700	28600
		1985 BOATS														
30	5	VOYAGER 26 MKII	CUT	SA/CR	FBG	KL	IB	10D	BMW	8	3	6700	3	4	24200	26800
30	6	VOYAGER 26 MKII	CUT	SA/CR	FBG	KL	IB	12D	BMW	8	3	6700	3	4	24200	26900

OCEAN YACHTS INC

EGG HARBOR CITY NJ 0821 COAST GUARD MFG ID- XYU See inside cover to adjust price for area

For more recent years, see the BUC Used Boat Price Guide, Volume 1

LOA FT	LOA IN	NAME AND/ OR MODEL	TOP/ RIG	BOAT TYPE	HULL MTL	HULL TP	ENGINE TP	ENGINE # HP	ENGINE MFG	BEAM FT	BEAM IN	WGT LBS	DRAFT FT	DRAFT IN	RETAIL LOW	RETAIL HIGH
		1996 BOATS														
44		MOTOR YACHT 44	FB	MY	FBG	SV	IB	T425D	CAT	15		42500	3	7	243000	267000
44		MOTOR YACHT 44	FB	MY	FBG	SV	IB	T430D	VLVO	15		42500	3	7	238500	262000
44		MOTOR YACHT 44	FB	MY	FBG	SV	IB	T485D	DD	15		42500	3	7	251500	276500
44	8	SUPER SPORT 45	FB	SF	FBG	SV	IB	T485D	DD	15	2	37000	3	7	234500	257500
44	8	SUPER SPORT 45	FB	SF	FBG	SV	IB	T600D	MAN	15	2	37000	3	7	251000	276000
44	8	SUPER SPORT 45	FB	SF	FBG	SV	IB	T625D	DD	15	2	37000	3	7	261500	287000
48		COCKPIT MY 48	FB	MYCPT	FBG	SV	IB	T430D	VLVO	15		42500	3	7	229000	251500
48		COCKPIT MY 48	FB	MYCPT	FBG	SV	IB	T435D	CAT	15		42500	3	7	232000	255000
48		COCKPIT MY 48	FB	MYCPT	FBG	SV	IB	T485D	DD	15		42500	3	7	241500	265500
48	8	SUPER SPORT 48	FB	SF	FBG	SV	IB	T600D	MAN	16		45000	4	2	286000	314000
		IB T625D DD 291000 320000, IB T760D DD 317000 348000, IB T800D MAN 324000 356000														
		IB T820D MAN 327500 360000														
53		SUPER SPORT 53	FB	SF	FBG	SV	IB	T760D	DD	16	4	52000	4	4	365500	401500
53		SUPER SPORT 53	FB	SF	FBG	SV	IB	T10CD	MAN	16	4	52000	4	4	412500	453500
53		SUPER SPORT 53	FB	SF	FBG	SV	IB	T12CD	MAN	16	4	52000	4	4	448000	492500
60		SUPER SPORT 60	FB	SF	FBG	SV	IB	T12CD	MAN	17		75000	4	8	555500	610500
60		SUPER SPORT 60	FB	SF	FBG	SV	IB	T13CD	CAT	17		75000	4	8	574500	631500
66		SUPER SPORT 66	FB	SF	FBG	SV	IB	T12CD	MAN	17	8	80000	5		603500	663000
66		SUPER SPORT 66	FB	SF	FBG	SV	IB	T13CD	CAT	17	8	80000	5		640000	703000
		1995 BOATS														
32		SUPER SPORT 32	FB	SF	FBG	SV	IB	T300D	CUM	12	4	17043	2	6	101000	111000
38	9	SUPER SPORT 38	FB	SF	FBG	SV	IB	T430D	VLVO	14	2	27000	3	8	166500	183000
38	9	SUPER SPORT 38	FB	SF	FBG	SV	IB	T435D	CAT	14	2	27000	3	8	177500	195000
42		SUPER SPORT 42	FB	SF	FBG	SV	IB	T430D	VLVO	15		35466	3	7	219000	241000
42		SUPER SPORT 42	FB	SF	FBG	SV	IB	T435D	CAT	15		35466	3	7	228000	251000
42		SUPER SPORT 42	FB	SF	FBG	SV	IB	T485D	DD	15		35466	3	7	236000	259000
44		MOTOR YACHT 44	FB	MY	FBG	SV	IB	T430D	VLVO	15		40000	3	7	219000	240500
44		MOTOR YACHT 44	FB	MY	FBG	SV	IB	T435D	CAT	15		40000	3	7	224500	247000
44		MOTOR YACHT 44	FB	MY	FBG	SV	IB	T485D	DD	15		40000	3	7	231500	254500
48		COCKPIT MY 48	FB	MYCPT	FBG	SV	IB	T430D	VLVO	15		42500	3	7	219500	241000
48		COCKPIT MY 48	FB	MYCPT	FBG	SV	IB	T435D	CAT	15		42500	3	7	222000	244000
48		COCKPIT MY 48	FB	MYCPT	FBG	SV	IB	T485D	DD	15		42500	3	7	231500	254000
48		SUPER SPORT 48	FB	SF	FBG	SV	IB	T550D	DD	15	2	40000	3	6	246500	271000
48		SUPER SPORT 48	FB	SF	FBG	SV	IB	T735D	DD	15	2	40000	3	6	281500	309500
48		SUPER SPORT 48	FB	SF	FBG	SV	IB	T760D	DD	15	2	40000	3	6	286000	314500
53		SUPER SPORT 53	FB	SF	FBG	SV	IB	T735D	DD	16	4	52000	4	4	345000	379000
53		SUPER SPORT 53	FB	SF	FBG	SV	IB	T760D	DD	16	4	52000	4	4	350000	385000
53		SUPER SPORT 53	FB	SF	FBG	SV	IB	T820D	MAN	16	4	54000	4	4	369500	406000
56		COCKPIT MY 56	FB	MYCPT	FBG	SV	IB	T485D	DD	16	4	54500	4		325000	357000
56		COCKPIT MY 56	FB	MYCPT	FBG	SV	IB	T550D	DD	16	4	54500	4		343500	377500
58		SUPER SPORT 58	FB	SF	FBG	SV	IB	T10CD	DD	17	6	72215	4	10	563500	619000
58		SUPER SPORT 58	FB	SF	FBG	SV	IB	T11CD	MAN	17	6	72215	4	10	566500	622500
58		SUPER SPORT 58	FB	SF	FBG	SV	IB	T11CD	DD	17	6	72215	4	10	569000	625000
66		SUPER SPORT 66	FB	SF	FBG	SV	IB	T10CD	DD	17	8	80000	5		569500	625500
66		SUPER SPORT 66	FB	SF	FBG	SV	IB	T11CD	MAN	17	8	80000	5		563000	618500
66		SUPER SPORT 66	FB	SF	FBG	SV	IB	T11CD	DD	17	8	80000	5		574500	631000
		1994 BOATS														
35		SUPER SPORT 35	FB	SF	FBG	SV	IB	T300D	CAT	13		19800	2	11	119000	131000
38	9	SUPER SPORT 38	FB	SF	FBG	SV	IB	T430D	VLVO	14	2	27000	3	8	159500	175000
38	9	SUPER SPORT 38	FB	SF	FBG	SV	IB	T435D	CAT	14	2	27000	3	8	170000	186500
42		SUPER SPORT 42	FB	SF	FBG	SV	IB	T430D	VLVO	15		35466	3	7	210000	230500
42		SUPER SPORT 42	FB	SF	FBG	SV	IB	T435D	CAT	15		35466	3	7	218500	240000
42		SUPER SPORT 42	FB	SF	FBG	SV	IB	T485D	DD	15		35466	3	7	226000	248000
44		MOTOR YACHT 44	FB	MY	FBG	SV	IB	T430D	VLVO	15		40000	3	7	209500	230500
44		MOTOR YACHT 44	FB	MY	FBG	SV	IB	T435D	CAT	15		40000	3	7	215000	236500
44		MOTOR YACHT 44	FB	MY	FBG	SV	IB	T485D	DD	15		40000	3	7	222000	244000
48		COCKPIT MY 48	FB	MYCPT	FBG	SV	IB	T430D	VLVO	15		42500	3	7	210000	231000
48		COCKPIT MY 48	FB	MYCPT	FBG	SV	IB	T435D	CAT	15		42500	3	7	212500	233500
48		COCKPIT MY 48	FB	MYCPT	FBG	SV	IB	T485D	DD	15		42500	3	7	221500	243500
48		SUPER SPORT 48	FB	SF	FBG	SV	IB	T550D	DD	15	2	40000	3	6	236000	259500
48		SUPER SPORT 48	FB	SF	FBG	SV	IB	T735D	DD	15	2	40000	3	6	270000	296500
48		SUPER SPORT 48	FB	SF	FBG	SV	IB	T760D	DD	15	2	40000	3	6	274000	301000
48	6	MOTOR YACHT 48	FB	MY	FBG	SV	IB	T485D	DD	16	4	51000	4	1	294000	323000
48	6	MOTOR YACHT 48	FB	MY	FBG	SV	IB	T550D	DD	16	4	51000	4	1	305500	336000
53		SUPER SPORT 53	FB	SF	FBG	SV	IB	T735D	DD	16	4	52000	4	4	330500	363500
53		SUPER SPORT 53	FB	SF	FBG	SV	IB	T760D	DD	16	4	52000	4	4	335500	369000
53		SUPER SPORT 53	FB	SF	FBG	SV	IB	T850D	MAN	16	4	54000	4	4	359500	395000
56		COCKPIT MY 56	FB	MYCPT	FBG	SV	IB	T485D	DD	16	4	54500	4		311000	342000
56		COCKPIT MY 56	FB	MYCPT	FBG	SV	IB	T550D	DD	16	4	54500	4		329000	361500
58		SUPER SPORT 58	FB	SF	FBG	SV	IB	T10CD	DD	17	6	72215	4	10	540000	593500
58		SUPER SPORT 58	FB	SF	FBG	SV	IB	T11CD	MAN	17	6	72215	4	10	543000	597000
58		SUPER SPORT 58	FB	SF	FBG	SV	IB	T11CD	DD	17	6	72215	4	10	545500	599500
66		SUPER SPORT 66	FB	SF	FBG	SV	IB	T10CD	DD	17	8	80000	5		545500	599500
66		SUPER SPORT 66	FB	SF	FBG	SV	IB	T11CD	MAN	17	8	80000	5		539500	592500
66		SUPER SPORT 66	FB	SF	FBG	SV	IB	T11CD	DD	17	8	80000	5		550500	604500
		1993 BOATS														
35		SPORT FISH/CRUISER	FB	SF	FBG	SV	IB	T300D	CAT	13		18000	2	11	107500	118000
35		SPORT FISH/CRUISER	FB	SF	FBG	SV	IB	T300D	CUM	13		18000	2	11	106000	116500
35		SUPER SPORT 35	FB	SF	FBG	SV	IB	T300D	CAT	13		19800	2	11	113500	124500
35		SUPER SPORT 35	FB	SF	FBG	SV	IB	T300D	CUM	13		19800	2	11	112000	123000
38	9	SUPER SPORT 38	FB	SF	FBG	SV	IB	T425D	CAT	14	2	27000	3	8	160500	176500
38	9	SUPER SPORT 38	FB	SF	FBG	SV	IB	T430D	VLVO	14	2	27000	3	8	152000	167000
42		SUPER SPORT 42	FB	SF	FBG	SV	IB	T430D	VLVO	15		35466	3	7	200000	219500
42		SUPER SPORT 42	FB	SF	FBG	SV	IB	T435D	CAT	15		35466	3	7	208000	229000
42		SUPER SPORT 42	FB	SF	FBG	SV	IB	T485D	DD	15		35466	3	7	215000	236500
44		MOTOR YACHT 44	FB	MY	FBG	SV	IB	T430D	VLVO	15		40000	3	7	199500	219500
44		MOTOR YACHT 44	FB	MY	FBG	SV	IB	T435D	CAT	15		40000	3	7	205000	225000
44		MOTOR YACHT 44	FB	MY	FBG	SV	IB	T485D	DD	15		40000	3	7	211500	232500
48		SUPER SPORT 48	FB	SF	FBG	SV	IB	T485D	DD	15	2	40000	3	6	213000	234500
48		SUPER SPORT 48	FB	SF	FBG	SV	IB	T550D	DD	15	2	40000	3	6	225000	247500
48	6	MOTOR YACHT 48	FB	MY	FBG	SV	IB	T485D	DD	16	4	51000	4	1	280000	307500
53		SUPER SPORT 53	FB	SF	FBG	SV	IB	T735D	DD	16	4	50000	4	4	308500	339500
53		SUPER SPORT 53	FB	SF	FBG	SV	IB	T760D	DD	16	4	50000	4	4	313500	344500
53		SUPER SPORT 53	FB	SF	FBG	SV	IB	T850D	MAN	16	4	54000	4	4	342500	376500
56		COCKPIT MOTOR YACHT	FB	MYCPT	FBG	SV	IB	T485D	DD	16	4	54500	4		296500	326000
56		COCKPIT MOTOR YACHT	FB	MYCPT	FBG	SV	IB	T550D	DD	16	4	54500	4		313500	344500
58		SUPER SPORT 58	FB	SF	FBG	SV	IB	T10CD	DD	17	6	72215	4	10	514500	565500
58		SUPER SPORT 58	FB	SF	FBG	SV	IB	T11CD	MAN	17	6	72215	4	10	517500	568500
66		SUPER SPORT 66	FB	SF	FBG	SV	IB	T10CD	DD	17	8	80000	4	8	520000	571000
66		SUPER SPORT 66	FB	SF	FBG	SV	IB	T11CD	MAN	17	8	80000	4	8	514000	565000
66		SUPER SPORT 66	FB	SF	FBG	SV	IB	T11CD	DD	17	8	80000	4	8	524500	576500
		1992 BOATS														
29		SPORT FISH/CRUISER	FB	SPTCR	FBG	SV	IB	T240-T320		11	6	12257	2	5	43700	50800
29		SPORT FISH/CRUISER	FB	SPTCR	FBG	SV	IB	T250D	CUM	11	6	12257	2	5	65400	71900
29		SUPER SPORT 29	FB	SF	FBG	SV	IB	T240-T320		11	6	13500	2	5	47500	54200
29		SUPER SPORT 29	FB	SF	FBG	SV	IB	T250D	CUM	11	6	13500	2	5	70800	77800
32		SUPER SPORT 32	FB	SF	FBG	SV	IB	T320	CRUS	12	4	17043	2	6	63300	69600
32		SUPER SPORT 32	FB	SF	FBG	SV	IB	T300D	CUM	12	4	17043	2	6	87400	96000
35		SPORT FISH/CRUISER	FB	SF	FBG	SV	IB	T320	CRUS	13		18000	2	11	81400	89400
35		SPORT FISH/CRUISER	FB	SF	FBG	SV	IB	T300D	CAT	13		18000	2	11	102500	112500
35		SPORT FISH/CRUISER	FB	SF	FBG	SV	IB	T300D	CUM	13		18000	2	11	101000	111000
35		SUPER SPORT 35	FB	SF	FBG	SV	IB	T320	CRUS	13		19800	2	11	85000	93400
35		SUPER SPORT 35	FB	SF	FBG	SV	IB	T300D	CAT	13		19800	2	11	108000	119000
35		SUPER SPORT 35	FB	SF	FBG	SV	IB	T300D	CUM	13		19800	2	11	106500	117000
38	9	SUPER SPORT 38	FB	SF	FBG	SV	IB	T425D	CAT	14	2	26000	3	8	149000	164000
42		SUPER SPORT 42	FB	SF	FBG	SV	IB	T425D	CAT	15		35466	3	7	197000	216500
42		SUPER SPORT 42	FB	SF	FBG	SV	IB	T485D	DD	15		35466	3	7	205000	225500
48		MOTOR YACHT 48	FB	MY	FBG	SV	IB	T485D	DD	16	2	45932	4	1	248000	272500
48		SUPER SPORT 48	FB	SF	FBG	SV	IB	T485D	DD	15	2	40000	3	6	203000	223500
53		SUPER SPORT 53	FB	SF	FBG	SV	IB	T760D	DD	16	4	54000	4	4	311000	342000
53		SUPER SPORT 53	FB	SF	FBG	SV	IB	T820D	MAN	16	4	54000	4	4	321500	353500
56		COCKPIT MOTOR YACHT	FB	MYCPT	FBG	SV	IB	T485D	DD	16	4	54500	4		282500	310500
56		COCKPIT MOTOR YACHT	FB	MYCPT	FBG	SV	IB	T550D	DD	16	4	54500	4		299000	328500
58		SUPER SPORT 58	FB	SF	FBG	SV	IB	T10CD	MAN	17	6	72215	4	10	485500	533500
58		SUPER SPORT 58	FB	SF	FBG	SV	IB	T10CD	DD	17	6	72215	4	10	490500	539000
63		SUPER SPORT 63	FB	SF	FBG	SV	IB	T10CD	MAN	17	8	74000	4	8	448500	493000
63		SUPER SPORT 63	FB	SF	FBG	SV	IB	T10CD	DD	17	8	74000	4	8	456000	501000
		1991 BOATS														
29		SPORT FISH/CRUISER	FB	SPTCR	FBG	SV	IB	T240-T320		11	6	12257	2	5	41500	48200
29		SPORT FISH/CRUISER	FB	SPTCR	FBG	SV	IB	T250D	CUM	11	6	12257	2	5	62400	68600
29		SUPER SPORT 29	FB	SF	FBG	SV	IB	T240-T320		11	6	13500	2	5	44600	51700
29		SUPER SPORT 29	FB	SF	FBG	SV	IB	T250D	CUM	11	6	13500	2	5	67500	74200
32		SUPER SPORT 32	FB	SF	FBG	SV	IB	T320	CRUS	12	4	17043	2	6	60100	66100
32		SUPER SPORT 32	FB	SF	FBG	SV	IB	T300D	CUM	12	4	17043	2	6	83400	91700
35		SPORT FISH/CRUISER	FB	SF	FBG	SV	IB	T320	CRUS	13		18000	2	11	77300	85000
35		SPORT FISH/CRUISER	FB	SF	FBG	SV	IB	T300D	CAT	13		18000	2	11	97800	107500
35		SPORT FISH/CRUISER	FB	SF	FBG	SV	IB	T300D	CUM	13		18000	2	11	96300	106000
35		SUPER SPORT 35	FB	SF	FBG	SV	IB	T320	CRUS	13		19800	2	11	80800	88800
35		SUPER SPORT 35	FB	SF	FBG	SV	IB	T300D	CAT	13		19800	2	11	103000	113500
35		SUPER SPORT 35	FB	SF	FBG	SV	IB	T300D	CUM	13		19800	2	11	101500	111500
38	4	SUPER SPORT 38	FB	SF	FBG	SV	IB	T375D	CAT	13	8	23000	3	2	125500	138000
42		SUPER SPORT 42	FB	SF	FBG	SV	IB	T425D	CAT	15		35466	3	7	188000	206500

CONTINUED ON NEXT PAGE

LOA FT	LOA IN	NAME AND/ OR MODEL	TOP/ RIG	BOAT TYPE	-HULL- MTL	-HULL- TP	TP	ENGINE # HP	ENGINE MFG	BEAM FT	BEAM IN	WGT LBS	DRAFT FT	DRAFT IN	RETAIL LOW	RETAIL HIGH
1991 BOATS																
42		SUPER SPORT 42	FB	SF	FBG	SV	IB	T485D	DD	15		35466	3	7	195500	215000
48		MOTOR YACHT 48	FB	MY	FBG	SV	IB	T485D	DD	16	2	45932	4	1	236500	260000
48		MOTOR YACHT 48	FB	MY	FBG	SV	IB	T550D	DD	16	2	45932	4	1	247000	271500
48		SUPER SPORT 48	FB	SF	FBG	SV	IB	T485D	DD	15	2	40000	3	6	194000	213000
53		SUPER SPORT 53	FB	SF	FBG	SV	IB	T760D	DD	16	4	54000	4	4	297000	326000
53		SUPER SPORT 53	FB	SF	FBG	SV	IB	T820D	MAN	16	4	54000	4	4	306500	337000
53		SUPER SPORT 53	FB	SF	FBG	SV	IB	T10CD	MAN	16	4	54000	4	4	341000	375000
56		COCKPIT MOTOR YACHT	FB	MYCPT	FBG	SV	IB	T485D	DD	16	4	54500	4		270000	296500
56		COCKPIT MOTOR YACHT	FB	MYCPT	FBG	SV	IB	T550D	DD	16	4	54500	4		285500	313500
58		SUPER SPORT 58	FB	SF	FBG	SV	IB	T10CD	MAN	17	6	72215	4	10	463000	508500
58		SUPER SPORT 58	FB	SF	FBG	SV	IB	T10CD	DD	17	6	72215	4	10	468000	514000
63		SUPER SPORT 63	FB	SF	FBG	SV	IB	T10CD	MAN	17	8	74000	4	8	428000	470500
63		SUPER SPORT 63	FB	SF	FBG	SV	IB	T10CD	DD	17	8	74000	4	8	435000	478500
1990 BOATS																
29		SPORT FISH/CRUISER	FB	SPTCR	FBG	SV	IB	T240-T320		11	6	12257	2	5	39500	45900
29		SPORT FISH/CRUISER	FB	SPTCR	FBG	SV	IB	T250D	CUM	11	6	12257	2	5	59600	65500
29		SUPER SPORT 29	FB	SF	FBG	SV	IB	T240-T320		11	6	13500	2	5	42500	49100
29		SUPER SPORT 29	FB	SF	FBG	SV	IB	T250D	CUM	11	6	13500	2	5	64500	70900
32		SUPER SPORT 32	FB	SF	FBG	SV	IB	T350	CRUS	12	4	17043	2	6	58000	63800
32		SUPER SPORT 32	FB	SF	FBG	SV	IB	T300D	CUM	12	4	17043	2	6	79700	87600
35		SPORT CRUISER 35	FB	SPTCR	FBG	SV	IB	T320	CRUS	13		18000	2	11	73700	81000
35		SPORT CRUISER 35	FB	SPTCR	FBG	SV	IB	T300D	CUM	13		18000	2	11	92200	101500
35		SPORT FISH 35	FB	SF	FBG	SV	IB	T320	CRUS	13		18000	2	11	73500	80800
35		SPORT FISH 35	FB	SF	FBG	SV	IB	T300D	CUM	13		18000	2	11	92000	101000
35		SUPER SPORT 35	FB	SF	FBG	SV	IB	T350	CRUS	13		19800	2	11	77700	85400
35		SUPER SPORT 35	FB	SF	FBG	SV	IB	T300D	CUM	13		19800	2	11	97100	106500
42		SUPER SPORT 42	FB	SF	FBG	SV	IB	T425D	CAT	15		35466	3	7	179500	197000
42		SUPER SPORT 42	FB	SF	FBG	SV	IB	T485D	GM	15		35466	3	7	184000	202500
44		SUPER SPORT 44	FB	SF	FBG	SV	IB	T485D	GM	15	2	36000	3	6	167500	184000
48		MOTOR YACHT 48	FB	MY	FBG	SV	IB	T485D	GM	16	2	45932	4	1	226000	248500
48		MOTOR YACHT 48	FB	MY	FBG	SV	IB	T550D	GM	16	2	45932	4	1	236000	259000
48		SUPER SPORT 48	FB	SF	FBG	SV	IB	T485D	GM	15	2	40000	3	6	184500	202500
48		SUPER SPORT 48	FB	SF	FBG	SV	IB	T550D	GM	15	2	40000	3	6	195000	214000
53		MOTOR YACHT 53	FB	MY	FBG	SV	IB	T735D	GM	17	2	64000	4	6	298500	328500
53		SUPER SPORT 53	FB	SF	FBG	SV	IB	T760D	GM	16	4	54000	4	4	283500	311500
53		SUPER SPORT 53	FB	SF	FBG	SV	IB	T820D	MAN	16	4	54000	4	4	292500	321500
53		SUPER SPORT 53	FB	SF	FBG	SV	IB	T10CD	MAN	16	4	54000	4	4	325500	358000
56		COCKPIT MOTOR YACHT	FB	MYCPT	FBG	SV	IB	T485D	GM	16	4	54500	4		257000	282500
56		COCKPIT MOTOR YACHT	FB	MYCPT	FBG	SV	IB	T550D	GM	16	4	54500	4		272000	299000
58		SUPER SPORT 58	FB	SF	FBG	SV	IB	T10CD	MAN	17	6	72215	4	10	442000	485500
58		SUPER SPORT 58	FB	SF	FBG	SV	IB	T10CD	GM	17	6	72215	4	10	449000	493500
63		SUPER SPORT 63	FB	SF	FBG	SV	IB	T10CD	MAN	17	8	74000	4	8	408500	449000
63		SUPER SPORT 63	FB	SF	FBG	SV	IB	T10CD	GM	17	8	74000	4	8	423000	465000
1989 BOATS																
32		SUPER SPORT 32	FB	SF	FBG	DV	IB	T350	CRUS	12	4	17043	2	6	55200	60700
32		SUPER SPORT 32	FB	SF	FBG	DV	IB	T250D-T300D		12	4	17043	2	6	73600	83700
35		SUPER SPORT 35	FB	SF	FBG	DV	IB	T350	CRUS	13		19800	2	11	73900	81300
35		SUPER SPORT 35	FB	SF	FBG	DV	IB	T300D	GM	13		19800	2	11	93100	102500
35		SUPER SPORT 35	FB	SF	FBG	DV	IB	T400D	GM	13		19800	2	11	99800	109500
38		SUPER SPORT 38	FB	SF	FBG	SV	IB	T350	CRUS	13	8	23000	3	2	91400	100500
38		SUPER SPORT 38	FB	SF	FBG	SV	IB	T375D	CAT	13	8	23000	3	2	112500	124000
38		SUPER SPORT 38	FB	SF	FBG	SV	IB	T400D	GM	13	8	23000	3	2	111500	122500
44		SUPER SPORT 44	FB	SF	FBG	SV	IB	T485D	GM	15	2	36000	3	6	160000	175500
48		MOTOR YACHT 48	FB	MY	FBG	SV	IB	T485D	GM	16	2	45932	4		216000	237000
48		SUPER SPORT 48	FB	SF	FBG	SV	IB	T485D	GM	15	2	40000	3	6	176000	193500
53		MOTOR YACHT 53	FB	SF	FBG	SV	IB	T735D	GM	17	2	64000	4	6	302000	331500
55		SUPER SPORT 55	FB	SF	FBG	SV	IB	T735D	GM	16	4	58000	4	4	291000	320000
63		SUPER SPORT 63	FB	SF	FBG	SV	IB	T900D	GM	17	8	74000	4	8	380500	418000
63		SUPER SPORT 63	FB	SF	FBG	SV	IB	T11CD	GM	17	8	74000	4	8	406500	447000
63		SUPER SPORT 63	FB	SF	FBG	SV	IB	T11CD	MAN	17	8	74000	4	8	396500	435500
1988 BOATS																
35		SUPER SPORT 35	FB	SPTCR	FBG	DV	IB	T350	CRUS	13		19800	2	4	70600	77600
35		SUPER SPORT 35	FB	SPTCR	FBG	DV	IB	T300D	GM	13		19800	2	4	89300	98100
38		SUPER SPORT 38	FB	SF	FBG	DV	IB	T350	CRUS	13	8	23000	3	2	87400	96000
38		SUPER SPORT 38	FB	SF	FBG	DV	IB	T375D	CAT	13	8	23000	3	2	107500	118500
38		SUPER SPORT 38	FB	SF	FBG	DV	IB	T400D	GM	13	8	23000	3	2	106500	117000
44		SUPER SPORT 44	FB	SF	FBG	SV	IB	T485D	GM	15	2	36000	3	6	153000	168000
48		SUPER SPORT 48	FB	SF	FBG	SV	IB	T485D	GM	15	2	40000	3	6	168000	185000
53		MOTOR YACHT 53	FB	MY	FBG	SV	IB	T735D	GM	17	2	64000	4	6	272500	299500
55	8	SUPER SPORT 55	FB	SF	FBG	SV	IB	T735D	GM	16	4	58000	4	4	284000	312000
63		SUPER SPORT 63	FB	SF	FBG	SV	IB	T D	GM	17	8	74000	4	8	**	**
63		SUPER SPORT 63	FB	SF	FBG	SV	IB	T10CD	GM	17	8	74000	4	8	386500	424500
1987 BOATS																
38	4	SUPER SPORT	FB	SF	FBG	SV	IB	T350		13	8	23000	3	2	84300	92700
38	4	SUPER SPORTFISH	FB	SF	FBG	SV	IB	T355D	CAT	13	8	23000	3	2	103000	113000
44		SUPER-SPORT	FB	SF	FBG	DS	IB	T450D	GM	15	2	36000	3	6	146000	160500
48		SUPER SPORT 48	FB	SF	FBG	SV	IB	T450D	GM	15	2	40000	3	6	156000	171500
55	8	SUPER SPORT 55	FB	SF	FBG	SV	IB	T710D	GM	16	4	58000	4	4	267500	294000
1986 BOATS																
38	4	SUPER SPORT	FB	SF	FBG	SV	IB	T355D	CAT	13	8	23000	3	2	98600	108500
38	4	SUPER-SPORT	FB	SF	FBG	SV	IB	T350	CRUS	13	8	23000	3	2	81400	89400
44		SUPER-SPORT	FB	SF	FBG	SV	IB	T450D	GM	15	2	36000	3	6	137000	150500
46		SUN-LINER	FB	CR	FBG	SV	IB	T450D	GM	15	2	40000	3	6	144500	159000
46		SUPER-SPORT	FB	SF	FBG	SV	IB	T450D	GM	15	2	40000	3	6	146500	161000
46		SUPER-SPORT	FB	SF	FBG	SV	IB	T475D	GM	15	2	40000	3	6	149500	164500
48		SUPER SPORT	FB	SF	FBG	SV	IB	T450D	GM	15	2	40000	3	6	144500	159000
48		SUPER SPORT	FB	SF	FBG	SV	IB	T525D	GM	15	2	40000	3	6	152500	167500
55	8	SUPER-SPORT	FB	SF	FBG	SV	IB	T570D	GM	16	4	58000	4	4	234000	257000
63		SUPER-SPORT	FB	SF	FBG	SV	IB	T650D	GM	17	8	70000	4	8	285000	313000
1985 BOATS																
38	4	SUPER SPORT	FB	SF	FBG	SV	IB	T355D	CAT	13	8	23000	3	2	94400	104000
38	4	SUPER-SPORT	FB	SF	FBG	SV	IB	T300		13	8	23000	3	2	76300	83800
38	4	SUPER-SPORT	FB	SF	FBG	SV	IB	T350	CRUS	13	8	23000	3	2	77900	85600
38	4	SUPER-SPORT	FB	SF	FBG	SV	IB	T355D	CAT	13	8	23000	3	2	94400	104000
42		SUN-LINER	FB	CR	FBG	SV	IB	T300D	J&T	14	4	28000	3	6	110000	121000
42		SUN-LINER	FB	CR	FBG	SV	IB	T410D	J&T	14	4	28000	3	6	117500	129000
42		SUPER-SPORT	FB	SF	FBG	SV	IB	T300D	J&T	14	4	30000	3	6	114000	125000
42		SUPER-SPORT	FB	SF	FBG	SV	IB	T410D	J&T	14	4	30000	3	6	125000	137500
44		SUPER-SPORT	FB	SF	FBG	SV	IB	T450D	GM	15	2	36000	3	6	131000	144000
46		SUN-LINER	FB	CR	FBG	SV	IB	T450D	J&T	15	2	40000	3	6	138500	152500
46		SUPER-SPORT	FB	SF	FBG	SV	IB	T450D	J&T	15	2	40000	3	6	140500	154500
46		SUPER-SPORT	FB	SF	FBG	SV	IB	T475D	GM	15	2	40000	3	6	143000	157500
50		SUPER-SPORT	FB	SF	FBG	SV	IB	T570D	GM	16		50000	4	2	182000	200000
50		SUPER-SPORT	FB	SF	FBG	SV	IB	T675D	S&S	16		50000	4	2	195000	214500
55	8	SUN-LINER	FB	MY	FBG	SV	IB	T570D	GM	16	4	58000	4	4	217500	239000
55	8	SUPER-SPORT	FB	SF	FBG	SV	IB	T570D	GM	16	4	58000	4	4	224000	246500
63		SUPER-SPORT	FB	SF	FBG	SV	IB	T650D	GM	17	8	66000	4	8	267000	293500
1984 BOATS																
38	4	SUPER-SPORT	FB	SF	FBG	SV	IB	T355D	CAT	13	8	23000	3	6	90500	99400
42		SUN-LINER	FB	CR	FBG	SV	IB	T300D	J&T	14	4	28000	3	6	105500	115500
42		SUN-LINER	FB	CR	FBG	SV	IB	T410D	J&T	14	4	28000	3	6	112500	124000
42		SUPER-SPORT	FB	SF	FBG	SV	IB	T300D	J&T	14	4	30000	3	6	109000	120000
42		SUPER-SPORT	FB	SF	FBG	SV	IB	T410D	J&T	14	4	30000	3	6	120000	132000
46		SUN-LINER	FB	CR	FBG	SV	IB	T450D	GM	15	2	40000	3	9	132500	146000
46		SUN-LINER	FB	CR	FBG	SV	IB	T475D	GM	15	2	40000	3	9	134000	147000
46		SUPER-SPORT	FB	SF	FBG	SV	IB	T450D	GM	15	2	40000	3	9	134500	147500
46		SUPER-SPORT	FB	SF	FBG	SV	IB	T475D	GM	15	2	40000	3	9	137000	151000
50		SUPER-SPORT	FB	SF	FBG	SV	IB	T570D	GM	16		50000	4	2	174500	191500
50		SUPER-SPORT	FB	SF	FBG	SV	IB	T675D	S&S	16		50000	4	2	187000	205500
55		SUN-LINER	FB	MY	FBG	SV	IB	T600D	S&S	16	4	62000	4	4	222000	244000
55		SUN-LINER	FB	MY	FBG	SV	IB	T675D	S&S	16	4	62000	4	4	232000	255000
55	8	SUPER-SPORT	FB	SF	FBG	SV	IB	T570D	GM	16	4	58000	4	4	215000	236000
55	8	SUPER-SPORT	FB	SF	FBG	SV	IB	T675D	S&S	16	4	58000	4	4	230500	253500

....For earlier years, see the BUC Used Boat Price Guide, Volume 3

OCEANA MARINE MFG INC

CAPE CANAVERAL FL 32920

See inside cover to adjust price for area

LOA FT	LOA IN	NAME AND/ OR MODEL	TOP/ RIG	BOAT TYPE	-HULL- MTL	-HULL- TP	TP	ENGINE # HP	ENGINE MFG	BEAM FT	BEAM IN	WGT LBS	DRAFT FT	DRAFT IN	RETAIL LOW	RETAIL HIGH
1986 BOATS																
40		BAYSIDE	HT	HB		FL	IB			20		9000			39800	44200
40		CYPRESS	HT	HB		FL	IB			14		6000			20900	23200
40		HOMEPORT	HT	HB		FL	IB			14		6000			21600	24000
40		NEWPORTER	HT	HB		FL	IB			20		9000			22700	25200
40		RIVERVIEW	HT	HB		FL	IB			18		8000			32300	35900
40		RIVIERA	HT	HB		FL	IB			20		9000			56600	62200
1985 BOATS																
40		BAYSIDE	HT	HB	FBG	FL	OB			20		9000			33900	37700
40		CYPRESS	HT	HB	FBG	FL	OB			14		6000			16200	18500
40		HARBOUR-HOUSE	HT	HB	FBG	FL	OB			18		8000			25200	28000
40		HOMEPORT	HT	HB	FBG	FL	OB			14		6000			12600	14300
40		NEWPORTER	HT	HB	FBG	FL	OB			20		9000			12300	14000
40		RIVERVIEW	HT	HB	FBG	FL	OB			18		8000			24600	27300
40		RIVIERA	HT	HB	FBG	FL	OB			20		9000			53500	58800
1984 BOATS																
40		BAYSIDE	HT	HB	F/W	FL	OB			20		9000			31200	34700
40		CYPRESS	HT	HB	F/W	FL	OB			14		6000			15100	17100

OCEANA MARINE MFG INC   -CONTINUED   See inside cover to adjust price for area

LOA FT IN	NAME AND/ OR MODEL	TOP/ RIG	BOAT TYPE	-HULL- MTL TP	TP	----ENGINE--- # HP MFG	BEAM FT IN	WGT LBS	DRAFT FT IN	RETAIL LOW	RETAIL HIGH
--- 1984 BOATS ---										
40	HARBOUR-HOUSE	HT	HB	F/W FL	OB		18	8000		23600	26200
40	HOMEPORT	HT	HB	F/W FL	OB		14	6000		11600	13200
40	NEWPORTER	HT	HB	F/W FL	OB		20	9000		11400	13000
40	RIVERVIEW	HT	HB	F/W FL	OB		18	8000		23000	25600
40	RIVIERA	HT	HB	F/W FL	OB		20	9000		50200	55200

OFFSHORE BOAT CORP
MIAMI FL 33150   See inside cover to adjust price for area

LOA FT IN	NAME AND/ OR MODEL	TOP/ RIG	BOAT TYPE	-HULL- MTL TP	TP	----ENGINE--- # HP MFG	BEAM FT IN	WGT LBS	DRAFT FT IN	RETAIL LOW	RETAIL HIGH
--- 1986 BOATS ---										
25	WHITEWATER	OP	CTRCN	FBG DV	OB		8	5000	2 8	10400	11800
25	WHITEWATER	OP	CTRCN	FBG DV	SE	205 OMC	8	5000	2 8	10400	11800
25	WHITEWATER	OP	CTRCN	FBG DV	IB	255-350	8	5000	2 8	13700	16500
25	WHITEWATER	OP	CTRCN	FBG DV	IB	200D PERK	8	5000	2 8	19400	21500
25	WHITEWATER	OP	CTRCN	FBG DV	SE	T115-T205	8	5000	2 8	10400	11800
25	WHITEWATER	OP	CTRCN	FBG DV	IB	T110D VLVO	8	5000	2 8	20300	22600
31 7	WHITEWATER 32	OP	CUD	FBG DV	OB		8 5	4500	1 6	18800	20900
--- 1984 BOATS ---										
25	WHITEWATER	OP	CTRCN	FBG DV	OB		8	5000	2 8	9950	11300
25	WHITEWATER	OP	CTRCN	FBG DV	SE	205 OMC	8	5000	2 8	9950	11300
25	WHITEWATER	OP	CTRCN	FBG DV	IB	255-350	8	5000	2 8	12500	15100
25	WHITEWATER	OP	CTRCN	FBG DV	IB	200D-230D	8	5000	2 8	18000	20000
25	WHITEWATER	OP	CTRCN	FBG DV	IB	T115 OMC	8	5000	2 8	9950	11300
25	WHITEWATER	OP	CTRCN	FBG DV	IB	T138 VLVO	8	5000	2 8	13200	15000
25	WHITEWATER	OP	CTRCN	FBG DV	SE	T155-T205	8	5000	2 8	9950	11300

....For earlier years, see the BUC Used Boat Price Guide, Volume 3

OFFSHORE CONCEPTS CORP
FANTOM MARINE   See inside cover to adjust price for area
WINCHESTER MA 01890   COAST GUARD MFG ID- OFC

LOA FT IN	NAME AND/ OR MODEL	TOP/ RIG	BOAT TYPE	-HULL- MTL TP	TP	----ENGINE--- # HP MFG	BEAM FT IN	WGT LBS	DRAFT FT IN	RETAIL LOW	RETAIL HIGH
--- 1987 BOATS ---										
32	OPEN FISHERMAN		CTRCN	FBG DV	OB		8		3	20000	22200
32	RAISED DECK/SPORT	OVNTR	FBG DV	OB			8		3	20000	22300
32	SPORT/RACER	OFF	FBG DV	OB			8		3	20100	22300

OFFSHORE YACHT BUILDERS INC
DIV OF BASIC INDUSTRIES   See inside cover to adjust price for area
PALMETTO FL 34220

LOA FT IN	NAME AND/ OR MODEL	TOP/ RIG	BOAT TYPE	-HULL- MTL TP	TP	----ENGINE--- # HP MFG	BEAM FT IN	WGT LBS	DRAFT FT IN	RETAIL LOW	RETAIL HIGH
--- 1995 BOATS ---										
17	CENTER CONSOLE	OP	CTRCN	FBG SV	OB		8	1235	8	4950	5700
18 2	FLATS BOAT	OP	CTRCN	FBG SV	OB		7 6		10	4750	5450
18 6	CENTER CONSOLE LINER	OP	CTRCN	FBG SV	OB		8	1800	11	6600	7600
19	STALKER	OP	CTRCN	FBG TR	OB		7 4	1325	1	5450	6250
21 4	CENTER CONSOLE	OP	CTRCN	FBG SV	OB		8	2550	10	8100	9350
21 4	WALK AROUND	OP	RNBT	FBG SV	OB		8	2570	10	8150	9400
22	CENTER CONSOLE	OP	CTRCN	FBG SV	OB		8	2340	1 11	7950	9150
24	CENTER CONSOLE LINER	OP	OFF	FBG DV	OB		9 6	3100	1 2	10700	12200
26	CABIN CENTER CONSOLE	OP	OFF	FBG DV	OB		9 6		2	13900	15800
26 4	CENTER CONSOLE LINER	OP	CTRCN	FBG DV	OB		8 6	3200	2	13800	15600
28	SPORT DECK	OP	OFF	FBG DV	OB		8 6	2700	1 6	14200	16200
28	SPORT DECK	OP	OFF	FBG DV	OB		8 6	4200	2	16600	18900
--- 1994 BOATS ---										
18 2	FLATS BOAT	OP	CTRCN	FBG SV	OB		7 6	1150	10	4550	5250
18 6	CENTER CONSOLE LINER	OP	CTRCN	FBG SV	OB		8	1400	11	5300	6100
19	STALKER	OP	CTRCN	FBG TR	OB		7 4	1325	1	5150	5950
22	CENTER CONSOLE	OP	CTRCN	FBG SV	OB		8	1300	1 11	4650	5350
23 4	CENTER CONSOLE LINER	OP	CTRCN	FBG DV	OB		8	1700	1 2	6000	6900
26	CABIN CENTER CONSOLE	OP	OFF	FBG DV	OB		9 6	3700	2	13500	15400
26	SPORT DECK	OP	OFF	FBG DV	OB		8 6	3200	2	13000	14800
26 4	CENTER CONSOLE LINER	OP	CTRCN	FBG DV	OB		8 6	2700	1 6	13500	15300
28	SPORT DECK	OP	OFF	FBG DV	OB		8 6	4200	2	15800	17900
--- 1992 BOATS ---										
18	OFFSHORE CTR CONSOLE	OP	CTRCN	FBG SV	OB		8	1100		3900	4550
21	OFFSHORE CTR CONSOLE	OP	CTRCN	FBG SV	OB		8	1700		5100	5900
21	OFFSHORE WALKAROUND	OP	CUD	FBG SV	OB		8	1900		5550	6400
22	OFFSHORE CTR CONSOLE	OP	CTRCN	FBG SV	OB		8	1400		4500	5200
22	OFFSHORE SD CONSOLE	OP	OPFSH	FBG SV	OB		8	1400		4500	5200
24	OFFSHORE CTR CONSOLE	OP	CUD	FBG DV	OB		8 5	2300		7200	8300
24	OFFSHORE SPORT CUDDY	OP	CTRCN	FBG DV	OB		8 5	2800		8550	9800
26	OFFSHORE CTR CONSOLE	OP	CTRCN	FBG DV	OB		8 5	2500		11000	12600
26	OFFSHORE CTR CONSOLE	OP	CUD	FBG DV	OB		8 5	3000		11600	13100
26	OFFSHORE SPORT CUDDY	OP	CUD	FBG DV	OB		8 5	3000		11600	13200
28	OFFSHORE CTR CONSOLE	OP	CTRCN	FBG DV	OB		8 5	2700		13800	15600
28	OFFSHORE CTR CONSOLE	OP	CUD	FBG DV	OB		8 5	3000		14000	15900
28	OFFSHORE SPORT CUDDY	OP	CUD	FBG DV	OB		8 5	3200		14000	15900
--- 1989 BOATS ---										
21 4	OFFSHORE 21	OP	CTRCN	DV	OB		8	1700		4600	5250
22	OFFSHORE 22	OP	CTRCN	SV	OB		8	1400		3900	4550
24	OFFSHORE 24	OP	CTRCN	DV	OB		8 5	2300		6300	7250
24	OFFSHORE 24	OP	CUD	DV	OB		8 5	2300		6300	7250
26	OFFSHORE 26	OP	CTRCN	DV	OB		8 5	2500		4250	4950
26	OFFSHORE 26	OP	CUD	DV	OB		8 5	2500		5750	6600
26	OFFSHORE 26 SPORT	OP	CTRCN	DV	OB		8 5	2500		6300	7250
28	OFFSHORE 28	ST	CTRCN	DV	OB		8 5	3200		6850	7850
28	OFFSHORE 28	ST	CUD	DV	OB		8 5	3200		9400	10700
28	OFFSHORE 28 SPORT	ST	CTRCN	DV	OB		8 5	3200		9850	11200

OFFSHORE YACHTS
S NORWALK CT 06854   See inside cover to adjust price for area

LOA FT IN	NAME AND/ OR MODEL	TOP/ RIG	BOAT TYPE	-HULL- MTL TP	TP	----ENGINE--- # HP MFG	BEAM FT IN	WGT LBS	DRAFT FT IN	RETAIL LOW	RETAIL HIGH
--- 1986 BOATS ---										
33 1	OFFSHORE 33	SA/CR	FBG SK				11	13000	4	25000	27800
39 3	OFFSHORE 39	SA/RC	FBG SK				12 9	18000	4 1	40100	44600
43 2	OFFSHORE 43	KTH	SA/RC FBG	SK	IB	D	13 1	20216	4 10	53400	58700
--- 1985 BOATS ---										
33 1	OFFSHORE 33	SA/CR	FBG KL				11	13000	4	23400	26000
39 3	OFFSHORE 39	KTH	SA/RC FBG	KL			12 9	18200	4 10	39900	44300
43 2	OFFSHORE 43	KTH	SA/RC FBG	SK	IB	D	13 1	20216	4 10	50000	55000

OLD WHARF DORY COMPANY
WELLFLEET MA 02667   COAST GUARD MFG ID- XWC   See inside cover to adjust price for area
          For more recent years, see the BUC Used Boat Price Guide, Volume 1

LOA FT IN	NAME AND/ OR MODEL	TOP/ RIG	BOAT TYPE	-HULL- MTL TP	TP	----ENGINE--- # HP MFG	BEAM FT IN	WGT LBS	DRAFT FT IN	RETAIL LOW	RETAIL HIGH
--- 1984 BOATS ---										
17 2	SWAMPSCOTT DORY	SLP	SAIL	CDR CB			4 5	350	4	3200	3700
20	ELVER	YWL	SA/CR	CDR CB			7 3	800	4	5250	6000
25 3	BLACK-SKIMMER	YWL	SA/CR	PLY CB			7	1200	10	8600	9900

....For earlier years, see the BUC Used Boat Price Guide, Volume 3

OLDPORT MARINE
NEWPORT RI 02840   See inside cover to adjust price for area
          For more recent years, see the BUC Used Boat Price Guide, Volume 1

LOA FT IN	NAME AND/ OR MODEL	TOP/ RIG	BOAT TYPE	-HULL- MTL TP	TP	----ENGINE--- # HP MFG	BEAM FT IN	WGT LBS	DRAFT FT IN	RETAIL LOW	RETAIL HIGH
--- 1996 BOATS ---										
18	OMS 18	OP	LNCH	FBG DS	IB	18D- 27D	7 3	4000	1 10	19400	22500
25 10	OMS 26	OP	LNCH	FBG DS	IB	50D-110D	9 2	5000	3	24600	25900
25 10	OMS 26	OP	LNCH	FBG DS	IB	140D-170D	9 2	5000	3	27900	32100
25 10	OMS BASS BOAT	OP	BASS	FBG DS	IB	88D YAN	9 2	5000	3	25900	28800
--- 1995 BOATS ---										
18	OMS 18	OP	LNCH	FBG SV	IB	27D YAN	7 3		1 10	20100	22400
20	OMS 20	OP	LNCH	FBG SV	IB	27D YAN	7 11		2 9	22700	25200
25 10	OMS 26	OP	BASS	FBG SV	IB	75D YAN	9 2		3 2	30500	33900
25 10	OMS 26	OP	LNCH	FBG SV	IB	66D YAN	9 2		3	29700	33000
--- 1994 BOATS ---										
18	OMS 18	OP	LNCH	FBG SV	IB	27D YAN	7 3		1 10	19500	21700
20	OMS 20	OP	LNCH	FBG SV	IB	27D YAN	7 11		2 9	22000	24400
25 10	OMS 26	OP	LNCH	FBG SV	IB	66D YAN	9 2		3	28200	31300
--- 1993 BOATS ---										
18	OMS 18	OP	LNCH	FBG SV	IB	27D YAN	7 3		1 10	18500	20600
20	OMS 20	OP	LNCH	FBG SV	IB	27D YAN	7 11		2 9	20900	23200
25 10	OMS 26	OP	LNCH	FBG SV	IB	66D YAN	9 2		3	26800	29800

OLDPORT MARINE -CONTINUED See inside cover to adjust price for area

LOA FT	IN	NAME AND/ OR MODEL	TOP/ RIG	BOAT TYPE	-HULL- MTL	TP	ENGINE TP	# HP	MFG	BEAM FT	IN	WGT LBS	DRAFT FT	IN	RETAIL LOW	RETAIL HIGH
		1992 BOATS														
18		OMS 18	OP	LNCH	FBG	SV	IB	27D	YAN	7	3		1	10	17300	19600
20		OMS 20	OP	LNCH	FBG	SV	IB	27D	YAN	7	11		2	9	19900	22100
25	10	OMS 26	OP	LNCH	FBG	SV	IB	66D	YAN	9	2		3		25600	28400
		1991 BOATS														
18		OMS 18	OP	LNCH	FBG	SV	IB	27D	YAN						16500	18700
20		OMS 20	OP	LNCH	FBG	SV	IB	27D	YAN						19400	21500
25	10	OMS 26	OP	LNCH	FBG	SV	IB	66D	YAN	9	2		3		24400	27100
		1990 BOATS														
18		OMS 18	OP	LNCH	FBG	SV	IB	27D	YAN						15700	17900
20		OMS 20	OP	LNCH	FBG	SV	IB	27D	YAN						18500	20500
25	10	OMS 26	OP	LNCH	FBG	SV	IB	48D	YAN	9	2		3		23300	25900
		1989 BOATS														
26		PASSENGER LAUNCH		LNCH	FBG		IB	66D	YAN	9	3	4300	2	10	22100	24600

OLYMPIC BOAT CO

RAY MARINE DISTRIBUTING
MONROE WA 98272 COAST GUARD MFG ID- OLP

See inside cover to adjust price for area

For more recent years, see the BUC Used Boat Price Guide, Volume 1

LOA FT	IN	NAME AND/ OR MODEL	TOP/ RIG	BOAT TYPE	-HULL- MTL	TP	ENGINE TP	# HP	MFG	BEAM FT	IN	WGT LBS	DRAFT FT	IN	RETAIL LOW	RETAIL HIGH
		1996 BOATS														
17	7	EVOLUTION 18	ST	RNBT	F/S	DV	OB			7	4	1300			5050	5800
17	7	EVOLUTION 18	HT	RNBT	F/S	DV	OB			7	4	1400			5350	6150
17	7	EVOLUTION 18 BULKHD	HT	RNBT	F/S	DV	OB			7	4	1500			5650	6450
19	5	DELUXE 2000	ST	RNBT	F/S	DV	OB			7	5	1940			7150	8200
19	5	DELUXE 2000	HT	RNBT	F/S	DV	OB			7	5	2040			7350	8450
19	5	DELUXE 2000 BULKHD	HT	RNBT	F/S	DV	OB			7	5	2140			7550	8650
21	6	NORTHWEST 22	HT	CUD	F/S	DV	IO	220	VLVO	8		3500			18400	20400
21	6	RESORTER 22	HT	CUD	F/S	DV	IO	220	VLVO	8		3500			16000	18200
23	8	NORTHWEST 24	HT	CUD	F/S	DV	IO	250	VLVO	8	6	4500			22700	25300
23	8	WALKAROUND 24XL	HT	CUD	F/S	DV	IO	250	VLVO	8	6	4500			24500	27200
23	8	WALKAROUND 24XL	HT	CUD	F/S	DV	IO	130D	VLVO	8	6	4500			26500	29400
25	4	SUPER 26XL	HT	CUD	F/S	DV	IO	250	VLVO	8	6	5250			29300	32600
25	4	SUPER 26XL	HT	CUD	F/S	DV	IO	200D	VLVO	8	6	5250			34200	38000
25	4	SUPER 26XLF	HT	CUD	F/S	DV	IO	250	VLVO	8	6	5400			28300	31500
25	4	SUPER SPORT 26	HT	CUD	F/S	DV	IO	250	VLVO	8	6	5250			26300	29200
25	4	SUPER SPORT 26	HT	CUD	F/S	DV	IO	200D	VLVO	8	6	5250			31200	34700
		1995 BOATS														
17	7	EVOLUTION 18	ST	RNBT	FBG	DV	OB			7	4	1350			4950	5700
17	7	EVOLUTION 18	HT	RNBT	FBG	DV	OB			7	4	1350			4950	5700
19	5	DELUXE 2000	HT	RNBT	FBG	DV	OB			7	5	2460			7550	8700
19	5	RUNABOUT 20	ST	RNBT	FBG	DV	OB			7	5	1940			6700	7750
24	6	NORTHWEST W/A 22	HT	CUD	FBG	DV	OB			8		3550			15200	17300
24	6	NORTHWEST W/A 22	HT	CUD	FBG	DV	IO	185-250		8		3550			16400	19300
24	6	RESORTER 22	HT	CUD	FBG	DV	OB			8		3500	3	6	12100	13800
24	6	RESORTER 22	HT	CUD	FBG	DV	IO	185-250		8		3550	3	6	14600	17400
26	1	NORTHWEST W/A 24	HT	CUD	FBG	SV	OB			8	6	4720			17400	19800
26	1	NORTHWEST W/A 24	HT	CUD	FBG	SV	IO	225-250		8	6	4720			21900	24700
26	1	NORTHWEST W/A 24	HT	CUD	FBG	SV	IB	130D-230D		8	6	4720			28200	34000
26	1	WALKAROUND XL 24	HT	RNBT	FBG	DV	OB			8	6	5100			20300	22600
26	1	WALKAROUND XL 24	HT	RNBT	FBG	DV	IO	225-250		8	6	5100			23700	26800
26	1	WALKAROUND XL 24	HT	RNBT	FBG	DV	IB	130D-200D		8	6	5100			30000	36800
26	1	WALKAROUND XL 24	HT	RNBT	FBG	DV	IB	230D	VLVO	8	6	5100			34400	38200
27	8	SUPER SPORT 26	HT	CUD	FBG	SV	OB			8	6	5000			18300	20400
27	8	SUPER SPORT 26	HT	CUD	FBG	SV	IO	225-250		8	6	5000			24000	26700
27	8	SUPER SPORT 26	HT	CUD	FBG	SV	IB	130D-230D		8	6	5000			30200	36400
27	8	SUPER XL 26	HT	CUD	FBG	SV	OB			8	6	5250			20800	23100
27	8	SUPER XL 26	HT	CUD	FBG	SV	IO	250	VLVO	8	6	5250			26400	29400
27	8	SUPER XL 26	HT	CUD	FBG	SV	IB	200D-230D		8	6	5250			35700	41000
37		MOTOR YACHT 33	HT	CR	FBG	SV	IB	280D	VLVO	11	6	16000			98300	108000
37		MOTOR YACHT 33	HT	CR	FBG	SV	IB	400D	VLVO	11	6	16000			102500	113000
		1994 BOATS														
16	3	NORWESTER 17	OP	RNBT	FBG	DV	OB			6	8	950			3300	3850
17	7	EVOLUTION 18	ST	RNBT	FBG	DV	OB			7	4	1350			4700	5400
19	5	RUNABOUT 20	ST	RNBT		DV	OB			7	5	1940			6400	7350
19	5	RUNABOUT 20	ST	RNBT	FBG	DV	OB			7	5	1940			6400	7350
23		RESORTER 22	HT	CUD	FBG	DV	OB			8		3500	3	6	11500	13100
23	10	NORTHWEST W/A 22	HT	CUD	FBG	DV	IO	185-250		8		3500			15200	17900
23	10	RESORTER 22	HT	CUD	FBG	DV	IO	185-250		8		3500	3	6	13500	16000
24	6	NORTHWEST W/A 22	HT	CUD	FBG	DV	OB			8		3500			14200	16200
26		NORTHWEST W/A 24	HT	CUD	FBG	SV	OB			8	6	4500			16300	18500
26		NORTHWEST W/A 24	HT	CUD	FBG	SV	IO	225-250		8	6	4500			19900	22500
26		NORTHWEST W/A 24	HT	CUD	FBG	SV	IB	130D-230D		8	6	4500			26000	31400
27	8	SUPER SPORT 26	HT	CUD	FBG	SV	OB			8	6	5250			17300	19700
27	8	SUPER SPORT 26	HT	CUD	FBG	SV	IO	225-250		8	6	5250			23500	26100
27	8	SUPER SPORT 26	HT	CUD	FBG	SV	IB	130D-230D		8	6	5250			29900	35800
27	8	SUPER XL 26	HT	CUD	FBG	SV	OB			8	6	5250			19700	21900
27	8	SUPER XL 26	HT	CUD	FBG	SV	IO	245-250		8	6	5250			24800	27600
27	8	SUPER XL 26	HT	CUD	FBG	SV	IB	200D-230D		8	6	5250			34000	38900
		1993 BOATS														
17	7	EVOLUTION 18	ST	RNBT	FBG	DV	OB			7	4	1350			4450	5150
17	7	EVOLUTION 18 DELUXE	HT	RNBT	FBG	DV	OB			7	4	1510			4850	5600
17	7	EVOLUTION 18 POPTOP	HT	RNBT	FBG	DV	OB			7	4	1825			5500	6350
19	5	OV 2000 DELUXE	HT	RNBT	F/S	DV	OB			7	5				6300	7200
19	5	OV 2000 DELUXE	HT	RNBT	F/S	DV	IO	110-135		7	5	2560			7550	8700
23	5	OMV 2300 SPORT SEDAN	HT	CUD	FBG	SV	OB			8		3050			11700	13300
23	5	OMV 2300 SPORT SEDAN	HT	CUD	FBG	SV	IO	155-240		8		3930			15900	18600
23	5	OMV 2300 SPORT SEDAN	HT	CUD	FBG	SV	IO	130D	VLVO	8		3930			19300	21400
23	10	NORTHWEST W/A 21	HT	CUD	FBG	DV	OB			8		3200			10600	12000
23	10	NORTHWEST W/A 21	HT	CUD	FBG	DV	IO	155-245		8		3500			14400	17000
23	10	RESORTER 22 DELUXE	HT	CUD	FBG	DV	OB			8		3485	3	6	10900	12400
23	10	RESORTER 22 DELUXE	HT	CUD	FBG	DV	IO	155-245		8		3500	3	6	12200	14500
26		NORTHWEST W/A 24	HT	CUD	FBG	SV	OB			8	6	4025			14400	16300
26		NORTHWEST W/A 24	HT	CUD	FBG	SV	IO	190-245		8	6	4525			18600	21200
26		NORTHWEST W/A 24	HT	CUD	FBG	SV	IB	130D-230D		8	6	4525			25100	30000
26		NORTHWEST W/A 24	HT	CUD	FBG	SV	IO	T270	VLVO	8	6	4525			22600	25100
27	8	SUPER SPORT 26	HT	CUD	FBG	SV	OB			8	6	4750			17200	19500
27	8	SUPER SPORT 26	HT	CUD	FBG	SV	IO	205-245		8	6	4750			20800	23800
		IB 130D-200D 26100 32100, IB 230D VLVO 30000 33400, IO T270 VLVO													25800	28700
27	8	SUPER XFL SPORT 26	FB	CUD	FBG	SV	OB			8	6	5250			17500	19900
27	8	SUPER XFL SPORT 26	FB	CUD	FBG	SV	IO	245	VLVO	8	6	5450			23100	25700
27	8	SUPER XFL SPORT 26	FB	CUD	FBG	SV	IB	200D-230D		8	6	5450			32000	36800
27	8	SUPER XFL SPORT 26	FB	CUD	FBG	SV	IO	T270	VLVO	8	6	5450			27600	30600
27	8	SUPER XL SPORT 26	HT	CUD	FBG	SV	OB			8	6	5250			18100	20100
27	8	SUPER XL SPORT 26	HT	CUD	FBG	SV	IO	245	VLVO	8	6	5250			22600	25100
27	8	SUPER XL SPORT 26	HT	CUD	FBG	SV	IB	200D-230D		8	6	5250			31100	35800
27	8	SUPER XL SPORT 26	HT	CUD	FBG	SV	IO	T270	VLVO	8	6	5250			27000	30100
		1992 BOATS														
16	3	RUNABOUT 17	ST	RNBT	FBG	SV	OB			7	4				2950	3450
17	5	EVOLUTION	ST	RNBT	FBG	SV	OB			7	4	1350			4200	4900
17	5	EVOLUTION DLX	HT	RNBT	FBG	SV	OB			7	4	1510			4600	5300
19	1	RUNABOUT 2000	ST	RNBT	FBG	SV	OB			7	5	1840			5500	6300
19	1	RUNABOUT 2000	ST	RNBT	FBG	SV	IO	110-155		7	5	2456			6400	7350
19	1	RUNABOUT 2000 DLX	HT	RNBT	FBG	SV	IO			7	5	1940			**	**
19	1	RUNABOUT 2000 DLX	HT	RNBT	FBG	SV	IO	110-155		7	5	2560			6550	7550
19	6	NORTHWEST W/A 20	ST	CUD	FBG	SV	OB			8		2900			6800	7850
19	6	NORTHWEST W/A 20	ST	CUD	FBG	SV	IO	155-245		8		3200			8300	9950
19	6	NORTHWEST W/A 20	HT	CUD	FBG	SV	OB			8		3200			6800	7850
19	6	NORTHWEST W/A 20	HT	CUD	FBG	SV	IO	155-245		8		3200			8300	9950
21	4	RESORTER 21 DXL	HT	CUD	FBG	SV	OB			8					9400	10700
21	4	RESORTER 21 DXL	HT	CUD	FBG	SV	IO	155-245		8					11400	13400
21	6	NORTHWEST W/A 21	HT	CUD	FBG	SV	OB			8					10400	11900
21	6	NORTHWEST W/A 21	HT	CUD	FBG	SV	IO	155-245		8					12200	14300
25	8	SUPER SPORT 26	HT	CUD	FBG	SV	IO	225		8	6	4750			19200	21300
26		NORTHWEST W/A 24	HT	CUD	FBG	SV	OB			8	6	4500			14600	16500
26		NORTHWEST W/A 24	HT	CUD	FBG	SV	IO	155-245		8	6	4500			16600	19300
26		NORTHWEST W/A 24	HT	CUD	FBG	SV	IO	120D-216D		8	6	4500			20500	24600
27	8	SUPER SPORT 26	HT	CUD	FBG	SV	OB			8	6	4750			16000	18200
27	8	SUPER SPORT 26	HT	CUD	FBG	SV	IO	155-245		8	6	4750			18500	21700
27	8	SUPER SPORT 26	HT	CUD	FBG	SV	IO	120D-140D		8	6	4750			21300	24100
27	8	SUPER SPORT 26	HT	CUD	FBG	SV	IO	216D		8	6	4750			24000	26700
27	8	SUPER XL SPORT 26	HT	CUD	FBG	SV	OB			8	6	5250			16700	19000
27	8	SUPER XL SPORT 26	HT	CUD	FBG	SV	IO	155-245		8	6	5250			19700	23000
27	8	SUPER XL SPORT 26	HT	CUD	FBG	SV	IO	120D-216D		8	6	5250			22900	28200
27	8	SUPER XLF 26	HT	CUD	FBG	SV	IO	245		8	6	5750			21800	24200
		1986 BOATS														
16	3	OV 1700 RUNABOUT	ST	RNBT	F/S	DV	OB			6	7	950			2400	2800
16	3	OV 1700 SKI	ST	SKI	F/S	DV	OB			6	7	965			2400	2800
16	3	OV 1700 SPECIAL	ST	FSH	F/S	DV	OB			6	7	920			2300	2700
16	3	OV 1700 STANDARD	HT	RNBT	F/S	DV	OB			6	7	1050			2600	3050
17	5	OV 1800 BOWRIDER	ST	RNBT	F/S	DV	OB			7	3	1395			3400	3950
17	5	OV 1800 BOWRIDER	ST	RNBT	F/S	DV	IO	120-175		7	3	2045			3700	4500
17	5	OV 1800 DELUXE	HT	RNBT	F/S	DV	OB			7	3	1510			3600	4200
17	5	OV 1800 DELUXE	HT	RNBT	F/S	DV	IO	120-175		7	3	2160			3800	4650
17	5	OV 1800 RUNABOUT	ST	RNBT	F/S	DV	OB			7	3	1350			3350	3850
17	5	OV 1800 RUNABOUT	ST	RNBT	F/S	DV	IO	120-190		7	3	2000			3650	4550

CONTINUED ON NEXT PAGE

LOA FT	LOA IN	NAME AND/ OR MODEL	TOP/ RIG	BOAT TYPE	HULL MTL	HULL TP	ENGINE TP	ENGINE # HP	ENGINE MFG	BEAM FT	BEAM IN	WGT LBS	DRAFT FT	DRAFT IN	RETAIL LOW	RETAIL HIGH
1986 BOATS																
17	5	OV 1800 SPECIAL	ST	FSH	F/S	DV	OB			7	3	1330			3250	3800
17	5	OV 1800 SPECIAL	ST	FSH	F/S	DV	IO	120-146		7	3	1980			3850	4650
17	5	OV 1800 STANDARD	HT	RNBT	F/S	DV	OB			7	3	1450			3500	4100
19	1	OV 2000 DELUXE	HT	RNBT	F/S	DV	OB			7	4	2220			4850	5550
19	1	OV 2000 DELUXE	HT	RNBT	F/S	DV	SE	115	OMC	7	4	2605			5100	5850
19	1	OV 2000 DELUXE	HT	RNBT	F/S	DV	IO	120-190		7	4	2870			5000	6100
19	1	OV 2000 RUNABOUT	ST	RNBT	F/S	DV	OB			7	4	1540			3850	4500
19	1	OV 2000 RUNABOUT	ST	RNBT	F/S	DV	IO	120-205		7	4	2190			4350	5300
19	1	OV 2000 SPECIAL	ST	FSH	F/S	DV	SE	115	OMC	7	4	1895			4450	5100
19	1	OV 2000 SPECIAL	ST	FSH	F/S	DV	IO	120-146		7	4	2160			4700	5550
21		OV 2200 CUDDY	ST	CUD	F/S	DV	OB			8		2550			6750	7750
21		OV 2200 CUDDY	ST	CUD	F/S	DV	SE	115	OMC	8		2935			7250	8350
21		OV 2200 CUDDY	ST	CUD	F/S	DV	IO	140		8		3230			8050	9250
21		OV 2200 CUDDY	ST	CUD	F/S	DV	IO	146-190		8		3601			9000	10200
21		OV 2200 CUDDY	ST	CUD	F/S	DV	SE	205	OMC	8		3085			7400	8500
21		OV 2200 CUDDY	ST	CUD	F/S	DV	IO	225-260		8		3954			9800	11500
21		OV 2200 DELUXE	HT	CBNCR	F/S	DV	OB			8		2750			7000	8050
21		OV 2200 DELUXE	HT	CBNCR	F/S	DV	SE	115	OMC	8		3135			7450	8550
21		OV 2200 DELUXE	HT	CBNCR	F/S	DV	IO	140-190		8		3430			9150	10900
21		OV 2200 DELUXE	HT	CBNCR	F/S	DV	SE	205	OMC	8		3285			7550	8700
21		OV 2200 DELUXE	HT	CBNCR	F/S	DV	IO	225-260		8		3654			10000	11800
23	2	OMV 2300 SPORT SEDAN	HT	EXP	F/S	SV	OB			8					9700	11000
23	2	OMV 2300 SPORT SEDAN	HT	EXP	F/S	SV	SE	115	OMC	8		4010			10400	11900
23	2	OMV 2300 SPORT SEDAN	HT	EXP	F/S	SV	IO	170-190		8		4050			10700	12400
23	2	OMV 2300 SPORT SEDAN	HT	EXP	F/S	SV	SE	205	OMC	8		3775			10100	11500
23	2	OMV 2300 SPORT SEDAN	HT	EXP	F/S	SV	IO	230-260		8		4280			11400	13200
25	6	OMV 2600 COMMERCIAL	HT	FSH	F/S	SV	IO	170-190		8		4060			12700	14800
25	6	OMV 2600 COMMERCIAL	HT	FSH	F/S	SV	SE	205	OMC	8		3785			11500	13100
25	6	OMV 2600 COMMERCIAL	HT	FSH	F/S	SV	IO	225-260		8		4154			13700	16000
25	6	OMV 2600 COMMERCIAL	HT	FSH	F/S	SV	IO	110D	VLVO	8		4191			16400	18600
25	6	OMV 2600 COMMERCIAL	HT	FSH	F/S	SV	SE	T115	OMC	8		4020			11800	13400
25	6	OMV 2600 COMMERCIAL	HT	FSH	F/S	SV	IO	T120-T146		8		4550			15100	17600
25	6	OMV 2600 SPORT SEDAN	HT	FSH	F/S	SV	IO	170-190		8		4660			13900	16100
25	6	OMV 2600 SPORT SEDAN	HT	FSH	F/S	SV	SE	205	OMC	8		4385			12200	13900
25	6	OMV 2600 SPORT SEDAN	HT	FSH	F/S	SV	IO	225-260		8		4754			14800	17300
25	6	OMV 2600 SPORT SEDAN	HT	FSH	F/S	SV	IO	110D	VLVO	8		4791			18800	20900
25	6	OMV 2600 SPORT SEDAN	HT	FSH	F/S	SV	SE	T115	OMC	8		4620			12500	14200
25	6	OMV 2600 SPORT SEDAN	HT	FSH	F/S	SV	IO	T120-T146		8		5150			16300	18900
25	6	OMV 2600 XL	HT	SPTCR	F/S	SV	IO	190-260		8		4820			13600	16600
25	6	OMV 2600 XL	HT	SPTCR	F/S	SV	IO	110D	VLVO	8		4881			14900	17000
25	6	OMV 2600 XL	HT	SPTCR	F/S	SV	IO	T120-T146		8		4990			15500	18100
25	6	OMV 2600 XLC		SDNSF	F/S	SV	SE	205	OMC	8		4947			12800	14500
25	6	OMV 2600 XLC		SDNSF	F/S	SV	IO	225-260		8		4877			15900	18600
25	6	OMV 2600 XLC		SDNSF	F/S	SV	SE	T115	OMC	8		4663			12500	14200
25	6	OMV 2600XL	HT	SPTCR	F/S	SV	IO	170	MRCR	8		4750			13300	15100
25	6	OMV 2600XL	HT	SPTCR	F/S	SV	SE	205	OMC	8		4475			12400	14100
25	6	OMV 2600XL	HT	SPTCR	F/S	SV	IO	230-260		8		4798			13900	16100
25	6	OMV 2600XL	HT	SPTCR	F/S	SV	SE	T115	OMC	8		4710			12700	14400
25	6	OMV 2600XL	HT	SPTCR	F/S	SV	IO	T120-T140		8		5240			15600	18100
1985 BOATS																
16	3	OV 1700 RUNABOUT	ST	RNBT	F/S	DV	OB			6	7	950			2350	2700
16	3	OV 1700 SKI	ST	SKI	F/S	DV	OB			6	7	965			2350	2700
16	3	OV 1700 SPECIAL	ST	FSH	F/S	DV	OB			6	7	920			2250	2650
16	3	OV 1700 STANDARD	HT	RNBT	F/S	DV	OB			6	7	1050			2550	2950
17	5	OV 1800 BOWRIDER	ST	RNBT	F/S	DV	OB			7	3	1395			3300	3850
17	5	OV 1800 BOWRIDER	ST	RNBT	F/S	DV	IO	120-185		7	3	2045			3550	4300
17	5	OV 1800 DELUXE	HT	RNBT	F/S	DV	OB			7	3	1510			3500	4100
17	5	OV 1800 DELUXE	HT	RNBT	F/S	DV	IO	120-185		7	3	2160			3650	4400
17	5	OV 1800 RUNABOUT	ST	RNBT	F/S	DV	OB			7	3	1350			3250	3750
17	5	OV 1800 RUNABOUT	ST	RNBT	F/S	DV	IO	120-190		7	3	2000			3500	4350
17	5	OV 1800 SPECIAL	ST	FSH	F/S	DV	OB			7	3	1330			3200	3700
17	5	OV 1800 SPECIAL	ST	FSH	F/S	DV	IO	120-140		7	3	1980			3650	4400
17	5	OV 1800 STANDARD	HT	RNBT	F/S	DV	OB			7	3	1450			3400	3950
19	1	OV 2000 DELUXE	HT	RNBT	F/S	DV	OB			7	4	2220			4700	5400
19	1	OV 2000 DELUXE	HT	RNBT	F/S	DV	SE	115	OMC	7	4	2605			4950	5700
19	1	OV 2000 DELUXE	HT	RNBT	F/S	DV	IO	120-140		7	4	2870			4800	5600
19	1	OV 2000 DELUXE	HT	RNBT	F/S	DV	SE	155	OMC	7	4	2740			5000	5750
19	1	OV 2000 DELUXE	HT	RNBT	F/S	DV	IO	170-190		7	4	3030			4950	5850
19	1	OV 2000 RUNABOUT	ST	RNBT	F/S	DV	OB			7	4	1540			3750	4350
19	1	OV 2000 RUNABOUT	ST	RNBT	F/S	DV	SE	115	OMC	7	4	1895			4300	5000
19	1	OV 2000 RUNABOUT	ST	RNBT	F/S	DV	IO	120-140		7	4	2190			4100	4900
19	1	OV 2000 RUNABOUT	ST	RNBT	F/S	DV	SE	155	OMC	7	4	2060			4550	5250
19	1	OV 2000 RUNABOUT	ST	RNBT	F/S	DV	IO	170-190		7	4	2350			4300	5100
19	1	OV 2000 SPECIAL	ST	FSH	F/S	DV	OB			7	4	1510			3700	4300
19	1	OV 2000 SPECIAL	ST	FSH	F/S	DV	SE	115	OMC	7	4	1895			4300	4950
19	1	OV 2000 SPECIAL	ST	FSH	F/S	DV	IO	120-140		7	4	2160			4500	5300
19	1	OV 2000 SPECIAL	ST	FSH	F/S	DV	SE	155	OMC	7	4	2030			4500	5150
21		OV 2200 CUDDY	ST	CUD	F/S	DV	OB			8		2550			6550	7500
21		OV 2200 CUDDY	ST	CUD	F/S	DV	SE	115	OMC	8		2935			7050	8100
21		OV 2200 CUDDY	ST	CUD	F/S	DV	IO	138-140		8		3601			8550	9800
21		OV 2200 CUDDY	ST	CUD	F/S	DV	SE	155	OMC	8		3070			7200	8250
21		OV 2200 CUDDY	ST	CUD	F/S	DV	IO	170-190		8		3360			7950	9300
21		OV 2200 CUDDY	ST	CUD	F/S	DV	SE	205	OMC	8		3085			7200	8300
21		OV 2200 CUDDY	ST	CUD	F/S	DV	IO	225-260		8		3954			9400	11000
21		OV 2200 CUDDY	ST	CUD	F/S	DV	IO	110D	VLVO	8		3991			10900	12400
21		OV 2200 DELUXE	HT	CBNCR	F/S	DV	OB			8		2750			6800	7850
21		OV 2200 DELUXE	HT	CBNCR	F/S	DV	SE	115	OMC	8		3135			7250	8300
21		OV 2200 DELUXE	HT	CBNCR	F/S	DV	IO	138-140		8		3301			8700	10000
21		OV 2200 DELUXE	HT	CBNCR	F/S	DV	SE	155	OMC	8		3270			7350	8450
21		OV 2200 DELUXE	HT	CBNCR	F/S	DV	IO	170-190		8		3560			9000	10400
21		OV 2200 DELUXE	HT	CBNCR	F/S	DV	SE	205	OMC	8		3285			7350	8450
21		OV 2200 DELUXE	HT	CBNCR	F/S	DV	IO	225-260		8		3654			9600	11300
21		OV 2200 DELUXE	HT	CBNCR	F/S	DV	IO	110D	VLVO	8		3691			11900	13600
23	2	OMV 2300 SPORT SEDAN	HT	EXP	F/S	SV	SE	115-155		8		4010			10100	11500
23	2	OMV 2300 SPORT SEDAN	HT	EXP	F/S	SV	IO	170-190		8		4050			10300	11900
23	2	OMV 2300 SPORT SEDAN	HT	EXP	F/S	SV	SE	205	OMC	8		3775			9800	11100
23	2	OMV 2300 SPORT SEDAN	HT	EXP	F/S	SV	IO	230-260		8		4280			10900	12600
25	6	OMV 2600 COMMERCIAL	HT	FSH	F/S	SV	SE	155	OMC	8		3770			11200	12700
25	6	OMV 2600 COMMERCIAL	HT	FSH	F/S	SV	IO	170-190		8		4060			12200	14200
25	6	OMV 2600 COMMERCIAL	HT	FSH	F/S	SV	SE	205	OMC	8		3785			11200	12700
25	6	OMV 2600 COMMERCIAL	HT	FSH	F/S	SV	IO	225-260		8		4154			13100	15400
25	6	OMV 2600 COMMERCIAL	HT	FSH	F/S	SV	IO	110D	VLVO	8		4191			15700	17800
25	6	OMV 2600 COMMERCIAL	HT	FSH	F/S	SV	SE	T115	OMC	8		4020			11500	13000
25	6	OMV 2600 COMMERCIAL	HT	FSH	F/S	SV	IO	T120-T140		8		4550			14500	16900
25	6	OMV 2600 SPORT SEDAN	HT	FSH	F/S	SV	SE	155	OMC	8		4370			11900	13500
25	6	OMV 2600 SPORT SEDAN	HT	FSH	F/S	SV	IO	170-190		8		4660			13300	15500
25	6	OMV 2600 SPORT SEDAN	HT	FSH	F/S	SV	SE	205	OMC	8		4385			11900	13500
25	6	OMV 2600 SPORT SEDAN	HT	FSH	F/S	SV	IO	225-260		8		4754			14200	16600
25	6	OMV 2600 SPORT SEDAN	HT	FSH	F/S	SV	IO	110D	VLVO	8		4791			18000	20000
25	6	OMV 2600 SPORT SEDAN	HT	FSH	F/S	SV	SE	T115	OMC	8		4620			12100	13800
25	6	OMV 2600 SPORT SEDAN	HT	FSH	F/S	SV	IO	T120-T140		8		5150			15600	18000
25	6	OMV 2600 SPORT SEDAN	HT	FSH	F/S	SV	SE	T155-T205		8		4890			12400	14100
25	6	OMV 2600 XL	HT	SPTCR	F/S	SV	IO	190-260		8		4820			13000	15900
25	6	OMV 2600 XL	HT	SPTCR	F/S	SV	IO	110D	VLVO	8		4881			14300	16300
25	6	OMV 2600 XL	HT	SPTCR	F/S	SV	IO	T120-T138		8		4990			14900	17200
25	6	OMV 2600XL	HT	SPTCR	F/S	SV	SE	155	OMC	8		4460			12000	13700
25	6	OMV 2600XL	HT	SPTCR	F/S	SV	IO	170-185		8		4750			12700	14500
25	6	OMV 2600XL	HT	SPTCR	F/S	SV	SE	205	OMC	8		4475			12100	13700
25	6	OMV 2600XL	HT	SPTCR	F/S	SV	IO	230-260		8		4798			13300	15400
25	6	OMV 2600XL	HT	SPTCR	F/S	SV	SE	T115	OMC	8		4710			12300	14000
25	6	OMV 2600XL	HT	SPTCR	F/S	SV	IO	T120-T140		8		5240			14900	17300
25	6	OMV 2600XL	HT	SPTCR	F/S	SV	SE	T155-T205		8		4980			12500	14300

OMEGA YACHTS
NEW LONDON NH 03257

See inside cover to adjust price for area

LOA FT	LOA IN	NAME AND/ OR MODEL	TOP/ RIG	BOAT TYPE	HULL MTL	HULL TP	ENGINE TP	ENGINE # HP	ENGINE MFG	BEAM FT	BEAM IN	WGT LBS	DRAFT FT	DRAFT IN	RETAIL LOW	RETAIL HIGH
1987 BOATS																
30	8	OMEGA 30	SLP	SA/RC	FBG	KL	IB	10D	YAN	9	8	6950	5	1	27600	30700
33	8	OMEGA 34	SLP	SA/RC	FBG	KL	IB	18D	YAN	9	8	9920	5	1	39600	44000
36		OMEGA 36	SLP	SA/RC	FBG	KL	IB	27D	YAN	11		11240	5	6	46700	51300
42	5	OMEGA 42	SLP	SA/RC	FBG	KL	IB	35D	YAN	10	3	15000	5	5	80600	88500
1985 BOATS																
30	8	OMEGA 30	SLP	SA/RC	FBG	KL				9	8	6950	5	1	21800	24200
33	8	OMEGA 34	SLP	SA/RC	FBG	KL				9	8	9920	5	1	33100	36800

OMNI BY HARRISKAYOT

DIV OF HARRISKAYOT INC
FORT WAYNE IN 46808
See inside cover to adjust price for area
COAST GUARD MFG ID- HAM
FORMERLY HARRIS FLOTE-BOTE

For more recent years, see the BUC Used Boat Price Guide, Volume 1

LOA FT IN	NAME AND/OR MODEL	TOP/RIG	BOAT TYPE	HULL MTL TP	ENGINE TP # HP MFG	BEAM FT IN	WGT LBS	DRAFT FT IN	RETAIL LOW	RETAIL HIGH
					1996 BOATS					
18	CORSO 180	OP	RNBT	FBG TR	IO 180-185	8	2930		8100	9350
21 6	FLOTEDECK 2000LSI	OP	RNBT	FBG TR	IO 210-265	8	3400		10800	13300
22 6	SUPERDEK	ST	RNBT	FBG TR	IO 190-265	8 6	4500		14400	17100
23 11	LEGEND	OP	B/R	FBG TH	OB	8 6	3460		13100	14900
23 11	LEGEND	OP	B/R	FBG TH	IO 235-300	8 6	4900		16600	19400
					1995 BOATS					
18	CORSO 180	OP	RNBT	FBG TR	IO 185	8	2930		7250	8700
20	FLOTEDECK 200LS	OP	RNBT	FBG TR	IO 190-275	7 9	3380	3	9400	11600
21 6	FLOTEDECK 2000LSI	OP	RNBT	FBG TR	IO 190-300	8	3400	3	10300	12600
21 6	SUPERDEK	ST	RNBT	FBG TR	OB	8	3030		9700	11000
21 6	SUPERDEK	ST	RNBT	FBG TR	IO 180-275	8	4020		11200	14000
23 11	LEGEND	OP	B/R	FBG TH	OB	8 6	3460		12400	14200
23 11	LEGEND	OP	B/R	FBG TH	IO 235-300	8 6	4350		13800	16600
					1994 BOATS					
18	CORSO 180	OP	RNBT	FBG TR	OB	8	1605		5550	6400
18	CORSO 180	OP	RNBT	FBG TR	IO 160-185	8	1605		5150	6300
20	FLOTEDECK 200LS	OP	RNBT	FBG TR	IO 180-255	7 9	2700	3	7350	8800
21 6	FLOTEDECK 2000LSI	OP	RNBT	FBG TR	IO 190-255	8	2750	3	8100	9700
21 6	SUPERDEK	ST	RNBT	FBG TR	OB	8	2075		7150	8250
21 6	SUPERDEK	ST	RNBT	FBG TR	IO 190-255	8	3015		8500	10200
23 11	LEGEND	OP	B/R	FBG TH	OB	8 6	3460		11700	13400
23 11	LEGEND	OP	B/R	FBG TH	IO 205-300	8 6	4300		12600	15400
					1993 BOATS					
18	CORSO 180	OP	RNBT	FBG TR	OB	8	1605		5350	6150
18	CORSO 180	OP	RNBT	FBG TR	IO 160-180	8	1605		4800	5550
20	FLOTEDECK 200LS	OP	RNBT	FBG TR	IO 180-260	7 9	2700	3	6850	8250
21 6	FLOTEDECK 2000LSI	OP	RNBT	FBG TR	IO 190-260	8	2750	3	7550	9100
21 6	SUPERDEK	ST	RNBT	FBG TR	OB	8	2075		6850	7850
21 6	SUPERDEK	ST	RNBT	FBG TR	IO 180-240	8	3015		8000	9450
					1992 BOATS					
18	CORSO 180	OP	RNBT	FBG TR	IO 150-180	8	1605		4450	5250
20	FLOTEDECK 200LS	OP	RNBT	FBG TR	IO 200-260	7 9	2700	3	6400	7800
21 6	FLOTEDECK 2000LSI	OP	RNBT	FBG TR	IO 230-285	8	2750	3	7250	8800
21 6	SUPERDEK	ST	RNBT	FBG TR	OB	8	2075		6550	7550
21 6	SUPERDEK	ST	RNBT	FBG TR	IO 200-260	8	3015		7500	9050
					1991 BOATS					
18	FLOTEDECK 180DLX	OP	RNBT	FBG TR	IO 175-205	8	1605		4200	5000
20	FLOTEDECK 200LS	OP	RNBT	FBG TR	IO 205-260	7 9	2700	3	6100	7350
21 6	FLOTEDECK 2000LSI	OP	RNBT	FBG TR	IO 230-260	8	2750	3	6800	8050
					1990 BOATS					
18	FLOTEDECK 180DLX	OP	RNBT	FBG TR	IO 175-205	8	1605		3950	4700
20	FLOTEDECK 200LS	OP	RNBT	FBG TR	IO 205-260	7 9	2700	3	5700	6900
21 6	FLOTEDECK 2000LSI	OP	RNBT	FBG TR	IO 230-260	8	2750	3	6400	7600
					1989 BOATS					
18	CORSO 180 DLX	OP	RNBT	FBG TR	IO 165-205	8	2230	3	4250	5000
18	CORSO 180 DXL	OP	RNBT	FBG TR	IO 175	8	2230	3	4250	4950
20	FLOTEDECK 200LS	OP	RNBT	FBG TR	OB	7 9	1400	3	4000	4650
20	FLOTEDECK 200LS	OP	RNBT	FBG TR	IO 185-260	7 9	2700	3	5300	6500
21 6	FLOTEDECK 2000LSI	OP	RNBT	FBG TR	IO 230-260	8	2750	3	6100	7350
21 6	FLOTEDECK 2000LSJ	OP	RNBT	FBG TR	IO 230-260	8	2750	3	6000	7150
					1988 BOATS					
17	FLOTEDEK 170LS	OP	RNBT	FBG TR	OB	7 9	1250		3550	4100
17	FLOTEDEK 170LS	OP	RNBT	FBG SV	OB	7 9	2200		3700	4500
17	LIMITED K 170	OP	RNBT	FBG SV	OB 165-205	7 9	1250	3 1	3550	4100
17	LIMITED K 170	OP	RNBT	FBG SV	IO 165-205	7 9	2200	3 1	3700	4500
18	FLOTEDEK 180	OP	RNBT	AL TR	128-175	8	2230		3950	4800
18	K 18	OP	RNBT	AL	128-175	8	2230		3950	4800
20	FLOTEDEK 200LS	OP	RNBT	FBG TR	OB	7 9	1400		3850	4500
20	FLOTEDEK 200LS	OP	RNBT	FBG PN	OB 200-260	7 9	2700		5100	6350
20	LIMITED K 200	OP	RNBT	FBG PN	OB	7 9	1400		3850	4500
20	LIMITED K 200	OP	RNBT	FBG SV	IO 200-260	7 9	2700		5100	6350
20	ULTIMA 2000	OP	RNBT	FBG PN	IO 230-260	7 9	2750		5350	6350
21 6	FLOTEDEK 2000LSI	OP	RNBT	FBG TR	IO 230-260	8	2750		5750	6800
					1987 BOATS					
16 7	CRUSADER	OP	RNBT	FBG TR	OB	7 3	1100	3 4	3050	3550
16 7	CRUSADER	OP	RNBT	FBG TR	IO 165-205	7 3	2000	3 4	3300	3700
16 7	CURSADER	OP	RNBT	FBG TR	130	7 3	2000		3100	3650
16 7	FLOTEDEK 160	OP	RNBT	FBG TR	OB	7 3	1100		3050	3550
16 7	FLOTEDEK 160	OP	RNBT	FBG SV	IO 130-205	7 3	2000		3100	3700
17	FLOTEDEK 170LS	OP	RNBT	FBG TR	OB	7 9	1250		3450	4000
17	FLOTEDEK 170LS	OP	RNBT	FBG SV	IO 130-205	7 9	2200		3500	4150
17	LIMITED K 170	OP	RNBT	FBG TR	OB	7 9	1250	3 1	3400	4000
17	LIMITED K 170	OP	RNBT	FBG SV	IO 130-205	7 9	2200	3 1	3500	4250
20	FLOTEDEK 200LS	OP	RNBT	FBG TR	OB	7 9	1400		3750	4350
20	FLOTEDEK 200LS	OP	RNBT	FBG SV	IO 65-260	7 9	2700		4750	5850
20	LIMITED K 200	OP	RNBT	FBG SV	OB	7 9	1400		3750	4350
20	LIMITED K 200	OP	RNBT	FBG SV	IO 165-260	7 9	2700		4800	5850
21 6	FLOTEDEK 2000LSI	OP	RNBT	FBG TR	IO 230-260	8	2750		5450	6450
					1986 BOATS					
16 7	CRUSADER K 167	OP	RNBT	FBG TR	OB	7 3	1100		2950	3450
16 7	CRUSADER K 167	OP	RNBT	FBG SV	IO 140-175	7 3	2000		3000	3500
16 7	FLOTEDEK 160	OP	RNBT	FBG TR	OB 140-175	7 3	1100		2950	3450
16 7	FLOTEDEK 160	OP	RNBT	FBG TR	OB 190 MRCR	7 3	2000		3000	3500
16 7	FLOTEDEK 160	OP	RNBT	FBG SV	IO 205 MRCR	7 3	2200		3400	3950
17	FLOTEDEK 170LS	OP	RNBT	FBG TR	OB	7 9	1250		3350	3850
17	FLOTEDEK 170LS	OP	RNBT	FBG SV	IO 140-205	7 9	2200		3300	3900
17	LIMITED K 170	OP	RNBT	FBG TR	OB	7 9	1250		3350	3850
17	LIMITED K 170	OP	RNBT	FBG SV	IO 140-205	7 9	2200		3300	3950
20	FLOTEDEK 200LS	OP	RNBT	FBG TR	OB 260 MRCR	7 9	2700		4900	5650
20	FLOTEDEK 200LS	OP	RNBT	FBG TR	OB	7 9	1400		3600	4200
20	FLOTEDEK 200LS	OP	RNBT	FBG SV	IO 185-260	7 9	2700		4600	5550
20	LIMITED K 200	OP	RNBT	FBG TR	OB	7 9	1400		3600	4200
20	LIMITED K 200	OP	RNBT	FBG SV	IO 260	7 9	2700		4900	5600
21 6	FLOTEDEK 2000LSI	OP	RNBT	FBG TR	IO 230-260	8	2750		5150	6150
21 6	FLOTEDEK 2000LSI	OP	RNBT	FBG TR	IO 230 OMC	8	2750		5150	5950
					1985 BOATS					
16 7	FLOTEDEK 160	OP	RNBT	FBG SV	IO 140-185	7 3	2000		2850	3350
16 7	FLOTEDEK 160	OP	RNBT	FBG TR	OB	7 3	1100		2850	3350
16 7	FLOTEDEK 160	OP	RNBT	FBG TR	OB 190 MRCR	7 3	2000		2900	3350
17	FLOTE-DEK 170	OP	RNBT	FBG TR	OB	7 9	1250		3250	3750
17	FLOTEDEK 170	OP	RNBT	FBG TR	IO 140-190	7 9	2200		3200	3750
17	FLOTEDEK 170LS	OP	RNBT	FBG SV	IO 190 MRCR	7 9	2200		3300	3850
17	FLOTEDEK 170LS	OP	RNBT	FBG SV	IO 185 OMC	7 9	2200		3300	3800
20	FLOTE-DEK 200	OP	RNBT	FBG TR	OB	7 9	1400		3500	4050
20	FLOTEDEK 200LS	OP	RNBT	FBG SV	IO 185-260	7 9	2700		4400	5350
20	FLOTEDEK 200LS	OP	RNBT	FBG SV	IO 260 MRCR	7 9	2700		4800	5550
20	FLOTEDEK 200LS	OP	RNBT	FBG SV	IO 260 OMC	7 9	2700		4700	5400
					1984 BOATS					
17	FLOTE-DEK 170	OP	RNBT	FBG SV	OB	7 9	1250		3150	3650
17	FLOTE-DEK 170	OP	RNBT	FBG SV	IO 198	7 9	2200		3150	3650
20	FLOTE-DEK 200	OP	RNBT	FBG SV	OB	7 9	1400		3400	3950
20	FLOTE-DEK 200	OP	RNBT	FBG SV	IO 260	7 9	2700		4550	5200

....For earlier years, see the BUC Used Boat Price Guide, Volume 3

ONTARIO YACHTS CO LTD

BURLINGTON ONTARIO CANA COAST GUARD MFG ID- ZTY See inside cover to adjust price for area

For more recent years, see the BUC Used Boat Price Guide, Volume 1

LOA FT IN	NAME AND/OR MODEL	TOP/RIG	BOAT TYPE	HULL MTL TP	ENGINE TP # HP MFG	BEAM FT IN	WGT LBS	DRAFT FT IN	RETAIL LOW	RETAIL HIGH
					1996 BOATS					
17 11	IDEAL 18	SLP	SAROD	FBG KL		6 2	1240	3 3	7550	8650
23	SONAR 23	SLP	SARCC	FBG CB		7 10	2100	3 11	11700	13300
					1993 BOATS					
18	IDEAL 18	SLP	SACAC	FBG		6 2	1200	3 3	6150	7100
23	SONAR 23	SLP	SACAC	FBG		7 8	2000	3 9	9450	10700
30	ETCHELL 22	SLP	SACAC	FBG		7	3400	4 3	18200	20300
					1992 BOATS					
18	IDEAL 18	SLP	SAIL	FBG		6 2	1200	3 3	5800	6650
23	OSPREY	OP	RNBT	FBG	IO 260 MRCR	8 10	3300	1 10	12900	14600
23	SONAR 23	SLP	SAIL	FBG		7 8	2000	3 9	8950	10200
30	ETCHELL 22	SLP	SAIL	FBG		7	3400	4 3	16800	19000
					1987 BOATS					
23	SONAR 23	SLP	SAIL	FBG KL		7 8	2100	3 9	6650	7650
30	ETCHELLS 22	SLP	SAIL	FBG KL		7 3	3400	3 6	12200	13900
32 6	GREAT-LAKES 33		TRWL	FBG SV	IO 110D	11 6	11000	3 2	48600	53400
32 6	ONTARIO 32	SLP	SA/CR	FBG KL	IB D	11	9800	4 3	37700	41900
					1986 BOATS					
28 7	ONTARIO 28	SLP	SA/CR	FBG KL	IB D	10	6800	4	23600	26200
30 6	ETCHELLS 22	SLP	SA/OD	FBG KL		6 11	3400	4 6	11000	12400
32 6	GREAT-LAKES 33		TRWL	FBG SV	IO 110D	11 6	11000	3 2	46600	51200
33 7	VIKING 34	SLP	SA/RC	FBG KL	IB D	9 10	8800	3 2	33500	35500
38 3	ONTARIO 38	CUT	SA/CR	FBG KL		12	14675	5 6	57700	63400

LOA FT IN	NAME AND/ OR MODEL	TOP/ RIG	BOAT TYPE	-HULL- MTL TP	TP	----ENGINE--- # HP	MFG	BEAM FT IN	WGT LBS	DRAFT FT IN	RETAIL LOW	RETAIL HIGH
				--- 1985 **BOATS** ---								
22 3	GAZELLE 22	SLP	SAIL	FBG KL				7 3	2018	3 8	5550	6400
28 2	VIKING 28	SLP	SA/RC	FBG KL IB		D		8 4	4755	4 6	15300	17400
28 7	ONTARIO 28	SLP	SA/CR	FBG KL IB		D		10	6800	4	22200	24700
32	ONTARIO 32	SLP	SA/CR	FBG KL IB		D		11	9800	4 6	33400	37100
32 6	GREAT-LAKES 33		TRWL	FBG SV	IO	110D		11 6	11000	3 2	44200	49100
33 7	VIKING 34	SLP	SA/RC	FBG KL IB		D		9 10	8807	6	30100	33400
38 3	ONTARIO 38	SLP	SA/CR	FBG KL				12	14675	5 6	54600	60000
38 3	ONTARIO 38	CUT	SA/CR	FBG KL				12	14675	5 6	54300	59700
				--- 1984 **BOATS** ---								
19 3	MARK 19		SAIL	FBG KL	OB			7 11	1050	4	3400	3950
22 3	GAZELLE 22	SLP	SAIL	FBG KL				7 3	2018	3 8	5250	6000
28 2	VIKING 28	SLP	SA/RC	FBG KL IB		D		8 4	4755	4 6	14400	16400
28 7	ONTARIO 28	SLP	SA/CR	FBG KL IB		15D	YAN	10	6800	4	20900	23200
30 6	ETCHELLS 22	SLP	SA/OD	FBG KL				6 11	3400	4	10400	11800
32	ONTARIO 32	SLP	SA/CR	FBG KL IB		15D-	20D	11	10000	4 6	32000	35600
32 6	GREAT-LAKES 33	FB	TRWL	FBG DS IB		124D	VLVO	11 6	11000	3 2	59100	65000
32 6	GREAT-LAKES TRAWLER	FB	TRWL	FBG SV IB		117D	VLVO	11 6	11000	3 2	58700	64600
33 7	VIKING 34	SLP	SA/RC	FBG KL IB		15D	YAN	9 10	8807	6	28300	31400

....For earlier years, see the BUC Used Boat Price Guide, Volume 3

ORCA YACHTS LLC
CHESAPEAKE VA 23323   See inside cover to adjust price for area

For more recent years, see the BUC Used Boat Price Guide, Volume 1

LOA FT IN	NAME AND/ OR MODEL	TOP/ RIG	BOAT TYPE	-HULL- MTL TP	TP	----ENGINE--- # HP	MFG	BEAM FT IN	WGT LBS	DRAFT FT IN	RETAIL LOW	RETAIL HIGH
				--- 1994 **BOATS** ---								
32 8	ORCA 28	FB	SF	FBG DV	IB	T100D-T170D		11 3	7000	2 3	63200	77400
32 8	ORCA 28	FB	SF	FBG DV	IB	T192D-T225D		11 3	7000	2 3	72300	83100
32 8	ORCA 28 EXPRESS		SF	FBG DV	IB	T100D-T170D		11 3	7000	2 3	63200	77400
32 8	ORCA 28 EXPRESS		SF	FBG DV	IB	T192D-T225D		11 3	7000	2 3	72300	83100
36	ORCA 36 EXPRESS		SF	FBG DV	IB	T250D CUM		13	15000	3	150500	165500
	IB T300D CAT 160000 176000, IB T300D CUM 156500 172000, IB T350D CAT 167000 183500											
				--- 1993 **BOATS** ---								
32 8	ORCA 28	FB	SF	FBG DV	IB	T100D-T170D		11 3	7000	2 3	60200	73700
32 8	ORCA 28	FB	SF	FBG DV	IB	T192D-T225D		11 3	7000	2 3	68900	79200
32 8	ORCA 28 EXPRESS		SF	FBG DV	IB	T100D-T170D		11 3	7000	2 3	60200	73700
32 8	ORCA 28 EXPRESS		SF	FBG DV	IB	T192D-T225D		11 3	7000	2 3	68900	79200
36	ORCA 36 EXPRESS		SF	FBG DV	IB	T250D CUM		13	15000	3	143500	157500
	IB T300D CAT 152500 167500, IB T300D CUM 149000 163500, IB T350D CAT 159000 175000											

OSPREY MARINE & ENG CO INC
MIMS FL 32754   COAST GUARD MFG ID- XSP See inside cover to adjust price for area

LOA FT IN	NAME AND/ OR MODEL	TOP/ RIG	BOAT TYPE	-HULL- MTL TP	TP	----ENGINE--- # HP	MFG	BEAM FT IN	WGT LBS	DRAFT FT IN	RETAIL LOW	RETAIL HIGH
				--- 1984 **BOATS** ---								
33	RUM-RUNNER	HT	CR	FBG SV	IB	300D CAT		11 6	9000	3	36200	40200
33	RUM-RUNNER	HT	FSH	FBG SV	IB	300D-355D		11 6	9000	3	34000	39100
33	RUM-RUNNER	HT	SF	FBG SV	IB	355D CAT		11 6	9000	3	35100	39000
40 1	RUM-RUNNER	HT	CR	FBG SV	IB	300D CAT		12	14000	3 9	69400	76200
40 1	RUM-RUNNER	HT	CR	FBG SV	IB	350D CAT		12	14000	3 9	71100	78200
40 1	RUM-RUNNER	HT	FSH	FBG SV	IB	355D CAT		12	14000	3 9	71400	78500
40 1	RUM-RUNNER	FB	SF	FBG SV	IB	355D CAT		12	14000	3 9	71400	78500
40 1	RUM-RUNNER	FB	SF	FBG SV	IB	355D CAT		12	16000	3 9	77000	84600

....For earlier years, see the BUC Used Boat Price Guide, Volume 3

OUTER LIMITS YACHTS
CLEVELAND OH 44107   COAST GUARD MFG ID- OLY See inside cover to adjust price for area

LOA FT IN	NAME AND/ OR MODEL	TOP/ RIG	BOAT TYPE	-HULL- MTL TP	TP	----ENGINE--- # HP	MFG	BEAM FT IN	WGT LBS	DRAFT FT IN	RETAIL LOW	RETAIL HIGH
				--- 1988 **BOATS** ---								
16 4	INTERNATIONAL	SLP	SA/OD	WD	CB			4 8	175	4 6	2900	3400
16 6	FIREBALL	SLP	SA/OD	WD	CB			4 8			2950	3450
				--- 1987 **BOATS** ---								
16 4	INTERNATL-FIREBALL	SLP	SA/OD	WD	CB			4 6	175	4 6	2750	3200
16 6	FIREBALL	SLP	SA/OD	WD	CB			4 6		5	2800	3250
				--- 1986 **BOATS** ---								
16 6	FIREBALL	SLP	SA/OD	WD	CB			4 6		5	2650	3050
				--- 1985 **BOATS** ---								
16 6	FIREBALL	SLP	SA/OD	WD	CB			4 6		5	2450	2850
19 10	FLYING-DUTCHMAN	SLP	SA/OD	WD	CB			5 8		8	5450	6250

OUTER REEF MARINE
PALMETTO FL 33561   COAST GUARD MFG ID- XRJ See inside cover to adjust price for area

LOA FT IN	NAME AND/ OR MODEL	TOP/ RIG	BOAT TYPE	-HULL- MTL TP	TP	----ENGINE--- # HP	MFG	BEAM FT IN	WGT LBS	DRAFT FT IN	RETAIL LOW	RETAIL HIGH
				--- 1984 **BOATS** ---								
26 6	OUTER-REEF 26	HT	TRWL	FBG DS IB		50D	LEHM	9	7500	2 6	26100	29000
26 6	OUTER-REEF 26	FB	TRWL	FBG DS IB		50D	LEHM	9	7500	2 6	26100	29000
26 6	OUTER-REEF WORKBOAT		TRWL	FBG DS IB		50D	LEHM	9	7500	2 6	26100	29000
26 6	OUTER-REEF WORKBOAT	HT	UTL	FBG DS IB		50D	LEHM	9	7500	2 6	26100	29000
26 6	OUTER-REEF YACHT		TRWL	FBG DS IB		50D	LEHM	9	7500	2 6	26100	29000
32	OUTER-REEF WORKBOAT		FSH	FBG DS IB		80D	LEHM	12	17000	3 8	66800	73400
32	OUTER-REEF WORKBOAT	HT	UTL	FBG DS IB		80D	LEHM	12	17000	3 8	66800	73400
32	OUTER-REEF YACHT		TRWL	FBG DS IB		80D	LEHM	12	17000	3 8	66800	73400
32	OUTER-REEF YACHT	HT	TRWL	FBG DS IB		80D	LEHM	12	17000	3 8	66800	73400
36	OUTER-REEF 36	HT	TRWL	FBG DS IB		120D	LEHM	12	20000	3 10	90500	99500
36	OUTER-REEF 36 WB	HT	TRWL	FBG DS IB		120D	LEHM	12	20000	3 10	62400	68500
36	OUTER-REEF WORKBOAT		FSH	FBG DS IB		120D	LEHM	12	20000	3 10	74800	82200
36	OUTER-REEF YACHT		TRWL	FBG DS IB		120D	LEHM	12	20000	3 10	76400	84000

....For earlier years, see the BUC Used Boat Price Guide, Volume 3

OVERSEAS YACHTS EAST INC
DEFEVER
HYANNIS MA 02601   See inside cover to adjust price for area

FOR LATER YEARS SEE FAR EAST & ATLANTIC

LOA FT IN	NAME AND/ OR MODEL	TOP/ RIG	BOAT TYPE	-HULL- MTL TP	TP	----ENGINE--- # HP	MFG	BEAM FT IN	WGT LBS	DRAFT FT IN	RETAIL LOW	RETAIL HIGH
				--- 1984 **BOATS** ---								
35	PT-35	FB	TRWL	FBG DS IB		215D	PERK				83100	91300
35	PT-35	FB	TRWL	FBG DS IB		T 85D	PERK				83500	91700
36	MONK PT-36	FB	TRWL	FBG DS IB		120D	LEHM	13		4	86600	95200
	IB 135D PERK 86800 95400, IB T 85D PERK 89000 97900, IB T120D LEHM 89400 98400											
	IB T135D PERK 91200 100000											
38	PT-38 DC	FB	TRWL	FBG DS IB		120D	LEHM				102500	113000
	IB 135D PERK 103500 114000, IB T 85D PERK 108000 119000, IB T120D LEHM 108000 119000											
	IB T135D PERK 110500 121500											
38	PT-38 SEDAN	FB	TRWL	FBG DS IB		120D	LEHM				102500	113000
	IB 135D PERK 103500 113500, IB T 85D PERK 108000 119000, IB T120D LEHM 108000 119000											
	IB T135D PERK 110500 121500											
38	PT-38 SPORTFISH	FB	TRWL	FBG DS IB		T240D	PERK				116000	127500
38	PT-38 SUNDECK	FB	TRWL	FBG DS IB		120D	LEHM				102500	113000
	IB 135D PERK 103500 114000, IB T 85D PERK 108000 119000, IB T120D LEHM 108000 119000											
	IB T135D PERK 110500 121500											
40 6	DEFEVER 41	FB	TRWL	FBG DS IB		120D	LEHM	14 2	27000	4	125500	138000
	IB 135D LEHM 125500 138000, IB T 85D PERK 131500 144500, IB T120D LEHM 131500 144500											
	IB T135D PERK 134000 147500											
40 7	PT-41 DC	FB	TRWL	FBG DS IB		120D	LEHM	14 2	23000	4	110500	121500
	IB 135D PERK 111500 122500, IB T 85D PERK 116500 128000, IB T135D PERK 119000 131000											
40 7	PT-41 SPORTFISH	FB	TRWL	FBG DS IB		T120D	LEHM	14 2	23000	4	117000	129000
40 7	PT-41 SPORTFISH	FB	TRWL	FBG DS IB		T215D	PERK	14 2	23000	4	121500	134000
43 10	DEFEVER 44 AFT DECK	FB	TRWL	FBG DS IB		T120D	LEHM	15	38000	4 7	180000	198000
	IB T135D PERK 182000 200000, IB T200D PERK 186000 204500, IB T215D PERK 187000 205500											
	IB T350D 195000 214500											
47 3	DEFEVER 48 DC	FB	TRWL	FBG DS IB		T120D	LEHM	15	56000	4 9	184000	202000
	IB T135D PERK 185000 203000, IB T200D PERK 188500 207000, IB T215D PERK 189500 208000											
	IB T350D 197500 217000											
49	DEFEVER 49 PH	FB	TRWL	FBG DS IB		T120D	LEHM	15	60000		180000	198000
	IB T135D PERK 182000 200000, IB T200D PERK 189000 207500, IB T215D PERK 190500 209500											
	IB T350D 203500 223500											
51 7	DEFEVER 52 MY	FB	TRWL	FBG DS IB		T215D	GM	16 8	77253	4 9	242500	266000
51 7	DEFEVER 52 MY	FB	TRWL	FBG DS IB		T215D	PERK	16 8	77253	4 9	244500	268500

LOA FT	LOA IN	NAME AND/ OR MODEL	TOP/ RIG	BOAT TYPE	-HULL- MTL	-HULL- TP	ENGINE TP	ENGINE #	ENGINE HP	ENGINE MFG	BEAM FT	BEAM IN	WGT LBS	DRAFT FT	DRAFT IN	RETAIL LOW	RETAIL HIGH
		1984 BOATS															
60		DEFEVER 60 MY	FB	TRWL	FBG	DS	IB	T	D	CAT						**	**
66		DEFEVER 66 CPTMY	FB	TRWL	FBG	DS	IB	T	D	CAT						**	**

OY AVANCE YACHTS AB

LARSMO FINLAND

See inside cover to adjust price for area

SPARKMAN & STEPHENS INC
NEW YORK NY 10016

LOA FT	LOA IN	NAME AND/ OR MODEL	TOP/ RIG	BOAT TYPE	-HULL- MTL	-HULL- TP	ENGINE TP	ENGINE #	ENGINE HP	ENGINE MFG	BEAM FT	BEAM IN	WGT LBS	DRAFT FT	DRAFT IN	RETAIL LOW	RETAIL HIGH
		1986 BOATS															
24	6	AVANCE 245	SLP	SAIL	FBG	KL					8	4	3850	4	8	11500	13100
33	10	AVANCE 33	SLP	SA/RC	FBG	KL					8	7	8800	5	6	33400	37100
35	5	AVANCE 36	SLP	SA/RC	FBG	KL					9		11000	5	10	43900	48800
40		AVANCE 40	SLP	SA/RC	FBG	KL					12	7	19600	7	5	83600	91800
		1985 BOATS															
24	6	AVANCE 245	SLP	SAIL	FBG	KL					8	4	3850	4	8	10800	12300
33	10	AVANCE 33	SLP	SA/RC	FBG	KL					8	7	8800	5	6	31400	34900
35	5	AVANCE 36	SLP	SA/RC	FBG	KL					9		11000	5	10	41300	45900
40		AVANCE 40	SLP	SA/RC	FBG	KL					12	7	19600	7	5	78600	86400
		1984 BOATS															
33	7	AVANCE 33	SLP	SA/RC	F/S	KL					8	5	8800	5	5	29400	32600
35	4	AVANCE 36	SLP	SA/RC	F/S	KL					9		11000	5	8	38800	43100
40		AVANCE 40	SLP	SA/RC	F/S	KL					12	6	18700	7	4	71600	78700

OY NYKRA AB

NYKARLEBY FINLAND

See inside cover to adjust price for area

LOA FT	LOA IN	NAME AND/ OR MODEL	TOP/ RIG	BOAT TYPE	-HULL- MTL	-HULL- TP	ENGINE TP	ENGINE #	ENGINE HP	ENGINE MFG	BEAM FT	BEAM IN	WGT LBS	DRAFT FT	DRAFT IN	RETAIL LOW	RETAIL HIGH
		1986 BOATS															
30	9	SUNWIND 31		SAIL	FBG	KL					9	6	7269	5		21100	23400
		1985 BOATS															
30	9	SUNWIND 31		SAIL	FBG						9	6	7269	5		19800	22000

OYSTER MARINE LTD

IPSWICH SUFFOLK UNITED KINGDOM

See inside cover to adjust price for area

OYSTER USA
NEWPORT RI 02840

For more recent years, see the BUC Used Boat Price Guide, Volume 1

LOA FT	LOA IN	NAME AND/ OR MODEL	TOP/ RIG	BOAT TYPE	-HULL- MTL	-HULL- TP	ENGINE TP	ENGINE #	ENGINE HP	ENGINE MFG	BEAM FT	BEAM IN	WGT LBS	DRAFT FT	DRAFT IN	RETAIL LOW	RETAIL HIGH
		1996 BOATS															
41	11	OYSTER 42	SLP	SACAC	FBG	KL	IB		59D	VLVO	12	10	24000	6		273500	300500
44	4	OYSTER 45	SLP	SACAC	FBG	KL	IB		59D	VLVO	14		32000	6	6	341000	374500
48	6	OYSTER 485	SLP	SACAC	FBG	KL	IB		80D	PERK	14		37550	7	2	411500	452500
49		OYSTER 49 PH	SLP	SACIS	FBG	KL	IB		80D	PERK	14		38000	7		423500	465500
55	3	OYSTER 55	SLP	SACAC	FBG	KL	IB		80D	PERK	15	9	46000	7	6	623500	685500
55	3	OYSTER 55 PH	SLP	SACIS	FBG	KL	IB		80D	PERK	15	9	50000	7	8	631500	693500
61		OYSTER 61	CUT	SACAC	FBG	KL	IB		130D	PERK	16	10	62000	8	4	953000	1.035M
70	7	OYSTER 70	SLP	SACAC	FBG	KL	IB		225D	PERK	17	3	90000	9	1	1.350M	1.470M
79	6	OYSTER 80	CUT	SACAC	FBG	KL	IB		275D	FORD	19		58T	9	7	**	**
79	6	OYSTER 80 PH	CUT	SACIS	FBG	KL	IB		275D	FORD	19		58T	9	7	**	**
		1995 BOATS															
43	5	OYSTER 435	CUT	SACAC	FBG	KL	IB		50D	PERK	13	8	30000	6	5	294500	323500
43	5	OYSTER 435	KTH	SACAC	FBG	KL	IB		59D	PERK	13	9	30000	6	5	310000	341000
48	6	OYSTER 485	SLP	SACAC	FBG	KL	IB		82D	PERK	14		37550	7		385500	423500
48	6	OYSTER 485	CUT	SACAC	FBG	KL	IB		82D	PERK	14		37550	7		377000	414000
48	9	OYSTER 49 PH	SLP	SACIS	FBG	KL	IB		82D	PERK	14		42000	7		406500	446500
55	3	OYSTER 55	SLP	SACAC	FBG	KL	IB		82D	PERK	15	9	50000	7	7	590500	648500
55	3	OYSTER 55 PH	SLP	SACIS	FBG	KL	IB		82D	PERK	15	9	55000	7	8	599000	658500
61		OYSTER 61	SLP	SACAC	FBG	KL	IB		130D	PERK	16	10	62000	8	3	887000	974500
61		OYSTER 61	CUT	SACAC	FBG	KL	IB		130D	PERK	16	10	62000	8	3	881500	968500
61		OYSTER 61 PH	SLP	SACIS	FBG	KL	IB		130D	PERK	16	10	62000	8	3	887000	974500
67	6	OYSTER 68	SLP	SACAC	FBG	KL	IB		150D	PERK	17	3	85500	8	11	1.205M	1.305M
67	6	OYSTER 68	CUT	SACAC	FBG	KL	IB		150D	PERK	17	3	85500	8	11	1.205M	1.305M
69	6	OYSTER 70 PH	SLP	SACIS	FBG	KL	IB		150D	PERK	17	3	90000	9		1.260M	1.370M
69	6	OYSTER 70 PH	CUT	SACIS	FBG	KL	IB		150D	PERK	17	3	90000	9		1.260M	1.370M
79	6	OYSTER 80	CUT	SACAC	FBG	KL	IB		275D	FORD	19		58T	9	6	**	**
79	6	OYSTER 80	SLP	SACIS	FBG	KL	IB		275D	FORD	19		58T	9	6	**	**
79	6	OYSTER 80 PH	SLP	SACIS	FBG	KL	IB		275D	FORD	19		58T	9	6	**	**
79	6	OYSTER 80 PH	CUT	SACIS	FBG	KL	IB		275D	FORD	19		58T	9	6	**	**
		1994 BOATS															
55	3	OYSTER 55 PH	SLP	SACAC	FBG	KL	IB		82D	PERK	15	9	55000	7	8	560000	615500
61		OYSTER 61 DH	SLP	SACAC	FBG	KL	IB		130D	PERK	16	10	62000	8	3	829500	911500
69	6	OYSTER 70 PH	SLP	SACAC	FBG	KL	IB		150D	PERK	17	3	90000	9		1.180M	1.285M
		1993 BOATS															
46		OYSTER 461 DECKHOUSE	SLP	SACAC	FBG	KL	IB		60D	PERK	14		37250	7		312500	343500
48	6	OYSTER 485 DECKHOUSE	SLP	SACAC	FBG	KL	IB		60D	PERK	14		37550	7		337000	370000
		1990 BOATS															
49		OYSTER 49 PILOTHOUSE	SLP	SACAC	FBG	KL	IB		60D	PERK	14		42000	7		293000	322000
		1989 BOATS															
48		OYSTER 48	SLP	SACAC	FBG	KL	IB		60D	PERK	14	4	32000	6	3	238500	262000
68		OYSTER 68 DECKHOUSE	SLP	SACAC	FBG	KL	IB		60D	PERK	17	3	85500	8	11	816000	897000
		1986 BOATS															
34	8	HUSTLER SJ35	SLP	SA/RC	FBG	KL	IB		15D	YAN	11	5	7620	6	3	38900	43300
37		OYSTER-HERITAGE 37	SLP	SA/CR	FBG	KC	IB		36D	VLVO	12		15500	4	3	80800	88700
37		OYSTER-HERITAGE 37	SLP	SA/CR	FBG	KL	IB		36D	VLVO	12		15500	5	3	80500	88500
37		OYSTER-HERITAGE 37PH	SLP	SA/CR	FBG	KC	IB		36D	VLVO	12		15500	4	3	91400	100500
37		OYSTER-HERITAGE 37PH	SLP	SA/CR	FBG	KL	IB		36D	VLVO	12		15500	5	3	91100	100000
39	8	OYSTER 41	SLP	SA/RC	FBG	KL	SD		23D	VLVO	13	7	13000	6	10	86800	95300
39	8	OYSTER 41	SLP	SA/RC	FBG	KL	SD		35D	VLVO	13	7	13000	6	10	87200	95900
40	6	OYSTER 406	SLP	SA/CR	FBG	KC	IB		51D	PERK	12	9	22000	4	3	129000	142000
40	6	OYSTER 406	SLP	SA/CR	FBG	KL	IB		51D	PERK	12	9	22000	5	9	129000	142000
42		OYSTER 42	SLP	SA/CR	FBG	CB	SD		61D	VLVO	13	8	22600	4	6	137000	150500
42		OYSTER 42	SLP	SA/CR	FBG	KL	SD		61D	VLVO	13	8	22600	6		137000	150500
42	5	OYSTER 43	SLP	SA/RC	FBG	KL	SD		35D	VLVO	14	1	16600	7	6	115500	127000
43	5	OYSTER 435	SLP	SA/CR	FBG	KL					13	8	27500	6		155000	170500
43	5	OYSTER 435	KTH	SA/CR	FBG	CB	SD		61D	VLVO	13	8	22600	4	6	149500	164500
43	5	OYSTER 435	KTH	SA/CR	FBG	KL	SD		61D	VLVO	13	8	22600	6		149500	164500
46	2	OYSTER 46	KTH	SA/CR	FBG	KL	IB		85D	PERK	14		32000	6	6	192500	211500
53		OYSTER 53	SLP	SA/CR	FBG	KC	IB		85D	PERK	15	9	40800	5	9	271500	298500
53		OYSTER 53	SLP	SA/CR	FBG	KL	IB		85D	PERK	15	9	40800	7		271500	298500
53		OYSTER 53	KTH	SA/CR	FBG	KC	IB		85D	PERK	15	9	40800	5	9	279000	307000
53		OYSTER 53	KTH	SA/CR	FBG	KL	IB		85D	PERK	15	9	40800	7		279000	307000
55		OYSTER 55 DECKHOUSE	SLP	SACAC	FBG	KL	IB		60D	PERK	15	9	50000	7	7	317500	349000
		1985 BOATS															
34	8	OYSTER SJ35	SLP	SA/RC	FBG	KL	IB		15D	YAN	11	5	8550	6	3	41200	45700
35	1	OYSTER-MARINER 35	SLP	SA/CR	FBG	KL	IB				12	5	17116	5	3	80100	88000
37		OYSTER-HERITAGE 37	SLP	SA/CR	FBG	KC	IB		28D	VLVO	12		15500	4	3	80600	88500
37		OYSTER-HERITAGE 37	SLP	SA/CR	FBG	KL	IB		28D	VLVO	12		15500	5	3	80300	88200
37		OYSTER-HERITAGE 37PH	SLP	SA/CR	FBG	KC	IB		36D	VLVO	12		15500	4	3	80800	88800
37		OYSTER-HERITAGE 37PH	SLP	SA/CR	FBG	KL	IB		36D	VLVO	12		15500	5	3	80500	88500
39	6	OYSTER 39	KTH	SA/CR	FBG	KL	IB				12	10	23000	5	10	124500	137000
39	8	OYSTER 41	SLP	SA/RC	FBG	KL	IB		28D	VLVO	13	7	13000	6	10	81400	89400
39	8	OYSTER 41	SLP	SA/RC	FBG	KL	IB		36D	VLVO	13	7	13000	6	10	81700	89700
40	6	OYSTER 406	SLP	SA/CR	FBG	KC	IB		51D	PERK	12	9	20500	4	3	115500	127000
40	6	OYSTER 406	SLP	SA/CR	FBG	KL	IB		51D	PERK	12	9	20500	5	9	115500	127000
42		OYSTER 42	SLP	SA/CR	FBG	CB	SD		51D	PERK	13	8	27500	4	6	143000	157000
42		OYSTER 42	SLP	SA/CR	FBG	KL	SD		51D	PERK	13	8	27500	6		143000	157000
42	5	OYSTER 43	SLP	SA/RC	FBG	KL	IB		36D	VLVO	14	1	16600	7	6	108000	119000
43	5	OYSTER 435	KTH	SA/CR	FBG	CB	SD		61D	VLVO	13	8	27500	4	6	155500	171000
43	5	OYSTER 435	KTH	SA/CR	FBG	KL	SD		61D	VLVO	13	8	27500	6		155500	171000
46	2	OYSTER 46	KTH	SA/CR	FBG	KL	IB		85D	PERK	14		34500	6	6	186000	204500
53		OYSTER 53	SLP	SA/CR	FBG	KC	IB		85D	PERK	15	9	40800	5	9	254000	279000
53		OYSTER 53	SLP	SA/CR	FBG	KL	IB		85D	PERK	15	9	40800	7		254000	279000
53		OYSTER 53	KTH	SA/CR	FBG	KC	IB		85D	PERK	15	9	40800	5	9	261000	287000
53		OYSTER 53	KTH	SA/CR	FBG	KL	IB		85D	PERK	15	9	40800	7		261000	287000
		1984 BOATS															
34	8	HUSTLER SJ35	SLP	SA/RC	FBG	KL	IB		12D	YAN	11	5	7620	6	3	34400	38200
35	1	OYSTER-MARINER 35	SLP	SA/CR	FBG	KL	SD		23D	VLVO	12	5	16000	5	3	71400	78400
35	1	OYSTER-MARINER 35	SLP	SA/CR	FBG	KL	SD		35D	VLVO	12	5	16000	5	3	71500	78600
35	1	OYSTER-MARINER 35	SLP	SA/CR	FBG	KL	IB		40D	PERK	12	5	16000	5	3	71400	78400
35	1	OYSTER-MARINER 35	KTH	SA/CR	FBG	KL	SD		23D	VLVO	12	5	16000	5	3	72400	79600
35	1	OYSTER-MARINER 35	KTH	SA/CR	FBG	KL	SD		35D	VLVO	12	5	16000	5	3	72600	79800
35	1	OYSTER-MARINER 35	KTH	SA/CR	FBG	KL	IB		40D	PERK	12	5	16000	5	3	72400	79600
37		OYSTER-HERITAGE 37	SLP	SA/CR	FBG	KC	IB		30D	VLVO	12		15500	4	3	73600	80800
37		OYSTER-HERITAGE 37	SLP	SA/CR	FBG	KL	IB		36D	VLVO	12		15500	5	3	73400	80700
37		OYSTER-HERITAGE 37PH	SLP	SA/CR	FBG	KC	IB		30D	VLVO	12		15500	4	3	77800	85500
37		OYSTER-HERITAGE 37PH	SLP	SA/CR	FBG	KL	IB		36D	VLVO	12		15500	5	3	77700	85300
39	6	OYSTER 39	KTH	SA/CR	FBG	KL	SD		61D	VLVO	12	10	19500	5	10	106500	117000
39	6	OYSTER 39	KTH	SA/CR	FBG	KL	IB		85D	PERK	12	10	19500	5	10	102500	112500
39	8	OYSTER 41	SLP	SA/RC	FBG	KL	SD		23D	VLVO	13	7	13000	6	10	76100	83600
39	8	OYSTER 41	SLP	SA/RC	FBG	KL	SD		35D	VLVO	13	7	13000	6	10	76500	84100
42		OYSTER 435	SLP	SA/CR	FBG	CB	SD		61D	VLVO	13	8	22600	4	6	120000	132000

CONTINUED ON NEXT PAGE

LOA FT	LOA IN	NAME AND/ OR MODEL	TOP/ RIG	BOAT TYPE	-HULL- MTL	-HULL- TP	ENGINE TP	ENGINE # HP	ENGINE MFG	BEAM FT	BEAM IN	WGT LBS	DRAFT FT	DRAFT IN	RETAIL LOW	RETAIL HIGH
		1984 BOATS														
42		OYSTER 435	SLP	SA/CR	FBG	KL	SD	61D	VLVO	13	8	22600	6		120000	132000
42	5	OYSTER 43	SLP	SA/RC	FBG	KL	SD	35D	VLVO	14	1	16600	7	6	101500	111500
43	5	OYSTER 435	KTH	SA/CR	FBG	CB	SD	61D	VLVO	13	8	22600	4	6	131500	144500
43	5	OYSTER 435	KTH	SA/CR	FBG	KL	SD	61D	VLVO	13	8	22600	6		131500	144500
43	6	OYSTER 435 DECKHOUSE	SLP	SACAC	FBG	KL	IB	60D	PERK	13	9	30000	6	5	145500	160000
46	2	OYSTER 46	KTH	SA/CR	FBG	KL	IB	85D	PERK	14		32000	6	6	169000	185500

....For earlier years, see the BUC Used Boat Price Guide, Volume 3

OZARK BOAT WORKS INC

MOUNTAIN VIEW MO 65548 COAST GUARD MFG ID- XBW See inside cover to adjust price for area

LOA FT	LOA IN	NAME AND/ OR MODEL	TOP/ RIG	BOAT TYPE	-HULL- MTL	-HULL- TP	ENGINE TP	ENGINE # HP	ENGINE MFG	BEAM FT	BEAM IN	WGT LBS	DRAFT FT	DRAFT IN	RETAIL LOW	RETAIL HIGH
		1993 BOATS														
16		PANFISHER 1630V	OP	BASS	FBG	DV	OB			6		595			1800	2150
16		PANFISHER 1640V	OP	BASS	FBG	DV	OB			6		605			1850	2200
16	2	SPORTFISHER 1630MV	OP	BASS	FBG	SV	OB			6	5	725			2250	2600
16	2	SPORTFISHER 1640MV	OP	BASS	FBG	SV	OB			6	5	760			2350	2700
16	7	SPORTFISHER 1670V	OP	BASS	FBG	SV	OB			6	10	1025			3050	3550
16	7	SPORTFISHER 1680V	OP	BASS	FBG	SV	OB			6	10	1025			3200	3700
16	10	FISH & SKI	OP	RNBT	FBG	SV	OB			6	9	1060			3250	3750
17		FISH & SKI	OP	RNBT	FBG	DV	OB			7	1	1150			3500	4050
17		NORSEMAN	OP	UTL	FBG	DV	OB			7	1	1050			3200	3700
17		WALLEYE	OP	UTL	FBG	DV	OB			7	1	1050			3100	3600
18	2	1830 MV	OP	BASS	FBG	SV	OB			6	8	1250			3650	4250
18	2	1840 MV	OP	BASS	FBG	SV	OB			6	8	1250			4050	4700
		1992 BOATS														
16		PANFISHER 1630V	OP	BASS	FBG	DV	OB			6		595			1750	2050
16	2	SPORTFISHER 1610MV	OP	BASS	FBG	SV	OB			6	5	625			1850	2200
16	2	SPORTFISHER 1620MV	OP	CTRCN	FBG	SV	OB			6	5	750			2250	2600
16	2	SPORTFISHER 1630MV	OP	BASS	FBG	SV	OB			6	5	725			2150	2500
16	2	SPORTFISHER 1640MV	OP	BASS	FBG	SV	OB			6	5	760			2250	2650
16	2	SPORTFISHER 1670V	OP	BASS	FBG	SV	OB			6	5	1025			2950	3450
16	10	FISH & SKI	OP	RNBT	FBG	SV	OB			6	9	1060			3100	3600
17		FISH & SKI	OP	RNBT	FBG	DV	OB			7	1	1150			3350	3900
17		MUSKIE 1740V	OP	UTL	FBG	DV	OB			7	1	1050			3000	3500
17		NORSEMAN	OP	UTL	FBG	DV	OB			7	1	1050			3050	3550
17		WALLEYE	OP	CTRCN	FBG	DV	OB			7	1	1040			3050	3550
17		WALLEYE	OP	UTL	FBG	DV	OB			7	1	990			2850	3350
18	2	1830 MV DELUXE	OP	BASS	FBG	SV	OB			6	8	1250			3950	4600
18	2	1830 MV STANDARD	OP	BASS	FBG	SV	OB			6	8	1250			3250	3800
18	2	1840 MV DELUXE	OP	BASS	FBG	SV	OB			6	8	1250			4100	4750
18	2	1840 MV STANDARD	OP	BASS	FBG	SV	OB			6	8	1250			3500	4100
		1991 BOATS														
16		PANFISHER 1600V	OP	BASS	FBG	DV	OB			6		495			1400	1650
16		PANFISHER 1610V	OP	BASS	FBG	DV	OB			6		525			1500	1750
16		PANFISHER 1620V	OP	CTRCN	FBG	DV	OB			6		575			1600	1900
16		PANFISHER 1630V	OP	BASS	FBG	DV	OB			6		595			1650	2000
16		PANFISHER 1640V	OP	BASS	FBG	DV	OB			6		605			1700	2000
16	2	SPORTFISHER 1610MV	OP	BASS	FBG	SV	OB			6	5	625			1750	2100
16	2	SPORTFISHER 1620MV	OP	CTRCN	FBG	SV	OB			6	5	750			2150	2500
16	2	SPORTFISHER 1630MV	OP	BASS	FBG	SV	OB			6	5	725			2050	2450
16	2	SPORTFISHER 1640MV	OP	BASS	FBG	SV	OB			6	5	760			2200	2550
16	10	FIERA 1760MV	OP	RNBT	FBG	SV	IO	150	OMC	6	9	1800			4050	4700
16	10	FIERA 1760MV	OP	RNBT	FBG	SV	IO	175-185		6	9	1800			4150	5100
16	10	FIERA 1760MV	OP	RNBT	FBG	SV	IO	200		6	9	1800			4200	5200
16	10	FISH & SKI	OP	RNBT	FBG	SV	OB			6	9	1060			3000	3500
17		CIELO 1760V	OP	RNBT	FBG	SV	IO	150-200		7	1	2000			4500	5600
17		FISH & SKI	OP	RNBT	FBG	DV	OB			7	1	1150			3200	3750
17		MUSKIE 1740V	OP	UTL	FBG	DV	OB			7	1	1050			2900	3400
17		NORSEMAN	OP	UTL	FBG	DV	OB			7	1	1050			2950	3400
17		WALLEYE	OP	CTRCN	FBG	DV	OB			7	1	1040			2950	3450
17		WALLEYE	OP	UTL	FBG	DV	OB			7	1	990			2750	3200
		1990 BOATS														
16		COMBINATION V-162	OP	BASS	FBG	SV	OB			6		605			1650	1950
16		FISHERMAN F-161	OP	BASS	FBG	SV	OB			6		595			1600	1900
16	2	COMBINATION F-166	OP	BASS	FBG	TR	OB			6	5	750			2050	2400
16	2	FISHERMAN V-161	OP	BASS	FBG	TR	OB			6	5	725			1950	2350
16	10	FIERRA T-174	OP	RNBT	FBG	TR	IO	120-209		6	9	1800			4100	4900
16	10	FISH AND SKI T-174	OP	RNBT	FBG	SV	OB			6	9	1060			2950	3450
16	10	RUNABOUT T-174RA	OP	RNBT	FBG	SV	OB			6	9	1060			2800	3300
17		CIELO V-174	OP	RNBT	FBG	SV	IO	120-209		7	1	1950			4450	5250
17		FISH AND SKI V-174	OP	RNBT	FBG	SV	OB			7	1	1150			3200	3700
17		MUSKIE V-171	OP	BASS	FBG	SV	OB			7	1	1050			2850	3350
17		NORSEMAN V-171	OP	BASS	FBG	SV	OB			7	1	1050			2900	3350
17		RUNABOUT V-174RA	OP	RNBT	FBG	SV	OB			7	1	1150			3050	3550
		1989 BOATS														
16		CLASSIC V-161	OP	BASS	FBG	SV	OB			6		595			1550	1850
16		COMBINATION V-162	OP	BASS	FBG	SV	OB			6		605			1600	1900
16		FISHERMAN V-161	OP	BASS	FBG	SV	OB			6		595			1550	1850
16	2	CALIENTE	OP	RNBT	FBG	TR	OB			6	5	1020			2650	3100
16	2	COMBINATION F-162	OP	BASS	FBG	TR	OB			6	5	795			2100	2500
16	2	F-166	OP	BASS	FBG		OB			6	5	750			1950	2350
16	2	FISHERMAN F-162	OP	BASS	FBG	TR	OB			6	5	725			1900	2250
16	10	FIERA	OP	RNBT	FBG	TR	IO	128-130		7	8	1800			3900	4500
16	10	FISH AND SKI	OP	RNBT	FBG	TR	OB			6	9	1060			2850	3350
16	10	RUNABOUT T-174RA	OP	RNBT	FBG	TR	OB			6	9	1060			2750	3200
17		CIELO	OP	RNBT	FBG	SV	IO	128-130		7	1	2000			3900	4550
17		FISH AND SKI	OP	RNBT	FBG	SV	OB			7	1	1150			3100	3600
17		MARAUDER	OP	BASS	FBG	SV	OB			7	1	930			2550	2950
17		MUSKIE	OP	BASS	FBG	SV	OB			7	1	1050			2750	3250
17		NORSEMAN	OP	BASS	FBG	SV	OB			7	1	1050			2800	3250
17		RENEGADE	OP	BASS	FBG	SV	OB			7	1	930			2500	2900
17		RENEGADE II XV-172	OP	BASS	FBG	SV	OB			7	1	985			2650	3050
17		RUNABOUT V-174RA	OP	RNBT	FBG	SV	OB			7	1	1150			2950	3450
18	1	REGENCY	OP	RNBT	FBG	SV	IO	175-260		7	8	2500			4950	6100
		1988 BOATS														
16		CLASSIC V-161	OP	BASS	FBG	SV	OB			6		595			1500	1800
16		COMBINATION V-161	OP	BASS	FBG	SV	OB			6		605			1550	1850
16		FISHERMAN V-161	OP	BASS	FBG	SV	OB			6		595			1500	1800
16	2	COMBINATION F-162	OP	BASS	FBG	TR	OB			6	5	725			1950	2350
16	2	F-166	OP	BASS	FBG		OB			6	5	725			1850	2200
16	2	FISHERMAN F-161	OP	BASS	FBG	TR	OB			6	5	725			1750	2050
16	2	T-164 CALIENTE	OP	RNBT	FBG	TR	OB			6	5	1020			2600	3000
16	10	FIERA	OP	RNBT	FBG	TR	IO	128-130		7	8	1800			3700	4300
16	10	FISH AND SKI	OP	RNBT	FBG	TR	OB			6	9	1060			2800	3250
16	10	RUNABOUT T-174RA	OP	RNBT	FBG	TR	OB			6	9	1060			2650	3100
17		CIELO	OP	RNBT	FBG	SV	IO	128-130		7	1	2000			3750	4350
17		FISH AND SKI	OP	RNBT	FBG	SV	OB			7	1	1150			3000	3500
17		MARAUDER	OP	BASS	FBG	SV	OB			7	1	930			2450	2850
17		MUSKIE	OP	BASS	FBG	SV	OB			7	1	1050			2700	3100
17		NORSEMAN	OP	BASS	FBG	SV	OB			7	1	1050			2750	3150
17		RENEGADE	OP	BASS	FBG	SV	OB			7	1	930			2400	2800
17		RENEGADE II XV-172	OP	BASS	FBG	SV	OB			7	1	985			2550	3000
17		RUNABOUT V-174RA	OP	RNBT	FBG	SV	OB			7	1	1150			2850	3350
18		REGENCY	OP	RNBT	FBG	SV	IO	175-260		7	8	2500			4700	5800
		1987 BOATS														
16		CLASSIC V-161	OP	BASS	FBG	SV	OB			6		595			1450	1750
16		COMBINATION V-162	OP	BASS	FBG	SV	OB			6	5	1010			2500	2900
16		FISHERMAN V-161	OP	BASS	FBG	SV	OB			6		595			1450	1750
16		MUSKIE	OP	FSH	FBG	SV	OB			6		485			1200	1450
16	2	CALIENTE	OP	RNBT	FBG	TR	OB			6	4	1020			2500	2900
16	2	CLASSIC T-164	OP	RNBT	FBG	TR	OB			6	4	990			2450	2850
16	2	COMBINATION F-162	OP	BASS	FBG	TR	OB			6	5	725			1900	2300
16	2	F-163 CENTER CONSOLE	OP	CTRCN	FBG	TR	OB			6	5	750			1850	2200
16	2	FISHERMAN V-161	OP	BASS	FBG	TR	OB			6	5	725			1700	2000
16	10	FISH AND SKI	OP	RNBT	FBG	TR	OB			6	9	1060			2650	3050
17		MARAUDER	OP	BASS	FBG	SV	OB			7	1	930			2400	2800
17		RENEGADE	OP	BASS	FBG	SV	OB			7	1	930			2350	2700
18		FIERA	OP	RNBT	FBG	TR	IO	120-175		7	8	2500			4450	5150
18		REGENCY	OP	RNBT	FBG	SV	IO	175-260		7	8	2500			4800	5550
18		REGENCY V-180	OP	RNBT	FBG	SV	IO	200		7	8	2500			4550	5250
		1985 BOATS														
16		V-161	OP	BASS	FBG	SV	OB			6		595			1400	1650
16		V-162	OP	BASS	FBG	SV	OB			6		605			1400	1700
16		V-165	OP	FSH	FBG	SV	OB			6		485			1150	1350
16	2	F-161	OP	BASS	FBG	TR	OB			6	5	725			1700	2050
16	2	F-163	OP	CTRCN	FBG	TR	OB			6	5	750			1750	2100
16	2	F-165	OP	FSH	FBG	TR	OB			6	5	580			1350	1650
16	2	T-164	OP	RNBT	FBG	TR	OB			6	4	990			2300	2700
16	10	T-174	OP	RNBT	FBG	TR	OB			6	9	1060			2500	2900
17		MARAUDER XV-170	OP	BASS	FBG	SV	OB			7	1	930			2300	2650
17		SV-17	OP	BASS	FBG	SV	OB			6		710			1750	2050
18		V-180	ST	RNBT	FBG	SV	IO	170-260		7	8	2500			4100	5050
		1984 BOATS														
16		V-161	OP	BASS	FBG	SV	OB			5	10	595			1350	1650
16		V-162	OP	BASS	FBG	SV	OB			5	10	605			1400	1650
16		V-165	OP	FSH	FBG	SV	OB			5	10	450			1050	1250
16	2	F-161	OP	BASS	FBG	TR	OB			6	5	725			1650	2000

 CONTINUED ON NEXT PAGE

OZARK BOAT WORKS INC -CONTINUED See inside cover to adjust price for area

LOA FT	IN	NAME AND/ OR MODEL	TOP/ RIG	BOAT TYPE	HULL MTL	HULL TP	ENGINE TP	# HP	MFG	BEAM FT	BEAM IN	WGT LBS	DRAFT FT	DRAFT IN	RETAIL LOW	RETAIL HIGH
		1984 BOATS														
16	2	F-163	OP	CTRCN	FBG	TR	OB			6	5	750			1700	2050
16	2	F-165	OP	FSH	FBG	TR	OB			6	5	545			1250	1500
16	2	T-164	OP	RNBT	FBG	TR	OB			6	4	990			2300	2650
17		SV-17	OP	BASS	FBG	SV	OB			6		710			1700	2050
18		V-180	ST	RNBT	FBG	SV	IO	170-230		7	8	2500			3950	4700

....For earlier years, see the BUC Used Boat Price Guide, Volume 3

PACE YACHT CORP

ANNAPOLIS MD 21401

See inside cover to adjust price for area

LOA FT	IN	NAME AND/ OR MODEL	TOP/ RIG	BOAT TYPE	HULL MTL	HULL TP	ENGINE TP	# HP	MFG	BEAM FT	BEAM IN	WGT LBS	DRAFT FT	DRAFT IN	RETAIL LOW	RETAIL HIGH
		1989 BOATS														
33		PACE 33	FB	EXP	FBG	SV	IB	T350	CRUS	13	2	17000	2	5	51900	57000
33		PACE 33	FB	EXP	FBG	SV	IB	T250D-T320D		13	2	17000	2	5	65600	76200
36		PACE 36	FB	SDNSF	FBG	SV	IB	T350	CRUS	13	3	20000	2	9	70500	77400
		IB T250D CUM 79300 87100, IB T300D CUM 81700 89800, IB T320D CAT													84600	92900
40		PACE 40	FB	DCMY	FBG	SV	IB	T350	CRUS	14	1	30000	2	11	118500	130500
40		PACE 40	FB	DCMY	FBG	SV	IB	T320D	CAT	14	1	30000	2	11	135000	148500
40		PACE 40	FB	SDNSF	FBG	SV	IB	T375D	CAT	14		28000	2	9	133500	146500
40		PACE 40	FB	SDNSF	FBG	SV	IB	T400D	J&T	14		28000	2	9	133000	146000
40		PACE 40	FB	SDNSF	FBG	SV	IB	T450D	J&T	14		30000	2	9	144500	158500
48		PACE 48	FB	SDNSF	FBG	SV	IB	T550D	J&T	15		40000	4	4	173500	190500
48		PACE 48	FB	SDNSF	FBG	SV	IB	T750D	J&T	15		40000	4	4	201000	220500
57		PACE 57	FB	MY	FBG	SV	IB	T750D	J&T	19	8	62000	4	8	296000	325500
		1988 BOATS														
33		PACE 33	FB	EXP	FBG	SV	IB	T350	CRUS	13	2	15000	2	5	47800	52500
33		PACE 33	FB	EXP	FBG	SV	IB	T250D-T320D		13	2	15000	2	5	58400	68200
36		PACE 36	FB	SDNSF	FBG	SV	IB	T350	CRUS	13	3	20000	2	9	67400	74000
36		PACE 36	FB	SDNSF	FBG	SV	IB	T250D	CUM	13	3	20000	2	9	75800	83300
36		PACE 36	FB	SDNSF	FBG	SV	IB	T320D	CAT	13	3	20000	2	9	80800	88800
40		40		SF	FBG		IB			14	1	30000	2	11	**	**
40		PACE 40	FB	DCMY	FBG	SV	IB	T320D	CAT	14	1	30000	2	11	129000	142000
40		PACE 40	FB	SDNSF	FBG	SV	IB	400D	J&T	14		28000	2	9	114000	125000
40		PACE 40	FB	SDNSF	FBG	SV	IB	T375D	CAT	14		28000	2	9	127500	140000
40		PACE 40	FB	SDNSF	FBG	SV	IB	T450D	J&T	14		30000	2	9	138000	151500
48		PACE 48	FB	SDNSF	FBG	SV	IB	T550D	J&T	15		40000	4	4	166000	182000
48		PACE 48	FB	SDNSF	FBG	SV	IB	T750D	J&T	15		40000	4	4	192000	211000
57		PACE 57	FB	MY	FBG	SV	IB	750D	J&T	19	8	62000	4	8	216500	237500
		1987 BOATS														
33		PACE 33	FB	EXP	FBG	SV	IB	T350	CRUS	13	2	15000	2	5	45600	50100
33		PACE 33	FB	EXP	FBG	SV	IB	T320D	CAT	13	2	15000	2	5	59400	65300
33		PACE 33	FB	SDNSF	FBG	SV	IB	T350	CRUS	13	2	17000	2	5	47400	52000
36		PACE 36	FB	SDNSF	FBG	SV	IB	T350	CRUS	13	3	20000	2	9	64400	70800
36		PACE 36	FB	SDNSF	FBG	SV	IB	T320D	CAT	13	3	20000	2	9	77300	84900
36		PACE 36	FB	SDNSF	FBG	SV	IB	T375D	CAT	13	3	20000	2	9	80600	88600
40		PACE 40	FB	DCMY	FBG	SV	IB	T225D	CAT	14	1	30000	2	11	118000	129500
40		PACE 40	FB	DCMY	FBG	SV	IB	T320D	CAT	14	1	30000	2	11	123500	136000
40		PACE 40	FB	SDNSF	FBG	SV	IB	T375D	CAT	14		28000	2	9	122000	134000
40		PACE 40	FB	SDNSF	FBG	SV	IB	T450D	J&T	14		30000	2	9	132000	145000
48		PACE 48	FB	SDNSF	FBG	SV	IB	T750D	J&T	15		40000	4	4	183500	201500

PACEMAKER

DIV OF SEIDELMANN YACHTS
BERLIN NJ 08009 COAST GUARD MFG ID- XFR

See inside cover to adjust price for area

LOA FT	IN	NAME AND/ OR MODEL	TOP/ RIG	BOAT TYPE	HULL MTL	HULL TP	ENGINE TP	# HP	MFG	BEAM FT	BEAM IN	WGT LBS	DRAFT FT	DRAFT IN	RETAIL LOW	RETAIL HIGH
		1992 BOATS														
16		PACE CRAFT	OP	UTL	FBG	FL	OB			6	3	700	1	4	1250	1500
18		PACE CRAFT	OP	UTL	FBG	FL	OB			7	6	1200	1	4	2050	2450
21		PACE CRAFT	OP	UTL	FBG	FL	OB			7	8	1600	1	4	2650	3050
22		PACE CRAFT	OP	UTL	FBG	FL	OB			8	6	1800	1	4	3000	3500
33	10	PACEMAKER 34	FB	CNV	FBG	SV	IB	T365		14	3	16000	3	6	72000	79100
33	10	PACEMAKER 34	FB	DC	FBG	SV	IB	T300D		14	3	16000	3	6	83900	92200
33	10	PACEMAKER 34	FB	SF	FBG	SV	IB	T350D		14	3	16000	3	6	87200	95800
36	10	PACEMAKER 37	FB	CNV	FBG	SV	IB	T365		14	3	20000	3	8	84800	93100
36	10	PACEMAKER 37	FB	DC	FBG	SV	IB	T400D		14	3	20000	3	8	105000	115500
36	10	PACEMAKER 37	FB	SF	FBG	SV	IB	T450D		14	3	22000	3	8	116000	127500
39	10	PACEMAKER 40	FB	SF	FBG	SV	IB	T365		14	3	30000	3	10	136000	149500
39	10	PACEMAKER 40	FB	SF	FBG	SV	IB	T450D		14	3	30000	3	10	165000	181000
39	10	PACEMAKER 40	FB	SF	FBG	SV	IB	T600D		14	3	30000	3	10	182500	200500
		1991 BOATS														
33	10	PACEMAKER 34 CNV	FB	CNV	FBG	SV	IB	T350-T365		13	10	15000	3	6	67000	74100
33	10	PACEMAKER 34 S/F	FB	SF	FBG	SV	IB	T350	CRUS	13	10		3	6	53800	59200
33	10	PACEMAKER 34 S/F	FB	SF	FBG	SV	IB	T300D-T400D		13	10		3	6	71700	85600
36	10	PACEMAKER 37 CNV	FB	CNV	FBG	SV	IB	T350	CRUS	14		20000	4		81900	89900
36	10	PACEMAKER 37 CNV	FB	CNV	FBG	SV	IB	T365	MPC	14		20000	4		81700	89800
36	10	PACEMAKER 37 S/F	FB	SF	FBG	SV	IB	T350	CRUS	14			3	6	83600	91900
36	10	PACEMAKER 37 S/F	FB	SF	FBG	SV	IB	T300D	CUM	14			3	6	95700	105000
36	10	PACEMAKER 37 S/F	FB	SF	FBG	SV	IB	T400D	GM	14			3	6	103500	113500
		1990 BOATS														
33	10	PACEMAKER 33 CNV	FB	CNV	FBG	SV	IB	T340-T350		13	10	15000	3	6	63200	69800
33	10	PACEMAKER 34 S/F	FB	SF	FBG	SV	IB	T350	CRUS	13	10		3	6	51200	56300
33	10	PACEMAKER 34 S/F	FB	SF	FBG	SV	IB	T300D-T400D		13	10		3	6	68600	81700
36	10	PACEMAKER 36	FB	CNV	FBG	SV	IB	T340	MRCR	14		20000	4		77200	84800
36	10	PACEMAKER 36	FB	CNV	FBG	SV	IB	T350	CRUS	14		20000	4		78100	85900
36	10	PACEMAKER 37 S/F	FB	SF	FBG	SV	IB	T350	CRUS	14			3	6	79800	87700
36	10	PACEMAKER 37 S/F	FB	SF	FBG	SV	IB	T300D	CUM	14			3	6	91400	100500
36	10	PACEMAKER 37 S/F	FB	SF	FBG	SV	IB	T400D	GM	14			3	6	98700	108500
		1989 BOATS														
25	10	PACEMAKER 26 FB	FB	SF	FBG	SV	IB	260	MRCR	9	10	7500	2	6	20000	22200
30	8	PACEMAKER 31	FB	SF	FBG	SV	IB	T260	MRCR	11	6	12000	2	6	40100	44500
33	10	PACEMAKER 33 CNV	FB	CNV	FBG	SV	IB	T340	MRCR	13	10	15000	3	6	60100	66100
36	10	PACEMAKER 36	FB	CNV	FBG	SV	IB	T340	MRCR	14		29000	4		97100	106500
		1988 BOATS														
25	10	PACEMAKER 26 FB	FB	SF	FBG	SV	IB	260	MRCR	9	10	7500	2	6	19200	21400
30	8	PACEMAKER 31	FB	SF	FBG	SV	IB	T260	MRCR	11	6	12000	2	6	38200	42400
36	10	PACEMAKER 36	FB	CNV	FBG	SV	IB	T340	MRCR	14		29000	4		92800	102000
		1987 BOATS														
25	10	PACEMAKER 26	FB	SF	FBG	SV	IB	230-340		9	10	7000	2	2	16900	20100
25	10	WAHOO 26	OP	CTRCN	FBG	SV	IB	230-340		9	10	6400	1	8	15800	18900
25	10	WAHOO 26	OP	CTRCN	FBG	SV	IB	165D-260D		9	10	6400	1	8	20200	25000
25	10	WAHOO 26	OP	CTRCN	FBG	SV	IB	T130	MPC	9	10	6400	1	8	16400	18600
30	8	PACEMAKER 31	FB	SF	FBG	SV	IB	D	GM	11	6	12000	2	6	**	**
30	8	PACEMAKER 31	FB	SF	FBG	SV	IB	T230-T340		11	6	12000	2	6	35800	42400
30	8	PACEMAKER 31	FB	SF	FBG	SV	IB	T D	GM	11	6	12000	2	6	**	**
36	10	PACEMAKER 36	FB	CNV	FBG	SV	IB	D		14			4		**	**
36	10	PACEMAKER 36	FB	CNV	FBG	SV	IB	T340	MRCR	14			4		70900	77900
		1986 BOATS														
24	2	SEIDELMANN 245	SLP	SA/RC	FBG	KL	OB			8		3000	4	5	5600	6400
25	10	WAHOO 26	OP	CTRCN	FBG	SV	IB	165D		9	10	6400	1	8	19800	22000
29	5	SEIDELMANN 295	SLP	SA/RC	FBG	KL	OB			10	2	7200	6	2	15100	17200
29	11	SEIDELMANN 30T	SLP	SA/RC	FBG	KL	IB	D		11		8800	5	5	19200	21300
34		SEIDELMANN S34	SLP	SA/RC	FBG	KL	IB	D		11	10	11000	5	5	23500	26200
36	10	SEIDELMANN S37	SLP	SA/RC	FBG	KL	IB	D		12		13500	6		29900	33200
		1985 BOATS														
19	2	WAHOO 20	OP	CTRCN	FBG	SV	OB			7	11	2300	1	7	2800	3250
24	2	SEIDELMANN 245	SLP	SA/RC	FBG	KC	OB			8		3000	1	11	5250	6050
25	10	WAHOO 26	OP	CTRCN	FBG	SV	IB	165D		9	10	6400	1	8	19100	21300
29	5	SEIDELMANN 295	SLP	SA/CR	FBG	KC	OB			10	2	7200	3	3	14200	16200
29	5	SEIDELMANN 295 DEEP	SLP	SA/CR	FBG	KL	IB	15D	YAN	10	2	7400	5	5	14900	17000
29	5	SEIDELMANN 295 MID	SLP	SA/CR	FBG	KL	IB	15D		10	2	7400	4		14900	16900
29	5	SEIDELMANN 295 SHOAL	SLP	SA/CR	FBG	KC	IB	15D	YAN	10	2	7400	3	3	14900	17000
29	11	SEIDELMANN 30T DEEP	SLP	SA/CR	FBG	KL	IB	15D	YAN	11		8800	5	5	18200	20200
29	11	SEIDELMANN 30T SHOAL	SLP	SA/CR	FBG	KL	IB	15D	YAN	11		8800	4	2	18200	20200
34		SEIDELMANN 34 DEEP	SLP	SA/CR	FBG	KL	IB	19D	YAN	11	10	11000	5	5	22100	24600
34		SEIDELMANN 34 SHOAL	SLP	SA/CR	FBG	KL	IB	19D	YAN	11	10	11000	3	11	22100	24600
36	10	SEIDELMANN 37 DEEP	SLP	SA/CR	FBG	KL	IB	19D	YAN	12		13500	6	4	28000	31100
36	10	SEIDELMANN 37 SHOAL	SLP	SA/CR	FBG	KL	IB	19D	YAN	12		13900	4	5	28700	31900
		1984 BOATS														
24	2	SEIDELMANN 245	SLP	SA/CR	FBG	KL	OB			8		3000	1	11	4950	5650
24	6	SEIDELMANN 25 DEEP	SLP	SA/CR	FBG	KL	IB	8D	YAN	9	6	4600	4	4	7950	9150
24	6	SEIDELMANN 25 SHOAL	SLP	SA/CR	FBG	KL	OB			9	6	4600	3	3	7350	8450
28	5	SEIDELMANN 285	SLP	SA/CR	FBG	KL	OB			10		5400	5	1	9800	11200
29	5	SEIDELMANN 295	SLP	SA/CR	FBG	KC	OB			10	2	7200	3	3	13400	15200
29	5	SEIDELMANN 295	SLP	SA/CR	FBG	KC	IB	15D	YAN	10	2	7400	3	3	14000	15900
29	11	SEIDELMANN 299 DEEP	SLP	SA/CR	FBG	KL	IB	15D	YAN	11		8800	5	5	13900	15800
29	11	SEIDELMANN 30T	SLP	SA/CR	FBG	KL	IB	15D	YAN	11		8800	5	5	18600	20700
29	11	SEIDELMANN 30T SHOAL	SLP	SA/CR	FBG	KL	IB	15D	YAN	11		8800	4	2	18600	20700
34		SEIDELMANN 34 DEEP	SLP	SA/CR	FBG	KL	IB	23D	YAN	11	10	11000	5	5	20800	23200
34		SEIDELMANN 34 MID	SLP	SA/CR	FBG	KL	IB	23D	YAN	11	10	11000	4	9	20800	23200
34		SEIDELMANN 34 SHOAL	SLP	SA/CR	FBG	KL	IB	23D	YAN	11	10	11000	3	11	20800	23200
35	7	SEIDELMANN 375 DEEP	SLP	SA/CR	FBG	KL	IB	20D	YAN	12		11500	6	3	22100	24600
36	10	SEIDELMANN 37 DEEP	SLP	SA/CR	FBG	KL	IB	23D	YAN	12		13500	5	11	26400	29300
36	10	SEIDELMANN 37 MID	SLP	SA/CR	FBG	KL	IB	23D	YAN	12		13500	4	11	26400	29300
36	10	SEIDELMANN 37 SHOAL	SLP	SA/CR	FBG	KL	IB	23D	YAN	12		13900	4		27100	30100

....For earlier years, see the BUC Used Boat Price Guide, Volume 3

PACIFIC BOATS INC

SANTA CRUZ CA 95062 COAST GUARD MFG ID- PCX See inside cover to adjust price for area

LOA FT	LOA IN	NAME AND/ OR MODEL	TOP/ RIG	BOAT TYPE	HULL MTL	HULL TP	ENGINE TP	ENGINE # HP	ENGINE MFG	BEAM FT	BEAM IN	WGT LBS	DRAFT FT	DRAFT IN	RETAIL LOW	RETAIL HIGH
		1986 BOATS														
25		OLSON 25	SLP	SA/RC	F/S	KL	OB			9		2900	4	6	10500	11900
25		OLSON 25	SLP	SA/RC	FBG	KL	IB	D		9		2900	4	6	11700	13300
29	8	OLSON 29	SLP	SA/RC	F/S	KL	IB	8D	YAN	9	4	3700	5	7	16500	18700
29	11	OLSON 911-S	SLP	SA/RC	F/S	KL	IB	18D	YAN	10	4	7200	5	5	32700	36300
30		OLSON 30	SLP	SA/RC	FBG	KL	IB	D		9	3	3600	5	1	16200	18400
34		OLSON 34	SLP	SA/RC	F/S	KL	IB	15D	YAN	10	10	7500	6		35800	39800
40	4	OLSON 40	SLP	SA/RC	F/S	KL	IB	23D	YAN	11	6	10350	6	6	69500	76400
		1985 BOATS														
25		OLSON 25	SLP	SA/RC	F/S	KL	OB			9		2900	4	6	9950	11300
30		OLSON 30	SLP	SA/RC	F/S	KL	OB			9	3	3600	5	1	14900	16900
40	4	OLSON 40	SLP	SA/RC	F/S	KL	IB	23D	YAN	11	6	10350	6	6	65900	72400
		1984 BOATS														
25		OLSON 25	SLP	SA/RC	F/S	KL	OB			9		2800	4	6	9250	10500
30		OLSON 30	SLP	SA/RC	F/S	KL	OB			9	3	3600	5	1	14100	16100
30		OLSON 30	SLP	SA/RC	F/S	KL	IB	7D	YAN	9	3	3600	5	1	14400	16400
40	4	OLSON 40	SLP	SA/RC	F/S	KL	IB	23D	YAN	11	6	10350	6	6	62400	68600

....For earlier years, see the BUC Used Boat Price Guide, Volume 3

PACIFIC SEACRAFT CORP

FULLERTON CA 92831 COAST GUARD MFG ID- PCS See inside cover to adjust price for area

For more recent years, see the BUC Used Boat Price Guide, Volume 1

LOA FT	LOA IN	NAME AND/ OR MODEL	TOP/ RIG	BOAT TYPE	HULL MTL	HULL TP	ENGINE TP	ENGINE # HP	ENGINE MFG	BEAM FT	BEAM IN	WGT LBS	DRAFT FT	DRAFT IN	RETAIL LOW	RETAIL HIGH
		1996 BOATS														
24		FLICKA 20	SLP	SACAC	FBG	KL	IB	10D	YAN	8		6000	3	3	32200	35800
24		FLICKA 20	CUT	SACAC	FBG	KL	IB	10D	YAN	8		6000	3	3	32200	35800
27	3	DANA 24	SLP	SACAC	FBG	KL	IB	18D	YAN	8	7	8000	3	10	48900	53700
27	3	DANA 24	CUT	SACAC	FBG	KL	IB	18D	YAN	8	7	8000	3	10	48900	53700
31	10	PS CLASSIC 31	SLP	SACAC	FBG	KL	IB	30D		9	10	11000	4		82700	90900
31	10	PS VOYAGEMAKER 31	SLP	SACAC	FBG	KL	IB	30D		9	10	11000	4		87500	96200
31	10	PS VOYAGEMAKER 31	CUT	SACAC	FBG	KL	IB	30D		9	10	11000	4		83900	92200
32	10	PS PILOTHOUSE 32	SLP	SACIS	FBG	KL	IB	38D		9	10	12600	4	1	97300	107000
32	10	PS PILOTHOUSE 32	CUT	SACIS	FBG	KL	IB	38D		9	10	12600	4	1	97300	107000
34	1	PS CLASSIC 34	SLP	SACAC	FBG	KL	IB	38D		10		13500	4	1	98400	108000
34	1	PS VOYAGEMAKER 34	SLP	SACAC	FBG	KL	IB	38D	YAN	10		13500	4	1	112500	123500
34	1	PS VOYAGEMAKER 34	CUT	SACAC	FBG	KL	IB	38D		10		13500	4	1	105000	115000
34	1	PS VOYAGER 34	SLP	SACAC	FBG	KL	IB	38D	YAN	10		13500	4	11	111000	122000
36	11	PS CLASSIC 37	SLP	SACAC	FBG	KL	IB	50D	YAN	10	10	16000	4	5	128500	141000
36	11	PS CLASSIC 37	SLP	SACAC	FBG	KL	IB	50D	YAN	10	10	16000	5	6	127500	140000
36	11	PS VOYAGEMAKER 37	CUT	SACAC	FBG	KL	IB	50D	YAN	10	10	16000	4	5	128500	141000
36	11	PS VOYAGEMAKER 37	CUT	SACAC	FBG	KL	IB	50D	YAN	10	10	16000	5	6	126000	138500
42	2	PS PILOTHOUSE 40	CUT	SACIS	FBG	KL	IB	62D	YAN	12	5	24500	5	1	210500	231000
42	2	PS PILOTHOUSE 40	CUT	SACIS	FBG	KL	IB	62D	YAN	12	5	24500	6		210500	231000
42	2	PS VOYAGEMAKER 40	SLP	SACAC	FBG	KL	IB	50D	YAN	12	5	23000	5	1	202000	222000
42	7	PS VOYAGER 40	CUT	SACAC	FBG	KL	IB	50D	YAN	12	5	23000	6		189500	208000
44	1	PS 44 CR ED	CUT	SACAC	FBG	KL	IB	50D	YAN	12	8	27500	6	3	239500	263500
44	1	PS VOYAGEMAKER 44 CR	CUT	SACAC	FBG	KL	IB	50D	YAN	12	8	27500	5	3	241500	265500
		1995 BOATS														
24		FLICKA 20	SLP	SACAC	FBG	KL	IB	10D	YAN	8		5500	3	3	27700	30800
24		FLICKA 20	CUT	SACAC	FBG	KL	IB	10D	YAN	8		5500	3	3	27700	30800
27	3	DANA 24	SLP	SACAC	FBG	KL	IB	18D	YAN	8	7	8000	3	10	46500	51200
27	3	DANA 24	CUT	SACAC	FBG	KL	IB	18D	YAN	8	7	8000	3	10	46500	51200
31	10	PACIFIC-SEACRAFT 31	SLP	SACAC	FBG	KL	IB	30D	YAN	9	10	11000	4	11	78900	86700
31	10	PACIFIC-SEACRAFT 31	CUT	SACAC	FBG	KL	IB	30D	YAN	9	10	11000	4	11	78800	86600
32	10	PACIFIC-SEACRAFT PH	SLP	SACAC	FBG	KL	IB	38D		9	10	11600	4	1	84900	93300
32	10	PACIFIC-SEACRAFT PH	CUT	SACAC	FBG	KL	IB	38D	YAN	9	10	10000	4	1	73800	81100
34	1	CREALOCK 34	SLP	SACAC	FBG	KL	IB	38D	YAN	10		13500	4	11	97200	107000
34	1	CREALOCK 34	CUT	SACAC	FBG	KL	IB	38D	YAN	10		13500	4	11	98600	108500
34	1	CREALOCK 34 VOYAGER	SLP	SACAC	FBG	KL	IB	38D	YAN	10		13500	4	11	101500	111500
36	11	CREALOCK 37	SLP	SACAC	FBG	KL	IB	50D	YAN	10	10	16000	5	6	121000	133000
36	11	CREALOCK 37	CUT	SACAC	FBG	KL	IB	50D	YAN	10	10	16000	5	6	119500	131000
36	11	CREALOCK 37 VOYAGER	CUT	SACAC	FBG	KL	IB	50D	YAN	10	10	16000	5	6	124000	136000
41	7	CREALOCK 40 VOYAGER	CUT	SACAC	FBG	KL	IB	50D	YAN	12	5	23000	6	1	179500	197000
44		CREALOCK 44 CR ED	CUT	SACAC	FBG	KL	IB	50D	YAN	12	8	27500	6	3	226000	248500
		1994 BOATS														
24		FLICKA 20	SLP	SACAC	FBG	KL	IB	10D	YAN	8		6000	3	3	28900	32100
24		FLICKA 20	CUT	SACAC	FBG	KL	IB	10D	YAN	8		6000	3	3	28900	32100
27	3	DANA 24	SLP	SACAC	FBG	KL	IB	18D	YAN	8	7	8000	3	10	43600	48400
27	3	DANA 24	CUT	SACAC	FBG	KL	IB	18D	YAN	8	7	8000	3	10	43600	48400
30	11	ORION 27	SLP	SACAC	FBG	KL	IB	27D	YAN	9	3	10000	3	10	63700	70000
30	11	ORION 27	CUT	SACAC	FBG	KL	IB	27D	YAN	9	3	10000	3	10	63700	70000
31	10	PACIFIC-SEACRAFT 31	SLP	SACAC	FBG	KL	IB	30D	YAN	9	10	11000	4	11	74700	82100
31	10	PACIFIC-SEACRAFT 31	CUT	SACAC	FBG	KL	IB	30D	YAN	9	10	11000	4	11	74600	82000
32	10	PACIFIC-SEACRAFT PH	SLP	SACAC	FBG	KL	IB	38D		9	10	11600	4	1	80400	88300
32	10	PACIFIC-SEACRAFT PH	CUT	SACAC	FBG	KL	IB	38D	YAN	9	10	10000	4	1	69900	76800
34	1	CREALOCK 34	SLP	SACAC	FBG	KL	IB	38D	YAN	10		13200	4	11	90300	99200
34	1	CREALOCK 34	CUT	SACAC	FBG	KL	IB	38D	YAN	10		13200	4	11	91500	100500
34	1	CREALOCK 34 VOYAGER	SLP	SACAC	FBG	KL	IB	38D	YAN	10		13200	4	11	93800	103000
36	11	CREALOCK 37	SLP	SACAC	FBG	KL	IB	50D	YAN	10	10	16000	5	6	114500	126000
36	11	CREALOCK 37	CUT	SACAC	FBG	KL	IB	50D	YAN	10	10	13200	5	6	96900	106500
36	11	CREALOCK 37 VOYAGER	CUT	SACAC	FBG	KL	IB	50D	YAN	10	10	16000	5	6	115000	126500
44		CREALOCK 44 CR ED	CUT	SACAC	FBG	KL	IB	50D	YAN	12	8	27500	6	3	214000	235000
		1993 BOATS														
24		FLICKA 20	SLP	SACAC	FBG	KL	IB	10D	YAN	8		5500	3	3	24900	27600
24		FLICKA 20	CUT	SACAC	FBG	KL	IB	10D	YAN	8		5500	3	3	24900	27600
27	3	DANA 24	SLP	SACAC	FBG	KL	IB	18D	YAN	8	7	8000	3	10	41300	45900
27	3	DANA 24	CUT	SACAC	FBG	KL	IB	18D	YAN	8	7	8000	3	10	41300	45900
30	11	ORION 27	SLP	SACAC	FBG	KL	IB	27D	YAN	9	3	10000	3	10	60400	66300
30	11	ORION 27	CUT	SACAC	FBG	KL	IB	27D	YAN	9	3	10000	3	10	60400	66300
31	10	PACIFIC-SEACRAFT 31	SLP	SACAC	FBG	KL	IB	27D	YAN	9	10	11000	4	11	69400	76300
31	10	PACIFIC-SEACRAFT 31	CUT	SACAC	FBG	KL	IB	27D	YAN	9	10	11000	4	11	69400	76300
31	10	PACIFIC-SEACRAFT SHL	SLP	SACAC	FBG	KL	IB	27D	YAN	9	10	11000	4		73100	80300
31	10	PACIFIC-SEACRAFT SHL	CUT	SACAC	FBG	KL	IB	27D	YAN	9	10	11000	4		73100	80300
32	10	PACIFIC-SEACRAFT PH	SLP	SACAC	FBG	KL	IB	43D	VLVO	9	10	11600	5		75800	83300
32	10	PACIFIC-SEACRAFT PS	SLP	SACAC	FBG	KL	IB	43D	VLVO	9	10	11600	4	1	76500	84100
34	1	CREALOCK 34	SLP	SACAC	FBG	KL	IB	34D	YAN	10		13200	4	11	86100	94700
34	1	CREALOCK 34	CUT	SACAC	FBG	KL	IB	34D	YAN	10		13200	4	11	85000	93400
34	1	CREALOCK 34 SHOAL	SLP	SACAC	FBG	KL	IB	34D	YAN	10		13200	4	1	87200	95800
34	1	CREALOCK 34 SHOAL	CUT	SACAC	FBG	KL	IB	34D	YAN	10		13200	4	1	86100	94700
34	1	CREALOCK 34 VOYAGER	SLP	SACAC	FBG	KL	IB	34D	YAN	10		13200	4	11	87000	95600
34	1	CREALOCK 34 VOYAGER	CUT	SACAC	FBG	KL	IB	34D	YAN	10		13200	4	11	88100	96800
34	1	CREALOCK 34 VYGR SH	SLP	SACAC	FBG	KL	IB	34D	YAN	10		13200	4	1	88100	96800
34	1	CREALOCK 34 VYGR SH	CUT	SACAC	FBG	KL	IB	34D	YAN	10		13200	4	1	89200	98000
36	11	CREALOCK 37	SLP	SACAC	FBG	KL	IB	40D	YAN	10	10	16000	5	6	106000	116500
36	11	CREALOCK 37	CUT	SACAC	FBG	KL	IB	40D	YAN	10	10	13200	5	6	91500	100500
36	11	CREALOCK 37	YWL	SACAC	FBG	KL	IB	40D	YAN	10	10	16000	5	6	106000	116500
36	11	CREALOCK 37 SHOAL	SLP	SACAC	FBG	KL	IB	40D	YAN	10	10	16000	4	5	111500	122500
36	11	CREALOCK 37 SHOAL	CUT	SACAC	FBG	KL	IB	40D	YAN	10	10	16000	4	5	109500	120500
36	11	CREALOCK 37 SHOAL	YWL	SACAC	FBG	KL	IB	40D	YAN	10	10	16000	4	5	111500	122500
36	11	CREALOCK 37 VOYAGER	CAT	SACAC	FBG	KL	IB	50D	YAN	10	10	16000	5	6	109000	120000
36	11	CREALOCK 37 VOYAGER	SLP	SACAC	FBG	KL	IB	50D	YAN	10	10	16000	5	6	108500	119000
36	11	CREALOCK 37 VYGR SH	SLP	SACAC	FBG	KL	IB	50D	YAN	10	10	16000	4	5	109500	120500
36	11	CREALOCK 37 VYGR SH	CUT	SACAC	FBG	KL	IB	50D	YAN	10	10	16000	4	5	109000	120000
44		CREALOCK 44	CUT	SACAC	FBG	KL	IB	50D	YAN	12	8	27500	6	3	199000	218500
44		CREALOCK 44 SHOAL	CUT	SACAC	FBG	KL	IB	50D	YAN	12	8	27500	5	3	208500	229000
		1992 BOATS														
24		FLICKA 20	SLP	SAIL	FBG	KL	IB	10D	YAN	8		5500	3	3	25500	28300
24		FLICKA 20	CUT	SAIL	FBG	KL	IB	10D	YAN	8		5500	3	3	25500	28300
27	3	DANA 24	SLP	SAIL	FBG	KL	IB	18D	YAN	8	7	8000	3	10	44400	49300
27	3	DANA 24	CUT	SAIL	FBG	KL	IB	18D	YAN	8	7	8000	3	10	44400	49300
30	11	ORION 27	SLP	SAIL	FBG	KL	IB	27D	YAN	9	3	10000	4		61700	67800
30	11	ORION 27	CUT	SAIL	FBG	KL	IB	27D	YAN	9	3	10000	4		61700	67800
31	10	PACIFIC-SEACRAFT 31	SLP	SAIL	FBG	KL	IB	27D	YAN	9	10	11000	4	11	68200	74900
31	10	PACIFIC-SEACRAFT 31	CUT	SAIL	FBG	KL	IB	27D	YAN	9	10	11000	4	11	68100	74900
31	10	PACIFIC-SEACRAFT SHL	SLP	SAIL	FBG	KL	IB	27D	YAN	9	10	11000	4		69200	76000
31	10	PACIFIC-SEACRAFT SHL	CUT	SAIL	FBG	KL	IB	27D	YAN	9	10	11000	4		69200	76100
34	1	CREALOCK 34	SLP	SAIL	FBG	KL	IB	34D	YAN	10		13500	4	11	83800	92000
34	1	CREALOCK 34	CUT	SAIL	FBG	KL	IB	34D	YAN	10		13500	4	11	83800	92000
34	1	CREALOCK 34 SHOAL	SLP	SAIL	FBG	KL	IB	34D	YAN	10		13500	4	1	84800	93200
34	1	CREALOCK 34 SHOAL	CUT	SAIL	FBG	KL	IB	34D	YAN	10		13500	4	1	84800	93200
36	11	CREALOCK 37	SLP	SAIL	FBG	KL	IB	40D	YAN	10	10	16000	5	6	102500	112500
36	11	CREALOCK 37	CUT	SAIL	FBG	KL	IB	40D	YAN	10	10	16000	5	6	102000	112000
36	11	CREALOCK 37	YWL	SAIL	FBG	KL	IB	40D	YAN	10	10	16000	5	6	102500	112500
36	11	CREALOCK 37 SHOAL	SLP	SAIL	FBG	KL	IB	40D	YAN	10	10	16000	4	5	103500	114000
36	11	CREALOCK 37 SHOAL	CUT	SAIL	FBG	KL	IB	40D	YAN	10	10	16000	4	5	104000	114000
36	11	CREALOCK 37 SHOAL	YWL	SAIL	FBG	KL	IB	40D	YAN	10	10	16000	4	5	103500	114000
44		CREALOCK 44	CUT	SAIL	FBG	KL	IB	50D	YAN	12	8	27500	6	3	192000	211000
44		CREALOCK 44 SHOAL	CUT	SAIL	FBG	KL	IB	50D	YAN	12	8	27500	5	3	194000	213000
		1991 BOATS														
24		FLICKA 20	SLP	SAIL	FBG	KL	IB	10D	YAN	8		5500	3	3	24100	26800
24		FLICKA 20	CUT	SAIL	FBG	KL	IB	10D	YAN	8		5500	3	3	24100	26800
27	3	DANA 24	SLP	SAIL	FBG	KL	IB	18D	YAN	8	7	8000	3	10	42100	46700
27	3	DANA 24	CUT	SAIL	FBG	KL	IB	18D	YAN	8	7	8000	3	10	42100	46700
30	11	ORION 27	SLP	SAIL	FBG	KL	IB	27D	YAN	9	3	10000	4		58400	64200

LOA FT	LOA IN	NAME AND/ OR MODEL	TOP/ RIG	BOAT TYPE	-HULL- MTL	-HULL- TP	ENGINE TP	# HP	MFG	BEAM FT	BEAM IN	WGT LBS	DRAFT FT	DRAFT IN	RETAIL LOW	RETAIL HIGH
		1991 BOATS														
30	11	ORION 27	CUT	SAIL	FBG	KL	IB	27D	YAN	9	3	10000	4		58400	64200
31	10	PACIFIC-SEACRAFT 31	SLP	SAIL	FBG	KL	IB	27D	YAN	9	10	11000	4	11	64600	71000
31	10	PACIFIC-SEACRAFT 31	CUT	SAIL	FBG	KL	IB	27D	YAN	9	10	11000	4	11	64500	70900
31	10	PACIFIC-SEACRAFT SHL	SLP	SAIL	FBG	KL	IB	27D	YAN	9	10	11000	4		65500	72000
31	10	PACIFIC-SEACRAFT SHL	CUT	SAIL	FBG	KL	IB	27D	YAN	9	10	11000	4		65600	72100
34	1	CREALOCK 34	SLP	SAIL	FBG	KL	IB	34D	YAN	10		13500	4	11	79300	87200
34	1	CREALOCK 34	CUT	SAIL	FBG	KL	IB	34D	YAN	10		13500	4	11	79300	87200
34	1	CREALOCK 34 SHOAL	SLP	SAIL	FBG	KL	IB	34D	YAN	10		13500	4	1	80300	88200
34	1	CREALOCK 34 SHOAL	CUT	SAIL	FBG	KL	IB	34D	YAN	10		13500	4	1	80300	88200
36	11	CREALOCK 37	SLP	SAIL	FBG	KL	IB	40D	YAN	10	10	16000	5	6	97000	106500
36	11	CREALOCK 37	CUT	SAIL	FBG	KL	IB	40D	YAN	10	10	16000	5	6	96700	106500
36	11	CREALOCK 37	YWL	SAIL	FBG	KL	IB	40D	YAN	10	10	16000	5	6	97000	106500
36	11	CREALOCK 37 SHOAL	SLP	SAIL	FBG	KL	IB	40D	YAN	10	10	16000	4	5	98200	108000
36	11	CREALOCK 37 SHOAL	CUT	SAIL	FBG	KL	IB	40D	YAN	10	10	16000	4	5	98500	108000
36	11	CREALOCK 37 SHOAL	YWL	SAIL	FBG	KL	IB	40D	YAN	10	10	16000	4	5	98200	108000
44		CREALOCK 44	CUT	SAIL	FBG	KL	IB	50D	YAN	12	8	27500	6	3	182000	200000
44		CREALOCK 44 SHOAL	CUT	SAIL	FBG	KL	IB	50D	YAN	12	8	27500	5	3	183500	202000
		1990 BOATS														
24		FLICKA 20	SLP	SAIL	FBG	KL	IB	10D	YAN	8		5500	3	3	22900	25400
24		FLICKA 20	CUT	SAIL	FBG	KL	IB	10D	YAN	8		5500	3	3	22900	25400
27	3	DANA 24	SLP	SAIL	FBG	KL	IB	18D	YAN	8	7	8000	3	10	39800	44300
27	3	DANA 24	CUT	SAIL	FBG	KL	IB	18D	YAN	8	7	8000	3	10	39800	44300
30	11	ORION 27	SLP	SAIL	FBG	KL	IB	27D	YAN	9	3	10000	4		55400	60800
30	11	ORION 27	CUT	SAIL	FBG	KL	IB	27D	YAN	9	3	10000	4		55400	60800
31	10	PACIFIC-SEACRAFT 31	SLP	SAIL	FBG	KL	IB	27D	YAN	9	10	11000	4	11	61100	67200
31	10	PACIFIC-SEACRAFT 31	CUT	SAIL	FBG	KL	IB	27D	YAN	9	10	11000	4	11	61200	67200
31	10	PACIFIC-SEACRAFT SHL	SLP	SAIL	FBG	KL	IB	27D	YAN	9	10	11000	4		62100	68300
31	10	PACIFIC-SEACRAFT SHL	CUT	SAIL	FBG	KL	IB	27D	YAN	9	10	11000	4		62100	68200
34	1	CREALOCK 34	SLP	SAIL	FBG	KL	IB	34D	YAN	10		13500	4	11	75100	82500
34	1	CREALOCK 34	CUT	SAIL	FBG	KL	IB	34D	YAN	10		13500	4	11	75100	82500
34	1	CREALOCK 34 SHOAL	SLP	SAIL	FBG	KL	IB	34D	YAN	10		13500	4	1	76100	83700
34	1	CREALOCK 34 SHOAL	CUT	SAIL	FBG	KL	IB	34D	YAN	10		13500	4	1	76100	83700
36	11	CREALOCK 37	SLP	SAIL	FBG	KL	IB	40D	YAN	10	10	16000	5	4	91800	101000
36	11	CREALOCK 37	CUT	SAIL	FBG	KL	IB	40D	YAN	10	10	16000	5	4	91500	100500
36	11	CREALOCK 37	YWL	SAIL	FBG	KL	IB	40D	YAN	10	10	16000	5	4	91800	101000
36	11	CREALOCK 37 SHOAL	SLP	SAIL	FBG	KL	IB	40D	YAN	10	10	16000	4	5	93100	102500
36	11	CREALOCK 37 SHOAL	CUT	SAIL	FBG	KL	IB	40D	YAN	10	10	16000	4	5	93400	102500
36	11	CREALOCK 37 SHOAL	YWL	SAIL	FBG	KL	IB	40D	YAN	10	10	16000	4	5	93100	102500
		1989 BOATS														
23	7	FLICKA 20	SLP	SAIL	FBG	KL	IB	9D	YAN	8		5500	3	3	21400	23800
27	3	DANA 24	SLP	SAIL	FBG	KL	IB	18D	YAN	8	7	7200	3	10	33800	37600
27	3	DANA 24	CUT	SAIL	FBG	KL	IB	18D	YAN	8	7	7200	3	10	33800	37600
30	11	ORION 27 MKII	SLP	SAIL	FBG	KL	IB	27D	YAN	9	3	10000	4		52500	57600
30	11	ORION 27 MKII	CUT	SAIL	FBG	KL	IB	27D	YAN	9	3	10000	4	3	52500	57600
31	10	PACIFIC-SEACRAFT 31	SLP	SAIL	FBG	KL	IB	27D	YAN	9	10	11000	4	11	58000	63800
31	10	PACIFIC-SEACRAFT 31	CUT	SAIL	FBG	KL	IB	27D	YAN	9	10	11000	4	11	58000	63800
31	10	PACIFIC-SEACRAFT SHL	SLP	SAIL	FBG	KL	IB	27D	YAN	9	10	11000	4		58700	64500
31	10	PACIFIC-SEACRAFT SHL	CUT	SAIL	FBG	KL	IB	27D	YAN	9	10	11000	4		58700	64500
34	1	CREALOCK 34	SLP	SAIL	FBG	KL	IB	34D	YAN	10		13500	4	11	71200	78300
34	1	CREALOCK 34	CUT	SAIL	FBG	KL	IB	34D	YAN	10		13500	4	11	71200	78300
34	1	CREALOCK 34 SHOAL	SLP	SAIL	FBG	KL	IB	34D	YAN	10		13500	4	1	72100	79200
34	1	CREALOCK 34 SHOAL	CUT	SAIL	FBG	KL	IB	34D	YAN	10		13500	4	1	72100	79200
36	11	CREALOCK 37	SLP	SAIL	FBG	KL	IB	44D	YAN	10	10	16000	5	4	87200	95800
36	11	CREALOCK 37	CUT	SAIL	FBG	KL	IB	44D	YAN	10	10	16000	5	4	87200	95800
36	11	CREALOCK 37	YWL	SAIL	FBG	KL	IB	44D	YAN	10	10	16000	5	4	87200	95800
36	11	CREALOCK 37 SHOAL	SLP	SAIL	FBG	KL	IB	44D	YAN	10	10	16000	4	5	88200	96900
36	11	CREALOCK 37 SHOAL	CUT	SAIL	FBG	KL	IB	44D	YAN	10	10	16000	4	5	88200	96900
36	11	CREALOCK 37 SHOAL	YWL	SAIL	FBG	KL	IB	44D	YAN	10	10	16000	4	5	88200	96900
		1988 BOATS														
23	7	FLICKA 20	SLP	SAIL	FBG	KL	IB	9D	YAN	8		5500	3	3	20300	22600
27	3	DANA 24	SLP	SAIL	FBG	KL	IB	18D	YAN	8	7	7200	3	10	32000	35600
27	3	DANA 24	CUT	SAIL	FBG	KL	IB	18D	YAN	8	7	7200	3	10	32000	35600
30	11	ORION 27 MKII	SLP	SAIL	FBG	KL	IB	27D	YAN	9	3	10000	4		49700	54600
30	11	ORION 27 MKII	CUT	SAIL	FBG	KL	IB	27D	YAN	9	3	10000	4	3	49700	54600
31	10	PACIFIC-SEACRAFT 31	SLP	SAIL	FBG	KL	IB	27D	YAN	9	10	11000	4	11	55000	60400
31	10	PACIFIC-SEACRAFT 31	CUT	SAIL	FBG	KL	IB	27D	YAN	9	10	11000	4	11	55000	60400
31	10	PACIFIC-SEACRAFT SHL	SLP	SAIL	FBG	KL	IB	27D	YAN	9	10	11000	4		55700	61200
31	10	PACIFIC-SEACRAFT SHL	CUT	SAIL	FBG	KL	IB	27D	YAN	9	10	11000	4		55700	61200
34	1	CREALOCK 34	SLP	SAIL	FBG	KL	IB	34D	YAN	10		13500	4	11	67500	74100
34	1	CREALOCK 34	CUT	SAIL	FBG	KL	IB	34D	YAN	10		13500	4	11	67500	74100
34	1	CREALOCK 34 SHOAL	SLP	SAIL	FBG	KL	IB	34D	YAN	10		13500	4	1	68300	75000
34	1	CREALOCK 34 SHOAL	CUT	SAIL	FBG	KL	IB	34D	YAN	10		13500	4	1	68300	75000
36	11	CREALOCK 37	SLP	SAIL	FBG	KL	IB	44D	YAN	10	10	16000	5	4	82600	90700
36	11	CREALOCK 37	CUT	SAIL	FBG	KL	IB	44D	YAN	10	10	16000	5	4	82600	90700
36	11	CREALOCK 37	YWL	SAIL	FBG	KL	IB	44D	YAN	10	10	16000	5	4	82600	90700
36	11	CREALOCK 37 SHOAL	SLP	SAIL	FBG	KL	IB	44D	YAN	10	10	16000	4	5	83600	91800
36	11	CREALOCK 37 SHOAL	CUT	SAIL	FBG	KL	IB	44D	YAN	10	10	16000	4	5	83600	91800
36	11	CREALOCK 37 SHOAL	YWL	SAIL	FBG	KL	IB	44D	YAN	10	10	16000	4	5	83600	91800
		1987 BOATS														
24		FLICKA 20	SLP	SAIL	FBG	KL	IB	9D	YAN	8		5000	3	3	17500	19800
27	3	DANA 24	SLP	SAIL	FBG	KL	IB	18D	YAN	8	7	7200	3	10	30300	33700
27	3	DANA 24	CUT	SAIL	FBG	KL	IB	18D	YAN	8	7	7200	3	10	30300	33700
30	11	ORION 27 MKII	SLP	SAIL	FBG	KL	IB	27D	YAN	9	3	10000	4		47400	52000
30	11	ORION 27 MKII	CUT	SAIL	FBG	KL	IB	27D	YAN	9	3	10000	4	3	47400	52000
31	10	PACIFIC-SEACRAFT 31	SLP	SAIL	FBG	KL	IB	27D	YAN	9	10	11000	4	11	52100	57300
31	10	PACIFIC-SEACRAFT 31	CUT	SAIL	FBG	KL	IB	27D	YAN	9	10	11000	4	11	52100	57300
31	10	PACIFIC-SEACRAFT SHL	SLP	SAIL	FBG	KL	IB	27D	YAN	9	10	11000	4		52700	57900
31	10	PACIFIC-SEACRAFT SHL	CUT	SAIL	FBG	KL	IB	27D	YAN	9	10	11000	4		52700	57900
34	1	CREALOCK 34	SLP	SAIL	FBG	KL	IB	34D	YAN	10		13500	4	11	63900	70200
34	1	CREALOCK 34	CUT	SAIL	FBG	KL	IB	34D	YAN	10		13500	4	11	63900	70200
34	1	CREALOCK 34 SHOAL	SLP	SAIL	FBG	KL	IB	34D	YAN	10		13500	4	1	64800	71200
34	1	CREALOCK 34 SHOAL	CUT	SAIL	FBG	KL	IB	34D	YAN	10		13500	4	1	64800	71200
36	11	CREALOCK 37	SLP	SAIL	FBG	KL	IB	44D	YAN	10	10	16000	5	4	78200	85900
36	11	CREALOCK 37	CUT	SAIL	FBG	KL	IB	44D	YAN	10	10	16000	5	4	78200	85900
36	11	CREALOCK 37	YWL	SAIL	FBG	KL	IB	44D	YAN	10	10	16000	5	4	78200	86000
36	11	CREALOCK 37 SHOAL	SLP	SAIL	FBG	KL	IB	44D	YAN	10	10	16000	4	5	79300	87100
36	11	CREALOCK 37 SHOAL	CUT	SAIL	FBG	KL	IB	44D	YAN	10	10	16000	4	5	79300	87100
36	11	CREALOCK 37 SHOAL	YWL	SAIL	FBG	KL	IB	44D	YAN	10	10	16000	4	5	79200	87000
		1986 BOATS														
24		FLICKA 20	SLP	SAIL	FBG	KL	OB			8		6000	3	3	19000	21100
24		FLICKA 20	SLP	SAIL	FBG	KL	IB	10D	YAN	8		6000	3	3	20200	22400
24		FLICKA 20	CUT	SAIL	FBG	KL	IB	10D	YAN	8		6000	3	3	20200	22400
27	3	DANA 24	SLP	SAIL	FBG	KL	IB	15D	YAN	8	7	7200	3	10	28700	31900
27	3	DANA 24	CUT	SAIL	FBG	KL	IB	15D	YAN	8	7	7200	3	10	28700	31900
30	11	ORION 27 MKII	SLP	SAIL	FBG	KL	IB	15D- 23D		9	3	10000	4		44300	49300
30	11	ORION 27 MKII	CUT	SAIL	FBG	KL	IB	15D- 23D		9	3	10000	4	3	44300	49300
34	1	CREALOCK 34	SLP	SAIL	FBG	KL	IB	30D	WEST	10		12000	4	11	54200	59500
34	1	CREALOCK 34	CUT	SAIL	FBG	KL	IB	30D	WEST	10		12000	4	11	54200	59500
34	1	CREALOCK 34 SHOAL	SLP	SAIL	FBG	KL	IB	30D	WEST	10		12000	4	1	54800	60200
34	1	CREALOCK 34 SHOAL	CUT	SAIL	FBG	KL	IB	30D	WEST	10		12000	4	1	54800	60200
36	11	CREALOCK 37	SLP	SAIL	FBG	KL	IB	46D	WEST	10	10	16000	5	4	74400	81700
36	11	CREALOCK 37	CUT	SAIL	FBG	KL	IB	46D	WEST	10	10	16000	5	4	74400	81700
36	11	CREALOCK 37	YWL	SAIL	FBG	KL	IB	46D	WEST	10	10	16000	5	4	74400	81700
36	11	CREALOCK 37 SHOAL	SLP	SAIL	FBG	KL	IB	46D	WEST	10	10	16000	4	5	75000	82400
36	11	CREALOCK 37 SHOAL	CUT	SAIL	FBG	KL	IB	46D	WEST	10	10	16000	4	5	75000	82400
36	11	CREALOCK 37 SHOAL	YWL	SAIL	FBG	KL	IB	46D	WEST	10	10	16000	4	5	75000	82400
		1985 BOATS														
24		FLICKA 20	SLP	SAIL	FBG	KL	OB			8		6000	3	3	17600	20000
24		FLICKA 20	SLP	SAIL	FBG	KL	IB	10D	YAN	8		6000	3	3	19100	21200
24		FLICKA 20	CUT	SAIL	FBG	KL	IB	10D	YAN	8		6000	3	3	19100	21200
27	3	DANA 24	SLP	SAIL	FBG	KL	IB	15D	YAN	8	7	8000	3	10	30400	33700
27	3	DANA 24	CUT	SAIL	FBG	KL	IB	15D	YAN	8	7	8000	3	10	30400	33700
30	11	ORION 27 MKII	SLP	SAIL	FBG	KL	IB	15D- 23D		9	3	10000	4		42000	46700
30	11	ORION 27 MKII	CUT	SAIL	FBG	KL	IB	15D- 23D		9	3	10000	4	3	42000	46700
34	1	CREALOCK 34	SLP	SAIL	FBG	KL	IB	30D	WEST	10		12000	4	11	51300	56400
34	1	CREALOCK 34	CUT	SAIL	FBG	KL	IB	30D	WEST	10		12000	4	11	51300	56400
34	1	CREALOCK 34 SHOAL	SLP	SAIL	FBG	KL	IB	30D	WEST	10		12000	4	1	52000	57100
34	1	CREALOCK 34 SHOAL	CUT	SAIL	FBG	KL	IB	30D	WEST	10		12000	4	1	52000	57100
36	11	CREALOCK 37	SLP	SAIL	FBG	KL	IB	32D	UNIV	10	10	16000	5	4	70100	77100
36	11	CREALOCK 37	CUT	SAIL	FBG	KL	IB	32D	UNIV	10	10	16000	5	4	70100	77100
36	11	CREALOCK 37	YWL	SAIL	FBG	KL	IB	32D	UNIV	10	10	16000	5	4	70100	77100
36	11	CREALOCK 37 SHOAL	SLP	SAIL	FBG	KL	IB	32D	UNIV	10	10	16000	4	5	70700	77700
36	11	CREALOCK 37 SHOAL	CUT	SAIL	FBG	KL	IB	32D	UNIV	10	10	16000	4	5	70700	77700
36	11	CREALOCK 37 SHOAL	YWL	SAIL	FBG	KL	IB	32D	UNIV	10	10	16000	4	5	70700	77700
		1984 BOATS														
24		FLICKA 20	SLP	SAIL	FBG	KL	OB			8		5500	3	3	15100	17200
24		FLICKA 20	SLP	SAIL	FBG	KL	IB	10D	YAN	8		5500	3	3	16400	18600
24		FLICKA 20	CUT	SAIL	FBG	KL	IB	10D	YAN	8		5500	3	3	16400	18600
30	11	ORION 27 MKII	SLP	SAIL	FBG	KL	IB	15D	YAN	9	3	10000	4		39800	44200
30	11	ORION 27 MKII	CUT	SAIL	FBG	KL	IB	15D	YAN	9	3	10000	4	3	39800	44200
34	1	CREALOCK 34	SLP	SAIL	FBG	KL	IB	34D	UNIV	10		12000	4	11	48900	53800
34	1	CREALOCK 34	CUT	SAIL	FBG	KL	IB	34D	UNIV	10		12000	4	11	48900	53800
36	11	CREALOCK 37	SLP	SAIL	FBG	KL	IB	32D	UNIV	10	10	16000	5	4	66700	73300
36	11	CREALOCK 37	CUT	SAIL	FBG	KL	IB	32D	UNIV	10	10	16000	5	4	66700	73300
36	11	CREALOCK 37	YWL	SAIL	FBG	KL	IB	32D	UNIV	10	10	16000	5	4	66700	73300

....For earlier years, see the BUC Used Boat Price Guide, Volume 3

PACIFIC TRAWLERS

BELLINGHAM WA 98225 COAST GUARD MFG ID- PTL See inside cover to adjust price for area

For more recent years, see the BUC Used Boat Price Guide, Volume 1

LOA FT	LOA IN	NAME AND/ OR MODEL	TOP/ RIG	BOAT TYPE	HULL MTL	HULL TP	ENGINE TP	ENGINE # HP	ENGINE MFG	BEAM FT	BEAM IN	WGT LBS	DRAFT FT	DRAFT IN	RETAIL LOW	RETAIL HIGH
		1996 BOATS														
37		PACIFIC TRAWLER	EPH	MY	FBG	DS	IB	150D	CUM			16000	3	10	99600	109500
		1995 BOATS														
36	9	PACIFIC TRAWLER		MY	FBG	DS	IB	210D	CUM	13	3	28000	3	10	147000	162000

PACIFIC YACHTS INC

LAKE PARK FL 33403 See inside cover to adjust price for area

LOA FT	LOA IN	NAME AND/ OR MODEL	TOP/ RIG	BOAT TYPE	HULL MTL	HULL TP	ENGINE TP	ENGINE # HP	ENGINE MFG	BEAM FT	BEAM IN	WGT LBS	DRAFT FT	DRAFT IN	RETAIL LOW	RETAIL HIGH
		1994 BOATS														
62		PACIFIC 62	FB	MY	FBG	DS	IB	T14CD	DD	17	6	67000	4	6	590000	648500
		1993 BOATS														
62		PACIFIC 62	FB	MY	FBG	DS	IB	T14CD	DD	17	6	67000	4	6	563000	618500
		1992 BOATS														
62		PACIFIC 62	FB	MY	FBG	DS	IB	T14CD		17	6		4	6	527000	579500
		1989 BOATS														
62		WIDEBODY	FB	MY	FBG	SV	IB	T600D	GM	17	6	77600	4	6	375000	412000
68		WIDEBODY W/COCKPIT	FB	MYCPT	FBG	SV	IB	T600D	GM	17	6	79800	4	6	427000	469000
		1988 BOATS														
62		WIDEBODY	FB	MY	FBG	SV	IB	T600D	GM	17	6	77600	4	6	358500	394000
62		WIDEBODY W/COCKPIT	FB	MYCPT	FBG	SV	IB	T600D	GM	17	6	79800	4	6	374500	411500
		1987 BOATS														
62		WIDEBODY	FB	MY	FBG	DV	IB	T650D		17	8	77700	4	6	347500	382000
62		WIDEBODY	FB	MY	FBG	DV	IB	T950D	GM	17	6		4	6	352500	387000
68		WIDEBODY	FB	MY	FBG	DV	IB	T650D		17	8	83400	4	8	403000	442500

PACIFICA YACHTS

HONOLULU HI 96822-4667 COAST GUARD MFG ID- PYU See inside cover to adjust price for area
FORMERLY PACIFICA BY KIPPER YACHTS

LOA FT	LOA IN	NAME AND/ OR MODEL	TOP/ RIG	BOAT TYPE	HULL MTL	HULL TP	ENGINE TP	ENGINE # HP	ENGINE MFG	BEAM FT	BEAM IN	WGT LBS	DRAFT FT	DRAFT IN	RETAIL LOW	RETAIL HIGH
		1996 BOATS														
44		PACIFICA 44 CNV	FB	SF	FBG	SV	IB	T485D	DD	15		33000	4	2	317500	349000
47		PACIFICA 47 CNV	FB	SF	FBG	SV	IB	T550D	DD	15		36500	4	2	360500	396000
54	10	PACIFICA 54 CNV	FB	SF	FBG	SV	IB	T735D	DD	18		46000	4	7	505500	555500
58	10	PACIFICA 58 CNV	FB	SF	FBG	SV	IB	T10CD	DD	18		55000	4	7	659500	724500
		1994 BOATS														
41		SPORTFISHER	FB	SF	FBG	SV	IB	T485D	DD	14		29000	3		302000	332000
44		SPORTFISHER	FB	SF	FBG	SV	IB	T550D	DD	15		33000	4	2	304500	334500
52		SPORTFISHER	FB	SF	FBG	SV	IB	T750D	DD	15		44000	4	7	437000	480000
		1991 BOATS														
36		PACIFICA 36	FB	SF	FBG	SV	IB	T300D	GM	13		16000	3	4	125500	138000
36		PACIFICA 36	FB	SF	FBG	SV	IB	T375D	CAT	13		16000	3	4	136000	149500
36		SUPER FISHERMAN 36	FB	SDNSF	FBG	SV	IB	T300D	GM	13		16000	3	4	125500	138000
36		SUPER FISHERMAN 36	FB	SDNSF	FBG	SV	IB	T375D	CAT	13		16000	3	4	136000	149500
41		PACIFICA 41	FB	SF	FBG	SV	IB	T485D	GM	14		24000	3	11	228500	251500
41		PACIFICA 41	FB	SF	FBG	SV	IB	T550D	GM	14		24000	3	11	242500	266500
44		PACIFICA 44	FB	SF	FBG	SV	IB	T485D	GM	15		33000	4		242000	266000
44		PACIFICA 44	FB	SF	FBG	SV	IB	T550D	GM	15		33000	4		256500	281500
50		PACIFICA 50	FB	SF	FBG	SV	IB	T735D	GM	15		45000	4	7	335500	368500
52		PACIFICA 52	FB	SF	FBG	SV	IB	T750D	GM	15		55000	4	7	393000	432000
52		PACIFICA 52	FB	SF	FBG	SV	IB	T870D	GM	15		55000	4	7	417500	459000
52		PACIFICA 52	FB	SF	FBG	SV	IB	T11CD	GM	15		55000	4	7	460500	506000
67		PACIFICA 67	FB	MY	FBG	SV	IB	T870D	GM	22		90000	5		770000	846500
67		PACIFICA 67	FB	MY	FBG	SV	IB	T11CD	GM	22		90000	5		817500	898500
67		PACIFICA 67	FB	SF	FBG	SV	IB	T870D	GM	20	6	77000	5		651000	715500
67		PACIFICA 67	FB	SF	FBG	SV	IB	T11CD	GM	20	6	87000	5		738000	811000
67		PACIFICA 67	FB	YTFS	FBG	SV	IB	T870D	GM	21	6	83000	5		729000	801000
67		PACIFICA 67	FB	YTFS	FBG	SV	IB	T11CD	GM	21	6	83000	5		778000	855000
77		PACIFICA 77	FB	MY	FBG	SV	IB	T870D	GM	22			5		**	**
77		PACIFICA 77	FB	MY	FBG	SV	IB	T11CD	GM	22			5		**	**
77		PACIFICA 77	FB	YTFS	FBG	SV	IB	T870D	GM	21	6	95000	5		**	**
77		PACIFICA 77	FB	YTFS	FBG	SV	IB	T11CD	GM	21	6	95000	5		**	**
		1990 BOATS														
36		PACIFICA 36	FB	SF	FBG	SV	IB	T300D	GM	13		16000	3	4	119500	131500
36		PACIFICA 36	FB	SF	FBG	SV	IB	T375D	CAT	13		16000	3	4	130000	143000
36		SUPER FISHERMAN 36	FB	SDNSF	FBG	SV	IB	T300D	GM	13		16000	3	4	119500	131500
36		SUPER FISHERMAN 36	FB	SDNSF	FBG	SV	IB	T375D	CAT	13		16000	3	4	130000	143000
41		PACIFICA 41	FB	SF	FBG	SV	IB	T485D	GM	14		24000	3	11	218500	240000
41		PACIFICA 41	FB	SF	FBG	SV	IB	T550D	GM	14		24000	3	11	231500	254500
44		PACIFICA 44	FB	SF	FBG	SV	IB	T485D	GM	15		33000	4		231000	254000
44		PACIFICA 44	FB	SF	FBG	SV	IB	T550D	GM	15		33000	4		244500	269000
50		PACIFICA 50	FB	SF	FBG	SV	IB	T735D	GM	15		45000	4	7	320000	352000
52		PACIFICA 52	FB	SF	FBG	SV	IB	T750D	GM	15		55000	4	7	375000	412500
52		PACIFICA 52	FB	SF	FBG	SV	IB	T870D	GM	15		55000	4	7	398500	438000
52		PACIFICA 52	FB	SF	FBG	SV	IB	T11CD	GM	15		55000	4	7	439500	483000
67		PACIFICA 67	FB	MY	FBG	SV	IB	T870D	GM	22		80000	5		684500	752500
67		PACIFICA 67	FB	MY	FBG	SV	IB	T11CD	GM	22		80000	5		732000	804000
67		PACIFICA 67	FB	SF	FBG	SV	IB	T870D	GM	20	6	77000	5		621500	683000
67		PACIFICA 67	FB	SF	FBG	SV	IB	T11CD	GM	20	6	77000	5		660500	725500
67		PACIFICA 67	FB	YTFS	FBG	SV	IB	T870D	GM	21	6	73000	5		647500	711500
67		PACIFICA 67	FB	YTFS	FBG	SV	IB	T11CD	GM	21	6	73000	5		696000	765000
70		PACIFICA 70	FB	SF	FBG	SV	JT	T13CD	MTU	20	6		5		1.025M	1.110M
77		PACIFICA 77	FB	MY	FBG	SV	IB	T870D	GM	22			5		**	**
77		PACIFICA 77	FB	MY	FBG	SV	IB	T11CD	GM	22			5		**	**
77		PACIFICA 77	FB	YTFS	FBG	SV	IB	T870D	GM	21	6	85000	5		**	**
77		PACIFICA 77	FB	YTFS	FBG	SV	IB	T11CD	GM	21	6	85000	5		**	**
		1989 BOATS														
36		PACIFICA 36	FB	SF	FBG	SV	IB	T300D	GM	13		16000	3	4	114500	125500
36		PACIFICA 36	FB	SF	FBG	SV	IB	T375D	CAT	13		16000	3	4	124000	136500
36		SUPER FISHERMAN 36	FB	SDNSF	FBG	SV	IB	T300D	GM	13		16000	3	4	114500	125500
36		SUPER FISHERMAN 36	FB	SDNSF	FBG	SV	IB	T400D	GM	13		16000	3	4	124000	136500
41		PACIFICA 41	FB	SF	FBG	SV	IB	T400D	GM	14		24000	3	11	193500	212500
41		PACIFICA 41	FB	SF	FBG	SV	IB	T485D	GM	14		24000	3	11	208500	229000
41		PACIFICA 41	FB	SF	FBG	SV	IB	T560D	GM	14		24000	3	11	223000	245000
44		PACIFICA 44	FB	SF	FBG	SV	IB	T485D	GM	15		33000	4		220500	242500
44		PACIFICA 44	FB	SF	FBG	SV	IB	T560D	GM	15		33000	4		235500	259000
50		PACIFICA 50	FB	SF	FBG	SV	IB	T650D	GM	15		45000	4	7	289500	318500
52		PACIFICA 52	FB	SF	FBG	SV	IB	T750D	GM	15		55000	4	7	358500	394000
52		PACIFICA 52	FB	SF	FBG	SV	IB	T870D	GM	15		55000	4	7	381000	418500
52		PACIFICA 52	FB	SF	FBG	SV	IB	T11CD	GM	15		55000	4	7	420000	461500
60		PACIFICA 60	FB	SF	FBG	SV	IB	T870D	GM						401000	441000
60		PACIFICA 60	FB	SF	FBG	SV	IB	T11CD	GM						446500	491000
60		PACIFICA 60	FB	SF	FBG	SV	IB	T13CD	MTU						535500	588500
65		PACIFICA 65	FB	SF	FBG	SV	IB			21	6		5		**	**
67		PACIFICA 67	FB	MY	FBG	SV	IB	T870D	GM	22		80000	5		654000	718500
67		PACIFICA 67	FB	MY	FBG	SV	IB	T11CD	GM	22		80000	5		699000	768000
67		PACIFICA 67	FB	SF	FBG	SV	IB	T870D	GM	20	6	77000	5		593500	652500
67		PACIFICA 67	FB	SF	FBG	SV	IB	T11CD	GM	20	6	77000	5		630500	693000
67		PACIFICA 67	FB	YTFS	FBG	SV	IB	T870D	GM	21	6	73000	5		618500	679500
67		PACIFICA 67	FB	YTFS	FBG	SV	IB	T11CD	GM	21	6	73000	5		665000	730500
70		PACIFICA 70	FB	SF	FBG	SV	JT	T13CD	MTU	20	6		5		977500	1.060M
77		PACIFICA 77	FB	MY	FBG	SV	IB	T870D	GM	22			5		**	**
77		PACIFICA 77	FB	MY	FBG	SV	IB	T11CD	GM	22			5		**	**
77		PACIFICA 77	FB	YTFS	FBG	SV	IB	T870D	GM	21	6	85000	5		**	**
77		PACIFICA 77	FB	YTFS	FBG	SV	IB	T11CD	GM	21	6	85000	5		**	**
		1988 BOATS														
36		PACIFICA 36	FB	SF	FBG	SV	IB	T300D	GM	13		16000	3	4	109500	120000
36		PACIFICA 36	FB	SF	FBG	SV	IB	T375D	CAT	13		16000	3	4	118500	130500
36		SUPER FISHERMAN 36	FB	SDNSF	FBG	SV	IB	T300D	GM	13		16000	3	4	109500	120000
36		SUPER FISHERMAN 36	FB	SDNSF	FBG	SV	IB	T400D	GM	13		16000	3	4	118500	130500
41		PACIFICA 41	FB	SF	FBG	SV	IB	T400D	GM	14		24000	3	11	184500	203000
41		PACIFICA 41	FB	SF	FBG	SV	IB	T485D	GM	14		24000	3	11	199500	219000
41		PACIFICA 41	FB	SF	FBG	SV	IB	T560D	GM	14		24000	3	11	213000	234000
44		PACIFICA 44	FB	SF	FBG	SV	IB	T485D	GM	15		33000	4		211000	232000
44		PACIFICA 44	FB	SF	FBG	SV	IB	T560D	GM	15		33000	4		225000	247500
50		PACIFICA 50	FB	SF	FBG	SV	IB	T650D	GM	15		45000	4	7	277000	304000
52		PACIFICA 52	FB	SF	FBG	SV	IB	T750D	GM	15		55000	4	7	342500	376500
52		PACIFICA 52	FB	SF	FBG	SV	IB	T870D	GM	15		55000	4	7	364000	400000
52		PACIFICA 52	FB	SF	FBG	SV	IB	T11CD	GM	15		55000	4	7	401500	441000
60		PACIFICA 60	FB	SF	FBG	SV	IB	T870D	GM						383500	421500
60		PACIFICA 60	FB	SF	FBG	SV	IB	T11CD	GM						427000	469500
60		PACIFICA 60	FB	SF	FBG	SV	IB	T13CD	MTU						512000	562500
65		PACIFICA 65	FB	SF	FBG	SV	IB			21	6		5		**	**
67		PACIFICA 67	FB	MY	FBG	SV	IB	T870D	GM	22		80000	5		625000	687000
67		PACIFICA 67	FB	MY	FBG	SV	IB	T11CD	GM	22		80000	5		668000	734000
67		PACIFICA 67	FB	SF	FBG	SV	IB	T870D	GM	20	6	77000	5		567500	623500
67		PACIFICA 67	FB	SF	FBG	SV	IB	T11CD	GM	20	6	77000	5		603000	662500
67		PACIFICA 67	FB	YTFS	FBG	SV	IB	T870D	GM	21	6	73000	5		591000	649500
67		PACIFICA 67	FB	YTFS	FBG	SV	IB	T11CD	GM	21	6	73000	5		635500	698500
70		PACIFICA 70	FB	SF	FBG	SV	JT	T13C	MTU	20	6		5		**	**
77		PACIFICA 77	FB	MY	FBG	SV	IB	T870D	GM	22			5		**	**

CONTINUED ON NEXT PAGE

LOA FT IN	NAME AND/ OR MODEL	TOP/ RIG	BOAT TYPE	MTL	-HULL- TP	TP	ENGINE #	HP	MFG	BEAM FT IN	WGT LBS	DRAFT FT IN	RETAIL LOW	RETAIL HIGH
--- 1988 BOATS ---
77	PACIFICA 77	FB	MY	FBG	SV	IB	T11CD		GM	22			**	**
77	PACIFICA 77	FB	YTFS	FBG	SV	IB	T870D		GM	21 6	85000	5	**	**
77	PACIFICA 77	FB	YTFS	FBG	SV	IB	T11CD		GM	21 6	85000	5	**	**
--- 1987 BOATS ---
36	PACIFICA 36	FB	SF	FBG	SV	IB	T300D		GM	13	16000	3 4	104500	115000
36	PACIFICA 36	FB	SF	FBG	SV	IB	T375D		CAT	13	16000	3 4	113500	125000
36	SUPER FISHERMAN 36	FB	SDNSF	FBG	SV	IB	T300D		GM	13	16000	3 4	104500	115000
36	SUPER FISHERMAN 36	FB	SDNSF	FBG	SV	IB	T375D		CAT	13	16000	3 4	113500	125000
41	PACIFICA 41	FB	SF	FBG	SV	IB	T485D		GM	14	24000	3 11	197000	194500
41	PACIFICA 41	FB	SF	FBG	SV	IB	T485D		GM	15			195000	214000
44	PACIFICA 44	FB	SF	FBG	SV	IB	T565D		GM	15			202000	221500
44	PACIFICA 44	FB	MY	FBG	SV	IB	T565D		GM	15	33000	4	216500	237500
50	PACIFICA 50	FB	SF	FBG	SV	IB	T565D		GM	15	45000	4 7	249500	274500
50	PACIFICA 50	FB	SF	FBG	SV	IB	T650D		GM	15	45000	4 7	264500	291000
52	PACIFICA 52	FB	SF	FBG	SV	IB	T870D		GM	15	55000	4 7	327500	360000
52	PACIFICA 52	FB	SF	FBG	SV	IB	T870D		GM	15	55000	4 7	348000	382500
52	PACIFICA 52	FB	SF	FBG	SV	IB	T11CD		GM	15	55000	4 7	384000	422000
60	PACIFICA 60	FB	SF	FBG	SV	IB	T870D		GM				367000	403500
60	PACIFICA 60	FB	SF	FBG	SV	IB	T11CD		GM				408500	449000
60	PACIFICA 60	FB	SF	FBG	SV	IB	T13CD		MTU				490000	538500
67	PACIFICA 67	FB	MY	FBG	SV	IB	T870D		GM	20 6	80000	5	588000	646500
67	PACIFICA 67	FB	MY	FBG	SV	IB	T11CD		GM	20 6			650000	714500
67	PACIFICA 67	FB	MY	FBG	SV	IB	T11CD		GM	20 6	77000	5	543000	596500
67	PACIFICA 67	FB	SF	FBG	SV	IB	T870D		GM	20 6			585500	643500
67	PACIFICA 67	FB	SF	FBG	SV	IB	T13CD		MTU	20 6			666500	732500
67	PACIFICA 67	FB	YTFS	FBG	SV	IB	T870D		GM	20 6	73000	5	559000	614000
67	PACIFICA 67	FB	YTFS	FBG	SV	IB	T11CD		GM	20 6			621000	682500
77	PACIFICA 77	FB	MY	FBG	SV	IB	T870D		GM	20 6		5	**	**
77	PACIFICA 77	FB	MY	FBG	SV	IB	T11CD		GM	20 6			**	**
77	PACIFICA 77	FB	YTFS	FBG	SV	IB	T870D		GM	20 6	85000	5	**	**
77	PACIFICA 77	FB	YTFS	FBG	SV	IB	T11CD		GM	20 6			**	**
--- 1986 BOATS ---
36	PACIFICA 36	FB	SF	FBG	SV	IB	T300D		J&T	13	16000	3	100500	110500
36	PACIFICA 36	FB	SF	FBG	SV	IB	T355D		CAT	13	16000	3 4	106500	117500
36	SUPER FISHERMAN 36		SDNSF	FBG	SV	IB	T300D		J&T	13		3 4	100500	110500
36	SUPER FISHERMAN 36		SDNSF	FBG	SV	IB	T355D		CAT	13		3 4	106500	117500
41	PACIFICA 41	FB	SF	FBG	SV	IB	T410D		J&T	14	24000	3 11	171500	188500
44	PACIFICA 44	FB	SF	FBG	SV	IB	T535D		GM	15	33000	4 2	202000	222000
44	PACIFICA 44	FB	MY	FBG	SV	IB	T600D		GM	15	45000	4 7	241500	265000
50	PACIFICA 50	FB	SF	FBG	SV	IB	T600D		GM	15	45000	4 7	245000	269000
67	PACIFICA 67	FB	MY	FBG	SV	IB	T750D		GM	20 6	80000	5	542500	596500
67	PACIFICA 67	FB	SF	FBG	SV	IB	T750D		GM	20 6	77000	5	506000	556000
67	PACIFICA 67	FB	YTFS	FBG	SV	IB	T750D		GM	20 6	73000	5	514000	565000
77	PACIFICA 77	FB	MY	FBG	SV	IB	T750D		GM	20 6		5	**	**
77	PACIFICA 77	FB	YTFS	FBG	SV	IB	T750D		GM	20 6	85000	5	**	**
--- 1985 BOATS ---
36	PACIFICA 36	FB	SF	FBG	SV	IB	T300D		J&T	13	16000	3 4	96200	106000
36	PACIFICA 36	FB	SF	FBG	SV	IB	T355D		CAT	13	16000	3 4	102000	112500
36	SUPER FISHERMAN 36		SDNSF	FBG	SV	IB	T300D		J&T	13		3 4	96200	106000
36	SUPER FISHERMAN 36		SDNSF	FBG	SV	IB	T355D		CAT	13		3 4	102000	112500
41	PACIFICA 41	FB	SF	FBG	SV	IB	T410D		J&T	14	24000	3 11	164500	180500
44	PACIFICA 44	FB	SF	FBG	SV	IB	T450D		GM	15	33000	4 2	179000	196500
44	PACIFICA 44	FB	SF	FBG	SV	IB	T535D		GM	15	33000	4 2	193000	212500
50	PACIFICA 50	FB	MY	FBG	SV	IB	T600D		GM	15	45000	4 7	231000	254000
50	PACIFICA 50	FB	SF	FBG	SV	IB	T550D		GM	15	50000	4 7	239500	263000
50	PACIFICA 50	FB	SF	FBG	SV	IB	T600D		GM	15	45000	4 7	234500	257500
64	PACIFICA 64	FB	YTFS	FBG	SV	IB	T750D		GM				421000	463000
67	PACIFICA 67	FB	MY	FBG	SV	IB	T675D			21	91000	6 5	549000	603000
67	PACIFICA 67	FB	MY	FBG	SV	IB	T750D		GM	20 6	80000	5	519500	571000
67	PACIFICA 67	FB	SF	FBG	SV	IB	T750D		GM	20 6	77000	5	485000	532500
67	PACIFICA 67	FB	YTFS	FBG	SV	IB	T750D		GM	20 6	73000	5	492500	541000
77	PACIFICA 77	FB	MY	FBG	SV	IB	T750D		GM	20 6		5	**	**
77	PACIFICA 77	FB	SF	FBG	SV	IB	T750D		GM	20 6		5	**	**
77	PACIFICA 77	FB	YTFS	FBG	SV	IB	T750D		GM	20 6	85000	5	**	**
--- 1984 BOATS ---
36	PACIFICA 36	FB	SF	FBG	SV	IB	T300D		J&T	13	16000	3 4	92200	101500
41	PACIFICA 41	FB	SF	FBG	SV	IB	T410D		J&T	14	24000	3 11	157500	173000
44	PACIFICA 44	FB	SF	FBG	SV	IB	T525D		GM	15	33000	4 2	183500	201500
50	PACIFICA 50	FB	SF	FBG	SV	IB	T570D		GM	15	45000	4 7	219500	241500
63	PACIFICA 63	FB	SF	FBG	SV	IB	T675D		GM	20 6	75000	5	409500	450000
67	PACIFICA 67	FB	MY	FBG	SV	IB	T675D		GM	20 6	80000	5	486500	534500
67	PACIFICA 67	FB	SF	FBG	SV	IB	T675D		GM	20 6	77000	5	458000	503000
67	PACIFICA 67	FB	YTFS	FBG	SV	IB	T675D		GM	20 6	73000	5	460000	505500
77	PACIFICA 77	FB	YTFS	FBG	SV	IB	T675D		GM	20 6	85000	5	**	**

....For earlier years, see the BUC Used Boat Price Guide, Volume 3

PACKARD INC
CAPE CORAL FL 33904-421 COAST GUARD MFG ID- PCK See inside cover to adjust price for area

For more recent years, see the BUC Used Boat Price Guide, Volume 1

LOA FT IN	NAME AND/ OR MODEL	TOP/ RIG	BOAT TYPE	MTL	-HULL- TP	TP	ENGINE #	HP	MFG	BEAM FT IN	WGT LBS	DRAFT FT IN	RETAIL LOW	RETAIL HIGH
--- 1996 BOATS ---
21	CLASSIC		RNBT	FBG	SV	IB		205		6 6	2700		8600	9850
21	CLASSIC		RNBT	FBG	SV	IB		150D		6 6	2850		13100	14800
21	CUB VACATION		RNBT	FBG	SV	IB		200		6 6	2680		8550	9800
27	HERITAGE		RNBT	FBG	SV	IB		265		7 6	3000		16600	18900
27	SPORTSMAN		RNBT	FBG	SV	IB		265		7 6	3200		16900	19200
--- 1995 BOATS ---
21	CLASSIC		RNBT	FBG	SV	IB		205		6 6	2700		8100	9350
21	CLASSIC		RNBT	FBG	SV	IB		150D		6 6	2850		12400	14100
21	CUB VACATION		RNBT	FBG	SV	IB		200		6 6	2680		8050	9300
27	HERITAGE		RNBT	FBG	SV	IB		265		7 5	3000		15700	17900
27	SPORTSMAN		RNBT	FBG	SV	IB		265		7 6	3200		16000	18200
--- 1994 BOATS ---
21	CLASSIC		RNBT	FBG	SV	IO		160		6 6	2830		6250	7200
21	CLASSIC		RNBT	FBG	SV	IO		180		6 6	2700		7650	8800
21	CLASSIC		RNBT	FBG	SV	IO		140D		6 6	2910		9000	10200
27	HERITAGE		RNBT	FBG	SV	IO		235		7 5	3140		11600	13200
27	HERITAGE		RNBT	FBG	SV	IB		265		7 5	3000		14900	16900
27	HERITAGE		RNBT	FBG	SV	IB		150D		7 5	3090		13500	15400
--- 1993 BOATS ---
21	CLASSIC		RNBT	FBG	SV	IO		160		6 6	2830		5850	6700
21	CLASSIC		RNBT	FBG	SV	IO		180		6 6	2700		7250	8300
21	CLASSIC		RNBT	FBG	SV	IO		140D		6 6	2910		8300	9550
27	HERITAGE		RNBT	FBG	SV	IB		235		7 5	3140		10800	12300
27	HERITAGE		RNBT	FBG	SV	IB		265		7 5	3000		14100	16000
--- 1992 BOATS ---
21	CLASSIC		RNBT	FBG	SV	IO		160		6 6	2830		5450	6300
21	CLASSIC		RNBT	FBG	SV	IO		180		6 6	2700		6850	7900
21	CLASSIC		RNBT	FBG	SV	IO		140D		6 6	2910		7800	8950
27	HERITAGE		RNBT	FBG	SV	IB		235		7 5	3140		10100	11500
27	HERITAGE		RNBT	FBG	SV	IB		265		7 5	3000		13400	15200
--- 1991 BOATS ---
20	CRICKET		RNBT	FBG	SV	IO		200		6 4	2600		6000	6900
21	CLASSIC		RNBT	FBG	SV	IO		205		6 6	2830		5200	6000
21	CLASSIC		RNBT	FBG	SV	IO		150D		6 6	2910		7400	8500
27	HERITAGE		RNBT	FBG	SV	IB		235		7 5	3140		9500	10800
27	HERITAGE		RNBT	FBG	SV	IB		265		7 5	3000		12700	14400

PALAMOS BOATBUILD LTD
TORPOINT CORNWALL ENGLAND   See inside cover to adjust price for area

WORLD CATAMARANS
FT LAUDERDALE FL

LOA FT IN	NAME AND/ OR MODEL	TOP/ RIG	BOAT TYPE	MTL	-HULL- TP	TP	ENGINE #	HP	MFG	BEAM FT IN	WGT LBS	DRAFT FT IN	RETAIL LOW	RETAIL HIGH
--- 1989 BOATS ---
24	STRIDER	SLP	SA/RC	F/S	CT	OB				14 2	1800	1 10	20900	23200
30	FLICA 30	SLP	SA/CR	F/S	CT	OB				16 5	6050	3	56400	61900
35	BANSHEE	SLP	SA/RC	F/S	CT	OB				20 6	6720	1 6	87900	96500
35	FLICA 35	SLP	SA/CR	F/S	CT	OB				19 4	8960	3	94900	104500
37	BANSHEE EXPRESS	SLP	SA/RC	F/S	CT	OB	T	18D	YAN	20 6	7700	3	104500	115000
37	FLICA 37	SLP	SA/CR	F/S	CT	OB	T	18D	YAN	19 4	9000	3 4	109000	120000

PALM BEACH MARINECRAFT INC
NEW ULM MN 56073   COAST GUARD MFG ID- SBP See inside cover to adjust price for area
FORMERLY PALM BEACH PONTOON BOAT CO

For more recent years, see the BUC Used Boat Price Guide, Volume 1

LOA FT IN	NAME AND/ OR MODEL	TOP/ RIG	BOAT TYPE	MTL	-HULL- TP	TP	ENGINE #	HP	MFG	BEAM FT IN	WGT LBS	DRAFT FT IN	RETAIL LOW	RETAIL HIGH
--- 1996 BOATS ---
16 4	WHITECAP 165 CC	OP	CTRCN	FBG	DV	OB				7 3	800	10	2400	2750
17 2	PALM BEACH 1700 CC	OP	CTRCN	FBG	DV	OB				6 10	900	8	2750	3200

LOA FT IN	NAME AND/ OR MODEL	TOP/ RIG	BOAT TYPE	-HULL- MTL TP	TP	----ENGINE--- # HP	MFG	BEAM FT IN	WGT LBS	DRAFT FT IN	RETAIL LOW	RETAIL HIGH
			1996 BOATS									
17 2	PALM BEACH 1700 DUAL	OP	UTL	FBG DV	OB			6 10	950	8	2800	3250
17 2	PALM BEACH 1700 SIDE	OP	UTL	FBG DV	OB			6 10	900	8	2650	3100
18 6	BAYDANCER 185 CC	OP	CTRCN	FBG DV	OB			7 7	1150		3550	4100
19 6	BAYDANCER 1950 CC	OP	CTRCN	FBG SV	OB			8	1700	1	4950	5700
20 1	WHITECAP 200 CC	OP	CTRCN	FBG SV	OB			8 6	1800	1	5350	6150
21 6	BAYDANCER 215 CC	OP	CTRCN	FBG SV	OB			7 10	1800	10	5750	6600
21 6	BAYDANCER 2150 CC	OP	CTRCN	FBG SV	OB			7 10	2150	10	6600	7550
21 8	WHITECAP 222 CC	OP	CTRCN	FBG DV	OB			8 6	2200	1 6	6750	7750
21 8	WHITECAP 222 WI	OP	CTRCN	FBG DV	OB			8 6	2300	1 6	7000	8000

....For earlier years, see the BUC Used Boat Price Guide, Volume 3

PALMER JOHNSON INC
STURGEON BAY WI 54235   COAST GUARD MFG ID- PAJ See inside cover to adjust price for area

For more recent years, see the BUC Used Boat Price Guide, Volume 1

LOA FT IN	NAME AND/ OR MODEL	TOP/ RIG	BOAT TYPE	-HULL- MTL TP	TP	----ENGINE--- # HP	MFG	BEAM FT IN	WGT LBS	DRAFT FT IN	RETAIL LOW	RETAIL HIGH
			1995 BOATS									
65	EXPRESS 65		EXP	AL DV	IB	D	DD	19	66000	4 6	**	**
72 11	PJ 72 SF	FB	SF	AL DV	IB	T	D GM	20 6	85000	4 8	**	**
77	PJ 77 SF	FB	SF	AL DV	IB	T	D GM	20 6		4 8	**	**
			1994 BOATS									
65	EPXRESS 65		EXP	AL DV	IB	D	DD	19	66000	4 6	**	**
72 11	EAGLE 72 SF	FB	SF	AL DV	IB	T11CD	GM	20 6	85000	4 8	**	**
77	EAGLE 77 SF	FB	SF	AL DV	IB	T11CD	GM	20 6		4 8	**	**
			1993 BOATS									
72 11	EAGLE 72	FB	SF	AL DV	IB	T11CD	GM	20 6	85000	4 8	**	**
77	EAGLE 77	FB	SF	AL DV	IB	T11CD	GM	20 6		4 8	**	**
			1992 BOATS									
53	PJ 53 EXPRESS	HT	EXP	AL DV	IB	T11CD	MAN	15 11	43000	3 6	583000	640500
72 11	EAGLE 72	FB	SF	AL DV	IB	T11CD	GM	20 6	85000	4 8	**	**
75	PJ ALDEN 75	KTH	SA/CR	AL KC	IB	286D	VLVO	18	50T	6 6	**	**
77	EAGLE 77	FB	SF	AL DV	IB	T11CD	GM	20 6		4 8	**	**
			1991 BOATS									
72 11	EAGLE 72	FB	SF	AL DV	IB	T11CD	GM	20 6	85000	4 8	**	**
75	PJ ALDEN 75	KTH	SA/CR	AL KC	IB	286D	VLVO	18	50T	6 6	**	**
77	EAGLE 77	FB	SF	AL DV	IB	T11CD	GM	20 6		4 8	**	**
			1990 BOATS									
72 11	EAGLE 72	FB	SF	AL DV	IB	T11CD	GM	20 6	85000	4 8	**	**
75	PJ ALDEN 75	KTH	SA/CR	AL KC	IB	286D	VLVO	18	50T	6 6	**	**
77	EAGLE 77	FB	SF	AL DV	IB	T11CD	GM	20 6		4 8	**	**
			1989 BOATS									
72 11	EAGLE 72	FB	SF	AL DV	IB	T11CD	GM	20 6		4 8	**	**
72 11	EAGLE 77	FB	SF	AL DV	IB	T11CD	GM	20 6		4 8	**	**
			1984 BOATS									
45	P-J FRERS 45	SLP	SA/RC	AL KL	IB	D		13 6	19800	8	96300	106000
46	P-J HOLLAND 46	SLP	SA/RC	AL KL	IB	D		13	26000	8 3	116000	127500
56	P-J ALDEN 56	SLP	SA/RC	AL KL	IB	158D	VLVO		44000	5 6	307000	337000
62	FRERS 62	SLP	SA/RC	AL KL	IB	135D	PERK	17	42700	10	350000	384500
65	P-J DUBOIS 65	KTH	SA/RC	AL TK	IB	D		17	65000	7	448500	493000
68 9	P-J FRERS 69	SCH	SA/RC	AL KL	IB	D		18 2	90000	7 8	643500	707000
75	P-J ALDEN 75	KTH	SA/RC	AL KC	IB	286D	VLVO		50T	6 6	**	**
77	P-J FRERS 77	SLP	SA/RC	AL KL	IB	200D	GM		80000	10 4	**	**
77 6	ALDEN 78	KTH	SA/RC	AL KC	IB	D	CAT	18	95000	6	**	**
77 10	HOLLAND MAXI	SLP	SA/RC	AL KL	IB	384D	VLVO	18 1	69750	12 6	**	**

....For earlier years, see the BUC Used Boat Price Guide, Volume 3

PAMLICO YACHTS LTD
ROCKY MT NC 27801   See inside cover to adjust price for area

LOA FT IN	NAME AND/ OR MODEL	TOP/ RIG	BOAT TYPE	-HULL- MTL TP	TP	----ENGINE--- # HP	MFG	BEAM FT IN	WGT LBS	DRAFT FT IN	RETAIL LOW	RETAIL HIGH
			1986 BOATS									
28	PAMLICO 28	SLP	SA/RC	FBG KL	IB	D		9 6	9000	4 10	21400	23800
			1985 BOATS									
28	PAMLICO 28	SLP	SA/RC	FBG KL	IB	D		9 6	9000	4 10	20100	22300

PAN OCEANIC MARINE INC
MIAMI FL 33136   COAST GUARD MFG ID- FSL See inside cover to adjust price for area

LOA FT IN	NAME AND/ OR MODEL	TOP/ RIG	BOAT TYPE	-HULL- MTL TP	TP	----ENGINE--- # HP	MFG	BEAM FT IN	WGT LBS	DRAFT FT IN	RETAIL LOW	RETAIL HIGH
			1986 BOATS									
37 11	OCEANIC 38	SLP	SA/CR	FBG KL	IB	D		11 11	22000	5 6	76500	84100
42 11	OCEANIC 43	CUT	SA/CR	FBG KL	IB	D		13 1	27000	5 7	98700	108500
45 11	OCEANIC 46	CUT	SA/CR	FBG KL	IB	D		13 6	33000	5 10	118000	129500
			1984 BOATS									
37 11	OCEANIC 38	SLP	SA/CR	FBG KL	IB	D		11 11	22000	5 6	67700	74400
42 11	OCEANIC 43	CUT	SA/CR	FBG KL	IB	D		13 1	27000	5 7	87300	96000
45 10	OCEANIC 46	CUT	SA/CR	FBG KL	IB	D		13 6	33000	5 10	104000	114500

....For earlier years, see the BUC Used Boat Price Guide, Volume 3

PAN PACIFIC YACHTS LTD
TARZANA CA 91356   See inside cover to adjust price for area

LOA FT IN	NAME AND/ OR MODEL	TOP/ RIG	BOAT TYPE	-HULL- MTL TP	TP	----ENGINE--- # HP	MFG	BEAM FT IN	WGT LBS	DRAFT FT IN	RETAIL LOW	RETAIL HIGH
			1985 BOATS									
27	VANCOUVER	CUT	SA/CR	FBG KL	IB	20D	YAN	8 8	8900	4 6	28800	32000
32	VANCOUVER AFT COCKPT	CUT	SA/CR	FBG KL	IB	30D	YAN	10 7	14000	4 6	47700	52400
32	VANCOUVER PILOT	CUT	SA/CR	FBG KL	IB	23D- 30D		10 7	14000	4 6	48500	54400

PANTERA USA INC
N MIAMI BEACH FL 33180 COAST GUARD MFG ID- WCW See inside cover to adjust price for area

LOA FT IN	NAME AND/ OR MODEL	TOP/ RIG	BOAT TYPE	-HULL- MTL TP	TP	----ENGINE--- # HP	MFG	BEAM FT IN	WGT LBS	DRAFT FT IN	RETAIL LOW	RETAIL HIGH
			1993 BOATS									
23 7	PANTERA	OP	OFF	FBG DV	IO	365	MRCR	7	3700	1 6	12100	13700
28	PANTERA	OP	OFF	FBG DV	IO	T365	MRCR	7	5700	1 10	22900	25400
38	PANTERA	OP	OFF	FBG DV	IO	T390	MRCR	8 4	8000	1 8	44300	49200
			1992 BOATS									
24	PANTERA	OP	OFF	FBG DV	IO	365	MRCR	7	4000	1 6	12000	13700
28	PANTERA	OP	OFF	FBG DV	IO	T365	MRCR	7	5500	1 8	21500	23900
38	PANTERA	OP	OFF	FBG DV	IO	T575	MRCR	8 4	8000	1 8	54400	59800
			1991 BOATS									
23 7	PANTERA 24		OFF	FBG DV	IO	365	MRCR	7	3950	1 5	11100	12600
28	PANTERA 28		OFF	FBG DV	IO	T365	MRCR	8	5600	1 6	19900	22100
38	PANTERA 38		OFF	FBG DV	IO	T575	MRCR	8 2	8000	1 8	52100	57200

....For earlier years, see the BUC Used Boat Price Guide, Volume 3

PARAMOUNT POWERBOATS
DANIA FL 33004   COAST GUARD MFG ID- PPJ See inside cover to adjust price for area

For more recent years, see the BUC Used Boat Price Guide, Volume 1

LOA FT IN	NAME AND/ OR MODEL	TOP/ RIG	BOAT TYPE	-HULL- MTL TP	TP	----ENGINE--- # HP	MFG	BEAM FT IN	WGT LBS	DRAFT FT IN	RETAIL LOW	RETAIL HIGH
			1996 BOATS									
21	SUPER FISHERMAN	OP	CTRCN	FBG SV	OB			7 2	1800		6700	7700
26	SPORT FISHERMAN	OP	CTRCN	FBG DV	OB			8	3200		14900	17000
			1995 BOATS									
21	SUPER FISHERMAN	OP	CTRCN	FBG SV	OB			7 2	1800		6350	7300
26	SPORT FISHERMAN	OP	CTRCN	FBG DV	OB			8	3200		14200	16100
			1994 BOATS									
21	SUPER FISHERMAN	OP	CTRCN	FBG SV	OB			7 2	1800		6050	6950
26	SPORT FISHERMAN	OP	CTRCN	FBG DV	OB			8	3200		13500	15300
			1988 BOATS									
16	PARAMOUNT 4.9M	OP	CTRCN	FBG SV	OB			7 2	1400		3250	3750
18 3	PARAMOUNT 5.5M	OP	CTRCN	FBG SV	OB			7 9	1600		3650	4250
21	PARAMOUNT 6.4M	OP	CTRCN	FBG SV	OB			7 2	1900		4650	5350
21	PARAMOUNT 6.4MSE	OP	CTRCN	FBG SV	OB			7 2	1900		5350	6150
			1987 BOATS									
16	PARAMOUNT 4.9M	OP	CTRCN	FBG SV	OB			7 2	1100		2500	2950
21	PARAMOUNT 6.4M	OP	CTRCN	FBG SV	OB			7 2	1500		3700	4300
21	PARAMOUNT 6.4MSE	OP	CTRCN	FBG SV	OB			7 2	1500		4300	5000
			1985 BOATS									
21	PARAMOUNT 6.4M	OP	CTRCN	FBG SV	OB			7 2	1500		3600	4200
21	PARAMOUNT 6.4MSE	OP	CTRCN	FBG SV	OB			7 2	1500		4000	4650
			1984 BOATS									
21	PARAMOUNT 6.4M	OP	CTRCN	FBG SV	OB			7 2	1500	11	3100	3650
21	PARAMOUNT 6.4MSE	OP	CTRCN	FBG SV	OB			7 2	1500	11	4350	5000

PARKER DAWSON CORP

HINGHAM MA 02043 COAST GUARD MFG ID- PHR See inside cover to adjust price for area
FOR OLDER MODELS SEE PARKER HOPKINS

LOA FT	IN	NAME AND/ OR MODEL	TOP/ RIG	BOAT TYPE	HULL MTL	HULL TP	ENGINE TP	# HP	MFG	BEAM FT	IN	WGT LBS	DRAFT FT	IN	RETAIL LOW	RETAIL HIGH
1984 BOATS																
21	1	POACHER	KTH	SA/RC	FBG	DB	OB			7	6	1792	1		3350	3850
25	7	PARKER-DAWSON	SLP	SA/CR	FBG	SK	IB	D		8		5700	1	8	11400	13000

....For earlier years, see the BUC Used Boat Price Guide, Volume 3

PARKER MARINE ENTERPRISES

BEAUFORT NC 28516-2129 COAST GUARD MFG ID- PXM See inside cover to adjust price for area

For more recent years, see the BUC Used Boat Price Guide, Volume 1

LOA FT	IN	NAME AND/ OR MODEL	TOP/ RIG	BOAT TYPE	HULL MTL	HULL TP	ENGINE TP	# HP	MFG	BEAM FT	IN	WGT LBS	DRAFT FT	IN	RETAIL LOW	RETAIL HIGH
1996 BOATS																
18		CENTER CONSOLE 18	OP	CTRCN	FBG	SV	OB			7	6	1725		7	6000	6900
21		DV CC 21	OP	CTRCN	FBG	DV	OB			8	6	2525	1	3	11300	12800
21		DV WALKAROUND 21	OP	CUD	FBG	DV	OB			8	6	2975	1	3	12300	14000
23		DV CC 23	OP	CTRCN	FBG	DV	OB			8	6	2975	1	3	14300	16200
23		DV WALKAROUND 23	OP	CUD	FBG	DV	OB			9	6	3375	1	5	15600	17700
23	2	DV EXTENDED CABIN 23	HT	CUD	FBG	DV	OB			8	6	4000	1	4	17400	19800
23	2	DV EXTENDED CABIN 23	HT	CUD	FBG	DV	IO	220-250		8	6	5075	1	4	22500	25400
23	2	DV EXTENDED CABIN 23	HT	CUD	FBG	DV	IO	188D	VLVO	8	6	5075	1	4	26700	29700
23	4	DV SPORT CABIN 23	HT	CUD	FBG	DV	OB			8	6	3575	1	3	16500	18800
25	4	CENTER CONSOLE 25	HT	CTRCN	FBG	SV	OB			9	6	2700	1		16200	18400
25	4	CENTER CONSOLE 25	HT	CTRCN	FBG	SV	IO	220-265		9	6	3610	1		21100	24600
25	4	DV CC 25	OP	CTRCN	FBG	DV	OB			9	6	3600	1	5	18900	21000
25	4	DV CC 25	OP	CTRCN	FBG	DV	IO	235-300		9	6	4675	1	5	25200	29900
25	4	DV EXTENDED CABIN 25	HT	CUD	FBG	DV	OB			9	6	5000	1	6	21600	24000
25	4	DV EXTENDED CABIN 25	HT	CUD	FBG	DV	IO	235-300		9	6	6125	1	6	29400	34500
25	4	DV EXTENDED CABIN 25	HT	CUD	FBG	DV	IO	188D	VLVO	9	6	6125	1	6	35100	39100
25	4	DV SPORT CABIN 25	HT	CUD	FBG	DV	OB			9	6	4500	1	5	20700	23000
25	4	DV SPORT CABIN 25	HT	CUD	FBG	DV	IO	235-300		9	6	5625	1	5	27000	31700
25	4	DV SPORT CABIN 25	HT	CUD	FBG	DV	IO	188D	VLVO	9	6	5625	1	5	31800	35300
25	4	DV WALKAROUND 25	OP	CUD	FBG	DV	OB			9	6	4250	1	5	20200	22400
25	4	DV WALKAROUND 25	OP	CUD	FBG	DV	IO	235-300		9	6	5375	1	5	26100	30800
25	4	DV WALKAROUND 25	OP	CUD	FBG	DV	IO	180D	VLVO	9	6	5375	1	5	30400	33800
25	4	EXTENDED CABIN 25	HT	CUD	FBG	SV	OB			9	6	3875	1		19500	21600
25	4	EXTENDED CABIN 25	HT	CUD	FBG	SV	IO	235-300		9	6	5375	1		26600	31300
25	4	EXTENDED CABIN 25	HT	CUD	FBG	SV	IO	188D	VLVO	9	6	5375	1		31200	34700
25	4	SPORT CABIN 25	OP	CUD	FBG	SV	OB			9	6	3375	1		18400	20400
25	4	SPORT CABIN 25	OP	CUD	FBG	SV	IO	220-250		9	6	4285	1		22400	25500
25	4	SPORT CABIN 25	OP	CUD	FBG	SV	IO	188D	VLVO	9	6	4285	1		26000	28900
25	4	WALKAROUND 25	OP	CUD	FBG	SV	OB			9	6	3275	1		18100	20200
25	4	WALKAROUND 25	OP	CUD	FBG	SV	IO	220-250		9	6	4457	1		22700	25800
25	4	WALKAROUND 25	OP	CUD	FBG	SV	IO	188D	VLVO	9	6	4457	1		26500	29400
1995 BOATS																
18		CENTER CONSOLE 18	OP	CTRCN	FBG	SV	OB			7	6	1725		7	5700	6550
21		DV CC 21	OP	CTRCN	FBG	DV	OB			8	6	2525	1	3	10700	12200
21		DV WALKAROUND 21	OP	CUD	FBG	DV	OB			8	6	2975	1	3	11700	13300
23		DV CC 23	OP	CTRCN	FBG	DV	OB			8	6	2975	1	3	13600	15500
23		DV WALKAROUND 23	OP	CUD	FBG	DV	OB			9	6	3375	1	3	14800	16900
23	2	DV EXTENDED CABIN 23	HT	CUD	FBG	DV	OB			8	6	4000	1	4	16600	18900
23	2	DV EXTENDED CABIN 23	HT	CUD	FBG	DV	IO	185-255		8	6	5075	1	4	20800	23800
23	4	DV SPORT CABIN 23	HT	CUD	FBG	DV	OB			8	6	3525	1	3	15600	17700
25	4	CENTER CONSOLE 25	HT	CTRCN	FBG	SV	OB			9	6	2700	1		15500	17600
25	4	CENTER CONSOLE 25	HT	CTRCN	FBG	SV	IO	220-275		9	6	3610	1		19700	23200
25	4	DV CC 25	OP	CTRCN	FBG	DV	OB			9	6	3600	1	5	17600	20000
25	4	DV CC 25	OP	CTRCN	FBG	DV	IO	250-300		9	6	4675	1	5	23800	27900
25	4	DV EXTENDED CABIN 25	HT	CUD	FBG	DV	OB			9	6	5000	1	6	20600	22900
25	4	DV EXTENDED CABIN 25	HT	CUD	FBG	DV	IO	250-300		9	6	6125	1	6	27700	32200
25	4	DV EXTENDED CABIN 25	HT	CUD	FBG	DV	IO	185D	VLVO	9	6	6125	1	6	32700	36300
25	4	DV SPORT CABIN 25	HT	CUD	FBG	DV	OB			9	6	4500	1	5	19800	22000
25	4	DV SPORT CABIN 25	HT	CUD	FBG	DV	IO	250-300		9	6	5625	1	5	25400	29600
25	4	DV SPORT CABIN 25	HT	CUD	FBG	DV	IO	185D	VLVO	9	6	5625	1	5	29600	32900
25	4	DV WALKAROUND 25	OP	CUD	FBG	DV	OB			9	6	4250	1	5	19300	21400
25	4	DV WALKAROUND 25	OP	CUD	FBG	DV	IO	185-300		9	6	5375	1	5	23400	28100
25	4	EXTENDED CABIN 25	HT	CUD	FBG	SV	OB			9	6	3875	1		18700	20800
25	4	EXTENDED CABIN 25	HT	CUD	FBG	SV	IO	250-300		9	6	5375	1		25000	29200
25	4	EXTENDED CABIN 25	HT	CUD	FBG	SV	IO	185D	VLVO	9	6	5375	1		29000	32200
25	4	SPORT 25	OP	CTRCN	FBG	SV	OB			9	6	3375	1		17100	19400
25	4	SPORT 25	OP	CTRCN	FBG	SV	IO	225-255		9	6	4285	1		22100	25200
25	4	SPORT 25	OP	CTRCN	FBG	SV	IO	185D	VLVO	9	6	4285	1		30100	33500
25	4	WALKAROUND 25	OP	CUD	FBG	SV	OB			9	6	3275	1		16900	19200
25	4	WALKAROUND 25	OP	CUD	FBG	SV	IO	220-250		9	6	4350	1		20800	23700
25	4	WALKAROUND 25	OP	CUD	FBG	SV	IO	185D	VLVO	9	6	4350	1		24200	26900
1994 BOATS																
21		SPORT 21	OP	CTRCN	FBG	DV	OB			8	6	2125		10	9200	10500
21		SPORT 21	OP	CTRCN	FBG	DV	IO	160-235		8	6	2125		10	10300	12100
21		WALKAROUND 21	OP	CUD	FBG	DV	OB			8	6	2525		10	10300	11700
21		WALKAROUND 21	OP	CUD	FBG	DV	IO	160-235		8	6	2525		10	10500	12300
23		DV SPORT 23	OP	CTRCN	FBG	DV	OB			8	6	2975	1	3	13000	14800
23		DV SPORT 23	OP	CTRCN	FBG	DV	IO	160-250		8	6	2975	1	3	13300	15800
23		DV SPORT 23	OP	CTRCN	FBG	DV	IO	300	MRCR	8	6	2975	1	3	14800	16800
23		SPORT 23	OP	CTRCN	FBG	SV	OB			8	6	2350		10	10800	12300
23		SPORT 23	OP	CTRCN	FBG	SV	IO	160-250		8	6	2350		10	11800	14100
23	2	DV SPORT CABIN 23	HT	CUD	FBG	DV	OB			8	6	4000	1	4	15900	18000
23	2	DV SPORT CABIN 23	HT	CUD	FBG	DV	IO	160-300		8	6	4000	1	4	15500	19200
25	4	DV EXTENDED CABIN 25	HT	CUD	FBG	DV	OB			9	6	5000	1	6	19700	21900
25	4	DV EXTENDED CABIN 25	HT	CUD	FBG	DV	IO	190-300		9	6	5000	1	6	21400	25900
25	4	DV SPORT 25	OP	CTRCN	FBG	DV	OB			9	6	3600	1	5	16800	19100
25	4	DV SPORT 25	OP	CTRCN	FBG	DV	IO	190-300		9	6	3600	1	5	18100	22200
25	4	DV SPORT CABIN 25	HT	CUD	FBG	DV	OB			9	6	4500	1	5	19100	21200
25	4	DV SPORT CABIN 25	HT	CUD	FBG	DV	IO	190-235		9	6	4500	1	5	19400	22200
		IO 250 MRCR 20200 22400, IB 250 23700 26500, IO 300 MRCR													21200	23600
		IB 310 24500 27500, IB 250D-275D 33200 38200														
25	4	DV WALKAROUND 23	OP	CUD	FBG	DV	OB			9	6	4500	1	5	16600	18900
25	4	DV WALKAROUND 23	OP	CUD	FBG	DV	IO	160-300		9	6	4500	1	5	17500	21200
25	4	DV WALKAROUND 25	OP	CUD	FBG	DV	OB			9	6	4250	1	5	18600	20600
25	4	DV WALKAROUND 25	OP	CUD	FBG	DV	IO	190-235		9	6	4250	1	5	18900	21400
		IO 250 MRCR 19500 21700, IB 250 22900 25600, IO 300 MRCR													20600	22900
		IB 310 23700 26600, IB 250D-275D 32100 37100														
25	4	EXTENDED CABIN 25	HT	CUD	FBG	SV	OB			9	6	3750	1		17200	19600
25	4	EXTENDED CABIN 25	HT	CUD	FBG	SV	IO	160-250		9	6	3750	1		17100	20800
25	4	EXTENDED CABIN 25	HT	CUD	FBG	SV	IO	300	MRCR	9	6	3750	1		19700	21800
25	4	SPORT 25	OP	CTRCN	FBG	SV	OB			9	6	2700	1		14700	16700
25	4	SPORT 25	OP	CTRCN	FBG	SV	IO	160-250		9	6	2700	1		15200	18900
25	4	SPORT 25	OP	CTRCN	FBG	SV	IO	300	MRCR	9	6	2700	1		18200	20200
25	4	SPORT CABIN 25	HT	CUD	FBG	SV	OB			9	6	3375	1		16400	18600
25	4	SPORT CABIN 25	HT	CUD	FBG	SV	IO	160-250		9	6	3375	1		15900	19500
25	4	SPORT CABIN 25	HT	CUD	FBG	SV	IO	300	MRCR	9	6	3375	1		18600	20700
25	4	WALKAROUND 23	OP	CUD	FBG	SV	OB			9	6	3750	1		15200	17300
25	4	WALKAROUND 23	OP	CUD	FBG	SV	IB	160-250		9	6	3750	1		18500	20800
25	4	WALKAROUND 25	OP	CUD	FBG	SV	OB			9	6	3275	1		16100	18300
25	4	WALKAROUND 25	OP	CUD	FBG	SV	IO	160-250		9	6	3275	1		15500	19000
25	4	WALKAROUND 25	OP	CUD	FBG	SV	IO	300	MRCR	9	6	3275	1		18200	20200
1993 BOATS																
17		SPORT 17		CTRCN	FBG	DV	OB			7		1050		7	3450	4050
18		SPORT 18		CTRCN	FBG	DV	OB			7	6	1450		7	4650	5350
21		CUDDY 21		CUD	FBG	DV	OB			8	6	2525		10	9850	11200
21		SPORT 21		CTRCN	FBG	DV	OB			8	6	2125		10	8850	10000
21		SPORT 21		CTRCN	FBG	DV	IO	155-235		8	6	3025		10	11800	13800
21		WALKAROUND 21		CUD	FBG	SV	IO	155-235		8	6	3525		10	12300	14300
23		CENTER CONSOLE 23		CTRCN	FBG	SV	OB			8	6	2300		10	10200	11600
23		CUDDY 23		CUD	FBG	SV	OB			8	6	2700		10	11600	13200
23		DV CUDDY CABIN 23		CUD	FBG	DV	OB			8	6	3375	1	3	13600	15400
23		DV SPORT 23		CTRCN	FBG	DV	OB			8	6	3175	1	3	13000	14800
23		DV SPORT 23		CTRCN	FBG	DV	IO	155-300		8	6	3882	1	3	15200	18400
23		DV SPORT 23		CTRCN	FBG	DV	IO	120D-185D		8	6	3882	1	3	21500	26000
23		DV SPORT 23		CTRCN	FBG	DV	IO	200D	MRCR	8	6	3882	1	3	24200	26900
23		DV SPORT CABIN 23		CUD	FBG	DV	IO	155-300		8	6	5175	1	5	18300	21200
23		DV SPORT CABIN 23		CUD	FBG	DV	IO	120D-200D		8	6	5175	1	5	20800	25500
23		DV WALKAROUND 23		CUD	FBG	DV	IO	155-300		8	6	4282	1	3	15500	18700
23		DV WALKAROUND 23		CUD	FBG	DV	IO	120D-200D		8	6	4282	1	3	18500	22700
23		DV WALKAROUND 23		CUD	FBG	SV	IO	140D	VLVO	8	6	4282	1	3	18800	20900
23		SPORT 23		CTRCN	FBG	SV	IO	155-260		8	6	3207		10	13400	15900
23		SPORT 23		CTRCN	FBG	SV	IO	120D-185D		8	6	3207		10	19300	22900
23		SPORT CABIN 23		CUD	FBG	SV	OB			8	6	4000	1	4	15000	17000
23		WALKAROUND 23		CUD	FBG	SV	IO	155-260		8	6	3707		10	14000	16500
23		WALKAROUND 23		CUD	FBG	SV	IO	120D-185D		8	6	3707		10	16500	20000
25	4	CUDDY 25		CUD	FBG	SV	OB			9	6	3275	1		15500	17600
25	4	DV EXT CABIN 25		CUD	FBG	DV	OB			9	6	4250	1	5	17400	21200
25	4	DV EXT CABIN 25		CUD	FBG	DV	IO	170-330		9	6	6125	1	6	22200	27500
		IO 350 MRCR 25500 28300, IO 140D-216D 26500 31900, IO T135-T240													24200	28700

LOA FT IN	NAME AND/ OR MODEL	TOP/ RIG	BOAT TYPE	HULL MTL TP	TP	ENGINE # HP MFG	BEAM FT IN	WGT LBS	DRAFT FT IN	RETAIL LOW	RETAIL HIGH
1993 BOATS											
25 4	DV SPORT 25		CTRCN FBG	DV	OB		9 6	3600	1 5	16100	18300
25 4	DV SPORT 25		CTRCN FBG	DV	IO	170-295	9 6	4675	1 5	19300	23500
	IO 300-350 21400	25500, IO 140D-216D	26300	32600, IO T135-T240						21500	25900
25 4	DV SPORT CABIN 25		CUD FBG	DV	IO	170-330	9 6	4500	1 5	18300	20300
	IO 350 MRCR 24200	26900, IO 140D-216D	24600	29900, IO T135-T240						22900	27200
25 4	DV WALKAROUND 25		CUD FBG	DV	IO	170-300	9 6	5375	1 5	19300	24200
	IO 330-350 22000	25200, IO 140D-216D	22700	28000, IO T135-T240						21700	25700
25 4	EXT CABIN 25		CUD FBG	SV	OB		9 6	3875	1 1	16700	19000
25 4	EXT CABIN 25		CUD FBG	SV	IO	155-295	9 6	5375	1 1	20400	25200
	IO 300-350 22500	27000, IO 140D-216D	24200	29800, IO T135-T240						23100	27300
25 4	SPORT 25		CTRCN FBG	SV	OB		9 6	2700	1	14100	16000
25 4	SPORT 25		CTRCN FBG	SV	IO	155-260	9 6	3607	1	16500	20100
	IO 295-350 18700	22500, IO 140D-187D	21800	27200, IO 200D-216D						25000	27800
	IO T135-T240 18900	23000									
25 4	SPORT CABIN 25		CUD FBG	SV	IO	155-295	9 6	3375	1	15700	17800
	IO 300-350 19300	23100, IO 140D-216D	19700	24700, IO T135-T240						19400	23500
25 4	WALKAROUND 25		CUD FBG	SV	IO	155-295	9 6	4457	1	17500	21400
	IO 300-350 19500	23300, IO 140D-216D	20200	25100, IO T135-T240						19600	23700
1992 BOATS											
17	SPORT 17	OP	CTRCN FBG	DV	OB		7	1050	7	3350	3850
18	SPORT 18	OP	CTRCN FBG	DV	OB		7 6	1450	7	4500	5150
21	CUDDY 21	OP	CUD FBG	DV	OB		8 6	2525	10	9450	10700
21	SPORT 21	OP	CTRCN FBG	DV	OB		8 6	2125	10	8400	9650
23	23	OP	CUD FBG	SV	IO	250	8 6	2700	10	10900	12400
23	DV 23	OP	CTRCN FBG	DV	OB		8 6	2300	10	9800	11100
23	DV CUDDY CABIN 23	OP	CUD FBG	DV	IO		8 6	3375	1 3	13100	14800
23	DV SPORT 23	OP	CTRCN FBG	DV	OB		8 6	3175	1 3	12500	14200
23	SPORT CABIN 23	OP	CUD FBG	DV	IO		8 6	4000	1 4	14400	16400
25	CUDDY 25	OP	CUD FBG	DV	IO		9 6	3275	1	14900	16900
25 4	DV CUDDY CABIN 25	OP	CUD FBG	DV	IO	400	9 6	4250	1 5	21200	23600
25 4	DV EXT CABIN 25	OP	CUD FBG	DV	IO		9 6	5000	1 6	18300	20300
25 4	DV SPORT 25	OP	CTRCN FBG	DV	OB		9 6	3600	1 5	15400	17500
25 4	DV SPORT 25	OP	CUD FBG	DV	IO	400	9 6	4500	1 5	21800	24200
25 4	EXT CABIN 25	OP	CUD FBG	SV	OB		9 6	3875	1 1	16100	18300
25 4	SPORT CABIN 25	OP	CUD FBG	SV	IO	325	9 6	2700	1	16200	18500
25 4	SPORT CABIN 25	OP	CUD FBG	SV	IO	325	9 6	3375	1	16500	18800
1991 BOATS											
17	SPORT 17	OP	CTRCN FBG	DV	OB		7	1050	7	3200	3750
18	SPORT 18	OP	CTRCN FBG	DV	OB		7 6	1450	7	4250	4950
21	CUDDY CABIN	ST	FSH FBG	DV	OB		8 6	3550	10	10500	11900
21	CUDDY CABIN	ST	FSH FBG	DV	IO	235	8 6	3550	10	11400	13000
21	SPORT 21	OP	FSH FBG	DV	OB		8 6	2125	10	8100	9300
21	SPORT 21	OP	FSH FBG	DV	IO	235	8 6	2125	10	8700	10000
23	CUDDY CABIN DEEP VEE	ST	FSH FBG	DV	OB		8 6	3375	10	12500	14300
23	SPORT 23	ST	FSH FBG	DV	OB		8 6	2300	10	9450	10700
23	SPORT 23	ST	FSH FBG	DV	IO	250	8 6	2300	10	10100	11500
23	SPORT 23 DEEP VEE	ST	CTRCN FBG	DV	OB		8 6	2976	1 3	11500	13000
23	SPORT CABIN 23	ST	FSH FBG	DV	OB		8 6	2700	1	10700	12200
23	SPORT CABIN 23	ST	FSH FBG	DV	IO		8 6	2700	10	**	**
23	SPORT CABIN 23	ST	FSH FBG	DV	IB		8 6	2700	10	**	**
25 4	CUDDY CABIN	ST	FSH FBG	DV	OB		9 6	3550	10	14900	16900
25 4	CUDDY CABIN	ST	FSH FBG	DV	IO	325	9 6	3550	10	16800	19000
25 4	CUDDY CABIN DEEP VEE	ST	FSH FBG	DV	OB		9 6	4250	10	16100	18300
25 4	CUDDY CABIN DEEP VEE	ST	FSH FBG	DV	IO	400	9 6	4250	10	21000	23300
25 4	SPORT 25	OP	CTRCN FBG	DV	OB		9 6	2700	1	13000	14700
25 4	SPORT 25	ST	FSH FBG	DV	IO	325	9 6	2700	1	15200	17300
25 4	SPORT 25 DEEP VEE	ST	FSH FBG	DV	OB		9 6	3550	10	14900	16900
25 4	SPORT 25 DEEP VEE	ST	FSH FBG	DV	IO	400	9 6	3550	10	19600	21700
25 4	SPORT CABIN 25	OP	FSH FBG	DV	IO		9 6	3375	1	14500	16400
25 4	SPORT CABIN 25	ST	FSH FBG	DV	IO	325	9 6	3375	1	16400	18600
25 4	SPORT 25 DEEP VEE	ST	FSH FBG	DV	OB		9 6	4500	10	16500	18800
25 4	SPORT CABIN DEEP VEE 25	ST	FSH FBG	DV	IO	400	9 6	4500	10	21600	24000
1990 BOATS											
17	SPORT 17	OP	CTRCN FBG	DV	OB		7	1050	7	3100	3600
18	SPORT 18	OP	CTRCN FBG	DV	OB		7 6	1450	7	4100	4800
21	SPORT 21	OP	FSH FBG	DV	OB		8 6	2125	10	7800	8950
21	SPORT 21	OP	FSH FBG	DV	IO	235	8 6	2125	10	8150	9400
23	SPORT 23	ST	FSH FBG	DV	OB		8 6	2300	10	9150	10400
23	SPORT 23	ST	CTRCN FBG	DV	IO	250	8 6	2300	10	9500	10800
23	SPORT 23 DEE VEE	ST	CTRCN FBG	DV	OB		8 6	2976	1 3	11100	12600
23	SPORT 23 DEE VEE	ST	CTRCN FBG	DV	IO	250	8 6	2976	1 3	10700	12200
23	SPORT CABIN 23	ST	FSH FBG	DV	IO		8 6	2700	10	10300	11800
23	SPORT CABIN 23	ST	FSH FBG	DV	IB		8 6	2700	10	**	**
25 4	SPORT 25	OP	CTRCN FBG	DV	OB		9 6	2700	1	12500	14200
25 4	SPORT 25	OP	CTRCN FBG	DV	OB	325	9 6	2700	1	14300	16300
25 4	SPORT CABIN 25	OP	FSH FBG	DV	OB		9 6	3375	1	13900	15800
25 4	SPORT CABIN 25	OP	FSH FBG	DV	OB	325	9 6	3375	1	15400	17500

PARKER YACHTS

WINGA BOATS
ROCKLAND ME 04841-2546
See inside cover to adjust price for area

LOA FT IN	NAME AND/ OR MODEL	TOP/ RIG	BOAT TYPE	HULL MTL TP	TP	ENGINE # HP MFG	BEAM FT IN	WGT LBS	DRAFT FT IN	RETAIL LOW	RETAIL HIGH
1989 BOATS											
21	PARKER 21	SLP	SA/RC FBG	SK	OB		8 2	1950	3 9	7650	8800
27	PARKER 27	SLP	SA/RC FBG	SK	IB	9D YAN	9 3	5000	5 3	23500	26100
31	PARKER 31	SLP	SA/RC FBG	SK	IB	18D YAN	10	6000	6	31700	35300
1988 BOATS											
21	PARKER 21	SLP	SA/RC FBG	KL	OB		8 2	1950	3 9	7150	8200
27	PARKER 27	SLP	SA/RC FBG	KL	IB	18D YAN	9 3	5000	5 3	22300	24800
31	PARKER 31	SLP	SA/RC FBG	KL	IB	18D YAN	10	6000	6	29500	32700
1987 BOATS											
21	PARKER 21	SLP	SA/RC FBG	KL	OB		8 2	1950	3 9	6700	7750
27	SUPER-SEAL	SLP	SA/RC FBG	KL	IB	D	9 3	5000	5 3	20600	22900
31	PARKER 31	SLP	SA/RC FBG	KL	IB	18D	10	6000	6	27500	30600
1985 BOATS											
32	U-S-SOUTHERLY 100	SLP	SA/CR FBG	SK	IB	D	9 11	9500	5 10	39600	44000
36 10	U-S-SOUTHERLY 115	SLP	SA/CR FBG	SK	IB	D	11 11	14600	6 8	61700	67800
48	U-S-SOUTHERLY 145	SLP	SA/CR FBG	SK	IB	D	13 11	23000	7 8	120500	132500

....For earlier years, see the BUC Used Boat Price Guide, Volume 3

PARKINS MARINE INC

FT LAUDERDALE FL 33315   COAST GUARD MFG ID- PKN See inside cover to adjust price for area

LOA FT IN	NAME AND/ OR MODEL	TOP/ RIG	BOAT TYPE	HULL MTL TP	TP	ENGINE # HP MFG	BEAM FT IN	WGT LBS	DRAFT FT IN	RETAIL LOW	RETAIL HIGH
1987 BOATS											
22 9	H-23	SLP	SA/CR FBG	KL	IB	D	8	6900	3	17400	19800
29 5	H-28	SLP	SA/CR FBG	KL	IB	18D YAN	9	9600	3 6	31000	34400
37	H-37	KTH	SA/CR FBG	KL	IB	300 YAN	9 3	20000	4 11	68500	75200
1986 BOATS											
22 9	H-23	SLP	SA/CR FBG	KL	IB	D	8	6900	3	16400	18600
28	H-28	SLP	SA/CR FBG	KL	IB	18D YAN	9	9600	3 6	28600	31800
1985 BOATS											
23	H-23	SLP	SA/CR FBG	KL	IB	15D	8	6900	3	15500	17600
33	SCHEHERAZADE H-28	SLP	SA/CR FBG	KL	IB	15D YAN	9	10500	3 6	31400	34900
1984 BOATS											
32 9	SPIRIT H-28	SLP	SA/CR FBG	KL	IB	13D VLVO	8 11	10500	3 6	29500	32800

....For earlier years, see the BUC Used Boat Price Guide, Volume 3

PASSPORT YACHTS EAST INC

ANNAPOLIS MD 21403   COAST GUARD MFG ID- PAS See inside cover to adjust price for area

For more recent years, see the BUC Used Boat Price Guide, Volume 1

LOA FT IN	NAME AND/ OR MODEL	TOP/ RIG	BOAT TYPE	HULL MTL TP	TP	ENGINE # HP MFG	BEAM FT IN	WGT LBS	DRAFT FT IN	RETAIL LOW	RETAIL HIGH
1996 BOATS											
41 8	ROYAL PASSPORT 41 AC	CUT	SACAC FBG	KL	IB	51D YAN	12 8	22690	5 9	224500	247000
45 6	ROYAL PASSPORT 44 AC	CUT	SACAC FBG	KL	IB	62D YAN	14 2	25611	6 6	273000	300000
45 6	ROYAL PASSPORT 44 CC	CUT	SACAC FBG	KL	IB	62D YAN	14 2	25611	6 6	295500	324500
47 4	ROYAL PASSPORT 47 AC	KTH	SACAC FBG	KL	IB	62D YAN	14 2	25611	6 6	310500	341500
47 4	ROYAL PASSPORT 47 AC	CUT	SACAC FBG	KL	IB	62D YAN	14 2	25611	6 6	299000	328500
47 4	ROYAL PASSPORT 47 CC	CUT	SACAC FBG	KL	IB	62D YAN	14 2	25611	6 6	322500	354500
56 6	ROYAL PASSPORT 56 DS	CUT	SACIS FBG	KL	IB	110D YAN	16 3	41500	6 11	688000	756000
58 9	ROYAL PASSPORT 58 DS	CUT	SACIS FBG	KL	IB	110D YAN	16 3	41500	6 11	727500	799500

LOA FT	LOA IN	NAME AND/ OR MODEL	TOP/ RIG	BOAT TYPE	HULL MTL	HULL TP	ENGINE TP	#	HP	MFG	BEAM FT	BEAM IN	WGT LBS	DRAFT FT	DRAFT IN	RETAIL LOW	RETAIL HIGH
1994 BOATS																	
45	6	ROYAL PASSPORT 44	CUT	SACAC	FBG	KL	IB		62D	YAN	14	2	25611	5	4	255000	280000
47	3	ROYAL PASSPORT 47	CUT	SACAC	FBG	KL	IB		62D	YAN	14	2	26000	6		279000	306500
49		ROYAL PASSPORT 49	CUT	SACAC	FBG	KL	IB		75D	YAN	13	6	33000	6		334000	367000
50		ROYAL PASSPORT 50	CUT	SACAC	FBG	KL	IB		75D	YAN	13	6	33000	6		354000	389000
1993 BOATS																	
45	2	ROYAL PASSPORT 44	CUT	SACAC	FBG	KL	IB		62D	YAN	14		22000	5		222000	243500
46	7	ROYAL PASSPORT 47	CUT	SACAC	FBG	KL	IB		77D	YAN	13	6	34000	6		286500	315000
49		ROYAL PASSPORT 49	CUT	SACAC	FBG	KL	IB		77D	YAN	13	6	32000	6		313000	344000
50		ROYAL PASSPORT 50	CUT	SACAC	FBG	KL	IB		77D	YAN	13	6	32000	6		332500	365500
1992 BOATS																	
46	7	ROYAL PASSPORT 47	CUT	SAIL	FBG	KL	IB		77D	YAN	13	6	34000	6		271500	298500
49		ROYAL PASSPORT 49	CUT	SAIL	FBG	KL	IB		77D	YAN	13	6	32000	6		296500	326000
50		ROYAL PASSPORT 50	CUT	SAIL	FBG	KL	IB		77D	YAN	13	6	32000	6		315000	346000
1991 BOATS																	
49		ROYAL PASSPORT 49	CUT	SAIL	FBG	KL	IB		77D	YAN	13	6	33000	6		283500	311500
50		ROYAL PASSPORT 50	CUT	SAIL	FBG	KL	IB		77D	YAN	13	6	33000	6		300500	330500

PASSPORT YACHTS INC

TIEN MOU TAPEI TAIWAN ROC See inside cover to adjust price for area

LOA FT	LOA IN	NAME AND/ OR MODEL	TOP/ RIG	BOAT TYPE	HULL MTL	HULL TP	ENGINE TP	#	HP	MFG	BEAM FT	BEAM IN	WGT LBS	DRAFT FT	DRAFT IN	RETAIL LOW	RETAIL HIGH
1988 BOATS																	
37		PASSPORT 37	SLP	SA/RC	FBG	KL	IB		33D		11	11	17360	5	10	97000	106500
39	5	PASSPORT 40	SLP	SA/CR	FBG	KL	IB		50D		12	8	22771	5	9	129500	142500
41	9	PASSPORT 42	CUT	SA/CR	FBG	KL	IB		50D		12	10	25500	6	4	150000	165000
46	7	PASSPORT 47	CUT	SA/CR	FBG	KL	IB		85D		13	6	34000	6	6	205500	225500
46	7	PASSPORT 47 CC	CUT	SA/CR	FBG	KL	IB		85D		13	6	34000	6	6	213000	234000
51	1	PASSPORT 51 CC	KTH	SA/CR	FBG	KL	IB		D		14	5	38000	7	2	271500	298500
1986 BOATS																	
37		PASSPORT 37	SLP	SA/RC	FBG	KL	IB		33D		11	11	17360	5	10	87100	95700
39	5	PASSPORT 40	SLP	SA/CR	FBG	KL	IB		50D		12	8	22771	5	9	116500	128000
41	9	PASSPORT 42	CUT	SA/CR	FBG	KL	IB		50D		12	10	25500	6	4	134500	148000
46	7	PASSPORT 47	CUT	SA/CR	FBG	KL	IB		85D		13	6	34000	6	6	187500	206000
51	1	PASSPORT 51	CUT	SA/CR	FBG	KL	IB		D		14	5	38000	7	2	243000	267000
51	1	PASSPORT 51	KTH	SA/CR	FBG	KL	IB		D		14	5	38000	7	2	244000	268000
1985 BOATS																	
39	5	PASSPORT 40	SLP	SA/CR	FBG	KL	IB		50D		12	8	22771	5	9	110500	121500
41	9	PASSPORT 42	CUT	SA/CR	FBG	KL	IB		50D		12	10	25500	6	4	127500	140000
46	7	PASSPORT 47	CUT	SA/CR	FBG	KL	IB		85D		13	6	34000	6	6	178000	195500
51	1	PASSPORT 51	KTH	SA/CR	FBG	KL	IB		D		14	5	38000	7	2	231000	254000
1984 BOATS																	
39	5	PASSPORT 40	SLP	SA/CR	FBG	KL	IB		50D		12	8	22771	5	9	104500	115000
41	9	PASSPORT 42	CUT	SA/CR	FBG	KL	IB		50D		12	10	25500	6	4	121000	133000
46	7	PASSPORT 47	CUT	SA/CR	FBG	KL	IB		85D		13	6	34000	6	6	168500	185000
51	1	PASSPORT 51	KTH	SA/CR	FBG	KL	IB		D		14	5	38000	7	2	219000	241000

G A PATTEN BOATBUILDING INC

KITTERY ME 03904 COAST GUARD MFG ID- GAP See inside cover to adjust price for area

LOA FT	LOA IN	NAME AND/ OR MODEL	TOP/ RIG	BOAT TYPE	HULL MTL	HULL TP	ENGINE TP	#	HP	MFG	BEAM FT	BEAM IN	WGT LBS	DRAFT FT	DRAFT IN	RETAIL LOW	RETAIL HIGH
1986 BOATS																	
36	6	PIPEDREAM 36	SLP	SA/CR	FBG	KL	IB		D		10	6	13450	5	8	60800	66800
1985 BOATS																	
36	6	PIPE-DREAM 36.6	SLP	SA/CR	F/S	KL	IB		30D	WEST	10	6	15000	5	7	62800	69000
1984 BOATS																	
36	6	PIPE-DREAM 36.6	SLP	SA/CR	F/S	KL	IB		27D	WEST	10	6	15000	5	7	59000	64900

....For earlier years, see the BUC Used Boat Price Guide, Volume 3

PDQ YACHTS INC

WHITBY ONTARIO CANADA L COAST GUARD MFG ID- QPQ See inside cover to adjust price for area

For more recent years, see the BUC Used Boat Price Guide, Volume 1

LOA FT	LOA IN	NAME AND/ OR MODEL	TOP/ RIG	BOAT TYPE	HULL MTL	HULL TP	ENGINE TP	#	HP	MFG	BEAM FT	BEAM IN	WGT LBS	DRAFT FT	DRAFT IN	RETAIL LOW	RETAIL HIGH
1996 BOATS																	
31	7	PDQ 32 CLASSIC	SLP	SACAC	F/S	CT	IB	T	10	YAMA	16		7200	2	6	91300	100500
31	7	PDQ 32 LRC	SLP	SACAC	F/S	CT	IB	T	9D	YAN	16		7800	2	8	93300	102500
31	7	PDQ 32 PACIFICA	SLP	SACAC	F/S	CT	IB	T	10	YAMA	16		7300	2	6	91600	100500
36	5	PDQ 36 CLASSIC	SLP	SACAC	F/S	CT	IB	T	10	YAMA	18	3	8000	2	10	140500	154500
36	5	PDQ 36 LRC	SLP	SACAC	F/S	CT	IB	T	20D	YAN	18	3	8700	2	11	143500	158000
1995 BOATS																	
31	7	PDQ 32 CLASSIC	SLP	SACAC	FBG	CT	OB				16		5200	2	6	78700	86500
31	7	PDQ 32 LRC	SLP	SACAC	FBG	CT	OB				16		5600	2	6	80400	88300
31	7	PDQ 32 S/C	SLP	SACAC	FBG	CT	OB				16		4800	2	6	77000	84600
36	5	PDQ 36 CLASSIC	SLP	SACAC	FBG	CT	OB				18	3	8000	2	10	132000	145000
36	5	PDQ 36 LRC	SLP	SACAC	FBG	CT	SD	T	18D	YAN	18	3	8700	2	11	135000	148500
36	5	PDQ 36 S/C	SLP	SACAC	FBG	CT	OB				18	3	7200	2	9	128500	141000
1994 BOATS																	
31	7	PDQ 32 CLASSIC	SLP	SACAC	FBG	CT	OB				16		5200	2	6	74000	81300
31	7	PDQ 32 LRC	SLP	SACAC	FBG	CT	OB				16		5600	2	6	75500	83000
31	7	PDQ 32 S/C	SLP	SACAC	FBG	CT	OB				16		4800	2	6	72400	79600
36	5	PDQ 36 CLASSIC	SLP	SACAC	FBG	CT	OB				18	3	8000	2	10	124000	136500
36	5	PDQ 36 LRC	SLP	SACAC	FBG	CT	SD	T	18D	YAN	18	3	8700	2	11	127000	139500
36	5	PDQ 36 S/C	SLP	SACAC	FBG	CT	OB				18	3	7200	2	9	120500	132500
1993 BOATS																	
36	5	PDQ 36	SLP	SACAC	F/S	CT	OB				18	3	7000	2	10	112500	124000
1992 BOATS																	
36	5	PDQ 36	SLP	SA/CR	F/S	CT	OB				18	3	7000	2	10	106000	116500

PEARSON YACHT CORP

PORTSMOUTH RI 02871 COAST GUARD MFG ID- PEA See inside cover to adjust price for area

LOA FT	LOA IN	NAME AND/ OR MODEL	TOP/ RIG	BOAT TYPE	HULL MTL	HULL TP	ENGINE TP	#	HP	MFG	BEAM FT	BEAM IN	WGT LBS	DRAFT FT	DRAFT IN	RETAIL LOW	RETAIL HIGH
1991 BOATS																	
26	11	PEARSON 27	SLP	SA/CR	FBG	KL	IB		12D	UNIV	9	2	5800	3	4	23400	26000
30	10	PEARSON 31	SLP	SA/CR	FBG	KL	IB		18D	YAN	10	9	10000	5	9	43100	47900
32	6	PEARSON 33	SLP	SA/CR	FBG	WK	IB		18D	YAN	11		11750	3	7	50800	55800
33	9	PEARSON 34	FB	CNV	FBG		IB	T	320D	CAT	13		19000	3	4	94800	104000
34	6	PEARSON 34	SLP	SA/CR	FBG	KL	IB		34D	YAN	11	6	11500	4		50700	55700
37		PEARSON 38	SLP	SA/CR	FBG	KL	IB		34D	YAN	12	4	15175	4	9	69300	76200
37	5	PEARSON 37	SLP	SA/CR	FBG	KL	IB		34D	YAN	12	4	16000	4	8	73500	80800
37	6	PEARSON 38	FB	CNV	FBG	SV	IB	T	375D	CAT	13	10	24000	3	9	133000	146500
39	3	PEARSON 39	SLP	SA/CR	FBG	WK	IB		34D	YAN	12	5	16800	6	10	83100	91400
1990 BOATS																	
26	11	PEARSON 27	SLP	SA/CR	FBG	KL	IB		12D	UNIV	9	2	5800	3	4	22200	24600
30	10	PEARSON 31	SLP	SA/CR	FBG	KL	IB		18D	YAN	10	9	10000	5	9	40800	45400
32	6	PEARSON 33	SLP	SA/CR	FBG	WK	IB		18D	YAN	11		11750	3	7	48100	52900
33	9	PEARSON 34	FB	CNV	FBG		IB	T	320D	CAT	13		19000	3	4	90600	99500
34	6	PEARSON 34	SLP	SA/CR	FBG	KL	IB		34D	YAN	11	6	11500	4		48000	52800
36	6	PEARSON 36	SLP	SA/CR	FBG	KC	IB		30D	YAN	12	4	15000	6	6	64000	70300
37		PEARSON 38	SLP	SA/CR	FBG	KL	IB		34D	YAN	12	4	15175	4	9	65700	72200
37	5	PEARSON 37	SLP	SA/CR	FBG	KL	IB		34D	YAN	12	4	16000	4	8	69700	76600
37	6	PEARSON 38	FB	CNV	FBG	SV	IB	T	375D	CAT	13	10	24000	3	9	127000	139500
39	3	PEARSON 39	SLP	SA/CR	FBG	WK	IB		34D	YAN	12	5	16800	6	10	78800	86600
1989 BOATS																	
26	11	PEARSON 27	SLP	SA/CR	FBG	KL	IB		12D	WEST	9	1	5800	3	4	21000	23400
28	5	PEARSON 28	SLP	SA/CR	FBG	KL	IB		18D		9	10	7350	3	6	27700	30700
30	9	PEARSON 31	SLP	SA/CR	FBG	KL	IB		18D		10	9	10200	3	11	39500	43800
32	6	PEARSON 33	SLP	SA/CR	FBG	KC	IB		18D	YAN	11		11750	3	7	45800	50300
32	6	PEARSON 33	SLP	SA/CR	FBG	KL	IB		18D	YAN	11		11000	5	11	42500	47200
34	6	PEARSON 34	SLP	SA/CR	FBG	KL	IB		34D	YAN	11	6	11500	4		45700	50300
36	6	PEARSON 36	SLP	SA/CR	FBG	KC	IB		30D	YAN	12	4	15850	4	2	63500	69800
36	6	PEARSON 36	SLP	SA/CR	FBG	KL	IB		30D	YAN	12	4	15200	4	8	61300	67300
36	6	PEARSON 36	SLP	SA/CR	FBG	KL	IB		30D	YAN	12	4	15000	6	6	60600	66600
37	5	PEARSON 37	SLP	SA/CR	FBG	KL	IB		34D	YAN	12	4	16000	4	8	66000	72500
37	6	PEARSON 38	FB	CNV	FBG	SV	IB		350	CRUS	13	10	24000	3	9	93600	103000
37	6	PEARSON 38	FB	CNV	FBG	SV	IB		375D	CAT	13	10	24000	3	9	106500	117000
37	6	PEARSON 38	FB	DC	FBG	SV	IB		350	CRUS	13	10	24000	3	9	93300	102500
37	6	PEARSON 38	FB	DC	FBG	SV	IB		260D	CAT	13	10	24000	3	9	102000	112000
39	3	PEARSON 39	SLP	SA/CR	FBG	KC	IB		34D	YAN	12	5	17500	4	8	76900	84500
39	3	PEARSON 39	SLP	SA/CR	FBG	KL	IB		34D	YAN	12	5	16800	6	10	74600	82000
1988 BOATS																	
26	11	PEARSON 27	SLP	SA/CR	FBG	KL	IB		12D	UNIV	9	1	5800	3	4	19900	22100
28	5	PEARSON 28	SLP	SA/CR	FBG	KL	IB		18D		9	10	7350	3	6	26200	29100
30	9	PEARSON 31	SLP	SA/CR	FBG	KL	IB		18D		10	9	10200	3	11	37400	41500
32	6	PEARSON 33	SLP	SA/CR	FBG	KC	IB		18D	YAN	11		11750	3	7	42900	47700
32	6	PEARSON 33	SLP	SA/CR	FBG	KL	IB		18D	YAN	11		11000	5	11	40300	44700
36	6	PEARSON 36	SLP	SA/CR	FBG	KC	IB		30D	YAN	12	4	15850	4	2	60200	66200
36	6	PEARSON 36	SLP	SA/CR	FBG	KL	IB		30D	YAN	12	4	15000	6	6	57400	63100
37	5	PEARSON 37	SLP	SA/CR	FBG		IB		34D	YAN	12	4	16000	4	8	62500	68700
37	6	PEARSON 38	FB	CNV	FBG		IB	T	350	CRUS	13	10	24000	3	9	93500	103000
37	6	PEARSON 38	FB	CNV	FBG		IB	T	375D	CAT	13	10	24000	3	9	116000	127500
37	6	PEARSON 38	FB	DC	FBG		IB	T	350	CRUS	13	10	25000	3	9	96000	105500
37	6	PEARSON 38	FB	DC	FBG		IB	T	260D	CAT	13	10	25000	3	9	109500	120000
39	3	PEARSON 39	SLP	SA/CR	FBG	KC	IB		34D	YAN	12	5	17650	4	8	73300	80500

LOA FT	LOA IN	NAME AND/ OR MODEL	TOP/ RIG	BOAT TYPE	-HULL- MTL	-HULL- TP	ENGINE TP	ENGINE # HP	ENGINE MFG	BEAM FT	BEAM IN	WGT LBS	DRAFT FT	DRAFT IN	RETAIL LOW	RETAIL HIGH
		1988 BOATS														
39	3	PEARSON 39	SLP	SA/CR	FBG	KL	IB	34D	YAN	12	5	16800	6	10	70700	77700
		1987 BOATS														
26	11	PEARSON 27	SLP	SA/CR	FBG	KL	OB			9	1	5800	3	4	18200	20300
26	11	PEARSON 27	SLP	SA/CR	FBG	KL	IB	12D	UNIV	9	1	5800	3	4	19100	21200
28	5	PEARSON 28	SLP	SA/CR	FBG	KL	IB	15D		9	10	7350	3	6	24800	27600
30	9	PEARSON 31	SLP	SA/CR	FBG	KL	IB	18D		10	9	10200	3	11	35400	39400
32	6	PEARSON 33	SLP	SA/CR	FBG	KC	IB	18D		11		11750	3	7	40700	45200
32	6	PEARSON 33	SLP	SA/CR	FBG	KL	IB	18D		11		11000	5	11	38100	42400
36	6	PEARSON 36	SLP	SA/CR	FBG	KC	IB	30D	YAN	12	4	15850	4	2	57000	62700
36	6	PEARSON 36	SLP	SA/CR	FBG	KL	IB	30D	YAN	12	4	15000	6	6	54400	59800
39	3	PEARSON 39	SLP	SA/CR	FBG	KC	IB	46D		12	5	17650	4	8	69600	76400
39	3	PEARSON 39	SLP	SA/CR	FBG	KL	IB	46D		12	5	16800	6	10	67100	73800
42	2	PEARSON 422	SLP	SA/CR	FBG	KL	IB	58D	YAN	13		22200	5	3	91700	100500
43		PEARSON 43	FB	MY	FBG	SV	VD	T165D	PERK	14	10	22000	3		97100	106500
		1986 BOATS														
17	11	PEARSON 18	SLP	SA/CR	FBG	CB				6	10	800			3300	3850
23		PEARSON 23	SLP	SA/CR	FBG	KC				8		3500			8600	9900
25		PEARSON 25	SLP	SA/CR	FBG	KL				8		3750	4	3	9900	11200
28	5	PEARSON 28	SLP	SA/CR	FBG	KL	IB	15D		9	10	7350	3	6	23500	26100
30	4	PEARSON 303	SLP	SA/CR	FBG	KL	IB	15D	YAN	10	11	10400	4	4	34200	38000
32	6	PEARSON 33	SLP	SA/CR	FBG	KC	IB	18D		11		11750	3	7	38500	42800
32	6	PEARSON 33	SLP	SA/CR	FBG	KL	IB	18D		11		11000	5	11	36100	40200
33	9	PEARSON 34	SLP	SA/CR	FBG	KC	IB	23D	YAN	11	2	11750	3	10	38800	43200
33	9	PEARSON 34	SLP	SA/CR	FBG	KL	IB	23D	YAN	11	2	11240	5	11	37200	41300
36	6	PEARSON 36	SLP	SA/CR	FBG	KC	IB	30D	YAN	12	4	15850	4	2	54100	59400
36	6	PEARSON 36	SLP	SA/CR	FBG	KL	IB	30D	YAN	12	4	15000	6	6	51500	56600
38	4	PEARSON 385	SLP	SA/CR	FBG	KC	IB	D		11	7	20575			70900	77900
38	4	PEARSON 385	SLP	SA/CR	FBG	KL	IB	D		11	7	19100	5	6	66900	73600
39	3	PEARSON 39	SLP	SA/CR	FBG	KC	IB	46D		12	5	17650	4	8	65900	72400
39	3	PEARSON 39	SLP	SA/CR	FBG	KL	IB	46D		12	5	16800	6	10	63600	69900
42	2	PEARSON 422	SLP	SA/CR	FBG	KL	IB	58D	YAN	13		22200	5	3	86900	95400
43		PEARSON 43	FB	MY	FBG	SV	VD	T310	CRUS	14	10	22000	3		90800	99800
43		PEARSON 43	FB	MY	FBG	SV	VD	T165D	PERK	14	10	22000	3		92800	102000
		1985 BOATS														
22	6	ENSIGN 22	SLP	SA/RC	FBG	KL	OB			7		3000	3		7100	8150
23		PEARSON CAT	CAT	SAIL	FBG	KL	OB			8		3000	4		7200	8300
28	5	PEARSON 28	SLP	SA/CR	FBG	KL	IB	15D		9	10	7350	3	6	22300	24700
29	11	FLYER 30	SLP	SA/RC	FBG	KL	IB	D		11	1	6135	5	9	19100	21300
30	4	PEARSON 303	SLP	SA/CR	FBG	KL	IB	15D	YAN	10	11	10400	4	4	32400	36000
32	3	PEARSON 323	SLP	SA/CR	FBG	KL	IB	D		10	3	12000	4	5	37300	41400
33	9	PEARSON 34	SLP	SA/CR	FBG	KC	IB	23D	YAN	11	2	11750	3	10	36800	40900
33	9	PEARSON 34	SLP	SA/CR	FBG	KL	IB	23D	YAN	11	2	11240	5	11	35300	39200
36	5	PEARSON 367	SLP	SA/CR	FBG	KL	IB	D		11	6	17100	5	6	54600	60000
36	6	PEARSON 36	SLP	SA/CR	FBG	KC	IB	30D	YAN	12	4	15850	4	2	51200	56300
36	6	PEARSON 36	SLP	SA/CR	FBG	KL	IB	30D	YAN	12	4	15000	6	6	48800	53700
37		PEARSON 37	SLP	SA/RC	FBG	KL	IB	D		11	10	12800	6	6	43100	47800
37		PEARSON 37 SHOAL	SLP	SA/RC	FBG	KL	IB	D		11	10	12800	4	11	43100	47800
38	3	PEARSON 385	SLP	SA/CR	FBG	KC	IB	44D	YAN	11	7	20575	4	4	67100	73700
38	3	PEARSON 385	SLP	SA/CR	FBG	KL	IB	44D	YAN	11	7	19100	5	6	63400	69600
38	3	PEARSON 386	SLP	SA/CR	FBG	KC	IB	44D	YAN	11	7	19590	4	4	64600	71000
38	3	PEARSON 386	SLP	SA/CR	FBG	KL	IB	44D	YAN	11	7	17000	5	6	57900	63700
42	2	PEARSON 422	SLP	SA/CR	FBG	KL	IB	58D	YAN	13		22000	5	3	81900	90000
42	4	PEARSON 424	SLP	SA/CR	FBG	KL	IB	D		13		21000	5	3	80000	87900
43		PEARSON 43	FB	MY	FBG	SV	VD	T310	CRUS	14	10	22000	3		87000	95600
43		PEARSON 43	FB	MY	FBG	SV	VD	T165D	PERK	14	10	22000	3		88900	97600
53	7	PEARSON 530	KTH	SA/CR	F/S	KC	IB	85D	PERK	14	11	45000	5	9	193500	212500
53	7	PEARSON 530	KTH	SA/CR	F/S	KL	IB	85D	PERK	14	11	43000	6	10	192000	211000
		1984 BOATS														
22	6	ENSIGN	SLP	SA/OD	FBG	KL	OB			7		3000	3		6700	7700
30	3	PEARSON 303	SLP	SA/CR	FBG	KL	IB	15D	YAN	10	11	10000	4	4	29500	32800
33	10	PEARSON 34	SLP	SA/CR	FBG	KC	IB	16D	UNIV	11	3	11750	3	10	34900	38700
33	10	PEARSON 34	SLP	SA/RC	FBG	KL	IB	16D	UNIV	11	3	11240	5	11	33400	37100
36	11	PEARSON 37	SLP	SA/RC	F/S	KL	IB	21D	UNIV	11	10	12800	6	5	40500	45000
38	6	PEARSON 385	SLP	SA/CR	FBG	KL	IB	40D	PERK	11	6	18800			59500	65400
38	6	PEARSON 385	SLP	SA/CR	FBG	KL	IB	42D	PERK	11	7		5	6	55400	60900
38	6	PEARSON 386	SLP	SA/CR	FBG	KL	IB	42D	PERK	11	7	16915	5	6	54900	60300
38	6	PEARSON 386	SLP	SA/CR	FBG	KL	VD	50D	PERK			18800			59600	65500
42	2	PEARSON 422	SLP	SA/CR	FBG	KL	IB	58D	WEST	13		22000	5	3	77600	85300
42	4	PEARSON 424	CUT	SA/CR	F/S	KL	IB	58D	WEST	13		23000	5	3	80200	88100
42	4	PEARSON 424	KTH	SA/CR	F/S	KL	IB	58D	WEST	13		23000	5	3	80200	88200
42	4	PEARSON 424 PLANC	CUT	SA/CR	FBG	KL	IB	58D	WEST	13		23000	5	3	80200	88100
42	4	PEARSON 424 PLANC	KTH	SA/CR	FBG	KL	IB	58D	WEST	13		23000	5	3	80200	88200
53		PEARSON 530	KTH	SA/CR	F/S	KC	IB	85D	PERK	15		43000	5	9	175000	192500
53		PEARSON 530	KTH	SA/CR	F/S	KL	IB	85D	PERK	15		43000	6	10	175000	192500

....For earlier years, see the BUC Used Boat Price Guide, Volume 3

PELORUS YACHT SALES INC

ROCK HALL MD 21661 COAST GUARD MFG ID- POY See inside cover to adjust price for area

LOA FT	LOA IN	NAME AND/ OR MODEL	TOP/ RIG	BOAT TYPE	-HULL- MTL	-HULL- TP	ENGINE TP	ENGINE # HP	ENGINE MFG	BEAM FT	BEAM IN	WGT LBS	DRAFT FT	DRAFT IN	RETAIL LOW	RETAIL HIGH
		1986 BOATS														
30	10	SCANMAR 31 DEEP	SLP	SA/RC	FBG	KL	IB	18D	VLVO	9	10	7400	5	5	30800	34200
30	10	SCANMAR 31 SHOAL	SLP	SA/RC	FBG	KL	IB	18D	VLVO	9	10	7400	4	7	31100	34600
33	2	SCANMAR 33 DEEP	SLP	SA/RC	FBG	KL	IB	28D	VLVO	10	9	10140	5	9	41500	46100
33	2	SCANMAR 33 SHOAL	SLP	SA/RC	FBG	KL	IB	28D	VLVO	10	9	10140	4	11	41800	46500
35	1	SCANMAR 35 DEEP	SLP	SA/CR	FBG	KL	IB	28D	VLVO	10	9	10582	5	10	42200	46900
35	1	SCANMAR 35 SHOAL	SLP	SA/CR	FBG	KL	IB	28D	VLVO	10	9	10582	4	11	42600	47300
40	1	SCANMAR 40 DEEP	SLP	SA/CR	FBG	KL	IB	40D	VLVO	12	9	17700	6	6	71600	78700
40	1	SCANMAR 40 SHOAL	SLP	SA/CR	FBG	KL	IB	40D	VLVO	12	9	18300	5		73300	80500
		1985 BOATS														
30	10	SCANMAR 31 DEEP	SLP	SA/RC	FBG	KL	IB	18D	VLVO	9	10	7400	5	5	29100	32400
30	10	SCANMAR 31 SHOAL	SLP	SA/RC	FBG	KL	IB	18D	VLVO	9	10	7400	4	7	29100	32400
33	2	SCANMAR 33 DEEP	SLP	SA/RC	FBG	KL	IB	28D	VLVO	10	9	10140	5	9	39200	43500
33	2	SCANMAR 33 SHOAL	SLP	SA/RC	FBG	KL	IB	28D	VLVO	10	9	10140	4	9	39200	43500
35	1	SCANMAR 35 DEEP	SLP	SA/CR	FBG	KL	IB	28D	VLVO	10	9	10582	5	10	39900	44300
35	1	SCANMAR 35 SHOAL	SLP	SA/CR	FBG	KL	IB	28D	VLVO	10	9	10582	4	10	39900	44300

PENN YAN BOAT CO

OAK HALL VA 23416-0127 COAST GUARD MFG ID- PYB See inside cover to adjust price for area

For more recent years, see the BUC Used Boat Price Guide, Volume 1

LOA FT	LOA IN	NAME AND/ OR MODEL	TOP/ RIG	BOAT TYPE	-HULL- MTL	-HULL- TP	ENGINE TP	ENGINE # HP	ENGINE MFG	BEAM FT	BEAM IN	WGT LBS	DRAFT FT	DRAFT IN	RETAIL LOW	RETAIL HIGH
		1996 BOATS														
16		SWIFT 160	OP	RNBT	FBG	DV	IO	135	MRCR	6	5	1330	1	2	4300	5000
16		SWIFT 160 B/R	OP	RNBT	FBG	DV	IO	135	MRCR	6	5	1330	1	2	4450	5100
16		SWIFT 1600	OP	RNBT	FBG	DV	OB			6	5	880	1	2	1350	1600
16		SWIFT 1600 DC	OP	RNBT	FBG	DV	OB			6	5	880	1	2	1450	1700
17		SURF RESCUE	OP	ROW	FBG					5	6	360			**	**
18		GAMEFISH 180	OP	RNBT	FBG	DV	IO	135-205		7	4	2095	1	2	6500	7750
18		GAMEFISH 180 DC	OP	RNBT	FBG	DV	IO	135-205		7	4	2095	1	2	6650	7650
18		GAMEFISH 1800	OP	RNBT	FBG	SV	OB			7	4	1545	1	2	2600	3000
18		GAMEFISH 1800 DC	OP	RNBT	FBG	DV	OB			7	4	1545	1	2	2600	3000
18		STORM 1901	OP	CTRCN	FBG	SV	OB			8		1600	1	6	2500	2950
18	7	SAVAGE 1902 DC	OP	RNBT	FBG	DV	OB			8		1600	2	5	2650	3100
20	1	SPECTOR 2001 CC	OP	CTRCN	FBG	SV	OB			8		2285	1	4	3150	3650
20	6	ADVENTURER 202	OP	FSH	FBG	SV	IO	135-210		8		2985	1	4	8600	10100
20	6	ADVENTURER 202	OP	FSH	FBG	SV	IO	220D	MRCR	8		2985	1	4	15500	17600
20	6	EXPLORER 2000	OP	FSH	FBG	SV	OB			8		2185	1	2	3200	3750
20	6	SPECTOR 202 CC	OP	RNBT	FBG	SV	IO	135-250		8			1	4	7550	9100
20	6	SPECTOR 202 CC	OP	RNBT	FBG	SV	IO	220D	MRCR	8			1	4	11600	13100
22	7	OUTRAGE 225	HT	FSH	FBG	SV	IO	190-280		8	6	3600	2	6	10900	13200
22	7	OUTRAGE 225	HT	FSH	FBG	SV	IO	180D	MRCR	8	6	3600	2	6	17400	19800
22	7	RAGE 223	ST	FSH	FBG	SV	IO	190-280		8	6	3600	2	6	10900	13200
22	7	RAGE 223	ST	FSH	FBG	SV	IO	180D	MRCR	8	6	3600	2	6	17400	19800
22	8	AVENGER 232	OP	FSH	FBG	SV	IB	155	CRUS	9	5	3850	1	4	13500	15400
		IO 190-220 12400 14200, IO 250 MRCR 12700 14400, IB 250-260													13800	15700
		IO 280 MRCR 13100 14800, IO 180D MRCR 19500 21600, IB 180D-210D													18700	21200
		IO 220D MRCR 20300 22600, IB 262D MRCR 20300 22600														
22	8	AVENGER 235	HT	FSH	FBG	SV	IB	155	CRUS	9	5	4150	1	4	14300	16200
		IO 190-220 13000 15000, IO 250 MRCR 13400 15200, IB 250-260													14500	16500
		IO 280 MRCR 13700 15600, IO 180D MRCR 20300 22500, IB 180D-210D													19300	22100
		IO 220D MRCR 21100 23500, IB 262D MRCR 21100 23400														
22	8	AVENGER 239	FB	SF	FBG	SV	IB	155	CRUS	9	5	4350	1	4	14800	16800
		IO 190-220 14600 16700, IO 250 MRCR 14500 16400, IB 250-260													15000	17100
		IO 280 MRCR 14900 16900, IO 180D MRCR 20900 23300, IB 180D-210D													19800	22700
		IO 220D MRCR 21800 24200, IB 262D MRCR 21600 24000														
25		AGGRESSOR 257	OP	CR	FBG	DV	IB	155	CRUS	9	4	5100	2	3	18300	20300
		IO 210-220 15800 18000, IO 250 MRCR 16200 18400, IB 250-260													19100	21200
		IO 280 MRCR 16600 18800, IO 180D MRCR 19800 22000, IB 180D-210D													23500	27000
		IO 220D MRCR 20700 23000, IB 262D MRCR 25800 28700, IO 270D MRCR													21900	24400
25		AGRESSOR 257	OP	CR	FBG	DV	IO	300	MRCR	9	4	5100	2	3	16900	19200

LOA FT	LOA IN	NAME AND/ OR MODEL	TOP/ RIG	BOAT TYPE	-HULL- MTL	-HULL- TP	ENGINE TP	ENGINE # HP	ENGINE MFG	BEAM FT	BEAM IN	WGT LBS	DRAFT FT	DRAFT IN	RETAIL LOW	RETAIL HIGH
		1996 BOATS														
25		SHADOW 2500	TH	SF	FBG	SV	OB			9	4	5400	2		7950	9150
26		C-TRACKER 267	OP	SF	FBG	DV	IB	155	CRUS	10		5950	2	5	20900	23200
		IO 210-250 20700 23500, IB 260-265 21900 24600, IO 280 MRCR													21900	24300
		IO 300 MRCR 21900 24300, IB 300-320 22500 25300, IO 330 MRCR													23100	25600
		IO 180D MRCR 28200 31300, IB 180D-210D 26700 30700, IO 220D MRCR													29400	32700
		IB 262D MRCR 29200 32500, IO 270D MRCR 30500 33800, IB T155 CRUS													23400	25900
		IO T190-T220 22900 26100, IB T260-T320 24800 29300, IB T150D MRCR													32200	35800
		IO T180D MRCR 35500 39400, IBT180D-T210D 33700 39300, IB T262D MRCR													38300	42600
26		COMPETITOR 262	OP	SF	FBG	DV	IB	155	CRUS	10		5950	2	5	20800	23100
		IO 210-250 20600 23600, IB 260-265 21700 24500, IO 280 MRCR													21700	24100
		IO 300 MRCR 21800 24200, IB 300-320 22400 25100, IO 330 MRCR													22900	25500
		IO 180D MRCR 28000 31100, IB 210D MRCR 27500 30500, IO 220D MRCR													29300	32500
		IB 262D MRCR 29100 32300, IO 270D MRCR 30300 33600, IB T155 CRUS													23200	25800
		IO T190-T220 22800 25900, IB T260-T320 24600 29100, IB T150D MRCR													32000	35600
		IO T180D MRCR 35300 39200, IBT180D-T210D 33500 39000, IB T262D MRCR													38100	42300
26		LEGACY 269	FB	CR	FBG	DV	IB	155	CRUS	10		6800	2	5	22700	25200
		IO 210-250 20200 22600, IB 260-320 23600 27200, IO 180D MRCR													24900	27700
		IB 180D-210D 29500 33800, IO 220D MRCR 25900 28700, IB 262D MRCR													31900	35500
		IO 270D MRCR 27500 30500, IB T155 CRUS 25000 27800, IO T190-T205													21500	24200
		IB T260-T320 26400 31100, IB T150D MRCR 34800 38600, IO T180D MRCR													30600	33900
		IBT180D-T210D 36300 42000														
26		LEGEND 269	FB	CR	FBG	DV	IB	155-220		10		6800	2	5	23100	26100
		IO 250 MRCR 20400 22700, IB 250-265 23800 27000, IO 280 MRCR													21100	23500
		IB 280 MRCR 24100 26800, IO 300 MRCR 21500 23900, IB 300-320													23100	27700
		IO 330 MRCR 22100 24500, IB 330 MRCR 24700 27400, IO 180D MRCR													25300	28100
		IB 180D-210D 30000 34300, IO 220D MRCR 26200 29200, IB 262D MRCR													32400	36000
		IO 270D MRCR 27200 30200, IB T155 CRUS 25400 28300, IO T190-T220													21900	25300
		IB T260-T320 26800 31500, IB T150D MRCR 35200 39100, IO T180D MRCR													30900	34400
		IBT180D-T262D 36700 45600														
26		PRO-HUNTER 265	HT	SF	FBG	DV	IB	155	CRUS	10		6300	2	5	21700	24100
		IO 210-250 21900 24900, IB 260-265 22800 25300, IO 280 MRCR													22900	25400
		IO 300 MRCR 23300 25800, IB 300-320 23100 26000, IO 330 MRCR													24000	26600
		IO 180D MRCR 29300 32600, IB 180D-210D 27700 31700, IO 220D MRCR													30600	33900
		IB 262D MRCR 30000 33400, IO 270D MRCR 32200 35800, IB T155 CRUS													24000	26700
		IO T190-T220 24200 27500, IB T260-T320 25700 29900, IB T150D MRCR													33100	36800
		IO T180D MRCR 36500 40600, IBT180D-T210D 34600 40100, IB T262D MRCR													39000	43400
26	2	INTRUDER 255	HT	SF	FBG	SV	IO	190-280		8	6	4600	2	9	15700	18800
26	2	INTRUDER 255	HT	SF	FBG	SV	IO	180D-270D		8	6	4600	2	9	22300	27200
26	2	INVECTOR 253	OP	SF	FBG	DV	IO	270D	MRCR	8	6	4350	2	9	23700	26400
26	2	INVECTOR 253	OP	SF	FBG	SV	IO	190-280		8	6	4350	2	9	15100	18000
26	2	INVECTOR 253	OP	SF	FBG	SV	IO	180D-270D		8	6	4350	2	9	21500	26400
28		C-HUNTER 278	ST	SF	FBG	DV	IB	155-320		10		6800	1	5	23300	27900
		IB T155-T320 25700 31900, IB T150D MRCR 35600 39500, IB T262D MRCR													41600	46200
28		C-HUNTER 278	ST	SF	FBG	SV	IO	210-250		10		6800	1	5	23500	26200
		IB 260-265 24400 27200, IO 280 MRCR 24500 27200, IO 300 MRCR													24900	27600
		IB 300-310 24900 27600, IO 330 MRCR 25600 28400, IO 180D MRCR													31900	35400
		IB 180D-210D 30200 34500, IO 220D MRCR 33100 36800, IB 262D MRCR													32600	36300
		IO 270D MRCR 34800 38600, IO T190-T250 25800 30100, IB T260-T265													27500	30600
		IO T180D MRCR 39100 43400, IB T180D MRCR 37100 41300, IO T205D MRCR													40500	45000
		IB T210D MRCR 38700 43000														
28		C-STALKER 275	HT	OFF	FBG	SV	IB	155	CRUS	10		7200	1	5	24400	27100
		IO 210-250 21200 24000, IB 260-265 25100 27900, IO 280 MRCR													22000	24500
		IO 300 MRCR 22300 24800, IB 300-310 25500 28300, IO 330 MRCR													22900	25500
		IO 180D MRCR 26400 29300, IB 210D MRCR 31900 35400, IO 220D MRCR													27100	30100
		IB 262D MRCR 33300 37000, IO 270D MRCR 28300 31400, IB T155 CRUS													26300	29200
		IO T190-T210 23100 25900, IB T260-T310 27800 31700, IB T150D MRCR													36000	40000
		IO T180D MRCR 31500 35000, IBT180D-T262D 37400 46200														
28	3	PERSUADER 299	FB	CR	FBG	DV	IB	320	CRUS	11		9400	1	11	30700	34100
		IB 180D MRCR 37700 41900, IB T155-T320 31000 38400, IBT140D-T230D													41400	51200
		IB T262D MRCR 48000 52700														
28	3	PREDATOR 298	HT	SF	FBG	DV	IB	T155-T300		11		8400	1	11	29200	36000
		IB T310-T320 32900 37500, IBT140D-T210D 39000 46400, IBT230D-T262D													44000	50800
28	3	PROWLER 295	HT	SF	FBG	DV	IB	T260-T320		11		8900	1	11	34100	39600
28	3	PROWLER 295	HT	SF	FBG	DV	IB	T140D-T230D		11		8900	1	11	40900	50900
28	3	PROWLER 295	HT	SF	FBG	DV	IB	T262D	MRCR	11		8900	1	11	47800	52500
32	8	COMMANDER 339	FB	CR	FBG	DV	IB	T155-T320		11	3	13500	2	5	46100	55000
32	8	COMMANDER 339	FB	CR	FBG	DV	IB	T140D-T262D		11	3	13500	2	5	54300	65600
		1995 BOATS														
16		SWIFT 160	OP	RNBT	FBG	DV	IO	135	MRCR	6	5	1330	1	2	4000	4650
16		SWIFT 160 B/R	OP	RNBT	FBG	DV	IO	135	MRCR	6	5	1330	1	2	4100	4750
16		SWIFT 1600	OP	RNBT	FBG	DV	OB			6	5	880	1	2	1250	1500
16		SWIFT 1600 DC	OP	RNBT	FBG	DV	OB			6	5	880	1	2	1300	1550
17		SURF RESCUE	OP	ROW	FBG					5	6	360			**	**
18		GAMEFISH 180	OP	RNBT	FBG	DV	IO	135-180		7	4	2095	1	2	6050	7100
18		GAMEFISH 180 DC	OP	RNBT	FBG	DV	IO	135-175		7	4	2095	1	2	6200	7150
18		GAMEFISH 1800	OP	RNBT	FBG	SV	OB			7	4	1545	1	2	2450	2800
18		GAMEFISH 1800 DC	OP	RNBT	FBG	DV	OB			7	4	1545	1	2	2450	2800
18		QUEST 182	OP	RNBT	FBG	SV	IO	135-180		7	4	2150	2	5	6200	7200
19	4	STORM 1901	OP	CTRCN	FBG	SV	OB			8		1700	1	8	2500	2900
20	6	ADVENTURER 202	OP	FSH	FBG	SV	IO	135-205		8		2985	1	4	8000	9350
20	6	ADVENTURER 202	OP	FSH	FBG	SV	IO	220D	MRCR	8		2985	1	4	14500	16500
20	6	EXPLORER 2000	OP	FSH	FBG	SV	OB			8		2185	1	2	3000	3450
21	3	CLASSIC 218	OP	CR	FBG	SV	IO	160-250		8		3600	1	4	9100	10700
21	3	CLASSIC 218	OP	CR	FBG	SV	IO	220D	MRCR	8		3600	1	4	13000	14800
21	3	TORRENT 213	OP	FSH	FBG	SV	IO	135-250		8		3250	1	4	8900	10600
21	3	TORRENT 213	OP	FSH	FBG	SV	IO	220D	MRCR	8		3250	1	4	15700	17800
21	3	TOURNAMENT 212	OP	FSH	FBG	DV	IO	155-250		8		3250	1	4	8500	10300
21	3	TOURNAMENT 212	OP	FSH	FBG	DV	IO	220D	MRCR	8		3250	1	4	15400	17500
22	7	CONQUEST 222	OP	CR	FBG	DV	IO	190-250		8		2600	1	4	7700	9400
22	7	CONQUEST 222	OP	CR	FBG	DV	IO	350	MRCR	8		2600	1	4	9750	11100
22	7	OUTRAGE 225	HT	FSH	FBG	SV	IO	160-250		8	6	3600	2	6	10500	12300
22	7	OUTRAGE 225	HT	FSH	FBG	SV	IO	180D	MRCR	8	6	3600	2	6	16800	19100
22	7	RAGE 223	ST	FSH	FBG	SV	IO	160-250		8	6	3300	2	6	9900	11700
22	7	RAGE 223	ST	FSH	FBG	SV	IO	180D	MRCR	8	6	3300	2	6	16100	18300
22	8	AVENGER 232	OP	FSH	FBG	SV	IB	155	CRUS	9	5	3850	1	4	12800	14500
		IO 160 MRCR 11500 13000, IB 180 MRCR 12700 14400, IO 190-205													11500	13200
		IB 210 CRUS 13000 14700, IO 235 MRCR 11700 13300, IB 235 MRCR													12800	14500
		IO 250 MRCR 11900 13500, IB 250 CRUS 13000 14800, IO 180D MRCR													18400	20400
		IB 220D MRCR 18600 20600, IO 229D MRCR 19100 21300, IB 270D MRCR													19500	21700
22	8	AVENGER 235	HT	FSH	FBG	SV	IB	155	CRUS	9	5	4150	1	4	13500	15300
		IO 160-210 12100 13900, IO 235 MRCR 12400 14100, IB 235 MRCR													13500	15300
		IO 250 MRCR 12500 14200, IB 250 CRUS 13700 15600, IO 180D MRCR													19100	21300
		IB 180D MRCR 18500 20600, IO 220D MRCR 19700 21900, IB 220D-270D													19100	22500
22	8	AVENGER 239	FB	SF	FBG	SV	IB	155	CRUS	9	5	4350	1	4	14000	15900
		IO 160-205 13500 15500, IB 210 CRUS 14100 16100, IO 235 MRCR													13800	15700
		IB 235 MRCR 14000 15900, IO 250 MRCR 14000 15900, IB 250 CRUS													14200	16200
		IO 180D MRCR 19500 21700, IB 180D MRCR 19000 21200, IO 220D MRCR													20300	22600
		IB 220D-270D 19600 23000														
23	10	CHALLENGER 242	OP	CR	FBG	DV	IO	160-250		8		4100	1	4	11400	13400
23	10	CHALLENGER 242	OP	CR	FBG	DV	IO	180D-220D		8		4100	1	4	15000	17800
23	10	CHARGER 243	OP	FSH	FBG	SV	IO	160-250		6	10	4100	1	4	11600	13600
23	10	CHARGER 243	OP	FSH	FBG	SV	IO	180D-220D		6	10	4100	1	4	18700	21400
23	10	CONTENDER 245	HT	FSH	FBG	SV	IO	160-250		8		4350	1	4	12600	14800
23	10	CONTENDER 245	HT	FSH	FBG	SV	IO	180D-220D		8		4350	1	4	19600	22700
23	10	HERITAGE 248	OP	CR	FBG	SV	IO	160-250		8		4600	1	4	12500	14600
23	10	HERITAGE 248	OP	CR	FBG	SV	IO	180D-220D		8		4600	1	4	16100	19000
25		AGGRESSOR 257	OP	CR	FBG	DV	IB	155	CRUS	9	4	5100	2	3	16900	19200
		IO 205 MRCR 14700 16700, IB 210 CRUS 17400 19700, IO 235 MRCR													14900	17000
		IB 235 MRCR 17300 19700, IO 250 MRCR 15100 17100, IB 250 CRUS													18000	20000
		IO 180D MRCR 18700 20700, IB 180D MRCR 22300 24800, IO 220D MRCR													19300	21500
		IB 220D MRCR 23300 25900, IO 270D MRCR 20500 22700, IB 270D MRCR													24700	27500
25		SHADOW 2500	TH	SF	FBG	SV	OB			9	4	5400	2		7250	8350
26		COMPETITOR 262	OP	SF	FBG	DV	IO	155	CRUS	10		5950	2	5	19000	21100
		IB 210 CRUS 20300 22500, IO 235 MRCR 19900 22100, IB 235-250													20400	23000
		IO 300 MRCR 21000 23300, IB 300-320 21000 23800, IO 180D MRCR													26100	29000
		IO 220D MRCR 27300 30300, IB 220D-262D 26400 30700, IO 270D MRCR													28900	32100
		IB 270D MRCR 27800 30900, IO T155-T205 21300 24500, IB T210-T300													22900	26700
		IO T180D MRCR 32900 36600, IB T220D MRCR 33900 37600														
26		LEGACY 269	FB	CR	FBG	DV	IB	155-210		10		6800	2	5	21600	24700
		IO 235 MRCR 19100 21200, IB 235 MRCR 22300 24800, IO 250 MRCR													19300	21400
		IO 300 MRCR 20000 22200, IB 300-355 23100 26400, IO 180D MRCR													23400	26000
		IB 180D MRCR 28300 31400, IO 220D MRCR 24300 27000, IB 220D MRCR													29300	32600
		IO 270D MRCR 25500 28300, IB 270D MRCR 30800 34200, IB T155 CRUS													23800	26500
		IO T160-T205 20300 23300, IB T210-T355 24800 30500, IO T180D MRCR													28600	31800
		IBT180D-T220D 34600 40700														
26		PRO-HUNTER 265	HT	SF	FBG	DV	IB	155-210		10		6300	2	5	20500	23400
		IO 235 MRCR 26500 29400, IB 235 MRCR 21200 23500, IO 250 MRCR													26700	29600

 CONTINUED ON NEXT PAGE

LOA FT	LOA IN	NAME AND/ OR MODEL	TOP/ RIG	BOAT TYPE	-HULL- MTL	-HULL- TP	ENGINE TP	ENGINE # HP	ENGINE MFG	BEAM FT	BEAM IN	WGT LBS	DRAFT FT	DRAFT IN	RETAIL LOW	RETAIL HIGH
		1995 BOATS														
26		PRO-HUNTER 265	HT	SF	FBG	DV	IO	300	MRCR	10		8900	2	5	27400	30500
		IB 300-355 21900 25100, IO 180D MRCR 36900 41000, IB 180D MRCR 26300 29200														
		IO 220D MRCR 28500 31700, IB 220D MRCR 27300 30400, IO 270D MRCR 30000 33400														
		IB 270D MRCR 28800 32000, IB T155 CRUS 22700 25200, IO T160-T205 22100 25300														
		IB T210-T355 23600 29100, IO T180D MRCR 34100 37900, IBT180D-T220D 32900 38700														
26	2	INTRUDER 255	HT	SF	FBG	SV	IO	160-250		8	6	4600	2	9	15700	19200
26	2	INTRUDER 255	HT	SF	FBG	SV	IO	180D-220D		8	6	4600	2	9	21000	24800
26	2	INTRUDER 255	HT	SF	FBG	SV	IO	270D	MRCR	8	6	4600	2	9	24100	26700
26	2	INVECTOR 253	OP	SF	FBG	SV	IO	160-250		8	6	4350	2	9	15100	18400
		IO 300 MRCR 17100 19400, IO 180D-220D 20000 23800, IO 270D MRCR 23100 25700														
28		C-HUNTER 278	ST	SF	FBG	DV	IB	155	CRUS	10		6800	2	6	22500	25000
		IB T155 CRUS 25200 28000, IB T300-T355 28300 33300, IB T270D MRCR 39300 43700														
28		C-HUNTER 278	ST	SF	FBG	SV	IB	210-230		10		6800	2	6	23400	26300
		IO 235-250 23000 25800, IO 300 MRCR 24100 26800, IB 300-355 24600 28300														
		IO 180D MRCR 28600 31700, IB 180D-210D 27700 31900, IO 220D MRCR 29900 33200														
		IO 270D MRCR 31600 35100, IB 270D MRCR 30600 34000, IO T160-T205 24500 28400														
		IB T210-T230 26500 29900, IO T250 MRCR 26600 29600, IO T160D MRCR 34100 37800														
		IO T180D MRCR 35200 39100, IBT180D-T210D 34100 39800														
28		C-STALKER 275	HT	OFF	FBG	SV	IB	155-210		10		7200	2	9	23100	25900
		IO 250 MRCR 20200 22400, IB 250-270 23500 26500, IO 330 MRCR 21400 23800														
		IB 330-350 24300 27400, IO 150D MRCR 24400 27200, IB 150D MRCR 29600 32800														
		IO 210D MRCR 25100 27900, IB 210D MRCR 30300 33700, IO 270D MRCR 26400 29300														
		IB 270D MRCR 31900 35400, IB T155 CRUS 24800 27600, IO T160-T205 21200 24100														
		IB T210 CRUS 25700 28500, IO T250 MRCR 22400 24900, IB T250-T340 25900 30900														
		IO T150D MRCR 28300 31500, IBT150D-T210D 34200 41000, IB T270D MRCR 39900 44400														
28	3	PERSUADER 299	FB	CR	FBG	DV	IB	T155-T235		11		9400	1	11	29300	34200
28	3	PERSUADER 299	FB	CR	FBG	DV	IB	T355	CRUS	11		9400	1	11	33500	37200
28	3	PERSUADER 299	FB	CR	FBG	DV	IB	T180D-T270D		11		9400	1	11	41200	50800
28	3	PREDATOR 298	HT	SF	FBG	DV	IB	T210-T300		11		8400	1	11	28800	35100
		IB T355 CRUS 32600 36300, IBT180D-T220D 38300 46300, IB T270D MRCR 45800 50400														
28	3	PROWLER 295	HT	SF	FBG	DV	IB	T210-T355		11		8900	1	11	31200	38500
28	3	PROWLER 295	HT	SF	FBG	DV	IB	T155D-T220D		11		8900	1	11	40400	48800
28	3	PROWLER 295	HT	SF	FBG	DV	IB	T272D	MRCR	11		8900	1	11	46200	50800
32	8	COMMANDER 339	FB	CR	FBG	DV	IB	T210-T355		12		13500	2	5	44500	53100
32	8	COMMANDER 339	FB	CR	FBG	DV	IB	T155D-T270D		12		13500	2	5	52200	62900
		1994 BOATS														
16		SWIFT 160	OP	RNBT	FBG	DV	IO	135	MRCR	6	5	1330	1	2	3750	4350
16		SWIFT 160 B/R	OP	RNBT	FBG	DV	IO	135	MRCR	6	5	1330	1		3800	4400
16		SWIFT 1600	OP	RNBT	FBG	DV	OB			6	5	880	1	2	1200	1400
18		GAMEFISH 180	OP	RNBT	FBG	DV	IO	155-187		7	4	2095	1	2	5750	7000
18		GAMEFISH 180	OP	RNBT	FBG	DV	IO	135D		7	4	2095	1	2	8500	9800
18		GAMEFISH 1800	OP	RNBT	FBG	SV	OB			7	4	1545	1	2	2250	2650
18		QUEST 182	OP	RNBT	FBG	SV	IO	135-187		7	4	2150	2	5	5800	7100
18		QUEST 182	OP	RNBT	FBG	SV	IO	135D	VLVO	7	4	2150	2	5	8050	9250
20	6	ADVENTURER 202	OP	FSH	FBG	SV	IO	135-225		8		2985	1	4	7500	9200
20	6	ADVENTURER 202	OP	FSH	FBG	SV	IO	245	VLVO	8		2985	1	4	8150	9400
20	6	ADVENTURER 202	OP	FSH	FBG	SV	IO	135D-150D		8		2985	1	4	11500	14100
20	6	EXPLORER 2000	OP	FSH	FBG	SV	OB			8		2185	1	2	2800	3250
21	3	CLASSIC 218	OP	CR	FBG	SV	IO	160-250		8		3600	1	4	8400	10300
21	3	CLASSIC 218	OP	CR	FBG	SV	IO	135D-150D		8		3600	1	4	10600	12800
21	3	TEMPEST 215	HT	FSH	FBG	SV	IO	135-250		8		3600	1	4	8950	10900
21	3	TEMPEST 215	HT	FSH	FBG	SV	IO	135D-150D		8		3600	1	4	13200	15900
21	3	TORRENT 213	OP	FSH	FBG	SV	IO	135-235		8		3250	1	4	8250	10300
21	3	TORRENT 213	OP	FSH	FBG	SV	IO	245-250		8		3250	1	4	9100	10400
21	3	TORRENT 213	OP	FSH	FBG	SV	IO	135D-150D		8		3250	1	4	12500	15300
21	3	TOURNAMENT 212	OP	FSH	FBG	DV	IO	155-225		8		3250	1	4	7950	9750
21	3	TOURNAMENT 212	OP	FSH	FBG	DV	IO	230-250		8		3250	1	4	8400	10100
21	3	TOURNAMENT 212	OP	FSH	FBG	DV	IO	135D-150D		8		3250	1	4	12200	15000
22	7	CONQUEST 222	OP	CR	FBG	DV	IO	190-250		8		2600	1	4	7200	8750
22	7	CONQUEST 222	OP	CR	FBG	DV	IO	300	MRCR	8		2600	1	4	8000	9200
22	7	CONQUEST 222	OP	CR	FBG	DV	IO	350	MRCR	8		2600	1	4	9150	10400
22	7	OUTRAGE 225	HT	FSH	FBG	SV	IO	160-250		8	6	3600	2	6	9800	11900
22	7	OUTRAGE 225	HT	FSH	FBG	SV	IO	135D-185D		8	6	3600	2	6	14300	17800
22	7	RAGE 223	ST	FSH	FBG	SV	IO	160-235		8	6	3300	2	6	9300	11100
		IO 245 VLVO 9900 11200, IO 250 MRCR 9600 10900, IO 135D-185D 13700 17000														
22	8	AVENGER 232	OP	FSH	FBG	SV	IO	160-205		9	5	3850	1	4	10700	12600
		IB 210 CRUS 12300 13900, IO 225-245 11200 12900, IO 250 MRCR 11100 12600														
		IB 250 CRUS 12300 14000, IO 300 VLVO 12100 13800, IB 110D-130D 15600 17700														
		IO 135D VLVO 15400 17500, IB 140D YAN 16000 18200, IO 150D MRCR 16300 18500														
		IB 150D-170D 16100 18800, IO 180D MRCR 16800 19100, IB 180D MRCR 16600 18800														
		IO 185D VLVO 16100 18300, IB 195D VLVO 16100 18300, IO 216D VLVO 16600 18900														
		IO 220D MRCR 17500 19900, IB 220D-270D 17300 20900														
22	8	AVENGER 235	HT	FSH	FBG	SV	IO	160-205		9	5	4150	1	4	11300	13200
		IB 210 CRUS 12900 14700, IO 225-230 11800 13400, IO 235 MRCR 11500 13100														
		IB 235 MRCR 12800 14500, IO 245 VLVO 12000 13600, IO 250 MRCR 11700 13200														
		IB 250 CRUS 13000 14800, IO 300 VLVO 12700 14500, IB 110D-130D 16300 18500														
		IO 135D VLVO 16100 18300, IB 140D YAN 16700 19000, IO 150D MRCR 17000 19300														
		IB 150D-170D 16800 19600, IO 180D MRCR 17500 19800, IB 180D MRCR 17300 19600														
		IO 185D VLVO 16800 19100, IB 195D VLVO 16800 19000, IO 216D VLVO 17300 19700														
		IO 220D MRCR 18600 20700, IB 220D-270D 18400 21400														
22	8	AVENGER 239	FB	SF	FBG	SV	IO	160-205		9	5	4350	1	4	12600	14800
		IB 210 CRUS 13400 15200, IO 225-230 13200 15000, IO 235 MRCR 12900 14700														
		IB 235 MRCR 13200 15000, IO 245 VLVO 13400 15200, IO 250 MRCR 13000 14800														
		IB 250 CRUS 13500 15300, IO 300 VLVO 14200 16100, IB 110D-130D 16700 19000														
		IO 135D VLVO 16700 19000, IB 140D YAN 17200 19500, IO 150D MRCR 17500 19900														
		IB 150D-170D 17200 20100, IO 180D MRCR 18400 20400, IB 180D MRCR 18100 20100														
		IO 185D VLVO 17300 19700, IB 195D VLVO 17200 19600, IO 216D VLVO 18200 20200														
		IO 220D MRCR 19100 21300, IB 220D-270D 18800 21900														
23	10	CHALLENGER 242	OP	CR	FBG	DV	IO	160-250		8		4100	1	4	10700	12700
23	10	CHALLENGER 242	OP	CR	FBG	DV	IO	300	VLVO	8		4100	1	4	12000	13600
23	10	CHALLENGER 242	OP	CR	FBG	DV	IO	135D-216D		8		4100	1	4	12900	15900
23	10	CHARGER 243	OP	FSH	FBG	SV	IO	160-250		6	10	4100	1	4	10900	13100
		IO 300 VLVO 12300 14000, IO 135D-216D 15700 19400, IO 220D MRCR 18200 20200														
23	10	CONTENDER 245	HT	FSH	FBG	SV	IO	160-250		8		4350	1	4	11800	14100
		IO 300 VLVO 13200 15000, IO 135D-216D 16800 20600, IO 220D MRCR 19100 21200														
23	10	HERITAGE 248	OP	CR	FBG	SV	IO	160-250		8		4600	1	4	11700	13900
		IO 300 VLVO 13000 14800, IO 135D-216D 13900 17100, IO 220D MRCR 15600 17800														
25		AGGRESSOR 257	OP	CR	FBG	DV	IO	205	MRCR	9	4	5100	2	3	13700	15600
		IB 210 CRUS 16400 18700, IO 215-230 14000 16100, IO 235 MRCR 13900 15800														
		IB 235 MRCR 16400 18700, IO 245 VLVO 14300 16200, IO 250 MRCR 14100 16000														
		IB 250 CRUS 16700 18900, IO 300 14700 17100, IB 110D-125D 19600 21800														
		IO 135D VLVO 15800 17900, IB 140D YAN 20400 22700, IO 150D MRCR 16500 18700														
		IB 150D MRCR 20500 22800, IO 170D VLVO 16400 18600, IB 170D YAN 21100 23400														
		IO 180D MRCR 17000 19400, IB 180D MRCR 21200 23600, IO 185D VLVO 16600 18900														
		IB 195D VLVO 21000 23300, IO 210D MRCR 18000 20000, IB 220D 22200 24700														
		IO 262D MRCR 19100 21300, IB 270D MRCR 23500 26200														
25		SHADOW 2500	TH	SF	FBG	SV	OB			9	4	5400	2		6650	7650
26		COMPETITOR 262	OP	SF	FBG	DV	IB	210	CRUS	10		5950	2	5	19200	21300
		IO 225-230 18900 21100, IO 235 MRCR 18800 20900, IB 235 MRCR 19300 21400														
		IO 245 VLVO 19200 21300, IO 250 MRCR 19000 21100, IB 250 CRUS 19600 21700														
		IO 255 VLVO 19100 21200, IO 300 MRCR 19600 21700, IO 300 VLVO 19900 22100														
		IB 300-320 19900 22500, IB 110D-125D 22200 24600, IO 135D VLVO 22700 25200														
		IB 140D YAN 23000 25600, IO 150D MRCR 23600 26200, IB 150D-170D 23200 26500														
		IO 180D MRCR 24400 27100, IB 180D MRCR 24000 26700, IO 185D VLVO 24000 26700														
		IB 195D VLVO 23900 26500, IO 220D MRCR 25500 28300, IO 220D VLVO 24900 27700														
		IB 220D-262D 25100 29200, IO 270D MRCR 26900 29900, IO T160-T205 19900 23100														
		IB T210 CRUS 21700 24100, IO T225-T230 21400 23900, IB T235 MRCR 21800 24200														
		IO T245 VLVO 21900 24300, IB T250 CRUS 22200 24700, IBT110D-T125D 27100 30200														
		IO T135D VLVO 27700 30800, IB T140D YAN 28600 31800, IO T150D MRCR 29300 32600														
		IB T150D MRCR 28900 32100, IO T180D MRCR 30700 34100, IB T180D MRCR 30300 33700														
		IO T185D VLVO 30000 33300, IB T195D VLVO 30000 33300, IO T220D VLVO 31600 35100														
		IB T220D MRCR 32200 35800														
26		LEGACY 269	FB	CR	FBG	DV	IB	210	CRUS	10		6800	2	5	21000	23400
		IO 225-230 18100 20200, IO 235 MRCR 18000 20000, IB 235 MRCR 21100 23500														
		IO 245-250 18400 20500, IO 300 MRCR 18900 21000, IO 300 VLVO 19200 21300														
		IB 300-355 21900 25000, IB 110D YAN 25400 28200, IO 135D VLVO 20600 22800														
		IB 135D-140D 25300 28800, IO 150D MRCR 21200 23600, IB 150D-170D 26100 29700														
		IO 180D MRCR 21800 24200, IB 180D MRCR 26900 29900, IO 185D VLVO 21500 23900														
		IB 195D VLVO 26800 29700, IO 220D MRCR 22700 25200, IO 220D VLVO 22200 24700														
		IB 220D MRCR 27900 31000, IO 270D MRCR 23800 26400, IB 270D MRCR 29300 32500														
		IO T160-T205 19200 21900, IB T210 CRUS 23400 26000, IO T225-T230 20200 22600														
		IB T235 MRCR 23500 26100, IO T245 VLVO 20600 22900, IB T300 CRUS 24800 27500														
		IB T110D YAN 29900 33200, IO T135D VLVO 24400 27100, IBT135D-T140D 30100 34800														
		IO T150D MRCR 25600 28500, IB T150D MRCR 31600 35100, IO T180D MRCR 26700 29700														
		IB T180D MRCR 33000 36600, IO T185D VLVO 26100 29000, IB T195D VLVO 32600 36200														
		IO T220D VLVO 27400 30400, IB T220D 34800 38700														
26		PRO-HUNTER 265	HT	SF	FBG	DV	IB	210	CRUS	10		6300	2	5	19900	22200

CONTINUED ON NEXT PAGE

```
 LOA  NAME AND/                TOP/ BOAT  -HULL- ----ENGINE--- BEAM   WGT  DRAFT RETAIL RETAIL
 FT IN  OR MODEL                RIG TYPE  MTL TP TP # HP   MFG  FT IN  LBS  FT IN   LOW    HIGH
---------------------- 1994 BOATS ------------------------------------------------------------
 26     PRO-HUNTER 265          HT   SF    FBG DV IO 225-230     10       8900  2  5  24900  27700
    IO  235  MRCR  24700  27500, IB  235  MRCR  20000  22200, IO 245-250           25100  27900
    IO  300  MRCR  25600  28500, IO  300  VLVO  26000  28800, IB 300-355           20700  23800
    IB 110D-125D   23400  26000, IO  135D VLVO  33300  37000, IB  140D YAN         24100  26800
    IO  150D MRCR  33800  37600, IB 150D-170D   24300  27600, IO  180D MRCR        34400  38200
    IB  180D MRCR  25000  27800, IO  185D VLVO  34000  37800, IB  195D VLVO        24800  27600
    IO  220D MRCR  26600  29600, IO  220D VLVO  26000  28900, IB  220D MRCR        26000  28900
    IO  270D MRCR  28000  31100, IB  270D MRCR  27300  30400, IO T160-T205         20600  23800
    IB T210  CRUS  22400  24900, IO T225-T230   22100  24700, IB T235  MRCR        22400  24900
    IO T245  VLVO  22500  25000, IB T300  CRUS  23600  26300, IBT110D-T125D        28200  31400
    IO T135D VLVO  28800  32000, IB T140D YAN   29600  32900, IO T150D MRCR        30400  33800
    IB T150D MRCR  29900  33200, IO T180D MRCR  31800  35300, IB T180D MRCR        31200  34700
    IO T185D VLVO  31000  34500, IB T195D VLVO  30900  34300, IO T220D VLVO        32600  36200
    IB T220D MRCR  33100  36800

 26   2 INTRUDER 255            HT   SF    FBG SV IO 160-250      8  6  4600  2  9  14700  18200
    IO  300  VLVO  16900  19200, IO 135D-185D   17500  21800, IO 220D-270D         20900  25000

 26   2 INVECTOR 253            OP   SF    FBG SV IO 160-250      8  6  4350  2  9  14100  17400
    IO  300        16000  18500, IO 135D-150D   16600  19900, IO 180D-220D         18900  22200
    IO  270D MRCR  21600  24000

 28     C-HUNTER 268            ST   SF    FBG SV IB  210  CRUS 10        6800  2  6  21700  24100
    IO  230  VLVO  21100  23400, IB  230        21900  24300, IO 235-270           21000  24100
    IO  300  MRCR  22000  24400, IO  300  VLVO  22200  24700, IB 300-355           22700  26200
    IB  110D YAN   24000  26700, IO  135D VLVO  24400  27100, IB 135D-140D         24100  [illegible]
    IO  150D MRCR  25200  28000, IB 150D-170D   24900  28400, IO  180D MRCR        26100  29000
    IB  180D MRCR  25800  28600, IO  195D VLVO  26200  29100, IB 195D-210D         25900  29600
    IO  216D VLVO  26800  29800, IB  218D VLVO  26600  29500, IO  220D MRCR        27300  30300
    IO  270D MRCR  28800  32000, IB  270D MRCR  28500  31600, IO T160-T205         22300  25900
    IB T210  CRUS  24500  27300, IO T225  VLVO  24000  26600, IO T230  VLVO        24100  26800
    IB T230        24900  27700, IO T245  VLVO  24400  27200, IB T110D YAN         28100  31300
    IO T135D VLVO  29300  32500, IBT135D-T140D  28900  33100, IO T150D MRCR        30600  34000
    IB T150D MRCR  30200  33600, IO T160D MRCR  31100  34500, IO T180D MRCR        32100  35700
    IB T180D MRCR  31800  35300, IO T195D VLVO  32300  35900, IBT195D-T210D        31900  37000
    IO T216D VLVO  33400  37100

 28   3 PERSUADER 299           FB   CR    FBG DV IB T210-T355  11        9400  1 11  28800  35200
 28   3 PERSUADER 299           FB   CR    FBG DV IBT110D-T195D 11        9400  1 11  36100  43700
 28   3 PERSUADER 299           FB   CR    FBG DV IBT220D-T270D 11        9400  1 11  41100  48400
 28   3 PREDATOR 298            HT   SF    FBG DV IB T210-T355  11        8400  1 11  27300  33400
    IBT110D-T195D  33100  40700, IB T220D       37900  45700, IB T270D MRCR        43100  47900

 28   3 PROWLER 295             HT   SF    FBG DV IB T210-T300  11        8900  1 11  29500  35000
    IB T355  CRUS  33600  37400, IBT110D-T195D  36200  44200, IBT220D-T272D        39600  48400

 32   8 COMMANDER 339           FB   CR    FBG DV IB T210-T355  12       13500  2  5  42100  50500
 32   8 COMMANDER 339           FB   CR    FBG DV IBT110D-T270D 12       13500  2  5  48400  59800
---------------------- 1993 BOATS ------------------------------------------------------------
 16     SWIFT 160               OP  RNBT   FBG DV IO  115  MRCR  6  5  1330  1  2   3500   4050
 16     SWIFT 160 B/R           OP  RNBT   FBG DV IO  115  MRCR  6  5  1330  1      3550   4150
 16     SWIFT 1600              OP  RNBT   FBG DV OB             6  5   880  1  2   1150   1350
 18     GAMEFISH 180            OP  RNBT   FBG DV IO 115-205     7  4  2095  1  2   5350   6650
 18     GAMEFISH 180            OP  RNBT   FBG DV IO  130D VLVO  7  4  2095  1  2   7400   8500
 18     GAMEFISH 1800           OP  RNBT   FBG SV OB             7  4  1545  1  2   2250   2600
 18     QUEST 182               OP  RNBT   FBG SV IO 115-205     8     2095  2  5   5650   7000
 18     QUEST 182               OP  RNBT   FBG SV IO  130D VLVO  8     2095  2  5   7700   8900
 20   6 ADVENTURER 202          OP   FSH   FBG SV IO 115-229     8     2685  1  4   6550   8150
 20   6 ADVENTURER 202          OP   FSH   FBG SV IO  130D VLVO  8     2685  1  4  10200  11600
 20   6 ADVENTURER 202          OP   FSH   FBG SV IO  183D MRCR  8     2685  1  4  11500  13100
 20   6 EXPLORER 2000           OP   FSH   FBG SV OB             8     2185  1  2   2500   2950

 21   3 CLASSIC 218             OP   CR    FBG SV IO 155-230     8     3600  1  4   7850   9550
 21   3 CLASSIC 218             OP   CR    FBG SV IO  130D VLVO  8     3600  1  4   9850  11200
 21   3 CLASSIC 218             OP   CR    FBG SV IO  183D MRCR  8     3600  1  4  10900  12400
 21   3 TEMPEST 215             HT   FSH   FBG SV IO 135-230     8     3600  1  4   8250  10100
 21   3 TEMPEST 215             HT   FSH   FBG SV IO  130D VLVO  8     3600  1  4  12300  13900
 21   3 TEMPEST 215             HT   FSH   FBG SV IO  183D MRCR  8     3600  1  4  13600  15400
 21   3 TORRENT 213             OP   FSH   FBG SV IO 135-230     8     3250  1  4   7700   9500
 21   3 TORRENT 213             OP   FSH   FBG SV IO  130D VLVO  8     3250  1  4  11600  13200
 21   3 TORRENT 213             OP   FSH   FBG SV IO  183D MRCR  8     3250  1  4  13000  14800
 21   3 TOURNAMENT 212          OP   FSH   FBG DV IO 155-205     8     3250  1  4   7400   9100
    IO 210-230      8050   9350, IO  130D VLVO  11500  13000, IO  183D MRCR        12800  14600

 22   7 CONQUEST 222            OP   CR    FBG DV IO 180-240     8     2600  1  4   6700   8100
 22   7 CONQUEST 222            OP   CR    FBG DV IO  300  MRCR  8     2600  1  4   7500   8600
 22   7 CONQUEST 222            OP   CR    FBG DV IO  360  MRCR  8     2600  1  4   8700  10000
 22   7 OUTRAGE 225             HT   FSH   FBG SV IO 155-250     8  6  3600  2  6   9200  11100
 22   7 OUTRAGE 225             HT   FSH   FBG SV IO 130D-150D   8  6  3600  2  6  13300  15400
 22   7 OUTRAGE 225             HT   FSH   FBG SV IO 183D-219D   8  6  3600  2  6  14700  17400
 22   7 RAGE 223                ST   FSH   FBG SV IO 155-250     8  6  3300  2  6   8550  10600
 22   7 RAGE 223                ST   FSH   FBG SV IO 130D-150D   8  6  3300  2  6  12700  14700
 22   7 RAGE 223                ST   FSH   FBG SV IO 183D-219D   8  6  3300  2  6  14100  16700

 22   8 AVENGER 232             OP   FSH   FBG SV IO 155-205      9  5  5100  1  4  12300  14400
    IO  210  VLVO  12700  14500, IB  210  CRUS  11600  13200, IO 225-229           12800  14600
    IO  230  MRCR  12500  14300, IB  230  MRCR  11500  13000, IO  275  VLVO        13300  15100
    IB  300  CRUS  11900  13500, IB  110D YAN   14900  16900, IO  130D VLVO        17100  19400
    IB 130D-140D   14500  17400, IO  150D VLVO  17400  19700, IB  170D YAN         15700  17900
    IO 183D-219D   18900  21400

 22   8 AVENGER 235             HT   FSH   FBG SV IO 155-205      9  5  4150  1  4  10600  12400
    IO  210  VLVO  10900  12400, IB  210  CRUS  12300  13900, IO 225-229           11000  12600
    IO  230  MRCR  10800  12200, IB  230  MRCR  12100  13700, IO  275  VLVO        11500  13100
    IB  300  CRUS  12500  14200, IB  110D YAN   15500  17600, IO  130D VLVO        15000  17100
    IB 130D-140D   15100  18100, IO  150D VLVO  15300  17300, IB  170D YAN         16400  18600
    IO 183D-219D   16400  19300

 22   8 AVENGER 239             FB   SF    FBG SV IO 155-205      9  5  4350  1  4  11800  13900
    IO  210  VLVO  12200  13900, IB  210  CRUS  12700  14400, IO 225-229           12300  14000
    IO  230  MRCR  12000  13700, IB  230  MRCR  12500  14200, IO  275  VLVO        12800  14600
    IB  300  CRUS  13000  14700, IB  110D YAN   15900  18100, IO  130D VLVO        15500  17700
    IB 130D-140D   15600  18600, IO  150D VLVO  15800  17900, IB  170D YAN         16800  19100
    IO 183D-219D   16900  19800

 23 10 CHALLENGER 242           OP   CR    FBG DV IO 155-275     8     4100  1  4   9950  12300
 23 10 CHALLENGER 242           OP   CR    FBG DV IO 130D-183D   8     4100  1  4  12000  14900
 23 10 CHALLENGER 242           OP   CR    FBG DV IO  219D MRCR  8     4100  1  4  13600  15500
 23 10 CHARGER 243              OP   FSH   FBG SV IO 155-275     6 10  4100  1  4  10100  12600
 23 10 CHARGER 243              OP   FSH   FBG SV IO 130D-183D   6 10  4100  1  4  14600  18200
 23 10 CHARGER 243              OP   FSH   FBG SV IO  219D MRCR  6 10  4100  1  4  16600  18900
 23 10 CONTENDER 245            HT   FSH   FBG SV IO 155-275     8     4350  1  4  11000  13600
 23 10 CONTENDER 245            HT   FSH   FBG SV IO 130D-183D   8     4350  1  4  15600  19300
 23 10 CONTENDER 245            HT   FSH   FBG SV IO  219D MRCR  8     4350  1  4  18000  20000
 23 10 HERITAGE 248             OP   CR    FBG SV IO 155-275     8     4600  1  4  10900  13400
 23 10 HERITAGE 248             OP   CR    FBG SV IO 130D-183D   8     4600  1  4  13000  16000
 23 10 HERITAGE 248             OP   CR    FBG SV IO  219D MRCR  8     4600  1  4  14600  16600

 25     AGGRESSOR 257           OP   CR    FBG DV IO  205  MRCR  9  4  5100  2  3  12800  14600
    IO  210  VLVO  13100  14800, IB  210  CRUS  15600  17700, IO 225-230           13200  15000
    IB  260  MRCR  15700  17800, IO  275  VLVO  13700  15600, IB  300  CRUS        16200  18400
    IB  110D YAN   18900  21000, IO  130D VLVO  14700  16700, IB 130D-170D         18800  22300
    IO  183D MRCR  16000  18200, IBT183D-T219D  26300  30900

 25     SHADOW 2500             TH   SF    FBG SV OB             9  4  5300  2      5450   6300

 26     COMPETITOR 262          OP   SF    FBG DV IO  225  VLVO 10        5950  2  5  17300  19600
    IO  230  MRCR  17100  19500, IB  230  MRCR  18400  20500, IO  275  VLVO        18400  20400
    IO  300  MRCR  18500  20500, IB  300        19000  21200, IO  330  VLVO        19300  21400
    IB  355  CRUS  19600  21800, IB  110D YAN   21100  23500, IO  130D VLVO        21100  23400
    IB 130D-140D   21200  24400, IO  150D VLVO  21600  24000, IB 150D-170D         21700  25200
    IO  183D MRCR  22900  25400, IB  183D MRCR  23000  25500, IO  219D MRCR        23800  26400
    IB  219D MRCR  23900  26500, IO T155-T205   18800  21800, IO T210  VLVO        19700  21900
    IB T210  CRUS  20600  22900, IO T225-T229   20000  22300, IB T230  MRCR        20600  22900
    IO T275  VLVO  21200  23600, IB T300  CRUS  21900  24300, IB T110D YAN         25900  28700
    IO T130D VLVO  25700  28500, IBT130D-T140D  25800  30300, IO T150D VLVO        26500  29500
    IBT150D-T170D  26700  31800, IO T183D MRCR  28900  32100, IB T183D MRCR        29000  32200
    IO T219D MRCR  30500  33900

 26     LEGACY 269              FB   CR    FBG DV IO  225  VLVO 10        6800  1 11  16600  18800
    IO  230  MRCR  16400  18700, IB  230  MRCR  20000  22200, IO  275  VLVO        17100  19500
    IO  300  MRCR  17200  19600, IB  300        20700  23000, IO  330  VLVO        18500  20500
    IB  355  CRUS  21300  23700, IB  110D YAN   24200  26900, IO  130D VLVO        19100  21200
    IB 130D-140D   24000  27500, IO  150D VLVO  19500  21700, IB 150D-170D         24500  28300
    IO  183D MRCR  20500  22700, IB  183D MRCR  25700  28500, IO  219D MRCR        21200  23500
    IB  219D MRCR  26600  29500, IO T155-T205   17500  20900, IO T210  VLVO        18900  21000
    IB T210  CRUS  22200  24700, IO T225-T229   19100  21300, IB T230  MRCR        22200  24700
    IO T275  VLVO  19900  22100, IB T300  CRUS  23500  26100, IB T110D YAN         28500  31600
    IO T130D VLVO  22600  25200, IBT130D-T140D  28400  33100, IO T150D VLVO        23300  25900
    IBT150D-T170D  29200  34600, IO T183D MRCR  25100  27900, IB T183D MRCR        31500  35000
    IO T219D MRCR  26400  29300

 26     PRO-HUNTER 265          HT   SF    FBG DV IO  225  VLVO 11        8900  1 11  23600  26200
    IO  230  MRCR  23400  26000, IB  230  MRCR  19100  21300, IO  275  VLVO        24200  26900
    IO  300  MRCR  24300  27000, IB  300        19700  21900, IO  330  VLVO        25200  28000
    IB  355  CRUS  20300  22600, IB  110D YAN   22300  24800, IO  130D VLVO        31600  35100
```

 CONTINUED ON NEXT PAGE

LOA FT	LOA IN	NAME AND/ OR MODEL	TOP/ RIG	BOAT TYPE	-HULL- MTL	-HULL- TP	ENGINE TP	ENGINE # HP	ENGINE MFG	BEAM FT	BEAM IN	WGT LBS	DRAFT FT	DRAFT IN	RETAIL LOW	RETAIL HIGH
		1993 BOATS														
26		PRO-HUNTER 265	HT	SF	FBG	DV	IB	130D-140D		10		6300	2	5	22300	25500
		IO 150D VLVO 31600 35100, IB 150D-170D 22800 26300, IO 183D MRCR													32600	36300
		IB 183D MRCR 23900 26500, IO 219D MRCR 33400 37100, IB 219D MRCR													24700	27500
		IO T155-T205 19200 22600, IO T210 VLVO 20400 22600, IB T210 CRUS													21200	23600
		IO T225-T229 20700 23000, IB T230 MRCR 21200 23600, IO T275 VLVO													21800	24200
		IB T300 CRUS 22500 25000, IB T110D YAN 26900 29900, IO T130D VLVO													26700	29700
		IBT130D-T140D 26800 31300, IO T150D VLVO 27600 30600, IBT150D-T170D													27600	32800
		IO T183D MRCR 29900 33200, IB T183D MRCR 29900 33200, IO T219D MRCR													31500	35000
		IB T219D MRCR 31500 35000														
26	2	INTRUDER 255	HT	SF	FBG	SV	IO	155-260		8	6	4600	2	9	13600	16900
26	2	INTRUDER 255	HT	SF	FBG	SV	IO	275	VLVO	8	6	4600	2	9	15300	17400
26	2	INTRUDER 255	HT	SF	FBG	SV	IO	130D-150D		8	6	4600	2	9	16200	19100
26	2	INVECTOR 253	OP	SF	FBG	SV	IO	155-260		8	6	4350	2	9	13100	16200
		IO 275 VLVO 14800 16800, IO 130D-150D 15400 18200, IO 183D-219D													17400	20900
28		C-HUNTER 268	ST	SF	FBG	SV	IO	230	MRCR	10		6800	2	6	19600	21700
		IO 230 VLVO 19700 21900, IB 230 20800 23100, IO 250													19800	22200
		IO 300 MRCR 20600 22800, IB 300 MRCR 21500 23900, IO 330 VLVO													21300	23700
		IB 110D YAN 22700 25200, IO 130D VLVO 22700 25200, IB 130D-140D													22800	25800
		IO 150D VLVO 23300 25800, IB 150D-170D 23300 26800, IO 183D MRCR													24500	27200
		IB 183D MRCR 24600 27400, IO 218D VLVO 25100 27900, IB 218D VLVO													25100	27900
		IO 219D MRCR 25500 28300, IB 219D-245D 25700 29300, IO T155-T225													21000	24900
		IB T230 CRUS 23400 26000, IO T250 VLVO 23000 25500, IB T300 MRCR													24600	27400
		IB T110D YAN 26600 29600, IO T130D VLVO 27100 30100, IBT130D-T140D													27100	31300
		IO T150D VLVO 28100 31200, IB T150D VLVO 28100 31200, IO T155D MRCR													28800	32000
		IB T170D YAN 29600 32900, IO T175D MRCR 29800 33100, IO T183D MRCR													30200	33500
		IB T183D MRCR 30200 33500, IOT185D-T205D 30300 34700, IO T218D VLVO													31300	34800
		IB T218D VLVO 31300 34800, IO T219D MRCR 32000 35500, IBT219D-T245D													32000	37000
28	3	PERSUADER 299	FB	CR	FBG	DV	IB	T210-T230		11		9400	1	11	27300	30700
28	3	PERSUADER 299	FB	CR	FBG	DV	IB	T110D-T183D		11		9400	1	11	34400	41600
28	3	PERSUADER 299	FB	CR	FBG	DV	IB	T219D	MRCR	11		9400	1	11	39100	43400
28	3	PREDATOR 298	HT	SF	FBG	DV	IB	T210-T230		11		8900	1	11	24500	29800
		IB T300 CRUS 28200 31400, IBT110D-T183D 33000 40200, IB T219D MRCR													37800	42000
28	3	PROWLER 295	HT	SF	FBG	DV	IB	T210-T300		11		8900	1	11	30100	33400
28	3	PROWLER 295	HT	SF	FBG	DV	IB	T110D-T183D		11		8900	1	11	34500	42100
28	3	PROWLER 295	HT	SF	FBG	DV	IB	T219D	MRCR	11		8900	1	11	39600	44000
32	8	COMMANDER 339	FB	CR	FBG	DV	IB	T210-T355		12		13500	2	5	39900	47900
32	8	COMMANDER 339	FB	CR	FBG	DV	IB	T110D-T219D		12		13500	2	5	46400	54600
		1992 BOATS														
16		SWIFT 160	OP	RNBT	FBG	DV	IO	115	MRCR	6	5	1330	1		3250	3800
16		SWIFT 160 B/R	OP	RNBT	FBG	DV	IO	115	MRCR	6	5	1330	1		3350	3900
16		SWIFT 1600	OP	RNBT	FBG	DV	OB			6	5	880	1		1050	1250
18		GAMEFISH 180	OP	RNBT	FBG	DV	IO	115-205		7	4	2095	1	2	5000	6200
18		GAMEFISH 180	OP	RNBT	FBG	DV	IO	130D	VLVO	7	4	2095	1	2	6900	7950
18		GAMEFISH 1800	OP	RNBT	FBG	SV	OB			7	4	1545	1	2	2000	2400
18		QUEST 182	OP	RNBT	FBG	SV	IO	115-205		8		2095	2	5	5300	6550
18		QUEST 182	OP	RNBT	FBG	SV	IO	130D	VLVO	8		2095	2	5	7250	8300
20	6	ADVENTURER 202	OP	FSH	FBG	SV	IO	115-229		8		2685	1	4	6150	7650
20	6	ADVENTURER 202	OP	FSH	FBG	SV	IO	130D	VLVO	8		2685	1	4	9550	10900
20	6	ADVENTURER 202	OP	FSH	FBG	SV	IO	183D	MRCR	8		2685	1	4	10800	12300
20	6	EXPLORER 2000	OP	FSH	FBG	SV	OB			8		2185	1	2	2450	2850
21	3	CLASSIC 218	OP	CR	FBG	SV	IO	155-230		8		3600	1	4	7350	8950
21	3	CLASSIC 218	OP	CR	FBG	SV	IO	130D	VLVO	8		3600	1	4	9250	10500
21	3	CLASSIC 218	OP	CR	FBG	SV	IO	183D	MRCR	8		3600	1	4	10200	11600
21	3	TEMPEST 215	HT	FSH	FBG	SV	IO	135-230		8		3600	1	4	7700	9450
21	3	TEMPEST 215	HT	FSH	FBG	SV	IO	130D	VLVO	8		3600	1	4	11500	13000
21	3	TEMPEST 215	HT	FSH	FBG	SV	IO	183D	MRCR	8		3600	1	4	12700	14500
21	3	TORRENT 213	OP	FSH	FBG	SV	IO	135-230		8		3250	1	4	7200	8800
21	3	TORRENT 213	OP	FSH	FBG	SV	IO	130D	VLVO	8		3250	1	4	10900	12300
21	3	TORRENT 213	OP	FSH	FBG	SV	IO	183D	MRCR	8		3250	1	4	12100	13800
21	3	TOURNAMENT 212	OP	FSH	FBG	DV	IO	155-230		8		3250	1	4	6950	8700
21	3	TOURNAMENT 212	OP	FSH	FBG	DV	IO	130D	VLVO	8		3250	1	4	10700	12200
21	3	TOURNAMENT 212	OP	FSH	FBG	DV	IO	183D	MRCR	8		3250	1	4	12100	13800
22	7	CONQUEROR 224	OP	CR	FBG	DV	IO	180-240		8		2600	1	4	6700	7850
22	7	CONQUEROR 224	OP	CR	FBG	DV	IO	300	MRCR	8		2600	1	4	7450	8600
22	7	CONQUEROR 224	OP	CR	FBG	DV	IO	360	MRCR	8		2600	1	4	8600	9900
22	7	CONQUEST 222	OP	CR	FBG	DV	IO	180-240		8		2600	1	4	6250	7600
22	7	CONQUEST 222	OP	CR	FBG	DV	IO	300	MRCR	8		2600	1	4	7000	8050
22	7	CONQUEST 222	OP	CR	FBG	DV	IO	360	MRCR	8		2600	1	4	8150	9350
22	8	AVENGER 232	OP	FSH	FBG	SV	IO	155-205		9	5	5100	1	4	11600	13500
		IO 210 VLVO 11900 13500, IB 210 CRUS 11000 12500, IO 225-229													12000	13700
		IO 230 MRCR 11700 13400, IB 230 MRCR 10900 12400, IO 275 VLVO													12400	14100
		IB 300 CRUS 11300 12800, IB 110D YAN 14200 16100, IO 130D VLVO													16000	18200
		IB 130D-140D 13800 16600, IO 150D VLVO 16300 18500, IB 170D YAN													15000	17100
		IO 183D-219D 17300 20300														
22	8	AVENGER 235	HT	FSH	FBG	SV	IO	155-205		9	5	4150	1	4	9900	11600
		IO 210 VLVO 10200 11600, IB 210 CRUS 11600 13200, IO 225-229													10300	11800
		IO 230 MRCR 10100 11500, IB 230 MRCR 11500 13000, IO 275 VLVO													10800	12200
		IB 300 CRUS 11900 13500, IB 110D YAN 14800 16800, IO 130D VLVO													14000	16000
		IB 130D-140D 14400 17300, IO 150D VLVO 14300 16200, IB 170D YAN													15600	17800
		IO 183D-219D 15300 18100														
22	8	AVENGER 239	FB	SF	FBG	SV	IO	155-205		9	5	4350	1	4	11100	13000
		IO 210 VLVO 11500 13000, IB 210 CRUS 12000 13700, IO 225-229													11500	13100
		IO 230 MRCR 11300 12800, IB 230 MRCR 11900 13500, IO 275 VLVO													12000	13600
		IB 300 CRUS 12300 14000, IB 110D YAN 15200 17300, IO 130D VLVO													14500	16500
		IB 130D-140D 14800 17800, IO 150D VLVO 14700 16700, IB 170D YAN													16100	18200
		IO 183D-219D 15800 18600														
23	10	CHALLENGER 242	OP	CR	FBG	DV	IO	155-275		8		4100	1	4	9350	11500
23	10	CHALLENGER 242	OP	CR	FBG	DV	IO	130D-183D		8		4100	1	4	11300	14000
23	10	CHALLENGER 242	OP	CR	FBG	DV	IO	219D	MRCR	8		4100	1	4	12800	14500
23	10	CHARGER 243	OP	FSH	FBG	SV	IO	155-275		6	10	4100	1	4	9500	11800
23	10	CHARGER 243	OP	FSH	FBG	SV	IO	130D-183D		6	10	4100	1	4	13700	17000
23	10	CHARGER 243	OP	FSH	FBG	SV	IO	219D	MRCR	6	10	4100	1	4	15500	17700
23	10	CONTENDER 245	HT	FSH	FBG	SV	IO	155-275		8		4350	1	4	10300	12700
23	10	CONTENDER 245	HT	FSH	FBG	SV	IO	130D-183D		8		4350	1	4	14600	18100
23	10	CONTENDER 245	HT	FSH	FBG	SV	IO	219D	MRCR	8		4350	1	4	16500	18700
23	10	HERITAGE 248	OP	CR	FBG	SV	IO	155-275		8		4600	1	4	10200	12500
23	10	HERITAGE 248	OP	CR	FBG	SV	IO	130D-183D		8		4600	1	4	12200	15000
23	10	HERITAGE 248	OP	CR	FBG	SV	IO	219D	MRCR	8		4600	1	4	13700	15500
25		AGGRESSOR 257	OP	CR	FBG	DV	IO	205	MRCR	9	4	5100	2	3	12000	13600
		IO 210 VLVO 12200 13900, IB 210 CRUS 14800 16800, IO 225-230													12300	14000
		IB 260 MRCR 14900 16900, IO 275 VLVO 12800 14600, IB 300 CRUS													15300	17400
		IB 110D YAN 18100 20100, IO 130D VLVO 13700 15600, IB 130D-170D													17600	21300
		IO 183D MRCR 15000 17000, IBT183D-T219D 25000 29400														
26		COMPETITOR 262	OP	SF	FBG	DV	IO	225	VLVO	10		5950	2	5	16200	18400
		IO 230 MRCR 16000 18200, IB 230 MRCR 17100 19500, IO 275 VLVO													16800	19100
		IO 300 MRCR 16900 19200, IB 300 18200 20300, IO 330 VLVO													18200	20300
		IB 355 CRUS 18800 20900, IB 110D YAN 20200 22400, IO 130D VLVO													19700	21900
		IB 130D-140D 20200 23300, IO 150D VLVO 20200 22500, IB 150D-170D													20700	24100
		IO 183D MRCR 21400 23800, IB 183D MRCR 21900 24400, IO 219D MRCR													22300	24700
		IB 219D MRCR 22700 25300, IO T155-T205 17200 20700, IO T210 VLVO													18700	20800
		IB T210 CRUS 19500 21700, IO T225-T229 18900 21100, IB T230 MRCR													19500	21700
		IO T275 VLVO 19800 22000, IB T300 CRUS 20800 23100, IB T110D YAN													24700	27400
		IO T130D VLVO 24100 26700, IBT130D-T140D 24600 28900, IO T150D VLVO													24800	27600
		IBT150D-T170D 25400 30300, IO T183D MRCR 27000 30000, IB T183D MRCR													27700	30700
		IO T219D MRCR 28600 31700														
26		LEGACY 269	FB	CR	FBG	DV	IO	225	VLVO	10		6800	1	11	15500	17600
		IO 230 MRCR 15400 17500, IB 230 MRCR 19200 21300, IO 275 VLVO													16000	18200
		IO 300 MRCR 16100 18300, IB 300 19700 21800, IO 330 VLVO													16900	19200
		IB 355 CRUS 20300 22500, IB 110D YAN 23100 25600, IO 130D VLVO													18100	20100
		IB 130D-140D 22900 26200, IO 150D VLVO 18400 20500, IB 150D-170D													23300	27000
		IO 183D MRCR 19200 21300, IB 183D MRCR 24500 27200, IO 219D MRCR													19800	22000
		IB 219D MRCR 25300 28100, IO T155-T205 16400 19600, IO T210 VLVO													17300	19700
		IB T210 CRUS 21100 23400, IO T225-T229 17500 20000, IB T230 MRCR													21100	23400
		IO T275 VLVO 18900 21000, IB T300 CRUS 22300 24800, IB T110D YAN													27200	30200
		IO T130D VLVO 21200 23500, IBT130D-T140D 27100 31600, IO T150D VLVO													21800	24200
		IBT150D-T170D 27900 33000, IO T183D MRCR 23500 26100, IB T183D MRCR													30100	33400
		IO T219D MRCR 24700 27400														
26		PRO-HUNTER 265	HT	SF	FBG	DV	IO	225	VLVO	11		8900	1	11	22100	24500
		IO 230 MRCR 21900 24300, IB 230 MRCR 18200 20200, IO 275 VLVO													22600	25200
		IO 300 MRCR 22700 25300, IB 300 18900 21000, IO 330 VLVO													23600	26200
		IB 355 CRUS 19300 21400, IB 110D YAN 21300 23700, IO 130D VLVO													29500	32800
		IB 130D-140D 21300 24400, IO 150D VLVO 29600 32900, IB 150D-170D													21700	25200
		IO 183D MRCR 30500 33900, IB 183D MRCR 22900 25400, IO 219D MRCR													31200	34700
		IB 219D MRCR 23600 26200, IO T155-T205 18200 21100, IO T210 VLVO													19100	21200
		IB T210 CRUS 20100 22400, IO T225-T229 19300 21600, IB T230 MRCR													20100	22400
		IO T275 VLVO 20400 22700, IB T300 CRUS 21300 23700, IB T110D YAN													25600	28500
		IO T130D VLVO 25000 27800, IBT130D-T140D 25500 29900, IO T150D VLVO													25800	28700
		IBT150D-T170D 26300 31200, IO T183D MRCR 28000 31100, IB T183D MRCR													28500	31600
		IO T219D MRCR 29500 32800														
26	2	INTRUDER 255	HT	SF	FBG	SV	IO	155-260		8	6	4600	2	9	12800	15800
		IO 275 VLVO 14300 16300, IO 130D-150D 15200 17900, IO 183D-219D													17100	20500

CONTINUED ON NEXT PAGE

LOA FT	LOA IN	NAME AND/ OR MODEL	TOP/ RIG	BOAT TYPE	HULL MTL	HULL TP	ENGINE TP	ENGINE # HP	ENGINE MFG	BEAM FT	BEAM IN	WGT LBS	DRAFT FT	DRAFT IN	RETAIL LOW	RETAIL HIGH
		1992 BOATS														
26	2	INVECTOR 253	OP	SF	FBG	SV	IO	155-260		8	6	4350	2	9	12300	15200
		IO 275 VLVO 13800 15700, IO 130D-150D 14400 17000, IO 183D-219D													16300	19600
28	3	PERSUADER 299	FB	CR	FBG	DV	IB	T210-T230		11		9400	1	11	25900	29200
28	3	PERSUADER 299	FB	CR	FBG	DV	IB	T110D-T183D		11		9400	1	11	32800	39700
28	3	PERSUADER 299	FB	CR	FBG	DV	IB	T219D	MRCR	11		9400	1	11	37300	41400
28	3	PREDATOR 298	HT	SF	FBG	DV	IB	T210-T300		11		8900	1	11	25200	29800
28	3	PREDATOR 298	HT	SF	FBG	DV	IB	T110D-T183D		11		8900	1	11	31500	38300
28	3	PREDATOR 298	HT	SF	FBG	DV	IB	T219D	MRCR	11		8900	1	11	36100	40100
28	3	PROWLER 295	HT	SF	FBG	DV	IB	T210-T300		11		8900	1	11	26500	31300
28	3	PROWLER 295	HT	SF	FBG	DV	IB	T110D-T183D		11		8900	1	11	32900	40200
28	3	PROWLER 295	HT	SF	FBG	DV	IB	T219D	MRCR	11		8900	1	11	37800	42000
32	8	COMMANDER 339	FB	CR	FBG	DV	IB	T210-T355		12		13500	2	5	37900	45400
32	8	COMMANDER 339	FB	CR	FBG	DV	IB	T110D-T219D		12		13500	2	5	43800	52400
		1991 BOATS														
16		SWIFT 160	OP	RNBT	FBG	DV	IO	115	MRCR	6	5	1330	1		3050	3550
16		SWIFT 160 B/R	OP	RNBT	FBG	DV	IO	115	MRCR	6	5	1330	1		3100	3600
16		SWIFT 1600	OP	RNBT	FBG	DV	OB			6	5	880	1		1000	1200
18		GAMEFISH 180	OP	RNBT	FBG	DV	IO	115-175		7	4	2095	1	2	4700	5450
18		GAMEFISH 180	OP	RNBT	FBG	DV	IO	130D	VLVO	7	4	2095	1	2	6500	7450
18		GAMEFISH 1800	OP	RNBT	FBG	SV	OB			7	4	1545	1	2	1900	2250
20	6	ADVENTURER 202	OP	FSH	FBG	SV	IO	115-210		8		2685	1	4	5750	7050
20	6	ADVENTURER 202	OP	FSH	FBG	SV	IO	130D	VLVO	8		2685	1	4	9050	10300
20	6	ADVENTURER 202	OP	FSH	FBG	SV	IO	183D	MRCR	8		2685	1	4	10100	11500
20	6	EXPLORER 2000	OP	FSH	FBG	SV	OB			8		2185	1	2	2300	2650
21	3	CLASSIC 218	OP	CR	FBG	SV	IO	155-230		8		3600	1	4	6900	8400
21	3	CLASSIC 218	OP	CR	FBG	SV	IO	130D	VLVO	8		3600	1	4	8600	9850
21	3	CLASSIC 218	OP	CR	FBG	SV	IO	183D	MRCR	8		3600	1	4	9550	10900
21	3	TEMPEST 215	HT	FSH	FBG	SV	IO	135-230		8		3600	1	4	7250	8850
21	3	TEMPEST 215	HT	FSH	FBG	SV	IO	130D	VLVO	8		3600	1	4	10800	12200
21	3	TEMPEST 215	HT	FSH	FBG	SV	IO	183D-219D		8		3600	1	4	11900	14200
21	3	TORRENT 213	OP	FSH	FBG	SV	IO	135-230		8		3250	1	4	6750	8300
21	3	TORRENT 213	OP	FSH	FBG	SV	IO	130D	VLVO	8		3250	1	4	10200	11600
21	3	TORRENT 213	OP	FSH	FBG	SV	IO	183D	MRCR	8		3250	1	4	11400	12900
21	3	TOURNAMENT 212	ST	FSH	FBG	DV	IO	135-230		8		3250	1	4	6750	8300
21	3	TOURNAMENT 212	ST	FSH	FBG	DV	IO	130D	VLVO	8		3250	1	4	10200	11600
21	3	TOURNAMENT 212	ST	FSH	FBG	DV	IO	183D	MRCR	8		3250	1	4	11400	12900
22	7	CONQUEROR 224	OP	CR	FBG	DV	IO	180-240		8		2600	1	4	6300	7400
22	7	CONQUEROR 224	OP	CR	FBG	DV	IO	300	MRCR	8		2600	1	4	7000	8050
22	7	CONQUEROR 224	OP	CR	FBG	DV	IO	360	MRCR	8		2600	1	4	8100	9300
22	7	CONQUEST 222	OP	CR	FBG	DV	IO	180-240		8		2600	1	4	5900	7100
22	7	CONQUEST 222	OP	CR	FBG	DV	IO	300	MRCR	8		2600	1	4	6600	7550
22	7	CONQUEST 222	OP	CR	FBG	DV	IO	360	MRCR	8		2600	1	4	7650	8750
22	8	AVENGER 232	OP	FSH	FBG	SV	IO	155-229		9	5	3850	2	2	8850	10500
		IO 230 MRCR 9000 10300, IB 230 MRCR 10300 11800, IO 275 VLVO													9600	10900
		IB 305-360 10800 12600, IO 130D VLVO 15000 17000, IB 130D VLVO													13200	15000
		IO 150D VLVO 15200 17300, IB 150D VLVO 13400 15200, IO 183D MRCR													16200	18400
		IB 183D MRCR 14400 16400, IO 219D MRCR 16700 19000, IB 219D MRCR													15000	17000
22	8	AVENGER 235	HT	FSH	FBG	SV	IO	155-275		9	5	4150	2	2	9300	11500
22	8	AVENGER 235	HT	FSH	FBG	SV	IO	130D-183D		9	5	4150	1	4	13200	16300
22	8	AVENGER 235	HT	FSH	FBG	SV	IO	219D	MRCR	9	5	4150	1	4	14900	16900
22	8	AVENGER 239	FB	SF	FBG	SV	IO	155-229		9	5	4350	1	4	10400	12300
		IO 230 MRCR 10600 12000, IB 230 MRCR 11300 12800, IO 275 VLVO													11300	12800
		IB 305-360 11700 13700, IO 130D-183D 13600 16800, IO 219D MRCR													15300	17400
23	10	CHALLENGER 242	OP	CR	FBG	DV	IO	155-275		8		4100	1	4	8700	10800
23	10	CHALLENGER 242	OP	CR	FBG	DV	IO	130D-183D		8		4100	1	4	10600	13100
23	10	CHALLENGER 242	OP	CR	FBG	DV	IO	219D	MRCR	8		4100	1	4	12000	13600
23	10	CHARGER 243	OP	FSH	FBG	SV	IO	155-275		6	10	4100	1	4	8950	11100
23	10	CHARGER 243	OP	FSH	FBG	SV	IO	130D-183D		6	10	4100	1	4	12800	15900
23	10	CHARGER 243	OP	FSH	FBG	SV	IO	219D	MRCR	6	10	4100	1	4	14600	16600
23	10	CONTENDER 245	HT	FSH	FBG	SV	IO	155-275		8		4350	1	4	9650	11900
23	10	CONTENDER 245	HT	FSH	FBG	SV	IO	130D-183D		8		4350	1	4	13700	17000
23	10	CONTENDER 245	HT	FSH	FBG	SV	IO	219D	MRCR	8		4350	1	4	15500	17600
23	10	HERITAGE 248	OP	CR	FBG	SV	IO	155-275		8		4600	1	4	9550	11800
23	10	HERITAGE 248	OP	CR	FBG	SV	IO	130D-183D		8		4600	1	4	11400	14100
23	10	HERITAGE 248	OP	CR	FBG	SV	IO	219D	MRCR	8		4600	1	4	12800	14600
25		AGGRESSOR 257	OP	CR	FBG	DV	IO	205-275		9	4	5100	1	4	11300	13700
		IB 305-360 14600 17100, IO 130D VLVO 12900 14600, IB 130D VLVO													16800	19000
		IO 150D VLVO 13200 15000, IB 150D VLVO 17100 19500, IO 183D MRCR													14000	15900
		IB 183D-219D 18700 21400														
26		COMPETITOR 262	OP	SF	FBG	DV	IO	230	MRCR	10		8900	1	11	20300	22500
		IB 230 MRCR 16300 18500, IO 240-275 20300 23300, IO 300 MRCR													21000	23400
		IB 300-318 16800 19300, IO 330 VLVO 21900 24300, IB 350-460													17400	21200
		IB 130D-183D 19300 23300, IB 219D MRCR 21800 24200, IO T155-T229													16100	19800
26		LEGACY 269	FB	CR	FBG	DV	IO	230	MRCR	10		6800	1	11	14400	16400
		IB 230 MRCR 18200 20200, IO 240-275 14500 17100, IO 300 MRCR													15100	17200
		IB 300-305 18800 21000, IO 330 VLVO 15900 18000, IB 350-454													19200	22900
		IB 130D VLVO 21900 24300, IO 150D VLVO 16900 19200, IB 150D VLVO													22300	24700
		IO 183D MRCR 18200 20200, IB 183D MRCR 23400 26000, IO 219D MRCR													18800	20900
		IB 219D MRCR 24200 26900, IO T155-T229 15300 18700, IOT130D-T183D													19900	24500
26		PRO-HUNTER 265	HT	SF	FBG	DV	IO	230	MRCR	10		6300	2	5	15600	17800
		IB 230 MRCR 16900 19200, IO 240 MRCR 15700 17900, IB 275 VLVO													17300	19700
		IO 300 MRCR 16400 18700, IB 300-318 17400 20000, IO 330 VLVO													17300	19600
		IB 350-460 18400 21800, IB 130D-219D 20300 25200, IO T155-T229													21600	25300
28	3	PERSUADER 299	FB	CR	FBG	DV	IB	T230-T350		11		9400	1	11	24800	30000
28	3	PERSUADER 299	FB	CR	FBG	DV	IB	T150D-T219D		11		9400	1	11	32400	39500
28	3	PREDATOR 298	OP	SF	FBG	DV	IB	230-350		11		8400	1	11	21600	25600
28	3	PREDATOR 298	OP	SF	FBG	DV	IB	T130D-T183D		11		8400	1	11	29700	35900
28	3	PREDATOR 298	OP	SF	FBG	DV	IB	T219D	MRCR	11		8400	1	11	33900	37700
28	3	PROWLER 295	HT	SF	FBG	DV	IB	T230-T360		11		8900	1	11	24900	30200
28	3	PROWLER 295	HT	SF	FBG	DV	IB	T130D-T183D		11		8900	1	11	31200	37600
28	3	PROWLER 295	HT	SF	FBG	DV	IB	T219D	MRCR	11		8900	1	11	35400	39300
32	8	COMMANDER 339	FB	CR	FBG	DV	IB	T230-T360		12		13500	2	5	36300	43200
32	8	COMMANDER 339	FB	CR	FBG	DV	IB	T454-T460		12		13500	2	5	41100	45700
32	8	COMMANDER 339	FB	CR	FBG	DV	IB	T130D-T219D		12		13500	2	5	42000	50000
		1990 BOATS														
16		SWIFT 160	OP	RNBT	FBG	DV	IO	115	MRCR	6	5	1330	1		2900	3350
16		SWIFT 160 B/R	OP	RNBT	FBG	DV	IO	115	MRCR	6	5	1330	1		2950	3400
16		SWIFT 1600	OP	RNBT	FBG	SV	OB			6	5	880	1		945	1100
18		GAMEFISH 180	OP	RNBT	FBG	DV	IO	115-175		7	4	2095	1	2	4450	5150
18		GAMEFISH 180	OP	RNBT	FBG	DV	IO	130D	VLVO	7	4	2095	1	2	6100	7000
18		GAMEFISH 1800	OP	RNBT	FBG	SV	OB			7	4	1545	1	2	1750	2050
20	6	EXPLORER 2000	OP	FSH	FBG	SV	OB			8		2185	1	2	2200	2550
21	3	CLASSIC 218	OP	CR	FBG	SV	IO	155-230		8		3600	1	4	6450	7900
21	3	CLASSIC 218	OP	CR	FBG	SV	IO	130D	VLVO	8		3600	1	4	8050	9300
21	3	CLASSIC 218	OP	CR	FBG	SV	IO	183D	MRCR	8		3600	1	4	9050	10300
21	3	TEMPEST 215	HT	FSH	FBG	SV	IO	135-230		8		3600	1	4	6800	8300
21	3	TEMPEST 215	HT	FSH	FBG	SV	IO	130D	VLVO	8		3600	1	4	10100	11500
21	3	TEMPEST 215	HT	FSH	FBG	SV	IO	183D-219D		8		3600	1	4	11200	13300
21	3	TORRENT 213	OP	FSH	FBG	SV	IO	135-230		8		3250	1	4	6350	7800
21	3	TORRENT 213	OP	FSH	FBG	SV	IO	130D	VLVO	8		3250	1	4	9600	10900
21	3	TORRENT 213	OP	FSH	FBG	SV	IO	183D	MRCR	8		3250	1	4	10700	12100
21	3	TOURNAMENT 212	ST	FSH	FBG	DV	IO	135-230		8		3250	1	4	6350	7800
21	3	TOURNAMENT 212	ST	FSH	FBG	DV	IO	130D	VLVO	8		3250	1	4	9600	10900
21	3	TOURNAMENT 212	ST	FSH	FBG	DV	IO	183D	MRCR	8		3250	1	4	10700	12100
22	7	CONQUEROR 224	OP	CR	FBG	DV	IO	180-240		8		2600	1	4	5800	6900
22	7	CONQUEROR 224	OP	CR	FBG	DV	IO	300	MRCR	8		2600	1	4	6500	7500
22	7	CONQUEROR 224	OP	CR	FBG	DV	IO	360	MRCR	8		2600	1	4	7550	8650
22	7	CONQUEST 222	OP	CR	FBG	DV	IO	180-240		8		2600	1	4	5550	6750
22	7	CONQUEST 222	OP	CR	FBG	DV	IO	300	MRCR	8		2600	1	4	6250	7200
22	7	CONQUEST 222	OP	CR	FBG	DV	IO	360	MRCR	8		2600	1	4	7250	8350
22	8	AVENGER 232	OP	FSH	FBG	SV	IO	155-229		9	5	3850	2	2	8200	9900
		IO 230 MRCR 8400 9650, IB 230 MRCR 9850 11200, IO 275 VLVO													9100	10300
		IB 305-360 10200 12000, IO 130D VLVO 14100 16000, IB 130D VLVO													12600	14300
		IO 150D VLVO 14300 16300, IB 150D VLVO 12800 14500, IO 183D MRCR													15200	17300
		IB 183D MRCR 13800 15700, IO 219D MRCR 15700 17900, IB 219D MRCR													14300	16300
22	8	AVENGER 235	HT	FSH	FBG	SV	IO	155-229		9	5	4150	2	2	8650	10400
		IO 230 MRCR 8950 10200, IB 230 MRCR 10400 11800, IO 275 VLVO													9500	10800
		IB 305-360 10800 12600, IO 130D VLVO 11600 13200, IB 130D VLVO													13100	14900
		IO 150D VLVO 11800 13400, IB 150D VLVO 13400 15200, IO 183D MRCR													12700	14500
		IB 183D MRCR 14300 16300, IO 219D MRCR 13200 15100, IB 219D MRCR													14900	16900
22	8	AVENGER 239	FB	SF	FBG	SV	IO	155-229		9	5	4350	1	4	9750	11600
		IO 230 MRCR 9950 11300, IB 230 MRCR 10700 12200, IO 275 VLVO													10600	12000
		IB 305-360 11100 13000, IO 130D-183D 12800 15800, IO 219D MRCR													14400	16400
23	10	CHALLENGER 242	OP	CR	FBG	DV	IO	155-230		8		4100	1	4	8150	9850
		IO 275 VLVO 9000 10200, IO 130D-183D 9950 12300, IO 219D MRCR													11300	12800
23	10	CHARGER 243	OP	FSH	FBG	SV	IO	155-230		6	10	4100	1	4	8350	10000
		IO 275 VLVO 9200 10500, IO 130D-183D 12100 15000, IO 219D MRCR													13700	15600
23	10	CONTENDER 245	HT	FSH	FBG	SV	IO	155-275		8		4350	1	4	9150	11200
23	10	CONTENDER 245	HT	FSH	FBG	SV	IO	130D-183D		8		4350	1	4	12900	15900

CONTINUED ON NEXT PAGE

LOA FT	LOA IN	NAME AND/ OR MODEL	TOP/ RIG	BOAT TYPE	-HULL- MTL	-HULL- TP	ENGINE TP	ENGINE # HP	ENGINE MFG	BEAM FT	BEAM IN	WGT LBS	DRAFT FT	DRAFT IN	RETAIL LOW	RETAIL HIGH
		1990 BOATS														
23	10	CONTENDER 245	HT	FSH	FBG	SV	IO	219D	MRCR	8		4350	1	4	14500	16500
23	10	HERITAGE 248	OP	CR	FBG	SV	IO	155-275		8		4600	1	4	9050	11100
23	10	HERITAGE 248	OP	CR	FBG	SV	IO	130D-183D		8		4600	1	4	10700	13200
23	10	HERITAGE 248	OP	CR	FBG	SV	IO	219D	MRCR	8		4600	1	4	12100	13700
25		AGGRESSOR 257	OP	CR	FBG	DV	IO	205-229		9	4	5100	1	4	10600	12400
		IO 230 MRCR 10700 12200, IB 230 MRCR 13300 15100, IO 275 VLVO													11300	12900
		IB 305-360 13900 16200, IO 130D VLVO 12100 13800, IB 130D-150D													16000	18600
		IO 183D MRCR 13200 15000, IB 183D-219D 17500 20700														
26		COMPETITOR 262	OP	SF	FBG	DV	IO	230	MRCR	10		8900	1	11	19100	21200
		IB 230 MRCR 15500 17600, IO 240-275 19100 21900, IO 300 MRCR													19800	22000
		IB 300-318 16000 18400, IO 330 VLVO 20600 22800, IB 350-460													16600	20400
		IB 130D-219D 18700 23100, IO T155-T229 15100 18600														
26		PRO-HUNTER 265	HT	SF	FBG	DV	IO	230	MRCR	10		6300	2	5	14700	16700
		IB 230 MRCR 16000 18200, IO 240-275 14800 17500, IO 300 MRCR													15500	17600
		IB 300-318 16500 19000, IO 330 VLVO 16300 18500, IB 350-460													17100	21000
		IB 130D-219D 19400 24000, IO T155-T229 20300 23800														
28	3	PREDATOR 298	OP	SF	FBG	DV	IB	230-350		11		8400	1	11	20600	24300
28	3	PREDATOR 298	OP	SF	FBG	DV	IB	T130D-T183D		11		8400	1	11	28400	34300
28	3	PREDATOR 298	OP	SF	FBG	DV	IB	T219D	MRCR	11		8400	1	11	32400	36000
28	3	PROWLER 295	HT	SF	FBG	DV	IB	230-360		11		8900	1	11	21400	25200
28	3	PROWLER 295	HT	SF	FBG	DV	IB	T130D-T183D		11		8900	1	11	29800	35900
28	3	PROWLER 295	HT	SF	FBG	DV	IB	T219D	MRCR	11		8900	1	11	33800	37600
32	8	COMMANDER 339	FB	CR	FBG	DV	IB	230-460		12		13500	2	5	32200	38400
32	8	COMMANDER 339	FB	CR	FBG	DV	IB	T130D-T219D		12		13500	2	5	40100	47800
		1989 BOATS														
16		SWIFT 160	OP	RNBT	FBG	DV	IO	130		6	5	1330			2700	3150
16		SWIFT 160 BR	OP	RNBT	FBG	DV	IO	130		6	5	1330			2750	3200
16		SWIFT 1600 BR	OP	RNBT	FBG	DV	OB			6	5	1330			1400	1700
16		SWIFT 1600 CB	OP	RNBT	FBG	DV	OB			6	5	1330			1300	1550
18		GAMEFISH 180	OP	FSH	FBG	DV	IO	130-180		7	4	2095			4500	5250
18		GAMEFISH 1800	OP	FSH	FBG	DV	OB			7	4	2095			2000	2350
20	6	EXPLORER 2000	OP	RNBT	FBG	DV	OB			8		2185			2150	2500
21	3	CLASSIC 218	OP	CUD	FBG	DV	IO	165-260		8		3600			6100	7450
21	3	TOURNAMENT 212	OP	RNBT	FBG	DV	IO	165-260		8		3250			5400	6650
22	8	AVENGER 232	HT	FSH	FBG	DV	IO	175-211		9	5	3850			7800	9250
		IB 220 CRUS 9500 10800, IO 230-235 7900 9350, IO 260 MRCR													8100	9300
		IO 260 OMC 8050 9250, IB 260-270 9400 10900														
22	8	AVENGER 235	HT	FSH	FBG	DV	IO	175-211		9	5	4150			8200	9750
		IB 220 CRUS 10000 11400, IO 230-235 8350 9850, IO 260 MRCR													8500	9800
		IO 260 OMC 8450 9700, IB 260-270 9950 11500, IO 271 VLVO													8950	10200
22	8	AVENGER 239	FB	RNBT	FBG	DV	IO	175-211		9	5	4350			7600	9000
		IB 220 CRUS 10400 11800, IO 230-235 7700 9100, IO 260 MRCR													7850	9000
		IO 260 OMC 7800 8950, IB 260-270 10300 11900, IO 271 VLVO													8150	9400
23	10	CHALLENGER 242	OP	RNBT	FBG	DV	IO	175-271		8		4100			7250	9000
23	10	CONTENDER 245	HT	RNBT	FBG	DV	IO	175-271		8		4350			7600	9400
23	10	HERITAGE 248	OP	CUD	FBG	DV	IO	175-271		8		4600			8450	10400
25		AGGRESSOR 257	OP	CUD	FBG	DV	IO	211	VLVO	9	4	5100			10200	11600
		IB 220 CRUS 12800 14500, IO 230-235 10100 11700, IO 260 MRCR													10300	11700
		IO 260 OMC 10300 11700, IB 260-270 12800 14800, IO 271 VLVO													10600	12100
26		COMPETITOR 262	OP	FSH	FBG	DV	IB	220-350		10		5950			14800	18000
26		PRO-HUNTER 265	HT	FSH	FBG	DV	IB	220-350		10		6300			15400	18600
30	8	PREDATOR 298	OP	CUD	FBG	DV	IB	T220-T270				8400			23200	26800
32	8	COMMANDER 339	FB	CBNCR	FBG	DV	IB	T		12		13500			**	**
		1988 BOATS														
16		SWIFT 16	OP	RNBT	FBG	DV	IO	128-130		6	5	1600			2800	3300
16		SWIFT 16	OP	RNBT	FBG	DV	IO	146	VLVO	6	5	1600			3050	3550
18		GAMEFISH 180	OP	FSH	FBG	DV	IO	130-205		7	4	2250			4400	5350
21	3	CLASSIC 218	OP	CUD	FBG	DV	IO	165-260		8		3600			5800	7000
21	3	TOURNAMENT 212	OP	RNBT	FBG	DV	IO	165-260		8		3200			5100	6200
22	8	AVENGER 232	OP	FSH	FBG	DV	IO	175-210		9	5	3800			7300	8700
		IB 220 9050 10300, IO 225 VLVO 7600 8750, IB 225 VLVO													9000	10300
		IO 230 MRCR 7450 8550, IO 230 OMC 7400 8500, IB 230-250													8900	10100
		IO 260 MRCR 7600 8700, IO 260 OMC 7550 8650, IO 260 VLVO													7850	9000
		IB 260 8950 10300, IO 270 MRCR 7650 8800, IO 270 OMC													7600	8750
		IO 270 VLVO 7900 9100, IB 270 CRUS 9100 10400, IO 306 VLVO													8350	9600
22	8	AVENGER 235	HT	FSH	FBG	DV	IO	175-210		9	5	4100			7700	9150
		IB 220 9450 10800, IO 225 VLVO 8000 9200, IB 225 VLVO													9450	10800
		IO 230 MRCR 7850 9000, IO 230 OMC 7800 8950, IB 230-250													9400	10700
		IO 260 MRCR 8000 9200, IO 260 OMC 7950 9100, IO 260 VLVO													8250	9450
		IB 260 9450 10800, IO 270 MRCR 8050 9250, IO 270 OMC													8000	9200
		IO 270 VLVO 8300 9550, IB 270 CRUS 9550 10900, IO 306 VLVO													8850	10100
23	10	CHALLENGER 242	OP	RNBT	FBG	DV	IO	205-270		8		4100			6900	8500
23	10	HERITAGE 248	OP	CUD	FBG	DV	IO	205-270		8		4400			7800	9550
25		AGGRESSOR 257	OP	CUD	FBG	DV	IO	210	VLVO	9	4	5100			9650	11000
		IB 220 12200 13800, IO 225 VLVO 9700 11100, IB 225 VLVO													12200	13800
		IO 230 MRCR 9600 10900, IO 230 OMC 9550 10900, IB 230-250													12100	13800
		IO 260 MRCR 9800 11100, IO 260 OMC 9750 11100, IO 260 VLVO													10000	11300
		IB 260 12200 14000, IO 270 MRCR 9850 11200, IO 270 OMC													9850	11200
		IO 270 VLVO 10100 11400, IB 270 CRUS 12400 14100, IO 306 VLVO													10500	11900
26		COMPETITOR 262	OP	FSH	FBG	DV	IB	220-350		10		5500			13400	16400
27	11	PREDATOR 288	OP	CUD	FBG	DV	IB	T220-T280		11		7800			20700	23900
		1987 BOATS														
21	3	CLASSIC 210	OP	CUD	FBG	DV	IO	165-260		8		3600			5500	6650
21	3	TOURNAMENT 210	OP	FSH	FBG	DV	IO	165-260		8		3200			5350	6500
23	10	CHALLENGER 240	OP	FSH	FBG	DV	IO	175-260		8		4100			7350	8750
23	10	HERITAGE 240	OP	SF	FBG	DV	IO	175-260		8		4400			8400	9950
26		COMPETITOR 260	ST	SF	FBG	DV	IB	T220-T340		10		5500			14600	18000
26		COMPETITOR 260	ST	SF	FBG	DV	IB	T350	CRUS	10		5500			16200	18400
27	11	PREDATOR 280	OP	SF	FBG	DV	IB	T220-T350		11		7800			19700	24100
		1986 BOATS														
21	3	CLASSIC 210	OP	CUD	FBG	DV	IO	165-260		8		3600			5250	6350
21	3	TOURNAMENT 210	OP	FSH	FBG	DV	IO	165-260		8		3200			5100	6200
23	10	CHALLENGER 240	OP	FSH	FBG	DV	IO	175-260		8		4100			7000	8350
23	10	HERITAGE 240	OP	SF	FBG	DV	IO	175-260		8		4400			8000	9500
26		COMPETITOR 260	ST	SF	FBG	DV	IB	T220-T340		10		5500			14000	17200
26		COMPETITOR 260	ST	SF	FBG	DV	IB	T350	CRUS	10		5500			15400	17600
27	11	PREDATOR 280	OP	SF	FBG	DV	IB	T220-T350		11		7800			19000	23000
		1985 BOATS														
16		SPORT 16	OP	RNBT	FBG	DV	IO	120		6	4				2250	2650
18		GAMEFISHER	OP	FSH	FBG	DV	IO	140	MRCR	7	4	2250			3800	4400
18		SPORT	OP	SKI	FBG	DV	IO	140	MRCR	7	4	2250			3350	3900
20	6	PENN-YAN 205	OP	SF	FBG	DV	IB	220		8					5250	6050
21	3	CUDDY	OP	CUD	FBG	DV	IO	185	MRCR	8		3600			5050	5800
21	3	TOURNAMENT	OP	FSH	FBG	DV	IO	185	MRCR	8		3200			4950	5650
22	8	AVENGER	OP	FSH	FBG	DV	IB	220	CRUS	9	5	3800			7750	8900
22	8	AVENGER	OP	FSH	FBG	DV	TD	220	CRUS	9	5	3800			7750	8900
25		ANGLER 25	OP	CUD	FBG	DV	IO	230		9	4				8400	9650
26		TOURNAMENT	OP	SF	FBG	DV	IB	270	CRUS	10		5500			12000	13600
26		TOURNAMENT	OP	SF	FBG	DV	TD	270	CRUS	10		5500			12000	13600
27	11	SPORTFISH	OP	SF	FBG	DV	IB	T220	CRUS	11		7800			18200	20200
32	8	PENN-YAN 330	FB	SF	FBG	DV	IB	T270		12			1	10	25900	28700
		1984 BOATS														
16		BOWRIDER 16	OP	RNBT	FBG	DV	IO	120-140							2200	2550
16		SPORT 16 B/R		RNBT	FBG	DV	IO	120-140							2200	2550
18		GAMEFISHER	OP	RNBT	FBG	DV	IO	140-185		7	4		2	2	3300	3850
20	6	EXPLORER	OP	CUD	FBG	DV	TD	220-350		8			2	6	5150	6400
21	3	TOURNAMENT	OP	RNBT	FBG	DV	IO	185-230		8			2	6	3950	4700
22	8	AVENGER 23	OP	FSH	FBG	DV	TD	220-350		9	5	3800	1	2	7400	9000
22	8	AVENGER 23	HT	FSH	FBG	DV	TD	220-350		9	5	3800	1	2	7400	9000
23	10	24XE	OP	CR	FBG	DV	IO	228-260		8		4100			6250	7350
25		ANGLER 25 WALKAROUND	ST	CUD	FBG	DV	IO	228-260		10		6500	1	5	9750	11300
26		PENN-YAN 26	FB	SF	FBG	DV	TD	T220-T270		10			1	5	13000	15300
26		PENN-YAN 26	FB	SF	FBG	DV	TD	T350	CRUS	10			1	5	14400	16400
26		TOURNAMENT 26	OP	SF	FBG	DV	IB	270	CRUS	10			1	5	11700	13300
26		TOURNAMENT 26	OP	SF	FBG	DV	TD	270	CRUS	10			1	5	11700	13300
29	11	PENN-YAN 30	FB	SDN	FBG	DV	TD	T220-T350		11	10		1	10	20200	24000
		TD T D CAT ** **, TD T D CRUS ** **, TD T D CUM													**	**
		TD T D VLVO ** **														
29	11	PENN-YAN 30	FB	SF	FBG	DV	TD	T220-T350		11	10		1	10	17100	21200
		TD T D CAT ** **, TD T D CRUS ** **, TD T D CUM													**	**
		TD T D VLVO ** **														
32	8	PENN-YAN 33	FB	SDN	FBG	DV	TD	T270-T350		12			1	10	28400	33200
		TD T D CAT ** **, TD T D CRUS ** **, TD T D CUM													**	**
		TD T D VLVO ** **														
32	8	PENN-YAN 33	FB	SF	FBG	DV	TD	T270-T350		12			1	10	24700	28700
		TD T D CAT ** **, TD T D CRUS ** **, TD T D CUM													**	**
		TD T D VLVO ** **														

....For earlier years, see the BUC Used Boat Price Guide, Volume 3

PERFORMANCE CRUISING INC

TELSTAR
ANNAPOLIS MD 21403

See inside cover to adjust price for area

For more recent years, see the BUC Used Boat Price Guide, Volume 1

LOA FT IN	NAME AND/ OR MODEL	TOP/ RIG	BOAT TYPE	HULL MTL TP	TP	ENGINE # HP	MFG	BEAM FT IN	WGT LBS	DRAFT FT IN	RETAIL LOW	RETAIL HIGH
				1996 BOATS								
33 5	GEMINI 105M		SACAC	FBG CT				14	8000	1 6	67400	74100
34	GEMINI 3400		SACAC	FBG CT	OB			14	8000	1 6	70600	77600
34	GEMINI 3400		SACAC	FBG CT	IB	27D	WEST	14	8000	1 6	70600	77600
				1995 BOATS								
34	GEMINI 3400		SACAC	FBG CT	OB			14	8000	1 6	66400	73000
34	GEMINI 3400		SACAC	FBG CT	IB	27D	WEST	14	8000	1 6	66400	73000
				1994 BOATS								
32	GEMINI 3200	SLP	SACAC	FBG CT	OB			14	7000	1 6	51200	56300
34	GEMINI 3400		SACAC	FBG CT	OB			14	8000	1 6	62500	68700
34	GEMINI 3400		SACAC	FBG CT	IB	27D	WEST	14	8000	1 6	62500	68700
				1993 BOATS								
32	GEMINI 3200	SLP	SACAC	FBG CT	OB			14	7000	1 6	48200	52900
34	GEMINI 3400		SACAC	FBG CT	OB			14	8000	1 6	58800	64600
				1992 BOATS								
32	GEMINI 3200	SLP	SA/CR	FBG CT	OB			14	7000	1 6	45500	50100
				1991 BOATS								
32	GEMINI 3200	SLP	SA/CR	FBG CT	OB			14	8000	1 6	43900	48800
				1989 BOATS								
30 6	GEMINI	SLP	SA/CR	FBG CT	OB			14	7000	1 6	32900	36600
				1988 BOATS								
30 6	GEMINI	SLP	SA/CR	FBG CT	OB			14	7000	1 6	31000	34400
				1987 BOATS								
30 6	GEMINI	SLP	SA/CR	FBG CT	OB			14	7000	1 6	29100	32400
				1986 BOATS								
30 6	GEMINI	SLP	SA/CR	FBG CT	OB			14	7000	1 6	27400	30500
36 6	GEMINI	SLP	SA/CR	FBG CT	IB	T 15D	YAN	16	11000	3	50900	55900
36 6	GEMINI	SLP	SA/CR	FBG CT	IB	T 18D	VLVO	16	11000	3	50900	55900
36 6	GEMINI	SLP	SA/CR	FBG CT	IB	T 28D	VLVO	16	11000	3	50900	55900
				1985 BOATS								
30 6	GEMINI	SLP	SA/CR	FBG CT	OB			14	7000	1 6	25800	28600
36 6	GEMINI	SLP	SA/CR	FBG CT	IB	T 15D	YAN	16	11000	3	47800	52600
36 6	GEMINI	SLP	SA/CR	FBG CT	IB	T 18D	VLVO	16	11000	3	47800	52600
36 6	GEMINI	SLP	SA/CR	FBG CT	IB	T 28D	VLVO	16	11000	3	47800	52600
				1984 BOATS								
30 6	GEMINI 31	SLP	SA/RC	FBG CT				14	6520	1 6	23800	26400

....For earlier years, see the BUC Used Boat Price Guide, Volume 3

PERFORMANCE OFFSHORE CRUISER

TARGA YACHTS
OSTERVILLE MA 02655

See inside cover to adjust price for area

LOA FT IN	NAME AND/ OR MODEL	TOP/ RIG	BOAT TYPE	HULL MTL TP	TP	ENGINE # HP	MFG	BEAM FT IN	WGT LBS	DRAFT FT IN	RETAIL LOW	RETAIL HIGH
				1990 BOATS								
45 8	TARGA 13.4M	FB	MY	FBG SV	IB	T375D	CAT	15 3	27000	3	218000	240000
52	TARGA 16M	FB	TCMY	FBG SV	IB	T485D	GM	17 4	46100	3 10	336500	370000
52 7	DEFEVER 53	FB	TCMY	FBG SV	IB	T485D	CAT	16 6	55000	4 8	295000	324000
56 11	DEFEVER 57	FB	TCMY	FBG SV	IB	T485D	GM	16 9	56782	4 8	374500	411500
				1989 BOATS								
43 10	TARGA 44	FB	DC	FBG DV	IB	T375D	CAT	15 3	28000	3	165000	181000
46 11	DEFEVER 47	FB	MY	FBG DV	IB	T210D	CAT	16	44000	4 8	211000	232000
51 11	TARGA 52	FB	FDPH	FBG DV	IB	T485D	J&T	17 4	50000	3 11	290000	318500
52 6	DEFEVER 53	FB	MY	FBG DV	IB	T210D	CAT	16	48000	4 8	209000	230000
56 7	DEFEVER 57	FB	MY	FBG DV	IB	T485D	J&T	16	54000	4 8	325000	357000
56 7	DEFEVER 57	FB	YTFS	FBG DV	IB	T260D	CAT	16	54000	4 8	256000	281000
				1988 BOATS								
45 11	DEFEVER 46	FB	SPTCR	F/S DV	IB	T375D	CAT	15	30000	4 6	187500	206000
46 11	DEFEVER 47	FB	OFF	F/S DV	IB	T210D	CAT	16	43200	4 6	232000	255000
52 6	DEFEVER 53	FB	OFF	F/S DV	IB	T210D	CAT	16	48000	4 8	228500	251000
56 7	DEFEVER 57	FB	YTFS	FBG DV	IB	T260D	CAT	16	54000	4 8	245000	269000
				1987 BOATS								
45 11	DEFEVER 46	FB	SPTCR	F/S DV	IB	T375D	CAT	15	30000	4 6	179500	197000
46 11	DEFEVER 47	FB	OFF	F/S DV	IB	T210D	CAT	16	43200	4 6	222000	244000
52 6	DEFEVER 53	FB	OFF	F/S DV	IB	T210D	CAT	16	48000	4 8	218500	240000
52 6	DEFEVER 53	FB	OFF	F/S DV	IB	T375D	CAT	16	48000	4 8	261000	287000
56 7	DEFEVER 57	FB	YTFS	F/S DV	IB	T260D	CAT	16	54000	4 8	241500	265000
56 7	DEFEVER 57 CF	FB	YTFS	F/S DV	IB	T260D	CAT	16	54000	4 8	227000	249500
56 7	DEFEVER 57 MY	FB	MYDKH	F/S DV	IB	T260D	CAT	16	54000	4 8	216500	238000

PERFORMER YACHTS INC

RICHMOND VA 23229

See inside cover to adjust price for area

For more recent years, see the BUC Used Boat Price Guide, Volume 1

LOA FT IN	NAME AND/ OR MODEL	TOP/ RIG	BOAT TYPE	HULL MTL TP	TP	ENGINE # HP	MFG	BEAM FT IN	WGT LBS	DRAFT FT IN	RETAIL LOW	RETAIL HIGH
				1996 BOATS								
23 6	PERFORMER 24	OP	CTRCN	FBG DV	OB			8 3	4100	1 6	19800	22000
23 6	PERFORMER 24	OP	CTRCN	FBG DV	IO	250	MRCR	8 3	4200	1 6	16600	18800
23 6	PERFORMER 24	OP	CTRCN	FBG DV	IO	240D	MRCR	8 3	4200	1 6	26900	29900
23 6	PERFORMER 24	OP	CUD	FBG DV	OB			8	4700	1 6	21100	23500
23 6	PERFORMER 24	OP	CUD	FBG DV	IO	245-300		8	4500	1 6	16900	20400
23 6	PERFORMER 24	OP	CUD	FBG DV	IO	385-415		8	4700	1 6	21100	22000
23 6	PERFORMER 24	OP	CUD	FBG DV	IO	T135		8	4900	1 6	19100	22000
31 6	PERFORMER 32	OP	FSH	FBG DV	IB	T300D	GM	10 3	13500	2 5	87000	95600
				1995 BOATS								
23 6	PERFORMER 24	OP	CTRCN	FBG DV	OB			8 3	4100	1 6	19100	21200
23 6	PERFORMER 24	OP	CTRCN	FBG DV	IO	260	MRCR	8 3	4200	1 6	15600	17700
23 6	PERFORMER 24	OP	CTRCN	FBG DV	IO	200D	MRCR	8 3	4200	1 6	24000	26700
23 6	PERFORMER 24	OP	CUD	FBG DV	OB			8	4700	1 6	20100	22400
23 6	PERFORMER 24	OP	CUD	FBG DV	IO	215-250		8	4500	1 6	15000	18000
	IO 300	16600	18900, IO	390	MRCR	19800	21900, IO	T135			17500	20600
31 6	PERFORMER 32	OP	FSH	FBG DV	IB	T250D	GM	10 3	13500	2 5	79200	87000
				1994 BOATS								
23 6	PERFORMER 24	OP	CTRCN	FBG DV	OB			8 3	4100	1 6	18200	20300
23 6	PERFORMER 24	OP	CTRCN	FBG DV	IO	260	MRCR	8 3	4200	1 6	14500	16500
23 6	PERFORMER 24	OP	CTRCN	FBG DV	IO	200D	MRCR	8 3	4200	1 6	22400	24900
23 6	PERFORMER 24	OP	CUD	FBG DV	OB			8	4700	1 6	19300	21400
23 6	PERFORMER 24	OP	CUD	FBG DV	IO	215-250		8	4500	1 6	14000	16800
	IO 300	15500	17600, IO	390	MRCR	18600	20700, IO	T135			16300	19200
31 6	PERFORMER 32	OP	FSH	FBG DV	IB	T250D	GM	10 3	13500	2 5	75300	82800
				1993 BOATS								
23 6	PERFORMER 24	OP	CTRCN	FBG DV	OB			8 3	4100	1 6	17100	19400
23 6	PERFORMER 24	OP	CTRCN	FBG DV	IO	260	MRCR	8 3	4100	1 6	13600	15400
23 6	PERFORMER 24	OP	CTRCN	FBG DV	IO	200D	MRCR	8 3	4200	1 6	20900	23300
23 6	PERFORMER 24	OP	CUD	FBG DV	OB			8		1 6	18600	20700
23 6	PERFORMER 24	OP	CUD	FBG DV	IO	260-275		8	4500	1 6	13400	16000
23 6	PERFORMER 24	OP	CUD	FBG DV	IO	330-365		8	4700	1 6	15100	18300
23 6	PERFORMER 24	OP	CUD	FBG DV	IO	T145-T146		8	4900	1 6	15200	18000
31 6	PERFORMER 32	OP	FSH	FBG DV	IB	T250D	GM	10 3	13500	2 5	71800	78900
				1992 BOATS								
23 6	PERFORMER 24	OP	CTRCN	FBG DV	IO	260	MRCR	8 3	4100	1 6	16400	18600
23 6	PERFORMER 24	OP	CTRCN	FBG DV	IO	200D	MRCR	8 3	4200	1 6	12700	14400
23 6	PERFORMER 24	OP	CUD	FBG DV	OB			8		1 6	19600	21800
23 6	PERFORMER 24	OP	CUD	FBG DV	OB			8			17500	19900
23 6	PERFORMER 24	OP	CUD	FBG DV	IO	260-275		8	4500	1 6	12500	14900
23 6	PERFORMER 24	OP	CUD	FBG DV	IO	330-365		8	4700	1 6	14100	17200
23 6	PERFORMER 24	OP	CUD	FBG DV	IO	T145-T146		8	4900	1 6	14300	16800
31 6	PERFORMER 32	OP	FSH	FBG DV	IB	T250D	GM	10 3	13500	2 5	68400	75200
				1991 BOATS								
23 6	PERFORMER 24	OP	CTRCN	FBG DV	IO	260	MRCR	8 3	4200	1 6	16000	18200
23 6	PERFORMER 24	OP	CTRCN	FBG DV	IO	200D	MRCR	8 3	4200	1 6	11900	13500
23 6	PERFORMER 24	OP	CUD	FBG DV	OB			8			18600	20600
23 6	PERFORMER 24	OP	CUD	FBG DV	OB			8			16300	19100
23 6	PERFORMER 24	OP	CUD	FBG DV	IO	260-275		8	4500	1 6	11700	14000
23 6	PERFORMER 24	OP	CUD	FBG DV	IO	330-365		8	4700	1 6	13300	16100
23 6	PERFORMER 24	OP	CUD	FBG DV	IO	T145-T146		8	4900	1 6	13400	15800
31 6	PERFORMER 32	OP	FSH	FBG DV	IB	T250D	GM	10 3	13500	2 5	65300	71800
				1990 BOATS								
23 6	PERFORMER 24	OP	CUD	FBG DV	OB			8			16200	18500
23 6	PERFORMER 24	OP	CUD	FBG DV	IO	260-275		8	4500	1 6	11000	13200
23 6	PERFORMER 24	OP	CUD	FBG DV	IO	330-365		8	4700	1 6	12500	15100
23 6	PERFORMER 24	OP	CUD	FBG DV	IO	T146-T165		8	4900	1 6	13100	14800
31 6	PERFORMER 32	OP	FSH	FBG DV	IB	T250	GM	10 3	13500	2 5	44200	49100
				1989 BOATS								
23 6	PERFORMER 24		CUD	FBG DV	OB			8			15700	17800
23 6	PERFORMER 24		CUD	FBG DV	IO	260-311		8	4500	1 6	10500	13100
23 6	PERFORMER 24		CUD	FBG DV	IO	330-365		8	4700	1 6	11800	14300
23 6	PERFORMER 24		CUD	FBG DV	IO	T146-T165		8	5000	1 6	12500	14200
31 6	PERFORMER 32		FSH	FBG DV	IB	T250D	GM	10 3	13500	2 5	59700	65600
				1988 BOATS								
23 6	CENTER CONSOLE	ST	OPFSH	F/S DV	OB			8	4300	1 11	14600	16600
23 6	SEAHAWK CUDDY	ST	CUD	F/S DV	OB			8	4500	1 11	14900	17000
23 6	SEAHAWK CUDDY	ST	CUD	F/S DV	IO	260	MRCR	8	4300	1 11	9600	10900

PERSHING S P A
FERRETTI GROUP
61037 MONDOLFO (PU) ITALY

See inside cover to adjust price for area

For more recent years, see the BUC Used Boat Price Guide, Volume 1

LOA FT IN	NAME AND/ OR MODEL	TOP/ RIG	BOAT TYPE	-HULL- MTL TP	----ENGINE--- TP # HP MFG	BEAM FT IN	WGT LBS	DRAFT FT IN	RETAIL LOW	RETAIL HIGH
			1996 BOATS							
58 1	54		MY	FBG	IB T11CD	15 5		4 11	561000	616500
60	60		MY	FBG	IB T12CD				643000	707000
75 11	73		MY	FBG	IB T12CD	16 1		4 6	**	**
			1995 BOATS							
42 8	42		CBNCR	FBG	IB T435D	13 1			182000	199500
56	54		MY	FBG	IB T11CD	15 5		4 10	440000	483500

PETRICK SALES AGENCY
NORWALK CT 06850

See inside cover to adjust price for area

For more recent years, see the BUC Used Boat Price Guide, Volume 1

LOA FT IN	NAME AND/ OR MODEL	TOP/ RIG	BOAT TYPE	-HULL- MTL TP	----ENGINE--- TP # HP MFG	BEAM FT IN	WGT LBS	DRAFT FT IN	RETAIL LOW	RETAIL HIGH
			1996 BOATS							
35	TOUCAN 35	SLP	SARAC	F/S KL	OB	7	4400	5 3	40300	44800
			1995 BOATS							
35	TOUCAN 35	SLP	SARAC	F/S KL	OB	7	4400	5 3	37900	42100
			1994 BOATS							
35	TOUCAN 35	SLP	SARAC	F/S KL	OB	7	4400	5 3	35700	39600
			1993 BOATS							
35	TOUCAN 35	SLP	SARAC	F/S KL	OB	7	4400	5 3	33600	37300
			1992 BOATS							
35	TOUCAN 35	SLP	SA/OD	F/S KL	OB	7	4400	5 3	31600	35100
			1991 BOATS							
35	TOUCAN 35	SLP	SA/OD	F/S KL	OB	7	4400	5 3	29700	33000
			1990 BOATS							
35	TOUCAN 35	SLP	SA/OD	F/S KL	OB	7	4400	5 3	27900	31000
			1989 BOATS							
35	TOUCAN 35	SLP	SA/OD	F/S KL	OB	7	4400	5 3	26300	29200
			1988 BOATS							
35	TOUCAN 35	SLP	SA/RC	F/S KL	OB	7	4400	5 3	24700	27500
			1987 BOATS							
35	TOUCAN 35	SLP	SA/RC	FBG KL	OB	7	4400	5 3	23200	25800
			1986 BOATS							
35	TOUCAN 35	SLP	SA/RC	FBG KL	OB	7	4400	5 3	21900	24300
			1985 BOATS							
34 5	TOUCAN 35	SLP	SA/RC	FBG KL	OB	7	4410	5 2	20600	22900

PELLE PETTERSON A B
MOLNLYCKE MARIN A B
543600 ASKIM SWEDEN   COAST GUARD MFG ID- PFA

See inside cover to adjust price for area

SVEN-ERIK EKLUND
SAN DIEGO CA 92101

LOA FT IN	NAME AND/ OR MODEL	TOP/ RIG	BOAT TYPE	-HULL- MTL TP	----ENGINE--- TP # HP MFG	BEAM FT IN	WGT LBS	DRAFT FT IN	RETAIL LOW	RETAIL HIGH
			1985 BOATS							
34 7	MIXER CRUISING	SLP	SA/CR	FBG KL		10 8	9920	6 1	38900	43200

....For earlier years, see the BUC Used Boat Price Guide, Volume 3

PHANTOM BOATS
SARASOTA FL 34243   COAST GUARD MFG ID- PJI See inside cover to adjust price for area

For more recent years, see the BUC Used Boat Price Guide, Volume 1

LOA FT IN	NAME AND/ OR MODEL	TOP/ RIG	BOAT TYPE	-HULL- MTL TP	----ENGINE--- TP # HP MFG	BEAM FT IN	WGT LBS	DRAFT FT IN	RETAIL LOW	RETAIL HIGH
			1996 BOATS							
28 10	PHANTOM 29 TD FISH		OPFSH	FBG DV	IO 250D				39700	44100
29 10	PHANTOM SPEEDSTER		RACE	FBG DV	IO				**	**
33 10	PHANTOM 34 CANOPY		RACE	FBG DV	IO				**	**
33 10	PHANTOM 34 OPEN		OFF	FBG DV	IO				**	**
33 10	PHANTOM 34 TD FISH		OPFSH	FBG DV	IO T250D				119000	131000
			1995 BOATS							
28 10	PHANTOM 29 FISH		OPFSH	FBG DV	OB	8			26400	29400
28 10	PHANTOM 29 FISH		OPFSH	FBG DV	IO	8			**	**
28 10	PHANTOM 29 RACE		OFF	FBG DV	OB	8			27200	30300
28 10	PHANTOM 29 RACE		OFF	FBG DV	IO	8			**	**
33 10	PHANTOM 34 RACE		OFF	FBG DV	IO	8			**	**
			1994 BOATS							
28 10	PHANTOM 29 FISH		OPFSH	FBG DV	OB	8			25200	28000
28 10	PHANTOM 29 FISH		OPFSH	FBG DV	IO	8			**	**
28 10	PHANTOM 29 RACE		OFF	FBG DV	OB	8			25900	28700
28 10	PHANTOM 29 RACE		OFF	FBG DV	IO	8			**	**
33 10	PHANTOM 34 RACE		OFF	FBG DV	IO	8			**	**
			1993 BOATS							
28 10	PHANTOM 29 FISH		OPFSH	FBG DV	OB	8			24100	26800
28 10	PHANTOM 29 FISH		OPFSH	FBG DV	IO	8			**	**
28 10	PHANTOM 29 RACE		OFF	FBG DV	OB	8			24600	27400
28 10	PHANTOM 29 RACE		OFF	FBG DV	IO	8			**	**
33 10	PHANTOM 34 RACE		OFF	FBG DV	IO	8			**	**
			1992 BOATS							
28 10	PHANTOM 29 FISH		OPFSH	FBG DV	OB	8			23100	25700
28 10	PHANTOM 29 FISH		OPFSH	FBG DV	IO	8			**	**
28 10	PHANTOM 29 RACE		OFF	FBG DV	OB	8			23500	26100
28 10	PHANTOM 29 RACE		OFF	FBG DV	IO	8			**	**
33 10	PHANTOM 34 RACE		OFF	FBG DV	IO	8			**	**
			1991 BOATS							
28 10	OPEN FISHERMAN	OP	OPFSH	F/S SV	OB	8	3500	2	22200	24700
28 10	PHANTOM 29 LS		OFF	F/S SV	OB	8	3000	2	28200	31300
28 10	PHANTOM 29 LS		OFF	F/S SV	OB	8	5600	2 5	24400	27100
28 10	PHANTOM 29 RV		OFF	F/S SV	IO T260 MRCR	8	2400	2	22500	25000
28 10	PHANTOM 29 RV		OFF	F/S SV	IO	8	2400	2 5	**	**
28 10	TOURNAMENT FISHERMAN	OP	OPFSH	F/S SV	OB	8	3000	2	27800	30900
			1990 BOATS							
28 10	PHANTOM RACE	OP	OFF	FBG SV	OB	8	3300	1 7	21700	24100
28 10	PHANTOM RACE/PLEASR	OP	OFF	FBG SV	OB	8	4000	1 7	21700	24100
28 10	TOURNAMENT FISHERMAN	OP	OPFSH	FBG SV	OB	8	4500	1 7	21400	23800
			1986 BOATS							
17 2	V 172	OP	BASS	FBG DV	OB	6 10			2900	3400
17 2	V 172 FISH & SKI	OP	BASS	FBG DV	OB	6 10			2700	3150
17 4	V 174 DELUXE	OP	RNBT	FBG DV	OB	7	1166		3300	3850
17 4	V 174 DELUXE	OP	RNBT	FBG DV	IO 140-175	7	2050		2650	3100
17 4	V 174 SUPER DELUXE	OP	RNBT	FBG DV	OB	7	1166		3300	3850
17 4	V 174 SUPER DELUXE	OP	RNBT	FBG DV	IO 140-175	7	2050		2700	3150
18 8	190V DELUXE	OP	RNBT	FBG DV	IO 170-205	7 4	2520		3200	3800
18 8	190V SUPER DELUXE	OP	RNBT	FBG DV	IO 170-205	7 4	2520		3300	3850
20 4	STRIPER V204	ST	CTRCN	FBG DV	OB	8	1700		5250	6000
			1985 BOATS							
16 1	TRI 162 FISHER	OP	FSH	FBG TR	OB	5 7	520		1450	1700
16 1	TRI 162 PRO	OP	BASS	FBG TR	OB	5 7	700		1950	2300
17 2	V 172	OP	BASS	FBG DV	OB	6 10			2850	3300
17 2	V 172 FISH & SKI	OP	BASS	FBG TR	OB	6 10	920		2650	3050
17 3	SPIRIT 173		RNBT	FBG TR	OB	7	1150		3200	3700
17 3	SPIRIT 173		RNBT	FBG TR	IO 140	7	1040		1950	2350
17 4	V 174 DELUXE	OP	RNBT	FBG DV	OB	7	1166		3250	3750
17 4	V 174 DELUXE	OP	RNBT	FBG DV	IO 140-170	7	2050		2500	2900
17 4	V 174 SUPER DELUXE	OP	RNBT	FBG DV	OB	7	1166		3250	3750
17 4	V 174 SUPER DELUXE	OP	RNBT	FBG DV	IO 140-170	7	2050		2600	3000
20 4	STRIPER V174	ST	CTRCN	FBG DV	OB	8	1700		5100	5900
			1984 BOATS							
16	MYSTIC SUPER DELUXE	ST	RNBT	FBG DV	OB	6 9	935		2500	2950
16 2	FISHER		BASS	FBG TR	OB	5 7	475		1300	1550
16 2	PRO		BASS	FBG TR	OB	5 7	700		1900	2250
17 2	DEMON 172		BASS	FBG DV	OB	6 7	920		2600	3000
17 3	SPIRIT 173	ST	RNBT	FBG TR	OB	7	1500		3850	4500
17 3	SPIRIT 173	SLP	RNBT	FBG TR	IO 140	7	1040		1900	2250
17 3	SPIRIT 173	SLP	RNBT	FBG TR	IO 170	7	2150		2500	2900
17 4	SATAN 174	ST	RNBT	FBG DV	OB	7	1166		3200	3700
17 4	SATAN 174	ST	RNBT	FBG DV	IO 140	7	1050		1900	2250
17 4	SATAN 174	ST	RNBT	FBG DV	IO 170	7			2400	2750
17 4	SATAN SS 174	ST	RNBT	FBG DV	IO 170	7			2450	2850
20 4	STRIPER 204	OP	CTRCN	FBG DV	OB	8	1700		5000	5750

....For earlier years, see the BUC Used Boat Price Guide, Volume 3

PHEIL YACHTS
ST PETERSBURG FL 33705

See inside cover to adjust price for area

LOA FT IN	NAME AND/ OR MODEL	TOP/ RIG	BOAT TYPE	-HULL- MTL TP	----ENGINE--- TP # HP MFG	BEAM FT IN	WGT LBS	DRAFT FT IN	RETAIL LOW	RETAIL HIGH
			1985 BOATS							
37 6	PHEIL 37.5	SLP	SAIL	F/S CT	OB	22	3500	1	28800	32000

PHOENIX MARINE ENT INC

DIV OF AMERICAN MARINE HOLDING
HIALEAH FL 33010 COAST GUARD MFG ID- PMG

See inside cover to adjust price for area

For more recent years, see the BUC Used Boat Price Guide, Volume 1

LOA FT	LOA IN	NAME AND/ OR MODEL	TOP/ RIG	BOAT TYPE	HULL MTL	HULL TP	ENGINE TP	ENGINE # HP	ENGINE MFG	BEAM FT	BEAM IN	WGT LBS	DRAFT FT	DRAFT IN	RETAIL LOW	RETAIL HIGH
		1996 BOATS														
30	3	PHOENIX 27 TRN	OP	RNBT	FBG	DV	OB			9	10	6400	2		25500	28300
30	3	PHOENIX 27 TRN	OP	RNBT	FBG	DV	IB	T260		9	10	8200	2		42400	47100
30	3	PHOENIX 27 TRN	OP	RNBT	FBG	DV	IB	T200D	VLVO	9	10	8200	2		56200	61800
31	11	PHOENIX 29 SF CNV	FB	SF	FBG	DV	IB	T260		10		9450	2	4	47000	51700
31	11	PHOENIX 29 SF CNV	FB	SF	FBG	DV	IB	T200D-T230D		10		9450	2	4	60200	68700
31	11	PHOENIX 29 SFX	FB	SF	FBG	DV	IB	T260		10		9450	2	4	48900	53800
31	11	PHOENIX 29 SFX	FB	SF	FBG	DV	IB	T200D-T230D		10		9450	2	4	62600	71000
33	9	PHOENIX 34 SFX	FB	SF	FBG	DV	IB	T355		13		20810	2	9	98300	121500
33	9	PHOENIX 34 SFX	FB	SF	FBG	DV	IB	T350D-T435D		13		23890	2	9	142500	170500
33	9	PHOENIX 34 TRN	ST	CUD	FBG	DV	IB	T355	CRUS	13		19600	2	9	92700	102000
33	9	PHOENIX 34 TRN	ST	CUD	FBG	DV	IB	T350D-T435D		13		22680	2	9	133000	155000
33	9	PHOENIX 34 TRN	FB	SF	FBG	DV	IB	T355	MRCR	13		23890	2	9	95300	104500
33	9	PHOENIX 34 TRN	FB	SF	FBG	DV	IB	T420D	CAT	13		23890	2	9	139000	152500
37	10	PHOENIX 38 SFX CNV	FB	SF	FBG	DV	IB	T375D	CAT	14		30800	3	7	198500	218000
		IB T420D CAT 204500 225000, IB T435D CAT 207000 227500, IB T485D DD													212500	233500
37	10	PHOENIX 38 TRN	ST	CUD	FBG	DV	IB	T380	CRUS	14		28600	3	7	154500	169500
		IB T375D CAT 184500 203000, IB T435D CAT 193000 212000, IB T485D GM													194500	213500
37	10	PHOENIX 38 TRN	FB	SF	FBG	DV	IB	T420D	CAT	14		28600	3	7	190000	209000
		1995 BOATS														
30	3	PHOENIX 27 TRN	OP	RNBT	FBG	DV	OB			9	10	7200	1	10	24400	27100
30	3	PHOENIX 27 TRN	OP	RNBT	FBG	DV	IB	T260	CRUS	9	10	8200	2		40100	44500
30	3	PHOENIX 27 TRN	OP	RNBT	FBG	DV	IB	T200D	VLVO	9	10	8200	2		53400	58700
31	11	PHOENIX 29 SF CNV	FB	SF	FBG	DV	IB	T260	CRUS	10		9450	2	4	45000	50000
31	11	PHOENIX 29 SF CNV	FB	SF	FBG	DV	IB	T200D-T225D		10		9450	2	4	58300	66000
31	11	PHOENIX 29 SFX	FB	SF	FBG	DV	IO	T260	CRUS	10		9450	2	4	44200	49100
31	11	PHOENIX 29 SFX	FB	SF	FBG	DV	IO	T200D-T225D		10		9450	2	4	60400	68300
33	9	PHOENIX 33 SFX	FB	SF	FBG	DV	IB	T355	CRUS	13		20000	2	9	91400	100500
33	9	PHOENIX 33 SFX	FB	SF	FBG	DV	IB	T350D-T435D		13		23890	2	9	135500	158500
33	9	PHOENIX 33 TRN	ST	CUD	FBG	DV	IB	T355	CRUS	13		19600	2	9	90700	99700
33	9	PHOENIX 33 TRN	ST	CUD	FBG	DV	IB	T350D-T435D		13		22000	2	9	127500	150000
37	10	PHOENIX 33 SFX CNV	FB	SF	FBG	DV	IO	T375D	CAT	14		30800	3	7	163000	179000
37	10	PHOENIX 33 SFX CNV	FB	SF	FBG	DV	IO	T435D	CAT	14		30800	3	7	170000	187000
37	10	PHOENIX 33 SFX CNV	FB	SF	FBG	DV	IO	T485D	DD	14		30800	3	7	175000	192000
37	10	PHOENIX 37 TRN	ST	CUD	FBG	DV	IB	T380	CRUS	14		28600	3	7	148000	162500
		IB T375D CAT 176500 194000, IB T435D CAT 184500 203000, IB T485D GM													186000	204500
		1994 BOATS														
27	3	PHOENIX 27 TRN	OP	RNBT	FBG	DV	OB			9	10	8200	1	10	23400	26000
27	3	PHOENIX 27 WE	OP	RNBT	FBG	DV	IB	T260	CRUS	9	10	7200	1	10	35500	39400
27	3	PHOENIX 27 WE	OP	RNBT	FBG	DV	IB	T200D	VLVO	9	10	7200	1	10	46700	51400
27	3	WEEKENDER	OP	RNBT	FBG	DV	OB			9	10	7200	1	10	23300	25900
30	3	PHOENIX 27 TRN	OP	RNBT	FBG	DV	IB	T260	CRUS	9	10	8200	2		41100	45600
30	3	PHOENIX 27 TRN	OP	RNBT	FBG	DV	IB	T200D	VLVO	9	10	8200	2		48600	53400
31	11	PHOENIX 29 SF CNV	FB	SF	FBG	DV	IB	T200D-T260D		10		9450	2	4	54400	64000
32	5	BLACKHAWK 909	ST	EXP	FBG	DV	IO	T200D	VLVO	10		9150	2	7	56800	62400
32	5	BLACKHAWK 909	ST	EXP	FBG	DV	IB	T200D-T260D		10		9150	2	7	68300	80500
33	9	PHOENIX 33 SF CNV	FB	SF	FBG	DV	IB	T355	CRUS	13		20000	2	9	86500	95100
33	9	PHOENIX 33 SF CNV	FB	SF	FBG	DV	IB	T350D-T425D		13		26000	2	9	134500	148000
33	9	PHOENIX 33 SFX	FB	SF	FBG	DV	IB	T355	CRUS	13		20000	2	9	86500	95100
33	9	PHOENIX 33 SFX	FB	SF	FBG	DV	IB	T350D-T425D		13		22000	2	9	122500	142500
33	9	PHOENIX 33 TRN	ST	CUD	FBG	DV	IB	T355	CRUS	13		18000	2	9	83100	91300
33	9	PHOENIX 33 TRN	ST	CUD	FBG	DV	IB	T350D-T425D		13		22000	2	9	121500	141500
37	9	PHOENIX 37 TRN	ST	CUD	FBG	DV	IB	T380	CRUS	14		28000	3	7	138500	152000
		IB T375D CAT 166000 182000, IB T425D CAT 172000 189000, IB T485D GM													175000	192000
37	10	PHOENIX 37 SF CNV	FB	SF	FBG	DV	IB	T375D	CAT	14		30000	3	7	175000	192500
37	10	PHOENIX 37 SF CNV	FB	SF	FBG	DV	IB	T425D	CAT	14		30000	3	7	181500	199500
37	10	PHOENIX 37 SF CNV	FB	SF	FBG	DV	IB	T485D	GM	14		30000	3	7	184000	202500
		1993 BOATS														
27	3	PHOENIX 27 TRN	OP	RNBT	FBG	DV	OB			9	10	8200	1	10	22400	24900
27	3	PHOENIX 27 WE	OP	RNBT	FBG	DV	IB	T270	CRUS	9	10	7200	1	10	33800	37600
27	3	PHOENIX 27 WE	OP	RNBT	FBG	DV	IB	T200D	VLVO	9	10	7200	1	10	44100	49000
27	3	WEEKENDER	OP	RNBT	FBG	DV	OB			9	10	7200	1	10	22300	24800
30	3	PHOENIX 27 TRN	OP	RNBT	FBG	DV	IB	T210	CRUS	9	10	8200	2		37600	41700
30	3	PHOENIX 27 TRN	OP	RNBT	FBG	DV	IB	T200D	VLVO	9	10	8200	2		46500	51100
31	11	PHOENIX 29 SF CNV	FB	SF	FBG	DV	IB	T200D-T225D		10		9450	2	4	51800	58600
32	5	BLACKHAWK 909	ST	EXP	FBG	DV	IO	T200D	VLVO	10		9150	2	7	52900	58100
32	5	BLACKHAWK 909	ST	EXP	FBG	DV	IB	T200D-T270D		10		9150	2	7	65100	77600
33	9	PHOENIX 33 SF CNV	FB	SF	FBG	DV	IB	T454	CRUS	13		20000	2	9	86100	94600
33	9	PHOENIX 33 SF CNV	FB	SF	FBG	DV	IB	T306D-T425D		13		26000	2	9	125500	137500
33	9	PHOENIX 33 SFX	FB	SF	FBG	DV	IB	T454	CRUS	13		20000	2	9	86100	94600
33	9	PHOENIX 33 SFX	FB	SF	FBG	DV	IB	T306D-T425D		13		22000	2	9	112000	135500
33	9	PHOENIX 33 TRN	ST	CUD	FBG	DV	IB	T454	CRUS	13		18000	2	9	82900	91100
33	9	PHOENIX 33 TRN	ST	CUD	FBG	DV	IB	T306D-T425D		13		22000	2	9	112000	135000
37	9	PHOENIX 37 TRN	ST	CUD	FBG	DV	IB	T502	CRUS	14		28000	3	7	139500	153500
		IB T375D CAT 158000 173500, IB T425D CAT 164000 180000, IB T485D GM													166500	183000
37	10	PHOENIX 37 SF CNV	FB	SF	FBG	DV	IB	T375D	CAT	14		30000	3	7	167000	183500
37	10	PHOENIX 37 SF CNV	FB	SF	FBG	DV	IB	T425D	CAT	14		30000	3	7	173000	190000
37	10	PHOENIX 37 SF CNV	FB	SF	FBG	DV	IB	T485D	GM	14		30000	3	7	175500	193000
		1992 BOATS														
27	3	PHOENIX 27 TRN	OP	RNBT	FBG	DV	OB			9	10	8200	1	10	21500	23900
27	3	PHOENIX 27 WE	OP	RNBT	FBG	DV	IB	T270	CRUS	9	10	7200	1	10	32100	35700
27	3	PHOENIX 27 WE	OP	RNBT	FBG	DV	IB	T200D	VLVO	9	10	7200	1	10	42000	46700
27	3	WEEKENDER	OP	RNBT	FBG	DV	OB			9	10	7200	1	10	21400	23800
30	3	PHOENIX 27 TRN	OP	RNBT	FBG	DV	IB	T270	CRUS	9	10	8200	2		37200	41300
30	3	PHOENIX 27 TRN	OP	RNBT	FBG	DV	IB	T200D	VLVO	9	10	8200	2		43900	48800
30	8	PHOENIX 31 TRN	ST	CUD	FBG	DV	IB	T315	CRUS	12		10000	3	1	49100	53900
30	8	PHOENIX 31 TRN	ST	CUD	FBG	DV	IB	T300D-T320D		12		10000	3	1	62700	71100
31	11	PHOENIX 29 SF CNV	FB	SF	FBG	DV	IB	T270	CRUS	10		9450	2	4	42300	47100
31	11	PHOENIX 29 SF CNV	FB	SF	FBG	DV	IB	T200D-T225D		10		9450	2	4	49400	55900
32	5	BLACKHAWK 909	ST	EXP	FBG	DV	IB	T270	CRUS	10		9150	2	7	54600	60000
32	5	BLACKHAWK 909	ST	EXP	FBG	DV	IO	T200D	VLVO	10		9150	2	7	49400	54300
32	5	BLACKHAWK 909	ST	EXP	FBG	DV	IB	T200D	VLVO	10		9150	2	7	62100	68200
33	9	PHOENIX 33 SF CNV	FB	SF	FBG	DV	IB	T320-T380		13		20000	2	9	76700	86500
33	9	PHOENIX 33 SF CNV	FB	SF	FBG	DV	IB	T306D-T425D		13		26000	2	9	119500	131500
33	9	PHOENIX 33 SFX	FB	SF	FBG	DV	IB	T320-T380		13		20000	2	9	76700	86500
33	9	PHOENIX 33 SFX	FB	SF	FBG	DV	IB	T306D-T425D		13		22000	2	9	106500	130000
33	9	PHOENIX 33 TRN	ST	CUD	FBG	DV	IB	T320-T380		13		18000	2	9	73600	83100
33	9	PHOENIX 33 TRN	ST	CUD	FBG	DV	IB	T306D-T425D		13		22000	2	9	107000	128500
37	9	PHOENIX 37 TRN	ST	CUD	FBG	DV	IB	T380	CRUS	14		28000	3	7	125500	138000
		IB T375D CAT 150500 165500, IB T425D CAT 156500 171500, IB T485D GM													158500	174500
37	10	PHOENIX 37 SF CNV	FB	SF	FBG	DV	IB	T375D	CAT	14		30000	3	7	159000	175000
37	10	PHOENIX 37 SF CNV	FB	SF	FBG	DV	IB	T425D	CAT	14		30000	3	7	165000	181000
37	10	PHOENIX 37 SF CNV	FB	SF	FBG	DV	IB	T485D	GM	14		30000	3	7	167000	184000
		1991 BOATS														
27	3	PHOENIX 27 WE	OP	RNBT	FBG	DV	IB	T270	CRUS	9	10	7200	1	10	30500	33900
27	3	PHOENIX 27 WE	OP	RNBT	FBG	DV	IB	T200D	VLVO	9	10	7200	1	10	40100	44600
30	3	PHOENIX 27 TRN	OP	RNBT	FBG	DV	IB	T270	CRUS	9	10	8200	2		35400	39300
30	3	PHOENIX 27 TRN	OP	RNBT	FBG	DV	IB	T200D	VLVO	9	10	8200	2		41900	46500
30	8	PHOENIX 31 TRN	ST	CUD	FBG	DV	IB	T315	CRUS	12		11300	3	1	48100	52800
30	8	PHOENIX 31 TRN	ST	CUD	FBG	DV	IB	T300D-T320D		12		11300	3	1	63500	71700
31	11	PHOENIX 29 SF CNV	FB	SF	FBG	DV	IB	T270	CRUS	10		9450	2	4	40200	44700
31	11	PHOENIX 29 SF CNV	FB	SF	FBG	DV	IB	T200D-T260D		10		9450	2	4	47400	55500
32	5	BLACKHAWK 909	ST	EXP	FBG	DV	IB	T270	CRUS	10		9150	2	7	51900	57000
32	5	BLACKHAWK 909	ST	EXP	FBG	DV	IB	T200D	VLVO	10		9150	2	7	59300	65100
33	9	PHOENIX 33 SF CNV	FB	SF	FBG	DV	IB	T300-T355		13		20520	2	9	73100	82100
33	9	PHOENIX 33 SF CNV	FB	SF	FBG	DV	IB	T306D-T425D		13		23600	2	9	106500	128000
33	9	PHOENIX 33 SFX	FB	SF	FBG	DV	IB	T300-T355		13		20810	2	9	73500	82600
33	9	PHOENIX 33 SFX	FB	SF	FBG	DV	IB	T306D-T425D		13		23890	2	9	107500	129000
33	9	PHOENIX 33 TRN	ST	CUD	FBG	DV	IB	T300-T355		13		19600	2	9	71700	80600
33	9	PHOENIX 33 TRN	ST	CUD	FBG	DV	IB	T306D-T425D		13		22680	2	9	104000	125000
37	9	PHOENIX 33 TRN	ST	CUD	FBG	DV	IB	T375D	CAT	14		28600	3	7	146000	160500
37	9	PHOENIX 37 TRN	ST	CUD	FBG	DV	IB	T355	CRUS	14		28600	3	7	121000	133000
37	9	PHOENIX 37 TRN	ST	CUD	FBG	DV	IB	T425D	CAT	14		28600	3	7	151500	166500
37	9	PHOENIX 37 TRN	ST	CUD	FBG	DV	IB	T485D	GM	14		28600	3	7	153500	169000
37	10	PHOENIX 37 SF CNV	FB	SF	FBG	DV	IB	T355	CRUS	14		30800	3	7	129500	142500
		IB T375D CAT 154500 170000, IB T425D CAT 160000 176000, IB T485D GM													162500	178500
		1990 BOATS														
27	3	PHOENIX 27 WEEKENDER	OP	RNBT	FBG	DV	IB	T270	CRUS	9	10	7200	1	10	29000	32200
27	3	PHOENIX 27 WEEKENDER	OP	RNBT	FBG	DV	IB	T200D	VLVO	9	10	7200	1	10	38300	42600
30	3	PHOENIX 27 TOURNAMNT	OP	RNBT	FBG	DV	IB	T210	CRUS	9	10	8200	2		32200	35800
30	3	PHOENIX 27 TOURNAMNT	OP	RNBT	FBG	DV	IB	T200D	VLVO	9	10	8200	2		40000	44500
31	11	PHOENIX 29 SF CNV	FB	SF	FBG	DV	IB	T210	CRUS	10		9450	2	4	36700	40700
31	11	PHOENIX 29 SF CNV	FB	SF	FBG	DV	IB	T200D-T260D		10		9450	2	4	44800	53000
32	5	BLACKHAWK 909	ST	EXP	FBG	DV	IB	T270	CRUS	10		9150	2	7	49300	54200
32	5	BLACKHAWK 909	ST	EXP	FBG	DV	IB	T200D	VLVO	10		9150	2	7	56600	62200
33	9	PHOENIX 33 SF CNV	FB	SF	FBG	DV	IB	T300-T355		13		20520	2	9	69500	78100
33	9	PHOENIX 33 SF CNV	FB	SF	FBG	DV	IB	T306D-T425D		13		23600	2	9	102000	122500
33	9	PHOENIX 33 TRN	ST	CUD	FBG	DV	IB	T300-T355		13		19600	2	9	68200	76700
33	9	PHOENIX 33 TRN	ST	CUD	FBG	DV	IB	T306D-T400D		13		22680	2	9	99400	116500

CONTINUED ON NEXT PAGE

LOA FT	LOA IN	NAME AND/ OR MODEL	TOP/ RIG	BOAT TYPE	-HULL- MTL	-HULL- TP	TP	ENGINE # HP	ENGINE MFG	BEAM FT	BEAM IN	WGT LBS	DRAFT FT	DRAFT IN	RETAIL LOW	RETAIL HIGH
		1990 BOATS														
37	9	PHOENIX 37 TRN	ST	CUD	FBG	DV	IB	T300	CRUS	13		28600	3	7	119000	130500
		IB T355 CRUS 120500 132500, IB T425D CAT 149000 164000, IB T485D GM													151500	166500
37	10	PHOENIX 37 SF CNV	FB	SF	FBG	DV	IB	T355	CRUS	14		30800	3	7	124000	136000
		IB T375D CAT 147500 162500, IB T425D CAT 153000 168000, IB T485D GM													155000	170500
		1989 BOATS														
27	3	PHOENIX 27 FSHBUSTER	OP	RNBT	FBG	DV	IB	T260-T270		9	10	7200	1	10	27600	30900
27	3	PHOENIX 27 FSHBUSTER	OP	RNBT	FBG	DV	IB	T200D	VLVO	9	10	7200	1	10	36900	41000
27	3	PHOENIX 27 WKNDR	OP	RNBT	FBG	DV	IB	T260-T270		9	10	7200	1	10	27200	30500
27	3	PHOENIX 27 WKNDR	OP	RNBT	FBG	DV	IB	T200D	VLVO	9	10	7200	1	10	36400	40500
31	11	PHOENIX 29 SF CNV	FB	SF	FBG	DV	IB	T260-T270		10		9450	2	4	36200	40500
31	11	PHOENIX 29 SF CNV	FB	SF	FBG	DV	IB	T200D	VLVO	10		9450	2	4	42900	47600
32	5	BLACKHAWK 909	ST	EXP	FBG	DV	IB	T260-T270		10		9150	2	7	46900	51900
32	5	BLACKHAWK 909	ST	EXP	FBG	DV	IB	T200D	VLVO	10		9150	2	7	54200	59600
33	9	PHOENIX 33 SF CNV	FB	SF	FBG	DV	IB	T330-T502		13		14850	2	9	59400	72000
33	9	PHOENIX 33 SF CNV	FB	SF	FBG	DV	IB	T306D	VLVO	13		16000	2	9	77200	84800
33	9	PHOENIX 33 SF CNV	FB	SF	FBG	DV	IB	T375D-T400D		13		18200	2	9	88400	98100
37	10	PHOENIX 37 SF CNV	FB	SF	FBG	DV	IB	502	CRUS	14		27000	3	7	105500	116000
37	10	PHOENIX 37 SF CNV	FB	SF	FBG	DV	IB	375D	CAT	14		30800	3	7	127000	139500
37	10	PHOENIX 37 SF CNV	FB	SF	FBG	DV	IB	485D	GM	14		30800	3	7	130500	143000
		1988 BOATS														
27	3	PHOENIX 27 FSHBUSTER	OP	RNBT	FBG	DV	OB			9	10	5400	2	5	19000	21100
27	3	PHOENIX 27 FSHBUSTER	OP	RNBT	FBG	DV	IB	300D	GM	9	10	7000	2	5	31800	35400
27	3	PHOENIX 27 FSHBUSTER	OP	RNBT	FBG	DV	IB	375D	CAT	9	10	7500	2	5	36500	40500
27	3	PHOENIX 27 FSHBUSTER	OP	RNBT	FBG	DV	SE	T205	OMC	9	10	6000	1	6	19000	21100
27	3	PHOENIX 27 FSHBUSTER	OP	RNBT	FBG	DV	IB	T220-T270		9	10	7500	1	10	26200	30000
27	3	PHOENIX 27 FSHBUSTER	OP	RNBT	FBG	DV	IB	T200D	VLVO	9	10	8000	1	10	37700	41900
27	3	PHOENIX 27 WKNDR	OP	RNBT	FBG	DV	OB			9	10	5400	2	5	18500	20600
27	3	PHOENIX 27 WKNDR	OP	RNBT	FBG	DV	IB	300D-375D		9	10	7000	2	5	31400	38700
27	3	PHOENIX 27 WKNDR	OP	RNBT	FBG	DV	SE	T205	OMC	9	10	6000	1	6	18700	20800
27	3	PHOENIX 27 WKNDR	OP	RNBT	FBG	DV	IB	T220-T270		9	10	7500	1	10	25800	29600
27	3	PHOENIX 27 WKNDR	OP	RNBT	FBG	DV	IB	T200D	VLVO	9	10	7500	1	10	36000	40000
28	10	PHOENIX 29	FB	CR	FBG	DV	IB	T220-T270		10		8500	2	4	28900	33300
28	10	PHOENIX 29	FB	CR	FBG	DV	IB	T200D-T250D		10		8500	2	4	39000	46900
29	8	BLACKHAWK 909	ST	EXP	FBG	DV	IO	T260	MRCR	10		9150	2	7	26600	29500
		IO T260 VLVO 26700 29700, IB T260-T270 33800 37900, IO T200D VLVO													32200	35800
		IB T200D VLVO 43700 48500														
31	11	PHOENIX 29 SF CNV	FB	SF	FBG	DV	IB	T220-T270		10		8650	2	4	33100	38200
31	11	PHOENIX 29 SF CNV	FB	SF	FBG	DV	IB	T200D-T250D		10		8650	2	4	39700	47000
33	9	PHOENIX 33 CNV	FB	SF	FBG	DV	IB	T340-T350		13		14850	2	9	56700	62800
33	9	PHOENIX 33 CNV	FB	SF	FBG	DV	IB	T270D-T400D		13		17200	2	9	76000	91100
38		PHOENIX 38 CNV	FB	SF	FBG	DV	IB	T375D	CAT	14		23000	3	7	110000	121000
38		PHOENIX 38 CNV	FB	SF	FBG	DV	IB	T485D	S&S	14		25000	3	7	121500	134000
		1987 BOATS														
27	3	PHOENIX 27	OP	RNBT	FBG	DV	OB			9	10	5400	2	5	18200	20300
27	3	PHOENIX 27	OP	RNBT	FBG	DV	IB	300D	GM	9	10	7000	2	5	30300	33700
27	3	PHOENIX 27	OP	RNBT	FBG	DV	IB	375D	CAT	9	10	7500	2	5	34900	38800
27	3	PHOENIX 27	OP	RNBT	FBG	DV	SE	T205	OMC	9	10	6000	1	6	18300	20300
27	3	PHOENIX 27	OP	RNBT	FBG	DV	IB	T220-T270		9	10	7500	1	10	24800	28400
27	3	PHOENIX 27	OP	RNBT	FBG	DV	IB	T200D	VLVO	9	10	8000	1	10	36100	40100
28	10	PHOENIX 29	FB	CR	FBG	DV	IB	T220-T270		10		8500	2	4	27600	31800
28	10	PHOENIX 29	FB	CR	FBG	DV	IB	T200D-T250D		10		8500	2	4	37400	44900
29	8	BLACKHAWK 909	ST	EXP	FBG	DV	IO	T225-T230		10		9150	2	7	24700	27500
		IO T260 MRCR 25300 28100, IO T260 VLVO 25400 28200, IB T260-T270													32300	36100
		IO T200D VLVO 30600 34000, IB T200D VLVO 41800 46500														
33	9	PHOENIX 33 CNV	FB	SF	FBG	DV	IB	T330-T340		13		14850	2	9	54000	59500
33	9	PHOENIX 33 CNV	FB	SF	FBG	DV	IB	T270D-T375D		13		17200	2	9	72800	87200
38		PHOENIX 38 CNV	FB	SF	FBG	DV	IB	T375D	CAT	14		23000	3	7	105500	115500
38		PHOENIX 38 CNV	FB	SF	FBG	DV	IB	T450D	S&S	14		25000	3	7	113500	124500
		1986 BOATS														
27	3	PHOENIX 27	OP	RNBT	FBG	DV	OB			9	10	5400		1	17400	19700
27	3	PHOENIX 27	OP	RNBT	FBG	DV	IB	215D	GM	9	10	7000	2	5	26700	29700
27	3	PHOENIX 27	OP	RNBT	FBG	DV	IB	375D	CAT	9	10	7500	2	5	33500	37200
27	3	PHOENIX 27	OP	RNBT	FBG	DV	SE	T205	OMC	9	10	6000	1	6	17400	19800
27	3	PHOENIX 27	OP	RNBT	FBG	DV	IB	T220-T270		9	10	7500	1	10	23700	27200
27	3	PHOENIX 27	OP	RNBT	FBG	DV	IB	T165D	VLVO	9	10	8000	1	10	33100	36800
28	10	PHOENIX 29	FB	CR	FBG	DV	IB	T220-T270		10		8500	2	4	26300	30300
28	10	PHOENIX 29	FB	CR	FBG	DV	IB	T165D-T215D		10		8500	2	4	34200	41100
29	8	BLACKHAWK 909	ST	EXP	FBG	DV	IO	T225-T260		10		7800	2	7	22500	25800
38		PHOENIX 38 CNV	FB	SDNSF	FBG	DV	IB	T375D	CAT	14		25000	3	2	107000	117500
38		PHOENIX 38 CNV	FB	SDNSF	FBG	DV	IB	T415D	S&S	14		25000	3	2	105500	116000
		1985 BOATS														
27	3	PHOENIX 27		RNBT	FBG	DV	IB	350		9	10				21000	23300
27	3	PHOENIX 27	OP	RNBT	FBG	DV	OB			9	10	5400	1	6	16900	19200
27	3	PHOENIX 27	OP	RNBT	FBG	DV	IB	215D	S&S	9	10	7000	3		25500	28300
27	3	PHOENIX 27	OP	RNBT	FBG	DV	IB	355D	CAT	9	10	7500	3		31500	35000
27	3	PHOENIX 27	OP	RNBT	FBG	DV	SE	T205	OMC	9	10	6000	1	6	17000	19300
27	3	PHOENIX 27	OP	RNBT	FBG	DV	IB	T220-T270		9	10	7500	1	10	22600	25900
27	3	PHOENIX 27	OP	RNBT	FBG	DV	IB	T136D-T165D		9	10	8000	1	10	30600	35300
28	10	PHOENIX 29	FB	CR	FBG	DV	IB	T220-T270		10		8500	2	4	25200	29000
28	10	PHOENIX 29	FB	CR	FBG	DV	IB	T136D-T215D		10		8500	2	4	31500	39200
28	10	PHOENIX 29	FB	SF	FBG	DV	IB	T220-T270		10		8500	2	4	25200	29000
29	8	BLACKHAWK	ST	EXP	FBG	DV	IO	T220-T260		10			2	7	21700	24800
38		PHOENIX 38 CNV	FB	SDNSF	FBG	DV	IB	T350	CRUS	14		25000	3	7	83600	91900
		IB T355D CAT 101000 110500, IB T410D J&T 103000 113000, IB T410D S&S													101000	111000
		1984 BOATS														
27	3	PHOENIX 27	OP	RNBT	FBG	DV	OB			9	10	5400	1	6	16500	18800
27	3	PHOENIX 27	OP	RNBT	FBG	DV	IB	350	CRUS	9	10	6500	1	10	19100	21200
27	3	PHOENIX 27	OP	RNBT	FBG	DV	IB	300D	CAT	9	10	6500	1	10	25900	28700
27	3	PHOENIX 27	OP	RNBT	FBG	DV	SE	T205	OMC	9	10	6500	1	10	16600	18900
27	3	PHOENIX 27	OP	RNBT	FBG	DV	IB	T220-T270		9	10	7200	1	10	21100	24300
27	3	PHOENIX 27	OP	RNBT	FBG	DV	IB	T124D-T215D		9	10	7200	1	10	26600	32000
28	10	PHOENIX 29	FB	CR	FBG	DV	IB	T220-T270		10		8500	2	4	24000	27700
28	10	PHOENIX 29	FB	CR	FBG	DV	IB	T124D-T165D		10		8500	2	4	29800	35000
28	10	PHOENIX 29	FB	CR	FBG	DV	IB	T215D	S&S	10		8500	2	4	33900	37700
28	10	PHOENIX 29	FB	SF	FBG	DV	IB	T220-T270		10		8500	2	4	24100	27700
28	10	PHOENIX 29	FB	SF	FBG	DV	IB	T124D-T165D		10		8500	2	4	29800	35000
28	10	PHOENIX 29	FB	SF	FBG	DV	IB	T205D	J&T	10		8500	2	4	33800	37500
28	10	PHOENIX 29 CHARTER	FB	SF	FBG	DV	IB	T220-T270		10		8500	2	4	24100	27700
28	10	PHOENIX 29 CHARTER	FB	SF	FBG	DV	IB	T124D-T165D		10		8500	2	4	29800	35000
28	10	PHOENIX 29 CHARTER	FB	SF	FBG	DV	IB	T205D	J&T	10		8500	2	4	33800	37500
38		PHOENIX 38 CNV	FB	SDNSF	FBG	DV	IB	T350	CRUS	14		25000	3	7	80100	88100
		IB T300D CAT 92900 102000, IB T350D PERK 96300 106000, IB T410D S&S													96600	106000

....For earlier years, see the BUC Used Boat Price Guide, Volume 3

PIERCE ARROW MARINE INC

RICKFORD IL 61104

See inside cover to adjust price for area

LOA FT	LOA IN	NAME AND/ OR MODEL	TOP/ RIG	BOAT TYPE	-HULL- MTL	-HULL- TP	TP	ENGINE # HP	ENGINE MFG	BEAM FT	BEAM IN	WGT LBS	DRAFT FT	DRAFT IN	RETAIL LOW	RETAIL HIGH
		1988 BOATS														
16		PIERCE ARROW TURBO	SLP	SA/OD	F/S	KL				5	3	900	2	6	4200	4900
18	7	PIERCE ARROW 18	SLP	SA/RC	F/S	KL	OB			8	2	1400	3	6	5100	5850
18	7	PIERCE ARROW 18 RK	SLP	SA/RC	F/S	KL	OB			8	2	1200	4		4700	5400
31	3	PIERCE ARROW 31	SLP	SA/RC	F/S	KL	IB	18D	VLVO	10	2	6000	5		16600	18900
31	3	PIERCE ARROW 31 SK	SLP	SA/RC	F/S	KL	IB	18D	VLVO	10	2	6400	4		18200	20200

PLAY-CRAFT PONTOON CO

DIV RICHLAND DIVERSIFIED IND
RICHLAND MO 65556 COAST GUARD MFG ID- PLF

See inside cover to adjust price for area

For more recent years, see the BUC Used Boat Price Guide, Volume 1

LOA FT	LOA IN	NAME AND/ OR MODEL	TOP/ RIG	BOAT TYPE	-HULL- MTL	-HULL- TP	TP	ENGINE # HP	ENGINE MFG	BEAM FT	BEAM IN	WGT LBS	DRAFT FT	DRAFT IN	RETAIL LOW	RETAIL HIGH
		1996 BOATS														
36		3610	HT	HB	AL	PN	OB			13		9200			20400	22700
41		4110	HT	HB	AL	PN	OB			13		10800			20600	22900
43		4310	HT	HB	AL	PN	OB			13		11000			20200	22500
45		4511	HT	HB	AL	PN	OB			14		13800			23800	26400
49		4912	HT	HB	AL	PN	OB			15		15600			27800	30900
58		5812	HT	HB	AL	PN	OB			15		18100			39000	43300
		1995 BOATS														
36		3610	HT	HB	AL	PN	OB			13		9200			19300	21400
41		4110	HT	HB	AL	PN	OB			13		10800			19500	21600
43		4310	HT	HB	AL	PN	OB			13		11000			19000	21100
45		4511	HT	HB	AL	PN	OB			14		13800			22500	25000
49		4912	HT	HB	AL	PN	OB			15		15600			26100	28900
58		5812	HT	HB	AL	PN	OB			15		18100			36700	40700
		1994 BOATS														
17	4	RW175XL	OP	BASS	AL	SV	OB			5	10	1000			3150	3700
17	4	RW175XLA	OP	BASS	AL	SV	OB			5	10	1000			3350	3900
17	4	RW175XLB	OP	BASS	AL	SV	OB			5	10	1000			4450	5150
17	10	1860MVC	OP	JON	AL	SV	OB			7	2	360			1000	1200
17	10	1872MVC	OP	JON	AL	SV	OB			8		490			1450	1700
18		RW186	OP	BASS	AL	SV	OB			7	2	1250			3950	4600

LOA FT IN	NAME AND/ OR MODEL	TOP/ RIG	BOAT TYPE	HULL MTL TP	TP	#-ENGINE- HP	MFG	BEAM FT IN	WGT LBS	DRAFT FT IN	RETAIL LOW	RETAIL HIGH
——— 1994 **BOATS** ———												
18	RW186A	OP	BASS	AL SV	OB			7 2	1250		4100	4800
18	RW186B	OP	BASS	AL SV	OB			7 2	1250		5300	6100
21	2150 BR		RNBT	FBG DV	IO	260	MRCR	8	3350		9250	10500
22 5	2350 BR		RNBT	FBG DV	IO	260	MRCR	8	3900		10900	12300
33	MINI CABIN	HT	HB	AL PN	OB			8 4	5000		8850	10100
——— 1993 **BOATS** ———												
17	1700 BR		RNBT	FBG DV	IO			7 9	1150		3900	4500
17	1750 BR		RNBT	FBG DV	IO	135		7 9	2200		4650	5350
19 1	190 BR		RNBT	FBG DV	IO	205		8	2700		6050	6950
20	PM 20	ST	FD	AL PN	OB			8	1310		3800	4450
20 8	210 SBR		RNBT	FBG DV	IO	260	MRCR	8	2950		7800	8950
21	2150 BR		RNBT	FBG DV	IO	260	MRCR	8	3350		8550	9800
21	2150 CC		CUD	FBG DV	IO	260	MRCR	8	3600		9450	10800
22 5	2350 BR		RNBT	FBG DV	IO	260	MRCR	8	3900		10100	11500
22 5	2350 CC		CUD	FBG DV	IO	260	MRCR	8	4000		11000	12400
33	MINI CABIN	HT	HB	AL PN	OB			8 4	5000		8350	9600
——— 1992 **BOATS** ———												
17	1700 BR		RNBT	FBG DV	OB			7 9	1150		3700	4300
17	1750 BR		RNBT	FBG DV	OB	130		7 9	2200		4400	5050
19	190 SBR		RNBT	FBG DV	OB	230		8	2700		5750	6600
20	PM 20	ST	FD	AL PN	OB			8	1310		3600	4150
20 8	210 SBR		RNBT	FBG DV	IO	260	MRCR	8	2950		7300	8400
21	2150 BR		RNBT	FBG DV	IO	260	MRCR	8	3350		8000	9200
21	2150 CC		CUD	FBG DV	IO	260	MRCR	8	3600		8900	10100
22 5	2350 BR		RNBT	FBG DV	IO	260	MRCR	8	3900		9500	10900
22 5	2350 CC		CUD	FBG DV	IO	260	MRCR	8	4000		10300	11600
33	MINI CABIN		HB	AL PN	OB			8 4	5000		8000	9200
——— 1991 **BOATS** ———												
33	MINI CABIN		HB	AL PN	OB			8 4	5000		7700	8850
——— 1987 **BOATS** ———												
35	3510	HT	HB	AL PN	OB			10			10500	12000
40	4010	HT	HB	AL PN	OB			10			14800	16800
42	4210	HT	HB	AL PN	OB			10			16800	19100
——— 1986 **BOATS** ———												
35	3510	HT	HB	AL	OB			10			10200	11600
40	4010	HT	HB	AL	OB			10			13900	15800
42	4210	HT	HB	AL	OB			10			15900	18100
——— 1985 **BOATS** ———												
35	3510	HT	HB	AL	OB			10			9950	11300
40	4010	HT	HB	AL	OB			10			13600	15400

....For earlier years, see the BUC Used Boat Price Guide, Volume 3

PLUCKEBAUM CUSTOM BOATS
PROSPECT KY 40059   COAST GUARD MFG ID- PRP See inside cover to adjust price for area
FORMERLY PROSPECT BOAT WORKS INC

LOA FT IN	NAME AND/ OR MODEL	TOP/ RIG	BOAT TYPE	HULL MTL TP	TP	#-ENGINE- HP	MFG	BEAM FT IN	WGT LBS	DRAFT FT IN	RETAIL LOW	RETAIL HIGH
——— 1994 **BOATS** ———												
45	SPORT CRUISER	OP	SPTCR	AL SV	IB	T375D	CAT	15	18000	2 8	165500	182000
48	PLUCKEBAUM 48	FB	HB	AL SV	IB	T240	CHRY	14	18500	2 8	144500	159000
52	PLUCKEBAUM 52	FB	HB	AL SV	IB	T300D	CAT	16	20000	2 10	256000	281500
55	PLUCKEBAUM 55	FB	HB	AL SV	IB	T300D	CAT	17	22000	2 10	271500	298500
60	PLUCKEBAUM 60 MY	FB	MY	AL SV	IB	T375D	CAT	18	38000	3 4	267500	294000
60	PLUCKEBAUM 60 MYCPT	FB	MYCPT	AL SV	IB	T375D	CAT	18	38500	3 4	278500	306000
64	PLUCKEBAUM 64	FB	HB	AL SV	IB	T375D	CAT	18	28000	3	364500	400500
76	PLUCKEBAUM 76	FB	HB	AL SV	IB	T375D	CAT	18	34000	3	**	**
——— 1992 **BOATS** ———												
50	PLUCKEBACOASTAL	FB	HB	AL SV	IB	T300D	CUM	15	25000	3	194500	214000
56	PLUCKEBACOASTAL	FB	HB	AL SV	IB	T300D	CUM	15	28000	3	256500	282000
70	PLUCKEBACOASTAL	FB	HB	AL SV	IB	T320D	CUM	18	45000	3 6	337500	370500
——— 1986 **BOATS** ———												
30	PLUCKEBAUM	HT	SF	AL DV	IB	T210	CHRY	11	6000	2	21800	24200
54	APOLLO	ST	SPTCR	AL DV	IB	T570D	GM	16	25000	3 8	202000	222000
55	PLUCKEBAUM	HT	HB	AL SV	IB	T300D	CAT	17	40000	3 8	236500	260000
65	PLUCKEBAUM GBX-1	HT		AL SV	IB	T260D	CAT	19	60000	3 2	304000	334500
67	PLUCKEBAUM	HT	HB	AL SV	IB	T435D	GM	18	50000	3 8	297500	327000
75	PLUCKEBAUM	HT	HB	AL SV	IB	T570D	GM	19	60000	3 8	**	**
75	PLUCKEBAUM 301	HT	MY	AL DV	IB	R355D	CAT	20 6	67000	4 4	**	**
——— 1985 **BOATS** ———												
54	APOLLO	ST	SPTCR	AL DV	IB	T570D	GM	16	25000	3 8	193500	213000
55	PLUCKEBAUM	HT	HB	AL SV	IB	T300D	CAT	17	40000	3 6	220500	242500
65	PLUCKEBAUM GBX-1	HT		AL SV	IB	T260D	CAT	19	60000	3 2	292500	321500
67	PLUCKEBAUM	HT	HB	AL SV	IB	T435D	GM	18	50000	3 8	269500	296500
75	PLUCKEBAUM	HT	HB	AL SV	IB	T570D	GM	19	60000	3 8	**	**
75	PLUCKEBAUM 301	HT	MY	AL DV	IB	R355D	CAT	20 6	50T	5 6	**	**
——— 1984 **BOATS** ———												
54	APOLLO	ST	SPTCR	AL DV	IB	T570D	GM	16	25000	3 8	185500	204000
55	PLUCKEBAUM	HT	HB	AL SV	IB	T300D	CAT	17	40000	3 6	216000	237500
65	PLUCKEBAUM GBX-1	HT		AL SV	IB	T265D	CAT	19	60000	3 2	281500	309500
67	PLUCKEBAUM	HT	HB	AL SV	IB	T435D	GM	18	50000	3 8	264000	290000
75	PLUCKEBAUM	HT	HB	AL SV	IB	T570D	GM	19	60000	3 8	**	**
75	PLUCKEBAUM 301	HT	MY	AL DV	IB	R355D	CAT	20 6	67000	4 4	**	**

....For earlier years, see the BUC Used Boat Price Guide, Volume 3

PODCAT CATAMARANS
SANTA BARBARA CA 93109   See inside cover to adjust price for area

LOA FT IN	NAME AND/ OR MODEL	TOP/ RIG	BOAT TYPE	HULL MTL TP	TP	#-ENGINE- HP	MFG	BEAM FT IN	WGT LBS	DRAFT FT IN	RETAIL LOW	RETAIL HIGH
——— 1991 **BOATS** ———												
32	PODCAT 32	SLP	SA/RC	FBG CT	OB			22	5000	2 2	55200	60700
36	PODCAT 36	SLP	SA/RC	FBG CT	OB			22	4000	2 2	66700	73200
——— 1990 **BOATS** ———												
32	PODCAT 32		SA/CR	CT	OB			22	3500	1 6	47400	52100
32	PODCAT 32K		SA/RC	KEV CT	OB			22	2500	1 6	42900	47600
36	PODCAT 36		SA/RC	FBG CT	IB	50		23	4000	1 6	62700	68900
36	PODCAT 36K		SA/RC	KEV CT	IB	50		23	4000	1 6	62700	68900
——— 1989 **BOATS** ———												
32	PODCAT 32		SA/CR	CT	OB			22	3500	1 6	44100	49000
32	PODCAT 32K		SA/RC	KEV CT	OB			22	2500	1 6	40300	44800
36	PODCAT 36		SA/RC	FBG CT	IB	50		23	4000	1 6	59000	64800
36	PODCAT 36K		SA/RC	KEV CT	IB	50		23	3000	1 6	54600	60000
——— 1988 **BOATS** ———												
32	PODCAT 32		SA/CR	CT	OB			22	3500	1 6	41500	46100
32	PODCAT 32K		SA/RC	KEV CT	OB			22	2500	1 6	37900	42100
36	PODCAT 36		SA/CR	FBG CT	IB	50		23	4000	1 6	55500	61000
36	PODCAT 36K		SA/RC	KEV CT	IB	50		23	3000	1 6	51300	56400
——— 1987 **BOATS** ———												
32	PODCAT 32		SA/CR	CT	OB			22	3500	1 6	39000	43400
32	PODCAT 32		SA/RC	KEV CT	OB			22	2500	1 6	35700	39600
——— 1986 **BOATS** ———												
32	PODCAT 32	KTH	SA/CR	CT	OB			22	3500	4 6	36700	40800
32	PODCAT 32	KTH	SA/RC	KEV CT	OB			22	2500	4 6	33600	37300

POINTER MARINE CO INC
SIMSBURY CT 06070-0441   COAST GUARD MFG ID- PTR See inside cover to adjust price for area
FORMERLY POINTER CORP

LOA FT IN	NAME AND/ OR MODEL	TOP/ RIG	BOAT TYPE	HULL MTL TP	TP	#-ENGINE- HP	MFG	BEAM FT IN	WGT LBS	DRAFT FT IN	RETAIL LOW	RETAIL HIGH
——— 1994 **BOATS** ———												
16 6	EASTPOINT 17	OP	CTRCN	FBG SV	OB			6 7	700	5	2200	2550
16 6	EASTPOINT 17SC		CTRCN	FBG SV	OB			6 7	700	5	2200	2550
18	CLASSIC 18		CTRCN	FBG RB	OB			7 3	1200	6	3650	4250
18	CLASSIC 18		UTL	FBG RB	OB			7 3	1200	6	3400	3950
20 8	WESTPOINT 21		UTL	FBG RB	OB			8 3	1900	9	5150	5900
20 8	WESTPOINT 21 CUDDY		CUD	FBG	OB			8 3	1900	9	5750	6600
20 8	WESTPOINT 21V		CTRCN	FBG DV	OB			8 3	1900	9	5750	6600
20 8	WESTPOINT LOBSTER		UTL	FBG	OB			8 3	1900	9	5150	5900
——— 1993 **BOATS** ———												
16 6	POINTER 17		CTRCN	FBG SV	OB			6 7	700	5	2050	2450
16 6	POINTER 17	OP	CTRCN	FBG SV	OB			6 7	700	5	2050	2450
16 6	POINTER 17 SIDECNSL		OPFSH	FBG SV	OB			6 7	700	5	2050	2450
18	WESTPOINT 18		CTRCN	FBG RB	OB			7 3	1250	6	3550	4150
18	WESTPOINT 18		UTL	FBG RB	OB			7 3	1100	6	3000	3500
20 8	WESTPOINT 21		UTL	FBG RB	OB			8 3	1290	6	3400	4000
20 8	WESTPOINT 21 CUDDY		CUD	FBG	OB			8 3	1140	9	3650	4200
20 8	WESTPOINT 21CC		CTRCN	FBG RB	OB			8 3	1395	6	4300	5000
20 8	WESTPOINT 21V		CTRCN	FBG DV	OB			8 3	1395	9	4300	5000
20 8	WESTPOINT LOBSTER		UTL	FBG	OB			8 3	1520	9	4000	4650
——— 1990 **BOATS** ———												
16 6	POINTER 17	OP	CTRCN	FBG DS	OB			7	650	6	1650	1950
16 6	POINTER 17 SIDECNSL		OPFSH	FBG DS	OB			7	650	6	1650	1950
21	BLUEFISH	OP	CTRCN	FBG DS	OB			8 3	1575	6	4150	4850
21	OFFSHORE	OP	CTRCN	FBG DS	OB			8 3	1650	8	4500	5050
21	POINTER UTILITY	OP	UTL	FBG DS	OB			8 3	1475	9	3400	3950
21	WESTPORT 21 CUDDY	OP	CUD	FBG	OB				2100	8	5250	6000
——— 1989 **BOATS** ———												
16 6	POINTER 17	OP	CTRCN	FBG DS	OB			7	650	6	1600	1900
16 6	POINTER 17 SIDECNSL		OPFSH	FBG	OB			7	650	6	1550	1850

LOA FT	LOA IN	NAME AND/ OR MODEL	TOP/ RIG	BOAT TYPE	-HULL- MTL	-HULL- TP	ENGINE TP	# HP	MFG	BEAM FT	BEAM IN	WGT LBS	DRAFT FT	DRAFT IN	RETAIL LOW	RETAIL HIGH
		1989 BOATS														
21		BLUEFISH	OP	CTRCN	FBG	DS	OB			8	3	1575		8	4000	4650
21		OFFSHORE	OP	CTRCN	FBG	DS	OB			8	3	1650		8	4150	4850
21		POINTER UTILITY	OP	UTL	FBG	DS	OB			8	3	1475		8	3250	3800
21		WESTPORT 21 CUDDY	OP	CUD	FBG	DS	OB					2100		8	5000	5750
		1988 BOATS														
16	6	POINTER 17	OP	CTRCN	FBG	DS	OB			7		650		6	1500	1800
16	6	POINTER 17 SIDECNSL		OPFSH	FBG		OB			7		650		6	1500	1800
21		BLUEFISH	OP	CTRCN	FBG	DS	OB			8	3	1575		8	3850	4450
21		OFFSHORE	OP	CTRCN	FBG	DS	OB			8	3	1650		8	4000	4650
21		POINTER UTILITY	OP	UTL	FBG	DS	OB			8	3	1475		8	3150	3650
		1987 BOATS														
16	6	POINTER 17	OP	CTRCN	FBG	DS	OB			7		650		6	1450	1750
16	6	POINTER 17 SIDECNSL		OPFSH	FBG		OB			7		650		6	1450	1750
21		BLUEFISH	OP	CTRCN	FBG	DS	OB			8	3	1575		8	3700	4300
21		OFFSHORE	OP	CTRCN	FBG	DS	OB			8	3	1650		8	3850	4450
21		POINTER UTILITY	OP	UTL	FBG	DS	OB			8	3	1475		8	3000	3500
		1986 BOATS														
16	6	POINTER 17	OP	CTRCN	FBG	DS	OB			6	7	650		6	1400	1700
18	2	BLUEFISH	OP	CTRCN	FBG	DS	OB			7	3	1125		5	2050	2450
18	2	OFFSHORE	OP	CTRCN	FBG	DS	OB			7	3	1125		5	2850	3300
18	2	POINTER UTILITY	OP	UTL	FBG	DS	OB			7	3	1125		5	2350	2750
21		BLUEFISH	OP	CTRCN	FBG	DS	OB			8	3	1575		8	3550	4150
21		OFFSHORE	OP	CTRCN	FBG	DS	OB			8	3	1650		8	3700	4300
21		POINTER UTILITY	OP	UTL	FBG	DS	OB			8	3	1475		8	2900	3400
		1985 BOATS														
18	2	BLUEFISH	OP	CTRCN	FBG	DS	OB			7	3	1125		5	2000	2350
18	2	OFFSHORE	OP	CTRCN	FBG	DS	OB			7	3	1125		5	2750	3200
18	2	POINTER UTILITY	OP	UTL	FBG	DS	OB			7	3	1125		5	2250	2650
21		BLUEFISH	OP	CTRCN	FBG	DS	OB			8	3	1575		8	3450	4000
21		OFFSHORE	OP	CTRCN	FBG	DS	OB			8	3	1650		8	3600	4150
21		POINTER UTILITY	OP	UTL	FBG	DS	OB			8	3	1475		8	2800	3250
		1984 BOATS														
18	2	POINTER BLUEFISH		FSH	FBG	SV	OB			7	4	1200		5	2500	2900
18	2	POINTER OFFSHORE		SF	FBG	SV	OB			7	4	1300		5	2600	3000
18	2	POINTER UTILITY		UTL	FBG	SV	OB			7	4	1125		5	2200	2550
21		POINTER BLUEFISH		FSH	FBG	SV	OB			8	4	1550		8	3300	3850
21		POINTER OFFSHORE		SF	FBG	SV	OB			8	4	1650		8	3450	4050
21		POINTER UTILITY		UTL	FBG	SV	OB			8	4	1475		8	2750	3150

....For earlier years, see the BUC Used Boat Price Guide, Volume 3

POLAR KRAFT MFG CO

GODFREY MARINE
SYRACUSE IN 46567 COAST GUARD MFG ID- PLR

See inside cover to adjust price for area

For more recent years, see the BUC Used Boat Price Guide, Volume 1

LOA FT	LOA IN	NAME AND/ OR MODEL	TOP/ RIG	BOAT TYPE	-HULL- MTL	-HULL- TP	ENGINE TP	# HP	MFG	BEAM FT	BEAM IN	WGT LBS	DRAFT FT	DRAFT IN	RETAIL LOW	RETAIL HIGH
		1996 BOATS														
16		CRAPPIE 16T	OP	BASS	AL	SV	OB			5	8	527			1800	2150
16		CRAPPIE 16T AW	OP	BASS	AL	SV	OB			5	8	527			2150	2500
16		CRAPPIE CNSL	OP	BASS	AL	SV	OB			5	8	548			1900	2250
16		CRAPPIE CNSL AW	OP	BASS	AL	SV	OB			5	8	548			2250	2600
16		CRAPPIE S/S	OP	BASS	AL	SV	OB			5	8	535			1850	2200
16		CRAPPIE S/S AW	OP	BASS	AL	SV	OB			5	8	535			2200	2550
16		DAKOTA 1648	OP	JON	AL	SV	OB			5	8	257			980	1150
16		EAGLE 16	OP	BASS	AL	SV	OB			5	8	568			1950	2350
16		EAGLE 16 AW	OP	BASS	AL	SV	OB			5	8	568			2300	2700
16		JON-FB 1648	OP	JON	AL	SV	OB			5	8	287			1050	1300
16		JON-FB 1648 AW	OP	JON	AL	SV	OB			5	8	297			1100	1300
16		JON-FB 1651	OP	JON	AL	SV	OB			6		350			1300	1500
16		JON-FB 1651 AW	OP	JON	AL	SV	OB			6		370			1350	1600
16		JON-MV 1648	OP	JON	AL	SV	OB			5	8	291			1100	1300
16		JON-MV 1648 AW	OP	JON	AL	SV	OB			5	8	310			1150	1350
16		MARSH HUNTER 1645	OP	JON	AL	FL	OB			5	8	353			1300	1550
16		SPORTSMAN 16	OP	BASS	AL	SV	OB			5	8	569			1900	2250
16		SPORTSMAN 16 AW	OP	BASS	AL	SV	OB			5	8	569			2350	2750
16	8	V1700	OP	CTRCN	FBG	SV	OB			8	10				2450	2850
17		DS 1751	OP	JON	AL	SV	OB			6		397			1350	1600
17		EAGLE 17	OP	BASS	AL	SV	OB			5	8	580			2150	2500
17		EAGLE 17 AW	OP	BASS	AL	SV	OB			5	8	580			2450	2850
17		JON-MV 1751	OP	JON	AL	SV	OB			6		355			1200	1400
17		JON-MV 1751 AW	OP	JON	AL	SV	OB			6		375			1250	1500
17		MVT 1751	OP	JON	AL	TH	OB			6		378			1250	1500
17		PS 1780 STD	OP	CTRCN	FBG	SV	OB			6	8				2450	2900
17		PS 1796 COMM	OP	CTRCN	AL	SV	OB			8		1350			4850	5600
17		PS 1796 STD	OP	CTRCN	FBG	SV	OB			8					2450	2900
18		CHEROKEE 18	OP	BASS	AL	SV	OB			6		568			2200	2600
18		CHEROKEE 18 AW	OP	BASS	AL	SV	OB			6		568			2500	2900
18		JON-MV 1860	OP	JON	AL	SV	OB			6	10	440			1300	1550
18		JON-MV 1860 AW	OP	JON	AL	SV	OB			6	10	475			1400	1650
18		MVT 1860	OP	JON	AL	TH	OB			6	10	475			1500	1750
19		PS 1996 COMM	OP	CTRCN	AL	SV	OB			8		1600			5750	6650
19		PS 1996 STD	OP	CTRCN	FBG	SV	OB			8					2900	3350
20		JON-MV 2060	OP	JON	AL	SV	OB			6	10	475			1450	1750
20		JON-MV 2060 AW	OP	JON	AL	SV	OB			6	10	495			1700	2000
20		MVT 2060	OP	JON	AL	TH	OB			6	10	475			1500	1800
		1995 BOATS														
16		JON 1648	OP	JON	AL	FL	OB			5	8	277			995	1200
16		JON 1648 AW	OP	JON	AL	FL	OB			5	8	304			1050	1300
16		JON 1651	OP	JON	AL	SV	OB			6		305			1100	1300
16		JON 1651 AW	OP	JON	AL	SV	OB			6		355			1250	1450
16		JON-MV 1648	OP	JON	AL	SV	OB			5	8	278			995	1200
16		JON-MV 1648 AW	OP	JON	AL	SV	OB			5	8	317			1100	1350
16		MARSH HUNTER 1645	OP	JON	AL	FL	OB			5	8	353			1200	1450
16	8	V1700	OP	CTRCN	FBG	SV	OB			8	10				2300	2700
17		DS 1751	OP	JON	AL	SV	OB			6		397			1250	1500
17		EAGLE 17	OP	BASS	AL	SV	OB			6		430			1550	1850
17		JON-MV 1751	OP	JON	AL	SV	OB			6		297			950	1150
17		JON-MV 1751 AW	OP	JON	AL	SV	OB			6		338			1100	1300
17		MVT 1751	OP	JON	AL	TH	OB			6		363			1150	1400
17		X-STREAM 1780	OP	CTRCN	FBG	SV	OB			6	8				2350	2750
17		X-STREAM 1796	OP	CTRCN	FBG	SV	OB			8					2350	2750
18		CHEROKEE 18	OP	BASS	AL	SV	OB			6		568			2250	2650
18		JON-MV 1860	OP	JON	AL	SV	OB			6	8	437			1250	1450
18		JON-MV 1860 AW	OP	JON	AL	SV	OB			6	8	478			1350	1650
18		MVT 1860	OP	JON	AL	TH	OB			6	8	450			1300	1500
19		X-STREAM 1996	OP	CTRCN	FBG	SV	OB			8					2750	3200
20		JON-MV 2060	OP	JON	AL	SV	OB			7	8	470			1350	1600
20		JON-MV 2060 AW	OP	JON	AL	SV	OB			7	8	515			1700	2000
20		MVT 2060	OP	JON	AL	TH	OB			7	8	475			1450	1700
		1994 BOATS														
16		APACHE 16	OP	BASS	AL	SV	OB			5	8	514			1700	2000
16		APACHE 16 AW	OP	BASS	AL	SV	OB			5	8	514			1800	2150
16		JON 1648	OP	JON	AL	FL	OB			5	8	277			945	1150
16		JON 1648 AW	OP	JON	AL	FL	OB			5	8	304			1050	1200
16		JON 1651	OP	JON	AL	SV	OB			6		305			1050	1200
16		JON 1651 AW	OP	JON	AL	SV	OB			6		355			1150	1400
16		JON-MV 1648	OP	JON	AL	SV	OB			5	8	278			950	1150
16		JON-MV 1648 AW	OP	JON	AL	SV	OB			5	8	317			1050	1250
17		CHEROKEE 17	OP	BASS	AL	SV	OB			6		565			1950	2300
17		CHEROKEE 17 AW	OP	BASS	AL	SV	OB			6		565			2050	2450
17		JON-MV 1751	OP	JON	AL	SV	OB			6		297			905	1100
17		JON-MV 1751 AW	OP	JON	AL	SV	OB			6		338			1050	1200
17		MVT 1751	OP	JON	AL	TH	OB			6		363			1100	1300
18		BANSHEE 18	OP	BASS	AL	SV	OB			7	3	800			2900	3350
18		JON-MV 1860	OP	JON	AL	SV	OB			6	8	383			1000	1200
18		JON-MV 1860 AW	OP	JON	AL	SV	OB			6	8	437			1200	1400
18		MVT 1860	OP	JON	AL	TH	OB			6	8	393			1050	1250
20		JON-MV 2060	OP	JON	AL	SV	OB			7	8	470			1300	1550
20		JON-MV 2060 AW	OP	JON	AL	SV	OB			7	8	470			1400	1700
20		MVT 2060	OP	JON	AL	TH	OB			7	8	475			1350	1650
		1993 BOATS														
16		APACHE 16	OP	BASS	AL	SV	OB			5	8	514			1600	1900
16		APACHE 16 AW	OP	BASS	AL	SV	OB			5	8	514			1700	2050
16		JON 1648	OP	JON	AL	FL	OB			5	8	277			905	1100
16		JON 1648 AW	OP	JON	AL	FL	OB			5	8	304			980	1150
16		JON-MV 1648	OP	JON	AL	SV	OB			5	8	278			910	1100
16		JON-MV 1648 AW	OP	JON	AL	SV	OB			5	8	317			1000	1200
17		CHEROKEE 17	OP	BASS	AL	SV	OB			6		565			1850	2200
17		CHEROKEE 17 AW	OP	BASS	AL	SV	OB			6		565			1950	2350
17		JON-MV 1751	OP	JON	AL	SV	OB			6		297			865	1050
17		JON-MV 1751 AW	OP	JON	AL	SV	OB			6		338			980	1150
17		MVT 1751	OP	JON	AL	TH	OB			6		363			1050	1250
18		BANSHEE 18 AW	OP	BASS	AL	SV	OB			7	3	800			2750	3200
18		JON-MV 1860	OP	JON	AL	SV	OB			6	8	383			960	1150
18		JON-MV 1860 AW	OP	JON	AL	SV	OB			6	8	437			1100	1350
18		MVT 1860	OP	JON	AL	TH	OB			6	8	393			990	1200

LOA FT IN	NAME AND/ OR MODEL	TOP/ RIG	BOAT TYPE	-HULL- MTL TP	TP	----ENGINE--- # HP MFG	BEAM FT IN	WGT LBS	DRAFT FT IN	RETAIL LOW	RETAIL HIGH
					1990 BOATS						
16	BASS BOAT-SB160	OP	BASS	AL SV	OB		5 8	514		1450	1750
16	CRAPPIE BOAT-C16	OP	FSH	AL FL	OB		5 8	424		1200	1400
16	JOHN-CF1648	OP	JON	AL FL	OB		6	277		790	950
16	JOHN-CF1651	OP	JON	AL FL	OB		6	297		850	1000
16	JOHN-MV 1648	OP	JON	AL SV	OB		5 8	278		790	955
17	JOHN-MV 1751	OP	JON	AL SV	OB		6	297		755	910
18	JOHN-MV 1860	OP	JON	AL SV	OB		6 8	383		850	1000
					1986 BOATS						
16	160 BASS	OP	BASS	AL FL	OB		5 9	472		1150	1400
16	BEAR 48	OP	BASS	AL FL	OB		5 10	345		855	1000
16	CF1651AW	OP	BASS	AL FL	OB		6	345		825	995
16	KODIAK KS-I	OP	BASS	AL SV	OB		6 3	490		1200	1450
16	KODIAK KS-II	OP	BASS	AL SV	OB		6 3	530		1300	1550
16	SV1652	OP	UTL	AL SV	OB		6	415		1000	1200
17	CF-1760	OP	JON	AL FL	OB		6 8	560		1250	1450
17	CF1760AW	OP	JON	AL FL	OB		6 8	560		1600	1900
17	CGF-1760	OP	FSH	AL SV	OB		6 8	728		1450	1700
17 3	SUPER BASS 170	OP	BASS	AL FL	OB		6 1	514		1350	1600
17 11	CGF-1851	OP	JON	AL FL	OB		6	300		545	655
19	CF-1960	OP	JON	AL FL	OB		6 8	625		1250	1450
19	CGF-1960	OP	FSH	AL SV	OB		6 8	625		1750	2050
					1985 BOATS						
16 7	SUPER-BASS 170	OP	BASS	AL SV	OB		6	560		1350	1650
17 11	CGF-1851	OP	FSH	AL SV	OB		6	300		800	965
19	CGF-1960	OP	FSH	AL	OB		6 8	625		1700	2000
					1984 BOATS						
16 7	BEAR 48	OP	BASS	AL FL	OB		5 10	345		830	1000
16 7	SUPER-BASS 160	OP	BASS	AL FL	OB		5 6	500		1200	1400
16 7	SUPER-BEAR	OP	BASS	AL FL	OB			405		975	1150
17	CF-1760	OP	JON	AL FL	OB		6 8	560		1150	1350
17	CGF-1760	OP	FSH	AL SV	OB		6 8	560		1350	1600
17 4	SUPER-BASS 170	OP	BASS	AL FL	OB		6	640		1550	1850
17 11	CF-1851	OP	JON	AL FL	OB		6	290		495	595
17 11	CGF-1851	OP	JON	AL FL	OB		6	300		515	620
17 11	CGS-1851	OP	FSH	AL SV	OB		6	300		780	940
17 11	S-1851	OP	JON	AL FL	OB		6	300		515	620
18	PK1860	HT	UTL	AL SV	OB		6 8	680		1550	1850
19	CF-1960	OP	JON	AL FL	OB		6 8	625		1150	1400
19	CGF-1960	OP	FSH	AL SV	OB		6 8	625		1650	1950

....For earlier years, see the BUC Used Boat Price Guide, Volume 3

PORT CITY FIBERGLASS
WILMINGTON NC 28402   COAST GUARD MFG ID- POR See inside cover to adjust price for area

LOA FT IN	NAME AND/ OR MODEL	TOP/ RIG	BOAT TYPE	-HULL- MTL TP	TP	----ENGINE--- # HP MFG	BEAM FT IN	WGT LBS	DRAFT FT IN	RETAIL LOW	RETAIL HIGH
					1986 BOATS						
17 2	ALINDALE-SKIFF	OP	UTL	FBG FL	OB		5 2	420	4	650	785
17 4	SEA-MARK 1704	OP	UTL	FBG SV	OB		6 5	820	6	1250	1500
20 9	SEA-MARK 2100	OP	UTL	FBG SV	OB		8	1200	10	2000	2400
					1984 BOATS						
16 1	ALINDALE SKIFF	OP	UTL	FBG FL	OB		5 2	380	4	560	675
16 4	SEA-RAIDER 1604	OP	UTL	FBG TR	OB		6 6	730	10	1100	1300
16 11	ALINDALE SKIFF	OP	UTL	FBG SV	OB		5 2	450	5	665	805
17 4	SEA-MARK 1704	OP	UTL	FBG SV	OB		6 5	740	6	1100	1300
20 9	SEA-MARK 2009	OP	UTL	FBG SV	OB		8	1250	10	2000	2400

....For earlier years, see the BUC Used Boat Price Guide, Volume 3

PORTSMOUTH BOAT CO INC
WOLFESBORO NH 03894   See inside cover to adjust price for area

LOA FT IN	NAME AND/ OR MODEL	TOP/ RIG	BOAT TYPE	-HULL- MTL TP	TP	----ENGINE--- # HP MFG	BEAM FT IN	WGT LBS	DRAFT FT IN	RETAIL LOW	RETAIL HIGH
					1992 BOATS						
21 9	PORTSMOUTH 22 BASS	ST	SF	F/S RB	OB		7 10	2200	1 2	8200	9400
21 9	PORTSMOUTH 22 BASS	ST	SF	F/S RB	IB	185 CRUS	7 10	3600	2 3	20900	23200
21 9	PORTSMOUTH 22 BASS	ST	SF	F/S RB	IB	130D VLVO	7 10	3600	2 3	26700	29600
21 9	PORTSMOUTH 22 LBSTR	HT	SF	F/S RB	OB		7 10	2200	1 2	8200	9400
21 9	PORTSMOUTH 22 LBSTR	HT	SF	F/S RB	IB	185 CRUS	7 10	3600	2 3	20800	23200
21 9	PORTSMOUTH 22 LBSTR	HT	SF	F/S RB	IB	130D VLVO	7 10	3600	2 3	26400	29300
29 9	PORTSMOUTH 30 COMM	HT	FSH	F/S RB	IB	350 CRUS	10 6	10000	2 10	59200	65100
29 9	PORTSMOUTH 30 COMM	HT	FSH	F/S RB	IB	210D-320D	10 6	10000	2 10	68600	82200
29 9	PORTSMOUTH 30 CR	HT	CR	F/S RB	IB	350 CRUS	10 6	10000	2 10	59500	65400
29 9	PORTSMOUTH 30 CR	HT	CR	F/S RB	IB	210D-320D	10 6	10000	2 10	59200	82700
29 9	PORTSMOUTH 30 SPORT	HT	SF	F/S RB	IB	350 CRUS	10 4	10000	2 10	58100	63800
29 9	PORTSMOUTH 30 SPORT	HT	SF	F/S RB	IB	210D-320D	10 6	10000	2 10	67000	80700
					1991 BOATS						
21 9	PORTSMOUTH 22 BASS	ST	SF	F/S RB	OB		7 10	2200	1 2	7900	9050
21 9	PORTSMOUTH 22 BASS	ST	SF	F/S RB	IB	185 CRUS	7 10	3600	2 3	19800	22100
21 9	PORTSMOUTH 22 BASS	ST	SF	F/S RB	IB	130D VLVO	7 10	3600	2 3	25440	28300
21 9	PORTSMOUTH 22 LBSTR	HT	SF	F/S RB	OB		7 10	2200	1 2	7900	9050
21 9	PORTSMOUTH 22 LBSTR	HT	SF	F/S RB	IB	185 CRUS	7 10	3600	2 3	19800	22000
21 9	PORTSMOUTH 22 LBSTR	HT	SF	F/S RB	IB	130D VLVO	7 10	3600	2 3	25200	28000
29 9	PORTSMOUTH 30 COMM	HT	FSH	F/S RB	IB	350 CRUS	10 6	10000	2 10	56400	62000
29 9	PORTSMOUTH 30 COMM	HT	FSH	F/S RB	IB	210D-320D	10 6	10000	2 10	65500	78400
29 9	PORTSMOUTH 30 CR	HT	CR	F/S RB	IB	350 CRUS	10 6	10000	2 10	56600	62100
29 9	PORTSMOUTH 30 CR	HT	CR	F/S RB	IB	210D-320D	10 6	10000	2 10	66300	78900
29 9	PORTSMOUTH 30 SPORT	HT	SF	F/S RB	IB	350 CRUS	10 6	10000	2 10	55100	60600
29 9	PORTSMOUTH 30 SPORT	HT	SF	F/S RB	IB	210D-320D	10 6	10000	2 10	63900	76900
					1990 BOATS						
21 9	PORTSMOUTH 22 BASS	ST	SF	F/S RB	OB		7 10	2200	1 2	7600	8750
21 9	PORTSMOUTH 22 BASS	ST	SF	F/S RB	IB	185 CRUS	7 10	3600	2 3	19100	21200
21 9	PORTSMOUTH 22 BASS	ST	SF	F/S RB	IB	130D VLVO	7 10	3600	2 3	24400	27100
21 9	PORTSMOUTH 22 LOBSTR	HT	SF	F/S RB	OB		7 10	2200	1 2	7600	8750
21 9	PORTSMOUTH 22 LOBSTR	HT	SF	F/S RB	IB	185 CRUS	7 10	3600	2 3	19000	21100
21 9	PORTSMOUTH 22 LOBSTR	HT	SF	F/S RB	IB	130D VLVO	7 10	3600	2 3	24200	26900
29 9	PORTSMOUTH 30 COMM	HT	FSH	F/S RB	IB	350 CRUS	10 6	10000	2 10	54000	59300
29 9	PORTSMOUTH 30 COMM	HT	FSH	F/S RB	IB	210D-320D	10 6	10000	2 10	62900	75300
29 9	PORTSMOUTH 30 CR	HT	CR	F/S RB	IB	350 CRUS	10 6	10000	2 10	53900	59200
29 9	PORTSMOUTH 30 CR	HT	CR	F/S RB	IB	210D-320D	10 6	10000	2 10	63100	75400
29 9	PORTSMOUTH 30 SPORT	HT	SF	F/S RB	IB	350 CRUS	10 6	10000	2 10	52700	57900
29 9	PORTSMOUTH 30 SPORT	HT	SF	F/S RB	IB	210D-320D	10 6	10000	2 10	61000	73400

POST MARINE CO INC
MAYS LANDING NJ 08330   COAST GUARD MFG ID- PMC See inside cover to adjust price for area

For more recent years, see the BUC Used Boat Price Guide, Volume 1

LOA FT IN	NAME AND/ OR MODEL	TOP/ RIG	BOAT TYPE	-HULL- MTL TP	TP	----ENGINE--- # HP MFG	BEAM FT IN	WGT LBS	DRAFT FT IN	RETAIL LOW	RETAIL HIGH
					1996 BOATS						
43 10	POST 43	FB	SDNSF	FBG SV	IB	T550D GM	15 9	33000	4	263000	289000
43 10	POST 43	FB	SDNSF	FBG SV	IB	T565D GM	15 9	33000	4	266000	292500
46 9	POST 46	FB	SDNSF	FBG SV	IB	T550D GM	15 9	36000	4	281500	309000
50 7	POST 50	FB	SDNSF	FBG SV	IB	T735D GM	16 11	43000	4	391000	430000
					1995 BOATS						
43 10	POST 43	FB	SDNSF	FBG SV	IB	T550D GM	15 9	33000	4	252000	277000
43 10	POST 43	FB	SDNSF	FBG SV	IB	T565D GM	15 9	33000	4	255500	280500
43 10	POST 43	FB	SDNSF	FBG SV	IB	T735D GM	15 9	33000	4	286000	314500
46 9	POST 46	FB	SDNSF	FBG SV	IB	T550D GM	15 9	36000	4	269500	296000
50 7	POST 50	FB	SDNSF	FBG SV	IB	T735D GM	16 11	43000	4	375000	412000
					1994 BOATS						
43 10	POST 44	FB	SDNSF	FBG SV	IB	T550D GM	15 9	33000	4	240000	263500
46 9	POST 46	FB	SDNSF	FBG SV	IB	T550D GM	15 9	36000	4	258500	284000
50 7	POST 50	FB	SDNSF	FBG SV	IB	T735D GM	16 11	43000	4	359500	395000
					1993 BOATS						
43 10	POST 44	FB	SDNSF	FBG SV	IB	T485D GM	15 9	33000	4	228500	251000
46 9	POST 46	FB	SDNSF	FBG SV	IB	T485D GM	15 9	36000	4	232000	255000
50 7	POST 50	FB	SDNSF	FBG SV	IB	T735D GM	16 11	43000	4	342500	376000
					1992 BOATS						
43 10	POST 44	FB	SDNSF	FBG SV	IB	T485D GM	15 9	33000	4	218000	239500
46 9	POST 46	FB	SDNSF	FBG SV	IB	T485D GM	15 9	36000	4	221500	243000
50 7	POST 50	FB	SDNSF	FBG SV	IB	T735D GM	16 11	43000	4	326500	358500
					1991 BOATS						
43 10	POST 44	FB	SDNSF	FBG SV	IB	T485D GM	15 9	33000	4	208000	228500
46 9	POST 46	FB	SDNSF	FBG SV	IB	T485D GM	15 9	36000	4	211000	232000
50 7	POST 50	FB	SDNSF	FBG SV	IB	T735D GM	16 11	43000	4	311000	342000
					1990 BOATS						
43 10	POST 46	FB	SDNSF	FBG SV	IB	T485D GM	15 9	33000	4	198500	218000
46 9	POST 46	FB	SDNSF	FBG SV	IB	T485D GM	15 9	36000	4	201500	221500
46 9	POST 46	FB	SDNSF	FBG SV	IB	T550D GM	15 9	36000	4	233500	234500
50 7	POST 50	FB	SDNSF	FBG SV	IB	T735D GM	16 11	43000	4	297000	326500
					1989 BOATS						
43 8	POST 43	FB	SDNSF	FBG SV	IB	T485D GM	15 9	33000	4	180000	198000
46 9	POST 46	FB	SDNSF	FBG SV	IB	T485D GM	15 9	36000	4	192500	211500
50 7	POST 50	FB	SDNSF	FBG SV	IB	T735D GM	16 11	43000	4	283500	311500

LOA FT	IN	NAME AND/ OR MODEL	TOP/ RIG	BOAT TYPE	-HULL- MTL	TP	----ENGINE--- TP	# HP	MFG	BEAM FT	IN	WGT LBS	DRAFT FT	IN	RETAIL LOW	RETAIL HIGH
		1988 BOATS														
43	8	POST 43	FB	SDNSF	FBG	SV	IB	T450D	GM	15	9	33000	4		166500	183000
46	9	POST 46	FB	SDNSF	FBG	SV	IB	T485D	GM	15	9	36000	4		184000	202000
		1987 BOATS														
43	8	POST 43	FB	SDNSF	FBG	SV	IB	T450D	GM	15	9	33000	3		159500	175000
46	9	POST 46	FB	SDNSF	FBG	SV	IB	T450D	GM	15	9	36000	3	6	170000	187000
		1986 BOATS														
43	8	POST 43	FB	SDNSF	FBG	SV	IB	T450D	J&T	15	9	30000	3		145500	160000
46	9	POST 46	FB	SDNSF	FBG	SV	IB	T450D	J&T	15	9	33000	3	6	157000	172500
		1985 BOATS														
43	8	POST 43	FB	SDNSF	FBG	SV	IB	T450D	J&T	15	9	30000	3		139500	153500
46	9	POST 46	FB	SDNSF	FBG	SV	IB	T450D	J&T	15	9	33000	3	6	150500	165500
		1984 BOATS														
43	8	POST 43	FB	SDNSF	FBG	SV	IB	T450D	GM	15	9	30000	3		133000	146500
46	9	POST 46	FB	SDNSF	FBG	SV	IB	T450D	GM	15	9	33000	3	6	144000	158000

....For earlier years, see the BUC Used Boat Price Guide, Volume 3

POWERQUEST BOATS INC

PQ MARINE HOLDINGS
HOLLAND MI 49424

See inside cover to adjust price for area

FORMERLY POWER PLAY BOATS INC

For more recent years, see the BUC Used Boat Price Guide, Volume 1

LOA FT	IN	NAME AND/ OR MODEL	TOP/ RIG	BOAT TYPE	-HULL- MTL	TP	----ENGINE--- TP	# HP	MFG	BEAM FT	IN	WGT LBS	DRAFT FT	IN	RETAIL LOW	RETAIL HIGH
		1996 BOATS														
21	8	PRECEPT 220 SX	OP	CUD	FBG	DV	IO	235-300		8	2	3300	2	9	13600	16900
21	8	PRECEPT 220 SX	OP	CUD	FBG	DV	IO	330-350		8	2	3300	2	9	15000	18100
21	8	PRECEPT 221 BR	OP	B/R	FBG	DV	IO	235-300		8	2	3300	2	9	12700	15800
21	8	PRECEPT 221 BR	OP	B/R	FBG	DV	IO	330	MRCR	8	2	3300	2	9	14100	16000
23	7	STRYKER 237 BR	OP	B/R	FBG	DV	IO	235-300		8	6	3950	2	9	15500	18700
23	7	STRYKER 237 BR	OP	B/R	FBG	DV	IO	330-350		8	6	3950	2	9	17300	20400
23	7	STRYKER 237 BR	OP	B/R	FBG	DV	IO	385	MRCR	8	6	3950	2	9	19700	21900
23	7	STRYKER 237 XL	OP	CUD	FBG	DV	IO	235-300		8	6	3950	2	9	16500	20000
23	7	STRYKER 237 XL	OP	CUD	FBG	DV	IO	330-385		8	6	3950	2	9	18800	23300
23	9	PRECEPT 240 SX	OP	CUD	FBG	DV	IO	235-300		8	6	4000	3		17300	21000
23	9	PRECEPT 240 SX	OP	CUD	FBG	DV	IO	350-385		8	6	4000	3		19700	23700
25	7	LEGEND 257 BR	OP	B/R	FBG	DV	IO	235-330		8	6	4175	2	9	18100	22300
25	7	LEGEND 257 BR	OP	B/R	FBG	DV	IO	350-385		8	6	4179	2	9	20700	24500
25	7	LEGEND 257 BR	OP	B/R	FBG	DV	IO	415	MRCR	8	6	4200	2	9	23400	26000
25	7	LEGEND 257 XL	OP	CUD	FBG	DV	IO	235-330		8	6	4200	2	9	19600	24300
25	7	LEGEND 257 XL	OP	CUD	FBG	DV	IO	350-385		8	6	4200	2	9	22500	26700
25	7	LEGEND 257 XL	OP	CUD	FBG	DV	IO	415	MRCR	8	6	4200	2	9	25400	28200
27	1	LASER 270	OP	CUD	FBG	DV	IO	300-385		8	6	4800	2	9	25100	31000
27	1	LASER 270	OP	CUD	FBG	DV	IO	415	MRCR	8	6	4800	2	9	29100	32400
27	1	LASER 270	OP	CUD	FBG	DV	IO	T250	MRCR	8	6	5500	2	9	29800	33100
29	1	ENTICER 290	OP	OFF	FBG	DV	IO	T235-T330		8	6	6300	2	9	29800	36500
29	1	ENTICER 290	OP	OFF	FBG	DV	IO	T350-T415		8	6	6300	2	9	33600	40800
33	9	VYPER 340	OP	OFF	FBG	DV	IO	T300-T415		8	6	8200	3		56000	67400
33	9	VYPER 340	OP	OFF	FBG	DV	IO	T470-T490		8	6	8200	3		64500	72200
37	9	AVENGER 380	OP	OFF	FBG	DV	IO	T385	MRCR	8	6	9200	3		64800	71200
		IO T415 MRCR 67600 74300, IO T470 MRCR 73400 80600, IO T490 MRCR 75500 83000														
		1995 BOATS														
22	2	SPECTRA 222 BR	OP	B/R	FBG	DV	IO	235-300		8		3500	2	8	12100	14800
22	2	SPECTRA 222 BR	OP	B/R	FBG	DV	IO	350	MRCR	8		3500	2	8	14400	16400
22	2	SPECTRA 222 XL	OP	CUD	FBG	DV	IO	235-300		8		3500	2	8	12900	15800
22	2	SPECTRA 222 XL	OP	CUD	FBG	DV	IO	350-385		8		3500	2	8	15400	19200
23	7	STRYKER 237 BR	OP	B/R	FBG	DV	IO	235-300		8	6	3950	2	9	14400	17400
23	7	STRYKER 237 BR	OP	B/R	FBG	DV	IO	350-385		8	6	3950	2	9	16800	20600
23	7	STRYKER 237 XL	OP	CUD	FBG	DV	IO	235-300		8	6	3950	2	9	15400	18600
23	7	STRYKER 237 XL	OP	CUD	FBG	DV	IO	350-385		8	6	3950	2	9	18200	21800
25	7	LEGEND 257 BR	OP	B/R	FBG	DV	IO	235-300		8	6	4175	2	9	16600	20100
25	7	LEGEND 257 BR	OP	B/R	FBG	DV	IO	350-385		8	6	4179	2	9	19300	22800
25	7	LEGEND 257 XL	OP	CUD	FBG	DV	IO	235-300		8	6	4200	2	9	18400	21700
25	7	LEGEND 257 XL	OP	CUD	FBG	DV	IO	350-385		8	6	4200	2	9	21000	24900
25	7	LEGEND 257 XL	OP	CUD	FBG	DV	IO	415	MRCR	8	6	4200	2	9	23700	26300
27	1	LASER 270	OP	CUD	FBG	DV	IO	300-385		8	6	4800	2	9	23400	28900
27	1	LASER 270	OP	CUD	FBG	DV	IO	415	MRCR	8	6	4800	2	9	27200	30200
27	1	LASER 270	OP	CUD	FBG	DV	IO	T250	MRCR	8	6	5500	2	9	27800	30800
29	1	ENTICER 290	OP	OFF	FBG	DV	IO	T235-T300		8	6	6300	2	9	27800	32900
29	1	ENTICER 290	OP	OFF	FBG	DV	IO	T350-T415		8	6	6300	2	9	31400	38000
33	9	VYPER 340	OP	OFF	FBG	DV	IO	T300-T445		8	6	8200	3		52200	64600
33	9	VYPER 340	OP	OFF	FBG	DV	IO	T470-T490		8	6	8200	3		60200	67400
37	9	AVENGER 380	OP	OFF	FBG	DV	IO	T385	MRCR	8	6	9200	3		60400	66400
		IO T415 MRCR 63000 69300, IO T445 MRCR 65900 72500, IO T470 MRCR 68400 75200														
		IO T490 MRCR 70400 77400														
		1994 BOATS														
20	8	VIATE 208 BR	OP	RNBT	FBG	DV	IO	180-250		8		2830	2	8	9150	10800
20	8	VIATE 208 BR	OP	RNBT	FBG	SV	IO	160	MRCR	8		2830	2	8	9100	10300
20	8	VIATE 208 XL	OP	CUD	FBG	DV	IO	180-250		8		2800	2	8	9450	11200
20	8	VIATE 208 XL	OP	CUD	FBG	SV	IO	160	MRCR	8		2800	2	8	9450	10700
22	2	SPECTRA 222 BR	OP	RNBT	FBG	DV	IO	235-300		8		3500	2	8	11400	13900
22	2	SPECTRA 222 BR	OP	RNBT	FBG	DV	IO	350	MRCR	8		3500	2	8	13600	15400
22	2	SPECTRA 222 XL	OP	CUD	FBG	DV	IO	235-300		8		3500	2	8	12100	14700
22	2	SPECTRA 222 XL	OP	CUD	FBG	DV	IO	350-385		8		3500	2	8	14400	17900
23	7	STRYKER 237 BR	OP	B/R	FBG	DV	IO	235-300		8	6	3950	2	9	13500	16300
23	7	STRYKER 237 BR	OP	B/R	FBG	DV	IO	350-385		8	6	3950	2	9	15600	19300
23	7	STRYKER 237 BR	OP	RNBT	FBG	DV	IO	250	MRCR	8	6	3950	2	9	13600	15500
23	7	STRYKER 237 XL	OP	CUD	FBG	DV	IO	235	MRCR	8	6	3950	2	9	14400	16300
25	7	LEGEND 257 BR	OP	RNBT	FBG	DV	IO	235-300		8	6	4175	2	9	15500	18800
25	7	LEGEND 257 BR	OP	RNBT	FBG	DV	IO	350-385		8	6	4179	2	9	18200	21300
25	7	LEGEND 257 XL	OP	CUD	FBG	DV	IO	235-300		8	6	4200	2	9	16900	20400
25	7	LEGEND 257 XL	OP	CUD	FBG	DV	IO	350-385		8	6	4200	2	9	19600	23200
25	7	LEGEND 257 XL	OP	CUD	FBG	DV	IO	415	MRCR	8	6	4200	2	9	22100	24600
27	1	LASER 270	OP	CUD	FBG	DV	IO	300-385		8	6	4800	2	9	21800	27000
27	1	LASER 270	OP	CUD	FBG	DV	IO	415	MRCR	8	6	4800	2	9	25400	28200
27	1	LASER 270	OP	CUD	FBG	DV	IO	T250	MRCR	8	6	4800	2	9	24700	27500
29	1	ENTICER 290	OP	OFF	FBG	DV	IO	T235-T300		8	6	5975	2	9	25600	30300
29	1	ENTICER 290	OP	OFF	FBG	DV	IO	T350-T415		8	6	5975	2	9	28900	35200
		1993 BOATS														
18	4	PQXLT 185	OP	RNBT	FBG	DV	IO	235	MRCR	7	2	2650	2	7	7400	8500
20	8	VIATE 208 BR	OP	RNBT	FBG	SV	IO	160	MRCR	8		2830	2	8	8400	9650
20	8	VIATE 208 XL	OP	CUD	FBG	SV	IO	160	MRCR	8		2800	2	8	8850	10000
22	2	SPECTRA 222 BR	OP	RNBT	FBG	DV	IO	235	MRCR	8		3500	2	8	10700	12100
22	2	SPECTRA 222 XL	OP	CUD	FBG	DV	IO	235	MRCR	8		3500	2	8	11300	12800
23	1	CONQUEST 230	OP	CUD	FBG	DV	IO	235	MRCR	8		3975	2	8	12900	14700
25	7	LEGEND 257 XL	OP	CUD	FBG	DV	IO	235	MRCR	8	6	4200	2	9	15700	17900
27		LASER 270	OP	CUD	FBG	DV	IO	300	MRCR	8	6	4800	2	9	20300	22500
29	1	ENTICER 290	OP	OFF	FBG	DV	IO	T235	MRCR	8	6	5975	2	9	23900	26500
		1992 BOATS														
18	4	PQ XLT-185	OP	RNBT	FBG	DV	IO	175	MRCR	7	2	2650	2	7	6650	7650
20	8	VIATE 208 BR	OP	RNBT	FBG	SV	IO	155	MRCR	8		2830	2	7	7850	9050
20	8	VIATE 208 XL	OP	CUD	FBG	SV	IO	155	MRCR	8		2800	2	7	8150	9400
22	2	SPECTRA 222 BR	OP	RNBT	FBG	DV	IO	260	MRCR	8		3500	2	8	10200	11600
22	2	SPECTRA 222 XL	OP	CUD	FBG	DV	IO	260	MRCR	8		3500	2	8	10800	12200
23	1	CONQUEST 230	OP	CUD	FBG	DV	IO	260	MRCR	8		3975	2	8	12300	14000
27		LASER 270	OP	CUD	FBG	DV	IO	330	MRCR	8	6	4800	2	9	19600	21800
29	1	ENTICER 290	OP	OFF	FBG	DV	IO	T260	MRCR	8	6	5975	2	9	22900	25400
		1991 BOATS														
18	4	PQ INTEGRA	OP	RNBT	FBG	DV	IO	175	MRCR	7	2	2650	2	7	6350	7250
18	4	PQ XLT-185	OP	RNBT	FBG	DV	IO	175	MRCR	7	2	2650	2	7	6150	7100
22	2	SPECTRA 222 BR	OP	RNBT	FBG	DV	IO	260	MRCR	8		3500	2	8	9550	10900
22	2	SPECTRA 222 XL	OP	CUD	FBG	DV	IO	260	MRCR	8		3500	2	8	10100	11500
23	1	CONQUEST 230	OP	CUD	FBG	DV	IO	260	MRCR	8		3975	2	8	11600	13100
27		LASER 260	OP	CUD	FBG	DV	IO	330	MRCR	8	6	4800	2	9	18600	20600
29	1	ENTICER 290	OP	OFF	FBG	DV	IO	T260	MRCR	8	6	5975	2	9	21500	23900
		1990 BOATS														
18	4	INTEGRA	OP	B/R	FBG	DV	IO	175-260		7	2	2450			5400	6650
18	4	INTEGRA	OP	B/R	FBG	DV	IO	270	MRCR	7	2	2450			5900	6800
18	4	LUXURY SPORT	OP	RNBT	FBG	DV	IO	175-260		7	2	2650			5850	7200
18	4	LUXURY SPORT	OP	RNBT	FBG	DV	IO	270	MRCR	7	2	2650			6400	7350
18	4	XLT 185	OP	RNBT	FBG	DV	IO	175-260		7	2	2650			5850	7200
18	4	XLT 185	OP	RNBT	FBG	DV	IO	270	MRCR	7	2	2650			6400	7350
22	2	SPECTRA BR222	OP	B/R	FBG	DV	IO	260-270		8		3500			8950	10300
22	2	SPECTRA BR222	OP	B/R	FBG	DV	IO	330	MRCR	8		3500			9950	11300
22	2	SPECTRA XL222	OP	CUD	FBG	DV	IO	260-270		8		3500			9500	10900
22	2	SPECTRA XL222	OP	CUD	FBG	DV	IO	330-365		8		3500			10600	13100
23	1	CONQUEST 230	OP	CUD	FBG	DV	IO	260-270		8		3975			10900	12500
23	1	CONQUEST 230	OP	CUD	FBG	DV	IO	330-365		8		3975			12000	14600
29	1	ENTICER FX290	OP	OFF	FBG	DV	IO	T260-T330		8	6	5975			21100	25200
29	1	ENTICER FX290	OP	OFF	FBG	DV	IO	T365-T420		8	6	5975			23700	28400
		1989 BOATS														
18	4	INTEGRA	OP	B/R	FBG	DV	IO	175-260		7	2	2450			5100	6300
18	4	INTEGRA	OP	B/R	FBG	DV	IO	270	MRCR	7	2	2450			5550	6400
18	4	LUXURY SPORT	OP	RNBT	FBG	DV	IO	175-270		7	2	2650			5550	6900
18	4	XLT 185	OP	RNBT	FBG	DV	IO	175-270		7	2	2650			5550	6900
22	2	SPECTRA XL222	OP	RNBT	FBG	DV	IO	260-270		8		3500			8450	9800

 CONTINUED ON NEXT PAGE

LOA FT IN	NAME AND/ OR MODEL	TOP/ RIG	BOAT TYPE	-HULL- MTL TP	ENGINE TP # HP	MFG	BEAM FT IN	WGT LBS	DRAFT FT IN	RETAIL LOW	RETAIL HIGH
					1989 BOATS						
22 2	SPECTRA XL222	OP	RNBT	FBG DV	IO 320	MRCR	8	3500		9300	10600
23 1	ALTURA 230	OP	OFF	FBG DV	IO 260-330		8	4325		10900	13600
23 1	CONQUEST	OP	OFF	FBG DV	IO 260-320		8	3975		10300	12600
23 1	CONQUEST	OP	OFF	FBG DV	IO 330-365		8	3975		11300	13800

PRECISION BOAT WORKS
PALMETTO FL 34221   COAST GUARD MFG ID- PCW See inside cover to adjust price for area

For more recent years, see the BUC Used Boat Price Guide, Volume 1

LOA FT IN	NAME AND/ OR MODEL	TOP/ RIG	BOAT TYPE	-HULL- MTL TP	ENGINE TP # HP	MFG	BEAM FT IN	WGT LBS	DRAFT FT IN	RETAIL LOW	RETAIL HIGH
					1996 BOATS						
16 5	PRECISION 165	SLP	SACAC	FBG KL	OB		7 2	700	1 9	4750	5450
17 5	PRECISION 18	SLP	SARAC	FBG KC	OB		7 5	1100	1 3	6000	6850
20 9	PRECISION 21	SLP	SARAC	FBG KC	OB		8 3	1875	4 8	8200	9400
23 5	PRECISION 23	SLP	SARAC	FBG KC	OB		8 6	2450	5 4	10600	12000
28	PRECISION 28	SLP	SARAC	FBG KL	IB	12D WEST 10		5500	3 8	27600	30600
					1995 BOATS						
16 5	PRECISION 165	SLP	SACAC	FBG KL	OB		7 2	700	1 9	4500	5150
17 5	PRECISION 18	SLP	SARAC	FBG KC	OB		7 5	1100	1 3	5600	6450
20 9	PRECISION 21	SLP	SARAC	FBG KC	OB		8 3	1875	4 8	7700	8850
23 5	PRECISION 23	SLP	SARAC	FBG KC	OB		8 6	2450	5 4	9950	11300
28	PRECISION 28	SLP	SARAC	FBG KL	IB	12D WEST 10		5500	3 8	25900	28800
					1987 BOATS						
16 3	PRECISION 16	SLP	SA/OD	FBG CB			6 8	390	8	2000	2400
16 9	DAYSAILER I	SLP	SA/OD	FBG CB			6 3	575	7	2450	2850
17 5	PRECISION 18	SLP	SA/RC	FBG KC			7 5	1100	1 6	3450	4000
23 5	PRECISION 23	SLP	SA/RC	FBG KC			8 6	2450	1 11	6050	6950
					1986 BOATS						
16 3	PRECISION 16	SLP	SA/OD	FBG CB			6 8	390	8	1900	2250
16 9	DAYSAILER I	SLP	SA/OD	FBG CB			6 3	575	7	2300	2700
17 5	PRECISION 18	SLP	SA/RC	FBG KC			7 5	1100	1 6	3200	3750
23 5	PRECISION 23	SLP	SA/RC	FBG KC			8 6	2450	1 11	5700	6550
					1985 BOATS						
16 3	PRECISION 16	SLP	SA/OD	FBG CB			6 8	390	8	1750	2100
17 5	PRECISION 18	SLP	SA/RC	FBG KC			7 5	1100	1 6	3050	3500
					1984 BOATS						
16 3	PRECISION 16	SLP	SA/OD	FBG CB			6 8	388	8	1650	1950
24	SEAFORTH	SLP	SA/CR	FBG KL	IB	D	7 4	4000	2 6	8450	9750

....For earlier years, see the BUC Used Boat Price Guide, Volume 3

PREMIUM CUSTOM BOATS
PREMIUM PARASAIL BOATS INC   See inside cover to adjust price for area
FT MYERS FL 33907

For more recent years, see the BUC Used Boat Price Guide, Volume 1

LOA FT IN	NAME AND/ OR MODEL	TOP/ RIG	BOAT TYPE	-HULL- MTL TP	ENGINE TP # HP	MFG	BEAM FT IN	WGT LBS	DRAFT FT IN	RETAIL LOW	RETAIL HIGH
					1996 BOATS						
22	THRESHER 22	ST	CTRCN	FBG SV	OB		8	2800	6	6450	7400
28	PREMIUM PARASAIL	OP	COMM	FBG SV	IO 236D	VLVO 10	3	5100	2 8	**	**
28	THRESHER CABIN	HT	CUD	FBG SV	IO 236D	VLVO 10	3	5900	2 8	29400	32600
28	THRESHER CUDDY	OP	CUD	FBG SV	IO 236D	VLVO 10	3	5400	2 8	22300	24700
28	THRESHER DIVE EXP	OP	UTL	FBG SV	JT 390D	VLVO 10		6800	2 8	35600	39500
28	THRESHER OPEN	OP	CTRCN	FBG SV	IO 236D	VLVO 10	3	5100	2 8	24900	27600
28	THRESHER SPORT FISH	FB	SF	FBG SV	IO 236D	VLVO 10	3	6400	2 8	31000	34400
37	THRESHER 37 CREW	OP	COMM	FBG SV	IO T236D	VLVO 12		14400	2 8	**	**
					1995 BOATS						
22	THRESHER 22	ST	CTRCN	FBG SV	OB		8	2800	6	6050	6950
28	PREMIUM PARASAIL	OP	COMM	FBG SV	IO 236D	VLVO 10	3	5100	2 8	**	**
28	THRESHER CABIN	HT	CUD	FBG SV	IO 236D	VLVO 10	3	5900	2 8	27400	30500
28	THRESHER CUDDY	OP	CUD	FBG SV	IO 236D	VLVO 10	3	5400	2 8	20800	23100
28	THRESHER OPEN	OP	CTRCN	FBG SV	IO 236D	VLVO 10	3	5100	2 8	19900	22000
28	THRESHER SPORT FISH	FB	SF	FBG SV	IO 236D	VLVO 10	3	6400	2 8	28900	32100
					1994 BOATS						
22	THRESHER 22	ST	CTRCN	FBG SV	OB		8	2800	6	5700	6600
28	PREMIUM PARASAIL	HT	COMM	FBG SV	IO 236D	VLVO 10	3	5100	2 8	**	**
28	THRESHER CABIN	HT	CUD	FBG SV	IO 236D	VLVO 10	3	5900	2 8	20500	22800
28	THRESHER CUDDY	OP	CUD	FBG SV	IO 236D	VLVO 10	3	5400	2 8	19400	21600
28	THRESHER OPEN	OP	CTRCN	FBG SV	IO 236D	VLVO 10	3	5100	2 8	16200	18400
28	THRESHER SPORT FISH	FB	SF	FBG SV	IO 236D	VLVO 10	3	6400	2 8	27000	30000
					1993 BOATS						
22	THRESHER 22	ST	CTRCN	FBG SV	OB		8	2800	6	5450	6300
28	PREMIUM PARASAIL	OP	COMM	FBG SV	IO 236D	VLVO 10	3	5100	2 8	**	**
28	THRESHER CABIN	HT	CUD	FBG SV	IO 236D	VLVO 10	3	5900	2 8	19200	21300
28	THRESHER CUDDY	OP	CUD	FBG SV	IO 236D	VLVO 10	3	5400	2 8	18400	20400
28	THRESHER OPEN	OP	CTRCN	FBG SV	IO 236D	VLVO 10	3	5100	2 8	15100	17200
28	THRESHER SPORT FISH	FB	SF	FBG SV	IO 236D	VLVO 10	3	6400	2 8	25200	28000
37	THRESHER 37	OP	COMM	FBG SV	IO T236D	VLVO 12		14400	2 8	**	**
					1992 BOATS						
22	THRESHER 22	OP	COMM	FBG SV	IO D	YAN	8	3400	1 6	**	**
27 6	PREMIUM PARASAIL	OP	COMM	FBG SV	IO 200D	VLVO 10	3	6000	2 5	**	**
27 6	THRESHER CABIN	FB	CUD	FBG SV	IO 200D	VLVO 10	3	7000	2 5	18000	20000
27 6	THRESHER CUDDY	OP	CUD	FBG SV	IO 200D	VLVO 10	3	6500	2 5	16600	18400
27 6	THRESHER OPEN	OP	CTRCN	FBG SV	IO 200D	VLVO 10	3	6000	2 5	19700	21900
30	DIVE EXPRESS 3020	OP	CUD	FBG SV	IO 200D	VLVO 10	3	6500	2 5	18500	20500
30	FISH EXPRESS 3020	OP	CUD	FBG SV	IO 200D	VLVO 10	3	6000	2 5	17300	19700
37	THRESHER 37	OP	CUD	FBG SV	IO 472	VLVO 12		10000	2 6	34000	37800
					1991 BOATS						
27 6	PREMIUM PARASAIL	OP	COMM	FBG SV	IO 200D	VLVO 10	3	6000	2 5	**	**
27 6	THRESHER CABIN	FB	CUD	FBG SV	IO 200D	VLVO 10	3	7000	2 5	16500	18800
27 6	THRESHER CUDDY	OP	CUD	FBG SV	IO 200D	VLVO 10	3	6500	2 5	15600	17700
27 6	THRESHER OPEN	OP	CTRCN	FBG SV	IO 200D	VLVO 10	3	6000	2 5	18700	20800
30	DIVE EXPRESS 3020	OP	CUD	FBG SV	IO 200D	VLVO 10	3	6500	2 5	16900	19200
30	FISH EXPRESS 3020	OP	CUD	FBG SV	IO 200D	VLVO 10	3	6000	2 5	16200	18400

PRESENT YACHTS INC
ROCHESTER NY 14607-1619   See inside cover to adjust price for area

LOA FT IN	NAME AND/ OR MODEL	TOP/ RIG	BOAT TYPE	-HULL- MTL TP	ENGINE TP # HP	MFG	BEAM FT IN	WGT LBS	DRAFT FT IN	RETAIL LOW	RETAIL HIGH
					1987 BOATS						
38 2	SUNDECK 38 SERIES N	FB	DCMY	FBG SV	IB T200D	PERK 13	3	21000	3 4	100500	110500
38 2	SUNDECK 38 SERIES N	FB	DCMY	FBG SV	IB T225D	LEHM 13	3	21000	3 4	100000	110000
39 10	SUNDECK 40	FB	DCMY	FBG SV	IB T200D	VLVO 13	4	20000	3 7	103000	113500
39 10	SUNDECK 40	FB	DCMY	FBG DS	IB T135D	LEHM 13	8	20000	3 7	99800	109500
41 10	SUNDECK 42	FB	DCMY	FBG DS	IB T135D	LEHM 13	8	20000		99800	109500
	IB T200D VLVO 107000 118000, IB T225D LEHM 112000 123000, IB T306D VLVO 120500 132000										
46 3	SUNDECK 46	FB	DCMY	FBG DS	IB T225D	LEHM 14	6	26000	3 10	125500	138000
46 3	SUNDECK 46	FB	DCMY	FBG DS	IB T306D	VLVO 14	6	26000	3 10	136000	149500
					1986 BOATS						
34 4	SUNDECK 35	FB	DCMY	FBG DS	IB 120D		12			3 3	73600	80900
34 4	SUNDECK 35	FB	DCMY	FBG DS	IB 135D	PERK 12		18000	3 3	73300	80500
34 4	SUNDECK 35	FB	DCMY	FBG DS	IB 120D	VLVO 12		18000	3 3	74000	81300
37 11	SUNDECK 38	FB	DCMY	FBG DS	IB T135D	PERK 12	8	22000		97900	107500
38 2	SUNDECK 38 SERIES T	FB	DCMY	FBG SV	IB T200D	PERK 13	4	21000	3 4	96400	106000
38 2	SUNDECK 38 SERIES N	FB	DCMY	FBG SV	IB T200D	PERK 13	4	21000	3 4	95700	105500
39 10	SUNDECK 40	FB	DCMY	FBG SV	IB T200D	PERK 13	4	20000	3 7	99600	109500
41 10	SUNDECK 42	FB	DCMY	FBG DS	IB 120D		13	8		3 3	95900	105500
	IB T135D PERK 96900 106500, IB T200D PERK 105500 116000, IB T225D LEHM 107000 118000										
	IB T255D VLVO 122000 134000										
46 3	SUNDECK 46	FB	DCMY	FBG DS	IB T135D		14	6		3 10	114000	125000
	IB T200D PERK 119000 131000, IB T225D LEHM 120000 131500, IB T255D VLVO 122000 134000										
	IB T350D PERK 139500 153500										
54 10	MOTOR YACHT 55	FB	TCMY	FBG DS	IB T355D	CAT	17	52000	4	219500	241000
					1985 BOATS						
31	SEDAN	FB	TRWL	FBG DS	IB 120D		11 6			48800	53600
34 5	SUNDECK	FB	TRWL	FBG DS	IB T135D		12			67500	74200
37 10	SEDAN	FB	TRWL	FBG DS	IB 120D		12 10	18739	3 5	76600	84100
41 2	DOUBLE CABIN	FB	TRWL	FBG DS	IB 120D		13 8			101500	111500
41 2	TRI-CABIN		TRWL	FBG DS	IB 120D		13 8			105500	116000
41 10	SUNDECK	FB	TRWL	FBG DS	IB 120D		13 8	30864	4 2	126500	139000
44 10	PILOTHOUSE	FB	TRWL	FBG DS	IB T120D		15 10	30864	4 2	118000	130000
44 10	SEDAN	FB	TRWL	FBG DS	IB T120D		15 10	30864	4 2	114500	126000
					1984 BOATS						
31	SEDAN	FB	TRWL	FBG DS	IB 120D		11 6	14771	3 4	53000	58200
37 10	DOUBLE CABIN	FB	TRWL	FBG DS	IB 120D		12 10	18739	3 5	73400	80600
37 10	SEDAN	FB	TRWL	FBG DS	IB 120D		12 10	18739	3 5	73400	80600
40 6	SUNDECK	FB	TRWL	FBG DS	IB T120D		13 8			104500	115000
41 2	DOUBLE CABIN	FB	TRWL	FBG DS	IB 120D		13 8	25365	3 6	106500	117000
41 2	SEDAN	FB	TRWL	FBG DS	IB 120D		13 8	25365	3 6	90700	99400
41 10	SUNDECK	FB	TRWL	FBG DS	IB T120D		13 8			121500	133500
44 10	DOUBLE CABIN	FB	TRWL	FBG DS	IB T120D		15 10	30864	4 2	109500	120000
44 10	PH	FB	TRWL	MFBG DS	IB T120D		15 10	30864	4 2	107500	118000
44 10	SEDAN	FB	TRWL	FBG DS	IB T120D		15 10	30864	4 2	109500	120000

....For earlier years, see the BUC Used Boat Price Guide, Volume 3

PRESIDENT MARINE INT

N MIAMI BEACH FL 33180 COAST GUARD MFG ID- PRM See inside cover to adjust price for area

For more recent years, see the BUC Used Boat Price Guide, Volume 1

LOA FT	LOA IN	NAME AND/ OR MODEL	TOP/ RIG	BOAT TYPE	-HULL- MTL	-HULL- TP	ENGINE TP	ENGINE # HP	ENGINE MFG	BEAM FT	BEAM IN	WGT LBS	DRAFT FT	DRAFT IN	RETAIL LOW	RETAIL HIGH
		1996 BOATS														
48	9	PRESIDENT 485 MY	FB	MY	FBG	DS	IB	T375D	CAT	15	9	34400	3	2	234500	258000
54	9	PRESIDENT 545 CMY	FB	MY	FBG	DS	IB	T550D	DD	15	9	42000	3	4	291500	320500
54	9	PRESIDENT 545 MY	FB	MY	FBG	DS	IB	T550D	DD	15	9	42400	3	4	294000	323000
58	1	PRESIDENT 580 CMY	FB	MY	FBG	DS	IB	T550D	DD	15	8	44000	3	2	302500	332500
62	2	PRESIDENT 620 MY	FB	MY	FBG	DS	IB	T800D	CAT	16	7	60000	3	2	450000	494500
66	7	PRESIDENT 665 CMY	FB	MY	FBG	DS	IB	T735D	GM	17	10	73000	4	3	529500	582000
72	9	PRESIDENT 720 MY	FB	MY	FBG	DS	IB	T800D	CAT	20	2	76000	4		**	**
		1995 BOATS														
39	5	PRESIDENT 395 SD	FB	DC	FBG	DS	IB	T300D	CUM	13		24600	3	2	171500	188500
44	3	PRESIDENT 445 SD	FB	MY	FBG	DS	IB	T350D	CAT	14	5	31600	2	3	205000	225500
44	5	PRESIDENT 445 CONV	FB	MY	FBG	DS	IB	T375D	CAT	14	5	31600	2	3	207000	227500
48	9	PRESIDENT 485 CONV	FB	MY	FBG	DS	IB	T375D	CAT	15	9	34000	3	2	218500	240000
48	9	PRESIDENT 485 MY	FB	MY	FBG	DS	IB	T375D	CAT	15	9	34400	3	2	224500	246500
49	5	PRESIDENT 495 CMY	FB	MY	FBG	DS	IB	T375D	CAT	14	5	33800	2	3	224500	247000
51		PRESIDENT 510 MY	FB	MY	FBG	DS	IB	T550D	DD	15	8	42400	3	2	270500	297000
54	9	PRESIDENT 545 CMY	FB	MY	FBG	DS	IB	T550D	DD	15	9	42000	3	4	279500	307500
54	9	PRESIDENT 545 MY	FB	MY	FBG	DS	IB	T550D	DD	15	9	42400	3	4	281500	309500
58	1	PRESIDENT 580 CMY	FB	MY	FBG	DS	IB	T550D	DD	15	8	44000	3	2	290000	318500
58	1	PRESIDENT 580 MY	FB	MY	FBG	DS	IB	T550D	DD	15	8	44000	3	2	323500	355500
60	7	PRESIDENT 605 MY	FB	MY	FBG	DS	IB	T735D	GM	17	10	61000	3	4	386000	424500
66	7	PRESIDENT 665 CMY	FB	MY	FBG	DS	IB	T735D	GM	17	10	73000	4	3	505000	555000
		1994 BOATS														
39	5	PRESIDENT 395 SD	FB	DC	FBG	SV	IB	T300D	CUM	13		24600	3	2	164500	180500
42	10	PRESIDENT 425 SD	FB	MY	FBG	DV	IB	T350D	CAT	14	5	30000	2	3	207500	228000
44	3	PRESIDENT 445 SD	FB	MY	FBG	DV	IB	T350D	CAT	14	5	31600	2	3	195500	214500
44	5	PRESIDENT 445 CONV	FB	MY	FBG	DV	IB	T375D	CAT	14	5	31600	2	3	197000	216000
48	9	PRESIDENT 485 CONV	FB	MY	FBG	DV	IB	T375D	CAT	15	9	34000	3	2	207500	228000
48	9	PRESIDENT 485 MY	FB	MY	FBG	DV	IB	T375D	CAT	15	9	34400	3	2	213000	234000
49	5	PRESIDENT 495 CMY	FB	MY	FBG	DV	IB	T375D	CAT	14	5	33800	2	3	213500	234500
51		PRESIDENT 510 MY	FB	MY	FBG	DV	IB	T550D	DD	15	8	42400	3	2	258000	283500
54	9	PRESIDENT 545 CMY	FB	MY	FBG	DV	IB	T550D	DD	15	9	42000	3	4	270000	296500
54	9	PRESIDENT 545 MY	FB	MY	FBG	DV	IB	T550D	DD	15	9	42400	3	4	272000	298500
58	1	PRESIDENT 580 CMY	FB	MY	FBG	DV	IB	T550D	DD	15	8	44000	3	2	280000	308000
58	1	PRESIDENT 580 MY	FB	MY	FBG	SV	IB	T550D	DD	15	8	44000	3	2	309000	340000
60	7	PRESIDENT 605 MY	FB	MY	FBG	DV	IB	T735D	GM	17	10		3	4	365500	402000
66	7	PRESIDENT 665 CMY	FB	MY	FBG	DV	IB	T735D	GM	17	10	73000	4	3	482000	530000
70	7	PRESIDENT 705 MY	FB	MY	FBG	DV	IB	T800D	CAT	17	10		3	4	610500	671000
75		PRESIDENT 750 MY	FB	MY	FBG	DV	IB	T12CD	CAT						**	**
		1993 BOATS														
36	6	PRESIDENT 39 CNV	FB	CNV	FBG	SV	IB	T250D	CUM	12	10	21600	3	2	122500	134500
39	5	PRESIDENT 395 DC	FB	DC	FBG	SV	IB	T250D	CUM	13		24600	3	2	153000	168000
42	10	PRESIDENT 425 SD	FB	MY	FBG	DV	ID	T300D	CUM	14	5	30000	2	3	186500	205000
44	3	PRESIDENT 445 SD	FB	MY	FBG	DV	IB	T300D	CUM	14	5	31600	2	3	175500	192500
44	5	PRESIDENT 445 CONV	FB	MY	FBG	DV	IB	T300D	CUM	14	5	31600	2	3	172500	189500
44	5	PRESIDENT 445 MY	FB	MY	FBG	SV	IB	T300D	CAT	14	7	34500	3	6	180500	198500
46		PRESIDENT 46 MY	FB	MY	FBG	SV	IB	T300D	CUM	15	9	37400	4	2	189500	208000
48	6	PRESIDENT 49 COCKPIT	FB	MYCPT	FBG	SV	IB	T300D	CUM	15	9	41500	4	2	195000	214000
48	9	PRESIDENT 485 CONV	FB	MY	FBG	DV	IB	T375D	CAT	15	9	34000	3	2	198000	217500
48	9	PRESIDENT 485 SD	FB	MY	FBG	DV	IB	T375D	CAT	15	9	34400	3	2	197000	216500
48	9	PRESIDENT 488 SD	FB	MY	FBG	DV	IB	T375D	CAT	15	9	35400	3	3	199500	219000
49	5	PRESIDENT 495 CKPT	FB	MY	FBG	DV	IB	T375D	CAT	14	5	33800	2	3	197000	216500
51		PRESIDENT 510 MY	FB	MY	FBG	DV	IB	T435D	CAT	15	8	42400	3	2	224000	246500
52		PRESIDENT 52 COCKPIT	FB	MYCPT	FBG	SV	IB	T375D	CAT	15	9	44680	4	4	213500	234500
52		PRESIDENT 52 MY	FB	MY	FBG	SV	IB	T375D	CAT	15	9	46280	4	4	218000	239500
54	9	PRESIDENT 545 CMY	FB	MY	FBG	DV	IB	T375D	CAT	15	9	42000	3	4	209500	230500
54	9	PRESIDENT 545 MY	FB	MY	FBG	DV	IB	T375D	CAT	15	9	42400	3	4	211000	232000
57		PRESIDENT 57 MY	FB	MY	FBG	SV	IB	T735D	GM	17	10	66500	4	3	398000	437000
58	1	PRESIDENT 580 CMY	FB	MY	FBG	DV	IB	T435D	CAT	15	8	44000	3	2	244500	268500
60	7	PRESIDENT 605 MY	FB	MY	FBG	DV	IB	T735D	DD	17	10		3	4	354500	389500
65	7	PRESIDENT 655 MY	FB	MY	FBG	DV	IB	T735D	GM	17	10	72000	4	3	446000	490000
66	7	PRESIDENT 665 CP	FB	MY	FBG	DV	IB	T735D	GM	17	10	73000	4	3	460500	506000
70	7	PRESIDENT 705 MY	FB	MY	FBG	DV	IB	T735D	DD	17	10		3	4	571500	628500
		1992 BOATS														
36	6	PRESIDENT 37 CNV	FB	CNV	FBG	SV	IB	T250D	CUM	12	10	20400	3	1	112500	123500
39	5	PRESIDENT 395 DC	FB	DC	FBG	SV	IB	T250D	CUM	13		24600	3	2	145500	160000
41		PRESIDENT 41 COCKPIT	FB	MYCPT	FBG	SV	IB	T250D	CUM	13		24950	2	8	154000	169000
44	5	PRESIDENT 445 MY	FB	MY	FBG	SV	IB	T300D	CAT	14	7	34500	3	6	172000	189000
46		PRESIDENT 46 MY	FB	MY	FBG	SV	IB	T300D	CUM	15	9	37400	4	2	180500	198000
48	6	PRESIDENT 49 COCKPIT	FB	MYCPT	FBG	SV	IB	T300D	CUM	15	9	41500	4	2	185500	204000
52		PRESIDENT 52 COCKPIT	FB	MYCPT	FBG	SV	IB	T375D	CAT	15	9	44680	4	4	204000	224000
52		PRESIDENT 52 MY	FB	MY	FBG	SV	IB	T375D	CAT	15	9	46280	4	4	208500	229000
57		PRESIDENT 57 MY	FB	MY	FBG	SV	IB	T735D	GM	17	10	66500	4	3	379000	416500
65	7	PRESIDENT 655 MY	FB	MY	FBG	DV	IB	T735D	GM	17	10	72000	4	3	426500	468500
66	7	PRESIDENT 665 CP	FB	MY	FBG	DV	IB	T735D	GM	17	10	73000	4	3	440500	484000

PRESIDENT YACHTS

FT LAUDERDALE FL 33316 COAST GUARD MFG ID- MYI See inside cover to adjust price for area

LOA FT	LOA IN	NAME AND/ OR MODEL	TOP/ RIG	BOAT TYPE	-HULL- MTL	-HULL- TP	ENGINE TP	ENGINE # HP	ENGINE MFG	BEAM FT	BEAM IN	WGT LBS	DRAFT FT	DRAFT IN	RETAIL LOW	RETAIL HIGH
		1987 BOATS														
34	5	PRESIDENT 35 SF	FB	SF	FBG	SV	IB	T350	CRUS	12	10	18700	3		56900	62500
34	5	PRESIDENT 35 SF	FB	SF	FBG	SV	IB	T135D-T275D		12	10	18700	3		67300	79500
34	7	PRESIDENT 35 DC	FB	MY	FBG	SV	IB	T270-T350		12	10	18700	3		58000	66100
34	7	PRESIDENT 35 DC	FB	MY	FBG	SV	IB	T135D-T306D		12	10	18700	3		69900	85900
34	7	PRESIDENT 35 DC	FB	MY	FBG	SV	IB	T320D-T435D		12	10	18700	3		80000	95500
34	7	PRESIDENT 35 SF	FB	SF	FBG	SV	IB	T270	CRUS	12	10	18700	3		55900	61400
34	7	PRESIDENT 35 SF	FB	SF	FBG	SV	IB	T200D-T400D		12	10	18700	3		69700	86600
34	7	PRESIDENT 35 SF	FB	SF	FBG	SV	IB	T435D	GM	12	10	18700	3		81000	89000
36	6	PRESIDENT 37 DC	FB	MY	FBG	SV	IB	T270	CRUS	12	10	20400	3		72300	79400
		IB T350 CRUS 74200 81600, IB T135D LEHM 78900 86700, IB T200D PERK													82600	90700
		IB T200D VLVO 80300 88200, IB T225D LEHM 82500 90600, IB T240D PERK													84600	92900
		IB T250D GM 83700 92000, IB T275D LEHM 85000 93400, IB T300D J&T													86800	95400
		IB T306D VLVO 85200 93700, IB T320D CAT 89400 98200, IB T358D VLVO													88300	97000
		IB T375D CAT 93400 102500, IB T400D GM 93100 102500, IB T435D GM													95800	105500
36	6	PRESIDENT 37 SDN	FB	CR	FBG	SV	IB	T270	CRUS	12	10	20400	3		71200	78300
		IB T350 CRUS 73000 80200, IB T135D LEHM 78100 85900, IB T200D PERK													80900	88900
		IB T200D VLVO 78600 86300, IB T225D LEHM 80600 88600, IB T240D PERK													82600	90800
		IB T250D GM 81700 89800, IB T275D LEHM 82900 91100, IB T300D J&T													84600	93000
		IB T320D CAT 87100 95700, IB T358D VLVO 85800 94300, IB T360D VLVO													85900	94400
		IB T375D CAT 90800 99800, IB T400D GM 90400 99400, IB T435D GM													93000	102000
36	6	PRESIDENT 37 SF	FB	SF	FBG	SV	IB	T270	CRUS	12	10	20400	3		71200	78300
		IB T350 CRUS 73000 80200, IB T135D LEHM 78100 85900, IB T200D PERK													80900	88900
		IB T200D VLVO 78600 86300, IB T225D LEHM 80600 88600, IB T240D PERK													82600	90800
		IB T250D GM 81700 89800, IB T275D LEHM 82900 91100, IB T300D J&T													84600	93000
		IB T306D VLVO 83000 91200, IB T320D CAT 87000 95700, IB T358D VLVO													85800	94300
		IB T375D CAT 90800 99800, IB T400D GM 90400 99400, IB T435D GM													93000	102000
40	6	PRESIDENT 41 DC	FB	MY	FBG	SV	IB	T270	CRUS	13	10	22500	2	10	90900	99900
		IB T350 CRUS 93800 103000, IB T135D LEHM 95400 105000, IB T200D PERK													101000	111000
		IB T200D VLVO 97500 107000, IB T225D LEHM 100500 110500, IB T240D PERK													103500	114000
		IB T250D GM 102500 112500, IB T275D LEHM 104000 114500, IB T300D J&T													106500	117000
		IB T306D VLVO 104000 114500, IB T320D CAT 110000 121000, IB T358D VLVO													108000	118500
		IB T375D CAT 115000 126500, IB T400D GM 114000 125500, IB T435D GM													117500	129000
42	6	PRESIDENT 43 DC	FB	MY	FBG	SV	IB	T270	CRUS	13	10	28000	3	2	108000	118500
		IB T350 CRUS 114000 125000, IB T135D LEHM 115500 127000, IB T200D PERK													117000	129000
		IB T200D VLVO 114500 126000, IB T225D LEHM 118000 129500, IB T240D PERK													121000	133000
		IB T250D GM 120500 132500, IB T275D LEHM 123000 135000, IB T300D J&T													126000	138500
		IB T306D VLVO 124500 136500, IB T320D CAT 129500 142000, IB T358D VLVO													129500	142000
		IB T375D CAT 135500 149000, IB T400D GM 136000 149500, IB T435D GM													140000	154000
42	6	PRESIDENT 43 SDN	FB	SF	FBG	SV	IB	T270	CRUS	13	10	28000	3	2	106000	116500
		IB T350 CRUS 114500 125500, IB T135D LEHM 106500 117000, IB T200D PERK													114500	125500
		IB T200D VLVO 111500 122500, IB T225D LEHM 116000 127500, IB T240D PERK													119500	131000
		IB T250D GM 119000 131000, IB T275D LEHM 122500 134500, IB T300D J&T													126000	138500
		IB T306D VLVO 124500 137000, IB T320D CAT 130000 143000, IB T358D VLVO													131000	144000
		IB T375D CAT 140000 154000, IB T400D GM 139000 152500, IB T435D GM													143500	158000
54	5	PRESIDENT 54 MY	FB	MY	FBG	DV	IB	T462D	GM	16	2	47500	3	6	201500	221500
		1986 BOATS														
34		PRESIDENT 34 DC	FB	MY	FBG	SV	IB	T270	CRUS	12	10	18700	3		53100	58400
34		PRESIDENT 34 DC	FB	MY	FBG	SV	IB	T135D-T225D		12	10	18700	3		65900	76300
34		PRESIDENT 34 SF	FB	SF	FBG	SV	IB	T270	CRUS	12	10	18700	3		50900	56000
34		PRESIDENT 34 SF	FB	SF	FBG	SV	IB	T135D-T225D		12	10	18700	3		63700	71900
37		PRESIDENT 37 DC	FB	MY	FBG	SV	IB	T350	CRUS	12	10	20400	3		73500	80700
		IB T135D PERK 78900 86700, IB T200D PERK 81400 89500, IB T225D LEHM													81100	89100
37		PRESIDENT 37 SF	FB	SF	FBG	SV	IB	T350	CRUS	12	10	20400	3		72600	79800
		IB T135D PERK 78300 86100, IB T200D PERK 80300 88200, IB T225D LEHM													79900	87800
40	6	PRESIDENT 40 DC	FB	MY	FBG	SV	IB	T350	CRUS	13	5	22500	2	10	90100	99000
40	6	PRESIDENT 41 DC	FB	MY	FBG	SV	IB	T120D	LEHM	13	5	22500	2	10	92600	102000
		IB T135D LEHM 93500 102500, IB T160D LEHM 94900 104000, IB T225D LEHM													98500	108500

CONTINUED ON NEXT PAGE

LOA FT	LOA IN	NAME AND/ OR MODEL	TOP/ RIG	BOAT TYPE	-HULL- MTL	-HULL- TP	ENGINE TP	ENGINE # HP	ENGINE MFG	BEAM FT	BEAM IN	WGT LBS	DRAFT FT	DRAFT IN	RETAIL LOW	RETAIL HIGH
		1986 BOATS														
43		PRESIDENT 43 DC	FB	MY	FBG	SV	IB	T350	CRUS	13	11	28000	3		109500	120000
		IB T135D LEHM 111000 122000, IB T160D LEHM 107500 118000, IB T225D LEHM 113000 124000														
43		PRESIDENT 43 SDN	FB	SF	FBG	SV	IB	T350	CRUS	13	11	28000	3		110000	121000
43		PRESIDENT 43 SDN	FB	SF	FBG	SV	IB	T225D	LEHM	13	11	28000	3		111000	122000
54	5	PRESIDENT 54 MY	FB	MY	FBG	DV	IB	T462D	GM	16	2	47500	3	6	192500	212000
		1985 BOATS														
40	6	PRESIDENT 41 DC	FB	MY	FBG	SV	IB	T120D	YAN	13	5	22500	2	10	88900	97700
		IB T135D LEHM 89500 98400, IB T160D LEHM 90800 99800, IB T225D LEHM 94400 103500														
43		PRESIDENT 43 DC	FB	MY	FBG	SV	IB	T135D	LEHM	13	11	28000	3		106000	116500
43		PRESIDENT 43 DC	FB	MY	FBG	SV	IB	T160D	LEHM	13	11	28000	3		102500	113000
43		PRESIDENT 43 DC	FB	MY	FBG	SV	IB	T225D	LEHM	13	11	28000	3		108000	119000
43		PRESIDENT 43 SDN	FB	SF	FBG	SV	IB	T225D	LEHM	13	11	28000	3		106000	116500
43		PRESIDENT 43 SDN	FB	SF	FBG	SV	IB	T235D	VLVO	13	11	28000	3		106000	116500
54	5	PRESIDENT 54 MY	FB	MY	FBG	DV	IB	T462D	GM	16	2	47500	3	6	184500	203000
		1984 BOATS														
40	6	PRESIDENT 41 DC	FB	MY	FBG	SV	IB	T125D	LEYL	13	5	22500	2	10	85300	93700
		IB T135D LEHM 85800 94300, IB T160D LEHM 87000 95600, IB T225D LEHM 90400 99300														
43		PRESIDENT 43 DC	FB	MY	FBG	SV	IB	T135D	LEHM	13	11	28000	3		101500	111500
43		PRESIDENT 43 DC	FB	MY	FBG	SV	IB	T225D	LEHM	13	11	28000	3		103500	114000
43		PRESIDENT 43 SDN	FB	SF	FBG	SV	IB	T225D	LEHM	13	11	28000	3		101500	111500
43		PRESIDENT 43 SDN	FB	SF	FBG	SV	IB	T235D	VLVO	13	11	28000	3		101500	111500
54	5	PRESIDENT 54 MY	FB	MY	FBG	DV	IB	T462D	GM	16	2	47500	3	6	177000	194500

....For earlier years, see the BUC Used Boat Price Guide, Volume 3

PRINCECRAFT

KNOXVILLE TN 37914

See inside cover to adjust price for area

For more recent years, see the BUC Used Boat Price Guide, Volume 1

LOA FT	LOA IN	NAME AND/ OR MODEL	TOP/ RIG	BOAT TYPE	-HULL- MTL	-HULL- TP	ENGINE TP	ENGINE # HP	ENGINE MFG	BEAM FT	BEAM IN	WGT LBS	DRAFT FT	DRAFT IN	RETAIL LOW	RETAIL HIGH
		1996 BOATS														
16		PRO 162 BT	OP	FSH	AL	DV	OB			6	1	550			2250	2600
16		PRO 162 DLX	OP	FSH	AL	DV	OB			6	1	635			2550	2950
16		PRO 162 SC	OP	FSH	AL	DV	OB			6	1	580			2350	2750
16		STARFISH 15	OP	UTL	AL	SV	OB			6	1	293			1150	1400
16		STARFISH 20	OP	UTL	AL	SV	OB			6	1	300			1200	1400
16		STARFISH DLX	OP	UTL	AL	DV	OB			6	1	417			1650	2000
16	4	HOLIDAY	OP	UTL	AL	SV	OB			6	11	375			1500	1800
16	4	HOLIDAY DLX	OP	UTL	AL	DV	OB			6	11	505			2000	2400
16	6	PRO 167 BT	OP	FSH	AL	DV	OB			6	9	635			2600	3050
16	6	PRO 167 SC	OP	FSH	AL	DV	OB			6	9	710			2900	3400
16	6	PRO 169 DLX	OP	FSH	AL	DV	OB			6	8	780			3200	3700
16	9	PRO 166	OP	FSH	AL	DV	OB			6	11	809			3300	3850
17	1	PRO 177	OP	BASS	AL	DV	OB			7	1	940			3850	4500
17	4	SUPER PRO 175	OP	FSH	AL	DV	OB			7	1	900			3750	4350
17	5	SUPER PRO 176 F&P	OP	FSH	AL	DV	OB			7	3	1125			4550	5250
17	5	SUPER PRO 176 FISH	OP	FSH	AL	DV	OB			7	1	1075			4400	5100
17	5	SUPER PRO 176 PLAT	OP	FSH	AL	DV	OB			7	3	1110			4550	5200
17	7	PRO 178	OP	FSH	AL	DV	OB			7	1	950			3950	4600
19		VENTURA 190	ST	RNBT	AL	SV	OB			8		1685			6500	7450
19		VENTURA 191	ST	RNBT	AL	SV	OB			8		1625			6350	7300
19	4	HUDSON	OP	UTL	AL	SV	OB			7	1	465			1650	2000
19	4	HUDSON DLX	OP	UTL	AL	DV	OB			7	1	645			2450	2800
19	4	SUPER PRO 195	OP	FSH	AL	DV	OB			7	8	1150			4950	5700
19	4	SUPER PRO 196 F&P	OP	FSH	AL	DV	OB			7	10	1290			5400	6200
19	4	SUPER PRO 196 F&S	OP	FSH	AL	DV	IO	135-160		7	10				8500	9800
19	4	SUPER PRO 196 FISH	OP	FSH	AL	DV	OB			7	8	1075			4700	5400
19	4	SUPER PRO 196 PLAT	OP	FSH	AL	DV	OB			7	10	1275			5350	6150
22		VACANZA 220	ST	RNBT	AL	SV	OB			8		2000			9250	10500
22		VACANZA 220	ST	RNBT	AL	SV	IO	135-160		8		2000			8500	9800
22		VEN 221		RNBT	AL	SV	OB			8		1900			8900	10100
22		VENTURA 220	ST	RNBT	AL	SV	OB			8		1900			8900	10100
		1995 BOATS														
16		PRO 162 BT	OP	FSH	AL	SV	OB			6	1	550			2100	2500
16		PRO 162 SC	OP	FSH	AL	SV	OB			6	1	580			2250	2600
16		STARFISH 15	OP	UTL	AL	DV	OB			6	1	293			1100	1300
16		STARFISH 15	OP	UTL	AL	SV	OB			5	7	266			995	1200
16		STARFISH 20	OP	UTL	AL	DV	OB			6	1	300			1150	1350
16	1	PRO 162 DXL	OP	FSH	AL	SV	OB			6	1	615			2350	2750
16	4	HOLIDAY	OP	UTL	AL	DV	OB			6	11	375			1400	1700
16	4	HOLIDAY DXL	OP	UTL	AL	DV	OB			6	11	505			1900	2300
16	6	PRO 164 BT	OP	FSH	AL	SV	OB			6	8	590			2350	2700
16	6	PRO 164 SC	OP	FSH	AL	SV	OB			6	8	650			2550	2950
16	6	PRO 167 BT	OP	FSH	AL	SV	OB			6	8	635			2500	2900
16	6	PRO 167 SC	OP	FSH	AL	SV	OB			6	8	710			2750	3200
16	6	PRO 169 SC	OP	FSH	AL	SV	OB			6	8	780			3000	3500
16	9	HOLIDAY	OP	UTL	AL	SV	OB			6	4	330			1250	1500
17	2	PRO 1750 SC	OP	BASS	AL	SV	OB			5	10	718			2900	3350
17	4	SUPER PRO 175	OP	CTRCN	AL	SV	OB			7	1	900			3550	4150
17	4	SUPER PRO 176	OP	FSH	AL	SV	OB			7	1	1005			3900	4550
17	4	SUPER PRO 176 F & S	OP	RNBT	AL	SV	OB			7	1	970			3800	4400
17	7	PRO 177 SC	OP	BASS	AL	SV	OB			7	1	940			3750	4350
17	7	PRO 178 SC	OP	FSH	AL	SV	OB			7	1	950			3750	4350
18	4	JUMBO	OP	UTL	AL	DV	OB			6	8	335			1200	1400
18	4	JUMBO	OP	UTL	AL	SV	OB			6	8	335			1200	1400
19		VENTURA 190	OP	RNBT	AL	SV	OB			8		1685			6150	7100
19		VENTURA 191	OP	RNBT	AL	SV	OB			8		1625			6000	6900
19	4	SUPER PRO 195	OP	CTRCN	AL	SV	OB			7	10	1150			4700	5400
19	4	SUPER PRO 196	OP	FSH	AL	SV	OB			7	10	1170			4750	5500
19	4	SUPER PRO 196 F & S	OP	RNBT	AL	SV	OB			7	8	1160			4750	5450
19	4	SUPER PRO 196 F & S	OP	RNBT	AL	SV	IO	135-160		7	8	2125			7200	8250
19	5	SUPER PRO 196 F & S	OP	FSH	AL	SV	IO	160	OMC	7	10	2150			8050	9250
22		VACANZA	OP	RNBT	AL	SV	OB			8		2000			8650	9950
22		VACANZA	OP	RNBT	AL	SV	IO	135-160		8		2600			8950	10200
22		VENTURA 220	OP	RNBT	AL	SV	OB			8		1900			8300	9550
22	6	CORSICA	OP	CUD	AL	SV	OB			8		1800			8100	9300
22	6	CORSICA	OP	CUD	AL	SV	IO	135-175		8		2600			9650	11000
		1994 BOATS														
16		PRO 162 BT		FSH	AL	SV	OB			5	7	470			1700	2050
16		PRO 162 SC		FSH	AL	SV	OB			5	7	523			1900	2250
16		STARFISH		UTL	AL	SV	OB			5	7	266			950	1150
16	6	PRO 164 BT		FSH	AL	SV	OB			6	8	590			2250	2600
16	6	PRO 164 SC		FSH	AL	SV	OB			6	8	650			2450	2850
16	6	PRO 167 BT		FSH	AL	SV	OB			6	8	635			2400	2750
16	6	PRO 167 SC		FSH	AL	SV	OB			6	8	710			2650	3050
16	6	PRO 169 SC		FSH	AL	SV	OB			6	8	780			2850	3350
16	9	HOLIDAY		UTL	AL	SV	OB			6	4	330			1200	1400
17	2	PRO 1750 SC		BASS	AL	SV	OB			5	10	718			2750	3200
17	4	SUPER PRO 175		CTRCN	AL	SV	OB			7	1	940			3500	4100
17	4	SUPER PRO 176		FSH	AL	SV	OB			7	1	960			3550	4150
17	4	SUPER PRO 176 F & S		RNBT	AL	SV	OB			7	1	960			3600	4150
17	7	PRO 177 SC		BASS	AL	SV	OB			7	1	940			3550	4150
17	7	PRO 178 SC		FSH	AL	SV	OB			7	1	935			3550	4100
18	4	JUMBO		UTL	AL	SV	OB			6	8	335			1100	1350
19	4	SUPER PRO 195		CTRCN	AL	SV	OB			7	10	1125			4400	5050
19	4	SUPER PRO 196		FSH	AL	SV	OB			7	8	1160			4500	5200
19	4	SUPER PRO 196 F & S		RNBT	AL	SV	OB			7	8	1160			4550	5200
19	4	SUPER PRO 196 F & S		RNBT	AL	SV	IO	175	OMC	7	8	2125			6750	7750
22		VACANZA		RNBT	AL	SV	OB			8		2000			8200	9450
22		VACANZA		RNBT	AL	SV	IO	130	OMC	8		2715			8450	9700
22	6	CORSICA		CUD	AL	SV	OB			8		1800			7650	8800
22	6	CORSICA		CUD	AL	SV	IO	175	OMC	8		2600			9100	10300
		1993 BOATS														
16		PRO 162 BT		UTL	AL	SV	OB			5	7	470			1600	1900
16		PRO 162 SC		UTL	AL	SV	OB			5	7	523			1800	2150
16		STARFISH		UTL	AL	SV	OB			5	7	266			910	1100
16	6	PRO 164 BT		UTL	AL	SV	OB			6	8	590			2050	2400
16	6	PRO 164 SC		UTL	AL	SV	OB			6	8	650			2250	2650
16	6	PRO 167 BT		UTL	AL	SV	OB			6	8	635			2250	2600
16	6	PRO 167 SC		UTL	AL	SV	OB			6	8	710			2450	2850
16	6	PRO 169 SC		UTL	AL	SV	OB			6	8	780			2650	3100
16	9	HOLIDAY		UTL	AL	SV	OB			6	4	330			1150	1350
17	2	PRO 1750 SC		BASS	AL	SV	OB			5	10	718			2600	3050
17	4	SUPER PRO 175		CTRCN	AL	SV	OB			7	1	940			3350	3900
17	4	SUPER PRO 176		UTL	AL	SV	OB			7	1	960			3200	3750
17	4	SUPER PRO 176 F & S		RNBT	AL	SV	OB			7	1	960			3400	4000
17	4	SUPREME 176		RNBT	AL	SV	OB			7	1	940			3350	3900
17	7	PRO 177		BASS	AL	SV	OB			7	1	940			3400	3950
17	7	PRO 178 SC		UTL	AL	SV	OB			7	1	935			3150	3650
18	4	JUMBO		UTL	AL	SV	OB			6	8	335			1050	1250
19	4	SUPER PRO 196		UTL	AL	SV	OB			7	8	1160			3700	4300
19	4	SUPER PRO 196		UTL	AL	SV	IO	175	OMC	7	8	2125			6900	7900
19	4	SUPER PRO 196 F & S		RNBT	AL	SV	OB			7	8	1160			4300	5000
19	4	SUPER PRO 196 F & S		RNBT	AL	SV	IO	175	OMC	7	8	2125			6450	7400

LOA FT IN	NAME AND/ OR MODEL	TOP/ RIG	BOAT TYPE	HULL MTL TP	TP	ENGINE # HP MFG	BEAM FT IN	WGT LBS	DRAFT FT IN	RETAIL LOW	RETAIL HIGH
						1993 BOATS					
19 4	SUPREME 196		RNBT	AL SV	OB		7 8	1140		4200	4900
19 4	SUPREME 196		RNBT	AL SV	OB	175 OMC	7 8	2125		6200	7100
22	VACANZA		RNBT	AL SV	OB		8	2000		7800	8950
22	VACANZA		RNBT	AL SV	IO	130 OMC	8	2715		7900	9050
22 6	CORSICA		CUD	AL SV	OB		8	1800		7300	8400
22 6	CORSICA		CUD	AL SV	IO	175 OMC	8	2600		8400	9650

PRINDLE

PERFORMANCE CATAMARANS   See inside cover to adjust price for area
SANTA ANA CA 92705   COAST GUARD MFG ID- SUR
                  FORMERLY LEAR SIEGLER MARINE

For more recent years, see the BUC Used Boat Price Guide, Volume 1

LOA FT IN	NAME AND/ OR MODEL	TOP/ RIG	BOAT TYPE	HULL MTL TP	TP #	ENGINE HP MFG	BEAM FT IN	WGT LBS	DRAFT FT IN	RETAIL LOW	RETAIL HIGH
						1996 BOATS					
16	PRINDLE 16	SLP	SAROD	F/S	CT		7 11	300		3900	4500
18	PRINDLE 18	SLP	SAROD	F/S	CT		8 6	355		5000	5750
18	PRINDLE 18-2	SLP	SAROD	F/S	CT		8 6	375		5200	5950
18 3	PRINDLE ESCAPE	SLP	SAROD	F/S	CT		7 11	335		4850	5550
19 3	PRINDLE 19	SLP	SAROD	F/S	CT		8 6	385		5650	6500
						1995 BOATS					
16	PRINDLE 16	CAT	SAROD	F/S	CT			300		3650	4250
18	PRINDLE 18	CAT	SAROD	F/S	CT			355		4700	5400
18	PRINDLE 18-2	CAT	SAROD	F/S	CT			375		4900	5600
18 3	PRINDLE ESCAPE	CAT	SAROD	F/S	CT			335		4500	5200
19 3	PRINDLE 19	CAT	SAROD	F/S	CT			385		5300	6100
						1994 BOATS					
16	PRINDLE 16	CAT	SAROD	F/S	CT		7 11	300		3450	4000
18	PRINDLE 18	CAT	SAROD	F/S	CT		7 11	355		4450	5100
18	PRINDLE 18-2	CAT	SAROD	F/S	CT		8 6	375	2 1	4600	5300
18 3	PRINDLE ESCAPE	CAT	SAROD	F/S	CT		8 6	335	2 1	4200	4900
19 3	PRINDLE 19	CAT	SAROD	F/S	CT		8 6	385	2 1	5000	5750
						1993 BOATS					
18	PRINDLE 18-2	CAT	SAROD	F/S	CT		8 6	375	2 1	4300	5000
18 3	PRINDLE ESCAPE	CAT	SAROD	F/S	CT		8 6	335	2 1	3950	4600
19 3	PRINDLE 19	CAT	SAROD	F/S	CT		8 6	385	2 1	4700	5400
						1992 BOATS					
16	PRINDLE 16	CAT	SA/OD	F/S	CT		7 11	300	1 10	3050	3550
18	PRINDLE 18	CAT	SA/OD	F/S	CT		7 11	335		3700	4300
18	PRINDLE 18-2	CAT	SA/OD	F/S	CT		8 6	375	2 1	4050	4700
19 3	PRINDLE 19	CAT	SA/OD	F/S	CT		8 6	385	2 1	4450	5100
						1991 BOATS					
16	PRINDLE 16	CAT	SA/OD	F/S	CT		7 11	300	1 10	2850	3300
18	PRINDLE 18	CAT	SA/OD	F/S	CT		7 11	335		3500	4050
18	PRINDLE 18-2	CAT	SA/OD	F/S	CT		8 6	375	2 1	3800	4400
19 3	PRINDLE 19	CAT	SA/OD	F/S	CT		8 6	385	2 1	4150	4800
						1987 BOATS					
16	PRINDLE 16	CAT	SA/OD	F/S	CT		7 11	300	10	2250	2650
18	PRINDLE 18	CAT	SA/OD	F/S	CT		7 11	335	10	2750	3200
18	PRINDLE 18-2	CAT	SA/OD	F/S	CT		8 6	365	2 1	2900	3400
19 2	PRINDLE 19	CAT	SA/OD	F/S	CT		8 6	375		3150	3700
						1986 BOATS					
16	PRINDLE 16	CAT	SA/OD	F/S	CT		7 11	300	10	2100	2500
18	PRINDLE 18	CAT	SA/OD	F/S	CT		7 11	335	10	2600	3000
19 2	PRINDLE 19	CAT	SA/OD	F/S	CT		8 6	375		3000	3450
						1985 BOATS					
16	PRINDLE 16	SLP	SA/OD	F/S	CT		7 11	300	10	1950	2350
18	PRINDLE 18	SLP	SA/OD	F/S	CT		7 11	335	10	2400	2800
19 3	PRINDLE 19	SLP	SA/OD	F/S	CT		8 6	375	5	2800	3250

PRIORITY BOATS INC

MARATHON FL 33050   COAST GUARD MFG ID- PRY See inside cover to adjust price for area

LOA FT IN	NAME AND/ OR MODEL	TOP/ RIG	BOAT TYPE	HULL MTL TP	TP #	ENGINE HP MFG	BEAM FT IN	WGT LBS	DRAFT FT IN	RETAIL LOW	RETAIL HIGH
						1994 BOATS					
18 6	SHOTGUN	OP	FSH	FBG SV	OB			950	8	5300	6100
30	30-30	MT	SF	FBG SV	IB	T300D CAT	12 8	13000	3	70200	77200
32 7	32SS	F+T	EXP	FBG SV	IB	T300D CAT	12 11	14500	3	80800	88700
51	CANON BALL 51	EPH	COMM	FBG SV	IB	T475D DD	18 11	38000	4	**	**

PRIVATEER MFG CO INC

CHOCOWINITY NC 27817   COAST GUARD MFG ID- PVT See inside cover to adjust price for area

LOA FT IN	NAME AND/ OR MODEL	TOP/ RIG	BOAT TYPE	HULL MTL TP	TP #	ENGINE HP MFG	BEAM FT IN	WGT LBS	DRAFT FT IN	RETAIL LOW	RETAIL HIGH
						1984 BOATS					
18 4	RETRIEVER 1800	OP	CTRCN	FBG SV	OB		7 2	900	6	2300	2700
20 2	REVENGE 2002	OP	CTRCN	FBG SV	OB		7 10	1400	7	3550	4150
20 2	REVENGE 2002	ST	CBNCR	FBG SV	IO	117-140	7 10	2200	8	5850	6700
20 2	REVENGE 2002	OP	CTRCN	FBG SV	OB		7 10	1200	7	3150	3650
20 2	REVENGE 2002	OP	CTRCN	FBG SV	IO	117-140	7 10	2000	8	5650	6500
20 2	REVENGE II 2100	OP	CTRCN	FBG SV	OB		8 4	1600	10	3950	4600
20 2	REVENGE II 2100	OP	CTRCN	FBG SV	IO	117-260	8 4	2600	10	6450	7950
20 2	REVENGE II 2100	OP	CTRCN	FBG SV	IO	290 VLVO	8 4	2600	10	7300	8400
20 2	REVENGE II 2100	OP	CTRCN	FBG SV	IO	130D-165D	8 4	2600	10	9850	11500
24 4	RENEGADE 2400	HT	CTRCN	FBG SV	OB		9 1	2400	11	6500	7450
24 4	RENEGADE 2400	HT	CBNCR	FBG SV	IO	117-120	9 1	3900	2	10900	12400
IO 138 VLVO 11000			12500,	IB	138	VLVO	11700	13200,	IO	140-200	10800	12800
IO 225 VLVO 11200			12800,	IB	225	VLVO	12000	13700,	IO	228-230	11100	12600
IO 260 OMC 11200			12800,	IO	260	VLVO	11500	13800,	IB	260 VLVO	12100	13800
IO 290 VLVO 11900			13500,	IB	124D	VLVO	15200	17300,	IO	130D VLVO	14000	15900
IB 158D VLVO 15900			18000,	IO	165D	VLVO	14600	16600				
24 4	RENEGADE 2400	OP	CTRCN	FBG SV	OB		9 1	2000	11	5600	6450
24 4	RENEGADE 2400	OP	CTRCN	FBG SV	IO	117-120	9 1	3500	2	9800	11100
IO 138 VLVO 9850			11200,	IB	138	VLVO	11100	12600,	IO	140-200	9600	11300
IO 225 VLVO 10100			11500,	IB	225	VLVO	11400	13000,	IO	228-230	9950	11300
IO 260 OMC 10100			11400,	IO	260	VLVO	10400	11800,	IB	260 VLVO	11500	13100
IO 290 VLVO 10800			12300,	IB	124D	VLVO	14000	16000,	IO	130D VLVO	13300	15100
IB 158D VLVO 14600			16600,	IO	165D	VLVO	13800	15700				

....For earlier years, see the BUC Used Boat Price Guide, Volume 3

PRO-LINE BOATS INC

CRYSTAL RIVER FL 34423- COAST GUARD MFG ID- PLC See inside cover to adjust price for area

For more recent years, see the BUC Used Boat Price Guide, Volume 1

LOA FT IN	NAME AND/ OR MODEL	TOP/ RIG	BOAT TYPE	HULL MTL TP	TP	ENGINE # HP MFG	BEAM FT IN	WGT LBS	DRAFT FT IN	RETAIL LOW	RETAIL HIGH
						1996 BOATS					
17	STALKER 170	OP	CTRCN	FBG SV	OB		7	1750	1	4950	5700
18 2	STALKER 183 FLATS	OP	BASS	FBG SV	OB		8	1170	9	5700	6550
18 5	STALKER 190	OP	CTRCN	FBG SV	OB		7 6	2100	1	5500	6350
18 10	STALKER 180	OP	CTRCN	FBG SV	OB		8	1900	1 1	5300	6100
20 2	STALKER 200	OP	CUD	FBG DV	OB		8	2250	1 1	7650	8800
20 2	STALKER 201	OP	CTRCN	FBG SV	OB		8	2500	1 1	8100	9300
20 2	STALKER 202	OP	OPFSH	FBG SV	OB		8	2500	1 1	8100	9300
20 6	SPORTSMAN 210	OP	CTRCN	FBG SV	OB		8 6	3100	1 2	9500	10500
20 11	WALKAROUND 211	OP	CUD	FBG SV	OB		8 6	3100	1 2	9700	11000
20 11	WALKAROUND 211	OP	CUD	FBG SV	IO	180-220	8 6	3100	1 2	11600	13900
22 5	CUDDY 220	OP	CUD	FBG SV	OB		8 6	3450	1 3	11900	13500
22 5	CUDDY 220	OP	CUD	FBG SV	IO	180-250	8 6	3450	1 3	13400	16300
25 5	SPORTSMAN 240	OP	CTRCN	FBG SV	OB		8 6	3600	1 2	13300	15100
25 6	WALKAROUND 231	OP	CUD	FBG SV	OB		8 6	3650	1 2	14100	15300
25 6	WALKAROUND 231	OP	CUD	FBG SV	IO	210-265	8 6	3650	1 2	14900	18200
27 4	WALKAROUND 251	OP	CUD	FBG SV	OB		8 6	4250	1 5	15800	17900
27 4	WALKAROUND 251	OP	CUD	FBG SV	IO	235-300	8 6	4250	1 5	19200	22900
27 4	WALKAROUND 251	OP	CUD	FBG SV	IO	330 VLVO	8 6	4250	1 5	21600	24000
27 4	WALKAROUND 251	OP	CUD	FBG SV	IO	188D-240D	8 6	4250	1 5	22000	27200
27 5	SPORTSMAN 2700	OP	CTRCN	FBG SV	OB		9 10	4750	1 8	16400	18600
27 5	WALKAROUND 2510	OP	CUD	FBG SV	OB		9 10	5545	1 10	17400	19800
27 5	WALKAROUND 2510	OP	CUD	FBG SV	IO	235-330	9 10	5545	1 10	23300	28500
27 5	WALKAROUND 2510	OP	CUD	FBG SV	IO	188D-230D	9 10	5545	1 10	27400	32700
30	MID CABIN 2950	HT	WKNDR	FBG SV	OB		10 9	7500	1 10	30900	34300
30	MID CABIN 2950	HT	WKNDR	FBG SV	IO	240D MRCR	10 9	7500	1 10	40000	40000
30	MID CABIN 2950	HT	WKNDR	FBG SV	IO	T180-T265	10 9	7500	1 10	33800	40700
30	MID CABIN 2950	HT	WKNDR	FBG SV	IO	T188D VLVO	10 9	7500	1 10	44700	45200
34 10	BIMINI 3400	OP	CUD	FBG DV	OB		9 2	7500	2 1	36400	40500
						1995 BOATS					
17	SPORTSMAN 170		CTRCN	FBG DV	OB		7 6	1750	1	4700	5400
18 2	STALKER 183		FSH	FBG DV	OB		8	1170	9	5250	6000
18 6	SPORTSMAN 190		CTRCN	FBG DV	OB		8 6	1950	1	5050	5800
18 6	SPORTSMAN 192		RNBT	FBG DV	OB		7 6	1950	1	5250	6050
18 6	SPORTSMAN 192		RNBT	FBG DV	OB	175 MRCR	7 6	1950	1	5700	6600
20 11	SPORTSMAN 210		CTRCN	FBG DV	OB		8 6	2650	1 2	8550	9800

PRO-LINE BOATS INC -CONTINUED See inside cover to adjust price for area

LOA FT	LOA IN	NAME AND/ OR MODEL	TOP/ RIG	BOAT TYPE	HULL MTL	HULL TP	ENGINE TP	ENGINE # HP	ENGINE MFG	BEAM FT	BEAM IN	WGT LBS	DRAFT FT	DRAFT IN	RETAIL LOW	RETAIL HIGH
		1995 BOATS														
20	11	WALK AROUND 211		CUD	FBG	SV	OB			8	6	3100	1	2	9300	10600
25	5	SPORTSMAN 240	ST	FSH	FBG	DV	OB			8	6	3600	1	2	14000	15900
25	6	WALK AROUND 220		CUD	FBG	DV	OB			8	6	3650	1	2	11200	12700
25	6	WALK AROUND 220		CUD	FBG	DV	IO	175-230		8	6	3650	1	2	12700	14700
25	6	WALK AROUND 231		CUD	FBG	SV	OB			8	6	3650	1	2	12800	14600
27	4	WALK AROUND 251	ST	SF	FBG	DV	OB			8	6	4250	1	5	15000	17000
27	4	WALK AROUND 251	ST	SF	FBG	DV	IO	300	MRCR	8	6	4250	1	5	21200	23600
27	5	SPORTSMAN 2700		CTRCN	FBG	DV	OB			9	10	4730	1	6	15600	17700
27	5	WALK AROUND 2510		CUD	FBG	DV	OB			9	10	5545	1	10	16600	18900
27	5	WALK AROUND 2510		CUD	FBG	DV	IO	230-300		9	10	5545	1	10	21300	25100
27	5	WALK AROUND 2510		CUD	FBG	DV	IO	200D	MRCR	9	10	5545	1	10	26500	29500
30		MID CABIN 2950		CUD	FBG	DV	OB			10	9	7500	1	10	27900	31000
30		MID CABIN 2950		CUD	FBG	DV	IO	330	MRCR	10	9	7500	1	10	31100	34600
30		MID CABIN 2950		CUD	FBG	DV	IO	T175-T230		10	9	7500	1	10	31300	36600
30		MID CABIN 2950		CUD	FBG	DV	IO	T170D-T210D		10	9	7500	1	10	37200	43900
30		MID CABIN 2950		CUD	FBG	SV	IB			10	9	7500	1	10	**	**
30		MID CABIN 2950		CUD	FBG	SV	IB	T230		10	9	7500	1	10	38600	42900
		1994 BOATS														
17		SPORTSMAN 170		CTRCN	FBG	DV	OB			7	6	1750	1		4450	5100
18	2	STALKER 183		FSH	FBG	SV	OB			8		1170		9	4950	5700
18	6	SPORTSMAN 190		CTRCN	FBG	DV	OB			7	6	1950	1		4800	5500
18	6	SPORTSMAN 192		RNBT	FBG	DV	OB			7	6	1950	1		5000	5750
18	6	SPORTSMAN 192		RNBT	FBG	DV	IO	175	MRCR	7	6	1950	1		5350	6150
20	11	SPORTSMAN 210		CTRCN	FBG	DV	OB			8	6	2650	1	2	8150	9350
20	11	WALK AROUND 211		CUD	FBG	SV	OB			8	6	3100	1	2	8900	10100
25	6	SPORTSMAN 230		CTRCN	FBG	DV	OB			8	6	3300	1	2	12900	14700
25	6	WALK AROUND 220		CUD	FBG	DV	OB			8	6	3650	1	2	10700	12100
25	6	WALK AROUND 220		CUD	FBG	DV	IO	175-230		8	6	3650	1	2	11900	13700
25	6	WALK AROUND 231		CUD	FBG	SV	OB			8	6	3650	1	2	12200	13900
25	6	WALK AROUND 240		CUD	FBG	DV	OB			8	6	3780	1	2	12500	14200
25	6	WALK AROUND 240		CUD	FBG	DV	IO	205-230		8	6	3780	1	2	13300	15200
27	5	MID CABIN 2550		CUD	FBG	DV	OB			9	10	5845	1	10	16200	18400
27	5	MID CABIN 2550		CUD	FBG	DV	IO	230-330		9	10	5845	1	10	20700	25000
27	5	MID CABIN 2550		CUD	FBG	DV	IO	180D	MRCR	9	10	5845	1	10	25300	28100
27	5	MID CABIN 2550		CUD	FBG	DV	IO	T175-T205		9	10	5845	1	10	22500	25500
27	5	SPORTSMAN 2700		CTRCN	FBG	DV	OB			9	10	4730	1	6	14800	16900
27	5	WALK AROUND 2510		CUD	FBG	DV	OB			9	10	5545	1	10	15900	18100
27	5	WALK AROUND 2510		CUD	FBG	DV	IO	230-300		9	10	5545	1	10	19900	23400
27	5	WALK AROUND 2510		CUD	FBG	DV	IO	200D	MRCR	9	10	5545	1	10	25300	28100
27	5	WALK AROUND 2510		CUD	FBG	DV	IO	T175-T205		9	10	5545	1	10	21800	24700
27	10	WALK AROUND 260		CUD	FBG	DV	IO	205-230		8	6	3900	1	2	15700	18300
27	10	WALK AROUND 260		CUD	FBG	DV	IO	170D-200D		8	6	3900	1	2	18300	21300
27	10	WALK AROUND 260		CUD	FBG	SV	OB			8	6	3900	1	2	14800	16900
30		MID CABIN 2950		CUD	FBG	DV	OB			10	9	7500	1	10	26600	29600
30		MID CABIN 2950		CUD	FBG	DV	IO	330	MRCR	10	9	7500	1	10	29100	32300
30		MID CABIN 2950		CUD	FBG	DV	IO	T175-T230		10	9	7500	1	10	29300	34100
30		MID CABIN 2950		CUD	FBG	DV	IO	T170D-T210D		10	9	7500	1	10	34700	40900
30		MID CABIN 2950		CUD	FBG	SV	IB	T230		10	9	7500	1	10	36500	40600
30		MID CABIN 2950		CUD	FBG	SV	IB	T170D-T200D		10	9	7500	1	10	42700	49700
		1993 BOATS														
17		SPORTSMAN 170		CTRCN	FBG	DV	OB			7	6	1750	1		4200	4850
18	6	SPORTSMAN 190		CTRCN	FBG	DV	OB			7	6	1950	1		4550	5250
18	6	SPORTSMAN 192		RNBT	FBG	DV	OB			7	6	1950	1		4750	5450
18	6	SPORTSMAN 192		RNBT	FBG	DV	IO	175		7	6	1950	1		5000	5750
18	6	SPORTSMAN 19TC		RNBT	FBG	DV	OB			7	6	1850	1		4600	5300
20	1	CLASSIC 20		CTRCN	FBG	SV	OB			7	8	1780		9	5700	6550
20	11	SPORTSMAN 210		CTRCN	FBG	DV	OB			8	6	2650	1	2	7800	8950
20	11	WALKAROUND 210		CUD	FBG	DV	OB			8	6	3100	1	2	8450	9700
20	11	WALKAROUND 210		CUD	FBG	DV	IO	175		8	6	3100	1	2	9450	10700
22	5	CUDDY FISH 230		CUD	FBG	DV	OB			8	6	3450	1	3	10400	11800
22	5	CUDDY FISH 230		CUD	FBG	DV	IO	175-230		8	6	3450	1	3	10900	12600
25	6	SPORTSMAN 230		CTRCN	FBG	DV	OB			8	6	3300	1	2	10800	12300
25	6	WALKAROUND 220		CUD	FBG	DV	OB			8	6	3650	1	2	10200	11600
25	6	WALKAROUND 220		CUD	FBG	DV	IO	175-205		8	6	3650	1	2	11100	12700
25	6	WALKAROUND 220		CUD	FBG	DV	IO	230		8	6	3650	1	2	13900	15800
25	6	WALKAROUND 240		CUD	FBG	DV	OB			8	6	3780	1	2	12000	13600
25	6	WALKAROUND 240		CUD	FBG	DV	IO	205-230		8	6	3780	1	2	12400	14200
27	5	MID CABIN 2510		CUD	FBG	DV	OB			9	10	5545	1	10	15200	17300
27	5	MID CABIN 2510		CUD	FBG	DV	IO	230-300		9	10	5545	1	10	18800	21800
27	5	MID CABIN 2510		CUD	FBG	DV	IO	180D-210D		9	10	5545			22600	26000
27	5	MID CABIN 2510		CUD	FBG	DV	IO	T175-T205		9	10	5545	1	10	20300	23100
27	5	MID CABIN 2550		CUD	FBG	DV	OB			9	10	5845	1	10	15500	17600
27	5	MID CABIN 2550		CUD	FBG	DV	IO	230-330		9	10	5845	1	10	19300	23400
27	5	MID CABIN 2550		CUD	FBG	DV	IO	180D-210D		9	10	5845	1	10	23600	27100
27	5	MID CABIN 2550		CUD	FBG	DV	IO	T175-T205		9	10	5845	1	10	21000	23800
27	5	SPORTSMAN 2700		CTRCN	FBG	DV	OB			9	10	4730	1	6	14200	16100
27	10	WALKAROUND 260		CUD	FBG	DV	OB			8	6	3900	1	2	14200	16200
27	10	WALKAROUND 260		CUD	FBG	DV	IO	205-275		8	6	3900	1	2	14700	17900
27	10	WALKAROUND 260		CUD	FBG	DV	IO	300	MRCR	8	6	3900	1	2	16200	18400
27	10	WALKAROUND 260		CUD	FBG	DV	IO	180D-210D		8	6	3900	1	2	17000	20400
30		MID CABIN 2950		CUD	FBG	DV	OB			10	9	7500	1	10	25500	28300
30		MID CABIN 2950		CUD	FBG	DV	IO	275-330		10	9	7500	1	10	26200	30200
		IO 180D-210D 27600 31600, IO T175-T230 27300 31900, IOT180D-T210D													32900	38300
		1992 BOATS														
17		CLASSIC 17	OP	CTRCN	FBG	SV	OB			7	8	1450		8	3450	4050
18	6	MEDALLION 19 TWIN	OP	RNBT	FBG	SV	OB			7	6	1850	1		4400	5050
18	6	MEDALLION 19 TWIN	OP	RNBT	FBG	SV	IO	130-205		7	6	1850	1		4550	5650
18	6	SPORTSMAN 190	OP	CTRCN	FBG	DV	OB			7	6	1950	1		4300	5000
18	6	SPORTSMAN 192 TWIN	OP	B/R	FBG	DV	OB			7	6	1950	1		4550	5250
20	1	CLASSIC 20	OP	CTRCN	FBG	SV	OB			7	8	1780		9	5450	6250
20	11	SPORTSMAN 210	OP	CTRCN	FBG	DV	OB			8	6	2240	1	2	6700	7700
20	11	SPORTSMAN 210	OP	CTRCN	FBG	DV	IO	155-205		8	6	2240	1	2	7800	9500
20	11	SPORTSMAN 210	OP	CTRCN	FBG	DV	IO	130D	VLVO	8	6	2240	1	2	12200	13900
20	11	WALKAROUND 210	OP	FSH	FBG	DV	OB			8	6	2520	1	2	7250	8350
20	11	WALKAROUND 210	OP	FSH	FBG	DV	IO			8	6	2520	1	2	**	**
20	11	WALKAROUND 210	OP	FSH	FBG	DV	IO	130D	VLVO	8	6	2520	1	2	12800	14500
23	8	SPORTSMAN 230	OP	CTRCN	FBG	DV	OB			8	6	2560	1	2	8450	9750
23	8	SPORTSMAN 230	OP	CTRCN	FBG	DV	IO	205-260		8	6	2560	1	2	9700	11600
23	8	SPORTSMAN 230	OP	CTRCN	FBG	DV	IO	275	VLVO	8	6	2560	1	2	10700	12200
23	8	SPORTSMAN 230	OP	CTRCN	FBG	DV	IO	130D-200D		8	6	2560	1	2	14500	17800
23	8	WALKAROUND 230	OP	CUD	FBG	DV	OB			8	6	2800	1	2	8600	9900
23	8	WALKAROUND 230	OP	CUD	FBG	DV	IO	205-275		8	6	2800	1	2	9600	11300
23	8	WALKAROUND 230	OP	CUD	FBG	DV	IO	130D-200D		8	6	2800	1	2	11400	14000
23	8	WALKAROUND 240	OP	CUD	FBG	DV	OB			8	6	2800	1	2	9850	11200
23	8	WALKAROUND 240	OP	CUD	FBG	DV	IO	210-275		8	6	2800	1	2	10300	12800
23	8	WALKAROUND 240	OP	CUD	FBG	DV	IO	130D-200D		8	6	2800	1	2	12600	15400
25	5	2550 MC	OP	CUD	FBG	DV	OB			9	10	5845	2	10	14900	16900
25	5	2550 MC	OP	CUD	FBG	DV	IO	275	VLVO	9	10	5845	2	10	19100	21200
		IO 200D VLVO 22000 24500, IO T205-T210 19700 22400, IO T130D VLVO													25000	27800
25	5	2550 MC	OP	FSH	FBG	DV	OB			9	10	5845	2	10	14700	16800
25	5	MID-CABIN 2550	OP	CUD	FBG	DV	IO	275-330		9	10	5845	1	10	19100	22400
25	5	MID-CABIN 2550	OP	CUD	FBG	DV	IO	230D	VLVO	9	10	5845	1	10	22700	25200
25	5	MID-CABIN 2550	OP	CUD	FBG	DV	IO	T205-T229		9	10	5845	1	10	20900	23300
25	5	WALKAROUND 2510	HT	CUD	FBG	DV	OB			9	10	4700	1	10	13800	15700
25	5	WALKAROUND 2510	HT	CUD	FBG	DV	IO	260-300		9	10	4700	1	10	15800	18700
		IO 330 VLVO 17500 19900, IO 200D-230D 18800 21600, IO T205-T230													17500	20900
		IO T130D VLVO 21800 24200														
26		WALKAROUND 260	OP	CUD	FBG	DV	IO	229-275		8	6	3200	1	2	13200	15800
26		WALKAROUND 260	OP	CUD	FBG	DV	IO	330	VLVO	8	6	3200	1	2	15200	17300
26		WALKAROUND 260	ST	CUD	FBG	DV	OB			8	6	3200	1	2	13000	14800
26		WALKAROUND 260	ST	CUD	FBG	DV	IO	210-260		8	6	3200	1	2	12700	15200
26		WALKAROUND 260	ST	CUD	FBG	DV	IO	130D	VLVO	8	6	3200	1	2	12200	13900
26		WALKAROUND 260	ST	CUD	FBG	DV	IO	200D	VLVO	8	6	3200	1	2	14400	16400
30		MID-CABIN 2950	OP	CR	FBG	DV	OB			10	9	5900	1	10	24600	27400
30		MID-CABIN 2950	OP	CR	FBG	DV	IO	300-330		10	9	5900	1	10	25000	28500
		IO 200D-230D 24300 28000, IO T205-T229 26600 30400, IO T130D VLVO													26600	29500
		1991 BOATS														
17		CLASSIC 17	OP	CTRCN	FBG	SV	OB			7	8	1450			3300	3800
17		CLASSIC 17	OP	CTRCN	FBG	SV	IO	115		7	8	1450			3800	4400
18	6	MEDALLION 19TW	OP	RNBT	FBG	SV	OB			7	6	1850			4150	4800
18	6	MEDALLION 19TW	OP	RNBT	FBG	SV	IO		VLVO	7	6	1850			**	**
18	6	MEDALLION 19TW	OP	RNBT	FBG	SV	IO	130	YAMA	7	6	1850			4250	4900
18	6	SPORTSMAN 190	OP	CTRCN	FBG	DV	OB			7	6	1950			4100	4750
18	6	SPORTSMAN 190	OP	CTRCN	FBG	DV	IO	115		7	6	1950			4700	5400
20	1	CLASSIC 20	OP	CTRCN	FBG	SV	OB			7	8	1780			5200	6000
20	1	CLASSIC 20	OP	CTRCN	FBG	SV	IO	115		7	8	1780			6000	6850
20	11	SPORTSMAN 210	OP	CTRCN	FBG	DV	OB			8	6	2240			6450	7400
20	11	SPORTSMAN 210	OP	CTRCN	FBG	DV	IO	140		8	6	2240			7300	8400
20	11	WALKAROUND 210	OP	FSH	FBG	DV	OB			8	6	2520			6950	8000
23	8	SPORTSMAN 230	OP	CTRCN	FBG	DV	OB			8	6	2560			8100	9350
23	8	SPORTSMAN 230	OP	CTRCN	FBG	DV	IO	225		8	6	2560			9250	10500
23	8	SPORTSMAN 230	OP	CTRCN	FBG	DV	IO	130D-200D		8	6	2560			13600	16700
23	8	WALKAROUND 230	OP	CUD	FBG	DV	OB			8	6	2800			8300	9500
23	8	WALKAROUND 230	OP	CUD	FBG	DV	IO	205-210		8	6	2800			8550	9900
		IO 225 8500 9750, IO 230-260 8400 10000, IO 275 VLVO													9300	10600
		IO 130D VLVO 10600 12100, IO T115 9600 10900														

CONTINUED ON NEXT PAGE

LOA FT IN	NAME AND/ OR MODEL	TOP/ RIG	BOAT TYPE	-HULL- MTL TP	TP	----ENGINE--- # HP MFG	BEAM FT IN	WGT LBS	DRAFT FT IN	RETAIL LOW	RETAIL HIGH
				1991 BOATS							
23 8	WALKAROUND 240	OP	CUD	FBG DV	OB		8 6	2800		9500	10800
23 8	WALKAROUND 240	OP	CUD	FBG DV	IO	205-210	8 6	2800		10000	11400
	IO 225 9650			11000, IO		230-275 9800	12000, IO	130D VLVO		12000	13600
	IO T115 10700			12200							
25 5	2550 MC	OP	CUD	FBG DV	OB		9 10			12200	13900
25 5	2550 MC	OP	CUD	FBG DV	IO	260-275	9 10			13100	15500
	IO 200D VLVO 17200			19600, IO	T	VLVO **	**, IO	T130-T140		13700	15700
	IO T205-T230 15200			17300, IO	T130D VLVO	20300 22600					
25 5	SPORTSMAN 2500	TT	SF	FBG DV	OB		9 10	3700		11900	13500
25 5	SPORTSMAN 2500	TT	SF	FBG DV	IO	200 VLVO	9 10	3700		14300	16200
	IO T140 15600			17700, IO	T225	17000 19300, IO	T130D VLVO			22300	24800
25 5	WALKAROUND 2510	HT	CUD	FBG DV	OB		9 10	4700		13300	15100
25 5	WALKAROUND 2510	HT	CUD	FBG DV	IO	260-275	9 10	4700		14800	17400
	IO 200D VLVO 17300			19700, IO	T VLVO	** **, IO	T130	YAMA		15400	17500
	IO T140 15500			17700, IO	T205-T230	16800 19200, IO	T130D VLVO			20400	22700
26 3	WALKAROUND 260	ST	CUD	FBG DV	OB		8 6	3200		13200	14900
26 3	WALKAROUND 260	ST	CUD	FBG DV	IO	205-275	8 6	3200		12400	15300
	IO 130D VLVO 11500			13000, IO	200D VLVO	13700 15500, IO	T140			13600	15500
28 5	WALKAROUND 2800	OP	CUD	FBG DV	OB		10 6	5400		19900	22100
28 5	WALKAROUND 2800	OP	CUD	FBG DV	IO	275 VLVO	10 6	5400		20100	22300
	IO 200D VLVO 20400			22600, IO	T VLVO	** **, IO	T130	YAMA		20000	22200
	IO T140			, IO	T205-T275	22000 26200, IO	T130D VLVO			22900	25400
				1990 BOATS							
17	SPORT 17	OP	FSH	FBG SV	OB		7 8	1450	8	3100	3600
17	SPORT 17	OP	FSH	FBG SV	SE		7 8	1450	8	**	**
18 6	SPORT 190	OP	CTRCN	FBG DV	OB		7 6	1950	1	3950	4600
18 6	SPORT 190	OP	CTRCN	FBG DV	SE	OMC	7 6	1950	1	**	**
20 1	SPORT 20	OP	CTRCN	FBG SV	OB		7 8	1780	9	5000	5750
20 1	SPORT 20	OP	CTRCN	FBG SV	SE	OMC	7 8	1780	9	**	**
20 11	SPORT 210	OP	CTRCN	FBG DV	OB		8 6	2240	1 2	6200	7100
20 11	SPORT 210	OP	CTRCN	FBG DV	SE	OMC	8 6	2240	1 2	**	**
20 11	WALKAROUND 210	OP	FSH	FBG DV	OB		8 6	2520	1 2	6700	7700
20 11	WALKAROUND 210	OP	FSH	FBG DV	SE	OMC	8 6	2520	1 2	**	**
20 11	WALKAROUND 210	OP	FSH	FBG DV	IO	175-205	8 6	2520	1 2	7300	8500
23 8	CHINOOK 230	OP	FSH	FBG DV	OB		8 6	2800	1 2	8450	9700
23 8	CHINOOK 230	OP	FSH	FBG DV	SE	OMC	8 6	2800	1 2	**	**
23 8	CHINOOK 230	OP	FSH	FBG DV	SE	260 MRCR	8 6	2800	1 2	9400	10700
23 8	CHINOOK 230	OP	FSH	FBG DV	SE	T OMC	8 6	2800	1 2	**	**
23 8	SPORT 230	OP	CTRCN	FBG DV	OB		8 6	2560	1 2	7800	8950
23 8	SPORT 230	OP	CTRCN	FBG DV	SE	T OMC	8 6	2560	1 2	**	**
23 8	WALKAROUND 230	OP	CUD	FBG DV	OB		8 6	2800	1 2	8550	9800
23 8	WALKAROUND 230	OP	CUD	FBG DV	SE	OMC	8 6	2800	1 2	**	**
23 8	WALKAROUND 230	OP	CUD	FBG DV	IO	205-260	8 6	2800	1 2	8400	10100
23 8	WALKAROUND 230	OP	CUD	FBG DV	SE	T	8 6	2800	1 2	**	**
25 5	SPORT 250	TT	SF	FBG DV	OB		9 10	3700	1 10	11400	13000
25 5	SPORT 250	TT	SF	FBG DV	SE	T OMC	9 10	3700	1 10	**	**
25 5	WALKAROUND 250	HT	SF	FBG DV	OB		9 10	4700	1 10	12600	14400
25 5	WALKAROUND 250	HT	SF	FBG DV	IO	260-330	9 10	4700	1 10	15800	19400
25 5	WALKAROUND 250	HT	SF	FBG DV	SE	T OMC	9 10	4700	1 10	**	**
25 5	WALKAROUND 250	HT	SF	FBG DV	IO	T175-T205	9 10	4700	1 10	17000	19800
28	WALKAROUND 280	OP	CUD	FBG DV	OB		10 6	5400	1 10	18500	20500
28	WALKAROUND 280	OP	CUD	FBG DV	IO	260-330	10 6	5400	1 10	18000	21300
28	WALKAROUND 280	OP	CUD	FBG DV	SE	T OMC	10 6	5400	1 10	**	**
28	WALKAROUND 280	OP	CUD	FBG DV	IO	T175-T205	10 6	5400	1 10	19100	21900
				1986 BOATS							
17	PRO 17 SPORTSMAN	ST	CTRCN	FBG SV	OB		7 8	1490	8	2800	3250
17	PRO 17 SPORTSMAN	ST	CTRCN	FBG SV	SE	115 OMC	7 8	1490	8	2800	3250
17	PRO 17 SPORTSMAN	ST	CTRCN	FBG SV	OB	140	7 8	1490	8	2900	3400
20 1	PRO 20	ST	OPFSH	FBG SV	OB		7 8	1690	10	4200	4900
20 1	PRO 20	ST	OPFSH	FBG SV	SE	115 OMC	7 8	1690	10	4200	4900
20 6	PRO 21 CUDDY	ST	CUD	FBG SV	OB		8	2450	1 8	5650	6500
20 6	PRO 21 CUDDY	ST	CUD	FBG SV	SE	115-155	8	2450	1 8	5650	6500
20 6	PRO 21 CUDDY	ST	CUD	FBG SV	SE	170-190	8	2450	1 8	5650	6500
20 6	PRO 21 CUDDY	ST	CUD	FBG SV	SE	205 OMC	8	2450	1 8	5650	6500
20 6	PRO 21 CUDDY	ST	CUD	FBG SV	SE	205 OMC	8	2450	1 8	5200	6000
20 6	PRO 21 WALKAROUND	ST	CTRCN	FBG DV	OB	115-155	8	1930	1	4750	5450
20 6	PRO 21 WALKAROUND	ST	CTRCN	FBG DV	IO	170-190	8	2940	1	6050	7000
20 6	PRO 21 WALKAROUND	ST	CTRCN	FBG DV	SE	205 OMC	8	2940	1	5950	6850
20 6	PRO 21 WALKAROUND	ST	CTRCN	FBG DV	IO	205 OMC	8	2940	1	6100	7000
20 6	PRO 21 WALKAROUND	ST	CUD	FBG DV	OB		8	2350	1	5500	6350
20 6	PRO 21 WALKAROUND	ST	CUD	FBG DV	SE	115-155	8	2940	1	6150	7050
20 6	PRO 21 WALKAROUND	ST	CUD	FBG DV	IO	170-190	8	2940	1	5750	6650
20 6	PRO 21 WALKAROUND	ST	CUD	FBG DV	SE	205 OMC	8	2940	1	6150	7050
20 6	PRO 21 WALKAROUND	ST	CUD	FBG DV	IO	205 OMC	8	2940	1	5750	6650
23	PRO 23	ST	CTRCN	FBG DV	OB		8	2150	1 6	5700	6550
23	PRO 23	ST	CTRCN	FBG DV	SE	115-155	8	2430	1 8	6300	7250
23	PRO 23	ST	CTRCN	FBG DV	SE	170-190	8	2430	1 8	6300	7250
23	PRO 23	ST	CTRCN	FBG DV	SE	205 OMC	8	2430	1 8	6350	7250
23	PRO 23	ST	CTRCN	FBG DV	IO	205 OMC	8	2430	1 8	6300	7250
23	PRO 23 WALKAROUND	ST	CUD	FBG DV	OB		8	2470	1 8	6600	7550
23	PRO 23 WALKAROUND	ST	CUD	FBG DV	SE	115-155	8	2300	1 8	6200	7150
23	PRO 23 WALKAROUND	ST	CUD	FBG DV	IO	170-190	8	2300	1 8	6700	7150
23	PRO 23 WALKAROUND	ST	CUD	FBG DV	SE	205 OMC	8	2300	1 8	6200	7150
23	PRO 23 WALKAROUND	ST	CUD	FBG DV	IO	205 OMC	8	5850	1 8	5850	6700
28	PRO 28 WALKAROUND	ST	CUD	FBG DV	OB		10 6	5500		16100	18300
28	PRO 28 WALKAROUND	ST	CUD	FBG DV	IO	260	10 6	5500		14400	16300
28	PRO 28 WALKAROUND	ST	CUD	FBG DV	SE	T205 OMC	10 6	5500		16100	18300
28	PRO 28 WALKAROUND	ST	CUD	FBG DV	IO	T205 OMC	10 6	5500		15900	18000
				1985 BOATS							
17	PRO 17 SPORTSMAN	ST	CTRCN	FBG SV	OB		7 8	1490	8	2750	3150
20 1	PRO 20	ST	CTRCN	FBG SV	OB		7 8	1690	10	4050	4700
20 1	PRO 20 TWIN CONSOLE	ST	OPFSH	FBG SV	OB		7 8	1725	10	4150	4800
20 1	PRO 20A	ST	OPFSH	FBG SV	OB		7 8	1610	8	3900	4550
20 6	PRO 21 CUDDY	ST	CUD	FBG DV	OB		8	2450	1 8	5500	6300
20 6	PRO 21 WALKAROUND	ST	CTRCN	FBG DV	OB		8	1930	1	4600	5300
20 6	PRO 21 WALKAROUND	ST	CTRCN	FBG DV	IO	185 MRCR	8	2940	1	5850	6700
20 6	PRO 21 WALKAROUND	ST	CUD	FBG DV	OB		8	2350	1	5350	6150
20 6	PRO 21 WALKAROUND	ST	CUD	FBG DV	IO	140 MRCR	8	2940	1	5650	6300
23	PRO 23	ST	CTRCN	FBG DV	OB		8	2150	1 6	5550	6350
23	PRO 23	ST	CTRCN	FBG DV	IO	170 MRCR	8	2430	1 8	6050	6950
23	PRO 23 TWIN CONSOLE	ST	OPFSH	FBG DV	OB		8	2175	1 6	5700	6550
23	PRO 23 TWIN CONSOLE	ST	OPFSH	FBG DV	IO	170 MRCR	8	2720	1 6	6350	7350
23	PRO 23 TWIN CONSOLE	ST	OPFSH	FBG DV	IO	170 MRCR	8	2470	1 6	6400	7350
23	PRO 23 WALKAROUND	ST	CUD	FBG DV	IO	185 MRCR	8	2300	1 8	5600	6450
				1984 BOATS							
16 10	PRO 17	ST	CTRCN	FBG SV	OB		7 8	1410	8	2550	2950
16 10	PRO 17 TWIN CONSOLE	ST	OPFSH	FBG SV	OB		7 8	1430	8	2650	2950
17	PRO 17 SPORTSMAN	ST	CTRCN	FBG SV	OB		7 8	1490	8	2650	3100
20 1	PRO 20	ST	CTRCN	FBG SV	OB		7 8	1690	10	3950	4550
20 1	PRO 20	ST	CUD	FBG SV	OB		7 8	1780	10	4200	4850
20 1	PRO 20 TWIN CONSOLE	ST	OPFSH	FBG SV	OB		7 8	1725	10	4050	4700
20 6	PRO 21 WALKAROUND	ST	CTRCN	FBG DV	OB		8	1930	1	4500	5150
20 6	PRO 21 WALKAROUND	ST	CTRCN	FBG DV	IO	185 MRCR	8	2940	1	5650	6500
20 6	PRO 21 WALKAROUND	ST	CUD	FBG DV	OB		8	2350	1	5200	6000
20 6	PRO 21 WALKAROUND	ST	CUD	FBG DV	IO	140 MRCR	8	2940	1	5300	6100
23	PRO 23	ST	CUD	FBG DV	IO	115	8	1930	1	5000	5800
23	PRO 23	ST	CTRCN	FBG DV	OB		8	2150	1 6	5400	6200
23	PRO 23	ST	CTRCN	FBG DV	IO	170 MRCR	8	2430	1 8	5800	6700
23	PRO 23 TWIN CONSOLE	ST	OPFSH	FBG DV	OB		8	2175	1 6	5550	6350
23	PRO 23 TWIN CONSOLE	ST	OPFSH	FBG DV	IO	170 MRCR	8	2720	1 6	6150	7050
23	PRO 23 WALKAROUND	ST	CUD	FBG DV	OB		8	2470	1 6	6200	7150
23	PRO 23 WALKAROUND	ST	CUD	FBG DV	IO	140-185	8	2150	1 6	5250	6200

....For earlier years, see the BUC Used Boat Price Guide, Volume 3

PROCRAFT BOATS
DIV OF MARINE GROUP
SPRINGFIELD MO 65803

See inside cover to adjust price for area

For more recent years, see the BUC Used Boat Price Guide, Volume 1

LOA FT IN	NAME AND/ OR MODEL	TOP/ RIG	BOAT TYPE	-HULL- MTL TP	TP	----ENGINE--- # HP MFG	BEAM FT IN	WGT LBS	DRAFT FT IN	RETAIL LOW	RETAIL HIGH
				1995 BOATS							
16 10	170 PRO	OP	FSH	FBG DV	OB		7	1355		9100	10300
16 10	V-170C	OP	FSH	FBG DV	OB		7	1415		9450	10700
16 11	170CC	OP	FSH	FBG DV	OB		7 2	900		6350	7300
17 2	V-170B	OP	FSH	FBG DV	OB		6 10	1290		8800	10000
17 10	V-180B	OP	FSH	FBG DV	OB		7 3	1415		9650	10900
17 10	V-180C	OP	FSH	FBG DV	OB		7 3	1465		9850	11200
18 1	180 COMBO	OP	RNBT	FBG DV	OB		7 7	1720		11200	12700

LOA FT IN	NAME AND/ OR MODEL	TOP/ RIG	BOAT TYPE	-HULL- MTL TP	---ENGINE--- TP # HP MFG	BEAM FT IN	WGT LBS	DRAFT FT IN	RETAIL LOW	RETAIL HIGH
					1995 BOATS					
18 3	180 DUAL PRO	OP	FSH	FBG DV	OB	7 7	1630		10700	12200
18 3	180 PRO	OP	FSH	FBG DV	OB	7 7	1575		9800	11100
18 3	SUPER PRO 180	OP	FSH	FBG DV	OB	7 7	1575		10900	12400
19 2	190CC	OP	FSH	FBG DV	OB	7 4	1450		10200	11600
19 6	200 COMBO	OP	RNBT	FBG DV	OB	7 9	1900		12600	14300
19 6	210 DUAL PRO	OP	FSH	FBG DV	OB	7 9	1925		12600	14400
19 6	210 PRO	OP	FSH	FBG DV	OB	7 8	1900		12500	14300
19 8	V-200C	OP	FSH	FBG DV	OB	7	1355		9950	11300
20 1	SUPER PRO 200	OP	FSH	FBG DV	OB	7 7	1450		11100	12600
20 2	V-200B	OP	FSH	FBG DV	OB	7 7	1695		12500	14200
20 2	V-200DC	OP	FSH	FBG DV	OB	7 7	1715		12600	14300
20 6	210CC	OP	FSH	FBG DV	OB	8 6	1600		12100	13800
					1994 BOATS					
16 6	AP-1600	OP	FSH	FBG DV	OB	6 8	1155		7400	8500
16 10	PRO 170	OP	FSH	FBG DV	OB	7	1355		8550	9800
16 10	V-170C	OP	FSH	FBG DV	OB	7	1415		8950	10200
16 11	170CC	OP	FSH	FBG DV	OB	7 2	900		6000	6900
17 2	V-170B	OP	FSH	FBG DV	OB	6 10	1290		8250	9500
17 4	AP-1750	OP	FSH	FBG DV	OB	7 2	1390		8900	10100
17 4	AP-1760	OP	FSH	FBG DV	OB	7 2	1390		8900	10100
17 10	V-180B	OP	FSH	FBG DV	OB	7 3	1415		9150	10400
17 10	V-180C	OP	FSH	FBG DV	OB	7 3	1465		9350	10600
18 1	COMBO 180	OP	RNBT	FBG DV	OB	7 7	1720		10600	12000
18 3	DUAL 180	OP	FSH	FBG DV	OB	7 7	1630		10700	11600
18 3	PRO 180	OP	FSH	FBG DV	OB	7 7	1575		9300	10600
18 3	SUPER PRO 180	OP	FSH	FBG DV	OB	7 7	1575		10300	11700
19 2	190CC	OP	FSH	FBG DV	OB	7 4	1450		9700	11000
19 6	COMBO 200	OP	RNBT	FBG DV	OB	7 9	1900		11900	13500
19 6	DUAL 200	OP	FSH	FBG DV	OB	7 9	1825		11600	13200
19 6	PRO 200	OP	FSH	FBG DV	OB	7 8	1800		11500	13100
19 8	V-200C	OP	FSH	FBG DV	OB	7	1355		9450	10700
20 1	SUPER PRO 200	OP	FSH	FBG DV	OB	7 7	1450		10500	11900
20 2	V-200DC	OP	FSH	FBG DV	OB	7 7	1715		11900	13500
20 6	210CC	OP	FSH	FBG DV	OB	8 6	1600		11500	13100
					1993 BOATS					
16 10	COMBO 170	OP	RNBT	FBG DV	OB	7	1415		8550	9850
16 10	PRO 170	OP	FSH	FBG DV	OB	7	1355		8150	9350
17 2	V-170B	OP	FSH	FBG DV	OB	6 10	1290		7900	9050
17 4	1750PF	OP	FSH	FBG DV	OB	7 2	1390		8350	9600
17 10	V-180B	OP	FSH	FBG DV	OB	7 3	1415		8600	9850
17 10	V-180C	OP	FSH	FBG DV	OB	7 3	1465		8900	10100
18 1	COMBO 180	OP	RNBT	FBG DV	OB	7 7	1720		10100	11500
18 3	DUAL 180	OP	FSH	FBG DV	OB	7 7	1630		9700	11000
18 3	PRO 180	OP	FSH	FBG DV	OB	7 7	1575		9450	10700
19 6	COMBO 200	OP	RNBT	FBG DV	OB	7 9	1900		11300	12900
19 6	DUAL 200	OP	FSH	FBG DV	OB	7 9	1825		11000	12500
19 6	PRO 200	OP	FSH	FBG DV	OB	7 8	1800		10900	12400

PROFIL MARINE YACHT S P A
VIA PRIMO MAGGIO 27 ITALY   See inside cover to adjust price for area

CONTINENTAL CUSTOM YACHTS INC
POMPANO BEACH FL 33062

LOA FT IN	NAME AND/ OR MODEL	TOP/ RIG	BOAT TYPE	-HULL- MTL TP	----ENGINE--- TP # HP MFG	BEAM FT IN	WGT LBS	DRAFT FT IN	RETAIL LOW	RETAIL HIGH
					1984 BOATS					
49 5	CHEROKEE	OP	MY	FBG DV	IB T VLVO 13	9	24250	3 11	**	**
	**	**		IB T D PERK	** **		IB T220D FIAT		139500	153000
	IB T235D VLVO 139000	152500,	IB T270D FIAT	143500 158000,	IB T300D CAT		148500 163000			
	IB T300D CUM 145000	159500,	IB T350D IF	148500 163000,	IB T350E IF		152500 167500			
	IB T355D CAT 154500	170000,	IB T400D IF	159000 174500,	IB T500D CUM		172500 189500			

PROFILE CUSTOM POWERBOATS
RICHLAND CENTER WI 53581   See inside cover to adjust price for area

For more recent years, see the BUC Used Boat Price Guide, Volume 1

LOA FT IN	NAME AND/ OR MODEL	TOP/ RIG	BOAT TYPE	-HULL- MTL TP	----ENGINE--- TP # HP MFG	BEAM FT IN	WGT LBS	DRAFT FT IN	RETAIL LOW	RETAIL HIGH
					1993 BOATS					
25 6	PROFILE 26	OP	OFF	FBG DV	IO	7	3500	1 6	**	**
29 2	PROFILE 29	OP	OFF	FBG DV	IO	8	4450	1 10	**	**
30 8	PROFILE 31	OP	OFF	FBG DV	IO	8	6500	1 10	**	**
35	PROFILE 35	OP	OFF	FBG DV	IO	10 2	7500		**	**

PROGRESSION INDUSTRIES INC
COPIAGUE NY 11726   See inside cover to adjust price for area

LOA FT IN	NAME AND/ OR MODEL	TOP/ RIG	BOAT TYPE	-HULL- MTL TP	----ENGINE--- TP # HP MFG	BEAM FT IN	WGT LBS	DRAFT FT IN	RETAIL LOW	RETAIL HIGH
					1994 BOATS					
21 9	PROGRESSION 22	OP	OFF	F/S DV	OB	7 8	1250	2 3	11800	13400
21 9	PROGRESSION 22	OP	OFF	F/S DV	IO 250 MRCR	7 8	2550	2 5	13200	15000
21 9	PROGRESSION 22	OP	OFF	F/S DV	IO 350 MRCR	7 8	2750	2 5	17200	19500
21 9	REFLECTION 22	OP	OFF	F/S DV	OB	7 8	1250	2 3	11800	13400
21 9	REFLECTION 22	OP	OFF	F/S DV	IO 250 MRCR	7 8	1250	2 3	11400	12900
21 9	REFLECTION 22	OP	OFF	F/S DV	IO 350 MRCR	7 8	1250	2 3	14600	16600
23 7	PROGRESSION 237	OP	OFF	F/S DV	OB	7 9	1650	2 6	15700	18800
23 7	PROGRESSION 237	OP	OFF	F/S DV	IO 250 MRCR	7 9	3000	2 8	16300	18500
23 7	PROGRESSION 237	OP	OFF	F/S DV	IO 350 MRCR	7 9	3200	2 8	20400	22600
23 7	REFLECTION 237	OP	OFF	F/S DV	OB	7 9	1650	2 6	15700	17800
23 7	REFLECTION 237	OP	OFF	F/S DV	IO 250 MRCR	7 9	3000	2 8	16300	18500
23 7	REFLECTION 237	OP	OFF	F/S DV	IO 350 MRCR	7 9	3200	2 8	20400	22600
24	PROGRESSION 24	OP	OFF	F/S DV	OB	8	2575	2 6	23700	27200
24	PROGRESSION 24	OP	OFF	F/S DV	IO 350 MRCR	8	4025	2 6	23800	26500
27	PROGRESSION 27SC	OP	OFF	F/S DV	IO	8 2	2325	2	42400	47100
27	PROGRESSION 27SC	OP	OFF	F/S DV	IO 350 MRCR	8 2	3620	2	27300	30300
27	PROGRESSION 27SC	OP	OFF	F/S DV	IO T250 MRCR	8 2	4546	2 2	31700	35200
27	PROGRESSION 27SC	OP	OFF	F/S DV	IO T350 MRCR	8 2	4876	2 4	38300	42600
28 10	PROGRESSION 29	OP	OFF	F/S DV	OB	8 3	3500	2 6	52000	57200
28 10	PROGRESSION 29	OP	OFF	F/S DV	IO 445 MRCR	8 3	4300	2	40400	44900
28 10	PROGRESSION 29	OP	OFF	F/S DV	IO T350 MRCR	8 3	5600	2 8	47900	52700
					1993 BOATS					
20 10	PROGRESSION 21	OP	OFF	F/S DV	OB	7 8	1150	2	10300	11700
21 9	PROGRESSION 22	OP	OFF	F/S DV	OB	7 8	1250	2 3	11300	12800
21 9	PROGRESSION 22	OP	OFF	F/S DV	IO 250 MRCR	7 8	2550	2 5	12300	14000
21 9	PROGRESSION 22	OP	OFF	F/S DV	IO 350 MRCR	7 8	2750	2 5	16000	18200
23 7	PROGRESSION 237	OP	OFF	F/S DV	OB	7 9	1650	2 6	15000	18000
23 7	PROGRESSION 237	OP	OFF	F/S DV	IO 250 MRCR	7 9	3000	2 8	14900	16900
23 7	PROGRESSION 237	OP	OFF	F/S DV	IO 350 MRCR	7 9	3200	2 8	19000	21100
24	PROGRESSION 24	OP	OFF	F/S DV	OB	8	2575	2 6	22600	26000
24	PROGRESSION 24	OP	OFF	F/S DV	IO 350 MRCR	8	4025	2 6	22300	24700
24	PROGRESSION 24	OP	OFF	F/S DV	IO T250 MRCR	8	4800	2 8	25700	28500
27	PROGRESSION 27SC	OP	OFF	F/S DV	IO	8 2	2325	2	40600	45100
27	PROGRESSION 27SC	OP	OFF	F/S DV	IO T350 MRCR	8 2	3620	2	25500	28300
27	PROGRESSION 27SC	OP	OFF	F/S DV	IO T250 MRCR	8 2	4546	2 2	29600	32900
27	PROGRESSION 27SC	OP	OFF	F/S DV	IO T350 MRCR	8 2	4876	2 4	35400	39400
28 10	PROGRESSION 29	OP	OFF	F/S DV	OB	8 3	3500	2 6	49800	54800
28 10	PROGRESSION 29	OP	OFF	F/S DV	IO T350-T445	8 3	5600	2 8	44200	54300
					1992 BOATS					
21 9	PROGRESSION 22	OP	OFF	F/S DV	OB	7 8	1250	2 3	10800	12300
21 9	PROGRESSION 22	OP	OFF	F/S DV	IO 250 MRCR	7 8	2550	2 5	11500	13100
21 9	PROGRESSION 22	OP	OFF	F/S DV	IO 350 MRCR	7 8	2750	2 5	14800	16900
23 7	PROGRESSION 237	OP	OFF	F/S DV	OB	7 9	1650	2 6	14300	17200
23 7	PROGRESSION 237	OP	OFF	F/S DV	IO 250 MRCR	7 9	3000	2 8	13800	15700
23 7	PROGRESSION 237	OP	OFF	F/S DV	IO 350 MRCR	7 9	3200	2 8	17400	19700
24	PROGRESSION 24	OP	OFF	F/S DV	OB	8	2575	2 6	21700	24900
24	PROGRESSION 24	OP	OFF	F/S DV	IO 350 MRCR	8	4025	2 6	20800	23100
24	PROGRESSION 24	OP	OFF	F/S DV	IO T250 MRCR	8	4800	2 8	24000	26700
27	PROGRESSION 27SC	OP	OFF	F/S DV	IO	8 2	2325	2	38800	43200
27	PROGRESSION 27SC	OP	OFF	F/S DV	IO 350 MRCR	8 2	3620	2	23800	26500
27	PROGRESSION 27SC	OP	OFF	F/S DV	IO T250 MRCR	8 2	4546	2 2	27700	30700
27	PROGRESSION 27SC	OP	OFF	F/S DV	IO T350 MRCR	8 2	4876	2 4	33100	36800
28 10	PROGRESSION 29	OP	OFF	F/S DV	IO	8 3	3500	2 6	47800	52600
28 10	PROGRESSION 29	OP	OFF	F/S DV	IO T250 MRCR	8 3	5300	2 9	35800	39700
28 10	PROGRESSION 29	OP	OFF	F/S DV	IO T350-T445	8 3	5600	2 8	41400	50800
					1991 BOATS					
21 9	PROGRESSION 22	OP	OFF	F/S DV	OB	7 8	1250	2 3	10400	11800
21 9	PROGRESSION 22	OP	OFF	F/S DV	IO 270 MRCR	7 8	2550	2 5	11100	12600
21 9	PROGRESSION 22	OP	OFF	F/S DV	IO 360 MRCR	7 8	2750	2 5	14300	16300
23 7	PROGRESSION 237	OP	OFF	F/S DV	OB	7 9	1650	2 6	13300	15600
23 7	PROGRESSION 237	OP	OFF	F/S DV	IO 270 MRCR	7 9	3000	2 8	13200	15000
23 7	PROGRESSION 237	OP	OFF	F/S DV	IO 360 MRCR	7 9	3200	2 8	16700	19000
24	PROGRESSION 24	OP	OFF	F/S DV	OB	8	2575	2 6	20800	23800
24	PROGRESSION 24	OP	OFF	F/S DV	IO 360 MRCR	8	4025	2 6	19900	22100
24	PROGRESSION 24	OP	OFF	F/S DV	IO T270 MRCR	8	4800	2 8	23100	25600
27	PROGRESSION 27SC	OP	OFF	F/S DV	OB	8 2			37300	41400

LOA FT	LOA IN	NAME AND/ OR MODEL	TOP/ RIG	BOAT TYPE	-HULL- MTL	-HULL- TP	TP	ENGINE # HP	ENGINE MFG	BEAM FT	BEAM IN	WGT LBS	DRAFT FT	DRAFT IN	RETAIL LOW	RETAIL HIGH
		1991 BOATS														
27		PROGRESSION 27SC	OP	OFF	F/S	DV	IO	360-410		8	2				24000	28800
27		PROGRESSION 27SC	OP	OFF	F/S	DV	IO	T270	MRCR	8	2				26200	29100
27		PROGRESSION 27SC	OP	OFF	F/S	DV	IO	T360	MRCR	8	2				30600	34100
28	10	PROGRESSION 29	OP	OFF	F/S	DV	OB			8	3	3500	2	6	46300	50800
28	10	PROGRESSION 29	OP	OFF	F/S	DV	IO	T270	MRCR	8	3	5300	2	9	34200	38000
28	10	PROGRESSION 29	OP	OFF	F/S	DV	IO	T360-T410		8	3	5600	2	8	39100	47100
		1990 BOATS														
21	9	PROGRESSION 22	OP	OFF	F/S	DV	OB			7	8	1650			12700	14400
21	9	PROGRESSION 22	OP	OFF	F/S	DV	IO	270	MRCR	7	8	2550			10400	11800
21	9	PROGRESSION 22	OP	OFF	F/S	DV	IO	365	MRCR	7	8	2750			13400	15200
23	7	PROGRESSION 237	OP	OFF	F/S	DV	OB			7	9	1650	2	6	13200	15000
23	7	PROGRESSION 237	OP	OFF	F/S	DV	IO	270-300		7	9	3000	2	6	12400	14100
23	7	PROGRESSION 237	OP	OFF	F/S	DV	IO	365	MRCR	7	9	3200	2	6	15500	17700
24		PROGRESSION 24	OP	OFF	F/S	DV	OB			8					17100	19400
24		PROGRESSION 24	OP	OFF	F/S	DV	IO		MRCR	8					**	**
		IO 300 MRCR 14400 16400, IO 365 MRCR 16600 18900, IO T270 MRCR 16900 19200														
28	10	PROGRESSION 29	OP	OFF	F/S	DV	OB			8	3	3095			44100	49000
28	10	PROGRESSION 29	OP	OFF	F/S	DV	IO	T	MRCR	8	3	3095			**	**
28	10	PROGRESSION 29	OP	OFF	F/S	DV	IO	T270-T365		8	3	3095			30100	37100
		1989 BOATS														
23	7	PROGRESSION 237	OP	OFF	F/S	DV	OB			7	9	1650	2	6	12700	14500
23	7	PROGRESSION 237	OP	OFF	F/S	DV	IO		MRCR	7	9	2800			**	**
23	7	PROGRESSION 237	OP	OFF	F/S	DV	IO	270	MRCR	7	9	3000	2	6	11700	13200
23	7	PROGRESSION 237	OP	OFF	F/S	DV	IO	365	MRCR	7	9	3200	2	6	14800	16800
24		INSTIGATOR	OP	OFF	F/S	DV	OB			8		2575	2	6	17600	20000
24		INSTIGATOR	OP	OFF	F/S	DV	IO		MRCR	8		2575	2	6	**	**
24		INSTIGATOR	OP	OFF	F/S	DV	IO	365	MRCR	8		2575	2	6	12500	14200
24		INSTIGATOR SE	OP	OFF	F/S	DV	OB			8		2575	2	6	22000	24400
24		INSTIGATOR SE	OP	OFF	F/S	DV	IO		MRCR	8		2575	2	6	**	**
		IO 270 MRCR 11100 12600, IO 365 MRCR 14800 16800, IO T270 MRCR 13700 15600														
24		INSTIGATOR XL	OP	OFF	F/S	DV	OB			8		2575	2	6	18300	20300
24		INSTIGATOR XLSE	OP	OFF	F/S	DV	OB			8		2575	2	6	19400	21600
24		PROGRESSION 24	OP	OFF	F/S	DV	IO		MRCR	8		3450			**	**
24		PROGRESSION 24	OP	OFF	F/S	DV	IO	270	MRCR	8		3450			13100	14800
28	10	INTENSE 29	OP	OFF	F/S	DV	OB			8	3	4200	2	9	42400	47100
28	10	INTENSE 29	OP	OFF	F/S	DV	IO	T	MRCR	8	3	5500	2	9	**	**
28	10	INTENSE 29	OP	OFF	F/S	DV	IO	T270	MRCR	8	3	5500	2	9	28400	31600
28	10	INTENSE 29	OP	OFF	F/S	DV	IO	T365	MRCR	8	3	5500	2	9	32100	35700
28	10	INTENSE 29 SE	OP	OFF	F/S	DV	OB			8	3	5500	2	9	46100	50700
28	10	INTENSE 29 SE	OP	OFF	F/S	DV	IO	T	MRCR	8	3	5500	2	9	**	**
28	10	INTENSE 29 SE	OP	OFF	F/S	DV	IO	T270-T365		8	3	5500	2	9	32400	40400
28	10	PROGRESSION 29	OP	OFF	F/S	DV	OB			8	3	4200			42400	47100
28	10	PROGRESSION 29	OP	OFF	F/S	DV	IO	T	MRCR	8	3				**	**
28	10	PROGRESSION 29	OP	OFF	F/S	DV	IO	T270	MRCR	8	3				29400	32700
28	10	PROGRESSION 29	OP	OFF	F/S	DV	IO	T365	MRCR	8	3				33300	37000
31		PROGRESSION 31	OP	OFF	F/S	DV	IO	T270-T365		8	3				39100	47300
		1988 BOATS														
23	7	PROGRESSION 237	OP	OFF	F/S	DV	OB			7	9	1650			12300	14000
23	7	PROGRESSION 237	OP	OFF	F/S	DV	IO	270	MRCR	7	9	3000			11000	12500
23	7	PROGRESSION 237	OP	OFF	F/S	DV	IO	320-330		7	9	3200			12300	14300
23	7	PROGRESSION 237	OP	OFF	F/S	DV	IO	365	MRCR	7	9	3200			13700	15600
24		INSTIGATOR	OP	OFF	F/S	DV	OB			8		2250			14700	16700
24		INSTIGATOR	OP	OFF	F/S	DV	IO	330	MRCR	8		3450			12400	14100
24		INSTIGATOR	OP	OFF	F/S	DV	IO	365-420		8		3450			14900	18200
24		INSTIGATOR	OP	OFF	F/S	DV	IO	T270	MRCR	8		3450			14100	16100
24		INSTIGATOR SE	OP	OFF	F/S	DV	OB			8		2250			17500	19900
24		INSTIGATOR SE	OP	OFF	F/S	DV	IO	270	MRCR	8		3450			12300	14000
		IO 330-365 14800 16900, IO 420 MRCR 19100 21200, IO T270 MRCR 16300 18500														
24		INSTIGATOR XL	OP	OFF	F/S	DV	OB			8		2250			14700	16800
24		INSTIGATOR XL SE	OP	OFF	F/S	DV	OB			8		2250			15300	17400
28	10	INTENSE 29	OP	OFF	F/S	DV	OB			8	3	4200			37900	42100
28	10	INTENSE 29	OP	OFF	F/S	DV	IO	T		8	3				**	**
28	10	INTENSE 29	OP	OFF	F/S	DV	IO	T270-T330		8	3	4200			25500	30700
28	10	INTENSE 29	OP	OFF	F/S	DV	IO	T365-T420		8	3	4200			29200	34800
28	10	INTENSE 29 SE	OP	OFF	F/S	DV	OB			8	3	4200			43900	48800
28	10	INTENSE 29 SE	OP	OFF	F/S	DV	IO	T270-T330		8	3	4200			29100	34900
28	10	INTENSE 29 SE	OP	OFF	F/S	DV	IO	T365-T420		8	3	4200			33000	40400
31		PROGRESSION 31	OP	OFF	F/S	DV	IO	T275-T365		8	3				37200	44200
		1987 BOATS														
28	10	INTENSE 29	OP	OFF	F/S	DV	OB			8	3	4200			39500	43900
28	10	INTENSE 29	OP	OFF	F/S	DV	IO	365-420		8	3	4200			23700	27900
28	10	INTENSE 29	OP	OFF	F/S	DV	IO	T370-T420		8	3	4200			29700	35700
31		PROGRESSION 31	OP	OFF	F/S	DV	IO	T270-T365		8	3				34800	42100

PROUT CATAMARANS LTD

CANVEY ISLAND ESSEX ENG COAST GUARD MFG ID- PRV See inside cover to adjust price for area

For more recent years, see the BUC Used Boat Price Guide, Volume 1

LOA FT	LOA IN	NAME AND/ OR MODEL	TOP/ RIG	BOAT TYPE	-HULL- MTL	-HULL- TP	TP	ENGINE # HP	ENGINE MFG	BEAM FT	BEAM IN	WGT LBS	DRAFT FT	DRAFT IN	RETAIL LOW	RETAIL HIGH
		1996 BOATS														
34		PROUT 34	CUT	SACAC	FBG	CT	IB	20D	VLVO	15	7	9900	2	8	108500	119500
34		PROUT 34 EXCEL	CUT	SACAC	FBG	CT	IB	T 10D	VLVO	15	7	9900	2	8	108500	119500
37		PROUT 37	CUT	SACAC	FBG	CT	IB	30D	VLVO	16	3	12100	2	10	145000	159500
37		PROUT 37 EXCEL	CUT	SACAC	FBG	CT	IB	T 20D	VLVO	16	3	12100	2	10	145000	159500
39		PROUT 39 CHARTER	CUT	SACAC	FBG	CT	IB	T 20D	VLVO	18	3	17000	3	2	188500	207500
39		PROUT 39 FAMILY	CUT	SACAC	FBG	CT	IB	T 20D	VLVO	18	3	17000	3	2	181000	199000
39		PROUT 39 MASTER	CUT	SACAC	FBG	CT	IB	T 20D	VLVO	18	3	17000	3	2	188500	207500
39		PROUT 39 OPEN	CUT	SACAC	FBG	CT	IB	T 20D	VLVO	18	3	17000	3	2	175000	192000
43	3	PANTHER 44		MY	FBG	CT	IB	T320D		16		22000	3		183500	202000
45		PROUT 45 CHARTER	CUT	SACAC	FBG	CT	IB	T 30D	VLVO	20	10	22550	3	5	276500	304000
45		PROUT 45 FAMILY	CUT	SACAC	FBG	CT	IB	T 30D	VLVO	20	10	22550	3	5	268000	294500
45		PROUT 45 MASTER	CUT	SACAC	FBG	CT	IB	T 30D	VLVO	20	10	22550	3	5	276500	304000
45		PROUT 45 OPEN	CUT	SACAC	FBG	CT	IB	T 30D	VLVO	20	10	22550	3	5	260000	286000
49	11	PROUT 50	CUT	SACAC	FBG	CT	IB	T 40D	VLVO	23	5	26520	3	7	446500	490500
49	11	PROUT 50 DAY CHARTER	CUT	SACAC	FBG	CT	IB	T 40D	VLVO	23	5	26520	3	7	349500	384000
61	3	PANTHER 61		MY	FBG	CT	IB	T820D	MAN	21	11	52000	3		584000	642000
61	3	PANTHER 61		MY	FBG	CT	IB	T11CD	MTU	21	11	52000	3		710000	780000
70		PANTHER 70		MY	FBG	CT	IB	T12CD	MAN	21	11	64000	3		1.035M	1.125M
70		PANTHER 70		MY	FBG	CT	IB	T13CD	MTU	21	11	64000	3		1.195M	1.300M
		1995 BOATS														
25	11	SIROCCO 26	SLP	SACAC	FBG	CT	IB	15D	VLVO	12	9	5291	2	4	38200	42500
34		PROUT 34	CUT	SACAC	FBG	CT	IB	18D	VLVO	15	3	8800	2	6	98900	108500
37		PROUT 37	CUT	SACAC	FBG	CT	IB	27D	VLVO	16	3	11500	2	8	134500	148000
39		PROUT 39 CHARTER	CUT	SACAC	FBG	CT	IB	18D	VLVO	18	5	15646	3	2	168500	185500
39		PROUT 39 FAMILY	CUT	SACAC	FBG	CT	IB	18D	VLVO	18	5	15646	3	2	166000	182000
39		PROUT 39 MASTER	CUT	SACAC	FBG	CT	IB	18D	VLVO	18	5	15646	3	2	171500	188500
43	3	PANTHER 44		MY	FBG	CT	IB	T300D	SABR	16		18000	3		150500	165000
45		PROUT 45	CUT	SACAC	FBG	CT	IB	D		20	3	15679	3	1	235500	258500
50		PROUT 50	CUT	SACAC	FBG	CT	IB	T 27D	YAN	23	6	20000	3	4	374500	412000
		1994 BOATS														
25	11	SIROCCO 26	SLP	SACAC	FBG	CT	IB	15D	VLVO	12	9	5291	2	4	36000	39900
34		EVENT 34	CUT	SACAC	FBG	CT	IB	18D	VLVO	15	3	8000	2	6	90700	99600
37		SNOWGOOSE 37 ELITE	CUT	SACAC	FBG	CT	IB	27D	VLVO	16	3	11500	2	8	126500	139000
39		ESCALE 39 CHARTER	CUT	SACAC	FBG	CT	IB	18D	VLVO	18	5	14000	3	2	154000	169000
39		ESCALE 39 FAMILY	CUT	SACAC	FBG	CT	IB	18D	VLVO	18	5	14000	3	2	151500	166500
39		ESCALE 39 MASTER	CUT	SACAC	FBG	CT	IB	18D	VLVO	18	5	14000	3	2	156500	172000
42		ENCORE 43	CUT	SACAC	FBG	CT	IB	D		20	3	15679	3	1	194000	213000
43	3	PANTHER 44		MY	FBG	CT	IB	T300D	SABR	16		18000	3		144000	158500
50		QUASAR 50 ESPACE	CUT	SACAC	FBG	CT	IB	T 27D	YAN	23	6	20000	3	4	352500	387500
		1993 BOATS														
25	11	SIROCCO 26	SLP	SACAC	FBG	CT	IB	15D	YAN	12	9	5291	2	4	33800	37600
34		EVENT 34	CUT	SACAC	FBG	CT	IB	18D	YAN	15	3	8000	2	6	85300	93700
37		SNOWGOOSE 37 ELITE	CUT	SACAC	FBG	CT	IB	27D	YAN	16	3	11500	2	8	119000	131000
39		ESCALE 39 CHARTER	CUT	SACAC	FBG	CT	IB	18D	YAN	18	5	14000	3	2	145000	159000
39		ESCALE 39 FAMILY	CUT	SACAC	FBG	CT	IB	18D	YAN	18	5	14000	3	2	142500	156500
39		ESCALE 39 MASTER	CUT	SACAC	FBG	CT	IB	18D	YAN	18	5	14000	3	2	147500	162000
42		ENCORE 43	CUT	SACAC	FBG	CT	IB	D		20	3	15679	3	1	182500	200500
43	3	PANTHER 44		MY	FBG	CT	IB	T300D	SABR	16		18000	3		138000	151500
50		QUASAR 50 ESPACE	CUT	SACAC	FBG	CT	IB	T 27D	YAN	23	6	20000	3	4	331500	364500
		1992 BOATS														
25	11	SIROCCO 26	SLP	SA/CR	FBG	CT	IB	15D	YAN	12	9	5291	2	4	31800	35300
33		QUEST 33 CS	CUT	SA/CR	FBG	CT	IB	18D	YAN	14	4	8377	2	6	80000	88000
33		QUEST 33 SPORT	CUT	SA/CR	FBG	CT	IB	18D	YAN	14	4	8377	2	6	69800	76800
34		EVENT 34	CUT	SA/CR	FBG	CT	IB	18D	YAN	15	3	8000	2	6	80200	88200
37		SNOWGOOSE 37 ELITE	CUT	SA/CR	FBG	CT	IB	27D	YAN	16	3	11500	2	8	112000	123000
39		ESCALE 39 CHARTER	CUT	SA/CR	FBG	CT	IB	18D	YAN	18	5	14000	3	2	136000	149500
39		ESCALE 39 FAMILY	CUT	SA/CR	FBG	CT	IB	18D	YAN	18	5	14000	3	2	134000	147000
39		ESCALE 39 MASTER	CUT	SA/CR	FBG	CT	IB	18D	YAN	18	5	14000	3	2	138500	152000
42		ENCORE 43	CUT	SA/CR	FBG	CT	IB	D		20	3	15679	3	1	171500	188500
43	3	PANTHER 44		MY	FBG	CT	IB	T300D	SABR	16		18000	3		131500	144500
50		QUASAR 50 ESPACE	CUT	SA/CR	FBG	CT	IB	T 27D	YAN	23	6	20000	3	4	312000	342500
		1991 BOATS														
25	11	SIROCCO 26	SLP	SA/CR	FBG	CT	IB	15D	YAN	12	9	5000	2	4	29500	32700
26		SCAMPER 26	SLP	SA/OD	FBG	CT	IB	18D	YAN	14	3	1984	1	8	23200	25800
33		QUEST 33 CS	CUT	SA/CR	FBG	CT	IB	18D	YAN	14	3	7500	2	7	68400	75200
34		EVENT 34	CUT	SA/CR	FBG	CT	IB	18D	YAN	15	8	8000	2	6	75500	82900
37		SNOWGOOSE 37 ELITE	CUT	SA/CR	FBG	CT	IB	27D	YAN	16	3	9600	2	8	100500	110500
39		ESCALE 39	CUT	SA/CR	FBG	CT	IB	35D	YAN	18	5	12000	3	2	123000	135000

 CONTINUED ON NEXT PAGE

LOA FT	LOA IN	NAME AND/ OR MODEL	TOP/ RIG	BOAT TYPE	-HULL- MTL	-HULL- TP	TP	ENGINE # HP	ENGINE MFG	BEAM FT	BEAM IN	WGT LBS	DRAFT FT	DRAFT IN	RETAIL LOW	RETAIL HIGH
		1991 BOATS														
43	3	PANTHER 44		MY	FBG	CT	IB	T300D	SABR	16		18000	3		125000	137500
50		QUASAR 50 ESPACE	CUT	SA/CR	FBG	CT	IB	T 27D	YAN	24		20000	3		293500	322500
		1990 BOATS														
25	11	SIROCCO 26	SLP	SA/CR	FBG	CT	IB	15D	YAN	12	9	5000	2	4	27700	30800
26		SCAMPER 26	SLP	SA/OD	FBG	CT	OB			14	3	1984	1	8	21800	24200
33		QUEST 33 CS	CUT	SA/CR	FBG	CT	IB	18D	YAN	14	3	7500	2	7	64400	70700
34		EVENT 34	CUT	SA/CR	FBG	CT	IB	18D	YAN	15	3	8000	2	6	71000	78000
37		SNOWGOOSE 37 ELITE	CUT	SA/CR	FBG	CT	IB	27D	YAN	16	4	9600	2	8	94500	104000
43	3	PANTHER 44		MY	FBG	CT	IB	T300D	SABR	16		18000	3		119500	131500
50		QUASAR 50 ESPACE	CUT	SA/CR	FBG	CT	IB	T 27D	YAN	24		20000	3		276000	303000
		1989 BOATS														
25	11	SIROCCO 26	SLP	SA/CR	FBG	CT	IB	15D	YAN	12	9	5000	2	4	26100	29000
26		SCAMPER 26	SLP	SA/OD	FBG	CT	OB			14	3	1984	1	8	20500	22800
33		QUEST 33 CS	CUT	SA/CR	FBG	CT	IB	18D	YAN	14	3	7500	2	7	60500	66500
34		EVENT 34	CUT	SA/CR	FBG	CT	IB	18D	YAN	15	3	8000	2	6	66800	73400
37		SNOWGOOSE 37 ELITE	CUT	SA/CR	FBG	CT	IB	27D	YAN	15	3	9600	2	8	88900	97700
43	3	PANTHER 44		MY	FBG	CT	IB	T300D	SABR	16		18000	3		114000	125500
50		QUASAR 50 ESPACE	CUT	SA/CR	FBG	CT	IB	T 27D	YAN	24		20000	3		259500	285000
		1988 BOATS														
25	11	SIROCCO 26	SLP	SA/CR	FBG	CT	IB	15D	YAN	12	9	5000	2	4	24500	27200
26		SCAMPER 26	SLP	SA/OD	FBG	CT	OB			14	3	1984	1	8	19300	21400
33		QUEST 33 CS	CUT	SA/CR	FBG	CT	IB	18D	YAN	14	3	7500	2	7	56900	62600
37		SNOWGOOSE 37 ELITE	CUT	SA/CR	FBG	CT	IB	27D	YAN	15	3	9600	2	8	83600	91900
43	3	PANTHER 44		MY	FBG	CT	IB	T300D	SABR	16		18000	3		109000	119500
50		QUASAR 50 S2	CUT	SA/CR	FBG	CT	IB	T 23D	YAN	20		20000	3		244000	260000
		1987 BOATS														
25	11	SIROCCO 26	SLP	SA/CR	FBG	CT	IB	15D	YAN	12	9	5000	2	4	23000	25600
26		SCAMPER 26	SLP	SA/OD	FBG	CT	OB			14	3	1984	1	8	18300	20300
31		QUEST 31 PH	CUT	MS	FBG	CT	IB	T 15D	YAN	14	3	9620	2	7	48400	53200
31		QUEST 33 CS	CUT	SA/CR	FBG	CT	IB	18D	YAN	14	3	9520	2	7	48300	53000
33		QUEST 33 CS	CUT	SA/CR	FBG	CT	IB	18D	YAN	14	3	7500	2	7	53600	58900
37		SNOWGOOSE 37 ELITE	CUT	SA/CR	FBG	CT	IB	27D	YAN	15	3	9600	2	8	78600	86400
37		SNOWGOOSE 37 PH	CUT	MS	FBG	CT	IB	T 27D	YAN	15	3	9600	2	8	78600	86400
43	3	PANTHER 44		MY	FBG	CT	IB	T330D	SABR	16		18000	3		106500	117000
49	6	QUASAR 50	CUT	SA/CR	FBG	CT	IB	T 23D	YAN	20		20000	3		224000	246500
		1986 BOATS														
25	11	SIROCCO 26	SLP	SA/CR	FBG	CT	IB	15D	YAN	12	9	5000	2	4	21700	24100
26		SCAMPER 26	SLP	SA/OD	FBG	CT	OB			14	3	1984	1	8	16800	19100
31		QUEST 31	CUT	SA/CR	FBG	CT	IB	15D	YAN	14	3	7300	2	7	42000	46700
31		QUEST 31 PH	CUT	MS	FBG	CT	IB	T 35D	YAN	14	3	7300	2	7	42000	46700
33		QUEST 33 CS	CUT	SA/CR	FBG	CT	IB	15D	YAN	14	3	7500	2	7	50400	55400
37		SNOWGOOSE 37	CUT	SA/CR	FBG	CT	IB	23D	YAN	15	3	9600	2	8	74000	81300
37		SNOWGOOSE 37 PH	CUT	MS	FBG	CT	IB	T 35D	YAN	15	3	9600	2	8	74000	81300
40		PANTHER 40		MS	FBG	CT	IB	600D	SABR	16		20203	2	3	111500	122500
49	6	QUASAR 50	CUT	SA/CR	FBG	CT	IB	T 23D	YAN	20		20000	3		211000	231500
		1985 BOATS														
25	11	SIROCCO 26	SLP	SA/CR	FBG	CT	IB	15D	YAN	12	9	5000	2	4	20400	22700
26		SCAMPER 26	SLP	SA/OD	FBG	CT	OB			14	3	1984	1	8	15700	17900
33		QUEST 33 CS	CUT	SA/CR	FBG	CT	IB	15D	YAN	14	3	7500	2	7	47600	52400
37		SNOWGOOSE 37	CUT	SA/CR	FBG	CT	IB	23D	YAN	15	3	9600	2	8	69600	76400
37		SNOWGOOSE 37 PH	CUT	MS	FBG	CT	IB	T 36D	VW	15	3	9600	2	8	69600	76400
49	6	QUASAR 50	CUT	SA/CR	FBG	CT	IB	T 23D	YAN	20		20000	3		198500	218000
		1984 BOATS														
25	11	SIROCCO 26	SLP	SA/CR	FBG	CT	IB	15D	YAN	12	9	5000	2	4	19200	21300
31		QUEST 31	CUT	SA/CR	FBG	CT	IB	15D	YAN	14	3	7300	2	7	37200	41300
31		QUEST 31 PH	CUT	MS	FBG	CT	IB	T 36D	VW	14	3	7300	2	7	37200	41300
33		QUEST 33 CS	CUT	SA/CR	FBG	CT	IB	15D	YAN	14	3	7500	2	7	44300	49300
37		SNOWGOOSE 37	CUT	SA/CR	FBG	CT	IB	22D	YAN	15	3	9600	2	8	65400	71900
37		SNOWGOOSE 37 PH	CUT	MS	FBG	CT	IB	T 36D	VW	15	3	9600	2	8	65400	71900
49	6	QUASAR 50	CUT	SA/CR	FBG	CT	IB	T 22D	YAN	20		20000	3		186500	205000

....For earlier years, see the BUC Used Boat Price Guide, Volume 3

PT PERFORMANCE MOTOR YACHTS

MARINE YACHT SALES INC
SEAPORT YACHTS INC
LAUREL HOLLOW NY 11791

See inside cover to adjust price for area

LOA FT	LOA IN	NAME AND/ OR MODEL	TOP/ RIG	BOAT TYPE	-HULL- MTL	-HULL- TP	TP	ENGINE # HP	ENGINE MFG	BEAM FT	BEAM IN	WGT LBS	DRAFT FT	DRAFT IN	RETAIL LOW	RETAIL HIGH
		1989 BOATS														
35	4	PT35 SEDAN	FB	MY	FBG	DV	IB	T150D	CUM	12	6	19000	3		91600	100500
35	4	PT35 SUNDECK	FB	MY	FBG	DV	IB	T150D	CUM	12	6	19000	3		91600	100500
		IB T210D CUM 96300 106000, IB T250D CUM 100000 110000, IB T300D CUM													100500	110500
36		PT36 SPORTFISHERMAN	FB	MY	FBG	DV	IB	T250D	CUM	12	6	21000	3	3	106000	116500
36		PT36 SPORTFISHERMAN	FB	MY	FBG	DV	IB	T300D	CUM	12	6	20000	3	3	106500	117000
38		PT38 SEDAN	FB	MY	FBG	DV	IB	T150D	CUM	13	6		3	6	115000	126000
		IB T210D CUM 117500 129500, IB T250D CUM 120000 132000, IB T300D CUM													123500	135500
38		PT38 SUNDECK	FB	MY	FBG	DV	IB	T150D	CUM	13	6	22200	3	6	112500	123500
		IB T210D CUM 115000 126500, IB T250D CUM 117500 129000, IB T300D CUM													121000	133000
42		PT42 COCKPIT MOTORYT	FB	MY	FBG	DV	IB	T150D	CUM	13	6	25000	3	6	132000	145000
		IB T210D CUM 139000 153000, IB T250D CUM 144000 158000, IB T300D CUM													150000	165000
46	4	PT46	FB	MY	FBG	DV	IB	T250D	CUM	15	9	36500	3	7	160500	176500
		IB T270D CUM 163500 180000, IB T300D CUM 168500 185500, IB T320D CUM													172500	189500
		IB T375D CAT 183500 201500, IB T450D J&T 195500 215000, IB T485D J&T													201500	221500
52	2	PT52	FB	MY	FBG	DV	IB	T250D	CUM	15	9	39500	3	7	155000	170000
		IB T270D CUM 157000 172500, IB T300D CUM 160500 176000, IB T320D CUM													162500	179000
		IB T375D CAT 172500 189500, IB T450D J&T 185500 204000, IB T485D J&T													191500	210500
		1988 BOATS														
35	4	PT35 SEDAN	FB	MY	FBG	DV	IB	T150D	CUM	12	6	19000	3		87700	96400
35	4	PT35 SUNDECK	FB	MY	FBG	DV	IB	T150D	CUM	12	6	19000	3		87700	96400
35	4	PT35 SUNDECK	FB	MY	FBG	DV	IB	T210D	CUM	12	5	19500			92200	101500
35	4	PT35 SUNDECK	FB	MY	FBG	DV	IB	T250D	CUM	12	5	20000			95900	105500
36		PT36 SPORTFISHERMAN	FB	MY	FBG	DV	IB	T250	CUM	12	6	21000	3	3	86000	94500
36		PT36 SPORTFISHERMAN	FB	MY	FBG	DV	IB	T210D	CUM	12	6	20000	3	3	96200	105500
38		PT38 SEDAN	FB	MY	FBG	DV	IB	T150D	CUM	13	6		3	6	109500	120500
		IB T210D CUM 112500 123500, IB T250D CUM 114500 126000, IB T270D CUM													116000	127500
		IB T320D CUM 119500 131000														
38		PT38 SUNDECK	FB	MY	FBG	DV	IB	T150D	CUM	13	6	22200	3	6	107500	118000
		IB T210D CUM 113000 124500, IB T250D CUM 116000 127500, IB T270D CUM													118000	129500
		IB T320D CUM 122500 135000														
42		PT42 COCKPIT MOTORYT	FB	MY	FBG	DV	IB	T150D	CUM	13	6	22000	3	6	115000	126000
		IB T210D CUM 124500 137000, IB T250D CUM 129500 142000, IB T270D CUM													132500	146000
		IB T320D CUM 140500 154000														
46	4	PT46	FB	MY	FBG	DV	IB	T270D	CUM	15	9	29000	3	7	137500	151000
46	4	PT46	FB	MY	FBG	DV	IB	T320D	CUM	15	9	30000	3	7	146000	160500
52	2	PT52	FB	MY	FBG	DV	IB	T270D	CUM	15	9	32000	3	7	140500	154500
52	2	PT52	FB	MY	FBG	DV	IB	T320D	CUM	15	9	33000	3	7	147000	161500
		1987 BOATS														
35	4	PT35 SEDAN	FB	MY	FBG	DV	IB	T150D	CUM	12	6	19000	3		84000	92300
35	4	PT35 SUNDECK	FB	MY	FBG	DV	IB	T150D	CUM	12	6	19000	3		84000	92300
35	4	PT35 SUNDECK	FB	MY	FBG	DV	IB	T210D	CUM	12	5	19500			88300	97100
35	4	PT35 SUNDECK	FB	MY	FBG	DV	IB	T270D	CUM	12	5	20000			93000	102000
36		PT36 SPORTFISHERMAN	FB	MY	FBG	DV	IB	T210D	CUM	12	6	20000	3	3	92000	101000
36		PT36 SPORTFISHERMAN	FB	MY	FBG	DV	IB	T270D	CUM	12	6	21000	3	3	98100	108000
38		PT38 SEDAN	FB	MY	FBG	DV	IB	T150D	CUM	13	6		3	6	105000	115500
		IB T210D CUM 107500 118000, IB T270D CUM 111000 122000, IB T320D CUM													114000	125500
38		PT38 SUNDECK	FB	MY	FBG	DV	IB	T150D	CUM	13	6	22200	3	6	102500	113000
		IB T210D CUM 108000 119000, IB T270D CUM 113000 124000, IB T320D CUM													117500	129000
42		PT42 COCKPIT MOTORYT	FB	MY	FBG	DV	IB	T150D	CUM	13	6	22000	3	6	110000	120500
		IB T210D CUM 119000 131000, IB T270D CUM 127000 139500, IB T320D CUM													134000	147500
46	4	PT46	FB	MY	FBG	DV	IB	T270D	CUM	15	9	29000	3	7	131500	144500
46	4	PT46	FB	MY	FBG	DV	IB	T320D	CUM	15	9	30000	3	7	139500	153500
52	2	PT52	FB	MY	FBG	DV	IB	T270D	CUM	15	9	32000	3	7	135000	148000
52	2	PT52	FB	MY	FBG	DV	IB	T320D	CUM	15	9	33000	3	7	141500	155000

PURSUIT

DIV OF S2 YACHTS INC
FT PIERCE FL 34946

See inside cover to adjust price for area

ALSO TIARA YACHTS

For more recent years, see the BUC Used Boat Price Guide, Volume 1

LOA FT	LOA IN	NAME AND/ OR MODEL	TOP/ RIG	BOAT TYPE	-HULL- MTL	-HULL- TP	TP	ENGINE # HP	ENGINE MFG	BEAM FT	BEAM IN	WGT LBS	DRAFT FT	DRAFT IN	RETAIL LOW	RETAIL HIGH
		1996 BOATS														
20	6	PURSUIT 2150 CC	OP	CTRCN	FBG	SV	OB			8		2550	1	2	10800	12300
20	6	PURSUIT 2150 DUAL	OP	B/R	FBG	SV	OB			8		2550	1	2	11000	12500
20	6	PURSUIT 2150 WA	OP	CUD	FBG	SV	OB			8		2500	1	2	10800	12200
24	7	PURSUIT 2470 CC	OP	CTRCN	FBG	SV	OB			8	6	3200	1	3	16200	18400
24	7	PURSUIT 2470 WA	OP	CUD	FBG	SV	OB			8	6	3600	1	3	18100	20100
24	7	PURSUIT DENALI 24	OP	CUD	FBG	SV	IO	T250	VLVO	8	6		2	6	26200	29100
26	5	PURSUIT 2600 CC	OP	CTRCN	FBG	SV	IO	300	CRUS	9	7	6000	2	4	32600	36200

LOA FT	LOA IN	NAME AND/ OR MODEL	TOP/ RIG	BOAT TYPE	-HULL- MTL	-HULL- TP	ENGINE TP	ENGINE # HP	ENGINE MFG	BEAM FT	BEAM IN	WGT LBS	DRAFT FT	DRAFT IN	RETAIL LOW	RETAIL HIGH
		1996 BOATS														
26	5	PURSUIT 2600 CC	OP	CTRCN	FBG	SV	IO	170D-230D		9	7	6000	2	4	42800	51100
26	5	PURSUIT 2655 CC	OP	CTRCN	FBG	SV	OB			9	7	4550	1	5	22900	25400
28	7	PURSUIT 2800 CC	OP	CTRCN	FBG	SV	IB	T250	MRCR	9	6		2	6	59400	65300
28	7	PURSUIT 2800 WA	OP	CUD	FBG	SV	IB	T250	MRCR	9	6		2	6	59100	65000
28	7	PURSUIT 2870 CC	OP	CTRCN	FBG	SV	OB			9	6		2	6	34400	38200
30		PURSUIT 2870 WA	OP	CUD	FBG	SV	OB			9	6	5600	2	6	33000	36600
31	1	PURSUIT 3100 EXP FSH	OP	EXP	FBG	SV	IB	225D	VLVO	12		11000	2	9	76900	84500
31	1	PURSUIT 3100 EXP FSH	OP	EXP	FBG	SV	IO	T300	MRCR	12		11000	2	9	64600	71000
31	2	PURSUIT 3000 EXP	OP	EXP	FBG	SV	IB	T250	CRUS	12		10800	2	9	65400	71900
31	2	PURSUIT 3000 EXP	OP	EXP	FBG	SV	IB	T225D	VLVO	12		10800	2	9	78300	86000
		1995 BOATS														
18	6	PURSUIT 1950 CC	OP	CTRCN	FBG	SV	OB			8		1900	1	6	7000	8050
18	6	PURSUIT 1950 DUAL	OP	W/T	FBG	SV	OB			8		2000	1	6	7200	8300
20	6	PURSUIT 2150 CC	OP	CTRCN	FBG	SV	OB			8		2550	1	2	10300	11800
20	6	PURSUIT 2150 DUAL	OP	B/R	FBG	SV	OB			8		2550	1	2	10400	11900
20	6	PURSUIT 2150 WA	OP	CUD	FBG	SV	OB			8		2500	1	2	10300	11700
22	6	PURSUIT 2350 WA	ST	CUD	FBG	SV	OB			8	6	3400	1	3	14400	16400
24	7	PURSUIT 2470 CC	OP	CTRCN	FBG	SV	OB			8	6	3200	1	3	15500	17600
24	7	PURSUIT 2470 WA	OP	CTRCN	FBG	SV	OB			8	6	3600	1	3	16700	19000
24	7	PURSUIT 2470 WA	OP	CUD	FBG	SV	OB			8	6	3600	1	3	16800	19100
24	9	PURSUIT 2555 WA	OP	CUD	FBG	SV	OB			8	6	4300	1	3	19200	21400
24	9	PURSUIT 2560 WA	OP	CUD	FBG	SV	IO	250-300		8	6	5150	1	7	22800	27200
26	5	PURSUIT 2600 CC	OP	CTRCN	FBG	SV	IO	300	CRUS	9	7	6000	2	4	30400	33700
26	5	PURSUIT 2600 CC	OP	CTRCN	FBG	SV	IO	170D	YAN	9	7	6000	2	4	39900	44400
26	5	PURSUIT 2655 CC	OP	CTRCN	FBG	SV	OB			9	7	4550	1	5	21800	24300
28		PURSUIT 2855 EXP FSH	OP	CUD	FBG	SV	OB			10	3	6500	1	9	31200	34700
30		PURSUIT 2870 WA	OP	CUD	FBG	SV	OB			9	6	5600	2	6	31200	34700
31	1	PURSUIT 3100 EXP FSH	OP	EXP	FBG	SV	IB	225D	VLVO	12		11000	2	9	73100	80300
31	1	PURSUIT 3100 EXP FSH	OP	EXP	FBG	SV	IO	T300	MRCR	12		11000	2	9	60300	66300
31	2	PURSUIT 3000 EXP	OP	EXP	FBG	SV	IB	T250-T340		12		10800	2	9	61800	71900
31	2	PURSUIT 3000 EXP	OP	EXP	FBG	SV	IB	T225D	VLVO	12		10800	2	9	74400	81700
		1994 BOATS														
18	6	PURSUIT 1950	OP	CTRCN	FBG	SV	OB			8		1900	1	6	6700	7700
18	6	PURSUIT 1950 C/C	OP	CTRCN	FBG	SV	OB			8		1900	1	6	4550	5200
18	6	PURSUIT 1950 DUAL	OP	W/T	FBG	SV	OB			8		2000	1	6	6900	7900
20	6	PURSUIT 2150	OP	CTRCN	FBG	SV	OB			8		2550	1	2	9900	11200
20	6	PURSUIT 2150 C/C	OP	CTRCN	FBG	SV	OB			8		2550	1	2	9900	11200
20	6	PURSUIT 2150 DUAL	OP	B/R	FBG	SV	OB			8		2550	1	2	9950	11300
20	6	PURSUIT 2150 WA	OP	CUD	FBG	SV	OB			8		2550	1	2	9900	11200
22	6	PURSUIT 2350 C/C	OP	CTRCN	FBG	SV	OB			8	6	3000	1	3	12700	14500
22	6	PURSUIT 2350 WA	ST	CUD	FBG	SV	OB			8	6	3400	1	3	13800	15700
22	6	PURSUIT 2355 C/C	OP	CTRCN	FBG	SV	OB			8	6	3300	1	3	13500	15400
24	9	PURSUIT 2555 C/C	OP	CTRCN	FBG	SV	OB			8	6	4000	1	3	17100	19500
24	9	PURSUIT 2555 WA	OP	CUD	FBG	SV	OB			8	6	4300	1	3	18300	20400
24	9	PURSUIT 2560 WA	OP	CUD	FBG	SV	IO	240-300		8	6	5150	1	7	21200	24800
26	5	PURSUIT 2600 C/C	OP	CTRCN	FBG	SV	IO	300	MRCR	9	7	6000	2	4	28400	31500
26	5	PURSUIT 2655 C/C	OP	CTRCN	FBG	SV	OB			9	7	4550	1	5	20900	23200
26	5	PURSUIT 2655 EXP FSH	OP	CUD	FBG	SV	OB			9	7	4700	1	5	21200	23500
26	5	PURSUIT 2655 EXP FSH	ST	CUD	FBG	SV	OB			9	7	4700	1	5	21800	24200
28		PURSUIT 2855 EXP FSH	OP	CUD	FBG	SV	OB			10	3	6500	1	9	29700	33000
31	1	PURSUIT 3100 EXP FSH	OP	EXP	FBG	SV	IO	T300	MRCR	12		11000	2	9	56300	61900
		1993 BOATS														
18	6	PURSUIT 1850	OP	CTRCN	FBG	SV	OB			8		2000	1	4	6600	7600
20	6	PURSUIT 2150	OP	CUD	FBG	SV	OB			8		2600	1	2	9600	10900
20	6	PURSUIT 2150 EXP FSH	OP	CUD	FBG	SV	IO	205		8		2600	1	2	9600	11400
23		PURSUIT 2350 C/C	OP	CTRCN	FBG	SV	OB			8	6	3100	1	3	12900	14600
23		PURSUIT 2350 WA	ST	CUD	FBG	SV	OB			8	6	3200	1	3	13200	14900
24	9	PURSUIT 2550 C/C	OP	CTRCN	FBG	SV	OB			8	6	3700	1	3	15700	17800
24	9	PURSUIT 2550 EXP FSH	OP	CUD	FBG	SV	IO	260-275		8	6	4300	1	4	17500	20700
24	9	PURSUIT 2550 EXP FSH	OP	CUD	FBG	SV	IO	330		8	6	4300	1	4	19300	22200
26	5	PURSUIT 2650	ST	CUD	FBG	SV	IO	330		9	7	6100	1	5	26100	29600
26	5	PURSUIT 2650 C/C	OP	CTRCN	FBG	SV	OB			9	7	4800	1	5	20200	22400
27		PURSUIT 2700	ST	SF	FBG	SV	IB	T260	MRCR	10		7500	2		38400	42700
27		PURSUIT 2700	ST	SF	FBG	SV	IB	T170D	YAN	10		7500	2		51500	56600
		1992 BOATS														
18	6	PURSUIT 1850	OP	CTRCN	FBG	SV	OB			8		2000	1	4	6350	7300
20	6	PURSUIT 2100 C/C	OP	CTRCN	FBG	SV	OB			8		2500	1	2	9050	10300
20	6	PURSUIT 2150	OP	CUD	FBG	SV	OB			8		2600	1	2	9250	10500
20	6	PURSUIT 2150 EXP FSH	OP	CUD	FBG	SV	IO	205		8		2600	1	2	9050	10700
23		PURSUIT 2350 C/C	OP	CTRCN	FBG	SV	OB			8	6	3100	1	3	12400	14000
23		PURSUIT 2350 WA	ST	CUD	FBG	SV	OB			8	6	3200	1	3	12600	14400
23		PURSUIT 2350 WA	ST	CUD	FBG	SV	OB			8	6	4200	1	4	14800	16800
24	9	PURSUIT 2550 BROADBL	OP	CUD	FBG	SV	OB			8	6	3300	1	4	14100	16000
24	9	PURSUIT 2550 C/C	OP	CTRCN	FBG	SV	OB			8	6	3700	1	3	15100	17100
24	9	PURSUIT 2550 EXP FSH	OP	CUD	FBG	SV	OB			8	6	3300	1	4	14100	16000
24	9	PURSUIT 2550 EXP FSH	OP	CUD	FBG	SV	IO	260-275		8	6	4300	1	4	16400	19400
24	9	PURSUIT 2550 EXP FSH	OP	CUD	FBG	SV	IO	330		8	6	4300	1	4	18200	21000
24	9	PURSUIT 2550 WA	ST	CUD	FBG	SV	OB			8	6	3300	1	3	14100	16000
26	5	PURSUIT 2650	ST	CUD	FBG	SV	OB			9	7	5000	1	5	20000	22200
26	5	PURSUIT 2650	ST	CUD	FBG	SV	IO	330		9	7	6100	1	5	24400	27700
26	5	PURSUIT 2650 C/C	OP	CTRCN	FBG	SV	OB			9	7	4800	1	5	19400	21500
27		PURSUIT 2700	ST	SF	FBG	SV	IB	T235-T260		10		7500	2		36200	40500
27		PURSUIT 2700	ST	SF	FBG	SV	IB	T170D	YAN	10		7500	2		49100	54000
28	2	PURSUIT 2800 OPEN	ST	SF	FBG	SV	OB			10		5500	1	9	27500	30500
33		PURSUIT 3250 EXP FSH		SF	FBG	SV	IB	T300-T330		12	6	13000			72500	80800
33		PURSUIT 3250 EXP FSH		SF	FBG	SV	IB	T300D		12	6	13000	2	8	91100	100000
		1991 BOATS														
18	6	PURSUIT 1850	OP	CTRCN	FBG	SV	OB			8		2000	1	4	6100	7000
20	6	PURSUIT 2100 C/C	OP	CTRCN	FBG	SV	OB			8		2500	1	2	8650	9900
20	6	PURSUIT 2150		CUD	FBG	SV	IO	205	MRCR	8		2600	1	2	8400	9650
20	6	PURSUIT 2150	ST	CUD	FBG	SV	OB			8		2600	1	2	8900	10100
23		PURSUIT 2350	ST	CUD	FBG	SV	OB			8	6	3200	1	3	12200	13800
23		PURSUIT 2350	ST	CUD	FBG	SV	OB			8	6	4200	1	4	14200	16200
23		PURSUIT 2350 C/C	OP	CTRCN	FBG	SV	OB			8	6	3100	1	3	11900	13500
24	9	PURSUIT 2550	OP	CUD	FBG	SV	IO	260		8	6	4000	1	4	14700	17100
24	9	PURSUIT 2550	OP	CUD	FBG	SV	IO	330		8	6	4000	1	4	16000	18900
24	9	PURSUIT 2550 C/C	OP	CTRCN	FBG	SV	OB			8	6	3700	1	3	14500	16500
24	9	PURSUIT 2550 WA	ST	CUD	FBG	SV	OB			8	6	3300	1	3	13600	15400
26	5	PURSUIT 2650	ST	CUD	FBG	SV	OB			9	7	5000	1	5	19200	21400
26	5	PURSUIT 2650	ST	CUD	FBG	SV	IO	330		9	7	6100	1	5	22900	26000
27		PURSUIT 2700	ST	SF	FBG	SV	IB	T260	MRCR	10		7500	2		34700	38500
28	2	PURSUIT 2800 OPEN	ST	SF	FBG	SV	OB			10		5500	1	9	26500	29400
33		PURSUIT 3250		SF	FBG	SV	IB	T330	MRCR	12	6	13000	2	8	69800	76800
33		PURSUIT 3250		SF	FBG	SV	IB	T300D		12	6	13000	2	8	87000	95600
		1990 BOATS														
20	6	PURSUIT 2150	ST	CUD	FBG	SV	OB			8		2600	1	2	8500	9800
20	6	PURSUIT 2150 C/C	OP	CTRCN	FBG	SV	OB			8		2500	1	2	8350	9550
21	7	PURSUIT 2200	ST	CUD	FBG	SV	OB			8		3000	1	3	10200	11600
23		PURSUIT 2350	ST	CUD	FBG	SV	OB			8	6	3200	1	3	11800	13400
23		PURSUIT 2350	ST	CUD	FBG	SV	IO	260-275		8	6	4200	1	4	13000	15500
23		PURSUIT 2350 C/C	OP	CTRCN	FBG	SV	OB			8	6	3100	1	3	11500	13000
24	9	PURSUIT 2550 C/C	OP	CTRCN	FBG	SV	OB			8	6	3700	1	3	14000	15900
24	9	PURSUIT 2550 EXP FSH	ST	CUD	FBG	SV	OB			8	6	3300	1	3	13100	14900
26	5	PURSUIT 2650	ST	CUD	FBG	SV	OB			9	7	5000	1	5	18500	20600
26	5	PURSUIT 2650	ST	CUD	FBG	SV	IO	260-330		9	7	6100	1	5	20200	24400
28	2	PURSUIT 2800 OPEN	ST	SF	FBG	SV	OB			10		5500	1	9	25600	28400
		1989 BOATS														
20	2	PURSUIT 2000 CUDDY	ST	FSH	FBG	SV	OB			8		1950	1	3	6750	7750
20	6	PURSUIT 2100 C/C	OP	CTRCN	FBG	SV	OB			8		2500	1	2	8050	9250
21	7	PURSUIT 2200	ST	CUD	FBG	SV	OB			8		3000	1	3	9900	11200
21	7	PURSUIT 2200 C/C	OP	CTRCN	FBG	SV	OB			8		2850	1	3	9550	10900
23		PURSUIT 2350	ST	CUD	FBG	SV	OB			8	6	3200	1	3	11400	12900
23		PURSUIT 2350	ST	CUD	FBG	SV	IO	260-275		8	6	4200	1	4	12300	14600
23		PURSUIT 2350 C/C	OP	CTRCN	FBG	SV	OB			8	6	3100	1	3	11100	12600
24	9	PURSUIT 2550	ST	CUD	FBG	SV	IO	260-275		8	6	4300	1	4	13600	16100
24	9	PURSUIT 2550 C/C	OP	CTRCN	FBG	SV	OB			8	6	3700	1	3	13500	15400
24	9	PURSUIT 2550 EXP FSH	ST	CUD	FBG	SV	OB			8	6	3300	1	3	12700	14400
26	5	PURSUIT 2650	ST	CUD	FBG	SV	OB			9	7	5000	1	5	17500	19900
26	5	PURSUIT 2650	ST	CUD	FBG	SV	IO	260-330		9	7	6100	1	5	19100	22600
27		PURSUIT 2700	OP	SF	FBG	SV	IB	T260-T270		10		7500	2		31400	35400
28	2	PURSUIT 2800 OPEN	ST	SF	FBG	SV	OB			10		5500	1	9	24700	27500
		1988 BOATS														
20	2	PURSUIT 2000 CUDDY	OP	FSH	FBG	DV	OB			8		1950	1	3	6550	7500
20	6	PURSUIT 2100 C/C	OP	CTRCN	FBG	DV	OB			8		2300	1	2	7450	8550
21	7	PURSUIT 2200	OP	CUD	FBG	DV	OB			8		4000			10700	12100
21	7	PURSUIT 2200	OP	CUD	FBG	DV	IO	230-260		8		4000	1	4	10000	11600
21	7	PURSUIT 2200 C/C	OP	CTRCN	FBG	DV	OB			8		2800	1	3	9200	10500
23		PURSUIT 2350	OP	CUD	FBG	DV	OB			8	6	4200			12900	14700
23		PURSUIT 2350	OP	CUD	FBG	DV	IO	230-260		8	6	4200			11400	13200
24	7	PURSUIT 2500 C/C	OP	CTRCN	FBG	DV	OB			8		3200	1	4	11800	13400
24	9	PURSUIT 2550	ST	CUD	FBG	DV	OB			8	6	3200	1	4	12100	13700
24	9	PURSUIT 2550	ST	CUD	FBG	DV	SE		OMC	8	6	3200	1	4	**	**
24	9	PURSUIT 2550	ST	CUD	FBG	DV	IO	260		8	6	4200	1	4	12700	14400
24	9	PURSUIT 2550	ST	CUD	FBG	DV	SE	T	OMC	8	6	3200	1	4	**	**
24	9	PURSUIT 2550 C/C	TT	CTRCN	FBG	DV	OB			8	6	3000	1	3	11500	13100
25	6	PURSUIT 2600	ST	CUD	FBG	DV	OB			8	9	3800	1	6	14200	16100
25	6	PURSUIT 2600	ST	CUD	FBG	DV	IO	260		8	9	4600	1	6	14200	16100
25	6	PURSUIT 2600	ST	CUD	FBG	DV	SE	275	OMC	8	9	3800	1	6	14200	16100
25	6	PURSUIT 2600	ST	CUD	FBG	DV	IO	330-335		8	9	4600	1	6	15300	17500
25	6	PURSUIT 2600	ST	CUD	FBG	DV	SE	T	OMC	8	9	3800	1	6	**	**

CONTINUED ON NEXT PAGE

LOA FT	LOA IN	NAME AND/ OR MODEL	TOP/ RIG	BOAT TYPE	HULL MTL	HULL TP	ENGINE TP	ENGINE # HP	ENGINE MFG	BEAM FT	BEAM IN	WGT LBS	DRAFT FT	DRAFT IN	RETAIL LOW	RETAIL HIGH
		1988 BOATS														
27		PURSUIT 2700	OP	SF	FBG	DV	SE	T	OMC	10		5700	2		**	**
27		PURSUIT 2700 OFF	TT	CTRCN	FBG	DV	SE	T	OMC	10		7550	2		**	**
31	3	PURSUIT 3100	OP	SF	FBG	DV	IB	T270-T350		12		10500	2	9	48200	55800
31	3	PURSUIT 3100	OP	SF	FBG	DV	IB	T250D	GM	12		10500	2	9	60300	66300
31	3	PURSUIT 3100	FB	SF	FBG	DV	IB	T350	CRUS	12		13200	2	11	53700	59000
		1987 BOATS														
20	6	PURSUIT 2100 C/C	OP	CTRCN	FBG	DV	OB			8		2300	1	2	7200	8300
21	7	PURSUIT 2000 CUDDY	OP	CTRCN	FBG	DV	OB			8		1950	1	3	6850	7850
21	7	PURSUIT 2200	OP	CUD	FBG	DV	OB			8		2700	2	6	8800	10000
21	7	PURSUIT 2200	OP	CUD	FBG	DV	IO	230-260		8		3650	2	6	8950	10400
21	7	PURSUIT 2200 C/C	OP	CTRCN	FBG	DV	OB			8		3000	1	3	9300	10600
23		PURSUIT 2350	OP	CUD	FBG	DV	IO	230-260		8	6	4200			10800	12500
23		PURSUIT 2350	OP	CUD	FBG	DV	SE	T225	OMC	8	6	4200			12500	14300
24	7	PURSUIT 2500 C/C	OP	CTRCN	FBG	DV	OB			8		3200	1	4	11500	13000
24	7	PURSUIT 2500 C/C	OP	CTRCN	FBG	DV	SE	190	OMC	8		3200	1	4	11500	13000
24	7	PURSUIT 2500 C/C	OP	CTRCN	FBG	DV	SE	T115	OMC	8		3200	1	4	11500	13000
24	7	PURSUIT 2500 W/BRKT	OP	CTRCN	FBG	DV	OB			8		3200	1	4	11500	13000
24	9	PURSUIT 2550	ST	CUD	FBG	DV	OB			8	6	3200	2	6	11700	13300
24	9	PURSUIT 2550	ST	CUD	FBG	DV	IO	260		8	6	4200	2	6	12100	13700
24	9	PURSUIT 2550	ST	CUD	FBG	DV	SE	T140-T225		8	6	3200	2	6	11700	13300
24	9	PURSUIT 2550 C/C	TT	CTRCN	FBG	DV	OB			8	6	3000	1	3	11200	12700
24	9	PURSUIT 2550 W/BRKT	TT	CTRCN	FBG	DV	OB			8	6	3000	1	3	11200	12700
24	9	PURSUIT 2550 W/BRKT	ST	CUD	FBG	DV	OB			8	6	3200	2	6	11700	13300
25	6	PURSUIT 2600	ST	CUD	FBG	DV	OB			8	9	3800	2	6	13800	15700
25	6	PURSUIT 2600	ST	CUD	FBG	DV	IO	260		8	9	4600	2	6	13500	15300
25	6	PURSUIT 2600	ST	CUD	FBG	DV	SE	275	OMC	8	9	3800	2	6	13800	15700
25	6	PURSUIT 2600	ST	CUD	FBG	DV	IO	335	OMC	8	9	4600	2	6	14600	16600
25	6	PURSUIT 2600	ST	CUD	FBG	DV	SE	T140	OMC	8	9	3800	2	6	13800	15700
25	6	PURSUIT 2600 W/BRKT	ST	CUD	FBG	DV	OB			8	9	3800	2	6	13800	15700
27		PURSUIT 2700	OP	SF	FBG	DV	SE	T225	OMC	10		5700	2	8	17400	19800
27		PURSUIT 2700 C/C	OP	CTRCN	FBG	DV	OB			10		5700	2	8	17500	19800
27		PURSUIT 2700 OFF	TT	CTRCN	FBG	DV	OB			10		5550	2	8	18100	20100
27		PURSUIT 2700 OFF	TT	CTRCN	FBG	DV	SE	T225		10		7550	2	8	18400	20400
31	3	PURSUIT 3100	FB	SF	FBG	DV	IB	T350	CRUS	12		13200	2	11	51200	56300
		1986 BOATS														
20	2	PURSUIT 2000 C/C	OP	CTRCN	FBG	DV	OB			8		1950	1	3	6150	7050
20	2	PURSUIT 2000 CUDDY	ST	FSH	FBG	DV	OB			8		1950	1	3	6150	7100
20	2	PURSUIT 2000 CUDDY	ST	FSH	FBG	DV	IO	188-230		8		2950	2	3	7050	8600
21	7	PURSUIT 2200	OP	CUD	FBG	DV	OB			8		2700	2	6	8500	9750
21	7	PURSUIT 2200	OP	CUD	FBG	DV	IO	188-260		8		3650	2	6	8300	10300
21	7	PURSUIT 2200 C/C	OP	CTRCN	FBG	DV	OB			8		2400	1	3	7750	8900
24	7	PURSUIT 2500	ST	CUD	FBG	DV	OB			8		3200	1	4	11300	12800
24	7	PURSUIT 2500	ST	CUD	FBG	DV	SE	205	OMC	8		4200	1	4	13400	15200
24	7	PURSUIT 2500	ST	CUD	FBG	DV	SE	T115	OMC	8		4200	1	4	13400	15200
24	7	PURSUIT 2500	ST	FSH	FBG	DV	IO	228-260		8		4200	2	5	11600	13900
24	7	PURSUIT 2500 C/C	ST	CTRCN	FBG	DV	OB			8		3300	1	4	11400	12900
24	7	PURSUIT 2500 C/C	ST	CTRCN	FBG	DV	SE	205	OMC	8		3300	1	4	11400	12900
24	7	PURSUIT 2500 C/C	ST	CTRCN	FBG	DV	SE	T115	OMC	8		3300	1	4	11400	12900
25	6	PURSUIT 2600	ST	CUD	FBG	DV	OB			8	9	3675	2	7	13300	15100
25	6	PURSUIT 2600	ST	CUD	FBG	DV	IO			8	9	4600	2	7	**	**
25	6	PURSUIT 2600	ST	CUD	FBG	DV	SE	205	OMC	8	9	3675	2	7	13300	15100
25	6	PURSUIT 2600	ST	CUD	FBG	DV	IO	260		8	9	4600	2	7	12900	14900
25	6	PURSUIT 2600	ST	CUD	FBG	DV	SE	T155	OMC	8	9		2	7	13500	15300
27		PURSUIT 2700	OP	SF	FBG	DV	SE	T205	OMC	10		7500	1	9	17200	19500
27		PURSUIT 2700	OP	SF	FBG	DV	IB	T220-T270		10		7500	1	9	26700	30700
27		PURSUIT 2700	TT	SF	FBG	DV	SE	T205	OMC	10		7500	1	9	17400	19800
27		PURSUIT 2700	TT	SF	FBG	DV	IB	T220-T270		10		7500	1	9	26700	30700
31	3	PURSUIT 3100	OP	SF	FBG	DV	IB	T260-T350		12		9200	2	9	35300	41700
31	3	PURSUIT 3100	HT	SF	FBG	DV	IB	T260-T350		12		9500	2	9	35500	41900
31	3	PURSUIT 3100	FB	SF	FBG	DV	IB	T260-T350		12		10000	2	9	42900	50600
31	3	PURSUIT 3100	TT	SF	FBG	DV	IB	T260-T350		12		10500	2	9	43300	51100
36	8	PURSUIT 3600	OP	SF	FBG	DV	IB	T350	CRUS	13	9	16500	2	11	70300	77300
36	8	PURSUIT 3600	OP	SF	FBG	DV	IB	T D	CAT	13	9	16500	2	11	**	**
36	8	PURSUIT 3600	OP	SF	FBG	DV	IB	T235D	VLVO	13	9	16500	2	11	76500	84100
36	8	PURSUIT 3600	TT	SF	FBG	DV	IB	T350	CRUS	13	9	16500	2	11	70300	77300
36	8	PURSUIT 3600	TT	SF	FBG	DV	IB	T D	CAT	13	9	16500	2	11	**	**
36	8	PURSUIT 3600	TT	SF	FBG	DV	IB	T235D	VLVO	13	9	16500	2	11	76500	84100
		1985 BOATS														
20	2	PURSUIT 2000 C/C	OP	FSH	FBG	DV	OB			8		1950	1	3	6000	6900
20	2	PURSUIT 2000 CUDDY	ST	FSH	FBG	DV	OB			8		1950	1	3	6000	6900
20	2	PURSUIT 2000 CUDDY	ST	FSH	FBG	DV	IO	188-230		8		2950	2	3	6800	8250
21	7	PURSUIT 2200	OP	CUD	FBG	DV	OB			8		2700	2	6	8250	9500
21	7	PURSUIT 2200	OP	CUD	FBG	DV	IO	188-260		8		3650	2	6	7950	9900
21	7	PURSUIT 2200 C/C	OP	CTRCN	FBG	DV	OB			8		2400	1	3	7550	8650
24	7	PURSUIT 2500	ST	CUD	FBG	DV	OB			8		3200	1	4	11000	12500
24	7	PURSUIT 2500	ST	CUD	FBG	DV	SE	205	OMC	8		4200	1	4	13100	14800
24	7	PURSUIT 2500	ST	CUD	FBG	DV	SE	T115	OMC	8		4200	1	4	13100	14800
24	7	PURSUIT 2500	ST	FSH	FBG	DV	IO	228-260		8		4200	2	5	11200	13300
24	7	PURSUIT 2500 C/C	ST	CTRCN	FBG	DV	OB			8		3300	1	4	11100	12600
24	7	PURSUIT 2500 C/C	ST	CTRCN	FBG	DV	SE	205	OMC	8		3300	1	4	11100	12600
24	7	PURSUIT 2500 C/C	ST	CTRCN	FBG	DV	SE	T115	OMC	8		3300	1	4	11100	12600
25	6	PURSUIT 2600	ST	CUD	FBG	DV	OB			8	9	3675	2	7	13000	14700
25	6	PURSUIT 2600	ST	CUD	FBG	DV	IO			8	9	4600	2	7	**	**
25	6	PURSUIT 2600	ST	CUD	FBG	DV	SE	205	OMC	8	9	3675	2	7	13000	14700
25	6	PURSUIT 2600	ST	CUD	FBG	DV	IO	260		8	9	4600	2	7	12300	14300
25	6	PURSUIT 2600	ST	CUD	FBG	DV	SE	T155	OMC	8	9	3675	2	7	13000	14700
27		PURSUIT 2700	OP	SF	FBG	DV	SE	T205	OMC	10		7500	1	9	16700	18900
27		PURSUIT 2700	OP	SF	FBG	DV	IB	T220-T270		10		7500	1	9	25500	29300
27		PURSUIT 2700	TT	SF	FBG	DV	SE	T205	OMC	10		7500	1	9	16900	19200
27		PURSUIT 2700	TT	SF	FBG	DV	IB	T220-T270		10		7500	1	9	25500	29300
31	3	PURSUIT 3100	OP	SF	FBG	DV	IB	T260-T350		12		9200	2	9	33700	39800
31	3	PURSUIT 3100	HT	SF	FBG	DV	IB	T260-T350		12		9500	2	9	33900	40000
31	3	PURSUIT 3100	FB	SF	FBG	DV	IB	T260-T350		12		10000	2	9	41000	48400
31	3	PURSUIT 3100	TT	SF	FBG	DV	IB	T260-T350		12		10500	2	9	41400	48800
36	8	PURSUIT 3600	OP	SF	FBG	DV	IB	T350	CRUS	13	9	16500	2	11	67300	74000
36	8	PURSUIT 3600	OP	SF	FBG	DV	IB	T D	CAT	13	9	16500	2	11	**	**
36	8	PURSUIT 3600	OP	SF	FBG	DV	IB	T235D	VLVO	13	9	16500	2	11	73300	80500
36	8	PURSUIT 3600	TT	SF	FBG	DV	IB	T350	CRUS	13	9	16500	2	11	67300	74000
36	8	PURSUIT 3600	TT	SF	FBG	DV	IB	T D	CAT	13	9	16500	2	11	**	**
36	8	PURSUIT 3600	TT	SF	FBG	DV	IB	T235D	VLVO	13	9	16500	2	11	73300	80500
		1984 BOATS														
20	2	PURSUIT 2000 C/C	OP	FSH	FBG	DV	OB			8		1950	1	3	5850	6700
20	2	PURSUIT 2000 CUDDY	ST	FSH	FBG	DV	OB			8		1950	1	3	5850	6700
20	2	PURSUIT 2000 CUDDY	ST	FSH	FBG	DV	IO	170-230		8		2950	2	3	6500	8000
21	7	PURSUIT 2200	OP	CUD	FBG	DV	OB			8		2700	2	6	8050	9250
21	7	PURSUIT 2200	OP	CUD	FBG	DV	IO	170-185		8		3650	2	6	7650	9050
21	7	PURSUIT 2200	OP	CUD	FBG	DV	SE	205	OMC	8		2760	2	6	8150	9400
21	7	PURSUIT 2200	OP	CUD	FBG	DV	IO	225-260		8		3650	2	6	8050	9550
21	7	PURSUIT 2200 C/C	OP	CTRCN	FBG	DV	OB			8		2400	1	3	7350	8450
21	7	PURSUIT 2200 C/C	OP	CTRCN	FBG	DV	SE	205	OMC	8		2760			8050	9250
24	7	PURSUIT 2500	ST	CUD	FBG	DV	OB			8		3200	1	4	10800	12200
24	7	PURSUIT 2500	ST	CUD	FBG	DV	SE	205	OMC	8		4200	1	4	12800	14500
24	7	PURSUIT 2500	ST	CUD	FBG	DV	SE	T115	OMC	8		4200	1	4	12800	14500
24	7	PURSUIT 2500	ST	FSH	FBG	DV	IO	228-260		8		4200	2	5	10800	12800
24	7	PURSUIT 2500 C/C	ST	CTRCN	FBG	DV	OB			8		3300	1	4	10800	12300
24	7	PURSUIT 2500 C/C	ST	CTRCN	FBG	DV	SE	205	OMC	8		3300	1	4	10800	12300
24	7	PURSUIT 2500 C/C	ST	CTRCN	FBG	DV	SE	T115	OMC	8		3300	1	4	10800	12300
25	6	PURSUIT 2600	ST	CUD	FBG	DV	OB			8	9	3675	2	7	12700	14400
25	6	PURSUIT 2600	ST	CUD	FBG	DV	SE	205	OMC	8	9	3675	2	7	12700	14400
25	6	PURSUIT 2600	ST	CUD	FBG	DV	IO	260		8	9	4600	2	7	11900	13800
25	6	PURSUIT 2600	ST	CUD	FBG	DV	SE	T155	OMC	8	9	3675	2	7	12700	14400
25	6	PURSUIT 2600	ST	CUD	FBG	DV	IO	T170-T185		8	9	4600	2	7	12800	14900
25	6	PURSUIT 2600	ST	CUD	FBG	DV	SE	T205	OMC	8	9	3675	2	7	12700	14400
27		PURSUIT 2700	OP	SF	FBG	DV	SE	T205	OMC	10		7300	1	9	16200	18400
27		PURSUIT 2700	OP	SF	FBG	DV	IB	T220-T270		10		7500	1	9	24400	28000
27		PURSUIT 2700	TT	SF	FBG	DV	SE	T205	OMC	10		7500	1	9	16500	18700
27		PURSUIT 2700	TT	SF	FBG	DV	IB	T220-T270		10		7500	1	9	24400	28000
31	3	PURSUIT 3100	OP	SF	FBG	DV	SE	T205	OMC	12		10500	2	9	30300	33700
31	3	PURSUIT 3100	OP	SF	FBG	DV	IB	T260-T350		12		9200	2	9	32100	38000
31	3	PURSUIT 3100	HT	SF	FBG	DV	SE	T205	OMC	12		9500	2	9	30800	34200
31	3	PURSUIT 3100	HT	SF	FBG	DV	IB	T260-T350		12		9500	2	9	32300	38200
31	3	PURSUIT 3100	FB	SF	FBG	DV	IB	T260-T350		12		10000	2	9	39100	46200
31	3	PURSUIT 3100	TT	SF	FBG	DV	SE	T205	OMC	12		10500	2	9	30800	34200
31	3	PURSUIT 3100	TT	SF	FBG	DV	IB	T260-T350		12		10500	2	9	39500	46600

....For earlier years, see the BUC Used Boat Price Guide, Volume 3

PYRAMID INTERNATIONAL INC

HOUSTON TX 77086 COAST GUARD MFG ID- PYO See inside cover to adjust price for area

LOA FT	LOA IN	NAME AND/ OR MODEL	TOP/ RIG	BOAT TYPE	HULL MTL	HULL TP	ENGINE TP	ENGINE # HP	ENGINE MFG	BEAM FT	BEAM IN	WGT LBS	DRAFT FT	DRAFT IN	RETAIL LOW	RETAIL HIGH
		1985 BOATS														
19	11	EAGLE-TRIMARAN	SLP	SA/RC	F/S	TM	OB			14	9	1400	4		8100	9300
		1984 BOATS														
19	11	EAGLE-TRIMARAN	SLP	SA/RC	F/S	TM	OB			14	9	1400	4		7600	8750

PYTHON BOATS INC
BUFORD GA 30518   COAST GUARD MFG ID- PYH See inside cover to adjust price for area

For more recent years, see the BUC Used Boat Price Guide, Volume 1

LOA FT IN	NAME AND/ OR MODEL	TOP/ RIG	BOAT TYPE	-HULL- MTL TP TP	----ENGINE--- # HP MFG	BEAM FT IN	WGT LBS	DRAFT FT IN	RETAIL LOW	RETAIL HIGH
1996 BOATS										
18	VYPER		RNBT	FBG DV IO	265 MRCR	7	2200	2 3	7650	8800
21	VENOM		B/R	FBG DV JT	350 MPC	7	2100	1 6	9800	11100
21 6	SKI KATANA		SKI	FBG DV IB	265 MRCR	8	2500	1 8	10500	11900
24	PYTHON		CUD	FBG DV IO	330 MRCR	7	3100	3	13100	14900
1994 BOATS										
18	VYPER		RNBT	FBG DV IO	270 MRCR	7	2100	2 3	6600	7600
20 6	SKI KATANA		SKI	FBG DV IB	285 PCM	7 3	2250	1 2	8000	9200
23 6	SNAKE ATTACK		RNBT	FBG DV IO	365 MRCR	7	3400	1 10	11900	13600
1993 BOATS										
18	VYPER		RNBT	FBG DV IO	270 MRCR	7	2100	2 3	6150	7100
20 6	SKI KATANA		SKI	FBG SV IB	285 PCM	7 3	2250	1 2	7600	8700
23 6	SNAKE ATTACK		RNBT	FBG DV IO	365 MRCR	7	3400	1 10	11100	12700
1991 BOATS										
18	VENOM JET	OP	RNBT	F/S SV JT	390 BRKR	7			8000	9150
19 7	SUPER SNAKE	OP	RNBT	F/S SV IO	260 MRCR	7			6900	7950
19 7	SUPER SNAKE	OP	RNBT	F/S SV IO	330 MRCR	7			7950	9150
20 6	SKI KATANA	OP	SKI	F/S SV IB	255-285	6 3	2550		6700	7800
23 6	SNAKE ATTACK 24	OP	OFF	F/S SV IO	330-365	7	3200	1 10	9150	11300
23 6	SNAKE ATTACK 24	OP	OFF	F/S SV IO	410 MRCR	7	3200	1 10	11300	12900
23 6	SNAKE ATTACK SP24	OP	OFF	F/S SV IO	330-365	7	3200	1 10	9450	11700
23 6	SNAKE ATTACK SP24	OP	OFF	F/S SV IO	410 MRCR	7	3200	1 10	11700	13300
1984 BOATS										
18	PYTHON BUBBLE DECK	OP	RACE	FBG	JT				**	**
18	PYTHON BUBBLE DECK	OP	RACE	FBG	JT				4100	4800
20	PYTHON MINI	OP	OFF	FBG DV IO	290 CHEV				4600	5500
20	PYTHON MINI	OP	OFF	FBG DV JT	260-290				6000	6900
24	PYTHON	OP	OFF	FBG DV IO	330 CHEV	7	3550		6400	8000
24	PYTHON	OP	OFF	FBG DV IO	260-320	7	3550		7100	8150
24	PYTHON	OP	OFF	FBG DV IO	390 CHEV	7	3550		8200	9400

QUANTUM MARINE
US MARINE
EVERETT WA 98206   See inside cover to adjust price for area

For more recent years, see the BUC Used Boat Price Guide, Volume 1

LOA FT IN	NAME AND/ OR MODEL	TOP/ RIG	BOAT TYPE	-HULL- MTL TP TP	----ENGINE--- # HP MFG	BEAM FT IN	WGT LBS	DRAFT FT IN	RETAIL LOW	RETAIL HIGH
1996 BOATS										
16 8	QUANTUM 170XD	OP	BASS	FBG SV OB		6 9	1575	2 2	4700	5400
18 1	QUANTUM 180XD-FS	OP	BASS	FBG SV OB		7 2	1750	2 2	5050	5800
18 9	QUANTUM 190XS-FS	OP	BASS	FBG SV OB		7 4	2010	2 8	5550	6350
1995 BOATS										
16 8	QUANTUM 170XD	OP	BASS	FBG SV OB		6 9	1575	2 2	4450	5100
18 1	QUANTUM 180XD-F/S	OP	BASS	FBG SV OB		7 2	1750	2 2	4850	5550

QUEEN LONG MARINE CO LTD
KAOHSIUNG TAIWAN   See inside cover to adjust price for area

For more recent years, see the BUC Used Boat Price Guide, Volume 1

LOA FT IN	NAME AND/ OR MODEL	TOP/ RIG	BOAT TYPE	-HULL- MTL TP TP	----ENGINE--- # HP MFG	BEAM FT IN	WGT LBS	DRAFT FT IN	RETAIL LOW	RETAIL HIGH
1996 BOATS										
46 3	HYLAS 46 SCHEEL	SLP	SACAC	FBG WK IB	D	13 9	27777	4 10	253000	278000
46 3	HYLAS 46 STD	SLP	SACAC	FBG KL IB	D	13 9	27777	6	253000	278000

QUEENSHIP
MAPLE RIDGE BC CANADA V2W 1V9   See inside cover to adjust price for area
FORMERLY COOPER & QUEENSHIP

For more recent years, see the BUC Used Boat Price Guide, Volume 1

LOA FT IN	NAME AND/ OR MODEL	TOP/ RIG	BOAT TYPE	-HULL- MTL TP TP	----ENGINE--- # HP MFG	BEAM FT IN	WGT LBS	DRAFT FT IN	RETAIL LOW	RETAIL HIGH
1994 BOATS										
41 4	QUEENSHIP 40 SD	FB	MY	FBG SV IB	T340 CRUS	13 8	19000	3	108500	119500
	IB T300D CAT 126500 139000, IB T300D DD				126000 138000, IB T320D MTU				136000	149000
62 1	QUEENSHIP 62 MY	FB	MY	FBG SV IB	T550D DD	17 8	58000	4 6	444500	488500
	IB T600D MTU 468000 514500, IB T665D DD				490000 526000, IB T680D MAN				453000	497500
	IB T735D DD 471500 518000, IB T750D MTU				494000 543000					
70	QUEENSHIP 70 MY	FB	MY	FBG SV IB	T665D MTU	17 8	70000	4 6	643000	706500
	IB T680D MAN 613500 674000, IB T735D DD				633000 695500, IB T750D MTU				656000	721000
	IB T10CD MTU 706000 775500, IB T14CD DD				775500 852000					
1990 BOATS										
25 8	PROWLER 8M		CUD	FBG DV IO	260-330	9 3	4300	2 6	14000	17300
25 8	PROWLER 8M COMMAND		RNBT	FBG DV IO	260 MRCR	9 3	6000	2 6	15900	18100
25 8	PROWLER 8M COMMAND		RNBT	FBG DV IO	200D VLVO	9 3	6000	2 6	19000	21200
25 8	PROWLER 8M COMMAND		RNBT	FBG DV IO	T165-T180	9 3	6000	2 6	16800	19200
25 8	PROWLER 8M SUNBRIDGE		RNBT	FBG DV IO	260 MRCR	9 3	5850	2 6	15600	17800
25 8	PROWLER 8M SUNBRIDGE		RNBT	FBG DV IO	200D VLVO	9 3	5850	2 6	18900	21000
25 8	PROWLER 8M SUNBRIDGE		RNBT	FBG DV IO	T160-T180	9 3	5850	2 6	16500	18900
29 8	PROWLER 9M	FB	SDN	FBG DV IO	T165-T230	12	10000	2 4	28300	33400
29 8	PROWLER 9M	FB	SDN	FBG DV IO	T260 MRCR	12	10000	2 4	32800	36400
29 8	PROWLER 9M	FB	SDN	FBG DV IO	T D VLVO	12	10000	2 4	**	**
29 8	PROWLER 9M SUNBRIDGE	FB	SDN	FBG DV IO	T165-T260	12	10000	2 4	28300	32200
29 8	PROWLER 9M SUNBRIDGE	FB	SDN	FBG DV IO	T130D VLVO	12	10000	2 4	34400	38200
29 8	PROWLER 9M SUNDECK	FB	SDN	FBG DV IB	T165-T205	12	10000	2 4	28300	35000
29 8	PROWLER 9M SUNDECK	FB	SDN	FBG DV IB	T230-T260	12	10000	2 4	37700	42900
29 8	PROWLER 9M SUNDECK	FB	SDN	FBG DV IB	T D VLVO	12	10000	2 4	**	**
32 8	PROWLER 10M	FB	SDN	FBG DV IB	T260-T340	12 6	14000	2 8	51300	59300
32 8	PROWLER 10M	FB	SDN	FBG DV IB	T200D VLVO	12 6	14000	2 8	64400	70800
32 8	PROWLER 10M SUNDECK	FB	SDN	FBG DV IB	T260-T340	12 6	14000	2 8	53700	62000
32 8	PROWLER 10M SUNDECK	FB	SDN	FBG DV IB	T200D VLVO	12 6	14000	2 8	67100	73700
42 6	PROWLER 12M	FB	SDN	FBG DV IB	T260 VLVO	13 8	19000	3	108500	119500
42 6	PROWLER 12M	FB	SDN	F/S DV IB	T340 MRCR	13 8	19000	3	111500	122500
42 6	PROWLER 12M	FB	SDN	FBG DV IB	T200D VLVO	13 8	19000	3	115500	127000
	IB T250D GM 118000 129500, IB T275D GM				120000 132000, IB T300D J&T				124500	136500
42 6	PROWLER 12M	FB	SF	FBG DV IB	T260 MRCR	13 8	19000	3	101000	111000
	IB T340 MRCR 108000 118500, IB T200D VLVO				109000 120000, IB T250D GM				115500	126500
	IB T275D GM 118000 129500, IB T300D J&T				121500 133500					
42 6	PROWLER 12M SUNDECK	FB	SDN	FBG DV IB	T260 MRCR	13 8	19000	3	106000	116500
	IB T340 MRCR 112000 123000, IB T200D VLVO				113500 124500, IB T250D GM				120000	132000
	IB T275D GM 121500 133500, IB T300D J&T				124500 134000					
1989 BOATS										
25 8	PROWLER 8M		CUD	FBG DV IO	260-330	9 3	4300	2 6	13200	16300
25 8	PROWLER 8M COMMAND		RNBT	FBG DV IO	260 MRCR	9 3	6000	2 6	15000	17000
25 8	PROWLER 8M COMMAND		RNBT	FBG DV IO	200D VLVO	9 3	6000	2 6	18200	20200
25 8	PROWLER 8M COMMAND		RNBT	FBG DV IO	T165-T180	9 3	6000	2 6	15800	18200
25 8	PROWLER 8M SUNBRIDGE		RNBT	FBG DV IO	260 MRCR	9 3	5850	2 6	14700	16700
25 8	PROWLER 8M SUNBRIDGE		RNBT	FBG DV IO	200D VLVO	9 3	5850	2 6	17400	19800
25 8	PROWLER 8M SUNBRIDGE		RNBT	FBG DV IO	T160-T180	9 3	5850	2 6	15500	17900
29 8	PROWLER 9M	FB	SDN	FBG DV IO	T165-T205	12	10000	2 4	25700	29700
29 8	PROWLER 9M	FB	SDN	FBG DV IO	T230-T260	12	10000	2 4	34600	39400
29 8	PROWLER 9M	FB	SDN	FBG DV IO	T D VLVO	12	10000	2 4	**	**
29 8	PROWLER 9M SUNBRIDGE		SDN	FBG DV IO	T165-T260	12	10000	2 4	26700	32300
29 8	PROWLER 9M SUNBRIDGE		SDN	FBG DV IO	T130D VLVO	12	10000	2 4	43400	48200
29 8	PROWLER 9M SUNDECK	FB	SDN	FBG DV IO	T165-T205	12	10000	2 4	27700	31900
29 8	PROWLER 9M SUNDECK	FB	SDN	FBG DV IO	T230-T260	12	10000	2 4	37100	42200
29 8	PROWLER 9M SUNDECK	FB	SDN	FBG DV IO	T D VLVO	12	10000	2 4	**	**
32 8	PROWLER 10M	FB	SDN	FBG DV IB	T260-T340	12 6	14000	2 8	49400	57200
32 8	PROWLER 10M	FB	SDN	FBG DV IB	T200D VLVO	12 6	14000	2 8	62300	68500
32 8	PROWLER 10M SUNDECK	FB	SDN	FBG DV IB	T260-T340	12 6	14000	2 8	50500	58300
32 8	PROWLER 10M SUNDECK	FB	SDN	FBG DV IB	T200D VLVO	12 6	14000	2 8	63500	69700
42 6	PROWLER 12M	FB	SDN	FBG DV IB	T260 MRCR	13 8	19000	3	101000	111000
42 6	PROWLER 12M	FB	SDN	F/S DV IB	T340 MRCR	13 8	19000	3	106500	117000
42 6	PROWLER 12M	FB	SDN	FBG DV IB	T200D VLVO	13 8	19000	3	108500	119500
	IB T250D GM 113000 124500, IB T275D GM				115000 126500, IB T300D J&T				117000	128500
42 6	PROWLER 12M	FB	SF	FBG DV IB	T260 MRCR	13 8	19000	3	96400	106000
	IB T340 MRCR 103000 113500, IB T200D VLVO				104000 114500, IB T250D GM				110000	121000
	IB T275D GM 112500 124000, IB T300D J&T				116000 127500					
42 6	PROWLER 12M SUNDECK	FB	SDN	FBG DV IB	T260 MRCR	13 8	19000	3	103000	113500
	IB T340 MRCR 109000 114500, IB T200D VLVO				110000 121000, IB T250D GM				114000	125500
	IB T275D GM 116000 127500, IB T300D J&T				118000 129500					
1988 BOATS										
16 10	PROWLER 5.1M			F/S DV IO	130 MRCR	7	1900		3450	4000
19 8	PROWLER 6.0M			F/S DV IO	130 MRCR	7 10	2500		5050	5800
21 8	PROWLER 6.6M			F/S DV IO	130 MRCR	8	3080		6950	8000
21 8	PROWLER 6.6M		CUD	F/S DV IO	130 MRCR	8	2800		6900	7950

LOA FT IN	NAME AND/ OR MODEL	TOP/ RIG	BOAT TYPE	-HULL- MTL TP	----ENGINE--- TP # HP MFG	BEAM FT IN	WGT LBS	DRAFT FT IN	RETAIL LOW	RETAIL HIGH
					1988 BOATS					
25 8	PROWLER 8M		FBG	DV IO	260 MRCR	9 4	6000	1	15400	17500
25 8	PROWLER 8M	OFF	FBG	DV IO	260 MRCR	9 4	5850	1	15000	17000
31 6	PROWLER 9M		F/S	DV IO	T180 MRCR	12	10600	2 4	31400	34900
31 6	PROWLER 9M	SDN	F/S	DV IO	T180 MRCR	12	10600	2 4	30200	33500
35	PROWLER 10M		F/S	DV IB	T260 MRCR	12 6	14000	2 8	52800	58000
35	PROWLER 10M	SDN	F/S	DV IB	T260 MRCR	12 6	14000	2 8	55100	60600
38	PROWLER 12M		F/S	DV IB	T340 MRCR	13 10	20000	3	86100	94600
40	GULF COMMANDER	SDN	F/S	DS IB	T165 VLVO	13 3		3 6	81100	89100
					1987 BOATS					
25 8	PROWLER 8M		FBG	DV IO	260 MRCR	9 4	6000	1	14700	16700
25 8	PROWLER 8M	OFF	FBG	DV IO	260 MRCR	9 4	5850	1	14200	16200
31 6	PROWLER 9M		F/S	DV IO	T180 MRCR	12	10600	2 4	29900	33200
31 6	PROWLER 9M	SDN	F/S	DV IO	T180 MRCR	12	10600	2 4	28700	31900
35	PROWLER 10M		F/S	DV IB	T260 MRCR	12 6	14000	2 8	50300	55300
35	PROWLER 10M	SDN	F/S	DV IB	T260 MRCR	12 6	14000	2 8	52600	57800
38	PROWLER 12M		F/S	DV IB	T340 MRCR	13 10	20000	3	82300	90500
40	GULF COMMANDER	SDN	F/S	DS IB	T165 VLVO	13 3		3 6	77600	85200

QUEST
OMC FISHING BOAT GROUP
MURFEESBORO TN 37130

See inside cover to adjust price for area

LOA FT IN	NAME AND/ OR MODEL	TOP/ RIG	BOAT TYPE	-HULL- MTL TP	----ENGINE--- TP # HP MFG	BEAM FT IN	WGT LBS	DRAFT FT IN	RETAIL LOW	RETAIL HIGH
					1996 BOATS					
16 9	QUEST 170 CC		CTRCN	FBG SV	OB	7 5			5100	5650
17 9	QUEST 187 CC	OP	CTRCN	FBG SV	OB	7 8	2210	2 3	5000	5750
19	QUEST 190 CC		CTRCN	FBG SV	OB	8			5400	6200
20 1	QUEST 227 CC	OP	CTRCN	FBG SV	OB	8 6	3410	2 8	7000	8050
20 1	QUEST 227 WA	OP	CUD	FBG DV	OB	8 6	3850	2 9	7100	8150
21 8	QUEST 220 CC		CTRCN	FBG SV	OB	8			9500	10800
22 6	QUEST 250 CC	OP	CTRCN	FBG DV	OB	9	4390	2 10	10800	12300
25	QUEST 280 WA	OP	CUD	FBG DV	OB	9 5	5860	3	15300	17400
					1995 BOATS					
16 9	QUEST 170 CC		CTRCN	FBG SV	OB	7 5			4800	5550
17 9	QUEST 187 CC	OP	CTRCN	FBG SV	OB	7 8	2210	2 3	4700	5450
19	QUEST 190 CC		CTRCN	FBG SV	OB	8			5100	5900
20 1	QUEST 217 CC	OP	CTRCN	FBG SV	OB	8 6	3410	2 8	6600	7600
20 1	QUEST 217 WA	OP	CUD	FBG DV	OB	8 6	3850	2 9	6650	7650
21 8	QUEST 220 CC		CTRCN	FBG SV	OB	8			9000	10200
22 6	QUEST 237 CC	OP	CTRCN	FBG DV	OB	9	4390	2 10	10200	11600
25	QUEST 257 WA	OP	CUD	FBG DV	OB	9 5	5860	3	14600	16600
					1994 BOATS					
17 9	QUEST 187 CC	OP	CTRCN	FBG DV	OB	7 8	2210	2 3	4450	5150
19 3	QUEST 207 CC	OP	CTRCN	FBG DV	OB	8 2	2620	2 6	4950	5700
20 1	QUEST 217 CC	OP	CTRCN	FBG SV	OB	8 6	3410	2 8	6250	7200
20 1	QUEST 217 WA	OP	CUD	FBG DV	OB	8 6	3850	2 9	6300	7250
22 6	QUEST 237 CC	OP	CTRCN	FBG DV	OB	9	4390	2 10	9750	11100
25	QUEST 257 WA	OP	CUD	FBG DV	OB	9 5	5860	3	13600	15400
					1993 BOATS					
17 9	QUEST 187 CC	OP	CTRCN	FBG DV	OB	7 8	2210	2 3	4200	4900
19 3	QUEST 207 CC	OP	CTRCN	FBG DV	OB	8 2	2620	2 6	4700	5400
20 1	QUEST 217 CC	OP	CTRCN	FBG SV	OB	8 6	3410	2 8	5950	6850
20 1	QUEST 217 WA	OP	CUD	FBG DV	OB	8 6	3850	2 9	6000	6900
22 6	QUEST 237 CC	OP	CTRCN	FBG DV	OB	9	4390		9250	10500
25	QUEST 257 WA	OP	CUD	FBG DV	OB	9 5	5860		12900	14700

QUICKSTEP SAILBOATS
BRISTOL RI 02809

See inside cover to adjust price for area

LOA FT IN	NAME AND/ OR MODEL	TOP/ RIG	BOAT TYPE	-HULL- MTL TP	----ENGINE--- TP # HP MFG	BEAM FT IN	WGT LBS	DRAFT FT IN	RETAIL LOW	RETAIL HIGH
					1987 BOATS					
23 11	QUICKSTEP 24	SLP	SA/CR	FBG KL	OB	7 11	4000	3 5	8950	10200
23 11	QUICKSTEP 24 D	SLP	SA/CR	FBG KL	IB	9D YAN	7 11	4000	3 5	9900	11300

R & L YACHT CONSULTANTS
TORONTO ONTARIO CANADA

See inside cover to adjust price for area

LOA FT IN	NAME AND/ OR MODEL	TOP/ RIG	BOAT TYPE	-HULL- MTL TP	----ENGINE--- TP # HP MFG	BEAM FT IN	WGT LBS	DRAFT FT IN	RETAIL LOW	RETAIL HIGH
					1986 BOATS					
33 2	R & L 33	SLP	SA/RC	WD KL	IB D	11 2	9200	6	49400	54300
					1985 BOATS					
33 2	R & L 33	SLP	SA/RC	WD KL	IB D	11 2	9200	6	46700	51300
					1984 BOATS					
33 3	3/4 TON	SLP	SA/RC	WD KL	IB D	11 3	9200	6	43500	48300

....For earlier years, see the BUC Used Boat Price Guide, Volume 3

R & M MARINE PRODUCTS
RANDOLPH MA 02368

See inside cover to adjust price for area

LOA FT IN	NAME AND/ OR MODEL	TOP/ RIG	BOAT TYPE	-HULL- MTL TP	----ENGINE--- TP # HP MFG	BEAM FT IN	WGT LBS	DRAFT FT IN	RETAIL LOW	RETAIL HIGH
					1993 BOATS					
17 9	BUZZARDS BAY 14	SLP	SACAC	FBG KL		5 10	2000	2 6	9750	11100

R YACHT BUILDER INC
PT CLINTON OH 43452   COAST GUARD MFG ID- RYO   See inside cover to adjust price for area

LOA FT IN	NAME AND/ OR MODEL	TOP/ RIG	BOAT TYPE	-HULL- MTL TP	----ENGINE--- TP # HP MFG	BEAM FT IN	WGT LBS	DRAFT FT IN	RETAIL LOW	RETAIL HIGH
					1984 BOATS					
30	R-30-F	OP	SF	AL SV	IB 320 MRCR	11	7200	2 6	14400	16300
30	R-30-F	OP	SF	AL SV	IB T255 MRCR	11	8400	2 5	16300	18500
30	R-30-F	HT	SF	AL SV	IB 320 MRCR	11	7400	2 6	14500	16500
30	R-30-F	HT	SF	AL SV	IB T255 MRCR	11	8600	2 5	16400	18700
30	R-30-S		SPTCR	AL SV	IB 320 MRCR	11	7200	2 6	15300	17400
30	R-30-ST		SPTCR	AL SV	IB T255 MRCR	11	8400	2 5	17300	19700
31	R-30-SCR	CR		AL SV	IB T330 MRCR	11	9600	2 6	20600	22900

RABCO COMPETITION MARINE
ST PETERSBURG FL 33712   COAST GUARD MFG ID- RCT   See inside cover to adjust price for area

LOA FT IN	NAME AND/ OR MODEL	TOP/ RIG	BOAT TYPE	-HULL- MTL TP	----ENGINE--- TP # HP MFG	BEAM FT IN	WGT LBS	DRAFT FT IN	RETAIL LOW	RETAIL HIGH
					1996 BOATS					
28	CENTER CONSOLE		CTRCN	FBG SV	OB				25600	28500
28	DUAL CONSOLE OS		RNBT	FBG SV	OB				25600	28500
28	SIDE CONSOLE OS		RNBT	FBG SV	OB				25600	28500
35	CENTER CONSOLE		CTRCN	FBG SV	OB				**	**
35	DUAL CONSOLE OS		RNBT	FBG SV	OB				**	**
35	SIDE CONSOLE		RNBT	FBG SV	OB				**	**
					1995 BOATS					
28	CENTER CONSOLE		CTRCN	FBG SV	OB				24400	27100
28	DUAL CONSOLE OS		RNBT	FBG SV	OB				24400	27100
28	SIDE CONSOLE OS		RNBT	FBG SV	OB				24400	27100
35	CENTER CONSOLE		CTRCN	FBG SV	OB				**	**
35	DUAL CONSOLE OS		RNBT	FBG SV	OB				**	**
35	SIDE CONSOLE		RNBT	FBG SV	OB				**	**
					1994 BOATS					
28	CENTER CONSOLE		CTRCN	FBG SV	OB				23400	25900
28	DUAL CONSOLE OS		RNBT	FBG SV	OB				23400	25900
28	SIDE CONSOLE OS		RNBT	FBG SV	OB				23400	25900
35	CENTER CONSOLE		CTRCN	FBG SV	OB				**	**
35	DUAL CONSOLE OS		RNBT	FBG SV	OB				**	**
35	SIDE CONSOLE		RNBT	FBG SV	OB				**	**
					1993 BOATS					
28	CENTER CONSOLE		CTRCN	FBG SV	OB				22400	24900
28	DUAL CONSOLE OS		RNBT	FBG SV	OB				22400	24900
28	SIDE CONSOLE OS		RNBT	FBG SV	OB				22400	24900
35	CENTER CONSOLE		CTRCN	FBG SV	OB				**	**
35	DUAL CONSOLE OS		RNBT	FBG SV	OB				**	**
35	SIDE CONSOLE		RNBT	FBG SV	OB				**	**
					1992 BOATS					
28	CENTER CONSOLE		CTRCN	FBG SV	OB				21500	23900
28	DUAL CONSOLE OS		RNBT	FBG SV	OB				21500	23900
28	SIDE CONSOLE OS		RNBT	FBG SV	OB				21500	23900
35	CENTER CONSOLE		CTRCN	FBG SV	OB				**	**
35	DUAL CONSOLE OS		RNBT	FBG SV	OB				**	**
35	SIDE CONSOLE		RNBT	FBG SV	OB				**	**
					1991 BOATS					
28	CENTER CONSOLE		CTRCN	FBG SV	OB				20700	23000
28	DUAL CONSOLE OS		RNBT	FBG SV	OB				20700	23000
28	SIDE CONSOLE OS		RNBT	FBG SV	OB				20700	23000
35	CENTER CONSOLE		CTRCN	FBG SV	OB				**	**
35	DUAL CONSOLE OS		RNBT	FBG SV	OB				**	**
35	SIDE CONSOLE		RNBT	FBG SV	OB				**	**

LOA FT IN	NAME AND/ OR MODEL	TOP/ RIG	BOAT TYPE	-HULL- MTL TP	ENGINE TP # HP MFG	BEAM FT IN	WGT LBS	DRAFT FT IN	RETAIL LOW	RETAIL HIGH
			1990 BOATS							
28	CENTER CONSOLE		CTRCN	FBG SV	OB				20000	22300
28	DUAL CONSOLE OS		RNBT	FBG SV	OB				20000	22300
28	SIDE CONSOLE		RNBT	FBG SV	OB				20000	22300
35	CENTER CONSOLE		CTRCN	FBG SV	OB				**	**
35	DUAL CONSOLE OS		RNBT	FBG SV	OB				**	**
35	SIDE CONSOLE		RNBT	FBG SV	OB				**	**
			1989 BOATS							
28	CENTER CONSOLE		CTRCN	FBG SV	OB				19400	21500
28	DUAL CONSOLE OS		RNBT	FBG SV	OB				19400	21500
28	SIDE CONSOLE		RNBT	FBG SV	OB				19400	21500
35	CENTER CONSOLE		CTRCN	FBG SV	OB				**	**
35	DUAL CONSOLE OS		RNBT	FBG SV	OB				**	**
35	SIDE CONSOLE		RNBT	FBG SV	OB				**	**
			1988 BOATS							
28	CENTER CONSOLE		CTRCN	FBG SV	OB				19000	21100
28	DUAL CONSOLE OS		RNBT	FBG SV	OB				19000	21100
28	SIDE CONSOLE		RNBT	FBG SV	OB				19000	21100
35	CENTER CONSOLE		CTRCN	FBG SV	OB				**	**
35	DUAL CONSOLE OS		RNBT	FBG SV	OB				**	**
35	SIDE CONSOLE		RNBT	FBG SV	OB				**	**
			1987 BOATS							
28	CENTER CONSOLE		CTRCN	FBG SV	OB				18500	20600
28	DUAL CONSOLE OS		RNBT	FBG SV	OB				18500	20600
28	SIDE CONSOLE		RNBT	FBG SV	OB				18500	20600
35	CENTER CONSOLE		CTRCN	FBG SV	OB				**	**
35	DUAL CONSOLE OS		RNBT	FBG SV	OB				**	**
35	SIDE CONSOLE		RNBT	FBG SV	OB				**	**

RAIDER BOATS INC

COLVILLE WA 99114   COAST GUARD MFG ID- RBC See inside cover to adjust price for area

For more recent years, see the BUC Used Boat Price Guide, Volume 1

LOA FT IN	NAME AND/ OR MODEL	TOP/ RIG	BOAT TYPE	-HULL- MTL TP	ENGINE TP # HP MFG	BEAM FT IN	WGT LBS	DRAFT FT IN	RETAIL LOW	RETAIL HIGH
			1996 BOATS							
16	OSPREY		B/R	AL SV	OB	6 10	1000		2350	2700
16	OSPREY	OP	B/R	AL SV	OB	6 10	1000		2350	2700
18	OSPREY		B/R	AL SV	OB	7 3	1200		2900	3350
18	OSPREY	OP	B/R	AL SV	OB	7 3	1200		2900	3350
20	OSPREY		B/R	AL SV	OB	7 3	1325		3500	4050
20	OSPREY	OP	B/R	AL SV	OB	7 3	1325		3500	4050
20	SEA RAIDER		FSH	AL SV	OB	7 9	1400		3650	4250
20	SEA RAIDER		FSH	AL SV	OB	7 9	1400		3650	4250
22	SEA RAIDER	OP	B/R	AL SV	OB	7 10	1500		4150	4800
22	SEA RAIDER		FSH	AL SV	OB	7 10	1500		4150	4800
22	SEA RAIDER WT	HT	FSH	AL SV	OB	7 10	1875		5050	5800
			1995 BOATS							
16	OSPREY		B/R	AL SV	OB	6 10	1000		2250	2600
16	OSPREY	OP	B/R	AL SV	OB	6 10	1000		2250	2600
18	OSPREY		B/R	AL SV	OB	7 3	1200		2750	3200
18	OSPREY	OP	B/R	AL SV	OB	7 3	1200		2750	3200
20	OSPREY		B/R	AL SV	OB	7 3	1325		3350	3900
20	OSPREY	OP	B/R	AL SV	OB	7 3	1325		3350	3900

RAMPAGE SPORT FISHING YACHTS

DIV KCS INTERNATIONAL INC
OCONTO WI 54153   COAST GUARD MFG ID- RPG   See inside cover to adjust price for area
FORMERLY TILLOTSON PEARSON CO

For more recent years, see the BUC Used Boat Price Guide, Volume 1

LOA FT IN	NAME AND/ OR MODEL	TOP/ RIG	BOAT TYPE	-HULL- MTL TP	ENGINE TP # HP MFG	BEAM FT IN	WGT LBS	DRAFT FT IN	RETAIL LOW	RETAIL HIGH
			1995 BOATS							
29 6	RAMPAGE 28	HT	SF	F/S DV	IB T245-T250	11	8200	2 6	47900	52600
29 6	RAMPAGE 28	HT	SF	F/S DV	IB T170D YAN	11	8200	2 6	57200	62900
31 10	RAMPAGE 31	HT	SF	F/S DV	IB T330-T340	11 11	12000	2 9	78900	87200
31 10	RAMPAGE 31	HT	SF	F/S DV	IBT200D-T300D	11 11	12000	2 9	88500	101000
31 10	RAMPAGE 31	HT	SF	F/S DV	IB T350D CAT	11 11	12000	2 9	102000	112000
34 10	RAMPAGE 33	OP	SF	F/S DV	IB T330 VLVO	12 4	14250	2 8	103500	113500
34 10	RAMPAGE 33	HT	SF	F/S DV	IBT300D-T350D	12 4	14250	2 8	124000	142000
34 10	RAMPAGE 33	HT	SF	F/S DV	IB T340-T400	12 4	14250	2 8	103500	117000
34 10	RAMPAGE 33	HT	SF	F/S DV	IBT300D-T320D	12 4	14250	2 8	122000	138500
35 7	RAMPAGE 36	OP	SF	F/S DV	IB T375D CAT	13 9	19000	2 9	154500	170000
35 7	RAMPAGE 36	OP	SF	F/S DV	IB T400D DD	13 9	19000	2 9	157000	172500
35 7	RAMPAGE 36	OP	SF	F/S DV	IB T425D CAT	13 9	19000	2 9	161000	177000
			1994 BOATS							
29 6	RAMPAGE 28	HT	SF	F/S DV	IB T245-T250	11	8200	2 6	44800	49800
29 6	RAMPAGE 28	HT	SF	F/S DV	IB T170D YAN	11	8200	2 6	54400	59800
31 10	RAMPAGE 31	HT	SF	F/S DV	IB T330-T340	11 11	12000	2 9	74700	82600
31 10	RAMPAGE 31	HT	SF	F/S DV	IBT200D-T300D	11 11	12000	2 9	84200	101500
31 10	RAMPAGE 31	HT	SF	F/S DV	IB T350D CAT	11 11	12000	2 9	96800	106500
34 10	RAMPAGE 33	OP	SF	F/S DV	IB T330 VLVO	12 4	14250	2 8	97700	107500
34 10	RAMPAGE 33	HT	SF	F/S DV	IBT300D-T350D	12 4	14250	2 8	118000	135000
34 10	RAMPAGE 33	HT	SF	F/S DV	IB T340-T400	12 4	14250	2 8	97800	111000
34 10	RAMPAGE 33	HT	SF	F/S DV	IBT300D-T320D	12 4	14250	2 8	116000	131500
35 7	RAMPAGE 36	OP	SF	F/S DV	IB T375D CAT	13 9	19000	2 9	147000	161500
35 7	RAMPAGE 36	OP	SF	F/S DV	IB T400D DD	13 9	19000	2 9	149000	164000
35 7	RAMPAGE 36	OP	SF	F/S DV	IB T425D CAT	13 9	19000	2 9	153500	168500
			1993 BOATS							
29 6	RAMPAGE 28	HT	SF	F/S DV	IB T245-T250	11	8200	2 6	42500	47200
29 6	RAMPAGE 28	HT	SF	F/S DV	IB T170D YAN	11	8200	2 6	51900	57000
31 10	RAMPAGE 31	HT	SF	F/S DV	IB T330-T340	11 11	12000	2 9	70800	78300
31 10	RAMPAGE 31	HT	SF	F/S DV	IBT200D-T300D	11 11	12000	2 9	80200	96800
31 10	RAMPAGE 31	HT	SF	F/S DV	IB T350D CAT	11 11	12000	2 9	92200	101500
34 10	RAMPAGE 33	OP	SF	F/S DV	IB T330 VLVO	12 4	14250	2 8	92600	102000
34 10	RAMPAGE 33	HT	SF	F/S DV	IBT300D-T350D	12 4	14250	2 8	112000	128500
34 10	RAMPAGE 33	HT	SF	F/S DV	IB T340-T400	12 4	14250	2 8	92700	105000
34 10	RAMPAGE 33	HT	SF	F/S DV	IBT300D-T320D	12 4	14250	2 8	110500	125500
35 7	RAMPAGE 36	OP	SF	F/S DV	IB T375D CAT	13 9	19000	2 9	140000	154000
35 7	RAMPAGE 36	OP	SF	F/S DV	IB T400D DD	13 9	19000	2 9	142000	156000
35 7	RAMPAGE 36	OP	SF	F/S DV	IB T425D CAT	13 9	19000	2 9	146000	160500
			1992 BOATS							
29 6	RAMPAGE 28	HT	SF	F/S DV	IB T240-T250	11	8200	2 6	40200	44800
29 6	RAMPAGE 28	HT	SF	F/S DV	IB T170D YAN	11	8200	2 6	49500	54400
31 10	RAMPAGE 31	HT	SF	F/S DV	IB T305-T310	11 11	12000	2 9	66200	73000
31 10	RAMPAGE 31	HT	SF	F/S DV	IBT190D-T300D	11 11	12000	2 9	75800	92300
34 10	RAMPAGE 33	OP	SF	F/S DV	IB T305 VLVO	12 4	14250	2 8	86900	95500
34 10	RAMPAGE 33	HT	SF	F/S DV	IB T310-T400	12 4	14250	2 8	107000	117500
34 10	RAMPAGE 33	HT	SF	F/S DV	IB T300D CAT	12 4	14250	2 8	86800	99700
34 10	RAMPAGE 33	HT	SF	F/S DV	IBT300D-T320D	12 4	14250	2 8	105500	119500
35 7	RAMPAGE 36	OP	SF	F/S DV	IB T375D CAT	13 9	19000	2 9	133500	147000
35 7	RAMPAGE 36	OP	SF	F/S DV	IB T400D DD	13 9	19000	2 9	133500	149000
35 7	RAMPAGE 36	OP	SF	F/S DV	IB T425D CAT	13 9	19000	2 9	139500	153000
			1991 BOATS							
29 6	RAMPAGE 28	HT	SF	F/S DV	IB T250 MRCR	11	8200	2 6	38300	42600
29 6	RAMPAGE 28	HT	SF	F/S DV	IB T205D PEN	11	8200	2 6	49900	54900
31 10	RAMPAGE 31	HT	SF	F/S DV	IB T330 MRCR	11 11	12000	2 9	63800	70200
31 10	RAMPAGE 31	HT	SF	F/S DV	IBT200D-T300D	11 11	12000	2 9	73000	88100
34 10	RAMPAGE 33	HT	SF	F/S DV	IB T330-T410	12 4	14250	2 8	83200	95200
34 10	RAMPAGE 33	HT	SF	F/S DV	IBT300D-T320D	12 4	14250	2 8	100500	114000
35 7	RAMPAGE 36	OP	FSH	F/S DV	IB T375D CAT	13 9	19000	2 9	127500	140000
35 7	RAMPAGE 36	OP	FSH	F/S DV	IB T400D DD	13 9	19000	2 9	129500	142500
35 7	RAMPAGE 36	OP	FSH	F/S DV	IB T425D CAT	13 9	19000	2 9	133000	146000
			1990 BOATS							
24 6	EXPRESS 24	OP	FSH	F/S DV	OB	9 11	4400	2 2	19000	21100
24 6	EXPRESS 24	OP	FSH	F/S DV	IO 260 MRCR	9 11	4900	2 5	17500	19800
24 6	EXPRESS 24	OP	FSH	F/S DV	IB 260-275	9 11	4900	2 8	20500	22800
24 6	MARK II	OP	FSH	F/S DV	OB	9 11	4400	2 11	17400	19800
24 6	MARK II	OP	FSH	F/S DV	IB 260-330	9 11	4400	2 8	19000	21900
24 6	MARK II	OP	FSH	F/S DV	IB 200D VLVO	9 11	4400	2 11	24500	27200
29 6	RAMPAGE 28	HT	SF	F/S DV	IO T260 MRCR	11	8200	2 6	33500	37300
29 6	RAMPAGE 28	HT	SF	F/S DV	IB T260 VLVO	11	8200	2 6	36800	40900
29 6	RAMPAGE 28	HT	SF	F/S DV	IB T205D	11	8200	2 6	47500	52200
31 10	RAMPAGE 31	HT	SF	F/S DV	IB T330 CRUS	11 11	12000	2 9	60700	66700
31 10	RAMPAGE 31	HT	SF	F/S DV	IBT200D-T300D	11 11	12000	2 9	69800	84200
35 7	RAMPAGE 36	OP	FSH	F/S DV	IB T375D CAT	13 9	20000	2 9	122500	138000
35 7	RAMPAGE 36	OP	FSH	F/S DV	IB T400D J&T	13 9	20000	2 9	128000	138000
35 7	RAMPAGE 36	OP	FSH	F/S DV	IB T425D CAT	13 9	20000	2 9	130500	143500
41 9	CONVERTIBLE 40	FB	SF	F/S DV	IB T375D J&T	15 2	25000	3 6	152500	167500
41 9	CONVERTIBLE 40	FB	SF	F/S DV	IB T525D J&T	15 2	25000	3 6	168000	184500
			1989 BOATS							
24 6	EXPRESS 24	OP	FSH	F/S SV	IO 260 MRCR	9 11	4400	2 5	17300	19600
24 6	EXPRESS 24	OP	FSH	F/S SV	IO 260 MRCR	9 11	4900	2 5	16400	18700
24 6	EXPRESS 24	OP	FSH	F/S SV	IB 260-275	9 11	4900	2 8	19600	21700
24 6	MARK II	OP	FSH	F/S SV	IB 260-330	9 11	4400	2 8	18300	21100
24 6	MARK II	OP	FSH	F/S SV	IB 200D VLVO	9 11	4400	2 8	23400	26000
29 6	SPORTSMAN 28	OP	SF	F/S SV	IB T260-T275	11	8200	2 6	35100	39200

LOA FT	IN	NAME AND/ OR MODEL	TOP/ RIG	BOAT TYPE	-HULL- MTL	TP	----ENGINE--- TP	# HP	MFG	BEAM FT	IN	WGT LBS	DRAFT FT	IN	RETAIL LOW	RETAIL HIGH
		1989 BOATS														
31	10	SPORTSFISHERMAN 31	OP	SF	F/S	SV	IB	T330	CRUS	11	11	12000	2	9	57800	63500
31	10	SPORTSFISHERMAN 31	OP	SF	F/S	SV	IB	T200D-T300D		11	11	12000	2	9	66700	80500
35	7	RAMPAGE 36	OP	FSH	F/S	SV	IB	T375D	CAT	13	9	20000	2	9	120000	132000
35	7	RAMPAGE 36	OP	FSH	F/S	SV	IB	T400D	J&T	13	9	20000	2	9	120500	132500
41	9	CONVERTIBLE 40	FB	SF	F/S	SV	IB	T450D	J&T	15		25000	3	6	148500	163500
41	9	CONVERTIBLE 40	FB	SF	F/S	SV	IB	T565D	J&T	15		25000	3	6	166000	182000
		1988 BOATS														
24	6	EXPRESS 24	OP	FSH	F/S	SV	OB			9	11	4400	2	2	16800	19100
24	6	EXPRESS 24	OP	FSH	F/S	SV	IO	260	MRCR	9	11	4900	2	5	15600	17700
24	6	EXPRESS 24	OP	FSH	F/S	SV	IB	260	VLVO	9	11	4900	2	8	18800	20900
24	6	MARK II	OP	FSH	F/S	SV	IB	260-330		9	11	4400	2	8	17100	20100
24	6	MARK II	OP	FSH	F/S	SV	IB	200D	VLVO	9	11	4400	2	8	22400	24900
29	6	SPORTSMAN 28	OP	SF	F/S	SV	IB	T260	VLVO	11		8200	2	6	33400	37100
31	10	SPORTSFISHERMAN 31	OP	SF	F/S	SV	IB	T330	CRUS	11	11	12000	2	9	55100	60500
31	10	SPORTSFISHERMAN 31	OP	SF	F/S	SV	IB	T200D-T300D		11	11	12000	2	9	63900	77100
41	9	CONVERTIBLE 40	FB	SF	F/S	SV	IB	T375D	CAT	15		25000	3	6	134500	147500
41	9	CONVERTIBLE 40	FB	SF	F/S	SV	IB	T450D	J&T	15		25000	3	6	142000	156000
41	9	CONVERTIBLE 40	FB	SF	F/S	SV	IB	T565D	J&T	15		25000	3	6	158500	174000
		1987 BOATS														
24	6	EXPRESS	OP	FSH	F/S	SV	IO	260	MRCR	9	11	4900	2	11	14700	16700
24	6	EXPRESS	OP	FSH	F/S	SV	IB	260	VLVO	9	11	4900	2	8	17600	20000
24	6	MARK II	OP	FSH	F/S	SV	IB	260-330		9	11	4400	2	8	16300	19200
24	6	MARK II	OP	FSH	F/S	SV	IB	200D	VLVO	9	11	4400	2	8	21500	23900
29	6	SPORTSMAN	OP	SF	F/S	SV	IB	T260	VLVO	11		8200	2	6	31900	35400
31	10	SPORTSFISHERMAN	OP	SF	F/S	SV	IB	T330	CRUS	11	11	12000	2	9	52500	57700
31	10	SPORTSFISHERMAN	OP	SF	F/S	SV	IB	T200D-T300D		11	11	12000	2	9	61200	73800
		1986 BOATS														
19		RAMPAGE FISH	OP	FSH	FBG	SV	OB			7	8	1800			5150	5900
24	6	RAMPAGE EXPRESS	OP	EXP	FBG	SV	IO	260		9	11		1	8	13400	15200
24	6	RAMPAGE EXPRESS	OP	EXP	FBG	SV	IB	260		9	11	4900	1	8	16600	18800
24	6	RAMPAGE-MARK II	OP	SF	FBG	SV	IB	260		9	11	4400	1	8	15300	17400
29	6	RAMPAGE-SPORTSMAN	OP	SF	FBG	SV	IB	T260		11					33900	37700
31	10	RAMPAGE 31		SF	FBG	SV	IB	T165D		11	11				47800	52500
		1985 BOATS														
19		RAMPAGE FISH	OP	FSH	FBG	SV	OB			7	8	1800			5000	5750
24	6	RAMPAGE EXPRESS	OP	CUD	FBG	SV	OB			9	11	4000	1	8	14200	16200
24	6	RAMPAGE EXPRESS	OP	EXP	FBG	SV	IO	228		9	11	4900	1	8	12500	14200
24	6	RAMPAGE EXPRESS	OP	EXP	FBG	SV	IB	270		9	11	4900	1	8	15900	18000
24	6	RAMPAGE TOURNAMENT	OP	CTRCN	FBG	SV	OB			9	11	3500	1	8	13100	14800
24	6	RAMPAGE TOURNAMENT	OP	CTRCN	FBG	SV	IO	228		9	11	4400	1	8	12200	13900
24	6	RAMPAGE TOURNAMENT	OP	CTRCN	FBG	SV	IB	270		9	11	4400	1	8	14700	16700
29	10	RAMPAGE EXPRESS FISH	OP	EXP	FBG	SV	IB	T270		11		8200			34900	38800
		1984 BOATS														
19		RAMPAGE	OP	CTRCN	FBG	DV	OB			7	8	1800	1	3	4850	5600
24	6	RAMPAGE	OP	EXP	FBG	DV	OB			9	8	4000	1	6	13800	15700
24	6	RAMPAGE EXPRESS	OP	EXP	FBG	DV	IO	228-260		9	8	4900	1	6	12000	13900
24	6	RAMPAGE EXPRESS	OP	EXP	FBG	DV	IB	270-350		9	8	4900	1	8	15300	18100
24	6	RAMPAGE EXPRESS	OP	EXP	FBG	DV	IB	158D	VLVO	9	8	4900	1	8	19500	21600
24	6	RAMPAGE TOURNAMENT	OP	CTRCN	FBG	DV	OB			9	8	3500	1	6	12700	14400
24	6	RAMPAGE TOURNAMENT	OP	CTRCN	FBG	DV	IO	228-260		9	8	4400	1	6	11700	13600
24	6	RAMPAGE TOURNAMENT	OP	CTRCN	FBG	DV	IB	270-350		9	8	4400	1	8	14200	16800
24	6	RAMPAGE TOURNAMENT	OP	CTRCN	FBG	DV	IB	158D	VLVO	9	8	4400	1	8	18300	20300
24	6	RAMPAGE TOURNAMENT	TT	CTRCN	FBG	DV	OB			9	8	3500	1	6	12700	14500
24	6	RAMPAGE TOURNAMENT	TT	CTRCN	FBG	DV	IO	228-260		9	8	4400	1	6	11700	13600
24	6	RAMPAGE TOURNAMENT	TT	CTRCN	FBG	DV	IB	270-350		9	8	4400	1	8	14200	16800
24	6	RAMPAGE TOURNAMENT	TT	CTRCN	FBG	DV	IB	158D	VLVO	9	8	4400	1	8	18300	20300

RAMPONE BOATS

EAST COAST MARINE INC
MIAMI FL 33133

See inside cover to adjust price for area

LOA FT	IN	NAME AND/ OR MODEL	TOP/ RIG	BOAT TYPE	-HULL- MTL	TP	----ENGINE--- TP	# HP	MFG	BEAM FT	IN	WGT LBS	DRAFT FT	IN	RETAIL LOW	RETAIL HIGH
		1984 BOATS														
25		RAMPONE	OP	OPFSH	FBG	DV	SE			8			2	8	**	**
25		RAMPONE	TT	OPFSH	FBG	DV	OB			8			2	8	8100	9300
25		RAMPONE	TT	OPFSH	FBG	DV	IB	270-350		8			2	8	8700	10500
25		RAMPONE	TT	OPFSH	FBG	DV	IB	200D	PERK	8			2	8	12400	14100
25		RAMPONE	TT	OPFSH	FBG	DV	IB	T138-T170		8			2	8	9200	10600
25		RAMPONE 25	OP	OPFSH	FBG	DV	OB			8		3500	2	8	7050	8100
25		RAMPONE 25	OP	OPFSH	FBG	DV	IB	270-350		8		5000	2	8	9200	10900
25		RAMPONE 25	OP	OPFSH	FBG	DV	IB	200D	PERK	8		5000	2	8	12600	14400
25		RAMPONE 25	OP	OPFSH	FBG	DV	IB	T138-T170		8		5000	2	8	9550	11000
25		RAMPONE 25	ST	OPFSH	FBG	DV	OB			8		5000	2	8	8450	9700
25		RAMPONE 25	HT	OPFSH	FBG	DV	OB			8		5000	2	8	8450	9700
25		RAMPONE 25	HT	OPFSH	FBG	DV	IB	270-350		8		5000	2	8	9200	10900
25		RAMPONE 25	HT	OPFSH	FBG	DV	IB	200D	PERK	8		5000	2	8	12600	14400
25		RAMPONE 25	HT	OPFSH	FBG	DV	IB	T170	MRCR	8		5000	2	8	9700	11000

....For earlier years, see the BUC Used Boat Price Guide, Volume 3

RANGER BOAT CO

KENT WA 98032

COAST GUARD MFG ID- RFB See inside cover to adjust price for area
SEE MARTINI MARINE

For more recent years, see the BUC Used Boat Price Guide, Volume 1

LOA FT	IN	NAME AND/ OR MODEL	TOP/ RIG	BOAT TYPE	-HULL- MTL	TP	----ENGINE--- TP	# HP	MFG	BEAM FT	IN	WGT LBS	DRAFT FT	IN	RETAIL LOW	RETAIL HIGH
		1996 BOATS														
20		RANGER 20	SLP	SAROD	FBG	KC	OB			7	10	1550	3	1	5900	6750
21		RANGER 21 LAUNCH	HT	PH	F/S	DS	IB	18D	YAN	6	8	2025	1	6	10100	11500
23	11	RANGER 24	SLP	SARAC	FBG	KL	OB			8	4	2950	4	2	11500	13100
26		RANGER 26	SLP	SACAC	FBG	KC	OB			8		4750	4	10	22000	24400
		1995 BOATS														
20		RANGER 20	SLP	SAROD	FBG	KC	OB			7	10	1550	3	1	5550	6350
21		RANGER 21 LAUNCH	HT	PH	F/S	DS	IB	18D- 27D		6	8	2025	1	6	9650	11400
23	11	RANGER 24	SLP	SARAC	FBG	KL	OB			8	4	2950	4	2	10800	12200
26		RANGER 26	SLP	SACAC	FBG	KC	OB			8		4750	4	10	20600	22900
		1994 BOATS														
20		RANGER 20	SLP	SAROD	FBG	KC	OB			7	10	1550	3	1	5150	5950
21		RANGER 21 LAUNCH	HT	PH	F/S	DS	IB	18D- 27D		6	8	2025	1	6	9200	10900
23	11	RANGER 24	SLP	SARAC	FBG	KL	OB			8	4	2950	4	2	10100	11400
26		RANGER 26	SLP	SACAC	FBG	KC	OB			8		4750	4	10	19200	21400
		1993 BOATS														
20		RANGER 20	SLP	SAROD	FBG	KC	OB			7	10	1550	3	1	4850	5550
21		RANGER 21 LAUNCH	HT	PH	F/S	DS	IB	18D- 27D		6	8	2025	1	6	8650	10400
23	11	RANGER 24	SLP	SARAC	FBG	KL	OB			8	4	2950	4	2	9400	10700
26		RANGER 26	SLP	SACAC	FBG	KC	OB			8		4750	4	10	17600	20000
		1992 BOATS														
20		RANGER 20	SLP	SA/OD	FBG	CB	OB			7	10	1550	1	9	4550	5200
21		RANGER 21 LAUNCH	HT	PH	FBG	SV	IB	18D		6	8	2025	1	6	7950	9150
		1991 BOATS														
20		RANGER 20	SLP	SA/OD	FBG	CB	OB			7	10	1550	1	9	4200	4900
21		RANGER 21 LAUNCH	HT	PH	FBG	SV	IB	18D		6	8	2025	1	6	7500	8650
		1990 BOATS														
20		RANGER 20	SLP	SA/OD	FBG	CB	OB			7	10	1550	1	9	3950	4600
21		RANGER 21 LAUNCH	HT	PH	FBG	SV	IB	9D- 18D		6	8	2025	1	6	6800	8250
		1989 BOATS														
20		RANGER 20	SLP	SA/OD	FBG	CB	OB			7	10	1550	1	9	3650	4250
21		RANGER 21 LAUNCH	HT	PH	FBG	SV	IB	9D- 18D		6	8	2025	1	6	6500	7900
26		RANGER 26	SLP	SA/CR	FBG	KC	OB			8		4750	2	4	13200	15000
28		RANGER 8.5	SLP	SA/RC	FBG	KL	IB	8D		9	6	5000	5	1	16200	18400
		1988 BOATS														
20		RANGER 20	SLP	SA/OD	FBG	CB	OB			7	10	1550	1	9	3450	4000
21		RANGER 21 LAUNCH	HT	PH	FBG	SV	IB	9D- 18D		6	8	2025	1	6	6200	7550
26		RANGER 26	SLP	SA/CR	FBG	KC	OB			8		4750	2	4	12100	13800
28		RANGER 8.5	SLP	SA/RC	FBG	KL	IB	8D		9	6	5000	5	1	14900	16900
		1987 BOATS														
20		RANGER 20	SLP	SA/OD	FBG	CB	OB			7	10	1550	1	9	3200	3700
21		RANGER 21 LAUNCH	HT	PH	FBG	SV	IB	9D- 18D		6	8	2025	1	6	5950	7200
26		RANGER 26	SLP	SA/CR	FBG	KC	OB			8		4750	2	4	11300	12800
28		RANGER 8.5	SLP	SA/RC	FBG	KL	IB	8D		9	6	5000	5	1	13600	15500
		1986 BOATS														
16	8	RANGER 16	SLP	SAIL	FBG	CB				6		550		3	1750	2100
18	2	RANGER 18	LAT	SAIL	FBG	CB				6	8	1200	1	2	2500	2900
18	2	RANGER 18	SLP	SAIL	FBG	CB				6	8	1200	1	2	2750	3150
20		RANGER 20	SLP	SA/OD	FBG	CB	OB			7	10	1550	1	9	3000	3500
21		RANGER 21 LAUNCH	HT	PH	FBG	SV	IB	9D- 18D		6	8	2025	1	6	5700	6900
24		RANGER 24	SLP	SA/RC	FBG	KL	OB			8	4	3200	4	1	6150	7100
26		RANGER 26	SLP	SA/CR	FBG	KC	OB			8		4750	2	4	10600	12000
28		RANGER 8.5	SLP	SA/RC	FBG	KL	IB	8D		9	6	5000	5	1	12900	14600
		1985 BOATS														
16	8	RANGER 16	SLP	SAIL	FBG	CB				6		550		3	1650	2000
18	2	RANGER 18	LAT	SAIL	FBG	CB				6	8	1200	1	2	2350	2700
18	2	RANGER 18	SLP	SAIL	FBG	CB				6	8	1200	1	2	2550	3000
20		RANGER 20	SLP	SA/RC	FBG	KC	OB			7	10	1500	3	1	2750	3200
21		RANGER 21	HT	PH	FBG	DS	IB	D		6		2000			**	**
24		RANGER 24	SLP	SA/RC	FBG	KL	OB			8	4	3200	4	1	5700	6550
26		RANGER 26	SLP	SA/CR	FBG	KC	IB	D		8		4750	2	4	10400	11900
28		RANGER 28	SLP	SA/RC	FBG	KL	IB	D		9	6	5100	5	1	12200	13800

LOA FT IN	NAME AND/ OR MODEL	TOP/ RIG	BOAT TYPE	-HULL- MTL TP	----ENGINE--- TP # HP MFG	BEAM FT IN	WGT LBS	DRAFT FT IN	RETAIL LOW	RETAIL HIGH
					1984 BOATS					
20	RANGER 20	SLP	SA/RC	FBG KC	OB	7 10	1500	1 10	2550	3000
24	RANGER 24	SLP	SA/RC	FBG KL	OB	8 4	3200	4 1	5400	6200
26	RANGER 26	SLP	SA/CR	FBG KC	IB	8 4	4750	2 4	9850	11200
28	RANGER 8.5	SLP	SA/RC	FBG KL	IB D	9 6	5100	5 1	11400	13000

....For earlier years, see the BUC Used Boat Price Guide, Volume 3

RANGER BOATS

RANGER BOATS
WOOD MFG   See inside cover to adjust price for area
FLIPPIN AR 72634   COAST GUARD MFG ID- RNG
               FORMERLY WOOD MFG CO INC

For more recent years, see the BUC Used Boat Price Guide, Volume 1

LOA FT IN	NAME AND/ OR MODEL	TOP/ RIG	BOAT TYPE	-HULL- MTL TP	----ENGINE--- TP # HP MFG	BEAM FT IN	WGT LBS	DRAFT FT IN	RETAIL LOW	RETAIL HIGH
					1996 BOATS					
18	RANGER 180C	OP	CTRCN	FBG SV	OB	7 6	1350		6500	7450
18 11	RANGER 184 FLATS	OP	BASS	FBG SV	OB	7 9	1350		6700	7700
20 1	RANGER 210C	OP	CTRCN	FBG SV	OB	8 6	2850		11900	13500
22 8	RANGER 230C	OP	CTRCN	FBG SV	OB	8 6	3100		16100	18300
24 8	RANGER 250C	OP	CTRCN	FBG SV	OB	9	3990		21200	23500
					1995 BOATS					
18	RANGER 180C	OP	CTRCN	FBG SV	OB	7 6	1350		6150	7050
18 11	RANGER 184 FLATS	OP	BASS	FBG SV	OB	7 9	1350		6350	7300
20 1	RANGER 210C	OP	CTRCN	FBG SV	OB	8 6	2850		11200	12800
22 8	RANGER 230C	OP	CTRCN	FBG SV	OB	8 6	3100		15000	17000
24 8	RANGER 250C	OP	CTRCN	FBG SV	OB	9	3990		20000	22300
					1994 BOATS					
18	RANGER 180C	OP	CTRCN	FBG SV	OB	7 6	1350		5800	6700
18 11	RANGER 184 FLATS	OP	BASS	FBG SV	OB	7 9	1350		6000	6900
20 1	RANGER 210C	OP	CTRCN	FBG SV	OB	8 6	2850		10700	12100
20 8	RANGER 216WA	OP	CUD	FBG SV	OB	8 4	2800		11400	12900
22 8	RANGER 230C	OP	CTRCN	FBG SV	OB	8 6	3100		14200	16200
24 8	RANGER 250C	OP	CTRCN	FBG SV	OB	9	3990		19000	21100
					1993 BOATS					
17 10	RANGER 361V FLATS	OP	BASS	FBG SV	OB	7 4	1321		5450	6250
18	RANGER 180C	OP	CTRCN	FBG SV	OB	7 6	1350		5550	6350
20 1	RANGER 200C	OP	CTRCN	FBG SV	OB	8 6	2850		10100	11500
20 8	RANGER 216WA	OP	CUD	FBG SV	OB	8 4	2800		10800	12300
22 8	RANGER 230C	OP	CTRCN	FBG SV	OB	8 6	3375		14300	16200
24 8	RANGER 250C	OP	CTRCN	FBG SV	OB	9	3990		18000	20000
					1992 BOATS					
16 10	APACHE 330V	OP	BASS	FBG SV	OB	6 10	1025		4050	4750
16 11	FISHERMAN 680T	OP	FSH	FBG SV	OB	6 8	990		3900	4550
16 11	FISHERMAN 681C	OP	FSH	FBG SV	OB	6 8	1050		4100	4800
17 6	COMANCHE 451V	OP	BASS	FBG SV	OB	7	1210		4800	5550
17 10	APACHE 354V	OP	BASS	FBG SV	OB	6 10	1050		4250	4950
17 10	APACHE 372V	OP	BASS	FBG SV	OB	7 4	1200		4800	5550
17 10	APACHE 374V	OP	BASS	FBG SV	OB	7 4	1200		4800	5550
17 10	APACHE 375V	OP	BASS	FBG SV	OB	7 4	1200		4800	5550
17 10	COMANCHE 361V	OP	BASS	FBG SV	OB	7 4	1225		4900	5650
17 10	COMANCHE 362V	OP	BASS	FBG SV	OB	7 4	1225		4900	5650
17 10	COMANCHE 363V	OP	BASS	FBG SV	OB	7 4	1225		4900	5650
17 10	COMANCHE 364V	OP	BASS	FBG SV	OB	7 4	1190		4800	5500
17 10	COMANCHE 365V	OP	BASS	FBG SV	OB	7 4	1200		4800	5550
18	COMANCHE 481V	OP	BASS	FBG SV	OB	7 6	1250		5000	5750
18	COMANCHE 482V	OP	BASS	FBG SV	OB	7 6	1270		5050	5800
18	COMANCHE 485V	OP	BASS	FBG SV	OB	7 6	1270		5050	5800
18	FISHERMAN 690C	OP	FSH	FBG SV	OB	7 6	1380		5350	6150
18	FISHERMAN 690T	OP	FSH	FBG SV	OB	7 6	1350		5250	6050
18	FISHERMAN 692C	OP	FSH	FBG SV	OB	7 6	1390		5400	6200
19 4	APACHE 390V	OP	BASS	FBG SV	OB	7 6	1325		5450	6300
19 4	APACHE 397V	OP	BASS	FBG SV	OB	7 6	1465		5900	6800
19 4	COMANCHE 391V	OP	BASS	FBG SV	OB	7 6	1325		5450	6300
19 4	COMANCHE 392V	OP	BASS	FBG SV	OB	7 6	1350		5550	6400
19 4	COMANCHE 393V	OP	BASS	FBG SV	OB	7 6	1335		5500	6300
19 4	COMANCHE 396V	OP	BASS	FBG SV	OB	7 6	1350		5550	6400
20 1	COMANCHE 395V	OP	BASS	FBG SV	OB	7 6	2400		**	**
20 1	COMANCHE 395VS	OP	BASS	FBG SV	IO	7 6	1475		6450	7400
20 2	COMANCHE 491V	OP	BASS	FBG SV	OB	7 8	1460		6400	7350
20 2	COMANCHE 491VS	OP	BASS	FBG SV	IO	7 8	1530		6650	7650
20 2	COMANCHE 492V	OP	BASS	FBG SV	OB	7 8	1490		6500	7500
20 2	COMANCHE 492VS	OP	BASS	FBG SV	IO	7 8	1550		6700	7700
					1985 BOATS					
16	RANGER 340		FSH	FBG SV	OB	7 6	1050		3100	3600
16 10	RANGER 330		BASS	FBG SV	OB	6 10	1025		3000	3600
16 10	RANGER 335		BASS	FBG SV	OB	6 10	1045		3150	3650
17 10	RANGER 350		BASS	FBG SV	OB	6 10	1050		3250	3800
17 10	RANGER 370		BASS	FBG SV	OB	7 4	1190		3650	4200
17 10	RANGER 372		BASS	FBG SV	OB	7 4	1190		3650	4200
17 10	RANGER 375		BASS	FBG DV	OB	7 4	1200		3650	4250
17 10	RANGER 375		FSH	FBG DV	OB	7 4			3600	4150
18 8	CHIEF 380		FSH	FBG DV	OB 160	7 6	1350		4100	4750
18 8	CHIEF 380		SF	FBG DV	IO 160	7 6			4400	5050
20	RANGER 395		BASS	FBG SV	OB	7 6			5500	6300
20	RANGER 395		FSH	FBG SV	IO	7 6			**	**
22	RANGER 622	OFF	FBG	DV	OB	8	2700		8500	9800
					1984 BOATS					
16 10	RANGER 330		BASS	FBG DV	OB	6 10	1025		3000	3500
16 10	RANGER 335		BASS	FBG DV	OB	6 10	1045		3050	3550
17 10	RANGER 350		BASS	FBG DV	OB	6 10	1050		3200	3700
17 10	RANGER 370		BASS	FBG DV	OB	7 4	1190		3550	4100
17 10	RANGER 372		BASS	FBG DV	OB	7 4	1190		3550	4100
17 10	RANGER 375		BASS	FBG DV	OB	7 4	1200		3550	4150
17 10	RANGER 375		FSH	FBG DV	OB	7 4			3450	4000
18 8	RANGER 380 CHIEF		FSH	FBG DV	OB 160	7 6	1350		4000	4650
18 8	RANGER 380 CHIEF		FSH	FBG DV	IO 160	7 6			3850	4500
20	RANGER 395		BASS	FBG SV	OB	7 6			5350	6150
20	RANGER 395		FSH	FBG SV	IO	7 6			**	**
22	RANGER 622		FSH	FBG DV	OB	8	2700		8300	9550

....For earlier years, see the BUC Used Boat Price Guide, Volume 3

RANGER SAILBOATS

A BANGOR PUNTA COMPANY
JENSEN MARINE   See inside cover to adjust price for area
FALL RIVER MA 02722   COAST GUARD MFG ID- RAY

LOA FT IN	NAME AND/ OR MODEL	TOP/ RIG	BOAT TYPE	-HULL- MTL TP	----ENGINE--- TP # HP MFG	BEAM FT IN	WGT LBS	DRAFT FT IN	RETAIL LOW	RETAIL HIGH
					1985 BOATS					
23 4	FUN	SLP	SA/RC	FBG SK		8	1875	2 4	4100	4800
					1984 BOATS					
23 4	FUN	SLP	SAIL	FBG SK		8	1875	2 4	3850	4500

....For earlier years, see the BUC Used Boat Price Guide, Volume 3

RAPID CRAFT BOATS INC

BLACKFOOT ID 83221   COAST GUARD MFG ID- TAD   See inside cover to adjust price for area

LOA FT IN	NAME AND/ OR MODEL	TOP/ RIG	BOAT TYPE	-HULL- MTL TP	----ENGINE--- TP # HP MFG	BEAM FT IN	WGT LBS	DRAFT FT IN	RETAIL LOW	RETAIL HIGH
					1984 BOATS					
16	BASS 1600	OP	BASS	AL SV	OB	4 10	560	4	2350	2700
16	BASS 1600	OP	BASS	AL SV	IB 115 VLVO	4 10	1050	4	2450	2800
17	WHITEWATER 17	OP	CR	AL SV	IB 170 CHEV	6	1500	6	3550	4100
18	BASS 1800	OP	BASS	AL SV	OB	4 10	600	4	2750	3200
18	BASS 1800	OP	BASS	AL SV	IB 138 VLVO	4 10	1100	4	3450	4000
18	WHITEWATER 18	OP	CR	AL SV	IB 215 FORD	6	1700	8	4500	5200
20	WHITEWATER 20	OP	CR	AL SV	IB 215 FORD	6	1750	8	5700	6550

RON RAWSON INC

REDMOND WA 98052   COAST GUARD MFG ID- RRW   See inside cover to adjust price for area

LOA FT IN	NAME AND/ OR MODEL	TOP/ RIG	BOAT TYPE	-HULL- MTL TP	----ENGINE--- TP # HP MFG	BEAM FT IN	WGT LBS	DRAFT FT IN	RETAIL LOW	RETAIL HIGH
					1986 BOATS					
30 6	RAWSON PILOTHOUSE 30	SLP	SA/CR	FBG KL		9	12500	5	30800	34200
					1985 BOATS					
30 6	RAWSON CRUISING 30	SLP	SA/CR	FBG KL		9	12000	5	27500	30500
30 6	RAWSON PILOTHOUSE 30	SLP	SA/CR	FBG KL		9	12500	5	28900	32100
					1984 BOATS					
30 6	RAWSON CRUISING 30	SLP	SA/CR	FBG KL		9	12000	5	25800	28700
30 6	RAWSON PILOTHOUSE 30	SLP	SA/CR	FBG KL		9	12500	5	27200	30200

....For earlier years, see the BUC Used Boat Price Guide, Volume 3

RAY'S RIVER DORIES

WOODROW INC
PORTLAND OR 97219   COAST GUARD MFG ID- RXX   See inside cover to adjust price for area

LOA FT IN	NAME AND/ OR MODEL	TOP/ RIG	BOAT TYPE	-HULL- MTL TP	----ENGINE--- TP # HP MFG	BEAM FT IN	WGT LBS	DRAFT FT IN	RETAIL LOW	RETAIL HIGH
			1996 BOATS							
16 6	ROGUE 18X60		ROW	WD FL		7 1	350		**	**

....For earlier years, see the BUC Used Boat Price Guide, Volume 3

REBEL INDUSTRIES INC

TALLEVAST FL 33588   COAST GUARD MFG ID- RRR   See inside cover to adjust price for area
FORMERLY RAY GREENE & CO INC

LOA FT IN	NAME AND/ OR MODEL	TOP/ RIG	BOAT TYPE	-HULL- MTL TP	----ENGINE--- TP # HP MFG	BEAM FT IN	WGT LBS	DRAFT FT IN	RETAIL LOW	RETAIL HIGH
			1986 BOATS							
18 7	SPINDRIFT 19	SLP	SA/RC	FBG KC	OB	7 6	1350	1 6	3300	3850
18 7	STARWIND 190	SLP	SA/RC	FBG KC	OB	7 6	1350	1 6	3550	4100
21 6	SPINDRIFT 22	SLP	SA/RC	FBG KC	OB		1990	1 6	4350	5000
22 3	STARWIND 223	SLP	SA/RC	FBG KC	OB	8 6	2435	1 10	5000	5750
24	SPINDRIFT 24	SLP	SA/RC	FBG KC	OB	8	3000	2	5950	6850
26 8	STARWIND 270	SLP	SA/RC	FBG KL	OB	9 8	5500	3 7	12100	13700

....For earlier years, see the BUC Used Boat Price Guide, Volume 3

DAVE REED & CO

CHILOQUIN OR 97624-0336   COAST GUARD MFG ID- DVR   See inside cover to adjust price for area
For more recent years, see the BUC Used Boat Price Guide, Volume 1

LOA FT IN	NAME AND/ OR MODEL	TOP/ RIG	BOAT TYPE	-HULL- MTL TP	----ENGINE--- TP # HP MFG	BEAM FT IN	WGT LBS	DRAFT FT IN	RETAIL LOW	RETAIL HIGH
			1996 BOATS							
17 8	CONTENDER	OP	SKI	FBG SV	IB 255 PCM	6 3	2300	1 9	10400	11900
			1995 BOATS							
17 8	CONTENDER	OP	SKI	FBG SV	IB 255 PCM	6 3	2300	1 9	9850	11200
			1994 BOATS							
17 8	CONTENDER	OP	SKI	FBG SV	IB 255 PCM	6 3	2300	1 9	9400	10700
			1993 BOATS							
17 8	CONTENDER	OP	SKI	FBG SV	IB 255 PCM	6 3	2300	1 9	8900	10100
			1992 BOATS							
17 8	CONTENDER	OP	SKI	FBG SV	IB 255 PCM	6 3	2300	1 9	8350	9600
			1991 BOATS							
17 8	CONTENDER	OP	SKI	FBG SV	IB 255 PCM	6 3	2300	1 9	7950	9150
			1990 BOATS							
17 8	CONTENDER	OP	SKI	FBG SV	IB 255 PCM	6 3	2300	1 9	7550	8700
			1989 BOATS							
17 8	CONTENDER	OP	SKI	FBG SV	IB 255 PCM	6 3	2300	1 9	7200	8250
			1988 BOATS							
17 8	CONTENDER	OP	SKI	FBG SV	IB 255 PCM	6 3	2300	1 9	6850	7850
			1987 BOATS							
17 8	CONTENDER	OP	SKI	FBG SV	IB 255 PCM	6 3	2300	1 9	6550	7500
			1986 BOATS							
17 8	CONTENDER	OP	SKI	FBG SV	IB 255 PCM	6 3	2300	1 9	6250	7150
			1985 BOATS							
17 8	CONTENDER	OP	SKI	FBG SV	IB 255 PCM	6 3	2300	1	5950	6850
			1984 BOATS							
17 8	CONTENDER	OP	SKI	FBG SV	IB 250 PCM	6 3	2300	1 9	5700	6550

....For earlier years, see the BUC Used Boat Price Guide, Volume 3

REGAL MARINE INDS INC

ORLANDO FL 32809   COAST GUARD MFG ID- RGM   See inside cover to adjust price for area
For more recent years, see the BUC Used Boat Price Guide, Volume 1

LOA FT IN	NAME AND/ OR MODEL	TOP/ RIG	BOAT TYPE	-HULL- MTL TP	----ENGINE--- TP # HP MFG	BEAM FT IN	WGT LBS	DRAFT FT IN	RETAIL LOW	RETAIL HIGH
			1996 BOATS							
17 3	VALANTI 176SC	OP	RNBT	FBG SV	IO 135-190	7 4	2250	2 7	4150	5150
17 3	VALANTI 176SE	OP	B/R	FBG SV	IO 135-190	7 4	2250	2 7	3950	4900
18 2	VALANTI 182SE	OP	RNBT	FBG SV	IO 135-190	8 3	2575	2 7	6350	7700
19 10	VALANTI 202SC	OP	CUD	FBG SV	IO 180-210	8 3	2800	2 7	7600	9100
19 10	VALANTI 202SC	OP	CUD	FBG SV	IO 220-250	8 3	2800	2 7	8350	9900
19 10	VALANTI 202SE	OP	B/R	FBG SV	IO 180-220	8 3	2800	2 7	7100	8650
19 10	VALANTI 202SE	OP	B/R	FBG SV	IO 250	8 3	2800	2 7	7450	8950
20 1	DESTINY 200	OP	RNBT	FBG SV	IO 180-250	8 6	3400	2 9	10400	12800
21 9	VALANTI 222SC	OP	CUD	FBG SV	IO 190-250	8 3	3200	2 7	11700	13800
21 9	VALANTI 222SE	OP	B/R	FBG SV	IO 190 VLVO	8 3	3200	2 7	10900	12400
21 9	VALANTI 222SE	OP	B/R	FBG SV	IO 210-250	8 3	3200	2 7	10700	12500
22 7	VENTURA 6.8	OP	CUD	FBG SV	IO 190-250	8 6	4000	2 7	14300	16700
22 7	VENTURA 6.8	OP	CUD	FBG SV	IO 300	8 6	4000	2 7	15100	17800
22 7	VENTURA 6.8	OP	CUD	FBG SV	IO 330	8 6	4000	2 7	15800	18900
23 1	VENTURA 7.0SE	OP	B/R	FBG SV	IO 190-250	8 6	3800		13200	15500
23 1	VENTURA 7.0SE	OP	B/R	FBG SV	IO 300-330	8 6	3800		14000	16700
23 9	DESTINY 240	OP	RNBT	FBG SV	IO 190-250	8 6	3900	3	13900	16300
26	COMMODORE 258	OP	WKNDR	FBG SV	IO 220-300	9 1	5000	2 10	19000	22300
26	COMMODORE 258	OP	WKNDR	FBG SV	IO 188D VLVO	9 1	5000	2 10	22300	24800
26	COMMODORE 258	OP	WKNDR	FBG SV	IO T135	9 1	5000	2 10	19900	22800
26	LEISURECAT 26	OP	CTRCN	FBG CT	OB	8 4	3200	1 8	11200	12700
27 6	VENTURA 8.3SC	OP	EXP	FBG SV	IO 300-385	9 1	5600	2 10	24800	30200
27 6	VENTURA 8.3SC	OP	EXP	FBG SV	IO 216D VLVO	9 1	5600	2 10	26800	29700
27 6	VENTURA 8.3SE	OP	EXP	FBG SV	IO T165-T250	9 1	5600	2 10	25400	31300
27 6	VENTURA 8.3SE	OP	B/R	FBG SV	IO 300-385	9 1	5600	2 10	22700	27700
27 6	VENTURA 8.3SE	OP	B/R	FBG SV	IO 216D VLVO	9 1	5600	2 10	24200	26900
27 6	VENTURA 8.3SE	OP	B/R	FBG SV	IO T165 MRCR	9 1	5600	2 10	23300	25900
28 6	COMMODORE 272	OP	WKNDR	FBG SV	IO 300-330	9 2	6800	3 6	27100	31500
28 6	COMMODORE 272	OP	WKNDR	FBG SV	IO 216D VLVO	9 2	6800	3 6	32000	35500
28 6	COMMODORE 272	OP	WKNDR	FBG SV	IO T180-T190	9 2	6800	3 6	28100	31800
28 9	COMMODORE 292	OP	WKNDR	FBG DV	IO T180-T250	10 4	9500	3 2	36900	43200
28 9	COMMODORE 292	OP	WKNDR	FBG DV	IO T185D VLVO	10 4	9500	3 2	49100	54000
32	COMMODORE 322	OP	WKNDR	FBG DV	IO 225 MRCR	11 2	11800	2 10	47600	52300
	IO T225-T250 51400	57400,	IB T260	MRCR	61200 67200,	IO T300			53900	59200
	IB T310 MRCR 63100	69300,	IO T330		54900	60300,	IB T340		64200	70500
	IO T215D VLVO 60000	65900								
42	COMMODORE 402	OP	EXP	FBG SV	IB T310 MRCR	13 1	16000	3	100500	110500
	IB T310 VLVO 101500	111500,	IB T340	MRCR	101500 111500,	IB T340	VLVO		102500	112500
	IB T400 MRCR 104000	114500,	IO T315D	CUM	93000 102000,	IO T350D	CAT		99700	109500
			1995 BOATS							
17 3	VALANTI 176SC	OP	RNBT	FBG SV	IO 135-185	7 4	2250	2 7	3850	4800
17 3	VALANTI 176SE	OP	B/R	FBG SV	IO 135-180	7 4	2250	2 7	3700	4500
18 2	VALANTI 182SE	OP	RNBT	FBG SV	IO 135-185	8 3	2575	2 7	5950	7200
19 10	VALANTI 202SC	OP	CUD	FBG SV	IO 180 MRCR	8 3	2800	2 7	7100	8150
	IO 185 VLVO 7350	8450,	IO	190	MRCR 7100	8150,	IO 190	VLVO	7400	8500
	IO 220 VLVO 7800	9000,	IO	235	MRCR 7300	8400,	IO 250	MRCR	7650	8800
19 10	VALANTI 202SE	OP	B/R	FBG SV	IO 180-250	8 3	2800	2 7	6650	8100
21 9	VALANTI 222SC	OP	CUD	FBG SV	IO 190-250	8 3	3200	2 7	10500	12900
21 9	VALANTI 222SE	OP	B/R	FBG SV	IO 190 MRCR	8 3	3200	2 7	9850	11200
21 9	VALANTI 222SE	OP	B/R	FBG SV	IO 190 VLVO	8 3	3200	2 7	10200	11600
21 9	VALANTI 222SE	OP	B/R	FBG SV	IO 220-250	8 3	3200	2 7	10300	12100
22 7	VALANTI 230SE	OP	B/R	FBG DV	IO 220-250	8 6	3695	2 7	11900	13600
22 7	VALANTI 230SE	OP	B/R	FBG DV	IO 220-300	8 6	3695	2 7	11900	14800
22 7	VENTURA 6.8	OP	CUD	FBG SV	IO 190-275	8 6	4000	2 7	13000	16000
22 7	VENTURA 6.8	OP	CUD	FBG SV	IO 300	8 6	4000	2 7	14100	16600
22 7	VENTURA 6.8	OP	CUD	FBG SV	IO 140D VLVO	8 6	4000	2 7	15800	18000
23 9	DESTINY 240	OP	RNBT	FBG SV	IO 190-275	8 6	3500	3	11700	14500
23 9	DESTINY 240	OP	RNBT	FBG SV	IO 140D VLVO	8 6	3500	3	14500	16400
26	COMMODORE 256	OP	WKNDR	FBG SV	IO 220-300	8 6	5000	2 10	17200	20900
26	COMMODORE 256	OP	WKNDR	FBG SV	IO 185D VLVO	8 6	5000	2 10	20600	22900
26	COMMODORE 256	OP	WKNDR	FBG SV	IO T135	8 6	5000	2 10	18600	21300
26 6	CLASSIC 233	OP	WKNDR	FBG SV	IO 190-235	8 4	4500		14400	16900
26 6	CLASSIC 233	OP	WKNDR	FBG SV	IO 140D VLVO	8 4	4500		17300	19600
27 6	VENTURA 8.3SC	OP	EXP	FBG SV	IO 300-385	9 1	5600	2 10	23100	28200
	IO 216D VLVO 25000	27700,	IO	T180-T250	24100	28800,	IO T275	VLVO	27200	30200
27 6	VENTURA 8.3SE	OP	B/R	FBG SV	IO 300-385	9 1	5800	2 10	21500	26200
27 6	VENTURA 8.3SE	OP	B/R	FBG SV	IO 216D VLVO	9 1	5800	2 10	23600	25700
28 6	COMMODORE 272	OP	WKNDR	FBG SV	IO 300-330	9 2	6800	3 6	25300	28900
28 6	COMMODORE 272	OP	WKNDR	FBG SV	IO 216D VLVO	9 2	6800	3 6	29800	33100
28 6	COMMODORE 272	OP	WKNDR	FBG SV	IO T180-T185	9 2	6800	3 6	26200	29600
28 6	COMMODORE 272	OP	WKNDR	FBG SV	IO T275-T275	10 4	8500	3 2	32800	39800
28 9	COMMODORE 292	OP	WKNDR	FBG DV	IO 185D VLVO	10 4	8500	3 2	42400	47100
28 9	COMMODORE 292	OP	WKNDR	FBG DV	IO 235 MRCR	11 2	11800	2 10	44100	49000
32	COMMODORE 322	OP	WKNDR	FBG DV	IO 235 MRCR	11 2	11800	2 10	44100	49000
	IO T235 VLVO 53100,	IO	T250 MRCR	48800	53600,	IO T250	VLVO		57500	63100
	IO T275-T300 49500	55000,	IO T310	MRCR	59600	65500,	IO T330	VLVO	51200	56200
	IB T340 MRCR 60700	66700,	IO T215D	VLVO	56000	61500				
42	COMMODORE 402	OP	EXP	FBG SV	IB T310 MRCR	13 1	16000	3	96300	106000

LOA FT	LOA IN	NAME AND/ OR MODEL	TOP/ RIG	BOAT TYPE	-HULL- MTL	-HULL- TP	ENGINE TP	ENGINE # HP	ENGINE MFG	BEAM FT	BEAM IN	WGT LBS	DRAFT FT	DRAFT IN	RETAIL LOW	RETAIL HIGH
		1995 BOATS														
42		COMMODORE 402	OP	EXP	FBG	SV	IB	T310	VLVO	13	1	16000	3		97200	107000
		IB T340 MRCR 97200 107000, IB T340 VLVO 98200 108000, IB T400 MRCR 99900 109500														
		IB T400 VLVO 101000 111000, IO T315D CUM 86800 95400, IO T350D CAT 93000 102000														
		1994 BOATS														
17	3	VALANTI 176CD	OP	CUD	FBG	SV	IO	115-185		7	4	2250	2	7	3650	4550
17	3	VALANTI 176SE	OP	RNBT	FBG	SV	IO	115-180		7	4	2250	2	7	3600	4400
17	3	VALANTI 176SE	OP	RNBT	FBG	SV	IO	185	VLVO	7	4	2570	2	7	4150	4800
18	2	VALANTI 182SE	OP	RNBT	FBG	SV	IO	110-185		8	3	2575	2	7	5500	6700
19	10	VALANTI 202SC	OP	RNBT	FBG	SV	IO	180-210		8	3	2800	2	7	6350	7650
19	10	VALANTI 202SC	OP	RNBT	FBG	SV	IO	225-240		8	3	2800	2	7	7000	8000
19	10	VALANTI 202SE	OP	RNBT	FBG	SV	IO	180	MRCR	8	3	2800	2	7	6250	7150
		IO 180-205 6800 7850, IO 210 YAMA 6150 7100, IO 225-235 6750 7750														
		IO 240 YAMA 6350 7300														
20	2	VALANTI 206SC	OP	CUD	FBG	SV	IO	180-230		7	10	2960	2	7	8300	10200
21	9	VALANTI 222SE	OP	RNBT	FBG	SV	IO	180-250		8	3	3200	2	7	9350	11100
22	7	VALANTI 230SE	OP	B/R	FBG	DV	IO	240-300		8	6	3700	2	7	11000	13300
22	7	VALANTI 230SE	OP	D/R	FBG	SV	IO	225-300		8	6	3700	2	7	11200	13900
22	7	VENTURA 6.8	OP	CUD	FBG	SV	IO	190-250		8	6	4000	2	7	12400	14600
22	7	VENTURA 6.8	OP	CUD	FBG	SV	IO	300		8	6	4000	2	7	13100	15500
26		LEISURE CAT	OP	CTRCN	FBG	CT	OB			8	3	3200	1	8	10200	11600
26		VALANTI 256	OP	WKNDR	FBG	SV	IO	225-300		8	6	4800	2	10	15600	18900
26		VALANTI 256	OP	WKNDR	FBG	SV	IO	185D	VLVO	8	6	4800	2	10	18900	21000
26		VALANTI 256	OP	WKNDR	FBG	SV	IO	T135		8	6	4800	2	10	16400	19300
26	6	VALANTI 233	OP	WKNDR	FBG	SV	IO	205-225		8	4	4800	3		14200	16600
26	6	VALANTI 233XL	OP	WKNDR	FBG	SV	IO	190-240		8	4	4500	3		13700	15800
26	6	VALANTI 233XL	OP	WKNDR	FBG	SV	IO	120D	VLVO	8	4	4500	3		15900	18000
27	6	VENTURA 8.3SC	OP	EXP	FBG	SV	IO	300		9	1	5800	2	10	21900	24700
		IO 385-425 20500 24000, IO 216D VLVO 23900 26500, IO T180-T250 22800 27600														
		IO T360-T390 28400 34000														
27	6	VENTURA 8.3SE	OP	B/R	FBG	SV	IO	300-390		9	1	5800	2	10	20100	25100
27	6	VENTURA 8.3SE	OP	B/R	FBG	SV	IO	502	MRCR	9	1	5800	2	10	25300	28200
27	6	VENTURA 8.3SE	OP	B/R	FBG	SV	IO	216D	VLVO	9	1	5800	2	10	21600	24000
28	6	COMMODORE 272	OP	WKNDR	FBG	SV	IO	300		9	2	6200	3	6	22600	25500
		IO 185D-216D 25000 28800, IO T180-T185 23500 26600, IO T360 YAMA 29300 32600														
32		VENTURA 9.8	OP	EXP	FBG	SV	IO	T225	VLVO	11	2	11000	3	2	44000	48900
		IB T240-T245 53400 58800, IO T250 VLVO 44700 49700, IO T250 YAMA 44700 49700														
		IB T250 MRCR 53700 59000, IO T300 MRCR 46700 51300, IO T300 VLVO 46700 51300														
		IO T300 YAMA 46700 51300, IB T300 MRCR 55500 60900, IB T300-T305 55500 61100														
		IB T310 MRCR 55800 61300, IB T D GM ** ** , IO T216D VLVO 50600 55600														
		IB T225D VLVO 62900 69100														
32	5	COMMODORE 300	OP	WKNDR	FBG	SV	IO	T190-T250		10		9200	3	2	29700	34500
32	5	COMMODORE 300	OP	WKNDR	FBG	SV	IO	T185D	VLVO	10		9200	3	2	36200	40200
42		COMMODORE 400	OP	EXP	FBG	SV	IB	T300	VLVO	13	1	16000	3		92800	102000
		IB T305 VLVO 93000 102000, IB T310 MRCR 92300 101500, IB T300D CUM 109500 120500														
		IB T326D VLVO 109000 120000														
		1993 BOATS														
17	3	VALANTI 176SC	OP	CUD	FBG	SV	OB			7	4	1670	2	7	3150	3650
17	3	VALANTI 176SC	OP	CUD	FBG	SV	IO	110-180		7	4	2250	2	7	3600	4250
17	3	VALANTI 176SC	OP	RNBT	FBG	SV	OB			7	4	1670	2	7	3250	3800
17	3	VALANTI 176SE	OP	RNBT	FBG	SV	OB			7	4	1670	2	7	3150	3650
17	3	VALANTI 176SE	OP	RNBT	FBG	SV	IO	110-180		7	4	2250	2	7	3400	4150
17	3	VALANTI 176SSE	OP	RNBT	FBG	SV	IO	110-175		7	4	2250	2	7	3450	4200
17	3	VALANTI 176SSE	OP	RNBT	FBG	SV	IO	180	VLVO	7	4	2250	2	7	3950	4550
19	4	VALANTI 196SC	OP	CUD	FBG	SV	OB			7	4	2000	2	7	4700	5400
19	4	VALANTI 196SE	OP	RNBT	FBG	SV	OB			7	4	2000	2	7	4700	5400
19	6	VALANTI 196SC	OP	CUD	FBG	SV	OB			7	4	2750	2	7	5400	6200
19	6	VALANTI 196SC	OP	CUD	FBG	SV	IO	135-180		7	4	2750	2	7	5550	6700
19	6	VALANTI 196SE	OP	CUD	FBG	SV	OB			7	4	2750	2	7	5400	6200
19	6	VALANTI 196SE	OP	RNBT	FBG	SV	IO	135-180		7	4	2570	2	7	5150	6250
19	10	VALANTI 202SE	OP	RNBT	FBG	SV	IO	135-205		8	3	2550	2	7	5600	6850
20	2	VALANTI 206SC	OP	CUD	FBG	SV	IO	175-250		7	10	2960	2	7	7750	9550
20	2	VALANTI 206SE	OP	B/R	FBG	DV	IO	230	MRCR	7	10	2960	2	7	7450	8600
20	2	VALANTI 206SE	OP	B/R	FBG	SV	IO	175-250		7	10	2960	2	7	7250	8950
22	7	VALANTI 230SE	OP	B/R	FBG	DV	IO	205-300		8	6	3700	2	7	10100	12400
22	7	VALANTI 230SE	OP	B/R	FBG	SV	IO	225-300		8	6	3700	2	7	10500	12900
22	7	VENTURA 6.8	OP	CUD	FBG	SV	IO	205-250		8	6	4000	2	7	11400	13600
22	7	VENTURA 6.8	OP	CUD	FBG	SV	IO	300		8	6	4000	2	7	12300	14500
23	10	VALANTI 230SC	OP	CUD	FBG	DV	IO	205-250		8	6	4000	2	7	11500	13700
23	10	VALANTI 230SC	OP	CUD	FBG	DV	IO	300		8	6	4000	2	7	12400	14700
23	10	VALANTI 230SC	OP	CUD	FBG	DV	IO	120D	VLVO	8	6	4000	2	7	13700	15600
26		VALANTI 252	OP	WKNDR	FBG	SV	IO	230-300		8	6	4800	2	10	14300	17700
26		VALANTI 252	OP	WKNDR	FBG	SV	IO	185D-216D		8	6	4800	2	10	17300	20200
26		VALANTI 252	OP	WKNDR	FBG	SV	IO	T135		8	6	4800	2	10	15300	18100
26	6	AMBASSADOR 233XL	OP	WKNDR	FBG	SV	IO	225-245		8	4	4500	3		13000	15000
26	6	AMBASSADOR 233XL	OP	WKNDR	FBG	SV	IO	130D	VLVO	8	4	4600	3		15200	17200
26	6	VALANTI 233	OP	WKNDR	FBG	SV	IO	205		8	4	4800	3		13300	15400
26	6	VALANTI 233	OP	WKNDR	FBG	SV	IO	300	VLVO	8	4	4800	3		14700	16700
27	6	VENTURA 8.3SC	OP	EXP	FBG	SV	IO	300		9	1	5800	2	10	20500	23000
		IO 216D VLVO 22300 24800, IO T180-T250 21600 25700, IO T360 YAMA 26600 29500														
		IO T480 YAMA 31700 35200, IO T130D VLVO 25100 27900														
27	6	VENTURA 8.3SE	OP	B/R	FBG	SV	IO	300		9	1	5800	2	10	19000	21100
27	6	VENTURA 8.3SE	OP	B/R	FBG	SV	IO	216D	VLVO	9	1	5800	2	10	20200	22400
28	6	COMMODORE 272	OP	WKNDR	FBG	SV	IO	300		9	2	6200	3	6	21000	23900
		IO 200D-230D 23800 27300, IO T135-T180 21100 24700, IO T360 YAMA 27400 30500														
29	5	COMMODORE 276	OP	WKNDR	FBG	SV	IO	300		9	6	6500	2	8	21900	24700
		IO T175-T180 22600 25600, IO T360 YAMA 28200 31300, IO T130D VLVO 27700 30800														
32		VENTURA 9.8	OP	EXP	FBG	SV	IO	T225	VLVO	11	2	11000	3	2	41100	45700
		IB T240 VLVO 50600 55600, IO T245 VLVO 41600 46300, IO T250 MRCR 41800 46400														
		IB T250 MRCR 50900 56000, IO T300 43100 47900, IB T305-T310 52700 58100														
		IOT185D-T216D 46100 52200														
32	5	COMMODORE 300	OP	WKNDR	FBG	SV	IO	T225-T250		10		9200	3	2	28600	32300
32	5	COMMODORE 300	OP	WKNDR	FBG	SV	IO	T410		10		9200	3	2	33400	37700
32	5	COMMODORE 300	OP	WKNDR	FBG	SV	IO	T185D-T216D		10		9200	3	2	33800	39000
42		COMMODORE 400	OP	EXP	FBG	SV	IB	T300	VLVO	13	1	16000	3		88400	97200
		IB T310 MRCR 87900 96600, IB T400 MRCR 91100 100000, IB T295D CUM 104000 114500														
		IB T306D VLVO 102500 112500														
		1992 BOATS														
16	11	VALANTI 170 CUDDY	OP	CUD	FBG	SV	OB			7	4	1670	2	7	3750	4350
16	11	VALANTI 170VBR	OP	RNBT	FBG	SV	OB			7	4	1670	2	7	3750	4350
17	1	VALANTI 170 CUDDY	OP	CUD	FBG	SV	IO	110-180		7	2	2250	2	7	4150	4900
17	1	VALANTI 170VBR	OP	RNBT	FBG	SV	IO	110-180		7	2	2250	2	7	4050	4800
19	4	VALANTI 190 CUDDY	OP	CUD	FBG	SV	OB			7	4	2000	2	7	4500	5200
19	4	VALANTI 190VBR	OP	RNBT	FBG	SV	OB			7	4	2000	2	7	4500	5200
19	6	VALANTI 190 CUDDY	OP	CUD	FBG	SV	IO	135-175		7	4	2570	2	7	5000	6250
19	6	VALANTI 190 CUDDY	OP	CUD	FBG	SV	IO	180	VLVO	7	4	2750	2	7	5450	6300
19	6	VALANTI 190VBR	OP	RNBT	FBG	SV	IO	135-175		7	4	2570	2	7	4800	6000
19	6	VALANTI 190VBR	OP	RNBT	FBG	SV	IO	180	VLVO	7	4	2750	2	7	5250	6050
20	2	VALANTI 200 CUDDY	OP	CUD	FBG	SV	IO	155-250		7	10	2760	2	7	6950	8600
20	2	VALANTI 200VBR	OP	B/R	FBG	DV	IO	155-230		7	10	2760	2	7	6500	7700
20	2	VALANTI 200VBR	OP	B/R	FBG	SV	IO	155-250		7	10	2760	2	7	6750	8050
20	3	SEBRING 195 CUDDY	OP	CUD	FBG	SV	IO	135-180		7	10	2425	2	7	6500	7850
21	8	VELOCITY 22	OP	RACE	FBG	SV	OB			7	10	2000	1	9	4700	5400
22	7	VALANTI 220 CUDDY	OP	CUD	FBG	DV	IO	230-250		8	6	3900	2	7	10600	12500
22	7	VALANTI 220 CUDDY	OP	CUD	FBG	DV	IO	300		8	6	3900	2	7	11300	13400
22	7	VALANTI 220 CUDDY	OP	CUD	FBG	SV	IO	230	VLVO	8	6	3900	2	7	10900	12300
22	7	VALANTI 220VBR	OP	B/R	FBG	SV	IO	230-250		8	6	3700	2	7	9550	11300
22	7	VALANTI 220VBR	OP	B/R	FBG	SV	IO	300		8	6	3700	2	7	10200	12100
23	3	VELOCITY 23VEL	OP	RACE	FBG	SV	IO	245-250		8		3500	2	10	9750	11100
23	3	VELOCITY 23VEL	OP	RACE	FBG	SV	IO	300-350		8		3665	2	10	10300	12900
23	10	VALANTI 225SC	OP	SPTCR	FBG	SV	IO	175-250		8	6	4300	2	7	11800	14200
23	10	VALANTI 225SC	OP	SPTCR	FBG	SV	IO	300		8	6	4300	2	7	12800	15000
26		VALANTI 240	OP	WKNDR	FBG	SV	IO	230-250		8	6	4800	2	10	15000	17500
		IO 300 16500 19200, IO 200D-230D 17500 20800, IO T110-T135 15900 18600														
26	4	ROYAL 25LF	OP	SF	FBG	SV	IO	230-300		8		4600	3	1	16300	20200
26	4	ROYAL 25LF	OP	SF	FBG	SV	IO	T115-T135		8		4600	3	1	17000	20200
26	6	AMBASSADOR 233XL	OP	WKNDR	FBG	SV	IO	180-245		8	4	4500	3		14600	17600
26	6	AMBASSADOR 233XL	OP	WKNDR	FBG	SV	IO	300	MRCR	8	4	4600	3		16300	18600
26	6	AMBASSADOR 233XL	OP	WKNDR	FBG	SV	IO	130D	VLVO	8	4	4600	3		15100	17200
27	6	ROYAL 250XL	OP	WKNDR	FBG	SV	IO	230-300		8		4600	3	1	16800	20700
27	6	ROYAL 250XL	OP	WKNDR	FBG	SV	IO	T250	MRCR	8		4600	3	1	20800	23100
27	6	VENTURA 8.3SE	OP	EXP	FBG	SV	IO	230-300		9	1	5800	2	10	18300	21600
		IO 200D-230D 20500 23600, IO T130-T230 19200 23600, IO T245-T250 21600 24000														
28	6	VALANTI 260	OP	WKNDR	FBG	SV	IO	230-300		9	2	6100	3	6	20800	24600
28	6	VALANTI 260	OP	WKNDR	FBG	SV	IO	200D-230D		9	2	6100	3	6	22700	26300
28	6	VALANTI 260	OP	WKNDR	FBG	SV	IO	T135-T180		9	2	6100	3	6	21700	25600
29	5	COMMODORE 270	OP	WKNDR	FBG	SV	IO	245-300		9	6	6500	2	8	23900	27600
29	5	COMMODORE 270	OP	WKNDR	FBG	SV	IO	T155-T250		9	6	6500	2	8	25000	30600
29	5	COMMODORE 270	OP	WKNDR	FBG	SV	IO	T130D	VLVO	9	6	6500	2	8	27500	30600
32	5	COMMODORE 290	OP	WKNDR	FBG	SV	IO	T175-T250		10		9100	3	2	31000	36400
32	5	COMMODORE 290	OP	WKNDR	FBG	SV	IO	T200D-T230D		10		9100	3	2	36600	42100

CONTINUED ON NEXT PAGE

LOA FT	LOA IN	NAME AND/ OR MODEL	TOP/ RIG	BOAT TYPE	-HULL- MTL	-HULL- TP	ENGINE TP	ENGINE # HP	ENGINE MFG	BEAM FT	BEAM IN	WGT LBS	DRAFT FT	DRAFT IN	RETAIL LOW	RETAIL HIGH
		1992 BOATS														
34	2	COMMODORE 320	OP	WKNDR	FBG	SV	IO	T230-T300		11	2	11000	2	11	43000	50200
34	2	COMMODORE 320	OP	WKNDR	FBG	SV	IO	T200D-T230D		11	2	11000	2	11	48600	54700
42		COMMODORE 380	OP	EXP	FBG	SV	IB	T300	VLVO	13	1	16000	3		84300	92700
		IB T310 MRCR 83800 92100, IB T400 MRCR 86900 95500, IB T300D IVCO													100000	110000
		IB T306D VLVO 97800 107500														
		1991 BOATS														
17	10	VALANTI 190C	OP	RNBT	FBG	SV	IO	120-205		7	3	2250	2	7	4000	4750
18	10	SEBRING 195C	OP	CUD	FBG	DV	IO	120-205		7	10	2600	2	7	4900	5800
18	10	VALANTI 200C	OP	CUD	FBG	DV	IO	145-260		7	10	2400			4550	5600
18	10	VALANTI 200V	OP	B/R	FBG	DV	IO	145-260		7	10	2600			4450	5450
18	10	VALANTI 220C	OP	B/R	FBG	DV	IO	260-275		8	6	3600	2	7	6000	7400
18	10	VALANTI 220C	OP	B/R	FBG	DV	IO	330		8	6	3600	2	7	6800	8300
18	10	VALANTI 220C	OP	CUD	FBG	DV	IO	260-275		8	6	3900	2	7	6750	8250
18	10	VALANTI 220C	OP	CUD	FBG	DV	IO	330		8	6	3900	2	7	7600	9250
19	6	EMPRESS 200EMP	OP	CUD	FBG	DV	IO	175-260		8		3100	2	8	5550	6750
19	6	EMPRESS 200EMP	OP	CUD	FBG	DV	IO	275	VLVO	8		3100	2	8	6300	7250
22	5	VALANTI 225	OP	CUD	FBG	DV	IO	200-275		8	6	4500	2	7	10800	13200
22	5	VALANTI 225	OP	CUD	FBG	DV	IO	330		8	6	4500	2	7	12200	14500
23	2	AMBASSADOR 233	OP	CUD	FBG	DV	IO	275-330		8	4	3995	3		11000	13100
23	2	AMBASSADOR 233	OP	CUD	FBG	DV	IO	130D	VLVO	8	4	3995	3		12300	13900
23	2	AMBASSADOR 233	OP	CUD	FBG	DV	IO	260D	MRCR	8	4	3995	3		14600	16600
23	5	VELOCITY 23VL	OP	CUD	FBG	DV	IO	270-275		8		2948	2	10	8700	10500
23	5	VELOCITY 23VL	OP	CUD	FBG	DV	IO	330-365		8		2940	2	10	9650	12000
24	6	ROYAL 250	OP	CUD	FBG	DV	IO	T260-T275		8		4000	3	1	13100	15900
24	6	ROYAL 250	OP	CUD	FBG	DV	IO	T330		8		4000	3	1	14900	18100
24	6	ROYAL 25LF	OP	CUD	FBG	DV	IO	275-330		8		4175	3	1	12000	14900
24	6	ROYAL 25LF	OP	CUD	FBG	DV	IO	260D	MRCR	8		4175	3	1	15700	17900
24	6	ROYAL 25LF	OP	CUD	FBG	DV	IO	T145-T146		8		4175	3	1	12300	14500
26		VALANTI 240	OP	WKNDR	FBG	SV	IO	230-300		8	6	4800	2	10	12500	15000
26		VALANTI 240	OP	WKNDR	FBG	SV	IO	120D	VLVO	8	6	4800	2	10	14400	16400
26		VALANTI 260	OP	WKNDR	FBG	SV	IO	230-300		9	2	6200	3	6	15600	19000
26		VALANTI 260	OP	WKNDR	FBG	SV	IO	185D	VLVO	9	2	6200	3	6	18900	21000
26		VALANTI 260	OP	WKNDR	FBG	SV	IO	T135-T180		9	2	6200	3	6	16600	19600
26	10	COMMODORE 270	OP	OVNTR	FBG	DV	IO	275-330		9	6	6500	2	5	18500	21400
26	10	COMMODORE 270	OP	OVNTR	FBG	DV	IO	T175-T275		9	6	6500	2	5	19000	23700
26	10	COMMODORE 270	OP	OVNTR	FBG	DV	IO	T130D	VLVO	9	6	6500	2	5	23200	25800
27	1	COMMODORE 290	OP	OVNTR	FBG	DV	IO	T200-T260		10		8200	3	2	22400	26100
27	1	COMMODORE 290	OP	OVNTR	FBG	DV	IO	T200D	VLVO	10		8200	3	2	30400	33800
27	10	COMMODORE 290	OP	OVNTR	FBG	DV	IO	T270-T275		10		8200	3	2	24400	27600
31	10	COMMODORE 320	OP	OVNTR	FBG	DV	IO	T260-T330		11	2	11000	2	11	36300	42200
31	10	COMMODORE 320	OP	OVNTR	FBG	DV	IO	T200D	VLVO	11	2	11000	2	11	40300	44700
36	1	COMMODORE 360	OP	OVNTR	FBG	DV	IO	T340	MRCR	13	1	17000	2	10	46400	51000
36	1	COMMODORE 360	OP	OVNTR	FBG	DV	IO	T340	VLVO	13	1	17000	2	10	47200	51900
36	1	COMMODORE 360	OP	OVNTR	FBG	DV	IO	T420	MRCR	13	1	17000	2	10	50200	55100
		1990 BOATS														
17	10	SEBRING 185RAB	OP	RNBT	FBG	DV	IO	120-205		7	3	2250	2	7	3750	4500
17	10	SEBRING 185V	OP	RNBT	FBG	DV	IO	120-205		7	3	2250	2	7	3750	4550
17	10	VALANTI 190C	OP	RNBT	FBG	SV	IO	120-205		7	3	2250	2	7	3750	4550
17	10	VALANTI 190V	OP	RNBT	FBG	SV	IO	120-205		7	3	2250	2	7	3750	4550
18	10	SEBRING 195C	OP	CUD	FBG	DV	IO	46-205		7	10	2600	2	7	4650	5450
18	10	SEBRING 195V	OP	B/R	FBG	DV	IO	120-205		7	10	2400	2	7	4150	4900
18	10	VALANTI 200C	OP	CUD	FBG	DV	IO	145-209		7	10	2400			4250	5250
18	10	VALANTI 200C	OP	CUD	FBG	DV	IO	260-275		7	10	2400			4600	5750
18	10	VALANTI 200V	OP	B/R	FBG	DV	IO	145-260		7	10	2600			4150	5150
18	10	VALANTI 200V	OP	B/R	FBG	DV	IO	275	VLVO	7	10	2600			4850	5550
19	6	EMPRESS 200EMP	OP	CUD	FBG	DV	IO	167-260		8		3100	2	8	5400	6350
19	6	EMPRESS 200EMP	OP	CUD	FBG	DV	IO	275	VLVO	8		3100	2	8	5900	6800
21	8	VELOCITY 22VL	OP	CUD	FBG	DV	OB			7	10	1650	1	7	3700	4300
21	8	VELOCITY 22VL	OP	CUD	FBG	DV	IO	260-275		7	10	2600	1	7	6850	8400
21	8	VELOCITY 22VL	OP	CUD	FBG	DV	IO	330		7	10	2600	1	7	7800	9600
22	2	VALANTI 220C	OP	CUD	FBG	DV	IO	260-275		8	6	3900	2	7	9400	11200
22	2	VALANTI 220C	OP	CUD	FBG	DV	IO	330		8	6	3900	2	7	10300	12300
22	2	VALANTI 220C	OP	CUD	FBG	DV	IO	130D	VLVO	8	6	3900	2	7	10900	12400
22	2	VALANTI 220V	OP	B/R	FBG	DV	IO	260-275		8	6	3600	2	7	8250	10000
22	2	VALANTI 220V	OP	B/R	FBG	DV	IO	330		8	6	3600	2	7	9250	11000
22	2	VALANTI 220V	OP	B/R	FBG	DV	IO	130D	VLVO	8	6	3600	2	7	9750	11100
22	5	VALANTI 225	OP	CUD	FBG	DV	IO	200-275		8	6	4500	2	7	10100	12500
22	5	VALANTI 225	OP	CUD	FBG	DV	IO	330		8	6	4500	2	7	11400	13600
22	5	VALANTI 225	OP	CUD	FBG	DV	IO	130D	VLVO	8	6	4500	2	7	12100	13700
23	2	AMBASSADOR 233	OP	CUD	FBG	DV	IO	260-330		8	4	3995	3		9900	12300
23	2	AMBASSADOR 233	OP	CUD	FBG	DV	IO	130D	VLVO	8	4	3995	3		11500	13100
23	5	VELOCITY 23VL	OP	CUD	FBG	DV	IO	270-275		8		2948	2	10	8150	9850
23	5	VELOCITY 23VL	OP	CUD	FBG	DV	IO	330-365		8		2948	2	10	9150	11300
24	6	AMBASSADOR 255	OP	CUD	FBG	DV	IO	275-330		8	4	4550	3	3	12100	14900
		IO 130D VLVO 13100 14900, IO 260D-270D 15600 18000, IO T167-T205													12800	14900
24	6	ROYAL 250	OP	CUD	FBG	DV	IO	T260-T275		8		4000	3	1	10000	12200
24	6	ROYAL 250	OP	CUD	FBG	DV	IO	T330	MRCR	8		4000	3	1	11100	12600
24	6	ROYAL 250	OP	CUD	FBG	DV	IO	T330	VLVO	8		4000	3	1	12300	13900
24	6	ROYAL 250V	OP	CUD	FBG	DV	IO	260-275		8		4000	3	1	10500	12500
		IO 330-365 11500 14000, IO T200-T209 11600 13800, IO T260-T275													14600	17800
		IO T330 MRCR 16400 18700, IO T330 VLVO 18700 20800														
24	6	ROYAL 25LF	OP	CUD	FBG	DV	IO	275-330		8		4175	3	1	11300	14000
24	6	ROYAL 25LF	OP	CUD	FBG	DV	IO	260D	MRCR	8		4175	3	1	14800	16800
24	6	ROYAL 25LF	OP	CUD	FBG	DV	IO	T145-T146		8		4175	3	1	11500	13600
27		COMMODORE 265	OP	OVNTR	FBG	DV	IO	275-330		9	6	6500	2	5	17100	20500
27		COMMODORE 265	OP	OVNTR	FBG	DV	IO	T167-T275		9	6	6500	2	5	18300	22400
27		COMMODORE 265	OP	OVNTR	FBG	DV	IO	T130D	VLVO	9	6	6500	2	5	21900	24300
27	1	COMMODORE 290	OP	OVNTR	FBG	DV	IO	T200-T275		10		8200	3	2	21100	25300
27	1	COMMODORE 290	OP	OVNTR	FBG	DV	IO	T200D	VLVO	10		8200	3	2	28600	31800
30		VELOCITY 30VL	OP	CUD	FBG	DV	IO	T275-T365		8		6575	3	6	21500	26100
31	10	COMMODORE 320	OP	OVNTR	FBG	DV	IO	T260-T330		11	2	11000	2	11	34200	39700
31	10	COMMODORE 320	OP	OVNTR	FBG	DV	IO	T200D	VLVO	11	2	11000	2	11	37900	42100
36	1	COMMODORE 360	OP	OVNTR	FBG	DV	IB	T340	MRCR	13	1	17000	2	10	68800	75600
36	1	COMMODORE 360	OP	OVNTR	FBG	DV	IB	T340	VLVO	13	1	17000	2	10	69300	76100
36	1	COMMODORE 360	OP	OVNTR	FBG	DV	IB	T420	MRCR	13	1	17000	2	10	71500	78600
		1989 BOATS														
17	10	MEDALLION 185XL	ST	RNBT	FBG	DV	IO	130-205		7	3	2225	2	7	3350	4000
18	10	SEBRING 195XL CUDDY	ST	CUD	FBG	DV	IO	130-205		7	10	2600	2	7	4150	4950
18	10	SEBRING 195XL VBR	ST	RNBT	FBG	DV	IO	130-205		7	10	2400	2	7	3850	4600
19	6	EMPRESS 200XL	ST	CUD	FBG	DV	IO	165-260		8		3100	2	8	4900	6000
20	6	MAJESTIC 210 CUDDY	ST	CUD	FBG	DV	IO	180-260		8		3200	2	7	6550	7900
20	6	MAJESTIC 210 VBR	ST	RNBT	FBG	DV	IO	230-270		8		3100	2	7	6300	7500
20	6	MAJESTIC 210 VBR	ST	RNBT	FBG	DV	IO	330	MRCR	8		3100	2	7	7300	8400
21	8	VELOCITY 22	ST	OFF	FBG	DV	OB			7	10	1650	1	7	3500	4100
21	8	VELOCITY 22	ST	OFF	FBG	DV	IO	260-270		7	10	2600	1	7	6450	7500
21	8	VELOCITY 22	ST	OFF	FBG	DV	IO	330	MRCR	7	10	2600	1	7	7350	8450
22	2	VALANTI 220 CUDDY	ST	CUD	FBG	DV	IO	230-270		8	6	3900	2	7	8550	10200
22	2	VALANTI 220 CUDDY	ST	CUD	FBG	DV	IO	330-365		8	6	3900	2	7	9700	11900
22	2	VALANTI 220 VBR	ST	RNBT	FBG	DV	IO	230-270		8	6	3600	2	7	7650	9100
22	2	VALANTI 220 VBR	ST	RNBT	FBG	DV	IO	330-365		8	6	3600	2	7	8700	10800
22	5	VALANTI 225SC		CR	FBG	SV	IO	180-270		8	6	4500	2	7	9550	11300
22	5	VALANTI 225SC		CR	FBG	SV	IO	330-365		8	6	4500	2	7	10800	13200
23	2	AMBASSADOR 233XL	ST	CUD	FBG	DV	IO	230-260		8	4	3995	3		9200	10700
23	5	VELOCITY 23	ST	OFF	FBG	DV	IO	260-270		8		2948	2	10	7600	8850
23	5	VELOCITY 23	ST	OFF	FBG	DV	IO	330	MRCR	8		2948	2	10	8500	9800
23	5	VELOCITY 23	ST	OFF	FBG	DV	IO	365	MRCR	8		2948	2	10	9400	10700
24	6	AMBASSADOR 255XL	ST	OVNTR	FBG	DV	IO	260-330		8	4	4550	3	3	11000	13500
24	6	AMBASSADOR 255XL	ST	OVNTR	FBG	DV	IO	T165-T180		8	4	4550	3	3	11700	13400
24	6	ROYAL 250XL	ST	CUD	FBG	DV	IO	230-330		8		4000	3	1	9700	11900
24	6	ROYAL 250XL	ST	CUD	FBG	DV	IO	365	MRCR	8		4000	3	1	11100	12600
24	6	ROYAL 250XL VRS	ST	CUD	FBG	DV	IO	260-330		8		4000	3	1	10300	12800
		IO 365 MRCR 12200 13900, IO T175-T270 10700 13400, IO T330 MRCR													13300	15100
24	6	ROYAL 25LF	ST	FSH	FBG	DV	IO	230-260		8		4175	3	1	10600	12300
24	6	ROYAL 25LF	ST	FSH	FBG	DV	IO	T165	MRCR	8		4175	3	1	11600	13200
27	1	COMMODORE 280	ST	OVNTR	FBG	DV	IO	T180-T270		10		8200	3	2	19600	23400
27	1	COMMODORE 280	ST	OVNTR	FBG	DV	IO	T330	MRCR	10		8200	3	2	22500	25000
30		VELOCITY 30	ST	OFF	FBG	DV	OB			8		4200	3	6	18000	20000
30		VELOCITY 30	ST	OFF	FBG	DV	IO	T270-T365		8		6575	3	6	21900	26600
31	10	COMMODORE 320	ST	OVNTR	FBG	DV	IO	T260-T365		11	2	11000	2	11	32200	38300
36	1	COMMODORE 360	ST	OVNTR	FBG	DV	IB	T340	MRCR	13	1	17000	2	10	65800	72300
		1988 BOATS														
17	10	MEDALLION 185XL	ST	RNBT	FBG	DV	IO	130-205		7	3	2225	2	7	3150	3800
18	10	SEBRING 195XL CUDDY	ST	CUD	FBG	DV	IO	130-205		7	10	2600	2	7	3950	4650
18	10	SEBRING 195XL VBR	ST	RNBT	FBG	DV	IO	130-205		7	10	2400	2	7	3650	4350
19	6	EMPRESS 200XL CUDDY	ST	CUD	FBG	DV	IO	130-260		8		3100	2	8	4650	5650
20	6	MAJESTIC 210XL CUDDY	ST	CUD	FBG	DV	IO		MRCR	8		3200	2	5	**	**
20	6	MAJESTIC 210XL CUDDY	ST	CUD	FBG	DV	IO	165-270		8		3200	2	5	6200	7600
20	6	MAJESTIC 210XL CUDDY	ST	CUD	FBG	DV	IO	330	MRCR	8		3200	2	5	7400	8500
20	6	MAJESTIC 210XL VBR	ST	RNBT	FBG	DV	IO	165-270		8		3100	2	7	5800	7100
20	6	MAJESTIC 210XL VBR	ST	RNBT	FBG	DV	IO	330	MRCR	8		3100	2	7	6950	7950
21	8	VELOCITY 22	ST	RACE	FBG	DV	OB			7	10	1650	1	7	3450	4000
21	8	VELOCITY 22	ST	RACE	FBG	DV	IO	260-270		7	10	2800	1	7	5950	6950
21	8	VELOCITY 22	ST	RACE	FBG	DV	IO	330	MRCR	7	10	2800	1	7	6800	7800

CONTINUED ON NEXT PAGE

LOA FT	LOA IN	NAME AND/ OR MODEL	TOP/ RIG	BOAT TYPE	-HULL- MTL	-HULL- TP	ENGINE TP	ENGINE # HP	ENGINE MFG	BEAM FT	BEAM IN	WGT LBS	DRAFT FT	DRAFT IN	RETAIL LOW	RETAIL HIGH
		1988 BOATS														
22	2	VALANTI 220XL CUDDY	ST	CUD	FBG	DV	IO	165-270		8	6	3900	2	7	7950	9600
22	2	VALANTI 220XL CUDDY	ST	CUD	FBG	DV	IO	330	MRCR	8	6	3900	2	7	9250	10500
22	2	VALANTI 220XL VCR	ST	RNBT	FBG	DV	IO	205-270		8	6	3800	2	7	7450	8950
22	2	VALANTI 220XL VCR	ST	RNBT	FBG	DV	IO	330	MRCR	8	6	3800	2	7	8500	9750
23	2	AMBASSADOR 233XL	ST	CUD	FBG	DV	IO	230-260		8	4	3995	3		8600	10100
23	2	AMBASSADOR 233XL	ST	CUD	FBG	DV	IO	330	MRCR	8	4	3995	3		9700	11000
23	5	VELOCITY 23	ST	RACE	FBG	DV	IO	260-270		8		2948	2	10	6750	7850
23	5	VELOCITY 23	ST	RACE	FBG	DV	IO	330	MRCR	8		2948	2	10	7550	8700
23	5	VELOCITY 23	ST	RACE	FBG	DV	IO	365	MRCR	8		2948	2	10	8250	9500
24	6	AMBASSADOR 255XL	ST	OVNTR	FBG	DV	IO	230-270		8	4	4550	3	3	10200	11900
24	6	AMBASSADOR 255XL	ST	OVNTR	FBG	DV	IO	330	MRCR	8	4	4550	3	3	11300	12800
24	6	AMBASSADOR 255XL	ST	OVNTR	FBG	DV	IO	T165-T205		8	4	4550	3	3	11100	12900
24	6	ROYAL 250 VRS	ST	RNBT	FBG	DV	IO	260-270		8		4000	3	1	8800	10100
		IO T165-T260 9400 11600, IO T270 MRCR 10400 11800, IO T330 MRCR													11800	13400
24	6	ROYAL 250XL	ST	CUD	FBG	DV	IO	230-270		8		4000	3	1	9250	10800
24	6	ROYAL 250XL	ST	CUD	FBG	DV	IO	330	MRCR	8		4000	3	1	10300	11700
24	6	ROYAL 250XL	ST	CUD	FBG	DV	IO	T165-T205		8		4000	3	1	10100	11800
24	6	ROYAL 25FF	ST	FSH	FBG	DV	IO	230-260		8		4175	3	1	10000	11600
24	6	ROYAL 25FF	ST	FSH	FBG	DV	IO	T130-T175		8		4175	3	1	10800	12500
27	1	COMMODORE 280	ST	OVNTR	FBG	DV	IO	330	MRCR	10		8200	3	2	18700	20700
27	1	COMMODORE 280	ST	OVNTR	FBG	DV	IO	T165-T270		10		8200	3	2	18600	22100
27	1	COMMODORE 280	ST	OVNTR	FBG	DV	IO	T330	MRCR	10		8200	3	2	21300	23700
30		VELOCITY 30	ST	RACE	FBG	DV	OB			8		4200	3	6	16900	19300
30		VELOCITY 30	ST	RACE	FBG	DV	IO	T260-T350		8		6450	3	6	16400	20300
31	10	COMMODORE 320	ST	OVNTR	FBG	DV	IO	T260-T350		11	2	11000	2	11	30500	35900
36	1	COMMODORE 360	ST	OVNTR	FBG	DV	IB	T330	MRCR	13	2	17800	2	10	64000	70300
36	1	COMMODORE 360	ST	OVNTR	FBG	DV	IB	T340	MRCR	13	2	17800	2	10	64200	70600
		1987 BOATS														
17	10	MEDALLION 185XL	ST	RNBT	FBG	DV	IO	120-180		7	3	2225			3000	3550
18	10	SEBRING 195XL	ST	CUD	FBG	DV	IO	120-205		7	10	2306			3500	4150
18	10	SEBRING 195XL	ST	RNBT	FBG	DV	IO	120-205		7	4	2260			3250	3850
19	6	EMPRESS 200XL	ST	CUD	FBG	DV	IO	140-260		8		3100			4450	5400
19	6	EMPRESS 200XL VBR	ST	RNBT	FBG	DV	IO	130-260		8		3000			4100	5100
20	6	MAJESTIC 210XL	ST	CUD	FBG	DV	IO		MRCR	8		3200			**	**
20	6	MAJESTIC 210XL	ST	CUD	FBG	DV	IO	165-260		8		3200			5850	7150
20	6	MAJESTIC 210XL VBR	ST	RNBT	FBG	DV	IO		MRCR	8		3100			**	**
20	6	MAJESTIC 210XL VBR	ST	RNBT	FBG	DV	IO	165-260		8		3100			5500	6700
21	8	VELOCITY 22	ST	RACE	FBG	DV	OB			7	10	1650			3350	3900
21	8	VELOCITY 22	ST	RACE	FBG	DV	IO	260-270		7	10	2800			5650	6600
21	8	VELOCITY 22	ST	RACE	FBG	DV	IO	330	MRCR	7	10	2800			6450	7400
23	2	AMBASSADOR 233XL	ST	CUD	FBG	DV	IO		MRCR	8	4	3995			**	**
23	2	AMBASSADOR 233XL	ST	CUD	FBG	DV	IO	205-260		8	4	3995			8100	9600
23	5	VELOCITY 23	ST	RACE	FBG	DV	IO	260-270		8		2948			6450	7450
23	5	VELOCITY 23	ST	RACE	FBG	DV	IO	330	MRCR	8		2948			7200	8250
24	6	AMBASSADOR 255XL	ST	OVNTR	FBG	DV	IO		MRCR	8		4550			**	**
		IO 230-260 9600 11100, IO T MRCR ** **, IO T120-T260													10300	12800
24	6	ROYAL 25 FF	ST	FSH	FBG	DV	IO	230-260		8		4175			9500	11000
24	6	ROYAL 25 FF	ST	FSH	FBG	DV	IO	T120-T180		8		4175			10200	12000
24	6	ROYAL 250XL	ST	CUD	FBG	DV	IO		MRCR	8		4000			**	**
		IO 205-260 8550 10200, IO T MRCR ** **, IO T120-T230													9450	11500
		IO T260 10400 11900														
27	4	COMMODORE 277XL	ST	OVNTR	FBG	DV	IO	T	MRCR	10		8200			**	**
27	4	COMMODORE 277XL	ST	OVNTR	FBG	DV	IO	T165-T260		10		8200			17400	21200
30		VELOCITY 30	ST	RACE	FBG	DV	OB			8		4200			16300	18600
30		VELOCITY 30	ST	RACE	FBG	DV	IO	T260-T330		8		6450			15600	18900
30		VELOCITY 30	ST	RACE	FBG	DV	IO	T370-T420		8		6450			17400	20900
36	1	COMMODORE 360XL	ST	OVNTR	FBG	DV	IB	T340	MRCR	13		14083			54800	60300
		1986 BOATS														
17	10	MEDALLION 185	ST	RNBT	FBG	DV	OB			7	3	1530			2900	3350
17	10	MEDALLION 185	ST	RNBT	FBG	DV	SE	115	OMC	7	3	2225			3600	4150
17	10	MEDALLION 185	ST	RNBT	FBG	DV	IO	120-190		7	3	2225			2900	3400
18	8	SEBRING 195	ST	RNBT	FBG	DV	SE	115	OMC	7	4	2260			3650	4250
18	8	SEBRING 195	ST	RNBT	FBG	DV	IO	120-230		7	4	2260			3050	3700
18	8	SEBRING 195	ST	RNBT	FBG	DV	IO	260		7	4	2260			3300	3850
18	10	SEBRING 195XL	ST	CUD	FBG	DV	SE	115	OMC	7	10	2306			3700	4300
18	10	SEBRING 195XL	ST	CUD	FBG	DV	IO	120-230		7	10	2306			3350	4050
18	10	SEBRING 195XL	ST	CUD	FBG	DV	IO	260		7	10	2306			3600	4200
19	6	EMPRESS 200XL	ST	CUD	FBG	DV	SE	115	OMC	8		3100			4150	4800
19	6	EMPRESS 200XL	ST	CUD	FBG	DV	IO	140		8		3100			4200	4850
19	6	EMPRESS 200XL	ST	CUD	FBG	DV	SE	155	OMC	8		3100			4150	4800
19	6	EMPRESS 200XL	ST	CUD	FBG	DV	IO	170-260		8		3100			4200	5150
19	6	EMPRESS 200XL VBR	ST	RNBT	FBG	DV	SE	115	OMC	8		3000			4150	4850
19	6	EMPRESS 200XL VBR	ST	RNBT	FBG	DV	IO	140		8		3000			3950	4550
19	6	EMPRESS 200XL VBR	ST	RNBT	FBG	DV	SE	155	OMC	8		3000			4150	4800
19	6	EMPRESS 200XL VBR	ST	RNBT	FBG	DV	IO	170-260		8		3000			3950	4850
20	6	MAJESTIC 210XL	ST	CUD	FBG	DV	SE	155	OMC	8		3200			4550	5250
20	6	MAJESTIC 210XL	ST	CUD	FBG	DV	IO	170-260		8		3200			5600	6800
20	6	MAJESTIC 210XL VBR	ST	RNBT	FBG	DV	SE	155	OMC	8		3100			4550	5200
20	6	MAJESTIC 210XL VBR	ST	RNBT	FBG	DV	IO	170-260		8		3100			5250	6400
20	11	REGENCY 21FF	ST	FSH	FBG	DV	OB			8		2553			4200	4900
20	11	REGENCY 21FF	ST	FSH	FBG	DV	SE	155	OMC	8		3360			4800	5500
20	11	REGENCY 21FF	ST	FSH	FBG	DV	IO	170-260		8		3360			6250	7550
24	6	AMBASSADOR 255XL	ST	OVNTR	FBG	DV	IO	230-260		8		4550			9200	10700
24	6	AMBASSADOR 255XL	ST	OVNTR	FBG	DV	IO	T120-T205		8		4550			9800	11600
24	6	ROYAL 25 LF	ST	FSH	FBG	DV	SE	155	OMC	8		4175			7150	8200
24	6	ROYAL 25 LF	ST	FSH	FBG	DV	IO	230-260		8		4175			9150	10600
24	6	ROYAL 25 LF	ST	FSH	FBG	DV	IO	T120-T190		8		4175			9800	11500
24	6	ROYAL 250 XL	ST	CUD	FBG	DV	IO	230-260		8		4000			8300	9750
24	6	ROYAL 250 XL	ST	CUD	FBG	DV	IO	T120-T205		8		4000			9050	10700
25	2	AMBASSADOR 233XL	ST	CUD	FBG	DV	IO	185-260		8	4	3995			8450	10300
27	4	COMMODORE 277 XL	ST	OVNTR	FBG	DV	IO	T170-T185		10		8200			16700	19100
27	4	COMMODORE 277XL	ST	OVNTR	FBG	DV	IO	T190-T260		10		8200			16900	20300
35	11	COMMODORE 360XL	ST	OVNTR	FBG	DV	IB	T340	MRCR	13		14083			51800	56900
		1985 BOATS														
16	5	MEDALLION 175	ST	RNBT	FBG	DV	OB			6	10	1110			2100	2500
16	5	MEDALLION 175	ST	RNBT	FBG	DV	IO	120-190		6	10	1730			2200	2750
17	10	MEDALLION 185	ST	RNBT	FBG	DV	OB			7	3	1530			2800	3250
17	10	MEDALLION 185	ST	RNBT	FBG	DV	SE	115	OMC	7	3	2225			3500	4050
17	10	MEDALLION 185	ST	RNBT	FBG	DV	IO	120-190		7	3	2225			2750	3400
18	8	MEDALLION 195	ST	RNBT	FBG	DV	OB			7	4	1575			2900	3400
18	8	MEDALLION 195	ST	RNBT	FBG	DV	SE	115	OMC	7	4	2260			3550	4100
18	8	MEDALLION 195	ST	RNBT	FBG	DV	IO	120-205		7	4	2260			2950	3650
18	8	MEDALLION 195	ST	RNBT	FBG	DV	IO	225-260		7	4	2260			3200	3900
19	6	EMPRESS 200XL	ST	CUD	FBG	DV	SE	115	OMC	8		3100			4000	4650
19	6	EMPRESS 200XL	ST	CUD	FBG	DV	IO	120-140		8		3100			4000	4850
19	6	EMPRESS 200XL	ST	CUD	FBG	DV	SE	155	OMC	8		3100			4000	4650
19	6	EMPRESS 200XL	ST	CUD	FBG	DV	IO	170-230		8		3100			4050	5000
19	6	EMPRESS 200XL	ST	CUD	FBG	DV	IO	260		8		3100			4250	5200
19	6	EMPRESS 200XL VBR	ST	RNBT	FBG	DV	SE	115	OMC	8		3000			4000	4650
19	6	EMPRESS 200XL VBR	ST	RNBT	FBG	DV	IO	120-140		8		3000			3750	4550
19	6	EMPRESS 200XL VBR	ST	RNBT	FBG	DV	SE	155	OMC	8		3000			4000	4650
19	6	EMPRESS 200XL VBR	ST	RNBT	FBG	DV	IO	170-230		8		3000			3800	4700
19	6	EMPRESS 200XL VBR	ST	RNBT	FBG	DV	IO	260		8		3000			4000	4900
20	6	MAJESTIC 210XL	ST	CUD	FBG	DV	SE	155	OMC	8		3200			4450	5100
20	6	MAJESTIC 210XL	ST	CUD	FBG	DV	IO	170-230		8		3200			5400	6600
20	6	MAJESTIC 210XL	ST	CUD	FBG	DV	IO	260		8		3200			5700	6800
20	6	MAJESTIC 210XL	ST	CUD	FBG	DV	IO	330	MRCR	8		3200			6450	7400
20	6	MAJESTIC 210XL VBR	ST	RNBT	FBG	DV	SE	155	OMC	8		3100			4400	5050
20	6	MAJESTIC 210XL VBR	ST	RNBT	FBG	DV	IO	170-230		8		3100			5050	6150
20	6	MAJESTIC 210XL VBR	ST	RNBT	FBG	DV	IO	260		8		3100			5350	6400
20	6	MAJESTIC 210XL VBR	ST	RNBT	FBG	DV	IO	330	MRCR	8		3100			6050	6950
20	11	REGENCY 21FF	ST	FSH	FBG	DV	OB			8		2553			4100	4750
20	11	REGENCY 21FF	ST	FSH	FBG	DV	SE	155	OMC	8		3360			4650	5350
20	11	REGENCY 21FF	ST	FSH	FBG	DV	IO	170-230		8		3360			6000	7300
20	11	REGENCY 21FF	ST	FSH	FBG	DV	IO	260		8		3360			6300	7550
20	11	REGENCY 21FF	ST	FSH	FBG	DV	SE	T115	OMC	8		3360			4650	5350
24	6	AMBASSADOR 255XL	ST	OVNTR	FBG	DV	SE	155	OMC	8		4550			7300	8400
24	6	AMBASSADOR 255XL	ST	OVNTR	FBG	DV	IO	185-260		8		4550			8550	10500
24	6	AMBASSADOR 255XL	ST	OVNTR	FBG	DV	IO	T120-T205		8		4550			9400	11300
24	6	REGENCY 25FF		FSH	FBG	DV	OB			8		3100			5750	6600
24	6	ROYAL 25 LF/FF	ST	FSH	FBG	DV	IO	185-260		8		4175			8500	10500
24	6	ROYAL 25 LF/FF	ST	FSH	FBG	DV	IO	T120-T185		8		4175			9450	11300
24	6	ROYAL 250 XL	ST	CUD	FBG	DV	IO	205-260		8		4000			7850	9650
24	6	ROYAL 250 XL	ST	CUD	FBG	DV	IO	T120-T185		8		4000			8600	10500
24	6	ROYAL 250XL	ST	CUD	FBG	DV	SE	155	OMC	8		4000			6950	8000
24	6	ROYAL 250XL	ST	CUD	FBG	DV	IO	185-200		8		4000			7800	9200
24	6	ROYAL 250XL	ST	CUD	FBG	DV	IO	T190-T205		8		4000			9000	10300
24	6	ROYAL LF/FF	ST	FSH	FBG	DV	SE	155	OMC	8		4175			6950	7950
24	6	ROYAL LF/FF	ST	FSH	FBG	DV	IO	190	MRCR	8		4175			8500	9750
24	6	ROYAL LF/FF	ST	FSH	FBG	DV	SE	T115	OMC	8		4175			6950	8000
27	4	COMMODORE 277 XL	ST	OVNTR	FBG	DV	IO	330	MRCR	10		8200			16000	18200
27	4	COMMODORE 277 XL	ST	OVNTR	FBG	DV	IO	T170-T185		10		8200			16000	18400
27	4	COMMODORE 277XL	ST	OVNTR	FBG	DV	IO	T190-T260		10		8200			16200	19800
27	4	COMMODORE 277XL	ST	OVNTR	FBG	DV	IO	T330	MRCR	10		8200			18900	21000

 CONTINUED ON NEXT PAGE

LOA FT	LOA IN	NAME AND/ OR MODEL	TOP/ RIG	BOAT TYPE	-HULL- MTL	TP	TP	----ENGINE--- # HP	MFG	BEAM FT	BEAM IN	WGT LBS	DRAFT FT	DRAFT IN	RETAIL LOW	RETAIL HIGH
		1985 BOATS														
36	1	COMMODORE 360XL	ST	OVNTR	FBG	DV	IB	T260	MRCR	13		14083			48800	53600
		IB T330 PCM 50000 55000, IB T340 MRCR 50300 55200, IB T165D VLVO													52400	57500
		IB T210D CAT 55500 61000														
		1984 BOATS														
16	5	MEDALLION 175	ST	RNBT	FBG	DV	OB			6	10	1150			2150	2500
16	5	MEDALLION 175	ST	RNBT	FBG	DV	IO	120-188		6	10	1750			2100	2550
17	10	MEDALLION 185	ST	RNBT	FBG	DV	OB			7	3	1450			2600	3050
17	10	MEDALLION 185	ST	RNBT	FBG	DV	IO	117-188		7	3	2250			2800	3300
18	8	MEDALLION 195	ST	RNBT	FBG	DV	OB			7	4	1600			2850	3350
18	8	MEDALLION 195	ST	RNBT	FBG	DV	IO	117-230		7	4	2600			3200	3850
18	8	MEDALLION 195	ST	RNBT	FBG	DV	IO	260		7	4	2600			3300	4050
19	6	EMPRESS 200XL	ST	CUD	FBG	DV	IO	140-260		8		2425			3350	4200
20	6	MAJESTIC 210XL	ST	CUD	FBG	DV	IO	138-260		8		3075			5200	6450
20	6	MAJESTIC 210XL	ST	CUD	FBG	DV	IO	330	MRCR	8		3075			6100	7000
20	11	REGENCY 21FF	ST	FSH	FBG	DV	OB			8		2450			3900	4500
20	11	REGENCY 21FF	ST	FSH	FBG	DV	IO	138-200		8		3450			6050	7050
20	11	REGENCY 21FF	ST	FSH	FBG	DV	SE	205	OMC	8		3450			4550	5200
20	11	REGENCY 21FF	ST	FSH	FBG	DV	IO	225-260		8		3450			6250	7400
24		AMBASSADOR 245XL	ST	OVNTR	FBG	DV	IO	117-260		8		4200			7750	9350
		IO 330 MRCR 8600 9900, IO 130D-165D 9250 10800, IO T117-T188													8850	10100
24	6	ROYAL 25 LF	ST	FSH	FBG	DV	IO	170-200		8		4050			7950	9450
24	6	ROYAL 25 LF	ST	FSH	FBG	DV	SE	205	OMC	8		4050			6600	7600
24	6	ROYAL 25 LF	ST	FSH	FBG	DV	IO	225-260		8		4050			8350	9900
		IO 330 MRCR 9250 10500, IO 130D-165D 11200 13200, IO T117-T188													9250	10700
24	6	ROYAL 250 XL	ST	CUD	FBG	DV	IO	170-200		8		4050			7550	8950
24	6	ROYAL 250 XL	ST	CUD	FBG	DV	SE	205	OMC	8		4050			6800	7800
24	6	ROYAL 250 XL	ST	CUD	FBG	DV	IO	225-260		8		4050			7900	9350
		IO 330 MRCR 8700 10000, IO 130D-165D 9000 10700, IO T117-T188													8650	10200
26	8	AMBASSADOR 255XL	ST	OVNTR	FBG	DV	IO	260		8		4500			9900	11300
26	8	AMBASSADOR 255XL	ST	OVNTR	FBG	DV	IO	T188		8		4500			10900	12400
27	4	COMMODORE 277 XL	ST	OVNTR	FBG	DV	IO	260-330		10		8000			14500	17300
27	4	COMMODORE 277 XL	ST	OVNTR	FBG	DV	IO	T138-T188		10		8000			15000	17500

....For earlier years, see the BUC Used Boat Price Guide, Volume 3

REGULATOR MARINE INC

EDENTON NC 27932 COAST GUARD MFG ID- DJI See inside cover to adjust price for area

For more recent years, see the BUC Used Boat Price Guide, Volume 1

LOA FT	LOA IN	NAME AND/ OR MODEL	TOP/ RIG	BOAT TYPE	-HULL- MTL	TP	TP	----ENGINE--- # HP	MFG	BEAM FT	BEAM IN	WGT LBS	DRAFT FT	DRAFT IN	RETAIL LOW	RETAIL HIGH
		1996 BOATS														
20	6	REGULATOR 21	OP	CTRCN	FBG	DV	OB			8	2	2700	1	4	17100	19400
23	4	REGULATOR 23	OP	CTRCN	FBG	DV	OB			8	4	3800			26900	29900
25	10	REGULATOR 26	OP	CTRCN	FBG	DV	OB			8	6	5000	2		34000	37800
25	10	REGULATOR EXPRESS	OP	CUD	FBG	DV	OB			8	6	5400	2		35200	39100
		1995 BOATS														
23	4	REGULATOR 23	OP	CTRCN	FBG	DV	OB			8	4	3800	1	10	25400	28200
25	10	REGULATOR 26	OP	CTRCN	FBG	DV	OB			8	6	5000	2		32200	35700
25	10	REGULATOR 26	OP	CTRCN	FBG	DV	IO	330	VLVO	8	6	6100	3		32600	36300
25	10	REGULATOR 26	OP	CTRCN	FBG	DV	IO	200D-230D		8	6	6100	3		42200	48400
25	10	REGULATOR EXPRESS	OP	CUD	FBG	DV	OB			8	6	5400	2		33300	37000
25	10	REGULATOR EXPRESS	OP	CUD	FBG	DV	IO	330	VLVO	8	6	6500	3		32200	35700
25	10	REGULATOR EXPRESS	OP	CUD	FBG	DV	IO	200D-230D		8	6	6500	3		35700	40800
		1994 BOATS														
23	4	REGULATOR 23	OP	CTRCN	FBG	DV	OB			8	4	3800	1	10	24100	26800
25	10	REGULATOR 26	OP	CTRCN	FBG	DV	OB			8	6	5000	2		30500	33900
25	10	REGULATOR 26	OP	CTRCN	FBG	DV	IO	330	VLVO	8	6	6100	3		30500	33900
25	10	REGULATOR 26	OP	CTRCN	FBG	DV	IO	200D-230D		8	6	6100	3		39400	45100
25	10	REGULATOR EXPRESS	OP	CUD	FBG	DV	OB			8	6	5400	2		31500	35000
25	10	REGULATOR EXPRESS	OP	CUD	FBG	DV	IO	330	VLVO	8	6	6500	3		30000	33400
25	10	REGULATOR EXPRESS	OP	CUD	FBG	DV	IO	200D-230D		8	6	6500	3		33300	38100
		1993 BOATS														
23	4	REGULATOR 23	OP	FSH	FBG	SV	OB			8	4	3800	2	10	22900	25500
25	10	REGULATOR 26	OP	CTRCN	FBG	SV	OB			8	6	5000	2		28900	32100
25	10	REGULATOR 26	OP	CTRCN	FBG	SV	IO	330	VLVO	8	6	5000	2		25400	28300
25	10	REGULATOR 26	OP	CTRCN	FBG	SV	IO	200D-230D		8	6	5000	2		31500	36400
25	10	REGULATOR EXPRESS	OP	CUD	FBG	SV	OB			8	6	5400	2		30000	33300
25	10	REGULATOR EXPRESS	OP	CUD	FBG	SV	IO	330	VLVO	8	6	5400	2		25100	27900
25	10	REGULATOR EXPRESS	OP	CUD	FBG	SV	IO	200D-230D		8	6	5400	2		26800	30800

RELIANCE SAILING CRAFT CO LTD

BEACONSFIELD MON PQ CANADA See inside cover to adjust price for area

LOA FT	LOA IN	NAME AND/ OR MODEL	TOP/ RIG	BOAT TYPE	-HULL- MTL	TP	TP	----ENGINE--- # HP	MFG	BEAM FT	BEAM IN	WGT LBS	DRAFT FT	DRAFT IN	RETAIL LOW	RETAIL HIGH
		1996 BOATS														
39	4	RELIANCE 12	SLP	SAROD	F/S	KL	IB	18D	YAN	8	4	9000	6		70700	77600
44	4	RELIANCE 44	CUT	SARCC	F/S	KL	IB	40D	PERK	11	8	28000	6	2	178500	196000
44	4	RELIANCE 44	KTH	SARCC	F/S	KL	IB	40D	PERK	11	8	28000	6	2	191500	210500
		1995 BOATS														
39	4	RELIANCE 12	SLP	SAROD	F/S	KL	IB	18D	YAN	8	4	9000	6		66100	72600
44	4	RELIANCE 44	CUT	SARCC	F/S	KL	IB	40D	PERK	11	8	28000	6	2	167000	183500
44	4	RELIANCE 44	KTH	SARCC	F/S	KL	IB	40D	PERK	11	8	28000	6	2	179000	197000
		1994 BOATS														
39	4	RELIANCE 12	SLP	SAROD	F/S	KL	IB	18D	YAN	8	4	9000	6		62000	68100
44	4	RELIANCE 44	CUT	SARCC	F/S	KL	IB	40D	PERK	11	8	28000	6	2	156000	171500
44	4	RELIANCE 44	KTH	SARCC	F/S	KL	IB	40D	PERK	11	8	28000	6	2	167500	184000
		1993 BOATS														
39	4	RELIANCE 12	SLP	SAROD	F/S	KL	IB	18D	YAN	8	4	9000	6		58600	64400
44	4	RELIANCE 44	CUT	SARCC	F/S	KL	IB	40D	PERK	11	8	28000	6	2	146000	160500
44	4	RELIANCE 44	KTH	SARCC	F/S	KL	IB	40D	PERK	11	8	28000	6	2	156500	172000
		1992 BOATS														
39	4	RELIANCE 12	SLP	SA/OD	F/S	KL	IB	18D	YAN	8	4	9000	6		54600	60000
44	4	RELIANCE 44	CUT	SA/CR	F/S	KL	IB	40D	PERK	11	8	28000	6	2	135500	149000
44	4	RELIANCE 44	KTH	SA/CR	F/S	KL	IB	40D	PERK	11	8	28000	6	2	145500	160000
		1991 BOATS														
39	4	RELIANCE 12	SLP	SA/OD	F/S	KL	SD	18D	VLVO	8	4	9000	6		51000	56000
		SD 18D YAN 51100 56100, IB 18D VLVO 51000 56000, IB 18D YAN													51100	56100
44	4	RELIANCE 44	CUT	SA/CR	F/S	KL	IB	40D	PERK	11	8	28000	6	2	127000	139500
44	4	RELIANCE 44	KTH	SA/CR	F/S	KL	IB	40D	PERK	11	8	28000	6	2	136000	149500
		1990 BOATS														
39	4	RELIANCE 12	SLP	SA/OD	FBG	KL	IB	D		8	4	9000	6		48200	53000
44	4	RELIANCE 44	CUT	SA/RC	FBG	KL	IB	D		11	8	28000	6	2	119500	131500
44	4	RELIANCE 44	KTH	SA/RC	FBG	KL	IB	D		11	8	28000	6	2	128500	141000
		1989 BOATS														
39	4	RELIANCE 12	SLP	SA/OD	FBG	KL	IB	D		8	4	9000	6		44600	49600
44	4	RELIANCE 44	CUT	SA/RC	FBG	KL	IB	D		11	8	28000	6	2	112000	123000
44	4	RELIANCE 44	KTH	SA/RC	FBG	KL	IB	D		11	8	28000	6	2	120000	132000
		1988 BOATS														
39	4	RELIANCE 12	SLP	SA/OD	FBG	KL	IB	D		8	4	9000	6		41700	46400
44	4	RELIANCE 44	CUT	SA/RC	FBG	KL	IB	D		11	8	28000	6	2	104500	115000
44	4	RELIANCE 44	KTH	SA/RC	FBG	KL	IB	D		11	8	28000	6	2	112000	123500
		1987 BOATS														
39	4	RELIANCE 12	SLP	SA/OD	FBG	KL	IB	D		8	4	9000	6		39000	43400
44	4	RELIANCE 44	CUT	SA/RC	FBG	KL	IB	D		11	8	28000	6	2	97800	107500
44	4	RELIANCE 44	KTH	SA/RC	FBG	KL	IB	D		11	8	28000	6	2	105000	115500
		1986 BOATS														
39	4	RELIANCE 12	SLP	SA/RC	FBG	KL	IB	D		8	4	9000	6		36500	40600
44	4	RELIANCE 44	CUT	SA/RC	FBG	KL	IB	D		11	8	28000	6	2	91400	100500
44	4	RELIANCE 44	KTH	SA/RC	FBG	KL	IB	D		11	8	28000	6	2	98100	108000
		1985 BOATS														
39	4	RELIANCE 12	SLP	SA/OD	FBG	KL	IB	D		8	4	9000	6		34100	37900
44	4	RELIANCE 44	CUT	SA/RC	FBG	KL	IB	D		11	8	28000	6	2	85500	94000
44	4	RELIANCE 44	KTH	SA/RC	FBG	KL	IB	D		11	8	28000	6	2	91800	101000

....For earlier years, see the BUC Used Boat Price Guide, Volume 3

RENKEN

UNITED MARINE CORPORATION
WATSEKA IL 60907 COAST GUARD MFG ID- RBM See inside cover to adjust price for area

For more recent years, see the BUC Used Boat Price Guide, Volume 1

LOA FT	LOA IN	NAME AND/ OR MODEL	TOP/ RIG	BOAT TYPE	-HULL- MTL	TP	TP	----ENGINE--- # HP	MFG	BEAM FT	BEAM IN	WGT LBS	DRAFT FT	DRAFT IN	RETAIL LOW	RETAIL HIGH
		1996 BOATS														
16		CLASSIC 160	OP	B/R	FBG	SV	OB			6	10	1100			3050	3550
17	6	CLASSIC 170	OP	B/R	FBG	SV	IO	180	MRCR	7	3	1370			4150	4800
17	6	CLASSIC 170	OP	RNBT	FBG	SV	IO	180	MRCR	7	3	1370			4450	5100
20	1	CLASSIC 200	OP	B/R	FBG	SV	OB			7	4	1900			6250	7150
20	1	CLASSIC 200	OP	B/R	FBG	SV	IO	235	MRCR	7	4	1900			6300	7250
20	1	CLASSIC 200	OP	CUD	FBG	SV	IO	235	MRCR	7	4	1900			6700	7700
20	1	CLASSIC 200	OP	RNBT	FBG	SV	IO	235	MRCR	7	4	1900			6450	7450
23	6	CLASSIC 230	OP	CUD	FBG	DV	IO	300	MRCR	7	5	2200			9650	11000
25	5	CLASSIC 240	OP	CR	FBG	DV	IO	300	MRCR	8	6	4200			16000	18100
26		CLASSIC 260	OP	CR	FBG	DV	IO	300	MRCR	8	6	4475			17200	19500

LOA FT	LOA IN	NAME AND/ OR MODEL	TOP/ RIG	BOAT TYPE	-HULL- MTL	-HULL- TP	ENGINE TP	ENGINE # HP	ENGINE MFG	BEAM FT	BEAM IN	WGT LBS	DRAFT FT	DRAFT IN	RETAIL LOW	RETAIL HIGH
		1994 BOATS														
16		CLASSIC 160	OP	B/R	FBG	DV	OB			6	10	1100			2750	3200
17	1	CLASSIC 170 CB MBS	OP	RNBT	FBG	DV	IO	130	YAMA	7	5	1370			3700	4300
17	1	CLASSIC 170 MBS	OP	B/R	FBG	DV	IO	130	YAMA	7	5	1370			3500	4050
17	1	SEAMASTER 1780	OP	CTRCN	FBG	DV	OB			7		1000			2550	3000
17	6	SEAMASTER 1880	OP	CTRCN	FBG	DV	OB			7	5	1200			3000	3500
19	1	CLASSIC 190 LB	OP	B/R	FBG	DV	IO	130	YAMA	8		1835			4800	5500
19	1	CLASSIC 190 MBS	OP	B/R	FBG	DV	IO	130	YAMA	8		1825			4800	5500
19	5	CLASSIC 200 BR MBS	OP	B/R	FBG	DV	IO	180	YAMA	7	5	1625			4550	5200
19	5	CLASSIC 200 BR SD	OP	B/R	FBG	DV	IO	180	YAMA	7	5	1635			4550	5250
19	5	CLASSIC 200 CC SD	OP	CUD	FBG	DV	IO	180	YAMA	7	5	1870			5050	5800
19	9	SEAMASTER 2008	OP	CUD	FBG	DV	OB			8		2325			5150	5950
19	9	SEAMASTER 2008	OP	CUD	FBG	DV	IO	180	YAMA	8		3275			7200	8250
19	9	SEAMASTER 2080	OP	CTRCN	FBG	DV	OB			8		1875			4550	5250
21	3	SEAMASTER 2288	OP	CUD	FBG	DV	OB			8		2850			7850	9050
21	3	SEAMASTER 2288	OP	CUD	FBG	DV	IO	205	YAMA	8		3800			9400	10700
23	6	CLASSIC 230	OP	CUD	FBG	DV	IO	205	YAMA	7	5	2200			7500	8650
24		SEAMASTER 2488	OP	CUD	FBG	DV	IO	210	YAMA	8	6	4300			12100	13700
26		CLASSIC 260 AC	OP	CR	FBG	DV	IO	240	YAMA	8	6	5475			15900	18000
26		SEAMASTER 2688	OP	CUD	FBG	DV	IO	240	YAMA	9	6	5510			16200	18500
		1993 BOATS														
16		CLASSIC 160	OP	B/R	FBG	DV	OB			6	10	1100			2600	3050
17	1	CLASSIC 170 CB MBS	OP	RNBT	FBG	DV	IO	130	YAMA	7	5	1370			3450	4000
17	1	CLASSIC 170 CB SD	OP	RNBT	FBG	DV	IO	130	YAMA	7	5	1370			3500	4050
17	1	CLASSIC 170 MBS	OP	B/R	FBG	DV	IO	130	YAMA	7	5	1370			3250	3800
17	1	CLASSIC 170 SD	OP	B/R	FBG	DV	IO	130	YAMA	7	5	1380			3250	3800
17	1	SEAMASTER 1780	OP	CTRCN	FBG	DV	OB			7		1000			2500	2900
17	6	SEAMASTER 1880	OP	CTRCN	FBG	DV	OB			7	5	1200			2850	3300
19	1	CLASSIC 190 MBS	OP	B/R	FBG	DV	IO	130	YAMA	8		1825			4500	5150
19	1	CLASSIC 190 SD	OP	B/R	FBG	DV	IO	130	YAMA	8		1835			4500	5150
19	5	CLASSIC 200 BR MBS	OP	B/R	FBG	DV	IO	180	YAMA	7	5	1625			4200	4900
19	5	CLASSIC 200 BR SD	OP	B/R	FBG	DV	IO	180	YAMA	7	5	1635			4200	4900
19	5	CLASSIC 200 CC SD	OP	CUD	FBG	DV	IO	180	YAMA	7	5	1870			4700	5400
19	5	CLASSIC 200BR CL MBS	OP	CUD	FBG	DV	IO	180	YAMA	7	5	1860			4700	5400
19	9	SEAMASTER 2008	OP	CUD	FBG	DV	OB			8		2325			4950	5700
19	9	SEAMASTER 2008	OP	CUD	FBG	DV	IO	180	YAMA	8		3275			6700	7700
19	9	SEAMASTER 2008 GIL	OP	CUD	FBG	DV	OB			8		2375			4950	5700
19	9	SEAMASTER 2080	OP	CTRCN	FBG	DV	OB			8		1875			4250	4950
21		CLASSIC 210 CUD MBS	OP	CUD	FBG	DV	IO	210	YAMA	7	5	2825			6850	7850
21	3	SEAMASTER 2288	OP	CUD	FBG	DV	OB			8		2850			7500	8600
21	3	SEAMASTER 2288	OP	CUD	FBG	DV	IO	210	YAMA	8		3800			8800	10000
21	3	SEAMASTER 2288 GIL	OP	CUD	FBG	DV	OB			8		2900			7550	8700
23	6	CLASSIC 230	OP	CUD	FBG	DV	IO	205		7	5	2200			7050	8100
24		SEAMASTER 2488	OP	CUD	FBG	DV	IO	210	YAMA	8	6	4300			11300	12800
24		SEAMASTER 2488 GIL	OP	CUD	FBG	DV	OB			8	6	3400			10100	11500
26		CLASSIC 260 AC	OP	CR	FBG	DV	IO	240	YAMA	8	6	5475			14800	16800
26		SEAMASTER 2688	OP	CUD	FBG	DV	IO	240	YAMA	9	6	5510			15200	17300
26		SEAMASTER 2688	OP	CUD	FBG	DV	IO	T130	YAMA	9	6	5510			15900	18100
26		SEAMASTER 2688 DUAL	OP	CUD	FBG	DV	OB			9	6	4630			13200	15000
26		SEAMASTER 2688 GIL	OP	CUD	FBG	DV	OB			9	6	4610			13200	15000
		1992 BOATS														
16		CLASSIC 1600	OP	B/R	FBG	DV	OB			6	10	1100			2500	2900
17	1	CLASSIC 1700	OP	B/R	FBG	DV	OB			7	5	1370			3050	3500
17	1	CLASSIC 1700	OP	B/R	FBG	DV	IO	130	YAMA	7	5	1370			3050	3550
17	1	CLASSIC 1700 CB	OP	RNBT	FBG	DV	IO	130	YAMA	7	5	1370			3150	3650
17	1	CLASSIC 1700 CB SD	OP	RNBT	FBG	DV	IO	130	YAMA	7	5	1370			3300	3850
17	1	CLASSIC 1700 SD	OP	B/R	FBG	DV	IO	130	YAMA	7	5	1380			3050	3550
17	1	SEAMASTER 1780	OP	CTRCN	FBG	DV	OB			7		1000			2350	2750
17	6	SEAMASTER 1880	OP	CTRCN	FBG	DV	OB			7	5	1200			2700	3150
19	1	CLASSIC 1900	OP	B/R	FBG	DV	IO	130	YAMA	8		1825			4150	4850
19	1	CLASSIC 1900 SD	OP	B/R	FBG	DV	IO	130	YAMA	8		1835			4150	4850
19	5	CLASSIC 2000	OP	B/R	FBG	DV	OB			7	5	1575			3650	4250
19	5	CLASSIC 2000	OP	B/R	FBG	DV	IO	130	YAMA	7	5	1625			3900	4500
19	5	CLASSIC 2000 CB	OP	RNBT	FBG	DV	IO	130	YAMA	7	5	1625			4050	4700
19	5	CLASSIC 2000 CB SD	OP	RNBT	FBG	DV	IO	130	YAMA	7	5	1635			4050	4700
19	5	CLASSIC 2000 CUD	OP	CUD	FBG	DV	OB			7	5	1830			3950	4600
19	5	CLASSIC 2000 CUD	OP	CUD	FBG	DV	IO	130	YAMA	7	5	1860			4350	5050
19	5	CLASSIC 2000 CUD SD	OP	CUD	FBG	DV	IO	130	YAMA	7	5	1870			4400	5050
19	5	CLASSIC 2000 SD	OP	B/R	FBG	DV	IO	130	YAMA	7	5	1635			3900	4550
19	9	SEAMASTER 2008	OP	CUD	FBG	DV	OB			8		2325			4700	5450
19	9	SEAMASTER 2008	OP	CUD	FBG	DV	IO	130	YAMA	8		3275			6250	7150
19	9	SEAMASTER 2008 GIL	OP	CUD	FBG	DV	OB			8		2375			4750	5500
19	9	SEAMASTER 2080	OP	CTRCN	FBG	DV	OB			8		1875			4050	4750
20	9	CLASSIC 2100 AC	OP	CR	FBG	DV	IO	205	YAMA	8	3	3930			8250	9450
20	9	CLASSIC 2100 WE	OP	WKNDR	FBG	DV	IO	205	YAMA	8	3	4040			8400	9650
21		CLASSIC 210	OP	B/R	FBG	DV	IO	130	YAMA	7	5	2675			5550	6400
21		CLASSIC 210 CB	OP	RNBT	FBG	DV	IO	130	YAMA	7	5	2675			5650	6500
21		CLASSIC 210 CB SD	OP	RNBT	FBG	DV	IO	130	YAMA	7	5	2675			5950	6800
21		CLASSIC 210 CUD	OP	CUD	FBG	DV	IO	205	YAMA	7	5	2825			6250	7200
21		CLASSIC 210 CUD SD	OP	CUD	FBG	DV	IO	205	YAMA	7	5	2825			6500	7500
21		CLASSIC 210 SD	OP	B/R	FBG	DV	IO	130	YAMA	7	5	2675			5800	6700
21	3	SEAMASTER 2288	OP	CUD	FBG	DV	OB			8		2850			7150	8200
21	3	SEAMASTER 2288	OP	CUD	FBG	DV	IO	205	YAMA	8		3800			8150	9350
21	3	SEAMASTER 2288 GIL	OP	CUD	FBG	DV	OB			8		2900			7200	8300
23	6	CLASSIC 230	OP	CUD	FBG	DV	IO	205		7	5	2200			6600	7550
24		SEAMASTER 2488	OP	CUD	FBG	DV	IO	205	YAMA	8	6	4300			10500	12000
24		SEAMASTER 2488 GIL	OP	CUD	FBG	DV	OB			8	6	3400			9700	11000
24	4	CLASSIC 2500 AC	OP	CR	FBG	DV	IO	205	YAMA	8		4525			11000	12500
26		CLASSIC 2600 AC	OP	CR	FBG	DV	IO	205	YAMA	8	6	5475			13500	15400
26		SEAMASTER 2688	OP	CUD	FBG	DV	IO	205	YAMA	9	6	5510			13900	15800
26		SEAMASTER 2688	OP	CUD	FBG	DV	IO	T130	YAMA	9	6	5510			14900	16900
26		SEAMASTER 2688 DUAL	OP	CUD	FBG	DV	OB			9	6	4630			12600	14300
26		SEAMASTER 2688 GIL	OP	CUD	FBG	DV	OB			9	6	4610			12600	14300
		1991 BOATS														
16		CLASSIC 1600	OP	B/R	FBG	DV	OB			6	10	1100			2450	2800
17	1	CLASSIC 1700	OP	B/R	FBG	DV	OB			7	5	1370			2900	3350
17	1	CLASSIC 1700	OP	B/R	FBG	DV	IO	130	OMC	7	5	1370			2800	3300
17	1	CLASSIC 1700 CB	OP	RNBT	FBG	DV	IO	130	OMC	7	5	1370			2950	3400
17	1	CLASSIC 1700 CB SD	OP	RNBT	FBG	DV	IO	130	OMC	7	5	1370			3100	3600
17	1	CLASSIC 1700 SD	OP	B/R	FBG	DV	IO	130	OMC	7	5	1380			2850	3300
17	6	SEAMASTER 1880	OP	CTRCN	FBG	DV	OB			7	5	1200			2600	3050
19	1	CLASSIC 1900	OP	B/R	FBG	DV	IO	130	OMC	8		1825			3850	4500
19	1	CLASSIC 1900 SD	OP	B/R	FBG	DV	IO	130	OMC	8		1835			3850	4500
19	5	CLASSIC 2000	OP	B/R	FBG	DV	OB			7	5	1575			3450	4050
19	5	CLASSIC 2000	OP	B/R	FBG	DV	IO	130	OMC	7	5	1625			3600	4200
19	5	CLASSIC 2000 CB	OP	RNBT	FBG	DV	IO	130	OMC	7	5	1625			3750	4350
19	5	CLASSIC 2000 CB SD	OP	RNBT	FBG	DV	IO	130	OMC	7	5	1635			3750	4350
19	5	CLASSIC 2000 CUD	OP	CUD	FBG	DV	OB			7	5	1830			3800	4400
19	5	CLASSIC 2000 CUD	OP	CUD	FBG	DV	IO	130	OMC	7	5	1860			4000	4650
19	5	CLASSIC 2000 CUD SD	OP	CUD	FBG	DV	IO	130	OMC	7	5	1870			4000	4700
19	5	CLASSIC 2000 SD	OP	B/R	FBG	DV	IO	130	OMC	7	5	1635			3600	4200
19	9	SEAMASTER 2008	OP	CUD	FBG	DV	OB			8		2325			4500	5150
19	9	SEAMASTER 2008	OP	CUD	FBG	DV	IO	130	OMC	8		3275			5800	6700
19	9	SEAMASTER 2008 GIL	OP	CUD	FBG	DV	OB			8		2375			4550	5200
19	9	SEAMASTER 2080	OP	CTRCN	FBG	DV	OB			8		1875			3900	4500
20	9	CLASSIC 2100 AC	OP	CR	FBG	DV	IO	175	OMC	8	3	3930			7600	8750
20	9	CLASSIC 2100 CUD	OP	CUD	FBG	DV	IO	175	OMC	8	3	3760			7400	8500
20	9	CLASSIC 2100 WE	OP	WKNDR	FBG	DV	IO	175	OMC	8	3	4040			7800	8950
21		CLASSIC 210	OP	B/R	FBG	DV	IO	130	OMC	7	5	2675			5200	5950
21		CLASSIC 210 CB	OP	RNBT	FBG	DV	IO	130	OMC	7	5	2675			5300	6100
21		CLASSIC 210 CB SD	OP	RNBT	FBG	DV	IO	130	OMC	7	5	2675			5500	6350
21		CLASSIC 210 CUD	OP	CUD	FBG	DV	IO	175	OMC	7	5	2825			5750	6600
21		CLASSIC 210 CUD SD	OP	CUD	FBG	DV	IO	175	OMC	7	5	2825			6000	6900
21		CLASSIC 210 SD	OP	B/R	FBG	DV	IO	130	OMC	7	5	2675			5400	6250
21	3	SEAMASTER 2288	OP	CUD	FBG	DV	OB			8		2850			6850	7850
21	3	SEAMASTER 2288	OP	CUD	FBG	DV	IO	175	OMC	8		3800			7550	8650
21	3	SEAMASTER 2288 GIL	OP	CUD	FBG	DV	OB			8		2900			6900	7950
24		SEAMASTER 2488	OP	CUD	FBG	DV	IO	175	OMC	8	6	4300			9800	11100
24		SEAMASTER 2488 GIL	OP	CUD	FBG	DV	OB			8	6	3400			9300	10600
24	4	CLASSIC 2500 AC	OP	CR	FBG	DV	IO	175	OMC	8		4525			10100	11500
26		CLASSIC 2600 AC	OP	CR	FBG	DV	IO	175	OMC	8	6	5475			12400	14100
26		SEAMASTER 2688	OP	CUD	FBG	DV	IO	175	OMC	9	6	5510			12800	14500
26		SEAMASTER 2688	OP	CUD	FBG	DV	IO	T130	OMC	9	6	5510			13900	15800
26		SEAMASTER 2688 DUAL	OP	CUD	FBG	DV	OB			9	6	4630			12100	13700
26		SEAMASTER 2688 GIL	OP	CUD	FBG	DV	OB			9	6	4610			12000	13700
		1990 BOATS														
16		CLASSIC 1600 B/R	ST	RNBT	FBG	SV	OB			6	10	1100			2350	2700
17	1	CLASSIC 1700 B/R	ST	RNBT	FBG	SV	OB			7	6	1335			2750	3200
17	1	CLASSIC 1700 B/R	ST	RNBT	FBG	SV	IO	128-175		7	6	1335			2850	3300
17	1	SPITFIRE 1700	ST	RNBT	FBG	SV	IO	175	OMC	7	6	1370			2900	3350
17	6	SEAMASTER 1880	ST	CTRCN	FBG	SV	OB			7	5	1200			2500	2900
19	1	CLASSIC 1900 B/R	ST	RNBT	FBG	SV	IO	128-205		8		1825			3750	4500
19	5	CLASSIC 2000 B/R	ST	RNBT	FBG	SV	OB			7	6	1575			3450	4050
19	5	CLASSIC 2000 B/R	ST	RNBT	FBG	SV	IO	128-235		7	6	1575			3500	4300
19	5	CLASSIC 2000 B/R	ST	RNBT	FBG	SV	IO	260	OMC	7	6	1575			3850	4450
19	5	CLASSIC 2000 CUDDY	ST	CUD	FBG	SV	OB			7	6	1830			3600	4200
19	5	CLASSIC 2000 CUDDY	ST	CUD	FBG	SV	IO	128-205		7	6	1830			3800	4700
19	5	CLASSIC 2000 CUDDY	ST	CUD	FBG	SV	IO	235-260		8		1830			4150	5000

CONTINUED ON NEXT PAGE

LOA FT	LOA IN	NAME AND/ OR MODEL	TOP/ RIG	BOAT TYPE	-HULL- MTL	-HULL- TP	ENGINE TP	ENGINE # HP	ENGINE MFG	BEAM FT	BEAM IN	WGT LBS	DRAFT FT	DRAFT IN	RETAIL LOW	RETAIL HIGH
		1990 BOATS														
19	5	SPITFIRE 2000	ST	RNBT	FBG	SV	OB			7	6	1575			3100	3600
19	5	SPITFIRE 2000	ST	RNBT	FBG	SV	IO	260-270		7	6	1625			3850	4550
19	9	SEAMASTER 2080	ST	CTRCN	FBG	SV	OB			8		1875			3700	4300
19	9	WALKAROUND 2008	ST	SF	FBG	SV	IO	128-260		8		2325			5100	6300
20	9	AFT 2100	ST	CR	FBG	SV	IO	175-270		8	3				7150	8700
20	9	CLASSIC 2100 CUDDY	ST	CUD	FBG	SV	IO	175-270		8	3	2860			5800	7150
20	9	WEEKENDER 2100	ST	WKNDR	FBG	SV	IO	175-270		8	3	3140			6150	7500
21	3	CUDDY FISH 2282	ST	SF	FBG	SV	IO	175-260		8		2450			6150	7500
21	3	SEAMASTER 2280	ST	CTRCN	FBG	SV	OB			8		2350			5800	6700
21	3	SEAMASTER 2280	ST	CTRCN	FBG	SV	IO	225	OMC	8		2350			5750	6600
21	3	WALK-A-ROUND 2288	ST	SF	FBG	SV	IO	175-260		8		2900			6750	8150
21	3	WALK-A-ROUND 2288	ST	SF	FBG	SV	IO	270	OMC	8		2900			7200	8250
21	3	WALK-A-ROUND 2288	ST	SF	FBG	SV	IO	T270	OMC	8		2900			8850	10000
24		WALK-A-ROUND 2488	ST	SF	FBG	SV	IO	205-270		8	6	3400			8950	10600
		IO 330 OMC 10100 11500, IO T128-T130 9850 11200, IO T330 OMC 12500 14200														
24	4	AFT 2500 SUN BRIDGE	ST	CR	FBG	SV	IO	235-270		8		3525			8150	9650
26		AFT 2600	ST	CR	FBG	SV	IO	260-330		8	6	4475			11000	13600
26		AFT 2600	ST	CR	FBG	SV	IO	T130	OMC	8	6	4475			11400	13000
26		WALK-A-ROUND 2688	ST	SF	FBG	SV	IO	260-330		9	6	4610			13100	16000
		IO 370 OMC 14900 17000, IO T128-T175 13500 16000, IO T370 OMC 18600 20700														
		1986 BOATS														
17	11	1750	OP	RNBT	FBG	DV	IO	120		7	6	1370			2500	2900
17	11	1750 B/R	OP	RNBT	FBG	DV	IO	175		7	6	1370			2550	2950
17	11	1750 D/R LTD	OP	RNBT	FBG	DV	IO	175		7	6	1370			2550	2950
19	8	1950 ELITE	OP	RNBT	FBG	DV	IO	200		7	2	1400			2850	3300
19	8	1950 STANDARD	OP	RNBT	FBG	DV	IO	200		7	2	1400			2850	3300
20	5	2050 B/R	OP	RNBT	FBG	DV	IO	120		7	6	1625			3100	3600
20	5	2050 B/R	OP	RNBT	FBG	DV	IO	260		7	6	1625			3600	4200
20	5	2050 B/R LTD XL	OP	RNBT	FBG	DV	IO	120-260		7	6	1625			3500	4200
20	5	2052 CUDDY	OP	CUD	FBG	DV	IO	120		7	6	1625			3450	4000
20	5	2052 CUDDY	OP	CUD	FBG	DV	IO	260		7	6	1625			3750	4350
22	8	2280 CTR CONSOLE	OP	CTRCN	FBG	DV	IO	120-260		8		2350			4900	6000
22	8	2282 CUDDY	OP	CUD	FBG	DV	IO	120-200		8		2100			4500	5250
22	8	2282 CUDDY	OP	FSH	FBG	DV	IO	120		8		2300			4850	5600
22	8	2282 CUDDY FISH	OP	FSH	FBG	DV	IO	260		8		2300			5200	5950
22	8	2288 WALKAROUND	OP	FSH	FBG	DV	IO	120		8		2100			4700	5400
22	8	2288 WALKAROUND	OP	FSH	FBG	DV	IO	260		8		2350			5250	6000
25	1	SUNBRIDGE 2500	OP	CR	FBG	DV	IO	200-260		8		4400			7900	9450
		1985 BOATS														
16	8	179M5 B/R	OP	RNBT	FBG	SV	IO	120		6	11	1200			1950	2300
16	8	179M5 B/R	OP	RNBT	FBG	SV	IO	125	VLVO	6	11	1200			2050	2450
16	8	RENKEN 750	OP	RNBT	FBG	SV	IO	170		6	11	1200			1950	2350
17	4	1840M5 B/R	OP	RNBT	FBG	SV	OB			7	2	1160			2000	2400
17	6	RENKEN 18	SLP	SA/CR	FBG	KL	OB			6	4	1220	2		2600	3050
18	2	RENKEN 950	OP	CUD	FBG	DV	IO	260		7	9	1500			2900	3350
18	8	1970M5 FISH	OP	FSH	FBG	DV	OB			7		1220			2200	2550
18	8	197M5 FISH	OP	FSH	FBG	DV	IO	120-125		7		1500			2650	3300
18	8	1985M5 B/R	OP	RNBT	FBG	SV	IO	120	OMC	7	2	1400			2400	2800
18	8	198M5 B/R	OP	RNBT	FBG	SV	IO	120	MRCR	7	2	1400			2500	2900
18	8	198M5 B/R	OP	RNBT	FBG	SV	IO	125	VLVO	7		1900			2800	3250
18	8	RENKEN 1095	OP	RNBT	FBG	DV	IO	260		7	2	1400			2750	3150
18	8	RENKEN 900	OP	FSH	FBG	DV	IO	260		7		1500			2950	3450
19	7	209M5 B/R	OP	RNBT	FBG	SV	IO	120-125		8		1875			3050	3750
19	7	209M5 C/C	OP	CUD	FBG	SV	IO	120-125		8		1900			3200	3900
19	7	209M5 CAMPER	OP	RNBT	FBG	SV	SE	115	OMC	7		1900			3100	3600
19	7	209M5 FISH	OP	RNBT	FBG	SV	IO	120-125		7		1900			2850	3450
19	7	RENKEN 2095	OP	CTRCN	FBG	DV	IO	260		7	10	1900			3600	4200
19	7	RENKEN 2095	OP	CUD	FBG	DV	IO	260		7	10	1900			3400	3950
19	7	RENKEN 2095	OP	RNBT	FBG	DV	IO	260		7	10	1900			3300	3800
20	4	204M5 BR	OP	RNBT	FBG	SV	IO	120	OMC	7		1450			2950	3450
22	8	228M5 CC	OP	CR	FBG	SV	IO	140	OMC	8		2100			4250	4900
22	8	228M5 FISH	OP	CR	FBG	SV	IO	140	OMC	8		2500			4600	5300
22	8	228M5 WA	OP	CR	FBG	SV	IO	140	OMC	8		2300			4450	5100
23	1	245M5 CC	OP	CR	FBG	SV	IO	185	OMC	8		2900			5100	5850
23	1	245M5 FISH	OP	FSH	FBG	DV	IO	185	OMC	8		2900			5400	6200
25	1	SUNBRIDGE 250M5		CR	FBG	SV	IO	200	OMC	8		4400			7550	8650
		1984 BOATS														
16	8	750 B/R	OP	RNBT	FBG	SV	IO	120-170		6	11	1200			1850	2250
17	4	795 B/R	OP	RNBT	FBG	SV	OB			7	2	1160			1950	2350
17	4	895 B/R	OP	RNBT	FBG	SV	IO	260		7	2	1290			2350	2750
17	6	RENKEN 18	SLP	SA/CR	FBG	KL	OB			6	4	1220	2		2450	2850
18	2	950 B/R	OP	RNBT	FBG	SV	IO	120-228		7	9	1450			2450	3000
18	2	950 B/R	OP	RNBT	FBG	SV	IO	260	MRCR	7	9	1450			2700	3150
18	2	950 C/C	OP	CUD	FBG	SV	IO	120	OMC	7	9	1500			2500	2900
18	2	950 C/C	OP	RNBT	FBG	DV	IO	260		7	9	1500			2700	3150
18	8	1095 B/R	OP	RNBT	FBG	SV	IO	120	OMC	7	2	1400			2350	2750
18	8	900 FISH	OP	FSH	FBG	DV	OB			7		1220			2100	2500
18	8	900 FISH	OP	FSH	FBG	DV	IO	120-228		7		1500			2550	3150
18	8	900 FISH	OP	FSH	FBG	DV	IO	260	MRCR	7		1500			2850	3300
18	8	900 STD	OP	RNBT	FBG	SV	OB			7		1220			2150	2500
18	8	900 STD	OP	RNBT	FBG	SV	IO	120-228		7		1420			2350	2900
18	8	900 STD	OP	RNBT	FBG	SV	IO	260	MRCR	7		1500			2650	3050
18	8	995 B/R	OP	RNBT	FBG	SV	OB			7	2	1220			2150	2500
19	7	2095 B/R	OP	RNBT	FBG	SV	IO	120-228		8		1875			2950	3600
19	7	2095 B/R	OP	RNBT	FBG	SV	IO	260	MRCR	8		1875			3200	3750
19	7	2095 C/C	OP	CUD	FBG	SV	IO	120-228		8		1900			3100	3750
19	7	2095 C/C	OP	CUD	FBG	SV	IO	260	MRCR	8		1900			3350	3900
21	2	2100 C/C	OP	CUD	FBG	DV	IO	120-260		8		1900			3650	4400
21	2	2100 STD	OP	RNBT	FBG	DV	IO	120-228		8		1650			3350	4050
21	2	2100 STD	OP	RNBT	FBG	DV	IO	260	MRCR	8		1650			3650	4200
21	2	2200 FISH	OP	FSH	FBG	DV	IO	117-230		8		2300			4300	5150
21	2	2200 FISH	OP	FSH	FBG	DV	IO	260		8		2300			4450	5400
23	1	2400 FISH	OP	FSH	FBG	DV	IO	170-230		8		2900			5200	6300
23	1	2400 FISH	OP	FSH	FBG	DV	IO	260		8		2900			5450	6550

....For earlier years, see the BUC Used Boat Price Guide, Volume 3

REVENGE YACHTS

POMPANO BEACH FL 33069

See inside cover to adjust price for area

LOA FT	LOA IN	NAME AND/ OR MODEL	TOP/ RIG	BOAT TYPE	-HULL- MTL	-HULL- TP	ENGINE TP	ENGINE # HP	ENGINE MFG	BEAM FT	BEAM IN	WGT LBS	DRAFT FT	DRAFT IN	RETAIL LOW	RETAIL HIGH
		1992 BOATS														
55	4	REVENGE 55 SPORTFISH	FB	SF	C/S		IB	T11CD	MAN	15	3	40000	4		1.500M	1.630M
57	4	REVENGE 57 SPORTFISH	FB	SF	C/S		IB	T11CD	MAN	15	3	40000	4		1.535M	1.665M
60		REVENGE 60 SPORTFISH	FB	SF	C/S		IB	T14CD	MWM	17	5	48000	4	2	1.625M	1.765M
65		REVENGE 65 SPORTFISH	FB	SF	C/S		IB	T14CD	MWM	17	5	52000	4	2	1.665M	1.810M
71	5	REVENGE 72 EX CRUISE		EXP	C/S		IB	Q D	MTU	16		55000	4		**	**

RHODE ISLAND MRNE SERV INC

DIV OF U S YACHT CHARTERS
WAKEFIELD RI 02880 COAST GUARD MFG ID- RXD

See inside cover to adjust price for area

LOA FT	LOA IN	NAME AND/ OR MODEL	TOP/ RIG	BOAT TYPE	-HULL- MTL	-HULL- TP	ENGINE TP	ENGINE # HP	ENGINE MFG	BEAM FT	BEAM IN	WGT LBS	DRAFT FT	DRAFT IN	RETAIL LOW	RETAIL HIGH
		1984 BOATS														
20		CLASSIC 20 COMMODORE		CR	FBG		IB			4	4				**	**
20		CLASSIC 20 NANCY		CR	FBG	DS	IB			4	4				**	**
20		CLASSIC 20 SCHEHERAZ		CR	FBG		IB			4	4				**	**
20		CLASSIC 20 TARRAGON		CR	FBG		IB			4	4				**	**
21		NORTH-SEA 21		CR	FBG	SV	IB	16		8		3500			18100	20200
26		NORTH-SEA 26		CR	FBG	SV	IB	20		10		5500			34300	38100
29		ANNIE 29		SPTCR	FBG	SV	IB	300		9		6000			37000	41100
30		CLASSIC 30 STEAMTRIG		CR	STL		IB			10					**	**
30		CLASSIC 30 TORPEDO		CR	WD		IB			5					**	**
32		NORTH-SEA 32		CR	STL	SV	IB	80		10		12000			54900	60300
35		DEBBIE S35	SLP	SA/RC	STL	KL	IB	D		11		16500	5	2	50200	55200
37		BLOCK-ISLAND S37	KTH	SA/RC	AL	KL	IB	D		11		21000	4	10	64600	70900
38		NORTH-SEA 38		CR	STL	SV	IB	100		11		20000			149500	164500
40		MONOCO 40		RNBT	WD	SV	IB	530		9		16000			182000	200000
40		SPRAY S40	YWL	SA/CR	AL	KL	IB	D		14		26000	4	8	79300	87100
41		CLASSIC 41		CR	STL	SV	IB	225		12		32000			234500	257500
44		OCEAN S44	KTH	SA/RC	AL	KL	IB	D		12		30000	6	6	95300	104500
45		NORTH-SEA 45		CR	STL	SV	IB	250		14		35000			239500	263500
45		TERN 45		CR	STL	SV	IB	300		15		35000			239000	262500
47		NICOLE S47	SCH	SA/RC	AL	KL	IB	D		13		38000	6	10	104500	115000
48		CLASSIC 48		CR	STL	SV	IB	300		16		40000			277500	305000
48		CLASSIC 48 PHOEBE		CR	STL		IB			11					**	**
50		CLASSIC 50 STEAM		CR	STL		IB			12					**	**
54		WORLD S54	SCH	SA/RC	AL	KL	IB	D		14		52000	7	6	155500	170500
55		CLASSIC 55		CR	STL	SV	IB	325		16		50000			322000	354000
60		ATLANTIS S60	SCH	SA/RC	AL	KL	IB	D		14	6	70000	8	2	275000	302000
65		HOLLY 65		CR	STL	SV	IB	350		19		60000			723500	795000
70		BLACKBIRD 70		CR	STL	SV	IB	375		20		80000			964500	1.050M
70		CLASSIC 70		CR	WD	DS	IB	T120		14		50000			666500	732500

LOA FT IN	NAME AND/ OR MODEL	TOP/ RIG	BOAT TYPE	-HULL- MTL TP	TP	----ENGINE--- # HP MFG	BEAM FT IN	WGT LBS	DRAFT FT IN	RETAIL LOW	RETAIL HIGH
						--- 1984 **BOATS**					
70	CORMORANT 70		CR	STL SV	IB	375	21	85000		997500	1.085M
70	OSPREY 70		CR	STL SV	IB	375	19	75000		927500	1.010M

....For earlier years, see the BUC Used Boat Price Guide, Volume 3

RICKBORN INDUSTRIES INC
BAYVILLE NJ 08721   COAST GUARD MFG ID- RCK See inside cover to adjust price for area

LOA FT IN	NAME AND/ OR MODEL	TOP/ RIG	BOAT TYPE	-HULL- MTL TP	TP	----ENGINE--- # HP MFG	BEAM FT IN	WGT LBS	DRAFT FT IN	RETAIL LOW	RETAIL HIGH
						--- 1986 **BOATS**					
25 11	RICKBORN PARA-SPEED			FBG DV	OB		8			8300	9500
						--- 1985 **BOATS**					
21 6	BLUE-SHARK			FBG DV	OB		8	1500	1 4	3300	3950
21 6	SALTY-DOG			FBG DV	OB		8	1650	1 4	3650	4250
26	CANYON RUNNER	OP	CTRCN	FBG DV	IO	225	8	4750	2	14800	16800
						--- 1984 **BOATS**					
21	HOLIDAY 21		CBNCR	FBG	OB		8	1775	1 1	3750	4350
21	RIDGERUNNER 21	OP	CTRCN	FBG DV	OB		8	1450	1 6	3200	3700
25	STARFIRE		CBNCR	FBG DV	IO	205	8	4150	1 6	13400	15200
26	BARNEGAT CC	OP	CTRCN	FBG DV	OB		8	2400	1 6	7850	9050
26	BARNEGAT CC	OP	CTRCN	FBG DV	IO	138	VLVO	8	2900	1 6	10800	12200
26	CANYON RUNNER CC	OP	CTRCN	FBG DV	IO			8		2	8050	9250
26	STARFIRE		CBNCR	FBG DV	OB		8	3550	1 6	8650	9950
26	TIDERUNNER	OP	SF	FBG DV	OB		8	2450	1 6	7900	9100
26	TIDERUNNER	OP	SF	FBG DV	IO	138	VLVO	8	2950	1 6	11300	12800

....For earlier years, see the BUC Used Boat Price Guide, Volume 3

RICKER YACHTS INC
ASTILLEROS AMATIQUE SA
ZONA 11 GUATEMALA   COAST GUARD MFG ID- RIX   See inside cover to adjust price for area

LOA FT IN	NAME AND/ OR MODEL	TOP/ RIG	BOAT TYPE	-HULL- MTL TP	TP	----ENGINE--- # HP MFG	BEAM FT IN	WGT LBS	DRAFT FT IN	RETAIL LOW	RETAIL HIGH
						--- 1996 **BOATS**					
42	RICKER 42	FB	TRWL	FBG DS	IB	T150D CUM	14 4	27000	3 3	146000	160500
42	RICKER 42	FB	TRWL	FBG DS	IB	T210D CUM	14 4	27000	3 3	149000	164000
42	RICKER 42 SD	FB	TRWL	FBG DS	IB	T210D CUM	14 4	29000	3 3	158000	173500
42	RICKER 42 SD	FB	TRWL	FBG DS	IB	T300D CUM	14 4	29000	3 3	164000	180500
46	RICKER 46	FB	MY	FBG SV	IB	T400D CUM	15 9	36000	4 2	195000	214000
46	RICKER 46	FB	MY	FBG SV	IB	T455D VLVO	15 9	36000	4 2	203000	223000
46	RICKER 46	FB	MY	FBG SV	IB	T485D DD	15 9	36000	4 2	210500	231500
48	RICKER 48	FB	SF	FBG SV	IB	T550D DD	16 2	45000	4 6	255000	280000
48	RICKER 48	FB	SF	FBG SV	IB	T612D VLVO	16 2	45000	4 6	266000	292500
48	RICKER 48	FB	SF	FBG SV	IB	T760D DD	16 2	45000	4 6	292000	320500
51	RICKER 51	FB	SF	FBG SV	IB	T550D DD	16 2	50000	4 6	289500	318500
51	RICKER 51	FB	SF	FBG SV	IB	T735D DD	16 2	50000	4 6	328000	360000
51	RICKER 51	FB	SF	FBG SV	IB	T767D MTU	16 2	50000	4 6	334500	367500
52	RICKER 52	FB	YTFS	FBG SV	IB	T400D CUM	16 2	41000	4 1	211000	232000
52	RICKER 52	FB	YTFS	FBG SV	IB	T485D DD	15 9	41000	4 1	234500	257500
						--- 1992 **BOATS**					
44 5	RICKER 42 SUNDECK	FB	MY	FBG SV	IB	T400D GM	14 9	26000	3 6	152500	167500
44 5	TRAWLER 42	FB	TRWL	FBG DS	IB	T200D GM	14 9	26000	3 8	121500	133500
44 5	TRAWLER 42	FB	TRWL	FBG DS	IB	T200D PERK	14 9	26000	3 8	122500	134500
47 10	RICKER 46 SUNDECK	FB	MY	FBG SV	IB	T485D GM	16	36000	3 11	188000	206500
51 10	RICKER 48 SF	FB	SF	FBG SV	IB	T735D GM	16 2	38000	4 3	242500	267000
53 10	RICKER 52 MY COCKPIT	FB	MYCPT	FBG SV	IB	T485D GM	16	44000	3 11	217500	239000
54 10	RICKER 51 SF	FB	SF	FBG SV	IB	T900D GM	16 2	40000	4 6	298500	328000
						--- 1991 **BOATS**					
51 10	RICKER 48	FB	SF	FBG SV	IB	T550D GM	16 2	39000	4 3	204000	224000

RIEHL MFG CO
CLINTON STEEL BOATS
PT CLINTON OH 43452   COAST GUARD MFG ID- RHL   See inside cover to adjust price for area

LOA FT IN	NAME AND/ OR MODEL	TOP/ RIG	BOAT TYPE	-HULL- MTL TP	TP	----ENGINE--- # HP MFG	BEAM FT IN	WGT LBS	DRAFT FT IN	RETAIL LOW	RETAIL HIGH
						--- 1985 **BOATS**					
16	JOHN BOAT	OP	JON	STL FL	OB		5 2			330	405
16	SEAFLYTE DELUXE	OP	UTL	STL SV	OB		6			540	650
16	SEAFLYTE STANDARD	OP	UTL	STL SV	OB		5 8			540	650
16	UTILITY	OP	UTL	STL FL	OB		5 2			540	650
18	FISHERMAN	OP	FSH	STL SV	OB		6 6			1400	1650
20	FISHERMAN	OP	FSH	STL SV	OB		7			2200	2550
						--- 1984 **BOATS**					
16	JOHN BOAT	OP	JON	STL FL	OB		5 2			320	390
16	SEAFLYTE DELUXE	OP	UTL	STL SV	OB		6			520	625
16	SEAFLYTE STANDARD	OP	UTL	STL SV	OB		5 8			520	625
16	UTILITY	OP	UTL	STL FL	OB		5 2			520	625
18	FISHERMAN	OP	FSH	STL SV	OB		6 6			1350	1600
20	CLINTON 20	OP	UTL	STL SV	IB	225	8 2			5850	6700
20	FISHERMAN	OP	FSH	STL SV	OB		7			2050	2450
22	CLINTON 22	OP	UTL	STL SV	IB	225	8			5650	6500
24	CLINTON 24	OP	UTL	STL SV	IB	300	9 8			8850	10100

....For earlier years, see the BUC Used Boat Price Guide, Volume 3

RINKER BOAT CO INC
SYRACUSE IN 46567   COAST GUARD MFG ID- RNK See inside cover to adjust price for area

For more recent years, see the BUC Used Boat Price Guide, Volume 1

LOA FT IN	NAME AND/ OR MODEL	TOP/ RIG	BOAT TYPE	-HULL- MTL TP	TP	----ENGINE--- # HP MFG	BEAM FT IN	WGT LBS	DRAFT FT IN	RETAIL LOW	RETAIL HIGH
						--- 1996 **BOATS**					
18 1	180	ST	RNBT	FBG SV	IO	130	7 5	1980		5200	5950
19 2	CAPTIVA 192	ST	RNBT	FBG SV	IO	180	7 6	2590		6600	7600
20 6	CAPTIVA 212	ST	CUD	FBG SV	IO	180	8 2	2775		8150	9350
20 6	CAPTIVA 212	ST	RNBT	FBG SV	IO	180	8 2	2675		7650	8750
20 6	FESTIVA 212	ST	CUD	FBG SV	IO	190	8 2	2775		8350	9600
23 6	CAPTIVA 232	ST	CUD	FBG SV	IO	235	8 6	4215		13000	14800
23 6	CAPTIVA 232	ST	RNBT	FBG SV	IO	235	8 6	4100		12000	13600
23 8	FLOTILLA III-3	ST	RNBT	FBG TM	IO	180	8 6	3540		10700	12100
25 9	FIESTA-VEE 266	ST	CUD	FBG SV	IO	210	8 6	5875		19700	21900
28 11	FIESTA-VEE 265	ST	CUD	FBG SV	IO	250	8 6	5775		23700	26400
30 2	FIESTA-VEE 280	ST	CUD	FBG SV	IO	T180	10	8680		29500	32700
33 11	FIESTA-VEE 300	ST	CR	FBG SV	IO	T250	10 6	10000		41400	46000
						--- 1995 **BOATS**					
18 1	180	ST	RNBT	FBG SV	IO	130	7 5	1980		4850	5550
18 11	CAPTIVA 190	ST	RNBT	FBG SV	IO	180	7 6	2495		5750	6600
20 6	CAPTIVA 212	ST	CUD	FBG SV	IO	180	8 2	2775		7600	8700
20 6	CAPTIVA 212	ST	RNBT	FBG SV	IO	180	8 2	2675		7100	8200
23 5	SPORT 236	ST	RNBT	FBG SV	IO	250	8 6	3725		11200	12700
23 6	CAPTIVA 232	ST	CUD	FBG SV	IO	235	8 6	4000		11700	13300
23 6	CAPTIVA 232	ST	RNBT	FBG SV	IO	235	8 6	3900		10800	12300
23 8	FLOTILLA III-3	ST	RNBT	FBG TM	IO	180	8 6	3760		10400	11800
25 9	FESTIVA 240	ST	RNBT	FBG SV	IO	180	8 6	4000		12900	14600
28 11	FIESTA-VEE 265	ST	CUD	FBG SV	IO	250	8 6	5775		22100	24600
30 2	FIESTA-VEE 280	ST	CUD	FBG SV	IO	T180	10	8680		27500	30500
33 11	FIESTA-VEE 300	ST	CR	FBG SV	IO	T250	10 6	10000		38700	43000
						--- 1994 **BOATS**					
17	CAPTIVA 170	ST	RNBT	FBG SV	OB		7 4	1320		2650	3100
18 1	180	ST	RNBT	FBG SV	IO	130	7 5	1980		4550	5200
18 11	CAPTIVA 190	ST	CUD	FBG SV	IO	175	7 6	2495		5350	6150
20 1	FESTIVA 202	ST	CUD	FBG SV	IO	130	7 5	2785		6500	7500
20 6	CAPTIVA 209	ST	CUD	FBG SV	IO	175	8 2	2675		7050	8150
20 6	CAPTIVA 209	ST	RNBT	FBG SV	IO	175	8 2	2675		6650	7650
23	FESTIVA 230	ST	CUD	FBG SV	IO	175	8 6	3285		9150	10400
23 5	OPEN BOW 236	ST	RNBT	FBG SV	IO	260	8 6	3625		9700	11000
23 5	SPORT 236	ST	CUD	FBG SV	IO	260	8 6	3725		10500	12000
23 8	FLOTILLA III-3	ST	RNBT	FBG TM	IO	175	8 6	3760		9650	11000
25 9	FESTIVA 240	ST	RNBT	FBG SV	IO	180	8 6	4000		12000	13600
28 11	FIESTA-VEE 265	ST	CUD	FBG SV	IO	260	8 6	5775		20800	23100
30 2	FIESTA-VEE 280	ST	CUD	FBG SV	IO	T175	10	8680		25600	28400
33 11	FIESTA-VEE 300	ST	CR	FBG SV	IO	T260	10 6	10000		36300	40300
						--- 1993 **BOATS**					
17	CAPTIVA 170	ST	RNBT	FBG SV	OB		7 4	1320		2500	2900
18 1	180	ST	RNBT	FBG SV	IO	130	7 5	1980		4200	4850
18 6	CAPTIVA 186	ST	CUD	FBG SV	IO	175	7 6	2445		4800	5550
20 1	FESTIVA 202	ST	CUD	FBG SV	IO	130	7 5	2785		6100	7000
20 6	CAPTIVA 209	ST	CUD	FBG SV	IO	175	8 2	2775		6600	7600
20 6	CAPTIVA 209	ST	RNBT	FBG SV	IO	175	8 2	2675		6200	7150
23	FESTIVA 230	ST	CUD	FBG SV	IO	175	8 6	3285		8450	9750
23 5	OPEN BOW 236	ST	RNBT	FBG SV	IO	260	8 6	3625		9150	10400
23 5	SPORT 236	ST	CUD	FBG SV	IO	260	8 6	3725		9850	11200
23 8	FLOTILLA III-3	ST	RNBT	FBG TM	IO	175	8 6	3760		9100	10300
28	FIESTA-VEE 260	ST	CUD	FBG SV	IO	260	8 6	5625		17500	19900
30 2	FIESTA VEE 280	ST	CUD	FBG SV	IO	T175	10	8680		23900	26500

RINKER BOAT CO INC -CONTINUED See inside cover to adjust price for area

LOA FT	LOA IN	NAME AND/ OR MODEL	TOP/ RIG	BOAT TYPE	-HULL- MTL	-HULL- TP	ENGINE TP	ENGINE # HP	ENGINE MFG	BEAM FT	BEAM IN	WGT LBS	DRAFT FT	DRAFT IN	RETAIL LOW	RETAIL HIGH
		1993 BOATS														
33	11	FIESTA-VEE 300	ST	CR	FBG	SV	IO	T260		10	6	10000			33900	37700
		1992 BOATS														
17		CAPTIVA 170	ST	RNBT	FBG	SV	OB			7	4	1300			2350	2750
18	1	181	ST	RNBT	FBG	SV	IO	130		7	4	2000			3900	4550
18	6	CAPTIVA 186	ST	RNBT	FBG	SV	IO	175		7	6	2300			4400	5100
20	1	FESTIVA 202	ST	CUD	FBG	SV	IO	130		7	5	2450			5300	6100
20	6	CAPTIVA 206	ST	CUD	FBG	SV	IO	175		8	2	2800			6200	7150
20	6	CAPTIVA 206	ST	RNBT	FBG	SV	IO	175		8	2	2700			5850	6700
23		FESTIVA 230	ST	CUD	FBG	SV	IO	175		8	6	3100			7650	8800
23	5	FIESTA-VEE 235	ST	CUD	FBG	SV	IO	200		8	6	4100			9550	10900
23	5	OPEN BOW 236	ST	RNBT	FBG	SV	IO	260		8	6	3400			8100	9300
23	5	SPORT 236	ST	CUD	FBG	SV	IO	260		8	6	3500			8900	10100
28		FIESTA-VEE V260	ST	CUD	FBG	SV	IO	260		8	6	5100			15800	17900
33	11	FIESTA-VEE 300	ST	CR	FBG	SV	IO	T260		10	6	10000			31800	35300
		1991 BOATS														
18	1	181	ST	RNBT	FBG	SV	IO	130		7	4	2000			3650	4250
18	6	CAPTIVA 186	ST	RNBT	FBG	SV	IO	175		7	6	2300			4100	4750
18	11	V190	ST	CUD	FBG	SV	IO	130		7	5	2350			4300	5000
20	6	CAPTIVA 206	ST	CUD	FBG	SV	IO	175		8	2	2800			5850	6700
20	6	CAPTIVA 206	ST	RNBT	FBG	SV	IO	175		8	2	2700			5450	6300
23		FESTIVA 230	ST	CUD	FBG	SV	IO	175		8	6	3100			7150	8250
23	5	FIESTA-VEE 235	ST	CUD	FBG	SV	IO	200		8	6	4100			9000	10200
23	5	OPEN BOW 236	ST	RNBT	FBG	SV	IO	260		8	6	3400			7600	8750
23	5	SPORT 236	ST	CUD	FBG	SV	IO	260		8	6	3500			8250	9450
28		FIESTA-VEE V260	ST	CUD	FBG	SV	IO	260		8	6	5100			14800	16800
33	11	FIESTA-VEE 300	ST	CR	FBG	SV	IO	T260		10	6	10000			29800	33100
		1990 BOATS														
16	6	V170	ST	RNBT	FBG	SV	OB			7	2	950			1550	1800
17	7	V180	ST	RNBT	FBG	SV	IO	130		7	3	1990			3300	3850
18	6	CAPTIVA 186	ST	RNBT	FBG	SV	IO	130		7	6	2180			3750	4350
18	11	V190	ST	CUD	FBG	SV	IO	130		7	5	2350			4050	4700
20	6	CAPTIVA 206	ST	CUD	FBG	SV	IO	175		8	2	2650			5350	6100
20	6	CAPTIVA 206	ST	RNBT	FBG	SV	IO	175		8	2	2550			5000	5750
23		FESTIVA 230	ST	CUD	FBG	SV	IO	175		8	6	3000			6600	7600
23	4	SPORT 236	ST	CUD	FBG	SV	IO	260		8	6	3200			7300	8400
28		FIESTA-VEE V250	ST	CUD	FBG	SV	IO	260		8	6	4600			13500	15300
33	11	FIESTA-VEE 300	ST	CR	FBG	SV	IO	T175		10	6	8300			25600	28400
		1989 BOATS														
16	6	V170	ST	RNBT	FBG	SV	OB			7	2	950			1450	1750
17	7	V180	ST	RNBT	FBG	SV	IO	130		7	3	1900			3050	3550
18	6	CAPTIVA 186	ST	RNBT	FBG	SV	IO	130		7	6	2180			3500	4100
18	11	V190	ST	CUD	FBG	SV	IO	130		7	5	2350			3800	4450
20	6	CAPTIVA 206	ST	CUD	FBG	SV	IO	175		8	2	2650			5000	5750
20	6	CAPTIVA 206	ST	RNBT	FBG	SV	IO	175		8	2	2550			4700	5400
23		FESTIVA 230	ST	CUD	FBG	SV	IO	175		8	6	3000			6250	7150
23	4	SPORT 236	ST	CUD	FBG	DV	IO	260		8	6	3200			6900	7900
24		FESTIVA 240	ST	CUD	FBG	DV	IO	175		8	6	3500			7200	8300
28		FIESTA-VEE V250	ST	CUD	FBG	DV	IO	260		8	6	4600			12700	14500
		1988 BOATS														
16	6	V170	ST	RNBT	FBG	SV	OB			7	2	950			1400	1650
16	6	V170	ST	RNBT	FBG	SV	IO	130		7	2	1700			2550	3000
17	7	V180	ST	RNBT	FBG	SV	IO	130		7	3	1900			2900	3350
18	6	CAPTIVA 186	ST	RNBT	FBG	SV	OB			7	6	1200			1950	2300
18	6	CAPTIVA 186	ST	RNBT	FBG	SV	IO	130		7	6	2180			3350	3850
18	11	V190	ST	CUD	FBG	SV	IO	130		7	5	2350			3600	4200
20	6	CAPTIVA 206	ST	CUD	FBG	SV	IO	175		8	2	2650			4750	5450
20	6	CAPTIVA 206	ST	RNBT	FBG	SV	IO	175		8	2	2550			4500	5150
23		V230	ST	CUD	FBG	SV	IO	175		8	1	2850			5600	6450
24		FESTIVA 240	ST	CUD	FBG	DV	IO	270		8	6	3500			7200	8250
28		FIESTA-VEE V250	ST	CUD	FBG	DV	IO	260		8	6	4600			12000	13700
		1987 BOATS														
16	6	V170		RNBT	FBG	SV	IO	120		7	2	1700			2450	2850
16	6	V170	OP	RNBT	FBG	SV	OB			7	2	950			1350	1600
17	7	V180		RNBT	FBG	SV	IO	120		7	3	1900			2750	3200
18	11	V190CC		CUD	FBG	SV	IO	130		7	5	2350			3450	4000
20	6	V195	OP	RNBT	FBG	DV	IO	165		8	2	2550			4200	4900
23		V210CC	OP	CUD	FBG	SV	IO	165		8	1	2850			5350	6150
28		FIESTA-VEE V250	OP	CUD	FBG	DV	IO	260		8	6	4600			11500	13000
		1986 BOATS														
16	6	V170		RNBT	FBG	SV	OB			7	2	950			1300	1550
17	7	V180		RNBT	FBG	SV	OB			7	3	1900			2450	2800
18	11	V190		CUD	FBG	SV	OB			7	5	2350			2800	3250
18	11	V190		RNBT	FBG	SV	OB			7	5	2100			2700	3150
20	2	V205		CUD	FBG	SV	OB			8	1	2750			3550	4100
		1985 BOATS														
16	6	V170		RNBT	FBG	SV	OB			7	2	950			1250	1500
16	6	V170		RNBT	FBG	SV	IO	120		7	2	1700			2250	2600
17	7	V180		RNBT	FBG	SV	IO	120		7	3	1900			2500	2950
18	11	V190		RNBT	FBG	SV	IO	120		7	5	2100			2900	3350
18	11	V190CB		RNBT	FBG	SV	IO	120		7	5	2100			2900	3350
20	5	V205		CUD	FBG	SV	IO	140		8		2750			4100	4800
		1984 BOATS														
16	6	V170 BR	OP	RNBT	FBG	DV	OB			7	2	975			1250	1500
16	6	V170 BR	OP	RNBT	FBG	DV	IO	140		7	2	1725			2200	2550
17	7	V180 BR	OP	RNBT	FBG	DV	IO	185		7	4	1850			2450	2850
19		V190 BR	OP	RNBT	FBG	DV	IO	120		7	5	2000			2750	3200
19		V190 CB	OP	RNBT	FBG	DV	IO	120		7	5	2000			2750	3200
20	5	V205	OP	CUD	FBG	DV	IO	120		8		2800			4000	4650

....For earlier years, see the BUC Used Boat Price Guide, Volume 3

RIVA S P A

FERRETTI GROUP
24067 SARNICO ITALY

COAST GUARD MFG ID- RVA

See inside cover to adjust price for area

For more recent years, see the BUC Used Boat Price Guide, Volume 1

LOA FT	LOA IN	NAME AND/ OR MODEL	TOP/ RIG	BOAT TYPE	-HULL- MTL	-HULL- TP	ENGINE TP	ENGINE # HP	ENGINE MFG	BEAM FT	BEAM IN	WGT LBS	DRAFT FT	DRAFT IN	RETAIL LOW	RETAIL HIGH
		1995 BOATS														
28	7	AQUARAMA SPECIAL	OP	RNBT	MHG	SV	IB	T350	RIVA	8	5	6504	2	7	**	**
35	5	RIVA 32 SPECIAL	OP	RNBT	FBG	DV	IB	T400	BPM	8	7	8422	2	8	113000	124500
43	3	TROPICANA 43 SPECIAL	OP	CR	FBG	SV	IB	T400D	CUM	12	8	23148	3	9	252500	277500
45	1	ANTALYA 43	OP	CR	FBG	SV	IB	T400D	CUM	12	7	25485	3	9	292500	321500
55	5	THALASSA 52	FB	MY	FBG	SV	IB	T680D	MAN	15	6	44105	3	2	438000	481500
57	3	FURAMA 58	FB	MY	FBG	SV	IB	T635D	MAN	16	3	48942	4	8	517000	568000
59	9	BAHAMAS 58	OP	CR	FBG	DV	IB	T11CD	MAN	16	3	53285	5	1	632000	694000
61	7	BLACK CORSAIR 20	HT	MY	FBG	SV	IB	T11CD	MAN	17	6	57319	5	8	730000	802500
65	1	CORSARO 20	FB	MY	FBG	SV	IB	T10CD	MTU	17	6	62610	5	4	743500	817000
		1994 BOATS														
28	7	AQUARAMA SPECIAL	OP	RNBT	MHG	SV	IB	T350	RIVA	8	5	6504	2	7	**	**
35	5	GITANO 31	OP	RNBT	FBG	DV	IB	T350	RIVA	9		9107	2	10	106000	116500
35	5	RIVA 32 SPECIAL	OP	RNBT	FBG	DV	IB	T400	BPM	8	7	8422	2	8	107000	117500
43	3	TROPICANA 43 SPECIAL	OP	CR	FBG	SV	IB	T400D	CUM	12	8	23148	3	9	242000	266000
45	1	ANTALYA 43	OP	CR	FBG	SV	IB	T400D	CUM	12	7	25485	3	9	280500	308500
55	5	THALASSA 52	FB	MY	FBG	SV	IB	T680D	MAN	15	6	44105	3	2	419500	461500
57	3	FURAMA 58	FB	MY	FBG	SV	IB	T635D	MAN	16	3	48942	4	8	495000	544000
59	9	BAHAMAS 58	OP	CR	FBG	DV	IB	T11CD	MAN	16	3	53285	5	1	605000	665000
61	7	BLACK CORSAIR 20	HT	MY	FBG	SV	IB	T11CD	MAN	17	6	57319	5	8	699500	768500
65	1	CORSARO 20	FB	MY	FBG	SV	IB	T10CD	MTU	17	6	62610	5	4	712000	782500
		1993 BOATS														
28	8	AQUARAMA SP	OP	RNBT	MHG	SV	IB	T350	RIVA	8	5	6504	2		**	**
35	5	GITANO 31	OP	RNBT	FBG	DV	IB	T350	RIVA	9		9107	2	11	100500	110500
35	5	RIVA 32 SPECIAL	OP	RNBT	FBG	DV	IB	T400	BPM	8	7	8422	2	8	101500	111500
43	4	ANTALYA 43	OP	CR	FBG	SV	IB	T400D	CUM	12	8		3	9	12000	13700
43	4	TROPICANA 43	OP	CR	FBG	SV	IB	T400D	CUM	12	8		3	9	**	**
50	3	SUPERAMERICA 50	FB	MY	FBG	SV	IB	T510D	MAN	13	8		4	3	362000	398000
51	4	TURBOROSSO 51	OP	CR	FBG	SV	IB	T820D	MAN	13	8		4	4	325500	357500
57	4	FURAMA 58	FB	MY	FBG	SV	IB	T635D	MAN	16	3	48942	4	8	472000	518500
59	1	BAHAMAS 58	OP	CR	FBG	DV	IB	T11CD	MAN	16	3		5	1	549000	603500
64	1	CORSARO 20	FB	MY	FBG	SV	IB	T10CD	MTU	17	6		5	4	841500	924500
64	2	BLACK CORSAIR 20	HT	MY	FBG	SV	IB	T11CD	MAN	17	6		5	2	864500	950000
		1992 BOATS														
28	8	AQUARAMA SP	OP	RNBT	MHG	SV	IB	T350	RIVA	8	5	6504	2		**	**
35	5	GITANO 31	OP	RNBT	FBG	DV	IB	T350	RIVA	9		9107	2	11	95300	105000
35	5	RIVA 32	OP	RNBT	FBG	DV	IB	T400	BPM	8	7	8422	2	8	96300	106000
43	4	TROPICANA 43	OP	CR	FBG	SV	IB	T400D	CUM	12	8		3	9	210500	231500
43	4	TROPICANA 43	OP	CR	FBG	SV	IB	T400D	GM	12	8		3	9	211500	232500
50	3	SUPERAMERICA 50	FB	MY	FBG	SV	IB	T510D	MAN	13	8		4	3	345000	379500
51	4	TURBOROSSO 51	OP	CR	FBG	SV	IB	T820D	MAN	13	8		4	4	310500	341000
57	4	FURAMA 58	FB	MY	FBG	SV	IB	T635D	MAN	16	3	48942	4	8	449500	494000
59	1	BAHAMAS 58	OP	CR	FBG	DV	IB	T11CD	MAN	16	3		5	1	523500	575500
64	1	CORSARO 20	FB	MY	FBG	SV	IB	T10CD	MTU	17	6		5	4	802000	881500
64	2	BLACK CORSAIR 20	HT	MY	FBG	SV	IB	T11CD	MAN	17	6		5	2	824000	905500
		1991 BOATS														
28	8	AQUARAMA SP	OP	RNBT	MHG	DV	IO	T350		8	5	6504	2		**	**
35	5	RIVA 32	OP	RNBT	FBG	DV	IB	T400	BPM	8	7	8422	2	8	91500	100500
43	4	TROPICANA 43	FB	CR	FBG	DS	IB	T400D		12	8		3	9	205000	225000
50	3	SUPERAMERICA 50	FB	MY	FBG	DS	IB	T510D		13	8		4	3	341000	374500
51	4	TURBOROSSO 51	FB	MY	FBG	DS	IB	T820D		13	8		4	4	401000	440500
57	4	FURAMA 58	FB	MY	FBG	DS	IB	T635D		16	3	48942	4	8	437500	481000
64	1	CORSARA 20	FB	MY	FBG	DS	IB	T10CD		17	6		5	4	758000	833000
64	2	BLACK CORSAIR 20	HT	MY	FBG	DV	IB	T11CD		17	6		5	2	791500	870000

LOA FT	LOA IN	NAME AND/ OR MODEL	TOP/ RIG	BOAT TYPE	-HULL- MTL	-HULL- TP	ENGINE TP	ENGINE # HP	ENGINE MFG	BEAM FT	BEAM IN	WGT LBS	DRAFT FT	DRAFT IN	RETAIL LOW	RETAIL HIGH
		1987 BOATS														
28	8	AQUARAMA-SPECIAL	OP	RNBT	MHG	FL	IB	T350	RIVA	8	5	6614	2		**	**
31	3	ST-TROPEZ	OP	RNBT	FBG	DV	IB	T350	RIVA	8	10	7060	2	4	80900	88900
38	4	BRAVO SPECIAL	HT	EXP	FBG	DV	IB	T320D	CUM	12	6	15870	3	2	129500	142000
49	10	SUPERAMERICA	FB	MY	FBG	DV	IB	T425D	CUM	13	9	31000	4	3	244500	269000
50	2	DIABLE	HT	EXP	FBG	DV	IB	T500D		13	9	30000	4	3	262500	288500
60		CORSARO	FB	MY	FBG	DV	IB	T700D		17	4	66000	4	7	526000	578000
61	4	BLACK-CORSAIR	FB	MY	FBG	DV	IB	T13CD		17	4	60000	5	3	661500	726500
		1986 BOATS														
19	3	RUDY SUPER	OP	RNBT	FBG	FL	IB	210	RIVA	7	1	2425	1	6	8250	9500
28	8	AQUARAMA-SPECIAL	OP	RNBT	MHG	FL	IB	T350	RIVA	8	5	6614	2		**	**
31	3	ST-TROPEZ	OP	RNBT	FBG	DV	IB	T350	RIVA	8	10	7060	2	4	77200	84900
38	4	BRAVO SPECIAL	HT	CBNCR	FBG	DV	IB	T320D	CUM	12	6	15870	3	2	125500	138000
42	8	MALIBU	FB	MY	FBG	DV	IB	T320D	CUM	12	7	21000	3	4	180000	197500
49	10	SUPERAMERICA	FB	MY	FBG	DV	IB	T425D	CUM	13	9	31000	3	8	234000	257000
50		DIABLE	HT	CBNCR	FBG	DV	IB	T500D							**	**
60		BLACK-CORSAIR	FB	MY	FBG	DV	IB	T13CD							515000	566000
60		CORSARO	FB	MY	FBG	DV	IB	T700D		17	4				404500	444000
		1985 BOATS														
19	3	RUDY SUPER	OP	RNBT	FBG	FL	IB	210	RIVA	7	1	2425	1	6	7900	9050
21	6	OLYMPIC	OP	RNBT	MHG	FL	IO	270		7	4	2865	1	6	30700	34200
28	8	AQUARAMA-SPECIAL	OP	RNBT	MHG	FL	IB	T350	RIVA	8	5	6614	2		**	**
31	3	ST-TROPEZ	OP	RNBT	FBG	DV	IB	T350	RIVA	8	10	7060	2	4	73800	81100
38	4	BRAVO SPECIAL	HT	CBNCR	FBG	DV	IB	T320D	CUM	12	6	15870	3	2	120000	132000
42		CARIBE	FB	SF	FBG	DV	IO	T320D		12	6	19000			121500	133500
42	8	MALIBU	FB	MY	FBG	DV	IB	T320D	CUM	12	7	21000	3	4	172500	189500
50		DIABLE	FB	MY	FBG	DV	IO	T500D		13	9	30000			175000	192500
50	10	SUPERAMERICA SPECIAL	FB	MY	FBG	DV	IB	T425D	CUM	13	9	31000	3	8	208000	228500
60		BLACK-CORSAIR	OP	OFF	FBG	DV	IB	T13CD	MTU	17	4	28000	6		470000	516500
60		CORSARO	FB	MY	FBG	DV	IO	T650D		17	6	66120			362000	398000
60		CORSARO	FB	MY	FBG	DV	IB	T700D		17	4	26000	5	7	409000	449500
		1984 BOATS														
19	3	RUDY SUPER	OP	RNBT	FBG	FL	IB	210	RIVA	7	1	2425	1	6	7550	8650
28	8	AQUARAMA-SPECIAL	OP	RNBT	MHG	FL	IB	T350	RIVA	8	5	6614	2		**	**
31	3	ST-TROPEZ	OP	RNBT	FBG	DV	IB	T350	RIVA	8	10	7060	2	4	70500	77500
38	4	BRAVO SPECIAL	HT	CBNCR	FBG	DV	IB	T320D	CUM	12	6	15870	3	2	115000	126500
42	8	CARIBE	FB	SF	FBG	DV	IB	T320D	CUM	12	7	19000	3	4	154000	169000
42	8	MALIBU	FB	MY	FBG	DV	IB	T320D	CUM	12	7	21000	3	4	165000	181500
50	10	SUPERAMERICA	FB	MY	FBG	DV	IB	T425D	CUM	13	9	31000	3	8	213000	234500
60		CORSARO	FB	MY	FBG	DV	IB	T650D		17	4				360500	396500
76		SUPERMONTECARLO	FB	MY	FBG	DV	IB	T13CD	MTU	18		85120	5	1	**	**

....For earlier years, see the BUC Used Boat Price Guide, Volume 3

RIVAL BOWMAN YACHT LTD

SOUTHAMPTON ENGLAND SO14 5QY
ALSO SADLER INTL

See inside cover to adjust price for area

For more recent years, see the BUC Used Boat Price Guide, Volume 1

LOA FT	LOA IN	NAME AND/ OR MODEL	TOP/ RIG	BOAT TYPE	-HULL- MTL	-HULL- TP	ENGINE TP	ENGINE # HP	ENGINE MFG	BEAM FT	BEAM IN	WGT LBS	DRAFT FT	DRAFT IN	RETAIL LOW	RETAIL HIGH
		1996 BOATS														
28	5	SADLER 29	SLP	SACAC	FBG	KL	IB	18D	VLVO	9	6	8200	5		74600	82000
34	9	SADLER 34	SLP	SACAC	FBG	KL	IB	29D	VLVO	10	9	12800	5	10	125000	137500
35	10	RIVAL 36	SLP	SACAC	FBG	KL	IB	29D	VLVO	11		15450	4	11	151500	166500
36	1	STARLIGHT 35	SLP	SACAC	FBG	KL	IB	29D	VLVO	11	6	14000	4	9	139500	153500
39	11	BOWMAN 40	CUT	SACAC	FBG	KL	IB	50D	VLVO	12	7	19000	4	11	210000	230500
40	5	STARLIGHT 39	SLP	SACAC	FBG	KL	IB	40D	LIST	12	6	18000	5	3	206500	227000
45	2	BOWMAN 45	CUT	SACAC	FBG	KL	IB	59D	VLVO	13		24500	5	9	307000	337000
48	2	BOWMAN 48	CUT	SACAC	FBG	KL	IB	80D	PERK	14	2	31700	5	10	392000	431000
		1995 BOATS														
28	5	SADLER 29	SLP	SACAC	FBG	KL	IB	18D	VLVO	9	6	8200	5		66100	72600
28	5	SADLER 29 CP	SLP	SACAC	FBG	KL	IB	18D	VLVO	9	6	8200	5		74200	81600
34	9	SADLER 34	SLP	SACAC	FBG	KL	IB	29D	VLVO	10	9	12800	5	10	111000	122000
34	9	SADLER 34 CP	SLP	SACAC	FBG	KL	IB	29D	VLVO	10	9	12800	5	10	124000	136500
36	1	STARLIGHT 35	SLP	SACAC	FBG	KL	IB	29D	PERK	11	6	13200	4	9	116500	128000
36	1	STARLIGHT 35 CP	SLP	SACAC	FBG	KL	IB	29D	VLVO	11	6	13200	4	9	126500	139000
40	5	STARLIGHT 39	SLP	SACAC	FBG	KL	IB	40D	LIST	12	6	17500	5	3	178000	195500
		1994 BOATS														
28	5	SADLER 29	SLP	SACAC	FBG	KL	IB	18D	VLVO	9	6	8200	5		62200	68300
28	5	SADLER 29 CP	SLP	SACAC	FBG	KL	IB	18D	VLVO	9	6	8200	5		69800	76700
34	9	SADLER 34	SLP	SACAC	FBG	KL	IB	29D	VLVO	10	9	12800	5	10	104500	115000
34	9	SADLER 34 CP	SLP	SACAC	FBG	KL	IB	29D	VLVO	10	9	12800	5	10	116500	128000
36	1	STARLIGHT 35	SLP	SACAC	FBG	KL	IB	29D	PERK	11	6	13200	4	9	109500	120500
36	1	STARLIGHT 35 CP	SLP	SACAC	FBG	KL	IB	29D	VLVO	11	6	13200	4	9	119000	130500
40	5	STARLIGHT 39	SLP	SACAC	FBG	KL	IB	50D	WATE	12	6	17500	5	3	168000	184500
		1993 BOATS														
28	5	SADLER 29	SLP	SACAC	FBG	KL	IB	18D	VLVO	9	6	8200	5		62100	68200
34	9	SADLER 34	SLP	SACAC	FBG	KL	IB	28D	VLVO	10	9	12800	5	10	104000	114500
35	1	SADLER STARLIGHT 35	SLP	SACAC	FBG	KL	IB	29D	PERK	11	6	13200	4	9	107500	118000
39	1	SADLER STARLIGHT 39	SLP	SACAC	FBG	KL	IB	50D	WATE	12	6	17500	5	3	158000	173500
39	1	SADLER STARLIGHT 39	SLP	SACAC	FBG	KL	IB	56D	MAID	12	6	17500	5	3	158000	174000
39	1	SADLER STARLIGHT 39	SLP	SACAC	FBG	KL	IB	59D	PERK	12	6	17500	5	3	157500	173000
		1992 BOATS														
25	9	SADLER 26	SLP	SA/CR	FBG	KL	IB	9D	VLVO	9	5	4800	3	6	30700	34200
28	5	SADLER 29	SLP	SA/CR	FBG	KL	IB	18D	VLVO	9	6	8200	3	8	58400	64200
34	9	SADLER 34	SLP	SA/CR	FBG	KL	IB	28D	VLVO	10	9	12800	4		97900	107500
36	1	SADLER STARLIGHT 35	SLP	SA/CR	FBG	KL	IB	28D	VLVO	11	6	13500	4	9	106000	116500
40	5	SADLER PANORAMA 40	SLP	SA/CR	FBG	KL	IB	59D	VLVO	12	6	18000	5	3	162500	178500
40	5	SADLER STARLIGHT 39	SLP	SA/CR	FBG	KL	IB	56D	FORD	12	6	17500	5	3	159500	175000
		1991 BOATS														
25	9	SADLER 26	SLP	SA/CR	FBG	KL	IB	9D	VLVO	9	5	4800	3	6	28900	32100
28	5	SADLER 29	SLP	SA/CR	FBG	KL	IB	18D	VLVO	9	6	8200	3	8	54900	60300
34	9	SADLER 34	SLP	SA/CR	FBG	KL	IB	28D	VLVO	10	9	12800	4		92000	101000
36	1	SADLER STARLIGHT 35	SLP	SA/CR	FBG	KL	IB	28D	VLVO	11	6	13200	4	9	97600	107000
40	5	SADLER PANORAMA 40	SLP	SA/CR	FBG	KL	IB	59D	VLVO	12	6	18000	5	3	153000	168000
40	5	SADLER STARLIGHT 39	SLP	SA/CR	FBG	KL	IB	56D	FORD	12	6	17500	5	3	150000	165000
		1990 BOATS														
25	9	SADLER 26	SLP	SA/CR	FBG	KL	IB	9D	VLVO	9	5	4800	4	8	27200	30200
28	5	SADLER 29	SLP	SA/CR	FBG	KL	IB	18D	VLVO	9	6	8200	5	3	51700	56800
34	7	SADLER STARLIGHT 35	SLP	SA/CR	FBG	KL	IB	28D	VLVO	11	6	13500	4	9	90800	99700
34	9	SADLER 34	SLP	SA/CR	FBG	KL	IB	28D	VLVO	10	9	12800	5	8	86600	95100
38	8	SADLER STARLIGHT 38	SLP	SA/CR	FBG	KL	IB	56D	FORD	12	6	16500	5	3	123500	135500
		1989 BOATS														
25	9	SADLER 26	SLP	SA/RC	F/S	KL	IB	10D	VLVO	9	5	4800	4	8	25600	28500
28	5	SADLER 29	SLP	SA/RC	F/S	KL	IB	20D	VLVO	9	6	8200	5		48600	53400
31	6	SADLER 32	SLP	SA/RC	F/S	KL	IB	20D	VLVO	10	6	9500	5	6	59300	65100
34	9	SADLER 34	SLP	SA/RC	F/S	KL	IB	28D	VLVO	10	9	12800	5	8	81400	89500
38	9	SADLER 38	SLP	SA/RC	F/S	KL	IB	56D		12	6	16500	6	7	116500	128000
45		SADLER 45	SLP	SA/RC	F/S	KL	IB	80D	YAN	12	6		8		200500	220500
		1985 BOATS														
28	5	SADLER 29	SLP	SA/CR	FBG	KL	IB	D		9	6	8200	5		37800	42000
31	6	SADLER 32	SLP	SA/CR	FBG	KL	IB	D		10	6	9500	5	6	46700	51300
		1984 BOATS														
25	9	SADLER 26	SLP	SA/CR	FBG	KL	IB	D		9	5	4800	4	8	19200	21300
28	5	SADLER 29	SLP	SA/CR	FBG	KL	IB	D		9	6	8200	5		35600	39500
31	6	SADLER 32	SLP	SA/CR	FBG	KL	IB	D		10	6	9500	5	6	43400	48200

....For earlier years, see the BUC Used Boat Price Guide, Volume 3

RIVAL YACHTS INC

ANNAPOLIS MD 21403 COAST GUARD MFG ID- RYF See inside cover to adjust price for area

LOA FT	LOA IN	NAME AND/ OR MODEL	TOP/ RIG	BOAT TYPE	-HULL- MTL	-HULL- TP	ENGINE TP	ENGINE # HP	ENGINE MFG	BEAM FT	BEAM IN	WGT LBS	DRAFT FT	DRAFT IN	RETAIL LOW	RETAIL HIGH
		1986 BOATS														
34		RIVAL 34	SLP	SA/CR	FBG	KL	IB	D		9	8	10900	4	8	49900	54900
34		SEASTREAM 34	KTH	MS	FBG	KL	IB	D		11		16800	4	10	75300	82700
35	10	RIVAL 36	SLP	SA/CR	FBG	KL	IB	D		11		14250	6		65200	71700
41		RIVAL 41	SLP	SA/CR	FBG	KL	IB	D		12	3	22046	5	11	107000	117500
43	5	SEASTREAM 43	KTH	MS	FBG	KL	IB	D		14		31360	6		143500	157500
		1985 BOATS														
34		RIVAL 34	SLP	SA/CR	FBG	KL	IB	20D		9	8	10900	4	8	47200	51900
35	10	RIVAL 36D	SLP	SA/CR	FBG	KL	IB	20D	BUKH	11		14250	6		61300	67300
35	10	RIVAL 36D	CUT	SA/CR	FBG	KL	IB	20D	BUKH	11		14250	6		61300	67300
35	10	RIVAL 36S	SLP	SA/CR	FBG	KC	IB	20D	BUKH	11		13700	3	11	59200	65000
35	10	RIVAL 36S	CUT	SA/CR	FBG	KC	IB	20D	BUKH	11		13700	3	11	59100	65000
37	7	RIVAL 38	SLP	SA/CR	FBG	KL	IB	36D	BUKH	11	3	17196	5	4	74900	82300
37	7	RIVAL 38	CUT	SA/CR	FBG	KL	IB	36D	BUKH	11	3	17196	5	4	74900	82300
41		RIVAL 41	SLP	SA/CR	FBG	KL	IB	51D	PERK	12	3	22046	5	11	100000	110000
41		RIVAL 41	CUT	SA/CR	FBG	KL	IB	51D	PERK	12	3	22046	5	11	100000	110000
41		RIVAL 41	KTH	SA/CR	FBG	KL	IB	51D	PERK	12	3	22046	5	11	100000	110000

RIVERTON BOAT WORKS

RIVERTON NJ 08077 COAST GUARD MFG ID- LPP See inside cover to adjust price for area
FORMERLY LIPPINCOTT BOAT WORKS INC

LOA FT	LOA IN	NAME AND/ OR MODEL	TOP/ RIG	BOAT TYPE	-HULL- MTL	-HULL- TP	ENGINE TP	ENGINE # HP	ENGINE MFG	BEAM FT	BEAM IN	WGT LBS	DRAFT FT	DRAFT IN	RETAIL LOW	RETAIL HIGH
		1986 BOATS														
30	4	LIPPINCOTT 30	SLP	SA/CR	FBG	KL	IB	15D	YAN	10		8600	4	11	21000	23300
30	4	LIPPINCOTT 30 SHOAL	SLP	SA/CR	FBG	KL	IB	15D	YAN	10		8600	4	2	21000	23300
35	11	LIPPINCOTT 36	SLP	SA/CR	FBG	KL	IB	23D	YAN	11	1	12500	5		31700	35200

LOA FT IN	NAME AND/ OR MODEL		TOP/ RIG	BOAT TYPE	-HULL- MTL TP	TP #	ENGINE HP MFG	BEAM FT IN	WGT LBS	DRAFT FT IN	RETAIL LOW	RETAIL HIGH
				---- 1985 BOATS								
30 4	LIPPINCOTT 30		SLP	SA/CR	FBG KL	IB	15D YAN	10	8600	4 11	19600	21800
30 4	LIPPINCOTT 30	SHOAL	SLP	SA/CR	FBG KL	IB	15D YAN	10	8600	4 2	19600	21800
35 11	LIPPINCOTT 36		SLP	SA/CR	FBG KL	IB	23D YAN	11 1	12500	5	29600	32900
				---- 1984 BOATS								
30 4	LIPPINCOTT 30		SLP	SA/CR	FBG KL	IB	15D YAN	10	8600	4 11	18600	20600
30 4	LIPPINCOTT 30	SHOAL	SLP	SA/CR	FBG KL	IB	15D YAN	10	8600	4 2	18600	20600
35 11	LIPPINCOTT 36		SLP	SA/CR	FBG KL	IB	23D YAN	11 1	12500	5	27700	30800

....For earlier years, see the BUC Used Boat Price Guide, Volume 3

RIVIERA FIBER CORPORATION
RIVIERA BEACH FL 33404 COAST GUARD MFG ID- RVR See inside cover to adjust price for area
FORMERLY RIVIERA BOAT INC

For more recent years, see the BUC Used Boat Price Guide, Volume 1

LOA FT IN	NAME AND/ OR MODEL	TOP/ RIG	BOAT TYPE	-HULL- MTL TP	TP #	ENGINE HP MFG	BEAM FT IN	WGT LBS	DRAFT FT IN	RETAIL LOW	RETAIL HIGH
			---- 1996 BOATS								
18 2	CAPRICE 181	OP	FSH	TH	OB		7	1100		2450	2800
19 3	CAPRICE 20	OP	FSH	DV	OB		6 9	1550		3300	3800
			---- 1995 BOATS								
18 2	CAPRICE 181	OP	FSH	TH	OB		7	1100		3250	2700
19 3	CAPRICE 20	OP	FSH	DV	OB		6 9	1550		3150	3650
			---- 1993 BOATS								
19 3	CAPRICE 20	OP	FSH	FBG SV	OB		7 5	2150		3500	4100
			---- 1992 BOATS								
19 3	CAPRICE 20	OP	FSH	FBG SV	OB		7 5	2150		3350	3900
			---- 1991 BOATS								
19 3	CAPRICE 20	OP	FSH	FBG SV	OB		7 5	2150		3250	3800
			---- 1990 BOATS								
19 3	CAPRICE 20	OP	FSH	FBG SV	OB		7 5	2150		3150	3650
			---- 1989 BOATS								
19 3	CAPRICE 20	OP	FSH	FBG SV	OB		7 5	2150		3050	3550
			---- 1987 BOATS								
17 10	RIVIERA 18	ST	RNBT	FBG TR	OB		6 10	950	2 3	1500	1800

THE RIVIERA GROUP
COOMERA QLD AUSTRALIA 4209   See inside cover to adjust price for area
FORMERLY RIVIERA MARINE MFG PTY LTD

For more recent years, see the BUC Used Boat Price Guide, Volume 1

LOA FT IN	NAME AND/ OR MODEL	TOP/ RIG	BOAT TYPE	-HULL- MTL TP	TP #	ENGINE HP MFG	BEAM FT IN	WGT LBS	DRAFT FT IN	RETAIL LOW	RETAIL HIGH
			---- 1992 BOATS								
33	RIVIERA 3300	FB	SDN	FBG DS	IB	T210D CUM	12 6	17200	2 7	102000	112500

ROBALO BOATS LLC
DIV OF MARINE PRODUCTS CORP
NASHVILLE GA 31639   COAST GUARD MFG ID- FGBR See inside cover to adjust price for area
FORMERLY ROBALO MARINE

For more recent years, see the BUC Used Boat Price Guide, Volume 1

LOA FT IN	NAME AND/ OR MODEL		TOP/ RIG	BOAT TYPE	-HULL- MTL TP	TP #	ENGINE HP MFG	BEAM FT IN	WGT LBS	DRAFT FT IN	RETAIL LOW	RETAIL HIGH
				---- 1996 BOATS								
18 1	ROBALO 1820		OP	CTRCN	FBG SV	OB		8	2835	2 9	6500	7500
23 3	ROBALO 2140		OP	RNBT	FBG SV	OB		8 6	4260	2 10	11200	12700
23 6	ROBALO 2120		OP	CTRCN	FBG SV	OB		8	3540	2 10	11000	12500
23 2	ROBALO 2320		OP	CTRCN	FBG SV	OB		8	4313	2 10	14500	16500
26	ROBALO 2440		OP	RNBT	FBG SV	OB		8 6	5743	2 10	18200	20200
27 4	ROBALO 2520		OP	CTRCN	FBG SV	OB		8 6	5050	2 10	17400	19700
27 8	ROBALO 2660		OP	CUD	FBG DV	OB		8 6	5452	2 10	18600	20700
27 8	ROBALO 2660		OP	CUD	FBG DV	OB		8 6	5370	2 10	18500	20600
				---- 1995 BOATS								
18 1	ROBALO 1820		OP	CTRCN	FBG SV	OB		8	2790	2 10	6200	7100
21 4	ROBALO 2120		OP	CTRCN	FBG SV	OB		8	3540	2 10	10400	11900
23 2	ROBALO 2320		OP	CTRCN	FBG SV	OB		8	4313	2 10	13800	15700
23 3	ROBALO 2140		OP	RNBT	FBG SV	OB		8 6	4260	2 10	10700	12100
25 6	ROBALO 2520		OP	CTRCN	FBG SV	OB		8 6	5050	2 10	16500	18700
26	ROBALO 2660		OP	CUD	FBG DV	OB		8 6	5452	2 10	17300	19700
26	ROBALO 2660		OP	CUD	FBG DV	OB		8 6	5370	2 10	17300	19600
26 1	ROBALO 2440		OP	RNBT	FBG SV	OB		8 6	5395	2 11	16600	18900
				---- 1994 BOATS								
18	ROBALO 1820		OP	CTRCN	FBG SV	OB		8	2700	2 10	5850	6750
21 4	ROBALO 2120		OP	CTRCN	FBG SV	OB		8	3540	2 10	9950	11300
21 4	ROBALO 2160	CUDDY	OP	CUD	FBG SV	OB		8	3660	2 10	10100	11400
23 2	ROBALO 2320		OP	CTRCN	FBG SV	OB		8	4275	2 10	13200	15000
25 6	ROBALO 2520		OP	CTRCN	FBG SV	OB		8 6	5050	2 10	15800	17900
26	ROBALO 2660	CUDDY	OP	CUD	FBG DV	OB		8 6	5352	2 10	16500	18700
26	ROBALO 2660	CUDDY	OP	CUD	FBG DV	OB		8 6	5370	2 10	16500	18700
26 1	ROBALO 2440		OP	RNBT	FBG SV	OB		8 6	5125	2 11	16400	18600
				---- 1993 BOATS								
18	ROBALO 1820		OP	CTRCN	FBG SV	OB		8	2700	3 10	5600	6400
21 4	ROBALO 2120		OP	CTRCN	FBG SV	OB		8	3540	2 10	9550	10800
21 4	ROBALO 2160	CUDDY	OP	CUD	FBG SV	OB		8	3660	2 10	9650	10900
23 2	ROBALO 2320		OP	CTRCN	FBG SV	OB		8	4275	2 10	12600	14300
25 6	ROBALO 2520		OP	CTRCN	FBG SV	OB		8 6	5050	2 10	15100	17100
26	ROBALO 2660	CUDDY	OP	CUD	FBG DV	OB		8 6	5352	2 10	15800	17900
26	ROBALO 2660	CUDDY	OP	CUD	FBG DV	OB		8 6	5370	2 10	15800	17900
				---- 1992 BOATS								
18	ROBALO 1820		OP	CTRCN	FBG DV	OB		7	2715		5350	6150
21 4	ROBALO 2120		OP	CTRCN	FBG DV	OB		8	3540	2 10	9200	10500
21 4	ROBALO 2160	CUDDY	OP	CUD	FBG DV	OB		8	3660	2 10	9300	10600
23 2	ROBALO 2320		OP	CTRCN	FBG DV	OB		8	4275	2 10	12100	13800
25 6	ROBALO 2520		OP	CTRCN	FBG DV	OB		8 6	5050	2 10	14500	16500
26	ROBALO 2660	CUDDY	OP	CUD	FBG DV	OB		8 6	5370	2 10	15100	17200
				---- 1991 BOATS								
18	ROBALO R1800		OP	CTRCN	FBG SV	OB		7	2000		4600	5255
19 5	ROBALO R2020		OP	CTRCN	FBG SV	OB		8	2230		5150	5900
21 4	ROBALO R2120		OP	CTRCN	FBG DV	OB		8	2420		7250	8300
21 4	ROBALO R2160			CUD	FBG DV	OB		8	3070		8300	9550
23 2	ROBALO R2320		OP	CTRCN	FBG DV	OB		8	3100		9600	10900
25 6	ROBALO R2520		OP	CTRCN	FBG DV	OB		8 6	3350		11900	13500
26	ROBALO R2660			CUD	FBG DV	OB		8 6	4700		14100	16000
26	ROBALO R2680		OP	CTRCN	FBG DV	OB		8 6	4700		14100	16000
				---- 1990 BOATS								
18	R1800		OP	CTRCN	FBG SV	OB		7 9	2000	1 8	4400	5050
19 5	R2020		OP	CTRCN	FBG SV	OB		8	2230	2 1	4950	5650
21 4	R2120		OP	CTRCN	FBG DV	OB		8	2420	2 1	7000	8050
21 4	R2160		OP	CUD	FBG DV	OB		8	3070	2 1	8000	9200
21 4	R2165		OP	CUD	FBG DV	IO	180-205	8	4020		8450	9800
23 2	R2320		OP	CTRCN	FBG DV	OB		8	3100	2 1	9300	10600
25 6	R2520		OP	CTRCN	FBG DV	OB		8 6	3350	2 1	11500	13000
26	R2660			CUD	FBG DV	OB		8 6	4700	2 1	13600	15500
26	R2680		OP	CTRCN	FBG DV	OB		8 6	4700	2 1	13600	15500
				---- 1989 BOATS								
18	R1800		OP	CTRCN	FBG SV	OB		7 9	2000	1 8	4200	4900
19 5	R2020		OP	CTRCN	FBG SV	OB		8	2230	2 1	4750	5450
21 4	R2120		OP	CTRCN	FBG DV	OB		8	2420	2 1	6750	7800
21 4	R2160		OP	CUD	FBG DV	OB		8	3070	2 1	7750	8950
21 4	R2165		OP	CUD	FBG DV	IO	205-230	8	4020		8050	9350
23	R2365		ST	CUD	FBG DV	IO	230-270	8 6	4394		9700	11400
23	R2365		ST	CUD	FBG DV	IO	T130 MRCR	8 6	4394		10600	12000
23 2	R2320		OP	CTRCN	FBG DV	OB		8	3100	2 1	9050	10300
25	R2565		OP	CUD	FBG DV	IO	260-330	8 6	4774		11600	14200
25	R2565		OP	CUD	FBG DV	IO	T130-T175	8 6	4774		12200	14300
25 6	R2520		OP	CTRCN	FBG DV	OB		8 6	3350	2 1	11100	12600
26	R2660			CUD	FBG DV	OB		8 6	4700	2 1	11800	13500
26	R2680		OP	CTRCN	FBG DV	OB		8 6	4700	2 1	13200	15000
				---- 1988 BOATS								
18	R1800		OP	CTRCN	FBG SV	OB		7 9	2000	1 8	4050	4750
19 5	R2020		OP	CTRCN	FBG SV	OB		8	2230	2 1	4500	5300
21 4	R2120		OP	CTRCN	FBG DV	OB		8	2420	2 1	6550	7550
21 4	R2160		OP	CUD	FBG DV	OB		8	3070	2 1	7550	8650
21 4	R2165		OP	CUD	FBG DV	IO	200 MRCR	8	4020		7550	8650
23	R2365		ST	CUD	FBG DV	IO	230 MRCR	8 6	4394		9200	10400
23 2	R2320		OP	CTRCN	FBG DV	OB		8	3100	2 1	8700	10000
25	R2565		OP	CUD	FBG DV	IO	260 MRCR	8 6	4774		10900	12400
25 6	R2520		OP	CTRCN	FBG DV	OB		8 6	3350	2 1	10800	12300
26	R2660			CUD	FBG DV	OB		8 6	4700	2 1	12800	14500
26	R2680		OP	CTRCN	FBG DV	OB		8 6	4700	2 1	12800	14500
				---- 1987 BOATS								
18	R1800		OP	CTRCN	FBG SV	OB		7 9	1900		3850	4450
19 5	R2020		OP	CTRCN	FBG SV	OB		8	2230		4500	5150
21 4	R2120		OP	CTRCN	FBG DV	OB		8	2420		6400	7350
21 4	R2160		OP	CUD	FBG DV	OB		8	3070		7350	8450
21 4	R2165		SLP	CUD	FBG DV	IO	200-260	8	4020		7150	8250
23 2	R2320		OP	CTRCN	FBG DV	OB		8	3100		8450	9700
25 6	R2520		OP	CTRCN	FBG DV	OB		8	3350		10500	11900

LOA FT IN	NAME AND/ OR MODEL	TOP/ RIG	BOAT TYPE	-HULL- MTL TP	----ENGINE--- TP # HP MFG	BEAM FT IN	WGT LBS	DRAFT FT IN	RETAIL LOW	RETAIL HIGH
			1987 BOATS							
26	R2660	OP	CUD	FBG DV	OB	8 6	4700		12400	14100
26	R2680	OP	CTRCN	FBG DV	OB	8 6	4700		12400	14100
			1986 BOATS							
18	ROBALO 1800	OP	CTRCN	FBG DV	OB	7 9	1990		3850	4450
19 5	ROBALO 2020	OP	CTRCN	FBG DV	OB	8	2230		4350	5000
21 4	ROBALO 2120	OP	CTRCN	FBG DV	OB	8	2420		6200	7150
21 4	ROBALO 2160	OP	CUD	FBG DV	OB	8	3070		7150	8200
21 4	ROBALO 2160	OP	SF	FBG DV	OB	8	3070		7150	8200
21 4	ROBALO 2163	OP	CUD	FBG DS	SE 155 OMC	8	4020		7700	8850
21 4	ROBALO 2163	OP	CUD	FBG DV	SE 205 OMC	8	4020		7700	8850
21 4	ROBALO 2163	OP	CUD	FBG DV	SE T115 OMC	8	4040		7700	8900
21 4	ROBALO 2163	OP	SF	FBG DV	SE OMC	8	3520		**	**
21 4	ROBALO 2165	OP	CUD	FBG DV	IO 205 OMC	8	4020		6800	7800
21 4	ROBALO 2165	OP	SF	FBG DV	IO 205 OMC	8	4070		7800	9000
23 2	ROBALO 2320	OP	CTRCN	FBG DV	OB	8	3100		8200	9450
23 2	ROBALO 2323	OP	CTRCN	FBG DV	SE OMC	8	3700		**	**
25 6	ROBALO 2520	OP	CTRCN	FBG DV	OB	8	3350		10200	11600
25 6	ROBALO 2523	OP	CTRCN	FBG DV	SE 205 OMC	8	4050		11000	12500
25 6	ROBALO 2523	OP	CTRCN	FBG DV	SE T OMC	8	4550		**	**
25 6	ROBALO 2523	OP	CTRCN	FBG DV	SE T155-T205	8	4320		11300	13100
26	ROBALO 2660	OP	CUD	FBG DV	OB	8 6	4700		12100	13800
26	ROBALO 2660	OP	SF	FBG DV	OB	8 6	4700		12100	13800
26	ROBALO 2663	OP	CUD	FBG DS	SE T205 OMC	8	5600		12700	14400
26	ROBALO 2663	OP	CUD	FBG DV	SE T155 OMC	8	5600		12700	14400
26	ROBALO 2663	OP	SF	FBG DV	SE T OMC	8 6	5900		**	**
26	ROBALO 2680	OP	CTRCN	FBG DV	OB	8 6	4000		11600	13200
26	ROBALO 2683	OP	CTRCN	FBG DV	SE T OMC	8 6	5200		**	**
26	ROBALO 2683	OP	CTRCN	FBG DV	SE T115-T155	8 6	4000		11600	13200
			1985 BOATS							
18	ROBALO 1800	OP	CTRCN	FBG DV	OB	7 9	1990		3750	4350
18	ROBALO 1800SD	OP	CTRCN	FBG DV	OB 115 OMC	7 9	2440		4100	4750
19 5	ROBALO 2020	OP	CTRCN	FBG DV	OB	8	2230		4200	4900
21 4	ROBALO 2120	OP	CTRCN	FBG DV	OB	8	2420		6050	7000
21 4	ROBALO 2160	OP	CUD	FBG DV	OB	8	3070		6950	8000
21 4	ROBALO 2163	OP	CUD	FBG DS	SE 155 OMC	8	4020		7550	8650
21 4	ROBALO 2163	OP	CUD	FBG DV	SE 205 OMC	8	4020		7550	8650
21 4	ROBALO 2163	OP	CUD	FBG DV	SE T115 OMC	8	4040		7550	8650
21 4	ROBALO 2165	OP	CUD	FBG DV	IO 170-200	8	4020		6400	7450
23 2	ROBALO 2320	OP	CTRCN	FBG DV	OB	8	3100		8050	9250
25 6	ROBALO 2520	OP	CTRCN	FBG DV	OB	8	3350		9950	11300
25 6	ROBALO 2523	OP	CTRCN	FBG DV	SE 205 OMC	8	4050		10800	12200
25 6	ROBALO 2523	OP	CTRCN	FBG DV	SE T115-T155	8	4320		11000	12800
26	ROBALO 2660	OP	CUD	FBG DV	OB	8	4700		11800	13500
26	ROBALO 2663	OP	CUD	FBG DS	SE T205 OMC	8	5600		12400	14100
26	ROBALO 2663	OP	CUD	FBG DV	SE T155 OMC	8	5600		12400	14100
			1984 BOATS							
18 1	ROBALO 1820	OP	CTRCN	FBG DV	OB	7 3	2215		3850	4500
19 4	ROBALO 2020	OP	CTRCN	FBG DV	OB	8	2230		4100	4750
21 4	ROBALO 2120	OP	CTRCN	FBG DV	OB	8	2420		5950	6800
21 4	ROBALO 2160	OP	CUD	FBG DV	OB	8	3070		6800	7850
21 4	ROBALO 2163	OP	CUD	FBG DS	SE 155 OMC	8	4020		7350	8450
21 4	ROBALO 2163	OP	CUD	FBG DV	SE 205 OMC	8	4020		7350	8450
21 4	ROBALO 2165	OP	CUD	FBG DV	IO 170-200	8	4020		6200	7200
23 2	ROBALO 2320	OP	CTRCN	FBG DV	OB	8	3100		7850	9000
25 6	ROBALO 2520	OP	CTRCN	FBG DV	OB	8	3350		9750	11100
26	ROBALO 2660	OP	CUD	FBG DV	OB	8	4700		11600	13100
26	ROBALO 2660	OP	CUD	FBG DV	OB	8	4700		11600	13100
26	ROBALO 2663	OP	CUD	FBG DS	SE T205 OMC	8	5600		12100	13700
26	ROBALO 2663	OP	CUD	FBG DV	SE T155 OMC	8	5600		12100	13700
26 5	SPORTFISHERMAN	OP	SF	FBG DV	IB T225-T260	10 2	7780		13000	14700
26 5	SPORTFISHERMAN	OP	SF	FBG DV	IB	10 2	7780		19500	22000
26 5	SPORTFISHERMAN	OP	SF	FBG DV	IB T124D VLVO	10 2	7780		25600	28500

....For earlier years, see the BUC Used Boat Price Guide, Volume 3

ROBINHOOD MARINE CENTER
GEORGETOWN ME 04548   See inside cover to adjust price for area

For more recent years, see the BUC Used Boat Price Guide, Volume 1

LOA FT IN	NAME AND/ OR MODEL	TOP/ RIG	BOAT TYPE	-HULL- MTL TP	----ENGINE--- TP # HP MFG	BEAM FT IN	WGT LBS	DRAFT FT IN	RETAIL LOW	RETAIL HIGH
			1996 BOATS							
36 2	ROBINHOOD 36	CUT	SACAC	FBG KL	IB 38D YAN	10 8	16100	5	136000	149500

RODGERS YACHT & DESIGN
CLEARWATER FL 33520   COAST GUARD MFG ID- RYH See inside cover to adjust price for area

LOA FT IN	NAME AND/ OR MODEL	TOP/ RIG	BOAT TYPE	-HULL- MTL TP	----ENGINE--- TP # HP MFG	BEAM FT IN	WGT LBS	DRAFT FT IN	RETAIL LOW	RETAIL HIGH
			1984 BOATS							
24	RODGERS 24	SLP	SA/RC	FBG KC	IB	8	2200	1 4	3750	4350
26 6	RODGERS 26	SLP	SA/CR	FBG CB	IB 15D	9 7	5650		11400	13000
26 6	RODGERS 26	SLP	SA/RC	FBG KL	IB 15D	9 7	5650	4 9	11400	13000
26 6	RODGERS 26	SLP	SA/RC	FBG KL	IB 15D	9 7	5650		11400	13000
26 6	RODGERS 26	SLP	SA/RC	FBG KL	IB 15D YAN	9	5650	4 9	11400	13000
30	RODGERS 30 MORC	SLP	SA/CR	FBG KL	IB 15D YAN	11 2	8800	5 6	20600	22800
30	RODGERS 30 MORC	SLP	SA/RC	FBG KL	IB 15D YAN	11 2	8800	5 6	20500	22800
32 10	RODGERS 32 1/2	SLP	SA/RC	FBG KL	IB 15D YAN	11 2	8800		21700	24100
32 10	RODGERS 33	SLP	SA/RC	FBG KC	IB 15D YAN	11 2	7800	3 6	19800	22000
32 10	RODGERS 33	SLP	SA/RC	FBG KL	IB 15D YAN	11 2	8800	6	21600	24000

....For earlier years, see the BUC Used Boat Price Guide, Volume 3

ROGERS MARINE
ROCKLAND ME 04843   COAST GUARD MFG ID- ROG See inside cover to adjust price for area

LOA FT IN	NAME AND/ OR MODEL	TOP/ RIG	BOAT TYPE	-HULL- MTL TP	----ENGINE--- TP # HP MFG	BEAM FT IN	WGT LBS	DRAFT FT IN	RETAIL LOW	RETAIL HIGH
			1986 BOATS							
37	SCHEEL 36	CUT	SA/RC	WD KL	VD 21D UNIV	9 9	11400	4 8	94000	103500
			1985 BOATS							
37	SCHEEL 36	CUT	SA/RC	WD KL	VD 21D UNIV	9 9	11400	4 8	88200	97000
			1984 BOATS							
37	SCHEEL 36	CUT	SA/RC	WD KL	VD 21D UNIV	9 9	11400	4 8	83000	91200

ROSBOROUGH BOATS LTD
HALIFAX NS CANADA B3P 1B3   See inside cover to adjust price for area

LOA FT IN	NAME AND/ OR MODEL	TOP/ RIG	BOAT TYPE	-HULL- MTL TP	----ENGINE--- TP # HP MFG	BEAM FT IN	WGT LBS	DRAFT FT IN	RETAIL LOW	RETAIL HIGH
			1994 BOATS							
18 4	RF-18	CBNCR	FBG FL	OB		7 6	2500	10	7150	8200
22	RF-22	CBNCR	FBG DS	IO 150 VLVO	8	2500	1 6	13300	15200
24 10	RF-246	CBNCR	FBG DS	IO 150D VLVO	8 6	4000	2	30000	33300
28 4	RF-28	CBNCR	FBG DS	IB 200D VLVO	10 2	7000	3 2	63400	69700
32 6	GALAXSEA 32	CBNCR	FBG DS	IB 300D VLVO	11 2	11000	3 2	108500	119000
34 10	RF-35	CBNCR	FBG DS	IB 350D VLVO	13 2	15000	4 1	132000	145500
			1993 BOATS							
18 4	RF-18	CBNCR	FBG FL	OB			2500		6850	7850
22	RF-22	CBNCR	FBG DS	IO 150 VLVO	8	2500		12500	14200
24 10	RF-246	CBNCR	FBG DS	IO 150D VLVO	8 6	4000	2	28000	31200
28 4	RF-28	CBNCR	FBG DS	IB 200D VLVO	10 2	7000	2	60400	66400
32 6	GALAXSEA 32	CBNCR	FBG DS	IB 300D VLVO	11 2	11000	3 2	103000	113500
34 10	RF-35	CBNCR	FBG DS	IB 350D VLVO	13 2	15000	4 1	126000	138500
			1986 BOATS							
18 4	RF-18	HT	CUD	FBG SV	OB	7 5		7	5050	5800
18 4	RF-18	OP	UTL	FBG SV	OB	7 5		7	4600	5300
18 4	RF-18	OP	UTL	FBG SV	OB	7 5	1200	7	**	**
28 3	RF-28	OP	CR	FBG DS	IB 85D	9 8	6500		27400	30400
28 3	RF-28	OP	TRWL	FBG DS	IB D	9 8	6500		**	**
28 3	RF-28	HT	TRWL	FBG DS	IB D	9 8	6500	3 2	**	**
28 3	RF-28 BANKS-CRUISER	HT	TRWL	FBG DS	IB D	9 8	6500	3 2	**	**
28 3	RF-28 CRUISER	HT	TRWL	FBG DS	IB D	9 8	6500	3 2	**	**
28 3	RF-28 SEDAN	HT	TRWL	FBG DS	IB D	9 8	6500	3 2	**	**
30	R-30	KTH	SA/CR	WD KL	IB 13D WEST	8 10	9850	3 8	26500	29400
31 3	TERN	KTH	SA/CR	WD KL	IB 13D	9	13600	5	36800	40900
32	DESTINY	KTH	SA/CR	WD KL	IB 51D PERK	11	14000	4 5	37700	41900
34 4	PILGRIM	CUT	SA/CR	WD KL	IB 51D PERK	11	22000	5	56900	62600
37 8	JOLLY-ROGER	KTH	SA/CR	WD KL	IB 85D PERK	12	28000	5	69800	76700
39 7	NOMAD	KTH	SA/CR	WD KL	IB 85D PERK	12	36000	5	85200	93600
45 8	NOR'EASTER	KTH	SA/CR	WD KL	IB	12 9	36000	6 3	91400	100500
45 10	BUCCANEER	SCH	SA/CR	WD KL	IB 85D PERK	13	42000	5 11	98900	108500
45 10	DISTANT-STAR	SCH	SA/CR	WD KL	IB 85D PERK	13	46000	6	103500	113500
45 10	PRIVATEER	KTH	SA/CR	WD KL	IB 85D PERK	13	42000	5 11	99300	109000
45 10	SEA-SONG	SCH	SA/CR	WD KL	IB 85D PERK	13	42000	5 11	99700	109500
55	AQUARIUS	SQ	SA/CR	WD KL	IB 85D PERK	15	75000	6 3	170500	187500

LOA FT IN	NAME AND/ OR MODEL	TOP/ RIG	BOAT TYPE	HULL MTL	TP	ENGINE TP #	HP	MFG	BEAM FT IN	WGT LBS	DRAFT FT IN	RETAIL LOW	RETAIL HIGH
						----- 1986 BOATS -----							
56	LOYALIST	SQ	SA/CR	WD	KL	IB	85D	PERK	14 6	76000	6 6	176000	193000
64 6	VAGABOND	KTH	SA/CR	WD	KL	IB	85D	PERK	17	55T	7 2	316000	347500
79 6	VIKING	SQ	SA/CR	WD	KL	IB	85D	PERK	21 6	78T	9 9	**	**
						----- 1985 BOATS -----							
18 4	RF-18	HT	CUD	FBG	SV	OB			7 5	1200	7	4900	5650
18 4	RF-18	OP	UTL	FBG	SV	IO	100		7 5			4550	5250
18 4	RF-18	OP	UTL	FBG	SV	OB			7 5		7	4450	5150
18 4	RF-18	OP	UTL	FBG	SV	IB	100		7 5	1200		4800	5550
28 3	RF-28	OP	TRWL	FBG	DS	IB			9 8	6500	3 2	**	**
28 3	RF-28	HT	TRWL	FBG	DS	IB	85D	PERK	9 8	6500	3 2	22500	25000
28 3	RF-28 BANKS-CRUISER	HT	TRWL	FBG	DS	IB	85D	PERK	9 8	6500	3 2	38600	42900
28 3	RF-28 CRUISER	HT	TRWL	FBG	DS	IB	D		9 8	6500	3 2	**	**
28 3	RF-28 SEDAN	HT	TRWL	FBG	DS	IB	D		9 8	6500	3 2	**	**
30	R-30	KTH	SA/CR	WD	KL	IB	13D	WEST	8 10	9850	3 8	24900	27700
31 3	TERN	KTH	SA/CR	WD	KL	IB	D		9 8	13600	5	34600	38500
32	DESTINY	KTH	SA/CR	WD	KL	IB	51D	PERK	11	14000	4 5	35400	39400
34 4	PILGRIM	CUT	SA/CR	WD	KL	IB	51D	PERK	11	22000	5	53600	58900
34 10	ATLANTIC EXP RF-35	HT	CBNCR	F/S	DS	IB	130D	PERK	13 2		4	84400	92700
34 10	ATLANTIC TRWL RF-35	HT	CBNCR	F/S	DS	IB	130D	PERK	13 2		4	76800	84400
34 10	GURDYHOUSE RF-35	HT	SF	F/S	DS	IB	130D	PERK	13 2		4	71500	78600
37 8	JOLLY-ROGER	KTH	SA/CR	WD	KL	IB	85D	PERK	12	28000	5	65700	72200
39 7	NOMAD	KTH	SA/CR	WD	KL	IB	85D	PERK	12	36000	6 3	80100	88000
45 8	NOR'EASTER	KTH	SA/CR	WD	KL	IB			12 9	36000	6 3	86000	94500
45 10	BUCCANEER	SCH	SA/CR	WD	KL	IB	85D	PERK	13 3	42000	5 11	93400	102500
45 10	DISTANT-STAR	SCH	SA/CR	WD	KL	IB	85D	PERK	13 3	46000	5 11	97300	107000
45 10	PRIVATEER	KTH	SA/CR	WD	KL	IB	85D	PERK	13 3	42000	5 11	93400	102500
45 10	SEA-SONG	SCH	SA/CR	WD	KL	IB	85D	PERK	13 3	42000	5 11	93400	102500
55 6	AQUARIUS	SQ	SA/CR	WD	KL	IB	85D	PERK	15	75000	6 3	160000	176000
56	LOYALIST	SQ	SA/CR	WD	KL	IB	85D	PERK	14 6	76000	6 6	165000	181500
64 6	VAGABOND	KTH	SA/CR	WD	KL	IB	85D	PERK	17	55T	7 2	297500	327000
79 6	VIKING	SQ	SA/CR	WD	KL	IB	85D	PERK	21 6	78T	9 9	**	**
						----- 1984 BOATS -----							
18 4	RF-18	HT	CUD	FBG	SV	OB			7 5		7	4750	5450
18 4	RF-18	OP	UTL	FBG	SV	OB			7 5		7	4250	4950
28 3	RF-28	OP	TRWL	FBG	DS	IB			9 8	6500	3 2	**	**
28 3	RF-28	HT	TRWL	FBG	DS	IB			9 8	6500	3 2	**	**
28 3	RF-28 BANKS-CRUISER	HT	TRWL	FBG	DS	IB			9 8	6500	3 2	**	**
28 3	RF-28 CRUISER	HT	TRWL	FBG	DS	IB			9 8	6500	3 2	**	**
28 3	RF-28 SEDAN	HT	TRWL	FBG	DS	IB			9 8	6500	3 2	**	**
30	R-30	KTH	SA/CR	WD	KL	IB	12D	WEST	8 10	9850	3 8	23400	26000
31 3	TERN	KTH	SA/CR	WD	KL	IB	D		9 8	13600	5	32600	36200
32	DESTINY	KTH	SA/CR	WD	KL	IB	50D	PERK	11	14000	4 5	33300	37000
34 4	PILGRIM	CUT	SA/CR	WD	KL	IB	50D	PERK	11	22000	5	50400	55400
37 8	JOLLY-ROGER	KTH	SA/CR	WD	KL	IB	85D	PERK	12	28000	5	61800	67900
39 7	NOMAD	KTH	SA/CR	WD	KL	IB	85D	PERK	12	36000	6 3	75400	82800
45 8	NOR'EASTER	KTH	SA/CR	WD	KL	IB			12 9	36000	6 3	80800	88800
45 10	BUCCANEER	SCH	SA/CR	WD	KL	IB	85D	PERK	13 3	42000	5 11	87800	96500
45 10	DISTANT-STAR	SCH	SA/CR	WD	KL	IB	85D	PERK	13 3	46000	5 11	91500	100500
45 10	PRIVATEER	KTH	SA/CR	WD	KL	IB	85D	PERK	13 3	42000	5 11	87800	96500
45 10	SEA-SONG	SCH	SA/CR	WD	KL	IB	85D	PERK	13 3	42000	5 11	87800	96500
55 6	AQUARIUS	SQ	SA/CR	WD	KL	IB	85D	PERK	15	75000	6 3	150000	165000
56	LOYALIST	SQ	SA/CR	WD	KL	IB	85D	PERK	14 6	76000	6 6	154500	170000
64 6	VAGABOND	KTH	SA/CR	WD	KL	IB	85D	PERK	17	55T	7 2	280000	307500
79 6	VIKING	SQ	SA/CR	WD	KL	IB	85D	PERK	21 6	78T	9 9	**	**

....For earlier years, see the BUC Used Boat Price Guide, Volume 3

ROSS MARINE INC
OAK BLUFFS MA 02557-0776   See inside cover to adjust price for area

LOA FT IN	NAME AND/ OR MODEL	TOP/ RIG	BOAT TYPE	HULL MTL	TP	ENGINE TP #	HP	MFG	BEAM FT IN	WGT LBS	DRAFT FT IN	RETAIL LOW	RETAIL HIGH
						----- 1992 BOATS -----							
23	BLAZER 23	SLP	SA/RC	FBG	KL				7 11	2200	3 11	12200	13800
23	SONAR	SLP	SA/OD	FBG	KL				7 11	2100	3 11	11800	13400
						----- 1991 BOATS -----							
23	BLAZER 23	SLP	SA/RC	FBG	KL				7 11	2200	3 11	11400	13000
23	SONAR	SLP	SA/OD	FBG	KL				7 11	2100	3 11	11100	12600
						----- 1990 BOATS -----							
23	BLAZER 23	SLP	SA/RC	FBG	KL				7 11	2200	3 11	10700	12200
23	SONAR	SLP	SA/OD	FBG	KL				7 11	2100	3 11	10400	11900
						----- 1989 BOATS -----							
23	BLAZER 23	SLP	SA/RC	FBG	KL				7 11	2200	3 11	10100	11500
23	SONAR	SLP	SA/OD	FBG	KL				7 11	2100	3 11	9800	11100
						----- 1988 BOATS -----							
23	BLAZER 23	SLP	SA/RC	FBG	KL				7 11	2200	3 11	9500	10800
23	SONAR	SLP	SA/OD	FBG	KL				7 11	2100	3 11	9200	10500
						----- 1987 BOATS -----							
23	SONAR	SLP	SA/OD	FBG	KL	OB			7 10	2100	3 11	8600	9850
						----- 1986 BOATS -----							
23	KIRBY 23	SLP	SA/RC	FBG	KL				7 10	2400	3 11	8850	10000
23	SONAR	SLP	SA/OD	FBG	KL				7 10	2100	3 11	8050	9250
						----- 1985 BOATS -----							
23	KIRBY 23	SLP	SA/RC	FBG	KL				7 11	2400	3 11	8200	9400
23	SONAR	SLP	SA/OD	FBG	KL				7 11	2100	3 11	7550	8650
						----- 1984 BOATS -----							
23	SONAR	SLP	SA/OD	FBG	KL				7 10	2100	3 11	7100	8150

....For earlier years, see the BUC Used Boat Price Guide, Volume 3

ROSSITER YACHTS LTD
DORSET ENGLAND   COAST GUARD MFG ID- PUR See inside cover to adjust price for area
                        FORMERLY PURBROOK ROSSITER

LOA FT IN	NAME AND/ OR MODEL	TOP/ RIG	BOAT TYPE	HULL MTL	TP	ENGINE TP #	HP	MFG	BEAM FT IN	WGT LBS	DRAFT FT IN	RETAIL LOW	RETAIL HIGH
						----- 1993 BOATS -----							
32	CURLEW	SLP	SACAC	FBG	KC	IB	30D	LIST	10 4	16172	3 8	87300	95900
32	CURLEW	CUT	SACAC	FBG	KC	IB	30D	LIST	10 4	16172	3 8	87300	95900
						----- 1986 BOATS -----							
32	CURLEW	SLP	SA/CR	FBG	KC	IB	24D	BUKH	10 4	16240	3 8	57600	63300
						----- 1985 BOATS -----							
32	CURLEW	SLP	SA/CR	FBG	KC	IB	20D	BUKH	10 4	16240	3 8	54400	59700

....For earlier years, see the BUC Used Boat Price Guide, Volume 3

ROUGH WATER BOATS INC
MIAMI FL 33054   See inside cover to adjust price for area

LOA FT IN	NAME AND/ OR MODEL	TOP/ RIG	BOAT TYPE	HULL MTL	TP	ENGINE TP #	HP	MFG	BEAM FT IN	WGT LBS	DRAFT FT IN	RETAIL LOW	RETAIL HIGH
						----- 1989 BOATS -----							
17 6	180-EXP	OP	OPFSH	F/S	DV	OB			6 9	790	1 2	2850	3300
17 6	180-SP	OP	OPFSH	F/S	DV	OB			6 9	950	1 2	3350	3850

ROUGHNECK
DIV OF OMC ALUMINUM BOAT GROUP   See inside cover to adjust price for area
LEBANON MO 65536

For more recent years, see the BUC Used Boat Price Guide, Volume 1

LOA FT IN	NAME AND/ OR MODEL	TOP/ RIG	BOAT TYPE	HULL MTL	TP	ENGINE TP #	HP	MFG	BEAM FT IN	WGT LBS	DRAFT FT IN	RETAIL LOW	RETAIL HIGH
						----- 1996 BOATS -----							
16 11	PRO 1752VT	OP	JON	AL	SV	OB			6 2	370		1650	1950
17	BASS 170	OP	BASS	AL	SV	OB			6 1	735		3650	4250
17	HUSKY 1760MT	OP	JON	AL	SV	OB			6 11	460		2000	2400
17	TUNNEL JET 1768JC	OP	CTRCN	AL	SV	OB			6 10	880		4400	5100
17	TUNNEL JET 1768JW	OP	FSH	AL	SV	OB			6 10	980		4700	5400
19	HULK 1960MHT	OP	CTRCN	AL	SV	OB			6 11	610		3400	3950
19	HULK 1960MHTD	OP	CTRCN	AL	SV	OB			6 11	920		4850	5600
19	HUSKY 1960MT	OP	JON	AL	SV	OB			6 11	515		1850	2200
19	TUNNEL JET 1968JC	OP	CTRCN	AL	SV	OB			6 10	1025		5300	6100
						----- 1995 BOATS -----							
16 11	PRO 1752VT	OP	JON	AL	SV	OB			6 2	310		1300	1550
17	BASS 170	OP	BASS	AL	SV	OB			6 1	735		3450	4000
17	HUSKY 1760MT	OP	JON	AL	SV	OB			6 11	475		1950	2350
17	TUNNEL JET 1768JC	OP	CTRCN	AL	SV	OB			6 10	880		4150	4800
17	TUNNEL JET 1768JW	OP	FSH	AL	SV	OB			6 10	950		4450	5150
19	HULK 1960MHT	OP	CTRCN	AL	SV	OB			6 11	610		3200	3700
19	HUSKY 1960MT	OP	JON	AL	SV	OB			6 11	515		1800	2150
19	TUNNEL JET 1968JC	OP	CTRCN	AL	SV	OB			6 10	1025		5050	5800
						----- 1994 BOATS -----							
16 11	PRO 1752VT	OP	JON	AL	SV	OB			6 2	310		1250	1450
17	BASS 170	OP	BASS	AL	SV	OB			6 1	735		3350	3900
17	HUSKY 1760MT	OP	JON	AL	SV	OB			6 11	475		1850	2200
17	TUNNEL JET 1768JC	OP	CTRCN	AL	SV	OB			6 10	880		3950	4600
17	TUNNEL JET 1768JW	OP	FSH	AL	SV	OB			6 10	950		4200	4900
19	HULK 1960MHT	OP	CTRCN	AL	SV	OB			6 11	610		3050	3550

LOA FT IN	NAME AND/ OR MODEL	TOP/ RIG	BOAT TYPE	-HULL- MTL TP	----ENGINE--- TP # HP MFG	BEAM FT IN	WGT LBS	DRAFT FT IN	RETAIL LOW	RETAIL HIGH
					1994 BOATS					
19	HUSKY 1960MT	OP	JON	AL SV OB		6 11	515		1750	2050
19	TUNNEL JET 1968JC	OP	CTRCN	AL SV OB		6 10	1025		4800	5550
					1993 BOATS					
16 11	PRO 1752VT	OP	JON	AL SV OB			400		1500	1800
17	BASS 170	OP	BASS	AL SV OB		6 1	735		3200	3750
17	HUSKY 1760MT	OP	JON	AL SV OB		6 11	475		1800	2100
17	TUNNEL JET 1768JC	OP	CTRCN	AL SV OB		6 10	880		3750	4350
17	TUNNEL JET 1768JW	OP	FSH	AL SV OB		6 10	950		4000	4650
19	HULK 1960MHT	OP	CTRCN	AL SV OB		6 11	750		3500	4050
19	HUSKY 1960MT	OP	JON	AL SV OB		6 11	515		1650	1950
19	TUNNEL JET 1968JC	OP	CTRCN	AL SV OB		6 10	1025		4600	5300

ROUGHWATER BOATS
MARINE DEL REY CA 90292 COAST GUARD MFG ID- RWB See inside cover to adjust price for area
FORMERLY ROUGHWATER YACHTS INC

LOA FT IN	NAME AND/ OR MODEL	TOP/ RIG	BOAT TYPE	-HULL- MTL TP	----ENGINE--- TP # HP MFG	BEAM FT IN	WGT LBS	DRAFT FT IN	RETAIL LOW	RETAIL HIGH
					1986 BOATS					
37	ROUGHWATER 37	FB	CR	FBG DS	IB 260D GM	11 7	16400	4	62100	68300
37	ROUGHWATER 37	FB	CR	FBG DS	IB T220D GM	11 7	17900	4	70400	77300
41	ROUGHWATER 41	FB	DCMY	FBG DS	IB 260D GM	13	22000	4	82100	90300
42	ROUGHWATER 42	FB	DCMY	FBG DS	IB T220D GM	13 6	24500	3 6	95900	105500
					1985 BOATS					
32 1	ROUGHWATER 33	SLP	SA/CR	FBG KL	IB D	9	15000	4	31000	34500
37	ROUGHWATER 37	FB	CR	FBG DS	IB 215D	11 7	17000	4	60500	66400
37	ROUGHWATER 37	FB	EXP	FBG DS	IB T215D	11 7	19000	4	69800	76700
41	ROUGHWATER 41	FB	DCMY	FBG DS	IB 215D	13	21000	4	75200	82600
					1984 BOATS					
32 1	ROUGHWATER 33	SLP	SA/CR	FBG KL	IB D	9	15000	4	29200	32400
37	ROUGHWATER 37	FB	CR	FBG DS	IB 250D GM	11 7	16400	4	56900	62500
37	ROUGHWATER 37	FB	CR	FBG DS	IB T215D GM	11 7	17900	4	64400	70700
37	ROUGHWATER 37	HT	SDN	FBG DS	IB 250D GM	11 7	16400	4	57100	62700
41	ROUGHWATER 41	HT	DCMY	FBG DS	IB 250D GM	13	22000	4	75100	82500
41	ROUGHWATER 41	FB	DCMY	FBG DS	IB 250D GM	13	22000	4	75000	82400

....For earlier years, see the BUC Used Boat Price Guide, Volume 3

ROYCE YACHTS
ATLANTIC WEST SYSTEMS INC
LA CONNER WA 98257   COAST GUARD MFG ID- RXY   See inside cover to adjust price for area

LOA FT IN	NAME AND/ OR MODEL	TOP/ RIG	BOAT TYPE	-HULL- MTL TP	----ENGINE--- TP # HP MFG	BEAM FT IN	WGT LBS	DRAFT FT IN	RETAIL LOW	RETAIL HIGH
					1993 BOATS					
76 2	ROYCE 76	FB	MYFD	ARX SV	IB T12CD MTU	18 9	79000	3 11	**	**
					1986 BOATS					
61 9	ROYCE 60	FB	MY	F/S SV	IB T450D CUM	17 9	70000	5	311000	341500
					1985 BOATS					
61 9	ROYCE 60	FB	MY	F/S SV	IB T450D CUM	17 9	70000	6	297500	327000

DICK RUS YACHTIN BV
ENKHUIZEN HOLLAND   See inside cover to adjust price for area

LOA FT IN	NAME AND/ OR MODEL	TOP/ RIG	BOAT TYPE	-HULL- MTL TP	----ENGINE--- TP # HP MFG	BEAM FT IN	WGT LBS	DRAFT FT IN	RETAIL LOW	RETAIL HIGH
					1989 BOATS					
31 2	WINNER 9.50	SLP	SA/RC	FBG KL	IB 18D YAN	10 2	7700	5 7	44500	49400

RYBO RUNNER BOATS LLC
ROYAL PALM BEACH FL 334 COAST GUARD MFG ID- RBV See inside cover to adjust price for area
FORMERLY RYBOVICH BOAT WORKS INC

LOA FT IN	NAME AND/ OR MODEL	TOP/ RIG	BOAT TYPE	-HULL- MTL TP	----ENGINE--- TP # HP MFG	BEAM FT IN	WGT LBS	DRAFT FT IN	RETAIL LOW	RETAIL HIGH
					1995 BOATS					
39	FB DAY FISHERMAN	FB	SF	F/W SV	IB T375D CAT	13		3 10	600500	660000
44	EXPRESS	FB	EXP	F/W SV	IB T560D GM	15 1		3 9	519500	571000
45	FB SPORTFISH	FB	SF	F/W SV	IB T560D GM	15 5		4	715500	786500
48	FB SPORTFISH	FB	SF	F/W SV	IB T550D GM	15 2		4 4	774500	851500
54	FB SPORTFISH	FB	SF	F/W SV	IB T760D GM	16		4 4	973500	1.060M
58	FB SPORTFISH	FB	SF	F/W SV	IB T11CD GM	17 7		4 10	1.160M	1.260M
63	FB SPORTFISH	FB	SF	F/W SV	IB T11CD GM	17 9		5 2	1.345M	1.465M
72	ENCLOSED SPORTFISH	FB	SF	F/W SV	IB T14CD GM	20		4 9	**	**
72	FB SPORTFISH	FB	SF	F/W SV	IB T14CD GM	20			**	**
					1994 BOATS					
39	FB DAY FISHERMAN	FB	SF	F/W SV	IB T375D CAT	13		3 10	575000	632000
44	EXPRESS	FB	EXP	F/W SV	IB T560D GM	15 1		3 9	496000	545000
45	FB SPORTFISH	FB	SF	F/W SV	IB T560D GM	15 5		4	685500	753500
48	FB SPORTFISH	FB	SF	F/W SV	IB T550D GM	15 2		4 4	742000	815500
54	FB SPORTFISH	FB	SF	F/W SV	IB T760D GM	16		4 4	930500	1.010M
58	FB SPORTFISH	FB	SF	F/W SV	IB T11CD GM	17 7		4 10	1.115M	1.210M
63	FB SPORTFISH	FB	SF	F/W SV	IB T11CD GM	17 9		5 2	1.290M	1.400M
72	ENCLOSED SPORTFISH	FB	SF	F/W SV	IB T14CD GM	20		4 9	**	**
72	FB SPORTFISH	FB	SF	F/W SV	IB T14CD GM	20			**	**
					1993 BOATS					
39	FB DAY FISHERMAN	FB	SF	F/W SV	IB T375D CAT	13		3 10	547500	602000
44	EXPRESS	FB	EXP	F/W SV	IB T560D GM	15 1		3 9	472000	518500
45	FB SPORTFISH	FB	SF	F/W SV	IB T560D GM	15 5		4	653000	717500
48	FB SPORTFISH	FB	SF	F/W SV	IB T550D GM	15 2		4 4	707000	777000
54	FB SPORTFISH	FB	SF	F/W SV	IB T760D GM	16		4 4	878500	965000
58	FB SPORTFISH	FB	SF	F/W SV	IB T11CD GM	17 7		4 10	1.060M	1.155M
63	FB SPORTFISH	FB	SF	F/W SV	IB T11CD GM	17 9		5 2	1.230M	1.335M
70	ENCLOSED SPORTFISH	FB	SF	F/W SV	IB T14CD GM	19		5 6	1.835M	1.995M
					1992 BOATS					
39	FB DAY FISHERMAN	FB	SF	F/W SV	IB T375D CAT	13		3 10	522000	573500
39	RAISED BRIDGE	FB	SF	F/W SV	IB T375D CAT	13		3 10	418500	460000
44	RAISED BRIDGE	FB	SF	F/W SV	IB T560D GM	15 1		3 9	620000	681500
45	FB SPORTFISH	FB	SF	F/W SV	IB T560D GM	15 5		4	622500	684000
48	FB SPORTFISH	FB	SF	F/W SV	IB T550D GM	15 2		4 4	674000	740500
53	FB SPORTFISH	FB	SF	F/W SV	IB T760D GM	16		4 4	826000	908000
58	FB SPORT FISH	FB	SF	F/W SV	IB T11CD GM	17 7		4 10	1.010M	1.100M
63	ENCLOSED SPORTFISH	FB	SF	F/W SV	IB T11CD GM	17 9		5 2	1.170M	1.275M
70		FB	SF	F/W SV	IB T14CD GM	19		5 6	1.750M	1.905M
					1991 BOATS					
34	RAISED BRIDGE	FB	SF	F/W SV	IB T300D VLVO				198000	218000
39	FB DAY FISHERMAN	FB	SF	F/W SV	IB T400D GM				503000	552500
39	RAISED BRIDGE	FB	SF	F/W SV	IB T400D GM				385000	423000
44	RAISED BRIDGE	FB	SF	F/W SV	IB T485D GM	15 1		3 9	554500	609000
45	FB SPORTFISH	FB	SF	F/W SV	IB T485D GM				553500	608500
48	FB SPORTFISH	FB	SF	F/W SV	IB T550D GM	15 2		4 4	643000	706500
58	FB SPORT CRUISER	FB	SF	F/W SV	IB T750D GM	17 7		4 10	881500	969000
63	FB SPORT CRUISER	FB	SF	F/W SV	IB T900D GM				1.040M	1.130M
					1988 BOATS					
30	RYBO RUNNER	OP	CTRCN	FBG SV	IO 225 OMC	10 8	4500	3	49800	54800
30	RYBO RUNNER	OP	CTRCN	FBG SV	IB 250D GM	10 8	7000	3 6	79900	87800
30	RYBO RUNNER	OP	CTRCN	FBG SV	IB T450 CRUS	10 8	7000	3	88600	97400
30	RYBO RUNNER	OP	SPTCR	FBG SV	IB T450 CRUS	10 8	12000	3	111500	122500
					1987 BOATS					
30	RYBO RUNNER	OP	CTRCN	FBG SV	IB OB	10 8	4500	3	36000	39900
30	RYBO RUNNER	OP	CTRCN	FBG SV	IB 250D GM	10 8	7000	3 6	76600	84100
30	RYBO RUNNER	OP	CTRCN	FBG SV	IB T450 CRUS	10 8	7000	3	84500	92900
30	RYBO RUNNER	OP	SPTCR	FBG SV	IB T450 CRUS	10 8	12000	3	106000	116500
					1986 BOATS					
30	RYBO-RUNNER	OP	CTRCN	FBG SV	OB	10 8	6000		34900	38700
30	RYBO-RUNNER	OP	CTRCN	FBG SV	IB 215D GM	10 8	7000	3 5	70800	77800
30	RYBO-RUNNER	OP	CTRCN	FBG SV	IB 205 OMC	10 8	6500		34900	38700
30	RYBO-RUNNER	OP	CTRCN	FBG SV	IB 270 CRUS	10 8	7000		70400	77400
30	RYBO-RUNNER	MT	CTRCN	FBG SV	IB 220D GM	10 8	7000	3 5	71200	78200
30	RYBO-RUNNER	MT	CTRCN	FBG SV	IB 205 OMC	10 8	6500		34900	38700
30	RYBO-RUNNER	MT	CTRCN	FBG SV	IB T270 CRUS	10 8	7000		70400	77400
30	RYBO-RUNNER WLKCBN	OP	CUD	FBG SV	OB	10 8	7000		35200	39100
30	RYBO-RUNNER WLKCBN	OP	CUD	FBG SV	IB T205 OMC	10 8	7500	3	35200	39100
30	RYBO-RUNNER WLKCBN	OP	CUD	FBG SV	IB 270 CRUS	10 8	6500		68200	75000
30	RYBO-RUNNER WLKCBN	OP	CUD	FBG SV	IB T220D GM	10 8	8000	3 5	87400	96000
30	RYBO-RUNNER WLKCBN	MT	CUD	FBG SV	OB	10 8	7000		35300	39200
30	RYBO-RUNNER WLKCBN	MT	CUD	FBG SE	205 OMC	10 8	6500		35300	39200
30	RYBO-RUNNER WLKCBN	MT	CUD	FBG SV	270 CRUS	10 8	6500		60500	66400
30	RYBO-RUNNER WLKCBN	MT	CUD	FBG SV	IB 220D GM	10 8	8000	3 5	72800	79900
					1985 BOATS					
30	RYBO-RUNNER	OP	CTRCN	FBG SV	IB 215D OMC	10 8	6500	3 5	65200	71600
30	RYBO-RUNNER	OP	CTRCN	FBG SV	IB T270 CRUS	10 8	6500		33900	37600
30	RYBO-RUNNER	OP	CTRCN	FBG SV	IB T270 CRUS	10 8	6500		66400	73000
30	RYBO-RUNNER	TT	CTRCN	FBG SV	IB 215D GM	10 8	6500	3 5	65200	71700
30	RYBO-RUNNER	TT	CTRCN	FBG SV	IB T205 OMC	10 8	6500		34000	37900
30	RYBO-RUNNER	TT	CTRCN	FBG SV	IB T270 CRUS	10 8	6500		66400	73000
					1984 BOATS					
30	RYBO-RUNNER	OP	CTRCN	FBG SV	IB OB	10 8	6500		33000	36600
30	RYBO-RUNNER	OP	CTRCN	FBG SV	IB 215D GM	10 8	6500	3 5	62600	68800
30	RYBO-RUNNER	OP	CTRCN	FBG SV	IB T205 OMC	10 8	6500		33000	36600
30	RYBO-RUNNER	OP	CTRCN	FBG SV	IB T270 CRUS	10 8	6500		63500	69700

LOA FT IN	NAME AND/ OR MODEL	TOP/ RIG	BOAT TYPE	-HULL- MTL TP TP	----ENGINE--- # HP MFG	BEAM FT IN	WGT LBS	DRAFT FT IN	RETAIL LOW	RETAIL HIGH
					----1984 BOATS					
30	RYBO-RUNNER	HT	CTRCN FBG	SV IB	215D GM	10 8	6500	3 5	62600	68800
30	RYBO-RUNNER	HT	CTRCN FBG	SV SE	T205 OMC	10 8	6500	3	33000	36700
30	RYBO-RUNNER	HT	CTRCN FBG	SV IB	T270 CRUS	10 8	6500	3	63500	69700
30	RYBO-RUNNER	TT	CTRCN FBG	SV IB	215D GM	10 8	6500	3 5	62600	68800
30	RYBO-RUNNER	TT	CTRCN FBG	SV SE	T205 OMC	10 8	6500	3	33000	36700
30	RYBO-RUNNER	TT	CTRCN FBG	SV IB	T270 CRUS	10 8	6500	3	63500	69700

....For earlier years, see the BUC Used Boat Price Guide, Volume 3

RYBOVICH
WEST PALM BEACH FL 33407   See inside cover to adjust price for area

For more recent years, see the BUC Used Boat Price Guide, Volume 1

LOA FT IN	NAME AND/ OR MODEL	TOP/ RIG	BOAT TYPE	-HULL- MTL TP TP	----ENGINE--- # HP MFG	BEAM FT IN	WGT LBS	DRAFT FT IN	RETAIL LOW	RETAIL HIGH
					----1996 BOATS					
72	ENCLOSED PILOTHOUSE	F+T	SF	WCM IB	T14CD DD	20		4 10	**	**
					----1995 BOATS					
45	OPEN FISHERMAN	TT	SF	F/W SV IB	T D				**	**
					----1994 BOATS					
55	SPORTFISH	H+T	SDNSF WCM	SV IB	T D				**	**
					----1993 BOATS					
45	OPEN FISHERMAN	TT	SF	F/W SV IB	T D				**	**
					----1992 BOATS					
39		TT	EXPSF WCM	SV IB	T D				**	**
54	SPORTFISH	H+T	SDNSF WCM	SV IB	T760D DD	16		4 4	620500	682000
					----1991 BOATS					
44	OPEN FISHERMAN	TT	SF	F/W SV IB	T550D GM	15 1		3 9	412000	453000
58		TT	SF	WCM IB	T10CD GM	17 7		4 10	711500	782000
					----1990 BOATS					
44	EXPRESS SPORTFISH	H+T	EXPSF WCM	SV IB	T550D GM	15			416500	457500
					----1989 BOATS					
44	EXPRESS	TT	EXPSF FBG	SV IB	T485D GM	15		4	382500	420500
48	CONVERTIBLE	TT	SDNSF WCM	SV IB	T735D DD	15 2		4	487000	535000
					----1986 BOATS					
60	SPORTFISHERMAN	F+T		FBG DV IB	T11CD DD	17 6		5 6	643000	706500

....For earlier years, see the BUC Used Boat Price Guide, Volume 3

C E RYDER CORP
BRISTOL RI 02809   COAST GUARD MFG ID- CER See inside cover to adjust price for area

LOA FT IN	NAME AND/ OR MODEL	TOP/ RIG	BOAT TYPE	-HULL- MTL TP TP	----ENGINE--- # HP MFG	BEAM FT IN	WGT LBS	DRAFT FT IN	RETAIL LOW	RETAIL HIGH
					----1986 BOATS					
22 6	SEA-SPRITE 23	SLP	SAIL FBG	KL OB	7	3350	3	8150	9350
23 11	QUICKSTEP	SLP	SAIL FBG	KL OB	7 11	4000	3 4	10300	11700
27 11	SEA-SPRITE 27	SLP	SA/CR FBG	KL IB	7 10	7600	4 8	25200	28000
30 1	BLACK-WATCH 30	OP	SF	FBG SV IB	T245-T325	10 11	8900		48700	56600
30 1	BLACK-WATCH 30	OP	SF	FBG SV IB	IBT205D-T211D	10 11	8900		63500	70300
30 1	BLACK-WATCH 30	TT	SF	FBG SV IB	T245-T325	10 11	8900		48700	56600
30 1	BLACK-WATCH 30	TT	SF	FBG SV IB	IBT205D-T211D	10 11	8900		63500	70300
30 2	SEA-SPRITE 30	SLP	SA/CR FBG	KL IB	D	9 6	10000	4 9	34400	38300
30 5	SOUTHERN-CROSS 28	CUT	SA/CR FBG	KL IB	D	8 6	8500	4 8	29200	32400
33 10	SEA-SPRITE 34	SLP	SA/CR FBG	KL IB	D	10 3	12800	5	44000	48900
34 6	SOUTHERN-CROSS 31	CUT	SA/CR FBG	KL IB	D	9 6	13600	4 7	47400	52100
35	SPRINGER 35	SLP	SA/CR FBG	KL IB	34D YAN	11	13000	4 9	45900	50400
35 3	SOUTHERN-CROSS 35	CUT	SA/CR FBG	KL IB	D	11 5 14461		4 11	55500	61000
41	SOUTHERN-CROSS 39	CUT	SA/CR FBG	KL IB	D	12 1 21000		4	82400	90600
					----1985 BOATS					
22 6	SEA-SPRITE 23	SLP	SAIL FBG	KL OB	7	3350	3	7650	8800
22 6	SEA-SPRITE 23	SLP	SAIL FBG	KL OB	8D YAN	7	3350	3	9100	10300
23 11	QUICKSTEP	SLP	SAIL FBG	KL IB	7 11	4000	3 5	9700	11000
27 11	SEA SPRITE PRELUDE	SLP	SAIL FBG	KL IB	10 NANN	8 10	7600	4 3	23300	25800
27 11	SEA-SPRITE 28	SLP	SAIL FBG	KL IB	11D UNIV	8 10	7600	4 8	23600	26200
30 2	SEA-SPRITE 30	SLP	SA/CR FBG	KL IB	16D UNIV	9 6	10000	4 9	32400	36000
30 5	SOUTHERN-CROSS 28	CUT	SAIL FBG	KL VD	11D UNIV	8 6	8500	4 8	27400	30500
33 11	SEA-SPRITE 34	SLP	SAIL FBG	KL IB	24D UNIV	10 3	12800	5	41400	46000
34 6	SOUTHERN-CROSS 31	CUT	SA/CR FBG	KL IB	21D UNIV	9 6	13600	4 7	44100	49000
35 3	SOUTHERN-CROSS 35	CUT	SAIL FBG	KL IB	24D UNIV	11 5 14461		4 11	52100	57300
41	SOUTHERN-CROSS 39	CUT	SA/CR FBG	KL VD	32D UNIV	12 1 21000		4	77200	84800
					----1984 BOATS					
22 6	SEA-SPRITE 23	SLP	SAIL FBG	KL OB	7	3350	3	7200	8300
22 6	SEA-SPRITE 23	SLP	SAIL FBG	KL OB	8D YAN	7	3350	3	8450	9750
23	SONAR	SLP	SAIL FBG	KL OB	7 10	2100	3 11	5350	6150
23 11	QUICKSTEP	SLP	SAIL FBG	KL IB	7 11	4000	3 5	9150	10400
27 11	SEA-SPRITE 28	SLP	SAIL FBG	KL IB	11D UNIV	8 10	7600	4 3	22300	24700
30 2	SEA-SPRITE 30	SLP	SA/CR FBG	KL IB	16D UNIV	9 6	10000	4 9	30400	33800
30 5	SOUTHERN-CROSS 28	CUT	SA/CR FBG	KL VD	11D UNIV	8 6	8500	4 8	25800	28700
33 11	SEA-SPRITE 34	SLP	SAIL FBG	KL IB	24D UNIV	10 3	12800	5	39300	43800
34 6	SOUTHERN-CROSS 31	CUT	SA/CR FBG	KL IB	21D UNIV	9 6	13600	4 7	41500	46100
35 3	SOUTHERN-CROSS 35	CUT	SAIL FBG	KL IB	24D UNIV	11 5 14461		4 11	49000	53900
41	SOUTHERN-CROSS 39	CUT	SA/CR FBG	KL VD	50D PERK	12 1 21000		5 4	72500	79600

....For earlier years, see the BUC Used Boat Price Guide, Volume 3

S & S

LOA FT IN	NAME AND/ OR MODEL	TOP/ RIG	BOAT TYPE	-HULL- MTL TP TP	----ENGINE--- # HP MFG	BEAM FT IN	WGT LBS	DRAFT FT IN	RETAIL LOW	RETAIL HIGH
See inside cover to adjust price for area

					----1984 BOATS					
30	VELOCITY SPTCR	ST	OFF	F/S DV IO	330	8	6800	1 7	19100	21200
39	VELOCITY SPTCR	ST	OFF	F/S DV IO	T330	8 2	8200	2	47300	52000

SABER MARINE SALES
CROMSTOCK PD MI 49321   See inside cover to adjust price for area

LOA FT IN	NAME AND/ OR MODEL	TOP/ RIG	BOAT TYPE	-HULL- MTL TP TP	----ENGINE--- # HP MFG	BEAM FT IN	WGT LBS	DRAFT FT IN	RETAIL LOW	RETAIL HIGH
					----1994 BOATS					
24	SABER 24	OP	OFF	F/S DV OB		7 9	2300		12600	14300
24	SABER 24	OP	OFF	F/S DV IO	250-300	7 9	3500		10000	12000
	IO 350 MRCR 11600		13200, IO 385-415		12800	15700, IO 425	MRCR	14200	16100
	IO 470-490 16400		19600						
28	SABER 28 CYCLONE	OP	OFF	F/S DV IO	T425-T490	7 10	6210		29800	36900
28	SABER 28 OFFSHORE	OP	OFF	F/S DV IO	425-490	7 10	6000		23300	27800
28	SABER 28 OFFSHORE	OP	OFF	F/S DV IO	T385-T415	7 10	6000		27500	32300
28 1	SABER 28 OFFSHORE	OP	OFF	F/S DV OB		7 10	3900		26000	28900
28 1	SABER 28 OFFSHORE	OP	OFF	F/S DV IO	300-350	7 10	4900		19200	22400
	IO 385-415 22800		25300, IO T250-T300		23100	27400, IO T350-T415		26400	32700
					----1993 BOATS					
24	SABER 24	OP	OFF	F/S DV OB		7 9	2300		12100	13700
24	SABER 24	OP	OFF	F/S DV IO	250-300	7 9	3500		9350	11200
24	SABER 24	OP	OFF	F/S DV IO	350 MRCR	7 9	3500		10800	12300
24	SABER 24	OP	OFF	F/S DV IO	390 MRCR	7 9	3500		12000	13600
28 1	SABER 28 OFFSHORE	OP	OFF	F/S DV OB		7 10	3900		25000	27700
28 1	SABER 28 OFFSHORE	OP	OFF	F/S DV IO	300-390	7 10	4900		17500	21900
	IO T220D MRCR 17200		19600, IO T250-T300		21400	25400, IO T350-T390		24600	29100
	IO T220D MRCR 27000		30000						
					----1992 BOATS					
24	SABER 24	OP	OFF	F/S DV OB		7 9	2300		11600	13200
24	SABER 24	OP	OFF	F/S DV IO	250-300	7 9	3500		8650	10500
24	SABER 24	OP	OFF	F/S DV IO	350 MRCR	7 9	3500		10100	11500
24	SABER 24	OP	OFF	F/S DV IO	390 MRCR	7 9	3500		11200	12700
28 1	SABER 28 OFFSHORE	OP	OFF	F/S DV OB		7 10	3900		24000	26600
28 1	SABER 28 OFFSHORE	OP	OFF	F/S DV IO	300-390	7 10	4900		16300	20400
	IO T220D MRCR 16100		18300, IO T250-T300		20000	23700, IO T350-T390		23000	27200
	IO T220D MRCR 25200		28000						
					----1991 BOATS					
24	SABER 24	OP	OFF	F/S DV OB		7 9	2300		11200	12700
24	SABER 24	OP	OFF	F/S DV IO	260 MRCR	7 9	3500		8150	9400
24	SABER 24	OP	OFF	F/S DV IO	330-365	7 9	3500		9150	11200
24	SABER 24	OP	OFF	F/S DV IO	410 MRCR	7 9	3500		11100	12600
28 1	SABER 28 OFFSHORE	OP	OFF	F/S DV OB		7 10	3900		23100	25700
28 1	SABER 28 OFFSHORE	OP	OFF	F/S DV IO	260-410	7 10	6000		15800	19600
	IO T410-T420 17400		19800, IO		T220D MRCR 14900	16900, IO T330-T365		20700	24400
	IO T410-T420 23700		26800, IO		T220D MRCR 23600	26200			
					----1990 BOATS					
28 1	SABER 28 OFFSHORE	OP	OFF	F/S DV OB		7 10	3900		22300	24800
28 1	SABER 28 OFFSHORE	OP	OFF	F/S DV IO	330-365	7 10	4900		14600	17200
	IO 420 MRCR 16300		18600, IO T260		OMC 17300	19700, IO T330-T365		19600	22900
	IO T420 MRCR 21300		25100						
					----1989 BOATS					
28 1	SABER 28 OFFSHORE	OP	OFF	F/S DV IO	330-365	7 10	4900		13500	15900
	IO 420 MRCR 15100		17200, IO T260-T320		16200	19800, IO T330-T365		18400	21600
	IO T420 MRCR 21300		23700						

LOA FT	IN	NAME AND/ OR MODEL	TOP/ RIG	BOAT TYPE	-HULL- MTL	TP	TP	----ENGINE--- # HP	MFG	BEAM FT	IN	WGT LBS	DRAFT FT	IN	RETAIL LOW	RETAIL HIGH
		1989 BOATS														
28	1	SABRE 28 OFFSHORE	OP	OFF	F/S	DV	OB			7	10	3500			21500	23900

SABRE CORPORATION

SOUTH CASCO ME 04077 COAST GUARD MFG ID- HWS See inside cover to adjust price for area
FORMERLY SABRE YACHTS

For more recent years, see the BUC Used Boat Price Guide, Volume 1

LOA FT	IN	NAME AND/ OR MODEL	TOP/ RIG	BOAT TYPE	-HULL- MTL	TP	TP	----ENGINE--- # HP	MFG	BEAM FT	IN	WGT LBS	DRAFT FT	IN	RETAIL LOW	RETAIL HIGH
		1996 BOATS														
36		SABRELINE 36	FB	TRWL	FBG	DS	IB	T255D	CAT	12	6	20000	3	4	155000	170500
36		SABRELINE 36 EXP	ST	EXP	FBG	DV	IB	T300D	CAT	12	6	18000	3	4	143500	157500
36	2	SABRE 362	SLP	SARAC	FBG	CB	IB	35D	WEST	12		15000	4	2	126000	138500
36	2	SABRE 362	SLP	SARAC	FBG	KL	IB	35D	WEST	12		13800	6	6	117000	128500
37	6	SABRELINE 34	FB	TRWL	FBG	DS	IB	T210D	CUM	12	6	17800	3	3	146500	161500
38	8	SABRE 38	SLP	SARAC	FBG	CB	IB	38D	WEST	12	4	17400	4	3	155500	171000
38	8	SABRE 38	SLP	SARAC	FBG	KL	IB	38D	WEST	12	4	16800	6	6	151500	166500
38	8	SABRE 38	SLP	SARAC	FBG	WK	IB	38D	WEST	12	4	16800	4	11	151500	166500
40	2	SABRE 402 FIN	SLP	SARAC	FBG	KL	IB	50D	WEST	13	4	18800	6	3	178000	196000
40	2	SABRE 402 WING	SLP	SARAC	FBG	WK	IB	50D	WEST	13	4	19000	4	11	179500	197000
42	5	SABRE 425	SLP	SARAC	FBG	CB	IB	46D	WEST	12	10	19200	5		205500	226000
42	5	SABRE 425 FIN	SLP	SARAC	FBG	KL	IB	46D	WEST	12	10	18800	6	10	202000	222000
42	5	SABRE 425 WING	SLP	SARAC	FBG	WK	IB	46D	WEST	12	10	19200	5		203000	223000
43	6	SABRELINE 43	FB	TRWL	FBG	DS	IB	T350D	CAT	15		38500	4		303500	333500
47	6	SABRELINE 47	FB	TRWL	FBG	DS	IB	T350D	CAT	15		40000	4		299000	328500
		1995 BOATS														
36	2	SABRE 362	SLP	SARAC	FBG	CB	IB	35D	WEST	12		15000	4	2	117500	129500
36	2	SABRE 362	SLP	SARAC	FBG	KL	IB	35D	WEST	12		13800	6	6	109500	120000
36	2	SABRE 362	SLP	SARAC	FBG	WK	IB	35D	WEST	12		14000	4	8	111000	121500
37	6	SABRELINE 34	FB	TRWL	FBG	DS	IB	T210D	CUM	12	6	17800	3	3	148000	162500
38	8	SABRE 38	SLP	SARAC	FBG	CB	IB	38D	WEST	12	4	17400	4	3	145000	159500
38	8	SABRE 38	SLP	SARAC	FBG	KL	IB	38D	WEST	12	4	16800	6	6	141500	155500
38	8	SABRE 38	SLP	SARAC	FBG	WK	IB	38D	WEST	12	4	16800	4	11	141500	155500
38	8	SABRE 38 II	SLP	SARAC	FBG	WK	IB	37D	WEST	12	4	16900	6	6	142000	156000
40	1	SABRELINE 36	FB	TRWL	FBG	DS	IB	T255D	CAT	12	6	20000	3	4	148500	163500
42	5	SABRE 425	SLP	SARAC	FBG	WK	IB	46D	WEST	12	10	19200	5		190500	209500
42	5	SABRE 425	SLP	SARAC	FBG	WK	IB	46D	WEST	12	10	18800	6	10	188500	207000
43		SABRELINE 43	FB	TRWL	FBG	DS	IB	T350D	CAT	15		32500	4		258000	283500
		1994 BOATS														
34		SABRELINE 34	FB	CR	FBG	SV	IB	T210D	CUM	12	6	17800	3	3	125500	137500
36		SABRELINE 36	FB	CR	FBG	SV	IB	T255D	CAT	12	6	20000	3	4	136500	150000
36	2	SABRE 362	SLP	SARAC	FBG	CB	IB	35D	WEST	12		14980	4	2	110000	120500
36	2	SABRE 362	SLP	SARAC	FBG	KL	IB	35D	WEST	12		13800	6	6	102000	112000
36	2	SABRE 362	SLP	SARAC	FBG	WK	IB	35D	WEST	12		14060	4	8	104000	114000
38	8	SABRE 38	SLP	SARAC	FBG	CB	IB	38D	WEST	12	4	17300	4	3	135000	148500
38	8	SABRE 38	SLP	SARAC	FBG	KL	IB	38D	WEST	12	4	16900	6	6	132500	146000
38	8	SABRE 38	SLP	SARAC	FBG	WK	IB	38D	WEST	12	4	17300	4	11	135000	148500
42	5	SABRE 425	SLP	SARAC	FBG	CB	IB	46D	WEST	12	10	19200	4	9	178000	195500
42	5	SABRE 425	SLP	SARAC	FBG	KL	IB	46D	WEST	12	10	18800	6	10	176000	193500
42	5	SABRE 425	SLP	SARAC	FBG	WK	IB	46D	WEST	12	10	19200	5		178000	195500
		1993 BOATS														
34		SABRELINE 34	FB	CR	FBG	SV	IB	T210D	CUM	12	6	17800	3	3	119500	131000
34	2	SABRE 34 CLASSIC	SLP	SARAC	FBG	CB	IB	27D	WEST	11	2	11800	4		79300	87100
34	2	SABRE 34 CLASSIC	SLP	SARAC	FBG	KL	IB	27D	WEST	11	2	11500	6		76700	84200
34	2	SABRE 34 CLASSIC	SLP	SARAC	FBG	WK	IB	27D	WEST	11	2	11700	4	6	78000	85700
36		SABRELINE 36	FB	CR	FBG	SV	IB	T250D	DD	12	6	20000	3	4	128500	141500
38	8	SABRE 38	SLP	SARAC	FBG	CB	IB	33D	WEST	12	4	17300	4	3	126000	138500
38	8	SABRE 38	SLP	SARAC	FBG	KL	IB	33D	WEST	12	4	16900	6	6	123500	136000
38	8	SABRE 38	SLP	SARAC	FBG	WK	IB	33D	WEST	12	4	17300	4	11	126000	138500
42	5	SABRE 425	SLP	SARAC	FBG	CB	IB	46D	WEST	12	10	19200	4	9	166500	183000
42	5	SABRE 425	SLP	SARAC	FBG	KL	IB	46D	WEST	12	10	18800	6	10	164500	180500
42	5	SABRE 425	SLP	SARAC	FBG	WK	IB	46D	WEST	12	10	19200	5		166500	183000
		1992 BOATS														
34		SABRELINE 34	FB	CR	FBG	SV	IB	T210D	CUM	12	6	17800	3	3	114000	125000
34	2	SABRE 34 AFT-CABIN	SLP	SA/RC	FBG	KL	IB	27D	WEST	11	2	11500	6		72900	80100
34	2	SABRE 34 AFT-CABIN	SLP	SA/RC	FBG	WK	IB	27D	WEST	11	2	11700	4	6	74100	81400
34	2	SABRE 34 CLASSIC	SLP	SA/RC	FBG	CB	IB	27D	WEST	11	2	11800	4		74000	81300
34	2	SABRE 34 CLASSIC	SLP	SA/RC	FBG	KL	IB	27D	WEST	11	2	11500	6		71600	78600
34	2	SABRE 34 CLASSIC	SLP	SA/RC	FBG	WK	IB	27D	WEST	11	2	11700	4	6	72800	80000
36		SABRELINE 36	FB	CR	FBG	SV	IB	T250D	DD	12	6	20000	3	4	122500	134500
38	8	SABRE 38	SLP	SA/RC	FBG	CB	IB	33D	WEST	12	4	17300	4	3	117500	129000
38	8	SABRE 38	SLP	SA/RC	FBG	KL	IB	33D	WEST	12	4	16900	6	6	115500	127000
38	8	SABRE 38	SLP	SA/RC	FBG	WK	IB	33D	WEST	12	4	17300	4	11	117500	129000
39	7	SABRE 40 RS	SLP	SA/RC	FBG	CB	IB	50D	YAN	12	6	17600	4	11	125500	138000
39	7	SABRE 40 RS	SLP	SA/RC	FBG	KL	IB	50D	YAN	12	6	17200	6	6	123500	135500
39	7	SABRE 40 RS	SLP	SA/RC	FBG	WK	IB	50D	YAN	12	6	17600	4	11	125500	138000
42		SABRELINE 42	FB	TRWL	FBG	DS	IB	T375D	CAT	14	2	26000	3	9	193000	212000
42	5	SABRE 425	SLP	SA/RC	FBG	CB	IB	46D	WEST	12	10	19200	4	9	155500	170500
42	5	SABRE 425	SLP	SA/RC	FBG	KL	IB	46D	WEST	12	10	18800	6	10	153500	168500
42	5	SABRE 425	SLP	SA/RC	FBG	WK	IB	46D	WEST	12	10	19200	5		155500	170500
		1991 BOATS														
30	7	SABRE 30	SLP	SA/RC	FBG	KL	IB	18D	WEST	10	6	9400	5	3	54200	59500
34		SABRE 34 CLASSIC	SLP	SA/RC	FBG	CB	IB	27D	WEST	11	2	11800	4		69000	75900
34		SABRE 34 CLASSIC	SLP	SA/RC	FBG	KL	IB	27D	WEST	11	2	11500	4	6	67300	74000
34		SABRE 34 CLASSIC	SLP	SA/RC	FBG	WK	IB	27D	WEST	11	2	11700	6		68500	75300
34		SABRELINE 34	FB	CR	FBG	SV	IB	T210D	CUM	12	6	17800	3	3	108500	119500
34	2	SABRE 34 AFT-CABIN	SLP	SA/RC	FBG	KL	IB	27D	WEST	11	2	11500	6		67500	74100
36		SABRE 36	SLP	SA/RC	FBG	KL	IB	27D	WEST	11	3	13200	6	4	79400	87300
36		SABRELINE 36	FB	CR	FBG	SV	IB	T250D	GM	12	6	20000	3	4	115500	127000
38	8	SABRE 38	SLP	SA/RC	FBG	CB	IB	33D	WEST	12	4	17300	4	3	110000	120500
38	8	SABRE 38	SLP	SA/RC	FBG	KL	IB	33D	WEST	12	4	16900	6	6	108000	118500
38	8	SABRE 38	SLP	SA/RC	FBG	WK	IB	33D	WEST	12	4	17300	4	11	110000	120500
42	5	SABRE 425	SLP	SA/RC	FBG	CB	IB	46D	WEST	12	10	19200	4	9	145000	159500
42	5	SABRE 425	SLP	SA/RC	FBG	KL	IB	46D	WEST	12	10	18800	6	10	143500	157500
42	5	SABRE 425	SLP	SA/RC	FBG	WK	IB	46D	WEST	12	10	19200	5		145000	159500
		1990 BOATS														
30	7	SABRE 30 TARGA	SLP	SA/RC	FBG	KL	IB	18D	WEST	10	6	9400	5	3	50600	55600
34	2	SABRE 34 AFT-CABIN	SLP	SA/RC	FBG	KL	IB	27D	WEST	11	2	11500	6		63000	69300
34	2	SABRE 34 AFT-CABIN	SLP	SA/RC	FBG	WK	IB	27D	WEST	11	2	11700	4	6	64100	70500
34	2	SABRE 34 CLASSIC	SLP	SA/RC	FBG	KC	IB	27D	WEST	11	2	11800	4		64700	71100
34	2	SABRE 34 CLASSIC	SLP	SA/RC	FBG	KL	IB	27D	WEST	11	2	11500	6		63000	69300
34	2	SABRE 34 CLASSIC	SLP	SA/RC	FBG	WK	IB	27D	WEST	11	2	11700	4	6	64100	70500
36		SABRE 36	SLP	SA/RC	FBG	KC	IB	27D	WEST	11	3	13500	4	2	75700	83200
36		SABRE 36	SLP	SA/RC	FBG	KL	IB	27D	WEST	11	3	13200	6	4	74200	81500
36		SABRE 36	SLP	SA/RC	FBG	WK	IB	27D	WEST	11	3	13500	4	9	75700	83200
36		SABRELINE 36	FB	CR	FBG	DV	IB	T250D	GM	12	6	20000	3	4	110000	121000
36		SABRELINE 36	FB	CR	FBG	SV	IB	T250D	GM	12	6	20000	3	4	110000	121000
38	8	SABRE 38	SLP	SA/RC	FBG	KC	IB	33D	WEST	12	4	17300	4	3	102500	113000
38	8	SABRE 38	SLP	SA/RC	FBG	KL	IB	33D	WEST	12	4	16900	6	6	101000	111000
38	8	SABRE 38	SLP	SA/RC	FBG	WK	IB	33D	WEST	12	4	17300	7	11	102500	113000
41	9	SABRE 42	SLP	SA/RC	FBG	KC	IB	46D	WEST	12	8	19200	4	9	130000	143000
41	9	SABRE 42	SLP	SA/RC	FBG	WK	IB	46D	WEST	12	8	19200	5		130000	143000
42	5	SABRE 42	SLP	SA/RC	FBG	KL	IB	46D	WEST	12	8	18800	6	10	134000	147000
		1989 BOATS														
30	7	SABRE 30 TARGA	SLP	SA/RC	FBG	KL	IB	18D	WEST	10	6	9400	5	3	47500	52200
30	7	SABRE 30 TARGA SHOAL	SLP	SA/RC	FBG	KL	IB	18D	WEST	10	6	9600	4		48300	53100
34	2	SABRE 34 CLASSIC	SLP	SA/RC	FBG	KC	IB	27D	WEST	11	2	11800	4		60400	66400
34	2	SABRE 34 CLASSIC	SLP	SA/RC	FBG	KL	IB	27D	WEST	11	2	11500	6		58200	64000
34	2	SABRE 34 CLASSIC	SLP	SA/RC	FBG	WK	IB	27D	WEST	11	2	11700	4	6	59200	65100
34	2	SABRE 34 TARGA A-C	SLP	SA/RC	FBG	KL	IB	27D	WEST	11	2	11500	6		59600	65500
34	2	SABRE 34 TARGA A-C	SLP	SA/RC	FBG	WK	IB	27D	WEST	11	2	11700	4	6	60600	66600
36		SABRE 36	SLP	SA/RC	FBG	KL	IB	27D	WEST	11	3	13200	6	4	69300	76200
36		SABRE 36	SLP	SA/RC	FBG	WK	IB	27D	WEST	11	3	13500	4	2	70800	77800
36		SABRE 36 SHOAL	SLP	SA/RC	FBG	KC	IB	27D	WEST	11	3	13500	4	2	70800	77800
36		SABRELINE 36	FB	CR	FBG	SV	IB	T250D	DD	12	6	20000	3	4	106000	116500
38	8	SABRE 38	SLP	SA/RC	FBG	KC	IB	33D	WEST	12	4	17300	4	3	95900	105500
38	8	SABRE 38	SLP	SA/RC	FBG	KL	IB	33D	WEST	12	4	16900	6	6	94200	103500
38	8	SABRE 38	SLP	SA/RC	FBG	WK	IB	33D	WEST	12	4	17300	6	6	95900	105500
41	9	SABRE 42	SLP	SA/RC	FBG	KC	IB	46D	WEST	12	8	19200	4	9	121500	133500
41	9	SABRE 42	SLP	SA/RC	FBG	KL	IB	46D	WEST	12	8	18800	6	10	120000	132000
41	9	SABRE 42	SLP	SA/RC	FBG	WK	IB	46D	WEST	12	8	19200	6	10	121500	133500
		1988 BOATS														
30	7	SABRE 30 III	SLP	SA/RC	FBG	KL	IB	18D	WEST	10	6	9400	5	3	44000	48800
30	7	SABRE 30 SHOAL III	SLP	SA/RC	FBG	KL	IB	18D	WEST	10	6	9600	4		44900	49900
34	2	SABRE 34 II	SLP	SA/RC	FBG	KL	IB	27D	WEST	11	2	11500	6		55100	60500
34	2	SABRE 34 SHOAL II	SLP	SA/RC	FBG	KC	IB	27D	WEST	11	2	11900	4		56900	62600
36		SABRE 36 I	SLP	SA/RC	FBG	KL	IB	27D	WEST	11	3	13200	6	4	64800	71200
36		SABRE 36 SHOAL I	SLP	SA/RC	FBG	KC	IB	27D	WEST	11	3	13500	4	2	66200	72700
38	8	SABRE 38 AFT CABIN	SLP	SA/RC	FBG	KC	IB	33D	WEST	12	4	17300	4	3	89600	98500
38	8	SABRE 38 AFT CABIN	SLP	SA/RC	FBG	KL	IB	33D	WEST	12	4	16900	6	6	88100	96800
41	9	SABRE 42 AFT CABIN I	SLP	SA/RC	FBG	KC	IB	46D	WEST	12	8	19200	4	9	113500	125000
41	9	SABRE 42 AFT CABIN I	SLP	SA/RC	FBG	KL	IB	46D	WEST	12	8	18800	6	10	112500	123500
		1987 BOATS														
30	7	SABRE 30	SLP	SA/RC	FBG	KL	IB	18D	WEST	10	6	9400	5	3	41100	45700
30	7	SABRE 30 SHOAL	SLP	SA/RC	FBG	KL	IB	18D	WEST	10	6	9600	4		42000	46600
32	2	SABRE 32	SLP	SA/RC	FBG	KL	IB	21D	WEST	10	6	10500	5	7	45900	50400
32	2	SABRE 32 AFT-CABIN	SLP	SA/RC	FBG	KC	IB	21D	WEST	10	6	10800	3	8	48800	53600
32	2	SABRE 32 AFT-CABIN	SLP	SA/RC	FBG	KL	IB	21D	WEST	10	6	10500	5	7	47700	52400
32	2	SABRE 32 SHOAL	SLP	SA/RC	FBG	KC	IB	21D	WEST	10	6	10800	3	8	47200	51900

 CONTINUED ON NEXT PAGE

LOA FT IN	NAME AND/ OR MODEL	TOP/ RIG	BOAT TYPE	-HULL- MTL TP TP	----ENGINE--- # HP MFG	BEAM FT IN	WGT LBS	DRAFT FT IN	RETAIL LOW	RETAIL HIGH

----------- 1987 BOATS -----------

LOA FT IN	NAME AND/ OR MODEL	TOP/ RIG	BOAT TYPE	-HULL- MTL TP TP	----ENGINE--- # HP MFG	BEAM FT IN	WGT LBS	DRAFT FT IN	RETAIL LOW	RETAIL HIGH
34 2	SABRE 34	SLP	SA/RC	FBG KL IB	27D WEST	11 2	11500	6	51500	56600
34 2	SABRE 34 SHOAL	SLP	SA/RC	FBG KL IB	27D WEST	11 2	11900	4 3	53200	58500
36	SABRE 36	SLP	SA/RC	FBG KL IB	27D WEST	11 3	13200	6 4	60600	66600
36	SABRE 36 SHOAL	SLP	SA/RC	FBG KC IB	27D WEST	11 3	13500	4 2	61900	68000
37 10	SABRE 38	SLP	SA/RC	FBG KL IB	33D WEST	11 6	15200	4 3	73200	80400
37 10	SABRE 38	SLP	SA/RC	FBG KC IB	33D WEST	11 6	15200	6 5	71600	78700
37 10	SABRE 38 AFT-CABIN	SLP	SA/RC	FBG KL IB	33D WEST	11 6	15600	4 3	75900	83400
37 10	SABRE 38 AFT-CABIN	SLP	SA/RC	FBG KL IB	33D WEST	11 6	15200	6 5	74400	81700
41 9	SABRE 42 AFT-CABIN	SLP	SA/RC	FBG KL IB	46D WEST	12 8	19200	4 9	106500	117000
41 9	SABRE 42 AFT-CABIN	SLP	SA/RC	FBG KL IB	46D WEST	12 8	18800	6 10	105000	115500

----------- 1986 BOATS -----------

LOA FT IN	NAME AND/ OR MODEL	TOP/ RIG	BOAT TYPE	-HULL- MTL TP TP	----ENGINE--- # HP MFG	BEAM FT IN	WGT LBS	DRAFT FT IN	RETAIL LOW	RETAIL HIGH
28 5	SABRE 28	SLP	SA/RC	FBG KL IB	13D WEST	9 2	7800	4	30700	34100
28 5	SABRE 28 SHOAL	SLP	SA/RC	FBG KL IB	13D WEST	9 2	8000	3 10	31500	35000
30 7	SABRE 30	SLP	SA/RC	FBG KL IB	18D WEST	10	9400	5 3	38400	42700
30 7	SABRE 30 SHOAL	SLP	SA/RC	FBG KL IB	18D WEST	10	9600	4	39300	43600
32 2	SABRE 32	SLP	SA/RC	FBG KL IB	21D WEST	10	10500	5 7	44200	47100
32 2	SABRE 32	SLP	SA/RC	FBG KC IB	21D WEST	10	10500	3 8	45900	50400
32 2	SABRE 32 AFT-CABIN	SLP	SA/RC	FBG KL IB	21D WEST	10	10800	5 7	44200	49100
32 2	SABRE 32 SHOAL	SLP	SA/RC	FBG KC IB	21D WEST	10	10800	3 8	44800	48500
34 2	SABRE 34	SLP	SA/RC	FBG KL IB	27D WEST	11 2	11500	6	48100	52900
34 2	SABRE 34 SHOAL	SLP	SA/RC	FBG KL IB	27D WEST	11 2	11900	4 3	49800	54700
36	SABRE 36	SLP	SA/RC	FBG KL IB	27D WEST	11 3	13200	6 4	56700	62300
36	SABRE 36 SHOAL	SLP	SA/RC	FBG KC IB	27D WEST	11 3	13500	4 2	58100	63600

37 10	SABRE 38	SLP	SA/RC	FBG KL IB	33D WEST	11 6	15600	4 3	68400	75100
37 10	SABRE 38	SLP	SA/RC	FBG KC IB	33D WEST	11 6	15200	6 6	67000	73600
37 10	SABRE 38 AFT-CABIN	SLP	SA/RC	FBG KC IB	33D WEST	11 6	15600	4 3	71000	78100
37 10	SABRE 38 AFT-CABIN	SLP	SA/RC	FBG KL IB	33D WEST	11 6	15200	6 6	69500	76400

----------- 1985 BOATS -----------

LOA FT IN	NAME AND/ OR MODEL	TOP/ RIG	BOAT TYPE	-HULL- MTL TP TP	----ENGINE--- # HP MFG	BEAM FT IN	WGT LBS	DRAFT FT IN	RETAIL LOW	RETAIL HIGH
28 5	SABRE 28	SLP	SA/RC	FBG KL IB	13D WEST	9 2	7800	4	28700	31900
28 5	SABRE 28 SHOAL	SLP	SA/RC	FBG KL IB	13D WEST	9 2	8000	3 10	29500	32800
29 11	SABRE 30	SLP	SA/RC	FBG KL IB	13D WEST	10	8600	5 2	32600	36200
29 11	SABRE 30 SHOAL	SLP	SA/RC	FBG KL IB	13D WEST	10	8800	4	33300	37000
32 2	SABRE 32	SLP	SA/RC	FBG KC IB	22D WEST	10 4	10800	3 8	40700	45300
32 2	SABRE 32	SLP	SA/RC	FBG KL IB	22D WEST	10 4	10500	5 7	39600	44000
32 2	SABRE 32 AFT-CABIN	SLP	SA/RC	FBG KC IB	22D WEST	10 4	10800	3 8	41200	45700
32 2	SABRE 32 AFT-CABIN	SLP	SA/RC	FBG KL IB	22D WEST	10 4	10500	5 7	41400	46000
33 8	SABRE 34	SLP	SA/RC	FBG KC IB	30D WEST	10	11700	3 11	45800	50400
33 8	SABRE 34	SLP	SA/RC	FBG KL IB	30D WEST	10	11300	5 10	43800	48700
36	SABRE 36	SLP	SA/RC	FBG KL IB	30D WEST	11	13500	4 2	54100	59500
36	SABRE 36	SLP	SA/RC	FBG KC IB	30D WEST	11	13200	6 4	55300	58300

37 10	SABRE 38	SLP	SA/RC	FBG KC IB	33D WEST	11 6	15600	4 3	63800	70100
37 10	SABRE 38	SLP	SA/RC	FBG KL IB	33D WEST	11 6	15200	6 6	62400	68600
37 10	SABRE 38 AFT-CABIN	SLP	SA/RC	FBG KC IB	33D WEST	11 6	15600	4 3	66600	73200
37 10	SABRE 38 AFT-CABIN	SLP	SA/RC	FBG KL IB	33D WEST	11 6	15200	6 6	65200	71700

----------- 1984 BOATS -----------

LOA FT IN	NAME AND/ OR MODEL	TOP/ RIG	BOAT TYPE	-HULL- MTL TP TP	----ENGINE--- # HP MFG	BEAM FT IN	WGT LBS	DRAFT FT IN	RETAIL LOW	RETAIL HIGH
28 5	SABRE 28	SLP	SA/RC	FBG KL IB	13D WEST	9 2	7800	4	26900	29900
28 5	SABRE 28 SHOAL	SLP	SA/RC	FBG KL IB	13D WEST	9 2	8000	3 10	27600	30600
29 11	SABRE 30	SLP	SA/RC	FBG KL IB	13D WEST	10	8600	5 2	30500	33800
29 11	SABRE 30 SHOAL	SLP	SA/RC	FBG KL IB	13D WEST	10	8800	4	31200	34600
32 2	SABRE 32	SLP	SA/RC	FBG KC IB	21D WEST	10 4	10800	3 8	38900	43300
32 2	SABRE 32	SLP	SA/RC	FBG KL IB	21D WEST	10 4	10500	5 7	37900	42100
33 8	SABRE 34	SLP	SA/RC	FBG KC IB	27D WEST	10 4	11700	3 11	42400	47100
33 8	SABRE 34	SLP	SA/RC	FBG KL IB	27D WEST	10	11300	6	41000	45500
36	SABRE 36	SLP	SA/RC	FBG KL IB	27D WEST	11 3	13200	6 4	49600	54500
36	SABRE 36	SLP	SA/RC	FBG KC IB	27D WEST	11	13200	4	50700	53300
37 10	SABRE 38	SLP	SA/RC	FBG KC IB	33D WEST	11 6	15600	4 3	59600	65500
37 10	SABRE 38	SLP	SA/RC	FBG KL IB	33D WEST	11 6	15200	6 6	58300	64000
37 10	SABRE 38 AFT-CABIN	SLP	SA/RC	FBG KC IB	33D WEST	11 6	15600	4 3	62400	68600

| 37 10 | SABRE 38 AFT-CABIN | SLP | SA/RC | FBG KL IB | 33D WEST | 11 6 | 15200 | 6 6 | 61200 | 67200 |

....For earlier years, see the BUC Used Boat Price Guide, Volume 3

SAGA YACHT
FULLERTON CA 92831

FORMERLY SAGA MARINE   See inside cover to adjust price for area

For more recent years, see the BUC Used Boat Price Guide, Volume 1

LOA FT IN	NAME AND/ OR MODEL	TOP/ RIG	BOAT TYPE	-HULL- MTL TP TP	----ENGINE--- # HP MFG	BEAM FT IN	WGT LBS	DRAFT FT IN	RETAIL LOW	RETAIL HIGH

----------- 1996 BOATS -----------

| 43 | SAGA 43 | SLP | SACAC | FBG KL IB | 50D YAN | 12 | 18000 | 5 | 158500 | 174500 |

SAIL CRAFT OF CANADA
KIRKLAND QUE CANADA

See inside cover to adjust price for area

LOA FT IN	NAME AND/ OR MODEL	TOP/ RIG	BOAT TYPE	-HULL- MTL TP TP	----ENGINE--- # HP MFG	BEAM FT IN	WGT LBS	DRAFT FT IN	RETAIL LOW	RETAIL HIGH

----------- 1986 BOATS -----------

| 20 | TORNADO OLYMPIC | SLP | SA/OD | F/S CT | | 10 | 350 | 6 | 6100 | 7050 |

----------- 1985 BOATS -----------

| 20 | TORNADO OLYMPIC | SLP | SA/OD | F/S CT | | 10 | 350 | 6 | 5750 | 6600 |

----------- 1984 BOATS -----------

| 20 | TORNADO OLYMPIC | SLP | SA/OD | F/S CT | | 10 | 350 | 6 | 5400 | 6200 |

....For earlier years, see the BUC Used Boat Price Guide, Volume 3

SAIL SPORTS LTD
VERNON ROCKVILLE CT 06066-3729

See inside cover to adjust price for area

LOA FT IN	NAME AND/ OR MODEL	TOP/ RIG	BOAT TYPE	-HULL- MTL TP TP	----ENGINE--- # HP MFG	BEAM FT IN	WGT LBS	DRAFT FT IN	RETAIL LOW	RETAIL HIGH

----------- 1990 BOATS -----------

18	DART 18		SAIL	FBG CT		7 6	285		4650	5350
20	DART 20		SAIL	FBG CT		8	350		5400	6200
20	DART 20 TSX		SAIL	FBG CT		8	375		5650	6500

SAIL/POWER YACHTS LTD
SOLOMON IS MD 20688   COAST GUARD MFG ID- TVZ   See inside cover to adjust price for area

LOA FT IN	NAME AND/ OR MODEL	TOP/ RIG	BOAT TYPE	-HULL- MTL TP TP	----ENGINE--- # HP MFG	BEAM FT IN	WGT LBS	DRAFT FT IN	RETAIL LOW	RETAIL HIGH

----------- 1986 BOATS -----------

38	OCEAN 38 DC		TRWL	FBG DS IB	135D PERK	12 10	22000	3 6	87600	96200
39	OCEAN SUN DECK		TRWL	FBG DS IB	135D PERK	12 10	22000	3 6	91100	100000
39	OCEAN SUN DECK		TRWL	FBG DS IB	T135D PERK	12 10	22000	3 6	97300	107000
42	NOVA 42 OCEAN		MY	FBG DS IB	T200D PERK	14	26000	3 8	113000	124000

----------- 1985 BOATS -----------

38	OCEAN 38 DC		TRWL	FBG DS IB	135D PERK	12 10	22000	3 6	83800	92100
39	OCEAN SUN DECK		TRWL	FBG DS IB	135D PERK	12 10	22000	3 6	87200	95800
39	OCEAN SUN DECK		TRWL	FBG DS IB	T135D PERK	12 10	22000	3 6	93200	102500
42	NOVA 42 OCEAN		MY	FBG DS IB	T200D PERK	14	26000	3 8	108000	119000

----------- 1984 BOATS -----------

| 38 4 | OCEAN-NOVA DC | | TRWL | FBG DS IB | 135D PERK | 12 10 | 22000 | 3 6 | 81100 | 89100 |
| 42 | OCEAN-NOVA SUNDECK | | TRWL | FBG DS IB | T165D PERK | 13 8 | 26000 | 3 8 | 104000 | 114500 |

....For earlier years, see the BUC Used Boat Price Guide, Volume 3

SAN AUGUSTINE FBG PROD
RAY-CRAFT
SAN AUGUSTINE TX 75972   COAST GUARD MFG ID- SAG   See inside cover to adjust price for area

LOA FT IN	NAME AND/ OR MODEL	TOP/ RIG	BOAT TYPE	-HULL- MTL TP TP	----ENGINE--- # HP MFG	BEAM FT IN	WGT LBS	DRAFT FT IN	RETAIL LOW	RETAIL HIGH

----------- 1986 BOATS -----------

| 17 4 | V-174 B/S | OP | BASS | FBG TR OB | | 6 | 1000 | | 2000 | 2350 |
| 17 7 | V-177 PRO | OP | BASS | FBG DV OB | | 6 9 | 900 | | 1850 | 2150 |

----------- 1985 BOATS -----------

| 17 4 | V-174 B/S | OP | BASS | FBG TR OB | | 6 | 1000 | | 1950 | 2300 |
| 17 7 | V-177 PRO | OP | BASS | FBG DV OB | | 6 9 | 900 | | 1800 | 2100 |

----------- 1984 BOATS -----------

| 17 4 | V-174 B/S | OP | BASS | FBG TR OB | | 6 | 1000 | | 1900 | 2250 |
| 17 7 | V-177 PRO | OP | BASS | FBG DV OB | | 6 9 | 900 | | 1750 | 2100 |

....For earlier years, see the BUC Used Boat Price Guide, Volume 3

SAN JUAN MANUFACTURING
AUBURN WA 98001   COAST GUARD MFG ID- CLK   See inside cover to adjust price for area

LOA FT IN	NAME AND/ OR MODEL	TOP/ RIG	BOAT TYPE	-HULL- MTL TP TP	----ENGINE--- # HP MFG	BEAM FT IN	WGT LBS	DRAFT FT IN	RETAIL LOW	RETAIL HIGH

----------- 1986 BOATS -----------

20 6	SAN-JUAN 21	SLP	SA/RC	FBG KC OB		7	1250		3150	3650
20 6	SAN-JUAN 21	SLP	SA/RC	FBG KL OB		7	1250		3150	3650
23	SAN-JUAN 23	SLP	SA/RC	FBG KC OB		8	2700		5900	6750
23	SAN-JUAN 23	SLP	SA/RC	FBG KL OB		8	2700	3	6350	6250
23	SAN-JUAN 23 SHOAL	SLP	SA/RC	FBG KC OB		8	2700	1 11	5450	6250
25 9	SAN-JUAN 26PC	SLP	SA/RC	FBG KL OB		9 6	3200	4	7050	8100
28 8	SAN-JUAN 29	SLP	SA/RC	FBG KL IB	15D YAN	10	6200	4 6	14800	16900

LOA FT IN	NAME AND/ OR MODEL	TOP/ RIG	BOAT TYPE	-HULL- MTL TP	TP #	-ENGINE- HP MFG	BEAM FT IN	WGT LBS	DRAFT FT IN	RETAIL LOW	RETAIL HIGH
					1986 BOATS						
33 10	SAN-JUAN 34	SLP	SA/RC	FBG KL	KC OB	23D YAN	10 11	10500	5 11	25500	28300
33 10	SAN-JUAN 34 SHOAL	SLP	SA/RC	FBG KL	IB	23D YAN	10 11	11000	4 9	26700	29600
					1985 BOATS						
20 6	SAN-JUAN 21	SLP	SA/RC	FBG KC	OB		7	1250	1	2950	3450
20 6	SAN-JUAN 21	SLP	SA/RC	FBG KL	OB		7	1250		2950	3450
23	SAN-JUAN 23	SLP	SA/RC	FBG KL	OB		8	2700	4	5250	6000
23	SAN-JUAN 23 SHOAL	SLP	SA/RC	FBG KC	OB		8	2700	1 11	5000	5750
25 9	SAN-JUAN 7.7	SLP	SA/RC	FBG KL	OB		9 6	3200	4	6600	7600
28 8	SAN-JUAN 28	SLP	SA/RC	FBG KL	IB	12D	10	6200	4 6	13900	15800
33 10	SAN-JUAN 34	SLP	SA/RC	FBG KL	IB	23D YAN	10 11	10500	5 11	24000	26700
33 10	SAN-JUAN 34 SHOAL	SLP	SA/RC	FBG KL	IB	23D YAN	10 11	11000	4 9	25100	27900
					1984 BOATS						
20 6	SAN-JUAN 21	SLP	SA/RC	FBG KL	OB		7	1250	1	2800	3250
23	SAN-JUAN 23	SLP	SA/RC	FBG KL	OB		8	2700	4	4900	5650
23	SAN-JUAN 23 SHOAL	SLP	SA/RC	FBG KC	OB		8	2700	1 11	4750	5450
24	SAN-JUAN 24	SLP	SA/RC	FBG KL	OB		8	3200	4	5200	6000
25 9	SAN-JUAN 7.7	SLP	SA/RC	FBG KL	IB	7D	9 6	3200	4	5750	6650
28 8	SAN-JUAN 28	SLP	SA/RC	FBG KL	IB	12D	10	6200	4 8	6750	7750
33	SAN-JUAN 33S	SLP	SA/RC	FBG KL	IB	D	8	5700	5 8	13100	14900
33 10	SAN-JUAN 34	SLP	SA/RC	FBG KL	IB	20D YAN	10 11	10500	5 11	11900	13500
33 10	SAN-JUAN 34 SHOAL	SLP	SA/RC	FBG KL	IB	20D YAN	10 11	11000	4 9	22500	25100
										23600	26200

....For earlier years, see the BUC Used Boat Price Guide, Volume 3

SANFORD-WOOD
PT RICHMOND CA 94804   See inside cover to adjust price for area
FORMERLY SANFORD BOAT CO INC

LOA FT IN	NAME AND/ OR MODEL	TOP/ RIG	BOAT TYPE	-HULL- MTL TP	TP #	-ENGINE- HP MFG	BEAM FT IN	WGT LBS	DRAFT FT IN	RETAIL LOW	RETAIL HIGH
					1985 BOATS						
51 6	MAGIC CLASS	SLP	SA/RC	WD KL	IB	D	13 6	35000	7	279000	306500
					1984 BOATS						
26	ALERION CLASS SLOOP	SLP	SA/CR	WD KC		7	7 7	6100	2 5	30000	33300
26	ALERION CLASS SLOOP	SLP	SA/CR	WD KC	SD	7 VLVO	7 7	6100	2 5	31800	35300
43	SHADOW CLASS	SLP	SA/CR	KC	IB	30D	12	17000	4	120000	132000
51	MAGIC CLASS	SLP	SA/CR	KL	IB	50D BMW	13 6	36000	7	255000	280000

....For earlier years, see the BUC Used Boat Price Guide, Volume 3

SANGER BOAT
FRESNO CA 93725   COAST GUARD MFG ID- SAN See inside cover to adjust price for area

For more recent years, see the BUC Used Boat Price Guide, Volume 1

LOA FT IN	NAME AND/ OR MODEL	TOP/ RIG	BOAT TYPE	-HULL- MTL TP	TP #	-ENGINE- HP MFG	BEAM FT IN	WGT LBS	DRAFT FT IN	RETAIL LOW	RETAIL HIGH
					1994 BOATS						
20	BAREFOOT SKIER		SKI	F/W SV	OB		7 2	1750	2	6850	7900
20 2	20 DXII		SKI	F/W SV	IB	250 MRCR	7 4	2450	1 10	9250	10500
20 4	20 SE		SKI	F/W SV	IB	240 MRCR	7 4	2400	1 10	9150	10400
20 8	20 DLX		SKI	F/W SV	IB	265 MRCR	7 6	2700	2	10100	11500
21	21 TX		SKI	F/W SV	IO	240 MRCR	7 6	2500	2 3	8000	9150
22 5	22 FX		SKI	F/W SV	IO	250 MRCR	7 6	2950	2	11700	13300
					1993 BOATS						
20	BAREFOOT SKIER		SKI	F/W SV	OB		7 2	1750	2	6500	7500
20 2	20 DXII		SKI	F/W SV	IB	250 MRCR	7 4	2450	1 10	8700	10000
20 4	20 SE		SKI	F/W SV	IB	240 INDM	7 4	2400	1 10	8500	9800
21	21 TX		SKI	F/W SV	IO	240 OMC	7 6	2500	2 3	7400	8500
22 5	22 FX		SKI	F/W SV	IO	250 MRCR	7 6	2950	2	11100	12600
					1988 BOATS						
18	SKI TUG		OP	SKI	FBG SV	IO	175-205	7 1	2000		3500	4150
20	BAREFOOT SKIER		OP	SKI	FBG SV	OB		7	4200	4900
20 4	SANGER SKIER DX		OP	SKI	FBG SV	IO	260 CHEV	7 4	2300	5150	5900
21	SANGER SKIER		OP	SKI	FBG SV	IO	260 MRCR	7 4	2200	5300	6100
21	SANGER SKIER TX		OP	SKI	FBG SV	IO	260 MRCR	7 6		5950	6850

....For earlier years, see the BUC Used Boat Price Guide, Volume 3

SANTA BARBARA BOATWORKS
WILSON BOATS   See inside cover to adjust price for area
GOLETA CA 93117   COAST GUARD MFG ID- SBZ

LOA FT IN	NAME AND/ OR MODEL	TOP/ RIG	BOAT TYPE	-HULL- MTL TP	TP #	-ENGINE- HP MFG	BEAM FT IN	WGT LBS	DRAFT FT IN	RETAIL LOW	RETAIL HIGH
					1986 BOATS						
20 4	C V-200	OP	CTRCN	FBG DV	OB		7 8			6800	7800
20 4	C V-200	OP	CTRCN	FBG DV	IO	145-260	7 8			5900	7350
20 4	C V-200	OP	CTRCN	FBG DV	IO	130D VLVO	7 8			8650	9950
20 4	SI V-2000	OP	CUD	FBG DV	OB		7 8	4000	1 2	6800	7800
20 4	SI V-2000	OP	CUD	FBG DV	IO	145-260	7 8			5950	7350
20 4	SI V-2000	OP	CUD	FBG DV	IO	130D VLVO	7 8			8550	9800
26 6	HT-V2600	HT	PH	FBG DV	IO	225-330	8			16500	20100
26 6	HT-V2600	HT	PH	FBG DV	IO	165D VLVO	8			20700	23000
26 6	SI V-26000	OP	CUD	FBG DV	IO	225-330	8	7500	1 6	15600	18900
26 6	SI V-26000	OP	CUD	FBG DV	IO	165D VLVO	8	7500	1 6	19100	21200
26 6	STC-26000	OP	CR	FBG DV	IO	225-330	8	7500	1 6	15300	19200
26 6	STC-26000	OP	CR	FBG DV	IO	165D VLVO	8			19400	21500
29 8	HT V-3000	HT	CR	FBG DV	IO	330 MRCR 10	2			23100	25600
	IB 235D-270D	30800	35200,	IO T260	VLVO	24800 27500,	IOT130D-T165D	24700	28500
29 8	SI V-3000	OP	CUD	FBG DV	IO	330 MRCR 10	2 10000	1 8	23900	26600
	IB 235D-270D	23400	27100,	IO T260	VLVO	23500 26100,	IOT130D-T165D	19300	22600
29 8	STC V-3000	OP	CR	FBG DV	IO	330 MRCR 10	2			23000	25600
	IB 235D-270D	30800	35200,	IO T260	VLVO	24700 27500,	IOT130D-T165D	24700	28500
					1985 BOATS						
20 4	C V-200	OP	CTRCN	FBG DV	OB		7 8			6650	7600
20 4	C V-200	OP	CTRCN	FBG DV	IO	138-260	7 8			5700	7000
20 4	SI V-2000	OP	CUD	FBG DV	IO	130D VLVO	7 8			8250	9500
20 4	SI V-2000	OP	CUD	FBG DV	OB		7 8	4000	1 2	6650	7600
20 4	SI V-2000	OP	CUD	FBG DV	IO	138-260	7 8			5650	7000
26 6	HT-V2600	OP	CUD	FBG DV	IO	130D VLVO	7 8			8150	9350
26 6	HT-V2600	HT	PH	FBG DV	IO	225-330	8			15700	19100
26 6	SI V-26000	HT	PH	FBG DV	IO	165D VLVO	8			20100	22400
26 6	SI V-26000	OP	CUD	FBG DV	IO	225-330	8	7500	1 6	14800	18000
26 6	STC-26000	OP	CUD	FBG DV	IO	165D VLVO	8	7500	1 6	18200	20200
26 6	STC-26000	OP	CR	FBG DV	IO	225-330	8	7500	1 6	15200	18300
		OP	CR	FBG DV	IO	165D VLVO	8			18400	20500
29 8	HT V-3000	HT	CR	FBG DV	IO	330 MRCR 10	2			22300	24700
	IB 235D-270D	29600	33700,	IO T260	VLVO	23700 26300,	IOT130D-T165D	24100	27200
29 8	SI V-3000	OP	CUD	FBG DV	IO	330 MRCR 10	2 10000	1 8	22800	25400
	IB 235D-270D	22400	26000,	IO T260	VLVO	22100 24600,	IOT130D-T165D	18300	21900
29 8	STC V-3000	OP	CR	FBG DV	IO	330 MRCR 10	2			22200	24700
	IB 235D-270D	29600	33700,	IO T260	VLVO	23700 26300,	IOT130D-T165D	24100	27200

SANTA CRUZ YACHTS LLC
LA SELUA BEACH CA 95026 COAST GUARD MFG ID- SYM See inside cover to adjust price for area

For more recent years, see the BUC Used Boat Price Guide, Volume 1

LOA FT IN	NAME AND/ OR MODEL	TOP/ RIG	BOAT TYPE	-HULL- MTL TP	TP #	-ENGINE- HP MFG	BEAM FT IN	WGT LBS	DRAFT FT IN	RETAIL LOW	RETAIL HIGH
					1996 BOATS						
53	SANTA CRUZ 52	SLP	SARAC	FBG KL	IB	62D YAN	14	21000	9	243000	267000
					1995 BOATS						
53	SANTA CRUZ 52	SLP	SARAC	FBG KL	IB	62D YAN	14	21000	9	393500	432500
					1994 BOATS						
53	SANTA CRUZ 52	SLP	SARAC	FBG KL	IB	62D YAN	14	21000	9	372500	409500
					1993 BOATS						
53	SANTA CRUZ 52	SLP	SARAC	FBG KL	IB	62D YAN	14	20000	9	351000	385500
					1992 BOATS						
53	SANTA CRUZ 52	SLP	SA/RC	FBG KL	IB	62D YAN	14	20000	9	332500	365000
					1989 BOATS						
40	SANTA-CRUZ 40	SLP	SA/RC	FBG KL	IB	23D YAN	12	10000	7	74100	81500
50	SANTA-CRUZ 50	SLP	SA/RC	FBG KL	IB	41D VLVO	12	18000	8	206500	226500
67	SANTA-CRUZ 70	SLP	SA/RC	FBG KL	IB	55D YAN	15	27000	9	399000	438500
					1988 BOATS						
40	SANTA-CRUZ 40	SLP	SA/RC	FBG KL	IB	23D YAN	12	10000	7	70200	77200
50	SANTA-CRUZ 50	SLP	SA/RC	FBG KL	IB	41D VLVO	12	18000	8	195500	215500
67	SANTA-CRUZ 70	SLP	SA/RC	FBG KL	IB	55D YAN	15	27000	9	378000	415500
					1987 BOATS						
40	SANTA CRUZ 40	SLP	SA/RC	FBG KL	IB	23D YAN	12	10000	7	66600	73100
50	SANTA CRUZ 50	SLP	SA/RC	FBG KL	IB	42D PATH	12	16000	8	180000	198000
67	SANTA CRUZ 70	SLP	SA/RC	FBG KL	IB	136D YAN	15	27000	8 5	360500	396500

SANTA CRUZ YACHTS LLC -CONTINUED See inside cover to adjust price for area

LOA FT	LOA IN	NAME AND/ OR MODEL	TOP/ RIG	BOAT TYPE	HULL MTL	HULL TP	ENGINE TP	#	HP	MFG	BEAM FT	BEAM IN	WGT LBS	DRAFT FT	DRAFT IN	RETAIL LOW	RETAIL HIGH
		1986 BOATS															
40		SANTA-CRUZ 40	SLP	SA/RC	FBG	KL	IB		23D	YAN	12		10500	7		65300	71800
50		SANTA-CRUZ 50	SLP	SA/RC	FBG	KL	IB		41D	VLVO	12		17000	8		173000	190500
67		SANTA-CRUZ 70	SLP	SA/RC	FBG	KL	IB		136D	YAN	15		27000	8	5	342000	375500
		1985 BOATS															
40		SANTA-CRUZ 40	SLP	SA/RC	FBG	KL	IB		23D	YAN	12		10000	7		59800	65700
40		SANTA-CRUZ 40	SLP	SA/RC	FBG	KL	IB		42D	PATH	12		10000	7		60200	66200
50		SANTA-CRUZ 50	SLP	SA/RC	FBG	KL	IB		42D	PATH	12		16000	8		162000	178000
50		SANTA-CRUZ 50 MK II	SLP	SA/RC	FBG	KL	IB		82D	PATH	12		17100	8		165500	181500
67		SANTA CRUZ 70	SLP	SA/RC	FBG	KL	IB		136D	BMW	15		27000	8	5	323500	355500
		1984 BOATS															
40		SANTA-CRUZ 40	SLP	SA/RC	FBG	KL	IB		22D	YAN	12		10000	7		56600	62200
40		SANTA-CRUZ 40	SLP	SA/RC	FBG	KL	IB		42D	PATH	12		10000	7		57100	62700
50		SANTA-CRUZ 50	SLP	SA/RC	FBG	KL	IB		42D	PATH	12		16000	8		153500	168500
50		SANTA-CRUZ 50	SLP	SA/RC	FBG	KL	IB		82D	PATH	12		16000	8		154500	169500
67		SANTA CRUZ 70	SLP	SA/RC	FBG	KL	IB		138D	BMW	15		25800	8	5	303000	333000

....For earlier years, see the BUC Used Boat Price Guide, Volume 3

SCANAM INC
MT DESERT ME 04660 See inside cover to adjust price for area

LOA FT	LOA IN	NAME AND/ OR MODEL	TOP/ RIG	BOAT TYPE	HULL MTL	HULL TP	ENGINE TP	#	HP	MFG	BEAM FT	BEAM IN	WGT LBS	DRAFT FT	DRAFT IN	RETAIL LOW	RETAIL HIGH
		1985 BOATS															
32	6	BIANCA 101 APHRODITE	SLP	SA/RC	FBG	KL	IB		D		7	10	5500	5	4	19900	22200
36	6	BIANCA 111	SLP	SA/RC	FBG	KL	IB		D		10	6	12000	6	6	46700	51300

SCANDIA PLAST BOAT WORKS LTD
LITTLE COMPTON RI 02837 COAST GUARD MFG ID- SPS See inside cover to adjust price for area

LOA FT	LOA IN	NAME AND/ OR MODEL	TOP/ RIG	BOAT TYPE	HULL MTL	HULL TP	ENGINE TP	#	HP	MFG	BEAM FT	BEAM IN	WGT LBS	DRAFT FT	DRAFT IN	RETAIL LOW	RETAIL HIGH
		1987 BOATS															
20	9	YNGLING MK5	SLP	SA/RC	F/S	KL					5	8	1320	3	6	5500	6350
		1985 BOATS															
20	9	YNGLING	SLP	SA/OD		KL					5	8	1320	3	6	4900	5600
20	9	YNGLING	SLP	SA/OD	FBG	KL					5	8	1320	3	6	4900	5600

....For earlier years, see the BUC Used Boat Price Guide, Volume 3

SCANDINAVIAN YACHTS & MARINE
VICTORIA BC CANADA COAST GUARD MFG ID- VER See inside cover to adjust price for area

LOA FT	LOA IN	NAME AND/ OR MODEL	TOP/ RIG	BOAT TYPE	HULL MTL	HULL TP	ENGINE TP	#	HP	MFG	BEAM FT	BEAM IN	WGT LBS	DRAFT FT	DRAFT IN	RETAIL LOW	RETAIL HIGH
		1986 BOATS															
28		GREAT DANE 28	SLP	SA/OD	FBG	KL	IB				8	2	8500	4	9	32200	35700
32		APOLLO 32		MY	FBG	SV	IB	T	80D		10	6	12000	2	7	61800	67900
		1985 BOATS															
28		GREAT DANE 28	SLP	SA/OD	FBG	KL					8	2	8500	4	9	27900	31000
32		APOLLO 32		MY	FBG	SV	IB	T	80D		10	6	12000	2	7	59200	65100
		1984 BOATS															
28		GREAT DANE 28	SLP	SA/OD	FBG	KL	IB		25D	VLVO	8	2	8500	4	9	28900	32100
30		APOLLO 30	HT	MY	FBG	SV	IB		80D	FORD	10		9000	2	6	38100	42400
32		APOLLO 32	HT	MY	FBG	SV	IB		80D	FORD	10		10000	2	7	47200	51900
32		APOLLO 32	HT	MY	FBG	SV	IB	T	80D	FORD	10		10000	2	7	53900	59300

....For earlier years, see the BUC Used Boat Price Guide, Volume 3

SCANDINAVIAN YACHTS LTD
ANNAPOLIS MD 21403 COAST GUARD MFG ID- XCY See inside cover to adjust price for area

LOA FT	LOA IN	NAME AND/ OR MODEL	TOP/ RIG	BOAT TYPE	HULL MTL	HULL TP	ENGINE TP	#	HP	MFG	BEAM FT	BEAM IN	WGT LBS	DRAFT FT	DRAFT IN	RETAIL LOW	RETAIL HIGH
		1988 BOATS															
21	10	NORDSHIP 666	SLP	MS	F/S	KL	OB				7	10	3969	4	7	14100	16000
21	10	NORDSHIP 666 SHOAL	SLP	MS	F/S	KL	OB				7	10	3969	3	11	14100	16000
23	7	GRANADA 24	SLP	SAIL	F/S	KL	OB				8	4	3528	4	1	13300	15100
23	7	GRANADA 24	SLP	SAIL	F/S	KL	SD		8D	VLVO	8	4	3528	4	1	14800	16800
25		MASCOT	SLP	MS	F/S	KL	IB		D							15800	18000
25		NORDIC FOLKBOAT	SLP	SAIL	F/S	KL	OB				7	2	4322	3	9	17600	20000
25	3	DRAGONFLY	SLP	SAIL	F/S	TM					19	8	1653	1	2	18100	20100
26	6	NORDSHIP 808	SLP	MS	F/S	KL	OB				9	2	5733	4	3	24700	27400
26	6	NORDSHIP 808	SLP	MS	F/S	KL	IB		9D	VLVO	9	2	5733	4	3	25500	28400
27	2	GRANADA 27	SLP	SAIL	F/S	KL	OB				9	1	4851	5	9	22000	24500
27	2	GRANADA 27	SLP	SAIL	F/S	KL	IB		9D	VLVO	9	1	4851	5	9	22800	25300
27	2	GRANADA 27 SHOAL	SLP	SAIL	F/S	KL	OB				9	1	4851	4	9	22000	24500
27	2	GRANADA 27 SHOAL	SLP	SAIL	F/S	KL	IB		9D	VLVO	9	1	4851	4	9	22800	25300
27	10	MASCOT	SLP	MS	F/S	KL	IB		D		9	7	8800	4	3	41900	46500
28	5	NORDSHIP 28 MS	SLP	MS	F/S	KL	IB		25D	VLVO	9	6	7332	4	11	35300	39200
29	10	GRANADA 30	SLP	SAIL	F/S	KL	OB				9	6	7066	3	3	35100	39000
29	10	GRANADA 30	SLP	SAIL	F/S	KL	IB		17D	VLVO	9	6	7056	3	3	35500	39500
30	10	GRANADA 31	SLP	SAIL	F/S	KL	OB				10		7938	5	9	40800	45300
30	10	GRANADA 31	SLP	SAIL	F/S	KL	IB		17D	VLVO	10		7938	5	9	41000	45500
30	10	GRANADA 31 SHOAL	SLP	SAIL	F/S	KL	OB				10		7938	4	9	40800	45300
30	10	GRANADA 31 SHOAL	SLP	SAIL	F/S	KL	IB		17D	VLVO	10		7938	4	9	41000	45500
32	6	MASCOT	SLP	MS	F/S	KL	IB		28D	VLVO	11	2	13228	4	11	67400	74100
32	10	BB-10M FAMILY RACER	SLP	SAIL	F/S	KL	OB				7	6	4956	4	10	25400	28200
32	10	BB-10M FAMILY RACER	SLP	SAIL	F/S	KL	IB		9D	YAN	7	6	4956	4	10	25400	28300
33	6	GRANADA 33	SLP	SAIL	F/S	KL	IB		18D	VLVO	11		9700	4	5	51200	56300
33	8	NORDSHIP 34 MS	SLP	MS	F/S	KL	IB		36D	VLVO	11	8	12128	5	5	62000	68200
35	5	GRANADA 35 CRUISER	SLP	SA/CR	F/S	KL	IB		28D	VLVO	11	11	12138	5	1	63700	70000
35	5	GRANADA 35 RACER	SLP	SA/RC	F/S	KL	IB		28D	VLVO	11	11	12138	6	1	63600	69900
36	9	LUFFE 37	SLP	MS	F/S	KL	IB		9D	VLVO	9		7717	5	5	42900	47700
43	9	LUFFE 44	SLP	MS	F/S	KL	IB		18D	VLVO	10	7	9920	6	5	86000	94500
		1987 BOATS															
21	10	NORDSHIP 666	SLP	MS	F/S	KL	OB				7	10	3969	4	7	13300	15100
21	10	NORDSHIP 666 SHOAL	SLP	MS	F/S	KL	OB				7	10	3969	3	11	13300	15100
23	7	GRANADA 24	SLP	SAIL	F/S	KL	OB				8	4	3528	4	1	12600	14300
23	7	GRANADA 24	SLP	SAIL	F/S	KL	SD		8D	VLVO	8	4	3528	4	1	13900	15800
25		MASCOT	SLP	MS	F/S	KL	IB		D							14800	16800
25		NORDIC FOLKBOAT	SLP	SAIL	F/S	KL	OB				7	2	4322	3	9	16400	18700
25	3	DRAGONFLY	SLP	SAIL	F/S	TM					19	8	1653	1	2	16500	18800
26	6	NORDSHIP 808	SLP	MS	F/S	KL	OB				9	2	5733	4	3	23500	26100
26	6	NORDSHIP 808	SLP	MS	F/S	KL	IB		9D	VLVO	9	2	5733	4	3	24400	27100
27	2	GRANADA 27	SLP	SAIL	F/S	KL	OB				9	1	4851	5	9	20900	23300
27	2	GRANADA 27	SLP	SAIL	F/S	KL	IB		9D	VLVO	9	1	4851	5	9	21800	24200
27	2	GRANADA 27 SHOAL	SLP	SAIL	F/S	KL	OB				9	1	4851	4	9	20900	23300
27	2	GRANADA 27 SHOAL	SLP	SAIL	F/S	KL	IB		9D	VLVO	9	1	4851	4	9	21800	24200
27	10	MASCOT	SLP	MS	F/S	KL	IB		D		9	7	8800	4	3	39200	43500
28	5	NORDSHIP 28 MS	SLP	MS	F/S	KL	IB		25D	VLVO	9	6	7332	4	11	33000	36700
29	10	GRANADA 30	SLP	SAIL	F/S	KL	OB				9	6	7066	3	3	32800	36400
29	10	GRANADA 30	SLP	SAIL	F/S	KL	IB		17D	VLVO	9	6	7056	3	3	33200	36900
30	10	GRANADA 31	SLP	SAIL	F/S	KL	OB				10		7938	5	9	38100	42400
30	10	GRANADA 31	SLP	SAIL	F/S	KL	IB		17D	VLVO	10		7938	5	9	38300	42600
30	10	GRANADA 31 SHOAL	SLP	SAIL	F/S	KL	OB				10		7938	4	9	38100	42400
30	10	GRANADA 31 SHOAL	SLP	SAIL	F/S	KL	IB		17D	VLVO	10		7938	4	9	38300	42600
32	6	MASCOT	SLP	MS	F/S	KL	IB		28D	VLVO	11	2	13228	4	11	63100	69300
32	10	BB-10M FAMILY RACER	SLP	SAIL	F/S	KL	OB				7	6	4956	4	10	24200	26900
32	10	BB-10M FAMILY RACER	SLP	SAIL	F/S	KL	IB		9D	YAN	7	6	4956	4	10	24300	27000
33	6	GRANADA 33	SLP	SAIL	F/S	KL	IB		18D	VLVO	11		9700	4	5	48100	52800
33	8	NORDSHIP 34 MS	SLP	MS	F/S	KL	IB		36D	VLVO	11	8	12128	5	5	58600	64400
35	5	GRANADA 35 CRUISER	SLP	SA/CR	F/S	KL	IB		28D	VLVO	11	11	12138	5	1	59600	65500
35	5	GRANADA 35 RACER	SLP	SA/RC	F/S	KL	IB		28D	VLVO	11	11	12138	6	1	60100	66000
36	9	LUFFE 37	SLP	MS	F/S	KL	IB		9D	VLVO	9		7717	5	5	40100	44600
43	9	LUFFE 44	SLP	MS	F/S	KL	IB		18D	VLVO	10	7	9920	6	5	80500	88400
		1986 BOATS															
21	10	NORDSHIP 666	SLP	MS	F/S	KL	OB				7	10	3969	4	7	12500	14200
21	10	NORDSHIP 666 SHOAL	SLP	MS	F/S	KL	OB				7	10	3969	3	11	12500	14200
23	7	GRANADA 24	SLP	SAIL	F/S	KL	OB				8	4	3528	4	1	11800	13400
23	7	GRANADA 24	SLP	SAIL	F/S	KL	SD		8D	VLVO	8	4	3528	4	1	13000	14800
25		DRAGONFLY	SLP	SAIL	F/S	TM										19200	21300
25		MASCOT	SLP	MS	F/S	KL	IB		D							13900	15700
25		NORDIC FOLKBOAT	SLP	SAIL	F/S	KL	OB				7	2	4322	3	9	15400	17500
26	6	NORDSHIP 808	SLP	MS	F/S	KL	OB				9	2	5733	4	3	22400	24900
26	6	NORDSHIP 808	SLP	MS	F/S	KL	IB		9D	VLVO	9	2	5733	4	3	22800	25300
27	2	GRANADA 27	SLP	SAIL	F/S	KL	OB				9	1	4851	5	9	20000	22200
27	2	GRANADA 27	SLP	SAIL	F/S	KL	IB		9D	VLVO	9	1	4851	5	9	20300	22600
27	2	GRANADA 27 SHOAL	SLP	SAIL	F/S	KL	OB				9	1	4851	4	9	20000	22200
27	2	GRANADA 27 SHOAL	SLP	SAIL	F/S	KL	IB		9D	VLVO	9	1	4851	4	9	20300	22600
27	10	MASCOT	SLP	MS	F/S	KL	IB		D							32000	35600
28	5	NORDSHIP 28 MS	SLP	MS	F/S	KL	IB		25D	VLVO	9	6	7332	4	11	30900	34300
29	10	GRANADA 30	SLP	SAIL	F/S	KL	OB				9	6	7066	3	3	30700	34100
29	10	GRANADA 30	SLP	SAIL	F/S	KL	IB		17D	VLVO	9	6	7056	3	3	31100	34500
30	10	GRANADA 31	SLP	SAIL	F/S	KL	OB				10		7938	5	9	35700	39600
30	10	GRANADA 31	SLP	SAIL	F/S	KL	IB		17D	VLVO	10		7938	5	9	35900	39800
30	10	GRANADA 31 SHOAL	SLP	SAIL	F/S	KL	OB				10		7938	4	9	35700	39600

LOA FT	LOA IN	NAME AND/ OR MODEL	TOP/ RIG	BOAT TYPE	HULL MTL	HULL TP	ENGINE TP	# HP	ENGINE MFG	BEAM FT	BEAM IN	WGT LBS	DRAFT FT	DRAFT IN	RETAIL LOW	RETAIL HIGH
		1986 BOATS														
30	10	GRANADA 31 SHOAL	SLP	SAIL	F/S	KL	IB	17D	VLVO	10		7938	4	9	35900	39800
31	5	TARGA	SLP	SAIL	F/S	KL	IB	D	VLVO						36300	40300
32	6	MASCOT	SLP	MS	F/S	KL	IB								54800	60200
32	10	BB-10M FAMILY RACER	SLP	SAIL	F/S	KL	OB			7	6	4956	4	10	22500	25000
32	10	BB-10M FAMILY RACER	SLP	SAIL	F/S	KL	IB	9D	YAN	7	6	4956	4	10	22600	25100
33	8	NORDSHIP 34 MS	SLP	MS	F/S	KL	IB	36D	VLVO	11	8	12128	5	5	54500	59900
35	5	GRANADA 35 CRUISER	SLP	SA/CR	F/S	KL	IB	28D	VLVO	11	11	12138	5	1	56300	61900
35	5	GRANADA 35 RACER	SLP	SA/RC	F/S	KL	IB	28D	VLVO	11	11	12138	6	1	56200	61700
37	7	LUFFE 37	SLP	MS	F/S	KL	IB	D							68600	75400
43	9	LUFFE 44	SLP	MS	F/S	KL	IB	D							72400	79600
		1985 BOATS														
21	10	NORDSHIP 666	SLP	MS	F/S	KL	OB			7	10	3969	4	7	11700	13300
21	10	NORDSHIP 666 SHOAL	SLP	SAIL	F/S	KL	OB			7	10	3969	3	11	11700	13300
23	7	GRANADA 24	SLP	SAIL	F/S	KL	OB			8	4	3528	4	1	11100	12600
23	7	GRANADA 24	SLP	SAIL	F/S	KL	SD	8D	VLVO	8	4	3528	4	1	12300	14000
25		DRAGONFLY	SLP	SAIL	F/S	TM									17500	19900
25		MASCOT	SLP	MS	F/S	KL	IB	D							13000	14800
25		NORDIC FOLKBOAT	SLP	SAIL	F/S	KL	OB			7	2	4322	3	9	14400	16400
26	6	NORDSHIP 808	SLP	MS	F/S	KL	OB			9	2	5733	4	3	20900	23200
26	6	NORDSHIP 808	SLP	MS	F/S	KL	IB	9D	VLVO	9	2	5733	4	3	21700	24200
27	2	GRANADA 27	SLP	SAIL	F/S	KL	OB			9	1	4851	5	9	18700	20700
27	2	GRANADA 27	SLP	SAIL	F/S	KL	IB	9D	VLVO	9	1	4851	5	9	19400	21500
27	2	GRANADA 27 SHOAL	SLP	SAIL	F/S	KL	OB			9	1	4851	4	9	18700	20700
27	2	GRANADA 27 SHOAL	SLP	SAIL	F/S	KL	IB	9D	VLVO	9	1	4851	4	9	19400	21500
27	10	MASCOT	SLP	MS	F/S	KL	IB	D							29900	33300
28		MARINA 28	SLP	SA/CR	STL	KL	IB			9	9	8140	4	6	31700	35200
28	2	MARINA 28	SLP	SA/CR	STL	KL	IB			9	9	8140	4	6	31900	35400
28	5	NORDSHIP 28 MS	SLP	MS	F/S	KL	IB	25D	VLVO	9	6	7332	4	11	28900	32100
29	10	GRANADA 30	SLP	SAIL	F/S	KL	OB			9	6	7066	3	3	28700	31900
29	10	GRANADA 30	SLP	SAIL	F/S	KL	IB	17D	VLVO	9	6	7056	3	3	29100	32300
30	10	GRANADA 31	SLP	SAIL	F/S	KL	OB			10		7938	5	9	33400	37100
30	10	GRANADA 31	SLP	SAIL	F/S	KL	IB	17D	VLVO	10		7938	5	9	33500	37300
30	10	GRANADA 31 SHOAL	SLP	SAIL	F/S	KL	OB			10		7938	4	9	33400	37100
30	10	GRANADA 31 SHOAL	SLP	SAIL	F/S	KL	IB	17D	VLVO	10		7938	4	9	33500	37300
31	5	TARGA	SLP	SAIL	F/S	KL	IB	D	VLVO						33900	37700
32	6	MASCOT	SLP	MS	F/S	KL	IB								51900	57100
32	10	BB-10M FAMILY RACER	SLP	SA/RC	F/S	KL	OB			7	6	4956	4	10	21500	23900
32	10	BB-10M FAMILY RACER	SLP	SA/RC	F/S	KL	IB	7D	BMW	7	6	4956	4	10	21500	23900
33	8	NORDSHIP 34 MS	SLP	MS	F/S	KL	IB	36D	VLVO	11	8	12128	5	5	51600	56700
35	5	GRANADA 35 CRUISER	SLP	SA/CR	F/S	KL	IB	28D	VLVO	11	11	12138	5	1	53000	58200
35	5	GRANADA 35 RACER	SLP	SA/RC	F/S	KL	IB	28D	VLVO	11	11	12138	6	1	52900	58100
36	6	MOTIVA 36	SLP	SA/CR	STL	KL	IB	D		12		7710	5	10	35300	39200
37	6	CONCORDE 38	SLP	SA/RC	FBG	KL	IB			9	6	4510	5	11	21600	24000
37	7	LUFFE 37	SLP	MS	F/S	KL	IB	D							64200	70500
39		MOTIVA 39	SLP	SA/CR	FBG	KL	IB	D		10		6600	4	10	36800	40800
40		MOTIVA 40	SLP	SA/CR	FBG	KL	IB	D		12		8360	6	4	50200	55200
43	9	LUFFE 44	SLP	MS	F/S	KL	IB	D							67800	74500
		1984 BOATS														
21	10	NORDSHIP 666	SLP	MS	F/S	KL	OB			7	10	3969	3	11	11100	12600
23	7	GRANADA 24	SLP	SAIL	F/S	KL	OB			8	4	3528	4	1	10500	11900
23	7	GRANADA 24	SLP	SAIL	F/S	KL	IB	10D	VLVO	8	4	3528	4	1	11700	13300
25		NORDIC FOLKBOAT	SLP	SAIL	F/S	KL	OB			7	2	4322	3	9	13600	15400
26	6	NORDSHIP 808	SLP	MS	F/S	KL	OB			9	2	5733	4	3	20000	22200
26	6	NORDSHIP 808	SLP	MS	F/S	KL	IB	10D	VLVO	9	2	5733	4	3	20400	22700
27	2	GRANADA 27	SLP	SAIL	F/S	KL	OB			9	1	4851	4	9	17200	19500
27	2	GRANADA 27	SLP	SAIL	F/S	KL	IB	10D		9	1	4851	4	9	18300	20300
28	5	NORDSHIP 28 MS	SLP	MS	F/S	KL	IB	25D	VLVO	9	6	7332	4	11	27100	30100
29	10	GRANADA 30	SLP	SAIL	F/S	KL	OB			9	6	7066	3	3	26900	29900
29	10	GRANADA 30	SLP	SAIL	F/S	KL	IB	17D	VLVO	9	6	7056	3	3	27300	30300
30	10	GRANADA 31	SLP	SAIL	F/S	KL	OB			10		7938	4	9	31300	34800
30	10	GRANADA 31	SLP	SAIL	F/S	KL	IB	17D		10		7938	4	9	31500	35000
30	10	GRANADA 939	SLP	SAIL	F/S	KL	OB			10		7938	5	9	31300	34800
30	10	GRANADA 939	SLP	SAIL	F/S	KL	IB	17D	VLVO	10		7938	5	9	31500	35000
32	10	BB-10M FAMILY RACER	SLP	SAIL	F/S	KL	OB			7	6	4956	4	10	20100	22300
32	10	BB-10M FAMILY RACER	SLP	SAIL	F/S	KL	IB	7D	BMW	7	6	4956	4	10	20200	22400
33	8	NORDSHIP 34 MS	SLP	MS	F/S	KL	IB	36D	VLVO	11	8	12128	5	5	48600	53400
35	5	GRANADA 35 CRUISER	SLP	SA/CR	F/S	KL	IB	28D	VLVO	11	11	12138	5	1	49800	54700
35	5	GRANADA 35 RACER	SLP	SA/RC	F/S	KL	IB	28D	VLVO	11	11	12138	6	1	49700	54600

....For earlier years, see the BUC Used Boat Price Guide, Volume 3

SCEPTRE YACHTS LTD

W VANCOUVER BC CANADA V COAST GUARD MFG ID- ZSZ See inside cover to adjust price for area

LOA FT	LOA IN	NAME AND/ OR MODEL	TOP/ RIG	BOAT TYPE	HULL MTL	HULL TP	ENGINE TP	# HP	ENGINE MFG	BEAM FT	BEAM IN	WGT LBS	DRAFT FT	DRAFT IN	RETAIL LOW	RETAIL HIGH
		1993 BOATS														
41		SCEPTRE 41 PILOTHSE	SLP	MS	FBG	KL	IB	55D	YAN	12	8	21500	6	1	177500	195000
		1992 BOATS														
41		SCEPTRE 41 PILOTHSE	SLP	MS	FBG	KL	IB	55D	YAN	12	8	21500	6		167000	183500
		1985 BOATS														
35	6	SCEPTRE 36	SLP	SA/CR	FBG	KL	IB	23D	YAN	11	5	12000	6		51200	56200
41		SCEPTRE 41	SLP	SA/CR	F/S	KL	IB	45D	BMW	12	8	21500	6	1	108000	119000
		1984 BOATS														
35	6	SCEPTRE 36	SLP	SAIL	FBG	KL		20D		11	5	12000	6		47500	52100
41		SCEPTRE 41	SLP	SAIL	FBG	KL	IB	50D	BMW	12	8	21500	6	1	102000	112000

....For earlier years, see the BUC Used Boat Price Guide, Volume 3

W D SCHOCK CORP

CORONA CA 92883 COAST GUARD MFG ID- WDS See inside cover to adjust price for area

For more recent years, see the BUC Used Boat Price Guide, Volume 1

LOA FT	LOA IN	NAME AND/ OR MODEL	TOP/ RIG	BOAT TYPE	HULL MTL	HULL TP	ENGINE TP	# HP	ENGINE MFG	BEAM FT	BEAM IN	WGT LBS	DRAFT FT	DRAFT IN	RETAIL LOW	RETAIL HIGH
		1996 BOATS														
20	3	SANTANA 20	SLP	SACAC	FBG	KL				8		1350	4		6150	7050
33	9	SCHOCK 34 PERFM CR	SLP	SACAC	FBG	KL	IB	27D	YAN	11	6	10350	6	5	51600	56800
35		SCHOCK 35	SLP	SACAC	FBG	KL	IB	27D	YAN	11	9	10000	6	9	54500	59800
54	8	SCHOCK 55	SLP	SACAC	FBG	KL	IB	60D	GM	12	6	17600	9		345500	380000
		1995 BOATS														
20	3	SANTANA 20	SLP	SACAC	FBG	KL				8		1350	4		5800	6650
33	9	SCHOCK 34 PERFM CR	SLP	SACAC	FBG	KL	IB	27D	YAN	11	6	10350	6	5	48600	53400
35		SCHOCK 35	SLP	SACAC	FBG	KL	IB	27D	YAN	11	9	10000	6	9	51200	56300
54	8	SCHOCK 55	SLP	SACAC	FBG	KL	IB	60D	GM	12	6	17600	9		325000	357000
		1994 BOATS														
20	3	SANTANA 20	SLP	SACAC	FBG	KL				8		1350	4		5450	6250
33	9	SCHOCK 34 PERFM CR	SLP	SACAC	FBG	KL	IB	27D	YAN	11	6	10350	6	5	45900	50500
35		SCHOCK 35	SLP	SACAC	FBG	KL	IB	27D	YAN	11	9	10000	6	9	48200	52900
54	8	SCHOCK 55	SLP	SACAC	FBG	KL	IB	60D	GM	12	6	17600	9		306000	336000
		1993 BOATS														
20	4	SURF DORY		ROW	FBG					5	10	300			**	**
33	9	SCHOCK 34 PERFM CR	SLP	SACAC	FBG	KL	IB	27D	YAN	11	6	10350	6	5	42700	47400
35		SCHOCK 35	SLP	SACAC	FBG	KL	IB	27D	YAN	11	9	10000	6	9	45500	50000
54	8	SCHOCK 55	SLP	SACAC	FBG	KL	IB	60D	GM	12	6	17600	9		287500	316000
		1992 BOATS														
18		NEWPORT ELECTRIC PKT		RNBT	FBG		OB			6	6	1650	1	8	5450	6250
20	3	SANTANA 20	SLP	SAIL	FBG	KL				8		1350	4		4800	5550
20	4	SURF DORY		ROW	FBG					5	10	300			**	**
23	5	SCHOCK 23	SLP	SAIL	FBG	KL				8	6	2800	2	11	8850	10000
24		WAVELENGTH 24	SLP	SAIL	FBG	KL				9		2500	4	5	8350	9600
33	9	SCHOCK 34 PERFM CR	SLP	SAIL	FBG	KL	IB	27D	YAN	11	6	10350	6	5	40300	44700
35		SCHOCK 35	SLP	SAIL	FBG	KL	IB	27D	YAN	11	9	10000	6	9	42400	47100
54	8	SCHOCK 55	SLP	SAIL	FBG	KL	IB	60D	GM	12	6	17600	9		270500	297500
		1991 BOATS														
20	3	SANTANA 20	SLP	SAIL	FBG	KL				8		1350	4		4550	5250
23	5	SCHOCK 23	SLP	SAIL	FBG	KL				8	6	2800	2	11	8200	9450
24		WAVELENGTH 24	SLP	SAIL	FBG	KL				9		2500	4	5	7850	9050
33	9	SCHOCK 34 PERFM CR	SLP	SAIL	FBG	KL	IB	27D	YAN	11	6	9800	6	5	35900	39800
35		SCHOCK 35	SLP	SAIL	FBG	KL	IB	27D	YAN	11	9	10000	6	9	39900	44300
40	9	SCHOCK 41 GRAND PRIX	SLP	SAIL	FBG	KL	IB	42D	PATH	12	11	15800	7	6	94900	104500
55		SCHOCK 55	SLP	SAIL	FBG	KL	IB	60D	GM	12	6				287500	316000
		1990 BOATS														
20	3	SANTANA 20	SLP	SAIL	FBG	KL				8		1350	4		4250	4900
23	5	SCHOCK 23	SLP	SAIL	FBG	KL				8	6	2800	2	11	7750	8900
24		WAVELENGTH 24	SLP	SAIL	FBG	KL				9		2500	4	5	7400	8500
29	11	SANTANA 30/30	SLP	SAIL	FBG	KL	IB	18D	YAN	10	3	6800	5	6	21600	24000
29	11	SANTANA 30/30 G PRIX	SLP	SAIL	FBG	KL	IB	9D	YAN	10	3	6800	5	6	21500	23900
33	9	SCHOCK 34 PRFRMNC CR	SLP	SAIL	FBG	KL	IB	27D	YAN	11	6	9800	6	5	33700	37500
35		SCHOCK 35	SLP	SAIL	FBG	KL	IB	27D	YAN	11	9	10000	6	9	37500	41700
40	9	SCHOCK 41 GRAND PRIX	SLP	SAIL	FBG	KL	IB	42D	PATH	12	11	15800	7	6	89300	98100
		1989 BOATS														
20	3	SANTANA 20	SLP	SAIL	FBG	KL				8		1350	4		4000	4650
23	5	SCHOCK 23	SLP	SAIL	FBG	KL				8	6	2800	2	11	7250	8350
24		WAVELENGTH 24	SLP	SAIL	FBG	KL	OB			9		2500	4	5	6950	8000
29	11	SANTANA 30/30	SLP	SAIL	FBG	KL	IB	18D	YAN	10	3	6800	5	6	20300	22600
29	11	SANTANA 30/30 G PRIX	SLP	SAIL	FBG	KL	IB	9D	YAN	10	3	6800	5	6	20200	22500
33	9	SCHOCK 34 PRFRMNC CR	SLP	SAIL	FBG	KL	IB	27D	YAN	11	6	9800	6	5	31700	35200
35		SCHOCK 35	SLP	SAIL	FBG	KL	IB	27D	YAN	11	9	10000	6	9	35300	39200

LOA FT	LOA IN	NAME AND/ OR MODEL	TOP/ RIG	BOAT TYPE	-HULL- MTL	-HULL- TP	ENGINE TP	# HP	MFG	BEAM FT	BEAM IN	WGT LBS	DRAFT FT	DRAFT IN	RETAIL LOW	RETAIL HIGH
		1989 BOATS														
40	9	SCHOCK 41 GRAND PRIX	SLP	SAIL	FBG	KL	IB	42D	PATH	12	11	15800	7	6	84000	92300
		1988 BOATS														
20	3	SANTANA 20	SLP	SAIL	FBG	KL				8		1350	4		3750	4350
23	5	SCHOCK 23	SLP	SAIL	FBG	KL				8	6	2800	2	11	6850	7850
24		WAVELENGTH 24	SLP	SAIL	FBG	KL	OB			9		2500	4	5	6550	7550
29	11	SANTANA 30/30	SLP	SAIL	FBG	KL	IB	18D	YAN	10	3	6800	5	6	19100	21200
29	11	SANTANA 30/30 G PRIX	SLP	SAIL	FBG	KL	IB	9D	YAN	10	3	6800	5	6	19200	21300
33	9	SCHOCK 34 GRAND PRIX	SLP	SAIL	FBG	KL	IB	18D	YAN	11	6	8500	6	5	25800	28700
33	9	SCHOCK 34 PRFRMNC CR	SLP	SAIL	FBG	KL	IB	27D	YAN	11	6	9800	6	5	29800	33200
35		SCHOCK 35	SLP	SAIL	FBG	KL	IB	27D	YAN	11	9	10000	6	9	33200	36900
35	8	NEW YORK 36	SLP	SAIL	FBG	KL	IB	18D	YAN	11	8	10500	6	4	36400	40500
40	9	SCHOCK 41 GRAND PRIX	SLP	SAIL	FBG	KL	IB	42D	PATH	12	11	15800	7	6	79000	86800
		1986 BOATS														
18		EDISON 18	OP	LNCH	FBG	DS	EL	3		6	10	1500	1	2	**	**
18		NEWPORT ELEC PACKET	OP	LNCH	FBG	DS	EL	3		6	5	1650	1	2	**	**
20	2	SANTANA 20	SLP	SA/OD	FBG	KL	OB			8		1350	4		3300	3850
23	4	SANTANA 23D	SLP	SA/RC	FBG	KL				8	10		5	3	6450	7400
23	4	SANTANA 23K	SLP	SA/RC	FBG	KL				8	10		4	6	5650	6450
24		WAVELENGTH 24	SLP	SA/RC	FBG	KL	OB			9		2500	4	5	5800	6650
29	11	SANTANA 30/30	SLP	SA/RC	FBG	KL	IB	D		10	3	6800	5	6	18500	20500
29	11	SCHOCK 30/30 GP	SLP	SA/RC	FBG	KL	IB	D		10	3	6800	5	6	15300	17400
34		SCHOCK 34 GP	SLP	SA/RC	F/S	KL	IB	D		6	6				27300	30300
34		SCHOCK 34 GP PERFORM	SLP	SA/RC	F/S	KL	IB	D		6	6				27300	30300
35		SCHOCK 35	SLP	SA/RC	F/S	KL	IB	D		11	10	10000	6	10	29200	32500
35	8	NEW YORK 36	SLP	SA/RC	F/S	KL	IB	D		11	8	10500	6	4	32300	35800
40	9	SCHOCK 41 GP	SLP	SA/RC	F/S	KL	IB	D		12	11	15800	7	6	69900	76800
		1985 BOATS														
18		EDISON 18	OP	LNCH	FBG		EL	3		6	10	1500	1	2	**	**
18		NEWPORT ELEC PACKET	ST	LNCH	FBG		EL	3		6	5	1650	1	2	**	**
18		NEWPORT ELEC PACKET	HT	LNCH	FBG		EL	3		6	5	1650			**	**
20	2	SANTANA 20	SLP	SA/OD	FBG	KL	OB			8		1350	4		3100	3600
20	4	LIFEGUARD DORY	OP	ROW	FBG	FL				5	10	300			**	**
23	4	SANTANA 23	SLP	SA/RC	FBG	KL	OB			8	10	2450	4	6	5150	5900
23	4	SANTANA 23	SLP	SA/RC	FBG	SK						2600			5350	6150
24		WAVELENGTH 24	SLP	SA/RC	FBG	KL	OB			9		2500	4	5	5450	6250
24	7	SANTANA 525	SLP	SA/RC	FBG	KL	OB			9	4	2400	4	6	5400	6200
29	11	SANTANA 30/30	SLP	SA/RC	FBG	KL	IB	D		10	3	6800	5	6	15700	17800
29	11	SCHOCK 30/30 GP	SLP	SA/RC	FBG	KL	IB	D		10	3	6800	5	6	15700	17800
35		SCHOCK 35	SLP	SA/RC	F/S	KL	IB	22D		11	10	10000	6	10	27500	30500
35		WAVELENGTH 35	SLP	SA/RC	FBG	KL	IB	D		11	11	9000	6	3	24800	27600
35	8	NEW-YORK 36	SLP	SA/RC	F/S	KL	IB	15D	VLVO	11	8	10500	6	4	30200	33600
40	9	SCHOCK 41 GP	SLP	SA/RC	F/S	KL	IB	42D	PATH	12	11	15800	7	6	65700	72200
		1984 BOATS														
18		EDISON 18	OP	LNCH	FBG	DS	EL	5		6	5	1650			**	**
18		HARD TOP	HT	LNCH	FBG	DS	EL	5		6	5	1650			**	**
18		NEWPORT-PACKET	OP	LNCH	FBG	DS	EL	3		6	5	1650	1	8	**	**
18		SURREY	OP	LNCH	FBG	DS	EL	5		6	5	1650			**	**
20	3	SANTANA 20	SLP	SA/OD	FBG	KL				8		1350	4		2900	3400
23	4	SANTANA 23	SLP	SA/RC	FBG	DB				8	10	2600		10	5050	5800
23	4	SANTANA 23 K	SLP	SA/RC	FBG	KL				8	10	2450	4	6	4850	5550
24		WAVELENGTH 24	SLP	SA/RC	FBG	KL				9		2500	4	5	5150	5900
24	7	SANTANA 525	SLP	SA/RC	FBG	KL				9	4	2400	4	6	5150	5900
29	11	SANTANA 30/30 GP	SLP	SA/RC	FBG	KL	IB	7D	BMW	10	3	6000	5	6	12900	14700
29	11	SANTANA 30/30 PC	SLP	SA/CR	FBG	KL	IB	15D	VLVO	10	3	6800	5	6	14700	16700
29	11	SANTANA 30/30 RC	SLP	SA/RC	FBG	KL				10	3	6000	5	6	13000	14800
29	11	WAVELENGTH 30	SLP	SA/RC	FBG	KL	IB			10		7000	5	4	15000	17100
35		SANTANA 35	SLP	SA/RC	FBG	KL	IB	15D	VLVO	11	11	8500	6	3	22000	24400
35		WAVELENGTH 35	SLP	SA/RC	FBG	KL	IB			11	11	9000	6	9	23100	25600
35	8	NEW-YORK 36	SLP	SA/RC	FBG	KL	IB	15D	VLVO	11	8	10000	6	4	27200	30200
40	9	SCHOCK 41	SLP	SA/CR	FBG	KL	IB	42D	PATH	12	11	17300	7	6	65600	72100
40	9	SCHOCK 41 GP	SLP	SA/RC	FBG	KL	IB	42D	PATH	12	11	15800	7	6	61800	67900

....For earlier years, see the BUC Used Boat Price Guide, Volume 3

SCHOECHL YACHTS

AUSTRIA

See inside cover to adjust price for area

For more recent years, see the BUC Used Boat Price Guide, Volume 1

LOA FT	LOA IN	NAME AND/ OR MODEL	TOP/ RIG	BOAT TYPE	-HULL- MTL	-HULL- TP	ENGINE TP	# HP	MFG	BEAM FT	BEAM IN	WGT LBS	DRAFT FT	DRAFT IN	RETAIL LOW	RETAIL HIGH
		1996 BOATS														
25		SUNBEAM 25	SLP	SACAC	FBG	KC	IB	10D	YAN	8	2	3700	3	5	33600	37300
25		SUNBEAM 25	SLP	SACAC	FBG	KL	IB	10D	YAN	8	2	3700	3	5	33600	37300
27	4	SUNBEAM 27	SLP	SACAC	FBG	KC	IB	18D	YAN	8	4	4800	3	6	45600	50100
27	4	SUNBEAM 27	SLP	SACAC	FBG	KL	IB	9D	YAN	8	4	4800	3	6	44600	49600
29		SUNBEAM 29	SLP	SACAC	FBG	KL	IB	18D	YAN						72400	79600
34	3	SUNBEAM 34	SLP	SACAC	FBG	KL	IB	27D	YAN	11	4	13000	5	2	121000	133000
40		SUNBEAM 39	SLP	SACAC	FBG	KL	IB	36D	YAN	12		19000	5	6	188000	206500
44		SUNBEAM 44	SLP	SACAC	FBG	KL	IB	60D	YAN	13	1	18600	5	7	215500	236500
		1995 BOATS														
25		SUNBEAM 25	SLP	SACAC	FBG	KC	IB	10D	YAN	8	2	3700	3	5	31600	35100
25		SUNBEAM 25	SLP	SACAC	FBG	KL	IB	10D	YAN	8	2	3700	3	5	31600	35100
27	4	SUNBEAM 27	SLP	SACAC	FBG	KC	IB	18D	YAN	8	4	4800	3	6	42400	47100
27	4	SUNBEAM 27	SLP	SACAC	FBG	KL	IB	9D	YAN	8	4	4800	3	6	41900	46600
29		SUNBEAM 29	SLP	SACAC	FBG	KL	IB	18D	YAN						68100	74800
34	3	SUNBEAM 34	SLP	SACAC	FBG	KL	IB	27D	YAN	11	4	13000	5	2	113500	125000
36	5	SUNBEAM MSII	SLP	MS	FBG	KL	IB	48D	YAN	11	6	17000	4	9	146000	160000
37		SUNBEAM 37/40	SLP	SACAC	FBG	KL	IB	34D	YAN	11	4	14500	5	4	128000	140500
40		SUNBEAM 39	SLP	SACAC	FBG	KL	IB	36D	YAN	12		19000	5	6	176000	193500
44		SUNBEAM 44	SLP	SACAC	FBG	KL	IB	60D	YAN	13	1	18600	5	7	202000	222000
		1994 BOATS														
25		SUNBEAM 25	SLP	SACAC	FBG	KC	IB	10D	YAN	8	2	3700	3	5	29700	33000
25		SUNBEAM 25	SLP	SACAC	FBG	KL	IB	10D	YAN	8	2	3700	3	5	29700	33000
27	4	SUNBEAM 27	SLP	SACAC	FBG	KC	IB	18D	YAN	8	4	4800	3	6	39900	44300
27	4	SUNBEAM 27	SLP	SACAC	FBG	KL	IB	9D	YAN	8	4	4800	3	6	39400	43800
29		SUNBEAM 29	SLP	SACAC	FBG	KL	IB	18D	YAN						64000	70300
34	3	SUNBEAM 34	SLP	SACAC	FBG	KL	IB	27D	YAN	11	4	13000	5	2	107000	117500
36	5	SUNBEAM MSII	SLP	MS	FBG	KL	IB	48D	YAN	11	6	17000	4	9	137000	150500
37		SUNBEAM 37/40	SLP	SACAC	FBG	KL	IB	34D	YAN	11	4	14500	5	4	120000	132000
40		SUNBEAM 39	SLP	SACAC	FBG	KL	IB	36D	YAN	12		19000	5	6	165000	181000
44		SUNBEAM 44	SLP	SACAC	FBG	KL	IB	60D	YAN	13	1	18600	5	7	190000	208500
		1993 BOATS														
25		SUNBEAM 25	SLP	SACAC	FBG	KC	IB	10D	YAN	8	2	3700	3	5	28000	31100
25		SUNBEAM 25	SLP	SACAC	FBG	KL	IB	10D	YAN	8	2	3700	3	5	28000	31100
27	4	SUNBEAM 27	SLP	SACAC	FBG	KC	IB	18D	YAN	8	4	4800	3	6	37500	41700
27	4	SUNBEAM 27	SLP	SACAC	FBG	KL	IB	9D	YAN	8	4	4800	3	6	37100	41200
29		SUNBEAM 29	SLP	SACAC	FBG	KL	IB	18D	YAN						60200	66200
34	3	SUNBEAM 34	SLP	SACAC	FBG	KL	IB	27D	YAN	11	4	13000	5	2	100500	110500
36	5	SUNBEAM MSII	SLP	MS	FBG	KL	IB	48D	YAN	11	6	17000	4	9	128500	141000
37		SUNBEAM 37/40	SLP	SACAC	FBG	KL	IB	34D	YAN	11	4	14500	5	4	112500	124000
44		SUNBEAM 44	SLP	SACAC	FBG	KL	IB	60D	YAN						178500	196000
		1992 BOATS														
25		SUNBEAM 25	SLP	SA/CR	FBG	KC	IB	10D	YAN	8	2	3700	3	5	26300	29200
25		SUNBEAM 25	SLP	SA/CR	FBG	KL	IB	10D	YAN	8	2	3700	3	5	26300	29200
27	4	SUNBEAM 27	SLP	SA/CR	FBG	KC	IB	18D	VLVO	8	4	4800	3	6	35200	39100
27	4	SUNBEAM 27	SLP	SA/CR	FBG	KL	IB	9D	YAN	8	4	4800	3	6	34900	38800
34	3	SUNBEAM 34	SLP	SA/CR	FBG	KL	IB	27D-	34D	11	4	13000	5	2	94400	104000
37		SUNBEAM 37/40	SLP	SA/CR	FBG	KL	IB	34D	VLVO	11	4	14500	5	4	106000	116500
37		SUNBEAM 37/40	SLP	SA/CR	FBG	KL	IB	34D	YAN	11	4	14500	5	4	106000	116500
38	5	SUNBEAM MSII	SLP	MS	FBG	KL	IB	48D	YAN	11	6	17000	4	9	125500	138000
		1991 BOATS														
25		SUNBEAM 25	SLP	SA/CR	FBG	KC	IB	10D	YAN	8	2	3700	3	5	24700	27500
25		SUNBEAM 25	SLP	SA/CR	FBG	KL	IB	10D	YAN	8	2	3700	3	5	24700	27500
27	4	SUNBEAM 27	SLP	SA/CR	FBG	KC	IB	18D	VLVO	8	4	4800	3	6	33100	36800
27	4	SUNBEAM 27	SLP	SA/CR	FBG	KL	IB	9D	YAN	8	4	4800	3	6	32800	36500
30		SUNBEAM 30	SLP	SA/CR	FBG	KL	IB	18D-	27D	9	8	7500	4	10	53200	58600
34	3	SUNBEAM 34	SLP	SA/CR	FBG	KL	IB	27D-	34D	11	4	13000	5	2	88700	97700
37		SUNBEAM 37/40	SLP	SA/CR	FBG	KL	IB	34D	VLVO	11	4	14500	5	4	99400	109000
37		SUNBEAM 37/40	SLP	SA/CR	FBG	KL	IB	34D	YAN	11	4	14500	5	4	99500	109500
		1990 BOATS														
25		SUNBEAM 25	SLP	SA/CR	FBG	KC	IB	10D	YAN	8	2	3700	3	5	23300	25800
25		SUNBEAM 25	SLP	SA/CR	FBG	KL	IB	10D	YAN	8	2	3700	3	5	23300	25800
27	4	SUNBEAM 27	SLP	SA/CR	FBG	KC	IB	18D	VLVO	8	4	4800	3	6	31100	34600
27	4	SUNBEAM 27	SLP	SA/CR	FBG	KL	IB	9D	YAN	8	4	4800	3	6	30900	34300
30		SUNBEAM 30	SLP	SA/CR	FBG	KL	IB	18D-	27D	9	8	7500	4	10	50000	55100
32	3	SUNBEAM 32	SLP	SA/CR	FBG	KL	IB	20D	YAN	10		9500	4	1	63000	69200
34	3	SUNBEAM 34	SLP	SA/CR	FBG	KL	IB	27D-	34D	11	4	13000	5	2	83400	91800
37		SUNBEAM 37	SLP	SA/CR	FBG	KL	IB	34D	VLVO	11	4	14500	5	4	93300	102500
37		SUNBEAM 37	SLP	SA/CR	FBG	KL	IB	34D	YAN	11	4	14500	5	4	93500	102500
		1989 BOATS														
23		SUNBEAM 23	SLP	SA/CR	FBG	KC	IB	9D		8		3000	3	4	17400	19900
23		SUNBEAM 23	SLP	SA/CR	FBG	KL	IB	9D		8		3000	3	4	17400	19900
25		SUNBEAM 25	SLP	SA/CR	FBG	KC	IB	10D		8	2	3700	3	5	21800	24300
25		SUNBEAM 25	SLP	SA/CR	FBG	KL	IB	10D		8	2	3700	3	5	21800	24300
27		SUNBEAM 27	SLP	SA/CR	FBG	KL	IB	9D	VLVO	8	4	4800	3	6	28800	32000
27	4	SUNBEAM 27	SLP	SA/CR	FBG	KC	IB	18D		8	4	4800	3	6	29300	32600
27	4	SUNBEAM 27	SLP	SA/CR	FBG	KL	IB	9D	YAN	8	4	4800	3	6	29000	32300
30		SUNBEAM 30	SLP	SA/CR	FBG	KL	IB	18D-	27D	9	8	7500	4	10	47300	52100
32	3	SUNBEAM 32	SLP	SA/CR	FBG	KL	IB	20D	YAN	10		9500	4	1	59200	65100
34	3	SUNBEAM 34	SLP	SA/CR	FBG	KL	IB	27D-	34D	11	4	13000	5	2	78400	86300
37		SUNBEAM 37	SLP	SA/CR	FBG	KL	IB	34D	VLVO	11	4	14500	5	4	87700	96300

LOA FT	LOA IN	NAME AND/ OR MODEL	TOP/ RIG	BOAT TYPE	HULL MTL	HULL TP	ENGINE TP	# HP	ENGINE MFG	BEAM FT	BEAM IN	WGT LBS	DRAFT FT	DRAFT IN	RETAIL LOW	RETAIL HIGH
		1989 BOATS														
37		SUNBEAM 37	SLP	SA/CR	FBG	KL	IB	34D	YAN	11	4	14500	5	4	87800	96500
		1988 BOATS														
23		SUNBEAM 23	SLP	SA/CR	FBG	KC	IB	9D		8		3000	3	4	16400	18800
23		SUNBEAM 23	SLP	SA/CR	FBG	KL	IB	9D		8		3000	3	4	16400	18800
25		SUNBEAM 25	SLP	SA/CR	FBG	KC	IB	10D		8	2	3700	3	5	20500	22900
25		SUNBEAM 25	SLP	SA/CR	FBG	KL	IB	10D		8	2	3700	3	5	20500	22900
27		SUNBEAM 27	SLP	SA/CR	FBG	KL	IB	9D	VLVO	8	4	4800	3	6	27100	30100
27	4	SUNBEAM 27	SLP	SA/CR	FBG	KC	IB	18D		8	4	4800	3	6	27500	30700
27	4	SUNBEAM 27	SLP	SA/CR	FBG	KL	IB	9D	YAN	8	4	4800	3	6	27300	30300
30		SUNBEAM 30	SLP	SA/CR	FBG	KL	IB	18D-	27D	9	8	7500	4	10	44000	49000
34	3	SUNBEAM 34	SLP	SA/CR	FBG	KL	IB	27D-	34D	11	4	13000	5	2	73700	81200
37		SUNBEAM 37	SLP	SA/CR	FBG	KL	IB	34D	VLVO	11	4	14500	5	4	82400	90500
37		SUNBEAM 37	SLP	SA/CR	FBG	KL	IB	34D	YAN	11	4	14500	5	4	82500	90600
		1987 BOATS														
23		SUNBEAM 23	SLP	SA/CR	FBG	KC	IB	9	VLVO	8		3000	3	4	14000	15900
23		SUNBEAM 23	SLP	SA/CR	FBG	KC	IB	9D	YAN	8		3000	3	4	15500	17600
23		SUNBEAM 23	SLP	SA/CR	FBG	KL	IB	9D		8		3000	3	4	15400	17600
25		SUNBEAM 25	SLP	SA/CR	FBG	KC	IB	10D		8	2	3700	3	5	19300	21500
25		SUNBEAM 25	SLP	SA/CR	FBG	KL	IB	10D		8	2	3700	3	5	19300	21500
27		SUNBEAM 27	SLP	SA/CR	FBG	KL	IB	9D	VLVO	8	4	4800	3	6	25500	28300
27	4	SUNBEAM 27	SLP	SA/CR	FBG	KC	IB	18	YAN	8	4	4800	3	6	25100	27900
27	4	SUNBEAM 27	SLP	SA/CR	FBG	KC	IB	18D	VLVO	8	4	4800	3	6	25900	28800
27	4	SUNBEAM 27	SLP	SA/CR	FBG	KL	IB	9D	YAN	8	4	4800	3	6	25700	28500
30		SUNBEAM 30	SLP	SA/CR	FBG	KL	IB	18D-	27D	9	8	7500	4	10	41400	46100
34	3	SUNBEAM 34	SLP	SA/CR	FBG	KL	IB	27D-	34D	11	4	13000	5	2	69300	76300
37		SUNBEAM 37	SLP	SA/CR	FBG	KL	IB	34D	VLVO	11	4	14500	5	4	77400	85000
37		SUNBEAM 37	SLP	SA/CR	FBG	KL	IB	34D	YAN	11	4	14500	5	4	77500	85100

SCHULZ BOAT CO LLC

BRISTOL RI 02809 COAST GUARD MFG ID- NHN See inside cover to adjust price for area
FORMERLY SHANNON YACHTS

For more recent years, see the BUC Used Boat Price Guide, Volume 1

LOA FT	LOA IN	NAME AND/ OR MODEL	TOP/ RIG	BOAT TYPE	HULL MTL	HULL TP	ENGINE TP	# HP	ENGINE MFG	BEAM FT	BEAM IN	WGT LBS	DRAFT FT	DRAFT IN	RETAIL LOW	RETAIL HIGH
		1996 BOATS														
28	2	SHANNON 28	CUT	SACAC	FBG	KL	IB	27D	YAN	9	6	9300	4	3	97900	107500
35	7	VOYAGER 36	FB	SDN	FBG	DV	IB	T300D	CAT	13	3	17000	3		182000	200000
37	9	SHANNON 37CB	CUT	SACAC	FBG	KC	IB	50D	YAN	11	6	17500	4	3	194500	213500
37	9	SHANNON 37CB	KTH	SACAC	FBG	KC	IB	50D	YAN	11	6	17500	4	3	194500	213500
38	7	SHANNON 39	CUT	SACAC	FBG	KL	IB	50D	YAN	12	2	18000	5	6	205000	225000
47	6	SHANNON 43	CUT	SACAC	FBG	KC	IB	71D	WEST	13		27500	4	9	323500	355500
47	6	SHANNON 43	KTH	SACAC	FBG	KC	IB	71D	WEST	13		27500	4	9	323500	355500
47	6	SHANNON PILOT 43	CUT	SACAC	FBG	KL	IB	71D	WEST	13		29000	4	9	332500	365500
50	11	SHANNON 50	KTH	SACAC	FBG	KC	IB	110D	YAN	14	3	39000	5	8	490000	538500
50	11	SHANNON 51 CTRCPT	KTH	SACAC	FBG	KC	IB	110D	YAN	14	3	39000	5	8	494500	543500
50	11	SHANNON AEGEAN 51	KTH	SACAC	FBG	KC	IB	110D	YAN	14	3	39000	5	8	538500	592000
		1995 BOATS														
28	2	SHANNON 28	CUT	SACAC	FBG	KL	IB	27D	YAN	9	6	9300	4	3	92700	102000
35	7	VOYAGER 36	FB	SDN	FBG	DV	IB	T300D	CAT	13	3	17000	3		172500	189500
37	9	SHANNON 37CB	CUT	SACAC	FBG	KC	IB	50D	YAN	11	6	17500	4	3	184000	202500
37	9	SHANNON 37CB	KTH	SACAC	FBG	KC	IB	50D	YAN	11	6	17500	4	3	184000	202500
38	7	SHANNON 39	CUT	SACAC	FBG	KL	IB	50D	YAN	12	2	18000	5	6	194000	213000
47	6	SHANNON 43	CUT	SACAC	FBG	KC	IB	71D	WEST	13		27500	4	9	306500	337000
47	6	SHANNON 43	KTH	SACAC	FBG	KC	IB	71D	WEST	13		27500	4	9	306500	337000
47	6	SHANNON PILOT 43	CUT	SACAC	FBG	KL	IB	71D	WEST	13		29000	4	9	315000	346000
50	11	SHANNON 50	KTH	SACAC	FBG	KC	IB	110D	YAN	14	3	39000	5	8	462500	508000
50	11	SHANNON 51 CTRCPT	KTH	SACAC	FBG	KC	IB	110D	YAN	14	3	39000	5	8	466000	512000
50	11	SHANNON AEGEAN 51	KTH	SACAC	FBG	KC	IB	110D	YAN	14	3	39000	5	8	514000	564500
		1994 BOATS														
28	2	SHANNON 28	CUT	SACAC	FBG	KL	IB	27D	YAN	9	6	9300	4	3	87800	96500
35	7	VOYAGER 36	FB	SDN	FBG	DV	IB	T300D	CAT	13	3	17000	3		164000	180500
37	9	SHANNON 37CB	CUT	SACAC	FBG	KC	IB	50D	YAN	11	6	17500	4	3	174500	191500
37	9	SHANNON 37CB	KTH	SACAC	FBG	KC	IB	50D	YAN	11	6	17500	4	3	174500	191500
38	7	SHANNON 39	CUT	SACAC	FBG	KL	IB	50D	YAN	12	2	18000	5	6	183500	202000
47	6	SHANNON 43	CUT	SACAC	FBG	KC	IB	62D	WEST	14		27500	4	9	290000	318500
47	6	SHANNON 43	KTH	SACAC	FBG	KC	IB	62D	WEST	14		27500	4	9	290000	318500
50	11	SHANNON 50	KTH	SACAC	FBG	KC	IB	110D	YAN	14	3	39000	5	8	438000	481500
50	11	SHANNON 51 CTRCPT	KTH	SACAC	FBG	KC	IB	110D	YAN	14	3	39000	5	8	441000	485000
50	11	SHANNON AEGEAN 51	KTH	SACAC	FBG	KC	IB	110D	YAN	14	3	39000	5	8	486500	535000
		1993 BOATS														
28	2	SHANNON 28	CUT	SACAC	FBG	KL	IB	15D	YAN	9	6	9300	4	3	82700	90900
28	8	BRENDAN 28 SPORT FSH	OP	SF	FBG	DV	IB	T220	CRUS	11	3	9600	2	4	54800	60200
32	10	BRENDAN 32 SPORT FSH	OP	SF	FBG	DV	IB	T205D	GM	12		11500	2	9	98600	108500
32	10	BRENDAN 32 SPORT SDN	OP	SDNSF	FBG	DV	IB	T205D	GM	12		13500	2	9	108000	119000
35	7	VOYAGER 36	FB	SDN	FBG	DV	IB	T255D	CAT	13	3	17000	3		188000	207000
37	9	SHANNON 37CB	CUT	SACAC	FBG	KC	IB	44D	YAN	11	6	17500	4	3	165000	181000
37	9	SHANNON 37CB	KTH	SACAC	FBG	KC	IB	44D	YAN	11	6	17500	4	3	165000	181000
37	9	SHANNON 38	CUT	SACAC	FBG	KL	IB	44D	YAN	11	6	18500	5		155000	170500
37	9	SHANNON 38	KTH	SACAC	FBG	KL	IB	44D	YAN	11	6	18500	5		172500	189500
37	9	SHANNON PILOT 38	CUT	SACAC	FBG	KL	IB	44D	YAN	11	6	18500	5		189500	208500
47	6	SHANNON 43	CUT	SACAC	FBG	KC	IB	58D	WEST	14		27500	4	9	274000	301500
47	6	SHANNON 43	KTH	SACAC	FBG	KC	IB	58D	WEST	14		27500	4	9	274500	301500
50	11	SHANNON 50	KTH	SACAC	FBG	KC	IB	110D	YAN	14	3	39000	5	8	417000	458000
50	11	SHANNON 51 CTRCPT	KTH	SACAC	FBG	KC	IB	110D	YAN	14	3	39000	5	8	427000	469000
50	11	SHANNON AEGEAN 51	KTH	SACAC	FBG	KC	IB	110D	YAN	14	3	39000	5	8	449500	494000
		1992 BOATS														
28	2	SHANNON 28	CUT	SA/CR	FBG	KL	IB	15D	YAN	9	6	9300	4	3	78300	86100
28	8	BRENDAN 28 SPORT FSH	OP	SF	FBG	DV	IB	T220	CRUS	11	3	9600	2	4	52200	57400
32	10	BRENDAN 32 SPORT FSH	OP	SF	FBG	DV	IB	T205D	GM	12		11500	2	9	94000	103000
32	10	BRENDAN 32 SPORT SDN	OP	SDNSF	FBG	DV	IB	T205D	GM	12		13500	2	9	103000	113500
35	7	VOYAGER 36	FB	SDN	FBG	DV	IB	T250D	GM	13	3	17000	3		176500	194000
37	9	SHANNON 37CB	CUT	SA/CR	FBG	KC	IB	44D	YAN	11	6	17500	4	3	156000	171500
37	9	SHANNON 37CB	KTH	SA/CR	FBG	KC	IB	44D	YAN	11	6	17500	4	3	156000	171500
37	9	SHANNON 38	CUT	SA/CR	FBG	KL	IB	44D	YAN	11	6	18500	5		147000	161500
37	9	SHANNON 38	KTH	SA/CR	FBG	KL	IB	44D	YAN	11	6	18500	5		163000	179500
37	9	SHANNON PILOT 38	CUT	SA/CR	FBG	KL	IB	44D	YAN	11	6	18500	5		179500	197500
47	6	SHANNON 43	CUT	SA/CR	FBG	KC	IB	58D	WEST	13		27500	4	9	260000	285500
47	6	SHANNON 43	KTH	SA/CR	FBG	KC	IB	58D	WEST	13		27500	4	9	260000	285500
50	11	SHANNON 50	KTH	SA/CR	FBG	KC	IB	110D	YAN	14	3	39000	5	8	395000	434000
50	11	SHANNON 51 CTRCPT	KTH	SA/CR	FBG	KC	IB	110D	YAN	14	3	39000	5	8	404500	444500
50	11	SHANNON AEGEAN 51	KTH	SA/CR	FBG	KC	IB	110D	YAN	14	3	39000	5	8	426000	468000
		1991 BOATS														
28	2	SHANNON 28	CUT	SA/CR	FBG	KL	IB	15D	YAN	9	6	9300	4	3	74200	81500
28	8	BRENDAN 28 SPORT FSH	OP	SF	FBG	DV	IB	T220	CRUS	11	3	9600	2	4	49600	54500
32	10	BRENDAN 32 SPORT FSH	OP	SF	FBG	DV	IB	T205D	GM	12		11500	2	9	89600	98400
32	10	BRENDAN 32 SPORT SDN	OP	SDNSF	FBG	DV	IB	T205D	GM	12		13500	2	9	98400	108000
35	7	VOYAGER 36	FB	SDN	FBG	DV	IB	T250D	GM	13	3	17000	3		168000	185000
37	9	SHANNON 37CB	CUT	SA/CR	FBG	KC	IB	44D	YAN	11	6	17500	4	3	148000	162500
37	9	SHANNON 37CB	KTH	SA/CR	FBG	KC	IB	44D	YAN	11	6	17500	4	3	148000	162500
37	9	SHANNON 38	CUT	SA/CR	FBG	KL	IB	44D	YAN	11	6	18500	5		139000	153000
37	9	SHANNON 38	KTH	SA/CR	FBG	KL	IB	44D	YAN	11	6	18500	5		154500	170000
37	9	SHANNON PILOT 38	CUT	SA/CR	FBG	KL	IB	44D	YAN	11	6	18500	5		170000	187000
47	6	SHANNON 43	CUT	SA/CR	FBG	KC	IB	58D	WEST	13		27500	4	9	246000	270500
47	6	SHANNON 43	KTH	SA/CR	FBG	KC	IB	58D	WEST	13		27500	4	9	246000	270500
50	11	SHANNON 50	KTH	SA/CR	FBG	KC	IB	110D	YAN	14	3	39000	5	8	374000	411000
50	11	SHANNON 51 CTRCPT	KTH	SA/CR	FBG	KC	IB	110D	YAN	14	3	39000	5	8	383000	421000
50	11	SHANNON AEGEAN 51	KTH	SA/CR	FBG	KC	IB	110D	YAN	14	3	39000	5	8	403500	443500
		1990 BOATS														
28	2	SHANNON 28	CUT	SA/CR	FBG	KL	IB	15D	YAN	9	6	9300	4	3	70300	77200
28	8	BRENDAN 28 SPORT FSH	OP	SF	FBG	DV	IB	T220	CRUS	11	3	9600	2	4	47200	51900
32	10	BRENDAN 32 SPORT FSH	OP	SF	FBG	DV	IB	T205D	GM	12		11500	2	9	85500	94000
32	10	BRENDAN 32 SPORT SDN	FB	SDNSF	FBG	DV	IB	T205D	GM	12		13500	2	9	94500	104000
35	7	VOYAGER 36	FB	SDN	FBG	DV	IB	T250D	GM	13	3	17000	3		160500	176500
37	9	SHANNON 37CB	CUT	SA/CR	FBG	KC	IB	44D	YAN	11	6	17500	4	3	140000	154000
37	9	SHANNON 37CB	KTH	SA/CR	FBG	KC	IB	44D	YAN	11	6	17500	4	3	140000	154000
37	9	SHANNON 38	CUT	SA/CR	FBG	KL	IB	44D	YAN	11	6	18500	5		132000	145000
37	9	SHANNON 38	KTH	SA/CR	FBG	KL	IB	44D	YAN	11	6	18500	5		146500	161000
37	9	SHANNON PILOT 38	CUT	SA/CR	FBG	KL	IB	44D	YAN	11	6	18500	5		161000	177000
47	6	SHANNON 43	CUT	SA/CR	FBG	KC	IB	58D	WEST	13		27500	4	9	233000	256000
47	6	SHANNON 43	KTH	SA/CR	FBG	KC	IB	58D	WEST	13		27500	4	9	233000	256000
50	11	SHANNON 50	KTH	SA/CR	FBG	KC	IB	110D	YAN	14	3	39000	5	8	350500	385000
50	11	SHANNON 51 CTRCPT	KTH	SA/CR	FBG	KC	IB	110D	YAN	14	3	39000	5	8	353500	388500
50	11	SHANNON AEGEAN 51	KTH	SA/CR	FBG	KC	IB	110D	YAN	14	3	39000	5	8	396000	435000
		1989 BOATS														
28	2	SHANNON 28	CUT	SA/CR	FBG	KL	IB	15D	YAN	9	6	9300	4	3	66600	73200
28	8	BRENDAN 28 SPORT FSH	OP	SF	FBG	DV	IB	T220	CRUS	11	3	9600	2	4	44200	49100
32	10	BRENDAN 32 SPORT FSH	OP	SF	FBG	DV	IB	T205D	GM	12		11500	2	9	81700	89800
32	10	BRENDAN 32 SPORT SDN	FB	SDNSF	FBG	DV	IB	T205D	GM	12		13500	2	9	90300	99300
37	9	SHANNON 37CB	CUT	SA/CR	F/S	KC	IB	44D	YAN	11	6	17500	4	3	133000	146000
37	9	SHANNON 37CB	KTH	SA/CR	F/S	KC	IB	44D	YAN	11	6	17500	4	3	133000	146000
37	9	SHANNON 38	CUT	SA/CR	FBG	KL	IB	44D	YAN	11	6	18500	5		126500	139000
37	9	SHANNON 38	KTH	SA/CR	FBG	KL	IB	44D	YAN	11	6	18500	5		138500	152500
37	9	SHANNON PILOT 38	CUT	SA/CR	FBG	KL	IB	44D	YAN	11	6	18500	5		151000	166000
47	6	SHANNON 43	CUT	SA/CR	F/S	KC	IB	66D	YAN	13		27500	4	9	221000	243000
47	6	SHANNON 43	KTH	SA/CR	F/S	KC	IB	66D	YAN	13		27500	4	9	221000	243000
50	11	SHANNON 50	KTH	SA/CR	F/S	KC	IB	110D	YAN	14	3	39000	5	8	341500	375000

CONTINUED ON NEXT PAGE

LOA FT IN	NAME AND/ OR MODEL	TOP/ RIG	BOAT TYPE	-HULL- MTL TP	----ENGINE--- TP # HP MFG	BEAM FT IN	WGT LBS	DRAFT FT IN	RETAIL LOW	RETAIL HIGH
	--------------- 1989 BOATS									
50 11	SHANNON 51 CTRCPT	KTH	SA/CR	F/S KC	IB 110D YAN	14 3	39000	5 8	347500	381500
50 11	SHANNON AEGEAN 51	SA	SA/CR	F/S KC	IB 110D YAN	14 3	39000	5 8	353500	388500
	--------------- 1988 BOATS									
28 2	SHANNON 28	CUT	SA/CR	FBG KL	IB 15D YAN	9 6	9300	4 3	63100	69300
28 8	BRENDAN 28 SPORT FSH	OP	SF	FBG DV	IB T270 CRUS	11 3	9600	2 4	42800	47500
32 10	BRENDAN 32 SPORT FSH	OP	SF	FBG DV	IB T270 CRUS	12	11500	2 9	62200	68300
32 10	BRENDAN 32 SPORT SDN	FB	SDNSF	FBG DV	IB T270 CRUS	12	13500	2 9	70700	77700
37 9	SHANNON 37CB	CUT	SA/CR	F/S KC	IB 44D YAN	11 6	17500	4 3	126000	138000
37 9	SHANNON 37CB	KTH	SA/CR	F/S KC	IB 44D YAN	11 6	17500	4 3	126000	138000
37 9	SHANNON 38	CUT	SA/CR	FBG KL	IB 44D YAN	11 6	18500	5	131500	144500
37 9	SHANNON 38	KTH	SA/CR	FBG KL	IB 44D YAN	11 6	18500	5	131500	144500
37 9	SHANNON PILOT 38	CUT	SA/CR	FBG KL	IB 44D YAN	11 6	18500	5	131500	144500
47 6	SHANNON 43	CUT	SA/CR	F/S KC	IB 66D YAN	13	27500	4 9	209500	230000
47 6	SHANNON 43	KTH	SA/CR	F/S KC	IB 66D YAN	13	27500	4 9	209500	230000
50 11	SHANNON 50	KTH	SA/CR	F/S KC	IB 85D PERK	14 3	39000	5 8	321500	353500
50 11	SHANNON 51 CTRCPT	KTH	SA/CR	F/S KC	IB 85D PERK	14 3	39000	5 8	324500	356500
50 11	SHANNON AEGEAN 51	SA	SA/CR	F/S KC	IB 85D PERK	14 3	39000	5 8	334000	367000
	--------------- 1987 BOATS									
28 2	SHANNON 28	CUT	SA/CR	FBG KL	IB 15D YAN	9 6	9300	4 3	59800	65700
32 10	BRENDAN 32 SPORT FSH	OP	SF	FBG DV	IB T210D CUM	12	11500	2 9	74800	82200
32 10	BRENDAN 32 SPORT SDN	FB	SDNSF	FBG DV	IB T210D CUM	12	13500	2 9	83000	91200
37 9	SHANNON 37CB	CUT	SA/CR	F/S KC	IB 40D PERK	11 6	17500	4 3	118500	130000
37 9	SHANNON 37CB	KTH	SA/CR	F/S KC	IB 40D PERK	11 6	17500	4 3	118500	130000
37 9	SHANNON 38	CUT	SA/CR	FBG KL	IB 40D PERK	11 6	18500	5	116000	127500
37 9	SHANNON 38	KTH	SA/CR	FBG KL	IB 40D PERK	11 6	18500	5	123500	136000
37 9	SHANNON PILOT 38	CUT	SA/CR	FBG KL	IB 40D PERK	11 6	18500	5	131000	144000
47 6	SHANNON 43	CUT	SA/CR	F/S KC	IB 60D BENZ	13	27500	4 9	198000	217500
47 6	SHANNON 43	KTH	SA/CR	F/S KC	IB 60D BENZ	13	27500	4 9	198000	217500
50 11	SHANNON 50	KTH	SA/CR	F/S KC	IB 85D PERK	14 3	39000	5 8	305000	335500
50 11	SHANNON 51 CTRCPT	KTH	SA/CR	F/S KC	IB 85D PERK	14 3	39000	5 8	307500	337500
50 11	SHANNON AEGEAN 51	KTH	SA/CR	F/S KC	IB 85D PERK	14 3	39000	5 8	316000	347000
	--------------- 1986 BOATS									
28 2	SHANNON 28	CUT	SA/CR	FBG KL	IB 15D YAN	9 6	9300	4 3	56700	62300
37 9	SHANNON 37CB	CUT	SA/CR	F/S KC	IB 40D PERK	11 6	17500	4 3	112000	123000
37 9	SHANNON 37CB	KTH	SA/CR	F/S KC	IB 40D PERK	11 6	17500	4 3	112000	123000
37 9	SHANNON 38	CUT	SA/CR	FBG KL	IB 40D PERK	11 6	18500	5	110000	121000
37 9	SHANNON 38	KTH	SA/CR	FBG KL	IB 40D PERK	11 6	18500	5	117000	129000
37 9	SHANNON PILOT 38	CUT	SA/CR	FBG KL	IB 40D PERK	11 6	18500	5	124500	137000
47 6	SHANNON 43	CUT	SA/CR	F/S KC	IB 60D BENZ	13	27500	4 9	187500	206000
47 6	SHANNON 43	KTH	SA/CR	F/S KC	IB 60D BENZ	13	27500	4 9	187500	206000
50 11	SHANNON 50	KTH	SA/CR	F/S KC	IB 85D PERK	14 3	39000	5 8	292000	320500
50 11	SHANNON 51 CTRCPT	KTH	SA/CR	F/S KC	IB 85D PERK	14 3	39000	5 8	292000	320500
50 11	SHANNON AEGEAN 51	KTH	SA/CR	F/S KC	IB 85D PERK	14 3	39000	5 8	296000	325500
	--------------- 1985 BOATS									
28 2	SHANNON 28	CUT	SA/CR	FBG KL	IB 15D YAN	9 6	9300	4 3	53700	59000
37 9	SHANNON 38	CUT	SA/CR	FBG KL	IB 51D PERK	11 6	18500	5	107000	117500
37 9	SHANNON 38	KTH	SA/CR	FBG KL	IB 51D PERK	11 6	18500	5	111500	122500
37 9	SHANNON-PILOT 38	CUT	SA/CR	FBG KL	IB 51D PERK	11 6	18500	5	116000	127500
47 6	SHANNON 43	CUT	SA/CR	FBG KC	IB 62D PERK	13	27500		177000	194500
47 6	SHANNON 43	CUT	SA/CR	FBG KL	IB 62D PERK	13	27500	4 9	177000	194500
47 6	SHANNON 43	KTH	SA/CR	FBG KC	IB 62D PERK	13	27500		177000	194500
47 6	SHANNON 43	KTH	SA/CR	FBG KL	IB 62D PERK	13	27500		177000	194500
50 11	SHANNON 50 AFTCPT	SCH	SA/CR	FBG KC	IB 85D PERK	14 3	39000	5 8	277500	304500
50 11	SHANNON 50 AFTCPT	KTH	SA/CR	FBG KC	IB 85D PERK	14 3	39000	5 8	277000	304500
50 11	SHANNON 50 AFTCPT	KTH	SA/CR	FBG KC	IB 85D PERK	14 3	39000	5 8	275000	302500
50 11	SHANNON 51 CTRCPT	KTH	SA/CR	FBG KC	IB 85D PERK	14 3	39000	5 8	276000	303500
50 11	SHANNON AEGEAN 51	CUT	SA/CR	FBG KC	IB 85D PERK	14 3	39000	5 8	277000	304500
50 11	SHANNON AEGEAN 51	KTH	SA/CR	FBG KC	IB 85D PERK	14 3	39000	5 8	282500	310500
	--------------- 1984 BOATS									
28 2	SHANNON 28	CUT	SA/CR	FBG KL	IB 15D YAN	9 6	9300	4 3	50900	55900
37 9	SHANNON 38	CUT	SA/CR	FBG KL	IB 40D PERK	11 6	18500	5	102000	112500
37 9	SHANNON 38	KTH	SA/CR	FBG KL	IB 40D PERK	11 6	18500	5	105500	115500
37 9	SHANNON-PILOT 38	CUT	SA/CR	FBG KL	IB 40D PERK	11 6	18500	5	108500	119000
50 11	SHANNON 50	SCH	SA/CR	FBG KC	IB D	14 3	39000	5 8	264000	290000
50 11	SHANNON 50	KTH	SA/CR	FBG KC	IB 85D PERK	14 3	39000	5 8	262000	288000
50 11	SHANNON 51 CTRCPT	KTH	SA/CR	FBG KC	IB 85D PERK	14 3	39000	5 8	262000	288000
50 11	SHANNON AEGEAN 51	KTH	SA/CR	FBG KC	IB 85D PERK	14 3	39000	5 8	266500	292500

....For earlier years, see the BUC Used Boat Price Guide, Volume 3

SCORPIO YACHTS INC
EXETER ON CANADA   COAST GUARD MFG ID- ZBV See inside cover to adjust price for area

LOA FT IN	NAME AND/ OR MODEL	TOP/ RIG	BOAT TYPE	-HULL- MTL TP	----ENGINE--- TP # HP MFG	BEAM FT IN	WGT LBS	DRAFT FT IN	RETAIL LOW	RETAIL HIGH
	--------------- 1984 BOATS									
35	SCORPIO 35	SLP	SA/CR	F/S KL	IB 23D YAN	11 2	10000	5	35500	39500
36 2	KIRBY 36	SLP	SA/RC	F/S KL	IB 23D YAN	11 4	10200	6 9	37400	41500

SCORPION POWERBOAT MFG INC
MIAMI FL 33166   COAST GUARD MFG ID- SOP See inside cover to adjust price for area

LOA FT IN	NAME AND/ OR MODEL	TOP/ RIG	BOAT TYPE	-HULL- MTL TP	----ENGINE--- TP # HP MFG	BEAM FT IN	WGT LBS	DRAFT FT IN	RETAIL LOW	RETAIL HIGH
	--------------- 1987 BOATS									
23 10	SCORPION 24SS	OP	RACE	FBG DV	OB	7	3800	1 3	10200	11600
23 10	SCORPION 24SS	OP	RACE	FBG DV	IB 260-370	7	3800	1 3	10500	12600
23 10	SCORPION 24SS	OP	RACE	FBG DV	IB 420 MRCR	7	3800	1 3	13300	15200
32 3	ELEGANTE 32	OP	RACE	FBG DV	OB	8 3	5500	1 8	30400	33800
32 3	ELEGANTE 32	KTH	RACE	FBG DV	IB T260 MRCR	8 3	5500	1 8	42600	47300
32 3	ELEGANTE 32	OP	RACE	FBG DV	IB T330-T370	8 3	5500	1 8	51700	63800
32 3	ELEGANTE 32	OP	RACE	FBG DV	IB T420 MRCR	8 3	5500	1 8	65100	71500
32 3	SCORPION 32	HT	OPFSH	FBG DV	IB 300-330	8 3	5500	1 8	31100	35100
32 3	SCORPION 32	HT	OPFSH	FBG DV	IB T200-T330	8 3	5500	1 8	32700	40300
32 3	SCORPION 32	HT	OPFSH	FBG DV	IB T370-T420	8 3	5500	1 8	37400	42500
32 3	SCORPION 32	OP	RACE	FBG DV	OB	8 3	5500	1 8	28900	32100
32 3	SCORPION 32SS	OP	RACE	FBG DV	IB T260 MRCR	8 3	5500	1 8	40100	44600
32 3	SCORPION 32SS	OP	RACE	FBG DV	IB T330-T370	8 3	5500	1 8	49000	66800
32 3	SCORPION 32SS	OP	RACE	FBG DV	IB T420 MRCR	8 3	5500	1 8	62300	68400
37	BOSS 37SS	OP	RACE	FBG DV	IB T330 MRCR				66400	73000
37	BOSS 37SS	OP	RACE	FBG DV	IB T370 MRCR				68000	74800
37	BOSS 37SS	OP	RACE	FBG DV	IB T420 MRCR				70600	77500
37	SCORPION 37SS	HT	OPFSH	FBG DV	IB T330 MRCR				63500	69800
37	SCORPION 37SS	OP	OPFSH	FBG DV	IB T370 MRCR				64700	71100
37	SCORPION 37SS	HT	OPFSH	FBG DV	IB T420 MRCR				66600	73200

SCOUT BOATS INC
SUMMERVILLE SC 29483   COAST GUARD MFG ID- SLP See inside cover to adjust price for area

For more recent years, see the BUC Used Boat Price Guide, Volume 1

LOA FT IN	NAME AND/ OR MODEL	TOP/ RIG	BOAT TYPE	-HULL- MTL TP	----ENGINE--- TP # HP MFG	BEAM FT IN	WGT LBS	DRAFT FT IN	RETAIL LOW	RETAIL HIGH
	--------------- 1996 BOATS									
16 2	SCOUT 162 SF	OP	CTRCN	FBG SV	OB	6 10	770	8	3550	4100
16 2	SCOUT 162 STD	OP	CTRCN	FBG SV	OB	6 10	770	8	3400	3950
17 2	SCOUT 172 DORADO	OP	B/R	FBG SV	OB	7 4	1100	9	5000	5750
17 2	SCOUT 172 SF	OP	CTRCN	FBG SV	OB	7 4	950	9	4400	5100
18 8	SCOUT 192 SF	OP	CTRCN	FBG SV	OB	8	1300	10	6100	7000
18 8	SCOUT 192 STD	OP	CTRCN	FBG SV	OB	8	1300	10	5850	6700
19 10	SCOUT 202 DORADO	OP	B/R	FBG SV	OB	8 4	2100	11	8900	10100
19 10	SCOUT 202 SF	OP	CTRCN	FBG SV	OB	8 4	1980	1	8500	9750

SEA CAMPER INDS INC
HOLLAND MI 49423   COAST GUARD MFG ID- FAR See inside cover to adjust price for area

LOA FT IN	NAME AND/ OR MODEL	TOP/ RIG	BOAT TYPE	-HULL- MTL TP	----ENGINE--- TP # HP MFG	BEAM FT IN	WGT LBS	DRAFT FT IN	RETAIL LOW	RETAIL HIGH
	--------------- 1985 BOATS									
24	SEA-CAMPER		CAMPR	FBG DV	IO 190	8			6900	7950
	--------------- 1984 BOATS									
24	SEA-CAMPER		CAMPR	FBG DV	IO 190	8			6650	7650

....For earlier years, see the BUC Used Boat Price Guide, Volume 3

SEA CRAFT
FOREST CITY NC 28043   COAST GUARD MFG ID- SXC See inside cover to adjust price for area
FORMERLY SEACRAFT INDUSTRIES INC

For more recent years, see the BUC Used Boat Price Guide, Volume 1

LOA FT IN	NAME AND/ OR MODEL	TOP/ RIG	BOAT TYPE	-HULL- MTL TP	----ENGINE--- TP # HP MFG	BEAM FT IN	WGT LBS	DRAFT FT IN	RETAIL LOW	RETAIL HIGH
	--------------- 1987 BOATS									
18 2	SUPERFISHERMAN 18	OP	CTRCN	FBG DV	OB	7 5	1800		5000	5750
20 4	SUPERFISHERMAN 20	OP	CTRCN	FBG DV	OB	7 6	2100		6950	8000
23 3	SCEPTRE 23	OP	CUD	FBG DV	OB	8	3300		11900	13500

LOA FT IN	NAME AND/ OR MODEL	TOP/ RIG	BOAT TYPE	-HULL- MTL TP	----ENGINE--- TP # HP MFG	BEAM FT IN	WGT LBS	DRAFT FT IN	RETAIL LOW	RETAIL HIGH
					1987 BOATS					
23 3	SUPERFISHERMAN 23	OP	CTRCN	FBG DV	OB	8	3100		11100	12700
23 3	WALK-AROUND 23	OP	CUD	FBG DV	OB	8	3300		12300	13900
27	SUPERFISHERMAN 27	OP	CTRCN	FBG DV	OB	10	5000		18400	20500
27	TOURNAMENT 27	OP	CUD	FBG DV	OB	9 10	5000	1 10	19300	21500
					1986 BOATS					
18 2	SUPERFISHERMAN 18	OP	CTRCN	FBG DV	OB	7 5	1800		4800	5550
19 8	MASTER-ANGLER 20	OP	CTRCN	FBG DV	OB	7 6	2000		5600	6450
20 4	SUPERFISHERMAN 20	OP	CTRCN	FBG DV	OB	7 6	2100		6750	7750
23 3	SCEPTRE 23	OP	CUD	FBG DV	OB	8	3300		11500	13000
23 3	SUPERFISHERMAN 23	OP	CTRCN	FBG DV	OB	8	3100		10800	12300
23 3	WALK-AROUND 23	OP	CUD	FBG DV	OB	8	3300		11800	13400
27	SUPERFISHERMAN 27	OP	CTRCN	FBG DV	OB	10	5000		17500	19900
27	TOURNAMENT 27	OP	CUD	FBG DV	OB	9 10	5000	1 10	18700	20700
					1985 BOATS					
18 2	SUPERFISHERMAN 18	OP	CTRCN	FBG DV	OB	7 5	1800	1	4650	5350
19 8	MASTER-ANGLER 20	OP	CTRCN	FBG DV	OB	7 6	2000	1 1	5400	6250
20 4	SPORT DIVER 20	OP	CTRCN	FBG DV	OB	7 6	2100	1 2	6900	7950
20 4	SUPERFISHERMAN 20	OP	CTRCN	FBG DV	OB	7 6	2100	1 2	6200	7150
23 3	SCEPTRE 23	OP	CTRCN	FBG DV	IO	260	3100		13300	15100
23 3	SCEPTRE 23	OP	CUD	FBG DV	OB	8	3300	1 4	11300	12800
23 3	SPORT DIVER 23	OP	CTRCN	FBG DV	OB	8	3100	1 4	10900	12300
23 3	SUPERFISHERMAN 23	OP	CTRCN	FBG DV	OB	8	3100	1 4	10100	11500
23 3	SUPERFISHERMAN 23	OP	CTRCN	FBG DV	IO	260	3100		13300	15100
					1984 BOATS					
18 2	SUPERFISHERMAN 18	OP	CTRCN	FBG SV	OB	7 5	1800		4550	5200
19 8	MASTER-ANGLER 20	OP	CTRCN	FBG SV	OB	7 6	2000		5250	6050
20 4	BOW RIDER 20	OP	RNBT	FBG SV	OB	7 6	2100		6500	7450
20 4	SPORT DIVER 20	OP	CTRCN	FBG SV	OB	7 6	2100		6750	7750
20 4	SUPERFISHERMAN 20	OP	CTRCN	FBG SV	OB	7 6	2100		6050	7000
23 3	SCEPTRE 23	OP	CUD	FBG SV	OB	8	3300		10900	12400
23 3	SPORT DIVER 23	OP	CTRCN	FBG SV	OB	8	3100		10600	12000
23 3	SUPERFISHERMAN 23	OP	CTRCN	FBG SV	OB	8	3100		9800	11200

....For earlier years, see the BUC Used Boat Price Guide, Volume 3

SEA FEVER YACHTS
RANCHO PALOS VERDES CA 90732   See inside cover to adjust price for area

LOA FT IN	NAME AND/ OR MODEL	TOP/ RIG	BOAT TYPE	-HULL- MTL TP	----ENGINE--- TP # HP MFG	BEAM FT IN	WGT LBS	DRAFT FT IN	RETAIL LOW	RETAIL HIGH
					1985 BOATS					
28	SEA-FEVER 28		SDN	FBG SV	IB 65D	10			16800	19100
30	SEA-FEVER 30		SDN	FBG SV	IB 65D	11 6			24000	26700
32	SEA-FEVER 32	KTH	SA/CR	FBG KL	IB D	11 6	12400	3 8	33500	37200
32 6	SEA-FEVER 33	CUT	SA/RC	FBG KL	IB D	11 2	14200	5 4	37800	42000
33 6	SEA-FEVER 34		DC	FBG SV	IB 124D	11 9	16000		38000	42200
33 6	SEA-FEVER 34		PH	FBG SV	IB T120D	11 9	16000		39100	43500
33 6	SEA-FEVER 34		SDN	FBG SV	IB 120D	11 9	16000		37800	42000
33 11	SEA-FEVER 34	CUT	SA/RC	FBG KL	IB D	11 9	14250	5	37500	41700
34 5	SEA-FEVER 34		DC	FBG SV	IB 120D	12	18000		43400	47700
34 6	SEA-FEVER 35	KTH	SA/CR	FBG KL	IB D	11 6	16950	4 10	45700	50200
35 9	SEA-FEVER 36		DC	FBG SV	IB 120D	12 6	17200		43600	48500
35 10	SEA-FEVER 36	KTH	SA/RC	FBG KL	IB D	11 10	16300	4 7	44200	49200
36 2	SEA-FEVER 36	CUT	SA/RC	FBG KL	IB D	11 2	26000	6	63400	69700
36 6	SEA-FEVER 37		SDN	FBG SV	IB 120D	11 6	22500	5 8	56900	62500
36 8	SEA-FEVER 37	KTH	SA/RC	FBG KL	IB D	11 6	22500	5 8	59400	65300
37	SEA-FEVER 37		DC	FBG SV	IB 120D	13	15400		38700	43000
37	SEA-FEVER 37		SDN	FBG SV	IB 120D	13	15400		38100	42300
37 7	SEA-FEVER 38	CUT	SA/RC	FBG KL	IB D	12 2	20000	5 6	52600	57800
37 9	SEA-FEVER	SLP	SA/RC	FBG KL	IB D	11 6	16755	6 6	46500	51100
39	SEA-FEVER 39		DC	FBG SV	IB 120D	13	28000		64500	70900
39 9	SEA-FEVER	CUT	SA/CR	FBG KC	IB D	13 2	21700	5	59500	65400
40	SEA-FEVER	KTH	SA/RC	FBG KL	IB D	12 2	28000	6	76100	83600
41	SEA-FEVER 41		DC	FBG SV	IB 120D	13 6	29500		70800	77800
41	SEA-FEVER 41		SDN	FBG SV	IB 120D	13 6	29500		68800	75600
41 5	SEA-FEVER	CUT	SA/RC	FBG KL	IB D	11 4	19000	5 9	56400	62000
41 9	SEA-FEVER	CUT	SA/RC	FBG KL	IB D	12 9	29215	5 9	73300	80500
41 10	SEA-FEVER	KTH	SA/RC	FBG KL	IB D	12 2	29300	6	79100	86900
42	SEA-FEVER 42		SDN	FBG SV	IB 120D	13 2	29800		69900	76800
42 6	SEA-FEVER	KTH	SA/RC	FBG KL	IB D	11 2	30000	6	78500	86300
45	SEA-FEVER	CUT	SA/RC	FBG KL	IB D	15	30000		81400	89500
45	SEA-FEVER 45		PH	FBG SV	IB 120D	15	33300		76600	84200
45	SEA-FEVER 45		SDN	FBG SV	IB 120D	15	33300		80300	88200
46	SEA-FEVER	CUT	SA/RC	FBG KL	IB D	13	30000	6	86100	94600
46	SEA-FEVER 46	KTH	SA/RC	FBG KL	IB D	13	30000	6	78300	86000
47	SEA-FEVER	CUT	SA/RC	FBG KL	IB D	13 8	32300		82200	90300
47	SEA-FEVER	KTH	SA/RC	FBG KL	IB D	13 2	29950	6	88000	96300
48	SEA-FEVER	KTH	SA/RC	FBG KL	IB D	13 6	36000	6	96500	106000
49 9	SEA-FEVER 49		PH	FBG SV	IB T120D	15	50000		112500	123500
50 5	SEA-FEVER	CUT	SA/RC	FBG KL	IB D	14 2	39000	7 2	112500	113000
50 5	SEA-FEVER	KTH	SA/RC	FBG KL	IB D	14 2	39000	7	109000	120000
51 7	SEA-FEVER 52		TRWL	FBG SV	IB T210D	16 8	77200		133000	146000
51 7	SEA-FEVER 54		TRWL	FBG SV	IB T210D	15	50000		112500	123500
53 7	SEA-FEVER	KTH	SA/CR	FBG KL	IB 200D	15 1	54000	6 4	137000	150500
58	SEA-FEVER 58		PH	FBG SV	IB 200D	13	53200		115000	126000
59	SEA-FEVER	KTH	SA/RC	FBG KL	IB D	15 8	59000	6	212000	233000
60	SEA-FEVER 60		TRWL	FBG SV	IB T300D	18	86000		188500	207000
65	SEA-FEVER	KTH	SA/RC	FBG KL	IB D	17 6	77383	7	297000	326000
66	SEA-FEVER	KTH	SA/RC	FBG KL	IB D	16 8	66794	6 9	256500	282000

....For earlier years, see the BUC Used Boat Price Guide, Volume 3

SEA FOX YACHTS INC
VINELAND NJ 08360   See inside cover to adjust price for area

LOA FT IN	NAME AND/ OR MODEL	TOP/ RIG	BOAT TYPE	-HULL- MTL TP	----ENGINE--- TP # HP MFG	BEAM FT IN	WGT LBS	DRAFT FT IN	RETAIL LOW	RETAIL HIGH
					1988 BOATS					
29	SEAFOX 29	FB	CR	F/S SV	IB T240-T275	11	9000	2 6	25700	29100
33	SEAFOX 33	OP	SF	F/S SV	IB T275 CHRY	11 6	11000	2 6	40000	44500
33	SEAFOX 33	OP	SF	F/S SV	IB T205D GM	11 6	11000	2 6	46700	51300
					1987 BOATS					
29	FLYBRIDGE	FB	CR	F/S SV	IB T240 CHRY	11	10000	2 6	25800	28600
29	SPORT EXPRESS		CR	F/S SV	IB T240 CHRY	11	9000	2 6	24500	27200
33	OFFSHORE 33	OP	FSH	F/S SV	IB T275 CHRY	11 6	11000	2 6	38200	42500
					1986 BOATS					
29	FLYBRIDGE	FB	CR	F/S SV	IB T240 CHRY	11	10000	2	24600	27300
29	SPORT EXPRESS		CR	F/S SV	IB T240 CHRY	11	9000	2	23400	26000

SEA NYMPH BOATS
SYRACUSE IN 46567   COAST GUARD MFG ID- SEA See inside cover to adjust price for area

DIV OMC ALUMINUM BOAT GROUP
LEBANON MO 65536

For more recent years, see the BUC Used Boat Price Guide, Volume 1

LOA FT IN	NAME AND/ OR MODEL	TOP/ RIG	BOAT TYPE	-HULL- MTL TP	----ENGINE--- TP # HP MFG	BEAM FT IN	WGT LBS	DRAFT FT IN	RETAIL LOW	RETAIL HIGH
					1996 BOATS					
16	FISH MACHINE FM160	OP	FSH	AL DV	OB	5 9	650		2650	3050
16 1	BACKTROLLER BT165	OP	FSH	AL DV	OB	5 8	500		2050	2400
16	MUSKIE SV1666	OP	UTL	AL SV	OB	5 8	235		930	1100
16	MUSKIE SV1666T	OP	UTL	AL SV	OB	5 8	235		930	1100
16	MUSKIE SV1666WT	OP	UTL	AL SV	OB	5 8	395		1600	1900
16 5	FISH MACHINE FM161	OP	FSH	AL DV	OB	6	650		2700	3100
16 5	FISH MACHINE FM164	OP	FSH	AL DV	OB	6	610		2500	2950
16 8	SIDEWINDER SC170	OP	FSH	AL DV	OB	7	840		3400	3950
16 10	FISH MACHINE FM170	OP	FSH	AL DV	OB	6 8	960		3850	4500
17	LUNKER JON S1752VCT	OP	JON	AL FL	OB	6 2	330		1200	1450
17	TOURNAMENT PRO TX175	OP	BASS	AL SV	OB	7 1	715		3050	3550
17 4	BACKTROLLER BT175	OP	FSH	AL DV	OB	7 1	958		3950	4550
17 4	SIDEWINDER SC175	OP	FSH	AL DV	OB	7 1	998		4050	4750
17 4	SPORTFISHER GLS175	OP	FSH	AL DV	OB	7 1	970		3950	4600
17 11	KING SV1880T	OP	UTL	AL SV	OB	7 8	470		1850	2200
18	LUNKER JON S1848	OP	JON	AL FL	OB	5 10	300		905	1100
18	LUNKER JON S1852MT	OP	JON	AL FL	OB	6 3	360		1100	1350
18	LUNKER JON S1852T	OP	JON	AL FL	OB	6 3	360		1100	1350
18	TUNNEL JON S1852MTNN	OP	JON	AL FL	OB	6 3	385		1200	1450
19	STINGER SPORT ST190	OP	BASS	AL SV	OB	8	1500		6150	7050
19	STINGER ST190	ST	BASS	AL SV	OB	8	1500		5800	6650
19 1	SPORTFISHER GLS195	OP	FSH	AL DV	OB	7 2	1150		4900	5600
19 1	WALLEYE TC195	OP	FSH	AL DV	OB	7 2	1185		4950	5700
22 1	STINGER STS220	ST	BASS	AL SV	OB	8	1975		8850	10000
					1995 BOATS					
16	FISH MACHINE 160	OP	FSH	AL DV	OB	5 9	650		2500	2900
16	FISH MACHINE 160	OP	FSH	AL SV	OB	5 9	650		2700	3100

LOA FT	LOA IN	NAME AND/ OR MODEL	TOP/ RIG	BOAT TYPE	HULL MTL	HULL TP	ENGINE TP	# HP	MFG	BEAM FT	BEAM IN	WGT LBS	DRAFT FT IN	RETAIL LOW	RETAIL HIGH
		1995 BOATS													
16	1	BACKTROLLER 165	OP	FSH	AL	DV	OB			5	8	500		1900	2300
16	1	BACKTROLLER 165	OP	FSH	AL	SV	OB			5	8	500		1100	1350
16	1	BACKTROLLER 165T	OP	FSH	AL	DV	OB			5	8	500		2200	2550
16	1	MUSKIE 1666	OP	UTL	AL	SV	OB			5	8	235		880	1050
16	1	MUSKIE 1666T	OP	UTL	AL	SV	OB			5	8	235		880	1050
16	1	MUSKIE 1666WT	OP	UTL	AL	SV	OB			5	8	395		1500	1800
16	5	FISH MACHINE 161	OP	FSH	AL	DV	OB			6	1	650		2550	2950
16	5	FISH MACHINE 161	OP	FSH	AL	SV	OB			6	1	650		2500	2900
16	5	FISH MACHINE 164	OP	FSH	AL	DV	OB			6	1	610		2450	2850
16	5	FISH MACHINE 164	OP	FSH	AL	SV	OB			6	1	610		2450	2850
16	8	SIDEWINDER 170	OP	FSH	AL	DV	OB			7		840		3250	3750
16	8	SIDEWINDER 170	OP	FSH	AL	SV	OB			7		840		3250	3750
16	10	FISH MACHINE 170	OP	FSH	AL	DV	OB			6	8	960		3650	4250
17		LUNKER 1752VCT	OP	JON	AL	FL	OB			6	2	330		1150	1350
17		TX 175	OP	BASS	AL	SV	OB			6	1	715		2850	3350
17		TX 175	OP	BASS	FBG	SV	OB			6	1	715		2800	3250
17	4	BACKTROLLER 175	OP	FSH	AL	DV	OB			7	1	958		3700	4300
17	4	BACKTROLLER 175	OP	FSH	AL	SV	OB			7	1	958		3700	4300
17	4	GLS 175	OP	FSH	AL	SV	OB			7	1	970		3750	4350
17	4	SIDEWINDER 175	OP	FSH	AL	DV	OB			7	1	998		3850	4500
17	4	SIDEWINDER 175	OP	FSH	AL	SV	OB			7	1	998		3850	4500
17	4	SPORTFISHER 175GLS	OP	FSH	AL	DV	OB			7	1	825		3250	3800
17	4	SPROTFISHER 175 GLS	OP	FSH	AL	DV	OB			7	1	825		3250	3800
17	11	KING 1880T	OP	UTL	AL	SV	OB			6	8	470		1750	2100
18		LUNKER 1752VCT	OP	JON	AL	FL	OB			6	2	330		965	1150
18		LUNKER 1848	OP	JON	AL	FL	OB			5	10	300		855	1000
18		LUNKER 1848TLR	OP	JON	AL	FL	OB			5	10	300		845	1000
18		LUNKER 1852MT	OP	JON	AL	FL	OB			6	3	345		1000	1200
18		LUNKER 1852MTNN	OP	JON	AL	FL	OB			6	3	345		1100	1300
18		LUNKER 1852MTNNTLR	OP	JON	AL	FL	OB			6	3	385		1150	1350
18		LUNKER 1852T	OP	JON	AL	FL	OB			6	3	345		925	1100
19		STINGER 190	ST	BASS	AL	DV	OB			8		1500		5450	6300
19		STINGER SPORT 190	ST	BASS	AL	SV	OB			8		1500		5800	6700
19	1	SPORTFISHER 195GLS	OP	FSH	AL	DV	OB			7	2	1150		4450	5100
19	1	WALLEYE 195TC	OP	FSH	AL	DV	OB			7	2	1185		4750	5450
		1994 BOATS													
16	1	TX165	OP	BASS	AL	SV	OB			5	10	560		2100	2450
16	5	FISH MACHINE 160	OP	FSH	AL	SV	OB			6		650		2700	3150
16	5	FISH MACHINE 161	OP	FSH	AL	SV	OB			6		650		2050	2450
16	5	FISH MACHINE 164	OP	FSH	AL	SV	OB			6		610		2300	2700
16	9	SIDEWINDER 170	OP	FSH	AL	SV	OB			7		850		3100	3600
17		LUNKER 1752VCT	OP	JON	AL	FL	OB			6	2	330		1100	1300
17	2	TX175	OP	BASS	AL	SV	OB			5	10	670		2600	3000
17	4	BACKTROLLER 175	OP	FSH	AL	SV	OB			7	1	958		3500	4100
17	4	GLS175	OP	FSH	AL	SV	OB			7	1	970		3550	4150
17	4	SIDEWINDER 175	OP	FSH	AL	SV	OB			7	1	998		3650	4250
18		LUNKER 1848	OP	JON	AL	FL	OB			5	10	300		805	965
18		LUNKER 1852MT	OP	JON	AL	FL	OB			6	3	345		965	1150
18		LUNKER 1852MTN	OP	JON	AL	FL	OB			6	3	345		1050	1250
18		LUNKER 1852T	OP	JON	AL	FL	OB			6	3	345		875	1050
19		GL195	OP	FSH	AL	SV	OB			7	3	1125		4250	4950
19	1	GLS195	OP	FSH	AL	SV	OB			7	3	1150		4400	5050
		1993 BOATS													
16	1	CRAPPIE 160	OP	BASS	AL	SV	OB			5	10	520		1850	2200
16	1	CRAPPIE PRO 161	OP	BASS	AL	SV	OB			5	10	575		2000	2400
16	1	TX165	OP	BASS	AL	SV	OB			5	10	970		3350	3900
16	5	FISH MACHINE 160	OP	FSH	AL	SV	OB			6		598		2100	2500
16	5	FISH MACHINE 161	OP	FSH	AL	SV	OB			6		550		1950	2300
16	5	FISH MACHINE 164	OP	FSH	AL	SV	OB			6		512		1800	2150
16	9	SIDEWINDER 170	OP	FSH	AL	SV	OB			7		850		2950	3450
17		LUNKER 1752VCT	OP	JON	AL	FL	OB			6	2	370		1150	1350
17	2	TX175	OP	BASS	AL	SV	OB			5	10	715		2600	3050
17	4	BACKTROLLER 175	OP	FSH	AL	SV	OB			7	1	958		3350	3900
17	4	GLS175	OP	FSH	AL	SV	OB			7	1	970		3400	3950
17	4	SIDEWINDER 175	OP	FSH	AL	SV	OB			7	1	998		3450	4050
17	4	SS175	OP	FSH	AL	SV	OB			7	1	970		3400	3950
18		LUNKER 1848	OP	JON	AL	FL	OB			5	10	290		730	880
18		LUNKER 1852MT	OP	JON	AL	FL	OB			6	3	325		850	1000
18		LUNKER 1852T	OP	JON	AL	FL	OB			6	3	325		850	1000
19		GL195	OP	FSH	AL	SV	OB			7	3	1125		4050	4700
19		GLS195	OP	FSH	AL	SV	OB			7	3	1050		3850	4500
19		GLS195	OP	FSH	AL	SV	IO	130		7	3	1805		4950	5700
19		SS195	OP	FSH	AL	SV	OB			7	3	1050		3850	4500
19		SS195	OP	RNBT	AL	SV	IO	130		7	3	1805		4600	5300
19		STRIPER 191	OP	FSH	AL	SV	OB			7	3	1050		3700	4350
22		GLS220	OP	CUD	AL	SV	IO	130-175		8	6	2650		7600	8750
		1992 BOATS													
16	1	TX160 CRAPPIE	OP	BASS	AL	SV	OB			5	10	484		1650	1950
16	1	TX161 CRAPPIE PRO	OP	BASS	AL	SV	OB			5	10	538		1850	2150
16	1	TX165 TOURN PRO	OP	BASS	AL	SV	OB			5	10	618		2050	2450
16	3	BT165 BACKTROLLER	OP	FSH	AL	SV	OB			5	10	420		1400	1650
16	3	SV1670 MUSKIE	OP	FSH	AL	DV	OB			5	10	250		825	990
16	5	FM160 FISH MACHINE	OP	BASS	AL	SV	OB			6		598		2050	2400
16	5	FM161 FISH MACHINE	OP	FSH	AL	SV	OB			6		610		2050	2400
16	5	FM164 FISH MACHINE	OP	FSH	AL	SV	OB			6	8	550		1850	2200
17		S1768CC	OP	UTL	AL	TH	OB			6	10	900		2700	3150
17		S1768W	OP	UTL	AL	TH	OB			6	10	900		3050	3500
17	2	TX175 TOURN PRO	OP	BASS	AL	SV	OB			5	10	718		2500	2900
17	4	BT175 BACKTROLLER	OP	FSH	AL	DV	OB			7	1	890		3000	3450
17	4	GLS175 SPORTFISHER	OP	FSH	AL	DV	OB			7	1	964		3200	3750
17	4	SC175 FISH-N-SKI	OP	FSH	AL	DV	OB			7	1	964		3200	3700
17	4	SC175 SIDEWINDER	OP	FSH	AL	DV	OB			7	1	956		3200	3700
17	4	SS175 FISH-N-SKI	OP	FSH	AL	DV	OB			7	1	964		3200	3700
18		S1848	OP	JON	AL	FL	OB			5	10	290		695	835
19		CC191 STRIPER	OP	CTRCN	AL	DV	OB			7	3	1000		3500	4050
19		GLS195 SPORTFISHER	OP	FSH	AL	DV	OB			7	3	1125		3800	4450
19		GLS195 SPORTFISHER	OP	FSH	AL	DV	IO	130		7	3	1805		4650	5350
19		S1968CC	OP	UTL	AL	TH	OB			6	10	910		2800	3250
19		SS195 FISH-N-SKI	OP	FSH	AL	DV	OB			7	3	1125		3850	4500
19		SS195 FISH-N-SKI	OP	FSH	AL	DV	IO	130	EVIN	7	3	1805		4650	5350
19		SS195 FISH-N-SKI	OP	FSH	AL	DV	IO	130	JOHN	7	3	1805		4650	5350
19		SS195 FISH-N-SKI	OP	FSH	AL	DV	IB	130	OMC	7	3	1805		5300	6100
22		GLS220 SPORTFISHER	OP	CUD	AL	DV	OB			8	6	2000		7150	8200
22		GLS220 SPORTFISHER	OP	CUD	AL	DV	IO	130	OMC	8	6	2650		7050	8100
		1991 BOATS													
16		1648	OP	JON	AL	FL	OB			5	11	267		860	1050
16		MV1648	OP	JON	AL	FL	OB			5	11	252		810	975
16		MV1648LW	OP	JON	AL	FL	OB			5	11	270		870	1050
16	1	TX162	OP	JON	AL	FL	OB			6		500		1500	1750
16	1	TX175	OP	BASS	AL	SV	OB			6		604		1950	2300
16	3	16M	OP	UTL	AL	SV	OB			5	10	250		760	915
16	3	BT165-20	OP	FSH	AL	SV	OB			5	10	420		1350	1600
16	5	FM160	OP	FSH	AL	SV	OB			6		616		1950	2350
16	5	FM161	OP	FSH	AL	SV	OB			6		550		1750	2100
16	7	BT175	OP	FSH	AL	SV	OB			6	10	700		2300	2650
16	7	CC171	OP	CTRCN	AL	SV	OB			6	10	700		2300	2700
16	7	GLS175	OP	FSH	AL	SV	OB			6	10	700		2300	2650
16	7	SC175	OP	FSH	AL	SV	OB			6	10	720		2350	2750
16	7	SS175	OP	RNBT	AL	SV	OB			6	10	790		2600	3000
19		CC191	OP	CTRCN	AL	SV	OB			7	5	1000		3300	3850
19		GLS195	OP	FSH	AL	SV	OB			7	5	1125		3650	4250
19		GLS195	OP	FSH	AL	SV	IO	130	OMC	7	5	1125		3950	4600
19		SS195	OP	RNBT	AL	SV	OB			7	5	1125		3700	4350
19		SS195	OP	RNBT	AL	SV	IO	130	OMC	7	5	1805		4000	4650
22		GLS220	ST	CUD	AL	SV	IO	130	OMC	8	6	2000		5900	6750
22		GLS220	ST	CUD	AL	SV	IO	150-175		8	6	2650		6600	7650
22		GLS220 OB	OP	CUD	AL	SV	OB			8	6	2000		6800	7800
		1990 BOATS													
16		1648	OP	JON	AL	FL	OB			5	11	267		815	980
16		MV1648	OP	JON	AL	FL	OB			5	11	252		775	935
16		MV1648LW	OP	JON	AL	FL	OB			5	11	270		825	990
16	1	TX175	OP	BASS	AL	SV	OB			6		604		1850	2200
16	3	16M	OP	UTL	AL	SV	OB			5	10	250		730	875
16	3	BT162-20	OP	FSH	AL	SV	OB			5	10	420		1250	1450
16	3	BT165-20	OP	FSH	AL	SV	OB			5	10	420		1300	1600
16	5	FM160	OP	FSH	AL	SV	OB			6		616		1850	2250
16	5	FM161	OP	FSH	AL	SV	OB			6		550		1700	2000
16	7	BT175	OP	FSH	AL	SV	OB			6	10	700		2200	2550
16	7	CC171	OP	CTRCN	AL	SV	OB			6	10	700		2200	2550
16	7	GLS175	OP	FSH	AL	SV	OB			6	10	790		2450	2850
16	7	SC175	OP	FSH	AL	SV	OB			6	10	720		2250	2600
16	7	SS171	OP	RNBT	AL	SV	OB			6	10	790		2500	2900
16	7	SS175	OP	RNBT	AL	SV	OB			6	10	790		2500	2900
19		CC191	OP	CTRCN	AL	SV	OB			7	5	1000		3200	3700
19		GLS195	OP	FSH	AL	SV	OB			7	5	1125		3500	4050
19		GLS195	OP	FSH	AL	SV	IO	128	OMC	7	5	1125		3750	4350
19		SS191	OP	RNBT	AL	SV	OB			7	5	1125		3550	4100
19		SS191	OP	RNBT	AL	SV	IO	128	OMC	7	5	1805		3750	4350

CONTINUED ON NEXT PAGE

LOA FT	LOA IN	NAME AND/ OR MODEL	TOP/ RIG	BOAT TYPE	-HULL- MTL	-HULL- TP	ENGINE TP	ENGINE # HP	ENGINE MFG	BEAM FT	BEAM IN	WGT LBS	DRAFT FT	DRAFT IN	RETAIL LOW	RETAIL HIGH
		1990 BOATS														
19		SS195	OP	RNBT	AL	SV	OB			7	5	1125			3600	4150
19		SS195	OP	RNBT	AL	SV	IO	128	OMC	7	5	1805			3800	4400
22		GLS220	ST	CUD	AL	SV	IO	130-175		10	2	2650			6900	8000
		1986 BOATS														
16	4	BIG-JOHN JX16	OP	JON	AL	FL	OB			6		300			755	910
16	4	BIG-JOHN JXL 16	OP	JON	AL	FL	OB			6		330			825	990
16	5	COHO 16R	OP	FSH	AL	SV	OB			6		287			755	905
16	5	FISHING-MACHINE 160	OP	BASS	AL	SV	OB			6		616			1650	1950
16	5	FISHING-MACHINE 161	OP	FSH	AL	SV	OB			6		550			1450	1700
16	5	PIKE-ATTACKER FM164	OP	FSH	AL	SV	OB			6		495			1300	1550
16	7	BAY-STRIPER CC171	OP	CTRCN	AL	DV	OB			6	10	700			1850	2200
16	7	FISH-N-SKI SS175	OP	RNBT	AL	DV	OB			6	10	790			2150	2500
16	7	FISH-TRACKER SC170	OP	FSH	AL	DV	OB			6	10	655			1700	2050
16	7	SKI-SPORT SS171	OP	RNBT	AL	DV	OB			6	10	760			2050	2400
16	9	BASS-ATTACKER TX-170	OP	BASS	AL	SV	OB			6		650			1750	2050
19		FISH-N-SKI SS195	OP	RNBT	AL	DV	OB			7	2	1125			3050	3550
19		SUPER-STRIPER CC191	OP	CTRCN	AL	DV	OB			7	2	1000			2700	3150
		1985 BOATS														
16	4	BASS-ATTACKER JB164	OP	BASS	AL	SV	OB			6		595			1500	1800
16	4	BASS-ATTACKER JB165	OP	BASS	AL	SV	OB			6		610			1550	1850
16	4	TRAVELER JX16	OP	JON	AL	FL	OB			6		300			730	880
16	4	TRAVELER JXL16	OP	JON	AL	FL	OB			6		330			795	960
16	5	COHO 16R	OP	FSH	AL	SV	OB			6		287			725	875
16	5	FISHING-MACHINE 160	OP	BASS	AL	DV	OB			6		616			1600	1900
16	5	FISHING-MACHINE 161	OP	FSH	AL	DV	OB			6		550			1400	1650
16	5	PIKE-ATTACKER FM164	OP	FSH	AL	DV	OB			6		495			1250	1500
16	7	BASS-STRIPER CC170	OP	CTRCN	AL	DV	OB			6	10	745			1900	2250
16	7	BAY-STRIPER CC171	OP	CTRCN	AL	DV	OB			6	10	700			1800	2100
16	7	FISH-N-SKI SS175	OP	RNBT	AL	DV	OB			6	10	790			2050	2400
16	7	FISH-TRACKER SC170	OP	FSH	AL	DV	OB			6	10	655			1650	1950
16	7	SKI-SPORT SS171	OP	RNBT	AL	DV	OB			6	10	760			1950	2350
19		FISH-N-SKI SS195	OP	RNBT	AL	DV	OB			7	5	1125			2950	3400
19		SUPER-STRIPER CC191	OP	CTRCN	AL	DV	OB			7	5	1000			2650	3100
		1984 BOATS														
16	3	FISH-FUN-SKI SS165	OP	RNBT	AL	DV	OB			6	10	818			2000	2400
16	4	BASS-ATTACKER JB164	OP	BASS	AL	SV	OB			6		595			1450	1750
16	4	BASS-ATTACKER JB165	OP	BASS	AL	SV	OB			6		610			1500	1800
16	4	TRAVELER JX16	OP	JON	AL	FL	OB			6		300			705	850
16	4	TRAVELER JXL16	OP	JON	AL	FL	OB			6		330			770	930
16	5	COHO 16R	OP	FSH	AL	SV	OB			6		287			705	850
16	5	FISHING-MACHINE 160	OP	BASS	AL	DV	OB			6		616			1550	1800
16	5	FISHING-MACHINE 161	OP	FSH	AL	DV	OB			6		550			1350	1600
16	5	PIKE-ATTACKER FM164	OP	FSH	AL	DV	OB			6		495			1200	1450
16	7	BASS-STRIPER CC170	OP	CTRCN	AL	DV	OB			6	10	745			1850	2200
16	7	BAY-STRIPER CC171	OP	CTRCN	AL	DV	OB			6	10	700			1700	2050
16	7	FISH-N-SKI SS175	OP	RNBT	AL	DV	OB			6	10	790			1950	2350
16	7	FISH-TRACKER SC170	OP	FSH	AL	DV	OB			6	10	655			1600	1900
16	7	SKI-SPORT SS171	OP	RNBT	AL	DV	OB			6	10	760			1900	2250
19		FISH-N-SKI SS195	OP	RNBT	AL	DV	OB			7	5	1125			2850	3300
19		SUPER-STRIPER CC191	OP	CTRCN	AL	DV	OB			7	5	1000			2550	3000

....For earlier years, see the BUC Used Boat Price Guide, Volume 3

SEA RANGER YACHT SALES INC

WILMINGTON CA 90748

See inside cover to adjust price for area

LOA FT	LOA IN	NAME AND/ OR MODEL	TOP/ RIG	BOAT TYPE	-HULL- MTL	-HULL- TP	ENGINE TP	ENGINE # HP	ENGINE MFG	BEAM FT	BEAM IN	WGT LBS	DRAFT FT	DRAFT IN	RETAIL LOW	RETAIL HIGH
		1989 BOATS														
38	3	SEA RANGER 39		TRWL	FBG	DS	IB	T125D	LEHM	13	8	23000	3	3	113500	124500
38	3	SEA RANGER 39		TRWL	FBG	DS	IB	T305D	VLVO	13	8	23000	3	3	121000	133000
40		SEA RANGER 40 CNV		TRWL	FBG	DS	IB	T225D	CUM	14	4	24000	3	4	124500	136500
40		SEA RANGER 40 CNV		TRWL	FBG	DS	IB	T375D	CAT	14	4	24000	3	4	140500	154500
40		SEA RANGER 42 SD		TRWL	FBG	DS	IB	T225D	CUM	14	4	24000	3	4	129500	142000
40		SEA RANGER 42 SD		TRWL	FBG	DS	IB	T375D	CAT	14	4	24000	3	4	145500	160000
43		SEA RANGER 43 AFTCBN		MY	FBG	DS	IB	T225D	CUM	14	4	26000	3	4	141000	155000
43		SEA RANGER 43 AFTCBN		MY	FBG	DS	IB	T375D	CAT	14	4	26000	3	4	167500	184000
43		SEA RANGER 43 CNV		MY	FBG	DS	IB	T225D	CUM	14	4	26000	3	4	139500	153000
43		SEA RANGER 43 CNV		MY	FBG	DS	IB	T375D	CAT	14	4	26000	3	4	166000	182500
45		SEA RANGER 45 AFTCBN		TRWL	FBG	DS	IB	T125D	LEHM	15	3	37400	4		156000	171500
45		SEA RANGER 45 AFTCBN		TRWL	FBG	DS	IB	T400D	GM	15	3	37400	4		172000	189000
45		SEA RANGER 45 SEDAN		TRWL	FBG	DS	IB	T125D	LEHM	15	3	37400	4		154500	170000
45		SEA RANGER 45 SEDAN		TRWL	FBG	DS	IB	T400D	GM	15	3	37400	4		171000	187500
46	1	SEA RANGER 46 AFTCBN		MY	FBG	DS	IB	T225D	CUM	14	4	27000	3	4	137500	151500
46	1	SEA RANGER 46 AFTCBN		MY	FBG	DS	IB	T375D	CAT	14	4	27000	3	4	166500	183000
46	1	SEA RANGER 46 CNV		MY	FBG	DS	IB	T225D	CUM	14	4	27500	3	4	138000	152000
46	1	SEA RANGER 46 CNV		MY	FBG	DS	IB	T375D	CAT	14	4	27500	3	4	165500	181500
47	3	SEA RANGER 47 PH		TRWL	FBG	DS	IB	T125D	LEHM	14	8	27000	4	4	148000	162500
47	3	SEA RANGER 47 PH		TRWL	FBG	DS	IB	T375D	CAT	14	8	27000	4	4	164500	180500
48		SEA RANGER 48 SS		TRWL	FBG	DS	IB	T305D	VLVO	14	4	26000	3	4	154500	169500
48		SEA RANGER 48 SS		TRWL	FBG	DS	IB	T375D	CAT	14	4	26000	3	4	161500	177500
51		SEA RANGER 51		MY	FBG	DS	IB	T260D	CAT	16	8	55000	4	3	219500	241500
51		SEA RANGER 51		MY	FBG	DS	IB	T650D	GM	16	8	55000	4	3	285000	313500
52		SEA RANGER 52 DC		TRWL	FBG	DS	IB	T375D	CAT	15	3	42000	4		173000	190000
52		SEA RANGER 52 DC		TRWL	FBG	DS	IB	T400D	GM	15	3	42000	4		173500	191000
55		SEA RANGER 55		MY	FBG	DS	IB	T320D	CAT	18	7	64900	4	9	257000	282500
55		SEA RANGER 55		MY	FBG	DS	IB	T750D	GM	18	7	64900	4	9	341000	374500
58		SEA RANGER 58		MY	FBG	DS	IB	T375D	CAT	18	7	59000	4	3	253000	278000
58		SEA RANGER 58		MY	FBG	DS	IB	T750D	GM	18	7	59000	4	3	341000	375000
59	3	SEA RANGER 60		MY	FBG	DS	IB	T355D	CAT	18	7	72000	4	9	316000	347000
59	3	SEA RANGER 60		MY	FBG	DS	IB	T750D	GM	18	7	72000	4	9	400000	439500
65	3	SEA RANGER 65		MY	FBG	DS	IB	T355D	CAT	18	7	79400	4	9	367000	403500
65	3	SEA RANGER 65		MY	FBG	DS	IB	T750D	GM	18	7	79400	4	9	453000	498000
72		SEA RANGER 72		MY	FBG	DS	IB	T650D	GM	18	7	95000	4	9	**	**
72		SEA RANGER 72		MY	FBG	DS	IB	T750D	GM	18	7	95000	4	9	**	**
		1988 BOATS														
38	3	SEA RANGER 39		TRWL	FBG	DS	IB	T125D		13	8	23000	3	3	108500	119000
38	3	SEA RANGER 39		TRWL	FBG	DS	IB	T305D		13	8	23000	3	3	118500	130000
40		SEA RANGER 40 CNV		TRWL	FBG	DS	IB	T225D		14	4	24000	3	4	120500	132500
40		SEA RANGER 40 CNV		TRWL	FBG	DS	IB	T375D		14	4	24000	3	4	132000	145000
40		SEA RANGER 40 SD		TRWL	FBG	DS	IB	T225D		14	4	24000	3	4	123000	135000
40		SEA RANGER 40 SD		TRWL	FBG	DS	IB	T375D		14	4	24000	3	4	134000	147000
43		SEA RANGER 43 AFTCBN		TRWL	FBG	DS	IB	T255D		14	4	26000	3	4	145500	159500
43		SEA RANGER 43 AFTCBN		TRWL	FBG	DS	IB	T475D		14	4	26000	3	4	163500	179500
43		SEA RANGER 43 CNV		TRWL	FBG	DS	IB	T225D		14	4	26000	3	4	143500	157500
43		SEA RANGER 43 CNV		TRWL	FBG	DS	IB	T375D		14	4	26000	3	4	154500	169500
45		SEA RANGER 45 AFTCBN		TRWL	FBG	DS	IB	T125D		15	3	37400	4		149000	164000
45		SEA RANGER 45 AFTCBN		TRWL	FBG	DS	IB	T405D		15	3	37400	4		165000	181000
45		SEA RANGER 45 SEDAN		TRWL	FBG	DS	IB	T125D		15	3	37400	4		148000	162500
45		SEA RANGER 45 SEDAN		TRWL	FBG	DS	IB	T375D		15	3	37400	4		161500	177500
46	1	SEA RANGER 46 CNV		TRWL	FBG	DS	IB	T255D		14	4	27000	3	4	147000	161500
46	1	SEA RANGER 46 CNV		TRWL	FBG	DS	IB	T375D		14	4	27000	3	4	155000	170000
46	1	SEA RANGER 46 SD		TRWL	FBG	DS	IB	T255D		14	4	27500	3	4	145000	159500
46	1	SEA RANGER 46 SD		TRWL	FBG	DS	IB	T375D		14	4	27500	3	4	152500	167500
46	1	SEA RANGER 46 SS		TRWL	FBG	DS	IB	T255D		14	4	26000	3	4	143500	157500
46	1	SEA RANGER 46 SS		TRWL	FBG	DS	IB	T375D		14	4	26000	3	4	151000	166000
47	3	SEA RANGER 47 PH		TRWL	FBG	DS	IB	T125D		14	8	27000	4	4	141500	155500
47	3	SEA RANGER 47 PH		TRWL	FBG	DS	IB	T375D		14	8	27000	4	4	156500	172000
48		SEA RANGER 48 SS		TRWL	FBG	DS	IB	T305D		14	4	26000	3	4	148000	163000
48		SEA RANGER 48 SS		TRWL	FBG	DS	IB	T375D		14	4	26000	3	4	153000	168000
51		SEA RANGER 51		MY	FBG	DS	IB	T260D		16	8	55000	4	3	210000	231000
51		SEA RANGER 51		MY	FBG	DS	IB	T650D		16	8	55000	4	3	272500	299500
52		SEA RANGER 52 DC		TRWL	FBG	DS	IB	T125D		15	3	42000	4		143500	157500
52		SEA RANGER 52 DC		TRWL	FBG	DS	IB	T375D		15	3	42000	4		167000	183500
53	6	SEA RANGER 53		MY	FBG	DS	IB	T260D		16	8				189500	208000
53	6	SEA RANGER 53		MY	FBG	DS	IB	T650D		16	8				236000	259500
55		SEA RANGER 55		MY	FBG	DS	IB	T320D		18	7	64900	4	9	247000	271500
55		SEA RANGER 55		MY	FBG	DS	IB	T750D		18	7	64900	4	9	327000	359500
58		SEA RANGER 58		MY	FBG	DS	IB	T375D		18	7	59000	4	3	241500	265000
58		SEA RANGER 58		MY	FBG	DS	IB	T870D		18	7	59000	4	3	346000	380000
59	3	SEA RANGER 60		MY	FBG	DS	IB	T355D		18	7	72000	4	9	301500	331000
59	3	SEA RANGER 60		MY	FBG	DS	IB	T870D		18	7	72000	4	9	405000	445000
65	3	SEA RANGER 65		MY	FBG	DS	IB	T355D		18	7	79400	4	9	349000	383500
65	3	SEA RANGER 65		MY	FBG	DS	IB	T870D		18	7	79400	4	9	444000	488000
72		SEA RANGER 72		MY	FBG	DS	IB	T355D		18	7	95000	4	9	**	**
72		SEA RANGER 72		MY	FBG	DS	IB	T870D		18	7	95000	4	9	**	**
		1987 BOATS														
38	3	SEA RANGER 39		TRWL	FBG	DS	IB	T125D		13	8	23000	3	3	103500	114000
38	3	SEA RANGER 39		TRWL	FBG	DS	IB	T305D		13	8	23000	3	3	113000	124500
40		SEA RANGER 40 CNV		TRWL	FBG	DS	IB	T225D		14	4				115500	127000
40		SEA RANGER 40 CNV		TRWL	FBG	DS	IB	T475D		14	4				136500	150000
40		SEA RANGER 40 SD		TRWL	FBG	DS	IB	T225D		14	4				117000	128500
40		SEA RANGER 40 SD		TRWL	FBG	DS	IB	T475D		14	4				136500	150000
43		SEA RANGER 43 CNV		TRWL	FBG	DS	IB	T225D		14	4				137000	151000
43		SEA RANGER 43 CNV		TRWL	FBG	DS	IB	T475D		14	4				156500	172000
43		SEA RANGER 43 SD		TRWL	FBG	DS	IB	T255D		14	4				137500	151000

CONTINUED ON NEXT PAGE

LOA FT	LOA IN	NAME AND/ OR MODEL	TOP/ RIG	BOAT TYPE	-HULL- MTL	-HULL- TP	TP	ENGINE # HP	ENGINE MFG	BEAM FT	BEAM IN	WGT LBS	DRAFT FT	DRAFT IN	RETAIL LOW	RETAIL HIGH
		1987 BOATS														
43		SEA RANGER 43 SD		TRWL	FBG	DS	IB	T475D		14	4				154500	170000
45		SEA RANGER 45 AFTCBN		TRWL	FBG	DS	IB	T125D		15	3	37400	4		142500	156500
45		SEA RANGER 45 AFTCBN		TRWL	FBG	DS	IB	T475D		15	3	37400	4		162500	178500
45		SEA RANGER 45 SEDAN		TRWL	FBG	DS	IB	T125D		15	3				135500	148500
45		SEA RANGER 45 SEDAN		TRWL	FBG	DS	IB	T475D		15	3				155500	171000
46	1	SEA RANGER 46 CNV		TRWL	FBG	DS	IB	T255D		14	4				141500	155500
46	1	SEA RANGER 46 CNV		TRWL	FBG	DS	IB	T475D		14	4				156500	172000
46	1	SEA RANGER 46 SD		TRWL	FBG	DS	IB	T255D		14	4				140500	154500
46	1	SEA RANGER 46 SD		TRWL	FBG	DS	IB	T475D		14	4				153000	168000
46	1	SEA RANGER 46 SS		TRWL	FBG	DS	IB	T255D		14	4				141000	155000
46	1	SEA RANGER 46 SS		TRWL	FBG	DS	IB	T475D		14	4				155500	170500
47	3	SEA RANGER 47 PH		TRWL	FBG	DS	IB	T125D		14	8	27000	4	4	135000	148500
47	3	SEA RANGER 47 PH		TRWL	FBG	DS	IB	T475D		14	8	27000	4	4	156000	171500
48		SEA RANGER 48 SS		TRWL	FBG	DS	IB	T305D							141500	155500
48		SEA RANGER 48 SS		TRWL	FBG	DS	IB	T475D		14	4				153000	168500
51		SEA RANGER 51		MY	FBG	DS	IB	T260D		16	8	55000	4	3	201000	220500
51		SEA RANGER 51		MY	FBG	DS	IB	T650D		16	8	55000	4	3	260500	286500
52		SEA RANGER 52 DC		TRWL	FBG	DS	IB	T125D		15	3				140000	153500
52		SEA RANGER 52 DC		TRWL	FBG	DS	IB	T475D		15	3				172000	189000
53	6	SEA RANGER 53		MY	FBG	DS	IB	T260D		16	8				181000	199000
53	6	SEA RANGER 53		MY	FBG	DS	IB	T650D		16	8				226500	249000
55		SEA RANGER 55		MY	FBG	DS	IB	T320D		18	7	64900	4	9	236500	260000
55		SEA RANGER 55		MY	FBG	DS	IB	T750D		18	7	64900	4	9	313000	344000
58		SEA RANGER 58		MY	FBG	DS	IB	T355D		18	7				209500	230500
58		SEA RANGER 58		MY	FBG	DS	IB	T870D		18	7				272000	299000
59	3	SEA RANGER 60		MY	FBG	DS	IB	T355D		18	7	72000	4	9	288000	316500
59	3	SEA RANGER 60		MY	FBG	DS	IB	T870D		18	7	72000	4	9	387000	425500
65	3	SEA RANGER 65		MY	FBG	DS	IB	T355D		18	7	79400	4	9	333500	366500
65	3	SEA RANGER 65		MY	FBG	DS	IB	T870D		18	7	79400	4	9	424500	466500
72		SEA RANGER 72		MY	FBG	DS	IB	T355D		18	7				**	**
72		SEA RANGER 72		MY	FBG	DS	IB	T870D		18	7		4	9	**	**
		1986 BOATS														
35	8	SEA-RANGER		TRWL	FBG	DS	IB	T 80D	FORD	13	4	19000	3	3	84200	92500
35	8	SEA-RANGER		TRWL	FBG	DS	IB	T120D	FORD	13	4	19000	3	3	86000	94500
35	8	SEA-RANGER		TRWL	FBG	DS	IB	T124D	VLVO	13	4	19000	3	3	85500	93900
36	6	SEA-RANGER		TRWL	FBG	DS	IB	T120D	FORD	13	1	26000	3	10	102500	112500
36	6	SEA-RANGER		TRWL	FBG	DS	IB	T124D	VLVO	13	1	26000	3	10	101500	111500
38	3	SEA-RANGER		TRWL	FBG	DS	IB	T120D	FORD	13	8	23000	3	3	99000	109000
38	3	SEA-RANGER		TRWL	FBG	DS	IB	T124D	VLVO	13	8	23000	3	3	97800	107500
45		SEA-RANGER		SDN	FBG	DS	IB	T120D	FORD	15	3	35200	4		139500	153500
45		SEA-RANGER		SDN	FBG	DS	IB	T124D	VLVO	15	3	35200	4		139500	153500
45	10	SEA-RANGER		TRWL	FBG	DS	IB	T120D	FORD	14	6	30500	4	3	136000	149500
45	10	SEA-RANGER		TRWL	FBG	DS	IB	T124D	VLVO	14	6	30500	4	3	136000	149000
46	10	SEA-RANGER		TRWL	FBG	DS	IB	T120D	FORD	14	2	32300	4	4	144000	158500
46	10	SEA-RANGER		TRWL	FBG	DS	IB	T124D	VLVO	14	2	32300	4	4	144000	158500
51		SEA-RANGER		MY	FBG	DS	IB	T270D	VLVO	16	8	55000	4	3	195500	215000
55		SEA-RANGER		MY	FBG	DS	IB	T310D	GM	18	7	64900	4	9	221500	243500
59	3	SEA-RANGER		MY	FBG	DS	IB	T350D	GM	19		72000	4	9	277000	304500
65		SEA-RANGER		MY	FBG	DS	IB	T462D	GM	19		76000	4	9	331000	363500
68		SEA-RANGER		MY	FBG	DS	IB	T462D	GM	19		79000	4	9	373000	409500
72	3	SEA-RANGER		MY	FBG	DS	IB	T462D	GM	18	7	90000	4	9	**	**
		1984 BOATS														
35	8	SEA-RANGER		TRWL	FBG	DS	IB	T120D	FORD	13	10	19000	3	3	78200	86000
35	8	SEA-RANGER		TRWL	FBG	DS	IB	T124D	VLVO	13	10	19000	3	3	77800	85500
36	6	SEA RANGER		TRWL	FBG	DS	IB	T124D	VLVO	13	1	26000	3	10	93100	102500
36	6	SEA-RANGER		TRWL	FBG	DS	IB	T120D	FORD	13	1	26000	3	10	93800	103000
38	3	SEA-RANGER		TRWL	FBG	DS	IB	T120D	FORD	13	8	23000	3	3	90900	99800
38	3	SEA-RANGER		TRWL	FBG	DS	IB	T124D	VLVO	13	8	23000	3	3	89700	98600
44	10	SEA-RANGER		TRWL	FBG	DS	IB	T120D	FORD	14	2	31000	4	4	122500	135000
44	10	SEA-RANGER		TRWL	FBG	DS	IB	T124D	VLVO	14	2	31000	4	4	122500	134500
45		SEA-RANGER		TRWL	FBG	DS	IB	T120D	FORD	15	3	32400	4		125500	138000
45		SEA-RANGER		TRWL	FBG	DS	IB	T124D	VLVO	15	3	32400	4		125000	137500
45	3	EXPLORER 45		SA/CR	FBG	KL	IB	50D	PERK	13		30000	6	8	112000	123000
46	10	SEA-RANGER		TRWL	FBG	DS	IB	T120D	FORD	14	2	32400	4	4	132500	145500
46	10	SEA-RANGER		TRWL	FBG	DS	IB	T124D	VLVO	14	2	32400	4	4	132500	145500
47	3	SEA-RANGER		TRWL	FBG	DS	IB	T235D	VLVO	14	8	29000	4	4	132500	145500
51		SEA-RANGER		MY	FBG	DS	IB	T265D	GM	16	8	52000	4	3	161000	177000
55		SEA-RANGER		MY	FBG	DS	IB	T265D	GM	18	7	64900	4	9	195500	215000
59	3	SEA-RANGER		MY	FBG	DS	IB	T350D	GM	19		72000	4	9	254000	279500
65		SEA-RANGER		MY	FBG	DS	IB	T462D	GM	19		76000	4	9	303500	333500
68		SEA-RANGER		MY	FBG	DS	IB	T462D	GM			79000	4	9	342000	376000
72		SEA-RANGER		MY	FBG	DS	IB	T675D	GM	19		85000	4	9	**	**

....For earlier years, see the BUC Used Boat Price Guide, Volume 3

SEA RAY BOATS

KNOXVILLE TN 37914 COAST GUARD MFG ID- SER See inside cover to adjust price for area

SEA RAY BOATS
MERRITT ISLAND FL 32953

For more recent years, see the BUC Used Boat Price Guide, Volume 1

LOA FT	LOA IN	NAME AND/ OR MODEL	TOP/ RIG	BOAT TYPE	-HULL- MTL	-HULL- TP	TP	ENGINE # HP	ENGINE MFG	BEAM FT	BEAM IN	WGT LBS	DRAFT FT	DRAFT IN	RETAIL LOW	RETAIL HIGH
		1996 BOATS														
16	4	SEA RAYDER F-16	OP	RNBT	FBG	SV	JT	120	MRCR	6	11	1250		11	4750	5450
18		LAGUNA 18 CC	OP	CTRCN	FBG	DV	OB			7	6	2000	2	2	4750	5450
18	2	BOW RIDER 175	OP	B/R	FBG	DV	OB			7		1850	2	6	4700	5400
18	2	BOW RIDER 175	OP	B/R	FBG	DV	IO	135	MRCR	7		2050	3		5050	5800
18	2	BOW RIDER 175 XL	OP	B/R	FBG	DV	IO	160	MRCR	7		2250	3	2	5350	6150
18	2	CLOSED BOW 175	OP	RNBT	FBG	DV	OB			7		1850	2	6	4700	5400
18	2	CLOSED BOW 175	OP	RNBT	FBG	DV	IO	135	MRCR	7		2050	3		5300	6100
18	2	CLOSED BOW 175 XL	OP	RNBT	FBG	DV	IO	160	MRCR	7		2250	3	2	5550	6400
18	6	BOW RIDER 190	OP	B/R	FBG	DV	IO	160-210		7	6	2750	2	7	6350	7450
18	6	CLOSED BOW 190	OP	RNBT	FBG	DV	IO	160-210		7	6	2750	2	7	6600	7700
18	8	SKI RAY 190	OP	SKI	FBG	DV	OB			7	6	2250	2	6	4900	5600
18	8	SPORTSTER BR	OP	SKI	FBG	DV	IB	265	MRCR	7	8	2750	1	9	8150	9350
20	5	SPITFIRE	OP	SKI	FBG	DV	IB	265	MRCR	6	11	2500	1	9	7200	8300
20	6	BOW RIDER 210	OP	B/R	FBG	DV	IO	210-220		8		2900	2	6	7550	8850
20	6	BOW RIDER 210	OP	B/R	FBG	DV	IO	250	MRCR	8		2900	2	6	8200	9400
20	6	BOW RIDER 210 SELECT	OP	B/R	FBG	DV	IO	210-250		8		2900	2	6	10700	12600
21	6	EXPRESS CRUISER 215	OP	EXP	FBG	DV	IO	180-250		8	6	3700	2	9	12300	14500
21	6	LAGUNA 21 DC	OP	B/R	FBG	DV	OB			8	6	3200	2	7	9100	10300
21	11	SPORTSTER BR	OP	SKI	FBG	DV	IB	265	MRCR	7	8	2750	1	9	11600	13200
22	5	BOW RIDER 230	OP	B/R	FBG	DV	IO	210-300		8	2	3700	2	8	12100	14900
22	5	BOW RIDER 230 SELECT	OP	B/R	FBG	DV	IO	250-300		8	2	4200	2	8	13600	16200
22	5	BOW RIDER 230 SELECT	OP	B/R	FBG	DV	IO	330	MRCR	8	2	4200	2	8	15000	17100
22	5	BOW RIDER 230 SELECT	OP	B/R	FBG	DV	IO	385	MRCR	8	2	4200	2	8	17000	19300
22	5	OVERNIGHTER 230	OP	CUD	FBG	DV	IO	210-300		8	2	3600	2	10	12700	15600
22	5	OVERNIGHTER 230 SLT	OP	CUD	FBG	DV	IO	250-300		8	2	4100	2	10	14200	17000
22	5	OVERNIGHTER 230 SLT	OP	CUD	FBG	DV	IO	330	MRCR	8	2	4100	2	10	15800	17900
22	5	OVERNIGHTER 230 SLT	OP	CUD	FBG	DV	IO	385	MRCR	8	2	4100	2	10	18300	20300
22	8	LAGUNA 21 CC	OP	CTRCN	FBG	DV	OB			8		2900	2	6	8000	9200
22	8	LAGUNA 21 WA	OP	CUD	FBG	DV	OB			8		3400	2	6	8400	9650
23	6	SUNDANCER 240	OP	CUD	FBG	DV	IO	210-250		8	6	4300	2	9	15500	18000
23	6	SUNDANCER 240	OP	CUD	FBG	DV	IO	140D	MRCR	8	6	4300	2	9	19500	21700
23	6	SUNDECK 240	OP	RNBT	FBG	DV	IO	180-250		8	6	3650	3		12800	15000
23	10	BOW RIDER 240	OP	B/R	FBG	DV	IO	300-330		8	6	4300	3		15800	18800
23	10	OVERNIGHTER 240	OP	CUD	FBG	DV	IO	300-330		8	6	4300	3		16900	20000
25	9	LAGUNA 24 CC	OP	CTRCN	FBG	DV	OB			8	6	4300	2	7	13100	14900
25	9	LAGUNA 24 FDC	OP	CUD	FBG	DV	OB			8	6	4650	2	7	13700	15500
26	5	SUNDANCER 250	OP	CUD	FBG	DV	IO	210-300		8	6	5200	3		19300	22900
26	5	SUNDANCER 250	OP	CUD	FBG	DV	IO	200D-240D		8	6	5200	3		24700	28600
27	6	BOW RIDER 280	OP	B/R	FBG	DV	IO	330-415		8	6	6400	3	5	26400	32200
27	6	BOW RIDER 280	OP	B/R	FBG	DV	IO	240D	MRCR	8	6	6400	3	5	29700	33000
27	6	BOW RIDER 280	OP	B/R	FBG	DV	IO	T250	MRCR	8	6	6400	3	2	28400	31600
29	11	SUNDANCER 270	OP	EXP	FBG	DV	IO	300-330		8	6	6400	3		25400	29000
29	11	SUNDANCER 270	OP	EXP	FBG	DV	IO	240D	MRCR	8	6	6400	3		29900	33200
29	11	SUNDANCER 270	OP	EXP	FBG	DV	IO	T180	MRCR	8	6	6400	2	9	26300	29200
32	1	SUNDANCER 290	OP	EXP	FBG	DV	IO	300	MRCR	9	8	8500	3	9	33600	37300
32	1	SUNDANCER 290	OP	EXP	FBG	DV	IO	240D	MRCR	9	8	8500	3	9	39300	43700
32	1	SUNDANCER 290	OP	EXP	FBG	DV	IO	T180	MRCR	9	8	8500	3	1	34600	38400
33	1	SUNDANCER 300	OP	EXP	FBG	DV	IO	T210-T220		10	6	10200	3	6	42700	47800
		IO T250 MRCR 43400 48200, VD T250 MRCR 50500 55500, IO T200D MRCR													51500	56600
33	6	SUNDANCER 330	OP	EXP	FBG	DV	VD	T250	MRCR	11	5	10600	3		65800	72300
36	1	SUNDANCER 330	OP	EXP	FBG	DV	VD	T235	MRCR	11	5	11200	3		66100	72700
		IO T300 MRCR 59300 65200, VD T310 MRCR 68700 75500, IO T330 MRCR													60600	66600
		VD T340 MRCR 69800 76700, IO T200D MRCR 62700 68900, IO T240D MRCR													65000	71400
36	10	EXPRESS CRUISER 370	OP	EXP	FBG	DV	IB	T310	MRCR	12	4	13000	2	5	83100	91300
		IB T225D VLVO 93200 102500, IB T292D CAT 102500 113000, IB T306D CUM													100500	110500
36	10	SEDAN BRIDGE 370	FB	SDN	FBG	DV	IB	T310	MRCR	12	4	14600	2	7	87200	95900
		IB T225D VLVO 98700 108500, IB T292D CAT 108500 119000, IB T306D CUM													106500	117000

498 CONTINUED ON NEXT PAGE 96th ed. - Vol. II

```
       LOA  NAME AND/             TOP/ BOAT -HULL- ----ENGINE---  BEAM    WGT   DRAFT RETAIL RETAIL
       FT IN OR MODEL             RIG  TYPE MTL TP TP # HP  MFG   FT IN   LBS   FT IN  LOW   HIGH
-------------------------- 1996 BOATS --------------------------------------------------------------
37   6 SUNDANCER 370             OP  EXP  FBG DV VD T310  MRCR 12  7 15400  2  8 103500 114000
     IB T225D VLVO 105500 116000, IB T292D CAT  116000 127500, IB T306D CUM  113500 124500

38   5 SUNSPORT 380              OP  EXP  FBG DV IO T300  MRCR 11    11200  3    63900  70200
     IO T350  MRCR  67300  74000, IO T385  MRCR  70800  77800, IO T415  MRCR  74200  81600
     IO T216D VLVO  77300  84900

40   4 EXPRESS CRUISER 400       OP  EXP  FBG DV IB T310  MRCR 13    16200  3  3 108000 119000
     IB T292D CAT  131000 144000, IB T306D CUM  128000 140500, IB T340D CAT  136500 150000

44     EXPRESS BRIDGE 440        FB  SPTCR FBG DV VD T292D CAT 13 11 26600  3  5 176000 193000
     VD T306D CUM  173500 190500, VD T340D CAT  181500 199500, VD T364D CUM  185000 203500
     VD T407D CUM  187000 205500

44     SEDAN BRIDGE 400          FB  SDN  FBG DV IB T310  MRCR 14  3 21000  3  4 132500 146000
     IB T292D CAT  155000 170500, IB T306D CUM  153000 168000, IB T340D CAT  161000 177000

45   5 AFT CABIN 420             FB  CRCPT FBG DV IB T340  MRCR 14  3 27000  3  1 162500 178500
     IB T292D CAT  183500 201500, IB T340D CAT  192500 211500, IB T407D CAT  206500 227000

49  11 SEDAN BRIDGE 500          FB  SDN  FBG DV IB T535D DD  15    40000  4  2 270500 297000
     IB T545D DD  272000 299000, IB T635D DD  287000 315000, IB T705D DD  298000 327500
     IB T735D DD  303000 333000

50   1 SUNDANCER 500             OP  CR   FBG DV IB T465D DD  15    32200  4    233000 256000
     IB T525D DD  243000 267000, IB T535D DD  245000 269000, VD T705D DD  271500 298500
     VD T735D DD  276500 303500

50  10 SUNDANCER 450             OP  EXP  FBG DV IB T292D CAT 13 11 23500  3  7 174500 191500
50  10 SUNDANCER 450             OP  EXP  FBG DV IB T340D CAT 13 11 23500  3  7 180500 198000
50  10 SUNDANCER 450             OP  EXP  FBG DV IB T407D CAT 13 11 23500  3  7 189000 207500
54  10 SEDAN BRIDGE 550          FB  SDN  FBG DV IB T535D DD  15    45000  4  2 330500 363500
54  10 SEDAN BRIDGE 550          FB  SDN  FBG DV IB T545D DD  15    45000  4  2 338000 371500
     IB T635D DD  364500 400500, IB T705D DD  384500 422500, IB T735D DD  393000 431500

54  10 SPORTFISH 550             FB  SDNSF FBG DV IB T545D DD  15    45000  4  2 331000 363500
54  10 SPORTFISH 550             FB  SDNSF FBG DV IB T705D DD  15    45000  4  2 379500 417000
54  10 SPORTFISH 550             FB  SDNSF FBG DV IB T735D DD  15    45000  4  2 388000 426500
54  10 SPORTFISH 550             FB  SF   FBG DV IB T525D DD  15    45000  4  2 328500 360500
54  10 SPORTFISH 550             FB  SF   FBG DV IB T535D DD  15    45000  4  2 331500 364500
54  10 SPORTFISH 550             FB  SF   FBG DV IB T635D DD  15    45000  4  2 363000 399000
62   6 HARD TOP 630              HT  EXP  FBG DV IB T10CD CAT 15  9 52000  5    505000 555000
62   6 HARD TOP 630              HT  EXP  FBG DV IB T11CD CAT 15  9 52000  5    529500 582000
62   6 SUPER SUN SPORT 630       OP  EXP  FBG DV IB T10CD CAT 15  9 52000  5    532000 585000
62   6 SUPER SUN SPORT 630       OP  EXP  FBG DV IB T11CD CAT 15  9 52000  5    568000 613500
64   6 COCKPIT MY 650            FB  MYCPT FBG DV IB T10CD CAT 18  1 75000  4 10 796000 875000
64   6 COCKPIT MY 650            FB  MYCPT FBG DV IB T11CD CAT 18  1 75000  4 10 830000 912000
-------------------------- 1995 BOATS --------------------------------------------------------------
18     LAGUNA 18 CC              OP  CTRCN FBG DV OB         7  6  2000  2  2  4500   5200
18   2 BOW RIDER 175             OP  B/R  FBG DV OB          7     1850  2  2  4450   5100
18   2 BOW RIDER 175             OP  B/R  FBG DV IO 135  MRCR 7     2050  3     4700   5350
18   6 BOW RIDER 180             OP  B/R  FBG DV IO 180-190  7  6  2750  2  7  5900   6800
18   6 CLOSED BOW 180            OP  RNBT FBG DV IO 180-190  7  6  2750  2  7  6100   7050
18   7 SPITFIRE                  OP  SKI  FBG DV IB 250-265  6 11  2500  1  9  6700   7750
18   7 SKI RAY 190               OP  SKI  FBG DV OB          7  6  2250  2  2  4650   5300
18   8 SPORTSTER BR              OP  SKI  FBG DV IO 265  MRCR 7  8  2750  1  9  7600   8750
18   8 SPORTSTER BR              OP  SKI  FBG DV IO 395  MRCR 7  8  2750  1  9  8800  10000
20   2 BOW RIDER 195             OP  B/R  FBG DV IO 135-180  7  7  2350  2  9  6950   8100
20   2 OVERNIGHTER 200           OP  CUD  FBG DV IO 190  MRCR 7  7  2900  2  9  8450   9700
20   2 OVERNIGHTER 200 SLT       OP  CUD  FBG DV IO 205-250  7  7  3000  2  9  8700  10300

20   6 BOW RIDER 200             OP  B/R  FBG DV IO 190-250  8     3000  2  6  8500  10200
20   6 BOW RIDER 200 SELECT      OP  B/R  FBG DV IO 205-265  8     3300  2  6  9200  10900
20   6 BOW RIDER 200 SELECT      OP  B/R  FBG DV IO 23C  MRCR 8    3300  2  6    **     **
20  10 LAGUNA 21 CC              OP  CTRCN FBG DV OB         8     2900  2  6  7550   8650
20  10 LAGUNA 21 WA              OP  CUD  FBG DV OB          8     3400  2  6  8000   9200
22   5 BOW RIDER 220             OP  B/R  FBG DV IO 205-300  8  2  3700  2  8 11100  13800
22   5 BOW RIDER 220 SELECT      OP  B/R  FBG DV IO 235-300  8  2  4000  2  8 12000  14500
22   5 BOW RIDER 220 SELECT      OP  B/R  FBG DV IO 365-385  8  2  4000  2  8 14500  17300
22   5 OVERNIGHTER 220           OP  CUD  FBG DV IO 205-300  8  2  3600  2 10 11700  14400
22   5 OVERNIGHTER 220 SLT       OP  CUD  FBG DV IO 235-300  8  2  3900  2 10 12500  15200
22   5 OVERNIGHTER 220 SLT       OP  CUD  FBG DV IO 385  MRCR 8  2  3900  2 10 16000  18200

23   2 SUNDANCER 230             OP  CUD  FBG DV IO 180-250  8     4300  2  9 13700  16000
23   2 SUNDANCER 230             OP  CUD  FBG DV IO 140D MRCR 8     4300  2  9 17300  19600
23  10 BOW RIDER 240             OP  B/R  FBG DV IO 235-300  8  6  4000  2  6 13100  15800
23  10 OVERNIGHTER 240           OP  CUD  FBG DV IO 235-300  8  6  4000  2  6 14000  16800
24     LAGUNA 24 CC              OP  CTRCN FBG DV OB         8  6  4300  2  7 12400  14100
24     LAGUNA 24 FDC             OP  CUD  FBG DV OB          8  6  4650  2  7 12900  14700
24   7 SUNDANCER 250             OP  CUD  FBG DV IO 235-300  8  6  5000  3    17300  20800
24   7 SUNDANCER 250             OP  CUD  FBG DV IO 238D MRCR 8  6  5000  3    13300  25700
27   4 SUNDANCER 270             OP  EXP  FBG DV IO 300  MRCR 8  6  6100  3    23900  25400
27   4 SUNDANCER 270             OP  EXP  FBG DV IO 200D-250D 8  6  6100  3    25400  27000
27   4 SUNDANCER 270             OP  EXP  FBG DV IO T135-T180 8  6  6100  3    22700  26400

27   6 SR 280                    OP  CUD  FBG DV IO 300  MRCR 8  6  4500  3    21500  23900
     IO 238D MRCR  23200  25800, IO T160-T250  21900  27200, IO T265  MRCR  25000  27800

29   4 SUNDANCER 290             OP  EXP  FBG DV IO 300  MRCR 9  8  7700  3  9 29900  33200
     IO 200D-238D  32700  37700, IO T160-T180  30300  34300, IO T140D MRCR  35900  39900

29   9 WEEKENDER 300             OP  WKNDR FBG DV IO T250  MRCR 10  6 8200  2  8 32400  36000
     VD T250  MRCR  37900  42100, IO T200D MRCR  38800  43100, VD T210D MRCR  47800  52500

30   6 SUNDANCER 300             OP  EXP  FBG DV IO T235  MRCR 10  6 9700  3  6 39600  44000
     IO T250  MRCR  40100  44500, VD T250  MRCR  47600  52300, IO T200D MRCR  46500  51100

31   2 SUN SPORT 310             OP  EXP  FBG DV IO T300-T385 9  6 8200  3  1 44700  53000
31   2 SUN SPORT 310             OP  EXP  FBG DV IOT200D-T238D 9  6 8200  3  1 48600  56200
31   2 SUN SPORT 310             ST  EXP  FBG DV IO T415  MRCR 9  6 8200  3  1 49400  54300
32  10 EXPRESS CRUISER 330       OP  EXP  FBG DV IB T235  MRCR 11  5 10100  3    49300  54200
     IO T250  MRCR  49800  54700, IB T250  MRCR  58500  64300, IB T300  MRCR  51400  56500
     IB T310  MRCR  60600  66600, IB T200D MRCR  56100  61700, IB T225D VLVO  69300  76100
     IB T238D MRCR  58100  63900

33   6 SUNDANCER 330             OP  EXP  FBG DV IB T235  MRCR 11  5 10600  3    52000  57200
     IO T250  MRCR  52500  57700, VD T250  MRCR  61600  67700, IB T300  MRCR  54200  59500
     IOT200D-T238D  64300

36  10 EXPRESS CRUISER 370       OP  EXP  FBG DV IB T310  MRCR 12  4 13000  2  5 78900  86700
     IB T225D VLVO  88900  97700, IB T292D CAT  97900 107500, IB T306D CUM  96000 105500

36  10 SEDAN BRIDGE 370          FB  SDN  FBG DV IB T310  MRCR 12  4 14600  2  7 82900  91100
     IB T225D VLVO  93700 103000, IB T292D CAT  103000 113000, IB T306D CUM  101000 111000

37   6 SUNDANCER 370             OP  EXP  FBG DV IB T310  MRCR 12  7 15400  2  8 98500 108000
     IB T225D VLVO 100000 110000, IB T292D CAT  110000 121000, IB T306D CUM  107500 118000

38   5 SUN SPORT 380             OP  EXP  FBG DV IO T300  MRCR 11    11200  3    59000  64900
     IO T350  MRCR  62200  68400, IO T385  MRCR  65400  71800, IO T415  MRCR  68600  75400
     IO T216D VLVO  71400  78500

40   4 EXPRESS CRUISER 400       OP  EXP  FBG DV IB T310  MRCR 13    16100  3  3 102500 112500
     IB T292D CAT  124000 136500, IB T306D CUM  121000 133000, IB T340D CAT  129000 142000

44     EXPRESS BRIDGE 440        FB  SPTCR FBG DV VD T292D CAT 13 11 26600  3  5 165500 182000
     VD T306D CUM  163500 179500, VD T340D CAT  171000 188000, VD T364D CUM  174500 191500
     VD T407D CUM  176500 194000

44     SUNDANCER 440             OP  CR   FBG DV VD T292D CAT 13 11 20100  3  3 136500 150000
     IO T306D CUM  103000 113500, IB T340D CAT  141500 155500, VD T364D CAT  144000 158500
     VD T407D CUM  144500 159000, VD T422D CAT  151000 166000

49  11 SEDAN BRIDGE 500          FB  SDN  FBG DV IB T535D DD  15    40000  4  2 254500 279500
     IB T545D DD  256000 281500, IB T635D DD  270000 296500, IB T705D DD  280500 308500
     IB T735D DD  285000 313500

50   1 SUNDANCER 500             OP  CR   FBG DV IB T465D DD  15    32100  4    219000 240500
     IB T525D DD  228500 251000, IB T535D DD  230000 253000, VD T705D DD  255500 280500
     VD T735D DD  260000 285500

50  10 SUNDANCER 450             OP  EXP  FBG DV IB T292D CAT 13 11 23500  3  7 165000 181500
50  10 SUNDANCER 450             OP  EXP  FBG DV IB T340D CAT 13 11 23500  3  7 171000 188000
50  10 SUNDANCER 450             OP  EXP  FBG DV IB T407D CAT 13 11 23500  3  7 179000 196500
54  10 SEDAN BRIDGE 550          FB  SDN  FBG DV IB T535D DD  15    45000  4  2 320500 352000
54  10 SEDAN BRIDGE 550          FB  SDN  FBG DV IB T545D DD  15    45000  4  2 322500 355000
     IB T635D DD  346000 380000, IB T705D DD  364500 400500, IB T735D DD  372500 409500

54  10 SPORTFISH 550             FB  SDNSF FBG DV IB T545D DD  15    45000  4  2 314000 345500
54  10 SPORTFISH 550             FB  SDNSF FBG DV IB T705D DD  15    45000  4  2 360000 395500
54  10 SPORTFISH 550             FB  SDNSF FBG DV IB T735D DD  15    45000  4  2 368000 404500
54  10 SPORTFISH 550             FB  SF   FBG DV IB T525D DD  15    45000  4  2 311500 344500
54  10 SPORTFISH 550             FB  SF   FBG DV IB T535D DD  15    45000  4  2 313500 345500
54  10 SPORTFISH 550             FB  SF   FBG DV IB T635D DD  15    45000  4  2 344500 378500
62   6 HARD TOP 630              HT  EXP  FBG DV IB T10CD CAT 15  9 52000  5    488000 536000
62   6 HARD TOP 630              HT  EXP  FBG DV IB T10CD CAT 15  9 52000  5    495000 544000
```

LOA FT	LOA IN	NAME AND/ OR MODEL	TOP/ RIG	BOAT TYPE	-HULL- MTL	-HULL- TP	ENGINE TP	ENGINE # HP	ENGINE MFG	BEAM FT	BEAM IN	WGT LBS	DRAFT FT	DRAFT IN	RETAIL LOW	RETAIL HIGH
		1995 BOATS														
62	6	HARD TOP 630	HT	EXP	FBG	DV	IB	T11CD	CAT	15	9	52000	5		516000	567000
62	6	SUPER SUN SPORT 630	OP	EXP	FBG	DV	IB	T10CD	DD	15	9	52000	5		514500	565000
62	6	SUPER SUN SPORT 630	OP	EXP	FBG	DV	IB	T10CD	DD	15	9	52000	5		522000	573500
62	6	SUPER SUN SPORT 630	OP	EXP	FBG	DV	IB	T11CD	CAT	15	9	52000	5		543500	597500
64	6	COCKPIT MY 650	FB	MYCPT	FBG	DV	IB	T10CD	DD	18	1	75000	4	10	766500	842500
64	6	COCKPIT MY 650	FB	MYCPT	FBG	DV	IB	T10CD	DD	18	1	75000	4	10	776000	853000
64	6	COCKPIT MY 650	FB	MYCPT	FBG	DV	IB	T11CD	CAT	18	1	75000	4	10	804500	884000
		1994 BOATS														
16	9	BOW RIDER 170	OP	RNBT	FBG	DV	IO	115	MRCR	7	1	1900	2	7	3950	4600
18		LAGUNA 18	OP	FSH	FBG	DV	OB			7	6	2000	2	2	4200	4900
18	2	BOW RIDER 180	OP	RNBT	FBG	DV	OB			7		1950	2	6	4300	5000
18	2	CLOSED BOW 180	OP	RNBT	FBG	DV	OB			7		1950	2	6	4300	5000
18	6	BOW RIDER 180	OP	RNBT	FBG	DV	IO	155-190		7	6	2750	2	7	5600	6500
18	6	CLOSED BOW 180	OP	RNBT	FBG	DV	IO	155-190		7	6	2750	2	7	5600	6500
18	7	SPITFIRE 185 SK	OP	RNBT	FBG	DV	IB	240-265		6	11	2500	1	9	6500	7550
18	8	SKI RAY 190	OP	RNBT	FBG	DV	OB			7	6	2250	2	6	4650	5350
18	8	SKI RAY 190 BR	OP	RNBT	FBG	DV	IB	250	MRCR	7	6	2250	2	6	6500	7500
20	2	200 OV/LTD	OP	CUD	FBG	DV	OB			7	7	2800	2	9	6500	7500
20	6	BOW RIDER 200	OP	RNBT	FBG	DV	IO	190-270		8		3000	2	6	8000	9800
20	10	LAGUNA 21 CC	OP	CTRCN	FBG	DV	OB			8		2900	2	6	7150	8200
20	10	LAGUNA 21 WA	OP	CUD	FBG	DV	OB			8		3400	2	6	7550	8650
21	4	SUNRUNNER 220	OP	RNBT	FBG	DV	IO	175-230		8		3150	2	8	8600	10100
22	5	BOW RIDER 220	OP	RNBT	FBG	DV	IO	205-300		8	2	3700	2	8	10400	12800
22	5	BOW RIDER 220 SELECT	OP	RNBT	FBG	DV	IO	230-300		8	2	4000	2	8	11100	13500
22	5	OVERNIGHTER 220	OP	CUD	FBG	DV	IO	205-300		8	2	3600	2	10	10800	13300
22	5	OVERNIGHTER 220 SLT	OP	CUD	FBG	DV	IO	230-300		8	2	3900	2	10	11500	14000
23	2	SUNDANCER 230	OP	CUD	FBG	DV	IO	190-230		8		4200	2	9	12400	14400
23	2	SUNDANCER 230	OP	CUD	FBG	DV	IO	150D	MRCR	8		4200	2	9	15900	18000
23	2	SUNDANCER 230	OP	SDN	FBG	DV	IO	175	MRCR	8		4200	2	9	12400	14100
23	10	BOW RIDER 240	OP	RNBT	FBG	DV	IO	230-300		8	6	4000	3		12000	14600
23	10	OVERNIGHTER 240	OP	CUD	FBG	DV	IO	230-300		8	6	4000	3		12800	15500
24		LAGUNA 24 CC	OP	CTRCN	FBG	DV	OB			8	6	3800	2	7	10900	12300
24	7	EXPRESS CRUISER 250	ST	EXP	FBG	DV	IO	230-300		8	6	5000	3		15800	19000
26		SUNRUNNER 280	OP	CUD	FBG	DV	IO	300	MRCR	8	6	4500	3		17100	19400
26		SUNRUNNER 280	OP	CUD	FBG	DV	IO	T155-T230		8	6	4500	3		17400	21300
26		SUNRUNNER 280	OP	CUD	FBG	DV	IO	T238D	MRCR	8	6	4500	3		28200	31300
27	4	SUNDANCER 270	OP	EXP	FBG	DV	IO	240-300		8	6	6100	3		20100	23500
27	4	SUNDANCER 270	OP	EXP	FBG	DV	IO	200D-238D		8	6	6100	3		23400	27300
27	4	SUNDANCER 270	OP	EXP	FBG	DV	IO	T155-T175		8	6	6100	3		21400	24200
29	4	SUNDANCER 290	OP	EXP	FBG	DV	IO	300	MRCR	9	8	7700	3	9	27600	30600
		IO 200D-238D 30200 34800, IO T155-T175 27800 31500, IO T150D MRCR													33700	37400
30	6	SUNDANCER 300	OP	EXP	FBG	DV	IO	T230	MRCR	10	6	8700	3	6	35500	39500
30	6	SUNDANCER 300	OP	EXP	FBG	DV	IB	T250	MRCR	10	6	8700	3	6	43000	47800
30	6	SUNDANCER 300	OP	EXP	FBG	DV	IO	T210D	MRCR	10	6	8700	3	6	42900	47700
30	6	WEEKENDER 300	OP	WKNDR	FBG	DV	IB	T210	MRCR	10	6	8200	2	8	36500	40500
30	6	WEEKENDER 300	OP	WKNDR	FBG	DV	IO	T230-T250		10	6	8200	2	8	31100	35100
30	6	WEEKENDER 300	OP	WKNDR	FBG	DV	IB	T200D	MRCR	10	6	8200	2	8	45600	50100
31	2	AMBERJACK 310	OP	CUD	FBG	DV	IB	T230-T310		11	5	10500	3	1	50400	58400
31	2	AMBERJACK 310	ST	CUD	FBG	DV	IB	T262D	MRCR	11	5	10500	3	1	64100	70400
31	2	SUN SPORT 310	OP	EXP	FBG	DV	IO	T300-T350		9	6	8200	3	1	41300	47700
31	2	SUN SPORT 310	OP	EXP	FBG	DV	IO	T210D-T238D		9	6	8200	3	1	45700	52100
31	2	SUN SPORT 310	ST	EXP	FBG	DV	IO	T415	MRCR	9	6	8200	3	1	45900	50400
32	10	EXPRESS CRUISER 330	OP	WKNDR	FBG	DV	IO	T230	MRCR	11	5	10000	3		37800	42000
		IB T240 MRCR 45700 50200, IO T300 MRCR 39700 44100, IB T310 MRCR													47600	52300
		IO T210D MRCR 45800 50300, IB T225D VLVO 54300 59700, IO T238D MRCR													47000	51700
32	10	SUNDANCER 330	OP	EXP	FBG	DV	IO	T230	MRCR	11	5	10000	3		44200	49100
		IB T250 MRCR 53700 59000, IO T300-T310 46800 51800, IOT210D-T238D													51000	57900
36	10	EXPRESS CRUISER 370	OP	EXP	FBG	DV	IB	T310	MRCR	12	4	13000	2	5	74700	82100
36	10	EXPRESS CRUISER 370	OP	EXP	FBG	DV	IB	T300D	CUM	12	4	13000	2	5	99100	109000
36	10	SEDAN BRIDGE 370	FB	SDN	FBG	DV	IB	T310	MRCR	12	4	14500	2	7	78100	85900
36	10	SEDAN BRIDGE 370	FB	SDN	FBG	DV	IB	T300D	CAT	12	4	14500	2	7	107500	118000
36	10	SEDAN BRIDGE 370	FB	SDN	FBG	DV	IB	T300D	CUM	12	4	14500	2	7	104500	114500
36	10	SUNDANCER 370	OP	EXP	FBG	DV	IB	T310	MRCR	12	4	13500	3	6	77900	85600
		IB T225D VLVO 96000 105500, IB T300D CAT 106000 116500, IB T300D CUM													103000	113000
		IB T340D CAT 110000 121000														
38	5	SUN SPORT 380	OP	EXP	FBG	DV	IO	T350	MRCR	11		11100	3		57100	62800
38	5	SUN SPORT 380	OP	EXP	FBG	DV	IO	T415	MRCR	11		11100	3		63000	69300
38	5	SUN SPORT 380	OP	EXP	FBG	DV	IB	T238D	VLVO	11		11100	3		90800	99800
40	4	EXPRESS CRUISER 400	OP	EXP	FBG	DV	IB	T310	MRCR	13		16000	3	3	96400	106000
		IB T300D CAT 117500 129500, IB T300D CUM 113500 125000, IB T340D CAT													121500	134000
44		EXPRESS BRIDGE 440	FB	SPTCR	FBG	DV	IB	T300D	CAT	13	11	26500	3	5	156500	172000
		IB T300D CUM 153000 168000, IB T340D CAT 161000 177000, IB T364D CAT													164000	180500
44		SUNDANCER 440	OP	CR	FBG	DV	IB	T300D	CAT	13	11	20000	3	3	129500	142000
		IB T300D CUM 126500 139000, IB T340D CAT 133000 146500, IB T364D CAT													135500	149000
		IB T388D CAT 138000 152000, IB T425D CAT 142500 156500														
49	11	SEDAN BRIDGE 500	FB	SDN	FBG	DV	IB	T465D	DD	15		40000	4	2	229000	251500
		IB T525D DD 238000 261500, IB T535D DD 239500 263500, IB T635D DD													254000	279500
		IB T645D MTU 269500 296000, IB T720D DD 266000 292500														
50	1	SUNDANCER 500	OP	CR	FBG	DV	IB	T465D	DD	15		32000	4		206000	226500
		IB T525D DD 215000 236000, IB T535D DD 216500 238000, IB T720D DD													242500	266500
54	10	SEDAN BRIDGE 550	OP	SDN	FBG	DV	IB	T535D	DD	15		45000	4	2	297000	326500
54	10	SEDAN BRIDGE 550	OP	SDN	FBG	DV	IB	T720D	DD	15		45000	4	2	345000	379000
54	10	SEDAN BRIDGE 550	FB	SDN	FBG	DV	IB	T525D	DD	15		45000	4	2	298000	327500
		IB T635D DD 327500 360000, IB T645D MTU 333500 366500, IB T720D DD													349500	384000
54	10	SPORTFISH 550	FB	SF	FBG	DV	IB	T525D	DD	15		45000	4	2	295000	324500
		IB T535D DD 298000 327500, IB T635D DD 326500 359000, IB T645D MTU													331500	364000
		IB T720D DD 349500 384000														
62	6	HARD TOP 630	HT	EXP	FBG	DV	IB	T970D	MTU	15	9	52000	5		453000	498000
		IB T10CD DD 462000 507500, IB T10CD DD 469000 515000, IB T12CD CAT													495000	544000
62	6	SUPER SUN SPORT 630	OP	EXP	FBG	DV	IB	T970D	MTU	15	9	52000	5		477500	525000
		IB T10CD DD 487000 535000, IB T10CD DD 494000 543000, IB T12CD CAT													522000	573500
64	6	COCKPIT MY 650	FB	MYCPT	FBG	DV	IB	T900D	DD	18	1	75000	4	10	689500	758000
		IB T970D MTU 720000 791000, IB T10CD DD 726000 797500, IB T10CD DD													734500	807500
		IB T12CD CAT 770500 846500														
		1993 BOATS														
16	8	BOWRIDER 180	OP	RNBT	FBG	DV	IO	115-155		7		2200	2	7	3850	4550
16	8	BOWRIDER 180 LTD	OP	RNBT	FBG	DV	OB			7		2200	2	7	4500	5150
16	8	CLOSED BOW 180	OP	RNBT	FBG	DV	IO	155	MRCR	7		2150	2	7	3850	4500
16	8	CLOSED BOW 180 LTD	OP	RNBT	FBG	DV	OB			7		2150	2	7	4450	5100
16	8	CLOSED BOW 180 LTD	OP	RNBT	FBG	DV	IO	115-135		7		2150	2	7	3850	4500
16	9	BOWRIDER 170 LTD	OP	RNBT	FBG	DV	IO	115	MRCR	7	1	1900	2	7	3650	4250
17	10	LAGUNA 18	OP	FSH	FBG	DV	OB			8		2260	2	6	4200	4900
18	7	SPITFIRE 185 SK	OP	RNBT	FBG	DV	IO	250	MRCR	6	11	2350	1	9	4850	5600
18	8	BOW RIDER 180 LTD	OP	RNBT	FBG	DV	IO	115-135		7		2200	2	7	4550	5200
18	8	SKI RAY 190 BR	OP	RNBT	FBG	DV	OB			7	6	2150	2	6	4250	4950
18	8	SKI RAY 190 CB	OP	RNBT	FBG	DV	OB			7	6	2150	2	6	4400	5100
18	8	SPORTSTER 190 SK	OP	RNBT	FBG	DV	IO	250	MRCR	7	6	2250	2	6	5000	5750
18	8	SPORTSTER 190 SK/BR	OP	RNBT	FBG	DV	IO	250	MRCR	7	6	2250	2	6	5000	5750
20	2	200 OV/LTD	OP	CUD	FBG	DV	OB			7	7	2600	2	9	6000	6900
20	2	200 OV/LTD	OP	CUD	FBG	DV	IO	115-150		7	7	2600	2	9	6650	7700
20	2	BOW RIDER 200	OP	RNBT	FBG	DV	IO	155-230		7	7	2500	2	9	6300	7500
20	10	LAGUNA 21 CC	OP	CTRCN	FBG	DV	OB			8		2670	2	6	6550	7500
20	10	LAGUNA 21 WA	OP	CUD	FBG	DV	IO	155-230		8		3400	2	6	8450	10000
20	10	LAGUNA 21 WA	OP	CUD	FBG	DV	IO	126D	VLVO	8		3400	2	6	10700	12200
21	4	BOW RIDER 220 SR	OP	RNBT	FBG	DV	IO	175-230		8		3050	2	8	7750	9150
21	4	BOWRIDER 220	OP	RNBT	FBG	DV	IO	250-300		8		3050	2	8	8100	9950
21	7	OVERNIGHTER 220	OP	CUD	FBG	DV	IO	155-250		8		3050	2	10	8250	9900
21	7	OVERNIGHTER 220	OP	CUD	FBG	DV	IO	300	MRCR	8		3050	2	10	9350	10600
23	2	230 DA/LTD	OP	SDN	FBG	DV	IO	175	MRCR	8		3500	3		10000	11400
23	10	BOW RIDER 240	OP	RNBT	FBG	DV	IO	230-300		8	6	3900	3		10900	13200
23	10	OVERNIGHTER 240	OP	CUD	FBG	DV	IO	230-300		8	6	4200	3		12300	14800
24		LAGUNA 24 CC	OP	CTRCN	FBG	DV	OB			8	6	3800	2	7	10300	11700
24		LAGUNA 24 FDC	OP	CUD	FBG	DV	OB			8	6	4650	2	7	11600	13200
24	7	EXPRESS CRUISER 250	ST	EXP	FBG	DV	IO	230-300		8	6	5000	3		14500	17500
24	7	EXPRESS CRUISER 250	ST	EXP	FBG	DV	IO	185D-200D		8	6	5000	3		17600	21000
26	9	SUNDANCER 270	OP	EXP	FBG	DV	IO	240-300		8	6	5600	3		17000	20300
26	9	SUNDANCER 270	OP	EXP	FBG	DV	IO	T155-T175		8	6	5600	3		18500	21000
26	9	WEEKENDER 270	OP	WKNDR	FBG	DV	IO	240-300		8	6	5600	3		18800	21800
28	7	SUNDANCER 290	OP	EXP	FBG	DV	IO	300	MRCR	9		6400	3	1	22200	24600
		IO 200D MRCR 23500 26100, IO T155-T175 22400 25400, IO T150D MRCR													27100	30100
29	2	LAGUNA 29 WA	OP	CUD	FBG	SV	IO	T205-T250		10	6	10600	2	8	31300	35800
29	2	LAGUNA 29 WA	OP	CUD	FBG	SV	IO	T195D-T216D		10	6	10600	2	8	41400	47100
29	9	SUNDANCER 300	OP	EXP	FBG	DV	IO	T155-T230		10	6	8300	2	8	28500	33700
29	9	SUNDANCER 300	OP	EXP	FBG	DV	IO	T120D-T140D		10	6	8300	2	8	32600	37700
29	9	WEEKENDER 300	OP	WKNDR	FBG	DV	IO	T155-T230		9		8000	2	8	24700	29200
		VD T250 MRCR 32200 35800, IO T185D VLVO 30900 34300, IO T200D MRCR													31900	35400

CONTINUED ON NEXT PAGE

LOA FT	LOA IN	NAME AND/ OR MODEL	TOP/ RIG	BOAT TYPE	-HULL- MTL	-HULL- TP	ENGINE TP	ENGINE # HP	ENGINE MFG	BEAM FT	BEAM IN	WGT LBS	DRAFT FT	DRAFT IN	RETAIL LOW	RETAIL HIGH
		1993 BOATS														
29	9	WEEKENDER 300	OP	WKNDR	FBG	DV	VD	T200D	MRCR	9		8000	2	8	40000	44500
31	2	AMBERJACK 310	OP	CUD	FBG	DV	IB	T230-T340		11	5	10500	3	1	47400	55700
31	2	AMBERJACK 310	OP	CUD	FBG	DV	IB	T300D	CUM	11	5	10500	3	1	62600	68800
31	2	AMBERJACK 310	ST	CUD	FBG	DV	IB	T292D	CAT	11	5	10500	3	1	62400	68600
31	2	SPORT BRIDGE 310	OP	CUD	FBG	DV	IB	T340	MRCR	11	5	11500	3	1	51600	56700
31	2	SPORT BRIDGE 310	OP	CUD	FBG	DV	IB	T300D	CUM	11	5	11500	3	1	64600	71000
31	2	SUN SPORT 310	OP	EXP	FBG	DV	IO	T330-T390		9	6	8200	3	1	39000	45500
31	2	SUN SPORT 310	OP	EXP	FBG	DV	IO	T195D-T216D		9	6	8200	3	1	40700	46500
31	2	SUN SPORT 310	ST	EXP	FBG	DV	IO	T390	MRCR	9	6	8200	3	1	41000	45500
31	2	SUNBRIDGE 310	OP	CUD	FBG	DV	IB	T300D	CAT	11	5	11500	3	1	66200	72800
32	10	EXPRESS CRUISER 330	OP	WKNDR	FBG	DV	IO	T230-T300		11	5	10000	3		34900	40600
		IB T310 MRCR 44000 48900, IOT185D-T200D 40000 45700, IB T225D VLVO													51100	56100
32	10	SUNDANCER 330	OP	EXP	FBG	DV	IO	T230	MRCR	11	5	10000	3		40800	45300
		VD T250 MRCR 50200 55200, IO T300 MRCR 42700 47400, VD T310 MRCR													52000	57200
		IOT185D-T216D 46100 52200														
35	4	EXPRESS BRIDGE 350	OP	EXP	FBG	DV	IO	T240	MRCR	11	5	11500	3	1	53900	59200
		IO T300 MRCR 55800 61300, IO T185D VLVO 59100 64900, IO T200D MRCR													60400	66400
36	10	EXPRESS CRUISER 370	OP	EXP	FBG	DV	IB	T330	MRCR	12	4	12000	2	5	67800	74600
		IB T275D VLVO 86100 94600, IB T292D CAT 91900 101000, IB T300D CUM													89600	98400
36	10	SEDAN BRIDGE 370	FB	SDN	FBG	DV	IB	T340	MRCR	12	4	14000	2	7	72900	80100
36	10	SEDAN BRIDGE 370	FB	SDN	FBG	DV	IB	T300D	CUM	12	4	14000	2	7	96400	106000
36	10	SUNDANCER 370	OP	EXP	FBG	DV	IO	T300	MRCR	12	4	12000	3	6	44900	49900
		VD T330 MRCR 69300 76100, IO T216D VLVO 60400 66400, VD T216D VLVO													84200	92600
38	5	SUN SPORT 380	OP	EXP	FBG	DV	IO	T350	MRCR	11		10000	3		50000	55000
38	5	SUN SPORT 380	OP	EXP	FBG	DV	IO	T390	MRCR	11		10000	3		53100	58400
38	5	SUN SPORT 380	OP	EXP	FBG	DV	IB	T292D	CAT	11		10000	3		89800	98700
40	4	EXPRESS CRUISER 400	OP	EXP	FBG	DV	IB	T340	MRCR	13		16000	3	3	91600	100500
40	4	EXPRESS CRUISER 400	OP	EXP	FBG	DV	IB	T300D	CAT	13		16000	3	3	110500	121500
40	4	EXPRESS CRUISER 400	OP	EXP	FBG	DV	IB	T300D	CUM	13		16000	3	3	107000	117500
44		EXPRESS BRIDGE 440	FB	SPTCR	FBG	DV	IB	T292D	CAT	13	11	26500	3	5	146000	160500
44		EXPRESS BRIDGE 440	FB	SPTCR	FBG	DV	IB	T292D	CUM	13	11	26500	3	5	143000	157500
44		EXPRESS BRIDGE 440	FB	SPTCR	FBG	DV	IB	T364D	CAT	13	11	26500	3	5	154500	169500
44		SUNDANCER 440	OP	CR	FBG	DV	IB	T292D	CAT	13	11	20000	3	3	121000	133000
		VD T293D CUM 118500 130000, VD T364D CAT 127500 140000, VD T417D CAT													133000	146000
49	11	SEDAN BRIDGE 500	FB	SDN	FBG	DV	IB	T485D	DD	15		40000	4	2	218000	239500
		IB T550D DD 227500 250000, IB T650D DD 241000 264500, IB T665D MTU													256500	282000
		IB T735D DD 252500 277500														
50	1	SUNDANCER 500	OP	CR	FBG	DV	VD	T465D	GM	15		32000	4		191000	210000
50	1	SUNDANCER 500	OP	CR	FBG	DV	VD	T535D	GM	15		32000	4		200500	220500
50	1	SUNDANCER 500	OP	CR	FBG	DV	VD	T720D	GM	15		32000	4		223500	246000
54	10	SEDAN BRIDGE 550	OP	SDN	FBG	DV	IB	T550D	GM	15		45000	4	2	282500	310000
		IB T650D GM 306500 337000, IB T665D MTU 316000 347500, IB T735D GM													326500	359000
54	10	SEDAN BRIDGE 550	FB	SDN	FBG	DV	IB	T550D	DD	15		45000	4	2	287500	315500
		IB T550D MTU 290500 319000, IB T650D DD 312000 343000, IB T735D DD													332500	365500
62	6	SUPER SUN SPORT 630	OP	EXP	FBG	DV	IB	T10CD	MTU	15	9	52000	5		455500	500500
62	6	SUPER SUN SPORT 630	OP	EXP	FBG	DV	IB	T10CD	DD	15	9	52000	5		465500	511500
62	6	SUPER SUN SPORT 630	OP	EXP	FBG	DV	IB	T10CD	GM	15	9	52000	5		474500	521500
64	6	COCKPIT MY 650	FB	MYCPT	FBG	DV	IB	T10CD	MTU	18	1	75000	4	10	685000	752500
64	6	COCKPIT MY 650	FB	MYCPT	FBG	DV	IB	T10CD	DD	18	1	75000	4	10	692000	760500
		1992 BOATS														
16	8	CLOSED BOW 180 LTD	OP	RNBT	FBG	DV	IO	115-155		7		2150	2	7	3550	4150
17	10	LAGUNA 18	OP	FSH	FBG	DV	OB			8		2260	2	6	4000	4650
18	8	BOW RIDER 180 LTD	OP	RNBT	FBG	DV	IO	115-155		7		2200	2	7	4050	4750
18	8	SKI RAY 190	OP	RNBT	FBG	DV	IO	175	MRCR	7	6	2150	2	6	4250	4950
18	8	SKI RAY 190	OP	RNBT	FBG	DV	IO	260-270		7	6	2150	2	6	4600	5400
20	2	200 OV/LTD	OP	CUD	FBG	DV	IO	155	MRCR	7	7	2600	2	9	6150	7100
20	2	200 OV/LTD	OP	RNBT	FBG	DV	IO	125	MRCR	7	7	2600	2	9	5900	6800
20	2	200 SR	OP	CUD	FBG	DV	IO	155-230		7	7	2450	2	9	6000	7100
20	2	BOW RIDER 200	OP	RNBT	FBG	DV	IO	155-230		7	7	2500	2	9	5800	6900
20	10	LAGUNA 21	OP	FSH	FBG	DV	OB			8		2670	2	6	6250	7150
21	4	220 SR	OP	RNBT	FBG	DV	IO	175-230		8		3050	2	8	7150	8450
21	4	BOW RIDER 220 SR	OP	RNBT	FBG	DV	IO	175-230		8		3050	2	8	7150	8450
21	7	OVERNIGHTER 220	OP	CUD	FBG	DV	IO	155-230		8		3050	2	10	7600	9000
23	2	230 DA/LTD	OP	SDN	FBG	DV	IO	205	MRCR	8		3500	3		9350	10600
23	8	SUNDANCER 240	OP	EXP	FBG	DV	IO	205-230		8	6	4000	3		10700	12300
23	10	BOW RIDER 240	OP	RNBT	FBG	DV	IO	230-300		8	6	3900	3		10100	12200
23	10	OVERNIGHTER 240	OP	CUD	FBG	DV	IO	260	MRCR	8	6	4200	3		11500	13100
24		LAGUNA 24	OP	FSH	FBG	DV	OB			8	6	3800	2	7	9850	11200
24		LAGUNA 24 CC	OP	CTRCN	FBG	DV	OB			8	6	3800	2	7	9850	11200
24		LAGUNA 24 FDC	OP	CUD	FBG	DV	OB			8	6	4650	2	7	11100	12600
26	9	SUNDANCER 270	OP	EXP	FBG	DV	IO	230-300		8	6	5600	3		15500	18700
26	9	SUNDANCER 270	OP	EXP	FBG	DV	IO	T155-T175		8	6	5600	3		16700	19400
26	9	WEEKENDER 270	OP	WKNDR	FBG	DV	IO	230-300		8	6	5000	3		15800	19200
28	7	SUNDANCER 290	OP	EXP	FBG	DV	IO	300	MRCR	9		5800	3	1	19800	22000
28	7	SUNDANCER 290	OP	EXP	FBG	DV	IO	T155-T175		9		5800	3	1	20000	22700
29	9	SUNDANCER 300	OP	EXP	FBG	DV	IO	T155-T230		10	6	8000	2	8	25900	30800
29	9	SUNDANCER 300	OP	EXP	FBG	DV	IO	T120D-T140D		10	6	8000	2	8	29400	34000
29	9	WEEKENDER 300	OP	WKNDR	FBG	DV	IO	T155-T230		9		5800	2	8	20800	25100
		VD T250 MRCR 28100 31200, IO T185D VLVO 24800 27600, IO T200D MRCR													25900	28700
		VD T200D MRCR 33100 36700														
31	2	AMBERJACK 310	OP	CUD	FBG	DV	IB	T260-T340		11	5	10500	3	1	44700	52300
31	2	AMBERJACK 310	OP	CUD	FBG	DV	IB	T300D	CUM	11	5	10500	3	1	58800	64700
31	2	SPORT BRIDGE 310	OP	CUD	FBG	DV	IB	T260-T340		11	5	11500	3	1	46200	53100
31	2	SPORT BRIDGE 310	OP	CUD	FBG	DV	IB	T300D	CUM	11	5	11500	3	1	61300	67400
31	2	SUN SPORT 310	OP	EXP	FBG	DV	IO	T330-T365		9	6	8100	3	1	35900	41100
31	2	SUN SPORT 310	OP	EXP	FBG	DV	IO	T220D	MRCR	9	6	8100	3	1	38800	43100
32	10	EXPRESS CRUISER 330	OP	WKNDR	FBG	DV	IO	T230-T300		11	5	10000	3		32100	37500
32	10	EXPRESS CRUISER 330	OP	WKNDR	FBG	DV	IB	T330	MRCR	11	5	10000	2	1	41600	46300
32	10	EXPRESS CRUISER 330	OP	WKNDR	FBG	DV	IO	T185D-T200D		11	5	10000	3		36900	42200
32	10	SUNDANCER 330	OP	EXP	FBG	DV	IO	T230	MRCR	11	5	10000	3		37600	41800
		VD T250 MRCR 47200 51800, IO T300 MRCR 39400 43700, VD T330 MRCR													49200	54100
		IOT185D-T200D 42000 47600														
35	4	EXPRESS BRIDGE 350	OP	EXP	FBG	DV	IO	T260	MRCR	11	5	11500	3	1	50200	55100
		IO T300 MRCR 51400 56500, IO T340 VLVO 53800 59200, IO T220D MRCR													56600	62200
		IO T220D VLVO 55900 61400														
36	10	EXPRESS CRUISER 370	OP	EXP	FBG	DV	IB	T330	MRCR	12	4	12000	2	5	63700	70000
36	10	EXPRESS CRUISER 370	OP	EXP	FBG	DV	IB	T410	MRCR	12	4	12000	2	5	66600	73200
36	10	EXPRESS CRUISER 370	OP	EXP	FBG	DV	IB	T300D	CUM	12	4	12000	2	5	84100	92400
36	10	SEDAN BRIDGE 370	FB	SDN	FBG	DV	IB	T340	MRCR	12	4	14000	2	7	68500	75200
36	10	SEDAN BRIDGE 370	FB	SDN	FBG	DV	IB	T410	MRCR	12	4	14000	2	7	71100	78100
36	10	SEDAN BRIDGE 370	FB	SDN	FBG	DV	IB	T300D	CUM	12	4	14000	2	7	90500	99500
36	10	SUNDANCER 370	OP	EXP	FBG	DV	IO	T300	MRCR	12	4	12000	3	6	41400	46000
		VD T330 MRCR 65100 71500, IO T210D MRCR 56700 62300, VD T210D MRCR													80400	88400
38	5	SUN SPORT 380	OP	EXP	FBG	DV	IO	T350	MRCR	11		10000	3		46400	51000
38	5	SUN SPORT 380	OP	EXP	FBG	DV	IO	T390	MRCR	11		10000	3		49000	53900
38	5	SUN SPORT 380	OP	EXP	FBG	DV	IO	T210D	MRCR	11		10000	3		54100	59500
40	4	EXPRESS CRUISER 400	OP	EXP	FBG	DV	IB	T340	MRCR	13		16000	3	3	86000	94500
40	4	EXPRESS CRUISER 400	OP	EXP	FBG	DV	IB	T410	MRCR	13		16000	3	3	88900	97600
40	4	EXPRESS CRUISER 400	OP	EXP	FBG	DV	IB	T300D	CUM	13		16000	3	3	100500	110500
44		SUNDANCER 440	OP	CR	FBG	DV	VD	T293D	CUM	13	11	20000	3	3	111000	122000
44		SUNDANCER 440	OP	CR	FBG	DV	VD	T364D	CAT	13	11	20000	3	3	120000	131500
44		SUNDANCER 440	OP	CR	FBG	DV	VD	T417D	CAT	13	11	20000	3	3	125000	137500
49	11	SUNDANCER 500	OP	EXP	FBG	DV	IB	T485D	GM	15		40000	4	2	210500	231000
50	1	SUNDANCER 500	OP	CR	FBG	DV	VD	T465D	GM	15		32000	4		179500	197500
50	1	SUNDANCER 500	OP	CR	FBG	DV	VD	T535D	GM	15		32000	4		188500	207000
50	1	SUNDANCER 500	OP	CR	FBG	DV	VD	T720D	GM	15		32000	4		210000	231000
54	10	SEDAN BRIDGE 550	OP	SDN	FBG	DV	IB	T550D	GM	15		45000	4	2	265500	292000
		IB T650D GM 288500 317000, IB T665D MTU 298000 327500, IB T735D GM													307500	337500
62	6	SUPER SUN SPORT 630	OP	EXP	FBG	DV	IB	T10CD	MTU	15	9	52000	5		428500	471000
62	6	SUPER SUN SPORT 630	OP	EXP	FBG	DV	IB	T10CD	GM	15	9	52000	5		446000	490000
		1991 BOATS														
16	9	BOW RIDER 160	OP	RNBT	FBG	DV	OB			7	1	1530	2	2	3100	3600
16	9	CLOSED BOW 160	OP	RNBT	FBG	DV	OB			7	1	1495	2	2	3050	3550
17	10	LAGUNA 17	OP	FSH	FBG	DV	OB			8		2260	2	6	3800	4450
18	2	BOW RIDER 170	OP	RNBT	FBG	DV	IO	115-155		7		2200	2	7	3400	4000
18	2	BOW RIDER 170 LTD	OP	RNBT	FBG	DV	IO	115-155		7		2200	2	7	3200	3800
18	2	CLOSED BOW 170	OP	RNBT	FBG	DV	IO	115-155		7		2150	2	7	3350	3950
18	2	CLOSED BOW 170 LTD	OP	RNBT	FBG	DV	IO	115-155		7		2150	2	7	3200	3750
18	8	BOW RIDER 180	OP	RNBT	FBG	DV	OB			7	6	1760	2	2	3500	4100
18	8	CLOSED BOW 180	OP	RNBT	FBG	DV	OB			7	6	1725	2	2	3450	4050
18	8	SKI RAY 180	OP	RNBT	FBG	DV	OB			7	6	2150	2	6	3950	4550
20	2	BOW RIDER 185	OP	RNBT	FBG	DV	IO	155-230		7	7	2500	2	9	4200	5050
20	2	BOW RIDER 185 SR	OP	RNBT	FBG	DV	IO	155-230		7	7	2450	2	9	4150	5000
20	10	LAGUNA 20	OP	FSH	FBG	DV	OB			8		2670	2	6	6000	6850
21	4	BOW RIDER 200	OP	RNBT	FBG	DV	IO	175-230		8		3150	2	8	6250	7400
21	4	BOW RIDER 200 SR	OP	RNBT	FBG	DV	IO	175-230		8		3050	2	8	6150	7250
21	4	OVERNIGHTER 200	OP	CUD	FBG	DV	IO	175-230		8		3050	2	10	6450	7600
21	4	OVERNIGHTER 200 LTD	OP	CUD	FBG	DV	IO	155	MRCR	8		3050	2	10	6400	7350

96th ed. - Vol. II CONTINUED ON NEXT PAGE 501

SEA RAY BOATS -CONTINUED See inside cover to adjust price for area

LOA FT	LOA IN	NAME AND/ OR MODEL	TOP/ RIG	BOAT TYPE	-HULL- MTL	-HULL- TP	ENGINE TP	ENGINE # HP	ENGINE MFG	BEAM FT	BEAM IN	WGT LBS	DRAFT FT	DRAFT IN	RETAIL LOW	RETAIL HIGH
		1991 BOATS														
22	2	PACHANGA 22	OP	EXP	FBG	DV	IO	240-300		8		2900	2	8	9800	12100
23	6	CUDDY CABIN 230	OP	CUD	FBG	DV	IO	230-300		8		3650	2	6	8300	10300
23	8	CUDDY CABIN 220	OP	CUD	FBG	DV	IO	175-230		8	6	3500	3		7850	9200
23	8	OVERNIGHTER 220	OP	CUD	FBG	DV	IO	175-230		8	6	3500	3		8400	9850
23	8	SUNDANCER 220	OP	EXP	FBG	DV	IO	205-230		8	6	4000	3		9300	10700
23	8	SUNDANCER 220 LTD	OP	EXP	FBG	DV	IO	175-230		8	6	4000	3		9000	10200
23	10	BOW RIDER 225	OP	RNBT	FBG	DV	IO	230-300		8	6	3900	3		8600	10600
24		LAGUNA 23	OP	FSH	FBG	DV	OB			8	6	3800	2	7	9450	10700
24		LAGUNA 23 CC	OP	CUD	FBG	DV	OB			8	6	4650	2	7	10600	12100
27	6	CUDDY CABIN 260	OP	CUD	FBG	DV	IO	300	MRCR	8	6	4500	3		13400	15200
27	6	CUDDY CABIN 260	OP	CUD	FBG	DV	IO	T155-T230		8	6	4500	3		13600	16700
27	6	OVERNIGHTER 260	OP	OVNTR	FBG	DV	IO	300	MRCR	8	6	4500	3		13400	15200
27	6	OVERNIGHTER 260	OP	OVNTR	FBG	DV	IO	T155-T230		8	6	4500	3		13600	16700
27	6	PACHANGA 27	OP	EXP	FBG	DV	IO	T240-T300		8	6	5100	2	8	23400	28300
28	6	SUNDANCER 250	OP	EXP	FBG	DV	IO	230-300		8	6	5100	3		13300	16100
28	6	SUNDANCER 250	OP	EXP	FBG	DV	IO	T155-T175		8	6	5100	3		14400	16600
28	6	WEEKENDER 250	OP	WKNDR	FBG	DV	IO	230-300		8	6	5000	3		13100	15800
30	6	SUNDANCER 270	OP	EXP	FBG	DV	IO	300	MRCR	10		5800	3	1	16200	18400
30	6	SUNDANCER 270	OP	EXP	FBG	DV	IO	T155-T175		10		5800	3	1	16400	19000
31	7	PACHANGA 32	OP	EXP	FBG	DV	IO	T300-T350		8	6	6300	3	1	33800	39600
31	11	SUNDANCER 280	OP	EXP	FBG	DV	IO	T155-T230		10	6	8000	2	8	21200	25000
31	11	SUNDANCER 280	OP	EXP	FBG	DV	IO	T120D-T140D		10	6	8000	2	8	25800	30000
31	11	WEEKENDER 280	OP	WKNDR	FBG	DV	IO	T155-T230		9		5800	2	8	19000	22900
		VD T250 MRCR 25900 28800, IO T185D VLVO 24400 27200, IO T200D MRCR 25600 28500														
		VD T200D MRCR 33400 37100														
35	4	EXPRESS CRUISER 310	OP	WKNDR	FBG	DV	IO	T230	MRCR	11	5	10000	3		33700	37400
		IO T300 MRCR 35400 39300, IB T330 MRCR 44800 49700, IO T185D VLVO 37000 41100														
		IO T200D MRCR 37700 41800														
35	4	SUNDANCER 310	OP	EXP	FBG	DV	IO	T230	MRCR	11	2	12000	3		33800	37600
		VD T250 MRCR 42600 47300, IO T300 MRCR 35300 39300, VD T330 MRCR 44700 49600														
		IO T185D VLVO 39300 43600, IO T200D MRCR 39900 44300														
38	5	SUN SPORT 370	OP	EXP	FBG	DV	IO	T350	MRCR	11		11000	3		38600	42800
38	5	SUN SPORT 370	OP	EXP	FBG	DV	IO	T390	MRCR	11		11000	3		40600	45100
38	5	SUN SPORT 370	OP	EXP	FBG	DV	IO	T210D	MRCR	11		11000	3		45700	50200
39	5	EXPRESS CRUISER 350	OP	EXP	FBG	DV	IB	T330	MRCR	12	4	13000	2	5	61800	67900
39	5	EXPRESS CRUISER 350	OP	EXP	FBG	DV	IB	T293D	CUM	12	4	13000	2	5	73600	80900
39	5	SUNDANCER 350	OP	EXP	FBG	DV	IO	T300	MRCR	12	4	13500	3	6	50300	55300
		VD T330 MRCR 62600 68800, IO T210D MRCR 54100 59400, VD T210D MRCR 70400 77400														
40	11	SEDAN BRIDGE 370	FB	SDN	FBG	DV	IB	T340	MRCR	12	4	14500	2	7	65500	72000
40	11	SEDAN BRIDGE 370	FB	SDN	FBG	DV	IB	T410	MRCR	12	4	14500	2	7	68000	74700
40	11	SEDAN BRIDGE 370	FB	SDN	FBG	DV	IB	T300D	CUM	12	4	14500	2	7	78600	86400
42	7	AFT CABIN 380	FB	CR	FBG	DV	IB	T330	MRCR	13	11	20000	2	7	79100	87000
42	7	AFT CABIN 380	FB	CR	FBG	DV	IB	T400	MRCR	13	11	20000	2	7	81400	89500
42	7	AFT CABIN 380	FB	CR	FBG	DV	IB	T293D	CUM	13	11	20000	2	7	91900	101000
47	1	SUNDANCER 420	OP	CR	FBG	DV	VD	T293D	CUM	13	11	20000	3	3	107500	118500
47	1	SUNDANCER 420	OP	CR	FBG	DV	VD	T364D	CAT	13	11	20000	3	3	116500	128000
47	1	SUNDANCER 420	OP	CR	FBG	DV	VD	T417D	CAT	13	11	20000	3	3	122000	134000
49	1	AFT CABIN 440	FB	CR	FBG	DV	IB	T330	MRCR	13	11	23000	2	8	108500	119000
		IB T400 MRCR 112000 123000, IB T364D CAT 130000 143000, IB T412D CAT 135000 148000														
52	9	SUNDANCER 480	OP	CR	FBG	DV	VD	T465D	DD	15		32000	4		162500	178500
52	9	SUNDANCER 480	OP	CR	FBG	DV	VD	T535D	DD	15		32000	4		170000	187000
52	9	SUNDANCER 480	OP	CR	FBG	DV	VD	T720D	DD	15		32000	4		186500	205000
		1990 BOATS														
16	9	BOW RIDER 160	OP	RNBT	FBG	DV	OB			7	1	1530	2	2	3000	3500
16	9	BOW RIDER 160	OP	RNBT	FBG	DV	IO	130	MRCR	7	1	1900	2	7	2600	3000
17	10	LAGUNA 17	OP	FSH	FBG	DV	OB								3350	3900
18	8	BOW RIDER 180	OP	RNBT	FBG	DV	OB			7	6	1760	2	2	3350	3900
18	8	BOW RIDER 180	OP	RNBT	FBG	DV	IO	130-175		7	6	2120	2	6	3350	3950
20	8	BOW RIDER 190	OP	RNBT	FBG	DV	IO	205-260		8		2820	2	6	4550	5450
20	10	BOW RIDER 200	OP	RNBT	FBG	DV	IO	175-205		7	10	2360	2	8	4100	4850
20	10	CUDDY CABIN 200	OP	CUD	FBG	DV	IO	175-205		7	10	2315	2	6	4250	5000
20	10	LAGUNA 20	OP	FSH	FBG	DV	OB			8		2670	2	6	5750	6600
22	2	PACHANGA 22	OP	EXP	FBG	DV	IO	270	MRCR	8		2900	2	8	9400	10700
22	2	PACHANGA 22	OP	EXP	FBG	DV	IO	330	MRCR	8		2900	2	8	10600	12000
22	6	BOW RIDER 210	OP	RNBT	FBG	DV	IO	260	MRCR	8		3030	2	6	6300	7250
23	6	CUDDY CABIN 230	OP	CUD	FBG	DV	IO	260	MRCR	8		3650	2	6	7850	9050
23	6	CUDDY CABIN 230	OP	CUD	FBG	DV	IO	330	MRCR	8		3650	2	6	8850	10100
23	8	CUDDY CABIN 220	OP	CUD	FBG	DV	IO	175-260		8	6	3500	3		7500	9000
23	8	OVERNIGHTER 220	OP	OVNTR	FBG	DV	IO	175-260		8	6	3500	3		7500	9000
23	8	SUNDANCER 220	OP	EXP	FBG	DV	IO	175-260		9	6	4000	3		8650	10300
24		LAGUNA 23	OP	FSH	FBG	DV	OB			8	6	3800	2	7	9100	10300
26	9	SUNDANCER 250	OP	EXP	FBG	DV	IO	260-330		8	6	5100	3		14000	16000
26	9	SUNDANCER 250	OP	EXP	FBG	DV	IO	T175-T205		8	6	5100	3		13500	15700
26	9	WEEKENDER 250	OP	WKNDR	FBG	DV	IO	260-330		8		4060	2	8	10800	13400
27	1	SUNDANCER 270	OP	EXP	FBG	DV	IO	T330		9		5800	3	1	18600	20700
27	6	CUDDY CABIN 260	OP	CUD	FBG	DV	IO	260-330		8	6	4500	3		11900	14600
27	6	CUDDY CABIN 260	OP	CUD	FBG	DV	IO	T175	MRCR	8	6	4500	3		12800	14600
27	6	OVERNIGHTER 260	OP	OVNTR	FBG	DV	IO	260-330		8	6	4500	3		11800	14600
27	6	OVERNIGHTER 260	OP	OVNTR	FBG	DV	IO	T175-T205		8	6	4500	3		12800	15000
27	6	PACHANGA 27	OP	EXP	FBG	DV	IO	330-365		8	6	5100	2	8	20300	23700
27	6	PACHANGA 27	OP	EXP	FBG	DV	IO	T270-T330		8	6	5100	2	8	22500	27400
29	3	AMBERJACK 270	OP	CUD	FBG	DV	IO	T175-T260		10		7000	2	8	18500	22000
29	3	AMBERJACK 270	OP	CUD	FBG	DV	IB	T130D-T150D		10		7000	2	8	29100	33400
29	8	SUNDANCER 280	OP	EXP	FBG	DV	IO	T175-T260		10	6	8000	2	8	19900	23700
29	8	SUNDANCER 280	OP	EXP	FBG	DV	IB	T130D-T150D		10	6	8000	2	8	32000	36600
31	7	PACHANGA 32	OP	EXP	FBG	DV	IO	T270-T365		8	6	6300	3	1	30300	37200
35	4	EXPRESS CRUISER 310	OP	WKNDR	FBG	DV	IB	T260	MRCR	11		9600	2	4	32700	36300
35	4	EXPRESS CRUISER 310	OP	WKNDR	FBG	DV	IB	T340	MRCR	11		9600	2	4	34500	38300
35	4	SUNDANCER 310	OP	EXP	FBG	DV	IB	T260	MRCR	11	2	12000	2	11	40000	44400
38	5	SUN SPORT 370	OP	EXP	FBG	DV	IO	T365		11		11000			41800	46500
39	5	EXPRESS CRUISER 350	OP	EXP	FBG	DV	IB	T340	MRCR	11	11	12100	2	5	57300	63000
39	5	SUNDANCER 350	OP	EXP	FBG	DV	VD	T340	MRCR	11	11	12500	2	5	57900	63600
40	1	AFT CABIN 380	OP	CR	FBG	DV	IB	T340	MRCR	13	11	20000	2	7	74400	81800
40	1	AFT CABIN 380	OP	CR	FBG	DV	IB	T306D	VLVO	13	11	20000	2	7	85200	93700
41	10	EXPRESS CRUISER 390	OP	EXP	FBG	DV	IB	T340	MRCR	13	11	16400	2	4	67600	74300
41	10	EXPRESS CRUISER 390	OP	EXP	FBG	DV	IB	T375D	VLVO	13	11	16400	2	4	82900	91100
45	11	AFT CABIN 440	OP	CR	FBG	DV	IB	T340	MRCR	13	11	23000	2	8	101000	111000
45	11	AFT CABIN 440	OP	CR	FBG	DV	IB	T375D	VLVO	13	11	23000	2	8	116500	128000
47	1	SUNDANCER 420	OP	CR	FBG	DV	IO	T340		13	11	20000	3	3	58700	64500
53		SUNDANCER 480	OP	CR	FBG	DV	IO	T485D		15		32000			134000	147000
55	4	SEDAN BRIDGE 500	FB	CR	FBG	DV	IO	T550D		15		40000	4	2	160500	176500
		1989 BOATS														
16	9	BOW RIDER 160	OP	RNBT	FBG	DV	OB			7	1	1530	2	2	2900	3350
16	9	BOW RIDER 160	OP	RNBT	FBG	DV	IO	130	MRCR	7	1	1900	2	7	2400	2800
17	10	LAGUNA 17	OP	FSH	FBG	DV	OB								3250	3750
18	8	BOW RIDER 180	OP	RNBT	FBG	DV	OB			7	6	1760	2	2	3200	3700
18	8	BOW RIDER 180	OP	RNBT	FBG	DV	IO	130-175		7	6	2120	2	6	3100	3650
20	8	BOW RIDER 190	OP	RNBT	FBG	DV	IO	205-260		8		2820	2	6	4150	5100
20	10	BOW RIDER 200	OP	B/R	FBG	DV	IO	175	MRCR	7	10	2360	2	8	3700	4300
20	10	BOW RIDER 200	OP	RNBT	FBG	DV	IO	130-200		7	10	2360	2	8	3800	4450
20	10	CUDDY CABIN 200	OP	CUD	FBG	DV	IO	130-205		7	10	2315	2	6	3900	4600
20	10	LAGUNA 20	OP	FSH	FBG	DV	OB			8		2670	2	6	5550	6350
22		OVERNIGHTER 220	OP	OVNTR	FBG	DV	IO	175-260		8	6	3500	3		6950	8350
22	2	PACHANGA 22	OP	EXP	FBG	DV	IO	270	MRCR	8		2900	2	8	8600	9900
22	2	PACHANGA 22	OP	EXP	FBG	DV	IO	330	MRCR	8		2900	2	8	9750	11100
22	6	BOW RIDER 210	OP	RNBT	FBG	DV	IO	260	MRCR	8		3030	2	6	5800	6700
23	6	CUDDY CABIN 230	OP	CUD	FBG	DV	IO	260	MRCR	8		3650	2	6	7250	8350
23	6	CUDDY CABIN 230	OP	CUD	FBG	DV	IO	330	MRCR	8		3650	2	6	8100	9300
23	8	CUDDY CABIN 220	OP	CUD	FBG	DV	IO	175-260		8	6	3500	3		6950	8350
23	8	SUNDANCER 220	OP	EXP	FBG	DV	IO	175-260		9	6	4000	3		8000	9550
24		LAGUNA 23	OP	FSH	FBG	DV	OB			8	6	3800	2	7	8650	9950
24	8	WEEKENDER 230	OP	WKNDR	FBG	DV	IO	260	MRCR	8		4060	2	8	8300	9550
24	8	WEEKENDER 230	OP	WKNDR	FBG	DV	IO	330	MRCR	8		4060	2	8	9200	10500
26	8	SUNDANCER 250	OP	EXP	FBG	DV	IO	330	MRCR	8	6	5100	3		12500	14200
26	8	SUNDANCER 250	OP	EXP	FBG	DV	IB	150D	VLVO	8	6	5100	3		17300	19700
26	8	SUNDANCER 250	OP	EXP	FBG	DV	IO	T175-T205		8	6	5100	3		12500	14500
26	9	SUNDANCER 250	OP	EXP	FBG	DV	IO	260	MRCR	8	6	5100	3		11600	13200
26	9	SUNDANCER 250	OP	EXP	FBG	DV	IB	130D	VLVO	8	6	5100	3		16900	19200
27	1	SUNDANCER 270	OP	EXP	FBG	DV	IO	T330		9		5800	3	1	16800	19100
27	6	CUDDY CABIN 260	OP	CUD	FBG	DV	IO	260	MRCR	8	6	4500	3		11000	12500
		IO 330 MRCR 13600 15400, IB 130D-150D 14800 17400, IO T175 MRCR 11900 13500														
27	6	OVERNIGHTER 260	OP	OVNTR	FBG	DV	IO	260-330		8	6	4500	3		11000	13500
27	6	OVERNIGHTER 260	OP	OVNTR	FBG	DV	IO	130D-150D		8	6	4500	3		11000	13000
27	6	OVERNIGHTER 260	OP	OVNTR	FBG	DV	IO	T175-T205		8	6	4500	3		11900	13900
27	6	PACHANGA 27	OP	EXP	FBG	DV	IO	330-365		8	6	5100	2	8	19000	21900
27	6	PACHANGA 27	OP	EXP	FBG	DV	IO	T270-T330		8	6	5100	2	8	20800	25300
28	3	SUNDANCER 268	OP	EXP	FBG	DV	IO	330	MRCR	8	6	5475	2	10	13600	15400
28	3	SUNDANCER 268	OP	EXP	FBG	DV	IO	T175-T205		8	6	5475	2	10	13600	15900
29	3	AMBERJACK 270	OP	CUD	FBG	DV	IO	T175-T260		10		7000	2	8	16700	20600
29	3	AMBERJACK 270	OP	CUD	FBG	DV	IB	T130D-T150D		10		7000	2	8	27300	31300
29	8	SUNDANCER 280	OP	EXP	FBG	DV	IO	T175-T260		10	6	8000	2	8	18600	21900
29	8	SUNDANCER 280	OP	EXP	FBG	DV	IB	T130D-T150D		10	6	8000	2	8	30000	34300
29	11	PACHANGA 32	OP	EXP	FBG	DV	IO	T270	MRCR	8	6	6300	3	1	28000	31100

 CONTINUED ON NEXT PAGE

LOA FT	LOA IN	NAME AND/ OR MODEL	TOP/ RIG	BOAT TYPE	HULL MTL	HULL TP	ENGINE TP	ENGINE # HP	ENGINE MFG	BEAM FT	BEAM IN	WGT LBS	DRAFT FT	DRAFT IN	RETAIL LOW	RETAIL HIGH
		1989 BOATS														
31	4	SUNDANCER 300	OP	EXP	FBG	DV	IO	T260	MRCR	11		9600	2	11	23600	26200
31	4	SUNDANCER 300	OP	EXP	FBG	DV	IB	T180D-T200D		11		9600	2	11	36200	41100
31	4	WEEKENDER 300	OP	WKNDR	FBG	DV	IB	T260-T340		11		9600	2	4	31100	36500
31	4	WEEKENDER 300	OP	WKNDR	FBG	DV	IB	T180D-T200D		11		9600	2	4	37800	43000
31	6	SEDAN BRIDGE 300	FB	SDN	FBG	DV	IB	T260-T340		12		11500	2	6	36900	43500
31	6	SEDAN BRIDGE 300	FB	SDN	FBG	DV	IB	T130D-T180D		12		11500	2	6	45900	53300
31	7	PACHANGA 32	OP	EXP	FBG	DV	IO	T330-T365		8	6	6300	3	1	29800	34400
35	8	SEDAN BRIDGE 340	FB	SDN	FBG	DV	IB	T340	MRCR	12	6	16500	2	9	56900	62500
35	8	SEDAN BRIDGE 340	FB	SDN	FBG	DV	IB	T200D	VLVO	12	6	16500	2	9	68300	75000
35	11	EXPRESS CRUISER 340	OP	EXP	FBG	DV	IB	T340	MRCR	11	11	12100	2	5	48800	53600
35	11	EXPRESS CRUISER 340	OP	EXP	FBG	DV	IB	T200D	VLVO	11	11	12100	2	5	53900	59200
35	11	SUNDANCER 340	OP	EXP	FBG	DV	VD	T340	MRCR	11	11	12500	2	5	49200	54000
40	1	AFT CABIN 380	FB	CR	FBG	DV	IB	T340	MRCR	13	11	20000	2	7	69700	76500
40	1	AFT CABIN 380	FB	CR	FBG	DV	IB	T306D	VLVO	13	11	20000	2	7	79900	87800
41	10	EXPRESS CRUISER 390	OP	EXP	FBG	DV	IB	T340	MRCR	13	11	16400	2	4	63300	69600
41	10	EXPRESS CRUISER 390	OP	EXP	FBG	DV	IB	T375D	VLVO	13	11	16400	2	4	77600	85300
45	11	AFT CABIN 440	FB	CR	FBG	DV	IB	T340	MRCR	13	11	23000	2	8	95500	105000
45	11	AFT CABIN 440	FB	CR	FBG	DV	IB	T375D	VLVO	13	11	23000	2	8	110500	121500
45	11	CONVERTIBLE 440	FB	SF	FBG	DV	IB	T340	MRCR	13	11	23000	2	8	94300	103500
45	11	CONVERTIBLE 440	FB	SF	FBG	DV	IB	T375D	VLVO	13	11	23000	2	8	113000	124000
47	1	SUNDANCER 420	OP	CR	FBG	DV	IO	T340		13	11	20000	3	3	54300	59700
47	11	EXPRESS CRUISER 460	OP	CR	FBG	DV	IB	T375D	CAT	14	11	25000	3	2	115000	126500
47	11	EXPRESS CRUISER 460	OP	CR	FBG	DV	IB	T450D	CAT	14	11	25000	3	2	121500	133500
47	11	EXPRESS CRUISER 460	OP	CR	FBG	DV	IB	T550D	CAT	14	11	25000	3	2	131000	144000
		1988 BOATS														
17	10	SEVILLE 18BR	OP	RNBT	FBG	DV	OB			7	6	1760	2	6	2900	3400
17	10	SEVILLE 18BR	OP	RNBT	FBG	DV	IO	130-175		7	6	2120	2	6	2750	3250
17	10	SEVILLE 18CB	OP	RNBT	FBG	DV	OB			7	6	1760	2	6	3200	3750
17	10	SEVILLE 18CB	OP	RNBT	FBG	DV	IO	130-175		7	6	2120	2	6	3050	3550
19	2	PACHANGA 19	OP	EXP	FBG	DV	IO	205-270		7	10	2500	2	4	4950	6150
19	2	SORRENTO 19BR	OP	RNBT	FBG	DV	IO	175-205		7	10	2620	2	6	3300	3900
19	6	MONACO 195	OP	RNBT	FBG	DV	IO	205-260		8		2930	1	1	4000	4900
19	6	MONACO SRV197	OP	RNBT	FBG	DV	IO	205-260		8		2930	1	1	4000	4900
20	8	MONACO 210	OP	RNBT	FBG	DV	IO	260		8		3130	1	1	5400	6200
20	8	SORRENTO 21BR	OP	RNBT	FBG	DV	IO	205-260		8		2820	2	6	3850	4700
20	8	SORRENTO 21CB	OP	RNBT	FBG	DV	IO	205-260		8		2820	2	6	3850	4700
20	10	SEVILLE 20BR	OP	RNBT	FBG	DV	IO	130-205		7	10	2360	2	8	3500	4150
20	10	SEVILLE 20CC	OP	CUD	FBG	DV	IO	130-205		7	10	2315	2	6	3600	4250
20	10	SEVILLE 21BR	OP	B/R	FBG	DV	IO	175-205		8		2975	2	6	4900	5700
20	10	SEVILLE 21CC	OP	CUD	FBG	DV	IO	175-205		8		2944	2	6	5200	6050
20	10	SEVILLE 21MC	OP	RNBT	FBG	DV	IO	175-205		8		3289	2	6	5350	6200
22		CUDDY CABIN 230	OP	CUD	FBG	DV	IO	260		8		3440	2	8	6450	7450
22		CUDDY CABIN 230	OP	CUD	FBG	DV	IO	330		8		3440	2	8	7250	8300
22	2	PACHANGA 22	OP	EXP	FBG	DV	IO	270		8		2900	2	8	8000	9150
22	2	PACHANGA 22	OP	EXP	FBG	DV	IO	330		8		2900	2	8	9100	10300
22	6	SORRENTO 23BR	OP	RNBT	FBG	DV	IO	260		8		3030	2	6	5400	6200
23		WEEKENDER 230	OP	WKNDR	FBG	DV	IO	260		8		4060	2	8	7700	8850
23		WEEKENDER 230	OP	WKNDR	FBG	DV	IO	330		8		4060	2	8	8450	9700
23	6	SORRENTO 24CC	OP	CUD	FBG	DV	IO	260		8		3650	2	6	6750	7750
23	10	SORRENTO 25SD	OP	CUD	FBG	DV	IO	130-260		8	8	5518	2	9	10100	11900
23	10	SORRENTO 25SD	OP	CUD	FBG	DV	IO	330		8	8	5518	2	9	11200	12700
24		LAGUNA 23	OP	CTRCN	FBG	DV	OB			8	6	3800	2	7	8400	9650
25		CUDDY CABIN 250	OP	CUD	FBG	DV	IO	260		8		3910	2	8	8550	9800
25		CUDDY CABIN 250	OP	CUD	FBG	DV	IO	330		8		3910	2	8	9400	10700
25	9	SEDAN BRIDGE 265		SDN	FBG	DV	IO	330		9		6380	2	10	14100	16100
25	9	SEDAN BRIDGE 265		SDN	FBG	DV	IO	T175-T205		9		6380	2	10	14100	16500
26	7	SUNDANCER 268	OP	EXP	FBG	DV	IO	330		8	5	5475	2	10	12600	14300
26	7	SUNDANCER 268	OP	EXP	FBG	DV	IO	T175-T205		8	5	5475	2	10	12600	14700
26	7	WEEKENDER 268	OP	WKNDR	FBG	DV	IO	330		8	6	5425	2	10	13100	14800
26	7	WEEKENDER 268	OP	WKNDR	FBG	DV	IO	T175-T205		8	6	5425	2	10	13100	15300
27	7	AMBERJACK 270	OP	CUD	FBG	DV	IO	T175-T260		10		6750	2	8	15200	18800
27	7	AMBERJACK 270	OP	CUD	FBG	DV	IO	T130D		10		6750	2	8	18900	21000
27	7	SUNDANCER 270	OP	EXP	FBG	DV	IO	T175-T260		10		5894	1	4	13700	16900
27	7	SUNDANCER 270	OP	EXP	FBG	DV	IO	T130D		10		7360	1	3	19000	21100
29	10	SEDAN BRIDGE 305		SDN	FBG	DV	IB	T260		12		11500	2	6	34400	38300
29	10	SEDAN BRIDGE 305		SDN	FBG	DV	IB	T130D-T200D		12		11500	2	6	42700	51700
31	1	SUNDANCER 300	OP	EXP	FBG	DV	IO	T260		11		9800	2	11	22000	24400
31	1	WEEKENDER 300	OP	WKNDR	FBG	DV	IO	T260		11		9500	2	4	22700	25300
31	1	WEEKENDER 300	OP	WKNDR	FBG	DV	IB	T200D		11		9500	2	4	36300	40400
31	7	PACHANGA 32	OP	EXP	FBG	DV	IO	T270-T330		8	6	6300	3	1	25900	30700
31	8	SUNDANCER 300	OP	EXP	FBG	DV	IO	T200D		11		9800	2	11	26100	29000
33	7	EXPRESS CRUISER 340	OP	EXP	FBG	DV	IB	T340		11	11	10100	2	5	43700	48600
33	7	EXPRESS CRUISER 340	OP	EXP	FBG	DV	IB	T200D		11	11	10100	2	5	49600	54500
33	7	SEDAN BRIDGE 340	FB	SDN	FBG	DV	IB	T340		11	11	11500	2	5	48500	53300
33	7	SUNDANCER 340	OP	EXP	FBG	DV	VD	T340	MRCR	11	11	12500	2	5	46100	50600
33	9	SEDAN BRIDGE 345	FB	SDNSF	FBG	DV	IB	T340		12	6	14600	2	9	48200	53000
33	9	SEDAN BRIDGE 345	FB	SDNSF	FBG	DV	IB	T200D		12	6	14600	2	9	56000	61500
39		EXPRESS CRUISER 390	OP	EXP	FBG	DV	IB	T340		13	11	16400	2	4	59200	65100
39		EXPRESS CRUISER 390	OP	EXP	FBG	DV	IB	T320D		13	11	16400	2	4	71700	78800
39		EXPRESS CRUISER 390	OP	EXP	FBG	DV	IB	T375D		13	11	16400	2	4	75200	82600
40	7	AFT CABIN 415	FB	CR	FBG	DV	IB	T340		13	11	22500	2	7	81700	89800
40	7	AFT CABIN 415	FB	CR	FBG	DV	IB	T320D		13	11	22500	2	7	94500	104000
40	7	AFT CABIN 415	FB	CR	FBG	DV	IB	T375D		13	11	22500	2	7	98000	107500
43	6	CONVERTIBLE 430		SF	FBG	DV	IB	T340		13	11	25700	2	8	93000	102000
43	6	CONVERTIBLE 430		SF	FBG	DV	IB	T320D		13	11	25700	2	8	106500	117000
43	6	CONVERTIBLE 430		SF	FBG	DV	IB	T375D		13	11	25700	2	8	111500	122500
45	6	CONVERTIBLE 460	FB	SF	FBG	DV	IB	T375D		14	11	34000	3	2	126500	139000
45	6	CONVERTIBLE 460	FB	SF	FBG	DV	IB	T475D		14	11	34000	3	2	134000	147500
45	6	CONVERTIBLE 460	FB	SF	FBG	DV	IB	T560D		14	11	34000	3	2	141500	155500
45	6	EXPRESS CRUISER 460	OP	EXP	FBG	DV	IO	T375D		14	11	27500	3	2	76100	83600
45	6	EXPRESS CRUISER 460	OP	EXP	FBG	DV	IO	T475D		14	11	27500	3	2	81000	89000
45	6	EXPRESS CRUISER 460	OP	EXP	FBG	DV	IO	T560D		14	11	27500	3	2	85600	94100
		1987 BOATS														
16	6	SEVILLE 17BR	OP	RNBT	FBG	DV	IO	130		7		1850	1		2250	2600
16	6	SEVILLE 17CB	OP	RNBT	FBG	DV	IO	130		7		1850	1		2250	2600
17	6	MONACO 185	OP	RNBT	FBG	DV	IO	165-260		8		2540	1	1	2950	3700
17	6	MONACO 187	OP	RNBT	FBG	DV	IO	165-205		8		2540	1	1	3050	3600
17	6	MONACO 187	OP	RNBT	FBG	DV	IO	260		8		2540	1	1	3300	3850
17	9	PACHANGA 19	OP	EXP	FBG	DV	IO	205		7	10	2250	2	4	4400	5050
18	6	SEVILLE 19BR	OP	RNBT	FBG	DV	IO	130-175		7	6	1950	1		2750	3200
18	6	SEVILLE 19CB	OP	RNBT	FBG	DV	IO	130-175		7	6	1950	1		2650	3150
18	6	SEVILLE 19CC	OP	RNBT	FBG	DV	IO	130-175		7	6	2050	1	1	2750	3250
19	2	SORRENTO 19BR	OP	RNBT	FBG	DV	IO	175-205		7	10	2620	2	6	3350	3950
19	6	MONACO SRV195	OP	RNBT	FBG	DV	IO	165-260		8		2930	1	1	3600	4450
19	6	MONACO SRV197	OP	RNBT	FBG	DV	IO	165-260		8		2930	1	1	3750	4600
20	6	PACHANGA II	OP	EXP	FBG	DV	IO		MRCR	8		2800	1	4	**	**
20	6	PACHANGA II	OP	EXP	FBG	DV	IO	340	OMC	8		2800	1	4	8300	9550
20	8	MONACO SRV200	OP	RNBT	FBG	DV	IO	205-260		8		3130	1	1	4750	5700
20	8	MONACO SRV207	OP	RNBT	FBG	DV	IO	205-260		8		3130	1	1	4900	5850
20	8	SORRENTO 21BR	OP	B/R	FBG	DV	IO	260	OMC	8		2820	2	6	4600	5300
20	8	SORRENTO 21BR	OP	RNBT	FBG	DV	IO	205-260		8		2820	2	6	4550	5450
20	10	SEVILLE 21BR	OP	B/R	FBG	DV	IO	165-205		8		3289	1	2	4850	5650
20	10	SEVILLE 21CC	OP	CUD	FBG	DV	IO	165-205		8		2830	1	2	4700	5500
20	10	SEVILLE 21MC	OP	RNBT	FBG	DV	IO	165-205		8		3289	1	2	4950	5750
21		SRV210 CC	OP	CUD	FBG	DV	IO	260		8		3430	1	3	5650	6500
22	6	SORRENTO 21CB	OP	RNBT	FBG	DV	IO	205-260		8		2820	2	6	5000	5950
22	6	SORRENTO 23BR	OP	RNBT	FBG	DV	IO	260		8		3030	2	6	5400	6200
23		SRV230 CC	OP	CUD	FBG	DV	IO		MRCR	8		3910	1	3	**	**
23		SRV230 CC	OP	CUD	FBG	DV	IO	260		8		3910	1	3	6950	8000
23		SRV230 CC	OP	CUD	FBG	DV	IO	335	OMC	8		3910	1	3	7650	8800
23		SRV230 FSH	OP	FSH	FBG	DV	IO		MRCR	8			1	3	**	**
23		SRV230 FSH	OP	FSH	FBG	DV	IO	260		8			1	3	7500	8600
23		SRV230 FSH	OP	FSH	FBG	DV	IO	335	OMC	8			1	3	8250	9450
23		SRV230 WE	OP	WKNDR	FBG	DV	IO		MRCR	8		4060	1	3	**	**
23		SRV230 WE	OP	WKNDR	FBG	DV	IO	260		8		4060	1	3	7150	8200
23		SRV230 WE	OP	WKNDR	FBG	DV	IO	335	OMC	8		4060	1	3	7850	9000
23	6	SORRENTO 24CC	OP	CUD	FBG	DV	IO	260		8		3650	2	6	6800	7800
25		SRV250 CC	OP	CUD	FBG	DV	IO		MRCR	8		4120	1	3	**	**
25		SRV250 CC	OP	CUD	FBG	DV	IO	260		8		4120	1	3	8200	9400
25		SRV250 CC	OP	CUD	FBG	DV	IO	335	OMC	8		4120	1	3	9050	10300
25		SRV250 FSH	OP	FSH	FBG	DV	IO		MRCR	8			1	3	**	**
25		SRV250 FSH	OP	FSH	FBG	DV	IO	260-335		8			1	3	9150	11300
25		SUNDANCER SRV250	OP	CBNCR	FBG	DV	IO		MRCR	8		4690	1	3	**	**
		IO 165-260 10100 12000, IO 335 OMC 11200 12800, IO T175 OMC 11100 12600														
26	7	SUNDANCER 268	OP	EXP	FBG	DV	IO		MRCR	8	5	5465	1	4	**	**
26	7	SUNDANCER 268	OP	EXP	FBG	DV	IO	260-335		8	5		1	4	11300	13300
26	7	SUNDANCER 268	OP	EXP	FBG	DV	IO	T165-T205		8	5		1	4	11900	14000
26	7	WEEKENDER 268	OP	WKNDR	FBG	DV	IO		MRCR	8	5		1	4	**	**
26	7	WEEKENDER 268	OP	WKNDR	FBG	DV	IO	260-335		8	5		1	4	11700	14300
26	7	WEEKENDER 268	OP	WKNDR	FBG	DV	IO	T165-T205		8	5		1	4	12400	14700
27	7	270 HARDTOP		CUD	FBG	DV	IO	T165-T260		10		6800	2	9	14100	17500
27	7	270 SPORT FISH	OP	SF	FBG	DV	IO	205	OMC	10		6950	2	9	14900	16900
27	7	270 SPORT FISH	OP	SF	FBG	DV	IO	T165-T260		10		6950	2	9	16200	20100
27	7	AMBERJACK 270	OP	CUD	FBG	DV	IO	T165-T260		9	8	6400	1	3	13600	16500
27	7	SUNDANCER 270	OP	EXP	FBG	DV	IO	T165-T175		10		5720	1	4	12500	14500
27	7	SUNDANCER 270	OP	EXP	FBG	DV	IO	T205		10		5894	1	4	13100	16400

CONTINUED ON NEXT PAGE

LOA FT	IN	NAME AND/ OR MODEL	TOP/ RIG	BOAT TYPE	-HULL- MTL	TP	---ENGINE--- TP	# HP	MFG	BEAM FT	IN	WGT LBS	DRAFT FT	IN	RETAIL LOW	RETAIL HIGH
		1987 BOATS														
27	7	SUNDANCER 270	OP	EXP	FBG	DV	IO	T260		10		7380	1	3	15200	17300
29	1	SEDAN BRIDGE SRV300	FB	SDN	FBG	DV	VD	T260	MRCR	11		10500	2	5	28000	31200
29	1	SEDAN BRIDGE SRV300	FB	SDN	FBG	DV	IB	T270	CRUS	11		10500	2	5	28300	31500
29	8	SUNDANCER SRV300	OP	EXP	FBG	DV	IO	T260		11		9800	1	4	21300	23700
29	8	WEEKENDER 300	OP	WKNDR	FBG	DV	IO	T260	MRCR	11		9500	1	4	21100	23500
29	8	WEEKENDER 300	OP	WKNDR	FBG	DV	IB	T270	CRUS	11		9500	1	4	27200	30200
29	11	PACHANGA 32	OP	EXP	FBG	DV	IO	340	OMC	8	6	6300	3	1	21900	24300
29	11	PACHANGA 32	OP	EXP	FBG	DV	IO	T	MRCR	8	6	6300	3	1	**	**
33	7	EXPRESS CRUISER 340	OP	EXP	FBG	DV	IB	T260-T350		11	11	10100	2	5	38900	45600
33	7	EXPRESS CRUISER 340	OP	EXP	FBG	DV	IB	T250D	S&S	11	11	10100	2	5	48600	53400
33	7	SEDAN BRIDGE SRV340	FB	SDN	FBG	DV	IB	T260-T350		11	11	11400	2	6	42700	50300
33	7	SEDAN BRIDGE SRV340	FB	SDN	FBG	DV	IB	T250D	S&S	11	11	11400	2	6	53900	59200
33	7	SPORT FISHERMAN 340	FB	SDNSF	FBG	DV	IB	T260-T350		11	11	10600	2	5	39200	45900
33	7	SPORT FISHERMAN 340	FB	SDNSF	FBG	DV	IB	T250D	S&S	11	11	10600	2	5	47100	51800
33	7	SUNDANCER 340	OP	CBNCR	FBG	DV	IB	T260-T350		11	11	10500	2	5	41400	46900
36	3	AFT CABIN 360	FB	DC	FBG	DV	IB	T260	MRCR	12	6	15100	2	11	48900	53800
36	3	AFT CABIN 360	FB	DC	FBG	DV	IB	T270	CRUS	12	6	15100	2	11	49300	54200
36	3	AFT CABIN 360	FB	DC	FBG	DV	IB	T240D	S&S	12	6	15100	2	11	61100	67200
39		EXPRESS CRUISER 390	OP	EXP	FBG	DV	IB	T340	MRCR	13	11	16400	2	4	55300	60800
		IB T350 CRUS 56200 61700, IB T320D CAT 69200 76000, IB T400D CAT													74800	82200
40	7	AFT CABIN 410	FB	MY	FBG	DV	IB	T340	MRCR	14		23500	2	7	78100	85800
		IB T350 CRUS 79000 86800, IB T306D VLVO 87400 96000, IB T320D CAT													92300	101500
		IB T358D VLVO 90300 99200, IB T400D CAT 98400 108000														
45	6	CONVERTIBLE 460	FB	CNV	FBG	DV	IB	T400D	CAT	14	11	32000	3	2	120500	132500
45	6	CONVERTIBLE 460	FB	CNV	FBG	DV	IB	T475D	S&S	14	11	32000	3	2	122500	134500
45	6	CONVERTIBLE 460	FB	CNV	FBG	DV	IB	T560D	S&S	14	11	32000	3	2	129000	142000
45	6	EXPRESS CRUISER 460	OP	EXP	FBG	DV	IO	T400D	CAT	14	11	24500	3	2	69700	76600
45	6	EXPRESS CRUISER 460	OP	EXP	FBG	DV	IO	T475D	S&S	14	11	24500	3	2	71100	78100
45	6	EXPRESS CRUISER 460	OP	EXP	FBG	DV	IO	T560D	S&S	14	11	24500	3	2	75200	82600
		1986 BOATS														
17	6	SEVILLE 5.0	OP	RNBT	FBG	DV	IO	120		7		1850			2050	2400
17	6	SEVILLE 5.0 BR	OP	RNBT	FBG	DV	IO	140		7		1850	1		1950	2300
17	6	SEVILLE 5.0 CB	OP	RNBT	FBG	DV	IO	140		7		1850	1		1850	2250
17	6	SEVILLE II 5.0BR	OP	RNBT	FBG	DV	IO	140		7		1850	1		2250	2600
17	6	SEVILLE II 5.0CB	OP	RNBT	FBG	DV	IO	140		7		1850	1		2200	2550
17	6	SEVILLE II 5.6CC	OP	RNBT	FBG	DV	IO	175	OMC	7	6	2050	1	1	2300	2650
18	6	MONACO 187	OP	RNBT	FBG	DV	IO	185	MRCR	8		2540	1	1	2850	3350
18	7	MONACO 185	OP	RNBT	FBG	DV	IO	170-260		8		2540	1	1	2750	3450
18	7	MONACO 187	OP	RNBT	FBG	DV	IO	170-260		8		2540	1	1	2850	3550
19	8	SEVILLE 5.6 BR	OP	RNBT	FBG	DV	IO	140		7	6	1950	1		2400	2800
19	8	SEVILLE 5.6 CB	OP	RNBT	FBG	DV	IO	140		7	6	1950	1		2350	2750
19	8	SEVILLE 5.6 CC	OP	RNBT	FBG	DV	IO	120-140		7	6	2050			2550	3000
19	8	SEVILLE II 5.6BR	OP	RNBT	FBG	DV	IO	140-175		7	6	1950	1		2700	3150
19	8	SEVILLE II 5.6CB	OP	RNBT	FBG	DV	IO	140-175		7	6	1950	1		2600	3050
19	8	SEVILLE II 5.6CC	OP	RNBT	FBG	DV	IO	140-170		7	6	2050	1	1	2700	3150
20	6	MONACO SRV195	OP	RNBT	FBG	DV	IO	170-260		8		2930	1	1	3350	4150
20	6	MONACO SRV197	OP	RNBT	FBG	DV	IO	170-260		8		2930	1	1	3500	4300
21	9	MONACO SRV200	OP	RNBT	FBG	DV	IO	205-260		8		3130	1	1	4450	5300
21	9	MONACO SRV207	OP	RNBT	FBG	DV	IO	205-260		8		3130	1	1	4550	5450
22		PACHANGA II	OP	EXP	FBG	DV	IO	260		8		2800	1	4	7300	8350
22		SEVILLE II 6.3BR	OP	B/R	FBG	DV	IO	170-175		8		3289	1	2	4550	5250
22		SEVILLE II 6.3BR	OP	B/R	FBG	DV	IO	205		8		3289	1	2	5150	5900
22		SEVILLE II 6.3CC	OP	CUD	FBG	DV	IO	140-205		8		2830	1	2	4400	5150
22		SEVILLE II 6.3MB	OP	RNBT	FBG	DV	IO	170-205		8		3289	1	2	4650	5400
22	2	SRV210 CC	OP	CUD	FBG	DV	IO	205-260		8		3430	1	3	5050	6050
24	1	SRV230 CC	OP	CUD	FBG	DV	IO	205-260		8		3910	1	3	6250	7450
24	1	SRV230 FSH	OP	FSH	FBG	DV	IO	205-260		8		4120	1	3	6850	8000
24	1	SRV230 WE	OP	WKNDR	FBG	DV	IO	205-260		8		4060	1	3	6450	7650
25	5	AMBERJACK SRV255	OP	CUD	FBG	DV	IO	T175-T230		9	8	6500	1	3	11600	13500
26	1	SRV250 CC	OP	CUD	FBG	DV	IO	205-260		8		4120	1	3	7300	8750
26	1	SRV250 CC	OP	CUD	FBG	DV	IO	T140-T205		8		4120	1	3	8050	9700
26	1	SRV250 FSH	OP	FSH	FBG	DV	IO	205-260		8				1	8100	9700
26	1	SRV250 FSH	OP	FSH	FBG	DV	IO	T140-T185		8			1	3	9000	10500
26	1	SRV250 FSH	OP	FSH	FBG	DV	IO	T205	MRCR	8			1	3	10900	12400
26	1	SUNDANCER SRV250	OP	CBNCR	FBG	DV	IO	230-260		8		4690	1	3	9700	11200
26	1	SUNDANCER SRV250	OP	CBNCR	FBG	DV	IO	T140-T205		8		4690		1	10300	11900
28		268 WE	OP	WKNDR	FBG	DV	IO	205-260		8	5		1	4	10500	12400
28		268 WE	OP	WKNDR	FBG	DV	IO	T170-T205		8	5		1	4	11600	13600
28		SUNDANCER 268	OP	EXP	FBG	DV	IO	230-260		8	5	5465	1	4	9900	11900
28		SUNDANCER 268	OP	EXP	FBG	DV	IO	T140-T205		8	5		1	4	10900	13100
29	1	SEDAN BRIDGE SRV300	FB	SDN	FBG	DV	VD	T260-T270		11		10500		2	26100	29400
29	2	AMBERJACK 270	OP	CUD	FBG	DV	IO	T140-T230		9	8	6172	1	3	12200	14800
29	2	AMBERJACK 270	OP	CUD	FBG	DV	IO	T260-T330		9	8	5880	1	3	13500	16800
29	2	SUNDANCER 270	OP	EXP	FBG	DV	IO	330	MRCR	10		6500	1	3	12300	14000
		IO T140-T185 11100 13600, IO T205-T230 12200 15300, IO T260 OMC													14100	16100
29	5	SUNDANCER 270	OP	EXP	FBG	DV	IO	T260	MRCR	10		7380	1	3	14200	16100
31	1	300 WE	OP	WKNDR	FBG	DV	IO	T260		11		9500	1	4	19700	21800
31	1	300 WE	OP	WKNDR	FBG	DV	IB	T270		11		9500	1	4	25200	28100
31	1	SUNDANCER SRV300	OP	EXP	FBG	DV	IO	T260		11		9800		1	19900	22100
34	10	EXPRESS CRUISER 340	OP	EXP	FBG	DV	IB	T260-T350		11	11	10100	2	5	36200	42500
34	10	EXPRESS CRUISER 340	OP	EXP	FBG	DV	IB	T240D	S&S	11	11	10100	2	5	44800	49700
34	10	SEDAN BRIDGE SRV340	FB	SDN	FBG	DV	IB	T260-T350		11	11	11400	2	6	39700	46800
34	10	SEDAN BRIDGE SRV340	FB	SDN	FBG	DV	IB	T240D	S&S	11	11	11400	2	6	49800	54800
34	10	SPORT FISHERMAN 340	FB	SDNSF	FBG	DV	IB	T260-T350		11	11	10600	2	5	36500	42700
34	10	SPORT FISHERMAN 340	FB	SDNSF	FBG	DV	IB	T240D	S&S	11	11	10600	2	5	43200	48000
34	10	SUNDANCER 340	OP	CBNCR	FBG	DV	IB	T260-T350		11	11	10500	2	5	38600	43700
38	2	AFT CABIN 360	FB	DC	FBG	DV	IB	T260	MRCR	12	6	15100	2	11	45900	50500
38	2	AFT CABIN 360	FB	DC	FBG	DV	IB	T270	CRUS	12	6	15100	2	11	46300	50900
38	2	AFT CABIN 360	FB	DC	FBG	DV	IB	T240D	S&S	12	6	15100	2	11	51800	57000
40	6	EXPRESS CRUISER 390	OP	EXP	FBG	DV	IB	T340	MRCR	13	11	16400	2	4	51600	56700
		IB T350 CRUS 52400 57600, IB T320D CAT 64600 71000, IB T375D CAT													68000	74800
40	6	SRV390	FB	SDNSF	FBG	DV	IB	T340	MRCR	13	11	18400	2	7	56600	62200
		IB T350 CRUS 57400 63100, IB T320D CAT 69600 76500, IB T375D CAT													73100	80300
47	1	EXPRESS CRUISER 460	OP	EXP	FBG	DV	IO	T375D	S&S	14	11	24500		3	61900	68000
47	1	EXPRESS CRUISER 460	OP	EXP	FBG	DV	IO	T450D	S&S	14	11	24500		3	64900	71300
47	1	EXPRESS CRUISER 460	OP	EXP	FBG	DV	IO	T530D	S&S	14	11	24500		3	68400	75200
		1985 BOATS														
16	6	SEVILLE 5.0 BR	OP	RNBT	FBG	DV	IO	120		7		1850	1		1900	2300
16	6	SEVILLE 5.0 CB	OP	RNBT	FBG	DV	IO	120		7		1850	1		1850	2200
17	6	MONACO 185	OP	RNBT	FBG	DV	IO	170-230		8		2540	1	1	2550	3100
17	6	MONACO 185	OP	RNBT	FBG	DV	IO	260		8		2540	1	1	2750	3200
17	6	MONACO 187	OP	RNBT	FBG	DV	IO	170-230		8		2540	1	1	2650	3200
17	6	MONACO 187	OP	RNBT	FBG	DV	IO	260		8		2540	1	1	2850	3300
17	6	MONACO SXL185	OP	RNBT	FBG	DV	IO	170-260		8		2560	1	1	2650	3300
17	6	MONACO SXL187	OP	RNBT	FBG	DV	IO	170-260		8		2560	1	1	2650	3300
18	6	SEVILLE 5.6 BR	OP	RNBT	FBG	DV	IO	120-140		7	6	1950	1		2350	2750
18	6	SEVILLE 5.6 CB	OP	RNBT	FBG	DV	IO	120-140		7	6	1950	1		2300	2700
18	6	SEVILLE 5.6 CC	OP	RNBT	FBG	DV	IO	120-140		7	6	2050	1	1	2400	2800
19	6	MONACO SRV195	OP	RNBT	FBG	DV	IO	170-260		8		2930	1	1	3100	3900
19	6	MONACO SRV197	OP	RNBT	FBG	DV	IO	170-260		8		2930	1	1	3200	4000
20	8	MONACO SRV200	OP	RNBT	FBG	DV	IO	170-260		8		3130	1	1	4000	4950
20	8	MONACO SRV207	OP	RNBT	FBG	DV	IO	170-260		8		3130	1	1	4150	5100
21		SRV210 CC	OP	CUD	FBG	DV	IO	170-260		8		3430	1	3	4700	5650
23		SRV230 CC	OP	CUD	FBG	DV	IO	200-260		8		3910	1	3	5850	6950
23		SRV230 FSH	OP	FSH	FBG	DV	IO	200-260		8		4120	1	3	6400	7500
23		SRV230 WE	OP	WKNDR	FBG	DV	IO	200-260		8		4060	1	3	6000	7150
25		SRV250 CC	OP	CUD	FBG	DV	IO	200-260		8		4120	1	3	6800	8150
25		SRV250 CC	OP	CUD	FBG	DV	IO	T120-T190		8		4120	1	3	7400	8950
25		SRV250 FSH	OP	FSH	FBG	DV	IO	200-260		8			1	3	7550	9050
25		SRV250 FSH	OP	FSH	FBG	DV	IO	T120-T190		8			1	3	8200	9900
25		SUNDANCER SRV250	OP	CBNCR	FBG	DV	IO	200-260		8		4690	1	3	9050	10500
25		SUNDANCER SRV250	OP	CBNCR	FBG	DV	IO	T120-T190		8		4690	1	3	9600	11000
25	5	AMBERJACK SRV255	OP	CUD	FBG	DV	IO	260-330		9	8	5880	1	3	9600	11600
25	5	AMBERJACK SRV255	OP	CUD	FBG	DV	IO	T120-T230		9	8	6120	1	3	10100	12600
26	3	SRV260 WE	OP	EXP	FBG	DV	IO	200-260		8		5150	1	4	8450	10200
26	3	SRV260 WE	OP	EXP	FBG	DV	IO	T120-T170		8		5390	1	4	9350	11500
26	3	SRV260 WE	OP	EXP	FBG	DV	IO	T185-T190		8		5844	1	4	10300	11800
26	3	SUNDANCER SRV260	OP	CBNCR	FBG	DV	IO	200-260		8		5200	1	4	10600	12400
26	3	SUNDANCER SRV260	OP	CBNCR	FBG	DV	IO	T120-T190		8		5440	1	4	11600	13900
27	7	SUNDANCER SRV270	OP	EXP	FBG	DV	IO	260-330		10		6500	1	3	11400	13700
27	7	SUNDANCER SRV270	OP	EXP	FBG	DV	IO	T120-T190		10		6740	1	3	11700	14600
27	7	SUNDANCER SRV270	OP	EXP	FBG	DV	IO	T200-T260		10		7360	1	3	13100	15700
29	1	SRV300 SEDAN BRIDGE	FB	SDN	FBG	DV	VD	260-330		11		10500	2	5	21600	24800
29	1	SRV300 SEDAN BRIDGE	FB	SDN	FBG	DV	VD	T120-T230		11		10500	2	5	21400	26400
29	1	SRV300 SEDAN BRIDGE	FB	SDN	FBG	DV	VD	T260	MRCR	11		10500	2	5	24300	27000
29	8	SRV300 WE	OP	WKNDR	FBG	DV	IO	260-330		11		9500	2	5	16300	19200
29	8	SRV300 WE	OP	WKNDR	FBG	DV	IO	T120-T230		11		9500	2	5	16200	20200
29	8	SRV300 WE	OP	WKNDR	FBG	DV	IO	T260	MRCR	11		9500	2	5	18600	20600
29	8	SUNDANCER SRV300	OP	EXP	FBG	DV	IO	260-330		11		9800	1	4	16500	19500
29	8	SUNDANCER SRV300	OP	EXP	FBG	DV	IO	T120-T230		11		9800	1	4	16500	20400
29	8	SUNDANCER SRV300	OP	EXP	FBG	DV	IO	T260	MRCR	11		9800	1	4	18800	20900
33	7	EXPRESS CRUISER 340	OP	EXP	FBG	DV	IB	T260-T350		11	11	10100	2	5	33700	39500
33	7	EXPRESS CRUISER 340	OP	EXP	FBG	DV	IB	T240D	S&S	11	11	10100	2	5	41800	46400

 CONTINUED ON NEXT PAGE

LOA FT	IN	NAME AND/ OR MODEL	TOP/ RIG	BOAT TYPE	-HULL- MTL	TP	TP	----ENGINE--- # HP	MFG	BEAM FT	IN	WGT LBS	DRAFT FT	IN	RETAIL LOW	RETAIL HIGH
		1985 BOATS														
33	7	SEDAN BRIDGE SRV340	FB	SDN	FBG	DV	IB	T260-T350		11	11	11400	2	6	36900	43500
33	7	SPORT FISHERMAN 340	FB	SDNSF	FBG	DV	IB	T260-T350		11	11	10600	2	5	33900	39700
33	7	SPORT FISHERMAN 340	FB	SDNSF	FBG	DV	IB	T240D	S&S	11	11	10600	2	5	40300	44800
33	7	SRV340 SEDAN BRIDGE	FB	SDN	FBG	DV	IB	T270-T340		11	11	11400	2	6	37200	43100
33	7	SRV340 SEDAN BRIDGE	FB	SDN	FBG	DV	IB	T240D	S&S	11	11	11400	2	6	46800	51400
33	7	SUNDANCER 340	OP	CBNCR	FBG	DV	IB	T260-T350		11	11	10500	2	5	35800	40600
36	3	360 AFT CABIN	FB	DC	FBG	DV	IB	T165	CRUS	12	6	15100	2	11	41600	46200
		IB T260 MRCR 42300 47000, IB T270 CRUS 42700 47400, IB T135D PERK 51100 56200														
		IB T200D PERK 53100 58300														
39		EXPRESS CRUISER 390	OP	EXP	FBG	DV	IB	T340	MRCR	13	11	16400	2	4	48100	52900
		IB T350 CRUS 48900 53700, IB T300D CAT 59200 65000, IB T325D S&S 57700 63400														
		IB T350D PERK 61900 68100, IB T355D CAT 62200 68300														
39		SRV390	FB	SDNSF	FBG	DV	IB	T340	MRCR	13	11	18400	2	7	52800	58000
		IB T350 CRUS 53500 58800, IB T300D CAT 63800 70200, IB T325D S&S 62400 68600														
		IB T350D PERK 66600 73200, IB T355D CAT 66900 73500														
		1984 BOATS														
16	6	SEVILLE 5.0 BR	OP	RNBT	FBG	DV	IO	120		7		1850	1		1800	2150
16	6	SEVILLE 5.0 CB	OP	RNBT	FBG	DV	IO	120		7		1850	1		1750	2050
17	6	MONACO 185	OP	RNBT	FBG	DV	IO	170-230		8		2540	1	1	2400	2900
17	6	MONACO 185	OP	RNBT	FBG	DV	IO	260		8		2540	1	1	2550	3000
17	6	MONACO 187	OP	RNBT	FBG	DV	IO	170-260		8		2540	1	1	2500	3100
17	6	MONACO SXL185	OP	RNBT	FBG	DV	IO	170-230		8		2540	1	1	2400	2950
17	6	MONACO SXL185	OP	RNBT	FBG	DV	IO	260		8		2540	1	1	2600	3050
17	6	MONACO SXL187	OP	RNBT	FBG	DV	IO	170-260		8		2540	1	1	2550	3150
18	6	SEVILLE 5.6 BR	OP	RNBT	FBG	DV	IO	120-140		7	6	1950	1		2250	2600
18	6	SEVILLE 5.6 CB	OP	RNBT	FBG	DV	IO	120-140		7	6	1950	1		2200	2550
18	6	SEVILLE 5.6 CC	OP	RNBT	FBG	DV	IO	120-140		7	6	2000	1	1	2250	2600
19	6	MONACO SRV195	OP	RNBT	FBG	DV	IO	170-260		8		2930	1	1	2950	3650
19	6	MONACO SRV197	OP	RNBT	FBG	DV	IO	170-260		8		2930	1	1	3050	3750
20	5	SRV210 FSH	OP	CUD	FBG	DV	IO	170-260		8		3540	1	2	4350	5300
20	8	MONACO SRV200	OP	RNBT	FBG	DV	IO	170-260		8		3130	1	1	3800	4650
20	8	MONACO SRV207	OP	RNBT	FBG	DV	IO	170-260		8		3130	1	1	3900	4800
21		SRV210 CC	OP	CUD	FBG	DV	IO	170-260		8		3430	1	3	4400	5350
22	4	SRV225 CC	OP	CUD	FBG	DV	IO	170-260		8		3860	1	3	5200	6200
22	4	SRV225 EC	OP	EXP	FBG	DV	IO	198-260		8		4020	1	3	5350	6400
24	7	AMBERJACK 245	OP	CUD	FBG	DV	IO	198-260		8		4020	1	3	6100	7300
24	7	AMBERJACK 245	OP	CUD	FBG	DV	IO	T120-T170		8		4260	1	3	6950	8600
24	7	AMBERJACK 245	OP	CUD	FBG	DV	IO	T185-T188		8		4714	1	3	7650	8850
24	7	SRV245 CUDDY CRUISER	OP	CUD	FBG	DV	IO	198-260		8		4060	1	3	6150	7350
24	7	SRV245 CUDDY CRUISER	OP	CUD	FBG	DV	IO	T120-T170		8		4300	1	3	7000	8650
24	7	SRV245 CUDDY CRUISER	OP	CUD	FBG	DV	IO	T185-T188		8		4754	1	3	7700	8900
24	7	SRV245 FSH	OP	CUD	FBG	DV	IO	198-260		8		4130	1	3	6250	7450
24	7	SRV245 FSH	OP	CUD	FBG	DV	IO	T120-T170		8		4370	1	3	7100	8750
24	7	SRV245 FSH	OP	CUD	FBG	DV	IO	T185-T188		8		4824	1	3	7800	8950
24	7	SUNDANCER SRV245	OP	CBNCR	FBG	DV	IO	198-260		8		4650	1	3	8000	9450
24	7	SUNDANCER SRV245	OP	CBNCR	FBG	DV	IO	T120-T188		8		4890	1	3	9050	11000
25	5	AMBERJACK SRV255	OP	CUD	FBG	DV	IO	260-330		9	8	5880	1	3	9050	10900
25	5	AMBERJACK SRV255	OP	CUD	FBG	DV	IO	T120-T228		9	8	6120	1	3	9500	11800
26	3	SRV260 EC	OP	EXP	FBG	DV	IO	198-260		8		5150	1	4	7900	9550
26	3	SRV260 EC	OP	EXP	FBG	DV	IO	T120-T170		8		5390	1	4	8700	10700
26	3	SRV260 EC	OP	EXP	FBG	DV	IO	T185-T188		8		5844	1	4	9650	11000
26	3	SUNDANCER SRV260	OP	CBNCR	FBG	DV	IO	198-260		8		5200	1	4	9900	11700
26	3	SUNDANCER SRV260	OP	CBNCR	FBG	DV	IO	T120-T188		8		5440	1	4	10800	13000
27	7	SEADANCER 270	OP	CR	FBG	DV	IB	T165-T270		10		6200	2	5	13900	17300
27	7	SUNDANCER SRV270	OP	EXP	FBG	DV	IO	260-330		10		6500	1	3	10700	12800
27	7	SUNDANCER SRV270	OP	EXP	FBG	DV	IO	T120-T188		10		6740	1	3	11000	13600
27	7	SUNDANCER SRV270	OP	EXP	FBG	DV	IO	T198-T260		10		7360	1	3	12300	14800
33	7	EXPRESS CRUISER 340	OP	EXP	FBG	DV	IB	T260-T350		11	11	10100	2	5	31300	36700
33	7	EXPRESS CRUISER 340	OP	EXP	FBG	DV	IB	T240D	S&S	11	11	10100	2	5	39000	43300
33	7	SEDAN BRIDGE SRV340	FB	SDN	FBG	DV	IB	T350	CRUS	11	11	11400	2	6	36400	40400
33	7	SPORT FISHERMAN 340	FB	SDNSF	FBG	DV	IB	T260-T350		11	11	10600	2	5	31500	36900
33	7	SPORT FISHERMAN 340	FB	SDNSF	FBG	DV	IB	T240D	S&S	11	11	10600	2	5	37600	41800
33	7	SRV340 SEDAN BRIDGE	FB	SDN	FBG	DV	IB	T260-T340		11	11	11400	2	6	34300	40100
33	7	SRV340 SEDAN BRIDGE	FB	SDN	FBG	DV	IB	T240D	S&S	11	11	11400	2	6	43200	48000
33	7	SUNDANCER 340	OP	CBNCR	FBG	DV	IB	T260-T350		11	11	10500	2	5	33300	37700
36	3	360 AFT CABIN	FB	DC	FBG	DV	IB	T165	CRUS	12	6	14500	2	11	37900	42100
		IB T260 MRCR 38600 42900, IB T270 CRUS 38900 43200, IB T135D PERK 46700 51400														
		IB T200D PERK 48300 53100														
39		EXPRESS CRUISER 390	OP	EXP	FBG	DV	IB	T340	MRCR	13	11	16000	2	4	43700	48500
		IB T350 CRUS 44400 49300, IB T300D CAT 54200 59600, IB T325D PERK 55500 61000														
		IB T325D S&S 52800 58100, IB T355D CAT 57000 62700														
39		SRV390	FB	SDNSF	FBG	DV	IB	T340	MRCR	13	11	18400	2	7	49100	54000
		IB T350 CRUS 49800 54800, IB T300D CAT 59500 65300, IB T325D PERK 60700 66700														
		IB T325D S&S 58100 63800, IB T355D CAT 62300 68400														

....For earlier years, see the BUC Used Boat Price Guide, Volume 3

SEA SPORT

UNITED MARINE CORPORATION
WATSEKA IL 60970

See inside cover to adjust price for area

For more recent years, see the BUC Used Boat Price Guide, Volume 1

LOA FT	IN	NAME AND/ OR MODEL	TOP/ RIG	BOAT TYPE	-HULL- MTL	TP	TP	----ENGINE--- # HP	MFG	BEAM FT	IN	WGT LBS	DRAFT FT	IN	RETAIL LOW	RETAIL HIGH
		1996 BOATS														
17	1	SEA SPORT 1740		CTRCN	FBG	SV	OB			6	10	1000			4550	5250
19	1	SEA SPORT 1840		CTRCN	FBG	SV	OB			7	3	1370			5950	6850
19	1	SEA SPORT 1940		B/R	FBG	SV	OB			7	3	1370			6350	7300
19	1	SEA SPORT 1940		CTRCN	FBG	SV	OB			7	3	1370			6350	7300
19	1	SEA SPORT 1940 F&S		B/R	FBG	SV	OB			7	3	1370			6350	7300
19	9	SEA SPORT 2040		CTRCN	FBG	SV	OB			8		2200			8850	10000
19	9	SEA SPORT 2044		CUD	FBG	DV	OB			8		2375			9350	10600
19	9	SEA SPORT 2044		CUD	FBG	DV	IO	220	MRCR	8		2375			13500	15400
21	3	SEA SPORT 2344		CUD	FBG	DV	OB			8		2850			12200	13900
23	11	SEA SPORT 2444		CUD	FBG	DV	OB			8	3	3400			16300	18600
23	11	SEA SPORT 2444		CUD	FBG	DV	IO	235	MRCR	8	6	3400			23200	25800
24	8	SEA SPORT 2344		CUD	FBG	DV	IO	235	MRCR	8	6	2850			22500	25000
26		SEA SPORT 2644		CUD	FBG	DV	OB			9	6	4610			21300	23700
26		SEA SPORT 2644		CUD	FBG	DV	IO	300	MRCR	9	6	4610			35100	39000

SEA SPORT BOATS INC

BELLINGHAM WA 98226 COAST GUARD MFG ID- WMA See inside cover to adjust price for area

For more recent years, see the BUC Used Boat Price Guide, Volume 1

LOA FT	IN	NAME AND/ OR MODEL	TOP/ RIG	BOAT TYPE	-HULL- MTL	TP	TP	----ENGINE--- # HP	MFG	BEAM FT	IN	WGT LBS	DRAFT FT	IN	RETAIL LOW	RETAIL HIGH
		1984 BOATS														
18		SPORTSMAN	ST	CUD	FBG	SV	IO	170	MRCR	7	1	2250			3900	4550
18		SPORTSMAN	ST	RNBT	FBG	SV	IO	170	MRCR	7	1	1900			3550	4100
22		SEASPORT	HT	CR	FBG	SV	IO			8		2500			**	**

SEA SPRITE

UNITED MARINE CORP
WATSEKA IL 60970

COAST GUARD MFG ID- SSB See inside cover to adjust price for area

For more recent years, see the BUC Used Boat Price Guide, Volume 1

LOA FT	IN	NAME AND/ OR MODEL	TOP/ RIG	BOAT TYPE	-HULL- MTL	TP	TP	----ENGINE--- # HP	MFG	BEAM FT	IN	WGT LBS	DRAFT FT	IN	RETAIL LOW	RETAIL HIGH
		1996 BOATS														
17	8	1700	OP	B/R	FBG	SV	IO	135	MRCR	7	8	2050			5850	6750
19	6	1950	OP	B/R	FBG	SV	IO	250	MRCR	8	1	2600			8100	9300
21	6	2150	OP	B/R	FBG	SV	IO	250	MRCR	7	2	2800			7950	9150
21	9	225	OP	CUD	FBG	DV	IO	250	MRCR	8		3480			10400	11800
		1995 BOATS														
17	2	175BR	OP	RNBT	FBG	SV	OB			7	5	1350			4400	5050
17	2	175FS	OP	RNBT	FBG	SV	OB			7	5	1125			3600	4150
17	6	180BR	OP	RNBT	FBG	SV	IO	135-180		7	6	2000			5500	6400
17	8	1700ES BR	OP	RNBT	FBG	SV	IO	135-180		7	8	1870			5500	6400
17	8	1700ES CD	OP	CUD	FBG	SV	IO	135-180		7	8	2060			5850	6800
18	7	190BR	OP	RNBT	FBG	SV	IO	135-235		7	6	2200			6150	7600
19		195BR	OP	RNBT	FBG	SV	OB			7	9	2250			5450	6250
19		195CC	OP	CUD	FBG	SV	OB			7	9	2400			5450	6250
19		195CL	OP	CUD	FBG	SV	OB			7	9	1700			5450	6250
19	5	1900ES BR	OP	RNBT	FBG	SV	IO	135-250		7	8	2350			6700	8200
19	5	1900ES CD	OP	CUD	FBG	SV	IO	135-160		7	8	2400			7000	8100
19	6	210BR	OP	RNBT	FBG	SV	IO	135-235		8		2500			7150	8550
19	8	200BR	OP	RNBT	FBG	SV	IO	135-235		7	8	2120			6500	7800
19	8	200CC	OP	CUD	FBG	SV	IO	135-235		7	8	2240			6900	8300
19	9	210CC	OP	CUD	FBG	SV	IO	135-235		8		2700			7850	9350

LOA FT	LOA IN	NAME AND/ OR MODEL	TOP/ RIG	BOAT TYPE	-HULL- MTL	TP	TP	ENGINE # HP	MFG	BEAM FT	BEAM IN	WGT LBS	DRAFT FT IN	RETAIL LOW	RETAIL HIGH
		1995 BOATS													
21	1	2100ES BR	OP	RNBT	FBG	SV	IO	135-250		7	9	2600		7000	8450
21	1	2100ES BR	OP	RNBT	FBG	SV	IO	350	MRCR	7	9	2600		9100	10400
21	1	2100ES CC	OP	CUD	FBG	SV	IO	135-250		7	9	2750		7550	9150
21	9	225BR	OP	RNBT	FBG	SV	IO	160-250		8		3000		8000	9550
21	9	225CC	OP	CUD	FBG	SV	IO	160-250		8		3480		9050	10500
21	9	225CL	OP	CUD	FBG	SV	IO	160-250		8		3480		9600	11000
23	6	2300ES CC	OP	CUD	FBG	SV	IO	205-300		8	6	3700		11000	13500
23	6	2300ES CC	OP	CUD	FBG	SV	IO	350	MRCR	8	6	3700		13000	14800
24	5	2500ES CC	OP	CUD	FBG	SV	IO	205-300		8	6	3900		11900	14700
24	5	2500ES CC	OP	CUD	FBG	SV	IO	350	MRCR	8	6	3900		14000	16000
24	8	2350WA	OP	CUD	FBG	SV	OB			8	6	3680		13300	15100
24	8	2350WA	OP	CUD	FBG	SV	IO	160-235		8	6	3680		11400	13500
		1994 BOATS													
17	2	175BR	OP	RNBT	FBG	SV	OB			7	5	1350		4150	4850
17	2	175FS	OP	RNBT	FBG	SV	OB			7	5	1125		3450	4000
17	2	175FSL	OP	RNBT	FBG	SV	OB			7	5	1125		3750	4350
17	6	180BR	OP	RNBT	FBG	SV	IO	115-205		7	6	2000		5150	6350
		IO 225-250 5700 6700, IO 300 6150 7650, IO 350 MRCR												7300	8350
17	8	1700ES BR	OP	RNBT	FBG	SV	IO	115-205		7	8	1870		5100	6300
		IO 215-250 5600 6700, IO 300 6150 7600, IO 350 MRCR												7250	8350
17	8	1700ES CD	OP	CUD	FBG	SV	IO	115-205		7	8	2060		5450	6700
		IO 215-250 5950 7100, IO 300 6550 8100, IO 350 MRCR												7700	8900
18	7	190BR	OP	RNBT	FBG	SV	IO	115-160		7	6	2200		5700	6900
		IO 185-250 6250 7550, IO 300 MRCR 6750 7750, IO 300-350												7350	9000
19		195BR	OP	RNBT	FBG	SV	OB			7	9	2250		5200	6000
19		195CC	OP	CUD	FBG	SV	OB			7	9	2400		5200	6000
19		195CL	OP	CUD	FBG	SV	OB			7	9	1700		5200	6000
19	5	1900ES BR	OP	RNBT	FBG	SV	IO	120-250		7	8	2350		6500	8000
19	5	1900ES BR	OP	RNBT	FBG	SV	IO	300		7	8	2350		7250	8900
19	5	1900ES BR	OP	RNBT	FBG	SV	IO	350	MRCR	7	8	2350		8400	9650
19	5	1900ES CD	OP	CUD	FBG	SV	IO	115-205		7	8	2400		6550	8050
		IO 225-250 7100 8350, IO 300 7600 9350, IO 350 MRCR												8900	10100
19	6	210BR	OP	RNBT	FBG	SV	IO	115-235		8		2500		6650	8250
		IO 245-250 7350 8450, IO 300 7650 9350, IO 350 MRCR												8900	10100
19	8	200BR	OP	RNBT	FBG	SV	IO	115-205		7	8	2120		6050	7450
		IO 225-250 6600 7750, IO 300 7050 8650, IO 350 MRCR												8150	9400
19	8	200CC	OP	CUD	FBG	SV	IO	115-205		7	8	2240		6400	7900
		IO 225-250 7000 8250, IO 300 7500 9200, IO 350 MRCR												8700	10000
19	9	210CC	OP	CUD	FBG	SV	IO	115-225		8		2700		7300	9050
		IO 245-250 8050 9250, IO 300 8350 10200, IO 350 MRCR												9600	10900
21	1	2100ES BR	OP	RNBT	FBG	SV	IO	115-235		7	9	2600		6500	8050
		IO 245-250 7150 8200, IO 300 7400 9000, IO 350 MRCR												8400	9650
21	1	2100ES CC	OP	CUD	FBG	SV	IO	115-235		7	9	2750		7050	8700
		IO 245-250 7700 8850, IO 300 8000 9700, IO 350 MRCR												9150	10400
21	9	225BR	OP	RNBT	FBG	SV	IO	160-250		8		3000		7450	9250
21	9	225BR	OP	RNBT	FBG	SV	IO	300		8		3000		8300	10100
21	9	225BR	OP	RNBT	FBG	SV	IO	350	MRCR	8		3000		9400	10700
21	9	225CC	OP	CUD	FBG	SV	IO	160-250		8		3480		8450	10300
21	9	225CC	OP	CUD	FBG	SV	IO	300	MRCR	8		3480		9000	10200
21	9	225CC	OP	CUD	FBG	SV	IO	300-350		8		3480		10200	11900
21	9	225CL	OP	CUD	FBG	SV	IO	160-190		8		3480		8600	10500
		IO 205 MRCR 8600 9900, IO 205-250 9450 10900, IO 300 MRCR												9450	10800
		IO 300-350 10800 12400													
23	6	2300ES CC	OP	CUD	FBG	SV	IO	205-250		8	6	3700		10200	12200
23	6	2300ES CC	OP	CUD	FBG	SV	IO	300-350		8	6	3700		11100	13800
24	5	2500ES CC	OP	CUD	FBG	SV	IO	205-300		8	6	3900		11400	14200
24	5	2500ES CC	OP	CUD	FBG	SV	IO	350	MRCR	8	6	3900		13100	14900
24	8	2350WA	OP	CUD	FBG	SV	OB			8	6	3680		12700	14500
24	8	2350WA	OP	CUD	FBG	SV	IO	155-250		8	6	3680		10800	12800
24	8	2350WA	OP	CUD	FBG	SV	IO	300-350		8	6	3680		11900	14700
		1993 BOATS													
17	2	175BR	OP	RNBT	FBG	SV	OB			7	5	1350		4000	4650
17	2	175FS	OP	RNBT	FBG	SV	OB			7	5	1125		3300	3800
17	2	175FSL	OP	RNBT	FBG	SV	OB			7	5	1125		3600	4200
17	6	180BR	OP	RNBT	FBG	SV	IO	110-275		7	6	2000		5050	6300
17	6	180BR	OP	RNBT	FBG	SV	IO	300-310		7	6	2000		5750	7150
17	6	180BR	OP	RNBT	FBG	SV	IO	350	MRCR	7	6	2000		6800	7800
17	8	1700ES BR	OP	RNBT	FBG	SV	IO	110-275		7	8	1870		5050	6250
17	8	1700ES BR	OP	RNBT	FBG	SV	IO	300-310		7	8	1870		5750	7100
17	8	1700ES BR	OP	RNBT	FBG	SV	IO	350	MRCR	7	8	1870		6800	7800
17	8	1700ES CD	OP	CUD	FBG	SV	IO	110-275		7	8	2060		5350	6650
17	8	1700ES CD	OP	CUD	FBG	SV	IO	300-310		7	8	2060		6100	7550
17	8	1700ES CD	OP	CUD	FBG	SV	IO	350	MRCR	7	8	2060		7200	8300
18	7	190BR	OP	RNBT	FBG	SV	IO	110-235		7	6	2200		5600	6900
		IO 245 OMC 5600 6450, IO 245-275 6150 7050, IO 300 MRCR												6300	7250
		IO 300-350 6900 8450													
19		195BR	OP	RNBT	FBG	SV	OB			7	9	2250		5000	5750
19		195CC	OP	CUD	FBG	SV	OB			7	9	2400		5000	5750
19		195CL	OP	CUD	FBG	SV	OB			7	9	1700		5000	5750
19	5	1900ES BR	OP	RNBT	FBG	SV	IO	110-275		7	8	2350		6100	7450
19	5	1900ES BR	OP	RNBT	FBG	SV	IO	300-310		7	8	2350		6800	8300
19	5	1900ES BR	OP	RNBT	FBG	SV	IO	350	MRCR	7	8	2350		7850	9000
19	5	1900ES CD	OP	CUD	FBG	SV	IO	110-275		7	8	2400		6400	7850
19	5	1900ES CD	OP	CUD	FBG	SV	IO	300-310		7	8	2400		7100	8750
19	5	1900ES CD	OP	CUD	FBG	SV	IO	350	MRCR	7	8	2400		8250	9450
19	6	210BR	OP	RNBT	FBG	SV	IO	110-275		8		2500		6450	7900
19	6	210BR	OP	RNBT	FBG	SV	IO	300-310		8		2500		7150	8750
19	6	210BR	OP	RNBT	FBG	SV	IO	350	MRCR	8		2500		8200	9450
19	8	200BR	OP	RNBT	FBG	SV	IO	110-275		7	8	2120		5900	7250
19	8	200BR	OP	RNBT	FBG	SV	IO	300-310		7	8	2120		6600	8100
19	8	200BR	OP	RNBT	FBG	SV	IO	350	MRCR	7	8	2120		7650	8800
19	8	200CC	OP	CUD	FBG	SV	IO	110-275		7	8	2240		6250	7700
19	8	200CC	OP	CUD	FBG	SV	IO	300-310		7	8	2240		7000	8600
19	8	200CC	OP	CUD	FBG	SV	IO	350	MRCR	7	8	2240		8100	9350
19	9	210CC	OP	CUD	FBG	SV	IO	110-275		8		2700		7100	8650
19	9	210CC	OP	CUD	FBG	SV	IO	300-310		8		2700		7850	9550
19	9	210CC	OP	CUD	FBG	SV	IO	350	MRCR	8		2700		9050	10300
21	1	2100ES BR	OP	RNBT	FBG	SV	IO	110-275		7	9	2600		6300	7650
21	1	2100ES BR	OP	RNBT	FBG	SV	IO	300-310		7	9	2600		6950	8450
21	1	2100ES BR	OP	RNBT	FBG	SV	IO	350	MRCR	7	9	2600		7850	9050
21	1	2100ES CC	OP	CUD	FBG	SV	IO	110-275		7	9	2750		6800	8250
21	1	2100ES CC	OP	CUD	FBG	SV	IO	300-310		7	9	2750		7500	9100
21	1	2100ES CC	OP	CUD	FBG	SV	IO	350	MRCR	7	9	2750		8450	9750
21	9	225BR	OP	RNBT	FBG	SV	IO	150-235		8		3000		6900	8500
		IO 245-275 7150 8650, IO 300-310 7800 9400, IO 350 MRCR												8800	10000
21	9	225CC	OP	CUD	FBG	SV	IO	150-275		8		3480		7750	9600
21	9	225CC	OP	CUD	FBG	SV	IO	300	MRCR	8		3480		8350	9600
21	9	225CC	OP	CUD	FBG	SV	IO	300-350		8		3480		9500	11100
21	9	225CL	OP	CUD	FBG	SV	IO	150-275		8		3480		8300	10200
21	9	225CL	OP	CUD	FBG	SV	IO	300	MRCR	8		3480		8950	10200
21	9	225CL	OP	CUD	FBG	SV	IO	300-350		8		3480		10000	11600
23	6	2300ES CC	OP	CUD	FBG	SV	IO	175-275		8	6	3700		9450	11400
23	6	2300ES CC	OP	CUD	FBG	SV	IO	300-350		8	6	3700		10300	12900
24	5	2500ES CC	OP	CUD	FBG	SV	IO	175-275		8	6	3900		10200	12400
24	5	2500ES CC	OP	CUD	FBG	SV	IO	300-350		8	6	3900		11300	13900
24	8	2350WA	OP	CUD	FBG	SV	OB			8	6	3680		12200	13900
24	8	2350WA	OP	CUD	FBG	SV	IO	150-275		8	6	3680		9850	12100
24	8	2350WA	OP	CUD	FBG	SV	IO	300-350		8	6	3680		11100	13700
		1992 BOATS													
16	1	1600 FS	OP	RNBT	FBG	SV	OB			6	9			2400	2800
16	1	1600 PRO	OP	RNBT	FBG	SV	OB			6	9			2250	2600
16	2	165 BR	OP	RNBT	FBG	SV	IO	110-200		6	10	1700		3850	4600
		IO 205 MRCR 3500 4050, IO 205-270 4250 4900, IO 285-330												4700	5750
		IO 365-370 5900 6800													
16	2	165 CD	OP	RNBT	FBG	SV	IO	110-200		6	10	1700		3850	4600
		IO 205 MRCR 3500 4050, IO 205-285 4250 4900, IO 300-330												4950	5750
		IO 365-370 5900 6800													
17	2	175 BR	OP	RNBT	FBG	SV	OB			7	5	1350		3850	4450
17	2	175 BR	OP	RNBT	FBG	SV	IO	110-270		7	5	2000		4500	5650
		IO 285 OMC 4950 5700, IO 300-330 5600 6550, IO 365-370												6550	7550
17	2	175 FSL	OP	RNBT	FBG	SV	OB			7	5	1125		3300	3850
17	6	MARK I	OP	RNBT	FBG	SV	IO	110-270		7	6	2000		4650	5750
		IO 285 OMC 5050 5850, IO 300-330 5700 6700, IO 365-370												6650	7650
18	2	1800 FS	OP	RNBT	FBG	SV	OB			7	4			4050	4700

LOA FT	LOA IN	NAME AND/ OR MODEL	TOP/ RIG	BOAT TYPE	-HULL- MTL	-HULL- TP	TP	----ENGINE--- # HP	MFG	BEAM FT	BEAM IN	WGT LBS	DRAFT FT	DRAFT IN	RETAIL LOW	RETAIL HIGH
		1992 BOATS														
18	2	1800 PRO	OP	RNBT	FBG	SV	OB			7	4				3650	4250
18	7	MARK II	OP	RNBT	FBG	SV	IO	110-285		7	8	2200			5300	6550
18	7	MARK II	OP	RNBT	FBG	SV	IO	300-330		7	8	2200			6400	7350
18	7	MARK II	OP	RNBT	FBG	SV	IO	365-370		7	6	2200			7150	8200
18	8	1900 MC	OP	RNBT	FBG	SV	OB			8		1750			4800	5550
19		195 BR	OP	RNBT	FBG	SV	OB			7	9	1600			4650	5300
19		195 BR	OP	RNBT	FBG	SV	IO	110-285		7	9	2250			5400	6750
19		195 BR	OP	RNBT	FBG	SV	IO	300-330		7	9	2250			6500	7550
19		195 BR	OP	RNBT	FBG	SV	IO	365-370		7	9	2250			7400	8550
19		195 CC	OP	CUD	FBG	SV	OB			7	9	1750			4900	5600
19		195 CC	OP	CUD	FBG	SV	IO	110-285		7	9	2400			5850	7200
19		195 CC	OP	CUD	FBG	SV	IO	300-330		7	9	2400			7000	8200
19		195 CC	OP	CUD	FBG	SV	IO	365-370		7	9	2400			8000	9200
19		195 CL	OP	CUD	FBG	SV	OB			7	9	1700			4800	5500
19		195 CL	OP	CUD	FBG	SV	IO	110-285		7	9	2450			5950	7300
19		195 CL	OP	CUD	FBG	SV	IO	300-330		7	9	2450			7100	8250
19		195 CL	OP	CUD	FBG	SV	IO	365-370		7	9	2450			8100	9300
19	5	1900 ES BR	OP	RNBT	FBG	SV	IO	110-285		7	8	2350			5700	7000
19	5	1900 ES BR	OP	RNBT	FBG	SV	IO	300-330		7	8	2350			6800	7900
19	5	1900 ES BR	OP	RNBT	FBG	SV	IO	365-370		7	8	2350			7700	8850
19	5	1900 ES CD	OP	RNBT	FBG	SV	IO	110-285		7	8	2400			5750	7050
19	5	1900 ES CD	OP	RNBT	FBG	SV	IO	300-330		7	8	2400			6850	8000
19	5	1900 ES CD	OP	RNBT	FBG	SV	IO	365-370		7	8	2400			7800	8950
19	9	210 BR	OP	RNBT	FBG	SV	IO	110-285		8		2500			6150	7500
19	9	210 BR	OP	RNBT	FBG	SV	IO	300-330		8		2500			7200	8400
19	9	210 BR	OP	RNBT	FBG	SV	IO	365-370		8		2500			8150	9350
19	9	210 CC	OP	CUD	FBG	SV	IO	110-285		8		2700			6650	8150
19	9	210 CC	OP	CUD	FBG	SV	IO	300-330		8		2700			7750	9050
19	9	210 CC	OP	CUD	FBG	SV	IO	365-370		8		2700			8900	10200
21	1	2100 ES	OP	RNBT	FBG	SV	IO	110-285		7	9	2600			5900	7200
21	1	2100 ES	OP	RNBT	FBG	SV	IO	300-330		7	9	2600			6850	8000
21	1	2100 ES	OP	RNBT	FBG	SV	IO	365-370		7	9	2600			7700	8850
21	1	2100 ESC	OP	CUD	FBG	SV	IO	110-285		7	9	2750			6400	7750
21	1	2100 ESC	OP	CUD	FBG	SV	IO	300-330		7	9	2750			7400	8600
21	1	2100 ESC	OP	CUD	FBG	SV	IO	365-370		7	9	2750			8300	9550
21	9	225 AFT	OP	CUD	FBG	SV	IO	155-285		8		4200			9000	10600
21	9	225 AFT	OP	CUD	FBG	SV	IO	300-370		8		4200			9950	12300
21	9	225 BR	OP	RNBT	FBG	SV	IO	155-285		8		3000			6700	8100
21	9	225 BR	OP	RNBT	FBG	SV	IO	300-330		8		3000			7650	8900
21	9	225 BR	OP	RNBT	FBG	SV	IO	360-370		8		3000			8350	9750
21	9	225 CC	OP	CUD	FBG	SV	IO	155-285		8		3480			7550	9250
21	9	225 CC	OP	CUD	FBG	SV	IO	300-330		8		3480			8550	9900
21	9	225 CC	OP	CUD	FBG	SV	IO	360-370		8		3480			9450	10800
21	9	225 CL	OP	CUD	FBG	SV	IO	155-285		8		3480			8000	9800
21	9	225 CL	OP	CUD	FBG	SV	IO	300-370		8		3480			9100	11300
23	11	230 CL	OP	CUD	FBG	SV	IO	155-285		8	2	3400			8600	10300
23	11	230 CL	OP	CUD	FBG	SV	IO	300-370		8	2	3400			9650	12000
24	8	2350 WA	OP	CUD	FBG	SV	IO	155-285		8	6	3680			9450	11500
24	8	2350 WA	OP	CUD	FBG	SV	IO	300-370		8	6	3680			10700	13300
25	9	265 AFT	OP	CR	FBG	SV	IO	230-330		8		5850			13700	17000
25	9	265 AFT	OP	CR	FBG	SV	IO	365-370		8		5850			15700	17900
		1991 BOATS														
16	2	165 BR	OP	RNBT	FBG	SV	IO	110-240		6	10	1700			3600	4500
		IO 245-270 3950 4600, IO 300-340 4650 5550, IO 365-370													5550	6350
16	2	165 CB	OP	RNBT	FBG	SV	IO	110-240		6	10	1700			3600	4500
		IO 245-270 3950 4600, IO 300-340 4650 5550, IO 365-370													5550	6350
17	2	175 BR	OP	RNBT	FBG	SV	OB			7	5	1350			3700	4300
17	2	175 BR	OP	RNBT	FBG	SV	IO	110-240		7	5	2000			4200	5200
		IO 245-270 4600 5300, IO 300-340 5250 6250, IO 365-370													6150	7050
17	2	175 BR SD	OP	RNBT	FBG	SV	IO	110-270		7	5	2000			4450	5500
17	2	175 BR SD	OP	RNBT	FBG	SV	IO	300-340		7	5	2000			5450	6500
17	2	175 BR SD	OP	RNBT	FBG	SV	IO	365-370		7	5	2000			6350	7250
17	2	175 F/S	OP	RNBT	FBG	SV	OB			7	5	1125			3200	3700
17	6	MARK I	OP	RNBT	FBG	SV	IO	110-200		7	6	2000			4300	5100
		IO 205 MRCR 4150 4850, IO 205 OMC 4200 4850, IO 205-270													4700	5400
		IO 300-340 5350 6400, IO 365-370 6250 7200														
17	6	MARK I SD	OP	RNBT	FBG	SV	IO	110-270		7	6	2000			4600	5600
17	6	MARK I SD	OP	RNBT	FBG	SV	IO	300-340		7	6	2000			5550	6600
17	6	MARK I SD	OP	RNBT	FBG	SV	IO	365-370		7	6	2000			6450	7400
18	7	MARK II	OP	RNBT	FBG	SV	IO	110-270		7	8	2200			5000	6150
18	7	MARK II	OP	RNBT	FBG	SV	IO	300-340		7	8	2200			6000	6900
18	7	MARK II	OP	RNBT	FBG	SV	IO	365-370		7	6	2200			6700	7700
18	7	MARK II SD	OP	RNBT	FBG	SV	IO	110-270		7	6	2200			4900	6100
18	7	MARK II SD	OP	RNBT	FBG	SV	IO	300-340		7	6	2200			5900	7150
18	7	MARK II SD	OP	RNBT	FBG	SV	IO	365-370		7	6	2200			6900	7950
18	8	1900 MC	OP	RNBT	FBG	SV	OB			8		1750			4650	5350
19		195 BR	OP	RNBT	FBG	SV	OB			7	9	1600			4450	5100
19		195 BR	OP	RNBT	FBG	SV	IO	110-270		7	9	2250			5050	6250
19		195 BR	OP	RNBT	FBG	SV	IO	300-340		7	9	2250			6100	7200
19		195 BR	OP	RNBT	FBG	SV	IO	365-370		7	9	2250			6950	8000
19		195 BR SD	OP	RNBT	FBG	SV	IO	110-270		7	9	2250			5300	6450
19		195 BR SD	OP	RNBT	FBG	SV	IO	300-340		7	9	2250			6300	7450
19		195 BR SD	OP	RNBT	FBG	SV	IO	365-370		7	9	2250			7150	8250
19		195 CC	OP	CUD	FBG	SV	OB			7	9	1750			4700	5400
19		195 CC	OP	CUD	FBG	SV	IO	110-270		7	9	2400			5500	6750
19		195 CC	OP	CUD	FBG	SV	IO	300-340		7	9	2400			6600	7800
19		195 CC	OP	CUD	FBG	SV	IO	365-370		7	9	2400			7550	8650
19		195 CL	OP	CUD	FBG	SV	OB			7	9	1700			4650	5350
19		195 CL	OP	CUD	FBG	SV	IO	110-270		7	9	2450			5550	6850
19		195 CL	OP	CUD	FBG	SV	IO	300-340		7	9	2450			6650	7850
19		195 CL	OP	CUD	FBG	SV	IO	365-370		7	9	2450			7600	8700
19	5	1900 ES BR	OP	RNBT	FBG	SV	IO	110-270		7	8	2350			5350	6550
19	5	1900 ES BR	OP	RNBT	FBG	SV	IO	300-340		7	8	2350			6350	7550
19	5	1900 ES BR	OP	RNBT	FBG	SV	IO	365-370		7	8	2350			7250	8300
19	5	1900 ES CD	OP	RNBT	FBG	SV	IO	110-270		7	8	2400			5400	6600
19	5	1900 ES CD	OP	RNBT	FBG	SV	IO	300-340		7	8	2400			6400	7600
19	5	1900 ES CD	OP	RNBT	FBG	SV	IO	365-370		7	8	2400			7300	8400
19	9	210 BR	OP	RNBT	FBG	SV	IO	110-270		8		2500			5750	7000
19	9	210 BR	OP	RNBT	FBG	SV	IO	300-340		8		2500			6750	8000
19	9	210 BR	OP	RNBT	FBG	SV	IO	365-370		8		2500			7650	8800
19	9	210 CC	OP	CUD	FBG	SV	IO	110-270		8		2700			6200	7600
19	9	210 CC	OP	CUD	FBG	SV	IO	300-340		8		2700			7300	8700
19	9	210 CC	OP	CUD	FBG	SV	IO	365-370		8		2700			8250	9550
21	1	2100 ES	OP	RNBT	FBG	SV	IO	125-270		7	9	2600			5350	6650
		IO 271-330 6100 7500, IO 340 OMC 6600 7600, IO 365-370													7250	8300
21	1	2100 ESC	OP	CUD	FBG	SV	IO	125-270		7	9	2750			5800	7150
		IO 271-330 6550 8100, IO 340 OMC 7150 8200, IO 365-370													7800	8950
21	9	225 AFT	OP	CUD	FBG	SV	IO	155-270		8		4200			8350	9950
21	9	225 AFT	OP	CUD	FBG	SV	IO	300-370		8		4200			9350	11600
21	9	225 BR	OP	RNBT	FBG	SV	IO	155-270		8		3000			6300	7600
21	9	225 BR	OP	RNBT	FBG	SV	IO	300-340		8		3000			7200	8450
21	9	225 BR	OP	RNBT	FBG	SV	IO	360-370		8		3000			7850	9150
21	9	225 CC	OP	CUD	FBG	SV	IO	155-270		8		3480			7050	8500
21	9	225 CC	OP	CUD	FBG	SV	IO	300-340		8		3480			8000	9450
21	9	225 CC	OP	CUD	FBG	SV	IO	360-370		8		3480			8850	10200
21	9	225 CL	OP	CUD	FBG	SV	IO	155-270		8		3480			7500	9000
21	9	225 CL	OP	CUD	FBG	SV	IO	300-360		8		3480			8450	10500
21	9	225 CL	OP	CUD	FBG	SV	IO	370	OMC	8		3480			9350	10600
23	11	230 CL	OP	CUD	FBG	SV	IO	155-270		8	2	3400			8050	9650
23	11	230 CL	OP	CUD	FBG	SV	IO	300-370		8	2	3400			9100	11200
24	8	2350 WA	OP	CUD	FBG	SV	IO	155-270		8	6	3680			8950	10700
24	8	2350 WA	OP	CUD	FBG	SV	IO	300-370		8	6	3680			10100	12400
25	9	265 AFT	OP	CR	FBG	SV	IO	230-300		8		5250			12000	14700
25	9	265 AFT	OP	CR	FBG	SV	IO	340-370		8		5250			13300	15700
		1990 BOATS														
16		1600 FS	OP	BASS	FBG	SV	OB			7		1050			2800	3250
16		1600 MC	OP	BASS	FBG	SV	OB			7		900			2450	2850
16		1600 PRO	OP	BASS	FBG	SV	OB			7		900			2450	2850
16		1600 SE	OP	BASS	FBG	SV	OB								1900	2250
16	2	165 BR	OP	RNBT	FBG	SV	IO	125-235		6	10	1700			3200	3950
16	2	165 BR	OP	RNBT	FBG	SV	IO	260-270		6	10	1700			3550	4250
16	2	165 BR	OP	RNBT	FBG	SV	IO	330-340		6	10	1700			4500	5250
16	2	165 CD	OP	RNBT	FBG	SV	IO	125-235		7	10	1700			3450	4250
16	2	165 CD	OP	RNBT	FBG	SV	IO	260-270		7	10	1700			3850	4550
16	2	165 CD	OP	RNBT	FBG	SV	IO	330-340		7	10	1700			4750	5550
17	2	175 BR	OP	RNBT	FBG	SV	OB			7	5	1075			2950	3450
17	2	175 BR	OP	RNBT	FBG	SV	IO	125-235		7	5	1700			3600	4400
17	2	175 BR	OP	RNBT	FBG	SV	IO	260-270		7	5	1700			3950	4700
17	2	175 BR	OP	RNBT	FBG	SV	IO	330-340		7	5	1700			4850	5700
17	2	175 BR SD	OP	RNBT	FBG	SV	IO	125-235		7	5	2250			4100	4950
17	2	175 BR SD	OP	RNBT	FBG	SV	IO	260-270		7	5	2250			4500	5250

 CONTINUED ON NEXT PAGE

LOA FT	LOA IN	NAME AND/ OR MODEL	TOP/ RIG	BOAT TYPE	-HULL- MTL	-HULL- TP	ENGINE TP	ENGINE # HP	ENGINE MFG	BEAM FT	BEAM IN	WGT LBS	DRAFT FT	DRAFT IN	RETAIL LOW	RETAIL HIGH
		1990 BOATS														
17	2	175 BR SD	OP	RNBT	FBG	SV	IO	330-340		7	5	2250			5350	6250
17	2	175 FS/BR	OP	FSH	FBG	SV	OB			7	5	1125			3050	3550
17	6	MARK 1	OP	RNBT	FBG	SV	IO	125-235		7	6	1875			3750	4600
17	6	MARK 1	OP	RNBT	FBG	SV	IO	260-270		7	6	1875			4050	4750
17	6	MARK 1	OP	RNBT	FBG	SV	IO	330-340		7	6	1875			5050	5900
17	6	MARK 1 SD	OP	RNBT	FBG	SV	IO	125-235		7	6	1875			3900	4750
17	6	MARK 1 SD	OP	RNBT	FBG	SV	IO	260-270		7	6	1875			4150	4900
17	6	MARK 1 SD	OP	RNBT	FBG	SV	IO	330-340		7	6	1875			5150	6050
18	2	175 BR SI	OP	RNBT	FBG	SV	IO	125-235		7	4	2250			4300	5200
18	2	175 BR SI	OP	RNBT	FBG	SV	IO	260-270		7	4	2250			4700	5450
18	2	175 BR SI	OP	RNBT	FBG	SV	IO	330-340		7	4	2250			5550	6500
18	6	1800 FS	OP	BASS	FBG	SV	OB			7	8	1250			3700	4300
18	6	1800 MC	OP	BASS	FBG	SV	OB			7	8	1250			3300	3800
18	6	1800 PRO	OP	BASS	FBG	SV	OB			7	8	1100			3150	3650
18	7	MARK 2	OP	RNBT	FBG	SV	IO	125-235		7	6	1975			4050	5000
18	7	MARK 2	OP	RNBT	FBG	SV	IO	260-270		7	6	1975			4400	5300
18	7	MARK 2	OP	RNBT	FBG	SV	IO	330-340		7	6	1975			5350	6250
18	7	MARK 2SD	OP	RNBT	FBG	SV	IO	125-260		7	6	1975			4300	5350
18	7	MARK 2SD	OP	RNBT	FBG	SV	IO	270		7	6	1975			4700	5450
18	7	MARK 2SD	OP	RNBT	FBG	SV	IO	330-340		7	6	1975			5550	6500
19		195 BR	OP	RNBT	FBG	SV	OB			7	9	1300			3650	4250
19		195 BR	OP	RNBT	FBG	SV	IO	125-260		7	9	2075			4450	5500
19		195 BR	OP	RNBT	FBG	SV	IO	270		7	9	2075			4850	5650
19		195 BR	OP	RNBT	FBG	SV	IO	330-340		7	9	2075			5700	6050
19		195 BR SD	OP	RNBT	FBG	SV	IO	125-260		7	9	2075			4600	5600
19		195 BR SD	OP	RNBT	FBG	SV	IO	270		7	9	2075			4950	5750
19		195 BR SD	OP	RNBT	FBG	SV	IO	330-340		7	9	2075			5800	6750
19		195 CC	OP	CUD	FBG	SV	OB			7	9	1300			3500	4100
19		195 CC	OP	CUD	FBG	SV	IO	125-260		7	9	2175			4650	5700
19		195 CC	OP	CUD	FBG	SV	IO	270		7	9	2175			5050	5900
19		195 CC	OP	CUD	FBG	SV	IO	330-340		7	9	2175			5950	6950
19		195 CC LINER	OP	CUD	FBG	SV	IO	125-260		7	9	2175			4850	5950
19		195 CC LINER	OP	CUD	FBG	SV	IO	270		7	9	2175			5250	6100
19		195 CC LINER	OP	CUD	FBG	SV	IO	330-340		7	9	2175			6150	7200
19		195 CC W/LINER	OP	CUD	FBG	SV	OB			7	9	1300			3800	4400
19	5	1900 ES	OP	RNBT	FBG	SV	IO	125-260		7	8	2200			4700	5800
19	5	1900 ES	OP	RNBT	FBG	SV	IO	270		7	8	2200			5150	5900
19	5	1900 ES	OP	RNBT	FBG	SV	IO	330-340		7	8	2200			5950	6900
19	9	210 BR	OP	RNBT	FBG	SV	IO	125-260		8		2345			5050	6250
19	9	210 BR	OP	RNBT	FBG	SV	IO	270		8		2345			5500	6300
19	9	210 BR	OP	RNBT	FBG	SV	IO	330-340		8		2345			6300	7350
19	9	210 CC	OP	CUD	FBG	SV	IO	125-260		8		2345			5250	6500
19	9	210 CC	OP	CUD	FBG	SV	IO	270		8		2345			5700	6600
19	9	210 CC	OP	CUD	FBG	SV	IO	330-340		8		2345			6550	7650
21		200 BRSI	OP	RNBT	FBG	SV	IO	125-270		8		2850			5350	6600
21		200 BRSI	OP	RNBT	FBG	SV	IO	330-340		8		2850			6450	7550
21	1	2100 ES	OP	CUD	FBG	SV	IO	125-270		7	9	2300			4950	6200
21	1	2100 ES	OP	CUD	FBG	SV	IO	330-340		7	9	2300			6150	7150
21	1	2100 ES CC	OP	RNBT	FBG	SV	IO	125-270		7	3	2300			4600	5700
21	1	2100 ES CC	OP	RNBT	FBG	SV	IO	330-340		7	3	2300			5700	6600
21	9	225 AFT	OP	CR	FBG	SV	IO	175-270		7	11	4580			8150	9850
21	9	225 AFT	OP	CR	FBG	SV	IO	330-340		7	11	4580			9400	10800
21	9	225 BR	OP	RNBT	FBG	SV	IO	175-270		7	11	3560			6400	7800
21	9	225 BR	OP	RNBT	FBG	SV	IO	330-340		7	11	3560			7500	8700
21	9	225 CC	OP	CUD	FBG	SV	IO	175-270		7	11	3480			6450	8050
21	9	225 CC	OP	CUD	FBG	SV	IO	330-340		7	11	3480			7600	8800
21	9	225 CC LINER	OP	CUD	FBG	SV	IO	175-270		7	11	3480			6850	8500
21	9	225 CC LINER	OP	CUD	FBG	SV	IO	330-340		7	11	3480			8000	9300
23	11	230 CC LINER	OP	CUD	FBG	SV	IO	175-270		8	2	3260			7200	8750
23	11	230 CC LINER	OP	CUD	FBG	SV	IO	330-340		8	2	3260			8350	9700
24	8	2350 WA	OP	CUD	FBG	SV	IO			9	6	3680			**	**
24	8	2350 WA	OP	CUD	FBG	SV	IO	175-270		9	6	3680			8450	10400
24	8	2350 WA	OP	CUD	FBG	SV	IO	330-340		9	6	3680			9850	11300
25	9	265 AFT	OP	CR	FBG	SV	IO	230-270		8		5250			11200	13200
		IO 330-340 12400 14200, IO T175-T260 12400 15300, IO T270													13600	15500
28	5	285 AFT	OP	CR	FBG	SV	IO	T175-T270		10		8300			17200	21100
		1989 BOATS														
16		1600 FS	OP	RNBT	FBG	SV	OB			7		1050			3100	3650
16		1600 MC	OP	RNBT	FBG	SV	OB			7		900			2900	3350
16		1600 PRO	OP	RNBT	FBG	SV	OB			7		900			2900	3350
16		1600 SE	OP	RNBT	FBG	SV	OB			7		900			2550	2950
16	3	160 B/R	OP	RNBT	FBG	DV	OB			6	4	650			2300	2650
17	2	175 B/R	OP	RNBT	FBG	DV	OB			7	5	1075			1750	2050
17	2	175 B/R	OP	RNBT	FBG	SV	IO	120-230		7	5	1675			3300	4050
17	2	175 B/R	OP	RNBT	FBG	SV	IO	260	MRCR	7	5	1675			3500	4100
17	2	175 B/R	OP	RNBT	FBG	SV	IO	260	OMC	7	5	1675			3800	4400
17	2	175 B/R 125 T/T	OP	RNBT	FBG	DV	OB			7	5	1075			3300	3800
17	2	175 B/R 50	OP	RNBT	FBG	DV	OB			7	5	1075			2650	3100
17	2	175 B/R 85 T/T	OP	RNBT	FBG	DV	OB			7	5	1075			3150	3650
17	2	175 B/R SD	OP	RNBT	FBG	SV	IO	120-260		7	5	1675			3400	4150
17	2	175 F/S 125 T/T	OP	RNBT	FBG	DV	OB			7	5	1075			3600	4200
17	2	175 F/S 50	OP	RNBT	FBG	DV	OB			7	5	1075			2950	3450
17	2	175 F/S 85 T/T	OP	RNBT	FBG	DV	OB			7	5	1075			3450	4050
17	2	175 F/S B/R	OP	RNBT	FBG	DV	OB			7	5	1075			2000	2400
17	5	160 S/A	OP	RNBT	FBG	SV	IO	120-230		6	10	1840			3350	4150
17	5	160 S/A	OP	RNBT	FBG	SV	IO	260		6	10	1840			3700	4350
17	6	MARK I	OP	RNBT	FBG	SV	IO	120-230		7	6	1850			3550	4350
17	6	MARK I	OP	RNBT	FBG	SV	IO	260	MRCR	7	6	1850			3700	4300
17	6	MARK I	OP	RNBT	FBG	SV	IO	260	OMC	7	6	1850			4050	4700
17	6	MARK I SD	OP	RNBT	FBG	SV	IO	120-230		7	6	1850			3650	4450
17	6	MARK I SD	OP	RNBT	FBG	SV	IO	260	MRCR	7	6	1850			3800	4450
17	6	MARK I SD	OP	RNBT	FBG	SV	IO	260	OMC	7	6	1850			4150	4800
18	6	1800 FS	OP	RNBT	FBG	SV	OB			7	8	1250			2300	2700
18	6	1800 FS 125	OP	RNBT	FBG	SV	OB			7	8	1250			3950	4600
18	6	1800 FS 85	OP	RNBT	FBG	SV	OB			7	8	1250			3800	4450
18	6	1800 MC	OP	RNBT	FBG	SV	OB			7	8	1100			2000	2350
18	6	1800 MC 125	OP	RNBT	FBG	SV	OB			7	8	1100			3650	4200
18	6	1800 MC 85	OP	RNBT	FBG	SV	OB			7	8	1100			3500	4050
18	6	1800 PRO	OP	RNBT	FBG	SV	OB			7	8	1100			2000	2350
18	6	1800 PRO 125	OP	RNBT	FBG	SV	OB			7	8	1100			3650	4200
18	6	1800 PRO 85	OP	RNBT	FBG	SV	OB			7	8	1100			3500	4050
18	7	MARK II	OP	RNBT	FBG	SV	IO	120-230		7	6	1950			3850	4700
18	7	MARK II	OP	RNBT	FBG	SV	IO	260	MRCR	7	6	1950			4050	4700
18	7	MARK II	OP	RNBT	FBG	SV	IO	260	OMC	7	6	1950			4400	5050
18	7	MARK II SD	OP	RNBT	FBG	SV	IO	120-230		7	6	1950			4000	4850
18	7	MARK II SD	OP	RNBT	FBG	SV	IO	260	MRCR	7	6	1950			4150	4800
18	7	MARK II SD	OP	RNBT	FBG	SV	IO	260	OMC	7	6	1950			4550	5200
19		195 B/R	OP	RNBT	FBG	SV	IO	120-230		7	9	2050			4150	5050
19		195 B/R	OP	RNBT	FBG	SV	IO	260		7	9	2050			4350	5400
19		195 B/R SD	OP	RNBT	FBG	SV	IO	120-230		7	9	2050			4250	5150
19		195 B/R SD	OP	RNBT	FBG	SV	IO	260		7	9	2050			4450	5500
19		195 CC	OP	CUD	FBG	SV	OB			7	9	1225			2300	2650
19		195 CC	OP	CUD	FBG	SV	IO	120-230		7	9	2150			4300	5250
19		195 CC	OP	CUD	FBG	SV	IO	260		7	9	2150			4550	5550
19		195 CC 125 T/T	OP	CUD	FBG	SV	OB			7	9	1225			3850	4450
19		195 CC 125 T/T LINER	OP	CUD	FBG	SV	OB			7	9	1225			4050	4700
19		195 CC 85 LINER	OP	CUD	FBG	SV	OB			7	9	1225			3900	4550
19		195 CC 85 T/T	OP	CUD	FBG	SV	OB			7	9	1225			3700	4300
19		195 CC LINER	OP	CUD	FBG	SV	OB			7	9	1225			2500	2900
19		195 CC LINER	OP	CUD	FBG	SV	IO	120-230		7	9	2150			4600	5450
19		195 CC LINER	OP	CUD	FBG	SV	IO	260		7	9	2150			4750	5800
19	5	1900 ES	OP	RNBT	FBG	SV	IO	120-260		7	8				4700	5800
19	9	MARK 4	OP	RNBT	FBG	SV	IO	120-260		8		2320			4750	5850
19	9	MARK 5 CC	OP	CR	FBG	SV	IO	120-260		8		2320			4900	6100
21		200 B/R SI	OP	RNBT	FBG	SV	IO		MRCR	8		2850			**	**
21		200 B/R SI	OP	RNBT	FBG	SV	IO		OMC	8		2850			**	**
21		200 B/R SI	OP	RNBT	FBG	SV	IO	165-270		8		2850			5100	6250
21	1	2100 ES	OP	RNBT	FBG	SV	IO	120-260		7	9				5350	6500
21	9	225 AFT	OP	CR	FBG	SV	IO		MRCR	7	11	4500			**	**
21	9	225 AFT	OP	CR	FBG	SV	IO		OMC	7	11	4500			**	**
21	9	225 AFT	OP	CR	FBG	SV	IO	165-270		7	11	4500			7600	9150
21	9	225 CC	OP	CR	FBG	SV	IO		MRCR	7	11	3400			**	**
21	9	225 CC	OP	CR	FBG	SV	IO		OMC	7	11	3400			**	**
21	9	225 CC	OP	CR	FBG	SV	IO	165-270		7	11	3400			5950	7300
21	9	225 CC LINER	OP	CR	FBG	SV	IO		MRCR	7	11	3400			**	**
21	9	225 CC LINER	OP	CR	FBG	SV	IO		OMC	7	11	3400			**	**
21	9	225 CC LINER	OP	CR	FBG	SV	IO	165-270		7	11	3400			6400	7750
23	11	230 CC	OP	CR	FBG	SV	IO		MRCR	8	2	3350			**	**
23	11	230 CC	OP	CR	FBG	SV	IO		OMC	8	2	3350			**	**
23	11	230 CC	OP	CR	FBG	SV	IO	165-270		8	2	3350			6900	8400
25	9	265 AFT	OP	CR	FBG	SV	IO		MRCR	8		5250			**	**
		IO OMC ** **, IO 230-270 10600 12400, IO T OMC													**	**
		IO T165-T260 11600 14400, IO T270 MRCR 12800 14600														

 CONTINUED ON NEXT PAGE

LOA FT IN	NAME AND/ OR MODEL	TOP/ RIG	BOAT TYPE	HULL MTL TP	ENGINE TP # HP MFG	BEAM FT IN	WGT LBS	DRAFT FT IN	RETAIL LOW	RETAIL HIGH
					1989 BOATS					
28 6	285 AFT		OP	CR	FBG SV IO T OMC	8	8280		**	**
28 6	285 AFT		OP	CR	FBG SV IO T165-T270	8	8280		15600	19400
					1988 BOATS					
16	160 S/A		OP	RNBT	FBG SV IO 120-205	6 10		10	2850	3450
16 3	160 B/R		OP	RNBT	FBG DV OB	6 4	650		1650	2000
17	170 B/R		OP	RNBT	FBG SV IO 120-205	7 4		1 4	3450	4100
17	170 B/R SI		OP	RNBT	FBG DV OB	7 4		1 4	3350	4050
17 2	175 B/R		OP	RNBT	FBG DV OB	7 5	1075		2750	3200
17 2	175 B/R		OP	RNBT	FBG SV IO 120-205	7 5	1675		3150	3750
17 2	175 B/R SD		OP	RNBT	FBG SV IO 120-205	7 5	1675		3200	3850
17 2	175 F/S B/R		OP	RNBT	FBG DV OB	7 5	1075		2750	3200
17 6	MARK I		OP	RNBT	FBG SV IO 120-205	7 6	1850		3400	4050
18 7	MARK II		OP	RNBT	FBG SV IO 120-230	7 6	1950		3700	4550
18 7	MARK II		OP	RNBT	FBG DV OB 260 MRCR	7 6	1950		4050	4700
19 5	195 B/R		OP	RNBT	FBG DV OB	7 6	1225		3300	3850
19 5	195 B/R		OP	RNBT	FBG SV IO 120-230	7 9	2050		4000	4900
19 5	195 B/R		OP	RNBT	FBG SV IO 260 MRCR	7 9	2050		4400	5100
19 5	195 B/R SD		OP	RNBT	FBG SV IO 120-230	7 9	2050		4100	5000
19 5	195 B/R SD		OP	RNBT	FBG SV IO 260 MRCR	7 9	2050		4500	5150
19 5	195 CC		OP	CUD	FBG SV OB	7 9	1225		3300	3850
19 5	195 CC		OP	CUD	FBG SV IO 120-230	7 9	2150		4150	5100
19 5	195 CC		OP	CUD	FBG SV IO 260 MRCR	7 9	2150		4600	5300
19 5	195 CC LINER		OP	CUD	FBG SV IO 120-260	7 9	2150		4450	5450
19 5	200 B/R		OP	RNBT	FBG SV IO MRCR	8		1 6	4650	5650
19 5	200 B/R SI		OP	RNBT	FBG SV IO 165-260	8		1 6	**	**
19 5	200 B/R SI		OP	RNBT	FBG SV IO 165-260	8		1 6	4550	5550
19 5	200 CC		OP	CUD	FBG SV IO MRCR	8		1 6	**	**
19 5	200 CC		OP	CUD	FBG SV IO 165-260	8		1 6	4800	5850
19 5	200 CC SI		OP	CUD	FBG SV IO MRCR	8		1 6	**	**
19 5	200 CC SI		OP	CUD	FBG SV IO 165-260	8		1 6	4700	5800
19 8	MARK 5 CC		OP	CR	FBG SV IO 165-260	8	2320		4650	5750
21 9	225 AFT		OP	CR	FBG SV IO 165-260	7 11	4500		7200	8600
21 9	225 AFT		OP	CR	FBG SV IO 350 MRCR	7 11	4500		8550	9850
21 9	225 CC		OP	CR	FBG SV IO 165-260	7 11	3400		5650	6850
21 9	225 CC		OP	CR	FBG SV IO 350 MRCR	7 11	3400		7000	8050
21 9	225 CC LINER		OP	CR	FBG SV IO 165-260	7 11	3400		6050	7250
21 9	225 CC LINER		OP	CR	FBG SV IO 350 MRCR	7 11	3400		7400	8500
23 11	230 CC		OP	CR	FBG SV IO 165-260	8 2	3350		6550	7850
23 11	230 CC		OP	CR	FBG SV IO 350 MRCR	8 2	3350		7900	9100
25 9	265 AFT		OP	CR	FBG SV IO MRCR	8	5250		**	**
	IO 230-260	10000	11700, IO	350 MRCR	11400 12900, IO T		MRCR		**	**
	IO T165-T260	10900	13600, IO T						**	**
28 6	285 AFT		OP	CR	FBG SV IO T MRCR	8	8280		**	**
28 6	285 AFT		OP	CR	FBG SV IO T165-T260	8	8280		14700	18200
					1987 BOATS					
17 2	SEA-SPRITE 175 B/R	ST	RNBT	FBG DV OB		7 5			2450	2850
17 2	SEA-SPRITE 175 B/R	ST	RNBT	FBG DV IO 120		7 5			3250	3800
17 2	SEA-SPRITE 175 F/S	ST	RNBT	FBG DV OB		7 5			3050	3550
17 2	SEA-SPRITE 175 S/S	ST	RNBT	FBG DV IO 120		7 5			3350	3900
17 5	SEA-SPRITE 185 B/R	ST	RNBT	FBG DV IO 120		7 9			3400	3950
17 5	SEA-SPRITE 185 S/S	ST	RNBT	FBG DV IO 120		7 9			3500	4050
19 5	SEA-SPRITE 195 B/R	ST	RNBT	FBG DV OB		7 9			3850	4500
19 5	SEA-SPRITE 195 B/R	ST	RNBT	FBG DV IO 120		7 9			4150	4850
19 5	SEA-SPRITE 195 C/C	ST	CUD	FBG DV OB		7 9			4450	5150
19 5	SEA-SPRITE 195 C/C	ST	CUD	FBG DV IO 120		7 9			4400	5050
19 5	SEA-SPRITE 195 S/S	ST	RNBT	FBG DV IO 120		7 9			4250	4950
21 8	SEA-SPRITE 225 C/C	ST	CR	FBG DV IO 120		8			5050	5800
21 9	SEA-SPRITE 225 C/C	ST	CR	FBG DV IO 120		7 11			4950	5700
23 11	SEA-SPRITE 230 C/C	ST	CUD	FBG DV IO 120		8 2			7350	8450
25 9	SEA-SPRITE 265C	ST	DC	FBG DV IO 230		8			8950	10200
28 6	SEA-SPRITE 285C	ST	DC	FBG DV IO T165		10			13500	15300
					1986 BOATS					
17 2	SEA-SPRITE 175	ST	RNBT	FBG DV OB		7 5			2950	3450
17 2	SEA-SPRITE 175 B/R	ST	RNBT	FBG DV OB		7 5			2400	2750
17 2	SEA-SPRITE 175 B/R	ST	RNBT	FBG DV IO 120		7 5			3150	3650
17 5	SEA-SPRITE 185 B/R	ST	RNBT	FBG DV IO 120		7 9			3300	3850
19 5	SEA-SPRITE 195 B/R	ST	RNBT	FBG DV OB		7 9			3750	4350
19 5	SEA-SPRITE 195 B/R	ST	RNBT	FBG DV IO 120		7 9			4000	4700
19 5	SEA-SPRITE 195 C/C	ST	CUD	FBG DV IO 120		7 9			4300	5000
19 5	SEA-SPRITE 195 CUDDY	ST	CUD	FBG DV OB		7 9			4150	4850
21 8	SEA-SPRITE 228 C/C	ST	CUD	FBG DV IO 120		8			4800	5550
23 11	SEA-SPRITE 230 C/C	ST	CUD	FBG DV IO 120		8 2			7050	8100
25 9	SEA-SPRITE 260C	ST	DC	FBG DV IO 230		8			8450	9750
					1985 BOATS					
16 9	CONTINENTAL MARK I	OP	RNBT	FBG DV IO 120		6 6			2750	3200
16 9	SEA-SPRITE 175 XL	OP	RNBT	FBG DV OB		6 6			2600	3000
17 9	SEA-SPRITE 180 XL	OP	RNBT	FBG DV OB		7 4			3050	3550
17 9	SEA-SPRITE 180 XL	OP	RNBT	FBG DV IO 120		7 4			3100	3600
18 3	SEA-SPRITE 185 XL	OP	RNBT	FBG DV IO 120		8			3400	3950
18 7	CONTINENTAL MARK II	OP	RNBT	FBG DV IO 120		7 5			3450	4050
18 7	CONTINENTAL MARK III	OP	RNBT	FBG DV IO 120		7 7			3750	4350
19 3	SEA-SPRITE 195 XL	OP	RNBT	FBG DV IO 120		8			3800	4400
19 8	CONTINENTAL MARK IV	OP	RNBT	FBG DV IO 120		8			4000	4650
19 8	SEA-SPRITE 210 XL	OP	CUD	FBG DV IO 120		8			4300	5000
19 8	SEA-SPRITE 210 XL	OP	FSH	FBG DV IO 120		8			4550	5250
19 8	SEA-SPRITE 210 XL	OP	RNBT	FBG DV IO 120		8			4250	4950
23 11	SEA-SPRITE 225 XL	OP	CUD	FBG DV IO 120		8 1			6750	7750
25 9	SEA-SPRITE 260 XL	OP	CR	FBG DV IO 200		8			7400	8500
					1984 BOATS					
16	COUGAR 672	ST	RNBT	FBG TR OB		6	780		1750	2100
16 1	STINGER 678		SKI	FBG FBG OB		6	750		1700	2000
16 9	MARK I BR	OP	RNBT	FBG DV OB 120-140		6 6	1675		2450	2850
16 9	SEA-RAVEN 780 XL	ST	SKI	FBG DV OB		6 8	995		2300	2650
16 9	SEA-RAVEN 780 XL	ST	SKI	FBG DV IO 120		6 8	1690		2300	2700
17 2	FISH-N-SKI 784		RNBT	FBG TR OB		7 1	935		2250	2600
17 9	SANDPIPER 889 XL	ST	RNBT	FBG DV OB		7 5	1200		2750	3200
17 9	SANDPIPER 889 XL	ST	RNBT	FBG DV IO 120-170		7 5	1950		2950	3600
18 3	SANDPIPER 889 XL	ST	RNBT	FBG DV IO 198-200		7 5	2340		3300	3800
18 7	SEA-SPIRIT 895	ST	RNBT	FBG DV IO 120-170		7 11	2250		3400	4100
18 7	MARK II BR	OP	RNBT	FBG DV IO 120-170		7 6	1900		3100	3750
18 7	MARK III CUDDY	OP	RNBT	FBG DV IO 120-170		7 6	1925		3100	3800
19 8	MARK IV	OP	RNBT	FBG DV IO 120-170		7 11	2100		3550	4300
19 8	SEA-SKIFF 2095	ST	CUD	FBG DV IO 120-170		7 11	2315		3850	4650
19 8	SEA-SKIFF 2095 B/R	ST	RNBT	FBG DV IO 198-200		7 11	2705		4250	4900
22 3	ESCAPADE I 2298	OP	CR	FBG DV IO 120-170		8	2160		3600	4350
25 9	ESCAPADE III 2696		CR	FBG DV IO 198-260			3375		5100	6100
							5075		8550	9700

....For earlier years, see the BUC Used Boat Price Guide, Volume 3

SEA STAR YACHTS
HAMPTON VA 23669   See inside cover to adjust price for area

LOA FT IN	NAME AND/ OR MODEL	TOP/ RIG	BOAT TYPE	HULL MTL TP	ENGINE TP # HP MFG	BEAM FT IN	WGT LBS	DRAFT FT IN	RETAIL LOW	RETAIL HIGH
					1992 BOATS					
29 6	TUGBOAT 30	HT	TRWL	FBG DS IB 90D LEHM		11	9600	2 10	45900	50400
35 3	TRAWLER SUNDECK 36	FB	TRWL	FBG SV IB 210D CAT		13	19000	3 1	101000	111000
35 3	TRAWLER SUNDECK 36	FB	TRWL	FBG SV IB T 90D LEHM		13 2	19000	3 1	101500	111500
35	TUGBOAT 36	HT	TUG	FBG DS IB 135D LEHM		12	16500	3 4	**	**
36 6	SPORTFISHERMAN 37	FB	SF	FBG SV IB T150D VLVO		14 1	26000	3 6	118500	130000
36 6	SPORTFISHERMAN 37	FB	SF	FBG SV IB T180D CAT		14 1	26000	3 6	123000	135000
36 6	SUNDECK MY 37	FB	MY	FBG SV IB T150D VLVO		14 1	26000	3 6	119000	131000
36 6	SUNDECK MY 37	FB	MY	FBG SV IB T210D CAT		14 1	26000	3 6	125000	137000
39 5	SPORTFISHERMAN 40	FB	SF	FBG SV IB T150D VLVO		13 2	31000	3 1	162500	178500
	IB T210D CAT	170000	186500, IB	T210D CAT	170000 186500, IB T306D VLVO				171000	187500
39 5	SUNDECK MY 40	FB	MY	FBG SV IB T150D VLVO		13 2	31000	3 1	163500	179500
39 5	SUNDECK MY 40	FB	MY	FBG SV IB T210D CAT		13 2	31000	3 1	171000	188000
39 5	SUNDECK TRAWLER 40	FB	TRWL	FBG SV IB 210 CAT		13 2	31000	3 1	164500	181000
39 5	SUNDECK TRAWLER 40	FB	TRWL	FBG SV IB 210 CAT		13 2	31000	3 1	173000	190000
39 5	TRAWLER 40	FB	TRWL	FBG SV IB 210D CAT		13 2	31000	3 1	154500	170000
39 5	TRAWLER 40	FB	TRWL	FBG SV IB 210D CAT		13 2	31000	3 1	168000	184500
43 6	SUNDECK MY 43	FB	MY	FBG SV IB T375D CAT		15	31000		191000	210000
46 6	SUNDECK MY 47	FB	MY	FBG SV IB T375D CAT		15	35000	3 6	218000	239500
48 6	SUNDECK MY 49	FB	MY	FBG SV IB T375D CAT		15	35000		208500	229000
49	SUNDECK MY 50	FB	MY	FBG SV IB T375D CAT		15	38000		225500	248000
57 6	TWINDECK MY 58	FB	MY	FBG SV IB T375D CAT		18	67360	4 9	403000	443000
61 6	TWINDECK MY 62	FB	MY	FBG SV IB T375D CAT		18 5	70360	4 9	419000	460000
64 6	TWINDECK MY 65	FB	MY	FBG SV IB T375D CAT		18	72360	4 9	494500	543000
69 6	TWINDECK MY 70	FB	MY	FBG SV IB T375D CAT		18 5	75360	4 9	589000	647500
					1991 BOATS					
29 6	TUGBOAT 30	HT	TRWL	FBG DS IB 90D LEHM		11	9600	2 10	43300	48100
35 3	TRAWLER SUNDECK 36	HT	TRWL	FBG SV IB 210D CAT		13	19000	3 1	96400	106000
35 3	TRAWLER SUNDECK 36	FB	TRWL	FBG SV IB T 90D LEHM		13 2	19000	3 1	96700	106000
36	TUGBOAT 36	HT	TUG	FBG DS IB 135D LEHM		12	16500	3 4	**	**

LOA FT	LOA IN	NAME AND/ OR MODEL	TOP/ RIG	BOAT TYPE	-HULL- MTL	-HULL- TP	ENGINE TP	ENGINE # HP	ENGINE MFG	BEAM FT	BEAM IN	WGT LBS	DRAFT FT	DRAFT IN	RETAIL LOW	RETAIL HIGH
		1991 BOATS														
36	6	SPORTFISHERMAN 37	FB	SF	FBG	SV	IB	T150D	VLVO	14	1	26000	3	6	113000	124000
36	6	SPORTFISHERMAN 37	FB	SF	FBG	SV	IB	T210D	CAT	14	1	26000	3	6	117000	129000
36	6	SUNDECK MY 37	FB	MY	FBG	SV	IB	T150D	VLVO	14	1	26000	3	6	113500	125000
36	6	SUNDECK MY 37	FB	MY	FBG	SV	IB	T210D	CAT	14	1	26000	3	6	119000	131000
39	5	SPORTFISHERMAN 40	FB	SF	FBG	SV	IB	T150D	VLVO	13	2	31000	3	1	155000	170500
		IB T210D CAT 162000 178000, IB T210D CAT 162000 178000, IB T306D VLVO													163000	179000
39	5	SUNDECK MY 40	FB	MY	FBG	SV	IB	T150D	VLVO	13	2	31000	3	1	156000	171500
39	5	SUNDECK MY 40	FB	MY	FBG	SV	IB	T210D	CAT	13	2	31000	3	1	163000	179000
39	5	SUNDECK TRAWLER 40	FB	TRWL	FBG	SV	IB	210D	CAT	13	2	31000	3	1	157000	172500
39	5	SUNDECK TRAWLER 40	FB	TRWL	FBG	SV	IB	T210D	CAT	13	2	31000	3	1	165000	181500
39	5	TRAWLER 40	FB	TRWL	FBG	SV	IB	210D	CAT	13	2	31000	3	1	147500	162000
39	5	TRAWLER 40	FB	TRWL	FBG	SV	IB	T210D	CAT	13	2	31000	3	1	160000	176000
42	6	SUNDECK MY 43	FB	MY	FBG	SV	IB	T375D	CAT	15		31000	3	6	182500	200500
46	6	SUNDECK MY 47	FB	MY	FBG	SV	IB	T375D	CAT	15		35000	3	6	207500	228500
48	6	SUNDECK MY 49	FB	MY	FBG	SV	IB	T375D	CAT	15		35000	3	6	199000	218500
49	6	SUNDECK MY 50	FB	MY	FBG	SV	IB	T375D	CAT	15		38000	3	6	212500	233500
57	6	TWINDECK MY 58	FB	MY	FBG	SV	IB	T375D	CAT	18	5	67360	4	9	384500	422500
61	6	TWINDECK MY 62	FB	MY	FBG	SV	IB	T375D	CAT	18	5	70360	4	9	399500	439000
64	6	TWINDECK MY 65	FB	MY	FBG	SV	IB	T375D	CAT	18	5	72360	4	9	471500	518000
69	6	TWINDECK MY 70	FB	MY	FBG	SV	IB	T375D	CAT	18	5	75360	4	9	562000	617500

SEA VEE BOATS

MIAMI FL 33150 COAST GUARD MFG ID- SXJ See inside cover to adjust price for area

For more recent years, see the BUC Used Boat Price Guide, Volume 1

LOA FT	LOA IN	NAME AND/ OR MODEL	TOP/ RIG	BOAT TYPE	-HULL- MTL	-HULL- TP	ENGINE TP	ENGINE # HP	ENGINE MFG	BEAM FT	BEAM IN	WGT LBS	DRAFT FT	DRAFT IN	RETAIL LOW	RETAIL HIGH
		1996 BOATS														
25		CENTER CONSOLE	OP	CTRCN	FBG	DV	IB	330		8	4	3600	2	8	24100	26800
25		OPEN 250S	OP	OPFSH	FBG	DV	IB	T225D		8	3	4600			47700	52400
28		SEA 28 CONVERTIBLE	TTP	SF	FBG	DV	OB			8	4	4100	2	8	42300	47000
29	6	280I	OP	FSH	FBG	DV	IB	250D		8	3	4100	2	8	36700	40700
		1995 BOATS														
25		SEA 25 CONVERTIBLE	OP	CNV	FBG	DV	OB			8	4	3600	2	8	18400	20400
25		SEA 25 CONVERTIBLE	OP	CNV	FBG	DV	IB	260-330		8	4	3600	2	8	23400	26300
25		SEA 25 CONVERTIBLE	OP	CNV	FBG	DV	IB	200D	VLVO	8	4	3600	2	8	30000	33400
25		SEA 25 OPENFISHERMAN	OP	CTRCN	FBG	DV	OB			8	4	3600	2	8	18100	20100
25		SEA 25 OPENFISHERMAN	OP	CTRCN	FBG	DV	IB	260-330		8	4	3600	2	8	22000	25300
25		SEA 25 OPENFISHERMAN	OP	CTRCN	FBG	DV	IB	200D	VLVO	8	4	3600	2	8	27100	30200
28		SEA 28 CONVERTIBLE	OP	CNV	FBG	DV	OB			8	4	4100	2	8	30000	33300
28		SEA 28 CONVERTIBLE	OP	CNV	FBG	DV	IB	260-330		8	4	4100	2	8	32700	37100
28		SEA 28 CONVERTIBLE	OP	CNV	FBG	DV	IB	200D	VLVO	8	4	4100	2	8	36800	40900
28		SEA 28 OPENFISHERMAN	OP	CTRCN	FBG	DV	OB			8	4	4100	2	8	29100	32300
28		SEA 28 OPENFISHERMAN	OP	CTRCN	FBG	DV	IB	260-330		8	4	4100	2	8	28700	33700
28		SEA 28 OPENFISHERMAN	OP	CTRCN	FBG	DV	IB	200D	VLVO	8	4	4100	2	8	29200	32500
31		SEA 31 CONVERTIBLE	OP	CNV	FBG	DV	OB			8	4	4800	2	8	40000	44500
31		SEA 31 CONVERTIBLE	OP	CNV	FBG	DV	IB	260-330		8	4	4800	2	8	47500	54500
31		SEA 31 CONVERTIBLE	OP	CNV	FBG	DV	IB	200D	VLVO	8	4	4800	2	8	50100	55000
31		SEA 31 OPENFISHERMAN	OP	CTRCN	FBG	DV	OB			8	4	4800	2	8	38000	42200
31		SEA 31 OPENFISHERMAN	OP	CTRCN	FBG	DV	IB	260-330		8	4	4800	2	8	41800	48700
31		SEA 31 OPENFISHERMAN	OP	CTRCN	FBG	DV	IB	200D	VLVO	8	4	4800	2	8	39900	44300
		1994 BOATS														
25		MCGEE 25	OP	CTRCN	FBG	DV	OB			8	4	3600	2	8	16800	19100
25		MCGEE 25	OP	CTRCN	FBG	DV	IO	260-330		8	4	3600	2	8	18300	22900
25		MCGEE 25	OP	CTRCN	FBG	DV	IO	200D	VLVO	8	4	3600	2	8	23900	26500
25		MCGEE CNV	OP	CNV	FBG	DV	OB			8	4	3600	2	8	17200	19500
25		MCGEE CNV	OP	CNV	FBG	DV	IO	260-330		8	4	3600	2	8	20800	25600
25		MCGEE CNV	OP	CNV	FBG	DV	IO	200D	VLVO	8	4	3600	2	8	26500	29400
25		MCGEE CUD	OP	CUD	FBG	DV	OB			8	4	3600	2	8	18100	20100
25		MCGEE CUD	OP	CUD	FBG	DV	IO	260	VLVO	8	4	3600	2	8	17100	19400
25		MCGEE CUD	OP	CUD	FBG	DV	IO	330	CRUS	8	4	3600	2	8	19500	21700
25		MCGEE CUD	OP	CUD	FBG	DV	IO	200D	VLVO	8	4	3600	2	8	19200	21300
31		MCGEE 31	OP	CTRCN	FBG	DV	OB			8	4	4800			35900	39900
31		MCGEE 31	OP	CTRCN	FBG	DV	IO	330		8	4	4800			36900	41000
31		MCGEE 31	OP	CTRCN	FBG	DV	IO	200D	VLVO	8	4	4800			38500	42800
31		MCGEE 31 CNV	OP	CNV	FBG	DV	OB			8	4	4800			37800	42000
31		MCGEE 31 CNV	OP	CNV	FBG	DV	IO	330		8	4	4800			44800	49700
31		MCGEE 31 CNV	OP	CNV	FBG	DV	IO	200D	VLVO	8	4	4800			48200	53000
31		MCGEE 31 CUD	OP	CUD	FBG	DV	OB			8	4	4800			39600	44000
		1993 BOATS														
25		MCGEE 25	OP	CTRCN	FBG	DV	OB			8	4	3600	2	8	16000	18200
25		MCGEE 25	OP	CTRCN	FBG	DV	IO	260	VLVO	8	4	3600	2	8	16800	19100
25		MCGEE 25	OP	CTRCN	FBG	DV	IO	330	CRUS	8	4	3600	2	8	19300	21400
25		MCGEE 25	OP	CTRCN	FBG	DV	IO	200D	VLVO	8	4	3600	2	8	22300	24800
25		MCGEE CNV	OP	CNV	FBG	DV	OB			8	4	3600	2	8	16200	18400
25		MCGEE CNV	OP	CNV	FBG	DV	IO	260-330		8	4	3600	2	8	19400	23900
25		MCGEE CNV	OP	CNV	FBG	DV	IO	200D	VLVO	8	4	3600	2	8	24700	27500
25		MCGEE CUD	OP	CUD	FBG	DV	OB			8	4	3600	2	8	16700	19000
25		MCGEE CUD	OP	CUD	FBG	DV	IO	260	VLVO	8	4	3600	2	8	15900	18100
25		MCGEE CUD	OP	CUD	FBG	DV	IO	330	CRUS	8	4	3600	2	8	18500	20500
25		MCGEE CUD	OP	CUD	FBG	DV	IO	200D	VLVO	8	4	3600	2	8	18200	20200
31		MCGEE 31	OP	CTRCN	FBG	DV	OB			8	4	4800			34100	37900
31		MCGEE 31	OP	CTRCN	FBG	DV	IO	330		8	4	4800			34400	38300
31		MCGEE 31	OP	CTRCN	FBG	DV	IO	200D	VLVO	8	4	4800			36000	40000
31		MCGEE 31 CNV	OP	CNV	FBG	DV	OB			8	4	4800			35600	39600
31		MCGEE 31 CNV	OP	CNV	FBG	DV	IO	330		8	4	4800			41800	46500
31		MCGEE 31 CNV	OP	CNV	FBG	DV	IO	200D	VLVO	8	4	4800			44800	49800
		1991 BOATS														
25		SEA-VEE 25	OP	CTRCN	FBG	DV	OB			8		3600	2	8	14600	16600
25		SEA-VEE 25	OP	CTRCN	FBG	DV	IO	260	VLVO	8		3600	2	8	14600	16600
25		SEA-VEE 25	OP	CTRCN	FBG	DV	IO	454-460		8		3600	2	8	22000	24400
25		SEA-VEE 25	OP	CTRCN	FBG	DV	IO	200D		8		3600	2	8	25000	27800
25		SEA-VEE 25 DUO PROP	OP	CTRCN	FBG	DV	IO	260	VLVO	8		3600	2	8	16300	18500
25		SEA-VEE 25 DUO PROP	OP	CTRCN	FBG	DV	IO	200D	VLVO	8		3600	2	8	21400	23700
25		SEA-VEE CNV	OP	CNV	FBG	DV	OB			8		3600	2	8	14800	16800
25		SEA-VEE CNV	OP	CNV	FBG	DV	IO	260	VLVO	8		3600	2	8	16700	19000
25		SEA-VEE CNV	OP	CNV	FBG	DV	IO	454-460		8		3600	2	8	23700	26400
25		SEA-VEE CNV	OP	CNV	FBG	DV	IO	200D		8		3600	2	8	27400	30500
25		SEA-VEE CNV DUO PROP	OP	CNV	FBG	DV	IO	260	VLVO	8		3600	2	8	19000	21200
25		SEA-VEE CNV DUO PROP	OP	CNV	FBG	DV	IO	200D	VLVO	8		3600	2	8	23600	26300
25		SEA-VEE CUD	OP	CUD	FBG	DV	OB			8		3600	2	8	15100	17200
25		SEA-VEE CUD	OP	CUD	FBG	DV	IO	260	VLVO	8		3600	2	8	13900	15800
25		SEA-VEE CUD	OP	CUD	FBG	DV	IO	454-460		8		3600	2	8	20800	23100
25		SEA-VEE CUD	OP	CUD	FBG	DV	IO	200D		8		3600	2	8	20000	22200
25		SEA-VEE CUD DUO PROP	OP	CUD	FBG	DV	IO	260	VLVO	8		3600	2	8	15400	17500
25		SEA-VEE CUD DUO PROP	OP	CUD	FBG	DV	IO	200D	VLVO	8		3600	2	8	16900	19200
		1990 BOATS														
25		SEA-VEE 25	OP	CTRCN	FBG	DV	OB			8		3600	2	8	14100	16100
25		SEA-VEE 25	OP	CTRCN	FBG	DV	IO	260	VLVO	8		3600	2	8	13700	15600
25		SEA-VEE 25	OP	CTRCN	FBG	DV	IO	454-460		8		3600	2	8	20700	23000
25		SEA-VEE 25	OP	CTRCN	FBG	DV	IO	200D		8		3600	2	8	23500	26100
25		SEA-VEE 25 W/DUO PRP	OP	CTRCN	FBG	DV	IO	260	VLVO	8		3600	2	8	15300	17400
25		SEA-VEE 25 W/DUO PRP	OP	CTRCN	FBG	DV	IO	200D	VLVO	8		3600	2	8	20100	22300
25		SEA-VEE CNV	OP	CNV	FBG	DV	OB			8		3600	2	8	14200	16100
25		SEA-VEE CNV	OP	CNV	FBG	DV	IO	260	VLVO	8		3600	2	8	15700	17900
25		SEA-VEE CNV	OP	CNV	FBG	DV	IO	454-460		8		3600	2	8	22300	24800
25		SEA-VEE CNV	OP	CNV	FBG	DV	IO	200D		8		3600	2	8	25800	28600
25		SEA-VEE CNV W/DUO PR	OP	CNV	FBG	DV	IO	260	VLVO	8		3600	2	8	17500	19900
25		SEA-VEE CNV W/DUO PR	OP	CNV	FBG	DV	IO	200D	VLVO	8		3600	2	8	22200	24700
25		SEA-VEE CUD	OP	CUD	FBG	DV	OB			8		3600	2	8	14300	16300
25		SEA-VEE CUD	OP	CUD	FBG	DV	IO	260	VLVO	8		3600	2	8	13100	14800
25		SEA-VEE CUD	OP	CUD	FBG	DV	IO	454-460		8		3600	2	8	19600	21800
25		SEA-VEE CUD	OP	CUD	FBG	DV	IO	200D		8		3600	2	8	19000	21100
25		SEA-VEE CUD W/DUO PR	OP	CUD	FBG	DV	IO	260	VLVO	8		3600	2	8	14500	16500
25		SEA-VEE CUD W/DUO PR	OP	CUD	FBG	DV	IO	200D	VLVO	8		3600	2	8	15900	18100
		1989 BOATS														
25		SEA-VEE 25	OP	CTRCN	FBG	DV	OB			8		3600	2	8	13700	15600
25		SEA-VEE 25	OP	CTRCN	FBG	DV	IO	260	VLVO	8		3600	2	8	13000	14700
25		SEA-VEE 25	OP	CTRCN	FBG	DV	IO	454-460		8		3600	2	8	19500	21700
25		SEA-VEE 25	OP	CTRCN	FBG	DV	IO	200D		8		3600	2	8	22200	24700
25		SEA-VEE 25 W/DUO PRP	OP	CTRCN	FBG	DV	IO	260	VLVO	8		3600	2	8	14500	16400
25		SEA-VEE 25 W/DUO PRP	OP	CTRCN	FBG	DV	IO	200D	VLVO	8		3600	2	8	19200	21300
25		SEA-VEE CNV	OP	CNV	FBG	DV	OB			8		3600	2	8	13700	15600
25		SEA-VEE CNV	OP	CNV	FBG	DV	IO	260	VLVO	8		3600	2	8	14900	16900
25		SEA-VEE CNV	OP	CNV	FBG	DV	IO	454-460		8		3600	2	8	21100	23400
25		SEA-VEE CNV	OP	CNV	FBG	DV	IO	200D		8		3600	2	8	24300	27000
25		SEA-VEE CNV W/DUO PR	OP	CNV	FBG	DV	IO	260	VLVO	8		3600	2	8	16500	18800
25		SEA-VEE CNV W/DUO PR	OP	CNV	FBG	DV	IO	200D	VLVO	8		3600	2	8	21000	23300
25		SEA-VEE CUD	OP	CUD	FBG	DV	OB			8		3600	2	8	13800	15600
25		SEA-VEE CUD	OP	CUD	FBG	DV	IO	260	VLVO	8		3600	2	8	12300	14000
25		SEA-VEE CUD	OP	CUD	FBG	DV	IO	454-460		8		3600	2	8	18700	20800
25		SEA-VEE CUD	OP	CUD	FBG	DV	IO	200D		8		3600	2	8	17500	19900
25		SEA-VEE CUD W/DUO PR	OP	CUD	FBG	DV	IO	260	VLVO	8		3600	2	8	13700	15500
25		SEA-VEE CUD W/DUO PR	OP	CUD	FBG	DV	IO	200D	VLVO	8		3600	2	8	15000	17100

SEA VEE BOATS   -CONTINUED   See inside cover to adjust price for area

LOA FT IN	NAME AND/ OR MODEL	TOP/ RIG	BOAT TYPE	HULL MTL TP TP	ENGINE # HP MFG	BEAM FT IN	WGT LBS	DRAFT FT IN	RETAIL LOW	RETAIL HIGH
				---- 1988 BOATS ----						
25	SEA-VEE 25	OP	CTRCN	FBG DV	OB	8	3600	2 8	13300	15100
25	SEA-VEE 25	OP	CTRCN	FBG DV	IO 260 VLVO	8	3600	2 8	12300	13900
25	SEA-VEE 25	OP	CTRCN	FBG DV	IO 454-460	8	3600	2 8	18700	20700
25	SEA-VEE 25	OP	CTRCN	FBG DV	IO 200D	8	3600	2 8	21000	23300
25	SEA-VEE 25 W/DUO PRP	OP	CTRCN	FBG DV	IO 260 VLVO	8	3600	2 8	13700	15600
25	SEA-VEE 25 W/DUO PRP	OP	CTRCN	FBG DV	IO 200D VLVO	8	3600	2 8	18100	20200
25	SEA-VEE CNV	OP	CNV	FBG DV	OB	8	3600	2 8	13300	15100
25	SEA-VEE CNV	OP	CNV	FBG DV	IO 260 VLVO	8	3600	2 8	14100	16000
25	SEA-VEE CNV	OP	CNV	FBG DV	IO 454-460	8	3600	2 8	19900	22100
25	SEA-VEE CNV W/DUO PR	OP	CNV	FBG DV	IO 200D	8	3600	2 8	23000	25600
25	SEA-VEE CNV W/DUO PR	OP	CNV	FBG DV	IO 260 VLVO	8	3600	2 8	15600	17800
25	SEA-VEE CNV W/DUO PR	OP	CNV	FBG DV	IO 200D VLVO	8	3600	2 8	19900	22100
25	SEA-VEE CUD	OP	CUD	FBG DV	OB	8	3600	2 8	13300	15100
25	SEA-VEE CUD	OP	CUD	FBG DV	IO 260 VLVO	8	3600	2 8	11700	13200
25	SEA-VEE CUD	OP	CUD	FBG DV	IO 454-460	8	3600	2 8	17300	19700
25	SEA-VEE CUD	OP	CUD	FBG DV	IO 200D	8	3600	2 8	16600	18900
25	SEA-VEE CUD W/DUO PR	OP	CUD	FBG DV	IO 200D VLVO	8	3600	2 8	12900	14700
25	SEA-VEE CUD	OP	CUD	FBG DV	IO 200D VLVO	8	3600	2 8	14200	16200
				---- 1987 BOATS ----						
25	SEA-VEE 25	OP	CTRCN	FBG DV	OB	8	3600	2 8	12900	14700
25	SEA-VEE 25	OP	CTRCN	FBG DV	IO 260-270	8	3600	2 8	12300	14000
25	SEA-VEE 25	OP	CTRCN	FBG DV	IO 200D	8	3600	2 8	18600	20700
25	SEA-VEE CONVERTIBLE	OP	CNV	FBG DV	OB	8	3600	2 8	12900	14700
25	SEA-VEE CONVERTIBLE	OP	CNV	FBG DV	IO 260-270	8	3600	2 8	14100	16000
25	SEA-VEE CONVERTIBLE	OP	CNV	FBG DV	IO 200D	8	3600	2 8	20200	22500
25	SEA-VEE CUDDY	OP	CUD	FBG DV	OB	8	3600	2 8	12900	14700
25	SEA-VEE CUDDY	OP	CUD	FBG DV	IO 260-270	8	3600	2 8	11700	13300
25	SEA-VEE CUDDY	OP	CUD	FBG DV	IO 200D	8	3600	2 8	14600	16600
				---- 1986 BOATS ----						
25	SEA-VEE 25	OP	CTRCN	FBG DV	OB	8	3600	1 4	12500	14200
25	SEA-VEE 25	TT	CTRCN	FBG DV	OB	8			11600	13100
				---- 1985 BOATS ----						
25	SEA-VEE 25	OP	CTRCN	FBG DV	OB	8	3600	1 4	12200	13800
25	SEA-VEE 25	TT	CTRCN	FBG DV	OB	8			11300	12800
				---- 1984 BOATS ----						
25	SEA-VEE 25	OP	CTRCN	FBG DV	OB	8	3600	1 4	11900	13500
25	SEA-VEE 25	TT	CTRCN	FBG DV	OB	8			11000	12500

....For earlier years, see the BUC Used Boat Price Guide, Volume 3

SEA-PRO BOATS INC

BRUNSWICK CORPORATION
NEWBERRY SC 29108-6141   See inside cover to adjust price for area

For more recent years, see the BUC Used Boat Price Guide, Volume 1

LOA FT IN	NAME AND/ OR MODEL	TOP/ RIG	BOAT TYPE	HULL MTL TP TP	ENGINE # HP MFG	BEAM FT IN	WGT LBS	DRAFT FT IN	RETAIL LOW	RETAIL HIGH
				---- 1996 BOATS ----						
16 7	RENEGADE	OP	RNBT	FBG SV	JT 120	7 1	1100	10	4700	5450
17	SEA PRO 170 CC	OP	CTRCN	FBG SV	OB	6 10	950	6	2800	3250
17	SEA PRO 170 DC	OP	FSH	FBG SV	OB	6 10	950	6	2800	3250
17 3	SPORT 180 BR	OP	B/R	FBG DV	IO 185	7 10	1400		4350	5000
17 6	SEA PRO 180 CC	OP	CTRCN	FBG DV	OB	7 5	1500		4150	4850
18 5	SEA PRO 190 CC	OP	FSH	FBG DV	OB	8	1750		4750	5450
18 5	SEA PRO 190 DC	OP	FSH	FBG DV	OB	8	1750		4700	5400
18 5	SEA PRO 190 WA	OP	FSH	FBG DV	IO 135	8	2550		7000	8000
18 11	CLASSIC 1900 CC	OP	CUD	FBG DV	OB	7 8	1850		5000	5750
19 6	ROYALE 196 BR	OP	B/R	FBG DV	IO 260	8	1600		6100	6900
19 6	ROYALE 196 CC	OP	CUD	FBG DV	IO 260	8	1800		6600	7600
20 6	SEA PRO 210 CC	OP	CTRCN	FBG DV	OB	8 6	1950		6250	7200
20 6	SEA PRO 210 SPORT	OP	CUD	FBG DV	OB	8 6	2500		7300	8400
20 6	SEA PRO 210 SPORT	OP	CUD	FBG DV	IO 230	8 6	3500		10300	11700
21 2	ROYALE 220 CC	OP	CUD	FBG DV	IO 300	8 6	2750		9500	10800
21 2	ROYALE 220 LINER	OP	CUD	FBG DV	IO 300	8 6	2750		10700	12100
21 6	SEA PRO 230 SPORT	OP	CUD	FBG DV	IO	8 6	3000		8900	10100
21 6	SEA PRO 230 SPORT	OP	CUD	FBG DV	IO 280	8 6	3900		12200	13800
22 8	LAZER 230	OP	CUD	FBG DV	IO 350	8 2	2760		11900	13500
				---- 1995 BOATS ----						
16 7	RENEGADE	OP	RNBT	FBG DV	JT 120	7 1	1100	10	4500	5150
17	SEA PRO 170 CC	OP	CTRCN	FBG SV	OB	6 10	950	6	2650	3100
17	SEA PRO 170 DC	OP	FSH	FBG SV	OB	6 10	950	6	2650	3050
17 3	SPORT 180 BR	OP	B/R	FBG DV	IO 185	7 10	1400		4100	4750
17 6	SEA PRO 180 CC	OP	CTRCN	FBG DV	OB	7 5	1500		3950	4600
18 5	SEA PRO 190 CC	OP	CTRCN	FBG DV	OB	8	1750		4500	5150
18 5	SEA PRO 190 DC	OP	FSH	FBG DV	OB	8	1750		4500	5150
18 11	CLASSIC 1900 CC	OP	CUD	FBG DV	OB	7 10	1600		5650	6500
19 6	ROYALE 196 BR	OP	B/R	FBG DV	IO 260	8	1750		5700	6550
19 6	ROYALE 196 CC	OP	CUD	FBG DV	IO 260	8	1800		6150	7100
20 6	SEA PRO 210 CC	OP	CTRCN	FBG DV	OB	8 6	1950		5950	6850
20 6	SEA PRO 210 SPORT	OP	CUD	FBG DV	OB	8 6	2500		6950	8000
21 2	ROYALE 220 CC	OP	CUD	FBG DV	IO 300	8 6	2750		9450	10700
21 6	SEA PRO 230 SPORT	OP	CUD	FBG DV	IO 280	8 6	3000		9650	11000
22 8	LAZER 230	OP	CUD	FBG DV	IO 350	8 2	2760		11100	12600

SEA-SAFE BV

VEERHAVEN NETHERLANDS   See inside cover to adjust price for area

LOA FT IN	NAME AND/ OR MODEL	TOP/ RIG	BOAT TYPE	HULL MTL TP TP	ENGINE # HP MFG	BEAM FT IN	WGT LBS	DRAFT FT IN	RETAIL LOW	RETAIL HIGH
				---- 1985 BOATS ----						
54	TRIOMPHATOR 54	MY		FBG DV	IB	17 1	53000		**	**
				---- 1984 BOATS ----						
53	TRIOMPHATOR 53	MY		FBG DV	IB	17 1	53000		**	**

SEABIRD

DIV OF P & L INDUSTRIES
PEMBROKE PARK FL   COAST GUARD MFG ID- VSL   See inside cover to adjust price for area
                  FORMERLY SEABIRD INDUSTRIES

LOA FT IN	NAME AND/ OR MODEL	TOP/ RIG	BOAT TYPE	HULL MTL TP TP	ENGINE # HP MFG	BEAM FT IN	WGT LBS	DRAFT FT IN	RETAIL LOW	RETAIL HIGH
				---- 1984 BOATS ----						
23 6	SEA-HAWK 24+	OP	CTRCN	FBG DV	OB	8	3000	2 7	7700	8850
23 6	SEA-HAWK 24+	OP	RNBT	FBG DV	OB	8	3000	2 7	7700	8850
23 6	SEA-HAWK 24+	OP	RNBT	FBG DV	SE OMC	8	3900	2 7	**	**
23 6	SEA-HAWK 24+	OP	RNBT	FBG DV	SE 225-230	8	3900	2 7	6500	7450
	IO 260 MRCR 6450	7400,	IO 260 VLVO	6650	7650, IB 260-270				8500	9800
	IB 124D VLVO 11000	12500,	IO 130D VLVO	7550	8700, IO T138 VLVO				7200	8300
29 1	CONDOR 29+	FB	SF	FBG DV	SE T OMC	10 3	9500	2 4	**	**
29 1	CONDOR 29+	FB	SF	FBG DV	IB T225-T270	10 3	9500	2 4	22900	26200
29 1	CONDOR 29+	FB	SF	FBG DV	IBT124D-T210D	10 3	9500	2 4	29000	36000
29 1	CUSTOM 29+	OP	OPFSH	FBG DV	SE T OMC	10 3	7800	2 4	**	**
29 1	CUSTOM 29+	OP	OPFSH	FBG DV	IB T225-T270	10 3	7800	2 4	20400	23400
29 1	CUSTOM 29+	OP	OPFSH	FBG DV	IBT124D-T210D	10 3	7800	2 4	23900	28000
36	CUSTOM 29+	OP	OPFSH	FBG DV	IBT200D-T210D	10 3	7800	2 4	27100	30500
36	EAGLE 36+	FB	SF	FBG DV	T350 CRUS 13	6	22000	3 6	60200	66200
	IB T270D CUM 69700	76600,	IB T300D CAT	72300	79500, IB T320D CUM				71800	78900
42 1	GOLDEN-EAGLE	FB	CR	FBG DV	IB T300D CAT 14		28500	3 5	112000	123000
42 1	GOLDEN-EAGLE	FB	CR	FBG DV	IB T320D CUM 14		28500	3 5	111000	122000
42 1	GOLDEN-EAGLE	FB	CR	FBG DV	IB T435D GM 14		28500	3 5	119500	131000

....For earlier years, see the BUC Used Boat Price Guide, Volume 3

SEAFARER FIBERGLASS YACHTS

HUNTINGTON NY 11743   COAST GUARD MFG ID- SFR See inside cover to adjust price for area

LOA FT IN	NAME AND/ OR MODEL	TOP/ RIG	BOAT TYPE	HULL MTL TP TP	ENGINE # HP MFG	BEAM FT IN	WGT LBS	DRAFT FT IN	RETAIL LOW	RETAIL HIGH
				---- 1985 BOATS ----						
21 8	SEAFARER 22 HIGH PER	SLP	SA/RC	FBG KL	OB	7 5	2400	2 10	4300	5000
21 8	SEAFARER 22 SHOAL	SLP	SA/RC	FBG KL	OB	7 5	2400	3 1	4400	5050
22 8	SEAFARER 23 H PERF	SLP	SA/RC	FBG KL	OB	7 7	2750	2 4	4950	5700
22 8	SEAFARER 23 SHOAL	SLP	SA/RC	FBG KL	OB	7 7	2750	2 4	5000	5750
25 9	SEAFARER 26 HIGH PER	SLP	SA/RC	FBG KL	OB	8 3	5200	4	10400	11800
25 9	SEAFARER 26 HIGH PER	SLP	SA/RC	FBG KL	IB 9D YAN	8 3	5200	4	11000	12500
25 9	SEAFARER 26 SHOAL	SLP	SA/RC	FBG KL	OB	8 3	5200	3 6	10500	11900
25 9	SEAFARER 26 SHOAL	SLP	SA/RC	FBG KL	IB 9D YAN	8 3	5200	3 6	11100	12600
29 11	SEAFARER 30	SLP	SA/RC	FBG KL	IB 13D- 15D	10	8600	4 9	20500	22800
29 11	SEAFARER 30 SHOAL	SLP	SA/RC	FBG KL	IB 13D- 15D	10	8600	4	20300	22800
36 8	SEAFARER 37 H PERF	SLP	SA/RC	FBG KL	IB 30D WEST 11	9	16500	6 3	39500	43900
36 8	SEAFARER 37 H PERF	SLP	SA/RC	FBG KL	IB 30D YAN 11	9	16500	6 3	39500	43900
36 8	SEAFARER 37 SHOAL	SLP	SA/RC	FBG KL	IB 30D WEST 11	9	17100	5	40700	45200
36 8	SEAFARER 37 SHOAL	SLP	SA/RC	FBG KL	IB 30D YAN 11	9	17100	5	40700	45200

96th ed. - Vol. II   CONTINUED ON NEXT PAGE   511

LOA FT	LOA IN	NAME AND/ OR MODEL	TOP/ RIG	BOAT TYPE	-HULL- MTL	-HULL- TP	ENGINE TP	ENGINE # HP	ENGINE MFG	BEAM FT	BEAM IN	WGT LBS	DRAFT FT	DRAFT IN	RETAIL LOW	RETAIL HIGH
		1984 BOATS														
21	8	SEAFARER 22 HIGH PER	SLP	SA/RC	FBG	KL	OB			7	5	2400	2	10	4050	4700
21	8	SEAFARER 22 SHOAL	SLP	SA/RC	FBG	KL	OB			7	5	2400	2	1	4100	4750
22	8	SEAFARER 23 H PERF	SLP	SA/RC	FBG	KL	OB			7	7	2750	3	3	4700	5400
22	8	SEAFARER 23 SHOAL	SLP	SA/RC	FBG	KL	OB			7	7	2750	2	4	4700	5450
25	9	SEAFARER 26 HIGH PER	SLP	SA/RC	FBG	KL	OB			8	3	5200	4		9750	11100
25	9	SEAFARER 26 HIGH PER	SLP	SA/RC	FBG	KL	IB	8D	YAN	8	3	5200	4		10300	11700
25	9	SEAFARER 26 SHOAL	SLP	SA/RC	FBG	KL	OB			8	3	5200	3	6	9850	11200
25	9	SEAFARER 26 SHOAL	SLP	SA/RC	FBG	KL	IB	8D	YAN	8	3	5200	3	6	10400	11900
29	11	SEAFARER 30	SLP	SA/RC	FBG	KL	IB	13D- 15D		10		8600	4	9	19100	21300
29	11	SEAFARER 30 SHOAL	SLP	SA/RC	FBG	KL	IB	13D- 15D		10		8600	4		19300	21400
36	8	SEAFARER 37 H PERF	SLP	SA/RC	FBG	KL	IB	30D	WEST	11	9	16500	6	3	37200	41300
36	8	SEAFARER 37 H PERF	SLP	SA/RC	FBG	KL	IB	30D	YAN	11	9	16500	6	3	37100	41300
36	8	SEAFARER 37 SHOAL	SLP	SA/RC	FBG	KL	IB	30D	WEST	11	9	17100	5		38300	42500
36	8	SEAFARER 37 SHOAL	SLP	SA/RC	FBG	KL	IB	30D	YAN	11	9	17100	5		38300	42500

....For earlier years, see the BUC Used Boat Price Guide, Volume 3

SEAIR MARINE LTD

N VANCOUVER BC CANADA

See inside cover to adjust price for area

LOA FT	LOA IN	NAME AND/ OR MODEL	TOP/ RIG	BOAT TYPE	-HULL- MTL	-HULL- TP	ENGINE TP	ENGINE # HP	ENGINE MFG	BEAM FT	BEAM IN	WGT LBS	DRAFT FT	DRAFT IN	RETAIL LOW	RETAIL HIGH
		1985 BOATS														
27		ODAIR 27	SLP	SA/RC	FBG	KL	IB	D		8		7000	4		17500	19900
27		VANCOUVER 27	CUT	SA/CR	FBG	KL				9		10000	4	5	24300	27000

....For earlier years, see the BUC Used Boat Price Guide, Volume 3

SEAJAY BOATS INC

SPEEDLINER BOATS
ST JOSEPH MO 64505 COAST GUARD MFG ID- SEJ

See inside cover to adjust price for area

LOA FT	LOA IN	NAME AND/ OR MODEL	TOP/ RIG	BOAT TYPE	-HULL- MTL	-HULL- TP	ENGINE TP	ENGINE # HP	ENGINE MFG	BEAM FT	BEAM IN	WGT LBS	DRAFT FT	DRAFT IN	RETAIL LOW	RETAIL HIGH
		1994 BOATS														
17		CHALLENGER VBC176	OP	SKI	FBG	DV	OB			6	4	850			3350	3900
17		CHALLENGER VS-177	OP	SKI	FBG	DV	OB			6	4	850			3050	3550
17		RAJAH CUSTOM VB-174	OP	BASS	FBG	DV	OB			6	4	700			2850	3350
17		RAJAH VB-174	OP	BASS	FBG	DV	OB			6	4	700			2500	2900
17		SATELLITE VBS-178	OP	SKI	FBG	DV	OB			6	4	825			3100	3600
17		SUNRAY I V-179	ST	RNBT	FBG	DV	IO	128-205		7	3	1850			4150	4950
17		WILD ONE TR-182	OP	RNBT	FBG	TH	OB			7	4	850			3200	3750
20	1	PRESIDENT I V-201	OP	RNBT	FBG	DV	IO	175-260		7	7	2500			6500	7850
		1993 BOATS														
17		CHALLENGER VBC176	OP	SKI	FBG	DV	OB			6	4	850			3200	3750
17		CHALLENGER VS-177	OP	SKI	FBG	DV	OB			6	4	850			2950	3400
17		RAJAH CUSTOM VB-174	OP	BASS	FBG	DV	OB			6	4	700			2750	3200
17		RAJAH VB-174	OP	BASS	FBG	DV	OB			6	4	700			2400	2800
17		SATELLITE VBS-178	OP	SKI	FBG	DV	OB			6	4	825			3000	3450
17		SUNRAY I V-179	ST	RNBT	FBG	DV	IO	128-205		7	3	1850			3900	4650
17		WILD ONE TR-182	OP	RNBT	FBG	TH	OB			7	4	850			3050	3550
20	1	PRESIDENT I V-201	OP	RNBT	FBG	DV	IO	175-260		7	7	2500			6050	7350
		1992 BOATS														
17		CHALLENGER VBS-176	OP	SKI	FBG	DV	OB			6	4	850			3250	3800
17		CHALLENGER VS-177	OP	SKI	FBG	DV	OB			6	4	850			2650	3050
17		CHALLENGER VS-177C	OP	SKI	FBG	DV	OB			6	4	850			2950	3450
17		RAJAH CUSTOM VB-174	OP	BASS	FBG	DV	OB			6	4	850			2950	3450
17		RAJAH VB-174	OP	BASS	FBG	DV	OB			6	4	800			2800	3250
17		SATELLITE VBS-178	OP	SKI	FBG	DV	OB			6	5	850			2950	3450
17		SPORT FISHER V-170	OP	FSH	FBG	DV	OB			6	11				2900	3350
17		SUNRAY I V-179	ST	RNBT	FBG	DV	IO	128-205		7	3	1950			3700	4450
18	6	FANTASY V-186	OP	FSH	FBG	DV	OB			7	2				4600	5250
20	1	PRESIDENT I V-201	OP	RNBT	FBG	DV	IO	175-260		7	7	2500			5700	6950
		1991 BOATS														
17		CHALLENGER VBS-176	OP	SKI	FBG	DV	OB			6	4	850			3150	3650
17		CHALLENGER VS-177	OP	SKI	FBG	DV	OB			6	4	850			2550	2950
17		CHALLENGER VS-177C	OP	SKI	FBG	DV	OB			6	4	850			2850	3300
17		RAJAH CUSTOM VB-174	OP	BASS	FBG	DV	OB			6	4	850			2850	3300
17		RAJAH VB-174	OP	BASS	FBG	DV	OB			6	4	800			2700	3150
17		SATELLITE VBS-178	OP	SKI	FBG	DV	OB			6	5	850			2850	3300
17		SPORT FISHER V-170	OP	FSH	FBG	DV	OB			6	11				2800	3250
17		SUNRAY I V-179	ST	RNBT	FBG	DV	IO	128-205		7	3	1950			3500	4150
18	6	FANTASY V-186	OP	FSH	FBG	DV	OB			7	2				4400	5050
20	1	PRESIDENT I V-201	OP	RNBT	FBG	DV	IO	175-260		7	7	2500			5350	6500
		1990 BOATS														
17		CHALLENGER VBS-176	OP	SKI	FBG	DV	OB			6	4	850			3050	3500
17		CHALLENGER VS-177	OP	SKI	FBG	DV	OB			6	4	850			2450	2850
17		CHALLENGER VS-177C	OP	SKI	FBG	DV	OB			6	4	850			2750	3200
17		RAJAH CUSTOM VB-174	OP	BASS	FBG	DV	OB			6	4	850			2750	3200
17		RAJAH VB-174	OP	BASS	FBG	DV	OB			6	4	800			2600	3000
17		SATELLITE VBS-178	OP	SKI	FBG	DV	OB			6	5	850			2750	3200
17		SPORT FISHER V-170	OP	FSH	FBG	DV	OB			6	11				2700	3100
17		SUNRAY I V-179	ST	RNBT	FBG	DV	IO	128-235		7	3	1950			3300	4050
18	6	FANTASY V-186	OP	FSH	FBG	DV	OB			7	2				4200	4900
20	1	PRESIDENT I V-201	OP	RNBT	FBG	DV	IO	175-260		7	7	2500			5000	6150
		1989 BOATS														
17		CHALLENGER VBS-176	OP	SKI	FBG	DV	OB			6	4	850			2950	3400
17		CHALLENGER VS-177	OP	SKI	FBG	DV	OB			6	4	850			2350	2750
17		CHALLENGER VS-177C	OP	SKI	FBG	DV	OB			6	4	850			2650	3100
17		RAJAH CUSTOM VB-174	OP	BASS	FBG	DV	OB			6	4	850			2650	3100
17		RAJAH VB-174	OP	BASS	FBG	DV	OB			6	4	800			2500	2900
17		SATELLITE VBS-178	OP	SKI	FBG	DV	OB			6	5	850			2650	3100
17		SPORT FISHER V-170	OP	FSH	FBG	DV	OB			6	11				2600	3000
17		SUNRAY I V-179	ST	RNBT	FBG	DV	IO	140-205		7	3	1950			3100	3700
18	6	FANTASY V-186	OP	FSH	FBG	DV	OB			7	2				4100	4750
18	6	FANTASY V-186	OP	SKI	FBG	DV	OB			7	2				4100	4800
20	1	PRESIDENT I V-201	OP	RNBT	FBG	DV	IO	175-260		7	7	2500			4750	5800
		1988 BOATS														
17		CHALLENGER VBS-176	OP	SKI	FBG	DV	OB			6	4	850			2850	3300
17		CHALLENGER VS-177	OP	SKI	FBG	DV	OB			6	4	850			2300	2700
17		CHALLENGER VS-177C	OP	SKI	FBG	DV	OB			6	4	850			2600	3000
17		RAJAH CUSTOM VB-174	OP	BASS	FBG	DV	OB			6	4	850			2600	3000
17		RAJAH VB-174	OP	BASS	FBG	DV	OB			6	4	800			2450	2850
17		SATELLITE VBS-178	OP	SKI	FBG	DV	OB			6	5	850			2600	3000
17		SUNRAY I V-179	ST	RNBT	FBG	DV	IO	140-205		7	3	1950			2950	3500
20	1	PRESIDENT I V-201	OP	RNBT	FBG	DV	IO	175-260		7	7	2500			4500	5500
		1987 BOATS														
17			OP	SKI	FBG	DV	OB			6	5	850			2500	2900
17		CHALLENGER VBS-176	OP	SKI	FBG	DV	OB			6	4	850			2750	3200
17		CHALLENGER VS-177	OP	SKI	FBG	DV	OB			6	4	850			2300	2650
17		CHALLENGER VS-177C	OP	SKI	FBG	DV	OB			6	4	850			2500	2900
17		RAJAH CUSTOM VB-174	OP	BASS	FBG	DV	OB			6	4	850			2500	2900
17		RAJAH VB-174	OP	BASS	FBG	DV	OB			6	4	800			2350	2750
17		SUNRAY I V-179	ST	RNBT	FBG	DV	SE	115	OMC	7	3	1750			4550	5250
17		SUNRAY I V-179	ST	RNBT	FBG	DV	IO	140-205		7	3	1950			2800	3350
17		SUNRAY II V-178	ST	RNBT	FBG	DV	OB			7	3	920			2700	3150
20	1	PRESIDENT I V-201	OP	RNBT	FBG	DV	IO	175-260		7	7	2500			4250	5250
		1986 BOATS														
17		CHALLENGER VBS-176	OP	SKI	FBG	DV	OB			6	4	850			2700	3150
17		CHALLENGER VS-177	OP	SKI	FBG	DV	OB			6	4	850			2200	2550
17		CHALLENGER VS-177C	OP	SKI	FBG	DV	OB			6	4	850			2450	2850
17		RAJAH CUSTOM VB-174	OP	BASS	FBG	DV	OB			6	4	850			2450	2850
17		RAJAH VB-174	OP	BASS	FBG	DV	OB			6	4	800			2350	2700
17		SUNRAY I V-179	ST	RNBT	FBG	DV	SE	115	OMC	7	3	1750			4450	5100
17		SUNRAY I V-179	ST	RNBT	FBG	DV	IO	140-198		7	3	1950			2650	3150
17		SUNRAY II V-178	ST	RNBT	FBG	DV	OB			7	3	920			2600	3050
20	1	PRESIDENT I V-201	OP	RNBT	FBG	DV	IO	170-260		7	7	2500			4050	5000
		1985 BOATS														
16	1	MARINER T-160	OP	FSH	FBG	TR	OB			6	8	850			2350	2700
16	1	MARINER T-161	OP	RNBT	FBG	TR	SE	115	OMC	6	8	1700			4350	5000
16	1	MARINER T-161	OP	RNBT	FBG	TR	IO	120-140		6	8	1700			2200	2550
16	1	MARINER T-162	OP	RNBT	FBG	TR	OB			6	8	800			2400	2750
16	1	SUNTIME T-164	OP	RNBT	FBG	TR	OB			6	8	800			1950	2300
17		CHALLENGER VBS-176	OP	SKI	FBG	DV	OB			6	4	850			2650	3050
17		CHALLENGER VS-177	OP	SKI	FBG	DV	OB			6	4	850			2100	2500
17		CHALLENGER VS-177C	OP	SKI	FBG	DV	OB			6	4	850			2400	2800
17		RAJAH CUSTOM VB-174	OP	BASS	FBG	DV	OB			6	4	850			2400	2800
17		RAJAH VB-174	OP	BASS	FBG	DV	OB			6	4	800			2300	2650
17		SUNRAY I V-179	ST	RNBT	FBG	DV	SE	115	OMC	7	3	1750			4350	5000
17		SUNRAY I V-179	ST	RNBT	FBG	DV	IO	140-198		7	3	1950			2550	3050
17		SUNRAY II V-178	ST	RNBT	FBG	DV	OB			7	3	920			2550	3000
20	1	PRESIDENT I V-201	OP	RNBT	FBG	DV	IO	170-260		7	7	2500			3900	4800
		1984 BOATS														
16	1	MARINER T-160	OP	FSH	FBG	TR	OB			6	8	850			2300	2650
16	1	MARINER T-161	OP	RNBT	FBG	TR	IO	115-140		6	8	1700			2050	2450
16	1	MARINER T-162	OP	RNBT	FBG	TR	OB			6	8	800			2400	2750
16	1	SUNTIME	OP	RNBT	FBG	TR	OB			6	8	800			1850	2200
17		CHALLENGER VS-176	OP	SKI	FBG	DV	OB			6	4	850			2550	2950
17		CHALLENGER VS-177	OP	SKI	FBG	DV	OB			6	4	850			2100	2500
17		CHALLENGER VS-177C	OP	SKI	FBG	DV	OB			6	4	850			2350	2700
17		RAJAH CUSTOM VB-174	OP	BASS	FBG	DV	OB			6	4	850			2350	2700
17		RAJAH VB-174	OP	BASS	FBG	DV	OB			6	4	800			2250	2600

SEAJAY BOATS INC — CONTINUED See inside cover to adjust price for area

LOA FT IN	NAME AND/ OR MODEL	TOP/ RIG	BOAT TYPE	HULL MTL	TP	TP	ENGINE #	HP	MFG	BEAM FT IN	WGT LBS	DRAFT FT IN	RETAIL LOW	RETAIL HIGH
							1984 BOATS							
17	SEASAINT V-176	OP	RNBT	FBG	DV	OB				6 4	775		2150	2550
17	SUNRAY I V-179	ST	RNBT	FBG	DV	SE		115	OMC	7 3	1750		4200	4900
17	SUNRAY I V-179	ST	RNBT	FBG	DV	OB	140-198			7 3	1950		2450	2950
17	SUNRAY II V-178	ST	RNBT	FBG	DV	OB				7 3	920		2500	2900
20 1	PRESIDENT I V-201	OP	RNBT	FBG	DV	IO	170-260			7 7	2500		3700	4650

....For earlier years, see the BUC Used Boat Price Guide, Volume 3

SEAMASTER
UNITED MARINE COPRORATION See inside cover to adjust price for area
WATSEKA IL 60970

For more recent years, see the BUC Used Boat Price Guide, Volume 1

LOA FT IN	NAME AND/ OR MODEL	TOP/ RIG	BOAT TYPE	HULL MTL	TP	TP	ENGINE #	HP	MFG	BEAM FT IN	WGT LBS	DRAFT FT IN	RETAIL LOW	RETAIL HIGH
							1996 BOATS							
17 1	SEAMASTER 1780	CTRCN	FBG	SV	OB					6 10	1000		2750	3200
19 1	SEAMASTER 1880	CTRCN	FBG	SV	OB					7 3	1370		3650	4250
19 1	SEAMASTER 1980	B/R	FBG	SV	OB					7 3	1370		3900	4500
19 1	SEAMASTER 1980	CTRCN	FBG	SV	OB					7 3	1370		3950	4550
19 1	SEAMASTER 1980 F+S	B/R	FBG	SV	OB					7 3	1370		3900	4500
19 9	SEAMASTER 2080	CTRCN	FBG	DV	OB					8	2200		5450	6250
19 9	SEAMASTER 2088	CUD	FBG	DV	OB					8	2375		5700	6550
19 9	SEAMASTER 2088	CUD	FBG	DV	IO		235	MRCR		8	2375		5950	6800
23 11	SEAMASTER 2488	CUD	FBG	DV	IO		235	MRCR		8 6	3400		10100	11500
23 11	SEAMASTER 2488	CUD	FBG	DV	IO		235	MRCR		8 6	3400		10200	11600
24 8	SEAMASTER 2388	CUD	FBG	DV	IO		235	MRCR		8 3	2850		9250	10500
24 8	SEAMASTER 2388	CUD	FBG	DV	IO		235	MRCR		8 3	2850		9900	11300
26	SEAMASTER 2688	CUD	FBG	DV	OB					9 6	4610		13300	15100
26	SEAMASTER 2688	CUD	FBG	DV	IO		300	MRCR		9 6	4610		15800	17900
26	SEAMASTER 2688	CUD	FBG	DV	IO	T410	MRCR		9 6	4610		24400	27100

SEAMASTER YACHTS
FT LAUDERDALE FL 33312 COAST GUARD MFG ID- EYT See inside cover to adjust price for area

LOA FT IN	NAME AND/ OR MODEL	TOP/ RIG	BOAT TYPE	HULL MTL	TP	TP	ENGINE #	HP	MFG	BEAM FT IN	WGT LBS	DRAFT FT IN	RETAIL LOW	RETAIL HIGH
							1987 BOATS							
33	SEAMASTER 33	CUT	SA/RC	FBG	KL	IB	D			10 6	16000	5	54800	60300
33 2	SEAMASTER 33	SLP	SA/RC	FBG	KC	IB	22D	PERK	10	8 16000	4 6		55200	60600
45 3	SEAMASTER 45	KTH	SA/RC	F/S	KL	IB	62D	PERK	13	3 27000	5 2		120500	132500
47 4	SEAMASTER 47	CUT	SA/RC	F/S	KL	IB	85D	PERK	13	3 28000	5 2		127500	140000
47 4	SEAMASTER 47	KTH	SA/RC	F/S	KL	IB	D			13 3	28500	5	136500	150000
51	SEAMASTER 51	KTH	SA/CR	F/S	KL	IB	85D	PERK	14	6 43000	6		184500	202500
51	SEAMASTER 51	CUT	SA/CR	F/S	KL	IB	85D	PERK	14	6 43000	6		174500	191500
53	SEAMASTER 53	KTH	SA/CR	F/S	KL	IB	85D	PERK	14	6 43000	6		203500	223500
							1986 BOATS							
33	SEAMASTER 33	CUT	SA/RC	FBG	KL	IB	D			10 6	16000	5	51500	56600
45 1	SEAMASTER 45	KTH	SA/RC	FBG	KL	IB	D			13 3	28000	5 2	114500	126000
51 2	SEAMASTER 51	CUT	SA/RC	FBG	KL	IB	D			14	43000	5 8	165000	181500
							1985 BOATS							
33	SEAMASTER 33	CUT	SA/RC	FBG	KL	IB	D			10 6	16000	5	48200	52900
33 2	SEAMASTER 33	SLP	SA/RC	FBG	KC	IB	22D	PERK	10	8 16000	4 6		48400	53200
45 3	SEAMASTER 45	KTH	SA/RC	F/S	KL	IB	62D	PERK	13	3 27000	5 2		105500	116000
47 4	SEAMASTER 47	CUT	SA/RC	F/S	KL	IB	85D	PERK	13	3 28000	5 2		111500	122500
47 4	SEAMASTER 47	KTH	SA/RC	F/S	KL	IB	D			13 3	28500	5	120000	131500
							1984 BOATS							
30 2	SEAMASTER 30	CUT	SA/RC	F/S	KL	IB	20D	WEST	8	6 11000	4		29700	33000
33 3	SEAMASTER 33	CUT	SA/RC	FBG	KL	IB	20D			10 6	11000	4 6	30400	34400
45 1	SEAMASTER 45	KTH	SA/RC	F/S	KL	IB	62D	PERK	13	3 28000	5		99900	110000
47 4	SEAMASTER 47	KTH	SA/RC	F/S	KL	IB	85D	PERK	13	3 28000	5		111500	122500

....For earlier years, see the BUC Used Boat Price Guide, Volume 3

SEAMASTER YACHTS INC
NO MIAMI FL 33161 See inside cover to adjust price for area

LOA FT IN	NAME AND/ OR MODEL	TOP/ RIG	BOAT TYPE	HULL MTL	TP	TP	ENGINE #	HP	MFG	BEAM FT IN	WGT LBS	DRAFT FT IN	RETAIL LOW	RETAIL HIGH
							1996 BOATS							
47 11	MOTORYACHT 48	F+H	MY	FBG	DV	IB	T425D	CAT	15	9 44000	3 10		233000	256000
							1995 BOATS							
47 11	MOTORYACHT 48	F+H	MY	FBG	DV	IB	T425D	CAT	15	9 44000	3 10		223500	245500
							1994 BOATS							
47 11	MOTORYACHT 48	F+H	MY	FBG	DV	IB	T425D	CAT	15	9 44000	3 10		214000	235000
							1993 BOATS							
47 11	MOTOR YACHT 48	F+H	MYFD	F/S	DV	IB	T425D	CAT	15	9 44000	3 10		210000	230500
							1992 BOATS							
47 11	MOTOR YACHT 48	F+H	MYFD	F/S	DV	IB	T425D	CAT	15	9 44000	3 10		200000	220000
							1991 BOATS							
47 11	MOTOR YACHT 48	F+H	MYFD	F/S	DV	IB	T320D	CAT	15	9 44000	3 10		174000	191000
							1990 BOATS							
47 11	MOTOR YACHT 48	F+H	MYFD	F/S	DV	IB	T375D	CAT	15	9 44000	3 10		174500	192000
							1989 BOATS							
44	MOTOR YACHT 44	F+H	MYFD	F/S	DV	IB	T306D	VLVO	13	6 36000	3 6		138500	152000
44	MOTOR YACHT 44	F+H	MYFD	F/S	DV	IB	T320D	CAT	13	6 36000	3 6		142000	156500
47 11	MOTOR YACHT 48	F+H	MYFD	F/S	DV	IB	T375D	CAT	15	9 44000	3 10		167000	183500
							1988 BOATS							
44	MOTOR YACHT 44	F+H	MYFD	F/S	DV	IB	T306D	VLVO	13	6 36000	3 6		132000	145500
44	MOTOR YACHT 44	F+H	MYFD	F/S	DV	IB	T320D	CAT	13	6 36000	3 6		136000	149500
47 11	MOTOR YACHT 48	F+H	MYFD	F/S	DV	IB	T375D	CAT	15	9 44000	3 10		159500	175500
							1987 BOATS							
44	MOTOR YACHT 44	F+H	MYFD	F/S	DV	IB	T306D	VLVO	13	6 36000	3 6		126500	139000
44	MOTOR YACHT 44	F+H	MYFD	F/S	DV	IB	T320D	CAT	13	6 36000	3 6		130000	143000
47 11	MOTOR YACHT 48	F+H	MYFD	F/S	DV	IB	T375D	CAT	15	9 44000	3 10		152500	167500
							1986 BOATS							
47 11	MOTOR YACHT 48	F+H	MYFD	F/S	DV	IB	T375D	CAT	15	9 44000	3 10		146000	160500
							1985 BOATS							
47 11	MOTOR YACHT 48	F+H	MYFD	F/S	DV	IB	T375D	CAT	15	9 44000	3 10		140000	153500
							1984 BOATS							
47 11	MOTOR YACHT 48	F+H	MYFD	F/S	DV	IB	T355D	CAT	15	9 44000	3 10		131500	144500

....For earlier years, see the BUC Used Boat Price Guide, Volume 3

SEASWIRL BOATS INC
SEASWIRL BOATS See inside cover to adjust price for area
CULVER OR 97734
  COAST GUARD MFG ID- GSS
  FORMERLY BRAMCO INC

For more recent years, see the BUC Used Boat Price Guide, Volume 1

LOA FT IN	NAME AND/ OR MODEL	TOP/ RIG	BOAT TYPE	HULL MTL	TP	TP	ENGINE #	HP	MFG	BEAM FT IN	WGT LBS	DRAFT FT IN	RETAIL LOW	RETAIL HIGH
							1996 BOATS							
17 3	BOWRIDER 170	OP	B/R	FBG	SV	OB				7 6	1770	2 5	4400	5050
17 3	STRIPER 1730	OP	CTRCN	FBG	SV	OB				7 6	1770	2 5	4350	5050
17 5	SPYDER 170	OP	B/R	FBG	SV	OB				7 10	1795	2 5	4400	5100
17 5	SPYDER 174	OP	B/R	FBG	SV	OB	160	VLVO	7 10	2010	2 5	5350	6150
18 3	BOWRIDER 180	OP	B/R	FBG	SV	OB				7 7	2005	2 5	4750	5450
18 4	BOWRIDER 180	OP	B/R	FBG	SV	IO	130	VLVO	7 7	2410	2 6	6000	6900
18 9	STRIPER 1850 DC	OP	FSH	FBG	SV	OB				7 11	1800	2 7	4600	5250
18 9	STRIPER 1850 WA	OP	FSH	FBG	SV	OB				7 10	2010	2 6	4950	5700
19 8	SPYDER 198	OP	B/R	FBG	SV	OB				7 10	2010	2 6	5150	5900
19 8	SPYDER 198	OP	B/R	FBG	SV	IO	160	VLVO	7 11	2480	2 7	6700	7700
20 1	BOWRIDER 201 LE	OP	B/R	FBG	SV	IO	220	VLVO	7 11	2715	2 6	8400	9700
20 1	CUDDY 201	OP	CUD	FBG	DV	OB				7 11	2285	2 6	6600	7600
20 1	CUDDY 201	OP	CUD	FBG	DV	IO	130	VLVO	7 11	2780	2 6	8900	10100
20 1	CUDDY 201 LE	OP	CUD	FBG	DV	IO	220	VLVO	7 11	2780	2 6	9200	10500
20 7	BOWRIDER 208	OP	B/R	FBG	SV	OB				8	2340	2 6	7000	8050
20 8	BOWRIDER 208	OP	B/R	FBG	SV	IO	130	VLVO	8	2800	2 6	8700	9950
21	STRIPER 2100	OP	CTRCN	FBG	SV	OB				8	2350	2 6	7250	8300
21	STRIPER 2100 DC	OP	B/R	FBG	SV	OB				8 5	2490	2 6	7500	8650
21 4	STRIPER 2100 WA	OP	FSH	FBG	SV	OB				8 5	2570	2 6	7650	8800
21 4	STRIPER 2150 WA	OP	FSH	FBG	DV	OB				8	3160	1 9	8900	10100
21 4	STRIPER 2150 WA	OP	FSH	FBG	DV	IO	130	VLVO	8	3550	1 9	11700	13300
21 10	BOWRIDER 220	OP	B/R	FBG	SV	IO	190	VLVO	8	3550	2 9	11300	12800
21 10	SPYDER 220	OP	B/R	FBG	SV	IO	190	VLVO	8	2675	2 8	9250	10500
23 1	CUDDY 230	OP	CUD	FBG	DV	IO	190	VLVO	8 4	3670	2 7	12700	14400
25	CUDDY 250	OP	CUD	FBG	DV	IO	190	VLVO	8 6	4310	3 1	15600	17700
25 6	STRIPER 2600 WA	OP	FSH	FBG	DV	IO	190	VLVO	8 6	3850	3 4	13100	14900
25 6	STRIPER 2600 WA	OP	FSH	FBG	DV	IO	150	VLVO	8 6	4550	3 4	16900	19200
25 9	CUDDY 250 AFT	OP	CUD	FBG	DV	IO	190	VLVO	8 6	4770	3 4	16300	18600
							1995 BOATS							
17 5	SPYDER 170	OP	B/R	FBG	SV	OB				7 10	1795	2 5	4150	4850
20	STRIPER 200	OP	CUD	FBG	SV	OB	130			7 11	2565	2 5	7550	8650
21 4	STRIPER 2150 WA	OP	FSH	FBG	DV	IO	220			8	4310	2 10	10800	12300
25	CUDDY CABIN	OP	CUD	FBG	DV	IO				8 6	4310	3	**	**
25 6	25 WALKAROUND	OP	CUD	FBG	DV	IO	225			8 7	4690	3	15800	17900

LOA FT	LOA IN	NAME AND/ OR MODEL	TOP/ RIG	BOAT TYPE	-HULL- MTL	-HULL- TP	ENGINE TP	ENGINE # HP	ENGINE MFG	BEAM FT	BEAM IN	WGT LBS	DRAFT FT	DRAFT IN	RETAIL LOW	RETAIL HIGH
		1995 BOATS														
25	6	2600 WALK AROUND	OP	FSH	FBG	SV	OB			8	6	3850	2	11	12500	14200
		1994 BOATS														
17	3	175 SE	OP	RNBT	FBG	SV	OB			7	6	1500			3500	4100
17	3	STRIPER 182	OP	CTRCN	FBG	DV	OB			7	6	1570			3600	4200
18	2	180 SE	OP	RNBT	FBG	SV	IO	175	OMC	7	6	2250			4900	5650
18	9	STRIPER 205	OP	CUD	FBG	DV	OB			7	11	1850			4200	4850
19	8	SPYDER 188	OP	RNBT	FBG	SV	OB			7	10	1645			4100	4750
19	8	SPYDER 188	OP	RNBT	FBG	SV	IO	200	OMC	7	10	2325			5600	6450
19	10	STRIPER 192	OP	B/R	FBG	DV	OB			7	11	1750			4350	5000
19	10	STRIPER 200	OP	CUD	FBG	DV	IO	175	OMC	7	11	2565			6150	7100
19	10	STRIPER 205	OP	CUD	FBG	DV	OB			7	11	1850			4500	5200
20	1	190 SE	OP	RNBT	FBG	SV	IO	200	OMC	7	11	2460			6700	7700
20	1	190 SWL	OP	CUD	FBG	DV	IO	175	OMC	7	11	2500			6950	8000
20	1	195 SE	OP	RNBT	FBG	SV	OB			7	11	1910			5400	6200
20	1	195 SWL	OP	CUD	FBG	DV	OB			7	11	1920			5400	6200
22	4	STRIPER 210	OP	CUD	FBG	DV	OB			8		2835			8100	9350
22	4	STRIPER 210	OP	CUD	FBG	DV	IO	200	OMC	8		3295			9450	10700
22	4	STRIPER 212	OP	CUD	FBG	DV	IO	200	OMC	8		3405			9650	11000
23	1	220 SE	OP	B/R	FBG	DV	IO	200	OMC	8	4	3500			9750	11100
23	1	220 SWL	OP	CUD	FBG	DV	IO	200	OMC	8	4	3570			10500	12000
25		230 SWL	OP	CUD	FBG	DV	IO	200	OMC	8	6	4140			13000	14700
		1993 BOATS														
17		175 SE/LX	OP	RNBT	FBG	SV	OB			7	6				4000	4650
18	2	180 SE	OP	RNBT	FBG	SV	IO	175	OMC	7	6	2300			4750	5450
18	2	STRIPER 182	OP	CTRCN	FBG	DV	OB			7	6	1870			3950	4600
18	9	STRIPER 192	OP	B/R	FBG	DV	OB			7	11	2130			4350	5050
18	9	STRIPER 200	OP	CUD	FBG	DV	IO	175	OMC	7	11	2735			5600	6450
18	9	STRIPER 205	OP	CUD	FBG	DV	OB			7	11	2230			4450	5100
19	8	SPYDER 188	OP	RNBT	FBG	SV	OB			7	10	2024			4550	5200
19	8	SPYDER 188	OP	RNBT	FBG	SV	IO	265	OMC	7	10	2590			5850	6750
20	1	190 SE	OP	RNBT	FBG	SV	IO	200	OMC	7	11	2630			6500	7450
20	1	190 SWL	OP	CUD	FBG	DV	IO	175	OMC	7	11	2670			6750	7750
20	1	195 SE	OP	RNBT	FBG	SV	OB			7	11	2290			5750	6600
20	1	195 SWL	OP	CUD	FBG	DV	OB			7	11	2290			5750	6600
20	9	SPYDER 208	OP	RNBT	FBG	DV	IO	330	OMC	8	2	3105			8900	10100
21		SPYDER 209	OP	CUD	FBG	DV	IO	265	OMC	8	2	2990			8150	9400
22	4	STRIPER 210	OP	CUD	FBG	DV	OB			8		3220			8450	9700
22	4	STRIPER 210	OP	CUD	FBG	DV	IO	265	OMC	8		3220			9150	10400
22	4	STRIPER 212	OP	CUD	FBG	DV	IO	265	OMC	8		3620			9800	11200
23	1	220 SWL	OP	CUD	FBG	DV	IO	265	OMC	8	4	3570			10200	11600
25		230 SWL	OP	CUD	FBG	DV	IO	330	OMC	8	6	4320			14100	16000
25	5	250 SWL	OP	EXP	FBG	DV	IO	330	OMC	8	6	4690			15100	17200
		1992 BOATS														
18	2	180 SE	OP	RNBT	FBG	DV	IO	175		7	6	2380			4500	5150
18	2	185 SE	OP	RNBT	FBG	DV	OB			7	6	1933			3850	4500
18	2	STRIPER 182	OP	CTRCN	FBG	DV	OB			7	6	1870			3800	4400
18	9	STRIPER 200	OP	CUD	FBG	DV	IO	175		7	11	2735			5300	6100
18	9	STRIPER 205	OP	CUD	FBG	DV	OB			7	11	2230			4200	4900
19	8	SPYDER 188	OP	RNBT	FBG	DV	OB			7	10	2024			4300	5000
19	8	SPYDER 188	OP	RNBT	FBG	DV	IO	240		7	10	2590			5400	6200
20	1	190 SE	OP	RNBT	FBG	DV	IO	175		7	11	2630			6050	6950
20	1	190 SWL	OP	CUD	FBG	DV	IO	175		7	11	2670			6350	7300
20	1	195 SE	OP	RNBT	FBG	DV	OB			7	11	2290			5500	6350
20	1	195 SWL	OP	CUD	FBG	DV	OB			7	11	2390			5650	6450
20	9	208 SE	OP	RNBT	FBG	DV	IO	240		8	2	3105			7250	8300
20	9	SPYDER 208	OP	RNBT	FBG	DV	IO	240		8	2	3860			8300	9550
21		SPYDER 209	OP	CUD	FBG	DV	IO	240		8	2	2990			7500	8650
22	4	STRIPER 210	OP	CUD	FBG	DV	OB			8		3220			8050	9300
22	4	STRIPER 210	OP	CUD	FBG	DV	IO	240		8		3560			9000	10200
22	4	STRIPER 212	OP	CUD	FBG	DV	IO	240		8		3670			9200	10400
23	1	220 SWL	OP	CUD	FBG	DV	IO	240		8	4	3570			9450	10700
25		230 SWL	OP	CUD	FBG	DV	IO	285		8	6	4320			12500	14200
25	5	250 SWL	OP	EXP	FBG	DV	IO	285		8	6	4690			13500	15300
		1989 BOATS														
16	2	TAHOE	ST	RNBT	FBG	SV	OB			6	9	1000			2000	2350
16	2	TAHOE	ST	RNBT	FBG	SV	IO	130	OMC	6	9	1750			2600	3050
17	2	STRIPER 172			FBG	SV	OB			7	4	1250			2500	2900
17	2	TEMPO	ST	RNBT	FBG	SV	OB			7	4	1250			2500	2900
17	2	TEMPO	ST	RNBT	FBG	SV	IO	130-175		7	4	2025			3100	3750
17	8	SPYDER SPORT	ST	RNBT	FBG	SV	OB			7	4	1000			2100	2500
17	8	SPYDER SPORT	ST	SKI	FBG	SV	IO	175-235		7	4	2000			3100	3850
17	8	SPYDER SPORT	ST	SKI	FBG	SV	IO	260	OMC	7	4	2115			3400	4000
18		SIERRA CLASSIC CUDDY	ST	CUD	FBG	SV	IO	130-175		7	6	2165			3450	4200
18		SIERRA CLASSIC CUDDY	ST	CUD	FBG	SV	IO	200-260		7	6	2415			3750	4650
18		SIERRA CUDDY LINER	ST	CUD	FBG	SV	IO	130-175		7	6	2165			3550	4300
18		SIERRA CUDDY LINER	ST	CUD	FBG	SV	IO	200-260		7	6	2415			3850	4750
18	6	SIERRA CLASSIC	ST	RNBT	FBG	SV	OB			7	10	1600			3100	3600
18	6	SIERRA CLASSIC	ST	RNBT	FBG	SV	IO	130-175		7	10	2290			3650	4450
18	6	SIERRA CLASSIC	ST	RNBT	FBG	SV	IO	200-260		7	10	2615			4000	4900
18	6	SIERRA CLASSIC SPORT	ST	RNBT	FBG	SV	IO	130-175		7	10	2290			3800	4550
18	6	SIERRA CLASSIC SPORT	ST	RNBT	FBG	SV	IO	200-260		7	10	2615			4150	5050
20	1	STRIPER 202	ST	CUD	FBG	SV	IO	175-260		7	7	2750			5100	6300
20	1	TOPAZ CUDDY	ST	CUD	FBG	SV	IO	175-235		7	7	2750			5200	6350
20	1	TOPAZ CUDDY	ST	CUD	FBG	SV	IO	260	OMC	7	7	2865			5700	6550
20	1	TOPAZ CUDDY LINER	ST	CUD	FBG	SV	IO	175-235		7	7	2750			5350	6500
20	1	TOPAZ CUDDY LINER	ST	CUD	FBG	SV	IO	260	OMC	7	7	2865			5800	6700
20	2	SPYDER B/R 20	ST	RNBT	FBG	SV	IO	175-260		7	9	2475			4700	5850
20	2	SPYDER SPORT 202	ST	RNBT	FBG	SV	IO	175-260		7	9	2475			4950	6000
21	2	SABLE CUDDY	ST	CUD	FBG	DV	IO	175-260		8		3315			6300	7800
21	2	SABLE CUDDY LINER	ST	CUD	FBG	SV	IO	175-260		8		3315			6500	8000
23		CORDOVA AFT CBN 230	ST	CUD	FBG	SV	IO	200-260		8		3825			7850	9350
		1988 BOATS														
16	2	TAHOE	ST	RNBT	FBG	SV	OB			6	9	1000			1900	2300
16	2	TAHOE	ST	RNBT	FBG	SV	IO	128-130		6	9	1750			2450	2850
17	2	STRIKER 172			FBG	SV	OB			7	4	1250			2400	2800
17	2	STRIPER 172			FBG	SV	OB			7	4	1250			2400	2800
17	2	TEMPO	ST	RNBT	FBG	SV	OB			7	4	1250			2400	2800
17	2	TEMPO	ST	RNBT	FBG	SV	IO	128-175		7	4	2015			2950	3500
17	2	TEMPO SPORT	ST	RNBT	FBG	SV	IO	175	OMC	7	4	2150			3100	3650
17	4	SPYDER	ST	RNBT	FBG	SV	OB			7	4	1000			2000	2350
17	4	SPYDER	ST	SKI	FBG	SV	OB			7	4	1000			2000	2350
17	4	SPYDER	ST	SKI	FBG	SV	IO	175-230		7	4	2000			2850	3550
17	4	SPYDER	ST	SKI	FBG	SV	IO	260	OMC	7	4	2115			3200	3700
17	4	SPYDER 174	ST	RNBT	FBG	SV	IO	175-230		7	4	2000			3000	3700
17	4	SPYDER 174	ST	RNBT	FBG	SV	IO	260	OMC	7	4	2115			3350	3850
18		SIERRA CUDDY	ST	CUD	FBG	SV	IO	128-175		7	6	2165			3300	4000
18		SIERRA CUDDY	ST	CUD	FBG	SV	IO	200-260		7	6	2415			3550	4400
18		SIERRA CUDDY LINER	ST	CUD	FBG	SV	IO	128-175		7	6	2165			3350	4050
18		SIERRA CUDDY LINER	ST	CUD	FBG	SV	IO	200-260		7	6	2415			3600	4450
18	6	SIERRA II	ST	RNBT	FBG	SV	OB			7	10	1600			3000	3500
18	6	SIERRA II	ST	RNBT	FBG	SV	IO	128-175		7	10	2290			3450	4200
18	6	SIERRA II	ST	RNBT	FBG	SV	IO	200-260		7	10	2615			3800	4650
18	6	SIERRA II SPORT	ST	RNBT	FBG	SV	IO	128-175		7	10	2290			3600	4350
18	6	SIERRA II SPORT	ST	RNBT	FBG	SV	IO	200-260		7	10	2615			3900	4800
20	1	STRIKER 202	ST	CUD	FBG	SV	IO	175	OMC	7	7	2750			4850	5550
20	1	STRIKER 202	ST	CUD	FBG	SV	IO	200-260				2865			5250	6350
20	1	TOPAZ	ST	RNBT	FBG	SV	IO	175-260		7	7	2750			4700	5800
20	1	TOPAZ CUDDY	ST	CUD	FBG	SV	IO	175-260		7	7	2750			4950	6150
20	1	TOPAZ CUDDY LINER	ST	CUD	FBG	SV	IO	175-260		7	7	2750			5050	6150
20	1	TOPAZ SPORT	ST	RNBT	FBG	SV	IO	175-260		7	7	2750			4800	6000
20	2	SPYDER 202	ST	RNBT	FBG	SV	IO	175-260		7	9	2475			4600	5700
21	2	SABLE CUDDY	ST	CUD	FBG	DV	IO	175-260		8		3315			6000	7400
21	2	SABLE CUDDY LINER	ST	CUD	FBG	SV	IO	175-260		8		3315			6150	7600
22	2	CORSAIR	ST	CUD	FBG	SV	IO	200-260		8		3650			6800	8100
22	2	CORSAIR LINER	ST	CUD	FBG	SV	IO	200-260		8		3650			7000	8300
		1987 BOATS														
16	2	TAHOE	ST	RNBT	FBG	SV	OB			6	9	1000			1850	2200
16	2	TAHOE	ST	RNBT	FBG	SV	IO	120-130		6	9	1750			2350	2750
17	2	TEMPO	ST	RNBT	FBG	SV	OB			7	4	1250			2350	2750
17	2	TEMPO	ST	RNBT	FBG	SV	IO	120-205		7	4	2015			2850	3500
17	4	SPYDER CLOSED BOW	ST	SKI	FBG	SV	OB			7	4	1000			1900	2250
17	4	SPYDER CLOSED BOW	ST	SKI	FBG	SV	IO	175-230		7	4	2000			2700	3350
17	4	SPYDER CLOSED BOW	ST	SKI	FBG	SV	IO	260		7	4	2106			3050	3500
17	4	SPYDER OPEN BOW	ST	SKI	FBG	SV	OB			7	4	1000			1950	2350
17	4	SPYDER OPEN BOW	ST	SKI	FBG	SV	IO	175-230		7	4	2000			2750	3450
17	4	SPYDER OPEN BOW	ST	SKI	FBG	SV	IO	260		7	4	2106			3100	3600
18		SIERRA CUDDY	ST	CUD	FBG	SV	IO	120-175		7	6	2165			3150	3800
18		SIERRA CUDDY	ST	CUD	FBG	SV	IO	200-260		7	6	2388			3400	4200
18		SIERRA CUDDY LINER	ST	CUD	FBG	SV	IO	120-205		7	6	2165			3250	4000
18		SIERRA CUDDY LINER	ST	CUD	FBG	SV	IO	230-260		7	6	2411			3550	4300
18	6	SIERRA II	ST	RNBT	FBG	SV	OB			7	10	1600			2900	3400
18	6	SIERRA II	ST	RNBT	FBG	SV	IO	120-205		7	10	2290			3300	4150
18	6	SIERRA II	ST	RNBT	FBG	SV	IO	230-260		7	10	2620			3700	4450
18	6	SIERRA II SPORT	ST	RNBT	FBG	SV	IO	120-205		7	10	2290			3450	4250
18	6	SIERRA II SPORT	ST	RNBT	FBG	SV	IO	230-260		7	10	2620			3850	4600
20	1	TOPAZ B/R	ST	RNBT	FBG	SV	IO	175-230		7	7	2750			4500	5500
20	1	TOPAZ B/R	ST	RNBT	FBG	SV	IO	260		7	7	2940			4950	5650
20	1	TOPAZ B/R SPORT	ST	RNBT	FBG	SV	IO	175-230		7	7	2750			4650	5650

CONTINUED ON NEXT PAGE

LOA FT IN	NAME AND/ OR MODEL	TOP/ RIG	BOAT TYPE	-HULL- MTL TP	----ENGINE--- TP # HP MFG	BEAM FT IN	WGT LBS	DRAFT FT IN	RETAIL LOW	RETAIL HIGH
---	--- 1987 BOATS ---									
20 1	TOPAZ B/R SPORT	ST	RNBT	FBG SV	IO 260	7 7	2940		5100	5850
20 1	TOPAZ CUDDY	ST	CUD	FBG SV	IO 175-230	7 7	2750		4650	5750
20 1	TOPAZ CUDDY	ST	CUD	FBG SV	IO 260	7 7	2940		5150	5950
20 1	TOPAZ CUDDY LINER	ST	CUD	FBG SV	IO 175-230	7 7	2750		4800	5900
20 1	TOPAZ CUDDY LINER	ST	CUD	FBG SV	IO 260	7 7	2940		5300	6050
22 2	CORSAIR	ST	CUD	FBG SV	IO 175-260	8	3545		6300	7750
22 2	CORSAIR LINER	ST	CUD	FBG SV	IO 175-260	8	3545		6500	7950
---	--- 1985 BOATS ---									
16	SPIRIT	ST	RNBT	FBG SV	OB	6 9	1000		1750	2050
16	SPIRIT	ST	RNBT	FBG SV	IO 120-140	6 9	1730		2150	2550
16 8	SPITFIRE	ST	RNBT	FBG SV	IO 120-170	7	1845		2350	2850
16 8	SPITFIRE SPORT	ST	RNBT	FBG SV	IO 140-170	7	1865		2400	2950
17 4	SPYDER	OP	SKI	FBG SV	OB	7 1	1000		1800	2150
17 4	SPYDER	OP	SKI	FBG SV	IO 140-170	7 1	1860		2300	2800
17 4	SPYDER	ST	RNBT	FBG SV	IO 200-260	7 1	2140		2550	3200
18	SIERRA	ST	RNBT	FBG SV	IO	7 6	1450		2550	2950
18	SIERRA	ST	RNBT	FBG SV	IO 170-230	7 6	2150		2750	3450
18	SIERRA CUDDY	ST	RNBT	FBG SV	IO 260 OMC	7 6	2290		2800	3550
18	SIERRA CUDDY	ST	CUD	FBG SV	IO 120-190	7 6	2020		2850	3450
18	SIERRA CUDDY	ST	CUD	FBG SV	IO 120-230	7 6	2240		3050	3700
18	SIERRA CUDDY	ST	CUD	FBG SV	IO 260	7 6	2340		3300	3850
18	SIERRA SPORT	ST	RNBT	FBG SV	IO 120-190	7 6	1990		2750	3400
18	SIERRA SPORT	ST	RNBT	FBG SV	IO 200-260	7 6	2290		3100	3850
18 8	SIERRA	ST	RNBT	FBG SV	IO 120-190	7 6	1990		2850	3500
18 8	SIERRA	ST	RNBT	FBG SV	IO 200-260	7 6	2290		3100	3850
20 1	TOPAZ	ST	CUD	F/S DV	IO 140-205	7 7	2530		4100	5100
20 1	TOPAZ	ST	CUD	F/S DV	IO 230-260	7 7	2790		4500	5350
22 6	CORSAIR	ST	CUD	F/S DV	IO 170-260	8	3500		5900	7300

....For earlier years, see the BUC Used Boat Price Guide, Volume 3

SEAWAY BOATS INC

LOA FT IN	NAME AND/ OR MODEL	TOP/ RIG	BOAT TYPE	-HULL- MTL TP	----ENGINE--- TP # HP MFG	BEAM FT IN	WGT LBS	DRAFT FT IN	RETAIL LOW	RETAIL HIGH
---	--- 1986 BOATS ---									
16 6	COMMERCIAL	OP	UTL	FBG SV	OB	6 8	800	6	**	**
16 6	SEASPRAY DLX	OP	RNBT	FBG SV	OB	6 8	900	6	2950	3450
16 6	SKIFF	OP	UTL	FBG SV	OB	6 8	650	6	2150	2500
16 6	SPORTSMAN	OP	OPFSH	FBG SV	OB	6 8	825	6	2700	3150
18 10		ST	RNBT	FBG RB	IO	7 6	1250	5	4200	4900
18 10		ST	RNBT	FBG RB	IO OMC	7 6		5	**	**
18 10		ST	RNBT	FBG RB	IO 120-170	7 6		5	4900	5700
18 10	COMMERCIAL	OP	CTRCN	FBG RB	IO	7 6	1200	5	**	**
18 10	COMMERCIAL	OP	CTRCN	FBG RB	IO 120	7 6		5	**	**
18 10	COMMERCIAL CUDDY	ST	CBNCR	FBG RB	IO 120	7 6		5	**	**
18 10	OPEN FISHERMAN	OP	CTRCN	FBG RB	OB	7 6	1250	5	4150	4850
18 10	OPEN FISHERMAN	OP	CTRCN	FBG RB	IO	7 6		5	**	**
18 10	OPEN FISHERMAN	OP	CTRCN	FBG RB	IO 120-170	7 6		5	5800	6700
18 10	SEAFARER		CUD	FBG RB	OB	7 6	1350	5	4900	5150
18 10	SEAFARER		CUD	FBG RB	IO OMC	7 6		5	**	**
18 10	SEAFARER		CUD	FBG RB	IO 120-170	7 6		5	5000	5800
20	SALTY-DOG	OP	RNBT	FBG SV	OB	8	1700	9	6450	7450
20	SALTY-DOG	OP	RNBT	FBG SV	SE OMC	8		9	**	**
20	SALTY-DOG	OP	RNBT	FBG SV	SE OMC	8		9	**	**
20	SALTY-DOG	OP	RNBT	FBG SV	IO OMC	8		9	**	**
20	SALTY-DOG	OP	RNBT	FBG SV	IO 120-170	8		9	6350	7650
22 8	COMMERCIAL	OP	UTL	FBG RB	OB	7 9	1600		**	**
22 8	COMMERCIAL	OP	UTL	FBG RB	IO OMC	7 9			**	**
22 8	COMMERCIAL	OP	UTL	FBG RB	SE 115 OMC	7 9			**	**
22 8	COMMERCIAL	OP	UTL	FBG RB	IO 120-170	7 9			**	**
22 8	COMMERCIAL CUDDY	HT	CBNCR	FBG RB	IO	7 9	2000		**	**
22 8	COMMERCIAL CUDDY	HT	CBNCR	FBG RB	IO OMC	7 9			**	**
22 8	COMMERCIAL CUDDY	HT	CBNCR	FBG RB	SE 115 OMC	7 9			**	**
22 8	COMMERCIAL CUDDY	HT	CBNCR	FBG RB	IO 120-170	7 9			**	**
22 8	SEA-HAVEN	OP	CUD	FBG RB	OB	7 9	2200		9050	10300
22 8	SEA-HAVEN	OP	CUD	FBG RB	IO OMC	7 9			**	**
22 8	SEA-HAVEN	OP	CUD	FBG RB	SE 115 OMC	7 9			8350	9950
22 8	SEA-HAVEN	OP	CUD	FBG RB	IO 120-170	7 9			**	**
22 8	SPORT FISHERMAN	OP	CTRCN	FBG RB	OB	7 9	1900		7800	8950
22 8	SPORT FISHERMAN	OP	CTRCN	FBG RB	IO OMC	7 9			**	**
22 8	SPORT FISHERMAN	OP	CTRCN	FBG RB	SE 115 OMC	7 9			8350	9950
22 8	SPORT FISHERMAN	OP	CTRCN	FBG RB	IO 120-170	7 9			**	**
25 11	COMMERCIAL	OP	COMM	FBG	OB	10	4500	2 7	**	**
25 11	COMMERCIAL	OP	UTL	FBG	IO OMC	10		2 7	**	**
25 11	COMMERCIAL	OP	UTL	FBG	IO 120-140	10		2 7	**	**
25 11	COMMERCIAL	OP	UTL	FBG	SE 155 OMC	10		2 7	**	**
25 11	COMMERCIAL	OP	UTL	FBG	IO 170 MRCR	10		2 7	**	**
IB 225 VLVO **		** , IO	260	MRCR **	** , IO 260 OMC				**	**
IB 260 VLVO **		** , IB	124D	VLVO **	** , IO 130D-155D				**	**
IB 165D VLVO **		**								
25 11	COMMERCIAL	OP	UTL	FBG	SE T115 OMC	10	4500	2 7	16500	18800
25 11	EXPLORER		CTRCN FBG		OB	10		2 7	16500	18800
25 11	EXPLORER		CTRCN FBG		IO OMC	10		2 7	**	**
25 11	EXPLORER		CTRCN FBG		IO 120-140	10		2 7	16200	19000
25 11	EXPLORER		CTRCN FBG		SE 155 OMC	10		2 7	15900	18100
25 11	EXPLORER		CTRCN FBG		IO 170 MRCR	10		2 7	16900	19200
IB 225 VLVO 21500	23900, IO	260	MRCR 18500	20500, IO 260 OMC	18400	20500
IB 260 VLVO 22000	24400, IB	124D	VLVO 31300	34700, IO 130D-155D	28600	32700
IB 165D VLVO 32700	36300					
25 11	EXPLORER		CTRCN FBG		SE T115 OMC	10		2 7	15900	18100
25 11	FULL HOUSE COMM	PH	FBG		OB	10	4500	2 7	12600	14300
25 11	FULL HOUSE COMM	PH	FBG		IO OMC	10		2 7	**	**
25 11	FULL HOUSE COMM	PH	FBG		IO 120-140	10		2 7	13400	16300
25 11	FULL HOUSE COMM	PH	FBG		SE 155 OMC	10		2 7	14000	15900
25 11	FULL HOUSE COMM	PH	FBG		IO 170 MRCR	10		2 7	14600	16500
IB 225 VLVO 19500	21700, IO	260	MRCR 16000	18200, IO 260 OMC	16000	18100
IB 260 VLVO 20000	22200, IB	124D	VLVO 50700	55800, IO 130D-155D	40400	45000
IB 165D VLVO 51200	56300					
25 11	FULL HOUSE COMM	PH	FBG		SE T115 OMC	10		2 7	14300	16200
25 11	FULL HOUSE DLX	PH	FBG		OB	10	4500	2 7	21200	23600
25 11	FULL HOUSE DLX	PH	FBG		IO OMC	10		2 7	**	**
25 11	FULL HOUSE DLX	PH	FBG		IO 120-140	10		2 7	19500	23000
25 11	FULL HOUSE DLX	PH	FBG		SE 155 OMC	10		2 7	19300	21400
25 11	FULL HOUSE DLX	PH	FBG		IO 170 MRCR	10		2 7	20900	23200
IB 225 VLVO 25700	28500, IO	260	MRCR 21900	24300, IO 260 OMC	21800	24300
IB 260 VLVO 26200	29100, IB	124D	VLVO 64000	70300, IO 130D-155D	53000	58200
IB 165D VLVO 64000	70400					
25 11	FULL HOUSE DLX	PH	FBG		SE T115 OMC	10		2 7	19000	21100
25 11	NORTH-STAR		CUD FBG		OB	10	4500	2 7	17100	19400
25 11	NORTH-STAR		CUD FBG		IO OMC	10		2 7	**	**
25 11	NORTH-STAR		CUD FBG		IO 120-140	10		2 7	17500	20400
25 11	NORTH-STAR		CUD FBG		SE 155 OMC	10		2 7	16600	18900
25 11	NORTH-STAR		CUD FBG		IO 170 MRCR	10		2 7	18500	20500
IB 225 VLVO 24200	26800, IO	260	MRCR 19400	21500, IO 260 OMC	19300	21500
IB 260 VLVO 24600	27300, IB	124D	VLVO 27400	30400, IO 130D-155D	20200	23200
IB 165D VLVO 29000	32200					
25 11	NORTH-STAR		CUD FBG		SE T115 OMC	10		2 7	16600	18900
---	--- 1985 BOATS ---									
16 6	COMMERCIAL	OP	UTL	FBG SV	OB	6 8	800	6	**	**
16 6	SEASPRAY	OP	RNBT	FBG SV	OB	6 8	800	6	2800	3250
16 6	SEASPRAY DLX	OP	RNBT	FBG SV	OB	6 8	900	6	2950	3400
16 6	SKIFF	OP	UTL	FBG SV	OB	6 8	650	6	2050	2450
16 6	SPORTSMAN	OP	OPFSH	FBG SV	OB	6 8	825	6	2650	3050
18 10	COMMERCIAL	OP	CTRCN	FBG RB	OB	7 6	1200	5	**	**
18 10	COMMERCIAL	OP	CTRCN	FBG RB	IO	7 6		5	**	**
18 10	COMMERCIAL CUDDY	ST	CBNCR	FBG RB	IO 120	7 6	1250	5	**	**
18 10	COMMERCIAL CUDDY	ST	CBNCR	FBG RB	IO 120	7 6		5	**	**
18 10	OPEN FISHERMAN	OP	CTRCN	FBG RB	OB	7 6	1250	5	4050	4700
18 10	OPEN FISHERMAN	OP	CTRCN	FBG RB	IO 120-170	7 6		5	5300	6100
18 10	SEAFARER		CUD	FBG RB	OB	7 6	1350	5	4300	5000
18 10	SEAFARER	ST	CUD	FBG RB	IO 120-170	7 6		5	4800	5550
18 10	VOYAGER	ST	RNBT	FBG RB	OB	7 6	1250	5	4050	4700
18 10	VOYAGER	ST	RNBT	FBG RB	IO 120-170	7 6		5	4700	5450
20	SALTY-DOG	OP	RNBT	FBG SV	OB	8	1700	9	6250	7200
20	SALTY-DOG	OP	RNBT	FBG SV	SE 115 OMC	8		9	**	**
20	SALTY-DOG	OP	RNBT	FBG SV	IO 120-138	8		9	6100	7350
20	SALTY-DOG	OP	RNBT	FBG SV	SE 155 OMC	8		9	**	**
20	SALTY-DOG	OP	RNBT	FBG SV	IO 170 MRCR	8		9	6150	7050
22 8	COMMERCIAL	OP	UTL	FBG RB	OB	7 9	1600		**	**
22 8	COMMERCIAL	OP	UTL	FBG RB	SE 115 OMC	7 9			**	**
22 8	COMMERCIAL	OP	UTL	FBG RB	IO 120-170	7 9			**	**
22 8	COMMERCIAL CUDDY	HT	CBNCR	FBG RB	OB	7 9	2000		**	**

LOA FT	LOA IN	NAME AND/ OR MODEL	TOP/ RIG	BOAT TYPE	-HULL- MTL	-HULL- TP	ENGINE TP	ENGINE # HP	ENGINE MFG	BEAM FT	BEAM IN	WGT LBS	DRAFT FT	DRAFT IN	RETAIL LOW	RETAIL HIGH
		1985 BOATS														
22	8	COMMERCIAL CUDDY	HT	CBNCR	FBG	RB	SE	115	OMC	7	9				**	**
22	8	COMMERCIAL CUDDY	HT	CBNCR	FBG	RB	IO	120-170		7	9				**	**
22	8	SEA-HAVEN	OP	CUD	FBG	RB	OB					2200			8650	9950
22	8	SEA-HAVEN	OP	CUD	FBG	RB	SE	115	OMC	7	9				**	**
22	8	SEA-HAVEN	OP	CUD	FBG	RB	IO	120-170		7	9				8000	9550
22	8	SPORT FISHERMAN	OP	CTRCN	FBG	RB	OB			7	9	1900			7550	8650
22	8	SPORT FISHERMAN	OP	CTRCN	FBG	RB	SE	115	OMC	7	9				**	**
22	8	SPORT FISHERMAN	OP	CTRCN	FBG	RB	IO	120-170		7	9				8000	9550
25	11	COMMERCIAL		UTL	FBG		OB			10		4500	2	7	**	**
25	11	COMMERCIAL		UTL	FBG		SE	155	OMC	10			2	7	**	**
25	11	COMMERCIAL		UTL	FBG		IB	225	VLVO	10			2	7	**	**
		IO 260 MRCR ** **, IO 260 OMC ** **, IB 260 VLVO													**	**
		IB 124D VLVO ** **, IO 130D-155D ** **, IB 158D VLVO													**	**
25	11	COMMERCIAL		UTL	FBG		SE	T115	OMC	10			2	7	**	**
25	11	COMMERCIAL CUDDY		CUD	FBG	SV	IB	225		10		7415	2	7	**	**
25	11	EXPLORER		CTRCN	FBG		OB			10		4500	2	7	16000	18100
25	11	EXPLORER		CTRCN	FBG		SE	155	OMC	10			2	7	15400	17500
25	11	EXPLORER		CTRCN	FBG		IB	225	VLVO	10			2	7	20600	22800
		IO 260 MRCR 17400 19700, IO 260 OMC 17300 19700, IB 260 VLVO													21000	23300
		IB 124D VLVO 30000 33300, IO 130D-155D 27500 31400, IB 158D VLVO													31100	34600
25	11	EXPLORER		CTRCN	FBG		SE	T115	OMC	10			2	7	15400	17500
25	11	FULL HOUSE COMM		PH	FBG		OB			10		4500	2	7	12900	14700
25	11	FULL HOUSE COMM		PH	FBG		SE	155	OMC	10			2	7	14000	16000
25	11	FULL HOUSE COMM		PH	FBG		IB	225	VLVO	10			2	7	19200	21300
		IO 260 MRCR 16500 18800, IO 260 OMC 16500 18700, IB 260 VLVO													19600	21800
		IB 124D VLVO 49700 54600, IO 130D-155D 39800 44400, IB 158D VLVO													50100	55000
25	11	FULL HOUSE COMM		PH	FBG		SE	T115	OMC	10			2	7	14300	16200
25	11	FULL HOUSE DLX		PH	FBG		OB			10		4500	2	7	20200	22500
25	11	FULL HOUSE DLX		PH	FBG		IO		MRCR	10			2	7	**	**
25	11	FULL HOUSE DLX		PH	FBG		SE	155	OMC	10			2	7	18100	20100
25	11	FULL HOUSE DLX		PH	FBG		IB	225	VLVO	10			2	7	24000	26700
		IO 260 OMC 21400 23800, IB 260 VLVO 24500 27200, IB 124D VLVO													59800	65700
		IO 130D-155D 49800 54800, IB 158D VLVO 60100 66100														
25	11	FULL HOUSE DLX		PH	FBG		SE	T115	OMC	10			2	7	17500	19900
25	11	NORTH-STAR		CUD	FBG		OB			10		4500	2	7	16500	18800
25	11	NORTH-STAR		CUD	FBG		SE	155	OMC	10			2	7	16100	18300
25	11	NORTH-STAR		CUD	FBG		IB	225	VLVO	10			2	7	23100	25600
		IO 260 MRCR 18800 20900, IO 260 OMC 18700 20800, IB 260 VLVO													23500	26100
		IB 124D VLVO 26300 29200, IO 130D-155D 19300 22200, IB 158D VLVO													27500	30600
25	11	NORTH-STAR		CUD	FBG		SE	T115	OMC	10			2	7	16100	18300
		1984 BOATS														
16	6	COMMERCIAL	OP	UTL	FBG	SV	OB			6	8	800		6	**	**
16	6	SEASPRAY	OP	RNBT	FBG	SV	OB			6	8	825		6	2500	2900
16	6	SEASPRAY DLX	OP	RNBT	FBG	SV	OB			6	8	825		6	2650	3100
16	6	SKIFF	OP	UTL	FBG	SV	OB			6	8	650		6	2000	2350
16	6	SPORTSMAN	OP	OPFSH	FBG	SV	OB			6	8	825		6	2550	2950
18	10		OP	CUD	FBG	RB	OB			7	5	1300		5	4050	4700
18	10		ST	RNBT	FBG	RB	OB			7	5	1150		5	3700	4300
18	10		ST	RNBT	FBG	RB	IO	120	MRCR	7	5			5	4400	5050
18	10	COMMERCIAL	OP	CTRCN	FBG	RB	OB			7	5	1100		5	**	**
18	10	COMMERCIAL	OP	CTRCN	FBG	RB	IO	120-170		7	5			5	**	**
18	10	COMMERCIAL CUDDY	ST	CBNCR	FBG	RB	OB			7	5	1250		5	**	**
18	10	COMMERCIAL CUDDY	ST	CBNCR	FBG	RB	IO	120-170		7	5			5	**	**
18	10	OPEN FISHERMAN	OP	CTRCN	FBG	RB	OB			7	5	1250		5	3900	4550
18	10	OPEN FISHERMAN	OP	CTRCN	FBG	RB	IO	120-170		7	5			5	5100	5850
18	10	SEAFARER		CUD	FBG	RB	OB			7	5	1250		5	3950	4550
18	10	SEAFARER		CUD	FBG	RB	IO	120-170		7	5			5	4600	5350
18	10	VOYAGER	ST	RNBT	FBG	RB	OB			7	5	1250		5	3950	4600
18	10	VOYAGER	ST	RNBT	FBG	RB	IO	120-170		7	5			5	4600	5300
20		SALTY-DOG	OP	RNBT	FBG	SV	OB			8		1700		9	6050	6950
20		SALTY-DOG	OP	RNBT	FBG	SV	SE	115	OMC	8				9	**	**
20		SALTY-DOG	OP	RNBT	FBG	SV	IO	120-138		8				9	5900	7100
20		SALTY-DOG	OP	RNBT	FBG	SV	SE	155	OMC	8				9	**	**
20		SALTY-DOG	OP	RNBT	FBG	SV	IO	170	MRCR	8				9	5950	6800
22	10	COMMERCIAL	OP	UTL	FBG	RB	OB			7	9	1600			**	**
22	10	COMMERCIAL	OP	UTL	FBG	RB	SE	115	OMC	7	9				**	**
22	10	COMMERCIAL	OP	UTL	FBG	RB	IO	120-170		7	9				**	**
22	10	COMMERCIAL CUDDY	HT	CBNCR	FBG	RB	OB			7	9	2000			**	**
22	10	COMMERCIAL CUDDY	HT	CBNCR	FBG	RB	SE	115	OMC	7	9				**	**
22	10	COMMERCIAL CUDDY	HT	CBNCR	FBG	RB	IO	120-170		7	9				**	**
22	10	SEA-HAVEN	OP	CUD	FBG	RB	OB			7	9	2200			8400	9700
22	10	SEA-HAVEN	OP	CUD	FBG	RB	SE	115	OMC	7	9				**	**
22	10	SEA-HAVEN	OP	CUD	FBG	RB	IO	120-170		7	9				7800	9300
22	10	SPORT FISHERMAN	OP	CTRCN	FBG	RB	OB			7	9	1900			7350	8450
22	10	SPORT FISHERMAN	OP	CTRCN	FBG	RB	SE	115	OMC	7	9				**	**
22	10	SPORT FISHERMAN	OP	CTRCN	FBG	RB	IO	120-170		7	9				7800	9300
25	11	COMMERCIAL		UTL	FBG		OB			10		4500	2	7	**	**
25	11	COMMERCIAL		UTL	FBG		SE	155	OMC	10			2	7	**	**
25	11	COMMERCIAL		UTL	FBG		IB	220	CRUS	10			2	7	**	**
		IO 260 ** **, IB 270 CRUS ** **, IB 124D VLVO													**	**
		IO 130D-155D ** **, IB 158D VLVO ** **														
25	11	COMMERCIAL		UTL	FBG		SE	T115	OMC	10			2	7	**	**
25	11	EXPLORER		CTRCN	FBG		OB			10			2	7	15500	17600
25	11	EXPLORER		CTRCN	FBG		SE	155	OMC	10			2	7	14900	16900
25	11	EXPLORER		CTRCN	FBG		IB	220	CRUS	10			2	7	19600	21800
		IO 260 16800 19000, IB 270 CRUS 20200 22500, IB 124D VLVO													28800	32000
		IO 130D-155D 26500 30300, IB 158D VLVO 29900 33200														
25	11	EXPLORER		CTRCN	FBG		SE	T115	OMC	10			2	7	14900	16900
25	11	FULL HOUSE COMM		PH			OB			10		4500	2	7	7200	8300
25	11	FULL HOUSE COMM		PH	FBG		SE	155	OMC	10			2	7	15400	17500
25	11	FULL HOUSE COMM		PH	FBG		IB	220	CRUS	10			2	7	18700	20800
		IO 260 15500 17600, IB 270 CRUS 19100 21200, IB 124D VLVO													48400	53200
		IO 130D-155D 38900 43300, IB 158D VLVO 48700 53500														
25	11	FULL HOUSE COMM		PH	FBG		SE	T115	OMC	10			2	7	14000	15900
25	11	FULL HOUSE COMM DLX		PH	FBG		OB			10			2	7	15800	18000
25	11	FULL HOUSE COMM DLX		PH	FBG		SE	115	OMC	10			2	7	15400	17500
25	11	FULL HOUSE COMM DLX		PH	FBG		IB	220	CRUS	10			2	7	22700	25200
		IO 260 19600 21800, IB 270 CRUS 23300 25900, IB 124D VLVO													56800	62400
		IO 130D-155D 47800 52500, IB 158D VLVO 57200 62800														
25	11	FULL HOUSE COMM DLX		PH	FBG		SE	T115	OMC	10			2	7	16800	19100
25	11	NORTH-STAR		CUD	FBG		OB			10		4500	2	7	16000	18200
25	11	NORTH-STAR		CUD	FBG		SE	155	OMC	10			2	7	15600	17700
25	11	NORTH-STAR		CUD	FBG		IB	220	CRUS	10			2	7	22000	24400
		IO 260 18200 20200, IB 270 CRUS 22600 25100, IB 124D VLVO													25200	28000
		IO 130D-155D 18800 21400, IB 158D VLVO 26400 29400														
25	11	NORTH-STAR		CUD	FBG		SE	T115	OMC	10			2	7	15600	17700

....For earlier years, see the BUC Used Boat Price Guide, Volume 3

SEAWIND CATAMARANS

ROZELLE, SYDNEY NSW AUS COAST GUARD MFG ID- EAW See inside cover to adjust price for area

For more recent years, see the BUC Used Boat Price Guide, Volume 1

LOA FT	LOA IN	NAME AND/ OR MODEL	TOP/ RIG	BOAT TYPE	-HULL- MTL	-HULL- TP	ENGINE TP	ENGINE # HP	ENGINE MFG	BEAM FT	BEAM IN	WGT LBS	DRAFT FT	DRAFT IN	RETAIL LOW	RETAIL HIGH
		1988 BOATS														
24	3	SEA-WIND 24 CAT	SLP	SA/RC	FBG	CT	OB			16		2000	1		19900	22200
31		SEA-WIND 31 CAT	SLP	SA/CR	F/S	CT	OB			23		5200	1	3	52200	57300
31		SEA-WIND 31 CAT	SLP	SA/CR	F/S	CT	IB	D	YAN	23		5200	1	3	52500	57700
		1987 BOATS														
24	3	SEA-WIND 24	CAT	SA/RC	FBG	CT	OB			16		2000	1		18700	20800
31		SEA-WIND 31	CAT	SA/CR	F/S	CT	IB	D	YAN	23		5200	1	3	49400	54300
		1986 BOATS														
24	3	SEA-WIND 24	CAT	SA/RC	FBG	CT	OB			16		1600		8	16200	18400
31		SEA-WIND 31	CAT	SA/CR	F/S	CT	IB	D	YAN	23		4500	1	3	44400	49300
		1985 BOATS														
24	3	SEA-WIND 24	CAT	SA/RC	FBG	CT	OB			16		1600		8	15200	17300
31		SEA-WIND 31	CAT	SA/CR	F/S	CT	IB	D	YAN	23		4500	1	3	41700	46300

SEAWOLF

CLEARWATER FL 34622 See inside cover to adjust price for area

LOA FT	LOA IN	NAME AND/ OR MODEL	TOP/ RIG	BOAT TYPE	-HULL- MTL	-HULL- TP	ENGINE TP	ENGINE # HP	ENGINE MFG	BEAM FT	BEAM IN	WGT LBS	DRAFT FT	DRAFT IN	RETAIL LOW	RETAIL HIGH
		1990 BOATS														
22	2	SEA WOLF 22	OP	CTRCN	FBG	DV	OB			8	6	2700			8900	10100
22	2	SEA WOLF 22 WA	OP	CUD	FBG	DV	OB			8	6	2875			9300	10600
25	10	SEA WOLF 26	OP	CTRCN	FBG	DV	OB			8	6	3300			13400	15300
25	10	SEA WOLF 26 WA	HT	CUD	FBG	DV	OB			8	6	4150			14700	16700

LOA FT IN	NAME AND/ OR MODEL	TOP/ RIG	BOAT TYPE	-HULL- MTL TP	----ENGINE--- TP # HP MFG	BEAM FT IN	WGT LBS	DRAFT FT IN	RETAIL LOW	RETAIL HIGH
				1990 **BOATS**						
27 4	SEA WOLF 27		OP	CTRCN FBG DV	OB	8 6	3600		18300	20300

SENATOR YACHTS
BALTIMORE MD 21231   COAST GUARD MFG ID- JRY See inside cover to adjust price for area

FORMERLY J R YACHT SALES INC

LOA FT IN	NAME AND/ OR MODEL	TOP/ RIG	BOAT TYPE	-HULL- MTL TP	----ENGINE--- TP # HP MFG	BEAM FT IN	WGT LBS	DRAFT FT IN	RETAIL LOW	RETAIL HIGH
				1987 **BOATS**						
30 6	SENATOR 31 FISHERMAN	FB	TRWL	FBG DS IB	100D-135D	11 6	14300	3 4	50700	61500
32	SENATOR 32 SUNDECK	FB	DCMY	FBG DS IB	130D-165D	10 6	14900	3 3	54600	60000
34 4	SENATOR 35 CLASSIC	FB	TRWL	FBG DS IB	135D-165D	12	18700	3 3	74900	83200
34 4	SENATOR 35 CLASSIC	FB	TRWL	FBG DS IBT	100D-T135D	12	18700	3 3	76800	87200
34 4	SENATOR 35 FUTURA	HT	TRWL	FBG DS IB	135D-165D	12	18700	3 3	74900	83200
34 4	SENATOR 35 FUTURA	FB	TRWL	FBG DS IBT	100D-T135D	12	18700	3 3	76800	87200
35	SENATOR 35 FUTURA II	FB	DCMY	FBG SV	IB T130D VLVO	12	16000	3 2	71200	78300
	IB T165D PERK 74000	81300,	IB T200D PERK	75900	83400, IB T200D VLVO				74600	82000
	IB T240D PERK 78200	86000								
36	SENATOR 36 SF	FB	SF	FBG DV IB	T135D PERK 13	8	22000	3 3	84100	92500
	IB T200D PERK 85400	93800,	IB T200D VLVO	83400	91600, IB T240D PERK				87100	95800
	IB T250D GM 86400	95000,	IB T275D PERK	87600	96300, IB T306D VLVO				88000	96700
	IB T350D CRUS 91900	101500,	IB T355D VLVO	90700	99700					
36	SENATOR 36 SUNDECK	HT	MY	FBG DV IB	T135D PERK 13	1	22000	3 3	86300	94800
	IB T200D PERK 89000	97800,	IB T200D VLVO	87000	95600, IB T225D LEHM				89100	98000
	IB T240D PERK 91100	100000,	IB T250D GM	90400	99400, IB T275D LEHM				91800	101000
	IB T306D VLVO 92300	101500,	IB T350D CRUS	96500	106000, IB T358D VLVO				95500	105000
41	SENATOR 41 SUNDECK	HT	MY	FBG SV IB	T135D PERK 14		26400	3 3	114500	126000
	IB T200D PERK 119500	131500,	IB T200D VLVO	116000	127500, IB T240D PERK				123000	135000
	IB T306D VLVO 124000	136000								
42	SENATOR 42 PH	FB	PH	FBG SV IB	T135D PERK 14	8	16000	3 10	76400	83900
	IB T200D PERK 86200	94700,	IB T200D VLVO	83200	91400, IB T240D PERK				92000	101000
	IB T306D VLVO 97300	107000,	IB T358D VLVO	104000	114500, IB T375D CAT				111500	122500
42	SENATOR 42 DCMY	FB	DCMY	FBG DV IB	T200D VLVO 14	10	16000	3 6	83200	91500
	IB T306D VLVO 98000	107500,	IB T350D GM	106500	117000, IB T358D VLVO				105000	115500
	IB T375D CAT 112500	123500								
46 3	SENATOR 46 PH	FB	PH	FBG SV IB	T135D PERK 14	8	29000	4	125000	137500
	IB T200D PERK 124500	137000,	IB T200D VLVO	121500	133500, IB T240D PERK				127000	139500
	IB T306D VLVO 130000	142500,	IB T358D VLVO	136000	149500, IB T375D CAT				141000	155000
				1986 **BOATS**						
36	SENATOR 36 SF	HT	SF	FBG DV IB	T135D PERK 13	8	22000	3 3	80500	88500
	IB T145D PERK 80600	88600,	IB T165D YAN	80000	88000, IB T175D YAN				80200	88100
	IB T200D PERK 81700	89800,	IB T240D PERK	83400	91600, IB T350D CRUS				88000	96700
36	SENATOR 36 SUNDECK	HT	DCMY	FBG DV IB	T135D PERK 13	1	22000	3 3	82600	90700
	IB T145D YAN 82200	90300,	IB T165D PERK	83700	92000, IB T175D YAN				83300	91500
	IB T200D PERK 85200	93600,	IB T240D PERK	87200	95800, IB T270D CRUS				87600	96200
	IB T350D CRUS 92400	101500								
42	SENATOR 42 DCMY	FB	DCMY	FBG DV IB	135D PERK 14	10	16000	3 6	79800	87600
	IB T135D PERK 72600	79800,	IB T165D PERK	77200	84600, IB T175D YAN				77600	85200
	IB T200D PERK 82500	90700,	IB T240D PERK	88300	97000					
42 6	SENATOR 40 DCMY	HT	DCMY	FBG DV IB	135D PERK 13	6	22000	3 6	94600	104000
	IB T135D PERK 93800	103000,	IB T165D PERK	97300	107000, IB T175D YAN				97300	107000
	IB T200D PERK 101000	111000,	IB T240D PERK	105500	116000					
				1984 **BOATS**						
34 9	SENATOR 35 DC	FB	TRWL	FBG DS IB	120D-158D	12	18000	3 3	65500	72000
34 9	SENATOR 35 DC	FB	TRWL	FBG DS IB	T85D-T145D	12	18000	3 3	68300	76400
34 9	SENATOR 35 SUNDECK	FB	TRWL	FBG DS IB	120D-158D	12	18000	3 3	66300	72900
34 9	SENATOR 35 SUNDECK	FB	TRWL	FBG DS IB	T85D-T145D	12	18000	3 3	67600	77400
45	SENATOR 45 PH	FB	MY	FBG DS IB	T135D PERK 15	3		4	110000	121000
45	SENATOR 45 SUNDECK	FB	MY	FBG DS IB	T135D PERK 15	3		4	112500	123500
51	SENATOR 51 FD	FB	MY	FBG DS IB	T310D GM	16	8	4 3	143500	157500

SERENDIPITY YACHTS
CORTE MADERA CA 94925-1238   See inside cover to adjust price for area

LOA FT IN	NAME AND/ OR MODEL	TOP/ RIG	BOAT TYPE	-HULL- MTL TP	----ENGINE--- TP # HP MFG	BEAM FT IN	WGT LBS	DRAFT FT IN	RETAIL LOW	RETAIL HIGH
				1984 **BOATS**						
42 4	SERENDIPITY 43	SLP	SA/RC	FBG KL IB	D	13 3	17800	7 4	67800	74500

....For earlier years, see the BUC Used Boat Price Guide, Volume 3

SEVEN SEAS BOAT WORKS
FIBERGLASS FABRICATORS INC   See inside cover to adjust price for area

PASCAGOULA MS 39567-5245

LOA FT IN	NAME AND/ OR MODEL	TOP/ RIG	BOAT TYPE	-HULL- MTL TP	----ENGINE--- TP # HP MFG	BEAM FT IN	WGT LBS	DRAFT FT IN	RETAIL LOW	RETAIL HIGH
				1988 **BOATS**						
53	CRUISER 53	FB	MY	FBG DV IB	T280D GM	16	33000	3 8	123500	135500
53	FLYBRIDGE 53	FB	SF	FBG DV IB	T500D GM	16	33000	3 8	149000	164000
54	FLYBRIDGE_EXPRESS	FB	SF	FBG DV IO	R365 MRCR	14	18000	3	107000	117500
55	CRUISER 55	FB	MY	FBG DV IB	T450D S&S	19	44000	3 8	154500	170000
55	MARLIN-TAKER	FB	SF	FBG DV IB	T650D GM	19	44000	3 8	186000	204500
56	SUPER FISH	FB	SF	FBG DV IB	T710D GM	19	40000	3 8	195000	214500
				1987 **BOATS**						
30	HI-PERFORMANCE D-30	ST	RACE	FBG DV IB	T UNIV	4	6000		**	**
44	CRUISER 44	FB	MY	FBG DV IB	T210D CAT	16	27500	3	89000	97800
44	FLYBRIDGE 44	FB	SF	FBG DV IB	T300D CAT	16	27500	3	91400	100500
53	CRUISER 53	FB	MY	FBG DV IB	T280D GM	16	33000	3 8	118500	130000
53	FLYBRIDGE 53	FB	SF	FBG DV IB	T500D GM	16	33000	3 8	143500	157500
55	CRUISER 55	FB	MY	FBG DV IB	T450D S&S	19	44000	3 8	148500	163000
55	MARLIN-TAKER	FB	SF	FBG DV IB	T650D GM	19	44000	3 8	178500	196000
56	SUPER FISH	FB	SF	FBG DV IB	T710D GM	19	40000	3 8	187000	205500
				1985 **BOATS**						
30	HI-PERFORMANCE D-30	ST	RACE	FBG DV IB	T UNIV	4	6000		**	**
44	CRUISER 44	FB	MY	FBG DV IB	T210D CAT	16	27500	3	80900	88800
44	FLYBRIDGE 44	FB	SF	FBG DV IB	T300D CAT	16	27500	3	82900	91000
53	CRUISER 53	FB	MY	FBG DV IB	T280D GM	16	33000	3 8	109500	120500
53	FLYBRIDGE 53	FB	SF	FBG DV IB	T500D GM	16	33000	3 8	132500	145500
55	CRUISER 55	FB	MY	FBG DV IB	T450D S&S	19	44000	3 8	137500	151000
55	MARLIN-TAKER	FB	SF	FBG DV IB	T650D GM	19	44000	3 8	164500	180500
				1984 **BOATS**						
44		FB	CR	FBG DV IB	T210D CAT	16	27500	3	74800	82200
44		FB	CR	FBG DV IB	T300D CAT	16	27500	3	79200	87100
53		FB	CR	FBG DV IB	T280D GM	16	33000	3 8	98800	108500
53		FB	CR	FBG DV IB	T500D GM	16	33000	3 8	128000	140500
55		FB	CR	FBG DV IB	T450D S&S	19	44000	3 8	125500	137500
55		FB	SF	FBG DV IB	T650D GM	19	44000	3 8	160000	176000

....For earlier years, see the BUC Used Boat Price Guide, Volume 3

SEYLER MARINE INC
APOPKA FL 32703   COAST GUARD MFG ID- SIG See inside cover to adjust price for area

LOA FT IN	NAME AND/ OR MODEL	TOP/ RIG	BOAT TYPE	-HULL- MTL TP	----ENGINE--- TP # HP MFG	BEAM FT IN	WGT LBS	DRAFT FT IN	RETAIL LOW	RETAIL HIGH
				1986 **BOATS**						
20 6	OMNI 21	OP	RNBT	FBG DV OB		7 1		1 1	4200	4850
20 6	OMNI 21	OP	RNBT	FBG DV IO	220-260	7	2300	1 6	6700	7900
20 6	OMNI 21	OP	RNBT	FBG DV IO	280-300	7	2300	2	8450	9850
21 8	F-22	OP	CTRCN	FBG SV OB		8	2500	8	4550	5250
	SE 115 OMC **	**	**	** , SE 155-205	**	** , SE T115	OMC	**	**	**
21 8	F-22	OP	CUD	FBG SV OB		8		8	4650	5350
21 8	F-22	OP	CUD	FBG SV SE	115 OMC	8		1 4	**	**
21 8	F-22	OP	CUD	FBG SV SE	155 OMC	8		1 5	**	**
21 8	F-22	OP	CUD	FBG SV IO	170-185	8		1 7	7650	9100
21 8	F-22	OP	CUD	FBG SV SE	205 OMC	8		1 7	**	**
21 8	F-22	OP	CUD	FBG SV IO	225-260	8		1 7	8150	9750
21 8	F-22	OP	CUD	FBG SV SE	T115 OMC	8		1 5	**	**
22 4	OMNI 22	OP	RACE	DV IB	280	7 2		2	9800	11100
22 4	OMNI 22	OP	RACE	KEV IB	425 PCM	7 2	2500	2	11400	13000
				1985 **BOATS**						
20 6	OMNI 21	OP	RNBT	FBG DV IO		7 1		1 1	4100	4750
20 6	OMNI 21	OP	RNBT	FBG DV IO	195 BMW	7 1	2300	2 6	6300	7200
	IB 220 BMW 7950	9150,	IO 225-260	6300	7600, IO 280 PCM				6450	7450
	IB 280-300 8100	9450								
21 8	F-22	OP	CTRCN	FBG SV OB		8	2500	8	4450	5100
	SE 115 OMC **	**	**	** , SE 155-205	**	** , SE T115	OMC	**	**	**

LOA FT	LOA IN	NAME AND/ OR MODEL	TOP/ RIG	BOAT TYPE	HULL MTL	HULL TP	ENGINE TP	ENGINE # HP	ENGINE MFG	BEAM FT	BEAM IN	WGT LBS	DRAFT FT	DRAFT IN	RETAIL LOW	RETAIL HIGH
		1985 BOATS														
21	8	F-22	OP	CUD	FBG	SV	OB			8				8	4550	5200
21	8	F-22	OP	CUD	FBG	SV	SE	115	OMC	8			1	4	**	**
21	8	F-22	OP	CUD	FBG	SV	SE	155	OMC	8			1	5	**	**
21	8	F-22	OP	CUD	FBG	SV	IO	170-185		8			1	7	7350	8750
21	8	F-22	OP	CUD	FBG	SV	SE	205	OMC	8			1	5	**	**
21	8	F-22	OP	CUD	FBG	SV	IO	225-260		8			1	7	7800	9350
21	8	F-22	OP	CUD	FBG	SV	SE	T115	OMC	8			1	5	**	**
22	4	OMNI 22	OP	RACE	KEV	DV	IB	425	PCM	7	2		2		10900	12400
22	4	OMNI 22	OP	RNBT	FBG	DV	IB	280		7	2				9450	10700
		1984 BOATS														
20	6	OMNI 21	OP	RNBT	FBG	DV	IB	190	BMW	7		2300	2		7500	8600
		IO 220 BMW 6150 7100, IB 220 PCM 7550 8700, IO 228-280													5850	7200
		IB 165D BMW 12400 14000														
21	8	F-22		CTRCN	FBG	SV	OB			8		2700	2		4600	5250
21	8	F-22		CTRCN	FBG	SV	IO			8		2700	2		**	**
22	4	OMNI 22	OP	RACE	KEV	DV	IB	330		7	2	2500	2		9300	10600
22	4	OMNI 22	OP	RACE	KEV	DV	IB	425	PCM	7	2	2500	2		10400	11800
22	4	OMNI 22	OP	RACE	KEV	SV	IB	260		7	2	2500	2		8900	10100
22	4	OMNI 22	OP	RNBT	FBG	DV	IB	300	PCM	7	2	2500	2		9200	10400
22	4	OMNI 22	OP	RNBT	FBG	DV	IB	165D	BMW	7	2	2500	2		13900	15800

....For earlier years, see the BUC Used Boat Price Guide, Volume 3

SHALLOW SPORT BOATS INC

PT ISABEL TX 78578 COAST GUARD MFG ID- SZX See inside cover to adjust price for area

LOA FT	LOA IN	NAME AND/ OR MODEL	TOP/ RIG	BOAT TYPE	HULL MTL	HULL TP	ENGINE TP	ENGINE # HP	ENGINE MFG	BEAM FT	BEAM IN	WGT LBS	DRAFT FT	DRAFT IN	RETAIL LOW	RETAIL HIGH
		1992 BOATS														
17	10	SPRINT 18	OP	CTRCN	FBG	TH	OB			7		1000		6	3800	4400
18	7	SPORT 18	OP	CTRCN	FBG	TH	OB			7	2	1050		6	4050	4700
21		SUPER SPORT 21	OP	CTRCN	FBG	TH	OB			8				11	5150	5950
21	4	STRIKER 21	OP	CTRCN	FBG	TH	OB			7	6	1200		6	5200	6000
		1991 BOATS														
17	10	SPRINT 18	OP	CTRCN	FBG	TH	OB			7		1000		6	3600	4200
18	7	SPORT 18	OP	CTRCN	FBG	TH	OB			7	2	1050		6	3850	4500
20	7	SPORT 20	OP	CTRCN	FBG	TH	OB			7	6	1200		6	4900	5650
21		SUPER SPORT 21	OP	CTRCN	FBG	TH	OB			8				11	4950	5700
		1990 BOATS														
17	3	SPORT N 17	OP	CTRCN	FBG	TH	OB			5	6			8	3450	4000
17	3	SPORT N 17	OP	SF	FBG	TH	OB			5	6			8	3550	4100
17	3	SPORT N 17	OP	UTL	FBG	TH	OB			5	6			8	3400	3950
17	7	SNIPER 17 7	OP	CTRCN	FBG	TH	OB			7	3	1050		6	3600	4150
17	7	SNIPER 17 7	OP	RNBT	PLY	TH	OB			7	3	1050		6	3650	4250
17	7	SNIPER 17 7	OP	UTL	PLY	TH	OB			7	3	1050		6	3400	3950
18	7	SPORT 18	OP	CTRCN	FBG	TH	OB			7	8			6	3700	4300
18	7	SPORT 18	FB	RNBT	PLY	TH	OB			7	8			6	3750	4350
18	7	SPORT 18	FB	UTL	PLY	TH	OB			7	8			6	3350	3900
20	6	SPORT 20	OP	CTRCN	FBG	TH	OB			7	10			6	4700	5400
20	6	SPORT 20	FB	RNBT	PLY	TH	OB			7	10			6	4800	5500
20	6	SPORT 20	FB	UTL	PLY	TH	OB			7	10			6	4000	4700
21		SUPER SPORT 21	OP	SF	FBG	TH	OB			7	6	1300		11	5050	5850
21		SUPER SPORT 21	FB	SF	FBG	TH	OB			7	6	1300		11	5050	5850
		1989 BOATS														
18	5	SPORT 18		SF	FBG	TH	OB			7		1050		5	3500	4100
20	6	SPORT 20		SF	FBG	TH	OB			7	10	1150		5	4350	5000

SHAMROCK

BLADEN COMPOSITES LLC
DIV OF PALMBER MARINE OF WA
BLADENBORO NC 28320 COAST GUARD MFG ID- OPA

See inside cover to adjust price for area

For more recent years, see the BUC Used Boat Price Guide, Volume 1

LOA FT	LOA IN	NAME AND/ OR MODEL	TOP/ RIG	BOAT TYPE	HULL MTL	HULL TP	ENGINE TP	ENGINE # HP	ENGINE MFG	BEAM FT	BEAM IN	WGT LBS	DRAFT FT	DRAFT IN	RETAIL LOW	RETAIL HIGH
		1996 BOATS														
20	2	OPEN 200	OP	OPFSH	FBG	SV	IB	275	INDM	8	6	3520	2		14600	16500
20	2	OPEN 200	OP	OPFSH	FBG	SV	IB	140D	YAN	8	6	3520	2		20000	22200
20	2	WALKAROUND 200	ST	CUD	FBG	SV	IB	275	INDM	8	6	3900	2		15600	17700
20	2	WALKAROUND 200	ST	CUD	FBG	SV	IB	140D	YAN	8	6	3900	2		21000	23400
22	3	CUDDY CABIN 220	ST	CTRCN	FBG	SV	IB	275	INDM	8	6	4000	2		18100	20100
22	3	CUDDY CABIN 220	ST	CTRCN	FBG	SV	IB	170D	YAN	8	6	4000	2		24100	26800
22	3	WALKAROUND 220	ST	CUD	FBG	SV	IB	275	INDM	8	6	4100	2		18400	20500
22	3	WALKAROUND 220	ST	CUD	FBG	SV	IB	170D	YAN	8	6	4100	2		24500	27200
25	9	MACKINAW 260	HT	SF	FBG	SV	IB	275	INDM	8		5300			26100	29000
25	9	MACKINAW 260	HT	SF	FBG	SV	IB	170D-210D		8		5300			31400	37900
26		CUDDY CABIN 260	ST	CUD	FBG	SV	IB	275	INDM	8	8	5600			27900	31000
26		CUDDY CABIN 260	ST	CUD	FBG	SV	IB	170D-210D		8	8	5600			33300	38500
26		EXPRESS 260	ST	CUD	FBG	SV	IB	275	INDM	8	8	5600			27700	30800
26		EXPRESS 260	ST	CUD	FBG	SV	IB	170D-210D		8	8	5600			33200	38300
26		EXPRESS 260	ST	CUD	FBG	SV	IB	315D	CUM	8	8	5600			39200	43500
		1995 BOATS														
20	2	OPEN FISH 200	OP	OPFSH	FBG	SV	IB	240	INDM	8	6	3520	2		13600	15500
20	2	OPEN FISH 200	OP	OPFSH	FBG	SV	IB	140D	YAN	8	6	3520	2		19200	21300
20	2	PREDATOR 200	ST	CUD	FBG	SV	IB	240	INDM	8	6	3800	2		14400	16300
20	2	PREDATOR 200	ST	CUD	FBG	SV	IB	140D	YAN	8	6	3800	2		19700	21900
20	2	WALKAROUND 200	ST	CUD	FBG	SV	IB	240	INDM	8	6	3900	2		14600	16600
20	2	WALKAROUND 200	ST	CUD	FBG	SV	IB	140D	YAN	8	6	3900	2		20000	22200
22	3	220XF	ST	CUD	FBG	SV	IB	285	INDM	8	6	4200	2		17400	19700
22	3	220XF	ST	CUD	FBG	SV	IB	170D	YAN	8	6	4200	2		23600	26200
22	3	OPEN FISH 220	OP	OPFSH	FBG	SV	IB	285	INDM	8	6	3850	2		16300	18500
22	3	OPEN FISH 220	OP	OPFSH	FBG	SV	IB	170D	YAN	8	6	3850	2		22500	25000
22	3	RENEGADE 220	ST	RNBT	FBG	SV	IB	285	INDM	8	6	4000	2		16900	19200
22	3	RENEGADE 220	ST	RNBT	FBG	SV	IB	170D	YAN	8	6	4000	2		23100	25600
22	3	STALKER 220	ST	CTRCN	FBG	SV	IB	285	INDM	8	6	4000	2		16800	19100
22	3	STALKER 220	ST	CTRCN	FBG	SV	IB	170D	YAN	8	6	4000	2		22900	25500
22	3	WALKAROUND 220	ST	CUD	FBG	SV	IB	285	INDM	8	6	4100	2		17100	19400
22	3	WALKAROUND 220	ST	CUD	FBG	SV	IB	170D	YAN	8	6	4100	2		23300	25800
25	9	MAKINAW 260	HT	SF	FBG	SV	IB	240	INDM	8		5300			24300	27000
25	9	MAKINAW 260	HT	SF	FBG	SV	IB	170D-210D		8		5300			29800	36000
26		260XF	ST	CUD	FBG	SV	IB	240	INDM	8	8	5600			25800	28700
26		260XF	ST	CUD	FBG	SV	IB	170D-210D		8	8	5600			31600	36500
		1994 BOATS														
19	6	C20	OP	OPFSH	FBG	SV	IB	200	INDM	8		2850	2		9600	10900
19	6	C20	OP	OPFSH	FBG	SV	IB	140D	YAN	8		2850	2		14100	16100
19	6	CP20	EPH	FDPH	FBG	SV	IB	200	INDM	8		2950	2		9750	11100
19	6	CP20	EPH	FDPH	FBG	SV	IB	140D	YAN	8		2950	2		14200	16200
19	6	CUDDY CABIN 196	ST	CUD	FBG	SV	IB	200	INDM	8		3100	2		10100	11400
19	6	CUDDY CABIN 196	ST	CUD	FBG	SV	IB	140D	YAN	8		3100	2		14500	16500
20	2	OPEN FISH 200	OP	OPFSH	FBG	SV	IB	240	INDM	8	6	3520	2		12900	14700
20	2	OPEN FISH 200	OP	OPFSH	FBG	SV	IB	140D	YAN	8	6	3520	2		18200	20300
20	2	PREDATOR 200	ST	CUD	FBG	SV	IB	240	INDM	8	6	3800	2		13600	15400
20	2	WALKAROUND 200	ST	CUD	FBG	SV	IB	240	INDM	8	6	3900	2		13800	15700
20	2	WALKAROUND 200	ST	CUD	FBG	SV	IB	140D	YAN	8	6	3900	2		19000	21100
22	3	220XF	ST	CUD	FBG	SV	IB	285	INDM	8	6	4200	2		16500	18700
22	3	220XF	ST	CUD	FBG	SV	IB	170D	YAN	8	6	4200	2		22400	24900
22	3	OPEN FISH 220	OP	OPFSH	FBG	SV	IB	285	INDM	8	6	3850	2		15400	17500
22	3	OPEN FISH 220	OP	OPFSH	FBG	SV	IB	170D	YAN	8	6	3850	2		21400	23800
22	3	RENEGADE 220	ST	RNBT	FBG	SV	IB	285	INDM	8	6	4000	2		16000	18200
22	3	RENEGADE 220	ST	RNBT	FBG	SV	IB	170D	YAN	8	6	4000	2		22000	24400
22	3	STALKER 220	ST	CTRCN	FBG	SV	IB	285	INDM	8	6	4000	2		15900	18000
22	3	STALKER 220	ST	CTRCN	FBG	SV	IB	170D	YAN	8	6	4000	2		21800	24200
22	3	WALKAROUND 220	ST	CUD	FBG	SV	IB	285	INDM	8	6	4100	2		16200	18400
22	3	WALKAROUND 220	ST	CUD	FBG	SV	IB	170D	YAN	8	6	4100	2		22100	24600
24		GRAND SLAM 24	MT	SF	FBG	DV	IB	T240	INDM	9	2	7500	2	6	31300	34800
24		GRAND SLAM 24	MT	SF	FBG	DV	IB	T170D	YAN	9	2	7500	2	6	43600	48500
25	9	COMM PH 260	EPH	FDPH	FBG	SV	IB	240	INDM	8		4850			21700	24100
25	9	COMM PH 260	EPH	FDPH	FBG	SV	IB	170D-210D		8		4850			26500	32600
25	9	MAKINAW 260	HT	SF	FBG	SV	IB	240	INDM	8		5300			23000	25500
25	9	MAKINAW 260	HT	SF	FBG	SV	IB	170D-210D		8		5300			28400	34200
25	9	OPEN FISH 260 SE	OP	CTRCN	FBG	SV	IB	240	INDM	8		4750			21400	23800
25	9	OPEN FISH 260 SE	OP	CTRCN	FBG	SV	IB	170D-210D		8		4750			26100	32200
25	9	PILOT HOUSE 260	EPH	FDPH	FBG	SV	IB	240	INDM	8		4850			21700	24100
25	9	PILOT HOUSE 260	EPH	FDPH	FBG	SV	IB	170D-210D		8		4850			26500	32600
26		260XC	ST	CUD	FBG	SV	IB	240	INDM	8	8	5600			24500	27200
26		260XC	ST	CUD	FBG	SV	IB	170D-210D		8	8	5600			30000	33800
26		260XF	ST	CUD	FBG	SV	IB	240	INDM	8	8	5600			24500	27200
26		260XF	ST	CUD	FBG	SV	IB	170D-210D		8	8	5600			30000	34700
31		GRAND SLAM 31	MT	SF	FBG	DV	IB	T330	INDM	11	4	10600	3	4	59200	65100
31		GRAND SLAM 31	MT	SF	FBG	DV	IB	T170D	YAN	11	4	10600	3	4	64700	71100
31		GRAND SLAM 31	MT	SF	FBG	DV	IB	T300D	CUM	11	4	11200	3	4	76000	83500
		1993 BOATS														
19	6	CUDDY CABIN 196	ST	CUD	FBG	SV	IB	200	INDM	8		3100	2		9550	10800
19	6	CUDDY CABIN 196	ST	CUD	FBG	SV	IB	140D	YAN	8		3100	2		13800	15700
19	6	OPEN FISH 196	OP	OPFSH	FBG	SV	IB	200	INDM	8		2850	2		9150	10400
19	6	OPEN FISH 196	OP	OPFSH	FBG	SV	IB	140D	YAN	8		2850	2		13500	15300

LOA FT	LOA IN	NAME AND/ OR MODEL	TOP/ RIG	BOAT TYPE	-HULL- MTL	-HULL- TP	TP	----ENGINE--- # HP	MFG	BEAM FT	BEAM IN	WGT LBS	DRAFT FT	DRAFT IN	RETAIL LOW	RETAIL HIGH
		1993 BOATS														
19	6	PILOT HOUSE 196	EPH	FDPH	FBG	SV	IB	200	INDM	8		2950	2		9300	10600
19	6	PILOT HOUSE 196	EPH	FDPH	FBG	SV	IB	140D	YAN	8		2950	2		13500	15400
20	2	OPEN FISH 200 SE	OP	OPFSH	FBG	SV	IB	240	INDM	8	6	3520	2		12200	13900
20	2	OPEN FISH 200 SE	OP	OPFSH	FBG	SV	IB	140D	YAN	8	6	3520	2		17000	19300
20	2	PREDATOR 200	ST	CUD	FBG	SV	IB	240	INDM	8	6	3800	2		12900	14600
20	2	RENEGADE 200	ST	RNBT	FBG	SV	IB	240	INDM	8	6	3650	2		12800	14500
20	2	RENEGADE 200	ST	RNBT	FBG	SV	IB	140D		8	6	3650	2		17600	19900
20	2	WARRIOR 200	ST	CUD	FBG	SV	IB	240	INDM	8	6	3900	2		13100	14900
20	2	WARRIOR 200	ST	CUD	FBG	SV	IB	140D	YAN	8	6	3900	2		18300	20400
22	3	OPEN FISH 220 SE	OP	OPFSH	FBG	SV	IB	285	INDM	8	6	3850	2		14600	16600
22	3	OPEN FISH 220 SE	OP	OPFSH	FBG	SV	IB	170D	YAN	8	6	3850	2		20400	22600
22	3	PREDATOR 220	ST	CUD	FBG	SV	IB	285	INDM	8	6	4200	2		15600	17700
22	3	PREDATOR 220	ST	CUD	FBG	SV	IB	170D	YAN	8	6	4200	2		21400	23700
22	3	RENEGADE 220	ST	RNBT	FBG	SV	IB	285	INDM	8	6	4000	2		15200	17200
22	3	RENEGADE 220	ST	RNBT	FBG	SV	IB	170D	YAN	8	6	4000	2		20900	23200
22	3	STALKER 220	ST	CTRCN	FBG	SV	IB	285	INDM	8	6	4000	2		15000	17100
22	3	STALKER 220	ST	CTRCN	FBG	SV	IB	170D	YAN	8	6	4000	2		20800	23100
22	3	WARRIOR 220	ST	CUD	FBG	SV	IB	285	INDM	8	6	4100	2		15300	17400
22	3	WARRIOR 220	ST	CUD	FBG	SV	IB	170D	YAN	8	6	4100	2		21100	23400
24		GRAND SLAM 24	MT	SF	FBG	DV	IB	T225	INDM	9	2	7500	2	6	29600	32900
24		GRAND SLAM 24	MT	SF	FBG	DV	IB	T170D	YAN	9	2	7500	2	6	41600	46200
25	9	COMM PH 260	EPH	FDPH	FBG	SV	IB	240	INDM	8		4850			20600	22800
25	9	COMM PH 260	EPH	FDPH	FBG	SV	IB	170D-210D		8		4850			25200	31100
25	9	CUDDY CABIN 260 LE	ST	CUD	FBG	SV	IB	240	INDM	8		5000			21000	23300
25	9	CUDDY CABIN 260 LE	ST	CUD	FBG	SV	IB	170D-210D		8		5000			25900	31300
25	9	MAKINAW 260	HT	SF	FBG	SV	IB	240	INDM	8		5300			21800	24200
25	9	MAKINAW 260	HT	SF	FBG	SV	IB	170D-210D		8		5300			27000	32600
25	9	OPEN FISH 260 SE	OP	CTRCN	FBG	SV	IB	240	INDM	8		4750			20300	22600
25	9	OPEN FISH 260 SE	OP	CTRCN	FBG	SV	IB	170D-210D		8		4750			24900	30700
25	9	PILOT HOUSE 260	EPH	FDPH	FBG	SV	IB	240	INDM	8		4850			20600	22800
25	9	PILOT HOUSE 260	EPH	FDPH	FBG	SV	IB	170D-210D		8		4850			25200	31100
25	9	PREDATOR 260	ST	SF	FBG	SV	IB	240	INDM	8		5100			21200	23600
25	9	PREDATOR 260	ST	SF	FBG	SV	IB	170D-210D		8		5100			26200	31700
31		GRAND SLAM 31	MT	SF	FBG	DV	IB	T330	INDM	11	4	10600	3	4	56100	61700
31		GRAND SLAM 31	MT	SF	FBG	DV	IB	T170D	YAN	11	4	10600	3	4	61600	67700
31		GRAND SLAM 31	MT	SF	FBG	DV	IB	T300D	CUM	11	4	11200	3	4	72400	79600
		1992 BOATS														
19	6	CUDDY CABIN 196	OP	CUD	FBG	SV	IB	185	CRUS	8		2950	1	10	9050	10300
19	6	CUDDY CABIN 196	OP	CUD	FBG	SV	IB	140D	YAN	8		3150	1	10	13300	15100
19	6	OPEN FISH 196	OP	OPFSH	FBG	SV	IB	185	CRUS	8		2500	1	10	8200	9400
19	6	OPEN FISH 196	OP	OPFSH	FBG	SV	IB	140D	YAN	8		2700	1	10	12500	14300
20	2	OPEN FISH 200SE	OP	OPFSH	FBG	SV	IB	215	FORD	8	6	3050	2		10600	12000
20	2	OPEN FISH 200SE	OP	OPFSH	FBG	SV	IB	100D-140D		8	6	3050	2		14400	17200
20	2	PREDATOR 200	OP	CUD	FBG	SV	IB	215	FORD	8	6	3550	2		11700	13300
20	2	PREDATOR 200	OP	CUD	FBG	SV	IB	140D	YAN	8	6	3550	2		16300	18500
20	2	RENEGADE LE KNOT 200	OP	RNBT	FBG	SV	IB	215	FORD	8	6	3240	2		11200	12700
20	2	RENEGADE LE KNOT 200	OP	RNBT	FBG	SV	IB	140D	YAN	8	6	3390	2		16100	18300
20	2	WARRIOR 200	OP	CUD	FBG	SV	IB	215	FORD	8	6	3610	2		11800	13400
20	2	WARRIOR 200	OP	CUD	FBG	SV	IB	140D	YAN	8	6	3610	2		16400	18600
22	3	OPEN 220 SE	OP	OPFSH	FBG	SV	IB	240	FORD	8	6	3660	2	2	13300	15100
22	3	OPEN 220 SE	OP	OPFSH	FBG	SV	IB	170D	YAN	8	6	3860	2	2	19400	21600
22	3	PREDATOR 220	OP	CUD	FBG	SV	IB	240	FORD	8	3	4060	2	2	14200	16100
22	3	PREDATOR 220	OP	CUD	FBG	SV	IB	170D	YAN	8	3	4260	2	2	20400	22600
22	3	RENEGADE 220LE	OP	RNBT	FBG	SV	IB	240	FORD	8	6	3850	2	2	13900	15800
22	3	RENEGADE 220LE	OP	RNBT	FBG	SV	IB	170D	YAN	8	6	4050	2	2	20100	22300
22	3	STALKER 220	OP	CUD	FBG	SV	IB	240	FORD	8	6	3860	2	2	13800	15700
22	3	STALKER 220	OP	CUD	FBG	SV	IB	170D	YAN	8	6	4060	2	2	20000	22200
22	3	WARRIOR 220	OP	CUD	FBG	SV	IB	240	FORD	8	6	3980	2	2	14100	16000
22	3	WARRIOR 220	OP	CUD	FBG	SV	IB	170D	YAN	8	6	4180	2	2	20300	22600
25	9	CUDDY CABIN 260LE	OP	CUD	FBG	SV	IB	240	FORD	8		5300	2		20300	22500
25	9	CUDDY CABIN 260LE	OP	CUD	FBG	SV	IB	170D-210D		8		5900	2		27700	32100
25	9	CUDDY CABIN 260LE	OP	CUD	FBG	SV	IB	300D	CUM	8		5900	2		31800	35300
25	9	MACKINAW 260	HT	CUD	FBG	SV	IB	240	FORD	8		5600	2		21500	23900
25	9	MACKINAW 260	HT	CUD	FBG	SV	IB	170D-210D		8		6200	2		29400	33700
25	9	MACKINAW 260	HT	CUD	FBG	SV	IB	300D	CUM	8		6200	2		33400	37100
25	9	OPEN 260SE	OP	OPFSH	FBG	SV	IB	240	FORD	8		4800	2		19100	21200
25	9	OPEN 260SE	OP	OPFSH	FBG	SV	IB	170D-210D		8		5400	2		25600	29600
25	9	OPEN 260SE	OP	OPFSH	FBG	SV	IB	300D	CUM	8		5400	2		29700	33000
25	9	PREDATOR 260	OP	CUD	FBG	SV	IB	240	FORD	8		5300	2		21300	23700
25	9	PREDATOR 260	OP	CUD	FBG	SV	IB	170D-210D		8		5900	2		28900	33400
25	9	PREDATOR 260	OP	CUD	FBG	SV	IB	300D	CUM	8		5900	2		33000	36600
25	9	STALKER	OP	CUD	FBG	SV	IB	240	FORD	8		5300	2		20500	22800
25	9	STALKER	OP	CUD	FBG	SV	IB	170D-210D		8		5900	2		27900	31700
25	9	STALKER	OP	CUD	FBG	SV	IB	300D	CUM	8		5900	2		32000	35500
31		GRANDSLAM 31	OP	SF	FBG	SV	IB	T330	CHEV	11	4	9250	3	4	43200	48000
31		GRANDSLAM 31	OP	SF	FBG	SV	IB	T170D-T210D		11	4	10600	3	4	58700	67300
31		GRANDSLAM 31	OP	SF	FBG	SV	IB	T300D	CUM	11	4	10600	3	4	67300	74000
		1991 BOATS														
19	6	CUDDY CABIN 196		CUD	FBG	SV	IB	185	CRUS	7	11	2950	1	10	8450	9700
19	6	CUDDY CABIN 196		CUD	FBG	SV	IB	140D	YAN	7	11	3150	1	10	12600	14400
19	6	OPEN FISH 196		CTRCN	FBG	SV	IB	185	CRUS	7	11	2500	1	10	7700	8850
19	6	OPEN FISH 196		CTRCN	FBG	SV	IB	140D	YAN	7	11	3250	1	10	12800	14600
19	6	PILOT HOUSE 196		UTL	FBG	SV	IB	185	CRUS	7	11	2900	1	10	8350	9600
19	6	PILOT HOUSE 196		UTL	FBG	SV	IB	140D	YAN	7	11	3420	1	10	13200	15000
20	2	CUDDY CABIN 200		CUD	FBG	SV	IB	215	INDM	8	6	3550	2		11000	12500
20	2	CUDDY CABIN 200		CUD	FBG	SV	IB	140D-170D		8	6	3750	2		16000	18800
20	2	OPEN SE 200		CTRCN	FBG	SV	IB	215	INDM	8	6	3050	2		10000	11400
20	2	OPEN SE 200		CTRCN	FBG	SV	IB	140D-170D		8	6	3250	2		14900	17500
20	2	RENEGADE 200		RNBT	FBG	SV	IB	215	INDM	8	6	3240	2		10600	12100
20	2	RENEGADE 200		RNBT	FBG	SV	IB	140D	YAN	8	6	3390	2		15400	17500
20	2	WARRIOR 200		CUD	FBG	SV	IB	215	INDM	8	6	3610	2		11200	12700
20	2	WARRIOR 200		CUD	FBG	SV	IB	140D-170D		8	6	3810	2		16100	18900
22	3	CUDDY CABIN 220		CUD	FBG	SV	IB	240	INDM	8	6	4060	2	2	13300	15100
22	3	CUDDY CABIN 220		CUD	FBG	SV	IB	170D	YAN	8	6	4260	2	2	19300	21500
22	3	OPEN SE 220		CTRCN	FBG	SV	IB	240	INDM	8	6	3660	2	2	12600	14300
22	3	OPEN SE 220		CTRCN	FBG	SV	IB	170D	YAN	8	6	3860	2	2	18800	20900
22	3	PREDATOR 220		CUD	FBG	SV	IB	240	INDM	8	6	4060	2	2	13800	15700
22	3	PREDATOR 220		CUD	FBG	SV	IB	170D	YAN	8	6	4260	2	2	19900	22100
22	3	RENEGADE 220		RNBT	FBG	SV	IB	240	INDM	8	6	3800	2	2	13000	14800
22	3	RENEGADE 220		RNBT	FBG	SV	IB	170D	YAN	8	6	4050	2	2	19200	21300
22	3	STALKER 220		CUD	FBG	SV	IB	240	INDM	8	6	3860	2	2	13100	14900
22	3	STALKER 220		CUD	FBG	SV	IB	170D	YAN	8	6	4060	2	2	19100	21200
22	3	WARRIOR 220		CUD	FBG	SV	IB	240	INDM	8	6	3980	2	2	13400	15200
22	3	WARRIOR 220		CUD	FBG	SV	IB	170D	YAN	8	6	4180	2	2	19400	21600
25	9	CUDDY LE 260		CBNCR	FBG	SV	IB	240	INDM	8		5300	2		22100	24600
25	9	CUDDY LE 260		CBNCR	FBG	SV	IB	210D	CUM	8		5900	2		33000	36600
25	9	CUDDY LE 260		CUD	FBG	SV	IB	300D	CUM	8		5900	2		30400	33800
25	9	MACKINAW 250		CBNCR	FBG	SV	IB	210D	CUM	8		6200	2		33900	37700
25	9	MACKINAW 260		CBNCR	FBG	SV	IB	240	INDM	8		5600	2		22900	25500
25	9	MACKINAW 260		CBNCR	FBG	SV	IB	300D	CUM	8		6200	2		36900	41000
25	9	OPEN SE 260		CTRCN	FBG	SV	IB	240	INDM	8		4800	2		18600	20700
25	9	OPEN SE 260		CTRCN	FBG	SV	IB	210D-300D		8		5400	2		26000	32300
25	9	PILOT HOUSE 260		UTL	FBG	SV	IB	240	INDM	8		4300	2		17100	19400
25	9	PILOT HOUSE 260		UTL	FBG	SV	IB	210D-300D		8		5500	2		26400	32600
25	9	PREDATOR 260		CUD	FBG	SV	IB	240	INDM	8		5300	2		20100	22400
25	9	PREDATOR 260		CUD	FBG	SV	IB	210D-300D		8		5900	2		28400	35000
25	9	STALKER 260		CUD	FBG	SV	IB	240	INDM	8		5300	2		19200	21300
25	9	STALKER 260		CUD	FBG	SV	IB	210D-300D		8		5900	2		27300	33800
		1990 BOATS														
17		170 OF LIMITED	OP	OPFSH	FBG	SV	IB	140		6	10	1800	1		4500	5200
20		200 CC	OP	CUD	FBG	SV	IB	215		7	11	3100	1	11	9250	10500
20		200 CC	OP	CUD	FBG	SV	IB	130D	VLVO	7	11	3100	1	11	12500	14200
20		200 OF	OP	CTRCN	FBG	SV	IB	215		7	11	2650	1	10	8300	9550
20		200 OF	OP	CTRCN	FBG	SV	IB	130D	VLVO	7	11	2650	1	10	11600	13200
20		200 PH	HT	UTL	FBG	SV	IB	215		7	11	2900	1	10	8850	10100
20		200 PH	HT	UTL	FBG	SV	IB	130D	VLVO	7	11	2900	1	10	12100	13700
20		200 WT	OP	RNBT	FBG	SV	IB	215		7	11	2800	1	10	8900	10100
20		200 WT	OP	RNBT	FBG	SV	IB	130D	VLVO	7	11	2800	1	10	12100	13800
20		PREDATOR 200	OP	CUD	FBG	SV	IB	215		7	11	3100	1	11	9250	10500
20		PREDATOR 200	OP	CUD	FBG	SV	IB	130D	VLVO	7	11	3100	1	11	12500	14200
20		REEF RUNNER	OP	SF	FBG	SV	IB	25		7	11	2650	1	11	7000	8050
20		REEF RUNNER	OP	SF	FBG	SV	IB	130D	VLVO	7	11	2650	1	11	11600	13200
20		STALKER 200	OP	CTRCN	FBG	SV	IB	215		7	11	2800	1	10	8600	9850
20		STALKER 200	OP	CTRCN	FBG	SV	IB	130D	VLVO	7	11	2800	1	10	11900	13500
22		CUDDY CABIN	OP	SF	FBG	SV	IB	240		8	6	3600	2		11700	13300
22		PREDATOR	OP	SF	FBG	SV	IB	240		8	6	3600	2		12400	14100
22		STALKER	OP	SF	FBG	SV	IB	240		8	6	3600	2		11100	12600
25	9	260 CC	OP	CUD	FBG	SV	IB	240		8		4400	2		16200	18400
25	9	260 CC LE	OP	CUD	FBG	SV	IB	240		8		4400	2		16800	19100
25	9	260 CPH	HT	PH	FBG	SV	IB	240		8		4300	2		16300	18500
25	9	260 CPH	HT	PH	FBG	SV	IB	210D	CUM	8		4300	2		21200	23500
25	9	260 OF	ST	CTRCN	FBG	SV	IB	240		8		4000	2		15600	17800
25	9	260 OF	ST	CTRCN	FBG	SV	IB	210D	CUM	8		4000	2		20300	22500
25	9	260 PH	HT	UTL	FBG	SV	IB	240		8		4300	2		16300	18500
25	9	260 PH	HT	UTL	FBG	SV	IB	210D	CUM	8		4300	2		21200	23600

CONTINUED ON NEXT PAGE

LOA FT	IN	NAME AND/ OR MODEL	TOP/ RIG	BOAT TYPE	-HULL- MTL	TP	----ENGINE--- TP	# HP	MFG	BEAM FT	IN	WGT LBS	DRAFT FT	IN	RETAIL LOW	RETAIL HIGH
		------------------- 1990 BOATS														
25	9	260 SE	OP	OPFSH	FBG	SV	IB	240		8		4800	2		17100	19400
25	9	260 SE	OP	OPFSH	FBG	SV	IB	210D	CUM	8		5400	2		24300	27000
25	9	MACKINAW 260	HT	CR	FBG	SV	IB	240		8		5600	2		19400	21600
25	9	MACKINAW 260	HT	CR	FBG	SV	IB	210D	CUM	8		6200	2		27700	30700
25	9	PREDATOR 260	HT	CUD	FBG	SV	IB	240		8		4400	2		16500	18700
25	9	PREDATOR 260	HT	CUD	FBG	SV	IB	210D	CUM	8		4400	2		21500	23900
25	9	REEF RUNNER	OP	SF	FBG	SV	IB	240		8		4000	2		15600	17800
25	9	REEF RUNNER	OP	SF	FBG	SV	IB	210D	CUM	8		4000	2		20200	22500
25	9	STALKER 260	OP	CTRCN	FBG	SV	IB	240		8		4400	2		16500	18700
25	9	STALKER 260	OP	CTRCN	FBG	SV	IB	210D	CUM	8		4400	2		21500	23900
31		GRANDSLAM 31	TT	SF	FBG	DV	IB	T330		11	4	10600	3	4	48100	52900
31		GRANDSLAM 31	TT	SF	FBG	DV	IB	T250D	CUM	11	4	10600	3	4	58300	64000
31	9	GRANDSLAM 31	TT	SF	FBG	DV	IB	300D	CUM	11	4	10600	3	4	54100	59400
		------------------- 1989 BOATS														
20		200 CC	OP	CUD	FBG	SV	IB	215		7	11	3100	1	11	8700	10000
20		200 CC	OP	CUD	FBG	SV	IB	130D	VLVO	7	11	3150	1	11	12000	13700
20		200 CW	OP	CTRCN	FBG	SV	IB	215		7	11	2650	1	10	8350	9600
20		200 CW	OP	CTRCN	FBG	SV	IB	130D	VLVO	7	11	2650	1	10	11100	12600
20		200 OF	OP	CTRCN	FBG	SV	IB	215		7	11	2650	1	10	7500	8600
20		200 OF	OP	CTRCN	FBG	SV	IB	130D	VLVO	7	11	2700	1	10	11200	12700
20		200 PH	HT	UTL	FBG	SV	IB	215		7	11	2900	1	10	8350	9600
20		200 PH	HT	UTL	FBG	SV	IB	130D	VLVO	7	11	2950	1	10	11600	13200
20		200 WT	OP	RNBT	FBG	SV	IB	215		7	11	2800	1	10	8350	9600
20		200 WT	OP	RNBT	FBG	SV	IB	130D	VLVO	7	11	2850	1	10	11700	13300
20		PREDATOR 200		CUD	FBG	SV	IB	215		7	11	3100	1	11	8700	10000
20		PREDATOR 200		CUD	FBG	SV	IB	130D	VLVO	7	11	3150	1	11	12000	13700
20		REEF RUNNER	OP	SF	FBG	SV	IB	215		7	11	2650	1	11	7900	9100
20		REEF RUNNER	OP	SF	FBG	SV	IB	D	CUM	7	11	2700	1	11	**	**
20		STALKER 200	OP	CTRCN	FBG	SV	IB	215		7	11	2800	1	10	8150	9400
20		STALKER 200	OP	CTRCN	FBG	SV	IB	130D	VLVO	7	11	2850	1	10	11500	13000
22		CUDDY CABIN	OP	SF	FBG	SV	IB	240		8	6	3600	2		11200	12700
22		CUDDY CABIN	OP	SF	FBG	SV	IB	D	CUM	8	6	4200	2		**	**
22		PREDATOR	OP	SF	FBG	SV	IB	240		8	6	3600	2		11900	13500
22		PREDATOR	OP	SF	FBG	SV	IB	D	CUM	8	6	4200	2		**	**
22		STALKER	OP	SF	FBG	SV	IB	240		8	6	3600	2		10500	11900
22		STALKER	OP	SF	FBG	SV	IB	D	CUM	8	6	4200	2		**	**
25	9	260 CC	OP	CUD	FBG	SV	IB	240		8		4400	2		15700	17800
25	9	260 CPH	HT	PH	FBG	SV	IB	240		8		4300	2		15500	17600
25	9	260 CPH	HT	PH	FBG	SV	IB	210D	CUM	8		4900	2		22100	24600
25	9	260 HT	HT	CUD	FBG	SV	IB	240		8		4400	2		15700	17800
25	9	260 HT	HT	CUD	FBG	SV	IB	210D	CUM	8		5000	2		22500	25000
25	9	260 OF	ST	CTRCN	FBG	SV	IB	240		8		4000	2		14900	16900
25	9	260 OF	ST	CTRCN	FBG	SV	IB	210D	CUM	8		4600	2		21200	23600
25	9	260 PH	HT	UTL	FBG	SV	IB	240		8		4300	2		15500	17600
25	9	260 PH	HT	UTL	FBG	SV	IB	210D	CUM	8		4900	2		22100	24600
25	9	PREDATOR 260		CUD	FBG	SV	IB	240		8		4400	2		15700	17800
25	9	PREDATOR 260		CUD	FBG	SV	IB	210D	CUM	8		5000	2		22500	25000
25	9	REEF RUNNER	OP	SF	FBG	SV	IB	240		8		4000	2		14900	16900
25	9	REEF RUNNER	OP	SF	FBG	SV	IB	210D	CUM	8		4600	2		21200	23500
25	9	STALKER 260	OP	CTRCN	FBG	SV	IB	240		8		4400	2		15700	17800
25	9	STALKER 260	OP	CTRCN	FBG	SV	IB	210D	CUM	8		5000	2		22500	25000
31		GRANDSLAM 31	TT	SF	FBG	DV	IB	T330		11	4	10600	3	4	46100	50600
31		GRANDSLAM 31	TT	SF	FBG	DV	IB	T250D	CUM	11	4	11800	3	4	58900	64700
		------------------- 1988 BOATS														
17		170 OF	OP	CTRCN	FBG	SV	IB	140	PCM	6	10	1700	1	1	3900	4550
20		200 CC	OP	CUD	FBG	SV	IB	220	PCM	7	11	3100	1	11	8300	9550
20		200 CC	OP	CUD	FBG	SV	IB	130D	VLVO	7	11	3150	1	11	11500	13100
20		200 CW	OP	CTRCN	FBG	SV	IB	200-220		7	11	2650	1	10	7950	9150
20		200 CW	OP	CTRCN	FBG	SV	IB	130D	VLVO	7	11	2650	1	10	10600	12100
20		200 OF	OP	CTRCN	FBG	SV	IB	200-220		7	11	2650	1	10	7100	8200
20		200 OF	OP	CTRCN	FBG	SV	IB	130D	VLVO	7	11	2700	1	10	10700	12200
20		200 PH	HT	UTL	FBG	SV	IB	200-220		7	11	2900	1	10	7950	9150
20		200 PH	HT	UTL	FBG	SV	IB	130D	VLVO	7	11	2950	1	10	11100	12700
20		200 WT	OP	RNBT	FBG	SV	IB	220	PCM	7	11	2800	1	10	8000	9150
20		200 WT	OP	RNBT	FBG	SV	IB	130D	VLVO	7	11	2850	1	10	11200	12700
20		PREDATOR 200		CUD	FBG	SV	IB	220	PCM	7	11	3100	1	11	8300	9550
20		PREDATOR 200		CUD	FBG	SV	IB	130D	VLVO	7	11	3150	1	11	11500	13100
20		STALKER 200	OP	CTRCN	FBG		IB	200-220		7	11	2800	1	10	7750	8950
20		STALKER 200	OP	CTRCN	FBG		IB	130D	VLVO	7	11	2850	1	10	11000	12500
25	9	260 CC	OP	CUD	FBG	SV	IB	250	PCM	8		4400	2		15000	17100
25	9	260 CPH	HT	PH	FBG	SV	IB	250	PCM	8		4300	2		14800	16900
25	9	260 CPH	HT	PH	FBG	SV	IB	210D	CUM	8		4900	2		21200	23500
25	9	260 HT	HT	CUD	FBG	SV	IB	250	PCM	8		4400	2		15000	17100
25	9	260 HT	HT	CUD	FBG	SV	IB	210D	CUM	8		5000	2		21500	23900
25	9	260 OF	ST	CTRCN	FBG	SV	IB	250	PCM	8		4000	2		14300	16200
25	9	260 OF	ST	CTRCN	FBG	SV	IB	210D	CUM	8		4600	2		20300	22500
25	9	260 PH	HT	UTL	FBG	SV	IB	250	PCM	8		4300	2		14900	16900
25	9	260 PH	HT	UTL	FBG	SV	IB	210D	CUM	8		4900	2		21200	23600
25	9	260 SF	TT	SF	FBG	SV	IB	250	PCM	8		4900	2		16000	18200
25	9	260 SF	TT	SF	FBG	SV	IB	210D	CUM	8		5500	2		23100	25600
25	9	PREDATOR 260		CUD	FBG	SV	IB	250	PCM	8		4400	2		15000	17100
25	9	PREDATOR 260		CUD	FBG	SV	IB	210D	CUM	8		5000	2		21500	23900
25	9	STALKER 260	OP	CTRCN	FBG		IB	250	PCM	8		4400	2		15000	17100
25	9	STALKER 260	OP	CTRCN	FBG		IB	210D	CUM	8		5000	2		21500	23900
31		GRANDSLAM 31	TT	SF	FBG		IB	T330	PCM	11	4	10600	3	4	43400	48200
31		GRANDSLAM 31	TT	SF	FBG		IB	T250D	CUM	11	4	11800	3	4	56400	62000
		------------------- 1987 BOATS														
17		170 OF	OP	CTRCN	FBG	SV	IB	140	PCM	6	10	1700	1	1	3750	4350
20		200 CC	OP	CUD	FBG	SV	IB	220	PCM	7	11	3100	1	11	7900	9100
20		200 CC	OP	CUD	FBG	SV	IB	110D	VLVO	7	11	3150	1	11	10800	12200
20		200 CW	OP	CTRCN	FBG	SV	IB	200-220		7	11	2650	1	10	7550	8750
20		200 CW	OP	CTRCN	FBG	SV	IB	110D	VLVO	7	11	2650	1	10	9950	11300
20		200 OF	OP	CTRCN	FBG	SV	IB	200-220		7	11	2650	1	10	6800	7800
20		200 OF	OP	CTRCN	FBG	SV	IB	110D	VLVO	7	11	2700	1	10	10000	11400
20		200 PH	HT	UTL	FBG	SV	IB	200-220		7	11	2900	1	10	7550	8700
20		200 PH	HT	UTL	FBG	SV	IB	110D	VLVO	7	11	2950	1	10	10400	11900
20		200 WT	OP	RNBT	FBG	SV	IB	220	PCM	7	11	2800	1	10	7600	8750
20		200 WT	OP	RNBT	FBG	SV	IB	110D	VLVO	7	11	2850	1	10	10500	11900
20		STALKER 200	OP	CTRCN	FBG		IB	200-220		7	11	2800	1	10	7400	8550
20		STALKER 200	OP	CTRCN	FBG		IB	110D	VLVO	7	11	2850	1	10	10300	11700
25	9	260 CC	OP	CUD	FBG	SV	IB	250	PCM	8		4400	2		14300	16300
25	9	260 CPH	HT	PH	FBG	SV	IB	250	PCM	8		4300	2		14200	16100
25	9	260 CPH	HT	PH	FBG	SV	IB	210D	CUM	8		4900	2		20300	22500
25	9	260 HT	HT	CUD	FBG	SV	IB	250	PCM	8		4400	2		14300	16300
25	9	260 HT	HT	CUD	FBG	SV	IB	210D	CUM	8		5000	2		20600	22900
25	9	260 OF	ST	CTRCN	FBG	SV	IB	250	PCM	8		4000	2		13600	15500
25	9	260 OF	ST	CTRCN	FBG	SV	IB	210D	CUM	8		4600	2		19400	21600
25	9	260 PH	HT	UTL	FBG	SV	IB	250	PCM	8		4300	2		14200	16100
25	9	260 PH	HT	UTL	FBG	SV	IB	210D	CUM	8		4900	2		20300	22600
25	9	260 SF	TT	SF	FBG	SV	IB	250	PCM	8		4900	2		15300	17400
25	9	260 SF	TT	SF	FBG	SV	IB	210D	CUM	8		5500	2		22100	24500
25	9	STALKER 260	OP	CTRCN	FBG		IB	250	PCM	8		4400	2		14300	16300
25	9	STALKER 260	OP	CTRCN	FBG		IB	210D	CUM	8		5000	2		20600	22900
31		GRANDSLAM 31	TT	SF	FBG		IB	T330	PCM	11	4	10600	3	4	41400	46000
31		GRANDSLAM 31	TT	SF	FBG		IB	T210D-T250D		11	4	11800	3	4	52000	59400
		------------------- 1986 BOATS														
17		170 OF	OP	CTRCN	FBG	SV	IB	130	PCM	6	10	1700	1	1	3500	4050
20		200 CC	OP	CUD	FBG	SV	IB	220	PCM	7	11	3100	1	11	7550	8650
20		200 CC	OP	CUD	FBG	SV	IB	110D	VLVO	7	11	3150	1	11	10300	11700
20		200 CW	OP	CTRCN	FBG	SV	IB	200-220		7	11	2650	1	10	7200	8350
20		200 CW	OP	CTRCN	FBG	SV	IB	110D	VLVO	7	11	2650	1	10	9500	10800
20		200 OF	OP	CTRCN	FBG	SV	IB	200-220		7	11	2650	1	10	6450	7450
20		200 OF	OP	CTRCN	FBG	SV	IB	110D	VLVO	7	11	2700	1	10	9600	10900
20		200 PH	HT	UTL	FBG	SV	IB	200-220		7	11	2900	1	10	7200	8300
20		200 PH	HT	UTL	FBG	SV	IB	110D	VLVO	7	11	2950	1	10	10000	11400
20		200 WT	OP	RNBT	FBG	SV	IB	220	PCM	7	11	2800	1	10	7250	8350
20		200 WT	OP	RNBT	FBG	SV	IB	110D	VLVO	7	11	2850	1	10	10000	11400
25	9	259 CC	OP	CUD	FBG	SV	IB	240D	PERK	8		5000	2		21300	23700
25	9	260 CC	OP	CUD	FBG	SV	IB	250	PCM	8		4400	2		13700	15600
25	9	260 CPH	HT	PH	FBG	SV	IB	250	PCM	8		4300	2		13500	15300
25	9	260 CPH	HT	PH	FBG	SV	IB	210D	CUM	8		4900	2		19400	21600
25	9	260 HT	HT	CUD	FBG	SV	IB	250	PCM	8		4400	2		13700	15600
25	9	260 HT	HT	CUD	FBG	SV	IB	210D	CUM	8		5000	2		19700	21900
25	9	260 OF	ST	CTRCN	FBG	SV	IB	250	PCM	8		4000	2		13000	14800
25	9	260 OF	ST	CTRCN	FBG	SV	IB	210D	CUM	8		4600	2		18800	20900
25	9	260 PH	HT	UTL	FBG	SV	IB	250	PCM	8		4300	2		13500	15400
25	9	260 PH	HT	UTL	FBG	SV	IB	210D	CUM	8		4900	2		19500	21600
25	9	260 SF	TT	SF	FBG	SV	IB	250	PCM	8		4900	2		14600	16600
25	9	260 SF	TT	SF	FBG	SV	IB	210D-240D		8		5500	2		21200	25200
		------------------- 1985 BOATS														
17		170 OF	OP	CTRCN	FBG	SV	IB	130	PCM	6	10	1700	1	1	3350	3850
20		200 CC	OP	CUD	FBG	SV	IB	220	PCM	7	11	3100	1	11	7200	8300
20		200 CC	OP	CUD	FBG	SV	IB	110D	VLVO	7	11	3150	1	11	9900	11300
20		200 CW	OP	CTRCN	FBG	SV	IB	200-220		7	11	2650	1	10	6900	7950
20		200 CW	OP	CTRCN	FBG	SV	IB	110D	VLVO	7	11	2650	1	10	9200	10400
20		200 OF	OP	CTRCN	FBG	SV	IB	200-220		7	11	2650	1	10	6200	7150
20		200 OF	OP	CTRCN	FBG	SV	IB	110D	VLVO	7	11	2700	1	10	9250	10500

CONTINUED ON NEXT PAGE

SHAMROCK (continued)

LOA FT IN	NAME AND/ OR MODEL	TOP/ RIG	BOAT TYPE	HULL MTL TP	ENGINE TP # HP MFG	BEAM FT IN	WGT LBS	DRAFT FT IN	RETAIL LOW	RETAIL HIGH
1985 BOATS										
20	200 PH	HT	UTL	FBG SV	IB 200-220	7 11	2900	1 10	6900	7950
20	200 PH	HT	UTL	FBG SV	IB 110D VLVO	7 11	2950	1 10	9600	10900
20	200 WT	OP	RNBT	FBG SV	IB 220 PCM	7 11	2800	1 10	6950	7950
20	200 WT	OP	RNBT	FBG SV	IB 110D VLVO	7 11	2850	1 10	9600	10900
25 9	259 CC	OP	CUD	FBG SV	IB 250 PCM	8	4400	2	13100	14900
25 9	259 CC	OP	CUD	FBG SV	IB 200D-240D	8	5000	2	19400	22700
25 9	259 CC	HT	CUD	FBG SV	IB 250 PCM	8	4400	2	13100	14900
25 9	259 CC	HT	CUD	FBG SV	IB 200D-240D	8	5000	2	19400	22700
25 9	259 CPH	HT	PH	FBG SV	IB 250-330	8	4300	2	12900	15500
25 9	259 CPH	HT	PH	FBG SV	IB 200D-240D	8	4900	2	19100	22400
25 9	259 OF	ST	CTRCN	FBG SV	IB 250 PCM	8	4000	2	12400	14100
25 9	259 OF	ST	CTRCN	FBG SV	IB 200D-240D	8	4600	2	18500	21600
25 9	259 PH	HT	UTL	FBG SV	IB 250 PCM	8	4300	2	12900	14700
25 9	259 PH	HT	UTL	FBG SV	IB 200D-240D	8	4900	2	19100	22400
25 9	259 SF	TT	SF	FBG SV	IB 250 PCM	8	4900	2	13900	15800
25 9	259 SF	TT	SF	FBG SV	IB 200D-240D	8	5500	2	20700	24200
1984 BOATS										
20	CENTER CONSOLE	OP	CTRCN	FBG SV	IB 200-220	7 11	2400	1 10	5950	6850
20	CENTER CONSOLE	OP	CTRCN	FBG SV	IB 85D PERK	7 11	2400	1 10	9100	10300
20	CON-WALK	OP	OPFSH	FBG SV	IB 185-220	7 11	2650	1 10	6250	7200
20	CON-WALK	OP	OPFSH	FBG SV	IB 85D PERK	7 11	2650	1 10	9400	10700
20	CUDDY CABIN	OP	CUD	FBG SV	IB 220 PCM	7 11	3000	1 11	6750	7750
20	CUDDY CABIN	OP	CUD	FBG SV	IB 85D PERK	7 11	3000	1 11	9900	11300
20	PILOT-HOUSE	HT	UTL	FBG SV	IB 200 PCM	7 11	2650	1 10	6250	7200
20	PILOT-HOUSE	HT	UTL	FBG SV	IB 85D PERK	7 11	2650	1 10	9400	10700
20	WALK-THRU	OP	OPFSH	FBG SV	IB 220 PCM	7 11	2750	1 10	6400	7350
20	WALK-THRU	OP	OPFSH	FBG SV	IB 85D PERK	7 11	2750	1 10	9550	10800
25 9	CENTER CONSOLE	OP	CTRCN	FBG SV	IB 250 PCM	8	4000	2	11900	13500
25 9	CENTER CONSOLE	OP	CTRCN	FBG SV	IB 200D PERK	8	4000	2	15900	18100
25 9	CUDDY CABIN	OP	CUD	FBG SV	IB 250 PCM	8	4400	2	12500	14200
25 9	CUDDY CABIN	OP	CUD	FBG SV	IB 200D PCM	8	4400	2	16900	19200
25 9	PILOT-HOUSE	HT	UTL	FBG SV	IB 250 PCM	8	4300	2	12300	14200
25 9	PILOT-HOUSE	HT	UTL	FBG SV	IB 200D PERK	8	4300	2	16600	18900

....For earlier years, see the BUC Used Boat Price Guide, Volume 3

SHEARWATER BOATWORKS LLC

WOODBINE NJ 08270   COAST GUARD MFG ID- SHR See inside cover to adjust price for area
FORMERLY SHEARWATER YACHTS

LOA FT IN	NAME AND/ OR MODEL	TOP/ RIG	BOAT TYPE	HULL MTL TP	ENGINE TP # HP MFG	BEAM FT IN	WGT LBS	DRAFT FT IN	RETAIL LOW	RETAIL HIGH
1994 BOATS										
35 7	SHEARWATER 33	OP	SF	FBG SV	IB 300D CUM	12	14500	2 8	115000	126000
35 7	SHEARWATER 33	OP	SF	FBG SV	IB T350D CAT	12	14500	2 8	139000	153000
35 7	SHEARWATER 33	OP	SF	FBG SV	IB T400D CUM	12	14500	2 8	141000	154500
35 7	SHEARWATER 33 BRKT	OP	SF	FBG SV	OB	12	14500	2 8	112000	123000

SHIELDS AERO MARINE INC

FOUNTAIN VALLEY CA 9270 COAST GUARD MFG ID- AHH See inside cover to adjust price for area

LOA FT IN	NAME AND/ OR MODEL	TOP/ RIG	BOAT TYPE	HULL MTL TP	ENGINE TP # HP MFG	BEAM FT IN	WGT LBS	DRAFT FT IN	RETAIL LOW	RETAIL HIGH
1986 BOATS										
27	AERO FISHER	ST	OFF	FBG DV	IO 260 MRCR	8	4100		9900	11300
27	AERO RACER	ST	RACE	FBG DV	IO T300 MRCR	8	5200		13000	14700
27	AERO SKIER	ST	OFF	FBG DV	IO 260 MRCR	8	4100		10200	11600
40	AERO SPORTCRUISER	ST	OFF	FBG CT	IO T330 MRCR	12	9200		33500	37300
40	AERO TIGER CAT	ST	RACE	FBG CT	IO T700 MRCR	12	9800		52100	57300
40	AERO-CAT	ST	RACE	FBG CT	IO R700 MRCR	12	10800		65600	72100
45	AERO RACER	ST	RACE	FBG CT	IO T600 MRCR	12	9000		67700	74400
45	AERO SPORTCRUISER	ST	SPTCR	FBG CT	IO T440 MRCR	12	12000		60300	66300
45	AERO SUPERBOAT	ST	RACE	FBG CT	IO R700 MRCR	12	11700		85000	93400
45	AERO-CAT	ST	RACE	FBG CT	IO T700 MRCR	12	10775		69200	76000
1985 BOATS										
27	AERO FISHER	ST	OFF	FBG DV	IO 260 MRCR	8	4100		9500	10800
27	AERO RACER	ST	OFF	FBG DV	IO T300 MRCR	8	5200		12400	14100
27	AERO SKIER	ST	OFF	FBG DV	IO 260 MRCR	8	4100		9800	11100
40	AERO RACER	ST	RACE	FBG CT	IO T700 MRCR	12	9800		50000	55000
40	AERO SPORTCRUISER	ST	OFF	FBG CT	IO T330 MRCR	12	9200		32200	35800
40	AERO-CAT	ST	RACE	FBG CT	IO R700 MRCR	12	10800		62900	69200
45	AERO RACER	ST	RACE	FBG CT	IO T600 MRCR	12	9000		65000	71500
45	AERO SPORTCRUISER	ST	SPTCR	FBG CT	IO T440 MRCR	12	12000		57600	63300
45	AERO SUPERBOAT	ST	RACE	FBG CT	IO R700 MRCR	12	11700		81500	89600
45	AERO-CAT	ST	RACE	FBG CT	IO T700 MRCR	12	10775		66400	73000

SHOALWATER MARINE INC

BOATS BY SHOALWATER
PT O'CONNOR TX 77982   COAST GUARD MFG ID- SHQ See inside cover to adjust price for area

LOA FT IN	NAME AND/ OR MODEL	TOP/ RIG	BOAT TYPE	HULL MTL TP	ENGINE TP	BEAM FT IN	WGT LBS	DRAFT FT IN	RETAIL LOW	RETAIL HIGH
1995 BOATS										
17 5	FLATS 18 TS TUNNEL	OP	CTRCN	FBG FL	OB	8	750	6	3600	4200
18 8	STEALTH 19 TV TUNNEL	OP	CTRCN	FBG SV	OB	8	900	8	4500	5150
20 7	LAGUNA 20 SL TUNNEL	OP	CTRCN	FBG SV	OB	8 6	1250	7	6100	7000
21 2	SPORTSMAN CLASSIC 21	OP	CTRCN	FBG SV	OB	8	1350	8	6600	7600
21 2	SPTMN 21 SK TUNNEL	OP	CTRCN	FBG SV	OB	8	1400	8	6800	7850
21 8	LEGEND 22 SV TUNNEL	OP	CTRCN	FBG SV	OB	8 6	1400	7	6900	7900
1994 BOATS										
17 5	FLATS 18 TS TUNNEL	OP	CTRCN	FBG FL	OB	8	750	6	3450	4000
18 8	STEALTH 19 TV TUNNEL	OP	CTRCN	FBG SV	OB	8	900	8	4250	4950
21 2	SPORTSMAN CLASSIC 21	OP	CTRCN	FBG SV	OB	8	1350	8	6300	7250
21 2	SPTMN 21 SK TUNNEL	OP	CTRCN	FBG SV	OB	8	1400	8	6500	7450
21 8	LEGEND 22 SV TUNNEL	OP	CTRCN	FBG SV	OB	8 6	1400	7	6600	7550
1993 BOATS										
17 5	180 TS TUNNEL	OP	CTRCN	FBG FL	OB	8	750	6	3300	3850
18 8	190 TV TUNNEL	OP	CTRCN	FBG SV	OB	8	900	8	4050	4700
21 2	210 SK TUNNEL	OP	CTRCN	FBG SV	OB	8	1350	6	6900	7900
21 8	220 SV TUNNEL	OP	CTRCN	FBG SV	OB	8 6	1350	7	6100	7000
1992 BOATS										
17 5	1700 TUNNEL	OP	CTRCN	FBG FL	OB	8	800	7	3350	3900
18 8	190TV TUNNEL	OP	CTRCN	FBG SV	OB	8	950	7	4050	4700
21 2	21K	OP	CTRCN	FBG SV	OB	8	1520	8	6300	7250
21 8	22V TUNNEL	OP	CTRCN	FBG SV	OB	8 6	1520	9	6450	7450
1991 BOATS										
17 5	1700 TUNNEL	OP	JON	FBG FL	OB	7 10	675	5	2300	2650
17 5	1750 TUNNEL	OP	JON	FBG FL	OB	7 10	875	5	2900	3400
18 2	18K	OP	CTRCN	FBG SV	OB	8	1025	8	4050	4700
18 2	18T TUNNEL	OP	CTRCN	FBG SV	OB	8	1025	8	4150	4800
21 2	21K	OP	CTRCN	FBG SV	OB	8	1250	8	5150	5900
21 2	21T TUNNEL	OP	CTRCN	FBG SV	OB	8	1250	8	5250	6000
21 8	22V TUNNEL	OP	CTRCN	F/S SV	OB	8 6	1025	9	4400	5050
1990 BOATS										
17 5	1700 TUNNEL	OP	JON	FBG FL	OB	7 10	675	5	2200	2600
17 5	1750 TUNNEL	OP	JON	FBG FL	OB	7 10	875	5	2800	3250
18 2	18K	OP	CTRCN	FBG SV	OB	8	1025	8	3900	4500
18 2	18T TUNNEL	OP	CTRCN	FBG SV	OB	8	1025	8	3950	4600
19 2	19SR	OP	CTRCN	FBG SV	OB	8 3	1050	1 2	4150	4800
20 2	STEATH 20	OP	CTRCN	FBG FL	OB	8 2	800	8	3300	3800
21 2	21K (NO) TUNNEL	OP	CTRCN	FBG SV	OB	8	1250	8	4950	5700
21 2	21T TUNNEL	OP	CTRCN	FBG SV	OB	8	1250	8	5050	5800
21 8	22V TUNNEL	OP	CTRCN	FBG SV	OB	8 6	1025	9	4200	4900
21 9	22SR	OP	CTRCN	FBG SV	OB	8 6	1700	1 5	6600	7550
1989 BOATS										
17 5	SW 17T		CTRCN	FBG FL	OB	8	900	6	3300	3850
17 5	SW 17T		CTRCN	FBG TH	OB	8	900	6	3300	3850
17 6	SW 18J		JON	FBG FL	OB	8	550	5	1700	2000
17 6	SW 18J		JON	FBG TH	OB	8	550	5	1700	2000
18	SW 18V		CTRCN	FBG FL	OB	7 8	850	6	3200	3700
18	SW 18V		CTRCN	FBG TH	OB	7 8	850	6	3200	3700
20 1	SW 20V		CTRCN	FBG FL	OB	7 8	950	6	3650	4250
20 1	SW 20V		CTRCN	FBG TH	OB	7 8	950	6	3650	4250
20 4	SW 20L		CTRCN	FBG FL	OB	8	1050	6	4050	4700
20 4	SW 20L		CTRCN	FBG TH	OB	8	1050	6	4050	4700
21 2	SW 22V		CTRCN	FBG FL	OB	8 6	1025	9	4000	4650
21 2	SW 22V		CTRCN	FBG TH	OB	8 6	1025	9	4000	4650
24 1	SW 24W		CTRCN	FBG FL	OB	8 6	1175	6	4850	5600
24 1	SW 24W		CTRCN	FBG TH	OB	8 6	1175	6	4850	5550
24 11	SW 25CCV		CUD	FBG FL	OB	8 6	1800	1	8650	9950
24 11	SW 25CCV		CUD	FBG TH	OB	8 6	1800	1	8650	9950
24 11	SW 25V		CTRCN	FBG FL	OB	8 6	1800	1	8600	9900
24 11	SW 25V		CTRCN	FBG TH	OB	8 6	1800	1	8600	9900
1988 BOATS										
17 5	SW 17V	OP	FSH	F/S FL	OB	8 8	900	6	3150	3700
20 1	SW 20V	OP	FSH	F/S DV	OB	7 8	950	6	3550	4100
20 4	SW 20L	OP	FSH	F/S FL	OB	8	1050	6	3900	4500

SIGNATURE GROUP INC

PORTSMOUTH RI 02871 — See inside cover to adjust price for area

ALSO SAROCA

LOA FT IN	NAME AND/ OR MODEL	TOP/ RIG	BOAT TYPE	-HULL- MTL	TP	ENGINE TP	# HP	MFG	BEAM FT IN	WGT LBS	DRAFT FT IN	RETAIL LOW	RETAIL HIGH
	1988 BOATS												
16 6	SAROCA		MS				2		4 6		2 9	1550	1850

SILHOUETTE YACHTS INC

MIAMI FL 33125 — See inside cover to adjust price for area

LOA FT IN	NAME AND/ OR MODEL	TOP/ RIG	BOAT TYPE	-HULL- MTL	TP	ENGINE TP	# HP	MFG	BEAM FT IN	WGT LBS	DRAFT FT IN	RETAIL LOW	RETAIL HIGH
	1989 BOATS												
41 10	SILHOUETTE SEADCK 42		MY	F/S	DV	IB	T375D	CAT	14 6	28000	3 2	151000	166000
44	SILHOUETTE SPORT CNV		MY	F/S	DV	IB	T375D	CAT	14 6	29000	3 2	149500	164500
	1988 BOATS												
41 10	SEA DECK 42		CR	FBG	DV	IB	T375D	CAT	14 6	28000	3 2	145000	159500
44	SPORT CONVERTIBLE 44		CR	FBG	DV	IB	T375D	CAT	14 6	29000	3 2	145000	159500

SILVER KING BOAT CORP

ST PETERSBURG FL 33743- COAST GUARD MFG ID- SNX See inside cover to adjust price for area

LOA FT IN	NAME AND/ OR MODEL	TOP/ RIG	BOAT TYPE	-HULL- MTL	TP	ENGINE TP	# HP	MFG	BEAM FT IN	WGT LBS	DRAFT FT IN	RETAIL LOW	RETAIL HIGH
	1995 BOATS												
16 3	SIGNATURE SERIES 16	OP	FSH	FBG	DV	OB			7 2	975	8	6200	7100
16 4	SILVERFLASH	OP	FSH	FBG	DV	OB			7 2	875	8	5600	6450
18 8	GRANDEMASTER 18	OP	FSH	FBG	DV	OB			7 7	1150	10	7700	8850
	1994 BOATS												
16 3	SIGNATURE SERIES 16	OP	FSH	FBG	DV	OB			7 2	975	8	5900	6750
16 4	SILVERFLASH	OP	FSH	FBG	DV	OB			7 2	875	8	5350	6150
18 8	GRANDEMASTER 18	OP	FSH	FBG	DV	OB			7 7	1150	10	7300	8400
	1993 BOATS												
16 3	SIGNATURE SERIES 16	OP	FSH	FBG	DV	OB			7 2	975	8	5600	6450
16 4	SILVERFLASH	OP	FSH	FBG	DV	OB			7 2	875	8	5100	5850
18 8	GRANDEMASTER 18	OP	FSH	FBG	DV	OB			7 7	1150	10	6950	8000
	1992 BOATS												
16 5	SILVER FLASH 16	OP	FSH	FBG	DV	OB			7 2	900	8	5000	5750
16 5	SILVER KING 16	OP	FSH	FBG	DV	OB			7 2	850	8	4750	5450
18 7	GRANDE MASTER	OP	FSH	FBG	DV	OB			7 6	1000	9	5900	6800
	1991 BOATS												
16 5	SILVER KING 16	OP	FSH	FBG	DV	OB			7 2	850	8	4550	5200
	1990 BOATS												
16 5	SILVER KING 16	OP	FSH	FBG	DV	OB			7 2	850	8	4350	5000
	1989 BOATS												
16 5	SILVER KING 16	OP	FSH	FBG		OB			7 2	750	8	3700	4300

SILVERTON MARINE CORP

MILLVILLE NJ 08332 — COAST GUARD MFG ID- STN See inside cover to adjust price for area

For more recent years, see the BUC Used Boat Price Guide, Volume 1

LOA FT IN	NAME AND/ OR MODEL	TOP/ RIG	BOAT TYPE	-HULL- MTL	TP	ENGINE TP	# HP	MFG	BEAM FT IN	WGT LBS	DRAFT FT IN	RETAIL LOW	RETAIL HIGH
	1996 BOATS												
29 10	EXPRESS 271	OP	EXP	FBG	DV	IO	210		8 6	7643	3 1	32700	36400
32 1	EXPRESS 310	OP	EXP	FBG	DV	IO	T210		11 9	9202	2 8	50700	55700
32 1	SEDAN CRUISER 312	FB	CNV	FBG	DV	IB	T210		11 9	9937	2 8	46000	50600
36 1	EXPRESS 361	OP	EXP	FBG	DV	IB	T320		13	14314	3	77300	84900
36 1	SEDAN CRUISER 362	FB	CNV	FBG	DV	IB	T320		13	15058	3	81700	89800
39 10	MOTOR YACHT 34	FB	MY	FBG	DV	IB	T320		12 10	16368	3	89700	98500
41 3	CONVERTIBLE 37	FB	CNV	FBG	DV	IB	T320		14	21852	3 7	104000	114000
43 7	MOTOR YACHT 402	FB	MY	FBG	DV	IB	T380		14 2	23535	3 4	135500	149000
45 10	COCKPIT MY 442	FB	MYCPT	FBG	DV	IB	T380		14 4	27305	3 6	140000	154000
46 3	CONVERTIBLE 41	FB	CNV	FBG	DV	IB	T380		14 1	24975	3 7	136500	150000
51 6	MOTOR YACHT 46	FB	DC	FBG	DV	IB	T485D	DD	16 2	34470	3 9	208500	229000
	1995 BOATS												
29 10	EXPRESS 271	OP	EXP	FBG	DV	IO	300	MRCR	8 5	7643	3 1	32200	35800
29 10	EXPRESS 271	OP	EXP	FBG	DV	IO	216D	VLVO	8 5	7643	3 1	34800	38700
29 10	EXPRESS 271	OP	EXP	FBG	DV	IO	T280	MRCR	8 5	7643	3 1	36400	40400
32 1	EXPRESS 310	OP	EXP	FBG	DV	IO	T190-T300		11 9	9202	2 8	46800	55400
32 1	SEDAN CRUISER 312	FB	CNV	FBG	DV	IO	T190	MRCR	11 9	9937	2 8	41100	45700
32 1	SEDAN CRUISER 312	FB	CNV	FBG	DV	IB	T230	MRCR	11 9	9937	2 8	43700	48500
32 1	SEDAN CRUISER 312	FB	CNV	FBG	DV	IO	T185D	VLVO	11 9	9937	2 8	63300	69500
36	CONVERTIBLE 31	FB	CNV	FBG	DV	IB	T235	CRUS	11 8	12668	2 10	60000	65900
36	CONVERTIBLE 31	FB	CNV	FBG	DV	IB	T225D	VLVO	11 8	12668	2 10	79200	87100
36	MIDCABIN 31	FB	CR	FBG	DV	IB	T235	CRUS	11 8	12668	2 10	55400	60900
36	MIDCABIN 31	FB	CR	FBG	DV	IB	T225D	VLVO	11 8	12668	2 10	70400	77400
36 1	EXPRESS 361	OP	EXP	FBG	DV	IB	T300	VLVO	13	14314	3	74000	81300
	IB T320 CRUS 74600 82000, IB T225D VLVO 80900 88900, IB T300D CAT											88600	97400
36 1	SEDAN CRUISER 362	FB	CNV	FBG	DV	IB	T320	CRUS	13	15058	3	78800	86600
36 1	SEDAN CRUISER 362	FB	CNV	FBG	DV	IB	T225D	VLVO	13	15058	3	86800	95400
36 1	SEDAN CRUISER 362	FB	CNV	FBG	DV	IB	T300D	CAT	13	15058	3	95300	104500
39 10	AFT CABIN 34	FB	CR	FBG	DV	IB	T300	CRUS	12 10	16368	3	80400	88300
39 10	AFT CABIN 34	FB	CR	FBG	DV	IB	T220D	VLVO	12 10	16368	3	92900	102000
39 10	CONVERTIBLE 34	FB	CNV	FBG	DV	IB	T300	CRUS	12 10	16369	3	84200	92500
39 10	CONVERTIBLE 34	FB	CNV	FBG	DV	IB	T225D	VLVO	12 10	16369	3	99500	109500
39 10	MIDCABIN 34	FB	CR	FBG	DV	IO	T300	CRUS	12 10	16369	3	68800	75600
39 10	MIDCABIN 34	FB	CR	FBG	DV	IB	T300	CRUS	12 10	16369	3	80400	88300
39 10	MIDCABIN 34	FB	CR	FBG	DV	IB	T225D	VLVO	12 10	16369	3	93200	102500
41 3	CONVERTIBLE 37	FB	CNV	FBG	DV	IB	T300	CRUS	14	21852	3 7	99800	109500
41 3	CONVERTIBLE 37	FB	CNV	FBG	DV	IB	T355	CRUS	14	21852	3 7	101500	111500
41 3	CONVERTIBLE 37	FB	CNV	FBG	DV	IB	T375D	CAT	14	21852	3 7	127500	140000
41 3	MIDCABIN 37	FB	CR	FBG	DV	IB	T300	CRUS	14	21852	3 7	99000	109000
41 3	MIDCABIN 37	FB	CR	FBG	DV	IB	T355	CRUS	14	21852	3 7	101000	111000
41 3	MIDCABIN 37	FB	CR	FBG	DV	IB	T375D	CAT	14	21852	3 7	125500	138000
46 3	CONVERTIBLE 41	FB	CNV	FBG	DV	IB	T355	CRUS	14 1	24975	3 7	130000	143000
46 3	CONVERTIBLE 41	FB	CNV	FBG	DV	IB	T375D	CAT	14 1	24975	3 7	157500	173000
46 3	CONVERTIBLE 41	FB	CNV	FBG	DV	IB	T435D	CAT	14 1	24975	3 7	166500	183000
46 3	MOTOR YACHT 41	FB	DC	FBG	DV	IB	T355	CRUS	14 1	25643	3 7	136500	150000
46 3	MOTOR YACHT 41	FB	DC	FBG	DV	IB	T375D	CAT	14 1	25643	3 7	164500	180500
46 3	MOTOR YACHT 41	FB	DC	FBG	DV	IB	T425D	CAT	14 1	25643	3 7	171500	188500
51 6	MOTOR YACHT 46	FB	DC	FBG	DV	IB	T485D	DD	16 2	34470	3 9	200000	219500
	1994 BOATS												
31 2	CONVERTIBLE 31	FB	CNV	FBG	DV	IB	T235	CRUS	11 8	11000	3	55100	60600
31 2	CONVERTIBLE 31	FB	CNV	FBG	DV	IB	T225D	VLVO	11 8	11000	3	71000	78100
31 2	MIDCABIN 31	FB	CR	FBG	DV	IB	T235	CRUS	11 8	11000	3	50500	55500
31 2	MIDCABIN 31	FB	CR	FBG	DV	IB	T225D	VLVO	11 8	11000	3	62000	68100
31 10	EXPRESS 310	OP	EXP	FBG	DV	IO	T190-T300		11 6	9500	2 3	42200	50700
31 10	SEDAN CRUISER 312	FB	CNV	FBG	DV	IB	T190-T230		11 6	10120	2 4	40300	46200
31 10	SEDAN CRUISER 312	FB	CNV	FBG	DV	IB	T185D	VLVO	11 6	10120	2 4	58800	64600
34 3	EXPRESS 34	OP	EXP	FBG	DV	IB	T300	CRUS	12 8	16500	3 1	75100	82500
34 3	EXPRESS 34	OP	EXP	FBG	DV	IB	T400D		12 8	16500	3 1	101000	111000
34 6	AFT CABIN 34	FB	CR	FBG	DV	IB	T300	CRUS	12 11	19000	2 11	80700	88700
34 6	AFT CABIN 34	FB	CR	FBG	DV	IB	T220D	VLVO	12 11	19000	2 11	96400	106000
34 6	CONVERTIBLE 34	FB	CNV	FBG	DV	IB	T300	CRUS	12 11	18000	2 11	88900	97700
34 6	CONVERTIBLE 34	FB	CNV	FBG	DV	IB	T225D-T400D		12 11	19000	2 11	110500	136000
34 6	MIDCABIN 34	FB	CR	FBG	DV	IB	T300	CRUS	12 11	18000	2 11	83600	91900
34 6	MIDCABIN 34	FB	CR	FBG	DV	IB	T225D-T400D		12 11	18000	2 11	99200	124000
37 4	CONVERTIBLE 37	FB	CNV	FBG	DV	IB	T300	CRUS	13 11	21000	3 7	93000	102000
37 4	CONVERTIBLE 37	FB	CNV	FBG	DV	IB	T355	CRUS	13 11	21000	3 7	94800	104000
37 4	CONVERTIBLE 37	FB	CNV	FBG	DV	IB	T375D	CAT	13 11	21000	3 7	119000	131000
37 4	MIDCABIN 37	FB	CR	FBG	DV	IB	T300	CRUS	13 11	21000	3 7	92300	101500
37 4	MIDCABIN 37	FB	CR	FBG	DV	IB	T355	CRUS	13 11	21000	3 7	94000	103500
37 4	MIDCABIN 37	FB	CR	FBG	DV	IB	T375D	CAT	13 11	21000	3 7	117500	129000
37 7	EXPRESS 38	OP	EXP	FBG	DV	IB	T355	CRUS	13 11	21000	3 7	95300	104500
37 7	EXPRESS 38	OP	EXP	FBG	DV	IB	T375D	CAT	13 11	21000	3 7	119000	131000
41 3	CONVERTIBLE 41	FB	CNV	FBG	DV	IB	T355	CRUS	14 10	28000	3 7	132500	146000
41 3	CONVERTIBLE 41	FB	CNV	FBG	DV	IB	T375D	CAT	14 10	28000	3 7	159000	174500
41 3	CONVERTIBLE 41	FB	CNV	FBG	DV	IB	T425D	CAT	14 10	28000	3 7	166000	182000
41 3	MOTOR YACHT 41	FB	DC	FBG	DV	IB	T355	CRUS	14 10	28000	3 6	134500	148000
41 3	MOTOR YACHT 41	FB	DC	FBG	DV	IB	T375D	CAT	14 10	28000	3 6	161500	177000
41 3	MOTOR YACHT 41	FB	DC	FBG	DV	IB	T425D	CAT	14 10	28000	3 6	168000	185000
46 8	MOTOR YACHT 46	FB	DC	FBG	DV	IB	T485D	DD	16 2	40500	3 9	211000	232000
	1993 BOATS												
31 2	CONVERTIBLE 31	FB	CNV	FBG	DV	IB	T235	CRUS	11 8	11000	3	52300	57400
31 2	CONVERTIBLE 31	FB	CNV	FBG	DV	IB	T225D	VLVO	11 8	11000	3	67700	74400
31 2	MIDCABIN 31	FB	CR	FBG	DV	IB	T235	CRUS	11 8	11000	3	47800	52600
31 2	MIDCABIN 31	FB	CR	FBG	DV	IB	T225D	VLVO	11 8	11000	3	59000	64900
31 10	CONVERTIBLE 29	FB	CNV	FBG	DV	IB	T190-T230		11 6	10120	2 4	38200	43700
31 10	CONVERTIBLE 29	FB	CNV	FBG	DV	IB	T185D	VLVO	11 6	10120	2 4	56000	61500
34 3	EXPRESS 34	OP	EXP	FBG	DV	IB	T300	CRUS	12 8	16500	3 1	71200	78200
34 3	EXPRESS 34	OP	EXP	FBG	DV	IB	T300D	J&T	12 8	16500	3 1	89300	98100
34 6	AFT CABIN 34	FB	CR	FBG	DV	IB	T300	CRUS	12 11	19000	2 11	76500	84100
34 6	AFT CABIN 34	FB	CR	FBG	DV	IB	T220D	VLVO	12 11	19000	2 11	91800	101000
34 6	CONVERTIBLE 34	FB	CNV	FBG	DV	IB	T300	CRUS	12 11	18000	2 11	84300	92600
34 6	CONVERTIBLE 34	FB	CNV	FBG	DV	IB	T225D-T300D		12 11	19000	2 11	105000	119500

522

CONTINUED ON NEXT PAGE

96th ed. - Vol. II

LOA FT	LOA IN	NAME AND/ OR MODEL	TOP/ RIG	BOAT TYPE	-HULL- MTL	-HULL- TP	ENGINE TP	ENGINE # HP	ENGINE MFG	BEAM FT	BEAM IN	WGT LBS	DRAFT FT	DRAFT IN	RETAIL LOW	RETAIL HIGH
		1993 BOATS														
34	6	MIDCABIN 34	FB	CR	FBG	DV	IB	T300	CRUS	12	11	18000	2	11	79300	87100
34	6	MIDCABIN 34	FB	CR	FBG	DV	IB	T225D-T300D		12	11	18000	2	11	94500	110000
37	4	CONVERTIBLE 37	FB	CNV	FBG	DV	IB	T300	CRUS	13	11	21000	3	7	88600	97400
37	4	CONVERTIBLE 37	FB	CNV	FBG	DV	IB	T355	CRUS	13	11	21000	3	7	90300	99300
37	4	CONVERTIBLE 37	FB	CNV	FBG	DV	IB	T375D	CAT	13	11	21000	3	7	113500	125000
37	4	MIDCABIN 37	FB	CR	FBG	DV	IB	T300	CRUS	13	11	21000	3	7	87900	96600
37	4	MIDCABIN 37	FB	CR	FBG	DV	IB	T355	CRUS	13	11	21000	3	7	89500	98400
37	4	MIDCABIN 37	FB	CR	FBG	DV	IB	T375D	CAT	13	11	21000	3	7	112000	123000
37	7	EXPRESS 38	OP	EXP	FBG	DV	IB	T355	CRUS	13	11	21000	3	7	90800	99800
37	7	EXPRESS 38	OP	EXP	FBG	DV	IB	T375D	CAT	13	11	21000	3	7	113500	124500
41	3	CONVERTIBLE 41	FB	CNV	FBG	DV	IB	T355	CRUS	14	10	28000	3	7	126500	139000
41	3	CONVERTIBLE 41	FB	CNV	FBG	DV	IB	T375D	CAT	14	10	28000	3	7	151500	166000
41	3	CONVERTIBLE 41	FB	CNV	FBG	DV	IB	T425D	CAT	14	10	28000	3	7	158000	173500
41	3	MOTOR YACHT 41	FB	DC	FBG	DV	IB	T355	CRUS	14	10	28000	3	6	128000	141000
41	3	MOTOR YACHT 41	FB	DC	FBG	DV	IB	T375D	CAT	14	10	28000	3	6	153500	169000
41	3	MOTOR YACHT 41	FB	DC	FBG	DV	IB	T425D	CAT	14	10	28000	3	6	160000	176000
46	8	MOTOR YACHT 46	FB	DC	FBG	DV	IB	T485D	DD	16	2	40500	3	9	201000	221000
		1992 BOATS														
31	2	CONVERTIBLE 31	FB	CNV	FBG	DV	IB	T235	CRUS	11	8	11000	3		49600	54500
31	2	CONVERTIBLE 31	FB	CNV	FBG	DV	IB	T192D	VLVO	11	8	11000	3		61900	68100
31	2	MIDCABIN 31	FB	CR	FBG	DV	IB	T235	CRUS	11	8	11000	3		45600	50200
31	2	MIDCABIN 31	FB	CR	FBG	DV	IB	T192D	VLVO	11	8	11000	3		54400	59800
34	3	EXPRESS 34	OP	EXP	FBG	DV	IB	T300	CRUS	12	8	16500	3	1	67600	74200
34	3	EXPRESS 34	OP	EXP	FBG	DV	IB	T300D	J&T	12	8	16500	3	1	85100	93500
34	6	AFT CABIN 34	FB	CR	FBG	DV	IB	T300	CRUS	12	11	19000	2	11	72600	79800
34	6	AFT CABIN 34	FB	CR	FBG	DV	IB	T300D	J&T	12	11	19000	2	11	92800	102000
34	6	CONVERTIBLE 34	FB	CNV	FBG	DV	IB	T300	CRUS	12	11	18000	2	11	80000	87900
34	6	CONVERTIBLE 34	FB	CNV	FBG	DV	IB	T300D	J&T	12	11	18000	2	11	104000	114000
34	6	MIDCABIN 34	FB	CR	FBG	DV	IB	T300	CRUS	12	11	18000	2	11	75200	82700
34	6	MIDCABIN 34	FB	CR	FBG	DV	IB	T300D	J&T	12	11	18000	2	11	95400	105000
37	4	CONVERTIBLE 37	FB	CNV	FBG	DV	IB	T300	CRUS	13	11	21000	3	7	84500	92800
37	4	CONVERTIBLE 37	FB	CNV	FBG	DV	IB	T355	CRUS	13	11	21000	3	7	86100	94600
37	4	CONVERTIBLE 37	FB	CNV	FBG	DV	IB	T375D	CAT	13	11	21000	3	7	108500	119000
37	4	MIDCABIN 37	FB	CR	FBG	DV	IB	T300	CRUS	13	11	21000	3	7	83800	92100
37	4	MIDCABIN 37	FB	CR	FBG	DV	IB	T355	CRUS	13	11	21000	3	7	85400	93800
37	4	MIDCABIN 37	FB	CR	FBG	DV	IB	T375D	CAT	13	11	21000	3	7	106500	117500
37	7	EXPRESS 38	OP	EXP	FBG	DV	IB	T300	CRUS	13	11	21000	3	7	85000	93400
37	7	EXPRESS 38	OP	EXP	FBG	DV	IB	T375D	CAT	13	11	21000	3	7	108000	119000
41	3	CONVERTIBLE 41	FB	CNV	FBG	DV	IB	T355	CRUS	14	10	28000	3	7	120500	132500
41	3	CONVERTIBLE 41	FB	CNV	FBG	DV	IB	T425D	CAT	14	10	28000	3	7	150500	165500
41	3	MOTOR YACHT 41	FB	DC	FBG	DV	IB	T355	CRUS	14	10	28000	3	6	122500	134500
41	3	MOTOR YACHT 41	FB	DC	FBG	DV	IB	T375D	CAT	14	10	28000	3	6	146500	161000
41	3	MOTOR YACHT 41	FB	DC	FBG	DV	IB	T425D	CAT	14	10	28000	3	6	152500	168000
46	8	MOTOR YACHT 46	FB	DC	FBG	DV	IB	T485D	J&T	16	2	40500	3	9	191000	210000
		1991 BOATS														
34	3	EXPRESS 34	OP	EXP	FBG	DV	IB	T350	CRUS	12	10	16500	3	1	65500	72000
34	3	EXPRESS 34	OP	EXP	FBG	DV	IB	T250D	J&T	12	10	16500	3	1	78300	86100
34	6	CONVERTIBLE 34	FB	CNV	FBG	DV	IB	T350	CRUS	12	10	18000	2	11	77900	85600
34	6	CONVERTIBLE 34	FB	CNV	FBG	DV	IB	T250D	J&T	12	10	18000	2	11	95500	105000
37	4	CONVERTIBLE 37	FB	CNV	FBG	DV	IB	T350	CRUS	13	11	21000	3	7	82000	90100
37	4	CONVERTIBLE 37	FB	CNV	FBG	DV	IB	T320D	CAT	13	11	21000	3	7	98700	108500
37	7	EXPRESS 38	OP	EXP	FBG	DV	IB	T350	CRUS	13	11	21000	3	7	82400	90500
37	7	EXPRESS 38	OP	EXP	FBG	DV	IB	T425D	CAT	13	11	21000	3	7	108000	118500
41	3	AFT CABIN 41	FB	DC	FBG	DV	IB	T350	CRUS	14	10	28000	3	6	114500	126000
41	3	AFT CABIN 41	FB	DC	FBG	DV	IB	T375D	CAT	14	10	28000	3	6	137500	151000
41	3	CONVERTIBLE 41	FB	CNV	FBG	DV	IB	T350	CRUS	14	10	28000	3	7	114500	126000
41	3	CONVERTIBLE 41	FB	CNV	FBG	DV	IB	T375D	CAT	14	10	28000	3	7	137500	151000
46	9	AFT CABIN 46	FB	DC	FBG	DV	IB	T485D	J&T	16	2	38000	4		155000	170500
		1990 BOATS														
30	8	EXPRESS 30	OP	EXP	FBG	DV	IB	T270	CRUS	10	10	9100	3		37900	42200
34	6	CONVERTIBLE	FB	CNV	FBG	DV	IB	T270	CRUS	12	7	13500	3	2	60400	66400
34	6	CONVERTIBLE 34	FB	CNV	FBG	DV	IB	T300	CRUS	12	7	13500	3	2	66200	72800
34	6	CONVERTIBLE 34	FB	CNV	FBG	DV	IB	T250D	J&T	12	7	13500	3	2	80600	88600
34	6	EXPRESS 34	FB	CNV	FBG	DV	IB	T220D	J&T	12	7	13500	3	2	72700	79900
34	6	EXPRESS 34	OP	EXP	FBG	DV	IB	T300-T350		12	7	11000	3	2	54900	62300
37		CONVERTIBLE	FB	CNV	FBG	DV	IB	T350	CRUS	14		20000	3		74000	81300
37		CONVERTIBLE	FB	CNV	FBG	DV	IB	T320D	CAT	14		20000	3		89700	98500
37	4	CONVERTIBLE 37	FB	CNV	FBG	DV	IB	T300	CRUS	13	11	21000	3	7	76900	84500
37	4	CONVERTIBLE 37	FB	CNV	FBG	DV	IB	T320D	CAT	13	11	21000	3	7	94200	103500
37	6	MOTOR YACHT 37	FB	MY	FBG	DV	IB	T320D	CAT	13	10	22000	3	8	98200	108000
37	6	MOTOR YACHT 37	FB	MY	FBG	DV	IB	T350D	CRUS	13	10	22000	3	8	98000	107500
39	7	EXPRESS 40	OP	EXP	FBG	DV	IB	T330	CRUS	14		21000	3	5	85900	94400
		IB T355 CRUS 87800 96500, IB T360 CRUS 86800 95400, IB T250D GM													95900	105500
40		AFT CABIN	FB	DC	FBG	DV	IB	T350	CRUS	14		24000	3		98400	108000
40		AFT CABIN	FB	DC	FBG	DV	IB	T320D	CAT	14		24000	3		113500	124500
40		AFT CABIN 40	FB	DC	FBG	DV	IB	T300	CRUS	14		24000	3	5	97200	107000
40		AFT CABIN 40	FB	DC	FBG	DV	IB	T320D	CAT	14		24000	3	5	116000	127500
40		CONVERTIBLE	FB	CNV	FBG	DV	IB	T350	CRUS	14		22000	3		91700	101000
40		CONVERTIBLE	FB	CNV	FBG	DV	IB	T320D	CAT	14		22000	3		108000	119000
40		CONVERTIBLE 40	FB	CNV	FBG	DV	IB	T320	CRUS	14	9	21000	3	8	84400	92700
40		CONVERTIBLE 40	FB	CNV	FBG	DV	IB	T320D	CAT	14	9	21000	3	8	101500	111500
41	2	AFT CABIN 41	FB	DC	FBG	DV	IB	T355	CRUS	14	10	28000	3	7	109500	120500
41	2	AFT CABIN 41	FB	DC	FBG	DV	IB	T375D	CAT	14	10	28000	3	7	131000	144000
46	8	AFT CABIN 46	FB	DC	FBG	DV	IB	T485D	J&T	16	2	38000	4	2	147500	162500
		1989 BOATS														
30	8	EXPRESS 30	OP	EXP	FBG	DV	IB	T270	CRUS	10	10	9100	3		36100	40100
34	6	CONVERTIBLE	FB	CNV	FBG	DV	IB	T270	CRUS	12	7	13500	3	2	57500	63200
34	6	CONVERTIBLE	FB	CNV	FBG	DV	IB	T220D	J&T	12	7	13500	3	2	69500	76400
34	6	EXPRESS 34	OP	EXP	FBG		IB	T350	CRUS	12	3	11000	3	1	54000	59300
37		CONVERTIBLE	FB	CNV	FBG	DV	IB	T350	CRUS	14		20000	3		70700	77700
37		CONVERTIBLE	FB	CNV	FBG	DV	IB	T320D	CAT	14		20000	3		85600	94100
37	6	MOTOR YACHT 37	FB	MY	FBG	DV	IB	T350	CRUS	13	10	22000	3	8	78400	86200
37	6	MOTOR YACHT 37	FB	MY	FBG	DV	IB	T320D	CAT	13	10	22000	3	8	93800	103000
39	7	EXPRESS 40	FB	EXP	FBG	DV	IB	T330	CRUS	14		21000	3	5	82000	90200
39	7	EXPRESS 40	FB	EXP	FBG	DV	IB	T360	CRUS	14		21000	3	5	82900	91100
39	7	EXPRESS 40	FB	EXP	FBG	DV	IB	T250D	GM	14		21000	3	5	91600	100500
40		AFT CABIN	FB	DC	FBG	DV	IB	T350	CRUS	14		24000	3		94000	103500
40		AFT CABIN	FB	DC	FBG	DV	IB	T320D	CAT	14		24000	3		109500	120500
40		CONVERTIBLE	FB	CNV	FBG	DV	IB	T350	CRUS	14		22000	3		87600	96300
40		CONVERTIBLE	FB	CNV	FBG	DV	IB	T320D	CAT	14		22000	3		103500	113500
		1988 BOATS														
30	8	EXPRESS 30	OP	EXP	FBG	DV	IB	T270	CRUS	10	10	9100	3		34400	38200
34		CONVERTIBLE	FB	CNV	FBG	DV	IB	T270	CRUS	12	6	12500	3	1	52200	57400
34		CONVERTIBLE	FB	CNV	FBG	DV	IB	T220D	J&T	12	6	12500	3	1	63400	69600
34	6	EXPRESS 34	OP	EXP	FBG		IB	T350	CRUS	12	10	11000	3	1	50900	55900
37		CONVERTIBLE	FB	CNV	FBG	DV	IB	T350	CRUS	14		20000	3		67600	74300
37		CONVERTIBLE	FB	CNV	FBG	DV	IB	T320D	CAT	14		20000	3		81900	89900
37	6	MOTOR YACHT 37	FB	MY	FBG	DV	IB	T350	CRUS	13	10	22000	3	8	75000	82400
37	6	MOTOR YACHT 37	FB	MY	FBG	DV	IB	T320D	CAT	13	10	22000	3	8	89700	98600
40		AFT CABIN	FB	DC	FBG	DV	IB	T350	CRUS	14		24000	3		89800	98700
40		AFT CABIN	FB	DC	FBG	DV	IB	T320D	CAT	14		24000	3		105000	115000
40		CONVERTIBLE	FB	CNV	FBG	DV	IB	T350	CRUS	14		22000	3		83700	92000
40		CONVERTIBLE	FB	CNV	FBG	DV	IB	T320D	CAT	14		22000	3		98800	108500
		1987 BOATS														
29	2	SPORTCRUISER	FB	SPTCR	FBG	SV	IB	T195	CRUS	10	10	7800		1	25000	27700
31		CONVERTIBLE	FB	CNV	FBG	DV	VD	T220-T270		11	11	11400	2	11	37900	43800
34		CONVERTIBLE	FB	CNV	FBG	DV	IB	T270	CRUS	12	6	12500	3	1	49800	54700
34		CONVERTIBLE	FB	CNV	FBG	DV	IB	T220D	J&T	12	6	12500	3	1	60700	66700
34	6	EXPRESS 34	OP	EXP	FBG		IB	T350	CRUS	12	10	11000	3	1	48500	53300
37		CONVERTIBLE	FB	CNV	FBG	DV	IB	T350	CRUS	14		20000	3		64600	71000
37		CONVERTIBLE	FB	CNV	FBG	DV	IB	T320D	CAT	14		20000	3		78300	86000
40		AFT CABIN	FB	DC	FBG	DV	IB	T350	CRUS	14		24000	3		85900	94400
40		AFT CABIN	FB	DC	FBG	DV	IB	T320D	CAT	14		24000	3		100500	110000
40		CONVERTIBLE	FB	CNV	FBG	DV	IB	T350	CRUS	14		22000	3		80100	88000
40		CONVERTIBLE	FB	CNV	FBG	DV	IB	T320D	CAT	14		22000	3		94500	104000
		1986 BOATS														
29		LUHRS 290	OP	SF	FBG		IB	T270	CRUS	10	9	9000	2	5	26200	29100
29	2	SPORTCRUISER	FB	SPTCR	FBG	SV	IB	T195	CRUS	10	10	7800		1	23800	26500
31		CONVERTIBLE	FB	CNV	FBG	DV	VD	T220-T270		11	11	11400	2	11	36200	41800
31		GULFSTREAM	OP	CR	FBG	DV	IB	T270-T350		11	11	9500	2	10	29500	34600
34		CONVERTIBLE	FB	CNV	FBG	DV	VD	T270	CRUS	12	6	12500	3	1	47800	52500
34		CONVERTIBLE	FB	CNV	FBG	DV	VD	T220D	J&T	12	6	12500	3	1	58200	63900
34		LUHRS 340	OP	SF	FBG		IB	T350	CRUS	12	6	12100	3	4	46400	51000
34		LUHRS 340	OP	SF	FBG		IB	T220D	J&T	12	6	12100	3	4	52300	57500
34		LUHRS 342	FB	SF	FBG		IB	T350	CRUS	12	6	13500	3	2	47800	52500
34		LUHRS 342	FB	SF	FBG		IB	T260D	J&T	12	6	13500	3	2	56800	62400
37		CONVERTIBLE	FB	CNV	FBG	DV	VD	T350	CRUS	14		20000	3		61800	68000
37		CONVERTIBLE	FB	CNV	FBG	DV	IB	T D	CAT	14		20000	3		**	**
40		AFT CABIN	FB	DC	FBG	DV	IB	T350	CRUS	14		24000	3		82200	90400
40		AFT CABIN	FB	DC	FBG	DV	IB	T D	CAT	14		24000	3		**	**
40		CONVERTIBLE	FB	CNV	FBG	DV	VD	T350	CRUS	14		22000	3		76600	84200
40		CONVERTIBLE	FB	CNV	FBG	DV	IB	T D	CAT	14		22000	3		**	**
		1985 BOATS														
29	2	SPORTCRUISER	FB	SPTCR	FBG	SV	IB	T165	CRUS	10	10	7800	1	7	22200	24600
31		CONVERTIBLE	FB	CNV	FBG	DV	VD	T220-T270		11	11	11400	2	11	34600	40000
31		CONVERTIBLE	FB	CNV	FBG	DV	VD	T158D	VLVO	11	11	11400	2	11	43900	48800
31		GULFSTREAM	OP	CR	FBG	DV	IB	T270-T350		11	11	9500	2	10	28200	33100
34		CONVERTIBLE	FB	CNV	FBG	DV	VD	T250-T270		12	6	12500	3	1	44500	50100

 CONTINUED ON NEXT PAGE

LOA FT	LOA IN	NAME AND/ OR MODEL	TOP/ RIG	BOAT TYPE	-HULL- MTL	TP	ENGINE TP	# HP	MFG	BEAM FT	BEAM IN	WGT LBS	DRAFT FT	DRAFT IN	RETAIL LOW	RETAIL HIGH
		1985 BOATS														
34		CONVERTIBLE	FB	CNV	FBG	DV	VD	T205D	J&T	12	6	12500	3	1	55000	60400
34		LUHRS 340	OP	SF	FBG		IB	T350	CRUS	12	6	12100	3	4	43900	48700
34		LUHRS 340	OP	SF	FBG		IB	T205D	J&T	12	6	12100	3	4	49600	54500
37		CONVERTIBLE	FB	CNV	FBG	DV	VD	T350	CRUS	14		20000	3		59200	65100
37		CONVERTIBLE	FB	CNV	FBG	DV	IB	T240D	PERK	14		20000	3		67700	74400
40		AFT CABIN	FB	DC	FBG	DV	IB	T350	CRUS	14		24000	3		78700	86500
40		AFT CABIN	FB	DC	FBG	DV	IB	T240D	PERK	14		24000	3		87700	96400
40		CONVERTIBLE	FB	CNV	FBG	DV	VD	T350	CRUS	14		22000	3		**	**
40		CONVERTIBLE	FB	CNV	FBG	DV	IB	T D	CAT	14		22000	3		**	**
		1984 BOATS														
31		CONVERTIBLE	FB	CNV	FBG	DV	VD	T220-T270		11	11	11400	2	11	33100	38200
31		CONVERTIBLE	FB	CNV	FBG	DV	VD	T158D	VLVO	11	11	11400	2	11	42200	46800
31		GULFSTREAM	OP	CR	FBG	DV	IB	T270-T350		11	11	9500	2	10	27000	31600
34		CONVERTIBLE	FB	CNV	FBG	DV	VD	T250-T270		12	6	12500	3	1	42500	47900
34		CONVERTIBLE	FB	CNV	FBG	DV	VD	T205D	J&T	12	6	12500	3	1	52800	58000
34		LUHRS 340	OP	SF	FBG		IB	T350	CRUS	12	6	12100	3	4	41900	46600
34		LUHRS 340	OP	SF	FBG		IB	T205D	J&T	12	6	12100	3	4	47800	52500
37		CONVERTIBLE	FB	CNV	FBG	DV	VD	T350	CRUS	14		20000	3		56700	62400
37		CONVERTIBLE	FB	CNV	FBG	DV	IB	T240D	PERK	14		20000	3		64800	71300
40		AFT CABIN	FB	DC	FBG	DV	IB	T350	CRUS	14		24000	3		75400	82900
40		AFT CABIN	FB	DC	FBG	DV	IB	T240D	PERK	14		24000	3		84000	92300

....For earlier years, see the BUC Used Boat Price Guide, Volume 3

SIRENA YACHTS USA

ESSEX CT 06426 COAST GUARD MFG ID- RNV See inside cover to adjust price for area

LOA FT	LOA IN	NAME AND/ OR MODEL	TOP/ RIG	BOAT TYPE	-HULL- MTL	TP	ENGINE TP	# HP	MFG	BEAM FT	BEAM IN	WGT LBS	DRAFT FT	DRAFT IN	RETAIL LOW	RETAIL HIGH
		1985 BOATS														
38	2	SIRENA 38	SLP	SAIL	FBG	KL	SD	18D	VLVO	10	2	11000	5	9	37000	41100
38	2	SIRENA 38	SLP	SAIL	FBG	KL	IB	18D	VLVO	10	2	11000	5	9	37000	41100
44	5	SIRENA 44	SLP	SAIL	FBG	KL	SD	36D	VLVO	12	5	18700	7	3	73500	80800
44	5	SIRENA 44	SLP	SAIL	FBG	KL	IB	36D	BUKH	12	5	18700	7	3	73600	80900

SISU BOAT INC

DOVER NH 03820 COAST GUARD MFG ID- SGH See inside cover to adjust price for area

LOA FT	LOA IN	NAME AND/ OR MODEL	TOP/ RIG	BOAT TYPE	-HULL- MTL	TP	ENGINE TP	# HP	MFG	BEAM FT	BEAM IN	WGT LBS	DRAFT FT	DRAFT IN	RETAIL LOW	RETAIL HIGH
		1988 BOATS														
21	9	SISU 22 BASS	OP	BASS	F/S	SV	SE		OMC	7	10	2600	1	5	**	**
21	9	SISU 22 BASS	OP	FSH	F/S	SV	OB			7	10	2200	1	5	11600	13200
21	9	SISU 22 BASS	OP	FSH	F/S	SV	IB	185	CRUS	7	10	3600	2	3	13100	14900
21	9	SISU 22 BASS	OP	FSH	F/S	SV	IB	130D	VLVO	7	10	3600	2	3	17100	19500
21	9	SISU 22 LOBSTER	HT	FSH	F/S	SV	OB			7	10	2200	1	5	11600	13200
21	9	SISU 22 LOBSTER	HT	FSH	F/S	SV	SE		OMC	7	10	3600	1	5	**	**
21	9	SISU 22 LOBSTER	HT	FSH	F/S	SV	IB	185	CRUS	7	10	3600	2	3	13100	14900
21	9	SISU 22 LOBSTER	HT	FSH	F/S	SV	IB	130D	VLVO	7	10	3600	2	3	17100	19500
25	6	SISU 26 LOBSTER	HT	FSH	F/S	SV	IB	200-270		9	8	7500	3		28300	31400
25	6	SISU 26 OFFSHORE	HT	PH	F/S	SV	IB	200D	VLVO	9	8	7500	3		37800	42000
25	6	SISU 26 OFFSHORE ISL	HT	FSH	F/S	SV	IB	270	CRUS	9	8	7500	3		31900	35400
29	9	SISU 30 BASS	HT	BASS	F/S	SV	IB	350	CRUS	10	6	10000	3		39400	43800
29	9	SISU 30 BASS	HT	BASS	F/S	SV	IB	250D-320D		10	6	10000	3		48300	56000
29	9	SISU 30 ISLANDER CR	HT	CBNCR	F/S	SV	IB			10	6	10000	3		**	**
29	9	SISU 30 LOBSTER	HT	FSH	F/S	SV	IB	350	CRUS	10	6	10000	3		36600	40600
29	9	SISU 30 LOBSTER	HT	FSH	F/S	SV	IB	250D-320D		10	6	10000	3		44900	52600
29	9	SISU 30 OFFSHORE	HT	FSH	F/S	SV	IB	350	CRUS	10	6	10000	3		42300	47000
29	9	SISU 30 OFFSHORE	HT	FSH	F/S	SV	IB	250D-320D		10	6	10000	3		51600	59500
		1987 BOATS														
21	9	SISU 22 BASS	OP	FSH	F/S	SV	OB			7	10	2200	1	5	11200	12700
21	9	SISU 22 BASS	OP	FSH	F/S	SV	IB	185	CRUS	7	10	3600	2	3	12500	14200
21	9	SISU 22 BASS	OP	FSH	F/S	SV	IB	130D	VLVO	7	10	3600	2	3	16400	18600
21	9	SISU 22 BASS BOAT	OP	BASS	F/S	SV	OB			7	10	2600	1	5	12700	14400
21	9	SISU 22 ISLANDER	OP	BASS	F/S	SV	IB	185	CRUS	7	10	3600	1	5	12500	14200
21	9	SISU 22 ISLANDER LOB	HT	FSH	F/S	SV	IB	185	CRUS	7	10	3600	1	5	12500	14200
21	9	SISU 22 LOBSTER	HT	FSH	F/S	SV	OB			7	10	2200	1	5	11200	12700
21	9	SISU 22 LOBSTER	HT	FSH	F/S	SV	IB	185	CRUS	7	10	3600	2	3	12500	14200
21	9	SISU 22 LOBSTER	HT	FSH	F/S	SV	IB	130D	VLVO	7	10	3600	2	3	15000	17000
21	9	SISU 22 LOBSTER BOAT	HT	FSH	F/S	SV	OB			7	10	2600	1	5	12600	14300
21	9	SISU 22 LOBSTER BOAT	HT	FSH	F/S	SV	IB	130D	VLVO	7	10	3600	1	5	18200	20300
25	6	SISU 26 LOBSTER	HT	FSH	F/S	SV	IB	270	CRUS	9	8	7500	3		22100	24600
25	6	SISU 26 LOBSTER	HT	FSH	F/S	SV	IB	200D	PERK	9	8	7500	3		32000	35600
25	6	SISU 26 OFFSHORE	HT	PH	F/S	SV	IB	270	CRUS	9	8	7500	3		27600	30600
25	6	SISU 26 OFFSHORE	HT	PH	F/S	SV	IB	200D	VLVO	9	8	7500	3		36200	40300
25	6	SISU 26 OFFSHORE ISL	HT	FSH	F/S	SV	IB	270	CRUS	9	8	7500	3		33100	36700
25	6	SISU 26 OFFSHORE ISL	HT	FSH	F/S	SV	IB	200D	VLVO	9	8	7500	3		41800	46400
29	9	SISU 30 CR ISLANDER	HT	CBNCR	F/S	SV	IB	350	CRUS	10	6	10000	3		43600	48500
29	9	SISU 30 CR ISLANDER	HT	CBNCR	F/S	SV	IB	250D	GM	10	6	10000	3		56800	62400
29	9	SISU 30 CRUISER	HT	CBNCR	F/S	SV	IB	350	CRUS	10	6	10000	3		43600	48500
29	9	SISU 30 CRUISER	HT	CBNCR	F/S	SV	IB	250D	GM	10	6	10000	3		56800	62400
29	9	SISU 30 LOBSTER	HT	FSH	F/S	SV	IB	350	CRUS	10	6	10000	3		37600	41800
29	9	SISU 30 LOBSTER	HT	FSH	F/S	SV	IB	250D	GM	10	6	10000	3		46600	51200
29	9	SISU 30 OFF ISLANDER	HT	FSH	F/S	SV	IB	350	CRUS	10	6	10000	3		37600	41800
29	9	SISU 30 OFF ISLANDER	HT	FSH	F/S	SV	IB	250D	GM	10	6	10000	3		46600	51200
29	9	SISU 30 OFF ISLANDER	FB	FSH	F/S	SV	IB	350	CRUS	10	6	10000			37600	41800
29	9	SISU 30 OFF ISLANDER	FB	FSH	F/S	SV	IB	250D	GM	10	6	10000	3		46600	51200
29	9	SISU 30 OFFSHORE	HT	FSH	F/S	SV	IB	350	CRUS	10	6	10000	3		37600	41800
29	9	SISU 30 OFFSHORE	HT	FSH	F/S	SV	IB	250D	GM	10	6	10000	3		46600	51200
		1986 BOATS														
21	9	SISU 22	OP	CTRCN	F/S	RB	OB			7	10	2000	1	5	10100	11400
21	9	SISU 22 BASS	OP	FSH	F/S	RB	OB			7	10	2200	1	5	10800	12300
21	9	SISU 22 BASS	OP	FSH	F/S	RB	IB	185	CRUS	7	10	3600	2	3	11900	13500
21	9	SISU 22 BASS	OP	FSH	F/S	RB	IB	110D	VLVO	7	10	3600	2	3	15400	17500
21	9	SISU 22 LOBSTER	HT	FSH	F/S	RB	OB			7	10	2200	1	5	10800	12300
21	9	SISU 22 LOBSTER	HT	FSH	F/S	RB	IB	185	CRUS	7	10	3600	2	3	11900	13500
21	9	SISU 22 LOBSTER	HT	FSH	F/S	RB	IB	110D	VLVO	7	10	3600	2	3	15400	17500
25	6	SISU 26 BASS	OP	FSH	F/S	RB	OB			9	8	4500	2	4	20700	23000
25	6	SISU 26 BASS	OP	FSH	F/S	RB	IB	200D	PERK	9	8	7500	3		36200	40200
25	6	SISU 26 BASS	HT	FSH	F/S	RB	IB	270	CRUS	9	8	7500	3		29000	32300
25	6	SISU 26 LOBSTER	HT	FSH	F/S	RB	OB			9	8	4500	2	4	20800	23100
25	6	SISU 26 LOBSTER	HT	FSH	F/S	RB	IB	270	CRUS	9	8	7500	3		23600	26200
25	6	SISU 26 LOBSTER	HT	FSH	F/S	RB	IB	200D	PERK	9	8	7500	3		36200	40200
25	6	SISU 26 OFFSHORE	HT	PH	F/S	RB	OB			9	8	4500	2	4	20900	23200
25	6	SISU 26 OFFSHORE	HT	PH	F/S	RB	IB	270	CRUS	9	8	7500	3		26300	29200
25	6	SISU 26 OFFSHORE	HT	PH	F/S	RB	IB	200D	PERK	9	8	7500	3		36200	40200
29	9	SISU 30 LOBSTER	HT	FSH	F/S	RB	IB	350	CRUS	10	6	10000	3		35900	39900
29	9	SISU 30 LOBSTER	HT	FSH	F/S	RB	IB	200D	PERK	10	6	10000	3		43000	47800
29	9	SISU 30 OFFSHORE	HT	CBNCR	F/S	RB	IB	350	CRUS	10	6	10000	3		41700	46300
29	9	SISU 30 OFFSHORE	HT	CBNCR	F/S	RB	IB	200D	PERK	10	6	10000	3		52100	57300
		1985 BOATS														
21	9	SISU 22	OP	CTRCN	F/S	RB	OB			7	10	2000	1	5	9800	11100
21	9	SISU 22	OP	CTRCN	F/S	RB	IO	117	VLVO	7	10	3000	1	5	8450	9700
		IB 138-165 9800 11400, IB 51D- 85D 13800 17200, IO 110D VLVO													12200	13900
		IB 110D VLVO 13400 15200														
21	9	SISU 22 BASS	OP	FSH	F/S	RB	OB			7	10	2200	1	5	10500	11900
21	9	SISU 22 BASS	OP	FSH	F/S	RB	IO	117	VLVO	7	10	3600	1	5	9550	10900
		IB 138-165 11100 12800, IB 51D- 85D 14800 17800, IO 110D VLVO													13500	15300
		IB 110D VLVO 14800 16800														
21	9	SISU 22 LOBSTER	HT	FSH	F/S	RB	OB			7	10	2200	1	5	10500	11900
21	9	SISU 22 LOBSTER	HT	FSH	F/S	RB	IO	117	VLVO	7	10	3600	1	5	9550	10900
		IB 125-165 10900 12800, IB 51D- 85D 14800 17800, IO 110D VLVO													13500	15300
		IB 110D VLVO 14800 16800														
25	6	SISU 26 BASS	OP	FSH	F/S	RB	OB			9	8	4500	2	4	20100	22400
25	6	SISU 26 BASS	OP	FSH	F/S	RB	IB	85D-200D		9	8	7500	2	3	31600	38600
25	6	SISU 26 BASS	HT	FSH	F/S	RB	IB	225	CHRY	9	8	7500	3		27200	30200
25	6	SISU 26 LOBSTER	HT	FSH	F/S	RB	OB			9	8	4500	2	4	20300	22600
25	6	SISU 26 LOBSTER	HT	FSH	F/S	RB	IB	225	CHRY	9	8	7500	3		22000	24400
25	6	SISU 26 LOBSTER	HT	FSH	F/S	RB	IB	85D-200D		9	8	7500	3		31600	38600
25	6	SISU 26 OFFSHORE	HT	PH	F/S	RB	OB			9	8	4500	2	4	20400	22600
25	6	SISU 26 OFFSHORE	HT	PH	F/S	RB	IB	225	CHRY	9	8	7500	3		24600	27300
25	6	SISU 26 OFFSHORE	HT	PH	F/S	RB	IB	85D-200D		9	8	7500	3		31500	38600
29	9	SISU 30 LOBSTER	HT	FSH	F/S	RB	OB			10	6				27600	30700
29	9	SISU 30 LOBSTER	HT	FSH	F/S	RB	IB	225	CHRY	10	6	10000	3		32400	35900
29	9	SISU 30 LOBSTER	HT	FSH	F/S	RB	IB	200D-240D		10	6	10000	3		41200	47100
29	9	SISU 30 OFFSHORE	HT	CBNCR	F/S	RB	OB			10	6		3		27800	30800
29	9	SISU 30 OFFSHORE	HT	CBNCR	F/S	RB	IB	225	CHRY	10	6	10000	3		36600	40600
29	9	SISU 30 OFFSHORE	HT	CBNCR	F/S	RB	IB	200D-240D		10	6	10000	3		50000	57100
		1984 BOATS														
21	9	SISU 22	OP	CTRCN	F/S	RB	OB			7	10	2000	1	9	9500	10800
21	9	SISU 22	OP	CTRCN	F/S	RB	IO	117	VLVO	7	10	3000	1	9	8150	9350
21	9	SISU 22	OP	CTRCN	F/S	RB	IB	138	VLVO	7	10	3000	1	9	9400	10700
21	9	SISU 22	OP	CTRCN	F/S	RB	IB	50D- 85D		7	10	3200	1	9	13300	16600
21	9	SISU 22 BASS	OP	FSH	F/S	RB	OB			7	10	2200	1	9	10200	11600
21	9	SISU 22 BASS	OP	FSH	F/S	RB	IO	117	VLVO	7	10	3600	2	2	9300	10500

LOA FT	LOA IN	NAME AND/ OR MODEL	TOP/ RIG	BOAT TYPE	HULL MTL	HULL TP	ENGINE TP	ENGINE # HP	ENGINE MFG	BEAM FT	BEAM IN	WGT LBS	DRAFT FT	DRAFT IN	RETAIL LOW	RETAIL HIGH
		1984 BOATS														
21	9	SISU 22 BASS	OP	FSH	F/S	RB	IB	138	VLVO	7	10	3600	2	2	10600	12000
21	9	SISU 22 BASS	OP	FSH	F/S	RB	IO	145		7	10	3600			9050	10300
21	9	SISU 22 BASS	OP	FSH	F/S	RB	IB	50D- 85D		7	10	3600	2	2	14200	17100
21	9	SISU 22 LOBSTER	HT	FSH	F/S	RB	OB			7	10	2200	1	9	10200	11600
21	9	SISU 22 LOBSTER	HT	FSH	F/S	RB	IO	117	VLVO	7	10	3600	2	2	9300	10500
21	9	SISU 22 LOBSTER	HT	FSH	F/S	RB	IB	125	VLVO	7	10	3600	2	2	10500	11900
21	9	SISU 22 LOBSTER	HT	FSH	F/S	RB	IB	50D- 85D		7	10	3600	2	2	14200	17100
25	6	SISU 26 BASS	OP	FSH	F/S	RB	IB	85D-200D		9	8	7500	3		30300	37000
25	6	SISU 26 BASS	HT	FSH	F/S	RB	OB			9	8	4500	2	4	20000	22200
25	6	SISU 26 LOBSTER	OP	FSH	F/S	RB	OB			9	8	4500	2	4	19800	22000
25	6	SISU 26 LOBSTER	HT	FSH	F/S	RB	IB	225	CHRY	9	8	7500	3		23500	26100
25	6	SISU 26 LOBSTER	HT	FSH	F/S	RB	IB	85D-200D		9	8	7500	3		30300	37000
25	6	SISU 26 OFFSHORE	HT	PH	F/S	RB	OB			9	8	4500	2	4	20000	22200
25	6	SISU 26 OFFSHORE	HT	PH	F/S	RB	IB	225	CHRY	9	8	7500	3		23500	26100
25	6	SISU 26 OFFSHORE	HT	PH	F/S	RB	IB	85D-200D		9	8	7500	3		30300	37000
29	9	SISU 30	HT	CBNCR	F/S	RB	IB	225	CHRY	10	6	10000	3		35000	38800
29	9	SISU 30	HT	CBNCR	F/S	RB	IB	200D-240D		10	6	10000	3		48000	54900

....For earlier years, see the BUC Used Boat Price Guide, Volume 3

SKEETER BOATS INC

A SUBDIVISION OF GARLOCK
DIV OF STEMCO MARINE
KILGORE TX 75662

COAST GUARD MFG ID- STE

See inside cover to adjust price for area

For more recent years, see the BUC Used Boat Price Guide, Volume 1

LOA FT	LOA IN	NAME AND/ OR MODEL	TOP/ RIG	BOAT TYPE	HULL MTL	HULL TP	ENGINE TP	ENGINE # HP	ENGINE MFG	BEAM FT	BEAM IN	WGT LBS	DRAFT FT	DRAFT IN	RETAIL LOW	RETAIL HIGH
		1988 BOATS														
16	4	SKEETER SF-140	OP	RNBT	FBG		OB			7	1	900			1900	2250
17		SKEETER SD-125	OP	RNBT	FBG		OB			6	8	1000			2050	2450
17		SKEETER SD-125FS	OP	RNBT	FBG		OB			6	8	1000			2300	2650
17		SKEETER SF-150	OP	RNBT	FBG		OB			7	3	1050			2300	2650
17		SKEETER SF-150FS	OP	RNBT	FBG		OB			7	3	1000			2200	2550
17		SKEETER SF-150SX	OP	RNBT	FBG		OB			7	3	1050			2300	2650
18	5	SKEETER SF-175	OP	RNBT	FBG		OB			7	3	1200			2550	2950
18	5	SKEETER SF-175DX	OP	RNBT	FBG		OB			7	3	1225			2650	3100
18	5	SKEETER SF-175FS	OP	RNBT	FBG		OB			7	3	1250			2700	3150
18	5	SKEETER SF-175S	OP	RNBT	FBG		OB			7	3	1200			2650	3050
18	5	SKEETER SF-175SX	OP	RNBT	FBG		OB			7	3	1200			2700	3150
20	7	SKEETER SK-2000	OP	RNBT	FBG		OB			8		1400			5200	5950
		1987 BOATS														
16	2	SKEETER HP-150	OP		FBG		OB			6	11	925			1850	2200
16	2	SKEETER SW-150	OP		FBG		OB			6	11	975			1900	2300
16	4	SKEETER SF-115	OP		FBG		OB			7	1	900			1800	2150
17		SKEETER SF-150	OP		FBG		OB			7	3	1050			2150	2500
17		SKEETER SF-160	OP		FBG		OB			7	3	1050			2150	2500
18	5	SKEETER SF-175	OP		FBG		OB			7	3	1200			2500	2900
18	5	SKEETER SF-175D	OP		FBG		OB			7	3	1225			2550	2950
18	5	SKEETER SF-180	OP		FBG		OB			7	3	1250			2550	3000
		1985 BOATS														
16		SKEETER C-265	OP		FBG		OB			5	5	800			1500	1750
16	2	SKEETER HP-150	OP		FBG		OB			6	11	925			1700	2050
16	2	SKEETER SW-150	OP		FBG		OB			6	11	975			1800	2150
16	4	SKEETER SF-115	OP		FBG		OB			7	1	900			1650	2000
17		SKEETER SF-150	OP		FBG		OB			7	3	1050			2000	2400
17		SKEETER SF-160	OP		FBG		OB			7	3	1050			1900	2300
18	5	SKEETER SF-175	OP		FBG		OB			7	3	1200			2350	2750
18	5	SKEETER SF-175D	OP		FBG		OB			7	3	1225			2400	2800
18	5	SKEETER SF-180	OP		FBG		OB			7	3	1250			2450	2850
		1984 BOATS														
17	11	STARFIRE 18	OP	BASS	FBG	DV	OB			7	2	1400			2500	2900

....For earlier years, see the BUC Used Boat Price Guide, Volume 3

SKI-PRO INC

MCQUEENEY TX 78123

See inside cover to adjust price for area

For more recent years, see the BUC Used Boat Price Guide, Volume 1

LOA FT	LOA IN	NAME AND/ OR MODEL	TOP/ RIG	BOAT TYPE	HULL MTL	HULL TP	ENGINE TP	ENGINE # HP	ENGINE MFG	BEAM FT	BEAM IN	WGT LBS	DRAFT FT	DRAFT IN	RETAIL LOW	RETAIL HIGH
		1995 BOATS														
20		EXTREME STD	OP	SKI	FBG	SV	IO	180	VLVO	7	4	2300	2	9	8000	9150
20		SKI-PRO 2000	OP	SKI	FBG	SV	IO	180	VLVO	7	5	2450	2	9	8450	9750
20		SKI-PRO EXTREME FOOT	OP	SKI	FBG	SV	IO	250	VLVO	7	5	2300	2	9	9000	10200
20		SKI-PRO FOOTER	OP	SKI	FBG	SV	IO	250	VLVO	7	5	2400	2	9	9200	10400
21		SKI-PRO 2050	OP	SKI	FBG	SV	IO	180	VLVO	7	2	2600	2	9	9700	11000
21		SKI-PRO 2100 BR	OP	SKI	FBG	SV	IO	180	VLVO	7	2	2600	2	9	9900	11300
21		SKI-PRO 2100 EXTREME	OP	SKI	FBG	SV	IO	180	VLVO	7	2	2600	2	9	8450	9700
21		SKI-PRO EXTREME BR	OP	SKI	FBG	SV	IO	180	VLVO	7	2	2600	2	9	8650	9950
		1994 BOATS														
20		EXTREME COMPETITION	OP	SKI	FBG	SV	IO	187	VLVO	7	4	2300	2	9	7800	8950
20		EXTREME CONFORT	OP	SKI	FBG	SV	IO	187	VLVO	7	4	2300	2	9	7800	8950
20		EXTREME STD	OP	SKI	FBG	SV	IO	187	VLVO	7	4	2300	2	9	7450	8600
20		SKI-PRO 2000	OP	SKI	FBG	SV	IO	270	VLVO	7	5	2450	2	9	8650	9950
20		SKI-PRO 2000 FOOTER	OP	SKI	FBG	SV	IO	270	VLVO	7	3	2400	2	9	8650	9950
21		SKI-PRO 2100 BR	OP	SKI	FBG	SV	IO	230	MRCR	7	2	2600	2	9	8450	9700
		1993 BOATS														
20		EXTREME COMPETITION	OP	SKI	FBG	SV	IO	187	VLVO	7	4	2300	2	9	7300	8400
20		EXTREME CONFORT	OP	SKI	FBG	SV	IO	187	VLVO	7	4	2300	2	9	7300	8400
20		EXTREME STD	OP	SKI	FBG	SV	IO	187	VLVO	7	4	2300	2	9	7000	8050
20		SKI-PRO 2000	OP	SKI	FBG	SV	IO	270	VLVO	7	5	2450	2	9	8100	9300
20		SKI-PRO 2000 FOOTER	OP	SKI	FBG	SV	IO	270	VLVO	7	3	2400	2	9	8100	9300
21		SKI-PRO 2100 BR	OP	SKI	FBG	SV	IO	230	MRCR	7	2	2600	2	9	7900	9050
		1992 BOATS														
20	1	2000	OP	SKI	FBG	SV	IO	230		7	5	2500	2	9	6900	8350
20	1	BAREFOOT 2000	OP	SKI	FBG	SV	IO	230	MRCR	7	5	2500	2	9	7050	8150
21	1	2100 BOWRIDER	OP	SKI	FBG	SV	IO	230		7	5	2500	2	9	7400	8850
		1991 BOATS														
20		2000 I/O	OP	SKI	FBG	SV	IO	260	MRCR	7	5	2450	2	9	6650	7650
20		2000 I/O FOOTER	OP	SKI	FBG	SV	IO	275	VLVO	7	5	2450	2	9	7200	8300
21		2100 BOWRIDER	OP	SKI	FBG	SV	IO	260	MRCR	7	5	2500	2	9	7100	8200
		1990 BOATS														
18		1800 I/O	OP	SKI	FBG	SV	IB	175	MRCR	7	5	2300			6100	7000
20		2000 I/O	OP	SKI	FBG	SV	IO	260	MRCR	7	5	2450			6550	7500
20		SKI PRO 1800	OP	SKI	FBG	DV	IO	175	MRCR	7	5	2200	1	6	5550	6400
20		SKI PRO 2000	OP	SKI	FBG	DV	IO	260	MRCR	7	5	2450	1	6	6000	6900
20		SKI PRO BOW RIDER	OP	SKI	FBG	DV	IB	260	MRCR	7	5	2200	1	6	7500	8600
20		SKI PRO INBOARD	OP	SKI	FBG	DV	IB	260	MRCR	7	5	2300	1	6	7650	8800
20		SKI PRO PREDITOR	OP	SKI	FBG	DV	IO	320	MRCR	7	5	2450	1	6	7100	8150
21		2100 BOWRIDER	OP	SKI	FBG	SV	IO	260	MRCR	7	5	2500			6700	7700
		1989 BOATS														
20		SKI PRO 1800	OP	SKI	FBG	DV	IO	175	MRCR	7	5	2200	1	6	5250	6050
20		SKI PRO 2000	OP	SKI	FBG	DV	IO	260	MRCR	7	5	2450	1	6	5900	6800
20		SKI PRO PREDITOR	OP	SKI	FBG	DV	IO	320	MRCR	7	5	2450	1	6	6700	7700
20		SKI-PRO 1800	OP	SKI	FBG	DV	IO	175	MRCR	7	5	2300	1	4	4850	5600
20		SKI-PRO 2000	OP	SKI	FBG	DV	IO	175-260		7	5	2300	1	4	5850	6850
		1987 BOATS														
20		SKI-PRO 2000	ST	SKI	FBG	SV	OB			7	5	1700			4750	5500
20		SKI-PRO 2000	ST	SKI	FBG	SV	IO	260	MRCR	7	5	2660	1	6	5550	6400
		1986 BOATS														
20		SKI-PRO 2000	ST	SKI	FBG	SV	OB			7	5	1700			4650	5350
20		SKI-PRO 2000	ST	SKI	FBG	SV	IO	260	MRCR	7	5	2660	1	6	5300	6100
		1985 BOATS														
18	3	SKI-PRO 1800	ST	SKI	FBG	SV	OB			7	5	1750			4000	4700
18	3	SKI-PRO 1800	ST	SKI	FBG	SV	IO	140-205		7	5	2500	1	6	3800	4550
18	3	SKI-PRO 1800	ST	SKI	FBG	SV	IO	230-260		7	5	2650	1	6	4100	4950

SKIFF CRAFT

HENRY BOATS
PLAIN CITY OH 43064

COAST GUARD MFG ID- HEN
FORMERLY HENRY BOATS INC

See inside cover to adjust price for area

For more recent years, see the BUC Used Boat Price Guide, Volume 1

LOA FT	LOA IN	NAME AND/ OR MODEL	TOP/ RIG	BOAT TYPE	HULL MTL	HULL TP	ENGINE TP	ENGINE # HP	ENGINE MFG	BEAM FT	BEAM IN	WGT LBS	DRAFT FT	DRAFT IN	RETAIL LOW	RETAIL HIGH
		1994 BOATS														
16		PETITE FISHERMAN	OP	FSH	MHG	SV	OB			5	4	400		5	2250	2600
22		X220	OP	RNBT	WD	SV	IO	180		8	1	2960	2	7	13100	14900
22		X220	OP	RNBT	WD	SV	IB	205		8	1	2960	2	7	16600	18800
22		X220	HT	RNBT	WD	SV	IO	180		8	1	2960	2	7	13100	14900
22		X220	HT	RNBT	WD	SV	IB	205		8	1	2960	2	7	16600	18800
24	3	X240	OP	RNBT	WD	SV	IO	180		8	1	3960	2	9	18000	20100
24	3	X240	OP	RNBT	WD	SV	IB	205		8	1	3960	2	9	22700	25200
24	3	X240	HT	RNBT	WD	SV	IO	180		8	1	3960	2	9	18000	20100
24	3	X240	HT	RNBT	WD	SV	IB	205		8	1	3960	2	9	22700	25200
25	6	X260	OP	RNBT	WD	SV	IO	205		9	10	5600	2	6	25000	27800
25	6	X260	OP	RNBT	WD	SV	IB	205		9	10	5600	2	6	31600	35200
25	6	X260	OP	RNBT	WD	SV	IO	T170		9	10	5600	2	6	27400	30500

LOA FT IN	NAME AND/OR MODEL	TOP/RIG	BOAT TYPE	HULL MTL	HULL TP	ENG TP	#	HP	MFG	BEAM FT IN	WGT LBS	DRAFT FT IN	RETAIL LOW	RETAIL HIGH
1994 BOATS														
25 6	X260	HT	RNBT	WD	SV	IB		205		9 10	5600	2 6	25000	27800
25 6	X260	HT	RNBT	WD	SV	IB		205		9 10	5600	2 6	31600	35200
25 6	X260	HT	RNBT	WD	SV			T170		9 10	5600	2 6	27400	30500
25 6	X260	FB	SF	WD	SV	IB		205		9 10	5600	2 6	30900	34300
25 6	X260	FB	SF	WD	SV	IB		205		9 10	5600	2 6	32000	35600
25 6	X260	FB	SF	WD	SV			T170		9 10	5600	2 6	34100	37900
28 2	X280	OP	RNBT	WD	SV	IO		300		10 2	7050	3 9	29800	33100
28 2	X280	OP	RNBT	WD	SV	IB		300		10 2	7050	3 9	43000	47800
28 2	X280	OP	RNBT	WD	SV	IB		T205		10 2	7050	3 9	46300	50800
28 2	X280	HT	RNBT	WD	SV	IO		300		10 2	7050	3 9	29800	33100
28 2	X280	HT	RNBT	WD	SV	IB		300		10 2	7050	3 9	43000	47800
28 2	X280	HT	RNBT	WD	SV	IB		T205		10 2	7050	3 9	46300	50800
28 2	X280	FB	SF	WD	SV	IO		300		10 2	7050	3 9	42600	47300
28 2	X280	FB	SF	WD	SV	IB		300		10 2	7050	3 9	43900	48800
28 2	X280	FB	SF	WD	SV	IB		T205		10 2	7050	3 9	47400	52100
31 2	X310	OP	RNBT	WD	SV	IB		300		11 6	9500	2 8	40200	44600
31 2	X310	OP	RNBT	WD	SV	IB		T205		11 6	9500	2 8	58900	64700
31 2	X310	OP	RNBT	WD	SV	IB		300		11 6	9500	2 8	61600	67700
31 2	X310	HT	RNBT	WD	SV	IO		300		11 6	9500	2 8	40200	44600
31 2	X310	HT	RNBT	WD	SV	IB		300		11 6	9500	2 8	58900	64700
31 2	X310	HT	RNBT	WD	SV	IB		T205		11 6	9500	2 8	61600	67700
31 2	X310	FB	SF	WD	SV	IO		300		11 6	9500	2 8	53700	59000
31 2	X310	FB	SF	WD	SV	IB		300		11 6	9500	2 8	56100	61600
31 2	X310	FB	SF	WD	SV	IB		T205		11 6	9500	2 8	58800	64600
33	X330	OP	RNBT	WD	SV	IB		300					73400	80700
33	X330	OP	RNBT	WD	SV	IB		T205					76500	84100
33	X330	HT	RNBT	WD	SV	IO		300					54500	59900
33	X330	HT	RNBT	WD	SV	IB		300					73500	80700
33	X330	HT	RNBT	WD	SV	IB		T205					76500	84100
33	X330	FB	SF	WD	SV	IO		300					67000	73600
33	X330	FB	SF	WD	SV	IB		300					69800	76700
33	X330	FB	SF	WD	SV	IB		T205					72600	79800
1993 BOATS														
26	ELITE 26	OP	RNBT	MBG	SV	OB				9 10	5000	2 4	26500	29500
28 2	X280	OP	RNBT	WD	SV	IO		300		10 2	7050	3 9	40800	45300
28 2	X280	OP	RNBT	WD	SV	IB		T205		10 2	7050	3 9	43400	48200
28 2	X280	HT	RNBT	WD	SV	IO		300		10 2	7050	3 9	40800	45300
28 2	X280	HT	RNBT	WD	SV	IB		T205		10 2	7050	3 9	43400	48200
28 2	X280	FB	SF	WD	SV	IO		300		10 2	7050	3 9	41600	46200
28 2	X280	FB	SF	WD	SV	IB		T205		10 2	7050	3 9	44400	49300
31 2	X310	OP	RNBT	WD	SV	IB		300		11 6	9500	2 8	55800	61300
31 2	X310	OP	RNBT	WD	SV	IB		T205		11 6	9500	2 8	58300	64100
31 2	X310	HT	RNBT	WD	SV	IB		300		11 6	9500	2 8	55800	61400
31 2	X310	HT	RNBT	WD	SV	IB		T205		11 6	9500	2 8	58400	64100
31 2	X310	FB	SF	WD	SV	IB		300		11 6	9500	2 8	53100	58400
31 2	X310	FB	SF	WD	SV	IB		T205		11 6	9500	2 8	55700	61200
33	X330	OP	RNBT	WD	SV	IB		300					69600	76400
33	X330	OP	RNBT	WD	SV	IB		T205					72500	79600
33	X330	HT	RNBT	WD	SV	IB		300					69600	76500
33	X330	HT	RNBT	WD	SV	IB		T205					72500	79700
33	X330	FB	SF	WD	SV	IB		300					66200	72700
33	X330	FB	SF	WD	SV	IB		T205					68800	75600
1987 BOATS														
22	X-220	OP	RNBT	WD	SV	IO		120		8			8450	9700
24	X-240	OP	RNBT	WD	SV	IO		170		8			11300	12800
24	X-240	OP	RNBT	WD	SV	IO		235		8			15300	17400
25 10	X-260	OP	RNBT	WD	SV	IO		198		10			15700	17800
25 10	X-260	OP	RNBT	WD	SV	IO		235		10			22000	24400
25 10	X-260	FB	SF	WD	SV	IO		198		10			19700	21900
31 2	X-310	OP	RNBT	WD	SV	IB		T235		12			44100	49000
31 2	X-310	HT	RNBT	WD	SV	IB		T235		12			44100	49000
1986 BOATS														
22	X-220			L/P	SV	IO		120		8			8100	9300
24	X-240			L/P		IB		235		8			14600	16600
24	X-240			L/P		IO		170		8			10900	12400
25 10	X-260			L/P		IB		235		10			21300	23700
31 2	X-310			L/P		IB		T235		12			40200	44700
1985 BOATS														
21 10	X-220	OP	RNBT	L/P	SV	IO		170	MRCR	8	2700		7350	8450
22	X-220	HT	CBNCR	L/P	SV	IO		120	MRCR	8			9150	10400
22	X-220	HT	RNBT	L/P	SV	IO		170	MRCR	8			7750	8900
24	X-240	OP	CBNCR	L/P	SV	IO		170	MRCR	8			12500	14300
24	X-240	HT	CBNCR	L/P	SV	IO		235	MRCR	8			14500	16500
24 3	X-240	OP	RNBT	L/P	SV	IO		198	MRCR	8	3500		9750	11100
24 3	X-240	OP	RNBT	L/P	SV	IB		235	MRCR	8			14200	16100
24 3	X-240	HT	RNBT	L/P	SV	IO		198	MRCR	8	3500		9750	11100
25 10	X-260	HT	CBNCR	L/P	SV	IB		235	MRCR	10			23100	25600
25 10	X-260	OP	RNBT	L/P	SV	IB		198	MRCR	10	5500		14800	16800
25 10	X-260	OP	RNBT	L/P	SV	IB		235		10			20000	22200
25 10	X-260	HT	RNBT	L/P	SV	IO		198	MRCR	10	5500		14800	16800
25 10	X-260	FB	SF	L/P	SV	IO		198	MRCR	10	5500		18600	20700
25 10	X-260	FB	SF	L/P	SV	IB		235	MRCR	10			20400	22700
30	X-300	OP	RNBT	L/P	SV	IB		T225-T235		12	8200		35100	40900
30	X-300	HT	RNBT	L/P	SV	IB		T225-T235		12	8600		35500	40900
30	X-300	FB	SF	L/P	SV	IB		T225-T235		12	8900		34600	39500
1984 BOATS														
21 10	X-220	HT	CBNCR	L/P	SV	IO		170	MRCR	8	2700		8200	9450
21 10	X-220		RNBT	L/P	SV	IO		120	MRCR	8			7400	8500
21 10	X-220	OP	RNBT	L/P	SV	IO		170	MRCR	8	2700		7100	8150
24 3	X-240	OP	CBNCR	L/P	SV	IO		198	MRCR	8	3500		11700	13300
24 3	X-240	HT	CBNCR	L/P	SV	IB		198	MRCR	8	3500		11700	13300
24 3	X-240	HT	CBNCR	L/P	SV	IB		225		8			13900	15800
24 3	X-240	OP	RNBT	L/P	SV	IB		198	MRCR	8	3500		9450	10700
24 3	X-240	HT	RNBT	L/P	SV	IO		198	MRCR	8	3800		9950	11300
25 10	X-260	HT	CBNCR	L/P	SV	IB		198	MRCR	10	5500		22000	24400
25 10	X-260	HT	CBNCR	L/P	SV	IB		225		10			22000	24400
25 10	X-260	OP	RNBT	L/P	SV	IO		198	MRCR	10	5500		14300	16200
25 10	X-260	HT	RNBT	L/P	SV	IO		198	MRCR	10	5500		14300	16200
25 10	X-260	FB	SDNSF	L/P	SV	IO		198	MRCR	10	5500		17600	20000
25 10	X-260	FB	SF	L/P	SV	IO		198	MRCR	10	5500		17600	20000
30	X-300	OP	RNBT	L/P	SV	IB		T225	CHRY	12	8200		33500	37200
30	X-300	HT	RNBT	L/P	SV	IB		T225	CHRY	12	8600		34000	37700
30	X-300	FB	SF	L/P	SV	IB		T225	CHRY	12	8900		33100	36800

....For earlier years, see the BUC Used Boat Price Guide, Volume 3

SKIMMER BOATS

CREATIVE MARINE PRODUCTS
SOUTH CENTRAL GROUP INC
NATCHEZ MS 39120

See inside cover to adjust price for area

For more recent years, see the BUC Used Boat Price Guide, Volume 1

LOA FT IN	NAME AND/OR MODEL	TOP/RIG	BOAT TYPE	HULL MTL	HULL TP	ENG TP	#	HP	MFG	BEAM FT IN	WGT LBS	DRAFT FT IN	RETAIL LOW	RETAIL HIGH
1996 BOATS														
29 8	SKIMMER 25	SLP	SCFAC	FBG	CB	OB		9D	YAN	8 2	3000	3 10	21900	24300
29 8	SKIMMER 25 PH	SLP	SCFAC	FBG	CB	OB				8 2	3400	3 10	24400	27100

SKIPJACK OF FT LAUD FLA INC

COOPER CITY FL 33328

COAST GUARD MFG ID- PNL   See inside cover to adjust price for area
FORMERLY PANALBOAT CO

LOA FT IN	NAME AND/OR MODEL	TOP/RIG	BOAT TYPE	HULL MTL	HULL TP	ENG TP	#	HP	MFG	BEAM FT IN	WGT LBS	DRAFT FT IN	RETAIL LOW	RETAIL HIGH
1987 BOATS														
22		CUT	MS	F/S		OB				7 9			4700	5400
36		CUT	MS	F/S		IB		275		11			35700	39600
1985 BOATS														
22		CUT	MS	F/S		OB				7 9			4050	4700
36		CUT	MS	F/S		IB		275		11			30900	34300

SKIPPER BOATS LTD

QUAY WARRINGTON UK

See inside cover to adjust price for area

LOA FT IN	NAME AND/OR MODEL	TOP/RIG	BOAT TYPE	HULL MTL	HULL TP	ENG TP	#	HP	MFG	BEAM FT IN	WGT LBS	DRAFT FT IN	RETAIL LOW	RETAIL HIGH
1986 BOATS														
17	SKIPPER 17	SLP	SAIL	FBG	SK					7	1100	1 6	6450	7400
1985 BOATS														
17	SKIPPER 17	SLP	SA/CR	FBG	CB	OB				7	1000		5750	6600
1984 BOATS														
17	SKIPPER 17	SLP	SA/CR	FBG	CB	OB				7	1000	1 3	5400	6200

....For earlier years, see the BUC Used Boat Price Guide, Volume 3

SKIPPERLINER INDUSTRIES

LACROSSE WI 54603-1533   COAST GUARD MFG ID- SGU See inside cover to adjust price for area

```
     LOA  NAME AND/            TOP/ BOAT -HULL- ----ENGINE--- BEAM  WGT  DRAFT RETAIL RETAIL
     FT IN  OR MODEL           RIG  TYPE MTL TP TP # HP MFG   FT IN LBS  FT IN  LOW   HIGH
-------------------------- 1995 BOATS -------------------------------------------------------
     60    SKIPPERLINER 620    FB   MY   FBG DS IB T    D CAT  16   56500  3  6   **     **
     66    SKIPPERLINER 700    FB   MY   FBG DS IB T    D CAT  18   62000  3  4   **     **
-------------------------- 1994 BOATS -------------------------------------------------------
     60    SKIPPERLINER 620    FB   MY   FBG DS IB T    D CAT  16   56500  3  6   **     **
     66    SKIPPERLINER 700    FB   MY   FBG DS IB T    D CAT  18   62000  3  4   **     **
-------------------------- 1993 BOATS -------------------------------------------------------
     60    SKIPPERLINER 620    FB   MY   FBG DS IB T    D CAT  16   56500  3  6   **     **
     66    SKIPPERLINER 700    FB   MY   FBG DS IB T    D CAT  18   62000  3  4   **     **
-------------------------- 1992 BOATS -------------------------------------------------------
     59 10 600 COASTAL MY      FB   MY   FBG DS IB T425D CAT  16   56000  3  6  143000 157000
-------------------------- 1988 BOATS -------------------------------------------------------
     40    FANTASY ISLAND      HT   HB   STL DS IB  120       14             37000  41100
           IB  130     37100  41300, IB  170         37600  41800, IB  200   37700  41900
           IB  211 VLVO 38100  42400, IB T120        38900  43200, IB T130   39200  43500
           IB  170     40100  44600, IB T200         40400  44900
     45    FANTASY ISLAND      HT   HB   STL DS IB  120       14             41700  46300
           IB  130     41800  46500, IB  170         42300  47000, IB  200   42500  47200
           IB  211 VLVO 42800  47600, IB T120        43600  48500, IB T130   43900  48800
           IB T170     45100  49900, IB T200         45700  50200, IB T230   45900  50400
           IB T260     46100  50700
     49    FANTASY ISLAND      HT   HB   STL DS IB  120       14             53900  59200
           IB  130     54000  59400, IB  170         54500  59900, IB  200   54600  60100
           IB  211 VLVO 55000  60500, IB T120        55800  61300, IB T130   56100  61700
           IB T170     56800  62400, IB T200         57000  62900, IB T230   57200  62800
           IB T260     57400  63100, IB T330         58800  64700
     50    AQUAMINIUM          HT   HB   STL DS IB  120       14             56000  61600
           IB  130     56400  62000, IB  170         56600  62200, IB  200   56300  61900
           IB  230     57300  63000, IB  260         57400  63000, IB  330   58200  63900
           IB T120     56700  62300, IB T130         57500  63200, IB T170   57800  63500
           IB T200     59000  64900, IB T230         59700  65600, IB T260   59900  65800
           IB T330     62100  68200
     50    FANTASY ISLAND      HT   HB   STL DS IB  120       14             57200  62900
           IB  130     57200  62900, IB  170         57600  63300, IB  200   58200  63900
           IB  211 VLVO 57600  63300, IB T120        60100  66000, IB T130   59900  65900
           IB T170     61500  67600, IB T200         60800  66800, IB T230   60500  66500
           IB T260     60800  66800
     53    AQUAMINIUM          HT   HB   STL DS IB  120       14             71100  78200
           IB  130     71300  78400, IB  170         71900  79000, IB  200   72100  79200
           IB  230     72200  79300, IB T120        73500  80800, IB T130    73900  81300
           IB T170     75200  82600, IB T200         75500  83000, IB T230   75700  83200
           IB T260     76000  83500, IB T330         77800  85500
     55    AQUAMINIUM          HT   HB   STL DS IB  120       14             78200  85900
           IB  130     78500  86300, IB  170         79100  86900, IB  200   78900  86700
           IB  230     79700  87500, IB T120         80300  88200, IB T130   81100  89100
           IB T170     82600  90800, IB T200         82500  90600, IB T230   83300  91500
           IB T260     83900  92200, IB T330         86600  95200
     55    FANTASY ISLAND      HT   HB   STL DS IB  120       14             79000  86800
           IB  130     79000  86800, IB  170         79700  87600, IB  200   80200  88100
           IB  211 VLVO 80000  88000, IB T120        81700  89800, IB T130   81700  89800
           IB T170     82600  90800, IB T200         83500  91700, IB T230   83100  91200
           IB T260     83100  91300, IB T330         83900  92200
     58    FLAGSHIP EXECUTIVE  HT   HB   STL DS IB  271       16             84300  92600
           IB  130D    88700  97400, IB T190         87100  95800, IB T200   87100  95700
           IB T230     87600  96200, IB T260         87700  96400, IB T330   89000  97800
     58    FLAGSHIP TRI LEVEL  HT   HB   STL DS IB  271       16             87700  96400
           IB  130D    90100  99000, IB T190         90900  99900, IB T200   91000 100000
           IB T230     91000 100000, IB T260         91500 100500, IB T330   93800 103000
     60    AQUAMINIUM          HT   HB   STL DS IB  120       14             84800  93200
           IB  130     85000  93400, IB  170         85600  94000, IB  200   85700  94200
           IB  230     85800  94300, IB T120         87100  95700, IB T130   87500  96100
           IB T170     88600  97400, IB T200         89000  97700, IB T230   89100  98000
           IB T260     89400  98300, IB T330         91100 100000
     66    FLAGSHIP CRSNG YACHT HT  HB   STL DS IB  271       16             99000 109000
           IB  130D   108000 118500, IB T230        102500 112500, IB T260  102500 113000
           IB T330    104500 114500
     73    FLAGSHIP CRSNG YACHT HT  HB   STL DS IB  271       16              **     **
           IB  130D     **     **  , IB T260          **     **  , IB T330    **     **
-------------------------- 1986 BOATS -------------------------------------------------------
     36    FANTASY-ISLAND F1360 HT  HB   STL DS IO T120 MRCR 14    19200  2 10  46300  50800
           IO T120 OMC  46100  50600, IO T125 VLVO  47300  52000, IO T138 VLVO 47400 52100
           IO T140 OMC  46100  50700, IO T170 MRCR  46400  51000, IO T200 MRCR 46700 51300
           IO T200 OMC  46500  51100, IO T200 VLVO  47900  52600, IO T225 VLVO 48400 53200
           IO T230 MRCR 47300  52000, IO T230 OMC   47000  51700, IO T260 MRCR 48200 53300
           IO T260 OMC  47900  52700, IO T260 VLVO  49700  54600
     36    FANTASY-ISLAND F1360 FB  HB   STL DS IO T120 MRCR 14    19200  2 10  46300  50800
           IO T120 OMC  46100  50600, IO T125 VLVO  47300  52000, IO T138 VLVO 47400 52100
           IO T140 OMC  46100  50700, IO T170 MRCR  46400  51000, IO T200 MRCR 46700 51300
           IO T200 OMC  46500  51100, IO T200 VLVO  47900  52600, IO T225 VLVO 48400 53200
           IO T230 MRCR 47300  52000, IO T230 OMC   47000  51700, IO T260 MRCR 48200 53300
           IO T260 OMC  47900  52700, IO T260 VLVO  49700  54600
     36    FANTASY-ISLAND FI360 HT  HB   STL DS IO  120 MRCR 14    19200  2 10  43200  48000
           IO  120 OMC  43100  47900, IO  125 VLVO  43800  48600, IO  138 VLVO 43800 48600
           IO  140 OMC  43100  47900, IO  170 MRCR  43300  48100, IO  200 MRCR 43400 48300
           IO  200 OMC  43200  48200, IO  200 VLVO  44000  48900, IO  225 VLVO 44300 49200
           IO  230 MRCR 43700  48600, IO  230 OMC   43600  48400, IO  260 MRCR 44200 49100
           IO  260 OMC  44000  48900, IO  260 VLVO  44900  49900
     36    FANTASY-ISLAND FI360 FB  HB   STL DS IO  120 MRCR 14    19200  2 10  43200  48000
           IO  120 OMC  43100  47900, IO  125 VLVO  43800  48600, IO  138 VLVO 43800 48600
           IO  140 OMC  43100  47900, IO  170 MRCR  43300  48100, IO  200 MRCR 43400 48300
           IO  200 OMC  43200  48200, IO  200 VLVO  44000  48900, IO  225 VLVO 44300 49200
           IO  230 MRCR 43700  48600, IO  230 OMC   43600  48400, IO  260 MRCR 44200 49100
           IO  260 OMC  44000  48900, IO  260 VLVO  44900  49900
     42    FANTASY-ISLAND FI420 HT  HB   STL DS IO  120 MRCR 14    20500  2 10  43300  48100
           IO  120 OMC  43200  48000, IO  125 VLVO  43800  48700, IO  138 VLVO 43800 48700
           IO  140 OMC  43200  48200, IO  170 MRCR  43400  48300, IO  200 MRCR 43500 48300
           IO  200 OMC  43400  48200, IO  200 VLVO  44000  49000, IO  225 VLVO 44300 49300
           IO  230 MRCR 43800  48600, IO  230 OMC   43600  48500, IO  260 MRCR 44200 49100
           IO  260 OMC  44100  49000, IO  260 VLVO  44900  49900, IO T120 MRCR 46300 50900
           IO T120 OMC  46100  50600, IO T125 VLVO  47400  52000, IO T138 VLVO 47400 52100
           IO T140 OMC  46100  50700, IO T170 MRCR  46500  51100, IO T200 MRCR 46700 51400
           IO T200 OMC  46500  51100, IO T200 VLVO  47900  52600, IO T225 VLVO 48400 53200
           IO T230 MRCR 47300  52000, IO T230 OMC   47000  51700, IO T260 MRCR 48200 53000
           IO T260 OMC  47900  52700, IO T260 VLVO  49700  54600
     42    FANTASY-ISLAND FI420 FB  HB   STL DS IO  120 MRCR 14    20500  2 10  43300  48100
           IO  120 OMC  43200  48000, IO  125 VLVO  43800  48700, IO  138 VLVO 43800 48700
           IO  140 OMC  43200  48200, IO  170 MRCR  43400  48200, IO  200 MRCR 43500 48300
           IO  200 OMC  43400  48200, IO  200 VLVO  44000  49000, IO  225 VLVO 44300 49300
           IO  230 MRCR 43800  48600, IO  230 OMC   43600  48500, IO  260 MRCR 44200 49100
           IO  260 OMC  44100  49000, IO  260 VLVO  44900  49900, IO T120 MRCR 46300 50900
           IO T120 OMC  46100  50600, IO T125 VLVO  47400  52000, IO T138 VLVO 47400 52100
           IO T140 OMC  46100  50700, IO T170 MRCR  46500  51100, IO T200 MRCR 46700 51400
           IO T200 OMC  46500  51100, IO T200 VLVO  47900  52600, IO T225 VLVO 48400 53200
           IO T230 MRCR 47300  52000, IO T230 OMC   47000  51700, IO T260 MRCR 48200 53000
           IO T260 OMC  47900  52700
     44    AQUAMINIUM AQ440     HT  HB   STL DS IO  120 MRCR 14    22500  2 11  51300  56400
           IO  120 OMC  51200  56300, IO  125 VLVO  51900  57100, IO  138 VLVO 51200 56300
           IO  140 OMC  51300  56300, IO  170 MRCR  51400  56500, IO  200 MRCR 51600 56700
           IO  228 MRCR 51500  56600, IO  200 OMC   51500  56700, IO  225 VLVO 52500 57700
           IO  260 OMC  52300  57400, IO  260 VLVO  51800  56900, IO  260 MRCR 52400 57600
           IO  330 MRCR 54400  59800, IO T120 MRCR  53700  59000, IO T120 OMC  53800 59100
           IO T125 VLVO 54900  60300, IO T138 VLVO  54900  60300, IO T140 OMC  53500 58800
           IO T170 MRCR 53900  59200, IO T200 MRCR  54200  59600, IO T200 OMC  54000 59300
           IO T225 VLVO 55500  61000, IO T230 MRCR  55800  61300, IO T230 OMC  55500 61000
           IO T260 VLVO 57100  62700, IO T260 MRCR  55800  61300, IO T330 OMC  60400 66300
     44    AQUAMINIUM AQ440     FB  HB   STL DS IO  120 MRCR 14    22500  2 11  51300  56400
           IO  120 OMC  51200  56300, IO  125 VLVO  51900  57100, IO  130 VLVO 51900 57100
           IO  140 OMC  51300  56300, IO  170 MRCR  51400  56500, IO  200 MRCR 51600 56700
           IO  230 MRCR 51900  57000, IO  230 OMC   51800  56900, IO  225 VLVO 52500 57700
           IO  260 MRCR 52300  57400, IO  260 VLVO  53200  58500, IO  290 MRCR 52400 57600
           IO  330 MRCR 54400  59800, IO T120 MRCR  53700  59000, IO T120 OMC  53900 59200
           IO T125 VLVO 54900  60300, IO T138 VLVO  54900  60300, IO T140 OMC  53500 58800
```
```
96th ed. - Vol. II          CONTINUED ON NEXT PAGE                          527
```

LOA FT IN	NAME AND/ OR MODEL	TOP/ RIG	BOAT TYPE	-HULL- MTL	TP	----ENGINE--- TP	# HP	MFG	BEAM FT IN	WGT LBS	DRAFT FT IN	RETAIL LOW	RETAIL HIGH
	1986 BOATS												
44	AQUAMINIUM AQ440	FB	HB	STL	DS	IO	T170	MRCR	14	22500	2 11	53900	59200
	IO T200 MRCR 54200 59600, IO T200 OMC 54000 59300, IO T200 VLVO 55500 61000												
	IO T225 VLVO 56000 61600, IO T230 MRCR 54800 60200, IO T230 OMC 54500 59900												
	IO T260 MRCR 55800 61300, IO T260 OMC 55500 61000, IO T260 VLVO 57100 62700												
	IO T290 VLVO 59000 64800, IO T330 MRCR 60400 66300												
44	FANTASY-ISLAND FI440	HT	HB	STL	DS	IO	120	MRCR	14	21000	2 11	50100	55100
	IO 120 OMC 50000 55000, IO 125 VLVO 50200 55200, IO 138 VLVO 50200 55200												
	IO 140 OMC 50000 55000, IO 170 MRCR 50200 55200, IO 200 MRCR 49900 54800												
	IO 200 OMC 50300 55200, IO 200 VLVO 50500 55500, IO 225 VLVO 50800 55800												
	IO 230 MRCR 50200 55200, IO 230 OMC 50100 55000, IO 260 MRCR 50700 55700												
	IO 260 OMC 50500 55500, IO 260 VLVO 51500 56600, IO T120 MRCR 52400 57600												
	IO T120 OMC 52200 57400, IO T125 VLVO 53600 58900, IO T138 VLVO 53600 58900												
	IO T140 OMC 52200 57400, IO T170 MRCR 52600 57800, IO T200 MRCR 52900 58200												
	IO T200 OMC 52700 57900, IO T200 VLVO 53800 59100, IO T225 VLVO 54300 59700												
	IO T230 MRCR 53500 58800, IO T230 OMC 53300 58500, IO T260 MRCR 54100 59500												
	IO T260 OMC 53800 59100, IO T260 VLVO 55700 61200												
44	FANTASY-ISLAND FI440	FB	HB	STL	DS	IO	120	MRCR	14	21000	2 11	50100	55100
	IO 120 OMC 50000 55000, IO 125 VLVO 50200 55200, IO 138 VLVO 50200 55200												
	IO 140 OMC 50000 55000, IO 170 MRCR 50200 55200, IO 200 MRCR 49900 54800												
	IO 200 OMC 50300 55200, IO 200 VLVO 50500 55500, IO 225 VLVO 50800 55800												
	IO 230 MRCR 50200 55200, IO 230 OMC 50100 55000, IO 260 MRCR 50700 55700												
	IO 260 OMC 50500 55500, IO 260 VLVO 51500 56600, IO T120 MRCR 52400 57600												
	IO T120 OMC 52200 57400, IO T125 VLVO 53600 58900, IO T138 VLVO 53600 58900												
	IO T140 OMC 52200 57400, IO T170 MRCR 52600 57800, IO T200 MRCR 52900 58200												
	IO T200 OMC 52700 57900, IO T200 VLVO 53800 59100, IO T225 VLVO 54300 59700												
	IO T230 MRCR 53500 58800, IO T230 OMC 53300 58500, IO T260 MRCR 54100 59500												
	IO T260 OMC 53800 59100, IO T260 VLVO 55700 61200												
45	SUNDANCE 450	HT	HB	STL	CT	IO	120		14			42000	46600
47	COMMANDER CM470	HT	HB	STL	DS	IO	120	MRCR	14	26000	3	56400	62000
	IO 120 OMC 56300 61900, IO 125 VLVO 57000 62700, IO 138 VLVO 57000 62700												
	IO 140 OMC 56400 61900, IO 170 MRCR 56500 62100, IO 200 MRCR 56700 62300												
	IO 200 OMC 56600 62200, IO 200 VLVO 57300 63000, IO 225 VLVO 57600 63300												
	IO 230 MRCR 57000 62600, IO 230 OMC 56900 62500, IO 260 MRCR 57500 63200												
	IO 260 OMC 57300 63000, IO 260 VLVO 58300 64000, IO 290 VLVO 59200 65100												
	IO 330 MRCR 59900 65800, IO T120 MRCR 59200 65000, IO T120 OMC 59000 64800												
	IO T125 VLVO 60300 66300, IO T138 VLVO 60400 66300, IO T140 OMC 59000 64800												
	IO T170 MRCR 59400 65200, IO T200 MRCR 59700 65600, IO T200 OMC 59400 65300												
	IO T200 VLVO 60900 67000, IO T225 VLVO 61500 67600, IO T230 MRCR 60300 66200												
	IO T230 OMC 60000 65900, IO T260 MRCR 61300 67300, IO T260 OMC 61000 67000												
	IO T260 VLVO 62900 69100, IO T290 VLVO 64800 71200, IO T330 MRCR 66100 72600												
47	COMMANDER CM470	FB	HB	STL	DS	IO	120	MRCR	14	26000	3	56400	62000
	IO 120 OMC 56300 61900, IO 125 VLVO 57000 62700, IO 138 VLVO 57000 62700												
	IO 140 OMC 56400 61900, IO 170 MRCR 56500 62100, IO 200 MRCR 56700 62300												
	IO 200 OMC 56600 62200, IO 200 VLVO 57300 63000, IO 225 VLVO 57600 63300												
	IO 230 MRCR 57000 62600, IO 230 OMC 56900 62500, IO 260 MRCR 57500 63200												
	IO 260 OMC 57300 63000, IO 260 VLVO 58300 64000, IO 290 VLVO 59200 65100												
	IO 330 MRCR 59900 65800, IO T120 MRCR 59200 65000, IO T120 OMC 59000 64800												
	IO T125 VLVO 60300 66300, IO T138 VLVO 60400 66300, IO T140 OMC 59000 64800												
	IO T170 MRCR 59400 65200, IO T200 MRCR 59700 65600, IO T200 OMC 59400 65300												
	IO T200 VLVO 60900 67000, IO T225 VLVO 61500 67600, IO T230 MRCR 60300 66200												
	IO T230 OMC 60000 65900, IO T260 MRCR 61300 67300, IO T260 OMC 61000 67000												
	IO T260 VLVO 62900 69100, IO T290 VLVO 64800 71200, IO T330 MRCR 66100 72600												
48	FANTASY-ISLAND 480	HT	HB	STL	SV	IO	120		14			51500	56600
52	COMMANDER CM520	HT	HB	STL	DS	IO	120	MRCR	14	28000	3	78800	86600
	IO 120 OMC 78700 86500, IO 125 VLVO 79600 87400, IO 138 VLVO 79600 87400												
	IO 140 OMC 78700 86500, IO 170 MRCR 78900 86700, IO 200 MRCR 79100 87000												
	IO 200 OMC 79000 86800, IO 200 VLVO 79900 87800, IO 225 VLVO 80300 88200												
	IO 230 MRCR 79500 87400, IO 230 OMC 79300 87200, IO 260 MRCR 80100 88100												
	IO 260 OMC 79900 87900, IO 260 VLVO 81100 89200, IO 290 VLVO 82400 90500												
	IO 330 MRCR 83200 91400, IO T120 MRCR 82300 90400, IO T120 OMC 82000 90100												
	IO T125 VLVO 83700 92000, IO T138 VLVO 83800 92100, IO T140 OMC 82100 90200												
	IO T170 MRCR 82500 90700, IO T200 MRCR 82900 91100, IO T200 OMC 82600 90800												
	IO T200 VLVO 84500 92900, IO T225 VLVO 85200 93600, IO T230 MRCR 83700 91900												
	IO T230 OMC 83300 91600, IO T260 MRCR 84900 93300, IO T260 OMC 84500 92900												
	IO T260 VLVO 86900 95500, IO T290 VLVO 89300 98200, IO T330 MRCR 91100 100000												
52	COMMANDER CM520	FB	HB	STL	DS	IO	120	MRCR	14	28000	3	78800	86600
	IO 120 OMC 78700 86500, IO 125 VLVO 79600 87400, IO 138 VLVO 79600 87400												
	IO 140 OMC 78700 86500, IO 170 MRCR 78900 86700, IO 200 MRCR 79100 87000												
	IO 200 OMC 79000 86800, IO 200 VLVO 79900 87800, IO 225 VLVO 80300 88200												
	IO 230 MRCR 79500 87400, IO 230 OMC 79300 87200, IO 260 MRCR 80100 88100												
	IO 260 OMC 79900 87900, IO 260 VLVO 81100 89200, IO 290 VLVO 82400 90500												
	IO 330 MRCR 83200 91400, IO T120 MRCR 82300 90400, IO T120 OMC 82000 90100												
	IO T125 VLVO 83700 92000, IO T138 VLVO 83800 92100, IO T140 OMC 82100 90200												
	IO T170 MRCR 82500 90700, IO T200 MRCR 82900 91100, IO T200 OMC 82600 90800												
	IO T200 VLVO 84500 92900, IO T225 VLVO 85200 93600, IO T230 MRCR 83700 91900												
	IO T230 OMC 83300 91600, IO T260 MRCR 84900 93300, IO T260 OMC 84500 92900												
	IO T260 VLVO 86900 95500, IO T290 VLVO 89300 98200, IO T330 MRCR 91100 100000												
53	SUNDANCE 530	HT	HB	STL	CT	IO	120		14			72200	79300
54	AQUAMINIUM 540/542	HT	HB	STL	DS	IO	120	MRCR	14	28500	3	81300	89300
	IO 120 OMC 81100 89100, IO 125 VLVO 82000 90100, IO 138 VLVO 82000 90100												
	IO 140 OMC 81100 89200, IO 170 MRCR 81400 89400, IO 200 MRCR 81600 89600												
	IO 200 OMC 81400 89500, IO 200 VLVO 82400 90500, IO 225 VLVO 82700 90900												
	IO 230 MRCR 81900 90100, IO 230 OMC 81800 89900, IO 260 MRCR 82600 90700												
	IO 260 OMC 82400 90500, IO 260 VLVO 83600 91800, IO 290 VLVO 84800 93200												
	IO 330 MRCR 85600 94100, IO T120 MRCR 84700 93100, IO T120 OMC 84400 92800												
	IO T125 VLVO 86200 94700, IO T138 VLVO 86200 94800, IO T140 OMC 84500 92900												
	IO T170 MRCR 85000 93400, IO T200 MRCR 85400 93800, IO T200 OMC 85100 93500												
	IO T200 VLVO 86900 95500, IO T225 VLVO 87700 96300, IO T230 MRCR 86100 94600												
	IO T230 OMC 85800 94200, IO T260 MRCR 87400 96000, IO T260 OMC 87000 95600												
	IO T260 VLVO 89400 98200, IO T290 VLVO 91800 101000, IO T330 MRCR 93500 102500												
54	AQUAMINIUM 540/542	FB	HB	STL	DS	IO	120	MRCR	14	28500	3	81300	89300
	IO 120 OMC 81100 89100, IO 125 VLVO 82000 90100, IO 138 VLVO 82000 90100												
	IO 140 OMC 81100 89200, IO 170 MRCR 81400 89400, IO 200 MRCR 81600 89600												
	IO 200 OMC 81400 89500, IO 200 VLVO 82400 90500, IO 225 VLVO 82700 90900												
	IO 230 MRCR 81900 90100, IO 230 OMC 81800 89900, IO 260 MRCR 82600 90700												
	IO 260 OMC 82400 90500, IO 260 VLVO 83600 91800, IO 290 VLVO 84800 93200												
	IO 330 MRCR 85600 94100, IO T120 MRCR 84700 93100, IO T120 OMC 84400 92800												
	IO T125 VLVO 86200 94700, IO T138 VLVO 86200 94800, IO T140 OMC 84500 92900												
	IO T170 MRCR 85000 93400, IO T200 MRCR 85400 93800, IO T200 OMC 85100 93500												
	IO T200 VLVO 86900 95500, IO T225 VLVO 87700 96300, IO T230 MRCR 86100 94600												
	IO T230 OMC 85800 94300, IO T260 MRCR 87400 96000, IO T260 OMC 87000 95600												
	IO T260 VLVO 89400 98200, IO T290 VLVO 91800 101000, IO T330 MRCR 93500 102500												
55	FLAGSHIP FS550M	FB	HB	STL	DS	IO	T170	MRCR	16	30000	3	87500	96100
	IO T200 MRCR 85800 94300, IO T200 OMC 85500 93900, IO T200 VLVO 87300 96000												
	IO T225 VLVO 88100 96800, IO T230 MRCR 86600 95100, IO T230 OMC 86300 94800												
	IO T260 MRCR 88000 96700, IO T260 OMC 87600 96300, IO T260 VLVO 89600 98500												
	IO T290 VLVO 92200 101500, IO T330 MRCR 93900 103000, IO T110D VLVO 91200 100000												
55	FLAGSHIP FS550TL	FB	HB	STL	DS	IO	T200	MRCR	16	30000	3	90000	98900
	IO T200 OMC 89700 98500, IO T200 VLVO 91600 100500, IO T225 VLVO 92300 101500												
	IO T230 MRCR 90700 99600, IO T230 OMC 90300 99200, IO T260 MRCR 92000 101000												
	IO T260 OMC 91700 100500, IO T260 VLVO 93600 103000, IO T290 VLVO 96400 106000												
	IO T330 MRCR 98100 108000, IO T110D VLVO 95300 104500												
57	COMMANDER CM570	HT	HB	STL	DS	IO	120	MRCR	14	31000	3	86300	94900
	IO 120 OMC 86200 94700, IO 125 VLVO 87100 95700, IO 138 VLVO 87100 95700												
	IO 140 OMC 86200 94700, IO 170 MRCR 86400 95000, IO 200 MRCR 86600 95200												
	IO 200 OMC 86500 95000, IO 200 VLVO 87400 96100, IO 225 VLVO 87800 96500												
	IO 230 MRCR 87000 95600, IO 230 OMC 86800 95400, IO 260 MRCR 87600 96300												
	IO 260 OMC 87500 96100, IO 260 VLVO 88600 97400, IO 290 VLVO 89900 98700												
	IO 330 MRCR 90700 99700, IO T120 MRCR 89800 98700, IO T120 OMC 89500 98400												
	IO T125 VLVO 91300 100500, IO T138 VLVO 91300 100500, IO T140 OMC 89600 98400												
	IO T170 MRCR 90000 98900, IO T200 MRCR 90400 99400, IO T200 OMC 90100 99000												
	IO T200 VLVO 92000 101000, IO T225 VLVO 92700 102000, IO T230 MRCR 91200 100000												
	IO T230 OMC 90800 99800, IO T260 MRCR 92400 101500, IO T260 OMC 92000 101000												
	IO T260 VLVO 94400 104000, IO T290 VLVO 96900 106500, IO T330 MRCR 98600 108500												
57	COMMANDER CM570	FB	HB	STL	DS	IO	120	MRCR	14	31000	3	86300	94900
	IO 120 OMC 86200 94700, IO 125 VLVO 87100 95700, IO 138 VLVO 87100 95700												
	IO 140 OMC 86200 94700, IO 170 MRCR 86400 95000, IO 200 MRCR 86600 95200												
	IO 200 OMC 86500 95000, IO 200 VLVO 87400 96100, IO 225 VLVO 87800 96500												
	IO 230 MRCR 87000 95600, IO 230 OMC 86800 95400, IO 260 MRCR 87600 96300												
	IO 260 OMC 87500 96100, IO 260 VLVO 88600 97400, IO 290 VLVO 89900 98700												
	IO 330 MRCR 90700 99700, IO T120 MRCR 89800 98700, IO T120 OMC 89500 98400												
	IO T125 VLVO 91300 100500, IO T138 VLVO 91300 100500, IO T140 OMC 89600 98400												
	IO T170 MRCR 90000 98900, IO T200 MRCR 90400 99400, IO T200 OMC 90100 99000												
	IO T200 VLVO 92000 101000, IO T225 VLVO 92700 102000, IO T230 MRCR 91200 100000												
	IO T230 OMC 90800 99800, IO T260 MRCR 92400 101500, IO T260 OMC 92000 101000												
	IO T260 VLVO 94400 104000, IO T290 VLVO 96900 106500, IO T330 MRCR 98600 108500												
60	SUNDANCE 600	HT	HB	STL	CT	IO	120		14			85700	94200
62	FLAGSHIP FS620	FB	HB	STL	DS	IO	T225	VLVO	16	34000	3	94800	104000
	IO T230 MRCR 93200 102500, IO T230 OMC 93000 102000, IO T260 MRCR 94500 104000												
	IO T260 OMC 94100 103500, IO T260 VLVO 96400 106000, IO T290 VLVO 98600 108500												

 CONTINUED ON NEXT PAGE

```
       LOA  NAME AND/        TOP/ BOAT  -HULL---  ----ENGINE---  BEAM   WGT  DRAFT RETAIL RETAIL
       FT IN OR MODEL         RIG  TYPE  MTL TP TP  # HP MFG  FT IN  LBS  FT IN  LOW   HIGH
----------------------- 1986 BOATS -------------------------------------------------------------
62  FLAGSHIP FS620         FB  HB   STL DS IO T330 MRCR 16   34000  3    100500 110500
62  FLAGSHIP FS620         FB  HB   STL DS IO T110D VLVO 16  34000  3     97800 107500
70  FLAGSHIP FS700         FB  HB   STL DS IO T260 MRCR 16   41000  3    109500 120500
    IO T260 OMC 109000 120000,  IO T260 VLVO 111500 122500,  IO T290 VLVO 114000 125000
    IO T330 MRCR 115500 127000,  IO T110D VLVO 113000 124000

----------------------- 1985 BOATS -------------------------------------------------------------
36  FANTASY-ISLAND FI360   HT  HB   STL DS IO T120 MRCR 14  19200  2 10   44700 49600
    IO T140 OMC 44500 49400,  IO T125 VLVO 46200 50800,  IO T138 VLVO 46200 50800
    IO T140 OMC 44500 49400,  IO T170 VLVO 46800 49800,  IO T198 VLVO 45600 50100
    IO T200 OMC 44900 49900,  IO T200 VLVO 46800 51400,  IO T225 VLVO 47300 51900
    IO T228 MRCR 46100 50700,  IO T230 OMC 45900 50400,  IO T260 MRCR 47100 51700
    IO T260 OMC 46800 51400,  IO T260 VLVO 48500 53300

36  FANTASY-ISLAND FI360   FB  HB   STL DS IO T120 MRCR 14  19200  2 10   44700 49600
    IO T120 OMC 44500 49400,  IO T125 VLVO 46200 50800,  IO T138 VLVO 46200 50800
    IO T140 OMC 44500 49400,  IO T170 VLVO 46800 49800,  IO T198 VLVO 45600 50100
    IO T200 OMC 44900 49900,  IO T200 VLVO 46800 51400,  IO T225 VLVO 47300 51900
    IO T228 MRCR 46100 50700,  IO T230 OMC 45900 50400,  IO T260 MRCR 47100 51700
    IO T260 OMC 46800 51400,  IO T260 VLVO 48500 53300

36  FANTASY-ISLAND FI360   HT  HB   STL DS IO 120 MRCR 14   19200  2 10   42200 46900
    IO 120 OMC 42100 46800,  IO 125 VLVO 42700 47400,  IO 138 VLVO 42700 47500
    IO 140 OMC 42100 46800,  IO 170 VLVO 42300 47000,  IO 198 MRCR 42400 47100
    IO 200 OMC 42300 47000,  IO 200 VLVO 43000 47700,  IO 225 VLVO 43200 48000
    IO 228 MRCR 42600 47400,  IO 230 OMC 42600 47300,  IO 260 MRCR 43100 47900
    IO 260 OMC 43000 47800,  IO 260 VLVO 43800 48700

36  FANTASY-ISLAND FI360   FB  HB   STL DS IO 120 MRCR 14   19200  2 10   42200 46900
    IO 120 OMC 42100 46800,  IO 125 VLVO 42700 47400,  IO 138 VLVO 42700 47500
    IO 140 OMC 42100 46800,  IO 170 VLVO 42300 47000,  IO 198 MRCR 42400 47100
    IO 200 OMC 42300 47000,  IO 200 VLVO 43000 47700,  IO 225 VLVO 43200 48000
    IO 228 MRCR 42600 47400,  IO 230 OMC 42600 47300,  IO 260 MRCR 43100 47900
    IO 260 OMC 43000 47800,  IO 260 VLVO 43800 48700

40  FANTASY-ISLAND 40      HT  HB   STL SV IO 120       14                32300 35900
42  COMMANDER 42           HT  HB   STL SV IO 120       14                34800 38600
42  FANTASY-ISLAND FI420   HT  HB   STL DS IO 120 MRCR 14  20500  2 10    42200 46900
    IO 120 OMC 42100 46800,  IO 125 VLVO 42700 47500,  IO 140 OMC 42200 46800
    IB 145 VLVO 41800 46500,  IO 170 VLVO 41800 46400,  IO 198 MRCR 42400 47200
    IO 200 OMC 42400 47100,  IO 200 VLVO 43000 47800,  IO 225 VLVO 43300 48100
    IO 228 MRCR 42700 47400,  IO 230 OMC 42600 47300,  IO 260 MRCR 43200 48000
    IO 260 OMC 43000 47800,  IO 260 VLVO 43900 48700,  IO T120 MRCR 44700 49600
    IO T138 VLVO 46300 50800,  IO T140 OMC 44500 49500,  IO T170 VLVO 44800 49800
    IO T225 VLVO 47300 51900,  IO T198 MRCR 45600 50100,  IO T200 OMC 44900 49900
    IO T200 VLVO 46800 51400,  IO T228 MRCR 46100 50700,  IO T230 OMC 45900 50500
    IO T260 MRCR 47100 51700,  IO T260 OMC 46800 51400,  IO T260 VLVO 48500 53300

42  FANTASY-ISLAND FI420   FB  HB   STL DS IO 120 MRCR 14  20500  2 10    42200 46900
    IO 120 OMC 42100 46800,  IO 125 VLVO 42700 47500,  IO 140 OMC 42200 46800
    IB 145 VLVO 41800 46500,  IO 170 VLVO 41800 46400,  IO 198 MRCR 42400 47200
    IO 200 OMC 42400 47100,  IO 200 VLVO 43000 47800,  IO 225 VLVO 43300 48100
    IO 228 MRCR 42700 47400,  IO 230 OMC 42600 47300,  IO 260 MRCR 43200 48000
    IO 260 OMC 43000 47800,  IO 260 VLVO 43900 48700,  IO T120 MRCR 44700 49600
    IO T120 OMC 44500 49400,  IO T125 VLVO 46200 50800,  IO T138 VLVO 46300 50800
    IO T140 OMC 44500 49500,  IO T170 VLVO 44800 49800,  IO T198 MRCR 45600 50100
    IO T200 OMC 44900 49900,  IO T200 VLVO 46800 51400,  IO T225 VLVO 47300 51900
    IO T228 MRCR 46100 50700,  IO T230 OMC 45900 50700,  IO T260 MRCR 47100 51700
    IO T260 OMC 46800 51400,  IO T260 VLVO 48500 53300

42  SUNDANCE 42            HT  HB   STL CT IO 120       14                36600 40600
44  AQUAMINIUM AQ440       HT  HB   STL DS IO 120 MRCR 14  22500  2 11    50100 55100
    IO 120 OMC 50000 55000,  IO 125 VLVO 50700 55700,  IO 138 VLVO 50700 55700
    IO 140 OMC 50000 55000,  IO 170 VLVO 50200 55200,  IO 198 MRCR 50400 55300
    IO 200 OMC 50200 55200,  IO 200 VLVO 51000 55900,  IO 225 VLVO 50300 56300
    IO 228 MRCR 50600 55600,  IO 230 OMC 50500 55500,  IO 260 MRCR 51200 56200
    IO 260 OMC 51000 56000,  IO 260 VLVO 51900 57100,  IO 290 VLVO 52900 58100
    IO 330 MRCR 53600 58900,  IO T120 MRCR 52800 58100,  IO T120 OMC 52600 57800
    IO T125 VLVO 53600 58900,  IO T138 VLVO 53600 58900,  IO T140 OMC 52700 57900
    IO T170 MRCR 58300,       IO T198 VLVO 53300 58600,  IO T200 OMC 53100 58400
    IO T200 VLVO 54100 59500,  IO T225 VLVO 54700 60100,  IO T228 MRCR 53900 59200
    IO T230 OMC 53700 59000,  IO T260 MRCR 54500 59900,  IO T260 OMC 54200 59500
    IO T260 VLVO 56000 61600,  IO T290 VLVO 57600 63300,  IO T330 MRCR 58900 64800

44  FANTASY-ISLAND FI440   HT  HB   STL DS IO 120 MRCR 14  21000  2 11    48900 53800
    IO 120 OMC 48800 53700,  IO 125 VLVO 49500 54400,  IO 138 VLVO 49500 54400
    IO 140 OMC 48800 53700,  IO 170 MRCR 49000 53900,  IO 198 VLVO 49200 54000
    IO 200 OMC 49100 53900,  IO 200 VLVO 49800 54700,  IO 225 VLVO 50100 55100
    IO 228 MRCR 49500 54300,  IO 230 OMC 49300 54200,  IO 260 MRCR 50000 54900
    IO 260 OMC 49800 54800,  IO 260 VLVO 50300 55200,  IO T120 MRCR 51200 56200
    IO T120 OMC 51000 56000,  IO T125 VLVO 52300 57500,  IO T138 VLVO 52400 57500
    IO T140 OMC 51000 56000,  IO T170 MRCR 51400 56400,  IO T198 MRCR 51600 56700
    IO T200 OMC 51400 56500,  IO T200 VLVO 52900 58200,  IO T225 VLVO 53500 58800
    IO T228 MRCR 52200 57400,  IO T230 OMC 52000 57100,  IO T260 MRCR 53200 58500
    IO T260 OMC 52900 58200

44  FANTASY-ISLAND FI440   FB  HB   STL DS IO 120 MRCR 14  21000  2 11    48900 53800
    IO 120 OMC 48800 53700,  IO 125 VLVO 49500 54400,  IO 138 VLVO 49500 54400
    IO 140 OMC 48800 53700,  IO 170 MRCR 49000 53900,  IO 198 VLVO 49200 54000
    IO 200 OMC 49100 53900,  IO 200 VLVO 49800 54700,  IO 225 VLVO 50100 55100
    IO 228 MRCR 49500 54300,  IO 230 OMC 49300 54200,  IO 260 MRCR 50000 54900
    IO 260 OMC 49800 54800,  IO 260 VLVO 50300 55200,  IO T120 MRCR 51200 56200
    IO T120 OMC 51000 56000,  IO T125 VLVO 52300 57500,  IO T138 VLVO 52400 57500
    IO T140 OMC 51000 56000,  IO T170 MRCR 51400 56400,  IO T198 MRCR 51600 56700
    IO T200 OMC 51400 56500,  IO T200 VLVO 52900 58200,  IO T225 VLVO 53500 58800
    IO T228 MRCR 52200 57400,  IO T230 OMC 52000 57100,  IO T260 MRCR 53200 58500
    IO T260 OMC 52900 58200

47  COMMANDER CM470        HT  HB   STL DS IO 120 MRCR 14  26000  3      55400 60900
    IO 120 OMC 55300 60800,  IO 125 VLVO 56000 61500,  IO 138 VLVO 56000 61500
    IO 140 OMC 55300 60800,  IO 170 MRCR 55500 61000,  IO 198 MRCR 55600 61100
    IO 200 OMC 55500 61000,  IO 200 VLVO 56300 61800,  IO 225 VLVO 56200 61800
    IO 228 MRCR 55900 61400,  IO 230 OMC 55800 61300,  IO 260 MRCR 56100 61700
    IO 260 OMC 56300 61800,  IO 260 VLVO 56900 62500,  IO 290 VLVO 57800 63500
    IO 330 MRCR 58500 64300,  IO T120 MRCR 57800 63500,  IO T120 OMC 57600 63200
    IO T125 VLVO 58900 64700,  IO T138 VLVO 58900 64800,  IO T140 OMC 57600 63300
    IO T170 MRCR 58000 63700,  IO T198 MRCR 58200 64000,  IO T200 OMC 58000 63800
    IO T200 VLVO 59500 65400,  IO T225 VLVO 60000 66000,  IO T228 MRCR 58800 64600
    IO T230 OMC 58600 64400,  IO T260 MRCR 59800 65700,  IO T260 OMC 59500 65400
    IO T260 VLVO 61300 67400,  IO T290 VLVO 63200 69500,  IO T330 MRCR 64500 70900

47  COMMANDER CM470        FB  HB   STL DS IO 120 MRCR 14  26000  3      55400 60900
    IO 120 OMC 55300 60800,  IO 125 VLVO 56000 61500,  IO 138 VLVO 56000 61500
    IO 140 OMC 55300 60800,  IO 170 MRCR 55500 61000,  IO 198 MRCR 55600 61100
    IO 200 OMC 55500 61000,  IO 230 OMC 55800 61800,  IO 225 VLVO 56100 61700
    IO 228 MRCR 56300 61400,  IO 260 VLVO 56900 62500,  IO 260 MRCR 56100 61700
    IO 330 MRCR 56300 61800,  IO 260 OMC 56900 62500,  IO 290 VLVO 57800 63500
    IO T125 VLVO 58500 64300,  IO T120 MRCR 57800 63500,  IO T120 OMC 57600 63200
    IO T170 MRCR 58900 64700,  IO T138 VLVO 58900 64800,  IO T140 OMC 57600 63300
    IO T200 VLVO 58000 63700,  IO T198 MRCR 58200 64000,  IO T200 OMC 58000 63800
    IO T230 OMC 59500 65400,  IO T225 VLVO 60000 66000,  IO T228 MRCR 58800 64600
    IO T260 VLVO 58600 64400,  IO T260 MRCR 59800 65700,  IO T260 OMC 59500 65400
    IO T290 VLVO 61300 67400,  IO T330 MRCR 63200 69500,  IO T330 MRCR 64500 70900

47  FANTASY-ISLAND FI420   HT  HB   STL DS IO T120 MRCR 14  20500  2 10   52900 58200
50  FANTASY-ISLAND FI420   HT  HB   STL DS IO T120 MRCR 14  20500  2 10   55000 60400
50  SUNDANCE 50            HT  HB   STL CT IO 120       14                56300 61900
52  COMMANDER CM520        HT  HB   STL DS IO 120 MRCR 14  28000  3      76900 84500
    IO 120 OMC 76800 84400,  IO 125 VLVO 77600 85300,  IO 138 VLVO 77700 85300
    IO 140 OMC 76800 84400,  IO 170 MRCR 77100 84700,  IO 198 MRCR 77200 84900
    IO 200 OMC 77100 84700,  IO 200 VLVO 78000 85700,  IO 225 VLVO 78300 86100
    IO 228 MRCR 77600 85200,  IO 230 OMC 77400 85100,  IO 260 MRCR 78200 85900
    IO 260 OMC 78000 85700,  IO 260 VLVO 79200 87000,  IO 290 VLVO 80400 88300
    IO 330 MRCR 81200 89200,  IO T120 MRCR 80300 88200,  IO T120 OMC 80000 87900
    IO T125 VLVO 81700 89800,  IO T138 VLVO 81800 89900,  IO T140 OMC 80100 88000
    IO T170 MRCR 80500 88500,  IO T198 MRCR 80900 88900,  IO T200 OMC 80600 88600
    IO T200 VLVO 82500 90600,  IO T225 VLVO 83200 91400,  IO T228 MRCR 81600 89600
    IO T230 OMC 81300 89400,  IO T260 MRCR 82900 91100,  IO T260 OMC 82500 90700
    IO T260 VLVO 84800 93200,  IO T290 VLVO 87200 95800,  IO T330 MRCR 88900 97600

52  COMMANDER CM520        FB  HB   STL DS IO 120 MRCR 14  28000  3      76900 84500
    IO 120 OMC 76800 84400,  IO 125 VLVO 77600 85300,  IO 138 VLVO 77700 85300
    IO 140 OMC 76800 84400,  IO 170 MRCR 77100 84700,  IO 198 MRCR 77200 84900
    IO 200 OMC 77100 84700,  IO 200 VLVO 78000 85700,  IO 225 VLVO 78300 86100
    IO 228 MRCR 77600 85200,  IO 230 OMC 77400 85100,  IO 260 MRCR 78200 85900
    IO 260 OMC 78000 85700,  IO 260 VLVO 79200 87000,  IO 290 VLVO 80400 88300
    IO 330 MRCR 81200 89200,  IO T120 MRCR 80300 88200,  IO T120 OMC 80000 87900
    IO T125 VLVO 81700 89800,  IO T138 VLVO 81800 89900,  IO T140 OMC 80100 88000
    IO T170 MRCR 80500 88500,  IO T198 MRCR 80900 88900,  IO T200 OMC 80600 88600
    IO T200 VLVO 82500 90600,  IO T225 VLVO 83200 91400,  IO T228 MRCR 81600 89600
    IO T230 OMC 81300 89400,  IO T260 MRCR 82900 91100,  IO T260 OMC 82500 90700
    IO T260 VLVO 84800 93200,  IO T290 VLVO 87200 95800,  IO T330 MRCR 88900 97600

54  AQUAMINIUM 540/542     HT  HB   STL DS IO 120 MRCR 14  28500  3      79300 87100
```

 CONTINUED ON NEXT PAGE

```
     LOA  NAME AND/           TOP/ BOAT -HULL-  ----ENGINE--- BEAM    WGT  DRAFT RETAIL RETAIL
     FT IN OR MODEL           RIG  TYPE MTL TP TP # HP  MFG   FT IN   LBS  FT IN  LOW    HIGH
------------------------------- 1985 BOATS -----------------------------------------------------
54       AQUAMINIUM 540/542   HT  HB   STL DS IO 125  VLVO 14       28500  3    80000  87900
    IO 138  VLVO 80000  87900, IO 140  OMC  79200  87000, IO 170  MRCR 79400  87300
    IO 198  MRCR 79600  87500, IO 200  OMC  79500  87300, IO 200  VLVO 80400  88300
    IO 225  VLVO 80700  88700, IO 228  MRCR 79900  87800, IO 230  OMC  79800  87700
    IO 260  MRCR 80600  88600, IO 260  OMC  80400  88300, IO 260  VLVO 81600  89600
    IO 290  VLVO 82700  90900, IO 330  MRCR 83600  91800, IO 330  OMC  82700  90900
    IO T120 OMC  82400  90600, IO T125 VLVO 84100  92400, IO T138 MRCR 84200  92500
    IO T140 OMC  82500  90600, IO T170 MRCR 82900  91100, IO T198 MRCR 83330  91500
    IO T200 OMC  83000  91200, IO T225 VLVO 84800  93000, IO T225 VLVO 85500  94000
    IO T228 MRCR 84000  92300, IO T230 OMC  83700  92000, IO T260 MRCR 85300  93700
    IO T260 OMC  84900  93300, IO T260 VLVO 87200  95800, IO T290 VLVO 86900  95600
    IO T330 MRCR 91200 100500

54       AQUAMINIUM 540/542   HT  HB   STL DS IO 120  MRCR 14       28500  3    79300  87100
    IO 120  OMC  79200 87000, IO 125  VLVO 80000 87900, IO 138  VLVO 80000 87900
    IO 140  OMC  79200 87000, IO 170  MRCR 79400 87300, IO 198  MRCR 79600 87500
    IO 200  OMC  79500 87300, IO 200  VLVO 80400 88300, IO 225  VLVO 80700 88700
    IO 228  MRCR 79900 87800, IO 230  OMC  79800 87700, IO 260  OMC  80400 88300
    IO 260  VLVO 81600 89600, IO 290  OMC  82700 90900, IO 330  MRCR 83600 91800
    IO T120 MRCR 82700 90900, IO T120 OMC  82400 90600, IO T125 VLVO 84100 92400
    IO T138 MRCR 84200 92500, IO T140 OMC  82500 90600, IO T170 VLVO 82900 91100
    IO T198 MRCR 83330 91500, IO T200 OMC  83000 91200, IO T200 VLVO 84800 93200
    IO T225 MRCR 85500 94000, IO T228 OMC  84000 92300, IO T230 OMC  83700 92000
    IO T260 MRCR 85300 93700, IO T260 OMC  84900 93300, IO T260 VLVO 87200 95800
    IO T330 MRCR 98400 100500

55       FLAGSHIP FS550       FB  HB   STL DS IO T190 MRCR 16       30000  3    85600  94100
    IO T260 OMC  87400  96000, IO T260     89700  98500, IO T290 VLVO 92000 101000
    IO T330 MRCR 93700 103000

57       COMMANDER CM570      HT  HB   STL DS IO 120  MRCR 14       31000  3    84200  92600
    IO 120  OMC  84100 92400, IO 125  VLVO 85000 93400, IO 138  VLVO 85000 93400
    IO 140  OMC  84100 92400, IO 170  MRCR 84400 92700, IO 198  MRCR 84500 92900
    IO 200  OMC  84400 92700, IO 200  VLVO 85300 93800, IO 225  VLVO 85700 94100
    IO 228  MRCR 84900 93300, IO 230  OMC  84700 93100, IO 260  OMC  85300 93800
    IO 260  VLVO 86500 95100, IO 290  VLVO 87700 96400, IO 330  MRCR 88500 97300
    IO 330  OMC  87300 96000, IO T120 VLVO 87600 96300, IO T120 OMC  87400 96000
    IO T125 VLVO 89000 97900, IO T138 MRCR 89100 97900, IO T140 OMC  87400 96000
    IO T170 MRCR 87900 96500, IO T198 MRCR 88200 96900, IO T200 OMC  87900 96600
    IO T200 VLVO 89800 98700, IO T225 VLVO 90500 99400, IO T228 MRCR 88900 97700
    IO T230 OMC  88600 97400, IO T260 OMC  90200 99100, IO T260 MRCR 89800 98700
    IO T260 VLVO 92200 101500

60       FLAGSHIP 60          HT  HB   STL SV IO 228       16              3    79800  87700
62       FLAGSHIP FS620       FB  HB   STL DS IO T260 MRCR 16       34000  3    92100 101000
    IO T260 OMC  91700 101000, IO T290 VLVO 93900 103000, IO T330 MRCR 96100 105500
    IO T330 MRCR 97700 107500

65       FLAGSHIP 65          HT  HB   STL SV IO 228       16              3    86000  94500
70       FLAGSHIP FS700       FB  HB   STL DS IO T260 MRCR 16       41000  3   106500 117000
    IO T260 OMC 106000 116500, IO T290 VLVO 108500 119500, IO T330 MRCR 111000 122000
    IO T330 MRCR 112500 123500
------------------------------- 1984 BOATS -----------------------------------------------------
36       FANTASY-ISLAND FI 36 HT  HB   STL DS IO 120       14       19200 2 10  41300  45800
40       FANTASY-ISLAND FI 40 HT  HB   STL SV IO 120       14       20500 2 10  41500  46100
42       COMMANDER 42         HT  HB   STL SV IO 120       14             2 10  34000  37800
44       AQUAMINIUM AQ 44     HT  HB   STL DS IO T120      14       22500 2 11  51700  56800
44       FANTASY-ISLAND FI 44 HT  HB   STL    IO 120       14       21000 2 11  47900  52600
47       COMMANDER CM 47      HT  HB   STL    IO T120      14       26000 3     56500  62100
52       COMMANDER CM 52      HT  HB   STL    IO T120      14       28000 3     78500  86300
54       AQUAMINIUM AQ 54     HT  HB   STL DS IO T120      14       28500 3     80800  88800
55       FLAGSHIP FS 55       HT  HB   STL DS IO T260      16       30000 3     85800  94200
57       COMMANDER CM 57      HT  HB   STL    IO T120      14       31000 3     85700  94200
60       FLAGSHIP-ISLAND 60   HT  HB   STL SV IO 228       16             3     78000  85700
62       FLAGSHIP FS 62       HT  HB   STL DS IO 228       16       34000 3     89900  98800

65       FLAGSHIP-ISLAND 65   HT  HB   STL SV IO 228       16             3     84100  92400
70       FLAGSHIP FS 70       HT  HB   STL DS IO T260      16       41000 3    104000 114500
```

....For earlier years, see the BUC Used Boat Price Guide, Volume 3

SKOOKUM MARINE CONSTRUCTION

PORT TOWNSEND WA 98368   COAST GUARD MFG ID- SKK   See inside cover to adjust price for area

```
     LOA  NAME AND/           TOP/ BOAT  -HULL-  ----ENGINE--- BEAM    WGT  DRAFT RETAIL RETAIL
     FT IN OR MODEL           RIG  TYPE  MTL TP TP # HP  MFG   FT IN   LBS  FT IN  LOW    HIGH
------------------------------- 1985 BOATS -----------------------------------------------------
28       SKOOKUM 28          SLP SA/SD FBG     SD   15D VLVO  9       8450  4 6  32900  36400
34       CHINOOK                 CR   FBG SV IB    300D CAT   11     18000  3 6  54600  60100
34  2    SKOOKUM 34          SLP SA/CR FBG SV IB     30D      10 10  18000      69800  76700
42       CHINOOK                 CR   FBG SV IB    300D CAT   14     24000  4 6  88700  97500
42       CHINOOK                 CR   FBG SV IB   T300D CAT   14     24000      99500 109500
47       SKOOKUM 47          SLP SA/CR FBG KL IB     60D      13 2   38000  6  130500 143500
50       SKOOKUM 50          SLP SA/CR FBG KL IB     60D      13 6   38000  6 4 155000 170500
53       SKOOKUM 53          KTH SA/CR FBG KL IB    120D      15 6   55000  7  214000 235000
70       SKOOKUM 70          CUT SA/CR FBG KL IB    160D      18 2    55T   8  509000 559500
------------------------------- 1984 BOATS -----------------------------------------------------
28       SKOOKUM 28          SLP SA/CR FBG KL SD     15D VLVO  9      8450  4 6  31000  34400
34  2    SKOOKUM 34          SLP SA/CR FBG SV IB     30D      10 10  18000     65600  72100
47       SKOOKUM 47          SLP SA/CR FBG KL IB     60D      13 2   38000  6  123000 135000
50       SKOOKUM 50          SLP SA/CR FBG KL IB     60D      13 6   38000  6 4 146000 160500
53       SKOOKUM 53          KTH SA/CR FBG KL IB    120D      15 6   55000  7  201000 221000
70       SKOOKUM 70          CUT SA/CR FBG KL IB    160D      18 2    55T   8  478500 526000
```

....For earlier years, see the BUC Used Boat Price Guide, Volume 3

JIM SMITH TOURNAMENT BOATS

STUART FL 34997   See inside cover to adjust price for area

```
     LOA  NAME AND/           TOP/ BOAT -HULL-  ----ENGINE--- BEAM    WGT  DRAFT RETAIL RETAIL
     FT IN OR MODEL           RIG  TYPE MTL TP TP # HP  MFG   FT IN   LBS  FT IN  LOW    HIGH
------------------------------- 1993 BOATS -----------------------------------------------------
40       TOURNAMENT 40-45     FB  SF  F/W SV IB  T        15     18000 3 8    **     **
40       TOURNAMENT 40-45     FB  SF  F/W SV IB  T240D    15     18000 3 8 188500 207000
50       TOURNAMENT 50        FB  SF  F/W SV IB  T      16 6     30000 4      **     **
52       TOURNAMENT 52        FB  SF  F/W SV IB  T      16 6     30000 4      **     **
54       TOURNAMENT 54        FB  SF  F/W SV IB  T      16 6     30000 4      **     **
56       TOURNAMENT 56        FB  SF  F/W SV IB  T      16 6     36000 4      **     **
60       TOURNAMENT 60        FB  SF  F/W SV IB  T      17 6     36000 4 4    **     **
61       TOURNAMENT 61        FB  SF  F/W SV IB  T300   17 6     36000 4 4 402500 442500
```

SMOKER CRAFT INC

NEW PARIS IN 46553   COAST GUARD MFG ID- SMK   See inside cover to adjust price for area

For more recent years, see the BUC Used Boat Price Guide, Volume 1

```
     LOA  NAME AND/           TOP/ BOAT -HULL-  ----ENGINE--- BEAM    WGT  DRAFT RETAIL RETAIL
     FT IN OR MODEL           RIG  TYPE MTL TP TP # HP  MFG   FT IN   LBS  FT IN  LOW    HIGH
------------------------------- 1996 BOATS -----------------------------------------------------
16       JON 1644             OP  JON  AL SV OB           5 3   300          910   1100
16       JON 1644 SPLIT SEAT  OP  JON  AL SV OB           5 3   300         1000   1200
16       JON 1648             OP  JON  AL SV OB           6     295          915   1100
16       JON 1648 W/LIVEWELL  OP  JON  AL SV OB           6     295          965   1150
16  2    PRO BASS 162         OP  BASS AL SV OB           6 3   590         1900   2300
16  5    BIG FISHERMAN 16     OP  FSH  AL SV OB           5 11  350         1350   1600
16  5    KINGTROLLER 16 CNSL  OP  RNBT AL DV OB           6 8   620         2050   2450
16  5    PRO MAG 161          OP  RNBT AL DV OB           6 8   720         2400   2800
16  5    PRO MAG 162          OP  RNBT AL DV OB           6 8   780         2600   3050
16  5    PRO MAG 165 CONSOLE  OP  RNBT AL DV OB           6 11  420         1400   1650
16  5    PRO TILLER 160       OP  RNBT AL DV OB           6 8   725         2450   2850
16  5    STILLETO 161         OP  RNBT AL DV OB           6 8   755         2500   2950

16  5    STILLETO 162         OP  RNBT AL DV OB           6 8   775         2600   3000
16  5    VOYAGER 16           OP  FSH  AL DV OB           6 11  850         1150   1350
16  8    PHANTOM 170 SINGLE   OP  RNBT AL DV OB           7 1  1020         3250   3800
16  8    PHANTOM 170 DUAL     OP  RNBT AL DV OB           7 1  1020         3450   4000
16 10    PRO MAG 168          OP  FSH  AL DV OB           5 9   540         1800   2150
17       JON 1750             OP  JON  AL SV OB           6 2   365         1050   1250
17       JON 1750 SPLIT SEAT  OP  JON  AL SV OB           7 2   365         1050   1250
17  2    PRO BASS 172         OP  BASS AL SV OB           6 3   685         2350   2750
17  5    PRO ALASKAN 171      OP  RNBT AL DV OB           7 2   760         2650   3050
17  5    PRO ALASKAN 172      OP  RNBT AL DV OB           7 2   820         2800   3250
17  8    ULTIMA 175           OP  RNBT AL DV OB           7 2  1120         3650   4250
17  8    ULTIMA F+S 175       OP  RNBT AL DV OB           7 2  1120         3750   4350

18  3    SABRE 180            OP  RNBT AL DV OB           6 10 1120         3850   4500
18  5    PRO MAG 182          OP  RNBT AL DV OB           7    1310         4300   5000
18 10    FAZER 192            OP  RNBT AL DV OB           7 3  1375         4550   5200
------------------------------- 1993 BOATS -----------------------------------------------------
16       BASS 1644            OP  BASS AL SV OB           5 7   580         1600   1900
16       CRAPPIE              OP  BASS AL SV OB           5 7   435         1200   1450
16       JON 1672             OP  JON  AL FL OB           6     260          700   845
16       JON 1672 LIVEWELL    OP  JON  AL FL OB           6     260          745   895
```

LOA FT	IN	NAME AND/ OR MODEL	TOP/ RIG	BOAT TYPE	-HULL- MTL	TP	----ENGINE--- TP	# HP	MFG	BEAM FT	IN	WGT LBS	DRAFT FT	IN	RETAIL LOW	RETAIL HIGH
		1993 BOATS														
16	2	KING TROLLER W/CSL	OP	FSH	AL	SV	OB			6	6	620			1750	2100
16	2	KING TROLLER W/O CSL	OP	FSH	AL	SV	OB			6	6	620			1650	1950
16	5	BIG FISHERMAN 16	OP	FSH	AL	SV	OB			5	11	420	2	7	1150	1400
16	5	PRO MAGNUM 161	OP	RNBT	AL	SV	OB			6	8	720	3	2	2050	2400
16	5	PRO MAGNUM 162	OP	RNBT	AL	SV	OB			6	8	780	3	2	2250	2600
16	5	PRO TILLER 160	OP	RNBT	AL	SV	OB			6	9	725			2050	2450
16	5	STILLETO 161	OP	RNBT	AL	SV	OB			6	8	775	3	2	2100	2500
16	5	STILLETO 162	OP	RNBT	AL	SV	OB			6	8	775	3	2	2300	2700
16	5	VOYAGER 16	OP	FSH	AL	SV	OB			5	11	350	2	7	980	1150
16	10	PRO MAGNUM 168	OP	FSH	AL	SV	OB			5	10	540	2	9	1550	1850
17		PRO BASS 17	OP	BASS	AL	SV	OB			6	3	715			2050	2450
17	5	FAZER 171	OP	RNBT	AL	SV	OB			6	9	850	3	2	2500	2900
17	5	FAZER 172	OP	RNBT	AL	SV	OB			6	9	910	3	2	2650	3100
17	5	FAZER 172 F & S	OP	RNBT	AL	SV	OB			6	8	925	3	2	2700	3100
18	5	PRO MAGNUM 181	OP	RNBT	AL	SV	OB			7					3450	4000
18	5	PRO MAGNUM 182	OP	RNBT	AL	SV	OB			7			3	2	3700	4300
18	10	FAZER 192	OP	RNBT	AL	SV	OB			7		1100	3	6	3250	3750
		1992 BOATS														
16	2	KING TROLLER W/CSL	OP	FSH	AL	SV	OB			6	6	620			1700	2000
16	2	KING TROLLER W/O CSL	OP	FSH	AL	SV	OB			6	6	620			1550	1850
16	2	SPIRIT FISH & SKI	OP	FSH	AL	SV	OB			7	2	665	2	10	1750	2050
16	5	BIG FISHERMAN 16	OP	FSH	AL	SV	OB			5	7	420	2	7	1100	1350
16	5	MAGNUM 161	OP	RNBT	AL	SV	OB			6	8	720	3		1950	2300
16	5	MAGNUM 162	OP	RNBT	AL	SV	OB			6	8	780	3		2100	2500
16	5	STILLETO 160	OP	RNBT	AL	SV	OB			6	8	775	3	2	2100	2450
16	5	STILLETO 161	OP	RNBT	AL	SV	OB			6	8	775	3	2	2100	2450
16	5	STILLETO 162	OP	RNBT	AL	SV	OB			6	8	775	3	2	2100	2450
16	5	VOYAGER 16	OP	FSH	AL	SV	OB			5	6	350	2	7	935	1100
16	8	ALANTE 17	OP	RNBT	FBG	DV	OB			7	6	1100	3	4	2900	3350
16	8	ALANTE 17	OP	RNBT	FBG	DV	IO	125-128		7	6	1200	3	4	2700	3150
16	8	AVANTE 17	OP	RNBT	FBG	DV	IO	130-145		7	6	1200	3	4	2650	3150
16	8	AVANTI 17	OP	RNBT	FBG	DV	IO	175		7	6	1200	3	4	2750	3150
16	10	MAGNUM 168	OP	FSH	AL	SV	OB			5	9	540			1450	1750
17		BASS CATCHER 17	OP	BASS	AL	SV	OB			6		600	1	9	1650	1950
17	1	LAZER 171	OP	RNBT	AL	SV	OB			6	8	790	2	8	2200	2550
17	5	FAZER 171	OP	RNBT	AL	SV	OB			6	6	850	3	2	2400	2800
17	5	FAZER 172	OP	RNBT	AL	SV	OB			6	9	910	3	2	2550	2950
17	10	ALASKAN W/CSL	OP	FSH	AL	SV	OB			6	2	700	3		2050	2450
17	10	ALASKAN W/O CSL	OP	FSH	AL	SV	OB			6	2	700	3		1900	2250
18	5	MAGNUM 182	OP	RNBT	AL	SV	OB			7		1140	3	2	3150	3650
18	8	REGATTA 189	OP	RNBT	FBG	DV	IO	125-235		7	6	1400	2	10	3350	4050
18	10	FRAZER 192	OP	RNBT	AL	SV	OB			7	3	1100	3	6	3100	3600
20	9	REGATTA 209	OP	RNBT	FBG	DV	IO	125-260		8	2	1850	2	10	4750	5800
20	9	TITAN 21	OP	CUD	AL	SV	IO	125	MRCR	7	6	1300			4450	5100
21	3	REGATTA 220	OP	OVNTR	FBG	DV	IO	125-260		8					5200	6400
22	6	REGATTA 250	OP	OVNTR	FBG	DV	IO	125-260		8	6	4500			9150	10800
		1991 BOATS														
16	2	KING TROLLER W/CSL	OP	FSH	AL	SV	OB			6	6	620			1600	1950
16	2	KING TROLLER W/O CSL	OP	FSH	AL	SV	OB			6	6	620			1500	1800
16	2	MAGNUM 161	OP	RNBT	AL	SV	OB			6	4	720	3		1850	2200
16	2	MAGNUM 162	OP	RNBT	AL	SV	OB			6	4	780	3		2000	2350
16	2	SPIRIT FISH & SKI	OP	FSH	AL	SV	OB			7	2	665	2	10	1650	2000
16	5	BIG FISHERMAN 16	OP	FSH	AL	SV	OB			5	7	420	2	7	1100	1300
16	5	STILLETO 160	OP	RNBT	AL	SV	OB			6	8	775	3	2	2000	2350
16	5	STILLETO 161	OP	RNBT	AL	SV	OB			6	8	775	3	2	2000	2350
16	5	STILLETO 162	OP	RNBT	AL	SV	OB			6	8	775	3	2	2000	2350
16	5	VOYAGER 16	OP	FSH	AL	SV	OB			5	6	350	2	7	905	1100
16	8	ALANTE 17	OP	RNBT	FBG	DV	OB			7	6	1100	3	4	2750	3250
16	8	ALANTE 17	OP	RNBT	FBG	DV	IO	125-128		7	6	1200	3	4	2550	2950
16	8	AVANTE 17	OP	RNBT	FBG	DV	IO	130-145		7	6	1200	3	4	2500	2950
16	8	AVANTI 17	OP	RNBT	FBG	DV	IO	175		7	6	1200	3	4	2550	3000
17		BASS CATCHER 17	OP	BASS	AL	SV	OB			6		600	1	9	1600	1900
17	1	LAZER 171	OP	RNBT	AL	SV	OB			6	8	790	2	8	2100	2450
17	5	FAZER 171	OP	RNBT	AL	SV	OB			6	6	850	3	2	2300	2650
17	5	FAZER 172	OP	RNBT	AL	SV	OB			6	9	910	3	2	2400	2800
17	10	ALASKAN W/CSL	OP	FSH	AL	SV	OB			6	2	700	3		1950	2350
17	10	ALASKAN W/O CSL	OP	FSH	AL	SV	OB			6	2	700	3		1800	2150
18	5	MAGNUM 182	OP	RNBT	AL	SV	OB			7		1140	3	2	3000	3500
18	8	REGATTA 189	OP	RNBT	FBG	DV	IO	125-235		7	6	1400	2	10	3100	3800
18	10	FRAZER 19	OP	RNBT	AL	SV	OB			7	3	1100	3	6	2950	3450
20	9	REGATTA 209	OP	RNBT	FBG	DV	IO	125-260		8	2	1850	2	10	4450	5450
20	9	TITAN 21	OP	CUD	AL	SV	IO	125	MRCR	7	6	1300			4100	4800
21	3	REGATTA 220	OP	OVNTR	FBG	DV	IO	125-260		8					4850	6000
22	6	REGATTA 250	OP	OVNTR	FBG	DV	IO	125-260		8	6	4500			8500	10200
		1990 BOATS														
16	2	KING TROLLER W/CSL	OP	FSH	AL	SV	OB			6	6	620			1550	1850
16	2	KING TROLLOR W/O CSL	OP	FSH	AL	SV	OB			6	6	620			1450	1700
16	2	MAGNUM 161	OP	RNBT	AL	SV	OB			6	4	700	3		1700	2050
16	2	MAGNUM 162	OP	RNBT	AL	SV	OB			6	4	740	3		1800	2150
16	2	SPIRIT FISH & SKI	OP	FSH	AL	SV	OB			7	2	665			1600	1900
16	5	BIG FISHERMAN 16	OP	FSH	AL	SV	OB			5	6	420	2	7	1050	1250
16	5	VOYAGER 16	OP	FSH	AL	SV	OB			5	6	350	2	7	870	1050
16	8	ALANTE 17	OP	RNBT	FBG	DV	OB			7	6	1100	3	4	2650	3100
16	8	ALANTE 17	OP	RNBT	FBG	DV	IO	125		7	6	1200	3	4	2350	2750
16	8	ALANTE 17 TLP	OP	RNBT	FBG	DV	IO	128-175							2550	3050
16	8	AVANTI 17	OP	RNBT	FBG	DV	IO	128-175		7	6	1200	3	4	2350	2800
16	8	AVANTI 17 TLP	OP	RNBT	FBG	DV	OB			7	6	1100	3	4	2650	3100
16	10	ALASKAN 17	OP	FSH	AL	SV	OB			6	6	460	2	6	1150	1400
16	10	MAGNUM 168	OP	FSH	AL	SV	OB			5	10	540	2	9	1350	1600
17	1	LAZER 17	OP	RNBT	AL	SV	OB			6	8	790	2	8	2000	2400
17	1	PRO BASS 17	OP	BASS	FBG	SV	OB			7		850	2	2	2150	2500
17	5	FAZER 171	OP	RNBT	AL	SV	OB			6	6	800	3	2	2050	2450
17	5	FAZER 172	OP	RNBT	AL	SV	OB			6	9	860	3	2	2250	2600
18	5	MAGNUM 182	OP	RNBT	AL	SV	OB			7		1140	3	2	2900	3350
18	8	REGATTA 189	OP	RNBT	FBG	DV	IO	125-230		7	6	1400	2	10	3000	3650
18	8	REGATTA 189 TLP	OP	RNBT	FBG	DV	IO	125-230		7	6	1400	2	10	2850	3500
19	4	TITAN 19	OP	CUD	AL	SV	IO	125	MRCR	7	3	1235	3	2	3050	3550
20	9	REGATTA 209	OP	RNBT	FBG	DV	IO		MRCR	8	2	1850	2	10	**	**
20	9	REGATTA 209	OP	RNBT	FBG	DV	IO	125-260		8	2	1850	2	10	4250	5300
20	9	REGATTA 209 TLP	OP	RNBT	FBG	DV	IO		MRCR	8	2	1850	2	10	**	**
20	9	REGATTA 209 TLP	OP	RNBT	FBG	DV	IO	125-235		8	2	1850	2	10	4000	5000
20	9	REGATTA 209 TLP	OP	RNBT	FBG	DV	IO	260	MRCR	8	2	1850	2	10	4350	5000
21		TITAN 21	OP	CUD	AL	SV	IO	125	MRCR	7	6	1300			3950	4600
21	3	REGATTA 220	OP	OVNTR	FBG	DV	IO	125-260		8		3000			5450	6650
22	6	REGATTA 250	OP	OVNTR	FBG	DV	IO	125-260		8	6	4500			8000	9550
		1989 BOATS														
16		DRIFT BOAT		UTL	AL		OB			6	3	340			780	940
16	2	MAGNUM 161MG	OP	RNBT	AL	SV	OB			6	4	650	3		1550	1850
16	2	MAGNUM 162		RNBT	AL	SV	OB			6	4	700	3		1650	1950
16	2	SPIRIT 165		RNBT	AL		OB			6	4	665	2	10	1550	1850
16	5	BIG FISHERMAN		FSH	AL	SV	OB			5	6	420	2	7	1000	1200
16	5	VOYAGER		FSH	AL		OB			5	6	350	2	7	840	1000
16	8	ALANTE 17		RNBT	FBG	DV	OB			7	6	1100	3	4	2550	3000
16	8	ALANTE 17		RNBT	FBG	DV	IO	175	MRCR	7	6	1200	3	4	2300	2650
16	10	ALASKAN 17	OP	FSH	AL	SV	OB			6	6	460	2	6	1150	1350
16	10	MAGNUM 168		FSH	AL	SV	OB			5	10	540	2	9	1300	1550
17	1	LAZER 171		RNBT	AL		OB			6	8	790	2	8	1900	2300
17	1	PRO BASS		BASS	FBG		OB			7		850	2	2	2050	2450
17	5	FAZER 171		RNBT	AL	SV	OB			6	6	800	3	2	1950	2350
17	5	FAZER 172		RNBT	AL		OB			6	9	860	3	2	2150	2500
18	5	MAGNUM 182		RNBT	AL	SV	OB			7		1140	3	2	2800	3250
18	7	ALANTE 19		RNBT	FBG	DV	IO	260	MRCR	8		1650	3	10	3250	3800
19	4	TITAN 19		RNBT	AL		IO	120		7	3	665	3	2	3000	3500
		1988 BOATS														
16		DRIFT BOAT		UTL	AL		OB			6	3	340			755	910
16	2	CHALLENGER 168CR	OP	RNBT	AL	SV	OB			6	4	665			1500	1800
16	2	MAGNUM 160MG	OP	FSH	AL	SV	OB			6	4	620			1400	1650
16	2	MAGNUM 161MG	OP	FSH	AL	SV	OB			6	4	650			1450	1750
16	2	MAGNUM 162		RNBT	AL	SV	OB			6	4	700			1600	1900
16	5	BIG FISHERMAN		FSH	AL	SV	OB			5	6	420			975	1150
16	5	VOYAGER		FSH	AL		OB			5	6	320			735	885
16	8	ALANTE 17		RNBT	FBG	DV	OB			7	6	1100			2500	2900
16	8	ALANTE 17		RNBT	FBG	DV	IO	175		7	6	1200			2150	2500
16	10	ALASKAN	OP	FSH	AL	SV	OB			6	6	440			1050	1250
16	10	MAGNUM 165		FSH	AL	SV	OB			5	10	540			1300	1500
17		BASS CATCHER	OP	BASS	AL	SV	OB			6	1	600			1450	1700
17	1	PRO BASS		BASS	FBG		OB			7		850			2000	2350
17	2	FAZER 17		RNBT	AL	SV	OB			6	6	820			1950	2300
18	5	MAGNUM 181		RNBT	AL	SV	OB			7		1140			2450	2850
18	5	MAGNUM 182		RNBT	AL	SV	OB			7		1140			2950	3400
18	6	CHALLENGER 18CRO	OP	RNBT	AL	SV	OB			7		1020			2450	2850
18	7	ALANTE 19		RNBT	FBG	DV	IO	230		8		1650			2950	3450
		1987 BOATS														
16		DRIFT BOAT		UTL	AL		OB			6	3	340			735	885
16	2	ANGLER 16SCO	OP	CTRCN	AL	SV	OB			6	4	620			1350	1650
16	2	CENTER CONSOLE ANGLE		CTRCN	AL		OB			6	4	510			1150	1350
16	2	CHALLENGER 168CR	OP	RNBT	AL	SV	OB			6	4	665			1450	1750

CONTINUED ON NEXT PAGE

LOA FT IN	NAME AND/ OR MODEL	TOP/ RIG	BOAT TYPE	HULL MTL TP	ENGINE TP # HP MFG	BEAM FT IN	WGT LBS	DRAFT FT IN	RETAIL LOW	RETAIL HIGH
					1987 BOATS					
16 2	MAGNUM 160MG	OP	FSH	AL	SV OB	6 4	620		1350	1650
16 2	MAGNUM 161MG	OP	FSH	AL	SV OB	6 4	650		1450	1700
16 2	SPORT ANGLER		FSH	AL	SV OB	6 4	650		1450	1700
16 5	BIG FISHERMAN		FSH	AL	SV OB	5 6	420		945	1150
16 5	BIG FISHERMAN DLX		FSH	AL	SV OB	5 6	460		1050	1250
16 5	VOYAGER		FSH	AL	OB	5 6	320		715	860
16 9	PRO ANGLER	OP	FSH	AL	SV OB	6 1	620		1400	1700
16 10	ALASKAN	OP	FSH	AL	SV OB	6 6	440		1000	1200
17	BASS CATCHER	OP	BASS	AL	SV OB	6 1	600		1400	1650
17 1	PRO BASS		BASS	FBG	OB	7	850		1900	2300
18 3	V180I	OP	RNBT	AL	SV IO	MRCR 6 4	2150		**	**
18 3	V180I	OP	RNBT	AL	SV IO	OMC 6 4	2150		**	**
18 6	CHALLENGER 18CRO	OP	RNBT	AL	SV OB	7	1020		2400	2800
18 6	SPORT ANGLER 18SAU		RNBT	AL	SV OB	7	1020		2400	2800
					1986 BOATS					
16	DRIFT BOAT		UTL	AL	OB	6 3	340		715	865
16 2	CENTER CONSOLE ANGLE		CTRCN	AL	OB	6 4	510		1100	1300
16 2	CHALLENGER 168CR	OP	RNBT	AL	SV OB	6 4	665		1450	1700
16 2	SPORT-ANGLER	OP	FSH	AL	SV OB	6 4	650		1400	1650
16 5	BIG FISHERMAN		FSH	AL	SV OB	5 6	420		1000	1200
16 5	BIG FISHERMAN DLX		FSH	AL	SV OB	5 6	460		1000	1200
16 5	VOYAGER		FSH	AL	OB	5 6	320		695	840
16 9	PRO-ANGLER	OP	FSH	AL	SV OB	6 1	620		1350	1650
16 10	ALASKAN	OP	FSH	AL	SV OB	6 6	440		990	1200
17	BASS-CATCHER	OP	BASS	AL	SV OB	6 1	600		1350	1600
17 1	PRO-BASS		BASS	FBG	OB	7	850		1850	2200
18 5	ALASKAN 180AF	OP	FSH	AL	SV OB	6 3	350		885	1050
18 6	CHALLENGER 18CRO	OP	RNBT	AL	OB	7	1020		2350	2750
18 6	SPORT-ANGLER 18SAU		RNBT	AL	OB	7	1020		2350	2750
					1985 BOATS					
16	DRIFT BOAT		UTL	AL	OB	6 3	340		700	845
16 2	CENTER CONSOLE ANGLE		CTRCN	AL	OB	6 4	510		1050	1300
16 2	CHALLENGER 168CR	OP	RNBT	AL	SV OB	6 4	665		1400	1650
16 2	SPORT-ANGLER	OP	FSH	AL	SV OB	6 4	650		1350	1600
16 5	ALASKAN 160AF	OP	FSH	AL	SV OB	6 2	340		720	870
16 5	BIG FISHERMAN		FSH	AL	SV OB	5 6	420		905	1100
16 5	PRO-ANGLER 165PA	OP	FSH	AL	SV OB	6 1	620		1300	1550
16 5	VOYAGER		FSH	AL	OB	5 6	350		745	895
17	BASS-CATCHER	OP	BASS	AL	SV OB	6 1	600		1300	1550
17 1	PRO-BASS		BASS	FBG	OB	7	850		1800	2150
18 5	ALASKAN 180AF	OP	FSH	AL	SV OB	6 3	350		860	1050
18 6	CHALLENGER 18CRO	OP	RNBT	AL	OB	7	1020		2300	2650
18 6	SPORT-ANGLER 18SAU		RNBT	AL	OB	7	1020		2300	2650
					1984 BOATS					
16 2	CHALLENGER 168CR	OP	RNBT	AL	SV OB	6 4	665		1350	1600
16 2	SPORT-ANGLER	OP	FSH	AL	SV OB	6 4	650		1350	1600
16 5	ALASKAN 160AF	OP	FSH	AL	SV OB	6 2	340		705	850
16 5	BIG FISHERMAN		FSH	AL	SV OB	5 6	420		885	1050
16 5	PRO-ANGLER 165PA	OP	FSH	AL	SV OB	6 1	620		1300	1550
17	BASS-CATCHER	OP	BASS	AL	SV OB	6 1	600		1300	1550
18 5	ALASKAN 180AF	OP	FSH	AL	SV OB	6 3	350		845	1000
18 6	CHALLANGER	OP	RNBT	AL	SV OB	7	1020		2250	2600

....For earlier years, see the BUC Used Boat Price Guide, Volume 3

SNUG HARBOR BOAT WORKS
ST PETERSBURG FL 33702   COAST GUARD MFG ID- SNU See inside cover to adjust price for area

LOA FT IN	NAME AND/ OR MODEL	TOP/ RIG	BOAT TYPE	HULL MTL TP	ENGINE TP # HP MFG	BEAM FT IN	WGT LBS	DRAFT FT IN	RETAIL LOW	RETAIL HIGH
					1985 BOATS					
17	THUNDERBIRD	SLP	SA/CR	FBG	OB	6 6	750	8	1750	2100
					1984 BOATS					
23	SNUG-HARBOR 23	SLP	SA/CR	FBG KL	IB 10D	8	4500	3	7750	8900

....For earlier years, see the BUC Used Boat Price Guide, Volume 3

SOL CATAMARANS INC
SANTA ANA CA 92705   COAST GUARD MFG ID- SXL See inside cover to adjust price for area

LOA FT IN	NAME AND/ OR MODEL	TOP/ RIG	BOAT TYPE	HULL MTL TP	ENGINE TP # HP MFG	BEAM FT IN	WGT LBS	DRAFT FT IN	RETAIL LOW	RETAIL HIGH
					1984 BOATS					
18 3	SOLCAT 18	SLP	SA/OD	F/S CT		7 11	330	4	2850	3300

....For earlier years, see the BUC Used Boat Price Guide, Volume 3

SOLARIS YACHTS
SOUTHAMPTON ENGLAND   COAST GUARD MFG ID- SLY See inside cover to adjust price for area

LOA FT IN	NAME AND/ OR MODEL	TOP/ RIG	BOAT TYPE	HULL MTL TP	ENGINE TP # HP MFG	BEAM FT IN	WGT LBS	DRAFT FT IN	RETAIL LOW	RETAIL HIGH
					1994 BOATS					
24	SUNBEAM 24	SLP	SACAC	F/S CT	OB	14	4400	2 1	34300	38200
29 6	SUNCAT 30	SLP	SACAC	F/S CT	OB	18	5060	2 2	56500	62000
31 10	SUNSTAR 32	SLP	SACAC	F/S CT	SD T 9D-T18D	17 3	8360	3	81400	89700
34	LIMA 34	SLP	SACAC	F/S CT	IB	21		1 7	66500	73100
36	SPORT 36	SLP	SACAC	F/S CT	IB 18D YAN	15 10	11200	2 10	126000	138500
36	SUNRISE 36	SLP	SACAC	F/S CT	SD T 9D YAN	15 10	13200	2 10	134000	147000
36	SUNRISE 36	SLP	SACAC	F/S CT	IB T 18D YAN	15 10	13250	2 10	134000	147500
36	SUNSTAR 36	SLP	SACAC	F/S CT	IB T 9D YAN	17 3	8600	3	119500	131000
36	SUNSTAR 36	SLP	SACAC	F/S CT	IB T 20D PERK	17 3	8600	3	119500	131000
39 10	SUNSTREAM 40	CUT	SACAC	F/S CT	SD T 18D YAN	16	16500	3 6	181500	199500
39 10	SUNSTREAM 40	CUT	SACAC	F/S CT	SD T 27D YAN	16	16560	3 6	181500	199500
46	SUNCREST 46	SLP	SACAC	F/S CT	IB T D YAN	24 6	17600	3	228000	250500
					1993 BOATS					
24	SUNBEAM 24	SLP	SACAC	F/S CT	OB	14	4400	2 1	32300	35900
29 6	SUNCAT 30	SLP	SACAC	F/S CT	OB	18	5060	2 2	52800	58100
31 10	SUNSTAR 32	SLP	SACAC	F/S CT	SD T 9D-T18D	17 3	8360	3	76200	83900
36	SPORT 36	SLP	SACAC	F/S CT	IB 18D YAN	15 10	11200	2 10	118000	129500
36	SUNRISE 36	SLP	SACAC	F/S CT	SD T 9D YAN	15 10	13200	2 10	125500	138000
36	SUNRISE 36	SLP	SACAC	F/S CT	IB T 18D YAN	15 10	13250	2 10	126000	138000
36	SUNSTAR 36	SLP	SACAC	F/S CT	IB T 9D YAN	17 3	8600	3	112000	123000
36	SUNSTAR 36	SLP	SACAC	F/S CT	IB T 20D PERK	17 3	8600	3	112000	123000
39 10	SUNSTREAM 40	CUT	SACAC	F/S CT	SD T 18D YAN	16	16500	3 6	170000	186500
39 10	SUNSTREAM 40	CUT	SACAC	F/S CT	SD T 27D YAN	16	16560	3 6	170000	187000
46	SUNCREST 46	SLP	SACAC	F/S CT	IB T D YAN	24 6	17600	3 6	214500	235500
					1990 BOATS					
24	SOLARIS SUNBEAM	SLP	SA/CR	F/S CT	OB	14	4390	2 1	26900	29900
36	SOLARIS SUNRISE	SLP	SA/CR	F/S CT	IB T 18D YAN	15 10	9520	2 10	94900	104500
39 10	SOLARIS SUNSTREAM	CUT	SA/CR	FBG	CT IB T 30D YAN	16 6	13440	3 6	132000	145000
					1989 BOATS					
36	SOLARIS SUNRISE	SLP	SA/CR	F/S CT	IB T 18D YAN	15 10	9520	2 10	88900	97700
39 10	SOLARIS SUNRISE	CUT	SA/CR	FBG	CT IB T 30D YAN	16 6	13440	3 6	123500	135500
42	SOLARIS SUNRISE	KTH	SA/CR	FBG	CT IB T 35D YAN	17 9	17920	4	153500	168500
					1988 BOATS					
36	SOLARIS SUNRISE	CUT	SA/CR	F/S CT	SD T 27D YAN	15 10	8960	2 9	80500	88500

IB   27D YAN   80500   88500, SD   54D FORD   80500   88500, IB   54D FORD   80500   88500
SD T 9D YAN   82000   90100, IB T 9D YAN   82000   90100, SD T 18D YAN   82000   90100
IB T 18D YAN   82000   100100

LOA FT IN	NAME AND/ OR MODEL	TOP/ RIG	BOAT TYPE	HULL MTL TP	ENGINE TP # HP MFG	BEAM FT IN	WGT LBS	DRAFT FT IN	RETAIL LOW	RETAIL HIGH
					1987 BOATS					
39 10	SOLARIS SUNSTREAM	CUT	SA/CR	FBG	CT SD T 18D YAN	16 6	13440	3 6	108000	119000

IB T 18D YAN   108000   119000, SD T 27D YAN   108000   119000, IB T 27D YAN   108000   119000

LOA FT IN	NAME AND/ OR MODEL	TOP/ RIG	BOAT TYPE	HULL MTL TP	ENGINE TP # HP MFG	BEAM FT IN	WGT LBS	DRAFT FT IN	RETAIL LOW	RETAIL HIGH
42	SOLARIS SUNSET	SLP	SA/CR	FBG	CT SD T 34D YAN	17 9	17920	4	134500	147500

IB T 34D YAN   134500   147500, SD T 54D FORD   134500   147500, IB T 54D FORD   134500   147500

LOA FT IN	NAME AND/ OR MODEL	TOP/ RIG	BOAT TYPE	HULL MTL TP	ENGINE TP # HP MFG	BEAM FT IN	WGT LBS	DRAFT FT IN	RETAIL LOW	RETAIL HIGH
42	SOLARIS SUNSET	KTH	SA/CR	FBG	CT SD T 34D YAN	17 9	17920	4	134500	147500

IB T 34D YAN   134500   147500, SD T 54D FORD   134500   147500, IB T 54D FORD   134500   147500

....For earlier years, see the BUC Used Boat Price Guide, Volume 3

SOMERSET BOAT CO
SOMERSET KY 42501   See inside cover to adjust price for area

LOA FT IN	NAME AND/ OR MODEL	TOP/ RIG	BOAT TYPE	HULL MTL TP	ENGINE TP # HP MFG	BEAM FT IN	WGT LBS	DRAFT FT IN	RETAIL LOW	RETAIL HIGH
					1985 BOATS					
16	WORK BOAT	DGY	AL		OB	6	600		965	1150
36	INLAND-CRUISER	HT	HB	AL	SV IO	14	12000		33500	37300
46	INLAND-CRUISER	HT	HB	AL	SV IO	14	15000		42700	47500
58	INLAND-CRUISER	HT	HB	AL	SV IO	14	22000		62600	68800
62	INLAND-CRUISER	HT	HB	AL	SV IO	15	22000		66400	73000
70	INLAND-CRUISER	HT	HB	AL	SV IO	14	25000		74100	81500
					1984 BOATS					
16	WORK BOAT	DGY	AL		OB	6	600		945	1150
36	INLAND-CRUISER	HT	HB	AL	SV IO	14	12000		32800	36500
46	INLAND-CRUISER	HT	HB	AL	SV IO	14	15000		41800	46400

SOMERSET BOAT CO — CONTINUED

LOA FT IN	NAME AND/OR MODEL	TOP/RIG	BOAT TYPE	HULL (MTL TP TP)	ENGINE (# HP MFG)	BEAM FT IN	WGT LBS	DRAFT FT IN	RETAIL LOW	RETAIL HIGH
					1984 BOATS					
58	INLAND-CRUISER	HT	HB	AL SV IO		14	20000		61300	67400
62	INLAND-CRUISER	HT	HB	AL SV IO		15	22000		64900	71300
70	INLAND-CRUISER	HT	HB	AL SV IO		18	30000		76400	83900

....For earlier years, see the BUC Used Boat Price Guide, Volume 3

SOUTH DADE BOATS INC
PERRINE FL 33157   COAST GUARD MFG ID- SXE   See inside cover to adjust price for area

LOA FT IN	NAME AND/OR MODEL	TOP/RIG	BOAT TYPE	HULL (MTL TP TP)	ENGINE (# HP MFG)	BEAM FT IN	WGT LBS	DRAFT FT IN	RETAIL LOW	RETAIL HIGH
					1984 BOATS					
28 4	GULFSTREAM	OP	CTRCN	FBG DV IB	215 GM	10	5500	2 7	22900	25400
28 4	GULFSTREAM	OP	CTRCN	FBG DV IO	T260 VLVO	10	5500	2 7	19500	21600
28 4	GULFSTREAM	OP	CTRCN	FBG DV IO	T124D VLVO	10	5500	2 7	24400	27100
28 4	GULFSTREAM	OP	SPTCR	FBG DV IB	215 GM	10	5500	2 7	22900	25400
28 4	GULFSTREAM	OP	SPTCR	FBG DV IO	T260 VLVO	10	5500	2 7	18700	20700
28 4	GULFSTREAM	OP	SPTCR	FBG DV IO	T124D VLVO	10	5500	2 7	24400	27100

SOUTHERN CROSS
NORTH AMERICAN OPERATIONS
TAMARAC FL 33319-3140   See inside cover to adjust price for area

SOUTHERN CROSS
QUEENSLAND AUSTRLIA

LOA FT IN	NAME AND/OR MODEL	TOP/RIG	BOAT TYPE	HULL (MTL TP TP)	ENGINE (# HP MFG)	BEAM FT IN	WGT LBS	DRAFT FT IN	RETAIL LOW	RETAIL HIGH
					1988 BOATS					
44 2	SOUTHERN CROSS 44	FB	SF	C/S SV IB	T540D GM	14 6	28000	3	177500	195000
52	SOUTHERN CROSS 52	FB	SF	C/S SV IB	T740D GM	15	38000	3 6	270500	297000
53	SOUTHERN CROSS 53	FB	FD	FBG DS IB	T450D GM	16	50000	3 10	275500	302500
53	SOUTHERN CROSS 53	FB	MY	FBG DS IB	T450D GM	16	50000	3 10	236000	259500
					1987 BOATS					
44 2	SOUTHERN CROSS 44	FB	SF	C/S SV IB	T540D GM	14 6	28000	3	169500	186500
52	SOUTHERN CROSS 52	FB	SF	C/S SV IB	T740D GM	15 6	38000	3 6	259000	284500
53	SOUTHERN CROSS 53	FB	MY	FBG DS IB	T435D GM	16	50000	3 10	223500	246000

SOUTHERN OFFSHORE LTD
TARPON SPRINGS FL 34286   See inside cover to adjust price for area
FORMERLY SOUTHERN OFFSHORE YACHTS INC

LOA FT IN	NAME AND/OR MODEL	TOP/RIG	BOAT TYPE	HULL (MTL TP TP)	ENGINE (# HP MFG)	BEAM FT IN	WGT LBS	DRAFT FT IN	RETAIL LOW	RETAIL HIGH
					1993 BOATS					
55	OFFSHORE 55	FB	PH	IB	T550D	16 10		4 4	385500	424000
					1992 BOATS					
37 11	VAGABOND 38	SLP	SAIL	FBG KL IB	44D YAN	12	19200	4 11	101500	111500
39 2	VAGABOND 39	CUT	SAIL	FBG KL IB	51D PERK	11 6	23500	5 7	119000	130500
46 7	VAGABOND 47	KTH	SAIL	FBG KL IB	85D VLVO	13 5	40000	5 3	208000	228500
50 2	ULTIMATE 50	FB	MY	FBG SV IB	T450D GM	16 10	42000	3 6	308500	339000
52	VAGABOND 52	SCH	SAIL	FBG KL IB	135D VLVO	13 11	50000	5	318500	350000
					1991 BOATS					
37 11	VAGABOND 38	SLP	SAIL	FBG KL IB	44D YAN	12	19200	4 11	95500	105500
39 2	VAGABOND 39	CUT	SAIL	FBG KL IB	51D PERK	11 6	23500	5 7	112000	123000
43 9	ULTIMATE 42	FB	MY	FBG SV IB	T260D GM	13	22000	3	175500	193000
46 7	VAGABOND 47	KTH	SAIL	FBG KL IB	85D VLVO	13 5	40000	5 3	197000	216500
50 2	ULTIMATE 50	FB	MY	FBG SV IB	T450D GM	16 10	42000	3 6	293500	322500
52	VAGABOND 52	SCH	SAIL	FBG KL IB	135D VLVO	13 11	50000	6	302000	331500
					1990 BOATS					
37 11	VAGABOND 38	SLP	SAIL	FBG KL IB	44D YAN	12	19200	4 11	89900	98800
39 2	VAGABOND 39	CUT	SAIL	FBG KL IB	51D PERK	11 6	23500	5 7	105000	115500
42 8	RON HOLLAND 43	SLP	SA/CR	FBG KL IB	44D YAN	13	23780	6	114000	125500
43 9	ULTIMATE 42	FB	MY	FBG SV IB	T260D GM	13	22000	3	167500	184000
45 11	SURPRISE 45	SLP	SAIL	FBG KL IB	52D PEUG	13 5	26400	6 5	146000	160500
45 11	SURPRISE 45	SCH	SAIL	FBG KL IB	52D PEUG	13 5	26400	6 5	146000	160500
46 7	VAGABOND 47	KTH	SAIL	FBG KL IB	85D VLVO	13 5	40000	5 3	186500	205000
50 2	ULTIMATE 50	FB	MY	FBG SV IB	T450D GM	16 10	42000	3 6	280000	307500
52	VAGABOND 52	SCH	SAIL	FBG KL IB	135D VLVO	13 11	50000	6	286000	314000
					1989 BOATS					
34 11	CT-35 SUNDECK		TRAWL	FBG IB	120D FORD	12	19800	3 5	98700	108500
34 11	CT-T35 TRAWLER		TRWL	FBG IB	120D FORD	12	19800	3 5	94100	103500
37 11	VAGABOND 38	SLP	SAIL	FBG KL IB	44D YAN	12	19200	4 11	84600	93000
39 2	VAGABOND 39	CUT	SAIL	FBG KL IB	51D PERK	11 6	23500	5 7	99000	109000
42 8	RON HOLLAND 43	SLP	SA/CR	FBG KL IB	44D YAN	13	23780	6 8	107500	118500
43 9	ULTIMATE 42	FB	MY	FBG SV IB	T260D GM	13	22000	3	159500	175500
45 11	SURPRISE 45	SLP	SAIL	FBG KL IB	52D PEUG	13 5	26400	6 5	138500	152000
45 11	SURPRISE 45	SCH	SAIL	FBG KL IB	52D PEUG	13 5	26400	6 5	138500	152000
46 7	VAGABOND 47	KTH	SAIL	FBG KL IB	85D VLVO	13 5	40000	5 3	176500	194000
50 2	ULTIMATE 50	FB	MY	FBG SV IB	T450D GM	16 10	42000	3 6	267000	293500
52	VAGABOND 52	SCH	SAIL	FBG KL IB	135D VLVO	13 11	50000	6	271000	297500
					1988 BOATS					
34 11	CT-35 SUNDECK		TRWL	FBG IB	120D FORD	12	19800	3 5	92300	101500
34 11	CT-T35 TRAWLER		TRWL	FBG IB	120D FORD	12	19800	3 5	92300	101500
37 11	VAGABOND 38	SLP	SAIL	FBG KL IB	44D YAN	12	19200	4 11	79700	87600
39 2	VAGABOND 39	CUT	SAIL	FBG KL IB	51D PERK	11 6	23500	5 7	93100	102500
42 8	RON HOLLAND 43	SLP	SA/CR	FBG KL IB	44D YAN	13	23780	6 8	101500	112000
43 9	ULTIMATE 42	FB	MY	FBG SV IB	T260D GM	13	22000	3	152500	167500
45 11	SURPRISE 45	SLP	SAIL	FBG KL IB	52D PEUG	13 5	26400	6 5	131000	144000
45 11	SURPRISE 45	SCH	SAIL	FBG KL IB	52D PEUG	13 5	26400	6 5	131000	144000
46 7	VAGABOND 47	KTH	SAIL	FBG KL IB	85D VLVO	13 5	40000	5 3	167500	184000
50 2	ULTIMATE 50	FB	MY	FBG SV IB	T450D GM	16 10	42000	3 6	255000	280500
52	VAGABOND 52	SCH	SAIL	FBG KL IB	135D VLVO	13 11	50000	6	256500	282000
					1987 BOATS					
27	VANCOUVER 27	CUT	SAIL	FBG KL IB	22D YAN	8 8	8960	4 6	30900	34400
29 2	VANCOUVER 25	SLP	SAIL	FBG KL IB	22D YAN	8 6	7500	4	28100	31200
32	VANCOUVER 32	CUT	SAIL	FBG KL IB	T 22D YAN	10 7	14000	4 6	60000	66000
32	VANCOUVER 32 PH	CUT	SAIL	FBG KL IB	22D YAN	10 7	14000	4 6	56000	66000
38 9	MARINER 36	CUT	SAIL	FBG KL IB	44D YAN	11	21000	5	80500	88400
38 9	MARINER 36	KTH	SAIL	FBG KL IB	44D YAN	11	21000	5	85800	94300
39 2	VAGABOND 39	CUT	SAIL	FBG KL IB	51D PERK	11 6	23500	5 7	87700	96300
43 9	ULTIMATE 42	FB	MY	FBG SV IB	T260D GM	13	22000	3	145500	160000
45 11	SURPRISE 45	SLP	SAIL	FBG KL IB	52D PEUG	13 5	26400	6	124500	136500
45 11	SURPRISE 45	SCH	SAIL	FBG KL IB	52D PEUG	13 5	26400	6	124500	136500
46 7	VAGABOND 47	KTH	SAIL	FBG KL IB	85D VLVO	13 5	40000	5	158500	174500
50 2	ULTIMATE 50	FB	MY	FBG SV IB	T450D GM	16 10	42000	3	243500	268000
52	VAGABOND 52	SCH	SAIL	FBG KL IB	135D VLVO	13 11	50000	6	243000	267000
55	TAYANA 55	CUT	SAIL	FBG KL IB	135D PERK	16 1	48400	6	296500	326000
					1986 BOATS					
27	VANCOUVER 27	CUT	SAIL	FBG KL IB	22D YAN	8 8	8960	4 6	29200	32500
29 2	VANCOUVER 25	SLP	SAIL	FBG KL IB	8D- 15D	8 6	7500	4	26500	29600
32	VANCOUVER 32	CUT	SAIL	FBG KL IB	T 22D YAN	10 7	14000	4 6	56800	62400
32	VANCOUVER 32 PH	CUT	SAIL	FBG KL IB	22D YAN	10 7	14000	4 6	56800	62400
38 9	MARINER 36	CUT	SAIL	FBG KL IB	33D YAN	11	21000	5	75500	83100
38 9	MARINER 36	KTH	SAIL	FBG KL IB	33D YAN	11	21000	5	80600	88500
39 2	VAGABOND 39	CUT	SAIL	FBG KL IB	51D PERK	11 6	23500	5 7	82500	90700
43 9	ULTIMATE 42	FB	MY	FBG SV IB	T260D GM	13	22000	3	139000	153000
45 11	SURPRISE 45	SCH	SAIL	FBG KL IB	52D PEUG	13 5	26400	6	118000	129500
46 7	VAGABOND 47	KTH	SAIL	FBG KL IB	85D VLVO	13 5	40000	5	150500	165500
50 2	ULTIMATE 50	FB	MY	FBG SV IB	T450D GM	16 10	42000	3	232000	255000
52	VAGABOND 52	SCH	SAIL	FBG KL IB	135D VLVO	13 11	50000	6	230500	253000
					1985 BOATS					
29 2	VANCOUVER 25	SLP	SAIL	FBG KL IB	8D- 15D	8 6	7500	4	25100	28000
38 9	MARINER 36	CUT	SAIL	FBG KL IB	33D YAN	11	21000	5	71200	78300
38 9	MARINER 36	KTH	SAIL	FBG KL IB	33D YAN	11	21000	5	75900	83400
45 11	SURPRISE 45	SLP	SA/CR	FBG KL IB	D	13	26400	6	112000	123000
45 11	SURPRISE 45	SLP	SAIL	FBG KL IB	52D PERK	13 5	26400	6	111500	122500
45 11	SURPRISE 45	SCH	SAIL	FBG KL IB	52D PERK	13 5	26400	6	111000	122000

....For earlier years, see the BUC Used Boat Price Guide, Volume 3

SOUTHERN SAILS INC
SKIPPER YACHTS
SEMINOLE FL 33542   COAST GUARD MFG ID- XUT   See inside cover to adjust price for area

LOA FT IN	NAME AND/OR MODEL	TOP/RIG	BOAT TYPE	HULL (MTL TP TP)	ENGINE (# HP MFG)	BEAM FT IN	WGT LBS	DRAFT FT IN	RETAIL LOW	RETAIL HIGH
					1985 BOATS					
17 2	SKIPPER-MATE	SLP	SAIL	FBG CB OB		7 2	1300		2400	2800
19	SKIPPER COD	SLP	SAIL	FBG KL OB		6 9	1900	2	3050	3550
20	SKIPPER 20	SLP	SAIL	FBG KL OB		6 9	2000	2	3200	3750
					1984 BOATS					
17 2	SKIPPERS-MATE	SLP	SAIL	FBG CB OB		7 2	1300		2300	2650
19	SKIPPER CUDDY	SLP	SAIL	FBG KL OB		6 9	1900	2	2850	3350
20	SKIPPER 20	SLP	SAIL	FBG KL OB		6 9	2000	2	3050	3500

....For earlier years, see the BUC Used Boat Price Guide, Volume 3

SOUTHERN SKIMMER CO

ROBERT C RODECKER
BEAUFORT NC 28516   COAST GUARD MFG ID- ROD   See inside cover to adjust price for area
FORMERLY UNITED STATES SKIFFS

LOA FT IN	NAME AND/ OR MODEL	TOP/ RIG	BOAT TYPE	-HULL- MTL TP	TP	--ENGINE--- # HP MFG	BEAM FT IN	WGT LBS	DRAFT FT IN	RETAIL LOW	RETAIL HIGH
						1992 BOATS					
16 2	1650	OP	JON	FBG FL	OB		6 3	480	4	1350	1600
17 11	1860	OP	JON	FBG FL	OB		7 4	615	4	1600	1900
19 1	1970	OP	JON	FBG FL	OB		7 6	700	4	1750	2100
21	2170	OP	JON	FBG FL	OB		7 6	770	4	1900	2300
23 5	2480	OP	JON	FBG FL	OB		8 4	1030	4	2700	3100
						1986 BOATS					
16 1	SOUTHERN SKIMMER1650	OP	JON	FBG FL	OB		6 3	290	3	680	820
17 11	SOUTHERN SKIMMER1860	OP	JON	FBG FL	OB		7 4	607	3	1200	1450
18 11	SOUTHERN SKIMMER1970	OP	JON	FBG FL	OB		7 6	650	3	1250	1500
21	SOUTHERN SKIMMER2170	OP	JON	FBG FL	OB		7 6	710	3	1350	1600
						1985 BOATS					
16 1	CAROLINA-SKIFF 1650	OP	JON	FBG FL	OB		6 3	290	3	660	795
17 11	CAROLINA-SKIFF 1860	OP	JON	FBG FL	OB		7 4	607	3	1200	1400
18 11	CAROLINA-SKIFF 1970	OP	JON	FBG FL	OB		7 6	650	3	1200	1450
21	CAROLINA-SKIFF 2170	OP	JON	FBG FL	OB		7 6	710	3	1300	1550
						1984 BOATS					
16	16050	OP	JON	FBG FL	OB		6 5	275		610	735
17	17060	OP	JON	FBG FL	OB		7 2	475		965	1150
19	19060	OP	JON	FBG FL	OB		7 2	600		1100	1300
19	19060	OP	JON	FBG FL	OB		7 2	500		966	1050
19	19070	OP	JON	FBG FL	OB		7 4	600		1100	1300
21 6		OP	JON	FBG FL	OB		8 6	775		1400	1650
21 6	21678	OP	JON	FBG FL	OB		8	775		1400	1650
24	24078	OP	JON	FBG FL	OB		8	875		1600	1900

....For earlier years, see the BUC Used Boat Price Guide, Volume 3

SOUTHERN STAR

SYLACAUGA AL 35150   COAST GUARD MFG ID- VSV See inside cover to adjust price for area

For more recent years, see the BUC Used Boat Price Guide, Volume 1

LOA FT IN	NAME AND/ OR MODEL	TOP/ RIG	BOAT TYPE	-HULL- MTL TP	TP	--ENGINE--- # HP MFG	BEAM FT IN	WGT LBS	DRAFT FT IN	RETAIL LOW	RETAIL HIGH
						1996 BOATS					
16	OPEN FISHERMAN 16	OPFSH	FBG SV	OB			8	1500		5200	6000
17	OPEN FISHERMAN 17	OPFSH	FBG SV	OB			8	1550		5300	6100

SOUTHERN YACHTS

WICHITA KS 67216   COAST GUARD MFG ID- SDY See inside cover to adjust price for area

LOA FT IN	NAME AND/ OR MODEL	TOP/ RIG	BOAT TYPE	-HULL- MTL TP	TP	--ENGINE--- # HP MFG	BEAM FT IN	WGT LBS	DRAFT FT IN	RETAIL LOW	RETAIL HIGH
						1986 BOATS					
20	TORNADO	CAT	SA/OD	F/S	CT		10	300	2	4200	4900
						1985 BOATS					
18	DRAGBOAT	SKI	FBG FL	IB			8			**	**
20	TORNADO	CAT	SA/OD	F/S	CT		10	300	2 1	3950	4600
						1984 BOATS					
18	DRAGBOAT SK	SKI	FBG FL	IB			8			**	**
19	FLYING-SCOT	SA/OD	FBG DB				6 9	675	8	4450	5100
20	TORNADO CAT	SA/OD	FBG CT				10	350	5	4150	4800

....For earlier years, see the BUC Used Boat Price Guide, Volume 3

SOVEREIGN AMERICA INC

DIV OF WATER SPORTS DEPOT INC
ST PETERSBURG FL 33706- COAST GUARD MFG ID- XUP   See inside cover to adjust price for area
FORMERLY CUSTOM FBG PRODUCTS INTL INC

For more recent years, see the BUC Used Boat Price Guide, Volume 1

LOA FT IN	NAME AND/ OR MODEL	TOP/ RIG	BOAT TYPE	-HULL- MTL TP	TP	--ENGINE--- # HP MFG	BEAM FT IN	WGT LBS	DRAFT FT IN	RETAIL LOW	RETAIL HIGH
						1996 BOATS					
17 4	MUD HEN 17	GAF	SACAC FBG	SK	OB		6 3	650	3	7550	8700
18	SOVEREIGN 18	SLP	SACAC FBG	KL	OB		7	1350	1 10	11600	13200
20	SOVEREIGN 20 SHOAL	SLP	SACAC FBG	KL	OB		7 2	1700	2	13100	14900
21	BAY HEN 21	GAF	SACAC FBG	BB	OB		6 3	900	3 6	9950	11300
24	SOVEREIGN 24 SHOAL	SLP	SACAC FBG	KL	OB		8	3600	2 7	23600	26300
						1995 BOATS					
17 4	MUD HEN 17	GAF	SACAC FBG	SK	OB		6 3	750	9	7550	8700
18	SOVEREIGN 18	SLP	SACAC FBG	KL	OB		7	1350	1 10	10900	12400
20 3	SOVEREIGN 20 SHOAL	SLP	SACAC FBG	KL	OB		7 2	1700	2	12400	14100
21	BAY HEN 21	GAF	SACAC FBG	BB	OB		6 3	900	3 6	9350	10600
24	SOVEREIGN 24 SHOAL	SLP	SACAC FBG	KL	OB		8	3600	2 7	22200	24700
						1994 BOATS					
17 4	MUD HEN 17	GAF	SACAC FBG	SK	OB		6 3	750	9	7050	8150
18	SOVEREIGN 18	SLP	SACAC FBG	KL	OB		7	1350	1 10	10300	11700
20 3	SOVEREIGN 20 SHOAL	SLP	SACAC FBG	KL	OB		7 2	1700	2	11600	13200
21	BAY HEN 21	GAF	SACAC FBG	BB	OB		6 3	900	3 6	8800	10000
24	SOVEREIGN 24 SHOAL	SLP	SACAC FBG	KL	OB		8	3600	2 7	20900	23300
						1993 BOATS					
17 4	MUD HEN 17	GAF	SACAC FBG	SK	OB		6 3	750	3 6	6650	7650
18	SOVEREIGN 18	SLP	SACAC FBG	KL	OB		7	1350	1 10	9600	10900
20 3	SOVEREIGN 20 SHOAL	SLP	SACAC FBG	KL	OB		7 2	1700	2 4	10900	12400
21	BAY HEN 21	GAF	SACAC FBG	BB	OB		6 3	900	3 6	8200	9400
24	SOVEREIGN 24 SHOAL	SLP	SACAC FBG	KL	OB		8	3400	2 7	19000	21100
						1992 BOATS					
17 4	MUD HEN 17	GAF	SAIL	FBG			7	750	3 6	6250	7200
18	SOVEREIGN 18	SLP	SAIL	FBG	KL	OB	7	1350	1 10	9050	10300
20 3	SOVEREIGN 20 SHOAL	SLP	SAIL	FBG	KL	OB	7 2	1700	2 4	10300	11700
21	BAY HEN 21	GAF	SAIL	FBG	BB	OB	6 3	900	3 6	7700	8850
24	SOVEREIGN 24 SHOAL	SLP	SAIL	FBG	KL	OB	8	3400	2 7	17400	19800
						1991 BOATS					
17	ANTARES 17 DAYSAILOR	SLP	SAIL	FBG		OB	7	1150	1 10	7700	8850
18	SOVEREIGN 18 SAILBT	SLP	SAIL	FBG	KL	OB	7	1350	1 10	8400	9650
20 3	SOVEREIGN 20 SHOAL	SLP	SAIL	FBG	KL	OB	7 2	1700	2 4	9650	11000
24	SOVEREIGN 24 SHOAL	SLP	SAIL	FBG	KL	OB	8	3000	2 7	14800	16800
						1990 BOATS					
17	ANTARES 17 DAYSAILOR	SLP	SAIL	FBG		OB	7	1150	1 10	7200	8300
18	SOVEREIGN 18 SAILBT	SLP	SAIL	FBG	KL	OB	7	1350	1 10	7850	9050
20 3	SOVEREIGN 20 SHOAL	SLP	SAIL	FBG	KL	OB	7 2	1700	2 4	9100	10300
24	SOVEREIGN 24 SHOAL	SLP	SAIL	FBG	KL	OB	8	3000	2 7	13900	15800
						1989 BOATS					
17	ANTARES 17 DAYSAILOR	SLP	SAIL	FBG		OB	7	1150	4 13	6750	7800
18	SOVEREIGN 18 SAILBT	SLP	SAIL	FBG	KL	OB	7	1350	1 10	7350	8450
19 3	SOVEREIGN 20 SHOAL	SLP	SAIL	FBG		OB	7 2	1700	2 4	8400	9650
24	SOVEREIGN 24 SHOAL	SLP	SAIL	FBG	KL	OB	8	3000	2 7	13100	14900
						1988 BOATS					
17	ANTARES 17 DAYSAILOR	SLP	SAIL			OB	7	1150	2	6350	7300
18	SOVEREIGN 18 SAILBT	SLP	SAIL		KL		7	1350	2	6900	7950
19 3	EXPRESS 19 SWINGKEEL	SLP	SAIL		SK	OB	7 2	1550	1 4	7450	8600
19 3	EXPRESS 20 SHOAL	SLP	SAIL			OB	7 2	1700	2 4	7850	9050
						1987 BOATS					
19 3	EXPRESS 19 SHOAL	SLP	SAIL			OB	7 2	1700	2 4	7350	8450
19 3	EXPRESS 19 SWINGKEEL	SLP	SAIL		SK	OB	7 2	1550	1 4	7000	8050

SOVEREIGN YACHT CO INC

LARGO FL 33540   COAST GUARD MFG ID- XVG See inside cover to adjust price for area

LOA FT IN	NAME AND/ OR MODEL	TOP/ RIG	BOAT TYPE	-HULL- MTL TP	TP	--ENGINE--- # HP MFG	BEAM FT IN	WGT LBS	DRAFT FT IN	RETAIL LOW	RETAIL HIGH
						1986 BOATS					
17	SOVEREIGN 17	SLP	SA/CR FBG	KL	OB		7	1350	1 10	2500	2900
18	ANTARES 18	SLP	SA/CR FBG	KL	OB		7	1100	1 10	2250	2650
23	SOVEREIGN 23	SLP	SA/CR FBG	KL	OB		8	3250	2 4	5000	5750
24	ANTARES 24	SLP	SA/CR FBG	KL	OB		8	3000	2 4	4950	5700
28	SOVEREIGN 28	SLP	SA/CR FBG	KL	IB	D	8 4	6800	3 4	13200	14900
						1985 BOATS					
17	ADVENTURE 17-A	SLP	SA/CR FBG	KL	OB		7	1350	1 10	2300	2650
17	ADVENTURE 17-B	SLP	SA/CR FBG	KL	OB		7	1350	1 10	2400	2800
18	SOVEREIGN 18	SLP	SA/CR FBG	KL	OB		7	1900	2 4	2850	3300
23	ADVENTURE 23 DEEP	SLP	SA/CR FBG	KL	IB	7D BMW	8	3250	3 8	4750	5450
23	ADVENTURE 23 DEEP	SLP	SA/CR FBG	KL	IB	7D BMW	8	3350	3 8	5550	6350
23	ADVENTURE 23 SHOAL	SLP	SA/CR FBG	KL	IB		8	3250	2 4	4700	5450
23	ADVENTURE 23 SHOAL	SLP	SA/CR FBG	KL	IB	7D BMW	8	3600	2 4	5850	6700
24	PRINCESS 24 DEEP	SLP	SA/CR FBG	KL	IB		8	3350	3 8	5100	5850
24	PRINCESS 24 DEEP	SLP	SA/CR FBG	KL	IB	7D BMW	8	3600	3 8	6000	6900
24	PRINCESS 24 SHOAL	SLP	SA/CR FBG	KL	IB		8	3350	2 4	5100	5850
24	PRINCESS SHOAL 24	SLP	SA/CR FBG	KL	IB	7D BMW	8	3600	2 4	6000	6900
28	SOVEREIGN 28	SLP	SA/CR FBG	KL	IB	10D BMW	8 4	6200	3 4	11200	12700
						1984 BOATS					
17	ADVENTURE 17-A	SLP	SA/CR FBG	KL	OB		7	1350	1 10	2150	2500
17	ADVENTURE 17-B	SLP	SA/CR FBG	KL	OB		7	1350	1 10	2300	2650
18	SOVEREIGN 18	SLP	SA/CR FBG	KL	OB		7	1900	2 4	2650	3100
23	ADVENTURE 23	SLP	SA/CR FBG	KL	OB		8	3250	3 8	4450	5150
23	ADVENTURE 23	SLP	SA/CR FBG	KL	IB	7D BMW	8	3350	3 8	5200	6000

LOA FT IN	NAME AND/ OR MODEL	TOP/ RIG	BOAT TYPE	-HULL- MTL TP	----ENGINE--- TP # HP MFG	BEAM FT IN	WGT LBS	DRAFT FT IN	RETAIL LOW	RETAIL HIGH
---	--- 1984	BOATS								
23	ADVENTURE 23 SHOAL	SLP	SA/CR FBG	KL	OB	8	3250	2 4	4450	5150
23	ADVENTURE 23 SHOAL	SLP	SA/CR FBG	KL	IB 7D BMW	8	3600	2 4	5500	6300
24	PRINCESS 24	SLP	SA/CR FBG	KL	OB	8	3350	3 8	4800	5500
24	PRINCESS 24	SLP	SA/CR FBG	KL	IB 7D BMW	8	3600	3 8	5650	6450
24	PRINCESS SHOAL 24	SLP	SA/CR FBG	KL	OB	8	3350	2 4	4800	5500
24	PRINCESS SHOAL 24	SLP	SA/CR FBG	KL	IB 7D BMW	8	3600	2 4	5650	6450
28	SOVEREIGN 28	SLP	SA/CR FBG	KL	IB 12D BMW	8 4	6200	3 4	10500	12000
28	SOVEREIGN 28	CUT	SA/CR FBG	KL	IB D	8 4	5500	3 3	9400	10700

....For earlier years, see the BUC Used Boat Price Guide, Volume 3

SOVEREL MARINE INC
N PALM BEACH FL 33410   COAST GUARD MFG ID- SVM See inside cover to adjust price for area

LOA FT IN	NAME AND/ OR MODEL	TOP/ RIG	BOAT TYPE	-HULL- MTL TP	----ENGINE--- TP # HP MFG	BEAM FT IN	WGT LBS	DRAFT FT IN	RETAIL LOW	RETAIL HIGH
---	--- 1987	BOATS								
30	SOVEREL 30	SLP	SA/RC FBG	KL	IB D	11	7000	5 3	16600	18800
33	SOVEREL 33	SLP	SA/RC FBG	KL	IB D	11	11000	6	26800	29800
36	SOVEREL 36	SLP	SA/RC FBG	KL	IB D	11	14000	6 5	35300	39200
39	SOVEREL 39	SLP	SA/RC FBG	KL	IB D	12 1	11000	7 5	33600	37300
48	SOVEREL 48	KTH	SA/RC FBG	KC	IB D	13	28000	5	61500	67600
50	SOVEREL 50	SLP	SA/RC FBG	KL	IB D	15	23000	9	113000	124000
---	--- 1985	BOATS								
30	SOVEREL 30	SLP	SA/RC FBG	KL	IB D	11	7000	5 3	14900	16900
33	SOVEREL 33	SLP	SA/RC FBG	KL	IB D	11	11000	6	24000	26700
36	SOVEREL 36	SLP	SA/RC FBG	KL	IB D	11	14000	6 5	31700	35200
39	SOVEREL 39	SLP	SA/RC FBG	KL	IB D	12 1	11000	7 5	30100	33500
48	SOVEREL 48	KTH	SA/RC FBG	KC	IB D	13	28000	5	81700	89800
50	SOVEREL 50	SLP	SA/RC FBG	KL	IB D	15	23000	9	101500	111500
---	--- 1984	BOATS								
33	SOVEREL 33-15/16	SLP	SA/RC FBG	KL	IB D	11	10000	5 10	22800	25300
35 10	SOVEREL 36	SLP	SA/RC FBG	KC	IB 16D REN	10 8	14500	3 9	30700	34200
35 10	SOVEREL 36	SLP	SA/RC FBG	KC	IB 30D WEST	10 8	14500	3 9	30900	34300
35 10	SOVEREL 36	SLP	SA/RC FBG	KC	IB 16D REN	10 8	14500	6 6	30700	34200
48	SOVEREL 48	KTH	SA/RC FBG	KC	IB 85D LEHM	13	28000	5	77600	85300
50	SOVEREL 50	SLP	SA/CR FBG	KL	IB 85D LEHM	14	38000	8	96100	105500

....For earlier years, see the BUC Used Boat Price Guide, Volume 3

SOVEREL PERFORMANCE YACHTS
AND RIVER USA 44045   COAST GUARD MFG ID- BER See inside cover to adjust price for area

LOA FT IN	NAME AND/ OR MODEL	TOP/ RIG	BOAT TYPE	-HULL- MTL TP	----ENGINE--- TP # HP MFG	BEAM FT IN	WGT LBS	DRAFT FT IN	RETAIL LOW	RETAIL HIGH
---	--- 1988	BOATS								
26 6	SOVEREL 27	SLP	SA/RC F/S	KL	IB 9D YAN	8 9	4000	5	16200	18400
33	SOVEREL 33	SLP	SA/RC F/S	KL	IB 9D YAN	11	6000	5 10	26100	29000
38 5	SOVEREL 39	SLP	SA/RC F/S	KL	IB 27D YAN	12 6	11800	7 8	60400	66300
49 3	SOVEREL 50	SLP	SA/RC F/S	KL	IB D WEST	15	25200	9 2	175000	192500
---	--- 1987	BOATS								
26 6	SOVEREL 27	SLP	SA/RC F/S	KL	IB 11D YAN	8 9	4000	5	15300	17400
33	SOVEREL 33	SLP	SA/RC F/S	KL	IB 11D YAN	11	6000	5 10	24600	27300
38 5	SOVEREL 39	SLP	SA/RC F/S	KL	IB 27D YAN	12 6	11800	7 8	56800	62400
49 3	SOVEREL 50	SLP	SA/RC F/S	KL	IB D WEST	15	25200	9 2	164500	181000

SPACECRAFT BOATWORKS INC
MIAMI FL 33142   COAST GUARD MFG ID- SPA See inside cover to adjust price for area

LOA FT IN	NAME AND/ OR MODEL	TOP/ RIG	BOAT TYPE	-HULL- MTL TP	----ENGINE--- TP # HP MFG	BEAM FT IN	WGT LBS	DRAFT FT IN	RETAIL LOW	RETAIL HIGH
---	--- 1990	BOATS								
23 4	CAPTAIN	HT	CUD	FBG	SV OB	8	4200	1 7	12700	14500
23 4	CAPTAIN	HT	CUD	FBG	SV IO 167-209	8	4200	1 7	9700	11100
23 4	CAPTAIN	HT	CUD	FBG	SV SE 225	8	4200	1 7	12700	14500
23 4	CAPTAIN	HT	CUD	FBG	SV IO 229-275	8	4200	1 7	9900	11700
IO 330 VLVO 11300	12800, IO 180D-200D	12500	14100, IO	T120-T125					10900	12400
23 4	CAPTAIN	HT	CUD	FBG	SV IO T140	8	4200	1 7	12700	14500
23 4	CAPTAIN	HT	CUD	FBG	SV IO T146-T171	8	4200	1 7	11000	12500
23 4	COMMODORE	FB	SF	FBG	SV OB	8	4600	1 7	13300	15600
23 4	COMMODORE	FB	SF	FBG	SV IO 200-209	8	4600	1 7	11700	13600
23 4	COMMODORE	FB	SF	FBG	SV SE 225	8	4600	1 7	13300	15100
23 4	COMMODORE	FB	SF	FBG	SV IO 229-275	8	4600	1 7	12100	14300
IO 330 VLVO 13700	15500, IO 180D-200D	16400	18700, IO	T120-T125					13300	15100
23 4	COMMODORE	FB	SF	FBG	SV IO T140	8	4600	1 7	13300	15100
23 4	COMMODORE	FB	SF	FBG	SV IO T146-T171	8	4600	1 7	13300	15200
23 4	CONQUEROR	ST	CUD	FBG	SV OB	8	3800	1 3	12100	13700
23 4	CONQUEROR	ST	CUD	FBG	SV IO 140	8	3800	1 3	12100	13700
23 4	CONQUEROR	ST	CUD	FBG	SV SE 146-209	8	3800	1 3	9050	10400
23 4	CONQUEROR	ST	CUD	FBG	SV SE 225	8	3800	1 3	12100	13700
23 4	CONQUEROR	ST	CUD	FBG	SV IO 229-275	8	3800	1 3	9250	10900
IO 330 VLVO 10600	12000, IO 180D-200D	11800	13400, IO	T120-T125					10200	11600
23 4	CONQUEROR	ST	CUD	FBG	SV IO T140	8	3800	1 3	12100	13700
23 4	CONQUEROR	ST	CUD	FBG	SV IO T146 VLVO	8	3800	1 3	10300	11700
23 4	OLYMPIAN	ST	CUD	FBG	SV OB	8	3600	1 3	11700	13300
23 4	OLYMPIAN	ST	CUD	FBG	SV IO 140	8	3600	1 3	11700	13300
23 4	OLYMPIAN	ST	CUD	FBG	SV SE 146-209	8	3600	1 3	8600	10000
23 4	OLYMPIAN	ST	CUD	FBG	SV SE 226	8	3600	1 3	11700	13300
23 4	OLYMPIAN	ST	CUD	FBG	SV IO 229-275	8	3600	1 3	8950	10600
IO 330 VLVO 10200	11600, IO 180D-200D	11400	13000, IO	T120-T125					9900	11300
23 4	OLYMPIAN	ST	CUD	FBG	SV IO T140	8	3600	1 3	11700	13300
23 4	OLYMPIAN	ST	CUD	FBG	SV IO T146 VLVO	8	3600	1 3	9950	11300
23 4	SUPER SPORT	ST	CUD	FBG	DV OB	8	4100	1 3	12600	14300
23 4	SUPER SPORT	ST	CUD	FBG	DV IO 167-209	8	4100	1 3	9500	10900
23 4	SUPER SPORT	ST	CUD	FBG	DV SE 225	8	4100	1 3	12600	14300
23 4	SUPER SPORT	ST	CUD	FBG	DV IO 229-275	8	4100	1 3	9750	11500
IO 330 VLVO 11100	12600, IO 180D-200D	12300	14000, IO	T120-T125					10800	12200
23 4	SUPER SPORT	ST	CUD	FBG	DV IO T140	8	4100	1 3	12600	14300
23 4	SUPER SPORT	ST	CUD	FBG	DV IO T146-T171	8	4100	1 3	10800	12300
24 10	BRUTE CC	ST	CTRCN FBG	DV	OB	8	3600	1 2	12500	14200
24 10	BRUTE CC	ST	CTRCN FBG	DV	IO 167-209	8	3600	1 2	9850	11500
24 10	BRUTE CC	ST	CTRCN FBG	DV	SE 225	8	3600	1 2	12500	14200
24 10	BRUTE CC	ST	CTRCN FBG	DV	IO 229-275	8	3600	1 2	10200	12000
IO 330 VLVO 11800	13400, IO 180D-200D	14700	16700, IO	T120 VLVO					11200	12700
24 10	BRUTE CC	ST	CTRCN FBG	DV	IO T146-T225	8	3600	1 2	12500	14200
24 10	BRUTE TC	ST	OPFSH FBG	DV	OB	8	3600	1 2	11400	13300
24 10	BRUTE TC	ST	OPFSH FBG	DV	IO 167-209	8	3600	1 2	9700	11300
24 10	BRUTE TC	ST	OPFSH FBG	DV	SE 225	8	3600	1 2	12500	14200
24 10	BRUTE TC	ST	OPFSH FBG	DV	IO 229-275	8	3600	1 2	10100	12100
IO 330 VLVO 11600	13200, IO 180D-200D	14400	16400, IO	T120-T125					11100	12600
24 10	BRUTE TC	ST	OPFSH FBG	DV	SE T140	8	3600	1 2	12500	14200
24 10	BRUTE TC	ST	OPFSH FBG	DV	IO T146-T171	8	3600	1 2	12300	13000
---	--- 1989	BOATS								
23 4	CAPTAIN	HT	CUD	FBG	SV OB	8	4200	1 7	12300	14000
23 4	CAPTAIN	HT	CUD	FBG	SV IO 175-205	8	4200	1 7	8950	10500
23 4	CAPTAIN	HT	CUD	FBG	SV SE 225 OMC	8	4200	1 7	12300	14000
23 4	CAPTAIN	HT	CUD	FBG	SV IO 230-271	8	4200	1 7	9100	11000
23 4	CAPTAIN	HT	CUD	FBG	SV IO 200D VLVO	8	4200	1 7	11500	13000
23 4	CAPTAIN	HT	CUD	FBG	SV IO T130-T151	8	4200	1 7	9800	11800
23 4	COMMODORE	FB	SF	FBG	SV OB	8	4500	1 7	12100	14500
23 4	COMMODORE	FB	SF	FBG	SV IO 200-205	8	4500	1 7	11100	12600
23 4	COMMODORE	FB	SF	FBG	SV SE 225	8	4500	1 7	12700	14500
23 4	COMMODORE	FB	SF	FBG	SV IO 230-271	8	4500	1 7	10900	13200
23 4	COMMODORE	FB	SF	FBG	SV IO 200D VLVO	8	4500	1 7	14900	17000
23 4	COMMODORE	FB	SF	FBG	SV IO T130-T151	8	4500	1 7	11800	14100
23 4	CONQUEROR	ST	CUD	FBG	SV OB	8	3800	1 3	11700	13300
23 4	CONQUEROR	ST	CUD	FBG	SV IO 130-211	8	3800	1 3	8150	9850
23 4	CONQUEROR	ST	CUD	FBG	SV SE 225	8	3800	1 3	11700	13300
23 4	CONQUEROR	ST	CUD	FBG	SV IO 230-271	8	3800	1 3	8350	10300
23 4	CONQUEROR	ST	CUD	FBG	SV IO 200D VLVO	8	3800	1 3	10800	12300
23 4	CONQUEROR	ST	CUD	FBG	SV IO T131 VLVO	8	3800	1 3	9650	11000
23 4	CONQUEROR	ST	CUD	FBG	SV IO T140 OMC	8	3800	1 3	11700	13300
23 4	CONQUEROR	ST	CUD	FBG	SV IO T151 VLVO	8	3800	1 3	9700	11000
23 4	OLYMPIAN	ST	CUD	FBG	SV OB	8	3600	1 3	11300	12800
23 4	OLYMPIAN	ST	CUD	FBG	SV IO 130 OMC	8	3600	1 3	7850	9050
23 4	OLYMPIAN	ST	CUD	FBG	SV SE 225	8	3600	1 3	11300	12800
23 4	OLYMPIAN	ST	CUD	FBG	SV IO 151-211	8	3600	1 3	8100	9500
23 4	OLYMPIAN	ST	CUD	FBG	SV SE 225	8	3600	1 3	11300	12800
23 4	OLYMPIAN	ST	CUD	FBG	SV IO 230-271	8	3600	1 3	8050	9950
23 4	OLYMPIAN	ST	CUD	FBG	SV IO 200D VLVO	8	3600	1 3	10500	11900
23 4	OLYMPIAN	ST	CUD	FBG	SV IO T130-T151	8	3600	1 3	8900	10700
23 4	SUPER-SPORT V240	ST	CUD	FBG	DV OB	8	4100	1 3	12200	13800
23 4	SUPER-SPORT V240	ST	CUD	FBG	DV IO 175-211	8	4100	1 3	8700	10400

LOA FT	LOA IN	NAME AND/ OR MODEL	TOP/ RIG	BOAT TYPE	-HULL- MTL	-HULL- TP	ENGINE TP	ENGINE # HP	ENGINE MFG	BEAM FT	BEAM IN	WGT LBS	DRAFT FT	DRAFT IN	RETAIL LOW	RETAIL HIGH
		1989 BOATS														
23	4	SUPER-SPORT V240	ST	CUD	FBG	DV	SE	225		8		4100	1	3	12200	13800
23	4	SUPER-SPORT V240	ST	CUD	FBG	DV	IO	230-271		8		4100	1	3	8950	10800
23	4	SUPER-SPORT V240	ST	CUD	FBG	DV	IO	200D	VLVO	8		4100	1	3	11300	12800
23	4	SUPER-SPORT V240	ST	CUD	FBG	DV	IO	T130-T131		8		4100	1	3	9650	11500
23	4	SUPER-SPORT V240	ST	CUD	FBG	DV	SE	T140	OMC	8		4100	1	3	12200	13800
23	4	SUPER-SPORT V240	ST	CUD	FBG	DV	IO	T151-T175		8		4100	1	3	10200	11600
24	10	BRUTE CENTER CONSOLE	ST	CTRCN	FBG	DV	OB			8		3600	1	2	12100	13700
24	10	BRUTE CENTER CONSOLE	ST	CTRCN	FBG	DV	IO	175-211		8		3600	1	2	9150	10800
24	10	BRUTE CENTER CONSOLE	ST	CTRCN	FBG	DV	SE	225		8		3600	1	2	12100	13700
24	10	BRUTE CENTER CONSOLE	ST	CTRCN	FBG	DV	IO	230-271		8		3600	1	2	9400	11500
24	10	BRUTE CENTER CONSOLE	ST	CTRCN	FBG	DV	IO	200D	VLVO	8		3600	1	2	13700	15600
24	10	BRUTE CENTER CONSOLE	ST	CTRCN	FBG	DV	IO	T130-T175		8		3600	1	2	10200	12300
24	10	BRUTE TWIN CONSOLE	ST	OPFSH	FBG	DV	OB			8		3600	1	2	12100	13700
24	10	BRUTE TWIN CONSOLE	ST	OPFSH	FBG	DV	IO	175-211		8		3600	1	2	9050	10700
24	10	BRUTE TWIN CONSOLE	ST	OPFSH	FBG	DV	SE	225		8		3600	1	2	12100	13700
24	10	BRUTE TWIN CONSOLE	ST	OPFSH	FBG	DV	IO	230-271		8		3600	1	2	9400	11300
24	10	BRUTE TWIN CONSOLE	ST	OPFSH	FBG	DV	IO	200D	VLVO	8		3600	1	2	13500	15300
24	10	BRUTE TWIN CONSOLE	ST	OPFSH	FBG	DV	IO	T130-T131		8		3600	1	2	10100	12000
24	10	BRUTE TWIN CONSOLE	ST	OPFSH	FBG	DV	SE	T140	OMC	8		3600	1	2	12100	13700
24	10	BRUTE TWIN CONSOLE	ST	OPFSH	FBG	DV	IO	T151-T175		8		3600	1	2	10700	12100
		1988 BOATS														
23	4	CAPTAIN	HT	CUD	FBG	SV	OB			8		4300	1	7	12000	13600
23	4	CAPTAIN	HT	CUD	FBG	SV	IO	175-205		8		4200	1	7	8400	10000
23	4	CAPTAIN	HT	CUD	FBG	SV	SE	225		8		4200	1	7	12000	13600
23	4	CAPTAIN	HT	CUD	FBG	SV	IO	230-271		8		4200	1	7	8500	10500
23	4	CAPTAIN	HT	CUD	FBG	SV	IO	200D	VLVO	8		4200	1	7	10800	12300
23	4	CAPTAIN	HT	CUD	FBG	SV	IO	T130-T151		8		4200	1	7	9350	11100
23	4	COMMODORE	FB	SF	FBG	SV	OB			8		4500	1	7	12400	14000
23	4	COMMODORE	FB	SF	FBG	SV	IO	200-205		8		4500	1	7	10500	11900
23	4	COMMODORE	FB	SF	FBG	SV	SE	225		8		4500	1	7	12400	14000
23	4	COMMODORE	FB	SF	FBG	SV	IO	230-271		8		4500	1	7	10300	12500
23	4	COMMODORE	FB	SF	FBG	SV	IO	200D	VLVO	8		4500	1	7	14100	16100
23	4	COMMODORE	FB	SF	FBG	SV	IO	T130-T151		8		4500	1	7	11100	13300
23	4	CONQUEROR	ST	CUD	FBG	SV	OB			8		3800	1	3	11300	12900
23	4	CONQUEROR	ST	CUD	FBG	SV	IO	130-211		8		3800	1	3	7750	9300
23	4	CONQUEROR	ST	CUD	FBG	SV	SE	225		8		3800	1	3	11300	12900
23	4	CONQUEROR	ST	CUD	FBG	SV	IO	230-271		8		3800	1	3	7900	9750
23	4	CONQUEROR	ST	CUD	FBG	SV	IO	200D	VLVO	8		3800	1	3	10200	11600
23	4	CONQUEROR	ST	CUD	FBG	SV	IO	T131	VLVO	8		3800	1	3	9200	10500
23	4	CONQUEROR	ST	CUD	FBG	SV	SE	T140	OMC	8		3800	1	3	11300	12900
23	4	CONQUEROR	ST	CUD	FBG	SV	IO	T151	VLVO	8		3800	1	3	9250	10500
23	4	OLYMPIAN	ST	CUD	FBG	SV	OB			8		3600	1	3	11000	12500
23	4	OLYMPIAN	ST	CUD	FBG	SV	IO	130	OMC	8		3600	1	3	7450	8550
23	4	OLYMPIAN	ST	CUD	FBG	SV	SE	140	OMC	8		3600	1	3	11000	12500
23	4	OLYMPIAN	ST	CUD	FBG	SV	IO	151-211		8		3600	1	3	7700	9000
23	4	OLYMPIAN	ST	CUD	FBG	SV	SE	225		8		3600	1	3	11000	12500
23	4	OLYMPIAN	ST	CUD	FBG	SV	IO	230-271		8		3600	1	3	7600	9450
23	4	OLYMPIAN	ST	CUD	FBG	SV	IO	200D	VLVO	8		3600	1	3	9950	11300
23	4	OLYMPIAN	ST	CUD	FBG	SV	IO	T130-T151		8		3600	1	3	8350	10200
23	4	SUPER-SPORT V240	ST	CUD	FBG	DV	OB			8		4100	1	3	11800	13400
23	4	SUPER-SPORT V240	ST	CUD	FBG	DV	IO	175-211		8		4100	1	3	8250	9850
23	4	SUPER-SPORT V240	ST	CUD	FBG	DV	SE	225		8		4100	1	3	11800	13400
23	4	SUPER-SPORT V240	ST	CUD	FBG	DV	IO	230-271		8		4100	1	3	8350	10300
23	4	SUPER-SPORT V240	ST	CUD	FBG	DV	IO	200D	VLVO	8		4100	1	3	10700	12200
23	4	SUPER-SPORT V240	ST	CUD	FBG	DV	IO	T130-T131		8		4100	1	3	9200	10900
23	4	SUPER-SPORT V240	ST	CUD	FBG	DV	SE	T140	OMC	8		4100	1	3	11800	13400
23	4	SUPER-SPORT V240	ST	CUD	FBG	DV	IO	T151-T175		8		4100	1	3	9650	11000
24	10	BRUTE CENTER CONSOLE	ST	CTRCN	FBG	DV	OB			8		3600	1	2	11700	13300
24	10	BRUTE CENTER CONSOLE	ST	CTRCN	FBG	DV	IO	175-211		8		3600	1	2	8550	10300
24	10	BRUTE CENTER CONSOLE	ST	CTRCN	FBG	DV	SE	225		8		3600	1	2	11700	13300
24	10	BRUTE CENTER CONSOLE	ST	CTRCN	FBG	DV	IO	230-271		8		3600	1	2	8950	10900
24	10	BRUTE CENTER CONSOLE	ST	CTRCN	FBG	DV	IO	200D	VLVO	8		3600	1	2	13000	14800
24	10	BRUTE CENTER CONSOLE	ST	CTRCN	FBG	DV	IO	T130-T175		8		3600	1	2	9650	11600
24	10	BRUTE TWIN CONSOLE	ST	OPFSH	FBG	DV	OB			8		3600	1	2	11700	13300
24	10	BRUTE TWIN CONSOLE	ST	OPFSH	FBG	DV	IO	175-211		8		3600	1	2	8450	10200
24	10	BRUTE TWIN CONSOLE	ST	OPFSH	FBG	DV	SE	225		8		3600	1	2	11700	13300
24	10	BRUTE TWIN CONSOLE	ST	OPFSH	FBG	DV	IO	230-271		8		3600	1	2	8900	10700
24	10	BRUTE TWIN CONSOLE	ST	OPFSH	FBG	DV	IO	200D	VLVO	8		3600	1	2	12700	14500
24	10	BRUTE TWIN CONSOLE	ST	OPFSH	FBG	DV	IO	T130-T131		8		3600	1	2	9550	11300
24	10	BRUTE TWIN CONSOLE	ST	OPFSH	FBG	DV	SE	T140	OMC	8		3600	1	2	11700	13300
24	10	BRUTE TWIN CONSOLE	ST	OPFSH	FBG	DV	IO	T151-T175		8		3600	1	2	10100	11500
		1987 BOATS														
23	4	CAPTAIN	HT	CUD	FBG	SV	OB			8		4200	1	7	11600	13200
23	4	CAPTAIN	HT	CUD	FBG	SV	SE	120	OMC	8		4200	1	7	11600	13200
23	4	CAPTAIN	HT	CUD	FBG	SV	IO	175	OMC	8		4200	1	7	7950	9150
23	4	CAPTAIN	HT	CUD	FBG	SV	SE	190	OMC	8		4200	1	7	11600	13200
23	4	CAPTAIN	HT	CUD	FBG	SV	IO	200-205		8		4200	1	7	8250	9500
23	4	CAPTAIN	HT	CUD	FBG	SV	SE	225		8		4200	1	7	11600	13200
23	4	CAPTAIN	HT	CUD	FBG	SV	IO	225-275		8		4200	1	7	8350	10000
23	4	CAPTAIN	HT	CUD	FBG	SV	IO	200D	VLVO	8		4200	1	7	10300	11700
23	4	CAPTAIN	HT	CUD	FBG	SV	IO	T120-T151		8		4200	1	7	8900	10600
23	4	COMMODORE	FB	SF	FBG	SV	OB			8		4500	1	7	12000	13700
23	4	COMMODORE	FB	SF	FBG	SV	SE	190	OMC	8		4500			12000	13700
23	4	COMMODORE	FB	SF	FBG	SV	IO	200-205		8		4500	1	7	10000	11300
23	4	COMMODORE	FB	SF	FBG	SV	SE	225		8		4500	1	7	12000	13700
23	4	COMMODORE	FB	SF	FBG	SV	IO	225-275		8		4500	1	7	10100	11900
23	4	COMMODORE	FB	SF	FBG	SV	IO	200D	VLVO	8		4500	1	7	13400	15300
23	4	COMMODORE	FB	SF	FBG	SV	SE	T120	OMC	8		4500			12000	13700
23	4	COMMODORE	FB	SF	FBG	SV	IO	T130-T151		8		4500	1	7	10600	12700
23	4	CONQUEROR	ST	CUD	FBG	SV	OB			8		3800	1	3	11000	12500
23	4	CONQUEROR	ST	CUD	FBG	SV	IO	130-151		8		3800	1	3	7350	8700
23	4	CONQUEROR	ST	CUD	FBG	SV	SE	155		8		3800	1	3	11000	12500
23	4	CONQUEROR	ST	CUD	FBG	SV	IO	175	OMC	8		3800	1	3	7400	8500
23	4	CONQUEROR	ST	CUD	FBG	SV	SE	190	OMC	8		3800	1	3	11000	12500
23	4	CONQUEROR	ST	CUD	FBG	SV	IO	200-205		8		3800	1	3	7650	8800
23	4	CONQUEROR	ST	CUD	FBG	SV	SE	225		8		3800	1	3	11000	12500
23	4	CONQUEROR	ST	CUD	FBG	SV	IO	225-275		8		3800	1	3	7750	9350
23	4	CONQUEROR	ST	CUD	FBG	SV	IO	200D	VLVO	8		3800	1	3	9750	11100
23	4	CONQUEROR	ST	CUD	FBG	SV	SE	T120	OMC	8		3800	1	3	11000	12500
23	4	CONQUEROR	ST	CUD	FBG	SV	IO	T120-T151		8		3800	1	3	8200	10000
23	4	OLYMPIAN	ST	CUD	FBG	SV	OB			8		3600	1	3	10700	12100
23	4	OLYMPIAN	ST	CUD	FBG	SV	SE	120	OMC	8		3600	1	3	10700	12100
23	4	OLYMPIAN	ST	CUD	FBG	SV	IO	130-151		8		3600	1	3	7050	8400
23	4	OLYMPIAN	ST	CUD	FBG	SV	SE	155		8		3600	1	3	10700	12100
23	4	OLYMPIAN	ST	CUD	FBG	SV	IO	175	OMC	8		3600	1	3	7100	8150
23	4	OLYMPIAN	ST	CUD	FBG	SV	SE	190	OMC	8		3600	1	3	10700	12100
23	4	OLYMPIAN	ST	CUD	FBG	SV	IO	200-205		8		3600	1	3	7400	8500
23	4	OLYMPIAN	ST	CUD	FBG	SV	SE	225		8		3600	1	3	10700	12100
23	4	OLYMPIAN	ST	CUD	FBG	SV	IO	225-275		8		3600	1	3	7500	9000
23	4	OLYMPIAN	ST	CUD	FBG	SV	IO	200D	VLVO	8		3600	1	3	9450	10700
23	4	OLYMPIAN	ST	CUD	FBG	SV	IO	T120-T151		8		3600	1	3	7900	9650
23	4	SUPER-SPORT V240	ST	CUD	FBG	DV	OB			8		4100	1	3	11500	13100
23	4	SUPER-SPORT V240	ST	CUD	FBG	DV	IO	175	OMC	8		4100	1	3	7800	9000
23	4	SUPER-SPORT V240	ST	CUD	FBG	DV	SE	190	OMC	8		4100	1	3	11500	13100
23	4	SUPER-SPORT V240	ST	CUD	FBG	DV	IO	200-205		8		4100	1	3	8100	9300
23	4	SUPER-SPORT V240	ST	CUD	FBG	DV	SE	225		8		4100	1	3	11500	13100
23	4	SUPER-SPORT V240	ST	CUD	FBG	DV	IO	225-275		8		4100	1	3	8200	9850
23	4	SUPER-SPORT V240	ST	CUD	FBG	DV	IO	200D	VLVO	8		4100	1	3	10200	11600
23	4	SUPER-SPORT V240	ST	CUD	FBG	DV	SE	T120	OMC	8		4100	1	3	11500	13100
23	4	SUPER-SPORT V240	ST	CUD	FBG	DV	IO	T120-T175		8		4100	1	3	8650	10500
24	10	BRUTE CENTER CONSOLE	ST	CTRCN	FBG	DV	OB			8		3600	1	2	11400	12900
24	10	BRUTE CENTER CONSOLE	ST	CTRCN	FBG	DV	IO	175	OMC	8		3600	1	2	8150	9350
24	10	BRUTE CENTER CONSOLE	ST	CTRCN	FBG	DV	SE	190	OMC	8		3600	1	2	11400	12900
24	10	BRUTE CENTER CONSOLE	ST	CTRCN	FBG	DV	IO	200-205		8		3600	1	2	8450	9750
24	10	BRUTE CENTER CONSOLE	ST	CTRCN	FBG	DV	SE	225		8		3600	1	2	11400	12900
24	10	BRUTE CENTER CONSOLE	ST	CTRCN	FBG	DV	IO	225-275		8		3600	1	2	8600	10400
24	10	BRUTE CENTER CONSOLE	ST	CTRCN	FBG	DV	IO	200D	VLVO	8		3600	1	2	12400	14000
24	10	BRUTE CENTER CONSOLE	ST	CTRCN	FBG	DV	SE	T120	OMC	8		3600	1	2	11400	12900
24	10	BRUTE CENTER CONSOLE	ST	CTRCN	FBG	DV	IO	T120-T175		8		3600	1	2	9150	11000
24	10	BRUTE TWIN CONSOLE	ST	OPFSH	FBG	DV	OB			8		3600	1	2	11400	12900
24	10	BRUTE TWIN CONSOLE	ST	OPFSH	FBG	DV	IO	175	OMC	8		3600	1	2	8050	9250
24	10	BRUTE TWIN CONSOLE	ST	OPFSH	FBG	DV	SE	190	OMC	8		3600	1	2	11400	12900
24	10	BRUTE TWIN CONSOLE	ST	OPFSH	FBG	DV	IO	200-205		8		3600	1	2	8350	9600
24	10	BRUTE TWIN CONSOLE	ST	OPFSH	FBG	DV	SE	225		8		3600	1	2	11400	12900
24	10	BRUTE TWIN CONSOLE	ST	OPFSH	FBG	DV	IO	225-275		8		3600	1	2	8500	10300
24	10	BRUTE TWIN CONSOLE	ST	OPFSH	FBG	DV	IO	200D	VLVO	8		3600	1	2	12100	13800
24	10	BRUTE TWIN CONSOLE	ST	OPFSH	FBG	DV	SE	T120	OMC	8		3600	1	2	11400	12900
24	10	BRUTE TWIN CONSOLE	ST	OPFSH	FBG	DV	IO	T120-T175		8		3600	1	2	9050	10900
		1986 BOATS														
23	4	CAPTAIN	HT	CUD	FBG	SV	OB			8		3500	1	7	10200	11600
23	4	CAPTAIN	HT	CUD	FBG	SV	IO	175-200		8		4200	1	7	7600	9050
23	4	CAPTAIN	HT	CUD	FBG	SV	SE	205	OMC	8		4200	1	7	11300	12900
23	4	CAPTAIN	HT	CUD	FBG	SV	IO	205-260		8		4200	1	7	7650	9400
23	4	CAPTAIN	HT	CUD	FBG	SV	IO	165D	VLVO	8		4200	1	7	9550	10900
23	4	CAPTAIN	HT	CUD	FBG	SV	SE	T115	OMC	8		4200	1	7	11300	12900
23	4	CAPTAIN	HT	CUD	FBG	SV	IO	T120-T151		8		4200	1	7	8400	10200

LOA FT	IN	NAME AND/ OR MODEL	TOP/ RIG	BOAT TYPE	-HULL- MTL	TP	----ENGINE--- TP	# HP	MFG	BEAM FT	IN	WGT LBS	DRAFT FT	IN	RETAIL LOW	RETAIL HIGH
		1986 BOATS														
23	4	COMMODORE	FB	CUD	FBG	SV	OB			8		3800	1	7	10700	12200
23	4	COMMODORE	FB	CUD	FBG	SV	IO	200		8		4500	1	7	8100	9300
23	4	COMMODORE	FB	SF	FBG	SV	OB			8		4500	1	7	11700	13300
23	4	COMMODORE	FB	SF	FBG	SV	IO	200	VLVO	8		4500	1	7	9500	10800
23	4	COMMODORE	FB	SF	FBG	SV	SE	205	OMC	8		4500			11700	13300
23	4	COMMODORE	FB	SF	FBG	SV	IO	205-260		8		4500	1	7	9300	11200
23	4	COMMODORE	FB	SF	FBG	SV	IO	165D	VLVO	8		4500	1	7	12400	14100
23	4	COMMODORE	FB	SF	FBG	SV	SE	T115	OMC	8		4500			11700	13300
23	4	COMMODORE	FB	SF	FBG	SV	IO	T140-T151		8		4500	1	7	10100	12100
23	4	CONQUEROR		CUD	FBG	SV	OB			8		3100	1	3	9350	10600
23	4	CONQUEROR		CUD	FBG	SV	IO	200		8		3800	1	3	7150	8200
23	4	CONQUEROR	ST	CUD	FBG	SV	OB			8		3800	1	3	10700	12200
23	4	CONQUEROR	ST	CUD	FBG	SV	IO	140-200		8		3800	1	3	7050	8400
23	4	CONQUEROR	ST	CUD	FBG	SV	SE	205	OMC	8		3800	1	3	10700	12200
23	4	CONQUEROR	ST	CUD	FBG	SV	IO	205-260		8		3800	1	3	7100	8750
23	4	CONQUEROR	ST	CUD	FBG	SV	IO	165D	VLVO	8		3800	1	3	9050	10300
23	4	CONQUEROR	ST	CUD	FBG	SV	SE	T115	OMC	8		3800	1	3	10700	12200
23	4	CONQUEROR	ST	CUD	FBG	SV	IO	T120-T151		8		3800	1	3	7850	9550
23	4	OLYMPIAN		CUD	FBG	SV	OB			8		2900	1	3	8950	10200
23	4	OLYMPIAN		CUD	FBG	SV	IO	170		8		3600	1	3	6800	7850
23	4	OLYMPIAN	ST	CUD	FBG	SV	OB			8		3600	1	3	10400	11800
23	4	OLYMPIAN	ST	CUD	FBG	SV	IO	120-200		8		3600	1	3	6750	8100
23	4	OLYMPIAN	ST	CUD	FBG	SV	SE	205	OMC	8		3600	1	3	10400	11800
23	4	OLYMPIAN	ST	CUD	FBG	SV	IO	205-260		8		3600	1	3	6850	8450
23	4	OLYMPIAN	ST	CUD	FBG	SV	IO	165D	VLVO	8		3600	1	3	8650	9950
23	4	OLYMPIAN	ST	CUD	FBG	SV	SE	T115	OMC	8		3600	1	3	10400	11800
23	4	OLYMPIAN	ST	CUD	FBG	SV	IO	T125-T151		8		3600	1	3	8000	9200
23	4	SUPER-SPORT V240		CUD	FBG	DV	OB			8		3400	1	3	10000	11400
23	4	SUPER-SPORT V240		CUD	FBG	DV	IO	200		8		4100	1	3	7550	8650
23	4	SUPER-SPORT V240	ST	CUD	FBG	DV	OB			8		4100	1	3	11200	12700
23	4	SUPER-SPORT V240	ST	CUD	FBG	DV	IO	175-200		8		4100	1	3	7450	8900
23	4	SUPER-SPORT V240	ST	CUD	FBG	DV	SE	205	OMC	8		4100	1	3	11200	12700
23	4	SUPER-SPORT V240	ST	CUD	FBG	DV	IO	205-260		8		4100	1	3	7500	9250
23	4	SUPER-SPORT V240	ST	CUD	FBG	DV	IO	165D	VLVO	8		4100	1	3	9400	10700
23	4	SUPER-SPORT V240	ST	CUD	FBG	DV	SE	T115	OMC	8		4100	1	3	11200	12700
23	4	SUPER-SPORT V240	ST	CUD	FBG	DV	IO	T120-T175		8		4100	1	3	8250	10000
24	10	BRUTE CENTER CONSOLE	ST	CTRCN	FBG	DV	OB			8		3600	1	2	11100	12600
24	10	BRUTE CENTER CONSOLE	ST	CTRCN	FBG	DV	IO	175-200		8		3600	1	2	7750	9300
24	10	BRUTE CENTER CONSOLE	ST	CTRCN	FBG	DV	SE	205	OMC	8		3600	1	2	11100	12600
24	10	BRUTE CENTER CONSOLE	ST	CTRCN	FBG	DV	IO	205-260		8		3600	1	2	7900	9800
24	10	BRUTE CENTER CONSOLE	ST	CTRCN	FBG	DV	IO	165D	VLVO	8		3600	1	2	11200	12700
24	10	BRUTE CENTER CONSOLE	ST	CTRCN	FBG	DV	SE	T115	OMC	8		3600	1	2	11100	12600
24	10	BRUTE CENTER CONSOLE	ST	CTRCN	FBG	DV	IO	T120-T175		8		3600	1	2	8650	10600
24	10	BRUTE CENTER CONSOLE	TT	OPFSH	FBG	DV	OB			8		2900	1	2	9750	11100
24	10	BRUTE CENTER CONSOLE	TT	OPFSH	FBG	DV	IO	200		8		3600	1	2	7800	9000
24	10	BRUTE TWIN CONSOLE		OPFSH	FBG	DV	OB			8		2900	1	2	9750	11100
24	10	BRUTE TWIN CONSOLE		OPFSH	FBG	DV	IO	200		8		3600	1	2	7800	9000
24	10	BRUTE TWIN CONSOLE	ST	OPFSH	FBG	DV	OB			8		3600	1	2	11100	12600
24	10	BRUTE TWIN CONSOLE	ST	OPFSH	FBG	DV	IO	175-200		8		3600	1	2	7700	9200
24	10	BRUTE TWIN CONSOLE	ST	OPFSH	FBG	DV	SE	205	OMC	8		3600	1	2	11100	12600
24	10	BRUTE TWIN CONSOLE	ST	OPFSH	FBG	DV	IO	205-260		8		3600	1	2	7800	9650
24	10	BRUTE TWIN CONSOLE	ST	OPFSH	FBG	DV	IO	165D	VLVO	8		3600	1	2	11000	12500
24	10	BRUTE TWIN CONSOLE	ST	OPFSH	FBG	DV	SE	T115	OMC	8		3600	1	2	11100	12600
24	10	BRUTE TWIN CONSOLE	ST	OPFSH	FBG	DV	IO	T120-T175		8		3600	1	2	8550	10500
		1985 BOATS														
19		METEOR	ST	RNBT	FBG	SV	IO	120-170		7	6	2400	1	4	3400	4150
23	4	CAPTAIN	HT	CUD	FBG	SV	OB			8		4200	1	7	11100	12600
23	4	CAPTAIN	HT	CUD	FBG	SV	IO	165-200		8		4200	1	7	7500	8700
23	4	CAPTAIN	HT	CUD	FBG	SV	SE	205	OMC	8		4200	1	7	11100	12600
23	4	CAPTAIN	HT	CUD	FBG	SV	IO	225-260		8		4200	1	7	7650	9000
23	4	CAPTAIN	HT	CUD	FBG	SV	IO	165D	VLVO	8		4200	1	7	9200	10500
23	4	CAPTAIN	HT	CUD	FBG	SV	SE	T115	OMC	8		4200	1	7	11100	12600
23	4	CAPTAIN	HT	CUD	FBG	SV	IO	T120-T140		8		4200	1	7	8050	9750
23	4	COMMODORE	FB	SF	FBG	SV	OB			8		4500	1	7	11400	13000
23	4	COMMODORE	FB	SF	FBG	SV	IO	165-200		8		4500	1	7	9100	10400
23	4	COMMODORE	FB	SF	FBG	SV	SE	205	OMC	8		4500			11400	13000
23	4	COMMODORE	FB	SF	FBG	SV	IO	225-260		8		4500	1	7	9300	10800
23	4	COMMODORE	FB	SF	FBG	SV	IO	165D	VLVO	8		4500	1	7	11900	13600
23	4	COMMODORE	FB	SF	FBG	SV	SE	T115	OMC	8		4500			11400	13000
23	4	COMMODORE	FB	SF	FBG	SV	IO	T138-T140		8		4500	1	7	10200	11600
23	4	CONQUEROR	ST	CUD	FBG	SV	OB			8		3800	1	3	10500	11900
23	4	CONQUEROR	ST	CUD	FBG	SV	IO	138-200		8		3800	1	3	6950	8100
23	4	CONQUEROR	ST	CUD	FBG	SV	SE	205	OMC	8		3800	1	3	10500	11900
23	4	CONQUEROR	ST	CUD	FBG	SV	IO	225-260		8		3800	1	3	7100	8400
23	4	CONQUEROR	ST	CUD	FBG	SV	IO	165D	VLVO	8		3800	1	3	8600	9850
23	4	CONQUEROR	ST	CUD	FBG	SV	SE	T115	OMC	8		3800	1	3	10500	11900
23	4	CONQUEROR	ST	CUD	FBG	SV	IO	T120-T140		8		3800	1	3	7500	9150
23	4	OLYMPIAN	ST	CUD	FBG	SV	OB			8		3600	1	3	10100	11500
23	4	OLYMPIAN	ST	CUD	FBG	SV	IO	120-200		8		3600	1	3	6500	7800
23	4	OLYMPIAN	ST	CUD	FBG	SV	SE	205	OMC	8		3600	1	3	10100	11500
23	4	OLYMPIAN	ST	CUD	FBG	SV	IO	225-260		8		3600	1	3	6850	8100
23	4	OLYMPIAN	ST	CUD	FBG	SV	IO	165D	VLVO	8		3600	1	3	8300	9550
23	4	OLYMPIAN	ST	CUD	FBG	SV	SE	T115	OMC	8		3600	1	3	10100	11500
23	4	OLYMPIAN	ST	CUD	FBG	SV	IO	T120-T140		8		3600	1	3	7250	8850
23	4	SUPER-SPORT V240	ST	CUD	FBG	DV	OB			8		4100	1	3	10900	12400
23	4	SUPER-SPORT V240	ST	CUD	FBG	DV	IO	165-200		8		4100	1	3	7350	8550
23	4	SUPER-SPORT V240	ST	CUD	FBG	DV	SE	205	OMC	8		4100	1	3	10900	12400
23	4	SUPER-SPORT V240	ST	CUD	FBG	DV	IO	225-260		8		4100	1	3	7500	8850
23	4	SUPER-SPORT V240	ST	CUD	FBG	DV	IO	165D	VLVO	8		4100	1	3	9100	10300
23	4	SUPER-SPORT V240	ST	CUD	FBG	DV	SE	T115	OMC	8		4100	1	3	10900	12400
23	4	SUPER-SPORT V240	ST	CUD	FBG	DV	IO	T120-T170		8		4100	1	3	7900	9600
24	10	BRUTE CENTER CONSOLE	TT	OPFSH	FBG	DV	IO	T125	VLVO	8		3600	1	2	8600	9900
24	10	BRUTE TWIN CONSOLE	ST	OPFSH	FBG	DV	OB			8		3600	1	2	10800	12300
24	10	BRUTE TWIN CONSOLE	ST	OPFSH	FBG	DV	IO	165-200		8		3600	1	2	7500	8800
24	10	BRUTE TWIN CONSOLE	ST	OPFSH	FBG	DV	SE	205	OMC	8		3600	1	2	10800	12300
24	10	BRUTE TWIN CONSOLE	ST	OPFSH	FBG	DV	IO	225-260		8		3600	1	2	7800	9300
24	10	BRUTE TWIN CONSOLE	ST	OPFSH	FBG	DV	IO	165D	VLVO	8		3600	1	2	10600	12000
24	10	BRUTE TWIN CONSOLE	ST	OPFSH	FBG	DV	SE	T115	OMC	8		3600	1	2	10800	12300
24	10	BRUTE TWIN CONSOLE	ST	OPFSH	FBG	DV	IO	T120-T170		8		3600	1	2	8200	9950
		1984 BOATS														
19		METEOR	ST	RNBT	FBG	SV	IO	125	VLVO	7	6	2400	1	4	3450	4000
19		METEOR B/R	ST	RNBT	FBG	SV	IO	120	OMC	7	6	2400	1	4	3250	3800
23	4	CAPTAIN	HT	CUD	FBG	SV	OB			8					10400	11800
23	4	CAPTAIN	HT	CUD	FBG	SV	IO	200-225		8		4200	1	7	7300	8500
23	4	COMMODORE	FB	CUD	FBG	SV	IO	200-260		8		4500	1	7	7700	9150
23	4	CONQUEROR 24	ST	CUD	FBG	SV	OB			8					10000	11300
23	4	CONQUEROR 24	ST	CUD	FBG	SV	IO	145-230		8		3800	1	3	6700	7800
23	4	OLYMPIAN 24	ST	CUD	FBG	SV	IO	140-200		8		3600	1	3	6250	7500
23	4	SUPER-SPORT V240	ST	CUD	FBG	DV	OB			8					10900	12300
23	4	SUPER-SPORT V240	ST	CUD	FBG	DV	IO	200-260		8		4100	1	3	7150	8550
23	4	SUPER-SPORT V240	ST	CUD	FBG	DV	IO	165D	VLVO	8		4100	1	3	8650	9950
23	4	SUPER-SPORT V240	ST	CUD	FBG	DV	IO	T125	VLVO	8		4100	1	3	8050	9250
24	10	BRUTE V-25	OP	OPFSH	FBG	DV	OB			8					10600	12000
24	10	BRUTE V-25	OP	OPFSH	FBG	DV	IO	170-200		8		3600	1	2	7100	8500
24	10	BRUTE V-25	OP	OPFSH	FBG	DV	IO	260		8		3600	1	2	7550	8950

....For earlier years, see the BUC Used Boat Price Guide, Volume 3

SPECTRUM

DIV OF BRUNSWICK MARINE GROUP See inside cover to adjust price for area
TOPEKA IN 46571

FORMERLY SPECTRUM BY BLUE FIN

LOA FT	IN	NAME AND/ OR MODEL	TOP/ RIG	BOAT TYPE	-HULL- MTL	TP	----ENGINE--- TP	# HP	MFG	BEAM FT	IN	WGT LBS	DRAFT FT	IN	RETAIL LOW	RETAIL HIGH
		1996 BOATS														
16		1648	OP	JON	AL	FL	OB			5	7	264			790	950
16		1650MV	OP	JON	AL	FL	OB			6	3	327			960	1150
16	2	SF16 S&L	OP	UTL	AL	FL	OB			5	7	245			695	840
16	3	DOMINATOR 16DS	OP	BASS	AL	SV	OB			6		758			2350	2750
16	4	AVENGER 16SC	OP	FSH	AL	SV	OB			6	2	640			1950	2300
16	4	PRO AVENGER 16SC	OP	BASS	AL	SV	OB			6	5	640			2000	2350
16	4	PRO AVENGER 16T	OP	FSH	AL	SV	OB			6	2	565			1700	2050
16	4	SF CAMP 16	OP	FSH	AL	FL	OB			6	2	520			1550	1850
16	4	SF16 S&L WELD	OP	UTL	AL	FL	OB			6		410			1200	1450
16	4	SPORT 16	OP	FSH	AL	SV	OB			6	5	864			2600	3050
16	9	DOMINATOR 17	OP	BASS	AL	SV	OB			5	10	830			2600	3050
17	4	PRO AVENGER 17SC	OP	BASS	AL	SV	OB			7	3	840			2700	3150
18		1860MV	OP	JON	AL	FL	OB			6	8	417			985	1150
18	6	SPORT 18	OP	FSH	AL	SV	OB			7	2	1078			3400	3950
18	6	SPORT 18SD	OP	FSH	AL	SV	IO	135	MRCR	7	2	1150			5250	6050
19	4	PRO AVENGER 19	OP	BASS	AL	SV	OB			7	5	1300			4150	4800
19	4	PRO AVENGER 19SD	OP	BASS	AL	SV	IO	135-180		7	5	1325			5950	6900
20	1	SPECTRA 20	OP	RNBT	AL	SV	OB			8	4	1870			5850	6700

LOA FT IN	NAME AND/ OR MODEL	TOP/ RIG	BOAT TYPE	-HULL- MTL TP	----ENGINE--- TP # HP MFG	BEAM FT IN	WGT LBS	DRAFT FT IN	RETAIL LOW	RETAIL HIGH
	---------- 1995 BOATS ----------									
16	1648	OP	JON	AL FL	OB	5 7	264		750	905
16	1650MV	OP	JON	AL FL	OB	6 3	327		910	1100
16 2	SF16L	OP	UTL	AL FL	OB	5 7	245		660	795
16 2	SF16S	OP	UTL	AL FL	OB	5 7	245		660	795
16 4	AVENGER 16SC	OP	FSH	AL SV	OB	6 2	640		1800	2150
16 4	AVENGER 16T	OP	FSH	AL SV	OB	6 2	565		1600	1900
16 4	CAMP 16	OP	FSH	AL FL	OB	6 2	520		1500	1750
16 4	SPORT 16	OP	FSH	AL SV	OB	6 5	864		2500	2900
16 9	DOMINATOR 17	OP	BASS	AL SV	OB	5 10	830		2450	2900
17 4	PRO AVENGER 17SC	OP	BASS	AL SV	OB	7 3	840		2550	2950
18	1850MV	OP	JON	AL FL	OB	6 6	417		935	1100
18 6	SPORT 18	OP	FSH	AL SV	OB	7 2	1078		3200	3750
18 6	SPORT 18SD	OP	FSH	AL SV	IO	135 MRCR	7 2	1150		4900	5650
19 4	PRO AVENGER 19	OP	BASS	AL SV	IO	135 MRCR	7 5	1300		3900	4550
19 4	PRO AVENGER 19SD	OP	BASS	AL SV	IO	135 MRCR	7 5	1325		5550	6350
	---------- 1994 BOATS ----------									
16 2	SF16	OP	UTL	AL FL	OB		245		625	710
16 4	AVENGER 16SC	OP	FSH	AL SV	OB	6 2	610		1650	1950
16 4	AVENGER 16T	OP	FSH	AL SV	OB	6 2	550		1500	1750
16 4	PRO AVENGER 16	OP	FSH	AL SV	OB	6 5	717		1950	2300
16 4	SPORT 16	OP	FSH	AL SV	OB	6 5	864		2350	2750
17	DOMINATOR 17	OP	BASS	AL SV	OB	6 5	890		2500	2950
18 6	SPORT 18	OP	FSH	AL SV	OB	7 2	1078		3050	3550
18 6	SPORT 18 SD	OP	FSH	AL SV	IO	135 MRCR	7 2	1150		4600	5300
	---------- 1993 BOATS ----------									
16	1667	OP	JON	AL FL	OB	5 7	264		645	780
16	1667LW	OP	JON	AL FL	OB	5 7	264		705	845
16	1670MV	OP	JON	AL FL	OB	6 3	325		810	975
16 4	1603	OP	FSH	AL SV	OB	6 2	625		1600	1900
16 4	OPEN FISH 1606	OP	FSH	AL SV	OB	6 5	677		1750	2050
16 4	SPORTSTER 1600	OP	RNBT	AL SV	OB	6 5	845		2300	2650
16 6	HD1600	OP	UTL	AL SV	OB	5 7	245		595	715
16 6	HD1600 DXL C	OP	UTL	AL SV	OB	5 7	455		1400	1650
16 6	HD1600LW	OP	UTL	AL SV	OB	5 7	455		910	1100
16 7	1709	OP	BASS	AL SV	OB	5 6	843		2250	2600
17 4	1750	OP	B/R	AL SV	OB	115 MRCR	7 3	1206		3400	3950
17 4	CLOSED FISH 1706	OP	FSH	AL SV	OB	7 2	1045		2750	3200
17 4	FISH & SKI 1700	OP	RNBT	AL SV	OB	7 2	1045		2800	3250
19 4	CLOSED FISH 1906	OP	RNBT	AL SV	OB	7 5	1150		3150	3650
19 4	FISH & SKI 1900	OP	RNBT	AL SV	OB	7 5	1150		3200	3700
19 4	FISH & SKI 1950	OP	RNBT	AL SV	IO	115-155	7 5	1275		4200	4950
19 4	FISH & SKI 1956	OP	RNBT	AL SV	IO	115-155	7 5	1275		4400	5100
19 4	FISH & SKI 1957	OP	RNBT	AL SV	IO	115-155	7 5	1275		4750	5450
	---------- 1992 BOATS ----------									
16	1667	OP	JON	AL FL	OB	5 7	264		620	745
16	1667LW	OP	JON	AL FL	OB	5 7	264		670	810
16	1669MV	OP	JON	AL SV	OB	5 9	248		610	735
16 4	1603	OP	FSH	AL SV	OB	6 2	625		1550	1800
16 4	OPEN FISH 1606	OP	FSH	AL SV	OB	6 5	677		1650	1950
16 4	SPORTSTER 1600	OP	RNBT	AL SV	OB	6 5	770		1950	2300
16 6	HD1600	OP	UTL	AL SV	OB	5 7	455		570	685
16 6	HD1600 DXL C	OP	UTL	AL SV	OB	5 7	455		1300	1550
16 6	HD1600LW	OP	UTL	AL SV	OB	5 7	455		890	1050
16 7	1709	OP	BASS	AL SV	OB	5 6	550		1400	1650
17 4	1750	OP	B/R	AL SV	IO	115 MRCR	7 3	1175		3150	3650
17 4	CLOSED FISH 1706	OP	FSH	AL SV	OB	7 2	800		2000	2400
17 4	FISH & SKI 1700	OP	RNBT	AL SV	OB	7 2	930		2400	2800
19 4	1957	OP	RNBT	AL SV	IO	115-155	7 5	1275		4450	5100
19 4	CLOSED FISH 1906	OP	FSH	AL SV	OB	7 5	1050		2800	3250
19 4	FISH & SKI 1900	OP	RNBT	AL SV	OB	7 5	1100		2950	3400
19 4	FISH & SKI 1950	OP	RNBT	AL SV	IO	115-155	7 5	1275		3950	4650
19 4	FISH & SKI 1956	OP	RNBT	AL SV	IO	115-155	7 5	1275		4050	4750
	---------- 1991 BOATS ----------									
16	1667	OP	JON	AL FL	OB	5 7	264		595	715
16	1667LW	OP	JON	AL FL	OB	5 7	264		640	775
16	1669V	OP	JON	AL SV	OB	5 9	248		585	705
16 4	OPEN FISH 1606	OP	FSH	AL SV	OB	6 5	677		1600	1900
16 4	OPEN FISH 1608	OP	FSH	AL SV	OB	6 5	600		1400	1650
16 4	SPORTSTER 1600	OP	RNBT	AL SV	OB	6 5	770		1850	2200
16 6	HD1600	OP	UTL	AL SV	OB	5 7	245		545	655
16 6	HD1600 DXL C	OP	UTL	AL SV	OB	5 7	455		1150	1400
16 6	HD1600 LIVE WELL	OP	UTL	AL SV	OB	5 7	455		940	1100
16 7	1709	OP	BASS	AL SV	OB	5 6	550		1350	1600
17 4	1804	OP	BASS	AL SV	OB	5 6	1056		2550	2950
17 4	CLOSED FISH 1706	OP	FSH	AL SV	OB	7 2	800		1950	2300
17 4	FISH & SKI 1700	OP	RNBT	AL SV	OB	7 2	930		2300	2700
19 4	CLOSED FISH 1906	OP	FSH	AL SV	OB	7 5	1050		2650	3100
19 4	FISH & SKI 1900	OP	RNBT	AL SV	OB	7 5	1100		2800	3250
19 4	FISH & SKI 1950	OP	RNBT	AL SV	IO	115-155	7 5	1275		3850	4500
19 4	FISH & SKI 1956	OP	RNBT	AL SV	IO	115-155	7 5	1275		3900	4550
21 5	SPORT FISH 2152	OP	CUD	AL SV	IO	115-155	7 6	1400		5250	6050
	---------- 1990 BOATS ----------									
16 7	SPECTRUM 1704	OP	FSH	AL DV	OB	6 3	690		1550	1850
16 7	SPECTRUM 1709	OP	FSH	AL DV	OB	5 6	550		1250	1500
17 1	SPECTRUM 1700	OP	FSH	AL DV	OB	6 6	830		1900	2250
17 1	SPECTRUM 1706	OP	FSH	AL DV	OB	6 6	800		1850	2200
18 10	SPECTRUM 1900	OP	RNBT	AL DV	OB	7 1	1100		2650	3100
18 10	SPECTRUM 1906	OP	FSH	AL DV	OB	7 1	1050		2500	2900
18 10	SPECTRUM 1950	OP	RNBT	AL DV	IO	128 OMC	7 1	2150		3950	4550

SPECTRUM BOATS LTD

RICHMOND BC CANADA   COAST GUARD MFG ID- SBD See inside cover to adjust price for area

LOA FT IN	NAME AND/ OR MODEL	TOP/ RIG	BOAT TYPE	-HULL- MTL TP	----ENGINE--- TP # HP MFG	BEAM FT IN	WGT LBS	DRAFT FT IN	RETAIL LOW	RETAIL HIGH
	---------- 1986 BOATS ----------									
31	SPENCER 31	SLP	SA/CR	FBG KL	IB	D	9 2	9350	5	46200	50800
33 9	SPENCER 34	SLP	SA/RC	FBG KL	IB	D	11 2	10000	6	49500	54300
35	SPENCER 35 MARK II	SLP	SA/CR	FBG KL	IB	D	9 6	12000	5 3	59800	65700
35	SPENCER 35 MARK II	CUT	SA/CR	FBG KL	IB	D	9 6	12000	5 3	59800	65700
35	SPENCER 35 MARK II	KTH	SA/CR	FBG KL	IB	D	9 6	12000	5 3	59800	65700
42 3	SPENCER 42 MARK II	SLP	SA/CR	FBG KL	IB	D	11 4	19000	6	115000	126000
42 3	SPENCER 42 MARK II	CUT	SA/CR	FBG KL	IB	D	11 4	19000	6	113500	125000
42 3	SPENCER 42 MARK II	KTH	SA/CR	FBG KL	IB	D	11 4	19000	6	116000	127500
43 9	SPENCER 44	SLP	SA/CR	FBG KL	IB	D	11 6	24000	6 6	139500	153000
43 9	SPENCER 44	CUT	SA/CR	FBG KL	IB	D	11 6	24000	6 6	137500	151000
43 9	SPENCER 44	KTH	SA/CR	FBG KL	IB	D	11 6	24000	6 6	142500	156500
44	SPENCER 1330 CENTER	CUT	SA/RC	FBG KL	IB	D	13	24000	7	139000	152500
44	SPENCER 1330 PILTHSE	SLP	SA/CR	FBG KL	IB	D	13	24000	7	141000	155000
44	SPENCER 1330 PILTHSE	CUT	SA/CR	FBG KL	IB	D	13	24000	7	139000	152500
44	SPENCER 1331 AFT	SLP	SA/CR	FBG KL	IB	D	13	24000	7	141000	155000
45 7	SPENCER 46	SLP	SA/CR	FBG KL	IB	D	13	24000	7	150500	165000
45 7	SPENCER 46	CUT	SA/CR	FBG KL	IB	D	13	24000	7	147500	162000
45 7	SPENCER 46	KTH	SA/CR	FBG KL	IB	D	13	24000	7	155000	170500
53	SPENCER 53	SLP	SA/CR	FBG KL	IB	D	13 2	30000	7 6	229500	252000
53	SPENCER 53	CUT	SA/CR	FBG KL	IB	D	13 2	30000	7 6	224500	246500
53	SPENCER 53	KTH	SA/CR	FBG KL	IB	D	13 2	30000	7 6	234000	257000
	---------- 1985 BOATS ----------									
31	SPENCER 31	SLP	SA/CR	FBG KL	IB	D	9 2	9350		43300	48100
33 9	SPENCER 34	SLP	SA/RC	FBG KL	IB	D	11 2	10000		47100	51800
35	SPENCER 35 MARK II	SLP	SA/CR	FBG KL	IB	D	9 6	12000	5 3	56700	62300
42 3	SPENCER 42 MARK II	SLP	SA/CR	FBG KL	IB	D	11 4	19000	6	108500	119500
43 9	SPENCER 44	SLP	SA/CR	FBG KL	IB	D	11 6	24000	6	131500	144500
44 4	SPENCER 1330	SLP	SA/CR	FBG KL	IB	D	13	24000	7	135000	148000
45 6	SPENCER 46	SLP	SA/CR	FBG KL	IB	D	13	22000	7	136000	149500
52 7	SPENCER 53	SLP	SA/CR	FBG KL	IB	D	13 2	30000	7 6	211500	232000
	---------- 1984 BOATS ----------									
31	SPENCER 31	SLP	SA/CR	FBG KL	IB	D	9 2	9350		41100	45600
33 9	SPENCER 34	SLP	SA/RC	FBG KL	IB	D	11 2	10000		44800	49100
35	SPENCER MK II 35	SLP	SA/CR	FBG KL	IB	D	9 6	12000	5 3	53700	59000
42 3	SPENCER MK II 42	SLP	SA/CR	FBG KL	IB	D	11 4	19000	6	102500	113000
42 3	SPENCER MK II 42	KTH	SA/CR	FBG KL	IB	D	11 4	19000	6	104000	114500
43 9	SPENCER 44	SLP	SA/CR	FBG KL	IB	D	11 6	24000	6 6	123500	136500
43 9	SPENCER 44	KTH	SA/CR	FBG KL	IB	D	11 6	24000	6 6	127500	140000
44 4	SPENCER 1330	SLP	SA/CR	FBG KL	IB	D	13	24000	7	127500	140000
44 4	SPENCER 1330	KTH	SA/CR	FBG KL	IB	D	13	24000	7	131000	144000
45 6	SPENCER 46	SLP	SA/CR	FBG KL	IB	D	13	22000	7	128500	141000
45 6	SPENCER 46	KTH	SA/CR	FBG KL	IB	D	13	22000	7	132500	145500
52 7	SPENCER 53	SLP	SA/CR	FBG KL	IB	D	13 2	30000	7 6	199500	219500
52 7	SPENCER 53	KTH	SA/CR	FBG KL	IB	D	13 2	30000	7 6	204000	224500

....For earlier years, see the BUC Used Boat Price Guide, Volume 3

SPINDRIFT ONE DESIGNS

TALLEVAST FL 33588

See inside cover to adjust price for area

LOA FT IN	NAME AND/ OR MODEL	TOP/ RIG	BOAT TYPE	-HULL- MTL TP	TP	ENGINE # HP	MFG	BEAM FT IN	WGT LBS	DRAFT FT IN	RETAIL LOW	RETAIL HIGH
1985 BOATS												
16 1	REBEL	SLP	SA/OD	FBG CB				6 6	675	6	3000	3500
16 9	DAYSAILER I	SLP	SA/OD	FBG CB				6 3	575	7	2800	3250
21 6	SPINDRIFT 22	SLP	SA/OD	FBG KC	OB			8	1990	1 6	5850	6750
1984 BOATS												
16 1	REBEL	SLP	SA/OD	FBG CB				6 6	675	6	2800	3250
16 9	DAY SAILER ONE	SLP	SA/OD	FBG CB				6 3	575	7	2650	3100
21 6	SPINDRIFT 22	SLP	SA/OD	FBG				8	1990	1 6	5600	6400

....For earlier years, see the BUC Used Boat Price Guide, Volume 3

SPINDRIFT YACHTS

NEWPORT BEACH CA 92663   COAST GUARD MFG ID- SZG   See inside cover to adjust price for area

LOA FT IN	NAME AND/ OR MODEL	TOP/ RIG	BOAT TYPE	-HULL- MTL TP	TP	ENGINE # HP	MFG	BEAM FT IN	WGT LBS	DRAFT FT IN	RETAIL LOW	RETAIL HIGH
1987 BOATS												
34 10	RANGER CONVERTIBLE	FB	CNV	FBG DV	IB	T200D	VLVO	12 6	14900	2 4	75600	83100
34 10	RANGER SUNDECK	FB	MY	FBG DV	IB	T200D	VLVO	12 6	15400	2 4	84500	92900
40 4	CLASSIC	FB	MY	FBG SV	IB	T200D	VLVO	14 4	32300	4 1	130500	143500
42 10	RANGER CONVERTIBLE	FB	CNV	FBG DV	IB	T320D	CAT	15 4	31900	3 11	147500	162000
42 10	RANGER SUNDECK	FB	MY	FBG DV	IB	T320D	CAT	15 4	33200	3 11	162000	178000
46 6	CLASSIC	FB	MY	FBG SV	IB	T320D	CAT	15 4	42100	3 7	152000	167000
46 10	RANGER CONVERTIBLE	FB	CNV	FBG DV	IB	T375D	CAT	15 4	34900	3 11	166000	182500
46 10	RANGER SUNDECK	FB	MY	FBG DV	IB	T375D	CAT	15 4	36200	3 11	176000	193500
49	CLASSIC	FB	MY	FBG SV	IB	T320D	CAT	15 4	55100	3 8	188000	206500
52 2	CLASSIC	FB	MY	FBG SV	IB	T375D	CAT	15 4	60200	3 10	204000	224000
58	CLASSIC	FB	MY	FBG SV	IB	T375D	CAT	15 4	65300	3 10	234500	257500
1986 BOATS												
36	SPINDRIFT 36	FB	MY	FBG DS	IB	T270		14	19000		63200	69400
40	SPINDRIFT 40	FB	MY	FBG DS	IB	T165D		14	22800		95800	105500
42 6	SPINDRIFT PH	CUT	SA/CR	FBG KL	IB	D		13	34800	6 4	120500	132500
44	SPINDRIFT 44		SF	FBG SV	IB	T410D		14 9	39000		149500	164500
45 10	SPINDRIFT	CUT	SA/CR	FBG KL	IB	D		12 10	30700	6 4	123000	135000
46	SPINDRIFT 46	FB	MY	FBG DS	IB	T250D		15	41000		131500	144500
47	SPINDRIFT	CUT	SA/RC	FBG KL	IB	D		13 9	28990	7	124500	136500
49	SPINDRIFT 49	FB	MY	FBG DS	IB	T305D		15	46000		157000	172500
52	SPINDRIFT 52	FB	MY	FBG DS	IB	T305D		15	50000		157500	173000
58	SPINDRIFT 58	FB	SF	FBG DS	IB	T305D		15	65000		206500	227000
1985 BOATS												
40	SPINDRIFT 40	FB	MY	FBG DS	IB	T165D		14	22000		91800	101000
42 6	SPINDRIFT	CUT	SA/CR	FBG KL	IB	D		13	34000	6 4	112500	123500
44	SPINDRIFT 44		SF	FBG SV	IB	T410D		14 9	39000		117000	128500
45	SPINDRIFT 45		MY	FBG DS	IB	T250D		15	35200		121500	133500
45 10	SPINDRIFT	CUT	SA/CR	FBG KL	IB	D		12 10	30700	6 4	116000	127500
47	SPINDRIFT	CUT	SA/RC	FBG KL	IB	D		13 9	28990	7	117000	129000
49	SPINDRIFT 49	FB	MY	FBG DS	IB	T305D		15	40000		136500	150000
52	SPINDRIFT 52	FB	MY	FBG DS	IB	T305D		15	42000		133000	146500
58	SPINDRIFT 52+6	FB	SF	FBG DS	IB	T305D		15	48000		142000	156500
1984 BOATS												
42 6	SPINDRIFT 43 CTRCPT	SLP	SA/CR	FBG KL	IB	80D	FORD	13	34810	6 4	108500	119500
42 6	SPINDRIFT 43 PH	SLP	SA/CR	FBG KL	IB	80D	FORD	13	34810	6 4	108500	119500
45 10	SPINDRIFT 46	SLP	SA/CR	FBG KL	IB	90D	FORD	12 10	30700	6 4	112000	123000

SPOILER YACHTS INC

COSTA MESA CA 92626   COAST GUARD MFG ID- SPY   See inside cover to adjust price for area

LOA FT IN	NAME AND/ OR MODEL	TOP/ RIG	BOAT TYPE	-HULL- MTL TP	TP	ENGINE # HP	MFG	BEAM FT IN	WGT LBS	DRAFT FT IN	RETAIL LOW	RETAIL HIGH
1995 BOATS												
38 10	MOTOR YACHT	FB	TCMY	FBG SV	IB	T300D	CAT	14 8	23000	3 4	144500	158500

IB T350D CAT 150000 164500, IB T370D IVCO 147500 162500, IB T375D CAT 153000 168000
IB T425D CAT 159500 175500

| 38 10 | SPORTFISHER | FB | SF | FBG SV | IB | T300D | CAT | 14 8 | 23000 | 3 4 | 143500 | 157500 |

IB T350D CAT 149000 163500, IB T370D IVCO 147000 161500, IB T375D CAT 152000 167000
IB T425D CAT 158500 174500, IB T450D IVCO 156500 172000

| 39 | AFT CABIN SUN DECK | FB | SF | FBG DV | IB | T300D | CAT | 14 8 | 22000 | 3 2 | 140000 | 153500 |

IB T370D IVCO 143000 157500, IB T375D CAT 153000 168000, IB T425D CAT 155000 170500

| 39 | SPORTFISHER CNV | FB | SF | FBG DV | IB | T300D | CAT | 14 8 | 21000 | 3 2 | 135000 | 148500 |

IB T370D IVCO 138500 152000, IB T375D CAT 148500 163000, IB T425D CAT 150500 165500

| 45 | MOTOR YACHT | FB | MY | FBG SV | IB | T300D | CAT | 15 3 | 36000 | 3 8 | 187500 | 206500 |

IB T370D IVCO 201500 221500, IB T375D CAT 208000 228500, IB T425D CAT 215000 236500

| 45 | SPORTFISHER | FB | SF | FBG DV | IB | T300D | CAT | 15 3 | 35500 | 3 8 | 178000 | 196000 |

IB T370D IVCO 191500 210500, IB T375D CAT 197500 217000, IB T425D CAT 204500 225000

| 45 | YACHTFISHER | FB | YTFS | FBG DV | IB | T300D | CAT | 15 3 | 36000 | 3 8 | 178500 | 196000 |

IB T370D IVCO 192000 211000, IB T375D CAT 197500 217500, IB T425D CAT 204500 225000

| 48 | MOTOR YACHT | FB | MY | FBG SV | IB | T300D | CAT | 15 3 | 37000 | 3 8 | 185500 | 204000 |

IB T370D IVCO 199000 219000, IB T375D CAT 203500 224000, IB T425D CAT 210500 231000

| 48 | PILOT HOUSE | FB | PH | FBG SV | IB | T300D | CAT | 15 3 | 39000 | 3 8 | 189000 | 208000 |

IB T370D IVCO 199500 219500, IB T375D CAT 204500 224500, IB T425D CAT 210000 230500

| 48 | SPORTFISHER | FB | SF | FBG DV | IB | T300D | CAT | 15 3 | 38000 | 3 8 | 184000 | 202000 |

IB T370D IVCO 199000 219000, IB T375D CAT 203500 224000, IB T425D CAT 213000 234000

| 48 | YACHTFISHER | FB | YTFS | FBG DV | IB | T300D | CAT | 15 3 | 39000 | 3 8 | 180500 | 198500 |

IB T370D IVCO 199500 219000, IB T375D CAT 204000 224000, IB T425D CAT 213000 234000

| 51 | MOTOR YACHT | FB | MY | FBG SV | IB | T300D | CAT | 15 3 | 41000 | 3 8 | 196000 | 215500 |

IB T370D IVCO 214500 236000, IB T375D CAT 220000 241500, IB T425D CAT 229000 251500

| 51 | PILOT HOUSE | FB | PH | FBG SV | IB | T300D | CAT | 15 3 | 41000 | 3 8 | 197000 | 216500 |

IB T370D IVCO 215000 236000, IB T375D CAT 220000 242000, IB T425D CAT 229000 252000

| 51 | SPORTFISHER | FB | SF | FBG DV | IB | T300D | CAT | 15 3 | 39000 | 3 8 | 188000 | 206500 |

IB T370D IVCO 207000 227500, IB T375D CAT 212000 233000, IB T425D CAT 223500 246000

| 51 | YACHTFISHER | FB | YTFS | FBG DV | IB | T300D | CAT | 15 3 | 40000 | 3 8 | 186000 | 204500 |

IB T370D IVCO 208500 229000, IB T375D CAT 213500 234500, IB T425D CAT 224500 247000

| 52 | JSL SUPER SEDAN | FB | SDN | FBG SV | IB | T300D | GM | 16 4 | 42000 | 3 10 | 185000 | 203500 |

IB T370D IVCO 199000 218500, IB T375D CAT 200500 220500, IB T425D CAT 209500 230500

52	MOTOR YACHT	FB	MY	FBG SV	IB	T300D	GM	16 4	42000	3 10	184000	202000
52	MOTOR YACHT	FB	MY	FBG SV	IB	T375D	CAT	16 4	42000	3 10	201000	220500
52	MOTOR YACHT	FB	MY	FBG SV	IB	T425D	CAT	16 4	42000	3 10	212000	233000
55	MOTOR YACHT	FB	MY	FBG SV	IB	T300D	CAT	17	43000	3 10	183500	201500

IB T300D CAT 183500 201500, IB T370D IVCO 203000 223500, IB T375D CAT 208500 229000
IB T375D CAT 208500 229000, IB T425D CAT 242500 266500, IB T425D CAT 223500 245500
IB T700D MAN 309500 340000, IB T850D MAN 340500 374000

| 55 | SPORTFISHER | FB | SF | FBG DV | IB | T300D | CAT | 17 | 42000 | 3 10 | 187500 | 206000 |

IB T370D IVCO 210500 231000, IB T375D CAT 216000 237000, IB T425D CAT 247500 272000
IB T700D IVCO 323500 354500, IB T850D MAN 356000 391500

| 55 | SPORTFISHER | FB | SF | FBG SV | IB | T300D | CAT | 17 | 42000 | 3 10 | 185500 | 204000 |

IB T370D IVCO 207000 227500, IB T375D CAT 208500 229500, IB T425D CAT 224500 247000
IB T700D IVCO 311500 342500, IB T11CD MAN 400000 440000

| 55 | YACHTFISHER | FB | YTFS | FBG DV | IB | T300D | CAT | 17 | 43000 | 3 10 | 188500 | 207000 |

IB T370D IVCO 213000 234000, IB T375D CAT 218500 240000, IB T425D CAT 253500 278500
IB T700D IVCO 324500 356500, IB T850D MAN 360000 396000

| 55 | YACHTFISHER | FB | YTFS | FBG SV | IB | T300D | CAT | 17 | 43000 | 3 11 | 185500 | 203500 |

IB T370D IVCO 213000 234500, IB T375D CAT 215000 236000, IB T425D CAT 230500 253500
IB T700D IVCO 312500 343000, IB T11CD MAN 401000 440500

| 58 | JSL YACHTFISHER | FB | YTFS | FBG SV | IB | T300D | CAT | 16 | 4 53000 | 4 | 228500 | 251000 |

IB T370D IVCO 252000 277500, IB T375D CAT 254000 279500, IB T425D CAT 269500 296500
IB T700D IVCO 343500 377500, IB T850D IVCO 377500 415000

| 61 | MII MOTOR YACHT | FB | MY | FBG SV | IB | T300D | CAT | 17 | 54500 | 4 | 262000 | 288000 |

IB T370D IVCO 276500 304000, IB T375D CAT 278500 306000, IB T425D CAT 296500 326000
IB T700D IVCO 380000 417500, IB T850D MAN 415000 456000

| 61 | MOTOR YACHT | FB | MY | FBG DV | IB | T300D | CAT | 17 | 54000 | 4 | 259500 | 285000 |

IB T370D IVCO 266000 292500, IB T375D CAT 268500 295500, IB T425D CAT 277000 304000
IB T700D IVCO 359000 394500, IB T850D MAN 394000 433000

| 61 | YACHTFISHER | FB | YTFS | FBG DV | IB | T300D | CAT | 17 | 54000 | 4 | 255500 | 280500 |

IB T370D IVCO 263000 289000, IB T375D CAT 265500 291500, IB T425D CAT 275000 302500
IB T700D IVCO 363500 399500, IB T850D MAN 438000 480000

| 67 | MII MOTOR YACHT | FB | MY | FBG DV | IB | T300D | CAT | 17 | 59500 | 4 | 375000 | 412000 |

IB T370D IVCO 389000 427500, IB T375D CAT 391500 430000, IB T425D CAT 404000 444000
IB T700D IVCO 468500 515000, IB T850D IVCO 500000 549500

```
      LOA  NAME AND/          TOP/ BOAT  -HULL- ----ENGINE--- BEAM   WGT  DRAFT RETAIL RETAIL
      FT IN OR MODEL          RIG  TYPE  MTL TP TP # HP  MFG   FT IN  LBS  FT IN  LOW   HIGH
-------------------- 1995 BOATS ---------------------------------------------------------------
67    MII YACHTFISHER         FB  YTFS  FBG SV IB T300D CAT 17     59500 4  1 376500 414000
   IB T350D IVCO 391500 430500, IB T375D CAT 394000 433000, IB T425D CAT 407000 447500
   IB T700D IVCO 473000 519500, IB T850D MAN 497000 546000

-------------------- 1994 BOATS ---------------------------------------------------------------
38 10 MOTOR YACHT            FB  TCMY  FBG SV IB T300D CAT 14  8 23000 3  4 138500 152000
   IB T350D CAT 143500 158000, IB T370D IVCO 141500 155500, IB T375D CAT 146500 161000
   IB T425D CAT 153000 168500

38 10 SPORTFISHER            FB  SF    FBG SV IB T300D CAT 14  8 23000 3  4 137500 151000
   IB T350D CAT 142500 156500, IB T370D IVCO 140500 154500, IB T375D CAT 145500 160000
   IB T425D CAT 152000 167000, IB T450D IVCO 150000 164500

39    AFT CABIN SUN DECK     FB  SF    FBG DV IB T300D CAT 14  8 22000 3  2 134000 147000
   IB T370D IVCO 137000 150500, IB T375D CAT 146500 161000, IB T425D CAT 148500 163000

39    SPORTFISHER CNV        FB  SF    FBG DV IB T300D CAT 14  8 21000 3  2 129500 142000
   IB T370D IVCO 132500 145500, IB T375D CAT 142000 156000, IB T425D CAT 144000 158500

45    MOTOR YACHT            FB  YTFS  FBG SV IB T300D CAT 15  3 36000 3  8 179500 197000
   IB T370D IVCO 193000 212000, IB T375D CAT 199000 218500, IB T425D CAT 206000 226500

45    SPORTFISHER            FB  SF    FBG DV IB T300D CAT 15  3 35500 3  8 170500 197500
   IB T370D IVCO 183500 202000, IB T375D CAT 189500 208000, IB T425D CAT 196000 215500

45    YACHTFISHER            FB  YTFS  FBG DV IB T300D CAT 15  3 36000 3  8 171000 188000
   IB T370D IVCO 183500 202000, IB T375D CAT 189500 208000, IB T425D CAT 196000 215500

48    MOTOR YACHT            FB  MY    FBG SV IB T300D CAT 15  3 37000 3  8 178000 195500
   IB T370D IVCO 190500 209500, IB T375D CAT 195000 214500, IB T425D CAT 201500 221500

48    PILOT HOUSE            FB  PH    FBG SV IB T300D CAT 15  3 39000 3  8 181000 199000
   IB T370D IVCO 191000 210000, IB T375D CAT 195500 215000, IB T425D CAT 201000 221000

48    SPORTFISHER            FB  SF    FBG DV IB T300D CAT 15  3 38000 3  8 176000 193500
   IB T370D IVCO 191000 209500, IB T375D CAT 195000 214500, IB T425D CAT 204000 224500

48    YACHTFISHER            FB  YTFS  FBG DV IB T300D CAT 15  3 39000 3  8 173000 190000
   IB T370D IVCO 191000 210000, IB T375D CAT 195000 214500, IB T425D CAT 204000 224000

51    MOTOR YACHT            FB  MY    FBG SV IB T300D CAT 15  3 41000 3  8 187500 206500
   IB T370D IVCO 205500 226000, IB T375D CAT 210500 231500, IB T425D CAT 219000 241000

51    PILOT HOUSE            FB  PH    FBG SV IB T300D CAT 15  3 41000 3  8 188500 207500
   IB T370D IVCO 206000 226000, IB T375D CAT 211000 231500, IB T425D CAT 219500 241000

51    SPORTFISHER            FB  SF    FBG DV IB T300D CAT 15  3 39000 3  8 179500 197500
   IB T370D IVCO 198500 218000, IB T375D CAT 203000 223500, IB T425D CAT 214500 235500

51    YACHTFISHER            FB  YTFS  FBG DV IB T300D CAT 15  3 40000 3  8 178000 196000
   IB T370D IVCO 199500 219500, IB T375D CAT 204500 224500, IB T425D CAT 216000 236500

52    JSL SUPER SEDAN        FB  SDN   FBG SV IB T300D GM  16  4 42000 3 10 177500 195000
   IB T370D IVCO 190500 209500, IB T375D CAT 192000 211000, IB T425D CAT 201000 221000

52    MOTOR YACHT            FB  MY    FBG SV IB T300D GM  16  4 42000 3 10 176000 193500
52    MOTOR YACHT            FB  MY    FBG SV IB T375D CAT 16  4 42000 3 10 192500 211500
52    MOTOR YACHT            FB  MY    FBG SV IB T425D CAT 16  4 42000 3 10 203000 223000
55    MOTOR YACHT            FB  MY    FBG SV IB T300D CAT 17    43000 3 10 175500 193000
   IB T300D CAT 175500 193000, IB T375D CAT 195000 214000, IB T375D CAT 200000 219500
   IB T375D CAT 200000 219500, IB T425D CAT 232500 255500, IB T425D CAT 214000 235500
   IB T700D IVCO 296500 326000, IB T850D MAN 326500 358500

55    SPORTFISHER            FB  SF    FBG DV IB T300D CAT 17    42000 3 10 179500 197500
   IB T370D IVCO 201500 221500, IB T375D CAT 207000 227500, IB T425D CAT 237000 260500
   IB T700D IVCO 309000 340000, IB T850D MAN 341500 375000

55    SPORTFISHER            FB  SF    FBG DV IB T300D CAT 17    42000 3 10 177500 195500
   IB T370D IVCO 198500 218000, IB T375D CAT 200000 220000, IB T425D CAT 215500 236500
   IB T700D IVCO 298500 328000, IB T11CD MAN 383500 421500

55    YACHTFISHER            FB  YTFS  FBG SV IB T300D CAT 17    43000 3 10 180500 198500
   IB T370D IVCO 204000 224500, IB T375D CAT 209500 230000, IB T425D CAT 242500 266500
   IB T700D IVCO 310500 341500, IB T850D MAN 345000 379000

55    YACHTFISHER            FB  YTFS  FBG SV IB T300D CAT 17    43000 3 11 177500 195500
   IB T370D IVCO 204500 224500, IB T375D CAT 206000 226500, IB T425D CAT 221000 243000
   IB T700D IVCO 299000 328500, IB T11CD MAN 384500 422500

58    JSL YACHTFISHER        FB  YTFS  FBG SV IB T300D CAT 16  4 53000 4    219000 240500
   IB T370D IVCO 242000 266000, IB T375D CAT 243500 267500, IB T425D CAT 258500 284000
   IB T700D IVCO 329000 361500, IB T850D IVCO 361500 397500

61    MII MOTOR YACHT        FB  MY    FBG SV IB T300D CAT 17    54500 4    251500 276500
   IB T370D IVCO 265000 291500, IB T375D CAT 267000 293500, IB T425D CAT 284000 312500
   IB T700D IVCO 364000 400000, IB T850D MAN 397500 437000

61    MOTOR YACHT            FB  MY    FBG DV IB T300D CAT 17    54000 4    249000 273500
   IB T370D IVCO 255000 280500, IB T375D CAT 257500 283000, IB T425D CAT 265500 291500
   IB T700D IVCO 344000 378000, IB T850D MAN 377500 414500

61    YACHTFISHER            FB  YTFS  FBG DV IB T300D CAT 17    54000 4    245000 269000
   IB T370D IVCO 252000 277000, IB T375D CAT 254500 280000, IB T425D CAT 264000 290000
   IB T700D IVCO 348000 382500, IB T850D MAN 381500 419500

67    MII MOTOR YACHT        FB  MY    FBG DV IB T300D CAT 17    59500 4    359500 395500
   IB T370D IVCO 373000 409500, IB T375D CAT 375000 412500, IB T425D CAT 387000 425500
   IB T700D IVCO 449000 493500, IB T850D MAN 479000 526500

67    MII YACHTFISHER        FB  YTFS  FBG SV IB T300D CAT 17    59500 4  1 361000 397000
   IB T370D IVCO 375500 412500, IB T375D CAT 377500 415000, IB T425D CAT 390000 429000
   IB T700D IVCO 453000 498000, IB T850D MAN 476500 523000

-------------------- 1993 BOATS ---------------------------------------------------------------
38 10 MOTOR YACHT            FB  TCMY  FBG SV IB T300D CAT 14  8 23000 3  4 132000 145000
   IB T370D IVCO 135000 148500, IB T375D CAT 139500 153500, IB T425D CAT 146000 160500

38 10 SPORTFISHER            FB  SF    FBG SV IB T300D CAT 14  8 22000 3  4 126500 139000
   IB T370D IVCO 134000 147000, IB T375D CAT 138500 152500, IB T425D CAT 144500 159000
   IB T450D IVCO 142500 157000

39    AFT CABIN SUN DECK     FB  SF    FBG DV IB T300D CAT 14  8 22000 3  2 127500 140000
   IB T370D IVCO 130500 143500, IB T375D CAT 139500 153500, IB T425D CAT 141500 155500

39    SPORTFISHER CNV        FB  SF    FBG DV IB T300D CAT 14  8 21000 3  2 123000 135500
   IB T370D IVCO 126500 139000, IB T375D CAT 135500 148500, IB T425D CAT 137000 150500

45    MOTOR YACHT            FB  YTFS  FBG SV IB T300D CAT 15  3 36000 3  8 171000 188000
   IB T370D IVCO 184000 202000, IB T375D CAT 189500 208500, IB T425D CAT 196500 215500

45    SPORTFISHER            FB  SF    FBG DV IB T300D CAT 15  3 35500 3  8 162500 178500
   IB T370D IVCO 175000 192000, IB T375D CAT 180500 198000, IB T425D CAT 187000 205000

45    YACHTFISHER            FB  YTFS  FBG DV IB T300D CAT 15  3 36000 3  8 163000 179000
   IB T370D IVCO 175000 192500, IB T375D CAT 180500 198000, IB T425D CAT 186500 205000

48    MOTOR YACHT            FB  MY    FBG SV IB T300D CAT 15  3 37000 3  8 169500 186500
   IB T370D IVCO 181500 199500, IB T375D CAT 186000 204500, IB T425D CAT 192000 211000

48    PILOT HOUSE            FB  PH    FBG SV IB T300D CAT 15  3 39000 3  8 172500 190000
   IB T370D IVCO 182000 200000, IB T375D CAT 186500 205000, IB T425D CAT 191500 210500

48    SPORTFISHER            FB  SF    FBG DV IB T300D CAT 15  3 38000 3  8 167500 184500
   IB T370D IVCO 182000 199500, IB T375D CAT 186000 204000, IB T425D CAT 194500 213500

48    YACHTFISHER            FB  YTFS  FBG DV IB T300D CAT 15  3 39000 3  8 165000 181000
   IB T370D IVCO 182000 200000, IB T375D CAT 186000 204500, IB T425D CAT 194500 213500

51    MOTOR YACHT            FB  MY    FBG SV IB T300D CAT 15  3 41000 3  8 179000 196500
   IB T370D IVCO 196000 215500, IB T375D CAT 200500 220500, IB T425D CAT 208500 229500

51    PILOT HOUSE            FB  PH    FBG SV IB T300D CAT 15  3 41000 3  8 180000 197500
   IB T370D IVCO 196000 215500, IB T375D CAT 201000 220500, IB T425D CAT 209000 230000

51    SPORTFISHER            FB  SF    FBG DV IB T300D CAT 15  3 39000 3  8 171500 188500
   IB T370D IVCO 189000 208000, IB T375D CAT 193500 213000, IB T425D CAT 204000 224500

51    YACHTFISHER            FB  YTFS  FBG DV IB T300D CAT 15  3 40000 3  8 170000 186500
   IB T370D IVCO 190500 209000, IB T375D CAT 195000 214000, IB T425D CAT 205000 225500

52    JSL SUPER SEDAN        FB  SDN   FBG SV IB T300D GM  16  4 42000 3 10 169500 186000
   IB T370D IVCO 182000 199500, IB T375D CAT 183500 201500, IB T425D CAT 191500 210500

52    MOTOR YACHT            FB  MY    FBG SV IB T300D GM  16  4 42000 3 10 168500 185000
52    MOTOR YACHT            FB  MY    FBG SV IB T375D CAT 16  4 42000 3 10 183500 202000
52    MOTOR YACHT            FB  MY    FBG SV IB T425D CAT 16  4 42000 3 10 193500 213000
```

```
      LOA  NAME AND/           TOP/ BOAT  -HULL-  ----ENGINE---      BEAM   WGT   DRAFT  RETAIL RETAIL
      FT IN OR MODEL           RIG  TYPE  MTL TP TP # HP  MFG        FT IN  LBS   FT IN  LOW    HIGH
------------------ 1993 BOATS ------------------
55    MOTOR YACHT            FB  MY   FBG SV IB T300D CAT 17    43000 3 10 167500 184000
      IB T300D CAT 167500 184000, IB T370D IVCO 185500 204000, IB T375D CAT 190500 209500
      IB T375D CAT 190500 209500, IB T425D CAT 221500 243500, IB T425D CAT 204000 224000
      IB T700D IVCO 282500 310500, IB T850D MAN 311000 341500

55    SPORTFISHER           FB  SF   FBG DV IB T300D CAT 17    42000 3 10 171000 188000
      IB T370D IVCO 192000 211000, IB T375D CAT 197000 216500, IB T425D CAT 226000 248500
      IB T700D IVCO 294500 324000, IB T850D MAN 325500 357500

55    SPORTFISHER           FB  SF   FBG SV IB T300D CAT 17    42000 3 10 169500 186500
      IB T370D IVCO 189000 207500, IB T375D CAT 190500 209500, IB T425D CAT 205000 225500
      IB T700D IVCO 284500 312500, IB T11CD MAN 365500 401500

55    YACHTFISHER           FB  YTFS FBG DV IB T300D CAT 17    43000 3 10 172000 189000
      IB T370D IVCO 194500 214000, IB T375D CAT 199500 219500, IB T425D CAT 231000 254000
      IB T700D IVCO 296000 325000, IB T850D MAN 328500 361000

55    YACHTFISHER           FB  YTFS FBG SV IB T300D CAT 17    43000 3 11 169000 186000
      IB T370D IVCO 194500 214000, IB T375D CAT 196500 215500, IB T425D CAT 210500 231500
      IB T700D IVCO 285000 313000, IB T11CD MAN 366500 402500

58    JSL YACHTFISHER       FB  YTFS FBG SV IB T300D CAT 16  4 53000 4    208500 229000
      IB T370D IVCO 230500 253500, IB T375D CAT 232000 255000, IB T425D CAT 246000 270500
      IB T700D IVCO 313500 344500, IB T850D IVCO 344500 378500

61    MII MOTOR YACHT       FB  MY   FBG SV IB T300D CAT 17    54500 4    240000 264000
      IB T370D IVCO 253000 278000, IB T375D CAT 255000 280000, IB T425D CAT 271000 297500
      IB T700D IVCO 347000 381000, IB T850D MAN 378500 416000

61    MOTOR YACHT           FB  MY   FBG DV IB T300D CAT 17    54000 4    238000 261500
      IB T370D IVCO 244000 268000, IB T375D CAT 246500 270500, IB T425D CAT 253500 278500
      IB T700D IVCO 328000 360000, IB T850D MAN 359500 395000

61    YACHTFISHER           FB  YTFS FBG DV IB T300D CAT 17    54000 4    234000 257500
      IB T370D IVCO 241000 264500, IB T375D CAT 243000 267500, IB T425D CAT 252000 276500
      IB T700D IVCO 332000 364500, IB T850D MAN 363500 399500

67    MII MOTOR YACHT       FB  MY   FBG DV IB T300D CAT 17    59500 4    343500 377500
      IB T370D IVCO 355500 390500, IB T375D CAT 357500 393000, IB T425D CAT 369000 405500
      IB T700D IVCO 427500 470000, IB T850D IVCO 456500 501500

67    MII YACHTFISHER       FB  YTFS FBG SV IB T300D CAT 17    59500 4 1  344500 378500
      IB T370D IVCO 358000 393000, IB T375D CAT 360000 395500, IB T425D CAT 372000 408500
      IB T700D IVCO 431500 474500, IB T850D MAN 453500 498000

------------------ 1992 BOATS ------------------
38 10 MOTOR YACHT           FB  TCMY FBG SV IB T300D CAT 14  8 23000 3  4 125500 138000
      IB T370D IVCO 128500 141500, IB T375D CAT 133000 146500, IB T425D CAT 139000 153000

38 10 SPORTFISHER           FB  SF   FBG SV IB T300D CAT 14  8 22000 3  4 120500 132500
      IB T370D IVCO 127500 140000, IB T375D CAT 132000 145000, IB T425D CAT 138000 151500
      IB T450D IVCO 136000 149500

39    AFT CABIN SUN DECK    FB  SF   FBG SV IB T300D CAT 14  8 22000 3  2 121500 133500
      IB T370D IVCO 124500 136500, IB T375D CAT 133000 146000, IB T425D CAT 135000 148000

39    SPORTFISHER CNV       FB  SF   FBG DV IB T300D CAT 14  8 21000 3  2 117500 129000
      IB T370D IVCO 120500 132000, IB T375D CAT 129000 141500, IB T425D CAT 130500 143500

45    MOTOR YACHT           FB  YTFS FBG SV IB T300D CAT 15  3 36000 3  8 163000 179000
      IB T370D IVCO 175500 193000, IB T375D CAT 181000 198500, IB T425D CAT 187000 205500

45    SPORTFISHER           FB  SF   FBG DV IB T300D CAT 15  3 35500 3  8 155000 170500
      IB T370D IVCO 167000 183000, IB T375D CAT 172000 189000, IB T425D CAT 178000 195500

45    YACHTFISHER           FB  YTFS FBG DV IB T300D CAT 15  3 36000 3  8 155500 170500
      IB T370D IVCO 167000 183500, IB T375D CAT 172000 189000, IB T425D CAT 178000 195500

48    MOTOR YACHT           FB  MY   FBG SV IB T300D CAT 15  3 37000 3  8 161500 177500
      IB T370D IVCO 173000 190500, IB T375D CAT 177000 194500, IB T425D CAT 183000 201000

48    PILOT HOUSE           FB  PH   FBG SV IB T300D CAT 15  3 39000 3  8 164500 181000
      IB T370D IVCO 173500 191000, IB T375D CAT 177500 195500, IB T425D CAT 182500 200500

48    SPORTFISHER           FB  SF   FBG DV IB T300D CAT 15  3 38000 3  8 160000 175500
      IB T370D IVCO 173500 190500, IB T375D CAT 177000 194500, IB T425D CAT 185500 203500

48    YACHTFISHER           FB  YTFS FBG DV IB T300D CAT 15  3 39000 3  8 157000 172500
      IB T370D IVCO 173500 190500, IB T375D CAT 177500 195000, IB T425D CAT 185500 203500

51    MOTOR YACHT           FB  MY   FBG SV IB T300D CAT 15  3 41000 3  8 170500 187500
      IB T370D IVCO 187000 205000, IB T375D CAT 191000 210000, IB T425D CAT 199000 218500

51    PILOT HOUSE           FB  PH   FBG SV IB T300D CAT 15  3 41000 3  8 171500 188500
      IB T370D IVCO 187000 205500, IB T375D CAT 191500 210500, IB T425D CAT 199500 219000

51    SPORTFISHER           FB  SF   FBG DV IB T300D CAT 15  3 39000 3  8 163500 179500
      IB T370D IVCO 180500 198000, IB T375D CAT 184500 203000, IB T425D CAT 194500 214000

51    YACHTFISHER           FB  YTFS FBG DV IB T300D CAT 15  3 40000 3  8 162000 178000
      IB T370D IVCO 181500 199500, IB T375D CAT 185500 204000, IB T425D CAT 195500 215000

52    JSL SUPER SEDAN       FB  SDN  FBG SV IB T300D GM  16  4 42000 3 10 165500 177500
      IB T370D IVCO 173500 190500, IB T375D CAT 175000 192000, IB T425D CAT 182500 201000

52    MOTOR YACHT           FB  MY   FBG SV IB T300D GM  16  4 42000 3 10 160500 176500
52    MOTOR YACHT           FB  MY   FBG SV IB T375D GM  16  4 42000 3 10 175000 192500
52    MOTOR YACHT           FB  MY   FBG SV IB T425D GM  16  4 42000 3 10 184500 203000
55    MOTOR YACHT           FB  MY   FBG SV IB T300D CAT 17    43000 3 10 160000 175500
      IB T300D CAT 160000 175500, IB T370D IVCO 177000 194500, IB T375D CAT 181500 199500
      IB T375D CAT 181500 199500, IB T425D CAT 211000 232000, IB T425D CAT 194500 213500
      IB T700D IVCO 269500 296000, IB T850D MAN 296500 326000

55    SPORTFISHER           FB  SF   FBG DV IB T300D CAT 17    42000 3 10 163500 179500
      IB T370D IVCO 183000 201000, IB T375D CAT 188000 206500, IB T425D CAT 215500 236500
      IB T700D IVCO 281000 308500, IB T850D MAN 310000 340500

55    SPORTFISHER           FB  SF   FBG SV IB T300D CAT 17    42000 3 10 161500 177500
      IB T370D IVCO 180000 198000, IB T375D CAT 181500 199500, IB T425D CAT 195500 215000
      IB T700D IVCO 271000 298000, IB T11CD MAN 348500 383500

55    YACHTFISHER           FB  YTFS FBG DV IB T300D CAT 17    43000 3 10 164000 180000
      IB T370D IVCO 185500 204000, IB T375D CAT 190500 209000, IB T425D CAT 220500 242000
      IB T700D IVCO 282000 310000, IB T850D MAN 313500 344500

55    YACHTFISHER           FB  YTFS FBG SV IB T300D CAT 17    43000 3 11 161500 177500
      IB T370D IVCO 185500 204000, IB T375D CAT 187000 205500, IB T425D CAT 200500 220500
      IB T700D IVCO 271500 298500, IB T11CD MAN 349000 383500

58    JSL YACHTFISHER       FB  YTFS FBG SV IB T300D CAT 16  4 53000 4    198500 218500
      IB T370D IVCO 220000 241500, IB T375D CAT 221000 243000, IB T425D CAT 234500 258000
      IB T700D IVCO 298500 328000, IB T850D IVCO 328500 361000

61    MII MOTOR YACHT       FB  MY   FBG SV IB T300D CAT 17    54500 4    229000 251500
      IB T370D IVCO 241000 265000, IB T375D CAT 243000 267000, IB T425D CAT 258000 284000
      IB T700D IVCO 330500 363500, IB T850D MAN 361000 397000

61    MOTOR YACHT           FB  MY   FBG DV IB T300D CAT 17    54000 4    227000 249500
      IB T370D IVCO 232500 255500, IB T375D CAT 235000 258000, IB T425D CAT 241500 265500
      IB T700D IVCO 312500 343500, IB T850D MAN 342500 376500

61    YACHTFISHER           FB  YTFS FBG DV IB T300D CAT 17    54000 4    223000 245500
      IB T370D IVCO 229500 252500, IB T375D CAT 232000 255000, IB T425D CAT 240000 264000
      IB T700D IVCO 316500 347500, IB T850D MAN 346500 381000

67    MII MOTOR YACHT       FB  MY   FBG DV IB T300D CAT 17    59500 4    327500 359500
      IB T370D IVCO 339000 372500, IB T375D CAT 341000 374500, IB T425D CAT 351500 386500
      IB T700D IVCO 407500 448000, IB T850D IVCO 435000 478000

67    MII YACHTFISHER       FB  YTFS FBG SV IB T300D CAT 17    59500 4 1  328500 361000
      IB T370D IVCO 341000 375500, IB T375D CAT 343500 377500, IB T425D CAT 354500 389500
      IB T700D IVCO 411500 452000, IB T850D MAN 432500 475000

------------------ 1991 BOATS ------------------
39    AFT CABIN SUN DECK    FB  SF   FBG DV IB T300D GM  14  8 22000 3  2 113000 124000
      IB T370D IVCO 118500 130500, IB T375D CAT 127000 139500, IB T425D CAT 128500 141000

39    SPORTFISHER CNV       FB  SF   FBG DV IB T300D GM  14  8 21000 3  2 109000 119500
      IB T370D IVCO 114500 126000, IB T375D CAT 123000 135000, IB T425D CAT 124500 137000

45    MOTOR YACHT           FB  YTFS FBG SV IB T300D GM  15  3 36000 3  8 154500 169500
      IB T370D IVCO 167500 184000, TYB T375D CAT 172500 189500, IB T425D CAT 178500 196000

45    SPORTFISHER           FB  SF   FBG DV IB T300D GM  15  3 35500 3  8 147000 161500
      IB T370D IVCO 159000 175000, IB T375D CAT 164000 180000, IB T425D CAT 170000 186500
```

LOA FT IN	NAME AND/ OR MODEL	TOP/ RIG	BOAT TYPE	-HULL- MTL	TP	TP	----ENGINE--- # HP	MFG	BEAM FT IN	WGT LBS	DRAFT FT IN	RETAIL LOW	RETAIL HIGH
	1991 BOATS												
45	YACHTFISHER	FB	YTFS	FBG	DV	IB	T300D	GM	15 3	36000	3 8	147000	161500
	IB T370D IVCO 159000 175000, IB T375D CAT 164000 180500, IB T425D CAT 170000 186500												
48	MOTOR YACHT	FB	MY	FBG	SV	IB	T300D	GM	15 3	37000	3 8	153500	168500
	IB T370D IVCO 165000 181500, IB T375D CAT 169000 185500, IB T425D CAT 174500 191500												
48	PILOT HOUSE	FB	PH	FBG	SV	IB	T300D	GM	15 3	39000	3 8	156000	171000
	IB T370D IVCO 165500 182000, IB T375D CAT 169500 186000, IB T425D CAT 174000 191500												
48	SPORTFISHER	FB	SF	FBG	DV	IB	T300D	GM	15 3	38000	3 8	151500	166500
	IB T370D IVCO 165500 181500, IB T375D CAT 169000 185500, IB T425D CAT 177000 194500												
48	YACHTFISHER	FB	YTFS	FBG	DV	IB	T300D	GM	15 3	39000	3 8	150000	164500
	IB T370D IVCO 165500 182000, IB T375D CAT 169000 186000, IB T425D CAT 176500 194000												
51	MOTOR YACHT	FB	MY	FBG	SV	IB	T300D	GM	15 3	41000	3 8	162000	178500
	IB T370D IVCO 178000 196000, IB T375D CAT 182500 200500, IB T425D CAT 190000 208500												
51	PILOT HOUSE	FB	PH	FBG	SV	IB	T300D	GM	15 3	41000	3 8	162500	178500
	IB T370D IVCO 178500 196000, IB T375D CAT 182500 200500, IB T425D CAT 190000 209000												
51	SPORTFISHER	FB	SF	FBG	DV	IB	T300D	GM	15 3	39000	3 8	154500	170000
	IB T370D IVCO 172000 189000, IB T375D CAT 176000 193500, IB T425D CAT 185500 204000												
51	YACHTFISHER	FB	YTFS	FBG	DV	IB	T300D	GM	15 3	40000	3 8	154500	169500
	IB T370D IVCO 173000 190000, IB T375D CAT 177000 194500, IB T425D CAT 186500 205000												
52	JSL SUPER SEDAN	FB	SDN	FBG	SV	IB	T300D	GM	16 4	42000	3 10	154000	169500
	IB T370D IVCO 165500 181500, IB T375D CAT 167000 183500, IB T425D CAT 174500 191500												
52	MOTOR YACHT	FB	MY	FBG	SV	IB	T300D	GM	16 4	42000	3 10	153500	168500
52	MOTOR YACHT	FB	MY	FBG	SV	IB	T375D	CAT	16 4	42000	3 10	167000	183500
52	MOTOR YACHT	FB	MY	FBG	SV	IB	T425D	CAT	16 4	42000	3 10	176000	193500
55	MOTOR YACHT	FB	MY	FBG	SV	IB	T300D	GM	17	43000	3 10	151000	165500
	IB T370D IVCO 169000 185500, IB T375D CAT 173000 190500, IB T425D CAT 201500 221500												
	IB T700D IVCO 257000 282500, IB T850D MAN 283000 311000												
55	SPORTFISHER	FB	SF	FBG	DV	IB	T300D	GM	17	42000	3 10	154500	170000
	IB T370D IVCO 174500 192000, IB T375D CAT 179000 197000, IB T425D CAT 205500 226000												
	IB T700D IVCO 268000 294500, IB T850D MAN 296000 325000												
55	YACHTFISHER	FB	YTFS	FBG	DV	IB	T300D	GM	17	43000	3 10	156000	171500
	IB T370D IVCO 177000 194500, IB T375D CAT 181500 199500, IB T425D CAT 210500 231000												
	IB T700D MAN 269000 295500, IB T850D MAN 299000 328500												
58	JSL YACHTFISHER	FB	YTFS	FBG	SV	IB	T300D	GM	16 4	53000	4	190500	209000
	IB T370D IVCO 209500 230500, IB T375D CAT 211000 232000, IB T425D CAT 224000 246000												
	IB T700D IVCO 285000 313000, IB T850D IVCO 313500 344500												
61	MII MOTOR YACHT	FB	MY	FBG	SV	IB	T300D	GM	17	54500	4	216500	238000
	IB T370D IVCO 230000 252500, IB T375D CAT 232000 254500, IB T425D CAT 246500 270500												
	IB T700D IVCO 315500 346500, IB T850D IVCO 347500 382000												
61	MOTOR YACHT	FB	MY	FBG	DV	IB	T300D	GM	19 5	54000	4	233500	256500
	IB T370D IVCO 241000 264500, IB T375D CAT 243000 267000, IB T425D CAT 248500 273000												
	IB T700D IVCO 299000 328500, IB T850D MAN 327000 359500												
61	YACHTFISHER	FB	YTFS	FBG	DV	IB	T300D	GM	19 5	54000	4	229500	252500
	IB T370D IVCO 237000 260500, IB T375D CAT 239500 263000, IB T425D CAT 244500 269000												
	IB T700D IVCO 302000 332000, IB T850D MAN 331000 364000												
66	MOTOR YACHT	FB	MY	FBG		IB	T300D	GM	17	59500	4	292500	321000
	IB T370D IVCO 296500 325500, IB T375D CAT 299000 328500, IB T425D CAT 303000 333000												
	IB T700D IVCO 338000 371500, IB T850D IVCO 362500 398500												
66	YACHTFISHER	FB	YTFS	FBG	SV	IB	T300D	GM	17	59500	4 1	291000	320000
	IB T370D IVCO 295500 324500, IB T375D CAT 297500 327000, IB T425D CAT 302000 332000												
	IB T700D IVCO 338000 371500, IB T850D IVCO 362500 398500												
	1990 BOATS												
39	AFT CABIN SUN DECK	FB	SF	FBG	DV	IB	T300D	GM	14 8	22000	3 2	107500	118500
39	AFT CABIN SUN DECK	FB	SF	FBG	DV	IB	T370D	IVCO	14 8	22000	3 2	113000	124500
39	AFT CABIN SUN DECK	FB	SF	FBG	DV	IB	T375D	CAT	14 8	23000	3 2	121000	133000
39	SPORTFISHER CNV	FB	SF	FBG	DV	IB	T300D	GM	14 8	21000	3 2	104000	114500
39	SPORTFISHER CNV	FB	SF	FBG	DV	IB	T370D	IVCO	14 8	21000	3 2	109500	120500
39	SPORTFISHER CNV	FB	SF	FBG	DV	IB	T375D	CAT	14 8	22000	3 2	117500	129000
45	MOTOR YACHT	FB	YTFS	FBG	SV	IB	T300D	GM	15 3	36000	3 8	147500	162000
	IB T320D CAT 152000 167000, IB T370D IVCO 159500 175500, IB T375D CAT 164500 181000												
45	SPORTFISHER	FB	SF	FBG	DV	IB	T300D	GM	15 3	35500	3 8	140000	154000
45	SPORTFISHER	FB	SF	FBG	DV	IB	T370D	IVCO	15 3	35500	3 8	152000	167000
45	SPORTFISHER	FB	SF	FBG	DV	IB	T375D	CAT	15 3	36500	3 8	156500	172000
45	YACHTFISHER	FB	YTFS	FBG	DV	IB	T300D	GM	15 3	36000	3 8	140500	154500
45	YACHTFISHER	FB	YTFS	FBG	DV	IB	T370D	IVCO	15 3	36000	3 8	152000	167000
45	YACHTFISHER	FB	YTFS	FBG	DV	IB	T375D	CAT	15 3	37000	3 8	156500	172000
48	MOTOR YACHT	FB	MY	FBG	SV	IB	T300D	GM	15 3	37000	3 8	146500	161000
48	MOTOR YACHT	FB	MY	FBG	SV	IB	T370D	IVCO	15 3	37000	3 8	157500	173500
48	MOTOR YACHT	FB	MY	FBG	SV	IB	T375D	CAT	15 3	38000	3 8	161500	177500
48	PILOT HOUSE	FB	PH	FBG	SV	IB	T300D	GM	15 3	39000	3 8	148500	163500
48	PILOT HOUSE	FB	PH	FBG	SV	IB	T370D	IVCO	15 3	39000	3 8	158000	173500
48	PILOT HOUSE	FB	PH	FBG	SV	IB	T375D	CAT	15 3	40000	3 8	161500	177500
48	SPORTFISHER	FB	SF	FBG	DV	IB	T300D	GM	15 3	38000	3 8	144500	159000
48	SPORTFISHER	FB	SF	FBG	DV	IB	T370D	IVCO	15 3	38000	3 8	158000	173500
48	SPORTFISHER	FB	SF	FBG	DV	IB	T375D	CAT	15 3	39000	3 8	161500	177000
48	YACHTFISHER	FB	YTFS	FBG	DV	IB	T300D	GM	15 3	39000	3 8	143000	157000
48	YACHTFISHER	FB	YTFS	FBG	DV	IB	T370D	IVCO	15 3	39000	3 8	158000	173500
48	YACHTFISHER	FB	YTFS	FBG	DV	IB	T375D	CAT	15 3	40000	3 8	161500	177500
51	MOTOR YACHT	FB	MY	FBG	SV	IB	T300D	GM	15 3	41000	3 8	155000	170000
51	MOTOR YACHT	FB	MY	FBG	SV	IB	T370D	IVCO	15 3	41000	3 8	170000	187000
51	MOTOR YACHT	FB	MY	FBG	SV	IB	T375D	CAT	15 3	42000	3 8	174000	191500
51	PILOT HOUSE	FB	PH	FBG	SV	IB	T300D	GM	15 3	41000	3 8	155000	170500
51	PILOT HOUSE	FB	PH	FBG	SV	IB	T370D	IVCO	15 3	41000	3 8	170000	187000
51	PILOT HOUSE	FB	PH	FBG	SV	IB	T375D	CAT	15 3	42000	3 8	174500	191500
51	SPORTFISHER	FB	SF	FBG	DV	IB	T300D	GM	15 3	39000	3 8	147500	162000
51	SPORTFISHER	FB	SF	FBG	DV	IB	T370D	IVCO	15 3	39000	3 8	164000	180500
51	SPORTFISHER	FB	SF	FBG	DV	IB	T375D	CAT	15 3	40000	3 8	168000	184500
51	YACHTFISHER	FB	YTFS	FBG	DV	IB	T300D	GM	15 3	40000	3 8	147500	162000
51	YACHTFISHER	FB	YTFS	FBG	DV	IB	T370D	IVCO	15 3	40000	3 8	165000	181500
51	YACHTFISHER	FB	YTFS	FBG	DV	IB	T375D	CAT	15 3	41000	3 8	169000	186000
55	MOTOR YACHT	FB	MY	FBG	SV	IB	T300D	GM	17	43000	3 10	144000	158000
	IB T370D IVCO 161000 177000, IB T375D CAT 165500 181500, IB T700D IVCO 245500 269500												
	IB T700D MAN 245000 269500, IB T850D MAN 270000 296500												
55	SPORTFISHER	FB	SF	FBG	DV	IB	T300D	GM	17	42000	3 10	147500	162000
	IB T370D IVCO 166500 183000, IB T375D CAT 171000 188000, IB T680D MAN 249500 274000												
	IB T700D IVCO 256000 281000, IB T850D MAN 282500 310500												
55	YACHTFISHER	FB	YTFS	FBG	DV	IB	T300D	GM	17	43000	3 10	149000	164000
	IB T370D IVCO 169000 185500, IB T375D CAT 173000 190500, IB T680D MAN 253000 278000												
	IB T700D MAN 257000 282000, IB T850D MAN 285500 313500												
61	MOTOR YACHT	FB	MY	FBG	DV	IB	T425D	CAT	19 5	54000		237000	260500
	IB T680D MAN 279000 307000, IB T700D IVCO 285500 313500, IB T850D MAN 312000 343000												
61	YACHTFISHER	FB	YTFS	FBG	DV	IB	T425D	CAT	19 5	54000		233500	257000
	IB T680D MAN 282000 310000, IB T700D IVCO 288000 316500, IB T850D MAN 316000 347500												
	1989 BOATS												
39	SPORTFISHER CNV	FB	SF	FBG	DV	IB	T300D	GM	14 8	21000	3 2	99300	109000
	IB T320D CAT 103500 114000, IB T370D IVCO 104500 115000, IB T375D CAT 112000 123000												
39	SPORTFISHER SUN DECK	FB	SF	FBG	DV	IB	T300D	GM	14 8	22000	3 2	103000	113000
	IB T320D CAT 107000 117500, IB T370D IVCO 108000 119000, IB T375D CAT 115500 127000												
45	MOTOR YACHT	FB	YTFS	FBG	SV	IB	T300D	GM	15 3	36000	3 8	141000	154500
	IB T320D CAT 145000 159500, IB T370D IVCO 152500 167500, IB T375D CAT 157000 172500												
45	SPORTFISHER	FB	SF	FBG	DV	IB	T300D	GM	15 3	35500	3 8	134000	147000
	IB T320D CAT 138000 151500, IB T370D IVCO 145000 159500, IB T375D CAT 149500 164500												
45	YACHTFISHER	FB	YTFS	FBG	DV	IB	T300D	GM	15 3	36000	3 8	134000	147500
	IB T320D CAT 138500 152000, IB T370D IVCO 145000 159500, IB T375D CAT 149500 164500												
48	MOTOR YACHT	FB	MY	FBG	SV	IB	T300D	GM	15 3	37000	3 8	140000	153500
	IB T320D CAT 143000 157500, IB T370D IVCO 150500 165500, IB T375D CAT 154000 169500												
48	PILOT HOUSE	FB	PH	FBG	SV	IB	T300D	GM	15 3	39000	3 8	142000	156000
	IB T320D CAT 145000 159500, IB T370D IVCO 151000 166000, IB T375D CAT 154500 169500												
48	SPORTFISHER	FB	SF	FBG	DV	IB	T300D	GM	15 3	38000	3 8	138000	151500
	IB T320D CAT 142000 156000, IB T370D IVCO 150500 165500, IB T375D CAT 154000 169500												
48	YACHTFISHER	FB	YTFS	FBG	DV	IB	T300D	GM	15 3	39000	3 8	136500	150000
	IB T320D CAT 141000 154500, IB T370D IVCO 151000 166000, IB T375D CAT 154000 169500												

```
     LOA  NAME AND/        TOP/ BOAT  -HULL- ----ENGINE--- BEAM  WGT  DRAFT RETAIL RETAIL
  FT IN   OR MODEL         RIG  TYPE  MTL TP TP # HP  MFG  FT IN  LBS  FT IN  LOW    HIGH
------------------------- 1989 BOATS -------------------------
 51    MOTOR YACHT          FB   MY   FBG SV IB T300D GM  15  3 41000       3  8 148000 162500
        IB T320D CAT 152500 167500, IB T370D IVCO 162500 178500, IB T375D CAT 166500 183000
 51    PILOT HOUSE          FB   PH   FBG SV IB T300D GM  15  3 41000       3  8 148000 163000
        IB T320D CAT 152500 168000, IB T370D IVCO 162500 178500, IB T375D CAT 166500 183000
 51    SPORTFISHER          FB   SF   FBG DV IB T300D GM  15  3 39000       3  8 141000 155000
        IB T320D CAT 146000 160000, IB T370D IVCO 157000 172500, IB T375D CAT 160500 176500
 51    YACHTFISHER          FB   YTFS FBG DV IB T300D GM  15  3 40000       3  8 140500 154500
        IB T320D CAT 145500 160000, IB T370D IVCO 157500 173500, IB T375D CAT 161500 177500
 55    MOTOR YACHT          FB   MY   FBG SV IB T300D GM  17    43000       3  8 137500 151000
        IB T320D CAT 143500 157500, IB T370D IVCO 154000 169000, IB T375D CAT 158000 173500
        IB T630D IVCO 222500 244500, IB T630D MAN 222500 244500, IB T850D MAN 258000 283500
 55    SPORTFISHER          FB   SF   FBG DV IB T300D GM  17    42000       3 10 141000 155000
        IB T320D CAT 147000 161500, IB T370D IVCO 159000 175000, IB T375D CAT 163500 179500
        IB T630D IVCO 229000 252000, IB T630D MAN 229000 251500, IB T850D MAN 270000 296500
 55    YACHTFISHER          FB   YTFS FBG DV IB T300D GM  17    43000       3 10 142500 156500
        IB T320D CAT 148000 162500, IB T370D IVCO 161500 177000, IB T375D CAT 165500 182000
        IB T630D IVCO 233000 256000, IB T630D MAN 233000 256000, IB T850D MAN 272500 299500
 57    FLUSH DECK           FB   FD   FBG SV IB T300D GM  17    53000       3  8 172500 189500
        IB T320D CAT 177500 195000, IB T370D IVCO 189500 208500, IB T375D CAT 191000 210000
        IB T630D IVCO 243500 267500, IB T630D MAN 243000 267000, IB T850D MAN 280500 308500
 57    MOTOR YACHT          FB   MY   FBG SV IB T300D GM  17    53000       3  8 169000 185500
        IB T320D CAT 173500 191000, IB T370D IVCO 186000 204500, IB T375D CAT 187000 205500
        IB T630D IVCO 243500 262000, IB T630D MAN 238000 261500, IB T850D MAN 275000 302500
 61    FLUSH DECK           FB   FD   FBG SV IB T300D GM  17  1 58000       3  8 203500 224000
        IB T320D CAT 208000 228500, IB T370D IVCO 215000 236500, IB T375D CAT 217000 238000
        IB T630D IVCO 271000 297500, IB T630D MAN 268500 295000, IB T850D MAN 308500 339000
 61    FLUSH DECK W/COCKPIT FB  MYFD  FBG SV IB T300D GM  17  1 58000       3  8 202500 223000
        IB T320D CAT 207000 227500, IB T370D IVCO 214500 236000, IB T375D CAT 216000 237500
        IB T630D IVCO 271000 297500, IB T630D MAN 268500 295000, IB T850D MAN 308500 339000
------------------------- 1988 BOATS -------------------------
 39    SPORTFISHER CNV      FB   SF   FBG DV IB T300D GM  14  8 21000       3  4  94900 104000
 39    SPORTFISHER CNV      FB   SF   FBG DV IB T375D CAT 14  8 22500       3  4 108500 119500
 39    SUN DECK             FB   SF   FBG DV IB T300D GM  14  8 21500       3  4  96600 106000
 39    SUN DECK             FB   SF   FBG DV IB T375D CAT 14  8 23000       3  4 110500 121500
 51    MOTOR YACHT          FB   MY   FBG DV IB T375D CAT 15  3 43000       3  8 166000 182500
 51    PILOT HOUSE          FB   PH   FBG DV IB T375D CAT 15  3 42500       3  9 163500 180000
 51    SPORT FISHER         FB   SF   FBG DV IB T375D CAT 15  3 40500       3  8 152000 167000
 51    YACHT FISHER         FB   YTFS FBG DV IB T375D CAT 15  3 40000       3  8 155000 170000
 55    SPORT FISHER         FB   SF   FBG DV IB T375D CAT 17    43000       3 10 155500 171000
 55    SPORT FISHER         FB   SF   FBG DV IB T510D MAN  17    46500       3 11 194500 213500
 55    SPORT FISHER         FB   SF   FBG DV IB T630D IVCO 17    47000       3 11 218500 240000
 55    YACHT FISHER         FB   YTFS FBG DV IB T375D CAT 17    42500       3 10 154000 169500
 55    YACHT FISHER         FB   YTFS FBG DV IB T510D MAN  17    46000       3 11 192500 211500
 55    YACHT FISHER         FB   YTFS FBG DV IB T630D IVCO 17    46500       3 11 216500 238000
 60 10 FLUSH DECK W/COCKPIT FB   SF   FBG DV IB T375D CAT 17    52000       4  1 198000 217500
 60 10 FLUSH DECK W/COCKPIT FB   SF   FBG DV IB T510D MAN  17    55000       4  1 211000 231500
 60 10 FLUSH DECK W/COCKPIT FB   SF   FBG DV IB T630D IVCO 17    56000       4  1 230000 252500
------------------------- 1987 BOATS -------------------------
 39    SPORTFISHER CNV      FB   SF   FBG DV IB T300D GM  14  8 21000       3  4  90700  99700
 39    SPORTFISHER CNV      FB   SF   FBG DV IB T375D CAT 14  8 22500       3  4 104000 114000
 39    SUN DECK             FB   SF   FBG DV IB T300D GM  14  8 21500       3  4  92300 101500
 39    SUN DECK             FB   SF   FBG DV IB T375D CAT 14  8 23000       3  4 105500 116000
 51    MOTOR YACHT          FB   MY   FBG DV IB T375D CAT 15  3 42000       3  8 156000 171500
 51    PILOT HOUSE          FB   PH   FBG DV IB T375D CAT 15  3 42500       3  9 157500 173000
 51    SPORT FISHER         FB   SF   FBG DV IB T375D CAT 15  3 40500       3  8 148000 160000
 51    YACHT FISHER         FB   YTFS FBG DV IB T375D CAT 15  3 40000       3  8 148000 162500
 55    SPORT FISHER         FB   SF   FBG DV IB T375D CAT 17    43000       3 10 149000 163500
 55    SPORT FISHER         FB   SF   FBG DV IB T510D MAN  19    46000       3 11 186000 204500
 55    SPORT FISHER         FB   SF   FBG DV IB T630D IVCO 19    47000       3 11 209000 229500
 55    YACHT FISHER         FB   YTFS FBG DV IB T375D CAT 19    42500       3 10 147500 162000
 55    YACHT FISHER         FB   YTFS FBG DV IB T510D MAN  19    46000       3 11 184000 202000
 55    YACHT FISHER         FB   YTFS FBG DV IB T630D IVCO 19    46500       3 11 207000 227500
 60 10 FLUSH DECK W/COCKPIT FB   YTFS FBG DV IB T375D CAT 19    52000       4  1 193500 212500
 60 10 FLUSH DECK W/COCKPIT FB   YTFS FBG DV IB T510D MAN  19    55000       4  1 216000 237000
 60 10 FLUSH DECK W/COCKPIT FB   YTFS FBG DV IB T630D IVCO 19    56000       4  1 243500 267500
------------------------- 1986 BOATS -------------------------
 40 10 SPOILER CNV SDN      DCMY F/S SV IB T260D J&T  14  5 24000       3  8 103000 113000
        IB T300D VLVO 103000 113500, IB T320D CAT 109500 120000, IB T350D PERK 112000 123000
        IB T375D CAT 114500 125500
 40 10 SPOILER SUNBRIDGE    DCMY F/S SV IB T260D J&T  14  5 24000       3  8 102500 112500
        IB T300D VLVO 102500 113000, IB T320D CAT 109000 119500, IB T350D PERK 111500 122500
        IB T375D CAT 114000 125000
 44  2 SPOILER AFT CABIN    YTFS F/S SV IB T260D GM   14  9 29000       3  8 104000 114500
        IB T320D CAT 115000 126000, IB T350D PERK 119500 131500, IB T375D CAT 123000 135500
 44  2 SPOILER CNV SDN      DCMY F/S SV IB T260D GM   14  9 29000       3  8 109500 120500
        IB T320D CAT 118500 130500, IB T350D PERK 123000 135000, IB T375D CAT 126500 138500
 44  2 SPOILER SUNBRIDGE    DCMY F/S SV IB T260D GM   14  9 29000       3  8 106500 117000
        IB T320D CAT 115000 126500, IB T350D PERK 119000 130500, IB T375D CAT 122000 134000
 50  4 SPOILER AFT CABIN    YTFS F/S SV IB T260D GM   15    33000       4    110500 121500
        IB T320D CAT 126500 138500, IB T350D PERK 133500 147000, IB T375D CAT 139500 153500
 50  4 SPOILER CNV SDN      DCMY F/S SV IB T260D GM   15    33000       4    118500 130000
        IB T320D CAT 132000 145000, IB T350D PERK 138500 152000, IB T375D CAT 143500 157500
 50  4 SPOILER SUNBRIDGE    DCMY     SV IB T260D GM   15    33000       4    113500 124500
 50  4 SPOILER SUNBRIDGE    DCMY F/S    IB T320D CAT  15    33000       4    125500 138000
 50  4 SPOILER SUNBRIDGE    DCMY F/S SV IB T350D PERK 15    33000       4    131500 144500
 50  4 SPOILER SUNBRIDGE    DCMY F/S SV IB T375D CAT  15    33000       4    136500 150000
 53    SPOILER AFT CABIN    YTFS F/S SV IB T260D GM   17    42000       4  6 119000 130500
        IB T300D VLVO 128500 141000, IB T320D CAT 133000 146000, IB T350D PERK 139000 153500
        IB T375D CAT 145000 159500, IB T510D 171000 187500, IB T700D 202000 222000
 53    SPOILER CNV SDN      DCMY F/S SV IB T260D GM   17    42000       4  6 119500 131500
        IB T300D VLVO 124000 136500, IB T320D CAT 129000 141500, IB T350D PERK 133000 146000
        IB T375D CAT 137000 150500, IB T510D 158500 174500, IB T700D 186500 204500
 53    SPOILER FLUSH DECK   DCMY F/S SV IB T260D GM   17    42000       4  6 121500 133500
        IB T300D VLVO 128000 140500, IB T320D CAT 132500 146000, IB T350D PERK 138000 152000
        IB T375D CAT 143000 157000, IB T510D 167000 183500, IB T700D 196000 215500
 59  3 SPOILER AFT CABIN    YTFS F/S SV IB T375D CAT  17    48000       4  8 157500 173000
 59  3 SPOILER AFT DECK     YTFS F/S SV IB T260D GM   17    48000       4  8 140500 154000
        IB T300D VLVO 143500 158000, IB T320D CAT 149000 164000, IB T350D PERK 153500 168000
        IB T510D 185000 203500, IB T700D 221000 243000
 59  3 SPOILER CNV SDN      DCMY F/S SV IB T260D GM   17    48000       4  8 148500 163500
        IB T300D VLVO 151500 166500, IB T320D CAT 157000 172500, IB T350D PERK 159000 175000
        IB T375D CAT 162500 178500, IB T510D 182000 200000, IB T700D 211500 232500
 59  3 SPOILER FLUSH DECK   DCMY F/S SV IB T260D GM   17    48000       4  8 148500 163500
        IB T300D VLVO 151500 166500, IB T320D CAT 157000 172500, IB T350D PERK 159000 175000
        IB T375D CAT 162500 178500, IB T510D 182000 200000, IB T700D 211500 232500
------------------------- 1985 BOATS -------------------------
 40 10 SPOILER CNV SDN      DCMY F/S SV IB T250D J&T  14  5 24000       3  8  97800 107500
 40 10 SPOILER SUNBRIDGE    DCMY F/S SV IB T250D J&T  14  5 24000       3  8  97400 107000
 44  2 SPOILER AFT CABIN    YTFS F/S SV IB T300D CAT  14  9 29000       3  8 111000 117500
 44  2 SPOILER CNV SDN      DCMY F/S SV IB T300D CAT  14  9 29000       3  8 113000 122000
 44  2 SPOILER SUNBRIDGE    DCMY F/S SV IB T300D CAT  14  9 29000       3  8 107500 118500
 50  4 SPOILER AFT CABIN    YTFS F/S SV IB T355D CAT  15    33000       4    129000 142000
 50  4 SPOILER CNV SDN      DCMY F/S SV IB T300D CAT  15    33000       4    122000 134500
 50  4 SPOILER SUNBRIDGE    DCMY F/S SV IB T300D CAT  15    33000       4    116000 127500
 53    SPOILER AFT CABIN    YTFS F/S SV IB T355D CAT  17    42000       4  6 135000 148000
 53    SPOILER CNV SDN      DCMY F/S SV IB T355D CAT  17    42000       4  6 128500 141000
 53    SPOILER FLUSH DECK   DCMY F/S SV IB T355D CAT  17    42000       4  6 133500 146500
 59  3 SPOILER AFT CABIN    YTFS F/S SV IB T355D CAT  17    48000       4  8 154000 169000
 59  3 SPOILER CNV SDN      DCMY F/S SV IB T355D CAT  17    48000       4  8 154000 169000
 59  3 SPOILER FLUSH DECK   DCMY F/S SV IB T355D CAT  17    48000       4  8 154000 169000
```

....For earlier years, see the BUC Used Boat Price Guide, Volume 3

SPORT-CRAFT BOATS

PERRY FL 32347   COAST GUARD MFG ID- SXK See inside cover to adjust price for area

For more recent years, see the BUC Used Boat Price Guide, Volume 1

```
 LOA  NAME AND/                TOP/ BOAT  -HULL- ----ENGINE--- BEAM   WGT  DRAFT RETAIL RETAIL
FT IN  OR MODEL                 RIG TYPE  MTL TP TP # HP   MFG  FT IN  LBS  FT IN   LOW    HIGH
------------------------- 1996 BOATS ---------------------------------------------------------
16     FISHMASTER 160           OP  CTRCN FBG SV OB              7     1100            3200   3700
18     FISHMASTER 180           OP  CTRCN FBG DV OB              8     1250            3750   4350
19   8 AVANZA 1900              OP  B/R   FBG DV IO 160-235      8     2650            6750   8400
20   2 FISHMASTER 202           OP  CTRCN FBG DV OB              8     2150            6600   7550
20   2 FISHMASTER 202 WT        OP  FSH   FBG DV OB              8     2650            7350   8450
20   2 FISHMASTER 202 WT        OP  FSH   FBG DV IO 160-220      8     2650            8700  10700
20   6 AVANZA 2050 CC           OP  CUD   FBG DV IO 160-235      8     2650            8400  10400
20   8 AVANZA 2050              OP  B/R   FBG DV IO 160-235      8     2650            7950   9850
20   9 AVANZA 2100              OP  CUD   FBG DV IO 160-235      8  6  2850            9300  11300
23   2 FISHMASTER 232 CC        OP  CTRCN FBG DV OB              8  6  3500           10900  12400
23   2 FISHMASTER 232 CC        OP  CTRCN FBG DV IO 180-280      8  6  3500           12500  15600
23   2 FISHMASTER 232 CC        OP  CTRCN FBG DV IO 130D-230D    8  6  3500           18600  22500

23   2 FISHMASTER 232 FCC       OP  CTRCN FBG DV OB              8  6  3500           11400  13000
23   2 FISHMASTER 232 FWAC      OP  CUD   FBG DV OB              8  6  4450           13000  14800
23   2 FISHMASTER 232 SPT       OP  FSH   FBG DV OB              8  6  4250           12500  14200
23   2 FISHMASTER 232 SPT       OP  FSH   FBG DV IO 180-280      8  6  4250           14400  17700
23   2 FISHMASTER 232 SPT       OP  FSH   FBG DV IO 130D-230D    8  6  4250           20600  25000
23   2 FISHMASTER 232 WAC       OP  CUD   FBG DV OB              8  6  4450           12500  14200
23   2 FISHMASTER 232 WAC       OP  CUD   FBG DV IO 180-280      8  6  4450           14100  17300
23   2 FISHMASTER 232 WAC       OP  CUD   FBG DV IO 130D-230D    8  6  4450           16800  20800
24   2 FISHMASTER 250           HT  CUD   FBG DV IO 100-185      8     4050           13700  15900

24   2 FISHMASTER 250           HT  FSH   FBG DV IO 180-235      8     4050           14400  17800
       IO  250  MRCR  14900  17000, IO  250  VLVO  15300  17400, IB 250-260          16000  18200
       IO  265  VLVO  15600  17700, IB  270  MRCR  16100  18300, IO 275-280          15700  17900
       IO 130D-230D   20700  25400

24   2 FISHMASTER 250 CR        HT  CUD   FBG DV IO 180-250      8     4250           14100  16900
       IB  260  MRCR  16400  18700, IO 265-280       15100  17300, IO 130D-230D       16800  21000

25   2 FISHMASTER 252           OP  CTRCN FBG DV OB              8  6  4400           13900  15800
25   2 FISHMASTER 252 SPT       HT  FSH   FBG DV OB              8  6  4400           14000  15900
25   2 FISHMASTER 252 SPT       HT  FSH   FBG DV IO  180  MRCR   8  6  4450           16500  18800
       IO 180-235     19000  21200, IO  250  MRCR  16800  19100, IO  250  VLVO       17300  19700
       IB 250-260     19300  21600, IO  265  VLVO  19200  21300, IB  270  MRCR       19500  21700
       IO 275-280     19300  21400, IO 130D-200D   23300  28600, IO  230D VLVO       26700  29700

25   2 FISHMASTER 252 WAC       HT  FSH   FBG DV OB              8  6  4450           13800  15700
25   2 FISHMASTER 252 WAC       HT  FSH   FBG DV IO  180  MRCR   8  6  4450           14700  16700
       IO 180-280     16700  19500, IO 130D-200D   21300  26100, IO  230D VLVO       24400  27100

25   2 FISHMASTER 252F WAC      HT  FSH   FBG DV OB              8  6  4450           14300  16200
25   6 AVANZA 2500              OP  CUD   FBG DV IO 210-280      8  6  3200           13300  16600
       IO 300-330     14800  17600, IO 130D-150D   13600  16200, IO 200D-230D        15800  18900

25   6 AVANZA 2500 CR           OP  CR    FBG DV IO 210-280      8  6  3800           14500  17900
       IO 300-330     15900  18900, IO 130D-150D   15300  18000, IO 200D-230D        17300  20600

27     FISHMASTER 270           HT  CUD   FBG DV OB             10     4850           17400  19700
27     FISHMASTER 270           HT  CUD   FBG DV IB  215  MRCR  10     5650           23700  26300
       IO  220  MRCR  20500  22700, IO  250  MRCR  20700  23000, IO  250  VLVO       20900  23300
       IB 250-260     24100  26900, IO  265  VLVO  21400  23800, IB  270  MRCR       24400  27100
       IO 275-300     21600  24000, IB  310  MRCR  24500  27200, IO  330            22600  25200
       IB 340-405     25500  29700, IO 130D-200D   21500  26400, IO  230D VLVO       24700  27500
       IB 250D-300D   30600  36200, IO T190-T250   25400  28300

27     FISHMASTER 270 SPORT     HT  CUD   FBG DV OB             10     5650           17500  19900
27     FISHMASTER 270 SPORT     HT  CUD   FBG DV IB  215  MRCR  10     5650           24500  27300
       IO  220  MRCR  21300  23700, IO  250  MRCR  21600  24000, IO  250  VLVO       21800  24200
       IB 250-260     25100  28100, IO  265  VLVO  22300  24800, IB  270  MRCR       25400  28300
       IO 275-300     22500  25000, IB  310  MRCR  25500  28400, IO  330            23500  26100
       IB 340-405     26500  30800, IO 130D-200D   22200  27300, IO  230D VLVO       25500  28300
       IB 250D-300D   31400  37100, IO T190-T220   22100  27200, IO T235-T250        25300  29200

29   2 FISHMASTER 292 SPT       HT  CUD   FBG DV IO 250-260     11                    26100  29000
30     FISHMASTER 300 CR        HT  CUD   FBG DV OB             10     8335           25200  28000
30     FISHMASTER 300 CR        HT  CUD   FBG DV IB  215  MRCR  10     8335           31100  34500
       IO  300        28100  31400, IB  310  MRCR  32600  36300, IO  330            28600  32000
       IB  340  MRCR  33100  36800, IO 130D-230D   29400  35000, IO T190-T235        29300  33800
       IO T250  MRCR  30600  34000, IO T250  VLVO  30800  34200, IB T250-T310        35400  41100
       IOT200D-T230D  36100  41700

30     FISHMASTER 300 SPORT     HT  FSH   FBG DV OB             10     8495           24100  26800
30     FISHMASTER 300 SPORT     HT  FSH   FBG DV IB  215  MRCR  10     8495           31300  34800
       IO  220  MRCR  28500  31700, IO  250  MRCR  29000  32200, IO  250  VLVO       29100  32300
       IB 250-260     31900  35600, IO  265  VLVO  29400  32600, IB  270  MRCR       32200  35800
       IO 275-300     29500  33300, IB  310  MRCR  32800  36500, IO  330            30400  33900
       IB 340-405     33300  38200, IO 130D-230D   37400  44200, IB 250D-300D        38600  44600
       IO T190-T235   31100  35900, IO T250  MRCR  32500  36100, IO T250  VLVO       32700  36300
       IB T250-T310   35600  41300

31     AVANZA 3100              OP  CR    FBG DV IO T220-T250   11                    36800  41700
31     AVANZA 3100              OP  CR    FBG DV IOT190D-T250D 11                     44700  52600
36     FISHMASTER 360 CNV       FB  CUD   FBG DV IB T310  MRCR 13                     52700  57900
       IB T310  VLVO  53100  58300, IB T340  MRCR  53600  58900, IB T400  MRCR       55700  61200
       IB T415  MRCR  56300  61900, IB T250D CUM   72800  80000, IB T300D CAT        77800  85500
       IB T300D CUM   75800  83200, IB T350D CAT   81500  89600

36     FISHMASTER 360 EXP       HT  CUD   FBG DV IB T310  MRCR 13      16500          76100  83600
       IB T310  VLVO  76500  84100, IB T340  MRCR  77000  84600, IB T400  MRCR       79200  87000
       IB T405  MRCR  79400  87200, IB T415  MRCR  79800  87700, IB T250D CUM        86300  94900
       IB T300D CAT   91400 100500, IB T300D CUM   89400  98200, IB T350D CAT        95200 104500
------------------------- 1995 BOATS ---------------------------------------------------------
16     FISHMASTER 160           OP  CTRCN FBG SV OB              7     1100            3050   3550
16     SPRINT 1600 BR           OP  B/R   FBG DV IO 110-155      7     1750            3900   4550
16     SPRINT 1600 CB           OP  RNBT  FBG DV IO 110-155      7     1750            4150   4850
18     FISHMASTER 180           OP  CTRCN FBG SV OB              8                     4800   5500
18   2 SPRINT 1900 BR           OP  RNBT  FBG DV IO 110-180      7  8  2550            5900   6900
18   2 SPRINT 1900 CB           OP  RNBT  FBG DV IO 110-180      7  8  2450            5800   6750
18   2 SPRINT 1900 CC           OP  CUD   FBG DV IO 110-180      7  8  2450            5950   6950
19   8 AVANZA 1900 BR           OP  B/R   FBG DV IO 135-180      8     2650            6250   7550
20   2 FISHMASTER 202           OP  CTRCN FBG DV OB              8     2650            7000   8050
20   2 FISHMASTER 202 DUAL      OP  RNBT  FBG SV OB              8     2650            7000   8050
20   2 FISHMASTER 202 DUAL      OP  RNBT  FBG SV IO 135-180      8     2650            7350   8850
20   2 FISHMASTER 202 WAC       OP  FSH   FBG SV OB              8     2350            6600   7600

20   2 FISHMASTER 202 WAC       OP  FSH   FBG SV IO 135-180      8     2350            7600   9200
20   8 AVANZA 2050 BR           OP  B/R   FBG DV IO 135-230      8     2650            7350   8850
20   8 AVANZA 2050 BR           OP  B/R   FBG DV IO  245  VLVO   8     2650            8100   9300
20   8 AVANZA 2050 CC           OP  CUD   FBG SV IO 135-230      8     2650            7850   9450
20   8 AVANZA 2050 CC           OP  CUD   FBG SV IO  245  VLVO   8     2650            8600   9900
23   2 FISHMASTER 232           HT  CUD   FBG SV OB              8  6  4250           11900  13500
23   2 FISHMASTER 232           HT  CUD   FBG SV IO 175-245      8  6  4250           12700  15200
23   2 FISHMASTER 232 SPORT     OP  FSH   FBG SV OB              8  6  4250           11900  13500
23   2 FISHMASTER 232 WAC       OP  CUD   FBG SV OB              8  6  4450           11700  13300
23   2 FISHMASTER 232 WAC       OP  CUD   FBG SV IO 175-245      8  6  4450           13100  15700
23   2 FISHMASTER 232 WACBK     OP  CUD   FBG SV OB              8  6  4450           12500  14300

24   2 FISHMASTER 250           HT  FSH   FBG SV IO  205  MRCR   8     4250           14100  16000
       IO  205  VLVO  14400  16400, IB  205  VLVO  15200  17200, IO 225-245          14600  16800

25   2 FISHMASTER 252 BRKT      HT  FSH   FBG SV OB              8  6  4450           13400  15300
25   2 FISHMASTER 252 SPORT     HT  FSH   FBG SV OB              8  6  4400           13300  15100
25   2 FISHMASTER 252 SPORT     HT  FSH   FBG SV IO 205-245      8  6  4400           15200  18100
25   2 FISHMASTER 252 WAC       HT  FSH   FBG SV IO 175-245      8  6  4450           15000  18200
25   6 AVANZA 2500 CR           OP  CR    FBG DV IO 205-245      8  6  3800           13500  16100
25   6 AVANZA 2500 CUDDY        OP  CUD   FBG DV IO 205-245      8  6  3200           12400  14900
27     FISHMASTER 270           HT  CUD   FBG SV OB             10     5650           16600  18900
27     FISHMASTER 270           HT  CUD   FBG SV IB 230-245     10     5650           23000  25900
       IO  300        20800  23400, IB 305-400       24200  28500, IB  192D VLVO       27000  30000
       IO T135-T155   20700  23800

27     FISHMASTER 270 SPORT     HT  FSH   FBG SV OB             10     5650           16400  18700
27     FISHMASTER 270 SPORT     HT  FSH   FBG SV IO  230        10     5650           20700  23300
       IB  240  VLVO  23200  25800, IO  245  VLVO  21200  23500, IB  250  MRCR       23300  25900
       IO  300        22000  24800, IB 305-400       24200  28500, IB  192D VLVO       27000  30000
       IO T135-T155   21800  25100

29   2 FISHMASTER 292           FB  CR    FBG DV IB T305  VLVO 11                     33800  37600
29   2 FISHMASTER 292           FB  CR    FBG SV IO T205  VLVO 11                     26300  29200
       IB T205  VLVO  30700  34200, IO T240  VLVO  27300  30300, IB T240  VLVO       31800  35400
       IO T250  MRCR  27400  30400, IB T250  MRCR  32000  35600, IO T305  VLVO       29400  32700
       IO T310  MRCR  29300  32600, IB T310  MRCR  33800  37600, IO T124D VLVO       26000  28900
       IB T124D VLVO  31400  34900, IO T192D VLVO  30100  33500, IB T192D VLVO       36500  40500
       IO T230D VLVO  32400  36000, IB T230D VLVO  39100  43500

30     FISHMASTER 300 CR        HT  CUD   FBG SV IB 300-310     10     8335           30700  34300
       IO T180  VLVO  27100  30100, IB T205-T240   32400  37000, IB T250-T305        37500  41700
       IO T124D VLVO  30200  33600, IBT124D-T192D  36600  44800

30     FISHMASTER 300 SPORT     HT  FSH   FBG SV OB             10     8495           22900  25400
```


CONTINUED ON NEXT PAGE

LOA FT	IN	NAME AND/ OR MODEL	TOP/ RIG	BOAT TYPE	-HULL- MTL	TP	ENGINE TP	# HP	MFG	BEAM FT	IN	WGT LBS	DRAFT FT	IN	RETAIL LOW	RETAIL HIGH
		1995 BOATS														
30		FISHMASTER 300 SPORT	HT	FSH	FBG	SV	IO	230-400		10		8495			26800	33000
30		FISHMASTER 300 SPORT	HT	FSH	FBG	SV	IB	T205-T310		10		8495			32700	39100
30		FISHMASTER 300 SPORT	HT	FSH	FBG	SV	IB	T124D-T192D		10		8495			37000	45200
31		AVANZA 3100 CR	OP	CR	FBG	DV	IO	T175-T205		11		8700			31700	36200
31		AVANZA 3100 CR	OP	CR	FBG	DV	IO	T185D-T216D		11		8700			37700	43600
36		FISHMASTER 360	HT	CUD	FBG	DV	IO	T340	MRCR	13		16500			51100	56200
		1994 BOATS														
16		FISHMASTER 160	OP	CTRCN	FBG	SV	OB			7		1100			2900	3400
16		SPRINT 1600 BR	OP	B/R	FBG	DV	IO	110-155		7		1750			3650	4250
16		SPRINT 1600 CB	OP	RNBT	FBG	DV	IO	110-155		7		1750			3850	4550
18		FISHMASTER 180	OP	CTRCN	FBG	SV	OB			8					4600	5300
18	2	SPRINT 1900 BR	OP	RNBT	FBG	DV	IO	110-180		7	8	2550			5550	6450
18	2	SPRINT 1900 CB	OP	RNBT	FBG	DV	IO	110-180		7	8	2450			5400	6300
18	2	SPRINT 1900 CC	OP	CUD	FBG	DV	IO	110-180		7	8	2450			5550	6500
19	8	AVANZA 1900 BR	OP	B/R	FBG	DV	IO	135-180		8		2650			5850	7050
20	2	FISHMASTER 202	OP	CTRCN	FBG	DV	OB			8		2650			6650	7650
20	2	FISHMASTER 202 DUAL	OP	RNBT	FBG	SV	OB			8		2650			6700	7700
20	2	FISHMASTER 202 DUAL	OP	RNBT	FBG	SV	IO	135-180		8		2650			6850	8250
20	2	FISHMASTER 202 WAC	OP	FSH	FBG	SV	OB			8		2350			6300	7250
20	2	FISHMASTER 202 WAC	OP	FSH	FBG	SV	IO	135-180		8		2350			7100	8550
20	8	AVANZA 2050 BR	OP	B/R	FBG	DV	IO	135-230		8		2650			6900	8300
20	8	AVANZA 2050 BR	OP	B/R	FBG	DV	IO	245	VLVO	8		2650			7550	8650
20	8	AVANZA 2050 CC	OP	CR	FBG	SV	IO	135-230		8		2650			7350	8850
20	8	AVANZA 2050 CC	OP	CR	FBG	SV	IO	245	VLVO	8		2650			8050	9250
23	2	FISHMASTER 232	HT	CUD	FBG	SV	OB			8	6	4250			11400	12900
23	2	FISHMASTER 232	HT	CUD	FBG	SV	IO	175-245		8	6	4250			11800	14200
23	2	FISHMASTER 232 SPORT	OP	FSH	FBG	SV	OB			8	6	4250			11300	12900
23	2	FISHMASTER 232 WAC	OP	CUD	FBG	SV	OB			8	6	4450			11200	12700
23	2	FISHMASTER 232 WAC	OP	CUD	FBG	SV	IO	175-245		8	6	4450			12300	14700
23	2	FISHMASTER 232 WACBK	OP	CUD	FBG	SV	OB			8	6	4450			12000	13600
24	2	FISHMASTER 250	HT	CUD	FBG	SV	IO	205-245		8		4250			12500	14800
24	2	FISHMASTER 250	HT	FSH	FBG	SV	IO	205	MRCR	8		4050			12700	14400
		IO 205 VLVO 13000 14800, IB 205 VLVO 14400 16300, IO 230-245													12800	15100
25	2	FISHMASTER 252 BRKT	HT	FSH	FBG	SV	OB			8	6	4450			12800	14600
25	2	FISHMASTER 252 SPORT	HT	FSH	FBG	SV	OB			8	6	4400			12700	14400
25	2	FISHMASTER 252 SPORT	HT	FSH	FBG	SV	IO	205-245		8	6	4400			14200	16900
25	2	FISHMASTER 252 WAC	HT	FSH	FBG	SV	IO	175-245		8	6	4450			14000	17000
25	6	AVANZA 2500 CR	OP	CR	FBG	DV	IO	205-245		8	6	3800			12600	15100
25	6	AVANZA 2500 CUDDY	OP	CUD	FBG	DV	IO	205-245		8	6	3200			11600	13900
27		FISHMASTER 270	HT	CUD	FBG	SV	OB			10		5650			15900	18000
27		FISHMASTER 270	HT	CUD	FBG	SV	IB	230-245		10		5650			21800	24500
		IO 300 19400 21900, IB 305-400 22900 27000, IB 192D VLVO													25700	28500
		IO T135-T155													19300	22200
27		FISHMASTER 270 SPORT	HT	FSH	FBG	SV	OB			10		5650			15700	17900
27		FISHMASTER 270 SPORT	HT	FSH	FBG	SV	IO	230		10		5650			19400	21700
		IB 240 VLVO 22000 24500, IO 245 VLVO 19800 22000, IB 250 MRCR													22000	24500
		IO 300 20500 23100, IB 305-400 22900 27000, IB 192D VLVO													25700	28500
		IO T135-T155													20400	23500
29	2	FISHMASTER 292	FB	CR	FBG	DV	IB	T305	VLVO	11					32000	35600
29	2	FISHMASTER 292	FB	CR	FBG	SV	IO	T205	VLVO	11					24500	27200
		IB T205 VLVO 29100 32300, IO T240 VLVO 25500 28300, IB T240 VLVO													30100	33500
		IO T250 MRCR 25600 28400, IB T250 MRCR 30300 33700, IO T305 VLVO													27500	30500
		IO T310 MRCR 27300 30400, IB T310 MRCR 32000 35600, IO T124D VLVO													24300	27000
		IB T124D VLVO 29900 33200, IO T192D VLVO 28100 31300, IB T192D VLVO													34700	38500
		IO T230D VLVO 30200 33600, IB T230D VLVO 37200 41400														
30		FISHMASTER 300 CR	HT	FSH	FBG	SV	IB	300-310		10		8335			29100	32400
		IO T180 VLVO 26700 29700, IB T205-T240 30700 35100, IB T250-T305													35500	39500
		IO T124D VLVO 35200 39100, IBT124D-T192D 34800 42600														
30		FISHMASTER 300 SPORT	HT	FSH	FBG	SV	OB			10		8495			21800	24200
30		FISHMASTER 300 SPORT	HT	FSH	FBG	SV	IO	230-400		10		8495			25000	30800
30		FISHMASTER 300 SPORT	HT	FSH	FBG	SV	IB	T205-T310		10		8495			30900	37000
30		FISHMASTER 300 SPORT	HT	FSH	FBG	SV	IB	T124D-T192D		10		8495			35200	43000
31		AVANZA 3100 CR	OP	CR	FBG	DV	IO	T175-T205		11		8700			29600	33800
31		AVANZA 3100 CR	OP	CR	FBG	DV	IO	T185D-T216D		11		8700			35200	40700
		1993 BOATS														
16		FISHMASTER 160	OP	CTRCN	FBG	SV	OB			7		1100			2800	3250
16		SPRINT 1600 BR	OP	B/R	FBG	DV	IO	110-155		7		1750			3400	4000
16		SPRINT 1600 CB	OP	RNBT	FBG	DV	IO	110-155		7		1750			3600	4250
18		FISHMASTER 180	OP	CTRCN	FBG	SV	OB			8					4400	5100
18	2	SPRINT 1900 BR	OP	RNBT	FBG	DV	IO	110-180		7	8	2550			5150	6000
18	2	SPRINT 1900 CB	OP	RNBT	FBG	DV	IO	110-180		7	8	2450			5050	5900
18	2	SPRINT 1900 CC	OP	CUD	FBG	DV	IO	110-180		7	8	2450			5200	6050
19	8	AVANZA 1900 BR	OP	B/R	FBG	DV	IO	135-180		8		2650			5450	6600
20	2	FISHMASTER 202	OP	CTRCN	FBG	DV	OB			8		2650			6350	7300
20	2	FISHMASTER 202 DUAL	OP	RNBT	FBG	SV	OB			8		2650			6450	7400
20	2	FISHMASTER 202 DUAL	OP	RNBT	FBG	SV	IO	135-180		8		2650			6400	7700
20	2	FISHMASTER 202 WAC	OP	FSH	FBG	SV	OB			8		2350			6050	6950
20	2	FISHMASTER 202 WAC	OP	FSH	FBG	SV	IO	135-180		8		2350			6650	8000
20	8	AVANZA 2050 BR	OP	B/R	FBG	DV	IO	135-230		8		2650			6450	7750
20	8	AVANZA 2050 BR	OP	B/R	FBG	DV	IO	245	VLVO	8		2650			7050	8100
20	8	AVANZA 2050 CC	OP	CR	FBG	SV	IO	135-230		8		2650			6850	8250
20	8	AVANZA 2050 CC	OP	CR	FBG	SV	IO	245	VLVO	8		2650			7550	8650
23	2	FISHMASTER 232	HT	CUD	FBG	SV	OB			8	6	4250			10900	12400
23	2	FISHMASTER 232	HT	CUD	FBG	SV	IO	175-245		8	6	4250			11100	13300
23	2	FISHMASTER 232 SPORT	OP	FSH	FBG	SV	OB			8	6	4250			10900	12300
23	2	FISHMASTER 232 WAC	OP	CUD	FBG	SV	OB			8	6	4450			10700	12200
23	2	FISHMASTER 232 WAC	OP	CUD	FBG	SV	IO	175-245		8	6	4450			11500	13700
23	2	FISHMASTER 232 WACBK	OP	CUD	FBG	SV	OB			8	6	4450			11500	13100
24	2	FISHMASTER 250	HT	CUD	FBG	SV	IO	205-245		8		4250			11600	13900
24	2	FISHMASTER 250	HT	FSH	FBG	SV	IO	205	MRCR	8		4050			11900	13500
		IO 205 VLVO 12100 13800, IB 205 VLVO 13600 15500, IO 230-245													12000	14100
25	2	FISHMASTER 252 BRKT	HT	FSH	FBG	SV	OB			8	6	4450			12300	14000
25	2	FISHMASTER 252 SPORT	HT	FSH	FBG	SV	OB			8	6	4400			12200	13800
25	2	FISHMASTER 252 SPORT	HT	FSH	FBG	SV	IO	205-245		8	6	4400			13200	15800
25	2	FISHMASTER 252 WAC	HT	FSH	FBG	SV	IO	175-245		8	6	4450			13100	15900
25	6	AVANZA 2500 CR	OP	CR	FBG	DV	IO	205-245		8	6	3800			11700	14100
25	6	AVANZA 2500 CUDDY	OP	CUD	FBG	DV	IO	205-245		8	6	3200			10800	13000
27		FISHMASTER 270	HT	CUD	FBG	SV	OB			10		5650			15200	17200
27		FISHMASTER 270	HT	CUD	FBG	SV	IB	230-245		10		5650			20600	23200
		IO 300 18400 20700, IB 305-400 21700 25600, IB 192D VLVO													24500	27200
		IO T135-T155													18200	21000
27		FISHMASTER 270 SPORT	HT	FSH	FBG	SV	OB			10		5650			15100	17100
27		FISHMASTER 270 SPORT	HT	FSH	FBG	SV	IO	230		10		5650			18300	20500
		IB 240 VLVO 20900 23200, IO 245 VLVO 18700 20800, IB 250 MRCR													20900	23200
		IO 300 19200 21600, IB 305-400 21700 25600, IB 192D VLVO													24500	27200
		IO T135-T155													19100	21900
29	2	FISHMASTER 292	FB	CR	FBG	DV	IB	T305	VLVO	11					30400	33700
29	2	FISHMASTER 292	FB	CR	FBG	SV	IO	T205	VLVO	11					22900	25500
		IB T205 VLVO 27600 30600, IO T240 VLVO 23800 26500, IB T240 VLVO													28600	31700
		IO T250 MRCR 23900 26500, IB T250 MRCR 28700 31900, IO T305 VLVO													25700	28500
		IO T310 MRCR 25600 28400, IB T310 MRCR 30400 33700, IO T124D VLVO													22700	25200
		IB T124D VLVO 28500 31700, IO T192D VLVO 26300 29200, IB T192D VLVO													33000	36700
		IO T230D VLVO 28200 31400, IB T230D VLVO 35500 39400														
30		FISHMASTER 300 CR	HT	FSH	FBG	SV	IB	300-310		10		8335			27600	30800
		IO T180 VLVO 25000 27700, IB T205-T240 29100 33200, IB T250-T305													33700	37400
		IO T124D VLVO 32900 36600, IBT124D-T192D 33200 40600														
30		FISHMASTER 300 SPORT	HT	FSH	FBG	SV	OB			10		8495			20900	23200
30		FISHMASTER 300 SPORT	HT	FSH	FBG	SV	IO	230-400		10		8495			23400	28800
30		FISHMASTER 300 SPORT	HT	FSH	FBG	SV	IB	T205-T310		10		8495			29300	35000
30		FISHMASTER 300 SPORT	HT	FSH	FBG	SV	IB	T124D-T192D		10		8495			33600	41000
31		AVANZA 3100 CR	OP	CR	FBG	DV	IO	T175-T205		11		8700			27600	31600
31		AVANZA 3100 CR	OP	CR	FBG	DV	IO	T185D-T216D		11		8700			32900	38100
		1992 BOATS														
16		FISHMASTER 160	OP	CTRCN	FBG	SV	OB			7		1100			2700	3100
16		SPRINT 1600 BR	OP	B/R	FBG	DV	OB			7		1750			4050	4750
16		SPRINT 1600 BR	OP	B/R	FBG	DV	IO	110-155		7		1750			3200	3700
16		SPRINT 1600 CB	OP	RNBT	FBG	DV	IO	110-155		7		1750			3400	3950
18		FISHMASTER 180	OP	CTRCN	FBG	SV	OB			8					4200	4900
18	2	SPRINT 1900 BR	OP	CUD	FBG	DV	IO	110-180		7	8	2550			5000	5800
18	2	SPRINT 1900 CB	OP	RNBT	FBG	DV	IO	110-180		7	8	2450			4750	5500
18	2	SPRINT 1900 CC	OP	CUD	FBG	DV	IO	110-180		7	8	2450			4850	5700
19	8	AVANZA 1900 BR	OP	B/R	FBG	DV	IO	135-180		8		2650			5100	6200
20	2	FISHMASTER 202	OP	CTRCN	FBG	DV	OB			8		2650			6100	7000
20	2	FISHMASTER 202 DUAL	OP	RNBT	FBG	SV	OB			8		2650			6150	7100
20	2	FISHMASTER 202 DUAL	OP	RNBT	FBG	SV	IO	135-180		8		2650			6000	7200
20	2	FISHMASTER 202 WAC	OP	FSH	FBG	SV	OB			8		2350			5800	6650
20	2	FISHMASTER 202 WAC	OP	FSH	FBG	SV	IO	135-180		8		2350			6200	7500
20	8	AVANZA 2050 BR	OP	B/R	FBG	DV	IO	135-240		8		2650			6000	7250
20	8	AVANZA 2050 BR	OP	B/R	FBG	DV	IO	245	VLVO	8		2650			6600	7600
20	8	AVANZA 2050 CC	OP	CR	FBG	SV	IO	135-240		8		2650			6450	7750
20	8	AVANZA 2050 CC	OP	CR	FBG	SV	IO	245	VLVO	8		2650			7050	8100

 CONTINUED ON NEXT PAGE

LOA FT	IN	NAME AND/ OR MODEL	TOP/ RIG	BOAT TYPE	-HULL- MTL	TP	ENGINE TP	# HP	MFG	BEAM FT	IN	WGT LBS	DRAFT FT IN	RETAIL LOW	RETAIL HIGH
		1992 BOATS													
23	2	FISHMASTER 232	HT	CUD	FBG	SV	OB			8	6	4250		10400	11800
23	2	FISHMASTER 232	HT	CUD	FBG	SV	IO	175-245		8	6	4250		10400	12400
23	2	FISHMASTER 232 SPORT	OP	FSH	FBG	SV	OB			8	6	4250		10400	11800
23	2	FISHMASTER 232 SPORT	OP	FSH	FBG	SV	IO	175-245		8	6	4250		10900	13100
23	2	FISHMASTER 232 WAC	OP	CUD	FBG	SV	OB			8	6	4450		10300	11800
23	2	FISHMASTER 232 WAC	OP	CUD	FBG	SV	IO	175-245		8	6	4450		10700	12900
23	2	FISHMASTER 232 WACBK	OP	CUD	FBG	SV	OB			8	6	4450		11000	12500
24	2	FISHMASTER 250	HT	CUD	FBG	SV	IO	180-245		8		4250		10800	13000
24	2	FISHMASTER 250	HT	FSH	FBG	SV	IO	180-245		8		4050		11000	13200
25	2	FISHMASTER 252 BRKT	HT	FSH	FBG	SV	OB			8	6	4450		11800	13400
25	2	FISHMASTER 252 CUD	HT	CUD	FBG	SV	OB			8	6			10800	12300
25	2	FISHMASTER 252 CUD	HT	CUD	FBG	SV	IO	205-245		8	6			10900	13100
25	2	FISHMASTER 252 SPORT	HT	FSH	FBG	SV	OB			8	6	4400		11700	13300
25	2	FISHMASTER 252 SPORT	HT	FSH	FBG	SV	IO	205-245		8	6	4400		12400	14800
25	2	FISHMASTER 252 WAC	HT	FSH	FBG	SV	IO		OMC	8	6	4450		**	**
25	2	FISHMASTER 252 WAC	HT	FSH	FBG	SV	IO	175-245		8	6	4450		12300	14900
25	6	AVANZA 2500 CR	OP	CR	FBG	DV	IO	205-245		8	6	3800		11000	13200
25	6	AVANZA 2500 CUDDY	OP	CUD	FBG	DV	IO	205-245		8	6	3200		10100	12200
27		FISHMASTER 270	HT	CUD	FBG	SV	OB			10		5650		14500	16500
27		FISHMASTER 270	HT	CUD	FBG	SV	IB	230	MRCR	10		5650		19600	21800
		IO 240 YAMA 16000 18200, IB 240-245 19800 22100, IO 300												16800	19400
		IB 305-400 20600 24300, IB 192D VLVO 23300 25900, IO T135-T155												16700	19700
27		FISHMASTER 270	HT	FSH	FBG	SV	IO	230-245		10		4050		15600	18100
		IO 250 MRCR 15800 18000, IB 250 MRCR 19100 21200, IO 300-310												16600	19300
		IO 400 MRCR 19100 21200, IO 192D VLVO 20400 22600, IO 230D VLVO												21600	24000
		IB 230D VLVO 24500 27200, IO T135-T155 16500 19500													
27		FISHMASTER 270	FB	FSH	FBG	SV	IO	230-310		10		4850		15600	19300
		IO 400 MRCR 19100 21200, IO 192D-230D 20400 24000, IO T135-T155												16500	19500
27		FISHMASTER 270 BRKT	HT	FSH	FBG	SV	OB			10		4850		14300	16300
27		FISHMASTER 270 SPORT	HT	FSH	FBG	SV	OB			10		5650		14500	16400
27		FISHMASTER 270 SPORT	HT	FSH	FBG	SV	IO	230		10		5650		16700	19200
		IO 240 YAMA 16900 19200, IB 240 VLVO 19800 22000, IO 245 VLVO												17100	19400
		IB 250 MRCR 20800 23100, IO 300 18200 20400, IB 305-400												20600	24300
		IB 192D VLVO 23300 25900, IO T135-T155 18000 20800													
27		FISHMASTER 270 SPORT	FB	FSH	FBG	SV	IO	230-310		10		5650		16700	20600
		IO 400 MRCR 20200 22400, IO 192D-230D 22700 26500, IO T135-T155												18000	20800
29	2	FISHMASTER 292	FB	CR	FBG	DV	IB	T305	VLVO	11				28800	32000
29	2	FISHMASTER 292	FB	CR	FBG	SV	IO	T205	VLVO	11				21500	23800
		IB T205 VLVO 26200 29100, IO T240 VLVO 22300 24800, IB T240 VLVO												27100	30100
		IO T250 MRCR 22400 24800, IB T250 MRCR 27200 30300, IO T305 VLVO												24000	26700
		IO T310 MRCR 23900 26600, IB T310 MRCR 28800 32000, IO T124D VLVO												21200	23600
		IB T124D VLVO 27200 30200, IO T192D VLVO 24600 27400, IB T192D VLVO												31500	35000
		IO T230D VLVO 26400 29400, IB T230D VLVO 33800 37600													
29	2	FISHMASTER 292 CUD	HT	CUD	FBG	SV	IO	T205-T310		11				22000	27200
29	2	FISHMASTER 292 CUD	HT	CUD	FBG	SV	IO	T124D	VLVO	11				22600	25100
29	2	FISHMASTER 292 CUD	HT	CUD	FBG	SV	IO	T192D-T230D		11				25800	30600
30		FISHMASTER 300 CR	HT	FSH	FBG	SV	IO	300	VLVO	10		8335		22700	25200
		IB 300-310 26200 29200, IO T180 VLVO 23400 26000, IO T205 MRCR												23800	26400
		IO T205 VLVO 23900 26500, IB T205 27600 30700, IO T240 VLVO												24600	27300
		IB T240 VLVO 28400 31600, IO T250 MRCR 24600 27400, IB T250 MRCR												31400	34900
		IO T305 VLVO 26000 28900, IB T305 VLVO 29800 33100, IO T310 MRCR												26000	28800
		IO T124D VLVO 30800 34200, IB T124D VLVO 31600 35100, IO T192D VLVO												34000	37700
		IB T192D VLVO 34800 38700, IO T230D VLVO 35700 39700													
30		FISHMASTER 300 SPORT	HT	FSH	FBG	SV	OB			10		8495		20000	22200
30		FISHMASTER 300 SPORT	HT	FSH	FBG	SV	IO	230-400		10		8495		21900	26900
		IO T180 VLVO 23500 26100, IB T205-T310 27800 33300, IBT124D-T192D												32000	39100
		IO T230D VLVO 36000 40000													
30		FISHMASTER 360	HT	FSH	FBG	SV	IB	T310-T350		10		8335		35700	41200
30		FISHMASTER 360	HT	FSH	FBG	SV	IB	T296D-T367D		10		8335		39800	48300
31		AVANZA 3100 CR	OP	CR	FBG	DV	IO	210	YAMA	11		8700		24100	26800
31		AVANZA 3100 CR	OP	CR	FBG	DV	IO	T175-T216		11		8700		25900	29800
31		AVANZA 3100 CR	OP	CR	FBG	DV	IO	T185D	VLVO	11		8700		30800	34200
		1991 BOATS													
16		FISHMASTER 160	OP	CTRCN	FBG	SV	OB			7		1100		2600	3000
16		SPRINT 1600 BR	OP	B/R	FBG	DV	OB			7		1750		3900	4550
16		SPRINT 1600 BR	OP	B/R	FBG	DV	IO	110-155		7		1750		3000	3500
16		SPRINT 1600 CB	OP	RNBT	FBG	DV	IO	110-155		7		1750		3150	3700
18		FISHMASTER 180	OP	CTRCN	FBG	SV	OB			8				4050	4700
18	2	SPRINT 1900 BR	OP	CUD	FBG	DV	IO	110-180		7	8	2550		4650	5450
18	2	SPRINT 1900 CB	OP	RNBT	FBG	DV	IO	110-180		7	8	2450		4450	5200
18	2	SPRINT 1900 CC	OP	CUD	FBG	DV	IO	110-180		7	8	2450		4600	5300
19	8	AVANZA 1900 BR	OP	B/R	FBG	DV	IO	110-180		8		2650		5000	5800
20	2	FISHMASTER 202	OP	CTRCN	FBG	DV	OB			8		2650		5850	6750
20	2	FISHMASTER 202	OP	CTRCN	FBG	DV	IO		OMC	8		2650		**	**
20	2	FISHMASTER 202 WAC	OP	FSH	FBG	SV	OB			8		2350		5550	6400
20	2	FISHMASTER 202 WAC	OP	FSH	FBG	SV	IO		OMC	8		2350		**	**
20	2	FISHMASTER 202 WAC	OP	FSH	FBG	SV	IO	110-180		8		2350		6050	7050
20	2	FISHMASTER 202 WT	OP	RNBT	FBG	SV	OB			8		2650		5950	6850
20	2	FISHMASTER 202 WT	OP	RNBT	FBG	SV	IO		OMC	8		2650		**	**
20	2	FISHMASTER 202 WT	OP	RNBT	FBG	SV	IO	110-180		8		2650		5850	6800
20	8	AVANZA 2050 BR	OP	B/R	FBG	DV	IO	155-240		8		2650		5650	6800
20	8	AVANZA 2050 BR	OP	B/R	FBG	DV	IO	245	VLVO	8		2650		6200	7100
20	8	AVANZA 2050 CC	OP	CR	FBG	SV	IO	155-240		8		2650		6050	7250
20	8	AVANZA 2050 CC	OP	CR	FBG	SV	IO	245	VLVO	8		2650		6600	7600
23	2	FISHMASTER 232	HT	CTRCN	FBG	SV	OB			8	6	3500		8900	10100
23	2	FISHMASTER 232	HT	CTRCN	FBG	SV	IO		OMC	8	6	3500		**	**
23	2	FISHMASTER 232	HT	CTRCN	FBG	SV	IO	155-245		8	6	3500		8950	10800
23	2	FISHMASTER 232 BRKT	HT	CTRCN	FBG	SV	OB			8	6	3500		9050	10300
23	2	FISHMASTER 232 BRKT	OP	CUD	FBG	SV	OB			8	6	4450		10300	11800
23	2	FISHMASTER 232 BRKT	OP	FSH	FBG	SV	IO	155	MRCR	8	6	4250		10200	11500
23	2	FISHMASTER 232 SPORT	OP	FSH	FBG	SV	OB			8	6	4250		10000	11300
23	2	FISHMASTER 232 SPORT	OP	FSH	FBG	SV	IO		OMC	8	6	3770		**	**
23	2	FISHMASTER 232 SPORT	OP	FSH	FBG	SV	IO	155-245		8	6	4250		10600	12300
23	2	FISHMASTER 232 WAC	OP	CUD	FBG	SV	OB			8	6	4450		10200	11600
23	2	FISHMASTER 232 WAC	OP	CUD	FBG	SV	IO			8	6	4450		**	**
23	2	FISHMASTER 232 WAC	OP	CUD	FBG	SV	IO	155-245		8	6	4450		10100	12100
24	2	FISHMASTER 250	HT	FSH	FBG	SV	IO	155-250		8		4050		10300	12400
24	2	FISHMASTER 250 CR	HT	CR	FBG	SV	IO	155-245		8		4250		10000	12100
25	2	FISHMASTER 252 BRKT	HT	FSH	FBG	SV	OB			8	6	4450		11300	12900
25	2	FISHMASTER 252 SPORT	HT	FSH	FBG	SV	OB			8	6	4400		11200	12800
25	2	FISHMASTER 252 SPORT	HT	FSH	FBG	SV	IO		OMC	8	6	4000		**	**
25	2	FISHMASTER 252 SPORT	HT	FSH	FBG	SV	IO	155-245		8	6	4400		11300	13900
25	2	FISHMASTER 252 SPORT	HT	FSH	FBG	SV	IO	T	OMC	8	6	4000		**	**
25	2	FISHMASTER 252 WAC	HT	FSH	FBG	SV	OB			8	6	4450		11200	12800
25	2	FISHMASTER 252 WAC	HT	FSH	FBG	SV	IO		OMC	8	6	4450		**	**
25	2	FISHMASTER 252 WAC	HT	FSH	FBG	SV	IO	155-245		8	6	4450		11400	14000
25	2	FISHMASTER 252 WAC	HT	FSH	FBG	SV	IO	T	OMC	8	6	4450		**	**
25	6	AVANZA 2500 CR	OP	CR	FBG	DV	IO	180-245		8	6	3800		10300	12400
25	6	AVANZA 2500 CR	OP	CR	FBG	DV	IO	300	MRCR	8	6	3800		11400	12900
25	6	AVANZA 2500 CUDDY	OP	CUD	FBG	DV	IO	180-245		8	6	3200		9450	11400
25	6	AVANZA 2500 CUDDY	OP	CUD	FBG	DV	IO	300	MRCR	8	6	3200		10600	12000
27		FISHMASTER 270	HT	FSH	FBG	SV	OB			10		4850		13800	15700
27		FISHMASTER 270	HT	FSH	FBG	SV	IO	230	MRCR	10		4850		14600	16600
		IO 240 YAMA 14700 16700, IB 240 VLVO 17300 19600, IO 245 VLVO												14900	17000
		IB 250 MRCR 17300 19700, IO 300 15600 18000, IB 305-400												18500	21700
		IB 192D VLVO 19900 22200, IO T OMC ** **, IO T110-T155												15200	18300
27		FISHMASTER 270 SPORT	HT	FSH	FBG	SV	OB			10		5650		13900	15800
27		FISHMASTER 270 SPORT	HT	FSH	FBG	SV	IO	230	MRCR	10		5650		15700	17900
		IO 240 YAMA 15800 18000, IB 240 VLVO 19000 21100, IO 245 VLVO												16100	18200
		IB 250 MRCR 19000 21200, IO 300 16700 19200, IB 305-400												19600	23100
		IB 192D VLVO 22300 24700, IO T OMC ** **, IO T110-T155												16300	19500
29	2	FISHMASTER 292	FB	CR	FBG	DV	IB	305-400		11				23200	27300
		IB 296D VLVO 26900 29900, IB T205-T310 24900 30400, IB T124D VLVO												25900	28800
		IB T192D VLVO 30100 33400													
30		FISHMASTER 300 CR	HT	FSH	FBG	SV	OB			10		8335		19200	21400
30		FISHMASTER 300 CR	HT	FSH	FBG	SV	IO	230-300		10		8335		20400	23700
		IO T OMC ** **, IO T180 VLVO 21900 24400, IO T205 MRCR												22300	24800
		IB T205-T310 26300 30100, IBT124D-T192D 30200 37000													
30		FISHMASTER 300 SPORT	HT	FSH	FBG	SV	OB			10		8495		19200	21400
30		FISHMASTER 300 SPORT	HT	FSH	FBG	SV	IO	230	MRCR	10		8495		20500	22800
		IB 240 VLVO 24300 27000, IO 245 VLVO 20700 23100, IB 250 MRCR												24400	27100
		IO 300 21300 23800, IB 305-400 25100 29100, IO T OMC												**	**
		IO T205 MRCR 22400 24900, IB T205-T305 26400 31600, IBT124D-T192D												30500	37300
30		FISHMASTER 360	HT	FSH	FBG	SV	IB	T305-T400		10		8335		34000	37800
30		FISHMASTER 360	HT	FSH	FBG	SV	IB	T296D-T367D		10		8335		38000	46100
31		AVANZA 3100 CR	OP	CR	FBG	DV	IO	230-300		11		8700		22900	26400
		IO T155-T245 23900 28600, IO T300 VLVO 26900 29900, IO T185D VLVO												28900	32100

 CONTINUED ON NEXT PAGE

LOA FT	LOA IN	NAME AND/ OR MODEL	TOP/ RIG	BOAT TYPE	-HULL- MTL	-HULL- TP	ENGINE TP	ENGINE # HP	ENGINE MFG	BEAM FT	BEAM IN	WGT LBS	DRAFT FT IN	RETAIL LOW	RETAIL HIGH
		1990 BOATS													
16		FISHMASTER 160	OP	CTRCN	FBG	SV	OB			7		1100		2500	2900
16		SPRINT 1600 BR	OP	B/R	FBG	DV	IO	130-175		7		1750		2650	3250
16		SPRINT 1600 CB	OP	RNBT	FBG	DV	IO	130-175		7		1750		2800	3500
18	2	SPRINT 1900 BR	OP	B/R	FBG	DV	SE		OMC	7	8	2450		**	**
18	2	SPRINT 1900 BR	OP	B/R	FBG	DV	IO	130-230		7	8	2450		3850	4650
18	2	SPRINT 1900 BR	OP	B/R	FBG	DV	IO	231-260		7	8	2450		4200	4900
18	2	SPRINT 1900 CB	OP	RNBT	FBG	DV	SE		OMC	7	8	2450		**	**
18	2	SPRINT 1900 CB	OP	RNBT	FBG	DV	IO	130-230		7	8	2450		4000	4850
18	2	SPRINT 1900 CB	OP	RNBT	FBG	DV	IO	231-260		7	8	2450		4400	5100
18	2	SPRINT 1900 CC	OP	CUD	FBG	DV	SE		OMC	7	8	2550		**	**
18	2	SPRINT 1900 CC	OP	CUD	FBG	DV	IO	130-230		7	8	2550		4200	5100
18	2	SPRINT 1900 CC	OP	CUD	FBG	DV	IO	231-260		7	8	2550		4650	5350
20	2	FISHMASTER 200	OP	FSH	FBG	SV	SE		OMC	7	6	2400		**	**
20	2	FISHMASTER 202	OP	FSH	FBG	SV	OB			8				5500	6350
20	2	FISHMASTER 202	OP	FSH	FBG	SV	SE		OMC	8				**	**
20	2	FISHMASTER 202 WAC	OP	FSH	FBG	SV	OB			8		2350		5350	6150
20	2	FISHMASTER 202 WAC	OP	FSH	FBG	SV	SE		OMC	8		2350		**	**
20	2	FISHMASTER 202 WAC	OP	FSH	FBG	SV	IO	130-205		8		2350		5450	6700
20	2	FISHMASTER 202 WT	OP	RNBT	FBG	SV	SE		OMC	8		2650		**	**
20	2	FISHMASTER 202 WT	OP	RNBT	FBG	SV	IO	130-205		8		2650		5300	6450
20	8	AVANZA 2050	OP	CR	FBG	SV	IO	175-260		7	7	2620		5500	6700
20	8	AVANZA 2050	OP	CR	FBG	SV	IO	270	VLVO	7	7	2620		6250	7150
20	9	SPRINT 2100 CC	OP	CUD	FBG	DV	IO	130-230		8	1	2850		5950	7250
23	2	FISHMASTER 232	ST	CTRCN	FBG	SV	OB			8	6	3500		8550	9800
23	2	FISHMASTER 232	ST	CTRCN	FBG	SV	SE		OMC	8	6	3500		**	**
23	2	FISHMASTER 232	ST	CTRCN	FBG	SV	IO	175-260		8	6	3500		8350	10100
23	2	FISHMASTER 232	ST	CTRCN	FBG	SV	SE	T	OMC	8	6	3500		**	**
23	2	FISHMASTER 232	ST	CUD	FBG	SV	OB			8	6	4050		9500	10800
23	2	FISHMASTER 232	ST	CUD	FBG	SV	SE		OMC	8	6	4050		**	**
23	2	FISHMASTER 232	ST	CUD	FBG	SV	IO	175-260		8	6	4050		8850	10600
23	2	FISHMASTER 232	ST	CUD	FBG	SV	SE	T	OMC	8	6	4050		**	**
23	2	FISHMASTER 232 SPORT	HT	FSH	FBG	SV	OB			8	6	4250		9600	10900
23	2	FISHMASTER 232 SPORT	HT	FSH	FBG	SV	SE		OMC	8	6	4250		**	**
23	2	FISHMASTER 232 SPORT	HT	FSH	FBG	SV	IO	175-260		8	6	4250		9650	11500
23	2	FISHMASTER 232 WAC	OP	CUD	FBG	SV	OB			8	6	4450		9900	11300
23	2	FISHMASTER 232 WAC	OP	CUD	FBG	SV	SE		OMC	8	6	4450		**	**
23	2	FISHMASTER 232 WAC	OP	CUD	FBG	SV	IO	175-260		8	6	4450		9500	11200
23	2	FISHMASTER 232 WAC	OP	CUD	FBG	SV	SE	T	OMC	8	6	4450		**	**
24	2	FISHMASTER 250	HT	CUD	FBG	SV	IO	175	MRCR	8		4050		9250	10500
		IB 220 CRUS 11700 13300, IO 230-231 9400 10900, IO 260 MRCR												9600	10900
		IB 260 MRCR 11700 13200, IO 271 VLVO 10000 11300													
24	2	FISHMASTER 250 CR	HT	CR	FBG	SV	IO	175-271		8		4250		9450	11600
24	2	FISHMASTER 250 CR	HT	CR	FBG	SV	SE	T	OMC	8		4250		**	**
25	2	AVANZA 2650	OP	CR	FBG	SV	IO	260-300		8	6	6525		14200	16600
25	2	AVANZA 2650	OP	CR	FBG	SV	IO	T175-T205		8	6	6525		15000	17800
25	2	FISHMASTER 252	ST	CTRCN	FBG	SV	OB			8	6	3850		10100	11400
25	2	FISHMASTER 252	ST	CTRCN	FBG	SV	SE		OMC	8	6	3850		**	**
25	2	FISHMASTER 252	ST	CTRCN	FBG	SV	IB	200-260		8	6	3850		12000	13900
25	2	FISHMASTER 252	ST	CTRCN	FBG	SV	IB	200D	VLVO	8	6	3850		15500	17600
25	6	AVANZA 2500	OP	CUD	FBG	SV	IO	230-300		8	6	3200		9200	11300
25	6	AVANZA 2500 CR	OP	CR	FBG	SV	IO	230-300		8	6	3800		9900	12100
27		FISHMASTER 270	FB	FSH	FBG	SV	OB			10		4850		13100	14900
27		FISHMASTER 270	FB	FSH	FBG	SV	IO	260	MRCR	10		4850		14100	16000
		IB 260 MRCR 16600 18800, IO 271-300 14400 16700, IB 340 MRCR												17600	20000
		IB 502 MRCR 20200 22400, IO 740 VLVO 24200 26800, IB 200D VLVO												19300	21400
27		FISHMASTER 270	FB	FSH	FBG	SV	SE	T	OMC	10		4850		**	**
27		FISHMASTER 270	FB	FSH	FBG	SV	IO	T130-T175		10		4850		14400	17300
27		FISHMASTER 270 CR	ST	CR	FBG	SV	OB			10		4950		13500	15300
27		FISHMASTER 270 CR	ST	CR	FBG	SV	IO	260	MRCR	10		4950		13500	15300
		IB 260 MRCR 16700 19000, IO 271-330 13800 16700, IB 340-502												18100	22600
		IB 200D VLVO 19500 21700													
27		FISHMASTER 270 CR	ST	CR	FBG	SV	SE	T	OMC	10		4950		**	**
27		FISHMASTER 270 CR	ST	CR	FBG	SV	IO	T130-T175		10		4950		13800	16500
27		FISHMASTER 270 SPORT	HT	FSH	FBG	SV	OB			10		5650		13400	15300
27		FISHMASTER 270 SPORT	HT	FSH	FBG	SV	IO	260	MRCR	10		5650		15100	17200
		IB 260 MRCR 18200 20200, IO 271-330 15400 18600, IB 340-502												19200	23700
		IB 200D VLVO 21500 23900													
27		FISHMASTER 270 SPORT	HT	FSH	FBG	SV	SE	T	OMC	10		5650		**	**
27		FISHMASTER 270 SPORT	HT	FSH	FBG	SV	IO	T130-T175		10		5650		15500	18400
30		FISHMASTER 300 CR	FB	CR	FBG	SV	OB			10		8335		19000	21100
30		FISHMASTER 300 CR	FB	CR	FBG	SV	IO	260-300		10		8335		19500	22300
30		FISHMASTER 300 CR	FB	CR	FBG	SV	SE	T	OMC	10		8335		**	**
30		FISHMASTER 300 CR	FB	CR	FBG	SV	IB	T220	CRUS	10		8335		26800	29700
		IO T230 MRCR 21500 23800, IB T260-T340 27500 32400, IBT130D-T200D												30800	37700
30		FISHMASTER 300 SPORT	HT	FSH	FBG	SV	OB			10		8495		18800	20900
30		FISHMASTER 300 SPORT	HT	FSH	FBG	SV	IO	260	MRCR	10		8495		19600	21800
		IB 260 MRCR 23300 25900, IO 271-330 19800 22800, IB 340-502												24200	29100
30		FISHMASTER 300 SPORT	HT	FSH	FBG	SV	SE	T	OMC	10		8495		**	**
30		FISHMASTER 300 SPORT	HT	FSH	FBG	SV	IB	T220	CRUS	10		8495		25400	28200
		IO T230 MRCR 21500 23900, IB T260-T340 26100 30700, IBT130D-T200D												29400	36000
36		FISHMASTER 360	HT	CR	FBG	SV	IB	T340	MRCR	13		16500		58500	64300
		IB T502 MRCR 63800 70200, IB T306D VLVO 67300 73900, IB T380D VLVO												71100	78200
36		PESCA 360	OP	CR	FBG	SV	IB	T340	MRCR	13		16500		58500	64300
		IB T502 MRCR 63800 70200, IB T306D VLVO 67300 73900, IB T380D VLVO												71100	78100
36		PESCAMORE 360	FB	CR	FBG	SV	IB	T340	MRCR	13		17500		60300	66300
		IB T502 MRCR 65600 72100, IB T130D VLVO 63700 70000, IB T200D VLVO												65300	71800
		1989 BOATS													
16		FISHMASTER 160	OP	FSH	FBG	SV	OB			7		1200		2600	3050
16		SPRINT LINER 1600	OP	RNBT	FBG	DV	IO	131-260		7		1960		3000	3700
16		SPRINT LINER 1600	OP	RNBT	FBG	DV	IO	271	VLVO	7		1960		3450	4000
17	1	SPORTSMAN 180 BR	ST	RNBT	FBG	DV	IO	205	OMC	7	2	2110		3200	3700
18	2	SPRINT LINER 1900 BR	ST	RNBT	FBG	DV	SE		OMC	7	8	2690		**	**
18	2	SPRINT LINER 1900 BR	ST	RNBT	FBG	DV	IO		OMC	7	8	2690		**	**
		IO 130-205 3950 4900, IO 260-270 4250 5050, IO 271 VLVO												4650	5350
18	5	AVANZA 1850	OP	RNBT	FBG	DV	IO	130-260		7	8	2690		4200	5100
18	5	AVANZA 1850	OP	RNBT	FBG	DV	IO	271	VLVO	7	7	2620		4600	5300
18	5	SPRINT 1900 BR	OP	RNBT	FBG	DV	SE		OMC	7	8	2690		**	**
18	5	SPRINT 1900 BR	OP	RNBT	FBG	DV	IO	130-131		7	8	2690		3800	4600
18	5	SPRINT 1900 BR	OP	RNBT	FBG	DV	IO	151-270		7	8	2690		4200	5100
18	5	SPRINT 1900 BR	OP	RNBT	FBG	DV	IO	271	VLVO	7	8	2690		4700	5400
18	9	SPRINT 1900 BR	ST	FSH	FBG	DV	SE		OMC	7	8	2690		**	**
18	9	SPRINT 1900 CC	ST	CUD	FBG	DV	SE		OMC	7	6	2080		**	**
18	9	SPRINT 1900 CC	ST	CUD	FBG	DV	IO		OMC	7	6	2080		**	**
18	9	SPRINT 1900 CC	ST	CUD	FBG	DV	IO	130-175		7	6	2080		3650	4450
18	9	SPRINT LINER 1900 CC	OP	CUD	FBG	DV	SE			7	6	2080		**	**
18	9	SPRINT LINER 1900 CC	OP	CUD	FBG	DV	IO		OMC	7	6	2080		**	**
18	9	SPRINT LINER 1900 CC	OP	CUD	FBG	DV	IO	130-175		7	6	2080		3650	4250
20	2	FISHMASTER 200	ST	CTRCN	FBG	DV	SE		OMC	7	6	2400		**	**
20	2	FISHMASTER 202	OP	FSH	FBG	DV	OB			8		2450		5250	6050
20	2	FISHMASTER 202	OP	FSH	FBG	DV	SE		OMC	8		2450		**	**
20	2	FISHMASTER 202	OP	FSH	FBG	SV	SE		OMC	8		2450		**	**
20	2	FISHMASTER 205 WAC	ST	FSH	FBG	SV	OB			8		2645		5450	6250
20	2	FISHMASTER 205 WAC	ST	FSH	FBG	SV	SE		OMC	8		3015		**	**
20	2	FISHMASTER 205 WAC	ST	FSH	FBG	SV	IO	165-175		8		3015		5950	7100
20	2	FISHMASTER 205 WT	ST	FSH	FBG	DV	IO	205	VLVO	8		3020		6250	7200
20	2	FISHMASTER 205 WT	ST	FSH	FBG	SV	SE		OMC	8		3020		**	**
20	2	FISHMASTER 205 WT	ST	FSH	FBG	SV	IO	130-205		8		3020		5950	7200
20	9	SPRINT LINER 2100 CC	ST	CUD	FBG	DV	SE		OMC	8	1	3682		**	**
20	9	SPRINT LINER 2100 CC	ST	CUD	FBG	DV	IO		OMC	8	1	3682		**	**
20	9	SPRINT LINER 2100 CC	ST	CUD	FBG	DV	IO	130-231		8	1	3682		6650	8150
20	9	SPRINT LINER 2100 CC	ST	FSH	FBG	DV	SE		OMC	8	1	3682		**	**
20	9	SPRINT LINER 2100 CC	ST	FSH	FBG	DV	IO	130-231		8	1	3682		7000	8600
20	9	SPRINT LINER 2100 CC	ST	FSH	FBG	DV	IO	350	OMC	8	1	3682		8600	9850
22	2	FISHMASTER 222 WAC	ST	CUD	FBG	DV	OB			7	6	2710		6650	7600
22	2	FISHMASTER 222 WAC	ST	CUD	FBG	DV	SE		OMC	7	6	2710		**	**
22	2	FISHMASTER 222 WAC	ST	CUD	FBG	DV	IO	165-231		7	6	2710		5750	7050
23	2	FISHMASTER 232	OP	CUD	FBG	DV	IO			8	6	4350		**	**
		IO T ** ** , IO T205-T260 9900 12000, IO T271 VLVO												11200	12700
23	2	FISHMASTER 232	ST	CUD	FBG	DV	SE		OMC	8	6	4350		**	**
23	2	FISHMASTER 232	ST	CUD	FBG	DV	SE	T	OMC	8	6	4350		**	**
24	2	C-EAGLE 250	ST	CUD	FBG	DV	IB	220	CRUS	8		4050		11100	12600
		IO 230-231 8800 10300, IO 260 MRCR 9000 10200, IO 260 OMC												8950	10200
		IB 260-270 11000 12700, IO 271 VLVO 9400 10700, IO T												**	**
24	2	CAPRICE 250	ST	CUD	FBG	DV	SE		OMC	8		4820		**	**
24	2	CAPRICE 250	ST	CUD	FBG	DV	IO			8		4820		**	**
24	2	CAPRICE 250	ST	CUD	FBG	DV	IO	230-271		8		4820		10000	12000
24	2	CAPRICE 250	ST	CUD	FBG	DV	SE	T	OMC	8		4820		**	**
24	2	FISHERMAN 250	ST	FSH	FBG	DV	OB			8		4050		9650	11000

CONTINUED ON NEXT PAGE

SPORT-CRAFT BOATS   -CONTINUED   See inside cover to adjust price for area

LOA FT IN	NAME AND/ OR MODEL	TOP/ RIG	BOAT TYPE	HULL MTL TP	ENGINE TP # HP MFG	BEAM FT IN	WGT LBS	DRAFT FT IN	RETAIL LOW	RETAIL HIGH
					1989 BOATS					
24 2	FISHERMAN 250	ST	FSH	FBG DV	IO 230-271	8	4050		9300	11200
24 2	FISHMASTER 242 WAC	ST	FSH	FBG DV	OB	8	3060		7850	9050
24 2	FISHMASTER 242 WAC	ST	FSH	FBG DV	SE OMC	8	3060		**	**
24 2	FISHMASTER 242 WAC	ST	FSH	FBG DV	IO 230-271	8	3060		7650	9450
24 2	FISHMASTER 242 WAC	ST	FSH	FBG DV	SE T OMC	8	3060		**	**
25 2	CAPRICE 252	OP	CUD	FBG DV	IO MRCR	8 6	6925		**	**
25 2	CAPRICE 252	OP	CUD	FBG DV	IO OMC	8 6	6925		**	**
25 2	CAPRICE 252	OP	CUD	FBG DV	IO 260-271	8 6	6925		14000	16300
25 2	CAPRICE 252	OP	CUD	FBG DV	SE T OMC	8 6	6925		**	**
25 2	CAPRICE 252	OP	CUD	FBG DV	IO T165-T175	8 6	6925		14700	16700
25 2	FISHMASTER 252	OP	CTRCN	FBG DV	OB	8 6	4490		10200	11600
25 2	FISHMASTER 252	OP	CTRCN	FBG DV	SE OMC	8 6	4490		**	**
25 2	FISHMASTER 252	OP	CTRCN	FBG DV	IO 260-271	8 6	4490		10900	12800
25 2	FISHMASTER 252	OP	CTRCN	FBG DV	IB 340-350	8 6	4490		13400	15600
25 2	FISHMASTER 252	OP	CTRCN	FBG DV	IB 200D VLVO	8 6	4490		16300	18600
25 2	FISHMASTER 252	OP	CTRCN	FBG DV	SE T OMC	8 6	4490		**	**
25 2	FISHMASTER 252 W/BRC	OP	CTRCN	FBG DV	OB	8 6	4490		10300	11700
25 2	AVANZA 2400 CR	ST	CR	FBG DV	IO OMC	8 6	5300		**	**
25 6	AVANZA 2400 CR	ST	CR	FBG DV	IO 230-271	8	5300		11400	13600
25 6	AVANZA 2400 CUDDY	ST	CUD	FBG DV	IO 230-271	8	4960		10900	13100
25 6	AVANZA 2400 CUDDY	ST	CUD	FBG DV	IO 460 OMC	8	4960		14900	16900
27	CAPRICE 270	ST	CUD	FBG DV	IO	10	5725		**	**
	IO MRCR ** ** , IO 260-311 13600 16400, IB 340-350 19100 20500									
27	CAPRICE 270	ST	CUD	FBG DV	SE T OMC	10	5725		**	**
27	CAPRICE 270	ST	CUD	FBG DV	IO T171-T175	10	5725		14700	16700
27	COASTAL FISH 270	ST	FSH	FBG DV	IO	10	5650		**	**
	IO MRCR ** ** , IO 260 MRCR 14300 16200, IO 260 OMC 14200 16200									
	IB 260-350 17000 20500, IO 271D VLVO 20900 23200									
27	COASTAL FISH 270	ST	FSH	FBG DV	SE T OMC	10	5650		**	**
27	COASTAL FISH 270	ST	FSH	FBG DV	IO	10	5650		14600	18100
27	COASTAL FISH 270	ST	FSH	FBG DV	IO T130-T205	10	5650		**	**
27	COASTAL SF 270	HT	SF	FBG DV	IO	10	5650		16900	20500
27	COASTAL SF 270	HT	SF	FBG DV	IB 260-350	10	5650		23400	26000
27	COASTAL SF 270	HT	SF	FBG DV	IB 306D VLVO	10	5650		**	**
27	COASTAL SF 270	HT	SF	FBG DV	SE T OMC	10	5650		**	**
27	FISHERMAN 270	ST	FSH	FBG DV	IO	10	5510		**	**
	IO MRCR ** ** , IO 260 MRCR 14100 16000, IO 260 OMC 14100 16000									
	IB 260-270 16700 19300, IB 271 VLVO 14400 16300, IB 340-350 18000 20300									
27	FISHERMAN 270	ST	FSH	FBG DV	SE T OMC	10	5510		**	**
27	FISHERMAN 270	ST	FSH	FBG DV	IO T	10	5510		**	**
27	SPORT FISHERMAN 270	HT	SF	FBG DV	IO	10	5840		17200	20800
27	SPORT FISHERMAN 270	HT	SF	FBG DV	IB 260-350	10	5840		**	**
27	SPORT FISHERMAN 270	HT	SF	FBG DV	SE T OMC	10	5840		**	**
27	SPORT FISHERMAN 270	HT	SF	FBG DV	IO T	10	5840		**	**
30	CAPRICE 300	ST	CUD	FBG DV	IB	10	8335		**	**
30	CAPRICE 300	ST	CUD	FBG DV	IB T OMC	10	8335		24100	29400
30	CAPRICE 300	ST	CUD	FBG DV	IB T220-T350	10	8335		30700	34100
30	CAPRICE 300	ST	CUD	FBG DV	IB T200D VLVO	10	8335		**	**
30	CAPRICE 300 CB	FB	SF	FBG DV	IO	10	8665		20100	22400
30	CAPRICE 300 CB	FB	SF	FBG DV	IO 260 MRCR	10	8665		**	**
30	CAPRICE 300 CB	FB	SF	FBG DV	IO T OMC	10	8665		**	**
30	CAPRICE 300 CB	FB	SF	FBG DV	IO T	10	8665		22500	25000
	IB T220 CRUS 24300 27000, IO T230-T231 22000 24600, IO T260 OMC 22500 25000									
	IB T260-T270 25000 28000, IO T271 VLVO 22900 25400, IB T340-T350 26400 29600									
	IB T124D VLVO 28200 31400									
30	COASTAL FISH 300	ST	CUD	FBG DV	IB	10	8795		**	**
30	COASTAL FISH 300	ST	CUD	FBG DV	IB 340-350	10	8795		23300	26100
30	COASTAL FISH 300	ST	CUD	FBG DV	IB T OMC	10	8795		**	**
30	COASTAL FISH 300	ST	CUD	FBG DV	IB T	10	8795		**	**
30	COASTAL FISH 300	ST	CUD	FBG DV	IB T250-T350	10	8795		24400	29800
39	COASTAL FISH 300	ST	CUD	FBG DV	IB T124D VLVO	10	8795		28500	31700
39	PESCA 360	HT	CUD	FBG DV	IB T340 MRCR	13	19000	3 1	71200	78200
	IB T350 CRUS 72100 79300, IB T250D CUM 80000 88000, IB T250D GM 80500 88500									
	IB T306D VLVO 81200 89200, IB T358D VLVO 84000 92300, IB T375D CAT 90600 99500									
	IB T400D GM 89500 98300, IB T425D CUM 90600 99600									
39	PESCAMORE 360	HT	CUD	FBG DV	IB T340 MRCR				64800	71200
	IB T350 CRUS 65800 72300, IB T250D CUM 76900 84500, IB T250D GM 77300 85000									
	IB T306D VLVO 78000 85700, IB T358D VLVO 80800 88800, IB T375D CAT 87400 96000									
	IB T400D GM 86300 94800, IB T425D CUM 87400 96100									
					1988 BOATS					
16	FISHERMAN 160	OP	FSH	FBG SV	OB	7	1200		2550	2950
16	SKI KING 160	ST	RNBT	FBG SV	OB 120-180	7 4	1960		2650	3150
16 1	FISHERMAN 170	OP	FSH	FBG SV	OB	6 4	1170		2450	2900
17 1	FISHERMAN 172	ST	CTRCN	FBG DV	SE OMC	7 2	2140		**	**
17 1	SPORTSMAN 180 BR	ST	RNBT	FBG DV	SE	7 2	1470		3050	3500
17 1	SPORTSMAN 180 BR	ST	RNBT	FBG DV	SE OMC	7 2	2110		**	**
18 1	SPORTSMAN 180 BR	ST	RNBT	FBG DV	SE 120-205	7 2	2110		3000	3550
18 2	FISH'N SKI 190 BR	ST	RNBT	FBG DV	IO	7 8	1700		**	**
18 2	FISH'N SKI 190 BR	ST	RNBT	FBG DV	IO MRCR	7 8	1700		**	**
	IO OMC ** ** , IO 120-230 3050 3800, IO 260 3400 3950									
18 2	FISH'N SKI 190 CB	ST	RNBT	FBG DV	OB	7 8	1170		2600	3050
18 2	FISH'N SKI 190 CB	ST	RNBT	FBG DV	OMC	7 8	1700		**	**
18 2	FISH'N SKI 190 CB	ST	RNBT	FBG DV	MRCR	7 8	1700		**	**
	IO OMC ** ** , IO 120-230 3000 3750, IO 260 3400 3900									
18 2	SKI KING 185	OP	RNBT	FBG DV	IO 120-205	7 8	2690		3750	4450
18 5	SKI KING 190	OP	RNBT	FBG DV	IO OMC	7 7			**	**
18 5	SKI KING 190	OP	RNBT	FBG DV	SE	7 7			**	**
18 5	SKI KING 190	OP	RNBT	FBG DV	MRCR	7 7			**	**
18 5	SKI KING 190	OP	RNBT	FBG DV	IO 120-230	7 7			3350	4100
18 5	SKI KING 190	OP	RNBT	FBG DV	IO 260	7 7			3650	4250
18 9	C-EAGLE 190	ST	CUD	FBG DV	IO 120-205	7 6	2080		3450	4100
18 9	FISHERMAN 190	ST	CUD	FBG DV	IO	7 6	2080		**	**
18 9	FISHERMAN 190	OP	CUD	FBG DV	SE	7 6	2080		**	**
18 9	FISHERMAN 190	OP	CUD	FBG DV	IO MRCR	7 6	2080		**	**
18 9	FISHERMAN 190	OP	CUD	FBG DV	IO OMC	7 6	2080		**	**
18 9	FISHERMAN 190	OP	CUD	FBG DV	IO 230-260	7 6	2080		3600	4350
20 2	FISHERMAN 200	ST	CTRCN	FBG DV	SE OMC	8	2530		**	**
20 2	FISHERMAN 205 WT	ST	FSH	FBG DV	SE OMC	8	2900		**	**
20 2	FISHERMAN 205 WT	ST	FSH	FBG SV	IO 130-205	8	3020		5600	6550
20 2	OFFSHORE 205	ST	FSH	FBG SV	OB	8	2645		5250	6050
20 2	OFFSHORE 205	ST	FSH	FBG SV	OMC	8	3105		**	**
20 2	OFFSHORE 205	ST	FSH	FBG SV	IO 130-205	8	3105		5600	6650
20 9	C-EAGLE 210	ST	CUD	FBG DV	SE OMC	8 1	3682		**	**
20 9	C-EAGLE 210	ST	CUD	FBG DV	IO MRCR	8 1	3682		**	**
20 9	C-EAGLE 210	ST	CUD	FBG DV	IO OMC	8 1	3682		**	**
20 9	C-EAGLE 210	ST	CUD	FBG DV	IO 230-260	8 1	3682		6300	7650
20 9	FISHERMAN 210	ST	FSH	FBG DV	SE OMC	8 1	3682		**	**
20 9	FISHERMAN 210	ST	FSH	FBG DV	IO 130-260	8 1	3682		6650	8050
22 2	FISHERMAN 230	ST	FSH	FBG DV	IO 165-260	7 6	3450		6700	8050
22 2	OFFSHORE 222	ST	CUD	FBG DV	OB	7 6	2710		6400	7350
22 2	OFFSHORE 222	ST	CUD	FBG DV	OMC	7 6	4310		**	**
22 2	OFFSHORE 222	ST	CUD	FBG DV	IO 165-230	7 6	4310		700	7300
22 2	SPORTSMAN 230	ST	RNBT	FBG DV	IB CRUS	7 6	3450		**	**
	IO 165-205 6000 6950, IB 220 CRUS 8300 9500, IO 230 MRCR 6150 7050									
	IO 230 OMC 6100 7000, IB 230 MRCR 8150 9350, IO 260 6300 7200									
24 2	C-EAGLE 250	ST	CUD	FBG DV	IO OMC	8	4050		**	**
24 2	C-EAGLE 250	ST	CUD	FBG DV	IO MRCR	8	4050		**	**
	IO 230 OMC 8200 9450, IB 220 CRUS 10500 12000, IO 230 MRCR 8250 9500									
	IO 260 OMC 8400 9650, IB 230 MRCR 10400 11800, IO 260 MRCR 8450 9700									
	IB 260-270 10500 12100									
24 2	FISHERMAN 250	ST	CUD	FBG DV	SE T OMC	8	4050		**	**
24 2	FISHERMAN 250	ST	FSH	FBG DV	SE OMC	8	4050		**	**
24 2	FISHERMAN 250	ST	FSH	FBG DV	IO MRCR	8	4050		**	**
24 2	FISHERMAN 250	ST	FSH	FBG DV	IO	8	4050		**	**
24 2	FISHERMAN 250	ST	FSH	FBG DV	IO 230-260	8	4050		8800	10200
24 2	OFFSHORE 242	ST	FSH	FBG DV	OB	8	3060		7600	8700
24 2	OFFSHORE 242	ST	FSH	FBG DV	SE OMC	8	4400		**	**
24 2	OFFSHORE 242	ST	FSH	FBG DV	IO MRCR	8	4400		**	**
24 2	OFFSHORE 242	ST	FSH	FBG DV	IO	8	4400		**	**
24 2	OFFSHORE 242	ST	CUD	FBG DV	IO 230-260	8	4400		9400	10800
24 2	OFFSHORE 242	ST	CUD	FBG DV	IO OMC	8	4400		**	**
24 2	OFFSHORE 250	ST	CUD	FBG DV	SE OMC	8	4820		**	**
24 2	OFFSHORE 250	ST	CUD	FBG DV	IO MRCR	8	4820		**	**
24 2	OFFSHORE 250	ST	CUD	FBG DV	IO	8	4820		**	**
24 2	OFFSHORE 250	ST	CUD	FBG DV	IO 230-260	8	4820		9500	11000
24 2	OFFSHORE 250	ST	CUD	FBG DV	SE T OMC	8	4820		**	**
25 2	CAPRICE 252	OP	CUD	FBG DV	IO MRCR	8 6	6925		**	**
	IO OMC ** ** , IO 260 13300 15100, IO T130-T180 13700 16000									
25 2	FISHERMAN 252	OP	CTRCN	FBG DV	OB	8 6	4490		9900	11300

```
 LOA  NAME AND/                TOP/ BOAT  -HULL- ----ENGINE--- BEAM   WGT  DRAFT RETAIL RETAIL
 FT IN  OR MODEL                RIG TYPE  MTL TP TP # HP  MFG  FT IN  LBS  FT IN   LOW   HIGH
---------------------- 1988 BOATS -------------------------------------------------------------
 25   2 FISHERMAN 252          OP  CTRCN FBG DV SE        OMC   8  6  4490            **     **
 25   2 FISHERMAN 252          OP  CTRCN FBG DV IO        MRCR  8  6  4490            **     **
      IO       OMC      **     ** , IB 200-220      12000  13700, IO  230  MRCR  10100  11400
      IO  230  OMC   10000  11400, IB 230-350       12000  14800

 25   2 FISHERMAN 252          OP  CTRCN FBG DV SE T      OMC   8  6  4490            **     **
 27     C-EAGLE 270            ST  CUD   FBG DV SE        OMC  10     5510            **     **
 27     C-EAGLE 270            ST  CUD   FBG DV IO        MRCR 10     5510            **     **
      IO       OMC      **     ** , IO  260  MRCR  12600  14400, IO  260  OMC  12600  14300
      IB 260-350     16000  19400, IB  200D VLVO  19300  21500, IB  306D VLVO  22100  24600

 27     C-EAGLE 270            ST  CUD   FBG DV SE T      OMC  10     5510            **     **
 27     C-EAGLE 270            ST  CUD   FBG DV IO T130-T205   10     5510         12900  15900
 27     C-EAGLE 270            ST  CUD   FBG DV IO T230-T260   10     5510         14300  16800
 27     COASTAL FISH 270       ST  FSH   FBG DV SE        OMC  10     5650            **     **
 27     COASTAL FISH 270       ST  FSH   FBG DV IO        MRCR 10     5650            **     **
      IO       OMC      **     ** , IO  260  MRCR  13500  15400, IO  260  OMC  13500  15300
      IB 260-350     16200  19600, IB  200D VLVO  19700  21900, IB  306D VLVO  22400  24900

 27     COASTAL FISH 270       ST  FSH   FBG DV SE T      OMC  10     5650            **     **
 27     COASTAL FISH 270       ST  FSH   FBG DV IO T130-T205   10     5650         13800  16900
 27     COASTAL FISH 270       ST  FSH   FBG DV IO T230-T260   10     5650         15300  17900
 27     COASTAL SF 270         HT  SF    FBG DV SE        OMC  10     5650            **     **
 27     COASTAL SF 270         HT  SF    FBG DV IO        MRCR 10     5650            **     **
      IO       OMC      **     ** , IO  260  MRCR  14600  16600, IO  260  OMC  14500  16500
      IB 260-350     16100  19600, IB  200D VLVO  19600  21800, IB  306D VLVO  22400  24900

 27     COASTAL SF 270         HT  SF    FBG DV SE T      OMC  10     5650            **     **
 27     COASTAL SF 270         HT  SF    FBG DV IO T130-T205   10     5650         14900  18200
 27     COASTAL SF 270         HT  SF    FBG DV IO T230-T260   10     5650         16500  19300
 27     FISHERMAN 270          ST  FSH   FBG DV SE        OMC  10     5510            **     **
 27     FISHERMAN 270          ST  FSH   FBG DV IO        MRCR 10     5510            **     **
      IO       OMC      **     ** , IO  260  MRCR  13300  15200, IO  260  OMC  13300  15100
      IB 260-350     16000  19400, IB  200D VLVO  19300  21500, IB  306D VLVO  22100  24600

 27     FISHERMAN 270          ST  FSH   FBG DV SE T      OMC  10     5510            **     **
 27     FISHERMAN 270          ST  FSH   FBG DV IO T130-T205   10     5510         13700  16700
 27     FISHERMAN 270          ST  FSH   FBG DV IO T230-T260   10     5510         15100  17800
 27     OFFSHORE 270           ST  CUD   FBG DV SE        OMC  10     5725            **     **
 27     OFFSHORE 270           ST  CUD   FBG DV IO        MRCR 10     5725            **     **
      IO       OMC      **     ** , IO  260  MRCR  12900  14600, IO  260  OMC  12900  14600
      IB 260-350     16300  19600, IB  200D VLVO  19700  21900, IB  306D VLVO  22400  24900

 27     OFFSHORE 270           ST  CUD   FBG DV SE T      OMC  10     5725            **     **
 27     OFFSHORE 270           ST  CUD   FBG DV IO T175        10     5725         13800  15700
 27     SPORT FISHERMAN 270    HT  SF    FBG DV SE        OMC  10     5510            **     **
 27     SPORT FISHERMAN 270    HT  SF    FBG DV IO        MRCR 10     5510            **     **
      IO       OMC      **     ** , IO  260  MRCR  14400  16400, IO  260  OMC  14400  16300
      IB 260-350     15900  19300, IB  200D VLVO  19300  21400, IB  306D VLVO  22100  24500

 27     SPORT FISHERMAN 270    HT  SF    FBG DV SE T      OMC  10     5510            **     **
 27     SPORT FISHERMAN 270    HT  SF    FBG DV IO T130-T205   10     5510         14700  18100
 27     SPORT FISHERMAN 270    HT  SF    FBG DV IO T230-T260   10     5510         16300  19200
 30     COASTAL FISH 300       ST  CUD   FBG DV IB 260-350     10     8795         21400  24900
 30     COASTAL FISH 300       ST  CUD   FBG DV IB 200D-306D   10     8795         25900  31200
 30     COASTAL FISH 300       ST  CUD   FBG DV SE T      OMC  10     8795            **     **
 30     COASTAL FISH 300       ST  CUD   FBG DV IB T      CRUS 10     8795            **     **
 30     COASTAL FISH 300       ST  CUD   FBG DV IB T220-T270   10     8795         23300  26800
 30     COASTAL FISH 300       ST  CUD   FBG DV IB T124D VLVO  10     8795         27300  30300
 30     FISHERMAN 300          ST  FSH   FBG DV VD 260-350     10     8345         21000  24500
 30     FISHERMAN 300          ST  FSH   FBG DV VD T      CRUS 10     8345            **     **
 30     FISHERMAN 300          ST  FSH   FBG DV VD T220-T350   10     8345         22900  28100

 30     GREAT-LAKES SP 300     ST  SF    FBG DV IB 260-350     10     8795         21400  24800
 30     GREAT-LAKES SP 300     ST  SF    FBG DV IB 200D-306D   10     8795         25900  31200
 30     GREAT-LAKES SP 300     ST  SF    FBG DV SE T      OMC  10     8795            **     **
 30     GREAT-LAKES SP 300     ST  SF    FBG DV IB T      CRUS 10     8795            **     **
 30     GREAT-LAKES SP 300     ST  SF    FBG DV IB T220-T270   10     8795         23300  26800
 30     GREAT-LAKES SP 300     ST  SF    FBG DV IB T240D VLVO  10     8795         31700  35200
 30     OFFSHORE 300           ST  CUD   FBG DV VD 260-350     10     8665         21300  24700
 30     OFFSHORE 300           ST  CUD   FBG DV SE T      OMC  10     8665            **     **
 30     OFFSHORE 300           ST  CUD   FBG DV VD T      CRUS 10     8665            **     **
 30     OFFSHORE 300           ST  CUD   FBG DV IB T220-T270   10     8665         23200  26700
 30     OFFSHORE 300           ST  CUD   FBG DV IB T124D VLVO  10     8665         27100  30100
 30     OFFSHORE SF 300        FB  SF    FBG DV VD 260-350     10     8665         21300  24700

 30     OFFSHORE SF 300        FB  SF    FBG DV SE T      OMC  10     8665            **     **
 30     OFFSHORE SF 300        FB  SF    FBG DV IB T      CRUS 10     8665            **     **
 30     OFFSHORE SF 300        FB  SF    FBG DV IB T220-T270   10     8665         23200  26700
 30     OFFSHORE SF 300        FB  SF    FBG DV IB T124D VLVO  10     8665         27000  30000
 30     SPORT FISHERMAN 300    FB  SF    FBG DV VD 260-350     10     8345         21000  24400
 30     SPORT FISHERMAN 300    FB  SF    FBG DV VD T      CRUS 10     8345            **     **
 30     SPORT FISHERMAN 300    FB  SF    FBG DV VD T220-T350   10     8345         22900  28000
 39     PESCA 360              HT  CUD   FBG DV IB T340  MRCR 13     19000  3  1   68100  74800
      IB T350  CRUS  69000  75800, IB T250D CUM   76500  84100, IB T250D GM     76900  84500
      IB T270D CUM   77400  85000, IB T306D VLVO  77600  85300, IB T320D CUM    79900  87800
      IB T358D VLVO  80300  88200, IB T375D CAT   86600  95100, IB T400D GM     85500  94000
      IB T425D CUM   86600  95200
---------------------- 1987 BOATS -------------------------------------------------------------
 16     FISHERMAN 160          OP  FSH   FBG SV OB              7     1200          2450   2850
 16     SKI-KING 160           ST  RNBT  FBG DV IO 120-180      7     1960          2550   3000
 16   1 FISHERMAN 170          OP  FSH   FBG SV OB              6  4  1170          2400   2800
 17   1 FISHERMAN 172          OP  CTRCN FBG DV SE        OMC   7  2  2140            **     **
 17   1 SPORTSMAN 180 BR       ST  RNBT  FBG DV OB              7  2  2110          3750   4350
 17   1 SPORTSMAN 180 BR       ST  RNBT  FBG DV SE        OMC   7  2  2110            **     **
 17   1 SPORTSMAN 180 BR       ST  RNBT  FBG DV IO 120-205      7  2  2110          2850   3400
 18   2 FISH'N-SKI 190 BR      ST  RNBT  FBG DV SE        OMC   7  8  1700            **     **
 18   2 FISH'N-SKI 190 BR      ST  RNBT  FBG DV SE  115   OMC   7  8  1700          3350   3900
 18   2 FISH'N-SKI 190 BR      ST  RNBT  FBG DV IO 120-205      7  8  1700          2900   3450
 18   2 FISH'N-SKI 190 CB      ST  RNBT  FBG DV OB              7  8  1700          3350   3900
 18   2 FISH'N-SKI 190 CB      ST  RNBT  FBG DV IO 120-205      7  8  1700          2850   3450

 18   2 FISH'N-SKI BR          ST  RNBT  FBG DV IO  120   OMC   7  8  1700          2900   3350
 18   2 SPORTSMAN 190          ST  RNBT  FBG DV IO  120   OMC   7  8  2370          3350   3900
 18   2 SPORTSMAN 190 BR       ST  RNBT  FBG DV OB              7  8  2370          3950   4600
 18   2 SPORTSMAN 190 BR       ST  RNBT  FBG DV IO 120-260      7  8  2370          3400   4200
 18   2 SPORTSMAN 190 CB       ST  RNBT  FBG DV SE        OMC   7  8  2370            **     **
 18   2 SPORTSMAN 190 CB       ST  RNBT  FBG DV IO 120-130      7  8  2370          3200   3850
 18   2 SPORTSMAN 190 CB       ST  RNBT  FBG DV SE  165   MRCR  7  8  2370          3950   4600
 18   2 SPORTSMAN 190 CB       ST  RNBT  FBG DV IO 175-205      7  8  2370          3350   3950
 18   9 EAGLE 190 C            ST  CUD   FBG DV IO 120-205      7  6  2080          3250   3900
 20   2 FISHERMAN 200          ST  CTRCN FBG DV SE        OMC   7  6  2530            **     **
 20   2 FISHERMAN 202          OP  CTRCN FBG DV OB              8     2450          4850   5600
 20   2 FISHERMAN 205 WT       ST  FSH   FBG SV SE        OMC   8     3020            **     **

 20   2 FISHERMAN 205 WT       ST  FSH   FBG SV IO 130-205      8     2900          5150   6250
 20   2 OFFSHORE 205           ST  FSH   FBG SV OB              8     3105          5300   6100
 20   2 OFFSHORE 205           ST  FSH   FBG SV SE        OMC   8     3105            **     **
 20   2 OFFSHORE 205           ST  FSH   FBG SV IO 175-205      8     3105          5450   6350
 20   2 OFFSHORE FSH 205       ST  FSH   FBG SV SE        OMC   8     3015            **     **
 20   2 OFFSHORE FSH 205       ST  FSH   FBG SV IO 130-180      8     3015          5350   6150
 20   9 C-EAGLE 210            ST  CUD   FBG DV SE        OMC   8  1  3410            **     **
 20   9 C-EAGLE 210            ST  CUD   FBG DV IO 130-260      8  1  3410          5700   6900
 20   9 FISHERMAN 210          ST  FSH   FBG DV SE        OMC   8  1  3410            **     **
 20   9 FISHERMAN 210          ST  FSH   FBG DV IO 130-260      8  1  3410          6000   7300
 22   2 FISHERMAN 230          ST  FSH   FBG DV SE        OMC   7  6  3450            **     **

 22   2 FISHERMAN 230          ST  FSH   FBG DV IO 165-205      7  6  3450          6350   7350
      IO  230  MRCR   6500   7450, IO  230  OMC    6450   7400, IB  230  MRCR   7700   8850
      IO  260         6650   7650

 22   2 FISHERMAN 230          ST  FSH   FBG DV SE T      OMC   7  6  3450            **     **
 22   2 OFFSHORE 222           ST  CUD   FBG DV OB              7  6  4310          7800   9000
 22   2 OFFSHORE 222           ST  CUD   FBG DV SE        OMC   7  6  4310            **     **
 22   2 OFFSHORE 222           ST  CUD   FBG DV IO 165-230      7  6  4310          7100   8350
 22   2 SPORTSMAN 230          ST  RNBT  FBG DV SE        OMC   7  6  3450            **     **
 22   2 SPORTSMAN 230          ST  RNBT  FBG DV IO 165-180      7  6  3450          5700   6550
 22   2 SPORTSMAN 230          ST  RNBT  FBG DV SE  205   OMC   7  6  3450          7200   8250
 22   2 SPORTSMAN 230          ST  RNBT  FBG DV IO 205-260      7  6  3450          5750   6850
 22   2 SPORTSMAN 230          ST  RNBT  FBG DV IO T      OMC   7  6  3450            **     **
 24   2 C-EAGLE 250            ST  CUD   FBG DV SE        OMC   8     4050            **     **

 24   2 C-EAGLE 250            ST  CUD   FBG DV IO        MRCR  8     4050            **     **
      IO  205         7750   8900, IO  230  MRCR   7850   9000, IO  230  OMC    7800   9000
      IB  230  MRCR   9900  11300, IO  260  MRCR   8000   9200, IO  260  OMC    7950   9150
      IB  260  MRCR  10000  11300, IO 335-350       8850  10500

 24   2 C-EAGLE 250            ST  CUD   FBG DV SE T      OMC   8     4050            **     **
 24   2 FISHERMAN 250          ST  FSH   FBG DV SE        OMC   8     4050            **     **
 24   2 FISHERMAN 250          ST  FSH   FBG DV IO        MRCR  8     4050            **     **
 24   2 FISHERMAN 250          ST  FSH   FBG DV IO 205-260      8     4050          8200   9700
 24   2 FISHERMAN 250          HT  FSH   FBG DV IO        MRCR  8     4050            **     **
 24   2 FISHERMAN 250          HT  FSH   FBG DV IO  335   OMC   8     4050          9350  10600
 24   2 FISHERMAN 250          HT  FSH   FBG DV SE T      OMC   8     4050            **     **
 24   2 OFF FAMILY FSH 242     ST  FSH   FBG DV SE T      OMC   8     4400            **     **
 24   2 OFFSHORE 242           ST  FSH   FBG DV OB              8                   7950   9150
```


CONTINUED ON NEXT PAGE

SPORT-CRAFT BOATS -CONTINUED See inside cover to adjust price for area

LOA FT	IN	NAME AND/ OR MODEL	TOP/ RIG	BOAT TYPE	-HULL- MTL	TP	ENGINE TP	# HP	MFG	BEAM FT	IN	WGT LBS	DRAFT FT IN	RETAIL LOW	RETAIL HIGH
		1987 BOATS													
24	2	OFFSHORE 242	ST	FSH	FBG	DV	IO		MRCR	8		4400		**	**
24	2	OFFSHORE 242	ST	FSH	FBG	DV	IO	205-260		8		4400		8800	10300
24	2	OFFSHORE 242	ST	FSH	FBG	DV	IO	335-350		8		4400		9850	11600
24	2	OFFSHORE 242	ST	FSH	FBG	DV	SE	T	OMC	8		4400		**	**
24	2	OFFSHORE 250	ST	CUD	FBG	DV	SE		OMC	8		4820		**	**
24	2	OFFSHORE 250	ST	CUD	FBG	DV	IO		MRCR	8		4820		**	**
24	2	OFFSHORE 250	ST	CUD	FBG	DV	IO	205-260		8		4820		9000	10500
24	2	OFFSHORE 250	ST	CUD	FBG	DV	IO	335	OMC	8		4820		9950	11300
24	2	OFFSHORE 250	ST	CUD	FBG	DV	SE	T	OMC	8		4820		**	**
24	2	SPORTSMAN 250	ST	CUD	FBG	DV	SE		OMC	8		4820		**	**
24	2	SPORTSMAN 250	ST	CUD	FBG	DV	IO	205-260		8		4820		9000	10500
24	2	SPORTSMAN 250	ST	CUD	FBG	DV	IO	335-350		8		4820		9950	11700
24	2	SPORTSMAN 250	ST	CUD	FBG	DV	IO	454		8		4820		12800	14600
24	2	SPORTSMAN 250	ST	CUD	FBG	DV	SE	T	OMC	8		4820		**	**
25	2	FISHERMAN 252	OP	CTRCN	FBG	DV	OB			8	6	4490		9600	10900
25	2	FISHERMAN 252	OP	CTRCN	FBG	DV	SE		OMC	8	6	4490		**	**
25	2	FISHERMAN 252	OP	CTRCN	FBG	DV	IO	205		8	6	4490		9400	10700
		IO 230 MRCR 9550 10900, IO 230 OMC 9550 10800, IB 230-340												11500	13900
25	2	FISHERMAN 252	OP	CTRCN	FBG	DV	SE	T	OMC	8	6	4490		**	**
27		C-EAGLE 270	ST	CUD	FBG	DV	OB			10		5510		12300	14000
27		C-EAGLE 270	ST	CUD	FBG	DV	SE		OMC	10		5510		**	**
27		C-EAGLE 270	ST	CUD	FBG	DV	IO		MRCR	10		5510		**	**
		IO 260 MRCR 12000 13700, IO 260 OMC 12000 13600, IB 260 MRCR												15200	17300
		IO 330-335 12800 14600, IO 340 OMC 12900 14700, IB 340 MRCR												16000	18200
		IO 350 MRCR 13100 14900													
27		C-EAGLE 270	ST	CUD	FBG	DV	SE	T	OMC	10		5510		**	**
27		C-EAGLE 270	ST	CUD	FBG	DV	IO	T	MRCR	10		5510		**	**
		IO T130-T205 12300 15100, IO T230-T260 13600 16000, IO T330-T350												15500	18100
27		COASTAL FISH 270	ST	FSH	FBG	DV	SE		OMC	10		5650		**	**
27		COASTAL FISH 270	ST	FSH	FBG	DV	IO		MRCR	10		5650		**	**
		IO 260 MRCR 12800 14600, IO 260 OMC 12800 14600, IB 260 MRCR												15400	17500
		IO 330-335 13700 15600, IO 340 OMC 13800 15700, IB 340 MRCR												16200	18400
27		COASTAL FISH 270	ST	FSH	FBG	DV	SE	T	OMC	10		5650		**	**
27		COASTAL FISH 270	ST	FSH	FBG	DV	IO	T	MRCR	10		5650		**	**
		IO T130-T205 13100 16100, IO T230-T260 14500 17000, IO T335-T340												16600	19000
27		COASTAL FISH 270	HT	FSH	FBG	DV	IO	T330	MRCR	10		5650		16500	18800
27		COASTAL SF 270	ST	FSH	FBG	DV	IO	T	MRCR	10		5650		**	**
27		COASTAL SF 270	HT	SF	FBG	DV	SE		OMC	10		5650		**	**
27		COASTAL SF 270	HT	SF	FBG	DV	IO		MRCR	10		5650		**	**
		IO 260 MRCR 14100 16000, IO 260 OMC 14000 15900, IB 260 MRCR												15600	17700
		IO 330-335 15000 17000, IO 340 OMC 14900 16900, IB 340 MRCR												16400	18700
27		COASTAL SF 270	HT	SF	FBG	DV	SE	T	OMC	10		5650		**	**
27		COASTAL SF 270	HT	SF	FBG	DV	IO	T	MRCR	10		5650		**	**
		IO T130-T205 14400 17500, IO T230-T260 15800 18600, IO T330-T340												18400	20500
27		FISHERMAN 270	ST	FSH	FBG	DV	OB			10		5510		12200	13900
27		FISHERMAN 270	ST	FSH	FBG	DV	SE		OMC	10		5510		**	**
27		FISHERMAN 270	ST	FSH	FBG	DV	IO		MRCR	10		5510		**	**
		IO 260 MRCR 12700 14400, IO 260 OMC 12700 14400, IB 260 MRCR												15200	17300
		IO 330-335 13600 15400, IO 340 OMC 13700 15500, IB 340 MRCR												16000	18200
27		FISHERMAN 270	ST	FSH	FBG	DV	SE	T	OMC	10		5510		**	**
27		FISHERMAN 270	ST	FSH	FBG	DV	IO	T	MRCR	10		5510		**	**
		IO T130-T205 13000 15900, IO T230-T260 14400 16900, IO T330-T340												16400	18800
27		OFFSHORE 270	ST	CUD	FBG	DV	SE		OMC	10		5725		**	**
27		OFFSHORE 270	ST	CUD	FBG	DV	IO		MRCR	10		5725		**	**
		IO 260 MRCR 12300 13900, IO 260 OMC 12200 13900, IB 260 MRCR												15500	17600
		IO 330-335 13100 14900, IO 340 OMC 13200 15000, IB 340 MRCR												16300	18500
27		OFFSHORE 270	ST	CUD	FBG	DV	SE	T	OMC	10		5725		**	**
27		OFFSHORE 270	ST	CUD	FBG	DV	IO	T	MRCR	10		5725		**	**
		IO T130-T205 12500 15300, IO T230-T260 13800 16200, IO T330-T340												15700	18100
27		SPORT FISHERMAN 270	HT	SF	FBG	DV	OB			10		5650		11900	13500
27		SPORT FISHERMAN 270	HT	SF	FBG	DV	SE		OMC	10		5510		**	**
27		SPORT FISHERMAN 270	HT	SF	FBG	DV	IO	260	MRCR	10		5650		13700	15500
		IO 260 OMC 13600 15500, IB 260 MRCR 15200 17300, IO 330 MRCR												14600	16600
		IB 340 MRCR 16000 18100													
27		SPORT FISHERMAN 270	HT	SF	FBG	DV	SE	T	OMC	10		5510		**	**
27		SPORT FISHERMAN 270	HT	SF	FBG	DV	IO	T130-T205		10		5650		14000	17200
27		SPORT FISHERMAN 270	HT	SF	FBG	DV	IO	T230-T260		10		5650		15500	18200
27		SPORT FISHERMAN 270	HT	SF	FBG	DV	IO	T330	MRCR	10		5650		18100	20100
27		SPORT FISHERMAN 270	FB	SF	FBG	DV	IO		MRCR	10		5510		**	**
		IO 335-350 14700 17000, IO T MRCR ** **, IO T335-T350												18200	20700
30		COASTAL FSH 300	ST	CUD	FBG	DV	SE		OMC	10		8795		**	**
30		COASTAL FSH 300	ST	CUD	FBG	DV	IO		MRCR	10		8795		**	**
		IO 260 MRCR 15800 18000, IO 260 OMC 15800 17900, IB 260 MRCR												20400	22700
		IO 330-335 16400 18700, IO 340 OMC 16500 18800, IB 340 MRCR												21200	23600
		IO 350 MRCR 16600 18900													
30		COASTAL FSH 300	ST	CUD	FBG	DV	SE	T	OMC	10		8795		**	**
30		COASTAL FSH 300	ST	CUD	FBG	DV	IO	T	MRCR	10		8795		**	**
		IO T165-T205 16400 19300, IO T230 MRCR 17300 19600, IO T230 OMC												17300	19600
		IB T230 MRCR 22300 24800, IO T260 MRCR 18100 20100, IO T260 OMC												18100	20100
		IB T260 MRCR 22800 25300, IO T330-T350 19000 21500													
30		FISHERMAN 300	ST	FSH	FBG	DV	SE		OMC	10		8345		**	**
30		FISHERMAN 300	ST	FSH	FBG	DV	IO		MRCR	10		8345		**	**
		IO 260 MRCR 16400 18600, IO 260 OMC 16400 18600, VD 260 MRCR												20000	22300
		IO 330-335 17100 19400, IO 340 OMC 17200 19500, VD 340 MRCR												20800	23200
		IO 350 MRCR 17300 19600, IO T MRCR ** **, IO T165-T205												17000	20000
		IO T230 MRCR 18400 20400, IO T230 OMC 18400 20400, VD T230 MRCR												22000	24400
		IO T260 MRCR 18800 20900, IO T260 OMC 18800 20900, VD T260 MRCR												22500	25000
		IO T330-T335 19800 22100, IO T340 OMC 20000 22200, VD T340 MRCR												23800	26500
		IO T350 MRCR 20200 22500													
30		GREAT-LAKES SP 300	ST	SF	FBG	DV	SE		OMC	10		8795		**	**
30		GREAT-LAKES SP 300	ST	SF	FBG	DV	IO		MRCR	10		8795		**	**
		IO 260 MRCR 18400 20400, IO 260 OMC 18400 20400, IB 260 MRCR												20400	22700
		IO 330-335 19100 21300, IO 340 OMC 19000 21100, IB 340 MRCR												21200	23500
30		GREAT-LAKES SP 300	ST	SF	FBG	DV	SE	T	OMC	10		8795		**	**
30		GREAT-LAKES SP 300	ST	SF	FBG	DV	IO	T	MRCR	10		8795		**	**
		IO T165-T205 19100 21700, IO T230 MRCR 19900 22100, IO T230 OMC												19900	22100
		IB T230 MRCR 22300 24800, IO T260 MRCR 20400 22600, IO T260 OMC												20400	22600
		IB T260 MRCR 22800 25300, IO T330-T340 21600 24200													
30		OFFSHORE 300	ST	CUD	FBG	DV	IO		MRCR	10		8665		**	**
		IO 260 MRCR 14300 16300, IO 260 OMC 14300 16300, VD 260 MRCR												18700	20800
		IO 330-335 15000 18600, IO 340 OMC 16400 18700, VD 340 MRCR												19400	21500
		IO 350 MRCR 16600 18800													
30		OFFSHORE 300	ST	CUD	FBG	DV	SE	T	OMC	10				**	**
30		OFFSHORE 300	ST	CUD	FBG	DV	IO	T	MRCR	10		8665		**	**
		IO T165-T205 16300 18600, IO T230 MRCR 16000 18200, IO T230 OMC												16000	18200
		IB T230 MRCR 20700 22900, IO T260 MRCR 16500 18700, IO T260 OMC												16400	18700
		IB T260 MRCR 21200 23600, IO T330-T350 18100 21500													
30		OFFSHORE SF	FB	SF	FBG	DV	IO	260	MRCR	10				16300	18500
		IO 260 OMC 16300 18500, VD 260 MRCR 18700 20800, IO 330 MRCR												17100	19500
		VD 340 MRCR 19400 21500													
30		OFFSHORE SF	FB	SF	FBG	DV	SE	T165	OMC	10				16100	18200
30		OFFSHORE SF	FB	SF	FBG	DV	IO	T175-T205		10				17300	20200
		IO T230 MRCR 18600 20700, IO T230 OMC 18600 20700, IB T230 MRCR												20600	22900
		IO T260 MRCR 19200 21300, IO T260 OMC 19100 21300, IB T260 MRCR												21200	23500
		IO T330 MRCR 20400 22600													
30		OFFSHORE SF 300	FB	SF	FBG	DV	SE		OMC	10		8665		**	**
30		OFFSHORE SF 300	FB	SF	FBG	DV	IO		MRCR	10		8665		**	**
30		OFFSHORE SF 300	FB	SF	FBG	DV	IO	335-350		10		8665		19100	21300
30		OFFSHORE SF 300	FB	SF	FBG	DV	SE	T	OMC	10		8665		**	**
30		OFFSHORE SF 300	FB	SF	FBG	DV	IO	T	MRCR	10		8665		**	**
30		OFFSHORE SF 300	FB	SF	FBG	DV	IO	T335-T350		10		8665		21600	24400
30		SPORT FISHERMAN 300	FB	SF	FBG	DV	SE		OMC	10		8345		**	**
30		SPORT FISHERMAN 300	FB	SF	FBG	DV	IO		MRCR	10		8345		**	**
		IO 260 MRCR 17300 19600, IO 260 OMC 17300 19600, VD 260 MRCR												19600	21800
		IO 330 MRCR 18400 20500, IO 340 OMC 18900 21000, VD 340 MRCR												20400	22700
30		SPORT FISHERMAN 300	FB	SF	FBG	DV	SE	T	OMC	10		8345		**	**
30		SPORT FISHERMAN 300	FB	SF	FBG	DV	IO	T	MRCR	10		8345		**	**
		IO T165-T205 18800 21200, IO T230 MRCR 19300 21400, IO T230 OMC												19200	21400
		VD T230 MRCR 21600 24000, IO T260 MRCR 19800 22000, IO T260 OMC												19700	21900
		VD T260 MRCR 22100 24500, IO T330-T335 21100 23800, IO T340 OMC												21600	24000
		VD T340 MRCR 23400 26100													

CONTINUED ON NEXT PAGE

LOA FT	IN	NAME AND/ OR MODEL	TOP/ RIG	BOAT TYPE	-HULL- MTL	TP	----ENGINE--- TP	# HP	MFG	BEAM FT	IN	WGT LBS	DRAFT FT	IN	RETAIL LOW	RETAIL HIGH
		1986 BOATS														
16		SKI-KING 160	ST	RNBT	FBG	DV	IO	120-175		6	11	1210			1900	2300
16	1	FISH-N-SKI 170	ST	RNBT	FBG	DV	OB			6	4	1000			2000	2400
16	1	FISHERMAN 160	OP	FSH	FBG	SV	OB			7		1360			2650	3100
16	1	FISHERMAN 170	OP	FSH	FBG	SV	OB			6	2	1050			2100	2500
16	10	PLAY'N-SKI 170	ST	RNBT	FBG	SV	OB			7	8	1350			2700	3100
16	10	PLAY'N-SKI 170	ST	RNBT	FBG	SV	IO	120-190		7	8	1350			2350	2750
17	1	FISHERMAN 172	OP	CTRCN	FBG	DV	SE	115	OMC	7	2	2180			3700	4350
17	1	SPORTSMAN 180 BR	ST	RNBT	FBG	DV	OB			7	2	1300			2600	3050
17	2	SPORTSMAN 180 BR	ST	RNBT	FBG	DV	SE	115	OMC	7	2	1470			2900	3350
17	2	SPORTSMAN 180 BR	ST	RNBT	FBG	DV	IO	120-190		7	2	1470			2350	2750
18	2	FISH'N-SKI 190	ST	RNBT	FBG	DV	OB			7	8	1700			2750	3200
18	2	FISH'N-SKI 190	ST	RNBT	FBG	DV	IO	120-190		7	8	1700			2800	3300
18	2	FISH'N-SKI 190 BR/CB	ST	RNBT	FBG	DV	SE	115	OMC	7	8	1700			3300	3800
18	2	FISH'N-SKI 190 BR/CB	ST	RNBT	FBG	DV	IO	120	MRCR	7	8	1700			2800	3250
18	2	FISH'N-SKI 190 BR/CB	ST	RNBT	FBG	DV	SE	155	OMC	7	8	1700			3300	3850
18	2	FISH'N-SKI 190 BR/CB	ST	RNBT	FBG	DV	IO	170	MRCR	7	8	1700			2850	3300
18	2	SPORTSMAN 190 BR	ST	RNBT	FBG	DV	OB			7	8	1700			3500	4050
18	2	SPORTSMAN 190 BR	ST	RNBT	FBG	DV	IO	120-190		7	8	1700			2650	3200
18	2	SPORTSMAN 190 BR/CB	ST	RNBT	FBG	DV	SE	115	OMC	7	8	1700			3200	3750
18	2	SPORTSMAN 190 BR/CB	ST	RNBT	FBG	DV	IO	120	MRCR	7	8	1700			2750	3200
18	2	SPORTSMAN 190 BR/CB	ST	RNBT	FBG	DV	SE	155	OMC	7	8	1700			3200	3700
18	2	SPORTSMAN 190 BR/CB	ST	RNBT	FBG	DV	IO	170	MRCR	7	8	1700			2700	3150
18	2	SPORTSMAN 190 CB	ST	RNBT	FBG	DV	OB			7	8	1700			3500	4050
18	9	EAGLE 190 C	ST	CUD	FBG	DV	IO	140		7	6	2250			3250	3750
18	9	EAGLE 190 C	ST	CUD	FBG	DV	IO	170-205		7	6				3500	4150
20		FISHERMAN 200	OP	CTRCN	FBG	DV	OB			7	6	1800			3850	4450
20		FISHERMAN 200	ST	CTRCN	FBG	DV	SE	115-155		7	6	1800			3850	4450
20	2	FISHERMAN 205 WT	ST	FSH	FBG	SV	SE	115	OMC	8		2900			5050	5800
20	2	FISHERMAN 205 WT	ST	FSH	FBG	SV	IO	140		8		2900			4950	5700
20	2	FISHERMAN 205 WT	ST	FSH	FBG	SV	SE	155	OMC	8		2900			5050	5800
20	2	FISHERMAN 205 WT	ST	FSH	FBG	SV	IO	170-190		8		2900			5000	5800
20	2	FISHERMAN 205 WT	ST	FSH	FBG	SV	SE	205	OMC	8		2900			5050	5800
20	2	FISHERMAN 205 WT	ST	FSH	FBG	SV	IO	205		8		2900			5050	5800
20	5	OFF FAMILY FSH 205	ST	FSH	FBG	SV	SE	115	OMC	8		3105			5350	6150
20	5	OFF FAMILY FSH 205	ST	FSH	FBG	SV	IO	140		8		3105			5250	6050
20	5	OFF FAMILY FSH 205	ST	FSH	FBG	SV	SE	155	OMC	8		3105			5350	6150
20	5	OFF FAMILY FSH 205	ST	FSH	FBG	SV	IO	170-190		8		3105			5300	6100
20	5	OFF FAMILY FSH 205	ST	FSH	FBG	SV	SE	205	OMC	8		3105			5350	6150
20	9	C-EAGLE 210	ST	CUD	FBG	DV	SE	115	OMC	8	1	3300			5850	6700
20	9	C-EAGLE 210	ST	CUD	FBG	DV	IO	140		8	1	3300			5300	6100
20	9	C-EAGLE 210	ST	CUD	FBG	DV	SE	155	OMC	8	1	3300			5850	6700
20	9	C-EAGLE 210	ST	CUD	FBG	DV	IO	170-190		8	1	3300			5350	6150
20	9	C-EAGLE 210	ST	CUD	FBG	DV	SE	205	OMC	8	1	3300			5850	6700
20	9	C-EAGLE 210	ST	CUD	FBG	DV	IO	205-260		8	1	3300			5400	6450
20	9	FISHERMAN 210	ST	FSH	FBG	DV	SE	115	OMC	8	1	3300			5700	6550
20	9	FISHERMAN 210	ST	FSH	FBG	DV	IO	140		8	1	3300			5600	6450
20	9	FISHERMAN 210	ST	FSH	FBG	DV	SE	155	OMC	8	1	3300			5700	6550
20	9	FISHERMAN 210	ST	FSH	FBG	DV	IO	170-190		8	1	3300			5650	6500
20	9	FISHERMAN 210	ST	FSH	FBG	DV	SE	205	OMC	8	1	3300			5700	6550
20	9	FISHERMAN 210	ST	FSH	FBG	DV	IO	205-260		8	1	3300			5700	6800
22	2	FISHERMAN 230	ST	FSH	FBG	DV	SE	155	OMC	8		3434			6800	7800
22	2	FISHERMAN 230	ST	FSH	FBG	DV	IO	170-190		8		3434			6200	7150
22	2	FISHERMAN 230	ST	FSH	FBG	DV	SE	205	OMC	8		3434			6800	7800
22	2	FISHERMAN 230	ST	FSH	FBG	DV	IO	205-260		8		3434			6250	7450
22	2	FISHERMAN 230	ST	FSH	FBG	DV	SE	T115	OMC	8		3434			6800	7800
22	2	OFF FAMILY FSH 222	ST	CUD	FBG	DV	OB			7	6	2800			6150	7100
22	2	OFF FAMILY FSH 222	ST	CUD	FBG	DV	IO	170-230		7	6				4900	5800
22	2	OFF FAMILY FSH 222	ST	CUD	FBG	DV	SE	T115	OMC	7	6				**	**
22	2	OFFSHORE FAM FSH 222	ST	CUD	FBG	DV	SE	155-205		7	6	2800			6150	7100
22	2	SPORTSMAN 230	ST	RNBT	FBG	DV	SE	155	OMC	8		3434			6950	8000
22	2	SPORTSMAN 230	ST	RNBT	FBG	DV	IO	170-190		8		3434			5550	6400
22	2	SPORTSMAN 230	ST	RNBT	FBG	DV	SE	205	OMC	8		3434			6950	8000
22	2	SPORTSMAN 230	ST	RNBT	FBG	DV	IO	205-260		8		3434			5600	6700
22	2	SPORTSMAN 230	ST	RNBT	FBG	DV	SE	T115	OMC	8		3434			6950	8000
24	2	C-EAGLE 250	ST	CUD	FBG	DV	SE	205	OMC	8		5210			10200	11600
24	2	C-EAGLE 250	ST	CUD	FBG	DV	IO	205-330		8		5210			9150	11400
24	2	C-EAGLE 250	ST	CUD	FBG	DV	SE	T115-T205		8		5210			10200	11600
24	2	C-EAGLE 250	HT	CUD	FBG	DV	SE	205	OMC	8		5210			10200	11600
24	2	C-EAGLE 250	HT	CUD	FBG	DV	IO	230-330		8		5210			9200	11400
24	2	C-EAGLE 250	HT	CUD	FBG	DV	SE	T155-T205		8		5210			10200	11600
24	2	FISHERMAN 250	ST	FSH	FBG	DV	SE	205	OMC	8		5210			9950	11300
24	2	FISHERMAN 250	ST	FSH	FBG	DV	IO	205-260		8		5210			9600	11200
24	2	FISHERMAN 250	ST	FSH	FBG	DV	IO	330	MRCR	8		5210			10600	12000
24	2	FISHERMAN 250	ST	FSH	FBG	DV	SE	T115-T205		8		5210			9900	11300
24	2	FISHERMAN 250	HT	FSH	FBG	DV	IO	200	OMC	8		5210			9550	10800
24	2	FISHERMAN 250	HT	FSH	FBG	DV	SE	205	OMC	8		5210			9950	11300
24	2	FISHERMAN 250	HT	FSH	FBG	DV	IO	230-330		8		5210			9650	12000
24	2	FISHERMAN 250	HT	FSH	FBG	DV	SE	T115	OMC	8		5210			9900	11300
24	2	OFF FAMILY FSH 242	ST	FSH	FBG	DV	OB			8					7700	8850
24	2	OFF FAMILY FSH 242	ST	FSH	FBG	DV	SE	205	OMC	8		4400			9200	10500
24	2	OFF FAMILY FSH 242	ST	FSH	FBG	DV	IO	205-260		8		4400			8300	9850
24	2	OFF FAMILY FSH 242	ST	FSH	FBG	DV	IO	330	MRCR	8		4400			9400	10700
24	2	OFF FAMILY FSH 242	ST	FSH	FBG	DV	SE	T115-T205		8		4400			9200	10500
24	2	SPORTSMAN 250	ST	CUD	FBG	DV	SE	155	OMC	8		4820			9850	11200
24	2	SPORTSMAN 250	ST	CUD	FBG	DV	IO	205		8		4820			8500	9750
		IO 230 MRCR 8550 9850, IO 230 OMC 8500 9800, IB 230 MRCR 10800 12300														
		IO 260 MRCR 8800 10000, IO 260 OMC 8650 9950, IB 260 MRCR 10900 12400														
		IO 330 MRCR 9500 10800														
24	2	SPORTSMAN 250	ST	CUD	FBG	DV	SE	T115-T205		8		4820			9850	11200
27		C-EAGLE 270	ST	CUD	FBG	DV	OB			10					11800	13400
27		C-EAGLE 270	ST	CUD	FBG	DV	IO	260	MRCR	10		6800			12800	14600
		IO 260 OMC 12800 14600, IB 260 MRCR 16300 18500, IO 330 MRCR 13600 15400														
		IB 340 MRCR 17000 19300														
27		C-EAGLE 270	ST	CUD	FBG	DV	SE	T115	OMC	10		6800			12100	13800
27		C-EAGLE 270	ST	CUD	FBG	DV	IO	T140		10		6800			13200	15000
27		C-EAGLE 270	ST	CUD	FBG	DV	SE	T155	OMC	10		6800			12100	13800
27		C-EAGLE 270	ST	CUD	FBG	DV	IO	T170-T190		10		6800			13600	15700
27		C-EAGLE 270	ST	CUD	FBG	DV	SE	T205	OMC	10		6800			12100	13800
27		C-EAGLE 270	ST	CUD	FBG	DV	IO	T205-T260		10		6800			14000	16700
27		C-EAGLE 270	ST	CUD	FBG	DV	IO	T330	MRCR	10		6800			16000	18200
27		C-EAGLE 270	HT	CUD	FBG	DV	OB			10		6800			12100	13800
27		C-EAGLE 270	HT	CUD	FBG	DV	IO	260	MRCR	10		6800			12800	14600
		IO 260 OMC 12800 14600, IB 260 MRCR 16300 18500, IO 330 MRCR 13600 15400														
		IB 340 MRCR 17000 19300, IO T140 13200 15000														
27		C-EAGLE 270	HT	CUD	FBG	DV	SE	T155	OMC	10		6800			12100	13800
27		C-EAGLE 270	HT	CUD	FBG	DV	IO	T170-T190		10		6800			13600	15700
27		C-EAGLE 270	HT	CUD	FBG	DV	SE	T205	OMC	10		6800			12100	13800
27		C-EAGLE 270	HT	CUD	FBG	DV	IO	T205-T260		10		6800			14000	16700
27		C-EAGLE 270	HT	CUD	FBG	DV	IO	T330	MRCR	10		6800			16000	18200
27		FAMILY FISHERMAN 270	ST	CUD	FBG	DV	IO	260	MRCR	10		5740			11700	13300
		IO 260 OMC 11700 13300, IB 260 MRCR 14800 16800, IO 330 MRCR 12500 14200														
		IB 340 MRCR 15600 17700, IO T140 12100 13800														
27		FAMILY FISHERMAN 270	ST	CUD	FBG	DV	SE	T155	OMC	10		5740			12000	13700
27		FAMILY FISHERMAN 270	ST	CUD	FBG	DV	IO	T170-T190		10		5740			12500	14400
27		FAMILY FISHERMAN 270	ST	CUD	FBG	DV	SE	T205	OMC	10		5740			12000	13700
27		FAMILY FISHERMAN 270	ST	CUD	FBG	DV	IO	T205-T260		10		5740			12900	15500
27		FAMILY FISHERMAN 270	ST	CUD	FBG	DV	IO	T330	MRCR	10		5740			15000	17100
27		FAMILY FISHERMAN 270	ST	FSH	FBG	DV	SE	T115	OMC	10		6800			13200	15100
27		FISHERMAN 270	ST	FSH	FBG	DV	OB			10		6185			11900	13600
27		FISHERMAN 270	ST	FSH	FBG	DV	IO	260	MRCR	10		6800			13500	15400
		IO 260 OMC 13500 15400, IB 260 MRCR 16300 18500, IO 330 MRCR 14300 16300														
		IB 340 MRCR 17000 19300														
27		FISHERMAN 270	ST	FSH	FBG	DV	SE	T115	OMC	10		6800			10700	12200
27		FISHERMAN 270	ST	FSH	FBG	DV	IO	T140		10		6800			14000	15900
27		FISHERMAN 270	ST	FSH	FBG	DV	SE	T155	OMC	10		6800			12000	13600
27		FISHERMAN 270	ST	FSH	FBG	DV	IO	T170-T190		10		6800			14300	16500
27		FISHERMAN 270	ST	FSH	FBG	DV	SE	T205	OMC	10		6800			12000	13600
27		FISHERMAN 270	ST	FSH	FBG	DV	IO	T205-T260		10		6800			14700	17600
27		FISHERMAN 270	ST	FSH	FBG	DV	IO	T330	MRCR	10		6800			16900	19200
27		FISHERMAN 270	HT	FSH	FBG	DV	OB			10		6800			12000	13600
27		FISHERMAN 270	HT	FSH	FBG	DV	IO	260	MRCR	10		6800			13500	15400
		IO 260 OMC 13500 15400, IB 260 MRCR 16300 18500, IO 330 MRCR 14300 16300														
		IB 340 MRCR 17000 19300, IO T140 14000 15900														
27		FISHERMAN 270	HT	FSH	FBG	DV	SE	T155	OMC	10		6800			12000	13600
27		FISHERMAN 270	HT	FSH	FBG	DV	IO	T170-T190		10		6800			14300	16500
27		FISHERMAN 270	HT	FSH	FBG	DV	SE	T205	OMC	10		6800			12000	13600
27		FISHERMAN 270	HT	FSH	FBG	DV	IO	T205-T260		10		6800			14700	17600
27		FISHERMAN 270	HT	FSH	FBG	DV	IO	T330	MRCR	10		6800			16900	19200
27		SPORT FISHERMAN 270	FB	SF	FBG	DV	OB			10		6670			11200	12700
27		SPORT FISHERMAN 270	FB	SF	FBG	DV	IO	260	MRCR	10		6670			14500	16400
		IO 260 OMC 14400 16400, IB 260 MRCR 16100 18300, IO 330 MRCR 15300 17400														
		IB 340 MRCR 16800 19100														

CONTINUED ON NEXT PAGE

LOA FT	IN	NAME AND/ OR MODEL	TOP/ RIG	BOAT TYPE	-HULL- MTL	TP	ENGINE TP	# HP	MFG	BEAM FT	IN	WGT LBS	DRAFT FT IN	RETAIL LOW	RETAIL HIGH
		1986 BOATS													
27		SPORT FISHERMAN 270	FB	SF	FBG	DV	SE	T115	OMC	10		6670		11200	12700
27		SPORT FISHERMAN 270	FB	SF	FBG	DV	IO	T140		10		6670		14900	16900
27		SPORT FISHERMAN 270	FB	SF	FBG	DV	SE	T155	OMC	10		6670		11200	12700
27		SPORT FISHERMAN 270	FB	SF	FBG	DV	IO	T170-T190		10		6670		15300	17700
27		SPORT FISHERMAN 270	FB	SF	FBG	DV	SE	T205	OMC	10		6670		11200	12700
27		SPORT FISHERMAN 270	FB	SF	FBG	DV	IO	T205-T260		10		6670		15800	18800
27		SPORT FISHERMAN 270	FB	SF	FBG	DV	IO	T330	MRCR	10		6670		18500	20600
30		COASTAL FSH 300	ST	CUD	FBG	DV	IO	260	MRCR	10		9000		15200	17300
		IO 260 OMC 15200 17300, IB 260 MRCR 19600 21800, IO 330 MRCR												15800	18000
		IB 340 MRCR 20400 22700, IO T140 15500 17600													
30		COASTAL FSH 300	ST	CUD	FBG	DV	SE	T155	OMC	10		9000		16400	18600
30		COASTAL FSH 300	ST	CUD	FBG	DV	IO	T170-T190		10		9000		15900	18300
30		COASTAL FSH 300	ST	CUD	FBG	DV	SE	T205	OMC	10		9000		16400	18600
30		COASTAL FSH 300	ST	CUD	FBG	DV	IO	T205		10		9000		16300	18500
		IO T230 MRCR 16600 18900, IO T230 OMC 16600 18900, IB T230 MRCR												21400	23800
		IO T260 MRCR 17000 19300, IO T260 OMC 17000 19300, IB T260 MRCR												21900	24300
		IO T330 MRCR 18500 20500													
30		FISHERMAN 300	ST	FSH	FBG	DV	IO	260	MRCR	10		7255		15000	17000
		IO 260 OMC 15000 17000, VD 260 MRCR 18500 20600, IO 330 MRCR												15700	17800
		VD 340 MRCR 19100 21200, IO T140 15200 17300													
30		FISHERMAN 300	ST	FSH	FBG	DV	SE	T155	OMC	10		7255		16400	18600
30		FISHERMAN 300	ST	FSH	FBG	DV	IO	T170-T190		10		7255		15700	10200
30		FISHERMAN 300	ST	FSH	FBG	DV	SE	T205	OMC	10		7255		16400	18600
30		FISHERMAN 300	ST	FSH	FBG	DV	IO	T205		10		7255		16200	18400
		IO T230 MRCR 16600 18800, IO T230 OMC 16500 18800, VD T230 MRCR												20300	22500
		IO T260 MRCR 17000 19300, IO T260 OMC 17000 19300, VD T260 MRCR												20700	23000
		IO T330 MRCR 18600 20700, VD T340 MRCR 22100 24600													
30		FISHERMAN 300	HT	FSH	FBG	DV	IO	260	MRCR	10		7255		15000	17000
		IO 260 OMC 15000 17000, VD 260 MRCR 18500 20600, IO 330 MRCR												15700	17800
		VD 340 MRCR 19100 21200, IO T140 15200 17300													
30		FISHERMAN 300	HT	FSH	FBG	DV	SE	T155	OMC	10		7255		16400	18600
30		FISHERMAN 300	HT	FSH	FBG	DV	IO	T170-T190		10		7255		15700	18200
30		FISHERMAN 300	HT	FSH	FBG	DV	SE	T205	OMC	10		7255		16400	18600
30		FISHERMAN 300	HT	FSH	FBG	DV	IO	T205	OMC	10		7255		16200	18400
		IO T230 MRCR 16600 18800, IO T230 OMC 16500 18800, VD T230 MRCR												20300	22500
		IO T260 MRCR 17000 19300, IO T260 OMC 17000 19300, VD T260 MRCR												20700	23000
		IO T330 MRCR 18600 20700, VD T340 MRCR 22100 24600													
30		GREAT-LAKES SP 300	ST	SF	FBG	DV	IO	260	MRCR	10		9000		17300	19700
		IO 260 OMC 17300 19700, IB 260 MRCR 19600 21800, IO 330 MRCR												18400	20500
		IB 340 MRCR 20400 22600, IO T140 18000 20000													
30		GREAT-LAKES SP 300	ST	SF	FBG	DV	SE	T155	OMC	10		9000		16100	18300
30		GREAT-LAKES SP 300	ST	SF	FBG	DV	IO	T170-T190		10		9000		18500	20800
30		GREAT-LAKES SP 300	ST	SF	FBG	DV	SE	T205	OMC	10		9000		16100	18300
30		GREAT-LAKES SP 300	ST	SF	FBG	DV	IO	T205		10		9000		19000	21100
		IO T230 MRCR 19100 21300, IO T230 OMC 19100 21200, IB T230 MRCR												21400	23800
		IO T260 MRCR 19600 21800, IO T260 OMC 19600 21700, IB T260 MRCR												21900	24300
		IO T330 MRCR 20800 23100													
30		OFFSHORE FAM FSH 300	ST	CUD	FBG	DV	IO	260	MRCR	10				13700	15500
		IO 260 OMC 13700 15500, VD 260 MRCR 17500 19800, IO 330 MRCR												14400	16300
		VD 340 MRCR 18700 20800, IO T140 13900 15800													
30		OFFSHORE FAM FSH 300	ST	CUD	FBG	DV	SE	T155	OMC	10				16400	18600
30		OFFSHORE FAM FSH 300	ST	CUD	FBG	DV	IO	T170-T190		10				14400	16700
30		OFFSHORE FAM FSH 300	ST	CUD	FBG	DV	SE	T205	OMC	10				16400	18600
30		OFFSHORE FAM FSH 300	ST	CUD	FBG	DV	IO	T205		10		7200		15300	17400
		IO T230 MRCR 15300 17400, IO T230 OMC 15300 17300, IB T230 MRCR												19700	21900
		IO T260 MRCR 15700 17900, IO T260 OMC 15700 17900, IB T260 MRCR												20200	22500
		IO T330 MRCR 16900 19200													
30		OFFSHORE SF	FB	SF	FBG	DV	IO	260	MRCR					15800	17900
		IO 260 OMC 15700 17900, VD 260 MRCR 18000 20000, IO 330 MRCR												16500	18800
		VD 340 MRCR 18900 21000, IO T140 16100 18300													
30		OFFSHORE SF	FB	SF	FBG	DV	SE	T155	OMC	10				15500	17600
30		OFFSHORE SF	FB	SF	FBG	DV	IO	T170-T190						16600	19200
30		OFFSHORE SF	FB	SF	FBG	DV	SE	T205	OMC	10				15500	17600
30		OFFSHORE SF	FB	SF	FBG	DV	IO	T205						17200	19500
		IO T230 MRCR 18000 20000, IO T230 OMC 17600 20000, IB T230 MRCR												19900	22100
		IO T260 MRCR 18500 20600, IO T260 OMC 18500 20600, IB T260 MRCR												20500	22700
		IO T330 MRCR 19700 21900													
30		SPORT FISHERMAN 300	FB	SF	FBG	DV	IO	260	MRCR	10		7800		16500	18800
		IO 260 OMC 16500 18700, VD 260 MRCR 18900 21000, IO 330 MRCR												17200	19600
		VD 340 MRCR 19500 21600, IO T140 16800 19100													
30		SPORT FISHERMAN 300	FB	SF	FBG	DV	SE	T155	OMC	10		7800		15500	17600
30		SPORT FISHERMAN 300	FB	SF	FBG	DV	IO	T170-T190		10		7800		17300	20000
30		SPORT FISHERMAN 300	FB	SF	FBG	DV	SE	T205	OMC	10		7800		15500	17600
30		SPORT FISHERMAN 300	FB	SF	FBG	DV	IO	T205		10		7800		18200	20200
		IO T230 MRCR 18600 20700, IO T230 OMC 18600 20600, VD T230 MRCR												20600	22900
		IO T260 MRCR 19100 21200, IO T260 OMC 19100 21200, VD T260 MRCR												21100	23400
		IO T330 MRCR 20100 22400, VD T340 MRCR 22400 24900													
		1985 BOATS													
16		SKI-KING 160	ST	RNBT	FBG	DV	SE	115	OMC	6	11	1210		2350	2750
16		SKI-KING 160	ST	RNBT	FBG	DV	IO	120	MRCR	6	11	1210		1800	2150
16		SKI-KING 160	ST	RNBT	FBG	DV	IO	120	OMC	6	11	1210		1800	2150
16		SKI-KING 160	ST	RNBT	FBG	DV	IO	120-190		6	11	1210		1950	2400
16	1	ADVENTURER 170	ST	RNBT	FBG	DV	OB			6	4	955		1900	2250
16	1	ADVENTURER 170 SPEC		RNBT	FBG	DV	OB			6	4			2500	2950
16	1	FISH-N-SKI 170	ST	RNBT	FBG	DV	OB			6	4	1000		1950	2350
16	1	FISHERMAN 170	OP	FSH	FBG	SV	OB			6	2	1050		2050	2450
17	1	SPORTSMAN 180 B/R	ST	RNBT	FBG	DV	OB			7	2	1300		2550	2950
17	2	SPORTSMAN 180 BR	ST	RNBT	FBG	DV	SE	115	OMC	7	2	1470		2800	3250
17	2	SPORTSMAN 180 BR	ST	RNBT	FBG	DV	IO	120-190		7	2	1470		2250	2800
18	2	FISH'N-SKI 190	ST	RNBT	FBG	DV	OB			7	8	1700		3250	3750
18	2	FISH'N-SKI 190	ST	RNBT	FBG	DV	SE	115	OMC	7	8	1700		3200	3750
18	2	FISH'N-SKI 190	ST	RNBT	FBG	DV	IO	120-140		7	8	1700		2650	3300
18	2	FISH'N-SKI 190	ST	RNBT	FBG	DV	SE	155	OMC	7	8	1700		3200	3700
18	2	FISH'N-SKI 190	ST	RNBT	FBG	DV	IO	170-190		7	8	1700		2700	3150
18	2	SPORTSMAN 190 B/R	ST	RNBT	FBG	DV	OB			7	8	1700		3150	3650
18	2	SPORTSMAN 190 BR	ST	RNBT	FBG	DV	OB			7	8	1700		3150	3650
18	2	SPORTSMAN 190 BR	ST	RNBT	FBG	DV	SE	115	OMC	7	8	1700		3150	3650
18	2	SPORTSMAN 190 BR	ST	RNBT	FBG	DV	IO	120-140		7	8	1700		2600	3250
18	2	SPORTSMAN 190 BR	ST	RNBT	FBG	DV	SE	155	OMC	7	8	1700		3150	3650
18	2	SPORTSMAN 190 BR	ST	RNBT	FBG	DV	IO	170	MRCR	7	8	1700		2650	3100
18	2	SPORTSMAN 190 BR	ST	RNBT	FBG	DV	IO	170	OMC	7	8	1700		2650	3050
18	2	SPORTSMAN 190 BR	ST	RNBT	FBG	DV	IO	170-190		7	8	1700		2900	3400
20		FISHERMAN 200	OP	CTRCN	FBG	DV	OB			7	6	1800		3700	4300
20		FISHERMAN 200	ST	CTRCN	FBG	DV	SE	115-155		7	6	1800		3700	4300
20	5	OFF FAMILY FSH 205	ST	FSH	FBG	SV	SE	115	OMC	8		3105		5200	5950
20	5	OFF FAMILY FSH 205	ST	FSH	FBG	SV	IO	120-140		8		3105		5050	6000
20	5	OFF FAMILY FSH 205	ST	FSH	FBG	SV	SE	155	OMC	8		3105		5200	5950
20	5	OFF FAMILY FSH 205	ST	FSH	FBG	SV	IO	170-190		8		3105		5050	6050
20	5	OFF FAMILY FSH 205	ST	FSH	FBG	SV	SE	205	OMC	8		3105		5200	5950
20	9	C-EAGLE 210	ST	CUD	FBG	DV	SE	115	OMC	8	1	3300		5650	6500
20	9	C-EAGLE 210	ST	CUD	FBG	DV	IO	117-140		8	1	3300		5250	6050
20	9	C-EAGLE 210	ST	CUD	FBG	DV	SE	155	OMC	8	1	3300		5650	6500
20	9	C-EAGLE 210	ST	CUD	FBG	DV	IO	170-200		8	1	3300		5100	6150
20	9	C-EAGLE 210	ST	CUD	FBG	DV	SE	205	OMC	8	1	3300		5650	6500
20	9	C-EAGLE 210	ST	CUD	FBG	DV	IO	225-260		8	1	3300		5400	6450
20	9	C-EAGLE 210	ST	CUD	FBG	DV	IO	110D	VLVO	8	1	3300		6300	7250
20	9	FISHERMAN 210	ST	FSH	FBG	DV	SE	115	OMC	8	1	3300		5500	6350
20	9	FISHERMAN 210	ST	FSH	FBG	DV	IO	117-140		8	1	3300		5550	6400
20	9	FISHERMAN 210	ST	FSH	FBG	DV	SE	155	OMC	8	1	3300		5500	6350
20	9	FISHERMAN 210	ST	FSH	FBG	DV	IO	170-200		8	1	3300		5400	6500
20	9	FISHERMAN 210	ST	FSH	FBG	DV	SE	205	OMC	8	1	3300		5500	6350
20	9	FISHERMAN 210	ST	FSH	FBG	DV	IO	225-260		8	1	3300		5700	6800
20	9	FISHERMAN 210	ST	FSH	FBG	DV	IO	110D	VLVO	8	1	3300		7900	9050
22	2	FISHERMAN 230	ST	FSH	FBG	DV	IO	138-140		8		3434		6100	7000
22	2	FISHERMAN 230	ST	FSH	FBG	DV	SE	155	OMC	8		3434		6600	7600
22	2	FISHERMAN 230	ST	FSH	FBG	DV	IO	170-200		8		3434		5950	7100
22	2	FISHERMAN 230	ST	FSH	FBG	DV	SE	205	OMC	8		3434		6600	7600
22	2	FISHERMAN 230	ST	FSH	FBG	DV	IO	225-290		8		3434		6250	7750
22	2	FISHERMAN 230	ST	FSH	FBG	DV	IO	110D	VLVO	8		3434		8600	9900
22	2	FISHERMAN 230	ST	FSH	FBG	DV	SE	T115	OMC	8		3434		6600	7600
22	2	OFF FAMILY FSH 222	ST	CUD	FBG	DV	OB			7	6	2800		6000	6900
22	2	OFF FAMILY FSH 222	ST	CUD	FBG	DV	IO	138-260		7	6			4850	5950
22	2	OFF FAMILY FSH 222	ST	CUD	FBG	DV	IO	290	VLVO	7	6			5450	6300
22	2	OFF FAMILY FSH 222	ST	CUD	FBG	DV	IO	110D-165D		7	6			5950	7300
22	2	OFF FAMILY FSH 222	ST	CUD	FBG	DV	SE	T115	OMC	7	6			**	**
22	2	OFFSHORE FAM FSH 222	ST	CUD	FBG	DV	SE	155-205		7	6	2800		6000	6900
22	2	SPORTSMAN 230	ST	RNBT	FBG	DV	IO	138-140		8		3434		5450	6300
22	2	SPORTSMAN 230	ST	RNBT	FBG	DV	SE	155	OMC	8		3434		6750	7750

 CONTINUED ON NEXT PAGE

LOA FT	LOA IN	NAME AND/ OR MODEL	TOP/ RIG	BOAT TYPE	-HULL- MTL	-HULL- TP	ENGINE TP	ENGINE # HP	ENGINE MFG	BEAM FT IN	WGT LBS	DRAFT FT IN	RETAIL LOW	RETAIL HIGH
		1985 BOATS												
22	2	SPORTSMAN 230	ST	RNBT	FBG	DV	IO	170-200		8	3434		5350	6350
22	2	SPORTSMAN 230	ST	RNBT	FBG	DV	SE	205	OMC	8	3434		6750	7750
22	2	SPORTSMAN 230	ST	RNBT	FBG	DV	IO	225-290		8	3434		5600	6950
22	2	SPORTSMAN 230	ST	RNBT	FBG	DV	IO	110D	VLVO	8	3434		6500	7500
22	2	SPORTSMAN 230	ST	RNBT	FBG	DV	SE	T115	OMC	8	3434		6750	7750
24	2	C-EAGLE 250	ST	CUD	FBG	DV	SE	155	OMC	8	5210		9900	11200
24	2	C-EAGLE 250	ST	CUD	FBG	DV	IO	170-200		8	5210		8600	10100
24	2	C-EAGLE 250	ST	CUD	FBG	DV	SE	205	OMC	8	5210		9850	11200
24	2	C-EAGLE 250	ST	CUD	FBG	DV	IO	225	VLVO	8	5210		9000	10200
		IB 225-228 11100 12700, IO 230-330 8850 10900, IO 110D-165D 10000 11900												
24	2	C-EAGLE 250	ST	CUD	FBG	DV	SE	T115	OMC	8	5210		9850	11200
24	2	C-EAGLE 250	ST	CUD	FBG	DV	IO	T117-T140		8	5210		9700	11100
24	2	C-EAGLE 250	ST	CUD	FBG	DV	SE	T155	OMC	8	5210		9850	11200
24	2	C-EAGLE 250	ST	CUD	FBG	DV	IO	T170-T190		8	5210		9500	11200
24	2	C-EAGLE 250	ST	CUD	FBG	DV	SE	T205	OMC	8	5210		9900	11200
24	2	C-EAGLE 250	HT	CUD	FBG	DV	SE	155	OMC	8	5210		9850	11200
24	2	C-EAGLE 250	HT	CUD	FBG	DV	IO	170-200		8	5210		8600	10100
24	2	C-EAGLE 250	HT	CUD	FBG	DV	SE	205	OMC	8	5210		9900	11200
24	2	C-EAGLE 250	HT	CUD	FBG	DV	IO	225	VLVO	8	5210		9000	10200
		IB 225 VLVO 11100 12700, IO 228 MRCR 8850 10000, IB 228 MRCR 11000 12500												
		IO 230-330 8800 10900, IO 110D-165D 10000 11900, IO T117-T140 9700 11100												
24	2	C-EAGLE 250	HT	CUD	FBG	DV	SE	T155	OMC	8	5210		9850	11200
24	2	C-EAGLE 250	HT	CUD	FBG	DV	IO	T170-T188		8	5210		9500	11200
24	2	C-EAGLE 250	HT	CUD	FBG	DV	SE	T205	OMC	8	5210		9850	11200
24	2	FISHERMAN 250	ST	FSH	FBG	DV	SE	155	OMC	8	5210		9650	11000
24	2	FISHERMAN 250	ST	FSH	FBG	DV	IO	170-200		8	5210		9150	10700
24	2	FISHERMAN 250	ST	FSH	FBG	DV	SE	205	OMC	8	5210		9700	11000
24	2	FISHERMAN 250	ST	FSH	FBG	DV	IO	225	VLVO	8	5210		9450	10700
		IB 225 VLVO 11100 12700, IO 230-330 9350 11600, IO 110D-165D 12500 14800												
24	2	FISHERMAN 250	ST	FSH	FBG	DV	SE	T115	OMC	8	5210		9650	11000
24	2	FISHERMAN 250	ST	FSH	FBG	DV	IO	T117-T140		8	5210		10200	11700
24	2	FISHERMAN 250	ST	FSH	FBG	DV	SE	T155	OMC	8	5210		9700	11000
24	2	FISHERMAN 250	ST	FSH	FBG	DV	IO	T170-T190		8	5210		10000	11800
24	2	FISHERMAN 250	ST	FSH	FBG	DV	SE	T205	OMC	8	5210		9650	11000
24	2	FISHERMAN 250	HT	FSH	FBG	DV	SE	155	OMC	8	5210		9650	11000
24	2	FISHERMAN 250	HT	FSH	FBG	DV	IO	170-200		8	5210		9150	10700
24	2	FISHERMAN 250	HT	FSH	FBG	DV	SE	205	OMC	8	5210		9650	11000
24	2	FISHERMAN 250	HT	FSH	FBG	DV	IO	225-330		8	5210		9450	11600
24	2	FISHERMAN 250	HT	FSH	FBG	DV	IO	110D-165D		8	5210		12500	14800
24	2	FISHERMAN 250	HT	FSH	FBG	DV	SE	T115	OMC	8	5210		9700	11000
24	2	FISHERMAN 250	HT	FSH	FBG	DV	IO	T117-T188		8	5210		10200	11800
24	2	OFF FAMILY FSH 242	ST	FSH	FBG	DV	OB			8			7450	8550
24	2	OFF FAMILY FSH 242	ST	FSH	FBG	DV	SE	155	OMC	8	4400		8950	10200
24	2	OFF FAMILY FSH 242	ST	FSH	FBG	DV	IO	170-200		8	4400		7900	9400
24	2	OFF FAMILY FSH 242	ST	FSH	FBG	DV	SE	205	OMC	8	4400		8950	10200
24	2	OFF FAMILY FSH 242	ST	FSH	FBG	DV	IO	225-330		8	4400		8250	10300
24	2	OFF FAMILY FSH 242	ST	FSH	FBG	DV	IO	110D-165D		8	4400		11000	13200
24	2	OFF FAMILY FSH 242	ST	FSH	FBG	DV	SE	T115-T205		8	4400		8950	10200
27		C-EAGLE 270	ST	CUD	FBG	DV	OB			10			11500	13100
27		C-EAGLE 270	ST	CUD	FBG	DV	SE	205	OMC	10	6800		11800	13500
27		C-EAGLE 270	ST	CUD	FBG	DV	IO	260	MRCR	10	6800		12300	14000
		IO 260 OMC 12300 14000, IO 260 VLVO 12400 14100, IB 260 15500 17700												
		IO 290-330 12700 14800, IB 340 MRCR 16200 18400, IB 235D VLVO 20800 23100												
27		C-EAGLE 270	ST	CUD	FBG	DV	SE	T115	OMC	10	6800		11800	13500
27		C-EAGLE 270	ST	CUD	FBG	DV	IO	T138-T140		10	6800		12800	14600
27		C-EAGLE 270	ST	CUD	FBG	DV	SE	T155	OMC	10	6800		11800	13500
27		C-EAGLE 270	ST	CUD	FBG	DV	IO	T170-T200		10	6800		13000	15400
27		C-EAGLE 270	ST	CUD	FBG	DV	SE	T205	OMC	10	6800		11800	13500
27		C-EAGLE 270	ST	CUD	FBG	DV	IO	T225-T290		10	6800		13800	16900
27		C-EAGLE 270	ST	CUD	FBG	DV	IO	T330	MRCR	10	6800		15400	17500
27		C-EAGLE 270	HT	CUD	FBG	DV	OB			10	6800		11800	13500
27		C-EAGLE 270	HT	CUD	FBG	DV	SE	205	OMC	10	6800		11800	13500
27		C-EAGLE 270	HT	CUD	FBG	DV	IO	260	MRCR	10	6800		12300	14000
		IO 260 OMC 12300 14000, IO 260 VLVO 12400 14100, IB 260 15500 17700												
		IO 290-330 12700 14800, IB 340 MRCR 16200 18400, IB 235D VLVO 20800 23100												
		IO T138-T140 12800 14600												
27		C-EAGLE 270	HT	CUD	FBG	DV	SE	T155	OMC	10	6800		11800	13500
27		C-EAGLE 270	HT	CUD	FBG	DV	IO	T170-T200		10	6800		13000	15400
27		C-EAGLE 270	HT	CUD	FBG	DV	SE	T205	OMC	10	6800		11800	13500
27		C-EAGLE 270	HT	CUD	FBG	DV	IO	T225-T290		10	6800		13800	16900
27		C-EAGLE 270	HT	CUD	FBG	DV	IO	T330	MRCR	10	6800		15400	17500
27		FAMILY FISHERMAN 270	ST	CUD	FBG	DV	SE	205	OMC	10	5740		11700	13300
27		FAMILY FISHERMAN 270	ST	CUD	FBG	DV	IO	260	MRCR	10	5740		11200	12800
		IO 260 OMC 11200 12800, IO 260 VLVO 11400 12900, IB 260 14200 16200												
		IO 290-330 11700 13600, IB 340 MRCR 14900 16900, IB 235D VLVO 18500 20600												
		IO T138-T140 11800 13400												
27		FAMILY FISHERMAN 270	ST	CUD	FBG	DV	SE	T155	OMC	10	5740		11700	13300
27		FAMILY FISHERMAN 270	ST	CUD	FBG	DV	IO	T170-T200		10	5740		12000	14200
27		FAMILY FISHERMAN 270	ST	CUD	FBG	DV	SE	T205	OMC	10	5740		11700	13300
27		FAMILY FISHERMAN 270	ST	CUD	FBG	DV	IO	T225-T290		10	5740		12800	15800
27		FAMILY FISHERMAN 270	ST	CUD	FBG	DV	IO	T330	MRCR	10	5740		14400	16400
27		FAMILY FISHERMAN 270	ST	FSH	FBG	DV	SE	T115	OMC	10	6800		12900	14600
27		FISHERMAN 270	ST	FSH	FBG	DV	OB			10			11300	12800
27		FISHERMAN 270	ST	FSH	FBG	DV	SE	205	OMC	10	6800		11700	13200
27		FISHERMAN 270	ST	FSH	FBG	DV	IO	260	MRCR	10	6800		13000	14800
		IO 260 OMC 13000 14800, IO 260 VLVO 13100 14900, IB 260 15500 17700												
		IO 290-330 13400 15600, IB 340 MRCR 16200 18400, IB 235D VLVO 20800 23100												
27		FISHERMAN 270	ST	FSH	FBG	DV	SE	T115	OMC	10	6800		10400	11900
27		FISHERMAN 270	ST	FSH	FBG	DV	IO	T138-T140		10	6800		13600	15400
27		FISHERMAN 270	ST	FSH	FBG	DV	SE	T155	OMC	10	6800		11700	13200
27		FISHERMAN 270	ST	FSH	FBG	DV	IO	T170-T200		10	6800		13700	16200
27		FISHERMAN 270	ST	FSH	FBG	DV	SE	T205	OMC	10	6800		11700	13200
27		FISHERMAN 270	ST	FSH	FBG	DV	IO	T225-T290		10	6800		14600	17800
27		FISHERMAN 270	ST	FSH	FBG	DV	IO	T330	MRCR	10	6800		16200	18500
27		FISHERMAN 270	HT	FSH	FBG	DV	OB			10	6185		11600	13200
27		FISHERMAN 270	HT	FSH	FBG	DV	SE	205	OMC	10	6800		11600	13200
27		FISHERMAN 270	HT	FSH	FBG	DV	IO	260	MRCR	10	6800		13000	14800
		IO 260 OMC 13000 14800, IO 260 VLVO 13100 14900, IB 260 15500 17700												
		IO 290-330 13400 15600, IB 340 MRCR 16200 18400, IB 235D VLVO 20800 23100												
		IO T138-T140 13600 15400												
27		FISHERMAN 270	HT	FSH	FBG	DV	SE	T155	OMC	10	6800		11600	13200
27		FISHERMAN 270	HT	FSH	FBG	DV	IO	T170-T200		10	6800		13700	16200
27		FISHERMAN 270	HT	FSH	FBG	DV	SE	T205	OMC	10	6800		11600	13200
27		FISHERMAN 270	HT	FSH	FBG	DV	IO	T225-T290		10	6800		14600	17800
27		FISHERMAN 270	HT	FSH	FBG	DV	IO	T330	MRCR	10	6800		16200	18500
27		SPORT FISHERMAN 270	FB	SF	FBG	DV	OB			10	6670		10800	12300
27		SPORT FISHERMAN 270	FB	SF	FBG	DV	SE	205	OMC	10	6670		10800	12300
27		SPORT FISHERMAN 270	FB	SF	FBG	DV	IO	260	MRCR	10	6670		13900	15800
		IO 260 OMC 13900 15700, IO 260 VLVO 14000 15900, IB 260 15400 17500												
		IO 290-330 14400 16700, IB 340 MRCR 16000 18200, IB 235D VLVO 20400 22700												
27		SPORT FISHERMAN 270	FB	SF	FBG	DV	SE	T115	OMC	10	6670		10800	12300
27		SPORT FISHERMAN 270	FB	SF	FBG	DV	IO	T138-T140		10	6670		14500	16500
27		SPORT FISHERMAN 270	FB	SF	FBG	DV	SE	T155	OMC	10	6670		10800	12300
27		SPORT FISHERMAN 270	FB	SF	FBG	DV	IO	T170-T200		10	6670		14700	17300
27		SPORT FISHERMAN 270	FB	SF	FBG	DV	SE	T205	OMC	10	6670		10800	12300
27		SPORT FISHERMAN 270	FB	SF	FBG	DV	IO	T225-T290		10	6670		15600	19100
27		SPORT FISHERMAN 270	FB	SF	FBG	DV	IO	T330	MRCR	10	6670		17400	19800
30		COASTAL FSH 300	ST	CUD	FBG	DV	IO	260	MRCR	10	9000		14600	16600
		IO 260 OMC 14600 16600, IO 260 VLVO 14700 16700, IB 260 19000 21100												
		IO 290-330 14900 17300, IB 340 MRCR 19500 21600, IB 235D VLVO 23800 26500												
		IO T138-T140 14900 16900												
30		COASTAL FSH 300	ST	CUD	FBG	DV	SE	T155	OMC	10	9000		16000	18200
30		COASTAL FSH 300	ST	CUD	FBG	DV	IO	T170-T200		10	9000		15200	17800
30		COASTAL FSH 300	ST	CUD	FBG	DV	SE	T205	OMC	10	9000		16000	18200
30		COASTAL FSH 300	ST	CUD	FBG	DV	IO	T225	VLVO	10	9000		16000	18100
		IB T225 VLVO 20500 22700, IO T230 MRCR 15900 18100, IO T230 OMC 15900 18100												
		IB T230 MRCR 20500 22800, IO T260 MRCR 16300 18600, IO T260 OMC 16300 18500												
		IO T260 VLVO 16400 18700, IB T260 20900 23300, IO T290-T330 16800 19700												
		IOT130D-T165D 18200 21100												
30		FISHERMAN 300	ST	FSH	FBG	DV	IO	260	MRCR	10	7255		14400	16300
		IO 260 OMC 14400 16300, IO 260 VLVO 14400 16400, VD 260 MRCR 17300 19600												
		IO 290-330 14700 17100, VD 340 MRCR 18500 20500, IO T138-T140 14700 16700												
30		FISHERMAN 300	ST	FSH	FBG	DV	SE	T155	OMC	10	7255		15900	18100
30		FISHERMAN 300	ST	FSH	FBG	DV	IO	T170-T200		10	7255		15100	17700
30		FISHERMAN 300	ST	FSH	FBG	DV	SE	T205	OMC	10	7255		15900	18100
30		FISHERMAN 300	ST	FSH	FBG	DV	IO	T225	VLVO	10	7255		15900	18100
		IO T230 MRCR 15900 18100, IO T230 OMC 15900 18100, VD T230 MRCR 19300 21500												
		IO T260 MRCR 16300 18600, IO T260 OMC 16300 18500, IO T260 VLVO 16400 18700												
		VD T260 MRCR 19800 22000, IO T290-T330 16900 19800, VD T340 MRCR 21100 23400												
		IOT130D-T165D 19700 23300												

CONTINUED ON NEXT PAGE

LOA FT	LOA IN	NAME AND/ OR MODEL	TOP/ RIG	BOAT TYPE	-HULL- MTL	-HULL- TP	ENGINE TP	ENGINE # HP	ENGINE MFG	BEAM FT	BEAM IN	WGT LBS	DRAFT FT	DRAFT IN	RETAIL LOW	RETAIL HIGH
		1985 BOATS														
30		FISHERMAN 300	HT	FSH	FBG	DV	IO	260	MRCR	10		7255			14400	16300
		IO 260 OMC 14400 16300, IO 260 VLVO 14400 16400, VD 260 MRCR													17300	19600
		IO 290-330 14700 17100, VD 340 MRCR 18500 20500, VD 235D VLVO													20800	23200
		IO T138-T140 14700 16700														
30		FISHERMAN 300	HT	FSH	FBG	DV	SE	T155	OMC	10		7255			15900	18100
30		FISHERMAN 300	HT	FSH	FBG	DV	IO	T170-T200		10		7255			15100	17700
30		FISHERMAN 300	HT	FSH	FBG	DV	SE	T205	OMC	10		7255			15900	18100
30		FISHERMAN 300	HT	FSH	FBG	DV	IO	T225-T228		10		7255			15900	18100
		IO T230 OMC 15900 18100, VD T230 MRCR 19300 21500, IO T260 MRCR													16300	18600
		IO T260 OMC 16300 18500, IO T260 VLVO 16400 18700, VD T260 MRCR													19800	22000
		IO T290-T330 16900 19800, VD T340 MRCR 21100 23400, IOT130D-T165D													19700	23300
30		GREAT-LAKES SP 300	ST	SF	FBG	DV	IO	260	MRCR	10		9000			16600	18900
		IO 260 OMC 16600 18900, IO 260 VLVO 16700 19000, IB 260													19000	21100
		IO 290-330 17000 19700, IB 340 MRCR 19500 21600, IB 235D VLVO													23800	26500
		IO T138-T140 16900 19300														
30		GREAT-LAKES SP 300	ST	SF	FBG	DV	SE	T155	OMC	10		9000			15600	17700
30		GREAT-LAKES SP 300	ST	SF	FBG	DV	IO	T170-T200		10		9000			17300	20300
30		GREAT-LAKES SP 300	ST	SF	FBG	DV	SE	T205	OMC	10		9000			15600	17700
30		GREAT-LAKES SP 300	ST	SF	FBG	DV	IO	T225	VLVO	10		9000			18600	20700
		IB T225 VLVO 20400 22700, IO T228 MRCR 18500 20600, IO T230 OMC													18600	20600
		IB T230 MRCR 20500 22700, IO T260 MRCR 19000 21100, IO T260 OMC													19000	21100
		IO T260 VLVO 19100 21200, IB T260 20900 23300, IO T290-T330													19400	22200
		IOT130D-T165D 22400 26000														
30		OFFSHORE FAM FSH 300	ST	CUD	FBG	DV	IO	260	MRCR	10					13100	14900
		IO 260 OMC 13100 14900, IO 260 VLVO 13200 15000, IB 260 VLVO													16700	19000
		VD 260 MRCR 16700 18900, IO 290-330 13500 15700, VD 340 MRCR													17500	19900
		IB 235D VLVO 19200 21300, IO T138-T140 13400 15200														
30		OFFSHORE FAM FSH 300	ST	CUD	FBG	DV	SE	T155	OMC	10					16000	18200
30		OFFSHORE FAM FSH 300	ST	CUD	FBG	DV	IO	T170-T200		10					13800	16700
30		OFFSHORE FAM FSH 300	ST	CUD	FBG	DV	SE	T205	OMC	10					16000	18200
30		OFFSHORE FAM FSH 300	ST	CUD	FBG	DV	IO	T225	VLVO	10					14700	16700
		IB T225 VLVO 19000 21100, IO T230 MRCR 14700 16700, IO T230 OMC													14700	16600
		IB T230 MRCR 19000 21200, IO T260 MRCR 15100 17200, IO T260 OMC													15100	17100
		IO T260 VLVO 15200 17300, IB T260 19300 21500, IO T290-T330													15700	18400
		IOT130D-T165D 14500 17600														
30		OFFSHORE FAMILY SF	FB	SF	FBG	DV	IO	260	MRCR						15100	17200
		IO 260 OMC 15100 17200, IO 260 VLVO 15200 17200, VD 260 MRCR													16900	19100
		IO 290-330 15500 18000, VD 340 MRCR 18100 20100, IO T138-T140													15500	17600
30		OFFSHORE FAMILY SF	FB	SF	FBG	DV	SE	T155	OMC						15000	17100
30		OFFSHORE FAMILY SF	FB	SF	FBG	DV	IO	T170-T200							15900	18700
30		OFFSHORE FAMILY SF	FB	SF	FBG	DV	SE	T205	OMC						15000	17100
30		OFFSHORE FAMILY SF	FB	SF	FBG	DV	IO	T225	VLVO						16900	19200
		IB T225 VLVO 19000 21100, IO T230 MRCR 16900 19200, IO T230 OMC													16900	19200
		IB T230 MRCR 19000 21100, IO T260 MRCR 17400 19800, IO T260 OMC													17400	19700
		IO T260 VLVO 17500 19900, IB T260 19500 21800, IO T290-T330													18400	21200
		IOT130D-T165D 17000 21000														
30		SPORT FISHERMAN 300	FB	SF	FBG	DV	IO	260	MRCR	10		7800			15800	18000
		IO 260 OMC 15800 18000, IO 260 VLVO 15900 18100, VD 260 MRCR													18100	20100
		IO 290-330 16200 18800, VD 340 MRCR 18800 20900, IO T138-T140													16200	18400
30		SPORT FISHERMAN 300	FB	SF	FBG	DV	SE	T155	OMC	10		7800			15000	17100
30		SPORT FISHERMAN 300	FB	SF	FBG	DV	IO	T170-T200		10		7800			16600	19400
30		SPORT FISHERMAN 300	FB	SF	FBG	DV	SE	T205	OMC	10		7800			15000	17100
30		SPORT FISHERMAN 300	FB	SF	FBG	DV	IO	T225	VLVO	10		7800			17500	19800
		IO T230 MRCR 17500 19800, IO T230 OMC 17400 19800, VD T230 MRCR													19700	21800
		IO T260 MRCR 18300 20300, IO T260 OMC 18300 20300, IO T260 VLVO													18400	20500
		VD T260 MRCR 20100 22400, IO T290-T330 18900 21500, VD T340 MRCR													21400	23700
		IOT130D-T165D 20500 24100														
		1984 BOATS														
16	1	ADVENTURER 170	ST	RNBT	FBG	DV	OB			6	4	955			1850	2200
16	1	ADVENTURER 170 SPEC		RNBT	FBG	DV	OB			6	4				2450	2850
16	1	FISH-N-SKI 170	ST	RNBT	FBG	DV	OB			6	4	1000			1900	2300
16	1	FISHERMAN 170	OP	FSH	FBG	SV	OB			6	2	1050			2000	2350
16	4	C-GULL		RNBT	FBG	TR	OB			6	4	1150			2250	2600
16	4	C-GULL 170		RNBT	FBG	TR	IO	120		6	9				2150	2500
17	1	SPORTSMAN 180 B/R		RNBT	FBG	DV	IO	120		7	2				2450	2850
17	1	SPORTSMAN 180 B/R	ST	RNBT	FBG	DV	OB			7	2	1300			2500	2900
18	2	SPORTSMAN 190		RNBT	FBG	DV	IO	120		7	8				2800	3250
18	2	SPORTSMAN 190 B/R	ST	RNBT	FBG	DV	OB			7	8	1700			3100	3600
18	11	CAPRICE 190		CUD	FBG	DV	OB			7		1540			3000	3450
20		FISHERMAN 200	OP	CTRCN	FBG	DV	OB			7	6	1800			3600	4200
20	9	C-EAGLE 210	ST	CUD	FBG	DV	IO	117-260		8	1	3300			5050	6250
20	9	C-EAGLE 210	ST	CUD	FBG	DV	IO	110D	VLVO	8	1	3300			6100	7000
20	9	FISHERMAN 210	ST	FSH	FBG	DV	IO	117-260		8	1	3300			5350	6550
20	9	FISHERMAN 210	ST	FSH	FBG	DV	IO	110D	VLVO	8	1	3300			7600	8750
22	2	FISHERMAN 222 OSFF	ST	CUD	FBG	DV	OB			7	6	2800			5850	6700
22	2	FISHERMAN 222 OSFF	ST	CUD	FBG	DV	IO	138-260		7	6				4650	5750
22	2	FISHERMAN 222 OSFF	ST	CUD	FBG	DV	IO	290	VLVO	7	6				5300	6050
22	2	FISHERMAN 222 OSFF	ST	CUD	FBG	DV	IO	110D-165D		7	6				5750	7050
22	2	FISHERMAN 222 OSFF	ST	CUD	FBG	DV	SE	T115	OMC	7	6				**	**
22	2	FISHERMAN 230	ST	FSH	FBG	DV	IO	138-260		8		3434			5900	7200
22	2	FISHERMAN 230	ST	FSH	FBG	DV	IO	290	VLVO	8		3434			6500	7500
22	2	FISHERMAN 230	ST	FSH	FBG	DV	IO	110D	VLVO	8		3434			8300	9550
22	2	FISHERMAN 230	ST	FSH	FBG	DV	SE	T115	OMC	8		3434			6400	7350
22	2	SPORTSMAN 230	ST	RNBT	FBG	DV	IO	138-140		8		3434			5300	6050
22	2	SPORTSMAN 230	ST	RNBT	FBG	DV	SE	155	OMC	8		3434			6600	7550
22	2	SPORTSMAN 230	ST	RNBT	FBG	DV	IO	170-260		8		3434			5150	6450
22	2	SPORTSMAN 230	ST	RNBT	FBG	DV	IO	290	VLVO	8		3434			5850	6700
22	2	SPORTSMAN 230	ST	RNBT	FBG	DV	IO	110D	VLVO	8		3434			6300	7200
22	2	SPORTSMAN 230	ST	RNBT	FBG	DV	SE	T115	OMC	8		3434			6600	7550
24	2	C-EAGLE 250	ST	CUD	FBG	DV	SE	155	OMC	8		5210			9650	10900
24	2	C-EAGLE 250	ST	CUD	FBG	DV	IO	170-200		8		5210			8300	9800
24	2	C-EAGLE 250	ST	CUD	FBG	DV	SE	205	OMC	8		5210			9650	10900
24	2	C-EAGLE 250	ST	CUD	FBG	DV	IO	225	VLVO	8		5210			8600	9900
		IB 225 VLVO 10600 12100, IO 228 MRCR 8450 9700, IB 228 MRCR													10500	12000
		IO 230-290 8400 10400, IO 330 MRCR 9350 10600, IO 110D-165D													9650	11400
		IO T117-T140 9450 10700														
24	2	C-EAGLE 250	ST	CUD	FBG	DV	SE	T155	OMC	8		5210			9650	10900
24	2	C-EAGLE 250	ST	CUD	FBG	DV	IO	T170-T188		8		5210			9200	10800
24	2	C-EAGLE 250	ST	CUD	FBG	DV	SE	T205	OMC	8		5210			9650	11000
24	2	C-EAGLE 250	HT	CUD	FBG	DV	SE	155	OMC	8		5210			9650	11000
24	2	C-EAGLE 250	HT	CUD	FBG	DV	IO	170-200		8		5210			8300	9800
24	2	C-EAGLE 250	HT	CUD	FBG	DV	SE	205	OMC	8		5210			9650	11000
24	2	C-EAGLE 250	HT	CUD	FBG	DV	IO	225	VLVO	8		5210			8600	9900
		IB 225 VLVO 10600 12100, IO 228 MRCR 8450 9700, IB 228 MRCR													10500	12000
		IO 230-290 8400 10400, IO 330 MRCR 9350 10600, IO 110D-165D													9650	11400
		IO T117-T140 9450 10700														
24	2	C-EAGLE 250	HT	CUD	FBG	DV	SE	T155	OMC	8		5210			9650	10900
24	2	C-EAGLE 250	HT	CUD	FBG	DV	IO	T170-T188		8		5210			9200	10800
24	2	C-EAGLE 250	HT	CUD	FBG	DV	SE	T205	OMC	8		5210			9650	11000
24	2	FISHERMAN 242 OSFF	ST	FSH	FBG	DV	OB			8					7250	8300
24	2	FISHERMAN 242 OSFF	ST	FSH	FBG	DV	SE	155	OMC	8		4400			8600	9900
24	2	FISHERMAN 242 OSFF	ST	FSH	FBG	DV	IO	170-200		8		4400			7650	9050
24	2	FISHERMAN 242 OSFF	ST	FSH	FBG	DV	SE	205	OMC	8		4400			8550	9800
24	2	FISHERMAN 242 OSFF	ST	FSH	FBG	DV	IO	225-330		8		4400			7950	9950
24	2	FISHERMAN 242 OSFF	ST	FSH	FBG	DV	IO	110D-165D		8		4400			10600	12700
24	2	FISHERMAN 242 OSFF	ST	FSH	FBG	DV	SE	T115	OMC	8		4400			8550	9800
24	2	FISHERMAN 250	ST	FSH	FBG	DV	SE	155	OMC	8		5210			9350	10600
24	2	FISHERMAN 250	ST	FSH	FBG	DV	IO	170-200		8		5210			8850	10300
24	2	FISHERMAN 250	ST	FSH	FBG	DV	SE	205	OMC	8		5210			9350	10600
24	2	FISHERMAN 250	ST	FSH	FBG	DV	IO	225-330		8		5210			9200	11200
24	2	FISHERMAN 250	ST	FSH	FBG	DV	IO	110D-165D		8		5210			12000	14300
24	2	FISHERMAN 250	ST	FSH	FBG	DV	SE	T115	OMC	8		5210			9400	10700
24	2	FISHERMAN 250	ST	FSH	FBG	DV	IO	T117-T188		8		5210			9900	11400
24	2	FISHERMAN 250	HT	FSH	FBG	DV	SE	155	OMC	8		5210			9400	10700
24	2	FISHERMAN 250	HT	FSH	FBG	DV	IO	170-200		8		5210			8850	10300
24	2	FISHERMAN 250	HT	FSH	FBG	DV	SE	205	OMC	8		5210			9350	10600
24	2	FISHERMAN 250	HT	FSH	FBG	DV	IO	225-330		8		5210			9200	11200
24	2	FISHERMAN 250	HT	FSH	FBG	DV	IO	110D-165D		8		5210			12000	14300
24	2	FISHERMAN 250	HT	FSH	FBG	DV	SE	T115	OMC	8		5210			9400	10700
24	2	FISHERMAN 250	HT	FSH	FBG	DV	IO	T117-T188		8		5210			9900	11400
27		C-EAGLE 270	ST	CUD	FBG	DV	OB			10					11300	12800
27		C-EAGLE 270	ST	CUD	FBG	DV	SE	205	OMC	10		6800			11600	13200
27		C-EAGLE 270	ST	CUD	FBG	DV	IO	260	MRCR	10		6800			11900	13500
		IO 260 OMC 11900 13500, IO 260 VLVO 12000 13600, IB 260													14800	17000
		IO 290-330 12300 14300, IB 340 MRCR 15500 17600, IB 235D VLVO													19900	22200
		IO T138-T140 12400 14100														
27		C-EAGLE 270	ST	CUD	FBG	DV	SE	T155	OMC	10		6800			11600	13200
27		C-EAGLE 270	ST	CUD	FBG	DV	IO	T170-T200		10		6800			12600	14800
27		C-EAGLE 270	ST	CUD	FBG	DV	SE	T205	OMC	10		6800			11600	13200

```
      LOA  NAME AND/       TOP/ BOAT  -HULL-   ----ENGINE---  BEAM  WGT  DRAFT RETAIL RETAIL
      FT IN OR MODEL        RIG  TYPE MTL TP TP  # HP  MFG    FT IN LBS  FT IN  LOW   HIGH
-------------------- 1984 BOATS
27   C-EAGLE 270             ST  CUD  FBG DV IO T225-T290    10    6800          13400 16300
27   C-EAGLE 270             ST  CUD  FBG DV IO T330  MRCR   10    6800          14900 16900
27   C-EAGLE 270             HT  CUD  FBG DV OB              10    6800          11600 13200
27   C-EAGLE 270             HT  CUD  FBG DV SE 205  OMC     10    6800          11600 13200
27   C-EAGLE 270             HT  CUD  FBG DV IO 260  MRCR    10    6800          11900 13500
     IO 260  OMC  11900 13500, IO 260  VLVO 12000 13600, IB 260          14800 17000
     IO 290-330   12300 14300, IB 340  MRCR 15500 17600, IB 235D VLVO    19900 22200
     IO T138-T140 12400 14100

27   C-EAGLE 270             HT  CUD  FBG DV SE T155  OMC    10    6800          11600 13200
27   C-EAGLE 270             HT  CUD  FBG DV IO T170-T200    10    6800          12600 14800
27   C-EAGLE 270             HT  CUD  FBG DV IO T205  OMC    10    6800          11600 13200
27   C-EAGLE 270             HT  CUD  FBG DV IO T225-T290    10    6800          13400 16300
27   C-EAGLE 270             HT  CUD  FBG DV IO T330  MRCR   10    6800          14900 16900
27   FAMILY CRUISER 270      ST  CR   FBG DV SE 205  OMC     10    6800          11600 13200
27   FAMILY CRUISER 270      ST  CR   FBG DV IO 260  MRCR    10    6800          11900 13500
     IO 260  OMC  11900 13500, IO 260  VLVO 12000 13600, IB 260          14800 16900
     IO 330  MRCR 12600 14300, IB 340  MRCR 15500 17600, IB 235D VLVO    19900 22100
     IO T138-T140 12400 14100

27   FAMILY CRUISER 270      ST  CR   FBG DV SE T155  OMC    10    6800          11600 13200
27   FAMILY CRUISER 270      ST  CR   FBG DV IO T170-T200    10    6800          12500 14800
27   FAMILY CRUISER 270      ST  CR   FBG DV SE T205  OMC    10    6800          11600 13200
27   FAMILY CRUISER 270      ST  CR   FBG DV IO T225-T290    10    6800          13300 16300
27   FAMILY CRUISER 270      ST  CR   FBG DV IO T330  MRCR   10    6800          14800 16900
27   FAMILY CURISER 270      ST  CR   FBG DV IO 290  VLVO    10    6800          12300 14000
27   FAMILY FISHERMAN 270    ST  FSH  FBG DV SE 205  OMC     10    6800          12600 14300
27   FAMILY FISHERMAN 270    ST  FSH  FBG DV IO 260  MRCR    10    6800          13900 15800
     IO 260  OMC  13900 15800, IO 260  VLVO 14100 16000, IB 260          16500 18900
     IO 290-330   14400 16600, IB 340  MRCR 18300 20300, IB 235D VLVO    21300 23700
     IO T138-T140 14300 16300

27   FAMILY FISHERMAN 270    ST  FSH  FBG DV SE T155  OMC    10    6800          12400 14100
27   FAMILY FISHERMAN 270    ST  FSH  FBG DV IO T170-T200    10    6800          14400 16700
27   FAMILY FISHERMAN 270    ST  FSH  FBG DV SE T205  OMC    10    6800          12300 14000
27   FAMILY FISHERMAN 270    ST  FSH  FBG DV IO T225-T330    10    6800          15300 19000
27   FISHERMAN 270           ST  FSH  FBG DV OB              10    6185          11300 12800
27   FISHERMAN 270           ST  FSH  FBG DV SE 205  OMC     10    6800          10100 11500
27   FISHERMAN 270           ST  FSH  FBG DV IO 260  MRCR    10    6800          11200 12700
     IO 260  OMC  11200 12700, IO 260  VLVO 11300 12800, IB 260          13200 15000
     IO 290-330   11600 13600, IB 340  MRCR 13100 14900, IB 235D VLVO    18800 20900
     IO T138-T140 11800 13500

27   FISHERMAN 270           ST  FSH  FBG DV SE T155  OMC    10    6800          10300 11700
27   FISHERMAN 270           ST  FSH  FBG DV IO T170-T200    10    6800          12000 14300
27   FISHERMAN 270           ST  FSH  FBG DV SE T205  OMC    10    6800          10400 11800
27   FISHERMAN 270           ST  FSH  FBG DV IO T225-T290    10    6800          12900 15900
27   FISHERMAN 270           ST  FSH  FBG DV IO T330  MRCR   10    6800          14600 16600
27   FISHERMAN 270           HT  FSH  FBG DV OB              10    6185          11300 12800
27   FISHERMAN 270           HT  FSH  FBG DV SE 205  OMC     10    6800          11300 12900
27   FISHERMAN 270           HT  FSH  FBG DV IO 260  MRCR    10    6800          12600 14300
     IO 260  OMC  12500 14200, IO 260  VLVO 12700 14400, IB 260          14800 17000
     IO 290-330   13000 15100, IB 340  MRCR 15500 17600, IB 235D VLVO    19900 22200
     IO T138-T140 13100 14900

27   FISHERMAN 270           HT  FSH  FBG DV SE T155  OMC    10    6800          11300 12900
27   FISHERMAN 270           HT  FSH  FBG DV IO T170-T200    10    6800          13300 15700
27   FISHERMAN 270           HT  FSH  FBG DV SE T205  OMC    10    6800          11300 12900
27   FISHERMAN 270           HT  FSH  FBG DV IO T225-T290    10    6800          14100 17200
27   FISHERMAN 270           HT  FSH  FBG DV IO T330  MRCR   10    6800          15700 17800
27   SPORT FISHERMAN 270     FB  SF   FBG DV OB              10    6670          10500 11900
27   SPORT FISHERMAN 270     FB  SF   FBG DV SE 205  OMC     10    6670          10500 11900
27   SPORT FISHERMAN 270     FB  SF   FBG DV IO 260  MRCR    10    6670          15100 15200
     IO 260  OMC  13400 15200, IO 260  VLVO 13500 15400, IB 260          14700 16800
     IO 290-330   13900 16100, IB 340  MRCR 15300 17400, IB 235D VLVO    19600 21800
     IO T138-T140 14000 15900

27   SPORT FISHERMAN 270     FB  SF   FBG DV SE T155  OMC    10    6670          10500 11900
27   SPORT FISHERMAN 270     FB  SF   FBG DV IO T170-T200    10    6670          14200 16700
27   SPORT FISHERMAN 270     FB  SF   FBG DV SE T205  OMC    10    6670          10500 11900
27   SPORT FISHERMAN 270     FB  SF   FBG DV IO T225-T290    10    6670          15100 18400
30   C-EAGLE 300             ST  CUD  FBG DV IO T330  MRCR   10    6670          16800 19100
     IO 260  OMC  13100 14900, IO 260  VLVO 13200 15000, VD 260  MRCR    16500 18800
     IO 290-330   13400 15600, VD 340  MRCR 17300 19600, VD 235D VLVO    20000 22200
     IO T138-T140 13400 15200

30   C-EAGLE 300             ST  CUD  FBG DV SE T155  OMC    10    7255          15600 16200
30   C-EAGLE 300             ST  CUD  FBG DV IO T170-T200    10    7255          13800 16200
30   C-EAGLE 300             ST  CUD  FBG DV SE T205  OMC    10    7255          15600 17800
30   C-EAGLE 300             ST  CUD  FBG DV IO T225-T228    10    7255          14600 16500
     IO T230 OMC  14500 16500, VD T230 MRCR 18700 20800, IO T260  MRCR   14900 17000
     IO T260 OMC  14900 17000, IO T260 VLVO 15000 17100, IO T260  MRCR   19200 21300
     IO T290-T330 15500 18200, VD T340 MRCR 20200 22400, IOT130D-T165D   15100 18200

30   C-EAGLE 300             HT  CUD  FBG DV IO 260  MRCR    10    7255          13100 14900
     IO 260  OMC  13100 14900, IO 260  VLVO 13200 15000, VD 260  MRCR    16500 18800
     IO 290-330   13400 15600, VD 340  MRCR 17300 19600, VD 235D VLVO    20000 22200
     IO T138-T140 13400 15200

30   C-EAGLE 300             HT  CUD  FBG DV SE T155  OMC    10    7255          15600 17800
30   C-EAGLE 300             HT  CUD  FBG DV IO T170-T200    10    7255          13800 16200
30   C-EAGLE 300             HT  CUD  FBG DV SE T205  OMC    10    7255          15600 17800
30   C-EAGLE 300             HT  CUD  FBG DV IO T225-T228    10    7255          14600 16500
     IO T230 OMC  14500 16500, VD T230 MRCR 18700 20800, IO T260  MRCR   14900 17000
     IO T260 OMC  14900 17000, IO T260 VLVO 15000 17100, IO T260  MRCR   19200 21300
     IO T290-T330 15500 18200, VD T340 MRCR 20200 22400, IOT130D-T165D   15100 18200

30   FISHERMAN 300           ST  FSH  FBG DV IO 260         10    7255          13900 15800
     IO 260  OMC  13900 15700, IO 260  VLVO 13900 15800, VD 260  MRCR    16500 18800
     IO 290-330   14200 16500, VD 340  MRCR 17300 19600, VD 235D VLVO    20000 22200
     IO T138-T140 14200 16100

30   FISHERMAN 300           ST  FSH  FBG DV SE T155  OMC    10    7255          15600 17700
30   FISHERMAN 300           ST  FSH  FBG DV IO T170-T200    10    7255          14500 17100
30   FISHERMAN 300           ST  FSH  FBG DV SE T205  OMC    10    7255          15600 17700
30   FISHERMAN 300           ST  FSH  FBG DV IO T225-T228    10    7255          15400 17500
     IO T230 OMC  15300 17400, VD T230 MRCR 18700 20800, IO T260  MRCR   15800 17900
     IO T260 OMC  15700 17900, IO T260 VLVO 15900 18000, VD T260  MRCR   19200 21300
     IO T290-T330 16300 19200, VD T340 MRCR 20200 22400, IOT130D-T165D   19100 22500

30   FISHERMAN 300           HT  FSH  FBG DV IO 260  MRCR    10    7255          13900 15800
     IO 260  OMC  13900 15700, IO 260  VLVO 13900 15800, VD 260  MRCR    16500 18800
     IO 290-330   14200 16500, VD 340  MRCR 17300 19600, VD 235D VLVO    20000 22200
     IO T138-T140 14200 16100

30   FISHERMAN 300           HT  FSH  FBG DV SE T155  OMC    10    7255          15600 17700
30   FISHERMAN 300           HT  FSH  FBG DV IO T170-T200    10    7255          14500 17100
30   FISHERMAN 300           HT  FSH  FBG DV SE T205  OMC    10    7255          15600 17700
30   FISHERMAN 300           HT  FSH  FBG DV IO T225-T228    10    7255          15400 17500
     IO T230 OMC  15300 17400, VD T230 MRCR 18700 20800, IO T260  MRCR   15800 17900
     IO T260 OMC  15700 17900, IO T260 VLVO 15900 18000, VD T260  MRCR   19200 21300
     IO T290-T330 16300 19200, VD T340 MRCR 20200 22400, IOT130D-T165D   19100 22500

30   GREAT-LAKES 300 SP              FBG DV IO 260  MRCR                        14100 16000
     IO 260  OMC  14100 16000, IO 260  VLVO 14100 16100, IB 260          16100 18300
     IO 290-330   14500 16800, IB 340  MRCR 16900 19200, IB 235D VLVO    17400 19800
     IO T140-T145 14400 16500

30   GREAT-LAKES 300 SP              FBG DV IO T155  OMC                        15300 17400
30   GREAT-LAKES 300 SP              FBG DV IO T170-T200                        14900 17500
30   GREAT-LAKES 300 SP              FBG DV IO T205  OMC                        15300 17400
30   GREAT-LAKES 300 SP              FBG DV IO T225  VLVO                       15800 17900
     IB T225 VLVO 18400 20400, IO T228 MRCR 15800 17900, IO T230 OMC     15800 17900
     IB T230 MRCR 18400 20400, IO T228 VLVO 16200 18500, IO T260 OMC     16200 18400
     IO T260 VLVO 16300 18600, IB T260      18900 21000, IO T290-T330     16800 19800
     IOT130D-T165D 19500

30   OFFSHORE FAMILY CR             CR  FBG DV IO 260  MRCR 10                  13400 15300
     IO 260  OMC  13400 15200, IO 260  VLVO 13500 15300, IB 260          16900 19200
     IO 290-330   13700 15600, IB 340  MRCR 18100 20100, IB 235D VLVO    18700 20700
     IO T138-T140 13700 15600

30   OFFSHORE FAMILY CR             CR  FBG DV IO T155  OMC 10                  15600 17800
30   OFFSHORE FAMILY CR             CR  FBG DV IO T170-T188 10                  14100 16400
30   OFFSHORE FAMILY CR             CR  FBG DV IO T205  OMC 10                  15600 17800
30   OFFSHORE FAMILY CR             CR  FBG DV IO T225  VLVO 10                 15000 17100
     IB T225 VLVO 19100 21200, IO T228 MRCR 15000 17000, IB T228 MRCR   19100 21200
     IB T230 MRCR 19100 21200, IO T228 VLVO 15400 17600, IO T260 OMC     15400 17500
     IO T260 VLVO 15500 17700, IB T260      19600 21800, IO T290-T330     16000 18800
     IOT130D-T165D 14100 17300

30   OFFSHORE FAMILY SF      FB  SF   FBG DV IO 260  MRCR                       14600 16600
     IO 260  OMC  14600 16600, IO 260  VLVO 14600 16600, VD 260  MRCR    16100 18300
     IO 290-330   15000 17400, VD 340  MRCR 16900 19200, IO T140-T145    14900 17100
```

LOA FT	IN	NAME AND/ OR MODEL	TOP/ RIG	BOAT TYPE	-HULL- MTL	TP	ENGINE TP	# HP	MFG	BEAM FT	IN	WGT LBS	DRAFT FT	IN	RETAIL LOW	RETAIL HIGH
		1984 BOATS														
30		OFFSHORE FAMILY SF	FB	SF	FBG	DV	SE	T155	OMC						14600	16600
30		OFFSHORE FAMILY SF	FB	SF	FBG	DV	IO	T170-T200							15400	18100
30		OFFSHORE FAMILY SF	FB	SF	FBG	DV	SE	T205	OMC						14600	16600
30		OFFSHORE FAMILY SF	FB	SF	FBG	DV	IO	T225	VLVO						16300	18500
		IB T225 VLVO 18400 20400, IO T228 MRCR 16300 18500, IO T230 OMC													16300	18500
		IB T230 MRCR 18400 20400, IO T260 MRCR 16800 19100, IO T260 OMC													16800	19000
		IO T260 VLVO 16900 19200, IB T260 18900 21000, IO T290-T330													17400	20500
		IOT130D-T165D 16400 20200														
30		SPORT FISHERMAN 300	FB	SF	FBG	DV	IO	260	MRCR	10		7800			15300	17400
		IO 260 OMC 15300 17400, IO 260 VLVO 15300 17400, VD 260 MRCR													16900	19200
		IO 290-330 15600 18100, VD 340 MRCR 17600 20000, IB 235D VLVO													20800	23200
		IO T138-T140 15600 17700														
30		SPORT FISHERMAN 300	FB	SF	FBG	DV	SE	T155	OMC	10		7800			14600	16600
30		SPORT FISHERMAN 300	FB	SF	FBG	DV	IO	T170-T200		10		7800			16000	18700
30		SPORT FISHERMAN 300	FB	SF	FBG	DV	SE	T205	OMC	10		7800			14600	16600
30		SPORT FISHERMAN 300	FB	SF	FBG	DV	IO	T225-T228		10		7800			16900	19200
		IO T230 OMC 16800 19100, VD T230 MRCR 19000 21100, IO T260 MRCR													17300	19600
		IO T260 OMC 17300 19600, IO T260 VLVO 17400 19800, VD T260 MRCR													19200	21400
		IO T290-T330 18300 20900, VD T340 MRCR 20400 22700, IOT130D-T165D													19800	23200

....For earlier years, see the BUC Used Boat Price Guide, Volume 3

SPRINGER BOATS

RIO LINDA CA 95673 COAST GUARD MFG ID- XSI See inside cover to adjust price for area

LOA FT	IN	NAME AND/ OR MODEL	TOP/ RIG	BOAT TYPE	-HULL- MTL	TP	ENGINE TP	# HP	MFG	BEAM FT	IN	WGT LBS	DRAFT FT	IN	RETAIL LOW	RETAIL HIGH
		1987 BOATS														
18	1	TOURNAMENT	OP	BASS	FBG	SV	OB			7	7	1400			4100	4750
18	1	TOURNAMENT	OP	BASS	KEV	SV	OB			7	7	1400			4200	4900

STAMAS YACHTS INC

TARPON SPRINGS FL 34689 See inside cover to adjust price for area
FORMERLY STAMAS BOATS INC

For more recent years, see the BUC Used Boat Price Guide, Volume 1

LOA FT	IN	NAME AND/ OR MODEL	TOP/ RIG	BOAT TYPE	-HULL- MTL	TP	ENGINE TP	# HP	MFG	BEAM FT	IN	WGT LBS	DRAFT FT	IN	RETAIL LOW	RETAIL HIGH
		1996 BOATS														
25	9	TARPON 240	OP	CTRCN	FBG	SV	OB			8	6	3200	1	1	18500	20500
31	7	EXPRESS 290	OP	EXP	FBG	DV	IB	310-320		10	4	8600	2	4	51500	57000
31	7	EXPRESS 290	OP	EXP	FBG	DV	IB	230D	YAN	10	4	8600	2	4	61800	68000
31	7	TARPON 290	OP	CTRCN	FBG	DV	OB			10	4	5000	1	7	38200	42400
31	7	TARPON 290	OP	CTRCN	FBG	DV	IB	310-320		10	4	6000	2	4	43900	49300
31	7	TARPON 290	OP	CTRCN	FBG	DV	IB	230D	YAN	10	4	6000	2	4	47700	52400
32	6	EXPRESS 310	OP	EXP	FBG	DV	OB			11	2	8800	1	7	48000	52700
32	6	EXPRESS 310	OP	EXP	FBG	DV	IB	T250	CRUS	11	2	10500	1	7	62200	68400
32	6	EXPRESS 310	OP	EXP	FBG	DV	IB	T225D-T230D		11	2	10500	1	7	75300	83700
32	6	EXPRESS 310	OP	EXP	FBG	SV	OB			11	1	8800	1	7	48000	52700
32	6	EXPRESS 310	OP	EXP	FBG	SV	IB	T250	MRCR	11	2	10500	1	7	62100	68300
32	6	EXPRESS 310	OP	EXP	FBG	SV	IB	T170D	YAN	11	2	10500	1	7	71400	78400
38	6	EXPRESS 360	OP	EXP	FBG	DV	IB	T320	CRUS	13	2	16975	2	4	103500	114000
38	6	EXPRESS 360	OP	EXP	FBG	DV	IB	T380	CRUS	13	2	16975	2	4	106500	117000
38	6	EXPRESS 360	OP	EXP	FBG	DV	IB	T350D	CAT	13	2	16975	2	4	129000	141500
38	6	EXPRESS 360	OP	EXP	FBG	SV	IB	T310	MRCR	13	2	16975	2	4	102500	113000
38	6	EXPRESS 360	OP	EXP	FBG	SV	IB	T400	MRCR	13	2	16975	2	4	106500	117500
38	6	EXPRESS 360	OP	EXP	FBG	SV	IB	T300D	CAT	13	2	22500	2	4	146500	161000
		1995 BOATS														
24	4	TARPON 240		CTRCN	FBG	SV	OB			8	6	3200	1	1	17200	19500
25	4	TARPON 255	OP	CTRCN	FBG	DV	OB			8	6	3875	1	3	20600	22900
27	3	FAMILY FISHERMAN 255	OP	SF	FBG	DV	OB			8	6	4330	1	4	21800	24200
27	3	FAMILY FISHERMAN 255	OP	SF	FBG	DV	IO	245-250		8	6	5100	1	4	25700	28500
31	7	EXPRESS 290	OP	EXP	FBG	DV	OB			10	4	7010	1	7	38600	42900
31	7	EXPRESS 290	OP	EXP	FBG	DV	IB	170D	YAN	10	4	8600	2	4	55900	61400
31	7	TARPON 290	OP	CTRCN	FBG	DV	OB			10	4	5000	1	7	47000	51700
31	7	TARPON 290	OP	CTRCN	FBG	DV	IB	620		10	4	6000	1	7	61700	67800
32	6	EXPRESS 310	OP	EXP	FBG	SV	OB			11	2	8800	1	7	44900	49900
32	6	EXPRESS 310	OP	EXP	FBG	SV	IB	T250	MRCR	11	2	10500	1	7	58700	64500
32	6	EXPRESS 310	OP	EXP	FBG	SV	IB	T170D	YAN	11	2	10500	1	7	67800	74500
38	6	EXPRESS 360	OP	EXP	FBG	SV	IB	T310	MRCR	13	2	17000	2	4	98500	108500
38	6	EXPRESS 360	OP	EXP	FBG	SV	IB	T400	MRCR	13	2	17000	2	4	102500	112500
38	6	EXPRESS 360	OP	EXP	FBG	SV	IB	T300D	CAT	13	2	19000	2	4	126500	139000
		1994 BOATS														
24	4	TARPON 240		CTRCN	FBG	SV	OB			8	6	3200	1	1	16400	18600
25	4	TARPON 255	OP	CTRCN	FBG	DV	OB			8	6	3875	1	3	19600	21800
27	3	FAMILY FISHERMAN 255	OP	SF	FBG	DV	OB			8	6	4330	1	4	20700	23000
27	3	FAMILY FISHERMAN 255	OP	SF	FBG	DV	IO	245-250		8	6	5100	1	4	24000	26600
30	2	FAMILY FISHERMAN 288	OP	EXP	FBG	DV	IO	T205		11	2	9500	1	6	43600	48600
31	7	EXPRESS 290	OP	EXP	FBG	DV	OB			10	4	7010	1	7	36600	40700
32	6	EXPRESS 310	OP	EXP	FBG	SV	OB			11	2	8800	1	7	42800	47500
32	6	EXPRESS 310	OP	EXP	FBG	SV	IB	T250	MRCR	11	2	10500	1	7	55600	61100
32	6	EXPRESS 310	OP	EXP	FBG	SV	IB	T170D	YAN	11	2	10500	1	7	64500	70900
38	6	EXPRESS 360	OP	EXP	FBG	SV	IB	T310	MRCR	13	2	17000	2	4	94400	103500
38	6	EXPRESS 360	OP	EXP	FBG	SV	IB	T400	MRCR	13	2	17000	2	4	98200	108000
38	6	EXPRESS 360	OP	EXP	FBG	SV	IB	T300D	CAT	13	2	19000	2	4	121500	133500
		1993 BOATS														
24	4	TARPON 240		CTRCN	FBG	SV	OB			8	6	3200	1	1	15500	17600
25	4	TARPON 255	OP	CTRCN	FBG	DV	OB			8	6	3875	1	3	18900	21000
27	3	FAMILY FISHERMAN 255	OP	SF	FBG	DV	OB			8	6	5330	1	3	21500	23900
27	3	FAMILY FISHERMAN 255	OP	SF	FBG	DV	IO	240-245		8	6	5330	1	3	22600	25700
30	2	FAMILY FISHERMAN 288	OP	EXP	FBG	DV	OB			11	2	8150	1	6	38300	42500
30	2	FAMILY FISHERMAN 288	OP	EXP	FBG	DV	IO	T205		11	2	9500	1	6	40800	45500
31	7	EXPRESS 290	OP	EXP	FBG	DV	OB			10	4	7010	2	4	34800	38700
32	6	EXPRESS 310	OP	EXP	FBG	SV	OB			11	2	8800	1	6	40400	44900
32	6	EXPRESS 310	OP	EXP	FBG	SV	IB	T250	MRCR	11	2	10500	1	7	52700	57900
32	6	EXPRESS 310	OP	EXP	FBG	SV	IB	T170D	YAN	11	2	10500	1	7	61500	67600
38	6	EXPRESS 360	OP	EXP	FBG	SV	IB	T310	MRCR	13	2	16500	2	4	88400	97200
38	6	EXPRESS 360	OP	EXP	FBG	SV	IB	T400	MRCR	13	2	16500	2	4	92100	101000
38	6	EXPRESS 360	OP	EXP	FBG	SV	IB	T375D	CAT	13	2	16500	2	4	113500	125000
		1992 BOATS														
19		TARPON 180	OP	CTRCN	FBG	DV	OB			7		1800		11	7100	8150
22		TARPON 220	OP	CTRCN	FBG	SV	OB			8		3500	1		13600	15500
24	4	FREEDOM 244	OP	SPTCR	FBG	DV	OB			8	6	3900	1	1	17200	19500
25	4	TARPON 255	OP	CTRCN	FBG	DV	OB			8	6	3875	1	3	18200	20200
27	3	FAMILY FISHERMAN 255	OP	SF	FBG	DV	OB			8	6	5330	1	3	20500	22800
27	3	FAMILY FISHERMAN 255	OP	SF	FBG	DV	IO	240-245		8	6	5330	1	3	21200	24000
30	2	LIBERTY 288	HT	EXP	FBG	DV	OB			11	2	8150	1	6	36500	40600
30	2	LIBERTY 288	HT	EXP	FBG	DV	IO	T205		11	2	9500	1	6	38200	42500
38	6	EXPRESS 360	OP	EXP	FBG	DV	OB			13	2	16500	2	4	**	**
38	6	EXPRESS 360	OP	EXP	FBG	SV	IB	T310	MRCR	13	2	16500	2	4	84300	92700
		IB T400 MRCR 87800 96400, IB T375D CAT 108500 119000, IB T425D CAT													113500	125000
		1991 BOATS														
19		TARPON 180	OP	CTRCN	FBG	DV	OB			7		1800		11	6800	7800
24	4	FREEDOM 244	OP	SPTCR	FBG	DV	OB			8	6	3900	1	1	16500	18800
25	4	TARPON 255	OP	CTRCN	FBG	DV	OB			8	6	3875	1	3	17000	19400
27	3	FAMILY FISHERMAN 255	OP	SF	FBG	DV	OB			8	6	4330	1	3	18300	20400
27	3	FAMILY FISHERMAN 255	OP	SF	FBG	DV	IO	231-260		8	6	5330	1	3	20100	22400
30	2	LIBERTY 288	HT	EXP	FBG	DV	OB			11	2	8150	1	6	35000	38800
30	2	LIBERTY 288	HT	EXP	FBG	DV	IO	T205-T235		11	2	9500	1	6	35900	40700
38	6	EXPRESS 360	OP	EXP	FBG	SV	IB	T310	MRCR	13	2	16500	2	4	80400	88400
		IB T300D CAT 97000 106500, IB T375D CAT 103500 113500, IB T425D CAT													108500	119000
		1990 BOATS														
19		TARPON 180	OP	CTRCN	FBG	DV	OB			7		1800		11	6500	7500
24	4	FREEDOM 244	OP	SPTCR	FBG	DV	OB			8	6	3900	1	1	15800	17900
24	4	FREEDOM 244	OP	SPTCR	FBG	DV	IO	205	VLVO	8	6	4700	1	1	14300	16200
25	4	TARPON 255	OP	CTRCN	FBG	DV	OB			8	6	3875	1	3	16400	18600
27	3	FAMILY FISHERMAN 255	OP	SF	FBG	DV	OB			8	6	4330	1	3	17300	19600
27	3	FAMILY FISHERMAN 255	OP	SF	FBG	DV	IO	231-260		8	6	5330	1	3	19100	21300
30	2	LIBERTY 288	OP	SPTCR	FBG	DV	OB			11	2	8150	1	6	33500	37200
30	2	LIBERTY 288	OP	SPTCR	FBG	DV	IO	T205-T235		11	2	9500	1	6	30500	34500
		1989 BOATS														
19		TARPON 180	OP	CTRCN	FBG	DV	OB			7				11	6000	6900
22		TARPON 22	OP	CTRCN	FBG	SV	OB			8			1		9450	10700
24	4	FREEDOM 244	OP	SPTCR	FBG	SV	OB			8	6	3900	1	1	15200	17300
24	4	FREEDOM 244	OP	SPTCR	FBG	SV	IO	205-230		8	6	3900	1	1	11800	13400
25	4	TARPON 255	OP	CTRCN	FBG	SV	OB			8	6	4300	1	3	16600	18800
27	3	FISHERMAN 255	OP	FSH	FBG	SV	OB			8	6	4330	1	3	16700	19000
27	3	FISHERMAN 255	OP	FSH	FBG	SV	IO	231-260		8	6	4330	1	3	14300	16300
27	3	FISHERMAN 255	OP	FSH	FBG	SV	IO	T151	VLVO	8	6	4330	1	3	15700	17800
27	3	FISHERMAN 255	HT	FSH	FBG	SV	OB			8	6	4330	1	3	16800	19100
27	3	FISHERMAN 255	HT	FSH	FBG	SV	IO	231-260		8	6	4330	1	3	14300	16300
27	3	FISHERMAN 255	HT	FSH	FBG	SV	IO	T151	VLVO	8	6	4330	1	3	15700	17800
30	2	LIBERTY 288	OP	SPTCR	FBG	SV	OB			11	2	9500	1	6	32200	35800
30	2	LIBERTY 288	OP	SPTCR	FBG	SV	IO	T205-T230		11	2	9500	1	6	28800	32500
30	2	LIBERTY 288	HT	SPTCR	FBG	SV	OB			11	2	9500	1	6	32200	35800
30	2	LIBERTY 288	HT	SPTCR	FBG	SV	IO	T205-T230		11	2	9500	1	6	28800	32500

LOA FT	LOA IN	NAME AND/ OR MODEL	TOP/ RIG	BOAT TYPE	-HULL- MTL	-HULL- TP	ENGINE TP	ENGINE # HP	ENGINE MFG	BEAM FT	BEAM IN	WGT LBS	DRAFT FT	DRAFT IN	RETAIL LOW	RETAIL HIGH
		1988 BOATS														
18	3	TARPON 180	OP	CTRCN	FBG	DV	OB			7	3				5200	5950
22		TARPON 22	OP	CTRCN	FBG	SV	OB			8			1		9150	10400
23	3	TARPON 24	OP	OPFSH	FBG	SV	OB			8		3500	2	4	13000	14800
25	4	TARPON 255	OP	CTRCN	FBG	SV	OB			8	6	4300	1	3	16100	18200
25	4	TARPON 255	OP	CTRCN	FBG	SV	SE	205	OMC	8	6	4300	1	3	16100	18200
25	4	TARPON 255	OP	CTRCN	FBG	SV	SE	T		8	6				**	**
25	11	TARPON 26	OP	FSH	FBG	SV	OB			9	7	6400	2		19200	21300
25	11	TARPON 26	OP	FSH	FBG	SV	SE	205	OMC	9	7	6400	2		19200	21300
25	11	TARPON 26	OP	FSH	FBG	SV	IO	T260	MRCR	9	7	6400	2		21100	23400
27	3	FISHERMAN 255	OP	FSH	FBG	SV	OB			8	6	4330	1	3	16100	18300
27	3	FISHERMAN 255	OP	FSH	FBG	SV	SE	205	OMC	8	6	4330	1	3	16100	18300
27	3	FISHERMAN 255	OP	FSH	FBG	SV	IO	260		8	6	4330	1	3	13600	15400
27	3	FISHERMAN 255	HT	FSH	FBG	SV	OB			8	6	4330	1	3	16200	18400
27	3	FISHERMAN 255	HT	FSH	FBG	SV	SE	205	OMC	8	6	4330	1	3	16200	18400
27	3	FISHERMAN 255	HT	FSH	FBG	SV	IO	260		8	6	4330	1	3	13600	15400
30	2	LIBERTY 288	OP	SPTCR	FBG	SV	OB			11	2	9500	1	6	31000	34500
30	2	LIBERTY 288	OP	SPTCR	FBG	SV	SE	T230	OMC	11	2	9500	1	6	31000	34500
30	2	LIBERTY 288	OP	SPTCR	FBG	SV	IO	T230		11	2	9500	1	6	27700	30800
30	2	LIBERTY 288	HT	SPTCR	FBG	SV	OB			11	2	9500	1	6	31100	34500
30	2	LIBERTY 288	HT	SPTCR	FBG	SV	SE	T	OMC	11	2	9500	1	6	**	**
30	2	LIBERTY 288	HT	SPTCR	FBG	SV	IO	T230		11	2	9500	1	6	27700	30800
		1987 BOATS														
18	3	TARPON 180	OP	CTRCN	FBG	DV	OB			7	3				5050	5800
22		TARPON 22	OP	CTRCN	FBG	SV	OB			8			1		8850	10100
23	3	TARPON 24	OP	OPFSH	FBG	SV	OB			8		3500	2	4	12700	14400
23	3	TARPON 24	OP	OPFSH	FBG	SV	SE	205	OMC	8		3500	2	4	12700	14400
25	4	TARPON 255	OP	CTRCN	FBG	SV	OB			8	6	4300	1	3	15600	17700
25	4	TARPON 255	OP	CTRCN	FBG	SV	SE	205	OMC	8	6	4300	1	3	15600	17700
25	11	FISHERMAN 26	OP	FSH	FBG	SV	OB			9	7	6500	2	6	18700	20800
25	11	FISHERMAN 26	OP	FSH	FBG	SV	SE	205	OMC	9	7	6500	2	6	18700	20800
25	11	FISHERMAN 26	OP	FSH	FBG	SV	IO	260		9	7	6500	2	6	17600	20000
25	11	FISHERMAN 26	OP	FSH	FBG	SV	IB	340	MRCR	9	7	6500	2	6	22100	24600
25	11	FISHERMAN 26	OP	FSH	FBG	SV	SE	T	OMC	9	7	7500	2	6	**	**
25	11	FISHERMAN 26	OP	FSH	FBG	SV	IO	T175		9	7	7500	2	6	20700	23000
25	11	FISHERMAN 26	HT	FSH	FBG	SV	OB			9	7	6500	2	6	18700	20800
25	11	FISHERMAN 26	HT	FSH	FBG	SV	SE	205	OMC	9	7	6500	2	6	18700	20800
25	11	FISHERMAN 26	HT	FSH	FBG	SV	IO	260		9	7	6500	2	6	17600	20000
25	11	FISHERMAN 26	HT	FSH	FBG	SV	IB	340	MRCR	9	7	6500	2	6	22100	24600
25	11	FISHERMAN 26	HT	FSH	FBG	SV	SE	T	OMC	9	7	7500	2	6	**	**
25	11	FISHERMAN 26	HT	FSH	FBG	SV	IO	T175		9	7	7500	2	6	20700	23000
25	11	SPORTCRUISER 26	OP	SPTCR	FBG	SV	SE		OMC	9	7	7500	2	6	**	**
25	11	SPORTCRUISER 26	OP	SPTCR	FBG	SV	IO	260		9	7	6500	2	6	16700	18900
25	11	SPORTCRUISER 26	OP	SPTCR	FBG	SV	IB	340	MRCR	9	7	6500	2	6	22100	24600
25	11	SPORTCRUISER 26	OP	SPTCR	FBG	SV	IO	T175		9	7	7500	2	6	19600	21800
25	11	SPORTCRUISER 26	HT	SPTCR	FBG	SV	IO	260		9	7	6500	2	6	16700	18900
25	11	SPORTCRUISER 26	HT	SPTCR	FBG	SV	IB	340	MRCR	9	7	6500	2	6	22100	24600
25	11	SPORTCRUISER 26	HT	SPTCR	FBG	SV	IO	T175		9	7	7500	2	6	19600	21800
25	11	SPORTCRUISER 26	FB	SPTCR	FBG	SV	IO	260		9	7	6500	2	6	16700	18900
25	11	SPORTCRUISER 26	FB	SPTCR	FBG	SV	IB	340	MRCR	9	7	6500	2	6	22100	24600
25	11	SPORTCRUISER 26	FB	SPTCR	FBG	SV	SE	T	OMC	9	7	7900	2	6	**	**
25	11	SPORTCRUISER 26	FB	SPTCR	FBG	SV	IO	T175		9	7	7900	2	6	20300	22500
25	11	SPORTCURISER 26	HT	SPTCR	FBG	SV	SE	T	OMC	9	7	7500	2	6	**	**
25	11	TARPON 26	OP	FSH	FBG	SV	OB			9	7	6400	2		18600	20700
25	11	TARPON 26	OP	FSH	FBG	SV	SE	205	OMC	9	7	6400	2		18600	20700
25	11	TARPON 26	OP	FSH	FBG	SV	IO	260		9	7	6400	2		17400	19800
25	11	TARPON 26	OP	FSH	FBG	SV	IB	340	MRCR	9	7	6400	2		21900	24300
27	3	FISHERMAN 255	OP	FSH	FBG	SV	OB			8	6	4330	1	3	15700	17800
27	3	FISHERMAN 255	OP	FSH	FBG	SV	SE	205	OMC	8	6	4330	1	3	15700	17800
27	3	FISHERMAN 255	OP	FSH	FBG	SV	IO	260		8	6	4330	1	3	12900	14700
27	3	FISHERMAN 255	HT	FSH	FBG	SV	OB			8	6	4330	1	3	15700	17900
27	3	FISHERMAN 255	HT	FSH	FBG	SV	SE	205	OMC	8	6	4330	1	3	15700	17900
27	3	FISHERMAN 255	HT	FSH	FBG	SV	IO	260		8	6	4330	1	3	12900	14700
27	3	RIVIERA 255	OP	SPTCR	FBG	SV	OB			8	6	4330	1	3	20100	22400
27	3	RIVIERA 255	OP	SPTCR	FBG	SV	SE	205	OMC	8	6	4330	1	3	20100	22400
27	3	RIVIERA 255	OP	SPTCR	FBG	SV	IO	260		8	6	4330	1	3	14400	16300
27	3	RIVIERA 255	HT	SPTCR	FBG	SV	OB			8	6	4330	1	3	20200	22400
27	3	RIVIERA 255	HT	SPTCR	FBG	SV	SE	205	OMC	8	6	4330	1	3	20200	22400
27	3	RIVIERA 255	HT	SPTCR	FBG	SV	IO	260		8	6	4330	1	3	14400	16300
30		ARRIVAL 30	OP	SF	FBG	DV	IB	T340	MRCR	12					31200	34700
30		ARRIVAL 30	FB	SF	FBG	DV	IB	T340	MRCR	12					31200	34700
30	2	LIBERTY 288	OP	SPTCR	FBG	SV	OB			11	2	9500	1	6	30000	33400
30	2	LIBERTY 288	OP	SPTCR	FBG	SV	SE	T230	OMC	11	2	9500	1	6	30000	33400
30	2	LIBERTY 288	OP	SPTCR	FBG	SV	IO	T230		11	2	9500	1	6	26300	29200
30	2	LIBERTY 288	HT	SPTCR	FBG	SV	OB			11	2	9500	1	6	30100	33400
30	2	LIBERTY 288	HT	SPTCR	FBG	SV	SE	T	OMC	11	2	9500	1	6	**	**
30	2	LIBERTY 288	HT	SPTCR	FBG	SV	IO	T230		11	2	9500	1	6	26300	29200
32	3	CONTINENTAL 32	OP	CR	FBG	SV	IB	T340	MRCR	12		12000	12	9	51000	56100
32	3	CONTINENTAL 32	FB	CR	FBG	SV	IB	T340	MRCR	12		12000	2	9	51000	56100
32	3	SPORT SEDAN 32	OP	SDN	FBG	SV	IB	T340	MRCR	12		13300	2	9	56800	62500
32	3	SPORT SEDAN 32	FB	SDN	FBG	SV	IB	T340	MRCR	12		13300	2	9	56800	62500
32	3	SPORTFISHERMAN 32	OP	SF	FBG	DV	IB	T340	MRCR	12		12800	2	9	51700	56800
32	3	SPORTFISHERMAN 32	FB	SF	FBG	DV	IB	T340	MRCR	12		12800	2	9	51700	56800
		1986 BOATS														
18	3	TARPON 18	OP	CTRCN	FBG	DV	OB			7	3				4900	5650
21	3	STAMAS 21	OP	CR	FBG	SV	OB			7	9	3100	1	6	9750	11100
21	3	STAMAS 21	OP	CR	FBG	SV	IO	170		7	9	4100	1	6	8350	9600
23	3	STAMAS 24	OP	FSH	FBG	SV	OB			8		3500	2	4	12300	14000
23	3	STAMAS 24	OP	FSH	FBG	SV	SE	205	OMC	8		3500	2	4	12300	14000
23	3	STAMAS 24	OP	FSH	FBG	SV	IO	260		8		4500	2	4	11200	13100
23	3	STAMAS 24	OP	FSH	FBG	SV	SE	T115	OMC	8		4500	2	4	14100	16000
23	3	STAMAS 24	HT	FSH	FBG	SV	OB			8		3500	2	4	12300	14000
23	3	STAMAS 24	HT	FSH	FBG	SV	SE	205	OMC	8		3500	2	4	12300	14000
23	3	STAMAS 24	HT	FSH	FBG	SV	IO	260		8		4500	2	4	11200	13300
23	3	STAMAS 24	HT	FSH	FBG	SV	SE	T115	OMC	8		4600	2	4	14200	16100
23	3	STAMAS 24	OP	SPTCR	FBG	SV	SE	205	OMC	8		4600	2	4	14200	16200
23	3	STAMAS 24	OP	SPTCR	FBG	SV	IO	260		8		4600	2	4	10800	12600
23	3	STAMAS 24	OP	SPTCR	FBG	SV	SE	T115	OMC	8		4600	2	4	14200	16200
23	3	STAMAS 24	HT	SPTCR	FBG	SV	SE	205	OMC	8		4600	2	4	14200	16200
23	3	STAMAS 24	HT	SPTCR	FBG	SV	IO	260		8		4600	2	4	10800	12600
23	3	STAMAS 24	HT	SPTCR	FBG	SV	SE	T115	OMC	8		4600	2	4	14200	16200
23	3	STAMAS 24	HT	SPTCR	FBG	SV	IO	T138-T140		8		5000	2	4	12600	14400
23	3	TARPON 24	OP	OPFSH	FBG	SV	OB			8		3500	2	4	12300	14000
23	3	TARPON 24	OP	OPFSH	FBG	SV	SE	205	OMC	8		3500	2	4	12300	14000
23	3	TARPON 24	OP	OPFSH	FBG	SV	SE	T115	OMC	8		3500	2	4	12300	14000
25	4	STAMAS 25	OP	FSH	FBG	SV	OB			8	6		1	3	13300	15100
25	4	STAMAS 25	OP	FSH	FBG	SV	SE	205	OMC	8	6		1	3	14200	16200
25	4	STAMAS 25	OP	FSH	FBG	SV	IO	260		8	6		1	3	14200	16400
25	4	STAMAS 25	OP	FSH	FBG	SV	SE	T115-T155		8	6		1	3	14200	16200
25	4	STAMAS 25	OP	SPTCR	FBG	SV	OB			8	6		1	3	13400	15200
25	4	STAMAS 25	OP	SPTCR	FBG	SV	SE	205	OMC	8	6		1	3	14300	16200
25	4	STAMAS 25	OP	SPTCR	FBG	SV	IO	260		8	6		1	3	12500	14500
25	4	STAMAS 25	OP	SPTCR	FBG	SV	SE	T115-T155		8	6		1	3	14300	16200
25	4	TARPON 25	OP	CTRCN	FBG	SV	OB			8	6		1	3	13300	15100
25	4	TARPON 25	OP	CTRCN	FBG	SV	SE	205	OMC	8	6		1	3	14200	16100
25	4	TARPON 25	OP	CTRCN	FBG	SV	SE	T115-T155		8	6	4300	1	3	15200	17300
26		STAMAS 26		CBNCR	FBG	SV	OB			9	7	5500			17200	19600
26		STAMAS 26	OP	FSH	FBG	SV	SE	205	OMC	9	7		2	8	16000	18200
26		STAMAS 26	OP	FSH	FBG	SV	IO	260		9	7	6500	2	8	16800	19400
26		STAMAS 26	OP	FSH	FBG	SV	IB	340	MRCR	9	7	6500	2	8	21200	23500
26		STAMAS 26	OP	FSH	FBG	SV	SE	T155	OMC	9	7		2	8	16000	18200
26		STAMAS 26	OP	FSH	FBG	SV	IO	T170		9	7	7500	2	8	19700	21900
26		STAMAS 26	OP	FSH	FBG	SV	IB	T185	CRUS	9	7	6500	2	8	22100	24600
26		STAMAS 26	HT	FSH	FBG	SV	OB			9	7	5500			17200	19600
26		STAMAS 26	HT	FSH	FBG	SV	SE	205	OMC	9	7		2	8	16000	18200
26		STAMAS 26	HT	FSH	FBG	SV	IO	260		9	7		2	8	15000	17300
26		STAMAS 26	HT	FSH	FBG	SV	IB	340	MRCR	9	7		2	8	19200	21300
26		STAMAS 26	HT	FSH	FBG	SV	SE	T155	OMC	9	7		2	8	16000	18200
26		STAMAS 26	HT	FSH	FBG	SV	IO	T170		9	7		2	8	16000	18200
26		STAMAS 26	HT	FSH	FBG	SV	IB	T185	CRUS	9	7		2	8	19900	22100
26		STAMAS 26	OP	SPTCR	FBG	SV	IO	260	MRCR	9	7	7500	2	6	17600	20000
		IO 260 OMC 17600 19900, IO 260 VLVO 18200 20200, IB 260-340													22500	25900
26		STAMAS 26	OP	SPTCR	FBG	SV	SE	T115-T155		9	7	7500	2	6	18700	20800
26		STAMAS 26	OP	SPTCR	FBG	SV	IO	T170		9	7	7500	2	6	18900	21000
26		STAMAS 26	HT	SPTCR	FBG	SV	IO	260		9	7	7500	2	6	17600	20200
26		STAMAS 26	HT	SPTCR	FBG	SV	IB	340	MRCR	9	7	7500	2	6	23300	25900
26		STAMAS 26	HT	SPTCR	FBG	SV	SE	T115-T155		9	7	7500	2	6	18700	20800
26		STAMAS 26	HT	SPTCR	FBG	SV	IO	T170		9	7	7500	2	6	18900	21000
26		STAMAS 26	HT	SPTCR	FBG	SV	IB	T260	MRCR	9	7	7500	2	6	24900	27700
26		STAMAS 26	FB	SPTCR	FBG	SV	IO	260		9	7	6900	2	6	16600	18900
26		STAMAS 26	FB	SPTCR	FBG	SV	IB	340	MRCR	9	7	8400	2	6	25200	28000
26		STAMAS 26	FB	SPTCR	FBG	SV	SE	T115-T155		9	7	7500	2	6	18700	20800
26		STAMAS 26	FB	SPTCR	FBG	SV	IO	T170		9	7	8400	2	6	20200	22400
26		STAMAS 26	FB	SPTCR	FBG	SV	IB	T260	MRCR	9	7	6900	2	6	23700	26300
26		TARPON 26	OP	FSH	FBG	SV	OB			9	7	6400	2		18200	20200
26		TARPON 26	OP	FSH	FBG	SV	SE	205	OMC	9	7	6400	2		18200	20200
26		TARPON 26	OP	FSH	FBG	SV	IB	340	MRCR	9	7	6400	2		21000	23300

 CONTINUED ON NEXT PAGE

LOA FT IN	NAME AND/ OR MODEL	TOP/ RIG	BOAT TYPE	-HULL- MTL	TP	----ENGINE--- TP	# HP	MFG	BEAM FT IN	WGT LBS	DRAFT FT IN	RETAIL LOW	RETAIL HIGH
	1986 BOATS												
26	TARPON 26	OP	FSH	FBG	SV	SE	T155	OMC	9 7	6400	2	18200	20200
30	ARRIVAL 30	OP	SF	FBG	DV	IB	T260-T340		12			27800	33100
30	ARRIVAL 30	FB	SF	FBG	DV	IB	T260	MRCR	12			27800	30900
32 3	CONTINENTAL 32	ST	CR	FBG	SV	IB	T260-T340		12	12000	2 9	46700	53500
32 3	CONTINENTAL 32	FB	CR	FBG	SV	IB	T260-T340		12	12000	2 9	46700	53500
32 3	STAMAS 32	FB	SDN	FBG	SV	IB	T260-T340		12		2 9	41500	46600
32 3	STAMAS 32	OP	SF	FBG	SV	IB	T260-T340		12	12800	2 9	47400	54200
32 3	STAMAS 32	FB	SF	FBG	SV	IB	T260-T340		12		2 9	35700	42200
	1985 BOATS												
18 3	TARPON 18	OP	CTRCN	FBG	DV	OB			7 3			4800	5500
21 3	STAMAS 21	OP	CR	FBG	SV	OB			7 9	3100	1 6	9550	10800
21 3	STAMAS 21	OP	CR	FBG	SV	IO	170		7 9	4100	1 6	8050	9250
21 3	TARPON 21		CTRCN	FBG	DV	OB			7 9	2500		8400	9650
23 3	SPORTSMAN 24		RNBT	FBG	SV	IO	225-260		8			8150	9650
23 3	SPORTSMAN 24		RNBT	FBG	SV	IO	T138-T140		8			9250	10500
23 3	STAMAS 24	OP	FSH	FBG	SV	OB			8	3500	2 4	12000	13600
23 3	STAMAS 24	OP	FSH	FBG	SV	SE	205	OMC	8	3500	2 4	12000	13600
23 3	STAMAS 24	OP	FSH	FBG	SV	IO	225-260		8	4500	2 4	10800	12500
23 3	STAMAS 24	OP	FSH	FBG	SV	IO	T138-T140		8	4900	2 4	12600	14300
23 3	STAMAS 24	HT	FSH	FBG	SV	OB			8	3500	2 4	12000	13600
23 3	STAMAS 24	HT	FSH	FBG	SV	SE	205	OMC	8	3500	2 4	12000	13600
23 3	STAMAS 24	HT	FSH	FBG	SV	IO	225-260		8	4600	2 4	10900	12700
23 3	STAMAS 24	HT	FSH	FBG	SV	IO	T138-T140		8	4900	2 4	12600	14300
23 3	STAMAS 24	OP	SPTCR	FBG	SV	SE	205	OMC	8	4600	2 4	13900	15800
23 3	STAMAS 24	OP	SPTCR	FBG	SV	IO	225-260		8	4600	2 4	10400	12100
23 3	STAMAS 24	OP	SPTCR	FBG	SV	IO	T138-T140		8	5000	2 4	12100	13800
23 3	STAMAS 24	HT	SPTCR	FBG	SV	SE	205	OMC	8	4600	2 4	13900	15800
23 3	STAMAS 24	HT	SPTCR	FBG	SV	IO	225-260		8	4600	2 4	10400	12100
23 3	STAMAS 24	HT	SPTCR	FBG	SV	IO	T138-T140		8	5000	2 4	12100	13800
23 3	TARPON 24	OP	OPFSH	FBG	SV	OB			8	3500	2 4	12000	13700
23 3	TARPON 24	OP	OPFSH	FBG	SV	SE	205	OMC	8	3500	2 4	12000	13700
26	RIVIERA 26	ST	CR	FBG	SV	IO	260	MRCR	9 7	6500	2 6	15300	17400
	IO 260 OMC 15300 17300, IO 260 VLVO 15500 17600, IB 260-340											19400	22500
	IO T170 18100 20100												
26	STAMAS 26		CBNCR	FBG	SV	OB			9 7	5500		16800	19100
26	STAMAS 26	OP	FSH	FBG	SV	SE	205	OMC	9 7		2 8	15600	17700
26	STAMAS 26	OP	FSH	FBG	SV	IO	225-230		9 7	6500	2 8	16000	18200
	IO 260 MRCR 16100 18400, IO 260 OMC 16100 18300, IO 260 VLVO											16400	18600
	IB 260-340 19400 22500												
26	STAMAS 26	OP	FSH	FBG	SV	SE	T155	OMC	9 7		2 8	15600	17700
26	STAMAS 26	OP	FSH	FBG	SV	IO	T170		9 7	7500	2 8	19100	21300
26	STAMAS 26	HT	FSH	FBG	SV	OB			9 7	5500		16800	19100
26	STAMAS 26	HT	FSH	FBG	SV	SE	205	OMC	9 7		2 8	15600	17800
26	STAMAS 26	HT	FSH	FBG	SV	IO	260	MRCR	9 7		2 8	14400	16400
	IO 260 OMC 14300 16300, IO 260 VLVO 14600 16600, IB 260-340											17100	20400
26	STAMAS 26	HT	FSH	FBG	SV	SE	T155	OMC	9 7		2 8	15600	17800
26	STAMAS 26	HT	FSH	FBG	SV	IO	T170		9 7		2 8	15300	17400
26	STAMAS 26	OP	SPTCR	FBG	SV	IO	260	MRCR	9 7	7500	2 6	16900	19200
	IO 260 OMC 16800 19100, IO 260 VLVO 17100 19400, IB 260-340											21500	24700
	IO T170 18100 20100												
26	STAMAS 26	HT	SPTCR	FBG	SV	IO	260	MRCR	9 7	7500	2 6	16900	19200
	IO 260 OMC 16800 19100, IO 260 VLVO 17100 19400, IB 260-340											21500	24700
	IO T170 18100 20100												
26	STAMAS 26	FB	SPTCR	FBG	SV	IO	260	MRCR	9 7	6900	2 6	15900	18100
	IO 260 OMC 15900 18100, IO 260 VLVO 13800 15700, IB 260 MRCR											20200	22500
	IB 340 MRCR 24100 26700, IO T170 19400 21500												
26	TARPON 26	OP	FSH	FBG	SV	OB			9 7	6400	2	17400	19700
26	TARPON 26	OP	FSH	FBG	SV	SE	205	OMC	9 7	6400	2	17400	19700
26	TARPON 26	OP	FSH	FBG	SV	IO	260	VLVO	9 7	6400	2	16200	18400
26	TARPON 26	OP	FSH	FBG	SV	IB	340	MRCR	9 7	6400	2	20000	22200
26	TARPON 26	OP	FSH	FBG	SV	SE	T155	OMC	9 7	6400	2	17400	19700
30	ARRIVAL 30	OP	SF	FBG	DV	IB	T340	MRCR	12			28500	31600
30	ARRIVAL 30	HT	SF	FBG	DV	IB	T340	MRCR	12			28500	31600
30	ARRIVAL 30	FB	SF	FBG	DV	IB	T340	MRCR	12			28500	31600
32 3	CONTINENTAL 32	ST	CR	FBG	SV	IB	T260-T340		12	12000	2 9	44200	51400
32 3	CONTINENTAL 32	HT	CR	FBG	SV	IB	T260-T340		12	12000	2 9	44200	51400
32 3	CONTINENTAL 32	FB	CR	FBG	SV	IB	T260-T340		12	12000	2 9	44200	51400
32 3	STAMAS 32	FB	SDN	FBG	SV	IB	T260-T340		12		2 9	39600	44500
32 3	STAMAS 32	OP	SF	FBG	SV	IB	T260-T340		12	12800	2 9	44800	52000
32 3	STAMAS 32	HT	SF	FBG	SV	IB	T260-T340		12		2 9	34100	40300
32 3	STAMAS 32	FB	SF	FBG	SV	IB	T260-T340		12		2 9	34100	40300
44	STAMAS 44	KTH	SA/CR	FBG	KL	IB	62D	PERK	14	35000	5 1	127000	139500
	1984 BOATS												
18	STAMAS 18			FBG	DV	OB						3300	3850
21 3	STAMAS 21	OP	CR	FBG	SV	OB			7 9	3100	1 6	9350	10700
21 3	STAMAS 21	OP	CR	FBG	SV	IO	170		7 9	4100	1 6	7750	8900
21 3	TARPON 21		CTRCN	FBG	DV	OB			7 9	1500		5600	6400
23 3	SPORTSMAN 24		RNBT	FBG	SV	IO	225-260		8			7900	9350
23 3	SPORTSMAN 24		RNBT	FBG	SV	IO	T138-T140		8			8950	10200
23 3	STAMAS 24	OP	FSH	FBG	SV	OB			8	3500	2 4	11800	13400
23 3	STAMAS 24	OP	FSH	FBG	SV	SE	205	OMC	8	3500	2 4	11800	13400
23 3	STAMAS 24	OP	FSH	FBG	SV	IO	225-260		8	4500	2 4	10400	12100
23 3	STAMAS 24	OP	FSH	FBG	SV	IO	T138-T140		8	4900	2 4	12200	13800
23 3	STAMAS 24	HT	FSH	FBG	SV	OB			8	3500	2 4	11800	13400
23 3	STAMAS 24	HT	FSH	FBG	SV	SE	205	OMC	8	3500	2 4	11800	13400
23 3	STAMAS 24	HT	FSH	FBG	SV	IO	225-260		8	4600	2 4	10600	12300
23 3	STAMAS 24	HT	FSH	FBG	SV	IO	T138-T140		8	4900	2 4	12200	13800
23 3	STAMAS 24	OP	SPTCR	FBG	SV	IO	225-260		8	4600	2 4	10000	11700
23 3	STAMAS 24	OP	SPTCR	FBG	SV	IO	T138-T140		8	5000	2 4	11700	13300
23 3	STAMAS 24	HT	SPTCR	FBG	SV	IO	225-260		8	4600	2 4	10000	11700
23 3	STAMAS 24	HT	SPTCR	FBG	SV	IO	T138-T140		8	5000	2 4	11700	13300
23 3	TARPON 24	OP	OPFSH	FBG	SV	OB			8	3500	2 4	11800	13400
23 3	TARPON 24	OP	OPFSH	FBG	SV	SE	205	OMC	8	3500	2 4	11800	13400
26	RIVIERA 26	ST	CR	FBG	SV	IO	260	MRCR	9 7	6500	2 6	14800	16800
	IO 260 OMC 14700 16700, IO 260 VLVO 15000 17000, IB 260-340											18800	21500
	IO T138-T170 17100 19400												
26	STAMAS 26		CBNCR	FBG	SV	OB			9 7	5500		16400	18700
26	STAMAS 26	OP	FSH	FBG	SV	SE	205	OMC	9 7		2 8	15300	17400
26	STAMAS 26	OP	FSH	FBG	SV	IO	260	MRCR	9 7	6500	2 8	15600	17700
	IO 260 OMC 15500 17700, IO 260 VLVO 15800 17900, IB 260-340											18800	21500
26	STAMAS 26	OP	FSH	FBG	SV	SE	T155	OMC	9 7		2 8	15300	17400
26	STAMAS 26	OP	FSH	FBG	SV	IO	T170		9 7	7500	2 8	18500	20500
26	STAMAS 26	HT	FSH	FBG	SV	OB			9 7	5500		16400	18700
26	STAMAS 26	HT	FSH	FBG	SV	SE	205	OMC	9 7		2 8	15300	17400
26	STAMAS 26	HT	FSH	FBG	SV	IO	260	MRCR	9 7		2 8	13900	15800
	IO 260 OMC 13800 15700, IO 260 VLVO 14100 16000, IB 260-340											16300	19500
26	STAMAS 26	HT	FSH	FBG	SV	SE	T155	OMC	9 7		2 8	15300	17400
26	STAMAS 26	HT	FSH	FBG	SV	IO	T170		9 7		2 8	14800	16800
26	STAMAS 26	OP	SPTCR	FBG	SV	IO	260	MRCR	9 7	7500	2 6	16300	18500
	IO 260 OMC 16300 18500, IO 260 VLVO 16500 18700, IB 260-340											20500	23600
	IO T170 17100 19400												
26	STAMAS 26	HT	SPTCR	FBG	SV	IO	260	MRCR	9 7	7500	2 6	16300	18500
	IO 260 OMC 16300 18500, IO 260 VLVO 16500 18700, IB 260-340											20500	23600
	IO T170 17100 19400												
26	STAMAS 26	FB	SPTCR	FBG	SV	IO	260	MRCR	9 7	6900	2 6	15400	17500
	IO 260 OMC 15300 17400, IO 260 VLVO 13400 15200, IB 260 MRCR											19300	21500
	IB 340 MRCR 23000 25500, IO T170 18900 21000												
26	TARPON 26	OP	FSH	FBG	SV	OB			9 7	6400	2	17000	19300
26	TARPON 26	OP	FSH	FBG	SV	SE	205	OMC	9 7	6400	2	17000	19300
26	TARPON 26	OP	FSH	FBG	SV	IO	260	MRCR	9 7	6400	2	15400	17500
	IO 260 OMC 15400 17500, IO 260 VLVO 15600 17800, IB 260-340											18600	21300
26	TARPON 26	OP	FSH	FBG	SV	SE	T155	OMC	9 7	6400	2	17000	19300
30	ARRIVAL 30		SF	FBG	DV	IB	T260D	MRCR	12			32800	36500
32 3	CONTINENTAL 32	ST	CR	FBG	SV	IB	T260-T340		12	12000	2 9	42200	49100
32 3	CONTINENTAL 32	HT	CR	FBG	SV	IB	T260-T340		12	12000	2 9	42200	49100
32 3	CONTINENTAL 32	FB	CR	FBG	SV	IB	T260-T340		12	12000	2 9	42200	49100
32 3	STAMAS 32	HT	SDN	FBG	SV	IB	T260-T340		12	13300	2 9	47200	54400
32 3	STAMAS 32	FB	SDN	FBG	SV	IB	T260-T340		12		2 9	37900	42600
32 3	STAMAS 32	OP	SF	FBG	SV	IB	T260-T340		12	12800	2 9	42800	49700
32 3	STAMAS 32	HT	SF	FBG	SV	IB	T260-T340		12		2 9	32600	38500
32 3	STAMAS 32	FB	SF	FBG	SV	IB	T260-T340		12		2 9	32600	38500
44	STAMAS 44	KTH	SA/CR	FBG	KL	IB	62D	PERK	14	30000	5 1	110500	121000

....For earlier years, see the BUC Used Boat Price Guide, Volume 3

STAR CATAMARANS INC
JACKSON MI 49203   COAST GUARD MFG ID- XTJ See inside cover to adjust price for area

LOA FT IN	NAME AND/ OR MODEL	TOP/ RIG	BOAT TYPE	-HULL- MTL TP	----ENGINE--- TP # HP MFG	BEAM FT IN	WGT LBS	DRAFT FT IN	RETAIL LOW	RETAIL HIGH
			1984 BOATS							
18 4	STAR-CAT 5.6	SLP	SA/OD	FBG CT		7 10	425	6	2750	3200

....For earlier years, see the BUC Used Boat Price Guide, Volume 3

STARBOARD YACHT CO
STUART FL 34997   COAST GUARD MFG ID- SYX See inside cover to adjust price for area

LOA FT IN	NAME AND/ OR MODEL	TOP/ RIG	BOAT TYPE	-HULL- MTL TP	----ENGINE--- TP # HP MFG	BEAM FT IN	WGT LBS	DRAFT FT IN	RETAIL LOW	RETAIL HIGH
			1995 BOATS							
19 9	SEAWARD FOX	SLP	SAROD	FBG KL		8	1300	1 7	7400	8500
24 6	SEAWARD 23	SLP	SACAC	FBG KL IB	D YAN	8	2250	2 1	15600	17800
26 9	SEAWARD 25	SLP	SACAC	FBG KL IB	D YAN	8 3	3200	2 1	21300	23600
32 4	SEAWARD EAGLE 32	SLP	SACAC	FBG KL IB	D YAN	10 6	8500	3 6	59600	65500
			1994 BOATS							
19 9	SEAWARD FOX	SLP	SAROD	FBG KL		8	1300	1 7	6900	7950
24 6	SEAWARD 23	SLP	SACAC	FBG KL IB	D YAN	8 4	2250	2 1	18400	20400
26 9	SEAWARD 25	SLP	SACAC	FBG KL IB	D YAN	8 3	3200	2 1	19900	22100
			1993 BOATS							
19 9	SEAWARD FOX	SLP	SAROD	FBG KL		8	1300	1 7	6450	7400
24 6	SEAWARD 23	SLP	SACAC	FBG KL IB	D YAN	8 4	2250	2 1	16800	19000
26 9	SEAWARD 25	SLP	SACAC	FBG KL IB	D YAN	8 3	3200	2 1	18800	20900
			1991 BOATS							
17 4	SEAWARD FOX	SLP	SAIL	FBG	OB	8		1 7	5000	5750
24 6	SEAWARD 23	SLP	SAIL	FBG	OB	8 4		2 1	13000	14800
24 6	SEAWARD 23	SLP	SAIL	FBG	OB	8 4 10D YAN		2 1	14700	16700
26 9	SEAWARD 25	SLP	SAIL	FBG	IB	8 3		2 1	15000	17000
26 9	SEAWARD 25	SLP	SAIL	FBG	IB 10D YAN	8 3		2 1	16100	18400
			1990 BOATS							
17 4	SEAWARD FOX	SLP	SA/CR	FBG KL OB		8	1250	2 1	4700	5400
22 8	SEAWARD 23	SLP	SA/CR	FBG KL OB		8 4	2400	2 1	9000	10200
22 8	SEAWARD 23	SLP	SA/CR	FBG KL IB	10D YAN	8 4	2550	2 1	11300	12800
24 4	SEAWARD 24	SLP	SA/CR	FBG KL OB		8 3	3100	2 1	12100	13700
24 4	SEAWARD 24	SLP	SA/CR	FBG KL IB	10D YAN	8 3	3200	2 1	14000	15900
			1989 BOATS							
16 10	SEAWARD SEAFOX	SLP	SAIL	FBG WK OB		8	1250	1 7	4300	5000
21 8	SEAWARD 23	SLP	SAIL	FBG WK		8 4	2200	1 11	7350	8450
24 4	SEAWARD 24	SLP	SAIL	FBG WK OB		8 3	3100	2	11300	12800
24 4	SEAWARD 24	SLP	SAIL	FBG WK IB	D	8 3	3100	2	12600	14400
			1988 BOATS							
16 10	SEAWARD SEAFOX	SLP	SAIL	FBG WK OB		8	1250	1 7	4000	4650
21 8	SEAWARD 22	SLP	SAIL	FBG KC		8 3	2200	2	6900	7900
24 4	SEAWARD 24	SLP	SAIL	FBG KC OB		8	3100	2	10600	12000
			1987 BOATS							
16 10	SLIPPER 17 DH	SLP	SAIL	FBG KC OB		8	1250	1 7	3750	4350
21 8	SEAWARD 22	SLP	SAIL	FBG KC		8 3	2200	2	6450	7400
24 4	SEAWARD 24	SLP	SAIL	FBG KC OB		8	3100	2	9900	11200
			1986 BOATS							
16 10	SLIPPER 17 DH	SLP	SAIL	FBG KC OB		8	1250	1 7	3500	4050
21 8	SEAWARD 22	SLP	SAIL	FBG KC		8 3	2200	2	6000	6900
24 4	SEAWARD 24	SLP	SAIL	FBG KC OB		8	3100	2	9300	10500
			1985 BOATS							
16 10	SLIPPER 17 DH	SLP	SAIL	FBG KC OB		8	1250	1 7	3250	3800
21 8	SEAWARD 22	SLP	SAIL	FBG KC		8 3	2200	2	5650	6450
24 4	SEAWARD 24	SLP	SAIL	FBG KC OB		8	3100	2	8600	9850
			1984 BOATS							
16 10	SLIPPER 17 DH	SLP	SAIL	FBG CB OB		8	1250	1 7	3150	3700
16 10	SLIPPER 17 DH	SLP	SAIL	FBG KC OB		8	1250	1 7	3300	3850
16 10	SLIPPER 17 FD	SLP	SAIL	FBG KC OB		8	1250	1 7	2800	3250
16 10	SLIPPER 17 FD	SLP	SAIL	FBG KC OB		8	1250	1 7	3000	3450
24	STARBOARD 24	SLP	SAIL	FBG KC OB		8	3000	2	7650	8800
24 4	SEAWARD 24	SLP	SAIL	FBG KC OB		8	3100	2	8000	9200

....For earlier years, see the BUC Used Boat Price Guide, Volume 3

STARBOARD YACHTS INC
HOUSTON TX 77058   COAST GUARD MFG ID- TYA See inside cover to adjust price for area

LOA FT IN	NAME AND/ OR MODEL	TOP/ RIG	BOAT TYPE	-HULL- MTL TP	----ENGINE--- TP # HP MFG	BEAM FT IN	WGT LBS	DRAFT FT IN	RETAIL LOW	RETAIL HIGH
			1986 BOATS							
33 11	NASSAU 34	CUT	SA/CR	FBG KL IB	33D YAN	10 9	14250	5	57300	63000
41 10	NASSAU 42	SLP	SA/CR	FBG KL IB	51D PERK	12 9	21000	5 10	97100	106500
44 11	NASSAU 45	SLP	SA/CR	FBG KL IB	51D PERK	12 9	21250	5 10	111000	122000
			1985 BOATS							
33 11	NASSAU 34	CUT	SA/CR	FBG KL IB	33D YAN	10 9	14250	5	53900	59300
33 11	NASSAU 34	CUT	SAIL	FBG KL IB	30D YAN	10 9	14250	5	53900	59300
41 10	NASSAU 42	SLP	SA/CR	FBG KL IB	51D PERK	12 9	21000	5 10	91300	100500
41 10	NASSAU 42	SLP	SAIL	FBG KL IB	D PERK	12 9	21250	5 10	91900	101000
44 11	NASSAU 45	SLP	SA/CR	FBG KL IB	51D PERK	12 9	21250	5 10	104500	115000
			1984 BOATS							
29 2	VANCOUVER 25	SLP	SAIL	FBG KL IB	8D- 15D	8 6	7000	4	23000	25700
33 11	NASSAU 34	CUT	SAIL	FBG KL IB	36D YAN	10 9	14250	5	50800	55800
41 10	NASSAU 42	SLP	SAIL	FBG KL IB	50D PERK	12 9	21250	5 10	86500	95000

....For earlier years, see the BUC Used Boat Price Guide, Volume 3

STARCRAFT MARINE L L C
TOPEKA IN 46571   COAST GUARD MFG ID- STR See inside cover to adjust price for area

For more recent years, see the BUC Used Boat Price Guide, Volume 1

LOA FT IN	NAME AND/ OR MODEL	TOP/ RIG	BOAT TYPE	-HULL- MTL TP	----ENGINE--- TP # HP MFG	BEAM FT IN	WGT LBS	DRAFT FT IN	RETAIL LOW	RETAIL HIGH
			1996 BOATS							
16	1650 MV	OP	JON	AL FL OB		6 3	327		870	1050
16	1650 MV DLX	OP	JON	AL SV OB		6 3	655		1650	1950
16	SKIFF 16	OP	UTL	AL SV OB		5 5	400		525	630
16 2	SF 16L	OP	UTL	AL SV OB		5 7	245		615	740
16 4	FISHMASTER 160	OP	BASS	AL SV OB		6 2	654		1800	2150
16 4	FISHMASTER 160T	OP	BASS	AL SV OB		6 2	599		1650	1950
16 4	SF 16 CAMP	OP	UTL	AL SV OB		6 2	520		1400	1650
16 4	SUPER FISHERMAN 160	OP	RNBT	AL SV OB		6 2	710		2000	2350
16 6	SUPER SPORT 170	OP	RNBT	AL SV OB		6 9	1010		2800	3250
16 6	TOURNAMENT FISH 170	OP	RNBT	AL SV OB		6 9	910		2550	3000
16 9	STARCASTER 1700 LS	OP	BASS	AL SV OB		6	830		2350	2700
17	FISHMASTER 170	OP	RNBT	AL SV OB		7 1	1000		2800	3250
17	MARINER 170	OP	CTRCN	AL SV OB		7	975		2700	3150
17	STARCASTER 1700	OP	BASS	AL SV OB		6 3	915		2550	3000
17	SUPER FISHERMAN 170	OP	FSH	AL SV OB		7 1	1000		2750	3200
17 2	1700	OP	B/R	FBG SV OB		6 10	1250		3350	3900
17 2	1709	OP	RNBT	FBG SV OB		6 10	1200		3250	3800
17 2	1709	OP	RNBT	FBG SV OB		6 10	1290		3450	4050
17 2	1710	OP	B/R	FBG SV IO	135 MRCR	6 10	1490		3950	4600
17 4	TOURNAMENT PRO 170	OP	RNBT	FBG SV OB		7 2	1390		3700	4300
18	1860 MV	OP	JON	AL FL OB		7 8	890		890	1050
18 2	1800 SS	OP	B/R	AL SV OB		7 8	1599		4200	4850
18 2	1800 SS	OP	B/R	FBG SV OB		7 8	1599		4150	4850
18 2	1810	OP	B/R	FBG SV IO	135 MRCR	7 8	1658		5000	5750
18 2	1810 SS	OP	B/R	FBG SV IO	135 MRCR	7 8	1688		5100	5850
18 2	1811 SS	OP	RNBT	FBG SV IO	135 MRCR	7 8	1645		5300	6100
18 6	TOURNAMENT FISH 180	OP	RNBT	FBG SV OB		7 11	1090		3150	3650
18 6	TOURNAMENT PRO 180	OP	RNBT	FBG SV OB		7 11	1745		4500	5150
18 6	TOURNAMENT PRO 180	OP	RNBT	FBG SV OB		7 11	1745		4500	5150
18 6	SUPER FISHERMAN 190	OP	FSH	AL SV OB		7 6	1183		3350	4000
18 9	SUPER FISHERMAN 191	OP	RNBT	AL SV IO	135 MRCR	7 6	1183		5250	6000
18 10	FISHMASTER 190	OP	RNBT	AL SV OB		7 5	1158		3400	3850
19	ISLANDER 191	OP	CUD	AL SV IO	135 MRCR	7 8	1550		5900	6750
20	2010	OP	RNBT	FBG SV IO	180 MRCR	8 6	1968		6700	7700
20 2	2010 SS	OP	B/R	FBG SV IO	180 MRCR	8 6	2003		6500	7450
20 2	2012	OP	CUD	FBG SV IO	180 MRCR	8 6	2098		7050	8100
22	ISLANDER 220	OP	CUD	AL SV OB		8	1612		5000	5700
22	ISLANDER 221	OP	CUD	AL SV IO	135 MRCR	8	1612		7050	8100
22 2	2210 SS	OP	RNBT	FBG SV IO	180 MRCR	8 6	2490		8100	9300
22 2	2212	OP	CUD	FBG SV IO	230 MRCR	8 6	2535		8850	10100
26 7	CRUISER 2513	OP	CR	FBG SV IO	235 MRCR	8 6	3415		12500	14200
			1995 BOATS							
16	1648	OP	JON	AL FL OB		5 7	264		675	815
16	1650 MV	OP	JON	AL SV OB		6 3	327		815	985
16	TOURNAMENT PRO 160	OP	RNBT	FBG SV OB					3550	4150
16	TOURNAMENT PRO 160T	OP	RNBT	FBG SV OB					3550	4150
16	TOURNAMENT PRO 170	OP	RNBT	FBG SV OB					3550	4150
16 2	SF 16 S	OP	UTL	AL SV OB		5 7	245		600	720
16 2	SF 16L	OP	UTL	AL SV OB		5 7	245		585	700
16 4	CAMP 16	OP	UTL	AL SV OB		6 2	520		1350	1600
16 4	FISHMASTER 160	OP	BASS	AL SV OB		6 2	654		1700	2050
16 4	FISHMASTER 160T	OP	BASS	AL SV OB		6 2	599		1500	1850
16 4	SF 16WB	OP	UTL	AL SV OB		6 2	520		1300	1550

LOA FT	IN	NAME AND/ OR MODEL	TOP/ RIG	BOAT TYPE	-HULL- MTL	TP	----ENGINE--- TP	# HP	MFG	BEAM FT	IN	WGT LBS	DRAFT FT	IN	RETAIL LOW	RETAIL HIGH
		1995 BOATS														
16	4	SUPER FISHERMAN 160	OP	RNBT	AL	SV	OB			6	2	710			1900	2250
16	5	SUPER SPORT 170	OP	RNBT	AL	SV	OB			6	9	880			2350	2750
16	6	TOURNAMENT FISH 170	OP	RNBT	AL	SV	OB			6	9	910			2400	2800
17		FISHMASTER 170	OP	RNBT	AL	SV	OB			7	1	1000			2650	3100
17		MARINER 170	OP	CTRCN	AL	SV	OB			7		1050			2700	3150
17		STARCASTER 1700	OP	BASS	AL	SV	OB			6	3	915			2450	2850
17		SUPER FISHERMAN 170	OP	FSH	AL	SV	OB			7	1	1000			2600	3000
17		TOURNAMENT PRO 170	OP	RNBT	FBG	SV	OB								3850	4500
17	2	BOWRIDER 1700	OP	RNBT	FBG	SV	OB			6	10	1363			3400	4000
17	2	BOWRIDER 1710	OP	RNBT	FBG	SV	IO	135	MRCR	6	10	1330			3950	4600
17	2	CLOSED DECK 1701	OP	RNBT	FBG	SV	OB			6	10	1337			3350	3900
17	2	FISH N SKI 1709	OP	RNBT	FBG	SV	OB								3900	4500
18		1860 MV	OP	JON	AL	FL	OB			6	8	417			845	1000
18	2	BOWRIDER 1800	OP	RNBT	FBG	SV	OB								4250	4900
18	2	BOWRIDER 1810	OP	RNBT	FBG	SV	IO	135	MRCR	7	8	1565			4900	5600
18	2	BOWRIDER 1810 SS	OP	RNBT	FBG	SV	IO	135	MRCR	7	8	1550			4700	5400
18	2	CLOSED DECK 1811 SS	OP	RNBT	FBG	SV	IO	135	MRCR	7	8	1550			5000	5750
18	6	TOURNAMENT 180	OP	RNBT	FBG	SV	OB			7	11	1800			4300	4950
18	6	TOURNAMENT PRO 180	OP	RNBT	FBG	SV	OB			7	11	1555			3900	4550
18	9	SUPER FISHERMAN 190	OP	FSH	AL	SV	OB			7	6	1183			3150	3650
18	9	TOURNAMENT 180	OP	RNBT	FBG	SV	OB			7	6	1090			3000	3450
18	10	FISHMASTER 190	OP	RNBT	AL	SV	OB			7	5	1158			3150	3650
19		ISLANDER 191	OP	CUD	AL	SV	IO	135	MRCR	8		1369			5350	6150
20	2	BOWRIDER 2010	OP	RNBT	FBG	SV	IO	100	MRCR	8	6	1968			6200	7100
20	2	BOWRIDER 2010 SS	OP	RNBT	FBG	SV	IO	180	MRCR	8	6	2003			6200	7150
20	2	CUDDY CABIN 2012	OP	CUD	FBG	SV	IO	180	MRCR	8	6	2850			7600	8750
22		ISLANDER 220	OP	CUD	AL	SV	OB			8		1913			5450	6250
22		ISLANDER 221	OP	CUD	AL	SV	IO	135	MRCR	8		1612			6550	7550
22	2	BOWRIDER 2210	OP	RNBT	FBG	SV	IO	180	MRCR						9950	11300
22	2	BOWRIDER 2210 SS	OP	RNBT	FBG	SV	IO	180	MRCR	8	6				9950	11300
22	2	CUDDY CABIN 2212	OP	CUD	FBG	SV	IO	230	MRCR	8	6	2535			8150	9350
25		CRUISER 2513	OP	RNBT	FBG	SV	IO	235	MRCR						10600	12100
		1994 BOATS														
16		1648	OP	JON	AL	FL	OB			5	7	264			645	775
16		1650 MV	OP	JON	AL	FL	OB			6	3	327			780	940
16	2	CAMP 16	OP	UTL	AL	SV	OB			5	7	245			685	825
16	2	SF 16	OP	UTL	AL	SV	OB			5	7	245			455	550
16	4	FISHMASTER 160	OP	BASS	AL	SV	OB			6	2	510			1250	1500
16	4	PIKEMASTER 160	OP	BASS	AL	SV	OB			6	2	450			1100	1350
16	4	PIKEMASTER 160T	OP	BASS	AL	SV	OB			6	2	425			1050	1250
16	4	SF 16WB	OP	UTL	AL	SV	OB			6	2	520			1250	1500
16	5	SF 16WB	OP	RNBT	AL	SV	OB			6	9	880			2250	2600
16	5	SUPER SPORT 170	OP	RNBT	AL	SV	OB			6	2	880			2250	2600
16	6	WALLEYE 170	OP	FSH	AL	SV	OB			6	9	960			2350	2700
17		MARINER 170	OP	CTRCN	AL	SV	OB			7	1	1050			2600	3000
17		STAR CASTER 1700	OP	BASS	AL	SV	OB			6	2	1035			2550	3000
17		STARCASTER 1700	OP	BASS	AL	SV	OB			6	2	1035			2550	3000
17		SUPER FISHERMAN 170	OP	FSH	AL	SV	OB			7	1	1000			2450	2850
17	2	BOWRIDER 1700	OP	RNBT	FBG	SV	OB			6	10	1363			3250	3750
17	2	BOWRIDER 1710	OP	RNBT	FBG	SV	IO	135	MRCR	6	10	1330			3650	4250
17	2	CLOSED DECK 1701	OP	RNBT	FBG	SV	OB			6	10	1337			3200	3700
18	2	BOWRIDER 1810	OP	RNBT	FBG	SV	IO	135	MRCR	7	8	1565			4550	5250
18	2	BOWRIDER 1810 SS	OP	RNBT	FBG	SV	IO	135	MRCR	7	8	1550			4400	5100
18	2	CLOSED DECK 1811 SS	OP	RNBT	FBG	SV	IO	135	MRCR	7	8	1550			4650	5350
18	6	TOURNAMENT 180	OP	RNBT	FBG	SV	OB			7	11	1800			4050	4750
18	9	SUPER FISHERMAN 190	OP	FSH	AL	SV	OB			7	6	1155			2950	3400
18	9	SUPER FISHERMAN 191	OP	RNBT	AL	SV	IO	135	MRCR	7	6	1235			4500	5150
18	9	WALLEYE 180	OP	FSH	AL	SV	OB			7	11	1800			4050	4700
19		HOLIDAY 191	OP	FSH	AL	SV	IO	135	MRCR	7	8	1145			5000	5750
19		ISLANDER 191	OP	CUD	AL	SV	IO	135	MRCR	8		1260			4950	5700
20	2	2012 CC	OP	RNBT	FBG	SV	IO	180	MRCR	8	6	2850			6800	7800
20	2	BOWRIDER 2010	OP	RNBT	FBG	SV	IO	180	MRCR	8		2850			6400	7400
20	2	BOWRIDER 2010 SS	OP	RNBT	FBG	SV	IO	180	MRCR	8		2850			6700	7650
22		ISLANDER 221	OP	CUD	AL	SV	IO	135	MRCR	8		1600			6100	7050
22	2	CUDDY CABIN 2212	OP	CUD	FBG	SV	IO	230	MRCR	8	6	3470			9200	10500
		1993 BOATS														
16		1948-16	OP	JON	AL	FL	OB			5	7	264			590	710
16		1948-16LW	OP	JON	AL	FL	OB			5	7	264			640	770
16		2450-16V	OP	JON	AL	FL	OB			6	3	327			745	895
16		STARCASTER 1600DS	OP	BASS	AL	SV	OB			6	2	790			1800	2150
16		STARCASTER 1600SS	OP	BASS	AL	SV	OB			6	2	795			1850	2200
16	2	SEAFARER 16	OP	UTL	AL	SV	OB			5	7	245			545	655
16	2	SEAFARER 16DLX SC	OP	UTL	AL	SV	OB			5	7	455			1200	1450
16	2	SEAFARER 16LW	OP	UTL	AL	SV	OB			5	7	455			880	1050
16	4	FISHMASTER 160C	OP	BASS	AL	SV	OB			6	2	625			1450	1750
16	4	FISHMASTER 160T	OP	BASS	AL	SV	OB			6	2	625			1450	1750
16	4	SEAFARER SF 16WB	OP	UTL	AL	SV	OB			6	2				1000	1200
16	5	SUPERSPORT 170	OP	RNBT	AL	SV	OB			6	9	850			2000	2400
16	6	WALLEYE 170C	OP	FSH	AL	SV	OB			6	9				2500	2900
16	6	WALLEYE 170DC	OP	FSH	AL	SV	OB			6	9				2650	3100
16	6	WALLEYE 170T	OP	FSH	AL	SV	OB			6	9	870			2000	2400
16	6	WALLEYE TOURNAMENT	OP	FSH	FBG	SV	OB			6	8				2550	3000
17		MARINER 170	OP	CTRCN	AL	SV	OB			7	1	1050			2450	2850
17		STARCASTER 1700	OP	BASS	AL	SV	OB			6	2	930			2250	2600
17		SUPER FISHERMAN 170	OP	FSH	AL	SV	OB			7	1	930			2200	2550
17	3	ELITE 170	OP	RNBT	FBG	SV	OB			6	9	1180			2750	3200
17	3	ELITE 170CS	OP	RNBT	FBG	SV	OB			6	9	1100			2600	3000
17	3	ELITE 171	OP	RNBT	FBG	SV	IO	115-155		6	9	1140			3250	3800
17	3	ELITE 171CS	OP	RNBT	FBG	SV	IO	115-155		6	9	1167			3300	3850
17	3	ELITE 171CSS	OP	RNBT	FBG	SV	IO	115-155		6	9	1192			3400	3950
17	3	ELITE 171SS	OP	RNBT	FBG	SV	IO	115-155		6	9	1192			3200	3750
17	3	EUROSTAR 170 F&S	OP	RNBT	FBG	SV	OB			6	9	1180			2750	3200
17	3	EUROSTAR 171 F&S	OP	RNBT	FBG	SV	IO	115	MRCR	6	9	1120			3250	3750
18	8	SUPERSPORT 191	OP	RNBT	AL	SV	IO	115-155		7	4	1235			4050	4750
19		HOLIDAY 191	OP	FSH	AL	SV	IO	115-155		7	8	1145			4650	5400
19		ISLANDER 191V	OP	CUD	AL	SV	IO	115	MRCR	8		1280			4600	5300
19		MARINER 190	OP	CTRCN	AL	SV	OB			7	8	1300			3100	3600
19		SUPER FISHERMAN 190	OP	FSH	AL	SV	OB			7	8	1050			2600	3050
19		SUPER FISHERMAN 191	OP	RNBT	AL	SV	IO	115-155		7	8	930			4300	5000
19	1	ELITE 190	OP	B/R	FBG	SV	OB			8		1400			3350	3900
19	1	ELITE 190CS	OP	RNBT	FBG	SV	OB			8		1400			3300	3850
19	1	ELITE 191	OP	RNBT	FBG	SV	IO	115-205		8		1459			4550	5350
19	1	ELITE 191CS	OP	RNBT	FBG	SV	IO	115-205		8		1425			4550	5350
19	1	ELITE 191CSS	OP	RNBT	FBG	SV	IO	115-205		8		1425			4600	5450
19	1	ELITE 191SS	OP	RNBT	FBG	SV	IO	115-205		8		1459			4650	5500
19	1	EUROSTAR 191 F&S	OP	RNBT	FBG	SV	IO	115-205		8		1369			4550	5350
20	9	ELITE 211	OP	RNBT	FBG	SV	IO	155-230		8		1510			4950	5900
20	9	ELITE 211CC	OP	CUD	FBG	SV	IO	155-230		8		1910			5500	6550
20	9	ELITE 211DB	OP	RNBT	AL	SV	IO	155-255		8		1910			5300	6500
20	9	ELITE 211SS	OP	RNBT	FBG	SV	IO	155-230		8		1510			5050	6000
22		BLUEWATER 221 O/S	OP	CTRCN	FBG	SV	IO	155-230		8	6	2500			7200	8500
22		ISLANDER 221V	OP	CUD	AL	SV	IO	115-205		8	1	1600			5750	6750
		1992 BOATS														
16		1948-16	OP	JON	AL	FL	OB			5	7	264			565	680
16		1948-16LW	OP	JON	AL	FL	OB			5	7	264			615	740
16		2450-16V	OP	JON	AL	FL	OB			6	3	327			710	855
16		STARCASTER 1600	OP	BASS	AL	SV	OB			6	2	825			1800	2150
16		STARCASTER 1600DS	OP	BASS	AL	SV	OB			6	2	790			1750	2100
16		STARCASTER 1600FS	OP	BASS	AL	SV	OB			6	2	795			1750	2100
16	2	SEAFARER 16	OP	UTL	AL	SV	OB			5	7	245			520	625
16	2	SEAFARER 16DLX C	OP	UTL	AL	SV	OB			5	7	455			1200	1400
16	2	SEAFARER 16LW	OP	UTL	AL	SV	OB			5	7	455			805	970
16	4	FISHMASTER 160C	OP	BASS	AL	SV	OB			6	2	625			1400	1650
16	4	FISHMASTER 160T	OP	BASS	AL	SV	OB			6	2	625			1400	1650
16	4	SEAFARER SF 16WB	OP	UTL	AL	SV	OB			6	2				970	1150
16	5	SUPERSPORT 170	OP	RNBT	AL	SV	OB			6	9	850			1900	2300
16	6	WALLEYE 170C	OP	FSH	AL	SV	OB			6	9				2400	2800
16	6	WALLEYE 170DC	OP	FSH	AL	SV	OB			6	9				2550	2950
16	6	WALLEYE TOURNAMENT	OP	FSH	FBG	SV	OB			6	8				2450	2850
17		MARINER 170	OP	CTRCN	AL	SV	OB			7	1	1050			2350	2750
17		STARCASTER 1700	OP	BASS	AL	SV	OB			6	2	930			2100	2500
17		SUPER FISHERMAN 170	OP	FSH	AL	SV	OB			7	1	930			2050	2450
17	3	ELITE 170	OP	RNBT	FBG	SV	OB			6	9	1180			2650	3050
17	3	ELITE 170CS	OP	RNBT	FBG	SV	OB			6	9	1100			2500	2900
17	3	ELITE 171	OP	RNBT	FBG	SV	IO	115	MRCR	6	9	1140			3050	3550
17	3	ELITE 171CS	OP	RNBT	FBG	SV	IO	115	MRCR	6	9	1167			3050	3550
17	3	ELITE 171CSS	OP	RNBT	FBG	SV	IO	115	MRCR	6	9	1192			2950	3450
17	3	ELITE 171SS	OP	RNBT	FBG	SV	IO	115	MRCR	6	9	1192			3200	3700
17	3	EUROSTAR 170 F&S	OP	RNBT	FBG	SV	OB			6	9	1180			2650	3050
17	3	EUROSTAR 171 F&S	OP	RNBT	FBG	SV	IO	115	MRCR	6	9	1120			3000	3500
19		HOLIDAY 190	OP	FSH	AL	SV	OB			7	8	1305			2950	3450
19		HOLIDAY 191	OP	FSH	AL	SV	IO	115-155		7	8	1145			4300	5050
19		ISLANDER 191V	OP	CUD	AL	SV	IO	115	MRCR	8		1280			4250	4950
19		MARINER 190	OP	CTRCN	AL	SV	OB			7	8	1300			2950	3450
19		SUPER FISHERMAN 190	OP	FSH	AL	SV	OB			7	8	1050			2500	2900
19		SUPERSPORT 191	OP	RNBT	AL	SV	IO	115-155		7	8	930			4000	4700
19	1	ELITE 191	OP	RNBT	FBG	SV	IO	115-205		8		1459			4200	5050

 CONTINUED ON NEXT PAGE

LOA FT	LOA IN	NAME AND/ OR MODEL	TOP/ RIG	BOAT TYPE	-HULL- MTL	-HULL- TP	ENGINE TP	ENGINE # HP	ENGINE MFG	BEAM FT	BEAM IN	WGT LBS	DRAFT FT IN	RETAIL LOW	RETAIL HIGH
		1992 BOATS													
19	1	ELITE 191CS	OP	RNBT	FBG	SV	IO	115-205		8		1425		4200	5000
19	1	ELITE 191CSS	OP	RNBT	FBG	SV	IO	115-205		8		1425		4250	5100
19	1	ELITE 191SS	OP	RNBT	FBG	SV	IO	115-205		8		1459		4300	5100
19	1	EUROSTAR 191 F&S	OP	RNBT	FBG	SV	IO	115-205		8		1369		4200	5000
20	9	ELITE 211	OP	RNBT	FBG	SV	IO	155-230		8		1510		4650	5550
20	9	ELITE 211SS	OP	RNBT	FBG	SV	IO	155-230		8		1510		4750	5600
20	9	EUROSTAR 211FS	OP	RNBT	FBG	SV	OB			8		1400		3450	4050
20	9	EUROSTAR 211FS	OP	RNBT	FBG	SV	IO	230	MRCR	8		1400		4850	5600
22		BLUEWATER 221 O/S	OP	CTRCN	FBG	SV	IO	155-230		8	6	2500		6700	7950
22		ISLANDER 221V	OP	CUD	AL	SV	IO	115-205		8	1	1600		5350	6300
		1991 BOATS													
16		1948-16	OP	JON	AL	FL	OB			5	7	264		540	655
16		1948-16LW	OP	JON	AL	FL	OB			5	7	264		585	705
16		2448-16V	OP	JON	AL	SV	OB			5	9	248		535	645
16	2	SEAFARER 16	OP	UTL	AL	SV	OB			5	7	245		500	600
16	2	SEAFARER 16DLX C	OP	UTL	AL	SV	OB			5	7	455		1050	1250
16	2	SEAFARER 16LW	OP	UTL	AL	SV	OB			5	7	455		855	1000
16	4	FISHMASTER 165C	OP	BASS	AL	SV	OB			6	2	625		1350	1600
16	4	FISHMASTER 165T	OP	BASS	AL	SV	OB			6	2	625		1350	1600
16	7	STARCASTER 1700	OP	BASS	AL	SV	OB			5	6	550		1200	1450
17		FISHMASTER 170C	OP	BASS	AL	SV	OB			7	1	850		1850	2200
17		FISHMASTER 170T	OP	BASS	AL	SV	OB			7	1	850		1850	2200
17		MARINER 170	OP	CTRCN	AL	SV	OB			7	1	850		1850	2200
17		SUPER FISHERMAN 170	OP	FSH	AL	SV	OB			7	1	850		1850	2200
17		SUPERSPORT 170	OP	RNBT	AL	SV	OB			7	1	850		1850	2200
17	4	ELITE 1701	OP	RNBT	FBG	SV	IO	115-155		6	10	1140		2850	3300
17	4	ELITE 1701 S	OP	RNBT	FBG	SV	IO	115-155		6	10	1140		3050	3550
17	4	EUROSTAR 170 CB	OP	RNBT	FBG	SV	OB			6	10			3200	3700
17	4	EUROSTAR 170 F&S	OP	RNBT	FBG	SV	OB			6	10	1175		2500	2900
17	4	EUROSTAR 171 CB	OP	RNBT	FBG	SV	IO	115-155		6	10			3500	4100
17	4	EUROSTAR 171 F&S	OP	RNBT	FBG	SV	IO	115-155		6	10	1140		2850	3300
18	11	ISLANDER 191V	OP	CUD	AL	SV	IO	115-155		8		1280		3950	4650
19		MARINER 190	OP	CTRCN	AL	SV	OB			7	8	930		2150	2500
19		SUPER FISHERMAN 190	OP	FSH	AL	SV	OB			7	8	930		2150	2500
19		SUPERSPORT 191	OP	RNBT	AL	SV	IO	115-155		7	8	930		3750	4400
19	1	HOLIDAY 190	OP	FSH	AL	SV	OB			7	1	850		2000	2350
19	1	HOLIDAY 191	OP	FSH	AL	SV	IO	115-155		7	8	930		4100	4800
19	2	ELITE 1901	OP	RNBT	FBG	SV	IO	115-205		8		1140		3950	4650
19	2	ELITE 1901 S	OP	RNBT	FBG	SV	IO	115-205		8		1578		4200	4950
19	2	EUROSTAR 191 CB	OP	RNBT	FBG	SV	IO	115-205		8		1398		4000	4750
19	2	EUROSTAR 191 F&S	OP	RNBT	FBG	SV	IO	115-205		8		1578		3950	4700
20	9	EUROSTAR 2101 F&S	OP	RNBT	FBG	SV	IO	155-230		8		1648		4500	5350
22		MARINER 220V	OP	CTRCN	AL	SV	OB			8				5750	6600
22	1	BLUEWATER 221 O/S	OP	CTRCN	FBG	SV	IO	155-230		8	6	2860		6750	8000
22	1	ISLANDER 221V	OP	CUD	AL	SV	IO	115-180		8	1	1600		5050	5900
		1990 BOATS													
16		2048-16	OP	JON	AL	FL	OB			5	10	250		520	625
16		SPORTSMAN 16 PRO	OP	FSH	AL	FL	OB			5	10	420		850	1000
16		STARCASTER 160 PRO	OP	FSH	AL	FL	OB			5	10	540		1100	1300
16	1	FISHMASTER 160	OP	FSH	AL	DV	OB			6	5	610		1250	1450
16	1	MARINER 160	OP	FSH	AL	DV	OB			6	5	590		1200	1400
16	1	SUPER SPORT 160	OP	RNBT	AL	SV	OB			6	5	650		1350	1600
16	1	SUPERFISHERMAN 160	OP	FSH	AL	DV	OB			6	5	650		1300	1550
16	2	SELECT 160	OP	RNBT	FBG	DV	OB			6	10	800		1600	1950
16	3	SEAFARER 16	OP	FSH	AL	SV	OB			5	7	245		490	595
16	3	SEAFARER 16 DXL-C	OP	FSH	AL	SV	OB			5	7	455		935	1100
16	3	SEAFARER 16 DXL-T	OP	FSH	AL	SV	OB			5	7	435		895	1050
16	3	SEAFARER 16 F	OP	FSH	AL	SV	OB			5	7	335		680	820
16	4	FISHMASTER 165C	OP	FSH	AL	DV	OB			6	2	625		1300	1500
16	4	HERITAGE 1600	OP	RNBT	FBG	DV	OB			6	5	975		1950	2350
16	4	HERITAGE 1601	OP	RNBT	FBG	DV	IO			6	5	1060		**	**
17	6	HERITAGE 180	OP	RNBT	FBG	DV	OB			6	2	800		1700	2050
18	3	FISHMASTER 180C	OP	FSH	AL	DV	OB			6	5	960		2050	2450
18	3	FISHMASTER 180T	OP	FSH	AL	DV	OB			6	5	935		2000	2400
18	3	HOLIDAY 180	OP	FSH	AL	DV	OB			6	9	930		2000	2400
18	3	MARINER 180	OP	FSH	AL	DV	OB			6	7	850		1850	2200
18	3	SUPER SPORT 180	OP	RNBT	AL	SV	OB			6	7	930		2000	2400
18	3	SUPERFISHERMAN 180	OP	FSH	AL	DV	OB			6	8	900		1950	2300
18	6	SUPER SPORT 181	OP	RNBT	AL	DV	IO	115	MRCR	6	8	960		3000	3500
18	6	SUPER SPORT 181	OP	RNBT	AL	SV	IO	115	MRCR	6	7	960		3000	3450
18	7	HERITAGE 1900	OP	RNBT	FBG	DV	OB			7	2	1300		2700	3150
18	7	HERITAGE 1901	OP	RNBT	FBG	DV	IO			7	2	1330		**	**
18	11	ISLANDER 191V	OP	FSH	FBG	DV	IO	115	MRCR	8		1280		3900	4550
21	1	ISLANDER 221V	OP	FSH	FBG	SV	IO	115-155		8		1600		4750	5450
21	3	HERITAGE 210	OP	RNBT	FBG	DV	OB			7	2	900		2200	2550
21	5	HERITAGE 221	OP	RNBT	FBG	DV	IO			7	6	1440		**	**
22	1	HOLIDAY 220V	OP	FSH	AL	DV	OB			8		1500		3500	4100
22	1	ISLANDER 220V	OP	FSH	FBG	DV	OB			8		1600		3700	4300
22	1	MARINER 220V	OP	FSH	AL	DV	OB			8		1250		3000	3450
22	3	BLUEWATER 221 OF	OP	FSH	FBG	DV	IO			8		2860		**	**
		1989 BOATS													
16		2048-16	OP	JON	AL	FL	OB			5	10	250		470	565
16		2048-16 DELUXE	OP	JON	AL	FL	OB			5	10	335		645	775
16		2048-16 WELDED	OP	JON	AL	FL	OB			5	10	250		530	640
16		BB-160	OP	BASS	AL	FL	OB			5	10	540		1050	1250
16	1	FM-160	OP	FSH	AL	SV	OB			6	6	610		1200	1400
16	1	MR-160	OP	CTRCN	AL	SV	OB			6	6	590		1150	1400
16	1	SFM-160	OP	FSH	AL	SV	OB			6	5	650		1250	1500
16	1	SS-160	OP	RNBT	AL	SV	OB			6	5	650		1300	1550
16	2	ESCORT	OP	BASS	FBG	SV	OB			7	1	880		1700	2000
16	2	MEDALIST 1600	OP	RNBT	FBG	SV	OB			6	10	1000		1950	2300
16	2	MEDALIST 1601	OP	RNBT	FBG	SV	IO	120-130		6	10	1080		2250	2600
16	2	TF-160	OP	FSH	FBG	SV	OB			6	10	940		1800	2150
16	3	SF-16	OP	FSH	AL	SV	OB			5	7	245		475	570
16	3	SF-16 DELUXE	OP	FSH	AL	SV	OB			5	7	455		900	1050
16	3	SF-16 SPLIT SEAT	OP	FSH	AL	SV	OB			5	7	335		655	790
16	5	PM-160 CONSOLE STR	OP	FSH	AL	SV	OB			6	2	625		1350	1650
16	5	PM-160 TILLER STR	OP	FSH	AL	SV	OB			6	2	625		1100	1300
16	6	JUDGE	OP	BASS	FBG	SV	OB			6		845		1650	1950
16	11	BASS-BOSS BB170	OP	BASS	AL	FL	OB			5	10	640		1300	1550
16	11	GAMBLER	OP	BASS	FBG	SV	OB			7	1	1100		2150	2550
17	4	SELECT 170	OP	RNBT	FBG	DV	OB			7	10	1570		2900	3350
17	4	SELECT 171S	OP	RNBT	FBG	DV	IO	128-200		7	10	1570		3050	3700
17	6	BASS V180	OP	BASS	AL	SV	OB			6	2	800		1650	1950
17	8	STALKER 1800	OP	FSH	FBG	SV	OB			7	2	610		1250	1500
17	8	STALKER 1800 FSH	OP	FSH	FBG	SV	OB			7	2	610		1300	1550
18	3	BLUEWATER 180	OP	CTRCN	FBG	DV	OB			8		1000		2050	2450
18	3	SS-180	OP	RNBT	AL	SV	OB			6	7	930		1950	2300
18	4	MR-180	OP	CTRCN	AL	SV	OB			6	7	850		1800	2100
18	4	PM-180	OP	FSH	AL	SV	OB			6	7	935		1950	2300
18	4	SFM-180	OP	FSH	AL	SV	OB			6	7	900		1850	2200
18	4	SS-181	OP	RNBT	AL	SV	IO	120-130		6	7	960		2750	3200
18	5	HL-180	OP	RNBT	AL	SV	OB			6	9	930		1950	2300
18	6	MEDALIST 1900	OP	RNBT	FBG	SV	OB			7	2	1300		2600	3000
18	6	MEDALIST 1901	OP	RNBT	FBG	SV	IO	130-205		7	2	1330		3050	3650
18	9	SELECT 190S	OP	RNBT	FBG	DV	OB			7	10	1560		3000	3450
18	9	SELECT 191S	OP	RNBT	FBG	DV	IO	130-230		7	10	1560		3450	4150
18	9	SELECT 191S	OP	RNBT	FBG	DV	IO	260		7	10	1560		3750	4350
18	10	ISLANDER 190V	OP	CUD	AL	DV	OB			8		1280		2600	3000
18	10	ISLANDER 191V	OP	CUD	AL	DV	IO	120-205		8		1280		3450	4150
19	1	EAGLE	OP	RACE	FBG	SV	OB			7	2	1080		2300	2700
19	1	STALKER 1900	OP	BASS	FBG	SV	OB			7	2	1090		2300	2700
20	5	HL-200	OP	FSH	AL	DV	OB			8		1260		2800	3250
20	5	HL-200	OP	RNBT	AL	SV	OB			8		1260		2800	3250
20	5	STARTRON I	OP	RNBT	FBG	DV	IO	200-260		7	7	1725		3800	4700
20	8	SS-201	OP	RNBT	AL	DV	IO	130-205		8		1400		3800	4550
21	3	BLUEWATER 210	OP	CTRCN	FBG	SV	OB			8	6	1050		2450	2800
21	3	MR-210	OP	CTRCN	AL	SV	OB			7	2	900		2100	2500
21	4	ISLANDER 221	OP	CUD	AL	SV	IO	120-175		7	6	1438		4000	4700
22		CHIEFTAIN 221V	OP	CBNCR	AL	DV	IO	130-205		8		1840		5000	5850
22		ISLANDER 220V	OP	CUD	AL	DV	OB			8		1600		3550	4150
22		ISLANDER 221V	OP	CUD	AL	DV	IO	130-205		8		1600		4450	5200
22	2	BW-221 CUDDY	OP	CUD	FBG	DV	IO	165-260		8		2400		5050	6150
22	2	BW-221 OFFSHORE	OP	OFF	FBG	DV	IO	175-260		8		2860		5600	6750
22	3	MR-220V	OP	CTRCN	AL	DV	OB			8		1250		2900	3350
23	7	BLUEWATER 240	OP	CTRCN	FBG	SV	OB			8	6	1200		2800	3300
25	10	ISLANDER 261V	OP	CUD	AL	DV	IO	165-230		8		2400		6800	8450
		1988 BOATS													
16		2048-16	OP	JON	AL	FL	OB			5	10	250		455	550
16		2048-16 DELUXE	OP	JON	AL	FL	OB			5	10	335		625	750
16		2048-16 WELDED	OP	JON	AL	FL	OB			5	10	250		510	615
16		BB-160	OP	BASS	AL	FL	OB			5	10	540		1000	1200
16	1	FM-160	OP	FSH	AL	SV	OB			6	6	610		1150	1350
16	1	MR-160	OP	CTRCN	AL	SV	OB			6	6	590		1100	1350
16	1	SFM-160	OP	FSH	AL	SV	OB			6	5	650		1200	1450
16	1	SS-160	OP	RNBT	AL	SV	OB			6	5	650		1250	1500
16	2	ESCORT	OP	BASS	FBG	SV	OB			7	1	880		1650	1950
16	2	MEDALIST 1600	OP	RNBT	FBG	SV	OB			6	10	1000		1850	2200

CONTINUED ON NEXT PAGE

STARCRAFT MARINE L L C -CONTINUED See inside cover to adjust price for area

LOA FT	LOA IN	NAME AND/ OR MODEL	TOP/ RIG	BOAT TYPE	HULL MTL	HULL TP	ENGINE TP	ENGINE # HP	ENGINE MFG	BEAM FT	BEAM IN	WGT LBS	DRAFT FT	DRAFT IN	RETAIL LOW	RETAIL HIGH
		1988 BOATS														
16	2	MEDALIST 1601	OP	RNBT	FBG	SV	IO	120-130		6	10	1080			2050	2450
16	2	TF-160	OP	FSH	FBG	SV	OB			6	10	940			1750	2050
16	3	SF-16	OP	FSH	AL	SV	OB			5	7	245			460	555
16	3	SF-16 DELUXE	OP	FSH	AL	SV	OB			5	7	455			870	1050
16	3	SF-16 SPLIT SEAT	OP	FSH	AL	SV	OB			5	7	335			630	760
16	5	PM-160 CONSOLE STR	OP	FSH	AL	SV	OB			6	2	625			1300	1550
16	5	PM-160 TILEER STR	OP	FSH	AL	SV	OB			6	2	625			1050	1250
16	6	JUDGE	OP	BASS	FBG	SV	OB			6		845			1600	1900
16	11	BASS-BOSS BB170	OP	BASS	AL	FL	OB			5	10	640			1250	1500
16	11	GAMBLER	OP	BASS	FBG	SV	OB			7	1	1100			2050	2450
17	4	SELECT 170	OP	RNBT	FBG	DV	OB			7	10	1570			2800	3250
17	4	SELECT 171	OP	RNBT	FBG	DV	IO	128-200		7	10	1570			2900	3500
17	4	SELECT 171S	OP	RNBT	FBG	DV	IO	128-200		7	7	1570			2800	3400
17	6	BASS V180	OP	BASS	AL	SV	OB			6	2	800			1600	1900
17	8	STALKER 1800	OP	FSH	FBG	SV	OB			7	2				2300	2650
17	8	STALKER 1800 FSH	OP	FSH	FBG	SV	OB			7	2				2350	2700
18	3	BLUEWATER 180	OP	CTRCN	FBG	DV	OB			8					2500	2900
18	3	SS-180	OP	RNBT	AL	SV	OB			6	7	930			1850	2200
18	4	MR-180	OP	CTRCN	AL	SV	OB			6	7	850			1700	2050
18	4	PM-180	OP	FSH	AL	SV	OB			6	7	935			1850	2200
18	4	SFM-180	OP	FSH	AL	SV	OB			6	7	900			1800	2150
18	4	SS-181	OP	RNBT	AL	SV	IO	120-130		6	7	960			2600	3000
18	5	HL-180	OP	RNBT	AL	SV	OB			6	9	930			1850	2250
18	6	MEDALIST 1900	OP	RNBT	FBG	SV	OB			7	2	1300			2500	2900
18	6	MEDALIST 1901	OP	RNBT	FBG	SV	IO	130-205		7	2	1330			2850	3450
18	9	SELECT 190	OP	RNBT	FBG	DV	OB			7	10	1560			2900	3350
18	9	SELECT 191	OP	RNBT	FBG	DV	IO	130-230		7	10	1560			3200	3950
18	9	SELECT 191	OP	RNBT	FBG	DV	IO	260		7	10	1560			3550	4100
18	9	SELECT 191 CUDDY	OP	CUD	FBG	DV	IO	130-230		8		1975			3650	4400
18	9	SELECT 191S	OP	RNBT	FBG	DV	IO	130-230		7	10	1565			3200	3950
18	9	SELECT 191S	OP	RNBT	FBG	DV	IO	260		7	10	1565			3550	4100
18	10	ISLANDER 190V	OP	CUD	AL	DV	OB			8		1280			2500	2900
18	10	ISLANDER 191V	OP	CUD	AL	DV	IO	120-205		8		1280			3250	3900
19	1	EAGLE	OP	RACE	FBG	SV	OB			7	2	1080			2250	2600
19	1	STALKER 1900	OP	BASS	FBG	SV	OB			7	2	1090			2250	2600
19	2	XP-190	OP	RNBT	AL	DV	OB			7	2	1290			2550	2950
20	5	HL-200	OP	FSH	AL	DV	OB			8		1260			2700	3150
20	5	HL-200	OP	RNBT	AL	SV	OB			8		1260			2700	3150
20	5	STARTRON I	OP	RNBT	FBG	DV	IO	200-260		7	7	1725			3600	4450
20	8	SS-201	OP	RNBT	AL	DV	IO	130-205		8		1400			3600	4300
21	3	BLUEWATER 210	OP	CTRCN	FBG	SV	OB			8	6				4900	5600
21	3	MR-120	OP	CTRCN	AL	SV	OB			7	2	900			2000	2400
21	4	ISLANDER 221	OP	CUD	AL	SV	IO	120-175		7	6	1438			3800	4450
22		CHIEFTAIN 221V	OP	CBNCR	AL	DV	IO	130-205		8		1840			4700	5500
22		ISLANDER 220V	OP	CUD	AL	DV	OB			8		1600			3450	4000
22		ISLANDER 221V	OP	CUD	AL	DV	IO	130-205		8		1600			4150	4950
22	2	SF-221 OFFSHORE	OP	OFF	FBG	DV	IO	175-260		8		2860			5300	6400
22	2	SL-221 CUDDY	OP	CUD	FBG	DV	IO	165-260		8		2400			4800	5800
22	3	MR-220V	OP	CTRCN	AL	DV	OB			8		1250			2800	3250
23	7	BLUEWATER 240	OP	CTRCN	FBG	SV	OB			8	6				6300	7200
25	10	ISLANDER 261V	OP	CUD	AL	DV	IO	165-230		8		2400			6400	8000
		1987 BOATS														
16		2048-16	OP	JON	AL	FL	OB			5	10	250			445	535
16		2048-16 DELUXE	OP	JON	AL	FL	OB			5	10	335			605	725
16		2048-16 WELDED	OP	JON	AL	FL	OB			5	10	250			495	600
16	1	FISHMASTER 160	OP	FSH	AL	SV	OB			6	6	610			1100	1300
16	1	MARINER MR160	OP	CTRCN	AL	SV	OB			6	6	590			1100	1300
16	1	SFM-160	OP	FSH	AL	SV	OB			6	5	650			1200	1400
16	1	SUPER-SPORT 160	OP	RNBT	AL	SV	OB			6	5	650			1200	1450
16	2	CSS-160	OP	RNBT	FBG	SV	OB			6	4	1000			1800	2150
16	2	CSS-161	OP	RNBT	FBG	SV	IO	120-175		6	4	1080			1850	2250
16	2	SF-160	OP	FSH	FBG	SV	OB			6	10	940			1700	2000
16	3	DREAM	OP	BASS	FBG	SV	OB			6	5	1130			2000	2400
16	3	ESCORT	OP	BASS	FBG	SV	OB			7	1	880			1600	1900
16	3	MEDALIST 1600	OP	RNBT	FBG	SV	OB			6	5	980			1750	2100
16	3	MEDALIST 1601	OP	RNBT	FBG	SV	IO	120-130		6	5	1025			1850	2200
16	3	SEAFARER 16	OP	FSH	AL	SV	OB			5	7	245			445	535
16	3	SEAFARER DELUXE	OP	FSH	AL	SV	OB			5	7	455			845	1000
16	3	SEAFARER SPLIT SEAT	OP	FSH	AL	SV	OB			5	7	355			650	785
16	5	PM 160-CNSL STEERING	OP	FSH	AL	SV	OB			6	2	625			1150	1400
16	5	PM 160-TILLER	OP	FSH	AL	SV	OB			6	2	565			1050	1250
16	5	TROLLER 160	OP	BASS	AL	SV	OB			6	2	505			945	1150
16	6	JUDGE	OP	BASS	FBG	SV	OB			6	2	845			1550	1850
16	11	GAMBLER	OP	BASS	FBG	SV	OB			7	2	1100			2000	2350
16	11	MAGNUM 170	OP	BASS	FBG	SV	OB			7	2	1005			1850	2200
17	6	BASS V170	OP	BASS	AL	SV	OB			6	2	670			1300	1550
17	8	CSS-180	OP	RNBT	FBG	SV	OB			6	8	1100			2050	2450
18	3	22-180	OP	RNBT	AL	SV	OB			6	7	930			1800	2150
18	4	22-181	OP	RNBT	AL	SV	IO	120	MRCR	6	7	960			2450	2850
18	4	MARINER MR180	OP	CTRCN	AL	SV	OB			6	4	850			1650	2000
18	4	SFM 180	OP	FSH	AL	SV	OB			6	7	900			1750	2100
18	4	SS-181	OP	RNBT	AL	SV	IO	120-130		6	7	960			2450	2850
18	5	HOLIDAY HL180	OP	RNBT	AL	SV	OB			6	9	930			1800	2150
18	6	MEDALIST 1900	OP	RNBT	FBG	SV	OB			7	2	1310			2450	2850
18	6	MEDALIST 1901	OP	RNBT	FBG	SV	IO	130-205		7	2	1225			2700	3200
18	9	SELECT 190	OP	RNBT	FBG	DV	OB			7	10				3300	3850
18	9	SELECT 191	OP	RNBT	FBG	DV	IO	130-230		7	10	1560			3050	3700
18	9	SELECT 191	OP	RNBT	FBG	DV	IO	260		7	10	1560			3350	3900
18	9	SELECT 191 CUDDY	OP	CUD	FBG	DV	IO	130-230		8		1975			3450	4200
18	9	SELECT 191S	OP	RNBT	FBG	DV	IO	130-230		7	10	1565			3050	3700
18	9	SELECT 191S	OP	RNBT	FBG	DV	IO	260		7	10	1565			3350	3900
18	10	ISLANDER 190V	OP	CUD	AL	DV	OB			8		1280			2400	2800
18	10	ISLANDER 191V	OP	CUD	AL	DV	IO	120-205		8		1280			3100	3700
19	1	EAGLE	OP	RACE	FBG	SV	OB			7	2	1080			2200	2550
19	1	STALKER	OP	BASS	FBG	SV	OB			7	2	1080			2150	2500
19	2	XP-190	OP	RNBT	AL	DV	OB			7	2	1290			2450	2850
20	5	HL-200	OP	RNBT	AL	SV	OB			8		1260			2600	3050
20	8	SS-201	OP	RNBT	AL	DV	IO	130-205		8		1400			3400	4100
21	3	MARINER MR210	OP	CTRCN	AL	SV	OB			7	2	900			1950	2350
21	4	ISLANDER 221	OP	CUD	AL	SV	IO	120-175		7	6	1438			3600	4200
22		CHIEFTAIN 221V	OP	CBNCR	AL	DV	IO	130-205		8		1840			4500	5250
22		ISLANDER 220V	OP	CUD	AL	DV	OB			8		1600			3350	3900
22		ISLANDER 221V	OP	CUD	AL	DV	IO	130-205		8		1600			3950	4700
22	2	SC-221	OP	CUD	FBG	DV	IO	165-260		8		2350			4500	5500
22	2	SF-221 OFFSHORE	OP	OFF	FBG	DV	IO	175-260		8		2860			5000	6050
22	2	SL-221	OP	CUD	FBG	DV	IO	165-260		8		2400			4550	5550
22	3	MARINER MR220V	OP	CTRCN	AL	DV	OB			8		1250			2700	3150
25	10	ISLANDER 261V	OP	CUD	AL	DV	IO	165-230		8		2400			6100	7600
		1986 BOATS														
16		2048-16	OP	JON	AL	FL	OB			5	10	250			460	550
16		2048-16 DELUXE	OP	JON	AL	FL	OB			5	10	335			585	705
16		SS-160 SELECT	OP	RNBT	AL	SV	OB			6	4	650			1150	1400
16	1	FISHMASTER 160	OP	FSH	AL	SV	OB			6	4	640			1150	1350
16	1	MARINER MR160	OP	CTRCN	AL	SV	OB			6	5	650			1150	1350
16	1	SUPER-SPORT 160	OP	RNBT	AL	SV	OB			6	5	720			1300	1550
16	1	SUPER-SPORT 160SF	OP	FSH	AL	SV	OB			6	5	755			1350	1600
16	2	CCS-160 SELECT	OP	RNBT	FBG	DV	OB			6	4	1000			1800	2150
16	2	CSF-160	OP	CTRCN	FBG	DV	OB			6	10	1000			1750	2050
16	2	CSS-160	OP	RNBT	FBG	DV	OB			6	4	1000			1700	2000
16	2	CSS-161	OP	RNBT	FBG	DV	IO	120-175		6	4	1025			1750	2050
16	2	CSS-161 SELECT	OP	RNBT	FBG	DV	IO	120-140		6	4	1025			1800	2150
16	2	CSS-161SELECT	OP	RNBT	FBG	DV	IO	175	OMC	6	4	1025			1750	2100
16	2	CSS-166 SELECT	OP	RNBT	FBG	DV	IO	170	MRCR	6	4	1025			1800	2100
16	3	MEDALIST 1600	OP	RNBT	FBG	DV	OB			6	5	980			1700	2050
16	3	MEDALIST 1601	OP	RNBT	FBG	DV	IO	120-140		6	5	1025			1750	2100
16	3	SEAFARER 16	OP	FSH	AL	SV	OB			5	7	245			435	525
16	3	SEAFARER DELUXE	OP	FSH	AL	SV	OB			5	7	455			810	980
16	3	SEAFARER SPLIT SEAT	OP	FSH	AL	SV	OB			5	7	355			630	760
16	5	PIKEMASTER 160	OP	FSH	AL	SV	OB			6	2	565			1000	1200
16	5	PIKEMASTER TROLLER	OP	FSH	AL	SV	OB			6	2	625			1150	1350
17	1	CPS-17	OP	RNBT	FBG	DV	OB			6	5	1005			1800	2150
17	6	BASS V170	OP	BASS	AL	SV	OB			6	2	670			1250	1500
17	8	CSS-180	OP	RNBT	FBG	DV	OB			6	8	1000			1800	2100
17	8	CSS-180 SELECT	OP	RNBT	FBG	DV	OB			6	8	1000			1900	2250
17	8	CSS-181	OP	RNBT	FBG	DV	IO	120	MRCR	6	8	1140			2250	2600
17	10	CSS-181	OP	RNBT	FBG	DV	IO	120-175		6	8	1140			2150	2650
17	10	CSS-181 SELECT	OP	RNBT	FBG	DV	IO	120-175		6	8	1140			2350	2700
18	3	SS-180 SELECT	OP	RNBT	AL	SV	OB			6	7	930			1750	2100
18	4	MARINER MR180	OP	CTRCN	AL	SV	OB			6	4	745			1450	1700
18	4	SS-181 SELECT	OP	RNBT	AL	SV	IO	120-140		6	7	960			2350	2750
18	4	SUPER-SPORT 180	OP	RNBT	AL	SV	OB			6	7	950			1800	2150
18	4	SUPER-SPORT 180SF	OP	FSH	AL	SV	OB			6	7	930			1750	2100
18	5	HOLIDAY HL180	OP	RNBT	AL	SV	OB			6	9	960			1800	2150
18	6	MEDALIST 1901	OP	RNBT	FBG	DV	IO	140-205		7	2	1225			2550	3050
18	9	CSF-191	OP	CUD	AL	DV	IO	140-230		8		1975			3300	4000

562
CONTINUED ON NEXT PAGE
96th ed. - Vol. II

LOA FT	LOA IN	NAME AND/ OR MODEL	TOP/ RIG	BOAT TYPE	HULL MTL	HULL TP	ENGINE TP	ENGINE # HP	ENGINE MFG	BEAM FT	BEAM IN	WGT LBS	DRAFT FT	DRAFT IN	RETAIL LOW	RETAIL HIGH
		1986 BOATS														
18	9	CSS-1901 SELECT	OP	RNBT	FBG	DV	IO	140-230		7	10	1350			2800	3450
18	10	ISLANDER 190V	OP	CUD	AL	DV	OB			8		1280			2350	2750
18	10	ISLANDER 191V	OP	CUD	AL	DV	IO	140-205		8		1280			2950	3500
20	1	CPS 20	OP	RACE	FBG	TR	OB			7	11	1010			2050	2450
20	1	CPS-20	OP	RNBT	FBG	DV	OB			7	11	1170			2350	2750
20	2	CSF-200CC	OP	CTRCN	FBG	DV	OB			8		1550			2950	3450
20	8	SS-201 SELECT	OP	RNBT	AL	SV	IO	140-205		8		1400			3250	3900
21	3	MARINER MR210	OP	CTRCN	AL	SV	OB			7	2	1060			2250	2600
21	4	ISLANDER 221	OP	CUD	AL	DV	IO	120-175		7	6	1438			3400	4000
22		ISLANDER 220 V	OP	CUD	AL	DV	OB			8		1600			3250	3800
22		ISLANDER 221V	OP	CUD	AL	DV	IO	140-205		8		1600			3800	4450
22	2	CSF-221	OP	OFF	AL	DV	IO	170-230		8		2350			4300	5150
22	3	MARINER MR220V	OP	CTRCN	AL	DV	OB			8		1250			2650	3050
25	10	ISLANDER 261V	OP	CUD	AL	DV	IO	170-230		8		2400			5850	7250
		1985 BOATS														
16		2048-16	OP	JON	AL	FL	OB			5	10	250			445	540
16		2048-16 DELUXE	OP	JON	AL	FL	OB			5	10	335			570	690
16	1	FISHMASTER 160	OP	FSH	AL	SV	OB			6	4	640			1100	1300
16	1	MARINER MR160	OP	CTRCN	AL	SV	OB			6	5	650			1100	1350
16	1	SUPER-SPORT 160	OP	RNBT	AL	SV	OB			6	5	720			1250	1500
16	1	SUPER-SPORT 160SF	OP	FSH	AL	SV	OB			6	5	755			1300	1550
16	2	CSS160B	OP	RNBT	FBG	SV	OB			6	10	980			1650	2000
16	2	CSS161B	OP	RNBT	FBG	SV	IO			6	10	1065			**	**
16	2	CSS161B	OP	RNBT	FBG	SV	IO	140		6	10				2350	2750
16	3	SEAFARER 16	OP	FSH	AL	SV	OB			5	7	245			425	510
16	3	SEAFARER DELUXE	OP	FSH	AL	SV	OB			5	7	455			790	955
16	3	SEAFARER SPLIT SEAT	OP	FSH	AL	SV	OB			5	7	355			615	740
16	5	PIKEMASTER 160	OP	FSH	AL	SV	OB			6	2	565			995	1200
17	1	CPS 17	OP	RACE	FBG	SV	OB			6	5	890			1550	1800
17	6	BASS V170	OP	BASS	AL	SV	OB			6	2	670			1250	1450
17	9	CSS180B	OP	RNBT	FBG	SV	OB			6	10	1105			1950	2300
17	11	CSS181B	OP	RNBT	FBG	SV	IO		MRCR	6	10	1140			**	**
17	11	CSS181B	OP	RNBT	FBG	SV	IO		OMC	6	10	1140			**	**
18	3	HL181	OP	RNBT	AL	SV	IO	145		6	11				2800	3250
18	3	HOLIDAY HL181	OP	RNBT	AL	SV	IO	140		6	9	960			2250	2650
18	4	MARINER MR180	OP	CTRCN	AL	SV	OB			6	4	745			1400	1650
18	4	SUPER-SPORT 180	OP	RNBT	AL	SV	OB			6	7	950			1750	2050
18	4	SUPER-SPORT 180SF	OP	FSH	AL	SV	OB			6	7	930			1700	2050
18	4	SUPER-SPORT 181	OP	RNBT	AL	SV	IO	145		6	7				2750	3200
18	5	HOLIDAY HL180	OP	RNBT	AL	SV	OB			6	9	960			1750	2100
18	5	SUPER-SPORT 181	OP	RNBT	AL	SV	IO	140		6	7	960			2250	2650
18	9	CSS191B	OP	RNBT	FBG	SV	IO	240		8		1660			3050	3550
18	11	ISLANDER 190 V	OP	CUD	AL	DV	OB			8		1280			2300	2700
18	11	ISLANDER 191 V	OP	CUD	AL	DV	IO	150		8		1280			2850	3300
18	11	ISLANDER 191 V	OP	CUD	AL	DV	SE	155	OMC	8		1280			2300	2700
20	1	CPS 20	OP	RACE	FBG	TR	OB			7	11	1010			2000	2400
20	8	SUPER-SPORT 201	OP	RNBT	AL	SV	IO	140		8					3250	3800
21	3	MARINER MR210	OP	CTRCN	AL	SV	OB			7	2	1060			2200	2550
21	5	ISLANDER 221		CUD	AL	SV	IO	170		7	6				3450	4000
21	5	ISLANDER 221	OP	CUD	AL	SV	SE		OMC	7	6	1438			**	**
21	5	ISLANDER 221	OP	CUD	AL	SV	IO	120		7	6	1438			3300	3850
22		ISLANDER 220 V	OP	CUD	AL	DV	OB			8		1600			3150	3700
22		ISLANDER 221 V		CUD	AL	DV	SE		OMC	8		1600			**	**
22		ISLANDER 221 V		CUD	AL	DV	IO	470	MRCR	8		1600			7350	8500
22		ISLANDER 221V		CUD	AL	DV	IO	240		8					5450	6250
22	3	MARINER MR220V	OP	CTRCN	AL	DV	OB			8		1250			2550	3000
22	3	OFFSHORE SC221	OP	CUD	FBG	SV	IO			8		2420			**	**
22	3	SC221	OP	CUD	FBG		IO			8		2420			**	**
25	10	ISLANDER 261 V		CR	AL	DV	SE		OMC	8		2400			**	**
25	10	ISLANDER 261 V		CR	AL	DV	IO	240		8		2400			6150	7050
25	10	ISLANDER 261V		CR	AL	DV	IO	280		8					6950	8000
		1984 BOATS														
16		2048-16	OP	JON	AL	FL	OB			5	10	250			435	525
16		FISHMASTER 160	OP	FSH	AL	SV	OB			6	4	610			1050	1200
16		SUPER-SPORT 160	OP	RNBT	AL	SV	OB			6	5	650			1100	1300
16	2	CSS160B	OP	RNBT	FBG	SV	OB			6	10	1000			1650	1950
16	2	CSS161B	OP	RNBT	FBG	SV	IO	170		6	10	1025			1700	2000
16	2	SF 16	OP	ROW	AL	SV	OB			5	7	245			**	**
16	2	SF 16 DELUXE	OP	FSH	AL	SV	OB			5	7	370			625	750
16	3	V160	OP	RNBT	FBG	SV	OB			6	5	980			1650	1950
16	3	V160B	OP	RNBT	FBG	SV	OB			6	5	980			1650	1950
16	3	V161B	OP	RNBT	FBG	SV	IO	170		6	5	1025			1650	1950
16	5	PIKEMASTER 160	OP	FSH	AL	SV	OB			6	2	625			1050	1300
16	10	ST171		RNBT	FBG	TR	IO	200		6	10				2400	2800
17		CPS 17	OP	RACE	FBG	SV	OB			6	5				1450	1700
17	3	WV170B	OP	RNBT	FBG	SV	OB			6	11	1095			1850	2200
17	3	WV171B	OP	RNBT	FBG		IO	140-185		6	11	1170			1950	2400
17	3	WV171B	OP	RNBT	FBG	SV	IO	140-188		6	11	1170			2000	2400
17	6	BASS 170	OP	BASS	AL	SV	OB			6	2	670			1200	1450
18		CSS180B	OP	RNBT	FBG	SV	OB			6	10	1100			1900	2250
18		CSS181B	OP	RNBT	FBG	SV	IO	120-188		6	10	1140			2150	2550
18	1	MARINER 180	OP	CTRCN	AL	SV	OB			6	4	705			1300	1550
18	2	SUPER-SPORT 180	OP	RNBT	AL	SV	OB			6	7	930			1650	2000
18	3	HOLIDAY 180	OP	RNBT	AL	SV	OB			6	9	930			1650	2000
18	3	HOLIDAY 181	OP	RNBT	AL	SV	IO	120		6	9	960			2150	2550
18	3	HOLIDAY 181	OP	RNBT	AL	SV	JT	140	OMC	6	9	960			3250	3800
18	3	HOLIDAY 181	OP	RNBT	AL	SV	IO	140		6	9	960			2200	2550
18	3	SUPER-SPORT 181	OP	RNBT	AL	SV	IO	120		6	7	960			2100	2500
18	3	SUPER-SPORT 181	OP	RNBT	AL	SV	JT	140	OMC	6	7	960			3200	3750
18	3	SUPER-SPORT 181	OP	RNBT	AL	SV	IO	140		6	7	960			2100	2500
18	6	V190B	OP	RNBT	FBG	SV	OB			7	2	1325			2300	2650
18	6	V191B	OP	RNBT	FBG	SV	IO	140-230		7	2	1225			2350	2850
18	10	ISLANDER 190 V	OP	CUD	AL	DV	OB			8		1280			2250	2600
18	10	ISLANDER 191 V	OP	CUD	AL	DV	IO	185		8		1280			2750	3200
20		CPS 20	OP	RACE	FBG	TR	OB			7	11	1170			2300	2650
20		SF 201	OP	OPFSH	FBG	SV	IO	140-188		8		1780			3350	3950
21	2	MARINER 210	OP	CTRCN	AL	SV	OB			7	2	900			1800	2150
21	4	ISLANDER 221	OP	CUD	AL	SV	IO	120-188		7	6	1438			3150	3750
22		ISLANDER 220 V	OP	CUD	AL	DV	OB			8		1600			3100	3600
22		ISLANDER 221 V		CUD	AL	DV	IO	188		8		1600			3500	4100
22	2	SC221	OP	CBNCR	FBG		IO	228		8		2500			4650	5350
22	3	MARINER V220	OP	CTRCN	AL	DV	OB			8		1250			2500	2900
25	10	ISLANDER 261 V		CR	AL	DV	IO	230		8		2400			5850	6700
25	10	SF261V		SF	FBG	DV	IO	280		8					7600	8700

....For earlier years, see the BUC Used Boat Price Guide, Volume 3

STARDUST CRUISERS INC

MONTICELLO KY 43633-2111

See inside cover to adjust price for area

LOA FT	LOA IN	NAME AND/ OR MODEL	TOP/ RIG	BOAT TYPE	HULL MTL	HULL TP	ENGINE TP	ENGINE # HP	ENGINE MFG	BEAM FT	BEAM IN	WGT LBS	DRAFT FT	DRAFT IN	RETAIL LOW	RETAIL HIGH
		1995 BOATS														
54		STARDUST CR WB/SS	HT	HB	AL	PN				14			2	4	48300	53100
		IB 115 MRCR 55100 60500, IB 120 VLVO 55300 60800, IB 146 VLVO													55700	61200
		IB 155 MRCR 55500 61000, IB 175 VLVO 55900 61400, IB 180 MRCR													55600	61100
		IB 205 MRCR 55600 61100, IB 209 VLVO 56200 61700, IB 229 VLVO													55700	61200
		IB 230 MRCR 55700 61200, IB 240 MRCR 55700 61200, IB 275 VLVO													55900	61500
		IB 300 MRCR 56000 61500, IB 330 VLVO 56700 62300, IB 130D VLVO													57100	62800
		IB 140D MRCR 58800 64600, IB 170D MRCR 58300 64000, IB 200D VLVO													58600	64400
		IB 254D MRCR 60000 65900														
54		STARDUST CRUISER	HT	HB	AL	PN				14			2	4	43100	47900
		IB 115 MRCR 50600 55600, IB 120 VLVO 51000 56000, IB 146 VLVO													51400	56500
		IB 155 MRCR 51300 56300, IB 175 VLVO 51600 56700, IB 180 MRCR													51400	56500
		IB 205 MRCR 51500 56600, IB 209 VLVO 52000 57100, IB 229 VLVO													51700	56800
		IB 230 MRCR 51600 56700, IB 240 MRCR 51600 56800, IB 275 VLVO													51900	57000
		IB 300 MRCR 52000 57100, IB 330 VLVO 52700 57900, IB 130D VLVO													53200	58500
		IB 140D MRCR 53000 58200, IB 170D MRCR 54100 59500, IB 200D VLVO													54500	59900
		IB 254D MRCR 55800 61300														
60		STARDUST CR WB/SS	HT	HB	AL	PN				14			2	4	36100	40100
		IB 115 MRCR 51300 56300, IB 120 VLVO 51500 56600, IB 146 VLVO													51800	57000
		IB 155 MRCR 51700 56800, IB 175 VLVO 52000 57200, IB 180 MRCR													49800	54700
		IB 205 MRCR 51800 56900, IB 209 VLVO 52300 57400, IB 229 VLVO													51900	57000
		IB 230 MRCR 51800 56900, IB 240 MRCR 52700 57900, IB 275 VLVO													52100	57200
		IB 300 MRCR 52100 57200, IB 330 VLVO 52700 57900, IB 130D VLVO													**	**
		IB 140D MRCR ** ** , IB 170D MRCR ** ** , IB 200D VLVO													**	**
		IB 254D MRCR ** **														
60		STARDUST CRUISER	HT	HB	AL	PN				14			2	4	32500	36100
		IB 115 MRCR 46900 51500, IB 120 VLVO 47100 51700, IB 146 VLVO													47400	52100
		IB 155 MRCR 47300 52000, IB 175 VLVO 47600 52400, IB 180 MRCR													49800	54700
		IB 205 MRCR 47500 52300, IB 209 VLVO 48000 52700, IB 229 VLVO													47700	52400
		IB 230 MRCR 47600 52300, IB 240 MRCR 46800 51400, IB 275 VLVO													47800	52600
		IB 300 MRCR 48000 52700, IB 300 VLVO 49400 54300, IB 330 VLVO													48600	53400
		IB 130D VLVO ** ** , IB 140D MRCR ** ** , IB 170D MRCR													**	**

CONTINUED ON NEXT PAGE

```
        LOA  NAME AND/        TOP/ BOAT  -HULL- ----ENGINE---  BEAM  WGT  DRAFT RETAIL RETAIL
        FT IN  OR MODEL       RIG  TYPE  MTL TP TP # HP MFG    FT IN LBS  FT IN  LOW    HIGH
--------------------- 1995 BOATS ---------------------------------------------------------------
60      STARDUST CRUISER      HT  HB   AL  PN IB 200D VLVO 14              2  4    **     **
60      STARDUST CRUISER      HT  HB   AL  PN IB 254D MRCR 14              2  4    **     **
62      STARDUST CR WB/SS     HT  HB   AL  PN           14              2  4   42900  47700
   IB  115  MRCR  54600     60000, IB 120 VLVO 54800  60200, IB 146 VLVO 55100  60600
   IB  155  MRCR  55000     60400, IB 175 VLVO 55300  60800, IB 180 MRCR 55100  60600
   IB  205  MRCR  55100     60500, IB 209 VLVO 55500  61000, IB 229 VLVO 55200  60700
   IB  230  MRCR  55100     60600, IB 240 MRCR 55100  60600, IB 275 VLVO 55300  60800
   IB  300  MRCR  55400     60800, IB 330 VLVO 56000  61500, IB 130D VLVO  **     **
   IB  140D MRCR   **         **, IB 170D MRCR  **      **, IB 200D VLVO   **     **
   IB  254D MRCR   **         **

62      STARDUST CRUISER      HT  HB   AL  PN           14              2  4   38600  42900
   IB  115  MRCR  49900     54900, IB 120 VLVO 50300  55300, IB 146 VLVO 50700  55700
   IB  155  MRCR  50600     55500, IB 175 VLVO 50900  55900, IB 180 MRCR 50700  55700
   IB  205  MRCR  50800     55800, IB 209 VLVO 51200  56300, IB 229 VLVO 50900  55900
   IB  230  MRCR  50900     55900, IB 240 MRCR 50900  55900, IB 275 VLVO 51100  56100
   IB  300  MRCR  51200     56300, IB 330 VLVO 51800  56900, IB 130D VLVO  **     **
   IB  140D MRCR   **         **, IB 170D MRCR  **      **, IB 200D VLVO   **     **
   IB  254D MRCR   **         **

66      STARDUST CR WB/SS     HT  HB   AL  PN           14              2  4   54300  59700
   IB  115  MRCR  57800     63500, IB 120 VLVO 58000  63800, IB 146 VLVO 58300  64100
   IB  155  MRCR  58200     63900, IB 175 VLVO 58500  64300, IB 180 MRCR 58300  64100
   IB  205  MRCR  58300     64100, IB 209 VLVO 58800  64600, IB 229 VLVO 58400  64200
   IB  230  MRCR  58300     64100, IB 240 MRCR 58400  64100, IB 275 VLVO 58600  64400
   IB  300  MRCR  58600     64400, IB 330 VLVO 59200  65100, IB 130D VLVO 64900  71300
   IB  254D MRCR  63600     72100, IB 170D MRCR 66000 72600, IB 200D VLVO 63800  70100

66      STARDUST CRUISER      HT  HB   AL  PN           14              2  4   50500  55500
   IB  115  MRCR  53800     59100, IB 120 VLVO 54000  59400, IB 146 VLVO 54400  59700
   IB  155  MRCR  54300     59600, IB 175 VLVO 54600  60000, IB 180 MRCR 54400  59800
   IB  205  MRCR  54500     59900, IB 209 VLVO 54900  60300, IB 229 VLVO 54500  60000
   IB  230  MRCR  54500     59900, IB 240 MRCR 54600  60000, IB 275 VLVO 54800  60200
   IB  300  MRCR  54900     60300, IB 330 VLVO 55500  60900, IB 130D VLVO 57400  63100
   IB  140D MRCR  59700     65600, IB 170D MRCR 58300 64100, IB 200D VLVO 59800  65800
   IB  254D MRCR  61600     67700

70      STARDUST CR WB/SS     HT  HB   AL  PN IB 115  MRCR 14              2  4   57800  63600
   IB  120  VLVO  58100     63800, IB 146 VLVO 58400  64200, IB 155 MRCR 58200  64000
   IB  175  VLVO  58600     64400, IB 180 MRCR 58300  64100, IB 205 MRCR 58400  64100
   IB  209  VLVO  58800     64700, IB 229 VLVO 58600  64400, IB 230 MRCR 58400  64200
   IB  240  MRCR  58400     64200, IB 275 VLVO 58600  64400, IB 300 MRCR 58700  64500
   IB  330  VLVO  59300     65100, IB 130D VLVO 62600 68800, IB 140D MRCR 63300  69600
   IB  170D MRCR  63700     70000, IB 200D VLVO 63300 69500, IB 254D MRCR 65100  71600

70      STARDUST CRUISER      HT  HB   AL  PN IB 115  MRCR 14              2  4   53500  58800
   IB  120  VLVO  53800     59100, IB 146 VLVO 54100  59400, IB 155 MRCR 53900  59300
   IB  175  VLVO  54300     59700, IB 180 MRCR 54100  59500, IB 205 MRCR 54200  59600
   IB  209  VLVO  54600     60000, IB 229 VLVO 53900  59200, IB 230 MRCR 54300  59700
   IB  240  MRCR  54300     59700, IB 275 VLVO 54500  59900, IB 300 MRCR 54600  60000
   IB  330  VLVO  55200     60700, IB 20C VLVO 76500  84100, IB 130D VLVO 58200  64000
   IB  140D MRCR  58900     64700, IB 170D MRCR 59300 65200, IB 200D VLVO 59000  64900
   IB  254D MRCR  60800     66800

75      STARDUST CR WB/SS     HT  HB   AL  PN IB 130D VLVO 14              2  4    **     **
   IB  140D MRCR   **         **, IB 170D MRCR  **      **, IB 200D VLVO   **     **
   IB  254D MRCR   **         **

75      STARDUST CRUISER      HT  HB   AL  PN IB 130D VLVO 14              2  4    **     **
   IB  140D MRCR   **         **, IB 170D MRCR  **      **, IB 200D VLVO   **     **
   IB  254D MRCR   **         **
--------------------- 1994 BOATS ---------------------------------------------------------------
54      STARDUST CR WB/SS     HT  HB   AL  PN           14              2  4   45000  50000
   IB  115  MRCR  52200     57400, IB 120 VLVO 52500  57700, IB 146 VLVO 52800  58100
   IB  155  MRCR  52700     57900, IB 175 VLVO 53100  58300, IB 180 MRCR 52800  58000
   IB  205  MRCR  52800     58000, IB 209 VLVO 53300  58600, IB 229 VLVO 53000  58200
   IB  230  MRCR  52800     58100, IB 240 MRCR 52900  58100, IB 275 VLVO 53100  58400
   IB  300  MRCR  53100     58400, IB 330 VLVO 53800  59100, IB 130D VLVO 53700  59000
   IB  140D MRCR  55500     61000, IB 170D MRCR 54900 60400, IB 200D VLVO 55300  60700
   IB  254D MRCR  56500     62100

54      STARDUST CRUISER      HT  HB   AL  PN           14              2  4   40600  45100
   IB  115  MRCR  48200     53100, IB 120 VLVO 48400  53200, IB 146 VLVO 48800  53600
   IB  155  MRCR  48700     53500, IB 175 VLVO 49100  53900, IB 180 MRCR 48900  53700
   IB  205  MRCR  48900     53800, IB 209 VLVO 49400  54300, IB 229 VLVO 49100  53900
   IB  230  MRCR  49000     53900, IB 240 MRCR 49100  53900, IB 275 VLVO 49300  54100
   IB  300  MRCR  49400     54300, IB 330 VLVO 50000  54900, IB 130D VLVO 54500  54900
   IB  254D MRCR  52800     58100, IB 170D MRCR 51200 56300, IB 200D VLVO 51700  56800

60      STARDUST CR WB/SS     HT  HB   AL  PN           14              2  4   33700  37400
   IB  115  MRCR  48500     53200, IB 120 VLVO 48700  53500, IB 146 VLVO 49100  53800
   IB  155  MRCR  48800     53600, IB 175 VLVO 49200  54000, IB 180 MRCR 46700  51400
   IB  205  MRCR  49000     53800, IB 209 VLVO 49400  54300, IB 229 VLVO 49100  53900
   IB  230  MRCR  49000     53800, IB 240 MRCR 49800  54700, IB 275 VLVO 49200  54100
   IB  300  MRCR  49200     54100, IB 330 VLVO 49800  54700, IB 130D VLVO   **     **
   IB  140D MRCR   **         **, IB 170D MRCR  **      **, IB 200D VLVO   **     **

60      STARDUST CRUISER      HT  HB   AL  PN           14              2  4   30500  33900
   IB  115  MRCR  43400     48200, IB 120 VLVO 43600  48400, IB 146 VLVO 43900  48800
   IB  155  MRCR  43800     48700, IB 175 VLVO 44100  49000, IB 180 MRCR 46700  51400
   IB  205  MRCR  44000     48900, IB 209 VLVO 44400  49400, IB 229 VLVO 44100  49100
   IB  230  MRCR  44100     49000, IB 240 MRCR 43300  48200, IB 275 VLVO 44300  49200
   IB  300  MRCR  44100     49400, IB 300 VLVO 46300  50800, IB 330 VLVO 45000  50000
   IB  130D VLVO   **         **, IB 140D MRCR  **      **, IB 170D MRCR   **     **
   IB  200D VLVO   **         **, IB 254D MRCR  **      **

62      STARDUST CR WB/SS     HT  HB   AL  PN           14              2  4   40300  44700
   IB  115  MRCR  51600     56800, IB 120 VLVO 51900  57000, IB 146 VLVO 52200  57300
   IB  155  MRCR  52000     57200, IB 175 VLVO 52300  57500, IB 180 MRCR 52100  57300
   IB  205  MRCR  52100     57300, IB 209 VLVO 52600  57800, IB 229 VLVO 52200  57400
   IB  230  MRCR  52100     57300, IB 240 MRCR 52200  57300, IB 275 VLVO 52400  57500
   IB  300  MRCR  52400     57600, IB 330 VLVO 53000  58200, IB 130D VLVO   **     **
   IB  140D MRCR   **         **, IB 170D MRCR  **      **, IB 200D VLVO   **     **

62      STARDUST CRUISER      HT  HB   AL  PN           14              2  4   36200  40200
   IB  115  MRCR  47400     52100, IB 120 VLVO 47600  52300, IB 146 VLVO 47900  52600
   IB  155  MRCR  47800     52500, IB 175 VLVO 48100  52900, IB 180 MRCR 47900  52700
   IB  205  MRCR  48000     52800, IB 209 VLVO 48400  53200, IB 229 VLVO 48100  52900
   IB  230  MRCR  48100     52900, IB 240 MRCR 48100  52900, IB 275 VLVO 48300  53100
   IB  300  MRCR  48400     53200, IB 330 VLVO 49000  53800, IB 130D VLVO   **     **
   IB  140D MRCR   **         **, IB 170D MRCR  **      **, IB 200D VLVO   **     **

66      STARDUST CR WB/SS     HT  HB   AL  PN           14              2  4   51400  56500
   IB  115  MRCR  54400     59800, IB 120 VLVO 54600  60000, IB 146 VLVO 54900  60300
   IB  155  MRCR  54700     60100, IB 175 VLVO 55100  60500, IB 180 MRCR 54800  60300
   IB  205  MRCR  54900     60300, IB 209 VLVO 55300  60800, IB 229 VLVO 55000  60400
   IB  230  MRCR  54900     60300, IB 240 MRCR 54900  60300, IB 275 VLVO 55100  60500
   IB  300  MRCR  55100     60600, IB 330 VLVO 55700  61200, IB 130D VLVO 59200  65000
   IB  140D MRCR  59900     65800, IB 170D MRCR 60300 66200, IB 200D VLVO 59800  65700
   IB  254D MRCR  61600     67700

66      STARDUST CRUISER      HT  HB   AL  PN           14              2  4   47700  52400
   IB  115  MRCR  50900     56000, IB 120 VLVO 51100  56200, IB 146 VLVO 51500  56500
   IB  155  MRCR  51300     56400, IB 175 VLVO 51700  56800, IB 180 MRCR 51400  56600
   IB  205  MRCR  51600     56700, IB 209 VLVO 52000  57100, IB 229 VLVO 51600  56700
   IB  230  MRCR  51600     56700, IB 240 MRCR 51600  56700, IB 275 VLVO 51800  56900
   IB  300  MRCR  51900     57100, IB 330 VLVO 52500  57700, IB 130D VLVO 55600  61100
   IB  140D MRCR  56200     61700, IB 170D MRCR 56600 62200, IB 200D VLVO 56300  61900
   IB  254D MRCR  57800     63500

70      STARDUST CR WB/SS     HT  HB   AL  PN IB 115  MRCR 14              2  4   54500  59900
   IB  120  VLVO  54700     60200, IB 146 VLVO 55100  60500, IB 155 MRCR 54900  60300
   IB  175  VLVO  55200     60700, IB 180 MRCR 55000  60500, IB 205 MRCR 55000  60500
   IB  209  VLVO  55500     60900, IB 229 VLVO 55300  60800, IB 230 MRCR 55000  60600
   IB  240  MRCR  55100     60500, IB 275 VLVO 55300  60800, IB 300 MRCR 55300  60800
   IB  330  VLVO  55800     61400, IB 130D VLVO 58800 64400, IB 140D MRCR 59500  65400
   IB  170D MRCR  59900     65800, IB 200D VLVO 59400 65300, IB 254D MRCR 61200  67200

70      STARDUST CRUISER      HT  HB   AL  PN IB 115  MRCR 14              2  4   50600  55600
   IB  120  VLVO  50900     56000, IB 146 VLVO 51200  56300, IB 155 MRCR 51000  56200
   IB  175  VLVO  51300     56600, IB 180 MRCR 51100  56400, IB 205 MRCR 51100  56500
   IB  209  VLVO  51800     56900, IB 229 VLVO 51000  56100, IB 230 MRCR 51400  56500
   IB  240  MRCR  51300     56500, IB 275 VLVO 51700  56800, IB 300 MRCR 51500  56900
   IB  330  VLVO  52300     57500, IB 20C VLVO 71900  79000, IB 130D VLVO 54900  60300
   IB  140D MRCR  55600     61200, IB 170D MRCR 55900 61400, IB 200D VLVO 55600  61200
   IB  254D MRCR  57100     62800

75      STARDUST CR WB/SS     HT  HB   AL  PN IB 130D VLVO 14              2  4    **     **
   IB  140D MRCR   **         **, IB 170D MRCR  **      **, IB 200D VLVO   **     **
   IB  254D MRCR   **         **
```

STARDUST CRUISERS INC   -CONTINUED   See inside cover to adjust price for area

```
   LOA  NAME AND/             TOP/ BOAT  -HULL-  ----ENGINE---  BEAM  WGT  DRAFT RETAIL RETAIL
FT IN   OR MODEL              RIG  TYPE  MTL TP  TP #HP  MFG     FT IN LBS  FT IN LOW    HIGH
-------------------- 1994 BOATS --------------------------------------------------------------
75      STARDUST CRUISER      HT  HB   AL  PN IB  130D VLVO  14            2  4   **     **
     IB 140D MRCR    **       HT , IB  170D MRCR  **    **, IB 200D VLVO  200D   **     **
     IB 254D MRCR    **            **

--------------------- 1993 BOATS --------------------------------------------------------------
54      STARDUST CR WB/SS     HT  HB   AL  PN              14            2  4   42600  47300
     IB 115 MRCR 50000  54900, IB 120 VLVO 50200 55200, IB 146 VLVO 50000 55000
     IB 155 MRCR 49900  54800, IB 175 VLVO 50200 55200, IB 180 MRCR 50000 54900
     IB 205 MRCR 50000  55000, IB 209 VLVO 50500 55500, IB 229 VLVO 50100 55100
     IB 230 MRCR 50000  55000, IB 240 MRCR 50000 55000, IB 275 VLVO 50300 55200
     IB 300 MRCR 50300  55200, IB 330 VLVO 50900 55900, IB 130D VLVO 50300 56300
     IB 140D MRCR 53300  58200, IB 170D MRCR 52400 57600, IB 200D VLVO 52700 57900
     IB 254D MRCR 53900  59200

54      STARDUST CRUISER      HT  HB   AL  PN              14            2  4   38500  42700
     IB 115 MRCR 45700  50200, IB 120 VLVO 45900 50400, IB 146 VLVO 46200 50800
     IB 155 MRCR 46100  50700, IB 175 VLVO 46500 51100, IB 180 MRCR 46300 50900
     IB 205 MRCR 46400  50900, IB 209 VLVO 46600 51400, IB 229 VLVO 46500 51100
     IB 230 MRCR 46400  51000, IB 240 MRCR 46500 51100, IB 275 VLVO 46700 51300
     IB 300 MRCR 46800  51400, IB 330 VLVO 47400 52100, IB 130D VLVO 47700 52400
     IB 140D MRCR 47500  52200, IB 170D MRCR 48900 53800, IB 200D VLVO 49400 54200
     IB 254D MRCR 49900  54900

60      STARDUST CR WB/SS     HT  HB   AL  PN              14            2  4   31700  35200
     IB 115 MRCR 45700  50200, IB 120 VLVO 45900 50500, IB 146 VLVO 46200 50800
     IB 155 MRCR 46000  50600, IB 175 VLVO 46400 50900, IB 180 MRCR 43600 48400
     IB 205 MRCR 46200  50700, IB 209 VLVO 46600 51200, IB 229 VLVO 46300 50800
     IB 230 MRCR 46200  50700, IB 240 MRCR 46900 51800, IB 275 VLVO 46400 51000
     IB 300 MRCR 46400  51000, IB 330 VLVO 47000 51600, IB 130D VLVO  **    **
     IB 140D MRCR   **    **, IB 170D MRCR  **   **, IB 200D VLVO  **    **
     IB 254D MRCR   **

60      STARDUST CRUISER      HT  HB   AL  PN              14            2  4   28700  31900
     IB 115 MRCR 41000  45500, IB 120 VLVO 41200 45700, IB 146 VLVO 41400 46000
     IB 155 MRCR 41400  46000, IB 175 VLVO 41700 46300, IB 180 MRCR 43600 48400
     IB 205 MRCR 41600  46200, IB 209 VLVO 42000 46600, IB 229 VLVO 41700 46300
     IB 230 MRCR 41600  46300, IB 240 MRCR 40900 45500, IB 275 VLVO 41800 46500
     IB 300 MRCR 41900  46600, IB 300 VLVO 43300 48100, IB 330 VLVO 42400 47200
     IB 130D VLVO  **    **, IB 140D MRCR  **   **, IB 170D MRCR  **   **
     IB 200D VLVO  **    **, IB 254D MRCR  **   **

62      STARDUST CR WB/SS     HT  HB   AL  PN              14            2  4   38000  42200
     IB 115 MRCR 49200  54000, IB 120 VLVO 49400 54300, IB 146 VLVO 49700 54600
     IB 155 MRCR 49500  54400, IB 175 VLVO 49800 54800, IB 180 MRCR 49600 54500
     IB 205 MRCR 49600  54600, IB 209 VLVO 50000 55000, IB 229 VLVO 49700 54700
     IB 230 MRCR 49700  54600, IB 240 MRCR 49700 54600, IB 275 VLVO 49900 54800
     IB 300 MRCR 49900  54900, IB 330 VLVO 49900 54900, IB 130D VLVO  **    **
     IB 140D MRCR   **    **, IB 170D MRCR  **   **, IB 200D VLVO  **    **
     IB 254D MRCR   **

62      STARDUST CRUISER      HT  HB   AL  PN              14            2  4   34300  38100
     IB 115 MRCR 44200  49100, IB 120 VLVO 44400 49300, IB 146 VLVO 44700 49700
     IB 155 MRCR 44600  49500, IB 175 VLVO 44900 49900, IB 180 MRCR 44700 49700
     IB 205 MRCR 44800  49800, IB 209 VLVO 45700 50200, IB 229 VLVO 44900 49900
     IB 230 MRCR 44800  49900, IB 240 MRCR 44900 49900, IB 275 VLVO 45500 50100
     IB 300 MRCR 45700  50200, IB 330 VLVO 46200 50800, IB 130D VLVO  **    **
     IB 140D MRCR   **    **, IB 170D MRCR  **   **, IB 200D VLVO  **    **
     IB 254D MRCR   **

66      STARDUST CR WB/SS     HT  HB   AL  PN              14            2  4   49000  53800
     IB 115 MRCR 51800  56900, IB 120 VLVO 52100 57100, IB 146 VLVO 52300 57400
     IB 155 MRCR 52100  57300, IB 175 VLVO 52400 57600, IB 180 MRCR 52200 57400
     IB 205 MRCR 52200  57400, IB 209 VLVO 52700 57900, IB 229 VLVO 52300 57500
     IB 230 MRCR 52300  57400, IB 240 MRCR 52300 57500, IB 275 VLVO 52500 57700
     IB 300 MRCR 52500  57700, IB 330 VLVO 53100 58300, IB 130D VLVO 56100 61600
     IB 140D MRCR 56700  62300, IB 170D MRCR 56900 62500, IB 200D VLVO 56600 62200
     IB 254D MRCR 58100  63900

66      STARDUST CRUISER      HT  HB   AL  PN              14            2  4   44500  49500
     IB 115 MRCR 48500  53300, IB 120 VLVO 48700 53500, IB 146 VLVO 49000 53800
     IB 155 MRCR 48900  53700, IB 175 VLVO 49200 54000, IB 180 MRCR 49000 53900
     IB 205 MRCR 49100  54000, IB 209 VLVO 49500 54400, IB 229 VLVO 49200 54000
     IB 230 MRCR 49100  54000, IB 240 MRCR 49200 54000, IB 275 VLVO 49300 54200
     IB 300 MRCR 49400  54400, IB 330 VLVO 50000 54900, IB 130D VLVO 52900 58200
     IB 140D MRCR 53500  58800, IB 170D MRCR 53900 59200, IB 200D VLVO 53600 58900
     IB 254D MRCR 54800  60200

70      STARDUST CR WB/SS     HT  HB   AL  PN IB  115 MRCR 14            2  4   52000  57100
     IB 120 VLVO 52200  57400, IB 146 VLVO 52500 57700, IB 155 MRCR 52300 57500
     IB 175 VLVO 52700  57900, IB 180 MRCR 52400 57600, IB 205 MRCR 52500 57600
     IB 209 VLVO 52900  58100, IB 229 VLVO 52700 57900, IB 230 MRCR 52500 57700
     IB 240 MRCR 52500  57700, IB 275 VLVO 52700 57900, IB 300 MRCR 52700 57900
     IB 330 VLVO 53300  58600, IB 130D VLVO 55800 61300, IB 140D MRCR 56400 62000
     IB 170D MRCR 56600  62200, IB 200D VLVO 56400 62000, IB 254D MRCR 57900 63600

70      STARDUST CRUISER      HT  HB   AL  PN IB  115 MRCR 14            2  4   48400  53200
     IB 120 VLVO 48600  53400, IB 146 MRCR 48900 53700, IB 155 MRCR 48800 53700
     IB 175 VLVO 49100  54000, IB 180 MRCR 48900 53800, IB 205 MRCR 49000 53900
     IB 209 VLVO 49400  54300, IB 229 VLVO 48700 53600, IB 230 MRCR 49100 53900
     IB 240 MRCR 49100  54000, IB 275 VLVO 49300 54200, IB 300 MRCR 49400 54300
     IB 330 VLVO 49900  54900, IB 20C MRCR 68000 74700, IB 130D VLVO 52400 57500
     IB 140D MRCR 53000  58200, IB 170D MRCR 53300 58600, IB 200D VLVO 53100 58300
     IB 254D MRCR 54300  59600

75      STARDUST CR WB/SS     HT  HB   AL  PN IB  130D VLVO 14            2  4   **     **
     IB 140D MRCR    **       HT , IB  170D MRCR  **    **, IB 200D VLVO  200D   **     **
     IB 254D MRCR    **            **

75      STARDUST CRUISER      HT  HB   AL  PN IB  130D VLVO 14            2  4   **     **
     IB 140D MRCR    **       HT , IB  170D MRCR  **    **, IB 200D VLVO  200D   **     **
     IB 254D MRCR    **            **

--------------------- 1992 BOATS --------------------------------------------------------------
54      STARDUST CR WB/SS     HT  HB   AL  PN              14            2  4   40600  45100
     IB 115 MRCR 47600  52300, IB 120 VLVO 47800 52600, IB 146 VLVO 48100 52900
     IB 155 MRCR 48000  52700, IB 175 VLVO 48300 53100, IB 180 MRCR 48100 52800
     IB 205 MRCR 48100  52900, IB 209 VLVO 48600 53400, IB 229 VLVO 48300 53000
     IB 230 MRCR 48100  52900, IB 240 MRCR 48200 52900, IB 275 VLVO 48400 53200
     IB 300 MRCR 48400  53200, IB 330 VLVO 49000 53900, IB 130D VLVO 49000 54100
     IB 140D MRCR 50400  55400, IB 170D MRCR 49900 54800, IB 200D VLVO 50200 55100
     IB 254D MRCR 51300  56400

54      STARDUST CRUISER      HT  HB   AL  PN              14            2  4   36700  40700
     IB 115 MRCR 43200  47800, IB 120 VLVO 43200 48000, IB 146 VLVO 43600 48400
     IB 155 MRCR 43500  48300, IB 175 VLVO 43800 48600, IB 180 MRCR 43600 48500
     IB 205 MRCR 43700  48500, IB 209 VLVO 44100 49000, IB 229 VLVO 43800 48700
     IB 230 MRCR 43800  48600, IB 240 MRCR 43800 48700, IB 275 VLVO 44000 48900
     IB 300 MRCR 44100  49000, IB 330 VLVO 44700 49600, IB 130D VLVO 45000 50000
     IB 140D MRCR 44700  49700, IB 170D MRCR 46600 51200, IB 200D VLVO 47000 51700
     IB 254D MRCR 48000  52800

60      STARDUST CR WB/SS     HT  HB   AL  PN              14            2  4   30100  33500
     IB 115 MRCR 43000  47700, IB 120 VLVO 43200 48000, IB 146 VLVO 43500 48300
     IB 155 MRCR 43300  48100, IB 175 VLVO 43800 48500, IB 180 MRCR 41400 46000
     IB 205 MRCR 43500  48300, IB 209 VLVO 43800 48700, IB 229 VLVO 43500 48400
     IB 230 MRCR 43500  48300, IB 240 MRCR 44200 49100, IB 275 VLVO 43700 48500
     IB 300 MRCR 43700  48500, IB 330 VLVO 44200 49100, IB 130D VLVO  **    **
     IB 140D MRCR   **    **, IB 170D MRCR  **   **
     IB 200D VLVO   **

60      STARDUST CRUISER      HT  HB   AL  PN              14            2  4   27300  30300
     IB 115 MRCR 39000  43300, IB 120 VLVO 39200 43500, IB 146 VLVO 39500 43900
     IB 155 MRCR 39400  43800, IB 175 VLVO 39700 44100, IB 180 MRCR 41400 46000
     IB 205 MRCR 39600  44000, IB 209 VLVO 40000 44400, IB 229 VLVO 39700 44100
     IB 230 MRCR 39700  44100, IB 240 MRCR 38900 43300, IB 275 VLVO 39900 44300
     IB 300 MRCR 40000  44400, IB 300 VLVO 41200 45700, IB 330 VLVO 40500 44900
     IB 130D VLVO  **    **, IB 140D MRCR  **   **, IB 170D MRCR  **   **
     IB 200D VLVO  **    **, IB 254D MRCR  **   **

62      STARDUST CR WB/SS     HT  HB   AL  PN              14            2  4   36200  40200
     IB 115 MRCR 46700  51300, IB 120 VLVO 46900 51600, IB 146 VLVO 47200 51800
     IB 155 MRCR 47000  51700, IB 175 VLVO 47300 52100, IB 180 MRCR 47100 51800
     IB 205 MRCR 47200  51800, IB 209 VLVO 47600 52300, IB 229 VLVO 47200 51900
     IB 230 MRCR 47200  51800, IB 240 MRCR 47200 51800, IB 275 VLVO 47400 52000
     IB 300 MRCR 47400  52100, IB 330 VLVO 48000 52700, IB 130D VLVO  **    **
     IB 140D MRCR   **    **, IB 170D MRCR  **   **, IB 200D VLVO  **    **
     IB 254D MRCR   **

62      STARDUST CRUISER      HT  HB   AL  PN              14            2  4   32600  36200
     IB 115 MRCR 42000  46700, IB 120 VLVO 42200 46900, IB 146 VLVO 42500 47200
     IB 155 MRCR 42400  47100, IB 175 VLVO 42700 47400, IB 180 MRCR 42700 47400
     IB 205 MRCR 42600  47200, IB 209 VLVO 43000 47700, IB 229 VLVO 42700 47400
     IB 230 MRCR 42700  47400, IB 240 MRCR 42700 47400, IB 275 VLVO 42800 47600
     IB 300 MRCR 42900  47700, IB 330 VLVO 43500 48300, IB 130D VLVO  **    **
     IB 140D MRCR   **    **, IB 170D MRCR  **   **, IB 200D VLVO  **    **
     IB 254D MRCR   **
```

```
       LOA   NAME AND/        TOP/ BOAT   -HULL-   ----ENGINE---    BEAM   WGT   DRAFT RETAIL RETAIL
       FT IN  OR MODEL        RIG  TYPE   MTL TP   TP #  HP  MFG    FT IN  LBS   FT IN  LOW    HIGH
---------------------- 1992 BOATS -----------------------------------------------------------------
 66     STARDUST CR WB/SS     HT   HB     AL  PN                      14          2 4  46500  51100
    IB 115  MRCR 49600  54600, IB 120  VLVO 49800 54800, IB 146  VLVO 50100 55000
    IB 155  MRCR 50000  54900, IB 175  VLVO 50300 55200, IB 180  MRCR 50100 55000
    IB 205  MRCR 50100  55000, IB 209  VLVO 50000 54900, IB 229  VLVO 50200 55200
    IB 230  MRCR 50100  55100, IB 240  MRCR 50100 55100, IB 275  VLVO 49800 54700
    IB 300  MRCR 49800  54800, IB 330  VLVO 50400 55300, IB 130D VLVO 53700 59000
    IB 140D MRCR 53900  59200, IB 170D MRCR 54300 59600, IB 200D VLVO 53900 59200
    IB 254D MRCR 55400  60900

 66     STARDUST CRUISER      HT   HB     AL  PN                      14          2 4  42300  47000
    IB 115  MRCR 46000  50600, IB 120  VLVO 46200 50800, IB 146  VLVO 46500 51100
    IB 155  MRCR 46400  51000, IB 175  VLVO 46700 51300, IB 180  MRCR 46500 51100
    IB 205  MRCR 46600  51200, IB 209  VLVO 47000 51600, IB 229  VLVO 46700 51300
    IB 230  MRCR 46700  51300, IB 240  MRCR 46700 51300, IB 275  VLVO 46900 51500
    IB 300  MRCR 47000  51600, IB 330  VLVO 47500 52200, IB 130D VLVO 50200 55200
    IB 140D MRCR 50800  55800, IB 170D MRCR 51200 56300, IB 200D VLVO 50900 55900
    IB 254D MRCR 52500  57700

 70     STARDUST CR WB/SS     HT   HB     AL  PN IB 115 MRCR           14          2 4  49900  54900
    IB 120  VLVO 50100  55100, IB 146  VLVO 49900 54900, IB 155  MRCR 50300 55200
    IB 175  VLVO 50100  55100, IB 180  MRCR 49900 54800, IB 205  MRCR 49900 54800
    IB 209  VLVO 50300  55300, IB 229  VLVO 50000 54900, IB 230  MRCR 49900 54900
    IB 240  MRCR 49900  54900, IB 275  VLVO 50100 55100, IB 300  MRCR 50100 55100
    IB 330  VLVO 50700  55700, IB 130D VLVO 53600 58800, IB 140D MRCR 53700 59100
    IB 170D MRCR 54100  59500, IB 200D VLVO 53700 59000, IB 254D MRCR 55300 60700

 70     STARDUST CRUISER      HT   HB     AL  PN IB 115 MRCR           14          2 4  46100  50600
    IB 120  VLVO 46300  50800, IB 146  VLVO 46100 50600, IB 155  MRCR 46500 51000
    IB 175  VLVO 46700  51400, IB 180  MRCR 46600 51100, IB 205  MRCR 46700 51300
    IB 209  VLVO 47000  51700, IB 229  VLVO 46600 51300, IB 230  MRCR 46700 51300
    IB 240  MRCR 46700  51300, IB 275  VLVO 46900 51500, IB 300  MRCR 47000 51600
    IB 330  VLVO 47500  52200, IB 20C  VLVO 64600 71000, IB 130D VLVO 49800 54700
    IB 140D MRCR 50400  55400, IB 170D MRCR 50700 55700, IB 200D VLVO 50500 55500
    IB 254D MRCR 52100  57200

 75     STARDUST CR WB/SS     HT   HB     AL  PN IB 130D VLVO          14          2 4   **     **
    IB 140D MRCR  **    **, IB 170D MRCR  **   **, IB 200D VLVO  **   **
    IB 254D MRCR  **    **

 75     STARDUST CRUISER      HT   HB     AL  PN IB 130D VLVO          14          2 4   **     **
    IB 140D MRCR  **    **, IB 170D MRCR  **   **, IB 200D VLVO  **   **
    IB 254D MRCR  **    **

---------------------- 1991 BOATS -----------------------------------------------------------------
 54     STARDUST CR WB/SS     HT   HB     AL  PN                      14          2 4  38900  43200
    IB 115  MRCR 45600  50100, IB 120  VLVO 45800 50400, IB 146  VLVO 46100 50700
    IB 155  MRCR 46000  50500, IB 175  VLVO 46300 50900, IB 180  MRCR 46100 50600
    IB 205  MRCR 46100  50700, IB 209  VLVO 46500 51100, IB 229  VLVO 46200 50800
    IB 230  MRCR 46100  50700, IB 240  MRCR 46100 50700, IB 275  VLVO 46300 50900
    IB 300  MRCR 46400  51000, IB 330  VLVO 47000 51600, IB 130D VLVO 47200 51800
    IB 140D MRCR 48800  53600, IB 170D MRCR 48300 53000, IB 200D VLVO 48500 53300
    IB 254D MRCR 49700  54600

 54     STARDUST CRUISER      HT   HB     AL  PN                      14          2 4  35100  39000
    IB 115  MRCR 41200  45800, IB 120  VLVO 41400 46000, IB 146  VLVO 41700 46400
    IB 155  MRCR 41600  46300, IB 175  VLVO 41900 46600, IB 180  MRCR 41800 46400
    IB 205  MRCR 41800  46500, IB 209  VLVO 42200 46900, IB 229  VLVO 42000 46600
    IB 230  MRCR 41900  46600, IB 240  MRCR 41900 46600, IB 275  VLVO 42100 46800
    IB 300  MRCR 42200  46900, IB 330  VLVO 42800 47500, IB 130D VLVO 43100 47900
    IB 140D MRCR 42800  47600, IB 170D MRCR 44100 49000, IB 200D VLVO 44500 49500
    IB 254D MRCR 46000  50600

 60     STARDUST CR WB/SS     HT   HB     AL  PN                      14          2 4  28900  32100
    IB 115  MRCR 41100  45700, IB 120  VLVO 41300 45900, IB 146  VLVO 41600 46200
    IB 155  MRCR 41400  46000, IB 175  VLVO 41700 46400, IB 180  MRCR 39700 44100
    IB 205  MRCR 41600  46200, IB 209  VLVO 41900 46600, IB 229  VLVO 41600 46300
    IB 230  MRCR 41600  46200, IB 240  MRCR 42200 46900, IB 275  VLVO 41800 46400
    IB 300  MRCR 41800  46400, IB 330  VLVO 42300 46900, IB 130D VLVO  **   **
    IB 140D MRCR  **    **, IB 170D MRCR  **   **, IB 200D VLVO  **   **

 60     STARDUST CRUISER      HT   HB     AL  PN                      14          2 4  26000  28800
    IB 115  MRCR 37300  41500, IB 120  VLVO 37500 41700, IB 146  VLVO 37800 42000
    IB 155  MRCR 37700  41900, IB 175  VLVO 38000 42200, IB 180  MRCR 39700 44100
    IB 205  MRCR 37900  42100, IB 209  VLVO 38200 42500, IB 229  VLVO 38000 42200
    IB 230  MRCR 37900  42200, IB 240  MRCR 37300 41400, IB 275  VLVO 38000 42200
    IB 300  MRCR 38200  42500, IB 300  VLVO 39400 43700, IB 330  VLVO 38100 42300
    IB 130D VLVO  **    **, IB 140D MRCR  **   **, IB 170D MRCR 38700 43000
    IB 200D VLVO  **    **, IB 254D MRCR  **   **

 62     STARDUST CR WB/SS     HT   HB     AL  PN                      14          2 4  34600  38500
    IB 115  MRCR 44200  49100, IB 120  VLVO 44400 49300, IB 146  VLVO 44600 49600
    IB 155  MRCR 44500  49500, IB 175  VLVO 44800 49800, IB 180  MRCR 44600 49600
    IB 205  MRCR 44600  49600, IB 209  VLVO 45500 50000, IB 229  VLVO 44700 49700
    IB 230  MRCR 44600  49600, IB 240  MRCR 44600 49600, IB 275  VLVO 44800 49800
    IB 300  MRCR 44800  49800, IB 330  VLVO 45800 50400, IB 130D VLVO  **   **
    IB 140D MRCR  **    **, IB 170D MRCR  **   **, IB 200D VLVO  **   **

 62     STARDUST CRUISER      HT   HB     AL  PN                      14          2 4  31200  34700
    IB 115  MRCR 40400  44700, IB 120  VLVO 40400 44900, IB 146  VLVO 40700 45200
    IB 155  MRCR 40600  45100, IB 175  VLVO 40900 45400, IB 180  MRCR 40700 45200
    IB 205  MRCR 40800  45300, IB 209  VLVO 41100 45700, IB 229  VLVO 40900 45400
    IB 230  MRCR 40800  45400, IB 240  MRCR 40900 45400, IB 275  VLVO 41000 45600
    IB 300  MRCR 41100  45700, IB 330  VLVO 41600 46200, IB 130D VLVO  **   **
    IB 140D MRCR  **    **, IB 170D MRCR  **   **

 66     STARDUST CR WB/SS     HT   HB     AL  PN                      14          2 4  44000  48900
    IB 115  MRCR 47400  52100, IB 120  VLVO 47600 52300, IB 146  VLVO 47900 52600
    IB 155  MRCR 47700  52500, IB 175  VLVO 48000 52800, IB 180  MRCR 47800 52600
    IB 205  MRCR 47900  52600, IB 209  VLVO 48300 53100, IB 229  VLVO 48000 52700
    IB 230  MRCR 47900  52600, IB 240  MRCR 47900 52600, IB 275  VLVO 48100 52800
    IB 300  MRCR 48100  52900, IB 330  VLVO 48600 53500, IB 130D VLVO 51300 56400
    IB 140D MRCR 51900  57100, IB 170D MRCR 52300 57500, IB 200D VLVO 51900 57000
    IB 254D MRCR 53400  58700

 66     STARDUST CRUISER      HT   HB     AL  PN                      14          2 4  40500  45000
    IB 115  MRCR 43500  48800, IB 120  VLVO 43700 48600, IB 146  VLVO 44000 48900
    IB 155  MRCR 43900  48800, IB 175  VLVO 44200 49100, IB 180  MRCR 44000 48900
    IB 205  MRCR 44100  49000, IB 209  VLVO 44500 49400, IB 229  VLVO 44200 49100
    IB 230  MRCR 44200  49100, IB 240  MRCR 44200 49100, IB 275  VLVO 44300 49300
    IB 300  MRCR 44400  49400, IB 330  VLVO 44900 49900, IB 130D VLVO 48500 53300
    IB 140D MRCR 49100  55000, IB 170D MRCR 49400 54300, IB 200D VLVO 49200 54000
    IB 254D MRCR 50100  55100

 70     STARDUST CR WB/SS     HT   HB     AL  PN                      14          2 4   **     **
    IB 115  MRCR 47800  52500, IB 120  VLVO 48000 52700, IB 146  VLVO 48300 53000
    IB 155  MRCR 48100  52900, IB 175  VLVO 48400 53200, IB 180  MRCR 48200 53000
    IB 205  MRCR 48200  53000, IB 209  VLVO 48600 53400, IB 229  VLVO 48300 53100
    IB 230  MRCR 48200  53000, IB 240  MRCR 48300 53000, IB 275  VLVO 48500 53300
    IB 300  MRCR 48500  53300, IB 330  VLVO 49000 53800, IB 130D VLVO 51200 56300
    IB 140D MRCR 51800  56900, IB 170D MRCR 52200 57400, IB 200D VLVO 51800 56900
    IB 254D MRCR 53300  58600

 70     STARDUST CRUISER      HT   HB     AL  PN                      14          2 4  44000  48900
    IB 115  MRCR 43600  48500, IB 120  VLVO 43800 48700, IB 146  VLVO 44000 48900
    IB 155  MRCR 43900  48900, IB 175  VLVO 44200 49200, IB 180  MRCR 44100 49000
    IB 205  MRCR 44200  49100, IB 209  VLVO 44500 49500, IB 229  VLVO 44200 49100
    IB 230  MRCR 44200  49100, IB 240  MRCR 44200 49100, IB 275  VLVO 44400 49300
    IB 300  MRCR 44500  49500, IB 330  VLVO 45000 50000, IB 20C  VLVO 61800 67900
    IB 130D VLVO 48100  53000, IB 140D MRCR 48700 53600, IB 170D MRCR 49000 53900
    IB 200D VLVO 48800  53600, IB 254D MRCR 49800 54700

 75     STARDUST CR WB/SS     HT   HB     AL  PN                      14          2 4   **     **
    IB 115  MRCR  **    **, IB 120  VLVO  **   **, IB 146  VLVO  **   **
    IB 155  MRCR  **    **, IB 175  VLVO  **   **, IB 180  MRCR  **   **
    IB 205  MRCR  **    **, IB 209  VLVO  **   **, IB 229  VLVO  **   **
    IB 230  MRCR  **    **, IB 240  VLVO  **   **, IB 275  VLVO  **   **
    IB 300  MRCR  **    **, IB 330  VLVO  **   **, IB 130D VLVO  **   **
    IB 140D MRCR  **    **, IB 170D MRCR  **   **, IB 200D VLVO  **   **
    IB 254D MRCR  **    **

 75     STARDUST CRUISER      HT   HB     AL  PN                      14          2 4   **     **
    IB 115  MRCR  **    **, IB 120  VLVO  **   **, IB 146  VLVO  **   **
    IB 155  MRCR  **    **, IB 175  VLVO  **   **, IB 180  MRCR  **   **
    IB 205  MRCR  **    **, IB 209  VLVO  **   **, IB 229  VLVO  **   **
    IB 230  MRCR  **    **, IB 240  MRCR  **   **, IB 275  VLVO  **   **
    IB 300  MRCR  **    **, IB 330  VLVO  **   **, IB 130D VLVO  **   **
    IB 140D MRCR  **    **, IB 170D MRCR  **   **, IB 200D VLVO  **   **
    IB 254D MRCR  **    **

---------------------- 1990 BOATS -----------------------------------------------------------------
 54     STARDUST CRUISER      HT   HB     AL  PN IB 120                14          2 4  42100  46700
    IB 120  MRCR 40200  44700, IB 120  VLVO 40500 45000, IB 130  MRCR 40600 45200
    IB 146  VLVO 40700  45200, IB 165  MRCR 40600 45200, IB 167  VLVO 40900 45400
```

```
       LOA  NAME AND/          TOP/ BOAT  -HULL-  ----ENGINE---  BEAM  WGT  DRAFT RETAIL RETAIL
       FT IN  OR MODEL         RIG  TYPE  MTL TP  TP # HP  MFG   FT IN  LBS  FT IN  LOW   HIGH
--------------------------- 1990 BOATS ---------------------------
54      STARDUST CRUISER   HT   HB   AL  PN IB  175 MRCR 14               2  4  40700 45200
    IB  180  MRCR 40700 45300, IB  200  MRCR     45300, IB        205  MRCR 40800 45300
    IB  205  VLVO 41000 45600, IB  210  MRCR     45800, IB        225  VLVO 41100 45600
    IB  229  VLVO 41100 45600, IB  275  VLVO     46800, IB        307  VLVO 41400 46000
    IB  320  MRCR 41300 45800, IB  330  MRCR     46000, IB
    IB  130D VLVO 42000 46700, IB  200D VLVO     47100, IB       130D MRCR 42800 47600

54      STARDUST CUSTOM    HT   HB   AL  PN IB  120 VLVO 14               2  4  42100 46700
    IB  120  MRCR 42800 47600, IB  120  VLVO 43100 47800, IB  130  MRCR 43000 47700
    IB  146  VLVO 43300 48100, IB  165  VLVO 43300 48100, IB  167  VLVO 43500 48300
    IB  175  MRCR 43300 48100, IB  180  MRCR 43300 48100, IB  200  MRCR 43300 48100
    IB  205  MRCR 43300 48100, IB  205  VLVO 43600 48400, IB  210  MRCR 43800 48600
    IB  225  VLVO 43600 48400, IB  229  VLVO 43600 48400, IB  271  VLVO 42500 47200
    IB  275  VLVO 43900 48800, IB  307  VLVO 44000 48900, IB  320  MRCR 43800 48700
    IB  330  MRCR 43900 48700, IB   D   MRCR 45800 50300, IB 130D  VLVO 44300 49300
    IB  200D VLVO 44700 49600

54      STARDUST XL        FB   HB   AL  PN IB  120 VLVO 14               2  4  42100 46700
    IB  120  MRCR 41600 46200, IB  120  VLVO 41700 46400, IB  130  MRCR 41700 46300
    IB  146  MRCR 42000 46700, IB  165  VLVO 42000 46600, IB  167  VLVO 42200 46900
    IB  175  MRCR 42000 46700, IB  180  MRCR 42000 46700, IB  200  MRCR 42100 46700
    IB  205  MRCR 42100 46700, IB  205  VLVO 42300 47000, IB  210  MRCR 42300 47000
    IB  225  VLVO 42700 47400, IB  229  VLVO 42300 47000, IB  275  VLVO 42500 47200
    IB  307  VLVO 42700 47400, IB  320  MRCR 42500 47300, IB  330  MRCR 42600 47400
    IB   D   MRCR 44100 48900, IB 130D  VLVO 43200 48000, IB 200D  VLVO 44000 48900

60      STARDUST CRUISER   HT   HB   AL  PN IB  120 VLVO 14               2  4  38200 42400
    IB  120  MRCR 37800 41900, IB  120  VLVO 37900 42100, IB  130  MRCR 37800 42000
    IB  146  VLVO 38100 42400, IB  165  VLVO 38100 42400, IB  167  VLVO 38300 42500
    IB  175  MRCR 38100 42400, IB  180  MRCR 38100 42400, IB  200  MRCR 38200 42400
    IB  205  MRCR 38200 42400, IB  205  VLVO 38400 42600, IB  210  MRCR 38400 42600
    IB  225  VLVO 38400 42700, IB  229  VLVO 38400 42700, IB  275  VLVO 38500 42800
    IB  307  VLVO 38700 43000, IB  320  MRCR 38600 42900, IB  330  MRCR 38700 43000
    IB   D   MRCR  **   **  , IB  130D VLVO  **   **  , IB  200D MRCR  **   **

62      STARDUST CUSTOM    HT   HB   AL  PN IB  120 VLVO 14               2  4  41000 45600
    IB  120  MRCR 40700 45100, IB  120  VLVO 40800 45300, IB  130  MRCR 40700 45200
    IB  146  VLVO 41000 45600, IB  165  VLVO 40900 45500, IB  167  VLVO 41100 45700
    IB  175  MRCR 41000 45500, IB  180  MRCR 41000 45600, IB  200  MRCR 41000 45600
    IB  205  MRCR 41000 45600, IB  205  VLVO 41200 45800, IB  210  MRCR 41200 45800
    IB  225  VLVO 41300 45800, IB  229  VLVO 41300 45800, IB  275  VLVO 41400 45900
    IB  307  VLVO 41600 46200, IB  320  MRCR 41400 46000, IB  330  MRCR 41500 46100
    IB   D   MRCR  **   **  , IB  130D VLVO  **   **  , IB  200D MRCR  **   **

62      STARDUST XL        FB   HB   AL  PN OB  120 MRCR 14               2  4   **    **
    IB       MRCR 41000 45600, IB  120  MRCR 40600 45100, IB  120  VLVO 40800 45300
    IB  130  MRCR 40700 45200, IB  146  VLVO 40600 45100, IB  165  VLVO 40900 45500
    IB  167  VLVO 41100 45700, IB  175  MRCR 41000 45500, IB  180  MRCR 41000 45600
    IB  200  MRCR 41000 45600, IB  205  MRCR 41000 45600, IB  205  VLVO 41200 45800
    IB  210  MRCR 41200 45800, IB  225  VLVO 41300 45900, IB  229  VLVO 41300 45900
    IB  275  VLVO 41400 46000, IB  307  VLVO 41600 46200, IB  320  MRCR 41400 46000
    IB  330  MRCR 41500 46100, IB   D   MRCR  **   **  , IB  130D VLVO  **   **
    IB  200D VLVO  **   **

70      STARDUST CRUISER   HT   HB   AL  PN IB  120 VLVO 14               2  4  42100 46700
    IB  120  MRCR 41800 46400, IB  120  VLVO 42000 46700, IB  130  MRCR 42000 46700
    IB  146  MRCR 42200 46900, IB  165  VLVO 42200 46900, IB  171  VLVO 44300 49200
    IB  175  MRCR 42200 46900, IB  180  MRCR 42200 46900, IB  200  MRCR 42300 47000
    IB  205  MRCR 42300 47000, IB  205  VLVO 42500 47200, IB  210  MRCR 42700 47400
    IB  225  VLVO 42500 47300, IB  229  VLVO 42500 47200, IB  275  VLVO 43000 47800
    IB  307  VLVO 42800 47600, IB  320  MRCR 42700 47500, IB  330  MRCR 42800 47600
    IB   D   MRCR 46800 51500, IB  130D VLVO 46100 50700, IB  200D MRCR 46500 51100

70      STARDUST CUSTOM    HT   HB   AL  PN IB  120 VLVO 14               2  4  46800 51400
    IB  120  MRCR 46100 50700, IB  120  VLVO 46400 51000, IB  130  MRCR 46100 50700
    IB  146  MRCR 46600 51200, IB  165  VLVO 46500 51100, IB  167  VLVO 44300 49200
    IB  175  MRCR 46500 51100, IB  180  MRCR 46500 51100, IB  200  MRCR 46600 51200
    IB  205  MRCR 46500 51100, IB  205  VLVO 46800 51400, IB  210  MRCR 47000 51600
    IB  225  VLVO 46800 51400, IB  229  VLVO 46800 51500, IB  275  VLVO 47200 51900
    IB  307  VLVO 47100 51800, IB  307  VLVO 47000 51600, IB  330  MRCR 47000 51700
    IB   D   VLVO 50200 55200, IB  130D VLVO 49900 54800, IB  200D VLVO 50200 55200

70      STARDUST XL        FB   HB   AL  PN IB  120 VLVO 14               2  4  44200 49100
    IB  120  MRCR 43700 48600, IB  120  VLVO 43900 48700, IB  130  MRCR 43800 48700
    IB  146  MRCR 44100 49000, IB  165  VLVO 44100 49000, IB  167  VLVO 44300 49200
    IB  175  MRCR 44100 49000, IB  180  MRCR 44100 49000, IB  200  MRCR 44200 49100
    IB  205  MRCR 44200 49100, IB  205  VLVO 44400 49300, IB  210  MRCR 44400 49300
    IB  225  VLVO 44400 49300, IB  229  VLVO 44400 49300, IB  275  VLVO 44500 49500
    IB  307  VLVO 44700 49700, IB  320  MRCR 44600 49500, IB  330  MRCR 44700 49600
    IB   D   MRCR 48800 53600, IB  130D VLVO 48000 52800, IB  150D VLVO 48200 53000
    IB  200D VLVO 48700 53500

--------------------------- 1989 BOATS ---------------------------
54      STARDUST CRUISER        HB   AL  PN IB  120 VLVO 14               2  4  34100 37900
    IB       VLVO 40600 45100, IB  120  MRCR 38900 43200, IB  120  VLVO 39100 43400
    IB  130  MRCR 43300 48100, IB  146  VLVO 39300 43700, IB  165  MRCR 39100 43600
    IB  167  VLVO 39500 43800, IB  175  MRCR 39300 43700, IB  180  MRCR 39400 43700
    IB  200  MRCR 39400 43800, IB  205  MRCR 39400 43800, IB  210  MRCR 39600 44000
    IB  229  VLVO 39700 44100, IB  275  VLVO 39800 44200, IB  307  VLVO 40000 44400
    IB  320  MRCR 39800 44300, IB  330  MRCR 40000 44400, IB   D   MRCR 41300 45900
    IB  130D VLVO 40600 45100, IB  200D VLVO 40900 45500

54      STARDUST CUSTOM         HB   AL  PN IB  120 MRCR 14               2  4  36600 40700
    IB       VLVO 43100 47900, IB  120  MRCR 41300 45900, IB  120  VLVO 41600 46200
    IB  130  MRCR 41500 46100, IB  146  VLVO 41800 46500, IB  165  MRCR 41800 46400
    IB  167  VLVO 42000 46600, IB  175  MRCR 41800 46500, IB  180  MRCR 41800 46400
    IB  200  MRCR 41800 46500, IB  205  MRCR 41800 46500, IB  210  MRCR 42100 46700
    IB  229  VLVO 42100 46800, IB  275  VLVO 42300 47000, IB  307  VLVO 42500 47200
    IB  320  MRCR 42400 47100, IB  330  MRCR 42400 47100, IB   D   MRCR 43700 48600
    IB  130D VLVO 42800 47600, IB  200D VLVO 44000 48900

54      STARDUST XL        FB   HB   AL  PN IB  120 MRCR 14               2  4  40600 45100
    IB       VLVO 40800 45400, IB  120  MRCR 40100 44600, IB  120  VLVO 40300 44800
    IB  130  MRCR 40200 44700, IB  146  VLVO 40500 45000, IB  165  MRCR 40500 45000
    IB  167  VLVO 40700 45200, IB  175  MRCR 40600 45100, IB  180  MRCR 40600 45100
    IB  200  MRCR 40600 45100, IB  205  MRCR 40600 45100, IB  210  MRCR 40800 45400
    IB  229  VLVO 40900 45400, IB  275  VLVO 41200 45800, IB  307  VLVO 41200 45800
    IB  320  MRCR 41100 45600, IB  330  MRCR 41200 45700, IB   D   MRCR 42500 47300
    IB  130D VLVO 41700 46300, IB  200D VLVO 42500 47200

60      STARDUST CRUISER        HB   AL  PN IB  120 VLVO 14               2  4  36900 41000
    IB       VLVO 37000 41200, IB  120  MRCR 36400 40500, IB  120  VLVO 36600 40600
    IB  130  MRCR 36500 40600, IB  146  VLVO 36800 40900, IB  165  MRCR 36800 40900
    IB  167  VLVO 36900 41000, IB  175  MRCR 36800 40900, IB  180  MRCR 36800 40900
    IB  200  MRCR 36800 40900, IB  205  MRCR 36900 40900, IB  210  MRCR 37000 41200
    IB  229  VLVO 37100 41200, IB  275  VLVO 37200 41200, IB  307  VLVO 37400 41500
    IB  320  MRCR 37200 41400, IB  330  MRCR 37300 41500, IB   D   MRCR  **   **
    IB  130D VLVO  **   **  , IB  200D VLVO  **   **

62      STARDUST CUSTOM         HB   AL  PN IB  120 MRCR 14               2  4  39600 44000
    IB       VLVO 39800 44200, IB  120  MRCR 39200 43500, IB  120  VLVO 39300 43700
    IB  130  MRCR 39300 43600, IB  146  VLVO 39600 44000, IB  165  MRCR 39500 43900
    IB  167  VLVO 39700 44100, IB  175  MRCR 39500 43900, IB  180  MRCR 39600 44000
    IB  200  MRCR 39600 44000, IB  205  MRCR 39600 44000, IB  210  MRCR 39800 44200
    IB  229  VLVO 39900 44300, IB  275  VLVO 39900 44300, IB  307  VLVO 40100 44600
    IB  320  MRCR 40000 44400, IB  330  MRCR 40100 44500, IB   D   MRCR  **   **
    IB  130D VLVO  **   **  , IB  200D VLVO  **   **

62      STARDUST XL        FB   HB   AL  PN IB  120 MRCR 14               2  4  39600 44000
    IB       VLVO 39800 44200, IB  120  MRCR 39200 43500, IB  120  VLVO 39300 43700
    IB  130  MRCR 39300 43600, IB  146  VLVO 39600 44000, IB  165  MRCR 39500 43900
    IB  167  VLVO 39700 44100, IB  175  MRCR 39500 43900, IB  180  MRCR 39600 44000
    IB  200  MRCR 39600 44000, IB  205  MRCR 39600 44000, IB  210  MRCR 39800 44200
    IB  229  VLVO 39900 44300, IB  275  VLVO 39900 44300, IB  307  VLVO 40100 44600
    IB  320  MRCR 40000 44400, IB  330  MRCR 40100 44500, IB   D   MRCR  **   **
    IB  130D VLVO  **   **  , IB  200D VLVO  **   **

70      STARDUST CRUISER        HB   AL  PN IB  120 VLVO 14               2  4  36300 40400
    IB       VLVO 41500 46000, IB  120  MRCR 40300 44800, IB  120  VLVO 40500 45000
    IB  130  MRCR 40600 45100, IB  146  VLVO 40700 45300, IB  165  MRCR 40700 45200
    IB  171  VLVO 42700 47500, IB  175  MRCR 40800 45300, IB  180  MRCR 40800 45300
    IB  200  MRCR 40800 45300, IB  205  MRCR 40800 45300, IB  210  MRCR 41200 45800
    IB  229  VLVO 41200 45600, IB  275  VLVO 41200 45600, IB  307  VLVO 41400 46000
    IB  320  MRCR 41300 45800, IB  330  MRCR 41300 45800, IB   D   MRCR 44700 49700
    IB  130D VLVO 44000 48900, IB  200D VLVO 44400 49300

70      STARDUST CUSTOM         HB   AL  PN IB  120 VLVO 14               2  4  40000 44500
    IB       VLVO 46300 50900, IB  120  MRCR 44000 48900, IB  120  VLVO 44400 49300
    IB  130  MRCR 44600 49600, IB  146  VLVO 44400 49300, IB  165  MRCR 44400 49400
    IB  167  VLVO 42700 47500, IB  175  MRCR 44400 49300, IB  180  MRCR 44400 49300
    IB  200  MRCR 44400 49400, IB  205  MRCR 44500 49400, IB  210  MRCR 44600 49600
    IB  229  VLVO 44700 49700, IB  275  VLVO 44800 49800, IB  307  VLVO 45000 50000
    IB  320  MRCR 44900 49900, IB   D   MRCR 49000 53800, IB  130D VLVO 48200 52900
    IB  200D VLVO 48400 53200

70      STARDUST XL        FB 3 HB   AL  PN IB       14               2  4  42700 47400
```

LOA FT	LOA IN	NAME AND/ OR MODEL	TOP/ RIG	BOAT TYPE	-HULL- MTL	-HULL- TP	ENGINE TP	ENGINE # HP	ENGINE MFG	BEAM FT	BEAM IN	WGT LBS	DRAFT FT	DRAFT IN	RETAIL LOW	RETAIL HIGH
		1989 BOATS														
70		STARDUST XL	FB	HB	AL	PN	IB		VLVO	14			2	4	42800	47600
		IB 120 MRCR 42200 46900, IB 120 VLVO 42400 47100, IB 130 MRCR													42300	47000
		IB 146 VLVO 42600 47300, IB 165 MRCR 42600 47300, IB 167 VLVO													42700	47500
		IB 175 MRCR 42600 47300, IB 180 MRCR 42600 47300, IB 200 MRCR													42600	47400
		IB 205 MRCR 42600 47400, IB 210 VLVO 42800 47600, IB 229 VLVO													42900	47600
		IB 275 VLVO 43000 47800, IB 307 VLVO 43200 48000, IB 320 MRCR													43000	47800
		IB 330 MRCR 43100 47900, IB D MRCR 47100 51800, IB D VLVO													46600	51200

STARFIRE BOATS

WEST JORDAN UT 84088 COAST GUARD MFG ID- SRF See inside cover to adjust price for area

LOA FT	LOA IN	NAME AND/ OR MODEL	TOP/ RIG	BOAT TYPE	-HULL- MTL	-HULL- TP	ENGINE TP	ENGINE # HP	ENGINE MFG	BEAM FT	BEAM IN	WGT LBS	DRAFT FT	DRAFT IN	RETAIL LOW	RETAIL HIGH
		1992 BOATS														
17	4	STARFIRE 180SE	OP	B/R	FBG	SV	IO	135-180		7		2100			4650	5750
19	4	STARFIRE 200SE	OP	B/R	FBG	SV	IO	155-230		7	8	2550			6200	7600
19	4	STARFIRE 200SE	OP	B/R	FBG	SV	IO	275	VLVO	7	8	2550			7250	8350
20	7	STARFIRE 215F	OP	CUD	FBG	SV	OB			8		3750			3050	3550
20	7	STARFIRE 215F	OP	CUD	FBG	SV	IO	175-300		8		3750			11400	14200
20	7	STARFIRE 215SE	OP	CUD	FBG	SV	IO	175-275		8		3750			9950	11700
20	10	STARFIRE 210BR	OP	B/R	FBG	SV	IO	205-230		8	2	2700			7750	9300
20	10	STARFIRE 210BR	OP	B/R	FBG	SV	IO	275	VLVO	8	2	2700			8700	10000
21	2	STARFIRE 225CC	ST	CUD	FBG	SV	IO	180-240		8		3800			10400	12200
21	2	STARFIRE 225CC	ST	CUD	FBG	SV	IO	275-300		8		3800			11500	13600
22	3	STARFIRE 230BR	OP	B/R	FBG	SV	IO	205-300		8	2	3400			9650	12000
22	3	STARFIRE 230BR	OP	B/R	FBG	SV	IO	330	VLVO	8	2	3400			11800	13400
22	3	STARFIRE 230SSC	OP	CUD	FBG	SV	IO	205-275		8	2	3650			10800	13400
22	3	STARFIRE 230SSC	OP	CUD	FBG	SV	IO	300		8	2	3650			11800	14000
24	1	STARFIRE 245F	OP	CUD	FBG	SV	OB			8		4800			5250	6000
24	1	STARFIRE 245F	OP	CUD	FBG	SV	IO	205-275		8		4800			14500	17700
		IO 300 15600 18300, IO 185D-254D 18200 22400, IO T135-T230													16000	18900
		IO T275 VLVO 18700 20800														
25	7	STARFIRE 255F	OP	CUD	FBG	SV	OB			8	6	5100			5500	6350
25	7	STARFIRE 255F	OP	CUD	FBG	SV	IO	205-300		8	6	5100			16400	20300
		IO 185D-254D 19700 24500, IO T135-T230 18100 21700, IO T275 VLVO													21200	23500
26	3	STARFIRE 265	OP	CR	FBG	SV	IO	230-300		8	4	5650			18600	22200
26	3	STARFIRE 265	OP	CR	FBG	SV	IO	T135-T230		8	4	5650			19800	23800
26	3	STARFIRE 265	OP	CR	FBG	SV	IO	T275	VLVO	8	4	5650			23200	25700
31	8	STARFIRE 325	OP	CR	FBG	SV	IO	300	VLVO	11					36100	40100
		IO T240 MRCR 38200 42500, IB T240-T250 46800 51600, IO T275-T300													39400	44200
		IB T305-T310 48700 53600, IOT185D-T254D 45800 53900														
		1991 BOATS														
17	4	SPECIAL ED 180 BR	ST	RNBT	FBG	DV	IO	145-205		7		2100	2	4	4700	5800
19	4	SPECIAL ED 200 BR	ST	RNBT	FBG	DV	IO	145-260		7	7	2650	2	5	6150	7550
20	7	FISHERMAN 215	ST	CUD	F/S	DV	IO	200-260		7	11	3650	2	6	9350	11100
20	7	FISHERMAN 215	ST	CUD	F/S	DV	IO	275	VLVO	7	11	3650	2	6	10300	11700
20	7	FISHERMAN 215	ST	CUD	F/S	DV	IO	350		7	11	3650	2	6	11400	13000
20	7	SPECIAL ED 215 CC	ST	CUD	FBG	DV	IO	175-260		7	11	3350	2	6	8500	10300
20	7	SPECIAL ED 215 CC	ST	CUD	FBG	SV	IO	235	OMC	7	11	3350	2	6	8700	10000
20	10	STARCHASER 210 BR	ST	RNBT	FBG	DV	IO	175-270		8	2	2750	2	6	7450	9150
21	2	SANTA-CRUZ 225	ST	CUD	F/S	DV	IO	200-275		8		3800	2	6	9950	12400
21	2	SANTA-CRUZ 225	ST	CUD	F/S	DV	IO	350		8		3800	2	6	12100	13700
22	3	STARCHASER 230 BR	OP	RNBT	F/S	DV	IO	230-260		8	2	3400	2	6	9550	11100
		IO 330-350 10900 12900, IO 460 OMC 15400 17500, IO 570 VLVO													22800	25300
24	1	FISHERMAN 245	ST	CUD	F/S	DV	IO	230-260		8		4800	2	8	14100	16500
		IO 501 VLVO 24700 27500, IO 570 VLVO 28000 31100, IO T175-T260													15800	19500
		IO T570 VLVO 44200 49100														
24	1	STARCHASER 230 SSC	ST	CUD	F/S	DV	IO	260		8	2	3650	2	6	11800	13400
		IO 330-350 13000 15400, IO 460 OMC 17600 20000, IO 570 VLVO													25400	28200
25	7	FISHERMAN 255	ST	FSH	FBG	DV	IO	T150	VLVO	8	6	5500	2	4	19800	22000
26	3	WESTPORT AFT CABIN	ST	EXP	F/S	DV	IO	260-340		8	4	5650	2	4	18100	21600
		IO 570 VLVO 29300 32500, IO T175-T260 19500 23700, IO T570 VLVO													43000	47800
27	7	FISHERMAN 255	ST	FSH	FBG	DV	IO	205-340		8	6	5500	2	4	19600	24300
		IO D MRCR ** ** , IO D VLVO ** ** , IO T175-T260													21900	26700
32	10	WESTPORT 325 AFT CBN	ST	EXP	F/S	DV	IO	T260	MRCR	11		11000	2	6	42600	47300
		IB T260 MRCR 51900 57100, IO T330 MRCR 44900 49900, IB T330 MRCR													53700	59000
		1990 BOATS														
19	4	SPECIAL ED 200 BR	ST	RNBT	FBG	DV	IO	145-260		7	7	2650	2	5	5750	7100
20	7	FISHERMAN 215	ST	CUD	F/S	DV	IO	200-260		7	11	3650	2	6	8650	10500
20	7	FISHERMAN 215	ST	CUD	F/S	DV	IO	275	VLVO	7	11	3650	2	6	9650	11000
20	7	FISHERMAN 215	ST	CUD	F/S	DV	IO	350		7	11	3650	2	6	10700	12200
20	7	SPECIAL ED 215 CC	ST	CUD	FBG	DV	IO	175-205		7	11	3350	2	6	8000	9300
20	7	SPECIAL ED 215 CC	ST	CUD	FBG	SV	IO	200-260		7	11	3350	2	6	8100	9700
20	10	STARCHASER 210 BR	ST	RNBT	FBG	DV	IO	175-270		8	2	2750	2	6	7000	8600
21	2	SANTA-CRUZ 225	ST	CUD	F/S	DV	IO	200-275		8		3800	2	6	9350	11700
21	2	SANTA-CRUZ 225	ST	CUD	F/S	DV	IO	350		8		3800	2	6	11300	12900
22	3	STARCHASER 230 B/R	OP	RNBT	F/S	DV	IO	230-275		8	2	3400	2	6	8950	11000
22	3	STARCHASER 230 B/R	OP	RNBT	F/S	DV	IO	330-350		8	2	3400	2	6	10200	12100
22	3	STARCHASER 230 B/R	OP	RNBT	F/S	DV	IO	460	OMC	8	2	3400	2	6	14400	16400
24	1	FISHERMAN 245	ST	CUD	F/S	DV	IO	230-260		8		4800	2	8	13200	15300
		IO 501 VLVO 23200 25800, IO 570 VLVO 26300 29200, IO T175-T260													14800	18400
		IO T570 VLVO 41600 46200														
24	1	STARCHASER 230 SSC	ST	CUD	F/S	DV	IO	260		8	2	3650	2	6	11100	12600
		IO 330-350 12200 14400, IO 460 OMC 16600 18900, IO 570 VLVO													23800	26500
25	7	FISHERMAN 255	ST	FSH	FBG	DV	IO	205-340		8	6	5500	2	4	16500	20600
		IO D MRCR ** ** , IO D VLVO ** ** , IO T150-T260													18600	22300
26	3	WESTPORT AFT CABIN	ST	EXP	F/S	DV	IO	260-340		8	4	5650	2	4	16700	20300
		IO 570 VLVO 27400 30500, IO T175-T260 18300 22300, IO T570 VLVO													40400	44900
32	10	WESTPORT 325 AFT CBN	ST	EXP	F/S	DV	IO	T260	MRCR	11		11000	2	6	40000	44400
		IB T260 MRCR 49300 54200, IO T330 MRCR 42100 46800, IB T330 MRCR													51000	56100
		1989 BOATS														
19	4	DEL-REY 200 W/T	ST	RNBT	F/S	DV	IO	180-260		7	7	2650	2	6	5550	6900
19	4	DEL-REY 200 W/T	ST	RNBT	F/S	DV	IO	271	VLVO	7	7	2650	2	6	6350	7300
19	4	SALTAIRE 200 B/R	ST	RNBT	F/S	DV	IO	180-260		7	7	2650	2	6	5600	6950
19	4	SALTAIRE 200 B/R	ST	RNBT	F/S	DV	IO	271	VLVO	7	7	2650	2	6	6350	7350
19	4	SALTAIRE 200 B/R	ST	RNBT	F/S	DV	IO	350		7	7	2650	2	6	7350	8450
20	7	FISHERMAN 215	ST	CUD	F/S	DV	OB			7	11	3650	2	6	2750	3200
20	7	FISHERMAN 215	ST	CUD	F/S	DV	IO	200-260		7	11	3650	2	6	8200	9850
20	7	FISHERMAN 215	ST	CUD	F/S	DV	IO	271	VLVO	7	11	3650	2	6	9050	10300
20	7	FISHERMAN 215	ST	CUD	F/S	DV	IO	350		7	11	3650	2	6	10100	11500
21	2	SANTA-CRUZ 225	ST	CUD	F/S	DV	IO		MRCR	8		3800	2	6	**	**
		IO 230-271 8950 10900, IO 350 10700 12100, IO 460 OMC													14300	16200
22	3	STARCHASER 230 B/R	OP	RNBT	F/S	DV	IO		MRCR	8	2	3400	2	6	**	**
		IO 260-271 8550 10300, IO 350-365 10000 11900, IO 460 OMC													13400	15300
24	1	ENTERTAINER 245	ST	CUD	F/S	DV	IO	230-271		8		4650	2	8	12200	14600
24	1	FISHERMAN 245	ST	CUD	F/S	DV	IO	230-271		8		4800	2	8	12500	14900
24	1	FISHERMAN 245	ST	CUD	F/S	DV	IO	T165-T260		8		4800	2	8	13700	17000
24	1	FISHERMAN 245	ST	CUD	F/S	DV	IO	T271	VLVO	8		4800	2	8	15700	17900
24	1	STARCHASER 230 SSC	ST	CUD	F/S	DV	IO	260-271		8	2	3650	2	6	10400	12400
24	1	STARCHASER 230 SSC	ST	CUD	F/S	DV	IO	330-365		8	2	3650	2	6	11500	14000
24	1	STARCHASER 230 SSC	ST	CUD	F/S	DV	IO	460	OMC	8	2	3650	2	6	15700	17800
26	3	WESTPORT AFT CABIN	ST	EXP	F/S	DV	IO	260-340		8	4	5650	2	4	15700	19200
		IO T165-T260 16800 20800, IO T271 VLVO 19400 21600, IO T D VLVO													**	**
		IO T530D MRCR 41000 45500														
32	10	WESTPORT 325 AFT CBN	ST	EXP	F/S	DV	IO	T260	MRCR	11		11000	2	6	37600	41800
		IB T260 MRCR 47100 51800, IO T365 MRCR 41000 45600, IB T365 MRCR													49900	54800
		1988 BOATS														
17	4	LAGUNA 180 B/R	ST	RNBT	FBG	DV	IO	120-180		7		2150			4000	4950
17	4	MALIBU 180 W/T	ST	RNBT	FBG	DV	IO	120-180		7		2150			3850	4750
18	3	NEWPORT 190 B/R	ST	RNBT	F/S	DV	IO	175-260		7	6	2450			4700	5850
18	3	NEWPORT 190 B/R	ST	RNBT	F/S	DV	IO	271	VLVO	7	6	2450			5450	6250
19	4	DEL-REY 200 W/T	ST	RNBT	F/S	DV	IO	175-260		7	7	2650			5100	6300
19	4	DEL-REY 200 W/T	ST	RNBT	F/S	DV	IO	271	VLVO	7	7	2650			5850	6700
19	4	SALTAIRE 200 B/R	ST	RNBT	F/S	DV	IO	175-260		7	7	2650			5150	6350
19	4	SALTAIRE 200 B/R	ST	RNBT	F/S	DV	IO	271	VLVO	7	7	2650			5900	6750
19	4	SALTAIRE 200 B/R LTD	ST	RNBT	F/S	DV	IO	175-260		7	7	2650			5550	6800
19	4	SALTAIRE 200 B/R LTD	ST	RNBT	F/S	DV	IO	271	VLVO	7	7	2650			6300	7200
20	7	FISHERMAN 215	ST	CUD	F/S	DV	IO	200-260		7	11	3650			7750	9300
20	7	FISHERMAN 215	ST	CUD	F/S	DV	IO	271	VLVO	7	11	3650			8500	9750
20	7	FISHERMAN 215	HT	CUD	F/S	DV	IO	200-260		7	11	3600			7650	9200
20	7	FISHERMAN 215	HT	CUD	F/S	DV	IO	271	VLVO	7	11	3600			8400	9650
20	7	NEW-YORKER 215	ST	CUD	F/S	DV	IO	200-260		7	11	3400			7350	8900
20	7	NEW-YORKER 215	ST	CUD	F/S	DV	IO	271	VLVO	7	11	3400			8100	9350

CONTINUED ON NEXT PAGE

LOA FT	LOA IN	NAME AND/ OR MODEL	TOP/ RIG	BOAT TYPE	-HULL- MTL	-HULL- TP	ENGINE TP	ENGINE # HP	ENGINE MFG	BEAM FT	BEAM IN	WGT LBS	DRAFT FT	DRAFT IN	RETAIL LOW	RETAIL HIGH
		1988 BOATS														
20	7	NEW-YORKER 215	HT	CUD	F/S	DV	IO	200-260		7	11	3550			7600	9150
20	7	NEW-YORKER 215	HT	CUD	F/S	DV	IO	271	VLVO	7	11	3550			8350	9600
21	2	SANTA-CRUZ 225	ST	CUD	F/S	DV	IO	225-271		8		3800			8600	10300
21	2	SANTA-CRUZ 225	HT	CUD	F/S	DV	IO	225-271		8		4000			9000	10700
22	3	STARCHASER 220 B/R	OP	RNBT	F/S	DV	IO	260		8	2	3400	2	6	8100	9650
24	1	ENTERTAINER 245	ST	CUD	F/S	DV	IO	225-271		8		4650			11700	13800
24	1	ENTERTAINER 245	ST	CUD	F/S	DV	IO	T165-T260		8		4650			12600	15400
24	1	ENTERTAINER 245	ST	CUD	F/S	DV	IO	T271	VLVO	8		4650			14600	16500
24	1	ENTERTAINER 245	HT	CUD	F/S	DV	IO	225-271		8		4650			11700	13800
24	1	ENTERTAINER 245	HT	CUD	F/S	DV	IO	T165-T260		8		4650			12600	15400
24	1	ENTERTAINER 245	HT	CUD	F/S	DV	IO	T271	VLVO	8		4650			14600	16500
24	1	FISHERMAN 245	ST	CUD	F/S	DV	IO	225-271		8		4800			12000	14100
24	1	FISHERMAN 245	ST	CUD	F/S	DV	IO	T165-T260		8		4800			12900	15700
24	1	FISHERMAN 245	ST	CUD	F/S	DV	IO	T271	VLVO	8		4800			14900	16900
24	1	FISHERMAN 245	HT	CUD	F/S	DV	IO	225-271		8		5150			12700	14900
24	1	FISHERMAN 245	HT	CUD	F/S	DV	IO	T165-T260		8		5150			13600	16700
24	1	FISHERMAN 245	HT	CUD	F/S	DV	IO	T271	VLVO	8		5150			15600	17700
24	1	STARCHASER 220 SSC	ST	CUD	F/S	DV	IO	260		8	2	3650	2	6	9850	11200
26	3	WESTPORT AFT CABIN	ST	EXP	F/S	DV	IO	260-271		8	4	5650			14800	17300
26	3	WESTPORT AFT CABIN	ST	EXP	F/S	DV	IO	T175-T260		8	4	5650			16200	19600
26	3	WESTPORT AFT CABIN	ST	EXP	F/S	DV	IO	T271	VLVO	8	4	5650			18300	20400
		1987 BOATS														
17	4	LAGUNA 180 B/R	ST	RNBT	FBG	DV	OB			7		1280			1200	1450
17	4	LAGUNA 180 B/R	ST	RNBT	FBG	DV	IO	120-180		7		2100			3750	4600
17	4	MALIBU 180 W/T	ST	RNBT	FBG	DV	IO	120-180		7		2100			3550	4400
18	3	NEWPORT 190 B/R	ST	RNBT	F/S	DV	IO	175-260		7	6	2450			4450	5550
18	3	NEWPORT 190 B/R	ST	RNBT	F/S	DV	IO	271	VLVO	7	6	2450			5150	5950
19	4	DEL-REY 200 W/T	ST	RNBT	F/S	DV	IO	175-205		7	7	2600			4800	5550
19	4	DEL-REY 200 W/T	ST	RNBT	F/S	DV	IO	211-271		7	7	2600			5200	6450
19	4	SALTAIRE 200 B/R	ST	RNBT	F/S	DV	IO	175-205		7	7	2600			4800	5700
19	4	SALTAIRE 200 B/R	ST	RNBT	F/S	DV	IO	211-260		7	7	2600			5250	6200
19	4	SALTAIRE 200 B/R LTD	ST	RNBT	F/S	DV	IO	175-230		7	7	2600			5200	6400
19	4	SALTAIRE 200 B/R LTD	ST	RNBT	F/S	DV	IO	260		7	7	2600			5500	6650
20	7	FISHERMAN 215	ST	CUD	F/S	DV	IO	200-260		7	11	3600			7250	9050
20	7	FISHERMAN 215	HT	CUD	F/S	DV	IO	200-260		7	11	3600			7550	9400
20	7	NEW-YORKER 215	ST	CUD	F/S	DV	IO	200-230		7	11	3400			6950	8450
20	7	NEW-YORKER 215	ST	CUD	F/S	DV	IO	260		7	11	3400			7300	8750
20	7	NEW-YORKER 215	HT	CUD	F/S	DV	IO	200-230		7	11	3600			6950	8400
20	7	NEW-YORKER 215	HT	CUD	F/S	DV	IO	260		7	11	3600			7250	8700
21	2	SANTA-CRUZ 225	ST	CUD	F/S	DV	IO	225-260		8		3800			8150	9700
21	2	SANTA-CRUZ 225	HT	CUD	F/S	DV	IO	225-271		8		4000			8450	10200
24	1	ENTERTAINER 245	ST	CUD	F/S	DV	IO	225-260		8		4600			11000	12800
24	1	ENTERTAINER 245	ST	CUD	F/S	DV	IO	T165-T260		8		4600			11900	14500
24	1	ENTERTAINER 245	ST	CUD	F/S	DV	IO	T271	VLVO	8		4600			13500	15400
24	1	ENTERTAINER 245	HT	CUD	F/S	DV	IO	225-271		8		4800			10800	12700
24	1	ENTERTAINER 245	HT	CUD	F/S	DV	IO	T165-T260		8		4800			11800	14300
24	1	ENTERTAINER 245	HT	CUD	F/S	DV	IO	T271	VLVO	8		4800			13900	15800
24	1	FISHERMAN 245	ST	CUD	F/S	DV	IO	225-271		8		4800			11400	13400
24	1	FISHERMAN 245	ST	CUD	F/S	DV	IO	T165-T230		8		4800			12300	14900
24	1	FISHERMAN 245	ST	CUD	F/S	DV	IO	T260		8		4800			13000	15500
24	1	FISHERMAN 245	HT	CUD	F/S	DV	IO	225-271		8		4800			12000	14100
24	1	FISHERMAN 245	HT	CUD	F/S	DV	IO	T165-T230		8		4800			12800	15500
24	1	FISHERMAN 245	HT	CUD	F/S	DV	IO	T260		8		4800			13400	16000
26	3	WESTPORT AFT CABIN	ST	EXP	F/S	DV	IO	260-271		8	4	5600			13900	16200
26	3	WESTPORT AFT CABIN	ST	EXP	F/S	DV	IO	T175-T230		8	4	5600			15100	18500
26	3	WESTPORT AFT CABIN	ST	EXP	F/S	DV	IO	T260		8	4	5600			16400	19100
		1986 BOATS														
17	4	LAGUNA 180 B/R	ST	RNBT	FBG	DV	OB			6	2	1280			1150	1400
17	4	LAGUNA 180 B/R	ST	RNBT	FBG	DV	IO	117-190		6	2	2100			3550	4100
17	4	MALIBU 180 W/T	ST	RNBT	FBG	DV	IO	117-190		6	2	2100			3350	3900
18	3	MONTEREY 190 W/T	ST	RNBT	F/S	DV	IO	170-205		7	6				4100	5050
18	3	MONTEREY 190 W/T	ST	RNBT	F/S	DV	IO	225-260		7	6	2450			4500	5400
18	3	NEWPORT 190 B/R	ST	RNBT	F/S	DV	IO	170-205		7	6				4300	5250
18	3	NEWPORT 190 B/R	ST	RNBT	F/S	DV	IO	225-260		7	6	2450			4700	5650
19	4	DEL-REY 200 W/T	ST	RNBT	F/S	DV	IO	170-260		7	7				4700	5850
19	4	SALTAIRE 200 B/R	ST	RNBT	F/S	DV	IO	170-260		7	7				4750	5900
19	4	SALTAIRE 200 B/R LTD	ST	RNBT	F/S	DV	IO	185-230		7	7	2600			4950	6050
19	4	SALTAIRE 200 B/R LTD	ST	RNBT	F/S	DV	IO	260		7	7	2600			5250	6350
19	4	SKYLINER 200 HT	HT	RNBT	F/S	DV	IO	185-230		7	7	2750			4850	5950
19	4	SKYLINER 200 HT	HT	RNBT	F/S	DV	IO	260		7	7	2750			5150	6200
19	4	SKYLINER HT	HT	RNBT	F/S	DV	IO	170		7	7				4700	5400
20	7	FISHERMAN 215	ST	CUD	F/S	DV	IO	200-230		7	11	3600			6900	8350
20	7	FISHERMAN 215	ST	CUD	F/S	DV	IO	260		7	11	3600			7200	8600
20	7	FISHERMAN 215	HT	CUD	F/S	DV	IO	200-260		7	11	3600			7200	8950
20	7	NEW-YORKER 215	ST	CUD	F/S	DV	IO	200-230		7	11	3400			6650	8000
20	7	NEW-YORKER 215	ST	CUD	F/S	DV	IO	260		7	11	3400			6900	8300
20	7	NEW-YORKER 215	HT	CUD	F/S	DV	IO	200-230		7	11	3600			6600	7950
20	7	NEW-YORKER 215	HT	CUD	F/S	DV	IO	260		7	11	3600			6900	8250
21	2	SANTA-CRUZ 225	ST	CUD	F/S	DV	IO	225-260		8		3800			7800	9250
21	2	SANTA-CRUZ 225	HT	CUD	F/S	DV	IO	225-260		8		4000			8050	9550
24	1	ENTERTAINER 245	ST	CUD	F/S	DV	IO	225-260		8		4600			10500	12200
24	1	ENTERTAINER 245	ST	CUD	F/S	DV	IO	T170-T230		8		4600			11300	13800
24	1	ENTERTAINER 245	ST	CUD	F/S	DV	IO	T260		8		4600			12100	14400
24	1	ENTERTAINER 245	HT	CUD	F/S	DV	IO	200-260		8		4800			10700	12200
24	1	ENTERTAINER 245	HT	CUD	F/S	DV	IO	T170-T230		8		4800			11200	13700
24	1	ENTERTAINER 245	HT	CUD	F/S	DV	IO	T260		8		4800			12000	14200
24	1	FISHERMAN 245	ST	CUD	F/S	DV	IO	200-260		8		4800			10700	12600
24	1	FISHERMAN 245	ST	CUD	F/S	DV	IO	T170-T230		8		4800			11700	14200
24	1	FISHERMAN 245	ST	CUD	F/S	DV	IO	T260		8		4800			12400	14800
24	1	FISHERMAN 245	HT	CUD	F/S	DV	IO	225-260		8		4800			11400	13300
24	1	FISHERMAN 245	HT	CUD	F/S	DV	IO	T170-T230		8		4800			12100	14700
24	1	FISHERMAN 245	HT	CUD	F/S	DV	IO	T260		8		4800			12900	15300
25	7	WESTPORT 225	ST	EXP	F/S	DV	IO	260		8					12800	14600
26		AFT CABIN 265	ST	EXP	F/S	DV	IO	260		8		5600			13000	15000
26	3	AFT CABIN 265	ST	EXP	F/S	DV	IO	T185-T230		8		5600			14300	17300
26	3	AFT CABIN 265	ST	EXP	F/S	DV	IO	T260		8		5600			15500	18100
		1985 BOATS														
17	4	LAGUNA 180 B/R	ST	RNBT	FBG	DV	OB			6	2	1280			1150	1350
17	4	LAGUNA 180 B/R	ST	RNBT	FBG	DV	IO	117-200		6	2	2100			3350	4000
17	4	MALIBU 180 W/T	ST	RNBT	FBG	DV	IO	117-200		6	2	2100			3200	3850
18	3	MONTEREY 190 W/T	ST	RNBT	F/S	DV	IO	170-260		7	6	2450			4250	5200
18	3	NEWPORT 190 B/R	ST	RNBT	F/S	DV	IO	170		7	6	2450			3800	4600
18	3	NEWPORT 190 B/R	ST	RNBT	F/S	DV	IO	185-230		7	6	2450			4150	5150
18	3	NEWPORT 190 B/R	ST	RNBT	F/S	DV	IO	260		7	6	2450			4450	5400
19	4	DEL-REY 200 W/T	ST	RNBT	F/S	DV	IO	170-230		7	7	2600			4450	5500
19	4	DEL-REY 200 W/T	ST	RNBT	F/S	DV	IO	260		7	7	2600			4750	5750
19	4	SALTAIRE 200 B/R	ST	RNBT	F/S	DV	IO	170-230		7	7	2600			4500	5550
19	4	SALTAIRE 200 B/R	ST	RNBT	F/S	DV	IO	260		7	7	2600			4800	5800
19	4	SKYLINER 200 HT	HT	RNBT	F/S	DV	IO	170-230		7	7	2750			4600	5700
19	4	SKYLINER 200 HT	HT	RNBT	F/S	DV	IO	260		7	7	2750			4900	5950
20	7	FISHERMAN 215	ST	CUD	F/S	DV	IO	198-230		7	11	3600			6600	7950
20	7	FISHERMAN 215	ST	CUD	F/S	DV	IO	260		7	11	3600			6900	8250
20	7	FISHERMAN 215	ST	CUD	F/S	DV	IO	T170-T188		7	11	3600			7450	9050
20	7	FISHERMAN 215	HT	CUD	F/S	DV	IO	198-260		7	11	3600			6750	8450
20	7	FISHERMAN 215	HT	CUD	F/S	DV	IO	T170-T188		7	11	3600			7650	9250
20	7	NEW-YORKER 215	ST	CUD	F/S	DV	IO	198-230		7	11	3400			6350	7650
20	7	NEW-YORKER 215	ST	CUD	F/S	DV	IO	260		7	11	3400			6650	7950
20	7	NEW-YORKER 215	ST	CUD	F/S	DV	IO	T170-T188		7	11	3400			7200	8750
20	7	NEW-YORKER 215	HT	CUD	F/S	DV	IO	198-260		7	11	3600			6450	8050
20	7	NEW-YORKER 215	HT	CUD	F/S	DV	IO	T170-T188		7	11	3600			7300	8850
21	2	SANTA-CRUZ 225	ST	CUD	F/S	DV	IO	225-260		8		3800			7450	8850
21	2	SANTA-CRUZ 225	HT	CUD	F/S	DV	IO	225-260		8		4000			7750	9150
24	1	ENTERTAINER 245	ST	CUD	F/S	DV	IO	225-260		8		4600			10000	11700
24	1	ENTERTAINER 245	ST	CUD	F/S	DV	IO	T170-T230		8		4600			10800	13200
24	1	ENTERTAINER 245	ST	CUD	F/S	DV	IO	T260		8		4600			11500	13700
24	1	ENTERTAINER 245	HT	CUD	F/S	DV	IO	225-260		8		4800			10100	11700
24	1	ENTERTAINER 245	HT	CUD	F/S	DV	IO	T170-T230		8		4800			10700	13000
24	1	ENTERTAINER 245	HT	CUD	F/S	DV	IO	T260		8		4800			11600	13800
24	1	FISHERMAN 245	ST	CUD	F/S	DV	IO	225-260		8		4800			10400	12100
24	1	FISHERMAN 245	ST	CUD	F/S	DV	IO	T170-T230		8		4800			11200	13600
24	1	FISHERMAN 245	ST	CUD	F/S	DV	IO	T260		8		4800			11900	14100
24	1	FISHERMAN 245	HT	CUD	F/S	DV	IO	225-260		8		4800			10600	12400
24	1	FISHERMAN 245	HT	CUD	F/S	DV	IO	T170-T260		8		4800			11600	14400
24	7	EXPRESS 255		CBNCR	F/S	DV	IO	260	MRCR	8		5400	2	7	13400	15200
		IO 260 OMC 13300 15100, IO 260 VLVO 13600 15500, IO T260													13500	16000
26		EXPRESS 265	ST	EXP	F/S	DV	IO	260		8		5600			12400	14300
		1984 BOATS														
17	4	LAGUNA 180 B/R	ST	RNBT	FBG	DV	OB			6	2	1280			1100	1350
17	4	LAGUNA 180 B/R	ST	RNBT	FBG	DV	IO	117-200		6	2	2100			3250	3850
17	4	MALIBU 180 W/T	ST	RNBT	FBG	DV	IO	117-200		6	2	2100			3100	3700
18	3	MONTEREY 190 W/T	ST	RNBT	F/S	DV	IO	170-200		7	6	2450			3650	4550
18	3	MONTEREY 190 W/T	ST	RNBT	F/S	DV	IO	225-260		7	6	2450			4000	4900
18	3	NEWPORT 190 B/R	ST	RNBT	F/S	DV	IO	170-200		7	6	2450			3850	4750
18	3	NEWPORT 190 B/R	ST	RNBT	F/S	DV	IO	225-260		7	6	2450			4150	5050
18	3	SPORTSTER 190 SPR	ST	RNBT	F/S	DV	IO	170-230		7	6	2450			4100	5100
18	3	SPORTSTER 190 SPR	ST	RNBT	F/S	DV	IO	260		7	6	2450			4400	5350

CONTINUED ON NEXT PAGE

STARFIRE BOATS

–CONTINUED   See inside cover to adjust price for area

LOA FT IN	NAME AND/ OR MODEL	TOP/ RIG	BOAT TYPE	-HULL- MTL TP	----ENGINE--- TP # HP MFG	BEAM FT IN	WGT LBS	DRAFT FT IN	RETAIL LOW	RETAIL HIGH
					1984 BOATS					
19 4	DEL-REY 200 W/T	ST	RNBT	F/S DV	IO 170-230	7 7	2600		4250	5300
19 4	DEL-REY 200 W/T	ST	RNBT	F/S DV	IO 260	7 7	2600		4550	5500
19 4	SALTAIRE 200 B/R	ST	RNBT	F/S DV	IO 170-230	7 7	2600		4250	5350
19 4	SALTAIRE 200 B/R	ST	RNBT	F/S DV	IO 260	7 7	2600		4600	5550
19 4	SKYLINER 200 HT	ST	RNBT	F/S DV	IO 188 MRCR	7 7	2750		4450	5100
19 4	SKYLINER 200 HT	HT	RNBT	F/S DV	IO 170-230	7 7	2750		4450	5450
19 4	SKYLINER 200 HT	HT	RNBT	F/S DV	IO 260	7 7	2750		4700	5700
20 7	FISHERMAN 215	ST	CUD	F/S DV	IO 198-260	7 11	3600		6350	7900
20 7	FISHERMAN 215	ST	CUD	F/S DV	IO T170-T188	7 11	3600		7200	8750
20 7	FISHERMAN 215	HT	CUD	F/S DV	IO 198-260	7 11	3600		6500	8100
20 7	FISHERMAN 215	HT	CUD	F/S DV	IO T170-T188	7 11	3600		7350	8950
20 7	NEW-YORKER 215	ST	CUD	F/S DV	IO 198-230	7 11	3400		6100	7400
20 7	NEW-YORKER 215	ST	CUD	F/S DV	IO 260	7 11	3400		6400	7650
20 7	NEW-YORKER 215	ST	CUD	F/S DV	IO T170-T188	7 11	3400		6950	8450
20 7	NEW-YORKER 215	HT	CUD	F/S DV	IO 198-260	7 11	3600		6200	7750
20 7	NEW-YORKER 215	HT	CUD	F/S DV	IO T170-T188	7 11	3600		7050	8550
21 2	SANTA-CRUZ 225	ST	CUD	F/S DV	IO 225-260	8	3800		7200	8500
21 2	SANTA-CRUZ 225	HT	CUD	F/S DV	IO 225-260	8	4000		7450	8800
24 1	ENTERTAINER 245	ST	CUD	F/S DV	IO 225-260	8	4600		9650	11200
24 1	ENTERTAINER 245	ST	CUD	F/S DV	IO T170-T230	8	4600		10400	12700
24 1	ENTERTAINER 245	ST	CUD	F/S DV	IO T260	8	4600		11100	13200
24 1	ENTERTAINER 245	HT	CUD	F/S DV	IO 225-260	8	4800		9700	11300
24 1	ENTERTAINER 245	HT	CUD	F/S DV	IO T170-T230	8	4800		10300	12800
24 1	ENTERTAINER 245	HT	CUD	F/S DV	IO T260	8	4800		11200	13300
24 1	FISHERMAN 245	ST	CUD	F/S DV	IO 225-260	8	4800		10000	11600
24 1	FISHERMAN 245	ST	CUD	F/S DV	IO T170-T230	8	4800		10700	13000
24 1	FISHERMAN 245	HT	CUD	F/S DV	IO T260	8	4800		11400	13600
24 1	FISHERMAN 245	HT	CUD	F/S DV	IO 225-260	8	4800		10200	11900
24 1	FISHERMAN 245	HT	CUD	F/S DV	IO T170-T260	8	4800		11200	13800
26	EXPRESS 265	ST	EXP	F/S DV	IO 260	8	5600		12000	13800

....For earlier years, see the BUC Used Boat Price Guide, Volume 3

STARWIND SAILBOATS
DIV OF REBEL INDUSTRIES   See inside cover to adjust price for area
SARASOTA FL 34243

LOA FT IN	NAME AND/ OR MODEL	TOP/ RIG	BOAT TYPE	-HULL- MTL TP	----ENGINE--- TP # HP MFG	BEAM FT IN	WGT LBS	DRAFT FT IN	RETAIL LOW	RETAIL HIGH
					1987 BOATS					
18 7	STARWIND 190	SLP	SA/CR	FBG KC		7 6	1350	1 6	3350	3900
21 6	STARWIND 210	SLP	SA/CR	FBG KL		8	1890	4 8	4200	4850
22 3	STARWIND 223	SLP	SA/CR	FBG SK	OB	8 6	2435	1 10	5000	5750
					1985 BOATS					
18 7	STARWIND 19	SLP	SA/CR	FBG KC		7 6	1350	1 6	2950	3400
22 3	STARWIND 223	SLP	SA/CR	FBG SK	OB	8 6	2435	1 10	4400	5100
26 8	STARWIND 27	SLP	SA/CR	FBG KL	IB	9 8	5200	4 11	10400	11800
26 8	STARWIND 27	SLP	SA/CR	FBG KL	IB 10D	9 8	5200	4 11	11000	12500
26 8	STARWIND 27 SHOAL	SLP	SA/CR	FBG KL	IB	9 8	5500	3 7	11000	12500
26 8	STARWIND 27 SHOAL	SLP	SA/CR	FBG KL	IB 10D	9 8	5500	3 7	11600	13200
					1984 BOATS					
18	BUCCANEER	SLP	SA/OD	FBG CB		6	500	7	1600	1900
18	BUCCANEER CHAMPION	SLP	SA/OD	FBG CB		6	500	7	1800	2150
18 7	STARWIND 19	SLP	SA/CR	FBG KC		7 6	1350	1 6	2750	3200
22	STARWIND 22	SLP	SA/CR	FBG SK		7 9	2600	1 11	4250	4950
26 6	STARWIND 27	SLP	SA/CR	FBG KL	OB	9 7	5100	4 9	9500	10800
26 6	STARWIND 27	SLP	SA/CR	FBG KL	IB 10 YAN	9 7	5100	4 9	9700	11000
26 6	STARWIND 27 SHOAL	SLP	SA/CR	FBG KL	IB	9 7	5100	3 6	9500	10800
26 6	STARWIND 27 SHOAL	SLP	SA/CR	FBG KL	IB 10D YAN	9 7	5100	3 6	10000	11400

....For earlier years, see the BUC Used Boat Price Guide, Volume 3

STEALTH BASS BY VIP
VIVIAN INDUSTRIES INC   See inside cover to adjust price for area
VIVIAN LA 71082   COAST GUARD MFG ID- VVI

For more recent years, see the BUC Used Boat Price Guide, Volume 1

LOA FT IN	NAME AND/ OR MODEL	TOP/ RIG	BOAT TYPE	-HULL- MTL TP	----ENGINE--- TP # HP MFG	BEAM FT IN	WGT LBS	DRAFT FT IN	RETAIL LOW	RETAIL HIGH
					1996 BOATS					
16 9	BASS STEALTH SX165	OP	BASS	FBG SV	OB	6 11	1150		4300	5000
17 4	BASS STEALTH HT1780	OP	BASS	FBG FL	OB	6 8	1000		3850	4500
18	BASS STEALTH DX180	OP	BASS	FBG SV	OB	7 5	1550		5600	6450
18	BASS STEALTH SX180	OP	BASS	FBG SV	OB	7 5	1450		5350	6150
19 1	BASS STEALTH DX190	OP	BASS	FBG SV	OB	7 5	1550		5350	6150
19 1	BASS STEALTH SX190	OP	BASS	FBG SV	OB	7 5	1550		5700	6550
20 3	BASS STEALTH DX200	OP	BASS	FBG SV	OB	8	1875		7300	8400
20 3	BASS STEALTH SX200	OP	BASS	FBG SV	OB	8	1875		3950	4550
					1995 BOATS					
16 9	BASS STEALTH 16FFB	OP	FSH	FBG SV	OB	6 11	1050		3750	4400
16 9	BASS STEALTH FX165	OP	FSH	FBG SV	OB	6 11	1250		4450	5100
16 9	BASS STEALTH SX165	OP	BASS	FBG SV	OB	6 11	1150		4100	4750
18	BASS STEALTH DX180	OP	BASS	FBG SV	OB	7 5	1500		5350	6150
18	BASS STEALTH FX180	OP	FSH	FBG SV	OB	7 5	1500		5200	6000
18	BASS STEALTH SX180	OP	BASS	FBG SV	OB	7 5	1500		5100	5850
19 1	BASS STEALTH DX190	OP	BASS	FBG SV	OB	7 5	1550		5550	6350
19 1	BASS STEALTH FX190	OP	FSH	FBG SV	OB	7 5	1550		5550	6350
19 1	BASS STEALTH SX190	OP	BASS	FBG SV	OB	7 5	1500		5400	6200
20 3	BASS STEALTH SX200	OP	BASS	FBG SV	OB	8	1875		6750	7750
					1994 BOATS					
16 9	FFB 165	OP	FSH	FBG SV	OB	6 11	1050		3600	4200
16 9	FX 165 FISH & SKI	OP	FSH	FBG SV	OB	6 11	1250		4200	4850
16 9	SX 165	OP	BASS	FBG SV	OB	6 11	1150		3900	4550
18	FX 180	OP	FSH	FBG SV	OB	7 5	1500		5000	5750
18	SX 180	OP	BASS	FBG SV	OB	7 5	1450		4850	5600
19 1	DX 190	OP	BASS	FBG SV	OB	7 5	1550		5300	6100
20	DX 200	OP	BASS	FBG SV	OB	7 9	1875		6350	7300
					1993 BOATS					
16	FFB 161	OP	FSH	FBG SV	OB	5 4	790		2600	3000
16 9	FX 165 FISH & SKI	OP	FSH	FBG SV	OB	6 11	1320		4200	4900
16 9	SX 165	OP	BASS	FBG SV	OB	6 11	1320		4200	4900
17	FFB 171	OP	BASS	FBG SV	OB	6 8	1000		3350	3900
18	180 SX	OP	BASS	FBG SV	OB	7 5	1315		4350	5000
19 1	190 DX	OP	BASS	FBG SV	OB	7 5	1415		4750	5450
20	DX 200	OP	BASS	FBG SV	OB	7 9			6100	7000

STELLAR TECHNOLOGY INC
MIDDLETOWN RI 02840   See inside cover to adjust price for area

LOA FT IN	NAME AND/ OR MODEL	TOP/ RIG	BOAT TYPE	-HULL- MTL TP	----ENGINE--- TP # HP MFG	BEAM FT IN	WGT LBS	DRAFT FT IN	RETAIL LOW	RETAIL HIGH
					1987 BOATS					
29 11	STELLAR 30	SLP	SA/CR	FBG KL	IB 9D- 18D	10	5800	5 3	23200	25900
29 11	STELLAR 30	SLP	SA/CR	FBG SK	IB 9D YAN	10	5200	2 3	20800	23100
29 11	STELLAR SP	SLP	SA/CR	FBG	IB 77D YAN	10	6000	4	24500	27200
					1986 BOATS					
29 11	STELLAR	SLP	SA/CR	FBG SK	IB D	10	5600	2 3	21100	23500
29 11	STELLAR 30	SLP	SA/CR	FBG KL	IB D	10	5800	5 3	21900	24300
					1985 BOATS					
29 11	STELLAR 30	SLP	SA/CR	FBG KL	IB 9D YAN	10	5800	5 3	20500	22800
29 11	STELLAR 30	SLP	SA/CR	FBG SK	IB 9D YAN	10	5200	2 3	18600	20700

STINGRAY BOAT COMPANY
HARTSVILLE SC 29551   COAST GUARD MFG ID- PNY See inside cover to adjust price for area

For more recent years, see the BUC Used Boat Price Guide, Volume 1

LOA FT IN	NAME AND/ OR MODEL	TOP/ RIG	BOAT TYPE	-HULL- MTL TP	----ENGINE--- TP # HP MFG	BEAM FT IN	WGT LBS	DRAFT FT IN	RETAIL LOW	RETAIL HIGH
					1996 BOATS					
16 6	501	OP	RNBT	FBG DV	OB	6 2	864		2350	2750
17 10	551	OP	RNBT	FBG DV	OB	6	1160		3200	3700
18	556	OP	RNBT	FBG DV	IO 135 MRCR	7 1	1175		4100	4750
18	558	OP	RNBT	FBG DV	IO 135 MRCR	7 1	1175		4450	5100
19	586	OP	RNBT	FBG DV	IO 180 MRCR	7 1	1175		4750	5450
20 3	606	OP	RNBT	FBG DV	IO 180-250	7 8	1430		5900	7000
20 3	608	OP	RNBT	FBG DV	IO 210-250	7 8	1430		6300	7450
20 3	609	OP	RNBT	FBG DV	IO 180 MRCR	7 8	1575		6150	7050
21 6	656	OP	RNBT	FBG DV	IO 180-250	8	1933		7150	8650
21 6	658	OP	RNBT	FBG DV	IO 250-300	8 1	1966		7550	9400
21 6	659	OP	CUD	FBG DV	IO 180-250	8 1	2245		7900	9550
21 6	659	OP	RNBT	FBG DV	IO 250 MRCR	8 1	2245		7900	9050
22 8	698	OP	CUD	FBG DV	IO 300-330	8 1	2193		9500	11500
		IO 350 MRCR 10700	12200, IO	385 MRCR	12000 13600, IO	415 MRCR			13300	15100
23 6	719	OP	SPTCR	FBG DV	IO 180-250	8 6	3176		10800	12700
23 6	729	OP	SPTCR	FBG DV	IO 180-250	8 6	3576		11700	13700

STINGRAY BOAT COMPANY -CONTINUED See inside cover to adjust price for area

LOA FT	LOA IN	NAME AND/ OR MODEL	TOP/ RIG	BOAT TYPE	-HULL- MTL	-HULL- TP	ENGINE TP	ENGINE # HP	ENGINE MFG	BEAM FT	BEAM IN	WGT LBS	DRAFT FT	DRAFT IN	RETAIL LOW	RETAIL HIGH
1995 BOATS																
16	6	501	OP	RNBT	FBG	DV	OB			6	2	864			2250	2650
17	10	551	OP	RNBT	FBG	DV	OB			7		1160			3000	3500
18		556	OP	RNBT	FBG	DV	IO	135	MRCR	7	1	1175			3800	4450
18		558	OP	RNBT	FBG	DV	IO	135	MRCR	7	1	1175			4100	4750
19		586	OP	RNBT	FBG	DV	IO	135-180		7	1	1175			4400	5100
20	3	606	OP	RNBT	FBG	DV	IO	180-250		7	8	1430			5500	6600
20	3	608	OP	RNBT	FBG	DV	IO	180-250		7	8	1430			5800	6900
20	3	609	OP	RNBT	FBG	DV	IO	135-190		7	8	1575			5700	6600
21	6	656	OP	RNBT	FBG	DV	IO	180-265		8	1	1933			6700	8200
21	6	658	OP	RNBT	FBG	DV	IO	250-265		8	1	1966			7050	8250
21	6	659	OP	CUD	FBG	DV	IO	180-235		8	1	2245			7400	8650
21	6	659	OP	RNBT	FBG	DV	IO	250	MRCR	8	1	2245			7350	8450
22	8	696	OP	RNBT	FBG	DV	IO	250-300		8		2162			7650	9450
		IO 350 MRCR 9450 10700, IO 385 MRCR 10500 11900, IO 415 MRCR													11600	13200
22	8	698	OP	CUD	FBG	DV	IO	250-300		8	1	2193			8150	10100
		IO 350 MRCR 10000 11400, IO 385 MRCR 11200 12700, IO 415 MRCR													12400	14100
23	6	719	OP	SPTCR	FBG	DV	IO	180-250		8	6	3176			10100	11800
23	6	729	OP	SPTCR	FBG	DV	IO	180-250		8	6	3576			10900	12800
1994 BOATS																
16	6	501	OP	RNBT	FBG	DV	OB			6	2	864			2150	2500
17	10	551	OP	RNBT	FBG	DV	OB			7		1160			2850	3350
18		556	OP	RNBT	FBG	DV	IO	135	MRCR	7	1	1175			3550	4150
18		558	OP	RNBT	FBG	DV	IO	135	MRCR	7	1	1175			3850	4450
19		586	OP	RNBT	FBG	DV	IO	135-180		7	1	1175			4050	4750
20	3	606	OP	RNBT	FBG	DV	IO	180-235		7	8	1430			5300	6150
20	3	608	OP	RNBT	FBG	DV	IO	190-235		7	8	1430			5450	6450
20	3	609	OP	RNBT	FBG	DV	IO	180	MRCR	7	8	1575			5350	6150
21	6	656	OP	RNBT	FBG	DV	IO	180-250		8	1	1933			6250	7500
21	6	658	OP	RNBT	FBG	DV	IO	250	MRCR	8	1	1966			6600	7550
21	6	659	OP	CUD	FBG	DV	IO	180-235		8	1	2245			6900	8050
22	8	696	OP	RNBT	FBG	DV	IO	250-300		8		2162			7150	8850
22	8	696	OP	RNBT	FBG	DV	IO	350	MRCR	8		2162			8800	10000
22	8	696	OP	RNBT	FBG	DV	IO	415	MRCR	8		2162			10800	12300
22	8	698	OP	CUD	FBG	DV	IO	250-300		8	1	2193			7600	9450
22	8	698	OP	CUD	FBG	DV	IO	350	MRCR	8	1	2193			9400	10700
22	8	698	OP	CUD	FBG	DV	IO	415	MRCR	8	1	2193			11600	13100
23	6	719	OP	SPTCR	FBG	DV	IO	180-235		8	6	3176			9400	10900
1993 BOATS																
16	6	501	OP	RNBT	FBG	DV	OB			6	2	864			2000	2400
16	6	501S	OP	RNBT	FBG	DV	OB			6	2	864			2000	2400
17	10	551	OP	RNBT	FBG	DV	OB			7		1160			2750	3200
18		556	OP	RNBT	FBG	DV	IO	115	MRCR	7	1	1175			3300	3850
18		558	OP	RNBT	FBG	DV	IO	115	MRCR	7	1	1175			3550	4150
20	3	606	OP	RNBT	FBG	DV	IO	180	MRCR	7	8	1430			4650	5350
20	3	608	OP	RNBT	FBG	DV	IO	180	MRCR	7	8	1430			5250	6000
20	3	609	OP	RNBT	FBG	DV	IO	180	MRCR	7	8	1575			5000	5750
21	6	656	OP	RNBT	FBG	DV	IO	180-250		8	1	1933			5850	7050
21	6	658	OP	RNBT	FBG	DV	IO	250	MRCR	8	1	1966			6150	7050
21	6	659	OP	CUD	FBG	DV	IO	180-235		8	1	2245			6450	7550
22	8	696	OP	RNBT	FBG	DV	IO	250-300		8		2162			6650	8250
22	8	696	OP	RNBT	FBG	DV	IO	350	MRCR	8		2162			8150	9350
22	8	698	OP	CUD	FBG	DV	IO	250-300		8	1	2193			7100	8800
22	8	698	OP	CUD	FBG	DV	IO	350	MRCR	8	1	2193			8700	10000
22	8	698	OP	CUD	FBG	DV	IO	410	MRCR	8	1	2193			10600	12100
23	6	719	OP	SPTCR	FBG	DV	IO	235	MRCR	8	6	3176			9050	10300
23	6	719S	OP	SPTCR	FBG	DV	IO	180	MRCR	8	6	3176			8850	10000
1992 BOATS																
17	5	536 ZP	OP	RNBT	FBG	DV	IO	115-155		7	4	1345	2	6	3250	3800
17	5	537 ZP	OP	CUD	FBG	DV	IO	115-155		7	4	1290	2	6	3200	3750
19	5	596 ZP	OP	RNBT	FBG	DV	IO	115-175		7	10	1680	2	8	4150	5100
19	5	597 ZP	OP	CUD	FBG	DV	IO	115-175		7	10	1630	2	8	4250	5250
19	5	598 ZP	OP	RNBT	FBG	DV	IO	115-205		7	10	1690	2	8	4150	5100
19	5	598 ZP	OP	RNBT	FBG	DV	IO	240	VLVO	7	10	1690	2	8	4650	5350
19	5	599 ZP	OP	CUD	FBG	DV	IO	115-205		7	10	1780	2	8	4400	5350
21	5	656 ZP	OP	RNBT	FBG	DV	IO	115-230		8	1	2179	2	9	5600	6950
21	5	656 ZP	OP	RNBT	FBG	DV	IO	240-250		8	1	2179	2	9	6150	7050
21	5	657 ZP	OP	CUD	FBG	DV	IO	115-230		8	1	2119	2	9	5800	7200
21	5	657 ZP	OP	CUD	FBG	DV	IO	240-250		8	1	2119	2	9	6400	7350
21	5	658 ZP	OP	RNBT	FBG	DV	IO	155-250		8	1	2160	2	9	5850	7000
21	5	659 ZP	OP	CUD	FBG	DV	IO	135-230		8	1	2270	2	9	6000	7400
21	5	659 ZP	OP	CUD	FBG	DV	IO	240-250		8	1	2270	2	9	6550	7500
22	8	696 SVX	OP	RNBT	FBG	DV	IO	205-250		8		2190	3		6050	7450
22	8	696 SVX	OP	RNBT	FBG	DV	IO	300	MRCR	8		2190	3		6750	7750
22	8	698 SVX	OP	CUD	FBG	DV	IO	205-250		8		2180	3		6400	7850
22	8	698 SVX	OP	CUD	FBG	DV	IO	300		8		2180	3		7150	8700
22	8	698 SVX	OP	CUD	FBG	DV	IO	350	MRCR	8		2180	3		8100	9300
23	6	719 ZP	OP	SPTCR	FBG	DV	IO	175-250		8	6	3300	2	9	8400	10200
23	6	719 ZP	OP	SPTCR	FBG	DV	IO	300		8	6	3300	2	9	9300	11000
26	11	268 SVF	OP	FSH	FBG	DV	OB			8	6	4200	2	10	11800	13500
26	11	828 SVX	OP	CUD	FBG	DV	IO	T230-T300		8	6	4250	2	10	15400	18800
26	11	828 SVX	OP	CUD	FBG	DV	IO	T350	MRCR	8	6	4250	2	10	18000	20100
26	11	829 SVC	OP	CR	FBG	DV	IO	205-250		8	6	4850	3	2	13300	15700
26	11	829 SVC	OP	CR	FBG	DV	IO	300		8	6	4850	3	2	14500	16700
1991 BOATS																
17	5	536 ZP	OP	RNBT	FBG	DV	IO	125-175		7	4	1345	2	6	3050	3550
17	5	537 ZP	OP	CUD	FBG	DV	IO	125-175		7	4	1290	2	6	3000	3550
19	5	596 ZP	OP	RNBT	FBG	DV	IO	145-205		7	10	1680	2	8	3900	4800
19	5	597 ZP	OP	CUD	FBG	DV	IO	145-175		7	10	1630	2	8	4000	4900
19	5	597 ZP	OP	CUD	FBG	DV	IO	205	VLVO	7	10	1630	2	8	4350	5000
19	5	598 ZP	OP	RNBT	FBG	DV	IO	145-205		7	10	1690	2	8	3900	4900
19	5	598 ZP	OP	RNBT	FBG	DV	IO	260	MRCR	7	10	1690	2	8	4250	4950
19	5	598 ZP	OP	RNBT	FBG	DV	IO	270		7	10	1690	2	8	4350	5350
19	5	599 ZP	OP	CUD	FBG	DV	IO	145-205		7	10	1780	2	8	4100	5050
21	5	656 ZP	OP	RNBT	FBG	DV	IO	145-270		8	1	2179	2	9	5250	6550
21	5	656 ZP	OP	RNBT	FBG	DV	IO	275	VLVO	8	1	2179	2	9	6050	6950
21	5	657 ZP	OP	CUD	FBG	DV	IO	145-270		8	1	2119	2	9	5450	6800
21	5	657 ZP	OP	CUD	FBG	DV	IO	275	VLVO	8	1	2119	2	9	6300	7250
21	5	658 ZP	OP	RNBT	FBG	DV	IO	175-270		8	1	2160	2	9	5500	6550
21	5	658 ZP	OP	RNBT	FBG	DV	IO	275	VLVO	8	1	2160	2	9	6050	6950
21	5	659 ZP	OP	CUD	FBG	DV	IO	175-270		8	1	2270	2	9	5650	7000
21	5	659 ZP	OP	CUD	FBG	DV	IO	275	VLVO	8	1	2270	2	9	6450	7400
22	8	696 SVX	OP	RNBT	FBG	DV	IO	260-275		8		2190	3		5950	7300
22	8	696 SVX	OP	RNBT	FBG	DV	IO	330	MRCR	8		2190	3		6800	7800
22	8	698 SVX	OP	CUD	FBG	DV	IO	260-275		8		2180	3		6300	7750
22	8	698 SVX	OP	CUD	FBG	DV	IO	330		8		2180	3		7200	8800
22	8	698 SVX	OP	CUD	FBG	DV	IO	365	MRCR	8		2180	3		7950	9150
23	6	719 ZP	OP	SPTCR	FBG	DV	IO	175-275		8	6	3300	2	9	8100	9950
23	6	719 ZP	OP	SPTCR	FBG	DV	IO	330	MRCR	8	6	3300	2	9	9200	10500
26	11	268 SVF	OP	FSH	FBG	DV	OB			8	6	4200	2	10	11300	12900
26	11	828 SVX	OP	CUD	FBG	DV	IO	270-330		8	6	4250	2	10	12500	15600
26	11	828 SVX	OP	CUD	FBG	DV	IO	365	MRCR	8	6	4250	2	10	14100	16000
26	11	828 SVX	OP	CUD	FBG	DV	IO	T270-T365		8	6	4250	2	10	15500	19300
26	11	829 SVC	OP	CR	FBG	DV	IO	260-330		8	6	4850	3	2	13100	16000
1990 BOATS																
17	5	536 ZP	OP	RNBT	FBG	DV	IO	125-175		7	4	1345			2850	3350
17	5	537 ZP	OP	CUD	FBG	DV	IO	125-175		7	4	1290			2850	3350
19	3	SVB 198	OP	RNBT	FBG	DV	IO	125-200		7	9	1580			3550	4200
19	3	SVB 198	OP	RNBT	FBG	DV	IO	205	VLVO	7	9	1580			3850	4450
19	3	SVC 199	OP	CUD	FBG	DV	IO	125-200		7	9	1680			3700	4400
19	3	SVC 199	OP	CUD	FBG	DV	IO	205	VLVO	7	9	1680			4000	4650
19	3	SVC 200	OP	CR	FBG	DV	IO	125-200		7	9	1523			3600	4300
19	3	SVC 200	OP	CR	FBG	DV	IO	205-260		7	9	1523			3900	4600
19	5	596 ZP	OP	RNBT	FBG	DV	IO	125-175		7	10	1680			3650	4300
19	5	597 ZP	OP	CUD	FBG	DV	IO	125-200		7	10	1630			3750	4450
19	5	597 ZP	OP	CUD	FBG	DV	IO	205	VLVO	7	10	1630			4050	4700
20	1	SVC 210	OP	CUD	FBG	DV	IO	125-260		8		2270			4850	6000
21	5	656 ZP	OP	RNBT	FBG	DV	IO	125-270		8		2179			4900	6150
21	5	656 ZP	OP	RNBT	FBG	DV	IO	275	VLVO	8		2179			5650	6500
21	5	657 ZP	OP	CUD	FBG	DV	IO	125-260		8		2119			5100	6300
21	8	SVC 222	OP	CR	FBG	DV	IO	125-270		8		2043			5100	6400
21	8	SVC 222	OP	CR	FBG	DV	IO	275-330		8		2043			5900	7250
21	8	SVC 222	OP	CR	FBG	DV	IO	365	MRCR	8		2043			7050	8100
22	8	SVB 230	OP	CR	FBG	DV	IO	125-260		8		2073			5450	6650
		IO 275 VLVO 6200 7150, IO 330 MRCR 6500 7500, IO 330 VLVO													7250	8300
22	8	SVC 235	OP	CR	FBG	DV	IO	125-270		8		2073			5450	6750
		IO 275 VLVO 6250 7200, IO 330 MRCR 6550 7500, IO 330-365													7250	8450
26	11	SVC 270	OP	CR	FBG	DV	IO	125-205		8	6	4850			11000	13500
26	11	SVC 270	OP	CR	FBG	DV	IO	260-330		8	6	4850			12300	15300
26	11	SVC 275	OP	CR	FBG	DV	IO	270-330		8	6	4250			11800	14300
		IO 365 MRCR 13200 15100, IO T270-T330 14200 17200, IO T365 MRCR													15900	18100
29		SVF 268	OP	FSH	FBG	DV	OB			8	6	4200			13600	15400

CONTINUED ON NEXT PAGE

LOA FT	LOA IN	NAME AND/ OR MODEL	TOP/ RIG	BOAT TYPE	-HULL- MTL	-HULL- TP	ENGINE TP	ENGINE # HP	ENGINE MFG	BEAM FT	BEAM IN	WGT LBS	DRAFT FT	DRAFT IN	RETAIL LOW	RETAIL HIGH
		1986 BOATS														
16		SVB 160	OP	RNBT	FBG	DV	OB			6	9	1350			2300	2650
16		SVB 165	OP	RNBT	FBG	DV	IO	120-140		6	9	1700			2200	2600
17	3	SVB 170	OP	RNBT	FBG	SV	OB			7					2650	3050
17	3	SVB 175/176	OP	RNBT	FBG	DV	IO	140-170		7		1926			2550	3050
18	7	SVB 190	OP	RNBT	FBG	DV	IO	140	MRCR	7		1940			2750	3200
18	7	SVC 190	OP	RNBT	FBG	DV	IO	188	MRCR	7		2057			2850	3350
18	7	SVC 195	OP	CR	FBG	DV	IO	170	MRCR	7		2175			3000	3500
19	3	SVB 198	OP	RNBT	FBG	DV	IO	190	MRCR	7	9	2400			3400	3950
20	1	SVB 205	OP	RNBT	FBG	DV	IO	260	MRCR	8		2970			4650	5350
20	1	SVC 207	OP	RNBT	FBG	DV	IO	260	MRCR	8		2950			4650	5350
20	1	SVC 210	OP	CUD	FBG	DV	IO	260	MRCR	8		3177			5050	5800
21	8	SVC 220	OP	SPTCR	FBG	DV	IO	260	MRCR	8		2885			5150	5950
		1985 BOATS														
16		SVB 165		B/R	FBG	DV	OB			6	9	1800			2900	3350
17	3	SVB 175		RNBT	FBG	DV	OB			7		2100			3050	3550
18	7	SVB 190		RNBT	FBG	DV	OB			7		2200			3150	3650
18	7	SVC 190		RNBT	FBG	DV	OB			7		2200			3150	3650
18	7	SVC 195		RNBT	FBG	DV	OB			7		2200			3150	3650
20	1	SVB 205		RNBT	FBG	DV	OB			8		3000			4100	4800

....For earlier years, see the BUC Used Boat Price Guide, Volume 3

STOREBRO BRUKS AB

POMPANO BEACH FL 33062 COAST GUARD MFG ID- XBF See inside cover to adjust price for area

LOA FT	LOA IN	NAME AND/ OR MODEL	TOP/ RIG	BOAT TYPE	-HULL- MTL	-HULL- TP	ENGINE TP	ENGINE # HP	ENGINE MFG	BEAM FT	BEAM IN	WGT LBS	DRAFT FT	DRAFT IN	RETAIL LOW	RETAIL HIGH
		1987 BOATS														
30	6	STOREBRO-ROYAL ADRIA	OP	CBNCR	FBG	RB	IB	T130D-T200D		10	6	11000	3	3	68400	83500
30	6	STOREBRO-ROYAL BALTC	OP	CBNCR	FBG	RB	IB	T130D-T200D		10	6	11000	3	3	72100	87800
34		STOREBRO-ROYAL BISCA	HT	CBNCR	FBG	DS	IB	T200D-T306D		10	6	12000	3	1	90300	106500
34		STOREBRO-ROYAL BISCA	FB	CBNCR	FBG	DS	IB	T200D-T306D		10	6	12500	3	1	91500	108500
36	1	STOREBRO-ROYAL BALTC	HT	CBNCR	FBG	RB	IB	T306D	VLVO	12	6	19845	3	11	115500	127000
36	1	STOREBRO-ROYAL BALTC	FB	CBNCR	FBG	RB	IB	T306D	VLVO	12	6	19845	3	11	120000	132000
39	8	STOREBRO-ROYAL BALTC	HT	CBNCR	FBG	DS	IB	T306D	VLVO	12	10	25000	3	11	154500	169500
39	8	STOREBRO-ROYAL BALTC	HT	CBNCR	FBG	DS	IB	T386D	VLVO	12	10	26000	3	11	165500	181500
39	8	STOREBRO-ROYAL BALTC	FB	CBNCR	FBG	DS	IB	T306D	VLVO	12	10	26000	3	11	172000	189000
39	8	STOREBRO-ROYAL BALTC	FB	CBNCR	FBG	DS	IB	T386D	VLVO	12	10	27000	3	11	181000	199000
39	8	STOREBRO-ROYAL BISCY	HT	CBNCR	FBG	DS	IB	T306D	VLVO	12	10	25000	3	11	148000	162500
39	8	STOREBRO-ROYAL BISCY	HT	CBNCR	FBG	DS	IB	T386D	VLVO	12	10	26000	3	11	159000	175000
39	8	STOREBRO-ROYAL BISCY	FB	CBNCR	FBG	DS	IB	T300D	VLVO	12	10	27000	3	11	173000	190500
39	8	STOREBRO-ROYAL BISCY	FB	CBNCR	FBG	DS	IB	T306D	VLVO	12	10	26000	3	11	165500	182000
39	8	STOREBRO-ROYAL BISCY	FB	CBNCR	FBG	DS	IB	T386D	VLVO	12	10	26000	3	11	176000	193500
		1986 BOATS														
30	6	STOREBRO-ROYAL ADRIA	OP	CBNCR	FBG	RB	IB	T105D-T158D		10	6	11000	3	1	64600	77300
30	6	STOREBRO-ROYAL ADRIA	OP	CBNCR	FBG	RB	IB	T235D	VLVO	10	6	12000	3	1	80800	88800
30	6	STOREBRO-ROYAL BALTC	OP	CBNCR	FBG	RB	IB	T105D-T158D		10	6	11000	3	1	64600	77300
30	6	STOREBRO-ROYAL BALTC	OP	CBNCR	FBG	RB	IB	T235D	VLVO	10	6	12000	3	1	80800	88800
30	6	STOREBRO-ROYAL BALTC	HT	CBNCR	FBG	RB	IB	T105D-T158D		10	6	11500	3	1	66100	77300
30	6	STOREBRO-ROYAL BALTC	HT	CBNCR	FBG	RB	IB	T235D	VLVO	10	6	12500	3	1	82100	90200
30	6	STOREBRO-ROYAL BISCY	HT	CBNCR	FBG	RB	IB	T105D-T158D		10	6	12000	3	1	67700	80300
30	6	STOREBRO-ROYAL BISCY	HT	CBNCR	FBG	RB	IB	T235D	VLVO	10	6	13000	3	1	83400	91700
30	6	STOREBRO-ROYAL BISCY	FB	CBNCR	FBG	RB	IB	T105D-T158D		10	6	12500	3	1	69300	81900
30	6	STOREBRO-ROYAL BISCY	FB	CBNCR	FBG	RB	IB	T235D	VLVO	10	6	13500	3	1	84800	93200
30	6	STOREBRO-ROYAL PATRL	HT	CR	FBG		IB	T235D	VLVO	10	10	11000	3	1	61900	68000
33	7	STOREBRO-ROYAL 340		CR	FBG	DS	IB	T158D-T235D		12	4	14000	3	7	76600	88900
34		STOREBRO-ROYAL BALTC	HT	CBNCR	FBG	DS	IB	T105D-T158D		10	6	12000	3	1	77800	90800
34		STOREBRO-ROYAL BALTC	HT	CBNCR	FBG	DS	IB	T235D	VLVO	10	6	13000	3	1	91900	101000
34		STOREBRO-ROYAL BALTC	FB	CBNCR	FBG	DS	IB	T105D-T158D		10	6	12500	3	1	79200	92200
34		STOREBRO-ROYAL BALTC	FB	CBNCR	FBG	DS	IB	T235D	VLVO	10	6	13500	3	1	93000	102000
34		STOREBRO-ROYAL BISCA	FB	CBNCR	FBG	DS	IB	T105D-T158D		10	6	12500	3	1	79200	92200
34		STOREBRO-ROYAL BISCA	FB	CBNCR	FBG	DS	IB	T235D	VLVO	10	6	13500	3	1	93000	102000
34		STOREBRO-ROYAL BISCY	HT	CBNCR	FBG	DS	IB	T105D-T158D		10	6	12000	3	1	77800	90800
34		STOREBRO-ROYAL BISCY	HT	CBNCR	FBG	DS	IB	T235D	VLVO	10	6	13000	3	1	91900	101000
34		STOREBRO-ROYAL WORK	HT	PH	FBG	RB	IB	T105D-T235D		10	10	12000	3	3	70400	84200
36	1	STOREBRO-ROYAL BALTC	HT	CBNCR	FBG	RB	IB	T235D	VLVO	12	6	19845	3	11	105000	115500
36	1	STOREBRO-ROYAL BALTC	FB	CBNCR	FBG	RB	IB	T235D	VLVO	12	6	19845	3	11	109500	120000
39	8	STOREBRO-ROYAL BALTC	HT	CBNCR	FBG	DS	IB	T235D	VLVO	12	10	25000	3	11	140000	154000
39	8	STOREBRO-ROYAL BALTC	HT	CBNCR	FBG	DS	IB	T300D	VLVO	12	10	26000	3	11	148500	163000
39	8	STOREBRO-ROYAL BALTC	FB	CBNCR	FBG	DS	IB	T235D	VLVO	12	10	26000	3	11	156000	171500
39	8	STOREBRO-ROYAL BALTC	FB	CBNCR	FBG	DS	IB	T300D	VLVO	12	10	27000	3	11	165000	181500
39	8	STOREBRO-ROYAL BISCY	HT	CBNCR	FBG	DS	IB	T235D	VLVO	12	10	25000	3	11	140000	154000
39	8	STOREBRO-ROYAL BISCY	HT	CBNCR	FBG	DS	IB	T300D	VLVO	12	10	26000	3	11	148500	163000
39	8	STOREBRO-ROYAL BISCY	FB	CBNCR	FBG	DS	IB	T235D	VLVO	12	10	26000	3	11	156000	171500
39	8	STOREBRO-ROYAL BISCY	FB	CBNCR	FBG	DS	IB	T300D	VLVO	12	10	27000	3	11	165000	181500
		1985 BOATS														
30	6	STOREBRO-ROYAL ADRIA	OP	CBNCR	FBG	RB	IB	T105D-T158D		10	6	11000	3	1	62000	74100
30	6	STOREBRO-ROYAL ADRIA	OP	CBNCR	FBG	RB	IB	T235D	VLVO	10	6	12000	3	1	77500	85200
30	6	STOREBRO-ROYAL BALTC	OP	CBNCR	FBG	RB	IB	T105D-T158D		10	6	11000	3	1	62000	74100
30	6	STOREBRO-ROYAL BALTC	OP	CBNCR	FBG	RB	IB	T235D	VLVO	10	6	12000	3	1	77500	85200
30	6	STOREBRO-ROYAL BALTC	HT	CBNCR	FBG	RB	IB	T105D-T158D		10	6	11500	3	1	63400	74100
30	6	STOREBRO-ROYAL BALTC	HT	CBNCR	FBG	RB	IB	T235D	VLVO	10	6	12500	3	1	78800	86500
30	6	STOREBRO-ROYAL BISCY	HT	CBNCR	FBG	RB	IB	T105D-T158D		10	6	12000	3	1	65000	77100
30	6	STOREBRO-ROYAL BISCY	HT	CBNCR	FBG	RB	IB	T235D	VLVO	10	6	13000	3	1	80000	88000
30	6	STOREBRO-ROYAL BISCY	FB	CBNCR	FBG	RB	IB	T105D-T158D		10	6	12500	3	1	66500	78600
30	6	STOREBRO-ROYAL BISCY	FB	CBNCR	FBG	RB	IB	T235D	VLVO	10	6	13500	3	1	81400	89400
30	6	STOREBRO-ROYAL PATRL	HT	CR	FBG		IB	T235D	VLVO	10	10	11000	3	1	59400	65200
34		STOREBRO-ROYAL BALTC	HT	CBNCR	FBG	DS	IB	T105D-T158D		10	6	12000	3	1	74600	87100
34		STOREBRO-ROYAL BALTC	HT	CBNCR	FBG	DS	IB	T235D	VLVO	10	6	13000	3	1	88100	96800
34		STOREBRO-ROYAL BALTC	FB	CBNCR	FBG	DS	IB	T105D-T158D		10	6	12500	3	1	75900	88400
34		STOREBRO-ROYAL BALTC	FB	CBNCR	FBG	DS	IB	T235D	VLVO	10	6	13500	3	1	89200	98000
34		STOREBRO-ROYAL BISCA	FB	CBNCR	FBG	DS	IB	T105D-T158D		10	6	12500	3	1	75900	88400
34		STOREBRO-ROYAL BISCA	FB	CBNCR	FBG	DS	IB	T235D	VLVO	10	6	13500	3	1	89200	98000
34		STOREBRO-ROYAL BISCY	HT	CBNCR	FBG	DS	IB	T105D-T158D		10	6	12000	3	1	74600	87100
34		STOREBRO-ROYAL BISCY	HT	CBNCR	FBG	DS	IB	T235D	VLVO	10	6	13000	3	1	88100	96800
34		STOREBRO-ROYAL WORK	HT	PH	FBG	RB	IB	T105D-T235D		10	10	12000	3	3	67400	80800
36	1	STOREBRO-ROYAL BALTC	HT	CBNCR	FBG	RB	IB	T235D	VLVO	12	6	19845	3	11	100500	110500
36	1	STOREBRO-ROYAL BALTC	FB	CBNCR	FBG	RB	IB	T235D	VLVO	12	6	19845	3	11	104000	114500
39	8	STOREBRO-ROYAL BALTC	HT	CBNCR	FBG	DS	IB	T235D	VLVO	12	10	25000	3	11	134000	147500
39	8	STOREBRO-ROYAL BALTC	HT	CBNCR	FBG	DS	IB	T300D	VLVO	12	10	26000	3	11	142000	156000
39	8	STOREBRO-ROYAL BALTC	FB	CBNCR	FBG	DS	IB	T235D	VLVO	12	10	26000	3	11	149000	163500
39	8	STOREBRO-ROYAL BALTC	FB	CBNCR	FBG	DS	IB	T300D	VLVO	12	10	27000	3	11	157000	173000
39	8	STOREBRO-ROYAL BISCY	HT	CBNCR	FBG	DS	IB	T235D	VLVO	12	10	25000	3	11	134000	147500
39	8	STOREBRO-ROYAL BISCY	HT	CBNCR	FBG	DS	IB	T300D	VLVO	12	10	26000	3	11	142000	156000
39	8	STOREBRO-ROYAL BISCY	FB	CBNCR	FBG	DS	IB	T235D	VLVO	12	10	26000	3	11	149000	163500
39	8	STOREBRO-ROYAL BISCY	FB	CBNCR	FBG	DS	IB	T300D	VLVO	12	10	27000	3	11	157000	173000
		1984 BOATS														
30	6	STOREBRO-ROYAL ADRIA	OP	CBNCR	FBG	RB	IB	T129D-T158D		10	6	11000	3	1	61900	71200
30	6	STOREBRO-ROYAL ADRIA	OP	CBNCR	FBG	RB	IB	T240D	VLVO	10	6	12000	3	1	74900	82300
30	6	STOREBRO-ROYAL BALTC	OP	CBNCR	FBG	RB	IB	T129D-T158D		10	6	11000	3	1	61900	71200
30	6	STOREBRO-ROYAL BALTC	OP	CBNCR	FBG	RB	IB	T240D	VLVO	10	6	12000	3	1	74900	82300
30	6	STOREBRO-ROYAL BALTC	HT	CBNCR	FBG	RB	IB	T129D-T158D		10	6	11500	3	1	63200	71200
30	6	STOREBRO-ROYAL BALTC	HT	CBNCR	FBG	RB	IB	T240D	VLVO	10	6	12500	3	1	76000	83600
30	6	STOREBRO-ROYAL BISCY	HT	CBNCR	FBG	RB	IB	T129D-T158D		10	6	12000	3	1	64600	74000
30	6	STOREBRO-ROYAL BISCY	HT	CBNCR	FBG	RB	IB	T240D	VLVO	10	6	13000	3	1	77300	84900
30	6	STOREBRO-ROYAL BISCY	FB	CBNCR	FBG	RB	IB	T129D-T158D		10	6	12500	3	1	66000	75400
30	6	STOREBRO-ROYAL BISCY	FB	CBNCR	FBG	RB	IB	T240D	VLVO	10	6	13500	3	1	78500	86300
30	6	STOREBRO-ROYAL PATRL	HT	CR	FBG		IB	T240D	VLVO	10	10	11000	3	1	57300	62900
33	1	STOREBRO-ROYAL 33	SLP	SA/CR	FBG	KL	SD	35D	VLVO	11	2	10600	5	5	46400	51000
34		STOREBRO-ROYAL BALTC	HT	CBNCR	FBG	DS	IB	T129D-T158D		10	6	12000	3	1	73700	83600
34		STOREBRO-ROYAL BALTC	HT	CBNCR	FBG	DS	IB	T240D	VLVO	10	6	13000	3	1	85000	93400
34		STOREBRO-ROYAL BALTC	FB	CBNCR	FBG	DS	IB	T129D-T158D		10	6	12500	3	1	74800	84800
34		STOREBRO-ROYAL BALTC	FB	CBNCR	FBG	DS	IB	T240D	VLVO	10	6	13500	3	1	86100	94600
34		STOREBRO-ROYAL BISCY	HT	CBNCR	FBG	DS	IB	T129D-T158D		10	6	12000	3	1	73700	83600
34		STOREBRO-ROYAL BISCY	HT	CBNCR	FBG	DS	IB	T240D	VLVO	10	6	13000	3	1	85000	93400
34		STOREBRO-ROYAL BISCY	FB	CBNCR	FBG	DS	IB	T129D-T158D		10	6	12500	3	1	74800	84800
34		STOREBRO-ROYAL BISCY	FB	CBNCR	FBG	DS	IB	T240D	VLVO	10	6	13500	3	1	86100	94600
34		STOREBRO-ROYAL WORK	HT	PH	FBG	RB	IB	79D-240D		10	10	12000	3	3	60800	70100
34		STOREBRO-ROYAL WORK	HT	PH	FBG	RB	IB	T79D-T240D		10	10	12000	3	3	64700	77800
36	1	STOREBRO-ROYAL BALTC	HT	CBNCR	FBG	RB	IB	T240D	VLVO	12	6	19845	3	11	96700	106000
36	1	STOREBRO-ROYAL BALTC	FB	CBNCR	FBG	RB	IB	T240D	VLVO	12	6	19845	3	11	99800	109500
39	8	STOREBRO-ROYAL BALTC	HT	CBNCR	FBG	DS	IB	T240D	VLVO	12	10	25000	3	11	129000	141500
39	8	STOREBRO-ROYAL BALTC	HT	CBNCR	FBG	DS	IB	T291D	VLVO	12	10	26000	3	11	135500	149000
39	8	STOREBRO-ROYAL BALTC	FB	CBNCR	FBG	DS	IB	T240D	VLVO	12	10	26000	3	11	142000	156500
39	8	STOREBRO-ROYAL BALTC	FB	CBNCR	FBG	DS	IB	T291D	VLVO	12	10	27000	3	11	149500	164000
39	8	STOREBRO-ROYAL BISCY	HT	CBNCR	FBG	DS	IB	T240D	VLVO	12	10	25000	3	11	129000	141500
39	8	STOREBRO-ROYAL BISCY	HT	CBNCR	FBG	DS	IB	T291D	VLVO	12	10	26000	3	11	135500	149000
39	8	STOREBRO-ROYAL BISCY	FB	CBNCR	FBG	DS	IB	T240D	VLVO	12	10	26000	3	11	142000	156500
39	8	STOREBRO-ROYAL BISCY	FB	CBNCR	FBG	DS	IB	T291D	VLVO	12	10	27000	3	11	149500	164000

....For earlier years, see the BUC Used Boat Price Guide, Volume 3

STRATOS BOATS INC

MURFREESBORO TN 37127 COAST GUARD MFG ID- BNZ See inside cover to adjust price for area

For more recent years, see the BUC Used Boat Price Guide, Volume 1

LOA FT	LOA IN	NAME AND/ OR MODEL	TOP/ RIG	BOAT TYPE	HULL MTL	HULL TP	ENGINE TP	ENGINE #	ENGINE HP	ENGINE MFG	BEAM FT	BEAM IN	WGT LBS	DRAFT FT	DRAFT IN	RETAIL LOW	RETAIL HIGH
		1996 BOATS															
16	4	1700 FLATS	OP	FSH	FBG	SV	OB				7	3	995	1		3950	4600
16	8	268DC	OP	BASS	FBG	SV	OB				6	10	1090			4550	5250
16	8	268FS	OP	BASS	FBG	SV	OB				6	10	1180			4850	5600
16	8	268V	OP	BASS	FBG	SV	OB				6	8	1050			4400	5050
16	9	1700SP	OP	FSH	FBG	SV	OB				7	5	1350			5200	5950
17	4	1700CC	OP	CTRCN	FBG	SV	OB				7	3	995	1		4200	4850
17	5	217CF	OP	BASS	FBG	SV	OB				7	1	1290			5300	6100
17	9	278DC	OP	BASS	FBG	SV	OB				7	7	1370			5600	6450
17	9	278FS	OP	BASS	FBG	SV	OB				7	7	1390			5650	6500
17	9	278V	OP	BASS	FBG	SV	OB				7	6	1340			5500	6300
18		1850CC	OP	CTRCN	FBG	DV	OB				7	4	1880			6800	7800
18		1850DC	OP	FSH	FBG	DV	OB				7	4	1880			6700	7700
18	3	288DCR	OP	BASS	FBG	SV	OB				7	7	1390			5250	6050
18	3	288FS	OP	BASS	FBG	SV	OB				7	7	1390			6150	7100
18	3	288VF	OP	BASS	FBG	SV	OB				7	7	1340			5550	6400
18	3	288VR	OP	BASS	FBG	SV	OB				7	7	1370			5650	6500
18	10	280S/F	OP	BASS	FBG	SV	OB				7	6	1460			6050	6950
18	10	285XL	OP	BASS	FBG	SV	OB				7	5	1260			5400	6200
18	10	285XLDC	OP	BASS	FBG	SV	OB				7	5	1290			5500	6300
19	1	1900SP	OP	FSH	FBG	SV	OB				8		1725			6550	7500
19	1	1900SP-T	OP	FSH	FBG	SV	OB				8		1725			6650	7650
19	1	1900SP-V	OP	FSH	FBG	SV	OB				8		1725			6600	7600
19	3	219CF	OP	BASS	FBG	SV	OB				7	7	1300			5600	6450
19	3	219DC	OP	BASS	FBG	SV	OB				7	7	1330			5700	6550
19	8	2000CC	OP	CTRCN	FBG	DV	OB				8	3	2420			8300	9550
19	8	2000DC	OP	FSH	FBG	DV	OB				8	3	2420			8350	9600
20	1	201F/S	OP	BASS	FBG	SV	OB				7	9	1500			7050	8100
20	1	2050WA	OP	CUD	FBG	DV	OB				8	1	2600			10100	11500
20	4	201XL	OP	BASS	FBG	SV	OB				7	7	1440			6900	7900
20	4	201XLDC	OP	BASS	FBG	SV	OB				7	7	1470			7000	8050
20	4	201XLPD	OP	BASS	FBG	SV	OB				7	7	1490			7050	8150
20	7	290S/F	OP	BASS	FBG	SV	OB				7	11	1625			7750	8900
21	8	2100SP	OP	FSH	FBG	SV	OB				8		1400			6750	7800
21	8	2100SP-T	OP	FSH	FBG	SV	OB				8		1400			6700	7700
21	8	2100SP-V	OP	FSH	FBG	SV	OB				8		1400			6800	7850
22	1	2250CC	OP	CTRCN	FBG	DV	OB				8	6	2700			11500	13100
22	1	2250WA	OP	CUD	FBG	DV	OB				8	6	2900			12800	14500
24	1	2250CD	OP	FSH	FBG	SV	OB				8	6	2900			13500	15400
24	5	2300WA	OP	CUD	FBG	DV	OB				9		4200			18800	20900
26	5	2500WA	OP	CUD	FBG	DV	OB				9	10	5800			22800	25400
28	7	2700CC	OP	CTRCN	FBG	DV	OB				8	6	5200			23100	25700
28	7	2700CX	OP	CUD	FBG	DV	OB				8	6	5200			25600	28400
28	7	2700WA	OP	CUD	FBG	DV	OB				8	6	5400			25600	28400
32	5	3300CC	OP	CTRCN	FBG	DV	OB				9		5800			30800	34200
		1995 BOATS															
16	4	1700 FLATS	OP	FSH	FBG	SV	OB				7	3	995	1		3700	4300
16	8	268DC	OP	BASS	FBG	SV	OB				6	10	1090			4300	5000
16	8	268FS	OP	BASS	FBG	SV	OB				6	10	1180			4600	5300
16	8	268V	OP	BASS	FBG	SV	OB				6	8	1050			4150	4850
16	9	1700SP	OP	FSH	FBG	SV	OB				7	5	1250			4650	5300
17	4	1700CC	OP	CTRCN	FBG	SV	OB				7	3	995	1		3950	4600
17	5	217CF	OP	BASS	FBG	SV	OB				7	1	1290			5000	5750
17	9	275XL	OP	BASS	FBG	SV	OB				7		1200			4750	5500
17	9	278DC	OP	BASS	FBG	SV	OB				7	7	1370			5300	6050
17	9	278FS	OP	BASS	FBG	SV	OB				7	7	1390			5350	6150
17	11	284DCR	OP	BASS	FBG	SV	OB				7	7	1380			5100	5900
17	11	284FS	OP	BASS	FBG	SV	OB				7	7	1400			5600	6450
17	11	284VF	OP	BASS	FBG	SV	OB				7	7	1340			5150	5900
17	11	284VR	OP	BASS	FBG	SV	OB				7	7	1340			5300	6100
18		1850CC	OP	CTRCN	FBG	DV	OB				7	4	1880			6450	7400
18		1850DC	OP	FSH	FBG	DV	OB				7	4	1880			6350	7300
18	10	280S/F	OP	BASS	FBG	SV	OB				7	6	1460			5700	6550
18	10	285XL	OP	BASS	FBG	SV	OB				7	5	1260			5100	5850
19	1	1900SP	OP	FSH	FBG	SV	OB				8		1400			5400	6200
19	3	219CF	OP	BASS	FBG	SV	OB				7	7	1300			5300	6100
19	3	219DC	OP	BASS	FBG	SV	OB				7	7	1330			5400	6200
19	8	2000CC	OP	CTRCN	FBG	DV	OB				8	3	2420			7850	9000
19	8	2000DC	OP	FSH	FBG	DV	OB				8	3	2420			7900	9050
20	1	201F/S	OP	BASS	FBG	SV	OB				7	9	1500			6650	7650
20	1	2050WA	OP	CUD	FBG	DV	OB				8	1	2600			9550	10900
20	4	201SKI	OP	BASS	FBG	SV	OB				7	7	1350			6150	7100
20	4	201XL	OP	BASS	FBG	SV	OB				7	7	1440			6500	7450
20	4	201XLPD	OP	BASS	FBG	SV	OB				7	7	1490			6700	7650
20	7	290S/F	OP	BASS	FBG	SV	OB				7	11	1625			7250	8300
21	8	2100SP	OP	FSH	FBG	SV	OB				8		1650			7350	8450
22	1	2250CC	OP	CTRCN	FBG	DV	OB				8	6	2700			10900	12400
22	1	2250WA	OP	CUD	FBG	DV	OB				8	6	2900			12100	13700
24	1	2250CD	OP	FSH	FBG	SV	OB				8	6	2900			12800	14500
24	5	2300WA	OP	CUD	FBG	DV	OB				9		4200			18200	20200
26	5	2500WA	OP	CUD	FBG	DV	OB				9	10	5800			21600	24000
28	7	2700CC	OP	CTRCN	FBG	DV	OB				8	6	5200			21800	24300
28	7	2700CX	OP	CUD	FBG	DV	OB				8	6	5000			24200	26800
28	7	2700WA	OP	CUD	FBG	DV	OB				8	6	5400			24200	26800
32	5	3300CC	OP	CTRCN	FBG	DV	OB				9		5800			29100	32300
		1994 BOATS															
16		1500CC	OP	CTRCN	FBG	SV	OB				7	3	895			3250	3800
16	2	260F/S	OP	BASS	FBG	SV	OB				6	10	990			3650	4250
16	2	260V	OP	BASS	FBG	SV	OB				6	10	900			3350	3900
16	2	264DC	OP	BASS	FBG	SV	OB				6	10	1080			4000	4650
16	2	264V	OP	BASS	FBG	SV	OB				6	10	1050			3900	4550
16	4	1700 FLATS	OP	FSH	FBG	SV	OB				7	3	995	1		3500	4100
16	10	264F/S	OP	BASS	FBG	SV	OB				7		1280			4650	5350
17	4	1700CC	OP	CTRCN	FBG	SV	OB				7	3	995	1		3700	4300
17	5	217F	OP	BASS	FBG	SV	OB				7	1	1290			4750	5450
17	5	217TF	OP	BASS	FBG	SV	OB				7	1	1180			4450	5100
17	9	270DC	OP	BASS	FBG	SV	OB				7	5	1370			5000	5750
17	9	270FS	OP	BASS	FBG	SV	OB				7	5	1390			5050	5800
17	9	270VF	OP	BASS	FBG	SV	OB				7	5	1340			4900	5650
17	9	275XL	OP	BASS	FBG	SV	OB				7		1200			4550	5200
17	11	284DC	OP	BASS	FBG	SV	OB				7	7	1390			4900	5600
17	11	284FS	OP	BASS	FBG	SV	OB				7	7	1390			5300	6050
17	11	284VF	OP	BASS	FBG	SV	OB				7	7	1340			4850	5600
17	11	284VR	OP	BASS	FBG	SV	OB				7	7	1340			5000	5750
18		1850CC	OP	CTRCN	FBG	DV	OB				7	4	1880			6100	7000
18		1850DC	OP	FSH	FBG	DV	OB				7	4	1880			6000	6900
18	8	285XL	OP	BASS	FBG	SV	OB				7	5	1260			4800	5500
18	8	285XLDC	OP	BASS	FBG	SV	OB				7	5	1290			4900	5600
18	10	280S/F	OP	BASS	FBG	SV	OB				7	6	1460			5400	6200
19		219DC	OP	BASS	FBG	SV	OB				7	7	1330			5050	5800
19		219F	OP	BASS	FBG	SV	OB				7	7	1300			4950	5700
19	1	1900SP	OP	FSH	FBG	SV	OB				8		1200			4550	5250
19	6	289F/S	OP	BASS	FBG	SV	OB				7	11	1575			5850	6750
19	8	2000CC	OP	CTRCN	FBG	DV	OB				8	3	2420			7350	8450
19	8	2000DC	OP	FSH	FBG	DV	OB				8	3	2420			7400	8500
20	1	2050WA	OP	CUD	FBG	DV	OB				8	1	2600			9050	10300
20	3	201XL	OP	BASS	FBG	SV	OB				7	7	1440			6150	7050
20	3	201XLPD	OP	BASS	FBG	SV	OB				7	7	1490			6300	7250
20	4	201SKI	OP	BASS	FBG	SV	OB				7	7	1350			5850	6700
20	4	290S/F	OP	BASS	FBG	SV	OB				7	11	1625			6750	7750
21	8	2100SP	OP	FSH	FBG	SV	OB				8		1400			6050	6950
22	1	2250CC	OP	CTRCN	FBG	DV	OB				8	6	2700			10300	11700
22	1	2250WA	OP	CUD	FBG	DV	OB				8	6	2900			11400	13000
24	5	2300WA	OP	CUD	FBG	DV	OB				9		4200			16800	19100
26	5	2500WA	OP	CUD	FBG	DV	OB				9	10	5800			20600	22900
28	7	2700CC	OP	CTRCN	FBG	DV	OB				8	6	5200			20900	23200
28	7	2700CX	OP	CUD	FBG	DV	OB				8	6	5000			22900	25400
28	7	2700WA	OP	CUD	FBG	DV	OB				8	6	5400			22900	25400
32	5	3300CC	OP	CTRCN	FBG	DV	OB				9		5800			27600	30600
		1993 BOATS															
16	2	260F/S	OP	BASS	FBG	SV	OB				6	10	990			3450	4050
16	2	260V	OP	BASS	FBG	SV	OB				6	10	900			3200	3700
16	2	264DC	OP	BASS	FBG	SV	OB				6	10	1080			3800	4400
16	2	264V	OP	BASS	FBG	SV	OB				6	10	1050			3650	4250
16	10	364F/S	OP	BASS	FBG	SV	OB				7		1280			4450	5100
17	5	217F	OP	BASS	FBG	SV	OB				7	1	1290			4500	5200
17	5	217TF	OP	BASS	FBG	SV	OB				7	1	1180			4200	4900
17	9	274DCC	OP	BASS	FBG	SV	OB				7	7	1370			4750	5450
17	9	274F/S	OP	BASS	FBG	SV	OB				7	7	1390			4800	5500
17	9	274VF	OP	BASS	FBG	SV	OB				7	7	1340			4650	5350
17	9	275XL	OP	BASS	FBG	SV	OB				7		1200			4300	5000
18		1850CC	OP	CTRCN	FBG	DV	OB				7	4	1880			5700	6550
18		1850DC	OP	OFF	FBG	DV	OB				7	4	1880			5750	6600

CONTINUED ON NEXT PAGE

LOA FT	LOA IN	NAME AND/ OR MODEL	TOP/ RIG	BOAT TYPE	HULL MTL	HULL TP	ENGINE TP	ENGINE # HP	ENGINE MFG	BEAM FT	BEAM IN	WGT LBS	DRAFT FT	DRAFT IN	RETAIL LOW	RETAIL HIGH
		1993 BOATS														
18	8	285XL	OP	BASS	FBG	SV	OB			7	5	1260			4600	5250
18	8	285XLDC	OP	BASS	FBG	SV	OB			7	5	1290			4650	5350
18	10	280S/F	OP	BASS	FBG	SV	OB			7	6	1460			5100	5900
19		219DC	OP	BASS	FBG	SV	OB			7	7	1330			4800	5500
19		219F	OP	BASS	FBG	SV	OB			7	7	1300			4700	5450
19	4	295DCC	OP	BASS	FBG	SV	OB			7	7	1480			5250	6050
19	4	295DD	OP	BASS	FBG	SV	OB			7	7	1450			5200	5950
19	6	289F/S	OP	BASS	FBG	SV	OB			7	11	1575			5550	6400
19	8	2000CC	OP	CTRCN	FBG	DV	OB			8	3	2420			6800	7800
19	8	2000DC	OP	OFF	FBG	DV	OB			8	3	2420			7100	8200
20	1	2050WA	OP	OFF	FBG	DV	OB			8	1	2600			8150	9350
20	3	201SKI	OP	BASS	FBG	SV	OB			7	7	1350			5500	6350
20	3	201XL	OP	BASS	FBG	SV	OB			7	7	1440			5800	6700
20	3	201XLDC	OP	BASS	FBG	SV	OB			7	7	1470			5900	6800
20	3	201XLPD	OP	BASS	FBG	SV	OB			7	7	1490			5950	6850
20	4	290S/F	OP	BASS	FBG	SV	OB			7	11	1625			6400	7350
22	1	2250CC	OP	CTRCN	FBG	DV	OB			8	6	2700			9800	11200
22	1	2250WA	OP	CUD	FBG	DV	OB			8	6	2900			10800	12300
24	5	2300WA	OP	CUD	FBG	DV	OB			9		4200			16000	18100
26	5	2500WA	OP	CUD	FBG	DV	OB			9	10	5800			19600	21800
28	7	2700CC	OP	CTRCN	FBG	DV	OB			8	6	5200			20100	22400
28	7	2700CX	OP	CUD	FBG	DV	OB			8	6	5000			21700	24100
28	7	2700WA	OP	CUD	FBG	DV	OB			8	6	5400			21700	24100
32	5	3300CC	OP	CTRCN	FBG	DV	OB			9		5800			26100	29100
		1992 BOATS														
16	2	264V	OP	BASS	FBG	SV	OB			6	10	1050			3500	4050
16	10	264V F/S	OP	FSH	FBG	SV	OB			7		1285			4050	4700
17	5	TF-217	OP	FSH	FBG	SV	OB			7	1	1180			3850	4450
17	9	274 DCC	OP	BASS	FBG	SV	OB			7	7	1370			4250	4950
17	9	274 F/S	OP	FSH	FBG	SV	OB			7	7	1370			4350	5000
17	9	274 VF	OP	BASS	FBG	SV	OB			7	7	1340			4450	5150
17	9	275 PF	OP	BASS	FBG	SV	OB			7	7	1370			4800	5500
18		1850 CC	ST	CTRCN	FBG	DV	OB			7	4	1880			5400	6200
18		1850 DC	ST	FSH	FBG	DV	OB			7	4	1880			5500	6300
18	7	285 PF	OP	BASS	FBG	SV	OB			7	7	1390			4650	5350
18	7	285 SKI	OP	SKI	FBG	SV	OB			7	7	1257			4000	4650
18	8	285 XL	OP	BASS	FBG	SV	OB			7	1	1290			4350	5000
18	8	285 XLDC	OP	BASS	FBG	SV	OB			7	1	1290			4500	5200
19		F-219	OP	FSH	FBG	SV	OB			7	7	1300			4350	5000
19	4	295 DCC	OP	BASS	FBG	SV	OB			7	7	1450			5000	5750
19	4	295 PD	OP	BASS	FBG	SV	OB			7	7	1450			4900	5650
19	6	289 F/S	OP	FSH	FBG	SV	OB			7	11	1575			5100	5850
19	8	2000 CC	ST	CTRCN	FBG	DV	OB			8	3	2420			6450	7450
19	8	2000 DC	ST	FSH	FBG	DV	OB			8	3	2420			6850	7850
20	1	2050 WA	ST	CUD	FBG	DV	OB			8	1	2600			8150	9400
20	3	201 DCC	OP	BASS	FBG	SV	OB			7	7	1550			5900	6750
20	3	201 DCPD	OP	BASS	FBG	SV	OB			7	7	1550			5900	6800
20	3	201 PD	OP	BASS	FBG	SV	OB			7	7	1550			5800	6650
20	3	201 SKI	OP	SKI	FBG	SV	OB			7	7	1350			4900	5650
20	3	201 XL	OP	BASS	FBG	SV	OB			7	7	1470			5500	6350
20	3	201 XLDC	OP	BASS	FBG	SV	OB			7	7	1470			5700	6550
20	3	201P/201PF	OP	BASS	FBG	SV	OB			7	7	1495			5700	6550
20	4	290 SF	OP	SKI	FBG	SV	OB			7	11	1625			5700	6550
22	1	2250 CC	ST	CTRCN	FBG	DV	OB			8	6	2700			9350	10600
22	1	2250 WA	ST	CUD	FBG	DV	OB			8	6	2900			10300	11700
22	6	2260 WA	ST	CUD	FBG	DV	OB			9		4200			12900	14600
24	5	2450 WA	ST	CUD	FBG	DV	OB			9	10	5800			18000	20000
26	2	2600 CC	ST	CTRCN	FBG	DV	OB			8	6	5000			16900	19300
26	2	2600 CX	ST	CUD	FBG	DV	OB			8	6	5000			17400	19800
26	2	2600 WA	ST	CUD	FBG	DV	OB			8	6	5000			19800	22000
32	5	3300 CC	ST	CTRCN	FBG	DV	OB			9		5800			24900	27700

STREBLOW BOATS INC

KENOSHA WI 53143

See inside cover to adjust price for area

LOA FT	LOA IN	NAME AND/ OR MODEL	TOP/ RIG	BOAT TYPE	HULL MTL	HULL TP	ENGINE TP	ENGINE # HP	ENGINE MFG	BEAM FT	BEAM IN	WGT LBS	DRAFT FT	DRAFT IN	RETAIL LOW	RETAIL HIGH
		1984 BOATS														
20	1	STREBLOW	OP	RNBT	WD	DV	IB	330	CHRY	7	5	3400	2		17400	19800
23		STREBLOW	OP	RNBT	WD	DV	IB	330	CHRY	8		4300	2		23800	26400
23		STREBLOW	OP	RNBT	WD	DV	VD	330	CHRY	8		4300	2		24100	26800
26		STREBLOW	OP	RNBT	WD	DV	IB	330	CHRY	9	4	5600	2	4	33500	37300
26		STREBLOW	OP	RNBT	WD	DV	VD	330	CHRY	9	4	5600	2	4	33900	37700

....For earlier years, see the BUC Used Boat Price Guide, Volume 3

STRIKE YACHTS

DEERFIELD BEACH FL 33442

See inside cover to adjust price for area

For more recent years, see the BUC Used Boat Price Guide, Volume 1

LOA FT	LOA IN	NAME AND/ OR MODEL	TOP/ RIG	BOAT TYPE	HULL MTL	HULL TP	ENGINE TP	ENGINE # HP	ENGINE MFG	BEAM FT	BEAM IN	WGT LBS	DRAFT FT	DRAFT IN	RETAIL LOW	RETAIL HIGH
		1988 BOATS														
26		STRIKE	OP	CTRCN	FBG	SV	OB			8		5800	2	2	27600	30700
26		STRIKE	OP	CTRCN	FBG	SV	IB	220-350		8		5800	2	2	16600	20300
26		STRIKE	OP	CTRCN	FBG	SV	IB	200D-275D		8		5800	2	2	22600	26800
26		STRIKE	OP	RNBT	FBG	SV	OB			8		5800	2	2	27700	30800
26		STRIKE	OP	RNBT	FBG	SV	IB	220-350		8		5800	2	2	16400	19900
26		STRIKE	OP	RNBT	FBG	SV	IB	200D-275D		8		5800	2	2	22100	26100
29		STRIKE	OP	CTRCN	FBG	SV	IB	T220-T270		10	11	11280	2	6	29100	33300
29		STRIKE	OP	CTRCN	FBG	SV	IB	T200D-T250D		10	11	11280	2	6	42500	49200
29		STRIKE	OP	RNBT	FBG	SV	IB	T220-T270		10	11	11280	2	6	28700	32700
29		STRIKE	OP	RNBT	FBG	SV	IB	T200D-T275D		10	11	11280	2	6	41500	49000
		1987 BOATS														
26		STRIKE	OP	CUD	FBG	SV	OB			8			2	2	25300	28200
26		STRIKE	OP	CUD	FBG	SV	IB	220-350		8			2	2	13900	17300
26		STRIKE	OP	CUD	FBG	SV	IB	200D-275D		8			2	2	20300	24100
26		STRIKE		RNBT	FBG	SV	OB			8			2	2	23500	26100
26		STRIKE	OP	RNBT	FBG	SV	IB	220-350		8			2	2	13200	16400
26		STRIKE	OP	RNBT	FBG	SV	IB	200D-275D		8			2	2	19200	22900
29		STRIKE	OP	CUD	FBG	SV	IB	T220-T270		10	11		2	6	23400	27100
29		STRIKE	OP	CUD	FBG	SV	IB	T200D-T240D		10	11		2	6	28400	33900
29		STRIKE	OP	RNBT	FBG	SV	IB	T220-T270		10	11		2	6	22800	26300
29		STRIKE	OP	RNBT	FBG	SV	IB	T200D-T275D		10	11		2	6	27100	33600
		1985 BOATS														
26		OPENFISH CTR	OP	CTRCN	FBG	SV	IB	165D-240D		8		6500	2	2	21000	25300
26		OPENFISH CTR	TT	CTRCN	FBG	SV	IB	165D-240D		8		6500	2	2	21000	25300
26		RUNABOUT	OP	RNBT	FBG	SV	IB	165D-240D		8		6500	2	2	20600	24800
29		OPENFISH CTR	OP	CTRCN	FBG	SV	IB	T165D-T240D		10	11	13500	2	6	41500	49100
29		OPENFISH CTR	TT	CTRCN	FBG	SV	IB	T165D-T240D		10	11	13500	2	6	41500	49100

STRIK COAST GUARD MFG ID- SAY

See inside cover to adjust price for area

LOA FT	LOA IN	NAME AND/ OR MODEL	TOP/ RIG	BOAT TYPE	HULL MTL	HULL TP	ENGINE TP	ENGINE # HP	ENGINE MFG	BEAM FT	BEAM IN	WGT LBS	DRAFT FT	DRAFT IN	RETAIL LOW	RETAIL HIGH
		1987 BOATS														
36		STRIKER 36	FB	SDNSF	AL	SV	IB	T450D	GM	14	7	17000	2	8	128000	140500
50		STRIKER 50	FB	SDNSF	AL	SV	IB	T750D	GM	16	8	30000	3	10	285000	313500
58		STRIKER 58	FB	SDNSF	AL	SV	IB	T11CD	GM	19	6	51480	3	11	443000	487000
62		STRIKER 62	FB	SDNSF	AL	SV	IB	T11CD	GM	21		68000	3	10	523000	575000
70		STRIKER 70	FB	SDNSF	AL	SV	IB	T13CD	MTU	23	6	99000	3	11	926000	1.005M
		1986 BOATS														
62		STRIKER 62	FB	SDNSF	AL	SV	IB	T D	GM	20	8	65000	3	2	**	**
62		STRIKER 62	FB	SDNSF	AL	SV	IB	T870D	GM	20	8	65000	3	2	443500	487000
70		STRIKER 70	FB	SDNSF	AL	SV	IB	T13CD	MTU	23	6	80000	3	8	820500	901500
		1985 BOATS														
62		STRIKER 62	FB	SDNSF	AL	SV	IB	T840D	GM	20	8	45000	3	6	372500	409000
70		STRIKER 70	FB	SDNSF	AL	SV	IB	T13CD	MTU	23	6	80000	3	10	785500	863500
		1984 BOATS														
60		STRIKER 60	FB	SDNSF	AL	SV	IB	T840D	GM	20	8	45000	3	6	324000	356000
70		STRIKER 70	FB	SDNSF	AL	SV	IB	T13CD	MTU	23	6	80000	3	10	752500	827000

....For earlier years, see the BUC Used Boat Price Guide, Volume 3

STRINGARI SKIFFS

FIBERGLASSING SHOP
SAN DIEGO CA 92110

See inside cover to adjust price for area

COAST GUARD MFG ID- TFL
FORMERLY FIBERGLASS SHOP*THE

LOA FT	LOA IN	NAME AND/ OR MODEL	TOP/ RIG	BOAT TYPE	HULL MTL	HULL TP	ENGINE TP	ENGINE # HP	ENGINE MFG	BEAM FT	BEAM IN	WGT LBS	DRAFT FT	DRAFT IN	RETAIL LOW	RETAIL HIGH
		1986 BOATS														
18		STRINGARI CB		CTRCN	F/S	SV	IO	151	VLVO	8		2300	1	9	5650	6500
18		STRINGARI CTRCN		CTRCN	FBG	SV	IO	151	VLVO	8		2000	1	9	5300	6100
		1984 BOATS														
18		STRINGARI SKIFFS	OP	CTRCN	FBG	SV	IO	138	VLVO	8		1950	1	10	4850	5600

....For earlier years, see the BUC Used Boat Price Guide, Volume 3

STUART ANGLER CORP
MIAMI FL 33054   COAST GUARD MFG ID- XAL See inside cover to adjust price for area

For more recent years, see the BUC Used Boat Price Guide, Volume 1

LOA FT IN	NAME AND/ OR MODEL	TOP/ RIG	BOAT TYPE	-HULL- MTL TP	----ENGINE--- TP # HP MFG	BEAM FT IN	WGT LBS	DRAFT FT IN	RETAIL LOW	RETAIL HIGH
25 6	8 METER O/F	OP	OPFSH	FBG DV	OB	8	4500	3	12600	14300
30 6	9 METER O/F	OP	OPFSH	FBG DV	OB	8	6500	3 6	22400	24900
32 6	STUART ANGLER	OP	OPFSH	FBG DV	IO T300D	11	10500	3	52400	57600
32 6	STUART ANGLER	OP	OPFSH	FBG SV	OB	11	10000	3	30300	33700

....For earlier years, see the BUC Used Boat Price Guide, Volume 3

STUART MARINE CORP
ROCKLAND ME 04841   See inside cover to adjust price for area

For more recent years, see the BUC Used Boat Price Guide, Volume 1

LOA FT IN	NAME AND/ OR MODEL	TOP/ RIG	BOAT TYPE	-HULL- MTL TP	----ENGINE--- TP # HP MFG	BEAM FT IN	WGT LBS	DRAFT FT IN	RETAIL LOW	RETAIL HIGH
1996 BOATS										
19 2	MARINER 19	SLP	SAROD	FBG CB	OB	7	1305	10	9250	10500
19 2	MARINER 19	SLP	SAROD	FBG KL	OB	7	1430	3 3	9600	10900
19 2	RHODES 19	SLP	SAROD	FBG CB	OB	7	1030	10	8150	9400
19 2	RHODES 19	SLP	SAROD	FBG KL	OB	7	1325	3 3	9300	10500
1995 BOATS										
19 2	MARINER 19	SLP	SAROD	FBG CB	OB	7	1305	10	8600	9850
19 2	MARINER 19	SLP	SAROD	FBG KL	OB	7	1430	3 3	9100	10300
19 2	RHODES 19	SLP	SAROD	FBG CB	OB	7	1030	10	7650	8800
19 2	RHODES 19	SLP	SAROD	FBG KL	OB	7	1325	3 3	8650	9950
1994 BOATS										
19 2	MARINER	SLP	SAROD	FBG CB	OB	7	1305	10	8050	9250
19 2	MARINER	SLP	SAROD	FBG KL	OB	7	1430	3 3	8450	9700
19 2	RHODES 19	SLP	SAROD	FBG CB	OB	7	1030	10	7200	8300
19 2	RHODES 19	SLP	SAROD	FBG KL	OB	7	1325	3 3	8100	9350
1993 BOATS										
19 2	MARINER	SLP	SAROD	FBG CB	OB	7	1305	10	7600	8700
19 2	MARINER	SLP	SAROD	FBG KL	OB	7	1430	3 10	7950	9100
19 2	RHODES 19	SLP	SAROD	FBG CB	OB	7	1030	10	6750	7800
19 2	RHODES 19	SLP	SAROD	FBG KL	OB	7	1325	3 3	7650	8800
1992 BOATS										
19 2	MARINER	SLP	SA/OD	FBG CB	OB	7	1305	10	7100	8200
19 2	MARINER	SLP	SA/OD	FBG KL	OB	7	1430	3 10	7450	8600
19 2	RHODES 19	SLP	SA/OD	FBG CB	OB	7	1030	10	6350	7300
19 2	RHODES 19	SLP	SA/OD	FBG KL	OB	7	1325	3 3	7200	8250
1991 BOATS										
19 2	MARINER C/B	SLP	SA/OD	FBG CB	OB	7	1305	10	6700	7700
19 2	MARINER KEEL	SLP	SA/OD	FBG KL	OB	7	1430	3 10	7000	8050
19 2	RHODES 19 C/B	SLP	SA/OD	FBG CB	OB	7	1030	10	6000	6900
19 2	RHODES 19 KEEL	SLP	SA/OD	FBG KL	OB	7	1325	3 3	6750	7750
1990 BOATS										
19 2	MARINER C/B	SLP	SA/OD	FBG KC	OB	7	1305	10	6300	7250
19 2	MARINER KEEL	SLP	SA/OD	FBG KL	OB	7	1430	3 10	6600	7600
19 2	RHODES 19 C/B	SLP	SA/OD	FBG KC	OB	7	1030	10	5650	6500
19 2	RHODES 19 KEEL	SLP	SA/OD	FBG KL	OB	7	1325	3 3	6350	7300
1989 BOATS										
19 2	MARINER C/B	SLP	SA/OD	FBG KC	OB	7	1305	10	5900	6800
19 2	MARINER KEEL	SLP	SA/OD	FBG KL	OB	7	1430	3 10	6200	7150
19 2	RHODES 19 C/B	SLP	SA/OD	FBG KC	OB	7	1030	10	5300	6100
19 2	RHODES 19 KEEL	SLP	SA/OD	FBG KL	OB	7	1325	3 3	5950	6850
1988 BOATS										
19 2	MARINER	SLP	SA/OD	FBG CB	OB	7	1305	10	5600	6400
19 2	MARINER	SLP	SA/OD	FBG KL	OB	7	1430	3 3	5850	6700
19 2	RHODES 19	SLP	SA/OD	FBG CB	OB	7	1030	10	5000	5750
19 2	RHODES 19	SLP	SA/OD	FBG KL	OB	7	1325	3 3	5600	6450
1987 BOATS										
19 2	MARINER	SLP	SA/OD	FBG CB	OB	7	1305	10	5250	6050
19 2	MARINER	SLP	SA/OD	FBG CB	OB	7	1430	3 10	5500	6300
19 2	MARINER	SLP	SA/OD	FBG CB	OB	7	1030	10	4700	5400
19 2	RHODES 19	SLP	SA/OD	FBG KL	OB	7	1325	3 3	5300	6100
1986 BOATS										
19 2	MARINER	SLP	SA/OD	FBG CB	OB	7	1305	10	4950	5700
19 2	MARINER	SLP	SA/OD	FBG KL	OB	7	1430	3 10	5200	5950
19 2	RHODES 19	SLP	SA/OD	FBG CB	OB	7	1030	10	4450	5100
19 2	RHODES 19	SLP	SA/OD	FBG KL	OB	7	1325	3 3	5000	5750
1985 BOATS										
19 2	MARINER	SLP	SA/OD	FBG CB	OB	7	1305	10	4650	5350
19 2	MARINER	SLP	SA/OD	FBG KL	OB	7	1430	3 3	4900	5600
19 2	RHODES 19	SLP	SA/OD	FBG CB	OB	7	1030	10	4150	4800
19 2	RHODES 19	SLP	SA/OD	FBG KL	OB	7	1325	3 3	4700	5400

STUART YACHT BUILDERS
STUART FL 33497   See inside cover to adjust price for area

LOA FT IN	NAME AND/ OR MODEL	TOP/ RIG	BOAT TYPE	-HULL- MTL TP	----ENGINE--- TP # HP MFG	BEAM FT IN	WGT LBS	DRAFT FT IN	RETAIL LOW	RETAIL HIGH
1986 BOATS										
34	STUART 34		EXP	FBG SV	IO T300	11 4	12000		37800	42000
34	STUART 34		EXP	FBG SV	IO T300	11 4	12000		46900	51600
34	STUART 34		SF	FBG SV	OB	11 4	8000		56000	61600
34	STUART 34		SF	FBG SV	IO T300	11 4	12000		42500	47200
34 8	STUART 35	SLP	SA/CR	FBG KL	IB D	11 4	14250	4 2	63100	69300
43	STUART 43	KTH	SA/CR	FBG KL	IB D	12 6	30000	6	139000	153000
45	STUART 45		EXP	FBG SV	IO T410	15 3	27000		84100	92400
45	STUART 45		EXP	FBG SV	IB T410	15 3	24000		122500	135000
48	STUART 48		MY	FBG SV	IB T410	15 3	32000		169500	186000
55	STUART 55	CUT	SA/CR	FBG KL	IB D	15	33000	6 6	261500	287000
60	STUART 60		TRWL	FBG DS	IB T200	17	75000		284500	312500
63	STUART 63	KTH	SA/CR	FBG KL	IB D	16	80000	6 6	572000	629000
1985 BOATS										
34	STUART 34		EXP	FBG SV	IO T300	17	12000		31700	35200
34	STUART 34		EXP	FBG SV	IO T300	11 4	12000		44300	49200
34	STUART 34		SF	FBG SV	OB	11 4	8000		54700	60100
34	STUART 34		SF	FBG SV	IO T300	11 4	12000		40200	44700
34	STUART 34		SF	FBG SV	IO	11	12000		36000	40000
34 8	STUART 35	SLP	SA/RC	FBG KL	IB D	11 4	14250	4 2	59300	65100
43	STUART 43	KTH	SA/CR	FBG KL	IB D	12 6	30000	6	131000	144000
45	STUART 45		EXP	FBG SV	IO T410	15 3	24000		76200	83800
45	STUART 45		SF	FBG SV	IB T410	15 3	24000		119000	130500
48	STUART 48		MY	FBG SV	IB T410	15 3	32000		161500	177000
55	STUART 55	CUT	SA/RC	FBG KL	IB D	15	33000	6 6	244500	268500
58 6	STUART 60	SCH	SA/CR	FBG CT	IB D	24		4	310000	340500
60	STUART 60		TRWL	FBG DS	IB T200	17	75000		273500	300500
63	STUART 63	KTH	SA/CR	FBG KL	IB D	16	80000	6 6	536000	589500
1984 BOATS										
31	STUART 31	FB	SF	F/S SV	OB	11			33300	37000
31	STUART 31	FB	SF	F/S SV	IO T200	11			27900	31000
31	STUART 31	FB	SF	F/S SV	IB T140D	11			42500	47200
32	STUART 32		SF	F/S SV	OB	11			36100	40100
32	STUART 32		SF	F/S SV	IB 300D CAT	11			31900	35500
32	STUART 32		SF	F/S SV	SE T205 OMC	11			36100	40100
32	STUART 32		SF	F/S SV	IB T350 CRUS	11			30600	34000
32	STUART 32		SF	F/S SV	IB T CAT	11			**	**
34	STUART 34	FB	CR	F/S SV	IB T270 CAT	11			43200	48000
34	STUART 34	FB	CR	F/S SV	IB T158D VLVO	11			58200	63900
34	STUART 34		SF	F/S SV	OB	11			**	**
34	STUART 34		SF	F/S SV	IB 300D CAT	11			50500	55500
34	STUART 34		SF	F/S SV	SE T205 OMC	11			**	**
34	STUART 34		SF	F/S SV	IB T350 CRUS	11			39800	44200
34	STUART 34		SF	F/S SV	IB T CAT	11			**	**
36	STUART 36		SF	F/S SV	OB	11			**	**
36	STUART 36		SF	F/S SV	IB 300D CAT	11			53800	59100
36	STUART 36		SF	F/S SV	SE T205 OMC	11			**	**
36	STUART 36		SF	F/S SV	IB T350 CRUS	11			43300	48100
36	STUART 36		SF	F/S SV	IB T CAT	11			**	**
34 8	STUART 35	SLP	SA/CR	F/S SK	IB D	11 4	14250	4 2	55800	61300
35 11	SURPRISE	SLP	SA/CR	F/S KL	SD D	VLVO 11 4	14250	5 2	56800	62500
35 11	SURPRISE SCHEEL KL	SLP	SA/CR	F/S KL	SD D	VLVO 11 4	14250	4 2	56800	62500
36	STUART 36	FB	SF	F/S SV	IB T COMM	11			**	**
36	STUART 36	FB	CR	F/S SV	IB T158D VLVO	11			67700	74400
36	STUART 36	FB	CR	F/S SV	IB T235D VLVO	11			70200	77200
43	STUART 43	KTH	SA/CR	F/S KL	IB D	12 6	30000	6	123000	135000
46 6	STUART 45	HT	SA/CR	F/S SV	IB R300D SABR	15 3	27000	3 3	147000	161500
46 6	STUART 45	FB	SPTCR	F/S SV	IB R300D SABR	15 3	27000	3 3	137500	151500
55	STUART 55	CUT	SA/RC	FBG KL	IB D	15	33000	6	230500	253000
58 6	STUART 60	SCH	SA/CR	FBG CT	IB D	24	30000	4	292000	321000
63	STUART 63	KTH	SA/CR	FBG KC	IB D	16	80000	6 6	505000	555000

....For earlier years, see the BUC Used Boat Price Guide, Volume 3

SUMNER BOAT CO INC
AMITYVILLE NY 11701   COAST GUARD MFG ID- SBC See inside cover to adjust price for area

LOA FT IN	NAME AND/ OR MODEL	TOP/ RIG	BOAT TYPE	-HULL- MTL TP	----ENGINE--- TP # HP MFG	BEAM FT IN	WGT LBS	DRAFT FT IN	RETAIL LOW	RETAIL HIGH
				1996 BOATS						
16 9	ISLANDS 17	CUT	SAROD	FBG CB		6 6	575		4700	5400
18 8	ISLANDS 19	CUT	SAROD	FBG CB		7 7	950		6150	7100
				1995 BOATS						
16 9	ISLANDS 17	CUT	SAROD	FBG CB		6 6	575		4400	5050
18 8	ISLANDS 19	CUT	SAROD	FBG CB		7 7	950		5800	6650
				1992 BOATS						
16 9	ISLANDS 17		SA/OD	FBG CB		6 6	575	3 6	3600	4150
18 8	ISLANDS 19		SA/OD	FBG CB		7 7	950	4	4800	5500
				1986 BOATS						
16 7	ISLANDS 17	SLP	SA/OD	FBG	OB	6 7	475		2300	2700
18 8	ISLANDS 19	SLP	SA/OD	FBG	OB	7 8	800		3100	3600
				1985 BOATS						
16 7	ISLANDS 17	SLP	SA/OD	FBG	OB	6 7	475		2200	2550
18 8	ISLANDS 19	SLP	SA/OD	FBG	OB	7 8	800		2900	3350
				1984 BOATS						
16 7	ISLANDS 17	SLP	SAIL	FBG	OB	6 2	475		2000	2400

....For earlier years, see the BUC Used Boat Price Guide, Volume 3

SUN CHASER MARINE INC
ELKHART IN 46507   COAST GUARD MFG ID- SUN See inside cover to adjust price for area

LOA FT IN	NAME AND/ OR MODEL	TOP/ RIG	BOAT TYPE	-HULL- MTL TP	----ENGINE--- TP # HP MFG	BEAM FT IN	WGT LBS	DRAFT FT IN	RETAIL LOW	RETAIL HIGH
				1988 BOATS						
16 5	V170	ST	RNBT	FBG DV	IO 120-175	6 8	2000		2950	3550
16 5	V170 OB	OP	RNBT	FBG DV	OB	6 8	1050		2300	2700

SUN PATIO INC
MAPLE LAKE MN 55358   COAST GUARD MFG ID- POU See inside cover to adjust price for area

LOA FT IN	NAME AND/ OR MODEL	TOP/ RIG	BOAT TYPE	-HULL- MTL TP	----ENGINE--- TP # HP MFG	BEAM FT IN	WGT LBS	DRAFT FT IN	RETAIL LOW	RETAIL HIGH
				1993 BOATS						
16 2	WARRIOR LASER V160B	FSH	AL	SV OB		5 10	495		2200	2550
16 2	WARRIOR LASER V160S	FSH	AL	SV OB		5 10	550		2450	2800
16 3	WARRIOR LANCE V166B	FSH	AL	SV OB		6 8	550		2450	2850
16 3	WARRIOR LANCE V166S	FSH	AL	SV OB		6 8	595		2650	3050
16 6	WARRIOR PYTHON V116B	FSH	FBG	SV OB		6 8	975		4250	4900
16 6	WARRIOR PYTHON V166S	FSH	FBG	SV OB		6 8	975		4250	4900
16 7	WARRIOR LANCE V170B	FSH	AL	SV OB		7	950		4150	4800
16 7	WARRIOR LANCE V170S	FSH	AL	SV OB		7	1015		4450	5100
17 6	WARRIOR PYTHON V177	OP FSH	FBG	SV OB		6 11	1000		4500	5200
17 6	WARRIOR PYTHON V177B	FSH	FBG	SV OB		6 11	950		4300	5000
17 6	WARRIOR PYTHON V177S	FSH	FBG	SV OB		6 11	1000		4500	5200
18 2	WARRIOR PYTHON V182B	FSH	FBG	SV OB			1175		5250	6050
18 7	WARRIOR PYTHON V187D	FSH	FBG	DV OB			1350		5950	6800
18 7	WARRIOR PYTHON V187S	FSH	FBG	DV OB			1300		5750	6600
18 8	WARRIOR PYTHON V188D	FSH	FBG	DV OB		8	1150		5250	6050
18 8	WARRIOR PYTHON V188S	FSH	FBG	DV OB		8	1450		6250	7200
20 8	WARRIOR PYTHON V208	FSH	FBG	DV OB		8	1775		8300	9550
				1992 BOATS						
16 2	WARRIOR V160 LASER B	FSH	AL	SV OB		5 10	495		2050	2450
16 2	WARRIOR V160 LASER S	FSH	AL	SV OB		5 10	550		2350	2750
16 2	WARRIOR V160 LASERDX	FSH	AL	SV OB		5 10	495		2050	2450
16 3	WARRIOR V166 LANCE B	FSH	AL	SV OB		6 8	550		2350	2700
16 3	WARRIOR V166 LANCE S	FSH	AL	SV OB		6 8	595		2500	2950
16 7	WARRIOR V170 LANCE B	FSH	AL	SV OB		7	950		4000	4600
16 7	WARRIOR V170 LANCE D	FSH	AL	SV OB		7	1015		4200	4900
16 7	WARRIOR V170 LANCE S	FSH	AL	SV OB		7	985		4100	4800
17 6	WARRIOR PYTHON V117B	FSH	FBG	SV OB		6 11	950		4100	4800
17 6	WARRIOR PYTHON V117S	FSH	FBG	SV OB		6 11	1000		4300	5000
17 6	WARRIOR V177-BT	OP FSH	FBG	SV OB		6 11	950		4100	4800
17 6	WARRIOR V177-CONSOLE	OP FSH	FBG	SV OB		6 11	1000		4300	5000
17 6	WARRIOR V177-DUAL	OP FSH	FBG	SV OB		6 11	1025		4400	5050
17 6	WARRIOR V177-FISHSKI	OP FSH	FBG	SV OB		6 11	1025		4500	5150
18 8	WARRIOR PYTHON V188	FSH	FBG	SV OB		8	1500		6150	7100
20 8	WARRIOR PYTHON V208	FSH	FBG	SV OB		8	1500		6950	8000
				1991 BOATS						
17 6	WARRIOR V177-BT	OP FSH	FBG	SV OB		6 11	950		3950	4600
17 6	WARRIOR V177-CONSOLE	OP FSH	FBG	SV OB		6 11	1000		4150	4800
17 6	WARRIOR V177-DUAL	OP FSH	FBG	SV OB		6 11	1025		4100	4800
17 6	WARRIOR V177-FISHSKI	OP FSH	FBG	SV OB		6 11	1025		4350	5000

SUN RAY BOATS INC
PAYSON UT 84651   COAST GUARD MFG ID- BED See inside cover to adjust price for area
FORMERLY BEDOUIN BOAT MFG

For more recent years, see the BUC Used Boat Price Guide, Volume 1

LOA FT IN	NAME AND/ OR MODEL	TOP/ RIG	BOAT TYPE	-HULL- MTL TP	----ENGINE--- TP # HP MFG	BEAM FT IN	WGT LBS	DRAFT FT IN	RETAIL LOW	RETAIL HIGH
				1994 BOATS						
16 4	MIRAGE	OP	B/R	FBG DV	IO 120 OMC	6 10	1260	1 4	4500	5150
17 7	GENIE	ST	B/R	FBG DV	IO 175 OMC	7	1800	1 2	5950	6800
18 6	SUN RAY XLS	ST	B/R	FBG DV	IO 200 OMC	8	2300	1 4	7800	9000
20 3	CADIZ	ST	B/R	FBG DV	IO 260 OMC	8	3200	1 7	10300	11800
21	SHARIB	ST	CUD	FBG DV	IO 260 OMC	7 9	3600	1 7	12200	13900
				1993 BOATS						
17 7	GENIE	ST	RNBT	FBG DV	IO 175 OMC	7	1800	1 3	5850	6700
18 6	XLS	ST	RNBT	FBG DV	IO 200 OMC	8	2400	1 3	7750	8900
20 4	CADIZ	ST	RNBT	FBG DV	IO 260 OMC	8	3200	1 6	9900	11300
21	SHARIB	ST	OVNTR	FBG DV	IO 260 OMC	8	3600	1 6	11600	13200
				1985 BOATS						
16 4	MIRAGE	OP	RNBT	FBG DV	IO 117 VLVO	6 8	1200		3050	3500
17 7	GENIE	OP	RNBT	FBG DV	IO 170	7	1820		3750	4650
19 1	OASIS	OP	RNBT	FBG DV	IO 170	7 3	2670		5050	6100
20 3	CADIZ	OP	RNBT	FBG DV	IO 260 VLVO	7 8	3200		6500	7450
21 6	SHARIB	OP	OFF	FBG DV	IO 260 VLVO	7 8	3600		7800	9000
				1984 BOATS						
16 4	MIRAGE	OP	RNBT	FBG DV	IO 117 VLVO	6 8	1200		2900	3400
17 7	GENIE	OP	RNBT	FBG DV	IO 170	7	1820		3600	4500
19 1	OASIS	OP	RNBT	FBG DV	IO 170	7 3	2670		4900	5900
20 3	CADIZ	OP	RNBT	FBG DV	IO 260 VLVO	7 8	3200		6250	7200
21 6	SHARIB	OP	OFF	FBG DV	IO 260 VLVO	7 8	3600		7550	8650

....For earlier years, see the BUC Used Boat Price Guide, Volume 3

SUN RUNNER MARINE INC
SPOKANE WA 99205-3600   COAST GUARD MFG ID- XUE See inside cover to adjust price for area

LOA FT IN	NAME AND/ OR MODEL	TOP/ RIG	BOAT TYPE	-HULL- MTL TP	----ENGINE--- TP # HP MFG	BEAM FT IN	WGT LBS	DRAFT FT IN	RETAIL LOW	RETAIL HIGH
				1990 BOATS						
18 3	SUNSPORT 195 B	ST	RNBT	FBG DV	IO	7 8	2150		**	**
18 3	SUNSPORT 195 B	ST	RNBT	FBG DV	IO 131-231	7 8	2150		3250	4000
18 3	SUNSPORT 195 CV	ST	CUD	FBG DV	IO	7 8	2150		**	**
18 3	SUNSPORT 195 CV	ST	CUD	FBG DV	IO 131-231	7 8	2150		3300	4100
20 2	SPE 21	ST	CUD	FBG DV	IO 231-271	8	2700		5150	6250
20 2	SUNSPORT 215 B	ST	RNBT	FBG DV	IO	8	2700		**	**
20 2	SUNSPORT 215 B	ST	RNBT	FBG DV	IO 211-271	8	2700		4850	5950
20 2	SUNSPORT 215 CV	ST	CUD	FBG DV	IO	8	2700		**	**
20 2	SUNSPORT 215 CV	ST	CUD	FBG DV	IO 211-271	8	2700		5050	6250
20 8	GTS	ST	RNBT	FBG SV	IO	8	2600		**	**
20 8	GTS	ST	RNBT	FBG SV	IO 211-271	8	2600		4850	6000
24 3	SUNSPORT 235 WC	ST	CUD	FBG DV	IO	8	4100		8100	9750
24 3	SUNSPORT 235 WC	ST	CUD	FBG DV	IO 211-271	8	4100		8100	9750
24 3	SUNSPORT 235 WC	ST	CUD	FBG DV	IO 454 VLVO	8	4100		12800	14600
24 9	OFFSHORE 245	ST	CUD	FBG DV	IO	8	4100		**	**
24 9	OFFSHORE 245	ST	CUD	FBG DV	IO 211-271	8	4100		8300	10000
24 9	OFFSHORE 245	ST	CUD	FBG DV	IO 454 VLVO	8	4100		12900	14700
25 5	CLASSIC 230	ST	CR	FBG DV	IO	8 6	3500		**	**
25 5	CLASSIC 230	ST	CR	FBG DV	IO 211-271	8 6	4100		8900	10100
25 5	CLASSIC 230	ST	CR	FBG DV	IO 454 VLVO	8 6	3500		12700	14400
26 6	CLASSIC 238	ST	CR	FBG DV	IO 231-271	8 6	4000		9450	11200
26 6	CLASSIC 238	ST	CR	FBG DV	IO 454 VLVO	8 6	4000		13500	15400
28 2	CLASSIC 248	ST	CR	FBG DV	IO 231 VLVO	8 6	4400		10800	12200
28 4	CLASSIC 248	ST	CR	FBG DV	IO	8 6	4400		**	**
28 4	CLASSIC 248	ST	CR	FBG DV	IO 231-271	8 6	4400		11000	13000
28 4	CLASSIC 248	ST	CR	FBG DV	IO 454 VLVO	8 6	4400		14500	16400
28 7	ULTRA 252	ST	CR	FBG DV	IO	8 6	4800		**	**
29 7	SPE 29	ST	CR	FBG DV	IO T231-T271	8 6	6500		15400	18200
30 9	ULTRA 272	ST	CR	FBG DV	IO T231-T271	8 6	5500		**	**

| 24 | OI 271 VLVO | 12000 | 13600, IO | 454 VLVO | 15100 17100, IO | T131-T151 | | | 12200 | 14200 |
| 29 | IO 271 VLVO | 15300 | 17300, IO | 454 VLVO | 18100 20200, IO | T151-T211 | | | 15700 | 19000 |

576   CONTINUED ON NEXT PAGE   96th ed. - Vol. II

SUN RUNNER MARINE INC -CONTINUED See inside cover to adjust price for area

LOA FT	IN	NAME AND/ OR MODEL	TOP/ RIG	BOAT TYPE	-HULL- MTL	TP	TP	-ENGINE--- # HP	MFG	BEAM FT	IN	WGT LBS	DRAFT FT	IN	RETAIL LOW	RETAIL HIGH
		1990 BOATS														
31	11	CLASSIC 280	ST	CR	FBG	DV	IO			9	8	6975			**	**
31	11	CLASSIC 280	ST	CR	FBG	DV	IO	454	VLVO	9	8	6975			21000	23300
31	11	CLASSIC 280	ST	CR	FBG	DV	IO	T151-T271		9	8	6975			19400	23800
33	3	ULTRA 292	ST	CR	FBG	DV	IO			8	6	6500			**	**
		IO 271 VLVO 25700 28500, IO 454 VLVO 29300 32500, IO T151-T231 26400 30600														
34	3	ULTRA 302	ST	CR	FBG	DV	IO			10	5	8000			**	**
34	3	ULTRA 302	ST	CR	FBG	DV	IO	T211-T271		10	5	8000			26800	31000
34	3	ULTRA 302	ST	CR	FBG	DV	IO	T454	VLVO	10	5	8000			38200	42500
35	8	CLASSIC 320	ST	CR	FBG	DV	IO			11	6	9600			**	**
		IO T231 VLVO 30200 33600, IO T271 VLVO 30900 34400, IO T454 VLVO 42800 47500														
41	7	380 SB	ST	CR	FBG	DV	IO	T454	CRUS	14					64600	71000
41	7	380 SB	ST	CR	FBG	DV	IO	T502	CRUS	14					68400	75100
		1989 BOATS														
18	3	SUNSPORT 195 B	ST	RNBT	FBG	DV	IO	130-151		7	8	2150			2850	3550
18	3	SUNSPORT 195 B	ST	RNBT	FBG	DV	IO	205		7	8	2150			2950	3650
18	3	SUNSPORT 195 B	ST	RNBT	FBG	DV	IO	231-235		7	8	2150			3200	3750
18	3	SUNSPORT 195 CV	ST	CUD	FBG	DV	IO	130-151		7	8	2150			2950	3650
18	3	SUNSPORT 195 CV	ST	CUD	FBG	DV	IO	205		7	8	2150			3000	3750
18	3	SUNSPORT 195 CV	ST	CUD	FBG	DV	IO	231-235		7	8	2150			3300	3850
20	2	SUNSPORT 215 B	ST	RNBT	FBG	DV	IO	131-260		8		2700			4500	5350
20	2	SUNSPORT 215 B	ST	RNBT	FBG	DV	IO	271	VLVO	8		2700			4900	5600
20	2	SUNSPORT 215 CV	ST	CUD	FBG	DV	IO	131-260		8		2700			4650	5550
20	2	SUNSPORT 215 CV	ST	CUD	FBG	DV	IO	271	VLVO	8		2700			5100	5850
20	2	SUNSPORT 220 CV	ST	CUD	FBG	DV	IO	151-260		8		2900			4850	5800
20	2	SUNSPORT 220 CV	ST	CUD	FBG	DV	IO	271	VLVO	8		2900			5300	6100
20	8	GTS	ST	RNBT	FBG	SV	IO	205-260		8		2600			4400	5300
20	8	GTS	ST	RNBT	FBG	SV	IO	271	VLVO	8		2600			4900	5650
24	3	SUNSPORT 235 WC	ST	CUD	FBG	DV	IO	231-271		8		4100			7700	9200
24	7	CLASSIC 230	ST	CR	FBG	DV	IO	205-260		8	6	3500			6900	8300
24	7	CLASSIC 230	ST	CR	FBG	DV	IO	271	VLVO	8	6	3500			7500	8650
24	9	OFFSHORE 245	HT	CUD	FBG	SV	OB			8		4100			8450	9700
24	9	OFFSHORE 245	HT	CUD	FBG	SV	IO	231-271		8		4100			7900	9450
26	4	CLASSIC 238	ST	CR	FBG	DV	IO	231-271		8	6	4000			8950	10600
28	4	CLASSIC 248	ST	CR	FBG	DV	IO	231-271		8	6	4400			10300	12200
28	7	ULTRA 252	ST	CR	FBG	DV	IO	260-271		8	6	4800			11100	12800
28	7	ULTRA 252	ST	CR	FBG	DV	IO	T131-T151		8	6	4800			11400	13300
30	9	ULTRA 272	ST	CR	FBG	DV	IO	260-271		8	6	5500			14100	16200
30	9	ULTRA 272	ST	CR	FBG	DV	IO	T151-T205		8	6	5500			14600	17600
31	11	CLASSIC 280	ST	CR	FBG	DV	IO	T151-T271		9	6	6975			18000	22000
33	3	ULTRA 292	ST	CR	FBG	DV	IO	260-271		8	6	6500			23900	27200
33	3	ULTRA 292	ST	CR	FBG	DV	IO	T151-T235		8	6	6500			25200	29100
34	3	ULTRA 302	ST	CR	FBG	DV	IO	231-271		10	5	8000			23500	26500
34	3	ULTRA 302	ST	CR	FBG	DV	IO	T205-T271		10	5	8000			24800	29100
35	2	CLASSIC 320	ST	CR	FBG	DV	IO	T231	VLVO	11	6	9600			27400	30400
		IO T235 OMC 27100 30100, IO T260 OMC 27500 30500, IO T271 VLVO 28100 31200														
		1988 BOATS														
16	6	175 B	OP	RNBT	FBG	DV	IO	130-165		7	3	1950			2300	2850
18	3	195 B	ST	RNBT	FBG	DV	IO	130-205		7	8	2150			2750	3350
18	3	195 B	ST	RNBT	FBG	DV	IO	211-231		7	8	2150			2950	3500
18	3	195 CV	ST	CUD	FBG	DV	IO	130-205		7	8	2150			2800	3450
18	3	195 CV	ST	CUD	FBG	DV	IO	211-231		7	8	2150			3050	3600
19	8	211 SPORTSMAN	ST	FSH	FBG	SV	IO	131-231		8		2700			3900	4750
20	2	215 B	ST	RNBT	FBG	DV	IO	151-271		8		2900			4400	5500
20	2	215 CV	ST	CUD	FBG	DV	IO	151-260		8		2700			4450	5300
20	2	215 CV	ST	CUD	FBG	DV	IO	271	VLVO	8		2700			4850	5550
20	2	220 WEEKENDER	ST	CUD	FBG	DV	IO	151-271		8		2900			4600	5750
20	6	230 WEEKENDER	ST	SPTCR	FBG	DV	IO	151-271		8	6	3500			5450	6800
20	6	GTS	ST	RNBT	FBG	SV	IO		MRCR	8		2600			**	**
20	6	GTS	ST	RNBT	FBG	SV	IO	171-260		8		2600			4200	5000
20	6	GTS	ST	RNBT	FBG	SV	IO	271-311		8		2600			4650	5750
21	8	231 SPORTSMAN	ST	FSH	FBG	SV	IO	211-271		8		3400			5900	7150
21	8	231 SPORTSMAN	ST	FSH	FBG	SV	IO	T131-T180		8		3400			6750	7850
22	2	235 WEEKENDER	ST	CUD	FBG	DV	IO	165-260		8		4100			6250	7550
22	2	235 WEEKENDER	ST	CUD	FBG	DV	IO	271	VLVO	8		4100			6800	7850
22	4	230 CC SPORTSMAN	OP	FSH	FBG	DV	OB			8		2500			5250	6000
23	6	248 CLASSIC	ST	CR	FBG	DV	IO	165-271		8		4400			7100	8800
23	6	252 ULTRA	ST	CR	FBG	DV	IO	205-271		8	6	4800			7800	9550
23	6	252 ULTRA	ST	CR	FBG	DV	IO	T131-T180		8	6	4800			8900	10200
23	8	238 CLASSIC	ST	CR	FBG	DV	IO	211-271		8	6	4000			7000	8400
24	5	251 SPORTSMAN	HT	FSH	FBG	SV	IO	260-271		8		4000			7650	9150
24	5	251 SPORTSMAN	HT	FSH	FBG	SV	IO	T131-T180		8		4000			8500	9900
25	6	272 ULTRA	ST	CR	FBG	DV	IO	225-271		8	6	5500	3	2	9550	11300
25	6	272 ULTRA	ST	CR	FBG	DV	IO	T131-T180		8	6	5500	3	2	10300	12000
26	6	278 CLASSIC	ST	CR	FBG	DV	IO	T151-T260		9	7	6975			12700	15400
26	6	278 CLASSIC	ST	CR	FBG	DV	IO	T271	VLVO	9	7	6975			14000	15900
27	6	292 ULTRA	ST	CR	FBG	DV	IO	260-271		8	6	6500			11700	13600
27	6	292 ULTRA	ST	CR	FBG	DV	IO	T131-T231		8	6	6500			12200	15200
28		302 ULTRA	ST	CR	FBG	DV	IO	T180-T271		10		8000			13800	17100
29	6	318 CLASSIC	ST	CR	FBG	DV	IO	T225-T271		11	6	9600			18100	20800
31	11	3000 MOTOR YACHT	FB	MY	FBG	SV	IO	T151-T231		11		8500			23400	28200
		1987 BOATS														
16	6	170 B	OP	RNBT	FBG	DV	IO	120-171		7	3	1950			2150	2700
18	3	190 B	ST	RNBT	FBG	DV	OB			7	8	2150			3750	4350
18	3	190 B	ST	RNBT	FBG	DV	IO	130-205		7	8	2150			2600	3200
18	3	190 B	ST	RNBT	FBG	DV	IO	211-230		7	8	2150			2800	3300
18	3	190 CV	ST	CUD	FBG	DV	IO	130-205		7	8	2150			2650	3250
18	3	190 CV	ST	CUD	FBG	DV	IO	211-230		7	8	2150			2850	3400
20	2	210 B	ST	RNBT	FBG	DV	IO	151-260		8		2900			4150	5000
20	2	210 B	ST	RNBT	FBG	DV	IO	271	VLVO	8		2900			4600	5250
20	2	210 CV	ST	CUD	FBG	DV	IO	151-260		8		2700			4150	5000
20	2	210 CV	ST	CUD	FBG	DV	IO	271	VLVO	8		2700			4600	5300
20	2	220 CV	ST	CUD	FBG	DV	IO	151-271		8		2900			4400	5450
20	6	226 SB	ST	SPTCR	FBG	DV	IO	151-271		8	6	3500			5200	6400
22	2	225 CV	ST	CUD	FBG	DV	IO	165-260		8		4100			5950	7150
22	2	225 CV	ST	CUD	FBG	DV	IO	271	VLVO	8		4100			6500	7450
23	6	236 SB	ST	CR	FBG	DV	IO	165-271		8		4400			6750	8350
23	6	246 SB	ST	CR	FBG	DV	IO	151-271		8	6	4800	3	2	7500	9050
23	6	246 SB	ST	CR	FBG	DV	IO	T131-T180		8	6	4800	3	2	8350	9650
25	6	266 SB	ST	CR	FBG	DV	IO	225-271		8	6	5500			9150	10700
25	6	266 SB	ST	CR	FBG	DV	IO	T131-T180		8	6	5500	3	2	9750	11400
26	6	276 SB	ST	CR	FBG	DV	IO	T151-T260		9	7	6975			12000	14900
26	6	276 SB	ST	CR	FBG	DV	IO	T271	VLVO	9	7	6975			13500	15300
26	6	276 XL	ST	CR	FBG	DV	IO	T	MRCR	9	7	6975	3	2	**	**
26	6	276 XL	ST	CR	FBG	DV	IO	T225-T271		9	7	6975			12700	15100
26	6	276 XL	ST	CR	FBG	DV	IO	T311-T350		9	7	6975			14100	16600
27	6	286 SB	ST	CR	FBG	DV	IO	260-271		8	6	6500	3	2	11200	12900
27	6	286 SB	ST	CR	FBG	DV	IO	T131-T230		8	6	6500	3	2	11600	14300
28		296 SB	ST	CR	FBG	DV	IO	T180-T271		10		8000	3	2	13000	16100
29	6	316 SB	ST	CR	FBG	DV	IO	T225-T271		11	6	9600			16800	19700
		1986 BOATS														
16	6	170 B	OP	RNBT	FBG	DV	IO	120	MRCR	7	3	1950			2000	2350
16	6	170 B	OP	RNBT	FBG	DV	IO	131-170		7	3	1950			2100	2500
16	6	170 B SL	OP	RNBT	FBG	DV	IO	120	MRCR	7	3	1950			2050	2450
16	6	170 B SL	OP	RNBT	FBG	DV	IO	131-151		7	3	1950			2250	2600
16	6	175 F	OP	SF	FBG	DV	IO	131-181		7	3	1950			2500	2950
16	6	175 F	ST	SF	FBG	DV	OB			7	3	1150			2300	2700
18	3	190 B	ST	RNBT	FBG	DV	OB			7	8	1500			2950	3450
18	3	190 B	ST	RNBT	FBG	DV	IO	120-190		7	8	2150			2450	2950
18	3	190 B	ST	RNBT	FBG	DV	IO	225-230		7	8	2150			2650	3100
18	3	190 B SL	ST	RNBT	FBG	DV	IO	120-190		7	8	2150			2500	3050
18	3	190 B SL	ST	RNBT	FBG	DV	IO	225-230		7	8	2150			2750	3200
18	3	190 CV	ST	CUD	FBG	DV	IO	120-190		7	8	2150			2500	3100
18	3	190 CV	ST	CUD	FBG	DV	IO	225-230		7	8	2150			2750	3200
18	3	195 B SL	ST	CUD	FBG	DV	IO	225	VLVO	7	8	2700			3000	3500
18	3	195 XL	ST	CUD	FBG	DV	IO	151-230		7	8	2700			2900	3350
18	3	200 XL	ST	CUD	FBG	DV	IO	151-230		7	8	2700			3100	3650
18	3	2200 XL	ST	CUD	FBG	DV	IO	225	VLVO	7	8	2700			3200	3700
20	2	210 B	ST	RNBT	FBG	DV	IO	140-230							3700	4650
20	2	210 B	ST	RNBT	FBG	DV	IO	260							4150	4850
20	2	210 B SL	ST	RNBT	FBG	DV	IO	140-230							3800	4700
20	2	210 B SL	ST	RNBT	FBG	DV	IO	260							4250	4900
20	2	210 C SL	ST	CUD	FBG	DV	IO	140-190		8		2500			3650	4450
20	2	210 C SL	ST	CUD	FBG	DV	IO	225-260		8		2500			3950	4800
20	2	210 CV	ST	CUD	FBG	DV	IO	140-190		8		2700			3800	4600
20	2	210 CV	ST	CUD	FBG	DV	IO	225-260		8		2700			4100	5000
20	2	215 CF	ST	SF	FBG	DV	IO	151-260		8		3100			4950	6050
20	2	215 XL	ST	CUD	FBG	DV	IO	151-260		8		3100			4350	5350
20	2	22 ISL	ST	SF	FBG	DV	OB			8		2900			4500	5150
20	2	220 CV	ST	CUD	FBG	DV	IO	151-260		8		2900			4150	5150
20	6	220 SB	ST	SPTCR	FBG	DV	IO	140-230		8	6	3500			4800	5850
20	6	220 SB	ST	SPTCR	FBG	DV	IO	260		8	6	3500			5050	6050
22	2	225 S	ST	CUD	FBG	DV	IO	225-260		8		4100			5950	7050
22	2	230 CC	HT	CBNCR	FBG	DV	IO	151-260		8		4400			6800	8200
22	2	230 EXPRESS	ST	CR	FBG	DV	IO	151-260		8		4400			6200	7250
22	2	230 SB	ST	CR	FBG	DV	IO	151-230		8		4400			6050	7150

 CONTINUED ON NEXT PAGE

LOA FT	IN	NAME AND/ OR MODEL	TOP/ RIG	BOAT TYPE	-HULL- MTL	TP	ENGINE TP	# HP	MFG	BEAM FT	IN	WGT LBS	DRAFT FT	IN	RETAIL LOW	RETAIL HIGH
		1986 BOATS														
22	2	230 SB	ST	CR	FBG	DV	IO	260		8		4400			6150	7700
23	6	245 SB	ST	CR	FBG	DV	IO	151-260		8		4900			7150	8550
23	6	245 SD	ST	SPTCR	FBG	DV	IO	151-260		8		4900			7150	8600
26	6	275 SB	ST	CR	FBG	DV	IO	T151-T260		9	7	6975			11400	14200
26	6	275 SB	ST	CR	FBG	DV	IO	T155D	VLVO	9	7	6975			15000	17100
29	6	310 SB	ST	CR	FBG	DV	IO	T225-T260		11	6	9300			14900	17300
29	6	310 SB	ST	CR	FBG	DV	IO	T155D	VLVO	11	6	9300			17500	19900
		1985 BOATS														
16	6	170 B	OP	RNBT	FBG	DV	IO	120-170		7	3	1650			1750	2100
16	6	170 B SL	OP	RNBT	FBG	DV	IO	120-170		7	3	1650			1800	2150
16	6	175 B	ST	RNBT	FBG	DV	IO	140-170		7	3	1650			1800	2150
16	6	175 F	OP	SF	FBG	DV	IO	120-170		7	3	1650			2050	2450
16	6	175 F	ST	SF	FBG	DV	OB			7	3	970			1900	2250
18	3	190 B	ST	RNBT	FBG	DV	OB			7	8	1350			2650	3100
18	3	190 B	ST	RNBT	FBG	DV	IO	120-170		7	8	1900			2250	2600
18	3	190 B	ST	RNBT	FBG	DV	IO	225	VLVO	7	8	1900			2450	2850
18	3	190 CV	ST	CUD	FBG	DV	IO	120-170		7	8	1900			2300	2750
18	3	190 CV	ST	CUD	FBG	DV	IO	225	VLVO	7	8	1900			2500	2950
18	3	195 B	ST	RNBT	FBG	DV	OB			7	8	1700			3150	3650
18	3	195 B	ST	RNBT	FBG	DV	IO	170-230		7	8	2050			2500	2950
18	3	195 B SL	ST	CUD	FBG	DV	IO	140-190		7	8	2100			2400	2800
18	3	195 B SL	ST	CUD	FBG	DV	IO	225-230		7	8	2100			2600	3050
18	3	200 S	ST	CUD	FBG	DV	IO	170-190		7	8	2150			2400	2850
18	3	200 S	ST	CUD	FBG	DV	IO	225-230		7	8	2150			2650	3100
20	2	210 CV	ST	CUD	FBG	DV	IO	140-170		8		2400			3450	4000
20	2	210 CV	ST	CUD	FBG	DV	IO	225-260		8		2400			3700	4350
20	2	215 CF	ST	SF	FBG	DV	IO	170-230		8		2500			4050	5050
20	2	215 CF	ST	SF	FBG	DV	IO	260		8		2500			4300	5250
20	2	215 S	ST	CUD	FBG	DV	IO	170-260		8		2500			3850	4550
20	2	215 SL	ST	CUD	FBG	DV	IO	225-260		8		2500			3900	4800
20	2	220 S	ST	CUD	FBG	DV	IO	170-230		8		2750			3700	4650
20	2	220 S	ST	CUD	FBG	DV	IO	260		8		2750			3950	4800
20	6	220 SB	ST	SPTCR	FBG	DV	IO	140-230		8	6	2825			4000	4950
20	6	220 SB	ST	SPTCR	FBG	DV	IO	260		8	6	2825			4250	5150
22	2	225 S	ST	CUD	FBG	DV	IO	225-260		8		3225			4850	5750
22	2	230 CC	HT	CBNCR	FBG	DV	IO	170-260		8		3650			5550	6900
22	2	230 EXPRESS	ST	CR	FBG	DV	IO	190-260		8		3650			5050	6200
22	2	230 SB	ST	CR	FBG	DV	IO	190-260		8		3650			4950	6100
23	6	245 SB	ST	CR	FBG	DV	IO	225-260		8		3980			5950	7050
23	6	245 SD	ST	SPTCR	FBG	DV	IO	170-260		8		4000			5750	7100
26	3	275 SL	ST	CUD	FBG	DV	IO	T225-T290		9	7	7500			12000	14600
26	6	275 SB	ST	CR	FBG	DV	IO	T170-T260		9	7	7500			11400	14200
26	6	275 SB	ST	CR	FBG	DV	IO	T155D	VLVO	9	7	7500			15100	17200
29	6	310 SB	ST	CR	FBG	DV	IO	T190-T260		11	6	10000			15000	18000
29	6	310 SB	ST	CR	FBG	DV	IO	T155D	VLVO	11	6	10000			18400	20400
		1984 BOATS														
16	6	175 B	ST	RNBT	FBG	DV	IO	140-170		7	3	1650			1700	2050
16	6	175 F	OP	RNBT	FBG	DV	IO	120-170		7	3	1650			1700	2050
16	6	175 F	ST	RNBT	FBG	DV	OB			7	3	970			1850	2200
18		180 SL	OP	SKI	FBG	DV	IO	140-188		7	6	1650			1850	2250
18		180 SS	OP	SKI	FBG	DV	OB			7	6	850			1750	2050
18	3	190	ST	RNBT	FBG	DV	IO	120-140		7	8	1900			2150	2500
18	3	190	ST	RNBT	FBG	DV	IO	225	VLVO	7	8	1900			2350	2750
18	3	190 CU	ST	CUD	FBG	DV	IO	120-140		7	8	1900			2200	2550
18	3	190 CU	ST	CUD	FBG	DV	IO	225	VLVO	7	8	1900			2400	2800
18	3	195 B	ST	RNBT	FBG	DV	IO	170-185		7	8	2050			2250	2600
18	3	195 B	ST	RNBT	FBG	DV	IO	225-228		7	8	2050			2400	2800
18	3	200 S	ST	CUD	FBG	DV	IO	170-185		7	8	2150			2350	2750
18	3	200 S	ST	CUD	FBG	DV	IO	225-228		7	8	2150			2550	2950
20	2	210 CU	ST	CUD	FBG	DV	IO	140	MRCR	8		2400			3350	3850
20	2	210 CU	ST	CUD	FBG	DV	IO	225	VLVO	8		2400			3600	4200
20	2	215 CF	ST	CUD	FBG	DV	IO	170-228		8		2500			3300	4000
20	2	215 CF	ST	CUD	FBG	DV	IO	260		8		2500			3600	4150
20	2	215 S	ST	CUD	FBG	DV	IO	170-228		8		2500			3550	4300
20	2	215 S	ST	CUD	FBG	DV	IO	260		8		2500			3800	4400
20	2	215 SL	ST	CUD	FBG	DV	IO	185	MRCR	8		2500			3500	4100
20	2	215 SL	ST	CUD	FBG	DV	IO	225-260		8		2500			3850	4600
20	2	220 S	ST	CUD	FBG	DV	IO	185-228		8		2750			3600	4450
20	2	220 S	ST	CUD	FBG	DV	IO	260		8		2750			3800	4650
22	2	225 CF	ST	CUD	FBG	DV	IO	170-260		8		3225			4450	5300
22	2	225 S	ST	CUD	FBG	DV	IO	185	MRCR	8		3225			4450	5150
22	2	225 S	ST	CUD	FBG	DV	IO	225-260		8		3225			4900	5800
22	2	230 CC	HT	CBNCR	FBG	DV	IO	140-228		8		3650			5350	6450
22	2	230 CC	HT	CBNCR	FBG	DV	IO	110D	VLVO	8		3650			7000	8050
22	2	230 CC	HT	CBNCR	FBG	DV	IO	T140	MRCR	8		3650			6050	6950
22	2	230 EXPRESS	ST	CR	FBG	DV	IO	185-260		8		3650			4850	6000
22	2	230 SB	ST	CR	FBG	DV	IO	185-260		8		3650			4800	5950
22	2	230 SB	ST	CR	FBG	DV	IO	T140	MRCR	8		3650			5450	6250
23	6	245 CB	FB	CBNCR	FBG	DV	IO	225-260		8		4000			6550	7700
23	6	245 CB	FB	CBNCR	FBG	DV	IO	T140-T188		8		4000			6950	8100
23	6	245 SB	ST	CR	FBG	DV	IO	225-260		8		3980			5750	6800
26	6	275 SB	ST	CR	FBG	DV	IO	T170-T260		9	7	7500			11000	13700
26	6	275 SB	ST	CR	FBG	DV	IO	T110D-T155D		9	7	7500			13600	16500
29	6	310 SB	ST	CR	FBG	DV	IO	T170-T260		11	6	10000			14200	17300
29	6	310 SB	ST	CR	FBG	DV	IO	T155D	VLVO	11	6	10000			17300	19600

....For earlier years, see the BUC Used Boat Price Guide, Volume 3

SUN-RAY LTD

PAXTON IL 60957 COAST GUARD MFG ID- SZD See inside cover to adjust price for area

LOA FT	IN	NAME AND/ OR MODEL	TOP/ RIG	BOAT TYPE	-HULL- MTL	TP	ENGINE TP	# HP	MFG	BEAM FT	IN	WGT LBS	DRAFT FT	IN	RETAIL LOW	RETAIL HIGH
		1993 BOATS														
16	6	1700	OP	RNBT	FBG	DV	OB			7		1075			3000	3450
16	6	1700	OP	RNBT	FBG	DV	IO	145		7		1640			3550	4100
17		1750	OP	RNBT	FBG	DV	OB			7	3	1175			3250	3800
17		1750	OP	RNBT	FBG	DV	IO	175		7	3	1900			4000	4650
17	1	E 1700	OP	RNBT	FBG	DV	IO	145		7	3	1826			3950	4550
18		FISH & SKI	OP	SF	FBG	DV	OB			7	1	1150			3300	3850
18	7	1900	OP	RNBT	FBG	DV	IO	175		7	7	2100			4750	5450
18	9	1900 CC	OP	CUD	FBG	DV	IO	175		7	7	2350			5200	6000
21	1	2100 B-R	OP	RNBT	FBG	DV	IO	350		8		3050			8650	9950
21	1	Z212	OP	CUD	FBG	DV	IO	350		8		3250			9500	10800
21	2	2100 CUDDY	OP	CUD	FBG	DV	IO	350		8		3200			9450	10700
		1992 BOATS														
16	6	1700	OP	RNBT	FBG	DV	OB			7		1075			2850	3350
16	6	1700	OP	RNBT	FBG	DV	IO	145		7		1640			3300	3850
17		1750	OP	RNBT	FBG	DV	OB			7	3	1175			3150	3650
17		1750	OP	RNBT	FBG	DV	IO	175		7	3	1900			3750	4350
17	1	E 1700	OP	RNBT	FBG	DV	IO	145		7	3	1826			3700	4300
18		FISH & SKI	OP	SF	FBG	DV	OB			7	1	1150			3150	3700
18	7	1900	OP	RNBT	FBG	DV	IO	175		7	7	2100			4500	5150
18	9	1900 CC	OP	CUD	FBG	DV	IO	175		7	7	2350			4900	5600
21	1	2100 B-R	OP	RNBT	FBG	DV	IO	350		8		3050			8100	9350
21	1	Z212	OP	CUD	FBG	DV	IO	350		8		3250			8950	10200
21	2	2100 CUDDY	OP	CUD	FBG	DV	IO	350		8		3200			8900	10100
		1991 BOATS														
16	5	1700	OP	RNBT	FBG	DV	OB			7		1075			2750	3200
16	5	1700 IO	OP	RNBT	FBG	DV	IO	145		7		1640			3100	3600
17		1750	OP	RNBT	FBG	DV	OB			7	3	1175			3000	3500
17		1750 I/O	OP	RNBT	FBG	DV	IO	175		7	3	1900			3550	4100
17	1	E 1700 I/O	OP	RNBT	FBG	DV	IO	145		7	3	1826			3450	4000
18		FISH & SKI	OP	SF	FBG	DV	OB			7	1	1150			3050	3550
18	7	1900 I/O	OP	RNBT	FBG	DV	IO	175		7	7	2100			4150	4850
18	9	1900 CC I/O	OP	CUD	FBG	DV	IO	175		7	7	2350			4600	5300
21	1	2100 I/O B-R	OP	RNBT	FBG	DV	IO	350		8		3050			7600	8750
21	1	Z212 I/O	OP	CUD	FBG	DV	IO	350		8		3250			8300	9500
21	2	2100 I/O CUDDY	OP	CUD	FBG	DV	IO	350		8		3200			8250	9500
		1990 BOATS														
16	5	1700	OP	RNBT	FBG	DV	OB			7		1075			2650	3100
16	5	1700 I/O	OP	RNBT	FBG	DV	IO	145		7		1640			2900	3350
17	1	E 1700 I/O	OP	RNBT	FBG	DV	IO	145		7	3				3250	3750
18		FISH & SKI	OP	SF	FBG	DV	OB			7	1	1150			2950	3450
18	7	1900 I/O	OP	RNBT	FBG	DV	IO	175		7	7	2100			3900	4550
18	9	1900 CC I/O	OP	CUD	FBG	DV	IO	175		7	7	2350			4300	5000
21	1	2100 I/O B-R	OP	RNBT	FBG	DV	IO	350		8		3050			7150	8250
21	1	Z212 I/O	OP	CUD	FBG	DV	IO	350		8		3250			7800	8950
21	2	2100 I/O CUDDY	OP	CUD	FBG	DV	IO	350		8		3200			7750	8900
		1989 BOATS														
16	5	1700	OP	RNBT	FBG	DV	OB			7		1075			2550	3000
16	5	1700	OP	RNBT	FBG	DV	IO	130		7		1640			2750	3150
18		1800V FISH & SKI	OP	FSH	FBG	DV	OB			7	1	1150			2850	3300
18		1800V FISH & SKI	OP	SKI	FBG	DV	OB			7	1	1150			2850	3300
18	7	1900	OP	RNBT	FBG	DV	IO	205		7	7	2100			3750	4350
18	9	1900	OP	CUD	FBG	DV	IO	205		7	7	2350			4100	4750
20	2	2000	OP	RNBT	FBG	DV	IO	260		7	7	2400			4650	5350
21	1	2100	OP	CUD	FBG	DV	IO	260		8		3200			6150	7050
21	2	2100	OP	RNBT	FBG	DV	IO	260		8		3000			5650	6500

SUN-RAY LTD -CONTINUED See inside cover to adjust price for area

LOA FT	LOA IN	NAME AND/ OR MODEL	TOP/ RIG	BOAT TYPE	HULL MTL	HULL TP	ENGINE TP	# HP	MFG	BEAM FT	BEAM IN	WGT LBS	DRAFT FT	DRAFT IN	RETAIL LOW	RETAIL HIGH
		1989 BOATS														
21	2	Z212	OP	RNBT	FBG	DV	IO	260		8		3100			5750	6600
		1988 BOATS														
16	5	1700	OP	RNBT	FBG	DV	OB			7					2500	2900
16	5	1700	OP	RNBT	FBG	DV	IO	130		7					2600	3000
18		FISH & SKI 1800V			FBG	DV	OB			7	1	1150			2750	3200
18	7	1900	OP	RNBT	FBG	DV	IO	205		7	7	2100			3550	4100
18	9	1900	OP	CUD	FBG	DV	IO	205		7	7	2350			3900	4500
21	1	2100	OP	CUD	FBG	DV	IO	260		8		3200			5800	6700
21	2	2100	OP	RNBT	FBG	DV	IO	260		8		3000			5350	6150
		1987 BOATS														
16	5	1700	OP	RNBT	FBG	DV	OB			7		1075			2450	2800
16	5	1750	OP	RNBT	FBG	DV	IO	140		7		1640			2450	2850
18	7	1900	OP	RNBT	FBG	DV	IO	205		7	7	2100			3350	3900
18	9	1900	OP	CUD	FBG	DV	IO	205		7	7	2350			3700	4300
21		2100	OP	CUD	FBG	DV	IO	260		8		3200			5500	6300
21		2100	OP	RNBT	FBG	DV	IO	260		8		3000			5050	5800
		1985 BOATS														
16	5	1600V DELUXE	OP	RNBT	FBG	DV	OB			7		1075			2500	2900
16	5	1600V STANDARD	OP	RNBT	FBG	DV	OB			7		1075			2100	2500
16	5	1650V DELUXE	OP	RNBT	FBG	DV	IO	140		7		1640			2300	2650
18	7	1900V DELUXE	OP	RNBT	FBG	DV	IO	185		7	7	2100			3050	3550

SUNBIRD BOAT CO INC

DIV OF OUTBOARD MARINE CORP
COLUMBIA SC 29201

See inside cover to adjust price for area

For more recent years, see the BUC Used Boat Price Guide, Volume 1

LOA FT	LOA IN	NAME AND/ OR MODEL	TOP/ RIG	BOAT TYPE	HULL MTL	HULL TP	ENGINE TP	# HP	MFG	BEAM FT	BEAM IN	WGT LBS	DRAFT FT	DRAFT IN	RETAIL LOW	RETAIL HIGH
		1996 BOATS														
16	5	NEPTUNE 160 CC	OP	CTRCN	FBG	SV	OB			6	9	1227		11	3150	3700
17	2	SPIRIT 170 BR	ST	RNBT	FBG	SV	OB			7		1850		10	4400	5050
17	2	SPIRIT 170 FSH N SKI	ST	RNBT	FBG	SV	OB			7		1904		10	4500	5150
17	2	SPIRIT 170 SL	ST	RNBT	FBG	SV	IO	160	OMC	7		2218	1	6	4950	5650
17	2	SPIRIT 180 BR	ST	RNBT	FBG	SV	IO	135	OMC	7		1886	1	6	4550	5250
18		CORSAIR 180 BR	ST	RNBT	FBG	SV	IO	190	OMC	7	8	2475	1	5	5750	6600
18		CORSAIR 180 SL	ST	RNBT	FBG	SV	IO	190	OMC	7	8	2475	1	5	5900	6800
18	2	NEPTUNE 180 CC	OP	CTRCN	FBG	SV	OB			7		2009		11	4700	5400
18	2	NEPTUNE 181 DC	OP	RNBT	FBG	SV	OB			7		1995	1	1	4650	5350
18	10	CORSAIR 190 BR	ST	RNBT	FBG	SV	OB			7	6	2150	1	3	4900	5650
18	10	CORSAIR 190 CUDDY	ST	CUD	FBG	DV	OB			7	6	2590	1	3	5250	6000
19	6	NEPTUNE 200 CC	OP	CTRCN	FBG	SV	OB			7	6	2200	1	2	5200	6000
19	6	NEPTUNE 201 DC	OP	RNBT	FBG	SV	OB			7	6	2400	1	2	5450	6250
19	6	NEPTUNE 202 WA	OP	RNBT	FBG	SV	OB			7	6	2700	1		5650	6500
20	1	CORSAIR 200 BR	ST	RNBT	FBG	SV	IO	265	OMC	8	3	3143	1	6	9050	10300
20	1	CORSAIR 200 CUDDY	ST	CUD	FBG	SV	IO	265	OMC	8	3	3143	1	4	9500	10800
20	1	CORSAIR 200 SL	ST	RNBT	FBG	SV	IO	265	OMC	8	3	3143	1	6	9250	10500
22		CORSAIR 220 CUDDY	ST	CUD	FBG	SV	IO	265	OMC	8	3	3143	1	6	10500	11900
22		NEPTUNE 230 WA	OP	CUD	FBG	SV	IO	265	OMC	8	6	4590	1	6	13700	15600
22		NEPTUNE 230 WA	OP	RNBT	FBG	SV	OB			8	6	3820	1	6	8350	9600
		1994 BOATS														
16	4	CORSAIR 170	OP	B/R	FBG	SV	OB			6	8	1700			3800	4400
16	4	CORSAIR 170 FS	OP	FSH	FBG	DV	OB			6	8	1850			4050	4750
17	3	STINGER 175	OP	B/R	FBG	SV	IO	130	OMC	6	8	2000			3750	4350
18	2	NEPTUNE 180	OP	CTRCN	FBG	SV	OB			7		1600			3700	4250
18	7	CORSAIR 180	OP	RNBT	FBG	DV	IO	175	OMC	7	4	2350			4750	5450
18	7	CORSAIR 180 SL	OP	RNBT	FBG	DV	IO	175	OMC	7	4	2350			5100	5900
18	10	CORSAIR 190	OP	B/R	FBG	SV	OB			7	6	2200			4550	5250
18	10	CORSAIR 190 CUDDY	OP	CUD	FBG	SV	OB			7	6	2400			4700	5350
18	11	EUROSPORT 190 QR	OP	B/R	FBG	DV	OB			7	1	1950			4250	4950
19	2	CORSAIR 200	OP	CUD	FBG	SV	IO	200	OMC	7	6	2700			5800	6650
19	6	NEPTUNE 200	OP	CTRCN	FBG	SV	OB			7	6	2300			4850	5600
19	6	NEPTUNE 201 DUAL	OP	CTRCN	FBG	SV	OB			7	6	2500			5000	5750
19	6	NEPTUNE 202	OP	CUD	FBG	SV	OB			7	6	2550			5050	5800
19	10	CORSAIR 200	OP	B/R	FBG	SV	IO	235	OMC	7	8	2500			5600	6450
20	1	CORSAIR 200 SL	OP	RNBT	FBG	SV	IO	235	OMC	7	8	2500			6500	7450
		1993 BOATS														
16	6	CORSAIR 170	OP	B/R	FBG	SV	OB			6	11	1490			3250	3800
16	6	CORSAIR 170 SS	OP	B/R	FBG	DV	IO	90	OMC	6	11	1490			2900	3400
18	2	CORSAIR 185	OP	RNBT	FBG	DV	IO	175	OMC	7	1	2045			4050	4700
18	2	CORSAIR 185 SS	OP	RNBT	FBG	DV	IO	130	OMC	7	1	2045			4000	4650
18	2	CORSAIR 187 SL	OP	RNBT	FBG	DV	IO	130-175		7	1	2045			4100	4850
18	2	NEPTUNE 180	OP	CTRCN	FBG	SV	OB			6	11	1600			3500	4100
18	11	EUROSPORT 190 QR	OP	B/R	FBG	DV	IO	115	OMC	7	3	1800			3950	4550
19	1	REGENCY 195	OP	B/R	FBG	SV	IO	200-225		7	4	2300			4600	5400
19	2	CORSAIR 198	OP	CUD	FBG	SV	IO	175-200		7	8	2700			5450	6300
19	2	CORSAIR 198 SS	OP	CUD	FBG	SV	IO	130	OMC	7	8	2700			5400	6200
19	2	EUROSPORT 190 SS QR	OP	B/R	FBG	SV	IO	115	OMC	7	8	2700			5050	5800
19	6	NEPTUNE 200	OP	CTRCN	FBG	SV	OB			7	9	2300			4700	5350
19	6	NEPTUNE 202	OP	CTRCN	FBG	SV	OB			7	9	2700			4900	5650
20	1	CORSAIR 205 SL	OP	RNBT	FBG	SV	IO	200	OMC	7	8	2400			6000	6900
20	1	CORSAIR 205 SS STD	OP	RNBT	FBG	SV	IO	200	OMC	7	8	2400			5500	6300
20	1	CORSAIR 205 STD	OP	RNBT	FBG	SV	IO	200	OMC	7	8	2400			5900	6750
21	3	REGENCY 210 QR	OP	B/R	FBG	SV	IO	150	OMC	8		2500			6250	7150
21	3	REGENCY 210 QR	OP	CUD	FBG	SV	IO	150	OMC	8		2500			6650	7650
21	11	CORSAIR 218	OP	CUD	FBG	SV	IO	200	OMC	8	4	3500			8700	10000
		1992 BOATS														
16	6	CORSAIR 170 SS	OP	B/R	FBG	DV	IO	90	OMC	6	11	1490			2750	3150
18	2	CORSAIR 185	OP	RNBT	FBG	DV	IO	175	OMC	7	1	2045			3800	4400
18	2	CORSAIR 185 SS	OP	RNBT	FBG	DV	IO	130	OMC	7	1	2045			3750	4350
18	2	CORSAIR 187 SL	OP	RNBT	FBG	DV	IO	130-175		7	1	2045			3850	4550
18	11	EUROSPORT 190 QR	OP	B/R	FBG	DV	IO	115	OMC	7	3	1800			3700	4250
19	2	CORSAIR 190SS QR	OP	CUD	FBG	SV	IO	115	OMC	7	8	2700			5050	5800
19	2	CORSAIR 198 SS	OP	CUD	FBG	SV	IO	130	OMC	7	8	2700			5050	5800
19	6	NEPTUNE 200	OP	CTRCN	FBG	SV	OB			7	9	2300			4500	5150
20	1	CORSAIR 205 SL	OP	RNBT	FBG	SV	IO	200	OMC	7	8	2400			5600	6450
20	1	CORSAIR 205 STD	OP	RNBT	FBG	SV	IO	200	OMC	7	8	2400			5500	6350
20	1	CORSAIR 205SS STD	OP	RNBT	FBG	SV	IO	200	OMC	7	8	2400			5150	5900
21	11	CORSAIR 218	OP	CUD	FBG	SV	IO	200	OMC	8	4	3500			8150	9350
		1991 BOATS														
16	2	CORSAIR 160	OP	RNBT	FBG	DV	OB			6	8	1375			2850	3300
16	2	CORSAIR 160 FSH &SKI	OP	RNBT	FBG	DV	OB			6	8	1580			3200	3700
16	11	PROWLER	OP	BASS	FBG	SV	OB			6	2	900			1950	2300
17		SEACORE 173	OP	CTRCN	FBG	DV	OB			6	10	1600			3200	3700
17	4	SPL 174	OP	CUD	FBG	SV	OB			7	3	1615			3200	3750
17	6	CORSAIR 170	OP	RNBT	FBG	DV	OB			6	11	1680			3300	3850
17	6	CORSAIR 175	OP	RNBT	FBG	DV	IO	130-150		6	11	2000			3350	3900
18	4	CORSAIR 185	OP	RNBT	FBG	DV	IO	130-175		7	1	2150			3600	4350
18	4	CORSAIR 185SL	OP	RNBT	FBG	DV	IO	130-205		7	1	2150			3750	4500
18	6	BARLETTA 184	OP	CUD	FBG	DV	OB			7	8	1875			3600	4200
19		SPL 190	OP	RNBT	FBG	DV	OB			7	9	1900			3750	4350
19		SPL 194	OP	CUD	FBG	SV	OB			7	9	1975			3800	4450
19		SPL190	OP	RNBT	FBG	DV	OB			7	9	1900			3750	4350
19	2	CORSAIR 198	OP	CUD	FBG	SV	IO	130-205		7	8	2575			4650	5550
19	2	SWL 207	OP	FSH	FBG	SV	IO		OMC	8		3025			**	**
19	2	SWL 207	OP	FSH	FBG	SV	IO	175-185		8		3025			5550	6400
20		BARLETTA 204	OP	CUD	FBG	DV	OB			7	9	2165			4050	4700
20		SWL 203	OP	CTRCN	FBG	DV	OB			7	9	2300			4200	4850
20	1	BARLETTA 208	OP	CUD	FBG	SV	IO	130-200		7	8	2675			5500	6750
20	1	BARLETTA 208	OP	CUD	FBG	SV	IO	260	OMC	7	8	3007			6300	7250
20	1	CORSAIR 205	OP	RNBT	FBG	SV	IO	130-200		7	8	2174			4800	5750
20	1	CORSAIR 205	OP	RNBT	FBG	SV	IO	260	OMC	7	8	2405			5300	6100
20	1	CORSAIR 205 SL	OP	RNBT	FBG	SV	IO	175-260		7	8	2299			5000	6250
21	3	SWL 226	OP	FSH	FBG	SV	OB			8	6	3350			5650	6500
21	11	CORSAIR 218	OP	CUD	FBG	SV	IO	175-260		8	4	3329			7350	9100
21	11	CORSAIR 218	OP	CUD	FBG	SV	IO	270	OMC	8	4	3500			8000	9200
22	3	SWL 227	OP	FSH	FBG	SV	IO	185-260		8	6	4000			9150	10700
22	8	BARLETTA 229	OP	CUD	FBG	SV	IO	185-260		8	6	4140			9050	10700
24	8	SWL 246	OP	SF	FBG	SV	OB			9	3	4300			8350	9600
26	10	BARLETTA 279	OP	CUD	FBG	SV	IO	260-340		9		6600			15700	19000
26	10	BARLETTA 279	OP	CUD	FBG	SV	IO	T175-T205		9		7511			18300	20800
		1990 BOATS														
16	2	SPL 160	OP	RNBT	FBG	DV	OB			6	8	1375			2700	3150
16	2	SPL 160 FISH & SKI	OP	RNBT	FBG	DV	OB			6	8	1580			3050	3550
16	6	CORSICA 175	OP	RNBT	FBG	DV	IO	130-175		6	11	2000			2950	3500
16	6	SPL 170	OP	RNBT	FBG	DV	OB			6	11	1490			2900	3400
17	4	SPL 174	OP	CUD	FBG	SV	OB			7	3	1615			3100	3600
17	4	SWL 173	OP	CTRCN	FBG	DV	OB			7	3	1680			3200	3700
17	7	CORSICA 185	OP	RNBT	FBG	DV	IO	130-175		7	3	2075			3300	3900
17	7	CORSICA 188	OP	CUD	FBG	SV	IO	130-175		7	3	2165			3450	4050
18	4	CORSICA 185	OP	RNBT	FBG	DV	IO	130-175		7	1	2150			3450	4050
18	4	CORSICA 185SL	OP	RNBT	FBG	DV	IO	130-175		7	1	2150			3500	4100
18	6	BARLETTA 184	OP	CUD	FBG	DV	OB			7	8	1875			3500	4050
19		CORSICA 195	OP	RNBT	FBG	DV	IO	130-185		7	9	2175			3850	4500
19		CORSICA 198	OP	CUD	FBG	SV	IO	130-185		7	9	2210			4000	4700
19		SPL 190	OP	RNBT	FBG	DV	OB			7	9	1900			3600	4200
19		SPL 194	OP	CUD	FBG	SV	OB			7	9	1975			3650	4250
19	2	SWL 207	OP	FSH	FBG	SV	IO		OMC	8		3025			**	**

CONTINUED ON NEXT PAGE

LOA FT IN	NAME AND/ OR MODEL	TOP/ RIG	BOAT TYPE	-HULL- MTL TP	----ENGINE--- TP # HP MFG	BEAM FT IN	WGT LBS	DRAFT FT IN	RETAIL LOW	RETAIL HIGH
					1990 BOATS					
19 2	SWL 207	OP	FSH	FBG SV	IO 175-185	8	3025		5200	6000
20	BARLETTA 204	OP	CUD	FBG DV	OB	7 9	2165		3900	4500
20	SWL 203	OP	CTRCN	FBG DV	OB	7 9	2300		4000	4650
20 1	SUNBIRD SKIER	OP	SKI	FBG DV	OB	7 11	1715		3350	3900
20 5	CORSICA 218	OP	CUD	FBG SV	IO 175-235	8	2975		5800	6850
21 3	EUROSPORT 215	OP	RNBT	FBG DV	IO T200-T260	8	2750		6550	8100
21 3	EUROSPORT 215	OP	CUD	FBG DV	IO 200-270	8	2750		5850	7150
21 3	EUROSPORT 218	OP	RNBT	FBG DV	IO T270 OMC	8	2750		7200	8250
21 3	SWL 226	OP	FSH	FBG DV	OB	8	3350		5400	6250
22 8	BARLETTA 228	OP	CUD	FBG SV	IO 185-270	8 5	4020		8200	9900
22 8	BARLETTA 229	OP	CUD	FBG SV	IO 185-270	8 5	4140		8400	10100
23	EUROSPORT 238	OP	CUD	FBG SV	IO 340-370	8	4100		9800	11800
23 2	EUROSPORT 238CS	OP	CUD	FBG DV	OB	8	4100		7250	8300
26 10	BARLETTA 279	OP	CUD	FBG SV	IO 235-340	9	6600		14500	17900
26 10	BARLETTA 279	OP	CUD	FBG SV	IO T175 OMC	9	6600		15600	17800

SUNBIRD MARINE INC
FT LAUDERDALE FL 33312 COAST GUARD MFG ID- SON See inside cover to adjust price for area

LOA FT IN	NAME AND/ OR MODEL	TOP/ RIG	BOAT TYPE	-HULL- MTL TP	----ENGINE--- TP # HP MFG	BEAM FT IN	WGT LBS	DRAFT FT IN	RETAIL LOW	RETAIL HIGH
					1990 BOATS					
30	OPEN FISH IO		OPFSH	F/S DV	IB 350	8	4800	2	18500	20500
30	OPEN FISH IO		OPFSH	F/S DV	IB 350D	8	4800	2	21000	23300
30	OPEN FISH OB		OPFSH	F/S DV	IB	8	4300	2	27700	30800
30	SPORT IO		SPTCR	F/S DV	IB T350	8	5500	2	22900	25400
30	SPORT OB		SPTCR	F/S DV	IB	8	4800	2	27900	31000
35	OPEN FISH 35		OPFSH	F/S DV	IB	10 6	8500	2 3	43200	48000
35	OPEN FISH 35		OPFSH	F/S DV	IB T450D	10 6	8500	2 3	53500	58800
35	SPORT CRUISER 35		SPTCR	F/S DV	IB	10 6	9500	2 3	43200	48000
35	SPORT CRUISER 35		SPTCR	F/S DV	IB T450D	10 6	9500	2 3	59200	65100
35	SPORT FISH 35		SF	F/S DV	IB	10 6	10000	2 3	41500	46100
35	SPORT FISH 35		SF	F/S DV	IB T450D	10 6	10000	2 3	61400	67500
40	SPORT CRUISER 40		SPTCR	F/S DV	IB	9 6	10000	2 3	**	**
40	SPORT CRUISER 40		SPTCR	F/S DV	IB	9 6	10000	2 3	69600	76400
42	SPORT CRUISER 42		SPTCR	F/S DV	IB T600	10 6	10500	2 3	89000	97700
42	SPORT CRUISER 42		SPTCR	F/S DV	IB T600D	10 6	10500	2 3	111000	122000
44	SPORT CRUISER 44-B		SPTCR	F/S DV	IB T600	9 6	10500	2 3	95800	105500
44	SPORT CRUISER 44-B		SPTCR	F/S DV	IB T600D	10 6	10500	2 3	111500	122500
46	SPORT CRUISER 46		SPTCR	F/S DV	IB T700	10 6	13000	2 3	133000	146000
46	SPORT CRUISER 46-B		SPTCR	F/S DV	IB T600	10 6	11000	2 3	93600	103000
46	SPORT CRUISER 46-B		SPTCR	F/S DV	IB T600D	10 6	11000	2 3	120500	132500
					1989 BOATS					
30	BOW RIDER 30		B/R	F/S DV	IB	8	4000	2	**	**
30	BOW RIDER 30		B/R	F/S DV	IB T	8	4000	2	**	**
30	OPEN FISHERMAN 30		CTRCN	F/S DV	IB	8	4000	2	**	**
30	OPEN FISHERMAN 30		CTRCN	F/S DV	IB T	8	4000	2	**	**
30	SPORT 30		SPTCR	F/S DV	IB	8	4000	2	**	**
30	SPORT 30		SPTCR	F/S DV	IB T	8	4000	2	**	**
35	OPEN FISH 35		UTL	F/S DV	IB	10 6	7000	2 6	**	**
35	SPORT FISHERMAN 35		SF	F/S DV	IB T	10 6	9000	2 6	**	**
38	SPORT CRUISER 38B		SPTCR	F/S DV	IB T	10 6	9500	2 6	**	**
41	SPORT CRUISER 41		SPTCR	F/S DV	IB T	9	10000	2 6	**	**
42	SPORT CRUISER 42		SPTCR	F/S DV	IB T	10 6	11000	2 6	**	**
44 6	SPORT CRUISER 44B		SPTCR	F/S DV	IB T	9	10500	2 6	**	**
46	SPORT CRUISER 46		SPTCR	F/S DV	IB T500D	10 6	14000	2 9	99400	109500
46 6	SPORT CRUISER 46B		SPTCR	F/S DV	IB T	10 6	11500	2 6	**	**
					1988 BOATS					
28	SPORTCRUISER MGS 28	OP	B/R	FBG DV	IB T200	8		2	15500	17600
30	CORSA 30	OP	RNBT	FBG DV	IB T200	8		2	16700	19000
35	SPORTFISH 35	ST	SF	FBG DV	IB T330	10 6		2	33700	37500
39 4	CRUISER SPORTSMAN 39	OP	SF	FBG DV	IB T330	10 6		2	41100	45700
40	CORSA 40	OP	SPTCR	FBG DV	IB T330	9		2	53100	58400
42	SPORTCRUISER 42	OP	SPTCR	FBG DV	IB T330	9 6		2	59900	65800
43 6	CORSA 44	OP	SPTCR	FBG DV	IB T330	9 6		2	71800	79800
46	SPORTCRUISER 46	OP	SPTCR	FBG DV	IB T330	10 6		2	63000	69200
					1987 BOATS					
28	MAGUS 28 BOWRIDER		B/R	F/S DV	IB D	8	4000	1 6	**	**
28	MAGUS 28 CENTER CNSL		OPFSH	F/S DV	IB D	8	4000	1 6	**	**
28	MAGUS 28 SPORT		RACE	F/S DV	IB D	8	4000	1 6	**	**
30	CORSA 30 CENTER CNSL		OPFSH	F/S DV	IB D	8	4300	1 6	**	**
30	CORSA 30 SIDE CNSL		OPFSH	F/S DV	IB D	8	4300	1 6	**	**
30	CORSA 30 SPORT		RACE	F/S DV	IB D	8	4300	1 6	**	**
35	SPORT FISHERMAN 35		SF	F/S DV	IB T D	10 6	9000	2	**	**
42	OFFSHORE 42		SPTCR	F/S DV	IB T D	10 6	10500	2	**	**
44	CORSA 44 B		SPTCR	F/S DV	IB T D	10 6	10500	2	**	**
46	FALCON 46		SPTCR	F/S DV	IB T D	10 6	12000	2	**	**
46	OFFSHORE 46 B		SPTCR	F/S DV	IB T D	10 6	10800	2	**	**

SUNBIRD YACHTS LTD
HANTS ENGLAND   See inside cover to adjust price for area

LOA FT IN	NAME AND/ OR MODEL	TOP/ RIG	BOAT TYPE	-HULL- MTL TP	----ENGINE--- TP # HP MFG	BEAM FT IN	WGT LBS	DRAFT FT IN	RETAIL LOW	RETAIL HIGH
					1985 BOATS					
32 6	SUN-BIRD 32		SAIL	FBG KL		10 4		4	25300	28100

....For earlier years, see the BUC Used Boat Price Guide, Volume 3

SUNCHASER FLOATING HOMES
UVERPLANCK NY 10596   See inside cover to adjust price for area

LOA FT IN	NAME AND/ OR MODEL	TOP/ RIG	BOAT TYPE	-HULL- MTL TP	----ENGINE--- TP # HP MFG	BEAM FT IN	WGT LBS	DRAFT FT IN	RETAIL LOW	RETAIL HIGH
					1990 BOATS					
36	SUN SONG		FH	F/W FL		24	70000	1 6	**	**
40 6	MORNING STAR		FH	FBG FL		16 6	35000	10	**	**
42	AMINRA		FH	FBG FL			42000	1 1	**	**
42	DAWN LIGHT		FH	FBG FL			40000	1	**	**
					1989 BOATS					
37	SUN SONG		FH	FBG		24	70000	1 3	**	**
40 6	MORNING STAR		FH	FBG FL		16 6	35000	10	**	**
42	AMINRA		FH	FBG			42000	1 1	**	**
42	DAWN LIGHT		FH	FBG			40000	1	**	**
					1988 BOATS					
40 6	AMINRA		FH	FBG FL		16 6	35000	10	**	**
42	DAWN LIGHT		FH	FBG			42000	1 1	**	**
42			FH	FBG			40000	1	**	**

SUNCRUISER PONTOONS
DIV OF OMC ALUMINUM BOAT GROUP
SYRACUSE IN 46567   See inside cover to adjust price for area

For more recent years, see the BUC Used Boat Price Guide, Volume 1

LOA FT IN	NAME AND/ OR MODEL	TOP/ RIG	BOAT TYPE	-HULL- MTL TP	----ENGINE--- TP # HP MFG	BEAM FT IN	WGT LBS	DRAFT FT IN	RETAIL LOW	RETAIL HIGH
					1992 BOATS					
22 1	SD220 SPORT DECK	ST	RNBT	AL DV	OB	8	1800		4100	4750
22 1	SD220 SPORT DECK	ST	RNBT	AL PN	OB	8	1800		4100	4750

SUNDOWNER MARINE CORPORATION
ANNAPOLIS MD 21403   COAST GUARD MFG ID- XDO See inside cover to adjust price for area

LOA FT IN	NAME AND/ OR MODEL	TOP/ RIG	BOAT TYPE	-HULL- MTL TP	----ENGINE--- TP # HP MFG	BEAM FT IN	WGT LBS	DRAFT FT IN	RETAIL LOW	RETAIL HIGH
					1985 BOATS					
39 4	SCREAMER 12M	SLP	SA/RC	FBG KL	SD 15 OMC	10	3300	7 8	16200	18400

SUNRAY
ST ANNE DE LA PERADE QU COAST GUARD MFG ID- ZSU See inside cover to adjust price for area

LOA FT IN	NAME AND/ OR MODEL	TOP/ RIG	BOAT TYPE	-HULL- MTL TP	----ENGINE--- TP # HP MFG	BEAM FT IN	WGT LBS	DRAFT FT IN	RETAIL LOW	RETAIL HIGH
					1995 BOATS					
16	FISHERMAN	OP	UTL	FBG SV	OB	6	510		1350	1600
16	FISHERMAN DXL	OP	UTL	FBG SV	OB	6	510		1550	1800
16	SUPER FISHER	OP	FSH	FBG SV	OB	6	510		1450	1700
16 2	SKI	OP	RNBT	FBG SV	OB	6 6	675		1900	2250
16 3	XL-16	OP	B/R	FBG SV	OB	6 8	900		2550	2950
16 6	TAURUS	OP	B/R	FBG SV	OB	7	910		2600	3000
16 11	SUNKIFF	OP	FSH	FBG SV	OB	6	690		1950	2300
18	FISH N SKI	OP	UTL	FBG SV	OB	7	1288		3500	4050
18 6	ALLEGRO	OP	RNBT	FBG SV	OB	7 6	1450		4050	4700
18 6	ALLEGRO	OP	RNBT	FBG SV	IO	7 6	1450		**	**
18 6	ALLEGRO	OP	RNBT	FBG SV	IO 180	7 6	1450		5450	6300
20	PRELUDE	OP	B/R	FBG SV	IO	8	2600		**	**

LOA FT IN	NAME AND/ OR MODEL	TOP/ RIG	BOAT TYPE	-HULL- MTL TP	----ENGINE--- TP # HP MFG	BEAM FT IN	WGT LBS	DRAFT FT IN	RETAIL LOW	RETAIL HIGH
				---- 1995 BOATS ----						
20	PRELUDE	OP	B/R	FBG SV	IO 180-190	8	2600		7300	8450
21 10	EXCITER	OP	RNBT	FBG SV	IO	8	2451		**	**
21 10	EXCITER	OP	RNBT	FBG SV	IO 250	8	2451		9250	10500
21 10	EXCITER	OP	RNBT	FBG SV	IO 350	8	2451		11200	12700
23 3	INFINITY	OP	RNBT	FBG SV	IO 180-190	8 1	3300		**	**
23 3	INFINITY	OP	RNBT	FBG SV	IO 180-190	8 1	3300		10400	11900

....For earlier years, see the BUC Used Boat Price Guide, Volume 3

SUNSATION PERFORMANCE BOATS
ANCHORVILLE MI 48004   COAST GUARD MFG ID- SP3 See inside cover to adjust price for area
FORMERLY SUNSATION PRODUCTS

LOA FT IN	NAME AND/ OR MODEL	TOP/ RIG	BOAT TYPE	-HULL- MTL TP	----ENGINE--- TP # HP MFG	BEAM FT IN	WGT LBS	DRAFT FT IN	RETAIL LOW	RETAIL HIGH
				---- 1995 BOATS ----						
24 7	SUNSATION AGGRESSOR	OP	OFF	FBG DV	IO 300 MRCR	7 1	3100	3	14000	15900
24 7	SUNSATION AGGRESSOR	OP	OFF	FBG DV	IO 350-385	7 1	3100	3	15600	19300
24 7	SUNSATION AGGRESSOR	OP	OFF	FBG DV	IO 415	7 1	3100	3	18700	20800
28 6	SUNSATION INTIMIDATR	OP	OFF	FBG DV	IO 300-385	8	4500	3	25300	30600
IO 415 MRCR 28500	31600, IO 465-500				30100 34700, IO 525		MRCR		32000	35600
32	SUNSATION 32 DOM	OP	OFF	FBG DV	IO T300-T415	8 1	6200	3	49100	60000
32	SUNSATION 32 DOM	OP	OFF	FBG DV	IO T465 MRCR	8 1	6200	3	55300	60800
				---- 1994 BOATS ----						
24 7	SUNSATION AGGRESSOR	OP	OFF	FBG DV	IO 260-300	7 3	3000	2 9	12200	15000
24 7	SUNSATION AGGRESSOR	OP	OFF	FBG DV	IO 350-385	7 3	3150	3	14800	18200
24 7	SUNSATION AGGRESSOR	OP	OFF	FBG DV	IO 415 MRCR	7 3	3150	3	17200	19600
28	SUNSATION INTIMIDATR	OP	OFF	FBG DV	IO 300-385	8	4300	3	21800	24700
28	SUNSATION INTIMIDATR	OP	OFF	FBG DV	IO 415 MRCR	8	4300	3	24900	27700
28	SUNSATION INTIMIDATR	OP	OFF	FBG DV	IO 525 MRCR	8	4300	3	28400	31600
32	SUNSATION 32 DOM	OP	OFF	FBG DV	IO 465 MRCR	8	6100	3	43400	48200
32	SUNSATION 32 DOM	OP	OFF	FBG DV	IO T260-T415	8	6000	3	43900	54700
				---- 1993 BOATS ----						
24 7	SUNSATION AGGRESSOR	OP	OFF	FBG DV	IO 260-270	7 3	3000	2 9	11400	13100
IO 330-365	13000	16200, IO			420 MRCR 16400 18700, IO		465	MRCR	18700	20800
32	SUNSATION 32 DOM	OP	OFF	FBG DV	IO 330 MRCR	8	6100	3	38200	42500
32	SUNSATION 32 DOM	OP	OFF	FBG DV	IO T260-T420	8	6000	3	41300	51100
				---- 1992 BOATS ----						
24 7	SUNSATION AGGRESSOR	OP	OFF	FBG DV	IO 260-270	7 3	3000	2 9	10600	12200
IO 330-365	12100	14900, IO			420 MRCR 15400 17500, IO		465	MRCR	17100	19500
32	SUNSATION 32 DOM	OP	OFF	FBG DV	IO 330 MRCR	8	6100	3	35200	39100
32	SUNSATION 32 DOM	OP	OFF	FBG DV	IO T260-T365	8	6000	3	38100	46000
32	SUNSATION 32 DOM	OP	OFF	FBG DV	IO T420 MRCR	8	6100	3	43000	47800
				---- 1991 BOATS ----						
24 7	SUNSATION AGGRESSOR	OP	OFF	FBG DV	IO 260-270	7 3	3000	2 9	9950	11400
IO 330-365	11400	14000, IO			420 MRCR 14400 16400, IO		465	MRCR	16200	18400
30	SUNSATION 3200	OP	OFF	FBG DV	IO 330-420	8	3900	3	23200	28000
IO 465 MRCR 26200	29100, IO			T260-T365	26400 32900, IO		T420	MRCR	31600	35100
				---- 1990 BOATS ----						
23 7	SUNSATION	OP	OFF	FBG DV	IO 260-270	7 1	3000	2 9	8600	10000
23 7	SUNSATION MAGNUM	OP	OFF	FBG DV	IO 365 MRCR	7 1	3150	3	10900	12400
23 7	SUNSATION ROCKET	OP	OFF	FBG DV	IO 330 MRCR	7 1	3150	3	10000	11400
23 7	SUNSATION SP ED	OP	OFF	FBG DV	IO 420 MRCR	7 1	3150	3	12800	14500
				---- 1989 BOATS ----						
23 7	SUNSATION EX	OP	OFF	FBG DV	OB	7 1	2800	2 7	10900	12400
23 7	SUNSATION ROCKET	OP	OFF	FBG DV	IO 365 MRCR				10300	11700
23 7	SUNSATION SS	OP	OFF	FBG DV	IO 260 MRCR	7 1	3300	2 9	8550	9850
23 7	SUNSATION SS	OP	OFF	FBG DV	IO 320-330	7 1	3300	2 9	9450	11000
				---- 1988 BOATS ----						
23 7	SUNSATION EX	OP	OFF	FBG DV	OB	7 1	2800	2 7	10500	12000
23 7	SUNSATION SS	OP	OFF	FBG DV	IO 260-320	7 1	3300	2 9	8100	10100
23 7	SUNSATION SS	OP	OFF	FBG DV	IO 330 MRCR	7 1	3500	3	9450	10700
				---- 1986 BOATS ----						
23 7	EXTRAORDINARY	OP	RNBT	FBG DV	SE 205 OMC	7	2800		9900	11200

....For earlier years, see the BUC Used Boat Price Guide, Volume 3

SUNSEEKER
DANIA BEACH FL 33004   COAST GUARD MFG ID- QSU See inside cover to adjust price for area

HIDEAWAY YACHT GROUP
POMPANO BEACH FL 33062

For more recent years, see the BUC Used Boat Price Guide, Volume 1

LOA FT IN	NAME AND/ OR MODEL	TOP/ RIG	BOAT TYPE	-HULL- MTL TP	----ENGINE--- TP # HP MFG	BEAM FT IN	WGT LBS	DRAFT FT IN	RETAIL LOW	RETAIL HIGH
				---- 1992 BOATS ----						
29 11	HI-PERFORMANCE MHK	OP	OFF	FBG DV	IO T330-T365	10	7800	2 8	41100	47200
36 8	TOMAHAWK	OP	OFF	FBG DV	IO T330 VLVO	10 6	12320	3 7	58400	64200
36 8	TOMAHAWK	OP	OFF	FBG DV	IO T365 MRCR	10 6	12320	3 7	59300	65200
36 8	TOMAHAWK	OP	OFF	FBG DV	IO T410 MRCR	10 6	12320	3 7	62800	69000
38	MARTINIQUE	OP	SPTCR	FBG DV	IO T330 MRCR	12	15680	3 5	56800	61300
IO T330 VLVO 56700	62300, IO			T365	MRCR 57600 63300, IO		T200D	VLVO	67100	73700
44	LUXURY OFFSHORE	OP	OFF	FBG DV	IO T330 VLVO	11	16128	3 10	91000	100000
44	LUXURY OFFSHORE	OP	OFF	FBG DV	IO T410 MRCR	11	16128	3 10	97400	107000
44	LUXURY OFFSHORE	OP	OFF	FBG DV	IO T465 MRCR	11	16128	3 10	103000	113000
50	LUXURY OFFSHORE	OP	OFF	FBG DV	IB T680D MAN	13 2	31056	2 8	285500	314000
				---- 1991 BOATS ----						
29 11	HI-PERFORMANCE MHK	OP	OFF	FBG DV	IO T330-T365	10	7800	2 8	38500	44300
36	MARTINIQUE	OP	SPTCR	FBG DV	IO T330 MRCR	12	15680	3 5	52300	57500
IO T330 VLVO 53200	58400, IO			T365	MRCR 54000 59400, IO		T200D	VLVO	62900	69100
36 8	TOMAHAWK	OP	OFF	FBG DV	IO T330 VLVO	10 6	12320	3 7	54800	60200
36 8	TOMAHAWK	OP	OFF	FBG DV	IO T365 MRCR	10 6	12320	3 7	55600	61200
36 8	TOMAHAWK	OP	OFF	FBG DV	IO T410 MRCR	10 6	12320	3 7	58900	64700

SUNWARD YACHT CORP
WILMINGTON NC 28405   COAST GUARD MFG ID- SJW See inside cover to adjust price for area

LOA FT IN	NAME AND/ OR MODEL	TOP/ RIG	BOAT TYPE	-HULL- MTL TP	----ENGINE--- TP # HP MFG	BEAM FT IN	WGT LBS	DRAFT FT IN	RETAIL LOW	RETAIL HIGH
				---- 1995 BOATS ----						
48	SUNWARD 48	KTH	SACAC	FBG KL	IB 135D PERK	14 3	48000	5 7	333000	365500
63	SUNWARD 63	CUT	SACAC	FBG KL	IB 160D CAT	16 7	65000	7	647500	712000
				---- 1994 BOATS ----						
48	SUNWARD 48	KTH	SACAC	FBG KL	IB 135D PERK	14 3	48000	5 7	313000	344000
63	SUNWARD 63	CUT	SACAC	FBG KL	IB 160D CAT	16 7	65000	7	609500	669500
				---- 1993 BOATS ----						
48	SUNWARD 48	KTH	SA/CR	FBG KL	IB 135D PERK	14 3	48000	5 7	294500	323500
63	SUNWARD 63	CUT	SA/CR	FBG KL	IB 160D CAT	16 7	65000	7	573000	630000
				---- 1992 BOATS ----						
48	SUNWARD 48	KTH	SA/CR	FBG KL	IB 135D PERK	14 3	48000	5 7	277000	304500
63	SUNWARD 63	CUT	SA/CR	FBG KL	IB 160D CAT	16 7	65000	7	539000	592500
				---- 1991 BOATS ----						
48	SUNWARD 48	KTH	SA/CR	FBG KL	IB 135D PERK	14 3	48000	5 7	260500	286500
63	SUNWARD 63	CUT	SA/CR	FBG KL	IB 160D CAT	16 7	65000	7	507000	557000
				---- 1990 BOATS ----						
48	SUNWARD 48	KTH	SA/CR	FBG KL	IB 135D PERK	14 3	48000	5 7	245000	269500
63	SUNWARD 63	CUT	SA/CR	FBG KL	IB 160D CAT	16 7	65000	7	477000	524000
				---- 1989 BOATS ----						
48	SUNWARD 48	KTH	SA/CR	FBG KL	IB 135D PERK	14 3	48000	5 7	230500	253500
63	SUNWARD 63	CUT	SA/CR	FBG KL	IB 160D CAT	16 7	65000	7	448500	493000
				---- 1988 BOATS ----						
48	SUNWARD 48	KTH	SA/CR	FBG KL	IB 100D WEST	14 3	48000	5 8	217500	239000
63	SUNWARD 63	CUT	SA/CR	FBG KL	IB 160D CAT	16 7	65000	7	422000	463500
				---- 1987 BOATS ----						
48	SUNWARD 48	KTH	SA/CR	FBG KL	IB 100D WEST	14 3	48000	5 7	204500	224500
63	SUNWARD 63	CUT	SA/CR	FBG KL	IB 160D CAT	16 7	65000	7	397000	436000
				---- 1986 BOATS ----						
48	SUNWARD 48	KTH	SA/CR	FBG KL	IB 100D WEST	14 3	48000	5 8	192500	211500
63	SUNWARD 63	CUT	SA/CR	FBG KL	IB 160D CAT	16 7	65000	7	373500	410500
				---- 1985 BOATS ----						
48	SUNWARD 48	KTH	SA/CR	FBG KL	IB 100D WEST	14 3	48000	5 7	181000	199000
60 2	SUNWARD 60	CUT	SA/CR	FBG KL	IB 180D PERK	16 9	75023	5 9	377500	415000
				---- 1984 BOATS ----						
48	SUNWARD 48	KTH	SA/CR	FBG KL	IB 100D WEST	14 3	48000	5 7	170000	187000

....For earlier years, see the BUC Used Boat Price Guide, Volume 3

SUPERBOATS

LINDENHURST NY 11757-30 COAST GUARD MFG ID- SBY See inside cover to adjust price for area

For more recent years, see the BUC Used Boat Price Guide, Volume 1

LOA FT	LOA IN	NAME AND/ OR MODEL	TOP/ RIG	BOAT TYPE	-HULL- MTL	-HULL- TP	ENGINE TP	ENGINE # HP	ENGINE MFG	BEAM FT	BEAM IN	WGT LBS	DRAFT FT	DRAFT IN	RETAIL LOW	RETAIL HIGH
		1996 BOATS														
20	7	SUPERBOAT 21	OP	OFF	F/S	DV	OB			7	6	1250			8950	10200
20	7	SUPERBOAT 21	OP	OFF	F/S	DV	IO	250	MRCR	7	6	1250			15000	17000
23	7	FISHERMAN 24	OP	OFF	F/S	DV	OB			7		1800			12000	13600
23	7	SUPERBOAT 24	OP	OFF	F/S	DV	OB			7		1800			14000	15900
23	7	SUPERBOAT 24	OP	OFF	F/S	DV	IO	250-300		7		1800			19000	22600
23	7	SUPERBOAT 24	OP	OFF	F/S	DV	IO	350-385		7		1800			23100	28800
23	7	SUPERBOAT 24	OP	OFF	F/S	DV	IO	415	MRCR	7		1800			28800	32000
30		SUPERBOAT 30	OP	OFF	F/S	DV	OB			7		2500			42500	47200
30		SUPERBOAT 30	OP	OFF	F/S	DV	IO	250-350		7		2500			39600	48300
30		SUPERBOAT 30	OP	OFF	F/S	DV	IO	385-415		7		2500			45000	51500
31	7	SUPERCAT 32 HIGHDECK	OP	OFF	F/S	CT	OB			8	4	3900			55500	61000
31	7	SUPERCAT 32 HIGHDECK	OP	OFF	F/S	TH	IO			8	4	3900			**	**
31	7	SUPERCAT 32 SPORT	OP	OFF	F/S	CT	OB			8	4	3700			45600	50100
31	7	SUPERCAT 32 SPORT	OP	OFF	F/S	TH	IO			8	4	3700			**	**
33	7	SUPERBOAT 34	OP	OFF	F/S	DV	OB			8	6	3800			26700	29700
33	7	SUPERBOAT 34	OP	OFF	F/S	DV	IO			8	6	3800			**	**
		1995 BOATS														
20	7	SUPERBOAT 21	OP	OFF	F/S	DV	OB			7	6	1250			8350	9600
23	7	FISHERMAN 24	OP	OFF	F/S	DV	OB			7	6	1800			12300	13900
23	7	SUPERBOAT 24	OP	OFF	F/S	DV	OB			7		1800			12300	13900
23	7	SUPERBOAT 24	OP	OFF	F/S	DV	IO	235-300		7		1800			17100	21100
23	7	SUPERBOAT 24	OP	OFF	F/S	DV	IO	350-385		7		1800			21600	26800
23	7	SUPERBOAT 24	OP	OFF	F/S	DV	IO	415	MRCR	7		1800			26800	29800
30		SUPERBOAT 30	OP	OFF	F/S	DV	OB			7		2500			40100	44600
30		SUPERBOAT 30	OP	OFF	F/S	DV	IO	235-350		7		2500			36400	45100
30		SUPERBOAT 30	OP	OFF	F/S	DV	IO	385-415		7		2500			42000	48000
31	7	SUPERCAT 32 HIGHDECK	OP	OFF	F/S	CT	OB			8	4	3900			52500	57700
31	7	SUPERCAT 32 HIGHDECK	OP	OFF	F/S	CT	IB			8	4	3900			**	**
31	7	SUPERCAT 32 SPORT	OP	OFF	F/S	CT	OB			8	4	3700			42600	47400
31	7	SUPERCAT 32 SPORT	OP	OFF	F/S	CT	IB			8	4	3700			**	**
33	7	SUPERBOAT 34	OP	OFF	F/S	DV	OB			8	6	3800			25300	28100
33	7	SUPERBOAT 34	OP	OFF	F/S	DV	IB			8	6	3800			**	**
		1994 BOATS														
20	7	SUPERBOAT 21	OP	OFF	F/S	DV	OB			7	6	1250			7900	9100
23	7	FISHERMAN 24	OP	OFF	F/S	DV	OB			7	6	1800			11600	13200
23	7	SUPERBOAT 24	OP	OFF	F/S	DV	OB			7		1800			11600	13200
23	7	SUPERBOAT 24	OP	OFF	F/S	DV	IO	230-250		7		1800			15900	18400
		IO 300 MRCR 17500 19900, IO 350-385 20200 25100, IO 415-445													25000	30900
30		SUPERBOAT 30	OP	OFF	F/S	DV	OB			7		2500			38000	42200
30		SUPERBOAT 30	OP	OFF	F/S	DV	IO	230-350		7		2500			33800	42100
30		SUPERBOAT 30	OP	OFF	F/S	DV	IO	385-445		7		2500			39200	46100
31	7	SUPERCAT 32 HIGHDECK	OP	OFF	F/S	DV	OB			8	4	3900			47300	51900
31	7	SUPERCAT 32 HIGHDECK	OP	OFF	F/S	DV	IB			8	4	3900			**	**
31	7	SUPERCAT 32 SPORT	OP	OFF	F/S	DV	OB			8	4	3700			37800	42000
31	7	SUPERCAT 32 SPORT	OP	OFF	F/S	DV	IB			8	4	3700			**	**
		1993 BOATS														
20	7	SUPERBOAT 21	OP	OFF	F/S	DV	OB			7	6	1250			7550	8650
23	7	FISHERMAN 24	OP	OFF	F/S	DV	OB			7	6	1800			11100	12600
23	7	SUPERBOAT 24	OP	OFF	F/S	DV	OB			7		1800			11100	12600
23	7	SUPERBOAT 24	OP	OFF	F/S	DV	IO	230-250		7		1800			14800	17200
		IO 300 MRCR 16400 18600, IO 350 MRCR 19000 21200, IO 390-415													21500	26000
		IO 445 MRCR 26000 28900														
30		SUPERBOAT 30	OP	OFF	F/S	DV	OB			7		2500			36100	40100
30		SUPERBOAT 30	OP	OFF	F/S	DV	IO	230-350		7		2500			31600	39300
30		SUPERBOAT 30	OP	OFF	F/S	DV	IO	390-445		7		2500			36800	43100
31	7	SUPERCAT 32 HIGHDECK	OP	OFF	F/S	DV	OB			8	4	3900			44100	49000
31	7	SUPERCAT 32 HIGHDECK	OP	OFF	F/S	DV	IB			8	4	3900			**	**
31	7	SUPERCAT 32 SPORT	OP	OFF	F/S	DV	OB			8	4	3700			35900	39900
31	7	SUPERCAT 32 SPORT	OP	OFF	F/S	DV	IB			8	4	3700			**	**
		1992 BOATS														
20	7	SUPERBOAT 21	OP	OFF	F/S	DV	OB			7	6	1250			7150	8250
23	7	FISHERMAN 24	OP	OFF	F/S	DV	OB			7	6	1800			10600	12000
23	7	SUPERBOAT 24	OP	OFF	F/S	DV	OB			7		1800			10600	12000
23	7	SUPERBOAT 24	OP	OFF	F/S	DV	IO	260	MRCR	7		1800			14300	16300
23	7	SUPERBOAT 24	OP	OFF	F/S	DV	IO	365	MRCR	7		1800			18700	20800
30		SUPERBOAT 30	OP	OFF	F/S	DV	OB			7		2500			34300	38100
31	7	SUPERCAT 32 HIGHDECK	OP	OFF	F/S	DV	OB			8		3500			41700	46300
31	7	SUPERCAT 32 HIGHDECK	OP	OFF	F/S	DV	IO			8		3500			**	**
31	7	SUPERCAT 32 SPORT	OP	OFF	F/S	DV	OB			8		3500			33900	37700
31	7	SUPERCAT 32 SPORT	OP	OFF	F/S	DV	IO			8		3500			**	**
		1991 BOATS														
20	7	SUPERBOAT 21	OP	OFF	F/S	DV	OB			7	6	1250			6850	7850
23	7	SUPERBOAT 24	OP	OFF	F/S	DV	OB			7		1800			10100	11500
23	7	SUPERBOAT 24	OP	OFF	F/S	DV	IO			7		1800			**	**
23	7	SUPERBOAT 24	OP	OFF	F/S	DV	IO	T		7		1800			**	**
30		SUPERBOAT 30	OP	OFF	F/S	DV	OB			7		2500			32700	36400
31	7	SUPERCAT 32 HIGHDECK	OP	OFF	F/S		OB			8		3500			39800	44200
31	7	SUPERCAT 32 HIGHDECK	OP	OFF	F/S		IO			8		3500			**	**
31	7	SUPERCAT 32 SPORT	OP	OFF	F/S	DV	OB			8		3500			32200	35800
31	7	SUPERCAT 32 SPORT	OP	OFF	F/S	DV	IO			8		3500			**	**
		1990 BOATS														
20	7	SUPERBOAT 21	OP	OFF	F/S	DV	OB			7	6	1250			6550	7500
23	7	SUPERBOAT 24	OP	OFF	F/S	DV	OB			7		1800			9750	11100
23	7	SUPERBOAT 24	OP	OFF	F/S	DV	IO			7		1800			**	**
23	7	SUPERBOAT 24	OP	OFF	F/S	DV	IO	T		7		1800			**	**
30		SUPERBOAT 30	OP	OFF	F/S	DV	OB			7		2500			31300	34700
31	7	SUPERCAT 32 HIGHDECK	OP	OFF	F/S		OB			8		3500			38000	42300
31	7	SUPERCAT 32 HIGHDECK	OP	OFF	F/S		IO			8		3500			**	**
31	7	SUPERCAT 32 SPORT	OP	OFF	F/S	DV	OB			8		3500			30800	34200
31	7	SUPERCAT 32 SPORT	OP	OFF	F/S	DV	IO			8		3500			**	**
		1989 BOATS														
20	7	SUPERBOAT 21	OP	OFF	F/S	DV	OB			7	6	1250			6250	7200
23	7	SUPERBOAT 24	OP	OFF	F/S	DV	OB			7		1800			9350	10600
23	7	SUPERBOAT 24	OP	OFF	F/S	DV	IO			7		1800			**	**
23	7	SUPERBOAT 24	OP	OFF	F/S	DV	IO	T		7		1800			**	**
30		SUPERBOAT 30	OP	OFF	F/S	DV	OB			7		2500			30000	33300
31	7	SUPERCAT 32 HIGHDECK	OP	OFF	F/S		OB			8		3500			36400	40500
31	7	SUPERCAT 32 HIGHDECK	OP	OFF	F/S		IO			8		3500			**	**
31	7	SUPERCAT 32 SPORT	OP	OFF	F/S	DV	OB			8		3500			29500	32800
31	7	SUPERCAT 32 SPORT	OP	OFF	F/S	DV	IO			8		3500			**	**
		1988 BOATS														
20	7	SUPERBOAT 21	OP	OFF	F/S	DV	OB			7	6	1250			6000	6900
23	7	SUPERBOAT 24	OP	OFF	F/S	DV	OB			7		1800			9000	10200
23	7	SUPERBOAT 24	OP	OFF	F/S	DV	IO			7		1800			**	**
23	7	SUPERBOAT 24	OP	OFF	F/S	DV	IO	T		7		1800			**	**
30		SUPERBOAT 30	OP	OFF	F/S	DV	OB			7		2500			28700	31900
31	7	SUPERCAT 32 HIGHDECK	OP	OFF	F/S		OB			8		3500			35000	38900
31	7	SUPERCAT 32 HIGHDECK	OP	OFF	F/S		IO			8		3500			**	**
31	7	SUPERCAT 32 SPORT	OP	OFF	F/S	DV	OB			8		3500			28300	31400
31	7	SUPERCAT 32 SPORT	OP	OFF	F/S	DV	IO			8		3500	4		**	**
		1987 BOATS														
20	7	SUPERBOAT 21	OP	OFF	F/S	DV	OB			7	6	1250			5800	6650
23	7	SUPERBOAT 24	OP	OFF	F/S	DV	OB			7		1800			8550	9800
30		SUPERBOAT 30	OP	OFF	F/S	DV	OB			7		2500			27700	30700
31	7	SUPERCAT 32	OP	OFF	F/S	DV	OB			7		2500			29900	33200
31	7	SUPERCAT 32	OP	OFF	F/S	DV	IO			7		8500	4		**	**
		1986 BOATS														
20	7	SUPERBOAT 21	OP	RNBT	F/S	DV	OB			7	6	1250	1	6	5600	6450
23	7	SUPERBOAT 24	OP	OFF	F/S	DV	OB			7		1800	2		8250	9500
23	7	SUPERBOAT 24	OP	OFF	F/S	DV	IO	260	MRCR	7		3100	2	6	12800	14500
23	7	SUPERBOAT 24	OP	OFF	F/S	DV	IO	330	MRCR	7		3100	2	6	14300	16200
30		SUPERBOAT 30	OP	OFF	F/S	DV	OB			7		2500	2	5	26700	29600
30		SUPERBOAT 30	OP	OFF	F/S	DV	IO	330	MRCR	7		3800	2	6	22800	25300
30		SUPERBOAT 30	OP	OFF	F/S	DV	IO	T	CHEV	7		5000	2	10	**	**
31	7	CAT 32	OP	OFF	F/S	CT	OB			8		3500	2		31600	35100
31	7	CAT 32	OP	OFF	F/S	CT	IO	T280		8		5300	2	6	31800	35300
		1985 BOATS														
16		FISHERMAN	OP	CTRCN	FBG	SV	OB			6	6	750	1		2850	3300
20	7	SUPERBOAT 21	OP	RNBT	F/S	DV	OB			7	6	1250	1	6	5400	6200
23	6	FISHERMAN	OP	CTRCN	FBG	DV	OB			7		1700			7550	8700
23	7	SUPERBOAT 24	OP	OFF	F/S	DV	OB			7		1800	2		7950	9150
23	7	SUPERBOAT 24	OP	OFF	F/S	DV	IO	260	MRCR	7		3100	2	6	12200	13900
23	7	SUPERBOAT 24	OP	OFF	F/S	DV	IO	330	MRCR	7		3100	2	6	13700	15600
30		SUPERBOAT 30	OP	OFF	F/S	DV	OB			7		2500	2	5	25800	28600
30		SUPERBOAT 30	OP	OFF	F/S	DV	IO	330-400		7		3800	2	6	21600	25800
30		SUPERBOAT 30	OP	OFF	F/S	DV	IO	T300	MRCR	7		5000	2	10	25600	28500
31	7	CAT 32	OP	OFF	F/S	CT	OB			8		3500	2		30500	33900
31	7	CAT 32	OP	OFF	F/S	CT	IO	T280		8		5300	2	6	30300	33700
		1984 BOATS														
16		FISHERMAN	OP	CTRCN	FBG	SV	OB			6	6	750	1		2750	3200
20	7	SUPERBOAT 21	OP	RNBT	F/S	DV	OB			7	6	1250	1	6	5250	6050
23	6	FISHERMAN	OP	CTRCN	FBG	DV	OB			7		1700			7300	8400
23	7	SS 24	OP	OFF	F/S	DV	OB			7		1800	2		7750	8900
23	7	SS 24	OP	OFF	F/S	DV	IO	400		7		3100	2	6	15900	18100
30		SUPERBOAT 30	OP	OFF	F/S	DV	OB			7		2500	2	5	25000	27700
30		SUPERBOAT 30	OP	OFF	F/S	DV	IO	330-400		7		3800	2	6	21000	24900
30		SUPERBOAT 30	OP	OFF	F/S	DV	IO	T300		7		5000	2	10	24600	27300
31	7	CAT 32	OP	OFF	F/S	CT	OB			8		3500	2		29600	32800

CONTINUED ON NEXT PAGE

LOA FT IN	NAME AND/OR MODEL	TOP/RIG	BOAT TYPE	HULL MTL TP	ENGINE TP # HP MFG	BEAM FT IN	WGT LBS	DRAFT FT IN	RETAIL LOW	RETAIL HIGH
1984 BOATS										
31 7	CAT 32	OP	OFF	F/S CT	IO T280	8	5300	2 6	29100	32300

....For earlier years, see the BUC Used Boat Price Guide, Volume 3

SUPERCAT CATAMARANS
DIV OF ERICSON YACHTS
MAHTOMEDI MN 55115   COAST GUARD MFG ID- FMS   See inside cover to adjust price for area

LOA FT IN	NAME AND/OR MODEL	TOP/RIG	BOAT TYPE	HULL MTL TP	ENGINE TP # HP MFG	BEAM FT IN	WGT LBS	DRAFT FT IN	RETAIL LOW	RETAIL HIGH
1990 BOATS										
17	SUPERCAT 17	SLP	SA/OD	F/S CT		8	325	2	4150	4850
19	SUPERCAT 19XL	SLP	SA/OD	F/S CT		8 6	400	3 6	5850	6700
19	SUPERCAT 19XL PLTFRM	SLP	SA/OD	F/S CT		8 6	400	3 6	4950	5700
20	SUPERCAT 20	SLP	SA/OD	F/S CT		12	450	3 6	5950	6850
20	SUPERCAT 20 TALL	SLP	SA/OD	F/S CT		12	475	3 6	6150	7100
1989 BOATS										
17	SUPERCAT 17	SLP	SA/OD	F/S CT		8	325	2	3900	4550
17	SUPERCAT 17	SLP	SA/OD	F/S CT		8	325	2	3900	4550
19	SUPERCAT 19	SLP	SA/OD	F/S CT		8	385	3	4950	5700
19	SUPERCAT 19X	SLP	SA/OD	F/S CT		8 6	400	3 6	5000	5750
19	SUPERCAT 19XL	SLP	SA/OD	F/S CT		8 6	400	3 6	5200	5950
20	SUPERCAT 20	SLP	SA/OD	F/S CT		12	450	3 6	5600	6450
20	SUPERCAT 20 TALL	SLP	SA/OD	F/S CT		12	475	3 6	5800	6650
1988 BOATS										
17	SUPERCAT 17	SLP	SA/OD	F/S CT		8	325	2	3700	4300
17	SUPERCAT 17	SLP	SA/OD	F/S CT		8	325	2	3700	4300
18	SUPERCAT 18	CAT	SA/OD	F/S CT		12	370	3 6	4300	4950
19	SUPERCAT 19	SLP	SA/OD	F/S CT		8	385	3	4700	5400
20	SUPERCAT 20	SLP	SA/OD	F/S CT		12	450	3 6	5300	6050
20	SUPERCAT 20 TALL	SLP	SA/OD	F/S CT		12	465	3 6	5400	6200
1987 BOATS										
17	SUPERCAT 17	SLP	SA/OD	F/S CT		8	325	2	3450	4000
17	SUPERCAT 17	SLP	SA/OD	F/S CT		8	325	2	3450	4000
18	SUPERCAT 18	CAT	SA/OD	F/S CT		12	370	3 6	4000	4700
19	SUPERCAT 19	SLP	SA/OD	F/S CT		8	385	3	4400	5050
20	SUPERCAT 20	SLP	SA/OD	F/S CT		12	450	3 6	4950	5700
1986 BOATS										
18	SUPERCAT	SLP	SAIL	F/S CT					3800	4400
18	SUPERCAT 18	SLP	SA/OD	F/S CT					3800	4400
1985 BOATS										
17	SUPERCAT	SLP	SAIL	F/S CT		8	335	10	3150	3650
17	SUPERCAT 17	SLP	SA/OD	F/S CT		8	335	10	3150	3650
19	SUPERCAT	SLP	SAIL	F/S CT		8	375	6	3800	4400
19	SUPERCAT 19	SLP	SA/OD	F/S CT		8	375	6	3800	4400
20	SUPERCAT	SLP	SAIL	F/S CT		12	450	6	4400	5100
20	SUPERCAT 20	SLP	SA/OD	F/S CT		12	450	6	4400	5100
1984 BOATS										
17	SUPERCAT 17	SLP	SA/RC	FBG CT		8	335	10	2950	3450
19	SUPERCAT 19	SLP	SA/RC	FBG CT		8	375	6	3550	4150
20	SUPERCAT 20	SLP	SAIL	FBG CT		12	450	6	4100	4800
20	SUPERCAT 20 TALL RIG	SLP	SAIL	FBG CT		12	475	3 6	4250	4950

....For earlier years, see the BUC Used Boat Price Guide, Volume 3

SUPRA SPORTS INC
GREENBACK TN 37742   COAST GUARD MFG ID- XKB See inside cover to adjust price for area

LOA FT IN	NAME AND/OR MODEL	TOP/RIG	BOAT TYPE	HULL MTL TP	ENGINE TP # HP MFG	BEAM FT IN	WGT LBS	DRAFT FT IN	RETAIL LOW	RETAIL HIGH
1994 BOATS										
19 11	LABRISA	OP	SKI	F/S FL	IB 300 PCM	7 6	2900	2 2	9750	11100
20 10	MARIAH	OP	SKI	F/S FL	IB 300 PCM	7 11	3000	1 8	12900	14600
20 10	SUNSPORT	OP	SKI	F/S FL	IB 300 PCM	8	2950	2	12800	14600
22 8	SALTARE	OP	SKI	F/S FL	IB 300 PCM	8 3	3350	2 2	15500	17600
1993 BOATS										
19 9	ESPRIT	OP	SKI	F/S FL	IB 240 PCM	7 2	2445	1 10	7800	9000
19 9	IMPULSE	OP	SKI	F/S FL	IB 240 PCM	7 2	2445	1 10	7800	9000
19 9	SUPRA-COMP TS 6M	OP	SKI	F/S FL	IB 240 PCM	7 2	2460	1 10	7850	9000
19 11	LABRISA	OP	SKI	F/S FL	IB 240 PCM	7 5			8400	9650
20 4	MARAUDER	OP	SKI	F/S FL	IB 240 PCM	8	2950	2	11600	13100
20 4	SPIRIT	OP	SKI	F/S FL	IB 240 PCM	8	2950	2	11600	13100
20 4	SUNSPORT	OP	SKI	F/S FL	IB 240 PCM	8	2950	2	11600	13100
20 10	BRAVURA	OP	SKI	F/S FL	IB 240 PCM	7 11	3000	1 8	11900	13600
20 10	MARIAH	OP	SKI	F/S FL	IB 240 PCM	7 11	3000	1 8	11900	13600
22 8	PIRATA	OP	SKI	F/S FL	IB 240 PCM	8 3	3350	2 2	14400	16300
22 8	SALTARE	OP	SKI	F/S FL	IB 240 PCM	8 3	3350	2 2	14400	16300
1992 BOATS										
19 9	ESPRIT	OP	SKI	F/S FL	IB 240 PCM	7 2	2445	1 10	7400	8500
19 9	IMPULSE	OP	SKI	F/S FL	IB 240 PCM	7 2	2445	1 10	7400	8500
19 9	SUPRA-COMP TS 6M	OP	SKI	F/S FL	IB 240 PCM	7 2	2460	1 10	7400	8500
19 9	SUPRA-COMP TS 6M	OP	SKI	KEV FL	IB 240 PCM	7 2	2460	1 10	7400	8500
20 4	MARAUDER	OP	SKI	F/S FL	IB 240 PCM	8	2950	2	11000	12500
20 4	MARAUDER	OP	SKI	KEV FL	IB 240 PCM	8	2950	2	11000	12500
20 4	SPIRIT	OP	SKI	F/S FL	IB 240 PCM	8	2950	2	11000	12500
20 4	SPIRIT	OP	SKI	KEV FL	IB 240 PCM	8	2810	2	10600	12100
20 4	SUNSPORT	OP	SKI	F/S FL	IB 240 PCM	8	2950	2	11000	12500
20 4	SUNSPORT	OP	SKI	KEV FL	IB 240 PCM	8	2950	2	11000	12500
20 10	BRAVURA	OP	SKI	F/S FL	IB 240 PCM	7 11	3000	1 8	11300	12900
20 10	BRAVURA	OP	SKI	KEV FL	IB 240 PCM	7 11	3000	1 8	11300	12900
20 10	MARIAH	OP	SKI	F/S FL	IB 240 PCM	7 11	3000	1 8	11300	12900
20 10	MARIAH	OP	SKI	KEV FL	IB 240 PCM	7 11	3000	1 8	11300	12900
22 8	PIRATA	OP	SKI	F/S FL	IB 240 PCM	8 3	3350	2 2	13700	15500
22 8	PIRATA	OP	SKI	KEV FL	IB 240 PCM	8 3	3350	2 2	13600	15500
22 8	SALTARE	OP	SKI	F/S FL	IB 240 PCM	8 3	3350	2 2	13700	15500
22 8	SALTARE	OP	SKI	KEV FL	IB 240 PCM	8 3	3350	2 2	13600	15500
1989 BOATS										
19 9	CONBRIO	OP	SKI	FBG SV	IB 240	7 1	2350		6150	7050
19 9	SUPRA-COMP TS 6M	OP	SKI	FBG SV	IB 240-260	7 1	2200	2 1	5950	6900
20 3	MARAUDER		RNBT	FBG SV	IB 240 PCM	8	2950		9600	10900
20 3	SUNSPORT SKIER	OP	RNBT	FBG SV	IB 240-330	8	2800	2	9350	11100
20 10	BRAVURA		RNBT	FBG	IB 240-330	7 11	2800	2	9500	11300
20 10	BRAVURA		RNBT	FBG	IB 425 PCM	7 11	2800	2	11200	12700
20 10	MARIAH		RNBT	FBG	IB 240-330	7 11	2800	2	9500	11300
20 10	MARIAH		RNBT	FBG	IB 425 PCM	7 11	2800	2	11200	12700
22 8	PIRATA		RNBT	FBG	IB 240-330	8 3	2800	2 5	10600	12600
22 8	PIRATA		RNBT	FBG	IB 425 PCM	8 3	2800	2 5	12300	13900
22 8	SALTARE		RNBT	FBG SV	IB 240-330	8 3	2800	2 5	10600	13000
22 8	SALTARE	OP	RNBT	FBG SV	IB 425 PCM	8 3	3000	2 5	12700	14400
1988 BOATS										
19 6	SUNSPORT SKIER	OP	SKI	FBG SV	IB 240-330	7 11	2800	2	6800	8200
19 7	SUPRA-COMP TS 6M	OP	SKI	FBG SV	IB 240-260	7	2200	2 1	5550	6450
20 11	BRAVURA		RNBT	FBG	IB 240-330				9150	10800
20 11	BRAVURA		RNBT	FBG	IB 425 PCM				10700	12200
20 11	MARIAH		RNBT	FBG	IB 240-330				9150	10800
20 11	MARIAH		RNBT	FBG	IB 425 PCM				10700	12200
22 8	PIRATA		RNBT	FBG	IB 240-330	8 3	2800	2 5	10100	12000
22 8	PIRATA		RNBT	FBG	IB 425 PCM	8 3	2800	2 5	11700	13300
22 8	SALTARE		RNBT	FBG SV	IB 240-330	8 3	2800	2 5	10100	12400
22 8	SALTARE	OP	RNBT	FBG SV	IB 425 PCM	8 3	3000	2 5	12100	13700
1987 BOATS										
19 6	MARAUDER	OP	RNBT	FBG SV	IB 240-330	7 11	2800	2	6550	7900
19 6	MARAUDER SKIER	OP	SKI	FBG SV	IB 140-330	7 11	2800	2	6250	7700
19 6	SUNSPORT	OP	RNBT	FBG SV	IB 240-330	7 11	2800	2	6550	8150
19 6	SUNSPORT SKIER	OP	SKI	FBG SV	IB 240-330	7 11	2800	2	6450	7950
19 7	SUPRA-COMP TS 6M	OP	SKI	FBG SV	IB 240-260	7	2200	2 1	5300	6150
22 8	PIRATA		RNBT	FBG	OB	8 3	2800	2 5	14100	16000
22 8	SALTARE		RNBT	FBG SV	IB 240-330	8 3	2800	2 5	9650	11800
22 8	SALTARE	OP	RNBT	FBG SV	IB 425 PCM	8 3	3000	2 5	11500	13100
1986 BOATS										
19 6	MARAUDER	OP	RNBT	FBG SV	IB 255-330	7 11	2800	2	6500	7550
19 6	MARAUDER SKIER	OP	SKI	FBG SV	IB 255-330	7 11	2800	2	6100	7250
19 6	SUNSPORT	OP	RNBT	FBG SV	IB 255-330	7 11	2800	2	6500	7800
19 6	SUNSPORT SKIER	OP	SKI	FBG SV	IB 255-330	7 11	2800	2	6300	7600
19 6	SUPRA-BEAST	OP	SKI	FBG SV	IB 330 PCM	7 11	2875	2 3	6500	7450
19 6	SUPRA-RIDER	OP	SKI	FBG SV	IB 255-285	7 11	2750	2 3	6150	7350
19 6	SUPRA-RIDER	OP	SKI	FBG SV	IB 330 PCM	7 11	2875	2 3	6700	7700
19 6	SUPRA-STAR	OP	SKI	FBG SV	IB 255-285	7 11	2750	2 3	6150	7150
19 7	SUPRA-COMP TS 6M	OP	SKI	FBG SV	IB 255-285	7	2200	2 1	5300	6150
23	SALTARE	OP	RNBT	FBG SV	IB 255-330	8 3	2800	2 5	9400	11500
23	SALTARE	OP	RNBT	FBG SV	IB 454 PCM	8 3	3000	2 5	11600	13200
1985 BOATS										
19 6	MARAUDER	OP	RNBT	FBG SV	IB 250-330	7 11			6100	7300
19 6	MARAUDER SKIER	OP	SKI	FBG SV	IB 250-270	7 11			6200	7150
19 6	MARAUDER SKIER	OP	SKI	FBG SV	IB 280	7 11		2	5800	6650
19 6	SPORT-STAR	OP	SKI	FBG SV	IB 250-270	7 11			6000	6950
19 6	SUNSPORT	OP	B/R	FBG SV	IB 250-270	7 11			5700	6600
19 6	SUNSPORT	OP	B/R	FBG SV	IB 280 PCM	7 11	2800	2	6100	7050
19 6	SUNSPORT SKIER	OP	B/R	FBG SV	IB 250-270	7 11			5800	6700
19 6	SUNSPORT SKIER	OP	SKI	FBG SV	IB 280 PCM	7 11	2800	2	6000	6900
19 6	SUPRA-ALLEGRO	OP	CBNCR	FBG SV	IB 250-270	7 11			5750	6650
19 6	SUPRA-ALLEGRO	OP	CUD	FBG DV	IB 280-330	7 11	2950	2 4	6150	7550

LOA FT IN	NAME AND/ OR MODEL	TOP/ RIG	BOAT TYPE	-HULL- MTL TP	TP	----ENGINE--- # HP	MFG	BEAM FT IN	WGT LBS	DRAFT FT IN	RETAIL LOW	RETAIL HIGH
|------ 1985 BOATS ------												
19 6	SUPRA-ALLEGRO	HT	CUD	FBG DV	IB	250	PCM	7 11	2950	2 4	6100	7000
19 6	SUPRA-BEAST	OP	SKI	FBG SV	IB	330	PCM	7 11	2875	2 3	6200	7150
19 6	SUPRA-COMP TS6M	OP	SKI	FBG SV	IB	270	PCM	7 11			5750	6600
19 6	SUPRA-RIDER	OP	RNBT	FBG SV	IB	250-330		7 11			6200	7400
19 6	SUPRA-RIDER	OP	SKI	FBG SV	IB	250-330		7 11	2750	2 3	5950	7250
19 6	SUPRA-SPORT-STAR	OP	SKI	FBG SV	IB	250-280		7 11	2750	2 3	5750	6800
19 7	SUPRA-COMP TS 6M	OP	SKI	FBG SV	IB	250-280		7	2200	2 1	4850	5650
19 7	SUPRA-COMP TS 6M	OP	SKI	KEV SV	IB	351		7			5800	6650
|------ 1984 BOATS ------												
19 6	SUPRA-ALLEGRO	HT	CUD	FBG DV	IB	255-330		7 11	2950	2 4	5850	7200
19 6	SUPRA-BEAST	OP	SKI	FBG SV	IB	330		7 11	2875	2 3	5900	6900
19 6	SUPRA-RIDER	OP	SKI	FBG SV	IB	255-330		7 11	2750	2 3	5750	7000
19 6	SUPRA-SPORT	OP	SKI	FBG SV	IB	255-330		7 11	2750	2 3	5500	6900
19 6	SUPRA-STAR	OP	SKI	FBG SV	IB	255-330		7 11	2750	2 3	5500	6900
19 7	SUPRA-COMP TS 6M	OP	SKI	FBG SV	IB	255-330		7	2200	2 1	4650	5800

....For earlier years, see the BUC Used Boat Price Guide, Volume 3

SUPREME INDUSTRIES INC
LOUISVILLE TN 37777   COAST GUARD MFG ID- XTB See inside cover to adjust price for area

LOA FT IN	NAME AND/ OR MODEL	TOP/ RIG	BOAT TYPE	-HULL- MTL TP	TP	----ENGINE--- # HP	MFG	BEAM FT IN	WGT LBS	DRAFT FT IN	RETAIL LOW	RETAIL HIGH
|------ 1986 BOATS ------												
18 11	SKI-SUPREME	OP	SKI	FBG DV	IB	245		6 8	2275	2	5250	6000
20 2	SIERRA SUPREME	OP	B/R	FBG DV	IB	245		6 6	2640	2	7100	8150
|------ 1985 BOATS ------												
18 11	SKI-SUPREME	OP	SKI	FBG DV	IB			6 8	2275	2	**	**
18 11	SKI-SUPREME	OP	SKI	FBG DV	IB		INDM	6 8	2275	2	**	**
18 11	SKI-SUPREME	OP	SKI	FBG DV	IB	250	PCM	6 8	2275	2	5000	5750
20 2	SIERRA SUPREME	OP	B/R	FBG DV	IB		CHEV	7 6	2640	2	**	**
20 2	SIERRA SUPREME	OP	B/R	FBG DV	IB		INDM	7 6	2640	2	**	**
20 2	SIERRA SUPREME	OP	B/R	FBG DV	IB	250	PCM	7 6	2640	2	6750	7800
|------ 1984 BOATS ------												
18 11	SKI-SUPREME	OP	SKI	FBG SV	IB	255	PCM	6 8	2275	2	4800	5500

....For earlier years, see the BUC Used Boat Price Guide, Volume 3

SURF HUNTER CORP
FAIRHAVEN MA 02719   COAST GUARD MFG ID- SJJ See inside cover to adjust price for area
FORMERLY FAIRHAVEN MARINE INC

For more recent years, see the BUC Used Boat Price Guide, Volume 1

LOA FT IN	NAME AND/ OR MODEL		TOP/ RIG	BOAT TYPE	-HULL- MTL TP	TP	----ENGINE--- # HP	MFG	BEAM FT IN	WGT LBS	DRAFT FT IN	RETAIL LOW	RETAIL HIGH
|------ 1996 BOATS ------													
25	SURF-HUNTER			CTRCN	FBG DV	OB			9 2		2 6	22100	24600
25	SURF-HUNTER		OP	FSH	FBG DV	OB			9 2		2 6	22100	24600
25	SURF-HUNTER		OP	FSH	FBG DV	IO	271	VLVO	9 2	6100	2 6	48900	53800
25	SURF-HUNTER		OP	RNBT	FBG DV	IO	330	VLVO	9 2	6100	2 6	45900	50400
29 8	SURF-HUNTER			SDN	FBG DV	IO	T170D	VLVO	10 10	12000	3	125500	138000
|------ 1995 BOATS ------													
25	SURF-HUNTER			CTRCN	FBG DV	OB			9 2		2 6	21200	23500
25	SURF-HUNTER		OP	FSH	FBG DV	OB			9 2		2 6	21200	23500
25	SURF-HUNTER		OP	FSH	FBG DV	IO	271	VLVO	9 2	6100	2 6	45700	50200
25	SURF-HUNTER		OP	RNBT	FBG DV	IO	330	VLVO	9 2	6100	2 6	42200	46900
29 8	SURF-HUNTER			SDN	FBG DV	IO	T170D	VLVO	10 10	12000	3	117000	129000
|------ 1994 BOATS ------													
25	SURF-HUNTER			CTRCN	FBG DV	OB			9 2		2 6	20100	22300
25	SURF-HUNTER		OP	FSH	FBG DV	OB			9 2		2 6	20100	22300
25	SURF-HUNTER		OP	FSH	FBG DV	IO	271	VLVO	9 2	6100	2 6	42000	46600
25	SURF-HUNTER		OP	RNBT	FBG DV	IO	330	VLVO	9 2	6100	2 6	39400	43800
29 8	SURF-HUNTER			SDN	FBG DV	IO	T170D	VLVO	10 10	12000	3	109500	120000
|------ 1993 BOATS ------													
25	SURF-HUNTER			CTRCN	FBG DV	OB			9 2		2 6	19400	21600
25	SURF-HUNTER		OP	FSH	FBG DV	OB			9 2		2 6	19400	21600
25	SURF-HUNTER		OP	FSH	FBG DV	IO	271	VLVO	9 2	6100	2 6	39100	43400
25	SURF-HUNTER		OP	RNBT	FBG DV	IO	330	VLVO	9 2	6100	2 6	36800	40900
29 8	SURF-HUNTER			SDN	FBG DV	IO	T170D	VLVO	10 10	12000	3	102000	112000
|------ 1992 BOATS ------													
25	SURF-HUNTER			CTRCN	FBG DV	OB			9 2		2 6	18500	20600
25	SURF-HUNTER		OP	FSH	FBG DV	OB			9 2		2 6	18500	20600
25	SURF-HUNTER		OP	FSH	FBG DV	IO	271	VLVO	9 2	6100	2 6	36500	40600
25	SURF-HUNTER		OP	RNBT	FBG DV	IO	330	VLVO	9 2	6100	2 6	34400	38200
29 8	SURF-HUNTER			SDN	FBG DV	IO	T170D	VLVO	10 10	12000	3	94800	104000
|------ 1991 BOATS ------													
25	SURF-HUNTER			CTRCN	FBG DV	OB			9 2		2 6	17300	19600
25	SURF-HUNTER		OP	FSH	FBG DV	OB			9 2		2 6	17300	19600
25	SURF-HUNTER		OP	FSH	FBG DV	IO	271	VLVO	9 2	6100	2 6	34200	38000
25	SURF-HUNTER		OP	RNBT	FBG DV	IO	330	VLVO	9 2	6100	2 6	32200	35800
29 8	SURF-HUNTER			SDN	FBG DV	IO	T170D	VLVO	10 10	12000	3	89000	97800
|------ 1990 BOATS ------													
25	SURF-HUNTER			CTRCN	FBG DV	OB			9 2		2 6	16500	18800
25	SURF-HUNTER		OP	FSH	FBG DV	OB			9 2		2 6	16500	18800
25	SURF-HUNTER		OP	FSH	FBG DV	IO	271	VLVO	9 2	6100	2 6	32100	35700
25	SURF-HUNTER		OP	RNBT	FBG DV	IO	740	VLVO	9 2	6100	2 6	52200	57300
29 8	SURF-HUNTER			SDN	FBG DV	IO	T170D	VLVO	10 10	12000	3	83600	91900
|------ 1989 BOATS ------													
25	SURF-HUNTER			CTRCN	FBG DV	OB			9 2		2 6	15800	18000
25	SURF-HUNTER		OP	FSH	FBG DV	OB			9 2		2 6	15800	18000
25	SURF-HUNTER		OP	FSH	FBG DV	IO	271	VLVO	9 2	6100	2 6	30300	33700
29 8	SURF-HUNTER			SDN	FBG DV	IO	T170	VLVO	10 10	12000	3	59700	65700
|------ 1988 BOATS ------													
25	SURF-HUNTER			CTRCN	FBG DV	OB			9 2		2 6	15200	17300
25	SURF-HUNTER		OP	FSH	FBG DV	OB			9 2		2 6	15200	17300
25	SURF-HUNTER		OP	FSH	FBG DV	IO	271	VLVO	9 2	6100	2 6	28700	31900
29 8	SURF-HUNTER			SDN	FBG DV	IO	T170	VLVO	10 10	12000	3	56600	62200
|------ 1987 BOATS ------													
25	SURF-HUNTER		OP	CTRCN	FBG DV	OB			9 2		2 6	14600	16600
25	SURF-HUNTER		OP	FSH	FBG DV	OB			9 2		2 6	14600	16600
25	SURF-HUNTER		OP	FSH	FBG DV	IO	271	VLVO	9 2	6100	2 6	27300	30300
|------ 1986 BOATS ------													
25	SURF-HUNTER		OP	CTRCN	FBG DV	OB			9 2		2 6	14100	16000
25	SURF-HUNTER		OP	FSH	FBG DV	OB			9 2		2 6	14100	16000
25	SURF-HUNTER		OP	FSH	FBG DV	IB	225	CHRY	9 2	6250	2 6	30300	33700
25	IO 260 VLVO 24000		26600, IB	200D PERK	47100	51700, IO T170		MRCR		25000		27800	
25	SURF-HUNTER		OP	WKNDR	FBG DV	OB			9 2	5000	2 6	13300	15200
25	SURF-HUNTER		OP	WKNDR	FBG DV	IO	260	VLVO	9 2	7000	2 6	27500	30600
|------ 1985 BOATS ------													
25	SURF-HUNTER		OP	CTRCN	FBG DV	OB			9 2		2 6	13700	15500
25	SURF-HUNTER		OP	FSH	FBG DV	OB			9 2		2 6	13700	15500
25	SURF-HUNTER		OP	FSH	FBG DV	IB	225	CHRY	9 2	6250	2 6	28900	32200
25	IO 260 VLVO 23000		25500, IB	200D PERK	44700	49600, IO T170		MRCR		24000		26600	
25	SURF-HUNTER		OP	WKNDR	FBG DV	OB			9 2	5000	2 6	12900	14700
25	SURF-HUNTER		OP	WKNDR	FBG DV	IO	260	VLVO	9 2	7000	2 6	26400	29400
|------ 1984 BOATS ------													
25	SURF-HUNTER		OP	CTRCN	FBG DV	OB			9 2		2 6	13200	15000
25	SURF-HUNTER		OP	FSH	FBG DV	OB			9 2		2 6	13200	15000
25	SURF-HUNTER		OP	FSH	FBG DV	IB	225	CHRY	9 2	6250	2 6	27700	30700
25	IO 260 VLVO 22200		24600, IB	200D PERK	42900	47600, IO T170		MRCR		23100		25700	
25	SURF-HUNTER		OP	WKNDR	FBG DV	OB			9 2	5000	2 6	12500	14200
25	SURF-HUNTER		OP	WKNDR	FBG DV	IO	260	VLVO	9 2	7000	2 6	25500	28300

....For earlier years, see the BUC Used Boat Price Guide, Volume 3

SURFGLAS INC
PERFORMANCE CATAMARANS INC   See inside cover to adjust price for area
SANTA ANA CA 92705   COAST GUARD MFG ID- SUR
SEE STARCRAFT SAILBOAT PROD

LOA FT IN	NAME AND/ OR MODEL	TOP/ RIG	BOAT TYPE	-HULL- MTL TP	TP	----ENGINE--- # HP	MFG	BEAM FT IN	WGT LBS	DRAFT FT IN	RETAIL LOW	RETAIL HIGH
|------ 1985 BOATS ------												
16	PRINDLE 16	SLP	SA/OD	F/S	CT			7 11	300	10	2000	2350
18	PRINDLE 18	SLP	SA/OD	F/S	CT			7 11	335	10	2450	2850
|------ 1984 BOATS ------												
16	PRINDLE 16	SLP	SA/OD	F/S	CT			7 11	300	10	1850	2250
18	PRINDLE 18	SLP	SA/OD	F/S	CT			7 11	335	10	2350	2750

....For earlier years, see the BUC Used Boat Price Guide, Volume 3

SUTPHEN MARINE CORP

CAPE CORAL FL 33990   COAST GUARD MFG ID- SUT See inside cover to adjust price for area

For more recent years, see the BUC Used Boat Price Guide, Volume 1

LOA FT IN	NAME AND/OR MODEL	TOP/RIG	BOAT TYPE	HULL MTL TP	ENGINE TP	# HP	MFG	BEAM FT IN	WGT LBS	RETAIL LOW	RETAIL HIGH
1996 BOATS											
25 6	2700	OP	RNBT	FBG DV	OB			8		26000	28900
25 6	2700	OP	RNBT	FBG DV		415	MRCR	8		23000	25600
30 6	3200	OP	RNBT	FBG DV	IO			8		43200	48100
30 6	3200	OP	RNBT	FBG DV	IO	T350	MRCR	8		38100	42300
33 6	3500	OP	RNBT	FBG DV	IO	T415-T500		8		63900	77800
38 1	4000	OP	RNBT	FBG DV	IO	T415	MRCR	8		91800	101000
38 1	4000	OP	RNBT	FBG DV	IO	T350D	YAN	8		94200	103500
38 1	4000	OP	RNBT	FBG DV	IO	R415	MRCR	8		94500	104000
1995 BOATS											
25 6	260	OP	RNBT	FBG DV	OB			8		24800	27600
25 6	260	OP	RNBT	FBG DV	IO	T250	MRCR	8		19800	22000
30 6	310	OP	RNBT	FBG DV	IO			8		41200	45800
30 6	310	OP	RNBT	FBG DV	IO	T350	MRCR	8		35000	38900
33 6	340	OP	RNBT	FBG DV	IO	T415-T450		8		59900	69000
38 1	390	OP	RNBT	FBG DV	IO	T415	MRCR	8		85500	94000
38 1	390	OP	RNBT	FBG DV	IO	R415	MRCR	8		88100	96800
1994 BOATS											
25 6	260	OP	RNBT	FBG DV	OB			8		23700	26400
25 6	260	OP	RNBT	FBG DV	IO	T250	MRCR	8		18700	20800
30 6	310	OP	RNBT	FBG DV	IO			8		39300	43700
30 6	310	OP	RNBT	FBG DV	IO	T350	MRCR	8		32700	36300
33 6	340	OP	RNBT	FBG DV	IO	T415-T500		8		56100	67700
38 1	390	OP	RNBT	FBG DV	IO	T415	MRCR	8		79700	87600
38 1	390	OP	RNBT	FBG DV	IO	R415	MRCR	8		82200	90300
1993 BOATS											
25 6	260	OP	RNBT	FBG DV	OB			8		22700	25200
25 6	260	OP	RNBT	FBG DV	IO	T240	MRCR	8		16900	19200
30 6	310	OP	RNBT	FBG DV	OB			8		37500	41700
30 6	310	OP	RNBT	FBG DV	IO	T350	MRCR	8		30500	33900
33 6	340	OP	RNBT	FBG DV	IO	T390	MRCR	8		50200	55200
33 6	340	OP	RNBT	FBG DV	IO	T575	MRCR	8		62000	68200
38 1	390	OP	RNBT	FBG DV	IO	T390	MRCR	8		71800	78900
38 1	390	OP	RNBT	FBG DV	IO	R390	MRCR	8		73500	80800
1992 BOATS											
25 6	260	OP	RNBT	FBG DV	IO	T240	MRCR	8		21800	24200
25 6	260	OP	RNBT	FBG DV	OB			8		15800	18000
30 6	310	OP	RNBT	FBG DV	OB			8 2		36000	40000
30 6	310	OP	RNBT	FBG DV	IO	T350	MRCR	8 2		28700	31900
33 6	340	OP	RNBT	FBG DV	IO	T390	MRCR	8 2		46700	51300
33 6	340	OP	RNBT	FBG DV	IO	T575	MRCR	8		58200	63900
38 1	390	OP	RNBT	FBG DV	IO	T390	MRCR	8 2		66300	72800
38 1	390	OP	RNBT	FBG DV	IO	R390	MRCR	8 2		68000	74700
1991 BOATS											
25 6	260	OP	RNBT	FBG DV	OB			8		21000	23300
25 6	260	OP	RNBT	FBG DV	IO	T240	MRCR	8		14800	16800
30 6	310	OP	RNBT	FBG DV	OB			8		34500	38300
30 6	310	OP	RNBT	FBG DV	IO	T350	MRCR	8 2		26900	29900
33 6	340	OP	RNBT	FBG DV	IO	T390	MRCR	8 2		43500	48300
33 6	340	OP	RNBT	FBG DV	IO	T575	MRCR	8		54700	60100
38 1	390	OP	RNBT	FBG DV	IO	T390	MRCR	8 2		62300	68400
38 1	390	OP	RNBT	FBG DV	IO	R390	MRCR	8 2		63800	70100
1990 BOATS											
25 6	RUM-RUNNER 260	OP	RNBT	FBG DV	OB			8		20200	22500
25 6	RUM-RUNNER 260	OP	RNBT	FBG DV	IO	330-365		8	4000	12400	15000
	IO 425 MRCR 14900 16900, IO T270 MRCR 13800 15700, IO T330-T365 13500 18800										
30 6	SPIRIT 310	OP	EXP	FBG DV	IO			8 2	5980	33800	37500
30 6	SPIRIT 310	OP	EXP	FBG DV	IO	T270-T365		8 2	5980	30200	36900
30 6	SPIRIT 310	OP	EXP	FBG DV	IO	T425	MRCR	8 2	5980	34300	38100
33 6	OUTRAGEOUS 340	OP	EXP	FBG DV	OB			8 2	6600	43400	48200
33 6	OUTRAGEOUS 340	OP	EXP	FBG DV	IO	T330-T575		8 2	6600	46700	55100
38 1	DOMINATOR 380	OP	EXP	FBG DV	IO			8 2	6900	**	**
38 1	DOMINATOR 380	OP	EXP	FBG DV	IO	T365	MRCR	8 2	6900	46400	51000
	IO T575 MRCR 50700 55700, IO T575 MRCR 63400 69000, IO R420 MRCR 35900 39400										
1989 BOATS											
25 6	RUM-RUNNER 260	OP	RNBT	FBG DV	OB			8		19600	21700
25 6	RUM-RUNNER 260	OP	RNBT	FBG DV	IO	330-365		8	4000	11700	14100
	IO 420 MRCR 13900 15800, IO T270 MRCR 13700 15600, IO T330-T365 15300 18800										
30 6	SPIRIT 310	OP	EXP	FBG DV	IO			8 2		32600	36200
30 6	SPIRIT 310	OP	EXP	FBG DV	IO	T270-T365		8 2	5980	28400	34800
30 6	SPIRIT 310	OP	EXP	FBG DV	IO	T420	MRCR	8 2	5980	32300	35800
33 6	OUTRAGEOUS 340	OP	EXP	FBG DV	OB			8 2		41900	46600
33 6	OUTRAGEOUS 340	OP	EXP	FBG DV	IO	T330-T650		8 2	6600	43600	52100
38 1	DOMINATOR 380	OP	EXP	FBG DV	OB			8 2	6900	**	**
38 1	DOMINATOR 380	OP	EXP	FBG DV	IO	T365	MRCR	8 2	6900	43200	48000
	IO T420 MRCR 47900 52600, IO T575 MRCR 60700 66700, IO T650 34100 37900										
	IO R420 MRCR 33800 37600										
1988 BOATS											
25 6	RUM-RUNNER 260	OP	RNBT	FBG DV	OB			8		19000	21100
25 6	RUM-RUNNER 260	OP	RNBT	FBG DV	IO	330-370		8	4000	11100	13400
	IO 420 MRCR 13100 14900, IO 575 MRCR 17300 19600, IO T270 MRCR 13000 14800										
	IO T330-T365 14500 17800										
30 6	SPIRIT 310	OP	EXP	FBG DV	OB			8 2		31500	35000
30 6	SPIRIT 310	OP	EXP	FBG DV	IO	T270-T370		8 2	5980	26900	33000
30 6	SPIRIT 310	OP	EXP	FBG DV	IO	T420-T450		8 2	5980	30500	35000
33 6	OUTRAGEOUS 340	OP	EXP	FBG DV	OB			8 2		40500	45000
33 6	OUTRAGEOUS 340	OP	EXP	FBG DV	IO	T330-T650		8 2	6600	41200	50600
38 1	DOMINATOR 380	OP	EXP	FBG DV	OB			8 2	7200	**	**
38 1	DOMINATOR 380	OP	EXP	FBG DV	IO	T370	MRCR	8 2	7200	41500	46200
	IO T420 MRCR 44700 49700, IO T450 KAAM 48400 53100, IO T575 MRCR 57700 63400										
	IO T650 32100 35700, IO R420 MRCR 31900 35400										
1987 BOATS											
25 6	RUM-RUNNER 260	OP	RNBT	FBG DV	IO	330-370		8	4000	10500	12800
25 6	RUM-RUNNER 260	OP	RNBT	FBG DV	IO	420	MRCR	8	4000	12500	14200
25 6	RUM-RUNNER 260	OP	RNBT	FBG DV	IO	T260	MRCR	8	4000	13100	13100
29 5	OCEAN-PACER 300	OP	EXP	FBG DV	OB			8	3600	27400	30500
29 5	OCEAN-PACER 300	OP	EXP	FBG DV	IO	T260-T330		8	5800	21200	25500
29 5	OCEAN-PACER 300	OP	EXP	FBG DV	IO	T370-T425		8	5800	23900	28200
33	OUTRAGEOUS 330	OP	EXP	FBG DV	OB			8		37800	42000
33	OUTRAGEOUS 330	OP	EXP	FBG DV	IO	T330-T575		8	6600	37100	44500
33 10	MONTE-CARLO 340	OP	EXP	FBG DV	OB			8	7000	40200	44700
33 10	MONTE-CARLO 340	OP	EXP	FBG DV	IO	T330-T425		8	7000	40900	49800
38 1	DOMINATOR 380	OP	OFF	FBG DV	IO	T370	MRCR	8	7200	40800	45300
	IO T420 MRCR 44300 49200, IO T425 KAAM 45900 50500, IO T575 MRCR 57600 63400										
38 1	ELEGANTE 380	OP	OFF	FBG DV	IO	T370	MRCR	8	7700	42000	46700
	IO T375 MRCR 45600 50100, IO T425 KAAM 46800 51400, IO T575 MRCR 56200 61800										
1986 BOATS											
20 1	SUPER-PACER 200	OP	RNBT	FBG SV	OB			7	1800	7950	9150
20 1	SUPER-PACER 200	OP	RNBT	FBG SV	IO	260-300		7	2700	5150	6350
20 1	SUPER-PACER 200	OP	RNBT	FBG SV	JT	320-405		7	2700	7300	8400
25 6	RUM-RUNNER 260	OP	RNBT	FBG DV	OB			8	2800	16100	18300
25 6	RUM-RUNNER 260	OP	RNBT	FBG DV	IO	330-370		8	4000	10100	12300
	IO 400-440 11400 14100, IO T260-T300 11000 13400, IO T330-T370 12400 15500										
	IO T400 MRCR 14700 16700, IO T440 MRCR 16500 18700										
29 5	OCEAN-PACER 300	OP	EXP	FBG DV	OB			8	3600	26600	29500
29 5	OCEAN-PACER 300	OP	EXP	FBG DV	IO	T260-T330		8	5800	20200	24300
29 5	OCEAN-PACER 300	OP	EXP	FBG DV	IO	T370-T440		8	5800	22800	27000
33	OUTRAGEOUS	OP	EXP	FBG DV	OB			8		36700	40700
33	OUTRAGEOUS	OP	EXP	FBG DV	IO	T330-T440		8	6600	35500	42700
33	OUTRAGEOUS	OP	EXP	FBG DV	IO	T530-T550		8	6600	47000	56200
33 10	MONTE-CARLO 340	OP	EXP	FBG DV	OB			8	7000	39000	43900
33 10	MONTE-CARLO 340	OP	EXP	FBG DV	IO	T330-T440		8	7000	39100	47700
38 1	DOMINATOR 38	OP	OFF	FBG DV	IO	T550	KAAM	8	7200	52800	58000
38 1	DOMINATOR 380	OP	OFF	FBG DV	OB			8		**	**
38 1	DOMINATOR 380	OP	OFF	FBG DV	IO	T370	MRCR	8	7200	39000	43400
	IO T375 KAAM 39600 44900, IO T400 MRCR 40500 45000, IO T425 KAAM 43200 48100										
	IO T440 MRCR 43500 48300, IO T530 MRCR 50200 55100										
38 1	ELEGANTE 380	OP	OFF	FBG DV	IO	T370	MRCR	8	7700	39600	44000
	IO T375 KAAM 40400 44900, IO T400 MRCR 41700 46300, IO T425 KAAM 44000 48900										
	IO T440 MRCR 44300 49200, IO T530 MRCR 51000 56000, IO T550 KAAM 53600 58900										
1985 BOATS											
20 1	SUPER-PACER 200	OP	RNBT	FBG SV	OB			7	1800	7750	8900
20 1	SUPER-PACER 200	OP	RNBT	FBG SV	IO	260-300		7	2700	4950	6100
	JT 320 BERK 7000 8050, IO 330 MRCR 5700 6550, JT 333 BERK 7000 8050										
	IO 370 MRCR 6500 7450, IO 400 MRCR 7200 8300, JT 405 BERK 7000 8050										
	IO 440 MRCR 8350 9600										
25 6	RUM-RUNNER 260	OP	RNBT	FBG DV	OB			8	2800	15700	17800
25 6	RUM-RUNNER 260	OP	RNBT	FBG DV	IO	330-370		8	4000	9650	11800
25 6	RUM-RUNNER 260	OP	RNBT	FBG DV	IO	400-440		8	4000	11000	13600
25 6	RUM-RUNNER 260	OP	RNBT	FBG DV	IO	T260-T300		8	4000	10600	12800
29 5	OCEAN-PACER 300	OP	OFF	FBG DV	OB			8	3600	25500	28300
29 5	OCEAN-PACER 300	OP	OFF	FBG DV	IO	425	KAAM	8	5800	19100	21300
	IO T260-T330 19200 23000, IO T370-T440 21700 26500, IO T460-T475 24400 27700										

LOA FT	LOA IN	NAME AND/ OR MODEL	TOP/ RIG	BOAT TYPE	HULL MTL	HULL TP	ENGINE TP	# HP	MFG	BEAM FT	BEAM IN	WGT LBS	DRAFT FT	DRAFT IN	RETAIL LOW	RETAIL HIGH
		1985 BOATS														
33		OUTRAGEOUS	OP	OFF	FBG	DV	OB			8					35100	39000
33		OUTRAGEOUS	OP	OFF	FBG	DV	IO	T330-T460		8		6600			32000	39800
33		OUTRAGEOUS	OP	OFF	FBG	DV	IO	T475		8		6600			36600	40600
33	10	MONTE-CARLO 340	OP	OFF	FBG	DV	OB			8					37400	41500
33	10	MONTE-CARLO 340	OP	OFF	FBG	DV	IO	T330-T440		8		7000			35700	43700
33	10	MONTE-CARLO 340	OP	OFF	FBG	DV	IO	T460	MRCR	8		7000			40200	44700
38	1	DOMINATOR 380	OP	OFF	FBG	DV	OB			8					**	**
38	1	DOMINATOR 380	OP	OFF	FBG	DV	IO	375	KAAM	8		7200			33900	37600
		IO 425 KAAM 35500 39400, IO T370 MRCR 37300 41500, IO T400 MRCR													38900	43200
		IO T440 MRCR 41600 46200, IO T460 MRCR 42900 47700														
38	1	ELEGANTE 380	OP	OFF	FBG	DV	IO	375	KAAM	8		7700			34600	38500
		IO 425 KAAM 36200 40200, IO T370 MRCR 38100 42300, IO T400 MRCR													39500	43900
		IO T440 MRCR 42300 47100, IO T460 MRCR 43700 48500														
		1984 BOATS														
17	3	SPORT-PACER 173	OP	RNBT	FBG	SV	JT	360		6	8	1850			3200	3750
20	1	SPORT-PACER 200	OP	RNBT	FBG	SV	IO	260		7		2700			4750	5450
20	1	SUPER-PACER 200	OP	RNBT	FBG	SV	OB			8		1600			6950	7950
25	6	RUM-RUNNER 260	OP	RNBT	FBG	DV	OB			8		2800			15200	17300
25	6	RUM-RUNNER 260	OP	RNBT	FBG	DV	IO	330		8					9900	11200
25	6	RUM-RUNNER 260	OP	RNBT	FBG	DV	IO	T330		8					12200	13800
29	5	OCEAN-PACER 300	OP	RNBT	FBG	DV	OB			8		3600			24200	26800
29	5	OCEAN-PACER 300	OP	RNBT	FBG	DV	IO	T330		8		5800			15900	18000
33		OUTRAGEOUS 330	OP	RNBT	FBG	DV	IO	T330		8					25000	27800
34		MONTE-CARLO 340	OP	RNBT	FBG	DV	IO	T330		8					28500	31700
38	1	DOMINATOR 380	OP	RNBT	FBG	DV	IO	T370		8		7200			33000	36700
38	1	ELEGANTE 380	OP	RNBT	FBG	DV	IO	T370		8					42400	47100

....For earlier years, see the BUC Used Boat Price Guide, Volume 3

SWEDEN YACHTS

STENUNGSUND SWEDEN See inside cover to adjust price for area

For more recent years, see the BUC Used Boat Price Guide, Volume 1

LOA FT	LOA IN	NAME AND/ OR MODEL	TOP/ RIG	BOAT TYPE	HULL MTL	HULL TP	ENGINE TP	# HP	MFG	BEAM FT	BEAM IN	WGT LBS	DRAFT FT	DRAFT IN	RETAIL LOW	RETAIL HIGH
		1994 BOATS														
34		SWEDEN YACHT 340	SLP	SARAC	F/S	KL	SD	29D	VLVO	11	6	12600	6	5	113000	124000
34		SWEDEN YACHT 340	SLP	SARAC	F/S	WK	SD	29D	VLVO	11	6	12600	5	1	113000	124000
36	2	SWEDEN YACHT 370	SLP	SARAC	F/S	KL	SD	29D	VLVO	12		14300	6	8	130000	143000
36	2	SWEDEN YACHT 370	SLP	SARAC	F/S	WK	SD	29D	VLVO	12		14300	5	4	130000	143000
39		SWEDEN YACHT 390	SLP	SARAC	F/S	KL	SD	40D	VLVO	12	7	16800	7	4	163500	179500
39		SWEDEN YACHT 390	SLP	SARAC	F/S	WK	SD	40D	VLVO	12	7	16800	5	7	163500	179500
41		SWEDEN YACHT 41	SLP	SARAC	F/S	KL	SD	40D	VLVO	12	9	18700	7	4	189500	208500
41		SWEDEN YACHT 41	SLP	SARAC	F/S	WK	SD	40D	VLVO	12	9	18700	5	11	189500	208500
50		SWEDEN YACHT 50	SLP	SARAC	F/S	KL	SD	62D	VLVO	14	3	32000	8	6	346500	381000
50		SWEDEN YACHT 50	SLP	SARAC	F/S	WK	SD	62D	VLVO	14	3	32000	6	4	346500	381000
70		SWEDEN YACHT 70	SLP	SACAC	F/S	WK	SD	195D	VLVO	17		31000	8	5	593000	652000
		1993 BOATS														
34		SWEDEN YACHT 340	SLP	SARAC	F/S	KL	SD	18D	VLVO	11	6	12600	6	5	105500	115500
34		SWEDEN YACHT 340	SLP	SARAC	F/S	WK	SD	18D	VLVO	11	6	12600	5	1	105500	115500
36	2	SWEDEN YACHT 370	SLP	SARAC	F/S	KL	SD	28D	VLVO	12		14300	6	8	121500	133500
36	2	SWEDEN YACHT 370	SLP	SARAC	F/S	WK	SD	28D	VLVO	12		14300	5	4	121500	133500
39		SWEDEN YACHT 390	SLP	SARAC	F/S	KL	SD	28D	VLVO	12	7	16800	7	4	152000	167000
39		SWEDEN YACHT 390	SLP	SARAC	F/S	WK	SD	28D	VLVO	12	7	16800	5	7	152000	167000
41		SWEDEN YACHT 41	SLP	SARAC	F/S	KL	SD	43D	VLVO	12	9	18700	7	4	177000	194500
41		SWEDEN YACHT 41	SLP	SARAC	F/S	WK	SD	43D	VLVO	12	9	18700	5	11	177000	194500
50		SWEDEN YACHT 50	SLP	SARAC	F/S	KL	SD	62D	VLVO	14	3	32000	8	6	324000	356000
50		SWEDEN YACHT 50	SLP	SARAC	F/S	WK	SD	62D	VLVO	14	3	32000	6	4	324000	356000
		1992 BOATS														
34		SWEDEN YACHT 340	SLP	SA/RC	F/S	KL	SD	18D	VLVO	11	6	12600	6	5	98400	108000
34		SWEDEN YACHT 340	SLP	SA/RC	F/S	WK	SD	18D	VLVO	11	6	12600	5	1	98400	108000
36	2	SWEDEN YACHT 36	SLP	SA/RC	F/S	KL	SD	28D	VLVO	12		14300	6	8	113500	124500
36	2	SWEDEN YACHT 36	SLP	SA/RC	F/S	WK	SD	28D	VLVO	12		14300	5	4	113500	124500
39		SWEDEN YACHT 390	SLP	SA/RC	F/S	KL	SD	28D	VLVO	12	7	16800	7	4	142000	156000
39		SWEDEN YACHT 390	SLP	SA/RC	F/S	WK	SD	28D	VLVO	12	7	16800	5	7	142000	156000
41		SWEDEN YACHT 41	SLP	SA/RC	F/S	KL	SD	43D	VLVO	12	9	18700	7	4	165500	182000
41		SWEDEN YACHT 41	SLP	SA/RC	F/S	WK	SD	43D	VLVO	12	9	18700	5	11	165500	182000
50		SWEDEN YACHT 50	SLP	SA/RC	F/S	KL	SD	62D	VLVO	14	3	32000	8	6	302500	332500
50		SWEDEN YACHT 50	SLP	SA/RC	F/S	WK	SD	62D	VLVO	14	3	32000	6	4	302500	332500
		1990 BOATS														
34		SWEDEN 340	SLP	SA/RC	FBG	KL	IB	D	VLVO	11	5	12600	6	4	86000	94500
34		SWEDEN 340	SLP	SA/RC	FBG	WK	IB	D	VLVO	11	5	12600	5	2	86000	94500
36	1	SWEDEN 36	SLP	SA/RC	FBG	KL	IB	D	VLVO	12		14300	6	7	99000	109000
36	1	SWEDEN 36	SLP	SA/RC	FBG	WK	IB	D	VLVO	12		14300	5	4	99000	109000
38	7	SWEDEN 38	SLP	SA/RC	FBG	KL	IB	D	VLVO	12	6	16280	7	4	119500	131000
38	7	SWEDEN 38	SLP	SA/RC	FBG	WK	IB	D	VLVO	12	6	16280	5	8	119500	131000
39		SWEDEN 390	SLP	SA/RC	FBG	KL	IB	D	VLVO	12	7	16800	7	4	124500	137000
39		SWEDEN 390	SLP	SA/RC	FBG	WK	IB	D	VLVO	12	7	16800	5	8	124500	137000
41		SWEDEN 41	SLP	SA/RC	FBG	KL	IB	D	VLVO	12	9	18700	7	4	144500	159000
41		SWEDEN 41	SLP	SA/RC	FBG	WK	IB	D	VLVO	12	9	18700	5	9	144500	159000
50		SWEDEN 50	SLP	SA/RC	FBG	KL	IB	D		14	3	31500	8	6	263500	289500
50		SWEDEN 50	SLP	SA/RC	FBG	WK	IB	D		14	3	31500	6	6	263500	289500
		1989 BOATS														
34		SWEDEN 340	SLP	SA/RC	FBG	KL	IB	D	VLVO	11	5	12600	6	4	80400	88400
36	1	SWEDEN 36	SLP	SA/RC	FBG	KL	IB	D	VLVO	12		14300	6	7	92500	101500
36	1	SWEDEN 36	SLP	SA/RC	FBG	WK	IB	D	VLVO	12		14300	5	4	92500	101500
38	7	SWEDEN 38	SLP	SA/RC	FBG	KL	IB	D	VLVO	12	6	16280	6	7	111500	122500
41		SWEDEN 41	SLP	SA/RC	FBG	KL	IB	D	VLVO	12	9	18700	7	4	135000	148500
50		SWEDEN 50	SLP	SA/RC	FBG	KL	IB	D		14	3	31500	8	6	246000	270500
50		SWEDEN 50	SLP	SA/RC	FBG	WK	IB	D		14	3	31500	6	6	246000	270500
		1988 BOATS														
34		SWEDEN 340	SLP	SA/RC	FBG	KL	IB	D	VLVO	11	5	12600	6	4	75200	82600
36	1	SWEDEN 36	SLP	SA/RC	FBG	KL	IB	D	VLVO	12		14300	6	7	86500	95000
36	1	SWEDEN 36	SLP	SA/RC	FBG	WK	IB	D	VLVO	12		14300	5	4	86500	95000
38	7	SWEDEN 38	SLP	SA/RC	FBG	KL	IB	D	VLVO	12	6	16280	6	7	104500	114500
41		SWEDEN 41	SLP	SA/RC	FBG	KL	IB	D	VLVO	12	9	18700	7	4	126500	139000
50		SWEDEN 50	SLP	SA/RC	FBG	KL	IB	D		14	3	31500	8	6	230000	253000
50		SWEDEN 50	SLP	SA/RC	FBG	WK	IB	D		14	3	31500	6	6	230000	253000
		1987 BOATS														
34		SWEDEN 340	SLP	SA/RC	FBG	KL	IB	D	VLVO	11	5	12600	6	4	70300	77200
36	1	SWEDEN 36	SLP	SA/RC	FBG	KL	IB	D	VLVO	12		14300	6	7	80900	88900
36	1	SWEDEN 36	SLP	SA/RC	FBG	WK	IB	D	VLVO	12		14300	5	4	80900	88900
38	7	SWEDEN 38	SLP	SA/RC	FBG	KL	IB	D	VLVO	12	6	16280	6	7	97500	107000
41		SWEDEN 41	SLP	SA/RC	FBG	KL	IB	D	VLVO	12	9	18700	7	4	118000	130000
		1986 BOATS														
34		SWEDEN 340	SLP	SA/RC	FBG	KL	IB	D	VLVO	11	5	12600	6	4	65700	72200
36	1	SWEDEN 36	SLP	SA/RC	FBG	KL	IB	D	VLVO	12		14300	6	7	75600	83100
36	1	SWEDEN 36	SLP	SA/RC	FBG	WK	IB	D	VLVO	12		14300	5	4	75600	83100
38	7	SWEDEN 38	SLP	SA/RC	FBG	KL	IB	D	VLVO	12	6	16280	6	7	91200	100000
41		SWEDEN 41	SLP	SA/RC	FBG	KL	IB	D	VLVO	12	9	18700	7	4	110500	121500

....For earlier years, see the BUC Used Boat Price Guide, Volume 3

SWIFT MARINE INC

WRIGHTSVILLE BEACH NC 28480 See inside cover to adjust price for area

LOA FT	LOA IN	NAME AND/ OR MODEL	TOP/ RIG	BOAT TYPE	HULL MTL	HULL TP	ENGINE TP	# HP	MFG	BEAM FT	BEAM IN	WGT LBS	DRAFT FT	DRAFT IN	RETAIL LOW	RETAIL HIGH
		1986 BOATS														
30	1	THIRTY-PLUS	SLP	SA/RC	PLY	TM	OB			18	1	3000	1	3	26600	29600
		1984 BOATS														
30	1	THIRTY PLUS	SLP	SAIL	WD	TM	OB			18	2	2900	1	2	23500	26100

....For earlier years, see the BUC Used Boat Price Guide, Volume 3

SWITZER CRAFT INC

CRYSTAL LAKE IL 60014 COAST GUARD MFG ID- SWT See inside cover to adjust price for area

LOA FT	LOA IN	NAME AND/ OR MODEL	TOP/ RIG	BOAT TYPE	HULL MTL	HULL TP	ENGINE TP	# HP	MFG	BEAM FT	BEAM IN	WGT LBS	DRAFT FT	DRAFT IN	RETAIL LOW	RETAIL HIGH
		1989 BOATS														
17	11	SK175	OP	RNBT	FBG	DV	OB			7	3	850			2650	3100
17	11	SK175 OPEN BOW	OP	RNBT	FBG	DV	OB			7	3	850			2650	3100
20	1	GL21	OP	RNBT	FBG	DV	IO	260-270		8		2400			5450	6350
20	1	GL21	OP	RNBT	FBG	DV	IO	330	MRCR	8		2400			6300	7250
20	1	GL21	OP	RNBT	FBG	DV	IO	365	MRCR	8		2400			7050	8100
20	1	SS20-B	OP	RNBT	FBG	DV	OB			8		1250			4150	4800
20	1	SS20-B	OP	RNBT	FBG	DV	IO	180-270		8		2350			5100	6300
20	1	SS20-C	OP	CUD	FBG	DV	OB			8		1250			4150	4800
20	1	SS20-C	OP	CUD	FBG	DV	IO	180-260		8		2300			5250	6450
20	1	SS20-C	OP	CUD	FBG	DV	IO	270	MRCR	8		2350			5700	6550
20	1	SS220	OP	RNBT	FBG	DV	IO	260-270							5450	6350
20	1	SS220	OP	RNBT	FBG	DV	IO	330	MRCR						6300	7250
20	1	SS220	OP	RNBT	FBG	DV	IO	365	MRCR						7000	8050
24		SS240	OP	OFF	FBG	DV	OB			8	6	2200			7550	8650
24		SS240	OP	OFF	FBG	DV	IO	T260	MRCR	8	6	3200			9700	11000
24		SS240	OP	RNBT	FBG	DV	IO	270	MRCR	8	6	3200			7800	8950
24		SS240	OP	RNBT	FBG	DV	IO	330-365		8	6	3200			8550	10600

LOA FT IN	NAME AND/ OR MODEL	TOP/ RIG	BOAT TYPE	HULL MTL TP	ENGINE TP	# HP	MFG	BEAM FT IN	WGT LBS	DRAFT FT IN	RETAIL LOW	RETAIL HIGH
	1988 BOATS											
17 11	SK175	OP	RNBT	FBG DV	OB			7 3	850		2500	2950
17 11	SK175 OPEN BOW	OP	RNBT	FBG DV	OB			7 3	850		2650	3050
20 1	GL21	OP	RNBT	FBG DV	OB			8	1100		3600	4200
20 1	SS20-B	OP	RNBT	FBG DV	OB			8	1200		3850	4450
20 1	SS20-B	OP	RNBT	FBG DV	IO	260	MRCR	8	2400		5150	5900
20 1	SS20-C	OP	RNBT	FBG DV	OB			8	1200		3900	4550
20 1	SS20-C	OP	RNBT	FBG DV	IO	260	MRCR	8	2400		5200	5950
24	SS240	OP	OFF	FBG DV	OB			8 6	2800		9050	10300
24	SS240	OP	OFF	FBG DV	IO	T260	MRCR	8 6	3200		9200	10500
	1987 BOATS											
17 11	SK175	OP	RNBT	FBG DV	OB			7 3	850		2500	2900
20 1	GL 21	OP	RNBT	FBG DV	OB			8	1100		3500	4050
20 1	SS20-B	OP	RNBT	FBG DV	OB			8	1200		3700	4300
20 1	SS20-B	OP	RNBT	FBG DV	IO	260	MRCR	8	2400		4900	5600
20 1	SS20-C	OP	RNBT	FBG DV	OB			8	1200		3750	4400
20 1	SS20-C	OP	RNBT	FBG DV	IO	260	MRCR	8	2400		4950	5650
24	SS240	OP	OFF	FBG DV	OB			8 6	2800		8650	9950
24	SS240	OP	OFF	FBG DV	IO	T260	MRCR	8 6	3200		8650	9950
	1986 BOATS											
17 11	BOWRIDER 193-B	ST	RNBT	FBG TR	IO	185			2150		3250	3800
17 11	SKIER SK-175	OP	SKI	FBG SV	OB			7 4	900		2550	2950
20 1	BOWRIDER SS20-B	OP	RNBT	FBG SV	OB				1200		3650	4200
20 1	CUDDY CABIN SS20-C	OP	CUD	FBG SV	OB			7 10	1100		3350	3900
20 1	CUDDY CABIN SS20-C	OP	CUD	FBG SV	IO	190-205					4550	5250
20 1	GL-21	OP	RACE	FBG SV	OB			8	1000		3150	3650
	1984 BOATS											
17 11	BOW RIDER 193B	ST	RNBT	FBG TR	IO	185-188			2150		3000	3500
17 11	SKIER SK175	OP	SKI	FBG SV	OB			7 3	900		2400	2800
20 1	GL-21	OP	RACE	FBG SV	OB			8	1000		2950	3450
20 1	SS20B	OP	RNBT	FBG SV	OB				1100		3200	3700
20 1	SS20C	OP	CUD	FBG SV	OB			7 4	1100		3200	3700

....For earlier years, see the BUC Used Boat Price Guide, Volume 3

SYLVAN MARINE

SMOKER CRAFT INC
NEW PARIS IN 46553   COAST GUARD MFG ID- SYL   See inside cover to adjust price for area

For more recent years, see the BUC Used Boat Price Guide, Volume 1

LOA FT IN	NAME AND/ OR MODEL	TOP/ RIG	BOAT TYPE	HULL MTL TP	ENGINE TP	# HP	MFG	BEAM FT IN	WGT LBS	DRAFT FT IN	RETAIL LOW	RETAIL HIGH
	1996 BOATS											
16	JON 1644	OP	OPFSH	AL SV	OB			5 3	300		515	620
16	JON 1644 SPLIT	OP	OPFSH	AL SV	OB			5 3	300		570	685
16	JON 1648	OP	OPFSH	AL SV	OB			6	295		520	625
16	JON 1648 LIVEWELL	OP	OPFSH	AL SV	OB			6	295		545	660
16 2	BACK-TROLLER 16	OP	FSH	AL SV	OB			6 4	620		1150	1350
16 2	BASS SELECT 16	OP	BASS	AL DV	OB			6 3	590		1100	1350
16 2	SEA MONSTER 16	OP	FSH	AL SV	OB			6 4	610		1150	1350
16 2	SEA TROLLER 16	OP	FSH	AL SV	OB			6 4	650		1200	1400
16 3	BACK-TROLLER SLT 16	OP	RNBT	AL SV	OB			6 9	750		1450	1700
16 4	PRO SELECT 16 DUAL	OP	FSH	AL SV	OB			6 9	890		1600	1950
16 4	PRO SELECT 16 SGL	OP	FSH	AL SV	OB			6 9	840		1700	2050
16 4	SPORT SELECT 16 DUAL	OP	FSH	AL SV	OB			6 10	780		1450	1700
16 4	SUPER SELECT 16 SGL	OP	OPFSH	AL DV	OB			6 10	750		1200	1450
16 5	CLASSIC FISH 16	OP	FSH	AL DV	OB			5 11	420		785	945
16 5	SEA-SNAPPER 16	OP	FSH	AL FL	OB			6 10	660		660	840
16 5	SUPER-SNAPPER 16	OP	FSH	AL FL	OB			5 7	370		695	840
16 10	SPORT TROLLER 16	OP	FSH	AL	OB			5 10	540		1050	1250
17	JON 1750	OP	OPFSH	AL SV	OB			6 2	365		685	825
17	JON 1750 SPLIT	OP	OPFSH	AL SV	OB			6 2	365		740	890
17 2	BASS SELECT 17	OP	BASS	AL DV	OB			6 3	685		1350	1600
17 4	PRO SELECT 17 DUAL	OP	FSH	AL SV	OB			7	960		1800	2150
17 4	PRO SELECT 17 SGL	OP	FSH	AL SV	OB			7	930		1750	2100
17 4	SPORT SELECT 17 DUAL	OP	RNBT	AL SV	OB			7 4	960		1850	2200
17 4	SUPER SELECT 17 DUAL	OP	FSH	AL DV	OB			7	950		1750	2100
17 4	SUPER SELECT 17 SGL	OP	OPFSH	AL DV	OB			7	920		1700	2050
17 8	BARRITZ V178	OP	RNBT	FBG SV	IO	135-175		7 4	1200		5300	6150
17 8	V178	OP	SKI	FBG DV	OB			7 4	1100		2000	2400
17 8	V178 VIPER	OP	OPFSH	FBG DV	OB			7 4	1150		2100	2500
18 3	FALCON 180	OP	BASS	AL DV	OB			6 10	1150		2200	2600
18 5	SPACE SHIP 1800	OP	RNBT	FBG SV	IO	135	MRCR	7 3	1400		5800	6650
18 10	PRO SELECT 19 DUAL	OP	RNBT	AL SV	OB			7 3	1100		2200	2550
18 10	SPORT SELECT 19 DUAL	OP	OPFSH	AL SV	OB			7 3	1050		2000	2400
18 10	SUPER SELECT DUAL	OP	FSH	AL SV	OB			7 3	1050		2050	2400
20	SPACE SHIP 2001	OP	RNBT	FBG SV	IO	115-210		7 10	1800		7600	9000
20 7	PRO SELECT 21 DUAL	OP	OPFSH	AL DV	OB			7 6	1125		2550	3000
20 7	SPORT SELECT 21	OP	OPFSH	AL DV	IO	135	MRCR	7 6	1050		8150	9400
20 10	V210	OP	RNBT	FBG DV	IO	135-250		8	3035		10300	12200
21 3	SPACE DECK 2100	ST	RNBT	FBG DV	OB			8	1940		4100	4750
22 3	OFFSHORE FISHERMAN	OP	OPFSH	AL DV	OB			8 6	2360		5150	5900
23 4	SPACE DECK 2300	ST	RNBT	FBG DV	OB			8 8	2740		5850	6700
23 4	SPACE SHIP 2300	OP	RNBT	FBG DV	IO	135-250		8 3	2460		10500	12500
	1995 BOATS											
16	BIG JON 1648 WELL	OP	OPFSH	AL SV	OB			6	220		380	465
16	JON 1648	OP	OPFSH	AL SV	OB			6	220		360	440
16 2	BACK-TROLLER 16	OP	FSH	AL SV	OB			6 4	620		1100	1300
16 2	BASS SELECT 16		BASS	AL DV	OB			6 3	590		1050	1250
16 2	CRAPPIE SELECT 162		BASS	AL DV	OB			6 3	530		960	1150
16 2	SEA MONSTER 16	OP	FSH	AL SV	OB			5 6	610		1050	1250
16 2	SEA TROLLER 16	OP	FSH	AL SV	OB			6 4	650		1150	1350
16 3	BACK-TROLLER SLT 16	OP	RNBT	AL SV	OB			6 9	750		1350	1600
16 4	PRO SELECT 16 DUAL		FSH	AL SV	IO	T115		6 9	890		5450	6250
16 4	PRO SELECT 16 SINGLE		FSH	AL SV	IO	115		6 9	840		4200	4850
16 4	SPORT SEL 16 DL	OP	RNBT	AL SV	OB			6 9	840		1500	1800
16 4	SUPER SELECT 16 DUAL		FSH	AL SV	IO	T115					6750	7750
16 4	SUPER SELECT 16 SGN		FSH	AL SV	IO	115		6 9	840		3300	3800
16 5	CLASSIC FISH 16		OPFSH	AL DV	OB			5 11	420		740	895
16 5	SEA-SNAPPER 16	OP	FSH	AL FL	OB			6 6	225		400	485
16 5	SUPER-SNAPPER 16	OP	FSH	AL FL	OB			5 7	370		660	795
16 10	SPORT TROLLER 16	OP	FSH	AL SV	OB			5 9	420		770	925
17 2	BASS SELECT 17		BASS	AL DV	OB			6 3	685		1250	1500
17 4	PRO SELECT 17 DUAL		FSH	AL SV	IO	T150		7			6950	8000
17 4	PRO SELECT 17 SINGLE		FSH	AL SV	IO	150		7			5300	6100
17 4	SPORT SELECT 17	OP	RNBT	AL SV	OB			7 4	960		1750	2050
17 4	SUPER SELECT 17		OPFSH	AL SV	IO	150		7 4	950		4750	5450
17 8	BARRITZ V178		RNBT	FBG SV	IO	115-175		7 4	1200		4950	5750
17 8	V178		SKI	FBG DV	OB			7 4	1100		1900	2300
17 8	V178 VIPER		OPFSH	FBG DV	OB			7 4	1150		2000	2350
18 3	FALCON 180		BASS	AL DV	OB			6 10	1150		2050	2450
18 5	SPACE SHIP 1800	OP	RNBT	FBG SV	IO	115-175		7 3	1400		5400	6250
18 8	V188	OP	RNBT	FBG SV	IO	115-175		7 6	1200		5600	6550
18 10	PRO SELECT DUAL 19	OP	RNBT	AL SV	OB			7 3	1100		2000	2400
18 10	SPORT SELECT 19		OPFSH	AL SV	OB		175		7 3	1050		5950	6850
20	DECK BOAT 2001	OP	RNBT	FBG DV	IO	115-205		7 10	1800		7100	8350
20	ELITE CRUISE 820		OPFSH	AL PN	OB				1170		2500	2950
20	ELITE FISH 820		OPFSH	AL PN	OB				1170		2500	2950
20 7	PRO SELECT 21		OPFSH	AL DV	IO	115-175		7 6	1125		2500	2900
20 7	SPORT SELECT 21		OPFSH	AL DV	OB			7 6	1050		7600	8800
20 9	V209	OP	RNBT	FBG DV	IO	115-230		8 2	1850		7700	9200
21 3	SPACE DECK 2100	OP	RNBT	FBG SV	OB			8	1940		3850	4500
23 4	SPACE DECK 2300	OP	RNBT	FBG SV	OB			8 8	2360		5500	6350
23 4	SPACE SHIP 2300		RNBT	FBG SV	IO	115-230		8 8	2740		10500	12300
	1994 BOATS											
16	BASS 1644		FSH	AL SV	OB			5 7	550		920	1100
16	BIG JON 1648 WELL	OP	OPFSH	AL SV	OB			6	220		360	440
16	CRAPPIE 1544		FSH	AL SV	OB			5 7	410		675	815
16	JON 1648	OP	OPFSH	AL SV	OB			6	220		340	415
16 2	BACK-TROLLER 16		FSH	AL SV	OB			6 4	620		1050	1200
16 2	SEA MONSTER 16		FSH	AL SV	OB			6 4	610		1000	1200
16 2	SEA TROLLER 16		FSH	AL SV	OB			5 6	650		1100	1300
16 3	BACK-TROLLER SLT 16	OP	RNBT	AL SV	OB			6 9	750		1300	1500
16 3	SEA TROLLER SLT 16	OP	RNBT	AL SV	OB			6 9	790		1350	1600
16 4	PRO SELECT 16 DUAL		FSH	AL SV	IO	T115		6 9	890		5100	5850
16 4	PRO SELECT 16 SINGLE		FSH	AL SV	IO	115		6 9	840		3900	4500
16 4	SPORT SEL 16 DL	OP	RNBT	AL SV	OB			6 9	840		1450	1700
16 4	SUPER SELECT 16 DUAL		FSH	AL SV	IO	T115					6300	7250
16 4	SUPER SELECT 16 SGN		FSH	AL SV	IO	115		6 9	840		3100	3600
16 5	SEA-SNAPPER 16	OP	FSH	AL FL	OB			6 6	225		375	460
16 5	SUPER-SNAPPER 16	OP	FSH	AL FL	OB			5 7	370		625	755
16 8	VFC-175	OP	FSH	FBG SV	OB			7 6	1100		1750	2100
16 10	SPORT TROLLER 16	OP	FSH	AL SV	OB			5 9	420		730	880
17	PRO BASS 1750		FSH	AL SV	OB			6 3	710		1200	1450
17 4	PRO SELECT 17 DUAL		FSH	AL SV	IO	T150		7			6500	7450
17 4	PRO SELECT 17 SINGLE		FSH	AL SV	IO	150		7			4950	5700
17 4	SEA TROLLER SLT 17	OP	RNBT	AL SV	OB			7 4	950		1650	1950
17 4	SPORT SELECT 17	OP	RNBT	AL SV	OB			7 4	960		1650	1950

SYLVAN MARINE -CONTINUED See inside cover to adjust price for area

LOA FT	LOA IN	NAME AND/ OR MODEL	TOP/ RIG	BOAT TYPE	-HULL- MTL	-HULL- TP	ENGINE TP	ENGINE # HP	ENGINE MFG	BEAM FT	BEAM IN	WGT LBS	DRAFT FT	DRAFT IN	RETAIL LOW	RETAIL HIGH
		1994 BOATS														
17	4	SPORT SELECT 17 S	OP	RNBT	AL	SV	OB			7	4	920			1600	1900
17	8	BARRITZ V178		RNBT	FBG	SV	OB			7	4	1200			2000	2350
17	8	BARRITZ V178		RNBT	FBG	SV	IO	115-175		7	4	1200			4600	5400
18	5	SPACE SHIP 1800	OP	RNBT	FBG	SV	IO	115-175		7	3	1400			5000	5850
18	8	V188	OP	RNBT	FBG	DV	IO	115-205		7	6	1400			5250	6200
18	10	PRO SELECT DUAL 19	OP	RNBT	AL	SV	OB			7	3	1100			1900	2300
18	10	SUPER-SPORTSTER 19	OP	RNBT	AL	SV	OB			7	3	1045			1850	2200
20		DECK BOAT 2001	OP	RNBT	FBG	SV	IO	115-230		7	10	1800			6650	7950
20	7	SUPER-SPORTSTER 21	ST	RNBT	AL	SV	IO	135	MRCR	7	6	1150			6400	7350
20	9	V209	OP	RNBT	FBG	DV	IO	115-230		8	2	1850			7150	8550
21	3	SPACE DECK 2100	OP	RNBT	FBG	SV	OB			8		1940			3650	4250
21	7	OFFSHORE 22	ST	OFF	AL	SV	IO	115	MRCR	7	8	1540			7350	8450
21	7	OFFSHORE 22	HT	OFF	AL	SV	OB			7	8	1430			2850	3350
21	7	OFFSHORE 22	HT	OFF	AL	SV	IO	115-135		7	8	1540			7350	8450
21	7	PRO FISHERMAN DUAL	OP	FSH	AL	SV	OB			7	6	1100			2350	2750
21	7	SUPER-SPORTSTER 21	OP	RNBT	AL	SV	IO	115	MRCR	7	6	1150			6950	8000
21	7	SUPER-SPORTSTER 21	ST	RNBT	AL	SV	OB			7	6	1100			2350	2750
23	4	DECK BOAT 2300		RNBT	FBG	SV	IO	115-230		8	8	2740			9800	11500
23	4	SPACE DECK 2300	OP	RNBT	FBG	SV	OB			8	8	2740			5250	6050
		1993 BOATS														
16		BASS 1644		FSH	AL	SV	OB			5	7	550			870	1050
16		BIG JON 1672		JON	AL	FL	OB			5	8	260			405	495
16		BIG JON 1672 W/WELL		JON	AL	FL	OB			5	8	260			435	525
16		CRAPPIE 1544		FSH	AL	SV	OB			5	7	410			640	775
16	2	BACK-TROLLER 16	OP	FSH	AL	SV	OB			6	4	620			990	1200
16	2	PRO-FISHERMAN 16	OP	FSH	AL	SV	OB			6	4	650			990	1200
16	2	PRO-FISHERMAN 16 DUL	OP	FSH	AL	SV	OB			6	4	650			1050	1250
16	2	SEA MONSTER 16	OP	FSH	AL	SV	OB			5	6	610			975	1150
16	2	SEA TROLLER 16	OP	FSH	AL	SV	OB			5	6	650			1000	1200
16	2	SUPER-SPORTSTER 16	OP	RNBT	AL	SV	OB			6	4	690			1100	1350
16	4	PRO SELECT 16 DUAL		FSH	AL	SV	IO	T115		6	9	890			4750	5450
16	4	PRO SELECT 16 SINGLE		FSH	AL	SV	IO	115		6	9	840			3650	4250
16	4	SUPER SELECT 16 DUAL		FSH	AL	SV	IO	T115							5900	6750
16	4	SUPER SELECT 16 SGN		FSH	AL	SV	IO	115		6	9	840			2850	3350
16	5	SEA-SNAPPER 16	OP	FSH	AL	FL	OB			6	6	225			360	435
16	5	SUPER-SNAPPER 16	OP	FSH	AL	FL	OB			5	7	370			595	715
16	8	VFC-175	OP	FSH	FBG	SV	OB			7	6	1100			1650	2000
16	9	ELIMINATOR 17	OP	FSH	AL	SV	OB			6	11	800			1300	1550
16	9	ELIMINATOR 17 DUAL	OP	FSH	AL	SV	OB			6	11	825			1300	1550
16	9	PRO FISHERMAN 17 DUL	OP	FSH	AL	SV	OB			6	11	800			1250	1500
16	9	PRO FISHERMAN 17 SGN	OP	FSH	AL	SV	OB			6	11	800			1250	1500
16	9	SUPER-SPORTSTER 17	OP	RNBT	AL	SV	OB			6	11	800			1300	1550
16	10	SPORT TROLLER 16	OP	FSH	AL	SV	OB			5	9	420			690	835
17		PRO BASS 1750		FSH	AL	SV	OB			6	3	710			1150	1350
17		V170	OP	B/R	FBG	SV	OB			6	11	1150			1800	2150
17	4	PRO SELECT 17 DUAL		FSH	AL	SV	IO	T150		7					6050	7000
17	4	PRO SELECT 17 SINGLE		FSH	AL	SV	IO	150		7					4650	5350
18	6	SUPER-SPORTSTER 18	OP	RNBT	AL	SV	OB			6	10	990			1650	1950
18	8	V188	OP	RNBT	FBG	DV	IO	115-205		7	6	1400			4900	5800
18	8	V188	OP	RNBT	FBG	DV	IO	180D	YAN	7	6	1400			8200	9450
18	10	ELIMINATOR 19	OP	FSH	AL	SV	OB			7	3	1050			1750	2050
18	10	ELIMINATOR DUAL 19	OP	FSH	AL	SV	OB			7	3	1075			1750	2100
18	10	SUPER-SPORTSTER 19	OP	RNBT	AL	SV	OB			7	3	1045			1750	2100
18	10	SUPER-SPORTSTER 19	OP	RNBT	AL	SV	IO	110-135		7	3	1095			4750	5450
20	7	PRO FISHERMAN DUAL	OP	FSH	AL	SV	OB			7	6	1100			2200	2550
20	7	SUPER-SPORTSTER 21	OP	RNBT	AL	SV	IO	110-115		7	6	1150			5950	6850
20	7	SUPER-SPORTSTER 21	ST	RNBT	AL	SV	OB			7	6	1100			2200	2550
20	7	SUPER-SPORTSTER 21	ST	RNBT	AL	SV	IO	135	MRCR	7	6	1150			6000	6900
20	9	OFFSHORE 21	ST	OFF	AL	SV	OB			7	6	1330			2550	2950
20	9	OFFSHORE 21	ST	OFF	AL	SV	IO	115-175		7	6	1330			6300	7300
20	9	OFFSHORE 21	OP	RNBT	AL	SV	IO	110	YAMA	7	6	1330			6050	6950
20	9	V209	OP	RNBT	FBG	DV	IO	115-230		8	2	1850			6700	8000
21	7	OFFSHORE 22	ST	OFF	AL	SV	IO	115-135		7	8	1540			6850	7900
21	7	OFFSHORE 22	HT	OFF	AL	SV	OB			7	8	1430			2750	3150
21	7	OFFSHORE 22	HT	OFF	AL	SV	IO	115-135		7	8	1540			6850	7900
		1992 BOATS														
16	2	BACK-TROLLER 16	OP	FSH	AL	SV	OB			6	4	620			940	1100
16	2	PRO-FISHERMAN 16	OP	FSH	AL	SV	OB			6	4	650			945	1150
16	2	PRO-FISHERMAN DUAL16	OP	FSH	AL	SV	OB			6	4	650			1000	1200
16	2	SEA MONSTER 16	OP	FSH	AL	SV	OB			5	6	610			925	1100
16	2	SEA TROLLER 16	OP	FSH	AL	SV	OB			5	6	650			985	1150
16	2	SUPER-SPORTSTER 16	OP	RNBT	AL	SV	OB			6	4	690			1050	1250
16	5	SEA-SNAPPER 16	OP	FSH	AL	FL	OB			6	6	225			340	415
16	5	SUPER-SNAPPER 16	OP	FSH	AL	FL	OB			5	7	370			565	680
16	8	VFC-175	OP	FSH	FBG	SV	OB			7	6	1100			1600	1900
16	9	ELIMINATOR 17	OP	FSH	AL	SV	OB			6	11	800			1250	1500
16	9	ELIMINATOR DUAL 17	OP	FSH	AL	SV	OB			6	11	825			1250	1500
16	9	MASTER TROLLER 17	OP	FSH	AL	SV	OB			6	11	800			1100	1350
16	9	PRO FISHERMAN 17	OP	FSH	AL	SV	OB			6	11	800			1250	1500
16	9	SUPER-SPORTSTER 17	OP	RNBT	AL	SV	OB			6	11	800			1250	1500
16	10	SPORT TROLLER 16	OP	FSH	AL	SV	OB			5	9	420			660	795
17		BACKTROLLER 17	OP	FSH	AL	SV	OB			6	11	800			1200	1450
17		V170	OP	B/R	FBG	SV	OB			6	11	1150			1700	2000
18	3	SKI-TASTIC	OP	SKI	FBG	TH	IO	220-230		7	5	2850			6000	6950
18	5	PRO-FISHERMAN 18	OP	FSH	AL	SV	OB			6	10	850			1350	1600
18	5	PRO-FISHERMAN DUAL18	OP	FSH	AL	SV	OB			6	10	875			1400	1650
18	6	SUPER-SPORTSTER 18	OP	RNBT	AL	SV	OB			6	10	990			1550	1850
18	6	SUPER-SPORTSTER 18	OP	RNBT	AL	SV	IO	115-145		6	10	1040			4050	4750
18	8	V188	OP	RNBT	FBG	DV	IO	115-210		7	6	1400			4600	5450
18	10	ELIMINATOR 19	OP	FSH	AL	SV	OB			7	3	1050			1650	1950
18	10	ELIMINATOR DUAL 19	OP	FSH	AL	SV	OB			7	3	1075			1700	2000
18	10	SUPER-SPORTSTER 19	OP	RNBT	AL	SV	OB			7	3	1045			1650	2000
18	10	SUPER-SPORTSTER 19	OP	RNBT	AL	SV	IO	115-135		7	3	1095			4450	5100
19	2	SKI-TASTIC	OP	SKI	FBG	TH	IB	260	MRCR	6	8	2550			7150	8200
20	7	PRO FISHERMAN DUAL	OP	FSH	AL	SV	OB			7	6	1100			2050	2450
20	7	ROD MASTER 21	OP	CTRCN	AL	SV	OB			7	6	1070			2000	2350
20	7	SKIPPER 21	OP	FSH	AL	SV	OB			8	4	1150			2150	2500
20	7	SKIPPER 21	OP	FSH	AL	SV	IO	115-135		8	4	1160			6600	7600
20	7	SUPER-SPORTSTER 21	ST	RNBT	AL	SV	OB			7	6	1100			2050	2450
20	7	SUPER-SPORTSTER 21	ST	RNBT	AL	SV	IO	115-135		7	6	1150			5600	6450
20	9	OFFSHORE 21	ST	OFF	AL	SV	OB			7	6	1300			2400	2800
20	9	OFFSHORE 21	ST	OFF	AL	SV	IO	115-135		7	6	1330			5900	6750
20	9	V209	OP	RNBT	FBG	DV	IO	115-230		8	2	1850			6250	7500
20	9	V209 CUDDY	OP	CUD	FBG	DV	IO	115-230		8	2	1950			6650	7950
21	7	OFFSHORE 22	ST	OFF	AL	SV	OB			7	8	1430			2650	3050
21	7	OFFSHORE 22	ST	OFF	AL	SV	IO	115-135		7	8	1540			6400	7400
21	7	OFFSHORE 22	HT	OFF	AL	SV	IO	115-135		7	8	1540			6400	7400
24	8	LAGUNA 25	OP	SPTCR	FBG	SV	IO	115-230		8	6	4500			13100	15600
26	11	SPORT FISHERMAN	ST	FSH	FBG	DV	IO	115-220		8	6	4800			15700	19600
26	11	SPORT FISHERMAN	ST	FSH	FBG	DV	IO	230	MRCR	8	6	4800			17400	19800
		1991 BOATS														
16	2	BACK-TROLLER	OP	FSH	AL	SV	OB			6	4	620			895	1050
16	2	PRO-FISHERMAN	OP	FSH	AL	SV	OB			6	4	650			900	1050
16	2	PRO-FISHERMAN DUAL	OP	FSH	AL	SV	OB			6	4	650			975	1150
16	2	SEA MONSTER 16	OP	FSH	AL	SV	OB			5	6	610			880	1050
16	2	SEA TROLLER	OP	FSH	AL	SV	OB			5	6	650			940	1100
16	2	SUPER-SPORTSTER	OP	RNBT	AL	SV	OB			6	4	690			1000	1200
16	5	SEA-SNAPPER	OP	FSH	AL	FL	OB			6	6	225			325	395
16	5	SUPER-SNAPPER	OP	FSH	AL	FL	OB			5	7	370			540	650
16	8	VF-173	ST	FSH	FBG	SV	OB			7	6	1100			1500	1800
16	8	VFC-175	OP	FSH	FBG	SV	OB			7	6	1100			1500	1800
16	9	ELIMINATOR	OP	FSH	AL	SV	OB			6	11	800			1200	1400
16	9	ELIMINATOR DUAL	OP	FSH	AL	SV	OB			6	11	825			1200	1400
16	9	MASTER TROLLER	OP	FSH	AL	SV	OB			6	11	800			1050	1300
16	9	PRO FISHERMAN	OP	FSH	AL	SV	OB			6	11	800			1200	1400
16	9	SUPER-SPORTSTER	OP	RNBT	AL	SV	OB			6	11	800			1200	1400
16	10	SPORT TROLLER 16	OP	FSH	AL	SV	OB			5	9	420			630	755
17		BACKTROLLER 17	OP	FSH	AL	SV	OB			6	11	800			1150	1400
17		BASS HAWK 17	OP	BASS	AL	SV	OB			6	7	920			1350	1600
17		V170	OP	B/R	FBG	SV	OB			6	11	1150			1600	1950
18	3	SKI-TASTIC	OP	SKI	FBG	TH	IO	220-230		7	5	2850			5600	6500
18	5	PRO-FISHERMAN	OP	FSH	AL	SV	OB			6	10	850			1300	1550
18	5	PRO-FISHERMAN DUAL	OP	FSH	AL	SV	OB			6	10	875			1350	1600
18	6	SUPER-SPORTSTER	OP	RNBT	AL	SV	OB			6	10	990			1500	1800
18	6	SUPER-SPORTSTER	OP	RNBT	AL	SV	IO	115-145		6	10	1040			3800	4450
18	8	V188	OP	RNBT	FBG	DV	IO	115-210		7	6	1400			4250	5150
18	10	ELIMINATOR	OP	FSH	AL	SV	OB			7	3	1050			1550	1850
18	10	ELIMINATOR DUAL	OP	FSH	AL	SV	OB			7	3	1075			1600	1900
18	10	SUPER-SPORTSTER	OP	RNBT	AL	SV	OB			7	3	1045			1600	1900
18	10	SUPER-SPORTSTER	OP	RNBT	AL	SV	IO	115-135		7	3	1095			4100	4800
19	2	SKI-TASTIC	OP	SKI	FBG	TH	IB	260	MRCR	6	8	2550			6800	7800
20	7	PRO FISHERMAN DUAL	OP	FSH	AL	SV	OB			7	6	1100			1950	2300
20	7	ROD MASTER 21	OP	CTRCN	AL	SV	OB			7	6	1070			1900	2250
20	7	SKIPPER	OP	FSH	AL	SV	OB			8	4	1150			2000	2400
20	7	SKIPPER	OP	FSH	AL	SV	IO	115-135		8	4	1160			6200	7150
20	7	SUPER-SPORTSTER	ST	RNBT	AL	SV	OB			7	6	1100			1950	2300
20	7	SUPER-SPORTSTER	ST	RNBT	AL	SV	IO	115-135		7	6	1150			5250	6050

CONTINUED ON NEXT PAGE

LOA FT	LOA IN	NAME AND/ OR MODEL	TOP/ RIG	BOAT TYPE	-HULL- MTL	-HULL- TP	ENGINE TP	ENGINE # HP MFG	BEAM FT	BEAM IN	WGT LBS	DRAFT FT IN	RETAIL LOW	RETAIL HIGH
		1991 BOATS												
20	9	OFFSHORE	ST	OFF	AL	SV	OB		7	6	1300		2300	2700
20	9	OFFSHORE	ST	OFF	AL	SV	IO	115-135	7	6	1330		5500	6350
20	9	V209	OP	RNBT	FBG	DV	IO	115-230	8	2	1850		5900	7050
20	9	V209 CUDDY	OP	CUD	FBG	DV	IO	115-230	8	2	1950		6250	7450
21	3	LAGUNA 22	OP	CUD	FBG	SV	IO	115-230	8		3000		7750	9200
21	7	OFFSHORE	ST	OFF	AL	SV	OB		7	8	1430		2500	2900
21	7	OFFSHORE	ST	OFF	AL	SV	IO	115-135	7	8	1540		6000	6900
21	7	OFFSHORE	HT	OFF	AL	SV	IO	115-135	7	8	1540		6000	6900
24	8	LAGUNA 25	OP	SPTCR	FBG	SV	IO	115-230	8	6	4500		12300	14700
26	11	SPORT FISHERMAN	ST	FSH	FBG	DV	IO	115-220	8	6	4800		14700	18300
26	11	SPORT FISHERMAN	ST	FSH	FBG	DV	IO	230 MRCR	8	6	4800		16300	18500
		1990 BOATS												
16	2	BACK-TROLLER	OP	FSH	AL	SV	OB		6	4	450		615	745
16	2	PRO-FISHERMAN	OP	FSH	AL	SV	OB		6	4	650		895	1050
16	2	PRO-FISHERMAN DUAL	OP	FSH	AL	SV	OB		6	4	670		925	1100
16	2	RODMASTER	OP	FSH	AL	SV	OB		6	4	680		935	1100
16	2	SEA-MONSTER	OP	CTRCN	AL	SV	OB		6	4	610		850	1000
16	2	SEA-MONSTER	OP	FSH	AL	SV	OB		6	4	610		845	1000
16	2	SUPER-SPORTSTER	OP	RNBT	AL	SV	OB		6	4	690		980	1150
16	5	SEA-SNAPPER	OP	FSH	AL	FL	OB		6	4	225		310	380
16	5	SUPER TROLLER	OP	FSH	AL	SV	OB		5	9	420		585	705
16	5	SUPER-SNAPPER	OP	FSH	AL	FL	OB		5	7	370		515	625
16	8	VF-173	ST	FSH	FBG	SV	OB		7	6	1100		1450	1750
16	8	VFC-175	OP	FSH	FBG	SV	OB		7	6	1100		1450	1750
16	9	ELIMINATOR	OP	FSH	AL	SV	OB		6	11	800		1050	1250
16	9	ELIMINATOR DUAL	OP	FSH	AL	SV	OB		6	11	800		1150	1350
16	9	SUPER-SPORTSTER	OP	RNBT	AL	SV	OB		6	11	800		1150	1350
16	9	SUPER-SPORTSTER	OP	RNBT	AL	SV	IO	125-130	6	11	810		2850	3300
16	11	SCOUT	OP	FSH	AL	SV	OB		6	1	440		630	760
17	1	PRO-MISSILE	OP	BASS	FBG	SV	OB		7		850		1200	1400
18	3	SKI-TASTIC	OP	SKI	FBG	TH	IO	260	7	5	2850		5500	6350
18	5	PRO-FISHERMAN	OP	FSH	AL	SV	OB		6	10	850		1250	1450
18	5	PRO-FISHERMAN DUAL	OP	FSH	AL	SV	OB		6	10	875		1250	1500
18	6	RODMASTER	OP	CTRCN	AL	SV	OB		6	10	850		1250	1500
18	6	SUPER-SPORTSTER	OP	RNBT	AL	SV	OB		6	10	990		1450	1700
18	6	SUPER-SPORTSTER	OP	RNBT	AL	SV	IO	128-130	6	10	1040		3550	4150
18	8	V188	OP	RNBT	FBG	DV	IO	125-235	7	6	1400		4000	4900
18	8	V188	OP	RNBT	FBG	DV	IO	260	7	6	1400		4450	5150
18	8	V188 SPORT	OP	RNBT	FBG	DV	IO	260	7	6	1400		4450	5150
18	10	ELIMINATOR	OP	FSH	AL	SV	OB		7	3	1400		1900	2250
18	10	ELIMINATOR DUAL	OP	FSH	AL	SV	OB		7	3	1075		1550	1800
18	10	OFFSHORE	OP	OFF	AL	SV	IO	125 MRCR	7	3	1235		4050	4700
18	10	OFFSHORE	ST	OFF	AL	SV	IO	128-165	7	3	1235		4000	4700
18	10	SUPER-SPORTSTER	OP	RNBT	AL	SV	OB		7	3	1045		1500	1800
18	10	SUPER-SPORTSTER	OP	RNBT	AL	SV	IO	125-130	7	3	1095		3900	4500
19	2	SKI-TASTIC	OP	SKI	FBG	TH	IB	260 MRCR	6	8	2550		6450	7400
20	7	RODMASTER	OP	FSH	AL	SV	OB		7	6	1070		1800	2150
20	7	SKIPPER	OP	RNBT	AL	SV	OB		7	6	1150		1950	2300
20	7	SKIPPER	OP	RNBT	AL	SV	IO	125-165	7	6	1160		4950	5700
20	7	SPORTMASTER	OP	OPFSH	AL	SV	OB		7	6	1100		1850	2200
20	7	SUPER-SPORTSTER	ST	RNBT	AL	SV	OB		7	6	1100		1850	2200
20	7	SUPER-SPORTSTER	ST	RNBT	AL	SV	IO	128-130	7	6	1150		4900	5650
20	9	OFFSHORE	ST	OFF	AL	SV	OB		7	6	1300		2200	2550
20	9	OFFSHORE	ST	OFF	AL	SV	IO	125-130	7	6	1330		5200	5950
20	9	V209	OP	RNBT	FBG	DV	IO	125-260	8	2	1850		5550	6850
21	7	OFFSHORE	ST	OFF	AL	SV	OB		7	8	1430		2450	2850
21	7	OFFSHORE	ST	OFF	AL	SV	IO	125-130	7	8	1540		5650	6500
26	11	SPORT FISHERMAN	ST	FSH	FBG	DV	IO	125-230	8	6	4800		14000	17400
26	11	SPORT FISHERMAN	ST	FSH	FBG	DV	IO	260	8	6	4800		15700	17900
		1989 BOATS												
16	2	BACK-TROLLER	OP	FSH	AL	SV	OB		6	4	450		590	710
16	2	PRO-FISHERMAN	OP	FSH	AL	SV	OB		6	4	650		860	1000
16	2	PRO-FISHERMAN DUAL	OP	FSH	AL	SV	OB		6	4	670		885	1050
16	2	RODMASTER	OP	FSH	AL	SV	OB		6	4	680		900	1050
16	2	SEA-MONSTER	OP	CTRCN	AL	SV	OB		6	4	610		805	970
16	2	SEA-MONSTER	OP	FSH	AL	SV	OB		6	4	610		800	960
16	2	SUPER-SPORTSTER	OP	RNBT	AL	SV	OB		6	4	690		945	1100
16	5	SEA-SNAPPER	OP	FSH	AL	FL	OB		6	4	225		300	365
16	5	SPORT TROLLER	OP	FSH	AL	SV	OB		5	9	420		560	675
16	5	SUPER-SNAPPER	OP	FSH	AL	FL	OB		5	7	370		495	600
16	8	VF-173	ST	FSH	FBG	SV	OB		7	6	1100		1400	1650
16	8	VFC-175	OP	FSH	FBG	SV	OB		7	6	1100		1400	1650
16	9	ELIMINATOR	OP	FSH	AL	SV	OB		6	11	800		1000	1200
16	9	ELIMINATOR DUAL	OP	FSH	AL	SV	OB		6	11	800		1100	1300
16	9	SPORTSTER	OP	RNBT	AL	SV	OB		6	7	800		1100	1300
16	9	SPORTSTER	OP	RNBT	AL	SV	IO	120-130	6	7	810		2600	3000
16	9	SUPER-SPORTSTER	OP	RNBT	AL	SV	OB		6	11	800		1100	1300
16	9	SUPER-SPORTSTER	OP	RNBT	AL	SV	IO	120-130	6	11	810		2650	3100
16	11	SCOUT		FSH	AL	SV	OB		6	1	440		605	730
17	1	PRO-MISSILE	OP	BASS	FBG	SV	OB		7		850		1150	1350
18	3	SKI-TASTIC	OP	SKI	FBG	TH	IO	260	7	5	2850		5200	5950
18	5	PRO-FISHERMAN	OP	FSH	AL	SV	OB		6	10	850		1200	1400
18	5	PRO-FISHERMAN DUAL	OP	FSH	AL	SV	OB		6	10	875		1200	1450
18	6	RODMASTER	OP	CTRCN	AL	SV	OB		6	10	850		1200	1400
18	6	SPORTSTER	OP	RNBT	AL	SV	OB		6	10	990		1350	1650
18	6	SPORTSTER	OP	RNBT	AL	SV	IO	120-130	6	10	1040		3400	3950
18	6	SUPER-SPORTSTER	OP	RNBT	AL	SV	OB		6	10	990		1350	1650
18	6	SUPER-SPORTSTER	OP	RNBT	AL	SV	IO	128-130	6	10	1040		3350	3950
18	7	VFC-195	OP	CTRCN	FBG	SV	OB		8		1650		2000	2400
18	8	V188	OP	RNBT	FBG	DV	IO	120-235	7	6	1400		3800	4650
18	8	V188	OP	RNBT	FBG	DV	IO	260	7	6	1400		4150	4850
18	8	V188 SPORT	OP	RNBT	FBG	DV	IO	260	7	6	1400		4150	4850
18	10	ELIMINATOR	OP	FSH	AL	SV	OB		7	3	1400		1800	2150
18	10	ELIMINATOR DUAL	OP	FSH	AL	SV	OB		7	3	1075		1450	1750
18	10	OFFSHORE	OP	OFF	AL	SV	OB		7	3	1200		1600	1900
18	10	OFFSHORE	OP	OFF	AL	SV	IO	120 MRCR	7	3	1235		3800	4400
18	10	OFFSHORE	ST	OFF	AL	SV	IO	128-165	7	3	1235		3750	4450
18	10	SPORTSTER	OP	RNBT	AL	SV	OB		7	3	1075		1500	1750
18	10	SPORTSTER	OP	RNBT	AL	SV	IO	120-165	7	3	1125		3650	4300
18	10	SUPER-SPORTSTER	OP	RNBT	AL	SV	OB		7	3	1045		1450	1750
18	10	SUPER-SPORTSTER	OP	RNBT	AL	SV	IO	120-165	7	3	1095		3650	4300
19	2	SKI-TASTIC	OP	SKI	FBG	TH	IB	260 MRCR	6	8	2550		6150	7050
20	7	RODMASTER	OP	FSH	AL	SV	OB		7	6	1070		1750	2050
20	7	SKIPPER	OP	RNBT	AL	SV	OB		7	6	1150		1850	2200
20	7	SKIPPER	OP	RNBT	AL	SV	IO	120-165	7	6	1160		4700	5400
20	7	SPORTMASTER	OP	OPFSH	AL	SV	OB		7	6	1100		1800	2100
20	7	SPORTSTER	ST	RNBT	AL	SV	OB		7	6	1100		1800	2100
20	7	SPORTSTER	ST	RNBT	AL	SV	IO	120-165	7	6	1150		4700	5400
20	7	SUPER-SPORTSTER	ST	RNBT	AL	SV	OB		7	6	1100		1800	2100
20	7	SUPER-SPORTSTER	ST	RNBT	AL	SV	IO	128-165	7	6	1150		4650	5400
20	9	OFFSHORE	ST	OFF	AL	SV	OB		7	6	1300		2050	2450
20	9	OFFSHORE	ST	OFF	AL	SV	IO	120-165	7	6	1330		4900	5700
20	9	V209	OP	RNBT	FBG	DV	IO	120-260	8	2	1850		5200	6450
20	11	SPORT CRUISER	ST	CUD	FBG	SV	IO	120-260	8		3400		7350	8900
21	7	OFFSHORE	ST	OFF	AL	SV	OB		7	8	1430		2350	2750
21	7	OFFSHORE	ST	OFF	AL	SV	IO	120-165	7	8	1540		5350	6150
26	11	SPORT FISHERMAN	ST	FSH	FBG	DV	IO	120-200	8	6	4800		13100	16000
26	11	SPORT FISHERMAN	ST	FSH	FBG	DV	IO	230-260	8	6	4800		14400	16900
		1988 BOATS												
16	2	BACK-TROLLER	OP	FSH	AL	SV	OB		6	4	450		570	685
16	2	PRO-FISHERMAN	OP	FSH	AL	SV	OB		6	4	650		815	980
16	2	PRO-FISHERMAN DUAL	OP	FSH	AL	SV	OB		6	4	670		850	1000
16	2	RODMASTER	OP	FSH	AL	SV	OB		6	4	680		860	1050
16	2	SEAMONSTER	OP	CTRCN	AL	SV	OB		6	4	610		775	935
16	2	SEAMONSTER	OP	FSH	AL	SV	OB		6	4	610		765	925
16	2	SPORTSTER	OP	RNBT	AL	SV	OB		6	4	690		905	1100
16	2	SUPER-SPORTSTER	OP	RNBT	AL	SV	OB		6	4	690		905	1100
16	5	SEA-SNAPPER	OP	FSH	AL	FL	OB		6	4	225		285	350
16	5	SPORT TROLLER	OP	FSH	AL	SV	OB		5	9	420		540	650
16	5	SUPER-SNAPPER	OP	FSH	AL	FL	OB		5	7	370		480	580
16	8	VF-173	ST	FSH	FBG	SV	OB		7	6	1100		1350	1600
16	8	VFC-175	OP	FSH	FBG	SV	OB		7	6	1100		1350	1600
16	9	ELIMINATOR	OP	FSH	AL	SV	OB		6	11	800		1000	1200
16	9	ELIMINATOR DUAL	OP	FSH	AL	SV	OB		6	11			1150	1350
16	9	SPORTMASTER	ST	FSH	AL	SV	OB		6	11	800		1000	1200
16	9	SPORTSTER	OP	RNBT	AL	SV	OB		6	11	800		1050	1250
16	9	SPORTSTER	OP	RNBT	AL	SV	IO	120-130	6	11	800		2500	2950
16	9	SUPER-SPORTSTER	OP	RNBT	AL	SV	OB		6	11	800		1050	1250
16	9	SUPER-SPORTSTER	OP	RNBT	AL	SV	IO	120-130	6	11	800		2500	2950
16	10	SCOUT		FSH	AL	SV	OB		6		440		580	695
17	1	PRO-MISSILE	OP	BASS	FBG	SV	OB		7		850		1100	1300
18	3	SKI-TASTIC	OP	SKI	FBG	TH	IO	260	7	5	2850		4900	5650
18	5	PRO-FISHERMAN	OP	FSH	AL	SV	OB		6	10	850		1150	1350
18	5	PRO-FISHERMAN DUAL	OP	FSH	AL	SV	OB		6	10	875		1150	1400
18	6	RODMASTER	OP	CTRCN	AL	SV	OB		7		850		1150	1350
18	6	SPORTSTER	OP	RNBT	AL	SV	OB		6	10	990		1300	1550
18	6	SPORTSTER	OP	RNBT	AL	SV	IO	120-130	6	10	1040		3200	3750

 CONTINUED ON NEXT PAGE

LOA FT	LOA IN	NAME AND/ OR MODEL	TOP/ RIG	BOAT TYPE	-HULL- MTL	-HULL- TP	ENGINE TP	ENGINE # HP	ENGINE MFG	BEAM FT	BEAM IN	WGT LBS	DRAFT FT IN	RETAIL LOW	RETAIL HIGH
		1988 BOATS													
18	6	SUPER-SPORTSTER	OP	RNBT	AL	SV	OB			6	10	990		1300	1550
18	6	SUPER-SPORTSTER	OP	RNBT	AL	SV	IO	128-140		6	10	1040		3150	3750
18	7	VFC-195	OP	CTRCN	FBG	SV	OB			8		1650		1900	2300
18	8	V188	OP	RNBT	FBG	DV	IO	120-230		8		1400		3750	4600
18	8	V188	OP	RNBT	FBG	DV	IO	260		8		1400		4100	4800
18	8	V188 SPORT	OP	RNBT	FBG	DV	IO	260		8		1400		4100	4800
18	10	ELIMINATOR	OP	FSH	AL	SV	OB			7	3	1050		1400	1650
18	10	ELIMINATOR DUAL	OP	FSH	AL	SV	OB			7	3	1075		1400	1700
18	10	OFFSHORE	OP	CBNCR	AL	SV	OB			7		1200		1550	1850
18	10	OFFSHORE	OP	CBNCR	AL	SV	IO	120	MRCR	7		1235		3650	4250
18	10	OFFSHORE	ST	CBNCR	AL	SV	IO	128-165		7		1235		3600	4300
18	10	OFFSHORE 19	ST	CBNCR	AL	SV	IO	130	MRCR	7		1235		3650	4250
18	10	SPORTSTER	OP	RNBT	AL	SV	OB			7	3	1075		1450	1700
18	10	SPORTSTER	OP	RNBT	AL	SV	IO	120-165		7	3	1125		3450	4050
18	10	SUPER-SPORTSTER	OP	RNBT	AL	SV	OB			7	3	1045		1400	1650
18	10	SUPER-SPORTSTER	OP	RNBT	AL	SV	IO	120-165		7	3	1095		3450	4050
19	2	SKI-TASTIC	OP	SKI	FBG	TH	IB	260	MRCR	6	8	2550		5850	6700
20	7	OFFSHORE	ST	CUD	AL	SV	OB			7	7	1250		1900	2300
20	7	RODMASTER	OP	FSH	AL	SV	OB			7	6	1070		1650	2000
20	7	SKIPPER	OP	RNBT	AL	SV	OB			7	6	1150		1800	2100
20	7	SKIPPER	OP	RNBT	AL	SV	IO	120-165		7	6	1160		4450	5150
20	7	SPORTMASTER	OP	OPFSH	AL	SV	OB			6	10	1100		1700	2050
20	7	SPORTMASTER	ST	RNBT	AL	SV	OB			7	6	1160		1800	2150
20	7	SPORTSTER	ST	RNBT	AL	SV	OB			7	6	1100		1700	2050
20	7	SPORTSTER	ST	RNBT	AL	SV	IO	120-165		7	6	1150		4450	5150
20	7	SUPER-SPORTSTER	ST	RNBT	AL	SV	OB			7	6	1100		1700	2050
20	7	SUPER-SPORTSTER	ST	RNBT	AL	SV	IO	128-170		7	6	1150		4400	5150
20	9	OFFSHORE	ST	CBNCR	AL	SV	OB			7	6	1300		2000	2350
20	9	OFFSHORE	ST	CBNCR	AL	SV	IO	120-165		7	6	1330		5050	5850
20	9	V209	OP	RNBT	FBG	DV	IO	120-260		8	2	1850		4950	6100
20	9	V209 SPORT	OP	RNBT	FBG	DV	IO	260		8	2	1850		5300	6100
20	11	SPORT CRUISER	ST	CUD	FBG	SV	IO	120-260		8		3400		6950	8450
21	7	OFFSHORE	ST	CBNCR	AL	SV	OB			7	8	1430		2250	2600
21	7	OFFSHORE	ST	CBNCR	AL	SV	IO	120-165		7	8	1540		5550	6400
26	11	SPORT FISHERMAN	ST	FSH	FBG	DV	IO	120-200		8	6	4800		12400	15100
26	11	SPORT FISHERMAN	ST	FSH	FBG	DV	IO	230-260		8	6	4800		13700	16000
		1987 BOATS													
16	2	BACK-TROLLER	OP	FSH	AL	SV	OB			6	4	450		545	660
16	2	RODMASTER	OP	FSH	AL	SV	OB			6	4	680		820	985
16	2	SEAMONSTER	OP	CTRCN	AL	SV	OB			6	4	510		625	755
16	2	SEAMONSTER	OP	FSH	AL	SV	OB			6	4	510		620	745
16	2	SPORTSMASTER	OP	RNBT	AL	SV	OB			6	4	650		810	975
16	2	SPORTSTER	OP	RNBT	AL	SV	OB			6	4	690		870	1050
16	2	SUPER-SPORTSTER	OP	RNBT	AL	SV	OB			6	4	690		870	1050
16	5	SUPER-SNAPPER	OP	FSH	AL	FL	OB			5	7	420		520	625
16	7	BASS-HAWK II	OP	BASS	AL	FL	OB			6	4	635		795	955
16	8	V-171 B/R	ST	RNBT	FBG	DV	OB			7	6	1100		1300	1550
16	8	V-171 B/R	ST	RNBT	FBG	DV	IO	120-185		7	6	1450		2950	3500
16	8	VF173	ST	FSH	FBG	SV	OB			7	6	1100		1300	1550
16	8	VFC175	OP	FSH	FBG	SV	OB			7	6	1100		1300	1550
16	9	ELIMINATOR	OP	FSH	AL	SV	OB			6	11	800		990	1200
16	9	SEA-SNAPPER	OP	FSH	AL	FL	OB			6	2	340		435	525
16	9	SPORTMASTER	ST	FSH	AL	SV	OB			6	11	800		990	1200
16	9	SPORTSTER	ST	RNBT	AL	SV	OB			6	11	800		1000	1200
16	9	SPORTSTER	ST	RNBT	AL	SV	IO	120-140		6	11	800		2350	2800
16	9	SUPER SPORTSTER	ST	RNBT	AL	SV	OB			6	11	800		1000	1200
16	9	SUPER SPORTSTER	ST	RNBT	AL	SV	IO	120-140		6	11	800		2350	2800
16	10	SCOUT		FSH	AL	SV	OB			6		440		555	670
17	1	PRO-MISSILE	OP	BASS	FBG	SV	OB			7		850		1050	1250
18	6	OFFSHORE	ST	CBNCR	AL	SV	OB			7		1200		1450	1750
18	6	OFFSHORE	ST	CBNCR	AL	SV	IO	120-140		7		1840		3700	4350
18	6	RODMASTER	OP	CTRCN	AL	SV	OB			7		920		1200	1400
18	6	RODMASTER SIDE CNSL	OP	OPFSH	AL	SV	OB			7		920		1150	1400
18	6	SPORTSMASTER	ST	OPFSH	AL	SV	OB			7		1020		1300	1500
18	6	SPORTSTER	ST	RNBT	AL	SV	OB			7		1020		1300	1550
18	6	SPORTSTER	ST	RNBT	AL	SV	IO	120-140		7		1610		3300	3900
18	6	SUPER-SPORTSTER	ST	RNBT	AL	SV	OB			7		1020		1300	1550
18	6	SUPER-SPORTSTER	ST	RNBT	AL	SV	IO	120-140		7		1610		3300	3850
18	7	V-190 B/R	ST	RNBT	FBG	DV	IO	120-230		8		1750		3750	4600
18	8	VFC-195	OP	CTRCN	FBG	SV	OB			8		1650		1850	2200
19	2	SKI-TASTIC		SKI	FBG	TH	IB	250	PCM	6	8	1650		4600	5250
20	7	OFFSHORE	ST	CUD	AL	SV	OB			7	7	1250		1850	2200
20	7	ROOMASTER	OP	FSH	AL	SV	OB			7	6	1100		1650	1950
20	7	SKIPPER	ST	RNBT	AL	SV	OB			7	6	1100		1650	1950
20	7	SPORTMASTER	ST	RNBT	AL	SV	OB			7	6	1100		1650	1950
20	7	SPORTSTER	ST	RNBT	AL	SV	OB			7	6	1100		1650	1950
20	7	SPORTSTER	ST	RNBT	AL	SV	IO	120-140		7	6	1150		4150	4850
20	7	SUPER-SPORTSTER	ST	RNBT	AL	SV	OB			7	6	1100		1650	1950
20	7	SUPER-SPORTSTER	ST	RNBT	AL	SV	IO	120-140		7	6	1150		4150	4850
20	9	OFFSHORE	ST	CUD	AL	SV	IO	120-140		7	7			5000	5750
20	11	SPORT CRUISER	ST	CUD	FBG	SV	IO	120-205		8		3100		6200	7700
21	7	OFFSHORE	ST	CBNCR	AL	SV	OB			7	7	1300		1950	2300
21	7	OFFSHORE	ST	CBNCR	AL	SV	IO	120-140		7	10	1970		5600	6500
26	11	SPORT FISHERMAN	ST	FSH	FBG	DV	IO	140		8	6	4800		12000	13700
26	11	SPORT FISHERMAN	FB	FSH	FBG	DV	IO	120-205		8	6	4800		11800	14400
26	11	SPORT FISHERMAN	FB	FSH	FBG	DV	IO	230-260		8	6	4800		13000	15200
		1986 BOATS													
16	2	BACK-TROLLER	OP	FSH	AL	SV	OB			6	4	450		530	640
16	2	RODMASTER	OP	FSH	AL	SV	OB			6	4	680		790	955
16	2	SEAMONSTER	OP	CTRCN	AL	SV	OB			6	4	510		605	725
16	2	SEAMONSTER	OP	FSH	AL	SV	OB			6	4	510		595	720
16	2	SPORTSMASTER	OP	RNBT	AL	SV	OB			6	4	650		780	940
16	2	SPORTSTER	OP	RNBT	AL	SV	OB			6	4	690		830	995
16	2	SUPER-SPORTSTER	OP	RNBT	AL	SV	OB			6	4	690		830	995
16	5	SEA-SNAPPER	OP	FSH	AL	RB	OB			5	7	340		405	495
16	5	SPORT-TROLLER	OP	FSH	AL	RB	OB			5	9	420		500	605
16	5	SUPER-SNAPPER	OP	FSH	AL	FL	OB			5	7	420		500	605
16	7	BASS-HAWK II	OP	BASS	AL	FL	OB			6	1	635		765	925
16	8	V-171 B/R	ST	RNBT	FBG	DV	OB			7	6	1100		1250	1500
16	8	V-171 B/R	ST	RNBT	FBG	DV	IO	120-185		7	6	1450		2800	3300
16	8	VF173	ST	FSH	FBG	SV	OB			7	6	1100		1250	1500
16	8	VFC175	OP	FSH	FBG	SV	OB			7	6	1100		1250	1500
16	9	SEA-SNAPPER	OP	FSH	AL	FL	OB			6	2	340		420	505
16	10	SCOUT		FSH	AL	SV	OB			6		440		540	650
17	1	PRO-MISSILE	OP	BASS	FBG	SV	OB			7		850		1000	1200
18	6	OFFSHORE	ST	CBNCR	AL	SV	OB			7		1200		1400	1700
18	6	OFFSHORE	ST	CBNCR	AL	SV	IO	120-140		7		1840		3550	4150
18	6	RODMASTER	OP	CTRCN	AL	SV	OB			7		920		1150	1350
18	6	RODMASTER SIDE CNSL	OP	OPFSH	AL	SV	OB			7		920		1150	1350
18	6	SPORTSMASTER	ST	OPFSH	AL	SV	OB			7		1020		1250	1450
18	6	SPORTSTER	ST	RNBT	AL	SV	OB			7		1020		1250	1500
18	6	SPORTSTER	ST	RNBT	AL	SV	IO	120-140		7		1610		3150	3700
18	6	SUPER-SPORTSTER	ST	RNBT	AL	SV	OB			7		1020		1250	1500
18	6	SUPER-SPORTSTER	ST	RNBT	AL	SV	IO	120-140		7		1610		3150	3700
18	7	V-190 B/R	ST	RNBT	FBG	DV	IO	120-230		8		1750		3600	4400
18	8	VFC-195	OP	CTRCN	FBG	SV	OB			8		1650		1800	2150
19	2	SKI-TASTIC		SKI	FBG	TH	IB	250	PCM	6	8	1650		4350	5050
20	7	OFFSHORE	ST	CUD	AL	SV	OB			7	7	1250		1750	2100
20	7	ROOMASTER	OP	FSH	AL	SV	OB			7	6	1100		1600	1900
20	7	SKIPPER	ST	RNBT	AL	SV	OB			7	6	1100		1550	1850
20	7	SPORTMASTER	ST	RNBT	AL	SV	OB			7	6	1100		1600	1900
20	7	SPORTSTER	ST	RNBT	AL	SV	OB			7	6	1100		1600	1900
20	7	SPORTSTER	ST	RNBT	AL	SV	IO	120-140		7	6	1150		4000	4650
20	7	SUPER-SPORTSTER	ST	RNBT	AL	SV	OB			7	6	1100		1600	1900
20	7	SUPER-SPORTSTER	ST	RNBT	AL	SV	IO	120-140		7	6	1150		4000	4650
20	9	OFFSHORE	ST	CUD	AL	SV	IO	120-140		7	7			4750	5500
21	7	OFFSHORE	ST	CBNCR	AL	SV	OB			7	7	1300		1900	2250
21	7	OFFSHORE	ST	CBNCR	AL	SV	IO	120-140		7	10	1970		5350	6200
21	7	RODMASTER	OP	CTRCN	AL	SV	OB			7	7	1100		1600	1950
21	7	SPORTSTER	ST	RNBT	AL	SV	OB			7	7	1200		1750	2100
21	7	SPORTSTER	ST	RNBT	AL	SV	IO	120-170		7	7	1840		4500	5300
21	7	SUPER-SPORTSTER	ST	RNBT	AL	SV	OB			7	7	1200		1750	2100
		1985 BOATS													
16	2	BACK-TROLLER	OP	FSH	AL	SV	OB			6	4	450		510	615
16	2	RODMASTER	OP	FSH	AL	SV	OB			6	4	680		765	920
16	2	SEAMONSTER	OP	FSH	AL	SV	OB			6	4	510		580	695
16	2	SPORTSMASTER	OP	RNBT	AL	SV	OB			6	4	650		755	910
16	2	SPORTSTER	OP	RNBT	AL	SV	OB			6	4	690		795	960
16	2	SUPER-SPORTSTER	OP	RNBT	AL	SV	OB			6	4	690		805	970
16	5	SCOUT 16	OP	FSH	AL	SV	OB			5	6	420		490	590
16	5	SUPER-SNAPPER	OP	FSH	AL	FL	OB			5	7	420		490	590
16	7	BASS-HAWK II	OP	BASS	AL	FL	OB			6	1	635		740	890
16	8	V-171 B/R	ST	RNBT	FBG	DV	OB			7	6	1100		1250	1450
16	8	V-171 B/R	ST	RNBT	FBG	DV	IO	120-185		7	6	1450		2700	3200
16	9	SEA-SNAPPER	OP	FSH	AL	FL	OB			6	2	340		400	490
17		PRO-HAWK II	OP	BASS	FBG	FL	OB			6	5	750		885	1050

CONTINUED ON NEXT PAGE

LOA FT	LOA IN	NAME AND/ OR MODEL	TOP/ RIG	BOAT TYPE	-HULL- MTL	-HULL- TP	ENGINE TP	ENGINE # HP	ENGINE MFG	BEAM FT	BEAM IN	WGT LBS	DRAFT FT	DRAFT IN	RETAIL LOW	RETAIL HIGH
		1985 BOATS														
17	1	PRO-MISSILE	OP	BASS	FBG	SV	OB			7		850			995	1200
18	6	OFFSHORE	ST	CBNCR	AL	SV	OB			7		1200			1350	1650
18	6	OFFSHORE	ST	CBNCR	AL	SV	IO	120-140		7		1840			3400	4000
18	6	RODMASTER	OP	CTRCN	AL	SV	OB			7		920			1100	1300
18	6	RODMASTER SIDE CNSL	OP	OPFSH	AL	SV	OB			7		920			1100	1300
18	6	SKIPPER	ST	RNBT	AL	SV	OB			7		900			1100	1300
18	6	SPORTSMASTER	ST	OPFSH	AL	SV	OB			7		1020			1200	1400
18	6	SPORTSTER	ST	RNBT	AL	SV	OB			7		1020			1200	1450
18	6	SPORTSTER	ST	RNBT	AL	SV	IO	120-140		7		1610			3050	3550
18	6	SUPER-SPORTSTER	ST	RNBT	AL	SV	OB			7		1020			1200	1450
18	6	SUPER-SPORTSTER	ST	RNBT	AL	SV	IO	120-140		7		1610			3050	3550
18	7	V-190 B/R	ST	RNBT	FBG	DV	IO	120-230		8		1750			3450	4200
18	8	VFC-195	OP	CTRCN	FBG	SV	OB			8		1650			1750	2050
19	2	SKI-TASTIC		SKI	FBG	TH	IB	250	PCM	6	8	1650			4150	4800
20	7	OFFSHORE	ST	CUD	AL	SV	OB			7	7	1250			1700	2050
20	7	OFFSHORE	ST	CUD	AL	SV	IO	120-140		7	7	1870			4200	4950
21	7	OFFSHORE	ST	CBNCR	AL	SV	OB			7	7	1300			1800	2150
21	7	OFFSHORE	ST	CBNCR	AL	SV	IO	120-140		7	10	1970			5150	5950
21	7	RODMASTER	OP	CTRCN	AL	SV	OB			7	7	1100			1550	1850
21	7	SPORTSTER	ST	RNBT	AL	SV	OB			7	7	1200			1700	2000
21	7	SPORTSTER	ST	RNBT	AL	SV	IO	120-170		7	7	1840			4300	5050
21	7	SUPER-SPORTSTER	ST	RNBT	AL	SV	OB			7	7	1200			1700	2000
		1984 BOATS														
16	2	BACK-TROLLER	OP	FSH	AL	SV	OB			6	4	500			550	660
16	2	RODMASTER	OP	FSH	AL	SV	OB			6	4	680			740	890
16	2	SEAMONSTER	OP	FSH	AL	SV	OB			6	4	510			560	675
16	2	SPORTSMASTER	OP	RNBT	AL	SV	OB			6	4	650			730	880
16	2	SPORTSTER	OP	RNBT	AL	SV	OB			6	4	690			775	935
16	2	SUPER-SPORTSTER	OP	RNBT	AL	SV	OB			6	4	690			775	935
16	5	SEA-SNAPPER	OP	FSH	AL	FL	OB			5	7	340			380	465
16	5	SUPER-SNAPPER	OP	FSH	AL	FL	OB			5	7	420			475	570
16	6	BASS-HAWK II	OP	BASS	AL	FL	OB			6	1	635			715	860
16	8	V-171 B/R	ST	RNBT	FBG	DV	OB			7	6	1350			1400	1700
16	8	V-171 B/R	ST	RNBT	FBG	DV	IO	120-188		7	6	1450			2600	3100
17	1	PRO BASS MISSILE		BASS	FBG	SV	OB			7		850			965	1150
18	6	OFFSHORE	ST	CBNCR	AL	SV	OB			7		1200			1300	1600
18	6	OFFSHORE	ST	CBNCR	AL	SV	IO	120-140		7		1840			3300	3850
18	6	RODMASTER	OP	FSH	AL	SV	OB			7		920			1100	1300
18	6	RODMASTER SIDE CNSL	OP	FSH	AL	SV	OB			7		920			1050	1250
18	6	SKIPPER	ST	RNBT	AL	SV	OB			7		900			1050	1250
18	6	SKIPPER	ST	RNBT	AL	SV	IO	120-140		7		1594			2950	3450
18	6	SPORTSMASTER	ST	RNBT	AL	SV	OB			7		1020			1200	1400
18	6	SPORTSTER	ST	RNBT	AL	SV	OB			7		1020			1200	1400
18	6	SPORTSTER	ST	RNBT	AL	SV	IO	120-140		7		1610			2950	3450
18	6	SUPER-SPORTSTER	ST	RNBT	AL	SV	OB			7		1020			1200	1400
18	7	V-190 B/R	ST	RNBT	FBG	DV	IO	140-200		8		1650			3300	3900
18	7	V-190 B/R	ST	RNBT	FBG	DV	IO	228-230		8		2246			3800	4450
18	8	VFC-195	OP	FSH	FBG	SV	OB			8		1650			1700	2000
19	2	SKI-TASTIC		SKI	FBG	TH	IB	240	PCM	6	8	1650			3900	4550
21	7	OFFSHORE	ST	CBNCR	AL	SV	OB			7	10	1300			1750	2100
21	7	OFFSHORE	ST	CBNCR	AL	SV	IO	120-170		7	10	1970			4950	5850
21	7	RODMASTER	OP	CTRCN	AL	SV	OB			7	7	1100			1500	1800
21.	7	SPORTSTER	ST	RNBT	AL	SV	OB			7	7	1200			1650	1950
21	7	SPORTSTER	ST	RNBT	AL	SV	IO	120-170		7	7	1840			4150	4900
21	7	SUPER SPORTSTER	ST	RNBT	AL	SV	OB			7	7	1200			1650	1950

....For earlier years, see the BUC Used Boat Price Guide, Volume 3

SYMBOL YACHTS

WARWICK RI 02889

See inside cover to adjust price for area

For more recent years, see the BUC Used Boat Price Guide, Volume 1

LOA FT	LOA IN	NAME AND/ OR MODEL	TOP/ RIG	BOAT TYPE	-HULL- MTL	-HULL- TP	ENGINE TP	ENGINE # HP	ENGINE MFG	BEAM FT	BEAM IN	WGT LBS	DRAFT FT	DRAFT IN	RETAIL LOW	RETAIL HIGH
		1990 BOATS														
38	10	CONVERTIBLE SEDAN 39	FB	CNV	F/S	SV	IB	T350	MRCR	14	8	21000	3	2	83000	91200
		IB T250D CUM 93300 102500, IB T300D GM 103500 114000, IB T375D CAT 112500 124000														
38	10	MY 39 SUNDECK	FB	DCMY	F/S	SV	IB	T250D	CUM	14	8	22500	3	2	98500	108000
		IB T300D GM 105500 116000, IB T350D MRCR 102000 112000, IB T375D CAT 118000 129500														
44	2	MK# 44 SUNDECK	FB	DCMY	F/S	SV	IB	T375D	CAT	14	9	27000	3	10	140000	154000
44	2	MK# 44 SUNDECK	FB	DCMY	F/S	SV	IB	T485D	GM	14	9	28000	3	10	156500	172000
48	5	PILOT HOUSE	FB	PH	F/S	SV	IB	T375D	CAT	15		41000	3	10	180500	198500
48	5	PILOT HOUSE	FB	PH	F/S	SV	IB	T485D	GM	15		42000	3	10	190000	208500
48	5	YACHT FISHERMAN 48	FB	YTFS	F/S	SV	IB	T375D	CAT	15		39600	3	9	161500	177500
48	5	YACHT FISHERMAN 48	FB	YTFS	F/S	SV	IB	T485D	GM	15		41000	3	9	174000	191000
52	3	JSL 50	FB	DCMY	F/S	SV	IB	T375D	CAT	16	4	34000	3	6	183500	201500
52	3	JSL 50	FB	DCMY	F/S	SV	IB	T485D	GM	16	4	34000	3	6	201000	221000
52	10	YACHT FISHER 53	FB	YTFS	F/S	SV	IB	T375D	CAT	17		46500	3	9	204000	224500
52	10	YACHT FISHER 53	FB	YTFS	F/S	SV	IB	T485D	GM	17		47500	3	9	235000	258500
57	7	FLUSHDECK MY	FB	MY	F/S	SV	IB	T485D	GM	17		52000	3	9	272000	299000
57	10	FLUSHDECK MY	FB	MY	F/S	SV	IB	T550D	GM	17		54000	3	9	292500	321000
57	10	WIDEBODY FD MY	FB	MY	F/S	SV	IB	T485D	GM	17		53000	3	11	277500	305000
57	10	WIDEBODY FD MY	FB	MY	F/S	SV	IB	T550D	GM	17		54000	3	11	306000	336500
		1986 BOATS														
40	10	SYMBOL		MY	FBG	SV	IB	T350		14	9	25000			85400	93800
40	10	SYMBOL		SF	FBG	SV	IB	T350		14	9	23500			81600	89700
44	2	GT SPORTSMAN		SDNSF	FBG	SV	IB	T310D		14	9	27000			103500	113500
44	2	GT SPORTSMAN		SDNSF	FBG	SV	IB	T410D		14	9	27000			115000	126500
44	2	GT SPORTSMAN		SDNSF	FBG	SV	IB	T450D		14	9	27000			120000	132000
44	2	MOTORYACHT		MY	FBG	SV	IB	T310D		14	9	30000			111000	122000
44	2	MOTORYACHT		MY	FBG	SV	IB	T410D		14	9	30000			119500	131000
44	2	MOTORYACHT		MY	FBG	SV	IB	T450D		14	9	30000			123000	135500
		1985 BOATS														
34	8	UNIVERSAL 35	FB	DCMY	FBG	DS	IB	135D		14		18500	3	3	64500	70900
34	8	UNIVERSAL 35		TRWL	FBG	DS	IB	T 90D		14		18500	3	3	66200	72800
34	8	UNIVERSAL DBL CABIN		TRWL	FBG	DS	IB	135D		12		18000			65300	71700
34	8	UNIVERSAL GREAT CAB		TRWL	FBG	DS	IB	120D		12		18000			65400	71900
38		SYMBOL MOTOR YACHT		MY	FBG	SV	IB	T410D		14					87800	96500
38		SYMBOL MOTOR YACHT		MY	FBG	SV	IB	T450D		14					90800	99700
38		SYMBOL SPORTSMAN GT		SF	FBG	SV	IB	T410D		14					92400	101500
38		SYMBOL SPORTSMAN GT		SF	FBG	SV	IB	T450D		14					95300	105000
38		SYMBOL TRI CABIN		TCMY	FBG	SV	IB	T410D		14					97200	107000
38		SYMBOL TRI CABIN		TCMY	FBG	SV	IB	T450D		14					100000	110000
40	10	MOTOR YACHT 41	FB	MY	FBG	SV	IB	T330	CHRY	14	5	25500	3	8	84000	92300
40	10	SF-SEDAN 41 LTD ED	FB	SDNSF	FBG	SV	IB	D		14	5	25500	3	8	**	**
40	10	SYMBOL	FB	SDNSF	FBG	DV	IB	T350	CHRY	14	5	25500	3	8	84600	93000
		IB T350 CRUS 85500 93900, IB T350 MRCR 84800 93200, IB T130D LEHM 85200 93600														
		IB T135D PERK 86700 95300, IB T300D J&T 96000 105500, IB T310D J&T 96700 106500														
		IB T320D CUM 96400 106000, IB T375D J&T 102000 112000, IB T450D J&T 108500 119000														
40	10	SYMBOL SUN DECK	FB	MY	FBG	DV	IB	T350	CHRY	14	5	25500	3	8	84600	93000
		IB T350 CRUS 85500 94000, IB T350 MRCR 84900 93300, IB T130D LEHM 86500 95100														
		IB T135D PERK 88000 96700, IB T300D J&T 96500 106000, IB T310D J&T 97100 107000														
		IB T320D CUM 96800 106500, IB T375D J&T 102000 112000, IB T450D J&T 108000 119000														
40	10	TRI-CABIN	FB	TCMY	FBG	SV	IB	T330	CHRY	14	5	25500	3	8	85300	93800
44	2	GT SPORTSMAN	FB	SF	FBG	SV	IB	T460D		14	9	34000	3	8	128000	140500
44	2	MOTORYACHT	FB	MY	FBG	SV	IB	T410D		14	9	38000	3	8	131500	144500
44	2	SUN-DECK MARK II	FB	MY	FBG	SV	IB	T320D	CUM	14	9	36000	3	8	118000	129500
44	2	SUPER-SEDAN	FB	MY	FBG	SV	IB	320D	CUM	14	9	27000	3	8	90500	99400
44	2	SYMBOL	FB	TCMY	FBG	DV	IB	T300D	J&T	14	9	29000	3	8	109500	120000
		IB T310D J&T 110500 121500, IB T320D CUM 111000 122000, IB T375D J&T 117500 129500														
		IB T410D J&T 122000 134000, IB T450D J&T 126500 139000														
44	2	SYMBOL GT	FB	SDNSF	FBG	DV	IB	T300D	J&T	14	9	27000	3	8	100500	110500
		IB T310D J&T 102000 112000, IB T320D CUM 102500 112500, IB T375D J&T 110500 121500														
		IB T410D J&T 115000 126500, IB T450D J&T 120500 132500														
44	2	SYMBOL SUNDECK	FB	DCMY	FBG	DV	IB	T300D	J&T	14	9	29000	3	8	105000	115500
		IB T310D J&T 106000 116500, IB T320D CUM 106500 117000, IB T375D J&T 112500 123500														
		IB T410D J&T 116000 127500, IB T450D J&T 120500 132500														
44	2	TRI-CABIN MK I	FB	TCMY	FBG	SV	IB	T320D	CUM	14	9	34000	3	8	117000	128500
50	4	SYMBOL	FB	SDNSF	FBG	DV	IB	T462D	GM	15		45000	4		158000	173500
50	4	SYMBOL	FB	YTFS	FBG	DV	IB	T462D	GM	15		45000	4		159000	175000
50	4	YACHT FISH 50	FB	YTFS	FBG	SV	IB	T450		15		45000	4		143000	157000
53	6		FB	MY	FBG	SV	IB	T450		16	9	50000	4		182500	200500
53	6		FB	YTFS	FBG	SV	IB	T650		16	9	50000	4		212500	233500
53	6	EXT DECKHOUSE	FB	MY	FBG	SV	IB	T450		16	9	50000	4		188000	207000
53	8	MOTORYACHT 53	FB	MY	FBG	SV	IB	T650		17		54500	4		228000	250500
53	8	SYMBOL	FB	MY	FBG	DV	IB	T D		17		50000	4		**	**
58		SYMBOL	FB	MY	FBG	DV	IB	T462D	GM						212000	233000
58		SYMBOL	FB	YTFS	FBG	DV	IB	T D							**	**
		1984 BOATS														
40	10	SPORT SEDAN	FB	SF	FBG	SV	IB	T330	CHRY	14	5	25500	3	8	80700	88700
40	10	TRI-CABIN	FB	MY	FBG	SV	IB	T330	CHRY	14	5	25500	3	8	80400	88400
44	2	GT SPORTSMAN	FB	SF	FBG	SV	IB	T460D		14	9	34000	3	8	122500	134500

LOA FT IN	NAME AND/ OR MODEL	TOP/ RIG	BOAT TYPE	HULL MTL TP	ENGINE TP # HP MFG	BEAM FT IN	WGT LBS	DRAFT FT IN	RETAIL LOW	RETAIL HIGH
					1984 BOATS					
44 2	MARK II	FB	MY	FBG SV	IB T310D CUM	14 9	36000	3 8	113500	125000
44 2	MOTORYACHT	FB	MY	FBG SV	IB T410D CUM	14 9	38000	3 8	126000	138500
44 2	TRI-CABIN MK I	FB	TCMY	FBG SV	IB T310D CUM	14 9	34000	3 8	111000	122000
53 6		FB	MY	FBG SV	IB T450	16 9	50000	4	173000	190000
53 6		FB	YTFS	FBG SV	IB T650	16 9	50000	4	204000	224000
53 6	EXT DECKHOUSE	FB	MY	FBG SV	IB T450	16 9	50000	4	182500	200500

....For earlier years, see the BUC Used Boat Price Guide, Volume 3

SYMBOL YACHTS OF ILLINOIS INC
CHICAGO IL 60622   COAST GUARD MFG ID- XYI See inside cover to adjust price for area

LOA FT IN	NAME AND/ OR MODEL	TOP/ RIG	BOAT TYPE	HULL MTL TP	ENGINE TP # HP MFG	BEAM FT IN	WGT LBS	DRAFT FT IN	RETAIL LOW	RETAIL HIGH
					1989 BOATS					
58 8	SYMBOL 58	FB	TCMY	FBG SV	IB T355D CAT	17 1	59500	4	166000	182500
					1988 BOATS					
58 8	SYMBOL 58	FB	TCMY	FBG SV	IB T355D CAT	17 1	59500	4	159000	174500
					1987 BOATS					
51	YACHTFISH 51	FB	YTFS	FBG	IB T375D CAT	15	42000	3 10	109000	120000
58 8	SYMBOL 58	FB	TCMY	FBG SV	IB T355D CAT	17 1	54500	4	139500	153500
					1986 BOATS					
51	YACHTFISH 51	FB	YTFS	FBG	IB T375D CAT	15	42000	3 10	104500	115000
58 8	SYMBOL 58	FB	TCMY	FBG OV	IB T355D CAT	16 9	54500	4	133000	146500
					1985 BOATS					
51	YACHTFISH 51	FB	YTFS	FBG	IB T375D CAT	15	42000	3 10	100000	110000
58 8	SYMBOL 58	FB	TCMY	FBG SV	IB T355D CAT	16 9	54500	4	127500	140000

SYMONS CHOICE
ST PETERSBURG FL 33702   COAST GUARD MFG ID- SYM See inside cover to adjust price for area
FORMERLY SYMONS SAILING INC

LOA FT IN	NAME AND/ OR MODEL	TOP/ RIG	BOAT TYPE	HULL MTL TP	ENGINE TP # HP MFG	BEAM FT IN	WGT LBS	DRAFT FT IN	RETAIL LOW	RETAIL HIGH
					1996 BOATS					
30	C-CAT 3014 SERIES II	CAT	SACAC	F/S CT	OB		6200	2 10	69100	75900
					1995 BOATS					
30	C-CAT 3014	CAT	SACAC	F/S CT	OB		6000	2 10	64100	70500
					1994 BOATS					
30	C-CAT 3014	CAT	SACAC	F/S CT	OB		6200	2 10	58500	64300
					1993 BOATS					
30	AMERICAT 3014	CAT	SACAC	F/S CT	OB		6200	2 10	56700	62300
					1992 BOATS					
30	AMERICAT 3014	CAT	SACAC	FBG CT	OB		6200	2 10	53100	58400
					1985 BOATS					
25 11	SIROCCO 26	SLP	SA/RC	FBG CT	OB	12 9	5100	2 4	22000	24400
25 11	SIROCCO 26	SLP	SA/RC	FBG CT	IB D	12 9	5100	2 4	22000	24500
26 2	HEAVENLY-TWINS MKIV	SLP	SA/CR	FBG CT	OB	13 9		2 3	21700	24100
26 2	HEAVENLY-TWINS MKV	SLP	SA/CR	FBG CT	IB T 9D YAN	13 9		2 3	22900	25400
31	QUEST 31	SLP	SA/RC	FBG CT	IB 15D YAN	14 3	6500	2 8	37200	41300
32	CATFISHER 32	SLP	SA/CR	FBG CT	IB 15D YAN	13 1	7800	2 8	42900	47600
33	QUEST 33	SLP	SA/CR	FBG CT	IB 15D YAN	14 3	9500	2 8	49600	54500
37	SNOW-GOOSE 37	CUT	SA/CR	FBG CT	IB D	15	10000	2 8	66800	73400
37	SNOW-GOOSE 37	CUT	SA/CR	FBG CT	IB D	15	10000	2 8	66800	73400
46	LOGICAL 46	SLP	SA/RC	FBG CT	IB D	23 10	26000	3 3	164000	180000
49	QUASAR 50	CUT	SA/RC	FBG CT	IB 43D	19 8	14500	3	206000	226500
50	QUASAR 50	SLP	SA/CR	FBG CT	IB T 22D				217000	238500
					1984 BOATS					
25 11	SIROCCO 26	SLP	SA/RC	FBG CT	OB	12 9	5100	2 4	20700	23000
25 11	SIROCCO 26	SLP	SA/RC	FBG CT	IB D	12 9	5100	2 4	20700	23000
27	CATALAC 27	SLP	SA/CR	FBG CT	OB	13 8	6300	2 9	22900	25500
29 6	CATALAC 30	SLP	SA/CR	FBG CT	IB D	13 8	6300	2	29600	32900
30	IROQUOIS MK II	CUT	SA/RC	FBG CT	IB D	13 10	8000	2 6	33000	36700
31	QUEST 31	SLP	SA/RC	FBG CT	IB 15D YAN	14 3	6500	2 6	34900	38700
32	CATFISHER	SLP	SA/CR	FBG CT	IB 30D YAN	13 1	7800	2 4	40300	44700
35	CHEROKEE 35	SLP	SA/CR	FBG CT	IB D	17	11000	3 6	54800	60300
37	SNOW-GOOSE 37	CUT	SA/CR	FBG CT	IB 15D YAN	15	10000	2 8	62800	69000
37	SNOW-GOOSE 37	CUT	SA/CR	FBG CT	IB D	15	10000	2 8	62800	69000
40	CATALAC 40	CUT	SA/CR	FBG CT	IB D	17 6		3	94400	103500
45	APACHE 45 MKII	SLP	SA/CR	FBG CT	IB T D				146000	160500
45	APACHE 45 MKII	CUT	SA/CR	FBG CT	IB T D				146000	160500
45	APACHE 45 MKII	KTH	SA/CR	FBG CT	IB T D				146000	160500
49	QUASAR 50	CUT	SA/RC	FBG CT	IB D	19 8	14500	3	191500	210500
50	QUASAR 50	SLP	SA/CR	FBG CT	IB T 20D				204000	224500

....For earlier years, see the BUC Used Boat Price Guide, Volume 3

TA CHIAO BROS YACHT BLDG CO
TA CHIAO USA
SEABROOK TX 77586   COAST GUARD MFG ID- TAC See inside cover to adjust price for area
ALSO SEE SEABOARD MARINE

For more recent years, see the BUC Used Boat Price Guide, Volume 1

LOA FT IN	NAME AND/ OR MODEL	TOP/ RIG	BOAT TYPE	HULL MTL TP	ENGINE TP # HP MFG	BEAM FT IN	WGT LBS	DRAFT FT IN	RETAIL LOW	RETAIL HIGH
					1996 BOATS					
38 8	RN-38	SLP		FBG SV	IB T375D CAT	11	20305	3 6	147000	161500
41 3	RN-41	SF		FBG SV	IB T425D CAT	13 11	21715	3 6	181500	199500
42 8	CT-RH 43	SLP	SACAC	FBG KL	IB 50D PERK	13	23700	5 7	173500	190500
43 2	CT-44	CUT	SACAC	FBG KL	IB 50D PERK	13	20216	6	161500	177500
46 11	CT-47	CUT	SACAC	FBG KL	IB 62D PERK	13	29395	6	222500	244500
46 11	CT-47	KTH	SACAC	FBG KL	IB 62D PERK	13	29395	6	222500	244500
48	CT-48	CUT	SACAC	FBG KL	IB 85D PERK	14 6	40000	6 4	259000	285000
48	CT-48	KTH	SACAC	FBG KL	IB 85D PERK	14 6	40000	6 4	259500	285000
48 7	RN-48	SF		FBG SV	IB T735D GM	15	44000	3 6	264000	290000
51 6	CT-RH 52	SLP	SACAC	FBG KL	IB 85D PERK	14	38000	6	312500	343000
55 6	CT-56	KTH	SACAC	FBG KL	IB 135D LEHM	15	61500	6 5	451500	496500
64 10	CT-65	KTH	SACAC	FBG KL	IB 200D PERK	17	77383	7	874500	961000
					1995 BOATS					
37 9	CT-38	SLP	SACAC	FBG KL	IB 27D YAN	11 6	16755	6 7	112000	123000
38 8	RN-38	SF		FBG SV	IB T375D CAT	13 11	20305	3 6	139000	153000
41 3	RN-41	SF		FBG SV	IB T425D CAT	13 11	21715	3 6	172500	189500
42 8	CT-RH 43	SLP	SACAC	FBG KL	IB 50D PERK	13	23700	5 7	163000	179000
43 2	CT-44	CUT	SACAC	FBG KL	IB 50D PERK	13	20216	6	152000	167000
46 11	CT-47	CUT	SACAC	FBG KL	IB 62D PERK	13	29395	6	209000	230000
46 11	CT-47	KTH	SACAC	FBG KL	IB 62D PERK	13	29395	6	209000	230000
48	CT-48	CUT	SACAC	FBG KL	IB 85D PERK	14 6	40000	6 4	244000	268000
48	CT-48	KTH	SACAC	FBG KL	IB 85D PERK	14 6	40000	6 4	244000	268000
48 7	RN-48	SF		FBG SV	IB T735D GM	15	44000	3 6	251500	276500
51 6	CT-RH 52	SLP	SACAC	FBG KL	IB 85D PERK	14	38000	6	293500	323000
55 6	CT-56	KTH	SACAC	FBG KL	IB 135D LEHM	15	61500	6 5	424500	466500
64 10	CT-65	KTH	SACAC	FBG KL	IB 200D PERK	17	77383	7	819500	900500
					1994 BOATS					
37 9	CT-38	SLP	SACAC	FBG KL	IB 27D YAN	11 6	16755	6 7	105500	116000
38 8	RN-38	SF		FBG SV	IB T375D CAT	13 11	20305	3 6	132000	145000
41 3	RN-41	SF		FBG SV	IB T425D CAT	13 11	21715	3 6	163500	180000
42 8	CT-RH 43	SLP	SACAC	FBG KL	IB 50D PERK	13	23700	5 7	153500	168500
43 2	CT-44	CUT	SACAC	FBG KL	IB 50D PERK	13	20216	6	143000	157000
46 11	CT-47	CUT	SACAC	FBG KL	IB 62D PERK	13	29395	6	196500	216000
46 11	CT-47	KTH	SACAC	FBG KL	IB 62D PERK	13	29395	6	196500	216000
48	CT-48	CUT	SACAC	FBG KL	IB 85D PERK	14 6	40000	6 4	229500	252000
48	CT-48	KTH	SACAC	FBG KL	IB 85D PERK	14 6	40000	6 4	229500	252000
48 7	RN-48	SF		FBG SV	IB T735D GM	15	44000	3 6	240000	263500
55 6	CT-56	KTH	SACAC	FBG KL	IB 135D LEHM	15	61500	6 5	399500	439000
64 10	CT-65	KTH	SACAC	FBG KL	IB 200D PERK	17	77383	7	768000	844000
					1993 BOATS					
37 9	CT-38	SLP	SACAC	FBG KL	IB 27D YAN	11 6	16755	6 7	99100	109000
38 8	RN-38	SF		FBG SV	IB T375D CAT	13 11	20305	3 6	125500	138000
41 3	RN-41	SF		FBG SV	IB T425D CAT	13 11	21715	3 6	155500	171000
42 8	CT-RH 43	SLP	SACAC	FBG KL	IB 50D PERK	13	23700	5 7	144500	158500
43 2	CT-44	CUT	SACAC	FBG KL	IB 50D PERK	13	20216	6	134500	148000
46 11	CT-47	CUT	SACAC	FBG KL	IB 62D PERK	13	29395	6	185000	203500
46 11	CT-47	KTH	SACAC	FBG KL	IB 62D PERK	13	29395	6	185000	203500
48	CT-48	CUT	SACAC	FBG KL	IB 85D PERK	14 6	40000	6 4	215500	237000
48	CT-48	KTH	SACAC	FBG KL	IB 85D PERK	14 6	40000	6 4	215500	237000
48 7	RN-48	SF		FBG SV	IB T735D GM	15	44000	3 6	228500	251000
51 6	CT-RH 52	SLP	SACAC	FBG KL	IB 85D PERK	14	38000	6	259000	285500
55 6	CT-56	KTH	SACAC	FBG KL	IB 135D LEHM	15	61500	6 5	375500	412500
64 10	CT-65	KTH	SACAC	FBG KL	IB 200D PERK	17	77383	7	719500	790500
					1992 BOATS					
42 8	CT-RH 43	SLP	SAIL	FBG KL	IB 50D PERK	13	23700	5 7	135500	149000
46 11	CT-47	CUT	SAIL	FBG KL	IB 62D PERK	13	29395	6	174000	191000
46 11	CT-47	KTH	SAIL	FBG KL	IB 62D PERK	13	29395	6	174000	191000
48	CT-48	CUT	SAIL	FBG KL	IB 85D PERK	14 6	40000	6 4	203000	223000
48	CT-48	KTH	SAIL	FBG KL	IB 85D PERK	14 6	40000	6 4	203000	223000
51 6	CT-RH 52	SLP	SAIL	FBG KL	IB 85D PERK	14 7	38000	6 5	244500	268500

LOA FT	IN	NAME AND/ OR MODEL	TOP/ RIG	BOAT TYPE	-HULL- MTL	TP	TP	# HP	MFG	BEAM FT	IN	WGT LBS	DRAFT FT	IN	RETAIL LOW	RETAIL HIGH
		1992 BOATS														
55	6	CT-56	KTH	SAIL	FBG	KL	IB	135D	LEHM	15	6	61500	6	5	353000	388000
64	10	CT-65	KTH	SAIL	FBG	KL	IB	200D	PERK	17	6	77383	7		674000	740500
		1991 BOATS														
41	5	CT-42	KTH	SAIL	FBG	KL	IB	50D	PERK	12	2	29300	6	3	141500	155500
42	8	CT-RH 43	SLP	SAIL	FBG	KL	IB	50D	PERK	13		23700	5	7	127500	140500
43	2	CT-44	CUT	SAIL	FBG	KL	IB	50D	PERK	13	1	20200	6		119000	130500
46	11	CT-47	CUT	SAIL	FBG	KL	IB	62D	PERK	13	2	29395	6		163500	180000
46	11	CT-47	KTH	SAIL	FBG	KL	IB	62D	PERK	13	2	29395	6		163500	180000
48		CT-48	CUT	SAIL	FBG	KL	IB	85D	PERK	14	6	40000	6	4	191000	210000
48		CT-48	KTH	SAIL	FBG	KL	IB	85D	PERK	14	6	40000	6	4	191000	210000
51	6	CT-RH 52	SLP	SAIL	FBG	KL	IB	85D	PERK	14	7	38000	6	5	230000	252500
55	6	CT-56	KTH	SAIL	FBG	KL	IB	135D	LEHM	15	6	61500	6	5	332000	365000
64	10	CT-65	KTH	SAIL	FBG	KL	IB	200D	PERK	17	6	77383	7		631000	693500
		1989 BOATS														
33	3	CT-34	CUT	SA/CR	FBG	KL	IB	23D	YAN	10	3	16100	5		74000	81400
34	11	CT-T35 SUNDECK	FB	TRWL	FBG	DS	IB	135D	LEHM	12		19800	3	5	74900	82300
34	11	CT-T35 TRAWLER	FB	TRWL	FBG	DS	IB	135D	LEHM	12		19800	3	5	74600	81900
37	9	CT-38 PRINCESS	SLP	SA/CR	FBG	KL	IB	34D	YAN	11	6	16755	6	7	77700	85300
41	5	CT-42 AC	KTH	SA/CR	FBG	KL	IB	50D	PERK	12	2	29300	6	3	123000	135000
41	5	CT-42 CC	KTH	SA/CR	FBG	KL	IB	50D	PERK	12	2	29300	6	3	127000	139500
42	8	RH-43	SLP	SA/RC	FBG	KL	IB	50D	PERK	13		23780	6	8	113000	124500
43	2	CT-43	CAT	SA/CR	F/S	KL	IB	50D	PERK	13	2	20216	4	10	105500	116000
43	2	CT-44	CUT	SA/CR	F/S	KL	IB	50D	PERK	13	2	20216	6		105500	115500
46	11	CT-47	CUT	SA/RC	FBG	KL	IB	62D	PERK	13	2	29395	6		145000	159000
46	11	CT-47	KTH	SA/RC	FBG	KL	IB	62D	PERK	13	2	29395	6		145000	159000
48		CT-48	CUT	SA/CR	FBG	KL	IB	850D	PERK	14	6	40000	6	4	184000	202000
48		CT-48	KTH	SA/CR	FBG	KL	IB	85D	PERK	14	6	40000	6	4	169000	185500
48	11	CT-49	CUT	SA/RC	FBG	KL	IB	62D	PERK	13	2	29395	6		159000	175000
48	11	CT-49	KTH	SA/RC	FBG	KL	IB	62D	PERK	13	2	29395	6		159000	175000
51	6	RH-52	CUT	SA/RC	F/S	KL	IB	80D	PERK	14	7	38000	8	2	203000	223000
55	6	CT-56	KTH	SA/CR	FBG	KL	IB	135D	LEHM	15	6	61500	6	5	293500	322500
64	10	CT-65	KTH	SA/CR	FBG	KL	IB	200D	PERK	17	6	77383	7		553500	608000
		1988 BOATS														
33	3	CT-34	CUT	SA/CR	FBG	KL	IB	23D	YAN	10	3	16100	5		69600	76500
34	11	CT-T35 SUNDECK	FB	TRWL	FBG	DS	IB	135D	LEHM	12		19800	3	5	73400	80600
34	11	CT-T35 TRAWLER	FB	TRWL	FBG	DS	IB	135D	LEHM	12		19800	3	5	69600	76500
37	9	CT-38 PRINCESS	SLP	SA/CR	FBG	KL	IB	34D	YAN	11	6	16755	6	7	73000	80300
41	5	CT-42	KTH	SA/CR	FBG	KL	IB	50D	PERK	12	2	29300	6	3	117500	129000
42	8	RH-43	SLP	SA/RC	FBG	KL	IB	50D	PERK	13		23780	6	8	106500	117000
43	2	CT-43	CAT	SA/CR	F/S	KL	IB	50D	PERK	13	2	20216	4	10	99100	109000
43	2	CT-44	CUT	SA/CR	F/S	KL	IB	50D	PERK	13	2	20216	6		99000	109000
46	11	CT-47	CUT	SA/RC	FBG	KL	IB	62D	PERK	13	2	29395	6		136000	149500
46	11	CT-47	KTH	SA/RC	FBG	KL	IB	62D	PERK	13	2	29395	6		136000	149500
48		CT-48	CUT	SA/CR	FBG	KL	IB	850D	PERK	14	6	40000	6	4	173000	190000
48		CT-48	KTH	SA/CR	FBG	KL	IB	85D	PERK	14	6	40000	6	4	159000	174500
48	11	CT-49	CUT	SA/RC	FBG	KL	IB	62D	PERK	13	2	29395	6		149500	164500
48	11	CT-49	KTH	SA/RC	FBG	KL	IB	62D	PERK	13	2	29395	6		150000	164500
51	6	RH-52	CUT	SA/RC	F/S	KL	IB	80D	PERK	14	7	38000	8	2	190500	209500
55	6	CT-56	KTH	SA/CR	FBG	KL	IB	135D	LEHM	15	6	61500	6	5	276000	303000
64	10	CT-65	KTH	SA/CR	FBG	KL	IB	200D	PERK	17	6	77383	7		518000	569000
		1987 BOATS														
33	3	CT-34	CUT	SA/CR	FBG	KL	IB	23D	YAN	10	3	16100	5		65500	72000
34	11	CT-T35 SUNDECK	FB	TRWL	FBG	DS	IB	135D	LEHM	12		19800	3	4	70200	77100
34	11	CT-T35 TRAWLER	FB	TRWL	FBG	DS	IB	135D	LEHM	12		19800	3	4	66800	73400
37	9	CT-38 PRINCESS	SLP	SA/CR	FBG	KL	IB	34D	YAN	11	6	16755	6	7	68700	75500
41	5	CT-42	KTH	SA/CR	FBG	KL	IB	50D	PERK	12	2	29300	6	3	110500	121500
42	8	RON-HOLLAND 43	SLP	SA/RC	FBG	KL	IB	50D	PERK	13		23780	6	8	100000	110000
43	2	CT-43	CAT	SA/CR	F/S	KL	IB	50D	PERK	13	2	20216	4	10	93200	102500
43	2	CT-44	CUT	SA/CR	F/S	KL	IB	50D	PERK	13	2	20216	6		93200	102500
46	11	CT-47	CUT	SA/RC	FBG	KL	IB	62D	PERK	13	2	29395	6		128000	141000
46	11	CT-47	KTH	SA/RC	FBG	KL	IB	62D	PERK	13	2	29395	6		128000	141000
48		CT-48	KTH	SA/CR	FBG	KL	IB	86D	PERK	14	6	40000	6	4	149500	164000
48	11	CT-49	CUT	SA/RC	FBG	KL	IB	62D	PERK	13	2	29395	6		141000	154500
48	11	CT-49	KTH	SA/RC	FBG	KL	IB	62D	PERK	13	2	29395	6		141000	155000
51	6	RON-HOLLAND 52	CUT	SA/RC	F/S	KL	IB	80D	PERK	14	7	38000	8	2	179000	197000
55	6	CT-56	KTH	SA/CR	FBG	KL	IB	135D	LEHM	15	6	61500	6	5	259000	285000
64	10	CT-65	KTH	SA/CR	FBG	KL	IB	200D	PERK	17	6	77383	7		485000	533000
		1986 BOATS														
33	3	CT-34	CUT	SA/CR	FBG	KL	IB	20D	YAN	10	3	16000	5	2	61200	67300
34	11	CT-T35 SUNDECK	FB	TRWL	FBG	DS	IB	135D	LEHM	12		19800	3	4	69200	76100
34	11	CT-T35 TRAWLER	FB	TRWL	FBG	DS	IB	135D	LEHM	12		19800	3	4	62000	68200
37	9	CT-38	SLP	SA/CR	FBG	KL	IB	30D	YAN	11	6	16158	6	7	62700	68900
40		CT-T40 TRAWLER	FB	TRWL	FBG	RB	IB	135D	LEHM	13	1	22700	4		89200	98100
40	8	CT-41	KTH	SA/CR	FBG	KL	IB	50D	PERK	12	2	28000	6		100000	110000
40	10	CT-M41	FB	MY	FBG	SV	IB	T300D	CAT	13	9	25498	3		113000	124500
41	5	CT-42	KTH	SA/CR	FBG	KL	IB	50D	PERK	12	2	29300	6	3	103500	114000
42	8	RON-HOLLAND 43	SLP	SA/RC	FBG	KL	IB	50D	PERK	13		23780	6	8	94200	103500
43	2	CT-43	CAT	SA/CR	F/S	KL	IB	50D	PERK	13	2	20216	4	10	87700	96300
43	2	TANTON 44	CUT	SA/CR	F/S	KL	IB	50D	PERK	13	2	20216	6		87600	96300
46	11	CT-47	CUT	SA/RC	FBG	KL	IB	62D	PERK	13	2	29395	6		120500	132500
46	11	CT-47	KTH	SA/RC	FBG	KL	IB	62D	PERK	13	2	29395	6		120500	132500
49		CT-49	CUT	SA/CR	FBG	KL	IB	D		13	2	29395	6		134000	147000
51	6	RON-HOLLAND 52	CUT	SA/RC	F/S	KL	IB	80D	PERK	14	7	38000	8	2	168500	185000
53	7	CT-54	KTH	SA/CR	FBG	KL	IB	135D	LEHM	15	1	54000	6	6	210500	231500
55	6	CT-56	KTH	SA/CR	FBG	KL	IB	135D	LEHM	15	6	61500	6	5	243500	267500
64	10	CT-65	KTH	SA/CR	FBG	KL	IB	200D	PERK	17	6	77383	7		454000	498500
		1985 BOATS														
33	3	CT-34	CUT	SA/CR	FBG	KL	IB	20D		10	3	16100	5		58000	63700
34	11	CT-T35 SUNDECK	FB	TRWL	FBG	SV	IB	135D	LEHM	12		19800	3	5	62900	69200
34	11	CT-T35 TRAWLER	FB	TRWL	FBG	SV	IB	135D	LEHM	12		19800	3	5	62900	69200
37	9	CT-38	SLP	SA/CR	FBG	KL	IB	30D		11	6	16755	6	7	60600	66600
37	9	CT-38	SLP	SA/RC	FBG	KL	IB	30D	YAN	11	6	16158	6	7	58900	64800
40		CT-T40 TRAWLER	FB	TRWL	FBG	RB	IB	135D	LEHM	13	1	22700	4		85000	93400
40	8	CT-41	KTH	SA/CR	FBG	KL	IB	D		12	2	27500	6		93600	103000
40	8	CT-41	KTH	SA/CR	FBG	KL	IB	50D	PERK	12	2	28000	6		94000	103500
41	5	CT-42	KTH	SA/CR	FBG	KL	IB	D		12	2	23900	6		86600	95200
41	5	CT-42	KTH	SA/CR	FBG	KL	IB	50D	PERK	12	2	29300	6	3	97500	107000
42	8	RH-43	SLP	SA/RC	FBG	KL	IB	50D	PERK	13		23780	6	8	88600	97300
43	2	CT-43	CAT	SA/CR	F/S	KL	IB	50D	PERK	13	2	20216	4	10	82400	90600
43	2	CT-43	KTH	SA/CR	FBG	KL	IB	50D		13	2	20216	4	9	82900	91100
43	2	CT-44	CUT	SA/CR	F/S	KL	IB	50D	PERK	13	2	20216	6		82400	90600
46	11	CT-47	CUT	SA/CR	FBG	KL	IB	62D	PERK	13	2	29395	6		113500	124500
47		CT-47	CUT	SA/RC	FBG	KL	IB	62D	PERK	13	2	29395	6		113500	125000
49		CT-49	CUT	SA/CR	FBG	KL	IB	D		13	2	29395	6		126000	138500
51	6	CT-52	CUT	SA/CR	FBG	KL	IB	80D	PERK	14	7	38000	8	2	158500	174000
51	6	RH-52	CUT	SA/RC	F/S	KL	IB	80D	PERK	14	7	38000	8	2	158500	174000
53	7	CT-54	KTH	SA/CR	FBG	KL	IB	D		15	1	54000	6	6	197500	217000
53	7	CT-54	KTH	SA/CR	FBG	KL	IB	135D	LEHM	15	1	54000	6	6	198000	217500
64	10	CT-65	KTH	SA/CR	FBG	KL	IB	D		17	6	77383	7		425500	467500
64	10	CT-65	KTH	SA/CR	FBG	KL	IB	200D	PERK	17	6	77383	7		425000	467000
		1984 BOATS														
33	3	CT 34	CUT	SA/CR	FBG	KL	IB	D		10	3	16100	5		54500	59900
37	9	CT 38	SLP	SA/CR	FBG	KL	IB	D		11	6	16755	6	7	57100	62800
40	8	CT 41	KTH	SA/CR	FBG	KL	IB	D		12	2	27500	6		88000	96600
41	5	CT 42	KTH	SA/CR	FBG	KL	IB	D		12	2	23900	6		81400	89500
43	2	CT 43	KTH	SA/CR	FBG	KL	IB	D		13	2	20216	4	9	77900	85600
43	2	CT 44	CUT	SA/CR	FBG	KL	IB	D		13	2	20216	4	9	77900	85600
46	11	CT 47	CUT	SA/CR	FBG	KL	IB	D		13	2	29395	6		107000	117500
47	7	CT 48	KTH	SA/CR	FBG	KL	IB	D		13	4	39500	5		123000	135000
49		CT 49	CUT	SA/CR	FBG	KL	IB	D		13	2	29395	6		118500	130000

....For earlier years, see the BUC Used Boat Price Guide, Volume 3

TA SHING YACHT BLDG CO

AN PING INDUSTRIAL DIST
TAINAN TAIWAN

COAST GUARD MFG ID- TSQ

See inside cover to adjust price for area

For more recent years, see the BUC Used Boat Price Guide, Volume 1

LOA FT	IN	NAME AND/ OR MODEL	TOP/ RIG	BOAT TYPE	-HULL- MTL	TP	TP	# HP	MFG	BEAM FT	IN	WGT LBS	DRAFT FT	IN	RETAIL LOW	RETAIL HIGH
		1996 BOATS														
42	10	TASWELL 43	CUT	SACAC	FBG	KL	IB	50D	YAN	13	8	29000	6	6	300000	329500
42	10	TASWELL 43 AS	CUT	SACAC	FBG	KL	IB	75D	YAN	13	8	29000	4	10	301500	331500
48	10	TASWELL 49	CUT	SACAC	FBG	KL	IB	75D	YAN	15		40000	5	3	429000	471500
48	10	TASWELL 49 AS	CUT	SACAC	FBG	KL	IB	110D	YAN	15		40000	5	3	431000	473500
55	10	TASWELL 56	CUT	SACAC	FBG	KL	IB	110D	YAN	16	6	48500	6		635000	697500
58		TASWELL 58 AS	CUT	SACAC	FBG	KL	IB	140D	YAN	16	6	65000	6	3	876000	962500
58		TASWELL 58 TWIN CPT	CUT	SACAC	FBG	KL	IB	140D	YAN	16	6	63000	6	3	860500	945500
59	2	TASWELL 60 AS	CUT	SACAC	FBG	KL	IB	140D	YAN	16	6	65000	6	3	904500	994000
		1995 BOATS														
42	10	TASWELL 43	CUT	SACAC	FBG	KL	IB	50D	YAN	13	8	22000	6	3	242500	266500
42	10	TASWELL 43 AS	CUT	SACAC	FBG	KL	IB	75D	YAN	13	8	23500	4	10	252500	277500
48	10	TASWELL 49	CUT	SACAC	FBG	KL	IB	75D	YAN	15		32000	6	9	374000	411000
48	10	TASWELL 49 AS	CUT	SACAC	FBG	KL	IB	110D	YAN	15		32500	5	3	377500	415000
55	10	TASWELL 56	CUT	SACAC	FBG	KL	IB	110D	YAN	16	6	48500	7	6	597500	656500
58		TASWELL 58 AS	CUT	SACAC	FBG	KL	IB	140D	YAN	16	6	65000	6	3	824000	905500
58		TASWELL 58 TWIN CPT	CUT	SACAC	FBG	KL	IB	140D	YAN	16	6	67000	6	3	839000	922000
59	2	TASWELL 60 AS	CUT	SACAC	FBG	KL	IB	140D	YAN	16	6	65000	6	3	851000	935000

LOA FT	LOA IN	NAME AND/ OR MODEL	TOP/ RIG	BOAT TYPE	HULL MTL	HULL TP	TP	# HP	ENGINE MFG	BEAM FT	BEAM IN	WGT LBS	DRAFT FT	DRAFT IN	RETAIL LOW	RETAIL HIGH
1994 BOATS																
42	10	TASWELL 43	CUT	SACAC	FBG	KL	IB	50D	YAN	13	8	22000	6	3	228000	250500
42	10	TASWELL 43 AS	CUT	SACAC	FBG	KL	IB	75D	YAN	13	8	23500	4	10	237500	261000
48	10	TASWELL 49	CUT	SACAC	FBG	KL	IB	75D	YAN	15		32000	6	9	352000	386500
48	10	TASWELL 49 AS	CUT	SACAC	FBG	KL	IB	110D	YAN	15		32500	5	3	355500	390500
55	10	TASWELL 56	CUT	SACAC	FBG	KL	IB	110D	YAN	16	6	48500	7	6	561500	617000
58		TASWELL 58 AS	CUT	SACAC	FBG	KL	IB	140D	YAN	16	6	65000	6	3	775000	851500
58		TASWELL 58 TWIN CPT	CUT	SACAC	FBG	KL	IB	140D	YAN	16	6	67000	6	3	789500	867500
59	2	TASWELL 60 AS	CUT	SACAC	FBG	KL	IB	140D	YAN	16	6	65000	6	3	800500	879500
1993 BOATS																
42	10	TASWELL 43	CUT	SACAC	FBG	KL	IB	50D	YAN	13	8	22000	6	3	214500	235500
42	10	TASWELL 43 AS	CUT	SACAC	FBG	KL	IB	75D	YAN	13	8	22000	4	10	215500	237000
48	10	TASWELL 49	CUT	SACAC	FBG	KL	IB	75D	YAN	15		30000	6	9	324000	356000
48	10	TASWELL 49 AS	CUT	SACAC	FBG	KL	IB	110D	YAN	15		30000	5	3	325500	357500
55	10	TASWELL 56	CUT	SACAC	FBG	KL	IB	110D	YAN	16	6	44000	7	6	522000	573500
58		TASWELL 58 AS	CUT	SACAC	FBG	KL	IB	140D	YAN	16	6	60000	6	3	697000	766000
59	2	TASWELL 60 AS	CUT	SACAC	FBG	KL	IB	140D	YAN	16	6	60000	6	3	719000	790000
1992 BOATS																
42	10	TASWELL 43	CUT	SAIL	FBG	KL	IB	55D	YAN	13	8	23500	4	10	209500	230000
42	10	TASWELL 43 AS	CUT	SAIL	FBG	KL	IB	75D	YAN	13	8	23500	4	10	210500	231000
48	10	TASWELL 49	CUT	SAIL	FBG	KL	IB	75D	YAN	15		30000	6	9	304500	335000
48	10	TASWELL 49 AS	CUT	SAIL	FBG	KL	IB	110D	YAN	15		30000	5	3	306000	336500
55	10	TASWELL 56	CUT	SAIL	FBG	KL	IB	110D	YAN	16	6	44000	7	6	491000	539500
58		TASWELL 58 AS	CUT	SAIL	FBG	KL	IB	110D	YAN	16	6	60000	6	9	654500	719500
69	2	TASWELL 60 AS	CUT	SAIL	FBG	KL	IB	110D	YAN	16	6	60000	6	9	742000	815000
1990 BOATS																
30	9	TASHIBA 31	CUT	SAIL	FBG	KL	IB	33D	YAN	10	8	13790	5		88600	97300
35	11	TASHIBA 36	CUT	SAIL	FBG	KL	IB	44D	YAN	11	10	21820	5	6	139500	153500
39	11	TASHIBA 40	CUT	SAIL	FBG	KL	IB	44D	YAN	12	10	29000	6		193500	212500
42	10	TASWELL 43	CUT	SAIL	FBG	KL	IB	44D	YAN	13	8	23500	4	10	185000	203000
48	10	TASWELL 49	CUT	SAIL	FBG	KL	IB	55D	YAN	15		32000	5	3	274500	302000
48	10	TASWELL 49	CUT	SAIL	FBG	KL	IB	77D	YAN	15		32000	5	3	275500	303000
55	10	TASWELL 56	CUT	SAIL	FBG	KL	IB	66D	YAN	16	6	48500	6		437500	481000
1989 BOATS																
33	9	MASON 33	SLP	SA/CR	FBG	KL	IB	27D	YAN	10	10	14020	5		85000	93400
33	9	MASON 34	SLP	SA/CR	FBG	KL	IB	27D	YAN	10	10	14020	5		85300	93700
42	10	TASWELL 43	CUT	SAIL	FBG	KL	IB	44D	YAN	13	8	23500	4	10	174000	191000
43	11	MASON 44	CUT	SA/CR	FBG	KL	IB	55D	YAN	12	4	27400	6	5	197500	217000
43	11	MASON 44	KTH	SA/CR	FBG	KL	IB	55D	YAN	12	4	27400	6	5	197500	217000
45	9	NORDHAVN 46		CR	FBG	SV	IB	145D		15	5	48320	5		243000	267500
48	10	TASWELL 49	CUT	SAIL	FBG	KL	IB	55D	YAN	15		32000	5	3	258500	284000
48	10	TASWELL 49	CUT	SAIL	FBG	KL	IB	77D	YAN	15		32000	5	3	259000	285000
53	6	MASON 53	CUT	SA/CR	FBG	KL	IB	85D	PERK	14	10	43500	6	8	353000	387500
53	6	MASON 53 SHOAL	CUT	SA/CR	FBG	KL	IB	85D	PERK	14	10	43500	5	9	353000	387500
53	6	MASON 54	CUT	SA/CR	FBG	KL	IB	100D	WEST	14	10	43500	6	8	355000	390000
53	6	MASON 54 SHOAL	CUT	SA/CR	FBG	KL	IB	100D	WEST	14	10	43500	5	9	355000	390000
63	7	MASON 63	KTH	SA/CR	FBG	KL	IB	220D	GM	16	6	64400	7		629000	691000
63	7	MASON 64	CUT	SA/CR	FBG	KL	IB	220D	GM	16	6	64400	7		633500	696000
63	7	MASON 64	KTH	SA/CR	FBG	KL	IB	220D	GM	16	6	64400	7		638000	701000
1988 BOATS																
33	9	MASON 33	SLP	SA/CR	FBG	KL	IB	27D	YAN	10	10	14020	5		80100	88000
33	9	MASON 34	SLP	SA/CR	FBG	KL	IB	27D	YAN	10	10	14020	5		80100	88000
42	10	TASWELL 43	CUT	SAIL	FBG	KL	IB	44D	YAN	13	8	23500	4	10	163500	179500
43	11	MASON 43	CUT	SA/CR	FBG	KL	IB	55D	YAN	12	4	27400	6	5	185500	204000
43	11	MASON 43	KTH	SA/CR	FBG	KL	IB	55D	YAN	12	4	27400	6	5	186000	204000
43	11	MASON 44	CUT	SA/CR	FBG	KL	IB	55D	YAN	12	4	27400	6	5	185500	204000
43	11	MASON 44	KTH	SA/CR	FBG	KL	IB	55D	YAN	12	4	27400	6	5	186000	204000
48	10	TASWELL 49	CUT	SAIL	FBG	KL	IB	55D	YAN	15		32000	5	3	243000	267000
48	10	TASWELL 49	CUT	SAIL	FBG	KL	IB	77D	YAN	15		32000	5	3	243500	268000
53	6	MASON 53	CUT	SA/CR	FBG	KL	IB	85D	PERK	14	10	43500	6	8	332000	364500
53	6	MASON 53 SHOAL	CUT	SA/CR	FBG	KL	IB	85D	PERK	14	10	43500	5	9	332000	364500
53	6	MASON 54	CUT	SA/CR	FBG	KL	IB	100D	WEST	14	10	43500	6	8	334000	367000
53	6	MASON 54 SHOAL	CUT	SA/CR	FBG	KL	IB	100D	WEST	14	10	43500	5	9	334000	367000
63	7	MASON 63	KTH	SA/CR	FBG	KL	IB	220D	GM	16	6	64400	7		596000	654500
63	7	MASON 64	CUT	SA/CR	FBG	KL	IB	220D	GM	16	6	64400	7		596000	654500
63	7	MASON 64	KTH	SA/CR	FBG	KL	IB	220D	GM	16	6	64400	7		596000	654500
1987 BOATS																
33	9	MASON 33	SLP	SA/CR	FBG	KL	IB	27D	YAN	10	10	15000	5		80300	88200
43	11	MASON 43	CUT	SA/CR	FBG	KL	IB	55D	YAN	12	4	27400	6	3	174500	192000
43	11	MASON 43	KTH	SA/CR	FBG	KL	IB	55D	YAN	12	4	27400	6	3	175000	192000
43	11	MASON 44	CUT	SA/CR	FBG	KL	IB	55D	YAN	12	4	27400	6	5	174500	192000
43	11	MASON 44	KTH	SA/CR	FBG	KL	IB	55D	YAN	12	4	27400	6	5	175000	192000
53	6	MASON 53	CUT	SA/CR	FBG	KL	IB	100D	WEST	14	5	39600	6	8	308500	339000
53	6	MASON 53 SHOAL	CUT	SA/CR	FBG	KL	IB	100D	WEST	14	5	39600	5	9	308500	339000
54		MASON 54	CUT	SA/CR	FBG	KL	IB	100D	WEST	14	10	39600	6	8	318000	349500
63	7	MASON 63	KTH	SA/CR	FBG	KL	IB	140D	GM	16	6	64400	7		558500	613500
64		MASON 64	CUT	SA/CR	FBG	KL	IB	210D	GM	16	6	64400	7		560500	615500
1986 BOATS																
29	9	BABA 30	CUT	SA/CR	FBG	KL	IB	D		10	3	12500	4	9	62800	69000
33	9	MASON 33	SLP	SA/CR	FBG	KL	IB	21D	WEST	10	10	14020	5		70800	77800
34	10	BABA 35	CUT	SA/CR	FBG	KL	IB	D		11	2	21200	5	6	105000	115500
39	11	BABA 40	CUT	SA/CR	FBG	KL	IB	D		12	10	29000	6		151500	166500
40		NORSEMAN 400 AC	CUT	SA/CR	FBG	KL	IB	46D	WEST	13	3	19000	6	6	115000	126500
43	11	MASON 43	CUT	SA/CR	FBG	KL	IB	55D	YAN	12	4	27400	6	3	164500	180500
43	11	MASON 43	KTH	SA/CR	FBG	KL	IB	55D	YAN	12	4	27400	6	3	164500	180500
43	11	MASON 44	CUT	SA/CR	FBG	KL	IB	55D	YAN	12	4	27400	6	5	164500	180500
43	11	MASON 44	KTH	SA/CR	FBG	KL	IB	55D	YAN	12	4	27400	6	5	164500	180500
44	7	NORSEMAN 447 AC	CUT	SA/CR	FBG	KL	IB	61D	LEHM	13		28000	6	4	167000	183500
44	7	NORSEMAN 447 MC	CUT	SA/CR	FBG	KL	IB	61D	LEHM	13		28000	6	4	174000	191000
49	6	ORION 50	KTH	SA/RC	FBG	KL	IB	D		14	6	36600	6	6	232000	255000
53	6	MASON 53	CUT	SA/CR	FBG	KL	IB	100D	WEST	14	10	39600	6	8	289000	317500
53	6	MASON 53 SHOAL	CUT	SA/CR	FBG	KL	IB	100D	WEST	14	10	39600	5	9	291500	320500
63	7	MASON 63	KTH	SA/CR	FBG	KL	IB	140D	GM	16	6	64400	7		525500	577000
1985 BOATS																
29	9	BABA 30	CUT	SA/CR	FBG	KL	IB	27D	YAN	10	3	12500	4	9	59100	64900
33	9	MASON 33	CUT	SA/CR	FBG	KL	IB	22D	WEST	10	10	14020	5		66600	73200
34	11	BABA 35	CUT	SA/CR	FBG	KL	IB	32D	UNIV	11	2	21200	5	6	98600	108500
34	11	BABA 35 PH	CUT	SA/CR	FBG	KL	VD	32D	UNIV	11	2	21200	5	6	98600	108500
37	7	PANDA 38	CUT	SA/CR	FBG	KL	IB	36D		12		19000	5	10	95400	105000
39	11	BABA 40	CUT	SA/CR	FBG	KL	IB	44D	UNIV	12	10	29000	6		142000	156500
39	11	BABA 40	KTH	SA/CR	FBG	KL	IB	44D	UNIV	12	10	29000	6		142500	156500
43	11	MASON 43	CUT	SA/RC	FBG	KL	IB	51D	PERK	12	3	25000	6	3	146500	161000
43	11	MASON 43	KTH	SA/RC	FBG	KL	IB	51D	PERK	12	3	25000	6	3	146500	161000
44	7	NORSEMAN 447 AFT	CUT	SA/CR	FBG	KL	VD	61D	LEHM	13		28000	6	4	157000	172500
44	7	NORSEMAN 447 AFT SHL	CUT	SA/CR	FBG	KL	VD	61D	LEHM	13		28000	5	4	158500	174500
44	7	NORSEMAN 447 MID	CUT	SA/CR	FBG	KL	VD	61D	LEHM	13		28000	6	4	162000	178000
44	7	NORSEMAN 447 MID SHL	CUT	SA/CR	FBG	KL	VD	61D	LEHM	13		28000	5	4	163500	179500
49	6	ORION 50	CUT	SA/CR	FBG	KL	IB	85D	PERK	14	6	36600	6	6	217500	239000
49	6	ORION 50	KTH	SA/CR	FBG	KL	IB	85D	PERK	14	6	36600	6	6	217500	239000
53	9	MASON 53	CUT	SA/CR	FBG	KC	IB	85D	PERK	14	5	38600	5	9	274000	301500
53	9	MASON 53	KTH	SA/CR	FBG	KC	IB	85D	PERK	14	5	38600	5	9	274500	301500
63	7	MASON 63	KTH	SA/CR	FBG	KL	IB	140D	GM	16	6	64400	7		494000	543000
1984 BOATS																
29	9	BABA 30	CUT	SA/CR	FBG	KL	IB	23D	YAN	10	3	12500	4	9	55500	61000
33	5	PANDA 34	CUT	SA/CR	FBG	KL	IB	D		11		17500	5	5	76900	84600
34	11	BABA 35	CUT	SA/CR	FBG	KL	IB	33D	YAN	11	2	21200	5	6	92800	102000
34	11	BABA 35 PH	CUT	SA/CR	FBG	KL	SD	33D	YAN	11	2	21200	5	6	92800	102000
37	7	PANDA 38	CUT	SA/CR	FBG	KL	IB	D		12		19000	5	10	89900	98800
37	7	PANDA 38	CUT	SA/CR	FBG	KL	IB	36D		12		19000	5	10	89800	98600
38		PANDA 38	CUT	SA/CR	FBG	KL	IB								84200	92600
39	10	PANDA 40	CUT	SA/CR	FBG	KL	IB	D		12	10	29000	6		134000	147000
39	11	BABA 40	CUT	SA/CR	FBG	KL	IB	44D	UNIV	12	10	29000	6		134000	147000
41	10	TATOOSH 42	SCH	SA/CR	FBG	KL	IB	D		12	9	21500	5	10	117000	128500
43	11	MASON 43	CUT	SA/RC	FBG	KL	IB	50D	PERK	12	3	25000	6	3	138000	151500
43	11	MASON 43	KTH	SA/RC	FBG	KL	IB	50D	PERK	12	3	25000	6	3	138000	151500
44	7	NORSEMAN 447	CUT	SA/CR	FBG	KL	IB	61D	LEHM	13		28000	6	4	151000	165500
44	7	NORSEMAN 447 SHOAL	CUT	SA/CR	FBG	KL	IB	61D	LEHM	13		28000	5	4	151000	165500
49	6	ORION 50	KTH	SA/CR	FBG	KL	IB	85D	PERK	14	6	36600	6	6	204500	224500
50	7	TATOOSH 51	CUT	SA/CR	FBG	KL	IB	D		15	5	44000	6	4	227500	250000
53	9	MASON 53	CUT	SA/CR	FBG	KC	IB	85D	PERK	14	5	38600	5	9	258000	283500
53	9	MASON 53	KTH	SA/CR	FBG	KC	IB	85D	PERK	14	5	38600	5	9	258000	283500
63	7	MASON 63	KTH	SA/CR	FBG	KL	IB	140D	GM	16	6	64400	7		464500	510500

....For earlier years, see the BUC Used Boat Price Guide, Volume 3

TA YANG YACHT BUILDING CO LTD

LIN YAN KAOHSING HSN TA COAST GUARD MFG ID- TYA See inside cover to adjust price for area

For more recent years, see the BUC Used Boat Price Guide, Volume 1

LOA FT	LOA IN	NAME AND/ OR MODEL	TOP/ RIG	BOAT TYPE	HULL MTL	HULL TP	TP	# HP	ENGINE MFG	BEAM FT	BEAM IN	WGT LBS	DRAFT FT	DRAFT IN	RETAIL LOW	RETAIL HIGH
1996 BOATS																
36	8	TAYANA 37	CUT	SACAC	FBG	KL	IB	50D	YAN	11	6	22500	5	8	137000	150500
36	8	TAYANA 37 PH	KTH	SACAC	FBG	KL	IB	50D	YAN	11	6	22500	5	8	141000	155000
41	9	TAYANA 42	CUT	SACAC	FBG	KL	IB	44D	YAN	12	6	29147	5	10	180500	198500
41	9	TAYANA 42 CENTER	CUT	SACAC	FBG	KL	IB	44D	YAN	12	6	29147	5	10	186000	204500
47		TAYANA 47/48	CUT	SACAC	FBG	KL	IB	62D	YAN	14	6	35000	5	3	243500	267500
47		TAYANA 4748 CENTER	CUT	SACAC	FBG	KL	IB	62D	YAN	14	6	35000	5	3	214000	235000
52	6	TAYANA 52 AFT	CUT	SACAC	FBG	KL	IB	88D	YAN	15		38570	6	6	336500	370000
52	6	TAYANA 52 CC	CUT	SACAC	FBG	KL	IB	88D	YAN	15		38570	6	6	343500	377500

TA YANG YACHT BUILDING CO LTD -CONTINUED   See inside cover to adjust price for area

LOA FT	IN	NAME AND/ OR MODEL	TOP/ RIG	BOAT TYPE	-HULL- MTL	TP	TP	----ENGINE--- # HP	MFG	BEAM FT	IN	WGT LBS	DRAFT FT	IN	RETAIL LOW	RETAIL HIGH
		1996 BOATS														
55		TAYANA 55	CUT	SACAC	FBG	KL	IB	130D	PERK	16	1	48000	7	2	416000	457000
55		TAYANA 55	KTH	SACAC	FBG	KL	IB	130D	PERK	16	1	48000	7	2	416000	457000
58		TAYANA 58 PH	CUT	SACAC	FBG	KL	IB	140D	YAN	16	1	49500	6	4	507000	557000
64	8	TAYANA 65	CUT	SACAC	FBG	KL	IB	135D	PERK	17	9	74000	7	6	700000	769000
64	8	TAYANA 65 CENTER	CUT	SACAC	FBG	KL	IB	135D	PERK	17	9	74000	7	6	705500	775500
		1995 BOATS														
36	8	TAYANA 37	CUT	SACAC	FBG	KL	IB	50D	YAN	11	6	22500	5	8	139000	153000
41	9	TAYANA 42	CUT	SACAC	FBG	KL	IB	44D	YAN	12	6	29147	5	10	173500	190500
47		TAYANA 47/48	CUT	SACAC	FBG	KL	IB	62D	YAN	14	6	35000	5	3	233000	256000
52	6	TAYANA 52 AFT	CUT	SACAC	FBG	KL	IB	88D	YAN	15		38570	6	6	322000	354000
52	6	TAYANA 52 CC	CUT	SACAC	FBG	KL	IB	88D	YAN	15		38570	6	6	322000	354000
55		TAYANA 55	CUT	SACAC	FBG	KL	IB	130D	PERK	16	1	48000	7	2	394000	433000
55		TAYANA 55	KTH	SACAC	FBG	KL	IB	130D	PERK	16	1	48000	7	2	394000	433000
64	8	TAYANA 65	CUT	SACAC	FBG	KL	IB	135D	PERK	17	9	74000	7	6	665500	731500
		1994 BOATS														
36	8	TAYANA 37	CUT	SACAC	FBG	KL	IB	50D	YAN	11	6	22500	5	8	122000	134500
36	8	TAYANA 37	KTH	SACAC	FBG	KL	IB	50D	YAN	11	6	22500	5	8	125500	138000
41	9	TAYANA 42	CUT	SACAC	FBG	KL	IB	44D	YAN	12	6	29147	5	10	164500	180500
47		TAYANA 47/48	CUT	SACAC	FBG	KL	IB	62D	YAN	14	6	35000	5	3	220500	242500
52	6	TAYANA 52 AFT	CUT	SACAC	FBG	KL	IB	88D	YAN	15		38570	6	6	298500	328000
52	6	TAYANA 52 CC	CUT	SACAC	FBG	KL	IB	88D	YAN	15		38570	6	6	311500	342000
55		TAYANA 55	CUT	SACAC	FBG	KL	IB	130D	PERK	16	1	48000	7	2	373000	410000
55		TAYANA 55	KTH	SACAC	FBG	KL	IB	130D	PERK	16	1	48000	7	2	373000	410000
64	8	TAYANA 65	CUT	SACAC	FBG	KL	IB	135D	PERK	17	9	74000	7	6	630500	692500
		1993 BOATS														
36	8	TAYANA 37	CUT	SACAC	FBG	KL	IB	50D	YAN	11	6	22500	5	8	115500	127000
36	8	TAYANA 37	KTH	SACAC	FBG	KL	IB	50D	YAN	11	6	22500	5	8	118500	130000
41	9	TAYANA 42	CUT	SACAC	FBG	KL	IB	44D	YAN	12	6	29147	5	10	155500	171000
47		TAYANA 47/48	CUT	SACAC	FBG	KL	IB	62D	YAN	14	6	35000	5	3	209000	229500
52	6	TAYANA 52 AFT	CUT	SACAC	FBG	KL	IB	88D	YAN	15		38570	6	6	282500	310500
52	6	TAYANA 52 CC	CUT	SACAC	FBG	KL	IB	88D	YAN	15		38570	6	6	295000	324500
55		TAYANA 55	CUT	SACAC	FBG	KL	IB	130D	PERK	16	1	48000	7	2	353000	388000
55		TAYANA 55	KTH	SACAC	FBG	KL	IB	130D	PERK	16	1	48000	7	2	353500	388500
64	8	TAYANA 65	CUT	SACAC	FBG	KL	IB	135D	PERK	17	9	74000	7	6	597000	656000
		1992 BOATS														
36	8	TAYANA 37	CUT	SAIL	FBG	KL	IB	44D	YAN	11	6	22500	5	8	106000	116500
36	8	TAYANA 37	KTH	SAIL	FBG	KL	IB	44D	YAN	11	6	22500	5	8	112000	123000
36	8	TAYANA 37 PH	CUT	SAIL	FBG	KL	IB	44D	YAN	11	6	22500	5	8	113000	124000
41	9	TAYANA V-42 AFT	CUT	SAIL	FBG	KL	IB	44D	YAN	12	6	29147	5	10	141000	155000
41	9	TAYANA V-42 CTR	CUT	SAIL	FBG	KL	IB	44D	YAN	12	6	29147	5	10	146000	160500
41	9	TAYANA V-42 PH	CUT	SAIL	FBG	KL	IB	44D	YAN	12	6	29147	5	10	155000	170500
47		TAYANA 47	CUT	SAIL	FBG	KL	IB	55D	YAN	14	6	35000	6		197500	217000
52	6	TAYANA 52 AFT	CUT	SAIL	FBG	KL	IB	110D	YAN	15	1	38570	5	4	270500	297000
52	6	TAYANA 52 CTR	CUT	SAIL	FBG	KL	IB	110D	YAN	15	1	38570	5	4	278000	305500
55		TAYANA 55	CUT	SACAC	FBG	KL	IB	130D	PERK	16	1	48000	7	2	334500	367500
55		TAYANA 55	KTH	SACAC	FBG	KL	IB	130D	PERK	16	1	48000	7	2	334500	368000
64	8	TAYANA 65	CUT	SACAC	FBG	KL	IB	135D	PERK	17	9	74000	7	6	565500	621500
		1991 BOATS														
36	8	TAYANA 37	CUT	SAIL	FBG	KL	IB	44D	YAN	11	6	22500	5	8	100000	110000
36	8	TAYANA 37	KTH	SAIL	FBG	KL	IB	44D	YAN	11	6	22500	5	8	106000	116000
36	8	TAYANA 37 PH	CUT	SAIL	FBG	KL	IB	44D	YAN	11	6	22500	5	8	106500	117000
41	9	TAYANA V-42 AFT	CUT	SAIL	FBG	KL	IB	44D	YAN	12	6	29147	5	10	133500	146500
41	9	TAYANA V-42 CTR	CUT	SAIL	FBG	KL	IB	44D	YAN	12	6	29147	5	10	138500	152000
41	9	TAYANA V-42 PH	CUT	SAIL	FBG	KL	IB	44D	YAN	12	6	29147	5	10	147000	161500
47		TAYANA 47	CUT	SAIL	FBG	KL	IB	55D	YAN	14	6	35000	6		187000	205500
52	6	TAYANA 52 AFT	CUT	SAIL	FBG	KL	IB	110D	YAN	15	1	38570	5	4	256000	281500
52	6	TAYANA 52 CTR	CUT	SAIL	FBG	KL	IB	110D	YAN	15	1	38570	5	4	263500	289500
52	6	TAYANA 52 CTR	KTH	SAIL	FBG	KL	IB	110D	YAN	15	1	38570	5	4	259500	285500
55		TAYANA 55	SCH	SAIL	FBG	CB	IB	140D	YAN	16	1	48400	5	3	319000	350500
55		TAYANA 55	SCH	SAIL	FBG	KL	IB	140D	YAN	16	1	48400	6	7	319000	350500
55		TAYANA 55	CUT	SAIL	FBG	CB	IB	140D	YAN	16	1	48400	5	3	318500	350000
55		TAYANA 55	CUT	SAIL	FBG	KL	IB	140D	YAN	16	1	48400	6	7	318500	350000
64	8	TAYANA 65	CUT	SAIL	FBG	CB	IB	140D	YAN	18		74400	7		540000	593500
64	8	TAYANA 65	CUT	SAIL	FBG	KL	IB	140D	YAN	18		74400	7	6	540000	593500
		1990 BOATS														
36	8	TAYANA 37	CUT	SAIL	FBG	KL	IB	44D	YAN	11	6	22500	5	8	94100	103500
36	8	TAYANA 37	CUT	SAIL	FBG	KL	IB	49D	PERK	11	6	22500	5	8	93900	103000
36	8	TAYANA 37	KTH	SAIL	FBG	KL	IB	44D	YAN	11	6	22500	5	8	99800	109500
36	8	TAYANA 37	KTH	SAIL	FBG	KL	IB	49D	PERK	11	6	22500	5	8	99500	109500
36	8	TAYANA 37 PH	CUT	SAIL	FBG	KL	IB	44D	YAN	11	6	22500	5	8	101500	111500
36	8	TAYANA 37 PH	CUT	SAIL	FBG	KL	IB	49D	PERK	11	6	22500	5	8	101000	111000
41	9	TAYANA V-42 AFT	CUT	SAIL	FBG	KL	IB	44D	YAN	12	6	29147	5	10	130500	143000
41	9	TAYANA V-42 CTR	CUT	SAIL	FBG	KL	IB	44D	YAN	12	6	29147	5	10	134500	147500
47		TAYANA 47	CUT	SAIL	FBG	KL	IB	55D	YAN	14	6	35000	6		177500	195000
52	6	TAYANA 52 AFT	CUT	SAIL	FBG	KL	IB	72D	PERK	15	1	38570	5	4	241000	264500
52	6	TAYANA 52 CTR	CUT	SAIL	FBG	KL	IB	72D	PERK	15	1	38570	5	4	247000	271500
52	6	TAYANA 52 CTR	KTH	SAIL	FBG	KL	IB	72D	PERK	15	1	38570	5	4	244000	268000
55		TAYANA 55	SCH	SAIL	FBG	CB	IB	130D	PERK	16	1	48400	5	3	300500	330500
55		TAYANA 55	SCH	SAIL	FBG	KL	IB	130D	PERK	16	1	48400	6	7	300500	330500
55		TAYANA 55	CUT	SAIL	FBG	CB	IB	130D	PERK	16	1	48400	5	3	300000	330000
55		TAYANA 55	CUT	SAIL	FBG	KL	IB	130D	PERK	16	1	48400	6	7	300000	330000
		1989 BOATS														
36	8	TAYANA 37	CUT	SA/CR	FBG	KL	IB	44D	YAN	11	6	22500	5	8	92500	101500
41	9	TAYANA 42 AC	CUT	SA/CR	FBG	KL	IB	44D	YAN	12	6	29150	5	10	125000	137000
41	9	TAYANA 42 CC	CUT	SA/CR	FBG	KL	IB	44D	YAN	12	6	29150	5	10	126000	138500
47		TAYANA 47	CUT	SA/CR	FBG	KL	IB	55D	YAN	14	6	35000	6		168000	184500
52	5	TAYANA 52 AC	CUT	SA/CR	FBG	KL	IB	78D	PERK	15	1	38570	6	6	225500	248000
52	5	TAYANA 52 CC	CUT	SA/CR	FBG	KL	IB	78D	PERK	15	1	38570	6	6	234500	257500
55		TAYANA 55	CUT	SA/CR	FBG	KL	IB	135D	PERK	16	1	48400	7	2	284500	312500
		1988 BOATS														
36	8	TAYANA 37	CUT	SAIL	FBG	KL	IB	44D	YAN	11	6	22500	5	8	83100	91300
36	8	TAYANA 37	KTH	SAIL	FBG	KL	IB	44D	YAN	11	6	22500	5	8	89000	97800
36	8	TAYANA 37 PH	CUT	SAIL	FBG	KL	IB	44D	YAN	11	6	22500	5	8	91800	101000
41	9	TAYANA V-42 AFT	CUT	SAIL	FBG	KL	IB	44D	YAN	12	6	29147	5	10	117500	129000
41	9	TAYANA V-42 CTR	CUT	SAIL	FBG	KL	IB	44D	YAN	12	6	29147	5	10	120000	132000
45	3	TAYANA 41+2	FB	TRWL	FBG	SV	IB	T145D	ISUZ	14	11	33000	3	11	164500	181000
52	5	TAYANA 52 AFT	CUT	SAIL	FBG	KL	IB	85D	PERK	15	1	38570	5	4	215500	237000
52	5	TAYANA 52 CTR	CUT	SAIL	FBG	KL	IB	85D	PERK	15	1	38570	5	4	220500	242500
52	5	TAYANA 52 CTR	KTH	SAIL	FBG	KL	IB	85D	PERK	15	1	38570	5	4	218000	240000
55		TAYANA 55	SCH	SAIL	FBG	CB	IB	135D	PERK	16	1	48400	5	3	270000	296500
55		TAYANA 55	SCH	SAIL	FBG	KL	IB	135D	PERK	16	1	48400	6	7	270000	296500
55		TAYANA 55	CUT	SAIL	FBG	CB	IB	135D	PERK	16	1	48400	5	3	269000	295500
55		TAYANA 55	CUT	SAIL	FBG	KL	IB	135D	PERK	16	1	48400	6	7	269000	295500
		1987 BOATS														
36	8	TAYANA 37	CUT	SAIL	FBG	KL	IB	44D	YAN	11	6	22500	5	8	79400	87200
36	8	TAYANA 37	KTH	SAIL	FBG	KL	IB	44D	YAN	11	6	22500	5	8	80500	88400
36	8	TAYANA 37 PH	CUT	SAIL	FBG	KL	IB	44D	YAN	11	6	22500	5	8	86200	94700
36	8	TAYANA 37 PH	KTH	SAIL	FBG	KL	IB	44D	YAN	11	6	22500	5	8	87700	96400
41	9	TAYANA V-42 AFT	CUT	SAIL	FBG	KL	IB	44D	YAN	12	6	29147	5	10	110500	121000
41	9	TAYANA V-42 CTR	CUT	SAIL	FBG	KL	IB	44D	YAN	12	6	29147	5	10	115000	126000
45	3	TAYANA 41+2	FB	TRWL	FBG	SV	IB	T145D	ISUZ	14	11	33000	3	11	157500	173000
52	5	TAYANA 52 AFT	CUT	SAIL	FBG	KL	IB	85D	PERK	15	1	38570	5	4	204000	224000
52	5	TAYANA 52 CTR	CUT	SAIL	FBG	KL	IB	85D	PERK	15	1	38570	5	4	209500	230000
55		TAYANA 55	SCH	SAIL	FBG	CB	IB	135D	PERK	16	1	48400	5	3	255500	281000
55		TAYANA 55	SCH	SAIL	FBG	KL	IB	135D	PERK	16	1	48400	6	7	255500	281000
55		TAYANA 55	CUT	SAIL	FBG	CB	IB	135D	PERK	16	1	48400	5	3	255000	280000
		1986 BOATS														
36	8	TAYANA 37	CUT	SAIL	FBG	KL	IB	33D	YAN	11	6	22500	5	8	75600	83100
36	8	TAYANA 37	KTH	SAIL	FBG	KL	IB	33D	YAN	11	6	22500	5	8	76800	84300
36	8	TAYANA 37 PH	CUT	SAIL	FBG	KL	IB	33D	YAN	11	6	22500	5	8	80800	88700
36	8	TAYANA 37 PH	KTH	SAIL	FBG	KL	IB	33D	YAN	11	6	22500	5	8	81800	89900
41	9	TAYANA V-42 AFT	CUT	SAIL	FBG	KL	IB	33D	YAN	12	6	29147	5	10	104500	115000
41	9	TAYANA V-42 CTR	CUT	SAIL	FBG	KL	IB	33D	YAN	12	6	29147	5	10	108000	118500
45	3	TAYANA 41+2	FB	TRWL	FBG	SV	IB	T145D	ISUZ	14	11	33000	3	11	150500	165500
52	5	TAYANA 52	CUT	SAIL	FBG	KL	IB	85D	PERK	15	1	38570	5	4	196000	215000
52	5	TAYANA 52 CTR	SLP	SAIL	FBG	KL	IB	85D	PERK	15	1	38570	5	4	196000	215500
55		TAYANA 55	SCH	SAIL	FBG	CB	IB	135D	PERK	16	1	48400	5	3	242000	266000
55		TAYANA 55	SCH	SAIL	FBG	KL	IB	135D	PERK	16	1	48400	6	7	242000	266000
55		TAYANA 55	CUT	SAIL	FBG	CB	IB	135D	PERK	16	1	48400	5	3	241000	265000
55		TAYANA 55	CUT	SAIL	FBG	KL	IB	135D	PERK	16	1	48400	6	7	241000	265000
		1985 BOATS														
36	8	TAYANA 37	CUT	SAIL	FBG	KL	IB	33D	YAN	11	6	22500	5	8	74000	81300
36	8	TAYANA 37	KTH	SAIL	FBG	KL	IB	33D	YAN	11	6	22500	5	8	74900	82400
41	9	TAYANA V-42 AFT	CUT	SAIL	FBG	KL	IB	33D	YAN	12	6	29147	5	10	99200	109000
41	9	TAYANA V-42 CTR	CUT	SAIL	FBG	KL	IB	33D	YAN	12	6	29147	5	10	102500	112500
45	3	TAYANA 41+2	FB	TRWL	FBG	SV	IB	T145D	ISUZ	14	11	33000	3	11	143500	158000
52	5	TAYANA 52	CUT	SA/CR	FBG	KL	IB	D		15	1	38570	6	6	186500	205000
52	5	TAYANA 52	SLP	SAIL	FBG	KL	IB	85D	PERK	15	1	38570	5	4	185500	204000
55		TAYANA 55	SCH	SAIL	FBG	KL	IB	135D	PERK	16	1	48400	6	7	229500	252000
55		TAYANA 55	CUT	SAIL	FBG	KL	IB	135D	PERK	16	1	48400	6	7	228000	250500
		1984 BOATS														
30	6	TANTON 30	KTH	SA/CR	AL	KL	IB	D		10	9		5	2	32100	35600
34		TANTON 34	KTH	SA/CR	AL	KC	IB	D		12	6		5	6	44600	49500
35	10	TAYANA MARINER 36	CUT	SA/CR	FBG	KL	IB	33D	YAN	11		21000	5		65600	72100
35	10	TAYANA MARINER 36	KTH	SA/CR	FBG	KL	IB	33D	YAN	11		21000	5		66400	72900
36	8	TAYANA 37	CUT	SA/CR	FBG	KL	IB	33D	YAN	11	6	22500	5	8	70200	77100
36	8	TAYANA 37	KTH	SA/CR	FBG	KL	IB	33D	YAN	11	6	22500	5	8	71100	78100
36	8	TAYANA 37 PH	CUT	SAIL	FBG	KL	IB	36D	YAN	11	6	22500	5	8	70200	77200
36	8	TAYANA 37 PH	KTH	SAIL	FBG	KL	IB	36D	YAN	11	6	22500	5	8	71100	78200
37		TANTON 37	KTH	SA/CR	AL	KC	IB	D		13			5	6	74100	81500
40	4	TAYANA MARINER 40	KTH	SA/CR	FBG	KL	IB	D	YAN	11	5	26500	5	8	88100	96800
41		TANTON 41	KTH	SA/CR	AL	KL	IB	D		13	6		5	6	96500	106000

CONTINUED ON NEXT PAGE

LOA FT	LOA IN	NAME AND/ OR MODEL	TOP/ RIG	BOAT TYPE	-HULL- MTL	-HULL- TP	ENGINE TP	ENGINE # HP	ENGINE MFG	BEAM FT	BEAM IN	WGT LBS	DRAFT FT	DRAFT IN	RETAIL LOW	RETAIL HIGH
		1984 BOATS														
41	9	TAYANA V-42	CUT	SA/CR	FBG	KL	IB	D		12	6	29147	5	10	96000	105500
41	9	TAYANA V-42 AFT	SLP	SA/CR	FBG	KL	IB	33D	YAN	12	6	29147	5	10	92900	102000
41	9	TAYANA V-42 CTR	SLP	SA/CR	FBG	KL	IB	33D	YAN	12	6	29147	5	10	98100	108000
41	9	TAYANA V42 AFT CPT	CUT	SAIL	FBG	KL	IB	50D	PERK	12	6	29147	5	10	93800	103000
41	9	TAYANA V42 CTR CPT	CUT	SAIL	FBG	KL	IB	50D	PERK	12	6	29147	5	10	96900	106500
43		TANTON 43	KTH	SA/CR	FBG	KL	IB	D		13			4	10	102000	112000
45	11	SURPRISE 45	SLP	SA/CR	FBG	KL	IB	D		13	5	26400	6	5	108500	119500
45	11	SURPRISE 45	KTH	SA/CR	FBG	KL	IB	52D	PUEG	13	5	26400	6	5	108500	119000
52	6	TAYANA 52	CUT	SA/CR	FBG	KL	IB	85D	PERK			38570	5	4	176500	194000
52	6	TAYANA 52 SHOAL	CUT	SAIL	FBG	KL	IB	85D	PERK	15	1	38570	5	4	176500	194000
55		TAYANA 55	CUT	SA/CR	FBG	KL	IB	D		16	1	48400	6	6	217000	238000

....For earlier years, see the BUC Used Boat Price Guide, Volume 3

TAHITI CARIBBEAN BOATS

DIV OF HARDIN MARINE
ANAHEIM CA 92805 COAST GUARD MFG ID- HAO

See inside cover to adjust price for area

For more recent years, see the BUC Used Boat Price Guide, Volume 1

LOA FT	LOA IN	NAME AND/ OR MODEL	TOP/ RIG	BOAT TYPE	-HULL- MTL	-HULL- TP	ENGINE TP	ENGINE # HP	ENGINE MFG	BEAM FT	BEAM IN	WGT LBS	DRAFT FT	DRAFT IN	RETAIL LOW	RETAIL HIGH
		1996 BOATS														
18		180MR		SKI	FBG	SV	JT	333	HARD	6	7	1760	1	1	11500	13100
19		190SR		SKI	FBG	SV	JT	333	HARD	7	1	1850	1	1	12800	14500
19	1	190FR		SKI	FBG	SV	JT	333	HARD	6	11	1980	1	6	13000	14800
20		200AR		SKI	FBG	SV	JT	333	HARD	7	3	2340	1	6	16500	18800
20	2	200BR		SKI	FBG	SV	IO	235	MRCR	7	6	2360	1	6	13100	14900
20	2	200BR		SKI	FBG	SV	JT	333	HARD	7	6	2360	1	6	17000	19400
20	2	200SC		SKI	FBG	SV	IO	235	MRCR	7	6	2360	1	6	13100	14900
20	2	200SC		SKI	FBG	SV	JT	333	HARD	7	6	2360	1	6	17100	19400
21	2	210BR		SKI	FBG	SV	IO	235	MRCR	7	10	2840	1	11	15500	17700
21	2	210BR		SKI	FBG	SV	JT	333	HARD	7	10	2840	1	11	20300	22600
21	2	210SC		SKI	FBG	SV	IO	235	MRCR	7	10	2840	1	11	15500	17700
21	2	210SC		SKI	FBG	SV	JT	333	HARD	7	10	2840	1	11	19900	22200
23	7	240WR		CR	FBG	DV	IO	330	MRCR	7	9	3920	2	10	24800	27500
27	10	280WR		CR	FBG	DV	IO	330	MRCR	8		5400	1	6	39100	43500
		1995 BOATS														
18		180MR		SKI	FBG	SV	JT	333	HARD	6	7	1760	1	1	10900	12400
19		190SR		SKI	FBG	SV	JT	333	HARD	7	1	1850	1	1	12200	13800
19	1	190FR		SKI	FBG	SV	JT	333	HARD	6	11	1980	1	6	12400	14100
20		200AR		SKI	FBG	SV	JT	333	HARD	7	3	2340	1	6	15600	17700
20	2	200BR		SKI	FBG	SV	IO	235	MRCR	7	6	2360	1	6	12300	14000
20	2	200BR		SKI	FBG	SV	JT	333	HARD	7	6	2360	1	6	16100	18300
20	2	200SC		SKI	FBG	SV	IO	235	MRCR	7	6	2360	1	6	12300	14000
20	2	200SC		SKI	FBG	SV	JT	333	HARD	7	6	2360	1	6	16100	18300
21	2	210BR		SKI	FBG	SV	IO	235	MRCR	7	10	2840	1	11	14500	16500
21	2	210BR		SKI	FBG	SV	JT	333	HARD	7	10	2840	1	11	19600	21700
21	2	210SC		SKI	FBG	SV	IO	235	MRCR	7	10	2840	1	11	14500	16500
21	2	210SC		SKI	FBG	SV	JT	333	HARD	7	10	2840	1	11	19200	21300
23	7	240WR		CR	FBG	DV	IO	330	MRCR	7	9	3920	2	10	23500	26200
27	10	280WR		CR	FBG	DV	IO	330	MRCR	8		5400	1	6	36500	40500
		1993 BOATS														
18		180 MR	OP	RNBT	FBG	SV	IO	333	CHEV	6	7	1760			9400	10700
		IO 365 CHEV 10600 12100, IO 420 CHEV 13400 15200, IO 465 CHEV													16100	18300
18	10	190 TT	OP	RNBT	FBG	DV	IO	333	CHEV	6	11	1875			10100	11400
		IO 365 CHEV 11300 12800, IO 420 CHEV 14000 15900, IO 465 CHEV													16800	19100
19		190 SR	OP	RNBT	FBG	DV	IO	333	CHEV	7	1	1850			10200	11600
		IO 365 CHEV 11400 13000, IO 420 CHEV 14200 16100, IO 465 CHEV													16900	19200
19	1	190 FB	OP	RNBT	FBG	DV	IO	333	CHEV	6	11	1980			10300	11700
		IO 365 CHEV 11500 13100, IO 420 CHEV 14300 16200, IO 465 CHEV													17000	19400
20		200 AR	OP	RNBT	FBG	DV	IO	333	CHEV	7	3	2340			12600	14400
		IO 365 CHEV 14000 15900, IO 420 CHEV 17200 19500, IO 465 CHEV													20200	22500
20	2	200 BR	OP	RNBT	FBG	SV	IO	230	MRCR	7	6	2360			11100	12600
		IO 333 CHEV 13200 15000, IO 365 CHEV 14500 16500, IO 420 CHEV													18200	20200
		IO 465 CHEV 20900 23200														
20	2	200 SC	OP	RNBT	FBG	DV	IO	230	MRCR	7	6	2360			10800	12200
		IO 333 CHEV 12800 14500, IO 365 CHEV 14100 16000, IO 420 CHEV													17300	19600
		IO 465 CHEV 20300 22600														
20	3	200 GT	OP	RNBT	FBG	DV	OB			7	2	1360			6800	7850
21	2	210 BR	OP	RNBT	FBG	SV	IO	250	MRCR	7	10	2840			12900	14700
		IO 330-350 14800 17700, IO 365-390 16300 20000, IO 420-465													19900	24600
21	2	210 ER	OP	RNBT	FBG	SV	IO	250	MRCR	7	10	2840			12900	14700
		IO 330-350 14800 17700, IO 365-390 16300 20000, IO 420-465													19900	24600
21	2	210 SC	OP	RNBT	FBG	SV	IO	250	MRCR	7	10	2840			12900	14700
		IO 330-350 14800 17700, IO 365-390 16300 20000, IO 420-465													19900	24600
23	7	240 WR	OP	CUD	FBG	SV	IO	330-390		7	9	3920			20500	25600
25		HARDIN 250	OP	CUD	FBG	SV	IO	330-390							22100	27100
25		HARDIN 250	OP	CUD	FBG	SV	IO	210D	MRCR						27900	31000
27	10	280 WR	OP	CUD	FBG	SV	IO	250-350		8		5400			29100	35600
27	10	280 WR	OP	CUD	FBG	SV	IO	390	MRCR	8		5400			33500	37300
		1989 BOATS														
17	2	INVADER 17	OP	SKI	FBG	SV	IO		MRCR	6	11	2040			**	**
18		MARAUDER 18	OP	SKI	FBG	SV	JT	260-320		6	7	1800			7950	9150
19		FORMULA 19	OP	RNBT	FBG	DV	IO		BERK						**	**
19		FORMULA 19	OP	RNBT	FBG	DV	IO	320-333							7500	9000
19		FORMULA 19	OP	RNBT	FBG	DV	IO	405	HARD						10400	11900
19		RENEGADE 19	OP	SKI	FBG	SV	JT	260-405		7	1	1850			9000	10200
20		ARIES 20	OP	SPTCR	FBG	SV	IO	260	BERK	7	3	2340			9450	10700
20		ARIES 20	OP	SPTCR	FBG	SV	JT	280-405		7	3	2340			12100	13800
20	2	SPORT 20	OP	SPTCR	FBG	SV	OB			7	6	1658			6850	7900
20	2	SPORT 20 CL	OP	SPTCR	FBG	SV	IO		MRCR	7	6	2300			**	**
		JT 320-333 12300 14000, JT 405 BERK 12500 14200, IO 405 HARD													14100	16100
20	3	GMT 20	OP	RNBT	FBG	DV	OB			7	2	950			4400	5050
21	2	EMPRESS	OP	SPTCR	FBG	SV	OB			7	10	2298			9300	10600
21	2	EMPRESS CL	OP	SPTCR	FBG	SV	IO		MRCR	7	10	2840			**	**
		JT 320 BERK 14100 16000, IO 333 BERK 12800 14500, IO 405 BERK													15800	18000
21	2	EMPRESS OP	OP	SPTCR	FBG	SV	IO		MRCR	7	10	2840			**	**
21	2	EMPRESS OP	OP	SPTCR	FBG	SV	JT	320-405		7	10	2840			14500	16400
23	7	WARRIOR	OP	OVNTR	FBG	SV	IO		MRCR	7	9	3960			**	**
23	7	WARRIOR II	OP	OVNTR	FBG	SV	IO		MRCR	7	9	3920			**	**
24	3	EMPEROR	OP	OVNTR	FBG	SV	IO		MRCR	7	9	3520			**	**
24	3	EMPEROR	OP	OVNTR	FBG	SV	JT	333-405		7	9	3520			18500	20700
25	11	LIMITED-EDITION 26	OP	SPTCR	FBG	SV	IO		MRCR	8		3960			**	**
27	10	CONQUEROR 28	OP	SPTCR	FBG	SV	IO		MRCR	8		6000			**	**
27	10	WARRIOR III	OP	SPTCR	FBG	DV	IO		MRCR	8		5900			**	**
		1988 BOATS														
17	2	INVADER 17	OP	SKI	FBG	SV	IO		MRCR	6	11	2040			**	**
18		MARAUDER 18	OP	SKI	FBG	SV	JT	260-405		6	7	1800			7600	8700
19		RENEGADE 19	OP	SKI	FBG	SV	JT	260-405		7	1	1850			8450	9700
20		ARIES 20	OP	SPTCR	FBG	SV	IO	260	BERK	7	3	2340			8900	10100
20		ARIES 20	OP	SPTCR	FBG	SV	JT	280-405		7	3	2340			11500	13100
20	2	SPORT 20	OP	SPTCR	FBG	SV	OB			7	6	1658			6650	7650
20	2	SPORT 20 CL	OP	SPTCR	FBG	SV	IO		MRCR	7	6	2300			**	**
20	2	SPORT 20 CL	OP	SPTCR	FBG	SV	JT	260-405		7	6	2300			11700	13500
21	2	EMPRESS	OP	SPTCR	FBG	SV	OB			7	10	2298			9000	10200
21	2	EMPRESS CL	OP	SPTCR	FBG	SV	IO		MRCR	7	10	2840			**	**
		JT 320 BERK 13500 15300, IO 333 BERK 12100 13800, IO 405 BERK													14900	17000
21	2	EMPRESS OP	OP	SPTCR	FBG	SV	IO		MRCR	7	10	2840			**	**
21	2	EMPRESS OP	OP	SPTCR	FBG	SV	JT	320-405		7	10	2840			13700	15600
23	7	WARRIOR	OP	OVNTR	FBG	SV	IO		MRCR	8					**	**
23	7	WARRIOR II	OP	OVNTR	FBG	SV	IO		MRCR	7	9	3920			**	**
24	3	EMPEROR	OP	OVNTR	FBG	SV	IO		MRCR	7	9	3520			**	**
25	11	LIMITED-EDITION 26	OP	SPTCR	FBG	SV	IO		MRCR	8		3960			**	**
		1987 BOATS														
17	2	INVADER	OP	SKI	FBG	SV	IO	205-260		6	11	2040			4950	6050
18		MARAUDER 18	OP	SKI	FBG	SV	JT	260-405		6	7	1800			7200	8300
19		RENEGADE 19	OP	SKI	FBG	SV	JT	260-405		7	1	1850			8050	9250
20		ARIES 20	OP	SPTCR	FBG	SV	JT	260	BERK	7	3	2340			11100	12600
20		ARIES 20	OP	SPTCR	FBG	SV	IO	260		7	3	2340			8300	9550
20		ARIES 20	OP	SPTCR	FBG	SV	JT	280-405		7	3	2340			11100	12600
20	2	SPORT 20	OP	SPTCR	FBG	SV	OB			7	6	1658			6450	7450
20	2	SPORT 20	OP	SPTCR	FBG	SV	IO		MRCR	7	6	2300			**	**
		JT 260 BERK 11300 12800, IO 260 8500 9750, JT 280-333													11300	12800
		IO 335 OMC 10000 11400, JT 405 BERK 11300 12800														
21	2	EMPRESS	OP	SPTCR	FBG	SV	OB			7	10	2298			8650	9950
21	2	EMPRESS CLOSED BOW	OP	SPTCR	FBG	SV	IO		MRCR	7	10	2840			**	**
		IO 260 10000 11400, JT 320-333 12900 14700, IO 335 OMC													11300	12900
		JT 405 BERK 13000 14700														

CONTINUED ON NEXT PAGE

LOA FT IN	NAME AND/ OR MODEL	TOP/ RIG	BOAT TYPE	MTL	HULL TP	TP	#	ENGINE HP	MFG	BEAM FT IN	WGT LBS	DRAFT FT IN	RETAIL LOW	RETAIL HIGH
								1987	BOATS					
21 2	EMPRESS OPEN BOW	OP	SPTCR	FBG	SV	IO			MRCR	7 10	2840		**	**
	IO 260 10200 11600, JT 320-333 13200 15000, IO 335 OMC 11400 13000													
	JT 405 BERK 13100 14900													
23 7	WARRIOR	OP	OVNTR	FBG	SV	IO			MRCR	8			**	**
23 7	WARRIOR	OP	OVNTR	FBG	SV	IO		260-335		8			13200	16400
23 7	WARRIOR II	OP	OVNTR	FBG	SV	IO		260-335		7 9	3920		**	**
23 7	WARRIOR II	OP	OVNTR	FBG	SV	IO		260-335		7 9	3920		13100	16200
24 3	EMPEROR	OP	OVNTR	FBG	SV	IO				7 9	3520		**	**
24 3	EMPEROR	OP	OVNTR	FBG	SV	IO		260-335		7 9	3520		12700	15800
25 11	LIMITED-EDITION 26	OP	SPTCR	FBG	SV	IO			MRCR	8	3960		**	**
25 11	LIMITED-EDITION 26	OP	SPTCR	FBG	SV	IO		260-335		8	3960		15800	19600
25 11	LIMITED-EDITION 26	OP	SPTCR	FBG	SV	IO		T260		8	3960		19700	21800
27 10	CONQUEROR	OP	WKNDR	FBG	SV	IO				8	6000		**	**
27 10	CONQUEROR	OP	WKNDR	FBG	SV	IO		T260	MRCR	8	6000		26300	29300
								1986	BOATS					
17 4	INVADER	OP	SKI	FBG	SV	IO		185	MRCR	6 11	2040		4700	5350
21	EMPRESS	OP	SPTCR	FBG	SV	IO		260	MRCR	8	2715		9500	10800
21	EMPRESS	OP	SPTCR	FBG	SV	JT		333	HARD	8	2628		12100	13800
23 7	WARRIOR	OP	OVNTR	FBG	SV	IO		260	MRCR	8			12600	14400
28 2	CONQUEROR	OP	WKNDR	FBG	SV	IO		330	MRCR	8			23500	26200
28 2	CONQUEROR	OP	WKNDR	FBG	SV	IO		T260	MRCR	8			25700	28600
32	WARLORD	OP	OFF	FBG	DV	IO		T330	MRCR	8		9000	42700	47500
								1985	BOATS					
17 4	INVADER	OP	SKI	FBG	SV	IO		185	MRCR	6 11	2040		4450	5100
19	RENEGADE	OP	SKI	FBG	SV	JT		333	HARD	7 1	1850		7300	8400
21	EMPRESS	OP	SPTCR	FBG	SV	JT		260	MRCR	8	2715		9050	10300
21	EMPRESS	OP	SPTCR	FBG	SV	JT		333	HARD	8	2628		11600	13100
21	EMPRESS B/R	OP	RNBT	FBG	SV	IO		260	MRCR	8	2840		8300	9500
21	EMPRESS B/R	OP	RNBT	FBG	SV	JT		333	HARD	8	2753		11400	13000
23 7	WARRIOR	OP	OVNTR	FBG	SV	IO		260	MRCR	8			12400	13700
25 3	EMPEROR	OP	OVNTR	FBG	SV	IO		260	MRCR	8	3520		12700	14400
28 2	CONQUEROR	OP	WKNDR	FBG	SV	IO		330	MRCR	8			22400	24900
28 2	CONQUEROR	OP	WKNDR	FBG	SV	IO		T260	MRCR	8			24500	27300
32	WARLORD	OP	OFF	FBG	DV	IO		T260-T330		8		9000	38900	45100
								1984	BOATS					
17 4	INVADER	OP	SKI	FBG	SV	IO		185	MRCR	6 11	2040		4200	4900
19	RENEGADE	OP	SKI	FBG	SV	JT		333	HARD	7 1	1850		7000	8050
21	EMPRESS	OP	SPTCR	FBG	SV	IO		260	MRCR	8	2715		8550	9850
21	EMPRESS	OP	SPTCR	FBG	SV	JT		333	HARD	8	2628		11100	12700
21	EMPRESS B/R	OP	RNBT	FBG	SV	IO		260	MRCR	8	2840		7950	9100
21	EMPRESS B/R	OP	RNBT	FBG	SV	JT		333	HARD	8	2753		11000	12500
23 7	WARRIOR	OP	OVNTR	FBG	SV	IO		260	MRCR	8			11500	13100
25 3	EMPEROR	OP	OVNTR	FBG	SV	IO		260	MRCR	8	3520		12100	13800
28 2	CONQUEROR	OP	WKNDR	FBG	SV	IO		330	MRCR	8			22400	24900

TALBOT CONSTRUCTION CO INC
JEFFERSON LA 70121-3931   See inside cover to adjust price for area

LOA FT IN	NAME AND/ OR MODEL	TOP/ RIG	BOAT TYPE	MTL	HULL TP	TP	#	ENGINE HP	MFG	BEAM FT IN	WGT LBS	DRAFT FT IN	RETAIL LOW	RETAIL HIGH
								1994	BOATS					
48	TALBOT 48	KTH	SACAC	FBG	KL	IB		85D	PERK	13 4	40000	6 1	142000	156000
								1991	BOATS					
34	TALBOT 34	SLP	SAIL	FBG	KL	IB		25D	WEST	10 4	10500	5 6	42100	46800
48	TALBOT 48	KTH	SAIL	FBG	KL	IB		85D	PERK	13 4	38000	6	114500	126000
								1990	BOATS					
34	TALBOT 34	SLP	SAIL	FBG	KL	IB		25D	WEST	10 4	10500	5 6	39400	43800
48	TALBOT 48	KTH	SAIL	FBG	KL	IB		85D	PERK	13 4	33000	6	102000	112000
								1988	BOATS					
34	TALBOT 34	SLP	SA/RC	FBG	KL	IB		35D		9 8	14000	5 9	45800	50300
48	SUMMER WIND	KTH	SA/RC	FBG	KL	IB		85D	PERK	13 3	33500	6	90300	99200
								1985	BOATS					
48	TALBOT 48	KTH	SA/CR	FBG	KL	IB				13 4	28000	5 6	68900	75700

TALON MARINE CO
SARASOTA FL 33580   See inside cover to adjust price for area

LOA FT IN	NAME AND/ OR MODEL	TOP/ RIG	BOAT TYPE	MTL	HULL TP	TP	#	ENGINE HP	MFG	BEAM FT IN	WGT LBS	DRAFT FT IN	RETAIL LOW	RETAIL HIGH
								1995	BOATS					
22	TALON 22	OP	RNBT	FBG	PN	OB					1275		14000	15900
22	TALON 22	OP	RNBT	FBG	PN	OB		250-265		8	1275		12200	14100
	IO 350 MRCR 15200 17300, IO 385 MRCR 17100 19500, IO 415 MRCR 19300 21500													
	IO 465 MRCR 23100 25600													
25 4	TALON 25	OP	RNBT	FBG	PN	OB				8 4	2400		32600	36200
25 4	TALON 25	OP	RNBT	FBG	PN	IO		300-350		8 4	2500		19500	23800
25 4	TALON 25	OP	RNBT	FBG	PN	IO		415-465		8 4	2500		24800	30700
25 4	TALON 25 CARRIER	OP	RNBT	FBG	PN	OB				8 4	2250		31700	35200
								1993	BOATS					
17 6	TALON 18	OP	RNBT	FBG	PN	OB				8	900		9850	11200
21 6	TALON 21	OP	RNBT	FBG	PN	OB				8	1250		12300	14000
22	TALON 22	OP	RNBT	FBG	PN	OB				8	1275		12600	14300
25 4	TALON 25	OP	RNBT	FBG	PN	OB				8 4	2400		29400	32600
25 4	TALON 25	OP	RNBT	FBG	PN	IO		300	MRCR	8 4	2500		16800	19100
25 4	TALON 25	OP	RNBT	FBG	PN	IO		350-390		8 4	2500		18900	22800
25 4	TALON 25 CARRIER	OP	RNBT	FBG	PN	OB				8 4	2250		28600	31700
								1991	BOATS					
17 6	TALON 18	OP	RNBT	FBG	PN	OB				8	850		8450	9700
21 6	TALON 21	OP	RNBT	FBG	PN	OB				8	1000		9150	10400
22	TALON 22	OP	RNBT	FBG	PN	OB				8	1250		11300	12800
25 4	TALON 25	OP	RNBT	FBG	PN	OB				8 4	3100		29000	33200
25 4	TALON 25	OP	RNBT	FBG	PN	IO		300	MRCR	8 4	3100		15800	18000
37	TALON 37	OP	RNBT	FBG	PN	OB				10 4	3900		131000	144000
								1990	BOATS					
17 6	TALON 18	OP	RNBT	FBG	PN	OB				8	850		8100	9300
21 6	TALON 21	OP	RNBT	FBG	PN	OB				8	1000		8650	9950
22	TALON 22	OP	RNBT	FBG	PN	OB				8	1250		10800	12200
25 4	TALON 25	OP	RNBT	FBG	PN	OB				8 4	3100		28500	31700
25 4	TALON 25	OP	RNBT	FBG	PN	IO		300	MRCR	8 4	3100		14900	16900
								1989	BOATS					
17 6	TALON 21	OP	RNBT	FBG		OB				8	850		7750	8900
25 4	TALON 25	OP	RNBT	FBG		OB				8 4	1850		21900	24400

TANGO YACHTS
MIAMI BEACH FL 33139   See inside cover to adjust price for area

LOA FT IN	NAME AND/ OR MODEL	TOP/ RIG	BOAT TYPE	MTL	HULL TP	TP	#	ENGINE HP	MFG	BEAM FT IN	WGT LBS	DRAFT FT IN	RETAIL LOW	RETAIL HIGH
								1991	BOATS					
60	TANGO 60 WALKAROUND	FB	MY	FBG	SV	IB		T735D	GM	17 6	80000	4	295000	324000
60	TANGO 60 WIDEBODY	FB	MY	FBG	SV	IB		T735D	GM	17 6	80000	4	317000	348000
70	TANGO 70 COCKPIT	FB	MYCPT	FBG	SV	IB		T900D	GM	17 6	90000	4	377500	414500
70	TANGO 70 MOTORYACHT	FB	MY	FBG	SV	IB		T900D	GM	17 6	50T	4	391000	429500

TANTON INC
NEWPORT RI 02840   See inside cover to adjust price for area

LOA FT IN	NAME AND/ OR MODEL	TOP/ RIG	BOAT TYPE	MTL	HULL TP	TP	#	ENGINE HP	MFG	BEAM FT IN	WGT LBS	DRAFT FT IN	RETAIL LOW	RETAIL HIGH
								1985	BOATS					
39 2	TANTON 39	CUT	SA/CR	FBG	KL	IB				12 9		4 10	90300	99300
39 2	TANTON 39	KTH	SA/CR	FBG	KL	IB				12 9		4 10	90300	99300
43 2	TANTON 43	CUT	SA/CR	FBG	KL	IB				13 1		4 10	127500	140500
43 2	TANTON 43	KTH	SA/CR	FBG	KL	IB				13 1		4 10	128500	141000
44 3	TANTON 44	CUT	SA/CR	FBG	KL	IB				13		5 10	133500	147000
66 6	TANTON 70	CUT	SA/CR	FBG	KL	IB		120D		15	24980	8 6	206000	226000

....For earlier years, see the BUC Used Boat Price Guide, Volume 3

TANZER INDUSTRIES INC
DORION QUE CANADA   COAST GUARD MFG ID- ZTI See inside cover to adjust price for area

TANZER YACHTS INC
EDENTON NC 27932

LOA FT IN	NAME AND/ OR MODEL	TOP/ RIG	BOAT TYPE	MTL	HULL TP	TP	#	ENGINE HP	MFG	BEAM FT IN	WGT LBS	DRAFT FT IN	RETAIL LOW	RETAIL HIGH
								1986	BOATS					
16 4	TANZER 16	SLP	SA/OD	FBG	CB	OB				6 2	450	7	1700	2000
16 4	TANZER OVERNIGHTER	SLP	SA/OD	FBG	CB	OB				6 2	500	7	1800	2100
22 6	TANZER 22	SLP	SA/RC	FBG	KC	OB				7 10	3100	2	5500	6300
22	TANZER 22	SLP	SA/RC	FBG	KL	OB				7 10	3800	3 5	5200	6000
24 7	TANZER 7.5	SLP	SA/RC	FBG	KL	OB				8	3800	4	7250	8300
24 7	TANZER 7.5 SHOAL	SLP	SA/RC	FBG	KL	OB				8	4150	2 8	7850	9000
25 3	TANZER 25	SLP	SA/RC	FBG	KL	IB		D	YAN	9 7	4400	4 8	9500	10800
25 3	TANZER 25 SHOAL	SLP	SA/RC	FBG	KL	IB		D	YAN	9 7	4750	2 11	10200	11600
26 4	TANZER 26	SLP	SA/RC	FBG	KL	IB				8 8	4350	3 10	9200	10500
26 4	TANZER 26	SLP	SA/RC	FBG	KL	IB		8D	YAN	8 8	4350	3 10	9700	11000
26 7	TANZER 27	SLP	SA/RC	FBG	KL	OB				9 6	6200	4 6	13300	15100

LOA FT	LOA IN	NAME AND/ OR MODEL	TOP/ RIG	BOAT TYPE	-HULL- MTL	-HULL- TP	ENGINE TP	ENGINE # HP	ENGINE MFG	BEAM FT	BEAM IN	WGT LBS	DRAFT FT	DRAFT IN	RETAIL LOW	RETAIL HIGH
		1986 BOATS														
26	7	TANZER 27	SLP	SA/RC	FBG	KL	IB	15D	YAN	9	6	6200	4	6	13900	15800
26	7	TANZER 27 SHOAL	SLP	SA/CR	FBG	KL	IB	15D	YAN	9	6	6450	3	3	14500	16500
26	7	TANZER 27 SHOAL	SLP	SA/RC	FBG	KL	OB			9	6	6450	3	3	13800	15700
27	11	TANZER 8.5	SLP	SAIL	FBG	KL	OB			9	6	7400	4	4	16900	19200
27	11	TANZER 8.5	SLP	SAIL	FBG	KL	IB	12D-	15D	9	6	7400	4	4	17300	19700
29		TANZER 29	SLP	SA/RC	FBG	KL	IB	15D	YAN	10	3	6500	5	3	15600	17800
29		TANZER 29 SHOAL	SLP	SA/RC	FBG	KL	IB	15D	YAN	10	3	6800	4		16400	18600
30	7	TANZER 31	SLP	SA/RC	FBG	KL	IB	15D	YAN	10	6	8300	5	3	20800	23200
30	7	TANZER 31 SHOAL	SLP	SA/RC	FBG	KL	IB	15D	YAN	10	6	8700	4		21900	24300
34	5	TANZER 10.5 PH SHOAL	SLP	SAIL	FBG	KL	IB	30D	YAN	11	6	13000	4	6	32200	35800
34	5	TANZER 10.5PH	SLP	SAIL	FBG	KL	IB	30D	YAN	11	6	13000	5	10	33200	36900
34	5	TANZER 10.5PH	SLP	SAIL	FBG	SK	IB	30D	YAN	11	6	13000	2	1	34100	37900
		1985 BOATS														
16	4	TANZER 16	SLP	SA/OD	FBG	CB	OB			6	2	450		7	1600	1900
16	4	TANZER OVERNIGHTER	SLP	SA/OD	FBG	CB	OB			6	2	500		7	1700	2000
22	6	TANZER 22	SLP	SA/RC	FBG	KC	OB			7	10	3100	2		5150	5950
22	6	TANZER 22	SLP	SA/RC	FBG	KL	OB			7	10	2900	3	5	4900	5650
24	7	TANZER 7.5	SLP	SA/RC	FBG	KL	OB			8		3800	4		6800	7800
24	7	TANZER 7.5 SHOAL	SLP	SA/RC	FBG	KL	OB			8		4150	2	8	7400	8500
26	4	TANZER 26	SLP	SA/RC	FBG	KL	OB			8	8	4350	3	10	8550	9850
26	4	TANZER 26	SLP	SA/RC	FBG	KL	IB	8D	YAN	8	8	4350	3	10	9200	10400
26	7	TANZER 27	SLP	SA/RC	FBG	KL	OB			9	6	6200	4	6	12500	14200
26	7	TANZER 27	SLP	SA/RC	FBG	KL	IB	8D-	15D	9	6	6200	4	6	13000	14900
26	7	TANZER 27 SHOAL	SLP	SA/CR	FBG	KL	IB	15D	YAN	9	6	6450	3	3	13600	15500
26	7	TANZER 27 SHOAL	SLP	SA/RC	FBG	KL	OB			9	6	6450	3	3	13000	14800
26	7	TANZER 27 SHOAL	SLP	SA/RC	FBG	KL	IB	8D	YAN	9	6	6450	3	3	13500	15400
27	11	TANZER 8.5	SLP	SAIL	FBG	KL	OB			9	6	7400	4	4	15900	18100
27	11	TANZER 8.5	SLP	SAIL	FBG	KL	IB	15D	YAN	9	6	7400	4	4	16300	18600
30	7	TANZER 31	SLP	SA/RC	FBG	KL	IB	15D	YAN	10	6	8300	5	3	19600	21800
30	7	TANZER 31 SHOAL	SLP	SA/RC	FBG	KL	IB	15D	YAN	10	6	8700	4		20600	22800
34	5	TANZER 10.5 PH SHOAL	SLP	SAIL	FBG	KL	IB	30D	YAN	11	6	13000	4	6	30300	33600
34	5	TANZER 10.5PH	SLP	SAIL	FBG	KL	IB	30D	YAN	11	6	13000	5	10	31200	34700
34	5	TANZER 10.5PH	SLP	SAIL	FBG	SK	IB	30D	YAN	11	6	13000	2	1	32200	35700
		1984 BOATS														
16	4	TANZER 16	SLP	SA/OD	FBG	CB	OB			6	2	450		7	1500	1800
16	4	TANZER OVERNIGHTER	SLP	SA/OD	FBG	CB	OB			6	2	500		7	1600	1900
22	6	TANZER 22	SLP	SA/RC	FBG	KC	OB			7	10	3100	2		4850	5600
22	6	TANZER 22	SLP	SA/RC	FBG	KL	OB			7	10	2900	3	5	4650	5350
22	6	TANZER 22	SLP	SAIL	FBG	KC	OB			7	10	3100	2		4850	5600
22	6	TANZER 22	SLP	SAIL	FBG	KL	OB			7	10	2900	3	5	4650	5350
24	7	TANZER 7.5	SLP	SA/RC	FBG	KL	OB			8		3800	4		6400	7350
24	7	TANZER 7.5	SLP	SAIL	FBG	KL	OB			8		3800	4		6400	7350
24	7	TANZER 7.5 SHOAL	SLP	SA/RC	FBG	KL	OB			8		4150	2	8	6950	8000
24	7	TANZER 7.5 SHOAL	SLP	SAIL	FBG	KL	OB			8		4150	2	8	6950	8000
26	4	TANZER 26	SLP	SA/RC	FBG	KL	OB			8	8	4350	3	10	8050	9250
26	4	TANZER 26	SLP	SA/RC	FBG	KL	IB	8D		8	8	4350	3	10	8500	9750
26	4	TANZER 26	SLP	SAIL	FBG	KL	OB			8	8	4350	3	10	8050	9250
26	4	TANZER 26	SLP	SAIL	FBG	KL	IB	8D		8	8	4350	3	10	8500	9750
26	7	TANZER 27	SLP	SA/RC	FBG	KL	OB			9	6	6200	4	6	11700	13300
26	7	TANZER 27	SLP	SA/RC	FBG	KL	IB	8D		9	6	6200	4	6	12200	13800
26	7	TANZER 27	SLP	SAIL	FBG	KL	OB			9	6	6200	4	6	11700	13300
26	7	TANZER 27	SLP	SAIL	FBG	KL	IB	8D-	15D	9	6	6200	4	6	12200	13900
26	7	TANZER 27 SHOAL	SLP	SA/RC	FBG	KL	OB			9	6	6450	3	3	12200	13900
26	7	TANZER 27 SHOAL	SLP	SA/RC	FBG	KL	IB	8D		9	6	6450	3	3	12700	14400
26	7	TANZER 27 SHOAL	SLP	SAIL	FBG	KL	OB			9	6	6450	3	3	12200	13900
26	7	TANZER 27 SHOAL	SLP	SAIL	FBG	KL	IB	8D-	15D	9	6	6450	3	3	12700	14500
27	11	TANZER 8.5	SLP	SA/CR	FBG	KL	OB			9	6	7400	4	4	14900	17000
27	11	TANZER 8.5	SLP	SA/CR	FBG	KL	IB	12D-	15D	9	6	7400	4	4	15300	17400
27	11	TANZER 8.5	SLP	SAIL	FBG	KL	OB			9	6	7400	4	4	14900	17000
27	11	TANZER 8.5	SLP	SAIL	FBG	KL	IB	12D-	15D	9	6	7400	4	4	15300	17400
34	5	TANZER 10.5PH	SLP	SAIL	FBG	KL	IB	30D	YAN	11	6	13000	5	10	30400	33800
34	5	TANZER 10.5PH	SLP	SAIL	FBG	SK	IB	30D	YAN	11	6	13000	2	1	32200	35800
34	5	TANZER 10.5PH SHOAL	SLP	SAIL	FBG	KL	IB	30D	YAN	11	6	13000	4	6	25400	28200

....For earlier years, see the BUC Used Boat Price Guide, Volume 3

TARGA OY A B

HIMANKA FINLAND See inside cover to adjust price for area

FINNYACHT USA
S DARTMOUTH MA02748

LOA FT	LOA IN	NAME AND/ OR MODEL	TOP/ RIG	BOAT TYPE	-HULL- MTL	-HULL- TP	ENGINE TP	ENGINE # HP	ENGINE MFG	BEAM FT	BEAM IN	WGT LBS	DRAFT FT	DRAFT IN	RETAIL LOW	RETAIL HIGH
		1986 BOATS														
31	6	TARGA 96	SLP	SA/CR	FBG	KL	IB	D		9	10	9000	4	7	29400	32700
33	1	TARGA 101	SLP	SA/CR	FBG	KL	IB	D		10	2	9000	5	3	29500	32800
40	8	TARGA 42	SLP	SA/CR	FBG	KL	IB	D		9	5	1000	5	7	11300	12800
		1985 BOATS														
33	1	TARGA 101	SLP	SA/CR	FBG	KL	IB	D		10	2	9000	5	3	27700	30800
40	8	TARGA 42	SLP	SA/CR	FBG	KL	IB	D		9	5	10000	5	7	43400	48200
		1984 BOATS														
33	2	TARGA 101	SLP	SA/CR	FBG	KL	IB	D		10	2	9950	5	4	28800	32000
41	7	TARGA 42	SLP	SA/RC	FBG	KL	IB	D		9	5	10000	5	9	43700	48600

....For earlier years, see the BUC Used Boat Price Guide, Volume 3

TARTAN YACHTS INC

FAIRPORT HARBOR OH 4407 COAST GUARD MFG ID- TAR See inside cover to adjust price for area
SEE ALSO DOUGLASS & MCLEOD INC

For more recent years, see the BUC Used Boat Price Guide, Volume 1

LOA FT	LOA IN	NAME AND/ OR MODEL	TOP/ RIG	BOAT TYPE	-HULL- MTL	-HULL- TP	ENGINE TP	ENGINE # HP	ENGINE MFG	BEAM FT	BEAM IN	WGT LBS	DRAFT FT	DRAFT IN	RETAIL LOW	RETAIL HIGH
		1996 BOATS														
31	4	TARTAN 3100	SLP	SARAC	FBG	KL	IB	18D	WEST	10	11	9030	6		82100	90300
35	3	TARTAN 3500	SLP	SARAC	FBG	KL	IB	27D	WEST	11	9	11400	6	6	94600	104000
38		TARTAN 3800	SLP	SARAC	FBG	KL	IB	37D	WEST	12	5	16000	6	10	137000	150500
41	3	TARTAN 4100	SLP	SARAC	FBG	KL	IB	42D	WEST	13	6	19000	7		178500	196000
46	2	TARTAN 4600	SLP	SARAC	FBG	KL	IB	63D	WEST	14	4	24000	8	11	262500	288500
		1995 BOATS														
31	4	TARTAN 3100	SLP	SARAC	FBG	KL	IB	18D	WEST	10	11	9030	6		76700	84300
35	3	TARTAN 3500	SLP	SARAC	FBG	KL	IB	27D	WEST	11	9	11400	6	6	88400	97100
38		TARTAN 3800	SLP	SARAC	FBG	KL	IB	37D	WEST	12	5	16000	6	10	128000	140500
46	2	TARTAN 4600	SLP	SARAC	FBG	KL	IB	63D	WEST	14	4	24000	8	11	245000	269500
		1994 BOATS														
28	3	TARTAN 28 PIPER	SLP	SARAC	FBG	KL	IB	18D	YAN	9	11	6300	3	11	39400	43800
31	4	TARTAN 31 PIPER	SLP	SARAC	FBG	KL	IB	18D	YAN	10	11	9030	6		71600	78700
35	3	TARTAN 3500	SLP	SARAC	FBG	KL	IB	27D	YAN	11	9	11400	6	6	82500	90600
38		TARTAN 3800	SLP	SARAC	FBG	KL	IB	37D	YAN	12	5	16000	6	10	119500	131000
46	2	TARTAN 4600	SLP	SARAC	FBG	KL	IB	62D	YAN	14	4	24000	8	11	229000	251500
		1993 BOATS														
28	3	TARTAN PIPER	SLP	SARAC	FBG	KL	IB	13D	YAN	9	11	6300	3	11	36700	40800
31	4	TARTAN 31	SLP	SARAC	FBG	KL	IB	18D	YAN	10	11	9030	6		66900	73500
35	3	TARTAN 3500	SLP	SARAC	FBG	KL	IB	27D	YAN	11	9	11400	6	6	77000	84700
37	3	TARTAN 372	SLP	SARAC	FBG	KL	IB	43D	YAN	12	4	15200	6	10	104500	115000
46		TARTAN 4500	SLP	SARAC	FBG	KL	IB	27D	YAN	14	4	22900	8	11	206000	226500
		1992 BOATS														
28	3	TARTAN PIPER	SLP	SAIL	FBG	KL	IB	13D	VLVO	9	11	6300	3	11	34300	38100
31	4	TARTAN 31	SLP	SAIL	FBG	KL	IB	18D	VLVO	10	11	9030	6		62500	68600
35	3	TARTAN 3500	SLP	SAIL	FBG	KL	IB	27D		11	9	11400	6	6	71900	79000
37	3	TARTAN 372	SLP	SAIL	FBG	KL	IB	43D	VLVO	12	4	15200	6	10	97500	107000
41	2	TARTAN 412	SLP	SAIL	FBG	KL	IB	44D	UNIV	12	9	18500	7	6	133000	146000
45	9	TARTAN 4500	SLP	SAIL	FBG	KL	IB	27D		14	4	22900	8	11	189500	208500
		1991 BOATS														
28	3	TARTAN PIPER	SLP	SAIL	FBG	KL	IB	13D	VLVO	9	11	6300	3	11	32000	35600
31	4	TARTAN 31	SLP	SAIL	FBG	KL	IB	18D	VLVO	10	11	9030	6		58400	64100
37	3	TARTAN 372	SLP	SAIL	FBG	KL	IB	43D	VLVO	12	4	15200	6	10	91100	100000
41	2	TARTAN 412	SLP	SAIL	FBG	KL	IB	44D	UNIV	12	9	18500	7	6	124000	136500
		1989 BOATS														
28	3	TARTAN 28	SLP	SA/CR	FBG	KL	IB	18D	YAN	9	10	7450	4	11	33300	37000
28	3	TARTAN 28 SHOAL	SLP	SA/CR	FBG	KC	IB	18D	YAN	9	10	7450	3	11	33300	37000
31	4	TARTAN 31	SLP	SA/RC	FBG	KL	IB	18D	YAN	10	11	9030	6		51000	56000
31	4	TARTAN 31 SHOAL	SLP	SA/RC	FBG	KC	IB	18D	YAN	10	11	9030	4	4	51000	56000
34	5	TARTAN 34	SLP	SA/RC	FBG	KL	IB	27D	YAN	11		11000	6	3	56200	61800
34	5	TARTAN 34 SHOAL	SLP	SA/RC	FBG	KC	IB	27D	YAN	11		11000	4	6	56200	61800
37	3	TARTAN 372	SLP	SA/CR	FBG	KL	IB	34D	UNIV	12	5	15200	6	10	79400	87200
37	3	TARTAN 372 SHOAL	SLP	SA/CR	FBG	KC	IB	34D	UNIV	12	5	15200	4	9	79400	87200
40	3	TARTAN 40	SLP	SA/RC	FBG	KL	IB	44D	UNIV	12	8	17800	7	6	101500	111500
40	3	TARTAN 40 SHOAL	SLP	SA/RC	FBG	KC	IB	44D	UNIV	12	8	17800	4	9	101500	111500
40	3	TARTAN 40 SHOAL	SLP	SA/RC	FBG	KC	IB	44D	UNIV	12	8	17800	5	1	101500	111500
		1988 BOATS														
26	10	PRIDE 270	SLP	SA/RC	FBG	KL				8	6	3800	4	11	12000	13700
28	4	TARTAN 28	SLP	SA/CR	FBG	KL	IB	18D	YAN	9	10	7800	4	11	32700	36400
28	4	TARTAN 28 SHOAL	SLP	SA/CR	FBG	KC	IB	18D	YAN	9	10	7800	3	11	32700	36400
31	4	TARTAN 31	SLP	SA/RC	FBG	KL	IB	32D		10	11	9030	4	4	47900	52700
33	1	TARTAN TEN	SLP	SA/RC	FBG	KL	IB	15D	YAN	9	3	6700	5	10	25300	28100
34	5	TARTAN 34	SLP	SA/RC	FBG	KL	IB	27D	YAN	10	11	11000	6	3	52600	57800
34	5	TARTAN 34 SHOAL	SLP	SA/RC	FBG	KL	IB	27D	YAN	10	11	11000	4	5	52600	57800
37	4	TARTAN 37	SLP	SA/CR	FBG	KL	IB	32D	UNIV	11	9	15500	6	7	75600	83000

LOA FT	LOA IN	NAME AND/ OR MODEL	TOP/ RIG	BOAT TYPE	HULL MTL	HULL TP	TP	# HP	MFG	BEAM FT	BEAM IN	WGT LBS	DRAFT FT	DRAFT IN	RETAIL LOW	RETAIL HIGH
		1988 BOATS														
37	4	TARTAN 37 SHOAL	SLP	SA/CR	FBG	KC	IB	32D	UNIV	11	9	15500	4	2	75600	83000
40	3	TARTAN 40	SLP	SA/RC	FBG	KL	IB	44D	UNIV	12	8	17800	7	6	95000	104500
40	3	TARTAN 40 SHOAL	SLP	SA/RC	FBG	KC	IB	44D	UNIV	12	8	17800	4	9	95000	104500
40	3	TARTAN 40 SHOAL	SLP	SA/RC	FBG	KC	IB	44D	UNIV	12	8	17800	5	1	95000	104500
		1987 BOATS														
26	10	PRIDE 270	SLP	SA/RC	FBG	KL				8	6	3800	4	11	11300	12800
28	4	TARTAN 28	SLP	SA/CR	FBG	KL	IB	18D	YAN	9	10	7800	4	11	30400	33700
28	4	TARTAN 28 SHOAL	SLP	SA/CR	FBG	KC	IB	18D	YAN	9	10	7800	3	11	30800	34200
30		TARTAN 3000	SLP	SA/RC	FBG	KL	IB	15D	UNIV	10	1	7950	5	2	32800	36400
30		TARTAN 3000 SHOAL	SLP	SA/RC	FBG	KC	IB	15D	UNIV	10	1	7950	3	4	33800	37500
33	1	TARTAN TEN	SLP	SA/RC	FBG	KL	IB	15D	YAN	9	3	6700	5	10	23600	26300
34	5	TARTAN 34	SLP	SA/RC	FBG	KL	IB	27D	YAN	10	11	11000	6	3	49100	54000
34	5	TARTAN 34 SHOAL	SLP	SA/RC	FBG	KL	IB	27D	YAN	10	11	11000	4	5	49100	54000
37	4	TARTAN 37	SLP	SA/CR	FBG	KL	IB	32D	UNIV	11	9	15500	6	7	70600	77600
37	4	TARTAN 37 SHOAL	SLP	SA/CR	FBG	KC	IB	32D	UNIV	11	9	15500	4	2	70600	77600
40	3	TARTAN 40	SLP	SA/RC	FBG	KL	IB	32D	UNIV	12	8	17800	7	6	88100	96800
40	3	TARTAN 40	SLP	SA/RC	FBG	KL	IB	44D	UNIV	12	8	17800	7	6	88900	97700
40	3	TARTAN 40	SLP	SA/RC	FBG	KL	IB	44D	YAN	12	8	17800	7	6	88800	97600
40	3	TARTAN 40 SHOAL	SLP	SA/RC	FBG	KC	IB	32D	UNIV	12	8	17800	4	9	88800	97600
40	3	TARTAN 40 SHOAL	SLP	SA/RC	FBG	KC	IB	44D	UNIV	12	8	17800	4	9	88900	97700
40	3	TARTAN 40 SHOAL	SLP	SA/RC	FBG	KC	IB	44D	YAN	12	8	17800	4	9	88800	97600
		1986 BOATS														
26	10	PRIDE 270	SLP	SA/RC	FBG	KL				8	6	3800	4	11	10500	12000
28	4	TARTAN 28	SLP	SA/CR	FBG	KL	IB	17D	YAN	9	10	7800	4	11	28400	31500
28	4	TARTAN 28 SHOAL	SLP	SA/CR	FBG	KC	IB	17D	YAN	9	10	7800	3	11	28800	32000
30		TARTAN 3000	SLP	SA/RC	FBG	KL	IB	14D	UNIV	10	1	7950	5	2	30600	34000
30		TARTAN 3000 SHOAL	SLP	SA/RC	FBG	KC	IB	14D	UNIV	10	1	7950	3	4	31600	35100
33	1	TARTAN TEN	SLP	SA/RC	FBG	KL	IB	15D	YAN	9	3	6700	5	10	22100	24600
34	5	TARTAN 34	SLP	SA/RC	FBG	KL	IB	27D	YAN	10	11	11000	6	3	46200	50800
34	5	TARTAN 34 SHOAL	SLP	SA/RC	FBG	KL	IB	27D	YAN	10	11	11000	4	5	46200	50800
37	4	TARTAN 37	SLP	SA/CR	FBG	KL	IB	32D	UNIV	11	9	15500	6	7	66100	72600
37	4	TARTAN 37 SHOAL	SLP	SA/CR	FBG	KC	IB	32D	UNIV	11	9	15500	4	2	66100	72600
40	3	TARTAN 40	SLP	SA/RC	FBG	KL	IB	32D	UNIV	12	8	17800	7	6	82700	90900
40	3	TARTAN 40	SLP	SA/RC	FBG	KL	IB	44D	UNIV	12	8	17800	7	6	83100	91300
40	3	TARTAN 40	SLP	SA/RC	FBG	KL	IB	44D	WEST	12	8	17800	7	6	83200	91400
40	3	TARTAN 40 SHOAL	SLP	SA/RC	FBG	KC	IB	32D	UNIV	12	8	17800	4	9	82700	90900
40	3	TARTAN 40 SHOAL	SLP	SA/RC	FBG	KC	IB	44D	UNIV	12	8	17800	4	9	83100	91300
40	3	TARTAN 40 SHOAL	SLP	SA/RC	FBG	KC	IB	44D	WEST	12	8	17800	4	9	83200	91400
		1985 BOATS														
28	4	TARTAN 28	SLP	SA/CR	FBG	KL	IB	15D	YAN	9	10	7800	4	11	26700	29700
30		TARTAN 3000	SLP	SA/RC	FBG	KL	IB	14D	UNIV	10	1	7950	5	2	29100	32300
30		TARTAN 3000 SHOAL	SLP	SA/RC	FBG	KC	IB	14D	UNIV	10	1	7950	3	4	29100	32300
33	1	TARTAN TEN	SLP	SA/CR	FBG	KL	IB	15D	YAN	9	3	6700	5	10	20700	23000
34	5	TARTAN 34	SLP	SA/CR	FBG	KL	IB	24D	UNIV	10	11	10000	6	3	38900	43300
34	5	TARTAN 34 SHOAL	SLP	SA/CR	FBG	KL	IB	24D	UNIV	10	11	10000	4	5	38900	43300
37	4	TARTAN 37	SLP	SA/CR	FBG	KL	IB	32D	UNIV	11	9	15500	6	7	61800	67900
37	4	TARTAN 37 SHOAL	SLP	SA/CR	FBG	KC	IB	32D	UNIV	11	9	15500	4	2	61800	67900
40	3	TARTAN 40	SLP	SA/CR	FBG	KL	IB	40D	UNIV	12	8	17800	7	6	77600	85300
40	3	TARTAN 40 SHOAL	SLP	SA/CR	FBG	KC	IB	40D	UNIV	12	8	17800	4	9	77600	85300
		1984 BOATS														
28	4	TARTAN 28	SLP	SA/CR	FBG	KL	IB	15D	YAN	9	10	7800	4	11	25000	27700
30		TARTAN 3000	SLP	SA/RC	FBG	KC	IB	11D	UNIV	10	1	7950	5	2	27200	30200
33	1	TARTAN TEN	SLP	SA/RC	FBG	KL	IB	11D	UNIV	9	3	6700	5	10	19300	21500
33	8	TARTAN 33 SHOAL	SLP	SA/CR	FBG	KL	IB	24D	UNIV	11		10000	4	6	36300	40300
33	8	TARTAN 33R	SLP	SA/RC	FBG	KL	IB	24D	UNIV	11		9700	6	3	35200	39100
37	4	TARTAN 37	SLP	SA/CR	FBG	KL	IB	33D	WEST	11	9	15500	6	7	57900	63600
37	4	TARTAN 37 SHOAL	SLP	SA/CR	FBG	KC	IB	33D	WEST	11	9	15500	4	2	57900	63600
42		TARTAN 42	SLP	SA/CR	FBG	KL	IB	41D	WEST	12	3	22700	6	11	91100	100000
42		TARTAN 42 SHOAL	SLP	SA/CR	FBG	KL	IB	41D	WEST	12	3	22000	5		89400	98300

....For earlier years, see the BUC Used Boat Price Guide, Volume 3

TATOOSH MARINE

SEATTLE WA 98199

See inside cover to adjust price for area

LOA FT	LOA IN	NAME AND/ OR MODEL	TOP/ RIG	BOAT TYPE	HULL MTL	HULL TP	TP	# HP	MFG	BEAM FT	BEAM IN	WGT LBS	DRAFT FT	DRAFT IN	RETAIL LOW	RETAIL HIGH
		1985 BOATS														
33	11	PANDA 34	CUT	SA/CR	FBG	KL	IB	30D	UNIV	11		16500	5	6	82100	90200
37	7	PANDA 38	CUT	SA/CR	FBG	KL	IB	D		12		19000	5	10	97800	107500
39	10	PANDA 40	CUT	SA/CR	FBG	KL	IB	D		12	10	29000	6		143000	157000
39	10	PANDA 40	KTH	SA/CR	FBG	KL	IB	D		12	10	29000	6		143000	157000
41	10	TATOOSH 42	SCH	SA/CR	FBG	KL	IB	D		12	9	21500	5	10	125500	137500
50	7	TATOOSH 51	CUT	SA/CR	FBG	KL	IB	D		15	5	44000	6	4	255500	280500

TAYLOR BOATS

CUSHING OK 74023

See inside cover to adjust price for area

LOA FT	LOA IN	NAME AND/ OR MODEL	TOP/ RIG	BOAT TYPE	HULL MTL	HULL TP	TP	# HP	MFG	BEAM FT	BEAM IN	WGT LBS	DRAFT FT	DRAFT IN	RETAIL LOW	RETAIL HIGH
		1989 BOATS														
18	1	518 J		RNBT	FBG		JT	265		6	10	1950			4700	5400
18	1	518 WJ		RNBT	FBG		JT	265		6	10	1950			5400	6250
19	7	620 S		RNBT	FBG		SE	175		7	3	2730			5500	6300
20	2	720 J		RNBT	FBG		JT	330		7	4	1950			6550	7500
20	2	720 S		RNBT	FBG		SE	175		7	4	1950			5300	6050
20	2	820 J		RNBT	FBG		JT	330		7	4	1950			6250	7200
20	2	820 S		RNBT	FBG		SE	175		7	4	1950			5050	5850
23		923 S		RNBT	FBG		SE	260		6	5	2880			8050	9250
24	2	924 S		RNBT	FBG		SE	260		8		3450			9750	11100
24	2	925 S		RNBT	FBG		SE	260		8		3750			10300	11700
		1988 BOATS														
18	1	518 J		RNBT	FBG		JT	265		6	10	1950			4750	5450
18	1	518 WJ		RNBT	FBG		JT	265		6	10	1950			4900	5600
19	7	620 S		RNBT	FBG		SE	175		7	3	2730			5300	6100
20	2	720 J		RNBT	FBG		JT	330		7	4	1950			6200	7150
20	2	720 S		RNBT	FBG		SE	175		7	4	1950			5100	5900
20	2	820 J		RNBT	FBG		JT	330		7	4	1950			5950	6850
20	2	820 S		RNBT	FBG		SE	175		7	4	1950			4900	5650
23		923 S		RNBT	FBG		SE	260		6	5	2880			7800	8950
24	2	925 S		RNBT	FBG		SE	260		8		3750			10000	11400

TEAM SCARAB

VENTURA CA 93003

COAST GUARD MFG ID- TSC See inside cover to adjust price for area

LOA FT	LOA IN	NAME AND/ OR MODEL	TOP/ RIG	BOAT TYPE	HULL MTL	HULL TP	TP	# HP	MFG	BEAM FT	BEAM IN	WGT LBS	DRAFT FT	DRAFT IN	RETAIL LOW	RETAIL HIGH
		1991 BOATS														
50		SCARAB LONG RANGER		CR	FBG	DV	IO	10C	MRCR			15000			**	**
50		SCARAB LONG RANGER		CR	FBG	DV	IO	10C	VLVO			15000			**	**
50		SCARAB LONG RANGER		CR	FBG	DV	IO	10CD	CAT			15000			**	**

TECNOMAR SPA

PISA ITALY 56010

See inside cover to adjust price for area

For more recent years, see the BUC Used Boat Price Guide, Volume 1

LOA FT	LOA IN	NAME AND/ OR MODEL	TOP/ RIG	BOAT TYPE	HULL MTL	HULL TP	TP	# HP	MFG	BEAM FT	BEAM IN	WGT LBS	DRAFT FT	DRAFT IN	RETAIL LOW	RETAIL HIGH
		1990 BOATS														
36	8	BENETTI OFFSHORE 37	OP	OFF	FBG	DV	IO	T200D	VLVO	9	5	10600	1	8	50900	55900
40	9	BENETTI OFFSHORE 40	OP	OFF	FBG	DV	IB	T375D	CAT	9	7	15450	2	5	135000	148500
44	5	BENETTI OFFSHORE 45	OP	OFF	FBG	DV	IB	T425D	CAT	10		18100	3		151500	166500
49		BENETTI OFFSHORE 50	OP	OFF	FBG	DV	IB	T550D	GM	10		20300	3	9	209500	230000

TEMPEST YACHTS

S E Z MARINE
MIAMI BEACH FL 33280 COAST GUARD MFG ID- SZS

See inside cover to adjust price for area

LOA FT	LOA IN	NAME AND/ OR MODEL	TOP/ RIG	BOAT TYPE	HULL MTL	HULL TP	TP	# HP	MFG	BEAM FT	BEAM IN	WGT LBS	DRAFT FT	DRAFT IN	RETAIL LOW	RETAIL HIGH
		1992 BOATS														
42		TEMPEST 42	OP	SPTCR	FBG	SV	IB	T425D	CAT	13		17236	2	9	109000	120000
42		TEMPEST 42	OP	SPTCR	FBG	SV	IB	T550D	GM	13		17236	2	9	122500	134500
60		TEMPEST 60	OP	SPTCR	FBG	SV	IB	T10CD	CAT	16			3	6	306000	336000
74		TEMPEST 74	FB	MY	FBG	DS	IB	T10CD	CAT	19		90000	4		**	**
		1986 BOATS														
32	2	TEMPEST 32 EUROPA	OP	CR	FBG	DV	OB			8	2	6000	1	9	19100	21300
32	2	TEMPEST 32 SPORT	OP	SPTCR	FBG	DV	IB	T200-T330		8	2	6500	1	10	28800	35400
32	2	TEMPEST 32 SPORT	OP	SPTCR	FBG	DV	IO	T370	MRCR	8	2	6500	1	10	28000	31100
38		TEMPEST 38 SPORT	OP	SPTCR	FBG	DV	IB	T390	KAAM	9		8500	2	6	46500	51100
		IB T440 KAAM 47900 52600, IB T511 50200 55200, IB T540													51200	56300
		IB T330D 55900 61400, IB T355D CAT 59100 65000, IB R330D													62300	68500
43	6	TEMPEST 44 RIVIERA	OP	CR	FBG	DV	IB	T340	MRCR	9	6	15000	3	2	72800	80000
		IB T370 MRCR 73700 80900, IB T400 MRCR 75700 83200, IB T440 MRCR													79800	87700
		IB T D CAT ** ** , IB T355D CAT 87500 96200														
43	6	TEMPEST 44 SPORT	OP	SPTCR	FBG	DV	IB	T330	MRCR	9	6	14000	3	2	66100	72600

LOA FT IN	NAME AND/ OR MODEL	TOP/ RIG	BOAT TYPE	-HULL- MTL TP TP	----ENGINE--- # HP MFG	BEAM FT IN	WGT LBS	DRAFT FT IN	RETAIL LOW	RETAIL HIGH
--- 1986 BOATS ---
43 6	TEMPEST 44 SPORT	OP	SPTCR	FBG DV IB	T370 MRCR 9	6 14000	3 2	68500	75300
	IB T400 MRCR 70800	77800, IB	T440	MRCR	T420 81600, IB T	D CAT	**	**
	IB T355D CAT 81800	89900
43 6	TEMPEST MONTE CARLO	OP	CR	FBG DV IB	T340 MRCR 9	6 15000	3 2	66400	73200
	IB T370 MRCR 68200	75000, IB	T400	MRCR	T420 69400 76300, IB T440 MRCR	70700	77700
	IB T D CAT **	** , IB T355D CAT 82100	90200
43 6	TEMPEST MONTE CARLO	TT	CR	FBG DV IB	T340 MRCR 9	6 15000	3 2	71600	78700
	IB T370 MRCR 72700	79900, IB	T400	MRCR	T420 73900 81200, IB T440 MRCR	75900	83400
	IB T D CAT **	** , IB T355D CAT 87300	95900
43 6	TEMPEST SPORT FISH	OP	SF	FBG DV IB	T340 MRCR 9	6 16000	3 3	76000	83500
	IB T370 MRCR 77400	85000, IB	T400	MRCR	T420 79200 87000, IB T440 MRCR	82300	90400
	IB T D CAT **	** , IB T355D CAT 91200 100500
43 6	TEMPEST SPORT FISH	TT	SF	FBG DV IB	T340 MRCR 9	6 16000	3 3	78300	86100
	IB T370 MRCR 79400	87200, IB	T400	MRCR	T420 80600 88600, IB T440 MRCR	82700	90900
	IB T D CAT **	** , IB T355D CAT 93800 103000
--- 1985 BOATS ---
35 3	TEMPEST 35 SPORT		SPTCR	FBG DV IB	T340	8	8400		47400	52100
38 3	TEMPEST 38 SPORT	OP	SPTCR	FBG DV IB	T390 KAAM 9		8500	2 6	44700	49700
	IB T440 KAAM 46500	51100, IB		T511	48800 53600, IB T540		49800	54700
	IB T D CAT **	** , IB T330D	54200 59600, IB R330D		60600	66500
38 3	TEMPEST 38 TORNADO		SPTCR	FBG DV IB	T370	9	9200		50800	55800
43 6	TEMPEST 44		MY	FBG DV IB	T340	9	6 13500		68900	75700
43 6	TEMPEST 44		SF	FBG DV IB	T340	9	6 15000		72000	79100
43 6	TEMPEST 44 RIVIERA		CR	FBG DV IB	T340	9	6 14500		66000	72500
43 6	TEMPEST 44 RIVIERA	OP	CR	FBG DV IB	T340 MRCR 9	6 15000	3 2	66300	72800
	IB T370 MRCR 67500	74200, IB	T400	MRCR	T420 69100 76000, IB T440 MRCR	71700	78800
43 6	TEMPEST 44 SPORT	OP	SPTCR	FBG DV IB	T330 MRCR 9	6 14000	3 2	63000	69300
	IB T370 MRCR 65400	71900, IB	T400	MRCR	T420 67700 74400, IB T440 MRCR	71000	78100
	IB T D CAT **	** , IB T355D CAT 78000 85700
43 6	TEMPEST MONTE CARLO	OP	CTRCN	FBG DV IB	T340 MRCR 9	6 15000	3 2	71800	78900
	IB T370 MRCR 72500	79700, IB	T400	MRCR	T420 73300 80500, IB T440 MRCR	74500	81800
	IB T D CAT **	** , IB T355D CAT 85600 94100
43 6	TEMPEST MONTE CARLO	TT	CTRCN	FBG DV IB	T340 MRCR 9	6 15000	3 2	72300	79400
	IB T370 MRCR 72800	80100, IB	T400	MRCR	T420 73600 80800, IB T440 MRCR	74700	82100
	IB T D CAT **	** , IB T355D CAT 85800 94300
43 6	TEMPEST SPORT FISH	OP	SF	FBG DV IB	T340 MRCR 9	6 16000	3 3	72400	79600
	IB T370 MRCR 73800	81100, IB	T400	MRCR	T420 75600 83100, IB T440 MRCR	78700	86400
	IB T D CAT **	** , IB T355D CAT 87000 95600
43 6	TEMPEST SPORT FISH	TT	SF	FBG DV IB	T340 MRCR 9	6 16000	3 3	74600	82000
	IB T370 MRCR 75600	83000, IB	T400	MRCR	T420 76800 84400, IB T440 MRCR	78800	86600
	IB T D CAT **	** , IB T355D CAT 89300 98200
53	TEMPEST 53 CANNES	OP	EXP	FBG DV IB	D GM 15		32000	3	**	**
--- 1984 BOATS ---
35	TEMPEST 35 SPORT		SPTCR	FBG	IO T340	MRCR			38800	43100
38	TEMPEST 38 TORNADO		SPTCR	FBG	IO T370	MRCR			27800	30800
38	TEMPEST 38 TORNADO		SPTCR	FBG	IO T400	MRCR			29200	32400
43 6	TEMPEST 44	TT	SF	FBG DV IB	T340 MRCR 9	6 17000	3 4	83700	91900
43 6	TEMPEST 44	TT	SF	FBG DV IB	T355D CAT 9	6 17000	3 4	87000	95600
43 6	TEMPEST 44 OPEN FISH	OP	SF	FBG DV IB	T340 MRCR 9	6 17000	3 4	70400	77300
	IB T370 MRCR 71400	78400, IB	T400	MRCR	T420 72700 79900, IB T440 MRCR	74900	82400
	IB T300D CAT 80800	88700, IB T336D			CAT 82800 91000
43 6	TEMPEST 44 RIVIERA	OP	CR	FBG DV IB	T340 MRCR 9	6 15000	3 2	63200	69400
	IB T370 MRCR 64500	70800, IB	T400	MRCR	T420 66000 72600, IB T440 MRCR	68600	75400
	IB T300D CAT 73500	80800, IB T355D			CAT 77000 84600
43 6	TEMPEST 44 SPORT	OP	SPTCR	FBG DV IB	T330 MRCR 9	6 14000	3	60200	66100
	IB T370 MRCR 62500	68700, IB	T400	MRCR	T420 64800 71200, IB T440 MRCR	68000	74800
	IB T300D CAT 70500	77500, IB T355D			CAT 74500 81800

....For earlier years, see the BUC Used Boat Price Guide, Volume 3

THEURER SERVICES
CRAMCO INC
NEWARK NJ 07101
See inside cover to adjust price for area

LOA FT IN	NAME AND/ OR MODEL	TOP/ RIG	BOAT TYPE	-HULL- MTL TP TP	----ENGINE--- # HP MFG	BEAM FT IN	WGT LBS	DRAFT FT IN	RETAIL LOW	RETAIL HIGH
--- 1984 BOATS ---
18 6	SMALL-BEARD	SLP	SAIL	MHG CB		5 11	700	3	6000	6850
18 6	SMALL-BEARD 19	SLP	SAIL	WD CB OB		5 11	700		6000	6850
19 4	OYSTER	OP	LNCH	MHG DS IB	10D RUG	6 10	1100	2	8450	9700
19 4	OYSTER 20	OP	LNCH	WD RB IB	10D	6 10	1100		8450	9700

....For earlier years, see the BUC Used Boat Price Guide, Volume 3

THOMAS MARINE INC
ARLINGTON HEIGHTS IL 60005
See inside cover to adjust price for area

For more recent years, see the BUC Used Boat Price Guide, Volume 1

LOA FT IN	NAME AND/ OR MODEL	TOP/ RIG	BOAT TYPE	-HULL- MTL TP TP	----ENGINE--- # HP MFG	BEAM FT IN	WGT LBS	DRAFT FT IN	RETAIL LOW	RETAIL HIGH
--- 1996 BOATS ---
35 6	T 35	SLP	SACAC	FBG KL IB	28D YAN	11 6	9800	6 10	72000	79100
35 6	T 35C	SLP	SACAC	FBG KL IB	28D YAN	11 6	11500	4 11	83700	92000
--- 1995 BOATS ---
35 6	T 35	SLP	SACAC	FBG KL IB	28D YAN	11 6	9800	6 10	67700	74400
35 6	T 35C	SLP	SACAC	FBG KL IB	28D YAN	11 6	11500	4 11	78800	86600
--- 1994 BOATS ---
35 6	T 35	SLP	SACAC	FBG KL IB	28D YAN	11 6	9800	6 10	63700	70000
35 6	T35C	SLP	SACAC	FBG KL IB	28D YAN	11 6	11500	4 11	74100	81400
--- 1993 BOATS ---
35 6	T35C	SLP	SACAC	FBG KL IB	28D YAN	11 6	11500	4 11	69700	76600
--- 1992 BOATS ---
35 6	T35C	SLP	SA/CR	FBG KL IB	28D YAN	11 6	11500	4 11	65600	72000

THOMPSON MARINE PRODUCTS INC
ST CHARLES MI 48655   COAST GUARD MFG ID- TMS See inside cover to adjust price for area

For more recent years, see the BUC Used Boat Price Guide, Volume 1

LOA FT IN	NAME AND/ OR MODEL	TOP/ RIG	BOAT TYPE	-HULL- MTL TP TP	----ENGINE--- # HP MFG	BEAM FT IN	WGT LBS	DRAFT FT IN	RETAIL LOW	RETAIL HIGH
--- 1996 BOATS ---
17 5	CALAE 1800	OP	RNBT	FBG DV OB	135-205	8	2225		4700	5750
17 5	FISHERMAN 180	OP	CTRCN	FBG DV OB					7000	8050
19 5	CALAE 2000	OP	RNBT	FBG DV IO	135-250	8 1	2400		5500	6850
19 5	CALAE 2000	OP	RNBT	FBG DV IO	265-280	8 1	2400		6250	7200
19 5	CARRARA 2000	OP	CUD	FBG DV IO	135-220	8 1	2300		5550	6850
20 4	FISHERMAN 210	OP	FSH	FBG DV IO	180-265	8 4	3400		8100	9900
20 4	FISHERMAN 210	OP	FSH	FBG DV IO	300 VLVO	8 4	3400		9250	10500
20 4	FISHERMAN 210	OP	FSH	FBG DV IO	135D VLVO	8 4	3400		11700	13400
20 4	FISHERMAN 210	HT	FSH	FBG DV IO	205-220	8 4	3400		7900	9500
21 4	CALAE 2100	OP	RNBT	FBG DV IO	135-280	8 6	2750		6800	8400
21 4	CARRARA 2200	OP	CUD	FBG DV IO	180-280	8 6	2750		7200	8800
23 8	FISHERMAN 240	OP	FSH	FBG DV IO	200D VLVO	8 4	4550		17300	19600
23 8	FISHERMAN 240	HT	FSH	FBG DV IO	180-265	8 4	4550		11800	14200
	IO 300 MRCR 11800	13400, IO 300-330			13300 15100, IO 150D VLVO	16600	18800
25 5	FISHERMAN 260	OP	FSH	FBG DV IO	T190-T250	10 2	6200		18100	20600
25 5	FISHERMAN 260	HT	FSH	FBG DV IO	235-350	10 2	6200		16600	20500
	IO 385-415 19000	21900, IO 150D-230D			22600 27000, IO T135-T235	17200	21200
	IO T250 MRCR 15000	17000, IO T250-T300			19400 21800
26 2	CALAE 2600	OP	RNBT	FBG DV IO	180-280	8 6	4325		11100	13800
	IO 300-350 12400	14700, IO 385			13700 16300, IO T135		12200	14200
26 2	CARRARA 2600	OP	CUD	FBG DV IO	180-280	8 6	4325		12100	14800
	IO 300 12700	15100, IO 330-350			13700 16000, IO 385		14900	17800
	IO T135 13300	15400
26 2	SANTA CRUZ 2600	OP	SPTCR	FBG DV IO	235-300	8 6	5200		13900	17200
	IO 330-350 15000	17500, IO 385			16200 19200, IO 150D-200D	15100	18400
27 11	SANTA CRUZ 2700	OP	SPTCR	FBG DV IO	300-385	10	7225		19400	23600
	IO 415 MRCR 21900	24300, IO 230D VLVO			23000 25500, IO T160-T280	20400	25200
	IO T300 23000	26000, IOT150D-T200D			25200 30300
29 6	TORRENT 2900	OP	RNBT	FBG DV IO	300 MRCR	8 6	6200		15200	17300

LOA FT	IN	NAME AND/ OR MODEL	TOP/ RIG	BOAT TYPE	HULL MTL	HULL TP	ENGINE TP	# HP	MFG	BEAM FT	BEAM IN	WGT LBS	DRAFT FT IN	RETAIL LOW	RETAIL HIGH
		1996 BOATS													
29	6	TORRENT 2900	OP	RNBT	FBG	DV	IO	300-415		8	6	6200		16800	21000
		IO 230D VLVO 17400 19800, IO T160-T250 17100 21300, IO T265-T350												19500	23200
		IO T385-T390 20100 25100, IO T230D VLVO 22600 25100													
31	9	SANTA CRUZ 3100	OP	CR	FBG	DV	IO	T235-T330		11	4	11200		33400	40100
31	9	SANTA CRUZ 3100	OP	CR	FBG	DV	IO	T200D-T230D		11	4	11200		40300	46400
33	2	SANTA CRUZ 3400	OP	CR	FBG	DV	IO	T250-T350		12		12500		34500	41700
33	2	SANTA CRUZ 3400	OP	CR	FBG	DV	IO	T385-T390		12		12500		38300	44300
33	2	SANTA CRUZ 3400	OP	CR	FBG	DV	IO	T200D-T230D		12		12500		43500	49600
		1995 BOATS													
16	4	HERITAGE 170	OP	B/R	FBG	DV	IO	135	VLVO	8		2025		3900	4550
17	5	CALAE 1800	OP	RNBT	FBG	DV	IO	135-185		8		2225		4450	5350
17	5	FISHERMAN 1800	OP	CTRCN	FBG	DV	OB							6650	7650
18	4	HERITAGE 190	OP	B/R	FBG	DV	OB			8		1300		6900	7900
19	5	CALAE 2000	OP	RNBT	FBG	DV	IO	135-235		8	1	2400		5150	6300
19	5	CARRARA 2000	OP	CUD	FBG	DV	IO	135-185		8	1	2300		5200	6250
20	4	FISHERMAN 210	OP	FSH	FBG	DV	OB			8	4	3400		12700	14500
20	4	FISHERMAN 210	OP	FSH	FBG	DV	IO	160-250		8	4	3400		7300	8900
		IO 255 VLVO 7950 9150, IO 135D VLVO 11000 12500, IO T135												8350	10100
20	4	FISHERMAN 210	HT	FSH	FBG	DV	OB			8	4	3750		12600	14300
20	4	FISHERMAN 210	HT	FSH	FBG	DV	IO	160-215		8	4	3750		7800	9350
20	4	FISHERMAN 210	HT	FSH	FBG	DV	IO	235-255		8	4	3750		8450	9750
20	4	FISHERMAN 210	HT	FSH	FBG	DV	IO	T135	MRCR	8	4	3750		8950	10200
21	4	CALAE 2100	OP	RNBT	FBG	DV	IO	160-235		8	6	2750		6150	7400
21	4	CALAE 2100	OP	RNBT	FBG	DV	IO	250-255		8	6	2750		6450	7750
21	4	CARRARA 2200	OP	CUD	FBG	DV	IO	160-235		8	6	2750		6450	7900
21	4	CARRARA 2200	OP	CUD	FBG	DV	IO	250-255		8	6	2750		6750	8150
23	1	DECK BOAT 2200	OP	RNBT	FBG	TH	IO	160-255		8	2	3400		7600	9450
23	8	FISHERMAN 240	OP	FSH	FBG	DV	OB			8	4	4325		21100	23400
23	8	FISHERMAN 240	OP	FSH	FBG	DV	IO	180-255		8	4	4325		10400	12500
		IO 300 11200 13200, IO 135D-185D 14600 17300, IO T135 MRCR												11500	13000
		IO T135 VLVO 11900 13600, IO T135D VLVO 18900 20900													
23	8	FISHERMAN 240	HT	FSH	FBG	DV	OB			8	4	4550		21600	24000
23	8	FISHERMAN 240	HT	FSH	FBG	DV	IO	180-255		8	4	4550		10800	13000
		IO 300 11600 13600, IO 135D-185D 15100 18100, IO T135 MRCR												11800	13400
		IO T135 VLVO 12300 14000, IO T135D VLVO 19300 21500													
23	8	FISHERMAN 240	FB	FSH	FBG	DV	OB			8	4	5850		23300	25900
23	8	FISHERMAN 240	FB	FSH	FBG	DV	IO	180-300		8	4	5850		13300	16500
		IO 135D-185D 18400 21200, IO T135 MRCR 14400 16400, IO T135 VLVO												14900	17000
		IO T135D VLVO 22300 24800													
25	5	FISHERMAN 260	OP	FSH	FBG	DV	OB			10	2	4600		23100	25600
25	5	FISHERMAN 260	OP	FSH	FBG	DV	IO	250-300		10	2	4600		12600	15300
		IO 185D VLVO 17100 19400, IO T135-T235 13200 16400, IOT135D-T185D												20600	25000
25	5	FISHERMAN 260	HT	FSH	FBG	DV	OB			10	2	6200		25600	28400
25	5	FISHERMAN 260	HT	FSH	FBG	DV	IO	190-300		10	2	6200		15000	18400
		IO 135D-185D 20800 23900, IO T135-T235 16000 19600, IOT135D-T185D												25100	29600
25	5	FISHERMAN 260	FB	FSH	FBG	DV	OB			10	2	6350		25700	28600
25	5	FISHERMAN 260	FB	FSH	FBG	DV	IO	225-300		10	2	6350		15500	18600
		IO 185D VLVO 22000 24400, IO T135-T225 16200 19900, IOT135D-T185D												25300	30000
26	2	CARRARA 2600	OP	CUD	FBG	DV	IO	180-255		8	6	4325		11100	13700
26	2	CARRARA 2600	OP	CUD	FBG	DV	IO	300		8	6	4325		12400	14400
26	2	CARRARA 2600	OP	CUD	FBG	DV	IO	T135		8	6	4325		12400	14400
26	2	SANTA CRUZ 2600	OP	SPTCR	FBG	DV	IO	135-255		8	6	5200		12100	15100
		IO 300 13600 15800, IO 185D VLVO 14800 16800, IO T135												13600	15800
27	11	SANTA CRUZ 2700	OP	SPTCR	FBG	DV	IO	215-300		10		7225		17400	21000
27	11	SANTA CRUZ 2700	OP	SPTCR	FBG	DV	IO	T160-T235		10		7225		19000	22400
27	11	SANTA CRUZ 2700	OP	SPTCR	FBG	DV	IO	T135D-T185D		10		7225		22900	27500
29	6	TORRENT 2900	OP	RNBT	FBG	DV	IO	300	MRCR	8	6	5500		14000	15900
29	6	TORRENT 2900	OP	RNBT	FBG	DV	IO	350-415		8	6	5500		15500	18400
29	6	TORRENT 2900	OP	RNBT	FBG	DV	IO	T160-T300		8	6	5500		15200	18700
31	9	SANTA CRUZ 3100	OP	CR	FBG	DV	IO	T230-T300		11	4	11200		30900	36400
31	9	SANTA CRUZ 3100	OP	CR	FBG	DV	IO	T185D	VLVO	11	4	11200		35700	39700
33	2	SANTA CRUZ 3400	OP	CR	FBG	DV	IO	T250-T300		12		12500		32800	37900
33	2	SANTA CRUZ 3400	OP	CR	FBG	DV	IO	T185D-T216D		12		12500		38500	45400
		1994 BOATS													
17	5	CALAE 1800	OP	RNBT	FBG	DV	IO	120-185		8		2225		4100	5000
19	5	CALAE 2000	OP	RNBT	FBG	DV	IO	120-235		8	1	2400		4950	5900
19	5	CARRARA 2000	OP	CUD	FBG	DV	IO	120-180		8	1	2525		5300	6100
20	4	FISHERMAN 210	OP	FSH	FBG	DV	OB			8	4	3400		12200	13800
20	4	FISHERMAN 210	OP	FSH	FBG	DV	IO	135-215		8	4	3400		6800	8050
		IO 225-255 7400 8550, IO 135D VLVO 10200 11600, IO T135-T185												7800	9600
20	4	FISHERMAN 210	HT	FSH	FBG	DV	OB			8	4	3750		12400	14100
20	4	FISHERMAN 210	HT	FSH	FBG	DV	IO	135-215		8	4	3750		7450	8900
		IO 225-255 8150 9350, IO 135D VLVO 10400 11800, IO T135												8450	10000
20	4	FISHERMAN 210 LINER	HT	FSH	FBG	DV	OB			8	4	3750		11700	13300
20	4	FISHERMAN 210 LINER	HT	FSH	FBG	DV	IO	135-250		8	4	3750		7050	8500
		IO 255 VLVO 7700 8850, IO 135D VLVO 10000 11400, IO T135-T185												8100	9300
21	4	CALAE 2100	OP	RNBT	FBG	DV	IO	135-235		8	6	2750		5700	7050
21	4	CARRARA 2200	OP	CUD	FBG	DV	IO	135-235		8	6	2750		6000	7300
21	4	DAYTONA 2300	OP	CUD	FBG	DV	IO	160-300		8	4	4400		8150	10200
23	1	DECK BOAT 2200	OP	RNBT	FBG	DV	IO	160-235		8	2	3400		6900	8300
23	8	FISHERMAN 240	OP	FSH	FBG	DV	OB			8	4	4325		20100	22400
23	8	FISHERMAN 240	OP	FSH	FBG	DV	IO	160-300		8	4	4325		9900	12300
23	8	FISHERMAN 240	OP	FSH	FBG	DV	IO	125D-185D		8	4	4325		13700	16200
23	8	FISHERMAN 240	OP	FSH	FBG	DV	IO	T135		8	4	4325		10700	12700
23	8	FISHERMAN 240	HT	FSH	FBG	DV	OB			8	4	4550		21200	23600
23	8	FISHERMAN 240	HT	FSH	FBG	DV	IO	180-255		8	4	4550		10300	12300
		IO 300 11000 13000, IO 135D-185D 14400 17100, IO T135												11200	13300
		IO T125D VLVO 18100 20200													
23	8	FISHERMAN 240	FB	FSH	FBG	DV	OB			8	4	5850		22300	24800
23	8	FISHERMAN 240	FB	FSH	FBG	DV	IO	180-300		8	4	5850		12400	15400
23	8	FISHERMAN 240	FB	FSH	FBG	DV	IO	135D-185D		8	4	5850		17000	20000
23	8	FISHERMAN 240	FB	FSH	FBG	DV	IO	T135-T250		8	4	5850		13400	16600
23	8	FISHERMAN 240 LINER	HT	FSH	FBG	DV	OB			8	4	4550		20100	22300
23	8	FISHERMAN 240 LINER	HT	FSH	FBG	DV	IO	180-255		8	4	4550		9850	12000
		IO 300 10600 12500, IO 135D-185D 13900 16600, IO T135												10800	12800
		IO T125D VLVO 17300 19700													
25	5	FISHERMAN 260	OP	FSH	FBG	DV	OB			10	2	4600		22000	24500
25	5	FISHERMAN 260	OP	FSH	FBG	DV	IO	205-255		10	2	4600		11300	13600
		IO 300 12200 14300, IO 185D VLVO 15900 18100, IO T135-T205												12300	15000
		IO T215-T235 14900 16900, IOT135D-T185D 19400 23600													
25	5	FISHERMAN 260	HT	FSH	FBG	DV	OB			10	2	4950		22700	25200
25	5	FISHERMAN 260	HT	FSH	FBG	DV	IO	205-255		10	2	4950		11900	14200
		IO 300 12800 14900, IO 185D VLVO 16800 19100, IO T135-T205												12900	15600
		IO T215-T235 14300 16200, IOT135D-T185D 20300 24500													
25	5	FISHERMAN 260	FB	FSH	FBG	DV	OB			10	2	6125		24300	27100
25	5	FISHERMAN 260	FB	FSH	FBG	DV	IO	205-300		10	2	6125		13800	17000
		IO 185D VLVO 20100 22300, IO T135-T215 14800 18300, IO T225-T235												17100	19500
		IOT125D-T145D 22900 26200													
26	2	CARRARA 2600	OP	CUD	FBG	DV	IO	180-250		8	6	4325		10400	12700
26	2	CARRARA 2600	OP	CUD	FBG	DV	IO	300		8	6	4325		11600	13500
26	2	CARRARA 2600	OP	CUD	FBG	DV	IO	T135		8	6	4325		11600	13400
26	2	SANTA CRUZ 2600	OP	SPTCR	FBG	DV	IO	160-255		8	6	5200		11400	14100
		IO 300 12700 14700, IO 185D VLVO 13800 15700, IO T135												12700	14800
27	11	SANTA CRUZ 2700	OP	CBNCR	FBG	DV	IO	250	MRCR	10		7225		20300	22600
27	11	SANTA CRUZ 2700	OP	SPTCR	FBG	DV	IO	190-300		10		7225		15900	19300
		IO T115-T205 16600 20500, IO T215-T235 18800 21000, IOT135D-T185D												21400	25800
28	7	ADVENTURER 2900	FB	CBNCR	FBG	DV	IO	T260	MRCR	11		9200		26200	29100
28	7	ADVENTURER 2900	FB	CBNCR	FBG	DV	IO	T195D	VLVO	11		9200		37600	41700
31	9	SANTA CRUZ 3100	OP	CR	FBG	DV	IO	T160-T300		11	4	11200		29400	36100
31	9	SANTA CRUZ 3100	OP	CR	FBG	DV	IO	T185D	VLVO	11	4	11200		35500	39500
33	2	SANTA CRUZ 3400	OP	CR	FBG	DV	IO	T180-T330		12		12500		34900	42500
33	2	SANTA CRUZ 3400	OP	CR	FBG	DV	IO	T185D-T216D		12		12500		40800	46700
		1993 BOATS													
17	5	CALAE 1800	OP	RNBT	FBG	DV	IO	115-185		8		2225		3800	4700
17	5	CALAE 1800	OP	RNBT	FBG	DV	IO	205-210		8		2225		4100	4800
19	5	CALAE 2000	OP	RNBT	FBG	DV	IO	115-260		8	1	2400		4500	5550
19	5	CALAE 2000	OP	RNBT	FBG	DV	IO	275	VLVO	8	1	2400		5200	5950
19	5	CARRARA 2000	OP	CUD	FBG	DV	IO	115-225		8	1	2525		4750	5900
20	4	FISHERMAN 210	OP	FSH	FBG	DV	IO	115-270		8	4	3400		6350	7750
		IO 275 VLVO 7100 8200, IO 115D VLVO 9400 10700, IO T115-T146												7300	8850
20	4	FISHERMAN 210	HT	FSH	FBG	DV	IO	115-270		8	4	3750		6600	8050
		IO 275 VLVO 7400 8500, IO 115D VLVO 9250 10500, IO T115-T146												8050	9700
20	4	FISHERMAN 210 LINER	HT	FSH	FBG	DV	IO	115-270		8	4	3750		6950	8400
		IO 275 VLVO 7700 8850, IO 115D VLVO 9500 10800, IO T115-T135												7400	9050

CONTINUED ON NEXT PAGE

LOA FT	IN	NAME AND/ OR MODEL	TOP/ RIG	BOAT TYPE	-HULL- MTL	TP	ENGINE TP	# HP	MFG	BEAM FT	IN	WGT LBS	DRAFT FT	IN	RETAIL LOW	RETAIL HIGH
		1993 BOATS														
20	4	FISHERMAN 210 LINER	HT	FSH	FBG	DV	IO	T146	VLVO	8	4	3750			8300	9550
21	4	CALAE 2100	OP	RNBT	FBG	DV	IO	115-260		8	6	2750			5350	6550
21	4	CALAE 2100	OP	RNBT	FBG	DV	IO	275	VLVO	8	6	2750			6050	6950
21	4	CARRARA 2200	OP	CUD	FBG	DV	IO	115-260		8	6	2750			5600	6900
21	4	CARRARA 2200	OP	CUD	FBG	DV	IO	275	VLVO	8	6	2750			6350	7300
21	4	DAYTONA 2300	OP	CUD	FBG	DV	IO	155-270		8	4	4400			7650	9200
21	4	DAYTONA 2300	OP	CUD	FBG	DV	IO	275-300		8	4	4400			8350	9600
21	4	DAYTONA 2300	OP	CUD	FBG	DV	IO	330-370		8	4	4400			9300	10800
23	1	DECK BOAT 2200	OP	RNBT	FBG	DV	IO	155-260		8	2	3400			6450	7850
23	1	DECK BOAT 2200	OP	RNBT	FBG	DV	IO	275	VLVO	8	2	3400			7150	8200
23	8	FISHERMAN 240	OP	FSH	FBG	DV	IO	155-300		8	4	4325			9100	11100
		IO 330-370 10700 12400, IO 200D VLVO 13600 15400, IO T115-T146													10000	11900
		IO T130D VLVO 16200 18400														
23	8	FISHERMAN 240	HT	FSH	FBG	DV	IO	155-300		8	4	4550			9200	11300
		IO 330-370 10800 12600, IO 200D VLVO 13800 15600, IO T115-T146													10100	12000
		IO T130D VLVO 16300 18500														
23	8	FISHERMAN 240 LINER	HT	FSH	FBG	DV	IO	155-225		8	4	4550			9550	11300
		IO 230-370 11100 13500, IO 200D VLVO 14200 16100, IO T115-T146													10500	12400
		IO T130D VLVO 16700 18900														
23	8	FISHERMAN 240 LINER	FB	FSH	FBG	DV	IO	155-300		8	4	5850			11600	14000
		IO 330-370 13200 15300, IO 200D VLVO 16600 18900, IO T115-T146													12500	14800
		IO T130D VLVO 19500 21700														
25	5	FISHERMAN 260	OP	FSH	FBG	DV	IO	175-300		10	2	4600			10400	12900
		IO 330-370 12200 14300, IO 200D VLVO 15200 17200, IO T115-T200													11400	13800
		IO T205-T260 12200 14600, IO T275 VLVO 13600 15500, IOT130D-T200D													18100	22600
25	5	FISHERMAN 260	HT	FSH	FBG	DV	IO	175-300		10	2	4950			10900	13600
		IO 330-370 12700 14900, IO T115-T210 11900 14800, IO T225-T275													13200	16000
		IOT130D-T200D 18900 23400														
25	5	FISHERMAN 260	FB	FSH	FBG	DV	IO	175-300		10	2	6125			12700	15600
		IO 330-370 14500 16800, IO 200D VLVO 19200 21300, IO T115-T260													13600	17000
		IO T275 VLVO 15800 18000, IOT130D-T200D 21600 26400														
26	2	CARRARA 2600	OP	CUD	FBG	DV	IO	155-260		8	6	4325			9500	11800
26	2	CARRARA 2600	OP	CUD	FBG	DV	IO	270-275		8	6	4325			10500	12200
26	2	CARRARA 2600	OP	CUD	FBG	DV	IO	T130-T146		8	6	4325			10700	12700
26	2	SANTA CRUZ 2600	OP	SPTCR	FBG	DV	IO	155-275		8	6	5200			10600	13200
26	2	SANTA CRUZ 2600	OP	SPTCR	FBG	DV	IO	300-370		8	6	5200			11900	14700
26	2	SANTA CRUZ 2600	OP	SPTCR	FBG	DV	IO	200D	VLVO	8	6	5200			13200	15000
27	11	SANTA CRUZ 2700	OP	SPTCR	FBG	DV	IO	180-300		10		7225			14700	18100
		IO 330-370 16500 19200, IO T115-T205 15500 19400, IO T210-T275													17100	20700
		IOT130D-T200D 19900 24600														
28	7	ADVENTURER 2900	FB	CBNCR	FBG	DV	IO	T200-T275		11		9200			24300	27600
31	9	SANTA CRUZ 3100	OP	CR	FBG	DV	IO	T175-T330		11	4	11200			27700	34300
31	9	SANTA CRUZ 3100	OP	CR	FBG	DV	IO	T370	OMC	11	4	11200			31500	35000
31	9	SANTA CRUZ 3100	OP	CR	FBG	DV	IO	T200D	VLVO	11	4	11200			33400	37100
33	2	SANTA CRUZ 3400	OP	CR	FBG	DV	IO	T175-T330		12		12500			32500	40000
33	2	SANTA CRUZ 3400	OP	CR	FBG	DV	IO	T370	OMC	12		12500			36700	40700
33	2	SANTA CRUZ 3400	OP	CR	FBG	DV	IO	T250D	VLVO	12		12500			40100	44600
		1992 BOATS														
17	5	CALAE 1800	OP	RNBT	FBG	DV	IO	115-185		8		2225			3550	4400
17	5	CALAE 1800	OP	RNBT	FBG	DV	IO	205-210		8		2225			3850	4500
19	5	CALAE 2000	OP	RNBT	FBG	DV	IO	115-210		8	1	2400			4150	5150
19	5	CALAE 2000	OP	RNBT	FBG	DV	IO	225-275		8	1	2400			4550	5550
19	5	CARRARA 2000	OP	CUD	FBG	DV	IO	115-260		8	1	2525			4450	5500
19	5	CARRARA 2000	OP	CUD	FBG	DV	IO	275	VLVO	8	1	2525			5150	5900
19	8	FISHERMAN 200	OP	FSH	FBG	DV	IO	115-260		8	4	2525			4850	6000
19	8	FISHERMAN 200	OP	FSH	FBG	DV	IO	275	VLVO	8	4	2525			5600	6450
20	4	FISHERMAN 210	OP	FSH	FBG	DV	IO	115-270		8	4	3400			5900	7250
20	4	FISHERMAN 210	OP	FSH	FBG	DV	IO	275	VLVO	8	4	3400			6650	7650
20	4	FISHERMAN 210	OP	FSH	FBG	DV	IO	T115-T146		8	4	3400			6800	8300
20	4	FISHERMAN 210	HT	FSH	FBG	DV	IO	115-270		8	4	3750			6100	7500
20	4	FISHERMAN 210	HT	FSH	FBG	DV	IO	275	VLVO	8	4	3750			6850	7900
20	4	FISHERMAN 210	HT	FSH	FBG	DV	IO	T115-T146		8	4	3750			7050	8550
20	4	FISHERMAN 210 LINER	HT	FSH	FBG	DV	IO	115-270		8	4	3750			6550	7950
20	4	FISHERMAN 210 LINER	HT	FSH	FBG	DV	IO	275	VLVO	8	4	3750			7300	8350
20	4	FISHERMAN 210 LINER	HT	FSH	FBG	DV	IO	T115-T146		8	4	3750			7450	9000
21	4	CALAE 2100	OP	RNBT	FBG	DV	IO	115-260		8	6	2750			5000	6150
21	4	CALAE 2100	OP	RNBT	FBG	DV	IO	275	VLVO	8	6	2750			5650	6500
21	4	CARRARA 2100	OP	CUD	FBG	DV	IO	115-260		8	6	2750			5200	6350
21	4	CARRARA 2100	OP	CUD	FBG	DV	IO	275	VLVO	8	6	2750			5850	6750
21	4	CARRARA 2200	OP	CUD	FBG	DV	IO	115-260		8	6	2750			5300	6550
21	4	CARRARA 2200	OP	CUD	FBG	DV	IO	275	VLVO	8	6	2750			6050	6950
21	4	DAYTONA 2300	OP	CUD	FBG	DV	IO	155-275		8	4	4400			7150	8850
21	4	DAYTONA 2300	OP	CUD	FBG	DV	IO	300	MRCR	8	4	4400			7800	8950
21	4	DAYTONA 2300	OP	CUD	FBG	DV	IO	330-370		8	4	4400			8600	10200
23	4	CARRARA 2300	OP	CUD	FBG	DV	IO	115-260		8	4	3250			6350	7700
23	4	CARRARA 2300	OP	CUD	FBG	DV	IO	275	VLVO	8	4	3250			7050	8100
23	8	FISHERMAN 240	OP	FSH	FBG	DV	IO	155-300		8	4	4325			8400	10500
		IO 330-370 10000 11600, IO 200D VLVO 12700 14500, IO T115-T146													9400	11100
		IO T130D VLVO 15200 17200														
23	8	FISHERMAN 240	HT	FSH	FBG	DV	IO	155-300		8	4	4550			8450	10600
		IO 330-370 10000 11700, IO 200D VLVO 14800 16800, IO T115-T146													9400	11100
		IO T130D VLVO 15200 17300														
23	8	FISHERMAN 240 LINER	HT	FSH	FBG	DV	IO	155-300		8	4	4550			9100	11100
		IO 330-370 10600 12300, IO 200D VLVO 11400 12900, IO T115-T146													9900	11700
		IO T130D VLVO 15700 17800														
23	8	FISHERMAN 240 LINER	FB	FSH	FBG	DV	IO	155-300		8	4	5850			10800	13100
		IO 330-370 12400 14300, IO 200D VLVO 15600 17700, IO T115-T146													11700	13800
		IO T130D VLVO 18400 20500														
25	5	FISHERMAN 260	OP	FSH	FBG	DV	IO	175-275		10	2	4600			9750	11900
		IO 300-370 10700 13400, IO 200D VLVO 14200 16100, IO T115-T200													10600	13000
		IO T205-T260 11400 13600, IO T275 VLVO 12800 14500, IO T130D VLVO													16600	18900
		IO T200D VLVO 19200 21300														
25	5	FISHERMAN 260	HT	FSH	FBG	DV	IO	175-300		10	2	4950			10200	12700
		IO 330-370 11900 13900, IO T115-T210 11100 13900, IO T225-T275													12400	15000
		IO T130D VLVO 17300 19700, IO T200D VLVO 19700 21900														
25	5	FISHERMAN 260	FB	FSH	FBG	DV	IO	175-300		10	2	6125			11900	14600
		IO 330-370 13500 15700, IO 200D VLVO 17600 20000, IO T115-T260													12800	15900
		IO T275 VLVO 14800 16800, IOT130D-T200D 20200 24700														
26	2	CARRARA 2600	OP	CUD	FBG	DV	IO	155-270		8	6	4325			8950	11100
26	2	CARRARA 2600	OP	CUD	FBG	DV	IO	275	VLVO	8	6	4325			10000	11400
26	2	SANTA CRUZ 2600	OP	SPTCR	FBG	DV	IO	155-275		8	6	5200			9950	12400
26	2	SANTA CRUZ 2600	OP	SPTCR	FBG	DV	IO	300-370		8	6	5200			11100	13800
26	2	SANTA CRUZ 2600	OP	SPTCR	FBG	DV	IO	200D	VLVO	8	6	5200			12300	14000
27	1	SANTA CRUZ 2700	OP	SPTCR	FBG	DV	IO	180-300		10	1	7225			13300	16300
		IO 330-370 14900 17400, IO T115-T210 14100 17500, IO T225-T275													15600	18700
		IOT130D-T200D 18700 22800														
28	7	ADVENTURER 2900	FB	CBNCR	FBG	DV	IO	T200-T275		11		9200			22800	25800
30	7	SANTA CRUZ 3100	OP	CBNCR	FBG	DV	IO	T175-T370		11	4	11200			27500	33500
30	7	SANTA CRUZ 3100	OP	CBNCR	FBG	DV	IO	T200D	VLVO	11	4	11200			37700	41900
33	2	SANTA CRUZ 3400	OP	CR	FBG	DV	IO	T175-T330		12		12500			30400	37400
33	2	SANTA CRUZ 3400	OP	CR	FBG	DV	IO	T370	OMC	12		12500			34200	38000
33	2	SANTA CRUZ 3400	OP	CR	FBG	DV	IO	T250D	VLVO	12		12500			37300	41500
		1991 BOATS														
17		CUTLASS 170 BR	OP	RNBT	FBG	DV	IO	115-180		8		2025	1	3	3100	3650
17	8	CUTLASS 180 BR	OP	RNBT	FBG	DV	IO	115-180		8		2150	1	6	3350	3900
18	3	CALAE 175 BR	OP	RNBT	FBG	DV	IO	115-180		8		2225			3500	4100
19	2	CUTLASS 190 BR	OP	RNBT	FBG	DV	OB			8		2200	1	8	8250	9500
19	2	CUTLASS 190 BR	OP	RNBT	FBG	DV	IO	115-230		8		2200	1	8	3650	4400
19	2	CUTLASS 190 CB	OP	RNBT	FBG	DV	OB			8		2200	1	8	8250	9500
19	2	CUTLASS 190 CB	OP	RNBT	FBG	DV	IO	115-230		8		2200	1	8	3650	4400
20	3	CALAE 195 BR	OP	RNBT	FBG	DV	IO	115-230		8	1	2400			4000	4850
20	8	CARRARA 200	OP	CUD	FBG	DV	IO	115-230		8	4	2525	2		4550	5400
22		FISHERMAN 210	OP	FSH	FBG	DV	IO	115-240		8	4	3400			5900	7050
22		FISHERMAN 210	OP	FSH	FBG	DV	IO	T115-T135		8	4	3400			6750	7800
22		FISHERMAN 210	HT	FSH	FBG	DV	IO	115-240		8	4	3750			6350	7550
22		FISHERMAN 210	HT	FSH	FBG	DV	IO	T115-T135		8	4	3750			7200	8300
22		FISHERMAN 210 LINER	OP	FSH	FBG	DV	IO	115-240		8	4	3400			6200	7350
22		FISHERMAN 210 LINER	OP	FSH	FBG	DV	IO	T115-T135		8	4	3400			7000	8050
22		FISHERMAN 210 LINER	HT	FSH	FBG	DV	IO	115-240		8	4	3750			6600	7800
22		FISHERMAN 210 LINER	HT	FSH	FBG	DV	IO	T115-T135		8	4	3750			7450	8550
22	5	CALAE 205 BR	OP	RNBT	FBG	DV	IO	115-230		8	6	2750			4900	5800
22	5	CARRARA 205	OP	CUD	FBG	DV	IO	115-230		8	6	2750			5200	6150
23		CARRARA 220	OP	CUD	FBG	DV	IO	115-230		8		3250	2	1	5600	6650
23		CARRARA 220 LINER	OP	CUD	FBG	DV	IO	115-230		8		3250	2	1	5950	6950
23		DAYTONA 225	OP	CUD	FBG	DV	IO	155-300		8		4400			7200	9000
25		FISHERMAN 240	OP	FSH	FBG	DV	IO	155	MRCR	8	4	4325			8050	9250

CONTINUED ON NEXT PAGE

LOA FT	LOA IN	NAME AND/ OR MODEL	TOP/ RIG	BOAT TYPE	-HULL- MTL	-HULL- TP	ENGINE TP	ENGINE # HP	ENGINE MFG	BEAM FT	BEAM IN	WGT LBS	DRAFT FT	DRAFT IN	RETAIL LOW	RETAIL HIGH
		1991 BOATS														
25		FISHERMAN 240	OP	FSH	FBG	DV	IO	175-300		8	4	4325			9500	10900
		IO 200D VLVO 12200 13900, IO T115-T135 9050 10400, IO T130D VLVO													14700	16700
25		FISHERMAN 240	HT	FSH	FBG	DV	IO	155-240		8	4	4550			8550	10300
		IO 300 MRCR 9550 10800, IO 200D VLVO 12900 14600, IO T115-T135													9500	10900
		IO T130D VLVO 15200 17200														
25		FISHERMAN 240	FB	FSH	FBG	DV	IO	155-300		8	4	5850			10400	12800
		IO 200D VLVO 15600 17700, IO T115-T135 11300 13000, IO T130D VLVO													18200	20200
25		FISHERMAN 240 LINER	OP	FSH	FBG	DV	IO	155-240		8	4	4325			8400	10100
		IO 300 MRCR 9400 10700, IO 130D VLVO 11300 12900, IO 200D VLVO													12600	14300
		IO T115-T135 9400 10800														
25	5	CARRARA 245	OP	CUD	FBG	DV	IO	155-240		8	4	4125	2	4	7700	9400
25	5	CARRARA 245	OP	CUD	FBG	DV	IO	300	MRCR	8	4	4125	2	4	8800	10000
25	5	DAYTONA 250	OP	CUD	FBG	DV	IO	155-240		8	6	4925			8700	10500
25	5	DAYTONA 250	OP	CUD	FBG	DV	IO	300	MRCR	8	6	4925			9700	11000
25	5	DAYTONA 250	OP	CUD	FBG	DV	IO	200D	VLVO	8	6	4925			11000	12500
25	5	DAYTONA 260	OP	CUD	FBG	DV	IO	230-300		10		6250	2	5	11100	13300
		IO T115-T230 11600 14100, IO T130D VLVO 15300 17300, IO T200D VLVO													16800	19100
25	5	FISHERMAN 260	OP	FSH	FBG	DV	IO	175-300		10	2	4600			9150	11400
		IO 200D VLVO 13300 15100, IO T115-T230 9950 12400, IO T130D VLVO													15600	17700
		IO T200D VLVO 17600 20000														
25	5	FISHERMAN 260	HT	FSH	FBG	DV	IO	175-300		10	2	4950			9600	11900
		IO 200D VLVO 14000 15900, IO T115-T230 10400 12900, IO T130D VLVO													16200	18400
		IO T200D VLVO 18600 20700														
25	5	FISHERMAN 260	FB	FSH	FBG	DV	IO	175-300		10	2	6125			11100	13700
		IO 200D VLVO 16500 18700, IO T115-T230 12000 14600, IOT130D-T200D													19100	23100
26	2	SANTA CRUZ 260	OP	CBNCR	FBG	DV	IO	155-300		8	6	5200			11400	14200
26	2	SANTA CRUZ 260	OP	CBNCR	FBG	DV	IO	200D	VLVO	8	6	5200			16400	18600
27	1	SANTA CRUZ 270	OP	CBNCR	FBG	DV	IO	230-300		10		7225			15500	18700
27	1	SANTA CRUZ 270	OP	CBNCR	FBG	DV	IO	T115-T230		10		7225			15900	19200
27	1	SANTA CRUZ 270	OP	CBNCR	FBG	DV	IO	T130D-T200D		10		7225			23400	27600
27	3	CARRARA 255	OP	CUD	FBG	DV	IO	155-240		8	6	4325			9150	11200
27	3	CARRARA 255	OP	CUD	FBG	DV	IO	300	MRCR	8	6	4325			10500	11900
29	2	ADVENTURE 288	FB	CBNCR	FBG	DV	IO	T260	MRCR	11		9200	2	8	22100	24600
29	2	ADVENTURE 288	FB	CBNCR	FBG	DV	IO	T200D	VLVO	11		9200	2	8	31300	34700
29	7	DAYTONA 300	OP	CBNCR	FBG	DV	IO	T155-T300		10	2	8650	2	6	20800	24500
29	7	DAYTONA 300	OP	CBNCR	FBG	DV	IO	T130D-T200D		10	2	8650	2	6	27300	33400
30	7	SANTA CRUZ 310	OP	CBNCR	FBG	DV	IO	T175-T300		11	4	11200			25800	30700
30	7	SANTA CRUZ 310	OP	CBNCR	FBG	DV	IO	T200D	VLVO	11	4	11200			35400	39300
33	2	SANTA CRUZ 330	OP	CBNCR	FBG	DV	IO	T230-T330		12		12500			33000	38200
33	2	SANTA CRUZ 330	OP	CBNCR	FBG	DV	IO	T200D	VLVO	12		12500			39500	43900
		1990 BOATS														
17		CUTLASS 170 BR	OP	RNBT	FBG	DV	IO	125-205		8		2050	1	3	2950	3500
17	8	CUTLASS 180 BR	OP	RNBT	FBG	DV	IO	125-205		8		2150	1	6	3150	3750
18	6	SIDEWINDER 18 SS	OP	SKI	FBG	DV	IO	175-230		7		1900	1	10	2750	3350
18	6	SIDEWINDER 18 SS	OP	SKI	FBG	DV	IO	260-270		7		1900	1	10	3000	3550
18	6	SIDEWINDER 18 SS	OP	SKI	FBG	DV	IO	300	MRCR	7		1900	1	10	3300	3850
19	2	CUTLASS 190 BR	OP	RNBT	FBG	DV	IO	125-145		8		2200	1	8	3450	4000
19	2	CUTLASS 190 BR	OP	RNBT	FBG	DV	IO	175-260		8		2200	1	8	3950	4600
19	2	CUTLASS 190 CB	OP	RNBT	FBG	DV	IO	125-260		8		2200	1	8	3450	4200
19	2	CUTLASS 190 OB	OP	RNBT	FBG	DV	OB			8		1175	1	8	5200	6000
20	3	CUTLASS 195	ST	RNBT	FBG	DV	IO	125-260		8		2400			3750	4650
20	8	CARRARA 200	ST	CUD	FBG	DV	IO	125-260		8		2525	2		4100	5100
20	8	CARRARA 200	ST	CUD	FBG	DV	IO	270	MRCR	8		2525	2		4500	5150
20	8	FISHERMAN 200 V	OP	FSH	FBG	DV	IO	125-260		8		2525			4400	5400
22		FISHERMAN 210	OP	FSH	FBG	DV	IO	125-270		8		3400			5500	6750
22		FISHERMAN 210	OP	FSH	FBG	DV	IO	T125-T145		8		3400			6300	7300
22		FISHERMAN 210 L	OP	FSH	FBG	DV	IO	125-270		8		3400			5850	7150
22		FISHERMAN 210 L	OP	FSH	FBG	DV	IO	T125-T145		8		3400			6600	7600
22		FISHERMAN 210 V	OP	FSH	FBG	DV	IO	125-270		8		3400			5450	6650
22		FISHERMAN 210 V	OP	FSH	FBG	DV	IO	T125-T145		8		3400			6250	7200
22	5	CARRARA 205	ST	CUD	FBG	DV	IO	125-270		8	6	2750			4900	6000
23		CARRARA 220	ST	CUD	FBG	DV	IO	125-270		8		3250	2	1	5450	6650
23		DAYTONA 225 SPL	OP	CUD	FBG	DV	IO	175-300		8		4400			6800	8450
25		ADVENTURER 240	OP	CBNCR	FBG	DV	IO	175-300		8		4400			9050	10900
25		ADVENTURER 240	OP	CBNCR	FBG	DV	IO	T145	MRCR	8		4400			9750	11100
25		FISHERMAN 240	OP	FSH	FBG	DV	IO	125-230		8		4325			7400	9050
		IO 260-300 8050 9700, IO T125-T145 8450 9850, IO T205-T260													9350	11200
25		FISHERMAN 240 L	OP	FSH	FBG	DV	IO	125-270		8		4325			8000	9950
25		FISHERMAN 240 L	OP	FSH	FBG	DV	IO	300	MRCR	8		4325			9050	10300
25		FISHERMAN 240 L	OP	FSH	FBG	DV	IO	T125-T260		8		4325			9050	11000
25		FISHERMAN 240 V	OP	FSH	FBG	DV	IO	125-230		8		4325			7300	8900
		IO 260-300 7950 9550, IO T125-T205 8300 10200, IO T260 MRCR													9500	10800
25	5	CARRARA 245	ST	CUD	FBG	DV	IO	175-270		8		4125	2	4	7250	9000
25	5	CARRERA 245	ST	CUD	FBG	DV	IO	300	MRCR	8		4125	2	4	8100	9350
25	5	CARRERA 245	ST	CUD	FBG	DV	IO	T125-T205		8		4125	2	4	8100	9950
25	5	CARRERA 245	ST	CUD	FBG	DV	IO	T260	MRCR	8		4125	2	4	9350	10600
25	5	DAYTONA 250	ST	CBNCR	FBG	DV	IO	175-270		8	6	4925			10100	12000
25	5	DAYTONA 250 SPL	OP	CUD	FBG	DV	IO	240-300		8	6	4925			8600	10400
26	5	DAYTONA 260 SPL	ST	CUD	FBG	DV	IO	240-300		10		6250	2	5	10800	12900
26	5	DAYTONA 260 SPL	ST	CUD	FBG	DV	IO	T125-T230		10		6250	2	5	11200	13900
26	5	DAYTONA 260 SPL	ST	CUD	FBG	DV	IO	T260	MRCR	10		6250	2	5	12600	14300
26	5	FISHERMAN 260 L	OP	FSH	FBG	DV	IO	205-300		10		4950			9850	12200
26	5	FISHERMAN 260 L	OP	FSH	FBG	DV	IO	T125-T205		10		4950			10500	12900
26	5	FISHERMAN 260 L	OP	FSH	FBG	DV	IO	T230-T260		10		4950			11700	13800
26	5	FISHERMAN 260 V	OP	FSH	FBG	DV	OB			10		4950			20700	23000
26	5	FISHERMAN 260 V	OP	FSH	FBG	DV	IO	205-300		10		4950			9650	11900
26	5	FISHERMAN 260 V	OP	FSH	FBG	DV	IO	T125-T145		10		4950			10300	12000
26	5	FISHERMAN 260 V	OP	FSH	FBG	DV	IO	T175-T260		10		4950			12700	14400
27	5	MORITZ 250	ST	CBNCR	FBG	DV	IO	175-300		8	6	5200			12000	14700
29	2	ADVENTURER 288	FB	CBNCR	FBG	DV	IO	T260-T330		11		9200	2	8	20800	23800
29	6	DAYTONA 270	ST	CUD	FBG	DV	IO	240-300		10		7225	2	5	12900	15300
29	6	DAYTONA 270	ST	CUD	FBG	DV	IO	T125-T205		10		7225	2	5	13200	16100
29	6	DAYTONA 270	ST	CUD	FBG	DV	IO	T230-T260		10		7225	2	5	14500	17000
29	7	DAYTONA 300 SPL	ST	CBNCR	FBG	DV	IO	T175-T300		10	2	8650	2	6	20100	23100
32	6	ST TROPEZ 310	ST	CBNCR	FBG	DV	IO	T200-T300		11		11200			28500	33000
33	2	SANTA CRUZ 330	ST	CBNCR	FBG	DV	IO	T240-T340		12		12500			31300	36100
		1989 BOATS														
17		CUTLASS 170BR	OP	RNBT	FBG	DV	IO	120-180		8		2050	1	3	2800	3250
17	8	CUTLASS 180BR	OP	RNBT	FBG	DV	IO	120-180		8		2150	1	6	2950	3500
17	8	SIDEWINDER 18SS	OP	SKI	FBG	DV	IO	165-230		7		1900	1	10	2450	3000
17	8	SIDEWINDER 18SS	OP	SKI	FBG	DV	IO	260-270		7		1900	1	10	2700	3200
18	9	SEA-RAGE 196	OP	CUD	FBG	DV	IO	120-230		7	4	2450	1	9	3250	3950
18	9	SEA-RAGE 196	OP	CUD	FBG	DV	IO	260	MRCR	7	4	2450	1	9	3550	4100
19	2	CUTLASS 190BR	OP	RNBT	FBG	DV	IO	120-230		8		2200	1	8	3250	3950
19	2	CUTLASS 190BR	OP	RNBT	FBG	DV	IO	260	MRCR	8		2200	1	8	3500	4050
19	2	CUTLASS 190CB	OP	RNBT	FBG	DV	IO	120-230		8		2200	1	8	3250	3950
19	2	CUTLASS 190CB	OP	RNBT	FBG	DV	IO	260	MRCR	8		2200	1	8	3500	4050
19	2	CUTLASS 190OB	OP	RNBT	FBG	DV	OB			8		1175	1	8	5000	5750
19	4	CUTLASS 195	ST	RNBT	FBG	DV	IO	120-230		8		2400			3400	4100
19	4	CUTLASS 195	ST	RNBT	FBG	DV	IO	260	MRCR	8		2400			3650	4250
20	8	CARRARA 200	ST	CUD	FBG	DV	IO	120-260		8		2525	2		3850	4800
21		CARRARA 205	ST	CUD	FBG	DV	IO	120-260		8	4	2625			4100	5100
22		FISHERMAN 210L	ST	FSH	FBG	DV	IO	165-230		8		3400	1	10	5300	6250
22		FISHERMAN 210L	HT	FSH	FBG	DV	IO	165-230		8		3750	1	10	5700	6700
23		CARRARA 220	ST	CUD	FBG	DV	IO	130-270		8		3250	2	1	5100	6250
23		DAYTONA 225	ST	CBNCR	FBG	DV	IO	165-270		8		4400	2	3	7200	8650
25		FISHERMAN 240L	ST	FSH	FBG	DV	IO	165-260		8		4400	2	1	7350	9000
25		FISHERMAN 240L	HT	FSH	FBG	DV	IO	165-260		8		4550	2	1	7550	9200
25	5	CARRARA 245	ST	CUD	FBG	DV	IO	165-270		8		4125	2	4	6800	8500
25	5	CARRARA 245	ST	CUD	FBG	DV	IO	330	MRCR	8		4125	2	4	8000	9200
25	5	DAYTONA 250	ST	CBNCR	FBG	DV	IO	165-270		8	6	4925			9400	11300
26	5	DAYTONA 260	ST	CUD	FBG	DV	IO	260-330		10		6250	2	5	10400	12500
26	5	DAYTONA 260	ST	CUD	FBG	DV	IO	T165-T260		10		6250	2	5	10900	13500
26	5	FISHERMAN 260L	HT	FSH	FBG	DV	IO	230-270		10		5100			9550	11200
26	5	FISHERMAN 260L	HT	FSH	FBG	DV	IO	330	MRCR	10		5100			10500	11900
26	5	FISHERMAN 260L	HT	FSH	FBG	DV	IO	T165-T230		10		5100			10400	12600
29	2	ADVENTURER 288	FB	CBNCR	FBG	DV	IB	T260-T330		11		9200	2	8	23900	26800
29	6	DAYTONA 270	ST	CUD	FBG	DV	IO	260-330		10		7225	2	5	12400	14700
29	6	DAYTONA 270	ST	CUD	FBG	DV	IO	T165-T260		10		7225	2	5	12900	16000
29	7	DAYTONA 300	ST	CBNCR	FBG	DV	IO	T165-T260		10	2	8650	2	6	18900	21500
31	9	DAYTONA 310	ST	CBNCR	FBG	DV	IO	T165-T260		10	2	8950	2	6	22400	25800
		1988 BOATS														
16	4	CUTLASS 170BR	OP	RNBT	FBG	DV	IO	120-180		8		2050	1	3	2550	2950
17	4	CUTLASS 180BR	OP	RNBT	FBG	DV	IO	120-180		8		2150	1	6	2750	3250
17	8	SIDEWINDER 18SS	OP	SKI	FBG	DV	OB			7		1075	1	10	4200	4900
17	8	SIDEWINDER 18SS	OP	SKI	FBG	DV	JT			7		1900	1	10	**	**
		IO MRCR ** **, IO 165-230 2350 2850, IO 260													2550	2950
18	4	CUTLASS 190BR	OP	RNBT	FBG	DV	IO	120-230		8		2200	1	8	2950	3550

96th ed. - Vol. II
CONTINUED ON NEXT PAGE
603

THOMPSON MARINE PRODUCTS INC -CONTINUED See inside cover to adjust price for area

LOA FT	IN	NAME AND/ OR MODEL	TOP/ RIG	BOAT TYPE	-HULL- MTL	TP	TP	---ENGINE--- # HP	MFG	BEAM FT	IN	WGT LBS	DRAFT FT	IN	RETAIL LOW	RETAIL HIGH
		1988 BOATS														
18	4	CUTLASS 190BR	OP	RNBT	FBG	DV	IO	260		8		2200	1	8	3200	3700
18	4	CUTLASS 190CB	OP	RNBT	FBG	DV	IO	120-230		8		2200	1	8	2950	3550
18	4	CUTLASS 190CB	OP	RNBT	FBG	DV	IO	260		8		2200	1	8	3150	3700
18	4	CUTLASS 190OB	OP	RNBT	FBG	DV	OB			8		1175	1	8	4750	5450
18	9	SEA-RAGE 196CC	OP	CUD	FBG	DV	IO		MRCR	7	4	2450	1	9	**	**
18	9	SEA-RAGE 196CC	OP	CUD	FBG	DV	IO	120-230		7	4	2450	1	9	3100	3750
18	9	SEA-RAGE 196CC	OP	CUD	FBG	DV	IO	260		7	4	2450	1	9	3350	3900
19	8	CARRERA 200	OP	RNBT	FBG	DV	IO		MRCR	8		2525	2		**	**
19	8	CARRERA 200	OP	RNBT	FBG	DV	IO	130-260		8		2525	2		3350	4200
20	4	FISHERMAN I 210	OP	FSH	FBG	DV	IO		MRCR	8		3600	1	10	**	**
20	4	FISHERMAN I 210	OP	FSH	FBG	DV	IO	120-260		8		3600	1	10	4750	5750
20	4	FISHERMAN I 210	OP	FSH	FBG	DV	IO	T120-T180		8		3600	1	10	5300	6200
20	4	FISHERMAN I 210	HT	FSH	FBG	DV	IO	120-260		8		3600	1	10	4750	5750
20	4	FISHERMAN I 210L	OP	FSH	FBG	DV	IO		MRCR	8		3600	1	10	**	**
20	4	FISHERMAN I 210L	OP	FSH	FBG	DV	IO	120-260		8		3250	1	10	4450	5400
20	4	FISHERMAN I 210L	OP	FSH	FBG	DV	IO	T120-T180		8		3600	1	10	5600	6500
20	4	FISHERMAN I 210L	HT	FSH	FBG	DV	IO	120-260		8		3500	1	10	4700	5650
20	4	SPORTSMAN 210S	OP	CUD	FBG	DV	IO		MRCR	8		3400	1	10	**	**
20	4	SPORTSMAN 210S	OP	CUD	FBG	DV	IO	120-260		8		3400	1	10	4350	5300
20	4	SPORTSMAN 210S	HT	CUD	FBG	DV	IO	120-260		8		3450	1	10	4400	5350
21	4	CARRERA 220	OP	RNBT	FBG	DV	IO		MRCR	8		3250	2	1	**	**
21	4	CARRERA 220	OP	RNBT	FBG	DV	IO	120-260		8		3250	2	1	4200	5150
21	4	CARRERA 220L	OP	RNBT	FBG	DV	IO		MRCR	8		3400	2	1	**	**
21	4	CARRERA 220L	OP	RNBT	FBG	DV	IO	120-260		8		3400	2	1	4350	5300
21	4	DAYTONA 225	OP	SPTCR	FBG	DV	IO			8		4400	2	3	**	**
		IO MRCR ** **, IO 120-260 5550 6650, IO 460 OMC													8700	10000
23	4	ADVENTURER 240A	HT	CR	FBG	DV	IO		MRCR	8		5325	2	1	**	**
23	4	ADVENTURER 240A	HT	CR	FBG	DV	IO	165-260		8		5325	2	1	7200	8550
23	4	ADVENTURER 240A	HT	CR	FBG	DV	IO	T120-T180		8		5325	2	1	7850	9100
23	4	ADVENTURER 240A	FB	CR	FBG	DV	IO		MRCR	8		5880	2	1	**	**
23	4	ADVENTURER 240A	FB	CR	FBG	DV	IO	165-260		8		5880	2	1	7850	9300
23	4	ADVENTURER 240A	FB	CR	FBG	DV	IO	T120-T180		8		5880	2	1	8500	9850
23	4	FISHERMAN II 240	OP	FSH	FBG	DV	IO		MRCR	8		4325	2	1	**	**
23	4	FISHERMAN II 240	OP	FSH	FBG	DV	IO	120-260		8		4325	2	1	6100	7400
23	4	FISHERMAN II 240	OP	FSH	FBG	DV	IO	T120-T180		8		4325	2	1	6850	8000
23	4	FISHERMAN II 240	HT	FSH	FBG	DV	IO		MRCR	8		4550	2	1	**	**
23	4	FISHERMAN II 240	HT	FSH	FBG	DV	IO	120-260		8		4550	2	1	6700	7700
23	4	FISHERMAN II 240	HT	FSH	FBG	DV	IO	T120-T180		8		4550	2	1	7100	8300
23	4	FISHERMAN II 240	FB	FSH	FBG	DV	IO		MRCR	8		5850	2	1	**	**
23	4	FISHERMAN II 240	FB	FSH	FBG	DV	IO	120-260		8		5850	2	1	8250	9450
23	4	FISHERMAN II 240	FB	FSH	FBG	DV	IO	T120-T180		8		5850	2	1	8650	10000
23	4	FISHERMAN II 240L	OP	FSH	FBG	DV	IO		MRCR	8		4325	2	1	**	**
23	4	FISHERMAN II 240L	OP	FSH	FBG	DV	IO	120-260		8		4325	2	1	6700	8000
23	4	FISHERMAN II 240L	OP	FSH	FBG	DV	IO	T120-T180		8		4325	2	1	7400	8550
23	4	FISHERMAN II 240L	HT	FSH	FBG	DV	IO		MRCR	8		4550	2	1	**	**
23	4	FISHERMAN II 240L	HT	FSH	FBG	DV	IO	165-260		8		4550	2	1	7000	8300
23	4	FISHERMAN II 240L	HT	FSH	FBG	DV	IO	T120-T180		8		4550	2	1	7650	8850
23	4	FISHERMAN II 240L	FB	FSH	FBG	DV	IO	165-260		8		5850	2	1	8600	10100
23	4	FISHERMAN II 240L	FB	FSH	FBG	DV	IO	T120-T180		8		5850	2	1	9350	10700
23	4	SPORTSMAN 240S	OP	CUD	FBG	DV	IO		MRCR	8		4100	2	1	**	**
23	4	SPORTSMAN 240S	OP	CUD	FBG	DV	IO	165-260		8		4100	2	1	5850	7000
23	4	SPORTSMAN 240S	OP	CUD	FBG	DV	IO	T120-T180		8		4100	2	1	6500	7550
23	4	SPORTSMAN 240S	HT	WKNDR	FBG	DV	IO	165-260		8		5325	2	1	7200	8550
23	4	SPORTSMAN 240S	HT	WKNDR	FBG	DV	IO	T120-T180		8		5325	2	1	7850	9100
23	4	SPORTSMAN 240S	FB	WKNDR	FBG	DV	IO	165-260		8		5850	2	1	7950	9450
23	4	SPORTSMAN 240S	FB	WKNDR	FBG	DV	IO	T120-T180		8		5850	2	1	8800	10100
23	7	VACATIONER EXP 246A	OP	EXP	FBG	DV	IO		MRCR	8		4550	2	1	**	**
23	7	VACATIONER EXP 246A	OP	EXP	FBG	DV	IO	165-260		8		4550	2	1	6450	7650
24	4	CARRERA 245	OP	RNBT	FBG	DV	IO		MRCR	8		4125	2	4	**	**
24	4	CARRERA 245	OP	RNBT	FBG	DV	IO	120-260		8		4125	2	4	5650	6900
24	4	CARRERA 245	OP	RNBT	FBG	DV	IO	T120-T180		8		4125	2	4	6350	7450
25	5	DAYTONA 260	OP	SPTCR	FBG	DV	IO		MRCR	10		6250	2	5	**	**
		IO 260 9500 10800, IO 460 OMC 12100 13800, IO T120-T230													9750	11900
		IO T260 10800 12200														
27	3	DAYTONA 270	OP	SPTCR	FBG	DV	IO		MRCR	9		7225	2	5	**	**
		IO 260 10700 12100, IO T120-T230 10900 13400, IO T260													12200	13900
27	3	DAYTONA 275	OP	SPTCR	FBG	DV	IO		MRCR	9		7225	2	5	**	**
		IO 260 11100 12600, IO T120-T230 11200 13900, IO T260													12600	14300
28	7	ADVENTURER 288	OP	EXP	FBG	DV	IB	T230-T260		11		9200	2	8	19200	21900
28	8	DAYTONA 300	OP	SPTCR	FBG	DV	IO		MRCR	10	2	8650	2	6	**	**
		IO 260 13200 15000, IO T MRCR ** **, IO T165-T260													13700	16800
31	2	DAYTONA 275	OP	SPTCR	FBG	DV	IO	460	OMC	9		7225	2	6	16000	18200
31	2	DAYTONA 275	OP	SPTCR	FBG	DV	IO	T120	MRCR	9		7225	2	6	14200	16100
31	2	DAYTONA 310	OP	SPTCR	FBG	DV	IO		MRCR	10	2	8950	2	6	**	**
		IO 260 15200 17300, IO 460 OMC 16800 19100, IO T165-T260													15800	19300
		1987 BOATS														
16	4	CUTLASS 165BR	OP	RNBT	FBG	DV	IO	120-180		8		2050			2400	2800
17	4	CUTLASS 175BR	OP	RNBT	FBG	DV	IO	120-180		8		2150			2600	3050
17	8	SIDEWINDER 18SS	OP	SKI	FBG	DV	OB			7		1075			4050	4700
17	8	SIDEWINDER 18SS	OP	SKI	FBG	DV	JT			7		1900			**	**
		IO MRCR ** **, IO 165-230 2200 2700, IO 260													2400	2800
18	4	CUTLASS 185BR	OP	RNBT	FBG	DV	IO	120-230		8		2200			2800	3400
18	4	CUTLASS 185BR	OP	RNBT	FBG	DV	IO	260		8		2200			3000	3500
18	4	CUTLASS 185CB	OP	RNBT	FBG	DV	IO	120-230		8		2200			2800	3350
18	4	CUTLASS 185CB	OP	RNBT	FBG	DV	IO	260		8		2200			3000	3500
18	4	CUTLASS 185OB	OP	RNBT	FBG	DV	OB			8		1175			4550	5250
18	9	SEA-RAGE 196CC	OP	CUD	FBG	DV	IO		MRCR	7	4	2450			**	**
18	9	SEA-RAGE 196CC	OP	CUD	FBG	DV	IO	120-230		7	4	2450			2900	3550
18	9	SEA-RAGE 196CC	OP	CUD	FBG	DV	IO	260		7	4	2450			3150	3700
19	8	CARRERA 198	OP	RNBT	FBG	DV	IO		MRCR	8		2525			**	**
19	8	CARRERA 198	OP	RNBT	FBG	DV	IO	130-260		8		2525			3200	4000
20	4	FISHERMAN I 210	OP	FSH	FBG	DV	IO		MRCR	8		3600			**	**
20	4	FISHERMAN I 210	OP	FSH	FBG	DV	IO	120-260		8		3600			4550	5500
20	4	FISHERMAN I 210	OP	FSH	FBG	DV	IO	T120-T180		8		3600			5050	5900
20	4	FISHERMAN I 210	HT	FSH	FBG	DV	IO	120-260		8		3600			4550	5500
20	4	FISHERMAN I 210L	OP	FSH	FBG	DV	IO		MRCR	8		3600			**	**
20	4	FISHERMAN I 210L	OP	FSH	FBG	DV	IO	120-260		8		3250			4200	5150
20	4	FISHERMAN I 210L	OP	FSH	FBG	DV	IO	T120-T180		8		3600			5350	6200
20	4	FISHERMAN I 210L	HT	FSH	FBG	DV	IO	120-260		8		3500			4450	5400
20	4	SPORTSMAN 210S	OP	CUD	FBG	DV	IO		MRCR	8		3400			**	**
20	4	SPORTSMAN 210S	OP	CUD	FBG	DV	IO	120-260		8		3400			4100	5050
20	4	SPORTSMAN 210S	HT	CUD	FBG	DV	IO	120-260		8		3450			4150	5100
21	4	CARRERA 215	OP	RNBT	FBG	DV	IO		MRCR	8		3250			**	**
21	4	CARRERA 215	OP	RNBT	FBG	DV	IO	120-260		8		3250			4000	4900
21	4	CARRERA 215L	OP	RNBT	FBG	DV	IO		MRCR	8		3400			**	**
21	4	CARRERA 215L	OP	RNBT	FBG	DV	IO	120-260		8		3400			4100	5050
23	4	ADVENTURER 240A	HT	CR	FBG	DV	IO		MRCR	8		5325			**	**
23	4	ADVENTURER 240A	HT	CR	FBG	DV	IO	165-260		8		5325			6850	8150
23	4	ADVENTURER 240A	HT	CR	FBG	DV	IO	T120-T180		8		5325			7450	8650
23	4	ADVENTURER 240A	FB	CR	FBG	DV	IO		MRCR	8		5880			**	**
23	4	ADVENTURER 240A	FB	CR	FBG	DV	IO	165-260		8		5880			7450	8850
23	4	ADVENTURER 240A	FB	CR	FBG	DV	IO	T120-T180		8		5880			8050	9350
23	4	FISHERMAN II 240	OP	FSH	FBG	DV	IO		MRCR	8		4325			**	**
23	4	FISHERMAN II 240	OP	FSH	FBG	DV	IO	120-260		8		4325			5800	7000
23	4	FISHERMAN II 240	OP	FSH	FBG	DV	IO	T120-T180		8		4325			6500	7600
23	4	FISHERMAN II 240	HT	FSH	FBG	DV	IO		MRCR	8		4550			**	**
23	4	FISHERMAN II 240	HT	FSH	FBG	DV	IO	120-260		8		4550			6350	7300
23	4	FISHERMAN II 240	HT	FSH	FBG	DV	IO	T120-T180		8		4550			6800	7900
23	4	FISHERMAN II 240	FB	FSH	FBG	DV	IO		MRCR	8		5850			**	**
23	4	FISHERMAN II 240	FB	FSH	FBG	DV	IO	120-260		8		5850			7850	9000
23	4	FISHERMAN II 240	FB	FSH	FBG	DV	IO	T120-T180		8		5850			8200	9550
23	4	FISHERMAN II 240L	OP	FSH	FBG	DV	IO		MRCR	8		4325			**	**
23	4	FISHERMAN II 240L	OP	FSH	FBG	DV	IO	120-260		8		4325			6400	7600
23	4	FISHERMAN II 240L	OP	FSH	FBG	DV	IO	T120-T180		8		4325			7050	8100
23	4	FISHERMAN II 240L	HT	FSH	FBG	DV	IO		MRCR	8		4550			**	**
23	4	FISHERMAN II 240L	HT	FSH	FBG	DV	IO	165-260		8		4550			6600	7850
23	4	FISHERMAN II 240L	HT	FSH	FBG	DV	IO	T120-T180		8		4550			7250	8400
23	4	FISHERMAN II 240L	FB	FSH	FBG	DV	IO	165-260		8		5850			8150	9600
23	4	FISHERMAN II 240L	FB	FSH	FBG	DV	IO	T120-T180		8		5850			8900	10100
23	4	SPORTSMAN 240S	OP	CUD	FBG	DV	IO		MRCR	8		4100			**	**
23	4	SPORTSMAN 240S	OP	CUD	FBG	DV	IO	165-260		8		4100			5550	6650
23	4	SPORTSMAN 240S	OP	CUD	FBG	DV	IO	T120-T180		8		4100			6150	7150
23	4	SPORTSMAN 240S	HT	WKNDR	FBG	DV	IO	165-260		8		5325			6850	8150
23	4	SPORTSMAN 240S	HT	WKNDR	FBG	DV	IO	T120-T180		8		5325			7500	8650
23	4	SPORTSMAN 240S	FB	WKNDR	FBG	DV	IO	165-260		8		5850			7600	8950
23	4	SPORTSMAN 240S	FB	WKNDR	FBG	DV	IO	T120-T180		8		5850			8250	9550
23	7	VACATIONER EXP 246A	OP	EXP	FBG	DV	IO		MRCR	8		4550			**	**
23	7	VACATIONER EXP 246A	OP	EXP	FBG	DV	IO	165-260		8		4550			6100	7300
24	4	CARRERA 245	OP	RNBT	FBG	DV	IO		MRCR	8		4125			**	**

CONTINUED ON NEXT PAGE

LOA FT	LOA IN	NAME AND/ OR MODEL	TOP/ RIG	BOAT TYPE	HULL MTL	HULL TP	ENGINE TP	ENGINE # HP	ENGINE MFG	BEAM FT	BEAM IN	WGT LBS	DRAFT FT	DRAFT IN	RETAIL LOW	RETAIL HIGH
		1987 BOATS														
24	4	CARRERA 245	OP	RNBT	FBG	DV	IO	120-260		8		4125			5400	6550
24	4	CARRERA 245	OP	RNBT	FBG	DV	IO	T120-T180		8		4125			6050	7100
27	3	DAYTONA 270	OP	SPTCR	FBG	DV	IO		MRCR	9		7225			**	**
		IO 260 10300 11800, IO T120-T230 10500 13000, IO T260													11800	13400
28	7	ADVENTURER 288	OP	EXP	FBG	DV	IB	T230-T260		11		9200			18500	21100
28	8	DAYTONA 290	OP	SPTCR	FBG	DV	IO		MRCR	10	2	8650			**	**
		IO 260 12500 14200, IO T MRCR ** ** , IO T165-T330													13000	16200
		1986 BOATS														
17	8	SIDEWINDER 18SS	OP	SKI	FBG	DV	OB			7		1075			3900	4550
17	8	SIDEWINDER 18SS	OP	SKI	FBG	DV	JT			7		1900			**	**
17	8	SIDEWINDER 18SS	OP	SKI	FBG	DV	IO	185-230		7		1900			2100	2600
17	8	SIDEWINDER 18SS	OP	SKI	FBG	DV	IO	260		7		1900			2350	2700
18	4	CUTLASS 185BR	OP	RNBT	FBG	DV	IO	120-230		8		2200			2650	3250
18	4	CUTLASS 185BR	OP	RNBT	FBG	DV	IO	260		8		2200			2900	3350
18	4	CUTLASS 185CB	OP	RNBT	FBG	DV	IO	120-230		8		2200			2650	3200
18	4	CUTLASS 185CB	OP	RNBT	FBG	DV	IO	260		8		2200			2850	3350
18	4	CUTLASS 185OB	OP	RNBT	FBG	DV	OB			8		1175			4400	5050
18	9	SEA-RAGE 196BR	OP	RNBT	FBG	DV	IO	120-260		7	4	2450			2700	3350
18	9	SEA-RAGE 196CB	OP	RNBT	FBG	DV	IO	120-230		7	4	2450			2700	3350
18	9	SEA-RAGE 196CB	OP	RNBT	FBG	DV	IO	260		7	4	2450			3000	3500
18	9	SEA-RAGE 196CC	OP	CUD	FBG	DV	IO	120-230		7	4	2450			2800	3400
18	9	SEA-RAGE 196CC	OP	CUD	FBG	DV	IO	260		7	4	2450			3000	3500
20	4	FISHERMAN I 210	OP	FSH	FBG	DV	IO	120-260		8		3250			3850	4800
20	4	FISHERMAN I 210	HT	FSH	FBG	DV	IO	120-260		8		3500			4050	5000
20	4	FISHERMAN I 210L	OP	FSH	FBG	DV	IO	120-260		8		3250			4150	5100
20	4	FISHERMAN I 210L	HT	FSH	FBG	DV	IO	120-260		8		3500			4400	5350
20	4	HERITAGE 219	OP	RNBT	FBG	DV	IO	120-260		8		3300			3650	4500
20	4	SPORTSMAN 210S	OP	CUD	FBG	DV	IO	120-260		8		3250			3800	4700
20	4	SPORTSMAN 210S	HT	CUD	FBG	DV	IO	120-260		8		3450			3950	4850
20	4	SPORTSMAN 240S	OP	CUD	FBG	DV	IO	170-260		8		3300			3850	4700
21	4	CARRERA 215	OP	RNBT	FBG	DV	IO	120-260		8		3250			3700	4600
21	4	CARRERA 215L	OP	RNBT	FBG	DV	IO	120-260		8		3250			3900	4750
21	4	CARRERA 215L	OP	RNBT	FBG	DV	IO	T120-T190		8		3250			4400	5150
23	4	ADVENTURER 240A	HT	CR	FBG	DV	IO	170-260		8		5325			6550	7750
23	4	ADVENTURER 240A	HT	CR	FBG	DV	IO	T120-T190		8		5325			7150	8300
23	4	ADVENTURER 240A	FB	CR	FBG	DV	IO	170-260		8		5880			7150	8450
23	4	ADVENTURER 240A	FB	CR	FBG	DV	IO	T120-T170		8		5880			7700	8900
23	4	FISHERMAN II 240	OP	FSH	FBG	DV	IO	170-260		8		4325			5600	6700
23	4	FISHERMAN II 240	OP	FSH	FBG	DV	IO	T120-T170		8		4325			6450	7450
23	4	FISHERMAN II 240	HT	FSH	FBG	DV	IO	170-260		8		4550			5650	6950
23	4	FISHERMAN II 240	HT	FSH	FBG	DV	IO	T120-T170		8		4550			6450	7600
23	4	FISHERMAN II 240	FB	FSH	FBG	DV	IO	170-260		8		5850			7500	8850
23	4	FISHERMAN II 240	FB	FSH	FBG	DV	IO	T120-T170		8		5850			8100	9400
23	4	FISHERMAN II 240	OP	OFF	FBG	DV	IO	170-260		8		4326			5550	6600
23	4	FISHERMAN II 240	OP	OFF	FBG	DV	IO	T120	MRCR	8		4326			6100	7050
23	4	FISHERMAN II 240	FB	OFF	FBG	DV	IO	170-260		8		5850			7050	8400
23	4	FISHERMAN II 240	FB	OFF	FBG	DV	IO	T120-T190		8		5850			7700	8900
23	4	FISHERMAN II 240L	OP	FSH	FBG	DV	IO	170-260		8		4325			6100	7250
23	4	FISHERMAN II 240L	OP	FSH	FBG	DV	IO	T140-T170		8		4325			6700	7750
23	4	FISHERMAN II 240L	HT	FSH	FBG	DV	IO	170-260		8		4550			6500	7500
23	4	FISHERMAN II 240L	HT	FSH	FBG	DV	IO	T120-T190		8		4550			6950	8000
23	4	FISHERMAN II 240L	FB	FSH	FBG	DV	IO	170-260		8		5850			7500	8850
23	4	FISHERMAN II 240L	FB	FSH	FBG	DV	IO	T120-T170		8		5850			8100	9400
23	4	SPORTSMAN 240S	HT	WKNDR	FBG	DV	IO	170-260		8		5325			6550	7750
23	4	SPORTSMAN 240S	HT	WKNDR	FBG	DV	IO	T120-T190		8		5325			7150	8300
23	4	SPORTSMAN 240S	FB	WKNDR	FBG	DV	IO	170-260		8		5850			7250	8550
23	4	SPORTSMAN 240S	FB	WKNDR	FBG	DV	IO	T120-T175		8		5850			7850	9050
23	7	FAMILY EXPRESS 246	OP	EXP	FBG	DV	IO	170-260		8		4200			5500	6550
23	7	FAMILY EXPRESS 246	OP	EXP	FBG	DV	IO	T120-T175		8					6650	7700
23	7	FAMILY FLYBRIDGE 247	FB	EXP	FBG	DV	IO	170-260		8		4300			5600	6650
23	7	FAMILY FLYBRIDGE 247	FB	EXP	FBG	DV	IO	T120-T170		8					6650	7700
23	7	VACATIONER 246	OP	EXP	FBG	DV	IO	170-260		8		4550			5750	6800
23	7	VACATIONER 246	OP	EXP	FBG	DV	IO	T120-T190		8					6650	7750
23	7	VACATIONER EXP 246A	OP	EXP	FBG	DV	IO	170-260		8		4550			5950	7050
27	3	DAYTONA 270	OP	SPTCR	FBG	DV	IO	260-330		9		6250			9150	11000
27	3	DAYTONA 270	OP	SPTCR	FBG	DV	IO	T120-T230		9		7150			9900	12400
27	3	DAYTONA 270	OP	SPTCR	FBG	DV	IO	T260-T330		9		7150			11200	13800
28	7	ADVENTURER 288	OP	EXP	FBG	DV	IB	T230-T340		11		9200			17200	21300
28	8	DAYTONA 290	OP	SPTCR	FBG	DV	IO	260-330		10					12300	14600
28	8	DAYTONA 290	OP	SPTCR	FBG	DV	IO	T170-T260		10		7500			11700	14500
28	8	DAYTONA 290	OP	SPTCR	FBG	DV	IO	T330		10		7500			13700	15600
		1985 BOATS														
17	6	THOMPSON 8480		SKI	FBG	DV	OB			7		1175			4050	4700
17	8	SIDEWINDER 18SS	OP	SKI	FBG	DV	OB			7		1075			3800	4400
17	8	SIDEWINDER 18SS	OP	SKI	FBG	DV	JT			7		1900			**	**
17	8	SIDEWINDER 18SS	OP	SKI	FBG	DV	IO	185-230		7		1900			2000	2500
17	8	SIDEWINDER 18SS	OP	SKI	FBG	DV	IO	260		7		1900			2250	2600
18	4	CUTLASS 185	OP	RNBT	FBG	DV	OB			8		1175			4250	4900
18	4	CUTLASS 185	OP	RNBT	FBG	DV	IO	120-230		8		2200			2550	3100
18	4	CUTLASS 185	OP	RNBT	FBG	DV	IO	260		8		2200			2750	3200
18	9	SEA-COASTER 8491	OP	RNBT	FBG	DV	IO	260		7	4	2450			2800	3250
18	9	SEA-LANE 8495	OP	RNBT	FBG	DV	IO	260		7	4	2450			2800	3250
18	9	SEA-RAGE 195	OP	RNBT	FBG	DV	IO	120-230		7	4	2450			2600	3150
18	9	SEA-RAGE 195	OP	RNBT	FBG	DV	IO	260		7	4	2450			2800	3250
18	9	SEA-RAGE 196	OP	CUD	FBG	DV	IO	120-230		7	4	2450			2700	3250
18	9	SEA-RAGE 196	OP	CUD	FBG	DV	IO	260		7	4	2450			2900	3350
18	9	SEA-SPORT 191	OP	RNBT	FBG	DV	IO	120-230		7	4	2450			2600	3150
18	9	SEA-SPORT 191	OP	RNBT	FBG	DV	IO	260		7	4	2450			2800	3250
18	9	SIDEWINDER 195SS	OP	SKI	FBG	DV	IO	170-260		7	4	2600			2600	3250
18	9	THOMPSON 8491		RNBT	FBG	DV	OB			7	4	1300			4700	5400
20	4	FISHERMAN II 8532	OP	FSH	FBG	DV	IO	120-230		8		3250			3850	4600
20	4	FISHERMAN II 8532	OP	FSH	FBG	DV	IO	260		8		3250			4050	4950
20	4	FISHERMAN II 8532	HT	FSH	FBG	DV	IO	120-260		8		3500			4050	4950
20	4	FISHERMAN II 8532L	OP	FSH	FBG	DV	IO	120-260		8		3250			3850	4750
20	4	FISHERMAN II 8532L	HT	FSH	FBG	DV	IO	120-260		8		3500			4050	4950
20	4	SPORTSMAN 232	OP	CUD	FBG	DV	IO	120-260		8		3250			3650	4500
20	4	SPORTSMAN 232	HT	CUD	FBG	DV	IO	120-260		8		3450			3800	4650
20	4	WEEKENDER 252	OP	CUD	FBG	DV	IO	120-260		8		3300			3650	4550
21		THOMPSON 221			FBG	DV	IO	198		7	8	2750			3200	3750
		THOMPSON 8421			FBG	DV	IO	120		7	8	2500			3000	3500
23	4	ADVENTURER 252A	HT	CR	FBG	DV	IO	170-260		8		5325			6300	7450
23	4	ADVENTURER 252A	HT	CR	FBG	DV	IO	T120-T185		8		5325			6850	7950
23	4	ADVENTURER 252A	FB	CR	FBG	DV	IO	170-260		8		5880			6850	8100
23	4	ADVENTURER 252A	FB	CR	FBG	DV	IO	T120-T185		8		5880			7400	8600
23	4	EXPLORER 8552	OP	FSH	FBG	DV	IO	170-260		8		4325			5600	6700
23	4	EXPLORER 8552	OP	FSH	FBG	DV	IO	T120-T185		8		4325			6200	7200
23	4	EXPLORER 8552	HT	FSH	FBG	DV	IO	170-260		8		4550			5850	6950
23	4	EXPLORER 8552	HT	FSH	FBG	DV	IO	T120-T185		8		4550			6450	7450
23	4	EXPLORER 8552	FB	FSH	FBG	DV	IO	170-260		8		5850			7200	8500
23	4	EXPLORER 8552	FB	FSH	FBG	DV	IO	T120-T185		8		5850			7800	9050
23	4	EXPLORER 8552L	OP	FSH	FBG	DV	IO	170-260		8		4325			5600	6700
23	4	EXPLORER 8552L	OP	FSH	FBG	DV	IO	T140-T185		8		4325			6200	7200
23	4	EXPLORER 8552L	HT	FSH	FBG	DV	IO	170-260		8		4550			5850	6950
23	4	EXPLORER 8552L	HT	FSH	FBG	DV	IO	T120-T185		8		4550			6450	7450
23	4	EXPLORER 8552L	FB	FSH	FBG	DV	IO	170-260		8		5850			7200	8500
23	4	EXPLORER 8552L	FB	FSH	FBG	DV	IO	T120-T170		8		5850			7800	9000
23	4	OFFSHORE 8552	OP	OFF	FBG	DV	IO	170-260		8		4326			5300	6350
23	4	OFFSHORE 8552	OP	OFF	FBG	DV	IO	T120-T185		8		4326			5850	6850
23	4	OFFSHORE 8552	HT	OFF	FBG	DV	IO	170-260		8		4550			5550	6600
23	4	OFFSHORE 8552	HT	OFF	FBG	DV	IO	T120-T185		8		4550			6100	7050
23	4	OFFSHORE 8552	FB	OFF	FBG	DV	IO	170-260		8		5850			6800	8050
23	4	OFFSHORE 8552	FB	OFF	FBG	DV	IO	T120-T185		8		5850			7350	8550
23	4	WEEKENDER 252	OP	WKNDR	FBG	DV	IO	170-260		8		4400			5400	6400
23	4	WEEKENDER 252	OP	WKNDR	FBG	DV	IO	T120-T185		8		4400			5950	6900
23	4	WEEKENDER 252	HT	WKNDR	FBG	DV	IO	170-260		8		5325			6300	7450
23	4	WEEKENDER 252	HT	WKNDR	FBG	DV	IO	T120-T185		8		5325			6850	7950
23	4	WEEKENDER 252	FB	WKNDR	FBG	DV	IO	170-260		8		5850			6900	8150
23	4	WEEKENDER 252	FB	WKNDR	FBG	DV	IO	T120-T185		8		5850			7550	8700
23	7	FAMILY EXPRESS 246	OP	EXP	FBG	DV	IO	185-260		8		4200			5250	6300
23	7	FAMILY EXPRESS 246	OP	EXP	FBG	DV	IO	T120-T170		8					6400	7400
23	7	FAMILY FLYBRIDGE 247	FB	EXP	FBG	DV	IO	185-260		8		4300			5350	6400
23	7	FAMILY FLYBRIDGE 247	FB	EXP	FBG	DV	IO	T120-T170		8					6400	7400
23	7	VACATIONER EXP 246A	OP	EXP	FBG	DV	IO	185-260		8		4550			5600	6650
23	7	VACATIONER EXP 246A	OP	EXP	FBG	DV	IO	T120-T170		8					6400	7400
28	4	285	OP	SPTCR	FBG	DV	IO	260		10		6000	3	2	9550	10900
28	4	285	OP	SPTCR	FBG	DV	IO	T		10			3	2	**	**
28	7	EXPRESS FB 288	FB	EXP	FBG	DV	IO	260	MRCR	10	8	8000			11100	12600
		IO 260 OMC 11100 12600, IB 260 14000 15900, IB T165 CRUS													15700	17900
		IO T170-T200 12400 14400, IB T220 16400 18600, IO T225-T228													12800	14700
		IO T230 OMC 12900 14700, IB T230-T250 16400 18900, IO T255 COMM													13100	14900
		IO T260 MRCR 13200 15100, IO T260 OMC 13200 15000, IB T260-T270													16700	19200
		1984 BOATS														
17	6	SEA-FARER 8484	OP	RNBT	FBG	DV	IO	117-230		7		2200			2200	2650
17	6	SEA-FARER 8584	OP	RNBT	FBG	DV	OB			7		1175			4100	4750

 CONTINUED ON NEXT PAGE

LOA FT	IN	NAME AND/ OR MODEL	TOP/ RIG	BOAT TYPE	-HULL- MTL	TP	ENGINE TP	# HP	MFG	BEAM FT	IN	WGT LBS	DRAFT FT	IN	RETAIL LOW	RETAIL HIGH
		1984 BOATS														
17	6	SEA-FARER 8584	OP	RNBT	FBG	DV	IO	120		7		2200			2050	2500
17	6	SEA-FARER 8584	OP	RNBT	FBG	DV	IO	138-230		7		2200			2300	2800
17	6	SEA-FARER 8584	OP	RNBT	FBG	DV	IO	260		7		2200			2400	2900
17	6	SEA-LANCER 184	OP	RNBT	FBG	DV	IO	117-260		7		2200			2400	2950
17	6	SEA-RAIDER 8480	OP	RNBT	FBG	DV	OB			7		1175			3950	4600
17	6	SEA-RAIDER 8480	OP	RNBT	FBG	DV	IO	117-120		7		2200			2100	2500
17	6	SEA-RAIDER 8480	OP	RNBT	FBG	DV	IO	138-260		7		2200			2300	2800
17	6	SEA-RAIDER 8480	OP	RNBT	FBG	DV	IO	T140-T170		7		2200			2700	3150
17	6	SEA-RAIDER 8580	OP	RNBT	FBG	DV	OB			7		1175			4000	4650
17	6	SEA-RANGER 180	OP	RNBT	FBG	DV	IO	117-260		7		2200			2350	2950
17	8	SIDEWINDER 18SS	OP	SKI	FBG	DV	OB			7		1075			3700	4300
17	8	SIDEWINDER 18SS	OP	SKI	FBG	DV	JT		CHEV	7		1900			**	**
		IO 185-230 1950 2400, IO 260 2150 2500, JT 350 CHEV													3050	3550
18	4	CUTLASS 185	OP	RNBT	FBG	DV	OB			8					4500	5150
18	4	CUTLASS 185	OP	RNBT	FBG	DV	IO	117-188		8		2200			2550	3000
18	9	8491	OP	RNBT	FBG	DV	OB			7	4	1300			4550	5250
18	9	SEA-RAGE 195	OP	RNBT	FBG	DV	IO	117-138		7	4	2450			2550	3050
18	9	SEA-RAGE 195	OP	RNBT	FBG	DV	IO	140	MRCR	7	4	2450			900	1050
18	9	SEA-RAGE 195	OP	RNBT	FBG	DV	IO	140-260		7	4	2450			3050	3500
18	9	SEA-RAGE 196	OP	CUD	FBG	DV	IO	117-230		7	4				2700	3250
18	9	SEA-RAGE 196	OP	CUD	FBG	DV	IO	260		7	4				2800	3400
18	9	SEA-SPORT 191	OP	RNBT	FBG	DV	IO	117-138		7	4	2450			2700	3150
18	9	SEA-SPORT 191	OP	RNBT	FBG	DV	IO	140-260		7	4	2450			3050	3550
18	9	SIDEWINDER 195SS	OP	SKI	FBG	DV	IO	170-230		7	4				2400	2900
18	9	SIDEWINDER 195SS	OP	SKI	FBG	DV	IO	260		7	4				2600	3000
18	9	SIDEWINDER X-19	OP	SKI	FBG	DV	IO	170-230		7	4	2260			2350	2800
18	9	SIDEWINDER X-19	OP	SKI	FBG	DV	IO	260		7	4	2260			2500	2950
20	4	FISHERMAN 8422	OP	FSH	FBG	DV	IO	117-260		8		3125			3750	4650
20	4	FISHERMAN 8422	OP	FSH	FBG	DV	IO	T117-T188		8					4800	5550
20	4	FISHERMAN II 8432	OP	FSH	FBG	DV	IO	117-260		8		3250			3700	4500
20	4	FISHERMAN II 8432	OP	FSH	FBG	DV	IO	T117-T188		8					4800	5550
20	4	FISHERMAN II 8432	HT	FSH	FBG	DV	IO	117-260		8		3500			3850	4750
20	4	FISHERMAN II 8432	HT	FSH	FBG	DV	IO	T117-T188		8					4800	5550
20	4	FISHERMAN II 8432L	OP	FSH	FBG	DV	IO	117-260		8		3250			4000	4800
20	4	FISHERMAN II 8432L	OP	FSH	FBG	DV	IO	T117-T188		8					4800	5550
20	4	FISHERMAN II 8432L	HT	FSH	FBG	DV	IO	117-260		8		3500			4150	5000
20	4	FISHERMAN II 8432L	HT	FSH	FBG	DV	IO	T117-T188		8					4800	5550
20	4	HERITAGE 229	OP	CUD	FBG	DV	IO	117-260		8		3300			3650	4550
20	4	SPORTSMAN 232	OP	CUD	FBG	DV	IO	117-260		8		3250			3650	4500
20	4	SPORTSMAN 232	HT	CUD	FBG	DV	IO	117-260		8		3450			3750	4700
21		FISHMASTER 8421	OP	FSH	FBG	DV	IO	117-230		7	8	2500			3350	4050
21		FISHMASTER 8421	OP	FSH	FBG	DV	IO	260		7	8	2500			3450	4200
21		FISHMASTER 8421	OP	FSH	FBG	DV	IO	T117-T188		7	8	2500			4050	4700
21		FISHMASTER 8421L	OP	FSH	FBG	DV	IO	117-230		7	8	2750			3500	4250
21		FISHMASTER 8421L	OP	FSH	FBG	DV	IO	260		7	8	2750			3600	4400
21		FISHMASTER 8421L	OP	FSH	FBG	DV	IO	T117-T188		7	8				4500	5150
21		SUNDOWNER 221	OP	CUD	FBG	DV	IO	117-230		7	8	2750			3350	4000
21		SUNDOWNER 221	OP	CUD	FBG	DV	IO	260		7	8	2750			3450	4150
23	4	ADVENTURER 252A	HT	CR	FBG	DV	IO	170-260		8		5325			6050	7400
23	4	ADVENTURER 252A	HT	CR	FBG	DV	IO	130D	VLVO	8		5325			7100	8150
23	4	ADVENTURER 252A	HT	CR	FBG	DV	IO	T117-T188		8		5325			6850	7900
23	4	ADVENTURER 252A	FB	CR	FBG	DV	IO	170-260		8		5880			6600	8000
23	4	ADVENTURER 252A	FB	CR	FBG	DV	IO	130D	VLVO	8		5880			7650	8800
23	4	ADVENTURER 252A	FB	CR	FBG	DV	IO	T117-T188		8		5880			7350	8550
23	4	EXPLORER 8352L	OP	FSH	FBG	DV	IO	T138-T188		8		4325			6250	7150
23	4	EXPLORER 8352L	HT	FSH	FBG	DV	IO	117-140		8		4550			5750	6600
23	4	EXPLORER 8352L	HT	FSH	FBG	DV	IO	T188	MRCR	8		4550			6300	7200
23	4	EXPLORER 8452L	OP	FSH	FBG	DV	IO	117-260		8		4325			5500	6650
23	4	EXPLORER 8452L	OP	FSH	FBG	DV	IO	T117-T140		8		4325			6250	7150
23	4	EXPLORER 8452L	HT	FSH	FBG	DV	IO	138-260		8		4550			5750	6900
23	4	EXPLORER 8452L	HT	FSH	FBG	DV	IO	T117-T170		8		4550			6450	7450
23	4	EXPLORER 8452L	FB	FSH	FBG	DV	IO	117-260		8		5850			7050	8400
23	4	EXPLORER 8452L	FB	FSH	FBG	DV	IO	T117-T188		8		5850			7750	8950
23	4	OFFSHORE 8452	OP	OFF	FBG	DV	IO	117-260		8		4326			5200	6300
23	4	OFFSHORE 8452	OP	OFF	FBG	DV	IO	T117-T188		8		4326			5900	6800
23	4	OFFSHORE 8452	HT	OFF	FBG	DV	IO	117-260		8		4550			5450	6550
23	4	OFFSHORE 8452	HT	OFF	FBG	DV	IO	T117-T188		8		4550			6100	7050
23	4	OFFSHORE 8452	FB	OFF	FBG	DV	IO	117-260		8		5850			6650	7950
23	4	OFFSHORE 8452	FB	OFF	FBG	DV	IO	T117-T188		8		5850			7350	8450
23	4	WEEKENDER 252	OP	WKNDR	FBG	DV	IO	170-260		8		4400			5200	6400
23	4	WEEKENDER 252	OP	WKNDR	FBG	DV	IO	130D	VLVO	8		4400			6250	7150
23	4	WEEKENDER 252	OP	WKNDR	FBG	DV	IO	T117-T188		8		4400			5950	6900
23	4	WEEKENDER 252	HT	WKNDR	FBG	DV	IO	170-260		8		5325			6050	7400
23	4	WEEKENDER 252	HT	WKNDR	FBG	DV	IO	130D	VLVO	8		5325			7100	8150
23	4	WEEKENDER 252	HT	WKNDR	FBG	DV	IO	T117-T188		8		5325			6850	7900
23	4	WEEKENDER 252	FB	WKNDR	FBG	DV	IO	170-260		8		5850			6650	8050
23	4	WEEKENDER 252	FB	WKNDR	FBG	DV	IO	130D	VLVO	8		5850			7700	8850
23	4	WEEKENDER 252	FB	WKNDR	FBG	DV	IO	T117-T188		8		5850			7500	8700
23	7	FAMILY EXPRESS 246	OP	EXP	FBG	DV	IO	170-260		8		4200			5200	6250
23	7	FAMILY EXPRESS 246	OP	EXP	FBG	DV	IO	130D	VLVO	8		4200			6100	7050
23	7	FAMILY EXPRESS 246	OP	EXP	FBG	DV	IO	T117-T188		8					6400	7400
23	7	FAMILY FLYBRIDGE 247	FB	EXP	FBG	DV	IO	170-260		8		4300			5300	6350
23	7	FAMILY FLYBRIDGE 247	FB	EXP	FBG	DV	IO	130D	VLVO	8		4300			6200	7150
23	7	FAMILY FLYBRIDGE 247	FB	EXP	FBG	DV	IO	T117-T188		8					6400	7400
23	7	VACATIONER EXP 246A	OP	EXP	FBG	DV	IO	170-260		8		4550			5550	6600
23	7	VACATIONER EXP 246A	OP	EXP	FBG	DV	IO	130D	VLVO	8		4550			6450	7400
23	7	VACATIONER EXP 246A	OP	EXP	FBG	DV	IO	T117-T188		8					6400	7400
28	7	EXPRESS FB 288	FB	EXP	FBG	DV	IO	260		10	8	8000			10700	12200
		IB T165 CRUS 15000 17100, IO T170-T200 11900 13900, IB T220													15600	17800
		IO T225-T228 12400 14200, IO T230 OMC 12500 14200, IB T230-T250													15700	18000
		IO T255 COMM 12700 14400, IO T260 MRCR 12800 14500, IO T260 OMC													12800	14500
		IB T260-T270 16000 18300														

....For earlier years, see the BUC Used Boat Price Guide, Volume 3

THOROUGHBRED POWERBOATS INC

SANFORD FL 32771

See inside cover to adjust price for area

FORMERLY THOROUGHBRED OFFSHORE POWER

LOA FT	IN	NAME AND/ OR MODEL	TOP/ RIG	BOAT TYPE	-HULL- MTL	TP	ENGINE TP	# HP	MFG	BEAM FT	IN	WGT LBS	DRAFT FT	IN	RETAIL LOW	RETAIL HIGH
		1996 BOATS														
21	6	VELOCITY 22	OP	CUD	FBG	DV	OB			7	11	3100			18300	20300
21	6	VELOCITY 22	OP	CUD	FBG	DV	IO	300	MRCR	7	11	3100			14400	16400
21	6	VELOCITY 22	OP	CUD	FBG	DV	IO	350	MRCR	7	11	3100			16100	18300
21	6	VELOCITY 22	OP	CUD	FBG	DV	IO	385-415		7	11	3100			18300	22100
26	3	VELOCITY 26	OP	OFF	FBG	DV	OB			8	2	4650			30500	33900
26	3	VELOCITY 26	OP	OFF	FBG	DV	IO	300-385		8	2	4650			24200	30200
26	3	VELOCITY 26	OP	OFF	FBG	DV	IO	415	MRCR	8	2	4650			28600	31700
26	3	VELOCITY 26	OP	OFF	FBG	DV	IO	500-525		8	2	4650			32800	37800
32		VELOCITY 32	OP	OFF	FBG	DV	OB			8	4	5750			50300	55300
32		VELOCITY 32	OP	OFF	FBG	DV	IO	415-500		8	4	5750			44000	50500
32		VELOCITY 32	OP	OFF	FBG	DV	IO	T300-T500		8	4	6850			47900	59800
35		VELOCITY 35	OP	OFF	FBG	DV	IO	T350	MRCR	8	5	7900			72800	80000
		IO T415 MRCR 77400 85100, IO T500 MRCR 84700 93000, IO T525 MRCR													86700	95300
		IO T600 MRCR 92500 101500														
41		VELOCITY 41	OP	OFF	FBG	DV	IO	T350	MRCR	8	5	8950			58000	63700
		IO T415 MRCR 63100 69400, IO T500 MRCR 71300 78400, IO T525 MRCR													73600	80900
		IO T600 MRCR 79300 87200														
		1995 BOATS														
21	10	THOROUGHBRED 22 LTD	OP	CUD	FBG	DV	OB			7	11	3300			19300	21400
21	10	THOROUGHBRED 22 LTD	OP	CUD	FBG	DV	IO	260-300		7	11	3300			14200	16900
21	10	THOROUGHBRED 22 LTD	OP	CUD	FBG	DV	IO	350-385		7	11	3300			16500	19800
21	10	THOROUGHBRED 22 LTD	OP	CUD	FBG	DV	IO	415	MRCR	7	11	3300			19300	21400
21	10	VELOCITY 22	OP	CUD	FBG	DV	OB			7	11	3300			17100	19400
21	10	VELOCITY 22	OP	CUD	FBG	DV	IO	260-300		7	11	3300			12600	15200
21	10	VELOCITY 22	OP	CUD	FBG	DV	IO	350	MRCR	7	11	3300			15000	17100
26	3	THOROUGHBRED 26 LTD	OP	OFF	FBG	DV	OB			8	2	4950			29400	32600
26	3	THOROUGHBRED 26 LTD	OP	OFF	FBG	DV	IO	300-385		8	2	4950			24500	30300
26	3	THOROUGHBRED 26 LTD	OP	OFF	FBG	DV	IO	415	MRCR	8	2	4950			28600	31700
26	3	THOROUGHBRED 26 LTD	OP	OFF	FBG	DV	IO	450-500		8	2	4950			29000	34900
26	3	VELOCITY 26	OP	OFF	FBG	DV	OB			8	2	4825			29200	32500
26	3	VELOCITY 26	OP	OFF	KEV	DV	OB			8	2	4950			29400	32600
26	3	VELOCITY 26	OP	OFF	FBG	DV	IO	300-350		8	2	4950			22100	26300
26	3	VELOCITY 26	OP	OFF	FBG	DV	IO	385-415		8	2	4950			24900	29200
35		THOROUGHBRED 35 LTD	OP	OFF	FBG	DV	IO	T415	MRCR	8	5	7900			72200	79400
41		THOROUGHBRED 41 LTD	OP	OFF	FBG	DV	IO	T500	MRCR	8	5	9850			68500	75300
		1994 BOATS														
21	10	THOROUGHBRED 22 LTD	OP	CUD	FBG	DV	OB			7	11	3300			18800	20900
21	10	THOROUGHBRED 22 LTD	OP	CUD	FBG	DV	IO	260-300		7	11	3300			13000	15600
21	10	THOROUGHBRED 22 LTD	OP	CUD	FBG	DV	IO	350-385		7	11	3300			15200	18400
21	10	THOROUGHBRED 22 LTD	OP	CUD	FBG	DV	IO	415-445		7	11	3300			18200	21900
21	10	VELOCITY 22	OP	CUD	FBG	DV	OB			7	11	3300			16100	18300
21	10	VELOCITY 22	OP	CUD	FBG	DV	IO	260-300		7	11	3300			11900	14400

LOA FT	LOA IN	NAME AND/ OR MODEL	TOP/ RIG	BOAT TYPE	-HULL- MTL	-HULL- TP	ENGINE TP	ENGINE # HP	ENGINE MFG	BEAM FT	BEAM IN	WGT LBS	DRAFT FT	DRAFT IN	RETAIL LOW	RETAIL HIGH
		1994 BOATS														
21	10	VELOCITY 22	OP	CUD	FBG	DV	IO	350	MRCR	7	11	3300			14200	16100
26	3	THOROUGHBRED 26 LTD	OP	OFF	FBG	DV	OB			8	2	4950			28000	31100
26	3	THOROUGHBRED 26 LTD	OP	OFF	FBG	DV	IO	300-385		8	2	4950			21800	27100
		IO 415 MRCR 25600 28400, IO 445-500 26900 32500, IO T260 MRCR 24500 27200														
26	3	VELOCITY 26	OP	OFF	FBG	DV	OB			8	2	4825			27800	30900
26	3	VELOCITY 26	OP	OFF	KEV	DV	OB			8	2	4950			28000	31100
26	3	VELOCITY 26	OP	OFF	KEV	DV	IO	300-385		8	2	4950			21800	27100
26	3	VELOCITY 26	OP	OFF	KEV	DV	IO	415	MRCR	8	2	4950			25600	28400
		1993 BOATS														
26	3	VELOCITY 26	OP	OFF	FBG	DV	OB			8	2	4825			26500	29500
26	3	VELOCITY 26	OP	OFF	KEV	DV	IO	300-350		8	2	4950			20400	24000
		IO 390-445 23000 27900, IO 465-490 26000 30000, IO 575 MRCR 30100 33400														
		IO T240 MRCR 22400 24900														
35		MAJESTIC PRINCE	ST	OFF	KEV	DV	IO	T350	MRCR	8	5	7900	2		59300	65100
		IO T390 MRCR 61500 67500, IO T412 MRCR 62800 69100, IO T445 MRCR 65100 71500														
		IO T500 MRCR 69000 75800, IO T525 MRCR 70800 77800, IO T575 MRCR 74200 81600														
		IO T600 MRCR 75800 83300, IO T500D MRCR 76500 84100														
41		BOLD RULER	ST	OFF	KEV	DV	IO	T350	MRCR	8	5	9850	2	4	49600	54500
		IO T390 MRCR 52200 57400, IO T412 MRCR 53800 59200, IO T445 MRCR 56500 62100														
		IO T525 MRCR 63000 69300, IO T575 MRCR 66400 72900, IO T600 MRCR 67800 74500														
		IO T500D MRCR 74000 81400, IO R800 MRCR ** ** , IO R500D MRCR 80700 88600														
		1992 BOATS														
22		ALLSPORT	OP	CTRCN	FBG	DV	OB			8	1	1650		11	9600	10900
26		SUMMER SQUALL	ST	OFF	KEV	DV	IO	350-390		8	6	4450	1	6	19000	22600
		IO 445 MRCR 22400 24900, IO 525 MRCR 25500 28400, IO T240 MRCR 19700 21900														
		IO T350 MRCR 23800 26400														
35		MAJESTIC PRINCE	ST	OFF	KEV	DV	IO	T350	MRCR	8	6	7750	2		55200	60600
		IO T385 MRCR 57000 62600, IO T390 MRCR 57200 62900, IO T445 MRCR 60600 66600														
		IO T465 MRCR 61900 68000, IO T490 MRCR 63600 69900, IO T525 MRCR 65900 72400														
		IO T700 FORD 62700 68900, IO T500D MERL 71300 78300														
41		BOLD RULER	ST	OFF	KEV	DV	IO	T350	MRCR	8	6	9950	2	4	46500	51000
		IO T385 MRCR 48500 53300, IO T390 MRCR 48900 53700, IO T445 MRCR 52900 58200														
		IO T465 MRCR 54500 59900, IO T490 MRCR 56400 62000, IO T525 MRCR 59000 64800														
		IO T700 FORD 67000 73700, IO T500D MERL 69000 75800, IO R350 MRCR 46900 51500														
		IO R390 MRCR 50200 55100, IO R445 MRCR 55700 61200, IO R490 MRCR 60500 66500														
		IO R700 FORD 89600 98400, IO R500D MERL 75200 82700														
		1991 BOATS														
22		ALL SPORT	OP	CTRCN	FBG	DV	OB			8	1	1650		11	9250	10500
26		SUMMER SQUALL	ST	OFF	KEV	DV	IO	390	MRCR			4450	1	6	19100	21200
35		MAJESTIC PRINCE	ST	OFF	KEV	DV	IO	T400	MRCR	8	6	7750	2		54200	59600
41		BOLD RULER	ST	OFF	KEV	DV	IO	T700	FORD	8	6	9900	2	5	63100	69300
		1990 BOATS														
22		ALL SPORT	OP	CTRCN	FBG	DV	OB			8	7	1650	11		8900	10100
35		MAJESTIC PRINCE	ST	OFF	KEV	DV	IO	T500	MRCR	8	6	7750	2		56700	62300
41		BOLD RULER	ST	OFF	KEV	DV	IO	T500	MRCR	8	6	9800	2	3	50600	55700

THREE BUOYS HOUSEBOAT BLDRS

KELOWNA BC CANADA

See inside cover to adjust price for area

LOA FT	LOA IN	NAME AND/ OR MODEL	TOP/ RIG	BOAT TYPE	-HULL- MTL	-HULL- TP	ENGINE TP	ENGINE # HP	ENGINE MFG	BEAM FT	BEAM IN	WGT LBS	DRAFT FT	DRAFT IN	RETAIL LOW	RETAIL HIGH
		1989 BOATS														
46	3	SUNSEEKER 46 DELUXE	HT	HB		TR	IB	271	MRCR	12	6	19000	1	10	38700	42900
46	3	SUNSEEKER 46 EXEC	HT	HB		TR	IB	131	VLVO	12	6	20000	1	10	39200	43600
56	2	SUNSEEKER 56	HT	HB		TR	IB	131	VLVO	14		26000	1	6	57700	63400
56	2	SUNSEEKER 56	HT	HB		TR	IB	271	MRCR	14		26000	1	6	58200	64000
58		TORTOLA 58	HT	CR		DV	IB	T D	VLVO	14		32000	2	5	**	**
		1988 BOATS														
48	3	SUNSEEKER 46	HT	HB		TR	IB	131	VLVO	14		22000	1	5	41200	45700
48	3	SUNSEEKER 46	HT	HB		TR	IB	271	MRCR	14		22000	1	5	41600	46200
54	2	SUNSEEKER 52	HT	HB		TR	IB	131	VLVO	14		24000	1	5	53200	58400
58		TORTOLA 58	HT	CR		DV	IB	T D	VLVO	14		32000	2	5	**	**
58	2	SUNSEEKER 56	HT	HB		TR	IB	131	VLVO	14		26000	1	5	57200	62800
58	2	SUNSEEKER 56	HT	HB		TR	IB	271	MRCR	14		26000	1	5	57700	63400

THUNDER CRAFT BOATS INC

PIKEVILLE KY 41501 COAST GUARD MFG ID- TCT See inside cover to adjust price for area

LOA FT	LOA IN	NAME AND/ OR MODEL	TOP/ RIG	BOAT TYPE	-HULL- MTL	-HULL- TP	ENGINE TP	ENGINE # HP	ENGINE MFG	BEAM FT	BEAM IN	WGT LBS	DRAFT FT	DRAFT IN	RETAIL LOW	RETAIL HIGH
		1988 BOATS														
16		REGENCY 162		RNBT	FBG	DV	OB			6	8	1000			2250	2600
16		REGENCY 162		RNBT	FBG	DV	IO	120		6	8	2350			3350	3900
16	7	CITATION 170		RNBT	FBG	DV	IO	130		6	9	2350			3450	4050
17	7	LEGACY 180		RNBT	FBG	DV	IO	130		6	9	2400			3700	4300
17	9	NOVA 177		RNBT	FBG	DV	IO	130		7	6	2500			4050	4700
18	7	MALIBU 190		RNBT	FBG	DV	IO	130		6	9	2600			3750	4350
18	7	MALIBU CUDDY 195		RNBT	FBG	DV	IO	130		6	9	2600			4450	5100
		1987 BOATS														
16		REGENCY 162		RNBT	FBG	DV	OB			6	8	1000			2200	2550
16		REGENCY 162		RNBT	FBG	DV	IO	120		6	8	2350			3200	3700
16	7	CITATION 170		RNBT	FBG	DV	IO	130		6	9	2350			3300	3850
17	4	NOVA 177		RNBT	FBG	DV	IO	130		8		2500			3900	4550
17	7	LEGACY 180		RNBT	FBG	DV	IO	130		6	9	2400			3500	4100
18	7	MALIBU 190		RNBT	FBG	DV	IO	130		6	9	2600			3600	4150
18	7	MALIBU CUDDY 195		RNBT	FBG	DV	IO	130		6	9	2600			4200	4850
		1986 BOATS														
16		REGENCY 162		RNBT	FBG	DV	OB			6	8	1000			2050	2450
16		REGENCY 162		RNBT	FBG	DV	IO	140		6	8	2350			3050	3550
16	7	CITATION 170		RNBT	FBG	DV	OB			6	9	1000			2100	2500
16	7	CITATION 170		RNBT	FBG	DV	IO	140		6	9	2350			3150	3650
17	7	LEGACY 180		RNBT	FBG	DV	IO	140		6	9	2280			3250	3800
18	7	MALIBU 190		RNBT	FBG	DV	IO	140		6	9	2600			3700	4300
		1985 BOATS														
16		REGENCY 162		RNBT	FBG	DV	OB			6	8	1000			2000	2400
16		REGENCY 162		RNBT	FBG	DV	IO	140		6	8	2350			2900	3400
16	7	CITATION 170		RNBT	FBG	DV	OB			6	9	1000			2050	2450
16	7	CITATION 170		RNBT	FBG	DV	IO	140		6	9	2350			3050	3500
18	7	MALIBU		RNBT	FBG	DV	IO	190		6	9	2600			3600	4200
		1984 BOATS														
16		REGENCY 162		RNBT	FBG	DV	OB			6	8	1000			1950	2350
16		REGENCY 162		RNBT	FBG	DV	IO	120		6	8	2350			2800	3250
16	7	CITATION 170		RNBT	FBG	DV	OB			6	9	1000			2000	2350
16	7	CITATION 170		RNBT	FBG	DV	IO	120		6	9	2350			2900	3400
18	7	MALIBU 190		RNBT	FBG	DV	IO	120		6	9	2600			3450	4000

....For earlier years, see the BUC Used Boat Price Guide, Volume 3

THUNDERBIRD PROD CORP

FORMULA
DECATUR IN 46733 COAST GUARD MFG ID- TNR

See inside cover to adjust price for area

For more recent years, see the BUC Used Boat Price Guide, Volume 1

LOA FT	LOA IN	NAME AND/ OR MODEL	TOP/ RIG	BOAT TYPE	-HULL- MTL	-HULL- TP	ENGINE TP	ENGINE # HP	ENGINE MFG	BEAM FT	BEAM IN	WGT LBS	DRAFT FT	DRAFT IN	RETAIL LOW	RETAIL HIGH
		1996 BOATS														
18	2	FALCON 1800BR	OP	B/R	FBG	DV	OB			7	8	2550	2	6	6900	7900
18	2	FALCON 1800BR	OP	B/R	FBG	DV	IO	135-180		7	8	2550	2	6	6400	7350
18	2	FALCON 1800BR LE	OP	B/R	FBG	DV	OB			7	8	2550	2	6	6500	7500
18	2	FALCON 1800BR LE	OP	B/R	FBG	DV	IO	135-180		7	8	2550	2	6	5950	6850
18	2	FALCON 1800CB	OP	RNBT	FBG	DV	OB			7	8	2550	2	6	6650	7650
18	2	FALCON 1800CB	OP	RNBT	FBG	DV	IO	135-180		7	8	2500	2	6	6150	7100
18	2	FALCON 1800CB LE	OP	B/R	FBG	DV	OB			7	8	2550	2	6	6450	7450
18	2	FALCON 1800CB LE	OP	B/R	FBG	DV	IO	135-180		7	8	2550	2	6	5750	6700
20	2	FALCON 2000BR	OP	B/R	FBG	DV	IO	180-250		8		2825	2	6	9400	11100
20	2	FALCON 2000CD	OP	RNBT	FBG	DV	IO	180-250		8		2950	2	6	9800	11600
22	7	FALCON 2270BR	OP	B/R	FBG	DV	IO	210-300		8	6	3250	2	8	12000	14900
22	7	FALCON 2270CD	OP	RNBT	FBG	DV	IO	210-300		8	6	3400	2	8	12400	15400
23	2	F-232BR	OP	B/R	FBG	DV	IO	250-300		8	6	4300	2	4	14600	18300
23	2	F-232LS	OP	CUD	FBG	DV	IO	250-300		8	6	4300	2	4	16900	19700
25	2	F-252BR	OP	B/R	FBG	DV	IO	300-330		8	6	4525	2	8	18600	21300
25	2	F-252BR	OP	B/R	FBG	DV	IO	385	MRCR	8	6	4525	2	8	21200	23600
25	2	F-252LS	OP	CUD	FBG	DV	IO	300	MRCR	8	6	4525	2	4	19200	21300
25	2	F-252LS	OP	CUD	FBG	DV	IO	385	MRCR	8	6	4525	2	4	23000	25500
25	2	F-252SS	OP	CUD	FBG	DV	IO	300	MRCR	8	6	4525	2	4	19300	21400
25	2	F-252SS	OP	CUD	FBG	DV	IO	385	MRCR	8	6	4525	2	4	22700	25200
27		F-27PC	OP	OFF	FBG	DV	IO	300	MRCR	9	7	9500	3	5	35500	39400
27		F-27PC	OP	OFF	FBG	DV	IO	T180-T250		9	7	9500	3	5	36200	42000
27	1	F-271SR1	OP	OFF	FBG	DV	IO	385-415		8	3	5250	2	8	26400	30600
27	1	F-271SR1	OP	OFF	FBG	DV	IO	500	MRCR	8	3	5250	2	4	30900	34300
28		FORMULA 280 SUN SPT	OP	SPTCR	FBG	DV	IO	300		9	2	6300	3		28400	31600
28		FORMULA 280 SUN SPT	OP	SPTCR	FBG	DV	IO	T180-T250		9	2	6300	3		29500	35100
30	3	F-303SR1	OP	OFF	FBG	DV	IO	T300-T385		8	3	7250	2	10	40100	48400
31		F-31PC	OP	CR	FBG	DV	IO	T300-T330		11		11730	3	2	56400	63300
33		F-330SS	OP	CR	FBG	DV	IO	T300-T330		10	2	9700	2	11	50900	57200

LOA FT	IN	NAME AND/ OR MODEL	TOP/ RIG	BOAT TYPE	-HULL- MTL	TP	ENGINE TP	# HP	MFG	BEAM FT	IN	WGT LBS	DRAFT FT	IN	RETAIL LOW	RETAIL HIGH
		1996 BOATS														
33	6	F-336SR1	OP	OFF	FBG	DV	IO	T385-T510		8	3	8450	2	10	65700	80400
34		F-34PC	OP	CR	FBG	DV	IO	T300	MRCR	12		13000	2	6	73300	80500
34		F-34PC	OP	CR	FBG	DV	IB	T300-T310		12		13000	2	6	84400	93200
34		F-34PC	OP	CR	FBG	DV	IO	T330	MRCR	12		13000	2	6	74700	82100
38	2	F-382SR1	OP	OFF	FBG	DV	IO	T415	MRCR	8	3	10450	3	3	90400	99400
38	2	F-382SR1	OP	OFF	FBG	DV	IO	T470	MRCR	8	3	10450	3	3	97700	107500
38	2	F-382SR1	OP	OFF	FBG	DV	IO	T510	MRCR	8	3	10450	3	3	103000	113000
41		F-41PC	OP	CR	FBG	DV	IB	T410	MRCR	13	6	18520	2	9	127000	140000
41		F-41PC	OP	CR	FBG	DV	IB	T370D	CUM	13	6	21015	2	9	159500	175500
41	9	F-419SR1	OP	OFF	FBG	DV	IO	R415	MRCR	8	3	13100	3	2	116500	128000
41	9	F-419SR1	OP	OFF	FBG	DV	IO	R510	MRCR	8	3	13100	3	2	134000	147000
41	9	F-419SRI	OP	OFF	FBG	DV	IO	R500	MRCR	8	3	13100	3	2	132000	145000
		1995 BOATS														
18	2	FALCON 1800BR	OP	B/R	FBG	DV	OB			7	8	2550	2	6	6500	7500
18	2	FALCON 1800BR	OP	B/R	FBG	DV	IO	135-180		7	8	2550	2	6	5500	6700
18	2	FALCON 1800BR LE	OP	B/R	FBG	DV	OB			7	8	2550	2	6	6300	7200
18	2	FALCON 1800BR LE	OP	B/R	FBG	DV	IO	135-180		7	8	2550	2	6	5550	6450
18	2	FALCON 1800CB	OP	RNBT	FBG	DV	OB			7	8	2550	2	6	6300	7250
18	2	FALCON 1800CB	OP	RNBT	FBG	DV	IO	135-180		7	8	2500	2	6	5700	6650
18	2	FALCON 1800CB LE	OP	B/R	FBG	DV	OB			7	8	2550	2	6	6050	6950
18	2	FALCON 1800CB LE	OP	B/R	FBG	DV	IO	115-180		7	8	2550	2	6	5350	6200
20	2	FALCON 2000BR	OP	B/R	FBG	DV	IO	135-250		8		2825	2	6	8600	10400
20	2	FALCON 2000CD	OP	RNBT	FBG	DV	IO	135-250		8		2950	2	6	9150	10800
22	7	FALCON 2270BR	OP	B/R	FBG	DV	IO	205-250		8	6	3250	2	8	11200	13100
22	7	FALCON 2270BR	OP	B/R	FBG	DV	IO	330	MRCR	8	6	3250	2	8	12900	14700
22	7	FALCON 2270CD	OP	RNBT	FBG	DV	IO	205-300		8	6	3400	2	8	11600	14300
23	2	F-232BR	OP	B/R	FBG	DV	IO	250-300		8	6	4300	2	4	13700	17100
23	2	F-232LS	OP	B/R	FBG	DV	IO	250	MRCR	8	6	4300	2	4	14800	16800
23	2	F-232LS	OP	CUD	FBG	DV	IO	250-300		8	6	4300	2	4	15400	18400
23	2	F-232SS	OP	B/R	FBG	DV	IO	250	MRCR	8	6	4300	2	4	14500	16500
23	2	F-232SS	OP	CUD	FBG	DV	IO	250-300		8	6	4300	2	4	15100	18000
25	2	F-252BR	OP	B/R	FBG	DV	IO	300-350		8	6	4525	2	8	17000	20800
25	2	F-252BR	OP	B/R	FBG	DV	IO	385-415		8	6	4525	2	8	19800	23200
25	2	F-252LS	OP	B/R	FBG	DV	IO	385	MRCR	8	6	4525	2	4	19900	22100
25	2	F-252LS	OP	CUD	FBG	DV	IO	300-385		8	6	4525	2	4	18600	23000
25	2	F-252LS	OP	CUD	FBG	DV	IO	415	MRCR	8	6	4525	2	4	22600	25100
25	2	F-252SS	OP	CUD	FBG	DV	IO	300-350		8	6	4525	2	4	19000	21400
25	2	F-252SS	OP	CUD	FBG	DV	IO	385-415		8	6	4525	2	4	21700	25600
27		F-27PC	OP	OFF	FBG	DV	IO	300	MRCR	9	7	9500	3	5	33100	36800
27		F-27PC	OP	OFF	FBG	DV	IO	T180-T250		9	7	9500	3	5	33800	39200
27	1	F-271SR1	OP	OFF	FBG	DV	IO	350-415		8	3	5250	2	8	23600	28500
27	1	F-271SR1	OP	OFF	FBG	DV	IO	450-510		8	3	5250	2	8	26900	32400
28		FORMULA 280 SUN SPT	OP	SPTCR	FBG	DV	IO	300	MRCR	9	2	6300	3		26500	29500
28		FORMULA 280 SUN SPT	OP	SPTCR	FBG	DV	IO	T180-T250		9	2	6300	3		27500	32700
30	3	F-303SR1	OP	OFF	FBG	DV	IO	T300-T415		8	3	7250	2	10	37400	45100
30	3	F-303SR4	OP	OFF	FBG	DV	IO	T415	MRCR	8	3	7250	2	10	43600	48400
31		F-31PC	OP	CR	FBG	DV	IO	T300	MRCR	11		11730	3	2	52600	57800
33	6	F-336SR1	OP	OFF	FBG	DV	IO	T350-T500		8	3	8450	2	10	59600	74400
33	6	F-336SR1	OP	OFF	FBG	DV	IO	T510	MRCR	8	3	8450	2	10	68300	75000
34		F-34PC	OP	CR	FBG	DV	IB	T300-T410		12		13000	2	6	79800	92800
36		F-36PC	OP	CR	FBG	DV	IB	T410	MRCR	13	3	17600	3	8	94300	103500
38	2	F-382SR1	OP	OFF	FBG	DV	IO	T415	MRCR	8	3	10450	3	3	84400	92700
		IO T450 MRCR 88600 97400, IO T470 MRCR 91100 100000, IO T525 MRCR 97700 107500														
41	9	F-419SR1	OP	OFF	FBG	DV	IO	R415	MRCR	8	3	13100	3	2	108500	119500
41	9	F-419SR1	OP	OFF	FBG	DV	IO	R450	MRCR	8	3	13100	3	2	113000	124500
41	9	F-419SR1	OP	OFF	FBG	DV	IO	R525	MRCR	8	3	13100	3	2	127500	140500
41	9	F-419SRI	OP	OFF	FBG	DV	IO	R500	MRCR	8	3	13100	3	2	123000	135500
		1994 BOATS														
18	2	FALCON 1800BR	OP	B/R	FBG	DV	IO	135-180		7	8	2550	2	6	5200	6050
18	2	FALCON 1800CB	OP	RNBT	FBG	DV	IO	135-180		7	8	2500	2	6	5350	6200
20	2	FALCON 2000BR	OP	B/R	FBG	DV	IO	180-235		8		2825	2	6	8100	9600
20	2	FALCON 2000CD	OP	RNBT	FBG	DV	IO	180-235		8		2950	2	6	8500	10000
22	7	FALCON 2270BR	OP	B/R	FBG	DV	IO	205-270		8	6	3250	2	8	10400	12400
22	7	FALCON 2270BR	OP	B/R	FBG	DV	IO	330	MRCR	8	6	3250	2	8	12100	13700
23	2	F-232BR	OP	B/R	FBG	DV	IO	250	MRCR	8	6	4300	2	4	12700	14400
23	2	F-232BR	OP	B/R	FBG	DV	IO	300-350		8	6	4300	2	4	14000	17300
23	2	F-232LS	OP	B/R	FBG	DV	IO	250	MRCR	8	6	4300	2	4	14000	15900
23	2	F-232LS	OP	CUD	FBG	DV	IO	250-300		8	6	4300	2	4	14300	16900
23	2	F-232LS	OP	CUD	FBG	DV	IO	350	MRCR	8	6	4300	2	4	16400	18600
23	2	F-232SS	OP	B/R	FBG	DV	IO	250	MRCR	8	6	4300	2	4	13800	15700
23	2	F-232SS	OP	CUD	FBG	DV	IO	250-300		8	6	4300	2	4	14200	16700
23	2	F-232SS	OP	CUD	FBG	DV	IO	350	MRCR	8	6	4300	2	4	16200	18400
25	2	F-252BR	OP	B/R	FBG	DV	IO	250-300		8	6	4525	2	4	15100	18000
25	2	F-252BR	OP	B/R	FBG	DV	IO	385-415		8	6	4525	2	8	18100	21700
25	2	F-252LS	OP	B/R	FBG	DV	IO	385	MRCR	8	6	4525	2	4	18700	20700
25	2	F-252LS	OP	CUD	FBG	DV	IO	300-350		8	6	4525	2	4	16700	20800
25	2	F-252LS	OP	CUD	FBG	DV	IO	415	MRCR	8	6	4525	2	4	20900	23200
25	2	F-252SS	OP	B/R	FBG	DV	IO	385	MRCR	8	6	4525	2	4	19000	21100
25	2	F-252SS	OP	CUD	FBG	DV	IO	300-350		8	6	4525	2	4	17100	21200
25	2	F-252SS	OP	CUD	FBG	DV	IO	415	MRCR	8	6	4525	2	4	21300	23600
27		F-27PC	OP	OFF	FBG	DV	IO	300	MRCR	9	7	9500	3	5	30900	34300
27		F-27PC	OP	OFF	FBG	DV	IO	T180-T250		9	7	9500	3	5	31600	36600
27	1	F-271SR1	OP	OFF	FBG	DV	IO	300-385		8	3	5250	2	8	20900	25700
27	1	F-271SR1	OP	OFF	FBG	DV	IO	415-450		8	3	5250	2	4	24000	27900
27	1	F-271SR1	OP	OFF	FBG	DV	IO	510	MRCR	8	3	5250	2	4	27200	30200
30	3	F-303SR1	OP	OFF	FBG	DV	IO	T300-T415		8	3	7250	2	10	34900	43300
31		F-31PC	OP	CR	FBG	DV	IO	T300	MRCR	11		11730	3	2	49100	54000
33	6	F-336SR1	OP	OFF	FBG	DV	IO	T350-T450		8	3	8450	2	10	55700	66500
33	6	F-336SR1	OP	OFF	FBG	DV	IO	T510	MRCR	8	3	8450	2	10	63800	70100
34		F-34PC	OP	CR	FBG	DV	IB	T300	MRCR	12		13000	2	6	75500	83000
36		F-36PC	OP	CR	FBG	DV	IB	T410	MRCR	13	3	17600	3	8	90400	99300
38	2	F-382SR1	OP	OFF	FBG	DV	IO	T415	MRCR	8	3	10450	3	3	78800	86500
38	2	F-382SR1	OP	OFF	FBG	DV	IO	T525	MRCR	8	3	10450	3	3	91200	100500
41	9	F-419SR1	OP	OFF	FBG	DV	IO	R415	MRCR	8	3	13100	3	2	101500	111500
41	9	F-419SR1	OP	OFF	FBG	DV	IO	R525	MRCR	8	3	13100	3	2	119000	131000
41	9	F-419SRI	OP	OFF	FBG	DV	IO	R465	MRCR	8	3	13100	3	2	108500	119000
		1993 BOATS														
23	2	F-232BR	OP	B/R	FBG	DV	IO	270-330		8	6	4300	2	4	12700	15600
23	2	F-232BR	OP	B/R	FBG	DV	IO	365	MRCR	8	6	4300	2	4	14700	16700
23	2	F-232LS	OP	CUD	FBG	DV	IO	270-330		8	6	4300	2	4	13400	16300
23	2	F-232LS	OP	CUD	FBG	DV	IO	365	MRCR	8	6	4300	2	4	15600	17800
23	2	F-232SS	OP	CUD	FBG	DV	IO	270-330		8	6	4300	2	4	13600	16500
23	2	F-232SS	OP	CUD	FBG	DV	IO	365	MRCR	8	6	4300	2	4	15800	17900
25	2	F-252BR	OP	B/R	FBG	DV	IO	270-330		8	6	4525	2	8	14400	17600
25	2	F-252BR	OP	B/R	FBG	DV	IO	365-410		8	6	4525	2	8	16400	20300
25	2	F-252LS	OP	CUD	FBG	DV	IO	270-330		8	6	4525	2	4	15500	18700
25	2	F-252LS	OP	CUD	FBG	DV	IO	365-410		8	6	4525	2	4	18000	21600
25	2	F-252SS	OP	CUD	FBG	DV	IO	270-330		8	6	4525	2	4	15600	18900
25	2	F-252SS	OP	CUD	FBG	DV	IO	365-410		8	6	4525	2	4	18200	21800
26		F-26PC	OP	CR	FBG	DV	IO	330	MRCR	8	6	8200	2	11	25400	28200
26		F-26PC	OP	CR	FBG	DV	IO	T205	MRCR	8	6	8200	2	11	25800	28600
27	1	F-271SR1	OP	OFF	FBG	DV	IO	330-410		8	3	5250	2	8	20100	24700
27	1	F-271SR1	OP	OFF	FBG	DV	IO	465-525		8	3	5250	2	8	24000	28800
30	3	F-303SR1	OP	OFF	FBG	DV	IO	T270-T365		8	3	7250	2	10	31800	38400
30	3	F-303SR1	OP	OFF	FBG	DV	IO	T410	MRCR	8	3	7250	2	10	36200	40200
31		F-31PC	OP	CR	FBG	DV	IB	T330	MRCR	11		11730	3	2	56400	62000
33	6	F-336SR1	OP	OFF	FBG	DV	IO	T330-T465		8	3	8450	2	10	51300	63000
33	6	F-336SR1	OP	OFF	FBG	DV	IO	T500-T525		8	3	8450	2	10	59100	66300
34		F-34PC	OP	CR	FBG	DV	IB	T330		12		13000	2	6	72600	80000
36		F-36PC	OP	CR	FBG	DV	IB	T410	MRCR	13	3	17600	3	8	86100	94600
36		F-36PC	OP	CR	FBG	DV	IB	T306D	VLVO	13	3	17600	3	8	96300	106000
36		F-36PC	OP	CR	FBG	DV	IB	T340D	VLVO	13	3	17600	3	8	98600	108500
41	9	F-419SR1	OP	OFF	FBG	DV	IO	R410	MRCR	8	3	13100	3	2	94000	103500
41	9	F-419SR1	OP	OFF	FBG	DV	IO	R500	MRCR	8	3	13100	3	2	107500	118000
41	9	F-419SR1	OP	OFF	FBG	DV	IO	R525	MRCR	8	3	13100	3	2	111500	122500
41	9	F-419SRI	OP	OFF	FBG	DV	IO	R365	MRCR	8	3	13100	3	2	85400	93900
41	9	F-419SRI	OP	OFF	FBG	DV	IO	R410	MRCR	8	3	13100	3	2	90200	99100
41	9	F-419SRI	OP	OFF	FBG	DV	IO	R465	MRCR	8	3	13100	3	2	101500	111500
		1992 BOATS														
20	6	F-206LS	OP	CUD	FBG	DV	IO	270		7	10	3650	2	8	9600	11400
22	3	F-223LS	OP	CUD	FBG	DV	IO	270		8		4200	2	8	11700	13700
22	3	F-223LS	OP	CUD	FBG	DV	IO	330-365		8		4200	2	8	12700	15600
24	2	F-242LS	OP	OFF	FBG	DV	IO	270		8		4650	2	8	13900	16200
24	2	F-242LS	OP	OFF	FBG	DV	IO	330-365		8		4650	2	8	14900	18100
24	2	F-242LS	OP	OFF	FBG	DV	IO	410	MRCR	8		4650	2	8	17500	19900
24	2	F-242SS	OP	SPTCR	FBG	DV	IO	270		8		4750	2	8	14100	16500
24	2	F-242SS	OP	SPTCR	FBG	DV	IO	330-365		8		4750	2	8	15200	18400
25	2	F-252BR	OP	B/R	FBG	DV	IO	270	MRCR	8	6	4525	2	8	13500	15300
25	2	F-252BR	OP	B/R	FBG	DV	IO	330-365		8	6	4525	2	8	14500	17400
25	2	F-252BR	OP	B/R	FBG	DV	IO	410	MRCR	8	6	4525	2	8	16700	19000
26		F-26PC	OP	CR	FBG	DV	IO	330		8	6	8200	2	11	23800	26900
26		F-26PC	OP	CR	FBG	DV	IO	T205		8	6	8200	2	11	24100	27300
27	1	F-271SR1	OP	OFF	FBG	DV	IO	330-410		8	3	5150	2	8	18900	22900
27	1	F-271SR1	OP	OFF	FBG	DV	IO	465	MRCR	8	3	5150	2	8	22300	24800
29		F-29PC	OP	CR	FBG	DV	IO	T270-T330		10	7	11300	2	6	33300	39300
30	3	F-303SR1	OP	OFF	FBG	DV	IO	T270-T365		8	3	7250	2	10	29800	36000

 CONTINUED ON NEXT PAGE

LOA FT	LOA IN	NAME AND/ OR MODEL	TOP/ RIG	BOAT TYPE	-HULL- MTL	-HULL- TP	ENGINE TP	ENGINE # HP	ENGINE MFG	BEAM FT	BEAM IN	WGT LBS	DRAFT FT	DRAFT IN	RETAIL LOW	RETAIL HIGH
		1992 BOATS														
33	6	F-336SR1	OP	OFF	FBG	DV	IO	T330-T365		8	3	8450	2	10	48000	54100
33	6	F-336SR1	OP	OFF	FBG	DV	IO	T410-T465							55600	61100
34		F-34PC	OP	CR	FBG	DV	IB	T330		12		13000	2	6	68900	75900
35	7	F-357SRI	OP	OFF	FBG	DV	IO	T410	MRCR	8	6	9650	3		67700	74400
		IO T465 MRCR 71900 79000, IO T500 MRCR 74700 82100, IO T575 MRCR													80100	88000
36		F-36 EXPRESS	OP	CR	FBG	DV	IB	T340	MRCR	13	3	17200	3	8	78500	86200
36		F-36 EXPRESS	OP	CR	FBG	DV	IB	T410	MRCR	13	3	17200	3	8	81100	89100
36		F-36 EXPRESS	OP	CR	FBG	DV	IB	T300D	VLVO	13	3	17200	3	8	90200	99100
36		F-36PC	OP	CR	FBG	DV	IB	T340	MRCR	13	3	17600	3	8	79400	87300
36		F-36PC	OP	CR	FBG	DV	IB	T410	MRCR	13	3	17600	3	8	82100	90200
36		F-36PC	OP	CR	FBG	DV	IB	T306D	VLVO	13	3	17600	3	8	91800	101000
41	9	F-419SRI	OP	OFF	FBG	DV	IO	R365	MRCR	8	3	13100	3	2	80000	87900
41	9	F-419SRI	OP	OFF	FBG	DV	IO	R410	MRCR	8	3	13100	3	2	86200	94700
41	9	F-419SRI	OP	OFF	FBG	DV	IO	R465	MRCR	8	3	13100	3	2	94900	104500
		1991 BOATS														
20	6	F 206LS	OP	CUD	FBG	DV	IO	270		7	10	3650	2	8	9050	10700
22	3	F-223LS	OP	CUD	FBG	DV	IO	270		8		4200	2	8	11000	12900
22	3	F-223LS	OP	CUD	FBG	DV	IO	330-365		8		4200	2	8	11900	14600
24	2	F-242LS	OP	OFF	FBG	DV	IO	270		8		4650	2	8	13000	15200
24	2	F-242LS	OP	OFF	FBG	DV	IO	330-365		8		4650	2	8	14000	16900
24	2	F-242LS	OP	OFF	FBG	DV	IO	410	MRCR	8		4650	2	8	16400	18700
24	2	F-242SS	OP	SPTCR	FBG	DV	IO	270		8		4750	2	8	13300	15500
24	2	F-242SS	OP	SPTCR	FBG	DV	IO	330-365		8		4750	2	8	14200	17200
26		F-26PC	OP	CR	FBG	DV	IO	330		8	6	8200	2	11	22300	25200
26		F-26PC	OP	CR	FBG	DV	IO	T205		8	6	8200	2	11	22600	25600
27	2	F-272SRI	OP	OFF	FBG	DV	IO	T270-T330		8		7050	2	10	22300	26700
27	2	F-272SRI	OP	OFF	FBG	DV	IO	T365	MRCR	8		7050	2	10	25300	28200
29		F-29PC	OP	CR	FBG	DV	IO	T270-T330		10	7	11300	2	6	31200	36900
29	2	F-292SRI	OP	OFF	FBG	DV	IO	T330-T410		8		7400	2	10	27400	33500
31	1	F-311SRI	OP	OFF	FBG	DV	IO	T330-T465		8		7950	2	10	32300	40000
35	7	F-357SRI	OP	OFF	FBG	DV	IO	T410	MRCR	8	6	9650	3		63500	69800
		IO T420 MRCR 64200 70500, IO T465 MRCR 67500 74100, IO T500 MRCR													70000	77000
		IO T575 MRCR 75100 82600														
36		F-36 EXPRESS	OP	CR	FBG	DV	IB	T340	MRCR	13	3	17200	3	8	74900	82300
		IB T340 VLVO 75300 82800, IB T410 MRCR 77400 85000, IB T300D J&T													87900	96600
		IB T300D VLVO 86100 94600														
36		F-36PC	OP	CR	FBG	DV	IB	T340	MRCR	13	3	17600	3	8	75800	83300
		IB T340 VLVO 76200 83800, IB T410 MRCR 78300 86000, IB T300D J&T													89000	97800
		IB T300D VLVO 87200 95800														
41	9	F-419SRI	OP	OFF	FBG	DV	IO	R365	MRCR	8	3	13100	3	2	75000	82400
41	9	F-419SRI	OP	OFF	FBG	DV	IO	R410	MRCR	8	3	13100	3	2	80900	88900
41	9	F-419SRI	OP	OFF	FBG	DV	IO	R465	MRCR	8	3	13100	3	2	89100	97900
		1990 BOATS														
22	1	F 206LS	OP	CUD	FBG	DV	IO	270		7	10	3150	2	8	8300	9950
24	1	F-223LS	OP	CUD	FBG	DV	IO	270		8		3750	2	8	10400	12300
24	1	F-223LS	OP	CUD	FBG	DV	IO	330		8		3750	2	8	11400	13500
26		F-242SS	OP	SPTCR	FBG	DV	IO	270-330		8		4150	2	8	13100	16100
26	2	F-242LS	OP	OFF	FBG	DV	IO	330-365		8		4150	2	8	13600	16400
28	11	F-272SRI	OP	OFF	FBG	DV	IO	T270-T330		8		5750	2	10	22100	26300
30	5	F-26PC	OP	CR	FBG	DV	IO	330		8	6	7000	2	11	23400	26100
		IO 200D VLVO 23300 25900, IO T205 24300 27100, IO T130D VLVO													25100	27800
30	11	F-292SRI	OP	OFF	FBG	DV	IO	T330-T365		8		7000	2	10	25400	29400
33		F-311SRI	OP	OFF	FBG	DV	IO	T330-T420		8		7400	2	10	38900	46400
33	9	F-29PC	OP	CR	FBG	DV	IO	T270-T330		10	7	9700	2	6	39100	45700
33	9	F-29PC	OP	CR	FBG	DV	IO	T200D	VLVO	10	7	9700	2	6	42300	47000
36		F-36 EXPRESS	OP	CR	FBG	DV	IO	T340	VLVO	13	3	15000	3	8	42000	46700
36		F-36 EXPRESS	OP	CR	FBG	DV	IB	T340	MRCR	13	3	15000	3	8	65700	72200
36		F-36 EXPRESS	OP	CR	FBG	DV	IO	T300D	J&T	13	3	15000	3	8	52500	57700
36		F-36PC	OP	CR	FBG	DV	IO	T340	VLVO	13	3	15000	3	8	43200	48000
36		F-36PC	OP	CR	FBG	DV	IB	T340	MRCR	13	3	15000	3	8	67600	74300
36		F-36PC	OP	CR	FBG	DV	IO	T300D	J&T	13	3	15000	3	8	53800	59100
37	7	F-357SRI	OP	OFF	FBG	DV	IO	T420	MRCR	8	6	8950	3		54300	59600
37	7	F-357SRI	OP	OFF	FBG	DV	IO	T500	MRCR	8	6	8950	3		61000	67000
37	7	F-357SRI	OP	OFF	FBG	DV	IO	T575	MRCR	8	6	8950	3		66400	73000
		1989 BOATS														
20	6	FORMULA 206 LS	OP	CUD	FBG	DV	IO	205-270		7	10	3150	2	8	7100	8300
20	6	FORMULA 206 LS	OP	CUD	FBG	DV	IO	320	MRCR	7	10	3150	2	8	7900	9100
22	3	FORMULA 223 LS	OP	CUD	FBG	DV	IO	270-320		8		3750	2	8	9000	11000
22	3	FORMULA 223 LS	OP	CUD	FBG	DV	IO	330	MRCR	8		3900	2	8	10100	11500
22	3	FORMULA 223 SUNSPORT	OP	SPTCR	FBG	DV	IO	270-330		8		3750	2	8	9000	11200
24	2	FORMULA 242 LS	OP	OFF	FBG	DV	IO	330-365		8		4150	2	8	11500	14000
24	2	FORMULA 242 SUNSPORT	OP	SPTCR	FBG	DV	IO	271-330		8		4150	2	8	11000	13100
26		FORMULA 26 PC	OP	CR	FBG	DV	IO	271-330		8	6	7000	2	9	16900	20000
26		FORMULA 26 PC	OP	CR	FBG	DV	IO	T205-T271		8	6	7000	2	9	18300	21800
27	2	FORMULA 272 SR-1	OP	OFF	FBG	DV	IO	T270-T330		8		5750	2	10	18200	21700
29		FORMULA 29 PC	OP	CR	FBG	DV	IO	T270-T330		10	7	9700	2	5	26000	30500
29	2	FORMULA 292 SR-1	OP	OFF	FBG	DV	IO	T330-T365		8		7000	2	10	24000	27700
31	1	FORMULA 311 SR-1	OP	OFF	FBG	DV	IO	T330-T420		8		7400	2	10	28400	33900
35		FORMULA 35 PC	OP	CR	FBG	DV	IB	T340	MRCR	12		13750	2	8	62600	68800
35	7	FORMULA 357 SR-1	OP	OFF	FBG	DV	IO	T420	MRCR	8	6	8950	3		56000	61600
35	7	FORMULA 357 SR-1	OP	OFF	FBG	DV	IO	T575	MRCR	8	6	8950	3		65800	72300
36		FORMULA 36 EXPRESS	OP	CR	FBG	DV	IO	T340	MRCR	13	3	15000	2	8	39500	43900
		1988 BOATS														
20	6	FORMULA 206 LS	OP	CUD	FBG	DV	IO	260-270		7	10	3150	2	8	6700	7850
20	6	FORMULA 206 LS	OP	CUD	FBG	DV	IO	320	MRCR	7	10	3150	2	8	7500	8600
20	6	FORMULA 206 SPIDER	OP	RNBT	FBG	DV	IO	260-270		7	10	3250	2	8	6500	7650
20	6	FORMULA 206 SPIDER	OP	RNBT	FBG	DV	IO	320	MRCR	7	10	3250	2	8	7250	8350
22	3	FORMULA 223 LS	OP	CUD	FBG	DV	IO	260-270		8		3750	2	8	8300	9700
22	3	FORMULA 223 LS	OP	CUD	FBG	DV	IO	320-340		8		3750	2	8	9200	11000
22	3	FORMULA 223 SUNSPORT	OP	SPTCR	FBG	DV	IO	260-270		8		3750	2	8	8300	10100
22	3	FORMULA 223 SUNSPORT	OP	SPTCR	FBG	DV	IO	330	MRCR	8		3750	2	8	9400	10700
24	2	FORMULA 242 LS	OP	OFF	FBG	DV	IO	260-320		8		4150	2	8	9900	12100
24	2	FORMULA 242 LS	OP	OFF	FBG	DV	IO	330-365		8		4300	2	8	11100	13200
24	2	FORMULA 242 SR-1	OP	OFF	FBG	DV	IO	T270	MRCR	8		5050	2	8	13200	15000
24	2	FORMULA 242 SUNSPORT	OP	SPTCR	FBG	DV	IO	260-270		8		4150	2	8	9950	11800
24	2	FORMULA 242 SUNSPORT	OP	SPTCR	FBG	DV	IO	330	MRCR	8		4300	2	8	11200	12700
26	3	FORMULA 26 PC	OP	CR	FBG	DV	IO	260-330		8	6	7000	2	9	15800	19000
26	3	FORMULA 26 PC	OP	CR	FBG	DV	IO	T205	MRCR	8	6	7000	2	9	17100	19400
27	2	FORMULA 272 SR-1	OP	OFF	FBG	DV	IO	T270-T320		8		5750	2	10	16800	20500
27	2	FORMULA 272 SR-1	OP	OFF	FBG	DV	IO	T365	MRCR	8		5750	2	10	19600	21800
29	2	FORMULA 29 PC	OP	CR	FBG	DV	IO	T270		10	7	9700	2	5	24800	27800
31	1	FORMULA 311 SR-1	OP	OFF	FBG	DV	IO	T330-T450		8		7400	2	10	26900	33100
35		FORMULA 35 PC	OP	CR	FBG	DV	IB	T340	MRCR	12		13750	2	8	59600	65500
35	7	FORMULA 357 SR-1	OP	OFF	FBG	DV	IO	T405	KAAM	8	6	8950	3		52700	57900
35	7	FORMULA 357 SR-1	OP	OFF	FBG	DV	IO	T420	MRCR	8	6	8950	3		53100	58300
35	7	FORMULA 357 SR-1	OP	OFF	FBG	DV	IO	T450	KAAM	8	6	8950	3		55500	61000
		1987 BOATS														
20	6	FORMULA 206 LS	OP	RNBT	FBG	DV	IO	260		7	10	3150	2	8	6150	7050
20	6	FORMULA 206 SPIDER	OP	RNBT	FBG	DV	IO	260		7	10	3250	2	8	6250	7200
22	3	FORMULA 223 LS	OP	RNBT	FBG	DV	IO	260-320		8		3750	2	8	7500	9400
22	3	FORMULA 223 LS	OP	RNBT	FBG	DV	IO	330-340		8		3900	2	8	8550	9900
22	3	FORMULA 223 SUNSPORT	OP	WKNDR	FBG	DV	IO	260		8		3750	2	8	7950	9150
24	2	FORMULA 242 LS	OP	OFF	FBG	DV	IO	260-320		8		4150	2	8	9450	11500
24	2	FORMULA 242 LS	OP	OFF	FBG	DV	IO	330-340		8		4300	2	8	10600	12100
24	2	FORMULA 242 SR-1	OP	OFF	FBG	DV	IO	T260	MRCR	8		5050	2	8	12400	14100
24	2	FORMULA 242 SUNSPORT	OP	WKNDR	FBG	DV	IO	260		8		4150	2	8	9500	10800
24	2	FORMULA 242 SUNSPORT	OP	WKNDR	FBG	DV	IO	330	MRCR	8		4300	2	8	10700	12100
25		FORMULA 25 PC	OP	SPTCR	FBG	DV	IO	260		8		4550	2	8	10600	12100
25		FORMULA 25 PC	OP	SPTCR	FBG	DV	IO	330-340		8		4700	2	8	11800	13500
25		FORMULA 25 PC	OP	SPTCR	FBG	DV	IO	T180	MRCR	8		5050	2	8	12200	13900
27	2	FORMULA 272 SR-1	OP	OFF	FBG	DV	IO	T260	MRCR	8		5750	2	10	15800	18000
28		FORMULA 28 PC	OP	SPTCR	FBG	DV	IO	T260	MRCR	10		7850	2	10	20100	22300
31	1	FORMULA 311 SR-1	OP	OFF	FBG	DV	IO	T330-T450		8		7400	2	10	25500	31400
35		FORMULA 35 PC	OP	CR	FBG	DV	IB	T340	MRCR	12		13750	2	8	56900	62500
35	7	FORMULA 357 SR-1	OP	OFF	FBG	DV	IO	T370	MRCR	8	6	8950	3		47900	52600
		IO T405 KAAM 50100 55000, IO T420 MRCR 50400 55400, IO T450 KAAM													52800	58000
		1986 BOATS														
20	6	FORMULA 206 SPIDER	OP	RNBT	FBG	DV	IO			7	10	3250	2	8	**	**
20	6	FORMULA 206LS	OP	RNBT	FBG	DV	IO			7	10	3150	2	8	**	**
21	6	FORMULA 3 SUNSPORT	OP	CUD	FBG	DV	IO			8		3800	2	8	**	**
21	6	FORMULA 3LS	OP	CUD	FBG	DV	IO			8		3500	2	8	**	**
21	6	FORMULA 3SF	OP	SF	FBG	DV	IO			8		3800	2	8	**	**
24	2	FORMULA 242 SUNSPORT	OP	CUD	FBG	DV	IO			8		4200	2	8	**	**
24	2	FORMULA 242LS	OP	CUD	FBG	DV	IO			8		4200	2	8	**	**
24	2	FORMULA 242SF	OP	SF	FBG	DV	OB			8		3250	2	3	8100	9350
24	2	FORMULA 242SF	OP	SF	FBG	DV	IO			8		4200	2	8	**	**
25		FORMULA 25PC	OP	SPTCR	FBG	DV	IO			8		4550	2	8	**	**
27	2	FORMULA 272LS	OP	SPTCR	FBG	DV	IO			8		5750	2	10	**	**
28		FORMULA 28PC	OP	SPTCR	FBG	DV	IO			10		7850	2	10	**	**
30	2	FORMULA 302SR1	OP	SPTCR	FBG	DV	IO			8		6950	3		**	**
35		FORMULA 35 PC	OP	CR	FBG	DV	IO			12		13750	2	4	**	**
35	7	FORMULA 357 SR-1	OP	OFF	FBG	DV	IO			8	6	8950	3		**	**

 CONTINUED ON NEXT PAGE

LOA FT	LOA IN	NAME AND/ OR MODEL	TOP/ RIG	BOAT TYPE	HULL MTL	HULL TP	ENGINE TP	ENGINE # HP	ENGINE MFG	BEAM FT	BEAM IN	WGT LBS	DRAFT FT	DRAFT IN	RETAIL LOW	RETAIL HIGH
		1985 BOATS														
18	2	F-18	ST	RNBT	FBG	DV	OB			7	8	1650	2	7	3400	4000
18	2	F-18	ST	RNBT	FBG	DV	IO	170-260		7	8	2618	2	7	3300	4100
18	2	F-18 BOW RIDER	ST	RNBT	FBG	DV	IO	170-260		7	8	2698	2	7	3350	4150
19	6	FORMULA-TWO SF	ST	SF	FBG	DV	OB			8		2635	2	8	4700	5400
19	6	FORMULA-TWO SF	ST	SF	FBG	DV	IO	170-260		8		3050	2	8	4700	5750
19	6	FORMULA-TWO SS	ST	CUD	FBG	DV	IO	170-260		8		3050	2	8	4100	5050
21	6	FORMULA-THREE LS	ST	CUD	FBG	DV	IO	228-260		8		3500	2	8	6500	7700
21	6	FORMULA-THREE SF	ST	SF	FBG	DV	IO	198-260		8		3800	2	8	7750	9250
21	6	FORMULA-THREE SS	ST	CUD	FBG	DV	IO	198-260		8		3800	2	8	6800	8150
23		FORMULA 23 SC	ST	EXP	FBG	DV	IO	170-260		8		3900	2	8	7450	8800
24	2	FORMULA 242 LS	OP	CUD	FBG	DV	IO	260-330		8		4575	3	2	9400	11500
24	2	FORMULA 242 LS	OP	CUD	FBG	DV	IO	370-400		8		4575	3	2	10900	13300
24	2	FORMULA 242 LS	OP	CUD	FBG	DV	IO	T260	MRCR	8		4575	3	2	10700	12100
24	2	FORMULA 242 SF	OP	SF	FBG	DV	OB			8		3650			8600	9900
24	2	FORMULA 242 SF	OP	SF	FBG	DV	IO	260		8		4200	2	8	10000	11400
24	2	FORMULA 242 SS	ST	CUD	FBG	DV	IO	260	MRCR	8		4200	2	8	8850	10000
25		FORMULA 25 PC	OP	SPTCR	FBG	DV	IO	260		8		5300	2	11	10800	12300
25		FORMULA 25 PC	OP	SPTCR	FBG	DV	IO	T170-T188		8		5300	2	11	11500	13200
26	2	FORMULA 26 SF	OP	SF	FBG	DV	IO	T170-T260		9	6	6600	2	6	16200	19800
27	2	FORMULA 272 LS	OP	SPTCR	FBG	DV	IO	T260	MRCR	8		5750	3		14800	16800
28		FORMULA 28 PC	ST	SPTCR	FBG	DV	IO	T260	MRCR	10		7850	2	10	18600	20700
30	2	FORMULA 302 SRI	ST	SPTCR	FBG	DV	IO	T330-T425		8		6950	3	2	20600	25400
31	6	FORMULA 31 SC		EXP	FBG	DV	IB	T260		12		10500	2	6	35400	39400
31	6	FORMULA 31 SF		SF	FBG	DV	IB	T260		12		11600	2	6	36200	40200
31	6	FORMULA 31 SF	OP	SF	FBG	DV	IB	T340	MRCR	12		10500	2	6	37300	41400
31	6	FORMULA 31 SF	OP	SF	FBG	DV	IB	T240D	S&S	12		10500	2	6	44100	49100
31	6	FORMULA 31 SF	TT	SF	FBG	DV	IB	T340	MRCR	12		10500	2	6	37300	41400
31	6	FORMULA 31 SF	TT	SF	FBG	DV	IB	T240D	S&S	12		10500	2	6	44100	49100
31	6	FORMULA 31SC	OP	EXP	FBG	DV	IB	T340		12		10500	2	6	37300	41400
40	2	FORMULA 402 SRI	OP	SPTCR	FBG	DV	IO	T375	KAAM	9	4	10250	3		46600	51200
40	2	FORMULA 402 SRI	OP	SPTCR	FBG	DV	IO	T425	KAAM	9	4	10250	3		49900	54900
40	2	FORMULA F-402 SR1	OP	SPTCR	FBG	DV	IO	T330	MRCR	9	4	10250	3		43200	48000
		IO T370 MRCR 45700 50200, IO T400 MRCR 47600 52300, IO T440 MRCR 50100 55100														
		1984 BOATS														
16	9	FORMULA-ONE	OP	RNBT	FBG	DV	OB			7	3	1050	2	8	2300	2650
16	9	FORMULA-ONE	OP	RNBT	FBG	DV	IO	120-188		7	3	1950	2	8	2400	2850
18	2	F-18	ST	RNBT	FBG	DV	OB			7	8	1650	2	7	3350	3900
18	2	F-18	ST	RNBT	FBG	DV	IO	170-260		7	8	2618	2	7	3200	3950
18	2	F-18 BOW RIDER	ST	RNBT	FBG	DV	IO	170-260		7	8	2698	2	7	3250	4000
19	6	FORMULA-TWO B/R	ST	RNBT	FBG	DV	OB			8		1913	2	8	3900	4550
19	6	FORMULA-TWO B/R	ST	RNBT	FBG	DV	IO	170-260		8		2850	2	8	3650	4500
19	6	FORMULA-TWO SC	ST	CUD	FBG	DV	IO	170-260		8		3050	2	8	3950	4900
19	6	FORMULA-TWO SPTMN	ST	SF	FBG	DV	OB			8		2635	2	8	4600	5250
19	6	FORMULA-TWO SPTMN	ST	SF	FBG	DV	IO	170-260		8		3050	2	8	4550	5550
21	6	FORMULA-THREE LS	ST	CUD	FBG	DV	IO	198-260		8		3500	2	8	6200	7400
21	6	FORMULA-THREE SF	ST	SF	FBG	DV	IO	198-260		8		3800	2	8	7500	8950
23		F-23 SC EXPRESS	ST	EXP	FBG	DV	IO	170-260		8		3800	2	8	7050	8450
23		F-23 SC EXPRESS	HT	EXP	FBG	DV	IO	198-260		8		3800	2	8	7100	8450
23		FORMULA 23 SF		SF	FBG	DV	IO	175		8		3700			7900	9100
23		FORMULA 23 SF	OP	SF	FBG	DV	OB			8		3500	2	1	7700	8850
24	2	FORMULA 242 LS	OP	CUD	FBG	DV	IO	260-330		8		4575	3	2	9100	11100
24	2	FORMULA 242 LS	OP	CUD	FBG	DV	IO	370-400		8		4575	3	2	10600	12800
24	2	FORMULA 242 LS	OP	CUD	FBG	DV	IO	T260	MRCR	8		4575	3	2	10300	11700
24	2	FORMULA 242 SF		SF	FBG	DV	OB			8		3650			8450	9700
24	2	FORMULA 242 SF	OP	SF	FBG	DV	IO	260		8		4200	2	8	9650	11000
25		F-25 SC EXPRESS	ST	EXP	FBG	DV	IO	198-260		8		4350	2	11	8650	10400
25		F-25 SC EXPRESS	HT	EXP	FBG	DV	IO	198-260		8		4350	2	11	8650	10400
25		FORMULA 25 PC	OP	SPTCR	FBG	DV	IO	228-260		8		5300	2	11	10200	11900
25		FORMULA 25 PC	OP	SPTCR	FBG	DV	IO	T170-T188		8		5300	2	11	11100	12800
26	2	F-26 SC EXPRESS	ST	EXP	FBG	DV	IO	T170-T260		9	6	6600	2	6	13700	16800
26	2	FORMULA 26 SF	OP	SF	FBG	DV	IO	T170-T260		9	6	6600	2	6	15600	19100
27	2	FORMULA 272 LS	OP	SPTCR	FBG	DV	IO	T260-T300		8		5750	3		14300	17300
30	2	FORMULA 302 SR1	OP	SPTCR	FBG	DV	IO	T400	KAAM	8		6950	3	2	21500	23900
30	2	FORMULA 302 SR1	ST	SPTCR	FBG	DV	IO	T330-T425		8		6950	3	2	19900	24500
31	6	FORMULA 31 SF		SF	FBG	DV	IO	T260-T340		12		10500	2	6	30600	35900
31	6	FORMULA 31 SF		SF	FBG	DV	IO	T215D-T240D		12		10500	2	6	37800	43100
31	6	FORMULA 31 SF	FB	SF	FBG	DV	IO	T260-T340		12		10500	2	6	30600	35900
31	6	FORMULA 31 SF	FB	SF	FBG	DV	IO	T215D-T240D		12		10500	2	6	37800	43100
31	6	FORMULA 31SC	OP	EXP	FBG	DV	IO	T260	KAAM	12		10500	2	6	26900	29800
31	6	FORMULA 31SC	OP	EXP	FBG	DV	IO	T340D	KAAM	12		10500	2	6	34500	38300
40	2	FORMULA 402 SR1	OP	SPTCR	FBG	DV	IO	T330	MRCR	9	4	10250	3		41700	46400
		IO T370 MRCR 43700 48500, IO T375 KAAM 44500 49500, IO T400 KAAM 46700 51300														
		IO T400 MRCR 46000 50600, IO T425 KAAM 48300 53100, IO T440 MRCR 47200 51800														

....For earlier years, see the BUC Used Boat Price Guide, Volume 3

THUNDERCRAFT

THUNDERCRAFT
GRAND MERE QUE CANADA G COAST GUARD MFG ID- ZMC
FORMERLY CADORETTE MARINE

See inside cover to adjust price for area

For more recent years, see the BUC Used Boat Price Guide, Volume 1

LOA FT	LOA IN	NAME AND/ OR MODEL	TOP/ RIG	BOAT TYPE	HULL MTL	HULL TP	ENGINE TP	ENGINE # HP	ENGINE MFG	BEAM FT	BEAM IN	WGT LBS	DRAFT FT	DRAFT IN	RETAIL LOW	RETAIL HIGH
		1994 BOATS														
16	8	DIABLO 170	OP	B/R	F/S	DV	OB			6	11	1078			2600	3050
18	7	DIABLO 180	OP	B/R	F/S	DV	OB			7	4	1365			3350	3900
18	7	DIABLO 185	OP	B/R	F/S	DV	IO	135-180		7	4	2415			5300	6150
20	1	DIABLO 205	OP	CUD	F/S	DV	IO	180-235		7	9	2825	1	3	7350	8750
23	7	DIABLO 230	OP	CUD	F/S	DV	IO	180-235		8	6	3350	1	5	10300	12000
25		EXPRESS 240	ST	CR	F/S	DV	IO	250	MRCR	8	6	4806	1	8	14700	16700
27	10	EXPRESS 260	ST	CR	F/S	DV	IO	250-300		9		5700	1	10	19700	22800
27	10	EXPRESS 260	ST	CR	F/S	DV	IO	140D	MRCR	9		5700	1	10	20000	22300
27	10	EXPRESS 260	ST	CR	F/S	DV	IO	T135	MRCR	9		5700	1	10	20400	22600
30		EXPRESS 280	ST	CR	F/S	DV	IO	T180-T250		10		7210	1	11	26600	31500
30		EXPRESS 280	ST	CR	F/S	DV	IO	T140D	MRCR	12		11904	1	11	44000	48900
36	10	EXPRESS 350	ST	CR	F/S	DV	IO	T300	MRCR	12		11904	1	11	46200	50800
36	10	EXPRESS 350	ST	CR	F/S	DV	IO	T200D	MRCR	12		11904	1	11	56500	62100
		1993 BOATS														
17		NUOVA 170	ST	RNBT	F/S	SV	OB			7	3	1579			3450	4000
17		NUOVA 170	ST	RNBT	F/S	SV	IO	115-155		7	3	2204			4500	5200
17		STORM 170	ST	RNBT	F/S	DV	OB			6	10	1058			2500	2900
19		MAGNUM 195	ST	CUD	F/S	DV	IO	155-175		7	8	2422			5600	6500
19		NUOVA 190	ST	RNBT	F/S	DV	IO	155-175		7	8	2425			5450	6300
23	2	MAGNUM 215	ST	CUD	F/S	DV	IO	175-230		8		3572			9650	11200
25		EXPRESS 240	ST	CR	F/S	DV	IO	230-240		8	6	4740	1	8	13400	15400
27	10	EXPRESS 260	ST	CR	F/S	DV	IO	240-300		9		5250	1	10	17500	20900
27	10	EXPRESS 260	ST	CR	F/S	DV	IO	T115	MRCR	9		5250	1	10	18200	20200
30	1	EXPRESS 280	ST	CR	F/S	DV	IO	T175-T230		10		7552	1	11	25200	29400
36	10	EXPRESS 350	ST	CR	F/S	DV	IO	T300	MRCR	12		12000	3		42900	47700
36	10	EXPRESS 350	ST	CR	F/S	DV	IO	T210D	MRCR	12		12000	3		53400	58600
		1992 BOATS														
16		SKIMASTER 160	ST	SKI	F/S	DV	OB			6	5	904			2000	2350
17		NUOVA 170	ST	RNBT	F/S	SV	OB			7	3	1579			3300	3850
17		NUOVA 170	ST	RNBT	F/S	SV	IO	115-155		7	3	2204			4150	4850
19		MAGNUM 195	ST	CUD	F/S	DV	IO	155-175		7	8	2422			5250	6050
19		NUOVA 190	ST	RNBT	F/S	DV	IO	155-175		7	8	2425			5100	5900
20	10	EAGLE I	ST	OFF	F/S	DV	IO	175-230		8		3420			7700	9050
20	10	NUOVA 200	ST	RNBT	F/S	DV	IO	155-175		8		3572			7550	8700
23	2	MAGNUM 215	ST	CUD	F/S	DV	IO	175-230		8		3572			9100	10500
25		EXPRESS 240	ST	CR	F/S	DV	IO	230-240		8	6	4740	1	8	12600	14400
27		EAGLE III	ST	OFF	F/S	DV	IO	T300-T360				6211			20400	24900
27	10	EXPRESS 260	ST	CR	F/S	DV	IO	240-300		9		5250	1	10	16400	19600
27	10	EXPRESS 260	ST	CR	F/S	DV	IO	T115	MRCR	9		5250	1	10	16600	18900
30	1	EXPRESS 280	ST	CR	F/S	DV	IO	T175-T230		10		7552	1	11	23600	27500
36	10	EXPRESS 350	ST	CR	F/S	DV	IO	T300	MRCR	12		12000	3		40200	44600
36	10	EXPRESS 350	ST	CR	F/S	DV	IO	T210D	MRCR	12		12000	3		50000	54900
		1991 BOATS														
16		SKIMASTER	ST	SKI	F/S	DV	OB			6	5	904			1900	2300
16	6	SKIPPER 166	ST	RNBT	F/S	DV	OB			7	2	1150			2450	2850
17		NUOVA 170	ST	RNBT	F/S	SV	IO	130-175		7	3	2204			3900	4800
17		NUOVA 170 O/B	ST	RNBT	F/S	SV	OB			7	3	1579			3150	3700
19		NUOVA 190	ST	RNBT	F/S	DV	IO	175-205		7	8	2425			4800	5600
19		NUOVA 195	ST	CUD	F/S	DV	IO	175-205		7	8	2750			5300	6200
21	6	EAGLE II	ST	CUD	F/S	DV	IO	330-365				3572			9200	11300
23	2	HOLIDAY 210	ST	CUD	F/S	DV	IO	205-260		8		3572	1	6	8250	10200
23	2	HOLIDAY 210 GL	ST	CUD	F/S	DV	IO	205-260		8		3572	1	6	8900	10400
25		HOLIDAY 240	ST	CR	F/S	DV	IO	260-270		8	6	4740	1	8	12100	14000
27		EAGLE III	ST	CUD	F/S	DV	IO	365-420				5245			16300	20000
27		EAGLE III	ST	CUD	F/S	DV	IO	T330-T365				6260			20500	24200
27	10	HOLIDAY 260	ST	CR	F/S	DV	IO	260-330		9		5138	1	10	15500	19100
27	10	HOLIDAY 260	ST	CR	F/S	DV	IO	T130	MRCR	9		6045	1	10	16800	19100
30		HOLIDAY 280	ST	CR	F/S	DV	IO	T205-T270		10		7346	1	11	22400	26700

....For earlier years, see the BUC Used Boat Price Guide, Volume 3

TIARA YACHTS INC

DIV OF S2 YACHTS, INC
TIARA & S2 YACHTS
HOLLAND MI 49423

See inside cover to adjust price for area

COAST GUARD MFG ID- SSU
ALSO PURSUIT

For more recent years, see the BUC Used Boat Price Guide, Volume 1

LOA FT	LOA IN	NAME AND/ OR MODEL	TOP/ RIG	BOAT TYPE	-HULL- MTL	-HULL- TP	ENGINE TP	ENGINE # HP	ENGINE MFG	BEAM FT	BEAM IN	WGT LBS	DRAFT FT	DRAFT IN	RETAIL LOW	RETAIL HIGH
		1996 BOATS														
28	9	TIARA 2900 OPEN	OP	SPTCR	FBG	SV	IB	T250-T320		11	4	10000	2	2	61900	71200
28	9	TIARA 2900 OPEN	OP	SPTCR	FBG	SV	IO	T225D	GM	11	4	10000	2	2	72300	79400
31	6	TIARA 3100 OPEN	OP	EXP	F/S	SV	IB	T300	CRUS	12		11500	2	2	80000	87900
31	6	TIARA 3100 OPEN	OP	EXP	F/S	SV	IB	T230D-T315D		12		11500	2	2	93500	111500
32	10	TIARA 3300 OPEN	OP	EXP	F/S	SV	IB	T300	CRUS	12	6	13500	2	3	89300	98200
32	10	TIARA 3300 OPEN	OP	EXP	F/S	SV	IB	T315D	CUM	12	6	13500	2	3	112500	123500
35	8	TIARA 3500 EXP	OP	EXP	FBG	SV	IO	T380	CRUS	13	9	19800	2	10	103500	113500
35	8	TIARA 3500 EXP	OP	EXP	FBG	SV	IO	T420D	CUM	13	9	19800	2	10	125500	138000
35	8	TIARA 3500 EXP	OP	EXP	FBG	SV	IO	T435D	CAT	13	9	19800	2	10	132000	145000
36	8	TIARA 3600 OPEN	OP	EXP	F/S	SV	IB	T355	CRUS	13	9	16500	2	11	108000	118500
36	8	TIARA 3600 OPEN	OP	EXP	F/S	SV	IB	T375D	CAT	13	9	16500	2	11	138500	152500
37		TIARA 3700 OPEN	OP	EXP	F/S	SV	IB	T375D	CAT	14	2	21000	3	9	155500	171000
37	1	TIARA 3700 OPEN	OP	EXP	F/S	SV	IB	T420D	CUM	14	2	21000	3	9	156500	172000
37	1	TIARA 3700 OPEN	OP	EXP	F/S	SV	IB	T435D	CAT	14	2	21000	3	9	165000	181500
40	6	TIARA 4000 MID CABIN	OP	EXP	FBG	SV	IB	T420D	CUM	14	6	25000	3		197000	216500
40	6	TIARA 4000 MID CABIN	OP	EXP	FBG	SV	IB	T435D	CAT	14	6	25000	3		207000	227500
41	3	TIARA 4100 OPEN	OP	EXP	F/S	SV	IB	T435D	CAT	14	8	27500	3	6	204500	225000
41	3	TIARA 4100 OPEN	OP	EXP	F/S	SV	IB	T550D	DD	14	8	27500	3	6	221500	243500
43	2	TIARA 4300 CNV	FB	CNV	FBG	SV	IB	T550D	DD	15	2	31000	4		283000	311000
43	2	TIARA 4300 CNV	FB	CNV	FBG	SV	IB	T625D	DD	15	2	31000	4		298000	327500
43	2	TIARA 4300 OPEN	OP	EXP	FBG	SV	IB	T550D	DD	15	2	28000	4		245500	269500
43	2	TIARA 4300 OPEN	OP	EXP	FBG	SV	IB	T625D	DD	15	2	28000	4		256500	282000
		1995 BOATS														
28	9	TIARA 2900 OPEN	OP	SPTCR	FBG	SV	IB	T250-T320		11	4	10000	2	2	58500	67300
28	9	TIARA 2900 OPEN	OP	SPTCR	FBG	SV	IO	T225D	GM	11	4	10000	2	2	67400	74100
31	6	TIARA 3100 OPEN	OP	EXP	F/S	SV	IB	T300	CRUS	12		11500	2	2	75600	83100
31	6	TIARA 3100 OPEN	OP	EXP	F/S	SV	IB	T230D-T315D		12		11500	2	2	88900	106000
32	10	TIARA 3300 OPEN	OP	EXP	F/S	SV	IB	T300	CRUS	12	6	13500	2	3	84400	92800
32	10	TIARA 3300 OPEN	OP	EXP	F/S	SV	IB	T300D	DD	12	6	13500	2	3	106500	117000
35	8	TIARA 3500 EXP		EXP	FBG	SV	IO	T420D	CUM	13	9	19800	2	10	129000	141500
35	8	TIARA 3500 EXP		EXP	FBG	SV	IO	T435D	CAT	13	9	19800	2	10	136500	150000
35	8	TIARA 3500 EXP	OP	EXP	FBG	SV	IO	T380	CRUS	13	9	19800	2	10	96500	106000
36	8	TIARA 3600 CNV	FB	CNV	F/S	SV	IB	T355	CRUS	13	9	18300	3		112500	124000
36	8	TIARA 3600 CNV	FB	CNV	F/S	SV	IB	T375D	CAT	13	9	18300	3		144000	158500
36	8	TIARA 3600 OPEN	OP	EXP	F/S	SV	IB	T355	CRUS	13	9	16500	2	11	103500	114000
36	8	TIARA 3600 OPEN	OP	EXP	F/S	SV	IB	T375D	CAT	13	9	16500	2	11	132500	145500
40	6	TIARA 4000 OPEN	OP	EXP	FBG	SV	IB	T420D	CUM	14	6	25000	3		188500	207000
40	6	TIARA 4000 OPEN	OP	EXP	FBG	SV	IB	T435D	CAT	14	6	25000	3		198000	217500
43	2	TIARA 4300 CNV	FB	CNV	FBG	SV	IB	T550D	DD	15	2	31000	4		270500	297000
43	2	TIARA 4300 OPEN	OP	EXP	FBG	SV	IB	T550D	DD	15	2	28000	4		234000	257000
		1994 BOATS														
28	9	TIARA 2900 OPEN	OP	SPTCR	FBG	SV	IB	T250	CRUS	11	4	10000	2	2	55300	60800
28	9	TIARA 2900 OPEN	OP	SPTCR	FBG	SV	IO	T225D	GM	11	4	10000	2	2	62900	69100
31	6	TIARA 3100 OPEN	OP	EXP	F/S	SV	IB	T300	CRUS	12		11500	2	2	71600	78700
31	6	TIARA 3100 OPEN	OP	EXP	F/S	SV	IB	T230D-T300D		12		11500	2	2	84600	99900
32	10	TIARA 3300 OPEN	OP	EXP	F/S	SV	IB	T300	CRUS	12	6	13500	2	3	79900	87800
32	10	TIARA 3300 OPEN	OP	EXP	F/S	SV	IB	T300D	GM	12	6	13500	2	3	100500	110500
36	8	TIARA 3600 CNV	FB	CNV	F/S	SV	IB	T355	CRUS	13	9	18300	3		108000	118500
36	8	TIARA 3600 CNV	FB	CNV	F/S	SV	IB	T375D	CAT	13	9	18300	3		138000	151500
36	8	TIARA 3600 OPEN	OP	EXP	F/S	SV	IB	T355	CRUS	13	9	16500	2	11	99300	109000
36	8	TIARA 3600 OPEN	OP	EXP	F/S	SV	IB	T375D	CAT	13	9	16500	2	11	127000	139500
40	6	TIARA 4000 OPEN	OP	EXP	FBG	SV	IB	T400D	CUM	14	6	25000	3		178000	195500
40	6	TIARA 4000 OPEN	OP	EXP	FBG	SV	IB	T435D	CAT	14	6	25000	3		189500	208000
43	2	TIARA 4300 CNV	FB	CNV	FBG	SV	IB	T550D	GM	15	2	31000	4		254500	279500
43	2	TIARA 4300 OPEN	OP	EXP	FBG	SV	IB	T550D	GM	15	2	28000	4		219500	241000
		1993 BOATS														
22		TIARA 220	OP	CUD	FBG	SV	IO	260-275		8		3650	2	8	12300	14800
22		TIARA 220	OP	CUD	FBG	SV	IO	330		8		3650	2	8	13700	16400
22		TIARA 220 BR	OP	RNBT	FBG	SV	IO	260-275		8		3650	2	8	11600	14000
22		TIARA 220 BR	OP	RNBT	FBG	SV	IO	330		8		3650	2	8	12900	15500
25		TIARA 250	OP	OVNTR	FBG	SV	IO	330		8	11	4800	2	8	19500	22400
25		TIARA 250 BR	OP	RNBT	FBG	SV	IO	260-275		8	11	4800	2	8	16500	19500
25		TIARA 250 BR	OP	RNBT	FBG	SV	IO	330		8	11	4800	2	8	18300	21000
26		TIARA 260	OP	WKNDR	FBG	SV	IO	330		8	9	5200	2	8	22200	25200
27		TIARA 2700 OPEN	OP	CUD	FBG	SV	IB	T235	CRUS	10		7300	2		34900	38700
27		TIARA 2700 OPEN	OP	CUD	FBG	SV	IB	T170D	YAN	10		7300	2		47200	51800
27		TIARA 2700 OPEN	ST	CUD	FBG	SV	IB	T260	MRCR	10		7300	2		35200	39100
27	6	TIARA 270	OP	SPTCR	FBG	SV	IO	T205-T275		10	7	8000	1	10	30500	36500
27	6	TIARA 270	OP	SPTCR	FBG	SV	IO	T250D	VLVO	10	7	8000	1	10	43800	48700
29		TIARA 290	OP	SPTCR	FBG	SV	IO	T260-T275		11		8500	2	8	37600	42700
29		TIARA 290	OP	SPTCR	FBG	SV	IO	T250D	VLVO	11		8500	2	8	49300	54200
31	3	TIARA 3100 OPEN	OP	SPTCR	F/S	SV	IB	T300-T330		12		10500	2	9	65200	72900
31	3	TIARA 3100 OPEN	OP	SPTCR	F/S	SV	IB	T300D		12		10500	2	9	82500	90700
32	10	TIARA 3300 OPEN	OP	EXP	F/S	SV	IB	T300-T330		12	6	11500	2	3	73000	81400
32	10	TIARA 3300 OPEN	OP	EXP	F/S	SV	IB	T300D	GM	12	6	11500	2	3	89000	97800
36	8	TIARA 3600 CNV	FB	CNV	F/S	SV	IB	T355	CRUS	13	9	18300	3		103000	113000
36	8	TIARA 3600 CNV	FB	CNV	F/S	SV	IB	T360	MRCR	13	9	18300	3		102000	112500
36	8	TIARA 3600 CNV	FB	CNV	F/S	SV	IB	T375D	CAT	13	9	18300	3		131500	144500
36	8	TIARA 3600 OPEN	OP	EXP	F/S	SV	IB	T355	CRUS	13	9	16500	2	11	94600	104000
36	8	TIARA 3600 OPEN	OP	EXP	F/S	SV	IB	T360	MRCR	13	9	16500	2	11	94000	103000
36	8	TIARA 3600 OPEN	OP	EXP	F/S	SV	IB	T375D	CAT	13	9	16500	2	11	120500	132500
43	2	TIARA 4300 CNV	FB	CNV	FBG	SV	IB	T550D	GM	15	2	31000	4		242000	266000
43	2	TIARA 4300 OPEN	OP	EXP	FBG	SV	IB	T550D	GM	15	2	28000	4		209000	229500
		1992 BOATS														
22		TIARA 220	OP	CUD	FBG	SV	IO	260-275		8		3650	2	8	11500	13800
22		TIARA 220	OP	CUD	FBG	SV	IO	330-350		8		3650	2	8	12800	15400
22		TIARA 220 BR	OP	RNBT	FBG	SV	IO	260-275		8		3650	2	8	10900	13100
22		TIARA 220 BR	OP	RNBT	FBG	SV	IO	330		8		3650	2	8	12100	14500
25		TIARA 250	OP	OVNTR	FBG	SV	IO	330		8	11	4800	2	8	18500	21200
25		TIARA 250 B/R	OP	RNBT	FBG	SV	IO	260-275		8	11	4800	2	8	15500	18200
25		TIARA 250 B/R	OP	RNBT	FBG	SV	IO	330		8	11	4800	2	8	16700	19600
26		TIARA 260	OP	WKNDR	FBG	SV	IO	330		8	9	5200	2	8	20700	23600
27		TIARA 2700 OPEN	OP	CUD	FBG	SV	IB	T235	CRUS	10		7300	2		33100	36800
27		TIARA 2700 OPEN	OP	CUD	FBG	SV	IB	T170D	YAN	10		7300	2		44500	49500
27		TIARA 2700 OPEN	ST	CUD	FBG	SV	IB	T260	MRCR	10		7300	2		33400	37100
27	6	TIARA 270	OP	SPTCR	FBG	SV	IO	T205-T275		10	7	8000	1	10	28600	34200
27	6	TIARA 270	OP	SPTCR	FBG	SV	IO	T250D	VLVO	10	7	8000	1	10	40900	45400
29		TIARA 290	OP	SPTCR	FBG	SV	IO	T260-T275		11		8500	2	8	35100	39900
29		TIARA 290	OP	SPTCR	FBG	SV	IO	T250D	VLVO	11		8500	2	8	46400	51000
31	3	TIARA 3100 CNV	FB	CNV	F/S	SV	IB	T300-T330		12		13200	2	9	68300	76600
31	3	TIARA 3100 CNV	FB	CNV	F/S	SV	IB	T230D	VLVO	12		13200	2	9	88500	97300
31	3	TIARA 3100 FLYBRIDGB	FB	SDN	F/S	SV	IB	T300	CRUS	12		12500	2	9	67500	74200
31	3	TIARA 3100 FLYBRIDGB	FB	SDN	F/S	SV	IB	T230D	VLVO	12		12500	2	9	86300	94900
31	3	TIARA 3100 FLYBRIDGE	FB	SDN	F/S	SV	IB	T330	MRCR	12		12500	2	9	68900	75700
31	3	TIARA 3100 OPEN	OP	SPTCR	F/S	SV	IB	T300-T330		12		10500	2	9	61800	69200
31	3	TIARA 3100 OPEN	OP	SPTCR	F/S	SV	IB	T300D		12		10500	2	9	78700	86500
32	10	TIARA 3300 FLYBRIDGE	FB	SDNSF	F/S	SV	IB	T300D		12	6	13000	2	8	90000	98900
32	10	TIARA 3300 OPEN	OP	EXP	F/S	SV	IB	T300-T330		12	6	11500	2	3	69200	77300
32	10	TIARA 3300 OPEN	OP	EXP	F/S	SV	IB	T300D	GM	12	6	11500	2	3	84900	93300
36	8	TIARA 3600 CNV	FB	CNV	F/S	SV	IB	T300	CRUS	13	9	18300	3		95800	105500
		IB T330 MRCR 96200 105500, IB T355 CRUS 98000 107500, IB T360 MRCR 97400 107000														
		IB T375D CAT 125000 137500														
36	8	TIARA 3600 OPEN	OP	EXP	F/S	SV	IB	T300	CRUS	13	9	16500	2	11	88100	96800
		IB T330 MRCR 88400 97200, IB T355 CRUS 90200 99100, IB T360 MRCR 89600 98400														
		IB T300D CAT 107500 118000, IB T300D CUM 104000 114500, IB T375D CAT 115000 126500														
		IB T425D CAT 121000 133000														
43	2	TIARA 4300 CNV	FB	CNV	FBG	SV	IB	T550D	GM	15	2	31000	4		230500	253500
43	2	TIARA 4300 OPEN	OP	EXP	FBG	SV	IB	T425D	CAT	15	2	28000	4		187000	205500
43	2	TIARA 4300 OPEN	OP	EXP	FBG	SV	IB	T550D	GM	15	2	28000	4		199000	218500
		1991 BOATS														
22		TIARA 220	OP	CUD	FBG	SV	IO	260	MRCR	8		3650	2	8	10800	12300
22		TIARA 220	OP	CUD	FBG	SV	IO	330	MRCR	8		3650	2	8	12000	13700
25		TIARA 250	OP	OVNTR	FBG	SV	IO	330		8	11	4800	2	8	16900	19900
26		TIARA 260	OP	WKNDR	FBG	SV	IO	330		8	9	5200	2	8	19500	22100
27		TIARA 2700 OPEN	ST	CUD	FBG	SV	IB	T260	MRCR	10		7500	2		32100	35700
27	6	TIARA 270	OP	SPTCR	FBG	SV	IO	T205-T260		10	7	8000	1	10	26800	31200
27	6	TIARA 270	OP	SPTCR	FBG	SV	IO	T330	VLVO	10	7	8000	1	10	30900	34300
27	6	TIARA 270	OP	SPTCR	FBG	SV	IO	T250D	VLVO	10	7	8000	1	10	38300	42500
29		TIARA 290	OP	SPTCR	FBG	SV	IO	T260		11		8500	2	8	33000	36900
29		TIARA 290	OP	SPTCR	FBG	SV	IO	T250D	VLVO	11		8500	2	8	43000	47800
31	3	TIARA 3100 CNV	FB	CNV	F/S	SV	IB	T330	MRCR	12		13200	2	8	66200	72700
31	3	TIARA 3100 FLYBRIDGE	FB	SDN	F/S	SV	IB	T330	MRCR	12		12500	2	8	65500	71900
31	3	TIARA 3100 OPEN	OP	SPTCR	F/S	SV	IB	T330	MRCR	12		10500	2	8	59800	65700
31	3	TIARA 3100 OPEN	OP	SPTCR	F/S	SV	IB	T300D	GM	12		10500	2	8	74900	82300
32	10	TIARA 3300 OPEN	OP	EXP	F/S	SV	IB	T300-T330		12	6	11500	2	8	65800	73400
32	10	TIARA 3300 OPEN	OP	EXP	F/S	SV	IB	T300D	GM	12	6	11500	2	8	81000	89000
36	8	TIARA 3600 CNV	FB	CNV	F/S	SV	IB	T330	MRCR	13	9	18300	3		91700	101000
36	8	TIARA 3600 CNV	FB	CNV	F/S	SV	IB	T454	CRUS	13	9	18300	3		99000	109000
36	8	TIARA 3600 CNV	FB	CNV	F/S	SV	IB	T375D	CAT	13	9	18300	3		119500	131000

CONTINUED ON NEXT PAGE

LOA FT	IN	NAME AND/ OR MODEL	TOP/ RIG	BOAT TYPE	-HULL- MTL	TP	----ENGINE--- TP	# HP	MFG	BEAM FT	IN	WGT LBS	DRAFT FT	IN	RETAIL LOW	RETAIL HIGH
		1991 BOATS														
36	8	TIARA 3600 OPEN	OP	EXP	F/S	SV	IB	T330	MRCR	13	9	16500			84300	92700
		IB T454 CRUS 91300 100500, IB T375D CAT 109500 120500, IB T425D CAT													115500	127000
43	2	TIARA 4300 CNV	FB	CNV	FBG	SV	IB	T550D	GM	15	2	31000	4		220000	241500
43	2	TIARA 4300 OPEN	OP	EXP	FBG	SV	IB	T550D	GM	15	2	28000	3		189500	208500
		1990 BOATS														
23	7	SLICKCRAFT 237SC	ST	OVNTR	FBG	SV	IO	260-275		8		3650	2	8	11000	13200
23	7	SLICKCRAFT 237SC	ST	OVNTR	FBG	SV	IO	330	MRCR	8		3650	2	8	12200	13800
23	7	SLICKCRAFT 237SL	ST	CUD	FBG	SV	IO	260-275		8		3500	2	8	10700	12800
23	7	SLICKCRAFT 237SL	ST	CUD	FBG	SV	IO	330	MRCR	8		3500	2	8	11800	13500
23	7	SLICKCRAFT 237SS	ST	CUD	FBG	SV	IO	205-275		8		3550	2	8	10500	12900
26	8	SLICKCRAFT 268 SC	ST	SPTCR	FBG	SV	IO	330	VLVO	8	11	4800	2	8	18400	20400
26	8	SLICKCRAFT 268 SL	ST	SPTCR	FBG	SV	IO	330	VLVO	8	11	4800	2	8	18800	20800
26	8	SLICKCRAFT 268SC	ST	SPTCR	FBG	SV	IO	260-330		8	11	4800	2	8	16200	19600
26	8	SLICKCRAFT 268SL	ST	SPTCR	FBG	SV	IO	260-330		8	11	4800	2	8	16500	20000
26	8	SLICKCRAFT 268SL	ST	SPTCR	FBG	SV	IO	T205	MRCR	8	11	4800	2	8	18600	20700
27		SLICKCRAFT 2700 OPEN	ST	EXP	FBG	SV	IB	T260	MRCR	10		7500	2		30300	33700
27		TIARA 2700 OPEN	ST	CUD	FBG	SV	IB	T260	MRCR	10		7500	2		30800	34200
27	9	SLICKCRAFT 279SC	ST	SPTCR	FBG	SV	IO	260-330		8	9	5200	2	8	18900	22700
27	9	SLICKCRAFT 279SC	ST	SPTCR	FBG	SV	IO	T205		8	9	5200	2	8	20800	23400
31		SLICKCRAFT 310SC	ST	SPTCR	FBG	SV	IO	T260-T275		11		8500	2	8	34300	38700
31		SLICKCRAFT 310SC	ST	SPTCR	FBG	SV	IO	T200D	VLVO	11		8500	2	8	38800	43100
31	3	TIARA 3100 CNV	FB	CNV	F/S	SV	IB	T330-T454		12		13200	2	8	62900	71200
31	3	TIARA 3100 FLYBRIDGE	FB	SDN	F/S	SV	IB	T330-T454		12		12500	2	8	62300	72800
31	3	TIARA 3100 FLYBRIDGE	FB	SDN	F/S	SV	IB	T300D-T320D		12		12500	2	8	85100	95800
31	3	TIARA 3100 OPEN	OP	SPTCR	F/S	SV	IB	T260-T454		12		10500	2	8	54400	67900
31	3	TIARA 3100 OPEN	OP	SPTCR	F/S	SV	IB	T300D	GM	12		10500	2	8	71500	78600
32	10	TIARA 3300 OPEN	OP	EXP	F/S	SV	IB	T300-T330		11		11500	2	8	57200	63700
32	10	TIARA 3300 OPEN	OP	EXP	F/S	SV	IB	T300D	GM	11		11500	2	8	74700	82100
36	8	TIARA 3600 CNV	FB	CNV	F/S	SV	IB	T330	MRCR	13	9	18300	3		87600	96200
		IB T454 CRUS 94500 104000, IB T320D CAT 108500 119000, IB T375D CAT													114000	125000
36	8	TIARA 3600 OPEN	OP	EXP	F/S	SV	IB	T330	MRCR	13	9	16500	2	11	80500	88500
		IB T454 CRUS 87200 95800, IB T320D CAT 99500 109500, IB T375D CAT													104500	115000
43	2	TIARA 4300 CNV	FB	CNV	FBG	SV	IB	T550D	GM	15	2	31000	4		210000	230500
		1989 BOATS														
23	7	SLICKCRAFT 237SC	ST	OVNTR	FBG	SV	IO	260-275		8		3650	2	8	10400	12400
23	7	SLICKCRAFT 237SC	ST	OVNTR	FBG	SV	IO	330	MRCR	8		3650	2	8	11500	13000
23	7	SLICKCRAFT 237SL	ST	CUD	FBG	SV	IO	260-275		8		3500	2	8	10100	12100
23	7	SLICKCRAFT 237SL	ST	CUD	FBG	SV	IO	330	MRCR	8		3500	2	8	11200	12700
23	7	SLICKCRAFT 237SS	ST	CUD	FBG	SV	IO	205-275		8		3550	2	8	9850	12200
26	8	SLICKCRAFT 268SC	ST	SPTCR	FBG	SV	IO	260-330		8	11	4800	2	8	15200	18700
26	8	SLICKCRAFT 268SL	ST	SPTCR	FBG	SV	IO	260-330		8	11	4800	2	8	15600	19100
26	8	SLICKCRAFT 268SL	ST	SPTCR	FBG	SV	IO	T205	MRCR	8	11	4800	2	8	17200	19500
27		TIARA 2700 OPEN	ST	CUD	FBG	SV	IB	T260-T270		10		7500	2		29100	32800
27	9	SLICKCRAFT 279SC	ST	SPTCR	FBG	SV	IO	260-330		8	9	5200	2	8	17100	20700
27	9	SLICKCRAFT 279SC	ST	SPTCR	FBG	SV	IO	T205		8	9	5200	2	8	19100	21900
27	9	SLICKCRAFT 279SL	ST	SPTCR	FBG	SV	IO	260-330		8	9	5200	2	8	18200	21400
27	9	SLICKCRAFT 279SL	ST	SPTCR	FBG	SV	IO	T205		8	9	5200	2	8	19700	22700
30	10	SLICKCRAFT 310SC	OP	CBNCR	FBG	SV	IO	T260-T275		11		8500			38500	43000
31	3	TIARA 3100 CNV	FB	CNV	F/S	SV	IB	T330-T350		12		13200			59900	66800
31	3	TIARA 3100 FLYBRIDGE	FB	SDN	F/S	SV	IB	T330-T350		12		12500			59300	66100
31	3	TIARA 3100 OPEN	OP	SPTCR	F/S	SV	IB	T260-T350		12		10500			51800	60400
31	3	TIARA 3100 OPEN	OP	SPTCR	F/S	SV	IB	T300D	GM	12		10500			68400	75200
32	10	TIARA 3300 FLYBRIDGE	FB	SDNSF	F/S	SV	IB	T330-T350		12		13000			62100	69100
32	10	TIARA 3300 FLYBRIDGE	FB	SDNSF	F/S	SV	IB	T300D-T320D		12		13000			78000	88200
32	10	TIARA 3300 OPEN	OP	EXP	F/S	SV	IB	T330-T350				11500			59800	68000
32	10	TIARA 3300 OPEN	OP	EXP	F/S	SV	IB	T300D	GM			11500			73200	80500
36	8	TIARA 3600 CNV	FB	CNV	F/S	SV	IB	T330	MRCR	13	9	18300	3		83600	91900
		IB T350 CRUS 85000 93400, IB T320D CAT 103500 114000, IB T375D CAT													109000	119500
36	8	TIARA 3600 OPEN	OP	EXP	F/S	SV	IB	T330	MRCR	13	9	16500	2	11	76900	84500
		IB T350 CRUS 78200 86000, IB T320D CAT 95000 104500, IB T375D CAT													100000	110000
		1988 BOATS														
23	7	SLICKCRAFT 237SC	OP	CUD	FBG	DV	IO	230-260		8		3650	2	8	9650	11200
23	7	SLICKCRAFT 237SC	OP	CUD	FBG	DV	IO	330-335		8		3650	2	8	10900	12300
23	7	SLICKCRAFT 237SS	OP	CUD	FBG	SV	IO	205-260		8		3500	2	8	9300	10900
26	8	SLICKCRAFT 268SC	OP	CUD	FBG	DV	IO	260	MRCR	8	11	4800	2	8	14600	16600
26	8	SLICKCRAFT 268SC	OP	SPTCR	FBG	DV	IO	260-335		8	11	4800	2	8	14600	17900
27		TIARA 2700	OP	CUD	FBG	DV	SE	T	OMC	10		5700	2	8	**	**
27		TIARA 2700	OP	CUD	FBG	DV	IB	T220-T270		10		7500	2		27200	31300
27		TIARA 2700 OFFSHORE	TT	SF	FBG	DV	SE	T	OMC	10		5550	2		**	**
27		TIARA 2700 OFFSHORE	TT	SF	FBG	DV	IB	T220-T270		10		7500	2		27200	31200
27	6	SLICKCRAFT 270SC	OP	CBNCR	FBG	DV	IO	T260		9	10	7400	2	8	25800	28600
27	9	SLICKCRAFT 279SC	ST	SPTCR	FBG	DV	IO	260-335		8	9	5200	2	8	16500	20100
30	10	SLICKCRAFT 310SC	OP	CBNCR	FBG	DV	IO	T230-T260		11		8500	2	8	36200	40500
31	3	TIARA 3100	FB	SDN	FBG	DV	IB	T350	CRUS	12		12500	2	9	57300	63000
32	10	TIARA 3300	OP	SDNSF	FBG	DV	IB	T350	CRUS	12	6	11500	2	8	58400	64200
32	10	TIARA 3300	OP	SDNSF	FBG	DV	IB	T250D	GM	12	6	11500	2	8	67500	74200
32	10	TIARA 3300	FB	SDNSF	FBG	DV	IB	T350	CRUS	12	6	13000	2	8	59900	65900
32	10	TIARA 3300	FB	SDNSF	FBG	DV	IB	T300D-T320D		12	6	13000	2	8	74600	84100
36	8	TIARA 3600	OP	EXP	FBG	DV	IB	T350	CRUS	13	9	16500	2	11	73000	80200
36	8	TIARA 3600	OP	EXP	FBG	DV	IB	T320D	CAT	13	9	16500	2	11	88400	97200
36	8	TIARA 3600	OP	EXP	FBG	DV	IB	T375D	CAT	13	9	16500	2	11	93100	102500
36	8	TIARA 3600 CNV	FB	CNV	FBG	DV	IB	T350	CRUS	13	9	18300	3		81200	89300
36	8	TIARA 3600 CNV	FB	CNV	FBG	DV	IB	T320D	CAT	13	9	18300	3		99000	109000
36	8	TIARA 3600 CNV	FB	CNV	FBG	DV	IB	T375D	CAT	13	9	18300	3		104000	114000
		1987 BOATS														
17	6	SLICKCRAFT 180SL	OP	RNBT	FBG	DV	IO	230-260		7		2400	2	8	4100	5000
20	3	SLICKCRAFT 202SC	OP	B/R	FBG	DV	IO	230-260		7	10	2900	2	8	6100	7250
23	7	SLICKCRAFT 220SL	OP	RNBT	FBG	DV	IO	260		8		3100	2	8	7850	9050
23	7	SLICKCRAFT 220SL	OP	RNBT	FBG	DV	IO	330-340		8		3100	2	8	8850	10200
23	7	SLICKCRAFT 225SC	OP	CUD	FBG	DV	IO	260		8		3200	2	8	8550	9800
23	7	SLICKCRAFT 225SC	OP	CUD	FBG	DV	IO	330-335		8		3200	2	8	9550	10900
24	5	SLICKCRAFT 245SC	OP	CUD	FBG	DV	IO	260-335		8	10	4500	2	6	11600	14300
27		TIARA 2700	OP	CUD	FBG	DV	IB	T220	CRUS	10		7500	2		26000	28900
27		TIARA 2700	OP	CUD	FBG	DV	SE	T225	OMC	10		5700	2	8	25200	28000
27		TIARA 2700	OP	CUD	FBG	DV	IB	T270	CRUS	10		7500	2		26800	29800
27		TIARA 2700 OFFSHORE	TT	SF	FBG	DV	OB			10		5550	2	8	25100	27900
27		TIARA 2700 OFFSHORE	TT	SF	FBG	DV	IB	T220	CRUS	10		7500	2		26000	28800
27		TIARA 2700 OFFSHORE	TT	SF	FBG	DV	SE	T225	OMC	10		5550	2	8	25100	27900
27		TIARA 2700 OFFSHORE	TT	SF	FBG	DV	IB	T270	CRUS	10		7500	2		26800	29800
27		TIARA 2700 OFFSHORE	TT	SF	FBG	DV	IB	T215D	GM	10		7500	2		38400	42600
27		TIARA 2700 OPEN	OP	CUD	FBG	DV	OB			10		5700	2	8	25200	28000
27	6	SLICKCRAFT 270SC	OP	CBNCR	FBG	DV	IO	T230-T260		9	10	7400	2	8	24200	27200
27	9	SLICKCRAFT 265SC	OP	CBNCR	FBG	DV	IO	260-335		8	9	5200	2	8	19600	22400
31	3	TIARA 3100	FB	SDN	FBG	DV	IB	T350	CRUS	12		12500	2	9	54700	60100
31	3	TIARA 3100	OP	SPTCR	FBG	DV	IB	T270-T350		12		10500	2	9	45800	52700
31	3	TIARA 3100	OP	SPTCR	FBG	DV	IB	T215D	GM	12		10500	2	9	55100	60600
32	10	TIARA 3300	FB	SDNSF	FBG	DV	IB	T350	CRUS	12	6	13000	2	8	57100	62800
32	10	TIARA 3300	FB	SDNSF	FBG	DV	IB	T300D-T320D		12	6	13000	2	8	71500	80500
36	8	TIARA 3600	OP	EXP	FBG	DV	IB	T350	CRUS	13	9	16500	2	11	69800	76700
36	8	TIARA 3600	OP	EXP	FBG	DV	IB	T320D	CAT	13	9	16500	2	11	84600	92900
36	8	TIARA 3600	OP	EXP	FBG	DV	IB	T375D	CAT	13	9	16500	2	11	89000	97800
36	8	TIARA 3600 CNV	FB	CNV	FBG	DV	IB	T350	CRUS	13	9	18300	3		77700	85400
36	8	TIARA 3600 CNV	FB	CNV	FBG	DV	IB	T320D	CAT	13	9	18300	3		94600	104000
36	8	TIARA 3600 CNV	FB	CNV	FBG	DV	IB	T375D	CAT	13	9	18300	3		99400	109000
		1986 BOATS														
22		S2 6.9 METER	SLP	SA/RC	F/S	KC	OB			8		2200		10	5850	6750
22	6	CONTINENTAL 2300	ST	CUD	FBG	DV	IO	260		8		3750	2	4	8550	10200
23	10	S2 7.3 METER DEEP	SLP	SA/CR	FBG	KL	OB			8		3250	4		8050	9250
23	10	S2 7.3 METER DEEP	SLP	SA/CR	FBG	KL	SE	115	OMC	8		3250	4		9400	10700
23	10	S2 7.3 METER SHOAL	SLP	SA/CR	FBG	KL	OB			8		3250	3		8050	9250
23	10	S2 7.3 METER SHOAL	SLP	SA/CR	FBG	KL	SE	115	OMC	8		3250	3		9400	10700
25	11	S2 7.9 METER	SLP	SA/OD	FBG	KC	OB			9		4250	1	2	11300	12800
25	11	S2 7.9 METER	SLP	SA/OD	FBG	KC	IB	7D	BMW	9		4250	1	2	12000	13600
25	11	S2 7.9 METER F/K	SLP	SA/OD	FBG	KL	OB			9		4050	5		10700	12200
25	11	S2 7.9 METER F/K	SLP	SA/OD	FBG	KL	IB	7D	BMW	9		4050	5		11500	13000
26		CONTINENTAL 2600	ST	EXP	FBG	DV	IO	260		8	9	4600	2	8	12300	14200
26		CONTINENTAL 2600	ST	EXP	FBG	DV	IO	T190	MRCR	8	9	4600	2	8	13500	15300
26	7	S2 27 FT	SLP	SA/CR	F/S	KL	OB			9	3	5000	4	9	13500	15300
27	6	CONTINENTAL 2700	ST	EXP	FBG	DV	IO	T190-T260		9	10	7500	2	8	19300	23000
28		S2 8.6 METER DEEP	SLP	SA/CR	FBG	KL	IB	15D	YAN	9	6	7600	4	6	22600	25100
28		S2 8.6 METER SHOAL	SLP	SA/CR	FBG	KL	IB	15D	YAN	9	6	7600	3	11	22600	25100
29	10	S2 9.1 METER DEEP	SLP	SA/RC	F/S	KL	IB	15D- 23D		10	6	7850	5	6	23600	26300
29	10	S2 9.1 METER SHOAL	SLP	SA/RC	F/S	KL	IB	15D- 23D		10	6	7850	4	6	23600	26300
29	11	S2 30S	SLP	SA/CR	FBG	KC	IB	15D	YAN	10	3	9500	4	11	28700	31900
29	11	S2 30S SHOAL	SLP	SA/CR	FBG	KC	IB	15D	YAN	10	3	9500	3	11	28700	31900
29	11	S2 9.2 METER A DEEP	SLP	SA/CR	F/S	KL	IB	15D- 23D		10	3	9800	4	11	29600	33000
29	11	S2 9.2 METER A SHOAL	SLP	SA/CR	F/S	KL	IB	15D- 23D		10	3	9800	3	11	29600	33000
29	11	S2 9.2 METER C DEEP	SLP	SA/CR	F/S	KL	IB	15D- 23D		10	3	9800	4	11	29600	33000
29	11	S2 9.2 METER C SHOAL	SLP	SA/CR	F/S	KL	IB	15D- 23D		10	3	9800	3	11	29600	33000
31	3	CONTINENTAL 3100	OP	EXP	FBG	DV	IB	T260-T350		12		9200	2	9	41900	49600
31	3	CONTINENTAL 3100	HT	EXP	FBG	DV	IB	T260-T350		12		10500	2	9	42900	50500
31	3	CONTINENTAL 3100	FB	SDN	FBG	DV	IB	T260-T350		12		11500	2	11	48100	56600

LOA FT	LOA IN	NAME AND/ OR MODEL	TOP/ RIG	BOAT TYPE	-HULL- MTL	-HULL- TP	ENGINE TP	ENGINE # HP	ENGINE MFG	BEAM FT	BEAM IN	WGT LBS	DRAFT FT	DRAFT IN	RETAIL LOW	RETAIL HIGH
		1986 BOATS														
33	9	S2 10.3 DEEP	SLP	SA/RC	F/S	KL	IB	15D- 23D		11	4	10500	6	1	31400	35000
33	9	S2 10.3 SHOAL	SLP	SA/CR	F/S	KL	IB	15D- 23D		11	4	10500	4	11	31400	35000
35	2	WISHLIST	SLP	SA/CR	FBG	KC	IB	28D		11	6	14000	5	6	42000	46600
35	2	WISHLIST SHOAL	SLP	SA/CR	FBG	KC	IB	28D		11	6	14000	4	3	42000	46600
36		S2 11 A DEEP	SLP	SA/CR	F/S	KL	IB	30D	YAN	11	11	15000	5	6	45900	50400
36		S2 11 A SHOAL	SLP	SA/CR	F/S	KL	IB	30D	YAN	11	11	15000	4	8	45900	50400
36		S2 11 C DEEP	SLP	SA/CR	F/S	KL	IB	30D	YAN	11	11	15000	5	6	45900	50400
36		S2 11 METER C SHOAL	SLP	SA/CR	F/S	KL	IB	30D	YAN	11	11	15000	4	8	45900	50400
36	8	CONTINENTAL 3600	OP	EXP	FBG	DV	IB	T350	CRUS	13	9	16500	2	11	68100	74800
36	8	CONTINENTAL 3600	OP	EXP	FBG	DV	IB	T D	CAT	13	9	16500	2	11	**	**
36	8	CONTINENTAL 3600	OP	EXP	FBG	DV	IB	T235D	VLVO	13	9	16500	2	11	74200	81500
		1985 BOATS														
22		S2 6.9 METER	SLP	SA/RC	F/S	KC	OB			8		2200		10	5500	6350
22	6	CONTINENTAL 2300	ST	CUD	FBG	DV	IO	260		8		3750	2	4	8200	9800
23	10	S2 7.3 METER DEEP	SLP	SA/CR	FBG	KL	OB			8		3250	4		7550	8700
23	10	S2 7.3 METER DEEP	SLP	SA/CR	FBG	KL	IB	115	OMC	8		3250	4		8700	10000
23	10	S2 7.3 METER SHOAL	SLP	SA/CR	FBG	KL	OB			8		3250	3		7550	8700
23	10	S2 7.3 METER SHOAL	SLP	SA/CR	FBG	KL	IB	115	OMC	8		3250	3		8700	10000
25	11	S2 7.9 METER	SLP	SA/OD	FBG	KC	OB			9		4250	1	2	10600	12000
25	11	S2 7.9 METER	SLP	SA/OD	FBG	KC	IB	7D	BMW	9		4250	1	2	11300	12800
25	11	S2 7.9 METER F/K	SLP	SA/OD	FBG	KL	OB			9		4050	5		10100	11500
25	11	S2 7.9 METER F/K	SLP	SA/OD	FBG	KL	IB	7D	BMW	9		4050	5		10800	12300
26		CONTINENTAL 2600	ST	EXP	FBG	DV	IO	260		8	9	4600	2	8	11800	13600
26		CONTINENTAL 2600	ST	EXP	FBG	DV	IO	T190	MRCR	8	9	4600	2	8	12900	14700
26	7	S2 27 FT	SLP	SA/CR	F/S	KL	OB			9	3	5000	4	9	12700	14400
27	6	CONTINENTAL 2700	ST	EXP	FBG	DV	IO	T190-T260		9	10	7500	2	8	18700	22100
28		S2 8.6 METER DEEP	SLP	SA/CR	FBG	KL	IB	15D	YAN	9	6	7600	4	6	21200	23600
28		S2 8.6 METER SHOAL	SLP	SA/CR	FBG	KL	IB	15D	YAN	9	6	7600	3	11	21200	23600
29	10	S2 9.1 METER DEEP	SLP	SA/RC	F/S	KL	IB	15D- 23D		10	6	7850	5	6	22200	24700
29	10	S2 9.1 METER SHOAL	SLP	SA/RC	F/S	KL	IB	15D- 23D		10	6	7850	4	6	22200	24700
29	11	S2 9.2 METER A DEEP	SLP	SA/CR	F/S	KL	IB	15D- 23D		10	3	9800	4	11	27100	30200
29	11	S2 9.2 METER A SHOAL	SLP	SA/CR	F/S	KL	IB	15D- 23D		10	3	9800	3	11	27100	30200
29	11	S2 9.2 METER C DEEP	SLP	SA/CR	F/S	KL	IB	15D- 23D		10	3	9800	4	11	28700	31900
29	11	S2 9.2 METER C SHOAL	SLP	SA/CR	F/S	KL	IB	15D- 23D		10	3	9800	3	11	28700	31900
31	3	CONTINENTAL 3100	OP	EXP	FBG	DV	IB	T260-T350		12		9200	2	9	40000	47400
31	3	CONTINENTAL 3100	HT	EXP	FBG	DV	IB	T260-T350		12		10500	2	9	40900	48200
31	3	CONTINENTAL 3100	FB	SDN	FBG	DV	IB	T260-T350		12		11500	2	11	46200	54000
33	9	S2 10.3 DEEP	SLP	SA/RC	F/S	KL	IB	15D- 23D		11	4	10500	6	1	29600	32900
33	9	S2 10.3 SHOAL	SLP	SA/CR	F/S	KL	IB	15D- 23D		11	4	10500	4	11	29600	32900
36		S2 11 A DEEP	SLP	SA/CR	F/S	KL	IB	30D	YAN	11	11	15000	5	6	40900	45400
36		S2 11 A SHOAL	SLP	SA/CR	F/S	KL	IB	30D	YAN	11	11	15000	4	8	40900	45400
36		S2 11 C DEEP	SLP	SA/CR	F/S	KL	IB	30D	YAN	11	11	15000	5	6	44500	49400
36		S2 11 METER C SHOAL	SLP	SA/CR	F/S	KL	IB	30D	YAN	11	11	15000	4	8	44500	49400
36	8	CONTINENTAL 3600	OP	EXP	FBG	DV	IB	T350	CRUS	13	9	16500	2	11	65200	71700
36	8	CONTINENTAL 3600	OP	EXP	FBG	DV	IB	T D	CAT	13	9	16500	2	11	**	**
36	8	CONTINENTAL 3600	OP	EXP	FBG	DV	IB	T235D	VLVO	13	9	16500	2	11	71000	78100
		1984 BOATS														
22		GRAND-SLAM 6.9	SLP	SA/OD	FBG	KC	OB			8		2200		10	5200	5950
22	6	CONTINENTAL 2300	ST	CUD	FBG	DV	IO	260		8		3750	2	4	7950	9450
23	10	S2 7.3 METER DEEP	SLP	SAIL	FBG	KL	OB			8		3250	4		7100	8150
23	10	S2 7.3 METER DEEP	SLP	SAIL	FBG	KL	SE	115	OMC	8		3250	4		8250	9450
23	10	S2 7.3 METER SHOAL	SLP	SAIL	FBG	KL	OB			8		3250	3		7100	8150
23	10	S2 7.3 METER SHOAL	SLP	SAIL	FBG	KL	SE	115	OMC	8		3250	3		8250	9450
25	11	GRAND-SLAM 7.9	SLP	SA/OD	FBG	KC	OB			9		4250	1	2	9950	11300
25	11	GRAND-SLAM 7.9	SLP	SA/OD	FBG	KC	IB	7D	BMW	9		4250	1	2	10600	12000
25	11	GRAND-SLAM 7.9 F/K	SLP	SA/OD	FBG	KL	OB			9		4050	5		9500	10800
25	11	GRAND-SLAM 7.9 F/K	SLP	SA/OD	FBG	KL	IB	7D	BMW	9		4050	5		10100	11500
26		CONTINENTAL 2600	ST	EXP	FBG	DV	IO	260		8	9	4600	2	8	11400	13100
26		CONTINENTAL 2600	ST	EXP	FBG	DV	IO	T170-T185		8	9	4600	2	8	12200	14100
27	6	CONTINENTAL 2700	ST	EXP	FBG	DV	IO	260		9	10	7500	2	8	16500	18900
27	6	CONTINENTAL 2700	ST	EXP	FBG	DV	IO	T170-T260		9	10	7500	2	8	17400	21300
28		S2 8.6 METER DEEP	SLP	SAIL	FBG	KL	IB	15D		9	6	7600	4	6	20000	22200
28		S2 8.6 METER SHOAL	SLP	SAIL	FBG	KL	IB	15D		9	6	7600	3	11	20000	22200
29	10	S2 9.1 METER DEEP	SLP	SA/RC	FBG	KL	IB	15D	YAN	10	6	7850	5	6	20900	23200
29	10	S2 9.1 METER SHOAL	SLP	SA/RC	FBG	KL	IB	15D	YAN	10	6	7850	4	6	20900	23200
29	11	S2 9.2 METER A DEEP	SLP	SAIL	FBG	KL	IB	15D	YAN	10	3	9800	4	11	26200	29100
29	11	S2 9.2 METER A SHOAL	SLP	SAIL	FBG	KL	IB	15D	YAN	10	3	9800	3	11	26200	29100
29	11	S2 9.2 METER C DEEP	SLP	SAIL	FBG	KL	IB	15D	YAN	10	3	9800	4	11	26200	29100
29	11	S2 9.2 METER C SHOAL	SLP	SAIL	FBG	KL	IB	15D	YAN	10	3	9800	3	11	26200	29100
31	3	CONTINENTAL 3100	OP	EXP	FBG	DV	IB	T260-T350		12		9200	2	9	38200	45300
31	3	CONTINENTAL 3100	HT	EXP	FBG	DV	IB	T260-T350		12		10500	2	9	39100	46100
31	3	CONTINENTAL 3100	FB	SDN	FBG	DV	IB	T260-T350		12		11500	2	11	43700	51900
33	9	S2 10.3 DEEP	SLP	SA/RC	FBG	KL	IB	15D- 23D		11	4	10500	6	1	27800	30900
33	9	S2 10.3 SHOAL	SLP	SA/CR	FBG	KL	IB	15D- 23D		11	4	10500	4	11	27800	30900
36		S2 11 A DEEP	SLP	SA/CR	FBG	KL	IB	30D	YAN	11	11	15000	5	6	40100	44600
36		S2 11 A SHOAL	SLP	SA/CR	FBG	KL	IB	30D	YAN	11	11	15000	4	8	40100	44600
36		S2 11 C DEEP	SLP	SA/CR	FBG	KL	IB	30D	YAN	11	11	15000	5	6	40100	44600
36		S2 11 C SHOAL	SLP	SA/CR	FBG	KL	IB	30D	YAN	11	11	15000	4	6	40100	44600

....For earlier years, see the BUC Used Boat Price Guide, Volume 3

TIBERIAS MARINE INC

DENTON MD 21629 COAST GUARD MFG ID- GAK See inside cover to adjust price for area
FORMERLY GALILEE BOAT WORKS INC

LOA FT	LOA IN	NAME AND/ OR MODEL	TOP/ RIG	BOAT TYPE	-HULL- MTL	-HULL- TP	ENGINE TP	ENGINE # HP	ENGINE MFG	BEAM FT	BEAM IN	WGT LBS	DRAFT FT	DRAFT IN	RETAIL LOW	RETAIL HIGH
		1987 BOATS														
18	1	BOWRIDER 190	ST	B/R	FBG	DV	IO	120-175		7	4				2750	3250
18	1	FISHERMAN 180	ST	FSH	FBG	DV	IO	115-175		7	4				3100	3650
19	1	BOWRIDER 200	ST	B/R	FBG	DV	IO	120-230		7	6				3000	3600
19	1	BOWRIDER 200	ST	B/R	FBG	DV	IO	260	OMC	7	6				3250	3750
19	1	CUDDY CABIN	ST	CUD	FBG	DV	IO	205	OMC	7	6				3250	3800
19	1	CUDDY CABIN 200	ST	CUD	FBG	DV	IO	120-230		7	6				3200	3850
19	1	CUDDY CABIN 200	ST	CUD	FBG	DV	IO	260	OMC	7	6				3450	4000
		1986 BOATS														
19		BOWRIDER 190	OP	RNBT	FBG	DV	IO	131-151		7	3	2100			3000	3600

....For earlier years, see the BUC Used Boat Price Guide, Volume 3

TICON YACHTS

PT CREDIT ONTARIO CANADA See inside cover to adjust price for area

LOA FT	LOA IN	NAME AND/ OR MODEL	TOP/ RIG	BOAT TYPE	-HULL- MTL	-HULL- TP	ENGINE TP	ENGINE # HP	ENGINE MFG	BEAM FT	BEAM IN	WGT LBS	DRAFT FT	DRAFT IN	RETAIL LOW	RETAIL HIGH
		1985 BOATS														
29	11	TICON 30	SLP	SA/CR	FBG	KL	IB	11D	UNIV	11		9600	4	11	22200	24700

....For earlier years, see the BUC Used Boat Price Guide, Volume 3

TIDES BOAT WORKS

DIV OF THE TIDES INN INC See inside cover to adjust price for area
WHITE STONE VA 22578 COAST GUARD MFG ID- WXG

For more recent years, see the BUC Used Boat Price Guide, Volume 1

LOA FT	LOA IN	NAME AND/ OR MODEL	TOP/ RIG	BOAT TYPE	-HULL- MTL	-HULL- TP	ENGINE TP	ENGINE # HP	ENGINE MFG	BEAM FT	BEAM IN	WGT LBS	DRAFT FT	DRAFT IN	RETAIL LOW	RETAIL HIGH
		1996 BOATS														
18	10	TIDES 19	ST	CTRCN	FBG	SV	OB			7	4	1600		9	12400	14100
27	6	TIDES 27	HT	CTRCN	FBG	SV	IB	350		9	6	8000	2	6	46200	50800
27	6	TIDES 27	MT	CUD	FBG	SV	OB			9	6	8000	2	6	**	**
34	10	TIDES 34	HT	EXP	FBG	SV	IB	T350D		11	10	15000	2	8	138500	152500
34	10	TIDES 34	TT	EXP	FBG	SV	IB	T350D		11	10	15000	2	8	139000	153000
		1995 BOATS														
18	10	TIDES 19	OP	OPFSH	FBG	SV	OB			7	4	1500		10	11100	12600
27	6	TIDES 27	OP	OPFSH	FBG	SV	OB			9	6	8500	1	11	40800	45400
27	6	TIDES 27	OP	OPFSH	FBG	SV	IB	170D-300D		9	6	8500	1	11	53100	65400
27	6	TIDES 27	OP	OPFSH	FBG	SV	IB	350D	CAT	9	6	8500	1	11	62100	68200
27	6	TIDES 27	OP	OPFSH	FBG	SV	IB	T225D	VLVO	9	6	8500	1	11	64700	71100
31	10	TIDES 32	OP	OPFSH	FBG	SV	IB	T300D	CAT	11	6	12600	1	10	95700	105000
		1994 BOATS														
18	10	TIDES 19	OP	OPFSH	FBG	SV	OB			7	4	1500		10	10500	11900
27	6	TIDES 27	OP	OPFSH	FBG	SV	OB			9	6	7000	1	11	38800	43100
27	6	TIDES 27	OP	OPFSH	FBG	SV	IB	170D	YAN	9	6	7000	1	11	42100	46800
27	6	TIDES 27	OP	OPFSH	FBG	SV	IB	300D-350D		9	6	7000	1	11	49000	56700
27	6	TIDES 27	OP	OPFSH	FBG	SV	IB	T225D	VLVO	9	6	7000	1	11	54300	59700
31	10	TIDES 32	OP	OPFSH	FBG	SV	IB	T300D	CAT	11	6	12300	1	10	90000	98900
		1993 BOATS														
18	10	TIDES 19	OP	OPFSH	FBG	SV	OB			7	4	1500		10	9950	11300
27	6	TIDES 27	OP	OPFSH	FBG	SV	OB			9	6	7000	1	11	37100	41200
27	6	TIDES 27	OP	OPFSH	FBG	SV	IB	300D	CAT	9	6	7000	1	11	46900	51600
27	6	TIDES 27	OP	OPFSH	FBG	SV	IB	T200D	VLVO	9	6	7000	1	11	50000	54900
		1992 BOATS														
18	10	TIDES 19	OP	OPFSH	FBG	SV	OB			7	4	1500		10	9500	10800
27	6	TIDES 27	OP	OPFSH	FBG	SV	OB			9	6	7000	1	11	35500	39500
27	6	TIDES 27	OP	OPFSH	FBG	SV	IB	300D	CAT	9	6	7000	1	11	44300	49200
27	6	TIDES 27	OP	OPFSH	FBG	SV	IB	T200D	VLVO	9	6	7000	1	11	47900	52600

LOA FT	IN	NAME AND/ OR MODEL	TOP/ RIG	BOAT TYPE	-HULL- MTL	TP	----ENGINE--- TP	# HP	MFG	BEAM FT	IN	WGT LBS	DRAFT FT	IN	RETAIL LOW	RETAIL HIGH
		1991 BOATS														
18	10	TIDES 19	OP	OPFSH	FBG	SV	OB			7	4	1500		10	9050	10300
27	6	TIDESS 27	OP	OPFSH	FBG	SV	OB			9	6	7000	1	11	34200	38000
27	6	TIDESS 27	OP	OPFSH	FBG	SV	IB	D		9	6	7000	1	11	**	**
27	6	TIDESS 27	OP	OPFSH	FBG	SV	IB	T D		9	6	7000	1	11	**	**
		1990 BOATS														
27	6	TIDES 27	OP	OPFSH	FBG	SV	IB			9	6	7000	1	11	**	**
27	6	TIDES 27	OP	OPFSH	FBG	SV	IB	D		9	6	7000	1	11	**	**
27	6	TIDES 27	HT	SDN	FBG	DV	IO	260	MRCR	9	6	7500	2	6	26500	29400
27	6	TIDES 27	TT	SF	FBG	DV	IB	300D	CUM	9	6	7500	3	4	42600	47400
		1989 BOATS														
27	6	TIDES 27	OP	OPFSH	FBG	SV	IB	T D		9	6	7000	1	11	**	**
27	6	TIDES 27	TT	SF	FBG	DV	IB	T200D	VLVO	9	6	8500	2	6	48600	53400
		1988 BOATS														
27		TIDES 27	OP	OPFSH	FBG	SV	OB			9	6	6500	1	11	29400	32600
27	6	TIDES 27	TT	SF	F/W	DV	OB			9	6	7500	1	10	31300	34700

TIFFANY YACHTS INC

BURGESS VA 22432 COAST GUARD MFG ID- GPB See inside cover to adjust price for area
FORMERLY GLEBE POINT BOAT COMPANY

For more recent years, see the BUC Used Boat Price Guide, Volume 1

LOA FT	IN	NAME AND/ OR MODEL	TOP/ RIG	BOAT TYPE	-HULL- MTL	TP	----ENGINE--- TP	# HP	MFG	BEAM FT	IN	WGT LBS	DRAFT FT	IN	RETAIL LOW	RETAIL HIGH
		1995 BOATS														
40		TIFFANY 40	F+T	SF	F/S	SV	IB	T485D	DD	15		34000	3	2	234000	257000
56		TIFFANY 56	F+T	SF	F/S	SV	IB	T735D	DD	17	6	58000	4		662000	727500
72		TIFFANY 72	F+T	SF	FBG	SV	IB	T18CD	MWM	20		51T	5		**	**
		1994 BOATS														
40		TIFFANY 40	F+T	SF	F/S	SV	IB	T485D	DD	15		34000	3	2	223000	245000
56		TIFFANY 56	F+T	SF	F/S	SV	IB	T735D	DD	17	6	58000	4		633500	696500
72		TIFFANY 72	F+T	SF	FBG	SV	IB	T18CD	MWM	20		51T	5		**	**
		1993 BOATS														
40		TIFFANY 40	F+T	SF	F/S	SV	IB	T D	DD	15			3	2	**	**
56		TIFFANY 56	F+T	SF	F/S	SV	IB	T735D	DD	17	6		4		494000	543000
		1992 BOATS														
40		TIFFANY 40	F+T	SF	F/S	SV	IB	T450D	J&T	15		30000	3	2	178000	195500
46		TIFFANY 46	FB	SF	F/S	SV	IB	T550D	GM	16		38000	3	6	285000	313000
50		TIFFANY 50	FB	SF	F/S	SV	IB	T735D	GM	17		45000	3	8	360000	395500
56		TIFFANY 56	FB	SF	F/S	SV	IB	T735D	GM	17	6	52000	4		545500	599500
62		TIFFANY 62	FB	SF	F/S	SV	IB	T11CD	GM	18	6	74000	4		780500	858000
		1991 BOATS														
40		TIFFANY 40	F+T	SF	F/S	SV	IB	T450D	J&T	15		30000	3	2	169500	186500
46		TIFFANY 46	FB	SF	F/S	SV	IB	T550D	GM	16		38000	3	6	271500	298000
50		TIFFANY 50	FB	SF	F/S	SV	IB	T735D	GM	17		45000	3	8	343000	377000
56		TIFFANY 56	FB	SF	F/S	SV	IB	T735D	GM	17	6	52000	4		521500	573000
62		TIFFANY 62	FB	SF	F/S	SV	IB	T11CD	GM	18	6	74000	4		745500	819000
		1990 BOATS														
40		TIFFANY 40	F+T	SF	F/S	SV	IB	T450D	J&T	15		33000	3	2	173500	191000
46		TIFFANY 46	TT	SF	F/S	SV	IB	T550D	GM	16		38000	3	6	258000	283500
50		TIFFANY 50	FB	SF	F/S	SV	IB	T735D	GM	17		45000	3	8	327000	359500
56		TIFFANY 56	FB	SF	F/S	SV	IB	T735D	GM	17	6	52000	4		499000	548000
62		TIFFANY 62	FB	SF	F/S	SV	IB	T11CD	GM	18	6	74000	4		712000	782500
		1989 BOATS														
36		TIFFANY 36	TT	SF	F/S	SV	IB	T450D	J&T	14		26000	3	6	122500	134500
46		TIFFANY 46	TT	SF	F/S	SV	IB	T450D	CUM	16		38000	3	6	231500	254500
50		TIFFANY 50	FB	SF	F/S	SV	IB	T450D	CUM	17		45000	3	8	266500	293000
56		TIFFANY 56	FB	SF	F/S	SV	IB	T735D	GM	17	6	52000	4		477500	525000
62		TIFFANY 62	FB	SF	F/S	SV	IB	T11CD	GM	18	6	74000	4		681000	748000
		1988 BOATS														
36		TIFFANY 36	TT	SF	F/S	SV	IB	T450D	J&T	14		26000	3	6	117000	128500
46		TIFFANY 46	TT	SF	F/S	SV	IB	T450D	CUM	16		38000	3	6	221500	243000
50		TIFFANY 50	FB	SF	F/S	SV	IB	T450D	CUM	17		45000	3	8	254500	280000
56		TIFFANY 56	FB	SF	F/S	SV	IB	T735D	GM	16	6		4		393000	432000
62		TIFFANY 62	FB	SF	F/S	SV	IB	T11CD	GM	18	6	74000	4		651000	715500
		1987 BOATS														
36		TIFFANY 36	TT	SF	F/S	SV	IB	T450D	J&T	14		26000	3	6	111500	122500
46		TIFFANY 46	TT	SF	F/S	SV	IB	T450D	CUM	16		38000	3	6	211500	232500
50		TIFFANY 50	FB	SDN	F/S	SV	IB	T450D	CUM	17		45000	3	8	243000	267000
62		TIFFANY 62	FB	SF	F/S	SV	IB	T11CD	GM	18	6	74000	4		623000	684500
		1986 BOATS														
36		TIFFANY 36		SF	F/W	SV	IB	T450D	CUM	14		26000	3	6	102000	112500
46		TIFFANY 46		SF	F/W	SV	IB	T450D	CUM	16		38000	3	6	201500	221500
		1985 BOATS														
36		TIFFANY 36	TT	SF	F/W	SV	IB	T450D	J&T	14		26000	3	6	101500	111500
46		TIFFANY 46		SF	F/W	SV	IB	T450D	CUM	16		38000	3	6	192000	211500
50		TIFFANY 50	FB	SDNSF	F/W	SV	IB	T450D	CUM	17		45000	3	8	218500	240000
		1984 BOATS														
36		TIFFANY 36		SF	WD	SV	IB	T450D	CUM	14		26000	3	6	92600	102000
46		TIFFANY 46		SF	WD	SV	IB	T450D	CUM	16		38000	3	6	183500	201500

....For earlier years, see the BUC Used Boat Price Guide, Volume 3

TIGER FIBERGLASS & MARINE INC

MARYSVILLE MI 48040 COAST GUARD MFG ID- MZG See inside cover to adjust price for area

For more recent years, see the BUC Used Boat Price Guide, Volume 1

LOA FT	IN	NAME AND/ OR MODEL	TOP/ RIG	BOAT TYPE	-HULL- MTL	TP	----ENGINE--- TP	# HP	MFG	BEAM FT	IN	WGT LBS	DRAFT FT	IN	RETAIL LOW	RETAIL HIGH
		1996 BOATS														
28		TIGER VIPER 228		OFF	F/S	DV	IO	330	MRCR	7	8	4550			27900	31000
32		TIGER VIPER 232		OFF	F/S	DV	IO	330	MRCR	8		7200			49900	54900
		1994 BOATS														
28		TIGER VIPER		OFF	F/S	DV	IO	T250	MRCR	7	8	4500			26500	29500
32		TIGER VIPER 232		OFF	F/S	DV	IO	T300	MRCR	8		6000			47700	52400
		1993 BOATS														
28		TIGER VIPER 228		OFF	F/S	DV	IO	T350	MRCR	7	8	4500			28600	31800
32		TIGER VIPER 232		OFF	F/S	DV	IO	T300	MRCR	8		6000			44000	48900
		1990 BOATS														
27	10		OP	OFF	F/S	DV	IO	420	MRCR	7	8	3500	1	6	18500	20500

TILTON BOATWORKS INC

JENSEN BEACH FL 34957 See inside cover to adjust price for area

For more recent years, see the BUC Used Boat Price Guide, Volume 1

LOA FT	IN	NAME AND/ OR MODEL	TOP/ RIG	BOAT TYPE	-HULL- MTL	TP	----ENGINE--- TP	# HP	MFG	BEAM FT	IN	WGT LBS	DRAFT FT	IN	RETAIL LOW	RETAIL HIGH
		1993 BOATS														
18	11	FLORIDA SKIFF	OP	BASS	FBG	TH	OB			7	4	800		6	1350	1650

TOLLYCRAFT YACHT CORP

KELSO WA 98626 COAST GUARD MFG ID- TLY See inside cover to adjust price for area
FORMERLY TOLLYCRAFT CORPORATION

For more recent years, see the BUC Used Boat Price Guide, Volume 1

LOA FT	IN	NAME AND/ OR MODEL	TOP/ RIG	BOAT TYPE	-HULL- MTL	TP	----ENGINE--- TP	# HP	MFG	BEAM FT	IN	WGT LBS	DRAFT FT	IN	RETAIL LOW	RETAIL HIGH
		1996 BOATS														
45	3	COCKPIT MY 45	FB	MYCPT	FBG	SV	IB	T375D	CAT	14	11	28000	3		264000	290000
		IB T400D DD 271500 298500, IB T420D CAT 279500 307000, IB T435D CAT													284500	313000
48	2	COCKPIT MY 48	FB	MYCPT	FBG	SV	IB	T375D	CAT	15	5	32000	3	8	286500	315000
		IB T400D DD 297500 327000, IB T420D CAT 306000 336500, IB T435D CAT													312500	343500
63	7	COCKPIT MY 57	FB	MYCPT	FBG	DS	IB	T600D	CAT	17	3	58000	3	6	635000	698000
		IB T665D MTU 664500 730000, IB T680D MAN 668500 734500, IB T735D DD													692500	761000
		IB T800D CAT 719500 791000, IB T820D MAN 740500 814000														
67	10	MOTOR YACHT 65	FB	MY	FBG	DS	IB	T600D	CAT	17	11	68000	4		750000	824000
		IB T665D MTU 783000 860000, IB T680D MAN 770500 847000, IB T735D DD													799000	878000
		IB T800D CAT 828500 910500, IB T820D MAN 823000 904500														
		1995 BOATS														
40	2	SPORT SEDAN 40	FB	SDN	FBG	SV	IB	T375D	CAT	14	8	28000	3		231000	254000
40	2	SPORT SEDAN 40	FB	SDN	FBG	SV	IB	T400D	DD	14	8	28000	3		233000	256000
40	2	SPORT SEDAN 40	FB	SDN	FBG	SV	IB	T435D	CAT	14	8	28000	3		241500	265500
45	3	COCKPIT MY 45	FB	MYCPT	FBG	SV	IB	T375D	CAT	14	8	28000	3		253500	278500
45	3	COCKPIT MY 45	FB	MYCPT	FBG	SV	IB	T400D	DD	14	8	28000	3		261000	287000
45	3	COCKPIT MY 45	FB	MYCPT	FBG	SV	IB	T435D	CAT	14	8	28000	3		273500	300500
48	2	MOTOR YACHT 48	FB	MY	FBG	SV	IB	T375D	CAT	15	2	32000	3	8	264500	291000
48	2	MOTOR YACHT 48	FB	MY	FBG	SV	IB	T400D	DD	15	2	32000	3	8	269500	296500
48	2	MOTOR YACHT 48	FB	MY	FBG	SV	IB	T435D	CAT	15	2	32000	3	8	279000	306500
63	7	COCKPIT MY 57	FB	MYCPT	FBG	DS	IB	T680D	MAN	17	3	60000	3	6	663000	729000
63	7	COCKPIT MY 57	FB	MYCPT	FBG	DS	IB	T735D	DD	17	3	60000	3	6	691000	759500
63	7	COCKPIT MY 57	FB	MYCPT	FBG	DS	IB	T820D	MAN	17	3	60000	3	6	723500	795000
67	10	COCKPIT MY 57	FB	MYCPT	FBG	DS	IB	T820D	MAN	17	11	68000	4		873500	959500
67	10	MOTOR YACHT 65	FB	MY	FBG	DS	IB	T680D	MAN	17	11	68000	4		822000	903000
67	10	MOTOR YACHT 65	FB	MY	FBG	DS	IB	T735D	DD	17	11	68000	4		850000	934500

LOA FT	LOA IN	NAME AND/ OR MODEL	TOP/ RIG	BOAT TYPE	-HULL- MTL	-HULL- TP	ENGINE TP	ENGINE # HP	ENGINE MFG	BEAM FT	BEAM IN	WGT LBS	DRAFT FT	DRAFT IN	RETAIL LOW	RETAIL HIGH
		1995 BOATS														
78	9	COCKPIT MY 78	FB	MYCPT	ARX	DS	IB	T		21	6	50T	5		**	**
		1994 BOATS														
40	2	SPORT SEDAN 40	FB	SDN	FBG	SV	IB	T300D	CAT	14	8	28000	3		211000	231500
		IB T375D CAT 221500 243000, IB T400D DD 223000 245500, IB T435D CAT													231500	254000
40	2	SUNDECK CRUISER 40	FB	MY	FBG	SV	IB	T300D	CAT	14	8	28000	3		210500	231500
		IB T375D CAT 221500 243000, IB T400D DD 223500 245500, IB T435D CAT													231500	254500
45	3	COCKPIT MY 45	FB	MYCPT	FBG	SV	IB	T300D	CAT	14	8	28000	3		217500	239000
		IB T320D MTU 228500 251000, IB T375D CAT 242500 266500, IB T400D DD													250000	275000
		IB T435D CAT 262000 288000														
48	2	MOTOR YACHT 48	FB	MY	FBG	DS	IB	T320	MTU	15	2	32000	3	8	222000	244000
48	2	MOTOR YACHT 48	FB	MY	FBG	SV	IB	T300D	CAT	15	2	32000	3	8	240000	264000
		IB T375D CAT 253500 278500, IB T400D DD 258000 284000, IB T435D CAT													267000	293500
52	11	MOTOR YACHT 53	FB	MY	FBG	DS	IB	T550D	DD	16	11	60000	3	6	505500	555000
52	11	MOTOR YACHT 53	FB	MY	FBG	DS	IB	T680D	MAN	16	11	60000	3	6	544500	598500
55		MOTOR YACHT 55	FB	MY	FBG	DS	IB	T680D	MAN	16	11	60000	3	6	581000	638500
55		MOTOR YACHT 55	FB	MY	FBG	SV	IB	T550D	DD	16	11	60000	3	6	531000	583500
55		MOTOR YACHT 55	FB	MY	FBG	SV	IB	T665D	MTU	16	11	60000	3	6	571500	628000
55		MOTOR YACHT 55	FB	MY	FBG	SV	IB	T735D	DD	16	11	60000	3	6	594500	653000
57		COCKPIT MY 57	FB	MYCPT	FBG	DS	IB	T680D	MAN	16	11	60000	3	6	625500	687500
57		COCKPIT MY 57	FB	MYCPT	FBG	DS	IB	T735D	DD	16	11	60000	3	6	648500	713000
61	2	MOTOR YACHT 61	FB	MY	FBG	SV	IB	T485D	DD	17	11	66000	4		509000	559000
65		MOTOR YACHT 65	FB	MY	FBG	DS	IB	T680D	MAN	17	11	68000	4		704500	774000
65	2	MOTOR YACHT 65	FB	MY	FBG	DS	IB	T550D	DD	17	11	68000	4		666000	732000
		IB T665D MTU 719000 790500, IB T735D DD 734000 806500, IB T760D DD													742500	816000
		1993 BOATS														
32	6	SPORT CRUISER 32	FB	SPTCR	FBG	SV	IB	T260	MRCR	11	6	13000	2	9	70500	77500
32	6	SPORT CRUISER 32	FB	SPTCR	FBG	SV	IB	T200D-T225D		11	6	13000	2	9	83200	93400
34		SPORT SEDAN 34	FB	SDN	FBG	SV	IB	T400D	DD	14	8	28000	3		169000	186000
44	2	MOTOR YACHT 44	FB	MY	FBG	SV	IB	T320	MTU	14	8	28000	3		190000	209000
45	3	COCKPIT MY 45	FB	MYCPT	FBG	SV	IB	T300D	CAT	14	8	28000	3	9	207500	228000
		IB T320D MTU 217500 239000, IB T375D CAT 231000 254000, IB T400D DD													238000	262000
48	2	MOTOR YACHT 48	FB	MY	FBG	DS	IB	T320	MTU	15	2	42000	3	8	242000	265500
55		MOTOR YACHT 55	FB	MY	FBG	SV	IB	T550D	DD	16	11	60000	3	6	506000	556000
55		MOTOR YACHT 55	FB	MY	FBG	SV	IB	T665D	MTU	16	11	60000	3	6	544500	598500
55		MOTOR YACHT 55	FB	MY	FBG	SV	IB	T735D	DD	16	11	60000	3	6	566000	622000
57		COCKPIT MY 57	FB	MYCPT	FBG	SV	IB	T10CD	MTU	16	11	55000	3	6	682500	750000
65	2	MOTOR YACHT 65	FB	MY	FBG	DS	IB	T550D	DD	17	8	72000	4		664000	730000
		IB T665D MTU 715000 785500, IB T735D DD 728500 800500, IB T760D DD													736500	809500
		1992 BOATS														
30	6	SPORT CRUISER 30	FB	SPTCR	FBG	SV	IB	T200	VLVO	11	6	11500	2	9	53100	58400
34		SPORT SEDAN	FB	SDN	FBG	SV	IB	T390	MRCR	12	6	17000	2	10	91700	101000
34		SPORT SEDAN	FB	SDN	FBG	SV	IB	T200D-T300D		12	6	17000	2	10	105500	127000
40		SPORT SEDAN	FB	CNV	FBG	SV	IB	T425D	CAT	14	8	26000	3		197000	217000
40	2	SPORT SEDAN	FB	CNV	FBG	SV	IB	T340	MRCR	14	8	26000	3		156000	171500
40	2	SPORT SEDAN	FB	CNV	FBG	SV	IB	T375D	CAT	14	8	26000	3		191000	209500
40	2	SPORT SEDAN	FB	CNV	FBG	SV	IB	T400D	DD	14	8	26000	3		192500	212000
40	2	SUNDECK MOTOR YACHT	FB	MY	FBG	SV	IB	T340	MRCR	14	8	26000	3		156000	171000
		IB T375D CAT 190500 209500, IB T400D DD 192500 211500, IB T425D DD													196000	215500
44	2	COCKPIT MOTOR YACHT	FB	MYCPT	FBG	DS	IB	T340	MRCR	14	8	28000	3		171000	188000
		IB T375D CAT 211000 231500, IB T400D DD 216000 237500, IB T425D DD													222000	244000
48	2	COCKPIT MOTOR YACHT	FB	MYCPT	FBG	DS	IB	T300D	CAT	15	2	32000	3	8	227000	249000
52	11	MOTOR YACHT	FB	MY	FBG	DS	IB	T665D	MTU	16	11	55000	3	6	443500	487000
57		COCKPIT MY 57	FB	MYCPT	FBG	DS	IB	T550D	DD	16	11	55000	3	6	489500	538000
57		COCKPIT MY 57	FB	MYCPT	FBG	DS	IB	T665D	MTU	16	11	55000	3	6	534500	587500
61		MOTOR YACHT	FB	MY	FBG	DS	IB	T665D	MTU	17	8	64000	4		544000	598000
61	2	MOTOR YACHT	FB	MY	F/S	DS	IB	T550D	DD	17	8	65000	4		513000	563500
61	2	MOTOR YACHT	FB	MY	F/S	DS	IB	T735D	DD	17	8	65000	4		576000	632500
		1991 BOATS														
30	6	SPORT CRUISER 30	FB	SPTCR	FBG	SV	IB	T260	MRCR	11	6	11000	2	9	51600	56700
34		SPORT SEDAN	FB	SDN	FBG	SV	IB	T340	MRCR	12	6	17000	2	10	84800	93200
34		SPORT SEDAN	FB	SDN	FBG	SV	IB	T250D	DD	12	6	17000	2	10	105500	116000
38	6	SPORT YACHT	FB	MY	FBG	DS	IB	T340	MRCR	14	8	25500			136000	149500
38	6	SPORT YACHT	FB	MY	FBG	DS	IB	T250D	GM	14	8	25500			152000	167000
40	2	SPORT SEDAN	FB	CNV	FBG	SV	IB	T340	MRCR	14	8	26000	3		149000	163500
		IB T300D CUM 168000 184500, IB T375D CAT 182000 200000, IB T400D DD													184000	202000
40	2	SUNDECK MOTOR YACHT	FB	MY	FBG	SV	IB	T340	MRCR	14	8	26000	3		148500	163500
		IB T300D CUM 167500 184500, IB T375D CAT 182000 199500, IB T400D DD													183500	201500
44	2	COCKPIT MOTOR YACHT	FB	MYCPT	FBG	DS	IB	T340	MRCR	14	8	28000	3		163000	179500
		IB T300D CUM 180500 198500, IB T375D CAT 201000 221000, IB T400D DD													206000	226500
48	2	COCKPIT MOTOR YACHT	FB	MYCPT	FBG	DS	IB	T300D	CUM	15	2	42000	3	8	214000	235500
52	11	MOTOR YACHT	FB	MY	FBG	DS	IB	T550D	DD	16	11	52000	3	6	375500	413000
57		COCKPIT MY 57	FB	MY	FBG	DS	IB	T765D	DD	16	11	55000	3	6	514000	565000
57		COCKPIT MY 57	FB	MYCPT	FBG	DS	IB	T550D	DD	16	11	55000	3	6	467000	513000
57		COCKPIT MY 57	FB	MYCPT	FBG	DS	IB	T735D	DD	16	11	55000	3	6	533500	586000
61	2	MOTOR YACHT	FB	MY	F/S	DS	IB	T550D	DD	17	8	65000	4		489000	537500
61	2	MOTOR YACHT	FB	MY	F/S	DS	IB	T735D	DD	17	8	65000	4		549500	603500
61	2	MOTOR YACHT	FB	MY	F/S	DS	IB	T760D	DD	17	8	65000	4		557000	612000
		1990 BOATS														
30	6	SPORT CRUISER 30	FB	SPTCR	FBG	SV	IB	T260	MRCR	11	6	11000	2	9	49100	53900
34		SPORT SEDAN	FB	SDN	FBG	SV	IB	T340-T502		12	6	17000	2	10	80700	97300
34		SPORT SEDAN	FB	SDN	FBG	SV	IB	T250D	GM	12	6	17000	2	10	100500	110500
34		SUNDECK	FB	TCMY	FBG	SV	IB	T340	MRCR	12	6	17000	2	10	76600	84200
34		SUNDECK	FB	TCMY	FBG	SV	IB	T250D	GM	12	6	17000	2	10	93700	103000
38	11	SPORT YACHT	FB	MY	FBG	DS	IB	T340	MRCR	14	8	25500			132500	145500
38	11	SPORT YACHT	FB	MY	FBG	DS	IB	T502	MRCR	14	8	25500			142000	156000
38	11	SPORT YACHT	FB	MY	FBG	DS	IB	T250D	GM	14	8	25500			147500	162000
40	2	SPORT SEDAN	FB	CNV	FBG	SV	IB	T340	MRCR	14	8	26000	3		142000	156000
		IB T502 MRCR 152500 167500, IB T250D GM 156500 172000, IB T400D GM													172000	189000
40	2	SUNDECK MOTOR YACHT	FB	MY	FBG	SV	IB	T340	MRCR	14	8	26000	3		142000	156000
		IB T502 MRCR 152000 167000, IB T250D GM 156500 172000, IB T400D GM													171500	188500
44	2	COCKPIT MOTOR YACHT	FB	MYCPT	FBG	DS	IB	T340	MRCR	14	8	28000	3		156000	171000
		IB T502 MRCR 185500 204000, IB T250D GM 161500 177500, IB T400D GM													195000	214000
52	11	MOTOR YACHT	FB	MY	FBG	DS	IB	T550D	GM	16	11	52000	3	6	358500	394000
52	11	MOTOR YACHT	FB	MY	FBG	DS	IB	T735D	GM	16	11	52000	3	6	406000	446000
57		COCKPIT MY 57	FB	MYCPT	FBG	DS	IB	T550D	GM	16	11	55000	3	6	446500	490500
57		COCKPIT MY 57	FB	MYCPT	FBG	DS	IB	T735D	GM	16	11	55000	3	6	510000	560500
61	2	MOTOR YACHT	FB	MY	F/S	DS	IB	T735D	GM	17	8	65000	4		532500	585000
		1989 BOATS														
30	6	SPORT CRUISER 30	FB	SPTCR	FBG	SV	IB	T260	MRCR	11	6	11000	2	9	47000	51600
34		SPORT SEDAN	FB	SDN	FBG	SV	IB	T340	MRCR	12	6	17000	2	10	76800	84400
34		SPORT SEDAN	FB	SDN	FBG	SV	IB	T250D	GM	12	6	17000	2	10	96100	105500
34		SUNDECK	FB	TCMY	FBG	SV	IB	T340	MRCR	12	6	17000	2	10	72900	80100
34		SUNDECK	FB	TCMY	FBG	SV	IB	T250D	GM	12	6	17000	2	10	89600	98400
40	2	SPORT SEDAN	FB	CNV	FBG	SV	IB	T340	MRCR	14	8	26000	3		135500	149000
		IB T250D GM 149500 164500, IB T400D GM 164500 180500, IB T485D GM													175500	192500
40	2	SUNDECK MOTOR YACHT	FB	MY	FBG	SV	IB	T340	MRCR	14	8	26000	3		135500	149000
		IB T250D GM 149500 164500, IB T400D GM 164000 180500, IB T485D GM													175000	192500
44	2	COCKPIT MOTOR YACHT	FB	MYCPT	FBG	DS	IB	T340	MRCR	14	8	28000	3		149000	163500
		IB T250D GM 154000 169500, IB T400D GM 186000 204500, IB T485D GM													203500	224000
52	11	MOTOR YACHT	FB	MY	FBG	DS	IB	T400D	GM	16	11	52000	3	6	299500	329000
		IB T485D GM 324500 356500, IB T550D GM 342500 376000, IB T650D GM													367500	404000
		IB T735D GM 387500 426000														
57		COCKPIT MY 57	FB	MYCPT	FBG	DS	IB	T400D	GM	16	11	55000	3	6	369500	406500
		IB T485D GM 403000 443000, IB T650D GM 460500 506000, IB T735D GM													487500	535500
57		COCKPIT MY57	FB	MYCPT	FBG	DS	IB	T550D	GM	16	11	55000	3	6	427500	470000
61	2	MOTOR YACHT	FB	MY	F/S	DS	IB	T485D	GM	17	8	65000	4		431000	473500
		IB T550D GM 452500 497500, IB T650D GM 484000 531500, IB T735D GM													508500	558500
		1988 BOATS														
30	6	SPORT CRUISER 30	FB	SPTCR	FBG	SV	IB	T260	MRCR	11	6	11000	2	9	44300	49200
34		SPORT SEDAN	FB	SDN	FBG	SV	IB	T340	MRCR	12	6	17000	2	10	73200	80400
34		SPORT SEDAN	FB	SDN	FBG	SV	IB	T250D	GM	12	6	17000	2	10	92000	101000
34		SUNDECK	FB	TCMY	FBG	SV	IB	T340	MRCR	12	6	17000	2	10	69500	76300
34		SUNDECK	FB	TCMY	FBG	SV	IB	T250D	GM	12	6	17000	2	10	85700	94200
40	2	SPORT SEDAN	FB	CNV	FBG	SV	IB	T340	MRCR	14	8	26000	3		129500	142500
		IB T250D GM 143000 157000, IB T400D GM 157000 172500, IB T485D GM													167500	184000
40	2	SUNDECK MOTOR YACHT	FB	MY	FBG	SV	IB	T340	MRCR	14	8	26000	3		129500	142500
		IB T250D GM 143000 157000, IB T400D GM 157000 172500, IB T485D GM													167000	184000
44	2	COCKPIT MOTOR YACHT	FB	MYCPT	FBG	DS	IB	T340	MRCR	14	8	28000	3		142000	156500
		IB T250D GM 147500 162000, IB T400D GM 178000 195500, IB T485D GM													194500	214000
53		MOTOR YACHT	FB	MY	FBG	DS	IB	T400D	GM	16	11	52000	3	6	287000	315500
		IB T485D GM 311500 342000, IB T550D GM 328500 361000, IB T650D GM													352500	387500
		IB T735D GM 372000 409000														
57		COCKPIT MY 57	FB	MYCPT	FBG	DS	IB	T400D	GM	16	11	55000	3	6	353500	388500

CONTINUED ON NEXT PAGE

```
 LOA  NAME AND/                   TOP/ BOAT  -HULL- ----ENGINE--- BEAM   WGT  DRAFT RETAIL RETAIL
 FT IN  OR MODEL                   RIG TYPE  MTL TP TP # HP   MFG  FT IN  LBS  FT IN   LOW   HIGH
--------------------- 1988 BOATS ----------------------------------------------------------------
 57     COCKPIT MY 57              FB  MYCPT FBG DS IB T485D GM   16 11 55000  3  6 385500 423500
    IB T550D GM   408000 448000, IB T650D GM   440000 483500, IB T735D GM    466000 512000

 61  2 MOTOR YACHT                 FB  MY    F/S DS IB T485D GM   17  8 65000  4    412000 452500
    IB T550D GM   432500 475500, IB T650D GM   462500 508000, IB T735D GM    486000 534000
--------------------- 1987 BOATS ----------------------------------------------------------------
 30     SPORT CRUISER 30           FB  SPTCR FBG SV IB T    D GM  11  6 11000  2  9     **     **
 30  6 SPORT CRUISER 30            FB  SPTCR FBG SV IB T270  CRUS 11  6 11000  2  9  42600  47300
 34     CONVERTIBLE SF             FB  SDN   FBG SV IB T270-T350  12  6 17000  2 10  67600  77300
 34     CONVERTIBLE SF             FB  SDN   FBG SV IB T250D GM   12  6 17000  2 10  88100  96900
 34     SUNDECK                    FB  TCMY  FBG SV IB T270-T350  12  6 17000  2 10  64500  73300
 34     SUNDECK                    FB  TCMY  FBG SV IB T250D GM   12  6 17000  2 10  82100  90300
 40  2 CONVERTIBLE SF              FB  CNV   FBG SV IB T260D CAT  14  8                140500 154000
    IB T350D CRUS 145000 159500, IB T375D CAT  151500 166500, IB T485D GM    160500 176000

 40  2 SUNDECK MOTOR YACHT         FB  MY    FBG SV IB T350  CRUS 14  8 26000  3    125000 137500
    IB T250D GM   136500 150500, IB T260D CAT  140500 154000, IB T375D CAT   151500 166500

 44  2 COCKPIT MOTOR YACHT         FB  MYCPT FBG DS IB T350  CRUS 14  8 28000  3    138000 152000
    IB T260D CAT  144500 158500, IB T320D CAT  156500 172000, IB T370D GM    164500 180500
    IB T375D CAT  167500 184000

 48  2 COCKPIT MOTOR YACHT         FB  MYCPT FBG DS IB T210D CAT  15  2 42000  3  8 171000 187500
    IB T310D GM   180000 198000, IB T375D CAT  193000 212000, IB T410D GM    199500 219500

 61  2 MOTOR YACHT                 FB  MY    F/S DS IB T410D GM   17  8 65000  4    369500 406000
 61  2 MOTOR YACHT                 FB  MY    F/S DS IB T475D GM   17  8 65000  4    390500 429500
 61  2 MOTOR YACHT                 FB  MY    F/S DS IB T550D GM   17  8 65000  4    413500 454500
--------------------- 1986 BOATS ----------------------------------------------------------------
 30  6 SPORT CRUISER 30            FB  SDN   FBG SV IB T270  CRUS 11  6 11000  2  9  44500  49400
 34     CONVERTIBLE SEDAN          FB  SDN   FBG SV IB T270-T350  12  6 17000  2 10  64500  73800
 34     CONVERTIBLE SEDAN          FB  SDN   FBG SV IB T220D GM   12  6 17000  2 10  82600  90700
 34     SUNDECK                    FB  TCMY  FBG SV IB T270-T350  12  6 17000  2 10  61600  70000
 34     SUNDECK                    FB  TCMY  FBG SV IB T220D GM   12  6 17000  2 10  77200  84900
 40  2 SUN DECK MOTOR YACHT        FB  MY    FBG SV IB T270  CRUS 14  8 26000  3    117500 129000
    IB T350  CRUS 120000 131500, IB T210D CAT  130500 143500, IB T220D GM    129000 141500
    IB T320D CAT  139500 153000

 44  2 COCKPIT MOTOR YACHT         FB  MYCPT FBG DS IB T350  CRUS 14  8 28000  3    132000 145500
    IB T210D CAT  128500 141500, IB T220D GM   129000 142000, IB T320D CAT   150000 164500

 48  2 COCKPIT MOTOR YACHT         FB  MYCPT FBG DS IB T210D CAT  15  2 42000  3  8 163500 179500
    IB T300D CAT  172000 189000, IB T310D J&T  172500 189500, IB T355D CAT   180500 198500
    IB T410D J&T  191000 210000

 61  2 MOTOR YACHT                 FB  MY    F/S DS IB T355D CAT  17  8 65000  4    336000 369000
    IB T410D J&T  351500 386500, IB T475D GM   374000 411000, IB T550D GM    396000 435000

--------------------- 1985 BOATS ----------------------------------------------------------------
 25  1 SEDAN                       FB  SDN   FBG SV IO  260  MRCR  8        6400  2 10  14600  16600
 25  1 SEDAN                       FB  SDN   FBG SV IO  130D VLVO  8        6400  2 10  16800  19100
 26  8 SEDAN                       FB  SDN   FBG SV VD  270  CRUS 10        9000  2 10  25800  28700
    IO  330   MRCR   21300   23700, IB   220D GM     36900   41000, IO T170  MRCR  21300  23600

 30  6 SPORT CRUISER 30            FB  SDN   FBG SV IB T270  CRUS 11  6 11000  2  9  42500  47200
 34     CONVERTIBLE SEDAN          FB  SDN   FBG SV IB T270-T350  12  6 17000  2 10  61600  70500
 34     CONVERTIBLE SEDAN          FB  SDN   FBG SV IB T220D GM   12  6 17000  2 10  79200  87000
 34     SUNDECK                    FB  TCMY  FBG SV IB T270-T350  12  6 17000  2 10  58800  66900
 34     SUNDECK                    FB  TCMY  FBG SV IB T220D GM   12  6 17000  2 10  74100  81400
 37  4 CONVERTIBLE SEDAN           FB  SDN   FBG SV IB T270  CRUS 13  2 22000  3     91700 101000
    IB T350  CRUS  93800 103000, IB T210D CAT  104500 114500, IB T220D GM    103000 113000
    IB T300D CAT  110000 121000

 39  6 FAST-PASSAGE 39            CUT SA/CR FBG KL IB      D      11 10 21000  5  6 112500 124000
 40  2 SUN DECK MOTOR YACHT        FB  MY    FBG SV IB T270  CRUS 14  8 26000  3    112500 123500
    IB T350  CRUS 114500 126000, IB T210D CAT  125000 137500, IB T220D GM    123500 135500
    IB T300D CAT  131500 144500

 43  2 COCKPIT MOTOR YACHT         FB  MYCPT FBG DS IB T350  CRUS 14  2 30000  3  5 129000 141500
 43  2 COCKPIT MOTOR YACHT         FB  MYCPT FBG DS IB T220D GM   14  2 30000  3  5 129500 142500
 43  2 COCKPIT MOTOR YACHT         FB  MYCPT FBG DS IB T355D CAT  14  2 30000  3  5 151000 166000
 43  2 MOTOR YACHT                 FB  MY    FBG DS IB T210D CAT  14  2 30000  3  5 136000 149500
 43  2 MOTOR YACHT                 FB  MY    FBG DS IB T300D CAT  14  2 30000  3  5 147500 162000
 48  2 COCKPIT MOTOR YACHT         FB  MYCPT FBG DS IB T210D CAT  15  2 42000  3  8 156000 171500
    IB T300D CAT  164500 181000, IB T310D J&T  165000 181500, IB T355D CAT   173000 190000
    IB T410D J&T  183000 201000

 48  2 CONVERTIBLE SEDAN           FB  SDN   F/S DS IB T210D CAT  15  2 40000  3  8 160500 176500
    IB T300D CAT  168000 184500, IB T310D J&T  168500 185500, IB T355D CAT   172500 189500
    IB T410D J&T  176000 193500, IB T550D GM   185500 204000

 61  2 MOTOR YACHT                 FB  MY    F/S DS IB T310D      17  8 52000  4    288500 317000
    IB T355D CAT  292000 321000, IB T410D J&T  300500 330500, IB T475D GM    304500 334500
    IB T550D GM   319500 351000

--------------------- 1984 BOATS ----------------------------------------------------------------
 25  1 SEDAN                       FB  SDN   FBG SV IO  260  MRCR  8        6400  2 10  14100  16000
 25  1 SEDAN                       FB  SDN   FBG SV IO  130D VLVO  8        6400  2 10  16200  18400
 26  8 SEDAN                       FB  SDN   FBG SV VD  270  CRUS 10        9000  2 10  24700  27400
    IO  330   MRCR   20600   22800, IB   205D J&T    35100   39000, IO T170  MRCR  20500  22800

 29 11 SEDAN                       FB  SDN   FBG SV IB T270  CRUS 11  9 13500  2  6  41700  46300
 29 11 SEDAN                       FB  SDN   FBG SV IB T205D J&T  11  9 13500  2  6  59600  65500
 34     CONVERTIBLE SEDAN          FB  SDN   FBG SV IB T270  CRUS 12  6 17000  2 10  58900  64700
 34     CONVERTIBLE SEDAN          FB  SDN   FBG SV IB T205D J&T  12  6 17000  2 10  75300  82700
 34     TRI-CABIN                  FB  TCMY  FBG SV IB T270  CRUS 12  6 17000  2 10  56200  61800
 34     TRI-CABIN                  FB  TCMY  FBG SV IB T205D J&T  12  6 17000  2 10  70600  77600
 37  4 CONVERTIBLE SEDAN           FB  SDN   FBG SV IB T350  CRUS 13  2 22000  3     89900  98800
    IB T205D J&T   98400 108000, IB T210D CAT   99900 110000, IB T215D CUM    98000 107500
    IB T300D CAT  105500 116000, IB T320D CUM  104000 114500

 39  6 FAST-PASSAGE 39            CUT SA/CR FBG KL IB      D      11 10 21000  5  6 106000 116500
 43  2 MOTOR YACHT                 FB  MY    FBG DS IB T350  CRUS 14  2 30000  3  5 127000 139500
    IB T205D J&T  129000 141500, IB T210D CAT  130500 143500, IB T215D CUM   129500 142000
    IB T300D CAT  141000 155000, IB T320D CUM  141500 155500

 48  2 CONVERTIBLE SEDAN           FB  SDN   F/S DS IB T210D CAT  15  2 40000  3  8 154000 169000
    IB T215D CUM  154000 169000, IB T300D CAT  161000 177000, IB T310D GM    161500 177500
    IB T320D CUM  162500 178500, IB T410D J&T  168500 185500, IB T435D GM    170000 187000
    IB T570D GM   179000 197000

 48  2 MOTOR YACHT                 FB  MY    FBG DS IB T210D CAT  15  2 42000  3  8 158500 174000
    IB T215D CUM  157000 172500, IB T300D CAT  166000 182500, IB T310D GM    165500 182000
    IB T320D CUM  166500 183000, IB T410D J&T  178000 196000, IB T435D GM    181000 199000

 61  2 MOTOR YACHT                 FB  MY    F/S DS IB T300D CAT  17  8 52000  4    274500 301500
    IB T310D GM   271500 298500, IB T320D CUM  274000 301000, IB T355D CAT   280000 308000
    IB T410D J&T  288500 317000, IB T435D GM   286000 314000, IB T450D CUM   289500 318500
    IB T570D GM   310500 341000
```

....For earlier years, see the BUC Used Boat Price Guide, Volume 3

TOPAZ MARINE CORP

SWANSBORO NC 21584 COAST GUARD MFG ID- TPP See inside cover to adjust price for area
FORMERLY SEA HAWK MARINE

```
 LOA  NAME AND/                   TOP/ BOAT  -HULL- ----ENGINE--- BEAM   WGT  DRAFT RETAIL RETAIL
 FT IN  OR MODEL                   RIG TYPE  MTL TP TP # HP   MFG  FT IN  LBS  FT IN   LOW   HIGH
--------------------- 1991 BOATS ----------------------------------------------------------------
 32  8 ROYALE 32                   TT  SF    FBG SV IBT300D-T320D 12  2 16500  3  1 105000 117500
 32  8 TOPAZ 32                    TT  SF    FBG SV IBT300D-T320D 12  2 16500  3  1 104000 116000
 36     TOPAZ 36                   FB  SF    FBG SV IB T245D GM   13    22500  3  4 128000 140500
 37  6 TOPAZ 37                    TT  SF    FBG SV IB T375D CAT  13    19800  3  4 146000 160500
 39     ROYALE 39                  TT  SF    FBG SV IB T485D GM   13  2 22500  3  4 179000 196500
--------------------- 1990 BOATS ----------------------------------------------------------------
 32  8 TOPAZ 32                    OP  SF    FBG SV IBT306D-T320D 12  2 16500  3  1  99800 110500
 32  8 TOPAZ 32                    TT  SF    FBG SV IBT306D-T320D 12  2 16500  3  1  99800 111500
 32  8 TOPAZ 32 ROYALE             OP  SF    FBG SV IB T350  CRUS 12  2 16500  3  1  76000  83500
 32  8 TOPAZ 32 ROYALE             OP  SF    FBG SV IB T320D CAT  12  2 16500  3  1 102500 112500
 35  7 TOPAZ 35 FLYBRIDGE          FB  SF    FBG SV IB T425D GM                     129500 142000
 37  6 TOPAZ 37                    OP  SF    FBG SV IB T    D GM  13    16500  3  1     **     **
 37  6 TOPAZ 37                    OP  SF    FBG SV IB T375D CAT  13    19800  3  4 139500 153000
 37  6 TOPAZ 37                    TT  SF    FBG SV IB T    D GM  13    16500  3  1     **     **
 37  6 TOPAZ 37                    TT  SF    FBG SV IB T358D VLVO 13    19800  3  4 130000 143000
 39  1 TOPAZ 39 SPRT ROYALE        OP  SF    FBG SV IB T485D J&T  13    21900  3  1 171000 188000
--------------------- 1989 BOATS ----------------------------------------------------------------
 29     TOPAZ 29                   OP  SF    FBG SV IB T200D VLVO 10  3  8100  2  6  50800  55800
 29     TOPAZ 29                   TT  SF    FBG SV IB T200D VLVO 10  3  8100  2  6  50800  55800
 29     TOPAZ 29 SPORT             OP  SF    FBG SV IB T200D VLVO 10  3  7900  2  6  50100  55000
 29     TOPAZ 29 SPORT             TT  SF    FBG SV IB T200D VLVO 10  3  7900  2  6  50100  55000
 32  8 TOPAZ 32                    OP  SF    FBG SV IB T320D CAT  12  2 16500  3  1  97100 106500
 32  8 TOPAZ 32                    TT  SF    FBG SV IB T320D CAT  12  2 16500  3  1  97100 106500
 37  6 TOPAZ 37                    OP  SF    FBG SV IB T375D CAT  13    19800  3  4 133000 146000
 37  6 TOPAZ 37                    TT  SF    FBG SV IB T358D VLVO 13    19800  3  4 124000 136500
```

LOA FT	LOA IN	NAME AND/ OR MODEL	TOP/ RIG	BOAT TYPE	-HULL- MTL	-HULL- TP	ENGINE TP	ENGINE # HP	ENGINE MFG	BEAM FT	BEAM IN	WGT LBS	DRAFT FT	DRAFT IN	RETAIL LOW	RETAIL HIGH
		1989 BOATS														
38	2	TOPAZ 38 SPORT	OP	SF	FBG	SV	IB	T485D	J&T	13		20800	2	7	152500	167500
39	1	TOPAZ 39 FB	FB	SF	FBG	SV	IB	T485D	J&T	13		24500	3	5	175000	192500
39	1	TOPAZ 39 SPRT ROYALE	OP	SF	FBG	SV	IB	T485D	J&T	13		21900	3	1	163500	179500
44	3	TOPAZ 44 FB	FB	SF	FBG	SV	IB	T565D	J&T	15		38500	4	6	241500	265500
50	8	TOPAZ 50	FB	SF	FBG	SV	IB	T565D	J&T	15		45000	4	6	285500	313500
		1988 BOATS														
29		TOPAZ 29	OP	SF	FBG	SV	IB	T200D	VLVO	10	3	8100	2	6	48600	53400
29		TOPAZ 29	TT	SF	FBG	SV	IB	T200D	VLVO	10	3	8100	2	6	48600	53400
29		TOPAZ 29 SPORT	OP	SF	FBG	SV	IB	T200D	VLVO	10	3	7900	2	6	47900	52700
29		TOPAZ 29 SPORT	TT	SF	FBG	SV	IB	T200D	VLVO	10	3	7900	2	6	47900	52700
32	8	TOPAZ 32	OP	SF	FBG	SV	IB	T320D	CAT	12	2	16500	3	1	92900	102000
32	8	TOPAZ 32	TT	SF	FBG	SV	IB	T320D	CAT	12	2	16500	3	1	92900	102000
37	6	TOPAZ 37	OP	SF	FBG	SV	IB	T375D	CAT	13		19800	3	4	127000	139500
37	6	TOPAZ 37	TT	SF	FBG	SV	IB	T375D	J&T	13		19800	3	4	124500	136500
39	1	TOPAZ 39 FB	FB	SF	FBG	SV	IB	T450D	J&T	13		24500	3	5	163000	179000
44	3	TOPAZ 44 FB	FB	SF	FBG	SV	IB	T565D	J&T	15	6	38500	4	6	230000	253000
50	8	TOPAZ 50	FB	SF	FBG	SV	IB	T710D	J&T	15		45000	4	6	303500	333500
		1987 BOATS														
29		TOPAZ 29	OP	SF	FBG	SV	IB	T260	VLVO	10	3	8100	2	6	35800	39800
29		TOPAZ 29	OP	SF	FBG	SV	IB	T165D	VLVO	10	3	8100	2	6	44100	49000
29		TOPAZ 29	TT	SF	FBG	SV	IB	T260	VLVO	10	3	8100	2	6	35800	39800
29		TOPAZ 29	TT	SF	FBG	SV	IB	T165D	VLVO	10	3	8100	2	6	44100	49000
32		TOPAZ 32	OP	SF	FBG	SV	IB	T306D-T375D		12	2	16500	2	7	85800	99100
32		TOPAZ 32	TT	SF	FBG	SV	IB	T306D-T375D		12	2	16500	2	7	81500	94100
37	6	TOPAZ 37	OP	SF	FBG	SV	IB	T375D	CAT	13		17800	2	5	114000	125500
37	6	TOPAZ 37	OP	SF	FBG	SV	IB	T375D	J&T	13		17800	2	5	111500	122500
37	6	TOPAZ 37	TT	SF	FBG	SV	IB	T375D	CAT	13		17800	2	5	114000	125500
37	6	TOPAZ 37	TT	SF	FBG	SV	IB	T375D	J&T	13		17800	2	5	111500	122500
38	2	TOPAZ 38 FB	FB	SF	FBG	SV	IB	T450D	J&T	13		22700	2	7	143000	157000
44		TOPAZ 44 FB	FB	SF	FBG	SV	IB	T565D	J&T	15	6	37500	3	11	216500	237500
		1986 BOATS														
29		TOPAZ 29	OP	SF	FBG	SV	IB	T260	VLVO	10	3	8100	2	6	34200	38000
29		TOPAZ 29	OP	SF	FBG	SV	IB	T165D	VLVO	10	3	8100	2	6	42300	46900
29		TOPAZ 29	TT	SF	FBG	SV	IB	T260	VLVO	10	3	8100	2	6	34200	38000
29		TOPAZ 29	TT	SF	FBG	SV	IB	T165D	VLVO	10	3	8100	2	6	42300	46900
32		TOPAZ 32	OP	SF	FBG	SV	IB	T250D-T375D		12	2	16500	2	7	79000	95000
32		TOPAZ 32	TT	SF	FBG	SV	IB	T250D-T375D		12	2	16500	2	7	71100	85500
37	6	TOPAZ 37	OP	SF	FBG	SV	IB	T375D	CAT	13		17800	2	5	109000	120000
37	6	TOPAZ 37	OP	SF	FBG	SV	IB	T375D	VLVO	13		17800	2	5	102500	112500
37	6	TOPAZ 37	TT	SF	FBG	SV	IB	T375D	CAT	13		17800	2	5	109000	120000
37	6	TOPAZ 37	TT	SF	FBG	SV	IB	T375D	J&T	13		17800	2	5	106500	117000
38	2	TOPAZ 38 FB	FB	SF	FBG	SV	IB	T450D	J&T	13		22700	2	7	136500	150000
		1985 BOATS														
29		TOPAZ 29		SF	FBG	SV	IB	T165D		10		7900	2	6	40300	44700
36		TOPAZ 36		SF	FBG	SV	IB	T300D		13		17800	2	5	87400	96000
38		TOPAZ 38		SF	FBG	SV	IB	T300D		13		20800	2	7	108500	119500
38		TOPAZ 38	FB	SF	FBG	SV	IB	T410D		13		22700	2	7	124500	137000
		1984 BOATS														
29		TOPAZ 29	OP	SF	FBG	SV	IB	T260	VLVO	10	3	8100	2	6	31200	34600
29		TOPAZ 29	OP	SF	FBG	SV	IB	T124D-T165D		10	3	8100	2	6	36600	43200
29		TOPAZ 29	TT	SF	FBG	SV	IB	T260	VLVO	10	3	8100	2	6	31200	34600
29		TOPAZ 29	TT	SF	FBG	SV	IB	T124D-T165D		10	3	8100	2	6	36600	43200
29		TOPAZ 29 SPORT	OP	SPTCR	FBG	SV	IB	T138-T260		10	3	7900	2	6	27900	34400
29		TOPAZ 29 SPORT	OP	SPTCR	FBG	SV	IB	T124D-T158D		10	3	7900	2	6	36000	42200
29		TOPAZ 29 SPORT	TT	SPTCR	FBG	SV	IB	T138-T260		10	3	7900	2	6	27900	34400
29		TOPAZ 29 SPORT	TT	SPTCR	FBG	SV	IB	T124D-T158D		10	3	7900	2	6	36000	42200
36	2	TOPAZ 36	OP	SF	FBG	SV	IB	T235D	VLVO	13		17800	2	5	79900	87800
		IB T300D CAT 86200 94700, IB T300D J&T 85000 93400, IB T355D CAT 90000 98900														
36	2	TOPAZ 36	TT	SF	FBG	SV	IB	T235D	VLVO	13		17800	2	5	79900	87800
36	2	TOPAZ 36	TT	SF	FBG	SV	IB	T300D	CAT	13		17800	2	5	86200	94700
36	2	TOPAZ 36	TT	SF	FBG	SV	IB	T355D	CAT	13		17800	2	5	90000	98900
38	2	TOPAZ 38	OP	SF	FBG	SV	IB	T300D	CAT	13		20800	2	7	107500	118500
		IB T300D J&T 105500 116000, IB T355D CAT 112000 123500, IB T410D J&T 114500 126000														
		IB T450D GM 117500 129500														
38	2	TOPAZ 38	TT	SF	FBG	SV	IB	T300D	CAT	13		20800	2	7	107500	118500
		IB T300D J&T 105500 116000, IB T300D VLVO 102500 112500, IB T355D CAT 112000 123500														
		IB T410D J&T 114500 126000, IB T450D GM 117500 129500														
38	2	TOPAZ 38 FB	FB	SF	FBG	SV	IB	T355D	CAT	13		22700	2	7	119000	130500
38	2	TOPAZ 38 FB	FB	SF	FBG	SV	IB	T410D	J&T	13		22700	2	7	121500	133500
38	2	TOPAZ 38 FB	FB	SF	FBG	SV	IB	T450D	GM	13		22700	2	7	124500	136500
38	2	TOPAZ 38 FB	F+T	SF	FBG	SV	IB	T355D	CAT	13		22700	2	7	119000	130500
38	2	TOPAZ 38 FB	F+T	SF	FBG	SV	IB	T410D	J&T	13		22700	2	7	121500	133500
38	2	TOPAZ 38 FB	F+T	SF	FBG	SV	IB	T450D	GM	13		22700	2	7	124500	136500

....For earlier years, see the BUC Used Boat Price Guide, Volume 3

TORTOLA TRAWLERS

KEY LARGO FL 33037 COAST GUARD MFG ID- TTW See inside cover to adjust price for area
FORMERLY R H SPEAS

LOA FT	LOA IN	NAME AND/ OR MODEL	TOP/ RIG	BOAT TYPE	-HULL- MTL	-HULL- TP	ENGINE TP	ENGINE # HP	ENGINE MFG	BEAM FT	BEAM IN	WGT LBS	DRAFT FT	DRAFT IN	RETAIL LOW	RETAIL HIGH
		1985 BOATS														
38		TORTOLA 38	SLP	MS	F/W	KL	IB	100D	WEST	13		32000	4	4	63300	69600
40		TORTOLA 40	SLP	MS	F/W	KL	IB	100D	WEST	14		48000	4	6	84300	92600
40		TORTOLA 40	FB	TRWL	F/W	DS	IB	100D	WEST	14		48000	4	6	186000	204500
42		TORTOLA 42	FB	TRWL	F/W	DS	IB	100D	WEST	15		40000	4	4	155500	171000
45		TORTOLA 45	SLP	MS	F/W	KL	IB	175D	GM	16		49000	4	4	92500	101500
45		TORTOLA 45	FB	TRWL	F/W	DS	IB	175D	GM	16		48000	4	4	182000	200000
45		TORTOLA CHARTER	FB	TRWL	F/W	DS	IB	175D	GM	16		48000	4	4	182000	200000
48		TORTOLA 48	SLP	MS	F/W	KL	IB	175D	GM	16		64000	4	6	111500	122500
48		TORTOLA 48	FB	TRWL	F/W	DS	IB	175D	GM	16		62000	4	4	208500	229000
51		TORTOLA 51	FB	TRWL	F/W	DS	IB	265D	GM	18		72000	4	4	221500	243500
54		TORTOLA 54	SLP	MS	F/W	KL	IB	265D	GM	16		78000	4	10	147500	162000
54		TORTOLA 54	FB	TRWL	F/W	DS	IB	265D	GM	18		78000	4	4	247500	272000
57		TORTOLA 57	SLP	MS	F/W	KL	IB	265D	GM	18		87000	4	7	255000	280500
57		TORTOLA 57	FB	TRWL	F/W	DS	IB	265D	GM	18		85000	4	5	263500	289500
60		TORTOLA 60	SLP	MS	F/W	KL	IB	265D	GM	18		54T	4	8	366000	402000
60		TORTOLA 60	FB	TRWL	F/W	DS	IB	265D	GM	18		53T	4	8	362000	397500
		1984 BOATS														
36		TORTOLA 36	SLP	MS	F/W	KL	IB	100D	WEST	13		27000	4	4	51200	56300
36		TORTOLA 36	FB	TRWL	F/W	DS	IB	100D	WEST	13		27000	4	4	90900	99900
38		TORTOLA 38	SLP	MS	F/W	KL	IB	100D	WEST	13		32000	4	4	59300	65200
42		TORTOLA 42	FB	TRWL	F/W	DS	IB	100D	WEST	15		40000	4	4	148500	163500
45		TORTOLA 45	SLP	MS	F/W	KL	IB	175D	GM	16		49000	4	4	86700	95200
45		TORTOLA 45	FB	TRWL	F/W	DS	IB	175D	GM	16		48000	4	4	173500	190500
45		TORTOLA CHARTER	FB	TRWL	F/W	DS	IB	175D	GM	16		48000	4	4	173500	190500
48		TORTOLA 48	SLP	MS	F/W	KL	IB	175D	GM	16		64000	4	6	104500	115000
48		TORTOLA 48	FB	TRWL	F/W	DS	IB	175D	GM	16		62000	4	4	198500	218500
51		TORTOLA 51	FB	TRWL	F/W	DS	IB	265D	GM	18		72000	4	4	211000	232000
54		TORTOLA 54	SLP	MS	F/W	KL	IB	265D	GM	16		78000	4	10	138500	152000
54		TORTOLA 54	FB	TRWL	F/W	DS	IB	265D	GM	18		78000	4	4	237500	261000
57		TORTOLA 57	SLP	MS	F/W	KL	IB	265D	GM	18		87000	4	7	239000	262500
57		TORTOLA 57	FB	TRWL	F/W	DS	IB	265D	GM	18		85000	4	5	253000	278000
60		TORTOLA 60	SLP	MS	F/W	KL	IB	265D	GM	18		54T	4	8	343000	376500
60		TORTOLA 60	FB	TRWL	F/W	DS	IB	265D	GM	18		53T	4	8	347000	381500

....For earlier years, see the BUC Used Boat Price Guide, Volume 3

TRACKER MARINE

DIV OF TRACKER MARINE See inside cover to adjust price for area
SPRINGFIELD MO 65803

FORMERLY TRACKER BOATS

For more recent years, see the BUC Used Boat Price Guide, Volume 1

LOA FT	LOA IN	NAME AND/ OR MODEL	TOP/ RIG	BOAT TYPE	-HULL- MTL	-HULL- TP	ENGINE TP	ENGINE # HP	ENGINE MFG	BEAM FT	BEAM IN	WGT LBS	DRAFT FT	DRAFT IN	RETAIL LOW	RETAIL HIGH
		1996 BOATS														
16	1	PRO ANGLER V16	OP	FSH	AL	DV	OB			6	5	848			1800	2150
16	2	GRIZZLY 1648	OP	FSH	AL	SV	OB			5	10				2050	2450
16	2	GRIZZLY BASS SS	OP	BASS	AL	SV	OB			5	10				1650	1950
16	2	GRIZZLY BASS T	OP	BASS	AL	SV	OB			5	10				1650	1950
16	3	PRO DEEP V16 COMBO	OP	FSH	AL	DV	OB			6	6	986			2100	2500
16	4	BACK COUNTRY 16 CC	OP	BASS	AL	SV	OB			5	11	705			1550	1850
16	4	BACK COUNTRY 16T	OP	BASS	AL	SV	OB			5	11	705			1550	1850
16	5	PRO DEEP V16 SC	OP	FSH	AL	DV	OB			6	8	973			2050	2450
16	6	SUPER GUIDE V16	OP	BASS	AL	DV	OB			6	4	698			1550	1850
16	6	SUPER GUIDE V16 PRO	OP	BASS	AL	DV	OB			6	4	698			1550	1850
16	11	TARGA 17 COMBO	OP	W/T	AL	DV	OB			7	6	1193			2550	2950
16	11	TARGA 17 SC	OP	FSH	AL	DV	OB			7	6	1158			2500	2900
16	11	TARGA 17 TILLER	OP	FSH	AL	DV	OB			7	6	1158			2500	2900
17	2	PRO TEAM 175	OP	BASS	AL	SV	OB			6	2	1302			2750	3200
17	6	PRO DEEP V17	OP	FSH	AL	DV	OB			6	8	1058			2350	2750
17	11	SPORTSMAN 18	OP	FSH	AL	FL	OB			5	10	320			780	940
17	11	TARGA 18 SC	OP	FSH	AL	DV	OB			7	8	1263			2700	3100

TRACKER MARINE -CONTINUED See inside cover to adjust price for area

LOA FT	LOA IN	NAME AND/ OR MODEL	TOP/ RIG	BOAT TYPE	-HULL- MTL	-HULL- TP	----ENGINE--- TP	# HP	MFG	BEAM FT	BEAM IN	WGT LBS	DRAFT FT IN	RETAIL LOW	RETAIL HIGH
		1996 BOATS													
18		PRO TEAM 18 JET	OP	BASS	AL	DV	OB			6	5	1120		2500	2900
18		TOURNAMENT V18	OP	BASS	AL	DV	OB			7	1	772		1800	2150
18	1	GRIZZLY 1848	OP	FSH	AL	SV	OB			5	10			1850	2200
18	2	PRO TEAM 185	OP	BASS	AL	SV	OB			6	5	825		1900	2300
18	3	GRIZZLY 1860	OP	FSH	AL	SV	OB			7				1850	2200
18	6	TARGA 1900	OP	FSH	AL	DV	OB			7	10	1500		3100	3600
18	9	TARGA 19 SE	OP	FSH	AL	DV	OB			6	11	1255		2750	3150
20		TARGA 2000	OP	FSH	AL	DV	OB			8		1750		2550	3000
		1995 BOATS													
16		GUIDE V16	OP	FSH	AL	SV	OB			5	3	470		970	1150
16		NITRO 160 TF	OP	BASS	FBG	DV	OB			6	7	950		1900	2250
16		SUPER 16	OP	FSH	AL	DV	OB			6	2	575		1150	1400
16		SUPER 16 PRO	OP	FSH	AL	DV	OB			6	2	644		1300	1550
16		UTILITY V16	OP	FSH	AL	SV	OB			6	3	290		585	705
17		MAGNA 17 DC	OP	FSH	AL	DV	OB			6	9	953		1950	2350
17		MAGNA 17 FISH	OP	FSH	AL	DV	OB			6	11	980		2000	2400
17		NITRO 170 DC	OP	BASS	FBG	DV	OB			6	7	1189		2450	2850
17		NITRO 170 TF	OP	BASS	FBG	DV	OB			6	7	1189		2450	2850
17		PRO 17	OP	FSH	AL	SV	OB			5	11	720		1500	1800
17		PRO DEEP V17	OP	FSH	AL	DV	OB			6	6	871		1800	2150
17		TOURNAMENT TX17	OP	FSH	AL	SV	OB			5	11	730		1550	1850
17		TOURNAMENT V17	OP	FSH	AL	SV	OB			6		991		2000	2400
17	6	NITRO 180 FISH/SKI	OP	BASS	FBG	DV	OB			7	1	1305		2600	3050
17	6	NITRO 180 TF	OP	BASS	FBG	DV	OB			7	1	1205		2500	2900
18	10	MAGNA 19 BOW RIDER	OP	RNBT	AL	DV	OB			7	2	1315		2750	3200
18	10	MAGNA 19 CC	OP	FSH	AL	DV	OB			7	2	1340		2700	3150
18	10	MAGNA 19 SC	OP	FSH	AL	DV	OB			7	2	1290		2650	3100
19		NITRO 190 DC	OP	BASS	FBG	DV	OB			7	3	1420		2900	3350
19		NITRO 190 TF	OP	BASS	FBG	DV	OB			7	3	1420		2900	3350
19	8	SPORTSMAN 20	OP	FSH	AL	FL	OB			5	11	304		815	980
20		NITRO 2000DC	OP	BASS	FBG	DV	OB			7	10	1520		2250	2600
32		PARTY CRUISER	HT	HB	AL	PN	OB			8	6	5020		10900	12400
		1994 BOATS													
16		GUIDE V16	OP	FSH	AL	SV	OB			5	3	470		920	1100
16		NITRO 160 TF	OP	BASS	FBG	DV	OB			6	7	950		1800	2150
16		SUPER 16	OP	FSH	AL	DV	OB			6	2	575		1100	1300
16		SUPER 16 PRO	OP	FSH	AL	DV	OB			6	2	644		1250	1500
16		UTILITY V16	OP	FSH	AL	SV	OB			6	3	290		555	670
17		MAGNA 17 DC	OP	FSH	AL	DV	OB			6	9	953		1850	2200
17		MAGNA 17 FISH	OP	FSH	AL	DV	OB			6	11	980		1900	2250
17		NITRO 170 DC	OP	BASS	FBG	DV	OB			6	7	1189		2350	2700
17		NITRO 170 TF	OP	BASS	FBG	DV	OB			6	7	1189		2300	2650
17		PRO 17	OP	FSH	AL	SV	OB			5	11	720		1450	1700
17		PRO DEEP V17	OP	FSH	AL	DV	OB			6	6	871		1700	2050
17		TOURNAMENT TX17	OP	FSH	AL	SV	OB			5	11	730		1450	1750
17		TOURNAMENT V17	OP	FSH	AL	SV	OB			6		991		1900	2300
17	6	NITRO 180 FISH/SKI	OP	BASS	FBG	DV	OB			7	1	1305		2500	2900
17	6	NITRO 180 TF	OP	BASS	FBG	DV	OB			7	1	1205		2350	2750
18	10	MAGNA 19 BOW RIDER	OP	RNBT	AL	DV	OB			7	2	1315		2600	3050
18	10	MAGNA 19 CC	OP	FSH	AL	DV	OB			7	2	1340		2650	3100
18	10	MAGNA 19 SC	OP	FSH	AL	DV	OB			7	2	1290		2500	2950
19		NITRO 190 DC	OP	BASS	FBG	DV	OB			7	3	1420		2750	3200
19		NITRO 190 TF	OP	BASS	FBG	DV	OB			7	3	1420		2700	3150
19	8	SPORTSMAN 20	OP	FSH	AL	FL	OB			5	11	304		770	930
20		NITRO 2000DC	OP	BASS	FBG	DV	OB			7	10	1520		2050	2450
32		PARTY CRUISER	HT	HB	AL	PN	OB			8	6	5020		10700	12100
		1993 BOATS													
16		GUIDE V16	OP	FSH	AL	SV	OB			5	3	470		875	1050
16		NITRO 160 TF	OP	BASS	FBG	DV	OB			6	7	950		1700	2050
16		SWEET 16	OP	FSH	AL	DV	OB			6	2	575		1050	1250
16		SWEET 16 PRO	OP	FSH	AL	DV	OB			6	2	644		1200	1400
16		UTILITIES V16	OP	FSH	AL	SV	OB			6	3	290		530	640
17		MAGNA 17 DC	OP	FSH	AL	DV	OB			6	9	925		1700	2050
17		MAGNA 17 FISH	OP	FSH	AL	DV	OB			6	11	925		1700	2050
17		NITRO 170 DC	OP	BASS	FBG	DV	OB			6	7	1189		2200	2600
17		NITRO 170 TF	OP	BASS	FBG	DV	OB			6	7	1189		2150	2500
17		PRO 17	OP	FSH	AL	SV	OB			5	11	665		1250	1500
17		PRO DEEP V17	OP	FSH	AL	DV	OB			6	6	871		1650	1950
17		TOURNAMENT TX17	OP	FSH	AL	SV	OB			5	11	730		1400	1650
17		TOURNAMENT V17	OP	FSH	AL	SV	OB			6		991		1800	2150
17	6	NITRO 180 FISH/SKI	OP	BASS	FBG	DV	OB			7	1	1305		2400	2800
17	6	NITRO 180 TF	OP	BASS	FBG	DV	OB			7	1	1205		2250	2600
18	10	MAGNA 19 BOW RIDER	OP	RNBT	AL	DV	OB			7	2	1180		2350	2700
18	10	MAGNA 19 CC	OP	FSH	AL	DV	OB			7	2	1120		2300	2700
18	10	MAGNA 19 SC	OP	FSH	AL	DV	OB			7	2	1120		2000	2400
19		NITRO 190 DC	OP	BASS	FBG	DV	OB			7	3	1420		2650	3100
19		NITRO 190 TF	OP	BASS	FBG	DV	OB			7	3	1420		2600	3000
19	8	SPORTSMAN 20	OP	FSH	AL	FL	OB			5	11	304		730	880
20		NITRO 2000DC	OP	BASS	FBG	DV	OB			7	10	1520		1950	2350
32		PARTY CRUISER	HT	HB	AL	PN	OB			8	6	5020		10000	11400
		1992 BOATS													
16		GUIDE V16	OP	FSH	AL	SV	OB			5	4	470		820	990
16		NITRO 160 TF	OP	BASS	FBG	DV	OB			6	7	950		1650	1950
16		SWEET 16	OP	FSH	AL	DV	OB			6	6	575		1000	1200
16		SWEET 16 PRO	OP	FSH	AL	DV	OB			6	6	644		1100	1350
16		UTILITIES V16	OP	FSH	AL	SV	OB			5	10	290		505	610
17		MAGNA 17 CNV FISH	OP	FSH	AL	DV	OB			6	9	953		1700	2000
17		MAGNA 17 CNV FUN	OP	FSH	AL	DV	OB			6	9	953		1700	2000
17		MAGNA 17 FISH	OP	FSH	AL	DV	OB			6	9	925		1650	1950
17		NITRO 170 TF	OP	BASS	FBG	DV	OB			6	7	1189		2050	2450
17		PRO 17	OP	FSH	AL	SV	OB			5	11	665		1200	1450
17		PRO DEEP V 17	OP	FSH	AL	DV	OB			6	6	871		1550	1850
17		SUPER 17	OP	FSH	AL	DV	OB			6	6	675		1250	1450
17		SUPER 17 PRO	OP	FSH	AL	DV	OB			6	6	664		1200	1450
17		TOURNAMENT TX17	OP	FSH	AL	SV	OB			5	11	730		1300	1550
17		TOURNAMENT V 17	OP	FSH	AL	SV	OB			6		991		1750	2050
17	6	NITRO 180 FISH/SKI	OP	BASS	FBG	DV	OB			7	3	1205		2150	2500
17	6	NITRO 180 TF	OP	BASS	FBG	DV	OB			7	3	1205		2050	2450
18	10	MAGNA 19 BOW RIDER	OP	RNBT	AL	DV	OB			7	2	1180		2200	2550
18	10	MAGNA 19 CC	OP	FSH	AL	DV	OB			7	2	1120		2200	2550
18	10	MAGNA 19 SC	OP	FSH	AL	DV	OB			7	2	1120		1900	2300
19		NITRO 190 DC	OP	BASS	FBG	DV	OB			7	2	1420		2500	2900
19		NITRO 190 TF	OP	BASS	FBG	DV	OB			7	2	1463		2550	2950
19		NITRO ULTRA 190	OP	SKI	FBG	DV	OB			7	3	1463		2550	2950
19	8	SPORTSMAN 20	OP	FSH	AL	FL	OB			5	10	304		695	840
20		NITRO 2000DC	OP	BASS	FBG	DV	OB			7	10	1493		1850	2200
32		PARTY CRUISER	HT	HB	AL	PN	OB			8	6	5020		9650	10900
		1991 BOATS													
16		NITRO 160 TF	OP	BASS	FBG	DV	OB			6	6	950		1550	1850
16		SWEET 16	OP	FSH	AL	DV	OB			6	6	425		710	855
17		MAGNA 17 CNV FISH	OP	FSH	AL	DV	OB			7		950		1600	1900
17		MAGNA 17 CNV FUN	OP	FSH	AL	DV	OB			7		950		1600	1900
17		MAGNA 17 FISH	OP	FSH	AL	DV	OB			7		950		1600	1900
17		NITRO 170 TF	OP	BASS	FBG	DV	OB			6	6	1189		1950	2300
17		PRO 17	OP	FSH	AL	SV	OB			5	11	548		975	1150
17		PRO DEEP V17	OP	FSH	AL	DV	OB			6	6	675		1150	1400
17		SUPER 17	OP	FSH	AL	DV	OB			6	6	614		1100	1300
17		SUPER 17 PRO	OP	FSH	AL	DV	OB			6	6	664		1150	1350
17		TOURNAMENT TX17	OP	FSH	AL	SV	OB			5	11	700		1200	1450
17		TOURNAMENT V17	OP	FSH	AL	SV	OB			6		700		1200	1450
17	6	NITRO 175 SKI/FISH	OP	SKI	FBG	DV	OB			7	4	1200		1950	2350
17	6	NITRO 180 FS	OP	SKI	FBG	DV	OB			7	3	1305		2150	2500
17	6	NITRO 180 TF	OP	BASS	FBG	DV	OB			7	3	1205		2000	2400
18	10	MAGNA 19 CC	OP	FSH	AL	DV	OB			7	2	1120		1950	2300
18	10	MAGNA BOW RIDER	OP	RNBT	AL	DV	OB			7	2	1120		1950	2350
18	10	NITRO 185TF	OP	FSH	FBG	DV	OB			7	3	1480		2450	2850
18	10	NITRO ULTRA 190	OP	SKI	FBG	DV	OB			7	5	1463		2450	2850
20		NITRO 2000DC	OP	BASS	FBG	DV	OB			7	9	1550		1800	2150
32		PARTY CRUISER	HT	HB	AL	PN	OB			8	6	4450		7550	8700
		1990 BOATS													
16		SWEET 16	OP	FSH	AL	DV	OB			6	6	425		680	815
16	5	NITRO 165TF	OP	BASS	FBG	DV	OB			6	6	830		1350	1600
17		MAGNA 17 CNV FISH	OP	FSH	AL	DV	OB			7		950		1550	1850
17		MAGNA 17 CNV FUN	OP	FSH	AL	DV	OB			7		950		1550	1850
17		MAGNA 17 FISH	OP	FSH	AL	DV	OB			7		950		1500	1800
17		PRO 17	OP	FSH	AL	SV	OB			5	11	548		935	1100
17		PRO DEEP V17	OP	FSH	AL	DV	OB			6	6	675		1100	1350
17		TOURNAMENT TX17	OP	FSH	AL	SV	OB			5	11	700		1150	1400
17		TOURNAMENT V17	OP	FSH	AL	SV	OB			6		780		1300	1550
17		TRACKER 1600TF	OP	BASS	AL	SV	OB			7	2	830		1350	1650
17	6	NITRO 175FS	OP	BASS	FBG	DV	OB			7	1	1050		1700	2050
17	6	NITRO 175TF	OP	BASS	FBG	DV	OB			7	1	1050		1700	2050
17	6	NITRO SKI N FISH	OP	FSH	FBG	DV	OB			7	2	1200		1900	2250
18		TOURNAMENT 1800TF/FS	OP	BASS	FBG	SV	OB			7	2	1080		1750	2100
18	10	NITRO 185TF	OP	FSH	FBG	DV	OB			7	3	1480		2350	2750
20		NITRO 2000DC	OP	BASS	FBG	DV	OB			7	9	1550		1750	2050
		1989 BOATS													
17		MAGNA 17 CNV	OP	FSH	AL	SV	OB			7		950		1500	1800
17		MAGNA 17 FISH	OP	FSH	AL	SV	OB			7		950		1450	1700

LOA FT IN	NAME AND/ OR MODEL	TOP/ RIG	BOAT TYPE	-HULL- MTL TP	----ENGINE--- TP # HP MFG	BEAM FT IN	WGT LBS	DRAFT FT IN	RETAIL LOW	RETAIL HIGH
				1989 BOATS						
17	PRO 17	OP	FSH	AL TR OB		5 9	548		895	1050
17	PRO V17	OP	FSH	AL SV OB		6 6	695		1100	1300
17	TOURNAMENT TX17	OP	FSH	AL SV OB		5 9	700		1100	1300
17	TOURNAMENT V17	OP	FSH	AL SV OB		6 2	822		1300	1550
17	TRACKER 1600TF	OP	FSH	AL SV OB		6 2	830		1300	1550
17 6	NITRO SKI N FISH	OP	FSH	AL SV OB		7 2	1200		1800	2150
18	TOURNAMENT 1800TF/FS	OP	FSH	AL SV OB		7 2	1080		1700	2000
18 10	NITRO	OP	FSH	FBG DV OB		7 3	1350		2050	2450

TRANSPACIFIC MARINE CO LTD
TAIPEI TAIWAN ROC 248   COAST GUARD MFG ID- TMU See inside cover to adjust price for area

For more recent years, see the BUC Used Boat Price Guide, Volume 1

LOA FT IN	NAME AND/ OR MODEL	TOP/ RIG	BOAT TYPE	-HULL- MTL TP	----ENGINE--- TP # HP MFG	BEAM FT IN	WGT LBS	DRAFT FT IN	RETAIL LOW	RETAIL HIGH
				1996 BOATS						
32	EAGLE 32 PILOT HOUSE	FB	MY	FBG DS IB	135D	11 6	15500	3 4	107000	117500
32	EAGLE 32 SEDAN	FB	MY	FBG DS IB	135D	11 6	16500	3 4	112500	124000
40 6	EAGLE 40 PILOT HOUSE	FB	MY	FBG DS IB	210D CUM	14 6	26000	3 9	178500	196000
45 10	CORSICAN 46	FB	MY	FBG DS IB	T375D CAT	15	29000	3 6	300000	329500
48 6	TRANSPAC 49	KTH	SACAC	FBG KL IB	135D PERK	13 7	43000	6	348000	382500
48 6	TRANSPAC 49	KTH	SACAC	FBG KL IB	135D SABR	13 7	43000	6	349500	384000
51 9	CORSICAN 52	FB	MY	FBG DS IB	T375D CAT	15 6	31500	3 6	350000	385000
51 9	EAGLE 52	FB	MY	FBG DS IB	210D CUM	15	32000	3 6	287500	316000
				1994 BOATS						
32	EAGLE 32 PILOT HOUSE		MY	FBG DS IB	135D SABR	11 6	15500	3 4	96400	106000
32	EAGLE 32 SEDAN		MY	FBG DS IB	135D SABR	11 6	16500	3 4	101500	111500
40 6	EAGLE 40 PILOT HOUSE	FB	MY	FBG DS IB	210D CUM	14 6	26000	3 9	163500	179500
45 10	CORSICAN 46	FB	MY	FBG SV IB	T375D CAT	15	29000	3 6	270500	297000
48 6	TRANSPAC 49	KTH	SACAC	FBG KL IB	135D SABR	13 7	43000	6	313500	344500
50	EAGLE 50	FB	MY	FBG DS IB	210D CUM	15 3	46000	5 9	298000	327500
51	CORSICAN 51		MY	FBG SV IB	T375D CAT	15 6	31500	3 6	312500	343500
				1993 BOATS						
32	EAGLE 32 PILOT HOUSE		MY	FBG DS IB	90D SABR	11 6	15500	3 4	86400	94900
32	EAGLE 32 SEDAN		MY	FBG DS IB	90D SABR	11 6	16500	3 4	91000	100000
40 6	EAGLE 40 PILOT HOUSE	FB	MY	FBG DS IB	135D SABR	14 6	26000	3 9	152000	167000
45 10	CORSICAN 46	FB	MY	FBG SV IB	T375D CAT	15	29000	3 6	257500	282500
48 6	TRANSPAC 49	KTH	SACAC	FBG KL IB	90D SABR	13 7	43000	6	295500	325000
50	EAGLE 50	FB	MY	FBG DS IB	210D CUM	15 3	46000	5 9	283500	311500
51	CORSICAN 51		MY	FBG SV IB	T375D CAT	15 6	31500	3 6	297500	326500
				1992 BOATS						
32	EAGLE 32 PILOT HOUSE		MY	FBG DS IB	90D SABR	11 6	15500	3 4	82400	90500
32	EAGLE 32 SEDAN		MY	FBG DS IB	90D SABR	11 6	16500	3 4	86800	95400
45 10	CORSICAN 46	FB	MY	FBG SV IB	T375D CAT	15	29000	3 6	245000	269000
48 6	TRANSPAC 49	KTH	SAIL	FBG KL IB	90D SABR	13 7	43000	6	280000	307500
51	CORSICAN 51		MY	FBG SV IB	T375D CAT	15 6	31500	3 6	283000	310500
				1988 BOATS						
32	EAGLE	HT	TRWL	FBG DS IB	90D-135D	11 6	15500	3 4	68600	82600
46	CORSICAN 46	FB	MY	FBG SV IB	T375D CAT	15 6	26000	3	196000	215500
51	CORSICAN 51 CCKPT MY	FB	MY	FBG SV IB	T375D CAT				233500	257000
				1987 BOATS						
32	EAGLE	HT	TRWL	FBG DS IB	90D-135D	11 6	15500	3 4	65700	79100
				1986 BOATS						
32	EAGLE	HT	TRWL	FBG DS IB	80D- 90D	11 6	15500	3 4	63000	69300
48 6	TRANSPAC 49	KTH	SA/CR	FBG KL IB	D	13 7	43000	6	202500	222500
48 6	TRANSPAC 49 MKII	KTH	SA/CR	FBG KL IB	80D LEHM	13 7	43000	6	202000	222000
				1985 BOATS						
32	EAGLE	HT	TRWL	FBG DS IB	90D LEHM	11 6	17000	3 4	65300	71800
48 6	TRANSPAC 49	KTH	SA/CR	FBG KL IB	80D LEHM	13 7	43000	6	192000	211000
48 6	TRANSPAC 49 MKII	KTH	SA/CR	FBG KL IB	80D LEHM	13 7	43000	6	191500	210500
				1984 BOATS						
48 6	TRANSPAC 49 MKII	KTH	SA/CR	FBG KL IB	80D LEHM	13 7	43000	6	181500	199500

....For earlier years, see the BUC Used Boat Price Guide, Volume 3

TRAVELER BOATS INC
TIFTON GA 31794   COAST GUARD MFG ID- HPY See inside cover to adjust price for area

LOA FT IN	NAME AND/ OR MODEL	TOP/ RIG	BOAT TYPE	-HULL- MTL TP	----ENGINE--- TP # HP MFG	BEAM FT IN	WGT LBS	DRAFT FT IN	RETAIL LOW	RETAIL HIGH
				1989 BOATS						
16 9	SEA-LION 1700DSC	OP	RNBT	FBG SV OB		6 11	950		1850	2200
16 9	SEA-LION 1700CC-D	OP	CTRCN	FBG SV OB		6 11	950		1950	2350
16 9	SEA-LION 1700CC-S	OP	CTRCN	FBG SV OB		6 11	950		1700	2000
17	SEA-LION 1750CC	OP	CTRCN	FBG SV OB		7 11	950		1750	2100
17 5	SEA-LION 1750CC-D	OP	CTRCN	FBG SV OB		7 11	950		2000	2400
17 5	SEA-LION 1750FS-D	OP	BASS	FBG TR OB		7 11	1050		2000	2350
17 5	SEA-LION 1750FS-S	OP	BASS	FBG TR OB		7 11	1050		2150	2500
17 5	TRAVELER 1750SC-D	OP	RNBT	FBG TR OB		7 11	950		2050	2450
17 5	TRAVELER 1750SC-S	OP	RNBT	FBG TR OB		7 11	950		1700	2050
18 8	SEA-LION 1900CC-D	OP	CTRCN	FBG SV OB		7 7	1150		2500	2900
18 8	SEA-LION 1900CC-S	OP	CTRCN	FBG SV OB		7 7	1150		2200	2550
18 8	TRAVELER 1900DSC	OP	RNBT	FBG TR OB		7 7	1250		2500	2900
21 3	SEA-LION 2200CC-D	OP	CTRCN	FBG SV OB		8 6	2000		3650	4250
21 3	SEA-LION 2200CC-S	OP	CTRCN	FBG SV OB		8 6	2000		3300	3850
21 3	SEA-LION 2200WIC-D	OP	CTRCN	FBG SV OB		8 6	2000		4150	4850
21 3	SEA-LION 2200WIC-S	OP	CTRCN	FBG SV OB		8 6	2000		3800	4400
21 3	SEA-LION 2200WIC-XD	OP	CTRCN	FBG SV OB		8 6	2000		4600	5300
				1988 BOATS						
16 6	VANTAGE XL115	OP	RNBT	FBG TR OB		6 6	800		1500	1750
16 6	TRAVELER 1700FS	OP	RNBT	FBG SV OB		7	1200		2250	2600
16 9	SEA-LION 1700CC-D	OP	CTRCN	FBG SV OB		6 11	950		1900	2250
16 9	SEA-LION 1700CC-S	OP	CTRCN	FBG SV OB		6 11	950		1650	1900
17 5	TRAVELER 1750SC-D	OP	RNBT	FBG TR OB		7 11	950		2000	2350
17 5	SEA-LION 1750SC-D	OP	CTRCN	FBG SV OB		7 11	950		1650	1900
17	VANTAGE XL150	OP	RNBT	FBG TR OB		6 11	900		1750	2100
18 8	SEA-LION 1900CC-D	OP	CTRCN	FBG SV OB		7 7	1150		2400	2750
18 8	SEA-LION 1900CC-S	OP	CTRCN	FBG SV OB		7 7	1150		2150	2500
18 8	TRAVELER 1900DSC	OP	RNBT	FBG TR OB		7 7	1250		2400	2800
21 3	SEA-LION 2200CC-D	OP	CTRCN	FBG SV OB		8 6	2000		3550	4100
21 3	SEA-LION 2200CC-S	OP	CTRCN	FBG SV OB		8 6	2000		3200	3700
21 3	SEA-LION 2200CC-XD	OP	CTRCN	FBG SV OB		8 6	2000		3900	4550
21 3	SEA-LION 2200WIC-D	OP	CTRCN	FBG SV OB		8 6	2000		4000	4650
21 3	SEA-LION 2200WIC-S	OP	CTRCN	FBG SV OB		8 6	2000		3650	4250
21 3	SEA-LION 2200WIC-XD	OP	CTRCN	FBG SV OB		8 6	2000		4450	5100
				1987 BOATS						
16 6	FISH-&-SKI 1700FS	OP	RNBT	FBG SV OB		7	1200		2150	2500
16 9	SEA-LION 1700CC	OP	CTRCN	FBG SV OB		6 11	950		1750	2050
17 5	TRAVELER 1750SC	OP	BASS	FBG SV OB		7 11	1150		2100	2500
18 8	SEA-LION 1900CC	OP	CTRCN	FBG SV OB		7 7	1150		2200	2600
21 3	SEA-LION 2200WIC	OP	CTRCN	FBG SV OB		8 6	2200		3950	4600
				1985 BOATS						
16 6	FISH-&-SKI 1700FS	OP	RNBT	FBG SV OB		7	1200		2000	2400
16 9	SEA-LION 1700CC	OP	CTRCN	FBG SV OB		6 11	950		1650	1950
18 8	SEA-LION 1900CC	OP	CTRCN	FBG SV OB		7 7	1150		2050	2450

TRAWLER YACHTS INC
NEWPORT BEACH CA 92663   See inside cover to adjust price for area

LOA FT IN	NAME AND/ OR MODEL	TOP/ RIG	BOAT TYPE	-HULL- MTL TP	----ENGINE--- TP # HP MFG	BEAM FT IN	WGT LBS	DRAFT FT IN	RETAIL LOW	RETAIL HIGH
				1986 BOATS						
41	SPOILER 41	FB	TRWL	FBG DS IB	T260D J&T	14 5			92600	101500
	IB T300D VLVO 92300 101500, IB T320D CAT 97000 106500, IB T350D PERK 98800 108500									
	IB T375D CAT 100500 110500									
45	SPOILER 45	FB	TRWL	FBG DS IB	T260D J&T	15			110500 121500	
	IB T300D VLVO 111000 122500, IB T320D CAT 113500 125000, IB T350D PERK 116500 126500									
	IB T375D CAT 116500 128000									
51	SPOILER 51	FB	TRWL	FBG DS IB	T260D J&T	15 4			139500 153000	
	IB T300D VLVO 141500 155500, IB T320D CAT 142500 156500, IB T350D PERK 144000 158500									
	IB T375D CAT 145500 159500									
53	SPOILER 54	FB	TRWL	FBG DS IB	510D	17			142000 156000	
	IB 700D 147000 161500, IB T260D J&T 142000 156000, IB T320D CAT 145500 159500									
	IB T350D PERK 147000 161500, IB T375D CAT 148000 163000									
60	SPOILER 60	FB	TRWL	FBG DS IB	510D	17			205500 225500	
	IB 700D 218000 239500, IB T260D J&T 207000 227500, IB T320D CAT 215000 236000									
	IB T350D PERK 219000 240500, IB T375D CAT 222000 244000									
				1985 BOATS						
41	SPOILER 41	FB	TRWL	FBG DS IB	T260D GM	14 5			88100 96900	
	IB T308D VLVO 88600 97300, IB T320D CAT 92700 102000, IB T350D PERK 94500 104000									
	IB T375D CAT 96000 105500									
45	SPOILER 45	FB	TRWL	FBG DS IB	T250D VLVO	15			104500 115000	
	IB T260D GM 105500 116000, IB T308D VLVO 107000 117500, IB T320D CAT 109000 119500									
	IB T350D PERK 110500 121000, IB T375D CAT 111500 122500									

TRAWLER YACHTS INC — CONTINUED

LOA	NAME AND/OR MODEL	RIG	BOAT TYPE	MTL	TP	TP	#	HP	MFG	BEAM	WGT	DRAFT	RETAIL LOW	RETAIL HIGH
	— 1985 BOATS —													
51	SPOILER 51	FB	TRWL	FBG	DS	IB		T250D	VLVO	15 4			133000	146000
53	SPOILER 53	FB	TRWL	FBG	DS	IB		T260D	GM	17			136000	149500
60	SPOILER 60	FB	TRWL	FBG	DS	IB		T260D	GM	17			200000	220000

SPOILER 51 options: IB T260D GM 133500 146500, IB T308D VLVO 136000 149500, IB T320D CAT 136500 150000 / IB T350D CAT 138000 151500, IB T350D PERK 138000 151500

SPOILER 53 options: IB T308D VLVO 138500 152500, IB T320D CAT 139000 153000, IB T350D PERK 140500 154500 / IB T375D CAT 142000 156000

SPOILER 60 options: IB T308D VLVO 199500 219000, IB T320D CAT 206000 226000, IB T350D PERK 210000 230500 / IB T375D CAT 212500 233500

TREMOLINO BOAT CO
CHASKA MN 55318   COAST GUARD MFG ID- TMG See inside cover to adjust price for area

For more recent years, see the BUC Used Boat Price Guide, Volume 1

LOA	NAME AND/OR MODEL	RIG	BOAT TYPE	MTL	TP	TP	#	HP	MFG	BEAM	WGT	DRAFT	RETAIL LOW	RETAIL HIGH
	— 1985 BOATS —													
22 10	TREMOLINO	SLP	SA/OD	FBG	TM					16 6	800	1 2	6600	7600
	— 1984 BOATS —													
22 10	TREMOLINO	SLP	SA/OD	FBG	TM					16 6	800	1 1	6300	7200
22 10	TREMOLINO	SLP	SA/RC	FBG	TM					16 6	800	1 1	6300	7200

....For earlier years, see the BUC Used Boat Price Guide, Volume 3

TRESFJORD BOATS AS
VESTNES NORWAY   See inside cover to adjust price for area

LOA	NAME AND/OR MODEL	RIG	BOAT TYPE	MTL	TP	TP	#	HP	MFG	BEAM	WGT	DRAFT	RETAIL LOW	RETAIL HIGH
	— 1985 BOATS —													
31	NOVA 31	HT	CBNCR	FBG	DS	IB	T	D	VLVO				**	**

TREWORGY YACHTS INC
ST AUGUSTINE FL 32086   COAST GUARD MFG ID- TYI See inside cover to adjust price for area

LOA	NAME AND/OR MODEL	RIG	BOAT TYPE	MTL	TP	TP	#	HP	MFG	BEAM	WGT	DRAFT	RETAIL LOW	RETAIL HIGH
	— 1987 BOATS —													
34	ATLANTIS 34	CUT	MS	STL	KL	IB		62D	PERK	11 4	24000	4 6	46600	51200
	— 1986 BOATS —													
34	ATLANTIS 34	CUT	MS	STL	KL	IB		62D	PERK	11 4	24000	4 6	43400	48200
	— 1985 BOATS —													
34	ATLANTIS 34	CUT	MS	STL	KL	IB		62D	PERK	11 4	24000	4 6	40800	45300

TRIDENT MARINE LIMITED
FAREHM/HAMP ENGLAND   COAST GUARD MFG ID- TDS See inside cover to adjust price for area
                          FORMERLY TRIDENT MARINE SALES LIMITED

LOA	NAME AND/OR MODEL	RIG	BOAT TYPE	MTL	TP	TP	#	HP	MFG	BEAM	WGT	DRAFT	RETAIL LOW	RETAIL HIGH
	— 1991 BOATS —													
39 4	VOYAGER 40	SLP	SA/CR	FBG	KL	IB	T	43D	VLVO	13	18850	5	98100	108000
39 4	WARRIOR 40	CUT	SA/CR	FBG	KL	SD		43D	VLVO	13	19000	5	98500	108500
44	VOYAGER 45	SLP	SA/CR	FBG	KL	IB	T	59D	VLVO	14 3	25300	5 9	143000	157000
	— 1990 BOATS —													
39 4	VOYAGER 40	SLP	SA/CR	FBG	KL	IB	T	43D	VLVO	13	18850	5	91800	101000
39 4	WARRIOR 40	CUT	SA/CR	FBG	KL	SD		43D	VLVO	13	19000	5	92200	101500
44	VOYAGER 45	SLP	SA/CR	FBG	KL	IB	T	59D	VLVO	14 3	25300	5 9	133500	147000
	— 1989 BOATS —													
38	VOYAGER 38	KTH	SA/CR	FBG	KL	IB		65D	VLVO	13	18800	5	86500	95100
40	VOYAGER 40	SLP	SA/CR	FBG	KL	IB		65D	VLVO	13	18850	5	90700	99700
40	WARRIOR 40	CUT	SA/CR	FBG	KL	IB		43D	VLVO	13	19000	5	89000	97700
	— 1988 BOATS —													
38	VOYAGER 38	KTH	SA/CR	FBG	KL	IB		65D	VLVO	13	18800	5	81000	89000
40	VOYAGER 40	SLP	SA/CR	FBG	KL	IB		65D	VLVO	13	18850	5	84900	93300
40	WARRIOR 40	CUT	SA/CR	FBG	KL	IB		43D	VLVO	13	19000	5	83200	91400
	— 1987 BOATS —													
38	VOYAGER 38	KTH	SA/CR	FBG	KL	IB		65D	VLVO	13	18800	5	75800	83300
38	WARRIOR 38	CUT	SA/CR	FBG	KL	IB		43D	VLVO	13	18750	5	71200	78200
40	VOYAGER 40	SLP	SA/CR	FBG	KL	IB		65D	VLVO	13	18850	5	79400	87200
40	VOYAGER 40	SLP	SA/CR	FBG	KL	IB	T	43D	VLVO	13	18850	5	77600	85200
	— 1986 BOATS —													
36	SEAFORTH 36	KTH	SA/CR	FBG	KL	IB		65D	VLVO	11 2	13440	3 9	50800	55900
38	VOYAGER 38	KTH	SA/CR	FBG	KL	IB		65D	VLVO	13	18800	5	70900	77900
38	WARRIOR 38	CUT	SA/CR	FBG	KL	IB		36D	VLVO	13	18750	5	66500	73100
	— 1985 BOATS —													
38	VOYAGER 38	KTH	SA/CR	FBG	KL	IB		65D	VLVO	13	18800	5	66300	72900
38	WARRIOR 38	CUT	SA/CR	FBG	KL	IB		36D	VLVO	13	18750	5	62200	68300

....For earlier years, see the BUC Used Boat Price Guide, Volume 3

TRINITY YACHTS
GULFPORT MS 39505   See inside cover to adjust price for area

LOA	NAME AND/OR MODEL	RIG	BOAT TYPE	MTL	TP	TP	#	HP	MFG	BEAM	WGT	DRAFT	RETAIL LOW	RETAIL HIGH
	— 1993 BOATS —													
72 6	CUSTOM SPORT FISH	EPH	SF	AL	SV	IB		T14CD	DD	19 10	88000	4 6	**	**

TRINTELLA SHIPYARD
5231XA HERTOGENBOSCH   See inside cover to adjust price for area
                          FORMERLY ANN WEVER YACHTYARD BV

For more recent years, see the BUC Used Boat Price Guide, Volume 1

LOA	NAME AND/OR MODEL	RIG	BOAT TYPE	MTL	TP	TP	#	HP	MFG	BEAM	WGT	DRAFT	RETAIL LOW	RETAIL HIGH
	— 1996 BOATS —													
46	TRINTELLA 46A	SLP	SACAC	AL	KL	IB		63D	YAN	13 9	32000	6 2	395000	434500
47 3	TRINTELLA 47	SLP	SACAC	KEV	KL	IB		63D	YAN	14 9	33070	6 5	418000	459500
51 2	TRINTELLA 51A	SLP	SACAC	AL	KL	IB		80D	PERK	15 1	43210	6 9	531000	583500
58	TRINTELLA 58A	SLP	SACAC	AL	KL	IB		125D	PERK	16 3	60000	7 2	968000	1.050M
67 2	TRINTELLA 67D	SLP	SACAC	KEV	KL	IB		213D	CAT	18	88200	8 2	1.540M	1.675M
75 6	TRINTELLA 75A	SLP	SACAC	AL	KL	IB		233D	MTU	19 5	57T	9 2	**	**
	— 1995 BOATS —													
46	TRINTELLA 46A	SLP	SACAC	AL	KL	IB		63D	YAN	13 9	31750	6 2	368500	405000
47 3	TRINTELLA 47	SLP	SACAC	KEV	KL	IB		63D	YAN	14 9	33070	6 5	391000	430000
51 2	TRINTELLA 51A	SLP	SACAC	AL	KL	IB		80D	PERK	15 1	43210	6 9	496500	546000
58	TRINTELLA 58A	SLP	SACAC	AL	KL	IB		125D	PERK	16 3	56863	7 2	871000	957500
67 2	TRINTELLA 67D	SLP	SACAC	KEV	KL	IB		213D	CAT	18	88200	8 2	1.440M	1.565M
75 6	TRINTELLA 75A	SLP	SACAC	AL	KL	IB		233D	MTU	19 5	57T	9 2	**	**
	— 1984 BOATS —													
42 4	TRINTELLA 45	SLP	SA/RC	FBG	KL	IB		35D	VOVO	13 1	23841	6	135500	149000
45	TRINTELLA 45	SLP	SA/RC	FBG	KL	IB		72D	PERK	13 5	34000	7	176500	194000
53	TRINTELLA 53	SLP	SA/RC	FBG	KL	IB		124D		15 5	35400	7	252500	276000
53	TRINTELLA 53	SLP	SA/RC	FBG	KC	IB		124D	PERK	15 5	35400	7	251500	276000

....For earlier years, see the BUC Used Boat Price Guide, Volume 3

TRITON YACHTS
DIV OF GRUMMAN ALLIED IND INC
PORTSMOUTH RI 02871   See inside cover to adjust price for area

LOA	NAME AND/OR MODEL	RIG	BOAT TYPE	MTL	TP	TP	#	HP	MFG	BEAM	WGT	DRAFT	RETAIL LOW	RETAIL HIGH
	— 1985 BOATS —													
17 10	TRITON 18	SLP	SA/CR	FBG	CB					6 11	800	1 6	3350	3900
21 3	TRITON 21	SLP	SA/CR	FBG	KL					8	1700	1 4	5350	6150
23	TRITON 23	SLP	SA/CR	FBG	KL					7 11	3500	4	9500	10800
25	TRITON 25	SLP	SA/CR	FBG	KL					8	3750	4 3	11000	12500
25	TRITON 25 SHOAL	SLP	SA/CR	FBG	KL					8	3750	3	11000	12500
27	TRITON 27	SLP	SA/CR	FBG	KL	IB		D		9 6	6250	5 2	21600	24000
27	TRITON 27 SHOAL	SLP	SA/CR	FBG	KL	IB		D		9 6	6250	3 11	21600	24000
	— 1984 BOATS —													
21 3	TRITON 21	SLP	SA/OD	FBG	CB					8	1500	1 4	4750	5450
25	TRITON 25	SLP	SA/CR	FBG	KL	SD		15	OMC	8	3750	4 7	11100	12600
25	TRITON 25	SLP	SA/CR	FBG	SK	SD		15	OMC	8	3750	4 2	11100	12600
27	TRITON 27	SLP	SA/CR	FBG	KL	SD		15	OMC	9 6	6250	5 2	19900	22100
27	TRITON 27	SLP	SA/CR	FBG	KL	IB		15D	VLVO	9 6	6250	5 2	20400	22600
27	TRITON 27 SHOAL	SLP	SA/CR	FBG	KL	SD		15	OMC	9 6	6250	3 6	19900	22100
27	TRITON 27 SHOAL	SLP	SA/CR	FBG	KL	IB		15D	VLVO	9 6	6250	3 6	20400	22600

TROJAN EXPRESS YACHTS

CARVER BOAT CORP
PULASKI WI 54162

COAST GUARD MFG ID- CDR
FOR LATER YEARS SEE CARVER BOAT CORPORATION

See inside cover to adjust price for area

For more recent years, see the BUC Used Boat Price Guide, Volume 1

LOA FT IN	NAME AND/ OR MODEL	TOP/ RIG	BOAT TYPE	HULL MTL TP	ENGINE TP # HP MFG	BEAM FT IN	WGT LBS	DRAFT FT IN	RETAIL LOW	RETAIL HIGH
1996 BOATS
37 8	EXPRESS 350	OP	EXP	FBG DV	IB T320 CRUS	12	16403	2 10	92300	101500
	IB T355 CRUS 93600 103000, IB T380 CRUS 94700 104000, IB T300D CAT 112500 123500
	IB T315D CUM 109500 120500
39 4	EXPRESS 390	OP	EXP	FBG DV	IB T320 CRUS	6 19572	3 7	105500 116000
	IB T355 CRUS 107000 117500, IB T380 CRUS 108000 118500, IB T300D CAT 126500 139000
	IB T315D CUM 123500 135500, IB T350D CAT 131500 144500
44 9	EXPRESS 440	OP	EXP	FBG DV	IB T380 CRUS	15	28000	4	172500 190000
	IB T350D CAT 195500 214500, IB T420D CAT 204500 225000, IB T420D CUM 199500 219500
1995 BOATS
37 8	EXPRESS 350	OP	EXP	FBG DV	IB T315	12	16403	2 10	74300	81600
37 8	EXPRESS 350	OP	EXP	FBG DV	IB T392	12	16403	2 10	76900	84300
39 4	EXPRESS 390	OP	EXP	FBG DV	IB T350	13	6 19572	3 7	91300	100500
39 4	EXPRESS 390	OP	EXP	FBG DV	IB T392	13	6 19572	3 7	92900	102000
1994 BOATS
36 5	EXPRESS YACHT 370	FB	CR	FBG SV	IB T300 CRUS	13	6 16000	3 7	72800	80000
	IB T300 MRCR 72300 79400, IB T400 CRUS 76300 83900, IB T400 MRCR 75600 83000
	IB T300D CAT 88300 97100, IB T300D CUM 85800 94300
1993 BOATS
36 5	EXPRESS YACHT 370	FB	MY	FBG SV	IB T300 CRUS 13	2 16000	3 6	72000	79100
	IB T300 MRCR 71500 78600, IB T400 CRUS 75700 83200, IB T400 MRCR 75000 82400
	IB T300D CAT 88100 96800, IB T350D CAT 92100 101000
1992 BOATS
33	10-METER MID-CABIN	OP	EXP	FBG SV	IB T300 CRUS 13		12500	2 8	50000	55000
33	10-METER MID-CABIN	OP	EXP	FBG SV	IB T300D J&T 13		12500	2 8	62100	68200
35 4	10.8 METER CNV	FB	CNV	FBG SV	IB T300D CAT 13		15000	3 1	81500	89600
35 4	10.8-METER CNV	FB	CNV	FBG SV	IB T300 CRUS 13		15000	3 1	64200	70500
35 4	10.8-METER CNV	FB	CNV	FBG SV	IB T300D J&T 13		15000	3 1	80700	88700
36 5	10.8-METER EXPRESS	OP	EXP	FBG SV	IB T300 CRUS 13	2 17000	3 4	69500	76400
36 5	10.8-METER EXPRESS	OP	EXP	FBG SV	IB T300D CAT 13	2 17000	3 4	83800	92100
39	11-METER EXPRESS	OP	EXP	FBG SV	IB T300 CRUS 13	3 16800	3 3	72700	79900
	IB T355 CRUS 74300 81600, IB T375D CAT 96400 106000, IB T465D J&T 102500 112500
39 9	12-METER CONVERTIBLE	FB	CNV	FBG SV	IB T300 CRUS 14	3 19000	3 9	83900	92100
	IB T355 CRUS 85400 93800, IB T375D CAT 108500 119000, IB T465D J&T 114500 126000
39 9	12-METER MOTOR YACHT	FB	MY	FBG SV	IB T300 CRUS 14	3 22000	4 2	94700	104000
	IB T355 CRUS 96200 105500, IB T375D CAT 119000 131000, IB T465D J&T 125000 137500
41	12-METER EXPRESS	OP	EXP	FBG SV	IB T300 CRUS 14	3 18000	3 5	87400	96100
	IB T355 CRUS 89700 98600, IB T375D CAT 112000 123000, IB T425D CUM 117500 129000
	IB T465D J&T 119000 130500, IB T550D J&T 128500 141500
46 3	14-METER CONVERTIBLE	FB	CNV	FBG SV	IB T465D J&T 16	3 34000	3 6	207000 227500
46 3	14-METER CONVERTIBLE	FB	CNV	FBG SV	IB T550D J&T 16	3 34300	3 6	222000 244000
46 3	14-METER CONVERTIBLE	FB	CNV	FBG SV	IB T735D J&T 16	3 35100	3 6	254000 279000
1991 BOATS
32	CLASSIC 32 SEDAN	FB	SDN	FBG SV	IB T235 CRUS 13		12850	2 6	47000	51600
33	10-METER MID-CABIN	OP	EXP	FBG SV	IB T300 CRUS 13		12500	2 8	47800	52500
33	10-METER MID-CABIN	OP	EXP	FBG SV	IB T300D J&T 13		12500	2 8	59300	65100
35 4	10.8 METER CNV	FB	CNV	FBG SV	IB T300 CRUS 13		15000	3 1	77800	85500
35 4	10.8-METER CNV	FB	CNV	FBG SV	IB T300 CRUS 13		15000	3 1	61000	67000
35 4	10.8-METER CNV	FB	CNV	FBG SV	IB T300D J&T 13		15000	3 1	77100	84700
36 5	10.8-METER EXPRESS	OP	EXP	FBG SV	IB T300 CRUS 13	2 17000	3 4	66300	72900
36 5	10.8-METER EXPRESS	OP	EXP	FBG SV	IB T300D CAT 13	2 17000	3 4	79900	87900
37 6	11-METER EXPRESS	OP	EXP	FBG SV	IB T300 CRUS 14	3 16800	3 3	64900	71400
	IB T355 CRUS 66400 73000, IB T375D CAT 86000 94500, IB T465D J&T 91700 101000
39 9	12-METER CONVERTIBLE	FB	CNV	FBG SV	IB T300 CRUS 14	3 19000	3 9	80000	87900
	IB T355 CRUS 81500 89500, IB T375D CAT 103500 113500, IB T465D J&T 109000 120000
39 9	12-METER MOTOR YACHT	FB	MY	FBG SV	IB T300 CRUS 14	3 22000	4 2	90300	99200
	IB T355 CRUS 91800 101000, IB T375D CAT 113500 124500, IB T465D J&T 119500 131000
41	12-METER EXPRESS	OP	EXP	FBG SV	IB T300 CRUS 14	3 18000	3 5	83400	91700
	IB T355 CRUS 85600 94000, IB T375D CAT 107000 117500, IB T425D CAT 112000 123000
	IB T465D J&T 113500 124500, IB T550D J&T 123000 135000
46 3	14-METER CONVERTIBLE	FB	CNV	FBG SV	IB T465D J&T 16	3 34000	3 6	197000 216500
46 3	14-METER CONVERTIBLE	FB	CNV	FBG SV	IB T550D J&T 16	3 34300	3 6	211500 232500
46 3	14-METER CONVERTIBLE	FB	CNV	FBG SV	IB T735D J&T 16	3 35100	3 6	242500 266000
1990 BOATS
28 8	8.6 METER EXPRESS	OP	EXP	FBG SV	IO T230-T260 10	6 9500	2 2	21800	24800
32	CLASS 32 SEDAN	FB	SDN	FBG SV	IB T270 CRUS 13		12850	2 6	45800	50400
33	10-METER MID-CABIN	OP	EXP	FBG SV	IB T350-T400 13		12500	2 8	46700	52600
33	10-METER MID-CABIN	OP	EXP	FBG SV	IB T300D J&T 13		12500	2 8	56600	62200
35 4	10-METER CNV	FB	CNV	FBG SV	IB T350 CRUS 13		15000	3 1	59500	65300
35 4	10.8-METER CNV	FB	CNV	FBG SV	IB T350 CRUS 13		15000	3 1	73600	80900
37 6	11-METER EXPRESS	OP	EXP	FBG SV	IB T350 CRUS 14	3 16800	3 3	63200	69500
	IB T400 CRUS 65000 71500, IB T375D CAT 82000 90200, IB T450D J&T 86200 94700
39 9	12-METER CONVERTIBLE	FB	CNV	FBG SV	IB T350 CRUS 14	3 19000	3 9	77600	85300
	IB T400 CRUS 79500 87300, IB T375D CAT 98600 108500, IB T450D GM 101500 112000
	IB T485D J&T 106500 117000
39 9	12-METER MOTOR YACHT	FB	MY	FBG SV	IB T350 CRUS 14	3 22000	4 2	87400	96100
	IB T400 CRUS 89300 98100, IB T375D CAT 108500 119000, IB T450D J&T 112500 123500
	IB T485D J&T 116000 127500
41	12-METER EXPRESS	OP	EXP	FBG SV	IB T350 CRUS 14	3 18000	3 5	81500	89500
	IB T400 CRUS 83800 92100, IB T375D CAT 102000 112000, IB T425D CAT 107000 117500
	IB T450D J&T 106500 117000, IB T485D J&T 110000 121000
43 3	13-METER EXPRESS	OP	EXP	FBG SV	IB T400D J&T 14	3 24000	3 2	139000 153000
	IB T450D J&T 144000 158500, IB T485D J&T 148000 162500, IB T735D J&T 177000 194500
46 3	14-METER CONVERTIBLE	FB	CNV	FBG SV	IB T450D J&T 16	3 34000	3 6	185500 204000
	IB T485D J&T 191000 209500, IB T550D J&T 201500 221500, IB T735D J&T 231000 254000
1989 BOATS
28 8	8.6-METER EXPRESS	OP	EXP	FBG SV	IO T230-T260 10	6 9500	2 2	20600	23400
32	F-32 CONVERTIBLE	FB	SDN	FBG SV	IB T270 CRUS 13		12850	2 6	43200	48000
33	10-METER MID-CABIN	OP	EXP	FBG SV	IB T350 CRUS 13		12500	2	44000	48900
33	10-METER SPORT EXP	OP	EXP	FBG SV	IB T350 CRUS 13		11250	2	43000	47800
33	10-METER SPORT EXP	OP	EXP	FBG SV	IB T300D J&T 13		11250	2	54000	59100
33	10-METER SPORT SDN	FB	SDN	FBG SV	IB T350 CRUS 13		14250	2	49200	54600
33	10-METER SPORT SDN	FB	SDN	FBG SV	IB T300D J&T 13		14250	2	64000	70300
35 4	10.8-METER CNV	FB	CNV	FBG SV	IB T350 CRUS 13		15000	2 4	56600	62200
35 4	10.8-METER CNV	FB	CNV	FBG SV	IB T300D J&T 13		15000	2 4	70400	77400
36	F-36 CONVERTIBLE	FB	SDNSF	FBG SV	IB T350 CRUS 13		16900	2 11	60400	66400
37 6	11-METER SPORTYACHT	OP	EXP	FBG SV	IB T350 CRUS 14		16800	3 3	61300	67300
37 6	11-METER SPORTYACHT	OP	EXP	FBG SV	IB T375D CAT 14		16800	3 3	79200	87100
37 6	11-METER SPORTYACHT	OP	EXP	FBG SV	IB T450D J&T 14		16800	3 3	83200	91400
39 9	12-METER CONVERTIBLE	FB	CNV	FBG SV	IB T350 CRUS 14		19000	3 6	75100	82500
39 9	12-METER CONVERTIBLE	FB	CNV	FBG SV	IB T375D CAT 14		21100	3 6	102000 112000
39 9	12-METER CONVERTIBLE	FB	CNV	FBG SV	IB T450D GM 14		21900	3 6	107500 118000
39 9	12-METER MOTORYACHT	FB	MY	FBG SV	IB T350 CRUS 14		22000	3 8	84500 92900
39 9	12-METER MOTORYACHT	FB	MY	FBG SV	IB T375D CAT 14		24100	3 8	112000 122000
39 9	12-METER MOTORYACHT	FB	MY	FBG SV	IB T450D J&T 14		24900	3 8	117500 129500
41	12-METER EXPRESS	OP	EXP	FBG SV	IB T350 CRUS 14	3 18000	3 5	77800 85500
41	12-METER EXPRESS	OP	EXP	FBG SV	IB T375D CAT 14	3 18000	3 5	97400 107000
41	12-METER EXPRESS	OP	EXP	FBG SV	IB T450D J&T 14	3 18000	3 5	102000 112000
43	13-METER SPORT YACHT	OP	EXP	FBG SV	IB T450D J&T 16		24000	3 3	129500 142500
43	13-METER SPORT YACHT	OP	EXP	FBG SV	IB T550D J&T 16		26000	3 4	144500 158500
43	13-METER SPORT YACHT	OP	EXP	FBG SV	IB T735D J&T 16		26000	3 3	160000 176000
46 3	14-METER CONVERTIBLE	FB	CNV	FBG SV	IB T485D J&T 16		34000	3 6	182000 200000
46 3	14-METER CONVERTIBLE	FB	CNV	FBG SV	IB T550D J&T 16		34300	3 6	192500 211500
46 3	14-METER CONVERTIBLE	FB	CNV	FBG SV	IB T750D J&T 16		35100	3 6	223000 245000
1988 BOATS
28 8	8.6-METER EXPRESS	OP	EXP	FBG SV	IO T230-T260 10	6 9500	2 2	19500	22100
32	F-32 CONVERTIBLE	FB	SDN	FBG SV	IB T270 CRUS 13		12850	2 6	41100	45700
33	10-METER MID-CABIN	OP	EXP	FBG SV	IB T350 CRUS 13		12500	2	41400	46500
33	10-METER SPORT EXP	OP	EXP	FBG SV	IB T350 CRUS 13		11250	2	41000	45500
33	10-METER SPORT EXP	OP	EXP	FBG SV	IB T300D J&T 13		11250	2	49700	54600
33	10-METER SPORT SDN	FB	SDN	FBG SV	IB T350 CRUS 13		14250	2	47100	51700
33	10-METER SPORT SDN	FB	SDN	FBG SV	IB T300D J&T 13		14250	2	61300	67300
35 4	10.8-METER CNV	FB	CNV	FBG SV	IB T350 CRUS 13		15000	2 4	53900	59300
35 4	10.8-METER CNV	FB	CNV	FBG SV	IB T300D J&T 13		15000	2 4	67200	73800
36	F-36 CONVERTIBLE	FB	SDNSF	FBG SV	IB T350 CRUS 13		16900	2 11	57700	63400
36	F-36 TRI-CABIN	FB	TCMY	FBG SV	IB T270 CRUS 13		17500	2 11	57100	62800
37 6	11-METER SPORT SEDAN	FB	SDN	FBG SV	IB T350 CRUS 14		18000	3 3	62300	68400
37 6	11-METER SPORT SEDAN	FB	SDN	FBG SV	IB T375D CAT 14		18000	3 4	80100	88100
37 6	11-METER SPORT SEDAN	FB	SDN	FBG SV	IB T450D J&T 14		18000	3 4	84100	92400

LOA FT	LOA IN	NAME AND/ OR MODEL	TOP/ RIG	BOAT TYPE	-HULL- MTL	-HULL- TP	ENGINE TP	ENGINE # HP	ENGINE MFG	BEAM FT	BEAM IN	WGT LBS	DRAFT FT	DRAFT IN	RETAIL LOW	RETAIL HIGH
		1988 BOATS														
37	6	11-METER SPORTYACHT	OP	EXP	FBG	SV	IB	T350	CRUS	14		16800	3	3	58600	64400
37	6	11-METER SPORTYACHT	OP	EXP	FBG	SV	IB	T375D	CAT	14		16800	3	3	75700	83200
37	6	11-METER SPORTYACHT	OP	EXP	FBG	SV	IB	T450D	J&T	14		16800	3	3	79500	87400
39	9	12-METER CONVERTIBLE	FB	CNV	FBG	SV	IB	T350	CRUS	14		19000	3	6	71800	78900
39	9	12-METER CONVERTIBLE	FB	CNV	FBG	SV	IB	T375D	CAT	14		21100	3	6	97300	107000
39	9	12-METER CONVERTIBLE	FB	CNV	FBG	SV	IB	T450D	GM	14		21900	3	6	102500	112500
39	9	12-METER MOTORYACHT	FB	MY	FBG	SV	IB	T350	CRUS	14		22000	3	8	80800	88800
39	9	12-METER MOTORYACHT	FB	MY	FBG	SV	IB	T375D	CAT	14		24100	3	8	106000	116500
39	9	12-METER MOTORYACHT	FB	MY	FBG	SV	IB	T450D	J&T	14		24900	3	8	112500	123500
43		13-METER SPORT YACHT	OP	EXP	FBG	SV	IB	T450D	J&T	16		24000	3	3	124000	136000
43		13-METER SPORT YACHT	OP	EXP	FBG	SV	IB	T530D	J&T	16		26000	3	4	136000	149500
43		13-METER SPORT YACHT	OP	EXP	FBG	SV	IB	T750D	J&T	16		26000	3	3	154000	169500
46	3	14-METER CONVERTIBLE	FB	CNV	FBG	SV	IB	T450D	J&T	16		34000	3	6	169500	186000
46	3	14-METER CONVERTIBLE	FB	CNV	FBG	SV	IB	T550D	J&T	16	3	34300	3	6	184000	202000
46	3	14-METER CONVERTIBLE	FB	CNV	FBG	SV	IB	T750D	J&T	16	3	35100	3	6	213000	234000
		1987 BOATS														
28	8	8.6-METER EXPRESS	OP	EXP	FBG	SV	IO	T230-T260		10	6	9500	2	2	18700	21200
32		F-32 CONVERTIBLE	FB	SDN	FBG	SV	IB	T270	CRUS	13		12000	2	6	38800	43200
33		10-METER MID-CABIN	OP	EXP	FBG	SV	IB	T350	CRUS	13		12500	2		39900	44400
33		10-METER SPORT EXP	OP	EXP	FBG	SV	IB	T350	CRUS	13		11250	2		39100	43400
33		10-METER SPORT EXP	OP	EXP	FBG	SV	IB	T300D	J&T	13		11250	2		47800	52600
33		10-METER SPORT SDN	FB	SDN	FBG	SV	IB	T350	CRUS	13		14250	2		44400	49400
33		10-METER SPORT SDN	FB	SDN	FBG	SV	IB	T300D	J&T	13		14250	2		58700	64500
35	4	10.8-METER CNV	FB	CNV	FBG	SV	IB	T350	CRUS	13		15000	2	4	51400	56500
35	4	10.8-METER CNV	FB	CNV	FBG	SV	IB	T300D	GM	13		15000	2	4	64300	70700
36		F-36 CONVERTIBLE	FB	SDNSF	FBG	SV	IB	T350	CRUS	13		16000	2	11	53700	59000
36		F-36 TRI-CABIN	FB	TCMY	FBG	SV	IB	T270	CRUS	13		17500	2	11	54600	60000
37	6	11-METER SPORT SEDAN	FB	SDN	FBG	SV	IB	T350	CRUS	14		18000	3	3	59500	65400
37	6	11-METER SPORT SEDAN	FB	SDN	FBG	SV	IB	T375D	CAT	14		18000	3	3	76600	84200
37	6	11-METER SPORT SEDAN	FB	SDN	FBG	SV	IB	T450D	J&T	14		18000	3	4	80400	88300
37	6	11-METER SPORTYACHT	OP	EXP	FBG	SV	IB	T350	CRUS	14		16800	3	3	56000	61500
37	6	11-METER SPORTYACHT	OP	EXP	FBG	SV	IB	T375D	CAT	14		16800	3	3	72400	79600
37	6	11-METER SPORTYACHT	OP	EXP	FBG	SV	IB	T450D	J&T	14		16800	3	3	76000	83500
39	9	12-METER CONVERTIBLE	FB	CNV	FBG	SV	IB	T350	CRUS	14		19000	3	6	68700	75400
39	9	12-METER CONVERTIBLE	FB	CNV	FBG	SV	IB	T375D	CAT	14		19000	3	6	86900	95500
39	9	12-METER CONVERTIBLE	FB	CNV	FBG	SV	IB	T450D	GM	14		19000	3	6	89700	98600
43		13-METER SPORT YACHT	OP	EXP	FBG	SV	IB	T450D	J&T	16		24000	3	3	118500	130000
43		13-METER SPORT YACHT	OP	EXP	FBG	SV	IB	T530D	J&T	16		26000	3	4	130000	143000
43		13-METER SPORT YACHT	OP	EXP	FBG	SV	IB	T750D	J&T	16		26000	3	3	147500	162000
43	3	13-METER SEDAN	FB	SDN	FBG	SV	IB	T450D	GM	16	3	33000	3	4	145000	159500
43	3	13-METER SEDAN	FB	SDN	FBG	SV	IB	T530D	GM	16	3	33000	3	4	151500	167000
43	3	13-METER SEDAN	FB	SDN	FBG	SV	IB	T750D	GM	16	3	33000	3	4	168000	184500
		1986 BOATS														
26	6	270 EXPRESS	OP	EXP	FBG	SV	IB	T230	MRCR	10	1	6000	2	3	14800	16800
32		F-32 CONVERTIBLE	FB	SDN	FBG	SV	IB	T350	CRUS	13		12000	2	6	39300	43600
33		10-METER SPORT EXP	OP	EXP	FBG	SV	IB	T350	CRUS	13		11250	2		37300	41500
33		10-METER SPORT EXP	OP	EXP	FBG	SV	IB	T250D	J&T	13		11250	2		43300	48100
33		10-METER SPORT SDN	FB	SDN	FBG	SV	IB	T350	CRUS	13		14250	2		42400	47100
33		10-METER SPORT SDN	FB	SDN	FBG	SV	IB	T250D	J&T	13		14250	2		53700	59000
36		F-36 CONVERTIBLE	FB	SDNSF	FBG	SV	IB	T350	CRUS	13		16000	2	11	51400	56500
36		F-36 TRI CABIN	FB	TCMY	FBG	SV	IB	T270	CRUS	13		17500	2	11	52300	57400
37	6	11-METER SPORT SEDAN	FB	SDN	FBG	SV	IB	T350	CRUS	14		18000	3	3	57000	62600
37	6	11-METER SPORT SEDAN	FB	SDN	FBG	SV	IB	T450D	J&T	14		18000	3	4	76900	84500
37	6	11-METER SPORTYACHT	OP	EXP	FBG	SV	IB	T350	CRUS	14		16800	3	3	53600	58900
37	6	11-METER SPORTYACHT	OP	EXP	FBG	SV	IB	T450D	J&T	14		16800	3	3	72700	79900
43		13-METER SPORT YACHT	OP	EXP	FBG	SV	IB	T450D	J&T	16		24000	3	3	113000	124500
43		13-METER SPORT YACHT	OP	EXP	FBG	SV	IB	T530D	J&T	16		26000	3	4	124500	137000
		1985 BOATS														
29	5	9-METER	OP	EXP	FBG	SV	IB	T270-T350		11	8	11000	1	11	24700	28800
32		F-32 CONVERTIBLE	FB	SDN	FBG	SV	IB	T225		13			2	6	30100	33500
32		F-32 CONVERTIBLE	FB	SDN	FBG	SV	IB	T270	CRUS	13		12000	2	6	35400	39300
33		10-METER SPORT EXP	OP	EXP	FBG	SV	IB	T350	CRUS	13		11250	2		35600	39600
33		10-METER SPORT EXP	OP	EXP	FBG	SV	IB	T250D	J&T	13		11250	2		41500	46100
33		10-METER SPORT EXP	FB	EXP	FBG	SV	IB	T350	CRUS	13		11250	2		35600	39600
33		10-METER SPORT EXP	FB	EXP	FBG	SV	IB	T250D	J&T	13		11250	2		41500	46100
33		10-METER SPORT SDN	FB	SDN	FBG	SV	IB	T350	CRUS	13		14250	2		40500	45000
33		10-METER SPORT SDN	FB	SDN	FBG	SV	IB	T250D	J&T	13		14250	2		51500	56600
36		F-36 CONVERTIBLE	FB	SDNSF	FBG	SV	IB	T350	CRUS	13		16000	2	11	49200	54100
36		F-36 TRI CABIN	FB	TCMY	FBG	SV	IB	T250		13			2	11	38700	43000
36		F-36 TRI CABIN	FB	TCMY	FBG	SV	IB	T270	CRUS	13		17500	2	11	50000	55000
37	6	11-METER SPORT SEDAN	FB	SDN	FBG	SV	IB	T350	CRUS	14		18500	3	3	55700	61200
37	6	11-METER SPORT SEDAN	FB	SDN	FBG	SV	IB	T450D	J&T	14		19250	3	4	76600	84200
37	6	11-METER SPORTYACHT	OP	EXP	FBG	SV	IB	T350	CRUS	14		16800	3	3	51300	56400
37	6	11-METER SPORTYACHT	OP	EXP	FBG	SV	IB	T450D	J&T	14		16800	3	3	69600	76500
43		13-METER SPORT YACHT	OP	EXP	FBG	SV	IB	T450D	J&T	16		24000	3	3	108500	119000
43		13-METER SPORT YACHT	OP	EXP	FBG	SV	IB	T675D	J&T	16		26000	3	4	129500	142500
		1984 BOATS														
26	4	F-26		EXP	FBG	SV	IB	225		10	1	5450	2	3	11100	12600
29	5	9-METER	OP	EXP	FBG	SV	IB	T270-T350		11	8	11000	1	11	23600	27600
29	5	9-METER	OP	EXP	FBG	SV	IB	T158D-T205D		11	8	11000	1	11	31200	36800
29	5	9-METER	FB	EXP	FBG	SV	IB	T270-T350		11	8	11000	1	11	23600	27600
29	5	9-METER	FB	EXP	FBG	SV	IB	T158D-T205D		11	8	11000	1	11	31200	36800
32		F-32 CONVERTIBLE	FB	SDN	FBG	SV	IB	T270	CRUS	13		12000	2	6	33800	37600
33		10-METER AFT CABIN	OP	EXP	FBG	SV	IB	T350	CRUS	13		14250	2		35900	39900
33		10-METER AFT CABIN	OP	EXP	FBG	SV	IB	T205D-T250D		13		14250	2		43000	49400
33		10-METER AFT CABIN	FB	EXP	FBG	SV	IB	T350	CRUS	13		14250	2		35900	39900
33		10-METER AFT CABIN	FB	EXP	FBG	SV	IB	T205D-T250D		13		14250	2		43000	49400
33		10-METER AFT CABIN	FB	SDN	FBG	SV	IB	T350	CRUS	13		15750	2		39600	44000
33		10-METER AFT CABIN	FB	SDN	FBG	SV	IB	T205D-T250D		13		15750	2		49700	56800
33		10-METER SPORT EXP	OP	EXP	FBG	SV	IB	T270-T350		13		11250	2		32500	37800
33		10-METER SPORT EXP	OP	EXP	FBG	SV	IB	T205D-T250D		13		11250	2		38200	44200
33		10-METER SPORT EXP	FB	EXP	FBG	SV	IB	T270-T350		13		11250	2		32500	37800
33		10-METER SPORT EXP	FB	EXP	FBG	SV	IB	T205D-T250D		13		11250	2		38200	44300
33		10-METER SPORT SDN	FB	SDN	FBG	SV	IB	T350	CRUS	13		14250	2		38700	43000
33		10-METER SPORT SDN	FB	SDN	FBG	SV	IB	T205D-T250D		13		14250	2		47600	54300
36		F-36 CONVERTIBLE		SDNSF	FBG	SV	IB	T330		13		16000	2	11	46700	51300
36		F-36 CONVERTIBLE	FB	SDNSF	FBG	SV	IB	T350	CRUS	13		16000	2	11	47400	52100
36		F-36 TRI CABIN		TCMY	FBG	SV	IB	T250		13		17500	2	11	47700	52400
36		F-36 TRI CABIN	FB	TCMY	FBG	SV	IB	T270	CRUS	13		17500	2	11	47900	52700
37	6	11-METER SPORTYACHT	OP	EXP	FBG	SV	IB	T350	CRUS	14		16800	3	3	49200	54000
37	6	11-METER SPORTYACHT	OP	EXP	FBG	SV	IB	T300D	J&T	14		16800	3	3	58000	63700
37	6	11-METER SPORTYACHT	OP	EXP	FBG	SV	IB	T450D	J&T	14		16800	3	3	66700	73300
40	3	F-40	FB	MY	FBG	SV	IB	T330		14	2	27300	3	10	81100	89100
44	3	F-44	FB	MY	FBG	SV	IB	T330		14	11	32000	4		100500	110500

....For earlier years, see the BUC Used Boat Price Guide, Volume 3

TRUE WORLD MARINE

HOBY WORLD DEVELOPMENT INC
LITTLE FERRY NJ 07643 COAST GUARD MFG ID- TZO

See inside cover to adjust price for area

For more recent years, see the BUC Used Boat Price Guide, Volume 1

LOA FT	LOA IN	NAME AND/ OR MODEL	TOP/ RIG	BOAT TYPE	-HULL- MTL	-HULL- TP	ENGINE TP	ENGINE # HP	ENGINE MFG	BEAM FT	BEAM IN	WGT LBS	DRAFT FT	DRAFT IN	RETAIL LOW	RETAIL HIGH
		1996 BOATS														
16		GOOD GO ST-160		CTRCN	FBG	DV	OB			6		1410		10	5450	6250
20		GOOD GO TW-200		CTRCN	FBG	DV	OB			7		2340	1	4	8850	10000
24		GOOD GO TF-240		CTRCN	FBG	DV	OB			7	10	3820	1	7	16400	18600
24		GOOD GO TF-240		CTRCN	FBG	DV	IO	190-250		7	10	3820	1	7	21000	23400
24		GOOD GO TF-240		CTRCN	FBG	DV	IO	170D-230D		7	10	3820	1	7	32000	37900
28		GOOD GO TE-280		CTRCN	FBG	DV	OB			8		4520	1	10	**	**
28		GOOD GO TE-280		CTRCN	FBG	DV	IO	190-300		8		4520	1	10	32100	39400
28		GOOD GO TE-280		CTRCN	FBG	DV	IO	170D-230D		8		4520	1	10	39000	48500
28		GOOD GO TE-280		CTRCN	FBG	DV	IO	350D	YAN	8		4520	1	10	52900	58100

....For earlier years, see the BUC Used Boat Price Guide, Volume 3

TRUMP YACHTS

STONINGTON CT 06378 COAST GUARD MFG ID- TMP See inside cover to adjust price for area

LOA FT	LOA IN	NAME AND/ OR MODEL	TOP/ RIG	BOAT TYPE	-HULL- MTL	-HULL- TP	ENGINE TP	ENGINE # HP	ENGINE MFG	BEAM FT	BEAM IN	WGT LBS	DRAFT FT	DRAFT IN	RETAIL LOW	RETAIL HIGH
		1984 BOATS														
20	6	COMPANION	SLP	SA/CR	FBG	KL	OB			7	1	3000	2	9	7500	8650

....For earlier years, see the BUC Used Boat Price Guide, Volume 3

TSUNAMI MARINE INC

SEBRING FL 33870

See inside cover to adjust price for area

LOA FT	LOA IN	NAME AND/ OR MODEL	TOP/ RIG	BOAT TYPE	-HULL- MTL	-HULL- TP	ENGINE TP	ENGINE # HP	ENGINE MFG	BEAM FT	BEAM IN	WGT LBS	DRAFT FT	DRAFT IN	RETAIL LOW	RETAIL HIGH
		1985 BOATS														
23	3	TSUNAMI SF23		SF	FBG	DV	OB			8		3100	1	4	9250	10500

LOA FT IN	NAME AND/ OR MODEL	TOP/ RIG	BOAT TYPE	HULL MTL TP	TP	# HP	MFG	BEAM FT IN	WGT LBS	DRAFT FT IN	RETAIL LOW	RETAIL HIGH
					1984 BOATS							
23 3	TSUNAMI SF23	OP	SF	FBG DV	OB			8	3100	1 4	9050	10300
23 3	TSUNAMI SF23	TT	SF	FBG	OB			8		1 4	9050	10300

....For earlier years, see the BUC Used Boat Price Guide, Volume 3

TUFFY BOATS
LAKE MILLS WI 53551   See inside cover to adjust price for area

LOA FT IN	NAME AND/ OR MODEL	TOP/ RIG	BOAT TYPE	HULL MTL TP	TP	# HP	MFG	BEAM FT IN	WGT LBS	DRAFT FT IN	RETAIL LOW	RETAIL HIGH
					1995 BOATS							
16 5	MUSKIE RAMPAGE	OP	FSH	FBG DV	OB			6 2	950		3750	4350
16 5	RAMPAGE 160 C	OP	FSH	FBG DV	OB			6 2	850		3400	3950
16 5	RAMPAGE 160 T	OP	FSH	FBG DV	OB			6 2	800		3200	3750
16 9	STINGER 1700 C	OP	FSH	FBG DV	OB			6 8	1200		4700	5400
16 9	STINGER 1700 T	OP	FSH	FBG DV	OB			6 8	1200		4700	5400
17	WALLEYE MAST 1700	OP	FSH	FBG DV	OB			6 3	1485		5600	6400
18	PIKE RAMPAGE	OP	FSH	FBG DV	OB			6 3	1050		4350	5050
18	RAMPAGE 180 C	OP	FSH	FBG DV	OB			6 3	900		3800	4400
18	RAMPAGE 180 T	OP	FSH	FBG DV	OB			6 3	850		3600	4200
18	RENEGADE 1800 C	OP	CTFSH	FBG DV	OB			7 3	2000		6750	7750
18	RENEGADE 1800 CC	OP	FSH	FBG DV	OB			7 3	1250		5000	5750
18	RENEGADE 1800 DC	OP	FSH	FBG DV	OB			7 6	2000		7000	8050
18	RENEGADE 1800 T	OP	FSH	FBG DV	OB			7 6	2000		6900	7900
18 1	RAMPAGE MAGNUM 180	OP	FSH	FBG DV	OB			6 7	1000		4150	4850
18 1	RAMPAGE MAGNUM 180 C	OP	FSH	FBG DV	OB			6 7	1050		4400	5050
18 1	WALLEYE MAST 1800	OP	FSH	FBG DV	OB			6 9	1230		4950	5700
					1994 BOATS							
16 5	MUSKIE RAMPAGE	OP	FSH	FBG DV	OB			6 2	950		3600	4150
16 5	RAMPAGE 160 C	OP	FSH	FBG DV	OB			6 2	850		3250	3750
16 5	RAMPAGE 160 T	OP	FSH	FBG DV	OB			6 2	800		3050	3550
16 9	STINGER 1700 C	OP	FSH	FBG DV	OB			6 8	1200		4500	5150
16 9	STINGER 1700 T	OP	FSH	FBG DV	OB			6 8	1200		4500	5150
17	WALLEYE MAST 1700 C	OP	FSH	FBG DV	OB			6 3	1485		5350	6150
17	WALLEYE MAST 1700 CB	OP	FSH	FBG DV	OB			6 3	1485		5350	6150
17	WALLEYE MAST 1700 FS	OP	FSH	FBG DV	OB			6 3	1485		5350	6150
17	WALLEYE MAST 1700 T	OP	FSH	FBG DV	OB			6 3	1485		5350	6150
18	PIKE RAMPAGE	OP	FSH	FBG DV	OB			6 3	1050		4150	4800
18	RAMPAGE 180 C	OP	FSH	FBG DV	OB			6 3	900		3600	4200
18	RAMPAGE 180 T	OP	FSH	FBG DV	OB			6 3	850		3450	4000
18	RENEGADE 1800 C	OP	FSH	FBG DV	OB			7 6	2000		6450	7450
18	RENEGADE 1800 CC	OP	CTFSH	FBG DV	OB			7 3	1250		4800	5500
18	RENEGADE 1800 DC	OP	FSH	FBG DV	OB			7 6	2000		6700	7700
18	RENEGADE 1800 T	OP	FSH	FBG DV	OB			7 6	2000		6600	7550
18 1	RAMPAGE MAGNUM 180	OP	FSH	FBG DV	OB			6 7	1000		4000	4600
18 1	RAMPAGE MAGNUM 180 C	OP	FSH	FBG DV	OB			6 7	1050		4150	4800
18 1	WALLEYE MAST 1800 C	OP	FSH	FBG DV	OB			6 9	1230		4750	5450
18 1	WALLEYE MAST 1800 T	OP	FSH	FBG DV	OB			6 9	1230		4750	5450
					1993 BOATS							
16 5	160 C	OP	FSH	FBG DV	OB			6 2	850		3100	3600
16 5	160 XT	OP	FSH	FBG DV	OB			6 2	800		2950	3400
16 5	MUSKIE RAMPAGE	OP	FSH	FBG DV	OB			6 2	950		3450	4000
16 9	BASS N MARAUDER	OP	FSH	FBG SV	OB			5 10	1000		3650	4250
16 9	ESOX	OP	FSH	FBG SV	OB			5 10	850		3200	3750
16 9	ESOX C	OP	FSH	FBG SV	OB			5 10	900		3350	3900
16 9	ESOX MAGNUM	OP	FSH	FBG SV	OB			6 7	950		3500	4050
16 9	ESOX MAGNUM C	OP	FSH	FBG SV	OB			6 7	1000		3650	4250
16 9	MARAUDER	OP	FSH	FBG SV	OB			5 10	850		3100	3600
16 9	MARUDER C	OP	FSH	FBG SV	OB			5 10	900		3250	3800
16 9	STINGER 1700 C	OP	FSH	FBG DV	OB			6 8	1200		4250	4950
16 9	STINGER 1700 T	OP	FSH	FBG DV	OB			6 8	1200		4250	4950
18	180 C	OP	FSH	FBG DV	OB			6 3	900		3450	4050
18	180 XT	OP	FSH	FBG DV	OB			6 3	850		3300	3850
18	PIKE RAMPAGE	OP	FSH	FBG DV	OB			6 3	1050		3950	4600
18	RENEGADE 1800 CC	OP	CTFSH	FBG DV	OB			7 3	1250		4600	5300
18 1	MAGNUM 180	OP	FSH	FBG DV	OB			6 7	1000		3800	4450
18 1	MAGNUM 180 C	OP	FSH	FBG DV	OB			6 7	1050		3950	4600
18 1	WALLEYE MAST 1800 C	OP	FSH	FBG DV	OB			6 9	1230		4550	5250
18 1	WALLEYE MAST 1800 T	OP	FSH	FBG DV	OB			6 9	1230		4550	5250

TURNER MARINE
NEOGA IL 62447   COAST GUARD MFG ID- TUN See inside cover to adjust price for area

For more recent years, see the BUC Used Boat Price Guide, Volume 1

LOA FT IN	NAME AND/ OR MODEL	TOP/ RIG	BOAT TYPE	HULL MTL TP	TP	# HP	MFG	BEAM FT IN	WGT LBS	DRAFT FT IN	RETAIL LOW	RETAIL HIGH
					1996 BOATS							
18 2	Y-FLYER	SLP	SARAC	FBG CB				5 8	500	4	4600	5300
					1995 BOATS							
18 2	Y-FLYER	SLP	SARAC	FBG CB				5 8	500	4	4300	5000
					1994 BOATS							
18 2	Y-FLYER	SLP	SARAC	FBG CB				5 8	500	4	4050	4700
					1993 BOATS							
18 2	Y-FLYER	SLP	SACAC	FBG CB	OB			5 8	500	4	3800	4400
					1992 BOATS							
18 2	Y-FLYER	SLP	SAIL	FBG CB	OB			5 8	500	4	3550	4150
					1985 BOATS							
18 2	Y-FLYER	SLP	SA/OD	F/S CB				5 8	500	6	2350	2700
					1984 BOATS							
18 2	Y-FLYER	SLP	SA/OD	F/S CB				5 8	500	6	2200	2600

....For earlier years, see the BUC Used Boat Price Guide, Volume 3

ULTIMATE SAILBOATS INT'L
SANTA CRUZ CA 95061   See inside cover to adjust price for area

For more recent years, see the BUC Used Boat Price Guide, Volume 1

LOA FT IN	NAME AND/ OR MODEL	TOP/ RIG	BOAT TYPE	HULL MTL TP	TP	# HP	MFG	BEAM FT IN	WGT LBS	DRAFT FT IN	RETAIL LOW	RETAIL HIGH
					1996 BOATS							
20 10	ULTIMATE 20	SLP	SAROD	F/S CB	OB			8 6	1100	5	11700	13200
					1995 BOATS							
20	ULTIMATE 20	SLP	SAROD	F/S CB	OB			8 5	1000	2 2	10200	11600
					1994 BOATS							
20	ULTIMATE 20	SLP	SAROD	F/S CB	OB			8 5	1000	2 2	9550	10900
					1993 BOATS							
20	ULTIMATE 20	SLP	SAROD	F/S CB				8 5	1000	2 2	9050	10300
					1992 BOATS							
20	ULTIMATE 20	SLP	SA/OD	F/S CB				8 5	1000	5	8400	9650

UNIFLITE INC
BRADENTON FL 33506   COAST GUARD MFG ID- UNF See inside cover to adjust price for area
SEE ALSO CHRIS CRAFT

LOA FT IN	NAME AND/ OR MODEL	TOP/ RIG	BOAT TYPE	HULL MTL TP	TP	# HP	MFG	BEAM FT IN	WGT LBS	DRAFT FT IN	RETAIL LOW	RETAIL HIGH
					1984 BOATS							
28 2	MEGA	FB	SDN	FBG SV	IB	T220	CRUS	10 10	10500	2 4	22300	24800
28 2	SALTY-DOG	OP	SF	FBG SV	IB	T220	CRUS	10 10	9000	2 10	19200	21400
28 2	SALTY-DOG	FB	SF	FBG SV	IB	T158D	VLVO	10 10	9000	2 10	26000	28900
28 2	SALTY-DOG	HT	SF	FBG SV	IB	T220	CRUS	10 10	9000	2 10	19200	21400
28 2	SALTY-DOG	HT	SF	FBG SV	IB	T158D	VLVO	10 10	9000	2 10	26000	28900
31 8	SPORT SEDAN	FB	SDN	FBG SV	IB	T270	CRUS	11 11	15000	2 8	33300	37000
31 8	SPORT SEDAN	FB	SDN	FBG SV	IBT158D	T158D	J&T	11 11	15000	2 8	43500	51000
34 2	CONVERTIBLE	FB	SDN	FBG SV	IB	T270-T350		11 11	17000	2 9	41600	48100
34 2	CONVERTIBLE	FB	SDN	FBG SV	IB	T205D	J&T	11 11	17000	2 9	53100	58400
36	36 II SE	FB	MY	FBG SV	IB	T270	CRUS	12 4	17500	2 8	49600	54500
36	36 II SE	FB	MY	FBG SV	IB	T215D	GM	12 4	17500	2 8	55800	61100
36	SPORT SEDAN	FB	SDN	FBG SV	IB	T350	CRUS	12 4	20000	2 8	54700	60100
36	SPORT SEDAN	FB	SDN	FBG SV	IB	T215D	GM	12 4	20000	2 8	60800	66800
37 9	COASTAL-CRUISER	FB	SDN	FBG DS	IB	235D	VLVO	12 9	21000	3 10	62900	69100
37 9	COASTAL-CRUISER	FB	SDN	FBG DS	IB	T124D	VLVO	12 9	21000	3 10	64700	71100
37 9	COASTAL-CRUISER	FB	SDN	FBG DS	IB	T215D	GM	12 9	21000	3 10	68200	75000
38	CONVERTIBLE	FB	SDN	FBG SV	IB	T310D	GM	13 11	27000	2 8	83100	91300
38	CONVERTIBLE	FB	SDN	FBG SV	IB	T410D	J&T	13 11	27000	2 8	89300	98100
41 3	YACHT FISHERMAN	FB	YTFS	FBG SV	IB	T350	CRUS	14 2	20000	2 8	73300	80500
41 3	YACHT FISHERMAN	FB	YTFS	FBG SV	IB	T215D	GM	14 2	20000	2 8	75000	82400
41 3	YACHT FISHERMAN	FB	YTFS	FBG SV	IB	T235D	VLVO	14 2	20000	2 8	75300	82800
42	42 II SE	FB	MY	FBG SV	IB	T350	CRUS	14 9	30000	3 4	87100	95700
	IB T250D J&T	93100	102500,	IB T300D J&T	96600	106000,	IB T350D PERK	102000	112000			
42	CONVERTIBLE	FB	SDN	FBG SV	IB	T310D	GM	14 9	35000	3 9	110000	121000
42	CONVERTIBLE	FB	SDN	FBG SV	IB	T410D	J&T	14 9	35000	3 9	116500	128000
42	CONVERTIBLE	FB	SDN	FBG SV	IB	T425D	CUM	14 9	35000	3 9	116000	127500
45	YACHT HOME	FB	MY	FBG	IB	T270	CRUS	13 11	22000	3 4	73300	80600
45	YACHT HOME	FB	MY	FBG	IB	T215D	GM	13 11	22000	3 4	79300	87200

LOA FT	IN	NAME AND/ OR MODEL	TOP/ RIG	BOAT TYPE	HULL MTL	HULL TP	ENGINE TP	# HP	MFG	BEAM FT	IN	WGT LBS	DRAFT FT	IN	RETAIL LOW	RETAIL HIGH
		1984 BOATS														
46	3	MOTOR YACHT	FB	MY	FBG	SV	IB	T410D	J&T	15	3	46000	4	4	143500	158000
48		YACHT FISHERMAN	FB	YTFS	FBG	SV	IB	T310D	GM	14	9	38000	3	9	124500	136500
48		YACHT FISHERMAN	FB	YTFS	FBG	SV	IB	T410D	J&T	14	9	38000	3	9	142500	156500
48	10	CONVERTIBLE	FB	SDN	FBG	SV	IB	T425D	CUM	15	9	48000	4	9	163500	179500
48	10	CONVERTIBLE	FB	SDN	FBG	SV	IB	T570D	GM	15	9	48000	4	9	171000	188000
50	3	MOTOR YACHT 50	FB	MY	FBG		IB	T475D	GM	15	3	54000	4	4	158500	174500
53	3	COCKPIT MOTOR YACHT	FB	MYCPT	FBG		IB	T500D	GM	15	3	55200	4	4	179000	196500

....For earlier years, see the BUC Used Boat Price Guide, Volume 3

UNIVERSAL MARINE CO LTD

TAIPEI TAIWAN COAST GUARD MFG ID- LTV See inside cover to adjust price for area
FORMERLY RITTUN MARINE

LOA FT	IN	NAME AND/ OR MODEL	TOP/ RIG	BOAT TYPE	HULL MTL	HULL TP	ENGINE TP	# HP	MFG	BEAM FT	IN	WGT LBS	DRAFT FT	IN	RETAIL LOW	RETAIL HIGH
		1985 BOATS														
35	8	UNIVERSAL TRI-CABIN	FB	TRWL	FBG	DS	IB	120D	LEHM	12	8	24500	3	10	76300	83800
35	8	UNIVERSAL TRI-CABIN	FB	TRWL	FBG	DS	IB	135D		12	8	24500	3	10	75900	83400
38		UNIVERSAL 38	FB	SF	FBG	SV	IB	T136D	VLVO	13	6	20000			65100	71500
38		UNIVERSAL 38	FB	SF	FBG	SV	IB	T165D	VLVO	13	6	20000			65700	72100
40	10	PERRY 41	SLP	SA/CR	FBG	KL	IB	51D	PERK	12		22300	6		71400	78500
40	10	PERRY 41 SHOAL	SLP	SA/CR	FBG	KL	IB	51D	PERK	12					71400	78500
41		SUNDECK 41	FB	DCFD	FBG	DS	IB	136D	VLVO	13	8	30000			92400	101500
41		SUNDECK 41	FB	DCFD	FBG	DS	IB	T136D	VLVO	13	8	30000			96200	106000
41		UNIVERSAL SEDAN	FB	TRWL	FBG	DS	IB	120D	LEHM	13	8	29000	4		90400	99400
41		UNIVERSAL SEDAN	FB	TRWL	FBG	DS	IB	T120D	LEHM	13	8	29000	4		94500	104000
41		UNIVERSAL STUART	FB	TRWL	FBG	DS	IB	120D	LEHM	13	8	29000	4		90400	99400
41		UNIVERSAL STUART	FB	TRWL	FBG	DS	IB	T120D	LEHM	13	8	29000	4		94500	104000
45		UNIVERSAL 45	FB	DCCPT	FBG	SV	IB	T136D	VLVO	15		30000			91800	101000
45		UNIVERSAL 45	FB	DCCPT	FBG	SV	IB	T165D	VLVO	15		30000			92800	102000
46	7	PERRY 47	CUT	SA/CR	FBG	KL	SD	61D	VLVO	13	7		6	4	92600	101500
46	7	PERRY 47	CUT	SA/CR	FBG	KL	IB	80D	LEHM	13	7	30400	6	4	92800	102000
46	7	PERRY 47	CUT	SA/CR	FBG	KL	IB	120D	LEHM	13	7		6	4	93300	102500
46	7	PERRY 47	KTH	SA/CR	FBG	KL	IB	80D	LEHM	13	7	30400	6	4	92800	102000
46	7	PERRY 47	KTH	SA/CR	FBG	KL	IB	120D	LEHM	13	7		6	4	93300	102500
46	7	PERRY 47	KTH	SA/CR	FBG	KL	IB	124D	VLVO	13	7		6	4	93400	102500
46	7	PERRY 47 SHOAL	CUT	SA/CR	FBG	KL	IB	80D	LEHM	13	7				92800	102000
46	7	PERRY 47 SHOAL	KTH	SA/CR	FBG	KL	IB	80D	LEHM	13	7				92800	102000
		1984 BOATS														
35	8	RITTUN TRI-CABIN	FB	TRWL	FBG	DS	IB	120D	FORD	12	8	24500	3	10	73200	80400
35	8	RITTUN TRI-CABIN	FB	TRWL	FBG	DS	IB	T120D	FORD	12	8	24500	3	10	74200	81500
35	8	UNIVERSAL TRI-CABIN	FB	TRWL	FBG	DS	IB	120D	LEHM	12	8	24500	3	10	73200	80400
40	10	PERRY	SLP	SA/CR	FBG	KL	IB	50D	PERK	12		22300	6		67700	74400
40	10	PERRY	SLP	SA/CR	FBG	KL	IB	61D	LEHM	12		22300	6		68200	75000
40	10	PERRY 41	SLP	SA/CR	FBG	KL	IB	50D	PERK	12		22300	6		67700	74400
		SD 61D VLVO 68200 75000, IB 80D LEHM 68500 75300, IB 120D LEHM 69000 75900														
		IB 124D VLVO 69200 76000														
40	10	PERRY 41 SHOAL	SLP	SA/CR	FBG	KL	IB	50D	PERK	12					67700	74400
41		RITTUN SEDAN	FB	TRWL	FBG	DS	IB	120D	FORD	13	8	29000	4		87000	95600
41		RITTUN SEDAN	FB	TRWL	FBG	DS	IB	T120D	FORD	13	8	29000	4		90900	99900
41		RITTUN TRI-CABIN	FB	TRWL	FBG	DS	IB	120D	FORD	13	8	29000	4		87000	95600
41		RITTUN TRI-CABIN	FB	TRWL	FBG	DS	IB	T120D	FORD	13	8	29000	4		90900	99900
41		UNIVERSAL SEDAN	FB	TRWL	FBG	DS	IB	120D	LEHM	13	8	29000	4		86600	95200
41		UNIVERSAL SEDAN	FB	TRWL	FBG	DS	IB	T120D	LEHM	13	8	29000	4		90600	99500
41		UNIVERSAL STUART	FB	TRWL	FBG	DS	IB	120D	LEHM	13	8	29000	4		86600	95200
41		UNIVERSAL STUART	FB	TRWL	FBG	DS	IB	T120D	LEHM	13	8	29000	4		90600	99500
44	3	UNIVERSAL 45	FB	TRWL	FBG	DS	IB	T135D	LEHM	15		33400	3	6	104000	114500
46	7	PERRY	CUT	SA/CR	FBG	KL	IB	80D	LEHM	13	7	30400	6	4	87900	96600
46	7	PERRY	KTH	SA/CR	FBG	KL	IB	80D	LEHM	13	7	30400	6	4	88000	96700
46	7	PERRY 47	CUT	SA/CR	FBG	KL	SD	61D	VLVO	13	7		6	4	87700	96400
		IB 80D LEHM 87900 96600, IB 120D LEHM 88400 97100, IB 124D VLVO 88500 97200														
46	7	PERRY 47	KTH	SA/CR	FBG	KL	SD	61D	VLVO	13	7		6	4	87700	96400
		IB 80D LEHM 88000 96700, IB 120D LEHM 88400 97200, IB 124D VLVO 88500 97200														
46	7	PERRY 47 SHOAL	CUT	SA/CR	FBG	KL	IB	80D	LEHM	13	7				87900	96600
46	7	PERRY 47 SHOAL	KTH	SA/CR	FBG	KL	IB	80D	LEHM	13	7				88000	96700

....For earlier years, see the BUC Used Boat Price Guide, Volume 3

UNIVERSAL MARINE CORP

ST PETERSBURG FL 33701 COAST GUARD MFG ID- VMC See inside cover to adjust price for area

LOA FT	IN	NAME AND/ OR MODEL	TOP/ RIG	BOAT TYPE	HULL MTL	HULL TP	ENGINE TP	# HP	MFG	BEAM FT	IN	WGT LBS	DRAFT FT	IN	RETAIL LOW	RETAIL HIGH
		1986 BOATS														
19	3	MONTEGO 19	SLP	SAIL	FBG	SK	OB			7	2	2150		1	2450	2850
19	6	MONTEGO 20	SLP	SAIL	FBG	KL	OB			7	2	2300	2		2600	3000
25	3	MONTEGO 25	SLP	SA/RC	FBG	KL	OB			9	1	4550	4	6	6450	7400
25	3	MONTEGO 25	SLP	SA/RC	FBG	KL	SD	15	OMC	9	1	4550	4	6	6600	7600
25	3	MONTEGO 25	SLP	SA/RC	FBG	KL	SD	8D	YAN	9	1	4550	4	6	6850	7850
25	3	MONTEGO 25 SHOAL	SLP	SA/RC	FBG	KL	OB			9	1	4550	3	6	6000	6900
25	3	MONTEGO 25 SHOAL	SLP	SA/RC	FBG	KL	SD	15	OMC	9	1	4550	3	6	6250	7200
25	3	MONTEGO 25 SHOAL	SLP	SA/RC	FBG	KL	SD	8D	YAN	9	1	4550	3	6	6500	7450
27		UNIVERSAL 27	SLP	SAIL	FBG	KL	IB	28D	VLVO	9	2	3950	2	6	6400	7350
		1985 BOATS														
19	3	MONTEGO 19	SLP	SAIL	FBG	SK	OB			7	2	2150	1	2	2300	2700
19	6	MONTEGO 20	SLP	SA/CR	FBG	SK	OB			7	2	1700			2000	2350
19	6	MONTEGO 20	SLP	SAIL	FBG	KL	OB			7	2	2300	2		2400	2800
25	3	MONTEGO 25	SLP	SA/RC	FBG	KL	OB			9	1	4550	4	6	6000	6900
25	3	MONTEGO 25	SLP	SA/RC	FBG	KL	SD	15	OMC	9	1	4550	4	6	6200	7100
25	3	MONTEGO 25	SLP	SA/RC	FBG	KL	SD	8D	YAN	9	1	4550	4	6	6400	7350
25	3	MONTEGO 25 SHOAL	SLP	SA/RC	FBG	KL	OB			9	1	4550	3	6	5650	6500
25	3	MONTEGO 25 SHOAL	SLP	SA/RC	FBG	KL	SD	15	OMC	9	1	4550	3	6	5850	6750
25	3	MONTEGO 25 SHOAL	SLP	SA/RC	FBG	KL	SD	8D	YAN	9	1	4550	3	6	6050	6950
27		UNIVERSAL 27	SLP	SAIL	FBG	KL	IB	28D	VLVO	9	2	3950	2	6	6000	6900
		1984 BOATS														
19	3	MONTEGO 19	SLP	SAIL	FBG	SK	OB			7	2	2150	1	2	2200	2550
19	6	MONTEGO 20	SLP	SAIL	FBG	KL	OB			7	2	2300	2		2300	2650
25	3	MONTEGO 25	SLP	SA/RC	FBG	KL	OB			9	1	4500	4	6	5400	6200
25	3	MONTEGO 25	SLP	SA/RC	FBG	KL	SD	15	OMC	9	1	4700	4	6	5800	6700
25	3	MONTEGO 25	SLP	SA/RC	FBG	KL	SD	8D	YAN	9	1	4500	4	6	5950	6850
25	3	MONTEGO 25 SHOAL	SLP	SA/RC	FBG	KL	OB			9	1	4500	3	6	5400	6200
25	3	MONTEGO 25 SHOAL	SLP	SA/RC	FBG	KL	SD	15	OMC	9	1	4500	3	6	5600	6400
25	3	MONTEGO 25 SHOAL	SLP	SA/RC	FBG	KL	SD	8D	YAN	9	1	4500	3	6	5650	6500

....For earlier years, see the BUC Used Boat Price Guide, Volume 3

UNIVERSAL YACHTS

GLEN HEAD NY 11545 COAST GUARD MFG ID- MTI See inside cover to adjust price for area

LOA FT	IN	NAME AND/ OR MODEL	TOP/ RIG	BOAT TYPE	HULL MTL	HULL TP	ENGINE TP	# HP	MFG	BEAM FT	IN	WGT LBS	DRAFT FT	IN	RETAIL LOW	RETAIL HIGH
		1986 BOATS														
34	8	UNIVERSAL 35	FB	DCMY	FBG	DS	IB	120D-135D		12		18000	3	3	74600	81900
34	8	UNIVERSAL 35	FB	DCMY	FBG	DS	IB	T 80D	LEHM	13		18000	3	3	73400	80600
36	6	UNIVERSAL 37	FB	DCMY	FBG	DS	IB	120D	LEHM	13	1	23000	3	10	90300	99200
36	6	UNIVERSAL 37	FB	DCMY	FBG	DS	IB	T120D	LEHM	13	1	23000	3	10	92300	101500
38	3	UNIVERSAL 39	FB	DCMY	FBG	DS	IB	120D	LEHM	13	8	23000	3	3	93900	103000
38	3	UNIVERSAL 39	FB	TRWL	FBG	DS	IB	T120D	LEHM	13	8	23000	3	3	98700	108500
		1985 BOATS														
34	8	UNIVERSAL 35	FB	DCMY	FBG	DS	IB	120D	LEHM	12		18000	3	3	71500	78600
34	8	UNIVERSAL 35	FB	DCMY	FBG	DS	IB	T 90D	LEHM	13		18000	3	3	70000	76900
36	6	UNIVERSAL 37	FB	DCMY	FBG	DS	IB	120D	LEHM	13	1	23000	3	10	86300	94800
36	6	UNIVERSAL 37	FB	DCMY	FBG	DS	IB	T120D	LEHM	13	1	23000	3	10	88300	97000
38	3	UNIVERSAL 39	FB	DCMY	FBG	DS	IB	120D	LEHM	13	8	23000	3	3	89800	98700
38	3	UNIVERSAL 39	FB	TRWL	FBG	DS	IB	T120D	LEHM	13	8	23000	3	3	94400	103500
		1984 BOATS														
34	8	UNIVERSAL 35	FB	DCMY	FBG	DS	IB	120D	LEHM	12		18000	3	3	68600	75400
34	8	UNIVERSAL 35	FB	DCMY	FBG	DS	IB	T 90D	LEHM	13		18000	3	3	67100	73800
36	6	UNIVERSAL 37	FB	DCMY	FBG	DS	IB	120D	LEHM	13	1	23000	3	10	82600	90700
36	6	UNIVERSAL 37	FB	DCMY	FBG	DS	IB	T120D	LEHM	13	1	23000	3	10	84500	92800
38	3	UNIVERSAL 39	FB	DCMY	FBG	DS	IB	120D	LEHM	13	8	23000	3	3	85900	94400
38	3	UNIVERSAL 39	FB	TRWL	FBG	DS	IB	T120D	LEHM	13	8	23000	3	3	90300	99200

V I P BLUEWATER FISHING BOATS

VIVIAN INDUSTRIES INC
VIVIAN LA 71082 See inside cover to adjust price for area

ALSO V I P BOATS

For more recent years, see the BUC Used Boat Price Guide, Volume 1

LOA FT	IN	NAME AND/ OR MODEL	TOP/ RIG	BOAT TYPE	HULL MTL	HULL TP	ENGINE TP	# HP	MFG	BEAM FT	IN	WGT LBS	DRAFT FT	IN	RETAIL LOW	RETAIL HIGH
		1996 BOATS														
17	6	SEA STEALTH 180 CCF	OP	CTRCN	FBG	SV	OB			7	5	1580			6200	7100
20	6	SEA STEALTH 210 CCF	OP	CTRCN	FBG	SV	OB			8		2100			8000	9200
24	11	SEA STEALTH 236 CWAF	OP	CTRCN	FBG	SV	IO	250	MRCR	9		5100			14700	16800

V I P BLUEWATER FISHING BOATS -CONTINUED See inside cover to adjust price for area

LOA FT	LOA IN	NAME AND/ OR MODEL	TOP/ RIG	BOAT TYPE	HULL MTL	HULL TP	ENGINE TP	ENGINE # HP	ENGINE MFG	BEAM FT	BEAM IN	WGT LBS	DRAFT FT	DRAFT IN	RETAIL LOW	RETAIL HIGH
		1995 BOATS														
17	4	SEA STEALTH 176 CCF	OP	CTRCN	FBG	SV	OB			7	10	1390			5350	6150
17	6	SEA STEALTH 180 CCF	OP	CTRCN	FBG	SV	OB			7	5	1580			5900	6750
18	8	BAY STEALTH 1880 CCF	OP	CTRCN	FBG	SV	OB			8	6	1600			6100	7050
18	8	BAY STEALTH 1880 CCF	OP	CTRCN	FBG	TH	OB			8	6	1600			6100	7050
20	6	SEA STEALTH 210 CCF	OP	CTRCN	FBG	SV	OB			8		2100			7650	8750
21	8	BAY STEALTH 2180 CCF	OP	CTRCN	FBG	SV	OB			8	6	2180			8400	9650
21	8	BAY STEALTH 2180 CCF	OP	CTRCN	FBG	TH	OB			8	6	2180			8400	9650
22		SEA STEALTH 226 CCF	OP	CTRCN	FBG	SV	OB			8	8	2800			10300	11700
25		SEA STEALTH 250 CCF	OP	CTRCN	FBG	SV	OB			8		3220			13400	15200
		1993 BOATS														
17	4	BASS & BAY 172	OP	FSH	FBG	SV	OB			6	11	1075			3950	4600
17	4	CCF 176	OP	CTRCN	FBG	SV	OB			7	10	1400			4900	5650
17	6	CCF 180	OP	CTRCN	FBG	SV	OB			7	5	1580			5400	6200
20	6	CCF 210	OP	CTRCN	FBG	SV	OB			8		2100			7000	8050
20	6	SRT 206	OP	CTRCN	FBG	TH	OB			8	4	1650			5900	6750
23	10	CCF 240	OP	CTRCN	FBG	SV	OB			8		2520			9450	10700
25		CCF 250	OP	CTRCN	FBG	SV	OB			8		3220			12300	13900
27	4	WAC 267	OP	CR	FBG	SV	IO	250-300		8	6	5400			13300	15800
27	4	WAC 267 W/DB	OP	CR	FBG	SV	OB			8	6	5400			19200	21300
27	4	WAC 267 W/SB	OP	CR	FBG	SV	OB			8	6	5400			19200	21300

V I P BOATS

VIVIAN INDUSTRIES INC
VIVIAN LA 71082

See inside cover to adjust price for area

COAST GUARD MFG ID- VVI
formerly VIVIAN IND PLAST

For more recent years, see the BUC Used Boat Price Guide, Volume 1

LOA FT	LOA IN	NAME AND/ OR MODEL	TOP/ RIG	BOAT TYPE	HULL MTL	HULL TP	ENGINE TP	ENGINE # HP	ENGINE MFG	BEAM FT	BEAM IN	WGT LBS	DRAFT FT	DRAFT IN	RETAIL LOW	RETAIL HIGH
		1996 BOATS														
16	9	CONVERTIBLE 165	OP	RNBT	FBG	SV	OB			6	11	1250			2700	3150
18		CONVERTIBLE 180	OP	RNBT	FBG	SV	OB			7	5	1500			3200	3700
18		VISION 1886 SBR	OP	RNBT	FBG	SV	IO	135-205		7	2	2000			4450	5200
18		VISION 1886 SBR CMBO	OP	RNBT	FBG	SV	IO	135-205		7	2	2200			4600	5550
18		VISION 1886 XBR	OP	RNBT	FBG	SV	IO	135	MRCR	7	2	2000			4250	4950
19		VALIANT 1996 SBR	OP	RNBT	FBG	SV	IO	190-250		12		2550			7950	9250
19		VALIANT 1996 XBR	OP	RNBT	FBG	SV	IO	190-250		12		2550			7850	9150
19	1	CONVERTIBLE 190	OP	RNBT	FBG	SV	OB			7	5	1500			3300	3800
21		VICTORY 2102 SBR	OP	RNBT	FBG	SV	IO	190-300		12	6	3100			11200	13500
21		VICTORY 2102 SBR	OP	RNBT	FBG	SV	IO	330	MRCR	12	6	3100			13100	14800
21		VISCOUNT 2102 SCC	OP	CUD	FBG	SV	IO	190-250		12	6	3560			13000	15100
21		VISCOUNT 2102 SCC	OP	RNBT	FBG	SV	IO	220-300		12	6	3100			11900	14000
		1995 BOATS														
16	9	CONVERTIBLE 165	OP	RNBT	FBG	SV	OB			6	11	1250			2550	2950
16	9	SK 165	OP	RNBT	FBG	SV	OB			6	11	1150			2400	2750
17	4	VISION 1760 SBRCC	OP	RNBT	FBG	SV	IO	135	MRCR	7	1	1900			3900	4500
17	4	VISION 1760 XBRC	OP	RNBT	FBG	SV	IO	135	MRCR	7	1	1900			3650	4250
18		CONVERTIBLE 180	OP	RNBT	FBG	SV	OB			7	5	1500			3000	3500
18		SK 180	OP	RNBT	FBG	SV	OB			7	5	1450			2950	3400
18	3	CONVERTIBLE 183	OP	RNBT	FBG	SV	IO	180	MRCR	7	1	2100			4200	4900
18	10	VISION 1930 SBBCC	OP	RNBT	FBG	SV	IO	135-180		7	1	2000			4450	5150
18	10	VISION 1930 SBR	OP	RNBT	FBG	SV	IO	135-180		7	1	2000			4200	4900
18	10	VISION 1930 XBR	OP	RNBT	FBG	SV	IO	135-180		7	1	2000			4050	4800
19		VALIANT 1996 SBR	OP	RNBT	FBG	SV	IO	180-235		8		2550			5350	6250
19		VALIANT 1996 SPECIAL	OP	RNBT	FBG	SV	IO	180	MRCR	8		2550			5100	5900
19		VALIANT 1996 XBR	OP	RNBT	FBG	SV	IO	180-235		8		2550			5200	6150
19	1	CONVERTIBLE 190	OP	RNBT	FBG	SV	OB			7	5	1500			3100	3600
19	1	SK 190	OP	RNBT	FBG	SV	OB			7	5	1550			3200	3700
19	10	VERSAILLES 1950	OP	CUD	FBG	DV	IO	135-180		7	5	1910			4700	5450
21		VICTORY 2102 SBR	OP	RNBT	FBG	SV	IO	235	MRCR	8	6	2760			7600	8750
21		VICTORY 2102 XBR	OP	RNBT	FBG	SV	IO	235	MRCR	8	6	2760			8050	9250
21		VISCOUNT 2102 SCC	OP	RNBT	FBG	SV	IO	235	MRCR	8	6	3250			8600	9850
26	10	VINDICATOR 2700	OP	CUD	FBG	DV	IO	350	MRCR	9		5000			19100	21300
26	10	VINDICATOR 2700	OP	CUD	FBG	DV	IO	T235	MRCR	9		5000			19800	21900
		1994 BOATS														
16	9	1650	OP	RNBT	FBG	SV	OB			6	11				2650	3050
16	9	CONVERTIBLE 165	OP	RNBT	FBG	SV	OB			6	11	1250			2400	2800
17	4	CCF 176	OP	CTRCN	FBG	SV	OB			7	10	1400			2650	3050
17	4	VISION 1760 LXC	OP	RNBT	FBG	SV	IO	115	MRCR	7	1	1900			3500	4100
17	4	VISION 1760LX	OP	RNBT	FBG	SV	IO	115	YAMA	7	1	1900			3500	4100
18		CONVERTIBLE 180	OP	RNBT	FBG	SV	OB			7	5	1500			2850	3300
18	3	CONVERTIBLE 183 F/S	OP	RNBT	FBG	SV	IO	175-180		7	1	2100			3900	4550
18	10	VISION 1930LX	OP	RNBT	FBG	SV	IO	180		7	1	2000			3950	4550
18	10	VISION 1930SS	OP	RNBT	FBG	SV	IO	180		7	1	2000			4000	4650
19		VALIANT V1996 SBR	OP	RNBT	FBG	SV	IO	180		8		2550			4900	5600
19		VALIANT V1996 XBR	OP	RNBT	FBG	SV	IO	180		8		2550			4900	5600
19	10	VERSAILLES 1950LX	OP	CUD	FBG	DV	IO	180	MRCR	7	5	2500			5000	5750
19	10	VERSAILLES 1950LX	OP	CUD	FBG	SV	IO	180	YAMA	7	5	2500			5000	5750
20	6	SRT 206	OP	CTRCN	FBG	TH	OB			8	4	1650			3550	4100
21		VICTORY V2102 SBR	OP	RNBT	FBG	SV	IO	205	MRCR	8	6	3150			7750	8900
21		VICTORY V2102 XBR	OP	RNBT	FBG	SV	IO	205	MRCR	8	6	3150			7750	8900
22		CCF 226	OP	CR	FBG	SV	OB			8	8	2800			5700	6550
23	2	VINCENTE 2350SS	OP	CUD	FBG	DV	IO	204	MRCR	8		3800			10100	11400
23	2	VINDICATOR 2300	OP	CUD	FBG	DV	IO	300-350		8		4000			11300	14000
26	10	VINDICATOR 2700	OP	CUD	FBG	DV	IO	350	MRCR	9		5000			17500	19900
26	10	VINDICATOR 2700	OP	CUD	FBG	DV	IO	T235-T300		9		5000			18600	22300
		1993 BOATS														
16	9	1650	OP	RNBT	FBG	SV	OB			6	11				2500	2900
17	4	VISION 1760 LXC	OP	RNBT	FBG	SV	IO	115	MRCR	7	1	1900			3300	3800
18	3	CONVERTIBLE 183 F/S	OP	RNBT	FBG	SV	IO	175	MRCR	7	1	2100			3650	4250
18	3	CONVERTIBLE 185 F/S	OP	RNBT	FBG	SV	OB			7	1	1300			2450	2850
18	7	VALIANT 1850	OP	RNBT	FBG	SV	IB	150		7	2	1550			4150	4800
18	10	VISION 1930	OP	RNBT	FBG	SV	IO	175	MRCR	7	1	2000			3700	4300
19	10	VERSAILLES 1950	OP	CUD	FBG	DV	IO	175	MRCR	7	5	2500			4700	5400
19	10	VICTORY 2030	OP	RNBT	FBG	SV	IO	175-205		7	4	2400			4400	5100
19	10	VRESAILLES 1950	OP	CUD	FBG	DV	OB			7	5	2500			4000	4650
20	8	VINDICATOR 2100	OP	CUD	FBG	DV	IO	205-240		7	8	2800			6550	7750
20	8	VISCOUNT 2150	OP	CUD	FBG	DV	IO	175-230		7	8	2800			6500	7700
20	8	VIXEN 2130	OP	RNBT	FBG	SV	IO	205-230		7	8	2800			6300	7350
23	2	VINCENTE 2350	OP	CUD	FBG	DV	IO	204-240		8		3800			9400	10900
23	2	VINDICATOR 2300	OP	CUD	FBG	DV	IO	300	MRCR	8		4000			10600	12000
23	2	VINDICATOR 2300	OP	CUD	FBG	DV	IO	360	MRCR	8		4000			11800	13400
23	2	VOLANTE 2330	OP	RNBT	FBG	SV	IO	205-240		8		3800			8900	10300
26	10	VINDICATOR 2700	OP	CUD	FBG	DV	IO	300-360		9		5000			15400	18800
26	10	VINDICATOR 2700	OP	CUD	FBG	DV	IO	T240	MRCR	9		5000			17100	19500
30	1	VINDICATOR 3000	OP	CUD	FBG	DV	IO	T300-T360		8	6	7200			24600	29100
		1992 BOATS														
16		161 CONSOLE	OP	BASS	FBG	SV	OB			5	4				1500	1800
16		161 STICK	OP	BASS	FBG	SV	OB			5	4				1500	1800
16	2	162 F/S	OP	FSH	FBG	SV	OB			6	2	1060			1800	2150
16	9	1750		RNBT		SV	OB			6	10	1150			2050	2400
17		171 SC	OP	FSH	FBG	SV	OB			6	8	1050			1800	2150
17		BASS & BAY 171	OP	BASS	FBG	SV	OB			6	8	900			1600	1900
17		BASSLINER 171	OP	FSH	FBG	SV	OB			6	8	1100			1900	2250
17	4	176 CCF	OP	CTRCN	FBG	SV	OB			7	10	1400			2400	2750
17	4	VISION 1760 BR SS	OP	RNBT	FBG	SV	IO	115-135		7	1	1900			3050	3550
17	4	VISION 1760 LX	OP	CUD	FBG	SV	IO	115-135		7	1	1900			3100	3600
17	6	180 CCF	OP	CTRCN	FBG	SV	IB			7	5	1580			**	**
17	7	179 F/S	OP	FSH	FBG	SV	OB			7		1250			2200	2550
17	7	SK-18	OP	B/R	FBG	SV	OB			7	1	1130			2000	2400
18	3	183 F/S	OP	FSH	FBG	SV	IO	155-230		7	1	2100			3650	4450
18	3	185 F/S	OP	FSH	FBG	SV	OB			7	1	1300			2300	2650
18	3	SK-186	OP	B/R	FBG	SV	OB			7	1	1250			2250	2650
18	7	1850	OP	RNBT	FBG	SV	OB			7	2	1420			2550	3000
18	7	1850 CB	OP	RNBT	FBG	SV	OB			7	2	1420			2450	2850
18	8	VINDICATOR 1900	OP	RNBT	FBG	DV	IO	180	MRCR	7	3	2550			3950	4550
18	10	1930 MLS CD	OP	CUD	FBG	DV	IO	175	MRCR	7	8	2000			3750	4350
18	10	1930 MLX CD	OP	CUD	FBG	DV	IO	175	MRCR	7	8	2000			3750	4350
18	10	VERSAILLES 1950		RNBT	FBG	DV	OB			7	5	2500			3450	4000
18	10	VERSAILLES 1950 LX	OP	CUD	FBG	DV	IO	115-180		7	5	2500			4050	4750
18	10	VISION 1930 BR SS	OP	RNBT	FBG	SV	IO	155-205		7	1	2000			3450	4100
18	10	VISION 1930 LX	OP	CUD	FBG	DV	IO	115-180		7	1	2000			3500	4150
19	10	VICTORY 2030 BR SS	OP	RNBT	FBG	SV	IO	155-240		7	4	2400			4050	4900
19	10	VICTORY 2030 LX	OP	CUD	FBG	SV	IO	155-240		7	4	2400			4200	5100
20	6	210 CCF	OP	CTRCN	FBG	SV	IB			8		2100			**	**
20	8	VINDICATOR 2100	OP	RNBT	FBG	DV	IO	205-240		7	9	2800			5900	6950
20	8	VINDICATOR 2100	OP	RNBT	FBG	DV	IO	300	MRCR	7	9	2800			6600	7600
20	8	VISCOUNT 2150 LX	OP	CUD	FBG	DV	IO	180	MRCR	7	8	2800			5450	6250
20	8	VISCOUNT 2150 LX	OP	CUD	FBG	DV	IO	205-240		7	8	2800			6150	7250
20	8	VIXEN 2130 BR SS	OP	RNBT	FBG	SV	IO	180-240		7	8	2800			5850	6950
20	8	VIXEN 2130 LX	OP	CUD	FBG	SV	IO	180-240		7	8	2800			6750	7750
23	2	VINCENTE 2350 LX	OP	CUD	FBG	DV	IO	205-300		8		3800			8850	10800
23	2	VINDICATOR 2300	OP	CUD	FBG	DV	IO		MRCR	8		4000			**	**
23	2	VINDICATOR 2300	OP	CUD	FBG	DV	IO	240-300		8		4000			9350	11200
23	2	VOLANTE 2330 BR SS	OP	RNBT	FBG	SV	IO	205-300		8		3800			8250	10300
23	10	230 CCF	OP	CTRCN	FBG	SV	IB			8		2520			**	**
26	10	VINDICATOR 2700	OP	CUD	FBG	DV	IO		MRCR	9		5000			**	**
26	10	VINDICATOR 2700	OP	CUD	FBG	DV	IO	300	MRCR	9		5000			14400	16400

CONTINUED ON NEXT PAGE

LOA FT	LOA IN	NAME AND/ OR MODEL	TOP/ RIG	BOAT TYPE	-HULL- MTL	-HULL- TP	TP	----ENGINE--- # HP	MFG	BEAM FT	BEAM IN	WGT LBS	DRAFT FT	DRAFT IN	RETAIL LOW	RETAIL HIGH
		1992 BOATS														
26	10	VINDICATOR 2700	OP	CUD	FBG	DV	IO	T240	MRCR	9		5000			16000	18200
27	4	267 WAC	OP	CR	FBG	SV	IO	205-300		8	6	5400			14100	17400
27	4	267 WAC W/DB	OP	CR	FBG	SV	OB			8	6	5400			10800	12300
27	4	267 WAC W/SB	OP	CR	FBG	SV	OB			8	6	5400			10800	12300
30	1	VINDICATOR 3000	OP	CUD	FBG	DV	IO	T300	MRCR	8	6	7200			23000	25600
		1991 BOATS														
16		161 CONSOLE	OP	BASS	FBG	SV	OB			5	4				1450	1700
16		161 STICK	OP	BASS	FBG	SV	OB			5	4				1450	1700
16	2	162 F/S	OP	FSH	FBG	SV	OB			6	2	1060			1700	2050
16	5	VP-125	OP	FSH	FBG	SV	OB			6	6	1350			2200	2550
16	9	1750		RNBT		SV	OB			6	10	1150			1950	2300
16	10	174 CCF	OP	CTRCN	FBG	SV	IB			7	5	1200			**	**
17		171 SC	OP	FSH	FBG	SV	OB			6	8	1050			1750	2050
17		BASS & BAY 171	OP	BASS	FBG	SV	OB			6	8	900			1500	1800
17		BASSLINER 171	OP	FSH	FBG	SV	OB			6	8	1100			1800	2150
17	4	184 CCF	OP	CTRCN	FBG	SV	IB			7	10	1400			**	**
17	4	184 DCF	OP	FSH	FBG	SV	IB			7	10	1400			**	**
17	4	VISION 1760 BR SS	OP	RNBT	FBG	SV	IO	115-175		7	1	1900			2900	3350
17	4	VISION 1760 LX	OP	CUD	FBG	SV	IO	115-135		7	1	1900			2900	3400
17	6	180 CCF	OP	CTRCN	FBG	SV	IB			7	5	1580			**	**
17	7	179 F/S	OP	FSH	FBG	SV	OB			7		1250			2050	2450
17	7	SK-18	OP	B/R	FBG	SV	OB			7	1	1130			1900	2300
17	8	VP-150	OP	FSH	FBG	SV	OB			6	10	1400			2300	2650
18	3	183 F/S	OP	FSH	FBG	SV	IO	155-235		7	1	2100			3450	4200
18	3	183 F/S	OP	FSH	FBG	SV	IO	260	OMC	7	1	2100			3700	4300
18	3	185 F/S	OP	FSH	FBG	SV	OB			7	1	1300			2200	2550
18	3	SK-186	OP	B/R	FBG	SV	OB			7	1	1250			2150	2500
18	4	194 CCF	OP	CTRCN	FBG	SV	IB			8		1500			**	**
18	4	194 DCF	OP	FSH	FBG	SV	IB			8		1500			**	**
18	7	1850	OP	RNBT	FBG	SV	OB			7	2	1420			2350	2750
18	7	1850 CB	OP	RNBT	FBG	SV	OB			7	2	1420			2450	2850
18	7	VALIANT 1850 BR SS	OP	RNBT	FBG	DV	IO	155-175		7	2	2300			3400	4000
18	7	VANTAGE 1900 LX	OP	CUD	FBG	DV	IO	115-175		7	2	2350			3550	4150
18	8	VINDICATOR 1900	OP	RNBT	FBG	DV	IO	180-185		7	3	2550			3700	4300
18	10	VERSAILLES 1950		RNBT	FBG	DV	OB			7	5	2500			3300	3850
18	10	VERSAILLES 1950 BRSS	OP	RNBT	FBG	DV	IO	115-185		7	5	2500			3700	4350
18	10	VERSAILLES 1950 LX	OP	CUD	FBG	DV	IO	115-185		7	5	2500			3800	4450
18	10	VISION 1930 BR SS	OP	RNBT	FBG	SV	IO	155-235		7	1	2000			3250	3900
18	10	VISION 1930 LX	OP	CUD	FBG	DV	IO	115-185		7	1	2000			3300	3900
19	2	190 F/S	OP	FSH	FBG	SV	OB			7	6	1550			2600	3000
19	2	192 F/S	OP	FSH	FBG	SV	IO	155-260		7	6	2350			4000	4950
19	2	VP-190T	OP	FSH	FBG	SV	OB			7	6	1500			2500	2950
19	10	VICTORY 2030 BR SS	OP	RNBT	FBG	SV	IO	155-260		7	4	2400			3800	4700
19	10	VICTORY 2030 BR SS	OP	RNBT	FBG	SV	IO	270	OMC	7	4	2400			4100	4750
19	10	VICTORY 2030 LX	OP	CUD	FBG	SV	IO	155-260		7	4	2400			3950	4850
19	10	VICTORY 2030 LX	OP	CUD	FBG	SV	IO	270	OMC	7	4	2400			4250	4950
20	6	210 CCF	OP	CTRCN	FBG	SV	IB			8		2100			**	**
20	8	VINDICATOR 2100	OP	RNBT	FBG	DV	IO	205-270		7	9	2800			5550	6700
20	8	VINDICATOR 2100	OP	RNBT	FBG	DV	IO	300		7	9	2800			6200	7100
20	8	VISCOUNT 2150 LX	OP	CUD	FBG	DV	IO	180-270		7	8	2800			5800	7050
20	8	VIXEN 2130 BR SS	OP	RNBT	FBG	SV	IO	180-270		7	8	2800			5450	6650
20	8	VIXEN 2130 LX	OP	CUD	FBG	SV	IO	180-270		7	8	2800			5650	6900
23	2	VINCENTE 2350 LX	OP	CUD	FBG	DV	IO	205-300		8		3800			8200	10200
23	2	VINDICATOR 2300	OP	CUD	FBG	DV	IO		MRCR	8		4000			**	**
23	2	VINDICATOR 2300	OP	CUD	FBG	DV	IO		OMC	8		4000			**	**
23	2	VINDICATOR 2300	OP	CUD	FBG	DV	IO	240-300		8		4000			8700	10600
23	2	VOLANTE 2330 BR SS	OP	RNBT	FBG	SV	IO	205-300		8		3800			7750	9600
23	10	230 CCF	OP	CTRCN	FBG	SV	IB			8		2520			**	**
24	11	236 WAC	OP	CR	FBG	SV	IO	205-300		8	6	4800			10800	13200
24	11	236 WAC W/DB	OP	CR	FBG	SV	OB			8	6	4800			8050	9250
24	11	236 WAC W/SB	OP	CR	FBG	SV	OB			8	6	4800			8050	9250
25		250 CCF	OP	CTRCN	FBG	SV	IB			8		3220			**	**
26	10	VINDICATOR 2700	OP	CUD	FBG	DV	IO		MRCR	9		5000			**	**
		IO OMC ** ** , IO 300 13500 15400, IO T MRCR ** **														
		IO T OMC ** ** , IO T240-T300 15000 18500														
27	4	267 WAC	OP	CR	FBG	SV	IO	205-300		8	6	5400			13300	16300
27	4	267 WAC W/DB	OP	CR	FBG	SV	OB			8	6	5400			10300	11700
27	4	267 WAC W/SB	OP	CR	FBG	SV	OB			8	6	5400			10300	11700
30	1	VINDICATOR 3000	OP	CUD	FBG	DV	IO	T	MRCR	8	6	7200			**	**
30	1	VINDICATOR 3000	OP	CUD	FBG	DV	IO	T	OMC	8	6	7200			**	**
30	1	VINDICATOR 3000	OP	CUD	FBG	DV	IO	T240-T300		8	6	7200			20400	24000
		1990 BOATS														
16	2	FISH & SKI 162	OP	FSH	FBG	SV	OB			6		1100			1700	2000
16	5	VP 125	OP	FSH	FBG	SV	OB			6	6	1350			2050	2450
16	9	VISION 1750	OP	RNBT	FBG	DV	OB			6	10	1200			1900	2250
17		BASSLINER 171	OP	BASS	FBG	SV	OB			6	8	1250			1950	2350
17		FFB 171	OP	FSH	FBG	SV	OB			6	8	1000			1600	1900
17	4	VISION 1700 LX	OP	RNBT	FBG	DV	IO	128	OMC	7	1	1900			2600	3050
17	4	VISION 1700 SS	OP	RNBT	FBG	DV	IO	128	OMC	7	1	1900			2750	3200
17	6	CCF 180	OP	CTRCN	FBG	SV	OB			7	5	1550			2350	2750
17	7	FISH & SKI 179	OP	FSH	FBG	SV	OB			7		1400			2200	2550
17	8	VP 150	OP	FSH	FBG	SV	OB			6	10	1400			2200	2550
18	3	FISH & SKI 183	OP	FSH	FBG	SV	IO	130-235		7	1	2100			3200	3900
18	3	KONA 185	OP	RNBT	FBG	DV	IO	185-260		7	1	2500			3300	4050
18	7	VALIANT 1850	OP	RNBT	FBG	DV	OB			7	2	1550			2450	2850
18	7	VALIANT 1850 LX	OP	RNBT	FBG	SV	IO	130-175		7	2	2300			3200	3700
18	7	VALIANT 1850 SS	OP	RNBT	FBG	SV	IO	150-175		7	2	2300			3100	3650
18	7	VANTAGE 1850 LX	OP	RNBT	FBG	DV	IO	150-175		7	2	2300			3250	3800
18	7	VANTAGE 1850 SS	OP	RNBT	FBG	DV	IO	150-175		7	2	2300			3350	3900
18	7	VANTAGE 1900 LX	OP	CUD	FBG	DV	IO	130	OMC	7	2	2350			3300	3850
18	8	VINDICATORS 1900	OP	CUD	FBG	DV	IO	185	OMC	7	3	2550			3550	4100
19	2	FISH & SKI 190	OP	FSH	FBG	SV	OB			7	6	1550			2500	2900
19	2	FISH & SKI 192	OP	FSH	FBG	SV	IO	175-260		7	6	2700			4050	5000
19	2	KONA 205	OP	RNBT	FBG	DV	IO	235-260		7	6	2700			3850	4600
19	2	VP 190	OP	FSH	FBG	SV	OB			7	6	1500			2400	2800
19	10	VICTORY 1900 SS	OP	RNBT	FBG	SV	IO	175-260		7	4	2400			3600	4450
19	10	VICTORY 1960 LX	OP	RNBT	FBG	SV	IO	175-260		7	4	2400			3500	4350
20	6	CCF 210	OP	CTRCN	FBG	SV	OB			8		1850			3200	3750
20	8	VINDICATORS 2000	OP	CUD	FBG	DV	IO	235-270		7	8	2800			5550	6550
20	8	VINDICATORS 2000	OP	CUD	FBG	DV	IO	340	OMC	7	8	2800			6600	7600
20	8	VISCOUNT 2050 LX	OP	CUD	FBG	DV	IO	175-260		7	8	2800			5250	6350
20	8	VISCOUNT 2050 LX	OP	CUD	FBG	DV	IO	350	OMC	7	8	2800			6800	7800
20	8	VISCOUNT 2050 SS	OP	CUD	FBG	DV	IO	175-270		7	8	2800			5400	6550
20	8	VIXEN 2000 BR LX	OP	RNBT	FBG	SV	IO	175-260		7	8	2800			5050	6150
20	8	VIXEN 2000 BR LX	OP	RNBT	FBG	SV	IO	350	OMC	7	8	2800			6450	7450
20	8	VIXEN 2000 BR SS	OP	RNBT	FBG	SV	IO	175-270		7	8	2800			5150	6250
23	2	VINCENTE 2350 LX	OP	CUD	FBG	DV	IO	185-270		8		3800			7650	9200
23	2	VINCENTE 2350 LX	OP	CUD	FBG	DV	IO	340	OMC	8		3800			9000	10200
23	2	VINDICATORS 2300	OP	CUD	FBG	DV	IO	235-270		8		4000			8100	9550
23	2	VINDICATORS 2300	OP	CUD	FBG	DV	IO	330-370		8		4000			9200	11200
23	2	VOLANTE 2300 BR SS	OP	RNBT	FBG	SV	IO	185-270		8		3800			7200	8650
23	2	VOLANTE 2300 BR SS	OP	RNBT	FBG	SV	IO	340	OMC	8		3800			8350	9600
23	10	CCF 230	OP	CTRCN	FBG	SV	OB			8		2700			5050	5800
24	11	CWAF 236	OP	CUD	FBG	SV	OB			8	6	5100			7950	9100
24	11	CWAF 236	OP	CUD	FBG	SV	IO	185-270		8	6	5100			10500	12500
24	11	CWAF 236	OP	CUD	FBG	SV	IO	340	OMC	8	6	5100			11900	13600
25		CCF 250	OP	CTRCN	FBG	SV	OB			8		2700			5600	6450
27	4	CWAF 266	OP	CUD	FBG	SV	OB			8	6	5600			9650	11000
27	4	CWAF 266	OP	CUD	FBG	SV	IO	460	OMC	8	6	5600			16500	18800
30	1	VINDICATORS 3000	OP	CUD	FBG	DV	IO	T270-T370		8	6	7200			19700	24200
30	2	VISTA 302	OP	CR	FBG	SV	IO	460	OMC						22200	24700
30	2	VISTA 302	OP	CR	FBG	SV	IO	T175	OMC						20600	22900
		1989 BOATS														
16	2	FISH & SKI 162	OP	BASS	FBG	SV	OB			6	2	1060			1600	1900
16	5	VP125	OP	BASS	FBG	TR	OB			6	6	1025			1550	1850
16	9	VISION 1750	OP	RNBT	FBG	SV	OB			6	10	1150			1750	2050
17		BASSLINER 171	OP	BASS	FBG	SV	OB			6	8	1120			1700	2000
17		FFB171	OP	BASS	FBG	SV	OB			6	8	900			1400	1650
17	4	VISION LX1700	OP	RNBT	FBG	SV	IO	128	OMC	7	1	2175			2700	3150
17	6	CCF180	OP	CTRCN	FBG	SV	OB			7	5	1580			2300	2650
17	7	FISH & SKI 179	OP	SKI	FBG	SV	OB			7		1250			1900	2250
17	7	VELOCITY SK18	OP	RNBT	FBG	SV	OB			7		1130			1750	2100
18	3	FISH & SKI 183	OP	SKI	FBG	SV	IO	128-175		7	1	1850			2500	2950
18	6	VANTAGE 1850	OP	CUD	FBG	SV	IO	175	OMC	7	2	2500			3250	3750
18	7	VALIANT LX1850	OP	RNBT	FBG	SV	IO	128-175		7	2	2375			3000	3500
18	7	VALIANT SS1850	OP	RNBT	FBG	SV	IO	128-175		7	2	2375			3100	3650
18	7	VANTAGE 1850	OP	CUD	FBG	SV	IO	128	OMC	7	2	2500			3200	3750
18	8	VIND ANNIVERARY 1900	OP	RACE	FBG	SV	IO	185	OMC	7	3	2450			3250	3750
18	8	VINDICATOR 1900	OP	RACE	FBG	SV	IO	185	OMC	7	3	2450			3100	3600
19	2	FISH & SKI 190	OP	SKI	FBG	SV	OB			7	6	1400			2200	2550
19	2	FISH & SKI 192	OP	SKI	FBG	DV	IO	175-260		7	6	2350			3150	3900
19	2	FISH & SKI 192	OP	SKI	FBG	DV	IO	350	OMC	7	6	2350			4200	4900
19	2	VP190T	OP	BASS	FBG	DV	OB			7	6	1310			2050	2450
19	8	VISCOUNT LX1950	OP	CUD	FBG	SV	IO	128-185		7	4	2500			3450	4050
19	8	VISCOUNT SS1950	OP	CUD	FBG	SV	IO	128-185		7	4	2500			3550	4150
19	10	VICTORY LX1960	OP	RNBT	FBG	SV	IO	175-185		7	4	2550			3400	4000

LOA FT	LOA IN	NAME AND/ OR MODEL	TOP/ RIG	BOAT TYPE	HULL MTL	HULL TP	ENGINE TP	ENGINE # HP	ENGINE MFG	BEAM FT	BEAM IN	WGT LBS	DRAFT FT	DRAFT IN	RETAIL LOW	RETAIL HIGH
		1989 BOATS														
19	10	VICTORY SS1960	OP	RNBT	FBG	SV	IO	175-185		7	4	2550			3500	4100
20	6	CCF210	OP	CTRCN	FBG	SV	OB			8		2100			3400	3950
20	8	VINDICATOR 2000	OP	RACE	FBG	DV	IO	235-260		7	8	3000			5050	6000
20	8	VINDICATOR 2000	OP	RACE	FBG	DV	IO	350	OMC	7	8	3000			6250	7150
20	8	VIXEN 2000 LX	OP	RNBT	FBG	SV	IO	185-260		7	8	3000			4950	6050
20	8	VIXEN 2000 LX	OP	RNBT	FBG	SV	IO	350	OMC	7	8	3000			6300	7250
20	8	VIXEN 2000 SS	OP	RNBT	FBG	SV	IO	185-260		7	8	3000			5100	6050
20	8	VIXEN 2000 SS	OP	RNBT	FBG	SV	IO	350	OMC	7	8	3000			6300	7250
23	2	VINCENTE 2350	OP	CUD	FBG	SV	IO	185-260		8		3800			7200	8600
23	2	VINCENTE 2350	OP	CUD	FBG	SV	IO	350	OMC	8		3800			8550	9850
23	2	VINDICATOR 2300	OP	RACE	FBG	DV	IO	235-260		8		3600			6650	7750
23	2	VINDICATOR 2300	OP	RACE	FBG	DV	IO	T350	OMC	8		3600			9950	11300
23	2	VINDICATOR 2300	OP	RACE	FBG	DV	IO	T460	OMC	8		3600			15200	17200
23	10	CCF230	OP	CTRCN	FBG	SV	OB			8		2520			4600	5300
25		CCF250	OP	CTRCN	FBG	SV	OB			8		3220			5950	6850
27	4	WALKAROUND 266	OP	CR	FBG	SV	OB			8	6	5400			9450	10700
27	4	WALKAROUND 266	OP	CR	FBG	SV	IO	235-260		8	6	5400			12000	13900
27	4	WALKAROUND 266	OP	CR	FBG	SV	IO	460	OMC	8	6	5400			15400	17500
30	1	VINDICATOR 3000	OP	RACE	FBG	DV	IO	T350-T460		8	5	8000			18400	22600
30	3	SPORT CRUISER 2700	OP	SPTCR	FBG	SV	IO	260-350		8	6	6800			17000	20600
30	3	SPORT CRUISER 2700	OP	SPTCR	FBG	SV	IO	460	OMC	8	6	6800			19800	21900
30	3	SPORT CRUISER 2700	OP	SPTCR	FBG	SV	IO	T175	OMC	8	6	6800			18400	20400
		1988 BOATS														
16	2	HPV162 F/S	ST	BASS	FBG	TR	OB			6	2	1060			1500	1800
16	5	HS125	OP	BASS	FBG	TR	OB			6	6	985			1450	1700
16	9	VISION 1750	ST	RNBT	FBG	SV	OB			6	10	1150			1650	2000
16	9	VISION 1750	ST	RNBT	FBG	SV	IO	120		6	10	1650			2150	2500
17		BASSLINER 171	OP	BASS	FBG		OB			6	8	980			1450	1750
17		FAMILY FISHING 171		FSH	FBG	SV	OB			6	6	980			1450	1750
17	6	CCF180	OP	CTRCN	FBG	SV	OB			7	5	1580			2200	2550
17	6	HS150	OP	BASS	FBG	TR	OB			6	11	1075			1600	1900
17	7	HPV178 F/S	OP	BASS	FBG	TR	OB			7		1210			1750	2100
17	7	VELOCITY SK18	OP	RNBT	FBG	DV	OB			7		1130			1700	2000
18	7	VALIANT 1850		RNBT	FBG	DV	OB			7	2	1420			2050	2450
18	7	VALIANT 1850		RNBT	FBG	DV	IO	120		7	2	2180			2800	3250
18	7	VALIANT SS1850		RNBT	FBG	DV	IO	120		7	2	2220			2800	3250
18	8	VICTORY 1950	ST	RNBT	FBG	DV	OB			7	4				2250	2600
18	8	VICTORY 1950	ST	RNBT	FBG	DV	IO	120		7	4	2065			2750	3200
18	8	VICTORY 1950 CUDDY	OP	CR	FBG	DV	IO	120		7	4	1950			2750	3200
18	8	VICTORY SS1950	ST	RNBT	FBG	SV	IO	120		7	4	2110			2800	3250
18	8	VICTORY SS1950 CUDDY	OP	CR	FBG	SV	IO	120		7	4	2150			2900	3350
20	6	CCF 210		FSH	FBG	DV	OB			8		2100			3250	3800
20	8	VIXEN 2000 CB		RNBT	FBG	DV	IO	120		7	8	2920			4650	5350
20	8	VIXEN 2000 CUDDY		CR	FBG	DV	IO	120		7	8	2920			4900	5600
20	8	VIXEN 2000 OB		RNBT	FBG	DV	IO	120		7	8	2920			4650	5350
21		VINDICATOR 2250	OP	CR	FBG	SV	IO	120		8		2950			5100	5900
23	3	VINDICATOR 2300		CR	FBG	DV	IO	120		8		3560			6550	7500
23	10	CCF230	OP	CTRCN	FBG	SV	OB			8		2500			4400	5050
		1987 BOATS														
16	2	HPV162 F/S	ST	BASS	FBG	TR	OB			6	2	1090			1500	1800
16	2	SK-16	OP	RNBT	FBG	SV	OB			6	4	970			1350	1600
16	5	HS125	OP	BASS	FBG	TR	OB			6	6	985			1400	1650
16	9	VISION 1750	ST	RNBT	FBG	SV	OB			6	10	1150			1600	1900
16	9	VISION 1750	ST	RNBT	FBG	SV	IO	120-165		6	10				2450	2850
16	9	VISION SS1750	ST	RNBT	FBG	SV	IO	120-165		6	10	1850			2100	2550
16	9	VISION SUPER SPT1750	ST	RNBT	FBG	SV	IO	130-175		6	10	1850			2150	2550
17		BASSLINER 171	OP	BASS	FBG		OB			6	8	980			1400	1650
17	6	CCF180	OP	CTRCN	FBG	SV	OB			7	5	1490			1950	2300
17	6	CCSF180	OP	CTRCN	FBG	SV	OB			7	5	1490			2050	2450
17	6	HS150	OP	BASS	FBG	TR	OB			6	11	1075			1550	1850
17	7	HPV178FS	OP	BASS	FBG	TR	OB			7		1080			1550	1850
17	7	VELOCITY LUXURA SK18	OP	RNBT	FBG	DV	OB			7		1130			1600	1950
18	7	VIXEN LUXURA V192	ST	RNBT	FBG	SV	IO	175-260		7	8	2475			2950	3700
18	8	VICTORY 1950	ST	RNBT	FBG	SV	OB			7	6	1950			2500	2900
18	8	VICTORY 1950	ST	RNBT	FBG	SV	IO	120-205		7	6	1950			2500	3050
18	8	VICTORY 1950	ST	RNBT	FBG	SV	IO	260		7	6	1950			2800	3250
18	8	VICTORY SS1950	ST	RNBT	FBG	SV	IO	120-205		7	6	1950			2650	3200
18	8	VICTORY SS1950	ST	RNBT	FBG	SV	IO	260		7	6	1950			2900	3350
18	8	VISCOUNT 1950 CUDDY	OP	CUD	FBG	SV	IO	120-205				2150			2850	3400
18	8	VISCOUNT SS1950 CUD	OP	CUD	FBG	SV	IO	120-205				2150			2950	3550
19	2	HPV-190 F/S	OP	RNBT	FBG	SV	OB			7	6	1400			2050	2400
19	2	HPV-190T	OP	RNBT	FBG	SV	OB			7	6	1310			1950	2300
20	3	KONA 20	OP	RNBT	FBG	TR	OB			7	10	1535			2500	2900
20	3	KONA 20	OP	RNBT	FBG	TR	IO	260	MRCR	7	10	2535			4350	5050
20	3	KONA 20	OP	RNBT	FBG	TR	IO	350	MRCR	7	10	2535			5300	6100
20	6	CCF210	OP	CTRCN	FBG	SV	OB			8		1585			2600	3000
21		VINDICATOR 2250	OP	CUD	FBG	SV	IO		MRCR	8		2950			**	**
21		VINDICATOR 2250	OP	CUD	FBG	SV	IO		OMC	8		2950			**	**
21		VINDICATOR 2250	OP	CUD	FBG	SV	IO	200-260		8		2950			4950	5950
21		VOLANTE BOWRIDER	OP	B/R	FBG	SV	IO		MRCR	8		2825			**	**
21		VOLANTE BOWRIDER	OP	B/R	FBG	SV	IO		OMC	8		2825			**	**
21		VOLANTE BOWRIDER	OP	B/R	FBG	SV	IO	200-260		8		2825			4550	5450
23	10	CCF230	OP	CTRCN	FBG	SV	OB			8		2500			4250	4900
24	6	KONA 25	OP	CR	FBG	SV	IO		MRCR	7	11	3685			**	**
24	6	KONA 25	OP	CR	FBG	SV	IO		OMC	7	11	3685			**	**
24	6	KONA 25	OP	CR	FBG	SV	IO	200-260		7	11	3685			6900	8250
24	6	KONA 25	OP	CUD	FBG	SV	IO	260	MRCR	7	11	3685			7200	8250
25		CCF250	OP	CTRCN	FBG	SV	OB			8		2500			4800	5550
25		CWAFI	OP	CUD	FBG	SV	OB			8					6450	7400
		1986 BOATS														
16	2	HPV162F/S	ST	BASS	FBG	TR	OB			6	2	1090			1450	1750
16	2	HPV162T	OP	BASS	FBG	TR	OB			6	2	1060			1400	1700
16	9	VISION 1750	ST	RNBT	FBG	SV	OB			6	10	1150			1550	1850
16	9	VISION 1750	ST	RNBT	FBG	SV	IO	120-170		6	10				2350	2750
16	9	VISION SUPER SPT1750	ST	RNBT	FBG	SV	IO	140-170		6	10	1850			2050	2450
17		BASSLINER	OP	BASS	FBG		OB			6	8	980			1350	1600
17	7	HPV178DC	OP	BASS	FBG	TR	OB			7		1225			1650	2000
17	7	HPV178FS	OP	BASS	FBG	TR	OB			7		1080			1500	1800
17	7	HPV178T	OP	BASS	FBG	TR	OB			7		1180			1600	1950
17	7	VELOCITY LUXURA SK18	OP	RNBT	FBG	DV	OB			7		1130			1550	1850
17	8	KONA 18	OP	RNBT	FBG	TR	OB			7	1	980			1400	1650
18	6	VIXEN LUXURA V192	ST	RNBT	FBG	SV	IO	170-260		7	8	2475			2800	3500
18	8	VICTORY 1950	ST	RNBT	FBG	SV	IO	120-170		7	6	1950			2500	2900
19	2	HPV-190 F/S	OP	RNBT	FBG	SV	OB			7	6	1400			1950	2350
19	2	HPV-190T	OP	RNBT	FBG	SV	OB			7	6	1310			1850	2200
20	3	KONA 20	OP	RNBT	FBG	TR	OB			7	10	1450			2350	2700
20	3	KONA 20	OP	RNBT	FBG	TR	IO	230-260		7	10	2525			4000	4800
24	6	KONA 25	OP	CUD	FBG	SV	IO	260	MRCR	7	11	3685			6850	7900
		1985 BOATS														
16	2	HPV162F/S	ST	BASS	FBG	TR	OB			6	2	1090			1400	1700
16	2	HPV162T	OP	BASS	FBG	TR	OB			6	2	1060			1400	1650
16	2	VAMP 1620	ST	RNBT	FBG		OB			6	2	980			1300	1550
16	9	VICEROY 1750	ST	RNBT	FBG	SV	OB			6	10	1150			1450	1700
16	9	VICEROY 1750	ST	RNBT	FBG	SV	IO	120-140		6	10				2250	2650
16	9	VISION LUXURA 1750	ST	RNBT	FBG	SV	OB			6	10	1150			1600	1900
16	9	VISION LUXURA 1750	ST	RNBT	FBG	SV	IO	120-190		6	10	1850			1950	2350
17		BASSLINER	OP	BASS	FBG		OB			6	8	980			1300	1550
17	4	VENTURA LUXURA V172	ST	RNBT	FBG	SV	OB			7	8	1440			1850	2200
17	4	VENTURA LUXURA V172	ST	RNBT	FBG	SV	IO	170-190		7	8	2150			2350	2750
17	7	HPV178DC	OP	BASS	FBG	TR	OB			7		1225			1600	1950
17	7	HPV178FS	OP	BASS	FBG	TR	OB			7		1080			1450	1750
17	7	HPV178T	OP	BASS	FBG	TR	OB			7		1180			1550	1850
17	7	VELOCITY LUXURA SK18	OP	RNBT	FBG	DV	OB			7		1130			1500	1800
17	8	KONA 18	OP	RNBT	FBG	TR	OB			7	1	980			1350	1600
18	6	VIXEN LUXURA V192	ST	RNBT	FBG	SV	IO	170-260		7	8	2475			2700	3350
18	8	VICTORY 1950	ST	RNBT	FBG	SV	IO	120-190		7	6	1950			2400	2800
19	2	HPV-190 F/S	OP	RNBT	FBG	SV	OB			7	6	1400			1900	2250
19	2	HPV-190T	OP	RNBT	FBG	SV	OB			7	6	1310			1800	2150
20	3	KONA 20	OP	RNBT	FBG	TR	OB			7	10	1450			2250	2650
20	3	KONA 20	OP	RNBT	FBG	TR	IO	230-260		7	10	2525			3850	4600
24	6	KONA 25	OP	CUD	FBG	SV	IO	230-260		7	11	3685			6400	7550
		1984 BOATS														
16	2	COMPETITOR FISH/SKI	OP	RNBT	FBG	SV	OB			6	2	1060			1350	1600
16	2	HPV162F/S	OP	BASS	FBG	TR	OB			6	2	1090			1400	1650
16	2	HPV162T	OP	BASS	FBG	TR	OB			6	2	1060			1350	1600
16	2	LUXURA V162	ST	RNBT	FBG	SV	OB			6	2	1125			1400	1700
16	9	COMPETITOR 1750	ST	RNBT	FBG	SV	OB			6	10	1150			1450	1750
16	9	COMPETITOR 1750	ST	RNBT	FBG	SV	IO	120-140		6	10				2200	2550
16	9	LUXURA V169	OP	RNBT	FBG	SV	OB			6	10	1150			1450	1750
16	9	LUXURA V169	ST	RNBT	FBG	SV	IO	120-188		6	10	1850			1850	2250
17	4	LUXURA V172	ST	RNBT	FBG	SV	OB			7	8	1440			1800	2100
17	4	LUXURA V172	ST	RNBT	FBG	SV	IO	170-188		7	8	2150			2300	2700
17	7	HPV178DC	OP	BASS	FBG	TR	OB			7		1225			1600	1900
17	7	HPV178FS	OP	BASS	FBG	TR	OB			7		1080			1400	1700
17	7	HPV178T	OP	BASS	FBG	TR	OB			7		1180			1550	1800
17	7	LUXURA SK18	OP	RNBT	FBG	DV	OB			7		1130			1500	1750
17	8	KONA 18	OP	RNBT	FBG	TR	OB			7	1	980			1300	1550

CONTINUED ON NEXT PAGE

LOA FT IN	NAME AND/ OR MODEL	TOP/ RIG	BOAT TYPE	HULL MTL TP	ENGINE TP # HP MFG	BEAM FT IN	WGT LBS	DRAFT FT IN	RETAIL LOW	RETAIL HIGH
					1984 BOATS					
18 7	LUXURA V192	OP	RNBT	FBG SV IO	170-260	7 8	2475		2600	3250
18 8	COMPETITOR 1950	ST	RNBT	FBG SV IO	120-140	7 6	1950		2350	2700
19 2	HPV-190 F/S	OP	RNBT	FBG SV OB		7 6	1210		1650	1950
20 3	KONA 20BR		RNBT	FBG TR OB		7 10			2800	3250
20 3	KONA 20BR	OP	RNBT	FBG TR IO	228-260	7 10	2525		3700	4450
24 6	KONA 25	OP	CUD	FBG SV IO	228-260	7 11	3685		6200	7300

....For earlier years, see the BUC Used Boat Price Guide, Volume 3

V I P MARINE IND INC
MIAMI FL 33150 COAST GUARD MFG ID- VXP See inside cover to adjust price for area

For more recent years, see the BUC Used Boat Price Guide, Volume 1

LOA FT IN	NAME AND/ OR MODEL	TOP/ RIG	BOAT TYPE	HULL MTL TP	ENGINE TP # HP MFG	BEAM FT IN	WGT LBS	DRAFT FT IN	RETAIL LOW	RETAIL HIGH
					1996 BOATS					
17 1	SEASTRIKE 17CC	OP	RNBT	FBG SV OB		6 7	1000	1	3750	4350
17 1	SEASTRIKE 17SC	OP	RNBT	FBG SV OB		6 7	1000	1	4000	4650
18 3	SEASTRIKE 18CC	OP	CTRCN	FBG SV OB		6 11	1100	1	4000	4650
18 3	SEASTRIKE 18S	OP	CTRCN	FBG SV OB		6 11	1100	1	4550	5250
18 7	SEASTRIKE 190	OP	CTRCN	FBG SV OB		8	1500	1	5450	6300
20 4	SEASTRIKE 205	OP	CTRCN	FBG SV OB		8	1800	1 2	6500	7450
					1995 BOATS					
17 1	SEASTRIKE 17CC	OP	RNBT	FBG SV OB		6 7	1000	1	3650	4200
17 1	SEASTRIKE 17SC	OP	RNBT	FBG SV OB		6 7	1000	1	3750	4350
18 3	SEASTRIKE 18CC	OP	CTRCN	FBG SV OB		6 11	1100	1	3800	4450
18 3	SEASTRIKE 18S	OP	CTRCN	FBG SV OB		6 11	1100	1	4250	4950
18 7	SEASTRIKE 190	OP	CTRCN	FBG SV OB		8	1500	1 1	5200	5950
20 4	SEASTRIKE 205	OP	CTRCN	FBG SV OB		8	1800	1 2	6150	7050
					1994 BOATS					
17 1	SEASTRIKE 17CC	OP	RNBT	FBG SV OB		6 11	850		3000	3500
17 1	SEASTRIKE 17SC	OP	RNBT	FBG SV OB		6 11	850		3100	3600
18 3	SEASTRIKE 18	OP	CTRCN	FBG SV OB		6 11	1150		3950	4600
18 3	SEASTRIKE S	OP	CTRCN	FBG SV OB		6 11	1050		3650	4250
18 7	SEASTRIKE 190	OP	CTRCN	FBG SV OB		8	1500		4900	5650
20 4	SEASTRIKE 205	OP	CTRCN	FBG SV OB		8	1800		5850	6700
					1993 BOATS					
17 1	SEASTRIKE 17CC	OP	RNBT	FBG SV OB		6 11	850		2850	3300
17 1	SEASTRIKE 17SC	OP	RNBT	FBG SV OB		6 11	850		2950	3450
18 3	SEASTRIKE 18	OP	CTRCN	FBG SV OB		6 11	1150		3750	4400
18 3	SEASTRIKE S	OP	CTRCN	FBG SV OB		6 11	1050		3500	4050
18 7	SEASTRIKE 190	OP	CTRCN	FBG SV OB		8	1500		4700	5400
20 4	SEASTRIKE 205	OP	CTRCN	FBG SV OB		8	1800		5550	6400
23 10	SEASTRIKE	OP	CTRCN	FBG SV OB		8 6	3100		9950	11300
					1992 BOATS					
17 1	SEASQUIRT 17CC	OP	RNBT	FBG SV OB		6 11	850		2750	3150
17 1	SEASQUIRT 17SC	OP	RNBT	FBG SV OB		6 11	850		2800	3300
18 3	SEASQUIRT 18	OP	CTRCN	FBG SV OB		6 11	1150		3600	4200
18 3	SEASQUIRT HOOKER	OP	CTRCN	FBG SV OB		6 11	1050		3350	3900
18 7	SEAPLUS 18	OP	CTRCN	FBG SV OB		8	1500		4500	5200
20 4	SEAPLUS 20	OP	CTRCN	FBG SV OB		8	1800		5300	6100
23 10	SEAPLUS 24	OP	CTRCN	FBG SV OB		8 6	3100		9550	10900
					1991 BOATS					
17 1	SEASQUIRT	OP	RNBT	FBG SV OB					3050	3550
17 1	SEASQUIRT 17SC	OP	RNBT	FBG SV OB		6 11	1150		2650	3100
18 3	SEASQUIRT 18	OP	CTRCN	FBG SV OB		6 11	1150		3450	4000
18 3	SEASQUIRT HOOKER	OP	CTRCN	FBG SV OB		6 11	1050		3200	3700
18 7	SEAPLUS 18	OP	CTRCN	FBG SV OB		8	1500		4200	4900
20 4	SEAPLUS 20	OP	CTRCN	FBG SV OB		8	1800		5050	5800
23 10	SEAPLUS 24	OP	CTRCN	FBG SV OB		8 6	3100		9150	10400
					1990 BOATS					
16 6	SEASQUIRT 17	OP	CTRCN	FBG SV OB		6 7	850		2450	2850
18 3	SEASQUIRT 18	OP	CTRCN	FBG SV OB		6 11	1050		2850	3350
18 3	SEASQUIRT HOOKER	OP	CTRCN	FBG SV OB		6 11	1050		3250	3750
18 7	SEAPLUS 18	OP	CTRCN	FBG SV OB		8	1500		4050	4700
20 4	SEAPLUS 20	OP	CTRCN	FBG SV OB		8	1800		4850	5600
23 10	SEAPLUS 24	OP	CTRCN	FBG SV OB		8 6	3100		8600	9900
					1989 BOATS					
16 6	SEASQUIRT 17	OP	CTRCN	FBG SV OB		6 7	850		2350	2700
18 3	SEASQUIRT 18	OP	CTRCN	FBG SV OB		6 11	1050		2900	3400
18 7	SEAPLUS 18	OP	CTRCN	FBG SV OB		8	1500		3900	4500
20 4	SEAPLUS 20	OP	CTRCN	FBG SV OB		8	1800		4700	5400
23 10	SEAPLUS 24	OP	CTRCN	FBG DV OB		8 6			8250	9500
					1988 BOATS					
16 6	SEASQUIRT 17	OP	CTRCN	FBG SV OB		6 7	850		2250	2650
18 3	SEASQUIRT 18	OP	CTRCN	FBG SV OB		6 11	1050		2800	3250
18 7	SEAPLUS 18	OP	CTRCN	FBG SV OB		8	1500		3750	4350
20 4	SEAPLUS 20	OP	CTRCN	FBG SV OB		8	1800		4500	5200
					1987 BOATS					
16 6	SEASQUIRT 17	OP	CTRCN	FBG SV OB		6 7	830		2050	2450
18 3	SEASQUIRT 18	OP	CTRCN	FBG SV OB		6 11	1020		2700	3150
18 3	SEASQUIRT 18H	OP	CTRCN	FBG SV OB		6 11	1020		2600	3000
20 4	SEASQUIRT 20+	OP	CTRCN	FBG SV OB		8	1800		4250	4950
					1986 BOATS					
16 6	SEASQUIRT 17	OP	CTRCN	FBG SV OB		6 7	830		2000	2350
18 3	SEA DRIVE	OP	CTRCN	FBG SV SE		6 11	1020		**	**
18 3	SEASQUIRT 18	OP	CTRCN	FBG SV OB		6 11	1020		2850	3050
18 3	SEASQUIRT 18H	OP	CTRCN	FBG SV OB		6 11	1020		2450	2900
					1985 BOATS					
16 6	SEASQUIRT II	OP	CTRCN	FBG SV OB		6 7	750		1750	2100
18 3	BIG-HOOKER	OP	CTRCN	FBG SV OB		6 11	955		2350	2700
18 3	BIG-SEASQUIRT	OP	CTRCN	FBG SV OB		6 11	955		2400	2800
18 3	SEA DRIVE	OP	CTRCN	FBG SV OB		6 11	955		2350	2750
					1984 BOATS					
16 6	SEASQUIRT II	OP	CTRCN	FBG SV OB		6 7	750		1700	2000
18 3	BIG-HOOKER	OP	CTRCN	FBG SV OB		6 11	955		2250	2650
18 3	BIG-SEASQUIRT	OP	CTRCN	FBG SV OB		6 11	955		2350	2750

....For earlier years, see the BUC Used Boat Price Guide, Volume 3

VAGABOND YACHT CORPORATION
HOUSTON TX 77055 COAST GUARD MFG ID- VYC See inside cover to adjust price for area

LOA FT IN	NAME AND/ OR MODEL	TOP/ RIG	BOAT TYPE	HULL MTL TP	ENGINE TP # HP MFG	BEAM FT IN	WGT LBS	DRAFT FT IN	RETAIL LOW	RETAIL HIGH
					1986 BOATS					
37 11	WESTWIND 38	CUT	SA/CR	FBG KL IB	35D YAN	12	19200	4 11	86500	95100
41 8	WESTWIND 42	KTH	SA/CR	FBG KL IB	61D LEHM	12 10	28500	5 6	128500	141000
41 8	WESTWIND 42 SHOAL	KTH	SA/CR	FBG KL IB	61D LEHM	12 10	28500	4 10	128500	141000
					1985 BOATS					
37 11	WESTWIND 38	SLP	SA/CR	FBG KL IB	30D YAN	12	19200	4 11	81300	89300
37 11	WESTWIND 38	CUT	SA/CR	FBG KL IB	30D YAN	12	19200	4 11	81300	89300
41 8	WESTWIND 42	KTH	SA/CR	FBG KL IB	61D LEHM	12 10	28500	5 6	120500	132500
41 8	WESTWIND 42 SHOAL	KTH	SA/CR	FBG KL IB	61D LEHM	12 10	28500	4 10	120500	132500
					1984 BOATS					
37 11	WESTWIND 38	CUT	SA/CR	FBG KL IB	30D YAN	12	19200	4 11	76500	84000
41 8	WESTWIND 42	KTH	SA/CR	FBG KL IB	61D LEHM	12 10	28500	5 6	117000	128500
41 8	WESTWIND 42 SHOAL	KTH	SA/CR	FBG KL IB	61D LEHM	12 10	28500	4 10	110000	121000

....For earlier years, see the BUC Used Boat Price Guide, Volume 3

VALCO
HULLS INC
CLOVIS CA 93612 COAST GUARD MFG ID- HUL See inside cover to adjust price for area

LOA FT IN	NAME AND/ OR MODEL	TOP/ RIG	BOAT TYPE	HULL MTL TP	ENGINE TP # HP MFG	BEAM FT IN	WGT LBS	DRAFT FT IN	RETAIL LOW	RETAIL HIGH
					1985 BOATS					
16	ADVENTURER VA-16	OP	UTL	AL OB					990	1200
16	COASTLINER CL-16	OP	UTL	AL OB					740	895
16	DRIFT DB-16	OP	UTL	AL SV OB					730	880
16	SCOUT SC-16 ED	OP	PRAM	AL FL OB		5 11			1050	1250
16 4	COMMERCIAL U-16C	OP	UTL	AL SV OB		5 10	255		855	1000
16 4	RESORTER U-16R	OP	UTL	AL SV OB		5 7	240		790	950
16 6	EXPLORER VX-16	OP	UTL	AL SV OB		6 9	440		1500	1750
17	COASTLINER CL-17	OP	UTL	AL OB					1400	1700
17	DORY D-17	OP	UTL	AL OB					1550	1850
18	ADVENTURER VA-18	OP	UTL	AL OB					1650	1950
18 4	EXPLORER VX-18	OP	UTL	AL SV OB		6 9	495		1600	1900
19	DORY D-19	OP	UTL	AL OB					1550	1850
20 3	RIVER-RUNNER RR-20	OP	UTL	AL SV OB		6 11			1850	2200
20 6	EXPLORER VX-20	OP	UTL	AL SV OB		6 9	640		1850	2200
21 3	RIVER-RUNNER RR-21	OP	UTL	AL SV OB		6 11			1800	2150
24 6	EXPLORER VX-24	OP	UTL	AL SV OB		6 9	720		3350	3900
25 3	RIVER-RUNNER RR-25	OP	UTL	AL SV OB		6 11			6050	6950

....For earlier years, see the BUC Used Boat Price Guide, Volume 3

VALCO BOATS

WESTCOASTER-VALCO-BAYRUNNER
CLOVIS CA 93611

See inside cover to adjust price for area

FORMERLY HULLS INC

For more recent years, see the BUC Used Boat Price Guide, Volume 1

LOA FT	LOA IN	NAME AND/ OR MODEL	TOP/ RIG	BOAT TYPE	HULL MTL	HULL TP	ENGINE TP	# HP	MFG	BEAM FT	BEAM IN	WGT LBS	DRAFT FT	DRAFT IN	RETAIL LOW	RETAIL HIGH
		1996 BOATS														
16		BAYRUNNER BR-16	OP	FSH	AL	DV	OB			6	7	385			1500	1800
16	4	BAYRUNNER BR-16 OPEN	OP	UTL	AL	DV	OB			6	9	490			1900	2250
16	7	SCOUT SC-16 ED	OP	UTL	AL	TR	OB			5	10	390			1500	1800
17	2	WESTCOASTER WC-172WD	OP	FSH	AL	DV	OB			6	6	650			2650	3100
18		BAYRUNNER BR-18 VEE	OP	FSH	AL	DV	OB			6	7	435			1900	2250
18	4	BAYRUNNER BR-18	OP	FSH	AL	DV	OB			6	7	425			1900	2250
18	6	BAYRUNNER BR-18 OPD	OP	UTL	AL	DV	OB			7	1	690			2600	3000
20	6	BAYRUNNER MS-20 OPV	OP	FSH	AL	DV	OB			7	1	850			4000	4650
20	7	BAYRUNNER BR-20 OPD	OP	UTL	AL	DV	OB			7	1	720			2650	3050
22		CUDDY BR-22		CUD	AL	DV	OB			8		1170			5450	6250
22	2	BAYRUNNER BR-22 OPV	OP	FSH	AL	SV	OB			8		950			4550	5250
25	10	CUDDY WB-26		CUD	AL	DV	OB			8	6	2200			14700	16700
		1995 BOATS														
16		BAYRUNNER BR-16	OP	FSH	AL	DV	OB			6	7	385			1400	1700
16	4	BAYRUNNER BR-16 OPEN	OP	UTL	AL	DV	OB			6	9	490			1800	2100
16	7	SCOUT SC-16 ED	OP	UTL	AL	TR	OB			5	10	390			1400	1700
17	2	WESTCOASTER WC-172WD	OP	FSH	AL	DV	OB			6	6	650			2500	2950
18		BAYRUNNER BR-18 VEE	OP	FSH	AL	DV	OB			6	7	435			1800	2100
18	4	BAYRUNNER BR-18	OP	FSH	AL	DV	OB			6	7	425			1800	2100
18	6	BAYRUNNER BR-18 OPD	OP	UTL	AL	DV	OB			7	1	690			2500	2900
20	6	BAYRUNNER MS-20 OPV	OP	FSH	AL	DV	OB			7	1	850			3800	4400
20	7	BAYRUNNER BR-20 OPD	OP	UTL	AL	DV	OB			7	1	720			2500	2900
22		CUDDY BR-22		CUD	AL	DV	OB			8		1170			5150	5950
22	2	BAYRUNNER BR-22 OPV	OP	FSH	AL	SV	OB			8		950			4250	4950
25	10	CUDDY WB-26		CUD	AL	DV	OB			8	6	2200			13900	15800
		1994 BOATS														
16		BAYRUNNER BR-16	OP	FSH	AL	DV	OB			6	7	385			1350	1600
16	4	BAYRUNNER BR-16 OPEN	OP	UTL	AL	DV	OB			6	9	490			1700	2000
16	7	SCOUT SC-16 ED	OP	UTL	AL	TR	OB			5	10	390			1350	1600
17	2	WESTCOASTER WC-172WD	OP	FSH	AL	DV	OB			6	6	650			2450	2850
18		BAYRUNNER BR-18 VEE	OP	FSH	AL	DV	OB			6	7	435			1700	2000
18	4	BAYRUNNER BR-18	OP	FSH	AL	DV	OB			6	7	425			1700	2000
18	6	BAYRUNNER BR-18 OPD	OP	UTL	AL	DV	OB			7	1	690			2350	2750
20	6	BAYRUNNER MS-20 OPV	OP	FSH	AL	DV	OB			7	1	850			3600	4150
20	7	BAYRUNNER BR-20 OPD	OP	UTL	AL	DV	OB			7	1	720			2400	2800
22		CUDDY BR-22		CUD	AL	DV	OB			8		1170			4950	5700
22	2	BAYRUNNER BR-22 OPV	OP	FSH	AL	SV	OB			8		950			4050	4700
25	10	CUDDY WB-26		CUD	AL	DV	OB			8	6	2200			13200	15000
		1993 BOATS														
16		BAYRUNNER BR-16	OP	FSH	AL	DV	OB			6	7	385			1250	1500
16	4	BAYRUNNER BR-16 OPEN	OP	UTL	AL	DV	OB			6	9	490			1600	1900
16	7	SCOUT SC-16 ED	OP	UTL	AL	TR	OB			5	10	390			1300	1500
17	2	WESTCOASTER WC-172WD	OP	FSH	AL	DV	OB			6	6	650			2300	2700
18		BAYRUNNER BR-18	OP	FSH	AL	DV	OB			6	7	425			1550	1850
18		BAYRUNNER BR-18 VEE	OP	FSH	AL	DV	OB			6	7	435			1600	1900
18	4	BAYRUNNER BR-18 OPD	OP	UTL	AL	DV	OB			7	2	575			1850	2200
20	6	BAYRUNNER MS-20 OPV	OP	FSH	AL	DV	OB			7	1	850			3400	3950
20	7	BAYRUNNER BR-20 OPD	OP	UTL	AL	DV	OB			7	2	650			2000	2350
22		BAYRUNNER BR-22 OPV	OP	CTRCN	AL	SV	OB			8		950			3850	4450
22		CUDDY BR-22		CUD	AL	DV	OB			8		950			3850	4450
25	10	CUDDY WB-26		CUD	AL	DV	OB			8	6	2200			12500	14200
		1992 BOATS														
16		BAYRUNNER BR-16	OP	FSH	AL	DV	OB			6	7	385			1200	1450
16	4	BAYRUNNER BR-16 OPEN	OP	UTL	AL	DV	OB			6	9	490			1550	1800
16	7	SCOUT SC-16 ED	OP	UTL	AL	TR	OB			5	10	390			1200	1450
17	2	WESTCOASTER WC-172WD	OP	FSH	AL	DV	OB			6	6	650			2200	2550
18		BAYRUNNER BR-18	OP	FSH	AL	DV	OB			6	7	425			1500	1800
18		BAYRUNNER BR-18 VEE	OP	FSH	AL	DV	OB			6	7	435			1550	1800
18	4	BAYRUNNER BR-18 OPD	OP	UTL	AL	DV	OB			7	2	575			1750	2100
20	6	BAYRUNNER MS-20 OPV	OP	FSH	AL	DV	OB			7	1	850			3250	3750
20	7	BAYRUNNER BR-20 OPD	OP	UTL	AL	DV	OB			7	2	650			1900	2250
22		BAYRUNNER BR-22 OPV	OP	CTRCN	AL	SV	OB			8		950			3650	4250
22		CUDDY BR-22		CUD	AL	DV	OB			8		950			3650	4250
25	10	CUDDY WB-26		CUD	AL	DV	OB			8	6	2200			11900	13600
		1991 BOATS														
16		BAYRUNNER BR-16	OP	FSH	AL	DV	OB			6	7	385			1150	1350
16	4	BAYRUNNER BR-16 OPEN	OP	UTL	AL	DV	OB			6	9	490			1450	1750
17	2	WESTCOASTER WC-172HB	OP	FSH	AL	DV	OB			6	6	650			2050	2450
18		BAYRUNNER BR-18	OP	FSH	AL	DV	OB			6	7	425			1450	1700
18		BAYRUNNER BR-18V	OP	FSH	AL	DV	OB			6	7	435			1450	1750
18	4	BAYRUNNER BR-18 OPEN	OP	UTL	AL	DV	OB			7	2	575			1650	2000
20	6	BAYRUNNER MS-20 OV	OP	FSH	AL	DV	OB			7	1	850			3100	3600
20	7	BAYRUNNER BR-20	OP	UTL	AL	DV	OB			7	2	650			1800	2150
22		BAYRUNNER BR-22 OV	OP	CTRCN	AL	SV	OB			8		950			3500	4050
22		CUDDY BR-22		CUD	AL	DV	OB			8		950			3500	4050
25	10	CUDDY WB-26		CUD	AL	DV	OB			8	6	2200			11400	12900
		1990 BOATS														
16		ADVENTURER RB-16	OP	UTL	AL		OB			5	9	290			815	985
16		BAYRUNNER BR-16	OP	FSH	AL	DV	OB			6	7	385			1100	1300
16	4	BAYRUNNER BR-16 OPEN	OP	UTL	AL	DV	OB			6	9	490			1400	1650
16	4	COMMERCIAL U-16C	OP	FSH	AL	SV	OB			5	10	255			740	895
16	4	RESORTER U-16R	OP	FSH	AL	SV	OB			5	7	240			695	840
16	6	EXPLORER RB-16HD	OP	UTL	AL	TR	OB			5		440			1250	1500
16	7	SCOUT SC-16 ED	OP	UTL	AL	TR	OB			5	10	390			1100	1300
18		ADVENTURER RB-18	OP	UTL	AL		OB			5	9	315			860	1050
18		BAYRUNNER BR-18	OP	FSH	AL	DV	OB			6	7	425			1350	1600
18		BAYRUNNER BR-18V	OP	FSH	AL	DV	OB			6	7	435			1400	1650
18	4	BAYRUNNER BR-18 OPEN	OP	UTL	AL	DV	OB			7	2	575			1600	1900
18	4	EXPLORER RB-18HD	OP	UTL	AL	TR	OB			5		495			1350	1650
20	6	EXPLORER RB-20HD	OP	UTL	AL	TR	OB			6	9	640			1700	2050
20	7	BAYRUNNER BR-20 OPEN	OP	UTL	AL	DV	OB			7	2	650			1750	2050
22		BAYRUNNER BR-22V OPN	OP	CTRCN	AL	SV	OB			8		950			3350	3850
22		CUDDY 22		CUD	AL	DV	OB			8		950			3350	3900
25	10	CUDDY 26		CUD	AL	DV	OB			8	6	2200			10900	12400
		1989 BOATS														
16		ADVENTURER RB-16	OP	UTL	AL		OB			5	9	290			785	945
16		BAYRUNNER BR-16	OP	FSH	AL	DV	OB			6	7	385			1050	1250
16	3	WESTCOASTER WC-16	OP	FSH	AL	DV	OB			6	3	650			1800	2150
16	4	BAYRUNNER BR-16 OPEN	OP	UTL	AL	DV	OB			6	9	490			1350	1600
16	4	COMMERCIAL U-16C	OP	FSH	AL	SV	OB			5	10	255			710	855
16	4	RESORTER U-16R	OP	FSH	AL	SV	OB			5	7	240			670	805
16	6	EXPLORER RB-16HD	OP	UTL	AL	TR	OB			5		440			1200	1450
16	7	SCOUT SC-16 ED	OP	UTL	AL	TR	OB			5	10	390			1050	1250
18		ADVENTURER RB-18	OP	UTL	AL		OB			5	9	315			815	985
18		BAYRUNNER BR-18	OP	FSH	AL	DV	OB			6	7	425			1300	1550
18		BAYRUNNER BR-18V	OP	FSH	AL	DV	OB			6	7	435			1350	1600
18	4	BAYRUNNER BR-18 OPEN	OP	UTL	AL	DV	OB			7	2	575			1550	1850
18	4	EXPLORER RB-18HD	OP	UTL	AL	TR	OB			5		495			1300	1550
20	6	EXPLORER RB-20HD	OP	UTL	AL	TR	OB			6	9	640			1650	1950
20	7	BAYRUNNER BR-20 OPEN	OP	UTL	AL	DV	OB			7	2	650			1650	1950
22		BAYRUNNER B-22	ST	CUD	AL	DV	OB			8		1170			3850	4500
22		BAYRUNNER BR-22V OPN	OP	CTRCN	AL	SV	OB			8		950			3200	3700
		1988 BOATS														
16		ADVENTURER RB-16	OP	UTL	AL		OB			5	9	290			750	905
16		BAYRUNNER BR-16	OP	FSH	AL	DV	OB			6	5	385			1000	1200
16	2	DRIFT BOAT DB-16	OP	UTL	AL	SV	OB			5	11	300			780	940
16	4	BAYRUNNER BR-16 OPEN	OP	UTL	AL	DV	OB			6	7	490			1300	1550
16	4	COMMERCIAL U-16C	OP	FSH	AL	SV	OB			5	10	255			685	825
16	4	RESORTER U-16R	OP	FSH	AL	SV	OB			5	7	240			640	770
16	6	BASS BOAT SV-16BB	OP	UTL	AL	SV	OB			5	6	650			1700	2000
16	6	EXPLORER RB-16HD	OP	UTL	AL	TR	OB			5		440			1150	1350
16	7	SCOUT SC-16 ED	OP	UTL	AL	TR	OB			5	10	390			1050	1200
17	6	BASS BOAT SV-17BB	OP	UTL	AL	DV	OB			5	10	675			1750	2100
18		ADVENTURER RB-18	OP	UTL	AL		OB			5	9	315			785	945
18		BAYRUNNER BR-18	OP	FSH	AL	DV	OB			6	7	425			1250	1500
18		BAYRUNNER BR-18V	OP	FSH	AL	DV	OB			6	7	435			1300	1550
18	4	BAYRUNNER BR-18 OPEN	OP	UTL	AL	DV	OB			6	7	550			1400	1650
18	4	EXPLORER RB-18HD	OP	UTL	AL	TR	OB			5		495			1250	1500
20	3	RIVER-RUNNER RR-20	OP	UTL	AL	SV	OB			6	11				2000	2400
20	6	EXPLORER RB-20HD	OP	UTL	AL	TR	OB			6	9	640			1550	1850
20	7	BAYRUNNER BR-20	OP	UTL	AL	DV	OB			8		650			1600	1900
21	3	RIVER-RUNNER RR-21	OP	UTL	AL	SV	OB			6	11				2150	2500
22		BAYRUNNER BR-22	OP	UTL	AL	SV	OB			7	10	1170			3050	3500
24	6	EXPLORER RB-24HD	OP	UTL	AL	TR	OB			6	9	720			3650	4250
25	3	RIVER RUNNER RR-25	OP	UTL	AL	SV	OB			6	11				7850	9050
		1987 BOATS														
16		ADVENTURER RB-16	OP	UTL	AL		OB			5	9	290			725	870
16		BAYRUNNER BR-16	OP	FSH	AL	DV	OB			6	7	385			990	1200
16	2	DRIFT BOAT DB-16	OP	UTL	AL		OB			5	7	300			750	905
16	4	BAYRUNNER BR-16	OP	UTL	AL	DV	OB			6	9	490			1250	1450
16	4	COMMERCIAL U-16C	OP	FSH	AL	SV	OB			5	6	255			655	790
16	4	RESORTER U-16R	OP	FSH	AL	SV	OB			5	7	240			615	745
16	6	BASS BOAT SV-16BB	OP	UTL	AL	SV	OB			5	6	650			1650	1950
16	6	EXPLORER RB-16HD	OP	UTL	AL		OB			6	9	440			1100	1300
16	7	SCOUT SC-16 ED	OP	UTL	AL		OB			5	10	390			990	1200
17	6	BASS BOAT SV-17BB	OP	UTL	AL	DV	OB			5	10	675			1700	2050
18		ADVENTURER RB-18	OP	UTL	AL		OB			5	9	315			755	910

CONTINUED ON NEXT PAGE

LOA FT	LOA IN	NAME AND/ OR MODEL	TOP/ RIG	BOAT TYPE	HULL MTL	HULL TP	ENGINE TP	# HP	ENGINE MFG	BEAM FT	BEAM IN	WGT LBS	DRAFT FT	DRAFT IN	RETAIL LOW	RETAIL HIGH
		1987 BOATS														
18		BAYRUNNER BR-18	OP	FSH	AL	DV	OB			6	7	425			1200	1450
18	4	BAYRUNNER BR-18	OP	UTL	AL	DV	OB			6	9	550			1350	1600
18	4	EXPLORER RB-18AD	OP	UTL	AL	DV	OB			6	9	440			1050	1300
20	3	RIVER-RUNNER RR-20	OP	UTL	AL	SV	OB			6	11				1950	2300
20	6	EXPLORER RB-20HD	OP	UTL	AL		OB			6	9	640			1500	1800
20	7	BAYRUNNER BR-20	OP	UTL	AL	DV	OB			7	2	650			1550	1800
20	7	BAYRUNNER BR-20	OP	UTL	AL	SV	OB			7	2	650			1550	1800
21	3	RIVER-RUNNER RR-21	OP	UTL	AL	SV	OB			6	11				2050	2400
24	6	EXPLORER RB-24HD	OP	UTL	AL		OB			6	9	720			2600	3000
25	3	RIVER RUNNER	OP	UTL	AL	SV	OB			6	11				7600	8700
		1986 BOATS														
16		ADVENTURER VA-16	OP	UTL	AL		OB								1000	1200
16		BAYRUNNER BR-16	OP	FSH	AL	DV	OB			6	7	385			955	1150
16		BAYRUNNER BR-16	OP	UTL	AL	DV	OB								1200	1400
16		DRIFT BOAT DB-16	OP	UTL	AL		OB								740	895
16		EXPLORER VX-16	OP	UTL	AL		OB								1250	1500
16		RESORTER U-16R	OP	FSH	AL	SV	OB								765	920
16		SCOUT SC-16 ED	OP	UTL	AL		OB								790	950
16	7	VALCO SV-16	OP	BASS	AL	SV	OB			5	10				1450	1700
18		ADVENTURER VA-18	OP	UTL	AL		OB								1050	1250
18		BAYRUNNER BR-18	OP	FSH	AL	DV	OB			6	7	425			1150	1400
18		BAYRUNNER BR-18	OP	UTL	AL	DV	OB								1100	1350
18		EXPLORER VX-18	OP	UTL	AL		OB								1250	1500
20		BAYRUNNER BR-20	OP	UTL	AL	DV	OB								1600	1900
20		EXPLORER VX-20	OP	UTL	AL		OB								1850	2200
20		RIVER-RUNNER RR-20	OP	UTL	AL		OB								2250	2650
21		RIVER-RUNNER RR-21	OP	UTL	AL		OB								1950	2350
24		EXPLORER VX-24	OP	UTL	AL		OB								3400	3950
25		RIVER-RUNNER RR-25	OP	UTL	AL		OB								6800	7800
		1985 BOATS														
16		ADVENTURER VA-16	OP	UTL	AL		OB								985	1150
16		BAYRUNNER BR-16	OP	FSH	AL	DV	OB			6	7	385			925	1100
16		DAYRUNNER BR-16	OP	UTL	AL	DV	OB								1150	1350
16		DRIFT BOAT DB-16	OP	UTL	AL		OB								715	865
16		EXPLORER VX-16	OP	UTL	AL		OB								1200	1450
16		RESORTER U-16R	OP	FSH	AL	SV	OB								740	890
16		SCOUT SC-16 ED	OP	UTL	AL		OB								765	920
18		ADVENTURER VA-18	OP	UTL	AL		OB								1000	1200
18		BAYRUNNER BR-18	OP	FSH	AL	DV	OB			6	7	425			1150	1350
18		DAYRUNNER BR-18	OP	UTL	AL	DV	OB								1100	1300
18		EXPLORER VX-18	OP	UTL	AL		OB								1200	1450
20		DAYRUNNER BR-20	OP	UTL	AL	DV	OB								1550	1850
20		EXPLORER VX-20	OP	UTL	AL		OB								1750	2100
20		RIVER-RUNNER RR-20	OP	UTL	AL		OB								2200	2550
21		RIVER-RUNNER RR-21	OP	UTL	AL		OB								1900	2250
24		EXPLORER VX-24	OP	UTL	AL		OB								3300	3850
25		RIVER-RUNNER RR-25	OP	UTL	AL		OB								6550	7550

VALIANT YACHTS

GORDONVILLE TX 76245-37 COAST GUARD MFG ID- VAL See inside cover to adjust price for area

For more recent years, see the BUC Used Boat Price Guide, Volume 1

LOA FT	LOA IN	NAME AND/ OR MODEL	TOP/ RIG	BOAT TYPE	HULL MTL	HULL TP	ENGINE TP	# HP	ENGINE MFG	BEAM FT	BEAM IN	WGT LBS	DRAFT FT	DRAFT IN	RETAIL LOW	RETAIL HIGH
		1996 BOATS														
39		VALIANT 39	SLP	SACAC	FBG	KL	IB	35D	WEST	11	5	17000	5	9	164500	181000
42		VALIANT 42	CUT	SACAC	FBG	KL	IB	42D	WEST	12	6	24600	6		241500	265000
42		VALIANT 42 RS	CUT	SACAC	FBG	KL	IB	42D	WEST	12	6	25000	6		244000	268000
50		VALIANT 50	CUT	SACAC	FBG	KL	IB	63D	WEST	13	10	35500	6	3	369500	406500
		1995 BOATS														
39		VALIANT 39	SLP	SACAC	FBG	KL	IB	35D	WEST	11	5	17000	5	9	154500	170000
42		VALIANT 42	CUT	SACAC	FBG	KL	IB	42D	WEST	12	6	24600	6		227000	249500
42		VALIANT 42 RS	CUT	SACAC	FBG	KL	IB	42D	WEST	12	6	25000	6		229500	252000
50		VALIANT 50	CUT	SACAC	FBG	KL	IB	63D	WEST	13	10	35500	6	3	347500	382000
		1994 BOATS														
42		VALIANT 42	CUT	SACAC	FBG	KL	IB	43D	WEST	12	9	24000	6		217500	239000
42		VALIANT 42RS	CUT	SACAC	FBG	KL	IB	43D	WEST	12	9	24000	5	10	227000	249500
50		VALIANT 50	CUT	SACAC	FBG	KL	IB	50D	WEST	13	8	34000	6	3	372500	409000
		1993 BOATS														
37		VALIANT 37	SLP	SACAC	FBG	KL	IB	30D	VLVO	11	5	17000	5	9	136500	150000
40	2	VALIANT 42	CUT	SACAC	FBG	KL	IB	43D	VLVO	12	9	24600	6		201000	221000
47		VALIANT 47	CUT	SACAC	FBG	KL	IB	47D	VLVO	13	8	35500	6	3	306500	337000
47		VALIANT 47	CUT	SACAC	FBG	KL	IB	47D	WEST	13	8	34000	6	3	301500	331500
		1992 BOATS														
37		VALIANT 37	SLP	SACAC	FBG	KL	IB	30D	VLVO	11	5	17000	5	9	128500	141000
42		VALIANT 42RS	CUT	SACAC	FBG	KL	IB	43D	WEST	12	9	24000	5	10	196500	216000
47		VALIANT 47	CUT	SACAC	FBG	KL	IB	47D	WEST	13	8	35500	6	3	288500	317000
		1991 BOATS														
32	1	VALIANT 32	SLP	SACAC	FBG	KL	IB	18D	VLVO	10	5	11800	5	2	81600	89600
39	11	VALIANT 40	CUT	SACAC	FBG	KL	IB	43D	VLVO	12	4	23500	6		171500	188500
47	1	VALIANT 47	CUT	SACAC	FBG	KL	IB	59D	VLVO	13	10	30000	6	3	254500	280000
		1990 BOATS														
32	1	VALIANT 32	SLP	SACAC	FBG	KL	IB	D		10	5	11800	5	2	75700	83100
32	1	VALIANT 32 SHOAL	SLP	SACAC	FBG	KL	IB	D		10	5	11800	4	6	77800	85500
37		ESPRIT 37	SLP	SACAC	FBG	KL	IB	D		11	5	17000	5	9	107000	117500
37		ESPRIT 37 SHOAL	SLP	SACAC	FBG	KL	IB	D		11	5	17000	5	1	109500	120500
37		VALIANT 37	SLP	SACAC	FBG	KL	IB	D		11	5	17000	5	9	118000	129500
37		VALIANT 37 SHOAL	SLP	SACAC	FBG	KL	IB	D		11	5	17000	5	1	120500	132000
39	10	VALIANT 40	CUT	SACAC	FBG	KL	IB	D		12	4	22500	6		149000	164000
39	10	VALIANT 40 PH SHOAL	CUT	SACAC	FBG	KL	IB	D		12	4	22500	5	2	162000	178500
39	10	VALIANT 40 SHOAL	CUT	SACAC	FBG	KL	IB	D		12	4	22500	5	4	151500	166500
47		VALIANT 47	CUT	SACAC	FBG	KL	IB	D		13	10	30000	6	3	237500	261000
47		VALIANT 47 SHOAL	CUT	SACAC	FBG	KL	IB	D		13	10	30000	5	2	240500	264500
		1989 BOATS														
32	1	VALIANT 32	SLP	SACAC	FBG	KL	IB	D		10	5	11800	5	2	72200	79300
32	1	VALIANT 32 SHOAL	SLP	SACAC	FBG	KL	IB	D		10	5	11800	4	6	72200	79300
37		VALIANT 37	SLP	SACAC	FBG	KL	IB	D		11	5	17000	5	9	106000	116500
37		VALIANT 37 SHOAL	SLP	SACAC	FBG	KL	IB	D		11	5	17000	5	1	108000	118500
39	10	VALIANT 40	CUT	SACAC	FBG	KL	IB	D		12	4	22500	6		142500	156500
39	10	VALIANT 40 PH	CUT	SACAC	FBG	KL	IB	D		12	4	22500	6		152500	167500
39	10	VALIANT 40 SHOAL	CUT	SACAC	FBG	KL	IB	D		12	4	22500	5	4	146000	160500
47		VALIANT 47	CUT	SACAC	FBG	KL	IB	D		13	10	30000	6	3	223000	245000
47		VALIANT 47 SHOAL	CUT	SACAC	FBG	KL	IB	D		13	10	30000	5	2	226500	249000
		1988 BOATS														
32	1	VALIANT 32	SLP	SACAC	FBG	KL	IB	D		10	5	11800	5	2	67500	74100
32	1	VALIANT 32 SHOAL	SLP	SACAC	FBG	KL	IB	D		10	5	11800	4	6	68300	75000
37		VALIANT 37	SLP	SACAC	FBG	KL	IB	D		11	5	17000	5	9	99700	109500
37		VALIANT 37 SHOAL	SLP	SACAC	FBG	KL	IB	D		11	5	17000	5	1	101500	111500
39	10	VALIANT 40	CUT	SACAC	FBG	KL	IB	D		12	4	22500	6		133000	146000
39	10	VALIANT 40 PH	CUT	SACAC	FBG	KL	IB	D		12	4	22500	6		147000	161500
39	10	VALIANT 40 SHOAL	CUT	SACAC	FBG	KL	IB	D		12	4	22500	5	4	135000	148000
47		VALIANT 47	CUT	SACAC	FBG	KL	IB	D		13	10	30000	6	3	210000	230500
47		VALIANT 47 SHOAL	CUT	SACAC	FBG	KL	IB	D		13	10	30000	5	2	213500	234500
		1987 BOATS														
32	1	VALIANT 32	SLP	SACAC	FBG	KL	IB	30D	UNIV	10	5	11800	5	2	63500	69700
32	1	VALIANT 32 SHOAL	SLP	SACAC	FBG	KL	IB	30D	UNIV	10	5	11800	4	6	64200	70600
37		VALIANT 37	SLP	SACAC	FBG	KL	IB	40D	UNIV	11	5	17000	5	9	94700	104000
37		VALIANT 37 SHOAL	SLP	SACAC	FBG	KL	IB	40D	UNIV	11	5	17000	5	1	94700	104000
39	10	VALIANT 40	CUT	SACAC	FBG	KL	IB	50D	UNIV	12	4	22500	6		125000	137500
39	10	VALIANT 40 PH	CUT	SACAC	FBG	KL	IB	50D	UNIV	12	4	22500	6		138500	152000
39	10	VALIANT 40 SHOAL	CUT	SACAC	FBG	KL	IB	50D	UNIV	12	4	22500	5	4	127000	139500
47		VALIANT 47	CUT	SACAC	FBG	KL	IB	70D		13	10	30000	6	3	197000	216500
47		VALIANT 47 SHOAL	CUT	SACAC	FBG	KL	IB	70D		13	10	30000	5	2	200500	220500
		1986 BOATS														
32	1	VALIANT 32 SHOAL VM	SLP	SACAC	FBG	KL	IB	30D	UNIV	10	5	11800	4	6	60100	66000
32	1	VALIANT 32 VM	SLP	SACAC	FBG	KL	IB	30D	UNIV	10	5	11800	5	2	60100	66000
37		VALIANT 37 SHOAL VM	SLP	SACAC	FBG	KL	IB	40D	UNIV	11	5	17000	5	1	89100	97900
37		VALIANT 37 VM	SLP	SACAC	FBG	KL	IB	40D	UNIV	11	5	17000	5	9	89100	97900
39	10	VALIANT 40 PHVM	CUT	SACAC	FBG	KL	IB	50D	UNIV	12	4	22500	6		122500	134500
39	10	VALIANT 40 SHOAL VM	CUT	SACAC	FBG	KL	IB	50D	UNIV	12	4	22500	5	4	122500	134500
39	10	VALIANT 40 VM	CUT	SACAC	FBG	KL	IB	50D	UNIV	12	4	22500	6		122500	134500
47		VALIANT 47 SHOAL VM	CUT	SACAC	FBG	KL	IB	70D		13	10	30000	5	2	187000	205500
47		VALIANT 47 VM	CUT	SACAC	FBG	KL	IB	70D		13	10	30000	6	3	187000	205500
		1985 BOATS														
32	1	VALIANT 32	SLP	SACAC	FBG	KL	IB	22D	WEST	10	5	11800	5	2	55900	61400
32	1	VALIANT 32 SG	SLP	SACAC	FBG	KL	IB	22D	WEST	10	5	11800	5	2	55900	61400
32	1	VALIANT 32 SHOAL	SLP	SACAC	FBG	KL	IB	22D	WEST	10	5	11800	4	6	57700	63400
37		ESPRIT 37	SLP	SA/RC	FBG	KL	IB	D		11	6	17000	5	9	83700	92000
37		VALIANT 37	SLP	SACAC	FBG	KL	IB	33D	WEST	11	5	17000	5	9	82300	90500
37		VALIANT 37 SG	SLP	SACAC	FBG	KL	IB	33D	WEST	11	5	17000	5	9	82300	90500
37		VALIANT 37 SHOAL	SLP	SACAC	FBG	KL	IB	33D	WEST	11	5	17000	4	9	85200	93600
37		VALIANT 37 SHOAL	SLP	SACAC	FBG	KL	IB	33D	WEST	11	5	17000	5	1	85200	93600
39	10	VALIANT 40 PH	CUT	SACAC	FBG	KL	IB	46D	WEST	12	4	22500	6		114500	126000
39	10	VALIANT 40 SG	CUT	SACAC	FBG	KL	IB	46D	WEST	12	4	22500	6		114500	126000
39	10	VALIANT 40 SHOAL SG	CUT	SACAC	FBG	KL	IB	46D	WEST	12	4	22500	5	4	116500	128000
39	11	VALIANT 40	CUT	SACAC	FBG	KL	IB	46D	WEST	12	4	22500	6		114500	126000
39	11	VALIANT 40 SHOAL	CUT	SACAC	FBG	KL	IB	46D	WEST	12	4	22500	5	3	116500	128000
39	11	VALIANT PH	SLP	SACAC	FBG	KL	IB	46D	WEST	12	4	22500	6		114500	126000
39	11	VALIANT PH SHOAL	SLP	SACAC	FBG	KL	IB	46D	WEST	12	4	22500	5	3	116500	128000
47		VALIANT 47	CUT	SACAC	FBG	KL	IB	70D	WEST	13	10	30000	6	3	175000	192000
47		VALIANT 47 SG	CUT	SACAC	FBG	KL	IB	70D	WEST	13	10	30000	6	3	175000	192000

 CONTINUED ON NEXT PAGE

VALIANT YACHTS — CONTINUED

See inside cover to adjust price for area

LOA FT IN	NAME AND/ OR MODEL	TOP/ RIG	BOAT TYPE	HULL MTL TP	ENGINE TP # HP	MFG	BEAM FT IN	WGT LBS	DRAFT FT IN	RETAIL LOW	RETAIL HIGH
1985 BOATS											
47	VALIANT 47 SHOAL	CUT	SACAC	FBG KL IB	70D	WEST	13 10	30000	5 2	178000	195500
47	VALIANT 47 SHOAL SG	CUT	SACAC	FBG KL IB	70D	WEST	13 10	30000	6 4	178000	195500
1984 BOATS											
32 1	VALIANT 32 SG	SLP	SACAC	FBG KL IB	22D	WEST	10 5	11800	5 2	53100	58400
37	VALIANT 37 SG	SLP	SACAC	FBG KL IB	33D	WEST	11 5	17000	5 8	78800	86500
39 10	VALIANT 40 PH	SLP	SACAC	FBG KL IB	46D	WEST	12 4	22500	6	108500	119000
39 10	VALIANT 40 SG	SLP	SACAC	FBG KL IB	46D	WEST	12 4	22500	6	108500	119000
39 10	VALIANT 40 SHOAL SG	CUT	SACAC	FBG KL IB	46D	WEST	12 4	22500	4 11	108500	119000
47	VALIANT 47 SG	CUT	SACAC	FBG KL IB	70D	WEST	13 10	30000	6 3	166000	182500
47	VALIANT 47 SHOAL SG	CUT	SACAC	FBG KL IB	70D	WEST	13 10	30000	5 2	166000	182500

....For earlier years, see the BUC Used Boat Price Guide, Volume 3

VAN DER REST NAUTIC BV
ALKAMAAR HOLLAND

See inside cover to adjust price for area

LOA FT IN	NAME AND/ OR MODEL	TOP/ RIG	BOAT TYPE	HULL MTL TP	ENGINE TP # HP	MFG	BEAM FT IN	WGT LBS	DRAFT FT IN	RETAIL LOW	RETAIL HIGH
1984 BOATS											
24	FLYER 24	SLP	SA/OD	KL			8 2		4 7	7750	8900
27 10	FLYER 28	SLP	SA/OD	KL			9 6		4 7	11400	12900
31 2	FLYER 31	SLP	SA/OD	KL			10 8		5 5	11200	12800
35 2	FLYER 35	SLP	SA/OD	KL			11 5		5 5	**	**

VANCOUVER 25 YACHT CO INC
MARINA DEL REY CA 90291

See inside cover to adjust price for area

LOA FT IN	NAME AND/ OR MODEL	TOP/ RIG	BOAT TYPE	HULL MTL TP	ENGINE TP # HP	MFG	BEAM FT IN	WGT LBS	DRAFT FT IN	RETAIL LOW	RETAIL HIGH
1985 BOATS											
29 2	VANCOUVER 25	SLP	SA/RC	FBG KL IB	D		8 6	7000	4	27900	30900
1984 BOATS											
29 2	VANCOUVER 25	SLP	SA/RC	FBG KL IB	D		8 6	7000	4	26400	29300

VANDERHOEVEN
KE VLISSINGN HOLLAND

See inside cover to adjust price for area

LOA FT IN	NAME AND/ OR MODEL	TOP/ RIG	BOAT TYPE	HULL MTL TP	ENGINE TP # HP	MFG	BEAM FT IN	WGT LBS	DRAFT FT IN	RETAIL LOW	RETAIL HIGH
1991 BOATS											
28 3	VANDERHOEVEN 860C	FB	TRWL	STL DS IB	62D	PEUG	9 9		2 9	33500	37300
33 2	VANDERHOEVEN 1010	FB	MY	STL DS IB	105D	LEYL	10 9	15000	3 3	63800	70200
38 7	VANDERHOEVEN 1130	FB	MY	STL DS IB	120D	LEYL	11 5	22000	3 9	96400	106000
38 7	VANDERHOEVEN 1130	FB	MY	STL DS IB	T120D	LEYL	11 5	22000	3 9	102000	112000
41 9	VANDERHOEVEN 1230	FB	MY	STL DS IB	120D	LEYL	12 8	25000	4 3	109000	119500
41 9	VANDERHOEVEN 1230	FB	MY	STL DS IB	T120D	LEYL	12 8	25000	4 3	116000	127500
42 1	VANDERHOEVEN 1300	MS	MY	STL KL IB	160D	IVCO	14	40000	4 9	137000	150500
42 8	1300 T DELUXE	FB	TRWL	STL DS IB	160D	IVCO	13 8	36000	3 8	129000	142000
42 8	1300 T DELUXE	FB	TRWL	STL DS IB	T120D	IVCO	13 8	36000	3 8	136000	149500
42 8	1300 T ROYAL	FB	TRWL	STL DS IB	160D	IVCO	13 8	36000	3 8	148500	163500
42 8	1300 T ROYAL	FB	TRWL	STL DS IB	T120D	IVCO	13 8	36000	3 8	154500	169500
42 8	1300 TAC DELUXE	FB	TRWL	STL DS IB	160D	PEUG	13 8	36000	3 8	130500	143500
42 8	1300 TAC DELUXE	FB	TRWL	STL DS IB	T120D	IVCO	13 8	36000	3 8	137500	151000
42 8	1300 TAC ROYAL	FB	TRWL	STL DS IB	160D	IVCO	13 8	36000	3 8	150000	165000
42 8	1300 TAC ROYAL	FB	TRWL	STL DS IB	T120D	IVCO	13 8	36000	3 8	156000	171000
45 2	VANDERHOEVEN 1330	FB	MY	STL DS IB	145D	IVCO	12 8	29000	4 4	121500	134000
45 2	VANDERHOEVEN 1330	FB	MY	STL DS IB	T120D	IVCO	12 8	29000	4 4	128500	141000
46 7	1400 T DELUXE	FB	TRWL	STL DS IB	160D	IVCO	13 8	40000	3 9	147000	161500
46 7	1400 T DELUXE	FB	TRWL	STL DS IB	T120D	IVCO	13 8	40000	3 9	143000	157500
46 7	1400 T ROYAL	FB	TRWL	STL DS IB	160D	IVCO	13 8	40000	3 9	168000	184500
46 7	1400 T ROYAL	FB	TRWL	STL DS IB	T120D	IVCO	13 8	40000	3 9	161500	177500
46 7	1400 TAC DELUXE	FB	TRWL	STL DS IB	160D	IVCO	13 8	40000	3 9	146000	160500
46 7	1400 TAC ROYAL	FB	TRWL	STL DS IB	160D	IVCO	13 8	40000	3 9	168000	184500
46 7	1400 TAC ROYAL	FB	TRWL	STL DS IB	T120D	IVCO	13 8	40000	3 9	161500	177500
51 8	VANDERHOEVEN 1450	FB	MY	STL DS IB	T145D	IVCO	13 8	38000	4 6	139500	153500
51 8	VANDERHOEVEN 1555	FB	MY	STL DS IB	T145D	IVCO	13 8	38000	4 6	159000	174500

VANDESTADT & MC GRUER LTD
OWEN SOUND CANADA   COAST GUARD MFG ID- ZVM   See inside cover to adjust price for area

LOA FT IN	NAME AND/ OR MODEL	TOP/ RIG	BOAT TYPE	HULL MTL TP	ENGINE TP # HP	MFG	BEAM FT IN	WGT LBS	DRAFT FT IN	RETAIL LOW	RETAIL HIGH
1987 BOATS											
17 2	SIREN	SLP	SA/CR	FBG SK OB			6 8	750	8	2850	3300
22 1	SIRIUS 22	SLP	SA/CR	FBG KL OB			7 11	2500	3 6	6400	7350
22 1	SIRIUS 22	SLP	SA/CR	FBG SK OB			7 11	2100	1 4	5750	6600
28	SIRIUS	SLP	SA/CR	FBG KL IB	9D	YAN	9 8	6700	4 4	21900	24300
28	SIRIUS 28	SLP	SA/RC	FBG IB	9D	YAN	9 8	6700	3 6	22400	24800
28 5	SIRIUS 26	SLP	SA/RC	FBG KL OB			9 5	4500	3 2	14400	16300
1986 BOATS											
17 2	SIREN	SLP	SA/CR	FBG SK OB			6 8	750	8	2700	3150
22 1	SIRIUS 22	SLP	SA/CR	FBG KL OB			7 11	2500	3 6	6050	7000
22 1	SIRIUS 22	SLP	SA/CR	FBG SK OB			7 11	2100	1 4	5450	6250
28	SIRIUS	SLP	SA/CR	FBG KL IB	9D	YAN	9 8	6700	3 6	21000	23300
28	SIRIUS	SLP	SA/RC	FBG IB	9D	YAN	9 8	6700	3 6	21000	23300
1985 BOATS											
17 2	SIREN	SLP	SA/CR	FBG SK OB			6 8	750	8	2550	2950
21 2	SIRIUS	SLP	SA/CR	FBG KL OB			7 11	2000	1 4	4800	5500
22 1	SIRIUS	SLP	SA/CR	FBG KL OB			7 11	2000	3 6	5000	5750
22 1	SIRIUS	SLP	SA/CR	FBG SK OB			7 11	2000	1 4	5000	5750
28	SIRIUS	SLP	SA/RC	FBG KL IB	9D	YAN	9 8	6700		19900	22100
1984 BOATS											
17 2	SIREN	SLP	SA/CR	FBG SK OB			6 8	750	8	2400	2800
21 2	SIRIUS	SLP	SA/CR	FBG KL OB			7 11	2000	1 4	4550	5250
28	SIRIUS	SLP	SA/RC	FBG KL IB	8D	YAN	9 8	6700		19000	21100

....For earlier years, see the BUC Used Boat Price Guide, Volume 3

VANGUARD SAILBOATS
PORTSMOUTH RI 02871   COAST GUARD MFG ID- QQT   See inside cover to adjust price for area
FORMERLY VANGUARD INC

For more recent years, see the BUC Used Boat Price Guide, Volume 1

LOA FT IN	NAME AND/ OR MODEL	TOP/ RIG	BOAT TYPE	HULL MTL TP	ENGINE TP # HP	MFG	BEAM FT IN	WGT LBS	DRAFT FT IN	RETAIL LOW	RETAIL HIGH
1986 BOATS											
18	VANGUARD VOLANT	SLP	SA/OD	FBG CB			6	410	3 6	2250	2600
1985 BOATS											
18	VANGUARD VOLANT	SLP	SA/OD	FBG CB			6	410	3 6	2050	2450
1984 BOATS											
18	VANGUARD VOLANT	SLP	SA/OD	FBG CB			6	410	3 6	1950	2300

....For earlier years, see the BUC Used Boat Price Guide, Volume 3

VAUGHN BOATS
CANOGA PK CA 91304   COAST GUARD MFG ID- VAU   See inside cover to adjust price for area

LOA FT IN	NAME AND/ OR MODEL	TOP/ RIG	BOAT TYPE	HULL MTL TP	ENGINE TP # HP	MFG	BEAM FT IN	WGT LBS	DRAFT FT IN	RETAIL LOW	RETAIL HIGH
1984 BOATS											
22	OFFSHORE DAYCRUISER	OP	OFF	FBG DV OB			8			6950	8000
22	OFFSHORE DAYCRUISER	OP	OFF	FBG DV IB	330		8			6950	7950
22	OFFSHORE DAYCRUISER	OP	OFF	FBG DV IB	550	CHEV	8			9100	10300
25	OFFSHORE DAYCRUISER	OP	OFF	FBG DV OB			8			13500	15400
28	OFFSHORE CRUISER	OP	OFF	FBG DV IB	350	MRCR	8			14900	16900
28	OFFSHORE DAYCRUISER	OP	OFF	FBG DV OB			8			20100	22300
28	OFFSHORE DAYCRUISER	OP	OFF	FBG DV IB	T330		8			17000	19300

....For earlier years, see the BUC Used Boat Price Guide, Volume 3

VECTOR MARINE INC
BUFORD GA 30518

See inside cover to adjust price for area

LOA FT IN	NAME AND/ OR MODEL	TOP/ RIG	BOAT TYPE	HULL MTL TP	ENGINE TP # HP	MFG	BEAM FT IN	WGT LBS	DRAFT FT IN	RETAIL LOW	RETAIL HIGH
1989 BOATS											
24	OFFSHORE 24		OFF	FBG	IO 330-365		7	3200	2 11	11300	14000
24	OFFSHORE SPORT		OFF	FBG	IO 330-365		7	3200	2 11	11800	14500

VENTURA YACHT SERVICES INC
PT WASHINGTON NY 11050   See inside cover to adjust price for area

LOA FT IN	NAME AND/ OR MODEL	TOP/ RIG	BOAT TYPE	HULL MTL TP	TP #	ENGINE HP MFG	BEAM FT IN	WGT LBS	DRAFT FT IN	RETAIL LOW	RETAIL HIGH
			1985 BOATS								
35 1	KIWI 35	SLP	SA/OD	KEV SK	IB	D	8 4	2800	1 6	6300	7200
51 6	RON-HOLLAND 52	SLP	SA/CR	FBG KL	IB	88D	14 7	38000	8 2	120500	132000
			1984 BOATS								
51 6	RON-HOLLAND 52	CUT	SA/CR	FBG KC	IB	81D PERK	14 7	38000	5 11	110000	121000
51 6	RON-HOLLAND 52	CUT	SA/CR	FBG KL	IB	81D PERK	14 7	38000	8 2	110000	121000
51 6	RON-HOLLAND 52	KTH	SA/CR	FBG KC	IB	81D PERK	14 7	38000	5 11	116500	128000
51 6	RON-HOLLAND 52	KTH	SA/CR	FBG KL	IB	81D PERK	14 7	38000	8 2	116500	128000
51 6	RON-HOLLAND 52 SHOAL	CUT	SA/CR	FBG KL	IB	81D PERK	14 7	38000	6 5	110000	121000
51 6	RON-HOLLAND 52 SHOAL	KTH	SA/CR	FBG KL	IB	81D PERK	14 7	38000	6 5	116500	128000

VENTURE BOATS INC
WINCHESTER TN 37398   COAST GUARD MFG ID- VNB See inside cover to adjust price for area

LOA FT IN	NAME AND/ OR MODEL	TOP/ RIG	BOAT TYPE	HULL MTL TP	TP #	ENGINE HP MFG	BEAM FT IN	WGT LBS	DRAFT FT IN	RETAIL LOW	RETAIL HIGH
			1995 BOATS								
20 2	GRAND SPORT ELITE	BR	SKI	F/S SV	IB	310 PCM	7 6	2550	1 9	11100	12600

....For earlier years, see the BUC Used Boat Price Guide, Volume 3

VERSILCRAFT
55049 VIREGGIO ITALY   See inside cover to adjust price for area

LOA FT IN	NAME AND/ OR MODEL	TOP/ RIG	BOAT TYPE	HULL MTL TP	TP #	ENGINE HP MFG	BEAM FT IN	WGT LBS	DRAFT FT IN	RETAIL LOW	RETAIL HIGH
			1985 BOATS								
34	MOTOR YACHT	FB	MY	WD DV	IB	T200D MTM	7 2			80400	88400

VIA MARINE
CMPF
75008 PARIS FRANCE   See inside cover to adjust price for area

LOA FT IN	NAME AND/ OR MODEL	TOP/ RIG	BOAT TYPE	HULL MTL TP	TP #	ENGINE HP MFG	BEAM FT IN	WGT LBS	DRAFT FT IN	RETAIL LOW	RETAIL HIGH
			1984 BOATS								
41 7	VIA 42	SLP	SA/CR	AL KC	IB	36D VLVO	13 3	17416	3 3	62500	68600

....For earlier years, see the BUC Used Boat Price Guide, Volume 3

VICTORY CATAMARANS
BROOKLYN NY 11232   See inside cover to adjust price for area

For more recent years, see the BUC Used Boat Price Guide, Volume 1

LOA FT IN	NAME AND/ OR MODEL	TOP/ RIG	BOAT TYPE	HULL MTL TP	TP #	ENGINE HP MFG	BEAM FT IN	WGT LBS	DRAFT FT IN	RETAIL LOW	RETAIL HIGH
			1996 BOATS								
35	VICTORY 35	CAT	SACAC	FBG CT	IB	27D YAN	16	9000	2 10	104500	114500

VICTORY OFFSHORE POWERBOATS
SARASOTA FL 34230-0520   See inside cover to adjust price for area

LOA FT IN	NAME AND/ OR MODEL	TOP/ RIG	BOAT TYPE	HULL MTL TP	TP #	ENGINE HP MFG	BEAM FT IN	WGT LBS	DRAFT FT IN	RETAIL LOW	RETAIL HIGH
			1995 BOATS								
27	AERO-TEK 27	OP	OFF	FBG DV	IO	300-385	8	3900	2	34000	42400
27	AERO-TEK 27	OP	OFF	FBG DV	IO	415-465	8	3900	2	40000	48200
27	AERO-TEK 27	OP	OFF	FBG DV	IO	490 MRCR	8	3900	2	45500	50000
28	AERO-TEK 28	OP	OFF	FBG DV	OB		8	4020	2	31800	35400
28	AERO-TEK 28	OP	OFF	FBG DV	IO	300-385	8	4020	2	35600	43600
	IO 415-490 40800 49800, IO T235-T250 40000 45200, IO T385-T465 50700 62500										
	IO T490 MRCR 58900 64700, IOT180D-T220D 50300 60100										
28	AERO-TEK 28 CC	OP	OFF	FBG DV	OB		8	4020	2	31800	35400
28	AERO-TEK 28 CC 28	OP	OFF	FBG DV	IO	180D-220D	8	4020	2	27400	33200
28	SPIRIT 28	OP	OFF	FBG DV	IO	T235-T250	8	4020	2	33300	39900
28	SPIRIT 28	OP	OFF	FBG DV	IOT180D-T220D		8	4020	2	36100	44400
29	AERO-TEK 29	OP	OFF	FBG DV	OB		8	5100	2	38300	42500
29	AERO-TEK 29	OP	OFF	FBG DV	IO	T235-T250	8	5100	2	47900	53500
	IO T350-T415 54600 65400, IO T450-T490 62600 72900, IOT180D-T220D 50400 59700										
29	AERO-TEK 29 CC	OP	OFF	FBG DV	OB		8	5100	2	33300	37000
30	AERO-TEK 30	OP	OFF	FBG DV	OB		8	5300	2	42500	47200
30	AERO-TEK 30	OP	OFF	FBG DV	IO	T235-T350	8	5300	2	53300	65300
30	AERO-TEK 30	OP	OFF	FBG DV	IO	T385-T490	8	5300	2	61900	77000
30	AERO-TEK 30	OP	OFF	FBG DV	IOT180D-T220D		8	5300	2	54000	63400
30	AERO-TEK 30 CC	OP	OFF	FBG DV	OB		8	5300	2	37000	41100
31	AERO-TEK 31	OP	OFF	FBG DV	OB		8	5500		47100	51800
31	AERO-TEK 31	OP	OFF	FBG DV	IO	T235-T385	8	7500		63400	78200
31	AERO-TEK 31	OP	OFF	FBG DV	IO	T415-T490	8	7500		73000	86300
31	AERO-TEK 31	OP	OFF	FBG DV	IOT180D-T220D		8	7500		67100	77700
31	AERO-TEK 31 CC	OP	OFF	FBG DV	OB		8	5500		40800	45300
33	AERO-TEK 33	OP	OFF	FBG DV	OB		8	6020	2	43600	48500
33	AERO-TEK 33	OP	OFF	FBG DV	IO	T235-T385	8	6020	2	81500	100000
33	AERO-TEK 33	OP	OFF	FBG DV	IO	T415-T490	8	6020	2	93400	109500
33	AERO-TEK 33	OP	OFF	FBG DV	IOT180D-T220D		8	6020	2	80700	93100
33	AERO-TEK 33 CC	OP	OFF	FBG DV	OB		8	6020	2	38400	42600
34	AERO-TEK 34	OP	OFF	FBG DV	OB		8	6200		42900	47700
34	AERO-TEK 34	OP	OFF	FBG DV	IO	T235-T415	8	7900		94900	118500
34	AERO-TEK 34	OP	OFF	FBG DV	IO	T450-T490	8	7900		111000	127000
34	AERO-TEK 34	OP	OFF	FBG DV	IOT180D-T220D		8	7900		99400	113000
34	AERO-TEK 34 CC	OP	OFF	FBG DV	OB		8	6200		38000	42200
35	AERO-TEK 35	OP	OFF	FBG DV	OB		8	6460		44300	49200
35	AERO-TEK 35	OP	OFF	FBG DV	IO	T235 MRCR	8	6460		103000	113000
	IO T250 MRCR 103500 114000, IO T350 MRCR 111000 122000, IO T385 MRCR 114500 126000										
	IO T415 MRCR 118000 130000, IO T450 MRCR 122500 134500, IO T465 MRCR 124500 137000										
	IO T490 MRCR 128000 140500, IO T180D MRCR 108000 118500, IO T220D MRCR 111500 122500										
35	AERO-TEK 35 CC	OP	OFF	FBG DV	OB		8	6460		39300	43700
			1994 BOATS								
27	AERO-TEK 27	OP	OFF	FBG DV	IO	415 MRCR	8			36800	40800
28	AERO-TEK 28	OP	OFF	FBG DV	IO		8			30400	33800
28	AERO-TEK 28	OP	OFF	FBG DV	IO	300 MRCR	8			31000	34400
	IO 415 MRCR 35700 39600, IO T415 MRCR 47000 51600, IO T240D MRCR 45700 50200										
28	AERO-TEK 28 CC	OP	OFF	FBG DV	OB		8			30400	33800
28	SPIRIT 28	OP	OFF	FBG DV	IO	350 MRCR	8			32800	36500
28	SPIRIT 28	OP	OFF	FBG DV	IO	T250 MRCR	8			35100	38900
29	AERO-TEK 29	OP	OFF	FBG DV	OB		8			36600	40700
29	AERO-TEK 29	OP	OFF	FBG DV	IO	T415 MRCR	8			52300	57500
29	AERO-TEK 29	OP	OFF	FBG DV	IO	T240D MRCR	8			50800	55800
29	AERO-TEK 29 CC	OP	OFF	FBG DV	OB		8			31800	35400
30	AERO-TEK 30	OP	OFF	FBG DV	OB		8			40600	45100
30	AERO-TEK 30	OP	OFF	FBG DV	IO	T415 MRCR	8			55500	60900
30	AERO-TEK 30	OP	OFF	FBG DV	IO	T240D MRCR	8			52900	58100
30	AERO-TEK 30 CC	OP	OFF	FBG DV	OB		8			35400	39300
31	AERO-TEK 31	OP	OFF	FBG DV	OB		8			44500	49500
31	AERO-TEK 31	OP	OFF	FBG DV	IO	T415 MRCR	8			62600	68800
31	AERO-TEK 31	OP	OFF	FBG DV	IO	T240D MRCR	8			62400	68500
31	AERO-TEK 31 CC	OP	OFF	FBG DV	OB		8			39000	43400
33	AERO-TEK 33	OP	OFF	FBG DV	OB		8			49500	54500
33	AERO-TEK 33	OP	OFF	FBG DV	IO	T415 MRCR	8			89500	98400
33	AERO-TEK 33	OP	OFF	FBG DV	IO	T240D MRCR	8			82100	90200
33	AERO-TEK 33 CC	OP	OFF	FBG DV	OB		8			49600	54500
34	AERO-TEK 34	OP	OFF	FBG DV	OB		8			**	**
34	AERO-TEK 34	OP	OFF	FBG DV	IO	T415 MRCR	8			104000	114500
34	AERO-TEK 34	OP	OFF	FBG DV	IO	T240D MRCR	8			99200	109000
34	AERO-TEK 34 CC	OP	OFF	FBG DV	OB		8			**	**
35	AERO-TEK 35	OP	OFF	FBG DV	OB		8			**	**
35	AERO-TEK 35 CC	OP	OFF	FBG DV	OB		8			**	**
35	AERO-TEK 35 CC	OP	OFF	FBG DV	IO	T415 MRCR	8			114500	126000
35	AERO-TEK 35 CC	OP	OFF	FBG DV	IO	T240D MRCR	8			107500	118500
38	AERO-TEK 38	OP	OFF	FBG DV	IO	T415 MRCR	8			123500	136000
40	AERO-TEK 40	OP	OFF	FBG DV	IO	T490 MRCR	8			163000	179000
40	AERO-TEK 40	OP	OFF	FBG DV	IO	R415 MRCR	8			151500	166000
42	AERO-TEK 42	OP	OFF	FBG DV	IO	T490 MRCR	8			168000	184500
42	AERO-TEK 42	OP	OFF	FBG DV	IO	R415 MRCR	8			160000	176000
44	AERO-TEK 44	OP	OFF	FBG DV	IO	T490 MRCR	8			170500	187000
44	AERO-TEK 44	OP	OFF	FBG DV	IO	R415 MRCR	8			168000	184500

VIETTI CUSTOM BOATS

COSTA MESA CA 92626 COAST GUARD MFG ID- ECA See inside cover to adjust price for area
FORMERLY EMERSON CUSTOM BOATS

LOA FT	LOA IN	NAME AND/ OR MODEL	TOP/ RIG	BOAT TYPE	-HULL- MTL	-HULL- TP	ENGINE TP	ENGINE # HP	ENGINE MFG	BEAM FT	BEAM IN	WGT LBS	DRAFT FT	DRAFT IN	RETAIL LOW	RETAIL HIGH
		1985 BOATS														
16	10	SPLASH-CRAFT	ST	RNBT	FBG	TR	IO	117-200		7	2	2200		10	2850	3400
17		SPLASH-CRAFT DELUXE	ST	SKI	FBG	TR	IO	125-200		7	1	2200	1		2700	3250
		1984 BOATS														
16	10	SPLASH-CRAFT	ST	RNBT	FBG	TR	IO	117-200		7	2	2200		10	2750	3250

....For earlier years, see the BUC Used Boat Price Guide, Volume 3

VIKING

MIRAGE HOLDINGS INC
ARLINGTON WA 98223 COAST GUARD MFG ID- MCJ See inside cover to adjust price for area
ALSO MIRAGE

For more recent years, see the BUC Used Boat Price Guide, Volume 1

LOA FT	LOA IN	NAME AND/ OR MODEL	TOP/ RIG	BOAT TYPE	-HULL- MTL	-HULL- TP	ENGINE TP	ENGINE # HP	ENGINE MFG	BEAM FT	BEAM IN	WGT LBS	DRAFT FT	DRAFT IN	RETAIL LOW	RETAIL HIGH
		1996 BOATS														
17		VIKING 1701	OP	FSH	FBG	DV	OB			6	10	1750			7000	8050
18	9	VIKING 1901	ST	FSH	FBG	DV	OB			8		1900			7550	8700
19	10	VIKING 2000	ST	FSH	FBG	DV	OB			7	7	1900			8150	9350
		1995 BOATS														
17		VIKING 1701	OP	FSH	FBG	DV	OB			6	10	1750			6650	7650
18	9	VIKING 1901	ST	FSH	FBG	DV	OB			8		1900			7150	8250
18	9	VIKING 1901 LE	ST	FSH	FBG	DV	OB			8		1900			7250	8350
19	10	VIKING 200	ST	FSH	FBG	DV	OB			7	7	1800			7450	8550
		1994 BOATS														
17		VIKING 1701	OP	FSH	FBG	DV	OB			6	10	1750			6300	7250
18	9	VIKING 190	ST	FSH	FBG	DV	OB			8		1900			6800	7800
18	9	VIKING 190	ST	FSH	FBG	DV	IO	135-185		8		1900			6800	8300
18	9	VIKING 190 LE	ST	FSH	FBG	DV	OB			8		1900			6900	7950
18	9	VIKING 190 LE	ST	FSH	FBG	DV	IO	135-185		8		1900			6850	8350
19	10	VIKING 200	ST	FSH	FBG	DV	OB			7	7	1800			7050	8150

VIKING YACHT COMPANY

NEW GRETNA NJ 08244 COAST GUARD MFG ID- VKY See inside cover to adjust price for area

For more recent years, see the BUC Used Boat Price Guide, Volume 1

LOA FT	LOA IN	NAME AND/ OR MODEL	TOP/ RIG	BOAT TYPE	-HULL- MTL	-HULL- TP	ENGINE TP	ENGINE # HP	ENGINE MFG	BEAM FT	BEAM IN	WGT LBS	DRAFT FT	DRAFT IN	RETAIL LOW	RETAIL HIGH
		1996 BOATS														
39	4	CONVERTIBLE 38	FB	SDNSF	FBG	SV	IB	T485D	DD	14	2	32890	4	1	279000	306500
43		CONVERTIBLE 43	FB	SDNSF	FBG	SV	IB	T550D	DD	15	3	38595	4	3	330500	363000
43		CONVERTIBLE 43	FB	SDNSF	FBG	SV	IB	T600D	MAN	15	3	38595	4	3	334000	367000
43		SPORTFISH 43		SF	FBG	SV	IB	T550D	GM	15	3	34500	4	3	297500	326500
43		SPORTFISH 43		SF	FBG	SV	IB	T600D	MAN	15	3	34500	4	3	300000	329500
47	2	CONVERTIBLE 47	FB	SDNSF	FBG	SV	IB	T680D	MAN	15	6	46300	4	5	401000	440500
50		MOTOR YACHT 50	FB	MY	FBG	SV	IB	T735D	DD	15		65216	4	3	546000	600000
50	7	CONVERTIBLE 50	FB	SDNSF	FBG	SV	IB	T820D	MAN	16	4	58814	4	9	489000	537000
53	7	CONVERTIBLE 53	FB	SDNSF	FBG	SV	IB	T820D	MAN	16	7	68600	4	10	536500	589500
54	1	SPORTS YACHT 54	FB	MY	FBG	SV	IB	T820D	MAN	17	5	75000	4	10	532500	585000
57	7	MOTOR YACHT 57	FB	MY	FBG	SV	IB	T760D	DD	17	4	66000	4	5	588500	647000
58	11	CONVERTIBLE 58	FB	SDNSF	FBG	SV	IB	T12CD	MAN	18		81500	5	3	692000	760500
58	11	CONVERTIBLE 58	FB	SDNSF	FBG	SV	IB	T14CD	DD	18		81500	5	3	692500	761000
60	1	COCKPIT SPORTS YACHT	FB	MYCPT	FBG	SV	IB	T820D	MAN	17	5	68000	4	10	547000	601000
64	7	MOTOR YACHT 65	FB	MY	FBG	SV	IB	T10CD	DD	17	4	91000	4	9	783500	860500
68	8	CONVERTIBLE 68	FB	SDNSF	FBG	SV	IB	T14CD	DD	18	11	54T	5	6	1.065M	1.160M
72		COCKPIT MOTOR YACHT	FB	MYCPT	FBG	SV	IB	T10CD	MAN	17	5	54T	4	10	**	**
72		MOTOR YACHT 72	FB	MY	FBG	SV	IB	T10CD	MAN	17	5	54T	4	10	**	**
		1995 BOATS														
39	4	CONVERTIBLE 38	FB	SDNSF	FBG	SV	IB	T485D	DD	14	2	32890	4	1	267500	294000
43		CONVERTIBLE 43	FB	SDNSF	FBG	SV	IB	T550D	DD	15	3	38595	4	3	317000	348000
43		CONVERTIBLE 43	FB	SDNSF	FBG	SV	IB	T600D	MAN	15	3	38595	4	3	320000	352000
43		SPORTFISH 43		SF	FBG	SV	IB	T550D	GM	15	3	34500	4	3	285000	313500
43		SPORTFISH 43		SF	FBG	SV	IB	T600D	MAN	15	3	34500	4	3	287500	316000
47	2	CONVERTIBLE 47	FB	SDNSF	FBG	SV	IB	T680D	MAN	15	6	46300	4	5	384000	422000
50		MOTOR YACHT 50	FB	MY	FBG	SV	IB	T735D	DD	15		65216	4	3	523500	575000
50	7	CONVERTIBLE 50	FB	SDNSF	FBG	SV	IB	T820D	MAN	16	4	58814	4	9	468500	515000
53	7	CONVERTIBLE 53	FB	SDNSF	FBG	SV	IB	T820D	MAN	16	7	68600	4	10	514500	565500
54	1	SPORTS YACHT 54	FB	MY	FBG	SV	IB	T820D	MAN	17	5	75000	4	10	510500	561000
57	7	MOTOR YACHT 57	FB	MY	FBG	SV	IB	T760D	DD	17	4	66000	4	5	564500	620500
58	11	CONVERTIBLE 58	FB	SDNSF	FBG	SV	IB	T12CD	MAN	18		81500	5	3	663500	729500
58	11	CONVERTIBLE 58	FB	SDNSF	FBG	SV	IB	T14CD	DD	18		81500	5	3	664000	730000
60	1	COCKPIT SPORTS YACHT	FB	MYCPT	FBG	SV	IB	T820D	MAN	17	5	68000	4	10	525000	576500
64	7	MOTOR YACHT 65	FB	MY	FBG	SV	IB	T10CD	DD	17	4	91000	4	9	751500	825500
68	8	CONVERTIBLE 68	FB	SDNSF	FBG	SV	IB	T14CD	DD	18	11	54T	5	6	1.010M	1.095M
68	8	CONVERTIBLE 68	FB	SDNSF	FBG	SV	IB	T14CD	DD	18	11	54T	5	6	1.025M	1.115M
72		COCKPIT MOTOR YACHT	FB	MYCPT	FBG	SV	IB	T10CD	MAN	17	5	54T	4	10	**	**
72		MOTOR YACHT 72	FB	MY	FBG	SV	IB	T10CD	MAN	17	5	54T	4	10	**	**
		1994 BOATS														
39	4	CONVERTIBLE 38	FB	SDNSF	FBG	SV	IB	T485D	DD	14	2	32890	4	1	256500	281500
43		CONVERTIBLE 43	FB	SDNSF	FBG	SV	IB	T535D	DD	15	3	38595	4	3	300000	330000
43		SPORTFISH 43	FB	SF	FBG	SV	IB	T535D	GM	15	3	34500	4	3	270500	297500
47	2	CONVERTIBLE 47	FB	SDNSF	FBG	SV	IB	T680D	MAN	15	6	46300	4	5	368500	405000
50		MOTOR YACHT 50	FB	MY	FBG	SV	IB	T705D	DD	15		65216	4	3	496000	545000
50	7	CONVERTIBLE 50	FB	SDNSF	FBG	SV	IB	T820D	MAN	16	4	58814	4	9	449500	493500
53	7	CONVERTIBLE 53	FB	SDNSF	FBG	SV	IB	T820D	MAN	16	7	68600	4	10	492500	541500
54	1	SPORTS YACHT 54	FB	MY	FBG	SV	IB	T820D	MAN	17	5	75000	4	10	489000	537500
57	7	MOTOR YACHT 57	FB	MY	FBG	SV	IB	T820D	MAN	17	4	66000	4	5	556000	611000
58	11	CONVERTIBLE 58	FB	SDNSF	FBG	SV	IB	T11CD	MAN	18		81500	5	3	619000	680000
60	1	COCKPIT SPORTS YACHT	FB	MYCPT	FBG	SV	IB	T820D	MAN	17	5	68000	4	10	502500	552500
60	1	COCKPIT SPORTS YACHT	FB	MYCPT	FBG	SV	IB	T11CD	MAN	17	5	68000	4	10	562500	618500
64	7	COCKPIT MOTOR YACHT	FB	MYCPT	FBG	SV	IB	T10CD	MAN	17	4	91000	4	9	625000	686500
64	7	MOTOR YACHT 65	FB	MY	FBG	SV	IB	T10CD	MAN	17	4	91000	4	9	698500	767500
68	8	CONVERTIBLE 68	FB	SDNSF	FBG	SV	IB	T14CD	DD	18	11	54T	5	6	966500	1.050M
72		COCKPIT MOTOR YACHT	FB	MYCPT	FBG	SV	IB	T10CD	MAN	17	5	96813	4	10	**	**
72		MOTOR YACHT 72	FB	MY	FBG	SV	IB	T10CD	MAN	17	5	96813	4	10	**	**
		1993 BOATS														
39	4	CONVERTIBLE 38	FB	SDNSF	FBG	SV	IB	T485D	GM	14	2	32890	4	1	239000	263000
43		CONVERTIBLE 43	FB	SDNSF	FBG	SV	IB	T485D	GM	15	3	38595	4	3	272500	299000
45	5	CONVERTIBLE 45	FB	SDNSF	FBG	SV	IB	T550D	GM	15		39000	4		285500	313500
50		MOTOR YACHT 50	FB	MY	FBG	SV	IB	T735D	GM	15		65216	4	3	478000	525000
50	7	CONVERTIBLE 50	FB	SDNSF	FBG	SV	IB	T820D	MAN	16	4	58814	4	9	428000	470500
53	7	CONVERTIBLE 53	FB	SDNSF	FBG	SV	IB	T820D	MAN	16	7	68600	4	10	469500	516000
57	7	MOTOR YACHT 57	FB	MY	FBG	SV	IB	T820D	MAN	17	4	66000	4	5	529500	582000
58	11	CONVERTIBLE 58	FB	SDNSF	FBG	SV	IB	T11CD	MAN	18		81500	5	3	589500	648000
64	7	COCKPIT MOTOR YACHT	FB	MYCPT	FBG	SV	IB	T10CD	MAN	17	4	91000	4	9	596500	655500
64	7	MOTOR YACHT 65	FB	MY	FBG	SV	IB	T10CD	MAN	17	4	91000	4	9	664000	730000
72		COCKPIT MOTOR YACHT	FB	MYCPT	FBG	SV	IB	T10CD	MAN	17	5	96813	4	10	**	**
72		MOTOR YACHT 72	FB	MY	FBG	SV	IB	T10CD	MAN	17	5	96813	4	10	**	**
		1992 BOATS														
39	4	CONVERTIBLE 38	FB	SDNSF	FBG	SV	IB	T485D	GM	14	2	32890	4	1	228000	250500
43		CONVERTIBLE 43	FB	SDNSF	FBG	SV	IB	T485D	GM	15	3	38595	4	3	259500	285000
45	5	CONVERTIBLE 45	FB	SDNSF	FBG	SV	IB	T550D	GM	15		39000	4		272000	299000
50		MOTOR YACHT 50	FB	MY	FBG	SV	IB	T735D	GM	15		65216	4	3	455500	500500
50	7	CONVERTIBLE 50	FB	SDNSF	FBG	SV	IB	T735D	GM	16	4	58814	4	9	392000	431000
53	7	CONVERTIBLE 53	FB	SDNSF	FBG	SV	IB	T845D	MAN	16	7	68600	4	10	452000	496500
57	7	MOTOR YACHT 57	FB	MY	FBG	SV	IB	T735D	GM	17	4	66000	4	5	487000	535000
58	11	CONVERTIBLE 58	FB	SDNSF	FBG	SV	IB	T10CD	GM	18		81500	5	3	564500	620500
64	7	COCKPIT MOTOR YACHT	FB	MYCPT	FBG	SV	IB	T900D	GM	17	4	91000	4	9	567500	623500
64	7	MOTOR YACHT 65	FB	MY	FBG	SV	IB	T900D	GM	17	4	91000	4	9	634500	697000
72		COCKPIT MOTOR YACHT	FB	MYCPT	FBG	SV	IB	T10CD	GM	17	5	96813	4	10	**	**
72		MOTOR YACHT 72	FB	MY	FBG	SV	IB	T10CD	GM	17	5	96813	4	10	**	**
		1991 BOATS														
35		CONVERTIBLE 35	FB	SDNSF	FBG	SV	IB	T350	CRUS			20000			105000	115000
35		CONVERTIBLE 35	FB	SDNSF	FBG	SV	IB	T375D	CAT			20000			139500	153500
39	4	CONVERTIBLE 38	FB	SDNSF	FBG	SV	IB	T485D	GM	14	2	32890	4	1	217500	239000
43		CONVERTIBLE 43	FB	SDNSF	FBG	SV	IB	T485D	GM	15	3	38595	4	3	247500	272000
44		CONVERTIBLE 44	FB	MY	FBG	SV	IB	T485D	GM						262000	288000
45	5	CONVERTIBLE 45	FB	SDNSF	FBG	SV	IB	T550D	GM	15		39000	4		259500	285000
50		MOTOR YACHT 50	FB	MY	FBG	SV	IB	T735D	GM	15		65216	4	3	434500	477500
50	7	CONVERTIBLE 50	FB	SDNSF	FBG	SV	IB	T735D	GM	16	4	58814	4	9	374000	411000
53	7	CONVERTIBLE 53	FB	SDNSF	FBG	SV	IB	T845D	MAN	16	7	68600	4	10	431000	474000
57	7	MOTOR YACHT 57	FB	MY	FBG	SV	IB	T735D	GM	17	4	66000	4	5	464500	510500
58	11	CONVERTIBLE 58	FB	SDNSF	FBG	SV	IB	T11CD	GM	18		81500	5	3	554000	608500
64	7	MOTOR YACHT	FB	MY	FBG	SV	IB	T900D	GM	17	4	91000	4	9	523000	575000
64	7	MOTOR YACHT 65	FB	MY	FBG	SV	IB	T900D	GM	17	4	91000	4	9	604500	664500
72		COCKPIT MOTOR YACHT	FB	MYCPT	FBG	SV	IB	T10CD	GM	17	5	96813	4	10	**	**
72		MOTOR YACHT 72	FB	MY	FBG	SV	IB	T10CD	GM	17	5	96813	4	10	**	**
		1990 BOATS														
35		CONVERTIBLE 35	FB	SDNSF	FBG	SV	IB	T330	CRUS	13	1	20000	4	1	96600	106000
35		CONVERTIBLE 35	FB	SDNSF	FBG	SV	IB	T375D	CAT	13	1	20000	4	1	130000	143000
35		CONVERTIBLE 35	FB	SDNSF	FBG	SV	IB	T400D	GM	13	1	20000	4	1	130500	143500
39	4	CONVERTIBLE 38	FB	SDNSF	FBG	SV	IB	T330	CRUS	14	2	32890	4	1	168500	185500
39	4	CONVERTIBLE 38	FB	SDNSF	FBG	SV	IB	T425D	CAT	14	2	32890	4	1	205000	225500
39	4	CONVERTIBLE 38	FB	SDNSF	FBG	SV	IB	T425D	GM	14	2	32890	4	1	200000	219500

VIKING YACHT COMPANY -CONTINUED See inside cover to adjust price for area

LOA FT	LOA IN	NAME AND/ OR MODEL	TOP/ RIG	BOAT TYPE	-HULL- MTL	-HULL- TP	TP	ENGINE # HP	ENGINE MFG	BEAM FT	BEAM IN	WGT LBS	DRAFT FT	DRAFT IN	RETAIL LOW	RETAIL HIGH
		1990 BOATS														
41	2	CONVERTIBLE 41	FB	SDNSF	FBG	SV	IB	T330	CRUS	14	10	32000	4	3	166000	182000
41	2	CONVERTIBLE 41	FB	SDNSF	FBG	SV	IB	T375D	CAT	14	10	32000	4	3	197500	217000
41	2	CONVERTIBLE 41	FB	SDNSF	FBG	SV	IB	T485D	GM	14	10	32000	4	3	210000	230500
43		CONVERTIBLE 43	FB	SDNSF	FBG	SV	IB	T485D	GM	15	3	38595	4	3	239500	263500
44		DOUBLE CABIN MY	FB	DCMY	FBG	SV	IB	T485D	GM	15		40000	4		235500	258500
45	5	CONVERTIBLE 45	FB	SDNSF	FBG	SV	IB	T485D	GM	15		39000	4		236000	259500
45	5	CONVERTIBLE 45	FB	SDNSF	FBG	SV	IB	T550D	GM	15		39000	4		247500	272000
48	7	CONVERTIBLE	FB	SDNSF	FBG	SV	IB	T735D	GM	16		45500	4	7	298000	327500
50		COCKPIT MOTOR YACHT	FB	MYCPT	FBG	SV	IB	T485D	GM	15		43000	4		276000	303500
50		MOTOR YACHT 50	FB	MY	FBG	SV	IB	T735D	DD	15		65216	4	3	415000	456000
53	7	CONVERTIBLE 53	FB	SDNSF	FBG	SV	IB	T735D	GM	16	7	60000	4	10	357000	392500
53	7	CONVERTIBLE 53	FB	SDNSF	FBG	SV	IB	T845D	MAN	16	7	60000	4	10	377500	414500
55	7	WALK AROUND MY 55	FB	MY	FBG	SV	IB	T735D	GM	17	4	56000	4	5	396000	435500
55	7	WIDE BODY MY 55	FB	MY	FBG	SV	IB	T735D	GM	17	4	56000	4	5	388500	427000
57	2	CONVERTIBLE 57	FB	SDNSF	FBG	SV	IB	T11CD	GM	18		69000	5	3	510000	560500
62	6	COCKPIT MY 63	FB	MYCPT	FBG	SV	IB	T735D	GM	17	4	61500	4	9	435000	478000
62	6	EXTENDED FT DECK 63	FB	MY	FBG	SV	IB	T735D	GM	17	4	61500	4	9	437500	481000
62	6	EXTENDED FT DECK 63	FB	MY	FBG	SV	IB	T900D	GM	17	4	61500	4	9	479000	526000
62	6	WIDE BODY MY 63	FB	MY	FBG	SV	IB	T735D	GM	17	4	61500	4	9	422000	464000
62	6	WIDE BODY MY 63	FB	MY	FBG	SV	IB	T900D	GM	17	4	61500	4	9	463000	508500
72		MOTOR YACHT 72	FB	MY	FBG	SV	IB	T900D	GM	17	5	84000	4	9	**	**
72		MOTOR YACHT 72	FB	MY	FBG	SV	IB	T10CD	GM	17	5	84000	4	9	**	**
72	6	COCKPIT MOTOR YACHT	FB	MYCPT	FBG	SV	IB	T900D	GM	17	4	96813	4	10	**	**
72	6	COCKPIT MOTOR YACHT	FB	MYCPT	FBG	SV	IB	T10CD	GM	17	4	98613	4	10	**	**
		1989 BOATS														
35		CONVERTIBLE 35	FB	SDNSF	FBG	SV	IB	T330	CRUS	13	1	20000	4	1	92000	101000
35		CONVERTIBLE 35	FB	SDNSF	FBG	SV	IB	T375D	CAT	13	1	20000	4	1	124500	136500
35		CONVERTIBLE 35	FB	SDNSF	FBG	SV	IB	T400D	GM	13	1	20000	4	1	125000	137500
41	2	CONVERTIBLE 41	FB	SDNSF	FBG	SV	IB	T330	CRUS	14	10	32000	4	3	158500	174000
41	2	CONVERTIBLE 41	FB	SDNSF	FBG	SV	IB	T375D	CAT	14	10	32000	4	3	188500	207500
41	2	CONVERTIBLE 41	FB	SDNSF	FBG	SV	IB	T485D	GM	14	10	32000	4	3	200500	220000
44		DOUBLE CABIN MY	FB	DCMY	FBG	SV	IB	T485D	GM	15		40000	4		225000	247000
45	5	CONVERTIBLE 45	FB	SDNSF	FBG	SV	IB	T485D	GM	15		39000	4		225500	247500
45	5	CONVERTIBLE 45	FB	SDNSF	FBG	SV	IB	T550D	GM	15		39000	4		236500	259500
48	7	CONVERTIBLE	FB	SDNSF	FBG	SV	IB	T735D	GM	16		45500	4	7	284500	313000
50		COCKPIT MOTOR YACHT	FB	MYCPT	FBG	SV	IB	T485D	GM	15		43000	4		259000	284500
55	7	MOTOR YACHT 55	FB	MY	FBG	SV	IB	T735D	GM	17	4	56000	4	5	368000	404500
57	2	CONVERTIBLE 57	FB	SDNSF	FBG	SV	IB	T11CD	GM	18		69000	5	3	487000	535500
62	6	COCKPIT MY 63	FB	MYCPT	FBG	SV	IB	T735D	GM	17	4	61500	4	9	415500	456500
62	6	MOTOR YACHT 63	FB	MY	FBG	SV	IB	T735D	GM	17	4	61500	4	9	410500	451000
69	6	COCKPIT MY 70	FB	MYCPT	FBG	SV	IB	T900D	GM	17	4	73300	4	9	570500	627000
72		MOTOR YACHT 72	FB	MY	FBG	SV	IB	T900D	GM	17	5	79000	4	9	**	**
		1988 BOATS														
35		CONVERTIBLE	FB	SDNSF	FBG	SV	IB	T350	CRUS	13	1	20000	4	1	88300	97100
35		CONVERTIBLE	FB	SDNSF	FBG	SV	IB	T375D	CAT	13	1	20000	4	1	119000	131000
35		CONVERTIBLE	FB	SDNSF	FBG	SV	IB	T375D	GM	13	1	20000	4	1	117500	129000
41	2	CONVERTIBLE	FB	SDNSF	FBG	SV	IB	T350	CRUS	14	10	32000	4	3	151500	166500
41	2	CONVERTIBLE	FB	SDNSF	FBG	SV	IB	T375D	CAT	14	1	32000	4	3	181500	199500
41	2	CONVERTIBLE	FB	SDNSF	FBG	SV	IB	T485D	GM	14	10	32000	4	3	189500	208000
44		DOUBLE CABIN MY	FB	DCMY	FBG	SV	IB	T485D	GM	15		40000	4		215000	236000
45	5	CONVERTIBLE 45	FB	SDNSF	FBG	SV	IB	T485D	GM	15		39000	4		215500	236500
48	7	CONVERTIBLE	FB	SDNSF	FBG	SV	IB	T565D	GM	16		45500	4	7	247000	271500
48	7	CONVERTIBLE	FB	SDNSF	FBG	SV	IB	T735D	GM	16		45500	4	7	272000	299000
48	7	MOTORYACHT	FB	MY	FBG	SV	IB	T735D	GM	16		48500	4	7	279500	307000
50		COCKPIT MOTOR YACHT	FB	MYCPT	FBG	SV	IB	T450D	GM	15		43000	4		233500	257000
55	7	COCKPIT MOTOR YACHT	FB	MYCPT	FBG	SV	IB	T735D	GM	16		55570	4	7	360500	396000
57	2	CONVERTIBLE 57	FB	SDNSF	FBG	SV	IB	T D	GM	17	6	69000	5	6	**	**
		1987 BOATS														
35		CONVERTIBLE	FB	SDNSF	FBG	SV	IB	T350	CRUS	13	1	20000	4	1	84300	92600
35		CONVERTIBLE	FB	SDNSF	FBG	SV	IB	T375D	CAT	13	1	20000	4	1	114000	125500
35		CONVERTIBLE	FB	SDNSF	FBG	SV	IB	T375D	GM	13	1	20000	4	1	112500	123500
41	2	CONVERTIBLE	FB	SDNSF	FBG	SV	IB	T350	CRUS	14	10	32000	4	3	145000	159000
41	2	CONVERTIBLE	FB	SDNSF	FBG	SV	IB	T375D	CAT	14	1	32000	4	3	173500	191000
41	2	CONVERTIBLE	FB	SDNSF	FBG	SV	IB	T450D	GM	14	10	32000	4	3	176500	194000
44		DOUBLE CABIN MY	FB	DCMY	FBG	SV	IB	T450D	GM	15		40000	4		201000	220500
45	5	CONVERTIBLE 45	FB	SDNSF	FBG	SV	IB	T485D	GM	15		39000	4		206000	226000
48	7	CONVERTIBLE	FB	SDNSF	FBG	SV	IB	T565D	GM	16		45500	4	7	236000	259500
48	7	CONVERTIBLE	FB	SDNSF	FBG	SV	IB	T710D	GM	16		45500	4	7	256500	282000
48	7	MOTORYACHT	FB	MY	FBG	SV	IB	T565D	GM	16		48500	4	7	236500	260000
48	7	MOTORYACHT	FB	MY	FBG	SV	IB	T710D	GM	16		48500	4	7	251500	276500
50		COCKPIT MOTOR YACHT	FB	MYCPT	FBG	SV	IB	T450D	GM	15		43000	4		213000	234000
		1986 BOATS														
35		CONVERTIBLE	FB	SDNSF	FBG	SV	IB	T350	CRUS	13	1	20000	2	5	80400	88400
		IB T320D CAT 105000 115500, IB T375D CAT 109500 120000, IB T375D GM													108000	118500
35		SPORTFISHERMAN	OP	SF	FBG	SV	IB	T350	CRUS	13	1	19000	2	5	78600	86300
		IB T320D CAT 102000 112000, IB T375D CAT 106500 117000, IB T375D GM													105000	115500
35		SPORTFISHERMAN	TT	SF	FBG	SV	IB	T350	CRUS	13	1	19000	2	5	78600	86300
		IB T320D CAT 102000 112000, IB T375D CAT 104500 115000, IB T375D GM													106500	117000
41	2	CONVERTIBLE	FB	SDNSF	FBG	SV	IB	T350	CRUS	14	10	27900	3	10	124000	136000
41	2	CONVERTIBLE	FB	SDNSF	FBG	SV	IB	T375D	CAT	14	1	30000	3	10	159000	175000
41	2	CONVERTIBLE	FB	SDNSF	FBG	SV	IB	T450D	J&T	14	10	32000	3	10	170000	186500
44		DOUBLE CABIN MY	FB	DCMY	FBG	SV	IB	T350	CRUS	15		40000	3	10	160500	176500
44		DOUBLE CABIN MY	FB	DCMY	FBG	SV	IB	T375D	CAT	15		40000	3	10	185500	203500
44		MOTOR YACHT	FB	DCMY	FBG	SV	IB	T450D	J&T	15		40000	3	10	188500	207500
48	7	CONVERTIBLE	FB	SDNSF	FBG	SV	IB	T565D	J&T	16		45500	4	7	227000	249500
48	7	CONVERTIBLE	FB	SDNSF	FBG	SV	IB	T710D	J&T	16		45500	4	7	246000	270500
48	7	MOTORYACHT	FB	MY	FBG	SV	IB	T565D	GM	16		48500	4	7	226000	248500
48	7	MOTORYACHT	FB	MY	FBG	SV	IB	T710D	GM	16		48500	4	7	240500	264000
50		COCKPIT MOTOR YACHT	FB	MYCPT	FBG	SV	IB	T450D	J&T	15		43000	3	10	206000	226000
		1985 BOATS														
35		CONVERTIBLE	FB	SDNSF	FBG	SV	IB	T350	CRUS	13	1	20000	2	5	76800	84400
35		CONVERTIBLE	FB	SDNSF	FBG	SV	IB	T300D	CAT	13	1	20000	2	5	99400	109000
35		CONVERTIBLE	FB	SDNSF	FBG	SV	IB	T355D	CAT	13	1	20000	2	5	103500	113500
35		SPORTFISHERMAN	OP	SF	FBG	SV	IB	T350	CRUS	13	1	19000	2	5	75000	82500
35		SPORTFISHERMAN	OP	SF	FBG	SV	IB	T300D	CAT	13	1	19000	2	5	96500	106000
35		SPORTFISHERMAN	OP	SF	FBG	SV	IB	T355D	CAT	13	1	19000	2	5	100500	110500
41	2	CONVERTIBLE	FB	SDNSF	FBG	SV	IB	T350	CRUS	14	10	27900	3	10	118500	130000
		IB T300D 145500 160000, IB T355D CAT 147000 161500, IB T450D J&T													162500	178500
44		DOUBLE CABIN MY	FB	DCMY	FBG	SV	IB	T350	CRUS	15		40000	3	10	153500	169000
		IB T300D 167000 183500, IB T355D CAT 175000 192500, IB T450D J&T													184500	203000
46	6	CONVERTIBLE	FB	SDNSF	FBG	SV	IB	T450D		16		44000	4	7	195500	215000
46	6	CONVERTIBLE	FB	SDNSF	FBG	SV	IB	T565D	J&T	16		42400	4	7	208000	228500
46	6	CONVERTIBLE	FB	SDNSF	FBG	SV	IB	T675D	J&T	16		44000	4	7	225500	248000
48	7	CONVERTIBLE	FB	SDNSF	FBG	SV	IB	T565D	J&T	16		45500	4	7	217000	238500
48	7	CONVERTIBLE	FB	SDNSF	FBG	SV	IB	T710D	J&T	16		45500	4	7	235500	259000
50		COCKPIT MOTOR YACHT	FB	MYCPT	FBG	SV	IB	T300D		15		43000	3	10	177000	194500
50		COCKPIT MOTOR YACHT	FB	MYCPT	FBG	SV	IB	T355D	CAT	15		43000	3	10	184000	202000
50		COCKPIT MOTOR YACHT	FB	MYCPT	FBG	SV	IB	T450D	J&T	15		43000	3	10	197000	216500
		1984 BOATS														
35		CONVERTIBLE	FB	SDNSF	FBG	SV	IB	T350	CRUS	13	1	20000	2	5	73400	80700
		IB T300D CAT 95400 105000, IB T300D J&T 94600 104000, IB T355D CAT													99100	109000
35		SPORTFISHERMAN	OP	SF	FBG	SV	IB	T350	CRUS	13	1	19000	2	5	71700	78800
		IB T300D CAT 92600 102000, IB T300D J&T 91900 101000, IB T355D CAT													96400	106000
41	2	CONVERTIBLE	FB	SDNSF	FBG	SV	IB	T350	CRUS	14	10	32000	3	10	127000	139500
		IB T300D CAT 142000 156000, IB T300D J&T 140000 154000, IB T355D CAT													147500	162000
		IB T410D J&T 151500 166000, IB T450D J&T 156000 171000														
44		DOUBLE CABIN MY	FB	DCMY	FBG	SV	IB	T350	CRUS	15		40000	3	10	147000	161500
		IB T300D CAT 161500 177500, IB T300D J&T 160500 176500, IB T355D CAT													167500	184500
		IB T410D J&T 172500 189500, IB T450D J&T 177000 194500														
46	6	CONV TRIPLE STRM	FB	SDNSF	FBG	SV	IB	T450D	J&T	16		44000	4	7	185500	204000
46	6	CONVERTIBLE DBL STRM	FB	SDNSF	FBG	SV	IB	T450D	J&T	16		44000	4	7	181500	199500
46	6	CONVERTIBLE DBL STRM	FB	SDNSF	FBG	SV	IB	T530D	J&T	16		44000	4	7	190000	209000
46	6	CONVERTIBLE DBL STRM	FB	SDNSF	FBG	SV	IB	T675D	J&T	16		44000	4	7	204000	224500
46	6	CONVERTIBLE STRM	FB	SDNSF	FBG	SV	IB	T530D	J&T	16		44000	4	7	193500	213000
46	6	CONVERTIBLE TRI	FB	SDNSF	FBG	SV	IB	T675D	J&T	16		44000	4	7	207000	227000
50		COCKPIT MOTOR YACHT	FB	MYCPT	FBG	SV	IB	T300D	J&T	15		43000	3	10	170000	186500
		IB T355D CAT 176000 193500, IB T410D J&T 183000 201000, IB T450D J&T													188500	207000

....For earlier years, see the BUC Used Boat Price Guide, Volume 3

VINDICATOR BY VIP
DIV OF VIVIAN INDUSTRIES INC
VIVIAN LA 71082

See inside cover to adjust price for area

For more recent years, see the BUC Used Boat Price Guide, Volume 1

LOA FT IN	NAME AND/ OR MODEL	TOP/ RIG	BOAT TYPE	-HULL- MTL TP	----ENGINE--- TP # HP MFG	BEAM FT IN	WGT LBS	DRAFT FT IN	RETAIL LOW	RETAIL HIGH
				1996 BOATS						
19	VINDICATOR 1900	OP	CUD	FBG SV	IO 210-280	8	2550		6150	7600
21	VINDICATOR 2100	OP	CUD	FBG SV	IO 210-300	8 6	3950		9500	11700
21	VINDICATOR 2100	OP	CUD	FBG SV	IO 335 MRCR	8 6	3950		11000	12500
24 4	VINDICATOR 2400	OP	CUD	FBG SV	IO 250-300	8 6	4000		11300	13600
24 4	VINDICATOR 2400	OP	CUD	FBG SV	IO 330-350	8 6	4000		12500	14900
24 4	VINDICATOR 2400	OP	CUD	FBG SV	IO 385-415	8 6	4000		14000	17400
24 4	VINDICATOR 2440 BR	OP	RNBT	FBG SV	IO 250-300	8 6	4000		10700	12800
24 4	VINDICATOR 2440 BR	OP	RNBT	FBG SV	IO 330-350	8 6	4000		11800	13900
24 4	VINDICATOR 2440 BR	OP	RNBT	FBG SV	IO 385-415	8 6	4000		13400	16400

VINDO MARIN
VINDO NORTH AMERICA INC
NEW LONDON NH 03257

See inside cover to adjust price for area

LOA FT IN	NAME AND/ OR MODEL	TOP/ RIG	BOAT TYPE	-HULL- MTL TP	----ENGINE--- TP # HP MFG	BEAM FT IN	WGT LBS	DRAFT FT IN	RETAIL LOW	RETAIL HIGH
				1987 BOATS						
29 3	VINDO 32	SLP	SA/CR	FBG KL SD	13D VLVO	9 1	7040	4 3	37300	41400
33 8	VINDO 45	SLP	SA/CR	FBG KL SD	28D VLVO	11	13000	5 2	70700	77700
38 6	VINDO 65 MIX	KTH	SA/CR	FBG KL SD	65D VLVO	12 2	21000	6 3	117500	129000
				1985 BOATS						
29	VINDO 29	SLP	SA/CR	FBG KL IB	D	9 1	7040	4	33400	37100
29 3	VINDO 32	SLP	SA/CR	FBG KL SD	13D VLVO	9 1	7040	4 3	33500	37200
33 8	VINDO 45	SLP	SA/CR	FBG KL SD	35D VLVO	10 10		5 2	67300	74000
38	VINDO 38	KTH	SA/CR	FBG KL IB	D	12 2	21000	6 3	103500	113500
38 6	VINDO 65 MIX	KTH	MS	FBG KL SD	61D VLVO	12 2	21000	6 3	105500	116000
38 6	VINDO 65 MS	KTH	MS	FBG KL SD	61D VLVO	12 2	21000	6 3	105500	116000
38 6	VINDO 65 S	SLP	SA/CR	FBG KL SD	61D VLVO	12 2	21000	6 3	105500	116000
				1984 BOATS						
29 3	VINDO 32	SLP	SA/CR	FBG KL SD	13D VLVO	9 1	7040	4 3	31700	35200
33 9	VINDO 45	SLP	SA/CR	FBG KL SD	35D VLVO	10 11	13000	5 3	60200	66200
38 6	VINDO 65 MIX	KTH	SA/CR	FBG KL SD	51D VLVO	12 2	21000	6	99600	109500
38 6	VINDO 65 MS	KTH	MS	FBG KL SD	51D VLVO	12 2	21000	6	99600	109500
38 6	VINDO 65 S	SLP	SA/CR	FBG KL SD	51D VLVO	12 2	21000	6	99600	109500

....For earlier years, see the BUC Used Boat Price Guide, Volume 3

VISTA YACHT CO INC
PATCHAGUE NY 11772   COAST GUARD MFG ID- EEE See inside cover to adjust price for area

LOA FT IN	NAME AND/ OR MODEL	TOP/ RIG	BOAT TYPE	-HULL- MTL TP	----ENGINE--- TP # HP MFG	BEAM FT IN	WGT LBS	DRAFT FT IN	RETAIL LOW	RETAIL HIGH
				1994 BOATS						
42 10	VISTA 43	FB	TCMY	FBG SV	IB T210D CAT	15	32000	3 6	172000	189000
	IB T320D CAT 191500 210500,				IB T375D CAT 201000 221000,				IB T425D CAT 210500 231000	
46	VISTA 46 CONVERTIBLE	FB	SDN	FBG SV	IB T425D GM	15	36000	3 10	224500	246500
	IB T485D GM 230500 253000,				IB T550D GM 237000 260500,				IB T735D GM 253000 278000	
46 6	VISTA 46 MY	FB	TCMY	FBG SV	IB T210D CAT	15	36000	3 8	178500	196000
	IB T320D CAT 201000 220500,				IB T375D CAT 212500 233500,				IB T425D CAT 222500 244500	
48	VISTA 48 SPORTFISH	FB	SF	FBG DV	IB T425D CAT	16	36000	3 10	219500	241000
	IB T485D GM 235000 258000,				IB T550D GM 250500 275500,				IB T735D GM 291000 319500	
49 6	VISTA 49	FB	MY	FBG SV	IB T210D CAT	15	37500	3 10	183500	201500
	IB T320D CAT 196000 215500,				IB T375D CAT 205000 225000,				IB T425D CAT 214500 235500	
49 6	VISTA 49 COCKPIT MY	FB	TCMY	FBG SV	IB T210D CAT	15	38000	3 10	185500	203500
	IB T320D CAT 205500 225500,				IB T375D CAT 219000 240500,				IB T425D CAT 231000 254000	
49 6	VISTA 49 MY	FB	YTFS	FBG SV	IB T210D CAT	15	36000	3 10	167500	184000
	IB T320D CAT 198500 218000,				IB T375D CAT 217000 238500,				IB T425D CAT 232500 255500	
50 4	VISTA 50 TOURNAMENT	FB	SF	FBG DV	IB T485D GM	16	37000	3 10	240500	264500
50 4	VISTA 50 TOURNAMENT	FB	SF	FBG DV	IB T550D GM	16	37000	3 10	258000	283500
50 4	VISTA 50 TOURNAMENT	FB	SF	FBG DV	IB T735D GM	16	37000	3 10	303500	333500
52	VISTA 52	FB	MY	FBG SV	IB T210D CAT	15	40000	4	189500	208000
	IB T320D CAT 209000 229500,				IB T375D CAT 223500 245500,				IB T425D CAT 238000 261500	
52	VISTA 52 COCKPIT MY	FB	TCMY	FBG SV	IB T210D CAT	15 5	42000	4	198500	218000
	IB T320D CAT 227500 250000,				IB T375D CAT 245500 269500,				IB T425D CAT 261000 286500	
52	VISTA 52 MY	FB	YTFS	FBG SV	IB T210D CAT	15 5	42000	4	183000	201500
	IB T320D CAT 220000 242000,				IB T375D CAT 240000 263500,				IB T425D CAT 256500 281500	
				1993 BOATS						
42 10	VISTA 43	FB	TCMY	FBG SV	IB T210D CAT	15	32000	3 6	164000	180500
	IB T320D CAT 182500 200500,				IB T375D CAT 191500 210500,				IB T425D CAT 200500 220000	
46	VISTA 46 CONVERTIBLE	FB	SDN	FBG SV	IB T425D GM	15	36000	3 10	214000	235000
	IB T485D GM 219500 241000,				IB T550D GM 225500 248000,				IB T735D GM 241000 264500	
46 6	VISTA 46 MY	FB	TCMY	FBG SV	IB T210D CAT	15	36000	3 8	170000	187000
	IB T320D CAT 191500 210000,				IB T375D CAT 202000 222000,				IB T425D CAT 212000 232500	
48	VISTA 48 SPORTFISH	FB	SF	FBG DV	IB T425D CAT	16	36000	3 10	209000	230000
	IB T485D GM 224000 246000,				IB T550D GM 238500 262500,				IB T735D GM 277000 304500	
49 6	VISTA 49	FB	MY	FBG SV	IB T210D CAT	15	37500	3 10	174500	191500
	IB T320D CAT 186500 205000,				IB T375D CAT 195000 214500,				IB T425D CAT 204000 224500	
49 6	VISTA 49 COCKPIT MY	FB	TCMY	FBG SV	IB T210D CAT	15	38000	3 10	176500	194000
	IB T320D CAT 195500 215000,				IB T375D CAT 208500 229000,				IB T425D CAT 220000 242000	
49 6	VISTA 49 MY	FB	YTFS	FBG SV	IB T210D CAT	15	36000	3 10	159500	175000
	IB T320D CAT 189000 207500,				IB T375D CAT 206500 227000,				IB T425D CAT 221500 243500	
50 4	VISTA 50 TOURNAMENT	FB	SF	FBG DV	IB T485D GM	16	37000	3 10	229000	252500
50 4	VISTA 50 TOURNAMENT	FB	SF	FBG DV	IB T550D GM	16	37000	3 10	246000	270500
50 4	VISTA 50 TOURNAMENT	FB	SF	FBG DV	IB T735D GM	16	37000	3 10	289000	317500
52	VISTA 52	FB	MY	FBG SV	IB T210D CAT	15	40000	4	181000	199000
	IB T320D CAT 199500 219000,				IB T375D CAT 213000 234000,				IB T425D CAT 226500 249000	
52	VISTA 52 COCKPIT MY	FB	TCMY	FBG SV	IB T210D CAT	15 5	42000	4	189500	208000
	IB T320D CAT 216500 238000,				IB T375D CAT 234000 257000,				IB T425D CAT 248500 273000	
52	VISTA 52 MY	FB	YTFS	FBG SV	IB T210D CAT	15 5	42000	4	174500	192000
	IB T320D CAT 210000 230500,				IB T375D CAT 228500 251000,				IB T425D CAT 244000 268500	
				1992 BOATS						
42 10	VISTA 43	FB	TCMY	FBG SV	IB T210D CAT	15	32000	3 6	156500	172000
	IB T320D CAT 174000 191000,				IB T375D CAT 182500 201000,				IB T425D CAT 191000 210000	
46	VISTA 46 CONVERTIBLE	FB	SDN	FBG SV	IB T425D GM	15	36000	3 10	204000	224000
	IB T485D GM 209000 230000,				IB T550D GM 215000 236500,				IB T735D GM 229500 252500	
46 6	VISTA 46 MY	FB	TCMY	FBG SV	IB T210D CAT	15	36000	3 8	162000	178000
	IB T320D CAT 182500 200500,				IB T375D CAT 193000 212000,				IB T425D CAT 202000 222000	
48	VISTA 48 SPORTFISH	FB	SF	FBG DV	IB T425D CAT	16	36000	3 10	199500	219000
	IB T485D GM 213500 234500,				IB T550D GM 227500 250000,				IB T735D GM 264000 290000	
49 6	VISTA 49	FB	MY	FBG SV	IB T210D CAT	15 5	37500	3 10	166000	182500
49 6	VISTA 49	FB	MY	FBG SV	IB T375D CAT	15 5	37500	3 10	186000	204000
49 6	VISTA 49	FB	MY	FBG SV	IB T425D CAT	15 5	37500	3 10	194500	213500
49 6	VISTA 49	FB	YTFS	FBG SV	IB T210D CAT	15	36000	3 10	151000	166000
	IB T320D CAT 172500 189500,				IB T375D CAT 188500 207000,				IB T425D CAT 202000 222000	
49 6	VISTA 49 COCKPIT MY	FB	TCMY	FBG SV	IB T210D CAT	15	38000	3 10	168000	184500
	IB T320D CAT 186500 204500,				IB T375D CAT 198500 218500,				IB T425D CAT 210000 230500	
50 4	VISTA 50 TOURNAMENT	FB	SF	FBG DV	IB T485D GM	16	37000	3 10	218500	240000
50 4	VISTA 50 TOURNAMENT	FB	SF	FBG DV	IB T550D GM	16	37000	3 10	234500	257500
50 4	VISTA 50 TOURNAMENT	FB	SF	FBG DV	IB T735D GM	16	37000	3 10	275500	302500
52	VISTA 52	FB	MY	FBG SV	IB T210D CAT	15	40000	4	173000	190000
	IB T320D CAT 190500 209000,				IB T375D CAT 203500 223500,				IB T425D CAT 216000 237500	
52	VISTA 52 COCKPIT MY	FB	TCMY	FBG SV	IB T210D CAT	15 5	42000	4	181000	199000
	IB T320D CAT 206500 227000,				IB T375D CAT 223000 245000,				IB T425D CAT 237000 260500	
52	VISTA 52 MY	FB	YTFS	FBG SV	IB T210D CAT	15 5	42000	4	166500	183000
	IB T320D CAT 200000 220000,				IB T375D CAT 218000 239500,				IB T425D CAT 233000 256000	
				1991 BOATS						
36 6	VISTA 36	FB	TCMY	FBG SV	IB T150D CUM	14 1	26000	3 6	106000	116500
36 6	VISTA 36	FB	TCMY	FBG SV	IB T210D CUM	14 1	26000	3 6	107500	118000
36 6	VISTA 36	FB	TCMY	FBG SV	IB T250D CUM	14 1	26000	3 6	109000	120000

```
       LOA   NAME AND/         TOP/ BOAT  -HULL- ----ENGINE--- BEAM    WGT  DRAFT RETAIL RETAIL
       FT IN OR MODEL          RIG  TYPE  MTL TP TP # HP MFG   FT IN   LBS  FT IN  LOW    HIGH
-------------------- 1991 BOATS -----------------------------------------------------------------
       37 10 VISTA 38          FB   TCMY  FBG SV IB T150D CUM  14 1  27000  3  6 117500 129500
       37 10 VISTA 38          FB   TCMY  FBG SV IB T210D CUM  14 1  27000  3  6 119500 131500
       37 10 VISTA 38          FB   TCMY  FBG SV IB T250D CUM  14 1  27000  3  6 121500 133500
       37 10 VISTA 38 SPORT CNV FB  SDN   FBG SV IB T300D GM   14 5  25000  2  7 117000 129000
       37 10 VISTA 38 SPORT CNV FB  SDN   FBG SV IB T375D CAT  14 5  25000  2  7 126500 139000
       37 10 VISTA 38 SPORT CNV FB  SDN   FBG SV IB T400D GM   14 5  25000  2  7 128000 140000
       39  6 VISTA 40          FB   TCMY  FBG SV IB T150D CUM  14 1  31000  3  6 141500 155500
       39  6 VISTA 40          FB   TCMY  FBG SV IB T210D CUM  14 1  31000  3  6 144000 158500
       39  6 VISTA 40          FB   TCMY  FBG SV IB T250D CUM  14 1  31000  3  6 146000 160500
       42 10 VISTA 43          FB   TCMY  FBG SV IB T210D CAT  15 5  32000  3  6 149000 164000
          IB T320D CAT 166000 182500, IB T375D CAT 174500 191500, IB T425D CAT 182000 200000

       46    VISTA 46 CONVERTIBLE FB SDN  FBG SV IB T425D GM   15 5  36000  3 10 194500 213500
          IB T485D GM 199500 219500, IB T550D GM 205000 225500, IB T735D GM 219000 240500

       46  6 VISTA 46 MY       FB   TCMY  FBG SV IB T210D CAT  15    36000  3  8 154500 169500
          IB T320D CAT 174000 191500, IB T375D CAT 184000 202000, IB T425D CAT 192500 211500

       48    VISTA 48 SPORTFISH FB  SF    FBG DV IB T425D CAT  16    36000  3 10 190000 209000
          IB T485D GM 203500 223500, IB T550D GM 217000 238500, IB T735D GM 252000 277000

       49  6 VISTA 49          FB   MY    FBG SV IB T210D CAT  15 5  37500  3 10 158000 173500
          IB T320D CAT 169000 186000, IB T375D CAT 177000 194500, IB T425D CAT 185500 203500

       49  6 VISTA 49          FB   YTFS  FBG SV IB T210D CAT  15    36000  3 10 144000 158000
          IB T320D CAT 164500 181000, IB T375D CAT 180000 197500, IB T425D CAT 193000 212000

       49  6 VISTA 49 MY W/COCKPT FB TCMY FBG SV IB T210D CAT  15    38000  3 10 159500 175500
          IB T320D CAT 173000 190000, IB T375D CAT 183000 201000, IB T425D CAT 192500 211500

       50  4 VISTA 50 TOURNAMENT FB SF    FBG DV IB T425D GM   16    37000  3 10 193500 212500
          IB T485D GM 208500 229000, IB T550D GM 223500 246000, IB T735D GM 262500 288500

       52    VISTA 52          FB   MY    FBG SV IB T210D CAT  15    40000  4    165500 181500
          IB T320D CAT 182000 199500, IB T375D CAT 194000 213000, IB T425D CAT 206000 226500

       52    VISTA 52 MY       FB   YTFS  FBG SV IB T210D CAT  15 5  42000  4    159500 175000
          IB T320D CAT 191000 209500, IB T375D CAT 208000 228500, IB T425D CAT 220000 244000

       52    VISTA 52 MY W/COCKPT FB TCMY FBG SV IB T210D CAT  15 5  42000  4    172500 189500
          IB T320D CAT 192500 211500, IB T375D CAT 206500 227000, IB T425D CAT 219500 241000

       55    VISTA 55 MY W/COCKPT FB MY   FBG SV IB T270D CUM                    215000 236000
          IB T320D CUM 221000 242500, IB T375D CAT 236000 249500, IB T400D GM 229500 252500
          IB T425D GM 232000 255000, IB T485D GM 238000 261500

       55    VISTA 55 YACHTFISH FB  YTFS  FBG SV IB T270D CUM                    227500 250000
          IB T320D CUM 235000 258500, IB T375D CAT 243000 267500, IB T400D GM 245500 270000
          IB T425D GM 249000 273500, IB T485D GM 256000 281500

-------------------- 1990 BOATS -----------------------------------------------------------------
       36  6 VISTA 36          FB   TCMY  FBG SV IB T150D CUM  14 1  26000  3  6 101000 111000
       36  6 VISTA 36          FB   TCMY  FBG SV IB T210D CUM  14 1  26000  3  6 102500 112500
       36  6 VISTA 36          FB   TCMY  FBG SV IB T250D CUM  14 1  26000  3  6 104000 114500
       37 10 VISTA 38          FB   TCMY  FBG SV IB T150D CUM  14 1  27000  3  6 112000 123500
       37 10 VISTA 38          FB   TCMY  FBG SV IB T210D CUM  14 1  27000  3  6 114000 125500
       37 10 VISTA 38          FB   TCMY  FBG SV IB T250D CUM  14 1  27000  3  6 116000 127500
       37 10 VISTA 38 SPORT CNV FB  SDN   FBG SV IB T300D GM   14 5  25000  2  7 112000 123000
       37 10 VISTA 38 SPORT CNV FB  SDN   FBG SV IB T375D CAT  14 5  25000  2  7 121000 133000
       37 10 VISTA 38 SPORT CNV FB  SDN   FBG SV IB T400D GM   14 5  25000  2  7 120000 131500
       39  6 VISTA 40          FB   TCMY  FBG SV IB T150D CUM  14 1  31000  3  6 135000 148500
       39  6 VISTA 40          FB   TCMY  FBG SV IB T210D CUM  14 1  31000  3  6 137500 151000
       39  6 VISTA 40          FB   TCMY  FBG SV IB T250D CUM  14 1  31000  3  6 139500 153500

       42 10 VISTA 43          FB   TCMY  FBG SV IB T210D CAT  15 5  32000  3  6 142500 156500
          IB T320D CAT 158500 174000, IB T375D CAT 166500 183000, IB T425D CAT 174000 191000

       46    VISTA 46 CONVERTIBLE FB SDN  FBG SV IB T425D GM   15 5  36000  3 10 185500 204000
          IB T485D GM 190500 209500, IB T550D GM 196000 215000, IB T735D GM 209000 230000

       46  6 VISTA 46 MY       FB   TCMY  FBG SV IB T210D CAT  15    36000  3  8 147000 162000
          IB T320D CAT 166000 182500, IB T375D CAT 175500 193000, IB T425D CAT 184000 202000

       48    VISTA 48 SPORTFISH FB  SF    FBG DV IB T425D CAT  16    36000  3 10 181500 199500
          IB T485D GM 194000 213500, IB T550D GM 207000 227500, IB T735D GM 240500 264500

       49  6 VISTA 49          FB   MY    FBG SV IB T210D CAT  15 5  37500  3 10 150500 165500
          IB T320D CAT 161500 177500, IB T375D CAT 169000 185500, IB T425D CAT 177000 194500

       49  6 VISTA 49          FB   YTFS  FBG SV IB T210D CAT  15    36000  3 10 137500 151000
          IB T320D CAT 157000 172500, IB T375D CAT 171500 188500, IB T425D CAT 184000 202500

       49  6 VISTA 49 MY W/COCKPT FB TCMY FBG SV IB T210D CAT  15    38000  3 10 152000 167000
          IB T320D CAT 165000 181500, IB T375D CAT 174500 192000, IB T425D CAT 184000 202000

       50  4 VISTA 50 TOURNAMENT FB SF    FBG DV IB T425D GM   16    37000  3 10 184500 203000
          IB T485D GM 199000 218500, IB T550D GM 213500 234500, IB T735D GM 251000 275500

       52    VISTA 52          FB   MY    FBG SV IB T210D CAT  15    40000  4    158500 174000
          IB T320D CAT 174000 191000, IB T375D CAT 185500 203500, IB T425D CAT 197000 216000

       52    VISTA 52 MY       FB   YTFS  FBG SV IB T210D CAT  15 5  42000  4    152500 167500
          IB T320D CAT 182000 200000, IB T375D CAT 198500 218000, IB T425D CAT 212000 233000

       52    VISTA 52 MY W/COCKPT FB TCMY FBG SV IB T210D CAT  15 5  42000  4    165000 181500
          IB T320D CAT 184000 202000, IB T375D CAT 197000 216500, IB T425D CAT 209500 230000

       55    VISTA 55 MY W/COCKPT FB MY   FBG SV IB T270D CUM                    205000 225500
          IB T320D CUM 211000 231500, IB T375D CAT 216500 238000, IB T400D GM 219000 241000
          IB T425D CUM 221500 243500, IB T485D GM 227000 249500

       55    VISTA 55 YACHTFISH FB  YTFS  FBG SV IB T270D CUM                    217500 238500
          IB T320D CUM 224500 247000, IB T375D CAT 232000 255000, IB T400D GM 234500 257500
          IB T425D CAT 237500 261000, IB T485D GM 244500 268500

-------------------- 1989 BOATS -----------------------------------------------------------------
       36  6 VISTA 36          FB   TCMY  FBG SV IB T150D CUM  14 1  26000  3  6  96600 106000
       36  6 VISTA 36          FB   TCMY  FBG SV IB T210D CUM  14 1  26000  3  6  97800 107500
       36  6 VISTA 36          FB   TCMY  FBG SV IB T250D CUM  14 1  26000  3  6  99400 109000
       37 10 VISTA 38          FB   TCMY  FBG SV IB T150D CUM  14 1  27000  3  6 107000 117500
       37 10 VISTA 38          FB   TCMY  FBG SV IB T210D CUM  14 1  27000  3  6 109000 120000
       37 10 VISTA 38          FB   TCMY  FBG SV IB T250D CUM  14 1  27000  3  6 111000 122500
       37 10 VISTA 38 SPORT CNV FB  SDN   FBG SV IB T300D GM   14 5  25000  2  7 107000 117500
       37 10 VISTA 38 SPORT CNV FB  SDN   FBG SV IB T375D CAT  14 5  25000  2  7 115500 127000
       37 10 VISTA 38 SPORT CNV FB  SDN   FBG SV IB T400D GM   14 5  25000  2  7 114500 125500
       39  6 VISTA 40          FB   TCMY  FBG SV IB T150D CUM  14 1  31000  3  6 129000 142000
       39  6 VISTA 40          FB   TCMY  FBG SV IB T210D CUM  14 1  31000  3  6 131500 144500
       39  6 VISTA 40          FB   TCMY  FBG SV IB T250D CUM  14 1  31000  3  6 133500 146500

       39  6 VISTA 40 CNV/SDN  FB   SDN   FBG SV IB T150D CUM  14 1  31000  3  6 129000 141500
       39  6 VISTA 40 CNV/SDN  FB   SDN   FBG SV IB T210D CUM  14 1  31000  3  6 131500 144500
       39  6 VISTA 40 CNV/SDN  FB   SDN   FBG SV IB T250D CUM  14 1  31000  3  6 133500 146500
       42 10 VISTA 43          FB   TCMY  FBG SV IB T210D CAT  15 5  32000  3  6 136000 149500
          IB T270D CUM 142500 156500, IB T320D CAT 151000 166000, IB T375D CAT 159000 174500
          IB T425D CAT 166000 182500

       46    VISTA 46 CONVERTIBLE FB SDN  FBG DV IB T485D J&T  15 5  36000  3 10 186500 205000
       46    VISTA 46 CONVERTIBLE FB SDN  FBG DV IB T550D J&T  15 5  36000  3 10 191500 210500
       46    VISTA 46 CONVERTIBLE FB SDN  FBG DV IB T735D J&T  15 5  36000  3 10 204500 225000
       46    VISTA 46 CONVERTIBLE FB SDN  FBG DV IB T425D GM   15 5  36000  3 10 177000 195500
       46  6 VISTA 46          FB   TCMY  FBG SV IB T210D CAT  15    36000  3  8 143000 157000
          IB T270D CUM 153500 168500, IB T320D CAT 163000 179000, IB T375D CAT 172500 189500
          IB T435D CAT 182500 200500

       48    VISTA 48 SPORTFISH FB  SF    FBG DV IB T425D GM   16    36000  3 10 173500 190500
          IB T485D J&T 185500 204000, IB T550D J&T 198000 217500, IB T735D J&T 229500 252500

       49  6 VISTA 49             MY       FBG SV IB T210D CAT  15 5  37500  3 10 144000 158000
          IB T270D CUM 147000 161500, IB T320D CAT 154000 169000, IB T375D CAT 161000 177000
          IB T400D GM 163500 179500

       49  6 VISTA 49          FB   YTFS  FBG SV IB T210D CAT  15    36000  3 10 131000 144000
          IB T270D CUM 137500 151500, IB T320D CUM 150000 165000, IB T375D CAT 164000 180000
          IB T400D GM 170000 187000

       49  6 VISTA 49 MY W/COCKPT FB TCMY FBG SV IB T210D CAT  15    38000  3 10 145000 159500
          IB T270D CUM 149500 164000, IB T320D CAT 156500 172000, IB T375D CAT 166500 183000
          IB T400D GM 171000 187500

       50  4 VISTA 50 TOURNAMENT   SF     FBG DV IB T485D J&T  16    37000  3 10 189000 207500
       50  4 VISTA 50 TOURNAMENT   SF     FBG DV IB T550D J&T  16    37000  3 10 203000 223000
       50  4 VISTA 50 TOURNAMENT   SF     FBG DV IB T735D J&T  16    37000  3 10 238500 262000
       52    VISTA 52             MY       FBG SV IB T210D CAT  15    40000  4    151500 166500
          IB T270D CUM 157000 172500, IB T320D CUM 165000 181000, IB T375D CAT 176500 194500
          IB T400D GM 181000 199000
```

```
       LOA  NAME AND/        TOP/ BOAT  -HULL-  ----ENGINE---  BEAM   WGT  DRAFT RETAIL RETAIL
       FT IN OR MODEL         RIG  TYPE  MTL TP TP # HP MFG    FT IN  LBS  FT IN  LOW    HIGH
------------------- 1989 BOATS ------------------
52     VISTA 52               YTFS FBG SV IB T210D CAT 15 5 42000 4       145500 160000
       IB T270D CUM 156500 172000, IB T320D CUM 171000 188000, IB T375D CAT 186000 204500
       IB T400D GM  193000 212000

52     VISTA 52 MY W/COCKPT FB TCMY FBG SV IB T210D CAT 15 5 42000 4      158000 174000
       IB T270D CUM 165000 181500, IB T320D CUM 175000 192500, IB T375D CAT 188500 207000
       IB T400D GM  194000 213500

55     VISTA 55 MY W/COCKPT FB MY   FBG SV IB T270D CUM                   196000 215500
       IB T320D CUM 201500 221500, IB T375D CAT 207000 227500, IB T400D GM 209500 230000
       IB T425D GM  211500 232500, IB T485D GM 217000 238500

55     VISTA 55 YACHTFISH   FB YTFS FBG SV IB T270D CUM                   207500 228500
       IB T320D CUM 214500 236000, IB T375D CAT 222000 244000, IB T400D GM 224000 246500
       IB T425D GM  227000 249500, IB T485D GM 233500 256500

58     VISTA 58 TWIN DECK   FB MY   FBG SV IB T425D GM                    246500 271000
       IB T485D GM  255000 280000, IB T550D GM 263500 289500, IB T735D GM 285500 314000

58     VISTA 58 YACHTFISH   FB YTFS FBG SV IB T270D CUM                   222000 244000
       IB T320D CUM 231500 254500, IB T375D CAT 239500 263000, IB T400D GM 244000 268000
       IB T425D GM  248000 272500, IB T485D GM 257000 282500

62     VISTA 62 TWIN DECK   FB MY   FBG SV IB T425D GM                    339000 372500
       IB T485D GM  353000 388000, IB T550D GM 367000 403500, IB T735D GM 403500 443500

65     VISTA 65 TWIN DECK   FB MY   FBG SV IB T425D GM                    410000 450500
65     VISTA 65 TWIN DECK   FB MY   FBG SV IB T485D GM                    425500 467500
65     VISTA 65 TWIN DECK   FB MY   FBG SV IB T550D GM                    441500 485000
------------------- 1988 BOATS ------------------
36   6 VISTA 36             FB TCMY FBG SV IB T150D CUM 14 1 24000 3 6    86600 95200
36   6 VISTA 36             FB TCMY FBG SV IB T210D CUM 14 1 24000 3 6    87900 96600
36   6 VISTA 36             FB TCMY FBG SV IB T250D CUM 14 1 24000        89500 98400
37  10 VISTA 38             FB TCMY FBG SV IB T150D CUM 14 1 26000 3 6    99200 109000
37  10 VISTA 38             FB TCMY FBG SV IB T210D CUM 14 1 26000 3 6   101000 111000
37  10 VISTA 38             FB TCMY FBG SV IB T250D CUM 14 1 26000 3 6   103000 113000
37  10 VISTA 38 CNV/SDN     FB SDN  FBG SV IB T150D CUM 14 1 26000 3 6    99200 109000
37  10 VISTA 38 CNV/SDN     FB SDN  FBG SV IB T210D CUM 14 1 26000 3 6   101500 111500
37  10 VISTA 38 CNV/SDN     FB SDN  FBG SV IB T250D CUM 14 1 26000 3 6   103500 113500
39   6 VISTA 40             FB TCMY FBG SV IB T150D CUM 14 1 27000 3 6   110000 121000
       IB T210D CUM 112000 123000, IB T250D CUM 114000 125500, IB T270D CUM 115000 126500

39   6 VISTA 40 CNV/SDN     FB SDN  FBG SV IB T150D CUM 14 1 27000 3 6   110000 121000
       IB T210D CUM 112000 123000, IB T250D CUM 114000 125500, IB T270D CUM 115000 126500

42  10 VISTA 43                MY   FBG SV IB T300D J&T 15 5 32000 3 6   132500 145500
42  10 VISTA 43                MY   FBG SV IB T375D J&T 15 5 32000 3 6   141000 155000
42  10 VISTA 43             FB TCMY FBG SV IB T150D CUM 15 5 30000 3 6   131000 144000
       IB T270D CUM 129500 142000, IB T300D J&T 134000 147500, IB T320D CAT 138000 151500
       IB T320D CUM 136000 149000, IB T375D CAT 145500 160000, IB T375D J&T 144000 158000

46     VISTA 46 CONVERTIBLE FB SDN  FBG DV IB T375D CAT 16       3 10    131500 144500
       IB T450D J&T 136500 150000, IB T485D CUM 140000 154000, IB T550D J&T 148500 163000
       IB T650D J&T 162000 178000

46   6 VISTA 46             FB TCMY FBG SV IB T210D CUM 15 5 34000 3 8   128000 140500
       IB T270D CUM 136000 149500, IB T300D J&T 141500 155500, IB T320D CAT 145000 159500
       IB T320D CUM 144500 159000, IB T375D CAT 154500 169500, IB T375D J&T 154000 169000

48     VISTA 48 SPORTSFISH  FB SF   FBG DV IB T375D CAT 16       3 10    154000 169000
       IB T450D J&T 168000 184500, IB T485D CUM 174500 192000, IB T550D J&T 186500 205000
       IB T650D J&T 203000 223000

49   6 VISTA 49                MY   FBG SV IB T210D CUM 15 5 37000 3 10  135000 148500
       IB T270D CUM 139500 153500, IB T300D J&T 143500 158000, IB T320D CUM 146000 160500
       IB T320D CUM 144500 158500, IB T375D CAT 153000 168000, IB T375D J&T 152500 167500

49   6 VISTA 49             FB TCMY FBG SV IB T210D CUM 15 5 36000 3 10  137000 150500
       IB T270D CUM 149500 164500, IB T300D J&T 157000 172500, IB T320D CAT 162000 178000
       IB T320D CUM 162000 178000, IB T375D CAT 174500 191500, IB T375D J&T 174500 191500

49   6 VISTA 49                YTFS FBG SV IB T210  15 5 35000 3 10      120500 132000
       IB T270D CUM 129000 142000, IB T300D J&T 135500 149000, IB T320D CUM 140500 154000
       IB T320D CUM 140000 154000, IB T375D CAT 153500 168500, IB T375D J&T 153500 168500

49   6 VISTA 49 MY W/COCKPT FB TCMY FBG SV IB T210D CUM 15   36000 3 10  135000 148500
       IB T270D CUM 140000 154000, IB T300D J&T 144500 159000, IB T320D CUM 148500 163000
       IB T320D CUM 145500 159500, IB T375D CAT 155000 171000, IB T375D J&T 155500 171000

49   6 VISTA 49 YACHTFISH   FB TCMY FBG SV IB T210D CUM 15   36000 3 10  134000 147000
       IB T270D CUM 140000 153500, IB T300D J&T 145000 159500, IB T320D CUM 149000 163500
       IB T320D CUM 146500 161000, IB T375D CAT 157500 173000, IB T375D J&T 157500 173000

50   4 VISTA 50 TOURNAMENT     SF   FBG DV IB T450D J&T 16      3 10     173500 191000
       IB T485D J&T 179000 197000, IB T550D J&T 188500 207500, IB T650D J&T 202500 222500
       IB T735D J&T 213000 234000

52     VISTA 52                MY   FBG SV IB T210D CUM 15 5 39000 4     142500 156500
       IB T270D CUM 148500 163000, IB T300D J&T 155000 170500, IB T320D CUM 156500 172000
       IB T320D CUM 155000 170000, IB T375D CAT 165000 181500, IB T375D J&T 166000 182500

52     VISTA 52             FB TCMY FBG SV IB T210D CUM 15 5 37000 4     143500 158000
       IB T270D CUM 152000 167500, IB T300D J&T 160000 176000, IB T320D CAT 164500 180500
       IB T320D CUM 164000 180000, IB T375D CAT 179000 196500, IB T375D J&T 179000 196500

52     VISTA 52                YTFS FBG SV IB T210D CUM 15 5 38000 4     132500 145500
       IB T270D CUM 140000 154000, IB T300D J&T 148000 162500, IB T320D CUM 152000 167000
       IB T320D CUM 151500 166500, IB T375D CAT 166500 183000, IB T375D J&T 166500 183000

52     VISTA 52 MT W/COCKPT FB TCMY FBG SV IB T210D CUM 15   37000 4     144500 158500
52     VISTA 52 MT W/COCKPT FB TCMY FBG SV IB T300D J&T 15   37000 4     160000 175500
52     VISTA 52 MY W/COCKPT FB TCMY FBG SV IB T270D CUM 15   37000 4     150500 165500
       IB T320D CUM 160000 176000, IB T320D CUM 157000 172500, IB T375D CAT 170000 187000
       IB T375D J&T 170500 187500

52     VISTA 52 YACHTFISH   FB TCMY FBG SV IB T210D CUM 15   37000 4     142500 157000
       IB T270D CUM 149500 164000, IB T300D J&T 156500 172000, IB T320D CUM 160000 175500
       IB T320D CUM 157000 172500, IB T375D CAT 170500 187000, IB T375D J&T 171000 187500
------------------- 1987 BOATS ------------------
36   6 VISTA 36             FB TCMY FBG SV IB T150D CUM 14 1 18600 3 6    68100 74800
36   6 VISTA 36             FB TCMY FBG SV IB T210D CUM 14 1 18600 3 6    70000 76900
37  10 VISTA 38             FB TCMY FBG SV IB T135D FORD 14 1 22000 3 8   82600 90700
37  10 VISTA 38             FB TCMY FBG SV IB T150D CUM 14 1 22000 3 6    82600 90800
37  10 VISTA 38             FB TCMY FBG SV IB T210D CUM 14 1 22000 3 6    84500 92900
39   6 VISTA 40             FB TCMY FBG SV IB T150D CUM 14 1 22800 3 6    91700 101000
       IB T210D CAT 96100 105500, IB T210D CUM 93800 103000, IB T270D CUM 96500 106000

42  10 VISTA 43             FB TCMY FBG SV IB T270D CUM 15 5 26000 3 6   103500 114000
       IB T270D CUM 111500 122500, IB T300D J&T 116000 127500, IB T320D CUM 120000 132000
       IB T320D CUM 118000 129500, IB T375D CAT 127500 140500, IB T375D J&T 126000 138500

46     VISTA 46 CONVERTIBLE FB SDN  FBG DV IB T375D CAT 16       3 10    125500 138000
       IB T410D CUM 126000 138500, IB T450D J&T 130000 142500, IB T485D GM 133500 146500
       IB T550D GM  141000 155000, IB T485D GM 154500 169500

46   6 VISTA 46             FB TCMY FBG SV IB T210D CUM 15 5 34000 3 8   122000 134000
       IB T270D CUM 130000 143000, IB T300D J&T 135000 148500, IB T320D CUM 139000 152500
       IB T320D CUM 138000 152000, IB T375D CAT 147500 162000, IB T375D J&T 147000 161500

48     VISTA 48 SPORTSFISH  FB SF   FBG DV IB T375D CAT 16       3 10    147000 161500
       IB T410D CUM 153000 168500, IB T450D GM 160500 176500, IB T485D GM 167000 183500
       IB T550D GM  178000 196000, IB T650D GM 194000 213500

49   6 VISTA 49             FB TCMY FBG SV IB T210D CUM 15 5 36000 3 10  131000 144000
       IB T270D CUM 143000 157500, IB T320D CAT 155000 170000, IB T320D CUM 155000 170000
       IB T375D CAT 166500 183000

50     VISTA 50 TOURNAMENT     SF   FBG DV IB T450D GM 16        3 10    164500 180500
       IB T485D GM  169500 186500, IB T550D GM 179000 196500, IB T650D GM 192500 211500
       IB T735D GM  203000 223000

52     VISTA 52             FB TCMY FBG SV IB T210D CUM 15 5 37000 4     138000 151500
       IB T270D CUM 146000 160500, IB T320D CUM 157500 173000, IB T320D CUM 157000 172500
       IB T375D CAT 171000 188000
------------------- 1986 BOATS ------------------
36   6 VISTA 36             FB TCMY FBG SV IB T136D VLVO 14 1 18600 3 6   64400 70700
36   6 VISTA 36             FB TCMY FBG SV IB T165D VLVO 14 1 18600 3 6   64800 71200
39   6 VISTA 40             FB TCMY FBG SV IB T136D VLVO 14 1 22800 4 1   86300 94900
       LOA IB T165D VLVO 87100 95700, IB T210D CAT 92000 101000, IB T210D CUM 89800 98600
       IB T255D VLVO 90200 99200, IB T260D CAT 94500 104000

46     VISTA 46 CONVERTIBLE FB SDN  FBG DV IB T320D CUM 16       3 10    113500 125000
       IB T375D CUM 119500 131500, IB T410D J&T 121000 133000, IB T450D J&T 124500 136500
       IB T485D J&T 128000 140500, IB T530D J&T 133000 146000, IB T565D J&T 137500 151000
```

```
VISTA YACHT CO INC          -CONTINUED   See inside cover to adjust price for area
   LOA  NAME AND/          TOP/ BOAT  -HULL-  ----ENGINE---  BEAM   WGT  DRAFT RETAIL RETAIL
   FT IN OR MODEL          RIG  TYPE  MTL TP  TP # HP  MFG   FT IN  LBS  FT IN  LOW    HIGH
-------------------------- 1986 BOATS --------------------------------------------------
46    VISTA 46 CONVERTIBLE FB   SDN   FBG DV IB T600D J&T  16            3 10 141500 155500
46  9 VISTA 46             FB   TCMY  FBG SV IB T165D VLVO 15     34000  3  1 134000 147000
    IB T210D CAT  120000 132000, IB T210D CUM  119000 131000, IB T255D VLVO 126000 138500
    IB T260D CAT  127500 140000, IB T320D CAT  137500 151000, IB T320D CUM  137000 150500
    IB T375D CAT  146000 160500

47  6 VISTA 52             FB   TCMY  FBG SV IB T210D CAT  15   4 37000  4  2 128500 141500
    IB T210D CUM  128000 141000, IB T255D VLVO 136500 150000, IB T260D CAT  138000 151500
    IB T320D CAT  149000 163500, IB T320D CUM  148500 163500, IB T375D CAT  158000 173500

48    VISTA 48 SPORTSFISH  FB   SF    FBG DV IB T375D CAT  16            3  1 140500 154500
    IB T410D J&T  146500 161000, IB T450D J&T  154000 169000, IB T485D J&T  160000 175500
    IB T530D J&T  167500 184000, IB T565D J&T  173000 190000, IB T600D J&T  178500 196000

49  6 VISTA 49             FB   TCMY  FBG SV IB T210D CAT  15   4 36000  3 11 126000 138500
    IB T210D CUM  125500 138000, IB T255D VLVO 134500 147500, IB T260D CAT  135500 149000
    IB T320D CAT  149000 164000, IB T320D CUM  149000 164000, IB T375D CAT  160500 176500

50    VISTA 50 TOURNAMENT        SF    FBG DV IB T450D J&T  16            3  1 157500 173000
    IB T485D J&T  162500 178500, IB T530D J&T  168500 185500, IB T565D J&T  173500 190500
    IB T600D J&T  178000 195500, IB T710D J&T  191500 210500
-------------------------- 1985 BOATS --------------------------------------------------
36  6 VISTA 36                  TCMY  FBG SV IB T136D VLVO 14   1 18600  3  7  61600  67700
36  6 VISTA 36                  TCMY  FBG SV IB T165D VLVO 14   1 18600  3  7  62000  68100
39  6 VISTA 40                  TCMY  FBG SV IB T136D VLVO 14   1 18600  3  7  62700  68900
    IB T165D VLVO  83400  91700, IB T200D PERK  87700  96300, IB T250D VLVO  86200  94700

45 11 VISTA 46 CONVERTIBLE SF   SF    FBG SV IB T350D PERK 16     31000  3 10 122000 134000
    IB T355D CAT  122500 135000, IB T410D J&T  131000 144000, IB T450D J&T  137500 151000
    IB T485D J&T  143000 157000, IB T530D J&T  149500 164500, IB T565D J&T  155000 170000
    IB T610D J&T  161000 177000

46  9 VISTA 46             TCMY  FBG SV IB T165D VLVO 15     34000  3  8 127500 140500
    IB T200D PERK 113500 124500, IB T210D CAT  114500 126000, IB T250D VLVO 119000 131000
    IB T300D CAT  128000 140500, IB T300D CAT  127000 139500, IB T350D PERK 135500 149000
    IB T355D CAT  136000 149500

47 11 VISTA 48 SPORTSFISH  SF   SF    FBG SV IB T355D CAT  16     32000  3 10 123000 135000
    IB T410D J&T  129500 142500, IB T450D J&T  136000 149500, IB T485D J&T  142000 156000
    IB T530D J&T  149000 163500, IB T565D J&T  154500 169500, IB T610D J&T  161000 177000

49 11 VISTA 50 TOURNAMENT  SF   SF    FBG SV IB T450D J&T  16     34000  3 10 141500 155500
    IB T485D J&T  148000 162500, IB T530D J&T  156000 171500, IB T565D J&T  162000 178000
    IB T610D J&T  169500 186000, IB T710D J&T  185000 203000

52    VISTA 52             TCMY  FBG SV IB T165D VLVO 15     37000  4  2 124000 136000
    IB T200D PERK 127500 140000, IB T210D CAT  128500 141500, IB T250D VLVO 131000 144000
    IB T300D CAT  141500 155500, IB T300D VLVO 141000 155000, IB T350D PERK 153000 168000
    IB T355D CAT  154000 169500
-------------------------- 1984 BOATS --------------------------------------------------
36  6 VISTA 36             FB   DCMY  FBG SV IB T124D VLVO 14   1 18600  3  6  59600  65500
36  6 VISTA 36             FB   DCMY  FBG SV IB T158D VLVO 14   1 18600  3  6  60600  66600
36  6 VISTA 36             FB   DCMY  FBG SV IB T165D VLVO 14   1 18600  3  6  60800  66800
39  6 VISTA 40             FB   DCMY  FBG SV IB T124D VLVO 14   1 22800  4  1  78900  86700
    IB T158D VLVO  79800  87700, IB T165D VLVO  80000  87900, IB T200D PERK  86900  95500

46  9 VISTA 46             FB   MY    FBG SV IB T158D VLVO 15     32000  3  8 103000 113500
    IB T165D VLVO 106500 117000, IB T200D PERK 106000 116500, IB T235D VLVO 107000 117500
    IB T300D CAT  113500 124500, IB T350D PERK 119000 130500

52    VISTA 52             FB   MY    FBG SV IB T158D VLVO 15     37000  4  2 115000 126500
    IB T200D PERK 128500 141000, IB T235D VLVO 132500 145500, IB T300D CAT  130000 142500
    IB T350D PERK 137500 151000
```

VIVA YACHTS INC
FT LAUDERDALE FL 33316 COAST GUARD MFG ID- MQN See inside cover to adjust price for area

```
   LOA  NAME AND/          TOP/ BOAT  -HULL-  ----ENGINE---  BEAM   WGT  DRAFT RETAIL RETAIL
   FT IN OR MODEL          RIG  TYPE  MTL TP  TP # HP  MFG   FT IN  LBS  FT IN  LOW    HIGH
-------------------------- 1994 BOATS --------------------------------------------------
36    VIVA TOURNAMENT SF        SF    FBG SV IB T320D MTU  13   9       3  5  62300  68500
52    VIVA 52 EXPRESS           MY    FBG SV IB T65D  MTU  15   8       3  5 180000 198000
52    VIVA 52 EXPRESS      FB   MY    FBG SV IB T550D DD   15   8       3  5 161500 177500
60    MONTE CARLO 60 MY    FB   MY    FBG SV IB T550D DD   18   4       4  4 229000 251500
60    MONTE CARLO 60 MY    FB   MY    FBG SV IB T735D DD   18   4       4  4 249000 274000
62    VIVA 62 EXPRESS           MY    FBG SV IB T100D MTU  18   4       4  4 245500 270000
62    VIVA 62 EXPRESS           MY    FBG SV IB T735D DD   18   4       4  4 287500 315500
66    MONTE CARLO 66            MY    FBG SV IB T735D DD   18   4       4  4 325500 357500
66    MONTE CARLO 66 CP MY FB   MY    FBG SV IB T550D DD   18   4       4  4 314000 345500
70 10 MONTE CARLO 71 MY    FB   MY    FBG SV IB T100D MTU  18   4       4  4 385500 424000
72    VIVA 72 EXPRESS      FB   MY    FBG SV IB T10CD MTU  19           5     **     **
79  6 MONTE CARLO 80            MY    FBG SV IB T10CD MTU  19           5     **     **
-------------------------- 1993 BOATS --------------------------------------------------
36    VIVA TOURNAMENT SF        SF    FBG SV IB T320D MTU  13   9       3  5  59300  65100
52    VIVA 52 EXPRESS           MY    FBG SV IB T650D MTU  15   5       3  5 172000 189500
52    VIVA 52 EXPRESS      FB   MY    FBG SV IB T665D MTU  15   5       3  5 174000 191000
60    MONTE CARLO 60 MY    FB   MY    FBG SV IB T550D DD   18   4       4  4 219000 240500
60    MONTE CARLO 60 MY    FB   MY    FBG SV IB T735D DD   18   4       4  4 238000 261500
62    VIVA 62 EXPRESS           MY    FBG SV IB T735D DD   18   4       4  4 274500 301500
62    VIVA 62 EXPRESS           MY    FBG SV IB T10CD MTU  18   4       4  4 316000 347500
66    MONTE CARLO 66            MY    FBG SV IB T735D DD   18   4       4  4 311000 341500
66    MONTE CARLO 66 CP MY FB   MY    FBG SV IB T550D     18   4       4  4 298000 327500
70 10 MONTE CARLO 71 MY    FB   MY    FBG SV IB T735D DD   18   4       4  4 368500 405500
72    VIVA 72 EXPRESS      FB   MY    FBG SV IB T10CD MTU  19           5     **     **
79  6 MONTE CARLO 80            MY    FBG SV IB T10CD MTU  19           5     **     **
-------------------------- 1992 BOATS --------------------------------------------------
49  6 VIVA 50                   MY    FBG SV IB T385D VLVO 14   4       3  5 121000 133000
    IB T485D J&T  132500 145500, IB T500D DD   134000 147500, IB T550D DD   139000 152500

60    MONTE CARLO 60 MY    FB   MY    FBG SV IB T550D DD   18   4       4  4 209500 230000
60    MONTE CARLO 60 MY    FB   MY    FBG SV IB T735D DD   18   4       4  4 228000 250500
60    VIVA 60 EXPRESS           MY    FBG SV IB T735D DD   18   4       4  4 228000 250500
60    VIVA 60 EXPRESS           MY    FBG SV IB T10CD J&T  18   4       4  4 273000 300000
66    MONTE CARLO 66 CP MY FB   MY    FBG SV IB T550D J&T  18   4       4  4 286000 314000
66    MONTE CARLO 66 CP MY FB   MY    FBG SV IB T735D DD   18   4       4  4 297500 327000
70 10 MONTE CARLO 71 MY    FB   MY    FBG SV IB T735D DD   18   4       4  4 318000 349000
79  6 MONTE CARLO 80            MY    FBG SV IB T10CD MTU  18   4       4  4  **     **
-------------------------- 1991 BOATS --------------------------------------------------
49  6 VIVA 50                   MY    FBG SV IB T385D VLVO 14   4       3  5 115500 126500
    IB T485D J&T  126500 139000, IB T500D DD   127500 140500, IB T550D DD   132000 145500

60    MONTE CARLO 60 MY    FB   MY    FBG SV IB T550D DD   18   4       4  4 200500 220500
60    MONTE CARLO 60 MY    FB   MY    FBG SV IB T735D DD   18   4       4  4 218000 240000
60    VIVA 60 EXPRESS           MY    FBG SV IB T735D DD   18   4       4  4 218000 240000
60    VIVA 60 EXPRESS           MY    FBG SV IB T10CD J&T  18   4       4  4 261500 287000
66    MONTE CARLO 66 CP MY FB   MY    FBG SV IB T550D J&T  18   4       4  4 274000 301000
66    MONTE CARLO 66 CP MY FB   MY    FBG SV IB T735D DD   18   4       4  4 285000 313000
70 10 MONTE CARLO 71 MY    FB   MY    FBG SV IB T735D DD   18   4       4  4 304000 334500
79  6 MONTE CARLO 80            MY    FBG SV IB T10CD MTU  18   4       4  4  **     **
-------------------------- 1990 BOATS --------------------------------------------------
59  6 VIVA 60 EXPRESS           EXP   F/S DV IB T735D GM   18   4 45000  4  4 185000 203500
59  6 VIVA 60 MY                MY    F/S DV IB T735D GM   18   4 61000  4  4 199000 218500
66  6 VIVA 66 COCKPIT MY        MY    F/S DV IB T735D GM   18   4 67000  4  4 273500 300500
66  6 VIVA 66 MY                MY    F/S DV IB T735D GM   18   4 69000  4  4 275500 302500
70    VIVA 70 EXPRESS           EXP   F/S DV IB T10CD MTU  18   4 54000  4  4 313500 344500
71    VIVA 71 COCKPIT MY        MY    F/S DV IB T10CD MTU  18   4 71000  4  4 324500 356500
71    VIVA 71 MY                MY    F/S DV IB T10CD MTU  18   4 71000  4  4 326000 358000
79  8 VIVA 80 COCKPIT MY        MY    F/S DV IB T10CD MTU  18   4 82000  4  4  **     **
-------------------------- 1989 BOATS --------------------------------------------------
49  6 VIVA 50 EXPRESS           EXP   F/S DV IB T450D GM   14   6 30000  3  6 108500 119000
```

VOILIERS ELITE YACHT INT
BERNIERE QUE CANADA   See inside cover to adjust price for area

```
   LOA  NAME AND/          TOP/ BOAT  -HULL-  ----ENGINE---  BEAM   WGT  DRAFT RETAIL RETAIL
   FT IN OR MODEL          RIG  TYPE  MTL TP  TP # HP  MFG   FT IN  LBS  FT IN  LOW    HIGH
-------------------------- 1990 BOATS --------------------------------------------------
29  6 ELITE 286             SLP  SAIL  FBG KL IB    9D VLVO 10       5500  5  5  30000  33300
29  6 ELITE 286  SHOAL      SLP  SAIL  FBG KL IB    9D VLVO 10       5500  3  9  30000  33300
32  6 ELITE 326             SLP  SAIL  FBG KL IB   18D VLVO 11       7500  4  8  42000  46700
32  6 ELITE 326  SHOAL      SLP  SAIL  FBG KL IB   18D VLVO 11       7500  4  4  42000  46700
36  4 ELITE 364             SLP  SAIL  FBG KL IB   28D VLVO 11  9 11000  5  9  65300  71800
36  4 ELITE 364  SHOAL      SLP  SAIL  FBG KL IB   28D VLVO 11  9 11000  4  4  65300  71800
41  6 ELITE 416             SLP  SAIL  FBG KL IB   44D      13  9 15000  6  5 110000 121000
45  3 ELITE 446             SLP  SAIL  FBG KL IB   55D YAN  14  7 17000  6  8 149500 164000
45  3 ELITE 446  SHOAL      SLP  SAIL  FBG KL IB   55D YAN  14  7 17000  3 149500 164000
-------------------------- 1989 BOATS --------------------------------------------------
32  6 ELITE 326                  SAIL  FBG KL IB   18D VLVO 11       7500  5  5  39500  43900
32  6 ELITE 326  SHOAL           SAIL  FBG KL IB   18D VLVO 11       7500  4  4  39500  43900
```

VOYAGER MARINE
CAMDENTON MO 65020

See inside cover to adjust price for area

For more recent years, see the BUC Used Boat Price Guide, Volume 1

LOA FT IN	NAME AND/ OR MODEL	TOP/ RIG	BOAT TYPE	MTL	TP	TP	#	HP	MFG	BEAM FT IN	WGT LBS	DRAFT FT IN	RETAIL LOW	RETAIL HIGH
1996 BOATS														
16	JON 1656	OP	JON	AL	FL	OB				4 8			980	1150
16	JON 1670	OP	JON	AL	FL	OB				5 10	275		790	950
16	JON 1670 OPEN	OP	JON	AL	FL	OB				5 10	275		850	1000
16	JON 1670 W/T	OP	JON	AL	FL	OB				5 10	275		865	1050
16	JON 1685	OP	JON	AL	FL	OB				7 1	430		1200	1450
16	JON 1685 OPEN	OP	JON	AL	FL	OB				7 1	430		1250	1500
17	1770 BASS	OP	BASS	AL	FL	OB				5 10	645		2000	2400
18	JON 1870	OP	JON	AL	FL	OB				5 10			1150	1400
18	JON 1870 OPEN	OP	JON	AL	FL	OB				5 10			1250	1500
18	JON 1870 W/T	OP	JON	AL	FL	OB				5 10			1250	1500
18	JON 1885	OP	JON	AL	FL	OB				7 1	500		1200	1450
18	JON 1885 OPEN	OP	JON	AL	FL	OB				7 1	500		1250	1500
1995 BOATS														
16	JON 1656	OP	JON	AL	FL	OB				4 8			930	1100
16	JON 1670	OP	JON	AL	FL	OB				5 10	275		750	905
16	JON 1670 OPEN	OP	JON	AL	FL	OB				5 10	275		800	965
16	JON 1670 W/T	OP	JON	AL	FL	OB				5 10	275		810	980
16	JON 1685	OP	JON	AL	FL	OB				7 1	430		1150	1400
16	JON 1685 OPEN	OP	JON	AL	FL	OB				7 1	430		1200	1450
17	1770 BASS	OP	BASS	AL	FL	OB				5 10	645		1900	2300
18	JON 1870	OP	JON	AL	FL	OB				5 10			1100	1300
18	JON 1870 OPEN	OP	JON	AL	FL	OB				5 10			1200	1450
18	JON 1870 W/T	OP	JON	AL	FL	OB				5 10			1200	1400
18	JON 1885	OP	JON	AL	FL	OB				7 1	500		1150	1350
18	JON 1885 OPEN	OP	JON	AL	FL	OB				7 1	500		1200	1400
1994 BOATS														
16	JON 1656	OP	JON	AL	FL	OB				4 8			895	1050
16	JON 1670	OP	JON	AL	FL	OB				5 10	275		720	865
16	JON 1670 OPEN	OP	JON	AL	FL	OB				5 10	275		760	920
16	JON 1670 W/T	OP	JON	AL	FL	OB				5 10	275		775	935
16	JON 1685	OP	JON	AL	FL	OB				7 1	430		1100	1300
16	JON 1685 OPEN	OP	JON	AL	FL	OB				7 1	430		1150	1350
18	JON 1870	OP	JON	AL	FL	OB				5 10	275		525	630
18	JON 1870 OPEN	OP	JON	AL	FL	OB				5 10	275		525	630
18	JON 1870 W/T	OP	JON	AL	FL	OB				5 10	275		530	640
18	JON 1885	OP	JON	AL	FL	OB				7 1	275		525	630
18	JON 1885 OPEN	OP	JON	AL	FL	OB				7 1	500		1100	1300
1993 BOATS														
16	JON 1656	OP	JON	AL	FL	OB				4 8			855	1000
16	JON 1670	OP	JON	AL	FL	OB				5 10	275		685	830
16	JON 1670 OPEN	OP	JON	AL	FL	OB				5 10	275		730	880
16	JON 1670 W/T	OP	JON	AL	FL	OB				5 10	275		740	895
16	JON 1685	OP	JON	AL	FL	OB				7 1	430		1050	1250
16	JON 1685 OPEN	OP	JON	AL	FL	OB				7 1	430		1100	1300
18	JON 1870	OP	JON	AL	FL	OB				5 10	275		485	585
18	JON 1870 OPEN	OP	JON	AL	FL	OB				5 10	275		510	610
18	JON 1870 W/T	OP	JON	AL	FL	OB				5 10	275		515	620
18	JON 1885	OP	JON	AL	FL	OB				7 1	275		505	605
18	JON 1885 OPEN	OP	JON	AL	FL	OB				7 1	500		1050	1250
1992 BOATS														
16	JON 1656	OP	JON	AL	FL	OB				4 8			810	980
16	JON 1670	OP	JON	AL	FL	OB				5 10	275		660	795
16	JON 1670 OPEN	OP	JON	AL	FL	OB				5 10	275		700	845
16	JON 1670 W/T	OP	JON	AL	FL	OB				5 10	275		710	855
18	JON 1870	OP	JON	AL	FL	OB				5 10	275		465	560
18	JON 1870	OP	JON	AL	FL	OB				5 10	275		490	590
18	JON 1870 W/T	OP	JON	AL	FL	OB				5 10	275		495	595
18	JON 1885	OP	JON	AL	FL	OB				7 1	275		480	580

VOYAGER MARINE INC
CLEARWATER FL 33520 COAST GUARD MFG ID- SMF See inside cover to adjust price for area

LOA FT IN	NAME AND/ OR MODEL	TOP/ RIG	BOAT TYPE	MTL	TP	TP	#	HP	MFG	BEAM FT IN	WGT LBS	DRAFT FT IN	RETAIL LOW	RETAIL HIGH
1984 BOATS														
25 9	VOYAGER 26	CUT	SA/CR	FBG	KL	IB		10D	BMW	8 3	6600	3 4	19800	22000

....For earlier years, see the BUC Used Boat Price Guide, Volume 3

VOYAGER MOTOR YACHTS INC
CORNWALL ENGLAND

See inside cover to adjust price for area

LOA FT IN	NAME AND/ OR MODEL	TOP/ RIG	BOAT TYPE	MTL	TP	TP	#	HP	MFG	BEAM FT IN	WGT LBS	DRAFT FT IN	RETAIL LOW	RETAIL HIGH
1990 BOATS														
52	SPORTS ANGLER	FB	SF	AL	DS	IB		T275D	FORD	14 9	22500	3	225500	247500
52	SPORTS ANGLER	FB	SF	STL	DS	IB		T275D	FORD	14 9	35000	4	252000	277000
55	EXPRESS CRUISER	FB	CBNCR	AL	DS	IB		T350D	PERK	16	29000	3 3	286000	314500
55	EXPRESS CRUISER	FB	CBNCR	STL	DS	IB		T350D	PERK	16	49000	3 3	285500	313500
74 6	VOYAGER T S D Y	FB	MY	STL	DS	IB		T350D	PERK	20 3	86T	5 6	**	**
1989 BOATS														
52	SPORTS ANGLER	FB	SF	AL	DS	IB		T275D	FORD	14 9	22500	3	214000	235000
52	SPORTS ANGLER	FB	SF	STL	DS	IB		T275D	FORD	14 9	35000	4	240000	263500
55	EXPRESS CRUISER	FB	CBNCR	AL	DS	IB		T350D	PERK	16	29000	3	272000	299000
55	EXPRESS CRUISER	FB	CBNCR	STL	DS	IB		T350D	PERK	16	49000	3	271500	298000
74 6	VOYAGER T S D Y	FB	MY	STL	DS	IB		T350D	PERK	20 3	86T	5 6	**	**
1988 BOATS														
52	SPORTS ANGLER	FB	SF	AL	DS	IB		T275D	FORD	14 9	22500	3	203500	224000
52	SPORTS ANGLER	FB	SF	STL	DS	IB		T275D	FORD	14 9	35000	4	228500	251000
55	EXPRESS CRUISER	FB	CBNCR	AL	DS	IB		T350D	PERK	16	29000	3	259000	284500
55	EXPRESS CRUISER	FB	CBNCR	STL	DS	IB		T350D	PERK	16	49000	3	258000	283500
74 6	VOYAGER T S D Y	FB	MY	STL	DS	IB		T350D	PERK	20 3	73T	5 6	**	**

WAARSHIP INTERNATIONAL YACHTS
GRAND HAVEN MI 49417

See inside cover to adjust price for area

LOA FT IN	NAME AND/ OR MODEL	TOP/ RIG	BOAT TYPE	MTL	TP	TP	#	HP	MFG	BEAM FT IN	WGT LBS	DRAFT FT IN	RETAIL LOW	RETAIL HIGH
1987 BOATS														
21 7	WAARSHIP 660	SLP	SA/CR	PLY	KL	OB				8 2	2425	3 3	9000	10200
21 7	WAARSHIP 660	SLP	SA/CR	PLY	KL	IB		7		8 2	2425	3 3	9650	11000
25	WAARSHIP 740	SLP	SA/CR	PLY	KL	OB				9	3340	4 1	13300	15100
25	WAARSHIP 740	SLP	SA/CR	PLY	KL	IB		8		9	3340	4 1	13800	15700
26 6	WAARSHIP 740 OCEAN	SLP	SA/RC	PLY	KL	OB				9	3325	5 2	13700	15600
26 6	WAARSHIP 740 OCEAN	SLP	SA/RC	PLY	KL	IB		8		9	3325	5 2	14500	16400
29 5	WAARSHIP 900	SLP	SA/CR	PLY	KL	OB				10 8	6614	4 9	29000	32300
29 5	WAARSHIP 900	SLP	SA/CR	PLY	KL	IB		15D		10 8	6614	4 9	29500	32900
31 6	WAARSHIP 900 PLUS	SLP	SA/RC	PLY	KL	OB				10 8	6580	6	29300	32600
31 6	WAARSHIP 900 PLUS	SLP	SA/RC	PLY	KL	IB		15D		10 8	6580	6	29400	32700
34	WAARSHIP 10.10	SLP	SA/RC	PLY	KL	OB				8 2	4409	6 2	18300	20300
34	WAARSHIP 10.10	SLP	SA/RC	PLY	KL	IB		10D		8 2	4409	6 2	18500	20600
41 5	WAARSHIP 12.20	CUT	SA/CR	PLY	KL	OB				11 8	14330	5 2	81200	89300
41 5	WAARSHIP 12.20	CUT	SA/CR	PLY	KL	IB		35D		11 8	14330	5 2	81300	89400
41 5	WAARSHIP 12.20	SLP	SA/CR	FBG	KL	OB				11 8	14330	7 2	82800	91000
41 5	WAARSHIP 12.20	SLP	SA/RC	PLY	KL	IB		35D		11 8	14330	7 2	82900	91100
1986 BOATS														
30	WAARSHIP 900	SLP	SA/RC	WD	KL	IB		D		10 10	6614	4 11	27500	30600
1985 BOATS														
29 6	WAARSHIP 900	SLP	SA/RC	WD	KL	IB		15D	VLVO	10 10	6614	4 11	22400	24900

WACO MANUFACTURING INC
NORTH LITTLE ROCK AR 72 COAST GUARD MFG ID- WAC See inside cover to adjust price for area

For more recent years, see the BUC Used Boat Price Guide, Volume 1

LOA FT IN	NAME AND/ OR MODEL	TOP/ RIG	BOAT TYPE	MTL	TP	TP	#	HP	MFG	BEAM FT IN	WGT LBS	DRAFT FT IN	RETAIL LOW	RETAIL HIGH
1996 BOATS														
16	1836-16	OP	JON	AL	FL	OB				4 10	195		755	910
16	2048-16	OP	JON	AL	FL	OB				5 10	270		995	1200
16	2048-16 MV	OP	JON	AL	SV	OB				5 10	278		1000	1200
16	B16-DS	OP	BASS	AL	SV	OB				5 10	590		2150	2500
16	BMV-16	OP	BASS	AL	SV	OB				5 7	510		1850	2200
17 6	BIG BOY BASS	OP	BASS	AL	SV	OB				7 8	980		3650	4250
17 6	BIG BOY FISH-N-FOWL	OP	BASS	AL	SV	OB				7 8	900		3400	3950
20	BIG BOY BASS BOAT	OP	BASS	AL	SV	OB				7 8	1100		4650	5350
20	BIG BOY CC	OP	CTRCN	AL	SV	OB				7 8	1100		4650	5350
1995 BOATS														
16	1836-16	OP	JON	AL	FL	OB				4 6	195		720	865
16	2048-16	OP	JON	AL	FL	OB				5 10	270		950	1150
16	2048-16 MV	OP	JON	AL	SV	OB				5 10	278		975	1150
17	BASS BOAT	OP	BASS	AL						7 10	980		**	**
17	FISH-N-FOWL	OP	BASS	AL						7 10	900		**	**
20	BIG BOY BASS BOAT	OP	BASS	AL	SV	OB				7 8	1100		4400	5100
1994 BOATS														
16	1836-16	OP	JON	AL	FL	OB				4 6	195		690	830
16	2048-16	OP	JON	AL	FL	OB				5 10	270		915	1100

WACO MANUFACTURING INC -CONTINUED See inside cover to adjust price for area

LOA FT	LOA IN	NAME AND/ OR MODEL	TOP/ RIG	BOAT TYPE	-HULL- MTL	-HULL- TP	ENGINE TP	ENGINE # HP MFG	BEAM FT	BEAM IN	WGT LBS	DRAFT FT	DRAFT IN	RETAIL LOW	RETAIL HIGH
		1994 BOATS													
16		2048-16 MV	OP	JON	AL	SV	OB		5	10	278			930	1100
16		B-16 DS	OP	BASS	AL	SV	OB		5	7	587			1900	2300
16		BMV-16	OP	BASS	AL	SV	OB		5	7	570			1850	2200
16		C-16 DS	OP	BASS	AL	SV	OB		5	10	495			1600	1950
16		FISH N FOWL	OP	FSH	AL	SV	OB		5	10	430			1400	1700
18		WALLEYE 18	OP	FSH	AL	SV	OB		7		730			2600	3050
20		BIG BOY BASS BOAT	OP	BASS	AL	SV	OB		7	8	1100			4200	4850
		1993 BOATS													
16		1836-16	OP	JON	AL	FL	OB		4	6	195			660	795
16		2048-16	OP	JON	AL	FL	OB		5	10	270			875	1050
16		2048-16 MV	OP	JON	AL	SV	OB		5	10	278			900	1050
16		B-16 DS	OP	BASS	AL	SV	OB		5	7	587			1850	2200
16		BMV-16	OP	BASS	AL	SV	OB		5	7	570			1800	2150
16		C-16 DS	OP	BASS	AL	SV	OB		5	10	495			1550	1850
16		FISH N FOWL	OP	FSH	AL	SV	OB		5	10	430			1350	1600
		1992 BOATS													
16		1836-16	OP	JON	AL	FL	OB		4	6	195			635	765
16		2048-16	OP	JON	AL	FL	OB		5	10	270			845	1000
16		2048-16 MV	OP	JON	AL	SV	OB		5	10	278			865	1050
16		2050-16 FNF	OP	BASS	AL	FL	OB		5	10	430			1300	1550
16		B-16 DS	OP	BASS	AL	SV	OB		5	7	587			1750	2100
16		BMV-16	OP	BASS	AL	SV	OB		5	7	570			1700	2050
16		C-16 DS	OP	BASS	AL	SV	OB		5	10	495			1500	1800
18		WALLEYE 18	OP	BASS	AL	SV	OB		7		730			2100	2800

...,For earlier years, see the BUC Used Boat Price Guide, Volume 3

WAHOO BOATS

MARINE GROUP
SPRINGFIELD MO 65803 COAST GUARD MFG ID- MGI

See inside cover to adjust price for area

LOA FT	LOA IN	NAME AND/ OR MODEL	TOP/ RIG	BOAT TYPE	-HULL- MTL	-HULL- TP	ENGINE TP	ENGINE # HP MFG	BEAM FT	BEAM IN	WGT LBS	DRAFT FT	DRAFT IN	RETAIL LOW	RETAIL HIGH
		1996 BOATS													
16	2	1650 CC	OP	CTRCN	FBG	SV	OB		6	2	725		10	3450	4000
16	2	1650 DC	OP	RNBT	FBG	DV	OB		6	2	725		10	3450	4000
16	10	F 1600 EFS	OP	FSH	FBG	SV	OB		7	5	800			3700	4350
17		1750 CC	OP	CTRCN	FBG	SV	OB		6	8	890		11	4350	5000
18	5	1850 CC	OP	CTRCN	FBG	SV	OB		7	2	1470	1	1	6800	7800
18	5	1850 DC	OP	RNBT	FBG	SV	OB		7	2	1470	1	1	6900	7900
18	6	1900 CC EFS	OP	CTRCN	FBG	DV	OB		8		1690		11	7500	8600
18	10	F 1800 EFS	OP	FSH	FBG	SV	OB		7	9	900			4400	5100
20	1	2100 CC EFS	OP	CTRCN	FBG	DV	OB		8		1850		11	7350	8450
21		2150 CC	OP	CTRCN	FBG	SV	OB		7	8	1900	1	1	7950	9100
21		2150 DC	OP	RNBT	FBG	SV	OB		7	8	1900	1	1	7950	9150
21	10	F 2000 EFS	OP	FSH	FBG	SV	OB		8		1100			4900	5650
23		2400 W/A EFS	OP	SF	FBG	DV	OB		8	6	3400	1	5	13500	15300
23	6	2400 CC EFS	OP	CTRCN	FBG	DV	OB		8	6	3250	1	5	13400	15300
26		2600 CC EFS	OP	CTRCN	FBG	DV	OB		9		4100	1	5	18500	20600
26		2600 W/A EFS	OP	SF	FBG	DV	OB		9		4600	1	5	19100	21200
		1995 BOATS													
16	2	1650 LAZER	OP	RNBT	FBG	DV	OB		6	2	725		10	3350	3900
16	2	1650 LIGHTENING	OP	SF	FBG	SV	OB		6	2	975		10	4250	4950
16	2	1650 STRIPER LX	OP	CTRCN	FBG	SV	OB		6	2	725		10	3250	3750
16	2	1650 TWIN	OP	RNBT	FBG	DV	OB		6	2	725		10	3250	3750
17		1750 OFFSHORE	OP	CTRCN	FBG	SV	OB		6	8	890		11	4100	4750
18	5	1850 SPORTFISH	OP	RNBT	FBG	SV	OB		7	2	1470	1	1	6500	7500
18	5	1900 OFFSHORE	OP	CTRCN	FBG	SV	OB		7	2	1470	1	1	6450	7400
18	6	1860 EFS	OP	CTRCN	FBG	DV	OB		8		1650		11	7000	8050
20	1	2100 EFS	OP	CTRCN	FBG	DV	OB		8		1850		11	6950	8000
21		2100 OFFSHORE	OP	CTRCN	FBG	SV	OB		7	8	1900	1	1	7450	8600
21		2100 SPORTFISH	OP	RNBT	FBG	SV	OB		7	8	1900	1	1	7500	8600
23		2300 SPORTFISH	OP	SF	FBG	DV	OB		8	6	3450	1	5	12900	14600
23	6	2400 EFS	OP	CTRCN	FBG	DV	OB		8	6	3250	1	5	12700	14500
26		2600 EFS	OP	CTRCN	FBG	DV	OB		9		4300	1	5	17400	19800
26		2600 SPORTFISH	OP	SF	FBG	DV	OB		9		4600	1	5	18100	20100
		1994 BOATS													
16	2	1650 LAZER	OP	RNBT	FBG	DV	OB		6	2	725		10	3550	4150
16	2	1650 LX	OP	RNBT	FBG	SV	OB		6	2	725		10	3150	3650
16	2	1650 STRIPER LX	OP	CTRCN	FBG	SV	OB		6	2	725		10	3100	3600
16	2	1650 TWIN	OP	RNBT	FBG	DV	OB		6	2	725		10	3400	3950
17		1750 OFFSHORE	OP	CTRCN	FBG	SV	OB		6	8	890		11	3850	4500
18	5	1850 OFFSHORE	OP	CTRCN	FBG	SV	OB		7	2	1470	1	1	6100	7000
18	5	1850 SPORTFISH	OP	RNBT	FBG	SV	OB		7	2	1470	1	1	6150	7100
18	6	1860 EFS	OP	CTRCN	FBG	DV	OB		8		1650		11	6600	7600
20	1	2050 EFS	OP	CTRCN	FBG	DV	OB		8		1850		11	6600	7600
21		2100 OFFSHORE	OP	CTRCN	FBG	SV	OB		7	8	1900	1	1	7100	8150
21		2100 SPORTFISH	OP	RNBT	FBG	SV	OB		7	8	1900	1	1	7100	8150
23		2300 SPORTFISH	OP	SF	FBG	DV	OB		8	6	3450	1	5	12200	13900
23	6	2400 EFS	OP	CTRCN	FBG	DV	OB		8	6	3250	1	5	12100	13800
26		2600 EFS	OP	CTRCN	FBG	DV	OB		9		4300	1	5	16600	18900
26		2600 SPORTFISH	OP	SF	FBG	DV	OB		9		4600	1	5	16900	19200
		1993 BOATS													
16	2	1650 LX	OP	RNBT	FBG	SV	OB		6	2	725		10	2950	3450
16	2	1650 STRIPER	OP	CTRCN	FBG	SV	OB		6	2	725		10	2900	3400
16	2	1650 TWIN	OP	RNBT	FBG	DV	OB		6	2	725		10	3300	3800
17		1750 OFFSHORE	OP	CTRCN	FBG	SV	OB		6	8	890		11	3650	4250
18	5	1850 OFFSHORE	OP	CTRCN	FBG	SV	OB		7	2	1470	1	1	5800	6650
18	5	1850 SPORTFISH	OP	RNBT	FBG	SV	OB		7	2	1470	1	1	5850	6750
18	6	1860 EFS	OP	CTRCN	FBG	DV	OB		8		1650		11	6300	7250
20	1	2050 EFS	OP	CTRCN	FBG	DV	OB		8		1850		11	6300	7250
21		2100 OFFSHORE	OP	CTRCN	FBG	SV	OB		7	8	1900	1	1	6750	7800
21		2100 SPORTFISH	OP	RNBT	FBG	SV	OB		7	8	1900	1	1	6750	7800
23		2300 SPORTFISH	TT	SF	FBG	DV	OB		8	6	3450	1	5	11600	13200
26		2600 EFS	TT	CTRCN	FBG	DV	OB		9		4300	1	5	15700	17800
26		2600 SPORTFISH	TT	SF	FBG	DV	OB		9		4600	1	5	16100	18300
		1992 BOATS													
16	2	1650 LTD	OP	RNBT	FBG	SV	OB		6	2	725	1		2700	3150
16	2	1650 LX	OP	RNBT	FBG	SV	OB		6	2	725	1		2850	3300
16	2	1650 STRIPER	OP	CTRCN	FBG	SV	OB		6	2	725	1		2800	3250
16	2	1650 TWIN	OP	RNBT	FBG	DV	OB		6	2	725	1		3100	3650
16	2	PALM BEACH EDITION	OP	RNBT	FBG		OB		6	2	725	1		3250	3750
17		1750 OFFSHORE	OP	CTRCN	FBG	SV	OB		6	8	890		11	3450	4050
18	5	1850 OFFSHORE	OP	CTRCN	FBG	SV	OB		7	2	1470	1	1	5500	6350
18	5	1850 SPORTFISH	OP	RNBT	FBG	SV	OB		7	2	1470	1	1	5550	6400
21		2100 OFFSHORE	OP	CTRCN	FBG	SV	OB		7	8	1900	1	1	6450	7450
21		2100 SPORTFISH	OP	RNBT	FBG	SV	OB		7	8	1900	1	1	6450	7450
26		2600 EFS	TT	CTRCN	FBG	DV	OB		9		3800	1	6	14500	16500
26		2600 SPORTFISH	TT	SF	FBG	DV	OB		9		4400	1	6	15100	17100
		1991 BOATS													
16	2	1650 LTD	OP	RNBT	FBG	SV	OB		6	2	725	1		2650	3100
16	2	1650 LX	OP	RNBT	FBG	SV	OB		6	2	725	1		2700	3150
16	2	1650 STRIPER	OP	CTRCN	FBG	SV	OB		6	2	725	1		2650	3100
16	2	1650 TWIN	OP	RNBT	FBG	DV	OB		6	2	725	1		2950	3450
16	2	PALM BEACH EDITION	OP	RNBT	FBG		OB		6	2	725	1		3050	3550
17		1750 OFFSHORE	OP	CTRCN	FBG	SV	OB		6	8	890		11	3300	3850
18	5	1850 OFFSHORE	OP	CTRCN	FBG	SV	OB		7	2	1470	1	1	5250	6050
18	5	1850 SPORTFISH	OP	RNBT	FBG	SV	OB		7	2	1470	1	1	5300	6100
21		2100 OFFSHORE	OP	CTRCN	FBG	SV	OB		7	8	1900	1	1	6200	7100
21		2100 SPORTFISH	OP	RNBT	FBG	SV	OB		7	8	1900	1	1	6200	7100
26		2600 EFS	TT	CTRCN	FBG	DV	OB		9		3800	1	6	13900	15800
26		2600 SPORTFISH	TT	SF	FBG	DV	OB		9		4400	1	6	14400	16400
		1990 BOATS													
16	2	LTD 1650	OP	RNBT	FBG	SV	OB		6	2	725		9	2750	3150
16	2	SPECIAL 16.5	OP	RNBT	FBG	SV	OB		6	2	725		9	2050	2450
16	2	STRIPER 1650	OP	CTRCN	FBG	SV	OB		6	2	725		9	2550	2950
16	2	TWIN 1650	OP	RNBT	FBG	SV	OB		6	2	725		9	2950	3400
17		OFFSHORE 1750	OP	CTRCN	FBG	SV	OB		6	8	890		9	3150	3700
18	5	OFFSHORE 1850	OP	CTRCN	FBG	SV	OB		7	2	1470		10	5050	5800
18	5	SPORTFISH 1850	OP	RNBT	FBG	SV	OB		7	2	1470		10	5100	5850
21		OFFSHORE 2100	OP	CTRCN	FBG	SV	OB		7	8	1900	1		5950	6850
26		EFS 2600	OP	CTRCN	FBG	DV	OB		9		3700	1	6	13200	15000
		1989 BOATS													
16	2	16.2 LTD	OP	RNBT	FBG	DV	OB		6	2	725		9	2400	2800
16	2	16.2 STRIPER	OP	CTRCN	FBG	DV	OB		6	2	725		9	2450	2850
16	2	16.2 TWIN CONSOLE	OP	RNBT	FBG	DV	OB		6	2	725		9	2550	3000
18	5	18.5 OFFSHORE	OP	CTRCN	FBG	DV	OB		7	2	1470		10	4850	5550
18	5	18.5 SPORT FISH	OP	RNBT	FBG	DV	OB		7	2	1470		10	4900	5600
21		2100 OFFSHORE	OP	OFF	FBG	DV	OB		7	8	1900	1		5750	6600
		1988 BOATS													
16	2	16.2 LTD	OP	RNBT	FBG	DV	OB		6	2	725		9	2300	2650
16	2	16.2 STRIPER	OP	CTRCN	FBG	DV	OB		6	2	725		9	2350	2750
16	2	16.2 TWIN CONSOLE	OP	RNBT	FBG	DV	OB		6	2	725		9	2450	2850
18	5	18.5 OFFSHORE	OP	CTRCN	FBG	DV	OB		7	2	1470		10	4650	5350
18	5	18.5 TWIN CONSOLE	OP	RNBT	FBG	DV	OB		7	2	1470		10	4700	5400
21		2100 OFFSHORE	OP	OFF	FBG	DV	OB		7	8	1900	1		5550	6350
		1987 BOATS													
16	2	16.2 LTD	OP	RNBT	FBG	DV	OB		6	2	725			2250	2650
16	2	16.2 STRIPER	OP	CTRCN	FBG	DV	OB		6	2	725			2250	2650
16	2	16.2 TWIN CONSOLE	OP	RNBT	FBG	DV	OB		6	2	725			2300	2700
18	5	18.5 OFFSHORE	OP	CTRCN	FBG	DV	OB		7	2	1470			4500	5150

LOA FT	LOA IN	NAME AND/ OR MODEL	TOP/ RIG	BOAT TYPE	-HULL- MTL	-HULL- TP	ENGINE TP	# HP	MFG	BEAM FT	BEAM IN	WGT LBS	DRAFT FT IN	RETAIL LOW	RETAIL HIGH
		1987 BOATS													
18	5	18.5 TWIN CONSOLE	OP	RNBT	FBG	DV	OB			7	2	1470		4500	5200

WAITSBORO MFG CO INC

CORBIN KY 40701 COAST GUARD MFG ID- WMQ See inside cover to adjust price for area

LOA FT	LOA IN	NAME AND/ OR MODEL	TOP/ RIG	BOAT TYPE	-HULL- MTL	-HULL- TP	ENGINE TP	# HP	MFG	BEAM FT	BEAM IN	WGT LBS	DRAFT FT IN	RETAIL LOW	RETAIL HIGH
		1996 BOATS													
16	5	165 O/RX	OP	RNBT	FBG	DV	OB			6	10	1100		3350	3900
16	5	165 RX	OP	RNBT	FBG	DV	IO	125		6	10	1100		3400	3950
16	5	BASS SCALPER 165	OP	BASS	FBG	DV	OB			6	5	935		2900	3400
16	5	FISH & SKI 165 B/S	OP	BASS	FBG	DV	OB			6	5	980		3050	3550
17		170V	OP	BASS	FBG	DV	OB			7		800		2600	3000
17		EURO 170	OP	RNBT	FBG	DV	IO	125		6	10	1100		3650	4200
17	5	175 DO/RX	OP	RNBT	FBG	DV	OB			7	10	1440		4300	5000
17	5	175 DRX	OP	RNBT	FBG	DV	IO	125		7	1	1590		4350	5000
17	5	BASS SCALPER 175	OP	BASS	FBG	DV	OB			6	11	1050		3250	3750
17	5	FISH & SKI 175 B/S	OP	BASS	FBG	DV	OB			6	11	1050		3450	4000
18		180V	OP	BASS	FBG	DV	OB			7		925		3050	3550
18		EURO 190	OP	RNBT	FBG	DV	IO	125		7	1	1590		4550	5200
18	8	190 CC/RX	OP	CUD	FBG	DV	IO	125		7	11	1910		5550	6400
18	8	190 O/RX	OP	RNBT	FBG	DV	OB			7	4	1700		5000	5750
18	8	190 RX	OP	RNBT	FBG	DV	IO	125		7	4	1700		4950	5650
19	6	196FS	OP	BASS	FBG	DV	OB			7	11	1300		4250	4950
19	7	197 CC/RX	OP	CUD	FBG	DV	IO	125		7	4	2150		5900	6750
20		EURO 200	OP	RNBT	FBG	DV	IO	125		7	4	1700		5050	5800
20	2	210V	OP	BASS	FBG	DV	OB			7	9	1200		5100	5850
20	4	200RT	OP	BASS	FBG	DV	OB			7	5	925		4100	4750
20	4	200VT	OP	BASS	FBG	DV	OB			7	5	1000		4400	5100
21	2	210 CC/RX	OP	CUD	FBG	DV	IO	125		8		2120		6400	7350
22	6	WALK AROUND 220	OP	FSH	FBG	DV	IO	125		8		3600		9800	11100
24	2	242 CC/RX	OP	CUD	FBG	DV	IO	125		9		5000		13300	15100
		1995 BOATS													
16	5	165 O/RX	OP	RNBT	FBG	DV	OB			6	10	1100		3200	3750
16	5	165 RX	OP	RNBT	FBG	DV	IO	125		6	10	1100		3150	3700
16	5	BASS SCALPER 165	OP	BASS	FBG	DV	OB			6	5	935		2800	3250
16	5	FISH & SKI 165 B/S	OP	BASS	FBG	DV	OB			6	5	980		2900	3350
17		170V	OP	BASS	FBG	DV	OB			7		800		2450	2850
17		EURO 170	OP	RNBT	FBG	DV	IO	125		6	10	1100		3400	3950
17	5	175 DO/RX	OP	RNBT	FBG	DV	OB			7	10	1440		4100	4750
17	5	175 DRX	OP	RNBT	FBG	DV	IO	125		7	1	1590		4000	4650
17	5	BASS SCALPER 175	OP	BASS	FBG	DV	OB			6	11	1050		3100	3600
17	5	FISH & SKI 175 B/S	OP	BASS	FBG	DV	OB			6	11	1050		3300	3800
18		180V	OP	BASS	FBG	DV	OB			7		925		2900	3400
18		EURO 190	OP	RNBT	FBG	DV	IO	125		7	1	1590		4200	4850
18	8	190 CC/RX	OP	CUD	FBG	DV	IO	125		7	11	1910		5200	5950
18	8	190 O/RX	OP	RNBT	FBG	DV	OB			7	4	1700		4800	5500
18	8	190 RX	OP	RNBT	FBG	DV	IO	125		7	4	1700		4650	5300
19	6	196FS	OP	BASS	FBG	DV	OB			7	11	1300		4050	4700
19	7	197 CC/RX	OP	CUD	FBG	DV	IO	125		7	4	2150		5500	6300
20		EURO 200	OP	RNBT	FBG	DV	IO	125		7	4	1700		4700	5400
20	2	210V	OP	BASS	FBG	DV	OB			7	9	1200		4850	5600
20	4	200RT	OP	BASS	FBG	DV	OB			7	5	925		3900	4500
20	4	200VT	OP	BASS	FBG	DV	OB			7	5	1000		4150	4850
21	2	210 CC/RX	OP	CUD	FBG	DV	IO	125		8		2120		5950	6850
22	6	WALK AROUND 220	OP	FSH	FBG	DV	IO	125		8		3600		9200	10400
24	2	242 CC/RX	OP	CUD	FBG	DV	IO	125		9		5000		12400	14100
		1994 BOATS													
16	5	165 O/RX	OP	RNBT	FBG	DV	OB			6	10	1100		3050	3550
16	5	165 RX	OP	RNBT	FBG	DV	IO	125		6	10	1100		2950	3450
16	5	BASS SCALPER 165	OP	BASS	FBG	DV	OB			6	5	935		2650	3100
16	5	FISH & SKI 165 B/S	OP	BASS	FBG	DV	OB			6	5	980		2750	3200
17		170V	OP	BASS	FBG	DV	OB			7		800		2350	2750
17		EURO 170	OP	RNBT	FBG	DV	IO	125		6	10	1100		3150	3700
17	5	175 DO/RX	OP	RNBT	FBG	DV	OB			7	10	1440		3900	4550
17	5	175 DRX	OP	RNBT	FBG	DV	IO	125		7	1	1590		3750	4350
17	5	BASS SCALPER 175	OP	BASS	FBG	DV	OB			6	11	1050		2950	3400
17	5	FISH & SKI 175 B/S	OP	BASS	FBG	DV	OB			6	11	1050		3150	3650
18		180V	OP	BASS	FBG	DV	OB			7		925		2800	3250
18		EURO 190	OP	RNBT	FBG	DV	IO	125		7	1	1590		3900	4550
18	8	190 CC/RX	OP	CUD	FBG	DV	IO	125		7	11	1910		4850	5550
18	8	190 O/RX	OP	RNBT	FBG	DV	OB			7	4	1700		4600	5300
18	8	190 RX	OP	RNBT	FBG	DV	IO	125		7	4	1700		4250	4950
19	6	196FS	OP	BASS	FBG	DV	OB			7	11	1300		3900	4500
19	7	197 CC/RX	OP	CUD	FBG	DV	IO	125		7	4	2150		5100	5900
20		EURO 200	OP	RNBT	FBG	DV	IO	125		7	4	1700		4400	5100
20	2	210V	OP	BASS	FBG	DV	OB			7	9	1200		4700	5400
20	4	200RT	OP	BASS	FBG	DV	OB			7	5	925		3700	4300
20	4	200VT	OP	BASS	FBG	DV	OB			7	5	1000		4000	4650
21	2	210 CC/RX	OP	CUD	FBG	DV	IO	125		8		2120		5550	6400
22	6	WALK AROUND 220	OP	FSH	FBG	DV	IO	125		8		3600		8500	9750
24	2	242 CC/RX	OP	CUD	FBG	DV	IO	125		9		5000		11600	13100
		1993 BOATS													
16	5	165 O/RX	OP	RNBT	FBG	DV	OB			6	10	1100		2950	3450
16	5	165 RX	OP	RNBT	FBG	DV	IO	125		6	10	1100		2750	3200
16	5	BASS SCALPER 165	OP	BASS	FBG	DV	OB			6	5	935		2550	2950
16	5	FISH & SKI 165 B/S	OP	BASS	FBG	DV	OB			6	5	980		2650	3100
17		170V	OP	BASS	FBG	DV	OB			7		800		2300	2650
17		EURO 170	OP	RNBT	FBG	DV	IO	125		6	10	1100		2950	3450
17	5	175 DO/RX	OP	RNBT	FBG	DV	OB			7	10	1440		3750	4350
17	5	175 DRX	OP	RNBT	FBG	DV	IO	125		7	1	1590		3500	4100
17	5	175 ERX	OP	RNBT	FBG	DV	IO	125		7	1	1440		3400	3950
17	5	BASS SCALPER 175	OP	BASS	FBG	DV	OB			6	11	1050		2750	3200
17	5	FISH & SKI 175 B/S	OP	BASS	FBG	DV	OB			6	11	1050		3050	3550
18		180DC	OP	BASS	FBG	DV	OB			7		925		2750	3200
18		180V	OP	BASS	FBG	DV	OB			7		925		2600	3000
18		EURO 180	OP	RNBT	FBG	DV	IO	125		7	1	1590		3650	4250
18	8	190 CC/RX	OP	CUD	FBG	DV	IO	125		7	11	1910		4550	5250
18	8	190 O/RX	OP	RNBT	FBG	DV	OB			7	4	1700		4400	5050
18	8	190 RX	OP	RNBT	FBG	DV	IO	125		7	4	1700		4000	4650
19	6	196FS	OP	BASS	FBG	DV	OB			7	11	1300		3700	4300
19	7	197 CC/RX	OP	CUD	FBG	DV	IO	125		7	4	2150		4800	5500
19	7	197 CRX	OP	RNBT	FBG	DV	IO	125		7	4	1860		4400	5050
19	7	197 RX	OP	RNBT	FBG	DV	IO	125		7	4	1920		4450	5100
20		EURO 200	OP	RNBT	FBG	DV	IO	125		7	4	1700		4100	4750
20	2	210V	OP	BASS	FBG	DV	OB			7	9	1200		4500	5150
20	4	200RT	OP	BASS	FBG	DV	OB			7	5	925		3550	4150
20	4	200VT	OP	BASS	FBG	DV	OB			7	5	1000		3800	4450
21	2	210 CC/RX	OP	CUD	FBG	DV	IO	125		8		2120		5200	6000
22	6	WALK AROUND 220	OP	FSH	FBG	DV	IO	125		8		3600		7900	9100
24	2	242 CC/RX	OP	CUD	FBG	DV	IO	125		9		5000		10800	12300
		1992 BOATS													
16	5	165 O/RX	OP	RNBT	FBG	DV	OB			6	10	1100		2850	3300
16	5	165 RX	OP	RNBT	FBG	DV	IO	125		6	10	1100		2600	3000
16	5	BASS SCALPER 165	OP	BASS	FBG	DV	OB			6	5	935		2450	2850
16	5	FISH & SKI 165 B/S	OP	BASS	FBG	DV	OB			6	5	980		2550	2950
17		EURO 170	OP	RNBT	FBG	DV	IO	125		6	10	1100		2750	3200
17	5	175 DO/RX	OP	RNBT	FBG	DV	OB			7	10	1440		3600	4200
17	5	175 DRX	OP	RNBT	FBG	DV	IO	125		7	1	1590		3300	3800
17	5	175 ERX	OP	RNBT	FBG	DV	IO	125		7	1	1440		3150	3700
17	5	BASS SCALPER 175	OP	BASS	FBG	DV	OB			6	11	1050		2650	3100
17	5	FISH & SKI 175 B/S	OP	BASS	FBG	DV	OB			6	11	1050		2950	3450
18		EURO 180	OP	RNBT	FBG	DV	IO	125		7	1	1590		3400	3950
18	8	190 CC/RX	OP	CUD	FBG	DV	IO	125		7	11	1910		4200	4900
18	8	190 O/RX	OP	RNBT	FBG	DV	OB			7	4	1700		4200	4850
18	8	190 RX	OP	RNBT	FBG	DV	IO	125		7	4	1700		3750	4350
19	7	197 CC/RX	OP	CUD	FBG	DV	IO	125		7	4	2150		4500	5200
19	7	197 CRX	OP	RNBT	FBG	DV	IO	125		7	4	1860		4100	4750
19	7	197 RX	OP	RNBT	FBG	DV	IO	125		7	4	1920		4100	4800
20		EURO 200	OP	RNBT	FBG	DV	IO	125		7	4	1700		3850	4450
21	2	210 CC/RX	OP	CUD	FBG	DV	IO	125		8		2120		4850	5600
22	6	WALK AROUND 220	OP	FSH	FBG	DV	IO	125		8		3600		7400	8500
24	2	242 CC/RX	OP	CUD	FBG	DV	IO	125		9		5000		10100	11500
		1991 BOATS													
16	5	165 O/RX	OP	RNBT	FBG	DV	OB			6	10	1100		2700	3150
16	5	165 RX	OP	RNBT	FBG	DV	IO	125	MRCR	6	10	1100		2400	2750
16	5	165 RX/FS	OP	RNBT	FBG	DV	IO	125	MRCR	6	10	1100		2500	2900
16	5	BASS SCALPER 165	OP	BASS	FBG	DV	OB			6	5	935		2350	2750
16	5	BASS SCALPER 165 FS	OP	BASS	FBG	DV	OB			6	5	980		2450	2850
16	5	BASS SCALPER 165 FS	OP	SKI	FBG	DV	OB			6	5	980		2450	2850
17		EURO 170	OP	RNBT	FBG	DV	IO	125	MRCR					2850	3300
17	5	175 DRX	OP	RNBT	FBG	DV	IO	125	MRCR	7	1	1590		3200	3700
17	5	175 ERX	OP	RNBT	FBG	DV	IO	125	MRCR	7	1	1590		2950	3450
17	5	175 O/RX	OP	RNBT	FBG	DV	OB			7	1	1440		3450	4050
17	5	BASS SCALPER 175	OP	BASS	FBG	DV	OB			6	11	1050		2550	2950
17	5	BASS SCALPER 175 FS	OP	BASS	FBG	DV	OB			6	11	1050		2850	3300
18		EURO 180	OP	RNBT	FBG	DV	IO	125	MRCR	7	1	1440		3100	3600
18	8	190 CC/RX	OP	CUD	FBG	DV	IO	125	MRCR	6	11	1910		3600	4200

CONTINUED ON NEXT PAGE

LOA FT	IN	NAME AND/ OR MODEL	TOP/ RIG	BOAT TYPE	-HULL- MTL	TP	TP	----ENGINE--- # HP	MFG	BEAM FT	IN	WGT LBS	DRAFT FT	IN	RETAIL LOW	RETAIL HIGH
		1991 BOATS														
18	8	190 O/RX	OP	RNBT	FBG	DV	OB			7	4	1700			4000	4700
18	8	190 RX	OP	RNBT	FBG	DV	IO	125	MRCR	7	4	1700			3500	4100
19	7	197 CC/RX	OP	RNBT	FBG	DV	IO	125	MRCR	7	4	2150			4050	4700
19	7	197 CRX	OP	RNBT	FBG	DV	IO	125	MRCR	7	4	1860			3800	4450
19	7	197 RX	OP	RNBT	FBG	DV	IO	125	MRCR	7	4	1920			3850	4500
19	7	197 SRX	OP	RNBT	FBG	DV	IO	125	MRCR	7	4	1920			3850	4500
20		EURO 200	OP	RNBT	FBG	DV	IO	125	MRCR	7	4	1700			3600	4150
21	2	210 CC/RX	OP	CUD	FBG	DV	IO	125	MRCR	8		2120			4600	5300
24	2	242 CC/RX	OP	CR	FBG	DV	IO	260	MRCR	9		5000			9900	11200
		1990 BOATS														
16	5	165 BASS SCALPER	OP	BASS	FBG	DV	OB			6	5	935			2300	2650
16	5	165 BASS SCALPER FS	OP	BASS	FBG	DV	OB			6	5	980			2350	2750
16	5	165 BASS SCALPER FS	OP	SKI	FBG	DV	OB			6	5	980			2350	2750
16	5	165 O/RX	OP	RNBT	FBG	DV	OB			6	10	1100			2650	3050
16	5	165 RX	OP	RNBT	FBG	DV	IO	125	MRCR	6	10	1100			2250	2650
16	5	165 RX/FS	OP	RNBT	FBG	DV	IO	120-125		6	10	1100			2300	2700
17	5	175 BASS SCALPER	OP	BASS	FBG	DV	OB			6	11	1050			2450	2850
17	5	175 BASS SCALPER FS	OP	BASS	FBG	DV	OB			6	11	1050			2750	3200
17	5	175 DRX	OP	RNBT	FBG	DV	IO	125	MRCR	7	1	1590			3000	3500
17	5	175 ERX	OP	RNBT	FBG	DV	IO	125	MRCR	7	1	1590			2800	3250
17	5	175 O/RX	OP	RNBT	FBG	DV	OB			7	1	1440			3350	3900
18		EURO 180	OP	RNBT	FBG	DV	IO	125	MRCR	7	1	1440			2950	3400
18	8	190 CC/RX	OP	CUD	FBG	DV	IO	125	MRCR	6	11	1910			3400	3950
18	8	190 O/RX	OP	RNBT	FBG	DV	OB			7	4	1700			3900	4500
18	8	190 RX	OP	RNBT	FBG	DV	IO	125	MRCR	7	4	1700			3300	3850
19	7	197 CC/RX	OP	RNBT	FBG	DV	IO	125	MRCR	7	4	2150			3800	4400
19	7	197 CRX	OP	RNBT	FBG	DV	IO	125	MRCR	7	4	1860			3600	4200
19	7	197 RX	OP	RNBT	FBG	DV	IO	125	MRCR	7	4	1920			3650	4250
19	7	197 SRX	OP	RNBT	FBG	DV	IO	125	MRCR	7	4	1920			3650	4250
20		EURO 200	OP	RNBT	FBG	DV	IO	125	MRCR	7	4	1700			3400	3950
21	2	210 CC/RX	OP	CUD	FBG	DV	IO	125	MRCR	8		2120			4250	4950
24	2	242 CC/RX	OP	CR	FBG	DV	IO	260	MRCR	9		5000			9350	10600
		1989 BOATS														
16	5	165 BASS SCALPER		BASS	FBG	DV	OB			6	5	935			2200	2600
16	5	165 BASS SCALPER FS		BASS	FBG	DV	OB			6	5	980			2300	2700
16	5	165 BASS SCAPLER FS		SKI	FBG	DV	OB			6	5	980			2300	2700
16	5	165 O/RX		RNBT	FBG	DV	OB			6	10	1100			2550	2950
16	5	165 RX		RNBT	FBG	DV	IO	120	MRCR	6	10	1100			2150	2500
16	5	165 RX/FS		BASS	FBG	DV	IO	120	MRCR	6	10	1100			2250	2650
16	5	165 RX/FS		RNBT	FBG	DV	IO	120	MRCR	6	10	1100			2200	2550
17	5	175 BASS SCALPER		BASS	FBG	DV	OB			6	11	1050			2450	2850
17	5	175 BASS SCAPLER FS		BASS	FBG	DV	OB			6	11	1050			2550	2950
17	5	175 DRX		RNBT	FBG	DV	IO	120	MRCR	7	1	1590			2900	3400
17	5	175 ERX		RNBT	FBG	DV	IO	120	MRCR	7	1	1590			2550	2950
17	5	175 O/RX		RNBT	FBG	DV	OB			7	1	1440			3250	3750
18	8	190 CC/RX		CUD	FBG	DV	IO	120	MRCR	6	11	1910			3200	3700
18	8	190 O/RX		RNBT	FBG	DV	OB			7	4	1700			3750	4350
18	8	190 RX		RNBT	FBG	DV	IO	120	MRCR	7	4	1700			3100	3600
19	7	197 CC/RX		RNBT	FBG	DV	IO	120	MRCR	7	4	2150			3600	4150
19	7	197 CRX		RNBT	FBG	DV	IO	120	MRCR	7	4	1860			3400	3950
19	7	197 RX		RNBT	FBG	DV	IO	120	MRCR	7	4	1920			3450	4000
19	7	197 SRX		RNBT	FBG	DV	IO	120	MRCR	7	4	1920			3450	4000
21	2	210 CC/RX		CUD	FBG	DV	IO	120	MRCR	8		2120			4050	4700
24	2	242 CC/RX		CR	FBG	DV	IO	260	MRCR	9		5000			8800	10000
		1988 BOATS														
16	5	BASS-SCALPER 165	OP	BASS	FBG	SV	OB			6	5				1850	2200
16	5	FISH-&-SKI 165	OP	BASS	FBG	SV	OB			6	5				2050	2450
16	5	GLASSPORT 165	OP	RNBT	FBG	DV	OB			7	10	1150			2550	3000
17	5	BASS-SCALPER 175	OP	RNBT	FBG	DV	OB			7	6	1000			2350	2700
17	5	CLOSED BOW 175	ST	RNBT	FBG	DV	IO	120-200		7	1	1360			2450	2950
17	5	DELUXE B/R 175	ST	RNBT	FBG	DV	IO	120-230		7	1	1590			2600	3200
17	5	ECONOMY 175	OP	RNBT	FBG	DV	IO	120-175		7	1	1440			2500	2950
17	5	OB 175 EO/RX	OP	RNBT	FBG	DV	OB			7	1	1400			3050	3550
18	8	CC/RX 190	OP	RNBT	FBG	DV	IO	120-200		7	9	1910			3200	3800
18	8	CC/RX 190	OP	RNBT	FBG	DV	IO	260	MRCR	7	9	1910			3450	4050
18	8	GLASSPORT 190	OP	RNBT	FBG	DV	OB			7	4	1500			3350	3900
19	7	CLOSED BOW 197	ST	RNBT	FBG	DV	IO	120-200		7	4	1860			3200	3800
19	7	CLOSED BOW 197	ST	RNBT	FBG	DV	IO	260		7	4	1860			3500	4050
19	7	SS B/R 197	ST	RNBT	FBG	DV	IO	120-200		7	4	1920			3250	3850
19	7	SS B/R 197	ST	RNBT	FBG	DV	IO	260	MRCR	7	4	1920			3550	4100
19	7	VAN-LEAR 197	ST	CUD	FBG	DV	IO	120-200		7	4	2150			3500	4150
19	7	VAN-LEAR 197	ST	CUD	FBG	DV	IO	260	MRCR	7	4	2150			3800	4450
21	2	CC/RX 210	OP	RNBT	FBG	DV	IO	120-260		8		2120			3650	4550
		1987 BOATS														
16	5	BASS-SCALPER 165	OP	BASS	FBG	SV	OB			6	5				1800	2150
16	5	FISH-&-SKI 165	OP	BASS	FBG	SV	OB			6	5				2000	2350
16	5	GLASSPORT 165	OP	RNBT	FBG	DV	OB			7	10	1150			2500	2900
17	5	BASS-SCALPER 175	OP	RNBT	FBG	DV	OB			7	6	1000			2300	2650
17	5	CLOSED BOW 175	ST	RNBT	FBG	DV	IO	120-200		7	1	1360			2350	2800
17	5	DELUXE B/R 175	ST	RNBT	FBG	DV	IO	120-230		7	1	1590			2450	3000
17	5	ECONOMY 175	OP	RNBT	FBG	DV	IO	120-175		7	1	1440			2400	2800
17	5	OB 175 EO/RX	OP	RNBT	FBG	DV	OB			7	1	1400			3000	3450
18	8	GLASSPORT 190	OP	RNBT	FBG	DV	OB			7	4	1500			3250	3750
19	7	CLOSED BOW 197	ST	RNBT	FBG	DV	IO	120-200		7	4	1860			3050	3650
19	7	CLOSED BOW 197	ST	RNBT	FBG	DV	IO	260		7	4	1860			3300	3850
19	7	SS B/R 197	ST	RNBT	FBG	DV	IO	120-200		7	4	1920			3100	3650
19	7	SS B/R 197	ST	RNBT	FBG	DV	IO	260	MRCR	7	4	1920			3350	3900
19	7	VAN-LEAR 197	ST	CUD	FBG	DV	IO	120-200		7	4	2150			3350	3950
19	7	VAN-LEAR 197	ST	CUD	FBG	DV	IO	260	MRCR	7	4	2150			3600	4200
		1986 BOATS														
16	5	BASS-SCALPER 165	OP	BASS	FBG	SV	OB			6	5				1750	2050
16	5	FISH-&-SKI 165	OP	BASS	FBG	SV	OB			6	5				1950	2300
16	5	GLASSPORT 165	OP	RNBT	FBG	DV	OB			7	10	1150			2400	2800
17	5	BASS-SCALPER 175	OP	RNBT	FBG	DV	OB			7	6	1000			2250	2600
17	5	CLOSED BOW 175	ST	RNBT	FBG	DV	IO	120-228		7	1	1360			2250	2750
17	5	DELUXE B/R 175	ST	RNBT	FBG	DV	IO	120-230		7	1	1590			2350	2900
17	5	ECONOMY 175	OP	RNBT	FBG	DV	OB			7	1	1400			2500	2900
17	5	ECONOMY 175	OP	RNBT	FBG	DV	IO	120-170		7	1	1440			2300	2700
17	5	OB 175	OP	RNBT	FBG	DV	OB			7	1	1400			3300	3850
18	2	TRI-HULL 182	OP	RNBT	FBG	DV	IO	120-198		7	3	2500			3050	3600
18	2	TRI-HULL 182	OP	RNBT	FBG	DV	IO	260		7	3	2500			3300	3850
18	8	GLASSPORT 190	OP	RNBT	FBG	DV	OB			7	4	1500			3150	3650
19	7	CLOSED BOW 197	ST	RNBT	FBG	DV	IO	120-198		7	4	1860			2900	3450
19	7	CLOSED BOW 197	ST	RNBT	FBG	DV	IO	260		7	4	1860			3150	3700
19	7	SS B/R 197	ST	RNBT	FBG	DV	IO	120-198		7	4	1920			2950	3500
19	7	SS B/R 197	ST	RNBT	FBG	DV	IO	260	MRCR	7	4	1920			3200	3700
19	7	VAN-LEAR 197	ST	CUD	FBG	DV	IO	120-198		7	4	2150			3200	3800
19	7	VAN-LEAR 197	ST	CUD	FBG	DV	IO	260	MRCR	7	4	2150			3450	4000
		1985 BOATS														
16	5	BASS-SCALPER 165	OP	BASS	FBG	SV	OB			6	5				1700	2000
16	5	FISH-&-SKI 165	OP	BASS	FBG	SV	OB			6	5				1900	2250
17	5	CLOSED BOW 175	ST	RNBT	FBG	DV	IO	120-230		7	1	1360			2150	2650
17	5	DELUXE 175	ST	RNBT	FBG	DV	OB			7	1	1400			2800	3300
17	5	DELUXE B/R 175	ST	RNBT	FBG	DV	IO	170-230		7	1	1590			2300	2750
17	5	DELUXE BR 175	ST	RNBT	FBG	DV	IO	120-140		7	1	1590			2300	2650
17	5	ECONOMY 175	OP	RNBT	FBG	DV	OB			7	1	1400			2800	3300
17	5	ECONOMY 175	OP	RNBT	FBG	DV	IO	120-170		7	1	1440			2200	2600
18	2	TRI-HULL 182		RNBT	FBG	TR	IO	170		7	3	1600			2450	2850
19	7	CLOSED BOW 197	ST	RNBT	FBG	DV	IO	140-230		7	4	1860			2800	3400
19	7	CLOSED BOW 197	ST	RNBT	FBG	DV	IO	260		7	4	1860			3050	3550
19	7	SS B/R 197	ST	RNBT	FBG	DV	IO	140-230		7	4	1920			2850	3450
19	7	VAN-LEAR 197	ST	CUD	FBG	DV	IO	140-230		7	4	2150			3050	3700
19	7	VAN-LEAR 197	ST	CUD	FBG	DV	IO	260		7	4	2150			3300	3850
		1984 BOATS														
17	5	DELUXE 175	ST	RNBT	FBG	DV	OB			7	1	1400			2750	3200
17	5	DELUXE B/R 175	ST	RNBT	FBG	DV	IO	170-230		7	1	1590			2200	2700
17	5	ECONOMY 173		RNBT	FBG	DV	IO	120		7	1				2050	2450
17	5	ECONOMY 175	OP	RNBT	FBG	DV	OB			7	1	1400			2750	3200
17	5	ECONOMY 175	OP	RNBT	FBG	DV	IO	120-170		7	1	1440			2100	2500
18	2	TRI-HULL 182		RNBT	FBG	TR	IO	170-230		7	3	1600			2350	2850
19	7	SN 197		RNBT	FBG	DV	IO	170-230		7	4	1920			2750	3300
19	7	SS B/R 197		RNBT	FBG	DV	IO	170-230		7	4	1920			2750	3300
19	7	VAN-LEAR 197		CUD	FBG	DV	IO	170-230		7	4	2150			3000	3600

WALTERS BOAT CO INC

S NORWALK CT 06854

See inside cover to adjust price for area

LOA FT	IN	NAME AND/ OR MODEL	TOP/ RIG	BOAT TYPE	-HULL- MTL	TP	TP	----ENGINE--- # HP	MFG	BEAM FT	IN	WGT LBS	DRAFT FT	IN	RETAIL LOW	RETAIL HIGH
		1986 BOATS														
33	5	WALTERS 33	SLP	SA/RC	FBG	CB	IB			10	4	10584			37800	42000
		1985 BOATS														
33	5	WALTERS 33	SLP	SA/RC	FBG	CB	IB			10	4	8250			27700	30800

DAVID WALTERS

FT LAUDERDALE FL 33316 — See inside cover to adjust price for area

FORMERLY DAVID WALTERS YACHTS

LOA FT	LOA IN	NAME AND/ OR MODEL	TOP/ RIG	BOAT TYPE	HULL MTL	HULL TP	ENGINE TP	# HP	ENGINE MFG	BEAM FT	BEAM IN	WGT LBS	DRAFT FT	DRAFT IN	RETAIL LOW	RETAIL HIGH
		1991 BOATS														
41	5	CAMBRIA 40	CUT	SA/CR	FBG	KC	IB	46D	WEST	12	3	22200	5	2	199500	219000
45	11	CAMBRIA 44	CUT	SA/CR	FBG	KC	IB	58D	WEST	13	6	29400	5	3	284500	312500
46	2	CAMBRIA 46	CUT	SA/CR	FBG	KC	IB	58D	WEST	13	6	29400	5	3	287500	316000
48	1	CAMBRIA 48	CUT	SA/CR	FBG	KC	IB	58D	WEST	13	6	29800	5	3	317000	348500
50		CAMBRIA 50	CUT	SA/CR	FBG	KC	IB	58D	WEST	13	6	30200	5	3	358000	393500
		1990 BOATS														
41	5	CAMBRIA 40	CUT	SA/CR	FBG	KC	IB	46D	WEST	12	3	22200	5	2	187500	206000
45	11	CAMBRIA 44	CUT	SA/CR	FBG	KC	IB	58D	WEST	13	6	29400	5	3	267500	294000
46	2	CAMBRIA 46	CUT	SA/CR	FBG	KC	IB	58D	WEST	13	6	29400	5	6	270500	297500
48	1	CAMBRIA 48	CUT	SA/CR	FBG	KC	IB	58D	WEST	13	6	29800	5	3	298000	327500
50		CAMBRIA 50	CUT	SA/CR	FBG	KC	IB	58D	WEST	13	6	30200	5	3	337000	370000
		1989 BOATS														
41	5	CAMBRIA 40	CUT	SA/CR	FBG	KC	IB	46D	WEST	12	3	22200	5	2	176500	194000
45	11	CAMBRIA 44	CUT	SA/CR	FBG	KC	IB	58D	WEST	13	6	29400	5	3	251500	276500
46	5	CAMBRIA 48	CUT	SA/CR	FBG	KC	IB	58D	WEST	13	6	29800	5	3	259000	284500
50		CAMBRIA 50	CUT	SA/CR	FBG	KC	IB	58D	WEST	13	6	30200	5	3	317000	348000
		1988 BOATS														
41	5	CAMBRIA 40	CUT	SA/CR	FBG	KC	IB	46D	WEST	12	3	22200	5	2	166000	182500
45	11	CAMBRIA 44	CUT	SA/CR	FBG	KC	IB	58D	WEST	13	6	29400	5	3	236500	260000
46	5	CAMBRIA 46	CUT	SA/CR	FBG	KC	IB	58D	WEST	13	6	29800	5	3	243500	267500
50		CAMBRIA 50	CUT	SA/CR	FBG	KC	IB	58D	WEST	13	6	30200	5	3	298000	327500
		1987 BOATS														
41	5	CAMBRIA 40	CUT	SA/CR	F/S	KL	IB	46D	WEST	12	3	22200	4	11	156000	171500
45	10	CAMBRIA 44	CUT	SA/CR	F/S	KL	IB	58D	WEST	13	5	28600	5	3	219000	240500
46	5	CAMBRIA 46	CUT	SA/CR	F/S	KL	IB	58D	WEST	13	5	28600	5	3	225000	247500
		1985 BOATS														
45	11	CAMBRIA	SLP	SA/CR	F/S	KL	IB	D		13	6	28600	7	6	194500	213500
45	11	CAMBRIA SHOAL	SLP	SA/CR	F/S	KL	IB	D		13	6	28600	5	11	194500	213500

WARLOCK POWERBOATS INC

CORONA CA 91720 — COAST GUARD MFG ID- TPI See inside cover to adjust price for area

FORMERLY TEAM WARLOCK INC

LOA FT	LOA IN	NAME AND/ OR MODEL	TOP/ RIG	BOAT TYPE	HULL MTL	HULL TP	ENGINE TP	# HP	ENGINE MFG	BEAM FT	BEAM IN	WGT LBS	DRAFT FT	DRAFT IN	RETAIL LOW	RETAIL HIGH
		1994 BOATS														
22	7	SXT CAT 23		RNBT	F/S	CT	IO	330	MRCR	7	6	3500	1		13900	15800
23	6	WORLD CLASS 24		OFF	F/S	DV	IO	330	MRCR	6	8	3500	1	6	15600	17700
24	6	EURO CLASS 25		OFF	F/S	DV	IO	330	MRCR	6	8	3500	1	6	16400	18600
25		SXT CAT 25		RNBT	F/S	CT	IO	330	MRCR	8		4000	1	2	17200	19500
26	7	WORLD CLASS 27		OFF	F/S	DV	IO	330	MRCR	8		4000	1	8	20800	23100
28		SXT CAT 28		RNBT	F/S	CT	IO	T330	MRCR	8	6	5500	1	7	26700	29600
28	6	WORLD CLASS 29		OFF	F/S	DV	IO	T330	MRCR	8		5500	1	4	31300	34800
31		SXT CAT 31		RNBT	F/S	CT	IO	T330	MRCR	9		7500	2		37100	41300
32		EURO CLASS 32		OFF	F/S	DV	IO	T330	MRCR	8		7000	2		47600	52300
		1993 BOATS														
22		SXT CAT		RNBT	F/S	CT	IO	350	MRCR	7	9	2990	1		12500	14200
23		WORLD CLASS		OFF	F/S	DV	IO	350	MRCR	6	8	3000	1	6	13600	15500
24		EURO CLASS		OFF	F/S	DV	IO	350	MRCR	6	8	3000	1	6	14300	16200
25		SXT CAT		RNBT	F/S	CT	IO	390	MRCR	8		3500	1	2	16900	19200
26		WORLD CLASS		OFF	F/S	DV	IO	390	MRCR	7	8	3510	1	8	19800	22000
28		SXT CAT		RNBT	F/S	CT	IO	T390	MRCR	8	6	5500	1	7	27500	30500
28		WORLD CLASS		OFF	F/S	DV	IO	T390	MRCR	7	8	4800	1	4	30000	33300
31		SXT CAT		RNBT	F/S	CT	IO	T390	MRCR	9		6800	2		36600	40700
32		EURO CLASS		OFF	F/S	DV	IO	T390	MRCR	8		6700	2		46100	50600
		1990 BOATS														
20		SKI SPORT 20	OP	SKI	FBG	DV	IO								**	**
21		SXT CAT 21	OP	RNBT	FBG		IO								**	**
22		SPORT TUNNEL BR	OP	RNBT	FBG	TH	IO								**	**
22		SPORT TUNNEL CB	OP	RNBT	FBG	TH	IO								**	**
23		WORLD CLASS 23	OP	OFF	FBG	DV	IO								**	**
24		EURO CLASS 24	OP	OFF	FBG	DV	IO								**	**
25		PXT CAT 25	OP	RNBT	FBG		IO								**	**
25		PXT CAT 25	OP	RNBT	FBG		IO	T							**	**
25		RXT CAT 25	OP	RACE	FBG		IO								**	**
25		RXT CAT 25	OP	RACE	FBG		IO	T							**	**
25		SRT CAT 25	OP	RACE	FBG		IO								**	**
25		SRT CAT 25	OP	RACE	FBG		IO	T							**	**
25		SXT CAT 25	OP	RNBT	FBG		IO								**	**
25		SXT CAT 25	OP	RNBT	FBG		IO	T							**	**
26		WORLD CLASS 26	OP	OFF	FBG	DV	IO								**	**
26		WORLD CLASS 26	OP	OFF	FBG	DV	IO	T							**	**
28		WORLD CLASS 28	OP	OFF	FBG	DV	IO								**	**
28		WORLD CLASS 28	OP	OFF	FBG	DV	IO	T							**	**
31		FXT CAT 31	OP	RNBT	FBG		IO	T							**	**
31		FXT CAT 31	OP	RNBT	FBG		IO	R							**	**
31		RXT CAT 31	OP	RNBT	FBG		IO	T							**	**
31		RXT CAT 31	OP	RNBT	FBG		IO	R							**	**
31		SRT CAT 31	OP	RNBT	FBG		IO	T							**	**
31		SRT CAT 31	OP	RNBT	FBG		IO	R							**	**
31		SXT CAT 31	OP	RNBT	FBG		IO	T							**	**
31		SXT CAT 31	OP	RNBT	FBG		IO	R							**	**
32		EURO CLASS 32	OP	OFF	FBG	DV	IO								**	**
32		EURO CLASS 32	OP	OFF	FBG	DV	IO	T							**	**

WARREN CRAFT BOATS

MIAMI FL 33142 — COAST GUARD MFG ID- WDC See inside cover to adjust price for area

LOA FT	LOA IN	NAME AND/ OR MODEL	TOP/ RIG	BOAT TYPE	HULL MTL	HULL TP	ENGINE TP	# HP	ENGINE MFG	BEAM FT	BEAM IN	WGT LBS	DRAFT FT	DRAFT IN	RETAIL LOW	RETAIL HIGH
		1986 BOATS														
16		1600 SKI	OP	RNBT	FBG	DV	OB			6	8	800			1300	1550
16		BACKCOUNTRY 4-IN-1	OP	FSH	FBG	DV	OB			6	8	705			1150	1400
16	4	1750 B/R	OP	RNBT	FBG	DV	OB			6	9	1700			2650	3050
16	4	1750 B/R	OP	RNBT	FBG	DV	IO	120	OMC	6	9	1700			2600	3000
16	9	1800 B/R	OP	RNBT	FBG	DV	IO	120	OMC	6	11	1800			2800	3250
16	9	CARIBBEAN SKIFF	OP	FSH	FBG	TR	OB			6	4	850			1450	1700
18	2	1950 B/R	OP	RNBT	FBG	DV	IO	120	OMC	7	6	1900			3300	3800
19	2	2050 B/R	OP	RNBT	FBG	DV	OB			7	6	2000			3000	3500
19	2	2050 B/R	OP	RNBT	FBG	DV	IO	120	OMC	7	6	2000			3550	4150
20	5	2200 CC	OP	CUD	FBG	DV	IO	120	OMC	8		2550			5000	5750
		1985 BOATS														
16		1600 SKI	OP	RNBT	FBG	DV	OB			6	8	800			1300	1550
16		BACKCOUNTRY 4-IN-1	OP	FSH	FBG	DV	OB			6	8	705			1150	1350
16	4	1750 B/R	OP	RNBT	FBG	DV	OB			6	9	1700			2550	3000
16	4	1750 B/R	OP	RNBT	FBG	DV	IO	120	OMC	6	9	1700			2500	2900
16	9	1800 B/R	OP	RNBT	FBG	DV	IO	120	OMC	6	11	1800			2650	3100
16	9	CARIBBEAN SKIFF	OP	FSH	FBG	TR	OB			6	4	850			1400	1650
18	2	1950 B/R	OP	RNBT	FBG	DV	IO	120	OMC	7	6	1900			3150	3650
19	2	2050 B/R	OP	RNBT	FBG	DV	OB			7	6	2000			2950	3450
19	2	2050 B/R	OP	RNBT	FBG	DV	IO	120	OMC	7	6	2000			3400	3950
20	5	2200 CC	OP	CUD	FBG	DV	IO	120	OMC	8		2550			4800	5550
		1984 BOATS														
16		BACKCOUNTRY 4-IN-1	OP	FSH	FBG	DV	OB			6	8	705			1100	1300
16	4	1750 B/R	OP	RNBT	FBG	DV	OB			6	9	1700			2500	2900
16	4	1750 B/R	OP	RNBT	FBG	DV	IB	120	OMC	6	9	1700			3150	3650
16	9	1800 B/R	OP	RNBT	FBG	DV	IB	120	OMC	6	11	1800			3400	3950
16	9	CARIBBEAN SKIFF	OP	FSH	FBG	TR	OB			6	4	850			1350	1650
18	2	1950 B/R	OP	RNBT	FBG	DV	IB	120	OMC	7	6	1900			3950	4600
18	2	1950 SD	OP	RNBT	FBG	DV	IB	120	OMC	7	6	1900			4050	4700
19	2	2050 B/R	OP	RNBT	FBG	DV	OB			7	6	2000			2900	3350
19	2	2050 B/R	OP	RNBT	FBG	DV	IB	120	OMC	7	6	2000			4250	4950
19	2	2050 SD	OP	RNBT	FBG	DV	IB	120	OMC	7	6	2000			4450	5150
19	2	2200 CC	OP	CUD	FBG	DV	IB	120	OMC	7	6	2200			4400	5050
20	5	2200 CC	OP	CUD	FBG	DV	IB	120	OMC	8		2550			5750	6650

....For earlier years, see the BUC Used Boat Price Guide, Volume 3

WARRIOR BOATS

DIV OF SUN PATIO INC

MAPLE LAKE MN 55358 — COAST GUARD MFG ID- PUO — See inside cover to adjust price for area

For more recent years, see the BUC Used Boat Price Guide, Volume 1

LOA FT	LOA IN	NAME AND/ OR MODEL	TOP/ RIG	BOAT TYPE	HULL MTL	HULL TP	ENGINE TP	# HP	ENGINE MFG	BEAM FT	BEAM IN	WGT LBS	DRAFT FT	DRAFT IN	RETAIL LOW	RETAIL HIGH
		1995 BOATS														
16		LANCE V160 DC		FSH	AL	SV	OB			5	10	510			2600	3050
16		LANCE V160 SC		FSH	AL	SV	OB			5	10	470			2400	2800
16	1	LASER V160 BT		FSH	AL	SV	OB			5	8	440			2250	2650
16	2	LANCE V170 SC		FSH	AL	SV	OB			6	3	630			3250	3800
16	3	LASER V170 BT		FSH	AL	SV	OB			6	5	550			2850	3350
16	6	EAGLE V166 BT		FSH	FBG	SV	OB			7	11	975			5000	5750
16	6	EAGLE V166 SC		FSH	FBG	SV	OB			7	11	1015			5200	5950
16	6	FALCON V166 BT		FSH	FBG	SV	OB			7	11	725			3800	4400
16	6	FALCON V166 SC		FSH	FBG	SV	OB			7	11	825			4250	4950
16	7	LANCE V170 DC		FSH	AL	SV	OB			6	3	650			3400	3950
16	7	LANCE V180 SC		FSH	AL	SV	OB			6	6	970			5050	5800

LOA FT	LOA IN	NAME AND/ OR MODEL	TOP/ RIG	BOAT TYPE	-HULL- MTL	-HULL- TP	ENGINE TP	ENGINE # HP	ENGINE MFG	BEAM FT	BEAM IN	WGT LBS	DRAFT FT	DRAFT IN	RETAIL LOW	RETAIL HIGH
		1995 BOATS														
16	10	LANCE V180 DC		FSH	AL	SV	OB			6	8	970			5050	5850
17	1	LASER V180 BT		FSH	AL	SV	OB			7	11	950			5000	5750
17	6	EAGLE V177 BT		FSH	FBG	SV	OB			7	11	1075			5650	6450
17	6	EAGLE V177 DC		FSH	FBG	SV	OB			7	11	1195			6150	7050
17	6	EAGLE V177 SC		FSH	FBG	SV	OB			7	11	1125			5850	6700
17	6	FALCON V177 BT		FSH	FBG	SV	OB			7	11	850			4600	5300
17	6	FALCON V177 SC		FSH	FBG	SV	OB			7	11	950			5050	5800
17	6	V177 DC		FSH	FBG	SV	OB			7	11	1150			5800	6650
17	6	V177 DUAL FISH SKI		FSH	FBG	SV	OB			7	11	1150			6100	7050
18	2	EAGLE V1890 BT		FSH	FBG	SV	OB			7	6	1175			6200	7100
18	2	EAGLE V1890 DC		FSH	FBG	SV	OB			7	6	1325			6800	7800
18	2	EAGLE V1890 SC		FSH	FBG	SV	OB			7	6	1225			6400	7350
18	8	EAGLE V188 DC		FSH	FBG	SV	OB			8		1500			7550	8700
18	8	EAGLE V188 SC		FSH	FBG	SV	OB			8		1450			7400	8500
19		LANCE V190 DC		FSH	AL	SV	OB			8		1185			6400	7350
19	3	EAGLE V190 DC		FSH	FBG	SV	OB			8	1	1350			7150	8200
19	3	LANCE V190 SC		FSH	AL	SV	OB			8		1145			6300	7200
20	8	EAGLE V208 DC		FSH	FBG	SV	OB			8		1775			9800	11100
		1994 BOATS														
16	2	BACKTROLLER LASER		FSH	AL	SV	OB			5	10	495			2450	2850
16	2	SD CONSL LASER V160		FSH	AL	SV	OB			5	10	550			2700	3150
16	3	BACKTROLLER		FSH	AL	SV	OB			6	8	550			2700	3150
16	3	SIDE CNSLE LNCE V166		FSH	AL	SV	OB			6	8	595			2950	3400
16	6	BACKTROLLER EAGLE		FSH	FBG	SV	OB			6	11	975			4750	5450
16	6	BACKTROLLER FALCON		FSH	FBG	SV	OB			6	11	725			3550	4100
16	6	SIDE CNSLE FLCN V166		FSH	FBG	SV	OB			6	11	825			4050	4700
17		BACKTROLLER		FSH	AL	SV	OB			7		950			4750	5450
17		SIDE CNSLE LNCE V170		FSH	AL	SV	OB			7		985			4900	5650
17	6	BACKTROLLER EAGLE		FSH	FBG	SV	OB			6	11	1075			5350	6150
17	6	DL FISH/SKI STD V177		FSH	FBG	SV	OB			6	11	1150			5700	6550
17	6	DUAL CNSOLE STD V177		FSH	FBG	SV	OB			6	11	1150			5550	6400
17	6	SD CNSLE EAGLE V177		FSH	FBG	SV	OB			6	11	1125			5550	6350
18	2	BACKTROLLER EAGLE		FSH	FBG	SV	OB			7	6	1175			5850	6750
18	2	DL CNSLE EAGLE V1890		FSH	FBG	SV	OB			7	6	1275			6250	7200
18	2	SD CNSLE EAGLE V1890		FSH	FBG	SV	OB			7	6	1225			6050	6950
18	8	DL CNSLE EAGLE V188		FSH	FBG	DV	OB			7	6	1500			7150	8200
18	8	SD CNSLE EAGLE V188		FSH	FBG	DV	OB			8		1450			7000	8050
19	3	DL CNSLE EAGLE V190		FSH	FBG	DV	OB			8	1	1350			6800	7800
20	8	DL CNSLE EAGLE V208		FSH	FBG	DV	OB			8		1775			9250	10500

WARRIOR CATAMARANS INC

OXNARD CA 93030 COAST GUARD MFG ID- WAF See inside cover to adjust price for area

LOA FT	LOA IN	NAME AND/ OR MODEL	TOP/ RIG	BOAT TYPE	-HULL- MTL	-HULL- TP	ENGINE TP	ENGINE # HP	ENGINE MFG	BEAM FT	BEAM IN	WGT LBS	DRAFT FT	DRAFT IN	RETAIL LOW	RETAIL HIGH
		1984 BOATS														
29		WARRIOR 29	SLP	SA/OD	FBG	CT				16		2000	1		17300	19700

....For earlier years, see the BUC Used Boat Price Guide, Volume 3

WATKINS YACHTS INC

CLEARWATER FL 33520 COAST GUARD MFG ID- WYM See inside cover to adjust price for area

LOA FT	LOA IN	NAME AND/ OR MODEL	TOP/ RIG	BOAT TYPE	-HULL- MTL	-HULL- TP	ENGINE TP	ENGINE # HP	ENGINE MFG	BEAM FT	BEAM IN	WGT LBS	DRAFT FT	DRAFT IN	RETAIL LOW	RETAIL HIGH
		1989 BOATS														
22	2	WATKINS SEAWOLF 22CC	OP	FSH	FBG	SV	OB			8	6	2700			5150	5950
		SE OMC ** ** , SE 235 OMC 5150 5950, SE T300 OMC													5150	5950
22	2	WATKINS SEAWOLF 22WA	OP	FSH	FBG	SV	OB			8	6	2875			5400	6200
		SE OMC ** ** , SE 235 OMC 5400 6200, SE T300 OMC													5400	6200
24	11	WATKINS 25	SLP	SA/RC	FBG	KL	OB			8		4800	2	6	9300	10600
24	11	WATKINS 25	SLP	SA/RC	FBG	KL	IB	9D		8		4800	2	6	9900	11200
25	10	WATKINS SEAWOLF 26CC	OP	FSH	FBG	SV	OB			8	6	3100			7650	8800
25	10	WATKINS SEAWOLF 26CC	OP	FSH	FBG	SV	SE		OMC	8	6	3100			**	**
25	10	WATKINS SEAWOLF 26CC	OP	FSH	FBG	SV	SE	T	OMC	8	6	3100			**	**
25	10	WATKINS SEAWOLF 26CC	OP	FSH	FBG	SV	IO	T470	OMC	8	6	3100			15800	18000
25	10	WATKINS SEAWOLF 26WA	OP	FSH	FBG	SV	OB			8	6	3325			7800	9000
25	10	WATKINS SEAWOLF 26WA	OP	FSH	FBG	SV	SE		OMC	8	6	3325			**	**
25	10	WATKINS SEAWOLF 26WA	OP	FSH	FBG	SV	SE	T	OMC	8	6	3325			**	**
25	10	WATKINS SEAWOLF 26WA	OP	FSH	FBG	SV	IO	T470	OMC	8	6	3325			16100	18300
29	10	WATKINS 30	SLP	SA/RC	FBG	KL	IB	18D		10	4	9100	4		22300	24800
33	1	WATKINS 30	SLP	SA/RC	FBG	KL	IB	27D		10	2	11200	4		28100	31200
		1988 BOATS														
22	2	WATKINS SEAWOLF 22CC	OP	FSH	FBG	SV	OB			8	6	2700			5000	5750
		SE OMC ** ** , SE 235 OMC 5000 5750, SE T300 OMC													5000	5750
22	2	WATKINS SEAWOLF 22WA	OP	FSH	FBG	SV	OB			8	6	2875			5200	6000
		SE OMC ** ** , SE 235 OMC 5200 6000, SE T300 OMC													5200	6000
24	11	WATKINS SEAWOLF 25	SLP	SA/RC	FBG	KL	OB			8		4800	2	6	8650	9950
24	11	WATKINS SEAWOLF 25	SLP	SA/RC	FBG	KL	IB	9D		8		4800	2	6	9350	10600
25	10	WATKINS SEAWOLF 26CC	OP	FSH	FBG	SV	OB			8	6	3100			7400	8500
25	10	WATKINS SEAWOLF 26CC	OP	FSH	FBG	SV	SE		OMC	8	6	3100			**	**
25	10	WATKINS SEAWOLF 26CC	OP	FSH	FBG	SV	SE	T	OMC	8	6	3100			**	**
25	10	WATKINS SEAWOLF 26CC	OP	FSH	FBG	SV	IO	T470	OMC	8	6	3100			15000	17000
25	10	WATKINS SEAWOLF 26WA	OP	FSH	FBG	SV	OB			8	6	3325			7550	8700
25	10	WATKINS SEAWOLF 26WA	OP	FSH	FBG	SV	SE		OMC	8	6	3325			**	**
25	10	WATKINS SEAWOLF 26WA	OP	FSH	FBG	SV	SE	T	OMC	8	6	3325			**	**
25	10	WATKINS SEAWOLF 26WA	OP	FSH	FBG	SV	IO	T470	OMC	8	6	3325			15300	17300
28	11	WATKINS SEAWOLF 30	SLP	SA/RC	FBG	KL	IB	18D		10	4	9100	4		20700	23000
33	1	WATKINS SEAWOLF 33	SLP	SA/RC	FBG	KL	IB	27D		10	2	11200	4		26400	29400
		1987 BOATS														
24	11	WATKINS 25	SLP	SA/RC	FBG	KL	OB			8		4800	2	6	8100	9350
24	11	WATKINS 25	SLP	SA/RC	FBG	KL	IB	9D		8		4800	2	6	8800	10000
28	11	WATKINS 29	SLP	SA/RC	FBG	KL	IB	18D		10	4	8800	4		19000	21100
33	1	WATKINS 33	SLP	SA/RC	FBG	KL	IB	27D		10	2	11200	4		24900	27600
		1986 BOATS														
24	11	WATKINS 25	SLP	SA/RC	FBG	KL	OB			8		4500	2	6	7150	8250
24	11	WATKINS 25	SLP	SA/RC	FBG	KL	IB	8D		8		4400	2	6	7550	8650
28	11	WATKINS 29	SLP	SA/RC	FBG	KL	IB	15D		10	4	8800	4		17500	19900
33	1	WATKINS 33	SLP	SA/RC	FBG	KL	IB	15D-	22D	10	2	11200	4		23400	26000
36		WATKINS 36C	SLP	SA/CR	FBG	KL	IB	40D		10	6	17000	4	6	35600	39500
		1985 BOATS														
24	11	WATKINS 25	SLP	SA/RC	FBG	KL	OB			8		4300	2	6	6450	7400
24	11	WATKINS 25	SLP	SA/RC	FBG	KL	IB	9D		8		4400	2	6	7100	8150
28	11	WATKINS 29	SLP	SA/RC	FBG	KL	IB	18D		10	4	8800	4		16500	18700
33	1	WATKINS 33	SLP	SA/RC	FBG	KL	IB	28D		10	2	11200	4		22000	24400
36		WATKINS 36	SLP	SA/CR	FBG	KL	IB	40D		10	6	18000	4	6	35200	39100
		1984 BOATS														
24	11	WATKINS 25	SLP	SA/RC	FBG	KL	OB			8		4300	2	6	6050	6950
24	11	WATKINS 25	SLP	SA/RC	FBG	KL	IB	8D	YAN	8		4400	2	6	6700	7700
27		WATKINS 27	SLP	SA/RC	FBG	KL	IB	8D	YAN	10		7800	3	8	13000	14700
28	11	WATKINS 29	SLP	SA/RC	FBG	KL	IB	15D	YAN	10	4	8800	4		15500	17600
33	1	WATKINS 33	SLP	SA/RC	FBG	KL	IB	15D-	22D	10	2	11200	4		20700	23000
36		WATKINS 36	SLP	SA/CR	FBG	KL	IB	50D	PERK	10	6	18000	4	6	33000	36700

....For earlier years, see the BUC Used Boat Price Guide, Volume 3

WAUQUIEZ INTERNATIONAL

DIV OF GROUPE BENETEAU
NEUVILLE EN FERRAIN FRANCE See inside cover to adjust price for area
FORMERLY CHANTIER WAUQUIEZ

For more recent years, see the BUC Used Boat Price Guide, Volume 1

LOA FT	LOA IN	NAME AND/ OR MODEL	TOP/ RIG	BOAT TYPE	-HULL- MTL	-HULL- TP	ENGINE TP	ENGINE # HP	ENGINE MFG	BEAM FT	BEAM IN	WGT LBS	DRAFT FT	DRAFT IN	RETAIL LOW	RETAIL HIGH
		1991 BOATS														
35	7	CENTURION 36	SLP	SAIL	FBG	KL	IB	43D	VLVO	12	3	16100	4	6	102000	112500
37	6	CENTURION 38	SLP	SAIL	FBG	KL	IB	43D	VLVO	12	9	19700	4	9	115000	126500
39	6	CENTURION 40	SLP	SAIL	FBG	KL	IB	43D	VLVO	13	4	20900	5	2	129500	142500
44	6	AMPHITRITE	SLP	MS	FBG	KL	IB	100D	VLVO	13	8	31900	6	3	199000	218500
45		CENTURION 45	SLP	SAIL	FBG	KL	IB	50D	PERK	13	4	24200	5	7	175500	193000
49	5	CENTURION 49	SLP	SAIL	FBG	KL	IB	60D	PERK	14	7	30900	5	7	241500	265500
58	6	CENTURION 59	SLP	SAIL	FBG	KL	IB	110D	VLVO	16	6	55100	7	5	518000	569000
		1985 BOATS														
32	10	GLADIATEUR	SLP	SA/RC	FBG	KL	IB	D		11		11000	6		45800	50300
35	1	PRETORIEN	SLP	SA/RC	FBG	KL	IB	D		11	7	14000	6		64500	70800
38		HOOD 38	SLP	SA/RC	FBG	KC	IB	D		11	9	22000	4	6	92100	101000
42		CENTURION 42	SLP	SA/RC	FBG	KL	IB	D		13	3	24300	7	5	112500	124000
43		AMPHITRITE	SLP	MS	FBG	KL	IB	D		13	8	28700	5	10	128500	141000
47	7	CENTURION 47	SLP	SA/RC	FBG	KL	IB	D		14	8	30000	8	6	157500	173500
		1984 BOATS														
32	10	GLADIATEUR	SLP	SA/RC	FBG	KL	IB	D		11		11000	6		42900	47600
35	1	PRETORIEN	SLP	SA/RC	FBG	KL	IB	D		11	7	14000	6		61100	67100
38		HOOD 38	SLP	SA/CR	FBG	KC	IB	D		11	9	22000	4	6	87300	96000
43		AMPHITRITE	KTH	MS	FBG	KL	IB	D		13	8	28700	5	10	122000	134000

LOA FT IN	NAME AND/ OR MODEL	TOP/ RIG	BOAT TYPE	–HULL– MTL TP TP	––ENGINE–– # HP MFG	BEAM FT IN	WGT LBS	DRAFT FT IN	RETAIL LOW	RETAIL HIGH
			1984 BOATS							
47	CENTURION 47	SLP	SA/RC	FBG KL	IB D	14 6	30000	8 6	146000	160000

....For earlier years, see the BUC Used Boat Price Guide, Volume 3

WAVERIDER BOATS
STEVENS POINT WI 54481– COAST GUARD MFG ID– WAY See inside cover to adjust price for area

LOA FT IN	NAME AND/ OR MODEL	TOP/ RIG	BOAT TYPE	–HULL– MTL TP TP	––ENGINE–– # HP MFG	BEAM FT IN	WGT LBS	DRAFT FT IN	RETAIL LOW	RETAIL HIGH
			1994 BOATS							
25 2	ENTERPRISE 252	OP	B/R	FBG DV	IO 250–300	8 2	4500	3 7	15900	18900

....For earlier years, see the BUC Used Boat Price Guide, Volume 3

WEATHERLY YACHTS INC
SEATTLE WA 98121   See inside cover to adjust price for area

LOA FT IN	NAME AND/ OR MODEL	TOP/ RIG	BOAT TYPE	–HULL– MTL TP TP	––ENGINE–– # HP MFG	BEAM FT IN	WGT LBS	DRAFT FT IN	RETAIL LOW	RETAIL HIGH
			1985 BOATS							
31 8	WEATHERLY 32	SLP	SA/CR	FBG KL	IB 22D YAN	9 6	15000	4 9	39200	43600

WEBBCRAFT INC
WEBB BOATS INC
COLLINSVILLE OK 74021   COAST GUARD MFG ID– WBB   See inside cover to adjust price for area

For more recent years, see the BUC Used Boat Price Guide, Volume 1

LOA FT IN	NAME AND/ OR MODEL	TOP/ RIG	BOAT TYPE	–HULL– MTL TP TP	––ENGINE–– # HP MFG	BEAM FT IN	WGT LBS	DRAFT FT IN	RETAIL LOW	RETAIL HIGH
			1994 BOATS							
18 11	FALCON 1900 ES	OP	B/R	FBG DV	IO 135–155	7 4	2350	2 5	5250	6050
21	COBRA 1950	OP	B/R	FBG DV	IO 155–235	7 8	2800	3 4	6350	7550
21 4	COBRA II 2150	OP	B/R	FBG DV	IO 155–250	7 8	2950	3 4	6700	8050
23 2	VELOTA 7 METER	OP	SPTCR	FBG DV	IO 235–300	8	3800	3 7	9850	12000
23 2	VELOTA 7 METER	OP	SPTCR	FBG DV	IO 360–385	8	3800	3 7	11800	14300
23 2	VELOTA 7 METER	OP	SPTCR	FBG DV	IO 410 MRCR	8	3800	3 7	13400	15300
25 2	ENTERPRISE 252	OP	B/R	FBG DV	IO 250–300	8 2	4500	3 7	11800	14100
25 2	ENTERPRISE 252	OP	B/R	FBG DV	IO 360–385	8 2	4500	3 7	13600	16200
25 2	ENTERPRISE 252	OP	B/R	FBG DV	IO 415 MRCR	8 2	4500	3 7	15100	17200
25 2	ENTERPRISE 252 SPT	OP	SPTCR	FBG DV	IO 235–300	8 2		3 7	11400	13800
25 2	ENTERPRISE 252 SPT	OP	SPTCR	FBG DV	IO 385–415	8 2		3 7	14100	17400
26 10	DISCOVERY 270	OP	B/R	FBG DV	IO 300–360	8 6	4800	2 3	14300	17400
26 10	DISCOVERY 270	OP	B/R	FBG DV	IO 385–415	8 6	4800	2 3	15700	18700
27	VELOTA 8 METER	OP	SPTCR	FBG DV	IO 300–360	9	5000	4	16700	20400
	IO 385–410 19000	21700, IO T250–T300 19200	22900, IO T360–T415						22200	26900
28	EQUALIZER 2800	OP	SPTCR	FBG DV	IO 300–385	8	5640	3 10	17400	21500
	IO 410 MRCR 19800	22000, IO T250–T300 19900	23500, IO T360–T415						22900	27100
32 5	CONCORDE 3030	OP	SPTCR	FBG DV	IO T250–T385	9	7800	3 10	28800	35500
32 5	CONCORDE 3030	OP	SPTCR	FBG DV	IO T410–T415	9	7800	3 10	32600	36400
32 5	VELOTA 3300	OP	SPTCR	FBG DV	IO 300–415	9	7500	3 10	22200	26100
32 5	VELOTA 3300	OP	SPTCR	FBG DV	IO T250–T360	9	7500	3 10	24100	29100
32 5	VELOTA 3300	OP	SPTCR	FBG DV	IO T410 MRCR	9	7500	3 10	27300	30300
			1993 BOATS							
16 11	FALCON 1700 ES	OP	B/R	FBG DV	IO	7 4	2150	2 5	6250	7150
16 11	FALCON 1700 ES	OP	B/R	FBG DV	OB	7 4	2150	2 5	4100	4750
18 11	FALCON 1900 ES	OP	B/R	FBG DV	IO 115–155	7 4	2350	2 5	6600	7600
18 11	FALCON 1900 ES	OP	B/R	FBG DV	OB 115–155	7 4	2350	2 5	4900	5650
19 9	AMERICAN 1850	OP	B/R	FBG DV	IO 115–180	7 6	2450	3 4	7250	8350
19 9	AMERICAN 1850	OP	B/R	FBG DV	OB	7 6	2450	3 4	5300	6150
21	COBRA 1950	OP	B/R	FBG DV	IO 135–240	7 8	2800	3 4	9950	11300
21	COBRA 1950	OP	B/R	FBG DV	OB	7 8	2800	3 4	5900	7100
21 4	COBRA II 2150	OP	B/R	FBG DV	IO 135–240	7 8	2950		10500	12000
21 4	COBRA II 2150	OP	B/R	FBG DV	OB	7 8	2950		6250	7450
21 5	COBRA 2150 ES	OP	CUD	FBG DV	IO 135–240	7 8	3000	3 6	6750	8050
23 2	RIVIERA 232 ES	OP	B/R	FBG DV	OB	8	3200	2 3	12700	14400
23 2	RIVIERA 232 ES	OP	B/R	FBG DV	IO 155–240	8	3200	2 3	7400	8800
	IO 300 MRCR 8200	9400, IO 360 MRCR 10700, IO 410 MRCR							10800	12200
23 2	VELOTA 7 METER	OP	SPTCR	FBG DV	IO 180–300	8	3800	3 7	9050	11200
23 2	VELOTA 7 METER	OP	SPTCR	FBG DV	IO 360 MRCR	8	3800	3 7	11000	12500
23 2	VELOTA 7 METER	OP	SPTCR	FBG DV	IO 410 MRCR	8	3800	3 7	12600	14300
24 1	ENTERPRISE 249 ES	OP	B/R	FBG DV	OB	8	3700	2 3	14700	16700
24 1	ENTERPRISE 249 ES	OP	B/R	FBG DV	IO 155–240	8	3700	2 3	8550	10100
	IO 300 MRCR 9450	10700, IO 360 MRCR 10500 12000, IO 410 MRCR							11900	13600
24 1	ENTERPRISE 249 SPT	OP	SPTCR	FBG DV	IO 155–300	8	3900	2 3	9600	11900
24 1	ENTERPRISE 249 SPT	OP	SPTCR	FBG DV	IO 360 MRCR	8	3900	2 3	11700	13300
24 1	ENTERPRISE 249 SPT	OP	SPTCR	FBG DV	IO 410 MRCR	8	3900	2 3	13200	15000
26 10	DISCOVERY 270 ES	OP	B/R	FBG DV	OB	8 6	4800	2 3	20300	22600
26 10	DISCOVERY 270 ES	OP	B/R	FBG DV	IO 240–300	8 6	4800	2 3	12600	15200
26 10	DISCOVERY 270 ES	OP	B/R	FBG DV	IO 330–360	8 6	4800	2 3	14300	17500
26 10	DISCOVERY 270 SPT	OP	SPTCR	FBG DV	IO 240–300	8 6	5000	2 3	13900	16700
26 10	DISCOVERY 270 SPT	OP	SPTCR	FBG DV	IO 360–410	8 6	5000	2 3	15800	19300
26 10	DISCOVERY 270 SPT	OP	B/R	FBG DV	IO T240 MRCR	8 6	5000	2 3	16400	18600
27	VELOTA 8 METER ES	OP	SPTCR	FBG DV	IO 300–360	9	5000	4	15000	18300
	IO 410 MRCR 17300	19600, IO T240–T300 16800 20700, IO T360–T410							19900	24200
28	EQUALIZER 2800	OP	SPTCR	FBG DV	IO 300–360	8	5640	3 10	16200	19600
	IO 410 MRCR 18600	20700, IO T240–T300 18500 22000, IO T360–T410							21400	25200
32 5	CONCORDE 3030 ES	OP	SPTCR	FBG DV	IO T240–T360	9	7800	3 10	26800	32500
32 5	CONCORDE 3030 ES	OP	SPTCR	FBG DV	IO T410 MRCR	9	7800	3 10	30500	33800
32 5	VELOTA 3300	OP	SPTCR	FBG DV	IO 300–410	9	7500		20800	24300
32 5	VELOTA 3300	OP	SPTCR	FBG DV	IO T240–T360	9	7500		22300	27200
32 5	VELOTA 3300	OP	SPTCR	FBG DV	IO T410 MRCR	9	7500		33300	37000
			1992 BOATS							
16 11	FALCON 1700 ES	OP	B/R	FBG DV	IO	7 4	2150	2 5	5950	6850
16 11	FALCON 1700 ES	OP	B/R	FBG DV	OB	7 4	2150	2 5	3800	4750
18 11	FALCON 1900 ES	OP	B/R	FBG DV	IO 115–175	7 4	2350	2 5	6300	7250
18 11	FALCON 1900 ES	OP	B/R	FBG DV	OB 115–175	7 4	2350	2 5	4550	5550
19 9	AMERICAN 1850	OP	B/R	FBG DV	IO 115–210	7 6	2450	3 4	6900	7900
19 9	AMERICAN 1850	OP	B/R	FBG DV	OB	7 6	2450	3 4	4950	6150
21	COBRA 1950	OP	B/R	FBG DV	IO 135–240	7 8	2800	3 4	9550	10900
21	COBRA 1950	OP	B/R	FBG DV	OB	7 8	2800	3 4	5550	6750
21	COBRA 1950	OP	B/R	FBG DV	IO 275 VLVO	7 8	2800	3 4	6350	7300
21 4	COBRA II 2020 ES	OP	B/R	FBG DV	IO 135–240	7 8	2950	3 6	10100	11500
21 4	COBRA II 2020 ES	OP	B/R	FBG DV	OB	7 8	2950	3 6	5850	7100
21 4	COBRA II 2020 ES	OP	B/R	FBG DV	IO 275 VLVO	7 8	2950	3 6	6600	7600
21 5	COBRA 2150 ES	OP	CUD	FBG DV	IO 135–240	7 8	3000	3 6	6300	7700
21 5	COBRA 2150 ES	OP	CUD	FBG DV	IO 275 VLVO	7 8	3000	3 6	7150	8250
22 8	RIVIERA 2100 LS	OP	B/R	FBG DV	OB	8	3200	3 7	11800	13400
22 8	RIVIERA 2100 LS	OP	B/R	FBG DV	IO 155–240	8	3200	3 7	6750	8100
	IO 275–300 7500	8650, IO 330–360 8400 9800, IO 410 MRCR							9900	11300
22 8	RIVIERA 232 ES	OP	B/R	FBG DV	OB	8 4	3300	2 3	12000	13700
22 8	RIVIERA 232 ES	OP	B/R	FBG DV	IO 155–240	8 4	3300	2 3	7000	8400
	IO 275–300 7750	8900, IO 330–360 8650 10100, IO 410 MRCR							10200	11500
23 2	VELOTA 7 METER	OP	SPTCR	FBG DV	IO 180–240	8	3800	3 7	8400	10000
	IO 275–330 9300	11600, IO 360 MRCR 10300 11700, IO 410 MRCR							11800	13400
24 1	ENTERPRISE 2300	OP	B/R	FBG DV	OB	8	3700	3 7	14100	16000
24 1	ENTERPRISE 2300	OP	B/R	FBG DV	IO 155–240	8	3700	3 7	8000	9600
	IO 275–300 8900	10100, IO 360 MRCR 9850 11200, IO 410 MRCR							11200	12700
24 1	ENTERPRISE 2300 SPT	OP	SPTCR	FBG DV	IO 155–240	8	3700	3 7	8600	10200
	IO 275–330 9500	11800, IO 360 MRCR 10600 12000, IO 410 MRCR							12000	13600
24 9	ENTERPRISE 249 ES	OP	B/R	FBG DV	OB	8 4	3700	2 3	14400	16300
24 9	ENTERPRISE 249 ES	OP	B/R	FBG DV	IO 155–240	8 4	3700	2 3	8250	9950
	IO 275–330 9300	11500, IO 360 MRCR 10300 11700, IO 410 MRCR							11500	13100
24 9	ENTERPRISE 249 SPT	OP	SPTCR	FBG DV	IO 155–240	8 4	3900	2 3	9300	11100
	IO 275–330 10300	12800, IO 360 MRCR 11500 13000, IO 410 MRCR							12800	14500
26 10	DISCOVERY 2400	OP	B/R	FBG DV	OB	8 6	4800	3 7	19500	21600
26 10	DISCOVERY 2400	OP	B/R	FBG DV	IO 240–300	8 6	4800	3 7	11500	13500
26 10	DISCOVERY 2400	OP	B/R	FBG DV	IO 330–360	8 6	4800	3 7	12800	14900
26 10	DISCOVERY 2400	OP	B/R	FBG DV	IO 410 MRCR	8 6	4800	3 7	14100	16000
26 10	DISCOVERY 2400 LS	OP	SPTCR	FBG DV	IO 240–300	8 6	4800	3 7	12500	15000
	IO 330–360 13900	16200, IO 410 MRCR 15400 17500, IO T240–T275							15100	18400
26 10	DISCOVERY 270 ES	OP	B/R	FBG DV	OB	8 6	4800	2 3	19500	21700
26 10	DISCOVERY 270 ES	OP	B/R	FBG DV	IO 240–300	8 6	4800	2 3	11800	14200
26 10	DISCOVERY 270 ES	OP	B/R	FBG DV	IO 330–410	8 6	4800	2 3	13200	16400
26 10	DISCOVERY 270 SPT	OP	SPTCR	FBG DV	IO 240–300	8 6	5000	2 3	13000	15600
26 10	DISCOVERY 270 SPT	OP	SPTCR	FBG DV	IO 330–410	8 6	5000	2 3	14500	18100

```
       LOA  NAME AND/          TOP/ BOAT  -HULL- ----ENGINE--- BEAM   WGT  DRAFT RETAIL RETAIL
    FT IN   OR MODEL           RIG  TYPE  MTL TP TP # HP  MFG   FT IN  LBS  FT IN LOW    HIGH
--------------------------- 1992 BOATS ---------------------------------------------------------
 26 10 DISCOVERY 270 SPT       OP SPTCR FBG DV IO T240-T275   8  6 5000  2  3 15400 18500
 27    VELOTA 8 METER ES       OP SPTCR FBG DV IO 300-360     8  8 5000     4 14000 17000
       IO 410 MRCR 16100  18300, IO T240-T300 15600 19200, IO T330-T410 18400 22400

 28    EQUALIZER 2800          OP SPTCR FBG DV IO 300-360     8    5640 3 10 15200 18300
       IO 410 MRCR       19400, IO T240-T300 16900 20700, IO T330-T410 19700 23500

 32 5 CONCORDE 3030 ES         OP SPTCR FBG DV IO T240-T360   8  8 7800 3 10 25000 30300
 32 5 CONCORDE 3030 ES         OP SPTCR FBG DV IO T410-T490   8  8 7800 3 10 28400 33300
--------------------------- 1991 BOATS ---------------------------------------------------------
 16 11 FALCON 1700 ES          OP B/R   FBG DV IO 115-175     7  4 2150  2  5  3550  4450
 18 11 FALCON 1900 ES          OP B/R   FBG DV IO 115-175     7  4 2350  2  5  4250  5200
 19  9 AMERICAN 1850           OP B/R   FBG DV IO 115-210     7  6 2450  3  3  4650  5750
 21    COBRA 1950              OP B/R   FBG DV IO 135-240     7  8 2800  3  3  5200  6350
 21    COBRA 1950              OP B/R   FBG DV IO 275  VLVO   7  8 2800  3  4  5950  6850
 21  4 COBRA II 2020 ES        OP B/R   FBG DV IO 135-240     7  8 2950  3  6  5450  6650
 21  4 COBRA II 2020 ES        OP B/R   FBG DV IO 275  VLVO   7  8 2950  3  6  6200  7150
 21  5 COBRA 2150 ES           OP CUD   FBG DV IO 135-240     7  8 3000  3  6  5950  7200
 21  5 COBRA 2150 ES           OP CUD   FBG DV IO 275  VLVO   7  8 3000  3  6  6700  7700
 22  8 RIVIERA 2100            OP B/R   FBG DV IO 155-240     7    3200  3  7  6350  7600
       IO 300 MRCR 7000  8050, IO 330-360 7850 9200, IO 410 MRCR 9350 10600

 22  8 RIVIERA 232 ES          OP B/R   FBG DV IO 155-240     8  4 3300  2  3  6550  7900
       IO 275-300 7300  8350, IO 330-360 8100 9450, IO 410 MRCR 9500 10800

 23  2 VELOTA 7 METER          OP SPTCR FBG DV IO 155-240     8    3800  3  7  7850  9350
       IO 275-300 8600  9900, IO 330-360 9550 11000, IO 410 MRCR 11000 12500

 24  1 ENTERPRISE 2300         OP B/R   FBG DV IO 155-240     8    3700  3  7  7500  9000
       IO 275-300 8250  9500, IO 330-360 9150 10600, IO 410 MRCR 10500 11900

 24  1 ENTERPRISE 2300         OP SPTCR FBG DV IO 155-240     8    3700        8050  9650
       IO 275-330 8950  11100, IO 360 MRCR 9950 11300, IO 410 MRCR 11200 12800

 24  9 ENTERPRISE 249 ES       OP B/R   FBG DV IO 155-240     8  4 3700  2  3  7750  9350
       IO 275-330 8650  10800, IO 360 MRCR 9700 11000, IO 410 MRCR 10800 12300

 24  9 ENTERPRISE 249 ES       OP SPTCR FBG DV IO 155-240     8  4 3900  2  3  8650 10400
       IO 275-330 9700  12000, IO 360 MRCR 10800 12200, IO 410 MRCR 12000 13600

 26 10 DISCOVERY 2400          OP B/R   FBG DV IO 240-300     8  6 4800  3  7 10700 12800
       IO 330-360 11900  13900, IO 410 MRCR 13100 14900, IO T240-T275 12900 15600

 26 10 DISCOVERY 270 ES        OP B/R   FBG DV IO 240-300     8  6 4800  2  3 11000 13200
 26 10 DISCOVERY 270 ES        OP B/R   FBG DV IO 330-410     8  6 4800  2  3 12300 13600
 26 10 DISCOVERY 270 ES        OP SPTCR FBG DV IO 240-300     8  6 5000  2  3 12200 14600
 26 10 DISCOVERY 270 ES        OP SPTCR FBG DV IO 330-410     8  6 5000  2  3 13600 16900
 26 10 DISCOVERY 270 ES        OP SPTCR FBG DV IO T240-T275   8  6 5000  2  3 14400 17500
 27    VELOTA 8 METER ES       OP SPTCR FBG DV IO 300-360     8    5000     4 13100 16000
       IO 410 MRCR 15100  17100, IO T240-T300 14600 18000, IO T330-T360 16900 19400
       IO T410 MRCR 19000  21100

 28    EQUALIZER 2800          OP SPTCR FBG DV IO 300-360     8    5640 3 10 14200 17200
       IO 410 MRCR 15900  18100, IO T240-T300 15800 19400, IO T330-T410 18500 22200

 32 5 CONCORDE 3030 ES         OP SPTCR FBG DV IO T240-T360   8  8 7800 3 10 23400 28400
 32 5 CONCORDE 3030 ES         OP SPTCR FBG DV IO T410-T490   8  8 7800 3 10 26600 31200
--------------------------- 1990 BOATS ---------------------------------------------------------
 19  9 AMERICAN 1850 DELUXE    OP B/R   FBG DV IO 130-200     7  6 2450        4400  5300
 19  9 AMERICAN 1850 DELUXE    OP B/R   FBG DV IO 211  VLVO   7  6 2450        5750  6600
 21    COBRA 1950              OP B/R   FBG DV IO 130-260     7  8 2800        4900  6000
 21  4 COBRA II 2020           OP B/R   FBG DV IO 130-270     7  8 2950        5150  6350
 21  4 COBRA II 2020           OP B/R   FBG DV IO 271  VLVO   7  8 2950        5800  6650
 21  5 SUNSTAR 2150            OP RNBT  FBG DV IO 130-270     7  8 3000        5300  6550
 21  5 SUNSTAR 2150            OP RNBT  FBG DV IO 271  VLVO   7  8 3000        5950  6850
 22  8 RIVIERA 2100            OP B/R   FBG DV IO 171-271     8    3200        6150  7600
 22  8 RIVIERA 2100            OP B/R   FBG DV IO 330         8    3200        7000  8050
 22  8 RIVIERA 2100            OP B/R   FBG DV IO 350-365     8    3200        7800  8950
 22  9 ENTERPRISE 2300         OP B/R   FBG DV IO 171-271     8    3700        6800  8300
 22  9 ENTERPRISE 2300         OP B/R   FBG DV IO 330         8    3700        7650  8900

 22  9 ENTERPRISE 2300         OP B/R   FBG DV IO 350-365     8    3700        8450  9700
 23  2 VELOTA 7 METER SD       OP SPTCR FBG DV IO 200-300     8    3800        7450  9250
 23  2 VELOTA 7 METER SD       OP SPTCR FBG DV IO 330  MRCR   8    3800        8500  9750
 23  2 VELOTA 7 METER SD       OP SPTCR FBG DV IO 350-365     8    3800        9450 10700
 24  1 ENTERPRISE 2300         OP SPTCR FBG DV IO 171-271     8    3700        7800  9500
 24  1 ENTERPRISE 2300         OP SPTCR FBG DV IO 330-365     8    3700        8800 10700
 25  2 PHANTA-SEA 2500         OP SPTCR FBG DV IO 454  VLVO   8    3700       12900 14700
 25  2 PHANTA-SEA 2500         OP SPTCR FBG DV IO 270-330     9  6 4800       10600 12900
 25  2 PHANTA-SEA 2500         OP SPTCR FBG DV IO 365  MRCR   9  6 4800       12000 13600
 26 10 DISCOVERY 2400          OP SPTCR FBG DV IO 454  VLVO   8  6 4800       15000 17000
 26 10 DISCOVERY 2400          OP B/R   FBG DV IO 330-365     8  6 4800       11200 13400
 26 10 DISCOVERY 2400          OP B/R   FBG DV IO 454  VLVO   8  6 4800       14000 15900

 26 10 DISCOVERY 2400          OP B/R   FBG DV IO T270-T271   8  6 4800       12600 14000
 26 10 DISCOVERY 2400 SD       OP CUD   FBG DV IO 260-330     8  6 4800       11400 14000
       IO 365 MRCR 12900  14600, IO 454 VLVO 15300 17400, IO T270-T271 13800 16000

 27    VELOTA 8 SD             OP SPTCR FBG DV IO 330-365     9    5000       12800 15200
       IO 454 VLVO 15800  17900, IO T270-T330 14300 17700, IO T365 MRCR 16300 18500
       IO T454 VLVO 20500  22800

 28    EQUALIZER 2800          OP SPTCR FBG DV IO 330-365     8    5640       13700 16200
       IO 454 VLVO 16100  18300, IO T270-T330 15500 19000, IO T365 MRCR 17400 19800
       IO T454 VLVO 20600  22800

 32 5 CONCORDE 3030            OP SPTCR FBG DV IO T270-T365   9    7800       22600 26900
 32 5 CONCORDE 3030            OP SPTCR FBG DV IO T454  VLVO  9    7800       26200 29100
--------------------------- 1989 BOATS ---------------------------------------------------------
 18 8 SHADOW 1900 DELUXE       OP B/R   FBG DV IO 130-200     7  6 2450        3850  4700
 18 8 SHADOW 1900 DELUXE       OP B/R   FBG DV IO 205  MRCR   7  6 2450        3950  4600
 18 8 SHADOW 1900 DELUXE       OP B/R   FBG DV IO T205-T211   7  6 2450        5100  5900
 19 6 COBRA 1950 CLS           OP B/R   FBG DV IO 130-260     7  8 2800        4650  5650
 19 6 COBRA 1950 CLS           OP B/R   FBG DV IO T205-T211   7  8 2800        5900  6850
 19 6 COBRA 1950 DELUXE        OP B/R   FBG DV IO 130-205     7  8 2800        4200  5100
 19 6 COBRA 1950 DELUXE        OP B/R   FBG DV IO 260  MRCR   7  8 2800        4600  5250
 19 6 COBRA 1950 DELUXE        OP B/R   FBG DV IO T205-T211   7  8 2800        5450  6300
 21 2 RIVIERA 2100             OP B/R   FBG DV IO 175-260     8    3200        5600  6700
 21 2 RIVIERA 2100             OP CUD   FBG DV IO 175-260     8    3200        5550  6700

 21 2 RIVIERA 2100 CLS         OP B/R   FBG DV IO 171-270     8    3200        5750  6750
       IO 330 MRCR 6550  7500, IO 365 MRCR 7100 8200, IO T205-T211 6950 8050
       IO T271 VLVO 7650  8800

 21 2 RIVIERA 2100 CLS         OP CUD   FBG DV IO 171-270     8    3200        5750  6800
       IO 330 MRCR 6600  7550, IO 365 MRCR 7250 8300, IO T205-T211 6950 8000
       IO T271 VLVO 7700  8850

 21 2 RIVIERA 2100 DELUXE      OP B/R   FBG DV IO 171-270     8    3200        4950  5950
       IO 330 MRCR 5800  6650, IO 365 MRCR 6400 7400, IO T205-T211 6050 7000
       IO T271 VLVO 6750  7750

 21 4 COBRA II 2020 CLS        OP B/R   FBG DV IO 130-270     7  8 2800        4850  6000
 21 4 COBRA II 2020 CLS        OP B/R   FBG DV IO T205-T211   7  8 2800        6200  7200
 21 4 COBRA II 2020 CLS        OP B/R   FBG DV IO T271  VLVO  7  8 2800        6900  7950
 21 4 COBRA II 2020 DELUXE     OP B/R   FBG DV IO 130-270     7  8 2800        4550  5700
 21 4 COBRA II 2020 DELUXE     OP B/R   FBG DV IO T205-T211   7  8 2800        5850  6750
 21 4 COBRA II 2020 DELUXE     OP B/R   FBG DV IO T271  VLVO  7  8 2800        6550  7550
 22 4 COBRA II COMBO FSHMN     OP CUD   FBG DV IO 130-275     7  8 3000        5550  6850
 22 4 COBRA II COMBO FSHMN     OP CUD   FBG DV IO T205-T211   7  8 3000        6950  8050
 22 4 COBRA II COMBO FSHMN     OP CUD   FBG DV IO T271  VLVO  7  8 3000        7700  8850
 22 9 ENTERPRISE 2300 CLS      OP B/R   FBG DV IO 171-270     8    3700        6850  8000
 22 9 ENTERPRISE 2300 CLS      OP B/R   FBG DV IO 330-365     8    3700        7600  9400
 22 9 ENTERPRISE 2300 CLS      OP B/R   FBG DV IO T205-T271   8    3700        8050 10000

 22 9 ENTERPRISE 2300 CLS      OP SPTCR FBG DV IO 171-270     8    3700        6850  8100
       IO 330-365 7750  9600, IO T205-T211 8050 9300, IO T271 VLVO 8900 10100

 22 9 ENTERPRISE 2300 DLX      OP B/R   FBG DV IO 171-270     8    3700        5950  7100
       IO 330 MRCR 6800  7850, IO 365 MRCR 7450 8550, IO T205-T211 7050 8150
       IO T271 VLVO 8900

 22 9 ENTERPRISE 2300 DLX      OP CUD   FBG DV IO 171-270     8    3700        6850  8050
       IO 330-365 7700  9600, IO T205-T211 8050 9300, IO T271 VLVO 8900 10100

 23 2 VELOTA 7 METER CLS       OP SPTCR FBG DV IO 200-271     8    3800        7400  8850
 23 2 VELOTA 7 METER CLS       OP SPTCR FBG DV IO 330-365     8    3800        8400 10300
 23 2 VELOTA 7 METER CLS       OP SPTCR FBG DV IO T205-T211   8    3800        8900 10200
 23 2 VELOTA 7 METER DLX       OP SPTCR FBG DV IO 200-270     8    3800        6500  7850
       IO 330-365 9400  11200, IO T205-T211 7750 9000, IO T271 VLVO 9150 10400

 24 DISCOVERY 2400 CLS         OP B/R   FBG DV IO 260-270     8  6 4200        7700  8950
 24 DISCOVERY 2400 CLS         OP B/R   FBG DV IO 330-365     8  6 4200        8400 10300
 24 DISCOVERY 2400 CLS         OP B/R   FBG DV IO T211-T271   8  6 4200        8850 10800
 24 DISCOVERY 2400 CLS         OP CUD   FBG DV IO 260-270     8  6 4200        8200  9550
 24 DISCOVERY 2400 CLS         OP CUD   FBG DV IO 330-365     8  6 4200        9050 11000
```

LOA FT	LOA IN	NAME AND/ OR MODEL	TOP/ RIG	BOAT TYPE	-HULL- MTL	-HULL- TP	ENGINE TP	ENGINE # HP	ENGINE MFG	BEAM FT	BEAM IN	WGT LBS	DRAFT FT	DRAFT IN	RETAIL LOW	RETAIL HIGH
		1989 BOATS														
24		DISCOVERY 2400 CLS	OP	CUD	FBG	DV	IO	T211-T271		8	6	4200			9400	11500
27		CONCORDE 27	OP	SPTCR	FBG	DV	IO	T270-T330		9		7500			16100	19600
27		CONCORDE 27	OP	SPTCR	FBG	DV	IO	T365	MRCR	9		7500			18600	20700
27		VELOTA 8 METER CLS	OP	SPTCR	FBG	DV	IO	330-365		9		5000			12800	15100
27		VELOTA 8 METER CLS	OP	SPTCR	FBG	DV	IO	T270-T330		9		5000			14100	17400
27		VELOTA 8 METER CLS	OP	SPTCR	FBG	DV	IO	T365	MRCR	9		5000			15900	18100
27		VELOTA 8 METER DLX	OP	SPTCR	FBG	DV	IO	330-365		9		5000			11400	13600
27		VELOTA 8 METER DLX	OP	SPTCR	FBG	DV	IO	T270-T330		9		5000			12900	15900
27		VELOTA 8 METER DLX	OP	SPTCR	FBG	DV	IO	T365	MRCR	9		5000			14800	16800
28		EQUALIZER 2800	OP	SPTCR	FBG	DV	IO	330-365		8		5800			13100	15400
28		EQUALIZER 2800	OP	SPTCR	FBG	DV	IO	T270-T330		8		5800			14600	18000
28		EQUALIZER 2800	OP	SPTCR	FBG	DV	IO	T365	MRCR	8		5800			16600	18900
29	7	CONCORDE 30	OP	SPTCR	FBG	DV	IO	T270-T330		9		7800			15800	19100
29	7	CONCORDE 30	OP	SPTCR	FBG	DV	IO	T365	MRCR	9		7800			17500	19800
35		CONCORDE 35	OP	SPTCR	FBG	DV	IO	T270	MRCR	9		8000			28700	31900
		IO T271 VLVO 29000 32200, IO T330 MRCR 30000 33300, IO T365 MRCR													30900	34400
		1988 BOATS														
18	8	SHADOW 1900	OP	B/R	FBG	DV	IO		VLVO	7	6	2450			**	**
18	8	SHADOW 1900	OP	B/R	FBG	DV	IO	165	MRCR	7	6	2450			3450	4050
18	8	SPECTRUM 1900	OP	B/R	FBG	DV	IO	165-200		7	6	2450			3800	4450
19	6	COBRA 1950	OP	B/R	FBG	DV	IO		VLVO	7	8	2800			**	**
19	6	COBRA 1950	OP	B/R	FBG	DV	IO	165-260		7	8	2800			4200	5150
20	5	FUN N' SUN 2050	OP	B/R	FBG	TR	IO		VLVO	7	10	3100			**	**
20	5	FUN N' SUN 2050	OP	B/R	FBG	TR	IO	260	MRCR	7	10	3100			4850	5550
21	2	RIVIERA 2100	OP	B/R	FBG	DV	IO		VLVO	8		3200			**	**
		IO 200-270 4950 6000, IO 330 MRCR 5850 6700, IO 365 MRCR													6400	7350
22	9	ENTERPRISE 2300	OP	B/R	FBG	DV	IO		VLVO	8		3700			**	**
22	9	ENTERPRISE 2300	OP	B/R	FBG	DV	IO	260-270		8		3700			6150	7150
22	9	ENTERPRISE 2300	OP	B/R	FBG	DV	IO	330-365		8		3700			6850	8500
22	9	ENTERPRISE 2300	OP	CUD	FBG	DV	IO		VLVO	8		3750			**	**
22	9	ENTERPRISE 2300	OP	CUD	FBG	DV	IO	260-270		8		3750			6650	7700
22	9	ENTERPRISE 2300	OP	CUD	FBG	DV	IO	330-365		8		3750			7350	9150
23		VELOTA 7M EURO-SPORT	OP	SPTCR	FBG	DV	IO		VLVO	8		3800			**	**
23		VELOTA 7M EURO-SPORT	OP	SPTCR	FBG	DV	IO	260-270		8		3800			6800	7900
23		VELOTA 7M EURO-SPORT	OP	SPTCR	FBG	DV	IO	330-365		8		3800			7500	9350
23		VELOTA 8M EURO-SPORT	OP	SPTCR	FBG	DV	IO		VLVO	9		5000			**	**
23		VELOTA 8M EURO-SPORT	OP	SPTCR	FBG	DV	IO	330-365		9		5000			9450	11400
23		VELOTA 8M EURO-SPORT	OP	SPTCR	FBG	DV	IO	T270	MRCR	9		5000			9950	11300
24		DISCOVERY 2400	OP	B/R	FBG	DV	IO		VLVO	8	6	4200			**	**
24		DISCOVERY 2400	OP	B/R	FBG	DV	IO	330-365		8	6	4200			7950	9800
27		CONCORDE 27	OP	SPTCR	FBG	DV	IO		VLVO	9		7500			**	**
27		CONCORDE 27	OP	SPTCR	FBG	DV	IO	T270-T330		9		7500			15200	18500
27		CONCORDE 27	OP	SPTCR	FBG	DV	IO	T365	MRCR	9		7500			17300	19600
27		VELOTA 8M EURO-SPORT	OP	SPTCR	FBG	DV	IO	T330	MRCR	9		5000			13800	15700
29	7	CONCORDE 30	OP	SPTCR	FBG	DV	IO		VLVO	9		7800			**	**
29	7	CONCORDE 30	OP	SPTCR	FBG	DV	IO	T270-T330		9		7800			15000	18000
29	7	CONCORDE 30	OP	SPTCR	FBG	DV	IO	T365-T420		9		7800			16500	20100
35		CONCORDE 35	OP	SPTCR	FBG	DV	IO		VLVO	9		8000			**	**
		IO T270 MRCR 27200 30200, IO T330 MRCR 28400 31500, IO T365 MRCR													29300	32500
		IO T420 MRCR 31000 34500														
		1986 BOATS														
16	10	BASSBOSS	OP	BASS	FBG	DV	OB			7		1000			2650	3100
17	2	SCORPION II FSH&SKI	OP	BASS	FBG	DV	OB			7	6	1000			2700	3100
17	8	TEMPO 18	OP	RNBT	FBG	DV	IO	140-205		7		2600			3250	3850
18	2	SCORPION I PRO	OP	BASS	FBG	DV	OB			7	6	1050			2900	3350
18	8	ARIES 19	OP	CUD	FBG	DV	IO	140-205		7	6	2550			3600	4300
18	8	SPECTRUM 19	OP	RNBT	FBG	DV	IO	140-205		7	6	2350			3350	4000
19	6	COBRA 19 1/2	OP	RNBT	FBG	DV	IO	140-260		7	6	2800			3900	4800
19	10	EAGLE 20	OP	RNBT	FBG	DV	IO	140-260		8		3000			4250	5200
21	2	ODESSEY 21	OP	CUD	FBG	DV	IO	170-260		8		3850			5400	6500
21	2	ODESSEY 21	OP	CUD	FBG	DV	IO	330	MRCR	8		3850			6300	7250
21	2	RIVIERA 21 CL DECK	OP	RNBT	FBG	DV	IO	140		8		3000			4350	5000
21	2	RIVIERA 21 CL DECK	OP	RNBT	FBG	DV	IO	370	MRCR	8		3000			5800	6650
21	2	RIVIERA 21 OPEN BOW	OP	RNBT	FBG	DV	IO	170-260		8		3000			4400	5300
21	2	RIVIERA 21 OPEN BOW	OP	RNBT	FBG	DV	IO	330	MRCR	8		3000			5200	6000
22	9	ENTERPRISE 23	OP	CUD	FBG	DV	IO	200-260		8		3750			5800	6950
22	9	ENTERPRISE 23	OP	CUD	FBG	DV	IO	330	MRCR	8		3750			6650	7650
22	9	ENTERPRISE 23	OP	CUD	FBG	DV	IO	370	MRCR	8		3750			7300	8400
22	9	ENTERPRISE 23	OP	RNBT	FBG	DV	IO	200-260		8		3550			5300	6300
22	9	ENTERPRISE 23	OP	RNBT	FBG	DV	IO	330	MRCR	8		3550			6100	7000
22	9	ENTERPRISE 23	OP	RNBT	FBG	DV	IO	370	MRCR	8		3550			6700	7650
24		DISCOVERY 24	OP	RNBT	FBG	DV	IO	190-260		8	6	4100			6300	7500
24		DISCOVERY 24	OP	RNBT	FBG	DV	IO	330-370		8	6	4100			7100	8850
24		DISCOVERY 24	OP	RNBT	FBG	DV	IO	T140-T260		8	6	4100			6950	8550
24	2	DISCOVERY 24	OP	CUD	FBG	DV	IO	260		8	6	4100			7000	8050
24	2	DISCOVERY 24	OP	CUD	FBG	DV	IO	330-370		8	6	4100			7650	9500
24	2	DISCOVERY 24	OP	CUD	FBG	DV	IO	T140-T260		8	6	4100			7450	9300
27		COMCORDE 27	OP	SPTCR	FBG	DV	IO	175	OMC						9050	10300
27		CONCORDE 27	OP	SPTCR	FBG	DV	IO	170-260							9050	11000
29	7	CONCORDE 30	OP	SPTCR	FBG	DV	IO	T260-T330		9		8000			13500	16400
29	7	CONCORDE 30	OP	SPTCR	FBG	DV	IO	T370-T440		9		8000			15100	18700
29	7	SIRIUS 30	OP	CUD	FBG	DV	IO	140-190		9		8500			10800	12700
29	7	SIRIUS 30	OP	CUD	FBG	DV	IO	T200-T260		9		8500			12400	14800
35		CONCORDE 35	OP	RACE	FBG	DV	IO	T260	MRCR	9		8000			21000	23400
		IO T300 MRCR 20900 23200, IO T330 MRCR 21500 23900, IO T370 MRCR													22600	25100
		IO T400 MRCR 23600 26200, IO T440 MRCR 25100 27900, IO T496 MRCR													27700	30800
		1985 BOATS														
16	3	DYNASTY 1650-V B/R	OP	RNBT	FBG	DV	IO	120-140		7		2000			2500	2900
17		BASSMATE	OP	BASS	FBG	DV	OB								2300	2650
17		SCORPION II FSH&SKI	OP	BASS	FBG	DV	OB								2950	3450
18		SCORPION I PRO	OP	BASS	FBG	DV	OB								3250	3800
18	8	DYNASTY 1900-V	OP	CUD	FBG	DV	IO	120-205		7	6	2300			3250	3850
18	8	DYNASTY 1900-V B/R	OP	RNBT	FBG	DV	IO	120-205		7	6	2300			3150	3750
19	8	WILDCAT 20-V	OP	RNBT	FBG	DV	IO	140-260		8		3000			4000	4950
19	11	DYNASTY 2000-V B/R	OP	RNBT	FBG	DV	IO	120-260		8		3000			4050	5000
21	2	DYNASTY 2100-V	OP	RNBT	FBG	DV	IO	120-260		8					4050	5000
21	2	DYNASTY 2100-V SPORT	OP	CUD	FBG	DV	IO	120-260		8					4400	5350
21	2	RIVIERA 21-V	OP	CUD	FBG	DV	IO	140-260		8		3000			4400	5350
21	2	RIVIERA 21-V	OP	CUD	FBG	DV	IO	330	MRCR	8		3000			5250	6050
21	2	RIVIERA 21-V	OP	CUD	FBG	DV	IO	370	MRCR	8		3000			5850	6750
21	2	RIVIERA 21-V	OP	RNBT	FBG	DV	IO	140-260		8		3000			4150	5100
21	2	RIVIERA 21-V	OP	RNBT	FBG	DV	IO	330	MRCR	8		3000			5000	5750
21	2	RIVIERA 21-V	OP	RNBT	FBG	DV	IO	370	MRCR	8		3000			5550	6400
21	2	RIVIERA 21-V EXPRESS	OP	CUD	FBG	DV	IO	140-205		8		3000			4350	5150
23	9	ENTERPRISE 24 B/R	OP	RNBT	FBG	DV	IO	170-260		8		3200			4950	5900
		IO 330 MRCR 5700 6600, IO 370 MRCR 6300 7250, IO T170													5600	6450
		IO T185-T260 6200 7200														
23	9	ENTERPRISE 24 SPORT	OP	CUD	FBG	DV	IO	170-260		8		3200			5250	6300
		IO 330 MRCR 6100 7000, IO 370 MRCR 6700 7700, IO T170-T260													5950	7400
23	9	EXPRESS DAY CR 24	OP	CR	FBG	DV	IO	170-260		8					5850	7000
		IO 330 MRCR 6700 7700, IO 370 MRCR 7300 8400, IO T170-T260													6550	8100
28		OFFSHORE SPORT RACER		SPTCR	FBG	DV	IO	T260-T330		10					11100	13800
28		OFFSHORE SPORT RACER		SPTCR	FBG	DV	IO	T370-T440		10					12700	15800
35		CONCORDE	OP	SPTCR	FBG	DV	IB	T260	MRCR	9		8000			29700	33000
		IO T330 MRCR 24700 27400, IB T370 MRCR 31300 34800, IB T400 MRCR													31900	35400
		IO T440 MRCR 27600 30700														
		1984 BOATS														
16	3	DYNASTY 1650 B/R	OP	RNBT	FBG	DV	IO	120-140		7		2000			2400	2800
18	8	DYNASTY 1900-V	OP	CUD	FBG	DV	IO	120-188		7	6	2300			3150	3700
18	8	DYNASTY 1900-V B/R	OP	RNBT	FBG	DV	IO	120-188		7	6	2300			3050	3600
19	8	WILDCAT 20-V	OP	RNBT	FBG	DV	IO	140-260		8		3000			3900	4800
19	11	DYNASTY 2000-V B/R	OP	RNBT	FBG	DV	IO	120-260		8		3000			3950	4850
21	2	DYNASTY 2100-V SPORT	OP	CUD	FBG	DV	IO	140-260		8					4200	5150
21	2	RIVIERA 21-V	OP	CUD	FBG	DV	IO	140-260		8		3000			4200	5150
21	2	RIVIERA 21-V	OP	CUD	FBG	DV	IO	330	MRCR	8		3000			5050	5850
21	2	RIVIERA 21-V	OP	CUD	FBG	DV	IO	370	MRCR	8		3000			5650	6500
21	2	RIVIERA 21-V	OP	RNBT	FBG	DV	IO	140-260		8		3000			4000	4900
21	2	RIVIERA 21-V	OP	RNBT	FBG	DV	IO	330	MRCR	8		3000			4800	5550
21	2	RIVIERA 21-V	OP	RNBT	FBG	DV	IO	370	MRCR	8		3000			5350	6150
23	9	ENTERPRISE 23 B/R	OP	RNBT	FBG	DV	IO	170-260		8		3200			4750	5700
		IO 330 MRCR 5500 6350, IO 370 MRCR 6050 7000, IO T170-T260													5400	6700
23	9	ENTERPRISE 23 SPORT	OP	CUD	FBG	DV	IO	170-260		8		3200			5050	6100
		IO 330 MRCR 5900 6750, IO 370 MRCR 6500 7450, IO T170-T260													5750	7150
35		CONCORDE	OP	SPTCR	FBG	DV	IB	T260	MRCR	9		8000			28300	31500
		IO T330 MRCR 23800 26400, IB T370 MRCR 30000 33300, IB T400 MRCR													30500	33900
		IO T440 MRCR 26600 29600														

....For earlier years, see the BUC Used Boat Price Guide, Volume 3

WEBBERS COVE BOAT YARD INC

BLUE HILL ME 04614-0364 COAST GUARD MFG ID- WBR See inside cover to adjust price for area

LOA FT	LOA IN	NAME AND/ OR MODEL	TOP/ RIG	BOAT TYPE	-HULL- MTL	-HULL- TP	ENGINE TP	ENGINE # HP	ENGINE MFG	BEAM FT	BEAM IN	WGT LBS	DRAFT FT	DRAFT IN	RETAIL LOW	RETAIL HIGH
		1995 BOATS														
22		WEBCO 22 BASS	ST	CUD	FBG	SV	IO			8	4	3350	2		**	**
22		WEBCO 22 CC	OP	CUD	FBG	SV	IO			8	4	3350	2		**	**
22		WEBCO 22 LOBSTER	HT	CUD	FBG	SV	IO			8	4	3350	2		**	**
26	4	WEBCO 26 CRUISER	HT	CUD	FBG	SV	IO			10	6	3350	2	6	**	**
26	4	WEBCO 26 LOBSTER	HT	CUD	FBG	SV	IO			10	6	3350	2	6	**	**
28	11	WEBCO 29 CRUISER	HT	CUD	FBG	SV	IO			10	6		3		**	**
28	11	WEBCO 29 LOBSTER	HT	CUD	FBG	SV	IO			10	6		3		**	**
		1994 BOATS														
22		WEBCO 22 KIT	HT	CUD	FBG	SV	IO			8	4	3350	2		**	**
26	4	WEBCO 26	HT	CUD	FBG	SV	IO			10	6		2	6	**	**
		1992 BOATS														
22		WEBCO 22	OP	BASS	FBG	SV	IO			8	4	3300	11		**	**
22		WEBCO 22	OP	CTRCN	FBG	SV	IO			8	4	3300	11		**	**
22		WEBCO 22 LOBSTER	HT	RNBT	FBG	SV	IO			8	4	3300	11		**	**
		1988 BOATS														
22		WEBCO 22	OP	BASS	FBG	SV	IO			8	4	3300	1	10	**	**
22		WEBCO 22	OP	CTRCN	FBG	SV	IO			8	4	3300	1	10	**	**
22		WEBCO 22	HT	RNBT	FBG	SV	IO			8	4	3300	1	10	**	**

....For earlier years, see the BUC Used Boat Price Guide, Volume 3

WELLCRAFT MARINE

DIV OF GENMAR
SARASOTA FL 34243 COAST GUARD MFG ID- WEL See inside cover to adjust price for area

For more recent years, see the BUC Used Boat Price Guide, Volume 1

LOA FT	LOA IN	NAME AND/ OR MODEL	TOP/ RIG	BOAT TYPE	-HULL- MTL	-HULL- TP	ENGINE TP	ENGINE # HP	ENGINE MFG	BEAM FT	BEAM IN	WGT LBS	DRAFT FT	DRAFT IN	RETAIL LOW	RETAIL HIGH
		1996 BOATS														
16	1	CCF 16	OP	CTRCN	FBG	DV	OB			6		1100			2850	3350
17	8	EXCEL 18DX	OP	B/R	FBG	SV	OB			7	2	1900			4600	5300
17	8	EXCEL 18SX	OP	B/R	FBG	SV	IO	135		7	2	2000			4600	5550
18	2	CCF 190	OP	CTRCN	FBG	DV	OB			7	4	2350	2	11	5050	5800
18	8	ECLIPSE 1950D	OP	B/R	FBG	DV	OB			7	4	2400			5350	6100
18	8	ECLIPSE 1950S	OP	RNBT	FBG	DV	IO	190		7	4	2600			5950	7150
18	8	ECLIPSE 1950SC	OP	CUD	FBG	DV	IO	190		7	4	2700			6300	7550
18	8	ECLIPSE 1950SS	OP	B/R	FBG	DV	IO	190		7	4	2600			5750	6950
18	8	EXCEL 19 DX	OP	B/R	FBG	SV	OB			7	4	2100	2	6	5050	5800
18	8	EXCEL 19 SL	OP	CUD	FBG	SV	IO	135-180		7	4	2400	2	7	5800	7050
18	8	EXCEL 19 SX	OP	B/R	FBG	DV	IO	135-180		7	4	2300	2	7	5300	6500
18	11	SCARAB JET	OP	RACE	FBG	DV	IO	185	VLVO	7		2100			5450	6250
19	4	CCF 195	OP	CTRCN	FBG	DV	OB			7	4	2350			5400	6200
20	7	ECLIPSE 2150S	OP	B/R	FBG	DV	IO	190-250		7	5	2900			7750	9700
20	7	ECLIPSE 2150SC	OP	CUD	FBG	DV	IO	190-215		7	5	3000			8500	10300
20	7	ECLIPSE 2150SC	OP	CUD	FBG	DV	IO	250	VLVO	7	5	3000			9350	10600
20	7	ECLIPSE 2150SS	OP	B/R	FBG	DV	IO	190-250		7	5	2900			7900	9800
20	7	EXCEL 21 DX	OP	B/R	FBG	DV	OB			7	5	2200	2	10	9850	11200
20	7	EXCEL 21 SL	OP	CUD	FBG	DV	IO	135-190		7	5	2700	2	11	7850	9500
20	7	EXCEL 21 SX	OP	B/R	FBG	DV	IO	135-190		7	5	2600	2	11	7200	8750
21	4	COASTAL 210	OP	FSH	FBG	DV	OB			8	3	3200			12500	14200
21	4	V21 STEP LIFT	OP	FSH	FBG	SV	OB			8		2300	2	8	10300	11800
21	8	CCF 218	OP	CTRCN	FBG	DV	OB			8	6	3175	2	8	12900	14600
22	1	SCARAB 22	OP	RACE	FBG	DV	IO	250-300		8		3200	2	9	9750	11800
22	1	SCARAB 22	OP	RACE	FBG	DV	IO	330		8		3200			11100	13300
23	5	COASTAL 218	OP	FSH	FBG	DV	OB			8	6	3300	2	8	13100	14900
24	1	EXCEL 23 FISH	OP	CUD	FBG	DV	OB			8	4	3200	2	8	13800	15700
24	4	ECLIPSE 2400S	OP	B/R	FBG	DV	IO	250-300		8	6	4200			13300	16400
25	4	CCF 238	OP	CTRCN	FBG	DV	OB			8	6	3800	2	6	17100	19400
25	4	COASTAL 238	OP	FSH	FBG	DV	OB			8	6	4000	2	7	18100	20100
25	5	EXCEL 23 SE	OP	CUD	FBG	DV	IO	190-250		8	6	4500	3	4	14000	16100
25	9	ECLIPSE 2600S	OP	B/R	FBG	DV	IO	300		8	6	4500			15700	18200
26	3	SCARAB SPORT 26	OP	CTRCN	FBG	DV	OB			7	8	2700	3		19300	21400
26	9	SCARAB 26	OP	RACE	FBG	DV	IO	300-330		8		4700			18100	21200
26	9	SCARAB 26	OP	RACE	FBG	DV	IO	385-415		8		4700			19900	23200
27	5	EXCEL 26 SE	OP	CUD	FBG	DV	IO	225-300		8	6	5000	3	4	18000	21100
27	5	EXCEL 26SE	OP	CUD	FBG	DV	IO	300	VLVO	8	6	5000	3	4	19200	21300
27	5	MARTINIQUE 2650	OP	CR	FBG	DV	IO	250-300		8	6	5500			20400	24000
28		COASTAL 264	OP	CUD	FBG	DV	OB			8	6	6000	3	4	23000	25600
28		COASTAL 264	OP	CUD	FBG	DV	IO	T200	MRCR	8	6	6000	3	4	22000	24500
29	5	SCARAB 29	OP	RACE	FBG	DV	IO	385-470		7	6	5500	3		22300	26600
29	5	SCARAB 29	OP	RACE	FBG	DV	IO	T250-T300		7	6	5500	3		23300	27200
29	6	SCARAB SPORT 302	OP	CUD	FBG	DV	OB			8		5000	3		35000	38900
31	1	SCARAB 31	OP	RACE	FBG	DV	IO	T330-T470		8	6	7300	3		38800	46500
31	1	SCARAB 31	OP	RACE	FBG	DV	IO	T490	MRCR	8	6	7300	3		43900	48800
31	1	SCARAB 31LE	OP	RACE	FBG	DV	IO	T470	MRCR	8	6	7300	3		38300	42600
34	5	MARTINIQUE 3200	OP	CR	FBG	DV	IB	T250-T300		11	2	10300	3		46500	52500
36	6	COASTAL 3300	ST	SF	FBG	DV	IB	T300	MRCR	12	8	13800	3		54700	60100
36	6	COASTAL 3300	ST	SF	FBG	DV	IB	T300D	CAT	12	8	13800	3		67900	74600
37	10	SCARAB 38	OP	RACE	FBG	DV	IO	T330	VLVO	8	9	9100	3		54600	60000
		IO T415 MRCR 59300 65100, IO T415 VLVO 60500 66500, IO T470 MRCR													64100	70400
		IO T490 MRCR 66000 72500, IO T550 MRCR 72200 79300														
37	11	EXCALIBUR 38	OP	EXP	FBG	DV	IO	T300	MRCR	10	8	12200			64200	70500
37	11	EXCALIBUR 38	OP	EXP	FBG	DV	IO	T385	MRCR	10	8	12200			70400	77400
37	11	EXCALIBUR 38	OP	EXP	FBG	DV	IO	T216D	VLVO	10	8	12200			77200	84900
38		MARTINIQUE 3600	OP	EXP	FBG	DV	IB	T225	VLVO	12	6	15000	3		70500	77500
		IB T310 MRCR 72200 79300, IB T330 MRCR 72800 80000, IB T300D CAT													87900	96600
44	6	EXCALIBUR 45	OP	EXP	FBG	DV	IO	T415	MRCR	11	8	15000			106500	117000
44	6	EXCALIBUR 45	OP	EXP	FBG	DV	IO	T216D	VLVO	11	8	15000			90400	99300
45	7	PORTOFINO 4300	OP	EXP	FBG	DV	IB	T400	MRCR	14	6	18200	2	10	117000	128500
45	7	PORTOFINO 4300	OP	EXP	FBG	DV	IB	T350D	CAT	14	6	18200	2	10	136000	149500
45	7	PORTOFINO 4300	OP	EXP	FBG	DV	IB	T420D	CAT	14	6	18200	2	10	144500	159000
		1995 BOATS														
18	2	CCF 190	OP	CTRCN	FBG	DV	OB			7	4	2350	2	11	4800	5500
18	2	ECLIPSE 182 S	OP	B/R	FBG	DV	IO	135-160		7	5	2150	2	8	4650	5600
18	2	ECLIPSE 182 SS	OP	B/R	FBG	DV	IO	135-160		7	5	2150	2	8	4750	5700
18	3	SCARAB SPRINT	OP	RACE	FBG	DV	IO	160		7		1860	2	9	4350	5300
18	8	EXCEL 19 DX	OP	B/R	FBG	SV	OB			7	4	1900	2	6	4550	5250
18	8	EXCEL 19 SL	OP	CUD	FBG	SV	IO	135-160		7	4	2400	2	7	5400	6550
18	8	EXCEL 19 SX	OP	B/R	FBG	DV	IO	135-160		7	4	2300	2	7	4950	6000
19	6	ECLIPSE 196 S	OP	B/R	FBG	DV	IO	180-215		7	10	2685	2	8	5900	7200
19	6	ECLIPSE 196 SC	OP	CUD	FBG	DV	IO	180-215		7	10	2750	2	8	6400	7800
19	6	ECLIPSE 196 SCS	OP	CUD	FBG	DV	IO	180-215		7	10	2750	2	8	6500	7900
19	6	ECLIPSE 196 SS	OP	B/R	FBG	DV	IO	180-215		7	10	2685	2	8	6000	7300
20	7	EXCEL 21 DX	OP	B/R	FBG	DV	OB			7	5	2200	2	10	9350	10700
20	7	EXCEL 21 SL	OP	CUD	FBG	DV	IO	135-190		7	5	2700	2	11	7350	8900
20	7	EXCEL 21 SX	OP	B/R	FBG	DV	IO	135-205		7	5	2600	2	11	6750	8150
21		ECLIPSE 210 S	OP	B/R	FBG	DV	IO	190-255		8	2	2740	3		7800	9500
21		ECLIPSE 210 SC	OP	CUD	FBG	DV	IO	190-255		8	2	3100	3		9000	10700
21		ECLIPSE 210 SCS	OP	CUD	FBG	DV	IO	190-255		8	2	3100	3		9150	10700
21		ECLIPSE 210 SS	OP	B/R	FBG	DV	IO	190-255		8	2	2740	3		7900	9600
21	4	V21 STEP LIFT	OP	FSH	FBG	SV	OB			8		2300	2	8	9850	11200
21	8	CCF 218	OP	CTRCN	FBG	DV	OB			8	6	3175	2	8	12300	13900
22	1	SCARAB 22	OP	RACE	FBG	DV	IO	235-300		8		3000	2	9	8600	10700
23		EXCEL 23 SL	OP	CUD	FBG	DV	IO	190-235		8	6	3400	2	11	10700	12400
23		NOVA 23 XL	OP	CUD	FBG	DV	IO	250-300		8	3	4000	2	10	11900	14800
23	3	ECLIPSE 232 FL	OP	B/R	FBG	DV	IO	235-300		8	6	3900	3		11100	13400
23	5	COASTAL 218	OP	FSH	FBG	DV	OB			8	6	3300	2	8	12500	14200
23	6	ECLIPSE 236 SC	OP	CUD	FBG	DV	IO	235-300		8	6	3875	3		11900	14400
24	1	EXCEL 23 FISH	OP	CUD	FBG	DV	OB			8	4	3200	2	8	13100	14900
25	4	CCF 238	OP	CTRCN	FBG	DV	OB			8	6	3800	2	6	16300	18500
25	4	COASTAL 238	OP	FSH	FBG	DV	OB			8	6	4000	2	7	16900	19200
25	4	COASTAL 238	OP	FSH	FBG	DV	IO	180-185		8	6	4000	2	7	12900	15000
25	5	EXCEL 23 SE	OP	CUD	FBG	DV	IO	190-235		8	6	4500	3	4	13100	15100
25	9	ECLIPSE 260 S	OP	B/R	FBG	DV	IO	235-300		8	6	4500	3	2	13700	17000
26	2	MARTINIQUE 2400	OP	CR	FBG	DV	IO	230-275		8	6	4500	3		14000	16000
26	3	SCARAB 26	OP	RACE	FBG	DV	IO	300	MRCR	7	8	2700	3		12700	14400
26	3	SCARAB 26	OP	RACE	FBG	DV	IO	385-415		7	8	2700	3		14800	17800
26	3	SCARAB SPORTSTER 26	OP	CTRCN	FBG	DV	OB			7	8	2700	3		18600	20700
27	5	EXCEL 26 SE	OP	CUD	FBG	DV	IO	230-300		8	6	5000	3	4	16500	19700
28		COASTAL 264	OP	CUD	FBG	DV	OB			8	6	6000	3	4	21800	24300
28		COASTAL 264	OP	CUD	FBG	DV	IO	235-255		8	6	6000	3	4	18700	21100
28	4	MARTINIQUE 2700	OP	CR	FBG	DV	IO	300		9	6	6600	3		21200	23800
28	4	MARTINIQUE 2700	OP	CR	FBG	DV	IO	185D-216D		9	6	6600	3		23900	27400
28	4	MARTINIQUE 2700	OP	CR	FBG	DV	IO	T160-T180		9	6	7100	3		22800	25400
28	10	COASTAL 2600	OP	CUD	FBG	DV	OB			9	8	5500	3		21100	23500
28	10	COASTAL 2600	OP	CUD	FBG	DV	IO	300-305		9	8	5500	3		19000	21300
28	10	COASTAL 2600	OP	CUD	FBG	DV	IO	T160-T180		9	8	5500	3		19500	21700
29	5	SCARAB 29	OP	RACE	FBG	DV	IO	300-415		7	6	5500	3		19600	23700
29	5	SCARAB 29	OP	RACE	FBG	DV	IO	470	MRCR	7	6	5500	3		22300	24800
29	5	SCARAB 29	OP	RACE	FBG	DV	IO	T250-T270		7	6	5500	3		21700	24900
29	6	SCARAB SPORT 302	OP	CUD	FBG	DV	OB			8		5000	3		33100	36800
31	1	SCARAB 31	OP	RACE	FBG	DV	IO	T300-T415		8	6	7300	3		34700	42500

648 CONTINUED ON NEXT PAGE 96th ed. - Vol. II

LOA FT	IN	NAME AND/ OR MODEL	TOP/ RIG	BOAT TYPE	-HULL- MTL	TP	ENGINE TP	# HP	MFG	BEAM FT	IN	WGT LBS	DRAFT FT	IN	RETAIL LOW	RETAIL HIGH
		1995 BOATS														
31	1	SCARAB 31	OP	RACE	FBG	DV	IO	T470-T490		8	6	7300	3		40000	45200
34	5	MARTINIQUE 3200	OP	CR	FBG	DV	IO	T235	VLVO	11	2	10300	3		36500	40600
		IO T250 MRCR 36900 41000, IB T250-T255 43500 48500, IO T275 VLVO 37500 41700														
		IB T300-T330 44900 50900, IOT185D-T216D 39400 45300, IB T225D VLVO 50000 55000														
36	6	COASTAL 3300	ST	SF	FBG	DV	IB	T300	MRCR	12	8	13800	3		51700	56800
36	6	COASTAL 3300	ST	SF	FBG	DV	IB	T340	VLVO	12	8	13800	3		52900	58100
36	6	COASTAL 3300	ST	SF	FBG	DV	IB	T300D	CAT	12	8	13800	3		64500	70900
37	10	SCARAB 38	OP	RACE	FBG	DV	IO	T385	MRCR	8	9	9100	3		53300	58500
		IO T390 VLVO 54500 59900, IO T415 MRCR 55300 60800, IO T470 MRCR 59800 65700														
		IO T490 MRCR 61500 67600, IO T550 MRCR 67300 74000														
38		MARTINIQUE 3600	OP	EXP	FBG	DV	IB	T225	VLVO	12	6	15000	3		66600	73200
		IB T310 MRCR 68200 75000, IB T330 VLVO 69100 76000, IB T195D VLVO 75500 83000														
		IB T216D VLVO 76500 84000														
43	2	SCARAB 43	OP	RACE	FBG	DV	IO	R415	MRCR	8	9	10500	3		86100	94700
		IO R470 MRCR 95300 104500, IO R490 MRCR 98600 108500, IO R550 MRCR 108000 118500														
45	7	PORTOFINO 43	OP	EXP	FBG	DV	IB	T310	MRCR	14	6	18200	2	10	107500	118000
		IB T330 VLVO 109500 120500, IB T350D CAT 132000 145000, IB T430D VLVO 135000 148000														
		IB T435D CAT 142000 156000														
45	7	PORTOFINO 4350	OP	EXP	FBG	DV	IB	T410D	CAT	14	6	18200	2	10	149000	164000
51	9	CMY 4600	FB	MYCPT	FBG	DV	IB	T435D	CAT	14	6	29000	3	2	179500	197000
		1994 BOATS														
17	10	FISH 18	OP	CTRCN	FBG	SV	OB			7	9	1750	2	5	3900	4500
18		EXCEL 18 DX	OP	RNBT	FBG	SV	OB			7	2	1675	2	4	3850	4500
18		EXCEL 18 SL	OP	RNBT	FBG	SV	IO	135	MRCR	7	2	1900	2	4	4250	4950
18		EXCEL 18 SX	OP	RNBT	FBG	SV	IO	135	VLVO	7	2	1900	2	4	4250	4950
18	2	ECLIPSE 182 S	OP	RNBT	FBG	DV	IO	135-185		7	5	2150	2	8	4600	5500
18	2	ECLIPSE 182 SS	OP	RNBT	FBG	DV	IO	135-185		7	5	2150	2	8	4700	5650
18	3	SCARAB SPRINT	OP	RACE	FBG	SV	IO	135		7		1860	2	9	4000	4900
19	4	ECLIPSE 196 SC	OP	CUD	FBG	DV	IO	180-205		7	9	2750	2	8	6100	7050
19	4	ECLIPSE 196 SCS	OP	CUD	FBG	DV	IO	180-205		7	9	2750	2	8	5950	7200
19	4	ECLIPSE 196 SS	OP	RNBT	FBG	DV	IO	180-205		7	9	2700	2	8	5650	6800
19	9	NOVA 200	OP	CUD	FBG	SV	IO	185-250		8		2900	3		6400	7750
19	9	NOVA 202	OP	CUD	FBG	SV	IO	180-240		8		2900	3		6350	7850
20		EXCEL 20 DX	OP	RNBT	FBG	SV	OB			7	5	2000	2	10	7850	9000
20		EXCEL 20 SL	OP	CUD	FBG	SV	IO	185	VLVO	7	5	2400	2	10	6550	7550
20		EXCEL 20 SX	OP	RNBT	FBG	SV	IO	185	VLVO	7	5	2350	2	10	6250	7150
20	6	ECLIPSE 196 S	OP	RNBT	FBG	DV	IO	180-205		7	10	2850	3		7000	8350
20	6	FISH 20	OP	CTRCN	FBG	SV	OB			8		2140	2	8	8450	9700
20	8	V21 STEP LIFT	OP	RNBT	FBG	SV	OB			8		2300	2	8	9150	10400
21		ECLIPSE 210 S	OP	RNBT	FBG	DV	IO	190-250		8	2	2740	3		7400	8700
21		ECLIPSE 210 SC	OP	CUD	FBG	DV	IO	190-250		8	2	2610	3		7550	8950
21		ECLIPSE 210 SCS	OP	CUD	FBG	DV	IO	190-250		8	2	2610	3		7700	9450
21		ECLIPSE 210 SS	OP	RNBT	FBG	DV	IO	190-250		8	2	2740	3		7500	8850
21	8	COASTAL 21	OP		FBG	DV	OB			8	6	2600	2	8	10400	11900
22	3	SCARAB SPRINT 22	OP	RACE	FBG	DV	IO	230-250		8		3800	2	8	9750	11100
23		EXCEL 23 SE	OP	CUD	FBG	SV	IO	225-235		8	6	3500	3	2	10400	11800
23		EXCEL 23 SE	OP	CUD	FBG	SV	IO	190D	VLVO	8	6	3500	3	2	12900	14600
23		EXCEL 23 SL	OP	CUD	FBG	SV	IO	190-225		8	6	3300	2	11	9800	11300
23		NOVA 23	OP	RNBT	FBG	DV	IO	300		7	10	4000	3	2	10900	12800
23	3	236 SC	OP	RNBT	FBG	DV	IO		VLVO	8	6	3875	3		**	**
23	3	236 SC	OP	RNBT	FBG	DV	IO	235	MRCR	8	6	3875	3		10300	11700
23	3	ECLIPSE 232	OP	RNBT	FBG	DV	IO	225-300		8	6	3900	3		10600	12500
23	8	FISH 238	OP		FBG	DV	OB			8	6	3200	2	8	13500	15400
24	3	PRIMA 243	OP	CR	FBG	DV	IO	225-250		8	6	4500	3		12800	15100
24	3	PRIMA 243	OP	CR	FBG	DV	IO	115D	VLVO	8	6	4500	3		14700	16700
26		EXEL 26 SE			FBG	DV	IO		VLVO	8	6	4100	3	3	**	**
26		EXEL 26 SE			FBG	DV	IO	235	MRCR	8	6	4100	3	3	13800	15600
26	1	COASTAL 2600	OP	FSH	FBG	SV	OB			9	8	7100	3		20900	23300
26	3	SCARAB SPORTSTER 26	OP	CTRCN	FBG	DV	OB			7	8	2700	3		17400	19800
26	3	SCARAB SPORTSTER 26	OP	CTRCN	FBG	DV	IO	300-350		7	10	4200	3	2	15500	18900
27	7	COASTAL 2800	ST	SF	FBG	SV	OB			9	11	6400	2	4	23300	25900
27	7	COASTAL 2800	ST	SF	FBG	SV	IB	T230	MRCR	9	11	8200	2	4	29600	32900
28	7	MARTINIQUE 2700	OP	CR	FBG	SV	IO	300	MRCR	9	8	6500	3		21700	24100
28	7	MARTINIQUE 2700	OP	CR	FBG	SV	IO	T300	VLVO	9	8	6500	3		25700	28500
28	7	MARTINIQUE 2700	OP	CR	FBG	SV	IOT180D-T250D			9	8	6500	3		28000	34300
29	5	SCARAB 29	OP	RACE	FBG	DV	IO	300-350		7	6	4600	3		17200	20400
29	5	SCARAB 29	OP	RACE	FBG	DV	IO	415	MRCR	7	6	4600	3		19400	21600
29	5	SCARAB 29	OP	RACE	FBG	DV	IO	T235-T245		7	6	5500	3		19900	22600
29	6	SCARAB SPORT 30	OP	CUD	FBG	DV	OB			8		5000	3		31400	34900
31	1	SCARAB THUNDER 31	OP	RACE	FBG	DV	IO	T300-T490		8	6	7300	3		29800	35500
31	1	SCARAB THUNDER 31	OP	RACE	FBG	DV	IO	T115D	VLVO	8	6	7300	3		27300	30300
31	1	SCARAB THUNDER 31	OP	RACE	FBG	SV	IO	T300	VLVO	8	6	7300	3		28100	31200
31	8	MARTINIQUE 3200	OP	CR	FBG	SV	IB	T230-T300		11	8	10300	2	10	39700	46200
33	4	COASTAL 3300	ST	SF	FBG	SV	IB	T300	MRCR	12	8	13800	2	10	49000	53800
33	4	COASTAL 3300	ST	SF	FBG	SV	IB	T300	VLVO	12	8	13800	2	10	49100	53900
33	4	COASTAL 3300	ST	SF	FBG	SV	IB	T300D	CUM	12	8	13800	2	10	60800	66800
35	6	MARTINIQUE 3600	OP	EXP	FBG	SV	IB	T195	VLVO	12	6	14400	3		61400	67400
		IB T300 MRCR 63200 69500, IB T415 MRCR 66800 73400, IB T330D VLVO 77200 84900														
37	10	SCARAB THUNDER 38	OP	RACE	FBG	DV	IO	T350	MRCR	8	9	9100	3		52000	57100
		IO T390 MRCR 54100 59500, IO T445 MRCR 59000 64900, IO T490 MRCR 57500 63100														
		IO T600 MRCR 67500 74100														
42	10	PORTOFINO 4300	ST	EXP	FBG	SV	IB	T330	MRCR	14	6	18200	2	10	103500	113500
		IB T330 VLVO 104000 114000, IB T410 MRCR 108500 119000, IB T375D CAT 129000 141500														
43	2	SCARAB THUNDER 43	OP	RACE	FBG	DV	IO	T490	MRCR	8	9	10500	2	6	78800	86600
		IO T600 MRCR 88300 97100, IO R350 MRCR 74100 81500, IO R445 MRCR 87700 96300														
		IO R490 MRCR 95100 104500, IO R600 MRCR 110500 121500														
46	3	CMY 4600	FB	MYCPT	FBG	SV	IB	T375D	CAT	14	6	29000	3	2	163500	180000
46	3	CMY 4600	FB	MYCPT	FBG	SV	IB	T435D	CAT	14	6	29000	3	2	171000	188000
		1993 BOATS														
17	10	FISH 18	OP	CTRCN	FBG	SV	OB			7	9	1750	2	5	3700	4300
18		EXCEL 18 DX	OP	RNBT	FBG	SV	OB			7	2	1675	2	4	3700	4250
18		EXCEL 18 SL	OP	RNBT	FBG	SV	IO	110	VLVO	7	2	1900	2	4	4150	4800
18		EXCEL 18 SX	OP	RNBT	FBG	SV	IO	110	VLVO	7	2	1900	2	4	4050	4700
18	2	ECLIPSE 182 S	OP	RNBT	FBG	DV	IO	115-175		7	5	2150	2	8	4200	5150
18	2	ECLIPSE 182 SS	OP	RNBT	FBG	DV	IO	115-175		7	5	2150	2	8	4250	5250
18	3	SCARAB SPIRIT	OP	RACE	FBG	SV	IO	115-130		7		1860	2	9	3750	4600
19	4	ECLIPSE 196 SC	OP	CUD	FBG	DV	IO	175-229		7	9	2750	2	8	5450	6750
19	4	ECLIPSE 196 SCS	OP	CUD	FBG	DV	IO	175-229		7	9	2750	2	8	5550	6900
19	4	ECLIPSE 196 SS	OP	RNBT	FBG	DV	IO	175-229		7	9	2700	2	8	5250	6500
19	9	NOVA 200	OP	CUD	FBG	SV	IO	175-240		8		2900	3		5950	7300
19	9	NOVA 200	OP	CUD	FBG	SV	IO	245	VLVO	8		2900	3		6500	7450
19	9	NOVA 202	OP	CUD	FBG	SV	IO		VLVO	8		2900	3		**	**
19	9	NOVA 202	OP	CUD	FBG	SV	IO	175-240		8		2900	3		5950	7300
19	9	NOVA 202	OP	CUD	FBG	SV	IO	245	VLVO	8		2900	3		6500	7450
20		EXCEL 20 DX	OP	RNBT	FBG	SV	OB			7	5	2000	2	10	7500	8600
20		EXCEL 20 SL	OP	CUD	FBG	SV	IO	155	VLVO	7	5	2400	2	10	6050	6950
20		EXCEL 20 SX	OP	RNBT	FBG	SV	IO	155	VLVO	7	5	2350	2	10	5800	6650
20	6	ECLIPSE 196 S	OP	RNBT	FBG	DV	IO	175-229		7	10	2850	3		6550	8000
20	6	FISH 20	OP	CTRCN	FBG	SV	OB			8		2140	2	8	8100	9300
20	8	V21 STEP LIFT	OP	RNBT	FBG	SV	OB			8		2300	2	8	8650	9900
21		ECLIPSE 210 CS	OP	CUD	FBG	DV	IO	205-245		8	2	2610	3		6850	8500
21		ECLIPSE 210 S	OP	RNBT	FBG	DV	IO	205-245		8	2	2740	3		6700	8250
21		ECLIPSE 210 SCS	OP	CUD	FBG	DV	IO	205-245		8	2	2610	3		6950	8600
21		ECLIPSE 210 SCS	OP	CUD	FBG	DV	IO	300	MRCR	8	2	2610	3		7700	8850
21		ECLIPSE 210 SS	OP	RNBT	FBG	DV	IO	205-245		8	2	2740	3		6800	8400
21		ECLIPSE 210 SS	OP	RNBT	FBG	DV	IO	300	MRCR	8	2	2740	3		7500	8650
21		FISH 217	OP	CTRCN	FBG	SV	IB	229-245		8	6	3600	2		10500	11900
21		FISH 217	OP	CTRCN	FBG	SV	IB	130D-170D		8	6	3600	2		13300	16600
21	5	210 CCF	OP	CTRCN	FBG	SV	OB			8	4	2600	2	8	9850	11200
23		EXCEL 23 SE	OP	CUD	FBG	SV	IO	180-225		8	6	3500	3	2	9500	11000
23		EXCEL 23 SE	OP	CUD	FBG	SV	IO	120D	VLVO	8	6	3500	3	2	11300	12800
23		EXCEL 23 SL	OP	CUD	FBG	SV	IO	180-255		8	6	3300	2	11	9200	10900
23	3	COASTAL 236	OP	FSH	FBG	SV	OB			8	6	3400	2	8	13200	15000
23	3	COASTAL 236	OP	FSH	FBG	SV	IO	225-230		8	6	4350	2	8	12000	13700
23	3	ECLIPSE 232	OP	RNBT	FBG	DV	IO	225-300		8	6	3900	3		9900	11700
23	3	ECLIPSE 233	OP	CUD	FBG	DV	IO	225-300		8	6	3900	3		10500	12500
24	3	PRIMA 243	OP	CR	FBG	DV	IO	175-300		8	6	4500	3		11700	14400
24	3	PRIMA 243	OP	CR	FBG	DV	IO	330	VLVO	8	6	4500	3		13800	15700
24	3	PRIMA 243	OP	CR	FBG	DV	IO	200D	VLVO	8	6	4500	3		14800	16800
24	8	COASTAL 250	OP	FSH	FBG	SV	OB			8	3	3500	3		14300	16300
24	8	COASTAL 250	OP	FSH	FBG	SV	IO	225-230		8	3	4400	3		12800	14600
25	7	NOVA 26	OP	CUD	FBG	DV	IO	300-350		8	2	5500	3		15400	18600
		IO 390-445 17400 21400, IO T225-T245 16900 19600, IO T300 18500 21300														
25	7	NOVA 26	OP	CUD	FBG	SV	IO	T300	MRCR	8	2	5500	3		18500	20600
26	1	COASTAL 2600	OP	FSH	FBG	SV	IO	300		9	8	7100	3		20200	22800
26	1	COASTAL 2600	OP	FSH	FBG	SV	IO	T175-T180		9	8	7100	3		20800	23600
26	3	SCARAB SPORTSTER 26	OP	CTRCN	FBG	DV	OB			7	8	2700	3		16700	18900
27	7	COASTAL 2800	ST	SF	FBG	SV	OB			9	11	6400	2	4	22400	24800
27	7	COASTAL 2800	ST	SF	FBG	SV	IB	T230-T245		9	11	8200	2	4	28100	31700

CONTINUED ON NEXT PAGE

LOA FT	LOA IN	NAME AND/ OR MODEL	TOP/ RIG	BOAT TYPE	-HULL- MTL	-HULL- TP	ENGINE TP	ENGINE # HP	ENGINE MFG	BEAM FT	BEAM IN	WGT LBS	DRAFT FT	DRAFT IN	RETAIL LOW	RETAIL HIGH
		1993 BOATS														
27	7	COASTAL 2800	ST	SF	FBG	SV	IB	T130D-T165D		9	11	8200	2	4	35100	41700
28	7	PRIMA 287	OP	CR	FBG	SV	IO	240-330		9	8	6500	3		19400	23300
		IO 200D VLVO 21300 23700, IO T155-T187 20400 23700, IO T130D VLVO 23500 26100														
29	6	SCARAB SPORT 30	OP	CUD	FBG	DV	OB			8		5000	3		29900	33200
31	1	SCARAB 31	OP	RACE	FBG	DV	IO	T300-T445		8	6	7300	3		29800	33300
31	1	SCARAB 31	OP	RACE	FBG	DV	IO	T200D-T230D		8	6	7300	3		30300	35400
31	1	SCARAB THUNDER 31	OP	RACE	FBG	DV	IO	T350-T490		8	6	7300	3		29000	35200
31	1	SCARAB THUNDER 31	OP	RACE	FBG	SV	IO	T425-T490		8	6	7300	3		31100	34600
31	1	SCARAB VIPER 31	OP	RACE	FBG	DV	IO	T300-T425		8	6	7250	3		25300	31300
31	1	SCARAB VIPER 31	OP	RACE	FBG	DV	IO	T445	MRCR	8	6	7250	3		28600	31800
31	1	SCARAB VIPER 31	OP	RACE	FBG	DV	IO	T200D	VLVO	8	6	7250	3		25900	28700
31	8	ST TROPEZ 3200	OP	CR	FBG	SV	IB	T230-T300		11	8	10300	2	10	42400	49400
		IO T200D VLVO 39200 43600, IB T200D VLVO 49400 54300, IO T230D VLVO 40500 45000														
33	4	COASTAL 3300	ST	SF	FBG	SV	IB	T300	CRUS	12	8	13800	2	10	46800	51400
		IB T300 MRCR 46700 51300, IB T300 VLVO 46800 51400, IBT300D-T425D 57900 71800														
34		SEDAN 34	FB	SDN	FBG	SV	IB	T300-T330		12	6	15700	3		62900	70200
34		SEDAN 34	FB	SDN	FBG	SV	IB	T300D	CUM	12	6	15700	3		80800	88800
35	6	ST TROPEZ 3600	OP	EXP	FBG	SV	IB	T300	CRUS	12	6	14400	3		64300	70700
		IB T310 MRCR 64300 70600, IB T330 VLVO 65100 71600, IB T360 CRUS 66100 72600														
		IB T400 MRCR 67100 73700, IO T200D VLVO 57000 62700, IO T230D VLVO 58100 63900														
		IB T300D CUM 77500 85100														
37	10	SCARAB THUNDER 38	OP	RACE	FBG	DV	IO	T350	MRCR	8	9	9100	3		48600	53400
		IO T390 MRCR 50600 55600, IO T415 MRCR 48200 53000, IO T445 MRCR 55200 60600														
		IO T490 MRCR 53700 59000, IO T600 MRCR 63000 69300														
42	10	PORTOFINO 4300	ST	EXP	FBG	SV	IB	T300	CRUS	14	6	18200	2	10	97500	107000
		IB T330 MRCR 98500 108000, IB T330 VLVO 99100 109000, IB T355 CRUS 100500 110500														
		IB T410 MRCR 103000 113500, IB T375D CAT 123000 135000, IB T380D VLVO 118000 129500														
		IB T425D CAT 128500 141500														
43	2	SCARAB THUNDER 43	OP	RACE	FBG	DV	IO	T490	MRCR	8	9	10500	2	6	73700	80900
		IO T600 MRCR 82500 90700, IO R350 MRCR 69300 76200, IO R390 MRCR 74100 81400														
		IO R425 MRCR 78900 86700, IO R445 MRCR 81900 90000, IO R490 MRCR 88800 97600														
		IO R600 MRCR 103500 113500														
46	3	CMY 4600	FB	MYCPT	FBG	SV	IB	T375D	CAT	14	6	29000	3	2	156500	172000
46	3	CMY 4600	FB	MYCPT	FBG	SV	IB	T425D	CAT	14	6	29000	3	2	162000	178500
		1992 BOATS														
17	10	FISH 18	OP	CTRCN	FBG	SV	OB			7	9	1750	2	5	3550	4150
17	10	FISH 18 CF	OP	CTRCN	FBG	SV	OB			7	9	1750	2	5	3550	4150
19	6	ECLIPSE 186	OP	RNBT	FBG	DV	IO	135-180		7	10	2700	3		5000	6000
19	9	NOVA 202	OP	RNBT	FBG	SV	IO	155-240		8		2900	3		5350	6350
20	6	ECLIPSE 196	OP	RNBT	FBG	DV	IO	135-180		7	10	2850	3		6050	7300
20	6	ECLIPSE 197	OP	RNBT	FBG	DV	IO	135-180		7	10	2900	3		6150	7350
20	6	FISH 20	OP	CTRCN	FBG	SV	OB			8		2140	2	8	7750	8950
20	6	V20 STEP LIFT	OP	RNBT	FBG	SV	OB			8		1920	2	8	7250	8350
20	6	V20 STEP LIFT	OP	RNBT	FBG	SV	IO	175-230		8		3120	2	8	6500	7950
21	3	SCARAB 21	OP	RACE	FBG	DV	IO	225-245		8		3800	2	8	8050	9400
21	3	SCARAB 21	OP	RACE	FBG	DV	IO	300		8		3800	2	8	8450	10100
21	5	210 CCF	OP	CTRCN	FBG	SV	OB			8	4	2300	2	8	8650	9950
21	5	COASTAL 210	OP	RNBT	FBG	SV	OB			8	4	2500	3		9300	10600
21	5	COASTAL 210	OP	RNBT	FBG	SV	IO	175-230		8	4	3450	3		7400	8950
21	6	ECLIPSE 215	OP	RNBT	FBG	DV	IO	175-245		7	10	3050	3		6700	8300
21	6	ECLIPSE 215	OP	RNBT	FBG	DV	IO	300	MRCR	7	10	3050	3		7450	8550
21	6	ECLIPSE 216	OP	RNBT	FBG	DV	IO	175-245		8		3300	3		7100	8750
21	6	ECLIPSE 216	OP	RNBT	FBG	DV	IO	300	MRCR	8		3300	3		7850	9050
23	2	ECLIPSE 232	OP	RNBT	FBG	SV	IO	180-300		8	6	3900	3		8900	10900
23	3	COASTAL 236	OP	FSH	FBG	SV	OB			8	6	3400	2	8	12700	14400
23	3	COASTAL 236	OP	FSH	FBG	SV	IO	180-230		8	6	3400	2	8	9100	10800
23	3	ECLIPSE 233	OP	RNBT	FBG	SV	IO	180-300		8	6	3900	3		8950	11000
24	8	SPORTSMAN 250	OP	FSH	FBG	SV	OB			8	3	3380	3		13500	15300
24	8	SPORTSMAN 250	OP	FSH	FBG	SV	IO	225-230		8	3	4400	3		12000	13700
24	10	GENESIS 240 II	OP	RNBT	FBG	SV	OB			8	6	2550	2	6	11500	13100
24	10	GENESIS 240 II	OP	RNBT	FBG	SV	IO	155-180		8	6	3450	2	6	8600	10200
24	10	GENESIS 240 II	OP	RNBT	FBG	SV	IO	130D	VLVO	8	6	3450	2	6	9900	11200
25	6	ECLIPSE 250	OP	RNBT	FBG	SV	IO	225-300		8	6	4500	3		11200	13400
25	7	NOVA 26 ST	OP	RNBT	FBG	DV	IO	300-350		8	2	5500	3		13300	16000
		IO 390-445 15000 18700, IO T225-T245 14600 16900, IO T300 15600 18400														
26	1	COASTAL 2600	OP	FSH	FBG	SV	OB			9	8	5500	3		18600	20600
26	1	COASTAL 2600	OP	FSH	FBG	SV	IO	300		9	8	7100	3		19100	21400
26	1	COASTAL 2600	OP	FSH	FBG	SV	IO	T175-T180		9	8	7100	3		19500	22100
26	3	SCARAB SPORTSTER 26	OP	CTRCN	FBG	DV	OB			7	8	2700	3		16000	18200
27	7	COASTAL 2800	ST	SF	FBG	SV	OB			9	11	8200	2	4	21500	23900
27	7	COASTAL 2800	ST	SF	FBG	SV	IB	T230-T245		9	11	8200	2	4	26700	30100
27	7	COASTAL 2800	ST	SF	FBG	SV	IB	T165D	YAN	9	11	8200	2	4	35800	39800
28		SCARAB 28XLT	OP	RACE	FBG	DV	IO	T240-T300		8	2	5900	3		15000	18600
28		SCARAB 28XLT	OP	RACE	FBG	DV	IO	T350	MRCR	8	2	5900	3		17200	19600
28	7	EXPRESS 2600	ST	EXP	FBG	SV	IO	240-300		9	8	7200	3		18100	21100
		IO 200D VLVO 20500 22800, IO T155-T180 19100 21700, IO T130D VLVO 22600 25100														
28	7	PRIMA 2600	ST	EXP	FBG	SV	IO	240-300		9	8	7200	3		20000	23200
		IO 200D VLVO 22500 25000, IO T155-T180 20900 23900, IO T130D VLVO 24300 27000														
29	6	SCARAB SPORT 30	OP	CTRCN	FBG	DV	OB			8		5000	3		27500	30500
30	2	MONACO 3000	ST	EXP	FBG	SV	IO	T130-T245		10	8	9800	3		26000	31700
30	2	MONACO 3000	ST	EXP	FBG	SV	IO	T130D	VLVO	10	8	9800	3		30400	33800
31	1	SCARAB 31	OP	RACE	FBG	DV	IO	T300-T445		8	6	7300	3		27700	31300
31	1	SCARAB 31	OP	RACE	FBG	DV	IO	T200D	VLVO	8	6	7300	3		28500	31700
31	1	SCARAB THUNDER 31	OP	RACE	FBG	DV	IO	T350-T490		8	6	7300	3		26800	32800
33	4	COASTAL 3300	ST	SF	FBG	SV	IB	T300-T400		12	8	14000	2	10	44100	51500
33	4	COASTAL 3300	ST	SF	FBG	SV	IB	T165D-T300D		12	8	14000	2	10	50300	61100
33	4	COASTAL 3300	ST	SF	FBG	SV	IB	T375D-T425D		12	8	14000	2	10	59900	68800
33	4	SPORT BRIDGE 3300	FB	SF	FBG	SV	IB	T300-T355		12	8	12000	2	8	49800	56500
33	4	SPORT BRIDGE 3300	FB	SF	FBG	SV	IB	T165D-T300D		12	8	12000	2	8	54100	66800
33	7	ST TROPEZ 3300	ST	EXP	FBG	SV	IB	T230-T300		11	8	10000	2	10	47700	54300
33	7	ST TROPEZ 3300	ST	EXP	FBG	SV	IO	T200D	VLVO	11	8	10000	2	10	43100	47900
33	7	ST TROPEZ 3300	ST	EXP	FBG	SV	IB	T200D	VLVO	11	8	10000	2	10	55400	60800
33	10	SCARAB 34	OP	RACE	FBG	DV	IO	T300-T350		8	4	7750	3		28500	33900
33	10	SCARAB 34	OP	RACE	FBG	DV	IO	T390-T445		8	4	7750	3		32400	39900
33	10	SCARAB 34	OP	RACE	FBG	DV	IO	T200D	VLVO	8	4	7750	3		33600	37300
33	10	SCARAB 34 FITT	OP	RACE	FBG	DV	IO	T300-T390		8	4	7750	3		34200	42400
33	10	SCARAB 34 FITT	OP	RACE	FBG	DV	IO	T445	MRCR	8	4	7750	3		41500	46200
33	10	SCARAB SUPER SPT 34	OP	RACE	FBG	DV	OB			8	4	5100	3		53400	58700
34		TRIUMPH AMERICUS 34	ST	EXP	FBG	SV	IB	T300	CRUS	12	6	15000	3		55800	61300
		IB T300 MRCR 55600 61100, IB T300 VLVO 55700 61300, IB T300D CUM 69400 76200														
34		TRIUMPH BDS 34	ST	EXP	FBG	SV	IB	T300	CRUS	12	6	15700	3		56600	62200
		IB T300 MRCR 56500 62100, IB T300 VLVO 56600 62200, IB T300D CUM 71000 78000														
35	11	GRAN SPORT 3400	ST	EXP	FBG	SV	IB	T300	CRUS	12	6	12000	3		57800	63500
		IB T300 MRCR 57500 63200, IB T300 VLVO 57800 63500, IB T355 CRUS 59400 65300														
		IB T400 MRCR 60500 66500, IO T200D VLVO 49800 54800, IB T200D VLVO 63700 70000														
37	10	SCARAB 38	OP	RACE	FBG	DV	IO	T350	MRCR	8	9	9100	3		38000	42300
37	10	SCARAB 38	OP	RACE	FBG	DV	IO	T390	MRCR	8	9	9100	3		39900	44400
37	10	SCARAB 38	OP	RACE	FBG	DV	IO	T445	MRCR	8	9	9100	3		42200	46900
37	10	SCARAB THUNDER 38	OP	RACE	FBG	DV	IO	T350	MRCR	8	9	9100	3		45700	50200
		IO T390 MRCR 47600 52300, IO T445 MRCR 51600 56700, IO T490 MRCR 50300 55200														
		IO T600 MRCR 59000 64800														
42	10	PORTOFINO 4300	ST	EXP	FBG	SV	IB	T300	CRUS	14	6	18000	2	10	92400	101500
		IB T330 MRCR 93400 102500, IB T330 VLVO 93900 103000, IB T355 CRUS 95400 105000														
		IB T410 MRCR 97900 107500, IB T375D CAT 116500 128000, IB T380D VLVO 112000 123000														
		IB T425D CAT 122000 134000														
43	2	SCARAB THUNDER 43	OP	RACE	FBG	DV	IO	T490	MRCR	8	9	10500	3		68900	75800
		IO T600 MRCR 77300 84900, IO T800 MRCR ** **, IO R350 MRCR 64900 71300														
		IO R390 MRCR 69300 76200, IO R445 MRCR 76700 84300, IO R490 MRCR 83200 91400														
		IO R600 MRCR 96800 106500, IO R800 MRCR ** **														
43	7	EXCALIBUR 44	OP	OFF	FBG	DV	IO	T390	MRCR	9		12000	3	6	65400	71900
		IO T445 MRCR 70700 77700, IO R350 MRCR 65500 72000, IO R390 MRCR 70500 77500														
48	6	CMY 4600	FB	MYCPT	FBG	SV	IB	T355	CRUS	14	6	26000	3	2	139000	152500
		IB T400 MRCR 141000 155000, IB T375D CAT 154500 169500, IB T425D CAT 160000 175500														
48	8	SCARAB METEOR 5000	OP	RACE	FBG	DV	IO	R350	MRCR	9	4	16000	3	8	60200	66100
48	8	SCARAB METEOR 5000	OP	RACE	FBG	DV	IO	R389	MRCR	9	4	16000	3	8	68500	75300
48	8	SCARAB METEOR 5000	OP	RACE	FBG	DV	IO	R445	MRCR	9	4	16000	3	8	72500	79700
		1991 BOATS														
16	9	SPORT 170	OP	RNBT	FBG	SV	OB			7	3	1950	2	8	3700	4300
16	9	SPORT 170	OP	RNBT	FBG	SV	IO	115	MRCR	7	5	1950	2	8	3250	3800
17	10	FISH 18	OP	CTRCN	FBG	SV	OB			7	9	1750	2	5	3450	4000
17	10	SPORT 18	OP	CTRCN	FBG	SV	OB			7	9	1750	2	5	3450	4000
18	3	SCARAB SPRINT 164	OP	RACE	FBG	DV	IO	135-167		7		1800	2	9	3250	4000
19	2	ECLIPSE 186	OP	RNBT	FBG	DV	IO	135-205		7	10	2700	3		4600	5600
19	3	SPORT 192	OP	RNBT	FBG	SV	IO	155-167		7	7	2400	2	6	4250	5150
20	6	ECLIPSE 196	OP	RNBT	FBG	DV	IO	135-210		7	10	2850	3		5700	6950

 CONTINUED ON NEXT PAGE

LOA FT	IN	NAME AND/ OR MODEL	TOP/ RIG	BOAT TYPE	-HULL- MTL	TP	ENGINE TP	# HP	MFG	BEAM FT	IN	WGT LBS	DRAFT FT	IN	RETAIL LOW	RETAIL HIGH
		1991 BOATS														
20	6	ECLIPSE 197	OP	RNBT	FBG	DV	IO	115-210		7	10	2900	3		5750	7000
20	6	FISH 20	OP	CTRCN	FBG	SV	OB			8		2140	2	8	7500	8600
20	6	V20 STEP LIFT	OP	RNBT	FBG	SV	OB			8		1920	2	8	6950	8000
20	6	V20 STEP LIFT	OP	RNBT	FBG	SV	IO	155-230		8		3120	2	8	6100	7500
20	6	V20 STEP LIFT	OP	RNBT	FBG	SV	IO	275	VLVO	8		3120	2	8	6900	7900
21	3	SCARAB EXCEL 21	OP	RACE	FBG	DV	IO	230-300		8		3800	2	8	7300	9100
21	3	SCARAB EXCEL 21	OP	RACE	FBG	DV	IO	330	VLVO	8		3800	2	8	8950	10100
21	5	210 CCF	OP	CTRCN	FBG	SV	OB			8	4	2300	2	8	8350	9600
21	5	COASTAL 210	OP	RNBT	FBG	SV	OB			8	4	2500	3		8950	10200
21	5	COASTAL 210	OP	RNBT	FBG	SV	IO	180-230		8	4	3450	3		6950	8450
21	5	COASTAL 210	OP	RNBT	FBG	SV	IO	275	VLVO	8	4	3450	3		7700	8850
21	6	ECLIPSE 215	OP	RNBT	FBG	DV	IO	180-230		7	10	3050	3		6300	7650
21	6	ECLIPSE 215	OP	RNBT	FBG	DV	IO	300	MRCR	7	10	3050	3		7000	8050
21	6	ECLIPSE 216	OP	RNBT	FBG	DV	IO	180-240		8		3300	3		6650	8100
21	6	ECLIPSE 216	OP	RNBT	FBG	DV	IO	300	MRCR	8		3300	3		7400	8500
23		NOVA 23XL	OP	RNBT	FBG	SV	IO	230-300		8	3	4000	2	10	8400	10400
23		NOVA 23XL	OP	RNBT	FBG	SV	IO	330-360		8	3	4000	2	10	9950	11500
23		NOVA 23XL	OP	RNBT	FBG	SV	IO	200D	VLVO	8	3	4000	2	10	10700	12200
23	2	ECLIPSE 232	OP	RNBT	FBG	SV	IO	180-240		8	6	3900	3		8250	9950
23	2	ECLIPSE 232	OP	RNBT	FBG	SV	IO	275	VLVO	8	6	3900	3		9100	10300
23	3	COASTAL 236	OP	FSH	FBG	SV	OB			8	6	3400	2	8	12200	13900
23	3	COASTAL 236	OP	FSH	FBG	SV	IO	180-240		8	6	3400	2	8	8450	10200
23	3	COASTAL 236	OP	FSH	FBG	SV	IO	275	VLVO	8	6	3400	2	8	9400	10700
23	3	ECLIPSE 233	OP	RNBT	FBG	SV	IO	180-240		8	6	3900	3		8300	9950
23	3	ECLIPSE 233	OP	RNBT	FBG	SV	IO	275	VLVO	8	6	3900	3		9150	10400
24	8	SPORTSMAN 250	OP	RNBT	FBG	SV	OB			8	3	3380	3		13000	14800
24	9	EXCALIBER 23	OP	RNBT	FBG	DV	IO	230-300		7	10	3800	3		8800	10700
24	9	EXCALIBER 23	OP	RNBT	FBG	DV	IO	330-360		7	10	3800	3		10300	11900
24	10	GENESIS 20	OP	RNBT	FBG	SV	OB			8	6	2700	2	6	11500	13000
24	10	GENESIS 20	OP	RNBT	FBG	SV	IO	T155-T230		8	6	3600	2	6	9550	11700
24	10	GENESIS 20	OP	RNBT	FBG	SV	IO	T130D	VLVO	8	6	3600	2	6	12700	14500
25	6	ECLIPSE 250	OP	RNBT	FBG	SV	IO	230-300		8	6	4500	3		10300	12600
25	6	ECLIPSE 253	OP	SPTCR	FBG	SV	IO	230-300		8	6	4800	3		11700	14100
25	6	ECLIPSE 253	OP	SPTCR	FBG	SV	IO	330	VLVO	8	6	4800	3		13300	15100
25	7	NOVA 26 ST	OP	RNBT	FBG	DV	IO	300-360		8	2	5500	3		12500	15300
		IO 410-445 14600 17600, IO T180-T240 12900 15400, IO T275-T300													14500	16600
		IO T330 VLVO 16100 18300														
26	1	COASTAL 2600	OP	FSH	FBG	SV	OB			9	8	5500	3		17500	19900
26	1	COASTAL 2600	OP	FSH	FBG	SV	IO	240-330		9	8	7100	3		16800	20900
26	1	COASTAL 2600	OP	FSH	FBG	SV	IO	T135-T205		9	8	7100	3		17600	21300
26	3	SCARAB 26CV	OP	RACE	FBG	DV	IO	240-300		7	8	3200	3		9200	11200
26	3	SCARAB 26CV	OP	RACE	FBG	DV	IO	330-360		7	8	3200	3		10600	12300
26	3	SCARAB 26CV	OP	RACE	FBG	DV	IO	410-445		7	8	3200	3		11900	14500
26	3	SCARAB SPORTSTER 26	OP	CTRCN	FBG	DV	OB			7	8	2700	3		15400	17500
27	7	COASTAL 2800	ST	SF	FBG	SV	IB	T235-T275		9	11	8200	2	4	25600	29200
27	7	COASTAL 2800	ST	SF	FBG	SV	IB	T130D	VLVO	9	11	8200	2	4	32000	35500
28		SCARAB 28XLT	OP	RACE	FBG	DV	IO	T240-T300		8	2	5900	3		14000	17100
28		SCARAB 28XLT	OP	RACE	FBG	DV	IO	T330-T360		8	2	5900	3		16000	18600
28		SCARAB 28XLT	OP	RACE	FBG	DV	IO	T200D	VLVO	8	2	5900	3		16500	18800
28	7	EXPRESS 2600	ST	EXP	FBG	SV	IO	240-330		9	8	7200	3		16600	20300
		IO 200D VLVO 19300 21400, IO T135-T205 17100 21000, IO T130D VLVO													21200	23600
28	7	PRIMA 2600	ST	EXP	FBG	SV	IO	240-330		9	8	7200	3		18900	22300
		IO 200D VLVO 21100 23400, IO T135-T205 19300 23000, IO T130D VLVO													22700	25300
29	6	SCARAB SPORT 30	OP	CTRCN	FBG	DV	OB			8		5000	3		26400	29300
30	2	MONACO 3000	ST	EXP	FBG	SV	IO	T205-T275		10	8	9800	3		25900	30400
30	2	MONACO 3000	ST	EXP	FBG	SV	IO	T200D	VLVO	10	8	9800	3		31000	34500
31	1	SCARAB EXCEL 31	OP	RACE	FBG	DV	IO	T300-T445		8	6	7300	3		22100	27600
31	1	SCARAB EXCEL 31	OP	RACE	FBG	DV	IO	T200D	VLVO	8	6	7300	3		22600	25100
31	1	SCARAB VIPER 31	OP	RACE	FBG	DV	IO	T300-T445		8	6	7250	3		22100	27500
31	1	SCARAB VIPER 31	OP	RACE	FBG	DV	IO	T200D	VLVO	8	6	7250	3		22600	25100
33	4	COASTAL 3300	ST	SF	FBG	SV	IB	T300-T410		12	8	15300	2	10	43100	50500
33	4	COASTAL 3300	ST	SF	FBG	SV	IB	T300D-T425D		12	8	15300	2	10	55500	68300
33	4	SPORT BRIDGE 3300	FB	SF	FBG	SV	IB	T300-T355		12	8	13800	2	8	49100	55500
33	4	SPORT BRIDGE 3300	FB	SF	FBG	SV	IB	T300D	CUM	12	8	13800	2	8	61600	67700
33	7	ST TROPEZ 3300	ST	EXP	FBG	SV	IB	T235-T330		11	8	11200	2	10	46500	53400
33	7	ST TROPEZ 3300	ST	EXP	FBG	SV	IB	T200D	VLVO	11	8	11200	2	10	52400	57600
33	10	SCARAB 34 FITT	OP	RACE	FBG	DV	IO	T200-T300		8	4	7750	3		29400	35800
33	10	SCARAB 34 FITT	OP	RACE	FBG	DV	IO	T360-T410		8	4	7750	3		34400	41000
33	10	SCARAB 34 FITT	OP	RACE	FBG	DV	IO	T445	MRCR	8	4	7750	3		38900	43200
33	10	SCARAB EXCEL 34	OP	RACE	FBG	DV	IO	T300	MRCR	8	4	7750	3		26800	29800
33	10	SCARAB EXCEL 34	OP	RACE	FBG	DV	IO	T330-T445		8	4	7750	3		30700	37500
33	10	SCARAB EXCEL 34	OP	RACE	FBG	DV	IO	T200D	VLVO	8	4	7750	3		31500	35000
33	10	SUPER SPORT	OP	CTRCN	FBG	DV	OB			8	4	5100	3		29400	32600
35	11	GRAN SPORT 3400	ST	EXP	FBG	SV	IB	T300	CRUS	12	6	13400	3		57500	63200
		IB T330 MRCR 57900 63600, IB T330 VLVO 58200 64000, IB T355 CRUS													59000	64800
		IB T410 MRCR 60300 66300, IB T200D VLVO 64200 70600														
37	10	SCARAB EXCEL 38	OP	RACE	FBG	DV	IO	T350	MRCR	8	9	9100	3		39000	43400
		IO T385 MRCR 40600 45100, IO T390 MRCR 40800 45300, IO T445 MRCR													43900	48800
39		CORSICA 3700	ST	EXP	FBG	SV	IB	T300	CRUS	13	6	16800	3	1	75600	83100
		IB T330 MRCR 75600 83000, IB T330 VLVO 76300 83800, IB T355 CRUS													77100	84800
		IB T410 MRCR 78300 86100														
42	10	PORTOFINO 4300	ST	EXP	FBG	SV	IB	T300	CRUS	14	6	18200	2	10	88700	97400
		IB T330 MRCR 89500 98400, IB T330 VLVO 90100 99000, IB T355 CRUS													91400	100500
		IB T410 MRCR 93800 103000, IB T200D VLVO 94300 103500, IB T375D CAT													112000	123000
		IB T425D CAT 117000 128500														
48	6	CMY 4600	FB	MYCPT	FBG	SV	IB	T300	CRUS	14	6	27000	3	2	131500	144500
		IB T330 MRCR 133000 146000, IB T330 VLVO 133000 146000, IB T355 CRUS													134000	147000
		IB T410 MRCR 136500 150000, IB T200D VLVO 132000 145000, IB T375D CAT													148500	163500
		IB T425D CAT 153500 169000														
48	8	SCARAB METEOR 5000	OP	RACE	FBG	DV	IO	R360	MRCR	9	4	16000	3	8	62400	68600
		IO R400 MRCR 65000 71400, IO R410 MRCR 65700 72200, IO R445 MRCR													68000	74800
		1990 BOATS														
16	9	CLASSIC 170	ST	RNBT	FBG	SV	OB			7	3	1400	2	8	2800	3250
16	9	CLASSIC 170	ST	RNBT	FBG	SV	IO	120-165		7	3	2250	2	8	3450	4000
16	9	SPORT 17	ST	RNBT	FBG	SV	IO	125	MRCR	7	3	1950	2	8	3150	3650
17	10	FISH 18	ST	CTRCN	FBG	SV	OB			7	9	1750	2	5	3300	3850
17	10	SPORT 18	ST	CTRCN	FBG	SV	OB			7	9	2250	2	5	3800	4400
19	6	ECLIPSE 186	ST	RNBT	FBG	SV	IO	120-205		7	10	2700	3		4500	5300
19	6	ECLIPSE 187	ST	RNBT	FBG	SV	IO	120-205		7	10	2750	3		4700	5500
20	6	ECLIPSE 196	ST	RNBT	FBG	SV	IO	145-205		7	10	2850	3		5250	6400
20	6	ECLIPSE 197	ST	RNBT	FBG	SV	IO	145-205		7	10	2900	3		5500	6650
20	6	FISH 20	ST	CTRCN	FBG	SV	OB			8		2150	2	8	7250	8350
20	6	FISH 20	ST	CTRCN	FBG	SV	SE	140	OMC	8		2700	2	8	8250	9450
20	6	SPORT 20	ST	CTRCN	FBG	SV	OB			8		2550	2	8	8000	9200
20	6	SPORT V-20	ST	CUD	FBG	SV	OB			8		2750	3		8300	9550
20	6	STEP LIFT V-20	ST	CUD	FBG	SV	OB			8		1920	3		6700	7750
20	6	STEP LIFT V-20	ST	CUD	FBG	SV	SE	140	OMC	8		3120	3		8650	9950
20	6	STEP LIFT V-20	ST	CUD	FBG	SV	IO	167-260		8		3120	3		6200	7300
21	3	COASTAL 210	ST	FSH	FBG	SV	OB			8	4	2900	3		9300	10600
21	3	COASTAL 210	ST	FSH	FBG	SV	IO	167-210		8	4	3850	3		8000	9300
21	3	COASTAL 210	ST	FSH	FBG	SV	SE	225	OMC	8	4	3850	3		10200	11600
21	3	COASTAL 210	ST	FSH	FBG	SV	IO	260	MRCR	8	4	3850	3		8150	9350
21	3	SCARAB EXCEL 21	OP	RACE	FBG	SV	IO	260-270		8		3800	2	4	7050	8500
21	6	ECLIPSE 215	ST	RNBT	FBG	SV	IO	200-260		7	10	3050	3		5950	7150
21	6	ECLIPSE 216	ST	RNBT	FBG	SV	IO	200-260		8		3300	3		6300	7550
21	9	EXCALIBUR 20	OP	RNBT	FBG	SV	IO	260-275		7	2	3100	3		6100	7500
22	7	COASTAL 230	ST	FSH	FBG	SV	OB			8	3	2850	3		10100	11400
22	7	COASTAL 230	ST	FSH	FBG	SV	IO	200-210		8	3	3850	3		8350	9900
22	7	COASTAL 230	ST	FSH	FBG	SV	SE	225	OMC	8	3	3650	3		11700	13300
22	7	COASTAL 230	ST	FSH	FBG	SV	IO	260-275		8	3	3850	3		8650	10500
22	7	COASTAL 230	ST	FSH	FBG	SV	SE	T140	OMC	8	3	3950	3		12200	13800
23		NOVA 23	OP	RNBT	FBG	DV	IO	260-275		8	3	4000	2	8	8100	9750
23		NOVA 23	OP	RNBT	FBG	DV	IO	330		8	3	4000	2	8	9000	10700
23	3	ECLIPSE 233	ST	RNBT	FBG	SV	IO	200-275		8	6	3900	3		7850	9750
24	8	COASTAL 250	ST	FSH	FBG	SV	OB			8	3	3500	3		12800	14600
24	8	COASTAL 250	ST	FSH	FBG	SV	IO	200-210		8	3	4150	3		9850	11500
24	8	COASTAL 250	ST	FSH	FBG	SV	SE	225	OMC	8	3	3900	3		13700	15600
24	8	COASTAL 250	ST	FSH	FBG	SV	IO	260-275		8	3	4150	3		10200	12100
24	8	COASTAL 250	ST	FSH	FBG	SV	SE	T140	OMC	8	3	4150	3		14200	16200
24	8	SPORTSMAN 250	ST	FSH	FBG	SV	OB			8	3	3380	3		12500	14300
24	8	SPORTSMAN 250	ST	FSH	FBG	SV	IO	200-210		8	3	4400	3		10200	11900
24	8	SPORTSMAN 250	ST	FSH	FBG	SV	SE	225	OMC	8	3	4400	3		14700	16700
24	8	SPORTSMAN 250	ST	FSH	FBG	SV	IO	260-275		8	3	4400	3		10700	12600
24	8	SPORTSMAN 250	ST	FSH	FBG	SV	SE	T140	OMC	8	3	4400	3		14700	16700
24	8	SPORTSMAN 250	ST	FSH	FBG	SV	IO	T145	MRCR	8	3	4400	3		11300	12800
25	6	SANIBEL 253	ST	EXP	FBG	SV	IO	260-330		8	6	4800	3		11200	13800
25	7	NOVA 26 ST	OP	RNBT	FBG	SV	IO	330-365		8	2	5500	3		12100	14500
25	7	NOVA 26 ST	OP	RNBT	FBG	SV	IO	T260-T275		8	2	5500	3		13000	15500
26	1	COASTAL 2600	ST	FSH	FBG	SV	OB			9	8	5500	3		16900	19200
26	1	COASTAL 2600	ST	FSH	FBG	SV	IO	270-330		9	8	7000	3		16000	19500

CONTINUED ON NEXT PAGE

WELLCRAFT MARINE -CONTINUED See inside cover to adjust price for area

LOA FT	LOA IN	NAME AND/ OR MODEL	TOP/ RIG	BOAT TYPE	-HULL- MTL	TP	ENGINE TP	# HP	MFG	BEAM FT	BEAM IN	WGT LBS	DRAFT FT	DRAFT IN	RETAIL LOW	RETAIL HIGH
		1990 BOATS														
26	1	COASTAL 2600	ST	FSH	FBG	SV	IO	T145-T205		9	8	7000	3		16500	19800
26	1	COASTAL 2600	ST	FSH	FBG	SV	SE	T225	OMC	9	8	7000	3		18100	20100
26	3	SCARAB 26CV	OP	RACE	FBG	DV	IO	260-275		7	8	3200	3		8850	10400
26	3	SCARAB 26CV	OP	RACE	FBG	DV	IO	330-365		7	8	3200	3		9650	11700
26	3	SCARAB SPRINT 26	ST	RACE	FBG	DV	OB			7	8	2700	3		15000	17100
26	3	SCARAB SPRINT 26	ST	RACE	FBG	DV	SE	225	OMC	7	8	3850	3		16000	18200
26	3	SCARAB SPRINT 26	ST	RACE	FBG	DV	IO	260-275		7	8	3850	3		9500	11200
26	3	SCARAB SPRINT 26	ST	RACE	FBG	DV	IO	330		7	8	3850	3		10300	12100
27	7	COASTAL 2800	ST	FSH	FBG	SV	SE	T225	OMC	9	11	8200	2	4	20100	22300
27	7	COASTAL 2800	ST	FSH	FBG	SV	IB	T240	CRUS	9	11	8200	2	4	24400	27200
27	7	COASTAL 2800	ST	FSH	FBG	SV	IO	T260	MRCR	9	11	8200	2	4	21000	23300
27	7	COASTAL 2800	ST	FSH	FBG	SV	IB	T265	VLVO	9	11	8200	2	4	24800	27600
28	3	SCARAB EXCEL 28	OP	RACE	FBG	DV	IO	330-365		7	8	4600	3	2	11500	13500
28	7	PRIMA 2600	ST	EXP	FBG	SV	IO	275-330		9	8	7200	3		17000	20200
28	7	PRIMA 2600	ST	EXP	FBG	SV	IO	T120-T175		9	8	7200	3		16900	20100
29	6	SCARAB SPORT 30	OP	CUD	FBG	DV	OB			8		5000	3		26200	29100
29	6	SCARAB SPORT 30	OP	CUD	FBG	DV	SE	T225	OMC	8		5600	3		26200	29100
30	2	MONACO 3000	ST	EXP	FBG	SV	IO	T200-T275		10	8	9800	3		24200	28600
31	1	SCARAB EXCEL 31	OP	RACE	FBG	DV	IO	T330-T365		8	6	7300	3		21200	24200
33	4	COASTAL 3300	ST	SF	FBG	SV	IB	T320-T360		12	8	13800	2	8	40100	45500
33	4	COASTAL 3300	ST	SF	FBG	SV	IB	T375D-T425D		12	8	13800	2	8	54300	62400
33	7	ST TROPEZ 3300	ST	EXP	FBG	SV	IB	T240-T360		11	8	10300	2	10	43200	51300
33	10	SCARAB EXCEL 34	OP	RACE	FBG	DV	IO	T330-T365		8	4	7750	3		28700	33300
33	10	SCARAB EXCEL 34	OP	RACE	FBG	DV	IO	T425	MRCR	8	4	7750	3		33000	36600
33	10	SUPER SPORT 34	OP	CTRCN	FBG	DV	OB			8	4	5485	3		28500	31700
33	10	SUPER SPORT 34	OP	CTRCN	FBG	DV	SE	T300	OMC	8	4	7485	3		28500	31700
33	10	SUPER SPORT 34	OP	CTRCN	FBG	DV	IO	T330-T365		8	4	7885	3		33700	38500
35	11	GRAN SPORT 3400	ST	EXP	FBG	SV	IB	T320	CRUS	12	6	13400	3		55200	60600
35	11	GRAN SPORT 3400	ST	EXP	FBG	SV	IB	T340	MRCR	12	6	13400	3		55300	60800
35	11	GRAN SPORT 3400	ST	EXP	FBG	SV	IB	T360	CRUS	12	6	13400	3		56200	61800
37	10	SCARAB EXCEL 38	OP	RACE	FBG	SV	IO	T365	MRCR	8	9	9100	3		37300	41400
37	10	SCARAB EXCEL 38	OP	RACE	FBG	SV	IO	T425	MRCR	8	9	9100	3		40100	44600
39		CORSICA 3700	ST	EXP	FBG	SV	IB	T340	MRCR	13	6	16800	3	1	66100	72700
39		CORSICA 3700	ST	EXP	FBG	SV	IB	T360	CRUS	13	6	16800	3	1	67300	74000
42	10	PORTOFINO 4300	ST	EXP	FBG	SV	IB	T320	CRUS	14	6	18200	2	10	85500	94000
		IB T330 VLVO 86000 94500, IB T340 MRCR 85900 94400, IB T360 CRUS 87500 96200														
		IB T375D CAT 106500 117000, IB T425D CAT 111500 122500														
42	10	SAN REMO 4300	ST	EXP	FBG	SV	IB	T320	CRUS	14	6	25000	3	2	105500	116000
		IB T330 VLVO 106000 116500, IB T340 MRCR 106000 116500, IB T360 CRUS 107500 118500														
		IB T375D CAT 127000 139500, IB T425D CAT 131500 144500														
43	2	SCARAB EXCEL 43	OP	RACE	FBG	DV	IO	R425	MRCR	8	9	10500	3		61600	67700
48	6	CMY 46	FB	MYCPT	FBG	SV	IB	T320	CRUS	14	6	27000	3	2	126500	138500
		IB T330 VLVO 125500 138000, IB T340 MRCR 125500 138000, IB T360 CRUS 126500 139000														
		IB T375D CAT 140500 154500, IB T425D CAT 145000 159500														
48	8	SCARAB METEOR 5000	OP	RACE	FBG	DV	IO	R425	MRCR	9	4	16000	3	2	62700	68900
		1989 BOATS														
16	9	CLASSIC 170	ST	RNBT	FBG	SV	OB			7	3	1100	1	8	2250	2600
16	9	CLASSIC 170	ST	RNBT	FBG	SV	IO	130	MRCR	7	3	1950	1	8	2850	3300
17	7	CLASSIC 180	ST	RNBT	FBG	SV	IO	130-175		7	2	2100	1	6	3100	3650
17	10	FISHERMAN 18	ST	CTRCN	FBG	SV	OB			7	9	1750	1	4	3200	3750
17	10	FISHERMAN 18	ST	CTRCN	FBG	SV	SE	115	OMC	7	9	2100	1	4	3550	4150
19	3	CLASSIC 190	ST	RNBT	FBG	DV	IO	130-175		7	7	2350	1	6	3700	4350
19	3	CLASSIC 192	ST	RNBT	FBG	DV	IO	130-175		7	7	2400	1	6	3750	4400
19	6	ECLIPSE 186	ST	RNBT	FBG	DV	IO	130-160		7	10	2250	1	6	3750	4400
20	6	CLASSIC 210	ST	RNBT	FBG	DV	IO	200-260		8		2990	1	6	5350	6400
20	6	FISHERMAN 20	ST	CTRCN	FBG	SV	OB			8		1920	1	6	6500	7450
20	6	FISHERMAN 20	ST	CTRCN	FBG	SV	SE	115-140		8		2500	1	6	7650	8800
20	6	STEP LIFT V20	ST	CUD	FBG	DV	OB			8		1920	1	6	6500	7450
20	6	STEP LIFT V20	ST	CUD	FBG	DV	SE	115-140		8		2300	1	6	7300	8400
20	6	STEP-LIFT V20	ST	CUD	FBG	DV	IO	165-260		8		2300	1	6	4800	5900
21	3	COASTAL 210	ST	SPTCR	FBG	SV	OB			8	4	2500	1	6	8150	9400
21	3	COASTAL 210	ST	SPTCR	FBG	SV	SE	140	OMC	8	4	3420	1	6	9600	10900
21	3	COASTAL 210	ST	SPTCR	FBG	SV	IO	165-200		8	4	3420	1	6	6400	7400
21	3	COASTAL 210	ST	SPTCR	FBG	SV	SE	225	OMC	8	4	3420	1	6	9600	10900
21	3	COASTAL 210	ST	SPTCR	FBG	SV	IO	260	MRCR	8	4	3420	1	6	6700	7750
21	3	SCARAB 21XL	OP	RACE	FBG	DV	IO	260-270		8		3100	1	8	5850	6800
21	6	ECLIPSE 215	ST	RNBT	FBG	DV	IO	200-260		7	10	2900	1	6	5450	6550
22	7	COASTAL 230	ST	SPTCR	FBG	SV	OB			8	2	2850	1	6	9750	11100
22	7	COASTAL 230	ST	SPTCR	FBG	SV	IO	200	MRCR	8	2	3890	1	6	7500	8600
22	7	COASTAL 230	ST	SPTCR	FBG	SV	SE	225	OMC	8	2	3650	1	6	11400	12900
22	7	COASTAL 230	ST	SPTCR	FBG	SV	IO	260	MRCR	8	2	3890	1	6	7750	8900
22	7	COASTAL 230	ST	SPTCR	FBG	SV	SE	T140	OMC	8	2	3950	1	6	11800	13400
22	7	FISHERMAN 23	ST	CTRCN	FBG	DV	OB			8	2	2300	1	6	8250	9450
22	7	FISHERMAN 23	ST	CTRCN	FBG	DV	SE	225	OMC	8	2	2660	1	6	9300	10600
22	7	FISHERMAN 23	ST	CTRCN	FBG	DV	SE	T115	OMC	8	2	2660	1	6	9300	10600
22	10	ELITE 220	ST	RNBT	FBG	DV	IO	260-270		8		3600	1	6	6950	8100
22	10	ELITE 220	ST	RNBT	FBG	DV	IO	330	MRCR	8		3600	1	6	7700	8850
22	10	ELITE 222	ST	RNBT	FBG	DV	IO	260-270		8		3900	1	6	7350	8550
22	10	ELITE 222	ST	RNBT	FBG	DV	IO	330	MRCR	8		3900	1	6	8100	9350
23		NOVA 23 XL	ST	CUD	FBG	DV	IO	260-270		8	3	4000	1	4	8100	9400
23		NOVA 23 XL	ST	CUD	FBG	DV	IO	330	MRCR	8	3	4000	1	4	9000	10200
23	3	ECLIPSE 233	ST	RNBT	FBG	DV	IO	200-260		8	6	4000			7550	8950
23	11	ARUBA	ST	EXP	FBG	DV	IO	260-330		8	3	5100	1	5	10300	12600
24	8	COASTAL 250	ST	FSH	FBG	SV	OB			8	3	3500	1	6	12400	14100
24	8	COASTAL 250	ST	FSH	FBG	SV	IO	200	MRCR	8		4130			9250	10500
24	8	COASTAL 250	ST	FSH	FBG	SV	SE	225	OMC	8	3	3900	1	6	13300	15100
24	8	COASTAL 250	ST	FSH	FBG	SV	IO	260	MRCR	8		4130	1	6	9550	10900
24	8	COASTAL 250	ST	FSH	FBG	SV	SE	T115-T140		8	3	4130	1	6	13700	15600
24	8	SPORTSMAN 250	ST	SPTCR	FBG	DV	OB			8		3380	1	6	12100	13800
24	8	SPORTSMAN 250	ST	SPTCR	FBG	DV	IO	200	MRCR	8		4400	1	6	9150	10400
24	8	SPORTSMAN 250	ST	SPTCR	FBG	DV	SE	225	OMC	8		4400	1	6	14200	16200
24	8	SPORTSMAN 250	ST	SPTCR	FBG	DV	IO	260	MRCR	8		4400	1	6	9450	10700
24	8	SPORTSMAN 250	ST	SPTCR	FBG	DV	SE	T115	OMC	8		4400	1	6	14200	16200
24	8	SPORTSMAN 250	ST	SPTCR	FBG	DV	IO	T130	MRCR	8		4400	1	6	9950	11300
24	8	SPORTSMAN 250	ST	SPTCR	FBG	DV	SE	T140	OMC	8		4400	1	6	14200	16200
24	8	SPORTSMAN 250	ST	SPTCR	FBG	DV	IO	T165	MRCR	8		4400	1	6	10100	11500
25	9	NOVA SPYDER	ST	RNBT	FBG	DV	IO	330-365		8		5200	1	11	11100	13200
25	9	NOVA SPYDER	ST	RNBT	FBG	DV	IO	T260-T270		8		5200	1	11	12000	13800
25	9	NOVA SPYDER	ST	RNBT	FBG	DV	IO	T330	MRCR	8		5200	1	11	13400	15300
26	3	SCARAB 26 SPRINT	OP	RACE	FBG	DV	OB			7	8	2700	1	6	14400	16400
26	3	SCARAB 26 SPRINT	OP	RACE	FBG	DV	SE	225	OMC	7	8	2700	1	6	14400	16400
26	5	ANTIGUA	ST	CBNCR	FBG	DV	IO	260-330		8	3	5900	1	8	15400	18200
27	7	COASTAL 2800	ST	SF	FBG	SV	SE	T225	OMC	9	11	8200	2	4	19400	21600
27	7	COASTAL 2800	ST	SF	FBG	SV	IB	T260-T270		9	11	8200	2	4	23400	26300
27	7	MONTE CARLO	ST	EXP	FBG	SV	IO	330	MRCR	9	11	7200	1	6	16100	18300
27	7	MONTE CARLO	ST	EXP	FBG	SV	IO	T200-T260		9	11	7200	1	6	16500	19800
27	8	NOVA III	ST	RNBT	FBG	DV	IO	T260-T330		8	2	5600	2	2	14100	17600
28	2	MONACO	OP	SPTCR	FBG	SV	IO	T200-T260		10	8	9200	1	11	19100	22200
28	3	SCARAB 28 EXCEL	OP	RACE	FBG	DV	IO	330-365		7	8	4600	1	9	10800	12700
29	6	SCARAB PANTHER	OP	RACE	FBG	DV	IO	T330-T365		8		6400	1	11	15600	18400
29	6	SCARAB SPORT	ST	CUD	FBG	DV	OB			8		2985	2		25300	28100
29	6	SCARAB SPORT	ST	CUD	FBG	DV	SE	T225	OMC	8		4500	2		25300	28100
31	8	ST TROPEZ	ST	EXP	FBG	SV	IB	T260-T350		11	8	10300	2	10	35400	41700
33	4	COASTAL 3300	ST	SF	FBG	SV	IB	T340-T350		12	8	13800	2	8	38400	43000
33	4	COASTAL 3300	ST	SF	FBG	SV	IB	T375D	CAT	12	8	13800	2	8	52500	57600
33	7	GRAN SPORT	ST	SPTCR	FBG	DV	IB	T340-T350		12	6	13400	3		46000	51000
33	10	SCARAB 34 SUPERSPORT	OP	RACE	FBG	DV	OB			8	4	5100	2		48400	53200
33	10	SCARAB 34 SUPERSPORT	OP	RACE	FBG	DV	SE	T225-T300		8	4	6600	2		54100	59500
33	10	SCARAB III	OP	RACE	FBG	DV	IO	T330-T365		8	4	7750	2	1	27000	31400
33	10	SCARAB III	OP	RACE	FBG	DV	IO	T420	MRCR	8	4	7750	2	1	30800	34200
36	11	COZUMEL	ST	SDNSF	FBG	DV	IB	T340	MRCR	13	6	21000	3	3	73700	81000
36	11	COZUMEL	ST	SDNSF	FBG	DV	IB	T350	CRUS	13	6	21000	3	3	74500	81900
36	11	COZUMEL	ST	SDNSF	FBG	DV	IB	T375D	CAT	13	6	23500	3	3	100000	110000
37	10	SCARAB 38XL	OP	RACE	FBG	DV	IO	T365	MRCR	8	9	9100	2		35200	39100
37	10	SCARAB 38XL	OP	RACE	FBG	DV	IO	T420	MRCR	8	9	9100	2		37600	41800
42	10	PORTOFINO	ST	EXP	FBG	DV	IB	T340	MRCR	14	6	18200	3		79700	87600
42	10	PORTOFINO	ST	EXP	FBG	DV	IB	T350	CRUS	14	6	18200	3		80700	88700
42	10	PORTOFINO	ST	EXP	FBG	DV	IB	T375D	CAT	14	6	18200	3		99900	110000
42	10	SAN REMO	ST	EXP	FBG	DV	IB	T340	MRCR	14	6	25000	3	2	99200	109000
42	10	SAN REMO	ST	EXP	FBG	DV	IB	T350	CRUS	14	6	25000	3	2	100000	110000
42	10	SAN REMO	ST	EXP	FBG	DV	IB	T375D	CAT	14	6	25000	3	2	119000	131000
43	2	SCARAB 43DJSE	OP	RACE	FBG	DV	IO	T420	MRCR	8	9	10500	2		53400	58700
48	8	SCARAB 5000 METEOR	OP	RACE	FBG	DV	IO	R420	MRCR	9	4	16000	2	2	56000	61500
		1988 BOATS														
16	9	CLASSIC 170	ST	RNBT	FBG	SV	OB			7	3	1100	1	8	2150	2500
16	9	CLASSIC 170	ST	RNBT	FBG	SV	IO	120-130		7	3	1950	1	8	2700	3150
17	6	CLASSIC 180	ST	RNBT	FBG	SV	IO	130-175		7	2	2100	1	4	2900	3400
17	10	FISHERMAN 18	ST	CTRCN	FBG	SV	OB			7	9	1750	1	4	3100	3600
17	10	FISHERMAN 18	ST	CTRCN	FBG	SV	SE	115-140		7	9	2100	1	4	3450	4000
19	3	CLASSIC 190	ST	RNBT	FBG	DV	IO	130-175		7	7	2350	1	6	3500	4100
19	3	CLASSIC 192	ST	RNBT	FBG	DV	IO	130-175		7	7	2400	1	6	3550	4150
19	6	CLASSIC 200	ST	RNBT	FBG	DV	IO	200-260		8		2850	1	6	4150	5050
20	6	CLASSIC 210	ST	RNBT	FBG	DV	IO	200-260		8		2990	1	6	5050	6050

 CONTINUED ON NEXT PAGE

LOA FT	LOA IN	NAME AND/ OR MODEL	TOP/ RIG	BOAT TYPE	-HULL- MTL	-HULL- TP	ENGINE TP	ENGINE # HP	ENGINE MFG	BEAM FT	BEAM IN	WGT LBS	DRAFT FT	DRAFT IN	RETAIL LOW	RETAIL HIGH
		1988 BOATS														
20	6	DUAL CONSOLE 20	ST	CTRCN	FBG	SV	OB			8		1920	1	6	6400	7350
20	6	DUAL CONSOLE 20	ST	CTRCN	FBG	SV	SE	115-140		8		2500	1	6	7500	8600
20	6	FISHERMAN 20	ST	CTRCN	FBG	SV	OB			8		1920	1	6	6200	7150
20	6	FISHERMAN 20	ST	CTRCN	FBG	SV	SE	115-140		8		2500	1	6	7400	8500
20	6	STEP-LIFT V20	ST	CUD	FBG	DV	OB			8		1920	1	6	6300	7250
20	6	STEP-LIFT V20	ST	CUD	FBG	DV	SE	115-140		8		2620	1	6	7600	8750
20	6	STEP-LIFT V20	ST	CUD	FBG	DV	IO	165-260		8		2620	1	6	4850	5900
21	3	COASTAL 210	ST	SPTCR	FBG	SV	OB			8	4	2500	1	6	7900	9100
21	3	COASTAL 210	ST	SPTCR	FBG	SV	SE	140-225		8	4	3420	1	6	9350	10600
22	7	COASTAL 230	ST	SPTCR	FBG	SV	OB			8	2	2700	1	6	9150	10400
22	7	COASTAL 230	ST	SPTCR	FBG	SV	IO	200	MRCR	8	2	3680	1	6	6800	7850
22	7	COASTAL 230	ST	SPTCR	FBG	SV	SE	225	OMC	8	2	3326	1	6	10500	11900
22	7	COASTAL 230	ST	SPTCR	FBG	SV	IO	260		8	2	3680	1	6	7050	8100
22	7	COASTAL 230	ST	SPTCR	FBG	SV	SE	T140	OMC	8	2	3680	1	6	11100	12600
22	7	FISHERMAN 23	ST	CTRCN	FBG	DV	OB			8	2	2300	1	8	8000	9200
22	7	FISHERMAN 23	ST	CTRCN	FBG	DV	SE	225		8	2	2660	1	8	9050	10300
22	7	FISHERMAN 23	ST	CTRCN	FBG	DV	SE	T140	OMC	8	2	2200	1	8	7700	8850
22	10	ELITE 220	ST	RNBT	FBG	DV	IO	260-270		8		3600	1	6	6600	7650
22	10	ELITE 220	ST	RNBT	FBG	DV	IO	330	MRCR	8		3600	1	6	7300	8400
22	10	ELITE 222	ST	RNBT	FBG	DV	IO	260-270		8		3900	1	6	6950	8100
22	10	ELITE 222	ST	RNBT	FBG	DV	IO	330	MRCR	8		3900	1	6	7700	8850
23		NOVA 23 XL	ST	CUD	FBG	DV	IO	260-270		8		4000	1	4	7600	8800
23		NOVA 23 XL	ST	CUD	FBG	DV	IO	330-340		8		4000	1	4	8350	9700
23	3	CONCEPT	ST	RNBT	FBG	DV	IO	260-270		8		3400	2		6450	7500
23	3	CONCEPT	ST	RNBT	FBG	DV	IO	330		8		3400	2		7200	8250
23	11	ARUBA	ST	EXP	FBG	DV	IO	260-340		8	3	5100	1	5	9700	12000
24	8	COASTAL 250	ST	FSH	FBG	SV	OB			8	3	3500	1	6	12100	13700
24	8	COASTAL 250	ST	FSH	FBG	SV	SE	225	OMC	8	3	3900	1	6	12900	14600
24	8	COASTAL 250	ST	FSH	FBG	SV	IO	260		8		4550	1	6	9700	11000
24	8	COASTAL 250	ST	FSH	FBG	SV	SE	T140	OMC	8		4250	1	6	13500	15400
24	8	SPORTSMAN 250	ST	SPTCR	FBG	DV	OB			8		3750	1	6	11800	13400
24	8	SPORTSMAN 250	ST	SPTCR	FBG	DV	SE	225	OMC	8		4100	1	6	13300	15100
24	8	SPORTSMAN 250	ST	SPTCR	FBG	DV	IO	260		8		4750	1	6	9450	10700
24	8	SPORTSMAN 250	ST	SPTCR	FBG	DV	IO	T130		8		4750	1	6	9900	11300
24	8	SPORTSMAN 250	ST	SPTCR	FBG	DV	SE	T140	OMC	8		4500	1	6	14000	15900
24	8	SPORTSMAN 250	ST	SPTCR	FBG	SV	IO	T165	MRCR	8		4750	1	6	10100	11500
25	9	NOVA SPYDER	ST	RNBT	FBG	DV	IO	330-365		8		5200	2		10500	12500
		IO 420 MRCR 12100 13700, IO T260-T270 11300 13100, IO T330-T340													12700	14600
26		ANTIGUA 2650	ST	CBNCR	FBG	DV	IO	330	MRCR	8	3	5000	1	6	13400	15200
27	7	COASTAL 2800	ST	SF	FBG	SV	IB	T220	CRUS	9	11	8200	2	4	21900	24300
27	7	COASTAL 2800	ST	SF	FBG	SV	SE	T225	OMC	9	11	8200	2	4	19000	21100
27	7	COASTAL 2800	ST	SF	FBG	SV	IB	T230-T270		9	11	8200	2	4	21900	25100
27	7	MONTE CARLO 2800	ST	EXP	FBG	SV	IO	330-340		9	11	7200	1	6	15300	17500
27	7	MONTE CARLO 2800	ST	EXP	FBG	SV	IO	T200-T260		9	11	7200	1	6	15600	18800
27	8	NOVA III	ST	RNBT	FBG	DV	IO	T260-T270		8	2	5600	2	2	13400	15400
28	2	ANTIGUA AFT CABIN	ST	CBNCR	FBG	DV	IO	260	OMC	8	3	5900	1	8	16200	18500
28	2	ANTIGUA AFT CABIN	ST	CBNCR	FBG	SV	IO	260	MRCR	8	3	5900	1	8	16300	18500
28	2	ANTIQUA AFT CABIN	ST	CBNCR	FBG	DV	IO	270-340		8	3	5900	1	8	16300	18900
28	3	SCARAB 28 EXCEL	OP	RACE	FBG	DV	IO	330-365		7	8	4500	1	9	10200	12000
29	6	SCARAB PANTHER	OP	RACE	FBG	DV	IO	T330-T365		8		6400	1	11	14700	17400
29	6	SCARAB PANTHER	OP	RACE	FBG	DV	IO	T420	MRCR	8		6400	1	11	16700	18900
29	6	SCARAB SPORT		CUD	FBG	DV	SE	T225	OMC	8		4500	2		24300	27000
29	6	SCARAB SPORT	ST	CUD	FBG	DV	OB			8		2985	2		24400	27100
31	8	ST TROPEZ 3200	ST	EXP	FBG	SV	IB	T260-T350		11	8	10300	2	10	33700	39700
33	7	GRAN SPORT 3400	ST	SPTCR	FBG	DV	IB	T340-T350		12	6	13400	3		43400	48600
33	10	NINJA	ST	RNBT	FBG	DV	IO	T330-T420		8	4	5100	2	1	23600	28300
33	10	SCARAB 34 SUPERSPORT	OP	RACE	FBG	DV	OB			8	4	5100	2		46800	51400
33	10	SCARAB 34 SUPERSPORT	OP	RACE	FBG	DV	SE	T225-T275		8	4	6600	2		52300	58300
33	10	SCARAB III	OP	RACE	FBG	DV	IO	T330-T365		8	4	7750	2	1	25600	29800
33	10	SCARAB III	OP	RACE	FBG	DV	IO	T420	MRCR	8	4	7750	2	1	29200	32400
36	11	COZUMEL	ST	SDNSF	FBG	DV	IB	T340	MRCR	13	8	21000	3	3	69900	76800
36	11	COZUMEL	ST	SDNSF	FBG	DV	IB	T350	CRUS	13	8	21000	3	3	70700	77700
36	11	COZUMEL	ST	SDNSF	FBG	DV	IB	T375D	CAT	13	8	21000	3	3	88400	97200
37	7	SCARAB 38 KV	OP	RACE	FBG	DV	IO	T365	MRCR	8	6	9100	2		32900	36600
37	7	SCARAB 38 KV	OP	RACE	FBG	DV	IO	T420	MRCR	8	6	9100	2		35200	39100
41	6	EXCALIBUR 42 EAGLE	OP	OFF	FBG	DV	IO	T365	MRCR	9		10500	2		48700	53500
41	6	EXCALIBUR 42 EAGLE	OP	OFF	FBG	DV	IO	T420	MRCR	9		10500	2		52600	57800
42	10	PORTOFINO	ST	EXP	FBG	DV	IB	T340	MRCR	14	6	18200	2	10	76200	83700
42	10	PORTOFINO	ST	EXP	FBG	DV	IB	T350	CRUS	14	6	18200	2	10	77100	84700
42	10	PORTOFINO	ST	EXP	FBG	DV	IB	T375D	CAT	14	6	18200	2	10	95500	105000
42	10	SAN REMO	ST	EXP	FBG	DV	IB	T340	MRCR	14	6	29000	3	2	105000	115500
42	10	SAN REMO	ST	EXP	FBG	DV	IB	T350	CRUS	14	6	29000	3	2	106000	116500
42	10	SAN REMO	ST	EXP	FBG	DV	IB	T375D	CAT	14	6	29000	3	2	124000	136000
48	8	SCARAB 5000 METEOR	OP	RACE	FBG	DV	IO	T575	MRCR	9	4	14000	2	2	55600	61100
48	8	SCARAB 5000 METEOR	OP	RACE	FBG	DV	IO	R420	MRCR	9	4	14000	2	2	53800	59100
		1987 BOATS														
17	6	CLASSIC 180	ST	RNBT	FBG	SV	OB			7	2	1525			2750	3200
17	6	CLASSIC 180	ST	RNBT	FBG	SV	IO	130-175		7	2	1800	1	6	2600	3000
17	10	FISHERMAN 18	ST	CTRCN	FBG	SV	OB			7	9	1750	1	4	3050	3500
17	10	FISHERMAN 18	ST	CTRCN	FBG	SV	SE		OMC	7	9	2100	1	4	**	**
19		CLASSIC 190	ST	RNBT	FBG	DV	IO	130-175		7	7	2200	1	6	3200	3700
19		CLASSIC 192	ST	RNBT	FBG	DV	IO	130-175		7	7	2275	1	6	3250	3800
19	6	CLASSIC 200	ST	RNBT	FBG	DV	IO	165-200		8		2600	1	6	3700	4350
19	6	ELITE 196	ST	RNBT	FBG	SV	IO	165-200		8		2700	1	6	3750	4450
20	6	CLASSIC 210	ST	RNBT	FBG	DV	IO	165-200		8		2700	1	6	4500	5250
20	6	DUAL CONSOLE 20	ST	CTRCN	FBG	SV	OB			8		1920	1	6	6200	7150
20	6	DUAL CONSOLE 20	ST	CTRCN	FBG	SV	SE		OMC	8		2500	1	6	**	**
20	6	FISHERMAN 20	ST	CTRCN	FBG	SV	OB			8		1920	1	6	6050	6950
20	6	FISHERMAN 20	ST	CTRCN	FBG	SV	SE		OMC	8		2500	1	6	**	**
20	6	STEP-LIFT V20	ST	CUD	FBG	DV	OB			8		1920	1	6	6150	7050
20	6	STEP-LIFT V20	ST	CUD	FBG	DV	SE		OMC	8		2620	1	6	**	**
20	6	STEP-LIFT V20	ST	CUD	FBG	DV	IO	165-260		8		2620	1	6	4650	5650
21		SCARAB 21	OP	RACE	FBG	DV	IO		MRCR	8		3100	1	6	**	**
21		SCARAB 21	OP	RACE	FBG	SV	OB			8		1950			6400	7350
21		SCARAB 21	OP	RACE	FBG	SV	IO	260		8		3100			5200	5950
22	7	COASTAL 230	ST	SPTCR	FBG	SV	OB			8	2	2700	1	6	8900	10100
22	7	COASTAL 230	ST	SPTCR	FBG	SV	SE		OMC	8	2	3326	1	6	**	**
22	7	COASTAL 230	ST	SPTCR	FBG	SV	IO	200-260		8	2	3680	1	6	6500	8050
22	7	COASTAL 230	ST	SPTCR	FBG	SV	SE	T	OMC	8	2	3680	1	6	**	**
22	7	FISHERMAN 23	ST	CTRCN	FBG	DV	OB			8	2	2300	1	8	7700	8850
22	7	FISHERMAN 23	ST	CTRCN	FBG	DV	SE			8	2	2660	1	8	**	**
22	7	FISHERMAN 23	ST	CTRCN	FBG	SV	SE	T	OMC	8	2	2660	1	8	**	**
22	7	SPORTFISH 23	ST	CTRCN	FBG	DV	OB			8	2	2300	1	8	7800	9000
22	7	SPORTFISH 23	ST	CTRCN	FBG	DV	IO	T	OMC	8	2	2300	1	8	**	**
22	7	SPORTFISH 23	ST	SPTCR	FBG	DV	SE		OMC	8	2	2300	1	8	**	**
22	10	ELITE 220	ST	RNBT	FBG	DV	IO		MRCR	8		3600	1	6	**	**
22	10	ELITE 220	ST	RNBT	FBG	DV	IO		OMC	8		3600	1	6	**	**
22	10	ELITE 220	ST	RNBT	FBG	DV	IO	200-260		8		3600	1	6	6050	7200
22	10	ELITE 222	ST	RNBT	FBG	DV	IO		MRCR	8		3900	1	6	**	**
22	10	ELITE 222	ST	RNBT	FBG	DV	IO		OMC	8		3900	1	6	**	**
22	10	ELITE 222	ST	RNBT	FBG	DV	IO	200-260		8		3900	1	6	6400	7600
23		NOVA 23	ST	CUD	FBG	DV	IO			8		4000	1	4	**	**
		IO MRCR ** **, IO 260 7150 8200, IO 335-340													7850	9150
23		NOVA 23 XL	ST	CUD	FBG	DV	IO			8		4000	1	4	**	**
		IO MRCR ** **, IO 260 7300 8400, IO 335-340													8000	9300
23	11	ARUBA EXPRESS	ST	EXP	FBG	DV	IO		MRCR	8	3	4100	1	5	**	**
23	11	ARUBA EXPRESS	ST	EXP	FBG	DV	IO		OMC	8	3	4100	1	5	**	**
23	11	ARUBA EXPRESS	ST	EXP	FBG	DV	IO	200-260		8	3	4100	1	5	7500	8900
24	8	COASTAL 250	ST	FSH	FBG	SV	OB			8		3500	1	4	11700	13300
24	8	COASTAL 250	ST	FSH	FBG	SV	SE		OMC	8		3900	1	4	**	**
24	8	COASTAL 250	ST	FSH	FBG	SV	IO	260		8		4550	1	4	9250	10500
24	8	COASTAL 250	ST	FSH	FBG	SV	SE	T	OMC	8		4250	1	4	**	**
24	8	SPORTSMAN 250	ST	SPTCR	FBG	DV	OB			8		3750	1	4	11500	13000
24	8	SPORTSMAN 250	ST	SPTCR	FBG	DV	SE		OMC	8		4100	1	4	**	**
24	8	SPORTSMAN 250	ST	SPTCR	FBG	DV	IO	260		8		4750	1	4	9050	10300
24	8	SPORTSMAN 250	ST	SPTCR	FBG	DV	SE	T	OMC	8		4100	1	4	**	**
24	8	SPORTSMAN 250	ST	SPTCR	FBG	DV	IO	T130		8		4750	1	4	9450	10700
24	8	SPORTSMAN 250	ST	SPTCR	FBG	SV	IO	T165	MRCR	8		4750	1	4	9600	10900
26		ANTIGUA AFT CABIN	ST	CBNCR	FBG	DV	IO	260	OMC	8	3	5000	1	4	12100	13800
26		ANTIGUA AFT CABIN	ST	CBNCR	FBG	SV	IO	260	MRCR	8	3	5000	1	4	12200	13800
26		ANTIQUA AFT CABIN	ST	CBNCR	FBG	DV	IO	270-340		8	3	5000	1	5	12200	14500
26	3	NOVA SPYDER	ST	RNBT	FBG	DV	IO	330-370		8		5200	2		10200	12300
		IO 420 MRCR 11700 13300, IO T MRCR ** **, IO T260													11100	12600
26	3	SCARAB 26 EXCEL	OP	RACE	FBG	DV	IO			7	8	4500	2	9	**	**
26	3	SCARAB 26 EXCEL	OP	RACE	FBG	DV	IO		MRCR	7	8	4500	2	9	**	**
26	3	SCARAB 26 EXCEL	OP	RACE	FBG	DV	IO	335-370		7	8	4500	2	9	9450	11400
27	7	COASTAL 2800	ST	SF	FBG	SV	SE	T	OMC	9	11	8200	2	4	**	**
27	7	COASTAL 2800	ST	SF	FBG	SV	IB	T220-T270		9	11	8200	2	4	20800	23900
27	7	MONTE CARLO 2800	ST	EXP	FBG	SV	IO		MRCR	9	11	7200	1	9	**	**
27	7	MONTE CARLO 2800	ST	EXP	FBG	SV	IO		OMC	9	11	7200	1	9	**	**
27	7	MONTE CARLO 2800	ST	EXP	FBG	SV	IO	T200-T260		9	11	7200	1	9	14900	17800
27	8	NOVA III	ST	RNBT	FBG	DV	IO		MRCR	8	2	5600	2	2	**	**

 CONTINUED ON NEXT PAGE

LOA FT	LOA IN	NAME AND/ OR MODEL	TOP/ RIG	BOAT TYPE	-HULL- MTL	-HULL- TP	ENGINE TP	ENGINE # HP	ENGINE MFG	BEAM FT	BEAM IN	WGT LBS	DRAFT FT	DRAFT IN	RETAIL LOW	RETAIL HIGH
		1987 BOATS														
27	8	NOVA III	ST	RNBT	FBG	DV	IO	T260		8	2	5600	2	2	12700	14400
29	6	SCARAB II	OP	RACE	FBG	DV	IO	T	MRCR	8		6500	1	11	**	**
29	6	SCARAB II	OP	RACE	FBG	DV	IO	T330-T370		8		6500	1	11	14000	16800
29	6	SCARAB II	OP	RACE	FBG	DV	IO	T420	MRCR	8		6500	1	11	15800	17900
29	6	SCARAB PANTHER	OP	RACE	FBG	DV	IO	T	MRCR	8		6400	1	11	**	**
		IO T OMC ** **, IO T330-T370 14000 16800, IO T420 MRCR													15700	17900
29	6	SCARAB SPORT		CUD	FBG	DV	SE	T	OMC	8		4500	2		**	**
29	6	SCARAB SPORT	ST	CUD	FBG	DV	OB			8		2985	2		23600	26200
31	8	ST TROPEZ 3200	ST	EXP	FBG	SV	IB	T260-T350		11	8	10300	2	10	32100	37900
33	7	GRAN SPORT 3400	ST	SPTCR	FBG	DV	IB	T340-T350		12	6	13400	2	9	41400	46300
33	10	SCARAB 34 SUPERSPORT	OP	RACE	FBG	DV	IB			8	4	5100	2		**	**
33	10	SCARAB 34 SUPERSPORT	OP	RACE	FBG	DV	SE	T	OMC	8	4	6600	2		**	**
33	10	SCARAB III	OP	RACE	FBG	DV	IO	T	MRCR	8	4	7750	2	1	**	**
33	10	SCARAB III	OP	RACE	FBG	DV	IO	T330-T370		8	4	7750	2	1	24300	28500
33	10	SCARAB III	OP	RACE	FBG	DV	IO	T420	MRCR	8	4	7750	2	1	27700	30800
33	10	SCARAB SUPER SPORT	OP	RACE	FBG	DV	OB			8	4	5100	2		44600	49600
33	10	SCARAB SUPER SPORT	OP	RACE	FBG	DV	SE	T	OMC	8	4	5100	2		**	**
37	7	SCARAB 38 KV	OP	RACE	FBG	DV	IO	T370	KAAM	8	9	9100	2		31300	34800
37	7	SCARAB 38 KV	OP	RACE	FBG	DV	IO	T420	MRCR	8	6	9100	2		33400	37100
41	6	EXCALIBUR 42 EAGLE	OP	OFF	FBG	DV	IO	T370	MRCR	9		10500	2		46800	51500
41	6	EXCALIBUR 42 EAGLE	OP	OFF	FBG	DV	IO	T420	MRCR	9		10500	2		50000	54900
42	10	PORTOFINO	ST	EXP	FBG	DV	IB	T340	MRCR	14	6	18200	2	10	72800	80000
42	10	PORTOFINO	ST	EXP	FBG	DV	IB	T350	CRUS	14	6	18200	2	10	73700	81000
48	8	SCARAB 5000 METEOR	OP	RACE	FBG	DV	IO	T575	MRCR	12		23900	3		61800	67900
48	8	SCARAB 5000 METEOR	OP	RACE	FBG	DV	IO	R420	MRCR	12		23900	3		56800	62400
		1986 BOATS														
17	6	AMERICAN 180	ST	RNBT	FBG	SV	OB			7	2	1300			2350	2750
17	6	AMERICAN 180	ST	RNBT	FBG	SV	IO	140-175		7	2	2000			2600	3050
17	10	FISHERMAN 180	ST	CTRCN	FBG	SV	OB			7	9	1750			3350	3900
17	10	FISHERMAN 180	ST	CTRCN	FBG	SV	SE		OMC	7	9	2100			**	**
19		AMERICAN 190	ST	RNBT	FBG	SV	IO	140-175		7	7	2400		1	3150	3700
19		AMERICAN 192	ST	CUD	FBG	SV	IO	140-175		7	7	2525		1	3350	3950
19	6	ELITE 185	ST	RNBT	FBG	SV	IO	140-205		8		2800			3650	4350
19	6	ELITE 200	ST	RNBT	FBG	DV	IO	205-260		8		2900		1	3800	4600
19	8	ELAN 197	ST	RNBT	FBG	SV	IO	175-205		7	7	2900			3650	4300
20	6	ELITE 210	ST	RNBT	FBG	DV	IO	205-260		8		3100		1	4700	5650
20	6	FISHERMAN V20	ST	CTRCN	FBG	DV	OB			8		1920		1	5950	6850
20	6	FISHERMAN V20	ST	CTRCN	FBG	DV	SE		OMC	8		2500		1	**	**
20	6	STEP-LIFT V20	ST	CUD	FBG	DV	OB			8		1920		1	6000	6900
20	6	STEP-LIFT V20	ST	CUD	FBG	DV	SE		OMC	8		2546		1	**	**
20	6	STEP-LIFT V20	ST	CUD	FBG	DV	IO	170-260		8		2620		1	4450	5400
20	6	STEP-LIFT V20	ST	SF	FBG	DV	OB			8		1920		1	6000	6850
20	6	STEP-LIFT V20	ST	SF	FBG	DV	SE		MRCR	8		2546		1	**	**
20	6	STEP-LIFT V20	ST	SF	FBG	DV	SE		OMC	8		2546		1	**	**
21		SCARAB 21	OP	RACE	FBG	SV	OB			8		1950			6200	7150
21		SCARAB 21	OP	RACE	FBG	SV	IO	260		8		3100			4950	5700
22	7	230 FISHERMAN	ST	SPTCR	FBG	DV	OB			8		3680			10000	11400
22	7	230 FISHERMAN	ST	SPTCR	FBG	DV	SE		OMC	8		3326			**	**
22	7	SPORTSMAN 230	ST	SPTCR	FBG	DV	OB			8		3326			10400	11800
22	7	SPORTSMAN 230	ST	SPTCR	FBG	DV	SE		OMC	8		3680			**	**
22	7	SPORTSMAN 230	ST	SPTCR	FBG	DV	IO	205-260		8		2700			5050	6050
23		AFT CABIN 230	ST	WKNDR	FBG	DV	IO	260		8		4200	2	8	7150	8200
23		NOVA 230	ST	CUD	FBG	DV	IO	260		8		4000			6850	7850
23		NOVA 230 XL	ST	CUD	FBG	DV	IO	260		8		4000			6950	8000
24	8	COASTAL 250	ST	FSH	FBG	SV	OB			8		3550			11500	13100
24	8	COASTAL 250	ST	FSH	FBG	SV	SE		OMC	8		3900			**	**
24	8	COASTAL 250	ST	FSH	FBG	SV	IO	260		8		4550			8850	10000
24	8	COASTAL 250	ST	FSH	FBG	SV	SE	T	OMC	8		3900			**	**
24	8	COASTAL 250	ST	FSH	FBG	SV	IO	T140-T170		8		4550			9350	10700
24	8	OFFSHORE 250	ST	CUD	FBG	DV	OB			8		3750			11900	13600
24	8	OFFSHORE 250	ST	CUD	FBG	DV	SE		OMC	8		4000			**	**
24	8	OFFSHORE 250	ST	CUD	FBG	DV	IO	260	MRCR	8		4050			7650	8800
24	8	OFFSHORE 250	ST	CUD	FBG	DV	SE	T	OMC	8		4000			**	**
24	8	OFFSHORE 250	ST	CUD	FBG	DV	IO	T140-T170		8		4050			8100	9500
24	8	OFFSHORE 250	ST	SPTCR	FBG	DV	IO	260	OMC	8		4050			7600	8750
24	8	SPORTSMAN 250	ST	SPTCR	FBG	DV	OB			8		3750			11200	12700
24	8	SPORTSMAN 250	ST	SPTCR	FBG	DV	SE		OMC	8		4100			**	**
24	8	SPORTSMAN 250	ST	SPTCR	FBG	DV	IO	260	OMC	8		4750			8500	9750
24	8	SPORTSMAN 250	ST	SPTCR	FBG	DV	SE	T	OMC	8		4100			**	**
24	8	SPORTSMAN 250	ST	SPTCR	FBG	DV	IO	T140-T170		8		4750			9100	10500
24	8	SPORTSMAN 350	ST	SPTCR	FBG	DV	IO	260	MRCR	8		4750			8550	9800
26		AFT CABIN 260	ST	CBNCR	FBG	DV	IO	260		8		5000	2	10	11600	13100
26	3	NOVA II	ST	CUD	FBG	DV	IO	T260		8		5400	1	11	11800	13400
27	7	2800 MONTE CARLO	ST	EXP	FBG	SV	IO	T170-T260		9	11	7200			13800	17000
27	7	COASTAL 2800	ST	SF	FBG	SV	SE	T	OMC	9	11	8200			**	**
27	7	COASTAL 2800	ST	SF	FBG	SV	IB	T220-T270		9	11	8200			19900	22800
27	8	NOVA III	ST	CUD	FBG	DV	IO	T260		8	2	5600			13300	15100
28	8	EXPRESS 2900	ST	EXP	FBG	DV	IB	T220-T270		10	8	9000	2	6	21500	24600
28	8	SPORT BRIDGE 2900	FB	SDN	FBG	DV	IB	T220-T270		10	8	10100		2	24500	28300
29	6	EXCALIBUR CAT	OP	OFF	FBG	CT	IO	T	KAAM	9	8	7300		2	**	**
29	6	EXCALIBUR CAT	OP	OFF	FBG	CT	IO	T370-T400		9	8	7300		2	18600	21200
29	6	SCARAB II	OP	RACE	FBG	DV	IO	T	KAAM	8		6400		2	**	**
29	6	SCARAB II	OP	RACE	FBG	DV	IO	T330-T370		8		6500		2	13400	16000
29	6	SCARAB II	OP	RACE	FBG	DV	IO	T400	MRCR	8		6400		2	15200	17200
29	6	SCARAB PANTHER	OP	RACE	FBG	DV	IO	T330-T400		8		6400			13400	15900
29	6	SCARAB PANTHER	OP	RACE	FBG	DV	IO	T425	KAAM	8		6400			15100	17200
29	6	SCARAB SPORT		OPFSH	FBG	DV	SE	T	OMC	8		4500	1	10	**	**
29	6	SCARAB SPORT	ST	OPFSH	FBG	DV	OB			8		2985			22600	25100
31	8	ST TROPAZ 3200	ST	EXP	FBG	SV	IB	T340	MRCR	11	8	10300	2	10	32300	35900
31	8	ST TROPEZ 3200	ST	EXP	FBG	SV	IB	T260-T350		11	8	10300	2	10	30700	36100
32		COASTAL 3200	ST	SF	FBG	SV	IB	T260-T350		11	6	13000			33000	38600
32		SPORT BRIDGE 3200	FB	SF	FBG	SV	IB	T260-T350		11	6	14000	3		33600	39200
33	7	GRAND SPORT 3400	ST	SPTCR	FBG	DV	IB	T260-T350		12	6	13400	2	7	38000	44200
33	10	SCARAB III	OP	RACE	FBG	DV	IO	T330-T400		8	4	7750		2	23200	28500
33	10	SCARAB III	OP	RACE	FBG	DV	IO	T440	MRCR	8	4	7750		2	27400	30500
33	10	SCARAB RAIDER 34	OP	RACE	FBG	DV	OB			8	4	5100	1	10	43500	48300
33	10	SCARAB RAIDER 34	OP	RACE	FBG	DV	SE		OMC	8	4	5100	1	10	**	**
37	7	SCARAB 38 KV	OP	RACE	FBG	DV	IO	T	KAAM	8	9	9100		2	**	**
		IO T370 MRCR 29700 33000, IO T400 MRCR 30800 34200, IO T440 MRCR													32500	36100
37	7	SCARAB RAIDER	OP	RACE	FBG	DV	OB			8	9	5100			51700	56800
39	6	SCARAB 400	OP	RACE	FBG	DV	IO	T330	MRCR	8	6	9300		3	33800	37500
		IO T370 MRCR 35000 38900, IO T400 MRCR 36200 40200, IO T440 MRCR													38000	42200
41	6	EXCALIBUR EAGLE	OP	OFF	FBG	DV	IO	T370	MRCR	9		10500		3	45500	50000
41	6	EXCALIBUR EAGLE	OP	OFF	FBG	DV	IO	T400	MRCR	9		10500		3	47400	52100
41	6	EXCALIBUR EAGLE	OP	OFF	FBG	DV	IO	T440	MRCR	9		10500		3	50100	55000
45		SCARAB 45	OP	RACE	FBG	DV	IO	R370	MRCR	12		23900	3		58200	64000
45		SCARAB 45	OP	RACE	FBG	DV	IO	R400	MRCR	12		23900	3		60000	66000
		1985 BOATS														
16	4	AMERICAN 166	ST	RNBT	FBG	DV	IO	120	OMC	7	2	2020	1	6	2300	2700
16	4	AMERICAN 170	ST	RNBT	FBG	DV	OB			7	2	1300	1	6	2300	2650
16	4	AMERICAN 170	ST	RNBT	FBG	DV	IO	120-140		7	2	2020	1	6	2350	2750
17	7	ELITE 180	ST	RNBT	FBG	DV	OB			7	2	1500	1	6	2600	3000
17	7	ELITE 180	ST	RNBT	FBG	DV	IO	140-190		7	2	2125	1	6	2500	2950
17	7	ELITE 182 CD	ST	SKI	FBG	SV	IO	140-190		7	2	2200	1	6	2400	2850
17	7	ELITE XL 180	ST	RNBT	FBG	DV	IO	140-190		7	2	2125	1	6	2650	3100
17	7	ELITE XL 182	ST	SKI	FBG	SV	IO	140-190		7	2	2200	1	6	2550	3000
17	10	FISHERMAN 180	ST	CTRCN	FBG	SV	OB			7	9	1750			3250	3800
19		AMERICAN 190	ST	RNBT	FBG	SV	IO	120-170		7	7	2300	1	6	3000	3500
19		AMERICAN 192	ST	CUD	FBG	SV	IO	120-170		7	7	2300	1	6	3050	3600
19	6	ELITE 200	ST	RNBT	FBG	DV	IO	200-260		8		2900	1	6	3550	4350
19	6	ELITE XL 200	ST	RNBT	FBG	DV	IO	200-260		8		2900	1	6	3700	4500
20	6	ELITE 210	ST	RNBT	FBG	DV	IO	200-260		8		3000	1	6	4300	5250
20	6	ELITE XL 210	ST	RNBT	FBG	DV	IO	200-260		8		3000			4500	5400
20	6	FISHERMAN V20	ST	CTRCN	FBG	DV	OB			8		1920	1	6	5800	6700
20	6	FISHERMAN V20	ST	CTRCN	FBG	DV	SE	115-205		8		2500	1	6	6850	7900
20	6	STEP-LIFT V20	ST	CUD	FBG	DV	OB			8		1920	1	6	5850	6700
20	6	STEP-LIFT V20	ST	CUD	FBG	DV	SE	115	OMC	8		2620	1	6	7050	8100
20	6	STEP-LIFT V20	ST	CUD	FBG	DV	IO	170-200		8		2620	1	6	4200	4950
20	6	STEP-LIFT V20	ST	CUD	FBG	DV	SE	205	OMC	8		2620	1	6	7050	8100
20	6	STEP-LIFT V20	ST	CUD	FBG	DV	IO	230-260		8		2620	1	6	4350	5200
21		SCARAB 21	OP	RACE	FBG	SV	IO	260-300		8		2800			4500	5500
22	7	SPORTSMAN 228	ST	SPTCR	FBG	DV	OB			8		2700	2	4	8350	9600
22	7	SPORTSMAN 228	ST	SPTCR	FBG	DV	IO	200		8		3680	2	4	5900	6800
22	7	SPORTSMAN 228	ST	SPTCR	FBG	DV	SE	205	OMC	8		3680	2	4	10200	11600
22	7	SPORTSMAN 228	ST	SPTCR	FBG	DV	IO	230-260		8		3680	2	4	6000	7000
22	7	SPORTSMAN 228	ST	SPTCR	FBG	DV	SE	T115	OMC	8		3680	2	4	10200	11600
23		AFT CABIN 230	ST	WKNDR	FBG	DV	IO	230-260		8		4200	2	8	6750	7900
23		AFT CABIN 230	ST	WKNDR	FBG	DV	IO	T170		8		4200	2	8	7400	8500
23		NOVA 230	ST	CUD	FBG	DV	IO	200-300		8		4000			6450	7900
23		NOVA 230 XL	ST	CUD	FBG	DV	IO	200-260		8		4000			6350	7700
23		NOVA 230 XL	ST	CUD	FBG	DV	IO	300	MRCR	8		4000			7000	8050
23		NOVA 230 XL	ST	CUD	FBG	DV	IO	T185-T190		8		4000			7150	8250
24	8	FISHERMAN 248 CUD	ST	CTRCN	FBG	DV	OB			8		3150	2	4	10400	11800
24	8	FISHERMAN 248 CUD	ST	CTRCN	FBG	DV	IO	200		8		4150	1	6	7550	8700

 CONTINUED ON NEXT PAGE

LOA FT	LOA IN	NAME AND/ OR MODEL	TOP/ RIG	BOAT TYPE	HULL MTL	HULL TP	ENGINE TP	ENGINE # HP	ENGINE MFG	BEAM FT	BEAM IN	WGT LBS	DRAFT FT	DRAFT IN	RETAIL LOW	RETAIL HIGH
		1985 BOATS														
24	8	FISHERMAN 248 CUD	ST	CTRCN	FBG	DV	SE	205	OMC	8		4150	1	6	12300	14000
24	8	FISHERMAN 248 CUD	ST	CTRCN	FBG	DV	IO	230-260		8		4150	1	6	7700	9050
24	8	FISHERMAN 248 CUD	ST	CTRCN	FBG	DV	SE	T115	OMC	8		4150	1	6	12300	14000
24	8	FISHERMAN 248 CUD	ST	CTRCN	FBG	DV	IO	T140-T190		8		4150	1	6	8350	9850
24	8	OFFSHORE 248	ST	CUD	FBG	DV	OB			8		3750	2	4	11700	13200
24	8	OFFSHORE 248	ST	CUD	FBG	DV	IO	200		8		4050	2	4	7050	8100
24	8	OFFSHORE 248	ST	CUD	FBG	DV	SE	205	OMC	8		4050	2	4	12200	13900
24	8	OFFSHORE 248	ST	CUD	FBG	DV	IO	230-260		8		4050	2	4	7150	8450
24	8	OFFSHORE 248	ST	CUD	FBG	DV	SE	T115	OMC	8		4050	2	4	12200	13900
24	8	OFFSHORE 248	ST	CUD	FBG	DV	IO	T140-T190		8		4050	2	4	7800	9200
24	8	SPORTSMAN 248	ST	SPTCR	FBG	DV	OB			8		3750	2	4	11700	13200
24	8	SPORTSMAN 248	ST	SPTCR	FBG	DV	IO	200		8		4750	2	4	7900	9100
24	8	SPORTSMAN 248	ST	SPTCR	FBG	DV	SE	205	OMC	8		4750			13300	15100
24	8	SPORTSMAN 248	ST	SPTCR	FBG	DV	IO	230-260		8		4750	2	4	8000	9400
24	8	SPORTSMAN 248	ST	SPTCR	FBG	DV	SE	T115	OMC	8		4750	2	4	13300	15100
24	8	SPORTSMAN 248	ST	SPTCR	FBG	DV	IO	T140-T185		8		4750			8650	10100
26		AFT CABIN 260	ST	CBNCR	FBG	DV	IO	230-260		8		5000	2	10	11000	12600
26		AFT CABIN 260	ST	CBNCR	FBG	DV	IO	T170-T230		8		5000	2	10	11500	13300
26	3	NOVA II	ST	CUD	FBG	DV	IO	330-370		8		5200	1	11	10200	12200
26	3	NOVA II	ST	CUD	FBG	DV	IO	400	MRCR	8		5200	1	11	11300	12800
26	3	NOVA II	ST	CUD	FBG	DV	IO	T260-T300		8		5200	1	11	11100	13400
26	10	EXCALIBUR SPEEDSTER	OP	OFF	FBG	DV	OB			7		3000	2	2	15000	17000
26	10	EXCALIBUR SPEEDSTER	OP	OFF	FBG	DV	IO	330-370		7		4500	2	4	9500	11400
26	10	EXCALIBUR SPEEDSTER	OP	OFF	FBG	DV	IO	400	MRCR	7		4500	2	4	10500	11900
28	8	EXPRESS 2900	ST	EXP	FBG	DV	IO	T230		10	8	9000	2	6	16100	18300
		IO T260 MRCR 16500 18700, IO T260 OMC 16400 18700, IB T260 MRCR													21000	23300
28	8	EXPRESS CRUISER 2900	ST	EXP	FBG	DV	IB	T230	MRCR	10	8	9000	2	6	20600	22900
28	8	SPORT BRIDGE 2900	FB	SDN	FBG	DV	IB	T230-T260		10	8	9000	2	6	22500	25700
28	8	SPORT BRIDGE 2900	FB	SDN	FBG	DV	IB	T165D	VLVO	10	8	9000	2	6	30900	34400
29	6	EXCALIBUR CAT	OP	OFF	FBG	CT	IO	T370-T440		9	8	7300	2	4	17500	21300
29	6	SCARAB II	OP	RACE	FBG	DV	IO	T300-T375		8		6400	2		12400	15500
29	6	SCARAB II	OP	RACE	FBG	DV	IO	T400-T440		8		6400	2		13900	16700
29	6	SCARAB SPORT		OPFSH	FBG	DV	SE	T205	OMC	8		4500	1	10	21900	24400
29	6	SCARAB SPORT	ST	OPFSH	FBG	DV	OB			8		2985			22000	24500
31	8	ST TROPAZ 3200	ST	EXP	FBG	SV	IB	T260-T340		11	8	10300	2	10	29300	34300
32		COASTAL 3200	ST	SF	FBG	DV	IB	T260-T340		11	6	13200	2	10	31600	36800
32		COASTAL 3200	ST	SF	FBG	DV	IB	T210D-T235D		11	6	13200	2	10	40100	45500
32		SEDAN BRIDGE 3200	FB	SDN	FBG	SV	IB	T260-T340		11	6	14000	3		34700	40700
32		SEDAN BRIDGE 3200	FB	SDN	FBG	SV	IB	T210D-T235D		11	6	14000	3		46800	52700
32		SPORT BRIDGE 3200	FB	SF	FBG	SV	IB	T260-T340		11	6	14000	3		32100	37300
32		SPORT BRIDGE 3200	FB	SF	FBG	SV	IB	T210D-T235D		11	6	14000	3		41400	47000
33	7	GRAND SPORT 3400	ST	SPTCR	FBG	DV	IB	T260-T340		12	6	13400	2	7	36300	41900
33	10	SCARAB III	OP	RACE	FBG	DV	IO	T300-T375		8	4	7750	2	2	21600	26400
33	10	SCARAB III	OP	RACE	FBG	DV	IO	T400-T440		8	4	7750	2	2	24600	29200
33	10	SCARAB RAIDER	OP	RACE	FBG	DV	OB			8	4	5100	1	10	42600	47300
33	10	SCARAB RAIDER	OP	RACE	FBG	DV	SE	T205	OMC	8	4	5100	1	10	42600	47300
34	6	CALIFORNIAN CNV		SF	FBG	SV	IB	T210D		12	4	18000			54500	59900
34	6	CALIFORNIAN EXP		EXP	FBG	SV	IB	T210D		12	4	18000			54600	60000
34	6	CALIFORNIAN MY		MY	FBG	SV	IB	T210D		12	4	18000			57700	63400
37	7	SCARAB 380	OP	RACE	FBG	DV	IO	T330	MRCR	8	9	9100	2	2	27400	30400
		IO T370 MRCR 28500 31700, IO T400 MRCR 29600 32800, IO T440 MRCR													31200	34700
37	7	SPECIAL EDITION 380	ST	RACE	FBG	DV	IO	T370	MRCR	8	9	9900			28600	31700
		IO T375 KAAM 28900 32100, IO T400 MRCR 29500 32800, IO T425 KAAM													30600	34000
		IO T440 MRCR 30900 34400														
37	8	CALIFORNIAN		MY	FBG	SV	IB	T210D		13		28000			91400	100500
37	8	CALIFORNIAN CNV		SF	FBG	SV	IB	T210D		13		28000			91000	100000
39		EXCALIBUR HAWK	OP	OFF	FBG	DV	IO	T370	MRCR	9		8500	2	10	37000	41100
		IO T375 KAAM 37700 41900, IO T400 MRCR 38600 42900, IO T425 KAAM													40900	45400
		IO T440 MRCR 41100 45700														
39	6	SCARAB 400	OP	RACE	FBG	DV	IO	T330	MRCR	8	6	9300	3		32400	36000
		IO T370 MRCR 33600 37300, IO T400 MRCR 34700 38600, IO T440 MRCR													36400	40500
41	6	EXCALIBUR EAGLE	OP	OFF	FBG	DV	IO	T370	MRCR	9		10500	3	2	43200	48000
		IO T400 MRCR 45500 50000, IO T440 MRCR 48000 52800, IB T300D CAT													76900	84500
43	8	CALIFORNIAN CPT MY		MY	FBG	SV	IB	T210D		13	3				121500	133500
45		SCARAB 45	OP	RACE	FBG	DV	IO	R370	MRCR	12		17000	3		52400	57500
45		SCARAB 45	OP	RACE	FBG	DV	IO	R400	MRCR	12		17000	3		48200	52900
45		SCARAB 45	OP	RACE	FBG	DV	IO	R440	MRCR	12		17000	3		49800	54700
52		CALIFORNIAN CPT MY		OFF	FBG	SV	IB	T300D		15	6				161000	177000
		1984 BOATS														
16	4	AMERICAN 166	ST	RNBT	FBG	DV	IO	117-140		7	2	2020			2000	2400
16	4	ELITE 166	ST	RNBT	FBG	DV	OB			7	2	1300			2250	2600
16	4	ELITE 166	ST	RNBT	FBG	DV	IO	117-140		7	2	2020			2700	3150
17	7	AMERICAN 180	ST	RNBT	FBG	DV	IO	117-140		7	2	2125			2600	3000
17	7	ELITE 180	ST	RNBT	FBG	DV	OB			7	2	1500			2550	2950
17	7	ELITE 180	ST	RNBT	FBG	DV	IO	138-230		7	2	2125			2800	3250
17	7	ELITE XL 180	ST	RNBT	FBG	DV	IO	138-230		7	2	2125			2950	3450
17	10	FISHERMAN 180	ST	CTRCN	FBG	SV	OB			7	9	1750			3200	3700
19	6	ELITE 200	ST	RNBT	FBG	DV	IO	170-230		8		2900			3450	4300
19	6	ELITE 200	ST	RNBT	FBG	DV	IO	260		8		2900			3700	4500
19	6	SUN-HATCH 196	ST	CUD	FBG	DV	OB			8		1880			3150	3650
19	6	SUN-HATCH 196	ST	CUD	FBG	DV	IO	170-230		8		2900			3600	4500
19	6	SUN-HATCH 196	ST	CUD	FBG	DV	IO	260		8		2900			3850	4650
20	6	ELITE 210	ST	RNBT	FBG	DV	IO	170	MRCR	8		3000			4050	4700
20	6	ELITE 210	ST	RNBT	FBG	DV	IO	170	OMC	8		3000			4050	4700
20	6	ELITE 210	ST	RNBT	FBG	DV	IO	170-260		8		3000			4400	5300
20	6	ELITE XL 210	ST	RNBT	FBG	DV	IO	170	MRCR	8		3000			4200	4900
20	6	ELITE XL 210	ST	RNBT	FBG	DV	IO	170	OMC	8		3000			4200	4850
20	6	ELITE XL 210	ST	RNBT	FBG	DV	IO	170-260		8		3000			4600	5450
20	6	FISHERMAN V20	ST	CTRCN	FBG	DV	OB			8		1920			5700	6500
20	6	STEP-LIFT V20	ST	CUD	FBG	DV	OB			8		1920			5700	6550
20	6	STEP-LIFT V20	ST	CUD	FBG	DV	SE	115	OMC	8		2620			6900	7950
20	6	STEP-LIFT V20	ST	CUD	FBG	DV	IO	170-230		8		2620			4050	5050
20	6	STEP-LIFT V20	ST	CUD	FBG	DV	IO	260		8		2620			4350	5250
22	7	SPORTSMAN 228	ST	OPFSH	FBG	DV	OB			8		2700			8200	9400
23		AFT CABIN 230	ST	WKNDR	FBG	DV	IO	198-260		8		4200			6400	7850
23		NOVA 230	ST	CUD	FBG	DV	IO	198-260		8		4000			6100	7500
23		NOVA 230 XL	ST	CUD	FBG	DV	IO	198-260		8		4000			6250	7700
23		NOVA 230 XL	ST	CUD	FBG	DV	IO	T170-T185		8		4000			6900	8300
24	8	FISHERMAN 248 CUD	ST	CTRCN	FBG	DV	OB			8		3150			10200	11500
24	8	OFFSHORE 248	ST	CUD	FBG	DV	OB			8		3750			11400	13000
24	8	OFFSHORE 248	ST	CUD	FBG	DV	IO	225-230		8		4000			7000	8050
24	8	OFFSHORE 248	ST	CUD	FBG	DV	SE	255	OMC	8		4000			11900	13500
24	8	OFFSHORE 248	ST	CUD	FBG	DV	IO	260		8		4000			7000	8300
24	8	OFFSHORE 248	ST	CUD	FBG	DV	IO	T138-T185		8		4000			7700	9050
24	8	SPORTSMAN 248	ST	SPTCR	FBG	DV	OB			8		3750			11400	13000
24	8	SPORTSMAN 248	ST	SPTCR	FBG	DV	IO	225-230		8		4700			7800	9000
24	8	SPORTSMAN 248	ST	SPTCR	FBG	DV	SE	255	OMC	8		4750			13000	14800
24	8	SPORTSMAN 248	ST	SPTCR	FBG	DV	IO	260		8		4750			7900	9300
24	8	SPORTSMAN 248	ST	SPTCR	FBG	DV	IO	T138-T185		8		4750			8600	10000
26		AFT CABIN 260	ST	CBNCR	FBG	DV	IO	225-230		8		5000			10700	12200
26		AFT CABIN 260	ST	CBNCR	FBG	DV	SE	255	OMC	8		5000			14000	15900
26		AFT CABIN 260	ST	CBNCR	FBG	DV	IO	260		8		5000			10700	12300
26		AFT CABIN 260	ST	CBNCR	FBG	DV	IO	T138-T230		8		5000			11300	13100
26	2	EXPRESS CRUISER 2600	OP	EXP	FBG	DV	IO	330	MRCR	9	10	7000			12000	13600
26	2	EXPRESS CRUISER 2600	OP	EXP	FBG	DV	IO	T170-T260		9	10	7000			12100	14900
26	3	NOVA II	ST	CUD	FBG	DV	IO	T198-T260		8		5200			10000	12500
26	3	NOVA II	ST	CUD	FBG	DV	IO	T300	MRCR	8		5200			11400	12900
26	10	EXCALIBUR O/S	OP	CTRCN	FBG	DV	OB			7			1	11	15200	17300
26	10	EXCALIBUR SPEEDSTER	OP	OFF	FBG	DV	OB			7		3000	1	11	14600	16600
26	10	EXCALIBUR SPEEDSTER	OP	OFF	FBG	DV	IO	300-370		7			1	11	9450	11600
26	10	EXCALIBUR SPEEDSTER	OP	OFF	FBG	DV	IO	400	MRCR	7			1	11	10700	12200
28	8	EXPRESS CRUISER 2900	ST	EXP	FBG	DV	IB	T220-T230		10	8	9200			19800	22100
28	8	EXPRESS CRUISER 2900	ST	EXP	FBG	DV	SE	T255	OMC	10	8	9200			19800	22000
28	8	EXPRESS CRUISER 2900	ST	EXP	FBG	DV	IO	T260	MRCR	10	8	9200			16000	18200
		IO T260 OMC 16000 18200, IO T260 VLVO 16200 18400, IB T260-T270													20300	22800
		IB T158D VLVO 26500 29400														
28	8	SPORT BRIDGE 2900	FB	SDN	FBG	DV	IB	T220-T230		10	8	9000			21400	23900
28	8	SPORT BRIDGE 2900	FB	SDN	FBG	DV	SE	T255	OMC	10	8	9000			19700	21900
28	8	SPORT BRIDGE 2900	FB	SDN	FBG	DV	IB	T260-T270		10	8	9000			22100	24800
28	8	SPORT BRIDGE 2900	FB	SDN	FBG	DV	IB	T158D-T225D		10	8	9000			29400	35900
28	8	SPORT BRIDGE 2900	FB	SDN	FBG	DV	IB	T260D	VLVO	10	8	9000			33900	37700
29	6	EXCALIBUR CAT	OP	OFF	FBG	CT	IO	T300-T370		9	10	6300	1	11	15200	18600
29	6	EXCALIBUR CAT	OP	OFF	FBG	CT	IO	T400	MRCR	9	10	6300	1	11	17000	19300
29	6	SCARAB II	OP	RACE	FBG	DV	IO	T300-T370		8		6400			12300	15000
29	6	SCARAB II	OP	RACE	FBG	DV	IO	T400	MRCR	8		6400			13700	15600
29	6	SCARAB S TYPE	OP	RACE	FBG	DV	IO	T300-T370		8		6400			11700	14400
29	6	SCARAB S TYPE	OP	RACE	FBG	DV	IO	T400	MRCR	8		6400			13200	15000
29	6	SCARAB SPORT	ST	OPFSH	FBG	DV	OB			8		2985			21600	24000
31	3	EXPRESS CRUISER 3100	OP	EXP	FBG	DV	IB	T260-T350		11	6	10200			26800	31600

CONTINUED ON NEXT PAGE

LOA FT	LOA IN	NAME AND/ OR MODEL	TOP/ RIG	BOAT TYPE	-HULL- MTL	-HULL- TP	ENGINE TP	ENGINE # HP	ENGINE MFG	BEAM FT	BEAM IN	WGT LBS	DRAFT FT	DRAFT IN	RETAIL LOW	RETAIL HIGH
		1984 BOATS														
31	3	EXPRESS CRUISER 3100	OP	EXP	FBG	DV	IB	T260D	VLVO	11	6	10200			34300	38200
32		COASTAL 3200	ST	SF	FBG	DV	IB	T260-T350		11	6	13200			30200	35400
32		COASTAL 3200	ST	SF	FBG	DV	IB	T205D-T235D		11	6	13200			38300	43600
33	7	EXPRESS CRUISER 3400	OP	EXP	FBG	DV	IB	T260-T350		12	6	13400			34600	40300
33	7	EXPRESS CRUISER 3400	OP	EXP	FBG	DV	IB	T205D-T235D		12	6	13400			42100	47500
33	10	SCARAB III	OP	RACE	FBG	DV	IO	T300-T370		8	4	7750			20800	25200
33	10	SCARAB III	OP	RACE	FBG	DV	IO	T400	MRCR	8	4	7750			23700	26400
34	6	CALIFORNIAN CNV		SF	FBG	SV	IB	T210D		12	4	18000			52400	57500
34	6	CALIFORNIAN MX		EXP	FBG	SV	IB	T210D		12	4	18000			52400	57600
34	6	CALIFORNIAN SEDAN		SPTCR	FBG	SV	IB	T210D	CAT	12	4	18000			52800	58000
37	7	SCARAB 380	OP	RACE	FBG	DV	IO	T300	MRCR	8	9	9100			27600	30600
		IO T330 MRCR 26400 29400, IO T370 MRCR 27500 30600, IO T400 MRCR													28500	31700
37	7	SPECIAL EDITION 380	ST	RACE	FBG	DV	IO	T300	MRCR	8	9	9900			28500	31700
		IO T330 MRCR 29200 32500, IO T370 MRCR 27600 30600, IO T400 MRCR													28500	31600
37	8	CALIFORNIAN		MY	FBG	SV	IB	T210D		13		28000			87600	96300
37	8	CALIFORNIAN CNV		SF	FBG	SV	IB	T210D		13		28000			87200	95800
37	8	CALIFORNIAN LRC		OFF	FBG	SV	IB	T210D		13		28000			87300	96000
39	3	HAWK	OP	OFF	FBG	DV	IO	T300	MRCR	9			2	2	45600	50100
		IO T330 MRCR 46500 51100, IO T370 MRCR 47900 52700, IO T400 MRCR													49500	54400
39	3	HAWK O/S	OP	CTRCN	FBG	DV	OB			9			2	2	**	**
41	6	EAGLE	OP	OFF	FBG	DV	IO	T370	MRCR	9	2		2	2	43100	47900
41	6	EAGLE	OP	OFF	FBG	DV	IO	T400	MRCR	9	2		2	2	44000	49500
41	8	CALIFORNIAN LRC		OFF	FBG	SV	IB	T210D		13	0	31000			104500	114500
43	8	CALIFORNIAN COCKPIT		MYCPT	FBG	SV	IB	T210D		13	3				107000	117500
50		CALIFORNIAN		MY	FBG	SV	IB	T300D		14	2	39000			122000	134500

....For earlier years, see the BUC Used Boat Price Guide, Volume 3

WELLINGTON BOAT WORKS

WILSON NY 14172

See inside cover to adjust price for area

LOA FT	LOA IN	NAME AND/ OR MODEL	TOP/ RIG	BOAT TYPE	-HULL- MTL	-HULL- TP	ENGINE TP	ENGINE # HP	ENGINE MFG	BEAM FT	BEAM IN	WGT LBS	DRAFT FT	DRAFT IN	RETAIL LOW	RETAIL HIGH
		1985 BOATS														
16		SPEEDSTER		RNBT	FBG	SV	IB	165	CRUS	5	4	1800	2		4150	4850
		1984 BOATS														
16		SPEEDSTER		RNBT	FBG	SV	IB	165	CRUS	5	4	1800	1	4	3950	4600

WELLINGTON BOATS INC

JACKSONVILLE FL 32238-0 COAST GUARD MFG ID- WLN See inside cover to adjust price for area

LOA FT	LOA IN	NAME AND/ OR MODEL	TOP/ RIG	BOAT TYPE	-HULL- MTL	-HULL- TP	ENGINE TP	ENGINE # HP	ENGINE MFG	BEAM FT	BEAM IN	WGT LBS	DRAFT FT	DRAFT IN	RETAIL LOW	RETAIL HIGH
		1989 BOATS														
57			CUT	MS	FBG	KL	IB	130D	FORD	15		60000	5		442000	486000
		1985 BOATS														
44		WELLINGTON 44	CUT	SA/CR	FBG	KC	IB	61D	LEHM	13	6	28000	4	3	96500	106000
46	11	WELLINGTON 47	CUT	SA/CR	FBG	KC	IB	D		13	6	45000	4	10	133500	147000
46	11	WELLINGTON 47	KTH	SA/CR	FBG	KC	IB	D		13	6	45000	4	10	133500	147000
57		WELLINGTON 57	SLP	MS	FBG	CB	IB	D		14	6	45000	4	4	307000	337000
57		WELLINGTON 57	KTH	MS	FBG	CB	IB	D		14	6	45000	4	4	307000	337000
57		WELLINGTON 57		MY	FBG	DS	IB	120D		14	6	50000			154000	169000
57		WELLINGTON 57	CUT	SA/CR	FBG	KC	IB	D		14	6	50000	4	6	319000	350500
		1984 BOATS														
44		WELLINGTON 44	CUT	SA/CR	FBG	KC	IB	D		13	6	28000	4	3	90800	99800
46	11	WELLINGTON 47	CUT	SA/CR	FBG	KC	IB	D		13	6	45000	4	10	126000	138000
46	11	WELLINGTON 47	KTH	SA/CR	FBG	KC	IB	D		13	6	45000	4	10	126000	138000
57		WELLINGTON 57	SLP	MS	FBG	KC	IB	D		14	6	50000	4	3	300000	329500
57		WELLINGTON 57	KTH	MS	FBG	KC	IB	D		14	6	50000	4	3	300000	329500
57		WELLINGTON 57		MY	FBG	DS	IB	120D		14	6	50000			148000	162500

....For earlier years, see the BUC Used Boat Price Guide, Volume 3

WENZEL FIBERGLASS BOAT CO

C-CRAFT BOATS
MCHENRY MD 21541 COAST GUARD MFG ID- WEN

See inside cover to adjust price for area

LOA FT	LOA IN	NAME AND/ OR MODEL	TOP/ RIG	BOAT TYPE	-HULL- MTL	-HULL- TP	ENGINE TP	ENGINE # HP	ENGINE MFG	BEAM FT	BEAM IN	WGT LBS	DRAFT FT	DRAFT IN	RETAIL LOW	RETAIL HIGH
		1984 BOATS														
16	8	WISP B/R	OP	RNBT	FBG	DV	IO	120-230							2850	3450

....For earlier years, see the BUC Used Boat Price Guide, Volume 3

WESTERLY YACHTS INC

ANDREW GEMENY & SON
WESTERLY YACHTS LIMITED
HYATTSVILLE MD 21403 COAST GUARD MFG ID- AGS

See inside cover to adjust price for area

WESTERLY MARINE CONSTRUCTION
HANTS ENGLAND

LOA FT	LOA IN	NAME AND/ OR MODEL	TOP/ RIG	BOAT TYPE	-HULL- MTL	-HULL- TP	ENGINE TP	ENGINE # HP	ENGINE MFG	BEAM FT	BEAM IN	WGT LBS	DRAFT FT	DRAFT IN	RETAIL LOW	RETAIL HIGH
		1987 BOATS														
33	2	STORM 33	SLP	SA/RC	FBG	DV		D	VLVO	11	7	11310	5	6	48200	53000
		1986 BOATS														
26		GRIFFON CLUB 26	SLP	SAIL	FBG	KL	IB	20D	BUKH	9	3	6000	4	9	24300	27000
26		GRIFFON CLUB 26	SLP	SAIL	FBG	TK	IB	20D	BUKH	9	3	6000	3	3	24300	27000
27	1	MERLIN 28	SLP	SAIL	FBG	KL	IB	18D	VLVO	9	11	6600	5	1	27200	30200
27	1	MERLIN 28	SLP	SAIL	FBG	TK	IB	18D	VLVO	9	11	6600	3	4	27200	30200
28	10	KONSORT 29	SLP	SAIL	FBG	KL	IB	18D	VLVO	10	9	7900	5	4	33600	37300
28	10	KONSORT 29	SLP	SAIL	FBG	TK	IB	18D	VLVO	10	9	7900	3	3	33600	37400
28	10	KONSORT DUO	SLP	MS	FBG	TK	IB	28D	VLVO	10	9	8400	3	2	35900	39900
31	10	FULMAR 32	SLP	SAIL	FBG	KL	IB	18D	VLVO	10	11	9900	5	3	42100	46700
31	10	FULMAR 32	SLP	SAIL	FBG	TK	IB	18D	VLVO	10	11	9900	4		42100	46700
33	8	FALCON 34	SLP	SAIL	FBG	KL	IB	28D	VLVO	12	3	12500	4	10	52900	58100
33	8	FALCON 34	SLP	SAIL	FBG	TK	IB	28D	VLVO	12	3	12500	3	11	52900	58100
33	8	SEAHAWK 34	SLP	SAIL	FBG	KL	IB	28D	VLVO	12	3	12698	4	10	53700	59000
33	8	SEAHAWK 34	SLP	SAIL	FBG	TK	IB	28D	VLVO	12	3	12698	3	11	53700	59000
35	8	CORSAIR 36	SLP	SAIL	FBG	KL	IB	28D	VLVO	12	6	15500	4	11	65300	71800
35	8	CORSAIR 36	KTH	SAIL	FBG	KL	IB	28D	VLVO	12	6	15500	4	11	65400	71900
38	6	SEALORD 39	SLP	SAIL	FBG	KL	IB	34D	VLVO	13	2	18500	5	6	81100	89200
38	6	SEALORD 39	KTH	SAIL	FBG	KL	IB	34D	VLVO	13	2	18500	5	6	81300	89300
		1985 BOATS														
26		GRIFFON	SLP	SA/CR	FBG	KL	IB	18D	VLVO	9	3		4	9	20200	22500
26		GRIFFON	SLP	SA/CR	FBG	TK	IB	18D	VLVO	9	3		3	3	20200	22500
26		GRIFFON CLUB 26	SLP	SAIL	FBG	KL	IB	18D	VLVO	9	3	6000	4	9	22700	25200
26		GRIFFON CLUB 26	SLP	SAIL	FBG	TK	IB	18D	VLVO	9	3	6000	3	3	22700	25200
27	1	MERLIN 28	SLP	SAIL	FBG	KL	IB	18D	VLVO	9	11	6600	5	1	25400	28200
27	1	MERLIN 28	SLP	SAIL	FBG	TK	IB	18D	VLVO	9	11	6600	3	4	25400	28200
28	7	MERLIN	SLP	SA/CR	FBG	KL	IB	18D- 20D		9	11		5		31700	35300
28	7	MERLIN	SLP	SA/CR	FBG	TK	IB	18D- 20D		9	11		3	4	31700	35400
28	10	KONSORT	SLP	SA/CR	FBG	KL	IB	18D	VLVO	10	9		5	4	31800	35300
28	10	KONSORT	SLP	SA/CR	FBG	TK	IB	18D	VLVO	10	9		3	3	31800	35400
28	10	KONSORT 29	SLP	SAIL	FBG	KL	IB	18D	VLVO	10	9	7900	5	4	31400	34800
28	10	KONSORT 29	SLP	SAIL	FBG	TK	IB	18D	VLVO	10	9	7900	3	3	31400	34900
28	10	KONSORT DUO	SLP	MS	FBG	TK	IB	28D	VLVO	10	9	8400	3	2	33500	37200
31	10	FULMAR	SLP	SA/CR	FBG	KL	IB	18D	VLVO	10	11		5	3	39600	44000
31	10	FULMAR	SLP	SA/CR	FBG	TK	IB	18D	VLVO	10	11		4		39700	44100
31	10	FULMAR 32	SLP	SAIL	FBG	KL	IB	18D	VLVO	10	11	9900	5	3	39300	43700
31	10	FULMAR 32	SLP	SAIL	FBG	TK	IB	18D	VLVO	10	11	9900	4		39300	43700
33	8	SEAHAWK	SLP	SA/CR	FBG	KL	IB	28D	VLVO	12	3		4	11	60500	66500
33	8	SEAHAWK	SLP	SA/CR	FBG	TK	IB	28D	VLVO	12	3		4	11	60600	66600
33	8	SEAHAWK 34	SLP	SAIL	FBG	KL	IB	28D	VLVO	12	3	12698	4	10	50200	55100
33	8	SEAHAWK 34	SLP	SAIL	FBG	TK	IB	28D	VLVO	12	3	12698	3	11	50200	55200
33	8	SEAHAWK 34 AFTCOCKPT	SLP	SAIL	FBG	KL	IB	28D	VLVO	12	3	12500	4	10	49400	54300
33	8	SEAHAWK 34 AFTCOCKPT	SLP	SAIL	FBG	TK	IB	28D	VLVO	12	3	12500	2	7	49400	54300
35	8	CORSAIR	SLP	SA/CR	FBG	KL	IB	28D	VLVO	12	6	15500	4	11	61100	67100
35	8	CORSAIR	KTH	SA/CR	FBG	KL	IB	28D	VLVO	12	6	15500	4	11	61200	67200
35	8	CORSAIR 36	SLP	SAIL	FBG	KL	IB	28D	VLVO	12	6	15500	4	11	61100	67100
35	8	CORSAIR 36	KTH	SAIL	FBG	KL	IB	28D	VLVO	12	6	15500	4	11	61200	67200
38	6	SEALORD	SLP	SA/CR	FBG	KL	IB	36D	VLVO	13	2	18500	5	6	75900	83400
38	6	SEALORD	CUT	SA/CR	FBG	KL	IB	36D	VLVO	13	2	18500	5	6	75600	83100
38	6	SEALORD	KTH	SA/CR	FBG	KL	IB	36D	VLVO	13	2	18500	5	6	76100	83600
38	6	SEALORD 39	SLP	SAIL	FBG	KL	IB	34D	VLVO	13	2	18500	5	6	75800	83300
38	6	SEALORD 39	KTH	SAIL	FBG	KL	IB	34D	VLVO	13	2	18500	5	6	76000	83500
40		STORM 10	SLP	SA/OD	FBG	KL	IB	15D		10	1	7715	6		42700	47500
		1984 BOATS														
26		GRIFFON 26	SLP	SA/CR	FBG	KL	IB	D		9	4	5900	4	9	20900	23200
29	10	KONSORT 29	SLP	SA/CR	FBG	KL	IB	D		10	9	7900	5	4	29500	32800
31	10	FULMAR 32	SLP	SA/CR	FBG	KL	IB	D		10	11	9900	5	3	36800	40900
33	3	DISCUSS 33	SLP	SA/CR	FBG	KL	IB	D		11	2	13500	5	5	49800	54700
34		VULCAN 34 PH	SLP	SA/CR	FBG	KL	IB	D		11	6	15571	4	6	56900	62500
35	8	CORSAIR	SLP	SA/CR	FBG	KL	IB	D		12	6		4	11	58800	64600
35	9	CONWAY 36	SLP	SA/CR	FBG	KL	IB	D		11	2	15500	6		57300	63000

LOA FT IN	NAME AND/ OR MODEL	TOP/ RIG	BOAT TYPE	-HULL- MTL TP	TP #	----ENGINE--- HP MFG	BEAM FT IN	WGT LBS	DRAFT FT IN	RETAIL LOW	RETAIL HIGH
				----- 1984 BOATS -----							
38 6	SEA-LORD	SLP	SA/CR	FBG KL	IB	D	13 2	18500	5 6	71200	78200

....For earlier years, see the BUC Used Boat Price Guide, Volume 3

WESTERN MARINE INC
HUNTINGTON BEACH CA 926 COAST GUARD MFG ID- WIH See inside cover to adjust price for area

LOA FT IN	NAME AND/ OR MODEL	TOP/ RIG	BOAT TYPE	-HULL- MTL TP	TP #	----ENGINE--- HP MFG	BEAM FT IN	WGT LBS	DRAFT FT IN	RETAIL LOW	RETAIL HIGH
				----- 1985 BOATS -----							
37	G-&-S	SLP	SA/RC	F/S KL	IB	D	11 6	10250	6 7	47900	52700
38 3	WESTERN	FB	TRWL	F/S DS	IB	D VLVO	13 8	25000	4 4	**	**
40	WESTERN	SLP	SA/RC	F/S KL	IB	D	12	15000	7 9	77800	85500
55	WESTERN	CUT	SA/CR	F/S KL	IB	105D NISS	14	42000	5 9	244000	268000
60	WESTERN	FB	TRWL	F/S DS	IB T	D GM	20			**	**
72 3	WESTERN	F+T	SF	F/S DV	IB T	D GM	20 3			**	**

WESTIDE YACHT INT'L CO LTD
HSIAOKONG KAOHSIUNG   COAST GUARD MFG ID- HCL See inside cover to adjust price for area

LOA FT IN	NAME AND/ OR MODEL	TOP/ RIG	BOAT TYPE	-HULL- MTL TP	TP #	----ENGINE--- HP MFG	BEAM FT IN	WGT LBS	DRAFT FT IN	RETAIL LOW	RETAIL HIGH
				----- 1984 BOATS -----							
45 2	HARDIN 45	KTH	SA/CR	FBG KL	IB	65D LEHM	13 4	30000	5 6	87900	96600

WESTPORT MARINE INC
COSTA MESA CA 92627   COAST GUARD MFG ID- WPB See inside cover to adjust price for area
FORMERLY WESTPORT PACIFIC

For more recent years, see the BUC Used Boat Price Guide, Volume 1

LOA FT IN	NAME AND/ OR MODEL	TOP/ RIG	BOAT TYPE	-HULL- MTL TP	TP #	----ENGINE--- HP MFG	BEAM FT IN	WGT LBS	DRAFT FT IN	RETAIL LOW	RETAIL HIGH
				----- 1996 BOATS -----							
18 9	PACIFIC-CAT 2/18	SLP	SAROD	FBG CT	OB		7 11	450	7	5500	6350
18 9	PACIFIC-CAT 3/18	SLP	SAROD	FBG CT	OB		7 11	440	7	5450	6250
				----- 1995 BOATS -----							
18 9	PACIFIC-CAT 2/18	SLP	SAROD	FBG CT	OB		7 11	450	7	5200	5950
18 9	PACIFIC-CAT 3/18	SLP	SAROD	FBG CT	OB		7 11	440	7	5100	5900
				----- 1994 BOATS -----							
18 9	PACIFIC-CAT 2/18	SLP	SAROD	FBG CT	OB		7 11	450	7	4900	5600
18 9	PACIFIC-CAT 3/18	SLP	SAROD	FBG CT	OB		7 11	440	7	4800	5550
				----- 1993 BOATS -----							
18 9	PACIFIC-CAT 2/18	SLP	SAROD	FBG CT	OB		7 11	450	7	4600	5300
18 9	PACIFIC-CAT 3/18	SLP	SAROD	FBG CT	OB		7 11	440	7	4550	5250
				----- 1992 BOATS -----							
18 9	PACIFIC-CAT 2/18	SLP	SA/OD	FBG CT	OB		7 11	450	7	4300	5000
18 9	PACIFIC-CAT 3/18	SLP	SA/OD	FBG CT	OB		7 11	440	7	4250	4950
				----- 1991 BOATS -----							
18 9	PACIFIC-CAT 2/18	SLP	SA/OD	FBG CT	OB		7 11	450	7	4050	4700
18 9	PACIFIC-CAT 3/18	SLP	SA/OD	FBG CT	OB		7 11	440	7	4000	4650
				----- 1990 BOATS -----							
18 9	PACIFIC-CAT 2/18	SLP	SA/OD	FBG CT	OB		7 11	450	7	3800	4400
18 9	PACIFIC-CAT 3/18	SLP	SA/OD	FBG CT	OB		7 11	440	7	3750	4350
				----- 1989 BOATS -----							
18 9	PACIFIC-CAT 2/18	SLP	SA/OD	FBG CT	OB		7 11	450	7	3600	4150
18 9	PACIFIC-CAT 3/18	SLP	SA/OD	FBG CT	OB		7 11	440	7	3550	4100
				----- 1988 BOATS -----							
18 9	PACIFIC-CAT 2/18	SLP	SA/OD	FBG CT	OB		7 11	450	7	3350	3900
18 9	PACIFIC-CAT 3/18	SLP	SA/OD	FBG CT	OB		7 11	440	7	3300	3850
18 9	PACIFIC-CAT STANDARD	SLP	SA/OD	FBG CT	OB		9 8	520	7	3650	4250
				----- 1987 BOATS -----							
18 9	PACIFIC-CAT 2/18	SLP	SA/OD	FBG CT	OB		7 11	450	7	3150	3700
18 9	PACIFIC-CAT 2/18WIDE	SLP	SA/OD	FBG CT	OB		9 8	520	7	3450	4000
18 9	PACIFIC-CAT 3/18	SLP	SA/OD	FBG CT	OB		7 11	440	7	3100	3650
				----- 1986 BOATS -----							
18 9	PACIFIC-CAT 2/18	SLP	SA/OD	FBG CT	OB		7 11	450	7	3000	3450
18 9	PACIFIC-CAT 2/18WIDE	SLP	SA/OD	FBG CT	OB		9 8	520	7	3250	3800
18 9	PACIFIC-CAT 3/18	SLP	SA/OD	FBG CT	OB		7 11	440	7	2950	3650
				----- 1985 BOATS -----							
18 9	PACIFIC-CAT 2/18	SLP	SA/OD	FBG CT	OB		7 11	450	7	2800	3250
18 9	PACIFIC-CAT 3/18	SLP	SA/OD	FBG CT	OB		7 11	440	7	2750	3200
18 9	PACIFIC-CAT STANDARD	SLP	SA/OD	FBG CT	OB		7 11	540	7	3100	3650
				----- 1984 BOATS -----							
18 9	PACIFIC-CAT 2/18	SLP	SA/OD	FBG CT	OB		7 11	450	7	2650	3050
18 9	PACIFIC-CAT 3/18	SLP	SA/OD	FBG CT	OB		7 11	440	7	2600	3000
18 9	PACIFIC-CAT STANDARD	SLP	SA/OD	FBG CT	OB		7 11	540	7	2950	3400

....For earlier years, see the BUC Used Boat Price Guide, Volume 3

WESTPORT SHIPYARD
WESTPORT WA 98595   See inside cover to adjust price for area

For more recent years, see the BUC Used Boat Price Guide, Volume 1

LOA FT IN	NAME AND/ OR MODEL	TOP/ RIG	BOAT TYPE	-HULL- MTL TP	TP #	----ENGINE--- HP MFG	BEAM FT IN	WGT LBS	DRAFT FT IN	RETAIL LOW	RETAIL HIGH
				----- 1987 BOATS -----							
48	WESTSHIP/WESTPORT 48	HT	MY	FBG SV	IB	310D	15			225000	247000
65	WESTSHIP/WESTPORT 65	HT	MY	FBG SV	IB T	310D	20			567000	623500
				----- 1985 BOATS -----							
48	WESTSHIP/WESTPORT 48	HT	MY	FBG SV	IB	310D	15			203500	224000
65	WESTSHIP/WESTPORT 65	HT	MY	FBG SV	IB T	310D	20			524500	576000
				----- 1984 BOATS -----							
48	WESTPORT	HT	MY	FBG SV	IB	T270D CAT	15 1	45000	4 6	208500	229500
56	WESTPORT	HT	MY	FBG SV	IB	T500D GM	17	55000	4 6	268000	294500
64	CABO 649	FB	MY	F/S SV	IB	T370D GM	20	85000	4 6	499000	548500
	IB T375D GM	499500	549000,	IB T380D CUM	499000	548500,	IB T435D GM	504500	554500
	IB T450D S&S	504000	554000,	IB T463D CAT	511500	562000,	IB T500D GM	511000	561500
	IB T570D GM	518500	570000,	IB T675D GM	527500	580000
65	WESTPORT	HT	MY	FBG SV	IB	T500D CAT	20	50T	5	549500	603500
70	WESTPORT	HT	MY	FBG SV	IB	T500D CAT	20	53T	5	650000	714000

....For earlier years, see the BUC Used Boat Price Guide, Volume 3

WHISSTOCKS MARINE
WOODBRIDGE ENGLAND   See inside cover to adjust price for area

LOA FT IN	NAME AND/ OR MODEL	TOP/ RIG	BOAT TYPE	-HULL- MTL TP	TP #	----ENGINE--- HP MFG	BEAM FT IN	WGT LBS	DRAFT FT IN	RETAIL LOW	RETAIL HIGH
				----- 1986 BOATS -----							
35	WHISSTOCK 35	CUT	SA/RC	AL KL	IB	D	11 5	11900	5 3	41500	46100
40 6	WHISSTOCK 40	SLP	SA/RC	AL KL	IB	D	12 3	18390	5 9	79800	87700
45	WHISSTOCK 45	SLP	SA/RC	AL KL	IB	D	13	23430	5 11	109500	120500
47 6	WHISSTOCK 48	KTH	SA/RC	AL KL	IB	D	14	30865		139000	153000
52 6	WHISSTOCK 53	SLP	SA/RC	AL KL	IB	D	14 6	35123	7 3	181000	199000
62	WHISSTOCK 62	CUT	SA/RC	AL CB	IB	D	16 10	74800		404000	444000
75	WHISSTOCK 75	KTH	SA/RC	AL CB	IB	D	20 6	55T		**	**

WHITBY BOAT WORKS LTD
WHITBY ONTARIO CANADA   COAST GUARD MFG ID- WBW See inside cover to adjust price for area

LOA FT IN	NAME AND/ OR MODEL	TOP/ RIG	BOAT TYPE	-HULL- MTL TP	TP #	----ENGINE--- HP MFG	BEAM FT IN	WGT LBS	DRAFT FT IN	RETAIL LOW	RETAIL HIGH
				----- 1988 BOATS -----							
37 2	ALBERG 37	SLP	SA/RC	FBG KL	SD	28D VLVO	10 2	16800	5 6	66400	73000
37 2	ALBERG 37	YWL	SA/RC	FBG KL	SD	28D VLVO	10 2	16800	5 6	66400	73000
42	WHITBY 42	KTH	SA/CR	FBG KL	SD	62D VLVO	13	23500	5	110500	121500
42	WHITBY 42 CUTTER RIG	KTH	SA/CR	FBG KL	SD	62D VLVO	13	23500	5	114000	125000
45	WHITBY 45 MARK II	SLP	SA/RC	FBG KL	IB	51D PERK	12	23500	6	134000	147000
45 6	WHITBY 45 MARK II	SLP	SA/RC	FBG KL	IB	51D PERK	12	22100	8	130000	143000
55	WHITBY 55	KTH	SA/CR	FBG KL	SD	65D VLVO	15 5		5 4	300000	330000
				----- 1987 BOATS -----							
37 2	ALBERG 37	SLP	SA/RC	FBG KL	SD	28D VLVO	10 2	16800	5 6	63000	69200
37 2	ALBERG 37	YWL	SA/RC	FBG KL	SD	28D VLVO	10 2	16800	5 6	63000	69200
42	WHITBY 42	KTH	SA/CR	FBG KL	SD	62D VLVO	13	23500	5	104500	115000
42	WHITBY 42 CUTTER RIG	KTH	SA/CR	FBG KL	SD	62D VLVO	13	23500	5	108000	118500
45	WHITBY 45 MARK II	SLP	SA/RC	FBG KL	IB	51D PERK	12	23500	6	127000	139500
45 6	WHITBY 45 MARK II	SLP	SA/RC	FBG KL	IB	51D PERK	12	22100	8	123000	135500
55	WHITBY 55	KTH	SA/CR	FBG KL	SD	65D VLVO	15 5		5 4	284500	312500
				----- 1986 BOATS -----							
30	ALBERG 30	SLP	SA/RC	FBG KL	IB	18D VLVO	8 9	9000	4 3	26600	29500
37 2	ALBERG 37	SLP	SA/RC	FBG KL	SD	28D VLVO	10 2	16800	5 6	59700	65600
37 2	ALBERG 37	YWL	SA/RC	FBG KL	SD	28D VLVO	10 2	16800	5 6	59700	65600
42	WHITBY 42	CUT	SA/CR	FBG KL	SD	62D VLVO	13	23500	5	100500	110500
42	WHITBY 42	KTH	SA/CR	FBG KL	SD	62D VLVO	13	23500	5	99400	109000
42	WHITBY 42 CUTTER RIG	KTH	SA/CR	FBG KL	IB	62D VLVO	13	23500	5	102000	112000
45	WHITBY 45 MARK II	SLP	SA/RC	FBG KL	IB	51D PERK	12	23500	6	120000	132000
45 6	WHITBY 45 MARK II	SLP	SA/RC	FBG KL	IB	51D PERK	12	22100	8	117000	128500

WHITBY BOAT WORKS LTD   -CONTINUED   See inside cover to adjust price for area

LOA FT IN	NAME AND/ OR MODEL	TOP/ RIG	BOAT TYPE	-HULL- MTL TP	TP #	ENGINE HP MFG	BEAM FT IN	WGT LBS	DRAFT FT IN	RETAIL LOW	RETAIL HIGH
						1986 BOATS					
55	WHITBY 55	KTH	SA/CR	FBG KL	SD	65D VLVO	15 5		5 4	269500	296000
						1985 BOATS					
30 3	ALBERG 30	SLP	SA/RC	FBG KL	SD	18D VLVO	8 9	9000	4 3	25200	28000
37 2	ALBERG 37	SLP	SA/RC	FBG KL	SD	28D VLVO	10 2	16800	5 6	56500	62100
37 2	ALBERG 37	YWL	SA/RC	FBG KL	SD	28D VLVO	10 2	16800	5 6	56500	62100
42	WHITBY 42	CUT	SA/CR	FBG KL	IB	62D VLVO	13	23500	5	95400	105500
42	WHITBY 42	KTH	SA/CR	FBG KL	IB	62D VLVO	13	23500	5	93500	103000
42	WHITBY 42 CUTTER RIG	KTH	SA/CR	FBG KL	IB	62D VLVO	13	23500	5	97300	107000
45	WHITBY 45 MARK II	SLP	SA/CR	FBG KL	IB	51D PERK	12	23500	6	114000	125000
45	WHITBY 45 MARK II	SLP	SA/RC	FBG KL	IB	51D PERK	12	22100	8	110500	121500
55	WHITBY 55	KTH	SA/CR	FBG KL	SD	65D VLVO	15 5	42000	5 4	255000	280000
						1984 BOATS					
30 3	ALBERG 30	SLP	SA/RC	FBG KL	SD	18D VLVO	8 9	9000	4 3	23900	26500
37 2	ALBERG 37	SLP	SA/RC	FBG KL	SD	28D VLVO	10 2	16800	5 6	53600	58900
37 2	ALBERG 37	YWL	SA/RC	FBG KL	SD	28D VLVO	10 2	16800	5 6	53600	58900
42	WHITBY 42	CUT	SA/CR	FBG KL	IB	62D VLVO	13	23500	5	90400	99400
42	WHITBY 42	KTH	SA/CR	FBG KL	IB	62D VLVO	13	23500	5	88600	97400
42	WHITBY 42 CUTTER RIG	KTH	SA/CR	FBG KL	IB	62D VLVO	13	23500	5	92200	101500
45	WHITBY 45 MARK II	SLP	SA/CR	FBG KL	IB	50D PERK	12	23500	6	108000	118500
45	WHITBY 45 MARK II	SLP	SA/RC	FBG KL	IB	50D PERK	12	22100	8	105000	115000
55	WHITBY 55	KTH	SA/CR	FBG KL	SD	65D VLVO	15 5		5 4	241500	265500

....For earlier years, see the BUC Used Boat Price Guide, Volume 3

WIDEBEAM LIMITED
BELL WORKS
LEICESTER UNITED KINGDOM   See inside cover to adjust price for area

FORMERLY BELL WOODWORKING LTD

For more recent years, see the BUC Used Boat Price Guide, Volume 1

LOA FT IN	NAME AND/ OR MODEL	TOP/ RIG	BOAT TYPE	-HULL- MTL TP	TP #	ENGINE HP MFG	BEAM FT IN	WGT LBS	DRAFT FT IN	RETAIL LOW	RETAIL HIGH
						1985 BOATS					
16	MIRROR 16	SLP	SA/OD	PLY CB	OB			320	6	2550	3000
16 6	FIREBALL	SLP	SA/CR	PLY CB			4 6	180	5	2050	2450
18 6	SEAGULL	SLP	SA/CR	PLY KL	OB		6 9	1750	1 5	6350	7300
20	MIRADOR	SLP	SA/CR	PLY KL	OB		8 2	2000	9	7050	8100
						1984 BOATS					
16	MIRROR 16	SLP	SA/OD	PLY CB	OB			320	6	2400	2800
16 6	FIREBALL	SLP	SA/CR	PLY CB			4 6	180	5	1900	2300
18 6	SEAGULL	SLP	SA/CR	PLY KL	OB		6 9	1750	1 5	5950	6850
20	MIRADOR	SLP	SA/CR	PLY KL	OB		8 2	2000	9	6650	7650

....For earlier years, see the BUC Used Boat Price Guide, Volume 3

WIGGERS CUSTOM YACHTS
BOWMANVILLE ONTARIO CANADA   See inside cover to adjust price for area

For more recent years, see the BUC Used Boat Price Guide, Volume 1

LOA FT IN	NAME AND/ OR MODEL	TOP/ RIG	BOAT TYPE	-HULL- MTL TP	TP #	ENGINE HP MFG	BEAM FT IN	WGT LBS	DRAFT FT IN	RETAIL LOW	RETAIL HIGH
						1985 BOATS					
37	PETERSON 37	SLP	SA/RC	FBG KL	IB	D	11 11	12000	6 8	35000	38900
39 10	DIVA	SLP	SA/RC	FBG KL	IB	D	12 8	12320	7 1	41400	46000

LEE S WILBUR & CO
MANSET ME 04656   COAST GUARD MFG ID- LSW See inside cover to adjust price for area

LOA FT IN	NAME AND/ OR MODEL	TOP/ RIG	BOAT TYPE	-HULL- MTL TP	TP #	ENGINE HP MFG	BEAM FT IN	WGT LBS	DRAFT FT IN	RETAIL LOW	RETAIL HIGH
						1988 BOATS					
34 4	WILBUR 34	OP	BASS	FBG SV	IB	D	12	13000	3 8	**	**
34 4	WILBUR 34	HT	OVNTR	FBG SV	IB	D	12	14000	3 8	**	**
34 4	WILBUR 34 CRUISER	FB	CBNCR	FBG SV	IB	D	12	14000	3 8	**	**
34 4	WILBUR 34 WEEKENDER	FB	WKNDR	FBG SV	IB	D	12	14000	3 8	**	**
						1987 BOATS					
34	WILBUR 34	HT	OVNTR	FBG DS	IB	D	12	14000	3 8	**	**
34	WILBUR 34	OP	SF	FBG DS	IB	D	12	14000	3 8	**	**
34	WILBUR 34	OP	SF	FBG DS	IB	260D-350D	12	13000	3 8	112000	127500
34	WILBUR 34	FB	WKNDR	FBG DS	IB	D	12	14000	3 8	**	**
34	WILBUR 34 CRUISER	FB	CBNCR	FBG DS	IB	D	12	14000	3 8	**	**
34	WILBUR 34 CRUISER	FB	CBNCR	FBG DS	IB	265D-375D	12	14000	3 8	132000	154500
38	WILBUR 38	FB	SF	FBG DS	IB	410D GM	12 9	21500	4	184500	202500
38	WILBUR 38	FB	SF	FBG DS	IB	T300D VLVO	12 9	21500	4	190500	209000
38	WILBUR 38	FB	SF	FBG DS	IB	T375D CAT	12 9	21500	4	211000	232000
38	WILBUR 38	FB	SPTCR	FBG DS	IB	410D GM	12 9	22500	4	191000	209500
38	WILBUR 38	FB	SPTCR	FBG DS	IB	T300D VLVO	12 9	22500	4	197000	216000
38	WILBUR 38	FB	SPTCR	FBG DS	IB	T375D CAT	12 9	22500	4	217500	239000
46 2	WILBUR/NEWMAN 46	FB	CBNCR	FBG DS	IB	350D	15 5		4 6	235500	259000
46 2	WILBUR/NEWMAN 46	FB	CBNCR	FBG DS	IB	11CD	15 5		4 6	250500	275000
61	WILBUR/HUNT 60		CR	FBG DS	IB		17	60000	5 2	**	**
61	WILBUR/HUNT 60	FB	MY	FBG DS	IB	T D GM	16 9		3 2	**	**
						1986 BOATS					
34	WILBUR 34		SF	FBG DS	IB	260D-350D		13000	3 9	107500	122500
34	WILBUR 34 CRUISER		CBNCR	FBG DS	IB	260D-350D		14500	3 9	128500	148000
38	WILBUR 38		SPTCR	FBG DS	IB	410D GM	13	28000	4	215000	236000
38	WILBUR/HUNT 38		CR	FBG DV	IB	350D	13 6			180500	198500
61	WILBUR/HUNT 60		CR	FBG DS	IB		17	60000	5 2	**	**
						1985 BOATS					
34	WILBUR 34 CRUISER		CBNCR	FBG DS	IB	200	12	13500	3 8	91700	101000
38	WILBUR 38		SF	FBG DS	IB	410D	13	24000	4	182500	200500
46	WILBUR/NEWMAN 46		CR	FBG DS	IB	550D	15			225000	247500
						1984 BOATS					
34	WILBUR 34		SF	FBG DS	IB	200	12	14500		85400	93800
38	WILBUR 38		SF	FBG DS	IB	405	13	28000	4	179000	196500
38	WILBUR/HUNT 38		SF	FBG SV	IB	T350	13	20000		139500	153500
44	WILBUR/HUNT 44		SF	FBG SV	IB	T405	13	24000		192000	211000

....For earlier years, see the BUC Used Boat Price Guide, Volume 3

THE WILLARD COMPANY INC
ANAHEIM CA 92806   COAST GUARD MFG ID- WLD See inside cover to adjust price for area

LOA FT IN	NAME AND/ OR MODEL	TOP/ RIG	BOAT TYPE	-HULL- MTL TP	TP #	ENGINE HP MFG	BEAM FT IN	WGT LBS	DRAFT FT IN	RETAIL LOW	RETAIL HIGH
						1986 BOATS					
40	WILLARD 40	KTH	MS	FBG KL	IB	D	13 8	33000	4 3	110000	121000
40	WILLARD 40	FB	TRWL	FBG DS	IB	130D	13 8	33000		125500	138000
55	LAPWORTH 55	CUT	SA/CR	FBG KL	IB	D	14 6	45000	6	255000	280000
						1985 BOATS					
30	WILLARD 30	FB	TRWL	FBG KL	IB	50D	10 6	17000	4 8	52500	57700
40	WILLARD 40	KTH	MS	FBG KL	IB	D	13 8	33000	4 3	104000	114500
40	WILLARD 40	FB	TRWL	FBG DS	IB	130D	13 8	33000		120000	132000
55	LAPWORTH 55	CUT	SA/CR	FBG KL	IB	D	14 6	45000	6	241000	265000
						1984 BOATS					
30	WILLARD 30	FB	TRWL	FBG KL	IB	50D	10 6	17000		50400	55300
30	WILLARD 8 TON	CUT	SA/CR	FBG KL	IB	D	10 6	17000	4 8	43200	48100
39 9	WILLARD 40	KTH	MS	FBG KL	IB	D	13 8	33000	4 3	97400	107000
39 9	WILLARD 40	FB	TRWL	FBG DS	IB	130D	13 8	33000		114000	125500
55	LAPWORTH 55	CUT	SA/CR	FBG KL	IB	D	14 6	45000	6	228500	251000

....For earlier years, see the BUC Used Boat Price Guide, Volume 3

JOHN WILLIAMS COMPANY INC
MT DESERT ME 04660   COAST GUARD MFG ID- JMW See inside cover to adjust price for area

For more recent years, see the BUC Used Boat Price Guide, Volume 1

LOA FT IN	NAME AND/ OR MODEL	TOP/ RIG	BOAT TYPE	-HULL- MTL TP	TP #	ENGINE HP MFG	BEAM FT IN	WGT LBS	DRAFT FT IN	RETAIL LOW	RETAIL HIGH
						1996 BOATS					
28	STANLEY 28	HT	YTFS	FBG DS	IB	200D VLVO	9 6	8500	2 11	122500	134500
35 8	STANLEY 36	HT	YTFS	FBG DS	IB	350D CAT	12	14000	3 6	241500	265500
39 6	STANLEY 39.2	HT	YTFS	FBG DS	IB	425D CAT	13	18000	5	278500	306000
45 8	STANLEY 44	HT	YTFS	FBG DS	IB	620D GM	14 8	32000	5 7	409500	449500
						1995 BOATS					
28	STANLEY 28	HT	YTFS	FBG DS	IB	200D VLVO	9 6	8500	2 11	116000	127500
35 8	STANLEY 36	HT	YTFS	FBG DS	IB	350D CAT	12	14000	3 6	229500	252000
39 6	STANLEY 39.2	HT	YTFS	FBG DS	IB	425D CAT	13	18000	5	266500	293000
45 8	STANLEY 44	HT	YTFS	FBG DS	IB	620D GM	14 8	32000	5 7	391500	430500
						1994 BOATS					
28	STANLEY 28	HT	YTFS	FBG DS	IB	200D CAT	9 6	8500	2 11	110500	121500
35 8	STANLEY 36	HT	YTFS	FBG DS	IB	300D CAT	12	12500	3 6	198000	217500
39 6	STANLEY 39.2	HT	YTFS	FBG DS	IB	350D CAT	13	15000	5	215500	237000
45 8	STANLEY 44	HT	YTFS	FBG DS	IB	400D GM	14 8	30000	5 7	309500	340000
						1993 BOATS					
28	STANLEY 28	HT	YTFS	FBG DS	IB	200D	9 6	8500	2 11	106000	116500
35 8	STANLEY 36	HT	YTFS	FBG DS	IB	300D	12	12500	3 6	186500	205000

LOA FT	IN	NAME AND/OR MODEL	TOP/RIG	BOAT TYPE	HULL MTL	TP	ENGINE TP	#	HP	MFG	BEAM FT	IN	WGT LBS	DRAFT FT	IN	RETAIL LOW	RETAIL HIGH
		1993 BOATS															
39	6	STANLEY 39.2	HT	YTFS	FBG	DS	IB		350D		13	8	15000	5		201000	221000
45	8	STANLEY 44	HT	YTFS	FBG	DS	IB		400D		14	8	30000	5	7	294500	323500
		1992 BOATS															
28		STANLEY 28	HT	YTFS	FBG	DS	IB		200D		9	6	8500	2	11	101000	111000
35	8	STANLEY 36	HT	YTFS	FBG	DS	IB		300D		12		12500	3	6	178000	195500
39	6	STANLEY 39.2	HT	YTFS	FBG	DS	IB		350D		13	8	15000	5		191500	210500
45	8	STANLEY 44	HT	YTFS	FBG	DS	IB		400D		14	8	30000	5	7	280000	308000
		1991 BOATS															
28		STANLEY 28	HT	YTFS	FBG	DS	IB		200D		9	6	8500	2	11	96600	106000
35	8	STANLEY 36	HT	YTFS	FBG	DS	IB		300D		12		12500	3	6	170000	186500
39	6	STANLEY 39.2	HT	YTFS	FBG	DS	IB		350D		13	8	15000	5		182500	200500
45	8	STANLEY 44	HT	YTFS	FBG	DS	IB		400D		14	8	30000	5	7	267000	293000
		1990 BOATS															
28		STANLEY 28	HT	YTFS	FBG	DS	IB		160D		9	6	8500	2	11	88100	96800
35	8	STANLEY 36	HT	YTFS	FBG	DS	IB		160D		12		12500	3	6	151500	166500
39	6	STANLEY 39.2	HT	YTFS	FBG	DS	IB		160D		13	8	15000	5		162000	178000
45	8	STANLEY 44	HT	YTFS	FBG	DS	IB		250D		14	8	30000	5	7	213000	234000
		1989 BOATS															
28		STANLEY 28	HT	YTFS	FBG	DS	IB		160D		9	6	8500	2	11	84200	92500
35	8	STANLEY 36	HT	YTFS	FBG	DS	IB		160D		12		12500	3	6	144500	159000
39	6	STANLEY 39.2	HT	YTFS	FBG	DS	IB		160D		13	8	15000	5		154500	170000
45	8	STANLEY 44	HT	YTFS	FBG	DS	IB		250D		14	8	30000	5	7	203500	223500
		1988 BOATS															
28		STANLEY 28	HT	YTFS	FBG	DS	IB		160D		9	6	8500	2	11	80600	88500
35	8	STANLEY 36	HT	YTFS	FBG	DS	IB		160D		12		12500	3	6	138500	152000
39	6	STANLEY 39.2	HT	YTFS	FBG	DS	IB		160D		13	8	15000	5		147500	162000
45	8	STANLEY 44	HT	YTFS	FBG	DS	IB		250D		14	8	30000	5	7	194500	213500
		1987 BOATS															
28		STANLEY 28	HT	YTFS	FBG	DS	IB		160D		9	6	8500	2	10	77200	84800
36		STANLEY 36	HT	YTFS	FBG	DS	IB		160D		12		12500			122500	134500
38		STANLEY 38	HT	YTFS	FBG	DS	IB		160D		13		15000			138500	152000
44		STANLEY 44	HT	YTFS	FBG	DS	IB		250D		14	6	30000	5	7	198000	218000
		1986 BOATS															
28		STANLEY 28	HT	YTFS	FBG	DS	IB		200D		9	6	8500			77500	85200
36		STANLEY 36	HT	YTFS	FBG	DS	IB		300D		12		14800			135000	148500
38	2	STANLEY 38	HT	YTFS	FBG	DS	IB		400D		12	4	18000			165000	181500
44	6	STANLEY 44	HT	YTFS	FBG	DS	IB		400D		14	8	30000			209000	229500
		1985 BOATS															
36		STANLEY 36	HT	YTFS	FBG	DS	IB		160D		12		12500			112000	123000
38		STANLEY 38	HT	YTFS	FBG	DS	IB		160D		13		15000			126500	139000
44		STANLEY 44	HT	YTFS	FBG	DS	IB		250D		14	6	30000	5	7	181000	199000

....For earlier years, see the BUC Used Boat Price Guide, Volume 3

WILMETTE BOATWORKS INC
WILMETTE IL 60091   COAST GUARD MFG ID- WUL   See inside cover to adjust price for area

LOA FT	IN	NAME AND/OR MODEL	TOP/RIG	BOAT TYPE	HULL MTL	TP	ENGINE TP	#	HP	MFG	BEAM FT	IN	WGT LBS	DRAFT FT	IN	RETAIL LOW	RETAIL HIGH
		1984 BOATS															
16	6	WILMETTE 5.0 METER	SLP	SAIL		KL					6	11	800	2		2550	3000
23	11	ALLEGRA 24	CUT	SA/CR	FBG	KL	IB		8D	YAN	8		6500	3	6	14800	16800

WINDFAST MARINE
COSTA MESA CA 92627   See inside cover to adjust price for area

LOA FT	IN	NAME AND/OR MODEL	TOP/RIG	BOAT TYPE	HULL MTL	TP	ENGINE TP	#	HP	MFG	BEAM FT	IN	WGT LBS	DRAFT FT	IN	RETAIL LOW	RETAIL HIGH
		1986 BOATS															
32	6	WILDWIND		SAIL		CT	IB		D		16		1350	3	4	19100	21200
		1985 BOATS															
32	6	WILDWIND		SAIL		CT	IB		D		16		1350	3	4	17500	19900

WINDSHIPS INC
CLEARWATER FL 33520   COAST GUARD MFG ID- WZI   See inside cover to adjust price for area

LOA FT	IN	NAME AND/OR MODEL	TOP/RIG	BOAT TYPE	HULL MTL	TP	ENGINE TP	#	HP	MFG	BEAM FT	IN	WGT LBS	DRAFT FT	IN	RETAIL LOW	RETAIL HIGH
		1987 BOATS															
63	5	WINDSHIP	CUT	SA/CR	F/S KC		IB		210D	CAT	17		81000	5	9	592500	651000
72	1	WINDSHIP	CUT	SA/OD	F/S KC		IB		210D	CAT	18		89000	6	2	**	**
		1986 BOATS															
63	5	WINDSHIP	CUT	SA/CR	F/S KC		IB		210D	CAT	17		81000	5	9	557500	612500
72	1	WINDSHIP	CUT	SA/OD	F/S KC		IB		210D	CAT	18		89000	6		**	**
		1985 BOATS															
63	5	WINDSHIP 63	SLP	SA/CR	FBG	SK	IB		210D	CAT	17		81000	5	9	524000	576000

WINDSPEED CATAMARANS
SAN DIEGO CA 92109   See inside cover to adjust price for area

LOA FT	IN	NAME AND/OR MODEL	TOP/RIG	BOAT TYPE	HULL MTL	TP	ENGINE TP	#	HP	MFG	BEAM FT	IN	WGT LBS	DRAFT FT	IN	RETAIL LOW	RETAIL HIGH
		1985 BOATS															
18		WINDSPEED 18	SLP	SAIL	FBG	CT					8		380			2450	2850
		1984 BOATS															
18		WINDSPEED 18	SLP	SAIL	FBG	CT					7	11	358			2250	2600

WINDWARD MARINE INC
TACOMA WA 98409   COAST GUARD MFG ID- WME   See inside cover to adjust price for area

LOA FT	IN	NAME AND/OR MODEL	TOP/RIG	BOAT TYPE	HULL MTL	TP	ENGINE TP	#	HP	MFG	BEAM FT	IN	WGT LBS	DRAFT FT	IN	RETAIL LOW	RETAIL HIGH
		1985 BOATS															
28		SEARAKER 28	SLP	SAIL	FBG	KL	SD		13D	VLVO	9		8450	4	6	25000	27700
34		SEARAKER 34	CUT	SA/CR	FBG	KL	IB		22D	WEST	10	10	18000	5		55300	60800
34	2	SEARAKER 34 M/S	CUT	MS	FBG	KL	IB		35D	WEST	10	10	18000	5		55400	60900
50	4	SEARAKER 50	CUT	SA/CR	FBG	KL	IB		85D	PERK	13	6	38000	6	6	154500	170000
50		SEARAKER 50 M/S	CUT	MS	FBG	KL	IB		85D	PERK	13	6	38000	6	6	154500	170000
50	4	SEARAKER 50 M/S	KTH	MS	FBG	KL	IB		85D	PERK	13	6	38000	6	6	159000	175000
		1984 BOATS															
28		SEARAKER 28	SLP	SAIL	FBG	KL	SD		13D	VLVO	9		8450	4	6	23500	26100
34		SEARAKER 34	CUT	SA/CR	FBG	KL	IB		23D	WEST	10	10	18000	5		52100	57200
34	2	SEARAKER 34 M/S	CUT	MS	FBG	KL	IB		35D	WEST	10	10	18000	5		52100	57300
50	4	SEARAKER 50	CUT	SA/CR	FBG	KL	IB		85D	PERK	13	6	38000	6	6	145000	159000
50		SEARAKER 50 M/S	CUT	MS	FBG	KL	IB		85D	PERK	13	6	38000	6	6	145000	159500
50	4	SEARAKER 50 M/S	KTH	MS	FBG	KL	IB		85D	PERK	13	6	38000	6	6	149500	164500

....For earlier years, see the BUC Used Boat Price Guide, Volume 3

WINDY BOATS
EXPRESS CRUISERS LTD
LYMINGTON ENGLAND   See inside cover to adjust price for area

LOA FT	IN	NAME AND/OR MODEL	TOP/RIG	BOAT TYPE	HULL MTL	TP	ENGINE TP	#	HP	MFG	BEAM FT	IN	WGT LBS	DRAFT FT	IN	RETAIL LOW	RETAIL HIGH
		1990 BOATS															
24	6	WINDY 7500	OP	RNBT	FBG	SV	IO		180-270		8	2				8650	10500
		IO 275-330	9550	11700, IO 130D-200D	10600	13000, IO T146-T180	10300	11800									
25	7	WINDY 7800	OP	CUD	FBG	SV	IO		180-275		8	2				10600	13000
		IO 330	12000	14000, IO 130D-200D	12800	15700, IO T146-T180	12200	14100									
26	3	WINDY 8000	OP	CR	FBG	SV	IO		205-275		9	3				13400	16100
		IO 330	14700	17000, IO 180D-200D	17600	20000, IO T146-T205	14900	17700									
		IO T130D VLVO	19900	22100													
28	10	WINDY 8800	OP	CR	FBG	SV	IO		270-330		9	3				20200	22900
28	10	WINDY 8800	OP	CR	FBG	SV	IO		T180-T205		9	3				21000	23900
28	10	WINDY 8800	OP	CR	FBG	SV	IO		T130D VLVO		9	3				23200	25800
29	6	WINDY 9000	OP	CR	FBG	SV	IO		270-330		9	9				19200	22200
		IO T180-T275	19900	24200, IO T330	22300	25200, IOT130D-T200D	24000	28100									
32	6	WINDY 9900	OP	CR	FBG	SV	IO		270-330		9	7				35900	41100
		IO T180-T275	37100	43600, IO T330	40500	46400, IOT130D-T200D	46300	53400									

WINGA YACHTS INC
CLEARWATER FL 33515   See inside cover to adjust price for area

LOA FT	IN	NAME AND/OR MODEL	TOP/RIG	BOAT TYPE	HULL MTL	TP	ENGINE TP	#	HP	MFG	BEAM FT	IN	WGT LBS	DRAFT FT	IN	RETAIL LOW	RETAIL HIGH
		1986 BOATS															
28	3	WINGA 862	SLP	SAIL	FBG	KL	SD		10	VLVO	9	7	5700	4	9	22700	25200
29	7	WINGA-PRINCESS	SLP	SAIL	FBG	KL	SD		28D		9	7	8000	4	2	33500	37200
31		WINGA 31	SLP	SAIL	FBG	KL	SD		18		10		7200	4	2	30300	33700
33	2	WINGA-QUEEN	SLP	SAIL	FBG	KL	SD		38D	VLVO	10	7	10000	4	7	42600	47300

LOA FT	LOA IN	NAME AND/ OR MODEL	TOP/ RIG	BOAT TYPE	-HULL- MTL	-HULL- TP	TP	# HP	MFG	BEAM FT	BEAM IN	WGT LBS	DRAFT FT	DRAFT IN	RETAIL LOW	RETAIL HIGH
		1985 BOATS														
28	3	WINGA 860	SLP	SA/RC	FBG	KL	IB	D		9	7	5700	4	11	21800	24200
28	3	WINGA 862	SLP	SA/RC		KL	IB	D		9	7	5700	4	11	21800	24200
33		WINGA-QUEEN	SLP	MS	FBG	KL	IB	D		10	9	9900	4	9	39600	44000
33	2	WINGA-QUEEN	SLP	SA/RC		KL	IB	D	VLVO	10	9	9900	4	9	39600	44000

WINNER BOATS INC

HARBOR INC
FRANKLIN TN 37064-2613

See inside cover to adjust price for area

LOA FT	LOA IN	NAME AND/ OR MODEL	TOP/ RIG	BOAT TYPE	-HULL- MTL	-HULL- TP	TP	# HP	MFG	BEAM FT	BEAM IN	WGT LBS	DRAFT FT	DRAFT IN	RETAIL LOW	RETAIL HIGH
		1989 BOATS														
16	5	ALPHA III	OP	BASS	FBG	DV	OB			6	7	1000			1950	2350
16	10	INTRIGUE 1700	ST	RNBT	FBG	DV	IO	130	MRCR	8	5	2100			3550	4100
17	1	ESCAPE 1750	ST	RNBT	FBG	DV	IO	130-175		7	5	2200			3300	4050
17	1	ESCAPE 1750 OUTBOARD	ST	RNBT	FBG	DV	OB			7	5	1200			2350	2750
17	1	ESCAPE SPORT	ST	RNBT	FBG	DV	IO	175	OMC	7	5	2350			3500	4050
17	1	ESCAPE SPORT 1750	ST	RNBT	FBG	DV	IO	130-175		7	5	2200			3400	4150
17	7	MACH II ZZ880	OP	SKI	FBG	SV	OB			6	11	1000			2000	2400
17	9	TOURNAMENT 1790	OP	BASS	FBG	SV	OB			7	2	1100			2250	2650
18	1	1850 CC	OP	CTRCN	FBG	DV	OB			8		1950			3400	3950
18	1	THE STRIPER	OP	CTRCN	FBG	DV	OB			8		2000			3450	4000
18	3	CHAMELEON CNV	OP	SKI	FBG	DV	OB			7	4	1250			2500	2900
18	3	NIGHTHAWK	OP	BASS	FBG	SV	OB			7	4	1300			2600	3050
18	3	SPIRIT	OP	SKI	FBG	DV	OB			7	3	1300			2550	3000
18	3	TOURNAMENT FX	OP	BASS	FBG	SV	OB			7	4	1350			2700	3100
18	3	TOURNAMENT LEGEND	OP	BASS	FBG	SV	OB			7	4	1250			2550	2950
18	3	TWIN TOURNAMENT	OP	BASS	FBG	SV	OB			7	4	1150			2350	2750
19	1	ESCAPE 1950	ST	RNBT	FBG	DV	IO	130-230		8		2700			4400	5500
19	1	ESCAPE 1950	ST	RNBT	FBG	DV	IO	260		8		3000			4900	5650
19	1	ESCAPE CUDDY 1950	ST	OVNTR	FBG	DV	IO	130-230		8		2900			4750	5750
19	1	ESCAPE CUDDY 1950	ST	OVNTR	FBG	DV	IO	260		8		3000			5150	5950
19	1	ESCAPE SPORT 1950	ST	RNBT	FBG	DV	IO	130-260		8		3000			4700	5750
19	1	INTRIGUE 1900	ST	RNBT	FBG	DV	IO	130-175		7	4	2400			3800	4550
19	1	INTRIGUE SPORT 1900	ST	RNBT	FBG	DV	IO	130-175		7	4	2400			3900	4600
19	3	TOURNAMENT I 2000	OP	BASS	FBG	SV	OB			7	10	1300			2700	3150
19	3	TOURNAMENT II 2000	OP	BASS	FBG	SV	OB			7	10	1350			2750	3200
20	1	MARATHON 2050	ST	SF	FBG	DV	OB			8	1	2350			5150	5900
20	1	MARATHON 2050	ST	SF	FBG	DV	IO	175-200		8	1	2350			5400	6300
22	1	BROUGHAM 2280	ST	SF	FBG	DV	OB			8	6	3500			7600	8750
22	1	BROUGHAM 2280	ST	SF	FBG	DV	IO	175-260		8	6	4300			9050	10900
22	1	CENTER CONSOLE 2280	ST	SF	FBG	DV	OB			8	6	3200			7250	8350
22	1	CENTER CONSOLE 2280	ST	SF	FBG	DV	IO	175-260		8	6	4000			8500	10300
22	1	WINNER SPT CUD 2280	ST	SF	FBG	DV	OB			8	6	3400			7500	8600
22	1	WINNER SPT CUD 2280	ST	SF	FBG	DV	IO	175-260		8	6	4200			8900	10700
		1988 BOATS														
16	5	ALPHA III	OP	BASS	FBG	DV	OB			6	7	1000			1900	2250
16	10	INTRIGUE 1700	ST	RNBT	FBG	DV	IO	130	MRCR	8	5	2100			3350	3850
17	1	ESCAPE 1750	ST	RNBT	FBG	DV	OB			7	5	1200			2300	2700
17	1	ESCAPE 1750	ST	RNBT	FBG	DV	IO	120-175		7	5	2200			3150	3800
17	1	ESCAPE 1750 XL	ST	RNBT	FBG	DV	IO	120-130		7	5	2200			3050	3550
17	1	ESCAPE SPORT	ST	RNBT	FBG	DV	IO	175	OMC	7	5	2350			3250	3800
17	1	ESCAPE SPORT 1750	ST	RNBT	FBG	DV	IO	120-175		7	5	2200			3300	4000
17	7	MACH II ZZ880	OP	SKI	FBG	SV	OB			6	11	1000			1950	2300
17	9	TOURNAMENT 1790	OP	BASS	FBG	SV	OB			7	2	1100			2200	2550
18	1	1850 CC	OP	CTRCN	FBG	DV	OB			8		1950			3250	3800
18	1	THE STRIPER	OP	CTRCN	FBG	DV	OB			8		2000			3300	3850
18	3	CHAMELEON CNV	OP	SKI	FBG	DV	OB			7	4	1250			2400	2800
18	3	SPIRIT	OP	SKI	FBG	DV	OB			7	3	1300			2500	2900
18	3	TOURNAMENT	OP	BASS	FBG	SV	OB			7	4	1150			2300	2700
18	3	TWIN TOURNAMENT	OP	BASS	FBG	SV	OB			7	4	1150			2300	2700
19	1	ESCAPE 1950	ST	RNBT	FBG	DV	IO	128-175		8		2450			3850	4750
19	1	ESCAPE 1950	ST	RNBT	FBG	DV	IO	200-260		8		2700			4150	5150
19	1	ESCAPE CUDDY 1950	ST	OVNTR	FBG	DV	IO	128-175		8		2650			4200	5100
19	1	ESCAPE CUDDY 1950	ST	OVNTR	FBG	DV	IO	200-260		8		2900			4550	5500
19	1	ESCAPE SPORT 1950	ST	RNBT	FBG	DV	IO	128-200		8		2450			3950	4950
19	1	ESCAPE SPORT 1950	ST	RNBT	FBG	DV	IO	230-260		8		2700			4450	5250
19	3	TOURNAMENT I 2000	OP	BASS	FBG	SV	OB			7	10	1300			2600	3050
19	3	TOURNAMENT II 2000	OP	BASS	FBG	SV	OB			7	10	1350			2700	3100
22	1	BROUGHAM 2280	ST	SF	FBG	DV	OB			8	6	3500			7400	8500
22	1	BROUGHAM 2280	ST	SF	FBG	DV	IO	175-260		8	6	4300			8500	10300
22	1	CENTER CONSOLE 2280	ST	SF	FBG	DV	OB			8	6	3200			7050	8100
22	1	CENTER CONSOLE 2280	ST	SF	FBG	DV	IO	175-260		8	6	4000			8050	9800
22	1	WINNER SPT CUD 2280	ST	SF	FBG	DV	OB			8	6	3400			7250	8350
22	1	WINNER SPT CUD 2280	ST	SF	FBG	DV	IO	175-260		8	6	4200			8350	10100
22	1	WINNER SPT CUD 2280	ST	SF	FBG	DV	SE	T		8	6	3000			**	**
		1987 BOATS														
17	1	ESCAPE 1750	ST	RNBT	FBG	DV	OB			7	5	1200			2250	2600
17	1	ESCAPE 1750	ST	RNBT	FBG	DV	SE			7	5	2000			**	**
17	1	ESCAPE 1750	ST	RNBT	FBG	DV	IO	120-175		7	5	2000			2850	3350
17	1	ESCAPE 1750 XL	ST	RNBT	FBG	DV	IO	120		7	5	2000			2750	3200
17	1	ESCAPE SPORT	ST	RNBT	FBG	DV	IO	175	OMC	7	5	2000			2900	3350
17	1	ESCAPE SPORT 1750	ST	RNBT	FBG	DV	SE			7	5	2000			**	**
17	1	ESCAPE SPORT 1750	ST	RNBT	FBG	DV	IO	120-175		7	5	2000			2950	3450
17	1	ESCAPE XL 1750	ST	RNBT	FBG	DV	IO	130	OMC	7	5	2000			2700	3150
17	7	MACH II ZZ880	OP	SKI	FBG	SV	OB			6	11	950			1800	2150
17	9	TOURNAMENT 1790	OP	BASS	FBG	SV	OB			7	2				2100	2450
18	1	1850 CC	OP	CTRCN	FBG	DV	OB			8		1300			2400	2800
18	1	CC 1850	OP	CTRCN	FBG	DV	SE			8		1300			**	**
18	1	THE STRIPER	OP	CTRCN	FBG	DV	OB			8		1300			2400	2800
18	3	CHAMELEON CNV	ST	RNBT	FBG	DV	OB			7	4	1050			2050	2400
18	3	TOURNAMENT	OP	BASS	FBG	SV	OB			7	4	1050			2000	2400
18	3	TWIN TOURNAMENT	OP	BASS	FBG	SV	OB			7	4	1050			2000	2400
19	1	ESCAPE 1950	ST	RNBT	FBG	DV	SE			8		2500			**	**
19	1	ESCAPE 1950	ST	RNBT	FBG	DV	IO	120-230		8		2500			3700	4500
19	1	ESCAPE 1950	ST	RNBT	FBG	DV	IO	260		8		2500			4000	4650
19	1	ESCAPE CUD SPT 1950	ST	OVNTR	FBG	DV	SE			8		2700			**	**
19	1	ESCAPE CUD SPT 1950	ST	OVNTR	FBG	DV	IO	120-260		8		2700			4100	5100
19	1	ESCAPE CUDDY 1950	ST	OVNTR	FBG	DV	SE			8		2700			**	**
19	1	ESCAPE CUDDY 1950	ST	OVNTR	FBG	DV	IO	120-260		8		2700			4000	5000
19	1	ESCAPE SPORT 1950	ST	RNBT	FBG	DV	SE			8		2500			**	**
19	1	ESCAPE SPORT 1950	ST	RNBT	FBG	DV	IO	120-260		8		2500			3800	4750
19	3	TOURNAMENT II 2000	OP	BASS	FBG	SV	OB			7	10	1200			2350	2750
22	1	WINNER SPT CUD 2280	ST	SF	FBG	DV	OB			8	6	3000			6600	7600
22	1	WINNER SPT CUD 2280	ST	SF	FBG	DV	SE	T		8	6	3000			**	**
		1986 BOATS														
16	2	Z660	OP	BASS	FBG	SV	OB			6	6	810			1450	1700
17		ESCAPE 1700	ST	RNBT	FBG	DV	IO	120-175		7	4	2000			2700	3150
17		ESCAPE 1700 OB	ST	RNBT	FBG	DV	OB			7	4	1200			2200	2550
17	6	Z880	OP	BASS	FBG	SV	OB			6	11	900			1700	2000
17	6	ZZ880	OP	SKI	FBG	SV	OB			6	11	950			1750	2050
18		SEA QUEST 1800	OP	FSH	FBG	DV	OB			8		1800			2900	3400
18	2	TOURNAMENT	OP	BASS	FBG	SV	OB			7	4	1050			1950	2300
18	2	TOURNAMENT II	OP	BASS	FBG	SV	OB			7	4	1050			2000	2350
19		ESCAPE 1900	ST	RNBT	FBG	DV	IO	170-260		8		2500			3500	4350
19		ESCAPE 1900 CUDDY	ST	OVNTR	FBG	DV	IO	170-260		8		2700			3850	4800
19		ESCAPE 1900 SPORT	ST	RNBT	FBG	DV	IO	170-260		8		2500			3650	4550
19	3	TOURNAMENT 2000	OP	BASS	FBG	SV	OB			7	10	1200			2300	2700
		1985 BOATS														
16	2	Z660	OP	BASS	FBG	SV	OB			6	6	810			1400	1650
16	2	ZZ660	OP	RNBT	FBG	SV	OB			6	6	850			1500	1750
17		ESCAPE 17	OP	RNBT	FBG	DV	IO	120-170		7	4	2000			2600	3050
17	6	Z880	OP	BASS	FBG	SV	OB			6	11	900			1650	1950
17	6	ZZ880	OP	RNBT	FBG	SV	OB			6	11	950			1700	2050
18	2	TOURNAMENT	OP	BASS	FBG	SV	OB			7	4	1050			1900	2250
19		ESCAPE 19	OP	RNBT	FBG	DV	IO	170-260		8		2500			3400	4250
19		ESCAPE CUDDY	ST	CUD	FBG	DV	IO	170-260		8		2700			3700	4600
19		ESCAPE SPORT	ST	RNBT	FBG	DV	IO	170-260		8		2500			3400	4250
		1984 BOATS														
17		1700 ESCAPE	OP	RNBT	FBG	DV	IO	120-185		7	4				2550	3000
17	6	ZZ880	OP	SKI	FBG	DV	OB			6	11	930			1600	1900
18	2	TOURNAMENT	OP	BASS	FBG	DV	OB			7	4	1025			1800	2150
19		1900 CUDDY	OP	CUD	FBG	DV	IO	170-260		8		2700			3550	4400
19		1900 ESCAPE	OP	CUD	FBG	DV	IO	170	MRCR	8		2500			3400	3950
19		1900 ESCAPE	OP	RNBT	FBG	DV	IO	170-230		8		2500			3250	3950
19		1900 ESCAPE	OP	RNBT	FBG	DV	IO	260	MRCR	8		2500			3500	4100
19		1900 ESCAPE	OP	RNBT	FBG	DV	IB	260	OMC	8		2500			4750	5450
19		1900 SPORT	OP	RNBT	FBG	DV	IO	170-260		8		2500			3300	4100

WISNER BROTHERS BOAT BLDRS

S NORWALK CT 06854

See inside cover to adjust price for area

LOA FT	LOA IN	NAME AND/ OR MODEL	TOP/ RIG	BOAT TYPE	-HULL- MTL	-HULL- TP	TP	# HP	MFG	BEAM FT	BEAM IN	WGT LBS	DRAFT FT	DRAFT IN	RETAIL LOW	RETAIL HIGH
		1986 BOATS														
23	8	WISNER CAT	SLP	SA/CR	FBG	CT	IB	D		11	4	8900	2	6	11700	13300
37	10	WISNER	SLP	SA/RC	FBG	KC	IB	D		12	1	14900	5	6	48500	53300
55		WISNER	SLP	SA/RC	FBG	CT	IB	D		25		35000	4		188000	206500

WISNER BROTHERS BOAT BLDRS   -CONTINUED   See inside cover to adjust price for area

LOA FT IN	NAME AND/ OR MODEL	TOP/ RIG	BOAT TYPE	-HULL- MTL TP	TP	ENGINE # HP	MFG	BEAM FT IN	WGT LBS	DRAFT FT IN	RETAIL LOW	RETAIL HIGH
------- 1985 BOATS -------
23 8	WISNER CAT	SLP	SA/CR	FBG CT	IB	D		11 4	8900	2 6	11000	12500
37 10	WISNER	SLP	SA/RC	FBG KC	IB			12 1	14900	5 6	42200	49100
37 10	WISNER	SLP	SA/CR	FBG KC	IB	D		12 1	14900	5 6	44900	49900
55	WISNER	SLP	SA/CR	FBG CT				25	35000	4	176000	193500
55	WISNER	SLP	SA/CR	FBG CT	IB	D		25	35000	4	176000	193500
------- 1984 BOATS -------
23 8	CAT BOAT	SLP	SA/CR	FBG KC	IB	D		11 4	8900	2 6	17400	19800
37 10	COLD MOLDED	SLP	SA/CR	FBG KC	IB	D		12 1	14900	5 6	42100	46700
55	CATAMARAN	SLP	SA/CR	FBG KL	IB	D		25	35000	4	148000	162500

....For earlier years, see the BUC Used Boat Price Guide, Volume 3

WITNESS CATAMARANS
FT MYERS FL 33901   COAST GUARD MFG ID- GUS See inside cover to adjust price for area

LOA FT IN	NAME AND/ OR MODEL	TOP/ RIG	BOAT TYPE	-HULL- MTL TP	TP	ENGINE # HP	MFG	BEAM FT IN	WGT LBS	DRAFT FT IN	RETAIL LOW	RETAIL HIGH
------- 1986 BOATS -------
35 8	WITNESS 35	SLP	SA/CR	FBG CT	SD	T 13D		17	13500	2 6	75600	83100
36	WITNESS 36 C	SLP	SA/CR	FBG CT	SD	T 13D		17	13500	2 6	74000	81300
36	WITNESS 36 S	SLP	SA/RC	FBG CT	HD	19D		17	11500	2 6	70800	77800
------- 1985 BOATS -------
35 8	WITNESS 35	SLP	SA/CR	FBG CT	SD	T 13D		17	13500	2 6	71100	78100
36 1	WITNESS 36	SLP	SA/RC	FBG CT	HD	22D		17	11500	2 6	67000	73700
------- 1984 BOATS -------
34 8	WITNESS 35	SLP	SA/CR	FBG CT	SD	T 10D	BUKH	16 11	13500	2 6	61900	68100
34 8	WITNESS 35	SLP	SA/CR	FBG CT	SD	T 15	OMC	16 11	11500	2 2	59100	65000

....For earlier years, see the BUC Used Boat Price Guide, Volume 3

WOOD MARINE COMPANY
DIV OF BOAT BARN INC
COUPEVILLE WA 98239   COAST GUARD MFG ID- BXA   See inside cover to adjust price for area

LOA FT IN	NAME AND/ OR MODEL	TOP/ RIG	BOAT TYPE	-HULL- MTL TP	TP	ENGINE # HP	MFG	BEAM FT IN	WGT LBS	DRAFT FT IN	RETAIL LOW	RETAIL HIGH
------- 1986 BOATS -------
23 11	WOOD-MARINE	SLP	SA/CR	P/C KL	OB			7 10	3900	2 10	8350	9550
------- 1984 BOATS -------
23 7	WOOD-MARINE 24	SLP	SA/CR	P/C KL	IB			7 7	3950	2 3	7350	8450
25	WOOD-MARINE 25	SLP	SA/CR	P/C KL	IB	8D	REN	7 10	4280	2 9	9500	10800

....For earlier years, see the BUC Used Boat Price Guide, Volume 3

WORLDCRUISER YACHT CO
COSTA MESA CA 92626   COAST GUARD MFG ID- WUC See inside cover to adjust price for area

LOA FT IN	NAME AND/ OR MODEL	TOP/ RIG	BOAT TYPE	-HULL- MTL TP	TP	ENGINE # HP	MFG	BEAM FT IN	WGT LBS	DRAFT FT IN	RETAIL LOW	RETAIL HIGH
------- 1985 BOATS -------
32	WESTSAIL 32	SLP	SA/CR	FBG KL	IB	51D	PERK	11	19500	5	71300	78300
38 8	WESTSAIL 39	CUT	SA/CR	FBG KL	IB	51D	PERK	11 10	19200	5	83400	91700
42 11	WESTSAIL 42	SCH	SA/CR	FBG KL	IB	60D		13	31500	5 9	129500	142000
42 11	WESTSAIL 42	CUT	SA/CR	FBG KL	IB	60D		13	31500	5 9	128000	140500
42 11	WESTSAIL 42	KTH	SA/CR	FBG KL	IB	60D		13	31500	5 9	136000	149500
42 11	WESTSAIL 43	SCH	SA/CR	FBG KL	IB	60D		13	31500	5 9	129500	142000
42 11	WORLDCRUISER 43 PH	KTH	SA/CR	FBG KL	IB	85D	PERK	13	31500	5 9	136000	149500
43 11	TRADITIONAL SCHOONER	SCH	SA/CR	FBG KL	SD	25D	VLVO	11	23000	6 2	111000	122000
43 11	TRADITIONAL SCHOONER	SCH	SA/CR	FBG KL	IB	42D	PATH	11	23000	6 2	111500	122500
50	FLUSHDECK SCHOONER	SCH	SA/CR	FBG KL	IB	85D	PERK	13	32000	6 8	161000	177000
------- 1984 BOATS -------
32	WESTSAIL 32	SLP	SA/CR	FBG KL	IB	42D	PATH	11	19500	5	67000	73700
36 9	PILOTHOUSE	SLP	SA/CR	FBG KL	SD	25D	VLVO	10 10	15500	5 11	61100	67200
36 9	PILOTHOUSE	SLP	SA/CR	FBG KL	IB	27D	PISC	10 10	15500	5 11	61100	67200
38 8	WESTSAIL 39	CUT	SA/CR	FBG KL	IB	42D	PATH	11 10	19200	5	78400	86200
42 11	WESTSAIL 42	SCH	SA/CR	FBG KL	IB	50D	PERK	13	31500	5 9	120500	132500
42 11	WESTSAIL 42	CUT	SA/CR	FBG KL	IB	60D		13	31500	5 9	120000	131500
42 11	WESTSAIL 42	KTH	SA/CR	FBG KL	IB	60D		13	31500	5 9	127000	140000
42 11	WESTSAIL 43	SCH	SA/CR	FBG KL	IB	60D		13	31500	5 9	121000	133000
42 11	WORLDCRUISER 43 PH	KTH	SA/CR	FBG KL	IB	85D	PERK	13	31500	5 9	127500	140000
43 11	TRADITIONAL SCHOONER	SCH	SA/CR	FBG KL	SD	25D	VLVO	11	23000	6 2	104000	114500
43 11	TRADITIONAL SCHOONER	SCH	SA/CR	FBG KL	IB	42D	PATH	11	23000	6 2	104500	115000
50	FLUSHDECK SCHOONER	SCH	SA/CR	FBG KL	IB	85D	PERK	13	32000	6 8	151500	166000

....For earlier years, see the BUC Used Boat Price Guide, Volume 3

WORLDWIDE SAILING YACHTS CO
HIGHLND PK IL 60035   See inside cover to adjust price for area

LOA FT IN	NAME AND/ OR MODEL	TOP/ RIG	BOAT TYPE	-HULL- MTL TP	TP	ENGINE # HP	MFG	BEAM FT IN	WGT LBS	DRAFT FT IN	RETAIL LOW	RETAIL HIGH
------- 1985 BOATS -------
36	CRUISING 36	CUT	SA/CR	FBG KL	IB	D		12	17200	5 6	65200	71700
------- 1984 BOATS -------
36	CRUISING 36	CUT	SA/CR	FBG KL	IB	D		12	17200	5 6	61400	67400

X-YACHTS
STAMFORD CT 06902   COAST GUARD MFG ID- XYA See inside cover to adjust price for area

For more recent years, see the BUC Used Boat Price Guide, Volume 1

LOA FT IN	NAME AND/ OR MODEL	TOP/ RIG	BOAT TYPE	-HULL- MTL TP	TP	ENGINE # HP	MFG	BEAM FT IN	WGT LBS	DRAFT FT IN	RETAIL LOW	RETAIL HIGH
------- 1996 BOATS -------
29 8	X-302	SLP	SARAC	F/S KL	IB	18D	YAN	9 8	8370	5 5	71000	78000
32 8	X-99	SLP	SAROD	F/S KL	IB	10D	VLVO	9 8	6570	5 7	57000	62700
33	X-332	SLP	SARAC	F/S KL	IB	18D	YAN	10 8	9590	5 9	83300	91500
35 1	X-362	SLP	SARAC	F/S KL	IB	20D	YAN	11 4	11440	6 2	102000	112000
35 1	X-362 CLASSIC	SLP	SARAC	F/S KL	IB	20D	YAN	11 4	11440	6 2	99200	109000
37	IMX-38	SLP	SAROD	F/S KL	IB	28D	VLVO	12 1	11800	6 9	111000	122000
37 7	X-382	SLP	SARAC	F/S KL	IB	30D	YAN	12 2	14300	6 2	132000	145000
41	X-412 3 CABIN	SLP	SARAC	F/S KL	IB	43D	YAN	12 8	16314	6 9	170000	188000
41	X-412 4 CABIN	SLP	SARAC	F/S KL	IB	43D	YAN	12 8	16314	6 9	174000	191000
44 3	X-442 3 CABIN	SLP	SARAC	F/S KL	IB	51D	YAN	13 6	21300	7 5	234000	257000
44 3	X-442 4 CABIN	SLP	SARAC	F/S KL	IB	51D	YAN	13 6	21300	7 5	237000	260500
48	X-482 CLASSIC	SLP	SARAC	F/S KL	IB	75D	YAN	14	26455	8 2	307000	337500
48	X-482 CLASSIC 4 CAB	SLP	SARAC	F/S KL	IB	75D	YAN	14	26455	8 2	310000	341000
51 1	X-512	SLP	SARAC	F/S KL	IB	88D	YAN	14 8	30112	8	383000	421000
60	X-612	SLP	SARAC	F/S KL	IB	110D	YAN	16 7	49606	9 5	728000	800000
------- 1994 BOATS -------
30 4	X-312	SLP	SARAC	F/S KL	IB	18D	VLVO	9 10	7400	5 6	56000	61600
32 10	X-99	SLP	SAROD	F/S KL	IB	10D	VLVO	9 10	6280	5 9	48100	52800
33 6	X-342	SLP	SARAC	F/S KL	IB	18D	VLVO	10 9	9200	6 1	70500	77500
35 1	X-362	SLP	SAROD	F/S KL	IB	20D	VLVO	11 5	11440	6 2	88500	97300
37 5	IMX-38	SLP	SAROD	F/S KL	IB	28D	VLVO	12 1	14333	6 11	98500	108000
37 9	X-382	SLP	SARAC	F/S KL	IB	28D	VLVO	12 1	14333	6 2	117000	128500
41	X-412	SLP	SARAC	F/S KL	IB	43D	VLVO	12 10	16314	6 2	151500	166500
44 4	X-442	SLP	SARAC	F/S KL	IB	59D	VLVO	13 7	21300	7 6	208000	228500
51 1	X-512	SLP	SARAC	F/S KL	IB	88D	YAN	14 10	30112	8	335500	369000
------- 1993 BOATS -------
26 1	X-79	SLP	SACAC	F/S KL	OB			9 6	2960	4 4	18900	21000
30 4	X-312 FRAC RIG	SLP	SACAC	F/S KL	IB	18D	VLVO	9 10	7400	5 6	52900	58100
30 4	X-312 MH RIG	SLP	SACAC	F/S KL	IB	18D	VLVO	9 10	7400	5 6	52400	57600
32 10	X-99	SLP	SACAC	F/S KL	IB	10D	VLVO	9 10	6280	5 9	44600	49500
33	X-3/4 TON	SLP	SACAC	F/S KL	IB	18D	YAN	11 1	7275	6 3	52300	57500
33 6	X-342 FRAC RIG	SLP	SACAC	F/S KL	IB	18D	VLVO	10 9	9200	6 1	66000	72500
33 6	X0342 MH RIG	SLP	SACAC	F/S KL	IB	18D	VLVO	10 9	9200	6 1	65300	71800
36 4	X-372 PRESTIGE MH	SLP	SACAC	F/S KL	IB	28D	VLVO	10 9	11243	6 4	84900	93300
36 4	X-372 SPORT FRAC	SLP	SACAC	F/S KL	IB	28D	VLVO	12	11243	6 1	82900	91100
37 9	X-382	SLP	SACAC	F/S KL	IB	28D	VLVO	12	14333	6 2	109000	120000
39 5	X-119	SLP	SACAC	F/S KL	IB	18D	VLVO	11	11466	6	100500	110000
39 9	X-1 TON	SLP	SACAC	F/S KL	IB	24D	BUKH	13	12676	7 6	111500	122500
41	X-412	SLP	SACAC	F/S KL	SD	43D	VLVO	12 9	16314	7 3	141500	155500
44 3	X-452	SLP	SACAC	F/S KL	IB	55D	YAN	13 11	19730	8 2	186500	205000
51 1	X-512	SLP	SACAC	F/S KL	IB	62D	VLVO	14 9	30112	8	312000	343000
------- 1992 BOATS -------
26 1	X-79	SLP	SAIL	F/S KL	OB			9 6	2960	4 4	17400	19700
30 4	X-312 FRAC RIG	SLP	SA/RC	F/S KL	IB	18D	VLVO	9 10	7400	5 6	49700	54600
30 4	X-312 MH RIG	SLP	SAIL	F/S KL	IB	18D	VLVO	9 10	7400	5 6	49100	54000
32 10	X-99	SLP	SAIL	F/S KL	IB	10D	VLVO	9 10	6280	5 9	42000	46700
33	X-3/4 TON	SLP	SAIL	F/S KL	IB	18D	YAN	11 1	7275	6 3	49300	54200
33 6	X-342 FRAC RIG	SLP	SAIL	F/S KL	IB	18D	VLVO	10 9	9200	6 1	62300	68400
33 6	X0342 MH RIG	SLP	SAIL	F/S KL	IB	18D	VLVO	10 9	9200	6 1	61600	67700
36 4	X-372 PRESTIGE MH	SLP	SAIL	F/S KL	IB	28D	VLVO	10 9	11243	6 4	79900	87800
36 4	X-372 SPORT FRAC	SLP	SAIL	F/S KL	IB	28D	VLVO	12	11243	6 1	78100	85800
37 9	X-382	SLP	SAIL	F/S KL	IB	28D	VLVO	12	14333	6 2	102500	113000
39 5	X-119	SLP	SAIL	F/S KL	IB	18D	VLVO	11	11466	6	94200	103500
39 9	X-1 TON	SLP	SAIL	F/S KL	IB	24D	BUKH	13	12676	7 6	104500	115000

X-YACHTS (continued)

LOA FT	IN	NAME AND/ OR MODEL	TOP/ RIG	BOAT TYPE	HULL MTL	TP	TP	ENG #	HP	MFG	BEAM FT	IN	WGT LBS	DRAFT FT	IN	RETAIL LOW	RETAIL HIGH
		———— 1992 BOATS															
41		X-412	SLP	SAIL	F/S	KL	SD		43D	VLVO	12	9	16314	7	3	133000	146000
44	3	X-452	SLP	SAIL	F/S	KL	SD		55D	YAN	13	11	19730	8	2	174500	192000
51	1	X-512	SLP	SAIL	F/S	KL	IB		62D	VLVO	14	9	30112	6	6	292000	320500
		———— 1991 BOATS															
26	1	X-79	SLP	SAIL	F/S	KL	OB				9	6	2960	4	4	16300	18500
30	4	X-312 FRAC RIG	SLP	SA/RC	F/S	KL	SD		18D	VLVO	9	10	7400	5	6	46900	51500
30	4	X-312 MH RIG	SLP	SA/RC	F/S	KL	SD		18D	VLVO	9	10	7400	5	6	46300	50900
32	10	X-99	SLP	SAIL	F/S	KL	SD		10D	BUKH	9	10	6280	5	9	39500	43900
33		X-3/4 TON	SLP	SAIL	F/S	KL	IB		18D	YAN	11	1	7275	6	3	46500	51100
33	6	X-342 FRAC RIG	SLP	SAIL	F/S	KL	IB		18D	VLVO	10	9	9200	6	1	58600	64300
33	6	X0342 MH RIG	SLP	SAIL	F/S	KL	IB		18D	VLVO	10	9	9200	6	1	58000	63700
36	4	X-372 PRESTIGE MH	SLP	SAIL	F/S	KL	IB		28D	VLVO	11	9	11243	6	6	75000	82400
36	4	X-372 SPORT FRAC	SLP	SAIL	F/S	KL	IB		28D	VLVO	11	9	11243	6	6	73200	80400
39	5	X-119	SLP	SAIL	F/S	KL	IB		18D	VLVO	10	9	11466	6	6	88300	97100
39	9	X-1 TON	SLP	SAIL	F/S	KL	IB		24D	BUKH	13		12676	7	6	98200	108000
41		X-412	SLP	SAIL	F/S	KL	SD		43D	VLVO	12	9	16314	7	3	124500	137000
44	3	X-452	SLP	SAIL	F/S	KL	IB		55D	YAN	13	11	19730	8	2	163500	180000
51	1	X-512	SLP	SAIL	F/S	KL	IB		62D	VLVO	14	9	30112	6	6	273000	300000
		———— 1990 BOATS															
26	1	X-79	SLP	SAIL	F/S	KL	OB				9	6	2960	4	4	15300	17400
30	4	X-312 FRAC RIG	SLP	SA/RC	F/S	KL	SD		18D	VLVO	9	10	7400	5	6	43500	48300
30	4	X-312 M H RIG	SLP	SA/RC	F/S	KL	SD		18D	VLVO	9	10	7400	5	6	43000	47700
32	10	X-99	SLP	SAIL	F/S	KL	SD		10D	BUKH	9	10	6280	5	9	37100	41200
33		X-3/4 TON	SLP	SAIL	F/S	KL	IB		18D	YAN	11	1	7275	6	3	43200	48000
33	6	X-342 FRACTIONAL RIG	SLP	SAIL	F/S	KL	IB		18D	VLVO	10	9	9200	6	1	55200	60700
33	6	X-342 MASTHEAD RTG	SLP	SAIL	F/S	KL	IB		18D	VLVO	10	9	9200	6	1	54600	60000
36	4	X-372 PRESTIGE M H	SLP	SAIL	F/S	KL	IB		28D	VLVO	11	9	11243	6	6	70400	77400
36	4	X-372 SPORT FRACT	SLP	SAIL	F/S	KL	IB		28D	VLVO	11	9	11243	6	6	68500	75300
39	5	X-119	SLP	SAIL	F/S	KL	IB		18D	VLVO	10	9	11466	6	6	82800	91000
39	9	X-402 M H	SLP	SAIL	F/S	KL	IB		28D	VLVO	13		13200	7	3	94600	104000
44	3	X-452	SLP	SAIL	F/S	KL	IB		55D	YAN	13	11	19730	8	2	153500	168500
		———— 1989 BOATS															
26	1	X-79	SLP	SAIL	F/S	KL	OB				9	6	2960	4	4	14400	16300
32	10	X-99	SLP	SAIL	F/S	KL	SD		10D	BUKH	9	10	6280	5	9	34800	38700
33		X-3/4 TON	SLP	SAIL	F/S	KL	IB		18D	YAN	11	1	7275	6	3	40500	45100
33	6	X-342 FRACTIONAL RIG	SLP	SAIL	F/S	KL	IB		18D	VLVO	10	9	9200	6	1	52000	57200
33	6	X-342 MASTHEAD RIG	SLP	SAIL	F/S	KL	IB		18D	VLVO	10	9	9200	6	1	51400	56500
36	4	X-372 PRESTIGE M H	SLP	SAIL	F/S	KL	IB		28D	VLVO	11	9	11243	6	6	66100	72600
36	4	X-372 SPORT FRACT	SLP	SAIL	F/S	KL	IB		28D	VLVO	11	9	11243	6	6	64100	70500
39	5	X-119	SLP	SAIL	F/S	KL	IB		18D	VLVO	10	9	11466	6	6	77600	85300
39	9	X-1 TON	SLP	SAIL	F/S	KL	IB		24D	BUKH	13		12676	7	6	86200	94800
39	9	X-402 M H	SLP	SAIL	F/S	KL	IB		28D	VLVO	13		13200	7	3	88700	97500
44	3	X-452	SLP	SAIL	F/S	KL	IB		55D	YAN	13	11	19730	8	2	143500	157500
		———— 1988 BOATS															
26	1	X-79	SLP	SAIL	F/S	KL	OB				9	6	2960	4	4	13500	15300
32	10	X-99	SLP	SAIL	F/S	KL	SD		10D	BUKH	9	10	6280	5	9	32600	36300
33		X-3/4 TON	SLP	SAIL	F/S	KL	IB		18D	YAN	11	1	7275	6	3	38000	42300
33	6	X-342 FRACTIONAL RIG	SLP	SAIL	F/S	KL	IB		18D	VLVO	10	9	9200	6	1	48500	53300
33	6	X-342 MASTHEAD RIG	SLP	SAIL	F/S	KL	IB		18D	VLVO	10	9	9200	6	1	48500	53300
36	4	X-372 PRESTIGE M H	SLP	SAIL	F/S	KL	IB		28D	VLVO	11	9	11243	6	6	62000	68100
36	4	X-372 SPORT FRACT	SLP	SAIL	F/S	KL	IB		28D	VLVO	11	9	11243	6	6	60300	66200
39	9	X-1 TON	SLP	SAIL	F/S	KL	IB		24D	BUKH	13		12676	7	6	80600	88800
39	9	X-402 M.H.	SLP	SAIL	F/S	KL	IB		28D	VLVO	13		13200	7	3	83100	91300
44	3	X-452	SLP	SAIL	F/S	KL	IB		55D	YAN	13	11	19730	8	2	134500	147500
		———— 1985 BOATS															
26	1	X-79	SLP	SA/OD	F/S	KL	OB				9	6	2960	4	4	11200	12700
26	1	X-79	SLP	SA/RC		KL	OB				9	6	2960	4	3	11200	12700
30	3	X-95	SLP	SA/RC		KL	IB		D		10	6	6710	5	7	28400	31600
30	3	X-95	SLP	SA/RC	F/S	KL	IB		15D	YAN	10	6	6710	5	8	28300	31400
32	11	X 3/4 TON	SLP	SA/RC		KL	IB				11	1	7480	6	2	32400	36000
32	11	X-102	SLP	SA/RC		KL	IB				11	1	7700	6	2	33300	37000
32	11	X-102	SLP	SA/RC	F/S	KL	IB		15D	YAN	11	1	7700	6	2	33200	36900
33		X-3/4 TON	SLP	SA/RC	C/S	KL	IB		20D	BUKH	11	1	7275	6	2	31400	34900
39		X-1 TON	SLP	SA/RC	C/S	KL	IB		36D	BUKH	12	11	12676	7		65600	72100
39	8	X 1 TON	SLP	SA/RC		KL	IB		D		12	11	12760	6	11	66500	73000
39	8	X-402	SLP	SA/RC		KL	IB		D		12	11	13200	7	5	68200	74900
39	9	S-402	SLP	SA/RC	F/S	KL	IB		28D	VLVO	12	11	13200	6	11	68300	75100

YAMAHA MOTOR CORP LTD
KENNESAW GA 30144   COAST GUARD MFG ID- YAM See inside cover to adjust price for area

YAMAHA
SHIZVOKA JAPAN

For more recent years, see the BUC Used Boat Price Guide, Volume 1

LOA FT	IN	NAME AND/ OR MODEL	TOP/ RIG	BOAT TYPE	HULL MTL	TP	TP	ENG #	HP	MFG	BEAM FT	IN	WGT LBS	DRAFT FT	IN	RETAIL LOW	RETAIL HIGH
		———— 1986 BOATS															
16	3	YAMAHA 16 SEALARK	SLP	SAIL	FBG	CB					5	10	265			1950	2300
26		YAMAHA 26	SLP	SA/RC	FBG	KL	IB		D		9	2	4320	5	1	14700	16700
29	5	YAMAHA 30	SLP	SA/RC	FBG	KL	IB		D		10	7	7264	5	9	26700	29700
33	5	YAMAHA 33	SLP	SA/RC	FBG	KL	IB		D		11		10584	6	3	39400	43800
37	5	YAMAHA 37	SLP	SA/RC	FBG	KL	IB		D		11	10	14333	6	7	57000	62600
		———— 1985 BOATS															
16	3	YAMAHA 16 SEALARK	SLP	SAIL	FBG	CB					5	10	265			1800	2150
26		YAMAHA 26	SLP	SA/RC	FBG	KL	IB		D		9	2	4320	5	1	13800	15700
29	5	YAMAHA 30	SLP	SA/RC	FBG	KL	IB		D		10	7	7264	5	9	25100	27900
33	5	YAMAHA 33	SLP	SA/RC	FBG	KL	IB		D		11		10584	6	3	37100	41200
37	5	YAMAHA 37	SLP	SA/RC	FBG	KL	IB		D		11	10	14333	6	7	53600	58900
		———— 1984 BOATS															
16	3	YAMAHA 16 SEALARK	SLP	SAIL	FBG	CB					5	10	265			1700	2050
26	3	YAMAHA 26	SLP	SA/RC	FBG	KL	IB		8D		9	2	4344	5	1	13200	14900
29	5	YAMAHA 30	SLP	SA/RC	FBG	KL	IB		15D		10	7	7264	5	9	23600	26200
33	5	YAMAHA 33	SLP	SA/RC	FBG	KL	IB		D		11		10584	6	3	34900	38800
34	1	YAMAHA 35CS	SLP	SA/CR	FBG	KL	IB		D		11		13780	5	3	45600	50100
35	11	YAMAHA 36	SLP	SA/RC	FBG	KL	IB		D		11	10	14333	6	7	48200	53000

....For earlier years, see the BUC Used Boat Price Guide, Volume 3

YAR-CRAFT LLC
WAUSAU WI 54401   COAST GUARD MFG ID- YAR See inside cover to adjust price for area

For more recent years, see the BUC Used Boat Price Guide, Volume 1

LOA FT	IN	NAME AND/ OR MODEL	TOP/ RIG	BOAT TYPE	HULL MTL	TP	TP	ENG #	HP	MFG	BEAM FT	IN	WGT LBS	DRAFT FT	IN	RETAIL LOW	RETAIL HIGH
		———— 1996 BOATS															
16		1678 BACK TROLLER	OP	FSH	FBG	DV	OB				6	6	760			2750	3200
16		1678 SIDE CONSOLE	OP	FSH	FBG	DV	OB				6	6	800			2900	3400
17		WINNEBAGO 1778 WE	ST	FSH	FBG	DV	OB				6	6	1040			3850	4450
17	5	1785 BACK TROLLER	OP	FSH	FBG	DV	OB				7	1	950			3600	4200
17	5	1785 SIDE CONSOLE	OP	FSH	FBG	DV	OB				7	1	1000			3750	4350
18	2	1890 CRS B/T	OP	FSH	FBG	DV	OB				7	3	1300			4800	5550
18	2	1890 CRS S/C	OP	FSH	FBG	DV	OB				7	3	1300			4800	5550
19		MICHIGAN 1990	ST	FSH	FBG	DV	OB				7	6	1600			5700	6550
		———— 1995 BOATS															
16		1678 BACK TROLLER	OP	FSH	FBG	DV	OB				6	6	760			2650	3100
16		1678 SIDE CONSOLE	OP	FSH	FBG	DV	OB				6	6	800			2750	3200
17		WINNEBAGO 1778 WE	ST	FSH	FBG	DV	OB				6	6	1040			3600	4200
17	6	1785 BACK TROLLER	OP	FSH	FBG	DV	OB				7	1	950			3400	3950
17	6	1785 SIDE CONSOLE	OP	FSH	FBG	DV	OB				7	1	1000			3550	4150
18	2	1890 CRS B/T	OP	FSH	FBG	DV	OB				7	3	1300			4550	5250
18	2	1890 CRS S/C	OP	FSH	FBG	DV	OB				7	3	1300			4550	5250
19		MICHIGAN 1990	ST	FSH	FBG	DV	OB				7	6	1600			5350	6150
		———— 1994 BOATS															
16		BACK TROLLER 1678	OP	FSH	FBG	DV	OB				6	6	760			2500	2900
16		SIDE CONSOLE 1678	OP	FSH	FBG	DV	OB				6	6	800			2650	3050
17		ANNIVERSARY MODEL	ST	FSH	FBG	DV	OB				6	6	1040			3550	4150
17		BACK TROLLER 1781	OP	FSH	FBG	DV	OB				6	6	850			2850	3350
17		TOURNAMENT PRO SPCL	OP	FSH	FBG	DV	OB				6	6	900			3000	3500
17		WINNEBAGO/WALLEYE	ST	FSH	FBG	DV	OB				6	6	1040			3300	3850
18		CATCH & RELEASE B/T	OP	FSH	FBG	DV	OB				7	3	1300			4100	4750
18		CATCH & RELEASE S/C	OP	FSH	FBG	DV	OB				7	3	1300			4450	5150
19		MICHIGAN 2050	ST	FSH	FBG	DV	OB				7	6	1600			5100	5900
		———— 1993 BOATS															
16		BACK TROLLER 1678	OP	FSH	FBG	DV	OB				6	6	760			2450	2850
16		SIDE CONSOLE 1678	OP	FSH	FBG	DV	OB				6	6	800			2500	2900
17		BACK TROLLER 1781	OP	FSH	FBG	DV	OB				6	6	850			2750	3150
17		TOURNAMENT PRO SPCL	OP	FSH	FBG	DV	OB				6	6	900			2850	3350
17		WINNEBAGO/WALLEYE	ST	FSH	FBG	DV	OB				6	6	1040			3250	3800
18		CATCH & RELEASE B/T	OP	FSH	FBG	DV	OB				7	3	1300			3900	4550
18		CATCH & RELEASE S/C	OP	FSH	FBG	DV	OB				7	3	1300			4150	4800
19		CHINOOK 2090	OP	FSH	FBG	DV	OB				7	6	1700			5050	5650
19		MICHIGAN 2050	ST	FSH	FBG	DV	OB				7	6	1600			4900	5650
		———— 1992 BOATS															
16		BACK TROLLER 1678	OP	FSH	FBG	DV	OB				6	6	760			2300	2700
16		SIDE CONSOLE 1678	OP	FSH	FBG	DV	OB				6	6	800			2450	2850
16		BACK TROLLER 1781	OP	FSH	FBG	DV	OB				6	6	850			2600	3050
17		TOURNAMENT PRO SPCL	OP	FSH	FBG	DV	OB				6	6	900			2750	3250
17		WINNEBAGO/WALLEYE	ST	FSH	FBG	DV	OB				6	6	1040			3100	3600

LOA FT	IN	NAME AND/ OR MODEL	TOP/ RIG	BOAT TYPE	-HULL- MTL	TP	ENGINE TP	# HP	MFG	BEAM FT	IN	WGT LBS	DRAFT FT	IN	RETAIL LOW	RETAIL HIGH
		1992 BOATS														
18		CATCH & RELEASE B/T	OP	FSH	FBG	DV	OB			7	3	1300			3700	4300
18		CATCH & RELEASE S/C	OP	FSH	FBG	DV	OB			7	3	1300			4000	4600
19		CHINOOK 2090	ST	FSH	FBG	DV	OB			7	6	1700			4850	5600
19		MICHIGAN 2050	ST	FSH	FBG	DV	OB			7	6	1600			4650	5350
		1991 BOATS														
16		BACK TROLLER 1678	OP	FSH	FBG	DV	OB			6	6	760			2200	2550
16		SIDE CONSOLE 1678	OP	FSH	FBG	DV	OB			6	6	800			2300	2700
17		BACK TROLLER 1781	OP	FSH	FBG	DV	OB			6	6	850			2500	2900
17		TOURNAMENT PRO SPCL	OP	FSH	FBG	DV	OB			6	6	900			2650	3050
17		WINNEBAGO/WALLEYE	ST	FSH	FBG	DV	OB			6	6	1040			2950	3450
18		CATCH & RELEASE B/T	OP	FSH	FBG	DV	OB			7	3	1300			3550	4100
18		CATCH & RELEASE S/C	OP	FSH	FBG	DV	OB			7	3	1300			3800	4400
19		CHINOOK 2090	ST	FSH	FBG	DV	OB			7	6	1700			4650	5350
19		MICHIGAN 2050	ST	FSH	FBG	DV	OB			7	6	1600			4450	5100
		1990 BOATS														
16		1678-B/T	OP	FSH	FBG	DV	OB			6	6	760			2050	2450
16		1678-S/C	OP	FSH	FBG	DV	OB			6	6	800			2200	2600
17		1778 WINNEBAGO/WALLE	OP	FSH	FBG	DV	OB			6	6	1040			2850	3300
17		1781 TRNMNT PRO SPCL	OP	FSH	FBG	DV	OB			6	6	850			2650	3100
17		1781-B/T	OP	FSH	FBG	DV	OB			6	6	810			2350	2700
17		1781-S/C	OP	FSH	FBG	DV	OB			6	6	850			2150	2500
19		2050 MICHIGAN	OP	FSH	FBG	DV	OB			7	6	1600			4200	4900
19		2090 CHINOOK	ST	FSH	FBG	DV	OB			7	6	1700			4450	5100
		1989 BOATS														
16		B/T TRNMNT PRO 1678	OP	FSH	FBG	DV	OB			6	6	710			1850	2200
16		S/C TRNMNT PRO 1678	OP	FSH	FBG	DV	OB			6	6	740			1950	2300
17		1781 S/C GPS	OP	FSH	FBG	DV	OB			6	9	800			2200	2600
17		S/C TRNMNT PRO 1781	OP	FSH	FBG	DV	OB			6	9	790			2200	2550
17		WINNEBAGO-WALLEYE	OP	RNBT	FBG	DV	OB			6	6	1040			2800	3250
19		CHINOOK 1990	ST	FSH	FBG	DV	OB			7	6	1700			4200	4900
19		WINNEBAGO-WALLEYE	OP	RNBT	FBG	DV	OB			7	6	1400			3750	4350
		1988 BOATS														
16		B/T TRNMNT PRO 1678	OP	FSH	FBG	DV	OB			6	6	710			1800	2150
16		BACK-TROLLER 1678	OP	FSH	FBG	DV	OB			6	6	710			1750	2100
16		FISH-&-SKI 1678	OP	FSH	FBG	DV	OB			6	6	740			1850	2200
16		S/C TRNMNT PRO 1678	OP	FSH	FBG	DV	OB			6	6	740			1850	2200
16		SIDE-CONSOLE 1678	OP	FSH	FBG	DV	OB			6	6	740			1800	2150
17		BACK-TROLLER 1781	OP	FSH	FBG	DV	OB			6	9	760			2000	2350
17		S/C TRNMNT PRO 1781	OP	FSH	FBG	DV	OB			6	9	790			2050	2450
17		WINNEBAGO-WALLEYE	OP	RNBT	FBG	DV	OB			6	6	1040			2700	3100
19		CHINOOK 1990	ST	FSH	FBG	DV	OB			7	6	1700			4050	4700
		1987 BOATS														
16		AMERICANA 1683	OP	RNBT	FBG	DV	OB			6	6	900			2250	2600
16		BACK-TROLLER 1678	OP	FSH	FBG	DV	OB			6	6	710			1700	2050
16		FISH-&-SKI 1678	OP	FSH	FBG	DV	OB			6	6	920			2250	2600
16		SIDE-CONSOLE 1678	OP	FSH	FBG	DV	OB			6	6	740			1800	2100
17		BACK-TROLLER 1781	OP	FSH	FBG	DV	OB			6	8	790			2000	2350
17		FISH-&-SKI 1778	OP	FSH	FBG	DV	OB			6	6	1040			2450	2850
17		SIDE-CONSOLE 1781	OP	FSH	FBG	DV	OB			6	8	790			2000	2350
17		WINNEBAGO-WALLEYE	OP	FSH	FBG	DV	OB			6	6	1040			2650	3100
19		CHINOOK 1990	ST	FSH	FBG	DV	OB			7	6	1700			3900	4500
		1986 BOATS														
16		AMERICANA 1683	OP	RNBT	FBG	DV	OB			6	6	900			2150	2500
16		BACK-TROLLER 1678	OP	FSH	FBG	DV	OB			6	6	710			1650	1950
16		FISH-&-SKI 1678	OP	FSH	FBG	DV	OB			6	6	920			2150	2500
16		SIDE-CONSOLE 1678	OP	FSH	FBG	DV	OB			6	6	740			1700	2050
17		BACK-TROLLER 1781	OP	FSH	FBG	DV	OB			6	8	790			1900	2250
17		FISH-&-SKI 1778	OP	FSH	FBG	DV	OB			6	6	1040			2500	2900
17		PATRIOT 1783	OP	RNBT	FBG	DV	OB			6	6	1000			2450	2850
17		SIDE-CONSOLE 1781	OP	FSH	FBG	DV	OB			6	8	790			1900	2250
19		CHINOOK 1990	ST	FSH	FBG	DV	OB			7	6	1700			3750	4350
		1985 BOATS														
16		AMERICANA 1683	OP	RNBT	FBG	DV	OB			6	6	900			2050	2450
16		BACK-TROLLER 1678	OP	FSH	FBG	DV	OB			6	6	600			1350	1600
16		FISH-&-SKI 1678	OP	FSH	FBG	DV	OB			6	6	900			2000	2400
16		SIDE-CONSOLE 1678	OP	FSH	FBG	DV	OB			6	6	74			135	165
17		BACK-TROLLER 1781	OP	FSH	FBG	DV	OB			6	8	760			1800	2100
17		FISH-&-SKI 1778	OP	FSH	FBG	DV	OB			6	6	1040			2400	2800
17		PATRIOT 1783	OP	RNBT	FBG	DV	OB			6	6	1000			2400	2750
17		SIDE-CONSOLE 1781	OP	FSH	FBG	DV	OB			6	8	790			1850	2200
19		CHINOOK 1990	ST	FSH	FBG	DV	OB			7	6				3250	3750
19	4	FREEDOM 2073	OP	RNBT	FBG	DV	OB			7	3	1600			3600	4150
		1984 BOATS														
16		1678-VP		OPFSH	FBG	DV	OB			6	6	600			1300	1550
16		1678-VP-SC		OPFSH	FBG	DV	OB			6	6	630			1350	1650
16		AMERICANA 1683		RNBT	FBG	DV	OB			6	6	900			2000	2350
16		AMERICANA 1683		RNBT	FBG	DV	IO	140		6	7	2011			3000	3450
16		FISH-&-SKI 1678		FSH	FBG	DV	OB			6	6	920			2000	2350
16	6	EAGLE 1663		RNBT	FBG	TR	OB			6	5	900			2000	2400
17		1781-VP		OPFSH	FBG	DV	OB			6	8	800			1800	2150
17		1781-VP-SC		OPFSH	FBG	DV	OB			6	8	800			1800	2150
17		FISH-&-SKI 1778		FSH	FBG	DV	OB			6	6	1040			2350	2700
17		PATRIOT 1783		RNBT	FBG	DV	OB			6	6	1000			2300	2700
17		PATRIOT 1783		RNBT	FBG	DV	IO	140		6	5	1950			3050	3550
19	4	FREEDOM 2073		CUD	FBG	DV	OB			7	3	1600			3450	4050
19	4	FREEDOM 2073		RNBT	FBG	SV	IO	170		7	3	2600			4350	5050
19	4	LIBERTY 2083		RNBT	FBG	SV	IO	140		7		2300			3950	4600

....For earlier years, see the BUC Used Boat Price Guide, Volume 3

YARDWAY MARINE LTD

CONTAINER PORT RD KWAI COAST GUARD MFG ID- XIG See inside cover to adjust price for area
ALSO HALVORSEN MARINE LTD

For more recent years, see the BUC Used Boat Price Guide, Volume 1

LOA FT	IN	NAME AND/ OR MODEL	TOP/ RIG	BOAT TYPE	-HULL- MTL	TP	ENGINE TP	# HP	MFG	BEAM FT	IN	WGT LBS	DRAFT FT	IN	RETAIL LOW	RETAIL HIGH
		1996 BOATS														
32		ISLAND GYPSY 32 AC	FB	TRWL	FBG	SV	IB	135D	SABR	12		16500	3	8	112000	123500
32		ISLAND GYPSY 32 AC	FB	TRWL	FBG	SV	IB	T 90D	SABR	12		16500	3	8	113000	124500
32		ISLAND GYPSY 32 FB	FB	TRWL	FBG	SV	IB	135D-225D		12		16500	3	8	110500	123000
32		ISLAND GYPSY 32 FB	FB	TRWL	FBG	SV	IB	T90D-T200D		12		16500	3	8	111500	138000
32		ISLAND GYPSY 32 SDN	FB	TRWL	FBG	SV	IB	135D-225D		12		16500	3	8	105500	125000
32		ISLAND GYPSY 32 SDN	FB	TRWL	FBG	SV	IB	T90D-T200D		12		16500	3	8	106500	132500
32		ISLAND GYPSY 32 SF	FB	SF	FBG	SV	IB	135D-225D		12		14000	3	8	92700	102000
32		ISLAND GYPSY 32 SF	FB	SF	FBG	SV	IB	T90D-T200D		12		14000	3	8	90400	103500
32		ISLAND GYPSY 325 SDN	FB	TRWL	FBG	SV	IB	135D	SABR	12		16500	3	8	105500	115500
36		ISLAND GYPSY 36 FB	FB	TRWL	FBG	SV	IB	135D	SABR	13		25550	3	11	129000	142000
		IB 375D CAT 136500 150500, IB T135D SABR 131500 144500, IB T200D VLVO 136500 150000														
		IB T225D SABR 137000 150500														
36		ISLAND GYPSY 36 MKII	FB	TRWL	FBG	SV	IB	135D	SABR	13		25550	3	11	132000	145500
		IB 375D CAT 140500 154000, IB T135D SABR 134500 148000, IB T200D VLVO 139500 153500														
		IB T225D SABR 140000 154000														
36		ISLAND GYPSY 36 QC	FB	TRWL	FBG	SV	IB	135D	SABR	13		25550	3	11	130000	143000
		IB T135D SABR 132500 145500, IB T200D VLVO 137500 151000, IB T225D SABR 138000 151500														
36		ISLAND GYPSY 36 SDN	FB	TRWL	FBG	SV	IB	135D	SABR	13		25550	3	11	126500	139000
		IB 375D CAT 134000 147500, IB T135D SABR 129000 141500, IB T200D VLVO 133500 146500														
		IB T225D SABR 134000 147000														
36		ISLAND GYPSY 36 TC	FB	TRWL	FBG	SV	IB	135D	SABR	13		25550	3	11	136000	149500
		IB 375D CAT 143500 157500, IB T135D SABR 138500 152000, IB T200D VLVO 142500 156500														
		IB T225D SABR 143000 157500														
40		ISLAND GYPSY 40 CL	FB	TRWL	FBG	SV	IB	T135D	SABR	14	3	32000	3	6	184000	202000
40		ISLAND GYPSY 40 CL	FB	TRWL	FBG	SV	IB	T225D	SABR	14	3	32000	3	6	188000	206500
40		ISLAND GYPSY 40 CL	FB	TRWL	FBG	SV	IB	T375D	CAT	14	3	32000	3	6	211500	232500
40		ISLAND GYPSY 40 FD	FB	TRWL	FBG	SV	IB	T135D	SABR	14	3	34500	3	6	195500	215000
40		ISLAND GYPSY 40 FD	FB	TRWL	FBG	SV	IB	T225D	SABR	14	3	34500	3	6	199500	219500
40		ISLAND GYPSY 40 FD	FB	TRWL	FBG	SV	IB	T375D	CAT	14	3	34500	3	6	223000	245500
40		ISLAND GYPSY 40 MC	FB	MY	FBG	SV	IB	T135D	SABR	14	3	33500	3	6	190500	209500
40		ISLAND GYPSY 40 MC	FB	MY	FBG	SV	IB	T225D	SABR	14	3	33500	3	6	194500	214000
40		ISLAND GYPSY 40 MC	FB	MY	FBG	SV	IB	T375D	CAT	14	3	33500	3	6	218000	239500
44	3	ISLAND GYPSY 44 CL	FB	TRWL	FBG	SV	IB	T135D	SABR	15	4	38000	4	3	218000	239500
44	3	ISLAND GYPSY 44 CL	FB	TRWL	FBG	SV	IB	T225D	SABR	15	4	38000	4	3	223500	246000
44	3	ISLAND GYPSY 44 CL	FB	TRWL	FBG	SV	IB	T375D	CAT	15	4	38000	4	3	241500	265500
44	3	ISLAND GYPSY 44 FB	FB	TRWL	FBG	SV	IB	T135D	SABR	15	4	38000	4	3	216500	238000
44	3	ISLAND GYPSY 44 FB	FB	TRWL	FBG	SV	IB	T225D	SABR	15	4	38000	4	3	222000	244000
44	3	ISLAND GYPSY 44 FB	FB	TRWL	FBG	SV	IB	T375D	CAT	15	4	38000	4	3	240000	263500
44	3	ISLAND GYPSY 44 MC	FB	MY	FBG	SV	IB	T225D	SABR	15	4	38000	4	3	211000	232000
44	3	ISLAND GYPSY 44 MC	FB	MY	FBG	SV	IB	T375D	CAT	15	4	38000	4	3	244000	268000
44	3	ISLAND GYPSY 44 MC	FB	MY	FBG	SV	IB	T550D	GM	15	4	38000	4	3	274000	301000
44	3	ISLAND GYPSY 44 SC	FB	SF	FBG	SV	IB	T225D	SABR	15	4	38000	4	3	207500	228000
44	3	ISLAND GYPSY 44 SC	FB	SF	FBG	SV	IB	T375D	CAT	15	4	38000	4	3	246500	271000
44	3	ISLAND GYPSY 44 SC	FB	SF	FBG	SV	IB	T550D	GM	15	4	38000	4	3	282000	310000
49		ISLAND GYPSY 49 CL	FB	TRWL	FBG	SV	IB	T135D	SABR	15	4	38000	4	5	228000	250500
49		ISLAND GYPSY 49 CL	FB	TRWL	FBG	SV	IB	T225D	SABR	15	4	38000	4	5	237000	260500
49		ISLAND GYPSY 49 CL	FB	TRWL	FBG	SV	IB	T375D	CAT	15	4	38000	4	5	260000	285500
49		ISLAND GYPSY 49 FD	FB	TRWL	FBG	SV	IB	T135D	SABR	15	4	42000	4	5	235500	258500

LOA FT	IN	NAME AND/ OR MODEL	TOP/ RIG	BOAT TYPE	-HULL- MTL	TP	TP	----ENGINE--- # HP	MFG	BEAM FT	IN	WGT LBS	DRAFT FT	IN	RETAIL LOW	RETAIL HIGH
		1996 BOATS														
49		ISLAND GYPSY 49 FD	FB	TRWL	FBG	SV	IB	T225D	SABR	15	4	42000	4	5	243500	268000
49		ISLAND GYPSY 49 FD	FB	TRWL	FBG	SV	IB	T375D	CAT	15	4	42000	4	5	266000	292500
49		ISLAND GYPSY 49 FD	FB	TRWL	FBG	SV	IB	T550D	GM	15	4	42000	4	5	288000	316500
49		ISLAND GYPSY 49 MC	FB	MY	FBG	SV	IB	T135D	SABR	15	4	42000	4	5	238000	261500
		IB T225D SABR 245000 269500, IB T375D CAT 269000 296000, IB T550D GM 295000 324500														
49		ISLAND GYPSY 49 PH	FB	TRWL	FBG	SV	IB	T135D	SABR	15	4	46000	4	5	245500	269500
		IB T225D SABR 254500 280000, IB T375D CAT 276500 303500, IB T550D GM 298000 327500														
51		ISLAND GYPSY 51 CSTM	FB	MY	FBG	SV	IB	T375D	CAT	16	6	60000	4	2	424500	466500
51		ISLAND GYPSY 51 CSTM	FB	MY	FBG	SV	IB	T550D	GM	16	6	60000	4	2	475000	522000
51		ISLAND GYPSY 51 MY	FB	MY	FBG	SV	IB	T375D	CAT	16	6	60000	4	2	415500	456500
51		ISLAND GYPSY 51 MY	FB	MY	FBG	SV	IB	T550D	GM	16	6	60000	4	2	465500	511500
51		ISLAND GYPSY 51 PH	FB	TRWL	FBG	SV	IB	T135D	SABR	15	4	50000	4	5	261500	287000
		IB T225D SABR 273000 300000, IB T375D CAT 299000 328500, IB T435D CAT 310500 341500														
		IB T550D GM 330000 362500														
57		ISLAND GYPSY 57 CKPT	FB	MY	FBG	SV	IB	T375D	CAT	16	6	83000	4	3	560000	615500
57		ISLAND GYPSY 57 CKPT	FB	MY	FBG	SV	IB	T550D	GM	16	6	83000	4	3	614000	675000
57		ISLAND GYPSY 57 MY	FB	MY	FBG	SV	IB	T375D	CAT	16	6	83000	4	3	560000	615500
57		ISLAND GYPSY 57 MY	FB	MY	FBG	SV	IB	T550D	GM	16	6	83000	4	3	614000	675000
57		ISLAND GYPSY 57 PH	FB	TRWL	FBG	SV	IB	T375D	CAT	16	6	82000	4	3	550000	604500
57		ISLAND GYPSY 57 PH	FB	TRWL	FBG	SV	IB	T550D	CAT	16	6	82000	4	3	620000	681500
61		ISLAND GYPSY 61 PH	FB	TRWL	FBG	SV	IB	T375D	CAT	16	6	90000	4	8	650000	714500
61		ISLAND GYPSY 61 PH	FB	TRWL	FBG	SV	IB	T435D	CAT	16	6	90000	4	8	666500	732500
61		ISLAND GYPSY 61 PH	FB	TRWL	FBG	SV	IB	T550D	GM	16	6	90000	4	8	689000	757000
62		ISLAND GYPSY 62 MY	FB	MY	FBG	SV	IB	T750D	GM	19	9	97000	4	8	1.070M	1.160M
62		ISLAND GYPSY 62 MY	FB	MY	FBG	SV	IB	T10CD	GM	19	9	97000	4	8	977500	1.060M
62		ISLAND GYPSY 62 SC	FB	SF	FBG	SV	IB	T10CD	GM	19	9	99000	4	6	947500	1.030M
68		ISLAND GYPSY 68 CKPT	FB	MY	FBG	SV	IB	T750D	GM	19	9	53T	4	6	988000	1.075M
68		ISLAND GYPSY 68 CKPT	FB	MY	FBG	SV	IB	T10CD	GM	19	9	53T	4	6	1.060M	1.155M
		1995 BOATS														
32		ISLAND GYPSY 32 AC	FB	TRWL	FBG	SV	IB	135D	SABR	12		16500	3	8	106500	117000
32		ISLAND GYPSY 32 AC	FB	TRWL	FBG	SV	IB	T 90D	SABR	12		16500	3	8	107500	118000
32		ISLAND GYPSY 32 FB	FB	TRWL	FBG	SV	IB	135D-225D		12		16500	3	8	104500	116500
32		ISLAND GYPSY 32 FB	FB	TRWL	FBG	SV	IB	T90D-T200D		12		16500	3	8	106000	131000
32		ISLAND GYPSY 32 SDN	FB	TRWL	FBG	SV	IB	135D-225D		12		16500	3	8	100000	119000
32		ISLAND GYPSY 32 SDN	FB	TRWL	FBG	SV	IB	T90D-T200D		12		16500	3	8	101500	126000
32		ISLAND GYPSY 32 SF	FB	SF	FBG	SV	IB	135D-225D		12		14000	3	8	88100	96800
32		ISLAND GYPSY 32 SF	FB	SF	FBG	SV	IB	T90D-T200D		12		14000	3	8	85900	98200
32		ISLAND GYPSY 325 SDN	FB	TRWL	FBG	SV	IB	135D	SABR	12		16500	3	8	100000	110000
36		ISLAND GYPSY 36 FB	FB	TRWL	FBG	SV	IB	135D	SABR	13		25550	3	11	124000	136000
		IB 375D CAT 131500 144000, IB T135D SABR 126500 138500, IB T200D VLVO 130500 143500														
		IB T225D SABR 131000 144000														
36		ISLAND GYPSY 36 MKII	FB	TRWL	FBG	SV	IB	135D	SABR	13		25550	3	11	127000	139500
		IB 375D CAT 134500 147500, IB T135D SABR 129500 142500, IB T200D VLVO 133500 147000														
		IB T225D SABR 134500 147500														
36		ISLAND GYPSY 36 QC	FB	TRWL	FBG	SV	IB	135D	SABR	13		25550	3	11	125000	137500
		IB T135D SABR 127500 140000, IB T200D VLVO 131500 144500, IB T225D SABR 132000 145500														
36		ISLAND GYPSY 36 SDN	FB	TRWL	FBG	SV	IB	135D	SABR	13		25550	3	11	121000	133000
		IB 375D CAT 128500 141000, IB T135D SABR 123500 136000, IB T200D VLVO 128000 140500														
		IB T225D SABR 128500 141000														
36		ISLAND GYPSY 36 TC	FB	TRWL	FBG	SV	IB	135D	SABR	13		25550	3	11	130500	143500
		IB 375D CAT 138000 151500, IB T135D SABR 132500 146000, IB T200D VLVO 137000 150500														
		IB T225D SABR 137500 151000														
40		ISLAND GYPSY 40 CL	FB	TRWL	FBG	SV	IB	T135D	SABR	14	3	32000	3	6	176500	194000
40		ISLAND GYPSY 40 CL	FB	TRWL	FBG	SV	IB	T225D	SABR	14	3	32000	3	6	180000	198000
40		ISLAND GYPSY 40 CL	FB	TRWL	FBG	SV	IB	T375D	CAT	14	3	32000	3	6	203000	223000
40		ISLAND GYPSY 40 FD	FB	TRWL	FBG	SV	IB	T135D	SABR	14	3	34500	3	6	187500	206000
40		ISLAND GYPSY 40 FD	FB	TRWL	FBG	SV	IB	T225D	SABR	14	3	34500	3	6	191500	210500
40		ISLAND GYPSY 40 FD	FB	TRWL	FBG	SV	IB	T375D	CAT	14	3	34500	3	6	214000	235500
40		ISLAND GYPSY 40 MC	FB	MY	FBG	SV	IB	T135D	SABR	14	3	33500	3	6	183000	201000
40		ISLAND GYPSY 40 MC	FB	MY	FBG	SV	IB	T225D	SABR	14	3	33500	3	6	186500	205000
40		ISLAND GYPSY 40 MC	FB	MY	FBG	SV	IB	T375D	CAT	14	3	33500	3	6	209500	230000
44	3	ISLAND GYPSY 44 CL	FB	TRWL	FBG	SV	IB	T135D	SABR	15	4	38000	4	3	209000	229500
44	3	ISLAND GYPSY 44 CL	FB	TRWL	FBG	SV	IB	T225D	SABR	15	4	38000	4	3	214500	235500
44	3	ISLAND GYPSY 44 CL	FB	TRWL	FBG	SV	IB	T375D	CAT	15	4	38000	4	3	231500	254500
44	3	ISLAND GYPSY 44 FB	FB	TRWL	FBG	SV	IB	T135D	SABR	15	4	38000	4	3	207500	228000
44	3	ISLAND GYPSY 44 FB	FB	TRWL	FBG	SV	IB	T225D	SABR	15	4	38000	4	3	213000	234000
44	3	ISLAND GYPSY 44 FB	FB	TRWL	FBG	SV	IB	T375D	CAT	15	4	38000	4	3	230000	253000
44	3	ISLAND GYPSY 44 MC	FB	MY	FBG	SV	IB	T225D	SABR	15	4	38000	4	3	202000	222000
44	3	ISLAND GYPSY 44 MC	FB	MY	FBG	SV	IB	T375D	CAT	15	4	38000	4	3	234000	257000
44	3	ISLAND GYPSY 44 MC	FB	MY	FBG	SV	IB	T550D	GM	15	4	38000	4	3	263000	289000
44	3	ISLAND GYPSY 44 SC	FB	SF	FBG	SV	IB	T225D	SABR	15	4	38000	4	3	199000	218500
44	3	ISLAND GYPSY 44 SC	FB	SF	FBG	SV	IB	T375D	CAT	15	4	38000	4	3	236500	260000
44	3	ISLAND GYPSY 44 SC	FB	SF	FBG	SV	IB	T550D	GM	15	4	38000	4	3	270500	297500
49		ISLAND GYPSY 49 CL	FB	TRWL	FBG	SV	IB	T135D	SABR	15	4	38000	4	5	216500	237500
49		ISLAND GYPSY 49 CL	FB	TRWL	FBG	SV	IB	T225D	SABR	15	4	38000	4	5	225500	248000
49		ISLAND GYPSY 49 CL	FB	TRWL	FBG	SV	IB	T375D	CAT	15	4	38000	4	5	247000	271500
49		ISLAND GYPSY 49 FD	FB	TRWL	FBG	SV	IB	T135D	SABR	15	4	42000	4	5	223000	245000
		IB T225D SABR 231000 254000, IB T375D CAT 252500 277500, IB T550D GM 273500 300500														
49		ISLAND GYPSY 49 MC	FB	MY	FBG	SV	IB	T135D	SABR	15	4	42000	4	5	225500	247500
		IB T225D SABR 232000 255000, IB T375D CAT 255000 280500, IB T550D GM 280500 308500														
49		ISLAND GYPSY 49 PH	FB	TRWL	FBG	SV	IB	T135D	SABR	15	4	46000	4	5	233000	256000
		IB T225D SABR 242500 266500, IB T375D CAT 263000 289000, IB T550D GM 283500 311500														
51		ISLAND GYPSY 51 CSTM	FB	MY	FBG	SV	IB	T375D	CAT	16	6	60000	4	2	406500	446500
51		ISLAND GYPSY 51 CSTM	FB	MY	FBG	SV	IB	T550D	GM	16	6	60000	4	2	455500	500500
51		ISLAND GYPSY 51 MY	FB	MY	FBG	SV	IB	T375D	CAT	16	6	60000	4	2	398000	437500
51		ISLAND GYPSY 51 MY	FB	MY	FBG	SV	IB	T550D	GM	16	6	60000	4	2	446500	490500
51		ISLAND GYPSY 51 PH	FB	TRWL	FBG	SV	IB	T135D	SABR	15	4	50000	4	5	247500	272000
		IB T225D SABR 259500 285000, IB T375D CAT 285000 313000, IB T435D CAT 296000 325500														
		IB T550D GM 315000 346000														
56		ISLAND GYPSY 56 SC	FB	SF	FBG	SV	IB	T750D	GM	16	6	50000	4	2	509500	560000
57		ISLAND GYPSY 57 CKPT	FB	MY	FBG	SV	IB	T375D	CAT	16	6	83000	4	3	533500	586000
57		ISLAND GYPSY 57 CKPT	FB	MY	FBG	SV	IB	T550D	GM	16	6	83000	4	3	585000	643000
57		ISLAND GYPSY 57 MY	FB	MY	FBG	SV	IB	T375D	CAT	16	6	83000	4	3	533500	586000
57		ISLAND GYPSY 57 MY	FB	MY	FBG	SV	IB	T550D	GM	16	6	83000	4	3	585000	643000
57		ISLAND GYPSY 57 PH	FB	TRWL	FBG	SV	IB	T375D	CAT	16	6	82000	4	3	524000	576000
57		ISLAND GYPSY 57 PH	FB	TRWL	FBG	SV	IB	T550D	CAT	16	6	82000	4	3	591000	649500
61		ISLAND GYPSY 61 PH	FB	TRWL	FBG	SV	IB	T375D	CAT	16	6	90000	4	8	620000	681500
61		ISLAND GYPSY 61 PH	FB	TRWL	FBG	SV	IB	T435D	CAT	16	6	90000	4	8	636000	698500
61		ISLAND GYPSY 61 PH	FB	TRWL	FBG	SV	IB	T550D	GM	16	6	90000	4	8	656500	721500
62		ISLAND GYPSY 62 MY	FB	MY	FBG	SV	IB	T750D	GM	19	9	97000	4	8	1.020M	1.110M
62		ISLAND GYPSY 62 MY	FB	MY	FBG	SV	IB	T10CD	GM	19	9	97000	4	8	937500	1.020M
62		ISLAND GYPSY 62 SC	FB	SF	FBG	SV	IB	T10CD	GM	19	9	99000	4	6	899000	988000
68		ISLAND GYPSY 68 CKPT	FB	MY	FBG	SV	IB	T750D	GM	19	9	53T	4	6	952500	1.035M
68		ISLAND GYPSY 68 CKPT	FB	MY	FBG	SV	IB	T10CD	GM	19	9	53T	4	6	1.020M	1.105M
		1994 BOATS														
32		ISLAND GYPSY 32 AC	FB	TRWL	FBG	SV	IB	135D	SABR	12		16500	3	8	100500	110500
32		ISLAND GYPSY 32 AC	FB	TRWL	FBG	SV	IB	T 90D	SABR	12		16500	3	8	102000	112000
32		ISLAND GYPSY 32 FB	FB	TRWL	FBG	SV	IB	135D-225D		12		16500	3	8	100000	115000
32		ISLAND GYPSY 32 FB	FB	TRWL	FBG	SV	IB	T90D-T200D		12		16500	3	8	100500	125000
32		ISLAND GYPSY 32 SDN	FB	TRWL	FBG	SV	IB	135D-225D		12		16500	3	8	95400	109500
32		ISLAND GYPSY 32 SDN	FB	TRWL	FBG	SV	IB	T90D-T200D		12		16500	3	8	96800	119500
32		ISLAND GYPSY 32 SF	FB	SF	FBG	SV	IB	135D-225D		12		14000	3	8	83800	92100
32		ISLAND GYPSY 32 SF	FB	SF	FBG	SV	IB	T90D-T200D		12		14000	3	8	81700	93400
32		ISLAND GYPSY 325 SDN	FB	TRWL	FBG	SV	IB	135D	SABR	12		16500	3	8	95400	105000
36		ISLAND GYPSY 36 FB	FB	TRWL	FBG	SV	IB	135D	SABR	13		25550	3	11	118500	130000
		IB 375D CAT 126000 138500, IB T135D SABR 122500 135000, IB T200D VLVO 125000 137500														
		IB T225D SABR 125500 138000														
36		ISLAND GYPSY 36 MKII	FB	TRWL	FBG	SV	IB	135D	SABR	13		25550	3	11	122500	134500
		IB 375D CAT 129000 141500, IB T135D SABR 126000 138500, IB T200D VLVO 128500 141000														
		IB T225D SABR 129000 142000														
36		ISLAND GYPSY 36 QC	FB	TRWL	FBG	SV	IB	T135D	SABR	13		25550	3	11	114000	125500
36		ISLAND GYPSY 36 QC	FB	TRWL	FBG	SV	IB	T200D	VLVO	13		25550	3	11	126000	138500
36		ISLAND GYPSY 36 QC	FB	TRWL	FBG	SV	IB	T225D	SABR	13		25550	3	11	126500	139500
36		ISLAND GYPSY 36 SDN	FB	TRWL	FBG	SV	IB	135D	SABR	13		25550	3	11	114000	125500
		IB 375D CAT 122000 134000, IB T135D SABR 118500 130500, IB T200D VLVO 121500 133500														
		IB T225D SABR 122000 134000														
36		ISLAND GYPSY 36 TC	FB	TRWL	FBG	SV	IB	135D	SABR	13		25550	3	11	125500	138000
		IB 375D CAT 132500 146000, IB T135D SABR 129500 142500, IB T200D VLVO 132000 145000														
		IB T225D SABR 132500 145500														
40		ISLAND GYPSY 40 CL	FB	TRWL	FBG	SV	IB	T135D	SABR	14	3	32000	3	6	169000	185500
40		ISLAND GYPSY 40 CL	FB	TRWL	FBG	SV	IB	T225D	SABR	14	3	32000	3	6	172500	189500
40		ISLAND GYPSY 40 CL	FB	TRWL	FBG	SV	IB	T375D	CAT	14	3	32000	3	6	194500	213500
40		ISLAND GYPSY 40 FD	FB	TRWL	FBG	SV	IB	T135D	SABR	14	3	34500	3	6	179500	197500
40		ISLAND GYPSY 40 FD	FB	TRWL	FBG	SV	IB	T225D	SABR	14	3	34500	3	6	183500	201500
40		ISLAND GYPSY 40 FD	FB	TRWL	FBG	SV	IB	T375D	CAT	14	3	34500	3	6	205000	225500
40		ISLAND GYPSY 40 MC	FB	MY	FBG	SV	IB	T135D	SABR	14	3	33500	3	6	175000	192500

CONTINUED ON NEXT PAGE

LOA FT	IN	NAME AND/ OR MODEL	TOP/ RIG	BOAT TYPE	-HULL- MTL	TP	TP	ENGINE # HP	MFG	BEAM FT	IN	WGT LBS	DRAFT FT	IN	RETAIL LOW	RETAIL HIGH
		1994 BOATS														
40		ISLAND GYPSY 40 MC	FB	MY	FBG	SV	IB	T225D	SABR	14	3	33500	3	6	179000	196500
40		ISLAND GYPSY 40 MC	FB	MY	FBG	SV	IB	T375D	CAT	14	3	33500	3	6	200500	220500
44	3	ISLAND GYPSY 44 CL	FB	TRWL	FBG	SV	IB	T135D	SABR	15	4	38000	4	3	200000	220000
44	3	ISLAND GYPSY 44 CL	FB	TRWL	FBG	SV	IB	T225D	SABR	15	4	38000	4	3	205500	226000
44	3	ISLAND GYPSY 44 CL	FB	TRWL	FBG	SV	IB	T375D	CAT	15	4	38000	4	3	222000	244000
44	3	ISLAND GYPSY 44 FB	FB	TRWL	FBG	SV	IB	T135D	SABR	15	4	38000	4	3	199000	218500
44	3	ISLAND GYPSY 44 FB	FB	TRWL	FBG	SV	IB	T225D	SABR	15	4	38000	4	3	204000	224000
44	3	ISLAND GYPSY 44 FB	FB	TRWL	FBG	SV	IB	T375D	CAT	15	4	38000	4	3	220500	242000
44	3	ISLAND GYPSY 44 MC	FB	MY	FBG	SV	IB	T225D	SABR	15	4	38000	4	3	193500	212500
44	3	ISLAND GYPSY 44 MC	FB	MY	FBG	SV	IB	T375D	CAT	15	4	38000	4	3	224000	246500
44	3	ISLAND GYPSY 44 MC	FB	MY	FBG	SV	IB	T550D	GM	15	4	38000	4	3	252000	276500
44	3	ISLAND GYPSY 44 SC	FB	SF	FBG	SV	IB	T225D	SABR	15	4	38000	4	3	190500	209500
44	3	ISLAND GYPSY 44 SC	FB	SF	FBG	SV	IB	T375D	CAT	15	4	38000	4	3	226500	249000
44	3	ISLAND GYPSY 44 SC	FB	SF	FBG	SV	IB	T550D	GM	15	4	38000	4	3	259500	285000
49		ISLAND GYPSY 49 CL	FB	TRWL	FBG	SV	IB	T135D	SABR	15	4	38000	4	5	205500	226000
49		ISLAND GYPSY 49 CL	FB	TRWL	FBG	SV	IB	T225D	SABR	15	4	38000	4	5	214500	236000
49		ISLAND GYPSY 49 CL	FB	TRWL	FBG	SV	IB	T375D	CAT	15	4	38000	4	5	235000	258000
49		ISLAND GYPSY 49 FD	FB	TRWL	FBG	SV	IB	T135D	SABR	15	4	42000	4	5	212000	233000
		IB T225D SABR 220000 241500, IB T375D CAT 240000 263500, IB T425D CAT 246500 271000														
		IB T550D GM 259500 285500														
49		ISLAND GYPSY 49 MC	FB	MY	FBG	SV	IB	T135D	SABR	15	4	42000	4	5	214000	235000
		IB T225D SABR 220000 242000, IB T375D CAT 242000 266000, IB T425D CAT 250000 274500														
		IB T550D GM 267500 294000														
49		ISLAND GYPSY 49 PH	FB	TRWL	FBG	SV	IB	T135D	SABR	15	4	46000	4	5	222000	244000
		IB T225D SABR 231000 254000, IB T375D CAT 250500 275000, IB T425D CAT 257000 282000														
		IB T550D GM 270000 297000														
51		ISLAND GYPSY 51 CSTM	FB	MY	FBG	SV	IB	T375D	CAT	16	6	60000	4	2	389500	428000
51		ISLAND GYPSY 51 CSTM	FB	MY	FBG	SV	IB	T550D	GM	16	6	60000	4	2	436500	479500
51		ISLAND GYPSY 51 MY	FB	MY	FBG	SV	IB	T375D	CAT	16	6	60000	4	2	380500	418000
51		ISLAND GYPSY 51 MY	FB	MY	FBG	SV	IB	T550D	GM	16	6	60000	4	2	427000	469000
51		ISLAND GYPSY 51 PH	FB	TRWL	FBG	SV	IB	T135D	SABR	16	4	50000	4	5	235000	258000
		IB T225D SABR 246500 271000, IB T375D CAT 272000 298500, IB T435D CAT 282500 310500														
		IB T550D GM 301000 330500														
56		ISLAND GYPSY 56 SC	FB	SF	FBG	SV	IB	T750D	GM	16	6	50000	4	2	488000	536500
57		ISLAND GYPSY 57 CKPT	FB	MY	FBG	SV	IB	T375D	CAT	16	6	83000	4	3	508500	559000
57		ISLAND GYPSY 57 CKPT	FB	MY	FBG	SV	IB	T550D	GM	16	6	83000	4	3	558000	613000
57		ISLAND GYPSY 57 MY	FB	MY	FBG	SV	IB	T375D	CAT	16	6	83000	4	3	508500	559000
57		ISLAND GYPSY 57 MY	FB	MY	FBG	SV	IB	T550D	GM	16	6	83000	4	3	558000	613000
57		ISLAND GYPSY 57 PH	FB	TRWL	FBG	SV	IB	T375D	CAT	16	6	82000	4	3	500000	549000
57		ISLAND GYPSY 57 PH	FB	TRWL	FBG	SV	IB	T550D	CAT	16	6	82000	4	3	563500	619500
61		ISLAND GYPSY 61 PH	FB	TRWL	FBG	SV	IB	T375D	CAT	16	6	90000	4	8	592000	651000
61		ISLAND GYPSY 61 PH	FB	TRWL	FBG	SV	IB	T435D	CAT	16	6	90000	4	8	607000	667000
61		ISLAND GYPSY 61 PH	FB	TRWL	FBG	SV	IB	T550D	GM	16	6	90000	4	8	626500	688500
62		ISLAND GYPSY 62 MY	FB	MY	FBG	SV	IB	T750D	GM						746000	820000
62		ISLAND GYPSY 62 MY	FB	MY	FBG	SV	IB	T10CD	GM						814500	895000
62		ISLAND GYPSY 62 SC	FB	SF	FBG	SV	IB	T10CD	GM	19	9	99000	4	6	861000	946500
68		ISLAND GYPSY 68 CKPT	FB	MY	FBG	SV	IB	T750D	GM	19	9	53T	4	6	902000	991500
68		ISLAND GYPSY 68 CKPT	FB	MY	FBG	SV	IB	T10CD	GM	19	9	53T	4	6	975500	1.060M
		1993 BOATS														
32		ISLAND GYPSY 32 AC	FB	TRWL	FBG	SV	IB	135D	SABR	12		16500	3	8	96000	105500
32		ISLAND GYPSY 32 AC	FB	TRWL	FBG	SV	IB	T 90D	SABR	12		16500	3	8	97100	106500
32		ISLAND GYPSY 32 FB	FB	TRWL	FBG	SV	IB	135D-225D		12		16500	3	8	95300	109500
32		ISLAND GYPSY 32 FB	FB	TRWL	FBG	SV	IB	T90D-T200D		12		16500	3	8	96000	119000
32		ISLAND GYPSY 32 SDN	FB	TRWL	FBG	SV	IB	135D-225D		12		16500	3	8	90800	104000
32		ISLAND GYPSY 32 SDN	FB	TRWL	FBG	SV	IB	T90D-T200D		12		16500	3	8	92300	114000
32		ISLAND GYPSY 32 SF	FB	SF	FBG	SV	IB	135D-225D		12		14000	3	8	79800	87700
32		ISLAND GYPSY 32 SF	FB	SF	FBG	SV	IB	T90D-T200D		12		14000	3	8	77900	89000
32		ISLAND GYPSY 325 SDN	FB	TRWL	FBG	SV	IB	135D	SABR	12		16500	3	8	90800	99800
36		ISLAND GYPSY 36 FB	FB	TRWL	FBG	SV	IB	135D	SABR	13		25550	3	11	113000	124000
		IB 375D CAT 120000 132000, IB T135D SABR 115500 126500, IB T200D VLVO 119500 131000														
		IB T225D SABR 120000 131500														
36		ISLAND GYPSY 36 MKII	FB	TRWL	FBG	SV	IB	135D	SABR	13		25550	3	11	117000	128500
		IB 375D CAT 122500 135000, IB T135D SABR 118500 130000, IB T200D VLVO 122500 134500														
		IB T225D SABR 123000 135000														
36		ISLAND GYPSY 36 QC	FB	TRWL	FBG	SV	IB	135D	SABR	13		25550	3	11	114000	125500
		IB T135D SABR 116000 127500, IB T200D VLVO 120000 132000, IB T225D SABR 120500 132500														
36		ISLAND GYPSY 36 SDN	FB	TRWL	FBG	SV	IB	135D	SABR	13		25550	3	11	109000	119500
		IB 375D CAT 116000 127500, IB T135D SABR 111500 122500, IB T200D VLVO 115500 127000														
		IB T225D SABR 116000 127500														
36		ISLAND GYPSY 36 TC	FB	TRWL	FBG	SV	IB	135D	SABR	13		25550	3	11	119500	131500
		IB 375D CAT 126500 139000, IB T135D SABR 121500 134000, IB T200D VLVO 125500 138000														
		IB T225D SABR 126000 138500														
40		ISLAND GYPSY 40 CL	FB	TRWL	FBG	SV	IB	T135D	SABR	14	3	32000	3	6	161000	177000
40		ISLAND GYPSY 40 CL	FB	TRWL	FBG	SV	IB	T225D	SABR	14	3	32000	3	6	164500	180500
40		ISLAND GYPSY 40 CL	FB	TRWL	FBG	SV	IB	T375D	CAT	14	3	32000	3	6	185000	203500
40		ISLAND GYPSY 40 FD	FB	TRWL	FBG	SV	IB	T135D	SABR	14	3	34500	3	6	171000	188000
40		ISLAND GYPSY 40 FD	FB	TRWL	FBG	SV	IB	T225D	SABR	14	3	34500	3	6	175000	192000
40		ISLAND GYPSY 40 FD	FB	TRWL	FBG	SV	IB	T375D	CAT	14	3	34500	3	6	195500	214500
40		ISLAND GYPSY 40 MC	FB	MY	FBG	SV	IB	T135D	SABR	14	3	33500	3	6	167000	183500
40		ISLAND GYPSY 40 MC	FB	MY	FBG	SV	IB	T225D	SABR	14	3	33500	3	6	170500	187000
40		ISLAND GYPSY 40 MC	FB	MY	FBG	SV	IB	T375D	CAT	14	3	33500	3	6	191000	210000
44	3	ISLAND GYPSY 44 CL	FB	TRWL	FBG	SV	IB	T135D	SABR	15	4	38000	4	3	190500	209500
44	3	ISLAND GYPSY 44 CL	FB	TRWL	FBG	SV	IB	T225D	SABR	15	4	38000	4	3	190500	209000
44	3	ISLAND GYPSY 44 CL	FB	TRWL	FBG	SV	IB	T375D	CAT	15	4	38000	4	3	211500	232500
44	3	ISLAND GYPSY 44 FB	FB	TRWL	FBG	SV	IB	T135D	SABR	15	4	38000	4	3	189500	208000
44	3	ISLAND GYPSY 44 FB	FB	TRWL	FBG	SV	IB	T225D	SABR	15	4	38000	4	3	200000	219500
44	3	ISLAND GYPSY 44 FB	FB	TRWL	FBG	SV	IB	T375D	CAT	15	4	38000	4	3	210000	230500
44	3	ISLAND GYPSY 44 MC	FB	MY	FBG	SV	IB	T225D	SABR	15	4	38000	4	3	184500	202500
44	3	ISLAND GYPSY 44 MC	FB	MY	FBG	SV	IB	T375D	CAT	15	4	38000	4	3	213500	234500
44	3	ISLAND GYPSY 44 MC	FB	MY	FBG	SV	IB	T550D	GM	15	4	38000	4	3	240000	263500
44	3	ISLAND GYPSY 44 SC	FB	SF	FBG	SV	IB	T225D	SABR	15	4	38000	4	3	181500	199500
44	3	ISLAND GYPSY 44 SC	FB	SF	FBG	SV	IB	T375D	CAT	15	4	38000	4	3	216000	237000
44	3	ISLAND GYPSY 44 SC	FB	SF	FBG	SV	IB	T550D	GM	15	4	38000	4	3	247000	271500
49		ISLAND GYPSY 49 CL	FB	TRWL	FBG	SV	IB	T135D	SABR	15	4	38000	4	5	195500	214500
49		ISLAND GYPSY 49 CL	FB	TRWL	FBG	SV	IB	T225D	SABR	15	4	38000	4	5	204000	224500
49		ISLAND GYPSY 49 CL	FB	TRWL	FBG	SV	IB	T375D	CAT	15	4	38000	4	5	223500	245500
49		ISLAND GYPSY 49 FD	FB	TRWL	FBG	SV	IB	T135D	SABR	15	4	42000	4	5	201500	221000
		IB T225D SABR 209000 229500, IB T375D CAT 228000 250500, IB T425D CAT 234000 257500														
		IB T550D GM 247000 271000														
49		ISLAND GYPSY 49 MC	FB	MY	FBG	SV	IB	T135D	SABR	15	4	42000	4	5	203000	223500
		IB T225D SABR 209000 229500, IB T375D CAT 230000 253000, IB T425D CAT 237500 261000														
		IB T550D GM 254000 279500														
49		ISLAND GYPSY 49 PH	FB	TRWL	FBG	SV	IB	T135D	SABR	15	4	46000	4	5	211000	232000
		IB T225D SABR 220000 241500, IB T375D CAT 238000 261500, IB T425D CAT 244000 268500														
		IB T550D GM 257000 282500														
51		ISLAND GYPSY 51 CSTM	FB	MY	FBG	SV	IB	T375D	CAT	16	6	60000	4	2	371000	408000
51		ISLAND GYPSY 51 CSTM	FB	MY	FBG	SV	IB	T550D	GM	16	6	60000	4	2	416000	457000
51		ISLAND GYPSY 51 MY	FB	MY	FBG	SV	IB	T375D	CAT	16	6	60000	4	2	362500	398000
51		ISLAND GYPSY 51 MY	FB	MY	FBG	SV	IB	T550D	GM	16	6	60000	4	2	407000	447000
56		ISLAND GYPSY 56 SC	FB	SF	FBG	SV	IB	T750D	GM	16	6	50000	4	2	465000	511000
57		ISLAND GYPSY 57 CKPT	FB	MY	FBG	SV	IB	T375D	CAT	16	6	83000	4	3	485500	534000
57		ISLAND GYPSY 57 CKPT	FB	MY	FBG	SV	IB	T550D	GM	16	6	83000	4	3	533000	585500
57		ISLAND GYPSY 57 MY	FB	MY	FBG	SV	IB	T375D	CAT	16	6	83000	4	3	485500	534000
57		ISLAND GYPSY 57 MY	FB	MY	FBG	SV	IB	T550D	GM	16	6	83000	4	3	533000	585500
57		ISLAND GYPSY 57 PH	FB	TRWL	FBG	SV	IB	T375D	CAT	16	6	82000	4	3	477000	524500
57		ISLAND GYPSY 57 PH	FB	TRWL	FBG	SV	IB	T550D	CAT	16	6	82000	4	3	538000	591500
62		ISLAND GYPSY 62 MY	FB	MY	FBG	SV	IB	T750D	GM						711000	781000
62		ISLAND GYPSY 62 MY	FB	MY	FBG	SV	IB	T10CD	GM						776000	852500
62		ISLAND GYPSY 62 SC	FB	SF	FBG	SV	IB	T10CD	GM	19	9	99000	4	6	820500	901500
68		ISLAND GYPSY 68 CKPT	FB	MY	FBG	SV	IB	T750D	GM	19	9	53T	4	6	859500	944500
68		ISLAND GYPSY 68 CKPT	FB	MY	FBG	SV	IB	T10CD	GM	19	9	53T	4	6	934000	1.015M
		1992 BOATS														
32		ISLAND GYPSY 32 AC	FB	TRWL	FBG	SV	IB	135D	SABR	12		16500	3	8	92400	101500
32		ISLAND GYPSY 32 AC	FB	TRWL	FBG	SV	IB	T 90D	SABR	12		16500	3	8	93400	102500
32		ISLAND GYPSY 32 FB	FB	TRWL	FBG	SV	IB	135D-225D		12		16500	3	8	92400	105500
32		ISLAND GYPSY 32 FB	FB	TRWL	FBG	SV	IB	T 90D	SABR	12		16500	3	8	90700	99700
32		ISLAND GYPSY 32 FB	FB	TRWL	FBG	SV	IB	T200D	VLVO	12		16500	3	8	103500	113500
32		ISLAND GYPSY 32 SDN	FB	TRWL	FBG	SV	IB	135D-225D		12		16500	3	8	85100	98000
32		ISLAND GYPSY 32 SDN	FB	TRWL	FBG	SV	IB	T90D-T200D		12		16500	3	8	88000	108500
32		ISLAND GYPSY 32 SF	FB	SF	FBG	SV	IB	135D-375D		12		14000	3	8	76100	84000
32		ISLAND GYPSY 32 SF	FB	SF	FBG	SV	IB	T90D-T200D		12		14000	3	8	74300	84900
32		ISLAND GYPSY 325 SDN	FB	TRWL	FBG	SV	IB	135D	SABR	12		16500	3	8	85900	94400
36		ISLAND GYPSY 36 FB	FB	TRWL	FBG	SV	IB	135D	SABR	13		25550	3	11	108000	118500
		IB 375D CAT 114500 125500, IB T135D SABR 109500 120500, IB T200D VLVO 114000 125000														
		IB T225D SABR 114500 125500														
36		ISLAND GYPSY 36 MKII	FB	TRWL	FBG	SV	IB	135D	SABR	13		25550	3	11	111500	122500
		IB 375D CAT 118000 130000, IB T135D SABR 113500 124500, IB T200D VLVO 117500 129000														

 CONTINUED ON NEXT PAGE

LOA FT	IN	NAME AND/ OR MODEL	TOP/ RIG	BOAT TYPE	-HULL- MTL	TP	TP	----ENGINE--- # HP	MFG	BEAM FT	IN	WGT LBS	DRAFT FT	IN	RETAIL LOW	RETAIL HIGH
		1992 BOATS														
36		ISLAND GYPSY 36 MKII	FB	TRWL	FBG	SV	IB	T225D	SABR	13		25550	3	11	118000	130000
36		ISLAND GYPSY 36 QC	FB	TRWL	FBG	SV	IB	135D	SABR	13		25550	3	11	108000	118500
		IB T135D SABR 110000 121000, IB T200D VLVO 114000 125000, IB T225D SABR 114500 125500														
		IB T375D CAT 131000 144000														
36		ISLAND GYPSY 36 SDN	FB	TRWL	FBG	SV	IB	135D	SABR	13		25550	3	11	103500	113500
		IB 375D CAT 110000 121000, IB T135D SABR 105500 116000, IB T200D VLVO 110000 121000														
		IB T225D SABR 110000 121000														
36		ISLAND GYPSY 36 TC	FB	TRWL	FBG	SV	IB	135D	SABR	13		25550	3	11	114500	126000
		IB 375D CAT 120500 132000, IB T135D SABR 117500 129000, IB T200D VLVO 119500 131500														
		IB T225D SABR 120500 132000														
40		ISLAND GYPSY 40 CL	FB	TRWL	FBG	SV	IB	T135D	SABR	14	3	32000	3	6	153500	168500
40		ISLAND GYPSY 40 CL	FB	TRWL	FBG	SV	IB	T225D	SABR	14	3	32000	3	6	157000	172500
40		ISLAND GYPSY 40 CL	FB	TRWL	FBG	SV	IB	T375D	CAT	14	3	32000	3	6	176500	194000
40		ISLAND GYPSY 40 FD	FB	TRWL	FBG	SV	IB	T135D	SABR	14	3	34500	3	6	163000	179500
40		ISLAND GYPSY 40 FD	FB	TRWL	FBG	SV	IB	T225D	SABR	14	3	34500	3	6	166500	183000
40		ISLAND GYPSY 40 FD	FB	TRWL	FBG	SV	IB	T375D	CAT	14	3	34500	3	6	186500	204500
40		ISLAND GYPSY 40 MC	FB	MY	FBG	SV	IB	T135D	SABR	14	3	33500	3	6	159000	175000
40		ISLAND GYPSY 40 MC	FB	MY	FBG	SV	IB	T225D	SABR	14	3	33500	3	6	162500	178500
40		ISLAND GYPSY 40 MC	FB	MY	FBG	SV	IB	T375D	CAT	14	3	33500	3	6	182000	200000
44	3	ISLAND GYPSY 44 CL	FB	TRWL	FBG	SV	IB	T135D	SABR	15	4	38000	4	3	182000	200000
44	3	ISLAND GYPSY 44 CL	FB	TRWL	FBG	SV	IB	T225D	SABR	15	4	38000	4	3	186500	205000
44	3	ISLAND GYPSY 44 CL	FB	TRWL	FBG	SV	IB	T375D	CAT	15	4	38000	4	3	201500	221500
44	3	ISLAND GYPSY 44 FB	FB	TRWL	FBG	SV	IB	T135D	SABR	15	4	38000	4	3	180500	198500
44	3	ISLAND GYPSY 44 FB	FB	TRWL	FBG	SV	IB	T225D	SABR	15	4	38000	4	3	185500	203500
44	3	ISLAND GYPSY 44 FB	FB	TRWL	FBG	SV	IB	T375D	CAT	15	4	38000	4	3	200000	220000
44	3	ISLAND GYPSY 44 MC	FB	MY	FBG	SV	IB	T225D	SABR	15	4	38000	4	3	175500	193000
44	3	ISLAND GYPSY 44 MC	FB	MY	FBG	SV	IB	T375D	CAT	15	4	38000	4	3	203500	223500
44	3	ISLAND GYPSY 44 MC	FB	MY	FBG	SV	IB	T550D	GM	15	4	38000	4	3	228500	251500
44	3	ISLAND GYPSY 44 SC	FB	SF	FBG	SV	IB	T225D	SABR	15	4	38000	4	3	173000	190000
44	3	ISLAND GYPSY 44 SC	FB	SF	FBG	SV	IB	T375D	CAT	15	4	38000	4	3	205500	226000
44	3	ISLAND GYPSY 44 SC	FB	SF	FBG	SV	IB	T550D	GM	15	4	38000	4	3	235500	258500
49		ISLAND GYPSY 49 CL	FB	TRWL	FBG	SV	IB	T135D	SABR	15	4	38000	4	5	186000	204500
49		ISLAND GYPSY 49 CL	FB	TRWL	FBG	SV	IB	T225D	SABR	15	4	38000	4	5	194500	213500
49		ISLAND GYPSY 49 CL	FB	TRWL	FBG	SV	IB	T375D	CAT	15	4	38000	4	5	212500	233500
49		ISLAND GYPSY 49 FD	FB	TRWL	FBG	SV	IB	T135D	SABR	15	4	42000	4	5	191500	210500
		IB T225D SABR 198500 218500, IB T375D CAT 217000 238500, IB T425D CAT 223000 245000														
		IB T550D GM 235000 258000														
49		ISLAND GYPSY 49 MC	FB	MY	FBG	SV	IB	T135D	SABR	15	4	42000	4	5	193000	212500
		IB T225D SABR 198500 218500, IB T375D CAT 219000 240500, IB T425D CAT 226000 248500														
		IB T550D GM 242000 266000														
49		ISLAND GYPSY 49 PH	FB	TRWL	FBG	SV	IB	T135D	SABR	15	4	46000	4	5	200500	220500
		IB T225D SABR 209500 230000, IB T375D CAT 226500 249000, IB T425D CAT 232500 255500														
		IB T550D GM 244500 268500														
51		ISLAND GYPSY 51 CSTM	FB	MY	FBG	SV	IB	T375D	CAT	16	6	60000	4	2	363500	399500
51		ISLAND GYPSY 51 CSTM	FB	MY	FBG	SV	IB	T550D	GM	16	6	60000	4	2	397000	436500
51		ISLAND GYPSY 51 MY	FB	MY	FBG	SV	IB	T375D	CAT	16	6	60000	4	2	335500	369000
51		ISLAND GYPSY 51 MY	FB	MY	FBG	SV	IB	T550D	GM	16	6	60000	4	2	387000	425500
56		ISLAND GYPSY 56 SC	FB	SF	FBG	SV	IB	T750D	GM	16	6	50000	4	2	443500	487000
57		ISLAND GYPSY 57 CKPT	FB	MY	FBG	SV	IB	T375D	CAT	16	6	83000	4	3	464500	510000
57		ISLAND GYPSY 57 CKPT	FB	MY	FBG	SV	IB	T550D	GM	16	6	83000	4	3	509000	559500
57		ISLAND GYPSY 57 MY	FB	MY	FBG	SV	IB	T375D	CAT	16	6	83000	4	3	464500	510000
57		ISLAND GYPSY 57 MY	FB	MY	FBG	SV	IB	T550D	GM	16	6	83000	4	3	509000	559500
57		ISLAND GYPSY 57 PH	FB	TRWL	FBG	SV	IB	T375D	CAT	16	6	82000	4	3	456000	501000
62		ISLAND GYPSY 62 MY	FB	MY	FBG	SV	IB	T750D	GM						677500	744500
62		ISLAND GYPSY 62 MY	FB	MY	FBG	SV	IB	T10CD	GM						739500	812500
62		ISLAND GYPSY 62 SC	FB	SF	FBG	SV	IB	T10CD	GM	19	9	99000	4	6	782000	859500
68		ISLAND GYPSY 68 CKPT	FB	MY	FBG	SV	IB	T750D	GM	19	9	53T	4	6	819500	900500
68		ISLAND GYPSY 68 CKPT	FB	MY	FBG	SV	IB	T10CD	GM	19	9	53T	4	6	881000	968000
		1991 BOATS														
32		ISLAND GYPSY 32 AC	FB	TRWL	FBG	SV	IB	135D		12		16500	3	8	86800	95400
32		ISLAND GYPSY 32 AC	FB	TRWL	FBG	SV	IB	T 90D		12		16500	3	8	88300	97100
32		ISLAND GYPSY 32 FB	FB	TRWL	FBG	SV	IB	135D-225D		12		16500	3	8	86800	100000
32		ISLAND GYPSY 32 FB	FB	TRWL	FBG	SV	IB	T90D-T200D		12		16500	3	8	88300	108500
32		ISLAND GYPSY 32 SDN	FB	TRWL	FBG	SV	IB	135D-225D		12		16500	3	8	81300	94200
32		ISLAND GYPSY 32 SDN	FB	TRWL	FBG	SV	IB	T90D-T200D		12		16500	3	8	83200	103500
32		ISLAND GYPSY 32 SF	FB	SF	FBG	SV	IB	135D-375D		12		14000	3	8	72700	80200
32		ISLAND GYPSY 32 SF	FB	SF	FBG	SV	IB	T90D-T200D		12		14000	3	8	70900	81000
32		ISLAND GYPSY 325 SDN	FB	TRWL	FBG	SV	IB	135D	LEHM	12		16500	3	8	81300	89300
36		ISLAND GYPSY 36 FB	FB	TRWL	FBG	SV	IB	135D	LEHM	13		25550	3	11	104000	114500
		IB 135D SABR 103000 113500, IB 375D CAT 109000 119500, IB T135D LEHM 106000 116500														
		IB T135D SABR 104500 115000, IB T200D VLVO 108500 119500, IB T225D LEHM 111000 122000														
		IB T225D SABR 109000 119500														
36		ISLAND GYPSY 36 MKII	FB	TRWL	FBG	SV	IB	135D	LEHM	13		25550	3	11	107000	117500
		IB 135D SABR 106000 117000, IB 375D CAT 112500 123500, IB T135D LEHM 110000 121000														
		IB T135D SABR 108500 119000, IB T200D VLVO 112000 123000, IB T225D LEHM 114500 126000														
		IB T225D SABR 112500 123500														
36		ISLAND GYPSY 36 QC	FB	TRWL	FBG	SV	IB	135D	LEHM	13		25550	3	11	104000	114500
		IB 135D SABR 103000 113500, IB T135D LEHM 106500 117000, IB T135D SABR 105000 115500														
		IB T200D VLVO 109000 119500, IB T225D LEHM 111000 122000, IB T225D SABR 109000 120000														
		IB T375D CAT 125000 137500														
36		ISLAND GYPSY 36 SDN	FB	TRWL	FBG	SV	IB	135D	LEHM	13		25550	3	11	99200	109000
		IB 135D SABR 98400 108000, IB 375D CAT 105000 115500, IB T135D LEHM 102000 112000														
		IB T135D SABR 100500 110500, IB T200D VLVO 104500 115000, IB T225D LEHM 107000 117500														
		IB T225D SABR 105000 115500														
36		ISLAND GYPSY 36 TC	FB	TRWL	FBG	SV	IB	135D	LEHM	13		25550	3	11	110000	121000
		IB 135D SABR 109500 120000, IB 375D CAT 115000 126000, IB T135D LEHM 113000 124000														
		IB T135D SABR 111500 122500, IB T200D VLVO 114000 125500, IB T225D LEHM 117000 128500														
		IB T225D SABR 115000 126000														
40		ISLAND GYPSY 40 FD	FB	TRWL	FBG	SV	IB	T135D	LEHM	14	3	34500	3	6	158500	174500
		IB T135D SABR 155500 171000, IB T225D LEHM 163000 179000, IB T225D SABR 159000 174500														
		IB T375D CAT 177500 195000														
40		ISLAND GYPSY 40 MC	FB	TRWL	FBG	SV	IB	T135D	LEHM	14	3	33500	3	6	155000	170000
		IB T135D SABR 152000 167000, IB T225D LEHM 159000 174500, IB T225D SABR 155000 170500														
		IB T375D CAT 174000 191000														
44	3	ISLAND GYPSY 44 FB	FB	TRWL	FBG	SV	IB	T135D	LEHM	15	4	35000	4	3	164500	180500
		IB T135D SABR 163000 179000, IB T225D LEHM 169500 186000, IB T225D SABR 167500 184000														
		IB T375D CAT 181500 199500														
44	3	ISLAND GYPSY 44 MC	FB	MY	FBG	SV	IB	T225D	LEHM	15	4	35000	4	3	158500	174000
		IB T225D SABR 156000 171500, IB T375D CAT 183500 201500, IB T550D GM 208000 228500														
44	3	ISLAND GYPSY 44 SC	FB	SF	FBG	SV	IB	T225D	LEHM	15	4	35000	4	3	156000	171500
		IB T225D SABR 154000 169500, IB T375D CAT 186000 204500, IB T550D GM 215500 236500														
49		ISLAND GYPSY 49 FD	FB	TRWL	FBG	SV	IB	T135D	LEHM	15	4	40000	4	5	179500	197000
		IB T135D SABR 179000 196500, IB T225D LEHM 186500 205000, IB T225D SABR 185500 204000														
		IB T375D CAT 203000 223000, IB T425D CAT 208500 229500, IB T550D GM 220000 242000														
49		ISLAND GYPSY 49 MC	FB	MY	FBG	SV	IB	T135D	LEHM	15	4	43000	4	5	186500	204500
		IB T135D SABR 185500 204000, IB T225D LEHM 192000 211000, IB T225D SABR 191000 209500														
		IB T375D CAT 210500 231000, IB T425D CAT 217000 238500, IB T550D GM 233000 256000														
49		ISLAND GYPSY 49 PH	FB	TRWL	FBG	SV	IB	T135D	LEHM	15	4	46000	4	5	191500	210500
		IB T135D SABR 191000 210000, IB T225D LEHM 200000 220000, IB T225D SABR 199500 219000														
		IB T375D CAT 216000 237500, IB T425D CAT 221500 243500, IB T550D GM 233000 256000														
51		ISLAND GYPSY 51 CSTM	FB	MY	FBG	SV	IB	T375D	CAT	16	6	49000	4	2	290000	319000
51		ISLAND GYPSY 51 CSTM	FB	MY	FBG	SV	IB	T550D	GM	16	6	49000	4	2	327000	359000
51		ISLAND GYPSY 51 MY	FB	MY	FBG	SV	IB	T375D	CAT	16	6	49000	4	2	282500	310500
51		ISLAND GYPSY 51 MY	FB	MY	FBG	SV	IB	T550D	GM	16	6	49000	4	2	318500	350000
56		ISLAND GYPSY 56 SC	FB	SF	FBG	SV	IB	T750D	GM						350000	384500
57		ISLAND GYPSY 57 CKPT	FB	MY	FBG	SV	IB	T375D	CAT	16	6	83000	4	3	427500	470000
57		ISLAND GYPSY 57 CKPT	FB	MY	FBG	SV	IB	T750D	GM	16	6	83000	4	3	535000	588000
57		ISLAND GYPSY 57 MY	FB	MY	FBG	SV	IB	T375D	CAT	16	6	83000	4	3	461000	506500
57		ISLAND GYPSY 57 MY	FB	MY	FBG	SV	IB	T750D	GM	16	6	83000	4	3	571000	627500
62		ISLAND GYPSY 62 MY	FB	MY	FBG	SV	IB	T750D	GM						646500	710500
62		ISLAND GYPSY 62 MY	FB	MY	FBG	SV	IB	T10CD	GM						705500	775000
62		ISLAND GYPSY 62 SC	FB	SF	FBG	SV	IB	T10CD	GM	19	9	99000	4	6	746000	820000
68		ISLAND GYPSY 68 CKPT	FB	MY	FBG	SV	IB	T750D	GM	19	9	53T	4	6	781500	859000
68		ISLAND GYPSY 68 CKPT	FB	MY	FBG	SV	IB	T10CD	GM	19	9	53T	4	6	840000	923000
		1990 BOATS														
32		ISLAND GYPSY SEDAN	FB	TRWL	FBG	SV	IB	135D	LEHM	11	6	16500	3	8	80600	88600
32		ISLAND GYPSY SPTFSH	FB	SF	FBG	SV	IB	135D	LEHM	11	6	14000	3	8	69000	75800
36		ISLAND GYPSY EXFB	FB	TRWL	FBG	SV	IB	T135D	LEHM	12	6	25500	3	11	103500	113500
36		ISLAND GYPSY QUADCB	FB	TRWL	FBG	SV	IB	T135D	LEHM	12	6	25500	3	11	104000	114500
40		ISLAND GYPSY AFTCB	FB	TRWL	FBG	SV	IB	T135D	LEHM	14	3	33500	3	6	149000	164000
40		ISLAND GYPSY MTRCR	FB	TRWL	FBG	SV	IB	T135D	LEHM	14	3	33500	3	6	146500	160500
44	3	ISLAND GYPSY 44	FB	MY	FBG	SV	IB	T135D	LEHM	15	4	38500	4	3	155000	170500

 CONTINUED ON NEXT PAGE

1990 BOATS

LOA FT	IN	NAME AND/OR MODEL	TOP/RIG	BOAT TYPE	MTL	TP	ENG TP	# HP	MFG	BEAM FT	IN	WGT LBS	DRAFT FT	IN	RETAIL LOW	RETAIL HIGH
44	3	ISLAND GYPSY 44FD	FB	FD	FBG	SV	IB	T135D	LEHM	15	4	38500	4	3	156000	171500
49		ISLAND GYPSY MTRCR	FB	MY	FBG	SV	IB	T225D	LEHM	15	4	43000	4	5	183000	201000
51		MOTOR YACHT	FB	MY	FBG	SV	IB	T375D	CAT	16	6	74500	4	2	288500	317000
57		MOTOR YACHT	FB	MY	FBG	SV	IB	T375D	CAT	16	6	83000	4	3	425500	467500
62		SPORTS CONVERTIBLE	FB	SF	F/S	SV	IB	T10CD	GM	19	9	99000	4	6	716500	787000
68		COCKPIT MOTOR YACHT	FB	MYCPT	F/S	SV	IB	T750D	GM	19	9	53T	4	6	756500	831500

1987 BOATS

LOA FT	IN	NAME AND/OR MODEL	TOP/RIG	BOAT TYPE	MTL	TP	ENG TP	# HP	MFG	BEAM FT	IN	WGT LBS	DRAFT FT	IN	RETAIL LOW	RETAIL HIGH
29	6	ISLAND-GYPSY 29		CR	FBG	SV	IB		90	11	4	13000			36500	40600
30		ISLAND GYPSY SDN 30		CR	FBG	SV	IB		135	11	6	14500			39900	44300
32	1	ISLAND-GYPSY 32		CR	FBG	SV	IB		135D	11	6	15000	3	8	64200	70500
36		ISLAND-GYPSY 36	FB	CR	FBG	SV	IB	T135D		12	6	23500	3	11	84100	92400
40		ISLAND-GYPSY 40		CR	FBG	SV	IB	T135D		14	3	31500	3	6	122500	134500
41		DAWN 41	SLP	SA/RC	FBG	KL	IB		D	13		18000	7			95700
44	3	ISLAND-GYPSY 44	FB	FD	FBG	SV	IB	T135D		15		32000			115000	126000
44	3	KONG-&-HALVORSEN		CR	FBG	SV	IB	T135		14	6	34000			117500	129500
44	4	KONG-&-HALVORSEN 44		SF	FBG	SV	IB	T450		15		32000			138000	151500
48	6	DAWN 48	KTH	SA/RC	FBG	KL	IB		D	14	3	27000	6		154500	170000
51		KONG-&-HALVORSEN 51		MY	FBG	SV	IB	T235		16	6	56000			178500	196000
57		KONG-&-HALVORSEN 57		MY	FBG	SV	IB	T235		16	6	62000			253000	278000
62		KONG-&-HALVORSEN 62		MY	FBG	SV	IB	T355D		19		91000	4	6	459000	504500
68		KONG-&-HALVORSEN 68		YTFS	FBG	SV	IB	T355D		19		95000	4	6	534500	587500
68		KONG-&-HALVORSEN 72		MY	FBG	SV	IB	T	D	20		50T	5	2	**	**
68		KONG-&-HALVORSEN 90		MY	FBG	SV	IB	T	D	22	6	55T	5	6	**	**

1986 BOATS

LOA FT	IN	NAME AND/OR MODEL	TOP/RIG	BOAT TYPE	MTL	TP	ENG TP	# HP	MFG	BEAM FT	IN	WGT LBS	DRAFT FT	IN	RETAIL LOW	RETAIL HIGH
29	6	ISLAND-GYPSY		CR	FBG		IB		90	11	4	13000			34800	38700
30		ISLAND-GYPSY SDN 30		CR	FBG		IB		135	11	6	14500			38100	42300
32	1	ISLAND-GYPSY 32		CR	FBG		IB		135D	11	6	15000			61500	67600
36		ISLAND-GYPSY 36		CR	FBG		IB		T250	12	6	23500			70600	77600
40		ISLAND-GYPSY 40		CR	FBG		IB		T135	14	3	31500			109500	120000
41		DAWN 41	SLP	SA/RC	FBG	KL	IB		D	13		18000	7		81800	89800
44	3	ISLAND-GYPSY 44	FB	FD	FBG		IB	T135D		15		32000			109500	120500
44	3	KONG & HALVORSEN 44		CR	FBG		IB	T135		14	6	34000			112500	123500
44	3	KONG & HALVORSEN 44		SF	FBG		IB	T450		15		32000			132500	145000
48	6	DAWN 48	KTH	SA/RC	FBG	KL	IB		D	14	3	27000	6		145500	160000

1985 BOATS

LOA FT	IN	NAME AND/OR MODEL	TOP/RIG	BOAT TYPE	MTL	TP	ENG TP	# HP	MFG	BEAM FT	IN	WGT LBS	DRAFT FT	IN	RETAIL LOW	RETAIL HIGH
30		ISLAND-GYPSY SDN 30		SDN	FBG		IB		135D	11	6	14500	3	8	54400	59800
32	1	ISLAND-GYPSY AFT CBN		SDN	FBG		IB		135D	11	6	15500	3	8	60600	66600
32	1	ISLAND-GYPSY SDN 32		SDN	FBG		IB		135D	11	6	15500	3	8	60600	66600
36		ISLAND-GYPSY FB	FB	SDN	FBG		IB	T135D		12	6	23500			77200	84800
36		ISLAND-GYPSY QUAD 36		SDN	FBG		IB	T135D		12	6	23500			77200	84800
44	3	ISLAND-GYPSY 44	FB	FD	FBG		IB	T135D		15		32000	4	3	112500	124000
44	3	ISLAND-GYPSY CONV 44	FB	SDNSF	FBG		IB	T450D		15		32000	3		149000	164000
48	6	DAWN 48	KTH	SA/RC	FBG	KL	IB		D	14	3	27000	6		136500	150500
51		ISLAND-GYPSY 51		MY	FBG		IB	T235D		16	6	56000	4	6	178500	196000
57		ISLAND-GYPSY 57		MY	FBG		IB	T235D		16	6	62000	4	10	234500	258000

....For earlier years, see the BUC Used Boat Price Guide, Volume 3

YEHASSO INC
NEW YORK NY 10016   COAST GUARD MFG ID- EHA See inside cover to adjust price for area

1984 BOATS

LOA FT	IN	NAME AND/OR MODEL	TOP/RIG	BOAT TYPE	MTL	TP	ENG TP	# HP	MFG	BEAM FT	IN	WGT LBS	DRAFT FT	IN	RETAIL LOW	RETAIL HIGH
36		VOYAGER 36	FB	CNV	FBG	SV	IB	200D	PERK	13		20000	3	11	57900	63600
36		VOYAGER SUNDECK 36	FB	TRWL	FBG	SV	IB	T135D	PERK	13		20000	3	11	61100	67200
41	9	VOYAGER S-42 CRUS	FB	TRWL	FBG	DS	IB	T135D	PERK	13	8	26000	3	6	90900	99900
41	9	VOYAGER SUNDECK 42	FB	TRWL	FBG	DS	IB	T135D	PERK	13	8	24000	3	6	86200	94800
41	9	VOYAGER SUNDECK 42	FB	TRWL	FBG	DS	IB	T165D	PERK	13	8	24000	3	6	87300	96000

....For earlier years, see the BUC Used Boat Price Guide, Volume 3

YONDER YACHT SPECIALISTS
NEW SMYRNA FL 32069   COAST GUARD MFG ID- YYS See inside cover to adjust price for area

1985 BOATS

LOA FT	IN	NAME OR MODEL	TOP/RIG	BOAT TYPE	MTL	TP	ENG TP	# HP	MFG	BEAM FT	IN	WGT LBS	DRAFT FT	IN	RETAIL LOW	RETAIL HIGH
48		MAY-FLOWER 48	KTH	SA/RC	FBG	KL	IB	85D	PERK	13	6	37000	5	8	118000	130000

1984 BOATS

LOA FT	IN	NAME OR MODEL	TOP/RIG	BOAT TYPE	MTL	TP	ENG TP	# HP	MFG	BEAM FT	IN	WGT LBS	DRAFT FT	IN	RETAIL LOW	RETAIL HIGH
48		MAY-FLOWER 48	KTH	SA/RC	FBG	KL	IB	85D	PERK	13	6	37000	5	8	111000	122000

....For earlier years, see the BUC Used Boat Price Guide, Volume 3

YOUNG SUN YACHT CORP
KAOHSIUNG TAIWAN ROC   COAST GUARD MFG ID- ROC See inside cover to adjust price for area

WONDERLAND INTERNATIONAL INC
WOODBURY NY 11797

1987 BOATS

LOA FT	IN	NAME OR MODEL	TOP/RIG	BOAT TYPE	MTL	TP	ENG TP	# HP	MFG	BEAM FT	IN	WGT LBS	DRAFT FT	IN	RETAIL LOW	RETAIL HIGH
34	3	YOUNG SUN 35 AFT CPT	CUT	SA/CR	FBG	KL	IB	30D	YAN	11		19000	5	6	58200	64000

1985 BOATS

LOA FT	IN	NAME OR MODEL	TOP/RIG	BOAT TYPE	MTL	TP	ENG TP	# HP	MFG	BEAM FT	IN	WGT LBS	DRAFT FT	IN	RETAIL LOW	RETAIL HIGH
34	6	YOUNG-SUN 35	CUT	SA/CR	FBG	KL	IB	33D	YAN	11		19300	5	6	54800	60200
42	6	YOUNG-SUN 43	CUT	SA/CR	FBG	KL	IB	90D	VLVO	12	2	31500	6		88700	97400
53	9	YOUNG-SUN 54	KTH	SA/CR	FBG	KL	IB	130D	ISUZ	14	2	50000	6	8	161500	177500
53	9	YOUNG-SUN 54	CUT	SAIL	FBG	KL	IB	120D	BENZ	14	2	50000	6	8	162500	178500

1984 BOATS

LOA FT	IN	NAME OR MODEL	TOP/RIG	BOAT TYPE	MTL	TP	ENG TP	# HP	MFG	BEAM FT	IN	WGT LBS	DRAFT FT	IN	RETAIL LOW	RETAIL HIGH
34	3	YOUNG-SUN 35	CUT	SA/CR	FBG	KL	IB	30D	YAN	11		19300	5	6	51600	56700
42	6	YOUNG-SUN 43 CTR CPT	CUT	SA/CR	FBG	KL	IB	51D	PERK	12	2	29500	6		79100	87000
42	6	YOUNG-SUN 43 PH	CUT	SA/CR	FBG	KL	IB	51D	PERK	12	2	29500	6		79100	87000
53	9	YOUNG SUN 54 CTR CPT	CUT	SA/CR	FBG	KL	IB	120D	LEHM	14	2	50000	5	10	152500	168000
53	9	YOUNG SUN 54 PH	CUT	SA/CR	FBG	KL	IB	120D	LEHM	14	2	50000	5	10	153000	168000

ZEPPELIN TECHNOLOGIES INC
GRANBY QUE CANADA J2G 7 COAST GUARD MFG ID- QZT See inside cover to adjust price for area

ZEPPELIN INFLATABLES INC
FT LAUDERDALE FL 33315

1991 BOATS

LOA FT	IN	NAME OR MODEL	TOP/RIG	BOAT TYPE	MTL	TP	ENG TP	# HP	MFG	BEAM FT	IN	WGT LBS	DRAFT FT	IN	RETAIL LOW	RETAIL HIGH
16		CENTURION 16		DGY	FBG	DV	OB				6	8	385			3450	4000
16		TROPHY 16		DGY	FBG	DV	OB				6	8				2600	3050
18		CENTURION 18		DGY	FBG	SV	OB				7	10	594			5900	6800
24	5	CENTURION 24		DGY	FBG	SV	OB				8	8	1760			20700	23000

INDEX

A WORD OF EXPLANATION

The following is a combination of a manufacturers' index and a model name cross-reference index. It has been compiled in answer to the many requests from BUC Book users for a complete, easy-to-use reference index.

A **manufacturer name** is printed in boldface type followed by the first page on which it appears.

> **American Marine Sports**................22
> ⇒**American Multihulls Inc**................22
> **American Pleasure Prod Inc**................22

A **boat model name** is printed in upper case type. Indented under the model name is a list of manufacturers that made a boat with that name followed by the boat length

> Premier Marine Inc **(20'D)**................421
> ⇒ATLANTIC
> Cape Cod Shipbuilding Co **(31'S)**................81
> Giacomo Colombo **(38'P)**................213
> Huckins Yacht Corp **(P)**................258

(rounded to the nearest foot) and basic boat type (C—canoe, D—deckboat, H—houseboat, O—outboard boat, P—powerboat with IB, IO, VD, or JT engine, S—sailboat) printed within brackets in bold type. If a manufacturer uses the name for more than one length or type, then no indicator may be shown. It is also possible that one or the other of length or boat type is undeterminable. The last item on the line is the page number. Remember, if no length or boat type is printed after a company's name, you should check the listing before eliminating it as the manufacturer you are seeking.

A **parent company or trade name** is printed in boldface type without a page number. Indented under the name is a list of the manufacturers which are divisions of the parent company followed by their page numbers.

> C & C Yachts................72
> ⇒**C & C Manufacturing Inc**
> Century Boat Company................101
> Cobia Boat Company................130

BOAT MANUFACTURER, TRADE NAME AND MODEL NAME INDEX

BOAT MANUFACTURER, TRADE NAME AND MODEL NAME INDEX

BOAT MANUFACTURER, TRADE NAME AND MODEL NAME INDEX

BOAT MANUFACTURER, TRADE NAME AND MODEL NAME INDEX

BOAT MANUFACTURER, TRADE NAME AND MODEL NAME INDEX

BOAT MANUFACTURER, TRADE NAME AND MODEL NAME INDEX

BOAT MANUFACTURER, TRADE NAME AND MODEL NAME INDEX

BOAT MANUFACTURER, TRADE NAME AND MODEL NAME INDEX

BOAT MANUFACTURER, TRADE NAME AND MODEL NAME INDEX

BOAT MANUFACTURER, TRADE NAME AND MODEL NAME INDEX

BOAT MANUFACTURER, TRADE NAME AND MODEL NAME INDEX

BOAT MANUFACTURER, TRADE NAME AND MODEL NAME INDEX

BOAT MANUFACTURER, TRADE NAME AND MODEL NAME INDEX